PETERSON'S

www.petersons.com

2001

College Money Handbook

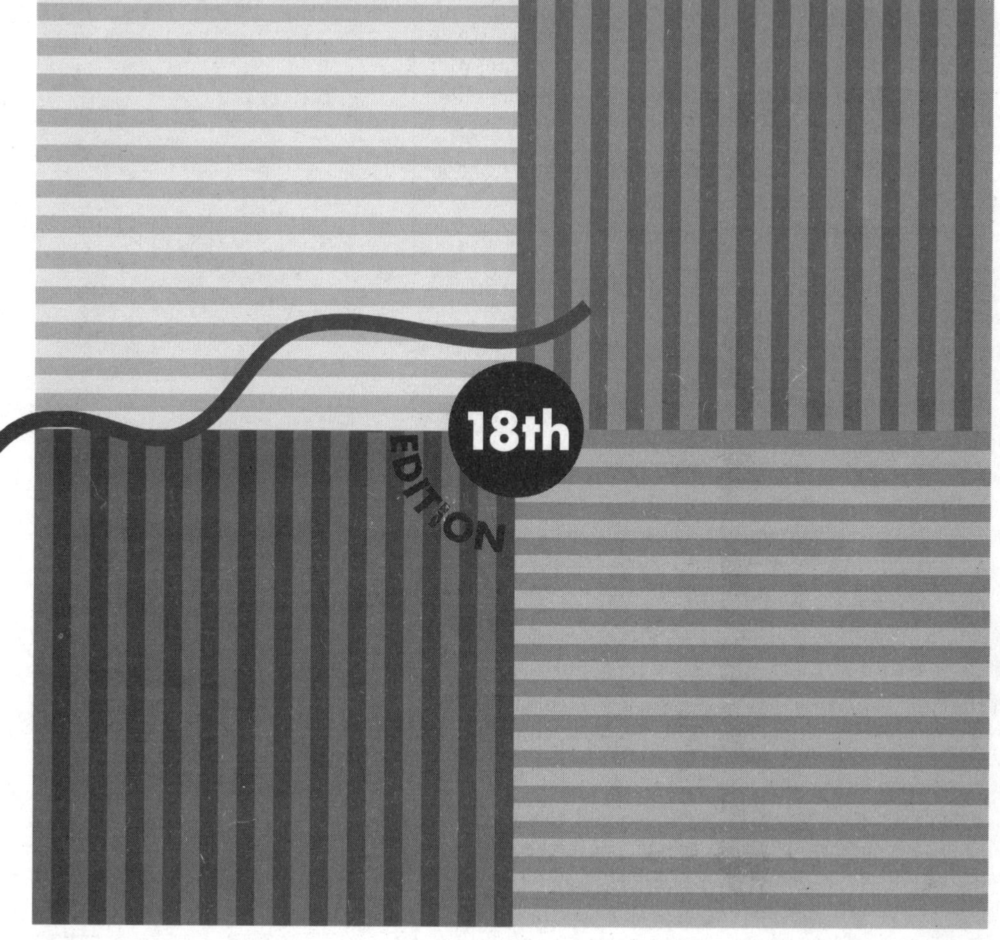

Billions of Dollars in Institutional, State, and Federal Aid

PETERSON'S
THOMSON LEARNING™

Australia • Canada • Mexico • Singapore • Spain • United Kingdom • United States

About Peterson's

Founded in 1966, Peterson's, a division of Thomson Learning, is the nation's largest and most respected provider of lifelong learning online resources, software, reference guides, and books. The Education Supersite[SM] at petersons.com—the Web's most heavily traveled education resource—has searchable databases and interactive tools for contacting U.S.-accredited institutions and programs. CollegeQuest[SM] (CollegeQuest.com) offers a complete solution for every step of the college decision-making process. GradAdvantage[TM] (GradAdvantage.org), developed with Educational Testing Service, is the only electronic admissions service capable of sending official graduate test score reports with a candidate's online application. Peterson's serves over 55 million education consumers annually.

Thomson Learning is among the world's leading providers of lifelong learning, serving the needs of individuals, learning institutions, and corporations with products and services for both traditional classrooms and for online learning. For more information about the products and services offered by Thomson Learning, please visit www.thomsonlearning.com. Headquartered in Stamford, Connecticut, with offices worldwide, Thomson Learning is part of The Thomson Corporation (www.thomson.com), a leading e-information and solutions company in the business, professional, and education marketplaces. The Corporation's common shares are listed on the Toronto and London stock exchanges.

Visit Peterson's Education Center on the Internet (World Wide Web) at www.petersons.com

Previous editions published as *Peterson's College Money Handbook* © 1983, 1984, 1985, 1986, 1987, 1988, 1989, 1990, 1991, 1996, 1997, 1998, 1999 and as *Paying Less for College*© 1992, 1993, 1994, 1995

ISSN 1098-831X
ISBN 0-7689-0425-0

Printed in the United States of America

10 9 8 7 6 5 4 3 2 1

CONTENTS

A Guide to the Financial Aid System

College Financial Aid Information

SECTION 8: COLLEGE FINANCIAL AID INDEXES

SECTION 1

Introduction

In most families, parents assume the major responsibility for paying college expenses while the child is the primary beneficiary of the education. We hope that students and parents will read this book together and participate in family discussions on how their education will be financed.

How to Use This Book

This book is both a quick resource and an in-depth reference that puts at your fingertips valuable information about college costs and financial aid opportunities. It contains:

- Easy-to-use charts, tables, and lists
- An overview of federal financial aid and the programs available
- A guide to help you through the maze of applying for financial aid
- A state-by-state description of each state-administered financial aid program
- Financial aid profiles of more than 1,800 individual colleges

The challenge of paying for college requires forethought, organization, and resourcefulness. However, there are many ways to manage college costs and many channels through which you can receive help. If typical financial aid packages are taken into consideration, the actual cost of four years of college is likely to be less than what most families spend on a new car, and, unlike a car, the value of a college education will increase as time goes on. We wish you success in your quest and hope that *Peterson's College Money Handbook* will prove to be helpful both in your college selection and in helping you finance the cost of your education.

Contents

A Guide to Financing Your Child's College Education

More and more families must count on financial aid. In this generation, financial aid is a basic and essential component of paying the costs of college. Most students and their families should plan on tapping the river of governmental and institutional financial aid subsidies that will supplement, and occasionally supersede, their personal saving and borrowing plans. If you do not consider how these sources may help you to pay for college costs, you are likely making a real mistake.

The financial aid system and its process can seem overwhelming, confusing, and complex, especially the first time you go through it. In "A Guide to Financing Your Child's College Education," Don Betterton, Director of Undergraduate Financial Aid at Princeton University, provides a clear, concise picture of what families need to know. A noted author, Betterton's twenty-five years of experience enable him to pinpoint the trouble areas and questions that most concern parents and students. Reading his article will give you the background and understanding necessary to make the best use of this book.

Common Questions Answered

In this section are the answers to the questions most often asked of financial aid administrators.

Federal Financial Aid Programs

This section provides a description of the federal programs that serve as the foundation of financial assistance. Included are descriptions of the two federal grant programs, the Federal Work-Study program, and the two families of loans, each of which has loan programs for both students and parents.

State Scholarship and Grant Programs

This section lists more than 400 specific grants and loans state by state. Eligibility requirements, award amounts, and contacts for further information are given for all programs.

College Cost and Financial Aid Metrics

The amount of aid available at colleges can vary widely. The table entitled "College Cost and Financial Aid Metrics" lists the percent of freshmen who applied for and received need-based gift aid and the percent of those whose need was fully met. Also listed are the average freshman financial aid package, the average cost after aid, and the average graduate indebtedness.

College Financial Aid Profiles

After the federal government, colleges provide the largest amount of financial aid to students. Colleges also control a great deal of federal and state money channeled to students. This section shows you the pattern and extent of each college's current awards.

Detailed profiles present facts and statistics on more than 1,800 undergraduate institutions of higher education. The profiles, which appear in alphabetical order by school name, contain data supplied by each college and university for full-time

Where Our Information Comes From

The college data were collected in fall and winter 1999 and spring 2000 through Peterson's Annual Survey of Undergraduate Institutions and the associated Annual Survey of Undergraduate Financial Aid. We sent detailed questionnaires to more than 1,800 institutions of higher education that are accredited in the U.S. and U.S. territories and offer full four- or five-year baccalaureate degrees via full-time on-campus programs of study. Officials at the colleges—usually the financial aid or admission officers but sometimes the registrars or institutional research staff members—completed and returned the forms. We entered the information we received into our database, verifying anything that seemed unusual. Because of the comprehensive editorial review that takes place in our offices, we have every reason to believe that the data presented in this book are accurate. However, you should always confirm costs and other facts with a specific school at the time of application, since colleges can and do change policies and fees whenever necessary.

The state aid data presented in *Peterson's College Money Handbook 2001* were submitted by state officials (usually the director of the state scholarship commission) to Peterson's in the spring of 2000. Because regulations for any government-sponsored program may be changed at any time, you should request written descriptive materials from the office administering a program in which you are interested.

students enrolled as of the fall of 1999 (unless otherwise noted). Each profile provides specific information on expenses, basic facts about the school, a summary of the school's undergraduate financial aid programs, detailed data on need-based and non-need-based awards for freshmen and undergraduates and what is required to apply for each, money-saving options to consider, and the name, title, address, telephone and fax numbers, and e-mail address of the person to contact for further information.

College Financial Aid Indexes

Five indexes in the back of the book provide valuable information from the college profiles for easy reference. Prospective students with special abilities, interests, characteristics, or circumstances will find these indexes helpful. A listing of colleges that offer money-saving options and tuition payment plans is also included.

Non-Need Scholarships for Undergraduates

Lists colleges that offer non-need-based scholarships to undergraduates with specific academic strengths, talents in the creative or performing arts, and special achievements or activities and to students in a wide variety of particular circumstances. Some of these circumstances are students with parents in specific professions; residents of particular geographic areas; spouses, children, and siblings of other students; and handicapped students.

Athletic Grants for Undergraduates

Lists colleges that award athletic scholarships in each of twenty-nine sports.

ROTC Programs

Lists colleges that offer Reserve Officers' Training Corps programs in one or more of the armed services.

Tuition Waivers

Lists colleges that offer full or partial tuition waivers for minority students, children of alumni, adult students, or senior citizens.

Tuition Payment Alternatives

Lists colleges that offer tuition payment alternatives (deferred payment plans, guaranteed tuition plans, installment payment plans, and tuition prepayment plans).

SECTION 2

A Guide to Financing Your Child's College Education

by Don Betterton, Director of Undergraduate Financial Aid, Princeton University

iven the lifelong benefit of a college degree (college graduates are projected to earn in a lifetime $800,000 to $1 million more than those with only a high school diploma), higher education is a worthwhile investment. However, it is also an expensive one made even harder to manage by cost increases that have outpaced both inflation and gains in family income. This reality of higher education economics means that parental concern about how to pay a child's college costs is a dilemma that shows no sign of getting easier.

Because of the high cost involved (even the most inexpensive four-year education at a public institution costs about $10,000 a year), good information about college budgets and strategies for reducing the "sticker price" is essential. You have made a good start by taking the time to read *Peterson's College Money Handbook.* In the chapters that follow, you will find valuable information about the four main sources of aid—federal, state, college, and private. Before you learn about the various programs, however, it will be helpful if you have an overview of how the college financial aid system operates and what long-range financing strategies are available.

Financial Aid

Financial aid refers to money that is awarded to a student, usually in a "package" that consists of gift aid (commonly called a scholarship or grant), a student loan, and a campus job.

College Costs

The starting point for organizing a plan to pay for your college education is to make a good estimate of the yearly cost of attendance. You can use the College Cost Worksheet on the next page to do this.

To estimate your college costs for 2001–2002, refer to the tuition and fees and room and board figures shown in Section 7, College Financial Aid Profiles, and inflate 1999–2000 costs by 10 percent. If 2000–2001 costs are listed, inflate those numbers by 5 percent. If you will commute from your home, use $2000 instead of the college's room and board charges and $900 for transportation. We have used $750 for books and $1300 for personal expenses. Finally, estimate the cost of two round trips if your home is more than a few hundred miles from the college. Add the items to calculate the total budget. You should now have a reasonably good estimate of college costs for 2001–2002. (To determine the costs for later years, adding 5 percent per year will probably give you a fairly accurate estimate.)

Do You Qualify for Need-Based Aid?

The next step is to evaluate whether or not you are likely to qualify for financial aid based on need. This step is critical, since more than 90 percent of the yearly total of $65 billion in student aid is awarded only after a determination is made that the family lacks sufficient financial resources to pay the full cost of college on its own. To judge your chance of receiving need-based aid, it is necessary to estimate an Expected Family Contribution (EFC) according to a government formula known as the Federal Methodology (FM). You can do

College Cost Worksheet

	College 1	College 2	College 3	Commuter College
Tuition and Fees	______	______	______	______
Room and Board	______	______	______	$2,000
Books	$ 750	$ 750	$ 750	$ 750
Personal Expenses	$1,300	$1,300	$1,300	$1,300
Travel	______	______	______	$ 900
Total Budget	______	______	______	______

so by referring to the Family Contribution Table in this section.

Applying for Need-Based Aid

Because the federal government provides about 75 percent of all aid awarded, the application and need evaluation process is controlled by Congress and the U.S. Department of Education. The application is the Free Application for Federal Student Aid, or FAFSA. In addition, nearly every state that offers student assistance uses the federal government's system to award its own aid. You apply for a state scholarship (see Section 5) by checking a box on the FAFSA. Furthermore, many colleges, besides arranging for the payment of federal and state aid, use the FAFSA to award their own funds to needy students. (Note: In addition to the FAFSA, some colleges also ask the family to complete the PROFILE application. See the box titled **What is PROFILE?** in this section.)

The FAFSA is your "passport" to receiving your share of the billions of dollars awarded annually in need-based aid. If comparing your cost of attendance to your EFC shows that you might qualify for aid, pick up a FAFSA from the high school guidance office after mid-November 2000. This form will ask for 2000 financial data, and it should be filed after January 1, 2001, in time to meet the earliest college or state scholarship deadline. Within two to four weeks after you submit the form, you will receive a summary of the FAFSA information, called the Student Aid Report, or SAR. The SAR will give you the EFC and also allow you to make corrections to the data you submitted.

You can also apply for federal student aid over the Internet using FAFSA on the Web. FAFSA on the Web can be accessed at http://www.fafsa.ed.gov with Netscape Navigator 4.0 or higher and Microsoft Internet Explorer 4.0 or higher. (Note: Many colleges provide the option to apply for early decision admission. If you apply for this before January 1, 2001 which is prior to when the FAFSA can be used, follow the college's instructions. Many

How Need Is Calculated and Aid Is Awarded

	COLLEGE X	COLLEGE Y
Total Cost of Attendance	$10,000	$24,000
– Expected Family Contribution	– 5,500	– 5,500
= Financial Need	$ 4,500	$18,500
– Grant Aid Awarded	– 675	–14,575
– Campus Job (Work-Study) Awarded	– 1,400	– 1,300
– Student Loan Awarded	– 2,425	– 2,625
= Unmet Need	0	0

Note: Sometimes a college is unable to meet all need. The amount of unmet need is called "the gap."

Family Contribution Table

Consult the following family contribution table using estimated 2000 income and likely asset holdings as of December 31, 2000. First, locate the approximate parental contribution in the table. If more than one family member will be in college at least half-time during 2001–2002, divide the parental contribution by the number in college. If you have savings, add 35 percent of that amount. If you earned in excess of $2200 in 2000, include 50 percent of the amount over $2200 in the income figure. To see whether or not you might qualify for need-based aid, subtract the family contribution from each college's budget. If the family contribution is only a few thousand dollars over the budget, it is still worthwhile to apply for aid since this procedure is only intended to give you a preliminary estimate of college costs and your family contribution.

If you may be eligible for aid at one or more of the colleges, pay close attention to the section **Applying for Need-Based Aid**. If, on the other hand, the possibility of showing need seems unlikely, you should concentrate on the sections describing merit aid and financial planning.

Approximate Expected Family Contribution for 2001–2002

	INCOME BEFORE TAXES								
ASSETS	$ 20,000	30,000	40,000	50,000	60,000	70,000	80,000	90,000	100,000
$ 20,000 (FAMILY SIZE)									
3	$ 220	2,100	3,200	5,400	8,700	11,800	14,800	17,600	20,400
4	0	1,400	2,000	4,000	7,400	10,500	13,400	15,900	19,300
5	0	300	1,300	3,000	6,200	9,300	12,200	15,100	18,100
6	0	0	600	2,100	5,000	7,800	10,800	13,700	16,600
$ 30,000 (FAMILY SIZE)									
3	$ 220	2,100	3,200	5,400	8,700	11,800	14,800	17,600	20,400
4	0	1,400	2,000	4,000	7,400	10,500	13,400	15,900	19,300
5	0	300	1,300	3,000	6,200	9,300	12,200	15,100	18,100
6	0	0	600	2,100	5,000	7,800	10,800	13,700	16,600
$ 40,000 (FAMILY SIZE)									
3	$ 220	2,200	3,300	5,600	8,900	11,900	14,900	14,700	21,700
4	0	1,500	2,100	4,100	7,500	10,700	13,600	16,000	20,400
5	0	400	1,400	3,100	6,300	9,400	12,300	15,200	18,100
6	0	0	600	2,200	5,100	8,000	11,000	13,900	16,700
$ 50,000 (FAMILY SIZE)									
3	$ 600	2,500	3,800	6,200	9,500	12,500	15,500	18,300	21,200
4	0	1,800	2,400	4,600	8,200	11,300	14,200	16,700	20,000
5	0	600	1,600	3,500	6,900	10,000	12,900	15,700	18,700
6	0	0	900	2,500	5,700	8,600	11,600	14,500	17,300
$ 60,000 (FAMILY SIZE)									
3	$ 800	2,900	4,200	6,700	10,100	13,100	16,000	18,900	21,800
4	140	2,000	2,700	5,100	8,700	11,900	14,800	17,600	20,600
5	0	900	1,900	3,900	7,500	10,600	13,500	16,300	19,300
6	0	0	1,200	2,900	6,300	9,200	12,200	15,100	17,900
$ 80,000 (FAMILY SIZE)									
3	$ 1,400	3,500	5,100	7,800	11,000	14,200	17,100	20,000	22,900
4	600	2,600	3,400	6,100	9,800	12,900	15,700	18,300	21,600
5	0	1,400	2,500	4,800	8,600	11,700	14,600	17,400	20,400
6	0	300	1,700	3,600	7,300	10,200	13,200	16,000	19,100
$100,000 (FAMILY SIZE)									
3	$ 1,800	4,400	6,100	8,900	12,300	15,300	18,200	21,100	24,000
4	1,200	3,300	4,200	7,200	10,900	14,000	16,800	15,400	22,700
5	100	1,900	3,200	5,800	9,700	12,800	15,600	18,500	21,500
6	0	900	2,300	4,400	8,400	11,400	14,400	17,200	20,100
$120,000 (FAMILY SIZE)									
3	$ 2,500	5,300	7,300	10,100	13,400	16,300	19,300	22,300	25,100
4	1,700	4,100	5,100	8,400	12,100	15,200	18,000	20,600	23,900
5	600	2,500	4,000	6,900	10,800	13,900	16,600	19,600	22,600
6	250	1,400	2,900	5,400	9,600	12,500	15,500	18,300	21,200
$140,000 (FAMILY SIZE)									
3	$ 3,200	6,500	8,400	11,200	14,500	17,400	20,400	23,300	26,200
4	2,300	5,100	6,200	9,500	13,200	16,200	19,100	21,700	25,000
5	1,200	3,200	4,900	8,100	11,900	15,100	17,900	20,800	23,800
6	800	1,900	3,700	6,500	10,700	13,600	16,500	19,400	22,400

colleges use either PROFILE or their own application form for early admission candidates.)

Awarding Aid

About the same time you receive the SAR, the colleges you list will receive the FAFSA information so they can calculate a financial aid award in a package that typically includes aid from at least one of the major sources—federal, state, college, or private. In addition, the award will probably consist of a combination of a scholarship or a grant, a loan, and a campus job. These last two pieces—loan and job—are called self-help aid because they require effort on your part (that is, the aid must be either earned through work or paid back later). Scholarships or grants are outright gifts that have no such obligation.

It is important that you understand each part of the package. You'll want to know, for example, how much is gift aid, the interest rate and repayment terms of the student loan, and how many hours per week the campus job requires. There should be an enclosure with the award letter that answers these kinds of questions. If not, make a list of your questions and call or visit the financial aid office.

Once you understand the terms of each item in the award letter, you should turn your attention to the "bottom line"—how much you will have to pay at each college where you were admitted. In addition to understanding the aid award, this means having a good estimate of the college budget so you can accurately calculate how much you and your family will have to contribute (often, an aid package does not cover the entire need). Colleges follow different practices in how much detail they include in their award notifications. Many colleges provide full information—types and amounts of aid, yearly costs, and the EFC divided between the parent and student shares. If these important items are missing or incomplete, you can do the work on your own. (See the Comparing Financial Aid Awards and Family Contribution worksheet on this page.) For example, if only the college's direct charges for tuition, room, and board are shown on the award letter, make your own estimate of indirect costs like books, personal expenses, and travel. Then subtract the total aid awarded from the yearly budget to get the EFC. A portion of that amount may be your contribution (35 percent of your savings and 50 percent of earnings over $2200), and the remainder is the parental share. If you can afford this amount at your first-choice college, the financial aid system has worked well for you, and your college attendance plans can go forward.

Worksheet

Comparing Financial Aid Awards and Family Contribution

	College 1	College 2	College 3
Cost of Attendance	______	______	______
Aid Awarded	______	______	______
Grant/Scholarship	______	______	______
Loan	______	______	______
Job	______	______	______
Total Aid	______	______	______
Expected Family Contribution	______	______	______
Student Contribution	______	______	______
Parent Contribution	______	______	______

But if you think your EFC is too high, you should contact the college's financial aid office and ask whether additional aid is available. Many colleges, private high-cost colleges in particular, are enrollment-oriented—they are willing to work with families to help make attendance at their institutions possible. Most colleges also allow applicants to appeal their financial aid awards, the budget used for you, or any of the elements used to determine the family contribution, especially if there are extenuating circumstances or if the information has changed since the application was submitted. Some colleges may also reconsider an award based on a "competitive appeal," the submission of a more favorable award letter from another college.

If your appeal is unsuccessful and there is still a gap between the expected parental contribution and what you feel you can pay from income and savings, you are left with two choices. One option is to attend a college where paying your share of the bill will not be a problem. (This assumes that an affordable option was included on the original list of colleges, a wise admission application strategy.) The second is to look into alternate methods of financing. At this stage, parental loans and tuition payment plans are the available financing options. A parental loan can bring the yearly cost down to a manageable level by spreading payments over a number of years. This is the type of financing that families use when purchasing a home or automobile. A tuition payment plan is essentially a short-term loan and allows you to pay the costs over ten to twelve months. It is an option for families who have the resources available but need help with managing their cash flow. See the section on financing for more information.

Non-Need-Based Aid

Regardless of whether or not you might qualify for a need-based award, it is always worthwhile to look into merit, or non-need, scholarships from sources such as foundations, agencies, religious groups, and service organizations. For a family that isn't eligible for need-based aid, merit scholarships are the only form of gift aid available. If you later qualify for a need-based award, a merit scholarship can be quite helpful in providing additional resources when the aid does not fully cover the costs. Even if the college meets 100 percent of need, a merit scholarship can benefit you by reducing the self-help (loan and job) portion of an award.

In searching for merit-based scholarships, keep in mind that there are relatively few awards (compared to those that are need-based), and most of them are highly competitive. Looking for a merit scholarship is like betting on a long shot in a horse race—the chances of winning are slim, but the payoff can be large. Use the following checklist when investigating merit scholarships.

- Take advantage of any scholarships for which you are automatically eligible based on parents' employer benefits, military service, association or church membership, other affiliations, or student or parent attributes (ethnic background, nationality, etc.). Company or union tuition remissions are the most common examples of these awards.
- Look for other awards for which you might be eligible based on the characteristics and affiliations indicated above, but where there is a selection process and an application is required. Free computerized searches are available on the Internet (you should not pay a fee for a scholarship search). Scholarship directories, such as *Peterson's Scholarships, Grants & Prizes*, which details some 2,000 scholarship programs, are useful resources and can be found in bookstores, high school guidance offices, or public libraries.

> The financial aid award letter tells you the amount of discount to subtract from the college's "sticker price." You don't know how much college will cost until you've completed this step.

- Read Section 5 to see if your state has a merit scholarship program.
- Look into national scholarship competitions. High school guidance counselors usually know about these scholarships. Examples of these awards are the National Merit Scholarship, Coca-Cola Scholarship, Aid Association for Lutherans, Intel Science Talent Search, and the U.S. Senate Youth Program. *Winning Money for College* (Peterson's, 4th ed., 1997) provides detailed profiles of fifty of the most lucrative and prestigious competitions open to high school students.
- ROTC (Reserve Officers' Training Corps) scholarships are offered by the Army, Navy, Air Force, and Marine Corps. A full ROTC scholarship covers tuition, fees, and textbook costs. Acceptance of an ROTC scholarship entails a commitment to take military science courses and to serve for a specific number of years as an officer in the sponsoring branch of the service. Competition is heavy, and preference may be given to students in certain fields of study, such as engineering science. Application procedures vary by service. Contact an armed services recruiter or high school guidance counselor for further information.
- Investigate community scholarships. High school guidance counselors usually have a list of these awards, and announcements are published in local newspapers. Most common are awards given by service organizations like the American Legion, Rotary International, and the local women's club.

If you are strong academically (for example, a National Merit Commended Scholar or better) or is very talented in fields such as athletics or performing/creative arts, you may want to consider colleges that offer their own merit awards to gifted students they wish to enroll. Refer to the Non-Need Scholarships for Undergraduates Index for lists of colleges that award non-need scholarships.

In addition to merit scholarships, there are loan and job opportunities for students who do not qualify for need-based aid. Federal loan programs include the unsubsidized Federal Stafford and Direct Loans. See **Section 4: Federal Financial Aid Programs** for more information. Some of

What is PROFILE?

There are many complexities in the financial aid process: knowing which aid is merit-based and which aid is need-based; understanding the difference between grants, loans, and work-study; and determining whether funds are from federal, state, college, or private sources.

In addition, the aid application process itself can be complex. It can involve more than the Free Application for Federal Student Aid (FAFSA) and Federal Methodology (FM). Among the approximately 2,000 four-year colleges, about 400 are private institutions with more than $2 billion of their own scholarship money. Many of these colleges feel that the federal aid system (FAFSA and FM) does not collect or evaluate information thoroughly enough for them to award their institutional funds. These colleges have made an arrangement with the College Scholarship Service, a branch of the College Board, to establish a separate application system.

The application is called the PROFILE, and need formula is the Institutional Methodology (IM). If you apply for financial aid at one of the colleges that use PROFILE, the admission material will state that PROFILE is required in addition to the FAFSA. You should read the information carefully and file PROFILE to meet the earliest college deadline. Before you can receive PROFILE, however, you must register, either by phone or through the Web (http://www.collegeboard.org/finaid/fastud/html/proform.html), providing enough basic information so the PROFILE package can be designed specifically for you. The FAFSA is free, but there is a charge for PROFILE. As with the FAFSA, PROFILE can be submitted via the Internet.

In addition to the requirement by certain colleges that you submit both the FAFSA and PROFILE (when used, PROFILE is always in addition to the FAFSA; it does not replace it), you should also realize that each system has its own method for analyzing family ability to pay for college. The main differences between PROFILE's Institutional Methodology and the FAFSA's Federal Methodology are as follows:

- PROFILE includes equity in the family home as an asset; the FAFSA doesn't.
- PROFILE expects a minimum student contribution, usually in the form of summer earnings. The FAFSA has no such minimum.
- PROFILE allows for more professional judgment than the FAFSA. Medical expenses, private secondary school costs, and a variety of special circumstances are considered under PROFILE, subject to the discretion of the aid counselor on campus.

To summarize: PROFILE's Institutional Methodology tends to be both more complete in its data collection and more rigorous in its analysis than the FAFSA's Federal Methodology. When IM results are compared to FM results for thousands of applicants, IM will usually come up with a somewhat higher expected parental contribution than FM.

Creditworthiness

If you will be borrowing to pay for your college education, making sure you qualify for a loan is critical. For the most part, that means your credit record must be free of default or delinquency. You can check your credit history with one or more of the following three major credit bureaus and clean up any adverse information that appears. The numbers below will provide specific information on what you need to provide in order to obtain a report. You will need to send a signed written request and a fee (usually $8 or less) that varies depending upon the state in which you reside. All of the credit bureaus accept credit report requests over their Web sites. You will usually be asked to provide your full name, phone number, social security number, birth date, and addresses for the last five years.

Equifax, Inc.
P.O. Box 105496
Atlanta, GA 30348-5496
800-997-2493
http://www.equifax.com

Trans Union LLC
Consumer Disclosure Center
P.O. Box 1000
Chester, PA 19022
800-888-4213
http://www.tuc.com

Experian National Consumer Assistance Center
P.O. Box 2104
Allen, TX 75013-2104
888-397-3742
800-972-0322 (TTY/TDD)
http://www.experian.com/product/consumer/index.html

NOTE:

A point of clarification about whether to put college savings in the parents' or your name: If you are certain that you will not be a candidate for need-based aid, there may be a tax advantage to accumulating money in the your name. However, when it comes to maximizing aid eligibility, it is important to understand that student assets are assessed at a 35 percent rate and parental assets at about 5 percent. Therefore, if your college savings are in your name, it is wise to reestablish title to these funds before applying for financial aid.

the organizations that sponsor scholarships—for example, the Air Force Aid Society—also provide loans.

Work opportunities during the academic year are another type of assistance that is not restricted to aid recipients. Many colleges will, after assigning jobs to students on aid, open campus positions to all students looking for work. In addition, there are usually off-campus employment opportunities available to everyone.

Financing Your Child's College Education

In this section, "financing" means putting together resources to pay the balance due the college over and above payments from the primary sources of aid—scholarships, student loans, and jobs. Financing strategies are important because the high cost of a college education today often requires a family, whether or not it receives aid, to think about stretching their college payment beyond the four-year period of enrollment. For high-cost colleges, it is not unreasonable to think about a 10-4-10 plan: ten years of saving; four years of paying college bills out of current income, savings, and borrowing; and ten years to repay a parental loan.

Savings

Although saving for college is always a good idea, many families are unclear about its advantages. Families do not save for two reasons. First, after expenses have been covered, many families do not have much money to set aside. An affordable but regular savings plan through a payroll deduction is usually the answer to the problem of spending your entire paycheck every month.

The second reason that saving for college is not a high priority is the belief that the financial aid system penalizes a family by lowering aid eligibility. The Federal Methodology of need determination is very kind to savers. In fact, savings are ignored completely for families that earn less than $50,000. Savings in the form of home equity and retirement plans are excluded from the calculation. And even when savings are counted, a maximum of 5.6 percent of the total is expected each year. In other words, if a family has $40,000 in savings after an asset protection allowance is considered, the contribution is no greater than $2240, an amount very close to the yearly interest that is accumulated. Therefore, it is possible for a family to meet its savings contribution without depleting the face value of its investments.

A sensible savings plan is important because of the financial advantage of saving compared to borrowing. The amount of money students borrow for college is now greater than the amount they receive in grants and scholarships. With loans becoming so widespread, savings should be carefully considered as an alternative to borrowing. Every dollar you save is a dollar plus interest that you will not have to borrow and repay.

Borrowing

Once you've calculated your "bottom-line" parental contribution and determined that the amount is not affordable out of your current income and assets, the most likely alternative is borrowing. First determine if you are eligible for a larger subsidized Federal Stafford or Direct Loan. Because no interest is due while you attend college, these are the most favorable loans. If this is not possible, look into the unsubsidized Stafford or Direct Loan, which is not based on need but where the interest is due each year. The freshman year limit (either subsidized or unsubsidized) is $2625.

After you have taken out the maximum amount of student loans, the next step is to look into parental loans. The federal government's parent loan program is called PLUS and is the standard against which other loans should be judged. A local bank that participates in the PLUS program can give you a schedule of monthly repayments per $1000 borrowed. Use this repayment figure to compare other parental loans available from commercial lenders (including home equity loans), state programs, or colleges themselves. Choose the one that offers the best terms after all up-front costs, tax advantages, and the amount of monthly payments are considered.

Make Financial Aid Work for You

This overview is intended to provide you with a road map to help you think about financing strategies and navigate through the complexities of the financial aid process. Much of the information you will need to help you determine your plan to pay for your education can be found within the pages of this publication. First use the parental contribution tables in conjunction with the college cost worksheet to estimate need eligibility. If there is a chance you will qualify for aid, complete the FAFSA (and PROFILE, if required). At the same time, look into merit scholarships. Once you are accepted, use the Comparing Financial Aid Awards and Family Contribution Worksheet to figure out your parents' obligation. If you can't afford the payment, present your arguments to the college's financial aid office before checking out the terms of PLUS and other parental loan options. And finally, if there are younger children at home, think about starting a college savings fund to get a head start on future costs.

If you are like millions of families that benefit from financial aid, it is likely that your college plans can go forward without undue worry about the costs involved. The key is to understand the financial aid system and to follow the best path for your family. The result of good information and good planning should be that you will receive your fair share of the billions of dollars available each year and that the cost of college will not prevent you from attending.

SECTION 3

Common Questions Answered

Q ***Are a student's chances of being admitted to a college reduced if the student applies for financial aid?***

A Generally not. Nearly all colleges have a policy of "need-blind" admissions, which means that a student's financial need is not taken into account in the admission decision. There are a few selective colleges, however, that do consider ability to pay before deciding whether or not to admit a student. Some colleges will mention this in their literature; others may not. The best advice is to apply for financial aid if the student needs assistance to attend college.

Q ***Are parents penalized for saving money for college?***

A No. As a matter of fact, families that have made a concerted effort to save money for college are in a much better position than those that have not. For example, a student from a family that has saved money may not have to borrow as much. Furthermore, the "taxing rate" on savings is quite low—only about 5 percent of the parents' assets are assessed and neither the home equity nor retirement savings are included. For example, a single 40-year-old parent who saved $40,000 for college expenses will have about $1900 counted as part of the parental contribution. Two parents, if the older one is 40 years old (a parent's age factors into the formula-tion), would have about $300 counted. (Note: The "taxing rate" for student assets is much higher—35 percent—compared to 5 percent for parents.)

Q ***How does the financial aid system work in cases of divorce or separation? How are step-parents treated?***

A In cases of divorce or separation, the financial aid application(s) should be completed by the parent with whom the student lived for the longest period of time in the last twelve months. If the custodial parent has remarried, the step-parent is considered a family member and must complete the application along with the natural parent. If your family has any special circumstances, you can discuss these directly with the financial aid office. (Note: Colleges that award their own aid may ask the noncustodial natural parent to complete a separate aid application and a contribu-tion will be calculated.)

Q ***When are students considered independent of parental support in applying for financial aid?***

A The student must be at least 24 years of age in order to be considered independent. If younger than 24, the student must be married, a graduate or professional student, have legal dependents other than a spouse, be an orphan or ward of the court, or a veteran of the armed forces.

Q ***What can a family do if a job loss occurs?***

A Financial aid eligibility is based on the previous year's income. So the family's 2000 income would be reported to determine eligibility for the 2001–2002 academic year. In that way, the family's income can be verified with an income tax return. But the previous year's income may not accurately reflect the cur-rent financial situation, particularly if a par-ent lost a job or retired. In these instances, the projected income for the coming year can be used instead. Families should discuss the situation directly with the financial aid office and be prepared to provide appropri-ate documentation.

Q ***When my daughter first went to college, we applied for financial aid and were denied because our expected family contribution was too high. Now, my son is a high school senior, and we will soon have two in college. Will we get the same results?***

A The results will definitely be different. Both your son and your daughter should apply. As we described earlier, need-based financial aid is based on your expected family contribution, or EFC. When you have two children in college, this amount is divided in half for each child.

Q ***I've heard about the "middle-income squeeze" in regard to financial aid. What is it?***

A The so-called "middle-income squeeze" is the idea that low-income families qualify for aid, high-income families have adequate resources to pay for education, and those in the middle are caught in between, not eligible for aid but without the ability to pay full college costs. There is no provision in the Federal Methodology that treats middle-income students differently than others (such as an income cutoff for eligibility). The Expected Family Contribution rises proportionately as income and assets increase. If a middle-income family does not qualify for aid, it is because the need analysis formula yields a contribution that exceeds college costs. But keep in mind that if a $60,000-income family does not qualify for aid at a public university with a $10,000 budget, the same family will likely be eligible for aid at a private college with a cost of $25,000 or more. Also, there are now loan programs available to parents and students that are not based on need. Middle-income families should realize, however, that many of the grant programs funded by federal and state governments are directed at lower-income families. It is therefore likely that a larger share of an aid package for a middle-income student will consist of loans rather than grants.

Q ***Given our financial condition, my daughter will be receiving financial aid. We will help out as much as we can, and, in fact, we ourselves will be borrowing. But I am concerned that she will have to take on a lot of loans in order to go to the college of her choice. Does she have any options?***

A She does. If offered a loan, she can decline all or part of it. One option is for her to ask in the financial aid office to have some of the loan changed to a work-study job. If this is not possible, she can find her own part-time work. Often there is an employment office on campus that can help her locate a job. In most cases, the more she works, the less she has to borrow.

Q ***Is it possible to change your financial aid package?***

A Yes. Most colleges have an appeal process. A request to change a need-based loan to a work-study job is usually approved if funds are available. A request to consider special financial circumstances may also be granted. At most colleges, a request for more grant money is rarely approved unless it is based on a change in the information reported. Applicants should speak with the financial aid office if they have reasons for a concern about their financial appeal. Some colleges may even respond to a competitive appeal, that is, a request to match another college's offer.

Q ***My son was awarded a Federal Stafford Loan as part of his financial aid package. His award letter also indicated that we could take out a PLUS loan. How do we go about choosing our lender? Do we go to our local bank?***

A Read the material that came with the financial aid award letter. It is likely that the college has an "approved lender" list for Stafford and PLUS Loans. Although you can borrow from any bank, your loan application will be processed more quickly if you use a lender approved by the college.

Q ***The cost of attending college seems to be going up so much faster than the Consumer Price Index. Why is that, and how can I plan for my child's four years?***

A The cost of higher education cannot be compared to the Consumer Price Index. The CPI does not take into account most of the costs faced by colleges. For example, the dollars that universities spend on grants and scholarships have risen at a rapid rate. Second, many universities have increased enrollment of students from less affluent families, further increasing the need for institutional financial aid. Third, colleges are expected to be on the cutting edge of technology, not only in research but also in the classroom and in the library. Last, during the high inflation years of the 1970s, most colleges deferred needed maintenance and repairs that can no longer be put off. In general, you can expect that college costs will rise about 2 to 3 percent faster than inflation.

Q ***I will be receiving a scholarship from my local high school. How will this scholarship be treated in my financial aid award?***

A Federal student aid regulations specify that all forms of aid must be included within the defined level of need. This means that additional aid such as outside scholarships must be combined with any need-based aid you receive; it may not be kept separate and used to reduce your family's contribution. If the college has not filled 100 percent of your need, it will usually allow outside scholarships to close the gap. Once your total need has been met, however, the college must reduce other aid and replace it with the outside award. Most colleges will allow you to use some, if not all, of an outside scholarship to replace self-help aid (loans and Federal Work-Study) rather than grant aid.

Q ***I know we're supposed to apply for financial aid as soon as possible after January 1. What if I don't have my W-2's yet and my tax return isn't done?***

A The first financial aid application deadlines usually fall in early February, and many are much later. Chances are you'll have your W-2 forms by then, but you won't have a completed tax return. If that is the case, complete the financial aid application using your best estimates. Then, when you receive the Student Aid Report (SAR), you can use your tax return to make corrections.

Q ***Is there enough aid available to make it worthwhile for me to consider colleges that are more expensive than I can afford?***

A Definitely. More than $65 billion in aid is awarded to undergraduates every year. With more than half of all enrolled students qualifying for some type of assistance, this totals more than $5500 per student. You should view financial aid as a large, national system of tuition discounts, some given according to a student's ability and talent, others based on what a student's family can afford to pay. If you qualify for need-based financial aid, you will essentially pay only your calculated family contribution, regardless of the cost of the college. You will not pay the "sticker price" (the cost of attendance listed in the college catalog) but a lower rate that is reduced by the amount of aid you receive. No college should be ruled out until after financial aid is considered. In addition, when deciding which college to attend, consider that the short-term cost of a college education is only one criterion. If the college meets your educational needs and you are convinced it can launch you on an exciting career, a significant up-front investment may turn out to be a bargain over the long run.

Q ***If I don't qualify for need-based aid, what options are available?***

A You should try to put together your own aid package to help reduce your parents' share. There are three sources to look into. First is to search for merit scholarships. Second is to seek employment, during both the summer and the academic year. The student employment office should be able to help you find a campus job. Third is borrowing. Even if you don't qualify for the need-based loan programs, the unsubsidized Federal Stafford and Direct Loans are available to all students. The terms and conditions are the same as the subsidized loan programs except that interest accrues while you are in college.

After you have contributed what you can through scholarships, employment, and loans, your parents will be faced with their share of the college bill. Many colleges have monthly payment plans that allow families to spread their payments over the academic year. If these monthly payments turn out to be more than your parents can afford, they can take out a parent loan. By borrowing from the college itself, from a commercial agency or lender, or through PLUS, parents can extend their college payments over a ten-year period or longer. Borrowing reduces the monthly obligation to its lowest level, but the total amount paid will be the highest due to principal and interest payments.

SECTION 4

Federal Financial Aid Programs

There are a number of sources of financial aid available to students: federal and state governments, private agencies, and the colleges themselves. In addition, as discussed earlier, there are three different forms of aid: grants, earnings, and loans.

The federal government is the single largest source of financial aid for students. In the 2000–2001 academic year, the U.S. Department of Education's student financial aid programs will make $46 billion available in loans, grants, and other aid to 8.8 million students. At the present time, there are two federal grant programs—the Federal Pell Grant and the Federal Supplemental Educational Opportunity Grant (FSEOG). There are three federal loan programs: the Federal Perkins Loan, the Direct Loan, and the Stafford Loan. The federal government also has a job program, Federal Work-Study, or FWS, that helps colleges provide employment for students. In addition to the student aid programs, there are also tuition tax credits. They are the HOPE Scholarship for freshmen and sophomores and the Lifetime Learning Tax Credit for undergraduate students after their second year and graduate students. Both programs work the same way. The federal tax bill is reduced by the amount of tuition paid up to specified limits.

Ninety-two percent of federal higher education loans are either Direct or Stafford. The difference between these loans is the lending source, but for the borrower, the difference is virtually invisible. Both Direct and Stafford programs make available two kinds of loans: Stafford Loans to students and PLUS Loans to parents. Stafford Loans are either subsidized or unsubsidized. Subsidized Stafford Loans are made on the basis of demonstrated student need and have their interest paid by the government during the time you are in school. For the non-need-based loans, the unsubsidized Stafford Loans and PLUS Loans, interest begins to accrue as soon as the money is received.

To qualify for the Pell and FSEOG programs, Federal Work-Study, the Perkins Loan, and the subsidized Stafford Loan, you must demonstrate financial need.

Federal Pell Grant

The Federal Pell Grant is the largest grant program; almost 4 million students received Pell Grants last year. This grant is intended to be the starting point of assistance for lower-income families. Eligibility for a Federal Pell Grant depends on the Expected Family Contribution (EFC). The amount you receive will depend on your EFC and the cost of education at the college you will attend. The highest award depends on how much the program is funded. The maximum for 2000–2001 is $3300, but this amount is expected to increase in 2001.

Table Used to Estimate Federal Pell Grants for 2000–2001

Adjusted Gross Income	Family Assets							
	$50,000	$55,000	$60,000	$65,000	$70,000	$75,000	$80,000	$85,000
$ 5,000	$3,300	$3,300	$3,300	$3,300	$3,300	$3,300	$3,300	$3,300
$10,000	3,300	3,300	3,300	3,300	3,300	3,300	3,300	3,300
$15,000	3,300	3,300	3,300	3,300	3,300	3,200	3,000	2,900
$20,000	2,900	2,700	2,500	2,400	2,300	2,200	2,100	2,000
$25,000	2,000	1,800	1,700	1,600	1,400	1,300	1,200	1,000
$30,000	1,000	900	700	600	600	0	0	0
$35,000	400	400	400	400	0	0	0	0

Note: Based on family of four, one child enrolled in college, oldest parent age 41.

To give you some idea of your possible eligibility for a Pell Grant, the table in this section may be helpful. The amounts shown are based on a family of 4, with one student in college, no emergency expenses, no contribution from student income or assets, and college costs of at least $3300 per year.

Federal Financial Aid Programs

Name of Program	Type of Program	Maximum Award Per Year
Federal Pell Grant	Need-based grant	$3300
Federal Supplemental Educational Opportunity Grant (FSEOG)	Need-based grant	$4000
Federal Work-Study	Need-based part-time job	no maximum
Federal Perkins Loan	Need-based loan	$4000
Subsidized Stafford/ Direct Loan	Need-based student loan	$2625 (first year)
Unsubsidized Stafford/ Direct Loan	Non-need-based student loan	$2625 (first year, dependent student)
PLUS Loans	Non-need-based parent loan	Up to the cost of education

Note: Both Direct and Stafford Loans have higher maximums after the freshman year.

Federal Supplemental Educational Opportunity Grant (FSEOG)

As its name implies, the Federal Supplemental Educational Opportunity Grant provides additional need-based federal grant money to supplement the Federal Pell Grant. Each participating college is given funds to award to especially needy students. The maximum award is $4000 per year, but the amount you receive depends on the college's policy, the availability of FSEOG funds, the total cost of education, and the amount of other aid awarded.

Federal Work-Study (FWS)

This program provides jobs for students who demonstrate need. Salaries are paid by funds from the federal government as well as the college. You work on an hourly basis on or off campus and must be paid at least the federal minimum wage. You may earn only up to the amount awarded in the financial aid package.

Federal Perkins Loan

This loan is a low-interest (5 percent) loan for students with exceptional financial need. Federal Perkins Loans are made through the college's financial aid office with the college as the lender. You can borrow a maximum of $4000 per year for up to five years of undergraduate study. Borrowers may take up to ten years to repay the loan, beginning nine months after they graduate, leave school, or drop below half-time status. No interest accrues while they are in school, and, under certain conditions (e.g., they teach in low-income areas, work in law enforcement, are full-time nurses or medical technicians, serve as Peace Corps or VISTA volunteers, etc.), some or all of the loan can be canceled. In addition, payments can be deferred under certain conditions such as unemployment.

Stafford and Direct Loans

Stafford and Direct Loans have the same interest rates, loan maximums, deferments, and cancellation benefits. A Stafford Loan may be borrowed from a commercial lender, such as a bank or credit union. A Direct Loan is borrowed directly from the U.S. Department of Education.

The interest rate varies annually (there is a maximum of 8.25 percent), and the rate for 1999–2000 was 6.92 percent during repayment and 6.32 percent while you are in college. If you qualify for a need-based subsidized Stafford Loan, the interest is paid by the federal government while you are enrolled in college. There is also an unsubsidized Stafford Loan that is not based on need for which you are eligible regardless of your family income.

The maximum amount dependent students may borrow in any one year is $2625 for freshmen, $3500 for sophomores, and $5500 for juniors and seniors, with a maximum of $23,000 for the total undergraduate program. The maximum amount independent students can borrow is $6625 for freshmen (of which no more than $2625 can be subsidized), $7500 for sophomores (of which no more than $3500 can be subsidized), and $10,500 for juniors and seniors (of which no more than $5500 can be subsidized). Borrowers must pay a 3 percent fee, which is deducted from the loan proceeds.

To apply for a Stafford Loan, you must first complete a FAFSA to determine eligibility for a subsidized loan and then complete a separate loan application that is submitted to a lender. The financial aid office can help in selecting a lender. The lender will send a promissory note where you agree to repay the loan. The proceeds of the loan, less the origination fee, will be sent to the college to be either credited to your account or released to you directly.

Once the repayment period starts, borrowers of both subsidized and unsubsidized Stafford or Direct Loans will have to pay a combination of interest and principal monthly for up to a ten-year period.

PLUS Loans

PLUS is for parents of dependent students to help families with cash-flow problems. There is no needs test to qualify. The loan has a variable interest rate that cannot exceed 9 percent (the rate for 1999-2000 was 7.7 percent). There is no yearly limit; you can borrow up to the cost of your education, less other financial aid received. Repayment begins sixty days after the money is advanced. A 3 or 4 percent fee is subtracted from the proceeds. Parent borrowers must generally have a good credit record to qualify. PLUS Loans may be processed under either the Direct or Stafford Loan system, depending on the type of loan program for which the college has contracted.

Tuition Tax Credits

Tuition tax credits allow families to reduce their tax bill by the amount of out-of-pocket college tuition expense. Unlike a tax deduction, which is modified according to your tax bracket, a tax credit is a dollar-for-dollar reduction in taxes paid.

There are two programs: the HOPE Scholarship and the Lifetime Learning Tax Credit. As is true of many federal programs, there are numerous rules and restrictions that apply. You should check with your tax preparer or financial adviser for information about your own particular situation.

HOPE Scholarship

The HOPE Scholarship offsets some of the expense for the first two years of college or vocational school. Students or the parents of dependent students can claim an annual income tax credit of up to $1500—100 percent of the first $1000 of tuition and required fees and 50 percent credit of the second $1000. Grants, scholarships, and other tax-free educational assistance must be deducted from the total tuition and fee payments.

This credit can be claimed for students who are in their first two years of college and who are enrolled on at least a half-time basis in a degree or certificate program for any portion of the year. This credit phases out for joint filers who have an income between $80,000 and $100,000 and for single filers who have between $40,000 and $50,000 of income. Parents may claim credits for more than one qualifying student.

Lifetime Learning Tax Credit

The Lifetime Learning Tax Credit is the counterpart of the HOPE Scholarship for college juniors, seniors, graduate students, and part-time students pursuing lifelong learning to improve or upgrade their job skills. The qualifying taxpayer can claim an annual tax credit of up to $1000—20 percent of the first $5000 of tuition. The credit is available for net tuition and fees, less grant aid. The total credit available is limited to $1000 per year per taxpayer (or joint-filing couple), and is phased out at the same income levels as the HOPE Scholarship.

AmeriCorps

AmeriCorps is a national umbrella group of service programs for students. Participants work in a public or private nonprofit agency and provide service to the community in one of four priority areas: education, human services, the environment, and public safety. In exchange, you earn a stipend (for living expenses) of between $7400 and $14,800 a year, health insurance coverage, and $4725 per year for up to two years to apply toward college expenses. Many student-loan lenders will postpone the repayment of student loans during service in AmeriCorps, and AmeriCorps will pay the interest that is accrued on qualified student loans for members who complete the service program. You can work before, during, or after you go to college and can use the funds to either pay current educational expenses or repay federal student loans. The AmeriCorps Web site is http://www.americorps.org. Speak to a college financial aid officer for more details about this program.

SECTION 5

State Scholarship and Grant Programs

Each state government has established one or more state-administered financial aid programs for qualified students. In many instances, these state programs are restricted to legal residents of the state. However, they often are available to out-of-state students who will be or are attending colleges or universities within the state. In addition to residential status, other qualifications frequently exist.

Gift aid and forgivable loan programs open to undergraduate and graduate students for all states and the District of Columbia are described on the following pages. They are arranged in alphabetical order, first by state name, then by program name. The annotation for each program provides information about the program, eligibility, and the contact addresses for applications or further information. Unless otherwise stated, this information refers to awards for 2000–2001. Information is provided by the state-sponsoring agency in response to Peterson's Annual Survey of Non-institutional Aid, which was conducted between November 1999 and April 2000. Information is accurate when Peterson's receives it. However, it is always advisable to check with the sponsor to ascertain that the information remains correct.

You should write to the address given for each program to request that award details for 2001–2002 be sent to them as soon as they are available. Descriptive information brochures and application forms for state scholarship programs are usually available from the financial aid offices of public colleges or universities within the specific state. High school guidance offices often have information and relevant forms for awards for which high school seniors may be eligible. Increasingly, state government agencies are putting state scholarship information on state government agency Web sites. In searching state government Web sites, however, you should be aware that the higher education agency in many states is separate from the state's general education office, which is often responsible only for elementary and secondary education. Also, the page at public university Web sites that provides information about student financial aid frequently has a list of state-sponsored scholarships and financial aid programs. College and university Web sites can be easily accessed through Peterson's CollegeQuest (http://www.CollegeQuest.com).

Names of scholarship programs are frequently used inconsistently or become abbreviated in popular usage. Many programs have variant names by which they are known. The program's sponsor has approved the title of the program that Peterson's uses in this guide, yet this name may differ from the program's official name or from its most commonly used name.

In addition to the grant aid and forgivable loan programs listed on the following pages, states may also offer internship or work-study programs, graduate fellowships and grants, or low-interest loans. If you are interested in learning more about these other kinds of programs, the state education office that supplies information or applications for the undergraduate scholarship programs listed here should be able to provide information about other kinds of higher education financial aid programs that are sponsored by the state.

ALABAMA

Nursing Scholarship Program-Alabama. For Alabama residents enrolled in approved nursing programs at colleges within the state. Must agree to practice nursing in Alabama for at least one year. Deadlines vary. Contact college financial aid office. Renewable. Applicant must remain in nursing program through its completion or scholarship must be repaid. *Academic/Career Areas:* Nursing. *Award:* Scholarship for use in any year; renewable. *Eligibility Requirements:* Applicant must be enrolled at a four-year institution; resident of Alabama and studying in Alabama. *Application Requirements:* Application.

Contact Dr. William Wall, Director of Grants and Scholarships, Alabama Commission on Higher Education, PO Box 302000, Montgomery, AL 36130. *Web site:* http://www.ache.state.al.us.

American Legion Auxiliary Department of Alabama Scholarship Program. Several scholarships for Alabama residents, preferably ages 17-25, who are children or grandchildren of veterans of World War I, World War II, Korea, Vietnam, Operation Desert Storm, Beirut, Grenada, or Panama. Submit proof of relationship and service record. Merit-based. Renewable awards of $850 each. Send self-addressed stamped envelope for application. *Award:* Scholarship for use in any year; renewable. *Award amount:* $850. *Number of awards:* 40. *Eligibility Requirements:* Applicant must be age 17-25; enrolled at a four-year institution; resident of Alabama and studying in Alabama. Applicant must have 3.5 GPA or higher. Applicant or parent must meet one or more of the following requirements: general military experience; retired from active duty; disabled or killed as a result of military service; prisoner of war; or missing in action. *Application Requirements:* Application, financial need analysis, photo, references, self-addressed stamped envelope, test scores, transcript. *Deadline:* April 1.

Contact Debora Stephens, Department Secretary, American Legion Auxiliary, Department of Alabama, 120 North Jackson Street, Montgomery, AL 36104-3811. *Phone:* 334-262-1176.

Alabama G.I. Dependents Scholarship Program. Full scholarship for dependents of Alabama disabled, prisoner of war, or missing-in-action veterans. Child or stepchild must initiate training before 26th birthday; age 30 deadline may apply in certain situations. No age deadline for spouses or widows. Contact for application procedures and deadline. *Award:* Scholarship for use in any year; renewable. *Eligibility Requirements:* Applicant must be enrolled at a two-year, four-year, or technical institution or university; resident of Alabama and studying in Alabama. Applicant or parent must meet one or more of the following requirements: general military experience; retired from active duty; disabled or killed as a result of military service; prisoner of war; or missing in action. *Application Requirements:* Application.

Contact Edward Minter, III, Scholarship Administrator, Alabama State Department of Veteran's Affairs, PO Box 1509, Montgomery, AL 36102-1509. *E-mail:* ed.minter@vaonline.va.gov. *Phone:* 334-242-5077. *Fax:* 334-242-5102.

Junior and Community College Performing Arts Scholarship-Alabama. Awards are for students of Alabama public junior and community colleges with talent in performing arts. Based on demonstrated ability. Must be Alabama resident enrolled full-time. Deadlines vary. One-time award. *Academic/Career Areas:* Performing Arts. *Award:* Scholarship for use in freshman or sophomore year; not renewable. *Eligibility Requirements:* Applicant must be enrolled at a two-year institution; resident of Alabama and studying in Alabama. *Application Requirements:* Application.

Contact Dr. William Wall, Director of Grants and Scholarships, Alabama Commission on Higher Education, PO Box 302000, Montgomery, AL 36130. *Web site:* http://www.ache.state.al.us.

Senior Adult Scholarship Program-Alabama. Available to Alabama residents over 60 for use at any two-year public institution in the state. Award is full tuition. Deadlines vary by institution. Award is renewable. *Award:* Scholarship for use in freshman or sophomore year; renewable. *Eligibility Requirements:* Applicant must be age 60; enrolled at a two-year or technical institution; resident of Alabama and studying in Alabama. *Application Requirements:* Application.

Contact Dr. William Wall, Director of Grants and Scholarships, Alabama Commission on Higher Education, PO Box 302000, Montgomery, AL 36130. *Web site:* http://www.ache.state.al.us.

Alabama National Guard Educational Assistance Program. Aids Alabama residents who are members of the Alabama National Guard and are enrolled in an accredited college in Alabama. Award is renewable. Forms must be signed by a representative of the Alabama Military Department and financial aid officer. Recipient must be in a degree-seeking program. *Award:* Scholarship for use in any year; renewable. *Award amount:* up to $1000. *Eligibility Requirements:* Applicant must be enrolled at a two-year or four-year institution; resident of Alabama and studying in Alabama. Applicant must have served in the Air Force National Guard or Army National Guard. *Application Requirements:* Application.

Contact Dr. William Wall, Director of Grants and Scholarships, Alabama Commission on Higher Education, PO Box 302000, Montgomery, AL 36130. *Web site:* http://www.ache.state.al.us.

Junior and Community College Athletic Scholarships-Alabama. Awards are for students of Alabama public junior and community colleges with talent in athletics. Renewable awards based on demonstrated ability. Must be Alabama resident enrolled full-time. Deadlines vary. *Award:* Scholarship for use in freshman or sophomore year; renewable. *Eligibility Requirements:* Applicant must be enrolled at a two-year institution; resident of Alabama; studying in Alabama and must have an interest in athletics/sports. *Application Requirements:* Application.

Contact Dr. William Wall, Director of Grants and Scholarships, Alabama Commission on Higher Education, PO Box

302000, Montgomery, AL 36130. *Web site:* http://www.ache.state.al.us.

Police Officers and Firefighters Survivors Education Assistance Program-Alabama. Provides tuition, fees, books, and supplies to dependents of full-time police officers and firefighters killed in the line of duty. Must attend any Alabama public college as an undergraduate. Must be Alabama resident. Renewable. *Award:* Scholarship for use in freshman, sophomore, junior, or senior year; renewable. *Eligibility Requirements:* Applicant must be enrolled at a two-year, four-year, or technical institution or university; single; resident of Alabama; studying in Alabama and have employment experience in police/firefighting. Restricted to U.S. citizens. *Application Requirements:* Application, transcript.

Contact Dr. William Wall, Director of Grants and Scholarships, Alabama Commission on Higher Education, PO Box 302000, Montgomery, AL 36130. *Web site:* http://www.ache.state.al.us.

Alabama Student Grant Program. Available to Alabama residents for undergraduate study at certain independent colleges within the state. Both full-time and half-time students are eligible. Deadlines: September 15, January 15, and February 15. Renewable award of up to $1200. *Award:* Scholarship for use in freshman, sophomore, junior, or senior year; renewable. *Award amount:* up to $1200. *Eligibility Requirements:* Applicant must be enrolled at a four-year institution; resident of Alabama and studying in Alabama. *Application Requirements:* Application.

Contact Dr. William Wall, Director of Grants and Scholarships, Alabama Commission on Higher Education, PO Box 302000, Montgomery, AL 36130. *Web site:* http://www.ache.state.al.us.

Two-Year College Academic Scholarship Program/Alabama. Award for Alabama residents enrolled in two-year post-secondary school in the state. Must have at least a 2.5 GPA. Awards are renewable if students maintain academic excellence. Deadlines vary from school to school. *Award:* Scholarship for use in freshman or sophomore year; renewable. *Eligibility Requirements:* Applicant must be enrolled at a two-year or technical institution; resident of Alabama and studying in Alabama. Applicant must have 2.5 GPA or higher. *Application Requirements:* Application, transcript.

Contact Dr. William Wall, Director of Grants and Scholarships, Alabama Commission on Higher Education, PO Box 302000, Montgomery, AL 36130. *Web site:* http://www.ache.state.al.us.

Technology Scholarship Program for Alabama Teachers. Scholarship not to exceed graduate tuition and fees at an approved Alabama institution. Must be full-time certified Alabama teacher enrolled in courses that incorporate new technology into curriculum. One-time award. Required courses must be completed or scholarship must be repaid. *Award:* Scholarship for use in graduate years; not renewable. *Eligibility Requirements:* Applicant must be resident of Alabama; studying in Alabama and have employment experience in teaching. Applicant must have 3.0 GPA or higher. *Application Requirements:* Application.

Contact Dr. William Wall, Director of Grants and Scholarships, Alabama Commission on Higher Education, PO Box 302000, Montgomery, AL 36130. *Web site:* http://www.ache.state.al.us.

Alabama Scholarships for Dependents of Blind Parents. Educational benefits in institutions of higher learning in Alabama for children from families in which the head of the family is blind and whose family income is insufficient to provide such educational benefits. Must be Alabama resident. *Award:* Scholarship for use in freshman, sophomore, junior, or senior year; renewable. *Award amount:* $500–$2500. *Eligibility Requirements:* Applicant must be age 18-23; enrolled at a two-year, four-year, or technical institution or university; resident of Alabama and studying in Alabama. Restricted to U.S. citizens. *Application Requirements:* Application, financial need analysis. *Deadline:* continuous.

Contact Terry Longest, Education Specialist, Alabama State Department of Education, Special Education Services, PO Box 302101, Montgomery, AL 36130. *E-mail:* tlongest@sdenet.alsde.edu. *Phone:* 334-242-8114. *Fax:* 334-242-9192.

ALASKA

Western Undergraduate Exchange (WUE) Program. Program allowing Alaska residents to enroll at two- or four-year institutions in participating states at a reduced tuition level, which is the in-state tuition plus 50% of that amount. To be used for full-time undergraduate studies. Contact for application procedures, requirements, deadlines, and further information. *Award:* Grant for use in freshman, sophomore, junior, or senior year; renewable. *Eligibility Requirements:* Applicant must be enrolled at a two-year or four-year institution and resident of Alaska.

Contact Fred Tolbert, Administrative Assistant, Special Programs, Alaska Commission on Postsecondary Education, 3030 Vintage Boulevard, Juneau, AK 99801-7109. *E-mail:* ftolbert@acpe.state.ak.us. *Phone:* 907-465-6741. *Fax:* 907-465-5316.

Michael Murphy Memorial Scholarship Loan Fund. Assists full-time undergraduate or graduate students enrolled in a program relating to law enforcement. Recipient receives forgiveness of 20 percent of the full loan amount for each year employed in law enforcement. Must be Alaska resident. *Academic/Career Areas:* Criminal Justice/Criminology; Law Enforcement/Police Administration; Social Services. *Award:* Forgivable loan for use in any year; renewable. *Award amount:* up to $1000. *Number of awards:* 3–6. *Eligibility Requirements:* Applicant must be enrolled at a two-year or four-year institution or university and resident of Alaska. *Application Requirements:* Application. *Deadline:* April 1.

Contact Ralph Reyes, First Sergeant, Alaska State Troopers, 5700 East Tudor Road, Anchorage, AK 99507. *Phone:* 907-269-5759. *Fax:* 907-269-5751. *Web site:* http://www.dps.state.ak.us/ast.

Alaska Commission on Postsecondary Education Teacher Education Scholarship Loan. Renewable loans for Alaska residents who are graduates of an Alaskan high school and pursuing teaching careers in rural elementary and secondary schools in Alaska. Must be nominated by rural school district. Eligible for 100% forgiveness if loan recipient teaches in Alaska upon graduation. Several awards of up to $7500 each. Must maintain good standing at institution. Contact for deadline. *Academic/Career Areas:* Education. *Award:* Forgivable loan for use in freshman, sophomore, junior, or senior year; renewable. *Award amount:* up to $7500. *Number of awards:* 200–220. *Eligibility Requirements:* Applicant must be enrolled at a four-year institution or university; resident of Alaska and studying in Alaska. *Application Requirements:* Application, transcript.

Contact Fred Tolbert, Administrative Assistant, Special Programs, Alaska Commission on Postsecondary Education, 3030 Vintage Boulevard, Juneau, AK 99801-7109. *E-mail:* ftolbert@acpe.state.ak.us. *Phone:* 907-465-6741. *Fax:* 907-465-5316.

ARIZONA

Tucson Osteopathic Medical Foundation Scholarship/Loan Program. Award for Arizona residents enrolled in osteopathic medical college. Preference given to residents of southeastern counties of Arizona. Must file Graduate and Professional Student Financial Aid application. Write for deadline and further information. One-time award of $6000 to $10,000. A percentage per year is forgiven for students who practice in a Southern Arizona county upon graduation. *Academic/Career Areas:* Health and Medical Sciences. *Award:* Forgivable loan for use in graduate years; not renewable. *Award amount:* $6000–$10,000. *Number of awards:* 6–10. *Eligibility Requirements:* Applicant must be resident of Arizona. *Application Requirements:* Application, financial need analysis, interview, references, transcript.

Contact Jenny Jones, Medical Education Manager, State of Arizona, 4280 North Campbell Avenue, Suite 200, Tucson, AZ 85718. *Phone:* 520-299-4545. *Fax:* 520-299-4609. *Web site:* http://www.tomf.org.

ARKANSAS

Governor's Scholars—Arkansas. Awards for outstanding Arkansas high school seniors. Must be an Arkansas resident and have a high school GPA of at least 3.6 or have scored at least 27 on the ACT. Award is $4000 per year for four years of full-time undergraduate study. Applicants who attain 32 or above on ACT, 1410 or above on SAT, or are selected as National Merit finalists will automatically receive an award equal to tuition, mandatory fees, room, and board at any Arkansas institution. *Award:* Scholarship for use in freshman, sophomore, junior, or senior year; renewable. *Award amount:* $4000–$15,000. *Eligibility Requirements:* Applicant must be high school student; enrolled at a two-year or four-year institution or university; resident of Arkansas and studying in Arkansas. Applicant must have 3.5 GPA or higher. *Application Requirements:* Application, test scores, transcript. *Deadline:* March 1.

Contact Melissa Goff, Manager of Student Financial Aid, Arkansas Department of Higher Education, 114 East Capitol, Little Rock, AR 72201. *E-mail:* melissag@adhe.arknet.edu. *Phone:* 501-371-2050. *Fax:* 501-371-2001. *Web site:* http://www.adhe.arknet.edu/finance/finsites.html.

Emergency Secondary Education Loan Program. Must be Arkansas resident enrolled full-time in approved Arkansas institution. Renewable award for students majoring in secondary math, science, special education, or foreign language. Must teach in Arkansas at least five years. Must rank in upper half of class or have a minimum 2.5 GPA. *Academic/Career Areas:* Biology; Education; Foreign Language; Physical Sciences and Math; Special Education. *Award:* Forgivable loan for use in sophomore, junior, senior, or graduate years; renewable. *Award amount:* up to $2500. *Number of awards:* up to 50. *Eligibility Requirements:* Applicant must be enrolled at a two-year or four-year institution or university; resident of Arkansas and studying in Arkansas. Applicant must have 2.5 GPA or higher. *Application Requirements:* Application, transcript. *Deadline:* April 1.

Contact Lillian Williams, Assistant Coordinator, Arkansas Department of Higher Education, 114 East Capitol, Little Rock, AR 72201. *E-mail:* lillianw@adhe.arknet.edu. *Phone:* 501-371-2050. *Fax:* 501-371-2001. *Web site:* http://www.adhe.arknet.edu/finance/finsites.html.

Minority Master's Fellows Program. Renewable award for graduate students who are African-Americans, Hispanics, or Asians, enrolled in full-time teacher certification program in math, science, or foreign language. Must be Arkansas resident, have 2.75 minimum GPA. Must teach two years following certification or repay scholarship. Must have received the Arkansas Minority Teachers' Scholarships as an undergraduate. *Academic/Career Areas:* Education; Foreign Language; Physical Sciences and Math; Science, Technology and Society. *Award:* Forgivable loan for use in graduate years; renewable. *Award amount:* up to $7500. *Number of awards:* up to 20. *Eligibility Requirements:* Applicant must be Asian, African American, or Hispanic; resident of Arkansas and studying in Arkansas. Applicant must have 2.5 GPA or higher. *Application Requirements:* Application, transcript. *Deadline:* June 1.

Contact Lillian Williams, Assistant Coordinator, Arkansas Department of Higher Education, 114 East Capitol, Little Rock, AR 72201. *E-mail:* lillianw@adhe.arknet.edu. *Phone:* 501-371-2050. *Fax:* 501-371-2001. *Web site:* http://www.adhe.arknet.edu/finance/finsites.html.

Arkansas Academic Challenge Scholarship Program. Awards for Arkansas residents who are graduating high school seniors. Must have at least a 2.5 GPA, score at least 19 on ACT, and have financial need. Award for undergraduate study at an Arkansas institution. Renewable up to three additional years. Inquire for details. *Award:* Scholarship for use in freshman, sophomore, junior, or senior year; renewable. *Award amount:* up to $2500. *Eligibility Requirements:* Applicant must be high school student; enrolled at a two-year or four-year institution or university; resident of Arkansas and studying in Arkansas. Applicant must have 2.5 GPA or higher. *Application Requirements:*

Application, financial need analysis, test scores, transcript. *Deadline:* October 1.

Contact Elyse Price, Assistant Coordinator, Arkansas Department of Higher Education, 114 East Capitol, Little Rock, AR 72201. *E-mail:* elysep@adhe.arknet.edu. *Phone:* 501-371-2050. *Fax:* 501-371-2001. *Web site:* http://www.adhe.arknet.edu/finance/finsites.html.

Arkansas Student Assistance Grant Program. Award for Arkansas residents attending a college within the state. Must be enrolled full-time, have financial need, and maintain satisfactory progress. One-time award for undergraduate use only. Deadline determined by each institution. Application is the FAFSA. *Award:* Grant for use in freshman, sophomore, junior, or senior year; not renewable. *Award amount:* $100–$600. *Number of awards:* 7000–10,000. *Eligibility Requirements:* Applicant must be enrolled at a two-year, four-year, or technical institution or university; resident of Arkansas and studying in Arkansas. *Application Requirements:* Application, financial need analysis.

Contact Phil Axelroth, Assistant Coordinator, Arkansas Department of Higher Education, 114 East Capitol, Little Rock, AR 72201. *E-mail:* phila@adhe.arknet.edu. *Phone:* 501-371-2050. *Fax:* 501-371-2001. *Web site:* http://www.adhe.arknet.edu/finance/finsites.html.

Faculty/Administrators Development Fellows Program—Arkansas. Renewable award for minority faculty per administrators of state-supported institutions of higher learning to pursue doctoral degrees. Must be a resident of Arkansas. Submit application and transcripts by June 1. Must teach at sponsoring institution for three years or repay loan. *Award:* Forgivable loan for use in ; renewable. *Award amount:* $12,000–$30,000. *Number of awards:* 1–2. *Eligibility Requirements:* Applicant must be Native American or Eskimo, Asian, African American, or Hispanic; resident of Arkansas and have employment experience in teaching. *Application Requirements:* Application, autobiography, references, transcript. *Deadline:* June 1.

Contact Phil Axelroth, Assistant Coordinator, Arkansas Department of Higher Education, 114 East Capitol, Little Rock, AR 72201. *E-mail:* phila@adhe.arknet.edu. *Phone:* 501-371-2050. *Fax:* 501-371-2001. *Web site:* http://www.adhe.arknet.edu/finance/finsites.html.

Arkansas Minority Teacher Scholars Program. Renewable award for African-American, Hispanic and Asian students who have completed at least 60 semester hours and are enrolled full-time in a teacher education program in Arkansas. Award may be renewed for one year. Must be Arkansas resident with minimum 2.5 GPA. Must teach for three to five years in Arkansas to repay scholarship funds received. Must pass PPST exam. *Academic/Career Areas:* Education. *Award:* Forgivable loan for use in junior or senior year; renewable. *Award amount:* up to $5000. *Number of awards:* up to 100. *Eligibility Requirements:* Applicant must be Asian, African American, or Hispanic; enrolled at a four-year institution or university; resident of Arkansas and studying in Arkansas. Applicant must have 2.5 GPA or higher. *Application Requirements:* Application, transcript. *Deadline:* June 1.

Contact Lillian Williams, Assistant Coordinator, Arkansas Department of Higher Education, 114 East Capitol, Little Rock, AR 72201. *E-mail:* lillianw@adhe.arknet.edu. *Phone:* 501-371-2050. *Fax:* 501-371-2001. *Web site:* http://www.adhe.arknet.edu/finance/finsites.html.

Law Enforcement Officers' Dependents Scholarship-Arkansas. For dependents, under 24 years old, of Arkansas law-enforcement officers killed or permanently disabled in the line of duty. Renewable award is a waiver of tuition, fees, and room at two- or four-year Arkansas institution. Deadlines: August 1, December 1, May 1, or July 1. Submit birth certificate, death certificate, and claims commission report of findings of fact. Proof of disability from State Claims Commission may also be submitted. *Award:* Scholarship for use in freshman, sophomore, junior, or senior year; renewable. *Eligibility Requirements:* Applicant must be age 23 or under; enrolled at a two-year or four-year institution or university; resident of Arkansas; studying in Arkansas and have employment experience in police/firefighting. *Application Requirements:* Application.

Contact Lillian Williams, Assistant Coordinator, Arkansas Department of Higher Education, 114 East Capitol, Little Rock, AR 72201. *E-mail:* lillianw@adhe.arknet.edu. *Phone:* 501-371-2050. *Fax:* 501-371-2001. *Web site:* http://www.adhe.arknet.edu/finance/finsites.html.

Freshman/Sophomore Minority Grant Program-Arkansas. Renewable award for college freshmen and sophomores who are African-American, Hispanic, and Asian, and pursuing a career in teacher education at an Arkansas institution. Must be Arkansas resident. Apply to education office on campus. *Academic/Career Areas:* Education. *Award:* Grant for use in freshman or sophomore year; renewable. *Award amount:* up to $1000. *Number of awards:* 200–300. *Eligibility Requirements:* Applicant must be Asian, African American, or Hispanic; enrolled at a two-year or four-year institution or university; resident of Arkansas and studying in Arkansas. *Application Requirements:* Application, transcript. *Deadline:* continuous.

Contact Lillian Williams, Assistant Coordinator, Arkansas Department of Higher Education, 114 East Capitol, Little Rock, AR 72201. *E-mail:* lillianw@adhe.arknet.edu. *Phone:* 501-371-2050. *Fax:* 501-371-2053. *Web site:* http://www.adhe.arknet.edu/finance/finsites.html.

Missing in Action/Killed in Action Dependent's Scholarship-Arkansas. Available to Arkansas residents whose parent or spouse was classified either as missing in action, killed in action or a prisoner-of-war. Must attend a state-supported institution. Renewable waiver of tuition, fees, room and board. Deadlines: August 1, December 1, May 1, or July 1. Submit proof of casualty. *Award:* Scholarship for use in any year; renewable. *Award amount:* up to $2500. *Eligibility Requirements:* Applicant must be enrolled at a two-year, four-year, or technical institution or university; resident of Arkansas and studying in Arkansas. Applicant or parent must meet one or more of the following requirements: general military experience; retired from active duty; disabled or killed as a result of military service; prisoner of war; or missing in action. *Application Requirements:* Application.

Contact Lillian Williams, Assistant Coordinator, Arkansas Department of Higher Education, 114 East Capitol, Little Rock, AR 72201. *E-mail:* lillianw@adhe.arknet.edu. *Phone:* 501-371-2050. *Fax:* 501-371-2001. *Web site:* http://www.adhe.arknet.edu/finance/finsites.html.

CALIFORNIA

Assumption Program of Loans for Education (APLE). Award for California residents enrolled full-time in teacher education programs within the state. Must teach for three years in California public school upon obtaining teaching credentials for loan assumption of up to $11,000 over the three-year period. Apply after March 1. *Academic/Career Areas:* Education. *Award:* Forgivable loan for use in junior or senior year; renewable. *Award amount:* up to $11,000. *Number of awards:* up to 4500. *Eligibility Requirements:* Applicant must be enrolled at a four-year institution; resident of California and studying in California. Applicant must have 2.5 GPA or higher. Restricted to U.S. citizens. *Application Requirements:* Application, essay, interview, references, test scores, transcript. *Deadline:* June 30.

Contact California Student Aid Commission, P O Box 419027, Rancho Cordova, CA 95741-9027 USA. *E-mail:* custsvcs@csac.ca.gov. *Phone:* 916-526-7590. *Fax:* 916-526-7977. *Web site:* http://www.csac.ca.gov.

University of California President's Postdoctoral Fellowship Program. One-year fellowship at the University of California to improve the quality and diversity of University faculty and to encourage minority and women Ph.D. holders to pursue academic careers. Must be sponsored by faculty or laboratory adviser. *Eligibility Requirements:* Applicant must be studying in California. *Application Requirements:* Application, essay, references, transcript. *Deadline:* December 1.

Contact Jane Gonzalez, Program Analyst, University of California, 300 Lakeside Drive, 18th Floor, Oakland, CA 94612-3550. *E-mail:* jane.gonzalez@ucop.edu. *Phone:* 510-987-9503. *Fax:* 510-987-9612.

Law Enforcement Personnel Dependents Grant-California. Renewable award for California residents who are dependents of California law enforcement officers killed or permanently disabled in the line of duty. Interview required. Submit application and financial aid form. *Award:* Grant for use in any year; renewable. *Eligibility Requirements:* Applicant must be resident of California and have employment experience in police/firefighting. *Application Requirements:* Application, financial need analysis, interview.

Contact California Student Aid Commission, P O Box 419027, Rancho Cordova, CA 95741-9027 USA. *E-mail:* custsvcs@csac.ca.gov. *Phone:* 916-526-7590. *Fax:* 916-526-7977. *Web site:* http://www.csac.ca.gov.

Child Development Teacher Loan Assumption Program. Assists California residents pursuing a teaching career in early childhood education. Must teach or supervise in a children's center for two years. For use at California institution. *Academic/Career Areas:* Education. *Award:* Grant for use in freshman, sophomore, junior, or senior year; renewable. *Award amount:* $1000–$2000. *Number of awards:* up to 100. *Eligibility Requirements:* Applicant must be enrolled at a two-year or four-year institution; resident of California and studying in California. Restricted to U.S. citizens. *Application Requirements:* Application. *Deadline:* July 31.

Contact California Student Aid Commission, P O Box 419027, Rancho Cordova, CA 95741-9027 USA. *E-mail:* custsvcs@csac.ca.gov. *Phone:* 916-526-7590. *Fax:* 916-526-7977. *Web site:* http://www.csac.ca.gov.

Law Enforcement Personnel Departments Scholarships (LEPD). Tuition award for dependents of California law enforcement personnel killed or permanently disabled in the line of duty. Must be a California resident. *Award:* Grant for use in any year; renewable. *Award amount:* $1584–$9422. *Eligibility Requirements:* Applicant must be enrolled at a two-year, four-year, or technical institution or university; resident of California and have employment experience in police/firefighting. Restricted to U.S. citizens. *Application Requirements:* Application, financial need analysis. *Deadline:* continuous.

Contact California Student Aid Commission, PO Box 419027, Rancho Cordova, CA 95741-9027. *E-mail:* custsvcs@csac.ca.gov. *Phone:* 916-526-7590. *Fax:* 916-526-8002. *Web site:* http://www.csac.ca.gov.

Cal Grant A. Award for California residents attending an approved college or university within the state. Must show financial need. Minimum GPA and applicable test score are sole basis for ranking applicants determined to be financially eligible. Renewable. Must provide GPA verification. *Award:* Grant for use in freshman, sophomore, or junior year; renewable. *Award amount:* $1430–$10,200. *Number of awards:* 27,866. *Eligibility Requirements:* Applicant must be enrolled at a two-year, four-year, or technical institution or university; resident of California and studying in California. Applicant must have 3.0 GPA or higher. Restricted to U.S. citizens. *Application Requirements:* Application, applicant must enter a contest, financial need analysis, test scores. *Deadline:* March 2.

Contact California Student Aid Commission, P O Box 41907, Rancho Cordova, CA 95741-9027 USA. *E-mail:* custsvcs@csac.ca.gov. *Phone:* 916-526-7590. *Fax:* 916-526-8002. *Web site:* http://www.csac.ca.gov.

Cal Grant B. Award for California residents who are seniors in high school. Award is to be used for non-tuition expenses for the freshman year. Based on financial need. Renewable for following three years with tuition coverage. Must attend California institution. *Award:* Grant for use in freshman year; renewable. *Award amount:* $1410–$9422. *Number of awards:* 25,000. *Eligibility Requirements:* Applicant must be high school student; enrolled at a two-year, four-year, or technical institution or university; resident of California and studying in California. Restricted to U.S. citizens. *Application Requirements:* Application, financial need analysis, transcript. *Deadline:* March 2.

Contact California Student Aid Commission, P O Box 419027, Rancho Cordova, CA 95741-9027 USA. *E-mail:* custsvcs@csac.ca.gov. *Phone:* 916-526-7590. *Fax:* 916-526-8002. *Web site:* http://www.csac.ca.gov.

Cal Grant T. One academic year award for California residents enrolled in post-baccalaureate teaching credential programs. Must already have a bachelor's degree and cannot already have teaching credentials. School must be approved by the State of California. Must rank in upper half of class or have minimum 2.5 GPA. *Academic/Career Areas:* Education. *Award:* Grant for use in graduate years; not renewable. *Award amount:* \$1868–\$9422. *Number of awards:* 3000. *Eligibility Requirements:* Applicant must be enrolled at a four-year institution or university; resident of California and studying in California. Applicant must have 2.5 GPA or higher. Restricted to U.S. citizens. *Application Requirements:* Application, financial need analysis. *Deadline:* June 1.

Contact California Student Aid Commission, PO Box 419027, Rancho Cordova, CA 95741-9027. *E-mail:* custsvcs@csac.ca.gov. *Phone:* 916-526-7590. *Fax:* 916-526-8002. *Web site:* http://www.csac.ca.gov.

Cal Grant C. Award for California residents who can profit most by short-term, vocational training. Program must lead to a recognized diploma, degree, or license. Course length must be between four months and two years. Award is renewable. Must attend a California institution. *Academic/Career Areas:* Trade/Technical Specialties. *Award:* Grant for use in any year; renewable. *Award amount:* \$530–\$2890. *Number of awards:* 2100. *Eligibility Requirements:* Applicant must be enrolled at a two-year or technical institution; resident of California and studying in California. Restricted to U.S. citizens. *Application Requirements:* Application, financial need analysis, transcript. *Deadline:* March 2.

Contact California Student Aid Commission, P O Box 419027, Rancho Cordova, CA 95741-9027 USA. *E-mail:* custsvs@csac.ca.gov. *Phone:* 916-526-7590. *Fax:* 916-526-8002. *Web site:* http://www.csac.ca.gov.

Robert C. Byrd Honors Scholarship Program-California. Award available to California high school seniors. Based on outstanding academic merit. Renewable up to four years. Must be enrolled full-time at any U.S. accredited post-secondary institution. Must be nominated. Inquire for information. *Award:* Scholarship for use in freshman, sophomore, junior, or senior year; renewable. *Award amount:* \$1500. *Number of awards:* 700–800. *Eligibility Requirements:* Applicant must be high school student and resident of California. Applicant must have 3.5 GPA or higher. *Application Requirements:* Application, test scores, transcript. *Deadline:* April 23.

Contact California Student Aid Commission, P O Box 419027, Rancho Cordova, CA 95741-9027 USA. *E-mail:* custsvcs@csa.ca.gov. *Phone:* 916-526-7590. *Fax:* 916-526-7977. *Web site:* http://www.csac.ca.gov.

California State University Real Estate Scholarship and Internship Grant Program. Targeted at low income and educationally disadvantaged undergraduate and graduate students at one of twenty-three California State University campuses. Must be enrolled at least half-time in a program related to land use or real estate. Minimum GPA is 2.5 for undergraduate students and 3.0 for graduate students. *Academic/Career Areas:* Architecture; Business/Consumer Services; Civil Engineering; Landscape Architecture; Real Estate. *Award:* Scholarship for use in any year; not renewable. *Award amount:* \$500–\$2350. *Number of awards:* 22–31. *Eligibility Requirements:* Applicant must be enrolled at a four-year institution or university and studying in California. Applicant must have 2.5 GPA or higher. Restricted to U.S. citizens. *Application Requirements:* Application, essay, financial need analysis, transcript. *Deadline:* April 30.

Contact Rebecca Saucedo-Ross, Project Manager, CSU Real Estate and Land Use Institute, 7700 College Town Drive, Suite 200, Sacramento, GA 95826-2304. *E-mail:* saucedorm@csus.edu. *Phone:* 916-278-6633. *Fax:* 916-278-4500.

Cooperative Agencies Resources for Education Program. Renewable award available to California resident attending a two-year California community college. Must have no more than 70 degree-applicable units, currently receive CAIWORKS/TANF, and have at least one child under 14 years old. Must be in EOPS, single head of household, and 18 or older. Contact local college EOPS-CARE office. *Award:* Grant for use in freshman or sophomore year; renewable. *Number of awards:* 11,000. *Eligibility Requirements:* Applicant must be age 18; enrolled at a two-year institution; single; resident of California; studying in California and member of Extended Opportunity Program Service. Restricted to U.S. citizens. *Application Requirements:* Application, financial need analysis, test scores, transcript. *Deadline:* continuous.

Contact Local Community College, California Community Colleges, 1102 Q Street, Sacramento, CA 95814. *Web site:* http://www.cccco.edu.

California State Psychological Association Foundation Minority Scholarships. Award for minority graduate students pursuing studies in the social sciences. Must attend a four-year institution in California. Submit application, transcript, financial aid form, essay, and references. One-time award of \$2500. *Academic/Career Areas:* Social Sciences. *Award:* Scholarship for use in graduate years; not renewable. *Award amount:* \$2500. *Number of awards:* 3. *Eligibility Requirements:* Applicant must be Native American or Eskimo, Asian, African American, or Hispanic; enrolled at a four-year institution and studying in California. Restricted to U.S. citizens. *Application Requirements:* Application, essay, financial need analysis, references, transcript. *Deadline:* October 15.

Contact Allyn M. Fernandez, Scholarship Coordinator, California State Psychological Association Foundation, 1022 G Street, Sacramento, CA 85814. *E-mail:* afernandez@calpsychlink.org. *Phone:* 916-325-9786. *Fax:* 916-325-9790. *Web site:* http://www.calpsychlink.org.

COLORADO

Colorado Nursing Scholarships. Renewable awards for Colorado residents pursuing nursing education programs at Colorado state-supported institutions. Applicant must agree to practice nursing in Colorado upon graduation. Contact colleges for complete information and deadlines. *Academic/Career Areas:* Nursing. *Award:* Scholarship for use in freshman, sophomore, junior, or senior year; renewable. *Eligibility Requirements:* Applicant must be enrolled at a two-year, four-year, or technical institution or university; resident of Colorado and studying in Colorado. *Application Requirements:* Application.

Contact Bridget Mullen, Financial Analyst, Colorado Commission on Higher Education, 1300 Broadway, 2nd Floor, Denver, CO 80203. *Phone:* 303-866-2723. *Fax:* 303-860-9750. *Web site:* http://www.state.co.us/cche_dir/hecche.html.

Colorado Student Incentive Grant. Renewable awards for Colorado residents who are attending Colorado state-supported post-secondary institutions at the undergraduate level. Must document financial need. Contact colleges for complete information and deadlines. *Award:* Grant for use in freshman, sophomore, junior, or senior year; renewable. *Eligibility Requirements:* Applicant must be enrolled at a two-year, four-year, or technical institution or university; resident of Colorado and studying in Colorado. *Application Requirements:* Application, financial need analysis.

Contact Bridget Mullen, Financial Analyst, Colorado Commission on Higher Education, 1300 Broadway, 2nd Floor, Denver, CO 80203. *Phone:* 303-866-2723. *Fax:* 303-860-9750. *Web site:* http://www.state.co.us/cche_dir/hecche.html.

Colorado Diversity Grants. Renewable awards for Colorado residents planning to pursue or currently pursuing post-secondary studies at a Colorado state-supported institution. Designed to increase participation of under-represented groups. Contact college for complete information and deadlines. *Award:* Grant for use in freshman, sophomore, junior, or senior year; renewable. *Eligibility Requirements:* Applicant must be enrolled at a two-year, four-year, or technical institution or university; resident of Colorado and studying in Colorado. *Application Requirements:* Application.

Contact Bridget Mullen, Financial Analyst, Colorado Commission on Higher Education, 1300 Broadway, 2nd Floor, Denver, CO 80203. *Phone:* 303-866-2723. *Fax:* 303-860-9750. *Web site:* http://www.state.co.us/cche_dir/hecche.html.

Colorado Undergraduate Merit Scholarships. Renewable awards for students attending Colorado state-supported institutions at the undergraduate level. Must demonstrate superior scholarship or talent. Contact college for complete information and deadlines. *Award:* Scholarship for use in freshman, sophomore, junior, or senior year; renewable. *Eligibility Requirements:* Applicant must be enrolled at a two-year, four-year, or technical institution or university and studying in Colorado. *Application Requirements:* Application.

Contact Bridget Mullen, Financial Analyst, Colorado Commission on Higher Education, 1300 Broadway, 2nd Floor, Denver, CO 80203. *Phone:* 303-866-2723. *Fax:* 303-860-9750. *Web site:* http://www.state.co.us/cche_dir/hecche.html.

Colorado Part-Time Grants. Renewable awards for Colorado residents who are less than full-time students attending Colorado state-supported post-secondary institutions. Contact colleges for complete information and deadlines. Need-based award. *Award:* Grant for use in freshman, sophomore, junior, or senior year; renewable. *Eligibility Requirements:* Applicant must be enrolled at a two-year, four-year, or technical institution or university; resident of Colorado and studying in Colorado. *Application Requirements:* Application, financial need analysis.

Contact Bridget Mullen, Colorado Commission on Higher Education, 1300 Broadway, 2nd Floor, Denver, CO 80203. *Phone:* 303-866-2723. *Fax:* 303-860-9750. *Web site:* http://www.state.co.us/cche_dir/hecche.html.

Colorado Part-Time Scholarships. Renewable awards for Colorado residents who are less than full-time students attending Colorado state-supported post-secondary institutions. Contact colleges for complete information and deadlines. Need-based award. *Award:* Scholarship for use in freshman, sophomore, junior, or senior year; renewable. *Eligibility Requirements:* Applicant must be enrolled at a two-year, four-year, or technical institution or university; resident of Colorado and studying in Colorado. *Application Requirements:* Application, financial need analysis.

Contact Bridget Mullen, Colorado Commission on Higher Education, 1300 Broadway, 2nd Floor, Denver, CO 80203. *Phone:* 303-866-2723. *Fax:* 303-860-9750. *Web site:* http://www.state.co.us/cche_dir/hecche.html.

Law Enforcement/POW/MIA Dependents Scholarship-Colorado. Aid available for Colorado residents who are dependents of Colorado law enforcement officers, fire or national guard personnel killed or disabled in the line of duty, and for dependents of prisoner-of-war or service personnel listed as missing in action. Award covers tuition only. Deadlines vary. Must attend Colorado school. *Award:* Scholarship for use in freshman, sophomore, junior, or senior year; renewable. *Eligibility Requirements:* Applicant must be enrolled at a two-year, four-year, or technical institution or university; resident of Colorado; studying in Colorado and have employment experience in police/firefighting. *Application Requirements:* Application.

Contact Bridget Mullen, Financial Analyst, Colorado Commission on Higher Education, 1300 Broadway, 2nd Floor, Denver, CO 80203. *Phone:* 303-866-2723. *Fax:* 303-860-9750. *Web site:* http://www.state.co.us/cche_dir/hecche.html.

Colorado Student Grant. Assists Colorado residents attending eligible public, private, or vocational institutions within the state. Application deadlines vary by institution. Renewable award for undergraduates. *Award:* Grant for use in freshman, sophomore, junior, or senior year; renewable. *Eligibility Requirements:* Applicant must be enrolled at a two-year, four-year, or technical institution or university; resident of Colorado and studying in Colorado. *Application Requirements:* Application, financial need analysis.

Contact Bridget Mullen, Colorado Commission on Higher Education, 1300 Broadway, 2nd Floor, Denver, CO 80203. *Phone:* 303-866-2723. *Fax:* 303-860-9750. *Web site:* http://www.state.co.us/cche_dir/hecche.html.

CONNECTICUT

Connecticut Independent College Student Grants. Award for Connecticut residents attending an independent college or university within the state on at least a half-time basis. Renewable awards based on financial need. Application deadline varies by institution. *Award:* Grant for use in any year; renewable. *Award amount:* up to $7777. *Eligibility Requirements:* Applicant must be enrolled at a two-year or four-year institution or university; resident of Connecticut and studying in Connecticut. *Application Requirements:* Application, financial need analysis, transcript.

Contact John Siegrist, Financial Aid Office, Connecticut Department of Higher Education, 61 Woodland Street, Hartford, CT 06105-2326. *Phone:* 860-947-1855. *Fax:* 860-947-1311. *Web site:* http://www.ctdhe.commnet.edu.

Connecticut Tuition Waiver for Senior Citizens. Renewable tuition waiver for a Connecticut senior citizen to use at an accredited two- or four-year institution in Connecticut. Must show financial need and prove senior citizen status. Award for undergraduate study only. *Award:* Grant for use in freshman, sophomore, junior, or senior year; renewable. *Eligibility Requirements:* Applicant must be enrolled at a two-year or four-year institution; resident of Connecticut and studying in Connecticut. *Application Requirements:* Application, financial need analysis. *Deadline:* continuous.

Contact John Siegrist, Financial Aid Office, Connecticut Department of Higher Education, 61 Woodland Street, Hartford, CT 06105-2326. *Phone:* 860-947-1855. *Fax:* 860-947-1311. *Web site:* http://www.ctdhe.commnet.edu.

Capitol Scholarship Program. Award for Connecticut residents attending eligible institutions in Connecticut or in a state with reciprocity with Connecticut (Delaware, Maine, Massachusetts, New Hampshire, Pennsylvania, Rhode Island, Vermont), or in Washington, DC. Must rank in top twenty percent of class or score at least 1200 on SAT and show financial need. *Award:* Scholarship for use in any year; renewable. *Award amount:* $300–$2000. *Eligibility Requirements:* Applicant must be enrolled at a two-year or four-year institution or university; resident of Connecticut and studying in Connecticut, Delaware, District of Columbia, Maine, Massachusetts, New Hampshire, Pennsylvania, Rhode Island, or Vermont. Applicant must have 3.5 GPA or higher. *Application Requirements:* Application, financial need analysis, test scores. *Deadline:* February 15.

Contact John Siegrist, Financial Aid Office, Connecticut Department of Higher Education, 61 Woodland Street, Hartford, CT 06105-2326. *Phone:* 860-947-1855. *Fax:* 860-947-1311. *Web site:* http://www.ctdhe.commnet.edu.

Robert C. Byrd Honors Scholarship-Connecticut. Renewable scholarship for Connecticut high school seniors in the top 2% of their class or scoring 1400 or above on the SAT. Acceptance letter from college required. *Award:* Scholarship for use in freshman, sophomore, junior, or senior year; renewable. *Award amount:* up to $1500. *Eligibility Requirements:* Applicant must be high school student; enrolled at a two-year or four-year institution and resident of Connecticut. Applicant must have 3.5 GPA or higher. Restricted to U.S. citizens. *Application Requirements:* Application, test scores. *Deadline:* continuous.

Contact John Siegrist, Financial Aid Office, Connecticut Department of Higher Education, 61 Woodland Street, Hartford, CT 06105-2326. *Phone:* 860-947-1855. *Fax:* 860-947-1311. *Web site:* http://www.ctdhe.commnet.edu.

Aid for Public College Students Grant Program/Connecticut. Award for students at Connecticut public institutions. Must be state residents and enrolled at least half-time. Renewable award based on financial need and academic progress. Application deadlines vary by institution. *Award:* Grant for use in any year; renewable. *Eligibility Requirements:* Applicant must be enrolled at a two-year or four-year institution; resident of Connecticut and studying in Connecticut. *Application Requirements:* Application, financial need analysis, transcript.

Contact John Siegrist, Financial Aid Office, Connecticut Department of Higher Education, 61 Woodland Street, Hartford, CT 06105-2326. *Phone:* 860-947-1855. *Fax:* 860-947-1311. *Web site:* http://www.ctdhe.commnet.edu.

DELAWARE

Librarian Incentive Scholarship Program. Renewable award for Delaware residents enrolled in graduate programs to pursue careers as librarians and archivists in Delaware libraries. Loan requires a service repayment in Delaware. Must have minimum 3.0 GPA. *Academic/Career Areas:* Library Sciences. *Award:* Forgivable loan for use in graduate years; renewable. *Award amount:* up to $10,000. *Number of awards:* up to 10. *Eligibility Requirements:* Applicant must be resident of Delaware. Applicant must have 3.0 GPA or higher. Restricted to U.S. citizens. *Application Requirements:* Application, essay, financial need analysis, test scores, transcript. *Deadline:* March 31.

Contact Maureen Laffey, Associate Director, Delaware Higher Education Commission, 820 North French Street, Wilmington, DE 19801. *E-mail:* mlaffey@

state.de.us. *Phone:* 302-577-3240. *Fax:* 302-577-6765. *Web site:* http://www.doe.state.de.us/high-ed.

Scholarship Incentive Program-Delaware. One-time award for Delaware residents with financial need. May be used at an institution in Delaware or Pennsylvania, or at another out-of-state institution if a program is not available at a publicly-supported school in Delaware. Must have minimum 2.5 GPA. *Award:* Grant for use in any year; not renewable. *Award amount:* \$700–\$2200. *Number of awards:* 1000–1300. *Eligibility Requirements:* Applicant must be enrolled at a two-year or four-year institution or university; resident of Delaware and studying in Delaware or Pennsylvania. Applicant must have 2.5 GPA or higher. Restricted to U.S. citizens. *Application Requirements:* Application, financial need analysis, transcript. *Deadline:* April 15.

Contact Maureen Laffey, Associate Director, Delaware Higher Education Commission, 820 North French Street, Wilmington, DE 19801. *E-mail:* mlaffey@state.de.us. *Phone:* 302-577-3240. *Fax:* 302-577-6765. *Web site:* http://www.doe.state.de.us/high-ed.

Speech Language Pathologist Incentive Program. Renewable loan for Delaware students pursuing graduate programs for speech or language pathology licenses. Must be U.S. citizen and demonstrate financial need. Must have minimum 3.0 GPA. Loan requires a service repayment in Delaware. *Academic/Career Areas:* Therapy/Rehabilitation. *Award:* Forgivable loan for use in graduate years; renewable. *Award amount:* up to \$10,000. *Number of awards:* 1–10. *Eligibility Requirements:* Applicant must be resident of Delaware. Applicant must have 3.0 GPA or higher. Restricted to U.S. citizens. *Application Requirements:* Application, essay, financial need analysis, test scores, transcript. *Deadline:* March 31.

Contact Maureen Laffey, Associate Director, Delaware Higher Education Commission, 820 North French Street, Wilmington, DE 19801. *E-mail:* mlaffey@state.de.us. *Phone:* 302-577-3240. *Fax:* 302-577-6765. *Web site:* http://www.doe.state.de.us/high-ed.

Diamond State Scholarship. Renewable award for Delaware high school seniors enrolling full-time at an accredited college or university. Must be ranked in upper quarter of class and score 1200 on SAT or 27 on the ACT. *Award:* Scholarship for use in freshman, sophomore, junior, or senior year; renewable. *Award amount:* \$1250. *Number of awards:* 50–200. *Eligibility Requirements:* Applicant must be high school student; enrolled at a four-year institution or university and resident of Delaware. Applicant must have 3.5 GPA or higher. Restricted to U.S. citizens. *Application Requirements:* Application, essay, test scores, transcript. *Deadline:* March 31.

Contact Maureen Laffey, Associate Director, Delaware Higher Education Commission, 820 North French Street, Wilmington, DE 19801. *E-mail:* mlaffey@state.de.us. *Phone:* 302-577-3240. *Fax:* 302-577-6765. *Web site:* http://www.doe.state.de.us/high-ed.

Educational Benefits for Children of Deceased Military and State Police. Renewable award for Delaware residents who are children of state or military police who were killed in the line of duty. Must attend a Delaware institution unless program of study is not available. Must submit proof of service and related death. Must be ages 16-24 at time of application. Deadline three weeks before classes begin. *Award:* Grant for use in freshman, sophomore, junior, or senior year; renewable. *Award amount:* \$2000–\$10,000. *Number of awards:* 1–10. *Eligibility Requirements:* Applicant must be age 16-24; enrolled at a two-year or four-year institution or university; resident of Delaware and have employment experience in police/firefighting. Restricted to U.S. citizens. Applicant or parent must meet one or more of the following requirements: general military experience; retired from active duty; disabled or killed as a result of military service; prisoner of war; or missing in action. *Application Requirements:* Application.

Contact Maureen Laffey, Associate Director, Delaware Higher Education Commission, 820 North French Street, Wilmington, DE 19801. *E-mail:* mlaffey@state.de.us. *Phone:* 302-577-3240. *Fax:* 302-577-6765. *Web site:* http://www.doe.state.de.us/high-ed.

Christa McAuliffe Teacher Scholarship Loan—Delaware. Award for Delaware residents who are pursuing teaching careers. Must agree to teach in Delaware public schools as repayment of loan. Minimum award is \$1000 and is renewable for up to four years. Available only at Delaware colleges. Based on academic merit. Must have minimum 2.5 GPA. *Academic/Career Areas:* Education. *Award:* Forgivable loan for use in freshman, sophomore, or junior year; renewable. *Award amount:* \$1000–\$5000. *Number of awards:* 1–50. *Eligibility Requirements:* Applicant must be enrolled at a four-year institution or university; resident of Delaware and studying in Delaware. Applicant must have 2.5 GPA or higher. Restricted to U.S. citizens. *Application Requirements:* Application, essay, test scores, transcript. *Deadline:* March 31.

Contact Maureen Laffey, Associate Director, Delaware Higher Education Commission, 820 North French Street, Wilmington, DE 19801. *E-mail:* mlaffey@state.de.us. *Phone:* 302-577-3240. *Fax:* 302-577-6765. *Web site:* http://www.doe.state.de.us/high-ed.

Delaware Nursing Incentive Scholarship Loan. Award for Delaware residents pursuing a nursing career. Must be repaid with nursing practice at a Delaware state-owned hospital. Based on academic merit. Must have minimum 2.5 GPA. Renewable for up to four years. *Academic/Career Areas:* Nursing. *Award:* Forgivable loan for use in freshman, sophomore, junior, or senior year; renewable. *Award amount:* \$1000–\$3000. *Number of awards:* 1–40. *Eligibility Requirements:* Applicant must be enrolled at a two-year or four-year institution or university and resident of Delaware. Applicant must have 2.5 GPA or higher. Restricted to U.S. citizens.

Application Requirements: Application, essay, test scores, transcript. *Deadline:* March 31.

Contact Maureen Laffey, Associate Director, Delaware Higher Education Commission, 820 North French Street, Wilmington, DE 19801. *E-mail:* mlaffey@state.de.us. *Phone:* 302-577-3240. *Fax:* 302-577-6765. *Web site:* http://www.doe.state.de.us/high-ed.

DISTRICT OF COLUMBIA

District of Columbia Commission on the Arts & Humanities Grants. Awards for artists in the District of Columbia to be used for community-based artistic projects and activities. Applicants must have interest in political science. *Academic/Career Areas:* Arts; Political Science. *Award:* Grant for use in any year; not renewable. *Award amount:* $1000–$2500. *Number of awards:* 125–200. *Eligibility Requirements:* Applicant must be enrolled at a two-year or four-year institution or university; resident of District of Columbia; studying in District of Columbia and must have an interest in art. Applicant must have 2.5 GPA or higher. Available to U.S. and non-U.S. citizens. *Application Requirements:* Application, interview. *Deadline:* continuous.

Contact Mary Liniger Hickman, Arts Education Coordinator, District of Columbia Commission on the Arts and Humanities, 410 Eighth Street N.W., 5th Floor, Washington, DC 20004. *E-mail:* mlhickman@hotmail.com. *Phone:* 202-724-5613. *Fax:* 202-727-4135. *Web site:* http://www.capaccess.org/dccah.

DC Leveraging Educational Assistance Partnership Program (LEAP). Available to Washington, DC, residents who have financial need. Must also apply for the Federal Pell Grant. Must attend an eligible college at least half-time. Award is renewable. Contact financial aid office or local library for more information. Proof of residency may be required. June deadline. *Award:* Scholarship for use in freshman, sophomore, junior, or senior year; renewable. *Award amount:* $400–$800. *Number of awards:* 1200. *Eligibility Requirements:* Applicant must be enrolled at a two-year or four-year institution or university and resident of District of Columbia. Restricted to U.S. citizens. *Application Requirements:* Application, financial need analysis.

Contact Ulysses S. Glee, Acting Chief, District of Columbia Office of Postsecondary Education Research and Assistance, 2100 Martin Luther King Jr. Avenue, SE, Suite 401, Washington, DC 20020. *Phone:* 202-727-3688.

OERI Visiting Scholars Fellowship Program. Opportunity to work at the OERI office of the U.S. Department of Education for one year, and do research related to education and learning. Applicant receives current salary. *Academic/Career Areas:* Communications; Computer Science/Data Processing; Economics; Education; History; Library Sciences; Literature/English/Writing; Physical Sciences and Math; Social Sciences. *Eligibility Requirements:* Restricted to U.S. citizens. *Application Requirements:* Application, applicant must enter a contest, essay, references, transcript.

Contact Craig Gidney, Program Specialist, National Research Council, Fellowships, TJ 2041, 2101 Constitution Avenue, Washington, DC 20418. *E-mail:* infofell@nas.edu. *Phone:* 202-334-2872. *Fax:* 202-334-3419. *Web site:* http://national-academies.org.

Dissertation Year Fellowship. Two $9000 awards to support scholarly research and writing among qualified civilian graduate students whose dissertations focus on the history of war on land. Topics submitted should complement the Center's existing projects. Contact for complete information. *Academic/Career Areas:* History; Peace and Conflict Studies. *Award:* Scholarship for use in graduate years; not renewable. *Award amount:* $9000. *Number of awards:* 2. *Eligibility Requirements:* Restricted to U.S. citizens. *Application Requirements:* Application, essay, references, transcript. *Deadline:* January 15.

Contact Dr. Birtle, Executive Secretary, United States Army Center of Military History, 103 3rd Avenue, SW, Washington, DC 20319-5058. *E-mail:* birtlaj@hqda.army.mil. *Phone:* 202-685-2278. *Fax:* 202-685-2077. *Web site:* http://www.army.mil/cmh-pg.

FLORIDA

Seminole and Miccosukee Indian Scholarship Program. Award for Florida Seminole and Miccosukee Indians attending approved Florida college or university full- or part-time. Eligibility based on need. The amount of the scholarship and renewal is determined by the respective tribe. Must maintain 2.0 GPA for renewal. Application deadlines are established by tribe. *Award:* Scholarship for use in any year; renewable. *Number of awards:* 23. *Eligibility Requirements:* Applicant must be Native American or Eskimo; enrolled at a two-year or four-year institution or university; resident of Florida and studying in Florida. *Application Requirements:* Application, financial need analysis.

Contact Theresa Antworth, Director of State Programs, Florida Department of Education, Office of Student Financial Assistance, Tallahassee, FL 32399-0400. *E-mail:* antwort@mail.doe.state.fl.us. *Phone:* 850-488-1034. *Fax:* 850-488-5966. *Web site:* http://www.firn.edu/doe.

Florida Resident Access Grant. Awards given to Florida residents attending an independent nonprofit college or university in Florida for undergraduate study. Cannot have previously received bachelor's degree. Must enroll minimum 12 credit hours. Deadline set by eligible post-secondary financial aid offices. Contact financial aid administrator for application information. Reapply for renewal. *Award:* Grant for use in freshman, sophomore, junior, or senior year; not renewable. *Award amount:* $1800. *Number of awards:* 23,425. *Eligibility Requirements:* Applicant must be enrolled at a four-year institution or university; resident of Florida and studying in Florida. *Application Requirements:* Application.

Contact Theresa Antworth, Director of State Programs, Florida Department of Education, Office of Student Financial Assistance, Tallahassee, FL 32399-0400. *E-mail:* antwort@mail.doe.state.fl.us.

Phone: 850-488-1034. *Fax:* 850-488-5966. *Web site:* http://www.firn.edu/doe.

Delores A. Auzenne Fellowship for Graduate Study. Available for minority students pursuing full-time graduate study at one of the four-year public institutions in the State University system. Must have at least a 3.0 GPA. Renewable award. Contact the Equal Opportunity Office at each of the ten public state universities. *Award:* Scholarship for use in graduate years; renewable. *Award amount:* $2500–$5000. *Number of awards:* 90. *Eligibility Requirements:* Applicant must be Native American or Eskimo, Asian, African American, or Hispanic; enrolled at a four-year institution and studying in Florida. Applicant must have 3.0 GPA or higher. *Application Requirements:* Application, transcript.

Contact Equal Opportunity/Academic Affairs Program Manager, Florida Board of Regents Office for Academic and Student Affairs, Florida Education Center, Suite 1548, Tallahassee, FL 32399-1950.

Florida Postsecondary Student Assistance Grant. Renewable grants for Florida residents, who are U.S. citizens or eligible non-citizens attending degree-granting private Florida colleges or universities, but not eligible under the Florida Private Student Assistance Grant. Must enroll full-time and have financial need. Application deadline set by eligible participating institutions. Allow at least 30 days for mailing and processing. *Award:* Grant for use in freshman, sophomore, junior, or senior year; renewable. *Award amount:* $200–$1500. *Number of awards:* 2800. *Eligibility Requirements:* Applicant must be enrolled at a two-year or four-year institution; resident of Florida and studying in Florida. *Application Requirements:* Application, financial need analysis.

Contact Theresa Antworth, Director of State Programs, Florida Department of Education, Office of Student Financial Assistance, Tallahassee, FL 32399-0400. *E-mail:* antwort@mail.doe.state.fl.us. *Phone:* 850-488-1034. *Fax:* 850-488-5966. *Web site:* http://www.firn.edu/doe.

Florida Public Student Assistance Grant. Grants for Florida resident and U.S. citizens attending a Florida public college or university full-time. Based on financial need. Renewable up to 9 semesters, 14 quarters, or until receipt of bachelor's degree. Deadline set by eligible participating institutions. *Award:* Grant for use in freshman, sophomore, junior, or senior year; renewable. *Award amount:* $200–$1500. *Number of awards:* 30,000. *Eligibility Requirements:* Applicant must be enrolled at a two-year or four-year institution; resident of Florida and studying in Florida. *Application Requirements:* Application, financial need analysis.

Contact Theresa Antworth, Director of State Programs, Florida Department of Education, Office of Student Financial Assistance, Tallahassee, FL 32399-0400. *E-mail:* antwort@mail.doe.state.fl.us. *Phone:* 850-488. *Fax:* 850-488-5966. *Web site:* http://www.firn.edu/doe.

"Chappie" James Most Promising Teacher Scholarship. Renewable scholarship for Florida high school senior in top 25 percent of class (with minimum 3.0 GPA) to enroll full-time as undergraduate at eligible Florida institution. Must intend to teach in Florida public schools. Must be nominated by high school principal. *Academic/Career Areas:* Education. *Award:* Scholarship for use in freshman or sophomore year; renewable. *Award amount:* $1500. *Number of awards:* 438. *Eligibility Requirements:* Applicant must be high school student; enrolled at a two-year or four-year institution or university; resident of Florida and studying in Florida. Applicant must have 3.0 GPA or higher. *Application Requirements:* Application, references, test scores, transcript. *Deadline:* March 1.

Contact Theresa Antworth, Director of State Programs, Florida Department of Education, Office of Student Financial Assistance, Tallahassee, FL 32399-0400. *E-mail:* antwort@mail.doe.state.fl.us. *Phone:* 850-487-1034. *Fax:* 850-488-5966. *Web site:* http://www.firn.edu/doe.

Critical Teacher Shortage Loan Forgiveness Program-Florida. Eligible Florida teachers may receive up to $10,000 for repayment of undergraduate and graduate educational loans which led to certification in critical teacher shortage subject area. Must teach full-time at a Florida public school in a critical area for a minimum of ninety days to be eligible for half of award. Contact for further information. *Academic/Career Areas:* Education. *Award:* Forgivable loan for use in graduate years; renewable. *Award amount:* $2500–$10,000. *Number of awards:* 1000. *Eligibility Requirements:* Applicant must be enrolled at a two-year or four-year institution or university; resident of Florida; studying in Florida and have employment experience in teaching. *Application Requirements:* Application. *Deadline:* July 15.

Contact Theresa Antworth, Director of State Programs, Florida Department of Education, Office of Student Financial Assistance, Tallahassee, FL 32399-0400. *E-mail:* antwort@mail.doe.state.fl.us. *Phone:* 850-488-1034. *Fax:* 850-488-5966. *Web site:* http://www.firn.edu/doe.

Critical Teacher Shortage Tuition Reimbursement-Florida. One-time awards for full-time Florida public school employees who are certified to teach in Florida and are teaching or preparing to teach in critical teacher shortage subject areas. Must earn minimum grade of 3.0 in approved courses. May receive tuition reimbursement up to 9 semester hours or equivalent per academic year, not to exceed $78 per semester hour, for maximum 36 hours. Contact for application and deadline. Must be resident of Florida. *Academic/Career Areas:* Education. *Award:* Scholarship for use in graduate years; not renewable. *Award amount:* up to $700. *Eligibility Requirements:* Applicant must be enrolled at a two-year or four-year institution or university; resident of Florida; studying in Florida and have employment experience in teaching. Applicant must have 3.0 GPA or higher. *Application Requirements:* Application. *Deadline:* May 30.

Contact Theresa Antwroth, Director of State Programs, Florida Department of Education, Office of Student Financial Assistance, Tallahassee, FL 32399-0400. *E-mail:* antwort@mail.doe.state.fl.us.

Phone: 850-488-1034. *Fax:* 850-488-5966. *Web site:* http://www.firn.edu/doe.

Florida Bright Futures Scholarship Program. Reward for Florida high school graduates who demonstrate high academic achievement and enroll in eligible Florida post-secondary institutions. There are three award levels. Each has different academic criteria and awards a different amount. Top ranked scholars from each county will receive additional $1500. *Award:* Scholarship for use in freshman, sophomore, junior, or senior year; renewable. *Award amount:* $1396–$2090. *Number of awards:* 70,263. *Eligibility Requirements:* Applicant must be high school student; enrolled at a two-year, four-year, or technical institution or university; resident of Florida and studying in Florida. *Application Requirements:* Application. *Deadline:* April 1.

Contact Theresa Antworth, Director of State Programs, Florida Department of Education, Office of Student Financial Assistance, Tallahassee, FL 32399-0400. *E-mail:* antwort@mail.doe.state.fl.us. *Phone:* 850-488-0049. *Fax:* 850-488-5966. *Web site:* http://www.firn.edu/doe.

Occupational and Physical Therapist Loan Forgiveness—Florida. Award is repayment of educational loans to occupational and physical therapists or assistants employed in Florida public schools. Must have Florida license and intend to work minimum three years in position, having already completed one full year. May reapply up to four academic years or a total of $10,000. *Academic/Career Areas:* Health and Medical Sciences; Therapy/Rehabilitation. *Award:* Forgivable loan for use in graduate years; not renewable. *Award amount:* $2500–$5000. *Number of awards:* 1–23. *Eligibility Requirements:* Applicant must be resident of Florida; studying in Florida and have employment experience in designated career field. *Application Requirements:* Application. *Deadline:* July 15.

Contact Theresa Antworth, Director of State Programs, Florida Department of Education, Office of Student Financial Assistance, Tallahassee, FL 32399-0400. *E-mail:* antwort@mail.doe.state.fl.us. *Phone:* 850-488-1034. *Fax:* 850-488-5966. *Web site:* http://www.firn.edu/doe.

Rosewood Family Scholarship Fund. Renewable award for eligible minority students to attend a Florida public post-secondary institution on a full-time-basis. Preference given to direct descendants of African-American Rosewood families affected by the incidents of January 1923. Must be black, Hispanic, Asian, Pacific Islander, American Indian, or Alaska native. Deadlines: Application due April 1; Free Application for Federal Student Aid (and Student Aid Report for nonresidents of Florida) must be processed by May 15. *Award:* Scholarship for use in freshman, sophomore, junior, or senior year; renewable. *Award amount:* $4000. *Number of awards:* 25. *Eligibility Requirements:* Applicant must be Native American or Eskimo, Asian, African American, or Hispanic; enrolled at a two-year, four-year, or technical institution or university and studying in Florida. *Application Requirements:* Application, financial need analysis. *Deadline:* April 1.

Contact Theresa Antworth, Director of State Programs, Florida Department of Education, Office of Student Financial Assistance, Tallahassee, FL 32399-0400. *E-mail:* antwort@mail.doe.state.fl.us. *Phone:* 850-488-1034. *Fax:* 850-488-5966. *Web site:* http://www.firn.edu/doe.

Florida Private Student Assistance Grant. Grants for Florida residents who are U.S. citizens or eligible non-citizens attending eligible independent nonprofit colleges or universities in Florida full-time with financial need. Renewable for up to nine semesters, fourteen quarters, or until receipt of bachelor's degree. Deadline May 15, or to be determined by individual eligible institutions. *Award:* Grant for use in freshman, sophomore, junior, or senior year; renewable. *Award amount:* $200–$1500. *Number of awards:* 7500. *Eligibility Requirements:* Applicant must be enrolled at a four-year institution or university; resident of Florida and studying in Florida. *Application Requirements:* Application, financial need analysis. *Deadline:* May 15.

Contact Theresa Antworth, Director of State Programs, Florida Department of Education, Office of Student Financial Assistance, Tallahassee, FL 32399-0400. *E-mail:* antwort@mail.doe.state.fl.us. *Phone:* 850-488. *Fax:* 850-488-5966. *Web site:* http://www.firn.edu/doe.

Occupational and Physical Therapist Tuition Reimbursement Program-Florida. Aid to eligible Florida public school occupational or physical therapists or assistants to improve skills and knowledge. Must provide proof of valid license or permit. Must be employed at Florida public school as full-time therapist for minimum of three years. Contact for deadlines. *Academic/Career Areas:* Health and Medical Sciences; Therapy/Rehabilitation. *Award:* Scholarship for use in graduate years; not renewable. *Eligibility Requirements:* Applicant must be enrolled at a two-year or four-year institution or university; resident of Florida; studying in Florida and have employment experience in designated career field. Applicant must have 3.0 GPA or higher. *Application Requirements:* Application, transcript. *Deadline:* May 30.

Contact Theresa Antworth, Director of State Programs, Florida Department of Education, Office of Student Financial Assistance, Tallahassee, FL 32399-0400. *E-mail:* antwort@mail.doe.state.fl.us. *Phone:* 850-488-1034. *Fax:* 850-488-5966. *Web site:* http://www.firn.edu/doe.

Limited Access Competitive Grant. Provides enrollment opportunities at participating private colleges and universities in Florida for qualified applicants who may be unable to obtain admission to designated state university limited-access programs due to lack of space. Grant equals 50% of state's cost to fund an undergraduate's public post-secondary education per academic year. Award may be received for maximum four semesters or six quarters. Must be graduate of Florida community college or transfer student from a state university in Florida. Application deadline established by each participating institution. *Academic/Career Areas:* Health and Medical Sciences; Special Education; Therapy/Rehabilitation. *Award:* Grant for use in freshman, sophomore, junior, or senior year; renewable. *Award amount:*

$2000. *Number of awards:* 705. *Eligibility Requirements:* Applicant must be enrolled at a four-year institution or university; resident of Florida and studying in Florida. *Application Requirements:* Application.

Contact Theresa Antworth, Director of State Programs, Florida Department of Education, Office of Student Financial Assistance, Tallahassee, FL 32399-0400. *E-mail:* antwort@mail.doe.state.fl.us. *Phone:* 850-488-1034. *Fax:* 850-488-5966. *Web site:* http://www.firn.edu/doe.

Jose Marti Scholarship Challenge Grant Fund. Award available to Hispanic-American students who were born in or whose parent was born in an Hispanic country. Must have lived in Florida for one year, be enrolled full-time in Florida at an eligible school, and have a GPA of 3.0 or above. Must be U.S. citizen or eligible non-citizen. Renewable award of $2000. Application must be postmarked by April 1. Free Application for Federal Student Aid must be processed by May 15. *Award:* Scholarship for use in any year; renewable. *Award amount:* $2000. *Number of awards:* 98. *Eligibility Requirements:* Applicant must be Latin American/Caribbean, Mexican, or Spanish; Hispanic; enrolled at a two-year or four-year institution or university; resident of Florida and studying in Florida. Applicant must have 3.0 GPA or higher. *Application Requirements:* Application, financial need analysis. *Deadline:* April 1.

Contact Theresa Antworth, Director of State Programs, Florida Department of Education, Office of Student Financial Assistance, Tallahassee, FL 32399-0400. *E-mail:* antwort@mail.doe.state.fl.us. *Phone:* 850-488-1034. *Fax:* 850-488-5966. *Web site:* http://www.firn.edu/doe.

Top Scholars Award. Renewable award for academically top-ranked Florida Bright Futures Scholarship Program recipients from each Florida school district. Must have attended a Florida high school during senior year and be enrolled at an eligible Florida institution. Minimum 3.5 GPA and 1270 SAT or 28 ACT required. *Award:* Scholarship for use in freshman, sophomore, junior, or senior year; renewable. *Award amount:* $1500–$4000. *Number of awards:* 200. *Eligibility Requirements:* Applicant must be high school student; enrolled at a two-year, four-year, or technical institution or university; resident of Florida and studying in Florida. Applicant must have 3.5 GPA or higher. *Application Requirements:* Application, test scores, transcript. *Deadline:* April 1.

Contact Theresa Antworth, Director of State Programs, Florida Department of Education, Office of Student Financial Assistance, Tallahassee, FL 32399-0400. *E-mail:* antwort@mail.doe.state.fl.us. *Phone:* 850-488-1034. *Fax:* 850-488-5966. *Web site:* http://www.firn.edu/doe.

Mary McLeod Bethune Scholarship. Available to Florida high school seniors with a GPA of 3.0 or above who will attend Florida Agricultural and Mechanical University, Bethune-Cookman College, Edward Waters College, or Florida Memorial College. Based on need. Reapply to renew. *Award:* Scholarship for use in freshman, sophomore, junior, or senior year; not renewable. *Award amount:* $3000. *Number of awards:* 265. *Eligibility Requirements:* Applicant must be high school student; enrolled at a four-year institution; resident of Florida and studying in Florida. Applicant must have 3.0 GPA or higher. *Application Requirements:* Application, financial need analysis, test scores, transcript. *Deadline:* April 30.

Contact Theresa Antworth, Director of State Programs, Florida Department of Education, Office of Student Financial Assistance, Tallahassee, FL 32399-0400. *E-mail:* antwort@mail.doe.state.fl.us. *Phone:* 850-488-1034. *Fax:* 850-488-5966. *Web site:* http://www.firn.edu/doe.

Nursing Scholarship Program. Provides financial assistance for full or part-time nursing students enrolled in upper division approved nursing program. Pays up to $8,000 per year undergraduate or $12,000 per year advanced degree. Loans repaid by working in medically underserved areas for each year of assistance. Must apply prior to start of semester or quarter for which applicant requests assistance. *Academic/Career Areas:* Nursing. *Award:* Forgivable loan for use in junior, senior, or graduate years; not renewable. *Award amount:* $8000–$12,000. *Eligibility Requirements:* Applicant must be enrolled at a four-year institution or university; resident of Florida and studying in Florida. *Application Requirements:* Application.

Contact Theresa Antworth, Director of State Programs, Florida Department of Education, Office of Student Financial Assistance, 325 West Gaines Street, Tallahassee, FL 32399-0400. *E-mail:* antwort@mail.doe.state.fl.us. *Phone:* 850-488-1034. *Fax:* 850-488-5966. *Web site:* http://www.firn.edu/doe.

Florida Teacher Scholarship and Forgivable Loan Program. Renewable two-year scholarship for Florida undergraduates in freshman or sophomore year in top 25% of their class. Renewable two-year loan for Florida upper division undergraduate and graduate students who intend to teach in a critical teacher shortage area in Florida. Undergraduates must have scored in at least 40th percentile on SAT or ACT, and have at least 2.5 GPA. Graduate applicants must have BA and at least 3.0 GPA or have scored at least 1000 on GRE. Up to $4000 awarded for undergraduate and $8000 for graduate. Deadline: April 1. Must be a Florida resident. *Academic/Career Areas:* Education. *Award:* Scholarship for use in freshman, sophomore, junior, senior, or graduate years; renewable. *Award amount:* $1500–$4000. *Number of awards:* 300. *Eligibility Requirements:* Applicant must be enrolled at a four-year institution or university; resident of Florida and studying in Florida. *Application Requirements:* Application, references, test scores, transcript. *Deadline:* April 1.

Contact Theresa Antworth, Director of State Programs, Florida Department of Education, Office of Student Financial Assistance, Tallahassee, FL 32399-0400. *E-mail:* antwort@mail.doe.state.fl.us. *Phone:* 850-488-1080. *Fax:* 850-488-5966. *Web site:* http://www.firn.edu/doe.

Scholarships for Children of Deceased or Disabled Veterans or Children of Servicemen Classified as POW or MIA-Florida. Renewable award for students between 16 and 22 years old enrolled full-time at a Florida public post-secondary institution. Provides full tuition and fees equal to the amount that would be required to pay for the average tuition and fees per credit hour, or equivalent, of a public post-secondary education institution at the comparable level for a maximum of 8 semesters of undergraduate study. Must be the child of a deceased, disabled, prisoner of war, or missing-in-action service member from specified wars or conflicts. Renewable for up to eight semesters. Must be a Florida resident. *Award:* Scholarship for use in freshman, sophomore, junior, or senior year; renewable. *Award amount:* \$1396–\$2090. *Number of awards:* 215. *Eligibility Requirements:* Applicant must be age 16-22; enrolled at a two-year, four-year, or technical institution or university; resident of Florida and studying in Florida. Applicant must have 3.0 GPA or higher. Applicant or parent must meet one or more of the following requirements: general military experience; retired from active duty; disabled or killed as a result of military service; prisoner of war; or missing in action. *Application Requirements:* Application, references, test scores, transcript. *Deadline:* April 1.

Contact Theresa Antworth, Director of State Programs, Florida Department of Education, Office of Student Financial Assistance, Tallahassee, FL 32399-0400. *E-mail:* antwort@mail.doe.state.fl.us. *Phone:* 850-488-1034. *Fax:* 850-488-5966. *Web site:* http://www.firn.edu/doe.

Nicaraguan and Haitian Scholarship Program. One-time award for one Nicaraguan and one Haitian student to attend a Florida state university system school. Must live in Florida and be a U.S. citizen or permanent resident. Permanent residents qualify provided they are either citizens of Nicaragua or Haiti. Minimum 3.0 GPA. Must demonstrate service to the community. May reapply. Deadline: July 1. *Award:* Scholarship for use in any year; not renewable. *Award amount:* \$4000–\$5000. *Number of awards:* 2. *Eligibility Requirements:* Applicant must be Haitian or Nicaraguan; enrolled at a four-year institution or university; resident of Florida; studying in Florida and have employment experience in community service. Applicant must have 3.0 GPA or higher. *Application Requirements:* Application, financial need analysis. *Deadline:* July 1.

Contact Theresa Antworth, Director of State Programs, Florida Department of Education, Office of Student Financial Assistance, Tallahassee, FL 32399-0400. *E-mail:* antwort@mail.doe.state.fl.us. *Phone:* 850-488-1034. *Fax:* 850-488-5966. *Web site:* http://www.firn.edu/doe.

Occupational and Physical Therapist Scholarship Loan Program-Florida. Renewable award for Florida residents enrolled full-time in occupational or physical therapy or assistant program at an eligible Florida institution. Must intend to work as therapist in Florida public schools for minimum of three years or repay loan. *Academic/Career Areas:* Therapy/Rehabilitation. *Award:* Forgivable loan for use in any year; renewable. *Award amount:* up to \$4000. *Number of awards:* 23. *Eligibility Requirements:* Applicant must be enrolled at a two-year or four-year institution or university; resident of Florida and studying in Florida. *Application Requirements:* Application, transcript. *Deadline:* April 15.

Contact Theresa Antwroth, Director of State Programs, Florida Department of Education, Office of Student Financial Assistance, Tallahassee, FL 32399-0400. *E-mail:* antwort@mail.doe.state.fl.us. *Phone:* 850-488-1034. *Fax:* 850-488-5966. *Web site:* http://www.firn.edu/doe.

GEORGIA

Georgia HOPE Teacher Scholarship Program. Forgivable loan program for Georgia residents who have been admitted into an advanced degree teacher education program leading to certification in a critical shortage field. Recipients are obligated to teach/serve in their area of study at a Georgia public school for one year for each \$2500 awarded, with a maximum of four years. Write for deadlines. *Academic/Career Areas:* Education; Special Education. *Award:* Forgivable loan for use in graduate years; renewable. *Award amount:* \$1000–\$10,000. *Eligibility Requirements:* Applicant must be resident of Georgia and studying in Georgia. *Application Requirements:* Application.

Contact William Flook, Director of Scholarships and Grants Division, Georgia Student Finance Commission, 2082 East Exchange Place, Suite 100, Tucker, GA 30084. *Web site:* http://www.gsfc.org.

HOPE—Helping Outstanding Pupils Educationally. Grant program for Georgia residents who are college undergraduates to attend an accredited two- or four-year Georgia institution. Tuition and fees not covered by federal aid may be covered by the grant. Minimum 3.0 GPA required. Renewable if student maintains grades and reapplies. Write for deadlines. *Award:* Scholarship for use in freshman, sophomore, junior, or senior year; renewable. *Award amount:* \$300–\$3000. *Number of awards:* 120,000–150,000. *Eligibility Requirements:* Applicant must be resident of Georgia and studying in Georgia. Applicant must have 3.0 GPA or higher. *Application Requirements:* Application.

Contact William Flook, Director of Scholarships and Grants Division, Georgia Student Finance Commission, 2082 East Exchange Place, Suite 100, Tucker, GA 30084. *Web site:* http://www.gsfc.org.

Georgia PROMISE Teacher Scholarship Program. Renewable, forgivable loans for junior undergraduates at Georgia colleges who have been accepted for enrollment into a teacher education program leading to initial certification. Minimum cumulative 3.6 GPA required. Recipient must teach at a Georgia public school for one year for each \$1500 awarded. Available to seniors for renewal only. Write for deadlines. *Academic/Career Areas:* Education; Special Education. *Award:* Forgivable loan for use in junior or senior year; renewable. *Award amount:* \$3000. *Number of awards:* 300–400. *Eligibility Requirements:* Applicant must be enrolled at a four-year institution or university and studying in Georgia. Applicant must have 3.5 GPA or higher. *Application Requirements:* Application, transcript.

Contact William Flook, Director of Scholarships and Grants Division, Georgia Student Finance Commission, 2082 East Exchange Place, Suite 100, Tucker, GA 30084. *Web site:* http://www.gsfc.org.

Georgia Regents Scholarship. Awards for exceptional students who show financial need and attend public colleges or universities in Georgia. Must be a Georgia resident. Applicant must contact his/her financial aid administrator for additional requirements, application procedures, and deadlines. *Award:* Scholarship for use in freshman, sophomore, junior, senior, or graduate years; not renewable. *Award amount:* $500–$1000. *Eligibility Requirements:* Applicant must be resident of Georgia and studying in Georgia. *Application Requirements:* Application, financial need analysis.

Contact William Flook, Director of Scholarships and Grants Division, Georgia Student Finance Commission, 2082 East Exchange Place, Suite 100, Tucker, GA 30084. *Web site:* http://www.gsfc.org.

Georgia Tuition Equalization Grant (GTEG). Award for Georgia residents pursuing undergraduate study at an accredited two- or four-year Georgia private institution. Complete the Georgia Student Grant Application. Award is $1000 per academic year. Deadlines vary. *Award:* Grant for use in freshman, sophomore, junior, or senior year; renewable. *Award amount:* $1000. *Number of awards:* 25,000–30,000. *Eligibility Requirements:* Applicant must be enrolled at a two-year or four-year institution or university; resident of Georgia and studying in Georgia. *Application Requirements:* Application.

Contact William Flook, Director of Scholarships and Grants Division, Georgia Student Finance Commission, 2082 East Exchange Place, Suite 100, Tucker, GA 30084. *Web site:* http://www.gsfc.org.

Georgia Public Safety Memorial Grant/ Law Enforcement Personnel Department Grant. Award for children of Georgia law enforcement officers, prison guards, or fire fighters killed or permanently disabled in the line of duty. Must attend an accredited post-secondary Georgia school. Complete the Law Enforcement Personnel Dependents application. *Award:* Grant for use in freshman, sophomore, junior, or senior year; renewable. *Award amount:* $2000–$7000. *Number of awards:* 20–40. *Eligibility Requirements:* Applicant must be enrolled at a two-year, four-year, or technical institution or university; resident of Georgia; studying in Georgia and have employment experience in police/ firefighting. *Application Requirements:* Application. *Deadline:* continuous.

Contact William Flook, Director of Scholarships and Grants Division, Georgia Student Finance Commission, 2082 East Exchange Place, Suite 100, Tucker, GA 30084. *Web site:* http://www.gsfc.org.

Service-Cancellable Stafford Loan-Georgia. To assist students enrolled in critical fields of study in allied health (e.g., nursing, physical therapy). For use at GSFA-approved schools. $3500 forgivable loan for dentistry students only. Contact school financial aid officer for more details. *Academic/Career Areas:* Dental Health/Services; Health and Medical Sciences; Nursing. *Award:* Forgivable loan for use in freshman, sophomore, junior, senior, or graduate years; not renewable. *Award amount:* $2000–$3500. *Eligibility Requirements:* Applicant must be enrolled at a two-year or four-year institution or university and resident of Georgia. Restricted to U.S. citizens. *Application Requirements:* Application, financial need analysis. *Deadline:* continuous.

Contact Grants Director, State of Georgia, 2082 East Exchange Place, Suite 100, Tucker, GA 30084. *Web site:* http://www.gsfc.org.

Georgia Regents Opportunity Grant. Need-based grants for Georgia residents attending public colleges and universities in Georgia. School's financial aid administrator must be contacted for application, application procedures, additional requirements, and application deadline. *Award:* Grant for use in graduate years; not renewable. *Award amount:* $2500–$5000. *Eligibility Requirements:* Applicant must be resident of Georgia and studying in Georgia. *Application Requirements:* Application.

Contact William Flook, Director of Scholarships and Grants Division, Georgia Student Finance Commission, 2082 East Exchange Place, Suite 100, Tucker, GA 30084. *Web site:* http://www.gsfc.org.

Robert C. Byrd Honors Scholarship-Georgia. Complete the application provided by the Georgia Department of Education. Nonrenewable awards for outstanding graduating Georgia high school seniors for full-time undergraduate study at eligible U.S. institution. Minimum 3.5 GPA required. *Award:* Scholarship for use in freshman year; not renewable. *Award amount:* $1121. *Number of awards:* 600–700. *Eligibility Requirements:* Applicant must be high school student; enrolled at a two-year or four-year institution or university and resident of Georgia. Applicant must have 3.5 GPA or higher. *Application Requirements:* Application, transcript. *Deadline:* April 1.

Contact William Flook, Director of Scholarships and Grants Division, Georgia Student Finance Commission, 2082 East Exchange Place, Suite 100, Tucker, GA 30084. *Web site:* http://www.gsfc.org.

State Medical Education Board Country Doctor Scholarship Program. Renewable loan of $10,000 per year for four years available to Georgia residents enrolled in U.S. medical school who display financial need. Repay by practicing one year for each year that loan is received. Payment begins upon graduation. *Academic/Career Areas:* Health and Medical Sciences. *Award:* Forgivable loan for use in graduate years; renewable. *Award amount:* $10,000. *Number of awards:* 25–30. *Eligibility Requirements:* Applicant must be resident of Georgia. *Application Requirements:* Application, financial need analysis, interview, photo, references, test scores, transcript. *Deadline:* May 15.

Contact Peggy Shull, Associate Director, State Medical Education Board of Georgia, 244 Washington Street, SW, 7th Floor, Room 7093, Atlanta, GA 30334.

Governor's Scholarship-Georgia. Award to assist students selected as Georgia scholars, STAR students, valedictorians, and salutatorians. For use at two- and four-year colleges and universities in Georgia. Recipients are selected as entering freshmen. Renewable award of up to $1575. *Award:* Scholarship for use in freshman year; renewable. *Award amount:* up to $1575. *Number of awards:* 2000–3000. *Eligibil-*

ity Requirements: Applicant must be high school student; enrolled at a two-year or four-year institution or university; resident of Georgia and studying in Georgia. Applicant must have 3.5 GPA or higher. *Application Requirements:* Application, transcript. *Deadline:* continuous.

Contact William Flook, Director of Scholarships and Grants Division, Georgia Student Finance Commission, 2082 East Exchange Place, Suite 100, Tucker, GA 30084. *Web site:* http://www.gsfc.org.

State Medical Education Board State Loan Repayment Program. Loan program to repay medical education debts. Participants must practice in underserved areas in Georgia. Loan of $25,000 per year for two years, may be renewed for two additional years, to four-year maximum. Minimum two-year repayment. Must submit disclosure of debt. Deadlines: quarterly, on 15th day of first month. *Academic/Career Areas:* Health and Medical Sciences. *Award:* Forgivable loan for use in graduate years; not renewable. *Award amount:* $25,000–$35,000. *Number of awards:* 10–12. *Eligibility Requirements:* Applicant must be studying in Georgia. *Application Requirements:* Application, references.

Contact Peggy Shull, Associate Director, State Medical Education Board of Georgia, 244 Washington Street, SW, 7th Floor, Room 7093, Atlanta, GA 30334. *E-mail:* smeb@mail.regents.peachnet.edu. *Phone:* 404-656-2226. *Fax:* 404-651-5788.

IDAHO

Leveraging Educational Assistance State Partnership Program (LEAP). Assists students attending participating Idaho colleges and universities majoring in any field except theology or divinity. Idaho residence is not required, but must be U.S. citizen or permanent resident. Must show financial need. Application deadlines vary by institution. One-time award. *Award:* Grant for use in any year; not renewable. *Award amount:* up to $5000. *Eligibility Requirements:* Applicant must be enrolled at a two-year or four-year institution or university and studying in Idaho. *Application Requirements:* Application, financial need analysis, self-addressed stamped envelope.

Contact Lynn Humphrey, Academic Program Coordinator, Idaho State Board of Education, PO Box 83720, Boise, ID 83720-0037. *E-mail:* scmith@osbe.state.id.us. *Phone:* 208-334-2270. *Fax:* 208-334-2632. *Web site:* http://www.sde.state.id.us/osbe/board.htm.

Idaho Commission on the Arts Fellowship Awards. Awards for Idaho residents displaying outstanding achievement in literature, visual arts media, or performing arts. Must be a U.S. citizen and at least 18 years of age. Award of $3500 plus possible show at Idaho gallery. Must submit resume and work samples. Write for deadline dates and more information. Three $1000 honorable mention awards available. *Academic/Career Areas:* Arts; Literature/English/Writing; Performing Arts. *Eligibility Requirements:* Applicant must be age 18 and resident of Idaho. Restricted to U.S. citizens. *Application Requirements:* Application, portfolio, self-addressed stamped envelope. *Deadline:* January 29.

Contact Barbara Garrett, Director of Artist Services, Idaho Commission on the Arts, PO Box 83720, Boise, ID 83720. *E-mail:* bgarrett@ica.state.id.us. *Phone:* 208-334-2119. *Fax:* 208-334-2488. *Web site:* http://www2.state.id.us/arts.

State of Idaho Scholarship Program. Available to Idaho residents who are graduating high school seniors. Must attend an approved Idaho college full-time. Based on class rank (must be verified by school official), GPA, and ACT scores. Vocational student applicants must take COMPASS. Award is renewable. *Award:* Scholarship for use in freshman, sophomore, junior, or senior year; renewable. *Award amount:* $2750. *Number of awards:* 25–30. *Eligibility Requirements:* Applicant must be high school student; enrolled at a two-year, four-year, or technical institution or university; resident of Idaho and studying in Idaho. Applicant must have 3.5 GPA or higher. Restricted to U.S. citizens. *Application Requirements:* Application, references, test scores. *Deadline:* January 31.

Contact Caryl Smith, Scholarship Assistant, Idaho State Board of Education, PO Box 83720, Boise, ID 83720-0037. *E-mail:* csmith@osbe.state.id.us. *Phone:* 208-334-2270. *Fax:* 208-334-2632. *Web site:* http://www.sde.state.id.us/osbe/board.htm.

Education Incentive Loan Forgiveness Contract-Idaho. Renewable award assists Idaho residents enrolling in teacher education or nursing programs within state. Must rank in top fifteen percent of high school graduating class, have a 3.0 GPA or above, and agree to work in Idaho for two years. Deadlines vary. Contact financial aid office at institution of choice. *Academic/Career Areas:* Education; Nursing. *Award:* Forgivable loan for use in freshman, sophomore, junior, or senior year; renewable. *Number of awards:* 29. *Eligibility Requirements:* Applicant must be enrolled at a four-year institution or university; resident of Idaho and studying in Idaho. Applicant must have 3.0 GPA or higher. Restricted to U.S. citizens. *Application Requirements:* Application, test scores, transcript.

Contact Caryl Smith, Scholarship Assistant, Idaho State Board of Education, PO Box 83720, Boise, ID 83720-0037. *E-mail:* csmith@osbe.state.id.us. *Phone:* 208-334-2270. *Fax:* 208-334-2632. *Web site:* http://www.sde.state.id.us/osbe/board.htm.

Idaho Minority and "At Risk" Student Scholarship. For Idaho residents who are disabled or members of a minority group and have financial need. Must attend one of eight post-secondary institutions in the state for undergraduate study. Deadlines vary by institution. Award is renewable. Must be a US citizen and be a graduate of an Idaho high school. Contact college financial aid office. *Award:* Scholarship for use in freshman, sophomore, junior, or senior year; renewable. *Award amount:* $2750. *Number of awards:* 40–45. *Eligibility Requirements:* Applicant must be enrolled at a two-year or four-year institution or university; resident of Idaho and studying in Idaho. *Application Requirements:* Application, financial need analysis.

Contact Caryl Smith, Scholarship Assistant, Idaho State Board of Education, PO Box 83720, Boise, ID 83720-0037. *E-mail:* csmith@osbe.state.id.us.

Phone: 208-334-2270. *Fax:* 208-334-2632. *Web site:* http://www.sde.state.id.us/osbe/board.htm.

ILLINOIS

Illinois National Guard Grant Program. Award for qualified National Guard personnel which pays tuition and fees at Illinois public universities and community colleges. Must provide documentation of service. Deadline: September 15. *Award:* Grant for use in any year; renewable. *Award amount:* up to $1350. *Number of awards:* 2300–2700. *Eligibility Requirements:* Applicant must be enrolled at a two-year or four-year institution or university; resident of Illinois and studying in Illinois. Applicant must have national guard experience. *Application Requirements:* Application. *Deadline:* September 15.

Contact Barb Levin, Client Information, Illinois Student Assistance Commission (ISAC), 1755 Lake Cook Road, Deerfield, IL 60015-5209. *Phone:* 847-948-8500 Ext. 2305. *Web site:* http://www.isac-online.org.

Merit Recognition Scholarship (MRS) Program. Award for Illinois high school seniors graduating in the top 5 percent of their class, and attending Illinois post-secondary institution. Deadline: June 15. Contact for application procedures. *Award:* Scholarship for use in freshman year; not renewable. *Award amount:* up to $1000. *Number of awards:* 1800–2200. *Eligibility Requirements:* Applicant must be high school student; enrolled at a two-year or four-year institution or university; resident of Illinois and studying in Illinois. Applicant must have 3.5 GPA or higher. *Application Requirements:* Application. *Deadline:* June 15.

Contact Barb Levin, Client Information, Illinois Student Assistance Commission (ISAC), 1755 Lake Cook Road, Deerfield, IL 60015-5209. *Phone:* 847-948-8500 Ext. 2305. *Web site:* http://www.isac-online.org.

Illinois Veteran Grant Program—IVG. Award for qualified veterans for tuition and fees at Illinois public universities', and community colleges. Must provide documentation of service (DD214). Deadline is continuous. *Award:* Grant for use in any year; renewable. *Award amount:* $1300–$1350. *Number of awards:* 13,000–16,000. *Eligibility Requirements:* Applicant must be enrolled at a two-year or four-year institution or university; resident of Illinois and studying in Illinois. Applicant must have general military experience. *Application Requirements:* Application. *Deadline:* continuous.

Contact Barb Levin, Client Information, Illinois Student Assistance Commission (ISAC), 1755 Lake Cook Road, Deerfield, IL 60015-5209. *Phone:* 847-948-8500 Ext. 2305. *Web site:* http://www.isac-online.org.

Grant Program for Descendents of Police, Fire, or Correctional Officers. Award for descendants of police, fire, and corrections officers killed or disabled in line of duty. Provides for tuition and fees at approved Illinois institutions. Must be resident of Illinois. Continuous deadline. Provide proof of status. *Award:* Grant for use in any year; renewable. *Award amount:* $3000–$4000. *Eligibility Requirements:* Applicant must be enrolled at a two-year, four-year, or technical institution or university; resident of Illinois; studying in Illinois and have employment experience in police/firefighting. Available to U.S. and non-U.S. citizens. *Application Requirements:* Application. *Deadline:* continuous.

Contact Barb Levin, Client Information, Illinois Student Assistance Commission (ISAC), 1755 Lake Cook Road, Deerfield, IL 60015-5209. *Phone:* 847-948-8500 Ext. 2305. *Web site:* http://www.isac-online.org.

Illinois Incentive for Access Program. Award for eligible first-time freshmen enrolling in approved Illinois institutions. One-time grant of up to $500 may be used for any educational expense. Deadline: October 1. *Award:* Grant for use in freshman year; not renewable. *Award amount:* up to $500. *Number of awards:* 19,000–21,000. *Eligibility Requirements:* Applicant must be enrolled at a two-year, four-year, or technical institution or university; resident of Illinois and studying in Illinois. *Application Requirements:* Financial need analysis. *Deadline:* October 1.

Contact Barb Levin, Client Information, Illinois Student Assistance Commission (ISAC), 1755 Lake Cook Road, Deerfield, IL 60015-5209. *Phone:* 847-948-8500 Ext. 2305. *Web site:* http://www.isac-online.org.

Illinois Minority Graduate Incentive Program Fellowship. Established in 1985 with Higher Education Cooperation Act funds provided by the Illinois Board of Higher Education. Purpose is to increase the number of minority members of the faculties and professional staffs at Illinois institutions of higher education where there is severe under-representation of minorities. Minimum GPA of 2.75. *Academic/Career Areas:* Electrical Engineering/Electronics; Engineering/Technology; Engineering-Related Technologies; Physical Sciences and Math; Science, Technology and Society. *Award:* Grant for use in graduate years; renewable. *Award amount:* $13,500–$15,000. *Number of awards:* 30. *Eligibility Requirements:* Applicant must be Native American or Eskimo, African American, or Hispanic and studying in Illinois. Restricted to U.S. citizens. *Application Requirements:* Application, applicant must enter a contest, essay, references, test scores, transcript. *Deadline:* February 15.

Contact Ms. Jane Meuth, IMGIP/ICEOP Administrator, Illinois Consortium for Educational Opportunity Program, Woody Hall C-224, Southern Illinois University, Carbondale, IL 62901. *E-mail:* jmeuth@www.imgip.siu.edu. *Phone:* 618-453-4558. *Fax:* 618-453-1800. *Web site:* http://www.imgip.siu.edu.

Higher Education License Plate Program—HELP. Need-based grants for students at institutions participating in program whose funds are raised by sale of special license plates commemorating the institutions. Deadline: June 30. *Award:* Grant for use in freshman, sophomore, junior, or senior year; not renewable. *Award amount:* up to $2000. *Number of awards:* up to 45. *Eligibility Requirements:* Applicant must be enrolled at a two-year or four-year institution or university; resident of Illinois and studying in Illinois. *Application Requirements:* Financial need analysis. *Deadline:* June 30.

Contact Barb Levin, Client Information, Illinois Student Assistance Commission (ISAC), 1755 Lake Cook Road, Deerfield, IL 60015-5209. *Phone:* 847-948-8500 Ext. 2305. *Web site:* http://www.isac-online.org.

Illinois Consortium for Educational Opportunity Program Fellowship. Established by the Illinois General Assembly and signed as Public Act 84-785 in September of 1985. Overall intent of ICEOP is to increase the number of underrepresented faculty and staff at Illinois institutions of higher education and higher education governing boards. Requires minimum GPA of 2.75. *Eligibility Requirements:* Applicant must be Native American or Eskimo, Asian, African American, or Hispanic; resident of Illinois and studying in Illinois. Restricted to U.S. citizens. *Application Requirements:* Application, applicant must enter a contest, essay, financial need analysis, references, test scores, transcript. *Deadline:* February 15.

Contact Ms. Jane Meuth, IMGIP/ICEOP Administrator, Illinois Consortium for Educational Opportunity Program, Woody Hall C-224, Southern Illinois University, Carbondale, IL 62901-4723. *E-mail:* jmeuth@www.imgip.siu.edu. *Phone:* 618-453-4558. *Fax:* 618-453-1800. *Web site:* http://www.imgip.siu.edu.

Illinois College Savings Bond Bonus Incentive Grant Program. Program offers holders of Illinois College Savings Bonds a $20 grant for each year of bond maturity payable upon bond redemption if at least 70 percent of proceeds are used to attend college in Illinois. May not be used by students attending religious or divinity schools. *Award:* Grant for use in any year; not renewable. *Award amount:* $40–$160. *Number of awards:* 1000–1200. *Eligibility Requirements:* Applicant must be enrolled at a two-year, four-year, or technical institution or university and studying in Illinois. Available to U.S. and non-U.S. citizens. *Application Requirements:* Application. *Deadline:* continuous.

Contact Barb Levin, Client Information, Illinois Student Assistance Commission (ISAC), 1755 Lake Cook Road, Deerfield, IL 60015-5209. *Phone:* 847-948-8500 Ext. 2305. *Web site:* http://www.isac-online.org.

MIA/POW Scholarships. One-time award for spouse, child, or step-child of veterans who are missing in action or were prisoner-of-war. Must be enrolled at a state-supported school in Illinois. Candidate must be U.S. citizen. High school students are not eligible. Must apply and be accepted before beginning of school. *Award:* Scholarship for use in any year; renewable. *Eligibility Requirements:* Applicant must be enrolled at a two-year or four-year institution or university and studying in Illinois. Applicant or parent must meet one or more of the following requirements: general military experience; retired from active duty; disabled or killed as a result of military service; prisoner of war; or missing in action. *Application Requirements:* Application. *Deadline:* continuous.

Contact Ms. Tracy Mahan, Grants Section, Illinois Department of Veterans' Affairs, 833 South Spring Street, Springfield, IL 62794-9432. *Phone:* 217-782-3564. *Fax:* 217-782-4161.

Illinois Student-to-Student Program of Matching Grants. Award provides matching funds for need-based grants at participating Illinois public universities and community colleges. Deadline: October 1. *Award:* Grant for use in freshman, sophomore, junior, or senior year; not renewable. *Award amount:* up to $1000. *Number of awards:* 2000–4000. *Eligibility Requirements:* Applicant must be enrolled at a two-year or four-year institution or university; resident of Illinois and studying in Illinois. *Application Requirements:* Financial need analysis. *Deadline:* October 1.

Contact Barb Levin, Client Information, Illinois Student Assistance Commission (ISAC), 1755 Lake Cook Road, Deerfield, IL 60015-5209. *Phone:* 847-948-8500 Ext. 2305. *Web site:* http://www.isac-online.org.

Minority Teachers of Illinois Scholarship Program. Award for minority students planning to teach at an approved Illinois preschool, elementary, or secondary school. Deadline: May 1. *Academic/Career Areas:* Education; Special Education. *Award:* Forgivable loan for use in sophomore, junior, or senior year; renewable. *Award amount:* $4000–$5000. *Number of awards:* 400–500. *Eligibility Requirements:* Applicant must be Native American or Eskimo, Asian, African American, or Hispanic; enrolled at a four-year institution or university; resident of Illinois and studying in Illinois. Applicant must have 2.5 GPA or higher. *Application Requirements:* Application. *Deadline:* May 1.

Contact Barb Levin, Client Information, Illinois Student Assistance Commission (ISAC), 1755 Lake Cook Road, Deerfield, IL 60015-5209. *Phone:* 847-948-8500 Ext. 2305. *Web site:* http://www.isac-online.org.

AAOS/OREF Fellowship in Health Services Research. Grant available to candidates who have completed an accredited North American orthopedic residency and are recommended by their department chair. Up to two two-year fellowships at up to $70,000 per year. *Academic/Career Areas:* Health and Medical Sciences; Therapy/Rehabilitation. *Application Requirements:* Application, references. *Deadline:* August 1.

Contact Jean McGuire, Vice President of Grants, Orthopaedic Research and Education Foundation, 6300 North River Road, Suite 700, Rosemont, IL 60018-4261. *E-mail:* mcguire@oref.org. *Phone:* 847-384-4348. *Fax:* 847-698-9767. *Web site:* http://www.oref.org.

David A. DeBolt Teacher Shortage Scholarship Program. Award to assist Illinois students planning to teach at an Illinois pre-school, elementary school, or high school in a teacher shortage discipline. Must agree to teach one year in teacher shortage area for each year of award assistance received. Deadline: May 1. *Academic/Career Areas:* Education; Special Education. *Award:* Forgivable loan for use in sophomore, junior, senior, or graduate years; not renewable. *Award amount:* $4000–$5000. *Number of awards:* 250–300. *Eligibility Requirements:* Applicant must be enrolled at a two-year or four-year institution or university; resident of Illinois and studying in Illinois. Applicant must have 2.5 GPA or higher. *Application Requirements:* Application, transcript. *Deadline:* May 1.

Contact Barb Levin, Client Information, Illinois Student Assistance Commission (ISAC), 1755 Lake Cook Road, Deerfield, IL 60015-5209. *Phone:* 847-948-8500 Ext. 2305. *Web site:* http://www.isac-online.org.

Veterans' Children Educational Opportunities. Renewable award is provided annually to each child age 19 or younger of a veteran who died or became totally disabled as a result of service during World War I, World War II, Korean, or Vietnam War. Must be an Illinois resident and studying in Illinois. *Award:* Grant for use in freshman year; renewable. *Award amount:* up to $250. *Eligibility Requirements:* Applicant must be age 10-18; resident of Illinois and studying in Illinois. Restricted to U.S. citizens. Applicant or parent must meet one or more of the following requirements: general military experience; retired from active duty; disabled or killed as a result of military service; prisoner of war; or missing in action. *Application Requirements:* Application.

Contact Ms. Tracy Mahan, Grants Section, Illinois Department of Veterans' Affairs, 833 South Spring Street, Springfield, IL 62794-9432. *Phone:* 217-782-3564. *Fax:* 217-782-4161.

Illinois Department of Children and Family Services Scholarships. Scholarship recipients will receive a medical card, a monthly check of $434 and a tuition waiver for those recipients who chose to attend one of nine Illinois public universities. Scholarship is prorated for a maximum of four years. Applicant must be 10 years of age, possess a diploma or GED accreditation. Must be a ward of the Department of Children and Family Services, or a former ward who has been adopted or placed in subsidized guardianship. ACT or SAT scores and letters of recommendation are required. Application deadline is April 30th. *Award:* Scholarship for use in any year; renewable. *Award amount:* $6000–$8250. *Number of awards:* 48. *Eligibility Requirements:* Applicant must be high school student; enrolled at a four-year institution or university; resident of Illinois and studying in Illinois. Restricted to U.S. citizens. *Application Requirements:* Application, autobiography, financial need analysis, references, test scores, transcript. *Deadline:* April 30.

Contact Dwight Lambert, Statewide Education Coordinator, Illinois Department of Children and Family Services, 406 East Monroe Street, #222, Springfield, IL 62701-1498. *E-mail:* dlambert@idcfs.state.il.us. *Phone:* 217-524-2030. *Fax:* 217-524-2101.

Illinois Monetary Award Program. Award for eligible students attending Illinois public universities, private colleges and universities, community colleges, and some proprietary institutions. Applicable only to tuition and fees. Based on financial need. Deadline: October 1. *Award:* Grant for use in freshman, sophomore, junior, or senior year; not renewable. *Award amount:* $300–$4320. *Number of awards:* 125,000–135,000. *Eligibility Requirements:* Applicant must be enrolled at a two-year, four-year, or technical institution or university; resident of Illinois and studying in Illinois. *Application Requirements:* Financial need analysis. *Deadline:* October 1.

Contact Barb Levin, Client Information, Illinois Student Assistance Commission (ISAC), 1755 Lake Cook Road, Deerfield, IL 60015-5209. *Phone:* 847-948-8500 Ext. 2305. *Web site:* http://www.isac-online.org.

INDIANA

Indiana Higher Education Grant. Assists full-time undergraduate students attending approved colleges or universities in Indiana. Renewable award based on financial need. Must be Indiana resident. Must complete Free Application for Federal Student Aid by the state's deadline, which is March 1, prior to the academic year expected to enroll. *Award:* Grant for use in freshman, sophomore, junior, or senior year; renewable. *Award amount:* $200–$4000. *Number of awards:* 35,000–40,000. *Eligibility Requirements:* Applicant must be resident of Indiana and studying in Indiana. *Application Requirements:* Application, financial need analysis. *Deadline:* March 1.

Contact Grant Counselors, Indiana State Student Assistance Commission (SSACI), 150 West Market Street, Suite 500, Indianapolis, IN 46204-2811. *E-mail:* grants@ssali.state.in.us. *Phone:* 317-232-2350. *Fax:* 317-232-3260. *Web site:* http://www.state.in.us/ssaci/.

National Guard Grant. Applicants must be active members of Indiana National Guard. Applicable to students attending public schools only. Covers 100% of tuition and fees at a public school. *Award:* Grant for use in freshman, sophomore, junior, or senior year; not renewable. *Eligibility Requirements:* Applicant must be enrolled at a two-year or four-year institution or university; resident of Indiana and studying in Indiana. Restricted to U.S. citizens. *Application Requirements:* Application. *Deadline:* March 1.

Contact Grants Counselor, Indiana State Student Assistance Commission (SSACI), 150 West Market Street, Suite 500, Indianapolis, IN 46204-2811. *Phone:* 317-232-2350. *Fax:* 317-232-2360. *Web site:* http://www.state.in.us/ssaci/.

Department of Veterans Affairs Free Tuition for Children of POW/MIA's in Vietnam. Renewable award for residents of Indiana who are the children of veterans declared missing in action or prisoner-of-war after January 1, 1960. Provides tuition at Indiana institutions for undergraduate study. *Award:* Scholarship for use in freshman, sophomore, junior, or senior year; renewable. *Eligibility Requirements:* Applicant must be resident of Indiana and studying in Indiana. Applicant or parent must meet one or more of the following requirements: general military experience; retired from active duty; disabled or killed as a result of military service; prisoner of war; or missing in action. *Application Requirements:* Application. *Deadline:* continuous.

Contact Jon Brinkley, State Service Officer, Indiana Department of Veterans' Affairs, 302 West Washington Street, Roome E-120, Indianapolis, IN 46204-2738. *E-mail:* jbrinley@dva.state.in.us. *Phone:* 317-232-3910. *Fax:* 317-232-7721. *Web site:* http://www.ai.org/veteran/index.html.

Hoosier Scholar Award. Scholarship for top prospective freshmen. Must attend approved Indiana college, or university. Open to students determined by high school to be academically qualified and in top twenty percent of class. One-time award for Indiana residents. *Award:* Scholarship for use in freshman year; not renewable. *Award amount:* $500. *Number of awards:* up to 800. *Eligibility Requirements:* Applicant must be high school student; enrolled at a two-year or four-year institution or university; resident of Indiana and studying in Indiana. Applicant must have 3.5 GPA or higher. Restricted to U.S. citizens. *Application Requirements:* Application, test scores, transcript. *Deadline:* March 1.

Contact Ada Davis, Program Coordinator, Indiana State Student Assistance Commission (SSACI), 150 West Market Street, Suite 500, Indianapolis, IN 46204-2811. *Phone:* 317-232-2355. *Fax:* 317-232-3260. *Web site:* http://www.state.in.us/ssaci/.

Indiana Remission of Fees for Child of Disabled Veteran. Renewable award for Indiana residents who are the children of veterans who received the Purple Heart Medal or are rated with a service-connected disability or died from a service-connected disease or injury. Pays partial tuition at Indiana state-supported institutions. Must submit paperwork as proof of decoration, not simply the medal. *Award:* Scholarship for use in any year; renewable. *Eligibility Requirements:* Applicant must be resident of Indiana and studying in Indiana. Applicant or parent must meet one or more of the following requirements: general military experience; retired from active duty; disabled or killed as a result of military service; prisoner of war; or missing in action. *Application Requirements:* Application. *Deadline:* continuous.

Contact Jon Brinkley, State Service Officer, Indiana Department of Veterans' Affairs, 302 West Washington Street, Room E-120, Indianapolis, IN 46204-2738. *E-mail:* jbrinkley@dva.state.in.us. *Phone:* 317-232-3910. *Fax:* 317-232-7721. *Web site:* http://www.ai.org/veteran/index.html.

Special Education Services Scholarship. Award for Indiana residents attending eligible Indiana institutions. Awards of $1000. Contact college or university for application deadline. *Academic/Career Areas:* Special Education; Therapy/Rehabilitation. *Award:* Scholarship for use in any year; not renewable. *Award amount:* $1000. *Eligibility Requirements:* Applicant must be enrolled at a four-year institution; resident of Indiana and studying in Indiana. Applicant must have 2.5 GPA or higher. *Application Requirements:* Application.

Contact Yvonne Heflin, Program Director, Indiana State Student Assistance Commission (SSACI), 150 West Market Street, Suite 500, Indianapolis, IN 46204-2811. *Phone:* 317-232-1178. *Fax:* 317-232-3260. *Web site:* http://www.state.in.us/ssaci/.

Indiana Minority Teacher Scholarship. Award for Indiana residents attending eligible Indiana institutions. Awards range from $1000 to $4000. Contact college or university for deadline and application details. *Academic/Career Areas:* Education. *Award:* Scholarship for use in any year; not renewable. *Award amount:* $1000–$4000. *Eligibility Requirements:* Applicant must be African American or Hispanic; enrolled at a four-year institution; resident of Indiana and studying in Indiana. Applicant must have 2.5 GPA or higher. *Application Requirements:* Application.

Contact Grant Counselor, Indiana State Student Assistance Commission (SSACI), 150 West Market Street, Suite 500, Indianapolis, IN 46204-2811. *E-mail:* grants@ssali.state.un.is. *Phone:* 317-232-2350. *Fax:* 317-232-3260. *Web site:* http://www.state.in.us/ssaci/.

Minority Teacher and Special Education Services Scholarship Program-Indiana. One-time award for black or Hispanic students seeking teacher certification in special education or physical or occupational therapy. Must be Indiana resident with minimum 2.0 GPA pursuing full-time study. Must agree to teach in an elementary or secondary school or practice in fields of occupational or physical therapy. *Academic/Career Areas:* Special Education; Therapy/Rehabilitation. *Award:* Scholarship for use in any year; not renewable. *Award amount:* $1000–$4000. *Number of awards:* 250–400. *Eligibility Requirements:* Applicant must be African American or Hispanic; enrolled at a four-year institution or university; resident of Indiana and studying in Indiana. *Application Requirements:* Application.

Contact Yvonne Heflin, Program Director, Indiana State Student Assistance Commission (SSACI), 150 West Market Street, Suite 500, Indianapolis, IN 46204-2811. *Phone:* 317-232-2350. *Fax:* 317-232-3260. *Web site:* http://www.state.in.us/ssaci/.

Indiana Nursing Scholarship Fund. Renewable award for Indiana students pursuing nursing degrees at eligible Indiana institutions. Must have minimum 2.0 GPA and show financial need. Must agree to work as a nurse in Indiana for at least two years. Contact for deadline. *Academic/Career Areas:* Nursing. *Award:* Scholarship for use in any year; not renewable. *Award amount:* up to $5000. *Eligibility Requirements:* Applicant must be enrolled at a two-year or four-year institution or university; resident of Indiana and studying in Indiana. *Application Requirements:* Application, financial need analysis.

Contact Yvonne Heflin, Program Director, Indiana State Student Assistance Commission (SSACI), 150 West Market Street, Suite 500, Indianapolis, IN 46204-2811. *Phone:* 317-232-2350. *Fax:* 317-232-3260. *Web site:* http://www.state.in.us/ssaci/.

Special Education Services and Occupational or Physical Therapy Scholarship. Renewable award for Indiana residents pursuing degrees in special education, or occupational or physical therapy in Indiana. Must have minimum 2.0 GPA. Must teach or practice full-time for three years in Indiana following certification. Contact individual institution for deadline. *Academic/Career Areas:* Special Education; Therapy/Rehabilitation. *Award:* Scholarship for use in freshman, sophomore, junior, or senior year; renewable. *Award amount:* $1000. *Number of awards:* 500–600. *Eligibility Requirements:* Applicant must be enrolled at a two-year or four-year institution; resident of Indiana and studying in Indiana. *Application Requirements:* Application.

Contact Yvonne Heflin, Program Director, Indiana State Student Assistance Commission (SSACI), 150 West Market Street, Suite 500, Indianapolis, IN 46204-2811. *Phone:* 317-232-2350. *Fax:* 317-232-3260. *Web site:* http://www.state.in.us/ssaci/.

Twenty-first Century Scholars Award. Renewable award for Indiana residents for use at two, or four-year post-secondary institutions in Indiana. Award based on need and renewable for each undergraduate year. Write for details and deadline. Must file FAFSA my March 1 prior to the academic year expected to enroll. *Award:* Scholarship for use in freshman, sophomore, junior, or senior year; renewable. *Award amount:* $1000. *Number of awards:* 2000–4000. *Eligibility Requirements:* Applicant must be enrolled at a two-year or four-year institution; resident of Indiana and studying in Indiana. Applicant must have 2.5 GPA or higher. Restricted to U.S. citizens. *Application Requirements:* Application, financial need analysis.

Contact Counselors, Indiana State Student Assistance Commission (SSACI), 150 West Market Street, Suite 500, Indianapolis, IN 46204-2811. *Phone:* 317-232-2100. *Fax:* 317-232-3260. *Web site:* http://www.state.in.us/ssaci/.

Child of Disabled Veteran Grant or Purple Heart Recipient, Grant. Reduction in tuition at Indiana state-supported colleges or universities for children of disabled veterans or Purple Heart recipients. Must submit Form DD214 or service record. *Award:* Grant for use in any year; renewable. *Eligibility Requirements:* Applicant must be enrolled at a four-year institution or university; resident of Indiana and studying in Indiana. Applicant or parent must meet one or more of the following requirements: general military experience; retired from active duty; disabled or killed as a result of military service; prisoner of war; or missing in action. *Application Requirements:* Application.

Contact Jon Brinkley, State Service Officer, Indiana Department of Veterans' Affairs, 302 West Washington Street, Room E-120, Indianapolis, IN 46204-2738. *E-mail:* jbrinley@dva.state.in.us. *Phone:* 317-232-3910. *Fax:* 317-232-7721. *Web site:* http://www.ai.org/veteran/index.html.

Indiana Freedom of Choice Grant. Renewable grants provide additional funds for students receiving the Indiana Higher Education Award. Must plan to attend an eligible private institution in Indiana. Recipients of IHEA automatically considered. Must be Indiana resident. Must complete Free Application for Federal Student Aid by the state's established deadline, which is March 1, prior to the academic year expected to enroll. *Award:* Grant for use in freshman, sophomore, junior, or senior year; renewable. *Award amount:* $200–$8518. *Number of awards:* 9000–11,000. *Eligibility Requirements:* Applicant must be enrolled at a two-year or four-year institution; resident of Indiana and studying in Indiana. Restricted to U.S. citizens. *Application Requirements:* Application, financial need analysis. *Deadline:* March 1.

Contact Grant Counselor, Indiana State Student Assistance Commission (SSACI), 150 West Market Street, Suite 500, Indianapolis, IN 46204-2811. *Phone:* 317-232-2350. *Fax:* 317-232-3260. *Web site:* http://www.state.in.us/ssaci/.

IOWA

Iowa Teacher Forgivable Loan Program. Forgivable loan assists students who will teach in Iowa secondary schools. Must be an Iowa resident attending an Iowa post-secondary institution. Contact for additional information. *Academic/Career Areas:* Education. *Award:* Forgivable loan for use in freshman, sophomore, junior, or senior year; not renewable. *Award amount:* $2686. *Eligibility Requirements:* Applicant must be enrolled at a four-year institution or university; resident of Iowa; studying in Iowa and have employment experience in teaching. *Application Requirements:* Application. *Deadline:* continuous.

Contact Julie Leeper, State Grants Administrator, Iowa College Student Aid Commission, 200 10th Street, 4th Floor, Des Moines, IA 50309-3609. *E-mail:* icsac@max.state.ia.us. *Phone:* 515-242-6703. *Fax:* 515-242-5996. *Web site:* http://www.iowacollegeaid.org.

State of Iowa Scholarship Program. Program provides recognition and financial honorarium to Iowa's academically talented high school seniors. Honorary scholarships are presented to all qualified candidates. Approximately 1,700 top-ranking candidates are designated State of Iowa Scholars every March, from an applicant pool of nearly 5,000 high school seniors. Must be used at an Iowa post-secondary institution. Minimum 3.5 GPA required. *Award:* Scholarship for use in freshman year; not renewable. *Number of awards:* up to 1700. *Eligibility Requirements:* Applicant must be high school student; enrolled at a two-year, four-year, or technical institution or university; resident of Iowa and studying in Iowa. Applicant must have 3.5 GPA or higher. *Application Requirements:* Application, test scores. *Deadline:* November 1.

Contact Julie Leeper, State Grants Administrator, Iowa College Student Aid Commission, 200 10th Street, 4th Floor, Des Moines, IA 50309-3609. *E-mail:* icsac@max.state.ia.us. *Phone:* 515-242-6703. *Fax:* 515-242-5996. *Web site:* http://www.iowacollegeaid.org.

Iowa Grants. Statewide need-based program to assist high-need Iowa residents. Recipients' must demonstrate a high level of financial need to receive awards ranging from $100 to $1,000. Awards are prorated for students enrolled for less than full-time. Awards must be used at Iowa post-secondary institutions. *Award:* Grant for use in freshman, sophomore, junior, or senior year; not renewable. *Award amount:* $100–$1000. *Eligibility Requirements:* Applicant must be enrolled at a two-year, four-year, or technical institution or university; resident of Iowa and studying in Iowa. *Application Requirements:* Application, financial need analysis. *Deadline:* continuous.

Contact Julie Leeper, State Grants Administrator, Iowa College Student Aid Commission, 200 10th Street, 4th Floor, Des Moines, IA 50309-3609. *E-mail:* icsac@max.state.ia.us. *Phone:* 515-242-6703. *Fax:* 515-242-5996. *Web site:* http://www.iowacollegeaid.org.

Iowa National Guard Education Assistance Program. Program provides post-secondary tuition assistance to members of Iowa National Guard Units. Must study at a post-secondary institution in Iowa. Contact for additional information. *Award:* Grant for use in freshman, sophomore, junior, or senior year; not renewable. *Award amount:* $1800. *Eligibility Requirements:* Applicant must be enrolled at a two-year, four-year, or technical institution or university; resident of Iowa; studying in Iowa and have employment experience in designated career field. Applicant must have served in the Air Force National Guard or Army National Guard. *Application Requirements:* Application. *Deadline:* continuous.

Contact Julie Leeper, State Grants Administrator, Iowa College Student Aid Commission, 200 10th Street, 4th Floor, Des Moines, IA 50309-3609. *E-mail:* icsac@max.state.ia.us. *Phone:* 515-242-6703. *Fax:* 515-242-5996. *Web site:* http://www.iowacollegeaid.org.

Iowa Tuition Grant Program. Program assists students' who attend independent post-secondary institutions in Iowa. Iowa residents currently enrolled, or planning to enroll, for at least three semester hours at one of the eligible Iowa post-secondary institutions' may apply. Awards currently range from $100 to $3900. Grants may not exceed the difference between independent college; and university tuition and fees and the average tuition and fees at the three public Regent universities. *Award:* Grant for use in freshman, sophomore, junior, or senior year; not renewable. *Award amount:* $100–$3900. *Eligibility Requirements:* Applicant must be enrolled at a two-year or four-year institution; resident of Iowa and studying in Iowa. *Application Requirements:* Application. *Deadline:* June 1.

Contact Julie Leeper, State Grants Administrator, Iowa College Student Aid Commission, 200 10th Street, 4th Floor, Des Moines, IA 50309-3609. *E-mail:* icsac@max.state.ia.us. *Phone:* 515-242-6703. *Fax:* 515-242-5996. *Web site:* http://www.iowacollegeaid.org.

Iowa Vocational-Technical Tuition Grant Program. Program provides need-based financial assistance to Iowa residents enrolled in career education (vocational-technical), and career option programs at Iowa area community colleges. Grants range from $150 to $650, depending on the length of program, financial need, and available funds. *Award:* Grant for use in freshman or sophomore year; not renewable. *Award amount:* $150–$650. *Eligibility Requirements:* Applicant must be enrolled at a technical institution; resident of Iowa and studying in Iowa. *Application Requirements:* Application. *Deadline:* June 1.

Contact Julie Leeper, State Grants Administrator, Iowa College Student Aid Commission, 200 10th Street, 4th Floor, Des Moines, IA 50309-3609. *E-mail:* icsac@max.state.ia.us. *Phone:* 515-242-6703. *Fax:* 515-242-5996. *Web site:* http://www.iowacollegeaid.org.

Iowa War Orphans Educational Aid. Renewable award for children of veterans who died as a result of service. Must be an Iowa resident for two years preceding application. Must attend post-secondary institution in the state. Copies of birth and death certificates required. *Award:* Scholarship for use in any year; renewable. *Award amount:* $600. *Number of awards:* 8. *Eligibility Requirements:* Applicant must be enrolled at a two-year or four-year institution or university; single; resident of Iowa and studying in Iowa. Applicant must have 2.5 GPA or higher. Applicant or parent must meet one or more of the following requirements: general military experience; retired from active duty; disabled or killed as a result of military service; prisoner of war; or missing in action. *Application Requirements:* Application.

Contact Brian Bales, Executive Director, Iowa Commission of Veterans Affairs, 7700 Northwest Beaver Drive, Camp Dodge, Johnston, IA 50131-1902. *E-mail:* brian.bales@icva.state.ia.us. *Phone:* 515-242-5331. *Fax:* 515-242-5659.

KANSAS

Kansas Educational Benefits for Children of MIA, POW, and Deceased Veterans of the Vietnam War. Full-tuition scholarship awarded to students who are children of veterans. Must show proof of parent's status as missing in action, prisoner of war, or killed in action in the Vietnam War. Kansas residence required. Must attend a state supported post secondary school. *Award:* Scholarship for use in any year; not renewable. *Eligibility Requirements:* Applicant must be studying in Kansas. Applicant or parent must meet one or more of the following requirements: general military experience; retired from active duty; disabled or killed as a result of military service; prisoner of war; or missing in action. *Application Requirements:* Application.

Contact Scholarship Administrator, Kansas Commission on Veterans Affairs, 700 Southwest Jackson, Jayhawk Tower, #701, Topeka, KS 66603.

Kansas Comprehensive Grant Program. Grants available for Kansas residents attending public or private baccalaureate colleges or universities in Kansas. Based on financial need. Must file Free Application for Federal Student Aid to apply. Renewable award of up to $2500 for undergraduate use. *Award:* Grant for use in freshman, sophomore, junior, or senior year; not renewable. *Award amount:* $1100–$3000. *Number of awards:* 7000–8000. *Eligibility Requirements:* Applicant must be enrolled at a two-year or four-year institution or university; resident of Kansas and studying in Kansas. *Application Requirements:* Financial need analysis. *Deadline:* April 1.

Contact Diane Lindeman, Associate Director of Fiscal Affairs, Kansas Board of Regents, 700 Southwest Harrison, Suite 1410, Topeka, KS 66603. *Phone:* 785-296-3517. *Fax:* 785-296-0983. *Web site:* http://www.ukans.edu/~kbor.

Vocational Education Scholarship Program-Kansas. Several scholarships for Kansas residents who graduated from a Kansas accredited high school. Must be enrolled in a vocational education program at an eligible Kansas institution. Based on ability and aptitude. Deadlines vary. Renewable award of $500. *Academic/Career Areas:* Trade/Technical Specialties. *Award:* Scholarship for use in freshman or sophomore year; renewable. *Award amount:* $500. *Number of awards:* 100–200. *Eligibility Requirements:* Applicant must be enrolled at a two-year or technical institution; resident of Kansas and studying in Kansas. *Application Requirements:* Application, test scores.

Contact Diane Lindeman, Associate Director of Fiscal Affairs, Kansas Board of Regents, 700 Southwest Harrison, Suite 1410, Topeka, KS 66603. *Phone:* 785-296-3517. *Fax:* 785-296-0983. *Web site:* http://www.ukans.edu/~kbor.

Kansas Teacher Scholarship. Several scholarships for Kansas residents pursuing teaching careers. Must teach in a "hard-to-fill" discipline in Kansas for one year for each award received. Renewable award of $5000. Application fee is $10. *Academic/Career Areas:* Education. *Award:* Forgivable loan for use in freshman, sophomore, junior, or senior year; renewable. *Award amount:* $5000. *Number of awards:* 60–80. *Eligibility Requirements:* Applicant must be enrolled at a two-year or four-year institution or university and resident of Kansas. *Application Requirements:* Application, references, test scores, transcript. *Fee:* $10. *Deadline:* April 1.

Contact Diane Lindeman, Associate Director of Fiscal Affairs, Kansas Board of Regents, 700 Southwest Harrison, Suite 1410, Topeka, KS 66603. *Phone:* 785-296-3517. *Fax:* 785-296-0983. *Web site:* http://www.ukans.edu/~kbor.

KENTUCKY

Department of Veterans Affairs Tuition Waiver-Kentucky. Renewable award for Kentucky residents who are dependents of veterans who were killed or totally disabled in the service. Must be a U.S. citizen under 25 years of age attending a Kentucky state school as an undergraduate. *Award:* Scholarship for use in freshman, sophomore, junior, or senior year; renewable. *Eligibility Requirements:* Applicant must be age 25 or under; resident of Kentucky and studying in Kentucky. Applicant or parent must meet one or more of the following requirements: general military experience; retired from active duty; disabled or killed as a result of military service; prisoner of war; or missing in action. *Application Requirements:* Application. *Deadline:* continuous.

Contact Larry Garrett, Coordinator, Kentucky Department of Veterans Affairs, 545 South Third Street, Louisville, KY 40202-9095. *Phone:* 800-928-4012. *Fax:* 502-595-4448.

Kentucky Educational Excellence Scholarship (KEES). Annual award based on each Kentucky high school year's GPA of 2.5 or higher and highest ACT or SAT score of 15 or higher received by high school graduation. Awards are renewable if required cumulative GPA maintained, or regained if eligibility is lost, at a Kentucky post-secondary school. Must be a Kentucky resident. *Award:* Scholarship for use in freshman, sophomore, junior, or senior year; renewable. *Award amount:* $125–$800. *Number of awards:* 30,000–35,000. *Eligibility Requirements:* Applicant must be high school student; enrolled at a two-year, four-year, or technical institution or university; resident of Kentucky and studying in Kentucky. Applicant must have 2.5 GPA or higher. Restricted to U.S. citizens. *Application Requirements:* Application.

Contact Tim Phelps, KEES Program Coordinator, Kentucky Higher Education Assistance Authority (KHEAA), 1050 U.S. 127 South, Frankfort, KY 40601-4323. *E-mail:* tphelps@kheaa.com. *Phone:* 502-696-7397. *Fax:* 502-696-7345. *Web site:* http://www.kheaa.com.

Kentucky Tuition Grant (KTG). Available to Kentucky residents who are full-time undergraduates at an independent college within the state. Must not be enrolled in a religion program. Based on financial need. Submit Free Application for Federal Student Aid. Priority deadline is March 15. *Award:* Grant for use in freshman, sophomore, junior, or senior year; not renewable. *Award amount:* $50–$1500. *Number of awards:* 9000–10,000. *Eligibility Requirements:* Applicant must be enrolled at a two-year or four-year institution or university; resident of Kentucky and studying in Kentucky. Restricted to U.S. citizens. *Application Requirements:* Application, financial need analysis. *Deadline:* continuous.

Contact Mark Wells, Program Coordinator, Kentucky Higher Education Assistance Authority (KHEAA), 1050 U.S. 127 South, Frankfort, KY 40601-4323. *E-mail:* mwells@kheaa.com. *Phone:* 502-696-7394. *Fax:* 502-696-7345. *Web site:* http://www.kheaa.com.

College Access Program (CAP) Grant. One-time award for U.S. citizen and Kentucky resident with no previous college degree. Provides $46 per semester hour for a minimum of six hours per semester. Applicants seeking degrees in religion are not eligible. Must demonstrate financial need and submit Free Application for Federal Student Aid. Priority deadline is March 15. *Award:* Grant for use in freshman, sophomore, junior, or senior year; not renewable. *Award amount:* up to $1100. *Number of awards:* 30,000–35,000. *Eligibility Requirements:* Applicant must be enrolled at a two-year, four-year, or technical institution or university; resident of Kentucky and studying in Kentucky. Restricted to U.S. citizens. *Application Requirements:* Application, financial need analysis. *Deadline:* continuous.

Contact Mark Wells, Program Coordinator, Kentucky Higher Education Assistance Authority (KHEAA), 1050 U.S. 127 South, Frankfort, KY 40601-4323. *E-mail:* mwells@kheaa.com. *Phone:* 502-696-7394. *Fax:* 502-696-7345. *Web site:* http://www.kheaa.com.

Kentucky Teacher Scholarship Program. Award for Kentucky residents attending Kentucky institutions and pursuing a teaching degree. Must teach one semester for each semester of award received. In critical shortage areas, must teach one semester for every two semesters of award received.

Repayment obligation if teaching requirement not met. Submit Free Application for Federal Student Aid and Teacher Scholarship Application. *Academic/Career Areas:* Education; Special Education. *Award:* Forgivable loan for use in any year; not renewable. *Award amount:* $100–$5000. *Number of awards:* 350–450. *Eligibility Requirements:* Applicant must be enrolled at a two-year or four-year institution or university; resident of Kentucky and studying in Kentucky. Restricted to U.S. citizens. *Application Requirements:* Application, financial need analysis. *Deadline:* May 8.

Contact Pam Polly, Program Coordinator, Kentucky Higher Education Assistance Authority (KHEAA), 1050 U.S. 127 South, Frankfort, KY 40601-4323. *E-mail:* ppolly@kheaa.com. *Phone:* 502-696-7392. *Fax:* 502-696-7345. *Web site:* http://www.kheaa.com.

Kentucky Department of Education Minority Educator Scholarship. Scholarship for minority teacher candidates who rank in the upper half of their class or have a minimum 2.5 GPA. *Academic/Career Areas:* Education. *Award:* Scholarship for use in any year; not renewable. *Number of awards:* 288. *Eligibility Requirements:* Applicant must be Native American or Eskimo, Asian, African American, or Hispanic; enrolled at a four-year institution; resident of Kentucky and studying in Kentucky. Applicant must have 2.5 GPA or higher. Restricted to U.S. citizens. *Application Requirements:* Application, references, transcript.

Contact Kathryn K. Wallace, Director, Kentucky Department of Education, 500 Mero Street, 17th Floor, Frankfort, KY 40601. *E-mail:* kwallace@kde.state.ky.us. *Phone:* 502-564-2672. *Fax:* 502-564-6952.

Nursing Incentive Scholarship Program-Kentucky. Awards offered to Kentucky residents who have been accepted into a nursing program. Recipients must work as a nurse in Kentucky one year for each year funded. Preference is given for financial need, LPNs pursuing RN education, and RNs pursuing graduate nursing education. Write or call for details. Renewable award of $2000. *Academic/Career Areas:* Nursing. *Award:* Scholarship for use in any year; renewable. *Award amount:* $2000. *Eligibility Requirements:* Applicant must be enrolled at a two-year, four-year, or technical institution or university and resident of Kentucky. *Application Requirements:* Application. *Deadline:* June 1.

Contact Darlene Chilton, Program Coordinator, Kentucky Board of Nursing, 313 Whittington Parkway, Suite 300, Louisville, KY 40222-5172. *E-mail:* darlene.chilton@mail.state.ky.us. *Phone:* 502-329-7000 Ext. 230. *Fax:* 502-329-8209.

Benefits for Veterans and their Dependents-Kentucky. Tuition waiver available to Kentucky dependents of veterans who were killed or totally disabled in the service. For use at a Kentucky state school. Renewable award is for undergraduate study. Student must be under 23 years of age. *Award:* Scholarship for use in freshman, sophomore, junior, or senior year; renewable. *Eligibility Requirements:* Applicant must be age 23 or under; enrolled at a two-year, four-year, or technical institution or university; resident of Kentucky and studying in Kentucky. Restricted to U.S. citizens. Applicant or parent must meet one or more of the following requirements: general military experience; retired from active duty; disabled or killed as a result of military service; prisoner of war; or missing in action. *Application Requirements:* Application. *Deadline:* continuous.

Contact Larry Garrett, Coordinator, Kentucky Department of Veterans Affairs, 545 South Third Street, Louisville, KY 40202-9095. *Phone:* 502-595-4447. *Fax:* 502-595-4448.

Environmental Protection Scholarships. Renewable awards for college juniors, seniors, and graduate students for tuition, fees, and room and board at a Kentucky state university. Awards of $3500 to $4500 per semester for up to four semesters. Five awards given in 1999 for a total of $15,912. Minimum 2.5 GPA required. Must agree to work full-time for the Kentucky Natural Resources and Environmental Protection Cabinet upon graduation. *Academic/Career Areas:* Agriculture; Chemical Engineering; Civil Engineering; Earth Science; Health and Medical Sciences. *Award:* Scholarship for use in junior, senior, or graduate years; renewable. *Award amount:* $3500–$4500. *Number of awards:* 3–5. *Eligibility Requirements:* Applicant must be enrolled at a four-year institution or university and studying in Kentucky. Applicant must have 2.5 GPA or higher. Available to U.S. and non-U.S. citizens. *Application Requirements:* Application, essay, interview, references, transcript. *Deadline:* February 15.

Contact Scholarship Program Coordinator, Kentucky Natural Resources and Environmental Protection Cabinet, 233 Mining/Mineral Resources Building, Lexington, KY 40506. *E-mail:* kipp@pop.uky.edu. *Phone:* 606-257-1299. *Fax:* 606-323-1049. *Web site:* http://www.uky.edu/waterresources.

LOUISIANA

TOPS Opportunity Award. Program awards an amount equal to tuition to students attending a Louisiana public institution, or an amount equal to the weighted average public tuition to students attending a LAICU private institution. Must have a minimum high school GPA of 2.5, the prior year's state average ACT score, and complete a 16.5 unit core curriculum. *Award:* Scholarship for use in freshman, sophomore, junior, or senior year; renewable. *Award amount:* $1056–$2708. *Eligibility Requirements:* Applicant must be high school student; enrolled at a two-year or four-year institution or university; resident of Louisiana and studying in Louisiana. Applicant must have 2.5 GPA or higher. Restricted to U.S. citizens. *Application Requirements:* Application, interview. *Deadline:* July 1.

Contact Public Information, Louisiana Office of Student Financial Assistance, PO Box 91202, Baton Rouge, LA 70821-9202. *E-mail:* custserv@osfa.state.la.us. *Phone:* 800-259-5626 Ext. 1012. *Web site:* http://www.osfa.state.la.us.

TOPS Performance Award. Program awards an amount equal to tuition plus a $400 annual stipend to students attending a Louisiana public institution, or an amount equal to the weighted average public tuition plus a $400 annual stipend to students attending a LAICU private institution. Must have a minimum high school GPA of 3.5, an ACT score of 23 and completion of a 16.5 unit core curriculum. *Award:* Scholarship for use in freshman, sophomore, junior, or senior year; renewable. *Award amount:* $1456–$3108. *Eligibility Requirements:* Applicant must be high school student; enrolled at a two-year or four-year institution or university; resident of Louisiana and studying in Louisiana. Applicant must have 3.5 GPA or higher. Restricted to U.S. citizens. *Application Requirements:* Application, test scores. *Deadline:* July 1.

Contact Public Information, Louisiana Office of Student Financial Assistance, PO Box 91202, Baton Rouge, LA 70821-9202. *E-mail:* custserv@osfa.state.la.us. *Phone:* 800-259-5626 Ext. 1012. *Web site:* http://www.osfa.state.la.us.

TOPS Teacher Award. High school graduates must have a 3.25 high school GPA, ACT score of 23 and completion of the core curriculum to be considered for this competitively awarded program. Undergraduate students with greater than 48 hours must have a 3.0 college GPA and graduate students must have an overall B average to be considered. Loan is forgiven if student receives certification and teaches one year at a Louisiana BESE approved school for each year of assistance received. *Academic/Career Areas:* Education. *Award:* Forgivable loan for use in freshman, sophomore, junior, senior, or graduate years; renewable. *Award amount:* $4000–$6000. *Number of awards:* 90. *Eligibility Requirements:* Applicant must be enrolled at a two-year or four-year institution or university; resident of Louisiana and studying in Louisiana. Restricted to U.S. citizens. *Application Requirements:* Application, test scores. *Deadline:* July 1.

Contact Public Information, Louisiana Office of Student Financial Assistance, PO Box 91202, Baton Rouge, LA 70821-9202. *E-mail:* custserv@osfa.state.la.us. *Phone:* 800-259-5626 Ext. 1012. *Web site:* http://www.osfa.state.la.us.

Rockefeller State Wildlife Scholarship. For Louisiana residents attending a public college within the state studying wildlife, forestry, or marine sciences full-time. Renewable up to five years as an undergraduate and two years as a graduate. Must have at least a 2.5 GPA and have taken the ACT or SAT. *Academic/Career Areas:* Animal/Veterinary Sciences; Applied Sciences; Natural Resources. *Award:* Scholarship for use in any year; renewable. *Award amount:* $1000. *Number of awards:* 60. *Eligibility Requirements:* Applicant must be enrolled at a two-year or four-year institution or university; resident of Louisiana and studying in Louisiana. Applicant must have 2.5 GPA or higher. Restricted to U.S. citizens. *Application Requirements:* Application, test scores, transcript. *Deadline:* March 31.

Contact Public Information, Louisiana Office of Student Financial Assistance, PO Box 91202, Baton Rouge, LA 70821-9202. *E-mail:* custserv@osfa.state.la.us. *Phone:* 800-259-5626 Ext. 1012. *Web site:* http://www.osfa.state.la.us.

Leveraging Educational Assistance Program (LEAP). LEAP program provides federal and state funds to provide need-based grants to academically qualified students. Individual award determined by Financial Aid Office and governed by number of applicants and availability of funds. File Free Application for Federal Student Aid by school deadline to apply each year. For Louisiana students attending Louisiana post-secondary institutions. *Award:* Grant for use in freshman, sophomore, junior, or senior year; not renewable. *Award amount:* $200–$2000. *Number of awards:* 3000. *Eligibility Requirements:* Applicant must be enrolled at a two-year, four-year, or technical institution or university; resident of Louisiana and studying in Louisiana. Restricted to U.S. citizens. *Application Requirements:* Application, financial need analysis.

Contact Public Information, Louisiana Office of Student Financial Assistance, PO Box 91202, Baton Rouge, LA 70821-9202. *E-mail:* custserv@osfa.state.la.us. *Phone:* 800-259-5626 Ext. 1012. *Web site:* http://www.osfa.state.la.us.

TOPS Tech Award. Program awards an amount equal to tuition for up to two years of technical training at a Louisiana public post-secondary institution that offers a vocational or technical education certificate or diploma program, or a non-academic degree program. Must have a 2.5 high school GPA, an ACT score of 19 and complete the TOPS-Tech core curriculum. *Award:* Scholarship for use in any year; renewable. *Eligibility Requirements:* Applicant must be high school student; enrolled at a technical institution; resident of Louisiana and studying in Louisiana. Applicant must have 2.5 GPA or higher. Restricted to U.S. citizens. *Application Requirements:* Application, test scores. *Deadline:* July 1.

Contact Public Information, Louisiana Office of Student Financial Assistance, PO Box 91202, Baton Rouge, LA 70821-9202. *E-mail:* custserv@osfa.state.la.us. *Phone:* 800-259-5626 Ext. 1012. *Web site:* http://www.osfa.state.la.us.

TOPS Honors Award. Program awards an amount equal to tuition plus an $800 per year stipend to students attending a Louisiana public institution, or an amount equal to the weighted average public tuition plus an $800 per year stipend to students attending a LAICU private institution. Must have a minimum high school GPA of 3.5, ACT score of 27, and complete a 16.5 unit core curriculum. *Award:* Scholarship for use in freshman, sophomore, junior, or senior year; renewable. *Award amount:* $1856–$3508. *Eligibility Requirements:* Applicant must be high school student; enrolled at a two-year or four-year institution or university; resident of Louisiana and studying in Louisiana. Applicant must have 3.5 GPA or higher. Restricted to U.S. citizens. *Application Requirements:* Application, test scores. *Deadline:* July 1.

Contact Public Information, Louisiana Office of Student Financial Assistance, PO Box 91202, Baton Rouge, LA 70821-9202. *E-mail:* custserv@osfa.state.la.us.

Phone: 800-259-5626 Ext. 1012. *Fax:* 225-922-0790. *Web site:* http://www.osfa.state.la.us.

Louisiana Department of Veterans Affairs Awards Program. Tuition exemption at any state supported college, university or technical institute for: children of veterans that are rated 90% or above service connected disabled by the U.S. Department of Veterans Affairs and: surviving spouse and children of veterans that died on active duty, in line of duty or where death was the result of a disability incurred in or aggravated by military service. *Award:* Scholarship for use in freshman, sophomore, junior, senior, or graduate years; renewable. *Award amount:* $12,000–$15,000. *Eligibility Requirements:* Applicant must be age 16-25; enrolled at a two-year, four-year, or technical institution or university; resident of Louisiana and studying in Louisiana. Restricted to U.S. citizens. Applicant or parent must meet one or more of the following requirements: general military experience; retired from active duty; disabled or killed as a result of military service; prisoner of war; or missing in action. *Application Requirements:* Application. *Deadline:* continuous.

Contact C. Ray Noland, V.A. Regional Manager, Louisiana Department of Veteran Affairs, PO Box 90495, Capitol Station, Baton Rouge, LA 70804. *E-mail:* rnoland@vetaffairs.com. *Phone:* 225-922-0507. *Fax:* 225-922-0511.

MAINE

Maine Student Incentive Scholarship Program. Scholarships for residents of Maine attending an eligible school, full-time, in Alaska, Connecticut, Delaware, the District of Columbia, Maine, Maryland, Massachusetts, New Hampshire, Pennsylvania, Rhode Island, or Vermont. Award based on need. Must reapply annually. Complete Free Application For Federal Student Aid to apply. One-time award of $500-$1000 for undergraduate study. *Award:* Grant for use in freshman, sophomore, junior, or senior year; not renewable. *Award amount:* $500–$1000. *Number of awards:* 8900–12,500. *Eligibility Requirements:* Applicant must be enrolled at a two-year, four-year, or technical institution or university; resident of Maine and studying in Alaska, Connecticut, Delaware, District of Columbia, Maine, Maryland, Massachusetts, New Hampshire, Pennsylvania, Rhode Island, or Vermont. *Application Requirements:* Application, financial need analysis. *Deadline:* May 1.

Contact Rochelle Bridgham, Program Officer, Finance Authority of Maine, 5 Community Drive, Augusta, ME 04332-0949. *E-mail:* rochelle@famemaine.com. *Phone:* 800-228-3734. *Fax:* 207-623-0095. *Web site:* http://www.famemaine.com.

Teachers for Maine Loan Program. Renewable loans for residents of Maine who are high school seniors with a minimum 3.0 GPA, preparing to study teacher education. Loan is forgivable if student teaches in Maine upon graduation. Awards are based on merit. *Academic/Career Areas:* Education. *Award:* Forgivable loan for use in freshman year; renewable. *Award amount:* $1500–$3000. *Eligibility Requirements:* Applicant must be high school student and resident of Maine. Applicant must have 3.0 GPA or higher. *Application Requirements:* Application, essay, test scores, transcript. *Deadline:* April 1.

Contact Rochelle Bridgham, Program Officer, Finance Authority of Maine, 5 Community Drive, Augusta, ME 04332-0949. *E-mail:* rochelle@famemaine.com. *Phone:* 800-228-3734. *Fax:* 207-623-0095. *Web site:* http://www.famemaine.com.

Veterans Dependents Educational Benefits-Maine. Award for dependents or spouses of veterans who were prisoner-of-war, missing in action, or permanently disabled as a result of service. Veteran must have been Maine resident at service entry for five years preceding application. For use at Maine institutions. Must be high school graduate. Must submit birth certificate. Award renewable for eight semesters for those under 22 years of age. *Award:* Scholarship for use in any year; renewable. *Eligibility Requirements:* Applicant must be age 21 or under; resident of Maine and studying in Maine. Applicant or parent must meet one or more of the following requirements: general military experience; retired from active duty; disabled or killed as a result of military service; prisoner of war; or missing in action. *Application Requirements:* Application. *Deadline:* continuous.

Contact Leslie Breton, Administrator, Maine Division of Veterans Services, State House Station 117, Augusta, ME 04333-0117. *E-mail:* mvs@me-arng.ngb.army.mil. *Phone:* 207-626-4464. *Fax:* 207-626-4471.

MARYLAND

Child Care Provider Program-Maryland. Provide assistance for Maryland undergraduates attending a Maryland institution and pursuing studies in child development. Must serve as a professional day care provider in Maryland for one year for each year award received. Must maintain minimum 2.0 GPA. Contact for further information. *Academic/Career Areas:* Education; Social Sciences; Social Services. *Award:* Forgivable loan for use in freshman, sophomore, junior, or senior year; not renewable. *Award amount:* $500–$2000. *Number of awards:* 37–90. *Eligibility Requirements:* Applicant must be enrolled at a two-year or four-year institution or university; resident of Maryland and studying in Maryland. *Application Requirements:* Application, transcript. *Deadline:* June 30.

Contact Scholarship Administration, Maryland State Higher Education Commission, 16 Francis Street, Annapolis, MD 21401-1781. *E-mail:* ssamail@mhec.state.5994. *Phone:* 410-974-5370. *Fax:* 410-974-5994. *Web site:* http://www.mhec.state.md.us.

Guaranteed Access Grant-Maryland. Award for Maryland resident enrolling full-time in an undergraduate program at a Maryland institution. Must be under 22 at time of first award and begin college within one year of completing high school in Maryland with a minimum 2.5 GPA. Must have an annual family income less than 130% of the federal poverty level guideline. *Award:* Grant for use in freshman, sophomore, junior, or senior year;

renewable. *Award amount:* $400–$8700. *Number of awards:* 401–763. *Eligibility Requirements:* Applicant must be age 21 or under; enrolled at a two-year or four-year institution or university; resident of Maryland and studying in Maryland. Applicant must have 2.5 GPA or higher. *Application Requirements:* Application, financial need analysis, transcript. *Deadline:* March 1.

Contact Scholarship Administration, Maryland State Higher Education Commission, 16 Francis Street, Annapolis, MD 21401-1781. *E-mail:* ssamail@mhec.state.md.us. *Phone:* 410-974-5370. *Fax:* 410-974-5994. *Web site:* http://www.mhec.state.md.us.

Science and Technology Scholarship. Provides assistance to full-time students in computer science, engineering, and information technology shortage areas. Must be high school senior at time of application. Must be Maryland resident. Must have cumulative unweighted 3.0 GPA in math, science, social studies, English, and foreign language. *Academic/Career Areas:* Biology; Chemical Engineering; Civil Engineering; Computer Science/Data Processing; Earth Science; Electrical Engineering/Electronics; Engineering/Technology; Engineering-Related Technologies; Fire Sciences; Physical Sciences and Math. *Award:* Forgivable loan for use in freshman, sophomore, junior, or senior year; renewable. *Award amount:* $1000–$3000. *Number of awards:* 800. *Eligibility Requirements:* Applicant must be high school student; enrolled at a two-year or four-year institution or university; resident of Maryland and studying in Maryland. Applicant must have 3.0 GPA or higher. *Application Requirements:* Application, transcript. *Deadline:* March 1.

Contact Scholarship Administration, Maryland State Higher Education Commission, 16 Francis Street, Annapolis, MD 21401-1781. *E-mail:* ssamail@mhec.state.md.us. *Phone:* 410-974-5370. *Fax:* 410-974-5994. *Web site:* http://www.mhec.state.md.us.

Distinguished Scholar-Teacher Education Awards. Award for Maryland high school seniors who have received a Distinguished Scholar Award and who will enroll as a full-time undergraduate in a Maryland institution and pursue a program of study leading to a Maryland teaching certificate. Must maintain 3.0 GPA in college for award to be renewed. $3000 award is given in addition to Distinguished Scholar Award. Must teach in a Maryland public school one year for each year you receive the scholarship. *Academic/Career Areas:* Education. *Award:* Forgivable loan for use in freshman, sophomore, junior, or senior year; renewable. *Award amount:* $3000. *Number of awards:* 23–53. *Eligibility Requirements:* Applicant must be high school student; enrolled at a two-year or four-year institution or university; resident of Maryland and studying in Maryland. *Application Requirements:* Application, test scores, transcript. *Deadline:* continuous.

Contact Scholarship Administration, Maryland State Higher Education Commission, 16 Francis Street, Annapolis, MD 21401-1781. *E-mail:* ssamail@mhec.state.md.us. *Phone:* 410-974-5370. *Fax:* 410-974-5994. *Web site:* http://www.mhec.state.md.us.

Delegate Scholarship Program-Maryland. Delegate scholarships help Maryland residents attending Maryland degree granting institution, certain career schools, or nursing diploma schools. May attend out-of-state institution if Maryland Higher Education Commission deems major to be unique and not offered at a Maryland institution. Free Application for Federal Student Aid may be required. *Award:* Scholarship for use in any year; not renewable. *Award amount:* $200–$9774. *Number of awards:* 244–2600. *Eligibility Requirements:* Applicant must be enrolled at a two-year, four-year, or technical institution or university and resident of Maryland. *Application Requirements:* Application, financial need analysis. *Deadline:* continuous.

Contact Scholarship Administration, Maryland State Higher Education Commission, 16 Francis Street, Annapolis, MD 21401-1781. *E-mail:* ssamail@mhec.state.md.us. *Phone:* 410-974-5370. *Fax:* 410-974-5994. *Web site:* http://www.mhec.state.md.us.

Edward T. Conroy Memorial Scholarship Program. Scholarship for dependents of deceased or 100% disabled U.S. Armed Forces personnel, Vietnam Missing in Action or prisoner-of-war, deceased State personnel, or deceased or disabled public safety personnel. Must be a Maryland resident at time of death or disability. Must attend Maryland institution. *Award:* Scholarship for use in any year; not renewable. *Award amount:* up to $3800. *Number of awards:* 46–140. *Eligibility Requirements:* Applicant must be enrolled at a two-year or four-year institution or university; resident of Maryland; studying in Maryland and have employment experience in designated career field. Applicant or parent must meet one or more of the following requirements: general military experience; retired from active duty; disabled or killed as a result of military service; prisoner of war; or missing in action. *Application Requirements:* Application. *Deadline:* July 15.

Contact Scholarship Administration, Maryland State Higher Education Commission, 16 Francis Street, Annapolis, MD 21401-1781. *E-mail:* ssamail@mhec.state.md.us. *Phone:* 410-974-5370. *Fax:* 410-974-5994. *Web site:* http://www.mhec.state.md.us.

Maryland State Nursing Scholarship and Living Expenses Grant. Renewable grant for Maryland residents enrolled in a two- or four-year Maryland institution nursing degree program. Recipients must agree to serve as a full-time nurse in a Maryland shortage area and must maintain a 3.0 GPA in college. Application deadlines are June 30 and March 1. Submit Free Application for Federal Student Aid. *Academic/Career Areas:* Nursing. *Award:* Forgivable loan for use in any year; renewable. *Award amount:* $200–$4800. *Number of awards:* 186–300. *Eligibility Requirements:* Applicant must be enrolled at a two-year or four-year institution or university; resident of Maryland and studying in Maryland. Applicant must have 3.0 GPA or higher. *Application Requirements:* Application, financial need analysis, transcript.

Contact Scholarship Administration, Maryland State Higher Education Commission, 16 Francis Street, Annapolis, MD 21401-1781. *E-mail:* ssamail@mhec.state.md.us. *Phone:* 410-974-5370. *Fax:* 410-974-5994. *Web site:* http://www.mhec.state.md.us.

Physical and Occupational Therapists and Assistants Scholarship Program. For Maryland residents training as physical and or occupational therapists' or therapy assistants at Maryland post-secondary institutions. Recipients must provide one year of service per year of award to handicapped school children or a hospital in Maryland. *Academic/Career Areas:* Therapy/Rehabilitation. *Award:* Forgivable loan for use in any year; not renewable. *Award amount:* up to $2000. *Number of awards:* 8–19. *Eligibility Requirements:* Applicant must be enrolled at a two-year or four-year institution; resident of Maryland and studying in Maryland. *Application Requirements:* Application, transcript. *Deadline:* July 1.

Contact Scholarship Administration, Maryland State Higher Education Commission, 16 Francis Street, Annapolis, MD 21401-1781. *E-mail:* ssamail@mhec.state.md.us. *Phone:* 410-974-5370. *Fax:* 410-974-5994. *Web site:* http://www.mhec.state.md.us.

Loan Assistance Repayment Program for Primary Care Physicians. Renewable loan repayment program for Maryland resident who is a primary care physician with valid license to practice medicine in Maryland. Must be working at an eligible practice site in Maryland and be willing to provide at least two years of service. *Academic/Career Areas:* Health and Medical Sciences. *Award:* Forgivable loan for use in ; renewable. *Award amount:* $25,000–$1.0. *Number of awards:* 10–20. *Eligibility Requirements:* Applicant must be resident of Maryland; studying in Maryland and have employment experience in designated career field. *Application Requirements:* Application. *Deadline:* continuous.

Contact Scholarship Administration, Maryland State Higher Education Commission, 16 Francis Street, Annapolis, MD 21401-1781. *E-mail:* ssamail@mhec.state.md.us. *Phone:* 410-974-5370. *Fax:* 410-974-5994. *Web site:* http://www.mhec.state.md.us.

Firefighter, Ambulance, and Rescue Squad Member Tuition Reimbursement Program-Maryland. Award intended to reimburse members of rescue organizations serving Maryland communities for tuition costs of course work towards a degree or certificate in fire service or medical technology. Must attend a two- or four-year school in Maryland. *Academic/Career Areas:* Health and Medical Sciences; Trade/Technical Specialties. *Award:* Scholarship for use in any year; not renewable. *Award amount:* $5500. *Number of awards:* 106–318. *Eligibility Requirements:* Applicant must be enrolled at a two-year or four-year institution; resident of Maryland; studying in Maryland and have employment experience in police/firefighting. *Application Requirements:* Application, transcript. *Deadline:* July 1.

Contact Scholarship Administration, Maryland State Higher Education Commission, 16 Francis Street, Annapolis, MD 21401-1781. *E-mail:* ssamail@mhec.state.md.us. *Phone:* 410-974-5370. *Fax:* 410-974-5994. *Web site:* http://www.mhec.state.md.us.

Senatorial Scholarships-Maryland. Renewable award for Maryland residents attending a Maryland degree-granting institution, nursing diploma school, or certain private career schools. May be used out-of-state only if Maryland Higher Education Commission deems major to be unique and not offered at Maryland institution. *Award:* Scholarship for use in any year; renewable. *Award amount:* $200–$2000. *Number of awards:* 5676–8666. *Eligibility Requirements:* Applicant must be enrolled at a two-year, four-year, or technical institution or university and resident of Maryland. *Application Requirements:* Financial need analysis, test scores. *Deadline:* March 1.

Contact Scholarship Administration, Maryland State Higher Education Commission, 16 Francis Street, Annapolis, MD 21401-1781. *E-mail:* ssamail@mhec.state.md.us. *Phone:* 410-974-5370. *Fax:* 410-974-5994. *Web site:* http://www.mhec.state.md.us.

Professional Scholarship Program-Maryland. Professional scholarships provide need-based financial assistance to full-time students attending a Maryland school of medicine, dentistry, law, pharmacy, social work, or nursing. Must be a Maryland resident. *Academic/Career Areas:* Dental Health/Services; Health and Medical Sciences; Law/Legal Services; Nursing; Social Services. *Award:* Scholarship for use in any year; renewable. *Award amount:* $200–$1000. *Number of awards:* 202–386. *Eligibility Requirements:* Applicant must be enrolled at a two-year or four-year institution or university; resident of Maryland and studying in Maryland. *Application Requirements:* Application, financial need analysis. *Deadline:* March 1.

Contact Scholarship Administration, Maryland State Higher Education Commission, 16 Francis Street, Annapolis, MD 21401-1781. *E-mail:* ssamail@mhec.state.md.us. *Phone:* 410-974-5370. *Fax:* 410-974-5994. *Web site:* http://www.mhec.state.md.us.

Sharon Christa McAuliffe Teacher Education-Critical Shortage Grant Program. Renewable awards for Maryland residents who are college juniors, seniors, or graduate students enrolled in a Maryland teacher education program. Must agree to enter profession in a subject designated as a critical shortage area. Must teach in Maryland for one year per award year. *Academic/Career Areas:* Education. *Award:* Forgivable loan for use in junior, senior, or graduate years; renewable. *Award amount:* $200–$11,500. *Number of awards:* 32–74. *Eligibility Requirements:* Applicant must be enrolled at a four-year institution or university; resident of Maryland and studying in Maryland. Applicant must have 3.0 GPA or higher. *Application Requirements:* Application, essay, transcript. *Deadline:* December 31.

Contact Scholarship Administration, Maryland State Higher Education Commission, 16 Francis Street, Annapolis, MD 21401-1781. *E-mail:* ssamail@mhec.state.

md.us. *Phone:* 410-974-5370. *Fax:* 410-974-5994. *Web site:* http://www.mhec.state.md.us.

Hope Scholarship. Student must be a high school senior at the time of application, must enroll in an eligible major. Family income may not exceed $80,000 annually. *Academic/Career Areas:* Business/Consumer Services; Health and Medical Sciences; Law Enforcement/Police Administration. *Award:* Grant for use in freshman, sophomore, junior, or senior year; renewable. *Award amount:* $1000–$3000. *Number of awards:* 1000–3000. *Eligibility Requirements:* Applicant must be high school student; enrolled at a two-year or four-year institution; resident of Maryland and studying in Maryland. Applicant must have 3.0 GPA or higher. Restricted to U.S. citizens. *Application Requirements:* Application, financial need analysis, transcript. *Deadline:* March 1.

Contact Scholarship Administration, Maryland State Higher Education Commission, 16 Francis Street, Annapolis, MD 21401-1781. *E-mail:* ssamail@mhec.state.md.us. *Phone:* 410-974-5370. *Fax:* 410-974-5994. *Web site:* http://www.mhec.state.md.us.

Maryland Teacher Scholarship. Available to Maryland residents attending a college in Maryland with a major in teacher education. *Academic/Career Areas:* Education; Special Education. *Award:* Grant for use in freshman, sophomore, junior, senior, or graduate years; renewable. *Award amount:* $1000–$3000. *Number of awards:* 500–1000. *Eligibility Requirements:* Applicant must be enrolled at a two-year or four-year institution or university; resident of Maryland and studying in Maryland. Applicant must have 3.0 GPA or higher. Restricted to U.S. citizens. *Application Requirements:* Application, transcript. *Deadline:* March 1.

Contact Scholarship Administration, Maryland State Higher Education Commission, 16 Francis Street, Annapolis, MD 21401-1781. *E-mail:* ssamail@mhec.state.md.us. *Phone:* 410-974-5370. *Fax:* 410-974-5994. *Web site:* http://www.mhec.state.md.us.

Developmental Disabilities Tuition Assistance Program. Provides tuition assistance to students who are service employees that provide direct support or care to individuals with Mental Health disabilities. *Award:* Grant for use in freshman, sophomore, junior, or senior year; renewable. *Award amount:* $1000–$3000. *Number of awards:* 300–500. *Eligibility Requirements:* Applicant must be enrolled at a two-year or four-year institution and have employment experience in designated career field. *Application Requirements:* Application.

Contact Scholarship Administration, Maryland State Higher Education Commission, 16 Francis Street, Annapolis, MD 21401-1781. *E-mail:* ssamail@mhec.state.md.us. *Phone:* 410-974-5370. *Fax:* 410-974-5994. *Web site:* http://www.mhec.state.md.us.

Distinguished Scholar Award-Maryland. Renewable award for Maryland students enrolled full-time at Maryland institutions. National Merit Scholar Finalists automatically receive award. Others may qualify for the award in satisfying criterions' of a 3.7+ GPA and, or in combination with high test scores, or for Talent in Arts competition in categories of music, drama, dance, or visual arts. Must maintain 3.0 GPA in college for award to be renewed. Contact for further details. *Award:* Scholarship for use in freshman, sophomore, junior, or senior year; renewable. *Award amount:* up to $3000. *Number of awards:* 350. *Eligibility Requirements:* Applicant must be high school student; enrolled at a two-year or four-year institution or university; resident of Maryland and studying in Maryland. *Application Requirements:* Application, test scores, transcript. *Deadline:* March 20.

Contact Scholarship Administration, Maryland State Higher Education Commission, 16 Francis Street, Annapolis, MD 21401-1781. *E-mail:* ssamail@mhec.state.md.us. *Phone:* 410-974-5370. *Fax:* 410-974-5994. *Web site:* http://www.mhec.state.md.us.

Loan Assistance Repayment Program for Medical Residents in Primary Care-Maryland. Renewable loan repayment assistance for medical residents specializing in primary care who agree to practice at an eligible site in Maryland for a minimum of two years. Must be Maryland resident and have a license to practice medicine in Maryland. *Academic/Career Areas:* Health and Medical Sciences. *Award:* Forgivable loan for use in graduate years; renewable. *Award amount:* up to $30,000. *Eligibility Requirements:* Applicant must be resident of Maryland; studying in Maryland and have employment experience in designated career field. *Application Requirements:* Application. *Deadline:* continuous.

Contact Scholarship Administration, Maryland State Higher Education Commission, 16 Francis Street, Annapolis, MD 21401-1781. *E-mail:* ssamail@mhec.state.md.us. *Phone:* 410-974-5370. *Fax:* 410-974-5994. *Web site:* http://www.mhec.state.md.us.

Part-Time Grant Program-Maryland. Funds provided to Maryland colleges and universities. Eligible students must be enrolled on a part-time basis (6-11 credits) in an undergraduate degree program. Must demonstrate financial need and also be Maryland resident. *Award:* Grant for use in freshman, sophomore, junior, or senior year; renewable. *Award amount:* $200–$1000. *Number of awards:* 2282–2707. *Eligibility Requirements:* Applicant must be enrolled at a two-year or four-year institution or university; resident of Maryland and studying in Maryland. Restricted to U.S. citizens. *Application Requirements:* Application, financial need analysis. *Deadline:* June 15.

Contact Scholarship Administration, Maryland State Higher Education Commission, 16 Francis Street, Annapolis, MD 21401-1781. *E-mail:* ssamail@mhec.state.md.us. *Phone:* 410-974-5370. *Fax:* 410-974-5994. *Web site:* http://www.mhec.state.md.us.

Educational Assistance Grants-Maryland. Award for Maryland residents accepted or enrolled in a full-time undergraduate degree or certificate program at a Maryland institution or hospital nursing school. Must submit financial aid form. Must earn 2.0 GPA in college to maintain award. *Award:* Grant for use in freshman, sophomore, junior, or senior year; renewable. *Award amount:* $200–$3000. *Number of awards:* 5903–18,893. *Eligibility Requirements:* Applicant must be enrolled at a two-year or four-year institution or university; resident of Maryland and studying in Maryland. Restricted to U.S. citizens. *Application Requirements:* Financial need analysis. *Deadline:* March 1.

Contact Scholarship Administration, Maryland State Higher Education Commission, 16 Francis Street, Annapolis, MD 21401-1781. *E-mail:* ssamail@mhec.state.md.us. *Phone:* 410-974-5370. *Fax:* 410-974-5994. *Web site:* http://www.mhec.state.md.us.

MASSACHUSETTS

Massachusetts Grant. Renewable award upon re-application and eligibility for Massachusetts residents to attend undergraduate post-secondary institutions in Connecticut, Maine, Maryland, Massachusetts, New Jersey, Pennsylvania, Rhode Island, Vermont, and District of Columbia. High school seniors may apply. Need-based award. Write for information. *Award:* Grant for use in freshman, sophomore, junior, or senior year; not renewable. *Award amount:* $200–$2500. *Number of awards:* 32,000–35,000. *Eligibility Requirements:* Applicant must be enrolled at a two-year, four-year, or technical institution or university; resident of Massachusetts and studying in Connecticut, District of Columbia, Maine, Maryland, Massachusetts, New Jersey, Pennsylvania, Rhode Island, or Vermont. *Application Requirements:* Application, financial need analysis. *Deadline:* May 1.

Contact Scholarship Director, Massachusetts Office of Student Financial Assistance, 330 Stuart Street, Boston, MA 02116.

Public Service Scholarship-Massachusetts. Scholarships for children and/or spouses of deceased members of fire, police, and corrections departments who were killed in the line of duty. Award also available to children of deceased veterans whose death was service-related, or prisoner-of-war or Missing in Action. For Massachusetts residents attending Massachusetts institutions. *Award:* Scholarship for use in freshman, sophomore, junior, or senior year; renewable. *Award amount:* $918–$1904. *Eligibility Requirements:* Applicant must be enrolled at a two-year or four-year institution or university; resident of Massachusetts; studying in Massachusetts and have employment experience in police/firefighting. Applicant or parent must meet one or more of the following requirements: general military experience; retired from active duty; disabled or killed as a result of military service; prisoner of war; or missing in action. *Application Requirements:* Application. *Deadline:* May 1.

Contact Jill McTague, Senior Counselor, Massachusetts Office of Student Financial Assistance, 330 Stuart Street, Boston, MA 02116.

Tomorrow's Teachers Scholarship Program. Tuition waver for graduating high school senior ranking in Top 25% of class. Must be a resident of Massachusetts and pursue a Bachelor's degree at a public college or university in the Commonwealth. Must commit to teach for four years in a Massachusetts Public School. Must maintain a 3.0 GPA. *Award:* Scholarship for use in freshman, sophomore, junior, or senior year; renewable. *Eligibility Requirements:* Applicant must be high school student; enrolled at a four-year institution or university; resident of Massachusetts and studying in Massachusetts. *Application Requirements:* Application.

Contact Scholarship Director, Massachusetts Office of Student Financial Assistance, 330 Stuart Street, Suite 304, Boston, MA 02116. *Phone:* 617-727-9420. *Fax:* 617-727-0667.

Gilbert Grant. Must be permanent Massachusetts resident for at least one year, attending full-time an independent, regionally accredited Massachusetts school. File the Free Application for Federal Student Aid after January 1. Contact college financial aid office for complete details. *Award:* Grant for use in freshman, sophomore, junior, or senior year; not renewable. *Award amount:* $200–$2500. *Eligibility Requirements:* Applicant must be enrolled at a two-year or four-year institution or university; resident of Massachusetts and studying in Massachusetts. *Application Requirements:* Application, financial need analysis.

Contact Scholarship Information, Massachusetts Office of Student Financial Assistance, 330 Stuart Street, Boston, MA 02116.

Tuition Waiver (General)-Massachusetts. Need-based tuition waiver for full-time-students. Must attend a Massachusetts public institution of higher education and be a permanent Massachusetts resident. File the Free Application For Federal Student Aid after January 1. Award is for undergraduate use. *Award:* Scholarship for use in freshman, sophomore, junior, or senior year; renewable. *Eligibility Requirements:* Applicant must be enrolled at a two-year or four-year institution or university; resident of Massachusetts and studying in Massachusetts. *Application Requirements:* Application, financial need analysis. *Deadline:* May 1.

Contact School Financial Aid Office, Massachusetts Office of Student Financial Assistance, 330 Stuart Street, Boston, MA 02116.

Higher Education Coordinating Council-Tuition Waiver Program. Renewable award is tuition exemption for up to four years. Available to active members of Air Force, Army, Navy, Marines, or Coast Guard who are residents of Massachusetts. For use at a Massachusetts college or university. Deadlines vary. Contact veterans coordinator at college. *Award:* Scholarship for use in freshman, sophomore, junior, or senior year; renewable. *Eligibility Requirements:* Applicant must be enrolled at a two-year or four-year institution or university; resident of Massachusetts and studying in Massachusetts. Applicant must have served in the Air Force, Army, Coast Guard, Marine Corp, or Navy. *Application Requirements:* Application, financial need analysis.

Contact Scholarship Director, Massachusetts Office of Student Financial Assistance, 330 Stuart Street, Boston, MA 02116.

Christian A. Herter Memorial Scholarship. Renewable award for Massachusetts residents who are in the 10th-11th grades. Must exhibit severe personal or family-related difficulties, medical problems, or have overcome a personal obstacle. Provides up to fifty percent of the student's calculated need, as determined by Federal methodology, at the college of their choice within the continental U.S. *Award:* Scholarship for use in freshman, sophomore, junior, or senior year; renewable. *Award amount:* \$2500–\$6500. *Number of awards:* 100–200. *Eligibility Requirements:* Applicant must be high school student; enrolled at a two-year or four-year institution or university and resident of Massachusetts. Applicant must have 2.5 GPA or higher. *Application Requirements:* Application, essay, financial need analysis, interview, transcript. *Deadline:* March 31.

Contact Cynthia Gray, Assistant Director, Massachusetts Office of Student Financial Assistance, 330 Stuart Street, Boston, MA 02116.

MICHIGAN

Tuition Incentive Program (TIP)-Michigan. Award for Michigan residents who receive or have received Medicaid through the Family Independence Agency. Scholarship provides two years tuition towards an associate degree at a Michigan college or university. Apply before graduating from high school or earning General Education Development diploma. *Award:* Scholarship for use in freshman or sophomore year; renewable. *Award amount:* \$6.0. *Eligibility Requirements:* Applicant must be high school student; age 12-19; enrolled at a two-year or four-year institution or university; resident of Michigan and studying in Michigan. *Application Requirements:* Application, financial need analysis. *Deadline:* continuous.

Contact Jennifer Wallace, Director, Family Independence Agency, 235 South Grand Avenue, Suite 1308, Lansing, MI 48909. *E-mail:* wallacej@state.mi.us. *Phone:* 800-243-2847. *Fax:* 517-241-8760.

Michigan Work-Study Program. Need-based work-study program for Michigan residents who are graduate or undergraduate students at Michigan school. Must maintain good academic standing. Amount of award varies. Deadlines determined by college. *Award:* Scholarship for use in any year; not renewable. *Eligibility Requirements:* Applicant must be enrolled at a two-year or four-year institution or university; resident of Michigan and studying in Michigan. *Application Requirements:* Financial need analysis.

Contact Scholarship and Grant Director, Michigan Higher Education Assistance Authority, PO Box 30466, Lansing, MI 48909.

Michigan Adult Part-Time Grant. Grant for part-time, needy, independent undergraduates at an approved, degree-granting Michigan college or university. Eligibility is limited to two years. Must be Michigan resident. Deadlines determined by college. *Award:* Grant for use in freshman, sophomore, junior, or senior year; not renewable. *Award amount:* up to \$600. *Eligibility Requirements:* Applicant must be enrolled at a two-year or four-year institution or university; resident of Michigan and studying in Michigan. *Application Requirements:* Application, financial need analysis.

Contact Scholarship and Grant Director, Michigan Higher Education Assistance Authority, PO Box 30466, Lansing, MI 48909-7966.

Michigan Competitive Scholarship. Awards limited to tuition. Must maintain a C average and meet the college's academic progress requirements. Must file Free Application For Federal Student Aid. Deadlines: February 21 and March 21. Must be Michigan resident. Renewable award of \$1200 for undergraduate study at a Michigan institution. *Award:* Scholarship for use in freshman, sophomore, junior, or senior year; renewable. *Award amount:* \$1200. *Eligibility Requirements:* Applicant must be enrolled at a two-year or four-year institution or university; resident of Michigan and studying in Michigan. *Application Requirements:* Application, financial need analysis, test scores.

Contact Scholarship and Grant Director, Michigan Higher Education Assistance Authority, PO Box 30466, Lansing, MI 48909.

Michigan Veterans Trust Fund Tuition Grant Program. Tuition grant of \$2800 for children of Michigan veterans who died on active duty or subsequently declared 100% disabled as the result of service-connected illness or injury. Must be 17 to 25 years old, be a Michigan resident, and attend a private or public institution in Michigan. *Award:* Grant for use in freshman, sophomore, junior, or senior year; renewable. *Award amount:* up to \$2800. *Eligibility Requirements:* Applicant must be age 17-25; enrolled at a two-year, four-year, or technical institution or university; resident of Michigan and studying in Michigan. Applicant or parent must meet one or more of the following requirements: general military experience; retired from active duty; disabled or killed as a result of military service; prisoner of war; or missing in action. *Application Requirements:* Application. *Deadline:* continuous.

Contact Mary Kay Bitten, Michigan Veterans Trust Fund, 611 West Ottawa, 3rd Floor, Lansing, MI 48913. *Phone:* 517-335-1634. *Fax:* 517-335-1631.

Michigan Tuition Grants. Students must attend a Michigan private, nonprofit, degree-granting college. Must file the Free Application For Student Aid and meet the college's academic progress requirements. Deadlines: February 21 and March 21. Must be Michigan resident. Renewable award of \$2500. *Award:* Grant for use in any year; renewable. *Award amount:* \$2500. *Eligibility Requirements:* Applicant must be enrolled at a two-year or four-year institution; resident of Michigan and studying in Michigan. *Application Requirements:* Application, financial need analysis.

Contact Scholarship and Grant Director, Michigan Higher Education Assistance Authority, PO Box 30466, Lansing, MI 48909-7966.

Michigan Educational Opportunity Grant. Need-based program for Michigan residents who are at least half-time undergraduates attending public Michigan colleges. Must maintain good academic standing. Deadline determined by college. Award of up to $1000. *Award:* Grant for use in freshman, sophomore, junior, or senior year; not renewable. *Award amount:* up to $1000. *Eligibility Requirements:* Applicant must be enrolled at a two-year or four-year institution or university; resident of Michigan and studying in Michigan. *Application Requirements:* Application, financial need analysis.

Contact Scholarship and Grant Director, Michigan Higher Education Assistance Authority, PO Box 30466, Lansing, MI 48909-7966.

MINNESOTA

Minnesota Reciprocal Agreement. Renewable tuition waiver for Minnesota residents. Waives all or part of non-resident tuition surcharge at public institutions in Iowa, Kansas, Michigan, Missouri, Nebraska, North Dakota, South Dakota, and Wisconsin. Deadline is last day of academic term. *Award:* Scholarship for use in any year; renewable. *Eligibility Requirements:* Applicant must be resident of Minnesota and studying in Iowa, Kansas, Michigan, Missouri, Nebraska, North Dakota, South Dakota, or Wisconsin. Restricted to U.S. citizens. *Application Requirements:* Application.

Contact Minnesota Higher Education Services Office, 1450 Energy Park Drive, Suite 350, St. Paul, MN 55108-5227. *Web site:* http://www.heso.state.mn.us.

Post-Secondary Child Care Grant Program-Minnesota. Renewable grant available for students not receiving AFDC or MFIP. Based on financial need. Cannot exceed actual child care costs or maximum award chart (based on income). Must be Minnesota resident. For use at Minnesota two- or four-year school. *Award:* Grant for use in freshman, sophomore, junior, or senior year; renewable. *Award amount:* $300–$2000. *Eligibility Requirements:* Applicant must be enrolled at a two-year or four-year institution; resident of Minnesota and studying in Minnesota. Restricted to U.S. citizens. *Application Requirements:* Application, financial need analysis. *Deadline:* continuous.

Contact Minnesota Higher Education Services Office, 1450 Energy Park Drive, Suite 350, St. Paul, MN 55108-5227. *Web site:* http://www.heso.state.mn.us.

Minnesota Summer Scholarships for Academic Enrichment. $1000 need-based scholarship for students in grades 9-12 who enroll in approved academic enrichment program during the summer. Must be Minnesota resident enrolled in Minnesota school. *Award:* Scholarship for use in any year; not renewable. *Eligibility Requirements:* Applicant must be high school student; age 19 or under; resident of Minnesota and studying in Minnesota. Applicant must have 3.0 GPA or higher. Restricted to U.S. citizens. *Application Requirements:* Application, financial need analysis, transcript.

Contact Minnesota Higher Education Services Office, 1450 Energy Park Drive, Suite 350, St. Paul, MN 55108-5227. *Web site:* http://www.heso.state.mn.us.

Minnesota State Veterans' Dependents Assistance Program. Tuition assistance to dependents of persons considered to be prisoner-of-war or missing in action after August 1, 1958. Must be Minnesota resident attending Minnesota two- or four-year school. *Award:* Scholarship for use in any year; renewable. *Eligibility Requirements:* Applicant must be enrolled at a two-year or four-year institution; resident of Minnesota and studying in Minnesota. Applicant or parent must meet one or more of the following requirements: general military experience; retired from active duty; disabled or killed as a result of military service; prisoner of war; or missing in action. *Application Requirements:* Application. *Deadline:* continuous.

Contact Minnesota Higher Education Services Office, 1450 Energy Park Drive, Suite 350, St. Paul, MN 55108-5227. *Web site:* http://www.heso.state.mn.us.

Minnesota Safety Officers' Survivor Program. Grant for eligible survivors of Minnesota public safety officer killed in the line of duty. Safety officers who have been permanently or totally disabled in the line of duty are also eligible. Must be used at a Minnesota institution participating in State Grant Program. Write for details. Must submit proof of death or disability and Public Safety Officers Benefit Fund Certificate. Must apply each year. Can be awarded for four years. *Award:* Scholarship for use in any year; not renewable. *Eligibility Requirements:* Applicant must be enrolled at a two-year or technical institution or university; studying in Minnesota and have employment experience in police/firefighting. Restricted to U.S. citizens. *Application Requirements:* Application. *Deadline:* continuous.

Contact Minnesota Higher Education Services Office, 1450 Energy Park Drive, Suite 350, St. Paul, MN 55108-5227. *Web site:* http://www.heso.state.mn.us.

Minnesota Indian Scholarship Program. One time award for Minnesota Native American Indian. Contact for deadline information. *Award:* Scholarship for use in any year; not renewable. *Eligibility Requirements:* Applicant must be Native American or Eskimo; enrolled at a two-year, four-year, or technical institution or university and resident of Minnesota. *Application Requirements:* Application.

Contact Joe Aitken, Director, Minnesota Indian Scholarship Office, 1819 Bemidji Avenue, Bemidji, MN 56601.

MN VA Educational Assistance for Veterans. One-time $350 stipend given to veterans who have used up all other federal funds, yet have time remaining on their delimiting period. Applicant must be a Minnesota resident and must be attending a Minnesota college or university, but not the University of Minnesota. *Award:* Grant for use in any year; not renewable. *Award amount:* $350. *Eligibility Requirements:* Applicant must be enrolled at a two-year, four-year, or technical institution or university; resident of Minnesota and studying in Minnesota. Restricted to U.S. citizens. Applicant must have general military experience. *Application Requirements:* Application, financial need analysis.

Contact Terrence Logan, Director of Veterans Benefits, Minnesota Department of Veterans' Affairs, 20 West 12th Street, Second Floor, St. Paul, MN 55155-2079. *Phone:* 651-296-2652. *Fax:* 651-296-3954.

Minnesota Educational Assistance for War Orphans. War orphans may qualify for $350 per year. Must have lost parent through service-related death. Children of deceased veterans may qualify for free tuition at State university, college, or vocational or technical schools, but not at University of Minnesota. Must have been resident of Minnesota for at least two years. *Award:* Grant for use in any year; renewable. *Award amount:* $350. *Eligibility Requirements:* Applicant must be enrolled at a two-year, four-year, or technical institution or university; resident of Minnesota and studying in Minnesota. Restricted to U.S. citizens. Applicant or parent must meet one or more of the following requirements: general military experience; retired from active duty; disabled or killed as a result of military service; prisoner of war; or missing in action. *Application Requirements:* Application, financial need analysis.

Contact Terrence Logan, Director of Veterans Benefits, Minnesota Department of Veterans' Affairs, 20 West 12th Street, Second Floor, St. Paul, MN 55155-2079. *Phone:* 651-296-2652. *Fax:* 651-296-3954.

MISSISSIPPI

Mississippi Health Care Professions Loan/Scholarship Program. Renewable award for junior, and senior undergraduates studying psychology, speech pathology or occupational therapy. Must be Mississippi residents attending four-year universities in Mississippi. Must fulfill work obligation in Mississippi or pay back as loan. Renewable award for graduate student enrolled in physical therapy. *Academic/Career Areas:* Health and Medical Sciences; Therapy/Rehabilitation. *Award:* Forgivable loan for use in junior, senior, or graduate years; renewable. *Eligibility Requirements:* Applicant must be enrolled at a four-year institution or university; resident of Mississippi and studying in Mississippi. *Application Requirements:* Application. *Deadline:* April 30.

Contact Board of Trustees, Mississippi State Student Financial Aid, 3825 Ridgewood Road, Jackson, MS 39211-6453.

Mississippi State Student Incentive Grant (SSIG). Award for Mississippi residents enrolled for full-time study at a Mississippi college, or university. Based on financial need. Deadline varies with each institution. Contact college financial aid office. *Award:* Grant for use in any year; not renewable. *Award amount:* $100–$1500. *Eligibility Requirements:* Applicant must be enrolled at a two-year or four-year institution or university; resident of Mississippi and studying in Mississippi. Restricted to U.S. citizens. *Application Requirements:* Application, financial need analysis. *Deadline:* continuous.

Contact Board of Trustees, Mississippi State Student Financial Aid, 3825 Ridgewood Road, Jackson, MS 39211-6453.

Nursing Education BSN Program-Mississippi. Renewable award for Mississippi undergraduates pursuing nursing programs in Mississippi in order to earn BSN degree. Include transcript and references with application. *Academic/Career Areas:* Nursing. *Award:* Forgivable loan for use in freshman, sophomore, junior, or senior year; renewable. *Eligibility Requirements:* Applicant must be enrolled at a two-year or four-year institution or university; resident of Mississippi and studying in Mississippi. *Application Requirements:* Application, driver's license, financial need analysis, references, transcript. *Deadline:* April 30.

Contact Board of Trustees, Mississippi State Student Financial Aid, 3825 Ridgewood road, Jackson, MS 39211-6453.

Southern Regional Education Board Loan/Scholarship. Award for Mississippi residents enrolled at accredited school of optometry or osteopathic medicine. Amount determined by Southern Regional Education Board. Renewable loan forgiven if student serves one year in Mississippi for each year loan is awarded. *Academic/Career Areas:* Health and Medical Sciences. *Award:* Forgivable loan for use in graduate years; renewable. *Eligibility Requirements:* Applicant must be enrolled at a four-year institution or university; resident of Mississippi and studying in Alabama, Florida, Tennessee, or Texas. *Application Requirements:* Application, transcript. *Deadline:* April 30.

Contact Board of Trustees, Mississippi State Student Financial Aid, 3825 Ridgewood Road, Jackson, MS 39211-6453.

Graduate and Professional Degree Loan/Scholarship-Mississippi. Renewable loan for Mississippi graduate students pursuing health-related degree programs not available at a Mississippi university. One year of service in Mississippi required for each year of loan. Eligible programs of study include the following: chiropractic medicine, podiatric medicine, orthotics or prosthetics. *Academic/Career Areas:* Health and Medical Sciences; Therapy/Rehabilitation. *Award:* Forgivable loan for use in graduate years; renewable. *Award amount:* $7000. *Eligibility Requirements:* Applicant must be resident of Mississippi. *Application Requirements:* Application, transcript. *Deadline:* April 30.

Contact Board of Trustees, Mississippi State Student Financial Aid, 3825 Ridgewood Road, Jackson, MS 39211-6453.

Law Enforcement Officer and Firemen Scholarship Program- Mississippi. Award for dependents of policemen or firemen who were fatally injured or permanently disabled in the line of duty. Must be a Mississippi resident and attend a state-supported college or university. The award is a full-tuition waiver. Renewable award for college undergraduates. *Award:* Scholarship for use in freshman, sophomore, junior, or senior year; renewable. *Eligibility Requirements:* Applicant must be enrolled at a two-year or four-year institution or university; resident of Mississippi and studying in Mississippi. *Application Requirements:* Application.

Contact Board of Trustees of State, Institutions of Higher Learning, State of Mississippi, 3825 Ridgewood Road, Jackson, MS 39211-6453.

Mississippi Law Enforcement Officers and Firemen Scholarship Program. Award for dependents and spouses of policemen or firemen who were killed or disabled in the line of duty. Must be a Mississippi resident and attend a state-supported college or university. The award is a full tuition waiver. Contact for deadline. *Award:* Scholarship for use in freshman, sophomore, junior, or senior year; renewable. *Eligibility Requirements:* Applicant must be enrolled at a two-year or four-year institution or university; resident of Mississippi and studying in Mississippi. *Application Requirements:* Application. *Deadline:* continuous.

Contact Board of Trustees, Mississippi State Student Financial Aid, 3825 Ridgewood Road, Jackson, MS 39211-6453.

William F. Winter Teacher Scholar Loan Program. Awarded to Mississippi residents pursuing a teaching career. Must be enrolled full-time in a program leading to a Class A certification and maintain a 2.5 GPA. Must agree to teach one year for each year award is received. *Academic/Career Areas:* Education. *Award:* Forgivable loan for use in freshman, sophomore, junior, or senior year; renewable. *Award amount:* $1000–$3000. *Eligibility Requirements:* Applicant must be enrolled at a two-year or four-year institution or university; resident of Mississippi and studying in Mississippi. Applicant must have 2.5 GPA or higher. *Application Requirements:* Application, transcript. *Deadline:* April 30.

Contact Board of Trustees, Mississippi State Student Financial Aid, 3825 Ridgewood Road, Jackson, MS 39211-6453.

Southeast Asia POW/MIA Scholarship Program. Award for the biological children of veterans currently or formerly listed as prisoner-of-war, or missing in action in Southeast Asia or as a result of action against the "Pueblo." The award is an eight-semester tuition waiver. Must be a Mississippi resident. *Award:* Scholarship for use in freshman, sophomore, junior, or senior year; renewable. *Eligibility Requirements:* Applicant must be enrolled at a two-year or four-year institution or university; resident of Mississippi and studying in Mississippi. Applicant or parent must meet one or more of the following requirements: general military experience; retired from active duty; disabled or killed as a result of military service; prisoner of war; or missing in action. *Application Requirements:* Application. *Deadline:* continuous.

Contact Board of Trustees, Mississippi State Student Financial Aid, 3825 Ridgewood Road, Jackson, MS 39211-6453.

Mississippi Nursing Education MSN Program. Renewable scholarship for Mississippi graduate nursing students attending Mississippi universities. Must fulfill work obligation in Mississippi or pay back as a loan. Write for further details. *Academic/Career Areas:* Nursing. *Award:* Forgivable loan for use in graduate years; renewable. *Eligibility Requirements:* Applicant must be resident of Mississippi and studying in Mississippi. *Application Requirements:* Application, driver's license, financial need analysis, references, transcript. *Deadline:* April 30.

Contact Board of Trustees, Mississippi State Student Financial Aid, 3825 Ridgewood Road, Jackson, MS 39211-6453.

MISSOURI

Advantage Missouri Program. Applicant must be seeking a program of instruction in a designated high demand field. High demand fields are determined each year. Borrower must work in Missouri in the high-demand field for one year for every year the loan is received to be forgiven. *Award:* Forgivable loan for use in freshman, sophomore, junior, or senior year; not renewable. *Award amount:* $2500. *Number of awards:* 1100. *Eligibility Requirements:* Applicant must be enrolled at a two-year, four-year, or technical institution or university; resident of Missouri and studying in Missouri. Restricted to U.S. citizens. *Application Requirements:* Application, financial need analysis. *Deadline:* April 1.

Contact Information Center, Missouri Coordinating Board for Higher Education, 3515 Amazonas Drive, Jefferson City, MO 65109. *Phone:* 800-473-6757. *Fax:* 573-751-6635. *Web site:* http://www.mocbhe.gov.

Charles Gallagher Student Assistance Program. Available to Missouri residents attending Missouri colleges or universities full-time. Must be undergraduates with financial need. May reapply for up to a maximum of ten semesters. Free Application for Federal Student Aid (FAFSA) or a renewal must be received by the central processor by April 1 to be considered. *Award:* Grant for use in freshman, sophomore, junior, or senior year; not renewable. *Award amount:* $100–$1500. *Number of awards:* up to 9000. *Eligibility Requirements:* Applicant must be enrolled at a two-year, four-year, or technical institution or university; resident of Missouri and studying in Missouri. Restricted to U.S. citizens. *Application Requirements:* Application, financial need analysis. *Deadline:* April 1.

Contact Information Center, Missouri Coordinating Board for Higher Education, 3515 Amazonas Drive, Jefferson City, MO 65109. *Phone:* 800-473-6757. *Fax:* 573-751-6635. *Web site:* http://www.mocbhe.gov.

Missouri Higher Education Academic Scholaship. Awards of $2000 for Missouri high school seniors. Must be in top 3% of Missouri SAT or ACT scorers. Must attend Missouri institution as full-time undergraduate. May reapply for up to ten semesters. *Award:* Scholarship for use in freshman, sophomore, junior, or senior year; not renewable. *Award amount:* $2000. *Number of awards:* 6000–6400. *Eligibility Requirements:* Applicant must be high school student; enrolled at a two-year, four-year, or technical institution or university; resident of Missouri and studying in Missouri. *Application Requirements:* Application, test scores. *Deadline:* July 31.

Contact Information Center, Missouri Coordinating Board for Higher Education, 3515 Amazonas Drive, Jefferson City, MO 65109. *Phone:* 800-473-6757. *Fax:* 573-751-6635. *Web site:* http://www.mocbhe.gov.

Missouri Minority Teaching Scholarship. Award may be used any year up to four years at an approved, participating Missouri institution. Scholarship is for minority Missouri residents with a minimum

3.5 GPA in teaching programs. Recipients must commit to teach for five years in a Missouri public elementary or secondary school. Graduate students must teach math or science. Otherwise, award must be repaid. *Academic/Career Areas:* Education. *Award:* Forgivable loan for use in any year; renewable. *Award amount:* $3000. *Number of awards:* 100. *Eligibility Requirements:* Applicant must be Native American or Eskimo, Asian, African American, or Hispanic; enrolled at a two-year or four-year institution or university; resident of Missouri and studying in Missouri. Applicant must have 3.5 GPA or higher. Restricted to U.S. citizens. *Application Requirements:* Application, essay, financial need analysis, references, test scores, transcript. *Deadline:* February 15.

Contact Laura Harrison, Program Specialist, Missouri Department of Elementary and Secondary Education, PO Box 480, Jefferson City, MO 65102-0480. *E-mail:* lharriso@mail.dese.state.mo.us. *Phone:* 573-751-1668. *Fax:* 573-526-3580. *Web site:* http://www.dese.state.mo.us.

Missouri Teacher Education Scholarship (General). Award for Missouri high school seniors or Missouri resident college freshmen or sophomores. Must attend approved teacher training program at Missouri four-year institution. Nonrenewable. Must rank in top fifteen percent of high school class or ACT/SAT. Merit-based award. *Academic/Career Areas:* Education. *Award:* Scholarship for use in freshman or sophomore year; not renewable. *Award amount:* $2000. *Number of awards:* 200. *Eligibility Requirements:* Applicant must be enrolled at a four-year institution; resident of Missouri and studying in Missouri. Applicant must have 3.5 GPA or higher. Restricted to U.S. citizens. *Application Requirements:* Application, essay, references, test scores, transcript. *Deadline:* February 15.

Contact Laura Harrison, Program Specialist, Missouri Department of Elementary and Secondary Education, PO Box 480, Jefferson City, MO 65102-0480. *E-mail:* lharriso@mail.dese.state.mo.us. *Phone:* 573-751-1668. *Fax:* 573-526-3580. *Web site:* http://www.dese.state.mo.us.

MONTANA

Life Member Montana Federation of Garden Clubs Scholarship. Applicant must be at least a sophomore, majoring in conservation, horticulture, park or forestry, floriculture, greenhouse management, land management, or related subjects. Must be in need of assistance. Must have a potential for a successful future. Must be ranked in upper half of class or have a minimum 2.5 GPA. Must be a Montana resident and all study must be done in Montana. Deadline: May 1. *Award:* Scholarship for use in sophomore year; not renewable. *Award amount:* $1000. *Number of awards:* 1. *Eligibility Requirements:* Applicant must be enrolled at a four-year institution or university; resident of Montana and studying in Montana. Applicant must have 2.5 GPA or higher. Restricted to U.S. citizens. *Application Requirements:* Autobiography, financial need analysis, photo, references, transcript. *Deadline:* May 1.

Contact Elizabeth Kehmeier, Life Members Scholarship Chairman, Montana Federation of Garden Clubs, 214 Wyant Lane, Hamilton, MT 59840. *Phone:* 406-363-5693.

NEBRASKA

Rural Health Scholarship Program. Must be enrolled, or accepted for enrollment in medical school at Creighton University or University of Nebraska Medical Center, or in Physician Assistant Program at UNMC. Students must agree to practice one year in shortage area for each year a scholarship is awarded, and to specialize in family practice, general surgery, internal medicine, pediatrics, obstetrics/gynecology, or psychiatry. *Academic/Career Areas:* Health and Medical Sciences. *Award:* Forgivable loan for use in graduate years; not renewable. *Award amount:* up to $10,000. *Eligibility Requirements:* Applicant must be studying in Nebraska and have employment experience in designated career field. *Application Requirements:* Application, interview.

Contact Nebraska Health and Human Services System, Office of Rural Health, 301 Centennial Mall South PO Box 95044, Lincoln, NE 68509. *Phone:* 402-471-2337.

American Legion Auxiliary Department of Nebraska Nurse's Gift Tuition Scholarship. One-time scholarship for Nebraska resident who is a veteran or a child of a veteran who served in the Armed Forces during dates of eligibility for American Legion membership. Proof of enrollment in nursing program at eligible institution required. Must rank in upper third of class or have a minimum 3.0 GPA. *Academic/Career Areas:* Nursing. *Award:* Scholarship for use in any year; not renewable. *Award amount:* $300–$500. *Number of awards:* 1–18. *Eligibility Requirements:* Applicant must be enrolled at a two-year or four-year institution or university and resident of Nebraska. Applicant must have 3.0 GPA or higher. Restricted to U.S. citizens. Applicant or parent must meet one or more of the following requirements: general military experience; retired from active duty; disabled or killed as a result of military service; prisoner of war; or missing in action. *Application Requirements:* Application, essay, financial need analysis, references, test scores, transcript. *Deadline:* April 17.

Contact Terry Walker, Department Secretary, American Legion Auxiliary, Department of Nebraska, PO Box 5227, Lincoln, NE 68505. *Phone:* 402-466-1808. *Fax:* 402-466-0182.

American Legion Auxiliary Department of Nebraska Practical Nurse Scholarship. Nonrenewable scholarship for a veteran or a child of a veteran who served in the Armed Forces during dates of eligibility for American Legion membership. For full-time undergraduate study toward nursing degree at eligible institution. Must be a Nebraska resident. Must rank in upper third of class or have a minimum 3.0 GPA. *Academic/Career Areas:* Nursing. *Award:* Scholarship for use in freshman, sophomore, junior, or senior year; not renewable. *Award amount:* $400–$1000. *Number of awards:* 1–3. *Eligibility Requirements:* Applicant must be enrolled at a two-year or four-year institution or university and resident of Nebraska. Applicant must have 3.0 GPA or higher. Applicant or parent must meet one or more of the following requirements: general military experience; retired from active duty; disabled or killed as a result of military service; prisoner of war; or missing in action. *Application Requirements:* Application, essay, financial need analysis, references, test scores, transcript. *Deadline:* April 16.

Contact Terry Walker, Department Secretary, American Legion Auxiliary, Department of Nebraska, PO Box 5227, Lincoln, NE 68505. *Phone:* 402-466-1808. *Fax:* 402-466-0182.

American Legion Auxiliary Department of Nebraska President's Scholarships. One-time award for Nebraska high school students who were entered into the national competition and did not win. Contact address below for more information. Must be child of a veteran. Must rank in the upper third of class or have minimum 3.0 GPA. *Award:* Scholarship for use in any year; not renewable. *Award amount:* $100–$300. *Number of awards:* 3. *Eligibility Requirements:* Applicant must be high school student; enrolled at a two-year, four-year, or technical institution or university and resident of Nebraska. Applicant must have 3.0 GPA or higher. Applicant or parent must meet one or more of the following requirements: general military experience; retired from active duty; disabled or killed as a result of military service; prisoner of war; or missing in action. *Application Requirements:* Application, essay, references, test scores, transcript. *Deadline:* April 16.

Contact Terry Walker, Department Secretary, American Legion Auxiliary, Department of Nebraska, PO Box 5227, Lincoln, NE 68505. *Phone:* 402-466-1808. *Fax:* 402-466-0182.

Roberta Marie Stretch Memorial Scholarship. One-time award for Nebraska residents who are children or grandchildren of veterans. Must be enrolled in an undergraduate or graduate program at a four-year institution. Preference given to former Nebraska Girls State Citizens. Must rank in upper third of class or have a minimum 3.0 GPA. *Academic/Career Areas:* Social Sciences. *Award:* Scholarship for use in freshman, sophomore, junior, senior, or graduate years; not renewable. *Award amount:* $400–$500. *Number of awards:* 1. *Eligibility Requirements:* Applicant must be enrolled at a four-year institution or university and resident of Nebraska. Applicant must have 3.0 GPA or higher. Applicant must have general military experience. *Application Requirements:* Application, financial need analysis, test scores, transcript. *Deadline:* April 16.

Contact Terry Walker, Department Secretary, American Legion Auxiliary, Department of Nebraska, PO Box 5227, Lincoln, NE 68505. *Phone:* 402-466-1808. *Fax:* 402-466-0182.

American Legion Auxiliary Department of Nebraska Student Aid Grants. One-time award for veteran or veteran's child in financial need. Must be a Nebraska resident of at least five years. Must be accepted or enrolled at an institution of higher learning. If in school, must rank in upper third of class or have a minimum 3.0 GPA. *Award:* Grant for use in any year; not renewable. *Award amount:* $200–$300. *Number of awards:* 1–20. *Eligibility Requirements:* Applicant must be enrolled at a two-year, four-year, or technical institution or university and resident of Nebraska. Applicant must have 3.0 GPA or higher. Applicant or parent must meet one or more of the following requirements: general military experience; retired from active duty; disabled or killed as a result of military service; prisoner of war; or missing in action. *Application Requirements:* Application, financial need analysis, test scores, transcript. *Deadline:* April 16.

Contact Terry Walker, Department Secretary, American Legion Auxiliary, Department of Nebraska, PO Box 5227, Lincoln, NE 68505. *Phone:* 402-466-1808. *Fax:* 402-466-0182.

American Legion Auxiliary Department of Nebraska President's Scholarship for Junior Members. One-time prize for female resident of Nebraska who has been entered into the National President's Scholarship for Junior Members and does not win at the national level. Must be in grades 9-12. Must rank in upper third of class or have a minimum 3.0 GPA. *Award:* Prize for use in freshman year; not renewable. *Award amount:* $100–$200. *Number of awards:* 3. *Eligibility Requirements:* Applicant must be high school student; enrolled at a two-year, four-year, or technical institution or university; female; resident of Nebraska and member of American Legion or Auxiliary. Applicant must have 3.0 GPA or higher. *Application Requirements:* Application, applicant must enter a contest, financial need analysis, references, transcript. *Deadline:* April 2.

Contact Terry Walker, Department Secretary, American Legion Auxiliary, Department of Nebraska, PO Box 5227, Lincoln, NE 68505. *Phone:* 402-466-1808. *Fax:* 402-466-0182.

Postsecondary Education Award Program-Nebraska. Available to undergraduates attending a participating private, nonprofit post-secondary institution in Nebraska. Available to Pell Grant recipients only. Nebraska residency required. Awards determined by each participating institution. Contact financial aid office at respective institution for more information. *Award:* Scholarship for use in freshman, sophomore, junior, or senior year; not renewable. *Eligibility Requirements:* Applicant must be enrolled at a two-year or four-year institution; resident of Nebraska and studying in Nebraska. Restricted to U.S. citizens. *Application Requirements:* Financial need analysis. *Deadline:* continuous.

Contact Contact institution of choice., State of Nebraska, 140 North 8th Street, Suite 300, PO Box 95005, Lincoln, NE 68509-9500. *Web site:* http://www.nol.org/nepostsecondaryed.

Nebraska Scholarship Assistance Program. Available to undergraduates attending a participating post-secondary institution in Nebraska. Available to Pell Grant recipients only. Nebraska residency required. Awards determined by each participating institution. Contact financial aid office at respective institution for more information. *Award:* Scholarship for use in freshman, sophomore, junior, or senior year; not renewable. *Eligibility Requirements:* Applicant must be resident of

Nebraska and studying in Nebraska. *Application Requirements:* Financial need analysis. *Deadline:* continuous.

Contact Contact institution of choice., State of Nebraska, 140 North 8th Street, Suite 300, PO Box 95005, Lincoln, NE 68509-9500. *Web site:* http://www.nol.org/nepostsecondaryed.

Nebraska State Scholarship Award Program. Available to undergraduates attending a participating post-secondary institution in Nebraska. Available to Pell Grant recipients only. Nebraska residency not required. Awards determined by each participating institution. Contact financial aid office at respective institution for more details. *Award:* Scholarship for use in freshman, sophomore, junior, or senior year; not renewable. *Eligibility Requirements:* Applicant must be studying in Nebraska. *Application Requirements:* Financial need analysis. *Deadline:* continuous.

Contact Contact institution of choice., State of Nebraska, 140 North 8th Street, Suite 300, PO Box 95005, Lincoln, NE 68509-9500. *Web site:* http://www.nol.org/nepostsecondaryed.

State of Nebraska Loan Repayment Program for Rural Health Professionals. Physicians, nurse practitioners, physician assistants practicing internal medicine, family practice, pediatrics, obstetrics, gynecology, general surgery, and psychiatry eligible. Therapists, mental health professionals, dentists and pharmacists also eligible. Must commit to practicing three years in approved shortage area. To be used toward repayment of commercial or government educational loans. *Academic/Career Areas:* Health and Medical Sciences; Nursing; Therapy/Rehabilitation. *Award:* Grant for use in ; not renewable. *Award amount:* up to $20,000. *Eligibility Requirements:* Applicant must have employment experience in designated career field. *Application Requirements:* Application.

Contact Nebraska Health and Human Services System, Office of Rural Health, 301 Centennial Mall South PO Box 95044, Lincoln, NE 68509-5044. *Phone:* 402-471-2337.

Nebraska National Guard Tuition Credit. Renewable award for members of the Nebraska National Guard. Pays 75% of enlisted soldier's tuition until he or she has received a baccalaureate degree. *Award:* Scholarship for use in freshman, sophomore, junior, or senior year; renewable. *Number of awards:* up to 1200. *Eligibility Requirements:* Applicant must be enrolled at a two-year, four-year, or technical institution or university; resident of Nebraska and studying in Nebraska. Applicant must have served in the Air Force National Guard or Army National Guard. *Application Requirements:* Application. *Deadline:* continuous.

Contact Cindy York, Staff Assistant, Nebraska National Guard, 1300 Military Road, Lincoln, NE 68508-1090. *Phone:* 402-471-7170. *Fax:* 402-471-7171.

Ruby Paul Campaign Fund Scholarship. One-time award for Nebraska residents who are children, grandchildren or great grandchildren of an American Legion Auxiliary member or who have been members of the American Legion, American Legion Auxiliary, or Sons of the American Legion or Auxiliary for two years prior to application. Must rank in upper third of class or have minimum 3.0 GPA. *Award:* Scholarship for use in any year; not renewable. *Award amount:* $100–$300. *Number of awards:* 1. *Eligibility Requirements:* Applicant must be enrolled at a two-year, four-year, or technical institution or university; resident of Nebraska and member of American Legion or Auxiliary. Applicant must have 3.0 GPA or higher. Applicant must have general military experience. *Application Requirements:* Application, essay, financial need analysis, references, test scores, transcript. *Deadline:* April 16.

Contact Terry Walker, Department Secretary, American Legion Auxiliary, Department of Nebraska, PO Box 5227, Lincoln, NE 68505. *Phone:* 402-466-1808. *Fax:* 402-466-0182.

American Legion Auxiliary Department of Nebraska Graduate Scholarships. One-time award for Nebraska resident who is a veteran or a child of a veteran during dates of eligibility for American Legion membership. For use at a Nebraska institution for training as a teacher of special education for the handicapped. Must rank in upper third of class or have a minimum 3.0 GPA. *Academic/Career Areas:* Education; Special Education. *Award:* Scholarship for use in graduate years; not renewable. *Award amount:* $200. *Eligibility Requirements:* Applicant must be resident of Nebraska and studying in Nebraska. Applicant must have 3.0 GPA or higher. Restricted to U.S. citizens. Applicant must have general military experience. *Application Requirements:* Application, test scores, transcript. *Deadline:* April 16.

Contact Terry Walker, Department Secretary, American Legion Auxiliary, Department of Nebraska, PO Box 5227, Lincoln, NE 68505. *Phone:* 402-466-1808. *Fax:* 402-466-0182.

NEVADA

Nevada Student Incentive Grant. Award available to Nevada residents for use at an accredited Nevada college or university. Must show financial need. Any field of study eligible. High school students may not apply. One-time award of up to $5000. Contact financial aid office at local college. *Award:* Grant for use in any year; not renewable. *Award amount:* $200–$5000. *Number of awards:* 400–800. *Eligibility Requirements:* Applicant must be enrolled at a two-year, four-year, or technical institution or university; resident of Nevada and studying in Nevada. *Application Requirements:* Application, financial need analysis.

Contact Contact the financial aid office at local college, Nevada Department of Education, 700 East 5th Street, Carson City, NV 89701.

NEW HAMPSHIRE

New Hampshire Career Incentive Program. Grants available to New Hampshire residents attending New Hampshire institutions in programs leading to certification in special education or foreign language education. Must work in shortage area following graduation. Deadlines: June 1 for fall or spring,

December 15 for spring. Must rank in upper third of class or have a minimum 3.0 GPA. *Academic/Career Areas:* Foreign Language; Special Education. *Award:* Forgivable loan for use in junior, senior, or graduate years; not renewable. *Award amount:* $2000–$3000. *Number of awards:* 1–25. *Eligibility Requirements:* Applicant must be enrolled at a four-year institution or university; resident of New Hampshire and studying in New Hampshire. Applicant must have 3.0 GPA or higher. *Application Requirements:* Application, financial need analysis. *Deadline:* June 1.

Contact Judith Knapp, Student Financial Assistant Coordinator, New Hampshire Postsecondary Education Commission, Two Industrial Park Drive, Concord, NH 03301-8512. *E-mail:* jknapp@nhsa.state.nh.us. *Phone:* 603-271-2555. *Fax:* 603-271-2696. *Web site:* http://www.state.nh.us/postsecondary.

New Hampshire Incentive Program (NHIP). Renewable grants for New Hampshire residents attending school in New Hampshire, Connecticut, Maine, Massachusetts, Rhode Island, or Vermont. Must be a full-time student with financial need. Deadline is May 1. Complete Free Application for Federal Student Aid. *Award:* Grant for use in freshman, sophomore, junior, or senior year; not renewable. *Award amount:* $450–$1000. *Number of awards:* 2500–3000. *Eligibility Requirements:* Applicant must be enrolled at a two-year, four-year, or technical institution or university; resident of New Hampshire and studying in Connecticut, Maine, Massachusetts, New Hampshire, Rhode Island, or Vermont. *Application Requirements:* Application, financial need analysis. *Deadline:* May 1.

Contact Judith Knapp, Student Financial Assistant Coordinator, New Hampshire Postsecondary Education Commission, Two Industrial Park Drive, Concord, NH 03301-8512. *E-mail:* jknapp@nhsa.state.nh.us. *Phone:* 603-271-2555. *Fax:* 603-271-2696. *Web site:* http://www.state.nh.us/postsecondary.

Scholarships for Orphans of Veterans-New Hampshire. Awards for New Hampshire residents whose parent died as a result of service in WWI, WWII, the Korean Conflict, or the Southeast Asian Conflict. Possible full tuition and $1000 per year with automatic renewal on reapplication. Contact department for application deadlines. Must be under 26. Must include proof of eligibility and proof of parent's death. *Award:* Grant for use in any year; renewable. *Award amount:* $1000. *Number of awards:* 1–10. *Eligibility Requirements:* Applicant must be age 26; enrolled at a two-year or four-year institution or university and resident of New Hampshire. Restricted to U.S. citizens. Applicant or parent must meet one or more of the following requirements: general military experience; retired from active duty; disabled or killed as a result of military service; prisoner of war; or missing in action. *Application Requirements:* Application.

Contact Patti Edes, Student Financial Assistant Coordinator, New Hampshire Postsecondary Education Commission, Two Industrial Park Drive, Concord, NH 03301-8512. *E-mail:* pedes@nhsa.state.nh.us. *Phone:* 603-271-2555. *Fax:* 603-271-2696. *Web site:* http://www.state.nh.us/postsecondary.

NEW JERSEY

New Jersey War Orphans Tuition Assistance. Renewable award for New Jersey residents who are high school seniors ages 16-21 and who are children of veterans killed or disabled in duty, missing in action, or prisoner-of-war. For use at a two- or four-year college or university. Write for more information. Deadlines: October 1 for fall semester and March 1 for spring semester. *Award:* Scholarship for use in any year; renewable. *Award amount:* $2000–$5000. *Eligibility Requirements:* Applicant must be high school student; age 16-21; enrolled at a two-year or four-year institution or university and resident of New Jersey. Applicant or parent must meet one or more of the following requirements: general military experience; retired from active duty; disabled or killed as a result of military service; prisoner of war; or missing in action. *Application Requirements:* Application, transcript.

Contact Barbara Gilsenan, Veterans Service Officer, New Jersey Department of Military and Veterans Affairs, PO Box 340, Trenton, NJ 08625. *Phone:* 609-530-6961. *Fax:* 609-530-6970.

Veterans' Tuition Credit Program-New Jersey. Award for veterans who served in the armed forces between December 31, 1960, and May 7, 1975. Must have been a New Jersey resident at time of induction or discharge or for one year prior to application. Apply by October 1 for fall, March 1 for spring. Renewable award of $200-$400. *Award:* Scholarship for use in any year; renewable. *Award amount:* $200–$400. *Eligibility Requirements:* Applicant must be enrolled at a two-year, four-year, or technical institution or university and resident of New Jersey. Applicant must have general military experience. *Application Requirements:* Application.

Contact Barbara Gilsenan, Veterans Service Officer, New Jersey Department of Military and Veterans Affairs, PO Box 340, Trenton, NJ 08625. *Phone:* 609-530-6961. *Fax:* 609-530-6970.

Tuition Assistance for Children of POW/MIAs. Assists children of military service personnel declared missing in action or prisoner-of-war after January 1, 1960. Must be a resident of New Jersey. Renewable grants provide tuition for undergraduate study in New Jersey. Apply by October 1 for fall, March 1 for spring. Must be high school senior to apply. *Award:* Scholarship for use in freshman, sophomore, junior, or senior year; renewable. *Eligibility Requirements:* Applicant must be high school student; enrolled at a two-year or four-year institution; resident of New Jersey and studying in New Jersey. Applicant or parent must meet one or more of the following requirements: general military experience; retired from active duty; disabled or killed as a result of military service; prisoner of war; or missing in action. *Application Requirements:* Application, transcript.

Contact Barbara Gilsenan, Veterans Service Officer, New Jersey Department of Military and Veterans Affairs, PO Box 340, Trenton, NJ 08625. *Phone:* 609-530-6961. *Fax:* 609-530-6970.

Martin Luther King Physician/Dentist Scholarships. Renewable award available to New Jersey residents enrolled full-time in a medicine or dentistry program. Must be from either disadvantaged background, minority; former or current EOF recipient. Several scholarships of varying number and amount. Must attend a New Jersey institution. *Academic/Career Areas:* Dental Health/Services; Health and Medical Sciences. *Award:* Scholarship for use in graduate years; renewable. *Eligibility Requirements:* Applicant must be resident of New Jersey and studying in New Jersey. Restricted to U.S. citizens. *Application Requirements:* Application, financial need analysis, references, transcript. *Deadline:* continuous.

Contact Sandra Rollins, Associate Director of Financial Aid, University of Medicine and Dentistry of NJ School of Osteopathic Medicine, 40 East Laurel Road, Primary Care Center 119, Stratford, NJ 08084 USA. *E-mail:* rollins@umdnj.edu. *Phone:* 856-566-6008. *Fax:* 856-566-6015. *Web site:* http://www3.umdnj.edu/faidweb.

New Jersey Educational Opportunity Fund Grants. Grants up to $4150 per year, not to exceed five years of eligibility. Must be a New Jersey resident for at least twelve consecutive months and attend a New Jersey institution. Must be from a disadvantaged background as defined by EOF guidelines. EOF recipients may qualify for the Martin Luther King Physician/Dentistry Scholarships' for graduate study at a professional institution. *Academic/Career Areas:* Dental Health/Services; Health and Medical Sciences. *Award:* Grant for use in freshman, sophomore, junior, senior, or graduate years; renewable. *Award amount:* up to $4150. *Eligibility Requirements:* Applicant must be enrolled at a four-year institution or university; resident of New Jersey and studying in New Jersey. Restricted to U.S. citizens. *Application Requirements:* Application.

Contact Sandra Rollins, Associate Director of Financial Aid, University of Medicine and Dentistry of NJ School of Osteopathic Medicine, 40 East Laurel Road, Primary Care Center 119, Stratford, NJ 08084. *E-mail:* rollins@umdnj.edu. *Phone:* 856-566-6008. *Fax:* 856-566-6015. *Web site:* http://www3.umdnj.edu/faidweb.

NJSA Scholarship Program. One-time award for permanent residents of New Jersey enrolled in an accredited architecture program. Minimum 2.5 GPA required. Must show evidence of financial need, scholarship, and promise in architecture. Submit portfolio and $5 application fee. *Academic/Career Areas:* Architecture. *Award:* Scholarship for use in sophomore, junior, senior, or graduate years; not renewable. *Award amount:* $250–$1500. *Eligibility Requirements:* Applicant must be enrolled at a four-year, or technical institution or university and resident of New Jersey. Applicant must have 2.5 GPA or higher. *Application Requirements:* Application, essay, financial need analysis, portfolio, references, transcript. *Fee:* $5. *Deadline:* April 29.

Contact Robert Zaccone, President, AIA New Jersey Scholarship Foundation, Inc., 212 White Avenue, Old Tappan, NJ 07675-7411.

NEW MEXICO

Lottery Success Scholarships. Awards equal to 100 percent of tuition at New Mexico public post-secondary institution. Must have New Mexico high school degree and be enrolled at New Mexico public college or university in first regular semester following high school graduation. Must obtain 2.5 GPA during this semester. May be eligible for up to eight consecutive semesters of support. Deadlines vary by institution. Apply through financial aid office of any New Mexico public post-secondary institution. *Award:* Scholarship for use in freshman, sophomore, junior, or senior year; not renewable. *Eligibility Requirements:* Applicant must be resident of New Mexico and studying in New Mexico. Applicant must have 2.5 GPA or higher. *Application Requirements:* Application.

Contact Monica Medrano, Program Officer, New Mexico Commission on Higher Education, PO Box 15910, Santa Fe, NM 87506-5910. *Phone:* 505-827-7383. *Fax:* 505-827-7392. *Web site:* http://www.nmche.org.

3% Scholarship Program. Award equal to tuition and required fees for New Mexico residents who are undergraduate students attending public post-secondary institutions in New Mexico. Contact financial aid office of any public post-secondary institution in New Mexico for deadline. *Award:* Scholarship for use in freshman, sophomore, junior, or senior year; not renewable. *Eligibility Requirements:* Applicant must be resident of New Mexico and studying in New Mexico. *Application Requirements:* Application.

Contact Monica Medrano, Program Officer, New Mexico Commission on Higher Education, PO Box 15910, Santa Fe, NM 87506-5910. *Phone:* 505-827-7383. *Fax:* 505-827-7392. *Web site:* http://www.nmche.org.

Children of Deceased Veterans Scholarship-New Mexico. Award for New Mexico residents who are children of veterans killed or disabled as a result of service, prisoner of war, or veterans missing in action. Must be between ages 16 to 26. For use at New Mexico schools for undergraduate study. Submit parent's death certificate and DD form 214. *Award:* Scholarship for use in freshman, sophomore, junior, or senior year; renewable. *Eligibility Requirements:* Applicant must be age 16-26; resident of New Mexico and studying in New Mexico. Applicant or parent must meet one or more of the following requirements: general military experience; retired from active duty; disabled or killed as a result of military service; prisoner of war; or missing in action. *Application Requirements:* Application, transcript. *Deadline:* continuous.

Contact Alan Martinez, Manager of State Benefits, New Mexico Veterans' Service Commission, PO Box 2324, Sante Fe, NM 87504. *Phone:* 505-827-6300. *Fax:* 505-827-6372. *Web site:* http://www.state.nm.us/veterans.

New Mexico Vietnam Veterans' Scholarship. Renewable award for Vietnam veterans who are New Mexico residents attending state-sponsored schools. Must have been awarded the Vietnam Campaign medal. Submit DD214. Must include discharge papers. *Award:* Scholarship for use in any year; renewable. *Award amount:* up to $1554. *Eligibility Requirements:* Applicant must be resident of New Mexico and studying in New Mexico. Applicant must have general military experience. *Application Requirements:* Application. *Deadline:* continuous.

Contact Alan Martinez, Manager State Benefits, New Mexico Veterans' Service Commission, PO Box 2324, Sante Fe, NM 87504. *Phone:* 505-827-6300. *Fax:* 505-827-6372. *Web site:* http://www.state.nm.us/veterans.

Children of Deceased Military/State Police Scholarship. Award for surviving children, ages 16-26, of military personnel, members of New Mexico National Guard, and New Mexico State Police who have been killed while on active duty. Award of $300 plus tuition waiver at any New Mexico public post-secondary institution. Contact financial aid office or New Mexico Veterans Service Commission for further information and deadlines. *Award:* Scholarship for use in any year; not renewable. *Award amount:* up to $300. *Eligibility Requirements:* Applicant must be age 16-26 and studying in New Mexico. Applicant or parent must meet one or more of the following requirements: general military experience; retired from active duty; disabled or killed as a result of military service; prisoner of war; or missing in action. *Application Requirements:* Application.

Contact Monica Medrano, Program Officer, New Mexico Commission on Higher Education, PO Box 15910, Santa Fe, NM 87506-5910. *Phone:* 505-827-7383. *Fax:* 505-827-7392. *Web site:* http://www.nmche.org.

Osteopathic Medical Student Loan Program-New Mexico. Renewable award for New Mexico residents enrolled in accredited program of osteopathic education in the U.S. Must practice full-time in New Mexico. Loan may be repaid through service. Priority given to those with financial need. To apply call the Commission at the CHE Student Helpline: 1-800-279-9777. *Academic/Career Areas:* Health and Medical Sciences. *Award:* Forgivable loan for use in graduate years; renewable. *Award amount:* up to $12,000. *Number of awards:* 1–10. *Eligibility Requirements:* Applicant must be resident of New Mexico. *Application Requirements:* Application, essay, financial need analysis, references, test scores, transcript. *Deadline:* July 1.

Contact Monica Medrano, Program Officer, New Mexico Commission on Higher Education, PO Box 15910, Santa Fe, NM 87506-5910. *Phone:* 505-827-7383. *Fax:* 505-827-7392. *Web site:* http://www.nmche.org.

New Mexico Competitive Scholarship. Scholarship available to encourage out-of-state students who have demonstrated high academic achievement to enroll in public institutions of higher education in New Mexico. One-time award for undergraduate students. Deadlines set by each institution. Contact financial aid office of any New Mexico public post-secondary institution to apply. *Award:* Scholarship for use in freshman, sophomore, junior, or senior year; not renewable. *Award amount:* $100. *Eligibility Requirements:* Applicant must be enrolled at a four-year institution or university and studying in New Mexico. Applicant must have 3.0 GPA or higher. *Application Requirements:* Application, essay, references, test scores.

Contact Monica Medrano, Program Officer, New Mexico Commission on Higher Education, PO Box 15910, Santa Fe, NM 87506-5910. *Phone:* 505-827-7383. *Fax:* 505-827-7392. *Web site:* http://www.nmche.org.

New Mexico Student Incentive Grant. Several grants available for resident undergraduate students attending public and private nonprofit institutions in New Mexico. Must demonstrate financial need. Several renewable awards of varying amounts. To apply contact financial aid office at any public or private non-profit post-secondary institution in New Mexico. *Award:* Grant for use in freshman, sophomore, junior, or senior year; renewable. *Award amount:* $200–$2500. *Eligibility Requirements:* Applicant must be enrolled at a two-year or four-year institution or university; resident of New Mexico and studying in New Mexico. *Application Requirements:* Application, financial need analysis.

Contact Monica Medrano, Program Officer, New Mexico Commission on Higher Education, PO Box 15910, Santa Fe, NM 87506-5910. *Phone:* 505-827-7383. *Fax:* 505-827-7392. *Web site:* http://www.nmche.org.

Nursing Student Loan-For-Service Program. Award for New Mexico residents accepted or enrolled in nursing program at New Mexico public post-secondary institution. Must practice as nurse in designated health professional shortage area in New Mexico. Award dependent upon financial need but may not exceed $12,000. Deadline: July 1. To apply call the Commission at the CHE Student Helpline: 1-800-279-9777. *Academic/Career Areas:* Nursing. *Award:* Forgivable loan for use in freshman, sophomore, junior, senior, or graduate years; not renewable. *Award amount:* up to $12,000. *Eligibility Requirements:* Applicant must be resident of New Mexico and studying in New Mexico. *Application Requirements:* Application, financial need analysis. *Deadline:* July 1.

Contact Monica Medrano, Program Officer, New Mexico Commission on Higher Education, PO Box 15910, Santa Fe, NM 87506-5910. *Phone:* 505-827-7383. *Fax:* 505-827-7392. *Web site:* http://www.nmche.org.

New Mexico Child Care Grants. Funds available to help undergraduate and graduate student parents enrolled at least half-time. Preference given to New Mexico residents. Several one-time awards of varying amounts. Must attend an institution in New Mexico. Apply through financial aid office of any New Mexico public post-secondary institution. *Award:* Scholarship for use in any year; not renewable. *Award amount:* up to $500. *Number of awards:* up to 1500. *Eligibility Requirements:* Applicant must be studying in New Mexico. *Application Requirements:* Application.

Contact Monica Medrano, Program Officer, New Mexico Commission on Higher Education, PO Box 15910, Santa Fe, NM 87506-5910. *Phone:* 505-827-7383. *Fax:* 505-827-7392. *Web site:* http://www.nmche.org.

Medical Student Loan-For-Service Program. Award for New Mexico residents accepted by or enrolled in public school of medicine in the U.S. Preference given to students attending UNM School of Medicine. Must practice as physician or physician assistant in designated health professional shortage area in New Mexico. Award dependent upon financial need but may not exceed $12,000 per year. Deadline: July 1. To apply call the Commission at the CHE Student Helpline: 1-800-279-9777. *Academic/Career Areas:* Health and Medical Sciences. *Award:* Forgivable loan for use in graduate years; not renewable. *Award amount:* up to $12,000. *Eligibility Requirements:* Applicant must be resident of New Mexico. *Application Requirements:* Application, financial need analysis. *Deadline:* July 1.

Contact Monica Medrano, Program Officer, New Mexico Commission on Higher Education, PO Box 15910, Santa Fe, NM 87506-5910. *Phone:* 505-827-7383. *Fax:* 505-827-7392. *Web site:* http://www.nmche.org.

New Mexico Scholars Program. Several scholarships to encourage New Mexico high school graduates to enroll in college full-time at a public or selected private nonprofit post-secondary institution in New Mexico before their 22nd birthday. Selected private colleges are College of Santa Fe, St. John's College in Santa Fe, and College of the Southwest. Must have graduated in top 5% of their class or obtained an ACT score of 25 or SAT score of 1140. One-time scholarship for tuition, books, and fees. Contact financial aid office at college to apply. *Award:* Scholarship for use in freshman, sophomore, junior, or senior year; not renewable. *Award amount:* $1000–$5000. *Eligibility Requirements:* Applicant must be enrolled at a two-year or four-year institution; resident of New Mexico and studying in New Mexico. *Application Requirements:* Application, financial need analysis, test scores.

Contact Monica Medrano, Program Officer, New Mexico Commission on Higher Education, PO Box 15910, Santa Fe, NM 87506-5910. *Phone:* 505-827-7383. *Fax:* 505-827-7392. *Web site:* http://www.nmche.org.

Minority Doctoral Assistance Loan-For-Service Program. Several loans available to increase the number of ethnic minorities and women available to teach in academic disciplines in which they are underrepresented. Must have a bachelor's or master's degree from New Mexico four-year public post-secondary institution and be accepted for enrollment as full-time doctoral student at eligible institution. As condition of the loan, recipient is required to teach at sponsoring New Mexico institution for a minimum of one year for each year loan is awarded. Several renewable loans for up to $25,000 per year. *Award:* Forgivable loan for use in graduate years; renewable. *Award amount:* up to $25,000. *Eligibility Requirements:* Applicant must be resident of New Mexico and studying in New Mexico. *Application Requirements:* Application, essay, references, transcript.

Contact Monica Medrano, Program Officer, New Mexico Commission on Higher Education, PO Box 15910, Santa Fe, NM 87506-5910. *Phone:* 505-827-7383. *Fax:* 505-827-7392. *Web site:* http://www.nmche.org.

New Mexico Health Professional Loan Repayment Program. Program to provide for repayment of outstanding student loans of practicing health professionals in return for two-year service commitment with optional one-year renewals in a designated medical shortage area in New Mexico. Deadline: July 1. To apply call the Commission at the CHE Student Helpline: 1-800-279-9777. *Academic/Career Areas:* Dental Health/Services; Health and Medical Sciences; Nursing. *Award:* Scholarship for use in graduate years; renewable. *Award amount:* up to $12,500. *Eligibility Requirements:* Applicant must be studying in New Mexico and have employment experience in designated career field. *Application Requirements:* Application, essay, references. *Deadline:* July 1.

Contact Monica Medrano, Program Officer, New Mexico Commission on Higher Education, PO Box 15910, Santa Fe, NM 87506-5910. *Phone:* 505-827-7383. *Fax:* 505-827-7392. *Web site:* http://www.nmche.org.

Vietnam Veterans Scholarship Program. Award for New Mexico residents who are Vietnam veterans enrolled in undergraduate or master-level course work at public or selected private New Mexico post-secondary institutions. Award may include tuition, required fees, and book allowance. Contact financial aid office of any public or eligible private New Mexico post-secondary institution for deadline. *Award:* Scholarship for use in freshman, sophomore, junior, senior, or graduate years; not renewable. *Eligibility Requirements:* Applicant must be resident of New Mexico and studying in New Mexico. Applicant or parent must meet one or more of the following requirements: general military experience; retired from active duty; disabled or killed as a result of military service; prisoner of war; or missing in action. *Application Requirements:* Application.

Contact Monica Medrano, Program Officer, New Mexico Commission on Higher Education, PO Box 15910, Santa Fe, NM 87506-5910. *Phone:* 505-827-7383. *Fax:* 505-827-7392. *Web site:* http://www.nmche.org.

Legislative Endowment Scholarships. Awards for undergraduate students with substantial financial need who are attending public post-secondary institutions in New Mexico. Preference given to returning adult students at two- and four-year institutions and students transferring from two-year to four-year institution. Deadline set by each institution. Must be resident of New Mexico. Contact financial aid office of any New Mexico public post-secondary institution to apply. *Award:* Scholarship for use in freshman, sophomore, junior, or senior year; not renewable. *Award amount:* up to $2500. *Eligibility Requirements:* Applicant must be resident of New Mexico and studying in New

Mexico. *Application Requirements:* Application, financial need analysis.

Contact Monica Medrano, Program Officer, New Mexico Commission on Higher Education, PO Box 15910, Santa Fe, NM 87506-5910. *Phone:* 505-827-7383. *Fax:* 505-827-7392. *Web site:* http://www.nmche.org.

Allied Health Student Loan Program-New Mexico. Renewable loans for New Mexico residents enrolled in an undergraduate allied health program. Loans can be forgiven through service in a medically underserved area or can be repaid. Penalties apply for failure to provide service. May borrow up to $12,000 per year for four years. Apply by calling the Commission at the CHE Student Helpline: 1-800-279-9777. *Academic/Career Areas:* Dental Health/Services; Health and Medical Sciences; Nursing; Social Sciences; Therapy/Rehabilitation. *Award:* Forgivable loan for use in freshman, sophomore, junior, or senior year; renewable. *Award amount:* up to $12,000. *Number of awards:* 1–40. *Eligibility Requirements:* Applicant must be enrolled at a two-year or four-year institution or university; resident of New Mexico and studying in New Mexico. *Application Requirements:* Application, essay, financial need analysis, references, transcript. *Deadline:* July 1.

Contact Monica Medrano, Program Officer, New Mexico Commission on Higher Education, PO Box 15910, Santa Fe, NM 87506-5910. *Phone:* 505-827-7383. *Fax:* 505-827-7392. *Web site:* http://www.nmche.org.

NEW YORK

New York Memorial Scholarships for Families of Deceased Police Officers and Fire Fighters. Renewable scholarship for dependents of New York police officers or firefighters who died in the line of duty. Must be a New York resident pursuing undergraduate study at a SUNY college or university. *Award:* Scholarship for use in freshman, sophomore, junior, or senior year; renewable. *Eligibility Requirements:* Applicant must be enrolled at a four-year institution or university; resident of New York; studying in New York and have employment experience in police/firefighting. *Application Requirements:* Application, financial need analysis. *Deadline:* May 1.

Contact Student Information, New York State Higher Education Services Corporation, 99 Washington Avenue, Room 1438, Albany, NY 12255. *Web site:* http://www.hesc.com.

Primary Care Service Corps Scholarship. The Primary Care Service Corps provides up to $15,000 per year for full-time study or up to $7500 per year for part-time study for students studying to become physician assistants, nurse practitioners, or midwives. In return, the student agrees to provide service in an underserved area of New York. *Academic/Career Areas:* Health and Medical Sciences; Nursing. *Award:* Scholarship for use in junior, senior, or graduate years; renewable. *Award amount:* $30,000. *Eligibility Requirements:* Applicant must be enrolled at a four-year institution or university and resident of New York. Restricted to U.S. citizens. *Application Requirements:* Application, essay, references, transcript. *Deadline:* April 3.

Contact Amy Pemberton, Program Administrator, New York State Department of Health, Corning Towers, Room 1084, ESP, Albany, NY 12237. *E-mail:* sch_loan@health.state.ny.us. *Phone:* 518-473-7019. *Fax:* 518-474-0572.

New York Educational Opportunity Program (EOP). Renewable award for New York resident attending New York college/university for undergraduate study. For educationally or economically disadvantaged students; includes educational assistance such as tutoring. *Award:* Scholarship for use in freshman, sophomore, junior, or senior year; renewable. *Eligibility Requirements:* Applicant must be enrolled at a two-year or four-year institution or university; resident of New York and studying in New York. *Application Requirements:* Application, financial need analysis, transcript.

Contact Student Information, New York State Higher Education Services Corporation, 99 Washington Avenue, Room 1438, Albany, NY 12255. *Web site:* http://www.hesc.com.

Regents Award for Children of Deceased Police Officers, Firefighters, or Correction Officers-New York. Award for children of New York police officers, firefighters, or correction officers killed in the line of duty. Must be a resident of New York and attend college full-time in New York. Renewable award of $450 for undergraduate study. *Award:* Scholarship for use in freshman, sophomore, junior, or senior year; renewable. *Award amount:* $450. *Eligibility Requirements:* Applicant must be enrolled at a four-year institution or university; resident of New York; studying in New York and have employment experience in police/firefighting. *Application Requirements:* Application. *Deadline:* May 1.

Contact Student Information, New York State Higher Education Services Corporation, 99 Washington Avenue, Room 1438, Albany, NY 12255. *Web site:* http://www.hesc.com.

Regents Award for Child of Veteran. Award for students whose parent, as a result of service in U.S. Armed Forces during war or national emergency, died; suffered a 40 percent or more disability; or is classified as missing in action or a prisoner-of-war. Veteran must be current New York State resident or have been so at time of death. Must be New York resident attending, or planning to attend, college in New York State. Must establish eligibility before applying for payment. *Award:* Scholarship for use in freshman, sophomore, junior, or senior year; not renewable. *Award amount:* $450. *Eligibility Requirements:* Applicant must be resident of New York and studying in New York. Applicant or parent must meet one or more of the following requirements: general military experience; retired from active duty; disabled or killed as a result of military service; prisoner of war; or missing in action. *Application Requirements:* Application. *Deadline:* May 1.

Contact Student Information, New York State Higher Education Services Corporation, 99 Washington Avenue, Room 1438, Albany, NY 12255. *Web site:* http://www.hesc.com.

Regents Professional Opportunity Scholarships. Award for New York State residents pursuing career in certain licensed professions. Must attend New York State college. Priority given to economically disadvantaged members of minority group underrepresented in chosen profession and graduates of SEEK, College Discovery, EOP, and HEOP. Must work in New York State in chosen profession one year for each annual payment. *Award:* Forgivable loan for use in freshman, sophomore, junior, senior, or graduate years; not renewable. *Award amount:* $1000–$5000. *Eligibility Requirements:* Applicant must be enrolled at a two-year or four-year institution or university; resident of New York and studying in New York. *Application Requirements:* Application. *Deadline:* May 1.

Contact Student Information, New York State Higher Education Services Corporation, 99 Washington Avenue, Room 1438, Albany, NY 12255. *Web site:* http://www.hesc.com.

New York Aid for Part-Time Study (APTS). Renewable scholarship provides tuition assistance to part-time students who are New York residents attending New York-accredited institutions. Deadlines and award amounts vary. *Award:* Grant for use in freshman, sophomore, junior, or senior year; renewable. *Award amount:* up to $2000. *Eligibility Requirements:* Applicant must be enrolled at a two-year or four-year institution; resident of New York and studying in New York. *Application Requirements:* Application.

Contact Student Information, New York State Higher Education Services Corporation, 99 Washington Avenue, Room 1438, Albany, NY 12255. *Web site:* http://www.hesc.com.

New York Vietnam Veterans Tuition Awards. Scholarship for veterans who served in Vietnam. Must be a New York resident attending a New York institution. Renewable award of $500-$1000. Deadline: May 1. Must establish eligibility by September 1. *Award:* Scholarship for use in any year; renewable. *Award amount:* $500–$1000. *Eligibility Requirements:* Applicant must be resident of New York and studying in New York. Applicant must have served in the Air Force, Army, Marine Corp, or Navy. *Application Requirements:* Application, financial need analysis. *Deadline:* May 1.

Contact Student Information, New York State Higher Education Services Corporation, 99 Washington Avenue, Room 1438, Albany, NY 12255. *Web site:* http://www.hesc.com.

Regents Professional Opportunity Scholarship Program—New York. Renewable award for New York residents in programs leading to a degree in a profession licensed by the Board of Regents. Priority given to minority or disadvantaged students. Must practice full time, professionally in New York for one year for each award received. *Academic/Career Areas:* Architecture; Business/Consumer Services; Civil Engineering; Dental Health/Services; Electrical Engineering/Electronics; Food Science/Nutrition; Interior Design; Landscape Architecture; Law/Legal Services; Nursing; Social Sciences; Therapy/Rehabilitation. *Award:* Forgivable loan for use in freshman, sophomore, junior, senior, or graduate years; renewable. *Award amount:* $1000–$5000. *Number of awards:* 220. *Eligibility Requirements:* Applicant must be Native American or Eskimo, African American, or Hispanic; enrolled at a two-year or four-year institution or university; resident of New York and studying in New York. Restricted to U.S. citizens. *Application Requirements:* Application. *Deadline:* May 1.

Contact Douglas Mercado, Chief, New York State Education Department, Room 1071 EBA, Albany, NY 12234. *E-mail:* dmercado@mail.nxsed.gov. *Phone:* 518-486-1319. *Fax:* 518-486-5346.

Primary Care Service Corps Scholarship Program (New York). Award for New York residents who are enrolled in, accepted to, or applied for study in an approved graduate, undergraduate, or certificate course of study. Must be within 24 months of completion of full-time training or within 48 months of completion of part-time training. Upon completion of training, recipient must be eligible to practice in New York state as a registered or certified physician assistant, nurse practitioner, or midwife. Recipient may accept up to two annual awards for full-time study or up to four awards for part-time study. Must fulfill service obligation by working in an underserved area for eighteen months per full-time award received, nine months per part-time award. *Academic/Career Areas:* Health and Medical Sciences; Nursing. *Award:* Forgivable loan for use in junior or senior year; renewable. *Award amount:* $7500–$15,000. *Eligibility Requirements:* Applicant must be enrolled at a four-year institution or university and resident of New York. *Application Requirements:* Application, references, transcript. *Deadline:* April 1.

Contact Student Information, New York State Higher Education Services Corporation, 99 Washington Avenue, Room 1438, Albany, NY 12255. *Web site:* http://www.hesc.com.

Regents Health Care Scholarships for Medicine and Dentistry-New York. Renewable award for New York residents enrolled in medical or dental program in New York. Priority for minorities or disadvantaged students. Must agree to practice in an area of New York with a shortage of physicians or dentists for a minimum of two years. *Academic/Career Areas:* Dental Health/Services; Health and Medical Sciences. *Award:* Forgivable loan for use in graduate years; renewable. *Award amount:* up to $10,000. *Number of awards:* 100. *Eligibility Requirements:* Applicant must be Native American or Eskimo, African American, or Hispanic; resident of New York and studying in New York. Restricted to U.S. citizens. *Application Requirements:* Application. *Deadline:* May 1.

Contact Douglas Mercado, Chief, New York State Education Department, Room 1071 EBA, Albany, NY 12234. *E-mail:* dmercado@mail.nxsed.gov. *Phone:* 518-486-1319. *Fax:* 518-486-5346.

Scholarships for Academic Excellence. Renewable awards of up to $1500 for academically outstanding New York State high school graduates planning to attend an approved post-secondary institution in New York State. For full-time study only. Contact high school guidance counselor to apply. *Award:* Scholarship for use in freshman, sophomore, junior, or senior year; renewable. *Award amount:* $500–$1500. *Number of awards:* 8000. *Eligibility Requirements:* Applicant must be high school student; resident of New York and studying in New York. *Application Requirements:* Application.

Contact Student Information, New York State Higher Education Services Corporation, 99 Washington Avenue, Room 1438, Albany, NY 12255. *Web site:* http://www.hesc.com.

Regents Physician Loan Forgiveness Award-New York. Renewable award for New York resident licensed to practice medicine in New York. Must be within two years of completing residency or have completed residency within last five years. Must be U.S. citizen or permanent resident. Must practice medicine in a designated area of New York. *Academic/Career Areas:* Health and Medical Sciences. *Award:* Forgivable loan for use in ; renewable. *Award amount:* up to $10,000. *Number of awards:* up to 80. *Eligibility Requirements:* Applicant must be resident of New York and studying in New York. Restricted to U.S. citizens. *Application Requirements:* Application. *Deadline:* May 1.

Contact Douglas Mercado, Chief, New York State Education Department, Room 1071 EBA, Albany, NY 12234. *E-mail:* dmercado@mail.nxsed.gov. *Phone:* 518-486-1319. *Fax:* 518-486-5346.

Scholarship for Academic Excellence. Each requested high school in NY State (public & non-public) will receive at least one $1500 scholarship. Remaining scholarships ($1500) and all $500 scholarships awarded based on size of the preceding year's graduating class. Scholarships can only be used at NY State colleges and universities. Scholarships awarded on academic excellence. Nominees for scholarships selected by high school and will be notified by State Education Department after budget is approved. *Award:* Scholarship for use in freshman, sophomore, junior, or senior year; renewable. *Award amount:* $500–$1500. *Number of awards:* 2000–6000. *Eligibility Requirements:* Applicant must be high school student; age 30 or under; enrolled at a two-year or four-year institution or university; resident of New York and studying in New York. Applicant must have 3.5 GPA or higher. Restricted to U.S. citizens. *Application Requirements:* Application, essay. *Deadline:* December 20.

Contact Mr. Douglas Mercado, Chief, New York State Education Department, Room 1071 EBA, Albany, NY 12234. *E-mail:* dmercado@mail.nysed.gov. *Phone:* 518-486-1319. *Fax:* 518-486-5346.

Native American Postsecondary Grant-in-Aid Program. Must be a New York resident and be on an official tribal roll of a New York state tribe, or be a child of a member. Deadlines are July 15 for fall semester, December 31 for the spring semester, and May 20 for the summer semester. Must maintain a minimum GPA of 2.0. *Award:* Grant for use in freshman, sophomore, junior, or senior year; renewable. *Award amount:* $1750. *Eligibility Requirements:* Applicant must be Native American or Eskimo; enrolled at a two-year, four-year, or technical institution or university; resident of New York and studying in New York. Restricted to U.S. citizens. *Application Requirements:* Application, essay, transcript.

Contact Adrian Cooke, Acting Coordinator, Native American Education Unit, New York State Education Department, Room 478 EBA, Albany, NY 12234. *Phone:* 518-474-0537. *Fax:* 518-474-3666.

New York State Tuition Assistance Program. Award for New York state residents attending New York post-secondary institution. Must be full-time-student in approved program with tuition over $200 per year. Must show financial need, and not be in default in any other state program. Renewable award of $275-$3900. *Award:* Grant for use in any year; renewable. *Award amount:* $275–$3900. *Number of awards:* 300,000–320,000. *Eligibility Requirements:* Applicant must be resident of New York and studying in New York. *Application Requirements:* Application, financial need analysis. *Deadline:* May 1.

Contact Student Information, New York State Higher Education Services Corporation, 99 Washington Avenue, Room 1438, Albany, NY 12255. *Web site:* http://www.hesc.com.

New York State Aid to Native Americans. Award for enrolled members of a New York State tribe and their children who are attending or planning to attend a New York State college and who are New York State residents. Award for full-time-students up to $1550 annually; part-time awards approximately $65 per credit hour. Deadlines: August 1, December 31, May 20. *Award:* Scholarship for use in freshman, sophomore, junior, or senior year; not renewable. *Award amount:* up to $1550. *Eligibility Requirements:* Applicant must be Native American or Eskimo; enrolled at a two-year, four-year, or technical institution or university; resident of New York and studying in New York. *Application Requirements:* Application.

Contact Student Information, New York State Higher Education Services Corporation, 99 Washington Avenue, Room 1438, Albany, NY 12255. *Web site:* http://www.hesc.com.

NORTH CAROLINA

North Carolina Student Loan Program for Health, Science, and Mathematics. Renewable award for North Carolina residents studying health-related fields, or science or math education. Based on merit, need, and promise of service as a health professional or educator in an underserved area of North Carolina. Need two co-signers. Submit surety statement. *Academic/Career Areas:* Dental Health/Services; Health Administration; Health and Medical Sciences; Nursing; Physical Sciences and Math; Therapy/Rehabilitation. *Award:* Forgivable loan for use in any year; renewable. *Award amount:* $3000–$8500. *Eligibility Requirements:* Applicant must be enrolled at a two-year or four-year institution or university; resident of North Carolina and studying in North Carolina.

Restricted to U.S. citizens. *Application Requirements:* Application, financial need analysis, transcript. *Deadline:* June 1.

Contact Manager of Scholarship and Grant Division, North Carolina State Education Assistance Authority, PO Box 13663, Research Triangle, NC 27709-3663. *Web site:* http://www.ncseaa.edu.

American Institute of Pakistan Studies Predoctoral Fellowships. One-time awards for pre-doctoral candidates to pursue research on Pakistan. Must be U.S. citizen and pursue a dissertation topic relevant to Pakistan studies. Submit application, transcripts, essay, and references by February 1. Award includes stipend of $2750 per month plus travel expenses of up to $2500. *Academic/Career Areas:* Humanities; Social Sciences. *Eligibility Requirements:* Applicant must have an interest in designated field specified by sponsor. Restricted to U.S. citizens. *Application Requirements:* Application, essay, references, transcript. *Deadline:* February 1.

Contact Charles Kennedy, Director, American Institute of Pakistan Studies, PO Box 7568, Winston-Salem, NC 27109. *E-mail:* ckennedy@wfu.edu. *Phone:* 336-758-5453. *Fax:* 336-758-6104.

North Carolina Teaching Fellows Program. Renewable award for North Carolina high school seniors pursuing teaching careers. Must agree to teach in a North Carolina public or government school for four years or repay award. Must attend one of the fourteen approved schools in North Carolina. Merit-based. Must interview at the local level and at the regional level as a finalist. *Academic/Career Areas:* Education. *Award:* Forgivable loan for use in freshman, sophomore, junior, or senior year; renewable. *Award amount:* $6500. *Number of awards:* up to 400. *Eligibility Requirements:* Applicant must be high school student; enrolled at a four-year institution; resident of North Carolina and studying in North Carolina. Applicant must have 3.5 GPA or higher. Restricted to U.S. citizens. *Application Requirements:* Application, essay, interview, references, test scores, transcript. *Deadline:* October 29.

Contact Ms. Sherry Woodruff, Program Officer, North Carolina Teaching Fellows Commission, Koger Center, Cumberland Building, Raleigh, NC 27612. *E-mail:* tfellows@ncforum.org. *Phone:* 919-781-6833. *Fax:* 919-781-6527. *Web site:* http://www.teachingfellows.org.

North Carolina Legislative Tuition Grant Program. Renewable aid for North Carolina residents attending approved private colleges or universities within the state. Must be enrolled full-time in an undergraduate program not leading to a religious vocation. Contact college financial aid office for deadlines. *Award:* Grant for use in freshman, sophomore, junior, or senior year; renewable. *Award amount:* up to $1600. *Eligibility Requirements:* Applicant must be enrolled at a two-year or four-year institution or university; resident of North Carolina and studying in North Carolina. Restricted to U.S. citizens. *Application Requirements:* Application.

Contact Manager of Scholarship and Grant Division, North Carolina State Education Assistance Authority, PO Box 13663, Research Triangle, NC 27709-3663. *Web site:* http://www.ncseaa.edu.

State Contractual Scholarship Fund Program-North Carolina. Renewable award for North Carolina residents already attending an approved private college or university in the state in pursuit of an undergraduate degree. Must have financial need. Contact college financial aid office for deadline and information. May not be enrolled in a program leading to a religious vocation. *Award:* Scholarship for use in freshman, sophomore, junior, or senior year; renewable. *Award amount:* up to $900. *Eligibility Requirements:* Applicant must be enrolled at a two-year or four-year institution or university; resident of North Carolina and studying in North Carolina. *Application Requirements:* Financial need analysis.

Contact Manager of Scholarship and Grant Division, North Carolina State Education Assistance Authority, PO Box 13663, Research Triangle, NC 27709-3663. *Web site:* http://www.ncseaa.edu.

Board of Governors Medical Scholarship Program. Renewable award for students accepted to one of four medical schools in North Carolina. Must be a resident of North Carolina and be nominated by medical school for the award. Stipend of $5000 per year plus tuition and required fees is provided. *Academic/Career Areas:* Health and Medical Sciences. *Award:* Scholarship for use in graduate years; renewable. *Award amount:* $12,000–$30,000. *Number of awards:* up to 20. *Eligibility Requirements:* Applicant must be resident of North Carolina and studying in North Carolina. *Application Requirements:* Application, essay, financial need analysis, references, test scores, transcript.

Contact Manager of Scholarship and Grant Division, North Carolina State Education Assistance Authority, PO Box 13663, Research Triangle, NC 27709-3663. *Web site:* http://www.ncseaa.edu.

North Carolina National Guard Tuition Assistance Program. For members of the North Carolina Air and Army National Guard who will remain in the service for two years following the period for which assistance is provided. Award is renewable. For use at approved North Carolina institutions. Deadline: 30 days before start of semester. *Award:* Grant for use in any year; renewable. *Award amount:* up to $1000. *Eligibility Requirements:* Applicant must be enrolled at a two-year, four-year, or technical institution or university; resident of North Carolina and studying in North Carolina. Applicant must have served in the Air Force National Guard or Army National Guard. *Application Requirements:* Application. *Deadline:* continuous.

Contact Mrs. Laura Sprayberry, Program Manager, North Carolina National Guard, 4105 Reedy Creek Road, Raleigh, NC 27607-6410. *E-mail:* spraybel@nc.arng.ngb.army.mil. *Phone:* 800-621-4136 Ext. 6488. *Fax:* 919-664-6439. *Web site:* http://www.ncguard.com/.

North Carolina Veterans Scholarships. Renewable awards for children of deceased or disabled veterans or veterans who were listed as prisoner-of-war or Missing In Action who were residents of North Carolina at time of entry into service.

Award covers up to four years of tuition, room and board, and fees at a North Carolina institution. Children do not have to be residents of North Carolina to qualify. *Award:* Scholarship for use in any year; renewable. *Award amount:* $1500–$4500. *Eligibility Requirements:* Applicant must be enrolled at a two-year, four-year, or technical institution or university and studying in North Carolina. Applicant or parent must meet one or more of the following requirements: general military experience; retired from active duty; disabled or killed as a result of military service; prisoner of war; or missing in action. *Application Requirements:* Application, financial need analysis, interview, transcript. *Deadline:* May 30.

Contact Charles Smith, Director, North Carolina Division of Veterans' Affairs, 325 North Salisbury Street, Raleigh, NC 27603. *Phone:* 919-733-3851. *Fax:* 919-733-2834.

North Carolina Rehabilitation Center for the Blind. Renewable award for North Carolina residents who are blind or visually impaired and require vocational rehabilitation to help find employment. Tuition and other assistance provided based on need. Submit documentation of impairment. *Award:* Scholarship for use in any year; renewable. *Eligibility Requirements:* Applicant must be enrolled at a two-year, four-year, or technical institution or university and resident of North Carolina. Applicant must be visually impaired. *Application Requirements:* Financial need analysis, interview.

Contact Jan Fesperman, Chief of Rehabilitation Programs and Facilities, North Carolina Division of Services for the Blind, 2601 Mail Service Center, Raleigh, NC 27699-2601. *E-mail:* jan.fesperman@ncmail.net. *Fax:* 919-715-8771.

Teacher Assistant Scholarship Loan-North Carolina. Available to North Carolina residents who are teacher assistants pursuing teacher certification, a two-year or associate's degree, or certification in special service areas including school psychology, school counseling, speech or language impaired, audiology, and library or media services. Must be or have been employed full-time as a teaching assistant in grades K-12. Must agree to teach in a North Carolina public school as repayment of loan. Renewable up to maximum accumulated award of $4800. Must maintain a 2.5 GPA to be eligible for renewal. Nominations must be made by the last Monday in January. *Academic/Career Areas:* Education. *Award:* Forgivable loan for use in any year; renewable. *Award amount:* up to $1200. *Eligibility Requirements:* Applicant must be enrolled at a two-year or four-year institution or university; resident of North Carolina; studying in North Carolina and have employment experience in designated career field or teaching. Applicant must have 2.5 GPA or higher. *Application Requirements:* Application, references, test scores, transcript.

Contact Division of Human Resource Management, North Carolina Department of Public Instruction, 301 North Wilmington Street, Raleigh, NC 27601-2825. *Web site:* http://www.dpi.state.nc.us.

Prospective Teacher Scholarship Loans-North Carolina. Renewable award for North Carolina residents for full-time undergraduate study in North Carolina leading to license in teaching or special services. May repay loan or work in a North Carolina public school by serving one year for each year award was received. Must have minimum 3.0 GPA and minimum 900 SAT. Applications may be obtained in December from high school counselors or financial aid administrators at colleges and universities with approved programs, and are due on the second Monday in February. *Academic/Career Areas:* Education; Library Sciences; Social Sciences; Special Education; Therapy/Rehabilitation. *Award:* Forgivable loan for use in freshman, sophomore, junior, or senior year; renewable. *Award amount:* up to $2500. *Number of awards:* 200. *Eligibility Requirements:* Applicant must be enrolled at a two-year or four-year institution or university; resident of North Carolina and studying in North Carolina. Applicant must have 3.0 GPA or higher. *Application Requirements:* Application, essay, references, test scores, transcript.

Contact Division of Human Resource Management, North Carolina Department of Public Instruction, 301 North Wilmington Street, Raleigh, NC 27601-2825. *Web site:* http://www.dpi.state.nc.us.

North Carolina Student Incentive Grant. Renewable award for North Carolina residents who are enrolled full-time at a North Carolina post-secondary institution. Must demonstrate substantial financial need. Must complete Free Application For Student Aid. Must be U.S. citizen and must maintain satisfactory academic progress. *Award:* Grant for use in freshman, sophomore, junior, or senior year; renewable. *Award amount:* $200–$1500. *Eligibility Requirements:* Applicant must be enrolled at a two-year or four-year institution or university; resident of North Carolina and studying in North Carolina. *Application Requirements:* Financial need analysis. *Deadline:* March 15.

Contact Manager of Scholarship and Grant Division, North Carolina State Education Assistance Authority, PO Box 13663, Research Triangle, NC 27709-3663. *Web site:* http://www.ncseaa.edu.

NORTH DAKOTA

North Dakota State Department of Transportation Engineering Grant. Educational grants for civil engineering, survey technology, and construction engineering are awarded to students who have completed one-year of course study at an institution of higher learning. Recipients must agree to work for the Department for a period time at least equal to the grant period or repay the grant at 6 percent interest. *Academic/Career Areas:* Civil Engineering; Engineering/Technology. *Award:* Grant for use in sophomore, junior, or senior year; renewable. *Award amount:* $1000. *Number of awards:* up to 4. *Eligibility Requirements:* Applicant must be enrolled at a four-year, or technical institution and studying in North Dakota. Applicant must have 2.5 GPA or higher. Restricted to U.S. citizens. *Application Requirements:* Application, financial need analysis, interview, transcript. *Deadline:* continuous.

Contact Patricia Frohlich, Personnel Officer, North Dakota State Department of Transportation, 608 East Boulevard Avenue, Bismarck, ND 58505-0700. *E-mail:* pfrohlic@state.nd.us. *Phone:* 701-328-2608. *Fax:* 701-328-1415. *Web site:* http://www.state.nd.us/dot/.

North Dakota Indian Scholarship Program. Assists Native American North Dakota residents in obtaining a college education. Priority given to full-time undergraduate students and those having a 3.5 GPA or higher. Certification of tribal enrollment required. For use at North Dakota institution. *Award:* Scholarship for use in freshman, sophomore, junior, senior, or graduate years; renewable. *Award amount:* $700–$2000. *Number of awards:* 120–150. *Eligibility Requirements:* Applicant must be Native American or Eskimo; enrolled at a two-year or four-year institution or university; resident of North Dakota and studying in North Dakota. Applicant must have 3.5 GPA or higher. *Application Requirements:* Application, financial need analysis, transcript. *Deadline:* July 15.

Contact Rhonda Schauer, Coordinator of American Indian Higher Education, North Dakota University System, 600 East Boulevard, Department 215, Bismarck, ND 58505-0230. *Phone:* 701-328-2166. *Web site:* http://www.ndus.nodak.edu.

North Dakota Student Financial Assistance Grants. Aids North Dakota residents attending an approved college or university in North Dakota. Must be enrolled in a program of at least nine months in length. *Award:* Grant for use in freshman, sophomore, junior, or senior year; not renewable. *Award amount:* up to $600. *Number of awards:* 3300–3600. *Eligibility Requirements:* Applicant must be enrolled at a two-year or four-year institution or university; resident of North Dakota and studying in North Dakota. *Application Requirements:* Application, financial need analysis. *Deadline:* April 15.

Contact Peggy Wipf, Director of Financial Aid, North Dakota University System, 600 East Boulevard, Department 215, Bismarck, ND 58505-0230. *Phone:* 701-328-4114. *Web site:* http://www.ndus.nodak.edu.

North Dakota Scholars Program. Provides scholarships equal to cost of tuition at the public colleges in North Dakota for North Dakota residents. Must score at or above the 95th percentile on ACT and rank in top twenty percent of high school graduation class. Must take ACT in fall. For high school seniors with a minimum 3.5 GPA. Application deadline is October ACT test date. *Award:* Scholarship for use in freshman, sophomore, junior, or senior year; renewable. *Number of awards:* 45–50. *Eligibility Requirements:* Applicant must be high school student; enrolled at a two-year or four-year institution or university; resident of North Dakota and studying in North Dakota. Applicant must have 3.5 GPA or higher. *Application Requirements:* Application, test scores.

Contact Peggy Wipf, Director of Financial Aid, North Dakota University System, 600 East Boulevard, Department 215, Bismarck, ND 58505-0230. *Phone:* 701-328-4114. *Web site:* http://www.ndus.nodak.edu.

OHIO

Physician Loan Repayment Program. Renewable award that offers repayment of student loans for Ohio physicians who agree to practice in specialized areas in Ohio with limited access to medical care. Up to four years of student loan indebtedness may be canceled. *Academic/Career Areas:* Health and Medical Sciences. *Award:* Forgivable loan for use in graduate years; renewable. *Award amount:* up to $20,000. *Eligibility Requirements:* Applicant must be resident of Ohio; studying in Ohio and have employment experience in designated career field. *Application Requirements:* Application. *Deadline:* continuous.

Contact Barb Closser, Program Administrator, Ohio Board of Regents, PO Box 182452, Columbus, OH 43218-2452. *E-mail:* barbara.closser@sgs.state.oh.us. *Phone:* 614-644-6629. *Fax:* 614-752-5903.

Ohio Student Choice Grant Program. Available to Ohio residents attending private colleges within the state. Must be enrolled full-time in a bachelor's degree program. Do not apply to state. Check with financial aid office of college. Renewable award. *Award:* Grant for use in freshman, sophomore, junior, or senior year; renewable. *Award amount:* up to $960. *Eligibility Requirements:* Applicant must be enrolled at a four-year institution; resident of Ohio and studying in Ohio. Restricted to U.S. citizens. *Application Requirements: Deadline:* continuous.

Contact Barbara Metheney, Program Administrator, Ohio Board of Regents, PO Box 182452, Columbus, OH 43218-2452. *E-mail:* barbara.metheney@sgs.state.oh.us. *Phone:* 614-752-9535. *Fax:* 614-752-5903.

Part-Time Student Instructional Grant-Ohio. Renewable grants for part-time undergraduates who are Ohio residents. Award amounts vary. Must attend an Ohio institution. *Award:* Grant for use in freshman, sophomore, or junior year; renewable. *Award amount:* up to $3750. *Eligibility Requirements:* Applicant must be enrolled at a two-year or four-year institution or university; resident of Ohio and studying in Ohio. Restricted to U.S. citizens. *Application Requirements:* Application, financial need analysis. *Deadline:* continuous.

Contact Barbara Metheney, Program Administrator, Ohio Board of Regents, PO Box 182452, Columbus, OH 43218-2452. *E-mail:* barbara.metheney@sgs.state.oh.us. *Phone:* 614-752-9535. *Fax:* 614-752-5903.

Ohio Missing in Action and Prisoners of War Orphans Scholarship. Aids children of Vietnam conflict servicemen who have been classified as missing in action or prisoner-of-war. Must be an Ohio resident, be 16-21, and be enrolled full-time at an Ohio college. Full tuition awards. Renewable award. *Award:* Scholarship for use in freshman, sophomore, junior, or senior year; renewable. *Number of awards:* 1–5. *Eligibility Requirements:* Applicant must be age 16-21; enrolled at a two-year or four-year institution; resident of Ohio and studying in Ohio. Restricted to U.S. citizens. Applicant or parent must meet one or more of the following requirements: general military experience; retired from active duty; disabled or killed as a result of military service; prisoner of war; or missing in action. *Application Requirements:* Application. *Deadline:* July 1.

Contact Sue Minturn, Program Administrator, Ohio Board of Regents, PO Box 182452, Columbus, OH 43218-2452. *E-mail:* sue.minturn@sgs.state.oh.us. *Phone:* 614-466-1190. *Fax:* 614-752-5903.

Regents Graduate/Professional Fellowship Program-Ohio. Available to Ohio residents pursuing a graduate or professional degree in Ohio immediately following graduation with a bachelor's degree. Must enroll full-time. Renewable for an additional year. *Eligibility Requirements:* Applicant must be resident of Ohio and studying in Ohio. Restricted to U.S. citizens. *Application Requirements:* Application, essay, interview, references, test scores, transcript. *Deadline:* March 1.

Contact Barbara Metheney, Program Administrator, Ohio Board of Regents, PO Box 182452, Columbus, OH 43218-2452. *E-mail:* barbara.metheney@sgs.state.oh.us. *Phone:* 614-752-9535. *Fax:* 614-752-5903.

Ohio Instructional Grant. Award for low- and middle-income Ohio residents attending an approved college or school of nursing in Ohio or Pennsylvania. Must be enrolled full-time and have financial need. Average award is $630. May be used for any course of study except theology. *Award:* Grant for use in freshman, sophomore, junior, or senior year; renewable. *Award amount:* $210–$3750. *Eligibility Requirements:* Applicant must be enrolled at a two-year or four-year institution or university; resident of Ohio and studying in Ohio or Pennsylvania. Restricted to U.S. citizens. *Application Requirements:* Application, financial need analysis. *Deadline:* October 1.

Contact David Bastian, Program Supervisor, Ohio Board of Regents, PO Box 182452, Columbus, OH 43218-2452. *E-mail:* david.bastian@sgs.state.oh.us. *Phone:* 614-752-9489. *Fax:* 614-752-5903.

Robert C. Byrd Honors Scholarship-Ohio. Renewable award for graduating high school seniors who demonstrate outstanding academic achievement. Each Ohio high school receives applications by January of each year. School can submit one application for each 200 students in the senior class. *Award:* Scholarship for use in freshman, sophomore, junior, or senior year; renewable. *Award amount:* $1500. *Eligibility Requirements:* Applicant must be high school student; enrolled at a two-year or four-year institution or university and resident of Ohio. Applicant must have 3.5 GPA or higher. *Application Requirements:* Application, test scores. *Deadline:* March 10.

Contact Program Coordinator, Ohio Board of Regents, PO Box 182452, Columbus, OH 43218-2452.

Ohio Academic Scholarship Program. Award for academically outstanding Ohio residents planning to attend an approved Ohio college. Must be a high school senior intending to enroll full-time. Award is renewable for up to four years. Must rank in upper quarter of class or have a minimum GPA of 3.5. *Award:* Scholarship for use in freshman, sophomore, junior, or senior year; renewable. *Award amount:* $2000. *Number of awards:* 1000. *Eligibility Requirements:* Applicant must be high school student; enrolled at a two-year or four-year institution; resident of Ohio and studying in Ohio. Applicant must have 3.5 GPA or higher. Restricted to U.S. citizens. *Application Requirements:* Application, test scores, transcript. *Deadline:* February 23.

Contact Sue Minturn, Program Administrator, Ohio Board of Regents, PO Box 182452, Columbus, OH 43218-2452. *E-mail:* sue.minturn@sgs.state.oh.us. *Phone:* 614-466-1190. *Fax:* 614-752-5903.

Ohio War Orphans Scholarship. Aids Ohio residents attending an eligible college in Ohio. Must be between the ages of 16-21, the child of a disabled or deceased veteran, and enrolled full-time. Renewable up to five years. Amount of award varies. Must include Form DD214. *Award:* Scholarship for use in freshman, sophomore, junior, or senior year; renewable. *Number of awards:* 300–450. *Eligibility Requirements:* Applicant must be age 16-21; enrolled at a two-year or four-year institution; resident of Ohio and studying in Ohio. Restricted to U.S. citizens. Applicant or parent must meet one or more of the following requirements: general military experience; retired from active duty; disabled or killed as a result of military service; prisoner of war; or missing in action. *Application Requirements:* Application. *Deadline:* July 1.

Contact Sue Minturn, Program Administrator, Ohio Board of Regents, PO Box 182452, Columbus, OH 43218-2452. *E-mail:* sue.minturn@sgs.state.oh.us. *Phone:* 614-466-1190. *Fax:* 614-752-5903.

Ohio National Guard Scholarship Program. Scholarships are for undergraduate studies at an approved Ohio postsecondary institution. Applicants must enlist for six years of Selective Service Reserve Duty in the Ohio National Guard. Scholarship pays 100% instructional and general fees for public institutions and an average of cost of public schools is available for private schools. Must be 18 years of age or older. Award is renewable. Deadlines : July 1, November 1, February 1, April 1. *Award:* Scholarship for use in freshman, sophomore, junior, or senior year; renewable. *Award amount:* $3000. *Number of awards:* 3500. *Eligibility Requirements:* Applicant must be age 18; enrolled at a two-year or four-year institution or university and studying in Ohio. Restricted to U.S. citizens. Applicant must have served in the Air Force National Guard or Army National Guard. *Application Requirements:* Application.

Contact Mrs. Toni Davis, Grants Administrator, Ohio National Guard, 2825 West Granville Road, Columbus, OH 43235-2787. *E-mail:* davist@tagoh.org. *Phone:* 614-336-7032. *Fax:* 614-336-7318.

Ohio Safety Officers College Memorial Fund. Available to children and surviving spouses of Ohio peace officers and fire fighters killed in the line of duty. Children must be under 26 years of age. Must be an Ohio resident and enroll full-time or part-time at an Ohio college or university. Renewable award. *Award:* Scholarship for use in freshman, sophomore, junior, or senior year; renewable. *Number of awards:* 50–65. *Eligibility Requirements:* Applicant must be age 25 or under; enrolled at a two-year or four-year institution or university; resident of Ohio; studying in Ohio and have employment experience in police/firefighting. Restricted to U.S. citizens. *Application Requirements: Deadline:* continuous.

Contact Barbara Metheney, Program Administrator, Ohio Board of Regents, PO Box 182452, Columbus, OH 43218-2452. *E-mail:* barbara.metheney@sgs.state.oh.us. *Phone:* 614-752-9535. *Fax:* 614-752-5903.

OKLAHOMA

Oklahoma Physician Manpower Training Rural Medical Education Scholarship Loan Program. Renewable award for Oklahoma residents enrolled or accepted in medical college who plan to do residency in primary care. Loan forgiveness if student practices in Oklahoma community with population of 7,500 or less for each year the loan was received. Scholarship totaling $42,000 for four years. *Academic/Career Areas:* Health and Medical Sciences. *Award:* Forgivable loan for use in graduate years; renewable. *Award amount:* $42,000. *Eligibility Requirements:* Applicant must be resident of Oklahoma. *Application Requirements:* Application, photo, references. *Deadline:* March 31.

Contact Charlotte Ward, Physician Placement Officer, State of Oklahoma, 1140 Northwest 63rd Street, Suite 302, Oklahoma City, OK 73116. *E-mail:* ptmc@klaosf.state.ok.us. *Phone:* 405-843-5667. *Fax:* 405-843-5792.

Academic Scholars Program. Encourages students of high academic ability to attend institutions in Oklahoma. Renewable up to five years. ACT or SAT scores must fall between 99.5 and 100th percentiles, or be designated as a National Merit Scholar or finalist. *Award:* Scholarship for use in any year; renewable. *Award amount:* $3500–$5500. *Eligibility Requirements:* Applicant must be enrolled at a two-year or four-year institution or university and studying in Oklahoma. Available to U.S. and non-U.S. citizens. *Application Requirements:* Application, test scores, transcript. *Deadline:* continuous.

Contact Oklahoma State Regents for Higher Education, 500 Education Building, Oklahoma City, OK 73105. *E-mail:* ppursifull@osrhe.edu. *Phone:* 405-524-9153. *Fax:* 405-524-9230. *Web site:* http://okhighered.org.

Future Teacher Scholarship Program-Oklahoma. Open to outstanding high school graduates who agree to teach in shortage areas. Must rank in top fifteen percent of graduating class or score above 85th percentile on ACT or similar test, or be accepted in an educational program. Students nominated by institution. Reapply to renew. *Academic/Career Areas:* Education. *Award:* Scholarship for use in any year; not renewable. *Award amount:* up to $1500. *Eligibility Requirements:* Applicant must be enrolled at a two-year or four-year institution or university; resident of Oklahoma and studying in Oklahoma. *Application Requirements:* Application, essay, test scores, transcript.

Contact Future Teachers Scholarship Program, Oklahoma State Regents for Higher Education, 500 Education Building, Oklahoma City, OK 73105. *Web site:* http://okhighered.org.

Oklahoma Physician Manpower Training Commission Resident Rural Scholarship Loan Program. Renewable loan for family practice residents who are in first or second year of family practice training in an Oklahoma family practice or medical program. Loan is forgivable if student practices after graduation for one month in rural community per each month the loan was received. Write for application deadlines. Loan is $36,000 to be used over three years. *Academic/Career Areas:* Health and Medical Sciences. *Award:* Forgivable loan for use in graduate years; renewable. *Award amount:* $36,000. *Eligibility Requirements:* Applicant must be studying in Oklahoma. *Application Requirements:* Application, references.

Contact Charlotte Ward, Physician Placement Officer, State of Oklahoma, 1140 Northwest 63rd Street, Suite 302, Oklahoma City, OK 73116. *E-mail:* ptmc@klaosf.state.ok.us. *Phone:* 405-843-5667. *Fax:* 405-843-5792.

Oklahoma Tuition Aid Grant. Award for Oklahoma residents enrolled at an Oklahoma institution at least part-time per semester in a degree program. May be enrolled in two- or four-year or nonprofit vocational-technical institution. File for federal student aid. Award of up to $1000 per year. *Award:* Grant for use in any year; renewable. *Award amount:* $200–$1000. *Number of awards:* 23,000. *Eligibility Requirements:* Applicant must be enrolled at a two-year, four-year, or technical institution or university; resident of Oklahoma and studying in Oklahoma. Restricted to U.S. citizens. *Application Requirements:* Application, financial need analysis. *Deadline:* April 30.

Contact Oklahoma Tuition Aid Grants Program, Oklahoma State Regents for Higher Education, PO Box 3020, Oklahoma City, OK 73101-3020. *E-mail:* otaginfo@otag.org. *Phone:* 405-858-4356. *Fax:* 405-858-4392. *Web site:* http://okhighered.org.

OREGON

Troutman's Emporium Scholarship. One scholarship available to Troutman's Emporium full, or part-time employees and dependents. Employee must have been employed for at least one year. Applicants must be planning to enroll at least half-time in an undergraduate course of study. Preference given to those planning to attend college in California, Idaho, Oregon, or Washington. One-time award. *Award:* Scholarship for use in freshman, sophomore, junior, or senior year; not renewable. *Number of awards:* 1. *Eligibility Requirements:* Applicant must be resident of Oregon; affiliated with Troutman's Emporium and have employment experience in designated career field. *Application Requirements:* Application, essay, financial need analysis, transcript. *Deadline:* March 1.

Contact Mr. James Beyer, Director of Grant Programs, Oregon Student Assistance Commission, 1500 Valley River Drive, Suite 100, Eugene, OR 97401. *Web site:* http://www.osac.state.or.us.

Pacific NW Federal Credit Union Scholarship. One scholarship available to graduating high school senior who is a member of Pacific NW Federal Credit Union. A special essay is required employing the theme, "Why is My Credit Union an Important Consumer Choice?". Employers and officials of the Credit Union and their dependents are not eligible. One-time award. *Award:* Scholarship for use in freshman year; not renewable. *Number of awards:* 1. *Eligibility Requirements:* Applicant must be high school student; resident of Oregon; affiliated with Pacific Northwest Federal Credit Union and must have an interest in designated field specified by sponsor. *Application Requirements:* Application, essay, financial need analysis, transcript. *Deadline:* March 1.

Contact Mr. James Beyer, Director of Grant Programs, Oregon Student Assistance Commission, 1500 Valley River Drive, Suite 100, Eugene, OR 97401. *Web site:* http://www.osac.state.or.us.

Oregon Public Employees Union Scholarship. Undergraduate awards available to current and former members of the Oregon Public Employees Union, their children, grandchildren, and spouses. Members must have been active for at least one year. Current or laid-off members and their spouses are eligible for part-time enrollment or for the graduate program. One-time award. Must attend an institution in Oregon. *Award:* Scholarship for use in any year; not renewable. *Eligibility Requirements:* Applicant must be enrolled at a four-year institution; resident of Oregon; studying in Oregon; affiliated with Oregon Public Employees Union and have employment experience in designated career field. *Application Requirements:* Application, essay, financial need analysis, transcript. *Deadline:* March 1.

Contact Mr. James Beyer, Director of Grant Programs, Oregon Student Assistance Commission, 1500 Valley River Drive, Suite 100, Eugene, OR 97401. *Web site:* http://www.osac.state.or.us.

Oregon Dungeness Crab Commission Scholarship. One scholarship available to graduating high school senior who is a dependent of licensed Oregon Dungeness Crab fisherman or crew member. One-time award. *Award:* Scholarship for use in freshman year; not renewable. *Number of awards:* 1. *Eligibility Requirements:* Applicant must be high school student; resident of Oregon; affiliated with Oregon Dungeness Crab Commission and have employment experience in designated career field. *Application Requirements:* Application, essay, financial need analysis, transcript. *Deadline:* March 1.

Contact Mr. James Beyer, Director of Grant Programs, Oregon Student Assistance Commission, 1500 Valley River Drive, Suite 100, Eugene, OR 97401. *Web site:* http://www.osac.state.or.us.

Oregon Metro Federal Credit Union Scholarship. One scholarship available to an Oregon high school graduate who is a Oregon Metro Federal Credit Union member. Preference given to graduating high school senior and applicant who plans to attend an Oregon college. One-time award. *Award:* Scholarship for use in freshman, sophomore, junior, or senior year; not renewable. *Number of awards:* 1. *Eligibility Requirements:* Applicant must be resident of Oregon; studying in Oregon; affiliated with Oregon Metro Federal Credit Union and must have an interest in designated field specified by sponsor. *Application Requirements:* Application, essay, financial need analysis, transcript. *Deadline:* March 1.

Contact Mr. James Beyer, Director of Grant Programs, Oregon Student Assistance Commission, 1500 Valley River Drive, Suite 100, Eugene, OR 97401-7020. *Web site:* http://www.osac.state.or.us.

Ida M. Crawford Scholarship. One-time scholarship awarded to Oregon high school seniors with a cumulative GPA of 3.5. Not available to applicants majoring in law, medicine, theology, teaching, or music. U.S. Bancorp employees, their children or near relatives, are not eligible. *Award:* Scholarship for use in freshman year; not renewable. *Eligibility Requirements:* Applicant must be high school student and resident of Oregon. Applicant must have 3.5 GPA or higher. *Application Requirements:* Application, essay, test scores, transcript. *Deadline:* March 1.

Contact Mr. James Beyer, Director of Grant Programs, Oregon Student Assistance Commission, 1500 Valley River Drive, Suite 100, Eugene, OR 97401. *Web site:* http://www.osac.state.or.us.

American Ex-Prisoner of War Scholarships: Peter Connacher Memorial Scholarship. Renewable award for American prisoner-of-war and their descendants. Written proof of prisoner-of-war status and discharge papers from the U.S. Armed Forces must accompany application. Statement of relationship between applicant and former prisoner-of-war is required. *Award:* Scholarship for use in any year; renewable. *Eligibility Requirements:* Applicant must be resident of Oregon. Applicant or parent must meet one or more of the following requirements: general military experience; retired from active duty; disabled or killed as a result of military service; prisoner of war; or missing in action. *Application Requirements:* Application, essay, transcript. *Deadline:* March 1.

Contact Mr. James Beyer, Director of Grant Programs, Oregon Student Assistance Commission, 1500 Valley River Drive, Suite 100, Eugene, OR 97401-7020. *Web site:* http://www.osac.state.or.us.

OSSC/Ben Selling Scholarship. Award for Oregon residents enrolling as sophomores or higher in college. College GPA 3.50 or higher required. Apply/compete annually. Must be U.S. citizen or permanent resident. *Award:* Scholarship for use in sophomore, junior, or senior year; not renewable. *Eligibility Requirements:* Applicant must be resident of Oregon. Applicant must have 3.5 GPA or higher. *Application Requirements:* Application, essay, financial need analysis, transcript. *Deadline:* March 1.

Contact Mr. James Beyer, Director of Grant Programs, Oregon Student Assistance Commission, 1500 Valley River Drive, Suite. 100, Eugene, OR 97401-7020. *Web site:* http://www.osac.state.or.us.

Ford Scholars. Award designed for Oregon graduating seniors, Oregon high school graduates not yet full-time undergraduates, or those who have completed two years of undergraduate study at an Oregon community college and will enter junior year at a four-year Oregon college. Required cumulative GPA of 3.0 unless accompanied by a counselor's recommendation. Applicant must plan to complete a four-year degree. *Award:* Scholarship for use in freshman, sophomore, or junior year; renewable. *Eligibility Requirements:* Applicant must be enrolled at a four-year institution; resident of Oregon and studying in Oregon. Applicant must have 3.0 GPA or higher. *Application Requirements:* Application, essay, test scores, transcript. *Deadline:* March 1.

Contact Mr. James Beyer, Director of Grant Programs, Oregon Student Assistance Commission, 1500 Valley River Drive, Suite 100, Eugene, OR 97401. *Web site:* http://www.osac.state.or.us.

Robert D. Forster Scholarship. One scholarship available to a dependent child of a Walsh Construction Co. employee who has completed 1,000 hours or more in each of three consecutive fiscal years. Award may be received for a maximum of twelve quarters of undergraduate study and may only be used at four-year colleges. *Award:* Scholarship for use in freshman, sophomore, junior, or senior year; renewable. *Number of awards:* 1. *Eligibility Requirements:* Applicant must be enrolled at a four-year institution; resident of Oregon; affiliated with Walsh Construction Company and have employment experience in designated career field. *Application Requirements:* Application, essay, financial need analysis, transcript. *Deadline:* March 1.

Contact Mr. James Beyer, Director of Grant Programs, Oregon Student Assistance Commission, 1500 Valley River Drive, Suite 100, Eugene, OR 97401. *Web site:* http://www.osac.state.or.us.

Roger W. Emmons Memorial Scholarship. One scholarship available to a graduating Oregon high school senior who is a child or grandchild of an employee (for at least three years) of member of the Oregon Refuse and Recycling Association. One-time award for use at an Oregon college. *Award:* Scholarship for use in freshman year; renewable. *Number of awards:* 1. *Eligibility Requirements:* Applicant must be high school student; resident of Oregon; studying in Oregon; affiliated with Oregon Refuse and Recycling Association and have employment experience in designated career field. *Application Requirements:* Application, essay, financial need analysis, transcript. *Deadline:* March 1.

Contact Mr. James Beyer, Director of Grant Programs, Oregon Student Assistance Commission, 1500 Valley River Drive, Suite 100, Eugene, OR 97401. *Web site:* http://www.osac.state.or.us.

Albina Fuel Company Scholarship. One scholarship available to a dependent child of a current Albina Fuel Company employee. The employee must have been employed for at least one full year as of October 1 prior to the scholarship deadline. One-time award. *Award:* Scholarship for use in freshman, sophomore, junior, or senior year; not renewable. *Number of awards:* 1. *Eligibility Requirements:* Applicant must be resident of Oregon; affiliated with Albina Fuel Company and have employment experience in designated career field. *Application Requirements:* Application, essay, financial need analysis, transcript. *Deadline:* March 1.

Contact Mr. James Beyer, Director of Grant Programs, Oregon Student Assistance Commission, 1500 Valley River Drive, Suite 100, Eugene, OR 97401-7020. *Web site:* http://www.osac.state.or.us.

Walter and Marie Schmidt Scholarship. One scholarship available to a student who is enrolled or planning to enroll in a program of training to become a registered nurse. Applicants must submit an additional essay describing their desire to pursue a nursing career in geriatrics. U.S. Bancorp employees and their relatives are not eligible. One-time award. *Academic/Career Areas:* Nursing. *Award:* Scholarship for use in freshman or sophomore year; not renewable. *Number of awards:* 1. *Eligibility Requirements:* Applicant must be resident of Oregon. *Application Requirements:* Application, essay, financial need analysis, transcript. *Deadline:* March 1.

Contact Mr. James Beyer, Director of Grant Programs, Oregon Student Assistance Commission, 1500 Valley River Drive, Suite 100, Eugene, OR 97401. *Web site:* http://www.osac.state.or.us.

Oregon Private 150 Scholarship. One scholarship available to a junior, senior, or graduate student who is a business major. Applicants must have a minimum cumulative 3.0 GPA. One-time award to be used at an Oregon college. Submit essay of 750 words or more describing an experience with a company that provides great customer service and what your experience tells you about running a business. *Academic/Career Areas:* Business/Consumer Services. *Award:* Scholarship for use in junior, senior, or graduate years; not renewable. *Number of awards:* 1. *Eligibility Requirements:* Applicant must be resident of Oregon and studying in Oregon. Applicant must have 3.0 GPA or higher. *Application Requirements:* Application, essay, financial need analysis, transcript. *Deadline:* March 1.

Contact Mr. James Beyer, Director of Grant Programs, Oregon Student Assistance Commission, 1500 Valley River Drive, Suite 100, Eugene, OR 97401. *Web site:* http://www.osac.state.or.us.

Mentor Graphics Scholarship. One-time award for computer science, computer engineering, or electrical engineering majors entering junior or senior year at a four-year institution. Preference for one award to female, African-American, or Hispanic applicant. *Academic/Career Areas:* Computer Science/Data Processing; Electrical Engineering/Electronics. *Award:* Scholarship for use in junior or senior year; not renewable. *Eligibility Requirements:* Applicant must be enrolled at a four-year institution and resident of Oregon. *Application Requirements:* Application, essay, transcript. *Deadline:* March 1.

Contact Mr. James Beyer, Director of Grant Programs, Oregon Student Assistance Commission, 1500 Valley River Drive, Suite 100, Eugene, OR 97401. *Web site:* http://www.osac.state.or.us.

OSSC Glenn Jackson Scholars Scholarships. Award for graduating high school seniors who are dependents of employees or retirees of Oregon Department of Transportation or Parks and Recreation Department. Employees must have worked in their department at least three years. Award for maximum twelve undergraduate quarters or 6 quarters at a two-year institution. Must be U.S. citizen or permanent resident. Contact for application and essay topics. *Award:* Scholarship for use in freshman, sophomore, junior, or senior year; renewable. *Eligibility Requirements:* Applicant must be high school student; resident of Oregon and have employment experience in designated career field. *Application Requirements:* Application, essay, financial need analysis, transcript. *Deadline:* March 1.

Contact Mr. James Beyer, Director of Grant Programs, Oregon Student Assistance Commission, 1500 Valley River Drive, Suite. 100, Eugene, OR 97401-7020. *Web site:* http://www.osac.state.or.us.

Lawrence R. Foster Memorial Scholarship. Awarded to students enrolled or planning to enroll in a public health degree program. First preference given to those working in the public health field and, those pursuing a graduate degree in public health. Undergraduates' entering junior or senior year health programs may apply if seeking a public health career, and not private practice. One-time award. *Academic/Career Areas:* Health and Medical Sciences. *Award:* Scholarship for use in any year; not renewable. *Eligibility Requirements:* Applicant must be enrolled at a four-year institution and resident of Oregon. *Application Requirements:* Application, essay, references, transcript. *Deadline:* March 1.

Contact Mr. James Beyer, Director of Grant Programs, Oregon Student Assistance Commission, 1500 Valley River Drive, Suite 100, Eugene, OR 97401. *Web site:* http://www.osac.state.or.us.

Woodard Family Scholarship. Scholarships are available to employees and children of employees of Kimwood Corporation or Middlefield Village. Applicants must have graduated from a U.S. high school. Awards may be used at Oregon four-year colleges only, and may be received for a maximum of twelve quarters of undergraduate study. *Award:* Scholarship for use in freshman, sophomore, junior, or senior year; renewable. *Eligibility Requirements:* Applicant must be enrolled at a four-year institution; resident of Oregon; studying in Oregon; affiliated with Kimwood Corporation or Middlefield Village and have employment experience in designated career field. *Application Requirements:* Application, essay, financial need analysis, transcript. *Deadline:* March 1.

Contact Mr. James Beyer, Director of Grant Programs, Oregon Student Assistance Commission, 1500 Valley River Drive, Suite 100, Eugene, OR 97401. *Web site:* http://www.osac.state.or.us.

Alpha Delta Kappa/Harriet Simmons Scholarship. One-time award for elementary and secondary education majors entering their senior year, or graduate students enrolled in a fifth-year program leading to a teaching certificate. Contact for additional information. *Academic/Career Areas:* Education. *Award:* Scholarship for use in senior or graduate years; not renewable. *Eligibility Requirements:* Applicant must be enrolled at a four-year institution or university and resident of Oregon. *Application Requirements:* Application, essay, transcript. *Deadline:* March 1.

Contact Mr. James Beyer, Director of Grant Programs, Oregon Student Assistance Commission, 1500 Valley River Drive, Suite 100, Eugene, OR 97401-7020. *Web site:* http://www.osac.state.or.us.

Oregon AFL-CIO Scholarship. One-time award for graduating Oregon high school seniors. Must write essay. Contact for guidelines. Preference given to applicants from union families. *Award:* Scholarship for use in freshman year; not renewable. *Eligibility Requirements:* Applicant must be high school student; resident of Oregon and have employment experience in designated career field. *Application Requirements:* Application, essay, test scores, transcript. *Deadline:* March 1.

Contact Mr. James Beyer, Director of Grant Programs, Oregon Student Assistance Commission, 1500 Valley River Drive, Suite 100, Eugene, OR 97401-7020. *Web site:* http://www.osac.state.or.us.

Oregon Trucking Association Scholarship. One scholarship available to a child of an Oregon Trucking Association member, or child of employee of member. Applicants must be Oregon residents who are graduating high school seniors from an Oregon high school. One-time award. *Award:* Scholarship for use in freshman year; not renewable. *Number of awards:* 1. *Eligibility Requirements:* Applicant must be high school student; resident of Oregon; affiliated with Oregon Trucking Association and have employment experience in designated career field. *Application Requirements:* Application, essay, financial need analysis, transcript. *Deadline:* March 1.

Contact Mr. James Beyer, Director of Grant Programs, Oregon Student Assistance Commission, 1500 Valley River Drive, Suite 100, Eugene, OR 97401. *Web site:* http://www.osac.state.or.us.

Clyde C. Crosby/Joseph M. Edgar Memorial Scholarship. One scholarship available for a graduating high school senior with a minimum 2.0 cumulative GPA who is a child, or dependent stepchild of an active, retired, disabled, or deceased member of local union affiliated with Teamsters #37. Member must have been active for at least one year. Award may be received for a maximum of twelve quarters. *Award:* Scholarship for use in freshman, sophomore, junior, or senior year; renewable. *Number of awards:* 1. *Eligibility Requirements:* Applicant must be high school student; resident of Oregon; member of Teamsters; affiliated with Teamsters #37 and have employment experience in designated career field. *Application Requirements:* Application, essay, financial need analysis, transcript. *Deadline:* March 1.

Contact Mr. James Beyer, Director of Grant Programs, Oregon Student Assistance Commission, 1500 Valley River Drive, Suite 100, Eugene, OR 97401-7020. *Web site:* http://www.osac.state.or.us.

David Family Scholarship. Award for residents of Clackamas, Lane, Linn, Marion, Multnomah, Washington, and Yamill counties. First preference to applicants enrolling at least half-time in upper-division or graduate programs at four-year colleges. Second preference to graduating high school seniors from West Linn-Wilsonville, Lake Oswego, Portland, Tigard-Tualatin, or Beaverton school districts. *Award:* Scholarship for use in any year;

renewable. *Eligibility Requirements:* Applicant must be enrolled at a four-year institution and resident of Oregon. Applicant must have 2.5 GPA or higher. *Application Requirements:* Application, essay, test scores, transcript. *Deadline:* March 1.

Contact Mr. James Beyer, Director of Grant Programs, Oregon Student Assistance Commission, 1500 Valley River Drive, Suite 100, Eugene, OR 97401-7020. *Web site:* http://www.osac.state.or.us.

Dorothy Campbell Memorial Scholarship. Renewable award for female Oregon high school senior with a minimum 2.75 GPA. Must have a strong and continuing interest in golf. *Award:* Scholarship for use in freshman, sophomore, junior, or senior year; renewable. *Eligibility Requirements:* Applicant must be high school student; enrolled at a four-year institution; female; resident of Oregon and must have an interest in golf. *Application Requirements:* Application, essay, test scores, transcript. *Deadline:* March 1.

Contact Mr. James Beyer, Director of Grant Programs, Oregon Student Assistance Commission, 1500 Valley River Drive, Suite 100, Eugene, OR 97401. *Web site:* http://www.osac.state.or.us.

Ford Opportunity Program. Award designed for Oregon residents who are single heads of household with custody of a dependent child or children. May be used only at Oregon colleges. GPA of 3.0 required unless accompanied by a counselor's recommendation. Must plan to complete a four-year degree. *Award:* Scholarship for use in freshman, sophomore, junior, or senior year; renewable. *Eligibility Requirements:* Applicant must be enrolled at a four-year institution; single; resident of Oregon and studying in Oregon. Applicant must have 3.0 GPA or higher. *Application Requirements:* Application, essay, test scores, transcript. *Deadline:* March 1.

Contact Mr. James Beyer, Director of Grant Programs, Oregon Student Assistance Commission, 1500 Valley River Drive, Suite 100, Eugene, OR 97401. *Web site:* http://www.osac.state.or.us.

Oregon Collectors Association Bob Hasson Memorial Scholarship. One-time award for graduating Oregon high school seniors and recent Oregon high school graduates, enrolling in college within one year of graduation. Children and grandchildren of owners and officers of collection agencies registered in Oregon are not eligible. Award is based on a 3-4 page essay titled "The Proper Use of Credit". *Award:* Scholarship for use in freshman year; not renewable. *Eligibility Requirements:* Applicant must be resident of Oregon and studying in Oregon. *Application Requirements:* Application, essay, test scores, transcript. *Deadline:* March 1.

Contact Mr. James Beyer, Director of Grant Programs, Oregon Student Assistance Commission, 1500 Valley River Drive, Suite 100, Eugene, OR 97401. *Web site:* http://www.osac.state.or.us.

PENNSYLVANIA

Prisoner of War/Missing in Action Dependents Grant-Pennsylvania. For dependent children of Pennsylvania military personnel classified as prisoner-of-war or Missing in Action. Awards are up to $1200 for in-state study and up to $800 for out-of-state study. Renewable award. Submit Free Application for Federal Student Aid. Parents must have been Pennsylvania residents prior to service. *Award:* Grant for use in any year; renewable. *Award amount:* up to $1200. *Eligibility Requirements:* Applicant must be enrolled at a two-year, four-year, or technical institution or university. Applicant or parent must meet one or more of the following requirements: general military experience; retired from active duty; disabled or killed as a result of military service; prisoner of war; or missing in action. *Application Requirements:* Application, financial need analysis. *Deadline:* continuous.

Contact Keith New, Director of Communications and Press Office, Pennsylvania Higher Education Assistance Agency, 1200 North Seventh Street, Harrisburg, PA 17102. *E-mail:* knew@pheaa.org. *Phone:* 717-720-2509. *Fax:* 717-720-3903. *Web site:* http://www.pheaa.org.

Veterans Grant-Pennsylvania. Renewable awards for Pennsylvania residents who are qualified veterans attending an approved undergraduate program full-time. Up to $3100 for in-state study or $800 for out-of-state study. Deadlines: May 1 for all renewal applicants, new applicants who plan to enroll in an undergraduate baccalaureate degree program, and those in college transfer programs at two-year public or junior colleges; August 1 for all first-time applicants who plan to enroll in a business, trade, or technical school; a hospital school of nursing; or a two-year terminal program at a community, junior, or four-year college. *Award:* Grant for use in freshman, sophomore, junior, or senior year; renewable. *Award amount:* up to $3100. *Eligibility Requirements:* Applicant must be resident of Pennsylvania. Applicant must have general military experience. *Application Requirements:* Application.

Contact Keith New, Director of Communications and Press Office, Pennsylvania Higher Education Assistance Agency, 1200 North Seventh Street, Harrisburg, PA 17102. *E-mail:* knew@pheaa.org. *Phone:* 717-720-2509. *Fax:* 717-720-3903. *Web site:* http://www.pheaa.org.

Pennsylvania State Grant. Award for Pennsylvania residents attending an approved post-secondary institution as undergraduates in a program of at least two years duration. Renewable for up to eight semesters if show continued need and academic progress. Submit Free Application for Federal Student Aid. *Award:* Grant for use in freshman, sophomore, junior, or senior year; renewable. *Award amount:* $300–$3100. *Number of awards:* up to 143,000. *Eligibility Requirements:* Applicant must be enrolled at a two-year, four-year, or technical institution or university and resident of Pennsylvania. *Application Requirements:* Application, financial need analysis. *Deadline:* May 1.

Contact Keith New, Director of Communications and Press Office, Pennsylvania Higher Education Assistance Agency, 1200 North Seventh Street, Harrisburg, PA 17102. *E-mail:* knew@pheaa.org. *Phone:*

717-720-2509. *Fax:* 717-720-3903. *Web site:* http://www.pheaa.org.

Scholars in Residence Program. Provides for four to twelve weeks of financial support for full time research and study in collections maintenance by the Commission on topics broadly related to Pennsylvania history. *Academic/Career Areas:* History. *Eligibility Requirements:* Applicant must be enrolled at a two-year, four-year, or technical institution or university. Available to Canadian and non-U.S. citizens. *Application Requirements:* Application, essay, references. *Deadline:* January 15.

Contact Ms. Linda Shopes, Historian, Pennsylvania Historical and Museum Commission, PO Box 1026, Harrisburg, PA 17108. *E-mail:* ishopes@phmc.state.pa.us. *Phone:* 717-772-3257. *Fax:* 717-787-4822. *Web site:* http://www.phmc.state.pa.us.

RHODE ISLAND

Burns and Haynes Textile Scholarship Fund. Award to benefit students studying textile technology. Preference given to children of members of National Association of Textile Supervisors. *Award:* Scholarship for use in any year; renewable. *Award amount:* $500. *Number of awards:* 1. *Eligibility Requirements:* Applicant must be enrolled at a four-year institution and must have an interest in designated field specified by sponsor. *Application Requirements: Deadline:* September.

Contact John Beardon, Rhode Island Foundation, PO Box 325 Village Station, Medway, MA 02053. *Web site:* http://www.rifoundation.org.

Rhode Island Higher Education Grant Program. Grants for residents of Rhode Island attending an approved school in U.S., Canada, or Mexico. Based on need. Renewable for up to four years if in good academic standing. Applications accepted January 1 through March 1. Several awards of variable amounts. *Award:* Grant for use in freshman, sophomore, junior, or senior year; renewable. *Award amount:* $250–$750. *Number of awards:* 10,000–12,000. *Eligibility Requirements:* Applicant must be enrolled at a two-year, four-year, or technical institution or university and resident of Rhode Island. Restricted to U.S. citizens. *Application Requirements:* Application, financial need analysis. *Deadline:* March 1.

Contact Mary Ann Welch, Director of Program Administration, Rhode Island Higher Education Assistance Authority, 560 Jefferson Boulevard, 222 21st. Avenue South, Warwick, RI 02886. *Phone:* 401-736-1100. *Fax:* 401-732-3541. *Web site:* http://www.riheaa.org.

SOUTH CAROLINA

Legislative Incentives for Future Excellence Program. The goals of the LIFE Scholarship Program are to increase access to higher education, improve the employability of South Carolina's students so as to attract business to the State, provide incentives for students to be better prepared for college, to improve SAT scores, and to graduate from college on time. Must have minimum 3.0 GPA. *Award:* Scholarship for use in freshman, sophomore, junior, or senior year; renewable. *Award amount:* $1000–$2000. *Eligibility Requirements:* Applicant must be enrolled at a two-year or four-year institution or university; resident of South Carolina and studying in South Carolina. Applicant must have 3.0 GPA or higher. Restricted to U.S. citizens. *Application Requirements:* Test scores, transcript.

Contact Tobi Swartz, Project Administrator, South Carolina Commission on Higher Education, 1333 Main Street, Suite 200, Columbia, SC 29201. *E-mail:* tswartz@che400.state.sc.us. *Phone:* 803-737-2293. *Fax:* 803-737-2297.

South Carolina Need-Based Grants Program. Need-based grant awarded based on results of Free Application for Federal Student Aid. A student may receive up to $1689 annually for full-time and up to $275 annually for part-time. The grant must be applied toward the cost of attendance at the college for up to eight full-time equivalent terms. Student must be degree-seeking. *Award:* Grant for use in freshman, sophomore, junior, or senior year; renewable. *Award amount:* $275–$1689. *Eligibility Requirements:* Applicant must be enrolled at a two-year, four-year, or technical institution or university; resident of South Carolina and studying in South Carolina. Restricted to U.S. citizens. *Application Requirements:* Financial need analysis. *Deadline:* continuous.

Contact Ms. Sherry Hubbard, Program Coordinator, South Carolina Commission on Higher Education, 1333 Main Street, Suite 200, Columbia, SC 29201. *E-mail:* shubbard@che400.state.sc.us. *Phone:* 803-737-2262. *Fax:* 803-737-2297.

South Carolina Tuition Grants Program. Assists South Carolina residents attending one of twenty approved South Carolina Independent colleges. Freshmen must be in upper 3/4 of high school class or have SAT score of at least 900. Upper-class students must complete twenty-four semester hours per year to be eligible. *Award:* Grant for use in freshman, sophomore, junior, or senior year; not renewable. *Award amount:* $1990–$3730. *Number of awards:* up to 10,000. *Eligibility Requirements:* Applicant must be enrolled at a two-year or four-year institution or university; resident of South Carolina and studying in South Carolina. Restricted to U.S. citizens. *Application Requirements:* Application, financial need analysis, test scores, transcript. *Deadline:* June 30.

Contact South Carolina Tuition Grants Commmission, 1310 Lady Street, Suite 811, Columbia, SC 29211-2159. *Phone:* 803-734-1200. *Fax:* 803-734-1426. *Web site:* http://www.state.sc.us/tuitiongrants.

Palmetto Fellows Scholarship Program. Renewable award for qualified high school seniors in South Carolina to attend a four-year South Carolina institution. Must rank in top five percent of class at the end of sophomore or junior year, earn a 3.5 GPA on a 4.0 scale, and score at least 1200 on the SAT or 27 on the ACT. Submit official transcript and test scores with application by established deadline (usually January of Senior year). *Award:* Scholarship for use in freshman, sophomore, junior, or senior year; renewable. *Award amount:* up to $5000. *Number of awards:* 600–700. *Eligibility Requirements:* Applicant must be high school student; enrolled at a four-year institution or university; resident of South Carolina and studying in South Carolina. Applicant must have 3.5 GPA or higher. Restricted to U.S. citizens. *Application Requirements:* Application, applicant must enter a contest, references, test scores, transcript. *Deadline:* January 15.

Contact Ms. Sherry Hubbard, Program Coordinator, South Carolina Commission on Higher Education, 1333 Main Street, Suite 200, Columbia, SC 29201. *E-mail:* shubbard@che400.state.sc.us. *Phone:* 803-737-2262. *Fax:* 803-737-2297.

South Carolina Teacher Loan Program. One-time awards for South Carolina residents attending four-year post-secondary institutions in South Carolina. Recipients must teach in the South Carolina public school system in a critical-need area after graduation. 20% of loan forgiven for each year of service. Write for additional requirements. *Academic/Career Areas:* Education; Special Education. *Award:* Forgivable loan for use in any year; not renewable. *Award amount:* $2500–$5000. *Number of awards:* up to 975. *Eligibility Requirements:* Applicant must be enrolled at a four-year institution or university; resident of South Carolina and studying in South Carolina. Applicant must have 3.0 GPA or higher. *Application Requirements:* Application, test scores. *Deadline:* June 1.

Contact Jennifer Jones-Gaddy, Vice President, South Carolina Student Loan Corporation, PO Box 21487, Columbia, SC 29221. *E-mail:* jgaddy@slc.sc.edu. *Phone:* 803-798-0916. *Fax:* 803-772-9410. *Web site:* http://www.slc.sc.edu.

Educational Assistance for Certain War Veteran's Dependents- South Carolina. Renewable aid to South Carolina Disabled Veterans' dependents under age 26. Veterans must have had wartime. For undergraduate study at any South Carolina state supported colleges. Must be South Carolina resident. *Award:* Scholarship for use in freshman, sophomore, junior, or senior year; renewable. *Eligibility Requirements:* Applicant must be age 18-26; enrolled at a two-year, four-year, or technical institution or university; resident of South Carolina and studying in South Carolina. Restricted to U.S. citizens. Applicant or parent must meet one or more of the following requirements: general military experience; retired from active duty; disabled or killed as a result of military service; prisoner of war; or missing in action. *Application Requirements:* Application.

Contact Ms. Barbara O'Connor, Free Tuition Assistant, South Carolina Division of Veterans Affairs, 1801 Assembly Street, Room 230, Columbia, SC 29201. *Phone:* 803-255-4317. *Fax:* 803-255-4257.

SOUTH DAKOTA

South Dakota Board of Regents Bjugstad Scholarship. Scholarship for graduating North or South Dakota high school senior who is a Native American. Must demonstrate academic achievement, character and leadership abilities. Submit proof of tribal enrollment. One-time award of $500. Must rank in upper half of class or have a minimum 2.5 GPA. Must be pursuing studies in agriculture, agribusiness, or natural resources. *Academic/Career Areas:* Agribusiness; Agriculture; Natural Resources. *Award:* Scholarship for use in freshman year; not renewable. *Award amount:* $500. *Number of awards:* 1. *Eligibility Requirements:* Applicant must be Native American or Eskimo; high school student; enrolled at a two-year or four-year institution; resident of North Dakota or South Dakota and must have an interest in leadership. Applicant must have 2.5 GPA or higher. *Application Requirements:* Application, references, transcript. *Deadline:* February 18.

Contact South Dakota Board of Regents, 207 East Capitol Avenue, Pierre, SD 57501-3159. *Web site:* http://www.ris.sdbor.edu.

Aid to Dependents of Deceased Veterans. For South Dakota residents under 25 who are children of veterans who died in service between June 25, 1950, and May 7, 1975, or August 2, 1990, and March 3, 1991. Must be enrolled full-time in a state educational institution under control of the Board of Regents. Contact financial aid office of any South Dakota college for further information and deadlines. *Award:* Scholarship for use in freshman, sophomore, junior, or senior year; not renewable. *Eligibility Requirements:* Applicant must be age 24 or under; enrolled at a two-year or four-year institution; resident of South Dakota and studying in South Dakota. Applicant or parent must meet one or more of the following requirements: general military experience; retired from active duty; disabled or killed as a result of military service; prisoner of war; or missing in action. *Application Requirements:* Application.

Contact South Dakota Board of Regents, 207 East Capitol Avenue, Pierre, SD 57501-3159. *Web site:* http://www.ris.sdbor.edu.

South Dakota Board of Regents Annis I. Fowler/Kaden Scholarship. Scholarship for graduating South Dakota high school seniors to pursue a career in elementary education at a South Dakota public university. One-time award. Minimum 3.0 GPA required. *Academic/Career Areas:* Education. *Award:* Scholarship for use in freshman year; not renewable. *Award amount:* $1000. *Number of awards:* 1. *Eligibility Requirements:* Applicant must be high school student; resident of South Dakota and studying in South Dakota. Applicant must have 3.0 GPA or higher. *Application Requirements:* Application, essay, references, transcript. *Deadline:* February 18.

Contact South Dakota Board of Regents, 207 East Capitol Avenue, Pierre, SD 57501-3159. *Web site:* http://www.ris.sdbor.edu.

Haines Memorial Scholarship. One-time scholarship for South Dakota public university students who are sophomores, juniors, or seniors having at least a 2.5 GPA and majoring in education. Include resume with application. Must be South Dakota resident. *Academic/Career Areas:* Education. *Award:* Scholarship for use in sophomore, junior, or senior year; not renewable. *Award amount:* $2150. *Number of awards:* 1. *Eligibility Requirements:* Applicant must be resident of South Dakota and studying in South Dakota. Applicant must have 2.5 GPA or higher.

Application Requirements: Application, autobiography, essay. *Deadline:* February 18.

Contact South Dakota Board of Regents, 207 East Capitol Avenue, Pierre, SD 57501-3159. *Web site:* http://www.ris.sdbor.edu.

South Dakota Board of Regents Marlin R. Scarborough Memorial Scholarship. One-time award for a student who is of junior standing at the time of receipt of funding at a South Dakota public university. Must be nominated by the university. Merit-based. Must have community service and leadership experience. *Award:* Scholarship for use in junior year; not renewable. *Award amount:* $1500. *Number of awards:* 1. *Eligibility Requirements:* Applicant must be resident of South Dakota; studying in South Dakota; have employment experience in community service and must have an interest in leadership. Applicant must have 3.5 GPA or higher. *Application Requirements:* Application, essay.

Contact South Dakota Board of Regents, 207 East Capitol Avenue, Pierre, SD 57501-3159. *Web site:* http://www.ris.sdbor.edu.

TENNESSEE

Tennessee Teaching Scholars Program. Forgivable loan for college juniors, seniors, and college graduates admitted to an education program in Tennessee with a minimum GPA of 2.75. Students must commit to teach in a Tennessee public school one year for each year of the award. *Academic/Career Areas:* Education. *Award:* Forgivable loan for use in junior, senior, or graduate years; not renewable. *Award amount:* $1000–$3000. *Number of awards:* 30–250. *Eligibility Requirements:* Applicant must be enrolled at a four-year institution or university; resident of Tennessee and studying in Tennessee. Restricted to U.S. citizens. *Application Requirements:* Application, references, test scores, transcript. *Deadline:* April 15.

Contact Mike McCormick, Scholarship Administrator, Tennessee Student Assistance Corporation, Suite 1950, Parkway Towers, Nashville, TN 37243-0820. *Phone:* 615-741-1346. *Fax:* 615-741-6101. *Web site:* http://www.state.tn.us/tsac.

Minority Teaching Fellows Program/ Tennessee. Forgivable loan for minority Tennessee residents pursuing teaching careers. Minimum 2.75 GPA. Must be in the top quarter of the class or score an 18 on ACT. Submit statement of intent, test scores, and transcripts with application and two letters of recommendation. Must teach one year per year of award or repay as a loan. *Academic/Career Areas:* Education; Special Education. *Award:* Forgivable loan for use in freshman, sophomore, junior, or senior year; renewable. *Award amount:* $5000. *Number of awards:* 19–29. *Eligibility Requirements:* Applicant must be Native American or Eskimo, Asian, African American, or Hispanic; enrolled at a two-year or four-year institution or university; resident of Tennessee and studying in Tennessee. Restricted to U.S. citizens. *Application Requirements:* Application, essay, references, test scores, transcript. *Deadline:* April 15.

Contact Michael Roberts, Grant and Scholarship Administrator, Tennessee Student Assistance Corporation, Suite 1950, Parkway Towers, Nashville, TN 37243-0820. *E-mail:* roberts@mail.state.tn.us. *Phone:* 615-741-1346. *Fax:* 615-741-6101. *Web site:* http://www.state.tn.us/tsac.

Tennessee Student Assistance Award Program. Assists Tennessee residents attending an approved college or university within the state. Complete a Free Application for Federal Student Aid form. Apply January 1 to May 1. *Award:* Grant for use in freshman, sophomore, junior, or senior year; renewable. *Award amount:* $1626. *Number of awards:* 19,500. *Eligibility Requirements:* Applicant must be enrolled at a two-year, four-year, or technical institution or university; resident of Tennessee and studying in Tennessee. Restricted to U.S. citizens. *Application Requirements:* Application, financial need analysis. *Deadline:* May 1.

Contact Naomi Derryberry, Grant and Scholarship Administrator, Tennessee Student Assistance Corporation, Suite 1950, Parkway Towers, Nashville, TN 37243-0820. *Phone:* 615-741-1346. *Fax:* 615-741-6101. *Web site:* http://www.state.tn.us/tsac.

Ned McWherter Scholars Program. Assists Tennessee residents with high academic ability. Must have high school GPA of at least 3.5 and have scored in top five percent of SAT or ACT. Must attend college in Tennessee. Only high school seniors may apply. *Award:* Scholarship for use in freshman, sophomore, junior, or senior year; renewable. *Award amount:* $6000. *Number of awards:* 55. *Eligibility Requirements:* Applicant must be high school student; enrolled at a two-year or four-year institution or university; resident of Tennessee and studying in Tennessee. Applicant must have 3.5 GPA or higher. Restricted to U.S. citizens. *Application Requirements:* Application, test scores, transcript. *Deadline:* February 15.

Contact Naomi Derryberry, Grant and Scholarship Administrator, Tennessee Student Assistance Corporation, Suite 1950, Parkway Towers, Nashville, TN 37243-0820. *Phone:* 615-741-1346. *Fax:* 615-741-6101. *Web site:* http://www.state.tn.us/tsac.

TEXAS

Early High School Graduation Scholarships. Award of $1000 for Texas residents who have completed the requirements for graduation from a Texas high school in no more than 36 consecutive months. Call 1-800-242-3062 Extension 6387 for a copy of form letter to be submitted by high school counselor. Eligibility continues until full $1000 tuition award is received. Must submit high school certificate of eligibility to Coordinating Board. *Award:* Scholarship for use in any year; not renewable. *Award amount:* $1000. *Eligibility Requirements:* Applicant must be high school student; enrolled at a two-year, four-year, or technical institution or university; resident of Texas and studying in Texas. *Application Requirements:* Application. *Deadline:* continuous.

Contact Texas Higher Education Coordinating Board, PO Box 12788, Austin,

TX 78711-2788. *E-mail:* grantinfo@thecb.state.tx.us. *Web site:* http://www.thecb.state.tx.us.

Tuition and Fee Exemption for Firemen Enrolled in Fire Science Courses-Texas. Assists firemen enrolled in fire science courses as part of a fire science curriculum. Award is exemption from tuition and laboratory fees at publicly supported Texas colleges. State residence not required. One-time award. *Academic/Career Areas:* Applied Sciences; Physical Sciences and Math; Trade/Technical Specialties. *Award:* Scholarship for use in freshman, sophomore, junior, or senior year; not renewable. *Award amount:* up to $222. *Eligibility Requirements:* Applicant must be enrolled at a two-year, four-year, or technical institution; studying in Texas and have employment experience in fire service or police/firefighting. *Application Requirements:* Application. *Deadline:* continuous.

Contact Admissions/Registrar, Texas Higher Education Coordinating Board, PO Box 12788, Austin, TX 78711-2788. *E-mail:* grantinfo@thecb.state.tx.us. *Web site:* http://www.thecb.state.tx.us.

Tuition and Fee Exemption for Blind or Deaf Students. Aids certain blind or deaf students by exempting them from payment of tuition and fees at public colleges or universities in Texas. Must be a resident of Texas. Deadlines vary. Renewable. Must submit certificate of deafness or blindness. *Award:* Scholarship for use in any year; renewable. *Award amount:* up to $951. *Eligibility Requirements:* Applicant must be enrolled at a two-year, four-year, or technical institution or university; resident of Texas and studying in Texas. Applicant must be hearing impaired or visually impaired. *Application Requirements:* Application.

Contact Texas Higher Education Coordinating Board, PO Box 12788, Austin, TX 78711-2788. *E-mail:* grantinfo@thecb.state.tx.us. *Web site:* http://www.thecb.state.tx.us.

Tuition and Fee Exemption for Children of Disabled Firemen and Peace Officers-Texas. Renewable award for children of firemen, game wardens, peace officers, or custodial employees of the Department of Corrections disabled or deceased while serving in Texas. Must attend a Texas institution. Must apply before 21st birthday. Must provide certification of parent's disability or death. *Award:* Scholarship for use in any year; renewable. *Award amount:* up to $1152. *Eligibility Requirements:* Applicant must be age 20 or under; enrolled at a two-year, four-year, or technical institution or university; resident of Texas; studying in Texas and have employment experience in designated career field, fire service, or police/firefighting. *Application Requirements:* Application. *Deadline:* continuous.

Contact Texas Higher Education Coordinating Board, Box 12788, Austin, TX 78711-2788. *E-mail:* grantinfo@thecb.state.tx.us. *Web site:* http://www.thecb.state.tx.us.

Tuition and Fee Exemption for Children of Prisoners of War or Persons Missing in Action-Texas. Assists children of prisoner-of-war or veterans classified as missing in action. Must be a Texas resident and attend a public college or university within Texas. Submit proof of service and proof of MIA/POW status. Award is exemption from tuition and fees. Must be under 21 years of age. Renewable. *Award:* Scholarship for use in any year; renewable. *Eligibility Requirements:* Applicant must be age 20 or under; enrolled at a two-year, four-year, or technical institution or university; resident of Texas and studying in Texas. Applicant or parent must meet one or more of the following requirements: general military experience; retired from active duty; disabled or killed as a result of military service; prisoner of war; or missing in action. *Application Requirements:* Application. *Deadline:* continuous.

Contact Texas Higher Education Coordinating Board, PO Box 12788, Austin, TX 78711-2788. *E-mail:* grantinfo@thecb.state.tx.us. *Web site:* http://www.thecb.state.tx.us.

State Tuition Exemption Program: Veterans and Dependents-Texas (Hazlewood Exemption). Renewable tuition and partial fee exemptions for Texas veterans who have been honorably discharged after at least 180 days of active duty. Must be a Texas resident at time of entry into service. Must have exhausted federal education benefits. Awards may go to dependents of Texas veterans if veteran is deceased from injury or illness related to service. *Award:* Scholarship for use in any year; renewable. *Award amount:* up to $467. *Eligibility Requirements:* Applicant must be enrolled at a two-year, four-year, or technical institution or university; resident of Texas and studying in Texas. Applicant or parent must meet one or more of the following requirements: general military experience; retired from active duty; disabled or killed as a result of military service; prisoner of war; or missing in action. *Application Requirements:* Application. *Deadline:* continuous.

Contact Texas Higher Education Coordinating Board, PO Box 12788, Austin, TX 78711-2788. *E-mail:* grantinfo@thecb.state.tx.us. *Web site:* http://www.thecb.state.tx.us.

Texas State Tuition Exemption Program: Highest Ranking High School Graduate. Award available to Texas residents who are the top ranked seniors of their high school. Must attend a public college or university within Texas. Recipient is exempt from certain charges for first two semesters. Deadlines vary. *Award:* Scholarship for use in freshman year; not renewable. *Award amount:* up to $1483. *Eligibility Requirements:* Applicant must be enrolled at a two-year, four-year, or technical institution or university; resident of Texas and studying in Texas. Applicant must have 3.5 GPA or higher. *Application Requirements:* Transcript.

Contact Texas Higher Education Coordinating Board, PO Box 12788, Austin, TX 78711-2788. *E-mail:* grantinfo@thecb.state.tx.us. *Web site:* http://www.thecb.state.tx.us.

Texas Public Educational/LEAP. Renewable aid for students currently enrolled in a public, college or university in Texas. Based on need. Amount of award is determined by the financial aid office of each school. Texas residence not necessary. Deadlines vary. *Award:* Grant for use in any year; renewable. *Award amount:* up to $372. *Eligibility Requirements:* Applicant must be enrolled at a two-year, four-year, or technical institution or university and studying in Texas. *Application Requirements:* Financial need analysis.

Contact Texas Higher Education Coordinating Board, PO Box 12788, Austin, TX 78711-2788. *E-mail:* grantinfo@thecb.state.tx.us. *Web site:* http://www.thecb.state.tx.us.

Toward Excellence, Access, and Success (TEXAS) Grant. Need and academic based grant program for Texas residents who have graduated from a Texas public high school or an accredited Texas private high school in Fall 1998 or later. The award is renewable. GED and home school students are not eligible. Applicants must have completed the recommended or advanced high school curriculum. Available only to students attending class 3/4 time or more. *Award:* Grant for use in freshman, sophomore, junior, or senior year; renewable. *Eligibility Requirements:* Applicant must be enrolled at a two-year or four-year institution or university; resident of Texas and studying in Texas. *Application Requirements:* Financial need analysis, transcript. *Deadline:* continuous.

Contact Texas Higher Education Coordinating Board, PO Box 12788, Austin, TX 78711-2788. *E-mail:* grantinfo@thecb.state.tx.us. *Web site:* http://www.thecb.state.tx.us.

Certified Educational Aides Exemption. Aids certain educational aides by exempting them from payment of tuition and fees at public colleges or universities in Texas. The educational aide must be certified by TEA and must have worked with students in the classroom for at least two years to apply. *Academic/Career Areas:* Education. *Award:* Scholarship for use in any year; not renewable. *Award amount:* up to $745. *Eligibility Requirements:* Applicant must be enrolled at a four-year institution or university; resident of Texas and studying in Texas. *Application Requirements:* Application, financial need analysis.

Contact Texas Higher Education Coordinating Board, PO Box 12788, Austin, TX 78711-2788. *E-mail:* grantinfo@thecb.state.tx.us. *Web site:* http://www.thecb.state.tx.us.

Good Neighbor Scholarship. Renewable aid for students residing in Texas who are citizens of another country of the Americas. Must attend public college in Texas. Student will be exempt from tuition. *Award:* Scholarship for use in any year; renewable. *Award amount:* up to $1504. *Eligibility Requirements:* Applicant must be enrolled at a two-year, four-year, or technical institution or university and studying in Texas. Available to Canadian and non-U.S. citizens. *Application Requirements:* Application, test scores, transcript. *Deadline:* continuous.

Contact Texas Higher Education Coordinating Board, PO Box 12788, Austin, TX 78711-2788. *E-mail:* grantinfo@thecb.state.tx.us. *Web site:* http://www.thecb.state.tx.us.

Tuition Equalization Grant (TEG)/LEAP. For Texas residents enrolled at least half-time at an independent college or university within the state. Based on financial need. Deadlines vary by institution. Award is renewable. Must not be in religion program or receiving athletic scholarship. *Award:* Grant for use in any year; renewable. *Award amount:* up to $1972. *Eligibility Requirements:* Applicant must be enrolled at a two-year or four-year institution or university; resident of Texas and studying in Texas. *Application Requirements:* Financial need analysis.

Contact Texas Higher Education Coordinating Board, PO Box 12788, Austin, TX 78711-2788. *E-mail:* grantinfo@thecb.state.tx.us. *Web site:* http://www.thecb.state.tx.us.

San Antonio International Piano Competition. International piano competition for 10 semi-finalists, ages 20-32. Cash awards, ranging from $500 for 5th prize to $10,000 for 1st prize, are determined through a series of daily concerts, with an additional award for the best performance of a commissioned work. Application fee: $50. Deadline: March 31. Additional awards: $350. *Academic/Career Areas:* Performing Arts. *Award:* Prize for use in any year; not renewable. *Award amount:* $350–$10,000. *Number of awards:* 6–11. *Eligibility Requirements:* Applicant must be age 20-32. Available to U.S. and non-U.S. citizens. *Application Requirements:* Application, applicant must enter a contest, autobiography, driver's license, photo, portfolio, references, self-addressed stamped envelope. *Fee:* $50. *Deadline:* March 31.

Contact Ms. Virginia Lawrence, Registrar, San Antonio International Piano Competition, PO Box 39636, San Antonio, TX 78218. *E-mail:* info@saipc.org. *Phone:* 210-655-0766. *Fax:* 210-824-5094. *Web site:* http://www.saipc.org.

General Scholarship Programs for Nursing Students. Several awards for Texas residents enrolled at least half-time in a nursing program leading to License of Vocational Nursing bachelor's, or master's degree at a Texas institution. ADN and BSN students must not be licensed to practice as a licensed RN. One-time award of up to $2000. *Academic/Career Areas:* Nursing. *Award:* Scholarship for use in freshman, sophomore, junior, senior, or graduate years; not renewable. *Award amount:* up to $2000. *Eligibility Requirements:* Applicant must be enrolled at a two-year or four-year institution or university; resident of Texas and studying in Texas. *Application Requirements:* Application, financial need analysis, test scores, transcript. *Deadline:* July 15.

Contact Texas Higher Education Coordinating Board, PO Box 12788, Austin, TX 78711-2788. *E-mail:* grantinfo@thecb.state.tx.us. *Web site:* http://www.thecb.state.tx.us.

Physician Education Loan Repayment Program. For physicians in allopathic or osteopathic medicine working in rural, or other medically underserved areas. Must be a Texas resident. Award is renewable up to five years. Applications taken on a continuous basis. *Academic/Career Areas:* Health and Medical Sciences. *Award:* Scholarship for use in graduate years; renewable. *Award amount:* up to $9000. *Eligibility Requirements:* Applicant must be resident of Texas and have employment experience in designated career field.

Application Requirements: Application. *Deadline:* continuous.

Contact Texas Higher Education Coordinating Board, Box 12788, Austin, TX 78711-2788. *E-mail:* grantinfo@thecb.state.tx.us. *Web site:* http://www.thecb.state.tx.us.

Texas Tuition Assistance Grant Program. Award for Texas residents enrolled full-time at a Texas institution. Must have received the award in the past to be eligible *Award:* Grant for use in any year; renewable. *Award amount:* up to $854. *Eligibility Requirements:* Applicant must be enrolled at a two-year, four-year, or technical institution or university; resident of Texas and studying in Texas. Applicant must have 3.0 GPA or higher. *Application Requirements:* Application, financial need analysis, test scores, transcript. *Deadline:* continuous.

Contact Texas Higher Education Coordinating Board, PO Box 12788, Austin, TX 78711-2788. *E-mail:* grantinfo@thecb.state.tx.us. *Web site:* http://www.thecb.state.tx.us.

Texas Physician Assistant Loan Reimbursement Program. Educational loan reimbursement program for physician assistants who have worked twelve consecutive months in a qualified rural Texas county. Submit a copy of diploma from accredited physician assistant school. *Academic/Career Areas:* Health and Medical Sciences. *Award:* Grant for use in any year; not renewable. *Award amount:* $2500–$5000. *Number of awards:* 18–36. *Eligibility Requirements:* Applicant must be resident of Texas. *Application Requirements:* Application. *Deadline:* June 30.

Contact Program Administrator, Texas Center for Rural Health Initiatives, 211 East 7th, Suite 915, Austin, TX 78767-1708. *Phone:* 512-479-8891. *Fax:* 512-479-8898. *Web site:* http://www.crhi.state.tx.us.

Teach for Texas Conditional Grant Program. This is a student loan with cancellation provisions for teaching. Prospective teachers must be enrolled in degree programs leading to certification in a teaching field designated as having a critical shortage of teachers, or, agree to teach in a Texas community certified as experiencing a critical shortage of teachers. For upper division college students only. *Academic/Career Areas:* Education. *Award:* Forgivable loan for use in junior or senior year; not renewable. *Eligibility Requirements:* Applicant must be enrolled at a four-year institution or university; resident of Texas and studying in Texas. *Application Requirements:* Application, financial need analysis, references. *Deadline:* continuous.

Contact Texas Higher Education Coordinating Board, PO Box 12788, Austin, TX 78711-2788. *E-mail:* grantinfo@thecb.state.tx.us. *Web site:* http://www.thecb.state.tx.us.

Texas Health Service Corps Program. Program providing stipends for primary care residents who agree to practice in rural Texas counties upon completion of residency program. Must provide medical school diploma. *Academic/Career Areas:* Health and Medical Sciences. *Award:* Grant for use in ; renewable. *Award amount:* $50,000. *Number of awards:* 3–4. *Eligibility Requirements:* Applicant must be resident of Texas and studying in Texas. *Application Requirements:* Application. *Deadline:* March 30.

Contact Program Administrator, Texas Center for Rural Health Initiatives, 211 East 7th, Suite 915, Austin, TX 78767-1708. *Phone:* 512-479-8891. *Fax:* 512-479-8898. *Web site:* http://www.crhi.state.tx.us.

Texas Outstanding Rural Scholar Recognition Program. Forgivable loan for Texas residents to pursue a health-related career in rural Texas. Need nomination by a sponsoring rural community. Sponsor applies for student. Must work one year for sponsoring community per award received. For use at Texas post-secondary institutions. Deadlines are the third Fridays in September, January, and May. Renewable award based on merit. College applicants must have minimum 3.0 GPA. High school applicants must be in upper quarter of class. *Academic/Career Areas:* Dental Health/Services; Health Administration; Health and Medical Sciences; Health Information Management/Technology; Nursing; Social Services; Therapy/Rehabilitation. *Award:* Forgivable loan for use in any year; renewable. *Award amount:* $2417–$40,882. *Eligibility Requirements:* Applicant must be enrolled at a two-year, four-year, or technical institution or university; resident of Texas; studying in Texas and must have an interest in designated field specified by sponsor. Applicant must have 3.0 GPA or higher. Restricted to U.S. citizens. *Application Requirements:* Application, essay, interview, references, test scores, transcript.

Contact Program Administrator, Texas Center for Rural Health Initiatives, 211 East 7th, Suite 915, Austin, TX 78767-1708. *Phone:* 512-479-8891. *Fax:* 512-479-8898. *Web site:* http://www.crhi.state.tx.us.

Community Scholarship Program. Selected nominees receive a forgiveness loan to cover costs of tuition and educational and living expenses. Student repays the loan by fulfilling a service obligation period. *Academic/Career Areas:* Health and Medical Sciences; Nursing. *Award:* Forgivable loan for use in graduate years; renewable. *Award amount:* $7312–$24,986. *Eligibility Requirements:* Applicant must be resident of Texas and studying in Texas. Restricted to U.S. citizens. *Application Requirements:* Application, essay, interview, references, test scores, transcript. *Deadline:* continuous.

Contact Program Administrator, Texas Center for Rural Health Initiatives, PO Drawer 1708, Austin, TX 78767. *Phone:* 512-479-8891 Ext. 230. *Fax:* 512-479-8898. *Web site:* http://www.crhi.state.tx.us.

Texas Tuition Exemption for AFDC (TANF) Students. Tuition and fee exemption for Texas residents who during last year of high school received financial assistance under Chap. 31, Human Resources Code (AFDC) for not less than 6 months. Must enroll at Texas institution within twelve months of high school graduation. Award is good for one year. *Award:* Scholarship for use in freshman year; not renewable. *Award amount:* up to $623. *Eligibility Requirements:* Applicant must be enrolled at a two-year, four-year, or technical institution or university; resident of Texas and studying in Texas. *Application Requirements:* Application, financial need analysis. *Deadline:* continuous.

Contact Texas Higher Education Coordinating Board, PO Box 12788, Austin, TX 78711-2788. *E-mail:* grantinfo@thecb.state.tx.us. *Web site:* http://www.thecb.state.tx.us.

Academic Common Market. For Texas residents who are graduate students pursuing a degree in a field of study not offered in Texas. May qualify for special tuition rates. Deadlines vary by institution. Must be studying in the South (excluding North Carolina). *Award:* Scholarship for use in graduate years; renewable. *Award amount:* up to $3224. *Eligibility Requirements:* Applicant must be resident of Texas and studying in Alabama, Arkansas, Florida, Georgia, Kentucky, Louisiana, Mississippi, Missouri, Oklahoma, South Carolina, Tennessee, or Virginia. *Application Requirements:* Application.

Contact Linda McDonough, Associate Program Director, Texas Higher Education Coordinating Board, PO Box 12788, Austin, TX 78711-2788. *E-mail:* grantinfo@thecb.state.tx.us. *Phone:* 512-483-6525. *Web site:* http://www.thecb.state.tx.us.

Scholarship Program for Licensed Vocational Nurses Becoming Professional Nurses-Texas. Scholarships available to Texas residents enrolled at least half-time in a nursing program leading to an associate, bachelor, or graduate degree in Texas. Must already be a licensed vocational nurse. Deadline varies. Renewable award of up to $2500. *Academic/Career Areas:* Nursing. *Award:* Scholarship for use in freshman, sophomore, junior, senior, or graduate years; renewable. *Award amount:* up to $2500. *Eligibility Requirements:* Applicant must be enrolled at a two-year or four-year institution or university; resident of Texas; studying in Texas and have employment experience in designated career field. *Application Requirements:* Application, financial need analysis, test scores, transcript.

Contact Texas Higher Education Coordinating Board, PO Box 12788, Austin, TX 78711-2788. *E-mail:* grantinfo@thecb.state.tx.us. *Web site:* http://www.thecb.state.tx.us.

Scholarship Program for Rural Bachelor of Science in Nursing or Graduate Nursing Students-Texas. Scholarships for Texas residents who are at least half-time undergraduate, or graduate students. Must be enrolled in a nursing program leading to a BSN or graduate degree at a Texas institution. Must be from a rural county in Texas. Deadline varies. One-time awards of up to $2500 each. *Academic/Career Areas:* Nursing. *Award:* Scholarship for use in freshman, sophomore, junior, senior, or graduate years; not renewable. *Award amount:* up to $2500. *Eligibility Requirements:* Applicant must be enrolled at a four-year institution or university; resident of Texas and studying in Texas. *Application Requirements:* Application, financial need analysis, test scores, transcript.

Contact Texas Higher Education Coordinating Board, PO Box 12788, Austin, TX 78711-2788. *E-mail:* grantinfo@thecb.state.tx.us. *Web site:* http://www.thecb.state.tx.us.

Scholarship Programs for Rural Professional or Vocational Nursing Students-Texas. Scholarships for Texas residents of rural counties. Must be enrolled in a nursing program at an institution in a non-metropolitan county of Texas. Maximum awards: $1500 for LVN/ADN students; $2500 for BSN or graduate students. Deadline varies. One-time award. *Academic/Career Areas:* Nursing. *Award:* Scholarship for use in freshman, sophomore, junior, senior, or graduate years; not renewable. *Award amount:* $1500–$2500. *Eligibility Requirements:* Applicant must be enrolled at a two-year or four-year institution or university; resident of Texas and studying in Texas. *Application Requirements:* Application, financial need analysis, test scores, transcript.

Contact Texas Higher Education Coordinating Board, PO Box 12788, Austin, TX 78711-2788. *E-mail:* grantinfo@thecb.state.tx.us. *Web site:* http://www.thecb.state.tx.us.

Scholarship Programs in Professional or Vocational Nursing- Texas. State scholarships for Texas residents enrolled in a nursing degree or licensure program. Maximum awards are $1500 for Licensed Vocational Nurse, $2000 for associate degree in nursing, and $3000 for Bachelor of Science in Nursing or graduate degree. Deadline varies. *Academic/Career Areas:* Nursing. *Award:* Scholarship for use in freshman, sophomore, junior, senior, or graduate years; not renewable. *Award amount:* $200–$3000. *Eligibility Requirements:* Applicant must be enrolled at a two-year or four-year institution or university; resident of Texas and studying in Texas. *Application Requirements:* Application, financial need analysis, test scores, transcript.

Contact Texas Higher Education Coordinating Board, PO Box 12788, Austin, TX 78711-2788. *E-mail:* grantinfo@thecb.state.tx.us. *Web site:* http://www.thecb.state.tx.us.

Texas Tuition Exemption for Senior Citizens. Tuition exemption for Texas residents over the age of 65 at eligible Texas institutions. Pays tuition for up to six semester credit hours per semester or summer term. Non-renewable. Awards made on a space-available basis. *Award:* Scholarship for use in any year; not renewable. *Award amount:* up to $138. *Number of awards:* 66. *Eligibility Requirements:* Applicant must be age 65; enrolled at a two-year, four-year, or technical institution or university; resident of Texas and studying in Texas. *Application Requirements:* Application. *Deadline:* continuous.

Contact Texas Higher Education Coordinating Board, PO Box 12788, Austin, TX 78711-2788. *E-mail:* grantinfo@thecb.state.tx.us. *Web site:* http://www.thecb.state.tx.us.

Texas Tuition Exemption for Foster Care Students. Exemption from tuition and fees at Texas institution. Must have been in foster care under the conservatorship of the Department of Protection and Regulatory Services on or after 18th birthday; or on the day of the student's 14th birthday, if the student was also eligible for adoption on or after that day; or the day the student graduated from high school or completed the equivalent of a high school diploma. Must enroll as undergraduate student within three years of discharge. *Award:* Scholarship for use in freshman, sophomore, junior, or senior year; renewable. *Award amount:* up to $449. *Eligibility Requirements:* Applicant must be enrolled at a two-year, four-year, or technical institution or university; resident of Texas and studying in Texas. *Application Requirements:* Application. *Deadline:* continuous.

Contact Texas Higher Education Coordinating Board, PO Box 12788, Austin, TX 78711-2788. *E-mail:* grantinfo@thecb.state.tx.us. *Web site:* http://www.thecb.state.tx.us.

Fifth-Year Accounting Student Scholarship Program. One-time award for students enrolled as fifth-year accounting students at a Texas institution. Must sign statement confirming intent to take the written exam for the purpose of being granted a certificate of CPA to practice in Texas. *Academic/Career Areas:* Business/Consumer Services. *Award:* Scholarship for use in senior or graduate years; not renewable. *Award amount:* up to $3000. *Eligibility Requirements:* Applicant must be enrolled at a four-year institution or university and studying in Texas. Available to U.S. and non-U.S. citizens. *Application Requirements:* Application, financial need analysis, transcript. *Deadline:* continuous.

Contact Texas Higher Education Coordinating Board, Po Box 12788, Austin, TX 78711-2788. *E-mail:* grantinfo@thecb.state.tx.us. *Web site:* http://www.thecb.state.tx.us.

State Student Incentive Grant-Texas. Available to residents of Texas attending public colleges or universities in Texas. Must be enrolled at least half-time and show financial need. Deadlines vary by institution. Award is renewable. *Award:* Grant for use in any year; renewable. *Award amount:* up to $828. *Eligibility Requirements:* Applicant must be enrolled at a two-year, four-year, or technical institution or university; resident of Texas and studying in Texas. *Application Requirements:* Financial need analysis. *Deadline:* continuous.

Contact Texas Higher Education Coordinating Board, PO Box 12788, Austin, TX 78711-2788. *E-mail:* grantinfo@thecb.state.tx.us. *Web site:* http://www.thecb.state.tx.us.

UTAH

Utah Tuition Waiver. Renewable awards ranging from partial to full tuition waivers at eligible Utah institutions. A limited number of waivers are available for nonresidents. Deadlines vary by institution. Contact financial aid office at participating institutions. *Award:* Scholarship for use in any year; renewable. *Eligibility Requirements:* Applicant must be enrolled at a two-year or four-year institution and studying in Utah. *Application Requirements:* Application, financial need analysis, interview.

Contact Information Specialist, Utah Higher Education Assistance Authority, PO Box 45202, Salt Lake City, UT 84145-0202. *E-mail:* uheaa@utahsbr.edu. *Phone:* 801-321-7188. *Fax:* 801-321-7299. *Web site:* http://www.uheaa.org.

Utah Tuition Waiver. Renewable awards ranging from partial to full tuition waivers at eligible Utah institutions. A limited number of waivers are available for nonresidents. Deadlines vary by institutions. Contact Financial Aid Office. *Award:* Scholarship for use in any year; renewable. *Eligibility Requirements:* Applicant must be enrolled at a two-year or four-year institution and studying in Utah. *Application Requirements:* Application, financial need analysis, interview.

Contact Utah State Board of Regents, 355 West North Temple, Triad 3, Suite 550, Salt Lake City, UT 84180-1205.

New Century Scholarship. Scholarship for qualified high school graduates of Utah. Must attend Utah operated state college. Award depends on number of hours student enrolled. Please contact for further eligibility requirements. *Award:* Scholarship for use in junior or senior year; renewable. *Award amount:* $500–$1000. *Eligibility Requirements:* Applicant must be high school student; enrolled at a four-year institution or university; resident of Utah and studying in Utah. *Application Requirements:* Application, test scores, transcript. *Deadline:* continuous.

Contact Angie Loving, Senior Officer for Programs/Administration, State of Utah, 3 Triad Center, Suite 500, Salt Lake City, UT 84180-1205.

Utah Educationally Disadvantaged Program. Renewable award for residents of Utah who are disadvantaged and attending an eligible institution in Utah. Must demonstrate need and satisfactory progress. Contact financial aid office of participating institution. *Award:* Scholarship for use in any year; renewable. *Eligibility Requirements:* Applicant must be enrolled at a two-year or four-year institution; resident of Utah and studying in Utah. Applicant must be hearing impaired, learning disabled, physically disabled, or visually impaired. *Application Requirements:* Application. *Deadline:* continuous.

Contact Utah State Board of Regents, 355 West North Temple, Triad 3, Suite 550, Salt Lake City, UT 84180-1205.

T.H. Bell Teaching Incentive Loan-Utah. Renewable awards for Utah residents who are high school seniors and wish to pursue teaching careers. Award pays for tuition and fees at a Utah state-supported institution. Must agree to teach in a Utah public school or pay back loan through monthly installments. Must be a U.S. citizen. *Academic/Career Areas:* Education; Special Education. *Award:* Forgivable loan for use in freshman, sophomore, junior, or senior year; renewable. *Number of awards:* 50. *Eligibility Requirements:* Applicant must be high school student; enrolled at a two-year or four-year institution or university; resident of Utah and studying in Utah. *Application Requirements:* Application, essay, test scores, transcript. *Deadline:* March 31.

Contact Diane DeMan, Executive Secretary, Utah State Office of Education, 250 East 500 South, Salt Lake City, UT 84111. *Phone:* 801-538-7741. *Fax:* 801-538-7973. *Web site:* http://www.usoe.k12.ut.us/cert/scholarships/scholars.htm.

Utah State Student Incentive Grant (SSIG). Available to students with substantial financial need for use at participating Utah schools. Contact Financial Aid Office of specific school for application requirements and deadlines. Must be Utah resident. *Award:* Grant for use in any year; renewable. *Award amount:* up to $2500. *Eligibility Requirements:* Applicant must be enrolled at a two-year, four-year, or technical institution or university; resident of Utah and studying in Utah. Restricted to U.S. citizens. *Application Requirements:* Application, financial need analysis.

Contact Information Specialist, Utah Higher Education Assistance Authority, PO Box 45202, Salt Lake City, UT 84145-0202. *E-mail:* uheaa@utahsbr.edu. *Phone:* 801-321-7188. *Fax:* 801-321-7299. *Web site:* http://www.uheaa.org.

Utah Educationally Disadvantaged Program. Renewable award for residents of Utah who are disadvantaged and attending an eligible institution in Utah. Must demonstrate need and satisfactory progress. Contact financial aid office of participating institution. *Award:* Scholarship for use in any year; renewable. *Eligibility Requirements:* Applicant must be enrolled at a two-year or four-year institution; resident of Utah and studying in Utah. Applicant must be hearing impaired, learning disabled, physically disabled, or visually impaired. *Application Requirements:* Application. *Deadline:* continuous.

Contact Information Specialist, Utah Higher Education Assistance Authority, PO Box 45202, Salt Lake City, UT 84145-0202. *E-mail:* uheaa@utahsbr.edu. *Phone:* 801-321-7188. *Fax:* 801-321-7299. *Web site:* http://www.uheaa.org.

VERMONT

Vermont Part-Time Student Grants. For undergraduates carrying less than twelve credits per semester who have not received a bachelor's degree. Must be Vermont resident. Based on financial need. Complete Vermont Financial Aid Packet to apply. May be used at any approved post-secondary institution. *Award:* Grant for use in freshman, sophomore, junior, or senior year; renewable. *Award amount:* $250–$5100. *Eligibility Requirements:* Applicant must be resident of Vermont. *Application Requirements:* Application, financial need analysis. *Deadline:* continuous.

Contact Grant Program, Vermont Student Assistance Corporation, PO Box 2000, Winooski, VT 05404-2000. *Phone:* 802-655-9602. *Fax:* 802-654-3765. *Web site:* http://www.vsac.org.

Vermont Non-Degree Student Grant Program. Renewable grants for Vermont residents enrolled in non-degree programs at colleges, vocational centers, and high school adult courses. May receive funds for two enrollment periods per year, up to $380 per course, per semester. Award based upon financial need. *Award:* Grant for use in any year; renewable. *Award amount:* up to $400. *Eligibility Requirements:* Applicant must be resident of Vermont. *Application Requirements:* Application, financial need analysis. *Deadline:* continuous.

Contact Grant Program, Vermont Student Assistance Corporation, PO Box 2000, Winooski, VT 05404-2000. *Phone:* 802-655-9602. *Fax:* 802-654-3765. *Web site:* http://www.vsac.org.

Vermont Incentive Grants. Renewable grants for Vermont residents based on financial need. Must meet needs test. Must be college undergraduate or graduate student enrolled full-time at an approved post-secondary institution. Only available to U.S. citizens or permanent residents. *Award:* Grant for use in freshman, sophomore, junior, senior, or graduate years; renewable. *Award amount:* $500–$6800. *Eligibility Requirements:* Applicant must be enrolled at a four-year institution or university and resident of Vermont. *Application Requirements:* Application, financial need analysis. *Deadline:* continuous.

Contact Grant Program, Vermont Student Assistance Corporation, PO Box 2000, Winooski, VT 05404-2000. *Phone:* 802-655-9602. *Fax:* 802-654-3765. *Web site:* http://www.vsac.org.

VIRGINIA

Virginia Tuition Assistance Grant Program. Several grants for undergraduate, graduate, and first professional degree students attending an approved private, non-profit college within Virginia. Must be a Virginia resident and be enrolled full-time. Not to be used for religious study. Preferred deadline July 31. Others are wait-listed. Renewable awards of approximately $2700 each. Contact college financial aid office. *Award:* Grant for use in any year; renewable. *Award amount:* $2700. *Eligibility Requirements:* Applicant must be enrolled at a four-year institution; resident of Virginia and studying in Virginia. *Application Requirements:* Application. *Deadline:* July 31.

Contact Financial Aid Office, VA State Council of Higher Education, James Monroe Building, 10th Floor, 101 North 14th Street, Richmond, VA 23219. *Web site:* http://www.schev.edu.

Mary Marshall Registered Nursing Program Scholarships. One-time award for registered nursing students who are Virginia residents. Must attend a full-time nursing program in Virginia. Recipient must agree to work in an underserved community in Virginia after graduation. Minimum 3.0 GPA required. *Academic/Career Areas:* Nursing. *Award:* Scholarship for use in any year; not renewable. *Award amount:* $1250. *Eligibility Requirements:* Applicant must be resident of Virginia and studying in Virginia. Applicant must have 3.0 GPA or higher. *Application Requirements:* Application, financial need analysis, transcript. *Deadline:* July 30.

Contact Program Coordinator, Virginia Department of Health,Center for Primary Care, Rural Health, and Health Policy, PO Box 2448, Richmond, VA 23218. *Phone:* 804-371-4090.

Mary Marshall Practical Nursing Scholarships. One-time award for practical nursing students who are Virginia residents. Must attend a full-time nursing program in Virginia. Recipient must agree to work in an underserved community in Virginia after graduation. Minimum 3.0 GPA required. *Academic/Career Areas:*

Nursing. *Award:* Scholarship for use in any year; not renewable. *Award amount:* $150–$500. *Eligibility Requirements:* Applicant must be enrolled at a two-year or technical institution; resident of Virginia and studying in Virginia. Applicant must have 3.0 GPA or higher. *Application Requirements:* Application, financial need analysis, transcript. *Deadline:* June 30.

Contact Program Coordinator, Virginia Department of Health,Center for Primary Care, Rural Health, and Health Policy, PO Box 2448, Richmond, VA 23218. *Phone:* 804-371-4090.

Nurse Practitioners/Nurse Midwife Program Scholarships. One-time award for nurse practitioner/nurse midwife students who are residents of Virginia. Must attend a full-time nursing program in Virginia. Recipient must agree to work in an underserved community in Virginia following graduation. Minimum 3.0 GPA required. *Academic/Career Areas:* Nursing. *Award:* Scholarship for use in any year; not renewable. *Award amount:* $5000. *Eligibility Requirements:* Applicant must be enrolled at a four-year institution or university; resident of Virginia and studying in Virginia. Applicant must have 3.0 GPA or higher. *Application Requirements:* Application, transcript. *Deadline:* June 30.

Contact Program Coordinator, Virginia Department of Health,Center for Primary Care, Rural Health, and Health Policy, PO Box 2448, Richmond, VA 23218. *Phone:* 804-371-4090.

Virginia Airport Operators Council Scholarship Award. One scholarship for a Virginia high school senior with a minimum 3.75 GPA who is planning a career in the aviation field. Must be accepted to an aviation program at an accredited institution. Submit letter of acceptance with application. One-time award of $2000. *Academic/Career Areas:* Aviation/Aerospace. *Award:* Scholarship for use in freshman year; not renewable. *Award amount:* $2000. *Number of awards:* 1. *Eligibility Requirements:* Applicant must be high school student; enrolled at a four-year, or technical institution or university and resident of Virginia. *Application Requirements:* Application, autobiography, essay, transcript. *Deadline:* February 17.

Contact Barbara Hutchinson, Scholarship Committee Chair, Virginia Airport Operators Council, 201 Bowen Loop, Charlottesville, VA 22911. *E-mail:* barbara@gocho.com. *Phone:* 904-973-8342. *Fax:* 904-974-7476.

WASHINGTON

Washington State Parent Teacher Association Scholarships Foundation. One-time grants for students who have graduated from a public high school in state of Washington, and who greatly need financial help to begin full-time post-secondary education. For entering freshmen only. *Award:* Grant for use in freshman year; not renewable. *Award amount:* $500–$1000. *Application Requirements:* Application, essay, financial need analysis, references, transcript. *Deadline:* March 1.

Contact Mr. Jim Carpenter, Executive Director, Washington State Parent Teacher Association Scholarships Foundation, 2003 65th Avenue West, Tacoma, WA 98466-6215. *Web site:* http://www.wastatepta.org.

WEST VIRGINIA

West Virginia Division of Veterans' Affairs War Orphans Education Program. Renewable waiver of tuition award for West Virginia residents who are children of deceased veterans. Parent must have died of service-connected disability. Must be ages 16-23. Minimum 2.6 GPA required. Must attend a state-supported West Virginia post-secondary institution. Deadline: July 1 and December 1. *Award:* Scholarship for use in any year; renewable. *Eligibility Requirements:* Applicant must be age 16-23; enrolled at a two-year, four-year, or technical institution or university; resident of West Virginia and studying in West Virginia. Applicant must have 2.5 GPA or higher. Applicant or parent must meet one or more of the following requirements: general military experience; retired from active duty; disabled or killed as a result of military service; prisoner of war; or missing in action. *Application Requirements:* Application.

Contact Ms. Susan Kerns, Secretary, West Virginia Division of Veterans' Affairs, 1321 Plaza East, Suite 101, Charleston, WV 25301-1400. *E-mail:* wvvetaff@aol.com. *Phone:* 304-668-3661. *Fax:* 304-668-3662.

West Virginia Higher Education Grant Program. For West Virginia residents attending an approved nonprofit degree-granting college or university in West Virginia or Pennsylvania. Must be enrolled full-time. Based on financial need and academic merit. Award covers tuition and fees. *Award:* Grant for use in freshman, sophomore, junior, or senior year; renewable. *Award amount:* $350–$2446. *Number of awards:* up to 10,072. *Eligibility Requirements:* Applicant must be enrolled at a two-year or four-year institution or university; resident of West Virginia and studying in Pennsylvania or West Virginia. *Application Requirements:* Application, financial need analysis, test scores, transcript. *Deadline:* March 1.

Contact Robert Long, Grant Program Coordinator, State College and University Systems of West Virginia, Central Office, 1018 Kanawha Boulevard East, Suite 700, Charleston, WV 25301. *E-mail:* long@scusco@wvnet.edu. *Phone:* 888-825-5707. *Fax:* 304-558-4622. *Web site:* http://www.scusco.wvnet.edu.

Underwood-Smith Teacher Scholarship Program. For West Virginia residents at West Virginia institutions, pursuing teaching careers. Must have a 3.25 GPA after completion of two years of course work. Must teach two years in West Virginia public schools for each year the award is received. *Academic/Career Areas:* Education. *Award:* Scholarship for use in junior, senior, or graduate years; renewable. *Award amount:* up to $5000. *Number of awards:* 65. *Eligibility Requirements:* Applicant must be enrolled at a four-year institution or university; resident of West Virginia and studying in West Virginia. Restricted to U.S. citizens. *Application Requirements:* Application, essay, references, test scores. *Deadline:* April 15.

Contact Michelle Wicks, Scholarship Coordinator, State College and University Systems of West Virginia, Central Office, 1018 Kanawha Boulevard East, Suite 700, Charleston, WV 25301. *E-mail:* wicks@scusco.wvnet.edu. *Phone:* 304-558-4618. *Fax:* 304-558-4622. *Web site:* http://www.scusco.wvnet.edu.

Tuition and Fee Waiver Program-West Virginia. Renewable award for students attending West Virginia public colleges or universities. Based on financial need and academic merit. Deadlines vary. Must contact specific college or university financial aid office for information and application. *Award:* Scholarship for use in any year; renewable. *Eligibility Requirements:* Applicant must be enrolled at a two-year or four-year institution or university and studying in West Virginia. Available to U.S. and non-U.S. citizens. *Application Requirements:* Application, financial need analysis, test scores, transcript.

Contact Michelle Wicks, Scholarship Coordinator, State College and University Systems of West Virginia, Central Office, 1018 Kanawha Boulevard East, Suite 700, Charleston, WV 25301. *E-mail:* wicks@scusco.wvnet.edu. *Phone:* 304-558-4618. *Fax:* 304-558-4622. *Web site:* http://www.scusco.wvnet.edu.

Health Sciences Scholarship Program. Award for students in final year of medical school or nurse practitioner or physician assistant programs. Must practice primary care for minimum of two years in underserved area of West Virginia. Available to students enrolled in West Virginia institutions, with preference given to West Virginia residents. One time award of $10,000. Deadline: October 31. Should be interested in primary care and rural practice. *Academic/Career Areas:* Health and Medical Sciences; Nursing. *Award:* Scholarship for use in graduate years; not renewable. *Award amount:* $10,000. *Number of awards:* 25. *Eligibility Requirements:* Applicant must be enrolled at a four-year institution or university; resident of West Virginia and studying in West Virginia. *Application Requirements:* Application, references. *Deadline:* October 31.

Contact Alicia Tyler, Program Coordinator, University System of West Virginia, 1018 Kanawha Boulevard East, Suite 1100, Charleston, WV 25301. *E-mail:* tyler@scusco.wvnet.edu. *Phone:* 304-558-0530. *Fax:* 304-558-0532. *Web site:* http://www.wvrhep.org.

WISCONSIN

Talent Incentive Program-Wisconsin. Assists residents of Wisconsin who are attending a nonprofit institution in Wisconsin and have substantial financial need. Must meet income criteria, be considered economically and educationally disadvantaged, be enrolled at least half-time, and be a first-time freshman. *Award:* Grant for use in freshman year; renewable. *Award amount:* $600–$1800. *Eligibility Requirements:* Applicant must be enrolled at a two-year, four-year, or technical institution or university; resident of Wisconsin and studying in Wisconsin. Available to U.S. and non-U.S. citizens. *Application Requirements:* Application, financial need analysis. *Deadline:* continuous.

Contact John Whitt, Wisconsin Higher Educational Aid Board, 131 West Wilson Street, Madison, WI 53707-7885. *E-mail:* john.whitt@heab.state.wi.us. *Phone:* 608-266-1665. *Fax:* 608-267-2808. *Web site:* http://heab.state.wi.us.

Wisconsin Higher Education Grants (WHEG). Grants for residents of Wisconsin attending a campus of the University of Wisconsin or Wisconsin Technical College. Must be enrolled at least half-time and show financial need. Renewable for up to five years. *Award:* Grant for use in freshman, sophomore, junior, or senior year; not renewable. *Award amount:* $250–$1800. *Eligibility Requirements:* Applicant must be enrolled at a two-year, four-year, or technical institution or university; resident of Wisconsin and studying in Wisconsin. Available to U.S. and non-U.S. citizens. *Application Requirements:* Financial need analysis. *Deadline:* continuous.

Contact Sandra Thomas, Program Coordinator, Wisconsin Higher Educational Aid Board, 131 West Wilson, Madison, WI 53707-7885. *E-mail:* sandy.thomas@heab.state.wi.us. *Phone:* 608-266-0888. *Fax:* 608-267-2808. *Web site:* http://heab.state.wi.us.

Minority Retention Grant-Wisconsin. Provides financial assistance to African-American, Native American, Hispanics, and former citizens of Laos, Vietnam, and Cambodia, for study in Wisconsin. Must be Wisconsin resident, enrolled at least half-time in a two- or four-year nonprofit college, and must show financial need. *Award:* Grant for use in sophomore, junior, senior, or graduate years; not renewable. *Award amount:* $250–$2500. *Eligibility Requirements:* Applicant must be Native American or Eskimo, Asian, African American, or Hispanic; enrolled at a two-year, four-year, or technical institution; resident of Wisconsin and studying in Wisconsin. Available to U.S. and non-U.S. citizens. *Application Requirements:* Application, financial need analysis. *Deadline:* continuous.

Contact Mary Lou Kuzdas, Program Coordinator, Wisconsin Higher Educational Aid Board, 131 West Wilson Street, Madison, WI 53707-7885. *E-mail:* mary.kuzdas@heab.state.wi.us. *Phone:* 608-267-2212. *Fax:* 608-267-2808. *Web site:* http://heab.state.wi.us.

Handicapped Student Grant-Wisconsin. One-time awards available to residents of Wisconsin who have severe or profound hearing or visual impairment. Must be enrolled at least half-time at a nonprofit institution. If the handicap prevents the student from attending a Wisconsin school, the award may be used out-of-state in a specialized college. *Award:* Grant for use in freshman, sophomore, junior, or senior year; not renewable. *Award amount:* $250–$1800. *Eligibility Requirements:* Applicant must be enrolled at a two-year, four-year, or technical institution or university and resident of Wisconsin. Applicant must be hearing impaired or visually impaired. Available to U.S. and non-U.S. citizens. *Application Requirements:* Application, financial need analysis. *Deadline:* continuous.

Contact Sandra Thomas, Wisconsin Higher Educational Aid Board, 131 West

Wilson Street, Madison, WI 53707-7885. *E-mail:* sandy.thomas@heab.state.wi.us. *Phone:* 608-266-0888. *Fax:* 608-267-2808. *Web site:* http://heab.state.wi.us.

Wisconsin Veterans Part-time Study Reimbursement Grant. Open only to Wisconsin veterans and dependents of deceased Wisconsin veterans. Renewable for continuing study. Contact office for more details. Application deadline is sixty days prior to course completion. Veterans may be reimbursed up to 65% of tuition and fees. *Award:* Grant for use in any year; renewable. *Award amount:* $300–$1100. *Eligibility Requirements:* Applicant must be resident of Wisconsin and studying in Wisconsin. Applicant or parent must meet one or more of the following requirements: general military experience; retired from active duty; disabled or killed as a result of military service; prisoner of war; or missing in action. *Application Requirements:* Application.

Contact Mr. Steve Olson, Public Relations Officer, Wisconsin Department of Veterans Affairs, PO Box 7843, Madison, WI 53707-7843. *Phone:* 608-266-1311.

Wisconsin Tuition Grant Program. Available to Wisconsin residents who are enrolled at least half-time in degree or certificate programs at independent, nonprofit colleges or universities in Wisconsin. Must show financial need. *Award:* Grant for use in freshman, sophomore, junior, or senior year; not renewable. *Award amount:* $250–$2172. *Eligibility Requirements:* Applicant must be enrolled at a four-year institution or university; resident of Wisconsin and studying in Wisconsin. Available to U.S. and non-U.S. citizens. *Application Requirements:* Application, financial need analysis.

Contact Mary Lou Kuzdas, Program Coordinator, Wisconsin Higher Educational Aid Board, 131 West Wilson Street, Madison, WI 53707-7885. *E-mail:* mary.kuzdas@heab.state.wi.us. *Phone:* 608-267-2212. *Fax:* 608-267-2808. *Web site:* http://heab.state.wi.us.

Minnesota-Wisconsin Reciprocity Program. Wisconsin residents may attend a Minnesota public institution and pay the reciprocity tuition charged by Minnesota institution. All programs are eligible except doctoral programs in medicine, dentistry, and veterinary medicine. *Award:* Scholarship for use in any year; renewable. *Eligibility Requirements:* Applicant must be enrolled at a two-year, four-year, or technical institution or university; resident of Wisconsin and studying in Minnesota. Restricted to U.S. citizens. *Application Requirements:* Application. *Deadline:* continuous.

Contact Cindy Lehrman, Wisconsin Higher Educational Aid Board, 131 West Wilson Street #902, Madison, WI 53707-7885. *E-mail:* cindy.lehrman@heab.state.wi.us. *Phone:* 608-267-2209. *Fax:* 608-267-2808. *Web site:* http://heab.state.wi.us.

Wisconsin Academic Excellence Scholarship. Renewable award for high school seniors with the highest GPA in graduating class. Must be a Wisconsin resident. Award covers tuition for up to four years. Must maintain 3.5 GPA for renewal. Scholarships of up to $2250 each. Must attend a nonprofit Wisconsin institution full-time. *Award:* Scholarship for use in freshman, sophomore, junior, or senior year; renewable. *Award amount:* up to $2250. *Eligibility Requirements:* Applicant must be high school student; enrolled at a two-year, four-year, or technical institution or university; resident of Wisconsin and studying in Wisconsin. Applicant must have 3.5 GPA or higher. Available to U.S. and non-U.S. citizens. *Application Requirements:* Transcript. *Deadline:* continuous.

Contact Alice Winters, Program Coordinator, Wisconsin Higher Educational Aid Board, 131 West Wilson Street, Madison, WI 53707-7885. *E-mail:* alice.winters@heab.state.wi.us. *Phone:* 608-267-2213. *Fax:* 608-267-2808. *Web site:* http://heab.state.wi.us.

Wisconsin Department of Veterans Affairs Retraining Grants. Renewable award for veterans, unmarried spouses of deceased veterans, or dependents of deceased veterans. Must be resident of Wisconsin and attend an institution in Wisconsin. Veteran must be recently unemployed and show financial need. Must enroll in a vocational or technical program that can reasonably be expected to lead to employment. Course work at four-year colleges or universities does not qualify as retraining. *Award:* Grant for use in any year; renewable. *Award amount:* up to $3000. *Eligibility Requirements:* Applicant must be enrolled at a technical institution; resident of Wisconsin and studying in Wisconsin. Applicant or parent must meet one or more of the following requirements: general military experience; retired from active duty; disabled or killed as a result of military service; prisoner of war; or missing in action. *Application Requirements:* Application, financial need analysis.

Contact Mr. Steve Olson, Public Relations Officer, Wisconsin Department of Veterans Affairs, PO Box 7843, Madison, WI 53707-7843. *Phone:* 608-266-1311.

Wisconsin National Guard Tuition Grant. Renewable award for active members of the Wisconsin National Guard who successfully complete a course of study at a qualifying school. Award covers full tuition, excluding fees, not to exceed undergraduate tuition charged by University of Wisconsin-Madison. *Award:* Grant for use in freshman, sophomore, junior, or senior year; renewable. *Award amount:* $1645. *Number of awards:* up to 4000. *Eligibility Requirements:* Applicant must be enrolled at a two-year, four-year, or technical institution or university. Restricted to U.S. citizens. Applicant must have served in the Air Force National Guard or Army National Guard. *Application Requirements:* Application. *Deadline:* continuous.

Contact Karen Behling, Tuition Grant Administrator, Department of Military Affairs, PO Box 14587, Madison, WI 53714-0587. *E-mail:* behlik@dma.state.wi.us. *Phone:* 608-242-3159. *Fax:* 308-242-3154.

Wisconsin Native American Student Grant. Grants for Wisconsin residents who are at least one-quarter American Indian. Must be attending a college or university within the state. Renewable for up to five years. Several grants of up to $1100. *Award:* Grant for use in any year; not renewable. *Award amount:* $250–$1100.

Eligibility Requirements: Applicant must be Native American or Eskimo; enrolled at a two-year, four-year, or technical institution or university; resident of Wisconsin and studying in Wisconsin. Available to U.S. and non-U.S. citizens. *Application Requirements:* Application, financial need analysis. *Deadline:* continuous.

Contact Sandra Thomas, Program Coordinator, Wisconsin Higher Educational Aid Board, 131 West Wilson, Madison, WI 53707-7885. *E-mail:* sandy.thomas@heab.state.wi.us. *Phone:* 608-266-0888. *Fax:* 608-267-2808. *Web site:* http://heab.state.wi.us.

WYOMING

Vietnam Veterans Award/Wyoming. Available to Wyoming residents who served in the armed forces between August 5, 1964, and May 7, 1975, and received a Vietnam service medal. Award is free tuition at the University of Wyoming or a state community college. *Award:* Scholarship for use in any year; renewable. *Eligibility Requirements:* Applicant must be enrolled at a two-year or four-year institution or university; resident of Wyoming and studying in Wyoming. Applicant must have general military experience. *Application Requirements:* Application. *Deadline:* continuous.

Contact JoelAnne Berrigan, Assistant Director, Scholarships, State of Wyoming/University of Wyoming, PO Box 3335, Laramie, WY 82071-3335. *E-mail:* finaid@uwyo.edu. *Phone:* 307-766-2117. *Fax:* 307-766-3800.

Wyoming State Student Incentive Grant. Award for Wyoming residents attending participating colleges and universities within the state. Based on financial need. Renewable up to four years. For undergraduate study. *Award:* Grant for use in freshman, sophomore, junior, or senior year; renewable. *Award amount:* up to $2000. *Eligibility Requirements:* Applicant must be enrolled at a two-year or four-year institution or university; resident of Wyoming and studying in Wyoming. *Application Requirements:* Application, financial need analysis. *Deadline:* March 1.

Contact JoelAnne Berrigan, Assistant Director, Scholarships, State of Wyoming/University of Wyoming, PO Box 3335, Laramie, WY 82071-3335. *E-mail:* finaid@uwyo.edu. *Phone:* 307-766-2117. *Fax:* 307-766-3800.

Superior Student in Education Scholarship-Wyoming. Available to Wyoming high school graduates who have demonstrated high academic achievement and plan to teach in Wyoming public schools. Award is for tuition at Wyoming institutions. Must maintain 3.0 GPA. *Academic/Career Areas:* Education. *Award:* Scholarship for use in freshman, sophomore, junior, or senior year; renewable. *Number of awards:* 16–80. *Eligibility Requirements:* Applicant must be enrolled at a two-year or four-year institution or university; resident of Wyoming; studying in Wyoming and must have an interest in leadership. Applicant must have 3.0 GPA or higher. *Application Requirements:* Application, references, test scores, transcript. *Deadline:* October 1.

Contact JoelAnne Berrigan, Assistant Director, Scholarships, State of Wyoming/University of Wyoming, PO Box 3335, Laramie, WY 82071-3335. *Phone:* 307-766-2117. *Fax:* 307-766-3800.

SECTION 

College Cost and Financial Aid Metrics

"It's important to remember that an investment in higher education is an investment for a lifetime. A wise choice will return far more than just the dollar value of the initial investment."

Michael Steidel
Director of Admissions
Carnegie Mellon University

The sticker-price cost of a private college education falls in the range of $7000 to $32,000 annually for tuition, room, and board. On average, the sticker price of public college education is about 38 percent of the private college cost. Your actual cost, however, depends upon your financial aid award, and private colleges often give more generous financial aid packages than public colleges. Regardless of your family's income level or your academic record, you are likely to be eligible for some form of financial aid. That's why it's important to look beyond the "sticker price" of attending the college of your choice and apply for financial aid before ruling out a college based on cost.

Your Expected Family Contribution is determined by a formulation of need that is based on your family's income and assets. Whether you demonstrate 100 percent financial need or hardly any, you can look to the financial aid office of the college that has accepted you to work with you to create a financial aid package that addresses your unique situation and makes your college education an investment that you can afford.

Whether it's in the form of scholarships, awards, grants, loans, or student employment, most colleges endeavor to provide financial assistance to admitted freshmen that will enable these students to enroll at their institution. The financial aid office in any college will guide you to the financial aid options available from a variety of sources—state and federal government programs, friends of the college, alumni, and the college itself. The actual amount and distribution of components of a financial aid package are determined from the evaluation of your personal financial situation and are also influenced by the unique financial resources, policies, and practices of each institution. Financial aid packages vary significantly from school to school.

To help shed some light on the typical patterns of financial aid by colleges, we have prepared the following table. This table can help you to better understand financial aid practices in general, form realistic expectations about the amounts of aid that might be provided by specific colleges or universities, and prepare for meaningful discussions with the financial aid officers at colleges you are considering. The data appearing in the table have been supplied by the schools themselves and are also shown in the individual college profiles.

Tuition and fees are based on the total of full-time tuition and mandatory fees for the 2000–2001 academic year (or estimated 2000–2001) or for the 1999–2000 academic year if 2000–2001 figures were not available. More information about these costs, as well as the costs of room and board and the year for which they are current, can be found in the individual college profiles. For institutions that have two or more tuition rates for different categories of students or types of programs, the lowest rate is used in figuring the cost.

The colleges are listed alphabetically by state. An "NR" in any individual column indicates that the applicable data element was "Not Reported."

The table is divided into seven columns of information for each college:

A. Institutional Control: whether the school is independent (ind.), including independent, independent–religious, and proprietary, or public, including federal, state, commonwealth, territory, county, district, city, state, local and state-related.

B. Tuition and fees: based on the total of full-time tuition and mandatory fees.

C. Room and board: the costs of room and board. If a school has room and board costs that vary according to the type of accommodation and meal plan, either the lowest figures are represented or the figures are for the most common room arrangement and a full meal plan. If a school has only housing arrangements, a dagger appears to the right of the number. An *"NA"* will appear in this column if no college-owned or -operated housing facilities are offered at all.

D. Percent of freshmen receiving need-based awards: calculated by dividing the number of freshman students determined to have need who received need-based gift aid by the number of full-time freshmen.

E. Percent of freshmen whose need was fully met: calculated by dividing the number of freshman students whose financial need was fully met by the number of full-time freshmen.

F. Average financial aid package for freshmen: the average dollar amount from all sources, including *gift aid* (scholarships and grants) and *self-help* (jobs and loans), awarded to aided freshmen. Note that this aid package may exceed tuition and fees if the average aid package included coverage of room and board expenses.

G. Average net cost after aid: average aid package subtracted from published costs (tuition, fees, room, and board) to produce what the average student will have to pay.

H. 1999 graduate's average indebtedness: average per-student indebtedness of graduating seniors.

Because personal situations vary widely, it is very important to note that an individual's aid package can be quite different from the averages. Moreover, the data shown for each school can fluctuate widely from year to year, depending on the number of applicants, the amount of need to be met, and the financial resources and policies of the college. Our intent in presenting this table is to provide you with useful facts and figures that can serve as general guidelines in your pursuit of financial aid. We caution you to use the data only as a jumping-off point for further investigation and analysis, not as a means to rank or select colleges.

After you have narrowed down the colleges in which you are interested based on academic and personal criteria, we recommend that you carefully study this table. From it, you can develop a list of questions for financial aid officers at the colleges you are seriously considering attending. Here are just a few questions you might want to ask:

- What specifically are the types and sources of the aid provided to freshmen at this school?
- What factors does this college consider in determining whether a financial aid applicant is qualified for its need-based aid programs?
- How does the college determine the combination of types of aid that make up an individual's package?
- How are non-need-based awards treated: as a part of the aid package or as a part of the parental/family contribution?
- Does this school "guarantee" financial aid and, if so, how is its policy implemented? Guaranteed aid means that by policy, 100 percent of need is met for all students judged to have need. Implementation determines *how* need is met and varies widely from school to school. For example, grade point average may determine the proportioning of scholarship, loan, and work-study aid. Rules for freshmen may be different from those for upperclass students.
- To what degree is the admission process "need-blind"? Need-blindness means that admission decisions are made without regard to the student's need for financial aid.
- What are the norms and practices for upperclass students? Our table presents information on *freshman* financial aid only; however, the financial aid office should be able and willing to provide you with comparable figures for upperclass students. A college might offer a wonderful package for the freshman year, then leave you mostly on your own to fund the remaining three years. Or the school may provide a higher proportion of scholarship money for freshmen, then rebalance its aid packages to contain more self-help aid (loans and work-study) in upperclass years. There is an assumption that, all other factors being equal, students who have settled into the pattern of college time management can handle more work-study hours than freshmen. Grade point average, tuition increases, changes in parental financial circumstances, and other factors may also affect the redistribution.

College Cost and Financial Aid Metrics

	Institutional Control ind.=independent; pub.=public	Tuition and fees	Room and board	Percent of freshmen receiving aid whose awards were need-based scholarships/grants	Percent of freshmen receiving aid whose need was fully met	Average financial aid package for freshmen	Average net cost after aid	1998 graduate's average indebtedness
Alabama								
Alabama Agricultural and Mechanical University	pub.	$2732	$2678	NR	NR	$5,244	$166	$17,021
Alabama State University	pub.	$2520	$3700	73%	28%	$5,750	$470	NR
Athens State University	pub.	$2400	$840†	NR	NR	NR	NR	NR
Auburn University	pub.	$2955	NR	38%	NR	$4,449	—	$17,236
Auburn University Montgomery	pub.	$2577	$2010†	NR	NR	NR	NR	NR
Birmingham-Southern College	ind.	$15,498	$5460	59%	95%	$9,598	$11,360	$13,226
Concordia College	ind.	$5642	$2900	15%	2%	$4,356	$4,186	NR
Faulkner University	ind.	$7500	$3990	71%	6%	$4,600	$6,890	$18,000
Huntingdon College	ind.	$11,910	$5740	95%	35%	$9,615	$8,035	$15,262
International Bible College	ind.	$5492	$1200†	NR	NR	NR	NR	NR
Jacksonville State University	pub.	$2440	$3080	NR	NR	NR	NR	$12,000
Judson College	ind.	$7640	$4600	100%	29%	$9,008	$3,232	$12,085
Miles College	ind.	$4630	$2940	NR	NR	NR	NR	NR
Oakwood College	ind.	$9058	$5292	NR	NR	NR	NR	NR
Samford University	ind.	$10,300	$4560	98%	32%	$8,403	$6,457	$14,228
Southeastern Bible College	ind.	$5740	$3240	98%	12%	$5,125	$3,855	$20,000
Southern Christian University	ind.	$8830	NA	100%	NR	$2,700	$6,130	$16,500
Spring Hill College	ind.	$16,254	$5768	100%	22%	$14,738	$7,284	NR
Stillman College	ind.	$5880	$3764	NR	NR	NR	NR	NR
Talladega College	ind.	$5873	$2964	89%	7%	NR	NR	NR
Troy State University	pub.	$2900	$3854	79%	NR	$2,056	$4,698	$17,125
Troy State University Dothan	pub.	$2832	NA	100%	NR	NR	NR	NR
Troy State University Montgomery	pub.	$2460	NA	100%	61%	NR	NR	NR
Tuskegee University	ind.	$9690	$5100	79%	40%	$11,832	$2,958	$17,125
The University of Alabama	pub.	$2872	$4154	53%	39%	$3,590	$3,436	$18,994
The University of Alabama at Birmingham	pub.	$3240	$2438†	65%	13%	NR	NR	$15,459
The University of Alabama in Huntsville	pub.	$3112	$3780	49%	17%	$4,599	$2,293	$15,146
University of Mobile	ind.	$7830	$4280	91%	NR	$7,550	$4,560	$14,000
University of Montevallo	pub.	$3290	$3354	51%	29%	$4,608	$2,036	$14,131
University of North Alabama	pub.	$2512	$3672	67%	28%	NR	NR	$16,466
University of South Alabama	pub.	$2670	$3114	56%	2%	$4,046	$1,738	NR
The University of West Alabama	pub.	$2688	$2740	NR	NR	NR	NR	NR
Virginia College at Birmingham	ind.	$7000	NA	NR	NR	NR	NR	NR
Alaska								
Alaska Bible College	ind.	$4750	$3900	38%	100%	NR	NR	NR
Sheldon Jackson College	ind.	$7250	NR	NR	NR	NR	NR	NR
University of Alaska Fairbanks	pub.	$3412	$4150	80%	14%	NR	NR	NR
Arizona								
Arizona State University	pub.	$2261	$5010	87%	22%	$6,135	$1,136	$17,385
Arizona State University East	pub.	$2211	$2440†	NR	NR	NR	NR	NR
Arizona State University West	pub.	$2191	NA	NR	NR	NR	NR	NR
DeVry Institute of Technology	ind.	$7778	NA	44%	4%	$6,204	$1,574	$13,147
Embry-Riddle Aeronautical University	ind.	$11,020	$4426	73%	NR	$9,463	$5,983	$17,125

*NA = not applicable; NR = not reported; * = includes room and board; † = room only.*

College Cost and Financial Aid Metrics

	Institutional Control ind.=independent; pub.=public	Tuition and fees	Room and board	Percent of freshmen receiving aid whose awards were need-based scholarships/grants	Percent of freshmen receiving aid whose need was fully met	Average financial aid package for freshmen	Average net cost after aid	1998 graduate's average indebtedness
Grand Canyon University	ind.	$8380	$4246	44%	11%	$7,987	$4,639	NR
International Baptist College	ind.	$4350	$3000	NR	NR	NR	NR	NR
Northern Arizona University	pub.	$2262	$3682	58%	28%	$5,987	—	$16,396
Prescott College	ind.	$13,450	NA	27%	NR	$3,996	$9,454	$16,787
Southwestern College	ind.	$7640	$2940	NR	NR	NR	NR	$10,000
The University of Arizona	pub.	$2264	$5548	NR	NR	$7,580	$232	$17,143
Arkansas								
Arkansas Baptist College	ind.	$2200	$3000	NR	NR	NR	NR	NR
Arkansas State University	pub.	$2972	$3020	97%	88%	$2,400	$3,592	$12,500
Arkansas Tech University	pub.	$2462	$3222	79%	30%	$2,958	$2,726	$15,849
Harding University	ind.	$8472	$4250	90%	75%	$7,832	$4,890	$22,420
Henderson State University	pub.	$2488	$2976	64%	26%	$3,722	$1,742	$13,000
Hendrix College	ind.	$11,615	$4415	65%	59%	$12,598	$3,432	NR
John Brown University	ind.	$11,492	$4478	96%	22%	$10,060	$5,910	$12,260
Lyon College	ind.	$10,622	$4703	100%	60%	$11,526	$3,799	$13,610
Ouachita Baptist University	ind.	$9010	$3450	99%	25%	$10,152	$2,308	$13,865
Philander Smith College	ind.	$3808	$2746	NR	NR	NR	NR	NR
Southern Arkansas University–Magnolia	pub.	$2232	$2800	94%	96%	$4,917	$115	$9259
University of Arkansas	pub.	$3660	$4358	80%	49%	$7,861	$157	$14,910
University of Arkansas at Little Rock	pub.	$2820	$2500†	NR	NR	NR	NR	NR
University of Arkansas at Monticello	pub.	$2530	$2580	NR	NR	NR	NR	$13,599
University of Arkansas at Pine Bluff	pub.	$2620	$3940	NR	NR	NR	NR	NR
University of Central Arkansas	pub.	$3402	$3290	NR	NR	NR	NR	NR
University of the Ozarks	ind.	$8530	$3924	100%	34%	$9,252	$3,202	$15,000
Williams Baptist College	ind.	$6270	$3200	100%	NR	NR	NR	$15,450
California								
Academy of Art College	ind.	$10,860	$6000†	50%	9%	$2,968	$13,892	$26,000
American InterContinental University	ind.	$11,850	$4245†	NR	NR	NR	NR	NR
Antioch Southern California/Santa Barbara	ind.	$9750	NA	NR	NR	NR	NR	NR
Art Center College of Design	ind.	$18,890	NA	72%	NR	$11,900	$6,990	NR
Art Institute of Southern California	ind.	$13,600	NA	NR	NR	NR	NR	NR
Art Institutes International at San Francisco	ind.	$14,160	NA	NR	NR	NR	NR	NR
Azusa Pacific University	ind.	$14,727	$4880	97%	19%	$8,185	$11,422	NR
Bethany College of the Assemblies of God	ind.	$10,280	$4580	NR	NR	NR	NR	$13,664
Biola University	ind.	$15,914	$5139	75%	18%	$12,324	$8,729	$19,521
Brooks Institute of Photography	ind.	$16,260	NA	NR	NR	$7,000	$9,260	NR
California Baptist University	ind.	$10,682	$4966	60%	90%	$8,600	$7,048	$15,800
California College of Arts and Crafts	ind.	$18,368	$5858	84%	NR	$23,301	$925	$22,500
California Institute of Integral Studies	ind.	$14,010	NR	NR	NR	NR	—	$15,000
California Institute of Technology	ind.	$19,959	$6180	89%	100%	$17,842	$8,297	$11,573
California Institute of the Arts	ind.	$19,950	$5150	87%	2%	$15,072	$10,028	$24,873
California Lutheran University	ind.	$16,200	$6240	95%	NR	$13,982	$8,458	$14,500
California Maritime Academy	pub.	$3206	$5750	73%	22%	$7,532	$1,424	$10,860
California Polytechnic State University, San Luis Obispo	pub.	$2210	$5553	92%	32%	$6,234	$1,529	$17,340

*NA = not applicable; NR = not reported; * = includes room and board; † = room only.*

College Cost and Financial Aid Metrics

	Institutional Control ind.=independent; pub.=public	Tuition and fees	Room and board	Percent of freshmen receiving aid whose awards were need-based scholarships/grants	Percent of freshmen receiving aid whose need was fully met	Average financial aid package for freshmen	Average net cost after aid	1998 graduate's average indebtedness
California State Polytechnic University, Pomona	pub.	$1875	$6278	83%	38%	$5,642	$2,511	$12,248
California State University, Bakersfield	pub.	$1875	$4345	89%	13%	$5,211	$1,009	$8911
California State University, Chico	pub.	$1994	$5860	NR	NR	NR	NR	NR
California State University, Dominguez Hills	pub.	$1730	$3436†	94%	49%	$5,860	—	$12,936
California State University, Fresno	pub.	$1746	$5816	81%	56%	$5,043	$2,519	$13,557
California State University, Fullerton	pub.	$1809	$3672†	88%	4%	$4,692	$789	$11,554
California State University, Hayward	pub.	$1683	$3100†	91%	9%	$4,624	$159	NR
California State University, Long Beach	pub.	$9082	$5400	88%	65%	$5,525	$8,957	NR
California State University, Los Angeles	pub.	$1722	$2979†	96%	NR	$6,114	—	NR
California State University, Northridge	pub.	$1814	$5865	89%	25%	$7,131	$548	$12,147
California State University, Sacramento	pub.	$1867	$5510	89%	16%	$6,382	$995	$15,529
California State University, San Marcos	pub.	$1694	$3924†	NR	NR	NR	NR	$11,293
California State University, Stanislaus	pub.	$1877	$6480	90%	32%	$5,236	$3,121	$13,228
Chapman University	ind.	$20,994	$7620	98%	26%	$17,340	$11,274	$18,893
Charles R. Drew University of Medicine and Science	ind.	$8400	NA	NR	NR	NR	NR	NR
Christian Heritage College	ind.	$10,840	$4725	NR	NR	NR	NR	NR
Claremont McKenna College	ind.	$20,760	$7060	99%	100%	$19,386	$8,434	$16,266
Cogswell Polytechnical College	ind.	$8420	NR	100%	NR	$3,448	—	$22,345
Columbia College–Hollywood	ind.	$10,725	NA	NR	NR	NR	NR	NR
Concordia University	ind.	$15,700	$5290	90%	47%	$8,500	$12,490	$16,000
Design Institute of San Diego	ind.	$10,200	NA	NR	NR	NR	NR	NR
DeVry Institute of Technology	ind.	$8776	NA	47%	5%	$7,892	$884	$10,344
DeVry Institute of Technology	ind.	$7778	NA	62%	7%	NR	NR	$15,493
DeVry Institute of Technology	ind.	$7778	NA	62%	8%	NR	NR	$16,431
DeVry Institute of Technology	ind.	$7778	NR	63%	10%	$7,347	—	$6125
Dominican University of California	ind.	$16,844	$7520	82%	24%	$17,018	$7,346	NR
Fresno Pacific University	ind.	$14,248	$4420	77%	46%	$16,464	$2,204	NR
Golden Gate University	ind.	$8592	NA	NR	NR	NR	NR	NR
Harvey Mudd College	ind.	$22,083	$8017	98%	100%	$17,939	$12,161	$17,544
Holy Names College	ind.	$15,070	$6400	94%	3%	$16,000	$5,470	$16,324
Hope International University	ind.	$11,220	$4500	NR	NR	NR	NR	NR
Humboldt State University	pub.	$1861	$5845	86%	3%	$6,038	$1,668	$14,000
Humphreys College	ind.	$6804	$2075†	NR	NR	NR	NR	NR
John F. Kennedy University	ind.	$10,251	NA	NR	NR	NR	NR	NR
LIFE Bible College	ind.	$5625	$3100	81%	6%	$4,076	$4,649	$5218
Loma Linda University	ind.	$14,220	$1983†	NR	NR	NR	NR	NR
Loyola Marymount University	ind.	$19,225	$7608	77%	28%	$18,484	$8,349	$18,426
The Master's College and Seminary	ind.	$13,400	$5300	95%	17%	$11,769	$6,931	$14,204
Menlo College	ind.	$16,800	$6800	100%	22%	$12,937	$10,663	NR
Mills College	ind.	$17,852	$7296	97%	57%	$19,395	$5,753	$17,083
Monterey Institute of International Studies	ind.	$19,500	NA	NR	NR	NR	NR	NR
Mount St. Mary's College	ind.	$17,328	$6634	NR	NR	NR	NR	NR
Musicians Institute	ind.	$12,000	NA	NR	NR	NR	NR	NR
The National Hispanic University	ind.	$3100	NA	NR	NR	NR	NR	NR
National University	ind.	$7485	NA	NR	NR	NR	NR	NR

*NA = not applicable; NR = not reported; * = includes room and board; † = room only.*

College Cost and Financial Aid Metrics

	Institutional Control ind.=independent; pub.=public	Tuition and fees	Room and board	Percent of freshmen receiving aid whose awards were need-based scholarships/grants	Percent of freshmen receiving aid whose need was fully met	Average financial aid package for freshmen	Average net cost after aid	1998 graduate's average indebtedness
Newschool of Architecture	ind.	$15,909	$6000	NR	NR	NR	NR	NR
Occidental College	ind.	$23,850	$6880	89%	100%	$23,507	$7,223	$14,049
Otis College of Art and Design	ind.	$19,294	NA	93%	NR	$6,800	$12,494	NR
Pacific Oaks College	ind.	$12,060	NA	NR	NR	NR	NR	$20,000
Pacific Union College	ind.	$14,475	$4425	100%	25%	$11,840	$7,060	$11,870
Pepperdine University	ind.	$23,070	$7010	NR	NR	NR	NR	NR
Pitzer College	ind.	$24,096	$6290	98%	100%	$21,942	$8,444	$20,530
Point Loma Nazarene University	ind.	$13,626	$5480	78%	24%	$9,860	$9,246	NR
Pomona College	ind.	$23,170	$7750	100%	100%	$21,310	$9,610	$15,800
St. John's Seminary College	ind.	$7555	$4000	NR	NR	NR	NR	NR
Saint Mary's College of California	ind.	$17,475	$7370	92%	51%	$16,133	$8,712	$16,500
Samuel Merritt College	ind.	$16,425	$3510†	NR	NR	NR	NR	NR
San Diego State University	pub.	$9156	$7110	80%	27%	$4,800	$11,466	$13,600
San Francisco Art Institute	ind.	$19,300	NA	100%	NR	$18,578	$722	NR
San Francisco Conservatory of Music	ind.	$18,670	NA	100%	47%	$12,922	$5,748	$17,582
San Francisco State University	pub.	$1826	$7380	60%	16%	$5,601	$3,605	$12,000
San Jose State University	pub.	$1939	$6248	85%	26%	$6,714	$1,473	$9981
Santa Clara University	ind.	$19,311	$7644	NR	NR	NR	NR	NR
Scripps College	ind.	$21,130	$7870	97%	100%	$20,177	$8,823	$18,278
Shasta Bible College	ind.	$4830	$1350†	NR	NR	NR	NR	NR
Simpson College and Graduate School	ind.	$10,540	$4680	92%	11%	$10,239	$4,981	NR
Sonoma State University	pub.	$7878	$6217	68%	89%	$6,589	$7,506	NR
Stanford University	ind.	$23,058	$7881	93%	99%	$20,920	$10,019	$15,892
Thomas Aquinas College	ind.	$14,900	$4300	90%	100%	$12,485	$6,715	$12,675
United States International University	ind.	$13,611	$5775	94%	82%	$12,482	$6,904	$16,210
University of California, Berkeley	pub.	$4046	$8266	78%	82%	$11,546	$766	NR
University of California, Davis	pub.	$4214	$7012	77%	35%	$10,412	$814	NR
University of California, Irvine	pub.	$3870	$6407	75%	98%	$9,244	$1,033	$13,199
University of California, Los Angeles	pub.	$3698	$7692	67%	79%	$8,409	$2,981	$16,187
University of California, Riverside	pub.	$4126	$6579	90%	45%	$8,927	$1,778	NR
University of California, San Diego	pub.	$3849	$7134	89%	99%	$9,094	$1,889	$11,000
University of California, Santa Barbara	pub.	$3844	$7156	79%	52%	$9,446	$1,554	NR
University of California, Santa Cruz	pub.	$4377	$7337	73%	75%	$9,539	$2,175	$13,569
University of La Verne	ind.	$16,860	NR	87%	16%	$14,912	—	NR
University of Redlands	ind.	$19,811	$7368	99%	46%	$19,271	$7,908	$22,072
University of San Diego	ind.	$19,128	$8440	93%	49%	$15,346	$12,222	$23,100
University of San Francisco	ind.	$19,060	$8242	82%	19%	$15,693	$11,609	$22,238
University of Southern California	ind.	$22,636	$7282	94%	100%	$22,354	$7,564	$14,722
University of the Pacific	ind.	$20,725	$6378	97%	42%	$20,141	$6,962	NR
University of West Los Angeles	ind.	$6030	NA	NR	NR	NR	NR	NR
Vanguard University of Southern California	ind.	$13,778	$5060	NR	NR	NR	NR	NR
Westmont College	ind.	$20,965	$7068	97%	23%	$13,798	$14,235	$18,319
Whittier College	ind.	$20,128	$6736	93%	72%	$17,240	$9,624	NR
Woodbury University	ind.	$16,710	$5990	85%	19%	$14,150	$8,550	NR

*NA = not applicable; NR = not reported; * = includes room and board; † = room only.*

College Cost and Financial Aid Metrics

	Institutional Control ind.=independent; pub.=public	Tuition and fees	Room and board	Percent of freshmen receiving aid whose awards were need-based scholarships/grants	Percent of freshmen receiving aid whose need was fully met	Average financial aid package for freshmen	Average net cost after aid	1998 graduate's average indebtedness
Colorado								
Adams State College	pub.	$2092	$5080	NR	NR	NR	NR	NR
The Art Institute of Colorado	ind.	$12,480	$6000	NR	NR	NR	NR	$30,000
Colorado Christian University	ind.	$10,790	$5160	92%	18%	$8,424	$7,526	NR
The Colorado College	ind.	$21,822	$5568	92%	39%	$18,894	$8,496	$13,418
Colorado School of Mines	pub.	$5211	$4920	67%	100%	$10,195	—	$17,500
Colorado State University	pub.	$3062	$5200	79%	37%	$5,450	$2,812	$14,253
Colorado Technical University	ind.	$6108	NA	29%	24%	$2,160	$3,948	NR
Colorado Technical University Denver Campus	ind.	$6108	NA	NR	NR	NR	$6,108	$29,000
Fort Lewis College	pub.	$2219	$4452	70%	37%	$4,685	$1,986	$13,432
Jones International University	ind.	$3750	NA	NR	NR	NR	NR	NR
Mesa State College	pub.	$2123	$5048	60%	75%	$6,007	$1,164	$13,600
Metropolitan State College of Denver	pub.	$2112	NA	NR	NR	$5,924	—	$23,000
Naropa University	ind.	$12,867	NR	65%	20%	NR	NR	$19,816
Nazarene Bible College	ind.	$5760	NA	88%	NR	NR	NR	NR
Regis University	ind.	$16,670	$6700	94%	28%	$12,010	$11,360	$20,000
Rocky Mountain College of Art & Design	ind.	$15,510	NA	56%	5%	$3,501	$12,009	NR
University of Colorado at Boulder	pub.	$3118	$5202	69%	19%	$6,826	$1,494	$16,422
University of Colorado at Colorado Springs	pub.	$3191	$5683	78%	19%	$5,086	$3,788	$15,067
University of Colorado at Denver	pub.	$2418	NA	65%	18%	$3,514	—	$15,275
University of Northern Colorado	pub.	$2754	$4796	66%	13%	$4,883	$2,667	NR
University of Southern Colorado	pub.	$2307	$4768	NR	NR	$5,268	$1,807	NR
Western State College of Colorado	pub.	$2208	$4890	85%	30%	$6,625	$473	$12,500
Westwood College of Technology	ind.	$8919	NA	NR	NR	NR	NR	NR
Connecticut								
Albertus Magnus College	ind.	$14,343	$6512	53%	47%	$10,000	$10,855	$15,625
Central Connecticut State University	pub.	$3772	$5652	47%	50%	$7,484	$1,940	$18,600
Connecticut College	ind.	$30,595*	NR	93%	100%	$20,158	—	$17,280
Eastern Connecticut State University	pub.	$4146	$5850	77%	75%	$4,950	$5,046	$10,200
Fairfield University	ind.	$20,435	$7380	85%	22%	$14,013	$13,802	$18,765
Holy Apostles College and Seminary	ind.	$5630	$5930	NR	NR	NR	$11,560	NR
Lyme Academy of Fine Arts	ind.	$10,550	NA	NR	NR	NR	NR	NR
Paier College of Art, Inc.	ind.	$10,835	NA	95%	NR	$4,892	$5,943	$20,044
Quinnipiac University	ind.	$17,780	$8175	95%	9%	$10,908	$15,047	$13,177
Sacred Heart University	ind.	$14,720	$7200	95%	32%	$10,595	$11,325	$16,880
Saint Joseph College	ind.	$16,150	$6610	100%	35%	$14,082	$8,678	$7541
Southern Connecticut State University	pub.	$3773	$5825	95%	100%	$4,525	$5,073	NR
Teikyo Post University	ind.	$13,400	$5900	60%	38%	$10,572	$8,728	NR
Trinity College	ind.	$24,490	$6890	95%	100%	$21,199	$10,181	$13,761
University of Bridgeport	ind.	$14,641	$6970	NR	NR	$17,527	$4,084	NR
University of Connecticut	pub.	$5404	$5694	66%	28%	$6,714	$4,384	$16,598
University of Hartford	ind.	$19,696	$7840	96%	NR	$13,814	$13,722	NR
University of New Haven	ind.	$14,550	$6560	90%	25%	$12,314	$8,796	$15,500
Wesleyan University	ind.	$25,120	$6510	88%	100%	$20,775	$10,855	$24,430

*NA = not applicable; NR = not reported; * = includes room and board; † = room only.*

College Cost and Financial Aid Metrics

	Institutional Control ind.=independent; pub.=public	Tuition and fees	Room and board	Percent of freshmen receiving aid whose awards were need-based scholarships/grants	Percent of freshmen receiving aid whose need was fully met	Average financial aid package for freshmen	Average net cost after aid	1998 graduate's average indebtedness
Western Connecticut State University	pub.	$3758	$5434	81%	2%	$4,493	$4,699	NR
Yale University	ind.	$24,500	$7440	NR	NR	NR	NR	NR
Delaware								
Delaware State University	pub.	$3256	$4880	70%	37%	$5,012	$3,124	NR
Goldey-Beacom College	ind.	$9398	$3490†	NR	NR	NR	NR	NR
University of Delaware	pub.	$4858	$5132	80%	54%	$7,500	$2,490	$14,000
Wesley College	ind.	$11,919	$5018	NR	NR	NR	NR	NR
District of Columbia								
American University	ind.	$21,399	$8392	88%	18%	$18,480	$11,311	NR
The Catholic University of America	ind.	$18,972	$7765	97%	76%	$16,105	$10,632	NR
The Corcoran College of Art and Design	ind.	$14,140	NA	74%	NR	$6,789	$7,351	NR
Gallaudet University	ind.	$7180	$7130	NR	NR	NR	NR	NR
Georgetown University	ind.	$23,295	$8693	96%	100%	$18,895	$13,093	$19,016
The George Washington University	ind.	$23,375	$8210	99%	76%	$21,700	$9,885	$18,953
Southeastern University	ind.	$7500	NA	68%	81%	$5,025	$2,475	NR
Strayer University	ind.	$7695	NA	NR	NR	NR	NR	NR
Trinity College	ind.	$14,025	$6500	95%	7%	$14,654	$5,871	NR
University of the District of Columbia	pub.	$2070	NA	83%	NR	NR	NR	$19,000
Florida								
Barry University	ind.	$15,530	$6220	89%	14%	$16,883	$4,867	$17,469
Bethune-Cookman College	ind.	$8988	$5534	99%	15%	$9,465	$5,057	$17,900
Carlos Albizu University	ind.	$6834	NA	NR	NR	NR	$6,834	NR
Clearwater Christian College	ind.	$8500	$3698	34%	5%	$6,621	$5,577	$13,051
Eckerd College	ind.	$18,220	$4960	100%	85%	$15,500	$7,680	$17,500
Edward Waters College	ind.	$6600	$4514	NR	NR	NR	NR	NR
Embry-Riddle Aeronautical University	ind.	$10,700	$5440	76%	NR	$10,723	$5,417	$17,125
Embry-Riddle Aeronautical University, Extended Campus	ind.	$1860	NA	NR	NR	NR	NR	$17,125
Flagler College	ind.	$6130	$3800	64%	15%	$6,271	$3,659	$13,763
Florida Agricultural and Mechanical University	pub.	$2187	$3942	NR	NR	NR	NR	NR
Florida Atlantic University	pub.	$2253	$4774	88%	15%	$5,311	$1,716	NR
Florida Baptist Theological College	ind.	$3960	$3150	NR	47%	$2,000	$5,110	$15,000
Florida College	ind.	$7250	$5540	NR	NR	NR	NR	NR
Florida Gulf Coast University	pub.	$2319	$5326	82%	27%	$4,833	$2,812	NR
Florida Institute of Technology	ind.	$17,300	$5270	100%	20%	$16,621	$5,949	$24,265
Florida International University	pub.	$2326	$5206	87%	9%	NR	NR	NR
Florida Memorial College	ind.	$7232	$3236	75%	60%	$11,000	—	$10,000
Florida Metropolitan University–Fort Lauderdale College	ind.	$6555	NA	NR	100%	$7,230	—	$21,085
Florida Metropolitan University–Orlando College, Melbourne	ind.	$6555	NA	NR	NR	NR	NR	NR
Florida Metropolitan University–Orlando College, North	ind.	$6555	NA	NR	NR	NR	NR	NR
Florida Metropolitan University–Orlando College, South	ind.	$4395	NA	NR	NR	NR	NR	NR
Florida Metropolitan University–Tampa College	ind.	$6879	NA	30%	96%	$6,000	$879	$12,000
Florida Metropolitan University–Tampa College, Brandon	ind.	$6555	NA	NR	NR	NR	NR	NR
Florida Metropolitan University–Tampa College, Lakeland	ind.	$6555	NA	NR	NR	NR	NR	NR
Florida Southern College	ind.	$12,950	$5550	99%	32%	$12,095	$6,405	$12,678

*NA = not applicable; NR = not reported; * = includes room and board; † = room only.*

College Cost and Financial Aid Metrics

	Institutional Control ind.=independent; pub.=public	Tuition and fees	Room and board	Percent of freshmen receiving aid whose awards were need-based scholarships/grants	Percent of freshmen receiving aid whose need was fully met	Average financial aid package for freshmen	Average net cost after aid	1998 graduate's average indebtedness
Florida State University	pub.	$2196	$4952	89%	5%	$2,946	$4,202	$15,458
Hobe Sound Bible College	ind.	$4080	$3010	90%	77%	$3,865	$3,225	$11,000
International Academy of Design	ind.	$10,260	NA	NR	NR	NR	NR	NR
International College	ind.	$6870	NA	62%	88%	$7,000	—	$20,000
Jacksonville University	ind.	$14,950	$5210	80%	38%	$14,144	$6,016	NR
Lynn University	ind.	$19,250	$6800	100%	35%	$13,206	$12,844	$14,200
New College of the University of South Florida	pub.	$2492	$4663	42%	60%	$9,945	—	$15,800
Northwood University, Florida Campus	ind.	$11,625	$6233	80%	NR	$13,229	$4,629	$13,378
Nova Southeastern University	ind.	$11,800	$6390	87%	2%	$15,510	$2,680	NR
Palm Beach Atlantic College	ind.	$11,120	$4470	100%	37%	$8,902	$6,688	$16,600
Ringling School of Art and Design	ind.	$15,600	$7288	25%	8%	$8,805	$14,083	$21,966
Rollins College	ind.	$21,852	$6700	93%	31%	$22,703	$5,849	$14,600
St. John Vianney College Seminary	ind.	$7000	$4000	NR	NR	NR	NR	NR
Saint Leo University	ind.	$11,650	$6050	94%	59%	$11,938	$5,762	$12,000
St. Thomas University	ind.	$13,320	$4400	61%	34%	$16,027	$1,693	NR
Southeastern College of the Assemblies of God	ind.	$6023	$3508	85%	29%	$6,410	$3,121	$9775
Stetson University	ind.	$18,385	$6070	99%	38%	$17,163	$7,292	$17,500
Trinity Baptist College	ind.	$3980	$3000	88%	37%	$4,130	$2,850	$6096
Trinity College of Florida	ind.	$4730	$3020	NR	NR	NR	NR	NR
Trinity International University, South Florida Campus	ind.	$8850	NA	84%	3%	$6,500	$2,350	$15,000
University of Central Florida	pub.	$2297	$5215	43%	NR	$2,650	$4,862	NR
University of Florida	pub.	$2141	$5040	54%	NR	$7,028	$153	NR
University of Miami	ind.	$21,344	$7782	98%	20%	$18,948	$10,178	$19,108
University of North Florida	pub.	$1820	$5100	65%	37%	$1,693	$5,227	$11,141
University of South Florida	pub.	$2256	$4606	52%	26%	$6,774	$88	$16,900
The University of Tampa	ind.	$15,542	$5175	93%	16%	$12,623	$8,094	$17,130
University of West Florida	pub.	$2294	$2310†	NR	NR	NR	NR	NR
Warner Southern College	ind.	$8980	$4358	NR	NR	NR	NR	NR
Webber College	ind.	$8160	$3570	100%	47%	$9,056	$2,674	$11,923
Georgia								
Agnes Scott College	ind.	$16,025	$6660	99%	95%	$17,410	$5,275	$14,580
Albany State University	pub.	$2700	$3256	NR	NR	NR	NR	NR
American InterContinental University	ind.	$11,430	$4350	NR	NR	NR	NR	NR
Armstrong Atlantic State University	pub.	$2388	$4460	NR	NR	NR	NR	NR
Atlanta Christian College	ind.	$8398	$3640	NR	NR	NR	NR	NR
Augusta State University	pub.	$2082	NA	NR	NR	$3,728	—	$12,041
Berry College	ind.	$11,550	$5272	92%	54%	$11,100	$5,722	$11,266
Beulah Heights Bible College	ind.	$3200	$1500†	100%	NR	NR	NR	$19,750
Brenau University	ind.	$11,730	$6876	100%	38%	$12,800	$5,806	$18,724
Clark Atlanta University	ind.	$11,120	$5974	NR	NR	NR	NR	NR
Clayton College & State University	pub.	$2702	NA	50%	38%	NR	NR	NR
Columbus State University	pub.	$2444	$3870	NR	NR	NR	NR	NR
Covenant College	ind.	$15,960	$4450	89%	19%	$11,580	$8,830	$17,214
Dalton State College	pub.	$1318	NA	NR	NR	NR	NR	NR

*NA = not applicable; NR = not reported; * = includes room and board; † = room only.*

College Cost and Financial Aid Metrics

	Institutional Control ind.=independent; pub.=public	Tuition and fees	Room and board	Percent of freshmen receiving aid whose awards were need-based scholarships/grants	Percent of freshmen receiving aid whose need was fully met	Average financial aid package for freshmen	Average net cost after aid	1998 graduate's average indebtedness
DeVry Institute of Technology	ind.	$7778	NA	84%	15%	NR	NR	NR
DeVry Institute of Technology	ind.	$7778	NA	88%	9%	NR	NR	NR
Emmanuel College	ind.	$7210	$3700	47%	18%	$5,879	$5,031	$17,093
Emory University	ind.	$23,130	$7750	88%	95%	$19,203	$11,677	$16,358
Fort Valley State University	pub.	$2294	$3432	NR	NR	NR	NR	NR
Georgia Baptist College of Nursing	ind.	$1508	$1500†	100%	NR	$9,125	—	$13,653
Georgia College and State University	pub.	$2214	$4170	34%	NR	NR	NR	$13,206
Georgia Institute of Technology	pub.	$3108	$5118	80%	38%	$6,226	$2,000	NR
Georgia Southern University	pub.	$2432	$4284	90%	26%	$4,452	$2,264	$13,021
Georgia Southwestern State University	pub.	$2312	$3484	53%	53%	NR	NR	$20,000
Georgia State University	pub.	$2886	$4190†	NR	NR	NR	NR	NR
Kennesaw State University	pub.	$2306	NA	38%	64%	NR	NR	NR
LaGrange College	ind.	$11,001	$4656	100%	36%	$10,728	$4,929	$16,000
Macon State College	pub.	$1322	NA	NR	NR	NR	NR	NR
Medical College of Georgia	pub.	$2700	$1302†	NR	NR	NR	NR	$13,186
Mercer University	ind.	$16,290	$5380	100%	81%	$15,820	$5,850	$12,833
North Georgia College & State University	pub.	$2210	$3526	NR	NR	NR	NR	NR
Oglethorpe University	ind.	$17,700	$5300	93%	42%	$16,108	$6,892	NR
Paine College	ind.	$7528	$3286	99%	11%	$7,151	$3,663	$19,750
Piedmont College	ind.	$9500	$4400	90%	84%	$7,621	$6,279	$13,048
Reinhardt College	ind.	$8800	$4750	NR	NR	NR	NR	NR
Savannah College of Art and Design	ind.	$16,200	$6750	72%	22%	$5,600	$17,350	$17,000
Savannah State University	pub.	$2356	$4084	NR	NR	NR	NR	NR
Shorter College	ind.	$9170	$4650	98%	35%	$9,087	$4,733	$16,700
Southern Polytechnic State University	pub.	$2134	$4452	41%	31%	$3,460	$3,126	$16,585
State University of West Georgia	pub.	$2212	$3806	NR	NR	$6,751	—	NR
Thomas University	ind.	$7870	NA	NR	NR	NR	NR	NR
Toccoa Falls College	ind.	$8424	$3896	NR	NR	NR	NR	NR
University of Georgia	pub.	$3024	$4902	98%	40%	$4,974	$2,952	$13,597
Valdosta State University	pub.	$2290	$3954	49%	51%	$5,683	$561	$12,725
Wesleyan College	ind.	$16,300	$6600	95%	96%	$13,623	$9,277	$16,250
Hawaii								
Brigham Young University–Hawaii Campus	ind.	$2875	$5125	NR	NR	NR	NR	NR
Chaminade University of Honolulu	ind.	$11,700	$5670	86%	59%	$7,419	$9,951	$21,805
Hawaii Pacific University	ind.	$8460	$8120	65%	37%	$12,108	$4,472	$15,600
University of Hawaii at Hilo	pub.	$1466	$4992	82%	33%	$5,492	$966	$7600
University of Hawaii at Manoa	pub.	$3141	$5297	84%	22%	$4,026	$4,412	$12,161
University of Hawaii–West Oahu	pub.	$1906	NA	NR	NR	NR	NR	$7700
Idaho								
Albertson College of Idaho	ind.	$16,280	$4200	100%	19%	$10,003	$10,477	$15,460
Boise Bible College	ind.	$4630	$3600	NR	6%	$5,485	$2,745	NR
Boise State University	pub.	$2283	$3558	NR	NR	NR	NR	NR
Idaho State University	pub.	$2398	$3780	39%	97%	$8,127	—	$17,657
Lewis-Clark State College	pub.	$2204	$3500	70%	100%	$3,336	$2,368	NR

*NA = not applicable; NR = not reported; * = includes room and board; † = room only.*

College Cost and Financial Aid Metrics

	Institutional Control ind.=independent; pub.=public	Tuition and fees	Room and board	Percent of freshmen receiving aid whose awards were need-based scholarships/grants	Percent of freshmen receiving aid whose need was fully met	Average financial aid package for freshmen	Average net cost after aid	1998 graduate's average indebtedness
Northwest Nazarene University	ind.	$13,500	$4020	99%	22%	$9,654	$7,866	$19,545
University of Idaho	pub.	$2348	$3952	61%	84%	$4,200	$2,100	$18,465
Illinois								
Augustana College	ind.	$17,187	$5037	99%	37%	$13,864	$8,360	$15,672
Aurora University	ind.	$12,480	$4662	87%	72%	$12,342	$4,800	NR
Barat College	ind.	$13,500	$5250	NR	NR	NR	NR	NR
Benedictine University	ind.	$14,060	$5180	NR	NR	NR	NR	NR
Blackburn College	ind.	$8275	$3670	NR	NR	NR	NR	NR
Blessing-Rieman College of Nursing	ind.	$10,400	$4570	NR	NR	NR	NR	$11,000
Bradley University	ind.	$13,960	$5300	98%	70%	$11,210	$8,050	$15,350
Chicago State University	pub.	$3151	$5825	NR	NR	NR	NR	NR
Columbia College Chicago	ind.	$10,830	$4988†	NR	NR	NR	NR	NR
Concordia University	ind.	$13,860	$5365	74%	78%	$12,000	$7,225	$14,400
DePaul University	ind.	$14,700	$6300	85%	NR	$14,000	$7,000	$16,700
DeVry Institute of Technology	ind.	$7778	NA	61%	8%	$5,777	$2,001	$11,095
DeVry Institute of Technology	ind.	$7778	NA	89%	2%	NR	NR	$12,247
Dominican University	ind.	$14,820	$5030	NR	NR	$12,105	$7,745	$12,013
Eastern Illinois University	pub.	$3962	$4104	48%	78%	$7,024	$1,042	$12,211
East-West University	ind.	$8190	NA	NR	NR	$7,500	$690	NR
Elmhurst College	ind.	$13,900	$5266	90%	81%	$13,832	$5,334	$12,850
Eureka College	ind.	$15,450	$4860	96%	84%	$11,921	$8,389	$14,202
Finch University of Health Sciences/The Chicago Medical School	ind.	$12,903	NA	NR	NR	NR	NR	NR
Governors State University	pub.	$2398	NA	NR	NR	NR	NR	NR
Greenville College	ind.	$12,586	$4850	100%	25%	$12,895	$4,541	NR
Harrington Institute of Interior Design	ind.	$11,086	NA	NR	NR	NR	NR	$20,714
Illinois College	ind.	$10,200	$4500	88%	58%	$10,473	$4,227	$12,801
The Illinois Institute of Art	ind.	$11,904	NA	NR	NR	NR	NR	$15,800
Illinois Institute of Technology	ind.	$17,600	$5250	52%	NR	$20,600	$2,250	$19,138
Illinois State University	pub.	$4340	$4238	67%	36%	$5,911	$2,667	$9283
Illinois Wesleyan University	ind.	$20,410	$5150	100%	78%	$15,033	$10,527	$16,258
International Academy of Merchandising & Design, Ltd.	ind.	$10,692	NA	NR	NR	NR	NR	NR
Judson College	ind.	$13,890	$5360	97%	21%	$11,884	$7,366	NR
Kendall College	ind.	$11,600	$5000	NR	NR	NR	NR	NR
Knox College	ind.	$21,174	$5436	100%	100%	$18,657	$7,953	$15,715
Lake Forest College	ind.	$21,190	$5000	100%	100%	$16,465	$9,725	$14,604
Lakeview College of Nursing	ind.	$7440	NA	NR	NR	NR	NR	NR
Lewis University	ind.	$12,810	$5730	86%	30%	$13,087	$5,453	NR
Lincoln Christian College	ind.	$6708	$3900	NR	NR	NR	NR	NR
Loyola University Chicago	ind.	$18,310	$7006	98%	31%	$17,876	$7,440	$18,300
MacMurray College	ind.	$12,375	$4430	100%	20%	$14,336	$2,469	$17,242
McKendree College	ind.	$11,250	$4250	91%	79%	$10,585	$4,915	$11,434
Millikin University	ind.	$16,008	$5593	91%	73%	$14,935	$6,666	$14,468
Monmouth College	ind.	$15,720	$4410	NR	NR	NR	NR	NR
Moody Bible Institute	ind.	$1225	$4770	NR	NR	$2,250	$3,745	$10,000

*NA = not applicable; NR = not reported; * = includes room and board; † = room only.*

College Cost and Financial Aid Metrics

	Institutional Control ind.=independent; pub.=public	Tuition and fees	Room and board	Percent of freshmen receiving aid whose awards were need-based scholarships/grants	Percent of freshmen receiving aid whose need was fully met	Average financial aid package for freshmen	Average net cost after aid	1998 graduate's average indebtedness
NAES College	ind.	$5140	NA	NR	NR	NR	NR	NR
The National College of Chiropractic	ind.	$17,203	$4281†	NR	NR	NR	NR	NR
National-Louis University	ind.	$13,095	NR	NR	NR	NR	NR	NR
North Central College	ind.	$15,216	$5250	98%	39%	$14,033	$6,433	$14,061
Northeastern Illinois University	pub.	$2890	NA	NR	NR	NR	NR	NR
Northern Illinois University	pub.	$4099	$4400	NR	NR	NR	NR	NR
Northwestern University	ind.	$23,562	$6970	95%	100%	$20,455	$10,077	$13,222
Olivet Nazarene University	ind.	$12,728	$4696	58%	24%	$13,179	$4,245	$15,300
Principia College	ind.	$15,984	$5784	100%	90%	$10,909	$10,859	$8764
Quincy University	ind.	$14,700	$4780	81%	78%	$14,015	$5,465	$13,475
Robert Morris College	ind.	$10,950	NA	98%	7%	$9,246	$1,704	$8511
Rockford College	ind.	$16,800	$5430	NR	NR	NR	NR	NR
Rush University	ind.	$12,270	$7284†	NR	NR	NR	NR	$19,230
Saint Anthony College of Nursing	ind.	$11,460	NA	NR	NR	NR	NR	$13,000
Saint Francis Medical Center College of Nursing	ind.	$9200	$1680†	NR	NR	NR	NR	NR
St. John's College	ind.	$7654	NA	NR	NR	NR	NR	NR
Saint Xavier University	ind.	$13,760	$5553	99%	25%	$10,716	$8,597	$15,787
School of the Art Institute of Chicago	ind.	$20,220	$5725†	NR	NR	NR	NR	NR
Shimer College	ind.	$14,180	$1950†	100%	14%	$11,146	$4,984	$16,631
Southern Illinois University Carbondale	pub.	$3936	$3889	66%	26%	$5,598	$2,227	$11,475
Southern Illinois University Edwardsville	pub.	$2827	$4290	86%	44%	$7,829	—	NR
Trinity Christian College	ind.	$12,730	$5010	75%	66%	$11,173	$6,567	NR
University of Chicago	ind.	$24,234	$7834	NR	NR	NR	NR	$13,770
University of Illinois at Chicago	pub.	$4780	$5856	86%	36%	$11,000	—	NR
University of Illinois at Springfield	pub.	$3042	$2376†	NR	NR	NR	NR	NR
University of Illinois at Urbana–Champaign	pub.	$4752	$5424	NR	NR	$7,500	$2,676	$10,394
University of St. Francis	ind.	$13,082	$5120	65%	63%	$12,388	$5,814	$11,506
Western Illinois University	pub.	$3610	$4392	79%	30%	$5,492	$2,510	$13,463
Wheaton College	ind.	$14,930	$5080	83%	6%	$13,280	$6,730	$14,496
Indiana								
Anderson University	ind.	$14,680	$4750	100%	44%	$13,533	$5,897	$17,650
Ball State University	pub.	$3686	$4520	61%	50%	$4,919	$3,287	$10,000
Bethel College	ind.	$11,950	$3950	70%	2%	$5,728	$10,172	$13,517
Butler University	ind.	$17,360	$5850	99%	33%	$11,880	$11,330	$18,700
Calumet College of Saint Joseph	ind.	$6750	NA	NR	NR	NR	NR	NR
DePauw University	ind.	$19,730	$6080	71%	100%	$19,570	$6,240	$13,218
Earlham College	ind.	$20,256	$4810	97%	42%	$19,982	$5,084	$10,366
Franklin College of Indiana	ind.	$13,635	$4160	100%	83%	$12,916	$4,879	$16,050
Goshen College	ind.	$13,140	$4640	100%	46%	$12,683	$5,097	$12,552
Grace College	ind.	$10,500	$4600	97%	45%	$10,224	$4,876	$11,985
Hanover College	ind.	$11,045	$4655	100%	50%	$10,084	$5,616	$11,735
Huntington College	ind.	$14,230	$5190	93%	99%	$11,470	$7,950	$18,125
Indiana Institute of Technology	ind.	$12,300	$4564	99%	8%	$9,998	$6,866	$16,500
Indiana State University	pub.	$3426	$4434	61%	16%	$4,460	$3,400	$4129

*NA = not applicable; NR = not reported; * = includes room and board; † = room only.*

College Cost and Financial Aid Metrics

	Institutional Control ind.=independent; pub.=public	Tuition and fees	Room and board	Percent of freshmen receiving aid whose awards were need-based scholarships/grants	Percent of freshmen receiving aid whose need was fully met	Average financial aid package for freshmen	Average net cost after aid	1998 graduate's average indebtedness
Indiana University Bloomington	pub.	$4212	$5492	58%	20%	$6,085	$3,619	NR
Indiana University East	pub.	$3104	NA	79%	29%	$5,257	—	NR
Indiana University Kokomo	pub.	$3104	NA	71%	11%	$3,691	—	NR
Indiana University Northwest	pub.	$3128	NA	79%	11%	$4,362	—	NR
Indiana University–Purdue University Fort Wayne	pub.	$2827	NA	68%	27%	NR	NR	$8088
Indiana University–Purdue University Indianapolis	pub.	$3713	$3450	74%	7%	$4,561	$2,602	NR
Indiana University South Bend	pub.	$3197	NA	67%	9%	$4,259	—	NR
Indiana University Southeast	pub.	$3092	NA	68%	11%	$3,857	—	NR
Indiana Wesleyan University	ind.	$11,760	$4580	NR	NR	NR	NR	NR
Manchester College	ind.	$13,930	$5110	100%	80%	$15,556	$3,484	$13,370
Marian College	ind.	$14,416	$4876	96%	53%	$15,039	$4,253	$15,674
Martin University	ind.	$6720	NA	90%	NR	NR	NR	$20,000
Oakland City University	ind.	$10,096	$3730	NR	NR	NR	NR	NR
Purdue University	pub.	$3724	$5500	61%	34%	$6,616	$2,608	$15,633
Purdue University Calumet	pub.	$2577	NA	61%	13%	$3,666	—	$10,309
Purdue University North Central	pub.	$3211	NA	71%	16%	$5,000	—	NR
Rose-Hulman Institute of Technology	ind.	$19,545	$5475	86%	29%	$14,017	$11,003	$22,000
Saint Joseph's College	ind.	$14,190	$5080	73%	35%	$12,500	$6,770	$16,730
Saint Mary-of-the-Woods College	ind.	$14,660	$5410	75%	38%	$12,000	$8,070	$15,000
Saint Mary's College	ind.	$16,994	$5962	98%	22%	$14,149	$8,807	$15,894
Taylor University	ind.	$15,118	$4630	94%	26%	$11,077	$8,671	$14,655
Taylor University, Fort Wayne Campus	ind.	$12,600	$4230	94%	14%	$12,450	$4,380	NR
Tri-State University	ind.	$13,700	$4950	100%	56%	$10,096	$8,554	$14,000
University of Indianapolis	ind.	$14,630	$5225	88%	24%	$11,576	$8,279	$16,418
University of Notre Dame	ind.	$22,187	$5750	95%	100%	$18,242	$9,695	$19,635
University of Saint Francis	ind.	$12,495	$4800	NR	NR	NR	NR	NR
University of Southern Indiana	pub.	$2920	$2286†	68%	23%	$3,925	$1,281	$13,695
Valparaiso University	ind.	$17,636	$4660	100%	63%	$15,189	$7,107	$17,435
Wabash College	ind.	$17,275	$5435	100%	100%	$17,569	$5,141	$13,925
Iowa								
Allen College	ind.	$8220	NA	94%	14%	NR	NR	$11,199
Briar Cliff College	ind.	$13,890	$4767	69%	56%	$12,956	$5,701	NR
Buena Vista University	ind.	$15,751	$4507	100%	17%	$16,295	$3,963	$15,960
Central College	ind.	$14,186	$4944	100%	28%	$14,349	$4,781	$20,665
Clarke College	ind.	$13,586	$5082	99%	32%	$12,688	$5,980	$16,838
Coe College	ind.	$17,540	$5020	80%	86%	$17,597	$4,963	$15,310
Cornell College	ind.	$18,995	$5140	100%	32%	$16,730	$7,405	$18,025
Dordt College	ind.	$12,650	$3600	100%	19%	$11,650	$4,600	$14,271
Drake University	ind.	$16,580	$4870	100%	37%	$13,632	$7,818	$19,630
Emmaus Bible College	ind.	$5390	$2780	100%	4%	$2,881	$5,289	$9400
Faith Baptist Bible College and Theological Seminary	ind.	$7886	$3350	83%	NR	$5,011	$6,225	$12,979
Graceland College	ind.	$11,810	$3830	80%	53%	$14,770	$870	$15,649
Grand View College	ind.	$12,520	$3832	100%	31%	$11,687	$4,665	$10,762
Grinnell College	ind.	$19,460	$5600	100%	100%	$17,528	$7,532	$12,148

*NA = not applicable; NR = not reported; * = includes room and board; † = room only.*

College Cost and Financial Aid Metrics

	Institutional Control ind.=independent; pub.=public	Tuition and fees	Room and board	Percent of freshmen receiving aid whose awards were need-based scholarships/grants	Percent of freshmen receiving aid whose need was fully met	Average financial aid package for freshmen	Average net cost after aid	1998 graduate's average indebtedness
Hamilton Technical College	ind.	$5850	NA	NR	NR	NR	NR	NR
Iowa State University of Science and Technology	pub.	$3132	$4171	68%	18%	$5,283	$2,020	$16,836
Iowa Wesleyan College	ind.	$12,700	$4370	100%	28%	$13,218	$3,852	$14,752
Loras College	ind.	$15,350	$5804	87%	33%	$15,389	$5,765	$14,728
Luther College	ind.	$17,290	$3810	100%	33%	$14,054	$7,046	$16,942
Maharishi University of Management	ind.	$15,630	$5200	100%	26%	$16,746	$4,084	$16,454
Marycrest International University	ind.	$12,760	$4840	NR	NR	NR	NR	NR
Morningside College	ind.	$13,146	$4636	91%	64%	$13,740	$4,042	$15,028
Mount Mercy College	ind.	$13,850	$4600	75%	41%	$12,631	$5,819	$16,382
Mount St. Clare College	ind.	$12,800	$4360	100%	39%	$10,674	$6,486	$13,219
Northwestern College	ind.	$12,270	$3500	100%	86%	$13,608	$2,162	$10,140
Palmer College of Chiropractic	ind.	$15,705	NA	NR	NR	NR	NR	NR
St. Ambrose University	ind.	$13,580	$5150	55%	25%	$12,000	$6,730	$13,000
Simpson College	ind.	$14,430	$4800	100%	30%	$15,084	$4,146	$16,851
University of Dubuque	ind.	$13,530	$4280	99%	48%	$16,286	$1,524	$14,157
The University of Iowa	pub.	$2998	$4370	58%	56%	$4,105	$3,263	$11,018
University of Northern Iowa	pub.	$3130	$4200	49%	26%	$4,270	$3,060	$16,983
Upper Iowa University	ind.	$10,752	$4156	91%	NR	$10,500	$4,408	$17,125
Wartburg College	ind.	$15,765	$4400	100%	15%	$13,630	$6,535	$14,826
William Penn University	ind.	$12,770	$4140	100%	93%	$9,271	$7,639	NR
Kansas								
Baker University	ind.	$11,750	$4700	NR	NR	NR	NR	NR
Barclay College	ind.	$6250	$3100	86%	71%	$7,500	$1,850	$10,000
Benedictine College	ind.	$12,316	$4800	91%	15%	$13,381	$3,735	$15,539
Bethany College	ind.	$12,304	$3780	80%	39%	$6,945	$9,139	$15,296
Bethel College	ind.	$11,800	$4700	87%	61%	$13,111	$3,389	$13,610
Emporia State University	pub.	$2086	$3656	NR	NR	NR	NR	$12,827
Fort Hays State University	pub.	$2063	$3770	NR	NR	NR	NR	NR
Friends University	ind.	$11,010	$3420	88%	14%	$8,329	$6,101	$10,132
Kansas State University	pub.	$2592	$3950	40%	14%	$4,801	$1,741	$15,927
Kansas Wesleyan University	ind.	$11,000	$4000	100%	100%	$10,851	$4,149	$10,911
Manhattan Christian College	ind.	$6870	$3610	45%	20%	$5,841	$4,639	NR
McPherson College	ind.	$11,700	$4900	86%	18%	$11,134	$5,466	$19,075
MidAmerica Nazarene University	ind.	$10,474	$5060	NR	NR	NR	NR	NR
Newman University	ind.	$10,268	$3950	80%	45%	$9,425	$4,793	NR
Ottawa University	ind.	$10,250	$4220	56%	NR	$5,735	$8,735	$14,000
Pittsburg State University	pub.	$2142	$3715	68%	11%	$4,635	$1,222	$10,433
Saint Mary College	ind.	$11,390	$4600	NR	NR	NR	NR	NR
Southwestern College	ind.	$10,560	$4270	72%	70%	$12,724	$2,106	$13,803
Sterling College	ind.	$11,030	$4586	100%	71%	$9,000	$6,616	$12,287
Tabor College	ind.	$12,410	$4480	89%	23%	$11,220	$5,670	$16,452
University of Kansas	pub.	$2518	$3941	72%	24%	$5,054	$1,405	NR
Washburn University of Topeka	pub.	$2934	$3320	58%	NR	$4,175	$2,079	NR
Wichita State University	pub.	$2573	$4070	58%	7%	$4,094	$2,549	NR

*NA = not applicable; NR = not reported; * = includes room and board; † = room only.*

College Cost and Financial Aid Metrics

	Institutional Control ind.=independent; pub.=public	Tuition and fees	Room and board	Percent of freshmen receiving aid whose awards were need-based scholarships/grants	Percent of freshmen receiving aid whose need was fully met	Average financial aid package for freshmen	Average net cost after aid	1998 graduate's average indebtedness
Kentucky								
Alice Lloyd College	ind.	$360	$2680	100%	30%	NR	NR	$3371
Asbury College	ind.	$13,784	$3566	97%	30%	$10,092	$7,258	$17,222
Bellarmine College	ind.	$12,650	$3940	100%	36%	$11,469	$5,121	$14,200
Berea College	ind.	$199	$3686	100%	NR	$19,454	—	NR
Brescia University	ind.	$9545	$4240	60%	25%	$8,720	$5,065	NR
Campbellsville University	ind.	$8240	$3990	NR	NR	$7,839	$4,391	NR
Centre College	ind.	$21,350*	NR	100%	29%	$14,691	—	$13,000
Clear Creek Baptist Bible College	ind.	$3170	$2740	100%	NR	$3,329	$2,581	NR
Cumberland College	ind.	$9920	$4276	74%	35%	$10,911	$3,285	$14,469
Eastern Kentucky University	pub.	$2390	$3676	66%	31%	$5,711	$355	$13,804
Georgetown College	ind.	$12,390	$4600	100%	35%	$11,619	$5,371	$14,393
Kentucky Christian College	ind.	$6880	$3914	56%	15%	$7,479	$3,315	$17,119
Kentucky Mountain Bible College	ind.	$4170	$2800	NR	NR	NR	NR	NR
Kentucky Wesleyan College	ind.	$10,020	$4770	100%	54%	$13,725	$1,065	$12,000
Mid-Continent College	ind.	$2960	$2988	100%	NR	$5,257	$691	$9960
Midway College	ind.	$9122	$4850	98%	31%	$8,908	$5,064	$15,946
Morehead State University	pub.	$2440	$3300	69%	32%	$4,722	$1,018	$13,230
Murray State University	pub.	$2606	$3570	64%	97%	$4,570	$1,606	$14,375
Northern Kentucky University	pub.	$2442	$3654	59%	NR	$3,835	$2,261	$20,400
Pikeville College	ind.	$7800	$3340	89%	59%	$8,500	$2,640	$12,000
Spalding University	ind.	$10,996	$2810	100%	34%	$9,737	$4,069	$11,620
Sullivan College	ind.	$9600	$2790†	NR	NR	NR	NR	NR
Thomas More College	ind.	$12,580	$3756	96%	95%	$11,343	$4,993	$18,931
Transylvania University	ind.	$14,600	$5350	100%	44%	$12,939	$7,011	$14,650
Union College	ind.	$11,320	NR	98%	61%	$8,764	—	$11,283
University of Louisville	pub.	$3246	$3400	59%	29%	$5,538	$1,108	NR
Western Kentucky University	pub.	$2390	$3460	60%	55%	$5,544	$306	NR
Louisiana								
Centenary College of Louisiana	ind.	$14,600	$4500	99%	35%	$12,066	$7,034	$16,500
Dillard University	ind.	$9200	$4800	NR	100%	$13,646	$354	$18,679
Grambling State University	pub.	$2301	$2636	83%	NR	NR	NR	$18,350
Louisiana College	ind.	$7413	$3160	NR	NR	NR	NR	NR
Louisiana State University and Agricultural and Mechanical College	pub.	$2881	$4220	47%	49%	$4,952	$2,149	$17,093
Louisiana State University in Shreveport	pub.	$2200	$4032†	NR	NR	NR	NR	NR
Louisiana Tech University	pub.	$2549	$3120	92%	19%	$4,983	$686	NR
Loyola University New Orleans	ind.	$15,481	$6116	61%	43%	$13,633	$7,964	$15,887
McNeese State University	pub.	$2113	$2328	34%	52%	$3,167	$1,274	NR
Northwestern State University of Louisiana	pub.	$2327	$2596	NR	NR	NR	NR	NR
Our Lady of Holy Cross College	ind.	$5950	NA	NR	NR	NR	NR	$18,500
Southeastern Louisiana University	pub.	$2217	$2770	89%	20%	$3,584	$1,403	NR
Southern University and Agricultural and Mechanical College	pub.	$2286	$3339	NR	NR	NR	NR	NR
Tulane University	ind.	$24,214	$7042	96%	68%	$21,980	$9,276	$20,040
University of Louisiana at Lafayette	pub.	$2013	$2656	57%	NR	$3,200	$1,469	NR

*NA = not applicable; NR = not reported; * = includes room and board; † = room only.*

College Cost and Financial Aid Metrics

	Institutional Control ind.=independent; pub.=public	Tuition and fees	Room and board	Percent of freshmen receiving aid whose awards were need-based scholarships/grants	Percent of freshmen receiving aid whose need was fully met	Average financial aid package for freshmen	Average net cost after aid	1998 graduate's average indebtedness
University of Louisiana at Monroe	pub.	$2052	$3660	NR	NR	NR	NR	NR
University of New Orleans	pub.	$2532	$3175	NR	NR	NR	NR	NR
Xavier University of Louisiana	ind.	$9700	$5100	NR	NR	NR	NR	NR
Maine								
Bates College	ind.	$31,400*	NR	97%	100%	$21,805	—	$15,129
Bowdoin College	ind.	$24,955	$6520	99%	100%	$20,321	$11,154	$16,077
Colby College	ind.	$31,580*	NR	87%	100%	$19,100	—	$16,300
College of the Atlantic	ind.	$19,485	$5220	94%	84%	$17,408	$7,297	$13,887
Husson College	ind.	$9310	$4990	NR	NR	$10,650	$3,650	$17,125
Maine College of Art	ind.	$16,718	$6389	100%	8%	$11,183	$11,924	NR
Maine Maritime Academy	pub.	$5092	$5022	99%	22%	$8,018	$2,096	$13,358
Saint Joseph's College	ind.	$13,735	$5950	99%	18%	$12,287	$7,398	$16,122
Thomas College	ind.	$12,290	$5550	NR	NR	$15,027	$2,813	$19,125
Unity College	ind.	$12,780	$5300	95%	69%	$9,406	$8,674	NR
University of Maine	pub.	$4656	$5256	89%	26%	$7,825	$2,087	$15,000
The University of Maine at Augusta	pub.	$3366	NA	85%	11%	NR	NR	NR
University of Maine at Farmington	pub.	$3776	$4614	92%	43%	$7,517	$873	$15,474
University of Maine at Fort Kent	pub.	$3375	$4000	89%	15%	$3,780	$3,595	$10,483
University of Maine at Machias	pub.	$3445	$4330	NR	NR	NR	NR	NR
University of Maine at Presque Isle	pub.	$3390	$4048	94%	44%	$5,710	$1,728	$10,186
University of New England	ind.	$15,500	$6200	NR	NR	NR	NR	NR
University of Southern Maine	pub.	$4192	$4926	81%	15%	$6,079	$3,039	NR
Maryland								
Baltimore Hebrew University	ind.	$5630	NA	NR	100%	$3,718	$1,912	NR
Bowie State University	pub.	$3664	$4012	40%	22%	$5,505	$2,171	NR
Capitol College	ind.	$12,308	$3240†	100%	NR	$7,600	$7,948	$12,000
College of Notre Dame of Maryland	ind.	$15,875	$6800	84%	76%	$15,957	$6,718	$17,000
Columbia Union College	ind.	$12,660	$4400	NR	NR	NR	NR	NR
Coppin State College	pub.	$3973	$5274	80%	11%	$4,487	$4,760	$12,000
Frostburg State University	pub.	$4132	$5214	76%	24%	$3,798	$5,548	$13,103
Goucher College	ind.	$20,485	$7380	99%	NR	$15,700	$12,165	$6928
Hood College	ind.	$17,600	$6900	99%	91%	$18,771	$5,729	$12,255
Johns Hopkins University	ind.	$23,660	$7870	80%	83%	$19,735	$11,795	$16,100
Loyola College in Maryland	ind.	$18,830	$7600	71%	93%	$14,020	$12,410	$15,020
Maryland Institute, College of Art	ind.	$18,710	$4400†	NR	NR	NR	NR	NR
Morgan State University	pub.	$3874	$5718	NR	NR	NR	NR	NR
Mount Saint Mary's College and Seminary	ind.	$16,720	$6650	100%	32%	$12,808	$10,562	$15,463
Peabody Conservatory of Music of The Johns Hopkins University	ind.	$21,975	$8060	88%	15%	$13,219	$16,816	NR
St. John's College	ind.	$23,490	$6360	79%	95%	$19,826	$10,024	$17,125
St. Mary's College of Maryland	pub.	$7360	$6325	87%	20%	$5,709	$7,976	$14,399
Salisbury State University	pub.	$4156	$5590	46%	24%	$4,259	$5,487	$14,000
Sojourner-Douglass College	ind.	$4470	NA	NR	NR	NR	NR	NR
Towson University	pub.	$4710	$5800	63%	30%	$7,878	$2,632	NR
University of Baltimore	pub.	$4122	NA	NR	NR	NR	NR	NR

*NA = not applicable; NR = not reported; * = includes room and board; † = room only.*

College Cost and Financial Aid Metrics

	Institutional Control ind.=independent; pub.=public	Tuition and fees	Room and board	Percent of freshmen receiving aid whose awards were need-based scholarships/grants	Percent of freshmen receiving aid whose need was fully met	Average financial aid package for freshmen	Average net cost after aid	1998 graduate's average indebtedness
University of Maryland, Baltimore County	pub.	$5160	$5694	NR	NR	$6,000	$4,854	$12,000
University of Maryland, College Park	pub.	$4939	$6306	67%	30%	$7,258	$3,987	$14,076
University of Maryland University College	pub.	$4416	NA	75%	NR	$1,201	$3,215	$1799
Villa Julie College	ind.	$10,980	$3650†	44%	45%	$10,265	$4,365	$13,344
Washington Bible College	ind.	$6460	$4250	NR	NR	NR	NR	NR
Washington College	ind.	$20,200	$5740	99%	70%	$16,113	$9,827	$17,278
Western Maryland College	ind.	$19,600	$5350	75%	33%	$18,028	$6,922	$15,799
Massachusetts								
American International College	ind.	$12,900	$6648	95%	21%	$12,300	$7,248	$17,000
Amherst College	ind.	$25,259	$6560	95%	100%	$23,605	$8,214	$12,340
Anna Maria College	ind.	$12,950	$5950	100%	21%	$11,022	$7,878	NR
Assumption College	ind.	$17,490	$6760	100%	36%	$12,969	$11,281	$16,400
Atlantic Union College	ind.	$12,634	$4020	99%	8%	$9,707	$6,947	$13,319
Babson College	ind.	$21,952	$8746	87%	100%	$17,150	$13,548	$20,000
Bay Path College	ind.	$13,010	$6864	100%	8%	$10,171	$9,703	NR
Becker College	ind.	$11,710	$5830	93%	25%	$7,407	$10,133	$16,410
Bentley College	ind.	$18,910	$8600	98%	35%	$16,579	$10,931	$17,438
Berklee College of Music	ind.	$16,627	$8890	NR	NR	NR	NR	NR
Boston Architectural Center	ind.	$6330	NA	NR	NR	NR	NR	NR
Boston College	ind.	$22,256	$8250	82%	98%	$18,793	$11,713	$16,417
Boston Conservatory	ind.	$18,135	$8200	43%	5%	$8,583	$17,752	$15,000
Boston University	ind.	$24,100	$8130	94%	66%	$21,214	$11,016	$18,702
Brandeis University	ind.	$25,174	$7040	98%	94%	$17,956	$14,258	NR
Bridgewater State College	pub.	$2123	$4704	85%	34%	$3,305	$3,522	$8693
Cambridge College	ind.	$7620	NA	NR	NR	$5,500	$2,120	NR
Clark University	ind.	$22,620	$4350	99%	18%	$17,067	$9,903	$17,224
College of Our Lady of the Elms	ind.	$14,720	$5566	97%	28%	$11,585	$8,701	$11,868
College of the Holy Cross	ind.	$23,815	$7540	82%	100%	$16,724	$14,631	$16,430
Curry College	ind.	$17,300	$6710	93%	NR	$12,500	$11,510	NR
Eastern Nazarene College	ind.	$14,060	$4550	97%	13%	$9,242	$9,368	NR
Emerson College	ind.	$19,316	$8734	89%	70%	$14,900	$13,150	$17,125
Emmanuel College	ind.	$16,612	$7390	90%	10%	$20,458	$3,544	$19,349
Endicott College	ind.	$14,556	$7410	98%	6%	$11,160	$10,806	$16,060
Fitchburg State College	pub.	$3018	$4540	NR	NR	NR	NR	NR
Framingham State College	pub.	$2830	$4154	72%	33%	$4,805	$2,179	$12,339
Gordon College	ind.	$16,420	$5050	86%	62%	$12,885	$8,585	$10,429
Hampshire College	ind.	$25,400	$6622	NR	NR	$19,925	$12,097	$16,000
Harvard University	ind.	$24,407	$7757	97%	100%	$21,390	$10,774	$14,744
Hellenic College	ind.	$8615	$6600	100%	50%	$6,000	$9,215	$15,000
Lasell College	ind.	$14,900	$7500	100%	12%	$15,816	$6,584	$17,209
Lesley College	ind.	$15,600	$7200	100%	7%	$12,285	$10,515	$13,378
Massachusetts College of Art	pub.	$3808	$7164	60%	53%	$7,780	$3,192	$16,760
Massachusetts College of Liberal Arts	pub.	$3357	$4290	74%	40%	$6,020	$1,627	$15,524
Massachusetts College of Pharmacy and Health Sciences	ind.	$17,320	$7900	99%	13%	$15,601	$9,619	$23,372

*NA = not applicable; NR = not reported; * = includes room and board; † = room only.*

College Cost and Financial Aid Metrics

College Cost and Financial Aid Metrics	Institutional Control ind.=independent; pub.=public	Tuition and fees	Room and board	Percent of freshmen receiving aid whose awards were need-based scholarships/grants	Percent of freshmen receiving aid whose need was fully met	Average financial aid package for freshmen	Average net cost after aid	1998 graduate's average indebtedness
Massachusetts Institute of Technology	ind.	$25,000	$6900	87%	100%	$23,365	$8,535	NR
Massachusetts Maritime Academy	pub.	$2873	$4560	76%	35%	$6,593	$840	NR
Merrimack College	ind.	$15,710	$7500	100%	72%	$13,360	$9,850	NR
Montserrat College of Art	ind.	$12,950	$3650†	76%	3%	$7,787	$8,813	$11,000
Mount Holyoke College	ind.	$24,354	$7110	98%	100%	$20,942	$10,522	$15,000
Mount Ida College	ind.	$15,830	$8950	NR	NR	NR	NR	NR
New England Conservatory of Music	ind.	$19,800	$8600	96%	21%	$14,808	$13,592	$19,000
Nichols College	ind.	$14,550	$6540	99%	35%	$11,576	$9,514	$18,799
Northeastern University	ind.	$18,867	$8610	94%	NR	$13,190	$14,287	NR
Pine Manor College	ind.	$11,440	$7160	100%	40%	$14,360	$4,240	$15,229
Regis College	ind.	$16,860	$7870	73%	81%	$15,156	$9,574	$18,443
Saint John's Seminary College of Liberal Arts	ind.	$5800	$3000	NR	NR	NR	NR	NR
Salem State College	pub.	$2958	$4044	88%	81%	$5,144	$1,858	NR
School of the Museum of Fine Arts	ind.	$18,580	NA	93%	3%	$8,324	$10,256	NR
Simmons College	ind.	$20,134	$8046	96%	44%	$19,618	$8,562	$19,650
Simon's Rock College of Bard	ind.	$23,300	$6410	96%	21%	$15,654	$14,056	NR
Smith College	ind.	$22,622	$7820	100%	100%	$21,320	$9,122	$15,142
Springfield College	ind.	$16,898	$5856	95%	25%	$12,600	$10,154	$16,500
Stonehill College	ind.	$16,336	$7852	94%	32%	$11,866	$12,322	$10,115
Suffolk University	ind.	$14,660	$9210	95%	12%	$11,254	$12,616	$20,384
Tufts University	ind.	$24,751	$7375	88%	100%	$19,765	$12,361	$14,834
University of Massachusetts Amherst	pub.	$5323	$4790	81%	21%	$6,965	$3,148	$16,255
University of Massachusetts Boston	pub.	$4307	NA	99%	36%	$6,676	—	$17,340
University of Massachusetts Dartmouth	pub.	$4129	$4992	NR	NR	NR	NR	$13,446
University of Massachusetts Lowell	pub.	$4255	$4726	88%	86%	$6,565	$2,416	$15,735
Wellesley College	ind.	$23,320	$7234	91%	100%	$18,657	$11,897	$17,664
Wentworth Institute of Technology	ind.	$12,450	$6500	30%	NR	$6,307	$12,643	$19,500
Western New England College	ind.	$15,504	$7050	99%	20%	$10,130	$12,424	$23,000
Westfield State College	pub.	$2974	$4174	65%	29%	$4,502	$2,646	NR
Wheaton College	ind.	$23,150	$6730	91%	51%	$16,559	$13,321	$16,193
Wheelock College	ind.	$17,410	$6945	99%	15%	$14,145	$10,210	$20,000
Williams College	ind.	$24,790	$6730	97%	100%	$22,099	$9,421	$14,328
Worcester Polytechnic Institute	ind.	$22,108	$6912	98%	50%	$15,944	$13,076	$18,596
Worcester State College	pub.	$2458	$4369	NR	NR	NR	NR	NR
Michigan								
Adrian College	ind.	$13,750	$4780	99%	24%	$14,552	$3,978	$15,187
Albion College	ind.	$18,160	$5220	100%	70%	$16,462	$6,918	$18,085
Alma College	ind.	$15,142	$5460	100%	34%	$14,122	$6,480	NR
Andrews University	ind.	$12,339	$3765	73%	14%	$11,594	$4,510	NR
Aquinas College	ind.	$14,034	$4884	100%	45%	$12,950	$5,968	$12,348
Calvin College	ind.	$14,040	$4890	100%	35%	$10,250	$8,680	$16,000
Center for Creative Studies—College of Art and Design	ind.	$16,526	$3200†	NR	NR	NR	NR	NR
Central Michigan University	pub.	$3630	$4620	84%	55%	$6,581	$1,669	$16,757
Cleary College	ind.	$7605	NA	NR	NR	NR	NR	NR

*NA = not applicable; NR = not reported; * = includes room and board; † = room only.*

College Cost and Financial Aid Metrics

	Institutional Control ind.=independent; pub.=public	Tuition and fees	Room and board	Percent of freshmen receiving aid whose awards were need-based scholarships/grants	Percent of freshmen receiving aid whose need was fully met	Average financial aid package for freshmen	Average net cost after aid	1998 graduate's average indebtedness
Concordia College	ind.	$13,800	$5800	NR	NR	$12,087	$7,513	$20,026
Cornerstone University	ind.	$10,344	$4712	NR	NR	NR	NR	NR
Davenport College of Business, Kalamazoo Campus	ind.	$8895	NA	NR	NR	NR	NR	NR
Davenport College of Business, Lansing Campus	ind.	$8111	NA	NR	NR	NR	NR	$3280
Detroit College of Business	ind.	$6768	NA	99%	9%	$6,497	$271	$5789
Detroit College of Business–Flint	ind.	$5004	NA	99%	9%	NR	NR	$5789
Detroit College of Business, Warren Campus	ind.	$6768	NA	99%	9%	$6,239	$529	$5789
Eastern Michigan University	pub.	$3754	$4842	71%	50%	$9,829	—	$11,719
Ferris State University	pub.	$4195	$5110	84%	5%	$6,237	$3,068	$13,000
Finlandia University	ind.	$12,260	$4340	NR	NR	NR	NR	NR
Grace Bible College	ind.	$7100	$4150	100%	8%	$5,297	$5,953	$15,632
Grand Valley State University	pub.	$4108	$4910	89%	100%	$5,674	$3,344	$11,600
Hillsdale College	ind.	$13,460	$5630	NR	29%	$10,090	$9,000	$13,385
Hope College	ind.	$16,024	$5030	92%	49%	$14,215	$6,839	$16,259
Kalamazoo College	ind.	$19,188	$5787	100%	88%	$15,625	$9,350	$17,100
Kendall College of Art and Design	ind.	$10,860	NA	92%	7%	$7,253	$3,607	$18,861
Kettering University	ind.	$14,775	$4020	94%	18%	$8,168	$10,627	$30,000
Lake Superior State University	pub.	$4034	$4930	42%	NR	$3,550	$5,414	NR
Lawrence Technological University	ind.	$10,340	$2385†	75%	15%	NR	NR	$15,400
Madonna University	ind.	$6610	$4676	NR	NR	NR	NR	NR
Michigan State University	pub.	$5590	$4298	78%	50%	$6,766	$3,122	$17,875
Michigan Technological University	pub.	$4491	$4726	94%	45%	$6,072	$3,145	$6397
Northern Michigan University	pub.	$3146	$4640	NR	NR	NR	NR	NR
Northwood University	ind.	$11,625	$5208	86%	21%	NR	NR	NR
Oakland University	pub.	$4292	$4715	57%	33%	$5,460	$3,547	NR
Olivet College	ind.	$13,158	$4252	NR	NR	NR	NR	NR
Reformed Bible College	ind.	$7371	$4100	98%	6%	$4,277	$7,194	$12,320
Rochester College	ind.	$8304	$4416	NR	NR	NR	NR	NR
Sacred Heart Major Seminary	ind.	$6114	$4390	NR	NR	NR	NR	NR
Saginaw Valley State University	pub.	$3512	$4800	NR	NR	NR	NR	NR
Saint Mary's College	ind.	$7524	$4500	100%	3%	$5,580	$6,444	$12,344
Siena Heights University	ind.	$12,400	$4502	NR	NR	$11,000	$5,902	NR
Spring Arbor College	ind.	$11,706	$4460	NR	NR	NR	NR	NR
University of Detroit Mercy	ind.	$14,332	$5470	100%	25%	$14,827	$4,975	$14,881
University of Michigan	pub.	$6333	$5614	70%	90%	$9,401	$2,546	$14,534
University of Michigan–Dearborn	pub.	$4361	NA	72%	23%	$3,450	$911	$14,314
University of Michigan–Flint	pub.	$3800	NA	100%	94%	$7,700	—	$10,600
Walsh College of Accountancy and Business Administration	ind.	$5275	NA	NR	NR	NR	NR	$12,700
Wayne State University	pub.	$3809	$4152†	48%	4%	$3,724	$4,237	$14,834
Western Michigan University	pub.	$3944	$4831	25%	NR	$4,078	$4,697	$16,000
William Tyndale College	ind.	$7050	$2800	52%	11%	$4,667	$5,183	$9500
Minnesota								
Augsburg College	ind.	$15,250	$5240	99%	68%	$10,280	$10,210	$20,846
Bemidji State University	pub.	$3579	$3778	66%	90%	$4,233	$3,124	$12,670

*NA = not applicable; NR = not reported; * = includes room and board; † = room only.*

College Cost and Financial Aid Metrics

	Institutional Control ind.=independent; pub.=public	Tuition and fees	Room and board	Percent of freshmen receiving aid whose awards were need-based scholarships/grants	Percent of freshmen receiving aid whose need was fully met	Average financial aid package for freshmen	Average net cost after aid	1998 graduate's average indebtedness
Bethel College	ind.	$15,335	$5410	100%	20%	$13,319	$7,426	$16,903
Carleton College	ind.	$23,469	$4761	98%	100%	$18,346	$9,884	$14,720
College of Saint Benedict	ind.	$16,441	$5040	100%	90%	$14,391	$7,090	$17,445
College of St. Catherine	ind.	$15,578	$4550	93%	61%	$17,479	$2,649	$17,341
The College of St. Scholastica	ind.	$15,510	$4760	88%	57%	$12,129	$8,141	$20,224
College of Visual Arts	ind.	$11,020	NA	68%	22%	$7,748	$3,272	$19,700
Concordia College	ind.	$14,020	$3900	100%	100%	$11,739	$6,181	$18,135
Concordia University at St. Paul	ind.	$14,752	$5160	100%	24%	$12,244	$7,668	$12,784
Crown College	ind.	$10,570	$4420	98%	74%	$11,273	$3,717	$17,067
Gustavus Adolphus College	ind.	$17,430	$4320	99%	NR	$16,290	$5,460	$16,952
Hamline University	ind.	$15,798	$5291	100%	17%	$15,507	$5,582	$18,887
Macalester College	ind.	$20,688	$5760	NR	NR	$16,295	$10,153	$14,350
Martin Luther College	ind.	$5145	$2340	90%	96%	$4,013	$3,472	$8694
Metropolitan State University	pub.	$2269	NA	NR	NR	NR	NR	NR
Minneapolis College of Art and Design	ind.	$18,190	$2900†	86%	45%	$10,034	$11,056	$22,250
Minnesota Bible College	ind.	$6056	$1800†	100%	77%	NR	NR	$18,558
Minnesota State University, Mankato	pub.	$3492	$5348	NR	NR	NR	NR	NR
Minnesota State University Moorhead	pub.	$3179	$3264	49%	8%	$3,925	$2,518	$13,100
Northwestern College	ind.	$14,982	$4448	75%	NR	NR	NR	$16,000
Oak Hills Christian College	ind.	$8590	$3100	NR	NR	NR	NR	NR
Saint John's University	ind.	$16,441	$4930	99%	88%	$13,719	$7,652	$16,487
St. Olaf College	ind.	$19,400	$4500	100%	100%	$13,970	$9,930	$15,991
Southwest State University	pub.	$3428	$3588	85%	62%	$6,521	$495	NR
University of Minnesota, Crookston	pub.	$5020	$4046	78%	60%	NR	NR	NR
University of Minnesota, Duluth	pub.	$4903	$4132	NR	NR	$5,818	$3,217	$11,500
University of Minnesota, Morris	pub.	$5312	$3910	88%	93%	$6,173	$3,049	$11,600
University of Minnesota, Twin Cities Campus	pub.	$4649	$4494	69%	42%	$6,934	$2,209	NR
University of St. Thomas	ind.	$16,340	$5180	99%	27%	$13,482	$8,038	$16,245
Winona State University	pub.	$3300	$3500	49%	27%	$4,275	$2,525	NR
Mississippi								
Alcorn State University	pub.	$2685	$2627	NR	NR	$5,750	—	NR
Belhaven College	ind.	$10,340	$3850	97%	11%	$10,218	$3,972	$10,255
Blue Mountain College	ind.	$5340	$2766	69%	18%	NR	NR	NR
Delta State University	pub.	$2596	$2730	NR	NR	NR	NR	$12,900
Magnolia Bible College	ind.	$4540	$1744	100%	NR	$2,175	$4,109	$5258
Millsaps College	ind.	$15,029	$6106	100%	48%	$16,527	$4,608	$18,743
Mississippi College	ind.	$9614	$4176	36%	45%	$10,424	$3,366	$22,588
Mississippi State University	pub.	$3329	$3690	95%	17%	$3,903	$3,116	$17,712
Mississippi University for Women	pub.	$2556	$2590	NR	NR	NR	NR	NR
Mississippi Valley State University	pub.	$2346	$2844	80%	96%	$8,493	—	NR
Rust College	ind.	$5200	$2400	NR	NR	NR	NR	NR
Tougaloo College	ind.	$7110	$3060	NR	NR	NR	NR	NR
University of Mississippi	pub.	$3053	$3414	91%	36%	$5,573	$894	$14,795
University of Mississippi Medical Center	pub.	$3168	$1530†	NR	NR	NR	NR	$9500

*NA = not applicable; NR = not reported; * = includes room and board; † = room only.*

College Cost and Financial Aid Metrics

	Institutional Control ind.=independent; pub.=public	Tuition and fees	Room and board	Percent of freshmen receiving aid whose awards were need-based scholarships/grants	Percent of freshmen receiving aid whose need was fully met	Average financial aid package for freshmen	Average net cost after aid	1998 graduate's average indebtedness
University of Southern Mississippi	pub.	$2870	$3345	62%	9%	$6,652	—	$16,558
Wesley College	ind.	$2800	$2450	NR	NR	NR	NR	NR
William Carey College	ind.	$5910	$1890	NR	NR	NR	NR	$15,000
Missouri								
Avila College	ind.	$11,960	$4800	96%	NR	NR	NR	$17,125
Baptist Bible College	ind.	$2888	$3612	NR	NR	$6,900	—	NR
Central Bible College	ind.	$6260	$3400	81%	8%	$5,510	$4,150	$10,330
Central Christian College of the Bible	ind.	$4500	$2600	72%	NR	$4,799	$2,301	$9692
Central Methodist College	ind.	$11,760	$4330	100%	90%	$12,353	$3,737	$16,252
Central Missouri State University	pub.	$2970	$4104	63%	80%	$5,750	$1,324	NR
College of the Ozarks	ind.	$150	$2500	71%	26%	NR	NR	NR
Columbia College	ind.	$9808	$4399	97%	13%	$6,219	$7,988	$13,576
Conception Seminary College	ind.	$8650	$5068	73%	55%	$13,543	$175	$11,302
Culver-Stockton College	ind.	$10,650	$4750	100%	41%	$8,406	$6,994	$8204
Deaconess College of Nursing	ind.	$8575	$3990	72%	22%	$6,703	$5,862	NR
DeVry Institute of Technology	ind.	$7778	NA	57%	6%	NR	NR	NR
Drury University	ind.	$10,695	$4130	99%	87%	$6,998	$7,827	$12,800
Evangel University	ind.	$9720	$3770	92%	13%	$7,034	$6,456	$10,555
Fontbonne College	ind.	$11,343	$4850	100%	43%	$8,500	$7,693	NR
Hannibal-LaGrange College	ind.	$8440	$3226	NR	NR	NR	NR	$14,563
Harris-Stowe State College	pub.	$2064	NA	68%	29%	NR	NR	$14,562
Jewish Hospital College of Nursing and Allied Health	ind.	$10,034	$2210†	NR	NR	$8,000	$4,244	$10,000
Kansas City Art Institute	ind.	$19,010	$5500	100%	18%	$12,827	$11,683	$17,125
Lincoln University	pub.	$2368	$3790	77%	70%	$5,750	$408	$17,125
Logan University of Chiropractic	ind.	$9360	NA	NR	NR	NR	NR	NR
Maryville University of Saint Louis	ind.	$12,280	$5400	100%	15%	$10,992	$6,688	$11,751
Messenger College	ind.	$3430	$2940	NR	NR	NR	NR	NR
Missouri Baptist College	ind.	$9408	$4480	NR	NR	NR	NR	NR
Missouri Southern State College	pub.	$2496	$3610	63%	7%	$3,667	$2,439	$11,571
Missouri Tech	ind.	$8850	$3600†	NR	NR	NR	NR	NR
Missouri Valley College	ind.	$11,900	$5000	NR	NR	NR	NR	$15,300
Missouri Western State College	pub.	$2774	$3600	NR	NR	$3,566	$2,808	$15,150
Northwest Missouri State University	pub.	$3330	$4150	52%	4%	$4,160	$3,320	$13,493
Ozark Christian College	ind.	$5325	$3480	NR	NR	NR	NR	NR
Park University	ind.	$4770	$4790	55%	42%	$6,449	$3,111	$10,500
Research College of Nursing	ind.	$12,840	$5230	NR	NR	NR	NR	NR
Rockhurst University	ind.	$13,845	$5020	79%	NR	$13,175	$5,690	$15,106
St. Louis Christian College	ind.	$4950	$3120	89%	14%	$5,627	$2,443	NR
St. Louis College of Pharmacy	ind.	$13,370	$5375	NR	NR	$10,654	$8,091	$45,108
Saint Louis University	ind.	$17,268	$5900	98%	30%	NR	NR	$19,058
Saint Luke's College	ind.	$8600	$3000	NR	NR	NR	NR	$21,000
Southeast Missouri State University	pub.	$3225	$4401	55%	38%	$3,410	$4,216	$14,090
Southwest Baptist University	ind.	$9290	$2830	46%	9%	$7,618	$4,502	$12,756
Southwest Missouri State University	pub.	$3564	$3846	54%	13%	$4,425	$2,985	$13,455

*NA = not applicable; NR = not reported; * = includes room and board; † = room only.*

College Cost and Financial Aid Metrics

	Institutional Control ind.=independent; pub.=public	Tuition and fees	Room and board	Percent of freshmen receiving aid whose awards were need-based scholarships/grants	Percent of freshmen receiving aid whose need was fully met	Average financial aid package for freshmen	Average net cost after aid	1998 graduate's average indebtedness
Stephens College	ind.	$15,770	$5870	76%	NR	NR	NR	NR
Truman State University	pub.	$3562	$4400	NR	NR	$5,319	$2,643	$15,357
University of Missouri–Columbia	pub.	$4581	$4545	87%	43%	$6,224	$2,902	$16,161
University of Missouri–Kansas City	pub.	$3852	NR	67%	95%	$12,227	—	$22,127
University of Missouri–Rolla	pub.	$4665	$4557	98%	52%	$9,011	$211	$15,000
University of Missouri–St. Louis	pub.	$4798	$4500	NR	NR	NR	NR	NR
Washington University in St. Louis	ind.	$24,745	$7724	99%	100%	$19,879	$12,590	NR
Webster University	ind.	$12,450	$5440	91%	NR	$12,910	$4,980	NR
Westminster College	ind.	$14,070	$4880	100%	45%	$12,300	$6,650	$12,600
William Jewell College	ind.	$13,020	$4010	86%	NR	NR	NR	$17,908
William Woods University	ind.	$13,050	$5400	NR	NR	NR	NR	NR
Montana								
Carroll College	ind.	$11,778	$4716	98%	24%	$11,090	$5,404	$21,364
Montana State University–Billings	pub.	$2922	$4200	71%	18%	$4,100	$3,022	$13,555
Montana State University–Bozeman	pub.	$2965	$4650	75%	34%	$5,841	$1,774	$17,000
Montana State University–Northern	pub.	$2691	$3800	NR	NR	NR	NR	NR
Montana Tech of The University of Montana	pub.	$2865	$4090	71%	50%	$4,500	$2,455	$11,500
Rocky Mountain College	ind.	$12,243	$4147	100%	20%	$9,311	$7,079	$16,606
University of Great Falls	ind.	$8420	$1500†	90%	36%	$9,771	$149	$20,750
The University of Montana–Missoula	pub.	$2967	$4496	71%	26%	NR	NR	NR
Western Montana College of The University of Montana	pub.	$2545	$3810	97%	NR	$4,532	$1,823	$13,867
Nebraska								
Bellevue University	ind.	$4030	NA	29%	100%	NR	NR	NR
Chadron State College	pub.	$2263	$3300	NR	NR	NR	NR	$11,000
Clarkson College	ind.	$7176	$2800†	85%	NR	NR	NR	NR
College of Saint Mary	ind.	$12,836	$4598	NR	NR	NR	NR	NR
Concordia University	ind.	$11,876	$3938	88%	73%	$12,148	$3,666	NR
Creighton University	ind.	$14,132	$5446	70%	50%	$12,581	$6,997	$19,441
Dana College	ind.	$12,700	$4074	66%	34%	$12,370	$4,404	$14,735
Doane College	ind.	$12,280	$3730	83%	38%	$11,833	$4,177	$15,716
Grace University	ind.	$7964	$3400	100%	16%	$3,627	$7,737	$11,000
Hastings College	ind.	$12,916	$4066	100%	20%	$10,472	$6,510	$15,778
Midland Lutheran College	ind.	$13,320	$3610	100%	25%	$12,419	$4,511	$18,491
Nebraska Christian College	ind.	$4930	$2960	100%	NR	NR	NR	NR
Nebraska Methodist College of Nursing and Allied Health	ind.	$8700	$1480†	100%	21%	$7,022	$3,158	NR
Nebraska Wesleyan University	ind.	$12,826	$3974	100%	18%	$9,695	$7,105	NR
Union College	ind.	$10,696	$3030	100%	12%	$7,548	$6,178	$10,736
University of Nebraska at Kearney	pub.	$2728	$3430	NR	NR	NR	NR	NR
University of Nebraska at Omaha	pub.	$2823	$5290	52%	NR	NR	NR	$14,200
University of Nebraska–Lincoln	pub.	$3338	$4070	77%	23%	$4,955	$2,453	$15,540
University of Nebraska Medical Center	pub.	$2838	NA	NR	NR	NR	NR	$24,100
Wayne State College	pub.	$2271	$3300	70%	34%	$2,842	$2,729	NR
York College	ind.	$8000	$3300	54%	23%	$7,311	$3,989	NR

*NA = not applicable; NR = not reported; * = includes room and board; † = room only.*

College Cost and Financial Aid Metrics

	Institutional Control ind.=independent; pub.=public	Tuition and fees	Room and board	Percent of freshmen receiving aid whose awards were need-based scholarships/grants	Percent of freshmen receiving aid whose need was fully met	Average financial aid package for freshmen	Average net cost after aid	1998 graduate's average indebtedness
Nevada								
Morrison University	ind.	$5580	NA	64%	82%	NR	NR	NR
Sierra Nevada College	ind.	$11,600	$5600	NR	NR	NR	NR	$12,250
University of Nevada, Las Vegas	pub.	$2386	$5694	76%	58%	$5,322	$2,758	$11,500
University of Nevada, Reno	pub.	$2259	$5295	62%	21%	$8,300	—	NR
New Hampshire								
Colby-Sawyer College	ind.	$19,110	$7240	90%	NR	$13,000	$13,350	$17,200
Daniel Webster College	ind.	$15,650	$6002	79%	NR	$12,000	$9,652	$20,875
Dartmouth College	ind.	$24,884	$6390	89%	100%	$24,081	$7,193	$14,818
Franklin Pierce College	ind.	$17,990	$6050	100%	15%	$14,379	$9,661	$18,000
Keene State College	pub.	$5046	$4938	71%	39%	$6,955	$3,029	$16,439
New England College	ind.	$18,097	$6214	96%	NR	$15,068	$9,243	$14,750
New Hampshire College	ind.	$15,848	$6790	NR	NR	NR	NR	NR
Notre Dame College	ind.	$14,378	$5713	NR	NR	NR	NR	NR
Plymouth State College	pub.	$5032	$5030	75%	10%	$7,480	$2,582	$16,343
Rivier College	ind.	$14,260	$5690	93%	32%	$12,377	$7,573	$16,555
Saint Anselm College	ind.	$17,640	$6520	86%	27%	$16,515	$7,645	$16,448
Thomas More College of Liberal Arts	ind.	$9600	$7400	81%	25%	$8,768	$8,232	$13,056
University of New Hampshire	pub.	$6939	$4798	71%	27%	$12,322	—	$19,712
University of New Hampshire at Manchester	pub.	$4684	NA	NR	NR	NR	NR	NR
White Pines College	ind.	$10,100	$5500	NR	NR	NR	NR	NR
New Jersey								
Bloomfield College	ind.	$10,450	$5150	98%	3%	$10,885	$4,715	$12,967
Caldwell College	ind.	$12,400	$5900	100%	NR	$8,125	$10,175	$11,350
Centenary College	ind.	$14,340	$6150	99%	37%	$13,627	$6,863	NR
The College of New Jersey	pub.	$5685	$6330	NR	NR	$7,000	$5,015	$13,000
College of Saint Elizabeth	ind.	$14,030	$6440	100%	12%	$17,752	$2,718	$14,261
DeVry Institute	ind.	$7778	NA	69%	10%	NR	NR	$10,431
Drew University	ind.	$23,008	$6564	NR	NR	NR	NR	$12,880
Fairleigh Dickinson University, Florham-Madison Campus	ind.	$15,593	$6600	84%	6%	$16,903	$5,290	$15,968
Fairleigh Dickinson University, Teaneck–Hackensack Campus	ind.	$15,330	$6536	87%	4%	$16,168	$5,698	$18,493
Felician College	ind.	$11,060	$5670	NR	75%	$10,500	$6,230	$18,000
Georgian Court College	ind.	$12,334	$4000	94%	74%	$11,867	$4,467	$14,047
Kean University	pub.	$4384	$4330†	81%	19%	$3,878	$4,836	NR
Monmouth University	ind.	$15,686	$6476	55%	13%	$10,242	$11,920	$18,750
Montclair State University	pub.	$4320	$6212	9%	38%	$7,197	$3,335	$11,198
New Jersey Institute of Technology	pub.	$6480	$7050	70%	43%	$8,874	$4,656	NR
Princeton University	ind.	$24,630	$6969	99%	100%	$22,300	$9,299	$15,500
Ramapo College of New Jersey	pub.	$5110	$6790	85%	44%	$5,967	$5,933	$11,498
The Richard Stockton College of New Jersey	pub.	$4400	$5381	100%	75%	$8,565	$1,216	$13,135
Rider University	ind.	$16,820	$6770	88%	40%	$15,351	$8,239	$12,500
Rowan University	pub.	$4921	$5766	47%	34%	$4,610	$6,077	NR
Rutgers, The State University of New Jersey, Camden College of Arts and Sciences	pub.	$5874	$5548	90%	37%	$7,811	$3,611	$15,709
Rutgers, The State University of New Jersey, College of Nursing	pub.	$5792	$6110	83%	28%	$8,943	$2,959	$17,701

*NA = not applicable; NR = not reported; * = includes room and board; † = room only.*

College Cost and Financial Aid Metrics

	Institutional Control ind.=independent; pub.=public	Tuition and fees	Room and board	Percent of freshmen receiving aid whose awards were need-based scholarships/grants	Percent of freshmen receiving aid whose need was fully met	Average financial aid package for freshmen	Average net cost after aid	1998 graduate's average indebtedness
Rutgers, The State University of New Jersey, College of Pharmacy	pub.	$6576	$6098	66%	27%	$8,916	$3,758	$16,760
Rutgers, The State University of New Jersey, Cook College	pub.	$6544	$6098	65%	30%	$8,231	$4,411	$16,078
Rutgers, The State University of New Jersey, Douglass College	pub.	$6017	$6098	68%	30%	$8,176	$3,939	$16,496
Rutgers, The State University of New Jersey, Livingston College	pub.	$6038	$6098	72%	25%	$8,051	$4,085	$15,942
Rutgers, The State University of New Jersey, Mason Gross School of the Arts	pub.	$6052	$6098	57%	22%	$8,264	$3,886	$18,141
Rutgers, The State University of New Jersey, Newark College of Arts and Sciences	pub.	$5814	$6110	89%	31%	$8,185	$3,739	$14,313
Rutgers, The State University of New Jersey, Rutgers College	pub.	$6052	$6098	68%	31%	$8,469	$3,681	$15,560
Rutgers, The State University of New Jersey, School of Engineering	pub.	$6576	$6098	72%	21%	$8,848	$3,826	$16,386
Saint Peter's College	ind.	$15,606	$6446	NR	NR	NR	NR	NR
Seton Hall University	ind.	$17,360	$7496	89%	10%	$10,841	$14,015	$15,824
Stevens Institute of Technology	ind.	$21,140	$7280	93%	27%	$19,137	$9,283	$12,900
Westminster Choir College of Rider University	ind.	$16,760	$7080	97%	30%	$14,724	$9,116	$12,500
William Paterson University of New Jersey	pub.	$4690	$5650	68%	30%	$6,558	$3,782	$11,728
New Mexico								
College of the Southwest	ind.	$4640	$3500	100%	6%	$7,268	$872	$11,687
Eastern New Mexico University	pub.	$1830	$3690	88%	11%	$5,038	$482	$16,511
Nazarene Indian Bible College	ind.	$4020	$1575	100%	25%	$3,074	$2,521	NR
New Mexico Highlands University	pub.	$1866	$2730	NR	NR	NR	NR	NR
New Mexico Institute of Mining and Technology	pub.	$2328	$3584	80%	90%	$7,405	—	$14,500
St. John's College	ind.	$22,200	$6386	91%	95%	$17,512	$11,074	$17,125
University of New Mexico	pub.	$2430	$4800	93%	28%	$6,402	$828	$15,896
Western New Mexico University	pub.	$1768	$2938	92%	10%	$4,356	$350	NR
New York								
Adelphi University	ind.	$14,920	$7180	65%	100%	$12,500	$9,600	$19,927
Albany College of Pharmacy of Union University	ind.	$12,173	$5100	100%	NR	$8,431	$8,842	$19,231
Alfred University	ind.	$19,074	$7174	100%	93%	$22,200	$4,048	$17,500
Audrey Cohen College	ind.	$14,480	NA	74%	NR	$4,420	$10,060	$24,000
Bard College	ind.	$24,000	$7220	99%	60%	$19,959	$11,261	$15,400
Barnard College	ind.	$22,316	$9084	94%	100%	$21,866	$9,534	$13,430
Bernard M. Baruch College of the City University of New York	pub.	$3340	NA	87%	35%	$5,412	—	$8100
Boricua College	ind.	$6600	NA	NR	NR	$3,150	$3,450	NR
Briarcliffe College	ind.	$9070	NA	NR	NR	NR	NR	NR
Canisius College	ind.	$15,548	$6340	95%	NR	$14,274	$7,614	NR
Cazenovia College	ind.	$12,140	$5928	NR	NR	NR	NR	NR
City College of the City University of New York	pub.	$3309	NA	NR	NR	NR	NR	NR
Clarkson University	ind.	$20,225	$7484	90%	26%	$14,980	$12,729	$18,110
Colgate University	ind.	$24,750	$6330	93%	96%	$22,011	$9,069	$12,777
College of Aeronautics	ind.	$8500	NR	100%	43%	$8,148	—	$18,000
College of Insurance	ind.	$14,612	$7900	57%	100%	$18,278	$4,234	$16,435
College of Mount Saint Vincent	ind.	$15,070	$7020	NR	NR	$13,300	$8,790	NR
The College of New Rochelle	ind.	$11,700	$6000	NR	NR	NR	NR	NR
The College of Saint Rose	ind.	$12,654	$6358	86%	20%	$10,468	$8,544	$16,379
College of Staten Island of the City University of New York	pub.	$3316	NA	NR	NR	NR	NR	NR

*NA = not applicable; NR = not reported; * = includes room and board; † = room only.*

College Cost and Financial Aid Metrics

	Institutional Control ind.=independent; pub.=public	Tuition and fees	Room and board	Percent of freshmen receiving aid whose awards were need-based scholarships/grants	Percent of freshmen receiving aid whose need was fully met	Average financial aid package for freshmen	Average net cost after aid	1998 graduate's average indebtedness
Columbia College	ind.	$24,974	$7732	86%	100%	$20,954	$11,752	NR
Columbia University, School of General Studies	ind.	$23,740	$9000	NR	NR	NR	NR	NR
Columbia University, The Fu Foundation School of Engineering and Applied Science	ind.	$24,974	$7732	82%	100%	$21,208	$11,498	$16,449
Concordia College	ind.	$14,350	$6200	NR	NR	NR	NR	NR
Cornell University	ind.	$23,848	$7827	90%	100%	$18,400	$13,275	$16,900
The Culinary Institute of America	ind.	$15,605	$5380	NR	NR	NR	NR	$18,500
Daemen College	ind.	$12,220	$6100	91%	13%	$8,597	$9,723	$19,500
DeVry Institute of Technology	ind.	$8776	NA	81%	5%	$8,644	$132	NR
Dominican College of Blauvelt	ind.	$12,370	$7000	NR	NR	NR	NR	NR
Dowling College	ind.	$14,070	$4800†	96%	24%	$8,505	$10,365	$13,500
D'Youville College	ind.	$11,250	$5380	94%	24%	$9,257	$7,373	NR
Elmira College	ind.	$22,540	$7280	100%	31%	$19,012	$10,808	NR
Eugene Lang College, New School University	ind.	$19,915	$9005	97%	3%	$14,566	$14,354	$17,125
Fashion Institute of Technology	pub.	$3195	$7339	89%	37%	$4,921	$5,613	NR
Five Towns College	ind.	$9620	NR	73%	13%	$4,000	—	$9000
Fordham University	ind.	$19,660	$6480	94%	15%	$16,570	$9,570	$15,379
Hamilton College	ind.	$25,050	$6200	98%	100%	$19,925	$11,325	$16,776
Hartwick College	ind.	$23,800	$6340	NR	NR	NR	NR	NR
Hilbert College	ind.	$10,800	$4540	98%	12%	$6,944	$8,396	NR
Hobart and William Smith Colleges	ind.	$24,342	$6882	99%	24%	$21,008	$10,216	$15,338
Hofstra University	ind.	$14,512	$7060	77%	NR	$11,362	$10,210	NR
Houghton College	ind.	$15,140	$5400	92%	22%	$10,118	$10,422	$16,850
Hunter College of the City University of New York	pub.	$3333	NR	NR	NR	$4,061	—	$7200
Iona College	ind.	$15,070	$8430	99%	63%	$15,488	$8,012	$16,086
Ithaca College	ind.	$18,410	$7956	97%	39%	$16,682	$9,684	$16,673
Jewish Theological Seminary of America	ind.	$8720	$5000†	100%	75%	NR	NR	$12,325
John Jay College of Criminal Justice of the City University of New York	pub.	$3312	NA	NR	NR	$4,800	—	$10,000
The Juilliard School	ind.	$16,600	$6850	85%	14%	$15,186	$8,264	$17,298
Keuka College	ind.	$13,085	$6370	NR	NR	$12,400	$7,055	NR
Laboratory Institute of Merchandising	ind.	$12,950	NA	59%	NR	$11,000	$1,950	$14,000
Lehman College of the City University of New York	pub.	$3320	NA	94%	NR	$4,800	—	$7200
Le Moyne College	ind.	$14,980	$6320	98%	85%	$11,900	$9,400	$16,000
Long Island University, Brooklyn Campus	ind.	$15,450	$5100	91%	51%	$11,205	$9,345	$19,380
Long Island University, Southampton College	ind.	$16,120	$7790	92%	NR	NR	NR	$15,235
Manhattan College	ind.	$15,810	$7450	89%	1%	$11,743	$11,517	NR
Manhattan School of Music	ind.	$19,580	$5250†	66%	5%	$17,081	$7,749	$17,125
Manhattanville College	ind.	$19,620	$8000	NR	20%	$18,974	$8,646	NR
Mannes College of Music, New School University	ind.	$18,000	$6875†	96%	11%	$10,808	$14,067	$18,380
Marist College	ind.	$14,754	$7418	73%	17%	$11,966	$10,206	$16,350
Marymount College	ind.	$15,130	$7800	NR	NR	NR	NR	NR
Marymount Manhattan College	ind.	$13,605	$6750†	90%	21%	$12,418	$7,937	NR
Medaille College	ind.	$11,450	$5300	NR	NR	NR	NR	NR
Medgar Evers College of the City University of New York	pub.	$3282	NA	NR	NR	NR	NR	NR

*NA = not applicable; NR = not reported; * = includes room and board; † = room only.*

College Cost and Financial Aid Metrics

	Institutional Control ind.=independent; pub.=public	Tuition and fees	Room and board	Percent of freshmen receiving aid whose awards were need-based scholarships/grants	Percent of freshmen receiving aid whose need was fully met	Average financial aid package for freshmen	Average net cost after aid	1998 graduate's average indebtedness
Mercy College	ind.	$7950	$7500	NR	NR	NR	NR	NR
Mount Saint Mary College	ind.	$11,470	$5700	NR	NR	$7,800	$9,370	$14,500
Nazareth College of Rochester	ind.	$14,046	$6376	99%	NR	$12,186	$8,236	$18,095
New School Bachelor of Arts, New School University	ind.	$13,068	$6310†	NR	NR	NR	NR	$14,500
New York Institute of Technology	ind.	$11,990	$6510	92%	NR	NR	NR	$17,125
New York School of Interior Design	ind.	$16,070	NA	100%	NR	$5,000	$11,070	$7500
New York University	ind.	$23,456	$8860	94%	NR	$16,534	$15,782	$17,985
Niagara University	ind.	$13,940	$6330	92%	18%	$13,074	$7,196	$12,743
Nyack College	ind.	$12,740	$5800	100%	19%	$12,502	$6,038	$17,000
Parsons School of Design, New School University	ind.	$21,790	NR	100%	12%	$11,628	—	$27,125
Plattsburgh State University of New York	pub.	$3957	$4850	89%	75%	$4,682	$4,125	$15,474
Polytechnic University, Brooklyn Campus	ind.	$20,810	$5470	97%	90%	$16,980	$9,300	$19,341
Practical Bible College	ind.	$6370	$3800	97%	9%	$3,020	$7,150	$4804
Pratt Institute	ind.	$20,084	$7800	80%	NR	$12,215	$15,669	NR
Purchase College, State University of New York	pub.	$3949	$5942	77%	98%	$7,505	$2,386	NR
Queens College of the City University of New York	pub.	$3403	NA	93%	57%	$3,500	—	$12,000
Rensselaer Polytechnic Institute	ind.	$22,955	$7692	100%	62%	$19,375	$11,272	$22,300
Roberts Wesleyan College	ind.	$13,614	$4614	99%	13%	$12,764	$5,464	$17,436
Rochester Institute of Technology	ind.	$17,637	$6852	93%	90%	$14,900	$9,589	NR
Russell Sage College	ind.	$15,300	$6350	99%	NR	$13,856	$7,794	$11,350
St. Bonaventure University	ind.	$14,430	$5800	100%	27%	$12,416	$7,814	$16,402
St. Francis College	ind.	$8410	NA	95%	NR	$8,226	$184	NR
St. John Fisher College	ind.	$14,140	$6050	78%	18%	$11,879	$8,311	$18,400
St. John's University	ind.	$14,420	$8550	94%	11%	$11,192	$11,778	$14,393
St. Joseph's College, New York	ind.	$8922	NA	100%	24%	$8,152	$770	$14,000
St. Joseph's College, Suffolk Campus	ind.	$9182	NA	83%	42%	$4,600	$4,582	$13,000
St. Lawrence University	ind.	$23,165	$7205	97%	42%	$23,664	$6,706	NR
St. Thomas Aquinas College	ind.	$12,120	$7150	NR	NR	NR	NR	NR
Sarah Lawrence College	ind.	$25,406	$8648	90%	73%	$18,134	$15,920	$16,362
School of Visual Arts	ind.	$15,320	$6400†	NR	NR	NR	NR	NR
Siena College	ind.	$14,130	$6215	99%	13%	$10,716	$9,629	$14,000
Skidmore College	ind.	$31,200*	$6950	91%	61%	$18,786	$19,364	$14,400
State University of New York at Albany	pub.	$4338	$5828	81%	12%	$6,750	$3,416	NR
State University of New York at Binghamton	pub.	$4416	$5516	81%	55%	$9,628	$304	$11,856
State University of New York at Buffalo	pub.	$4655	$5904	NR	NR	$5,501	$5,058	$15,250
State University of New York at Farmingdale	pub.	$4075	$6114	NR	NR	NR	NR	NR
State University of New York at New Paltz	pub.	$3985	$5368	80%	30%	$7,771	$1,582	NR
State University of New York at Oswego	pub.	$3975	$6160	84%	21%	$5,794	$4,341	$14,649
State University of New York at Stony Brook	pub.	$4141	$6421	95%	15%	$6,707	$3,855	NR
State University of New York College at Brockport	pub.	$9424*	$5410	75%	48%	$6,358	$8,476	$15,514
State University of New York College at Buffalo	pub.	$3909	$5170	NR	NR	NR	NR	NR
State University of New York College at Cortland	pub.	$4104	$5530	93%	44%	$5,425	$4,209	$18,279
State University of New York College at Fredonia	pub.	$4125	$5200	76%	68%	$5,329	$3,996	$12,691
State University of New York College at Geneseo	pub.	$4221	$4940	78%	80%	$6,080	$3,081	$12,500
State University of New York College at Oneonta	pub.	$4123	$5456	84%	28%	$7,210	$2,369	$15,100

*NA = not applicable; NR = not reported; * = includes room and board; † = room only.*

College Cost and Financial Aid Metrics

	Institutional Control ind.=independent; pub.=public	Tuition and fees	Room and board	Percent of freshmen receiving aid whose awards were need-based scholarships/grants	Percent of freshmen receiving aid whose need was fully met	Average financial aid package for freshmen	Average net cost after aid	1998 graduate's average indebtedness
State University of New York College at Potsdam	pub.	$3935	$5750	97%	82%	$8,607	$1,078	$15,303
State University of New York College of Environmental Science and Forestry	pub.	$3762	$8310	92%	97%	$7,550	$4,522	$15,000
State University of New York Institute of Technology at Utica/Rome	pub.	$3975	$6100	NR	NR	NR	NR	NR
State University of New York Maritime College	pub.	$4195	$5600	72%	60%	$12,000	—	$12,000
State University of New York Upstate Medical University	pub.	$3810	$6515	NR	NR	NR	NR	NR
Syracuse University	ind.	$19,784	$8400	90%	NR	$15,100	$13,084	$18,600
Touro College	ind.	$9250	NR	NR	NR	NR	NR	NR
Union College	ind.	$24,099	$6474	100%	100%	$22,348	$8,225	$17,650
University of Rochester	ind.	$22,864	$7512	99%	100%	$19,725	$10,651	NR
Utica College of Syracuse University	ind.	$16,410	$6350	100%	15%	NR	NR	NR
Vassar College	ind.	$24,030	$6770	100%	100%	$20,027	$10,773	$15,772
Wadhams Hall Seminary-College	ind.	$5525	$4775	67%	17%	$10,500	—	$6800
Wagner College	ind.	$18,000	$6500	99%	16%	$12,472	$12,028	NR
Webb Institute	ind.	$0	$6250	NR	100%	$4,700	$1,550	$16,600
Wells College	ind.	$12,300	$6100	100%	31%	$13,682	$4,718	$17,125
Yeshiva Karlin Stolin Rabbinical Institute	ind.	$5200	$3200	NR	NR	NR	NR	NR
Yeshiva University	ind.	$15,960	$5270	NR	NR	NR	NR	NR
York College of the City University of New York	pub.	$3292	NA	NR	NR	NR	NR	NR
North Carolina								
Appalachian State University	pub.	$2088	$3560	76%	41%	$4,555	$1,093	$9400
Barber-Scotia College	ind.	$7866	$3500	55%	84%	$8,180	$3,186	$12,125
Barton College	ind.	$10,834	$3892	80%	68%	$8,589	$6,137	$11,500
Belmont Abbey College	ind.	$12,712	$6528	85%	6%	$11,625	$7,615	$4000
Bennett College	ind.	$8460	$3702	NR	NR	NR	NR	NR
Brevard College	ind.	$12,310	$4820	93%	34%	$10,355	$6,775	$8618
Campbell University	ind.	$10,997	$3950	74%	84%	$15,117	—	$17,125
Catawba College	ind.	$12,600	$4840	100%	24%	$8,248	$9,192	NR
Chowan College	ind.	$11,520	$4600	100%	32%	$11,765	$4,355	$17,056
Davidson College	ind.	$22,228	$6340	87%	100%	$13,555	$15,013	$14,011
Duke University	ind.	$24,751	$7088	88%	100%	$18,566	$13,273	$16,098
East Carolina University	pub.	$1998	$4070	57%	31%	NR	NR	$14,105
Elon College	ind.	$12,896	$4551	82%	NR	$8,819	$8,628	$17,408
Fayetteville State University	pub.	$1702	$3800	NR	NR	NR	NR	NR
Gardner-Webb University	ind.	$11,660	$4760	99%	46%	$10,454	$5,966	NR
Greensboro College	ind.	$11,700	$4900	57%	27%	$8,900	$7,700	$12,229
Guilford College	ind.	$16,970	$5610	100%	85%	$14,742	$7,838	$14,260
Heritage Bible College	ind.	$4000	$2236	46%	NR	$3,167	$3,069	$15,152
High Point University	ind.	$12,440	$5770	NR	NR	NR	NR	NR
Johnson C. Smith University	ind.	$9974	$3875	38%	1%	$4,500	$9,349	$22,000
John Wesley College	ind.	$5556	$1750†	79%	7%	NR	NR	NR
Lees-McRae College	ind.	$11,200	$4100	NR	NR	NR	NR	NR
Mars Hill College	ind.	$11,600	$4300	NR	NR	NR	NR	NR
Meredith College	ind.	$9840	$4260	99%	36%	$8,054	$6,046	NR
Methodist College	ind.	$12,704	$4830	97%	NR	$9,625	$7,909	$17,944

*NA = not applicable; NR = not reported; * = includes room and board; † = room only.*

College Cost and Financial Aid Metrics

	Institutional Control ind.=independent; pub.=public	Tuition and fees	Room and board	Percent of freshmen receiving aid whose awards were need-based scholarships/grants	Percent of freshmen receiving aid whose need was fully met	Average financial aid package for freshmen	Average net cost after aid	1998 graduate's average indebtedness
Montreat College	ind.	$10,862	$4412	99%	NR	$9,227	$6,047	$16,274
Mount Olive College	ind.	$9210	$4000	100%	30%	$7,119	$6,091	$7453
North Carolina Agricultural and Technical State University	pub.	$1889	$4010	80%	24%	$5,719	$180	NR
North Carolina Central University	pub.	$1887	$3904	75%	33%	$5,447	$344	NR
North Carolina School of the Arts	pub.	$2517	$4462	82%	1%	$5,183	$1,796	$16,300
North Carolina State University	pub.	$2514	$4560	100%	23%	$6,314	$760	$14,801
North Carolina Wesleyan College	ind.	$8556	$5972	86%	NR	$9,325	$5,203	$11,250
Peace College	ind.	$9927	$5000	NR	NR	NR	NR	NR
Pfeiffer University	ind.	$10,844	$4367	95%	26%	$5,830	$9,381	NR
Piedmont Baptist College	ind.	$5750	$3400	100%	NR	$1,500	$7,650	$15,000
Queens College	ind.	$10,680	$5890	100%	28%	$9,938	$6,632	$15,300
Roanoke Bible College	ind.	$5610	$3460	100%	NR	$4,943	$4,127	$11,742
St. Andrews Presbyterian College	ind.	$13,735	$5300	61%	29%	$11,334	$7,701	NR
Saint Augustine's College	ind.	$7182	$4508	81%	70%	$9,453	$2,237	$18,000
Salem College	ind.	$13,415	$7920	NR	NR	NR	NR	NR
Shaw University	ind.	$6854	$4342	79%	17%	$5,775	$5,421	$17,125
The University of North Carolina at Asheville	pub.	$1960	$4179	76%	22%	$4,804	$1,335	$13,118
The University of North Carolina at Chapel Hill	pub.	$2365	$5280	94%	93%	$6,114	$1,531	$12,800
The University of North Carolina at Charlotte	pub.	$1920	$3816	69%	20%	$4,873	$863	$7848
The University of North Carolina at Greensboro	pub.	$2136	$4064	75%	53%	$4,600	$1,600	$10,026
The University of North Carolina at Pembroke	pub.	$1706	$3358	87%	36%	$4,277	$787	NR
The University of North Carolina at Wilmington	pub.	$2068	$4656	61%	29%	$6,694	$30	$12,559
Wake Forest University	ind.	$21,452	$5900	92%	54%	$17,400	$9,952	$17,661
Warren Wilson College	ind.	$13,600	$4444	88%	18%	$11,397	$6,647	$13,880
Western Carolina University	pub.	$2082	$3260	77%	93%	$5,400	—	$15,500
Wingate University	ind.	$13,050	$5200	83%	19%	$10,750	$7,500	$15,250
Winston-Salem State University	pub.	$1704	$3503	76%	10%	$3,125	$2,082	$10,900
North Dakota								
Dickinson State University	pub.	$2302	$2610	NR	NR	NR	NR	$8932
Jamestown College	ind.	$7550	$3300	100%	35%	$7,475	$3,375	$15,000
Mayville State University	pub.	$3106	$3042	79%	NR	$4,721	$1,427	$15,468
Medcenter One College of Nursing	ind.	$3236	$900†	NR	NR	NR	NR	NR
Minot State University	pub.	$2331	$2724	NR	NR	NR	NR	$11,884
North Dakota State University	pub.	$2886	$3408	73%	56%	$4,635	$1,659	$18,624
Trinity Bible College	ind.	$6294	$3680	67%	7%	$6,962	$3,012	NR
University of Mary	ind.	$8300	$3538	72%	52%	$7,700	$4,138	$15,691
University of North Dakota	pub.	$2956	$3406	34%	14%	$4,287	$2,075	$19,143
Valley City State University	pub.	$3097	$2800	97%	65%	$4,877	$1,020	NR
Ohio								
Antioch College	ind.	$19,231	$4876	95%	41%	$17,424	$6,683	$13,927
Art Academy of Cincinnati	ind.	$12,200	NA	97%	28%	$7,498	$4,702	$11,290
Ashland University	ind.	$14,676	$5450	100%	NR	$14,124	$6,002	$18,100
Baldwin-Wallace College	ind.	$15,340	$5460	92%	84%	$12,934	$7,866	$19,768
Bluffton College	ind.	$14,306	$5122	100%	86%	$13,232	$6,196	$16,587

*NA = not applicable; NR = not reported; * = includes room and board; † = room only.*

College Cost and Financial Aid Metrics

	Institutional Control ind.=independent; pub.=public	Tuition and fees	Room and board	Percent of freshmen receiving aid whose awards were need-based scholarships/grants	Percent of freshmen receiving aid whose need was fully met	Average financial aid package for freshmen	Average net cost after aid	1998 graduate's average indebtedness
Bowling Green State University	pub.	$4874	$5494	35%	30%	$5,002	$5,366	$15,000
Bryant and Stratton College	ind.	$9024	$3320†	58%	83%	$6,200	$6,144	$12,000
Capital University	ind.	$16,000	$4900	70%	89%	$13,666	$7,234	$16,200
Case Western Reserve University	ind.	$20,260	$5815	98%	73%	$18,843	$7,232	$19,375
Cedarville College	ind.	$10,740	$4788	39%	34%	$9,203	$6,325	$16,975
Central State University	pub.	$3443	$4860	NR	NR	NR	NR	NR
Cincinnati Bible College and Seminary	ind.	$6471	$3800	90%	25%	$5,000	$5,271	$14,589
Circleville Bible College	ind.	$6540	$4300	28%	16%	$7,200	$3,640	$15,000
Cleveland College of Jewish Studies	ind.	$6015	NA	NR	NR	NR	NR	NR
Cleveland Institute of Art	ind.	$15,015	$5076	100%	22%	$10,235	$9,856	$16,253
Cleveland Institute of Music	ind.	$18,625	$5590	100%	32%	$13,409	$10,806	$12,053
College of Mount St. Joseph	ind.	$13,090	$4950	98%	37%	$11,099	$6,941	$17,125
The College of Wooster	ind.	$20,530	$5420	100%	76%	$17,780	$8,170	$15,800
Columbus College of Art and Design	ind.	$13,440	$6000	NR	NR	NR	NR	NR
David N. Myers College	ind.	$8760	NA	75%	NR	NR	NR	$15,906
Defiance College	ind.	$14,550	$4230	NR	NR	NR	NR	$14,303
Denison University	ind.	$22,210	$6300	82%	73%	$9,069	$19,441	$14,021
DeVry Institute of Technology	ind.	$7778	NA	65%	6%	$6,215	$1,563	$11,451
Franciscan University of Steubenville	ind.	$12,270	$4970	88%	20%	$7,188	$10,052	$19,692
Franklin University	ind.	$5531	NA	75%	NR	NR	NR	NR
Heidelberg College	ind.	$16,672	$5264	100%	19%	$14,643	$7,293	$18,725
Hiram College	ind.	$17,710	$6024	85%	70%	$16,588	$7,146	$17,125
John Carroll University	ind.	$16,384	$6128	96%	43%	$13,942	$8,570	$12,695
Kent State University	pub.	$6016	$4530	77%	17%	$5,055	$5,491	$16,666
Kenyon College	ind.	$24,590	$4160	96%	61%	$17,391	$11,359	$16,650
Lake Erie College	ind.	$15,140	$5260	NR	NR	NR	NR	NR
Lourdes College	ind.	$9368	NA	90%	NR	$7,899	$1,469	NR
Malone College	ind.	$12,380	$5250	100%	82%	$11,257	$6,373	$15,114
Marietta College	ind.	$17,510	$4970	71%	5%	$15,910	$6,570	$16,077
The McGregor School of Antioch University	ind.	$10,176	NA	NR	NR	NR	NR	$18,000
Miami University	pub.	$6112	$5330	47%	25%	$5,603	$5,839	$16,710
Mount Union College	ind.	$14,880	$4370	100%	35%	$12,672	$6,578	$15,601
Mount Vernon Nazarene College	ind.	$11,926	$4203	76%	10%	$5,914	$10,215	$16,253
Muskingum College	ind.	$12,665	$5100	100%	46%	$11,937	$5,828	$14,872
Notre Dame College of Ohio	ind.	$13,618	$5248	100%	NR	$12,847	$6,019	$15,649
Oberlin College	ind.	$24,264	$6178	89%	100%	$21,919	$8,523	$13,926
Ohio Dominican College	ind.	$10,250	$5070	NR	NR	NR	NR	NR
Ohio Northern University	ind.	$21,435	$5265	100%	27%	$19,655	$7,045	$16,400
The Ohio State University	pub.	$4137	$5328	51%	27%	$6,533	$2,932	$11,800
Ohio University	pub.	$4800	$5484	36%	45%	$6,007	$4,277	$13,850
Ohio University–Chillicothe	pub.	$3192	NA	61%	41%	$5,519	—	NR
Ohio University–Eastern	pub.	$2128	NA	53%	34%	$4,817	—	NR
Ohio University–Lancaster	pub.	$2128	NA	62%	30%	$5,310	—	NR
Ohio University–Zanesville	pub.	$2128	NA	59%	38%	$5,217	—	NR
Ohio Wesleyan University	ind.	$20,940	$6560	80%	42%	$19,922	$7,578	$19,253

*NA = not applicable; NR = not reported; * = includes room and board; † = room only.*

College Cost and Financial Aid Metrics	Institutional Control ind.=independent; pub.=public	Tuition and fees	Room and board	Percent of freshmen receiving aid whose awards were need-based scholarships/grants	Percent of freshmen receiving aid whose need was fully met	Average financial aid package for freshmen	Average net cost after aid	1998 graduate's average indebtedness
Otterbein College	ind.	$16,260	$5121	NR	NR	NR	NR	NR
Pontifical College Josephinum	ind.	$7590	$4940	100%	NR	NR	NR	$15,000
Shawnee State University	pub.	$3294	$4431	91%	100%	$3,881	$3,844	$10,944
Tiffin University	ind.	$10,500	$4850	54%	15%	$3,561	$11,789	$16,670
The Union Institute	ind.	$6288	NA	NR	NR	NR	NR	NR
The University of Akron	pub.	$4152	$5010	53%	20%	$3,790	$5,372	$15,421
University of Cincinnati	pub.	$4998	$6399	62%	43%	$4,546	$6,851	NR
University of Dayton	ind.	$15,530	$4870	100%	64%	$9,904	$10,496	$16,357
The University of Findlay	ind.	$15,260	$5740	97%	8%	$11,200	$9,800	$17,500
University of Rio Grande	ind.	$2961	$4995	60%	25%	NR	NR	$13,750
University of Toledo	pub.	$4416	$4538	NR	NR	NR	NR	NR
Urbana University	ind.	$11,488	$5000	NR	NR	NR	NR	NR
Ursuline College	ind.	$13,760	$4560	NR	NR	NR	NR	NR
Walsh University	ind.	$11,728	$5400	100%	23%	$10,088	$7,040	$17,000
Wilberforce University	ind.	$9130	$4790	NR	NR	NR	NR	NR
Wilmington College	ind.	$14,666	$5220	95%	44%	$13,104	$6,782	$19,800
Wittenberg University	ind.	$20,906	$5206	85%	37%	$19,863	$6,249	NR
Xavier University	ind.	$15,880	$6680	99%	30%	$11,447	$11,113	$10,988
Youngstown State University	pub.	$3762	$4695	NR	NR	NR	NR	NR
Oklahoma								
Bartlesville Wesleyan College	ind.	$9700	$4100	51%	17%	$7,088	$6,712	NR
Cameron University	pub.	$2050	$2830	36%	48%	$3,600	$1,280	$6300
East Central University	pub.	$1962	$2226	77%	37%	$2,972	$1,216	$11,865
Hillsdale Free Will Baptist College	ind.	$5840	$3950	NR	NR	NR	NR	NR
Langston University	pub.	$1704	$2944	NR	NR	NR	NR	NR
Mid-America Bible College	ind.	$5552	$3196	NR	NR	NR	NR	NR
Northeastern State University	pub.	$1865	$2610	87%	60%	$3,903	$572	NR
Northwestern Oklahoma State University	pub.	$1987	$2316	86%	54%	$5,800	—	$9000
Oklahoma Baptist University	ind.	$9440	$3417	NR	NR	NR	NR	NR
Oklahoma Christian University of Science and Arts	ind.	$9590	$4100	86%	NR	$9,400	$4,290	$17,200
Oklahoma City University	ind.	$9558	$8800	87%	NR	$9,406	$8,952	$17,563
Oklahoma Panhandle State University	pub.	$1960	$2368	NR	NR	NR	NR	NR
Oklahoma State University	pub.	$2458	$4536	70%	26%	$6,198	$796	$14,113
Oral Roberts University	ind.	$11,650	$5076	98%	55%	$11,895	$4,831	$25,223
St. Gregory's University	ind.	$7866	$4070	93%	13%	NR	NR	NR
Southern Nazarene University	ind.	$9380	$4316	NR	NR	NR	NR	NR
Southwestern College of Christian Ministries	ind.	$5916	$3000	100%	12%	$7,450	$1,466	$12,250
Southwestern Oklahoma State University	pub.	$1873	$2440	93%	7%	$727	$3,586	$7500
University of Central Oklahoma	pub.	$1936	$2743	86%	86%	$3,200	$1,479	$10,000
University of Oklahoma	pub.	$2456	$4384	32%	89%	$5,089	$1,751	$18,976
University of Science and Arts of Oklahoma	pub.	$1878	$2320	92%	46%	$6,534	—	$11,120
University of Tulsa	ind.	$13,480	$4660	70%	28%	$13,705	$4,435	$21,376
Oregon								
The Art Institute of Portland	ind.	$12,060	NA	85%	3%	$1,900	$10,160	$10,490

*NA = not applicable; NR = not reported; * = includes room and board; † = room only.*

College Cost and Financial Aid Metrics

	Institutional Control ind.=independent; pub.=public	Tuition and fees	Room and board	Percent of freshmen receiving aid whose awards were need-based scholarships/grants	Percent of freshmen receiving aid whose need was fully met	Average financial aid package for freshmen	Average net cost after aid	1998 graduate's average indebtedness
Cascade College	ind.	$8590	$4700	NR	NR	NR	NR	NR
Concordia University	ind.	$15,500	$3820	100%	65%	$11,800	$7,520	$10,500
Eastern Oregon University	pub.	$3315	$4565	NR	NR	NR	NR	NR
Eugene Bible College	ind.	$5913	$3663	67%	7%	$5,000	$4,576	$17,500
George Fox University	ind.	$17,610	$5550	100%	47%	$15,561	$7,599	$15,708
Lewis & Clark College	ind.	$21,520	$6100	99%	26%	$19,670	$7,950	NR
Linfield College	ind.	$17,720	$5300	100%	56%	$14,200	$8,820	$17,600
Mount Angel Seminary	ind.	$8850	$4900	NR	NR	NR	NR	NR
Multnomah Bible College and Biblical Seminary	ind.	$8600	$3720	96%	14%	$6,590	$5,730	NR
Northwest Christian College	ind.	$13,905	$5157	100%	14%	$13,157	$5,905	$18,687
Oregon College of Art and Craft	ind.	$11,710	NA	100%	NR	$8,792	$2,918	$17,207
Oregon Health Sciences University	pub.	$5747	$2070†	NR	NR	NR	NR	NR
Oregon Institute of Technology	pub.	$3378	$4866	NR	NR	NR	NR	$17,000
Oregon State University	pub.	$3549	$5394	NR	NR	NR	NR	NR
Pacific Northwest College of Art	ind.	$13,200	$3825†	100%	NR	$9,856	$7,169	NR
Pacific University	ind.	$17,800	$4903	99%	34%	$15,957	$6,746	$18,500
Portland State University	pub.	$3468	$6150	NR	NR	$4,354	$5,264	NR
Reed College	ind.	$24,050	$6650	100%	100%	$22,208	$8,492	$14,010
Southern Oregon University	pub.	$3234	$4658	84%	20%	$5,819	$2,073	$13,404
University of Oregon	pub.	$3810	$5350	NR	NR	NR	NR	NR
University of Portland	ind.	$17,299	$5190	95%	42%	$14,205	$8,284	$19,319
Warner Pacific College	ind.	$135,000	$4567	53%	21%	$10,390	$129,177	$12,908
Western Baptist College	ind.	$13,690	$4940	78%	39%	$11,453	$7,177	$13,498
Western Oregon University	pub.	$3276	$5004	82%	39%	$5,904	$2,376	$14,301
Willamette University	ind.	$21,822	$5700	98%	59%	$18,850	$8,672	$16,800
Pennsylvania								
Albright College	ind.	$19,460	$5780	100%	24%	$17,488	$7,752	NR
Allegheny College	ind.	$20,690	$4970	100%	54%	$18,070	$7,590	$17,375
Allentown College of St. Francis de Sales	ind.	$13,640	$5860	97%	53%	$12,900	$6,600	NR
Alvernia College	ind.	$12,346	$5480	87%	10%	$9,374	$8,452	$12,000
Baptist Bible College of Pennsylvania	ind.	$8992	$4714	NR	NR	$6,778	$6,928	NR
Beaver College	ind.	$17,160	$7310	81%	14%	$16,339	$8,131	$17,125
Bloomsburg University of Pennsylvania	pub.	$4455	$3784	94%	90%	$6,643	$1,596	$13,300
Bryn Mawr College	ind.	$23,360	$8100	100%	100%	$21,246	$10,214	NR
Bucknell University	ind.	$22,881	$5469	80%	100%	$17,494	$10,856	$15,500
Cabrini College	ind.	$16,000	$7200	NR	NR	NR	NR	NR
California University of Pennsylvania	pub.	$4742	$4526	NR	NR	NR	NR	NR
Carlow College	ind.	$12,826	$5076	95%	75%	$11,970	$5,932	$15,000
Carnegie Mellon University	ind.	$22,300	$6810	98%	36%	$15,710	$13,400	$17,880
Cedar Crest College	ind.	$17,110	$6215	100%	31%	$16,708	$6,617	$19,095
Chatham College	ind.	$17,544	$6120	84%	5%	$15,357	$8,307	$17,000
Cheyney University of Pennsylvania	pub.	$4173	$4793	87%	58%	$7,400	$1,566	$20,000
Clarion University of Pennsylvania	pub.	$4600	$3984	50%	72%	$5,814	$2,770	$14,378
College Misericordia	ind.	$15,250	$6340	90%	13%	$10,036	$11,554	$16,900

*NA = not applicable; NR = not reported; * = includes room and board; † = room only.*

College Cost and Financial Aid Metrics

College	Institutional Control ind.=independent; pub.=public	Tuition and fees	Room and board	Percent of freshmen receiving aid whose awards were need-based scholarships/grants	Percent of freshmen receiving aid whose need was fully met	Average financial aid package for freshmen	Average net cost after aid	1998 graduate's average indebtedness
Delaware Valley College	ind.	$15,687	$6000	88%	42%	$14,235	$7,452	NR
Dickinson College	ind.	$24,450	$6450	98%	39%	$19,318	$11,582	$17,752
Drexel University	ind.	$16,150	$7842	94%	36%	$14,394	$9,598	NR
Duquesne University	ind.	$15,588	$6314	84%	32%	$13,854	$8,048	$17,842
East Stroudsburg University of Pennsylvania	pub.	$4492	$3938	74%	78%	$4,123	$4,307	$14,139
Edinboro University of Pennsylvania	pub.	$4358	$3788	100%	82%	$5,728	$2,418	$17,500
Elizabethtown College	ind.	$18,220	$5380	100%	22%	$15,187	$8,413	$15,644
Franklin and Marshall College	ind.	$23,720	$5730	91%	100%	$16,971	$12,479	$15,982
Gannon University	ind.	$13,408	$5440	100%	43%	$13,270	$5,578	$19,005
Geneva College	ind.	$12,650	$4952	97%	95%	$9,000	$8,602	$20,000
Gettysburg College	ind.	$24,032	$5644	100%	100%	$19,800	$9,876	$13,900
Grove City College	ind.	$7506	$4048	91%	26%	$3,320	$8,234	$11,383
Gwynedd-Mercy College	ind.	$13,540	$6500	100%	70%	$13,507	$6,533	$14,282
Haverford College	ind.	$23,780	$7620	90%	100%	$20,998	$10,402	$13,821
Holy Family College	ind.	$11,860	NA	92%	NR	$9,460	$2,400	$17,125
Immaculata College	ind.	$13,400	$6500	82%	27%	$11,723	$8,177	$17,125
Indiana University of Pennsylvania	pub.	$4397	$3782	59%	53%	$6,006	$2,173	$10,000
Juniata College	ind.	$19,360	$5290	100%	53%	$16,280	$8,370	$16,395
King's College	ind.	$15,910	$6620	100%	22%	$13,799	$8,731	$15,500
Kutztown University of Pennsylvania	pub.	$4448	$4082	74%	63%	$4,001	$4,529	$12,817
Lafayette College	ind.	$22,929	$7106	99%	97%	$20,195	$9,840	$13,875
Lancaster Bible College	ind.	$9430	$4300	81%	10%	$7,054	$6,676	$13,071
La Roche College	ind.	$11,450	$4130	NR	NR	NR	NR	NR
La Salle University	ind.	$17,260	$6602	85%	22%	$13,745	$10,117	$17,000
Lebanon Valley College	ind.	$17,260	$5490	100%	32%	$13,761	$8,989	$17,462
Lehigh University	ind.	$23,150	$6630	100%	100%	$19,650	$10,130	$15,178
Lincoln University	pub.	$5208	$5034	NR	NR	NR	NR	NR
Lock Haven University of Pennsylvania	pub.	$4244	$4136	65%	45%	$3,969	$4,411	$16,472
Lycoming College	ind.	$17,600	$4960	100%	24%	$13,605	$8,955	$14,900
Mansfield University of Pennsylvania	pub.	$4560	$3852	NR	14%	$1,559	$6,853	$20,862
Marywood University	ind.	$15,623	$6540	100%	NR	$12,205	$9,958	$19,170
MCP Hahnemann University	ind.	$10,225	$8526	NR	NR	NR	NR	NR
Mercyhurst College	ind.	$14,190	$5106	90%	76%	$6,036	$13,260	$16,781
Messiah College	ind.	$15,096	$5580	91%	14%	$11,726	$8,950	$16,999
Millersville University of Pennsylvania	pub.	$4595	$4730	81%	NR	$5,900	$3,425	$12,507
Moore College of Art and Design	ind.	$16,025	$6150	100%	8%	$12,664	$9,511	$25,000
Moravian College	ind.	$18,575	$5920	99%	23%	$14,898	$9,597	NR
Mount Aloysius College	ind.	$10,980	$4830	100%	NR	$4,650	$11,160	$17,000
Muhlenberg College	ind.	$20,085	$5390	96%	95%	$13,899	$11,576	NR
Neumann College	ind.	$13,920	$6500	NR	NR	NR	NR	NR
Peirce College	ind.	$8220	NA	25%	19%	$4,000	$4,220	$12,500
Pennsylvania School of Art & Design	ind.	$9290	NA	NR	NR	NR	NR	NR
Pennsylvania State University Abington College	pub.	$6312	NA	NR	NR	NR	NR	NR
Pennsylvania State University Altoona College	pub.	$6332	$4690	NR	NR	NR	NR	NR
Pennsylvania State University at Erie, The Behrend College	pub.	$6436	$4690	NR	NR	NR	NR	NR

*NA = not applicable; NR = not reported; * = includes room and board; † = room only.*

College Cost and Financial Aid Metrics

	Institutional Control ind.=independent; pub.=public	Tuition and fees	Room and board	Percent of freshmen receiving aid whose awards were need-based scholarships/grants	Percent of freshmen receiving aid whose need was fully met	Average financial aid package for freshmen	Average net cost after aid	1998 graduate's average indebtedness
Pennsylvania State University Berks Campus of the Berks–Lehigh Valley College	pub.	$6332	$4690	NR	NR	NR	NR	NR
Pennsylvania State University Harrisburg Campus of the Capital College	pub.	$6416	$4690	NR	NR	NR	NR	NR
Pennsylvania State University Lehigh Valley Campus of the Berks-Lehigh Valley College	pub.	$6242	NA	NR	NR	NR	NR	NR
Pennsylvania State University Schuylkill Campus of the Capital College	pub.	$6222	$4690	NR	NR	NR	NR	NR
Pennsylvania State University University Park Campus	pub.	$6436	$4690	72%	6%	$6,985	$4,141	$17,125
Philadelphia College of Bible	ind.	$10,355	$5073	96%	16%	$6,705	$8,723	$12,170
Philadelphia University	ind.	$14,738	$6576	100%	15%	$12,627	$8,687	$19,630
Point Park College	ind.	$12,454	$5334	100%	12%	$8,553	$9,235	NR
Robert Morris College	ind.	$9919	$6062	100%	NR	$6,300	$9,681	NR
Rosemont College	ind.	$15,270	$7030	NR	NR	NR	NR	NR
St. Charles Borromeo Seminary, Overbrook	ind.	$7950	$5550	NR	NR	NR	NR	NR
Saint Francis College	ind.	$15,040	$6480	92%	11%	$15,032	$6,488	$14,075
Saint Joseph's University	ind.	$18,430	$7514	88%	NR	$10,825	$15,119	NR
Saint Vincent College	ind.	$14,955	$5114	100%	12%	$12,337	$7,732	$19,842
Seton Hill College	ind.	$14,500	$4850	100%	78%	$13,550	$5,800	NR
Shippensburg University of Pennsylvania	pub.	$4550	$4120	NR	NR	$3,729	$4,941	NR
Slippery Rock University of Pennsylvania	pub.	$4484	$3810	82%	46%	$4,891	$3,403	$13,745
Susquehanna University	ind.	$19,670	$5550	99%	52%	$16,176	$9,044	$17,005
Swarthmore College	ind.	$24,190	$7500	100%	100%	$23,314	$8,376	$13,390
Talmudical Yeshiva of Philadelphia	ind.	$5100	$4500	100%	100%	$5,950	$3,650	NR
Temple University	pub.	$6622	$6302	100%	14%	$8,626	$4,298	$14,500
Thiel College	ind.	$10,785	$5490	100%	26%	$10,880	$5,395	$20,069
Thomas Jefferson University	ind.	$16,785	$2080†	NR	NR	NR	NR	NR
University of Pennsylvania	ind.	$24,230	$7362	92%	100%	$21,460	$10,132	$20,200
University of Pittsburgh	pub.	$6698	$5766	76%	14%	$8,185	$4,279	$16,000
University of Pittsburgh at Bradford	pub.	$6598	$5070	NR	NR	NR	NR	$16,000
University of Pittsburgh at Johnstown	pub.	$6630	$5460	80%	12%	$8,661	$3,429	$15,800
The University of Scranton	ind.	$17,740	$7710	98%	19%	$14,445	$11,005	$14,800
The University of the Arts	ind.	$16,800	$4500†	NR	NR	NR	NR	NR
University of the Sciences in Philadelphia	ind.	$15,204	$7600	67%	10%	$8,362	$14,442	NR
Ursinus College	ind.	$20,230	$5970	96%	68%	$16,217	$9,983	$16,000
Valley Forge Christian College	ind.	$6936	$3790	NR	NR	NR	NR	NR
Villanova University	ind.	$20,850	$8000	84%	15%	$15,033	$13,817	$16,652
Washington & Jefferson College	ind.	$19,000	$4750	99%	11%	$14,596	$9,154	NR
Waynesburg College	ind.	$11,430	$4590	99%	21%	$12,094	$3,926	$15,000
West Chester University of Pennsylvania	pub.	$4422	$4518	59%	45%	$5,359	$3,581	$17,000
Westminster College	ind.	$16,270	$4530	94%	42%	$14,954	$5,846	$14,896
Widener University	ind.	$16,750	$6920	100%	16%	$14,559	$9,111	$17,690
Wilkes University	ind.	$16,362	$7102	NR	NR	NR	NR	NR
Wilson College	ind.	$13,588	$6152	100%	98%	$13,425	$6,315	$14,667
York College of Pennsylvania	ind.	$6630	$4670	58%	23%	$5,167	$6,133	$14,350
Puerto Rico								
Bayamón Central University	ind.	$3570	NA	100%	NR	NR	NR	$7500

*NA = not applicable; NR = not reported; * = includes room and board; † = room only.*

College Cost and Financial Aid Metrics

	Institutional Control ind.=independent; pub.=public	Tuition and fees	Room and board	Percent of freshmen receiving aid whose awards were need-based scholarships/grants	Percent of freshmen receiving aid whose need was fully met	Average financial aid package for freshmen	Average net cost after aid	1998 graduate's average indebtedness
Escuela de Artes Plasticas de Puerto Rico	pub.	$4650	NA	NR	NR	NR	NR	NR
Inter American University of Puerto Rico, Arecibo Campus	ind.	$2940	NA	NR	NR	NR	NR	NR
Inter American University of Puerto Rico, Guayama Campus	ind.	$3700	NA	NR	NR	NR	NR	NR
Inter American University of Puerto Rico, San Germán Campus	ind.	$3996	$2200	100%	NR	$1,491	$4,705	NR
Polytechnic University of Puerto Rico	ind.	$4485	NA	NR	NR	NR	NR	NR
Universidad Adventista de las Antillas	ind.	$3690	$2150	100%	5%	$3,356	$2,484	NR
University of Puerto Rico, Humacao University College	pub.	$1095	NA	100%	NR	NR	NR	NR
University of Puerto Rico, Medical Sciences Campus	pub.	$1700	NA	100%	70%	$3,000	—	$4500
University of the Sacred Heart	ind.	$4660	$1800†	NR	NR	NR	NR	NR
Rhode Island								
Brown University	ind.	$25,186	$7094	96%	100%	$20,726	$11,554	$22,240
Bryant College	ind.	$17,330	$7250	96%	26%	$13,209	$11,371	$19,047
Johnson & Wales University	ind.	$13,845	$5970	84%	32%	$10,688	$9,127	$13,431
Providence College	ind.	$17,945	$7355	98%	25%	$13,175	$12,125	$19,125
Rhode Island School of Design	ind.	$21,405	$6490	NR	NR	NR	NR	NR
Roger Williams University	ind.	$17,980	$8200	78%	44%	$14,978	$11,202	$17,125
Salve Regina University	ind.	$16,850	$7500	95%	16%	$13,262	$11,088	$19,125
University of Rhode Island	pub.	$4928	$6378	NR	NR	NR	NR	NR
South Carolina								
Allen University	ind.	$4750	$4310	NR	NR	NR	NR	NR
Anderson College	ind.	$10,515	$4605	90%	3%	$6,954	$8,166	$13,379
Charleston Southern University	ind.	$10,410	$4002	NR	NR	$11,500	$2,912	$17,125
The Citadel, The Military College of South Carolina	pub.	$4258	$4340	77%	23%	$6,801	$1,797	$14,200
Claflin University	ind.	$7008	$3812	NR	NR	$10,505	$315	$13,141
Clemson University	pub.	$3470	$4122	41%	52%	$7,204	$388	$13,987
Coastal Carolina University	pub.	$3340	$4970	46%	13%	$5,305	$3,005	$12,000
Coker College	ind.	$14,552	$4720	93%	51%	$12,844	$6,428	$11,800
College of Charleston	pub.	$3520	$4070	77%	23%	$5,068	$2,522	$11,511
Columbia College	ind.	$15,060	$4990	100%	31%	$15,209	$4,841	NR
Columbia International University	ind.	$8630	$4380	82%	NR	NR	NR	NR
Converse College	ind.	$15,230	$4645	100%	50%	$15,335	$4,540	$14,886
Erskine College	ind.	$15,229	$4769	98%	63%	$14,325	$5,673	$13,125
Francis Marion University	pub.	$3470	$3550	NR	NR	NR	NR	$14,855
Furman University	ind.	$18,266	$4848	88%	85%	$12,630	$10,484	$11,750
Lander University	pub.	$3820	$3855	75%	60%	$4,430	$3,245	$16,450
Limestone College	ind.	$10,100	$4800	94%	23%	$6,312	$8,588	$6339
Medical University of South Carolina	pub.	$4626	NA	NR	NR	NR	NR	NR
Newberry College	ind.	$13,952	$4000	NR	NR	NR	NR	NR
North Greenville College	ind.	$7650	$4500	80%	85%	$8,100	$4,050	NR
Presbyterian College	ind.	$16,524	$4650	100%	17%	$15,684	$5,490	$13,113
Southern Wesleyan University	ind.	$11,498	$3852	100%	36%	$9,575	$5,775	$10,000
University of South Carolina	pub.	$3740	$4167	38%	25%	$2,720	$5,187	$16,200
University of South Carolina Aiken	pub.	$3358	$3940	NR	NR	NR	NR	NR
University of South Carolina Spartanburg	pub.	$3428	$3950	69%	NR	$2,762	$4,616	$13,597

*NA = not applicable; NR = not reported; * = includes room and board; † = room only.*

College Cost and Financial Aid Metrics

	Institutional Control ind.=independent; pub.=public	Tuition and fees	Room and board	Percent of freshmen receiving aid whose awards were need-based scholarships/grants	Percent of freshmen receiving aid whose need was fully met	Average financial aid package for freshmen	Average net cost after aid	1998 graduate's average indebtedness
Voorhees College	ind.	$5860	$3190	97%	6%	$8,468	$582	NR
Winthrop University	pub.	$4146	$4022	90%	36%	$5,177	$2,991	$14,751
Wofford College	ind.	$16,975	$5015	NR	NR	$13,898	$8,092	NR
South Dakota								
Augustana College	ind.	$14,754	$4260	100%	44%	$13,899	$5,115	$17,561
Black Hills State University	pub.	$3363	$2785	NR	NR	NR	NR	NR
Dakota State University	pub.	$3588	$2800	NR	NR	NR	NR	$13,840
Dakota Wesleyan University	ind.	$9916	$3640	85%	31%	$10,201	$3,355	NR
Huron University	ind.	$7500	$3900	57%	18%	$2,099	$9,301	NR
Mount Marty College	ind.	$10,128	$4020	100%	21%	$10,575	$3,573	$17,285
Presentation College	ind.	$7762	$3400	NR	NR	NR	NR	NR
South Dakota School of Mines and Technology	pub.	$3850	$3122	88%	59%	$4,126	$2,846	$12,709
South Dakota State University	pub.	$3357	$2868	45%	73%	$5,230	$995	$14,084
University of South Dakota	pub.	$3459	$3094	NR	NR	NR	NR	NR
Tennessee								
American Baptist College of American Baptist Theological Seminary	ind.	$2860	$1028†	NR	NR	NR	NR	NR
Aquinas College	ind.	$8800	NA	NR	NR	NR	NR	NR
Austin Peay State University	pub.	$2584	$3230	81%	NR	$5,703	$111	$16,108
Belmont University	ind.	$11,600	$5000	66%	32%	$10,913	$5,687	$20,469
Bethel College	ind.	$7800	$4380	NR	NR	NR	NR	NR
Bryan College	ind.	$11,200	$4000	75%	16%	$7,512	$7,688	$10,952
Carson-Newman College	ind.	$11,640	$3910	99%	23%	$11,177	$4,373	$14,591
Christian Brothers University	ind.	$13,490	$3950	NR	NR	NR	NR	NR
Crichton College	ind.	$7152	$2800†	57%	2%	$4,854	$5,098	$14,000
Cumberland University	ind.	$9900	$3500	NR	NR	NR	NR	NR
David Lipscomb University	ind.	$9689	$4344	70%	95%	NR	NR	$13,750
East Tennessee State University	pub.	$2532	$3070	61%	37%	$4,056	$1,546	NR
Fisk University	ind.	$8770	$4930	64%	55%	$12,500	$1,200	$20,000
Free Will Baptist Bible College	ind.	$6442	$3678	39%	NR	NR	NR	NR
Johnson Bible College	ind.	$5280	$3370	48%	NR	$2,988	$5,662	$11,980
King College	ind.	$10,750	$3850	100%	17%	$10,626	$3,974	$14,636
Lambuth University	ind.	$7918	$4220	98%	47%	$7,568	$4,570	$11,000
Lane College	ind.	$6150	$3800	NR	NR	NR	NR	NR
Lee University	ind.	$6862	$4020	79%	22%	$5,589	$5,293	$10,982
LeMoyne-Owen College	ind.	$6900	$4050	94%	1%	$7,014	$3,936	$10,500
Lincoln Memorial University	ind.	$9600	$3900	65%	69%	$7,490	$6,010	$11,200
Martin Methodist College	ind.	$8520	$3400	89%	75%	$6,514	$5,406	$7985
Maryville College	ind.	$16,025	$5080	100%	22%	$15,895	$5,210	$16,397
Memphis College of Art	ind.	$11,990	$3070†	13%	83%	$5,100	$9,960	$16,500
Middle Tennessee State University	pub.	$2516	$3096	56%	28%	$3,894	$1,718	$17,372
Milligan College	ind.	$11,480	$4000	64%	39%	$9,163	$6,317	$19,275
O'More College of Design	ind.	$8505	NR	NR	NR	NR	NR	NR
Rhodes College	ind.	$19,303	$5353	100%	55%	$18,393	$6,263	$15,598
Southern Adventist University	ind.	$10,620	$3730	94%	31%	$9,098	$5,252	$15,600

*NA = not applicable; NR = not reported; * = includes room and board; † = room only.*

College Cost and Financial Aid Metrics

	Institutional Control ind.=independent; pub.=public	Tuition and fees	Room and board	Percent of freshmen receiving aid whose awards were need-based scholarships/grants	Percent of freshmen receiving aid whose need was fully met	Average financial aid package for freshmen	Average net cost after aid	1998 graduate's average indebtedness
Tennessee State University	pub.	$2730	$3600	NR	NR	$7,405	—	NR
Tennessee Technological University	pub.	$2390	$4170	60%	21%	$4,506	$2,054	NR
Tennessee Temple University	ind.	$5250	$4750	89%	85%	$7,500	$2,500	$9000
Tennessee Wesleyan College	ind.	$7550	$4080	99%	25%	$6,940	$4,690	$11,746
Trevecca Nazarene University	ind.	$10,656	$4448	47%	21%	$9,775	$5,329	$19,532
Tusculum College	ind.	$12,500	$4100	62%	18%	$7,547	$9,053	$12,675
Union University	ind.	$11,900	$3850	88%	16%	$6,500	$9,250	$7800
The University of Memphis	pub.	$2818	$3320	65%	11%	$3,796	$2,342	$17,257
The University of Tennessee at Chattanooga	pub.	$2660	$2000†	80%	48%	$7,853	—	$12,445
The University of Tennessee at Martin	pub.	$2656	$3606	59%	17%	$5,253	$1,009	$10,500
The University of Tennessee Knoxville	pub.	$3104	$4030	66%	17%	$5,548	$1,586	$19,624
The University of Tennessee Memphis	pub.	$2634	$3600†	NR	NR	NR	NR	$15,545
University of the South	ind.	$19,080	$5230	100%	100%	$16,333	$7,977	$13,103
Vanderbilt University	ind.	$23,598	$8032	88%	98%	$24,073	$7,557	$19,900
Texas								
Abilene Christian University	ind.	$10,290	$4190	86%	39%	$8,878	$5,602	NR
Angelo State University	pub.	$2320	$4066	NR	NR	$3,247	$3,139	NR
Arlington Baptist College	ind.	$3610	$1700†	94%	NR	NR	NR	NR
Austin College	ind.	$15,219	$5891	100%	62%	$15,824	$5,286	$21,550
Baptist Missionary Association Theological Seminary	ind.	$2220	$3580†	NR	NR	NR	NR	NR
Baylor University	ind.	$11,938	$5238	99%	17%	$8,143	$9,033	NR
Concordia University at Austin	ind.	$11,570	$5200	100%	40%	$10,894	$5,876	$15,472
The Criswell College	ind.	$3910	NA	NR	NR	NR	NR	NR
Dallas Baptist University	ind.	$8700	$3680	60%	37%	$7,554	$4,826	NR
Dallas Christian College	ind.	$5690	$3700	42%	NR	$4,694	$4,696	NR
DeVry Institute of Technology	ind.	$7778	NA	66%	6%	NR	NR	$12,939
East Texas Baptist University	ind.	$8450	$3202	57%	95%	$8,433	$3,219	$20,000
Hardin-Simmons University	ind.	$9330	$3336	77%	NR	$8,258	$4,408	$12,080
Houston Baptist University	ind.	$10,828	$3900	NR	NR	NR	NR	NR
Howard Payne University	ind.	$9000	$3830	NR	NR	NR	NR	NR
Huston-Tillotson College	ind.	$6350	$4682	NR	NR	$8,456	$2,576	NR
Institute for Christian Studies	ind.	$1560	$1500†	NR	NR	NR	NR	$5500
Jarvis Christian College	ind.	$5200	$3750	86%	75%	$8,235	$715	NR
Lamar University	pub.	$2161	$3516	58%	NR	$1,222	$4,455	$8800
LeTourneau University	ind.	$12,240	$5250	80%	25%	$10,646	$6,844	$17,263
Lubbock Christian University	ind.	$9316	$3700	100%	42%	$10,314	$2,702	NR
McMurry University	ind.	$9695	$4244	84%	11%	$8,892	$5,047	$14,250
Midwestern State University	pub.	$2426	$3728	NR	NR	NR	NR	NR
Northwood University, Texas Campus	ind.	$11,625	$5146	84%	34%	$9,486	$7,285	$17,125
Our Lady of the Lake University of San Antonio	ind.	$11,408	$4352	89%	NR	$12,467	$3,293	$16,649
Paul Quinn College	ind.	$5670	$3800	NR	NR	NR	NR	NR
Rice University	ind.	$15,796	$6600	92%	100%	NR	NR	NR
St. Edward's University	ind.	$11,438	$5000	96%	20%	$9,607	$6,831	NR
St. Mary's University of San Antonio	ind.	$11,880	$5251	97%	25%	$11,864	$5,267	$16,415

*NA = not applicable; NR = not reported; * = includes room and board; † = room only.*

College Cost and Financial Aid Metrics

	Institutional Control ind.=independent; pub.=public	Tuition and fees	Room and board	Percent of freshmen receiving aid whose awards were need-based scholarships/grants	Percent of freshmen receiving aid whose need was fully met	Average financial aid package for freshmen	Average net cost after aid	1998 graduate's average indebtedness
Sam Houston State University	pub.	$1988	$3390	81%	NR	$4,666	$712	$8530
Schreiner College	ind.	$11,740	$6520	98%	6%	$9,333	$8,927	$9476
Southern Methodist University	ind.	$18,510	$6901	75%	31%	$19,479	$5,932	NR
Southwestern Adventist University	ind.	$9062	$4334	67%	18%	$7,779	$5,617	$17,375
Southwestern Assemblies of God University	ind.	$5858	$3946	68%	16%	$4,485	$5,319	$13,321
Southwestern University	ind.	$15,750	$6320	99%	100%	$13,264	$8,806	$18,879
Southwest Texas State University	pub.	$2756	$4583	59%	9%	$5,580	$1,759	$13,511
Stephen F. Austin State University	pub.	$2578	$4168	77%	26%	$2,817	$3,929	$9000
Sul Ross State University	pub.	$2150	$3530	NR	NR	NR	NR	NR
Tarleton State University	pub.	$2066	$3636	NR	NR	NR	NR	$10,000
Texas A&M International University	pub.	$2579	NR	95%	80%	$6,432	—	$10,000
Texas A&M University	pub.	$2639	$4898	89%	97%	$6,561	$976	$12,401
Texas A&M University at Galveston	pub.	$2855	$3977	NR	NR	NR	NR	NR
Texas A&M University–Commerce	pub.	$2526	$4055	NR	NR	NR	NR	NR
Texas A&M University–Corpus Christi	pub.	$2306	$5661	69%	22%	$5,378	$2,589	$11,000
Texas A&M University–Kingsville	pub.	$2542	$3484	96%	78%	$5,875	$151	$8500
Texas A&M University–Texarkana	pub.	$1692	NA	NR	NR	NR	NR	NR
Texas Chiropractic College	ind.	$13,935	NA	NR	NR	NR	NR	NR
Texas Christian University	ind.	$12,290	$3970	86%	36%	$12,111	$4,149	NR
Texas Lutheran University	ind.	$11,444	$4366	90%	22%	$11,527	$4,283	$18,519
Texas Tech University	pub.	$3107	$4787	69%	NR	$4,306	$3,588	NR
Texas Wesleyan University	ind.	$9250	$3886	NR	NR	NR	NR	NR
Texas Woman's University	pub.	$2072	$3872	96%	45%	$6,821	—	$18,912
Trinity University	ind.	$15,804	$6330	100%	100%	$15,258	$6,876	$14,272
University of Dallas	ind.	$14,420	$5446	100%	20%	$13,665	$6,201	$15,300
University of Houston	pub.	$2444	$4513	NR	NR	NR	NR	NR
University of Houston–Clear Lake	pub.	$2138	NA	NR	NR	NR	NR	NR
University of Houston–Downtown	pub.	$2316	NA	95%	14%	$4,756	—	NR
University of Houston–Victoria	pub.	$2004	NA	NR	NR	NR	$2,004	$12,530
University of Mary Hardin-Baylor	ind.	$8430	$3542	95%	46%	$6,546	$5,426	$15,300
University of North Texas	pub.	$2769	$4096	80%	26%	$4,901	$1,964	$14,955
University of St. Thomas	ind.	$12,416	$5050	83%	NR	$10,965	$6,501	NR
The University of Texas at Arlington	pub.	$2670	$1686†	66%	14%	$5,969	—	$13,055
The University of Texas at Austin	pub.	$3128	$4854	80%	85%	$7,260	$722	$17,000
The University of Texas at Brownsville	pub.	$1722	NA	NR	NR	NR	NR	NR
The University of Texas at Dallas	pub.	$2912	$1700†	29%	94%	$4,595	$17	NR
The University of Texas at El Paso	pub.	$2244	$2058†	90%	23%	$6,255	—	$5647
The University of Texas at San Antonio	pub.	$2974	$2832†	NR	NR	NR	NR	NR
The University of Texas at Tyler	pub.	$2240	$3199†	83%	100%	$5,300	$139	$6900
The University of Texas Health Science Center at San Antonio	pub.	$1520	NA	NR	NR	NR	NR	NR
The University of Texas–Houston Health Science Center	pub.	$3477	NR	NR	NR	NR	NR	$15,504
The University of Texas Medical Branch at Galveston	pub.	$1832	$1755†	NR	NR	NR	NR	$19,674
The University of Texas of the Permian Basin	pub.	$2320	NR	99%	27%	$5,373	—	$10,414
The University of Texas–Pan American	pub.	$2017	$2663	86%	NR	$1,987	$2,693	NR
The University of Texas Southwestern Medical Center at Dallas	pub.	$1940	NA	NR	NR	NR	NR	NR

*NA = not applicable; NR = not reported; * = includes room and board; † = room only.*

College Cost and Financial Aid Metrics

	Institutional Control ind.=independent; pub.=public	Tuition and fees	Room and board	Percent of freshmen receiving aid whose awards were need-based scholarships/grants	Percent of freshmen receiving aid whose need was fully met	Average financial aid package for freshmen	Average net cost after aid	1998 graduate's average indebtedness
University of the Incarnate Word	ind.	$12,140	$4870	98%	37%	$12,578	$4,432	NR
Wayland Baptist University	ind.	$7400	$3121	99%	26%	$7,878	$2,643	NR
West Texas A&M University	pub.	$1974	$3310	95%	40%	$4,750	$534	$17,125
Utah								
Brigham Young University	ind.	$2830	$4454	53%	29%	$1,938	$5,346	$11,350
Southern Utah University	pub.	$1965	$2520	66%	6%	$3,447	$1,038	$10,712
University of Utah	pub.	$2790	$5179	55%	16%	$6,193	$1,776	NR
Utah State University	pub.	$2314	$3938	68%	8%	$5,137	$1,115	$13,400
Weber State University	pub.	$2042	$3878	NR	NR	NR	NR	NR
Westminster College	ind.	$12,726	$4750	100%	25%	$11,569	$5,907	NR
Vermont								
Bennington College	ind.	$22,500	$5650	99%	6%	$17,125	$11,025	$19,300
Burlington College	ind.	$9066	NR	89%	11%	$7,585	—	$16,508
Castleton State College	pub.	$5030	$5346	NR	NR	NR	NR	NR
Champlain College	ind.	$10,585	$7450	85%	13%	$8,223	$9,812	NR
College of St. Joseph	ind.	$11,350	$6050	100%	6%	$10,723	$6,677	$14,585
Goddard College	ind.	$15,470	$5288	100%	NR	$18,100	$2,658	$17,125
Green Mountain College	ind.	$17,200	$4300	NR	NR	$15,500	$6,000	NR
Johnson State College	pub.	$5009	$5298	74%	39%	$7,538	$2,769	$16,910
Lyndon State College	pub.	$4864	$5298	53%	22%	$10,989	—	NR
Marlboro College	ind.	$19,560	$6750	100%	38%	$19,307	$7,003	$15,906
Middlebury College	ind.	$31,790*	NR	95%	100%	$23,354	—	$18,731
Norwich University	ind.	$15,156	$5718	NR	NR	NR	NR	NR
Saint Michael's College	ind.	$17,662	$7253	83%	NR	$12,634	$12,281	NR
Southern Vermont College	ind.	$10,990	$5350	92%	100%	$14,056	$2,284	$13,507
Sterling College	ind.	$13,355	$5670	84%	23%	$7,600	$11,425	NR
Trinity College of Vermont	ind.	$14,120	$6700	100%	13%	$14,821	$5,999	$16,462
University of Vermont	pub.	$8044	$5620	67%	92%	$15,000	—	$21,500
Virgin Islands								
University of the Virgin Islands	pub.	$4946	$5830	NR	NR	NR	NR	NR
Virginia								
Bluefield College	ind.	$7280	$4890	NR	NR	NR	NR	NR
Bridgewater College	ind.	$14,970	$6970	100%	42%	$14,804	$7,136	$17,630
Christendom College	ind.	$11,530	$4570	93%	88%	$8,617	$7,483	$8980
Christopher Newport University	pub.	$3048	$4950	73%	10%	$4,645	$3,353	NR
The College of William and Mary	pub.	$4610	$4897	82%	38%	$7,410	$2,097	NR
Community Hospital of Roanoke Valley–College of Health Sciences	ind.	$11,100	$4160	100%	17%	$10,782	$4,478	$13,240
Eastern Mennonite University	ind.	$13,480	$4950	99%	27%	$11,789	$6,641	$16,668
Emory & Henry College	ind.	$13,150	$5322	100%	31%	$12,696	$5,776	$18,000
Ferrum College	ind.	$10,990	$5000	99%	58%	$10,084	$5,906	$17,093
George Mason University	pub.	$3756	$5298	72%	54%	$5,720	$3,334	$13,826
Hampden-Sydney College	ind.	$16,531	$5898	100%	45%	$12,396	$10,033	$10,400
Hampton University	ind.	$10,580	$4754	NR	NR	NR	NR	NR
Hollins University	ind.	$16,710	$6125	100%	42%	$14,604	$8,231	$14,809

*NA = not applicable; NR = not reported; * = includes room and board; † = room only.*

College Cost and Financial Aid Metrics

	Institutional Control ind.=independent; pub.=public	Tuition and fees	Room and board	Percent of freshmen receiving aid whose awards were need-based scholarships/grants	Percent of freshmen receiving aid whose need was fully met	Average financial aid package for freshmen	Average net cost after aid	1998 graduate's average indebtedness
James Madison University	pub.	$3926	$5182	62%	14%	$4,522	$4,586	$12,000
Liberty University	ind.	$8750	$4800	NR	NR	NR	NR	$13,562
Longwood College	pub.	$3924	$4620	90%	26%	$5,934	$2,610	$14,197
Lynchburg College	ind.	$18,105	$4400	100%	29%	$13,556	$8,949	$17,992
Mary Baldwin College	ind.	$14,645	$7450	98%	20%	$15,168	$6,927	NR
Marymount University	ind.	$13,870	$6160	NR	NR	NR	NR	NR
Mary Washington College	pub.	$3204	$5298	80%	5%	$4,510	$3,992	$11,000
Norfolk State University	pub.	$2708	$5494	65%	35%	$5,900	$2,302	$17,000
Old Dominion University	pub.	$3796	$5114	74%	40%	$6,685	$2,225	$16,500
Radford University	pub.	$2887	$4770	63%	NR	$5,797	$1,860	$13,727
Randolph-Macon College	ind.	$17,660	$4520	100%	23%	$12,525	$9,655	$16,832
Randolph-Macon Woman's College	ind.	$17,080	$7010	100%	51%	$15,080	$9,010	$15,495
Roanoke College	ind.	$17,095	$5450	99%	30%	$14,725	$7,820	$14,784
Saint Paul's College	ind.	$8200	$4260	92%	1%	$10,340	$2,120	$22,000
Shenandoah University	ind.	$15,700	$5300	70%	43%	$10,080	$10,920	$13,618
Sweet Briar College	ind.	$17,150	$7000	100%	31%	$14,776	$9,374	$17,689
University of Richmond	ind.	$19,610	$4050	93%	41%	$14,667	$8,993	$14,300
University of Virginia	pub.	$4160	$4767	85%	52%	$9,197	—	$13,913
University of Virginia's College at Wise	pub.	$3192	$4938	NR	NR	NR	NR	NR
Virginia Commonwealth University	pub.	$3587	$4839	87%	17%	$4,839	$3,587	$22,379
Virginia Intermont College	ind.	$11,750	$5200	71%	94%	$3,744	$13,206	$17,125
Virginia Military Institute	pub.	$5014	$4376	72%	70%	$8,607	$783	$14,000
Virginia Polytechnic Institute and State University	pub.	$3620	$3722	83%	19%	$6,353	$989	$14,530
Virginia State University	pub.	$3086	$5096	65%	NR	$5,315	$2,867	$18,500
Virginia Union University	ind.	$9580	$4250	66%	9%	$8,368	$5,462	NR
Virginia Wesleyan College	ind.	$14,050	$5650	40%	15%	$10,852	$8,848	$16,292
Washington and Lee University	ind.	$17,105	$5547	89%	95%	$14,465	$8,187	NR
Washington								
Antioch University Seattle	ind.	$10,710	NA	NR	NR	NR	NR	$18,500
Bastyr University	ind.	$9825	$3500†	77%	NR	NR	NR	NR
Central Washington University	pub.	$3162	$4821	NR	NR	NR	NR	$18,929
City University	ind.	$6600	NA	71%	NR	$3,818	$2,782	$16,609
Cornish College of the Arts	ind.	$13,900	NA	91%	13%	$10,025	$3,875	$24,000
Eastern Washington University	pub.	$2907	$4399	78%	22%	$10,514	—	$14,509
The Evergreen State College	pub.	$2898	$4645	67%	50%	$9,197	—	$12,000
Gonzaga University	ind.	$16,860	$5350	98%	7%	$11,055	$11,155	$19,731
Henry Cogswell College	ind.	$10,800	NA	18%	NR	$2,818	$7,982	$16,432
Heritage College	ind.	$5190	NA	99%	3%	$4,336	$854	$4092
Northwest College	ind.	$9870	$5030	98%	31%	$10,743	$4,157	$10,722
Northwest College of Art	ind.	$8200	NA	NR	NR	NR	NR	NR
Pacific Lutheran University	ind.	$16,224	$5038	92%	43%	$14,649	$6,613	$19,267
Puget Sound Christian College	ind.	$6420	$4150	NR	NR	NR	NR	NR
Saint Martin's College	ind.	$14,180	$4768	100%	48%	$13,907	$5,041	$12,813
Seattle Pacific University	ind.	$14,934	$5724	95%	25%	$12,721	$7,937	$16,550

*NA = not applicable; NR = not reported; * = includes room and board; † = room only.*

College Cost and Financial Aid Metrics

	Institutional Control ind.=independent; pub.=public	Tuition and fees	Room and board	Percent of freshmen receiving aid whose awards were need-based scholarships/grants	Percent of freshmen receiving aid whose need was fully met	Average financial aid package for freshmen	Average net cost after aid	1998 graduate's average indebtedness
Seattle University	ind.	$16,110	$5870	97%	32%	$15,860	$6,120	NR
Trinity Lutheran College	ind.	$7746	$4525	NR	NR	NR	NR	NR
University of Puget Sound	ind.	$20,605	$5270	96%	42%	$16,392	$9,483	$20,259
University of Washington	pub.	$3638	$4905	54%	79%	$6,937	$1,606	NR
Walla Walla College	ind.	$13,941	$3021	87%	25%	$13,125	$3,837	$18,876
Washington State University	pub.	$3662	$4618	63%	46%	$7,972	$308	$15,000
Western Washington University	pub.	$2992	$5076	75%	69%	$5,134	$2,934	NR
Whitman College	ind.	$21,742	$6090	100%	61%	$13,761	$14,071	$12,431
Whitworth College	ind.	$16,924	$5500	99%	21%	$14,819	$7,605	NR
West Virginia								
Appalachian Bible College	ind.	$6132	$3310	100%	NR	$1,196	$8,246	NR
Bethany College	ind.	$18,574	$6122	97%	55%	$16,777	$7,919	$16,500
Bluefield State College	pub.	$2178	NA	100%	22%	$4,500	—	$6800
The College of West Virginia	ind.	$3840	$4376	93%	8%	$7,047	$1,169	$11,423
Concord College	pub.	$2538	$4018	72%	72%	$4,800	$1,756	$10,000
Davis & Elkins College	ind.	$12,280	$5330	90%	76%	$9,659	$7,951	$16,000
Fairmont State College	pub.	$2244	$3882	72%	40%	$3,558	$2,568	NR
Glenville State College	pub.	$2208	$3710	88%	29%	$5,638	$280	$12,116
Marshall University	pub.	$2886	$4652	75%	28%	$5,205	$2,333	$13,020
Ohio Valley College	ind.	$7528	$4000	83%	11%	$6,613	$4,915	$17,780
Salem-Teikyo University	ind.	$12,840	$4328	66%	97%	$14,600	$2,568	$17,000
Shepherd College	pub.	$2430	$4432	63%	16%	$4,918	$1,944	$12,381
University of Charleston	ind.	$13,200	$5530	72%	44%	$9,875	$8,855	$18,950
West Liberty State College	pub.	$2320	$3200	79%	39%	$4,998	$522	$10,890
West Virginia State College	pub.	$2836	$3600	NR	NR	NR	NR	NR
West Virginia University	pub.	$2748	$4990	64%	53%	$4,594	$3,144	$15,864
West Virginia University Institute of Technology	pub.	$2646	$4048	84%	18%	$4,900	$1,794	$9337
West Virginia Wesleyan College	ind.	$18,050	$4350	99%	62%	$16,844	$5,556	$15,787
Wheeling Jesuit University	ind.	$15,220	$5200	91%	50%	$16,294	$4,126	$15,000
Wisconsin								
Alverno College	ind.	$10,900	$4250	NR	NR	NR	NR	NR
Bellin College of Nursing	ind.	$9455	NA	NR	NR	NR	NR	$18,961
Beloit College	ind.	$20,440	$4628	100%	100%	$15,879	$9,189	$12,896
Cardinal Stritch University	ind.	$11,120	$4480	NR	NR	NR	NR	NR
Carroll College	ind.	$15,000	$4600	100%	100%	$13,811	$5,789	$15,772
Carthage College	ind.	$16,690	$4810	NR	NR	$13,941	$7,559	NR
Concordia University Wisconsin	ind.	$12,460	$4200	85%	71%	$11,506	$5,154	$15,247
Edgewood College	ind.	$11,650	$4380	100%	9%	$9,776	$6,254	$18,318
Lakeland College	ind.	$12,480	$4680	99%	30%	$10,323	$6,837	$10,301
Lawrence University	ind.	$21,012	$4697	100%	83%	$18,345	$7,364	$17,727
Maranatha Baptist Bible College	ind.	$6370	$3800	97%	6%	$5,525	$4,645	$10,829
Marian College of Fond du Lac	ind.	$12,256	$4364	81%	57%	$11,188	$5,432	$14,500
Marquette University	ind.	$17,336	$6086	99%	68%	$15,777	$7,645	NR
Milwaukee Institute of Art and Design	ind.	$15,080	$6458	100%	27%	$13,425	$8,113	$21,053

*NA = not applicable; NR = not reported; * = includes room and board; † = room only.*

College Cost and Financial Aid Metrics

	Institutional Control ind.=independent; pub.=public	Tuition and fees	Room and board	Percent of freshmen receiving aid whose awards were need-based scholarships/grants	Percent of freshmen receiving aid whose need was fully met	Average financial aid package for freshmen	Average net cost after aid	1998 graduate's average indebtedness
Milwaukee School of Engineering	ind.	$19,845	$4710	98%	10%	$13,400	$11,155	$21,500
Mount Mary College	ind.	$12,270	$4190	98%	27%	$9,710	$6,750	NR
Mount Senario College	ind.	$12,250	$4740	97%	NR	$10,816	$6,174	NR
Northland College	ind.	$14,675	$4470	99%	14%	$12,085	$7,060	NR
Ripon College	ind.	$18,240	$4400	100%	100%	$16,973	$5,667	$15,507
St. Norbert College	ind.	$16,770	$5162	99%	46%	$13,481	$8,451	$14,088
Silver Lake College	ind.	$11,150	$4365	71%	24%	$10,272	$5,243	$15,344
University of Wisconsin–Eau Claire	pub.	$3210	$3301	64%	70%	$5,089	$1,422	$13,252
University of Wisconsin–Green Bay	pub.	$3184	$2035†	49%	44%	$4,973	$246	NR
University of Wisconsin–La Crosse	pub.	$3242	$3300	53%	89%	$4,120	$2,422	$13,800
University of Wisconsin–Madison	pub.	$3738	$4206	45%	NR	NR	NR	$15,813
University of Wisconsin–Milwaukee	pub.	$3741	$2542†	72%	48%	NR	NR	NR
University of Wisconsin–Oshkosh	pub.	$3001	$3130	NR	NR	NR	NR	NR
University of Wisconsin–Parkside	pub.	$3200	$4230	52%	36%	$4,691	$2,739	$7725
University of Wisconsin–Platteville	pub.	$3132	$3338	NR	NR	NR	NR	$8500
University of Wisconsin–River Falls	pub.	$3102	$3350	71%	32%	$3,764	$2,688	$12,500
University of Wisconsin–Stevens Point	pub.	$3140	$3524	50%	20%	$4,200	$2,464	$12,921
University of Wisconsin–Stout	pub.	$3256	$3284	51%	23%	$4,630	$1,910	NR
University of Wisconsin–Superior	pub.	$2974	$3426	75%	40%	$4,318	$2,082	$12,500
University of Wisconsin–Whitewater	pub.	$3105	$3204	NR	NR	NR	NR	$10,451
Viterbo University	ind.	$12,490	$4400	100%	17%	$11,856	$5,034	$15,338
Wisconsin Lutheran College	ind.	$13,106	$4750	98%	28%	$11,899	$5,957	$13,830
Wyoming								
University of Wyoming	pub.	$2416	$4618	40%	66%	$4,959	$2,075	$16,168

*NA = not applicable; NR = not reported; * = includes room and board; † = room only.*

SECTION 7

College Financial Aid Profiles

After the federal government, colleges provide the largest amount of financial aid to students. In addition, they control most of the money channeled to students from the federal government. The amount and makeup of your financial aid package will depend on the institution's particular circumstances and its decisions concerning your application. The main section of this book shows you the pattern and extent of each college's current awards. The profiles present detailed factual and statistical data for each school in a uniform format to make easy, quick references and comparisons. Items that could not be collected in time for publication are designated as *N/A*. Items for which the specific figures could not be gathered in time are given as *available*. Colleges that supplied no data are listed by name and address only so that you do not overlook them in your search for colleges.

There is much anecdotal evidence that students and their families fail to apply for financial aid under the misapprehension that student aid goes only to poor families. Financial need in the context of college expenses is not the same as being needy in the broad social context. Middle-class families typically qualify for need-based financial aid; at expensive schools, even upper-middle-class families can qualify for need-based financial aid. We encourage you to apply for financial aid whether or not you think that you will qualify.

The following outline of the profile format explains what is covered in each section to help you understand the definition and significance of each item. The term *college* or *colleges* is frequently used below to refer to any institution of higher education, regardless of its official definition.

The College

The name of the college is the official name as it appears on the institution's charter. The city and state listed are the official location of the school. The subhead line shows tuition and required fees, as they were charged to the majority of full-time undergraduate students in the 1999–2000 academic year. Any exceptions to the 1999–2000 academic year figures are so noted. For a public institution, the tuition and fees shown are for state residents, and this is noted. If a college's annual expenses are expressed as a comprehensive fee (including full-time tuition, mandatory fees, and college room and board), this is noted, as are any unusual definitions, such as tuition only. The average undergraduate aid package is the average total package of grant, loan, and work-study aid that was awarded to defray the officially defined financial need of full-time undergraduates enrolled in fall 1999 (or fall 1998) who applied for financial aid, were determined to have need, and then actually received financial aid. This information appears in more detail below in each profile.

About the Institution

This paragraph gives the reader a brief introduction to a college. It contains the following elements:

Institutional control. Private institutions are designated as *independent* (nonprofit), *independent/religious* (sponsored by or affiliated with a religious group or having a nondenominational or interdenominational religious orientation), or *proprietary* (profit-making). Public institutions are designated by their primary source of support, such as *federal, state, commonwealth* (Puerto Rico), *territory* (U.S. territories), *county, district* (an administrative unit of public education, often having boundaries different from those of units of local government), *state- and locally-supported* ("locally" refers to county, district, or city), *state-supported* (funded by the state), or *state-related* (funded primarily by the state but administered autonomously).

Type of student body. The categories are *men* (100 percent of student body), *coed-primarily men, women* (100 percent of student body), *coed-primarily women,* and *coed.*

Degrees awarded. *Associate, bachelor's* (baccalaureate), *master's, doctoral* (doctorate), *first professional* (in such fields as law and medicine). There are no colleges in this book that award the associate degree only. Many award the bachelor's as their highest degree. You will need to talk to your family and guidance counselor to decide whether you want to attend a college that concentrates on undergraduate education or an institution with professional schools and research activities.

Number of undergraduate majors. This shows the number of academic fields in which the institution offers associate and/or bachelor's degrees. The purpose of this is to give you a brief indication of the range of subjects available. For a full list of each college's majors, visit http://www.CollegeQuest.com.

Enrollment. These figures are based on the actual number of full-time and part-time students enrolled in degree programs as of fall 1999. In most instances, they are designated as *total enrollment* (for the specific college or university) and *freshmen.* If the institution is a university and its total enrollment figure includes graduate students, a separate figure for *undergraduates* may be provided. If the profiled institution is a subunit of a university, the figures may be designated *total university enrollment* for the entire university and *total unit enrollment* for the specific subunit.

Methodology used for determining need. Private colleges usually have larger financial aid programs, but public colleges usually have lower sticker prices, especially for in-state or local students. At a public college, your financial need will be less, and you will receive a smaller financial aid package. The note on whether a college uses federal (FAFSA) or institutional methodology (usually PROFILE) will let you know whether you will have to complete one or two kinds of financial aid application forms. Federal Methodology is the needs-analysis formula used by the U.S. Department of Education to determine the Expected Family Contribution (EFC), which, when subtracted from the cost of attendance at an institution, determines the financial need of a student. There is no relative advantage or disadvantage to using one methodology over the other.

Undergraduate Expenses

If provided by the institution, the one-time application fee is listed. Costs are given for the 2000–2001 academic year (or estimated for the 2000–2001 academic year) or for the 1999–2000 academic year if 2000–2001 figures were not yet available. Annual expenses may be expressed as a comprehensive fee (including full-time tuition, mandatory fees, and college room and board) or may be given as separate figures for full-time tuition, fees, room and board, or room only. For public institutions where tuition differs according to state residence, separate figures are given for area or state residents and for nonresidents. Part-time tuition is expressed in terms of a per-unit rate (per credit, per semester hour, etc.), as specified by the institution.

The tuition structure at some institutions is complex. Freshmen and sophomores may be charged a different rate from the rate charged to juniors and seniors, a professional or vocational division may have a different fee structure from the liberal arts division of the same institution, or part-time tuition may be prorated on a sliding scale according to the number of credit hours taken. Tuition and fees may vary according to academic program, campus/location, class time (day, evening, weekend), course/credit load, course level, degree level, reciprocity agreements, and student level. If tuition and fees differ for international students, the rate charged is listed.

Room and board charges are reported as an average for one academic year and may vary according to board plan selected, campus/location, gender, type of housing facility, or student level. If no college-owned or -operated housing facilities are offered, the phrase *college housing not available* will appear.

If a college offers a *guaranteed tuition* plan, it promises that the tuition rate of an entering student will not increase for the entire term of enrollment, from entrance to graduation. Other payment plans might include *tuition prepayment,* which allows an entering student to lock in the current tuition rate for the entire term of enrollment by paying the full amount in advance rather than year by year, and *installment* and *deferred payment* plans, which allow students to delay the payment of the full tuition.

Guaranteed tuition and tuition prepayment help you to plan the total cost of your education and can save you from the financial distress sometimes caused by tuition hikes. Colleges that offer such plans may also help you to arrange financing, which in the long run can cost less than the total of four years of increasing tuition rates. Deferred payment or installment payments may better fit your personal financial situation, especially if you do not qualify for financial aid and, due to other financial commitments, find that obtaining the entire amount due is burdensome. Carefully investigate these plans, however, to see what premium you may pay at the end to allow you to defer immediate payment.

Freshman Financial Aid

Usually, these are actual figures for the 1999–2000 term, beginning in fall 1999; figures may also be estimated for that term, or they could be 1998–99 figures. The particular term for which these data apply is indicated. The figures are for degree-seeking full-time freshman students. The first figure is the percentage of freshmen who applied for any kind of financial aid. The next figure is the percentage of those freshmen financial aid applicants who were determined to have financial need—that is, through the formal needs-assessment process, had a calculated expected family contribution that was less than the total college cost. The next figure is the percentage of this group of eligible freshmen who received any financial aid. The next figure is the percentage of this preceding group of eligible aid recipients whose need was fully met by financial aid. The *Average need met* is the average percentage of financial need met for freshmen who received any need-based aid. The *Average financial aid package* is the average dollar amount awarded (need-based or non-need-based) to freshmen who applied for aid, were deemed eligible, and received any aid; awards used to reduce the expected family contribution are excluded from this average. The final line in most profiles is the percentage of freshmen who had no financial need but who received non-need-based aid other than athletic scholarships or special-group tuition benefits.

What do these data mean to you? If financial aid is important in your comparison of colleges, the relative percentage of students who received any aid, whose need was fully met, and the average percentage of need met have the most weight. These figures reflect the relative abundance of student aid available to the average eligible applicant. The average dollar amount of the aid package has real meaning, but only in relation to the college's expense; you will be especially interested in the difference between this figure and the costs figure, which is what the average student (in any given statistical group, there actually may be no average individual) will have to pay. Of course, if the financial aid package is largely loans rather than grants, you will have to pay this amount eventually. Relative differences in the figures of the number of students who apply for aid and who are deemed eligible can hinge on any number of factors: the relative sticker price of the college, the relative level of wealth of the students' families, the proportion of only children in college and students with siblings in college (families with two or more children in college are more likely to apply for aid and be considered eligible), or the relative sophistication in financial aid matters (or quality of college counseling they may have received) of the students and their families. While these may be interesting, they will not mean too much to most students and families. If you are among the unlucky (or, perhaps, lucky) students who do not qualify for need-based financial aid, the final sentence of this paragraph in the profile will be of interest because it reveals the relative policies that the college has in distributing merit-based aid to students who cannot demonstrate need.

Undergraduate Financial Aid

This is the parallel paragraph to the Freshman Financial Aid paragraph (see above). The same definitions apply, except that the group being considered is degree-seeking full-time undergraduate students (including freshmen).

There are cases of students who chose a particular college because they received a really generous financial aid package in their freshman year and then had to scramble to pay for the tuition bill in their later years. If a financial aid package is a key factor in your decision to attend a particular college, you want to be certain that the package offered to all undergraduates is not too far from that offered to freshmen. The key figures are those for the percentage of students who received any aid, the percentage of financial aid recipients whose need was fully met, the average percentage of need met, and the dollar figure of the average financial aid package. Generally, colleges assume that after the freshman year, students develop study habits and time-management skills that will allow them to take on part-time and summer employment without hurting their academic performance. So, the proportion of self-help aid (work-study and student loans) in the financial aid package tends to increase after the freshman year. This pattern, which is true of most colleges, can be verified below, in the freshman-undergraduate figures in the paragraph on Gift Aid (Need-Based).

Gift Aid (Need-Based)

Total amount is the total dollar figure in 1999–2000 (actual or estimated) or 1998–99 (actual) of need-based scholarships and grant (gift) aid awarded to degree-seeking full-time and part-time students that was used to meet financial need. The percentages of this aid from federal, state, institutional (college or university), and external (e.g., foundations, civic organizations, etc.) sources are shown. *Receiving aid* shows the percentages (and number, in parentheses) of freshmen and of all undergraduates who applied for aid, were considered eligible, and received any need-based gift aid. *Scholarships, grants, and awards* cites major categories of need-based gift aid provided by the college; these include Federal Pell Grants, Federal Supplemental Educational Opportunity Grants (FSEOG), state scholarships, private scholarships, college/university gift aid from institutional funds, United Negro College Fund aid, Federal Nursing Scholarships, and others.

Scholarships and grants are gifts awarded to students that do not need to be repaid. These are preferable to loans, which have to be repaid, or work-study wages, which may take time away from studies and personal pursuits. The total amount of need-based gift aid has to be placed into the context of the total number of undergraduate students (shown above, in the About the Institution paragraph) and the relative expense of the institution. Filing the FAFSA automatically puts you in line to receive any available federal grants for which you may qualify. However, if the college that you are considering has a higher than usual proportion of gift aid coming from state, institutional, or external sources, be sure to check with the financial aid office to find out what these sources may be and how to apply for them. For almost all colleges, the percentage of freshmen receiving need-based gift aid will be higher than the percentage of all undergraduates receiving need-based gift aid. However, if you are dependent on need-based gift aid, and the particular college you are considering shows a sharper drop from the freshman to undergraduate years than other colleges of a similar type, you might want to think about how this change will affect your ability to pay for later years at this college.

Gift Aid (Non-Need-Based)

Total amount is the total dollar figure in 1999–2000 (actual or estimated) or 1998–99 (actual) of non-need-based scholarships and grant (gift) aid awarded to degree-seeking full-time and part-time students. Non-need-based aid that was used to meet financial need is not included in this total. The percentages of this aid from federal, state, institutional (college or university), and external (e.g., National Merit Scholarships, civic, religious, fraternal organizations, etc.) sources are shown. *Receiving aid* shows the percentages (and number, in parentheses) of freshmen and of all undergraduates who did not receive need-based aid but who received non-need-based gift aid. *Average award* is the average dollar amount of awards to the students in this immediately preceding group. *Scholarships, grants, and awards by category* cites the major categories in which non-need-based awards are available and the number of awards made in that category (in parentheses, the total dollar value of these awards). The categories listed are *Academic Interests/Achievement,* which includes agriculture, business, communication, computer science, education, engineering/technologies, English, foreign languages, general academic interests/achievements, health fields, home economics, mathematics, military science, physical sciences, and social sciences; *Creative Arts/Performance,* which includes applied art and design, art/fine arts, creative writing, dance, debating, music, and theater/drama; *Special Achievements/Activities,* which includes general special achievements/activities, community service, leadership, religious involvement, and rodeo; and *Special Characteristics,* which includes adult students, children and siblings of alumni, disabilities, ethnic background, first-generation college students, international students, parents of current students, and veterans. *Tuition waivers* indicate special categories of students (minority students, children of alumni, college employees or children of employees, adult students, and senior citizens) who may qualify for full or partial waiver of tuition. *ROTC* indicates Army, Naval, and Air Force ROTC programs that are offered on campus; a program offered by arrangement on another campus is indicated by the word *cooperative.*

This section covers college-administered scholarships awarded to undergraduates on the basis of merit or personal attributes without regard to need. If you do not qualify for financial aid but nevertheless lack the resources to pay for college, non-need-based awards will be of special interest to you. Some personal characteristics are completely beyond an individual's control, and talents and achievements take a number of years to develop or attain. However, certain criteria for these awards, such as religious involvement, community service, and special academic interests can be attained in a relatively brief period of time. ROTC programs offer such benefits as tuition, the cost of textbooks, and living allowances. In return, you must fulfill a service obligation after graduating from college. Because they can be a significant help in paying for college, these programs have become quite competitive. Certain subject areas, such as nursing, health care, or technical fields, are in stronger demand than others. Among the obligations to consider about ROTC are that you must spend a regular portion of your available time in military training programs and that ROTC entails a multiyear commitment after your graduation to serve as an officer in the armed services branch sponsoring the program.

Loans

The figures here represent loans that are part of the financial aid award package. These are typically offered at rates lower than can be found in the normal loan marketplace. *Student loans* represents the total dollar amount of loans from all sources to full-time and part-time degree-seeking undergraduates or their parents. The percentage of these loans that goes to meet financial need and the percentage that goes to pay the non-need portion (the expected family contribution) are indicated. The percentage of the last graduating class who borrowed through any loan program (except parent loans) while enrolled at the college is shown, as is the average dollar figure per-borrower of cumulative undergraduate indebtedness of the last graduating class (this does not include loans from other institutions). *Parent loans* shows the total amount borrowed through parent loan programs as well as the percentages that were applied to the need-based and non-need-based portions of financial need. *Programs* indicates the major loan programs available to undergraduates. These include Direct and Stafford Loans (subsidized and unsubsidized and PLUS), Perkins Loans, Federal Nursing Loans, state loans, college/university loans, and other types.

Loans are forms of aid that must be repaid with interest. Most people will borrow money to pay college costs. The loans available through financial aid programs are offered at very favorable interest rates.

Student loans are preferable to parent loans because the payoff is deferred. In comparing colleges, the dollar amount of total indebtedness of the last class is a factor to be considered. Typically, this amount would increase proportionate to the tuition. However, if it does not, this could mean that the college provides relatively generous grant or work-study aid rather than loans in its financial aid package.

Work-Study

The total dollar amounts, number, and average dollar amount of *Federal Work-Study (FWS)* jobs appears first. The total dollar figure of *State or other work-study/jobs,* if available, is shown, as is the percentage of those dollars that go to meet financial need. The number of part-time jobs available on campus to undergraduates, other than work-study, is shown last.

FWS is a federally funded program that enables students with demonstrated need to earn money by working on or off campus, usually in a nonprofit organization. FWS jobs are a special category of jobs that are open to students only through the financial aid office. Other kinds of part-time jobs are routinely available at most colleges and may vary widely. In comparing colleges, you may find characteristic differences in how the "self-help" portions (loans and work-study) are proportioned. Families and students will differ as to how they ideally would proportion this self-help component. This preference may change as you mature and progress in class standing and your own ability to manage academic work and job responsibilities.

Athletic Awards

The total dollar amount of athletic scholarships given by the college to undergraduate students, whether or not it goes to meet financial need, is indicated, as are the average dollar amount of the athletic award that is non-need-based and the number of students who received non-need-based athletic awards.

If you are a serious student-athlete candidate, this may provide a broad context, but actual awards will depend upon your specific talents and the college's athletic needs at the particular time you want to attend. If you are a good athlete but not of starter caliber in a marquee sport, you might be able to secure a partial scholarship, depending on talent and the college's needs. In this case, the number of students receiving athletic awards in relation to the number of total undergraduates may be important.

Applying for Financial Aid

Required financial aid forms include the FAFSA (Free Application for Federal Student Aid), the institution's own form, PROFILE, a state aid form, a noncustodial (divorced/separated) parent's statement, a business/farm supplement, and others. The college's financial aid application deadline is noted as the *Financial aid deadline* and is shown in one of three ways: as a specific date if it is an absolute deadline; noted as *Continuous,* which means processing goes on without a deadline or until all available aid has been awarded; or as a date with the note *(priority),* meaning that you are encouraged to apply before that date in order to have the best chance of obtaining aid. *Notification date* is listed as either a specific date or continuous. The date by which you must reply to the college with your decision to accept or decline its financial aid package is listed as either a specific date or as a number of weeks from the date of notification.

Be prepared to check early with the colleges you are interested in as to exactly which forms will be required from you. All colleges require the FAFSA for students applying for federal aid. In most cases, colleges have a limited amount of funds set aside to use as financial aid. It is only natural that the first eligible students will get a larger share of what is available. The sooner you apply, the more likely it is that your financial need will be fully met and that a higher proportion of your financial aid package will consist of gift aid.

Contact

The name, title, address, telephone and fax numbers, and e-mail address of the person to contact for further information (student financial aid contact, chief financial aid officer, or office of financial aid) are given at the end of the profile. You should feel free to write or call for any materials you need or if you have questions.

How Schools Get into the Guide

Peterson's College Money Handbook 2001 covers accredited baccalaureate-degree-granting institutions in the United States and U.S. territories. Institutions have full accreditation or candidate-for-accreditation (preaccreditation) status granted by an institutional or specialized accrediting body recognized by the U.S. Department of Education or Council for Higher Education Accreditation. Recognized institutional accrediting bodies, which consider each institution as a whole, are the six regional associations of schools and colleges (Middle States, New England, North Central, Northwest, Southern, and Western), each of which is responsible for a specified portion of the United States and its territories; the Accrediting Association of Bible Colleges (AABC); the Accrediting Council for Independent Colleges and Schools (ACICS); the Accrediting Commission for Career Schools and Colleges of Technology (ACCSCT); the Distance Education and Training Council (DETC); the American Academy for Liberal Education; the Council on Occupational Education; and the Transnational Association of Christian Colleges and Schools (TRACS). Program registration by the New York State Board of Regents is considered to be the equivalent of institutional accreditation, since the Board requires that all programs offered by an institution meet its standards before recognition is granted. There are recognized specialized accrediting bodies in more than forty different fields, each of which is authorized to accredit specific programs in its particular field. This can serve as the equivalent of institutional accreditation for specialized institutions that offer programs in one field only (schools of art, music, optometry, theology, etc.).

Research Procedures

The data contained in the college chart, profiles, and indexes were collected between fall 1999 and spring 2000 through Peterson's Annual Survey of Undergraduate Financial Aid and Peterson's Annual Survey of Undergraduate Institutions. Questionnaires were sent to the more than 1,900 colleges and universities that meet the criteria for inclusion outlined above. All data included in this edition have been submitted by officials (usually financial aid officers, registrars, or institutional research personnel) at the schools themselves. In addition, the great majority of institutions that submitted data were contacted directly by Peterson's research staff members to verify unusual figures, resolve discrepancies, and obtain additional data. All usable information received in time for publication has been included. The omission of any particular item from an index or profile listing signifies that the item is either not applicable to that institution or that data were not available. Because of the comprehensive editorial review that takes place in our offices and because all material comes directly from college officials, we have every reason to believe that the information presented in this guide is accurate. However, you should check with a specific college or university at the time of application to verify such figures as tuition and fees, which may have changed since the publication of this volume.

ABILENE CHRISTIAN UNIVERSITY
Abilene, TX

Tuition & fees: $10,290 **Average undergraduate aid package: $10,694**

ABOUT THE INSTITUTION Independent religious, coed. Awards: associate, bachelor's, master's, doctoral, and first professional degrees. 93 undergraduate majors. Total enrollment: 4,650. Undergraduates: 4,078. Freshmen: 924. Federal methodology is used as a basis for awarding need-based institutional aid.

UNDERGRADUATE EXPENSES for 1999–2000 ***Application fee:*** $25. ***Comprehensive fee:*** $14,480 includes full-time tuition ($9810), mandatory fees ($480), and room and board ($4190). ***College room only:*** $1750. Full-time tuition and fees vary according to course load. Room and board charges vary according to board plan and housing facility. ***Part-time tuition:*** $327 per semester hour. ***Part-time fees:*** $16 per semester hour; $5 per term part-time. Part-time tuition and fees vary according to course load. ***Payment plans:*** tuition prepayment, installment.

FRESHMAN FINANCIAL AID (Fall 1998) 939 applied for aid; of those 84% were deemed to have need. 94% of freshmen with need received aid; of those 39% had need fully met. *Average percent of need met:* 78% (excluding resources awarded to replace EFC). *Average financial aid package:* $8878 (excluding resources awarded to replace EFC). 17% of all full-time freshmen had no need and received non-need-based aid.

UNDERGRADUATE FINANCIAL AID (Fall 1998) 3,238 applied for aid; of those 82% were deemed to have need. 88% of undergraduates with need received aid; of those 51% had need fully met. *Average percent of need met:* 92% (excluding resources awarded to replace EFC). *Average financial aid package:* $10,694 (excluding resources awarded to replace EFC). 11% of all full-time undergraduates had no need and received non-need-based aid.

GIFT AID (NEED-BASED) ***Total amount:*** $6,672,077 (40% Federal, 44% state, 16% institutional). ***Receiving aid:*** *Freshmen:* 64% (637); *all full-time undergraduates:* 52% (1,915). ***Average award:*** Freshmen: $3445; Undergraduates: $3395. ***Scholarships, grants, and awards:*** Federal Pell, FSEOG, state, private, college/university gift aid from institutional funds, United Negro College Fund.

GIFT AID (NON-NEED-BASED) ***Total amount:*** $5,855,344 (99% institutional, 1% external sources). ***Receiving aid:*** *Freshmen:* 62% (614); *Undergraduates:* 54% (1,996). ***Scholarships, grants, and awards by category:*** *Academic Interests/Achievement:* 2,311 awards ($5,766,071 total): agriculture, biological sciences, business, communication, education, English, foreign languages, general academic interests/achievements, home economics, mathematics, physical sciences, religion/biblical studies, social sciences. *Creative Arts/Performance:* 108 awards ($165,203 total): art/fine arts, debating, journalism/publications, music, theater/drama. *Special Achievements/Activities:* 153 awards ($129,400 total): cheerleading/drum major, leadership. *Special Characteristics:* 576 awards ($1,845,603 total): children of faculty/staff, ethnic background, first-generation college students, local/state students, members of minority groups, out-of-state students, previous college experience, relatives of clergy, religious affiliation. ***Tuition waivers:*** Full or partial for employees or children of employees.

LOANS ***Student loans:*** $19,011,933 (46% need-based, 54% non-need-based). 71% of past graduating class borrowed through all loan programs. ***Average need-based loan:*** Freshmen: $4905; Undergraduates: $6658. ***Parent loans:*** $3,314,237 (100% non-need-based). ***Programs:*** FFEL (Subsidized and Unsubsidized Stafford, PLUS), Perkins, state, college/university.

WORK-STUDY ***Federal work-study:*** *Total amount:* $540,441; 418 jobs averaging $1293. ***State or other work-study/employment:*** *Total amount:* $1,198,164 (4% need-based, 96% non-need-based). 902 part-time jobs averaging $1328.

ATHLETIC AWARDS *Total amount:* 1,743,305 (100% non-need-based).

APPLYING for FINANCIAL AID ***Required financial aid forms:*** FAFSA, institution's own form. ***Financial aid deadline (priority):*** 3/1. ***Notification date:*** Continuous beginning 4/1. Students must reply within 3 weeks of notification.

CONTACT Mr. Gary West, Director of Student Financial Services, Abilene Christian University, ACU Box 29007, Abilene, TX 79699-9007, 915-674-2643 or toll-free 800-460-6228 Ext. 2650. *E-mail:* westg@nicanor.acu.edu

ACADEMY OF ART COLLEGE
San Francisco, CA

Tuition & fees: $10,860 **Average undergraduate aid package: $4750**

ABOUT THE INSTITUTION Proprietary, coed. Awards: associate, bachelor's, and master's degrees. 17 undergraduate majors. Total enrollment: 5,638. Undergraduates: 4,987. Freshmen: 383. Federal methodology is used as a basis for awarding need-based institutional aid.

UNDERGRADUATE EXPENSES for 1999–2000 ***Application fee:*** $100. ***Tuition:*** full-time $10,860; part-time $450 per unit. ***Required fees:*** $30 per term part-time. Room and board charges vary according to housing facility. ***Payment plan:*** installment.

FRESHMAN FINANCIAL AID (Fall 1998) 460 applied for aid; of those 86% were deemed to have need. 95% of freshmen with need received aid; of those 9% had need fully met. *Average percent of need met:* 27% (excluding resources awarded to replace EFC). *Average financial aid package:* $2968 (excluding resources awarded to replace EFC). 7% of all full-time freshmen had no need and received non-need-based aid.

UNDERGRADUATE FINANCIAL AID (Fall 1998) 1,343 applied for aid; of those 88% were deemed to have need. 97% of undergraduates with need received aid; of those 13% had need fully met. *Average percent of need met:* 40% (excluding resources awarded to replace EFC). *Average financial aid package:* $4750 (excluding resources awarded to replace EFC). 6% of all full-time undergraduates had no need and received non-need-based aid.

GIFT AID (NEED-BASED) ***Total amount:*** $3,597,266 (69% Federal, 31% state). ***Receiving aid:*** *Freshmen:* 21% (186); *all full-time undergraduates:* 24% (671). ***Average award:*** Freshmen: $2720; Undergraduates: $3450. ***Scholarships, grants, and awards:*** Federal Pell, FSEOG, state, private.

LOANS ***Student loans:*** $16,263,310 (53% need-based, 47% non-need-based). 40% of past graduating class borrowed through all loan programs. Average indebtedness per student: $26,000. ***Average need-based loan:*** Freshmen: $2650; Undergraduates: $3350. ***Parent loans:*** $6,651,561 (100% non-need-based). ***Programs:*** Federal Direct (Subsidized and Unsubsidized Stafford, PLUS), FFEL (Subsidized and Unsubsidized Stafford, PLUS).

WORK-STUDY ***Federal work-study:*** *Total amount:* $75,556; 42 jobs averaging $1799.

APPLYING for FINANCIAL AID ***Required financial aid forms:*** FAFSA, institution's own form. ***Financial aid deadline (priority):*** 3/2. ***Notification date:*** 8/1.

CONTACT Mr. Joe Vollaro, Executive Vice President of Financial Aid and Compliance, Academy of Art College, 79 New Montgomery Street, San Francisco, CA 94105-3410, 415-274-8688 or toll-free 800-544-ARTS. *Fax:* 415-263-4130. *E-mail:* jvollaro@academyart.edu

ADAMS STATE COLLEGE
Alamosa, CO

Tuition & fees (CO res): $2092 **Average undergraduate aid package: $6460**

ABOUT THE INSTITUTION State-supported, coed. Awards: associate, bachelor's, and master's degrees. 68 undergraduate majors. Total enrollment: 2,512. Undergraduates: 2,025. Freshmen: 580. Federal methodology is used as a basis for awarding need-based institutional aid.

UNDERGRADUATE EXPENSES for 1999–2000 ***Application fee:*** $25. ***Tuition, state resident:*** full-time $1530; part-time $77 per semester hour. ***Tuition, nonresident:*** full-time $5740; part-time $287 per semester hour. ***Required fees:*** full-time $562; $21 per semester hour. Full-time tuition and fees vary according to reciprocity agreements. Part-time tuition and fees vary according to course load. ***College room and board:*** $5080; ***room only:*** $2580. Room and board charges vary according to board plan and housing facility. ***Payment plans:*** installment, deferred payment.

Adams State College (continued)

FRESHMAN FINANCIAL AID (Fall 1999) *Average percent of need met:* 84% (excluding resources awarded to replace EFC).

UNDERGRADUATE FINANCIAL AID (Fall 1999) *Average percent of need met:* 84% (excluding resources awarded to replace EFC). *Average financial aid package:* $6460 (excluding resources awarded to replace EFC).

GIFT AID (NEED-BASED) ***Total amount:*** $2,958,645 (77% Federal, 23% state). ***Scholarships, grants, and awards:*** Federal Pell, FSEOG, state, private, college/university gift aid from institutional funds.

GIFT AID (NON-NEED-BASED) ***Total amount:*** $1,754,598 (13% state, 49% institutional, 38% external sources). ***Scholarships, grants, and awards by category:*** *Academic Interests/Achievement:* biological sciences, business, communication, computer science, education, English, foreign languages, general academic interests/achievements, health fields, humanities, mathematics, premedicine, social sciences. *Creative Arts/Performance:* art/fine arts, music, performing arts, theater/drama. *Special Achievements/Activities:* community service, leadership, memberships. *Special Characteristics:* out-of-state students. ***Tuition waivers:*** Full or partial for employees or children of employees.

LOANS ***Student loans:*** $6,185,772 (67% need-based, 33% non-need-based). ***Parent loans:*** $256,301 (100% non-need-based). ***Programs:*** FFEL (Subsidized and Unsubsidized Stafford, PLUS), Perkins, college/university.

WORK-STUDY ***Federal work-study:*** *Total amount:* $324,959; jobs available. ***State or other work-study/employment:*** *Total amount:* $907,029 (70% need-based, 30% non-need-based). Part-time jobs available.

ATHLETIC AWARDS *Total amount:* 201,767 (100% non-need-based).

APPLYING for FINANCIAL AID ***Required financial aid form:*** FAFSA. ***Financial aid deadline (priority):*** 4/15. ***Notification date:*** Continuous beginning 4/30. Students must reply within 4 weeks of notification.

CONTACT Victor M. Vigil, Assistant Director of Financial Aid, Adams State College, 208 Edgemont Boulevard, Alamosa, CO 81102, 719-587-7306 or toll-free 800-824-6494. *Fax:* 719-587-7522.

ADELPHI UNIVERSITY

Garden City, NY

Tuition & fees: $14,920 **Average undergraduate aid package: $13,000**

ABOUT THE INSTITUTION Independent, coed. Awards: associate, bachelor's, master's, and doctoral degrees and post-bachelor's and post-master's certificates. 37 undergraduate majors. Total enrollment: 5,878. Undergraduates: 2,878. Freshmen: 554. Federal methodology is used as a basis for awarding need-based institutional aid.

UNDERGRADUATE EXPENSES for 1999–2000 ***Application fee:*** $35. ***Comprehensive fee:*** $22,100 includes full-time tuition ($14,750), mandatory fees ($170), and room and board ($7180). Full-time tuition and fees vary according to program. Room and board charges vary according to board plan and housing facility. ***Part-time tuition:*** $450 per credit. Part-time tuition and fees vary according to program. ***Payment plans:*** tuition prepayment, installment, deferred payment.

FRESHMAN FINANCIAL AID (Fall 1999, est.) 466 applied for aid; of those 100% were deemed to have need. 100% of freshmen with need received aid; of those 100% had need fully met. *Average financial aid package:* $12,500 (excluding resources awarded to replace EFC). 12% of all full-time freshmen had no need and received non-need-based aid.

UNDERGRADUATE FINANCIAL AID (Fall 1999, est.) 1,623 applied for aid; of those 100% were deemed to have need. 100% of undergraduates with need received aid. *Average financial aid package:* $13,000 (excluding resources awarded to replace EFC). 23% of all full-time undergraduates had no need and received non-need-based aid.

GIFT AID (NEED-BASED) ***Total amount:*** $5,566,219 (30% Federal, 32% state, 38% institutional). ***Receiving aid:*** *Freshmen:* 57% (304); *all full-time undergraduates:* 50% (1,043). ***Average award:*** Freshmen: $3588; Undergraduates: $4971. ***Scholarships, grants, and awards:*** Federal Pell, FSEOG, state, private, college/university gift aid from institutional funds, Scholarships for Disadvantaged Students (SDS).

GIFT AID (NON-NEED-BASED) ***Total amount:*** $4,857,335 (73% institutional, 27% external sources). ***Receiving aid:*** *Freshmen:* 50% (264); *Undergraduates:* 46% (976). ***Scholarships, grants, and awards by category:*** *Academic Interests/Achievement:* 783 awards ($3,976,502 total): foreign languages, general academic interests/achievements. *Creative Arts/Performance:* 157 awards ($744,650 total): art/fine arts, dance, music, performing arts, theater/drama. *Special Achievements/Activities:* 48 awards ($92,750 total): general special achievements/activities, memberships. *Special Characteristics:* 77 awards ($351,969 total): children and siblings of alumni, children of faculty/staff. ***Tuition waivers:*** Full or partial for employees or children of employees. ***ROTC:*** Army cooperative, Air Force cooperative.

LOANS ***Student loans:*** $9,349,876 (63% need-based, 37% non-need-based). 67% of past graduating class borrowed through all loan programs. Average indebtedness per student: $19,927. ***Parent loans:*** $1,566,364 (100% non-need-based). ***Programs:*** FFEL (Subsidized and Unsubsidized Stafford, PLUS), Perkins, Federal Nursing.

WORK-STUDY ***Federal work-study:*** *Total amount:* $1,339,373; 643 jobs available. ***State or other work-study/employment:*** *Total amount:* $440,690 (100% non-need-based). 346 part-time jobs averaging $1274.

ATHLETIC AWARDS *Total amount:* 950,000 (100% non-need-based).

APPLYING for FINANCIAL AID ***Required financial aid forms:*** FAFSA, state aid form. ***Financial aid deadline (priority):*** 2/15. ***Notification date:*** Continuous. Students must reply by 5/1.

CONTACT Mr. Joseph Posillico, Director of Admissions and Student Financial Services, Adelphi University, South Avenue, Garden City, NY 11530, 516-877-3080 or toll-free 800-ADELPHI.

ADRIAN COLLEGE

Adrian, MI

Tuition & fees: $13,750 **Average undergraduate aid package: $12,920**

ABOUT THE INSTITUTION Independent religious, coed. Awards: associate and bachelor's degrees. 45 undergraduate majors. Total enrollment: 1,060. Undergraduates: 1,060. Freshmen: 296. Both federal and institutional methodology are used as a basis for awarding need-based institutional aid.

UNDERGRADUATE EXPENSES for 1999–2000 ***Application fee:*** $20. ***Comprehensive fee:*** $18,530 includes full-time tuition ($13,650), mandatory fees ($100), and room and board ($4780). ***College room only:*** $2030. Room and board charges vary according to board plan. ***Payment plan:*** installment.

FRESHMAN FINANCIAL AID (Fall 1999) 279 applied for aid; of those 85% were deemed to have need. 100% of freshmen with need received aid; of those 24% had need fully met. *Average percent of need met:* 91% (excluding resources awarded to replace EFC). *Average financial aid package:* $14,552 (excluding resources awarded to replace EFC). 14% of all full-time freshmen had no need and received non-need-based aid.

UNDERGRADUATE FINANCIAL AID (Fall 1999) 916 applied for aid; of those 84% were deemed to have need. 100% of undergraduates with need received aid; of those 25% had need fully met. *Average percent of need met:* 92% (excluding resources awarded to replace EFC). *Average financial aid package:* $12,920 (excluding resources awarded to replace EFC). 14% of all full-time undergraduates had no need and received non-need-based aid.

GIFT AID (NEED-BASED) ***Total amount:*** $5,730,938 (12% Federal, 25% state, 60% institutional, 3% external sources). ***Receiving aid:*** *Freshmen:* 79% (236); *all full-time undergraduates:* 76% (758). ***Average award:*** Freshmen: $9587; Undergraduates: $8226. ***Scholarships, grants, and awards:*** Federal Pell, FSEOG, state, private, college/university gift aid from institutional funds.

GIFT AID (NON-NEED-BASED) ***Total amount:*** $1,040,277 (97% institutional, 3% external sources). ***Receiving aid:*** *Freshmen:* 9% (26); *Undergraduates:* 5% (50). ***Scholarships, grants, and awards by category:*** *Academic Interests/Achievement:* 495 awards ($2,858,360 total): business, general academic interests/achievements. *Creative Arts/Performance:* 123 awards ($123,000 total): art/fine arts, music, theater/drama. *Special Achievements/Activities:* 31 awards ($31,000 total): religious involvement. *Special*

Characteristics: 131 awards ($144,970 total): children and siblings of alumni, children of faculty/staff, children of workers in trades. ***Tuition waivers:*** Full or partial for employees or children of employees.

LOANS ***Student loans:*** $4,058,341 (73% need-based, 27% non-need-based). 81% of past graduating class borrowed through all loan programs. Average indebtedness per student: $15,187. ***Average need-based loan:*** Freshmen: $2958; Undergraduates: $3714. ***Parent loans:*** $6,718,106 (15% need-based, 85% non-need-based). ***Programs:*** FFEL (Subsidized and Unsubsidized Stafford, PLUS), Perkins, state, college/university, MI-Loan Program, Key Alternative Loans.

WORK-STUDY ***Federal work-study:*** *Total amount:* $563,390; 377 jobs averaging $1494.

APPLYING for FINANCIAL AID ***Required financial aid form:*** FAFSA. ***Financial aid deadline (priority):*** 3/15. ***Notification date:*** Continuous. Students must reply by 5/1 or within 2 weeks of notification.

CONTACT Mr. Christian Howard, Associate Director of Student Financial Services, Adrian College, 110 South Madison Street, Adrian, MI 49221-2575, 800-877-2246. *Fax:* 517-265-3331. *E-mail:* choward@adrian.edu

THE ADVERTISING ARTS COLLEGE

San Diego, CA

ABOUT THE INSTITUTION Proprietary, coed. Awards: associate and bachelor's degrees. 6 undergraduate majors. Total enrollment: 395. Undergraduates: 395. Freshmen: 160.

GIFT AID (NEED-BASED) ***Scholarships, grants, and awards:*** Federal Pell, FSEOG, state, private, college/university gift aid from institutional funds.

GIFT AID (NON-NEED-BASED) ***Scholarships, grants, and awards by category:*** *Academic Interests/Achievement:* communication, education. *Creative Arts/Performance:* applied art and design, art/fine arts, creative writing, general creative arts/performance.

LOANS ***Programs:*** Federal Direct (Subsidized and Unsubsidized Stafford, PLUS), FFEL (Subsidized and Unsubsidized Stafford, PLUS), Perkins.

WORK-STUDY Federal work-study jobs available.

APPLYING for FINANCIAL AID ***Required financial aid forms:*** FAFSA, institution's own form.

CONTACT Monica McCormick, Financial Aid Administrator, The Advertising Arts College, 10025 Mesa Rim Road, San Diego, CA 92121, 619-546-0602.

AGNES SCOTT COLLEGE

Decatur, GA

Tuition & fees: $16,025 | **Average undergraduate aid package: $16,335**

ABOUT THE INSTITUTION Independent religious, women only. Awards: bachelor's and master's degrees and post-bachelor's certificates. 27 undergraduate majors. Total enrollment: 887. Undergraduates: 879. Freshmen: 241. Both federal and institutional methodology are used as a basis for awarding need-based institutional aid.

UNDERGRADUATE EXPENSES for 1999–2000 ***Application fee:*** $35. ***Comprehensive fee:*** $22,685 includes full-time tuition ($15,880), mandatory fees ($145), and room and board ($6660). Room and board charges vary according to board plan and housing facility. ***Part-time tuition:*** $660 per credit hour. ***Part-time fees:*** $145 per year part-time. Part-time tuition and fees vary according to course load. ***Payment plans:*** installment, deferred payment.

FRESHMAN FINANCIAL AID (Fall 1998) 186 applied for aid; of those 80% were deemed to have need. 100% of freshmen with need received aid; of those 95% had need fully met. *Average percent of need met:* 99% (excluding resources awarded to replace EFC). *Average financial aid package:* $17,410 (excluding resources awarded to replace EFC). 26% of all full-time freshmen had no need and received non-need-based aid.

UNDERGRADUATE FINANCIAL AID (Fall 1998) 594 applied for aid; of those 85% were deemed to have need. 100% of undergraduates with need received aid; of those 94% had need fully met. *Average percent of need met:* 99% (excluding resources awarded to replace EFC). *Average financial aid package:* $16,335 (excluding resources awarded to replace EFC). 28% of all full-time undergraduates had no need and received non-need-based aid.

GIFT AID (NEED-BASED) ***Total amount:*** $5,556,170 (10% Federal, 14% state, 73% institutional, 3% external sources). ***Receiving aid:*** *Freshmen:* 72% (147); *all full-time undergraduates:* 68% (501). ***Average award:*** Freshmen: $12,448; Undergraduates: $11,041. ***Scholarships, grants, and awards:*** Federal Pell, FSEOG, state, private, college/university gift aid from institutional funds.

GIFT AID (NON-NEED-BASED) ***Total amount:*** $3,095,760 (12% state, 86% institutional, 2% external sources). ***Receiving aid:*** *Freshmen:* 39% (80); *Undergraduates:* 36% (268). ***Scholarships, grants, and awards by category:*** *Academic Interests/Achievement:* biological sciences, English, general academic interests/achievements, humanities, mathematics, physical sciences, social sciences. *Creative Arts/Performance:* music. *Special Achievements/Activities:* community service, general special achievements/activities. *Special Characteristics:* adult students, children of educators, children of faculty/staff, handicapped students, international students, local/state students. ***Tuition waivers:*** Full or partial for employees or children of employees. ***ROTC:*** Naval cooperative, Air Force cooperative.

LOANS ***Student loans:*** $2,153,347 (65% need-based, 35% non-need-based). 67% of past graduating class borrowed through all loan programs. Average indebtedness per student: $14,580. ***Average need-based loan:*** Freshmen: $2491; Undergraduates: $3786. ***Parent loans:*** $694,324 (100% non-need-based). ***Programs:*** FFEL (Subsidized and Unsubsidized Stafford, PLUS), college/university, Achiever Loans.

WORK-STUDY ***Federal work-study:*** *Total amount:* $406,225; 278 jobs averaging $1576. ***State or other work-study/employment:*** *Total amount:* $223,200 (21% need-based, 79% non-need-based). 152 part-time jobs averaging $1562.

APPLYING for FINANCIAL AID ***Required financial aid forms:*** FAFSA, institution's own form, noncustodial (divorced/separated) parent's statement, business/farm supplement. ***Financial aid deadline (priority):*** 3/1. ***Notification date:*** Continuous. Students must reply by 5/1 or within 2 weeks of notification.

CONTACT Melva Lord, Director of Financial Aid, Agnes Scott College, 141 East College Avenue, Atlanta/Decatur, GA 30030-3797, 404-471-6395 or toll-free 800-868-8602. *Fax:* 404-471-6159. *E-mail:* finaid@agnesscott.edu

ALABAMA AGRICULTURAL AND MECHANICAL UNIVERSITY

Normal, AL

Tuition & fees (AL res): $2732 | **Average undergraduate aid package: $4978**

ABOUT THE INSTITUTION State-supported, coed. Awards: bachelor's, master's, and doctoral degrees and post-master's certificates. 36 undergraduate majors. Total enrollment: 5,497. Undergraduates: 4,332. Freshmen: 1,121. Both federal and institutional methodology are used as a basis for awarding need-based institutional aid.

UNDERGRADUATE EXPENSES for 2000–2001 ***Application fee:*** $10. ***Tuition, state resident:*** full-time $2332; part-time $119 per semester hour. ***Tuition, nonresident:*** full-time $4264; part-time $219 per semester hour. ***Required fees:*** full-time $400. Part-time tuition and fees vary according to course load. ***College room and board:*** $2678. Room and board charges vary according to housing facility. ***Payment plan:*** deferred payment.

FRESHMAN FINANCIAL AID (Fall 1999, est.) 1373 applied for aid. *Average percent of need met:* 52% (excluding resources awarded to replace EFC). *Average financial aid package:* $5244 (excluding resources awarded to replace EFC). 4% of all full-time freshmen had no need and received non-need-based aid.

UNDERGRADUATE FINANCIAL AID (Fall 1999, est.) 3,848 applied for aid. *Average percent of need met:* 50% (excluding resources awarded to replace EFC). *Average financial aid package:* $4978 (excluding resources awarded to replace EFC). 8% of all full-time undergraduates had no need and received non-need-based aid.

Alabama Agricultural and Mechanical University (continued)

GIFT AID (NEED-BASED) ***Total amount:*** $10,478,667 (58% Federal, 1% state, 38% institutional, 3% external sources). ***Scholarships, grants, and awards:*** Federal Pell, FSEOG, state, private, college/university gift aid from institutional funds, United Negro College Fund.

GIFT AID (NON-NEED-BASED) ***Scholarships, grants, and awards by category:*** *Academic Interests/Achievement:* 558 awards ($1,831,322 total): general academic interests/achievements. *Creative Arts/Performance:* 326 awards ($1,053,633 total): music, theater/drama. *Special Characteristics:* 136 awards ($266,762 total): children of faculty/staff, parents of current students. ***Tuition waivers:*** Full or partial for minority students, employees or children of employees. ***ROTC:*** Army.

LOANS ***Student loans:*** $17,416,042 (100% need-based). 62% of past graduating class borrowed through all loan programs. Average indebtedness per student: $17,021. ***Parent loans:*** $835,762 (100% need-based). ***Programs:*** Federal Direct (Subsidized and Unsubsidized Stafford, PLUS), FFEL (Subsidized and Unsubsidized Stafford, PLUS), Perkins, state.

WORK-STUDY ***Federal work-study:*** *Total amount:* $234,861; 80 jobs averaging $2918. ***State or other work-study/employment:*** *Total amount:* $706,854 (100% non-need-based). 429 part-time jobs available.

ATHLETIC AWARDS *Total amount:* 1,027,998 (100% need-based).

APPLYING for FINANCIAL AID ***Required financial aid forms:*** FAFSA, institution's own form. ***Financial aid deadline (priority):*** 3/17. ***Notification date:*** Continuous. Students must reply within 2 weeks of notification.

CONTACT Mr. Carlos Clark, Director of Student Financial Aid, Alabama Agricultural and Mechanical University, PO Box 907, Normal, AL 35762-0907, 256-851-5400 or toll-free 800-553-0816. *Fax:* 256-851-5407.

ALABAMA STATE UNIVERSITY

Montgomery, AL

Tuition & fees (AL res): $2520 **Average undergraduate aid package: $7788**

ABOUT THE INSTITUTION State-supported, coed. Awards: associate, bachelor's, and master's degrees. 47 undergraduate majors. Total enrollment: 5,664. Undergraduates: 4,683. Freshmen: 1,203. Federal methodology is used as a basis for awarding need-based institutional aid.

UNDERGRADUATE EXPENSES for 1999–2000 ***Tuition, state resident:*** full-time $2520; part-time $105 per credit hour. ***Tuition, nonresident:*** full-time $5040; part-time $210 per credit hour. Full-time tuition and fees vary according to course load, degree level, and student level. Part-time tuition and fees vary according to course load, degree level, and student level. ***College room and board:*** $3700. Room and board charges vary according to housing facility. ***Payment plans:*** installment, deferred payment.

FRESHMAN FINANCIAL AID (Fall 1999) 1150 applied for aid; of those 99% were deemed to have need. 100% of freshmen with need received aid; of those 28% had need fully met. *Average percent of need met:* 65% (excluding resources awarded to replace EFC). *Average financial aid package:* $5750 (excluding resources awarded to replace EFC). 2% of all full-time freshmen had no need and received non-need-based aid.

UNDERGRADUATE FINANCIAL AID (Fall 1999) 4,503 applied for aid; of those 94% were deemed to have need. 100% of undergraduates with need received aid; of those 15% had need fully met. *Average percent of need met:* 75% (excluding resources awarded to replace EFC). *Average financial aid package:* $7788 (excluding resources awarded to replace EFC). 6% of all full-time undergraduates had no need and received non-need-based aid.

GIFT AID (NEED-BASED) ***Total amount:*** $8,191,908 (99% Federal, 1% state). ***Receiving aid:*** *Freshmen:* 71% (835); *all full-time undergraduates:* 60% (2,813). ***Average award:*** Freshmen: $2763; Undergraduates: $2772. ***Scholarships, grants, and awards:*** Federal Pell, FSEOG, state.

GIFT AID (NON-NEED-BASED) ***Total amount:*** $2,412,660 (1% state, 80% institutional, 19% external sources). ***Receiving aid:*** *Freshmen:* 25% (289); *Undergraduates:* 23% (1,058). ***Scholarships, grants, and awards by category:*** *Academic Interests/Achievement:* 421 awards: biological sciences, education, general academic interests/achievements, health fields, mathematics. *Creative Arts/Performance:* 100 awards: art/fine arts, music, performing arts, theater/drama. *Special Achievements/Activities:* 24 awards: cheerleading/drum major, general special achievements/activities, leadership. *Special Characteristics:* 414 awards: children of union members/company employees, ethnic background, general special characteristics, handicapped students, local/state students, members of minority groups, out-of-state students, religious affiliation, veterans, veterans' children. ***Tuition waivers:*** Full or partial for employees or children of employees. ***ROTC:*** Army cooperative, Naval.

LOANS ***Student loans:*** $14,868,512 (100% need-based). 90% of past graduating class borrowed through all loan programs. ***Average need-based loan:*** Freshmen: $2390; Undergraduates: $3096. ***Parent loans:*** $8,340,582 (100% need-based). ***Programs:*** FFEL (Subsidized and Unsubsidized Stafford, PLUS), Perkins, state, college/university.

WORK-STUDY ***Federal work-study:*** *Total amount:* $1,513,908; 853 jobs averaging $1775. ***State or other work-study/employment:*** *Total amount:* $225,000 (100% non-need-based). 185 part-time jobs averaging $1216.

ATHLETIC AWARDS *Total amount:* 1,112,462 (100% non-need-based).

APPLYING for FINANCIAL AID ***Required financial aid form:*** FAFSA. ***Financial aid deadline (priority):*** 5/1. ***Notification date:*** Continuous beginning 5/15.

CONTACT Mrs. Dorenda A. Adams, Director of Financial Aid, Alabama State University, PO Box 271, Montgomery, AL 36101-0271, 334-229-4323 or toll-free 800-253-5037. *Fax:* 334-299-4924. *E-mail:* dadams@asunet.alasu.edu

ALASKA BIBLE COLLEGE

Glennallen, AK

Tuition & fees: $4750 **Average undergraduate aid package: N/A**

ABOUT THE INSTITUTION Independent nondenominational, coed. Awards: associate and bachelor's degrees. 7 undergraduate majors. Total enrollment: 37. Undergraduates: 37. Freshmen: 8. Institutional methodology is used as a basis for awarding need-based institutional aid.

UNDERGRADUATE EXPENSES for 2000–2001 ***Application fee:*** $25. ***Comprehensive fee:*** $8650 includes full-time tuition ($4750) and room and board ($3900). ***Part-time tuition:*** $200 per credit. ***Payment plan:*** installment.

FRESHMAN FINANCIAL AID (Fall 1998) 13 applied for aid; of those 100% were deemed to have need. 100% of freshmen with need received aid; of those 100% had need fully met.

UNDERGRADUATE FINANCIAL AID (Fall 1998) 28 applied for aid; of those 100% were deemed to have need. 100% of undergraduates with need received aid; of those 100% had need fully met.

GIFT AID (NEED-BASED) ***Total amount:*** $39,500 (51% institutional, 49% external sources). ***Receiving aid:*** *Freshmen:* 31% (5); *all full-time undergraduates:* 25% (9). ***Scholarships, grants, and awards:*** private, college/university gift aid from institutional funds.

GIFT AID (NON-NEED-BASED) ***Total amount:*** $27,555 (100% institutional). ***Scholarships, grants, and awards by category:*** *Academic Interests/Achievement:* general academic interests/achievements, religion/biblical studies. *Creative Arts/Performance:* music. *Special Achievements/Activities:* religious involvement. *Special Characteristics:* children of faculty/staff, local/state students, religious affiliation, spouses of current students. ***Tuition waivers:*** Full or partial for employees or children of employees.

LOANS ***Student loans:*** $8500 (100% need-based). ***Programs:*** state.

WORK-STUDY ***State or other work-study/employment:*** *Total amount:* $11,994 (100% need-based). 10 part-time jobs averaging $1199.

APPLYING for FINANCIAL AID ***Required financial aid form:*** institution's own form. ***Financial aid deadline:*** 8/5 (priority: 5/31). ***Notification date:*** Continuous. Students must reply within 2 weeks of notification.

CONTACT Mr. James Folsom, Financial Aid Officer, Alaska Bible College, Box 289, Glennallen, AK 99588-0289, 907-822-3201 Ext. 222 or toll-free 800-478-7884. *Fax:* 907-822-5027. *E-mail:* jim_folsom@akbible.edu

ALASKA PACIFIC UNIVERSITY

Anchorage, AK

ABOUT THE INSTITUTION Independent, coed. Awards: associate, bachelor's, and master's degrees. 10 undergraduate majors. Total enrollment: 556. Undergraduates: 385. Freshmen: 34.

GIFT AID (NEED-BASED) ***Scholarships, grants, and awards:*** Federal Pell, FSEOG, state, college/university gift aid from institutional funds, Bureau of Indian Affairs Grants.

GIFT AID (NON-NEED-BASED) ***Scholarships, grants, and awards by category:*** *Academic Interests/Achievement:* general academic interests/achievements. *Special Achievements/Activities:* general special achievements/activities, leadership. *Special Characteristics:* ethnic background, international students, local/state students, out-of-state students, religious affiliation.

LOANS ***Programs:*** FFEL (Subsidized and Unsubsidized Stafford, PLUS), state.

WORK-STUDY Federal work-study jobs available.

APPLYING for FINANCIAL AID ***Required financial aid forms:*** FAFSA, financial aid transcript (for transfers), scholarship application form.

CONTACT Mr. Roger Frierson, Director of Financial Aid, Alaska Pacific University, 4101 University Drive, Anchorage, AK 99508-4672, 907-564-8342 or toll-free 800-252-7528.

ALBANY COLLEGE OF PHARMACY OF UNION UNIVERSITY

Albany, NY

Tuition & fees: $12,173 **Average undergraduate aid package: $8424**

ABOUT THE INSTITUTION Independent, coed. Awards: bachelor's and first professional degrees. 1 undergraduate major. Total enrollment: 656. Undergraduates: 621. Freshmen: 99. Federal methodology is used as a basis for awarding need-based institutional aid.

UNDERGRADUATE EXPENSES for 1999–2000 ***Application fee:*** $50. ***Comprehensive fee:*** $17,273 includes full-time tuition ($11,950), mandatory fees ($223), and room and board ($5100). ***College room only:*** $3500. Room and board charges vary according to student level. ***Part-time tuition:*** $398 per semester hour. ***Part-time fees:*** $223 per year part-time. Part-time tuition and fees vary according to course load. ***Payment plan:*** installment.

FRESHMAN FINANCIAL AID (Fall 1999, est.) 92 applied for aid; of those 96% were deemed to have need. 100% of freshmen with need received aid. *Average percent of need met:* 80% (excluding resources awarded to replace EFC). *Average financial aid package:* $8431 (excluding resources awarded to replace EFC). 17% of all full-time freshmen had no need and received non-need-based aid.

UNDERGRADUATE FINANCIAL AID (Fall 1999, est.) 562 applied for aid; of those 90% were deemed to have need. 100% of undergraduates with need received aid. *Average percent of need met:* 80% (excluding resources awarded to replace EFC). *Average financial aid package:* $8424 (excluding resources awarded to replace EFC). 20% of all full-time undergraduates had no need and received non-need-based aid.

GIFT AID (NEED-BASED) ***Total amount:*** $2,025,569 (21% Federal, 34% state, 40% institutional, 5% external sources). ***Receiving aid:*** *Freshmen:* 83% (88); *all full-time undergraduates:* 80% (503). ***Average award:*** Freshmen: $8201; Undergraduates: $8199. ***Scholarships, grants, and awards:*** Federal Pell, FSEOG, state, private, college/university gift aid from institutional funds.

GIFT AID (NON-NEED-BASED) ***Total amount:*** $77,376 (35% state, 64% institutional, 1% external sources). ***Receiving aid:*** *Freshmen:* 9% (10); *Undergraduates:* 4% (25). ***Scholarships, grants, and awards by category:*** *Academic Interests/Achievement:* general academic interests/achievements. *Special Characteristics:* children and siblings of alumni. ***Tuition waivers:*** Full or partial for employees or children of employees. ***ROTC:*** Army cooperative, Naval cooperative, Air Force cooperative.

LOANS ***Student loans:*** $4,482,302 (93% need-based, 7% non-need-based). 85% of past graduating class borrowed through all loan programs. Average indebtedness per student: $19,231. ***Average need-based loan:*** Freshmen: $5575; Undergraduates: $5587. ***Parent loans:*** $178,627 (94% need-based, 6% non-need-based). ***Programs:*** FFEL (Subsidized and Unsubsidized Stafford, PLUS), Perkins, college/university, Health Professions Student Loans (HPSL).

WORK-STUDY ***Federal work-study:*** *Total amount:* $86,012; 135 jobs averaging $637. ***State or other work-study/employment:*** *Total amount:* $50,600 (100% non-need-based). 50 part-time jobs averaging $1000.

APPLYING for FINANCIAL AID ***Required financial aid forms:*** FAFSA, state aid form. ***Financial aid deadline (priority):*** 2/1. ***Notification date:*** 3/15. Students must reply by 4/1.

CONTACT Tiffany M. Gutierrez, Director of Financial Aid, Albany College of Pharmacy of Union University, 106 New Scotland Avenue, Albany, NY 12208-3425, 518-445-7256. *Fax:* 518-445-7202.

ALBANY STATE UNIVERSITY

Albany, GA

Tuition & fees (GA res): $2700 **Average undergraduate aid package: N/A**

ABOUT THE INSTITUTION State-supported, coed. Awards: bachelor's and master's degrees and post-master's certificates. 29 undergraduate majors. Total enrollment: 3,356. Undergraduates: 2,935. Freshmen: 719. Federal methodology is used as a basis for awarding need-based institutional aid.

UNDERGRADUATE EXPENSES for 1999–2000 ***Application fee:*** $20. ***Tuition, state resident:*** full-time $2254; part-time $76 per credit. ***Tuition, nonresident:*** full-time $7678; part-time $302 per credit. ***Required fees:*** full-time $446; $446. Full-time tuition and fees vary according to course load. Part-time tuition and fees vary according to course load. ***College room and board:*** $3256; ***room only:*** $1480. Room and board charges vary according to housing facility.

GIFT AID (NEED-BASED) ***Total amount:*** $5,013,330 (99% Federal, 1% state). ***Scholarships, grants, and awards:*** Federal Pell, FSEOG, state, private, college/university gift aid from institutional funds, Federal Nursing.

GIFT AID (NON-NEED-BASED) ***Total amount:*** $1,262,721 (62% state, 30% institutional, 8% external sources). ***Scholarships, grants, and awards by category:*** *Academic Interests/Achievement:* biological sciences, computer science, education, general academic interests/achievements, health fields, mathematics, social sciences. *Creative Arts/Performance:* music. ***Tuition waivers:*** Full or partial for senior citizens. ***ROTC:*** Army.

LOANS ***Student loans:*** $9,865,341 (100% need-based). ***Parent loans:*** $325,686 (100% need-based). ***Programs:*** Federal Direct (Subsidized and Unsubsidized Stafford, PLUS), Perkins, state.

WORK-STUDY ***Federal work-study:*** *Total amount:* $387,106; 430 jobs averaging $900. ***State or other work-study/employment:*** *Total amount:* $269,168 (100% non-need-based). 165 part-time jobs averaging $1631.

ATHLETIC AWARDS *Total amount:* 332,250 (100% need-based).

APPLYING for FINANCIAL AID ***Required financial aid form:*** FAFSA. ***Financial aid deadline (priority):*** 4/15. ***Notification date:*** 5/15.

CONTACT Ms. Kathleen J. Caldwell, Director of Admissions and Financial Aid, Albany State University, 504 College Drive, Albany, GA 31705-2717, 912-430-4650 or toll-free 800-822-RAMS (in-state). *Fax:* 912-430-3936. *E-mail:* kcaldwel@asurams.edu

ALBERT A. LIST COLLEGE OF JEWISH STUDIES

New York, NY

See Jewish Theological Seminary of America

ALBERTSON COLLEGE OF IDAHO
Caldwell, ID

Tuition & fees: $16,280 **Average undergraduate aid package: $11,734**

ABOUT THE INSTITUTION Independent, coed. Awards: bachelor's degrees. 30 undergraduate majors. Total enrollment: 763. Undergraduates: 763. Freshmen: 211. Federal methodology is used as a basis for awarding need-based institutional aid.

UNDERGRADUATE EXPENSES for 1999–2000 ***Application fee:*** $25. ***Comprehensive fee:*** $20,480 includes full-time tuition ($16,000), mandatory fees ($280), and room and board ($4200). ***College room only:*** $2000. Room and board charges vary according to board plan and housing facility. ***Part-time tuition:*** $670 per credit. ***Part-time fees:*** $69 per term part-time. Part-time tuition and fees vary according to program. ***Payment plan:*** installment.

FRESHMAN FINANCIAL AID (Fall 1999, est.) 287 applied for aid; of those 73% were deemed to have need. 100% of freshmen with need received aid; of those 19% had need fully met. *Average percent of need met:* 62% (excluding resources awarded to replace EFC). *Average financial aid package:* $10,003 (excluding resources awarded to replace EFC). 24% of all full-time freshmen had no need and received non-need-based aid.

UNDERGRADUATE FINANCIAL AID (Fall 1999, est.) 751 applied for aid; of those 69% were deemed to have need. 100% of undergraduates with need received aid; of those 27% had need fully met. *Average percent of need met:* 78% (excluding resources awarded to replace EFC). *Average financial aid package:* $11,734 (excluding resources awarded to replace EFC). 26% of all full-time undergraduates had no need and received non-need-based aid.

GIFT AID (NEED-BASED) ***Total amount:*** $618,393 (84% Federal, 7% state, 9% institutional). ***Receiving aid:*** *Freshmen:* 73% (209); *all full-time undergraduates:* 69% (520). ***Average award:*** Freshmen: $5600; Undergraduates: $5220. ***Scholarships, grants, and awards:*** Federal Pell, FSEOG, state, private, college/university gift aid from institutional funds.

GIFT AID (NON-NEED-BASED) ***Total amount:*** $3,610,786 (94% institutional, 6% external sources). ***Receiving aid:*** *Freshmen:* 73% (209); *Undergraduates:* 69% (520). ***Scholarships, grants, and awards by category:*** *Academic Interests/Achievement:* 1,707 awards ($3,393,044 total): biological sciences, business, computer science, education, foreign languages, general academic interests/achievements, humanities, mathematics, physical sciences, premedicine, religion/biblical studies, social sciences. *Creative Arts/Performance:* 166 awards ($330,269 total): art/fine arts, debating, music, theater/drama. *Special Achievements/Activities:* 1 award ($2000 total): junior miss, rodeo. *Special Characteristics:* 127 awards ($494,687 total): children and siblings of alumni, children of faculty/staff, ethnic background, local/state students, members of minority groups, religious affiliation. ***Tuition waivers:*** Full or partial for children of alumni, employees or children of employees, adult students, senior citizens.

LOANS ***Student loans:*** $2,550,949 (60% need-based, 40% non-need-based). 81% of past graduating class borrowed through all loan programs. Average indebtedness per student: $15,460. ***Average need-based loan:*** Freshmen: $2106. ***Parent loans:*** $685,058 (100% need-based). ***Programs:*** FFEL (Subsidized and Unsubsidized Stafford, PLUS), Perkins, alternative loans.

WORK-STUDY ***Federal work-study:*** *Total amount:* $164,509; 158 jobs averaging $1041. ***State or other work-study/employment:*** *Total amount:* $229,732 (13% need-based, 87% non-need-based). 252 part-time jobs averaging $912.

ATHLETIC AWARDS *Total amount:* 830,414 (100% need-based).

APPLYING for FINANCIAL AID ***Required financial aid forms:*** FAFSA, institution's own form. ***Financial aid deadline (priority):*** 2/15. ***Notification date:*** 4/1. Students must reply within 3 weeks of notification.

CONTACT Mr. Ron E. Christianson, Director, Office of Student Financial Services, Albertson College of Idaho, 2112 Cleveland Boulevard, Campus Box 39, Caldwell, ID 83605-4432, 208-459-5308 or toll-free 800-AC-IDAHO. *Fax:* 208-459-5844. *E-mail:* rchristi@acofi.edu

ALBERTUS MAGNUS COLLEGE
New Haven, CT

Tuition & fees: $14,343 **Average undergraduate aid package: $8000**

ABOUT THE INSTITUTION Independent Roman Catholic, coed. Awards: associate, bachelor's, and master's degrees. 46 undergraduate majors. Total enrollment: 1,964. Undergraduates: 1,720. Federal methodology is used as a basis for awarding need-based institutional aid.

UNDERGRADUATE EXPENSES for 1999–2000 ***Application fee:*** $35. ***Comprehensive fee:*** $20,855 includes full-time tuition ($13,908), mandatory fees ($435), and room and board ($6512). ***Part-time tuition:*** $1,738 per course. ***Part-time fees:*** $15 per term part-time. Part-time tuition and fees vary according to class time. ***Payment plan:*** installment.

FRESHMAN FINANCIAL AID (Fall 1998) 210 applied for aid; of those 71% were deemed to have need. 100% of freshmen with need received aid; of those 47% had need fully met. *Average percent of need met:* 94% (excluding resources awarded to replace EFC). *Average financial aid package:* $10,000 (excluding resources awarded to replace EFC). 4% of all full-time freshmen had no need and received non-need-based aid.

UNDERGRADUATE FINANCIAL AID (Fall 1998) 950 applied for aid; of those 55% were deemed to have need. 100% of undergraduates with need received aid; of those 77% had need fully met. *Average percent of need met:* 85% (excluding resources awarded to replace EFC). *Average financial aid package:* $8000 (excluding resources awarded to replace EFC). 2% of all full-time undergraduates had no need and received non-need-based aid.

GIFT AID (NEED-BASED) ***Total amount:*** $1,595,127 (32% Federal, 60% state, 8% institutional). ***Receiving aid:*** *Freshmen:* 20% (80); *all full-time undergraduates:* 17% (210). ***Average award:*** Freshmen: $8000; Undergraduates: $7000. ***Scholarships, grants, and awards:*** Federal Pell, FSEOG, state.

GIFT AID (NON-NEED-BASED) ***Total amount:*** $732,536 (97% institutional, 3% external sources). ***Receiving aid:*** *Freshmen:* 33% (130); *Undergraduates:* 30% (380). ***Scholarships, grants, and awards by category:*** *Academic Interests/Achievement:* biological sciences, business, communication, computer science, education, English, foreign languages, general academic interests/achievements, humanities, international studies, mathematics, physical sciences, premedicine, religion/biblical studies, social sciences. *Creative Arts/Performance:* art/fine arts, performing arts, theater/drama. *Special Achievements/Activities:* community service, leadership. *Special Characteristics:* religious affiliation. ***Tuition waivers:*** Full or partial for employees or children of employees, senior citizens.

LOANS ***Student loans:*** $4,954,681 (54% need-based, 46% non-need-based). 85% of past graduating class borrowed through all loan programs. Average indebtedness per student: $15,625. ***Average need-based loan:*** Freshmen: $2625; Undergraduates: $4300. ***Parent loans:*** $171,456 (100% non-need-based). ***Programs:*** FFEL (Subsidized and Unsubsidized Stafford, PLUS), Perkins.

WORK-STUDY ***Federal work-study:*** *Total amount:* $75,803; jobs available. ***State or other work-study/employment:*** *Total amount:* $36,750 (100% need-based). Part-time jobs available.

APPLYING for FINANCIAL AID ***Required financial aid forms:*** FAFSA, institution's own form. ***Financial aid deadline (priority):*** 3/15. ***Notification date:*** 4/15. Students must reply within 2 weeks of notification.

CONTACT Director of Financial Aid, Albertus Magnus College, 700 Prospect Street, New Haven, CT 06511-1189, 203-773-8508 or toll-free 800-578-9160. *Fax:* 203-773-8972.

ALBION COLLEGE
Albion, MI

Tuition & fees: $18,160 **Average undergraduate aid package: $16,429**

ABOUT THE INSTITUTION Independent Methodist, coed. Awards: bachelor's degrees. 37 undergraduate majors. Total enrollment: 1,425. Undergraduates: 1,425. Freshmen: 409. Federal methodology is used as a basis for awarding need-based institutional aid.

UNDERGRADUATE EXPENSES for 1999–2000 ***Application fee:*** $20. ***One-time required fee:*** $100. ***Comprehensive fee:*** $23,380 includes full-time tuition ($17,984), mandatory fees ($176), and room and board ($5220). ***College room only:*** $2554. ***Part-time tuition:*** $3072 per unit. ***Payment plan:*** deferred payment.

FRESHMAN FINANCIAL AID (Fall 1999) 329 applied for aid; of those 80% were deemed to have need. 100% of freshmen with need received aid; of those 70% had need fully met. *Average percent of need met:* 97% (excluding resources awarded to replace EFC). *Average financial aid package:* $16,462 (excluding resources awarded to replace EFC). 30% of all full-time freshmen had no need and received non-need-based aid.

UNDERGRADUATE FINANCIAL AID (Fall 1999) 1,086 applied for aid; of those 87% were deemed to have need. 100% of undergraduates with need received aid; of those 77% had need fully met. *Average percent of need met:* 97% (excluding resources awarded to replace EFC). *Average financial aid package:* $16,429 (excluding resources awarded to replace EFC). 31% of all full-time undergraduates had no need and received non-need-based aid.

GIFT AID (NEED-BASED) ***Total amount:*** $11,646,591 (6% Federal, 15% state, 76% institutional, 3% external sources). ***Receiving aid:*** *Freshmen:* 64% (262); *all full-time undergraduates:* 63% (942). ***Average award:*** Freshmen: $13,221; Undergraduates: $12,638. ***Scholarships, grants, and awards:*** Federal Pell, FSEOG, state, private, college/university gift aid from institutional funds.

GIFT AID (NON-NEED-BASED) ***Total amount:*** $3,534,837 (94% institutional, 6% external sources). ***Receiving aid:*** *Freshmen:* 52% (214); *Undergraduates:* 48% (724). ***Scholarships, grants, and awards by category:*** *Academic Interests/Achievement:* business, general academic interests/achievements, mathematics. *Creative Arts/Performance:* art/fine arts, music, theater/drama. *Special Characteristics:* ethnic background, relatives of clergy. ***Tuition waivers:*** Full or partial for employees or children of employees.

LOANS ***Student loans:*** $4,736,914 (61% need-based, 39% non-need-based). 62% of past graduating class borrowed through all loan programs. Average indebtedness per student: $18,085. ***Average need-based loan:*** Freshmen: $2851; Undergraduates: $3676. ***Parent loans:*** $790,992 (100% non-need-based). ***Programs:*** FFEL (Subsidized and Unsubsidized Stafford, PLUS), Perkins, state.

WORK-STUDY ***Federal work-study:*** *Total amount:* $683,589; 522 jobs averaging $1309. ***State or other work-study/employment:*** *Total amount:* $9240 (97% need-based, 3% non-need-based). 8 part-time jobs averaging $1155.

APPLYING for FINANCIAL AID ***Required financial aid form:*** FAFSA. ***Financial aid deadline (priority):*** 2/15. ***Notification date:*** Continuous beginning 3/15.

CONTACT Kristi Schmidt, Director of Financial Aid, Albion College, Kellogg Center Box 4670, Albion, MI 49224-1831, 517-629-0440 or toll-free 800-858-6770. *Fax:* 517-629-0581. *E-mail:* kschmidt@albion.edu

ALBRIGHT COLLEGE

Reading, PA

Tuition & fees: $19,460 — **Average undergraduate aid package: $16,605**

ABOUT THE INSTITUTION Independent religious, coed. Awards: bachelor's degrees. 39 undergraduate majors. Total enrollment: 1,581. Undergraduates: 1,581. Freshmen: 393. Federal methodology is used as a basis for awarding need-based institutional aid.

UNDERGRADUATE EXPENSES for 1999–2000 ***Application fee:*** $25. ***Comprehensive fee:*** $25,240 includes full-time tuition ($18,910), mandatory fees ($550), and room and board ($5780). ***College room only:*** $3235. Room and board charges vary according to board plan and housing facility. ***Part-time tuition:*** $2185 per course. ***Part-time fees:*** $275 per term part-time. Part-time tuition and fees vary according to class time and program. ***Payment plan:*** installment.

FRESHMAN FINANCIAL AID (Fall 1999) 353 applied for aid; of those 93% were deemed to have need. 100% of freshmen with need received aid; of those 24% had need fully met. *Average percent of need met:* 88% (excluding resources awarded to replace EFC). *Average financial aid package:* $17,488 (excluding resources awarded to replace EFC). 16% of all full-time freshmen had no need and received non-need-based aid.

UNDERGRADUATE FINANCIAL AID (Fall 1999) 1,153 applied for aid; of those 90% were deemed to have need. 100% of undergraduates with need received aid; of those 30% had need fully met. *Average percent of need met:* 88% (excluding resources awarded to replace EFC). *Average financial aid package:* $16,605 (excluding resources awarded to replace EFC). 28% of all full-time undergraduates had no need and received non-need-based aid.

GIFT AID (NEED-BASED) ***Total amount:*** $11,530,493 (9% Federal, 13% state, 73% institutional, 5% external sources). ***Receiving aid:*** *Freshmen:* 84% (329); *all full-time undergraduates:* 69% (996). ***Average award:*** Freshmen: $12,283; Undergraduates: $11,112. ***Scholarships, grants, and awards:*** Federal Pell, FSEOG, state, private, college/university gift aid from institutional funds.

GIFT AID (NON-NEED-BASED) ***Total amount:*** $2,128,398 (1% state, 86% institutional, 13% external sources). ***Receiving aid:*** *Freshmen:* 8% (33); *Undergraduates:* 7% (97). ***Scholarships, grants, and awards by category:*** *Academic Interests/Achievement:* general academic interests/achievements. *Creative Arts/Performance:* art/fine arts, music, theater/drama. *Special Achievements/Activities:* junior miss, memberships. *Special Characteristics:* children and siblings of alumni, children of faculty/staff, international students, local/state students, members of minority groups, religious affiliation, siblings of current students. ***Tuition waivers:*** Full or partial for employees or children of employees, senior citizens.

LOANS ***Student loans:*** $7,135,185 (73% need-based, 27% non-need-based). ***Average need-based loan:*** Freshmen: $4342; Undergraduates: $4918. ***Parent loans:*** $951,927 (34% need-based, 66% non-need-based). ***Programs:*** FFEL (Subsidized and Unsubsidized Stafford, PLUS), Perkins, alternative loans.

WORK-STUDY ***Federal work-study:*** *Total amount:* $565,077; jobs available. ***State or other work-study/employment:*** *Total amount:* $223,550 (13% need-based, 87% non-need-based). Part-time jobs available.

APPLYING for FINANCIAL AID ***Required financial aid form:*** FAFSA. ***Financial aid deadline (priority):*** 3/1. ***Notification date:*** Continuous beginning 3/15. Students must reply by 5/1 or within 2 weeks of notification.

CONTACT Mary Ellen Duffy, Director of Financial Aid, Albright College, PO Box 15234, Reading, PA 19612-5234, 610-921-7515 or toll-free 800-252-1856. *Fax:* 610-921-7729. *E-mail:* finaid@alb.edu

AL COLLINS GRAPHIC DESIGN SCHOOL

Tempe, AZ

Tuition & fees: N/R — **Average undergraduate aid package: $7000**

ABOUT THE INSTITUTION Proprietary, coed. Awards: associate and bachelor's degrees. 4 undergraduate majors. Total enrollment: 1,577. Undergraduates: 1,577. Federal methodology is used as a basis for awarding need-based institutional aid.

UNDERGRADUATE EXPENSES for 1999–2000 ***One-time required fee:*** $100. ***Tuition:*** part-time $18,800 per degree program. Full-time tuition and fees vary according to program. ***Payment plans:*** tuition prepayment, installment, deferred payment.

FRESHMAN FINANCIAL AID (Fall 1999, est.) 1000 applied for aid; of those 99% were deemed to have need. 97% of freshmen with need received aid; of those 1% had need fully met. *Average percent of need met:* 60% (excluding resources awarded to replace EFC). *Average financial aid package:* $7000 (excluding resources awarded to replace EFC). 1% of all full-time freshmen had no need and received non-need-based aid.

UNDERGRADUATE FINANCIAL AID (Fall 1999, est.) 1,600 applied for aid; of those 97% were deemed to have need. 97% of undergraduates with need received aid; of those 3% had need fully met. *Average percent of need met:* 60% (excluding resources awarded to replace EFC). *Average financial aid package:* $7000 (excluding resources awarded to replace EFC). 1% of all full-time undergraduates had no need and received non-need-based aid.

GIFT AID (NEED-BASED) ***Total amount:*** $2,000,000 (100% Federal). ***Receiving aid:*** *Freshmen:* 29% (400); *all full-time undergraduates:* 28%

Al Collins Graphic Design School (continued)

(620). ***Average award:*** Freshmen: $1600; Undergraduates: $1600. ***Scholarships, grants, and awards:*** Federal Pell, FSEOG, private.

GIFT AID (NON-NEED-BASED) ***Total amount:*** $130,000 (38% institutional, 62% external sources). ***Receiving aid:*** *Freshmen:* 1% (20); *Undergraduates:* 1% (30). ***Scholarships, grants, and awards by category:*** *Creative Arts/Performance:* 18 awards ($50,000 total): applied art and design. ***Tuition waivers:*** Full or partial for employees or children of employees.

LOANS ***Student loans:*** $7,200,000 (49% need-based, 51% non-need-based). 70% of past graduating class borrowed through all loan programs. Average indebtedness per student: $13,825. ***Average need-based loan:*** Freshmen: $2600; Undergraduates: $7200. ***Parent loans:*** $2,800,000 (100% non-need-based). ***Programs:*** FFEL (Subsidized and Unsubsidized Stafford, PLUS), college/university.

WORK-STUDY ***Federal work-study:*** *Total amount:* $70,000; 45 jobs averaging $1555.

APPLYING for FINANCIAL AID ***Required financial aid forms:*** FAFSA, institution's own form. ***Financial aid deadline:*** Continuous. ***Notification date:*** Continuous beginning 3/1. Students must reply within 2 weeks of notification.

CONTACT Tina Newman, Director of Financial Aid, Al Collins Graphic Design School, 1140 South Priest Drive, Tempe, AZ 85281, 480-966-3000 Ext. 134 or toll-free 800-876-7070 (out-of-state). *Fax:* 480-446-1172. *E-mail:* tina@alcollins.com

ALCORN STATE UNIVERSITY

Alcorn State, MS

Tuition & fees (MS res): $2685 **Average undergraduate aid package: $8087**

ABOUT THE INSTITUTION State-supported, coed. Awards: associate, bachelor's, and master's degrees and post-master's certificates. 37 undergraduate majors. Total enrollment: 2,860. Undergraduates: 2,424. Freshmen: 513. Federal methodology is used as a basis for awarding need-based institutional aid.

UNDERGRADUATE EXPENSES for 1999–2000 ***Tuition, state resident:*** full-time $2685; part-time $104 per semester hour. ***Tuition, nonresident:*** full-time $5546; part-time $223 per semester hour. ***College room and board:*** $2627.

FRESHMAN FINANCIAL AID (Fall 1999) *Average percent of need met:* 80% (excluding resources awarded to replace EFC). *Average financial aid package:* $5750 (excluding resources awarded to replace EFC).

UNDERGRADUATE FINANCIAL AID (Fall 1999) *Average percent of need met:* 70% (excluding resources awarded to replace EFC). *Average financial aid package:* $8087 (excluding resources awarded to replace EFC).

GIFT AID (NEED-BASED) ***Total amount:*** $15,158,892 (100% Federal). ***Scholarships, grants, and awards:*** Federal Pell, FSEOG, state, private, college/university gift aid from institutional funds.

GIFT AID (NON-NEED-BASED) ***Total amount:*** $918,484 (79% state, 17% institutional, 4% external sources). ***Scholarships, grants, and awards by category:*** *Academic Interests/Achievement:* 236 awards: general academic interests/achievements. *Creative Arts/Performance:* 141 awards: music. *Special Characteristics:* 427 awards: children of faculty/staff, local/state students, members of minority groups. ***Tuition waivers:*** Full or partial for employees or children of employees. ***ROTC:*** Army.

LOANS ***Student loans:*** $8,812,417 (85% need-based, 15% non-need-based). 67% of past graduating class borrowed through all loan programs. ***Parent loans:*** $103,979 (100% non-need-based). ***Programs:*** Federal Direct (Subsidized and Unsubsidized Stafford, PLUS).

WORK-STUDY ***Federal work-study:*** *Total amount:* $442,628; 387 jobs averaging $1144.

ATHLETIC AWARDS *Total amount:* 1,125,666 (100% non-need-based).

APPLYING for FINANCIAL AID ***Required financial aid forms:*** FAFSA, institution's own form. ***Financial aid deadline (priority):*** 4/1. ***Notification date:*** Continuous.

CONTACT Juanita McKenzie-Russell, Director of Financial Aid, Alcorn State University, 1000 ASU Drive #28, Alcorn State, MS 39096-7500, 601-877-6190 or toll-free 800-222-6790 (in-state). *Fax:* 601-877-6110. *E-mail:* juanita@lorman.alcorn.edu

ALDERSON-BROADDUS COLLEGE

Philippi, WV

ABOUT THE INSTITUTION Independent religious, coed. Awards: associate, bachelor's, and master's degrees. 46 undergraduate majors. Total enrollment: 735. Undergraduates: 679. Freshmen: 240.

GIFT AID (NEED-BASED) ***Scholarships, grants, and awards:*** Federal Pell, FSEOG, state, private, college/university gift aid from institutional funds.

GIFT AID (NON-NEED-BASED) ***Scholarships, grants, and awards by category:*** *Academic Interests/Achievement:* education, general academic interests/achievements, health fields, humanities, physical sciences, social sciences. *Creative Arts/Performance:* art/fine arts, creative writing, debating, music, performing arts, theater/drama. *Special Achievements/Activities:* general special achievements/activities, leadership. *Special Characteristics:* children of faculty/staff, general special characteristics, international students, relatives of clergy, religious affiliation.

LOANS ***Programs:*** Federal Direct (Subsidized and Unsubsidized Stafford, PLUS), Perkins, Federal Nursing.

WORK-STUDY Federal work-study jobs available.

APPLYING for FINANCIAL AID ***Required financial aid form:*** FAFSA.

CONTACT Director of Financial Aid, Alderson-Broaddus College, College Hill, Box 2005, Philippi, WV 26416, 304-457-6354 or toll-free 800-263-1549. *Fax:* 304-457-6239. *E-mail:* bennett_pa@ab.edu

ALFRED UNIVERSITY

Alfred, NY

Tuition & fees: $19,074 **Average undergraduate aid package: $22,350**

ABOUT THE INSTITUTION Independent, coed. Awards: bachelor's, master's, and doctoral degrees. 67 undergraduate majors. Total enrollment: 2,437. Undergraduates: 2,113. Freshmen: 543. Both federal and institutional methodology are used as a basis for awarding need-based institutional aid.

UNDERGRADUATE EXPENSES for 1999–2000 ***Application fee:*** $40. ***One-time required fee:*** $300. ***Comprehensive fee:*** $26,248 includes full-time tuition ($18,498), mandatory fees ($576), and room and board ($7174). ***College room only:*** $3740. Full-time tuition and fees vary according to program and student level. Room and board charges vary according to board plan and housing facility. ***Part-time tuition:*** $494 per credit. ***Part-time fees:*** $29 per term part-time. ***Payment plans:*** tuition prepayment, installment, deferred payment.

FRESHMAN FINANCIAL AID (Fall 1999) 328 applied for aid; of those 95% were deemed to have need. 100% of freshmen with need received aid; of those 93% had need fully met. *Average percent of need met:* 98% (excluding resources awarded to replace EFC). *Average financial aid package:* $22,200 (excluding resources awarded to replace EFC). 7% of all full-time freshmen had no need and received non-need-based aid.

UNDERGRADUATE FINANCIAL AID (Fall 1999) 1,212 applied for aid; of those 95% were deemed to have need. 100% of undergraduates with need received aid; of those 92% had need fully met. *Average percent of need met:* 95% (excluding resources awarded to replace EFC). *Average financial aid package:* $22,350 (excluding resources awarded to replace EFC). 6% of all full-time undergraduates had no need and received non-need-based aid.

GIFT AID (NEED-BASED) ***Total amount:*** $13,295,000 (9% Federal, 11% state, 78% institutional, 2% external sources). ***Receiving aid:*** *Freshmen:* 88% (312); *all full-time undergraduates:* 89% (1,156). ***Average award:*** Freshmen: $17,300; Undergraduates: $16,600. ***Scholarships, grants, and awards:*** Federal Pell, FSEOG, state, private, college/university gift aid from institutional funds.

GIFT AID (NON-NEED-BASED) ***Total amount:*** $5,139,500 (1% state, 95% institutional, 4% external sources). ***Receiving aid:*** *Freshmen:* 42% (147);

Undergraduates: 34% (445). ***Scholarships, grants, and awards by category:*** *Academic Interests/Achievement:* biological sciences, business, communication, computer science, education, engineering/technologies, English, foreign languages, general academic interests/achievements, humanities, international studies, mathematics, military science, physical sciences, premedicine, social sciences. *Creative Arts/Performance:* art/fine arts, general creative arts/performance, performing arts. *Special Achievements/Activities:* leadership. *Special Characteristics:* children of educators, children of faculty/staff, international students. ***Tuition waivers:*** Full or partial for employees or children of employees. ***ROTC:*** Army cooperative.

LOANS ***Student loans:*** $6,574,000 (76% need-based, 24% non-need-based). 92% of past graduating class borrowed through all loan programs. Average indebtedness per student: $17,500. ***Average need-based loan:*** Freshmen: $3725; Undergraduates: $4850. ***Parent loans:*** $1,123,000 (100% non-need-based). ***Programs:*** FFEL (Subsidized and Unsubsidized Stafford, PLUS), Perkins, college/university.

WORK-STUDY ***Federal work-study:*** *Total amount:* $1,038,000; jobs available.

APPLYING for FINANCIAL AID ***Required financial aid forms:*** FAFSA, institution's own form, state aid form, noncustodial (divorced/separated) parent's statement, business/farm supplement. ***Financial aid deadline:*** Continuous. ***Notification date:*** Continuous beginning 2/1. Students must reply by 5/1 or within 2 weeks of notification.

CONTACT Mr. Earl Pierce, Director of Financial Aid, Alfred University, Alumni Hall, One Saxon Drive, Alfred, NY 14802-1205, 607-871-2159 or toll-free 800-541-9229. *Fax:* 607-871-2198. *E-mail:* pierce@alfred.edu

ALICE LLOYD COLLEGE

Pippa Passes, KY

Tuition & fees: $360 **Average undergraduate aid package: N/A**

ABOUT THE INSTITUTION Independent, coed. Awards: bachelor's degrees. 14 undergraduate majors. Total enrollment: 509. Undergraduates: 509. Freshmen: 170. Federal methodology is used as a basis for awarding need-based institutional aid.

UNDERGRADUATE EXPENSES for 1999–2000 includes mandatory fees ($360) and room and board ($2680). ***College room only:*** $1200. Full-time tuition and fees vary according to reciprocity agreements. ***Part-time tuition:*** $95 per credit hour. Full-time tuition: $0 for residents of 100 counties in Kentucky, Ohio, Tennessee, Virginia and West Virginia. Tuition for students who are not residents of participating counties: $4000. ***Payment plan:*** installment.

FRESHMAN FINANCIAL AID (Fall 1999, est.) 217 applied for aid; of those 58% were deemed to have need. 100% of freshmen with need received aid; of those 30% had need fully met. *Average percent of need met:* 80% (excluding resources awarded to replace EFC). 42% of all full-time freshmen had no need and received non-need-based aid.

UNDERGRADUATE FINANCIAL AID (Fall 1999, est.) 485 applied for aid; of those 56% were deemed to have need. 100% of undergraduates with need received aid; of those 30% had need fully met. *Average percent of need met:* 80% (excluding resources awarded to replace EFC). 44% of all full-time undergraduates had no need and received non-need-based aid.

GIFT AID (NEED-BASED) ***Total amount:*** $1,882,000 (33% Federal, 34% state, 33% institutional). ***Receiving aid:*** *Freshmen:* 58% (125); *all full-time undergraduates:* 56% (271). ***Average award:*** Freshmen: $7060; Undergraduates: $7079. ***Scholarships, grants, and awards:*** Federal Pell, FSEOG, state, private, college/university gift aid from institutional funds.

GIFT AID (NON-NEED-BASED) ***Total amount:*** $1,083,500 (99% institutional, 1% external sources). ***Scholarships, grants, and awards by category:*** *Special Achievements/Activities:* 39 awards ($258,000 total): general special achievements/activities. *Special Characteristics:* 7 awards ($42,476 total): members of minority groups. ***Tuition waivers:*** Full or partial for employees or children of employees.

LOANS ***Student loans:*** $162,000 (52% need-based, 48% non-need-based). 30% of past graduating class borrowed through all loan programs. Average indebtedness per student: $3371. ***Average need-based loan:*** Freshmen: $138; Undergraduates: $488. ***Programs:*** FFEL (Subsidized and Unsubsidized Stafford, PLUS), Perkins, college/university, Bagby Loans (for freshmen).

WORK-STUDY ***Federal work-study:*** *Total amount:* $547,700; 305 jobs averaging $1648. ***State or other work-study/employment:*** *Total amount:* $330,000 (100% non-need-based). 185 part-time jobs averaging $1648.

ATHLETIC AWARDS *Total amount:* 258,000 (100% non-need-based).

APPLYING for FINANCIAL AID ***Required financial aid form:*** FAFSA. ***Financial aid deadline (priority):*** 3/15. ***Notification date:*** Continuous beginning 4/15. Students must reply within 2 weeks of notification.

CONTACT Ms. Nancy M. Melton, Director of Financial Aid, Alice Lloyd College, 100 Purpose Road, Pippa Passes, KY 41844, 606-368-6059. *E-mail:* nancymelton@hotmail.com

ALLEGHENY COLLEGE

Meadville, PA

Tuition & fees: $20,690 **Average undergraduate aid package: $17,415**

ABOUT THE INSTITUTION Independent religious, coed. Awards: bachelor's degrees. 28 undergraduate majors. Total enrollment: 1,886. Undergraduates: 1,886. Freshmen: 565. Federal methodology is used as a basis for awarding need-based institutional aid.

UNDERGRADUATE EXPENSES for 1999–2000 ***Application fee:*** $30. ***One-time required fee:*** $200. ***Comprehensive fee:*** $25,660 includes full-time tuition ($20,410), mandatory fees ($280), and room and board ($4970). ***College room only:*** $2500. Room and board charges vary according to board plan and housing facility. ***Part-time tuition:*** $850 per credit hour. ***Part-time fees:*** $140 per term part-time. Part-time tuition and fees vary according to course load. ***Payment plans:*** tuition prepayment, installment.

FRESHMAN FINANCIAL AID (Fall 1999, est.) 490 applied for aid; of those 89% were deemed to have need. 100% of freshmen with need received aid; of those 54% had need fully met. *Average percent of need met:* 96% (excluding resources awarded to replace EFC). *Average financial aid package:* $18,070 (excluding resources awarded to replace EFC). 18% of all full-time freshmen had no need and received non-need-based aid.

UNDERGRADUATE FINANCIAL AID (Fall 1999, est.) 1,557 applied for aid; of those 91% were deemed to have need. 100% of undergraduates with need received aid; of those 52% had need fully met. *Average percent of need met:* 96% (excluding resources awarded to replace EFC). *Average financial aid package:* $17,415 (excluding resources awarded to replace EFC). 19% of all full-time undergraduates had no need and received non-need-based aid.

GIFT AID (NEED-BASED) ***Total amount:*** $16,528,182 (7% Federal, 11% state, 78% institutional, 4% external sources). ***Receiving aid:*** *Freshmen:* 77% (435); *all full-time undergraduates:* 77% (1,415). ***Average award:*** Freshmen: $12,841; Undergraduates: $11,802. ***Scholarships, grants, and awards:*** Federal Pell, FSEOG, state, private, college/university gift aid from institutional funds.

GIFT AID (NON-NEED-BASED) ***Total amount:*** $2,918,802 (94% institutional, 6% external sources). ***Receiving aid:*** *Freshmen:* 12% (69); *Undergraduates:* 9% (171). ***Scholarships, grants, and awards by category:*** *Academic Interests/Achievement:* 386 awards ($2,482,416 total): general academic interests/achievements. ***Tuition waivers:*** Full or partial for employees or children of employees. ***ROTC:*** Army cooperative.

LOANS ***Student loans:*** $7,197,618 (76% need-based, 24% non-need-based). 84% of past graduating class borrowed through all loan programs. Average indebtedness per student: $17,375. ***Average need-based loan:*** Freshmen: $4019; Undergraduates: $4301. ***Parent loans:*** $1,932,635 (100% non-need-based). ***Programs:*** FFEL (Subsidized and Unsubsidized Stafford, PLUS), Perkins, state.

WORK-STUDY ***Federal work-study:*** *Total amount:* $1,604,926; 1,191 jobs averaging $1348. ***State or other work-study/employment:*** *Total amount:* $362,005 (100% non-need-based). 246 part-time jobs averaging $1472.

APPLYING for FINANCIAL AID ***Required financial aid forms:*** FAFSA, federal income tax form (for verification). ***Financial aid deadline:*** 2/15. ***Notification date:*** 4/1. Students must reply by 5/1 or within 4 weeks of notification.

Allegheny College (continued)

CONTACT Ms. Robin Szitas, Director of Financial Aid, Allegheny College, 520 North Main Street, Meadville, PA 16335, 814-332-2701 or toll-free 800-521-5293. *Fax:* 814-337-0431. *E-mail:* fao@admin.alleg.edu

ALLEGHENY UNIVERSITY OF THE HEALTH SCIENCES

Philadelphia, PA

See MCP Hahnemann University

ALLEN COLLEGE

Waterloo, IA

Tuition & fees: $8220 **Average undergraduate aid package: N/A**

ABOUT THE INSTITUTION Independent, coed, primarily women. Awards: associate, bachelor's, and master's degrees (only offers nursing courses. General degree requirements must be taken at another institution). 2 undergraduate majors. Total enrollment: 237. Undergraduates: 219. Freshmen: 23. Federal methodology is used as a basis for awarding need-based institutional aid.

UNDERGRADUATE EXPENSES for 1999–2000 ***Application fee:*** $20. ***Tuition:*** full-time $8160; part-time $254 per credit hour. ***Required fees:*** full-time $60; $60 per year part-time. Full-time tuition and fees vary according to course load, location, program, and student level. Part-time tuition and fees vary according to program. ***Payment plan:*** installment.

FRESHMAN FINANCIAL AID (Fall 1999) 43 applied for aid; of those 86% were deemed to have need. 97% of freshmen with need received aid; of those 14% had need fully met. *Average percent of need met:* 59% (excluding resources awarded to replace EFC). 4% of all full-time freshmen had no need and received non-need-based aid.

UNDERGRADUATE FINANCIAL AID (Fall 1999) 101 applied for aid; of those 92% were deemed to have need. 92% of undergraduates with need received aid; of those 31% had need fully met. *Average percent of need met:* 74% (excluding resources awarded to replace EFC). 5% of all full-time undergraduates had no need and received non-need-based aid.

GIFT AID (NEED-BASED) ***Total amount:*** $583,059 (21% Federal, 64% state, 11% institutional, 4% external sources). ***Receiving aid:*** *Freshmen:* 71% (34); *all full-time undergraduates:* 76% (84). ***Average award:*** Freshmen: $2874; Undergraduates: $5062. ***Scholarships, grants, and awards:*** Federal Pell, FSEOG, state, private, college/university gift aid from institutional funds, Federal Nursing.

GIFT AID (NON-NEED-BASED) ***Total amount:*** $4300 (74% institutional, 26% external sources). ***Receiving aid:*** *Undergraduates:* 1% (1). ***Scholarships, grants, and awards by category:*** *Academic Interests/Achievement:* health fields. *Special Achievements/Activities:* community service, general special achievements/activities, leadership. *Special Characteristics:* local/state students. ***ROTC:*** Army cooperative.

LOANS ***Student loans:*** $782,757 (61% need-based, 39% non-need-based). 89% of past graduating class borrowed through all loan programs. Average indebtedness per student: $11,199. ***Average need-based loan:*** Freshmen: $2872; Undergraduates: $3880. ***Parent loans:*** $140,000 (18% need-based, 82% non-need-based). ***Programs:*** Federal Direct (Subsidized and Unsubsidized Stafford, PLUS), Perkins, Federal Nursing, college/university.

WORK-STUDY ***Federal work-study:*** *Total amount:* $9850; 6 jobs averaging $2000. ***State or other work-study/employment:*** *Total amount:* $2000 (100% need-based). 1 part-time job averaging $2000.

APPLYING for FINANCIAL AID ***Required financial aid forms:*** FAFSA, institution's own form. ***Financial aid deadline:*** Continuous. ***Notification date:*** Continuous beginning 4/1.

CONTACT Kathie S. Walters, Financial Aid Director, Allen College, 1825 Logan Avenue, Waterloo, IA 50703, 319-235-3983. *Fax:* 319-235-5280.

ALLENTOWN COLLEGE OF ST. FRANCIS DE SALES

Center Valley, PA

Tuition & fees: $13,640 **Average undergraduate aid package: N/A**

ABOUT THE INSTITUTION Independent Roman Catholic, coed. Awards: bachelor's and master's degrees (also offers adult program with significant enrollment not reflected in profile). 32 undergraduate majors. Total enrollment: 2,405. Undergraduates: 1,743. Freshmen: 366. Federal methodology is used as a basis for awarding need-based institutional aid.

UNDERGRADUATE EXPENSES for 1999–2000 ***Application fee:*** $30. ***Comprehensive fee:*** $19,500 includes full-time tuition ($13,350), mandatory fees ($290), and room and board ($5860). ***College room only:*** $3080. Full-time tuition and fees vary according to class time and course load. ***Part-time tuition:*** $555 per credit. Part-time tuition and fees vary according to class time and course load. ***Payment plans:*** installment, deferred payment.

FRESHMAN FINANCIAL AID (Fall 1999, est.) 320 applied for aid; of those 91% were deemed to have need. 100% of freshmen with need received aid; of those 53% had need fully met. *Average percent of need met:* 73% (excluding resources awarded to replace EFC). *Average financial aid package:* $12,900 (excluding resources awarded to replace EFC). 12% of all full-time freshmen had no need and received non-need-based aid.

GIFT AID (NEED-BASED) ***Total amount:*** $6,338,414 (12% Federal, 22% state, 66% institutional). ***Receiving aid:*** *Freshmen:* 81% (284). ***Average award:*** Freshmen: $5175. ***Scholarships, grants, and awards:*** Federal Pell, FSEOG, state, private, college/university gift aid from institutional funds.

GIFT AID (NON-NEED-BASED) ***Total amount:*** $1,765,448 (94% institutional, 6% external sources). ***Receiving aid:*** *Freshmen:* 47% (165). ***Scholarships, grants, and awards by category:*** *Academic Interests/Achievement:* biological sciences, business, communication, computer science, education, English, foreign languages, general academic interests/achievements, health fields, humanities, mathematics, military science, physical sciences, premedicine, religion/biblical studies, social sciences. *Creative Arts/Performance:* cinema/film/broadcasting, creative writing, dance, debating, general creative arts/performance, music, performing arts, theater/drama. *Special Achievements/Activities:* community service, general special achievements/activities, leadership, memberships, religious involvement. *Special Characteristics:* adult students, children of educators, children of faculty/staff, ethnic background, general special characteristics, international students, local/state students, members of minority groups, previous college experience, relatives of clergy, religious affiliation, siblings of current students, twins. ***Tuition waivers:*** Full or partial for employees or children of employees. ***ROTC:*** Army cooperative, Air Force cooperative.

LOANS ***Student loans:*** $5,388,328 (59% need-based, 41% non-need-based). ***Average need-based loan:*** Freshmen: $2625. ***Parent loans:*** $1,138,992 (100% non-need-based). ***Programs:*** FFEL (Subsidized and Unsubsidized Stafford, PLUS), Perkins, Federal Nursing, state, alternative loans.

WORK-STUDY ***Federal work-study:*** *Total amount:* $448,239; jobs available. ***State or other work-study/employment:*** *Total amount:* $154,755 (100% non-need-based). Part-time jobs available.

APPLYING for FINANCIAL AID ***Required financial aid forms:*** FAFSA, institution's own form, state aid form. ***Financial aid deadline (priority):*** 2/1. ***Notification date:*** Continuous beginning 2/15. Students must reply within 3 weeks of notification.

CONTACT Ms. Regina Sharpe, Director of Financial Aid, Allentown College of St. Francis de Sales, 2755 Station Avenue, Center Valley, PA 18034-9568, 610-282-1100 Ext. 1208 or toll-free 800-228-5114. *Fax:* 610-282-0131. *E-mail:* rs02@email.allencol.edu

ALLEN UNIVERSITY

Columbia, SC

Tuition & fees: $4750 **Average undergraduate aid package: N/A**

ABOUT THE INSTITUTION Independent African Methodist Episcopal, coed. Awards: bachelor's degrees. 15 undergraduate majors. Total enrollment: 320. Undergraduates: 320. Freshmen: 143. Federal methodology is used as a basis for awarding need-based institutional aid.

UNDERGRADUATE EXPENSES for 1999–2000 ***Application fee:*** $15. ***Comprehensive fee:*** $9060 includes full-time tuition ($4650), mandatory fees ($100), and room and board ($4310). ***Part-time tuition:*** $132 per credit hour.

GIFT AID (NEED-BASED) ***Total amount:*** $1,282,263 (78% Federal, 11% state, 9% institutional, 2% external sources). ***Scholarships, grants, and awards:*** Federal Pell, FSEOG, state, private, college/university gift aid from institutional funds.

GIFT AID (NON-NEED-BASED) ***Total amount:*** $478,800 (3% state, 94% institutional, 3% external sources). ***Scholarships, grants, and awards by category:*** *Academic Interests/Achievement:* 100 awards ($114,000 total): general academic interests/achievements. *Creative Arts/Performance:* 15 awards ($15,000 total): music. *Special Achievements/Activities:* 5 awards ($50,000 total): leadership. *Special Characteristics:* $200,000 total: religious affiliation. ***ROTC:*** Army cooperative.

LOANS ***Student loans:*** $324,000 (86% need-based, 14% non-need-based). ***Parent loans:*** $329,000 (100% non-need-based). ***Programs:*** FFEL (Subsidized and Unsubsidized Stafford, PLUS), Perkins.

WORK-STUDY ***Federal work-study:*** *Total amount:* $185,000; jobs available.

ATHLETIC AWARDS *Total amount:* 35,000 (100% need-based).

APPLYING for FINANCIAL AID ***Required financial aid form:*** FAFSA. ***Financial aid deadline (priority):*** 4/15. ***Notification date:*** Continuous beginning 5/1. Students must reply within 2 weeks of notification.

CONTACT Virginia M. Case, Director of Financial Aid, Allen University, 1530 Harden Street, Columbia, SC 29204-1085, 803-254-4165 Ext. 5736. *Fax:* 803-376-5733. *E-mail:* virginia.case@gte.net

ALMA COLLEGE

Alma, MI

Tuition & fees: $15,142 **Average undergraduate aid package: $13,635**

ABOUT THE INSTITUTION Independent Presbyterian, coed. Awards: bachelor's degrees. 57 undergraduate majors. Total enrollment: 1,383. Undergraduates: 1,383. Freshmen: 335. Federal methodology is used as a basis for awarding need-based institutional aid.

UNDERGRADUATE EXPENSES for 1999–2000 ***Application fee:*** $20. ***Comprehensive fee:*** $20,602 includes full-time tuition ($14,998), mandatory fees ($144), and room and board ($5460). ***College room only:*** $2704. Room and board charges vary according to board plan and housing facility. ***Part-time tuition:*** $576 per credit. Part-time tuition and fees vary according to course load. ***Payment plans:*** installment, deferred payment.

FRESHMAN FINANCIAL AID (Fall 1999, est.) 307 applied for aid; of those 85% were deemed to have need. 100% of freshmen with need received aid; of those 34% had need fully met. *Average percent of need met:* 90% (excluding resources awarded to replace EFC). *Average financial aid package:* $14,122 (excluding resources awarded to replace EFC). 24% of all full-time freshmen had no need and received non-need-based aid.

UNDERGRADUATE FINANCIAL AID (Fall 1999, est.) 1,149 applied for aid; of those 89% were deemed to have need. 100% of undergraduates with need received aid; of those 41% had need fully met. *Average percent of need met:* 90% (excluding resources awarded to replace EFC). *Average financial aid package:* $13,635 (excluding resources awarded to replace EFC). 24% of all full-time undergraduates had no need and received non-need-based aid.

GIFT AID (NEED-BASED) ***Total amount:*** $9,934,618 (7% Federal, 22% state, 68% institutional, 3% external sources). ***Receiving aid:*** *Freshmen:* 76% (261); *all full-time undergraduates:* 76% (1,016). ***Average award:*** Freshmen: $11,174; Undergraduates: $9977. ***Scholarships, grants, and awards:*** Federal Pell, FSEOG, state, private, college/university gift aid from institutional funds.

GIFT AID (NON-NEED-BASED) ***Total amount:*** $1,993,232 (1% state, 90% institutional, 9% external sources). ***Receiving aid:*** *Freshmen:* 11% (38); *Undergraduates:* 9% (122). ***Scholarships, grants, and awards by category:*** *Academic Interests/Achievement:* 924 awards ($5,007,463 total): general academic interests/achievements, humanities, premedicine. *Creative Arts/Performance:* 257 awards ($141,000 total): art/fine arts, dance, music, performing arts, theater/drama. *Special Characteristics:* 66 awards ($239,077 total): children of faculty/staff, previous college experience. ***Tuition waivers:*** Full or partial for employees or children of employees. ***ROTC:*** Army cooperative.

LOANS ***Student loans:*** $5,521,775 (67% need-based, 33% non-need-based). 87% of past graduating class borrowed through all loan programs. ***Average need-based loan:*** Freshmen: $2881; Undergraduates: $3587. ***Parent loans:*** $555,597 (25% need-based, 75% non-need-based). ***Programs:*** Federal Direct (Subsidized and Unsubsidized Stafford, PLUS), Perkins, state, college/university, alternative loans.

WORK-STUDY ***Federal work-study:*** *Total amount:* $155,000; 140 jobs averaging $1107. ***State or other work-study/employment:*** *Total amount:* $30,000 (100% need-based). 30 part-time jobs averaging $1000.

APPLYING for FINANCIAL AID ***Required financial aid form:*** FAFSA. ***Financial aid deadline (priority):*** 2/15. ***Notification date:*** Continuous beginning 3/1. Students must reply within 3 weeks of notification.

CONTACT Mr. Christopher A. Brown, Director of Financial Aid, Alma College, 614 West Superior, Alma, MI 48801-1599, 517-463-7347 or toll-free 800-321-ALMA. *Fax:* 517-463-7993. *E-mail:* cabrown@alma.edu

ALVERNIA COLLEGE

Reading, PA

Tuition & fees: $12,346 **Average undergraduate aid package: N/A**

ABOUT THE INSTITUTION Independent Roman Catholic, coed. Awards: associate, bachelor's, and master's degrees. 39 undergraduate majors. Total enrollment: 1,485. Undergraduates: 1,422. Freshmen: 244. Both federal and institutional methodology are used as a basis for awarding need-based institutional aid.

UNDERGRADUATE EXPENSES for 1999–2000 ***Application fee:*** $25. ***Comprehensive fee:*** $17,826 includes full-time tuition ($11,730), mandatory fees ($616), and room and board ($5480). Room and board charges vary according to board plan and housing facility. ***Part-time tuition:*** $400 per credit. ***Part-time fees:*** $28 per credit. Part-time tuition and fees vary according to class time and course load. ***Payment plans:*** installment, deferred payment.

FRESHMAN FINANCIAL AID (Fall 1999, est.) 169 applied for aid; of those 80% were deemed to have need. 100% of freshmen with need received aid; of those 10% had need fully met. *Average percent of need met:* 87% (excluding resources awarded to replace EFC). *Average financial aid package:* $9374 (excluding resources awarded to replace EFC). 10% of all full-time freshmen had no need and received non-need-based aid.

GIFT AID (NEED-BASED) ***Total amount:*** $4,767,190 (16% Federal, 27% state, 55% institutional, 2% external sources). ***Receiving aid:*** *Freshmen:* 50% (118). ***Average award:*** Freshmen: $4270. ***Scholarships, grants, and awards:*** Federal Pell, FSEOG, state, private, college/university gift aid from institutional funds.

GIFT AID (NON-NEED-BASED) ***Total amount:*** $534,000 (6% Federal, 17% state, 77% institutional). ***Receiving aid:*** *Freshmen:* 25% (59). ***Scholarships, grants, and awards by category:*** *Academic Interests/Achievement:* 20 awards ($90,000 total): general academic interests/achievements. *Special Achievements/Activities:* 20 awards ($50,000 total): community service, junior miss, religious involvement. *Special Characteristics:* 30 awards ($75,000 total): children and siblings of alumni, children of faculty/staff, international students, out-of-state students, previous college experience, religious affiliation, siblings of current students. ***Tuition waivers:*** Full or partial for employees or children of employees, senior citizens. ***ROTC:*** Army cooperative.

LOANS ***Student loans:*** $4,600,000 (60% need-based, 40% non-need-based). 85% of past graduating class borrowed through all loan programs. Average indebtedness per student: $12,000. ***Average need-based loan:***

Alvernia College (continued)

Freshmen: $2625. ***Parent loans:*** $350,000 (40% need-based, 60% non-need-based). ***Programs:*** FFEL (Subsidized and Unsubsidized Stafford, PLUS), Perkins, state, Health Professions Loans.

WORK-STUDY ***Federal work-study:*** *Total amount:* $108,693; 88 jobs averaging $1236. ***State or other work-study/employment:*** *Total amount:* $70,000 (100% non-need-based). 56 part-time jobs averaging $1236.

APPLYING for FINANCIAL AID ***Required financial aid form:*** FAFSA. ***Financial aid deadline (priority):*** 4/1. ***Notification date:*** Continuous. Students must reply within 3 weeks of notification.

CONTACT Ms. Vali G. Heist, Director of Financial Aid, Alvernia College, 400 Saint Bernardine Street, Reading, PA 19607-1799, 610-796-8215 or toll-free 888-ALVERNIA (in-state). *Fax:* 610-796-8336. *E-mail:* heistva@alvernia.edu

ALVERNO COLLEGE

Milwaukee, WI

Tuition & fees: $10,900 **Average undergraduate aid package: N/A**

ABOUT THE INSTITUTION Independent Roman Catholic, women only. Awards: associate, bachelor's, and master's degrees (also offers weekend program with significant enrollment not reflected in profile). 28 undergraduate majors. Total enrollment: 1,872. Undergraduates: 1,754. Freshmen: 156. Federal methodology is used as a basis for awarding need-based institutional aid.

UNDERGRADUATE EXPENSES for 1999–2000 ***Application fee:*** $20. ***One-time required fee:*** $15. ***Comprehensive fee:*** $15,150 includes full-time tuition ($10,800), mandatory fees ($100), and room and board ($4250). ***College room only:*** $1470. Full-time tuition and fees vary according to class time and program. Room and board charges vary according to board plan. ***Part-time tuition:*** $450 per credit hour. ***Part-time fees:*** $50 per term part-time. Part-time tuition and fees vary according to class time and program. ***Payment plans:*** installment, deferred payment.

GIFT AID (NEED-BASED) ***Total amount:*** $5,393,668 (31% Federal, 27% state, 41% institutional, 1% external sources). ***Scholarships, grants, and awards:*** Federal Pell, FSEOG, state, private, college/university gift aid from institutional funds.

GIFT AID (NON-NEED-BASED) ***Total amount:*** $51,200 (100% external sources). ***Scholarships, grants, and awards by category:*** *Academic Interests/Achievement:* general academic interests/achievements. *Creative Arts/Performance:* art/fine arts, music. *Special Achievements/Activities:* community service. *Special Characteristics:* children and siblings of alumni, siblings of current students. ***Tuition waivers:*** Full or partial for employees or children of employees. ***ROTC:*** Army cooperative, Air Force cooperative.

LOANS ***Student loans:*** $8,232,983 (55% need-based, 45% non-need-based). 80% of past graduating class borrowed through all loan programs. ***Parent loans:*** $246,390 (100% non-need-based). ***Programs:*** FFEL (Subsidized and Unsubsidized Stafford, PLUS), Perkins.

WORK-STUDY ***Federal work-study:*** *Total amount:* $57,154; 150 jobs averaging $381. ***State or other work-study/employment:*** *Total amount:* $36,898 (100% non-need-based). 95 part-time jobs averaging $388.

APPLYING for FINANCIAL AID ***Required financial aid forms:*** FAFSA, institution's own form, income tax forms, verification form. ***Financial aid deadline (priority):*** 4/15. ***Notification date:*** Continuous. Students must reply within 2 weeks of notification.

CONTACT Mark Levine, Director of Financial Aid, Alverno College, 3400 South 43rd Street, PO Box 343922, Milwaukee, WI 53234-3922, 414-382-6040 or toll-free 800-933-3401. *Fax:* 414-382-6354. *E-mail:* mark.levine@alverno.edu

AMERICAN ACADEMY OF ART

Chicago, IL

ABOUT THE INSTITUTION Proprietary, coed. Awards: associate and bachelor's degrees. 10 undergraduate majors. Total enrollment: 411. Undergraduates: 411. Freshmen: 106.

GIFT AID (NEED-BASED) ***Scholarships, grants, and awards:*** Federal Pell, FSEOG, private, college/university gift aid from institutional funds.

LOANS ***Programs:*** FFEL (Subsidized and Unsubsidized Stafford, PLUS).

WORK-STUDY Federal work-study jobs available.

APPLYING for FINANCIAL AID ***Required financial aid forms:*** FAFSA, institution's own form, state aid form.

CONTACT Ms. Debi Zoumis, Financial Services Director, American Academy of Art, 332 South Michigan Ave, Suite 300, Chicago, IL 60604-4302, 312-461-0600. *Fax:* 312-294-9570. *E-mail:* artfao@aol.com

AMERICAN BAPTIST COLLEGE OF AMERICAN BAPTIST THEOLOGICAL SEMINARY

Nashville, TN

Tuition & fees: $2860 **Average undergraduate aid package: N/A**

ABOUT THE INSTITUTION Independent Baptist, coed. Awards: associate and bachelor's degrees. 2 undergraduate majors. Total enrollment: 96. Undergraduates: 96. Federal methodology is used as a basis for awarding need-based institutional aid.

UNDERGRADUATE EXPENSES for 1999–2000 ***Application fee:*** $20. ***One-time required fee:*** $5. ***Tuition:*** full-time $2780; part-time $140 per credit hour. ***Required fees:*** full-time $80; $30 per term part-time. Room and board charges vary according to gender.

GIFT AID (NEED-BASED) ***Scholarships, grants, and awards:*** Federal Pell, state.

GIFT AID (NON-NEED-BASED) ***Scholarships, grants, and awards by category:*** *Special Characteristics:* religious affiliation.

APPLYING for FINANCIAL AID ***Required financial aid forms:*** FAFSA, institution's own form. ***Financial aid deadline:*** Continuous.

CONTACT Financial Aid Director, American Baptist College of American Baptist Theological Seminary, 1800 Baptist World Center Drive, Nashville, TN 37207, 615-228-7877.

AMERICAN BIBLE COLLEGE AND SEMINARY

Oklahoma City, OK

Tuition & fees: N/R **Average undergraduate aid package: N/A**

ABOUT THE INSTITUTION Independent interdenominational, coed. Awards: associate, bachelor's, and master's degrees. 2 undergraduate majors. Total enrollment: 227. Undergraduates: 167. Freshmen: 116. Federal methodology is used as a basis for awarding need-based institutional aid.

GIFT AID (NEED-BASED) ***Total amount:*** $158,438 (100% Federal). ***Scholarships, grants, and awards:*** Federal Pell, FSEOG.

LOANS ***Student loans:*** $180,123 (100% need-based). ***Programs:*** FFEL (Subsidized and Unsubsidized Stafford, PLUS).

WORK-STUDY ***Federal work-study:*** *Total amount:* $8160; jobs available.

APPLYING for FINANCIAL AID ***Required financial aid forms:*** FAFSA, noncustodial (divorced/separated) parent's statement, business/farm supplement. ***Financial aid deadline (priority):*** 5/15. ***Notification date:*** Continuous. Students must reply within 4 weeks of notification.

CONTACT Julia Williams, Financial Aid Director, American Bible College and Seminary, 4300 Highline Boulevard, Suite 202, Oklahoma City, OK 73108, 405-945-0100 Ext. 20 or toll-free 800-488-2528. *Fax:* 405-945-0311. *E-mail:* juliawil@excite.com

THE AMERICAN COLLEGE

Los Angeles, CA

See American InterContinental University

THE AMERICAN COLLEGE
Atlanta, GA

See American InterContinental University

AMERICAN COLLEGE OF PREHOSPITAL MEDICINE
Navarre, FL

CONTACT Financial Aid Office, American College of Prehospital Medicine, 7552 Navarre Parkway, Suite 1, Navarre, FL 32566-7312, 850-939-0840 or toll-free 800-735-2276.

AMERICAN INDIAN COLLEGE OF THE ASSEMBLIES OF GOD, INC.
Phoenix, AZ

ABOUT THE INSTITUTION Independent religious, coed. Awards: associate and bachelor's degrees. 3 undergraduate majors. Total enrollment: 76. Undergraduates: 76. Freshmen: 11.

GIFT AID (NEED-BASED) ***Scholarships, grants, and awards:*** Federal Pell, FSEOG, private, college/university gift aid from institutional funds.

GIFT AID (NON-NEED-BASED) ***Scholarships, grants, and awards by category:*** *Academic Interests/Achievement:* general academic interests/achievements.

LOANS ***Programs:*** FFEL (Subsidized and Unsubsidized Stafford, PLUS).

WORK-STUDY Federal work-study jobs available.

APPLYING for FINANCIAL AID ***Required financial aid form:*** FAFSA.

CONTACT Office of Student Financial Aid, American Indian College of the Assemblies of God, Inc., 10020 North Fifteenth Avenue, Phoenix, AZ 80521-2199, 800-933-3828. *E-mail:* aicweb@pop.goodnet.com

AMERICAN INTERCONTINENTAL UNIVERSITY
Los Angeles, CA

Tuition & fees: $11,850 **Average undergraduate aid package: N/A**

ABOUT THE INSTITUTION Proprietary, coed. Awards: associate, bachelor's, and master's degrees. 11 undergraduate majors. Total enrollment: 619. Undergraduates: 601. Federal methodology is used as a basis for awarding need-based institutional aid.

UNDERGRADUATE EXPENSES for 1999–2000 ***Application fee:*** $35. ***Tuition:*** full-time $11,850; part-time $1315 per course. Full-time tuition and fees vary according to location. Part-time tuition and fees vary according to location. ***Payment plans:*** installment, deferred payment.

GIFT AID (NEED-BASED) ***Scholarships, grants, and awards:*** Federal Pell, FSEOG, state, private.

GIFT AID (NON-NEED-BASED) ***Scholarships, grants, and awards by category:*** *Creative Arts/Performance:* applied art and design. *Special Achievements/Activities:* general special achievements/activities. ***Tuition waivers:*** Full or partial for employees or children of employees.

LOANS ***Programs:*** Federal Direct (Subsidized and Unsubsidized Stafford, PLUS), FFEL (Subsidized and Unsubsidized Stafford, PLUS), state.

WORK-STUDY Federal work-study jobs available.

APPLYING for FINANCIAL AID ***Required financial aid forms:*** FAFSA, institution's own form. ***Financial aid deadline:*** Continuous. ***Notification date:*** Continuous beginning 4/15.

CONTACT Mr. Joe Johnson, Financial Aid Counselor, American InterContinental University, 12655 West Jefferson Boulevard, Los Angeles, CA 90066, 310-302-2000 Ext. 2447. *Fax:* 310-302-2002.

AMERICAN INTERCONTINENTAL UNIVERSITY
Washington, DC

CONTACT Financial Aid Office, American InterContinental University, Suite 1C, 1776 G Street NW, Washington, DC 20006, 202-478-6212 or toll-free 800-295-9989.

AMERICAN INTERCONTINENTAL UNIVERSITY
Plantation, FL

CONTACT Financial Aid Office, American InterContinental University, 8151 West Peters Road, Suite 1000, Plantation, FL 33324, 954-835-0939.

AMERICAN INTERCONTINENTAL UNIVERSITY
Atlanta, GA

Tuition & fees: $11,430 **Average undergraduate aid package: N/A**

ABOUT THE INSTITUTION Proprietary, coed. Awards: associate and bachelor's degrees. 11 undergraduate majors. Total enrollment: 908. Undergraduates: 908. Freshmen: 122. Federal methodology is used as a basis for awarding need-based institutional aid.

UNDERGRADUATE EXPENSES for 1999–2000 ***Application fee:*** $35. ***Comprehensive fee:*** $15,780 includes full-time tuition ($11,430) and room and board ($4350). Full-time tuition and fees vary according to location. Room and board charges vary according to location. ***Part-time tuition:*** $1270 per course. Part-time tuition and fees vary according to location.

GIFT AID (NEED-BASED) ***Scholarships, grants, and awards:*** Federal Pell, FSEOG, state.

GIFT AID (NON-NEED-BASED) ***Tuition waivers:*** Full or partial for employees or children of employees.

LOANS ***Programs:*** Federal Direct (Subsidized and Unsubsidized Stafford, PLUS), state.

WORK-STUDY Federal work-study jobs available.

APPLYING for FINANCIAL AID ***Required financial aid forms:*** FAFSA, state aid form. ***Financial aid deadline:*** Continuous.

CONTACT Lillian Rice, Financial Aid Manager, American InterContinental University, 3330 Peachtree Road, NE, Atlanta, GA 30326-1016, 404-965-5700 or toll-free 888-999-4248 (out-of-state).

AMERICAN INTERCONTINENTAL UNIVERSITY
Atlanta, GA

CONTACT Financial Aid Office, American InterContinental University, 500 Embassy Row, 6600 Peachtree-Dunwoody Road, Atlanta, GA 30328, 404-965-6500 or toll-free 800-255-6839.

AMERICAN INTERNATIONAL COLLEGE
Springfield, MA

Tuition & fees: $12,900 **Average undergraduate aid package: $12,600**

ABOUT THE INSTITUTION Independent, coed. Awards: associate, bachelor's, master's, and doctoral degrees and post-master's certificates. 44 undergraduate majors. Total enrollment: 1,752. Undergraduates: 1,251. Freshmen: 253. Both federal and institutional methodology are used as a basis for awarding need-based institutional aid.

UNDERGRADUATE EXPENSES for 1999–2000 ***Application fee:*** $20. ***Comprehensive fee:*** $19,548 includes full-time tuition ($12,900) and

American International College (continued)

room and board ($6648). ***Part-time tuition:*** $315 per credit. ***Part-time fees:*** $25 per term part-time. ***Payment plans:*** tuition prepayment, installment, deferred payment.

FRESHMAN FINANCIAL AID (Fall 1999, est.) 230 applied for aid; of those 86% were deemed to have need. 100% of freshmen with need received aid; of those 21% had need fully met. *Average percent of need met:* 85% (excluding resources awarded to replace EFC). *Average financial aid package:* $12,300 (excluding resources awarded to replace EFC).

UNDERGRADUATE FINANCIAL AID (Fall 1999, est.) 663 applied for aid; of those 87% were deemed to have need. 100% of undergraduates with need received aid; of those 21% had need fully met. *Average percent of need met:* 85% (excluding resources awarded to replace EFC). *Average financial aid package:* $12,600 (excluding resources awarded to replace EFC).

GIFT AID (NEED-BASED) ***Total amount:*** $4,907,545 (24% Federal, 12% state, 62% institutional, 2% external sources). ***Receiving aid:*** *Freshmen:* 50% (188); *all full-time undergraduates:* 51% (548). ***Average award:*** Freshmen: $6100; Undergraduates: $6300. ***Scholarships, grants, and awards:*** Federal Pell, FSEOG, state, private, college/university gift aid from institutional funds.

GIFT AID (NON-NEED-BASED) ***Total amount:*** $512,427 (100% institutional). ***Receiving aid:*** *Freshmen:* 19% (71); *Undergraduates:* 19% (208). ***Scholarships, grants, and awards by category:*** *Academic Interests/Achievement:* general academic interests/achievements. *Special Achievements/Activities:* general special achievements/activities. ***Tuition waivers:*** Full or partial for employees or children of employees, senior citizens. ***ROTC:*** Army cooperative, Air Force cooperative.

LOANS ***Student loans:*** $5,901,342 (64% need-based, 36% non-need-based). 88% of past graduating class borrowed through all loan programs. Average indebtedness per student: $17,000. ***Average need-based loan:*** Freshmen: $4000; Undergraduates: $4400. ***Parent loans:*** $705,000 (85% need-based, 15% non-need-based). ***Programs:*** FFEL (Subsidized and Unsubsidized Stafford, PLUS), Perkins, Federal Nursing, state, college/university, alternative loans.

WORK-STUDY ***Federal work-study:*** *Total amount:* $534,550; 331 jobs averaging $1600. ***State or other work-study/employment:*** *Total amount:* $32,530 (100% non-need-based). Part-time jobs available.

ATHLETIC AWARDS *Total amount:* 1,705,000 (53% need-based, 47% non-need-based).

APPLYING for FINANCIAL AID ***Required financial aid forms:*** FAFSA, institution's own form. ***Financial aid deadline (priority):*** 4/1. ***Notification date:*** Continuous. Students must reply within 2 weeks of notification.

CONTACT Dr. Lee Sirois, Director of Financial Aid, American International College, 1000 State Street, Springfield, MA 01109-3189, 413-747-6259 or toll-free 800-242-3142. *Fax:* 413-737-2803.

AMERICAN UNIVERSITY

Washington, DC

Tuition & fees: $21,399 **Average undergraduate aid package: $19,470**

ABOUT THE INSTITUTION Independent Methodist, coed. Awards: associate, bachelor's, master's, doctoral, and first professional degrees. 70 undergraduate majors. Total enrollment: 10,894. Undergraduates: 5,533. Freshmen: 1,203. Both federal and institutional methodology are used as a basis for awarding need-based institutional aid.

UNDERGRADUATE EXPENSES for 2000–2001 ***Application fee:*** $45. ***Comprehensive fee:*** $29,791 includes full-time tuition ($21,144), mandatory fees ($255), and room and board ($8392). ***College room only:*** $5370. Room and board charges vary according to board plan and housing facility. ***Payment plans:*** tuition prepayment, installment, deferred payment.

FRESHMAN FINANCIAL AID (Fall 1999) 752 applied for aid; of those 78% were deemed to have need. 98% of freshmen with need received aid; of those 18% had need fully met. *Average percent of need met:* 77% (excluding resources awarded to replace EFC). *Average financial aid package:* $18,480 (excluding resources awarded to replace EFC). 16% of all full-time freshmen had no need and received non-need-based aid.

UNDERGRADUATE FINANCIAL AID (Fall 1999) 2,743 applied for aid; of those 85% were deemed to have need. 98% of undergraduates with need received aid; of those 27% had need fully met. *Average percent of need met:* 74% (excluding resources awarded to replace EFC). *Average financial aid package:* $19,470 (excluding resources awarded to replace EFC). 13% of all full-time undergraduates had no need and received non-need-based aid.

GIFT AID (NEED-BASED) ***Total amount:*** $25,473,546 (8% Federal, 1% state, 90% institutional, 1% external sources). ***Receiving aid:*** *Freshmen:* 42% (510); *all full-time undergraduates:* 42% (1,995). ***Average award:*** Freshmen: $12,970; Undergraduates: $12,258. ***Scholarships, grants, and awards:*** Federal Pell, FSEOG, state, private, college/university gift aid from institutional funds.

GIFT AID (NON-NEED-BASED) ***Total amount:*** $7,332,749 (100% institutional). ***Receiving aid:*** *Freshmen:* 10% (117); *Undergraduates:* 9% (428). ***Scholarships, grants, and awards by category:*** *Academic Interests/Achievement:* area/ethnic studies, biological sciences, business, communication, computer science, education, English, foreign languages, general academic interests/achievements, health fields, humanities, international studies, mathematics, social sciences. *Creative Arts/Performance:* music, performing arts, theater/drama. *Special Achievements/Activities:* leadership. *Special Characteristics:* children and siblings of alumni, ethnic background, members of minority groups. ***Tuition waivers:*** Full or partial for employees or children of employees, senior citizens. ***ROTC:*** Army cooperative, Air Force cooperative.

LOANS ***Student loans:*** $15,384,047 (64% need-based, 36% non-need-based). ***Average need-based loan:*** Freshmen: $3136; Undergraduates: $4285. ***Parent loans:*** $6,936,882 (100% non-need-based). ***Programs:*** Federal Direct (Subsidized and Unsubsidized Stafford, PLUS), Perkins, college/university.

WORK-STUDY ***Federal work-study:*** *Total amount:* $2,556,168; jobs available.

ATHLETIC AWARDS *Total amount:* 2,539,167 (100% non-need-based).

APPLYING for FINANCIAL AID ***Required financial aid forms:*** FAFSA, institution's own form. ***Financial aid deadline (priority):*** 3/1. ***Notification date:*** 4/1. Students must reply within 3 weeks of notification.

CONTACT Customer Relations Center, American University, 4400 Massachusetts Avenue, NW, Washington, DC 20016-8001, 202-885-6100. *Fax:* 202-885-1025. *E-mail:* afa@american.edu

AMERICAN UNIVERSITY OF PUERTO RICO

Bayamón, PR

Tuition & fees: N/R **Average undergraduate aid package: N/A**

ABOUT THE INSTITUTION Independent, coed. Awards: associate and bachelor's degrees. 9 undergraduate majors. Total enrollment: 4,091. Undergraduates: 4,091. Federal methodology is used as a basis for awarding need-based institutional aid.

UNDERGRADUATE EXPENSES for 1999–2000 ***Application fee:*** $15. ***Payment plan:*** guaranteed tuition.

GIFT AID (NEED-BASED) ***Scholarships, grants, and awards:*** Federal Pell, FSEOG, state, college/university gift aid from institutional funds.

GIFT AID (NON-NEED-BASED) ***ROTC:*** Army cooperative.

LOANS ***Programs:*** Federal Direct (Subsidized and Unsubsidized Stafford, PLUS).

WORK-STUDY Federal work-study jobs available.

APPLYING for FINANCIAL AID ***Required financial aid forms:*** FAFSA, institution's own form. ***Financial aid deadline:*** 5/30 (priority: 4/15). ***Notification date:*** Continuous beginning 6/30. Students must reply within 2 weeks of notification.

CONTACT Ms. Johanna Arroyo, Financial Aid Director, American University of Puerto Rico, PO Box 2037, Bayamón, PR 00960-2037, 787-798-2040 Ext. 201. *Fax:* 787-785-7377.

AMHERST COLLEGE

Amherst, MA

Tuition & fees: $25,259 **Average undergraduate aid package: $22,705**

ABOUT THE INSTITUTION Independent, coed. Awards: bachelor's degrees. 36 undergraduate majors. Total enrollment: 1,664. Undergraduates: 1,664. Freshmen: 422. Institutional methodology is used as a basis for awarding need-based institutional aid.

UNDERGRADUATE EXPENSES for 1999–2000 ***Application fee:*** $55. ***Comprehensive fee:*** $31,819 includes full-time tuition ($24,800), mandatory fees ($459), and room and board ($6560). ***College room only:*** $3280. ***Payment plans:*** installment, deferred payment.

FRESHMAN FINANCIAL AID (Fall 1999) 229 applied for aid; of those 80% were deemed to have need. 100% of freshmen with need received aid; of those 100% had need fully met. *Average percent of need met:* 100% (excluding resources awarded to replace EFC). *Average financial aid package:* $23,605 (excluding resources awarded to replace EFC). 16% of all full-time freshmen had no need and received non-need-based aid.

UNDERGRADUATE FINANCIAL AID (Fall 1999) 821 applied for aid; of those 88% were deemed to have need. 100% of undergraduates with need received aid; of those 100% had need fully met. *Average percent of need met:* 100% (excluding resources awarded to replace EFC). *Average financial aid package:* $22,705 (excluding resources awarded to replace EFC). 11% of all full-time undergraduates had no need and received non-need-based aid.

GIFT AID (NEED-BASED) ***Total amount:*** $13,065,108 (6% Federal, 91% institutional, 3% external sources). ***Receiving aid:*** *Freshmen:* 41% (173); *all full-time undergraduates:* 41% (676). ***Average award:*** Freshmen: $19,480; Undergraduates: $18,273. ***Scholarships, grants, and awards:*** Federal Pell, FSEOG, state, college/university gift aid from institutional funds.

GIFT AID (NON-NEED-BASED) ***Total amount:*** $685,338 (7% Federal, 93% external sources).

LOANS ***Student loans:*** $2,605,082 (87% need-based, 13% non-need-based). 52% of past graduating class borrowed through all loan programs. Average indebtedness per student: $12,340. ***Average need-based loan:*** Freshmen: $2682; Undergraduates: $3095. ***Parent loans:*** $1,149,220 (100% non-need-based). ***Programs:*** Federal Direct (Subsidized and Unsubsidized Stafford, PLUS), Perkins, college/university.

WORK-STUDY ***Federal work-study:*** *Total amount:* $853,655; 592 jobs averaging $1442. ***State or other work-study/employment:*** *Total amount:* $121,381 (100% need-based). 90 part-time jobs averaging $1349.

APPLYING for FINANCIAL AID ***Required financial aid forms:*** FAFSA, CSS Financial Aid PROFILE. ***Financial aid deadline (priority):*** 2/1. ***Notification date:*** 4/1. Students must reply by 5/1.

CONTACT Joe Paul Case, Director of Financial Aid, Amherst College, 202 Converse Hall, PO Box 5000, Amherst, MA 01002-5000, 413-542-2296. *Fax:* 413-542-2628. *E-mail:* finaid@amherst.edu

ANDERSON COLLEGE

Anderson, SC

Tuition & fees: $10,515 **Average undergraduate aid package: $8229**

ABOUT THE INSTITUTION Independent Baptist, coed. Awards: associate and bachelor's degrees. 31 undergraduate majors. Total enrollment: 1,216. Undergraduates: 1,216. Freshmen: 365. Both federal and institutional methodology are used as a basis for awarding need-based institutional aid.

UNDERGRADUATE EXPENSES for 2000–2001 ***Application fee:*** $20. ***Comprehensive fee:*** $15,120 includes full-time tuition ($9720), mandatory fees ($795), and room and board ($4605). Room and board charges vary according to board plan. ***Part-time tuition:*** $252 per credit hour. ***Payment plan:*** installment.

FRESHMAN FINANCIAL AID (Fall 1999) 280 applied for aid; of those 100% were deemed to have need. 100% of freshmen with need received aid; of those 3% had need fully met. *Average percent of need met:* 60% (excluding resources awarded to replace EFC). *Average financial aid package:* $6954 (excluding resources awarded to replace EFC).

UNDERGRADUATE FINANCIAL AID (Fall 1999) 887 applied for aid; of those 100% were deemed to have need. 100% of undergraduates with need received aid; of those 4% had need fully met. *Average percent of need met:* 57% (excluding resources awarded to replace EFC). *Average financial aid package:* $8229 (excluding resources awarded to replace EFC).

GIFT AID (NEED-BASED) ***Total amount:*** $6,929,893 (12% Federal, 21% state, 66% institutional, 1% external sources). ***Receiving aid:*** *Freshmen:* 85% (252); *all full-time undergraduates:* 81% (798). ***Scholarships, grants, and awards:*** Federal Pell, FSEOG, state, college/university gift aid from institutional funds.

GIFT AID (NON-NEED-BASED) ***Receiving aid:*** *Freshmen:* 19% (57); *Undergraduates:* 17% (167). ***Scholarships, grants, and awards by category:*** *Academic Interests/Achievement:* biological sciences, business, communication, computer science, education, English, general academic interests/achievements, physical sciences, religion/biblical studies. *Creative Arts/Performance:* applied art and design, art/fine arts, journalism/publications, music, theater/drama. *Special Achievements/Activities:* cheerleading/drum major, general special achievements/activities, leadership, religious involvement. *Special Characteristics:* adult students, children and siblings of alumni, children of current students, children of faculty/staff, general special characteristics, out-of-state students, parents of current students, relatives of clergy, religious affiliation, siblings of current students, spouses of current students, twins. ***Tuition waivers:*** Full or partial for employees or children of employees, adult students, senior citizens. ***ROTC:*** Army cooperative, Air Force cooperative.

LOANS ***Student loans:*** $2,950,824 (100% need-based). 76% of past graduating class borrowed through all loan programs. Average indebtedness per student: $13,379. ***Parent loans:*** $545,502 (100% need-based). ***Programs:*** FFEL (Subsidized and Unsubsidized Stafford, PLUS), Perkins, college/university.

WORK-STUDY ***Federal work-study:*** *Total amount:* $340,289; jobs available. ***State or other work-study/employment:*** *Total amount:* $274,566 (100% need-based). Part-time jobs available.

ATHLETIC AWARDS *Total amount:* 369,337 (100% non-need-based).

APPLYING for FINANCIAL AID ***Required financial aid forms:*** FAFSA, institution's own form, CSS Financial Aid PROFILE. ***Financial aid deadline:*** 7/31. ***Notification date:*** Continuous. Students must reply within 2 weeks of notification.

CONTACT Jason Moorhead, Consultant, Anderson College, 316 Boulevard, Box 1142, Anderson, SC 29621-4035, 864-231-2070 or toll-free 800-542-3594. *Fax:* 864-231-2008.

ANDERSON UNIVERSITY

Anderson, IN

Tuition & fees: $14,680 **Average undergraduate aid package: $13,530**

ABOUT THE INSTITUTION Independent religious, coed. Awards: associate, bachelor's, master's, doctoral, and first professional degrees. 59 undergraduate majors. Total enrollment: 2,251. Undergraduates: 1,988. Freshmen: 506. Federal methodology is used as a basis for awarding need-based institutional aid.

UNDERGRADUATE EXPENSES for 2000–2001 (est.) ***Application fee:*** $20. ***Comprehensive fee:*** $19,430 includes full-time tuition ($14,680) and room and board ($4750). ***College room only:*** $2750. Room and board charges vary according to board plan. ***Part-time tuition:*** $612 per credit. Part-time tuition and fees vary according to course load. ***Payment plan:*** installment.

FRESHMAN FINANCIAL AID (Fall 1999) 425 applied for aid; of those 84% were deemed to have need. 100% of freshmen with need received aid; of those 44% had need fully met. *Average percent of need met:* 95% (excluding resources awarded to replace EFC). *Average financial aid package:* $13,533 (excluding resources awarded to replace EFC). 24% of all full-time freshmen had no need and received non-need-based aid.

Anderson University (continued)

UNDERGRADUATE FINANCIAL AID (Fall 1999) 1,437 applied for aid; of those 87% were deemed to have need. 100% of undergraduates with need received aid; of those 48% had need fully met. *Average percent of need met:* 95% (excluding resources awarded to replace EFC). *Average financial aid package:* $13,530 (excluding resources awarded to replace EFC). 24% of all full-time undergraduates had no need and received non-need-based aid.

GIFT AID (NEED-BASED) ***Total amount:*** $9,881,772 (14% Federal, 23% state, 55% institutional, 8% external sources). ***Receiving aid:*** *Freshmen:* 75% (358); *all full-time undergraduates:* 73% (1,244). ***Average award:*** Freshmen: $8979; Undergraduates: $8284. ***Scholarships, grants, and awards:*** Federal Pell, FSEOG, state, private, college/university gift aid from institutional funds.

GIFT AID (NON-NEED-BASED) ***Total amount:*** $2,677,219 (1% Federal, 1% state, 82% institutional, 16% external sources). ***Receiving aid:*** *Freshmen:* 10% (47); *Undergraduates:* 8% (138). ***Scholarships, grants, and awards by category:*** *Academic Interests/Achievement:* 1,719 awards ($5,199,000 total): general academic interests/achievements. *Creative Arts/Performance:* 69 awards ($86,235 total): general creative arts/performance, music. *Special Achievements/Activities:* 11 awards ($27,000 total): leadership. *Special Characteristics:* 371 awards ($1,695,000 total): adult students, children of faculty/staff, international students, relatives of clergy. ***Tuition waivers:*** Full or partial for employees or children of employees, adult students.

LOANS ***Student loans:*** $7,300,577 (80% need-based, 20% non-need-based). 77% of past graduating class borrowed through all loan programs. Average indebtedness per student: $17,650. ***Average need-based loan:*** Freshmen: $3654; Undergraduates: $4558. ***Parent loans:*** $1,817,051 (24% need-based, 76% non-need-based). ***Programs:*** FFEL (Subsidized and Unsubsidized Stafford, PLUS), Perkins.

WORK-STUDY ***Federal work-study:*** *Total amount:* $1,619,035; 796 jobs averaging $2034. ***State or other work-study/employment:*** *Total amount:* $49,800 (100% non-need-based). Part-time jobs available.

APPLYING for FINANCIAL AID ***Required financial aid form:*** FAFSA. ***Financial aid deadline (priority):*** 3/1. ***Notification date:*** Continuous.

CONTACT Mr. Kenneth Nieman, Director of Financial Aid, Anderson University, 1100 East Fifth Street, Anderson, IN 46012-3495, 765-641-4180 or toll-free 800-421-3014 (in-state), 800-428-6414 (out-of-state). *Fax:* 765-641-3831. *E-mail:* knieman@anderson.edu

ANDREW JACKSON UNIVERSITY

Birmingham, AL

CONTACT Financial Aid Office, Andrew Jackson University, 10 Old Montgomery Highway, Birmingham, AL 35209, 205-871-9288.

ANDREWS UNIVERSITY

Berrien Springs, MI

Tuition & fees: $12,339 **Average undergraduate aid package: $13,593**

ABOUT THE INSTITUTION Independent Seventh-day Adventist, coed. Awards: associate, bachelor's, master's, doctoral, and first professional degrees. 93 undergraduate majors. Total enrollment: 2,968. Undergraduates: 1,825. Freshmen: 324. Federal methodology is used as a basis for awarding need-based institutional aid.

UNDERGRADUATE EXPENSES for 1999–2000 ***Application fee:*** $30. ***Comprehensive fee:*** $16,104 includes full-time tuition ($12,030), mandatory fees ($309), and room and board ($3765). ***College room only:*** $2235. ***Part-time tuition:*** $305 per quarter hour. ***Payment plan:*** installment.

FRESHMAN FINANCIAL AID (Fall 1998) 263 applied for aid; of those 72% were deemed to have need. 100% of freshmen with need received aid; of those 14% had need fully met. *Average percent of need met:* 82% (excluding resources awarded to replace EFC). *Average financial aid package:* $11,594 (excluding resources awarded to replace EFC). 26% of all full-time freshmen had no need and received non-need-based aid.

UNDERGRADUATE FINANCIAL AID (Fall 1998) 1,325 applied for aid; of those 71% were deemed to have need. 100% of undergraduates with need received aid; of those 22% had need fully met. *Average percent of need met:* 83% (excluding resources awarded to replace EFC). *Average financial aid package:* $13,593 (excluding resources awarded to replace EFC). 24% of all full-time undergraduates had no need and received non-need-based aid.

GIFT AID (NEED-BASED) ***Total amount:*** $4,518,796 (38% Federal, 13% state, 49% institutional). ***Receiving aid:*** *Freshmen:* 51% (138); *all full-time undergraduates:* 50% (716). ***Average award:*** Freshmen: $4844; Undergraduates: $5051. ***Scholarships, grants, and awards:*** Federal Pell, FSEOG, state, private, college/university gift aid from institutional funds.

GIFT AID (NON-NEED-BASED) ***Total amount:*** $2,558,155 (6% state, 93% institutional, 1% external sources). ***Receiving aid:*** *Freshmen:* 62% (169); *Undergraduates:* 45% (639). ***Scholarships, grants, and awards by category:*** *Academic Interests/Achievement:* general academic interests/achievements. *Creative Arts/Performance:* music. *Special Achievements/Activities:* community service, leadership, memberships, religious involvement. *Special Characteristics:* children and siblings of alumni, children of faculty/staff. ***Tuition waivers:*** Full or partial for employees or children of employees, senior citizens.

LOANS ***Student loans:*** $6,881,695 (100% need-based). 54% of past graduating class borrowed through all loan programs. ***Average need-based loan:*** Freshmen: $3227; Undergraduates: $7017. ***Parent loans:*** $2,664,378 (100% need-based). ***Programs:*** Federal Direct (Subsidized and Unsubsidized Stafford, PLUS), Perkins, college/university.

WORK-STUDY ***Federal work-study:*** *Total amount:* $600,495; 373 jobs averaging $1610. ***State or other work-study/employment:*** *Total amount:* $478,072 (100% need-based). 382 part-time jobs averaging $1251.

APPLYING for FINANCIAL AID ***Required financial aid forms:*** FAFSA, institution's own form. ***Financial aid deadline:*** Continuous. ***Notification date:*** Continuous beginning 3/15.

CONTACT R. Ellen Murdick, Assistant Director of Student Financial Services for Financial Aid, Andrews University, Student Financial Services Administration Building, Berrien Springs, MI 49104, 616-471-3221 or toll-free 800-253-2874. *Fax:* 616-471-3228.

ANGELO STATE UNIVERSITY

San Angelo, TX

Tuition & fees (TX res): $2320 **Average undergraduate aid package: $3833**

ABOUT THE INSTITUTION State-supported, coed. Awards: associate, bachelor's, and master's degrees. 37 undergraduate majors. Total enrollment: 5,859. Undergraduates: 5,859. Freshmen: 1,184. Federal methodology is used as a basis for awarding need-based institutional aid.

UNDERGRADUATE EXPENSES for 1999–2000 ***Tuition, state resident:*** full-time $1140; part-time $38 per semester hour. ***Tuition, nonresident:*** full-time $7620; part-time $254 per semester hour. ***Required fees:*** full-time $1180; $41 per semester hour; $71 per term part-time. Full-time tuition and fees vary according to course load. Part-time tuition and fees vary according to course load. ***College room and board:*** $4066; ***room only:*** $2566. Room and board charges vary according to board plan and housing facility. ***Payment plan:*** installment.

FRESHMAN FINANCIAL AID (Fall 1999, est.) *Average percent of need met:* 56% (excluding resources awarded to replace EFC). *Average financial aid package:* $3247 (excluding resources awarded to replace EFC).

UNDERGRADUATE FINANCIAL AID (Fall 1999, est.) *Average percent of need met:* 52% (excluding resources awarded to replace EFC). *Average financial aid package:* $3833 (excluding resources awarded to replace EFC).

GIFT AID (NEED-BASED) ***Total amount:*** $7,142,197 ***Scholarships, grants, and awards:*** Federal Pell, FSEOG, state, private, college/university gift aid from institutional funds.

GIFT AID (NON-NEED-BASED) ***Total amount:*** $1,249,700 ***Scholarships, grants, and awards by category:*** *Academic Interests/Achievement:* agriculture, biological sciences, business, communication, computer science, education, English, general academic interests/achievements, international studies, military science, physical sciences, premedicine. *Creative Arts/Performance:* music, theater/drama. *Special Achievements/Activities:* cheerleading/drum major. ***Tuition waivers:*** Full or partial for senior citizens. ***ROTC:*** Air Force.

WORK-STUDY Federal work-study jobs available. ***State or other work-study/employment:*** Part-time jobs available.

APPLYING for FINANCIAL AID ***Required financial aid forms:*** FAFSA, institution's own form. ***Financial aid deadline (priority):*** 6/1. ***Notification date:*** Continuous.

CONTACT Mr. James B. Parker, Director of Financial Aid, Angelo State University, PO Box 11015, ASU Station, San Angelo, TX 76909, 915-942-2246 or toll-free 800-946-8627. *E-mail:* jimmy.parker@angelo.edu

ANNA MARIA COLLEGE

Paxton, MA

Tuition & fees: $12,950 **Average undergraduate aid package: $11,354**

ABOUT THE INSTITUTION Independent Roman Catholic, coed. Awards: associate, bachelor's, and master's degrees and post-master's certificates. 24 undergraduate majors. Total enrollment: 1,293. Undergraduates: 719. Freshmen: 134. Federal methodology is used as a basis for awarding need-based institutional aid.

UNDERGRADUATE EXPENSES for 1999–2000 ***Application fee:*** $30. ***Comprehensive fee:*** $18,900 includes full-time tuition ($12,200), mandatory fees ($750), and room and board ($5950). Full-time tuition and fees vary according to program. ***Part-time tuition:*** $590 per course. ***Payment plans:*** guaranteed tuition, installment.

FRESHMAN FINANCIAL AID (Fall 1998) 152 applied for aid; of those 93% were deemed to have need. 100% of freshmen with need received aid; of those 21% had need fully met. *Average percent of need met:* 83% (excluding resources awarded to replace EFC). *Average financial aid package:* $11,022 (excluding resources awarded to replace EFC). 6% of all full-time freshmen had no need and received non-need-based aid.

UNDERGRADUATE FINANCIAL AID (Fall 1998) 440 applied for aid; of those 94% were deemed to have need. 100% of undergraduates with need received aid; of those 23% had need fully met. *Average percent of need met:* 85% (excluding resources awarded to replace EFC). *Average financial aid package:* $11,354 (excluding resources awarded to replace EFC). 6% of all full-time undergraduates had no need and received non-need-based aid.

GIFT AID (NEED-BASED) ***Total amount:*** $2,873,166 (14% Federal, 11% state, 74% institutional, 1% external sources). ***Receiving aid:*** *Freshmen:* 89% (141); *all full-time undergraduates:* 86% (385). ***Average award:*** Freshmen: $7455; Undergraduates: $7064. ***Scholarships, grants, and awards:*** Federal Pell, FSEOG, state, private, college/university gift aid from institutional funds.

GIFT AID (NON-NEED-BASED) ***Total amount:*** $157,912 (99% institutional, 1% external sources). ***Receiving aid:*** *Freshmen:* 3% (4); *Undergraduates:* 2% (10). ***Scholarships, grants, and awards by category:*** *Academic Interests/Achievement:* 126 awards ($439,600 total): general academic interests/achievements. *Creative Arts/Performance:* 9 awards ($8000 total): music. *Special Achievements/Activities:* 67 awards ($94,625 total): leadership, religious involvement. *Special Characteristics:* 150 awards ($143,000 total): children and siblings of alumni, children of faculty/staff, ethnic background, general special characteristics, members of minority groups, siblings of current students. ***Tuition waivers:*** Full or partial for children of alumni, employees or children of employees, senior citizens. ***ROTC:*** Army cooperative.

LOANS ***Student loans:*** $2,345,715 (74% need-based, 26% non-need-based). 95% of past graduating class borrowed through all loan programs. ***Average need-based loan:*** Freshmen: $3265; Undergraduates: $4065. ***Parent loans:*** $304,572 (29% need-based, 71% non-need-based). ***Programs:*** FFEL (Subsidized and Unsubsidized Stafford, PLUS), Perkins, state, alternative loans.

WORK-STUDY ***Federal work-study:*** *Total amount:* $107,707; 125 jobs averaging $1000.

APPLYING for FINANCIAL AID ***Required financial aid form:*** FAFSA. ***Financial aid deadline (priority):*** 3/15. ***Notification date:*** Continuous. Students must reply within 2 weeks of notification.

CONTACT Ms. Laurie Peltier, Director of Financial Aid and Admission, Anna Maria College, Sunset Lane, Paxton, MA 01612, 508-849-3366. *Fax:* 508-849-3362. *E-mail:* lpeltier@annamaria.edu

ANTIOCH COLLEGE

Yellow Springs, OH

Tuition & fees: $19,231 **Average undergraduate aid package: $17,564**

ABOUT THE INSTITUTION Independent, coed. Awards: bachelor's degrees. 57 undergraduate majors. Total enrollment: 628. Undergraduates: 618. Freshmen: 135. Federal methodology is used as a basis for awarding need-based institutional aid.

UNDERGRADUATE EXPENSES for 1999–2000 ***Application fee:*** $35. ***Comprehensive fee:*** $24,107 includes full-time tuition ($17,556), mandatory fees ($1675), and room and board ($4876). ***College room only:*** $2398. ***Part-time tuition:*** $375 per credit. ***Payment plan:*** installment.

FRESHMAN FINANCIAL AID (Fall 1999, est.) 122 applied for aid; of those 86% were deemed to have need. 100% of freshmen with need received aid; of those 41% had need fully met. *Average percent of need met:* 93% (excluding resources awarded to replace EFC). *Average financial aid package:* $17,424 (excluding resources awarded to replace EFC). 7% of all full-time freshmen had no need and received non-need-based aid.

UNDERGRADUATE FINANCIAL AID (Fall 1999, est.) 575 applied for aid; of those 97% were deemed to have need. 97% of undergraduates with need received aid; of those 63% had need fully met. *Average percent of need met:* 96% (excluding resources awarded to replace EFC). *Average financial aid package:* $17,564 (excluding resources awarded to replace EFC). 6% of all full-time undergraduates had no need and received non-need-based aid.

GIFT AID (NEED-BASED) ***Total amount:*** $2,918,920 (34% Federal, 4% state, 62% institutional). ***Receiving aid:*** *Freshmen:* 71% (100); *all full-time undergraduates:* 81% (483). ***Average award:*** Freshmen: $9951; Undergraduates: $9784. ***Scholarships, grants, and awards:*** Federal Pell, FSEOG, state, college/university gift aid from institutional funds.

GIFT AID (NON-NEED-BASED) ***Total amount:*** $1,137,801 (92% institutional, 8% external sources). ***Receiving aid:*** *Freshmen:* 32% (45); *Undergraduates:* 47% (281). ***Scholarships, grants, and awards by category:*** *Academic Interests/Achievement:* biological sciences, education, general academic interests/achievements, humanities, international studies, mathematics, physical sciences, social sciences. *Special Achievements/Activities:* community service. *Special Characteristics:* local/state students. ***Tuition waivers:*** Full or partial for employees or children of employees.

LOANS ***Student loans:*** $1,707,366 (86% need-based, 14% non-need-based). 75% of past graduating class borrowed through all loan programs. Average indebtedness per student: $13,927. ***Average need-based loan:*** Freshmen: $3195; Undergraduates: $3417. ***Parent loans:*** $582,431 (100% non-need-based). ***Programs:*** Federal Direct (Subsidized and Unsubsidized Stafford, PLUS), Perkins.

WORK-STUDY ***Federal work-study:*** *Total amount:* $810,788; 388 jobs averaging $2037.

APPLYING for FINANCIAL AID ***Required financial aid forms:*** FAFSA, institution's own form, noncustodial (divorced/separated) parent's statement, W-2 forms, federal income tax form(s). ***Financial aid deadline (priority):*** 3/1. ***Notification date:*** Continuous beginning 5/1.

CONTACT Mr. Larry Brickman, Financial Aid Director, Antioch College, 795 Livermore Street, Yellow Springs, OH 45387-1697, 937-767-6400 Ext. 6268 or toll-free 800-543-9436 (out-of-state). *Fax:* 937-767-6473. *E-mail:* lbobo@antioch-college.edu

ANTIOCH SOUTHERN CALIFORNIA/SANTA BARBARA

Santa Barbara, CA

Tuition & fees: $9750 **Average undergraduate aid package: N/A**

ABOUT THE INSTITUTION Independent, coed. Awards: bachelor's and master's degrees. 1 undergraduate major. Total enrollment: 253. Undergraduates: 101. Federal methodology is used as a basis for awarding need-based institutional aid.

UNDERGRADUATE EXPENSES for 1999–2000 ***Application fee:*** $60. ***Tuition:*** full-time $9750; part-time $325 per quarter hour. Part-time tuition and fees vary according to course load. ***Payment plan:*** installment.

GIFT AID (NEED-BASED) ***Total amount:*** $166,570 (47% Federal, 27% state, 18% institutional, 8% external sources). ***Scholarships, grants, and awards:*** Federal Pell, FSEOG, state, college/university gift aid from institutional funds.

GIFT AID (NON-NEED-BASED) ***Tuition waivers:*** Full or partial for employees or children of employees.

LOANS ***Student loans:*** $1,692,018 (73% need-based, 27% non-need-based). 70% of past graduating class borrowed through all loan programs. ***Programs:*** FFEL (Subsidized and Unsubsidized Stafford, PLUS), Perkins.

WORK-STUDY ***Federal work-study:*** *Total amount:* $69,389; jobs available.

APPLYING for FINANCIAL AID ***Required financial aid forms:*** FAFSA, institution's own form, income tax forms. ***Financial aid deadline:*** Continuous.

CONTACT Karen Morgan, Financial Aid Director, Antioch Southern California/Santa Barbara, 801 Garden Street, Santa Barbara, CA 93101-1580, 805-962-8179 Ext. 108. *Fax:* 805-962-4786.

ANTIOCH UNIVERSITY SEATTLE

Seattle, WA

Tuition & fees: $10,710 **Average undergraduate aid package: $9500**

ABOUT THE INSTITUTION Independent, coed. Awards: bachelor's and master's degrees. 1 undergraduate major. Total enrollment: 834. Undergraduates: 156. Both federal and institutional methodology are used as a basis for awarding need-based institutional aid.

UNDERGRADUATE EXPENSES for 1999–2000 ***Application fee:*** $50. ***Tuition:*** full-time $10,620; part-time $295 per credit hour. ***Required fees:*** full-time $90; $15 per term part-time. Full-time tuition and fees vary according to course load. Part-time tuition and fees vary according to course load and program. ***Payment plan:*** installment.

UNDERGRADUATE FINANCIAL AID (Fall 1999) 110 applied for aid; of those 81% were deemed to have need. 100% of undergraduates with need received aid; of those 94% had need fully met. *Average percent of need met:* 84% (excluding resources awarded to replace EFC). *Average financial aid package:* $9500 (excluding resources awarded to replace EFC).

GIFT AID (NEED-BASED) ***Total amount:*** $98,188 (100% Federal). ***Scholarships, grants, and awards:*** Federal Pell, FSEOG.

GIFT AID (NON-NEED-BASED) ***Tuition waivers:*** Full or partial for employees or children of employees.

LOANS ***Student loans:*** $801,000 (56% need-based, 44% non-need-based). Average indebtedness per student: $18,500. ***Average need-based loan:*** Undergraduates: $6000. ***Programs:*** FFEL (Subsidized and Unsubsidized Stafford, PLUS), Perkins.

WORK-STUDY ***Federal work-study:*** *Total amount:* $105,781; 17 jobs available.

APPLYING for FINANCIAL AID ***Required financial aid forms:*** FAFSA, institution's own form. ***Financial aid deadline:*** Continuous. ***Notification date:*** Continuous beginning 7/1. Students must reply within 2 weeks of notification.

CONTACT Kathy Battraw, Financial Aid Officer, Antioch University Seattle, 2326 Sixth Avenue, Seattle, WA 98121-1814, 206-441-5352 Ext. 5004. *Fax:* 206-441-3307. *E-mail:* kathy_battraw@antiochseattle.edu

APPALACHIAN BIBLE COLLEGE

Bradley, WV

Tuition & fees: $6132 **Average undergraduate aid package: $3116**

ABOUT THE INSTITUTION Independent nondenominational, coed. Awards: associate and bachelor's degrees. 2 undergraduate majors. Total enrollment: 303. Undergraduates: 303. Freshmen: 48. Both federal and institutional methodology are used as a basis for awarding need-based institutional aid.

UNDERGRADUATE EXPENSES for 2000–2001 ***Application fee:*** $10. ***Comprehensive fee:*** $9442 includes full-time tuition ($5112), mandatory fees ($1020), and room and board ($3310). ***Part-time tuition:*** $213 per credit hour. ***Part-time fees:*** $26 per credit hour. ***Payment plan:*** installment.

FRESHMAN FINANCIAL AID (Fall 1998) 98 applied for aid; of those 100% were deemed to have need. 96% of freshmen with need received aid. *Average percent of need met:* 96% (excluding resources awarded to replace EFC). *Average financial aid package:* $1196 (excluding resources awarded to replace EFC).

UNDERGRADUATE FINANCIAL AID (Fall 1998) 245 applied for aid; of those 100% were deemed to have need. 98% of undergraduates with need received aid. *Average percent of need met:* 85% (excluding resources awarded to replace EFC). *Average financial aid package:* $3116 (excluding resources awarded to replace EFC).

GIFT AID (NEED-BASED) ***Total amount:*** $696,460 (46% Federal, 6% state, 38% institutional, 10% external sources). ***Receiving aid:*** *Freshmen:* 96% (94); *all full-time undergraduates:* 84% (241). ***Average award:*** Freshmen: $1196; Undergraduates: $3116. ***Scholarships, grants, and awards:*** Federal Pell, FSEOG, state, private, college/university gift aid from institutional funds.

GIFT AID (NON-NEED-BASED) ***Scholarships, grants, and awards by category:*** *Academic Interests/Achievement:* 58 awards ($42,000 total): general academic interests/achievements. *Special Characteristics:* 123 awards ($111,767 total): children and siblings of alumni, children of faculty/staff, general special characteristics, international students, married students, relatives of clergy, veterans. ***Tuition waivers:*** Full or partial for employees or children of employees.

LOANS ***Student loans:*** $401,473 (100% need-based). ***Average need-based loan:*** Freshmen: $1500; Undergraduates: $2200. ***Parent loans:*** $51,694 (100% need-based). ***Programs:*** FFEL (Subsidized and Unsubsidized Stafford, PLUS).

WORK-STUDY ***Federal work-study:*** *Total amount:* $14,946; 32 jobs averaging $467.

APPLYING for FINANCIAL AID ***Required financial aid forms:*** FAFSA, institution's own form. ***Financial aid deadline (priority):*** 3/1. ***Notification date:*** Continuous beginning 6/15. Students must reply by 8/30 or within 4 weeks of notification.

CONTACT Mrs. Shirley Carfrey, Director of Financial Aid, Appalachian Bible College, PO Box ABC, Sandbranch Road, Bradley, WV 25818, 304-877-6428 Ext. 3244 or toll-free 800-678-9ABC. *Fax:* 304-877-5082. *E-mail:* financialaid@appbibco.edu

APPALACHIAN STATE UNIVERSITY

Boone, NC

Tuition & fees (NC res): $2088 **Average undergraduate aid package: $5164**

ABOUT THE INSTITUTION State-supported, coed. Awards: bachelor's, master's, and doctoral degrees and post-master's certificates. 99 undergraduate majors. Total enrollment: 12,779. Undergraduates: 11,570. Freshmen: 2,209. Federal methodology is used as a basis for awarding need-based institutional aid.

UNDERGRADUATE EXPENSES for 2000–2001 (est.) ***Application fee:*** $35. ***Tuition, state resident:*** full-time $962. ***Tuition, nonresident:*** full-time

$8232. ***Required fees:*** full-time $1126. Part-time tuition and fees vary according to course load. ***College room and board:*** $3560; ***room only:*** $2110. Room and board charges vary according to board plan and housing facility. ***Payment plan:*** installment.

FRESHMAN FINANCIAL AID (Fall 1998) 1121 applied for aid; of those 64% were deemed to have need. 90% of freshmen with need received aid; of those 41% had need fully met. *Average percent of need met:* 43% (excluding resources awarded to replace EFC). *Average financial aid package:* $4555 (excluding resources awarded to replace EFC). 24% of all full-time freshmen had no need and received non-need-based aid.

UNDERGRADUATE FINANCIAL AID (Fall 1998) 4,915 applied for aid; of those 75% were deemed to have need. 94% of undergraduates with need received aid; of those 57% had need fully met. *Average percent of need met:* 58% (excluding resources awarded to replace EFC). *Average financial aid package:* $5164 (excluding resources awarded to replace EFC). 20% of all full-time undergraduates had no need and received non-need-based aid.

GIFT AID (NEED-BASED) ***Total amount:*** $6,535,013 (63% Federal, 20% state, 8% institutional, 9% external sources). ***Receiving aid:*** *Freshmen:* 21% (489); *all full-time undergraduates:* 22% (2,379). ***Average award:*** Freshmen: $2954; Undergraduates: $2757. ***Scholarships, grants, and awards:*** Federal Pell, FSEOG, state, private, college/university gift aid from institutional funds.

GIFT AID (NON-NEED-BASED) ***Total amount:*** $3,309,187 (2% Federal, 47% state, 30% institutional, 21% external sources). ***Receiving aid:*** *Freshmen:* 6% (147); *Undergraduates:* 3% (324). ***Scholarships, grants, and awards by category:*** *Academic Interests/Achievement:* general academic interests/achievements. ***Tuition waivers:*** Full or partial for senior citizens. ***ROTC:*** Army.

LOANS ***Student loans:*** $16,976,098 (79% need-based, 21% non-need-based). 48% of past graduating class borrowed through all loan programs. Average indebtedness per student: $9400. ***Average need-based loan:*** Freshmen: $2679; Undergraduates: $4101. ***Parent loans:*** $4,265,918 (61% need-based, 39% non-need-based). ***Programs:*** FFEL (Subsidized and Unsubsidized Stafford, PLUS), Perkins, college/university.

WORK-STUDY ***Federal work-study:*** *Total amount:* $475,749; 476 jobs averaging $1000. ***State or other work-study/employment:*** *Total amount:* $2,999,162 (100% non-need-based). 2,428 part-time jobs averaging $1235.

ATHLETIC AWARDS *Total amount:* 1,309,821 (39% need-based, 61% non-need-based).

APPLYING for FINANCIAL AID ***Required financial aid form:*** FAFSA. ***Financial aid deadline (priority):*** 3/15. ***Notification date:*** Continuous. Students must reply within 3 weeks of notification.

CONTACT Kay Stroud, Associate Director of Student Financial Aid, Appalachian State University, Office of Student Financial Aid, PO Box 32059, Boone, NC 28608-2059, 828-262-2190. *Fax:* 828-262-2585. *E-mail:* stroudkn@appstate.edu

AQUINAS COLLEGE
Grand Rapids, MI

Tuition & fees: $14,034 **Average undergraduate aid package: $12,958**

ABOUT THE INSTITUTION Independent Roman Catholic, coed. Awards: associate, bachelor's, and master's degrees. 56 undergraduate majors. Total enrollment: 2,547. Undergraduates: 1,983. Freshmen: 354. Federal methodology is used as a basis for awarding need-based institutional aid.

UNDERGRADUATE EXPENSES for 2000–2001 ***Application fee:*** $25. ***Comprehensive fee:*** $18,918 includes full-time tuition ($14,034) and room and board ($4884). ***College room only:*** $2256. Full-time tuition and fees vary according to course load. Room and board charges vary according to board plan and housing facility. ***Part-time tuition:*** $280 per credit hour. Part-time tuition and fees vary according to course load. ***Payment plans:*** installment, deferred payment.

FRESHMAN FINANCIAL AID (Fall 1999) 319 applied for aid; of those 88% were deemed to have need. 100% of freshmen with need received aid; of those 45% had need fully met. *Average percent of need met:* 94% (excluding resources awarded to replace EFC). *Average financial aid package:* $12,950 (excluding resources awarded to replace EFC). 20% of all full-time freshmen had no need and received non-need-based aid.

UNDERGRADUATE FINANCIAL AID (Fall 1999) 1,076 applied for aid; of those 87% were deemed to have need. 100% of undergraduates with need received aid; of those 53% had need fully met. *Average percent of need met:* 96% (excluding resources awarded to replace EFC). *Average financial aid package:* $12,958 (excluding resources awarded to replace EFC). 23% of all full-time undergraduates had no need and received non-need-based aid.

GIFT AID (NEED-BASED) ***Total amount:*** $8,926,739 (8% Federal, 20% state, 72% institutional). ***Receiving aid:*** *Freshmen:* 80% (280); *all full-time undergraduates:* 75% (941). ***Average award:*** Freshmen: $11,249; Undergraduates: $9541. ***Scholarships, grants, and awards:*** Federal Pell, FSEOG, state, private, college/university gift aid from institutional funds.

GIFT AID (NON-NEED-BASED) ***Total amount:*** $1,471,714 (100% institutional). ***Receiving aid:*** *Freshmen:* 68% (239); *Undergraduates:* 51% (639). ***Scholarships, grants, and awards by category:*** *Academic Interests/Achievement:* general academic interests/achievements. *Special Achievements/Activities:* community service, leadership, memberships. *Special Characteristics:* children and siblings of alumni, children of faculty/staff. ***Tuition waivers:*** Full or partial for children of alumni, employees or children of employees.

LOANS ***Student loans:*** $2,525,158 (61% need-based, 39% non-need-based). 80% of past graduating class borrowed through all loan programs. Average indebtedness per student: $12,348. ***Average need-based loan:*** Freshmen: $1701; Undergraduates: $3417. ***Parent loans:*** $497,373 (100% non-need-based). ***Programs:*** FFEL (Subsidized and Unsubsidized Stafford, PLUS), Perkins.

WORK-STUDY ***Federal work-study:*** *Total amount:* $175,000; 183 jobs averaging $956. ***State or other work-study/employment:*** *Total amount:* $34,114 (100% need-based). 34 part-time jobs averaging $1000.

ATHLETIC AWARDS *Total amount:* 486,850 (78% need-based, 22% non-need-based).

APPLYING for FINANCIAL AID ***Required financial aid form:*** FAFSA. ***Financial aid deadline (priority):*** 2/15. ***Notification date:*** Continuous beginning 3/1. Students must reply within 2 weeks of notification.

CONTACT Mr. David J. Steffee, Director of Financial Aid, Aquinas College, 1607 Robinson Road, SE, Grand Rapids, MI 49506-1799, 616-459-8281 Ext. 5127 or toll-free 800-678-9593. *Fax:* 616-732-4547. *E-mail:* steffdav@aquinas.edu

AQUINAS COLLEGE
Nashville, TN

Tuition & fees: $8800 **Average undergraduate aid package: N/A**

ABOUT THE INSTITUTION Independent Roman Catholic, coed. Awards: associate and bachelor's degrees. 3 undergraduate majors. Total enrollment: 410. Undergraduates: 410. Federal methodology is used as a basis for awarding need-based institutional aid.

UNDERGRADUATE EXPENSES for 1999–2000 ***Application fee:*** $10. ***Tuition:*** full-time $8500; part-time $300 per semester hour. ***Required fees:*** full-time $300; $140 per term part-time. Full-time tuition and fees vary according to program. Part-time tuition and fees vary according to program. ***Payment plan:*** installment.

UNDERGRADUATE FINANCIAL AID (Fall 1998) 239 applied for aid; of those 76% were deemed to have need. 100% of undergraduates with need received aid.

GIFT AID (NEED-BASED) ***Total amount:*** $376,947 (49% Federal, 31% state, 10% institutional, 10% external sources). ***Receiving aid:*** *All full-time undergraduates:* 10% (36). ***Average award:*** Undergraduates: $1258. ***Scholarships, grants, and awards:*** Federal Pell, FSEOG, state, private, college/university gift aid from institutional funds.

GIFT AID (NON-NEED-BASED) ***Receiving aid:*** *Undergraduates:* 3% (11). ***Scholarships, grants, and awards by category:*** *Academic Interests/Achievement:* 18 awards ($15,850 total): business, education, general academic interests/achievements, health fields. *Special Achievements/*

Aquinas College (continued)

Activities: 14 awards ($21,000 total): leadership. *Special Characteristics:* 12 awards ($11,400 total): general special characteristics. ***ROTC:*** Army cooperative, Air Force cooperative.

LOANS ***Student loans:*** $983,811 (47% need-based, 53% non-need-based). ***Average need-based loan:*** Undergraduates: $2574. ***Parent loans:*** $42,404 (100% non-need-based). ***Programs:*** FFEL (Subsidized and Unsubsidized Stafford, PLUS), alternative loans.

WORK-STUDY ***Federal work-study:*** *Total amount:* $23,403; jobs available.

ATHLETIC AWARDS *Total amount:* 194,564 (100% need-based).

APPLYING for FINANCIAL AID ***Required financial aid forms:*** FAFSA, institution's own form. ***Financial aid deadline (priority):*** 5/1. ***Notification date:*** Continuous. Students must reply by 8/21 or within 3 weeks of notification.

CONTACT Bonnie Deese, Director of Financial Aid, Aquinas College, 4210 Harding Road, Nashville, TN 37205-2005, 615-297-7545 Ext. 431. *Fax:* 615-297-7970. *E-mail:* finaid@aquinas-tn.edu

ARIZONA STATE UNIVERSITY

Tempe, AZ

Tuition & fees (AZ res): $2261 **Average undergraduate aid package: $6794**

ABOUT THE INSTITUTION State-supported, coed. Awards: bachelor's, master's, doctoral, and first professional degrees and post-bachelor's and post-master's certificates. 90 undergraduate majors. Total enrollment: 44,215. Undergraduates: 33,948. Freshmen: 5,868. Federal methodology is used as a basis for awarding need-based institutional aid.

UNDERGRADUATE EXPENSES for 1999–2000 ***Application fee:*** $40 for nonresidents. ***Tuition, state resident:*** full-time $2188; part-time $115 per credit. ***Tuition, nonresident:*** full-time $9340; part-time $389 per credit. ***Required fees:*** full-time $73; $18 per term part-time. ***College room and board:*** $5010; ***room only:*** $3010. Room and board charges vary according to board plan and housing facility.

FRESHMAN FINANCIAL AID (Fall 1998) 3323 applied for aid; of those 54% were deemed to have need. 100% of freshmen with need received aid; of those 22% had need fully met. *Average percent of need met:* 71% (excluding resources awarded to replace EFC). *Average financial aid package:* $6135 (excluding resources awarded to replace EFC). 31% of all full-time freshmen had no need and received non-need-based aid.

UNDERGRADUATE FINANCIAL AID (Fall 1998) 16,617 applied for aid; of those 66% were deemed to have need. 100% of undergraduates with need received aid; of those 16% had need fully met. *Average percent of need met:* 70% (excluding resources awarded to replace EFC). *Average financial aid package:* $6794 (excluding resources awarded to replace EFC). 21% of all full-time undergraduates had no need and received non-need-based aid.

GIFT AID (NEED-BASED) ***Total amount:*** $32,194,820 (52% Federal, 2% state, 31% institutional, 15% external sources). ***Receiving aid:*** *Freshmen:* 33% (1,555); *all full-time undergraduates:* 32% (8,323). ***Average award:*** Freshmen: $4279; Undergraduates: $3561. ***Scholarships, grants, and awards:*** Federal Pell, FSEOG, state, private, college/university gift aid from institutional funds, Federal Nursing.

GIFT AID (NON-NEED-BASED) ***Total amount:*** $10,842,357 (45% institutional, 55% external sources). ***Receiving aid:*** *Freshmen:* 6% (269); *Undergraduates:* 2% (474). ***Scholarships, grants, and awards by category:*** *Academic Interests/Achievement:* architecture, area/ethnic studies, biological sciences, business, communication, computer science, education, engineering/technologies, English, foreign languages, general academic interests/achievements, health fields, home economics, humanities, mathematics, military science, physical sciences, premedicine, social sciences. *Creative Arts/Performance:* applied art and design, art/fine arts, cinema/film/broadcasting, creative writing, dance, debating, general creative arts/performance, journalism/publications, music, performing arts, theater/drama. *Special Achievements/Activities:* cheerleading/drum major, community service, general special achievements/activities, hobbies/interests, junior miss, leadership, memberships, rodeo. *Special Characteristics:* general special characteristics. ***Tuition waivers:*** Full or partial for employees or children of employees. ***ROTC:*** Army, Air Force.

LOANS ***Student loans:*** $72,793,003 (78% need-based, 22% non-need-based). Average indebtedness per student: $17,385. ***Average need-based loan:*** Freshmen: $2512; Undergraduates: $4080. ***Parent loans:*** $11,800,067 (31% need-based, 69% non-need-based). ***Programs:*** Federal Direct (Subsidized and Unsubsidized Stafford, PLUS), FFEL (PLUS), Perkins.

WORK-STUDY ***Federal work-study:*** *Total amount:* $1,291,238; 557 jobs averaging $2318. ***State or other work-study/employment:*** *Total amount:* $10,227,275 (19% need-based, 81% non-need-based). 4,157 part-time jobs averaging $2460.

ATHLETIC AWARDS *Total amount:* 3,891,651 (31% need-based, 69% non-need-based).

APPLYING for FINANCIAL AID ***Required financial aid form:*** FAFSA. ***Financial aid deadline (priority):*** 3/1. ***Notification date:*** Continuous beginning 3/15. Students must reply within 4 weeks of notification.

CONTACT Student Financial Assistance Office, Arizona State University, Box 870412, Tempe, AZ 85287-0412, 480-965-3355.

ARIZONA STATE UNIVERSITY EAST

Mesa, AZ

Tuition & fees (AZ res): $2211 **Average undergraduate aid package: $7125**

ABOUT THE INSTITUTION State-supported, coed. Awards: bachelor's and master's degrees. 17 undergraduate majors. Total enrollment: 1,466. Undergraduates: 1,105. Freshmen: 86. Federal methodology is used as a basis for awarding need-based institutional aid.

UNDERGRADUATE EXPENSES for 1999–2000 ***Application fee:*** $40. ***Tuition, state resident:*** full-time $2188; part-time $115 per semester hour. ***Tuition, nonresident:*** full-time $9340; part-time $389 per semester hour. ***Required fees:*** full-time $23; $13 per term part-time. Full-time tuition and fees vary according to location. Part-time tuition and fees vary according to course load and location. ***College room and board: room only:*** $2440. Room and board charges vary according to housing facility.

UNDERGRADUATE FINANCIAL AID (Fall 1998) 183 applied for aid; of those 76% were deemed to have need. 100% of undergraduates with need received aid; of those 13% had need fully met. *Average percent of need met:* 66% (excluding resources awarded to replace EFC). *Average financial aid package:* $7125 (excluding resources awarded to replace EFC). 12% of all full-time undergraduates had no need and received non-need-based aid.

GIFT AID (NEED-BASED) ***Total amount:*** $568,421 (58% Federal, 3% state, 24% institutional, 15% external sources). ***Receiving aid:*** *All full-time undergraduates:* 32% (100). ***Average award:*** Undergraduates: $3300. ***Scholarships, grants, and awards:*** Federal Pell, FSEOG, state, private, college/university gift aid from institutional funds.

GIFT AID (NON-NEED-BASED) ***Total amount:*** $105,026 (33% institutional, 67% external sources). ***Scholarships, grants, and awards by category:*** *Academic Interests/Achievement:* general academic interests/achievements. *Creative Arts/Performance:* general creative arts/performance. *Special Achievements/Activities:* general special achievements/activities. *Special Characteristics:* general special characteristics. ***Tuition waivers:*** Full or partial for employees or children of employees. ***ROTC:*** Army cooperative, Air Force cooperative.

LOANS ***Student loans:*** $1,746,172 (77% need-based, 23% non-need-based). ***Average need-based loan:*** Undergraduates: $4676. ***Parent loans:*** $86,569 (61% need-based, 39% non-need-based). ***Programs:*** Federal Direct (Subsidized and Unsubsidized Stafford, PLUS), FFEL (PLUS), Perkins.

WORK-STUDY ***Federal work-study:*** *Total amount:* $15,919; 4 jobs averaging $3980. ***State or other work-study/employment:*** *Total amount:* $308,902 (24% need-based, 76% non-need-based). 102 part-time jobs averaging $3028.

ATHLETIC AWARDS *Total amount:* 4556 (100% non-need-based).

APPLYING for FINANCIAL AID ***Required financial aid form:*** FAFSA. ***Financial aid deadline (priority):*** 3/1. ***Notification date:*** Continuous beginning 4/15. Students must reply within 4 weeks of notification.

CONTACT Karen Novak, Program Coordinator, Arizona State University East, 7001 East Williams Field Road, Building 20, Mesa, AZ 85212, 480-727-1042.

ARIZONA STATE UNIVERSITY WEST

Phoenix, AZ

Tuition & fees (AZ res): $2191 **Average undergraduate aid package: $8980**

ABOUT THE INSTITUTION State-supported, coed. Awards: bachelor's and master's degrees and post-bachelor's certificates. 22 undergraduate majors. Total enrollment: 4,943. Undergraduates: 3,737. Entering class: 13. Federal methodology is used as a basis for awarding need-based institutional aid.

UNDERGRADUATE EXPENSES for 1999–2000 ***Tuition, state resident:*** full-time $2118; part-time $115 per credit hour. ***Tuition, nonresident:*** full-time $9340; part-time $389 per credit hour. ***Required fees:*** full-time $73; $18 per term part-time. Part-time tuition and fees vary according to course load. ***Payment plan:*** installment.

UNDERGRADUATE FINANCIAL AID (Fall 1998) 1,057 applied for aid; of those 84% were deemed to have need. 100% of undergraduates with need received aid; of those 100% had need fully met. *Average percent of need met:* 100% (excluding resources awarded to replace EFC). *Average financial aid package:* $8980 (excluding resources awarded to replace EFC). 11% of all full-time undergraduates had no need and received non-need-based aid.

GIFT AID (NEED-BASED) ***Total amount:*** $3,107,108 (65% Federal, 30% institutional, 5% external sources). ***Receiving aid:*** *All full-time undergraduates:* 42% (665). ***Average award:*** Undergraduates: $3281. ***Scholarships, grants, and awards:*** Federal Pell, FSEOG, state, private, college/university gift aid from institutional funds, Federal Nursing.

GIFT AID (NON-NEED-BASED) ***Total amount:*** $152,280 (1% Federal, 35% institutional, 64% external sources). ***Receiving aid:*** *Undergraduates:* 1% (11). ***Tuition waivers:*** Full or partial for employees or children of employees.

LOANS ***Student loans:*** $9,259,817 (80% need-based, 20% non-need-based). ***Average need-based loan:*** Undergraduates: $4424. ***Parent loans:*** $68,819 (32% need-based, 68% non-need-based). ***Programs:*** Federal Direct (Subsidized and Unsubsidized Stafford, PLUS), FFEL (PLUS), Perkins, college/university.

WORK-STUDY ***Federal work-study:*** *Total amount:* $144,707; 63 jobs averaging $2297. ***State or other work-study/employment:*** *Total amount:* $654,818 (21% need-based, 79% non-need-based). 248 part-time jobs averaging $2640.

APPLYING for FINANCIAL AID ***Required financial aid form:*** FAFSA. ***Financial aid deadline:*** Continuous.

CONTACT Inez Moreno-Weinert, Assistant Director of Financial Aid Services, Arizona State University West, 4701 West Thunderbird Road, PO Box 37100, Phoenix, AZ 85069-7100, 602-543-8178.

ARKANSAS BAPTIST COLLEGE

Little Rock, AR

Tuition & fees: $2200 **Average undergraduate aid package: N/A**

ABOUT THE INSTITUTION Independent Baptist, coed. Awards: associate and bachelor's degrees. 8 undergraduate majors. Federal methodology is used as a basis for awarding need-based institutional aid.

UNDERGRADUATE EXPENSES for 1999–2000 ***Comprehensive fee:*** $5200 includes full-time tuition ($2200) and room and board ($3000). ***Part-time tuition:*** $89 per semester hour.

GIFT AID (NEED-BASED) ***Scholarships, grants, and awards:*** Federal Pell, FSEOG, state, private.

LOANS ***Programs:*** Federal Direct (Subsidized and Unsubsidized Stafford, PLUS).

WORK-STUDY Federal work-study jobs available.

APPLYING for FINANCIAL AID ***Required financial aid form:*** FAFSA. ***Financial aid deadline (priority):*** 4/15. ***Notification date:*** Continuous. Students must reply by 6/15.

CONTACT Ms. Evelyn Jones, Director of Financial Aid, Arkansas Baptist College, 1600 Bishop Street, Little Rock, AR 72202-6067, 501-374-7856.

ARKANSAS STATE UNIVERSITY

Jonesboro, AR

Tuition & fees (AR res): $2972 **Average undergraduate aid package: $2300**

ABOUT THE INSTITUTION State-supported, coed. Awards: associate, bachelor's, master's, and doctoral degrees and post-master's certificates. 75 undergraduate majors. Total enrollment: 10,461. Undergraduates: 9,398. Freshmen: 1,714. Federal methodology is used as a basis for awarding need-based institutional aid.

UNDERGRADUATE EXPENSES for 1999–2000 ***Application fee:*** $15. ***Tuition, state resident:*** full-time $2352; part-time $98 per credit hour. ***Tuition, nonresident:*** full-time $6024; part-time $251 per credit hour. ***Required fees:*** full-time $620; $19 per credit hour; $15 per term part-time. Full-time tuition and fees vary according to class time, course level, course load, degree level, location, and reciprocity agreements. Part-time tuition and fees vary according to class time, course load, degree level, location, and reciprocity agreements. ***College room and board:*** $3020. Room and board charges vary according to board plan and housing facility. ***Payment plan:*** installment.

FRESHMAN FINANCIAL AID (Fall 1998) 1480 applied for aid; of those 95% were deemed to have need. 100% of freshmen with need received aid; of those 88% had need fully met. *Average percent of need met:* 75% (excluding resources awarded to replace EFC). *Average financial aid package:* $2400 (excluding resources awarded to replace EFC). 15% of all full-time freshmen had no need and received non-need-based aid.

UNDERGRADUATE FINANCIAL AID (Fall 1998) 5,293 applied for aid; of those 93% were deemed to have need. 100% of undergraduates with need received aid; of those 78% had need fully met. *Average percent of need met:* 75% (excluding resources awarded to replace EFC). *Average financial aid package:* $2300 (excluding resources awarded to replace EFC). 34% of all full-time undergraduates had no need and received non-need-based aid.

GIFT AID (NEED-BASED) ***Total amount:*** $13,503,296 (51% Federal, 16% state, 29% institutional, 4% external sources). ***Receiving aid:*** *Freshmen:* 82% (1,367); *all full-time undergraduates:* 45% (3,351). ***Average award:*** Freshmen: $2000; Undergraduates: $2000. ***Scholarships, grants, and awards:*** Federal Pell, FSEOG, state, private, college/university gift aid from institutional funds.

GIFT AID (NON-NEED-BASED) ***Total amount:*** $991,186 (27% Federal, 49% state, 24% external sources). ***Receiving aid:*** *Freshmen:* 43% (711); *Undergraduates:* 43% (3,234). ***Scholarships, grants, and awards by category:*** *Academic Interests/Achievement:* 2,400 awards ($8,800,000 total): agriculture, biological sciences, business, communication, computer science, education, engineering/technologies, English, general academic interests/achievements, health fields, humanities, library science, mathematics, military science, physical sciences, premedicine, social sciences. *Creative Arts/Performance:* 200 awards ($175,000 total): art/fine arts, cinema/film/broadcasting, debating, journalism/publications, music, performing arts, theater/drama. *Special Achievements/Activities:* 30 awards ($75,000 total): cheerleading/drum major, community service, general special achievements/activities. *Special Characteristics:* adult students, children and siblings of alumni, children of current students, children of union members/company employees, children of workers in trades, children with a deceased or disabled parent, ethnic background, first-generation college students, general special characteristics, handicapped students, out-of-state students, veterans, veterans' children. ***Tuition waivers:*** Full or partial for children of alumni, employees or children of employees, senior citizens. ***ROTC:*** Army.

LOANS ***Student loans:*** $11,958,959 (71% need-based, 29% non-need-based). 51% of past graduating class borrowed through all loan programs.

Arkansas State University (continued)

Average indebtedness per student: $12,500. ***Average need-based loan:*** Freshmen: $1200; Undergraduates: $1600. ***Programs:*** FFEL (Subsidized and Unsubsidized Stafford, PLUS), Perkins.

WORK-STUDY ***Federal work-study:*** *Total amount:* $451,083; jobs available. ***State or other work-study/employment:*** *Total amount:* $2,970,288 (1% need-based, 99% non-need-based). Part-time jobs available.

ATHLETIC AWARDS *Total amount:* 1,141,514 (100% non-need-based).

APPLYING for FINANCIAL AID ***Required financial aid forms:*** FAFSA, institution's own form. ***Financial aid deadline (priority):*** 2/15. ***Notification date:*** Continuous beginning 6/1. Students must reply within 2 weeks of notification.

CONTACT Mr. Gregory Thornburg, Director of Financial Aid, Arkansas State University, PO Box 1620, State University, AR 72467, 870-972-2310 or toll-free 800-382-3030 (in-state), 800-643-0080 (out-of-state). *Fax:* 870-972-2794. *E-mail:* gthorn@chickasaw.astate.edu

ARKANSAS TECH UNIVERSITY

Russellville, AR

Tuition & fees (AR res): $2462 **Average undergraduate aid package: $4145**

ABOUT THE INSTITUTION State-supported, coed. Awards: associate, bachelor's, and master's degrees. 58 undergraduate majors. Total enrollment: 4,840. Undergraduates: 4,576. Freshmen: 1,149. Federal methodology is used as a basis for awarding need-based institutional aid.

UNDERGRADUATE EXPENSES for 1999–2000 ***Tuition, state resident:*** full-time $2352; part-time $104 per semester hour. ***Tuition, nonresident:*** full-time $4704; part-time $208 per semester hour. ***Required fees:*** full-time $110; $30 per term part-time. Full-time tuition and fees vary according to location. Part-time tuition and fees vary according to location. ***College room and board:*** $3222. Room and board charges vary according to board plan and housing facility. ***Payment plan:*** deferred payment.

FRESHMAN FINANCIAL AID (Fall 1998) 579 applied for aid; of those 80% were deemed to have need. 98% of freshmen with need received aid; of those 30% had need fully met. *Average percent of need met:* 52% (excluding resources awarded to replace EFC). *Average financial aid package:* $2958 (excluding resources awarded to replace EFC). 31% of all full-time freshmen had no need and received non-need-based aid.

UNDERGRADUATE FINANCIAL AID (Fall 1998) 2,165 applied for aid; of those 85% were deemed to have need. 98% of undergraduates with need received aid; of those 28% had need fully met. *Average percent of need met:* 55% (excluding resources awarded to replace EFC). *Average financial aid package:* $4145 (excluding resources awarded to replace EFC). 22% of all full-time undergraduates had no need and received non-need-based aid.

GIFT AID (NEED-BASED) ***Total amount:*** $4,081,685 (69% Federal, 31% state). ***Receiving aid:*** *Freshmen:* 40% (363); *all full-time undergraduates:* 39% (1,378). ***Average award:*** Freshmen: $2077; Undergraduates: $1990. ***Scholarships, grants, and awards:*** Federal Pell, FSEOG, state, private.

GIFT AID (NON-NEED-BASED) ***Total amount:*** $2,768,107 (2% state, 77% institutional, 21% external sources). ***Receiving aid:*** *Freshmen:* 25% (234); *Undergraduates:* 17% (596). ***Scholarships, grants, and awards by category:*** *Academic Interests/Achievement:* 622 awards ($1,249,285 total): agriculture, general academic interests/achievements. *Creative Arts/Performance:* 228 awards ($351,116 total): creative writing, journalism/publications, music. *Special Achievements/Activities:* 130 awards ($140,163 total): cheerleading/drum major, general special achievements/activities. *Special Characteristics:* 228 awards ($151,061 total): adult students, children of faculty/staff. ***Tuition waivers:*** Full or partial for employees or children of employees, senior citizens. ***ROTC:*** Army.

LOANS ***Student loans:*** $6,754,199 (64% need-based, 36% non-need-based). Average indebtedness per student: $15,849. ***Average need-based loan:*** Freshmen: $857; Undergraduates: $2053. ***Parent loans:*** $146,943 (100% non-need-based). ***Programs:*** FFEL (Subsidized and Unsubsidized Stafford, PLUS), Perkins, state.

WORK-STUDY ***Federal work-study:*** *Total amount:* $207,477; 192 jobs averaging $1148. ***State or other work-study/employment:*** *Total amount:* $398,831 (100% non-need-based). Part-time jobs available.

ATHLETIC AWARDS *Total amount:* 411,623 (100% non-need-based).

APPLYING for FINANCIAL AID ***Required financial aid forms:*** FAFSA, institution's own form. ***Financial aid deadline (priority):*** 4/15. ***Notification date:*** Continuous beginning 6/20. Students must reply within 2 weeks of notification.

CONTACT Ms. Sonya Jones, Student Aid Officer, Arkansas Tech University, Bryan Student Services Building, Room 117, Russellville, AR 72801-2222, 501-968-0377 or toll-free 800-582-6953 (in-state). *Fax:* 501-964-0857. *E-mail:* sonya.jones@mail.atu.edu

ARLINGTON BAPTIST COLLEGE

Arlington, TX

Tuition & fees: $3610 **Average undergraduate aid package: N/A**

ABOUT THE INSTITUTION Independent Baptist, coed. Awards: bachelor's degrees. 7 undergraduate majors. Total enrollment: 227. Undergraduates: 227. Freshmen: 61. Federal methodology is used as a basis for awarding need-based institutional aid.

UNDERGRADUATE EXPENSES for 1999–2000 ***Application fee:*** $15. ***Tuition:*** full-time $3360; part-time $105 per semester hour. ***Required fees:*** full-time $250; $125 per term part-time. ***Payment plans:*** installment, deferred payment.

FRESHMAN FINANCIAL AID (Fall 1998) 37 applied for aid; of those 86% were deemed to have need. 100% of freshmen with need received aid. *Average percent of need met:* 75% (excluding resources awarded to replace EFC).

UNDERGRADUATE FINANCIAL AID (Fall 1998) 129 applied for aid; of those 78% were deemed to have need. 100% of undergraduates with need received aid. *Average percent of need met:* 75% (excluding resources awarded to replace EFC).

GIFT AID (NEED-BASED) ***Total amount:*** $282,538 (57% Federal, 43% institutional). ***Receiving aid:*** *Freshmen:* 53% (30); *all full-time undergraduates:* 50% (94). ***Average award:*** Freshmen: $5811; Undergraduates: $5811. ***Scholarships, grants, and awards:*** Federal Pell, private, college/university gift aid from institutional funds.

GIFT AID (NON-NEED-BASED) ***Receiving aid:*** *Freshmen:* 4% (2); *Undergraduates:* 4% (7). ***Scholarships, grants, and awards by category:*** *Special Characteristics:* children of faculty/staff, spouses of current students. ***Tuition waivers:*** Full or partial for employees or children of employees.

LOANS ***Student loans:*** $386,613 (100% need-based). 60% of past graduating class borrowed through all loan programs. ***Programs:*** FFEL (Subsidized and Unsubsidized Stafford, PLUS).

WORK-STUDY Federal work-study jobs available.

APPLYING for FINANCIAL AID ***Required financial aid form:*** FAFSA. ***Financial aid deadline (priority):*** 8/1. ***Notification date:*** Continuous beginning 9/1.

CONTACT Mr. David B. Clogston Jr., Business Manager, Arlington Baptist College, 3001 West Division Street, Arlington, TX 76012-3425, 817-461-8741 Ext. 110. *Fax:* 817-274-1138.

ARMSTRONG ATLANTIC STATE UNIVERSITY

Savannah, GA

Tuition & fees (GA res): $2388 **Average undergraduate aid package: N/A**

ABOUT THE INSTITUTION State-supported, coed. Awards: associate, bachelor's, and master's degrees. 36 undergraduate majors. Total enrollment: 5,668. Undergraduates: 5,157. Freshmen: 750. Federal methodology is used as a basis for awarding need-based institutional aid.

UNDERGRADUATE EXPENSES for 1999–2000 ***Application fee:*** $20. ***Tuition, state resident:*** full-time $2098; part-time $76 per credit hour. ***Tuition,***

nonresident: full-time $7522; part-time $226 per credit hour. ***Required fees:*** full-time $290; $145 per term part-time. Part-time tuition and fees vary according to course load. ***College room and board:*** $4460; ***room only:*** $2610.

GIFT AID (NEED-BASED) ***Scholarships, grants, and awards:*** Federal Pell, FSEOG, state, private, college/university gift aid from institutional funds.

GIFT AID (NON-NEED-BASED) ***Scholarships, grants, and awards by category:*** *Academic Interests/Achievement:* biological sciences, computer science, education, engineering/technologies, English, general academic interests/achievements, health fields, humanities, mathematics, military science, physical sciences. *Creative Arts/Performance:* art/fine arts, music. ***Tuition waivers:*** Full or partial for employees or children of employees, senior citizens. ***ROTC:*** Army, Naval.

LOANS ***Programs:*** FFEL (Subsidized and Unsubsidized Stafford, PLUS).

WORK-STUDY Federal work-study jobs available. ***State or other work-study/employment:*** Part-time jobs available.

APPLYING for FINANCIAL AID ***Required financial aid form:*** FAFSA. ***Financial aid deadline (priority):*** 3/15. ***Notification date:*** Continuous. Students must reply within 2 weeks of notification.

CONTACT Mr. Brad Burnett, Director of Financial Aid, Armstrong Atlantic State University, 11935 Abercorn Street, Savannah, GA 31419-1997, 912-921-7498 or toll-free 800-633-2349. *Fax:* 912-921-7357. *E-mail:* financial_aid@mailgate.armstrong.edu

ARMSTRONG UNIVERSITY

Oakland, CA

CONTACT Ms. Patricia Fredette, Director of Financial Aid, Armstrong University, 1608 Webster Street, Oakland, CA 94612, 510-848-2500.

ARNOLD & MARIE SCHWARTZ COLLEGE OF PHARMACY AND HEALTH SCIENCES

Brooklyn, NY

See Long Island University, Brooklyn Campus

ART ACADEMY OF CINCINNATI

Cincinnati, OH

Tuition & fees: $12,200 **Average undergraduate aid package: $7886**

ABOUT THE INSTITUTION Independent, coed. Awards: associate, bachelor's, and master's degrees. 7 undergraduate majors. Total enrollment: 216. Undergraduates: 216. Freshmen: 50. Federal methodology is used as a basis for awarding need-based institutional aid.

UNDERGRADUATE EXPENSES for 2000–2001 ***Application fee:*** $25. ***Tuition:*** full-time $12,200; part-time $465 per credit hour. Part-time tuition and fees vary according to course load. ***Payment plan:*** installment.

FRESHMAN FINANCIAL AID (Fall 1999, est.) 44 applied for aid; of those 82% were deemed to have need. 100% of freshmen with need received aid; of those 28% had need fully met. *Average percent of need met:* 63% (excluding resources awarded to replace EFC). *Average financial aid package:* $7498 (excluding resources awarded to replace EFC).

UNDERGRADUATE FINANCIAL AID (Fall 1999, est.) 144 applied for aid; of those 87% were deemed to have need. 100% of undergraduates with need received aid; of those 24% had need fully met. *Average percent of need met:* 64% (excluding resources awarded to replace EFC). *Average financial aid package:* $7886 (excluding resources awarded to replace EFC).

GIFT AID (NEED-BASED) ***Total amount:*** $442,295 (20% Federal, 29% state, 44% institutional, 7% external sources). ***Receiving aid:*** *Freshmen:* 32% (35); *all full-time undergraduates:* 54% (116). ***Average award:*** Freshmen: $3343; Undergraduates: $3207. ***Scholarships, grants, and awards:*** Federal Pell, FSEOG, state, private, college/university gift aid from institutional funds.

GIFT AID (NON-NEED-BASED) ***Total amount:*** $184,987 (24% state, 54% institutional, 22% external sources). ***Receiving aid:*** *Freshmen:* 5% (5); *Undergraduates:* 4% (9). ***Scholarships, grants, and awards by category:*** *Creative Arts/Performance:* 92 awards ($249,198 total): applied art and design, art/fine arts. ***Tuition waivers:*** Full or partial for employees or children of employees. ***ROTC:*** Army cooperative, Naval cooperative, Air Force cooperative.

LOANS ***Student loans:*** $839,284 (77% need-based, 23% non-need-based). 64% of past graduating class borrowed through all loan programs. Average indebtedness per student: $11,290. ***Average need-based loan:*** Freshmen: $4154; Undergraduates: $4679. ***Parent loans:*** $496,281 (36% need-based, 64% non-need-based). ***Programs:*** FFEL (Subsidized and Unsubsidized Stafford, PLUS), state, college/university, alternative loans.

WORK-STUDY ***Federal work-study:*** *Total amount:* $20,439; 22 jobs averaging $929. ***State or other work-study/employment:*** *Total amount:* $29,936 (100% non-need-based). 28 part-time jobs averaging $1069.

APPLYING for FINANCIAL AID ***Required financial aid form:*** FAFSA. ***Financial aid deadline (priority):*** 3/1. ***Notification date:*** Continuous beginning 5/1. Students must reply within 2 weeks of notification.

CONTACT Ms. Karen Geiger, Director of Financial Aid, Art Academy of Cincinnati, 1125 Saint Gregory Street, Cincinnati, OH 45202-1700, 513-721-5205. *Fax:* 513-562-8778. *E-mail:* financialaid@artacademy.edu

ART CENTER COLLEGE OF DESIGN

Pasadena, CA

Tuition & fees: $18,890 **Average undergraduate aid package: $15,460**

ABOUT THE INSTITUTION Independent, coed. Awards: bachelor's and master's degrees. 8 undergraduate majors. Total enrollment: 1,438. Undergraduates: 1,345. Freshmen: 33. Federal methodology is used as a basis for awarding need-based institutional aid.

UNDERGRADUATE EXPENSES for 1999–2000 ***Application fee:*** $45. ***Tuition:*** full-time $18,890. ***Payment plan:*** installment.

FRESHMAN FINANCIAL AID (Fall 1999, est.) 173 applied for aid; of those 94% were deemed to have need. 98% of freshmen with need received aid. *Average percent of need met:* 45% (excluding resources awarded to replace EFC). *Average financial aid package:* $11,900 (excluding resources awarded to replace EFC). 2% of all full-time freshmen had no need and received non-need-based aid.

UNDERGRADUATE FINANCIAL AID (Fall 1999, est.) 972 applied for aid; of those 94% were deemed to have need. 96% of undergraduates with need received aid. *Average percent of need met:* 50% (excluding resources awarded to replace EFC). *Average financial aid package:* $15,460 (excluding resources awarded to replace EFC). 2% of all full-time undergraduates had no need and received non-need-based aid.

GIFT AID (NEED-BASED) ***Total amount:*** $4,916,745 (23% Federal, 40% state, 36% institutional, 1% external sources). ***Receiving aid:*** *Freshmen:* 51% (113); *all full-time undergraduates:* 52% (666). ***Average award:*** Freshmen: $6725; Undergraduates: $8325. ***Scholarships, grants, and awards:*** Federal Pell, FSEOG, state, private, college/university gift aid from institutional funds.

GIFT AID (NON-NEED-BASED) ***Tuition waivers:*** Full or partial for employees or children of employees.

LOANS ***Student loans:*** $8,737,669 (70% need-based, 30% non-need-based). 56% of past graduating class borrowed through all loan programs. ***Average need-based loan:*** Freshmen: $5028; Undergraduates: $6853. ***Parent loans:*** $1,170,814 (100% non-need-based). ***Programs:*** FFEL (Subsidized and Unsubsidized Stafford, PLUS), Perkins, college/university, alternative loans.

WORK-STUDY ***Federal work-study:*** *Total amount:* $275,000; 120 jobs averaging $2290.

APPLYING for FINANCIAL AID ***Required financial aid form:*** FAFSA. ***Financial aid deadline (priority):*** 3/1. ***Notification date:*** Continuous. Students must reply within 4 weeks of notification.

Art Center College of Design (continued)

CONTACT Clema McKenzie, Director of Financial Aid, Art Center College of Design, 1700 Lida Street, Pasadena, CA 91103-1999, 626-396-2215. *Fax:* 626-683-8684. *E-mail:* finaid@artcenter.edu

THE ART INSTITUTE OF BOSTON AT LESLEY

Boston, MA

ABOUT THE INSTITUTION Independent, coed. Awards: bachelor's degrees. 8 undergraduate majors. Total enrollment: 508. Undergraduates: 508. Freshmen: 112.

GIFT AID (NEED-BASED) ***Scholarships, grants, and awards:*** Federal Pell, FSEOG, state, private, college/university gift aid from institutional funds.

GIFT AID (NON-NEED-BASED) ***Scholarships, grants, and awards by category:*** *Academic Interests/Achievement:* general academic interests/achievements. *Creative Arts/Performance:* applied art and design, art/fine arts. *Special Achievements/Activities:* memberships. *Special Characteristics:* local/state students, members of minority groups.

LOANS ***Programs:*** FFEL (Subsidized and Unsubsidized Stafford, PLUS), state.

WORK-STUDY Federal work-study jobs available.

APPLYING for FINANCIAL AID ***Required financial aid forms:*** FAFSA, institution's own form, CSS Financial Aid PROFILE, financial aid transcript (for transfers), state income tax form.

CONTACT Ms. Atoosa Malekani, Assistant Financial Aid Officer, The Art Institute of Boston at Lesley, 700 Beacon Street, Boston, MA 02215-2598, 617-262-1223 Ext. 395 or toll-free 800-773-0494 (in-state). *Fax:* 617-437-1226.

THE ART INSTITUTE OF COLORADO

Denver, CO

Tuition & fees: $12,480 **Average undergraduate aid package: N/A**

ABOUT THE INSTITUTION Proprietary, coed. Awards: associate and bachelor's degrees. 11 undergraduate majors. Total enrollment: 1,977. Undergraduates: 1,977. Federal methodology is used as a basis for awarding need-based institutional aid.

UNDERGRADUATE EXPENSES for 2000–2001 ***Application fee:*** $50. ***Comprehensive fee:*** $18,480 includes full-time tuition ($12,480) and room and board ($6000). Full-time tuition and fees vary according to course load, degree level, and program. Room and board charges vary according to board plan, housing facility, and location. ***Part-time tuition:*** $260 per credit. Part-time tuition and fees vary according to course load and program. ***Payment plans:*** guaranteed tuition, installment.

UNDERGRADUATE FINANCIAL AID (Fall 1998) 1,621 applied for aid; of those 100% were deemed to have need. 100% of undergraduates with need received aid.

GIFT AID (NEED-BASED) ***Total amount:*** $2,164,230 (70% Federal, 12% state, 18% institutional). ***Receiving aid:*** *All full-time undergraduates:* 30% (591). ***Scholarships, grants, and awards:*** Federal Pell, FSEOG, state, private, college/university gift aid from institutional funds.

GIFT AID (NON-NEED-BASED) ***Total amount:*** $447,859 (17% state, 71% institutional, 12% external sources). ***Receiving aid:*** *Undergraduates:* 3% (65). ***Scholarships, grants, and awards by category:*** *Academic Interests/Achievement:* general academic interests/achievements. *Creative Arts/Performance:* applied art and design, art/fine arts, cinema/film/broadcasting, general creative arts/performance. *Special Achievements/Activities:* general special achievements/activities, junior miss. ***Tuition waivers:*** Full or partial for employees or children of employees.

LOANS ***Student loans:*** $9,668,153 (56% need-based, 44% non-need-based). 70% of past graduating class borrowed through all loan programs. Average indebtedness per student: $30,000. ***Parent loans:*** $3,232,127 (100% need-based). ***Programs:*** FFEL (Subsidized and Unsubsidized Stafford, PLUS), Perkins, state.

WORK-STUDY ***Federal work-study:*** *Total amount:* $51,006; 5 jobs averaging $6160. ***State or other work-study/employment:*** *Total amount:* $161,212 (91% need-based, 9% non-need-based). 34 part-time jobs averaging $6160.

APPLYING for FINANCIAL AID ***Required financial aid forms:*** FAFSA, institution's own form. ***Financial aid deadline:*** Continuous. ***Notification date:*** Continuous beginning 2/1. Students must reply within 2 weeks of notification.

CONTACT Deborah Spindler, Director of Student Financial Services, The Art Institute of Colorado, 200 East Ninth Avenue, Denver, CO 80203-2903, 303-837-0825 Ext. 575 or toll-free 800-275-2420. *Fax:* 303-860-8520. *E-mail:* spindled@aii.edu

THE ART INSTITUTE OF PHOENIX

Phoenix, AZ

ABOUT THE INSTITUTION Proprietary, coed, primarily men. Awards: associate and bachelor's degrees. 7 undergraduate majors. Total enrollment: 900. Undergraduates: 900.

GIFT AID (NEED-BASED) ***Scholarships, grants, and awards:*** Federal Pell, FSEOG, state, college/university gift aid from institutional funds.

LOANS ***Programs:*** FFEL (Subsidized and Unsubsidized Stafford, PLUS), Perkins.

WORK-STUDY Federal work-study jobs available.

APPLYING for FINANCIAL AID ***Required financial aid form:*** FAFSA.

CONTACT Paula A. Cady, Director of Student Financial Services, The Art Institute of Phoenix, 2233 West Dunlap Avenue, Phoenix, AZ 85021-2859, 800-474-2479 Ext. 109 or toll-free 800-474-2479 Ext. 114 (in-state). *Fax:* 602-997-0191. *E-mail:* cadyp@aii.edu

THE ART INSTITUTE OF PORTLAND

Portland, OR

Tuition & fees: $12,060 **Average undergraduate aid package: $2100**

ABOUT THE INSTITUTION Proprietary, coed. Awards: associate and bachelor's degrees. 5 undergraduate majors. Total enrollment: 443. Undergraduates: 443. Freshmen: 81. Federal methodology is used as a basis for awarding need-based institutional aid.

UNDERGRADUATE EXPENSES for 1999–2000 ***Application fee:*** $50. ***Tuition:*** full-time $12,060; part-time $268 per credit. ***Payment plans:*** guaranteed tuition, installment.

FRESHMAN FINANCIAL AID (Fall 1999, est.) 70 applied for aid; of those 90% were deemed to have need. 97% of freshmen with need received aid; of those 3% had need fully met. *Average percent of need met:* 3% (excluding resources awarded to replace EFC). *Average financial aid package:* $1900 (excluding resources awarded to replace EFC).

UNDERGRADUATE FINANCIAL AID (Fall 1999, est.) 275 applied for aid; of those 91% were deemed to have need. 97% of undergraduates with need received aid; of those 2% had need fully met. *Average percent of need met:* 2% (excluding resources awarded to replace EFC). *Average financial aid package:* $2100 (excluding resources awarded to replace EFC). 1% of all full-time undergraduates had no need and received non-need-based aid.

GIFT AID (NEED-BASED) ***Total amount:*** $507,000 (64% Federal, 35% institutional, 1% external sources). ***Receiving aid:*** *Freshmen:* 64% (52); *all full-time undergraduates:* 20% (73). ***Average award:*** Freshmen: $1100; Undergraduates: $1050. ***Scholarships, grants, and awards:*** Federal Pell, FSEOG, private, college/university gift aid from institutional funds.

GIFT AID (NON-NEED-BASED) ***Total amount:*** $80,000 (56% institutional, 44% external sources). ***Receiving aid:*** *Freshmen:* 12% (10); *Undergraduates:* 3% (12). ***Scholarships, grants, and awards by category:*** *Special Characteristics:* 4 awards ($46,620 total): children of faculty/staff. ***Tuition waivers:*** Full or partial for employees or children of employees.

LOANS ***Student loans:*** $3,200,000 (100% need-based). 50% of past graduating class borrowed through all loan programs. Average indebtedness per student: $10,490. ***Average need-based loan:*** Freshmen: $897;

Undergraduates: $1223. ***Parent loans:*** $1,400,000 (100% need-based). ***Programs:*** FFEL (Subsidized and Unsubsidized Stafford, PLUS).

WORK-STUDY ***Federal work-study:*** *Total amount:* $1393; 2 jobs averaging $1393.

APPLYING for FINANCIAL AID ***Required financial aid forms:*** FAFSA, financial aid transcript (for transfers). ***Financial aid deadline:*** Continuous. ***Notification date:*** Continuous beginning 2/1. Students must reply within 5 weeks of notification.

CONTACT Mr. Mickey Jacobson, Director of Student Financial Services, The Art Institute of Portland, 2000 Southwest Fifth Avenue, Portland, OR 97201-4907, 503-228-6528 Ext. 102 or toll-free 888-228-6528. *Fax:* 503-228-4227. *E-mail:* jacobsom@aii.edu

ART INSTITUTE OF SOUTHERN CALIFORNIA

Laguna Beach, CA

Tuition & fees: $13,600 **Average undergraduate aid package: N/A**

ABOUT THE INSTITUTION Independent, coed. Awards: bachelor's degrees. 3 undergraduate majors. Total enrollment: 244. Undergraduates: 244. Both federal and institutional methodology are used as a basis for awarding need-based institutional aid.

UNDERGRADUATE EXPENSES for 2000–2001 (est.) ***Application fee:*** $35. ***Tuition:*** full-time $13,400; part-time $560 per unit. ***Required fees:*** full-time $200. ***Payment plan:*** installment.

GIFT AID (NEED-BASED) ***Scholarships, grants, and awards:*** Federal Pell, FSEOG, state, private, college/university gift aid from institutional funds.

GIFT AID (NON-NEED-BASED) ***Scholarships, grants, and awards by category:*** *Academic Interests/Achievement:* general academic interests/achievements. *Creative Arts/Performance:* applied art and design, art/fine arts. ***Tuition waivers:*** Full or partial for employees or children of employees.

LOANS ***Programs:*** FFEL (Subsidized and Unsubsidized Stafford, PLUS).

WORK-STUDY Federal work-study jobs available.

APPLYING for FINANCIAL AID ***Required financial aid forms:*** FAFSA, institution's own form, CSS Financial Aid PROFILE.

CONTACT Christopher Brown, Assistant Dean, Financial Aid, Art Institute of Southern California, 2222 Laguna Canyon Road, Laguna Beach, CA 92651-1136, 949-376-6000 or toll-free 800-255-0762. *Fax:* 949-376-6009.

THE ART INSTITUTE OF WASHINGTON

Arlington, VA

CONTACT Financial Aid Office, The Art Institute of Washington, 1820 North Fort Meyer Drive, Ground Floor, Arlington, VA 22209, 703-358-9550 or toll-free 877-303-3771.

ART INSTITUTES INTERNATIONAL AT SAN FRANCISCO

San Francisco, CA

Tuition & fees: $14,160 **Average undergraduate aid package: N/A**

ABOUT THE INSTITUTION Independent, coed. Awards: associate and bachelor's degrees. 4 undergraduate majors. Total enrollment: 215. Undergraduates: 215. Freshmen: 69. Both federal and institutional methodology are used as a basis for awarding need-based institutional aid.

UNDERGRADUATE EXPENSES for 1999–2000 ***Application fee:*** $50. ***Tuition:*** full-time $14,160; part-time $295 per quarter hour. Full-time tuition and fees vary according to course load. Part-time tuition and fees vary according to course load. College housing is available through the California Culinary Academy. ***Payment plans:*** guaranteed tuition, installment.

GIFT AID (NEED-BASED) ***Scholarships, grants, and awards:*** Federal Pell, FSEOG, state, private.

GIFT AID (NON-NEED-BASED) ***Scholarships, grants, and awards by category:*** *Creative Arts/Performance:* general creative arts/performance. ***Tuition waivers:*** Full or partial for employees or children of employees.

LOANS ***Programs:*** FFEL (Subsidized and Unsubsidized Stafford, PLUS).

WORK-STUDY Federal work-study jobs available. ***State or other work-study/employment:*** Part-time jobs available.

APPLYING for FINANCIAL AID ***Required financial aid forms:*** FAFSA, institution's own form. ***Financial aid deadline (priority):*** 3/2.

CONTACT Brian Cronkright, Director of Student Financial Services, Art Institutes International at San Francisco, 1170 Market Street, San Francisco, CA 94102-4908, 415-865-0198 or toll-free 888-493-3261.

ASBURY COLLEGE

Wilmore, KY

Tuition & fees: $13,784 **Average undergraduate aid package: $10,010**

ABOUT THE INSTITUTION Independent nondenominational, coed. Awards: bachelor's degrees. 37 undergraduate majors. Total enrollment: 1,317. Undergraduates: 1,317. Freshmen: 328. Federal methodology is used as a basis for awarding need-based institutional aid.

UNDERGRADUATE EXPENSES for 2000–2001 ***Application fee:*** $25. ***Comprehensive fee:*** $17,350 includes full-time tuition ($13,644), mandatory fees ($140), and room and board ($3566). ***College room only:*** $1838. Full-time tuition and fees vary according to course load. Room and board charges vary according to board plan, gender, and housing facility. ***Part-time tuition:*** $560 per semester hour. Part-time tuition and fees vary according to course load. ***Payment plans:*** installment, deferred payment.

FRESHMAN FINANCIAL AID (Fall 1999) 270 applied for aid; of those 81% were deemed to have need. 100% of freshmen with need received aid; of those 30% had need fully met. *Average percent of need met:* 85% (excluding resources awarded to replace EFC). *Average financial aid package:* $10,092 (excluding resources awarded to replace EFC). 15% of all full-time freshmen had no need and received non-need-based aid.

UNDERGRADUATE FINANCIAL AID (Fall 1999) 963 applied for aid; of those 86% were deemed to have need. 99% of undergraduates with need received aid; of those 28% had need fully met. *Average percent of need met:* 83% (excluding resources awarded to replace EFC). *Average financial aid package:* $10,010 (excluding resources awarded to replace EFC). 11% of all full-time undergraduates had no need and received non-need-based aid.

GIFT AID (NEED-BASED) ***Total amount:*** $4,915,964 (14% Federal, 7% state, 65% institutional, 14% external sources). ***Receiving aid:*** *Freshmen:* 66% (214); *all full-time undergraduates:* 63% (797). ***Average award:*** Freshmen: $5363; Undergraduates: $5165. ***Scholarships, grants, and awards:*** Federal Pell, FSEOG, state, private, college/university gift aid from institutional funds.

GIFT AID (NON-NEED-BASED) ***Total amount:*** $999,912 (80% institutional, 20% external sources). ***Receiving aid:*** *Freshmen:* 28% (90); *Undergraduates:* 17% (209). ***Scholarships, grants, and awards by category:*** *Academic Interests/Achievement:* 339 awards ($1,069,689 total): general academic interests/achievements. *Creative Arts/Performance:* 22 awards ($24,439 total): music. *Special Characteristics:* 156 awards ($605,047 total): children and siblings of alumni, children of current students, children of faculty/staff, international students, siblings of current students. ***Tuition waivers:*** Full or partial for employees or children of employees, senior citizens. ***ROTC:*** Army cooperative, Air Force cooperative.

LOANS ***Student loans:*** $3,460,243 (91% need-based, 9% non-need-based). 69% of past graduating class borrowed through all loan programs. Average indebtedness per student: $17,222. ***Average need-based loan:*** Freshmen: $3318; Undergraduates: $3872. ***Parent loans:*** $783,051 (82% need-based, 18% non-need-based). ***Programs:*** FFEL (Subsidized and Unsubsidized Stafford, PLUS), Perkins, college/university.

WORK-STUDY ***Federal work-study:*** *Total amount:* $549,326; 484 jobs averaging $1135. ***State or other work-study/employment:*** *Total amount:* $84,546 (61% need-based, 39% non-need-based). 20 part-time jobs averaging $2562.

Asbury College (continued)

APPLYING for FINANCIAL AID ***Required financial aid forms:*** FAFSA, institution's own form. ***Financial aid deadline (priority):*** 3/1. ***Notification date:*** Continuous. Students must reply within 2 weeks of notification.

CONTACT Mr. Douglas B. Cleary, Director of Financial Aid, Asbury College, 1 Macklem Drive, Wilmore, KY 40390-1198, 606-858-3511 Ext. 2195 or toll-free 800-888-1818. *Fax:* 606-858-3921. *E-mail:* doug.cleary@asbury.edu

ASHLAND UNIVERSITY

Ashland, OH

Tuition & fees: $14,676 **Average undergraduate aid package: $14,415**

ABOUT THE INSTITUTION Independent religious, coed. Awards: associate, bachelor's, master's, doctoral, and first professional degrees. 70 undergraduate majors. Total enrollment: 6,102. Undergraduates: 2,850. Freshmen: 543. Federal methodology is used as a basis for awarding need-based institutional aid.

UNDERGRADUATE EXPENSES for 1999–2000 ***Application fee:*** $25. ***Comprehensive fee:*** $20,126 includes full-time tuition ($14,276), mandatory fees ($400), and room and board ($5450). ***College room only:*** $2873. Full-time tuition and fees vary according to class time, course load, and program. Room and board charges vary according to board plan and housing facility. ***Part-time tuition:*** $439 per credit hour. Part-time tuition and fees vary according to class time and program. ***Payment plan:*** installment.

FRESHMAN FINANCIAL AID (Fall 1999, est.) 529 applied for aid; of those 77% were deemed to have need. 100% of freshmen with need received aid. *Average percent of need met:* 90% (excluding resources awarded to replace EFC). *Average financial aid package:* $14,124 (excluding resources awarded to replace EFC). 14% of all full-time freshmen had no need and received non-need-based aid.

UNDERGRADUATE FINANCIAL AID (Fall 1999, est.) 1,990 applied for aid; of those 78% were deemed to have need. 100% of undergraduates with need received aid. *Average percent of need met:* 90% (excluding resources awarded to replace EFC). *Average financial aid package:* $14,415 (excluding resources awarded to replace EFC). 14% of all full-time undergraduates had no need and received non-need-based aid.

GIFT AID (NEED-BASED) ***Total amount:*** $18,486,645 (7% Federal, 19% state, 72% institutional, 2% external sources). ***Receiving aid:*** *Freshmen:* 76% (408); *all full-time undergraduates:* 71% (1,549). ***Average award:*** Freshmen: $8992; Undergraduates: $8251. ***Scholarships, grants, and awards:*** Federal Pell, FSEOG, state, college/university gift aid from institutional funds.

GIFT AID (NON-NEED-BASED) ***Total amount:*** $3,478,825 (14% state, 85% institutional, 1% external sources). ***Scholarships, grants, and awards by category:*** *Academic Interests/Achievement:* biological sciences, business, communication, computer science, education, English, foreign languages, general academic interests/achievements, home economics, humanities, international studies, mathematics, physical sciences, religion/biblical studies, social sciences. *Creative Arts/Performance:* art/fine arts, music, theater/drama. *Special Achievements/Activities:* leadership, religious involvement. *Special Characteristics:* 70 awards ($517,905 total): children and siblings of alumni, children of faculty/staff, religious affiliation, siblings of current students. ***Tuition waivers:*** Full or partial for employees or children of employees, senior citizens. ***ROTC:*** Air Force cooperative.

LOANS ***Student loans:*** $8,354,134 (90% need-based, 10% non-need-based). 63% of past graduating class borrowed through all loan programs. Average indebtedness per student: $18,100. ***Average need-based loan:*** Freshmen: $3169; Undergraduates: $4004. ***Parent loans:*** $1,800,000 (100% non-need-based). ***Programs:*** Federal Direct (Subsidized and Unsubsidized Stafford, PLUS), Perkins, college/university.

WORK-STUDY ***Federal work-study:*** *Total amount:* $1,142,364; 771 jobs averaging $1481. ***State or other work-study/employment:*** *Total amount:* $285,072 (76% need-based, 24% non-need-based). 63 part-time jobs available.

ATHLETIC AWARDS *Total amount:* 2,626,749 (69% need-based, 31% non-need-based).

APPLYING for FINANCIAL AID ***Required financial aid forms:*** FAFSA, institution's own form. ***Financial aid deadline:*** 3/15. ***Notification date:*** Continuous. Students must reply within 3 weeks of notification.

CONTACT Mr. Stephen C. Howell, Director of Financial Aid, Ashland University, 401 College Avenue, Room 312, Ashland, OH 44805-3702, 419-289-5002 or toll-free 800-882-1548. *E-mail:* showell@ashland.edu

ASSUMPTION COLLEGE

Worcester, MA

Tuition & fees: $17,490 **Average undergraduate aid package: $13,065**

ABOUT THE INSTITUTION Independent Roman Catholic, coed. Awards: associate, bachelor's, and master's degrees and post-master's certificates. 35 undergraduate majors. Total enrollment: 2,694. Undergraduates: 2,352. Freshmen: 492. Federal methodology is used as a basis for awarding need-based institutional aid.

UNDERGRADUATE EXPENSES for 1999–2000 ***Application fee:*** $40. ***Comprehensive fee:*** $24,250 includes full-time tuition ($17,320), mandatory fees ($170), and room and board ($6760). ***College room only:*** $4140. Full-time tuition and fees vary according to course load and reciprocity agreements. Room and board charges vary according to board plan and housing facility. ***Part-time tuition:*** $577 per credit. ***Part-time fees:*** $170 per year part-time. Part-time tuition and fees vary according to course load and student level. ***Payment plan:*** installment.

FRESHMAN FINANCIAL AID (Fall 1999, est.) 509 applied for aid; of those 87% were deemed to have need. 100% of freshmen with need received aid; of those 36% had need fully met. *Average percent of need met:* 82% (excluding resources awarded to replace EFC). *Average financial aid package:* $12,969 (excluding resources awarded to replace EFC). 18% of all full-time freshmen had no need and received non-need-based aid.

UNDERGRADUATE FINANCIAL AID (Fall 1999, est.) 1,513 applied for aid; of those 90% were deemed to have need. 100% of undergraduates with need received aid; of those 34% had need fully met. *Average percent of need met:* 82% (excluding resources awarded to replace EFC). *Average financial aid package:* $13,065 (excluding resources awarded to replace EFC). 15% of all full-time undergraduates had no need and received non-need-based aid.

GIFT AID (NEED-BASED) ***Total amount:*** $10,961,467 (5% Federal, 6% state, 86% institutional, 3% external sources). ***Receiving aid:*** *Freshmen:* 75% (443); *all full-time undergraduates:* 70% (1,336). ***Average award:*** Freshmen: $8894; Undergraduates: $8230. ***Scholarships, grants, and awards:*** Federal Pell, FSEOG, state, private, college/university gift aid from institutional funds.

GIFT AID (NON-NEED-BASED) ***Total amount:*** $2,166,364 (97% institutional, 3% external sources). ***Receiving aid:*** *Freshmen:* 10% (59); *Undergraduates:* 8% (146). ***Scholarships, grants, and awards by category:*** *Academic Interests/Achievement:* 885 awards ($5,660,000 total): general academic interests/achievements. *Special Characteristics:* 64 awards ($127,000 total): ethnic background, first-generation college students, local/state students, members of minority groups, siblings of current students. ***Tuition waivers:*** Full or partial for minority students, employees or children of employees. ***ROTC:*** Army cooperative, Naval cooperative, Air Force cooperative.

LOANS ***Student loans:*** $7,836,242 (73% need-based, 27% non-need-based). 77% of past graduating class borrowed through all loan programs. Average indebtedness per student: $16,400. ***Average need-based loan:*** Freshmen: $3694; Undergraduates: $4518. ***Parent loans:*** $3,098,653 (29% need-based, 71% non-need-based). ***Programs:*** FFEL (Subsidized and Unsubsidized Stafford, PLUS), Perkins, state, college/university.

WORK-STUDY ***Federal work-study:*** *Total amount:* $430,345; 451 jobs averaging $1023.

ATHLETIC AWARDS *Total amount:* 476,540 (5% need-based, 95% non-need-based).

APPLYING for FINANCIAL AID ***Required financial aid form:*** FAFSA. ***Financial aid deadline:*** 3/1 (priority: 2/1). ***Notification date:*** Continuous. Students must reply by 5/1 or within 2 weeks of notification.

CONTACT Carla Berg, Director of Financial Aid, Assumption College, 500 Salisbury Street, PO Box 15005, Worcester, MA 01615-0005, 508-767-7158 or toll-free 888-882-7786. *Fax:* 508-767-7376. *E-mail:* cberg@assumption.edu

ATHENS STATE UNIVERSITY

Athens, AL

Tuition & fees (AL res): $2400 **Average undergraduate aid package: N/A**

ABOUT THE INSTITUTION State-supported, coed. Awards: bachelor's degrees. 35 undergraduate majors. Total enrollment: 2,790. Undergraduates: 2,790. Federal methodology is used as a basis for awarding need-based institutional aid.

UNDERGRADUATE EXPENSES for 1999–2000 ***Application fee:*** $30. ***Tuition, state resident:*** full-time $2336; part-time $73 per semester hour. ***Tuition, nonresident:*** full-time $4672; part-time $146 per semester hour. ***Required fees:*** full-time $64; $2 per semester hour. Full-time tuition and fees vary according to course load. Part-time tuition and fees vary according to course load. ***College room and board: room only:*** $840.

UNDERGRADUATE FINANCIAL AID (Fall 1998) 2,751 applied for aid.

GIFT AID (NEED-BASED) ***Total amount:*** $1,854,443 (81% Federal, 19% state). ***Scholarships, grants, and awards:*** Federal Pell, FSEOG, state, private, college/university gift aid from institutional funds.

GIFT AID (NON-NEED-BASED) ***Total amount:*** $428,207 (33% institutional, 67% external sources). ***Scholarships, grants, and awards by category:*** *Academic Interests/Achievement:* 40 awards ($80,000 total): biological sciences, business, computer science, education, English, general academic interests/achievements, humanities, mathematics, physical sciences, social sciences. *Creative Arts/Performance:* 4 awards ($10,000 total): journalism/publications, music. *Special Achievements/Activities:* 10 awards ($20,000 total): cheerleading/drum major, general special achievements/activities, leadership. *Special Characteristics:* children and siblings of alumni, children of faculty/staff. ***ROTC:*** Army cooperative.

LOANS ***Student loans:*** $5,267,420 (68% need-based, 32% non-need-based). 50% of past graduating class borrowed through all loan programs. ***Programs:*** Federal Direct (Subsidized and Unsubsidized Stafford).

WORK-STUDY ***Federal work-study:*** *Total amount:* $100,000; 51 jobs averaging $2000.

ATHLETIC AWARDS *Total amount:* 72,432 (100% non-need-based).

APPLYING for FINANCIAL AID ***Required financial aid form:*** FAFSA. ***Financial aid deadline:*** Continuous. ***Notification date:*** Continuous beginning 5/1. Students must reply within 2 weeks of notification.

CONTACT Financial Aid Office, Athens State University, 300 North Beaty Street, Athens, AL 35611, 256-233-8122 or toll-free 800-522-0272. *Fax:* 256-233-8178. *E-mail:* huffmjs@athens.edu

ATLANTA CHRISTIAN COLLEGE

East Point, GA

Tuition & fees: $8398 **Average undergraduate aid package: N/A**

ABOUT THE INSTITUTION Independent Christian, coed. Awards: associate and bachelor's degrees. 9 undergraduate majors. Total enrollment: 377. Undergraduates: 377. Federal methodology is used as a basis for awarding need-based institutional aid.

UNDERGRADUATE EXPENSES for 1999–2000 ***Comprehensive fee:*** $12,038 includes full-time tuition ($7900), mandatory fees ($498), and room and board ($3640). Full-time tuition and fees vary according to course load and student level. Room and board charges vary according to board plan. ***Part-time tuition:*** $359 per semester hour. ***Part-time fees:*** $249 per term part-time. Part-time tuition and fees vary according to course load and student level. ***Payment plan:*** installment.

GIFT AID (NEED-BASED) ***Scholarships, grants, and awards:*** Federal Pell, FSEOG, state, college/university gift aid from institutional funds.

GIFT AID (NON-NEED-BASED) ***Scholarships, grants, and awards by category:*** *Academic Interests/Achievement:* general academic interests/achievements. *Creative Arts/Performance:* music. *Special Achievements/Activities:* memberships, religious involvement. *Special Characteristics:* children of faculty/staff, spouses of current students. ***Tuition waivers:*** Full or partial for employees or children of employees, senior citizens.

LOANS ***Programs:*** Federal Direct (Subsidized and Unsubsidized Stafford, PLUS), FFEL (Subsidized and Unsubsidized Stafford, PLUS), state.

WORK-STUDY Federal work-study jobs available.

APPLYING for FINANCIAL AID ***Required financial aid forms:*** FAFSA, institution's own form. ***Financial aid deadline (priority):*** 5/15. ***Notification date:*** Continuous.

CONTACT Blair Walker, Director of Financial Aid, Atlanta Christian College, 2605 Ben Hill Road, East Point, GA 30344, 404-761-8861 or toll-free 800-776-1ACC.

ATLANTA COLLEGE OF ART

Atlanta, GA

Tuition & fees: N/R **Average undergraduate aid package: $11,587**

ABOUT THE INSTITUTION Independent, coed. Awards: bachelor's degrees. 11 undergraduate majors. Total enrollment: 417. Undergraduates: 417. Freshmen: 65. Federal methodology is used as a basis for awarding need-based institutional aid.

FRESHMAN FINANCIAL AID (Fall 1999) 70 applied for aid; of those 87% were deemed to have need. 100% of freshmen with need received aid; of those 10% had need fully met. *Average percent of need met:* 69% (excluding resources awarded to replace EFC). *Average financial aid package:* $10,476 (excluding resources awarded to replace EFC). 10% of all full-time freshmen had no need and received non-need-based aid.

UNDERGRADUATE FINANCIAL AID (Fall 1999) 265 applied for aid; of those 88% were deemed to have need. 100% of undergraduates with need received aid; of those 11% had need fully met. *Average percent of need met:* 72% (excluding resources awarded to replace EFC). *Average financial aid package:* $11,587 (excluding resources awarded to replace EFC). 8% of all full-time undergraduates had no need and received non-need-based aid.

GIFT AID (NEED-BASED) ***Total amount:*** $1,392,316 (21% Federal, 16% state, 53% institutional, 10% external sources). ***Receiving aid:*** *Freshmen:* 63% (59); *all full-time undergraduates:* 56% (222). ***Scholarships, grants, and awards:*** Federal Pell, FSEOG, state, private, college/university gift aid from institutional funds.

GIFT AID (NON-NEED-BASED) ***Total amount:*** $196,729 (52% state, 35% institutional, 13% external sources). ***Receiving aid:*** *Freshmen:* 1% (1); *Undergraduates:* 2% (6). ***Scholarships, grants, and awards by category:*** *Academic Interests/Achievement:* 105 awards ($142,750 total): general academic interests/achievements. *Creative Arts/Performance:* 49 awards ($81,710 total): art/fine arts. ***Tuition waivers:*** Full or partial for employees or children of employees.

LOANS ***Student loans:*** $1,589,839 (83% need-based, 17% non-need-based). 59% of past graduating class borrowed through all loan programs. ***Parent loans:*** $572,918 (43% need-based, 57% non-need-based). ***Programs:*** FFEL (Subsidized and Unsubsidized Stafford, PLUS), college/university.

WORK-STUDY ***Federal work-study:*** *Total amount:* $85,425; 49 jobs averaging $1765.

APPLYING for FINANCIAL AID ***Required financial aid forms:*** FAFSA, institution's own form, need-based aid application form. ***Financial aid deadline (priority):*** 3/15. ***Notification date:*** 4/1. Students must reply within 2 weeks of notification.

CONTACT Ms. Teresa Tantillo, Director of Financial Aid, Atlanta College of Art, 1280 Peachtree Street, NE, Atlanta, GA 30309-3582, 404-733-5111 or toll-free 800-832-2104. *Fax:* 404-733-5107.

ATLANTIC COLLEGE

Guaynabo, PR

Tuition & fees: N/R **Average undergraduate aid package: N/A**

ABOUT THE INSTITUTION Independent. Federal methodology is used as a basis for awarding need-based institutional aid.

FRESHMAN FINANCIAL AID (Fall 1999) 99 applied for aid; of those 84% were deemed to have need. 100% of freshmen with need received aid; of those 5% had need fully met.

UNDERGRADUATE FINANCIAL AID (Fall 1999) 278 applied for aid; of those 90% were deemed to have need. 100% of undergraduates with need received aid; of those 4% had need fully met.

GIFT AID (NEED-BASED) ***Total amount:*** $945,000 (94% Federal, 6% state). ***Scholarships, grants, and awards:*** Federal Pell, FSEOG, state.

LOANS ***Student loans:*** $45,000 (100% need-based). 8% of past graduating class borrowed through all loan programs. Average indebtedness per student: $3000. ***Programs:*** Federal Direct (Subsidized and Unsubsidized Stafford), FFEL (Subsidized and Unsubsidized Stafford).

WORK-STUDY ***Federal work-study:*** *Total amount:* $24,835; 14 jobs averaging $588.

APPLYING for FINANCIAL AID ***Required financial aid forms:*** FAFSA, institution's own form. ***Financial aid deadline:*** Continuous. ***Notification date:*** Continuous. Students must reply within 2 weeks of notification.

CONTACT Ms. Irma M. Ramirez, Financial Aid Administrator, Atlantic College, PO Box 1774, Guaynabo, PR 00970, 787-789-4251. *Fax:* 787-720-1092.

ATLANTIC UNION COLLEGE

South Lancaster, MA

Tuition & fees: $12,634 **Average undergraduate aid package: $12,050**

ABOUT THE INSTITUTION Independent Seventh-day Adventist, coed. Awards: associate, bachelor's, and master's degrees. 45 undergraduate majors. Total enrollment: 785. Undergraduates: 704. Freshmen: 122. Federal methodology is used as a basis for awarding need-based institutional aid.

UNDERGRADUATE EXPENSES for 1999–2000 ***Application fee:*** $25. ***Comprehensive fee:*** $16,654 includes full-time tuition ($11,904), mandatory fees ($730), and room and board ($4020). ***College room only:*** $2160. Full-time tuition and fees vary according to class time and program. Room and board charges vary according to board plan and housing facility. ***Part-time tuition:*** $496 per hour. ***Payment plan:*** installment.

FRESHMAN FINANCIAL AID (Fall 1998) 79 applied for aid; of those 97% were deemed to have need. 100% of freshmen with need received aid; of those 8% had need fully met. *Average percent of need met:* 67% (excluding resources awarded to replace EFC). *Average financial aid package:* $9707 (excluding resources awarded to replace EFC). 50% of all full-time freshmen had no need and received non-need-based aid.

UNDERGRADUATE FINANCIAL AID (Fall 1998) 375 applied for aid; of those 98% were deemed to have need. 100% of undergraduates with need received aid; of those 10% had need fully met. *Average percent of need met:* 76% (excluding resources awarded to replace EFC). *Average financial aid package:* $12,050 (excluding resources awarded to replace EFC). 20% of all full-time undergraduates had no need and received non-need-based aid.

GIFT AID (NEED-BASED) ***Total amount:*** $2,056,172 (38% Federal, 7% state, 43% institutional, 12% external sources). ***Receiving aid:*** *Freshmen:* 48% (76); *all full-time undergraduates:* 77% (355). ***Average award:*** Freshmen: $5357; Undergraduates: $5605. ***Scholarships, grants, and awards:*** Federal Pell, FSEOG, state, private, college/university gift aid from institutional funds, Federal Nursing.

GIFT AID (NON-NEED-BASED) ***Total amount:*** $325,736 (56% institutional, 44% external sources). ***Receiving aid:*** *Freshmen:* 1% (1); *Undergraduates:* 1% (3). ***Scholarships, grants, and awards by category:*** *Academic Interests/Achievement:* general academic interests/achievements. *Creative Arts/Performance:* music. *Special Achievements/Activities:* leadership. ***Tuition waivers:*** Full or partial for employees or children of employees, senior citizens.

LOANS ***Student loans:*** $2,385,641 (94% need-based, 6% non-need-based). 81% of past graduating class borrowed through all loan programs. Average indebtedness per student: $13,319. ***Average need-based loan:*** Freshmen: $4039; Undergraduates: $6097. ***Parent loans:*** $411,552 (77% need-based, 23% non-need-based). ***Programs:*** FFEL (Subsidized and Unsubsidized Stafford, PLUS), Perkins, Federal Nursing, state, college/university, TERI Loans.

WORK-STUDY ***Federal work-study:*** *Total amount:* $128,616; 105 jobs averaging $2000.

ATHLETIC AWARDS *Total amount:* 48,682 (75% need-based, 25% non-need-based).

APPLYING for FINANCIAL AID ***Required financial aid forms:*** FAFSA, institution's own form. ***Financial aid deadline (priority):*** 4/1. ***Notification date:*** Continuous. Students must reply within 2 weeks of notification.

CONTACT Linda L. Mularczyk, Director of Financial Aid, Atlantic Union College, PO Box 1000, South Lancaster, MA 01561-1000, 978-368-2284 or toll-free 800-282-2030. *Fax:* 978-368-2283.

AUBURN UNIVERSITY

Auburn, AL

Tuition & fees (AL res): $2955 **Average undergraduate aid package: $5233**

ABOUT THE INSTITUTION State-supported, coed. Awards: bachelor's, master's, doctoral, and first professional degrees and post-master's certificates. 110 undergraduate majors. Total enrollment: 22,120. Undergraduates: 18,669. Freshmen: 3,692. Federal methodology is used as a basis for awarding need-based institutional aid.

UNDERGRADUATE EXPENSES for 1999–2000 ***Application fee:*** $25. ***Tuition, state resident:*** full-time $2895; part-time $80 per credit. ***Tuition, nonresident:*** full-time $8685; part-time $240 per credit. ***Required fees:*** full-time $60. Full-time tuition and fees vary according to program. Part-time tuition and fees vary according to program. Room and board charges vary according to housing facility. Part-time mandatory fees per term: $165 for state residents, $495 for nonresidents.

FRESHMAN FINANCIAL AID (Fall 1999, est.) 2053 applied for aid; of those 50% were deemed to have need. 91% of freshmen with need received aid. *Average percent of need met:* 50% (excluding resources awarded to replace EFC). *Average financial aid package:* $4449 (excluding resources awarded to replace EFC). 21% of all full-time freshmen had no need and received non-need-based aid.

UNDERGRADUATE FINANCIAL AID (Fall 1999, est.) 7,273 applied for aid; of those 70% were deemed to have need. 92% of undergraduates with need received aid. *Average percent of need met:* 56% (excluding resources awarded to replace EFC). *Average financial aid package:* $5233 (excluding resources awarded to replace EFC). 11% of all full-time undergraduates had no need and received non-need-based aid.

GIFT AID (NEED-BASED) ***Total amount:*** $7,874,582 (71% Federal, 1% state, 19% institutional, 9% external sources). ***Receiving aid:*** *Freshmen:* 10% (355); *all full-time undergraduates:* 12% (2,142). ***Average award:*** Freshmen: $2312; Undergraduates: $2289. ***Scholarships, grants, and awards:*** Federal Pell, FSEOG, state, private, college/university gift aid from institutional funds.

GIFT AID (NON-NEED-BASED) ***Total amount:*** $1,473,237 (69% institutional, 31% external sources). ***Receiving aid:*** *Freshmen:* 8% (298); *Undergraduates:* 6% (986). ***Scholarships, grants, and awards by category:*** *Academic Interests/Achievement:* agriculture, architecture, biological sciences, business, communication, computer science, education, engineering/technologies, English, foreign languages, general academic interests/achievements, health fields, humanities, international studies, mathematics, physical sciences, premedicine, social sciences. *Creative Arts/Performance:* music. *Special Achievements/Activities:* cheerleading/drum major, memberships. *Special Characteristics:* ethnic background, members of minority groups. ***Tuition waivers:*** Full or partial for children of alumni, employees or children of employees. ***ROTC:*** Army, Naval, Air Force.

LOANS ***Student loans:*** $29,978,478 (59% need-based, 41% non-need-based). Average indebtedness per student: $17,236. ***Average need-based loan:*** Freshmen: $2733; Undergraduates: $3779. ***Parent loans:*** $7,405,663 (100% non-need-based). ***Programs:*** Federal Direct (Subsidized and Unsubsidized Stafford, PLUS), Perkins, college/university.

WORK-STUDY ***Federal work-study:*** *Total amount:* $698,620; jobs available.

ATHLETIC AWARDS *Total amount:* 1,423,780 (66% need-based, 34% non-need-based).

APPLYING for FINANCIAL AID ***Required financial aid forms:*** FAFSA, institution's own form. ***Financial aid deadline (priority):*** 4/15. ***Notification date:*** 5/1. Students must reply within 2 weeks of notification.

CONTACT Mr. Mike Reynolds, Interim Director of Financial Aid, Auburn University, 203 Martin Hall, Auburn University, AL 36849-5144, 334-844-4723 or toll-free 800-AUBURN9 (in-state).

AUBURN UNIVERSITY MONTGOMERY

Montgomery, AL

Tuition & fees (AL res): $2577 **Average undergraduate aid package: N/A**

ABOUT THE INSTITUTION State-supported, coed. Awards: bachelor's, master's, and doctoral degrees. 24 undergraduate majors. Total enrollment: 5,354. Undergraduates: 4,539. Freshmen: 863. Federal methodology is used as a basis for awarding need-based institutional aid.

UNDERGRADUATE EXPENSES for 1999–2000 ***Application fee:*** $25. ***One-time required fee:*** $25. ***Tuition, state resident:*** full-time $2577; part-time $59 per quarter hour. ***Tuition, nonresident:*** full-time $7731; part-time $177 per quarter hour. Full-time tuition and fees vary according to course load. ***College room and board: room only:*** $2010. ***Payment plan:*** deferred payment.

GIFT AID (NEED-BASED) ***Total amount:*** $4,245,000 (99% Federal, 1% state). ***Scholarships, grants, and awards:*** Federal Pell, FSEOG, state.

GIFT AID (NON-NEED-BASED) ***Total amount:*** $900,000 (72% institutional, 28% external sources). ***Scholarships, grants, and awards by category:*** *Academic Interests/Achievement:* 280 awards ($650,000 total): general academic interests/achievements. *Special Achievements/Activities:* community service, leadership. ***Tuition waivers:*** Full or partial for employees or children of employees. ***ROTC:*** Army, Air Force cooperative.

LOANS ***Student loans:*** $15,000,000 (100% need-based). ***Parent loans:*** $500,000 (100% non-need-based). ***Programs:*** Federal Direct (Subsidized and Unsubsidized Stafford, PLUS), Perkins.

WORK-STUDY ***Federal work-study:*** *Total amount:* $200,000; 50 jobs averaging $3000.

APPLYING for FINANCIAL AID ***Required financial aid forms:*** FAFSA, institution's own form. ***Financial aid deadline (priority):*** 3/15. ***Notification date:*** 4/15. Students must reply within 4 weeks of notification.

CONTACT James V. Bradsher, Director of Financial Aid, Auburn University Montgomery, PO Box 244023, Montgomery, AL 36124-4023, 334-244-3570 or toll-free 800-227-2649 (in-state). *Fax:* 334-244-3913. *E-mail:* jbradshe@mickey.aum.edu

AUDREY COHEN COLLEGE

New York, NY

Tuition & fees: $14,480 **Average undergraduate aid package: $4550**

ABOUT THE INSTITUTION Independent, coed. Awards: associate, bachelor's, and master's degrees. 2 undergraduate majors. Total enrollment: 1,222. Undergraduates: 1,093. Freshmen: 173. Federal methodology is used as a basis for awarding need-based institutional aid.

UNDERGRADUATE EXPENSES for 1999–2000 ***Application fee:*** $20. ***Tuition:*** full-time $14,160; part-time $295 per credit. ***Required fees:*** full-time $320. Full-time tuition and fees vary according to program. ***Payment plans:*** guaranteed tuition, installment.

FRESHMAN FINANCIAL AID (Fall 1999, est.) 202 applied for aid; of those 100% were deemed to have need. 100% of freshmen with need received aid. *Average financial aid package:* $4420 (excluding resources awarded to replace EFC).

UNDERGRADUATE FINANCIAL AID (Fall 1999, est.) 1,054 applied for aid; of those 93% were deemed to have need. 100% of undergraduates with need received aid. *Average financial aid package:* $4550 (excluding resources awarded to replace EFC).

GIFT AID (NEED-BASED) ***Total amount:*** $2,461,456 (45% Federal, 55% state). ***Receiving aid:*** *Freshmen:* 67% (149); *all full-time undergraduates:* 68% (735). ***Average award:*** Freshmen: $1283; Undergraduates: $1276. ***Scholarships, grants, and awards:*** Federal Pell, FSEOG, state, college/university gift aid from institutional funds.

GIFT AID (NON-NEED-BASED) ***Total amount:*** $317,360 (99% institutional, 1% external sources). ***Receiving aid:*** *Freshmen:* 13% (28); *Undergraduates:* 12% (131). ***Scholarships, grants, and awards by category:*** *Academic Interests/Achievement:* general academic interests/achievements. ***Tuition waivers:*** Full or partial for employees or children of employees.

LOANS ***Student loans:*** $5,066,591 (59% need-based, 41% non-need-based). 80% of past graduating class borrowed through all loan programs. Average indebtedness per student: $24,000. ***Average need-based loan:*** Freshmen: $1945; Undergraduates: $2977. ***Programs:*** FFEL (Subsidized and Unsubsidized Stafford, PLUS).

WORK-STUDY ***Federal work-study:*** *Total amount:* $83,365; 24 jobs averaging $1895. ***State or other work-study/employment:*** *Total amount:* $43,500 (100% need-based). 29 part-time jobs averaging $1500.

APPLYING for FINANCIAL AID ***Required financial aid forms:*** FAFSA, state aid form, income information. ***Financial aid deadline:*** Continuous.

CONTACT Rosibel Gomez, Financial Aid Director, Audrey Cohen College, 75 Varick Street, New York, NY 10013-1919, 212-343-1234 Ext. 5004 or toll-free 800-33-THINK Ext. 5001 (in-state). *Fax:* 212-343-7399.

AUGSBURG COLLEGE

Minneapolis, MN

Tuition & fees: $15,250 **Average undergraduate aid package: $9428**

ABOUT THE INSTITUTION Independent Lutheran, coed. Awards: bachelor's and master's degrees and post-bachelor's certificates. 62 undergraduate majors. Total enrollment: 3,007. Undergraduates: 2,829. Freshmen: 323. Federal methodology is used as a basis for awarding need-based institutional aid.

UNDERGRADUATE EXPENSES for 1999–2000 ***Application fee:*** $25. ***Comprehensive fee:*** $20,490 includes full-time tuition ($15,084), mandatory fees ($166), and room and board ($5240). ***College room only:*** $2676. Room and board charges vary according to board plan and housing facility. ***Part-time tuition:*** $1630 per course. ***Part-time fees:*** $42 per term part-time. Part-time tuition and fees vary according to course load. ***Payment plans:*** installment, deferred payment.

FRESHMAN FINANCIAL AID (Fall 1999, est.) 277 applied for aid; of those 87% were deemed to have need. 98% of freshmen with need received aid; of those 68% had need fully met. *Average percent of need met:* 73% (excluding resources awarded to replace EFC). *Average financial aid package:* $10,280 (excluding resources awarded to replace EFC). 13% of all full-time freshmen had no need and received non-need-based aid.

UNDERGRADUATE FINANCIAL AID (Fall 1999, est.) 1,647 applied for aid; of those 86% were deemed to have need. 93% of undergraduates with need received aid; of those 49% had need fully met. *Average percent of need met:* 60% (excluding resources awarded to replace EFC). *Average financial aid package:* $9428 (excluding resources awarded to replace EFC). 10% of all full-time undergraduates had no need and received non-need-based aid.

GIFT AID (NEED-BASED) ***Total amount:*** $10,464,800 (17% Federal, 22% state, 54% institutional, 7% external sources). ***Receiving aid:*** *Freshmen:* 75% (234); *all full-time undergraduates:* 62% (1,264). ***Average award:*** Freshmen: $10,044; Undergraduates: $8146. ***Scholarships, grants, and awards:*** Federal Pell, FSEOG, state, private, college/university gift aid from institutional funds, Federal Nursing.

Augsburg College (continued)

GIFT AID (NON-NEED-BASED) ***Total amount:*** $457,668 (1% Federal, 74% institutional, 25% external sources). ***Receiving aid:*** *Freshmen:* 54% (168); *Undergraduates:* 35% (715). ***Scholarships, grants, and awards by category:*** *Academic Interests/Achievement:* biological sciences, business, communication, computer science, education, English, foreign languages, general academic interests/achievements, health fields, international studies, mathematics, physical sciences, religion/biblical studies, social sciences. *Creative Arts/Performance:* music, performing arts, theater/drama. *Special Achievements/Activities:* community service, general special achievements/activities, junior miss, leadership, religious involvement. *Special Characteristics:* children and siblings of alumni, international students, members of minority groups, relatives of clergy, siblings of current students. ***Tuition waivers:*** Full or partial for children of alumni, employees or children of employees, senior citizens. ***ROTC:*** Army cooperative, Naval cooperative, Air Force cooperative.

LOANS ***Student loans:*** $7,843,738 (92% need-based, 8% non-need-based). Average indebtedness per student: $20,846. ***Average need-based loan:*** Freshmen: $4539; Undergraduates: $6253. ***Parent loans:*** $790,009 (77% need-based, 23% non-need-based). ***Programs:*** FFEL (Subsidized and Unsubsidized Stafford, PLUS), Perkins, Federal Nursing, state.

WORK-STUDY ***Federal work-study:*** *Total amount:* $377,058; jobs available. ***State or other work-study/employment:*** *Total amount:* $383,017 (81% need-based, 19% non-need-based). Part-time jobs available.

APPLYING for FINANCIAL AID ***Required financial aid forms:*** FAFSA, institution's own form. ***Financial aid deadline:*** 4/15. ***Notification date:*** Continuous. Students must reply within 3 weeks of notification.

CONTACT Mr. Herald A. Johnson, Director of Enrollment and Financial Services, Augsburg College, 2211 Riverside Avenue, Minneapolis, MN 55454-1351, 612-330-1046 or toll-free 800-788-5678. *Fax:* 612-330-1308. *E-mail:* johnsonh@augsburg.edu

AUGUSTANA COLLEGE

Rock Island, IL

Tuition & fees: $17,187 **Average undergraduate aid package: $13,518**

ABOUT THE INSTITUTION Independent religious, coed. Awards: bachelor's degrees. 62 undergraduate majors. Total enrollment: 2,209. Undergraduates: 2,209. Freshmen: 565. Federal methodology is used as a basis for awarding need-based institutional aid.

UNDERGRADUATE EXPENSES for 1999–2000 ***Application fee:*** $25. ***Comprehensive fee:*** $22,224 includes full-time tuition ($16,866), mandatory fees ($321), and room and board ($5037). ***College room only:*** $2556. Room and board charges vary according to housing facility. ***Part-time tuition:*** $705 per credit. Part-time tuition and fees vary according to course load. ***Payment plans:*** tuition prepayment, installment.

FRESHMAN FINANCIAL AID (Fall 1999) 554 applied for aid; of those 73% were deemed to have need. 100% of freshmen with need received aid; of those 37% had need fully met. *Average percent of need met:* 90% (excluding resources awarded to replace EFC). *Average financial aid package:* $13,864 (excluding resources awarded to replace EFC). 25% of all full-time freshmen had no need and received non-need-based aid.

UNDERGRADUATE FINANCIAL AID (Fall 1999) 2,094 applied for aid; of those 74% were deemed to have need. 99% of undergraduates with need received aid; of those 35% had need fully met. *Average percent of need met:* 87% (excluding resources awarded to replace EFC). *Average financial aid package:* $13,518 (excluding resources awarded to replace EFC). 23% of all full-time undergraduates had no need and received non-need-based aid.

GIFT AID (NEED-BASED) ***Total amount:*** $14,373,852 (5% Federal, 24% state, 68% institutional, 3% external sources). ***Receiving aid:*** *Freshmen:* 71% (400); *all full-time undergraduates:* 69% (1,515). ***Average award:*** Freshmen: $10,064; Undergraduates: $9453. ***Scholarships, grants, and awards:*** Federal Pell, FSEOG, state, private, college/university gift aid from institutional funds.

GIFT AID (NON-NEED-BASED) ***Total amount:*** $3,278,281 (1% state, 94% institutional, 5% external sources). ***Receiving aid:*** *Freshmen:* 55% (313); *Undergraduates:* 47% (1,035). ***Scholarships, grants, and awards by category:*** *Academic Interests/Achievement:* 1,251 awards ($5,892,045 total): biological sciences, general academic interests/achievements. *Creative Arts/Performance:* 282 awards ($528,523 total): art/fine arts, creative writing, debating, music, theater/drama. *Special Characteristics:* 399 awards ($2,532,097 total): children and siblings of alumni, children of faculty/staff, international students, members of minority groups, religious affiliation, siblings of current students. ***Tuition waivers:*** Full or partial for employees or children of employees.

LOANS ***Student loans:*** $6,548,150 (100% need-based). 71% of past graduating class borrowed through all loan programs. Average indebtedness per student: $15,672. ***Average need-based loan:*** Freshmen: $3358; Undergraduates: $4073. ***Parent loans:*** $1,689,839 (100% need-based). ***Programs:*** FFEL (Subsidized and Unsubsidized Stafford, PLUS), Perkins.

WORK-STUDY ***Federal work-study:*** *Total amount:* $1,252,138; 1,012 jobs averaging $1237.

APPLYING for FINANCIAL AID ***Required financial aid forms:*** FAFSA, institution's own form. ***Financial aid deadline (priority):*** 4/1. ***Notification date:*** Continuous. Students must reply by 5/1.

CONTACT Sue Standley, Director of Financial Aid, Augustana College, 639 38th Street, Rock Island, IL 61201-2296, 309-794-7207 or toll-free 800-798-8100. *Fax:* 309-794-7174. *E-mail:* afass@augustana.edu

AUGUSTANA COLLEGE

Sioux Falls, SD

Tuition & fees: $14,754 **Average undergraduate aid package: $13,487**

ABOUT THE INSTITUTION Independent religious, coed. Awards: bachelor's and master's degrees. 49 undergraduate majors. Total enrollment: 1,774. Undergraduates: 1,728. Freshmen: 483. Federal methodology is used as a basis for awarding need-based institutional aid.

UNDERGRADUATE EXPENSES for 2000–2001 ***Application fee:*** $25. ***Comprehensive fee:*** $19,014 includes full-time tuition ($14,592), mandatory fees ($162), and room and board ($4260). ***College room only:*** $2160. Room and board charges vary according to board plan and housing facility. ***Part-time tuition:*** $200 per credit. Part-time tuition and fees vary according to course load. ***Payment plan:*** installment.

FRESHMAN FINANCIAL AID (Fall 1999) 401 applied for aid; of those 85% were deemed to have need. 100% of freshmen with need received aid; of those 44% had need fully met. *Average percent of need met:* 98% (excluding resources awarded to replace EFC). *Average financial aid package:* $13,899 (excluding resources awarded to replace EFC). 26% of all full-time freshmen had no need and received non-need-based aid.

UNDERGRADUATE FINANCIAL AID (Fall 1999) 1,313 applied for aid; of those 87% were deemed to have need. 100% of undergraduates with need received aid; of those 45% had need fully met. *Average percent of need met:* 98% (excluding resources awarded to replace EFC). *Average financial aid package:* $13,487 (excluding resources awarded to replace EFC). 26% of all full-time undergraduates had no need and received non-need-based aid.

GIFT AID (NEED-BASED) ***Total amount:*** $7,685,875 (17% Federal, 76% institutional, 7% external sources). ***Receiving aid:*** *Freshmen:* 74% (340); *all full-time undergraduates:* 73% (1,138). ***Average award:*** Freshmen: $9202; Undergraduates: $8233. ***Scholarships, grants, and awards:*** Federal Pell, FSEOG, private, college/university gift aid from institutional funds, need-linked special talent scholarships.

GIFT AID (NON-NEED-BASED) ***Total amount:*** $2,698,211 (90% institutional, 10% external sources). ***Receiving aid:*** *Freshmen:* 38% (176); *Undergraduates:* 36% (565). ***Scholarships, grants, and awards by category:*** *Academic Interests/Achievement:* biological sciences, business, communication, education, English, general academic interests/achievements, mathematics, physical sciences, premedicine, religion/biblical studies, social sciences. *Creative Arts/Performance:* art/fine arts, debating, music, theater/drama. *Special Achievements/Activities:* general special achievements/activities, leadership. *Special Characteristics:* children and siblings of alumni, children of current students, children of faculty/staff, international students, members of minority groups, religious affiliation, siblings of current students, spouses of current students, veterans. ***Tuition waivers:*** Full or partial for employees or children of employees, adult students, senior citizens.

LOANS ***Student loans:*** $6,433,504 (73% need-based, 27% non-need-based). 80% of past graduating class borrowed through all loan programs. Average indebtedness per student: $17,561. ***Average need-based loan:*** Freshmen: $4517; Undergraduates: $5116. ***Parent loans:*** $694,883 (26% need-based, 74% non-need-based). ***Programs:*** FFEL (Subsidized and Unsubsidized Stafford, PLUS), Perkins, Federal Nursing, Minnesota SELF Loans, alternative loans.

WORK-STUDY ***Federal work-study:*** *Total amount:* $568,589; 464 jobs averaging $1225. ***State or other work-study/employment:*** *Total amount:* $253,810 (28% need-based, 72% non-need-based). 169 part-time jobs averaging $1502.

ATHLETIC AWARDS *Total amount:* 1,451,661 (56% need-based, 44% non-need-based).

APPLYING for FINANCIAL AID ***Required financial aid form:*** FAFSA. ***Financial aid deadline (priority):*** 3/1. ***Notification date:*** Continuous beginning 4/1. Students must reply by 5/1 or within 2 weeks of notification.

CONTACT Ms. Brenda L. Murtha, Director of Financial Aid, Augustana College, 2001 South Summit Avenue, Sioux Falls, SD 57197, 605-336-5216 or toll-free 800-727-2844. *Fax:* 605-336-5295. *E-mail:* murtha@inst.augie.edu

AUGUSTA STATE UNIVERSITY

Augusta, GA

Tuition & fees (GA res): $2082 **Average undergraduate aid package: $6280**

ABOUT THE INSTITUTION State-supported, coed. Awards: associate, bachelor's, and master's degrees. 32 undergraduate majors. Total enrollment: 5,384. Undergraduates: 4,635. Freshmen: 854. Federal methodology is used as a basis for awarding need-based institutional aid.

UNDERGRADUATE EXPENSES for 1999–2000 ***Application fee:*** $20. ***Tuition, state resident:*** full-time $1808; part-time $76 per credit. ***Tuition, nonresident:*** full-time $7232; part-time $302 per credit. ***Required fees:*** full-time $274; $137 per term part-time.

FRESHMAN FINANCIAL AID (Fall 1998) 1183 applied for aid; of those 85% were deemed to have need. *Average percent of need met:* 65% (excluding resources awarded to replace EFC). *Average financial aid package:* $3728 (excluding resources awarded to replace EFC). 5% of all full-time freshmen had no need and received non-need-based aid.

UNDERGRADUATE FINANCIAL AID (Fall 1998) 3,140 applied for aid; of those 75% were deemed to have need. *Average percent of need met:* 65% (excluding resources awarded to replace EFC). *Average financial aid package:* $6280 (excluding resources awarded to replace EFC). 4% of all full-time undergraduates had no need and received non-need-based aid.

GIFT AID (NEED-BASED) ***Total amount:*** $3,638,571 (99% Federal, 1% external sources). ***Scholarships, grants, and awards:*** Federal Pell, FSEOG, state, private, college/university gift aid from institutional funds.

GIFT AID (NON-NEED-BASED) ***Total amount:*** $3,141,174 (72% state, 20% institutional, 8% external sources). ***Scholarships, grants, and awards by category:*** *Academic Interests/Achievement:* business, education, English, general academic interests/achievements, health fields, mathematics, military science, physical sciences. *Creative Arts/Performance:* art/fine arts, music, theater/drama. *Special Achievements/Activities:* hobbies/interests. *Special Characteristics:* 2,948 awards ($2,030,941 total): local/state students. ***Tuition waivers:*** Full or partial for employees or children of employees, senior citizens. ***ROTC:*** Army.

LOANS ***Student loans:*** $7,412,425 (59% need-based, 41% non-need-based). Average indebtedness per student: $12,041. ***Parent loans:*** $71,855 (100% non-need-based). ***Programs:*** FFEL (Subsidized and Unsubsidized Stafford, PLUS), Perkins, state, college/university, alternative loans.

WORK-STUDY ***Federal work-study:*** *Total amount:* $368,777; 169 jobs available. ***State or other work-study/employment:*** *Total amount:* $415,646 (100% non-need-based). Part-time jobs available.

ATHLETIC AWARDS *Total amount:* 367,022 (100% non-need-based).

APPLYING for FINANCIAL AID ***Required financial aid forms:*** FAFSA, institution's own form. ***Financial aid deadline (priority):*** 4/15. ***Notification date:*** Continuous beginning 5/1. Students must reply within 4 weeks of notification.

CONTACT Ms. Roxanne Padgett, Assistant Director of Financial Aid, Augusta State University, 2500 Walton Way, Augusta, GA 30904-2200, 706-737-1431. *Fax:* 706-737-1777. *E-mail:* rpadgett@aug.edu

AURORA UNIVERSITY

Aurora, IL

Tuition & fees: $12,480 **Average undergraduate aid package: $9111**

ABOUT THE INSTITUTION Independent, coed. Awards: bachelor's and master's degrees. 40 undergraduate majors. Total enrollment: 2,121. Undergraduates: 1,210. Freshmen: 183. Federal methodology is used as a basis for awarding need-based institutional aid.

UNDERGRADUATE EXPENSES for 1999–2000 ***Application fee:*** $25. ***Comprehensive fee:*** $17,142 includes full-time tuition ($12,480) and room and board ($4662). Full-time tuition and fees vary according to course load, location, and program. Room and board charges vary according to board plan and housing facility. ***Part-time tuition:*** $427 per credit hour. Part-time tuition and fees vary according to location and program. ***Payment plans:*** installment, deferred payment.

FRESHMAN FINANCIAL AID (Fall 1999) 147 applied for aid; of those 86% were deemed to have need. 100% of freshmen with need received aid; of those 72% had need fully met. *Average percent of need met:* 92% (excluding resources awarded to replace EFC). *Average financial aid package:* $12,342 (excluding resources awarded to replace EFC).

UNDERGRADUATE FINANCIAL AID (Fall 1999) 915 applied for aid; of those 82% were deemed to have need. 100% of undergraduates with need received aid; of those 59% had need fully met. *Average percent of need met:* 77% (excluding resources awarded to replace EFC). *Average financial aid package:* $9111 (excluding resources awarded to replace EFC).

GIFT AID (NEED-BASED) ***Total amount:*** $3,750,637 (20% Federal, 56% state, 24% institutional). ***Receiving aid:*** *Freshmen:* 111; *all full-time undergraduates:* 627. ***Scholarships, grants, and awards:*** Federal Pell, FSEOG, state, private, college/university gift aid from institutional funds.

GIFT AID (NON-NEED-BASED) ***Total amount:*** $2,401,427 (1% state, 89% institutional, 10% external sources). ***Receiving aid:*** *Freshmen:* 100; *Undergraduates:* 474. ***Scholarships, grants, and awards by category:*** *Academic Interests/Achievement:* 338 awards ($1,472,961 total): general academic interests/achievements. *Special Achievements/Activities:* 71 awards ($210,703 total): community service, leadership. *Special Characteristics:* 76 awards ($89,882 total): children and siblings of alumni, children of educators, children of faculty/staff, members of minority groups, out-of-state students, parents of current students, siblings of current students, spouses of current students. ***Tuition waivers:*** Full or partial for employees or children of employees, senior citizens. ***ROTC:*** Army cooperative.

LOANS ***Student loans:*** $4,080,582 (58% need-based, 42% non-need-based). ***Parent loans:*** $724,801 (100% non-need-based). ***Programs:*** FFEL (Subsidized and Unsubsidized Stafford, PLUS), Perkins, college/university.

WORK-STUDY ***Federal work-study:*** *Total amount:* $528,780; 335 jobs averaging $1578.

APPLYING for FINANCIAL AID ***Required financial aid form:*** FAFSA. ***Financial aid deadline (priority):*** 4/15. ***Notification date:*** Continuous. Students must reply within 4 weeks of notification.

CONTACT Office of Admissions and Financial Aid, Aurora University, 347 South Gladstone Avenue, Aurora, IL 60506-4892, 630-844-5149 or toll-free 800-742-5281. *Fax:* 630-844-5535.

AUSTIN COLLEGE

Sherman, TX

Tuition & fees: $15,219 **Average undergraduate aid package: $15,654**

Austin College (continued)

ABOUT THE INSTITUTION Independent Presbyterian, coed. Awards: bachelor's and master's degrees. 29 undergraduate majors. Total enrollment: 1,257. Undergraduates: 1,233. Freshmen: 324. Federal methodology is used as a basis for awarding need-based institutional aid.

UNDERGRADUATE EXPENSES for 2000–2001 ***Application fee:*** $35. ***Comprehensive fee:*** $21,110 includes full-time tuition ($15,094), mandatory fees ($125), and room and board ($5891). ***College room only:*** $2678. Room and board charges vary according to board plan. ***Payment plan:*** installment.

FRESHMAN FINANCIAL AID (Fall 1999) 311 applied for aid; of those 72% were deemed to have need. 100% of freshmen with need received aid; of those 62% had need fully met. *Average percent of need met:* 94% (excluding resources awarded to replace EFC). *Average financial aid package:* $15,824 (excluding resources awarded to replace EFC). 14% of all full-time freshmen had no need and received non-need-based aid.

UNDERGRADUATE FINANCIAL AID (Fall 1999) 1,172 applied for aid; of those 67% were deemed to have need. 100% of undergraduates with need received aid; of those 48% had need fully met. *Average percent of need met:* 90% (excluding resources awarded to replace EFC). *Average financial aid package:* $15,654 (excluding resources awarded to replace EFC). 19% of all full-time undergraduates had no need and received non-need-based aid.

GIFT AID (NEED-BASED) ***Total amount:*** $6,328,001 (13% Federal, 22% state, 60% institutional, 5% external sources). ***Receiving aid:*** *Freshmen:* 69% (223); *all full-time undergraduates:* 61% (773). ***Average award:*** Freshmen: $10,388; Undergraduates: $9666. ***Scholarships, grants, and awards:*** Federal Pell, FSEOG, state, private, college/university gift aid from institutional funds.

GIFT AID (NON-NEED-BASED) ***Total amount:*** $3,190,512 (95% institutional, 5% external sources). ***Receiving aid:*** *Freshmen:* 67% (218); *Undergraduates:* 60% (756). ***Scholarships, grants, and awards by category:*** *Academic Interests/Achievement:* biological sciences, business, communication, education, engineering/technologies, English, foreign languages, general academic interests/achievements, health fields, humanities, international studies, physical sciences, premedicine, religion/biblical studies, social sciences. *Creative Arts/Performance:* art/fine arts, journalism/publications, music, theater/drama. *Special Achievements/Activities:* general special achievements/activities, leadership, religious involvement. *Special Characteristics:* children of faculty/staff, ethnic background, first-generation college students, handicapped students, international students, local/state students, relatives of clergy. ***Tuition waivers:*** Full or partial for employees or children of employees.

LOANS ***Student loans:*** $5,419,157 (50% need-based, 50% non-need-based). 70% of past graduating class borrowed through all loan programs. Average indebtedness per student: $21,550. ***Average need-based loan:*** Freshmen: $3314; Undergraduates: $3967. ***Parent loans:*** $1,428,912 (100% non-need-based). ***Programs:*** Federal Direct (Subsidized and Unsubsidized Stafford, PLUS), Perkins, state, college/university.

WORK-STUDY ***Federal work-study:*** *Total amount:* $551,038; 375 jobs averaging $1600. ***State or other work-study/employment:*** *Total amount:* $197,645 (7% need-based, 93% non-need-based). Part-time jobs available.

APPLYING for FINANCIAL AID ***Required financial aid forms:*** FAFSA, institution's own form. ***Financial aid deadline (priority):*** 4/1. ***Notification date:*** Continuous. Students must reply by 5/1.

CONTACT Mrs. Laurie Coulter, Director of Financial Aid, Austin College, 900 North Grand Avenue, Wortham Center, Sherman, TX 75090-4400, 903-813-2900 or toll-free 800-442-5363. *Fax:* 903-813-3198. *E-mail:* finaid@austinc.edu

AUSTIN PEAY STATE UNIVERSITY

Clarksville, TN

Tuition & fees (TN res): $2584 **Average undergraduate aid package: $6924**

ABOUT THE INSTITUTION State-supported, coed. Awards: associate, bachelor's, and master's degrees and post-master's certificates. 34 undergraduate majors. Total enrollment: 7,440. Undergraduates: 6,985. Freshmen: 915. Federal methodology is used as a basis for awarding need-based institutional aid.

UNDERGRADUATE EXPENSES for 1999–2000 ***Application fee:*** $15. ***Tuition, state resident:*** full-time $2020; part-time $90 per semester hour. ***Tuition, nonresident:*** full-time $7136; part-time $314 per semester hour. ***Required fees:*** full-time $564; $20 per credit; $64 per term part-time. Part-time tuition and fees vary according to course load. ***College room and board:*** $3230; ***room only:*** $1800. Room and board charges vary according to board plan and housing facility. ***Payment plans:*** installment, deferred payment.

FRESHMAN FINANCIAL AID (Fall 1998) 620 applied for aid; of those 75% were deemed to have need. 82% of freshmen with need received aid. *Average percent of need met:* 70% (excluding resources awarded to replace EFC). *Average financial aid package:* $5703 (excluding resources awarded to replace EFC). 10% of all full-time freshmen had no need and received non-need-based aid.

UNDERGRADUATE FINANCIAL AID (Fall 1998) 3,429 applied for aid; of those 95% were deemed to have need. 75% of undergraduates with need received aid. *Average percent of need met:* 65% (excluding resources awarded to replace EFC). *Average financial aid package:* $6924 (excluding resources awarded to replace EFC). 5% of all full-time undergraduates had no need and received non-need-based aid.

GIFT AID (NEED-BASED) ***Total amount:*** $5,111,105 (87% Federal, 13% state). ***Receiving aid:*** *Freshmen:* 38% (307); *all full-time undergraduates:* 12% (570). ***Average award:*** Freshmen: $4100; Undergraduates: $3200. ***Scholarships, grants, and awards:*** Federal Pell, FSEOG, state, private.

GIFT AID (NON-NEED-BASED) ***Total amount:*** $3,639,206 (48% institutional, 52% external sources). ***Receiving aid:*** *Freshmen:* 39% (315); *Undergraduates:* 26% (1,182). ***Scholarships, grants, and awards by category:*** *Academic Interests/Achievement:* 343 awards ($367,997 total): general academic interests/achievements. *Creative Arts/Performance:* art/fine arts, creative writing, debating, music, theater/drama. *Special Achievements/Activities:* cheerleading/drum major, leadership. *Special Characteristics:* children of educators, children of faculty/staff. ***Tuition waivers:*** Full or partial for employees or children of employees, senior citizens. ***ROTC:*** Army.

LOANS ***Student loans:*** $12,735,847 (67% need-based, 33% non-need-based). 64% of past graduating class borrowed through all loan programs. Average indebtedness per student: $16,108. ***Average need-based loan:*** Freshmen: $2790; Undergraduates: $3875. ***Parent loans:*** $178,954 (100% non-need-based). ***Programs:*** FFEL (Subsidized and Unsubsidized Stafford, PLUS), Perkins, college/university.

WORK-STUDY ***Federal work-study:*** *Total amount:* $348,795; 353 jobs available. ***State or other work-study/employment:*** *Total amount:* $1,164,133 (100% non-need-based). 586 part-time jobs available.

ATHLETIC AWARDS *Total amount:* 739,473 (100% non-need-based).

APPLYING for FINANCIAL AID ***Required financial aid form:*** FAFSA. ***Financial aid deadline (priority):*** 4/1. ***Notification date:*** Continuous beginning 5/1. Students must reply within 2 weeks of notification.

CONTACT Brenda D. Burney, Associate Director, Austin Peay State University, PO Box 4546, Clarksville, TN 37044-0001, 931-221-7907 or toll-free 800-844-2778 (out-of-state). *Fax:* 931-221-6305. *E-mail:* burneyb@apsu.edu

AVERETT COLLEGE

Danville, VA

ABOUT THE INSTITUTION Independent Baptist, coed. Awards: associate, bachelor's, and master's degrees. 48 undergraduate majors. Total enrollment: 2,246. Undergraduates: 1,589. Freshmen: 272.

GIFT AID (NEED-BASED) ***Scholarships, grants, and awards:*** Federal Pell, FSEOG, state, private, college/university gift aid from institutional funds.

GIFT AID (NON-NEED-BASED) ***Scholarships, grants, and awards by category:*** *Academic Interests/Achievement:* general academic interests/achievements, health fields. *Special Characteristics:* general special characteristics, local/state students, relatives of clergy, religious affiliation.

LOANS ***Programs:*** FFEL (Subsidized and Unsubsidized Stafford, PLUS), Perkins.

WORK-STUDY ***Federal work-study:*** *Total amount:* $156,000; 142 jobs averaging $1200.

APPLYING for FINANCIAL AID ***Required financial aid form:*** FAFSA.

CONTACT Ms. Linda W. Gilliam, Director of Financial Aid, Averett College, 420 West Main Street, Danville, VA 24541-3692, 804-791-5646 or toll-free 800-AVERETT. *Fax:* 804-791-5647. *E-mail:* lgilliam@averett.edu

AVILA COLLEGE

Kansas City, MO

Tuition & fees: $11,960 **Average undergraduate aid package: N/A**

ABOUT THE INSTITUTION Independent Roman Catholic, coed. Awards: bachelor's and master's degrees. 38 undergraduate majors. Total enrollment: 1,438. Undergraduates: 1,247. Freshmen: 115. Federal methodology is used as a basis for awarding need-based institutional aid.

UNDERGRADUATE EXPENSES for 1999–2000 ***Comprehensive fee:*** $16,760 includes full-time tuition ($11,800), mandatory fees ($160), and room and board ($4800). Room and board charges vary according to housing facility. ***Part-time tuition:*** $260 per credit hour. ***Part-time fees:*** $3 per credit hour. ***Payment plans:*** guaranteed tuition, installment, deferred payment.

FRESHMAN FINANCIAL AID (Fall 1998) 107 applied for aid; of those 77% were deemed to have need. 100% of freshmen with need received aid.

UNDERGRADUATE FINANCIAL AID (Fall 1998) 439 applied for aid; of those 85% were deemed to have need. 100% of undergraduates with need received aid.

GIFT AID (NEED-BASED) ***Total amount:*** $1,464,970 (43% Federal, 17% state, 40% institutional). ***Receiving aid:*** *Freshmen:* 70% (79); *all full-time undergraduates:* 58% (343). ***Scholarships, grants, and awards:*** Federal Pell, FSEOG, state, private, college/university gift aid from institutional funds.

GIFT AID (NON-NEED-BASED) ***Total amount:*** $918,769 (1% state, 93% institutional, 6% external sources). ***Receiving aid:*** *Freshmen:* 62% (70); *Undergraduates:* 38% (223). ***Scholarships, grants, and awards by category:*** *Academic Interests/Achievement:* biological sciences, communication, general academic interests/achievements, humanities, premedicine. *Creative Arts/Performance:* art/fine arts, music, performing arts, theater/drama. *Special Characteristics:* children and siblings of alumni, children of current students, children of faculty/staff, religious affiliation, siblings of current students, spouses of current students. ***Tuition waivers:*** Full or partial for children of alumni, employees or children of employees, senior citizens. ***ROTC:*** Army cooperative.

LOANS ***Student loans:*** $3,886,529 (65% need-based, 35% non-need-based). Average indebtedness per student: $17,125. ***Parent loans:*** $189,464 (100% non-need-based). ***Programs:*** FFEL (Subsidized and Unsubsidized Stafford, PLUS), Perkins.

WORK-STUDY ***Federal work-study:*** *Total amount:* $141,915; 150 jobs averaging $946.

ATHLETIC AWARDS *Total amount:* 543,300 (100% non-need-based).

APPLYING for FINANCIAL AID ***Required financial aid form:*** FAFSA. ***Financial aid deadline:*** Continuous. ***Notification date:*** Continuous beginning 2/1. Students must reply within 3 weeks of notification.

CONTACT Ms. Cindy Butler, Director of Financial Aid, Avila College, 11901 Wornall Road, Kansas City, MO 64145-1698, 816-942-8400 Ext. 3600 or toll-free 800-GO-AVILA. *Fax:* 816-942-3362. *E-mail:* butlerca@mail.avila.edu

AZUSA PACIFIC UNIVERSITY

Azusa, CA

Tuition & fees: $14,727 **Average undergraduate aid package: $6859**

ABOUT THE INSTITUTION Independent nondenominational, coed. Awards: bachelor's, master's, doctoral, and first professional degrees. 37 undergraduate majors. Total enrollment: 5,982. Undergraduates: 3,092. Freshmen: 680. Federal methodology is used as a basis for awarding need-based institutional aid.

UNDERGRADUATE EXPENSES for 1999–2000 ***Application fee:*** $45. ***Comprehensive fee:*** $19,607 includes full-time tuition ($14,630), mandatory fees ($97), and room and board ($4880). ***College room only:*** $2380. ***Part-time tuition:*** $600 per unit. ***Part-time fees:*** $35 per term part-time. Part-time tuition and fees vary according to course load. ***Payment plan:*** installment.

FRESHMAN FINANCIAL AID (Fall 1998) 569 applied for aid; of those 68% were deemed to have need. 99% of freshmen with need received aid; of those 19% had need fully met. *Average percent of need met:* 75% (excluding resources awarded to replace EFC). *Average financial aid package:* $8185 (excluding resources awarded to replace EFC). 27% of all full-time freshmen had no need and received non-need-based aid.

UNDERGRADUATE FINANCIAL AID (Fall 1998) 2,086 applied for aid; of those 70% were deemed to have need. 99% of undergraduates with need received aid; of those 19% had need fully met. *Average percent of need met:* 74% (excluding resources awarded to replace EFC). *Average financial aid package:* $6859 (excluding resources awarded to replace EFC). 24% of all full-time undergraduates had no need and received non-need-based aid.

GIFT AID (NEED-BASED) ***Total amount:*** $9,663,867 (14% Federal, 37% state, 45% institutional, 4% external sources). ***Receiving aid:*** *Freshmen:* 63% (370); *all full-time undergraduates:* 60% (1,338). ***Average award:*** Freshmen: $8473; Undergraduates: $7413. ***Scholarships, grants, and awards:*** Federal Pell, FSEOG, state, private, college/university gift aid from institutional funds, Federal Nursing.

GIFT AID (NON-NEED-BASED) ***Total amount:*** $2,291,953 (96% institutional, 4% external sources). ***Receiving aid:*** *Freshmen:* 26% (150); *Undergraduates:* 16% (361). ***Scholarships, grants, and awards by category:*** *Academic Interests/Achievement:* 1,218 awards ($3,421,930 total): biological sciences, general academic interests/achievements, health fields, religion/biblical studies. *Creative Arts/Performance:* 543 awards ($484,693 total): debating, music, theater/drama. *Special Achievements/Activities:* 5 awards ($7000 total): cheerleading/drum major. *Special Characteristics:* 555 awards ($1,080,466 total): children of faculty/staff, ethnic background, international students, relatives of clergy, religious affiliation, siblings of current students. ***Tuition waivers:*** Full or partial for employees or children of employees. ***ROTC:*** Army cooperative.

LOANS ***Student loans:*** $8,808,267 (90% need-based, 10% non-need-based). 81% of past graduating class borrowed through all loan programs. ***Average need-based loan:*** Freshmen: $2985; Undergraduates: $4151. ***Parent loans:*** $3,285,284 (79% need-based, 21% non-need-based). ***Programs:*** FFEL (Subsidized and Unsubsidized Stafford, PLUS), Perkins.

WORK-STUDY ***Federal work-study:*** *Total amount:* $680,000; 453 jobs averaging $1500.

ATHLETIC AWARDS *Total amount:* 1,005,616 (63% need-based, 37% non-need-based).

APPLYING for FINANCIAL AID ***Required financial aid forms:*** FAFSA, institution's own form. ***Financial aid deadline:*** 8/1 (priority: 3/2). ***Notification date:*** Continuous. Students must reply within 3 weeks of notification.

CONTACT Director, Student Financial Services, Azusa Pacific University, 901 East Alosta Avenue, PO Box 7000, Azusa, CA 91702-7000, 626-812-3009 or toll-free 800-TALK-APU.

BABSON COLLEGE

Wellesley, MA

Tuition & fees: $21,952 **Average undergraduate aid package: $16,903**

ABOUT THE INSTITUTION Independent, coed. Awards: bachelor's and master's degrees. 11 undergraduate majors. Total enrollment: 3,431. Undergraduates: 1,701. Freshmen: 414. Both federal and institutional methodology are used as a basis for awarding need-based institutional aid.

UNDERGRADUATE EXPENSES for 2000–2001 (est.) ***Application fee:*** $50. ***Comprehensive fee:*** $30,698 includes full-time tuition ($21,952) and

Babson College (continued)

room and board ($8746). ***College room only:*** $5640. Full-time tuition and fees vary according to course load. Room and board charges vary according to board plan and housing facility. ***Payment plan:*** installment.

FRESHMAN FINANCIAL AID (Fall 1999, est.) 188 applied for aid; of those 91% were deemed to have need. 100% of freshmen with need received aid; of those 100% had need fully met. *Average percent of need met:* 100% (excluding resources awarded to replace EFC). *Average financial aid package:* $17,150 (excluding resources awarded to replace EFC). 6% of all full-time freshmen had no need and received non-need-based aid.

UNDERGRADUATE FINANCIAL AID (Fall 1999, est.) 702 applied for aid; of those 97% were deemed to have need. 100% of undergraduates with need received aid; of those 89% had need fully met. *Average percent of need met:* 99% (excluding resources awarded to replace EFC). *Average financial aid package:* $16,903 (excluding resources awarded to replace EFC). 4% of all full-time undergraduates had no need and received non-need-based aid.

GIFT AID (NEED-BASED) ***Total amount:*** $7,667,300 (8% Federal, 5% state, 87% institutional). ***Receiving aid:*** *Freshmen:* 36% (149); *all full-time undergraduates:* 33% (560). ***Average award:*** Freshmen: $13,094; Undergraduates: $11,054. ***Scholarships, grants, and awards:*** Federal Pell, FSEOG, state, private, college/university gift aid from institutional funds.

GIFT AID (NON-NEED-BASED) ***Total amount:*** $621,700 (100% institutional). ***Receiving aid:*** *Freshmen:* 7% (30); *Undergraduates:* 4% (61). ***Scholarships, grants, and awards by category:*** *Academic Interests/Achievement:* general academic interests/achievements. *Special Achievements/Activities:* 12 awards ($30,000 total): general special achievements/activities. ***Tuition waivers:*** Full or partial for employees or children of employees. ***ROTC:*** Army cooperative, Naval cooperative, Air Force cooperative.

LOANS ***Student loans:*** $4,473,500 (71% need-based, 29% non-need-based). 50% of past graduating class borrowed through all loan programs. Average indebtedness per student: $20,000. ***Average need-based loan:*** Freshmen: $2867; Undergraduates: $4508. ***Parent loans:*** $3,141,897 (100% non-need-based). ***Programs:*** FFEL (Subsidized and Unsubsidized Stafford, PLUS), Perkins, state, college/university.

WORK-STUDY ***Federal work-study:*** *Total amount:* $359,300; 338 jobs averaging $1063.

APPLYING for FINANCIAL AID ***Required financial aid forms:*** FAFSA, CSS Financial Aid PROFILE, noncustodial (divorced/separated) parent's statement, business/farm supplement. ***Financial aid deadline:*** 2/15. ***Notification date:*** 4/1. Students must reply by 5/1.

CONTACT Ms. Melissa Shaak, Director of Financial Aid, Babson College, Hollister Building, 3rd Floor, Babson Park, MA 02457-0310, 781-239-4219 or toll-free 800-488-3696. *Fax:* 781-239-5510.

BAKER UNIVERSITY

Baldwin City, KS

Tuition & fees: $11,750 **Average undergraduate aid package: N/A**

ABOUT THE INSTITUTION Independent United Methodist, coed. Awards: associate, bachelor's, and master's degrees. 40 undergraduate majors. Total enrollment: 2,659. Undergraduates: 1,741. Freshmen: 229. Federal methodology is used as a basis for awarding need-based institutional aid.

UNDERGRADUATE EXPENSES for 1999–2000 ***Application fee:*** $20. ***One-time required fee:*** $80. ***Comprehensive fee:*** $16,450 includes full-time tuition ($11,750) and room and board ($4700). Full-time tuition and fees vary according to location and program. Room and board charges vary according to board plan and housing facility. ***Part-time tuition:*** $455 per credit hour. Part-time tuition and fees vary according to course load. ***Payment plan:*** installment.

GIFT AID (NEED-BASED) ***Scholarships, grants, and awards:*** Federal Pell, FSEOG, state, private, college/university gift aid from institutional funds.

GIFT AID (NON-NEED-BASED) ***Scholarships, grants, and awards by category:*** *Academic Interests/Achievement:* biological sciences, business, communication, computer science, education, engineering/technologies, English, foreign languages, general academic interests/achievements, health fields, humanities, international studies, mathematics, physical sciences, premedicine, religion/biblical studies, social sciences. *Creative Arts/Performance:* art/fine arts, cinema/film/broadcasting, journalism/publications, music, theater/drama. *Special Achievements/Activities:* cheerleading/drum major, religious involvement. *Special Characteristics:* children of faculty/staff, ethnic background, international students, members of minority groups, out-of-state students, relatives of clergy. ***Tuition waivers:*** Full or partial for employees or children of employees, senior citizens. ***ROTC:*** Army cooperative.

LOANS ***Programs:*** FFEL (Subsidized and Unsubsidized Stafford, PLUS), Perkins.

WORK-STUDY Federal work-study jobs available.

APPLYING for FINANCIAL AID ***Required financial aid form:*** FAFSA. ***Financial aid deadline:*** 3/1.

CONTACT Mrs. Jeanne Mott, Financial Aid Director, Baker University, Box 65, Baldwin City, KS 66006-0065, 785-594-4595 or toll-free 800-873-4282. *Fax:* 785-594-8358.

BALDWIN-WALLACE COLLEGE

Berea, OH

Tuition & fees: $15,340 **Average undergraduate aid package: $11,828**

ABOUT THE INSTITUTION Independent Methodist, coed. Awards: bachelor's and master's degrees. 69 undergraduate majors. Total enrollment: 4,646. Undergraduates: 4,002. Freshmen: 714. Federal methodology is used as a basis for awarding need-based institutional aid.

UNDERGRADUATE EXPENSES for 2000–2001 ***Application fee:*** $15. ***Comprehensive fee:*** $20,800 includes full-time tuition ($15,340) and room and board ($5460). ***College room only:*** $2760. ***Part-time tuition:*** $490 per hour. Part-time tuition and fees vary according to class time. ***Payment plans:*** installment, deferred payment.

FRESHMAN FINANCIAL AID (Fall 1999) 669 applied for aid; of those 76% were deemed to have need. 100% of freshmen with need received aid; of those 84% had need fully met. *Average percent of need met:* 99% (excluding resources awarded to replace EFC). *Average financial aid package:* $12,934 (excluding resources awarded to replace EFC). 22% of all full-time freshmen had no need and received non-need-based aid.

UNDERGRADUATE FINANCIAL AID (Fall 1999) 2,530 applied for aid; of those 82% were deemed to have need. 100% of undergraduates with need received aid; of those 85% had need fully met. *Average percent of need met:* 98% (excluding resources awarded to replace EFC). *Average financial aid package:* $11,828 (excluding resources awarded to replace EFC). 19% of all full-time undergraduates had no need and received non-need-based aid.

GIFT AID (NEED-BASED) ***Total amount:*** $12,713,731 (13% Federal, 21% state, 64% institutional, 2% external sources). ***Receiving aid:*** *Freshmen:* 65% (467); *all full-time undergraduates:* 58% (1,723). ***Average award:*** Freshmen: $9145; Undergraduates: $6474. ***Scholarships, grants, and awards:*** Federal Pell, FSEOG, state, private, college/university gift aid from institutional funds.

GIFT AID (NON-NEED-BASED) ***Total amount:*** $6,878,312 (19% state, 74% institutional, 7% external sources). ***Scholarships, grants, and awards by category:*** *Academic Interests/Achievement:* 997 awards ($3,777,306 total): general academic interests/achievements. *Creative Arts/Performance:* 61 awards ($135,762 total): music. *Special Achievements/Activities:* 380 awards ($819,222 total): leadership. *Special Characteristics:* 97 awards ($365,725 total): children and siblings of alumni, members of minority groups, religious affiliation. ***Tuition waivers:*** Full or partial for children of alumni, employees or children of employees. ***ROTC:*** Army cooperative, Air Force cooperative.

LOANS ***Student loans:*** $12,366,731 (47% need-based, 53% non-need-based). 55% of past graduating class borrowed through all loan programs. Average indebtedness per student: $19,768. ***Average need-based loan:*** Freshmen: $2522; Undergraduates: $4306. ***Parent loans:*** $13,410,933 (5% need-based, 95% non-need-based). ***Programs:*** FFEL (Subsidized and Unsubsidized Stafford, PLUS), Perkins, college/university.

WORK-STUDY ***Federal work-study:*** *Total amount:* $2,229,882; 1,554 jobs averaging $1434. ***State or other work-study/employment:*** *Total amount:* $1,006,379 (100% non-need-based). Part-time jobs available.

APPLYING for FINANCIAL AID ***Required financial aid form:*** FAFSA. ***Financial aid deadline:*** 9/1 (priority: 5/1). ***Notification date:*** Continuous.

CONTACT Dr. George L. Rolleston, Director of Financial Aid, Baldwin-Wallace College, 275 Eastland Road, Berea, OH 44017-2088, 440-826-2108 or toll-free 877-BWAPPLY (in-state). *E-mail:* grollest@bw.edu

BALL STATE UNIVERSITY

Muncie, IN

Tuition & fees (IN res): $3686 **Average undergraduate aid package: $5656**

ABOUT THE INSTITUTION State-supported, coed. Awards: associate, bachelor's, master's, and doctoral degrees. 124 undergraduate majors. Total enrollment: 18,578. Undergraduates: 16,054. Freshmen: 3,649. Federal methodology is used as a basis for awarding need-based institutional aid.

UNDERGRADUATE EXPENSES for 1999–2000 ***Application fee:*** $25. ***Tuition, state resident:*** full-time $3576; part-time $1125 per term. ***Tuition, nonresident:*** full-time $9736; part-time $2885 per term. ***Required fees:*** full-time $110; $55 per term part-time. Part-time tuition and fees vary according to course load. ***College room and board:*** $4520. Room and board charges vary according to board plan and housing facility. ***Payment plan:*** installment.

FRESHMAN FINANCIAL AID (Fall 1999, est.) 3172 applied for aid; of those 68% were deemed to have need. 98% of freshmen with need received aid; of those 50% had need fully met. *Average percent of need met:* 70% (excluding resources awarded to replace EFC). *Average financial aid package:* $4919 (excluding resources awarded to replace EFC). 28% of all full-time freshmen had no need and received non-need-based aid.

UNDERGRADUATE FINANCIAL AID (Fall 1999, est.) 10,140 applied for aid; of those 71% were deemed to have need. 98% of undergraduates with need received aid; of those 61% had need fully met. *Average percent of need met:* 77% (excluding resources awarded to replace EFC). *Average financial aid package:* $5656 (excluding resources awarded to replace EFC). 24% of all full-time undergraduates had no need and received non-need-based aid.

GIFT AID (NEED-BASED) ***Total amount:*** $14,134,588 (50% Federal, 49% state, 1% institutional). ***Receiving aid:*** *Freshmen:* 32% (1,289); *all full-time undergraduates:* 30% (4,407). ***Average award:*** Freshmen: $3074; Undergraduates: $3064. ***Scholarships, grants, and awards:*** Federal Pell, FSEOG, state, private, college/university gift aid from institutional funds.

GIFT AID (NON-NEED-BASED) ***Total amount:*** $5,940,213 (13% state, 31% institutional, 56% external sources). ***Receiving aid:*** *Freshmen:* 21% (845); *Undergraduates:* 16% (2,285). ***Scholarships, grants, and awards by category:*** *Academic Interests/Achievement:* 2,266 awards ($4,581,640 total): architecture, biological sciences, business, communication, education, English, foreign languages, general academic interests/achievements, health fields, mathematics, social sciences. *Creative Arts/Performance:* 225 awards ($174,549 total): art/fine arts, dance, general creative arts/performance, journalism/publications, music, theater/drama. *Special Achievements/Activities:* 34 awards ($87,084 total): leadership. *Special Characteristics:* 224 awards ($393,364 total): children of faculty/staff. ***Tuition waivers:*** Full or partial for employees or children of employees. ***ROTC:*** Army.

LOANS ***Student loans:*** $45,986,111 (50% need-based, 50% non-need-based). 80% of past graduating class borrowed through all loan programs. Average indebtedness per student: $10,000. ***Average need-based loan:*** Freshmen: $2312; Undergraduates: $2992. ***Parent loans:*** $40,564,208 (100% non-need-based). ***Programs:*** Federal Direct (Subsidized and Unsubsidized Stafford, PLUS), Perkins, college/university.

WORK-STUDY ***Federal work-study:*** *Total amount:* $2,074,492; 991 jobs averaging $2093. ***State or other work-study/employment:*** *Total amount:* $10,526,000 (100% non-need-based). 6,700 part-time jobs averaging $1571.

ATHLETIC AWARDS *Total amount:* 2,231,845 (100% non-need-based).

APPLYING for FINANCIAL AID ***Required financial aid form:*** FAFSA. ***Financial aid deadline (priority):*** 3/1. ***Notification date:*** 4/15.

CONTACT Dr. Clarence L. Casazza, Director of Scholarships and Financial Aid, Ball State University, Financial Aid Office, Muncie, IN 47306-1099, 765-285-8924 or toll-free 800-482-4BSU. *Fax:* 765-285-2173. *E-mail:* ccasazza@bsu.edu

BALTIMORE HEBREW UNIVERSITY

Baltimore, MD

Tuition & fees: $5630 **Average undergraduate aid package: $2815**

ABOUT THE INSTITUTION Independent, coed. Awards: associate, bachelor's, master's, and doctoral degrees. 14 undergraduate majors. Total enrollment: 274. Undergraduates: 192. Both federal and institutional methodology are used as a basis for awarding need-based institutional aid.

UNDERGRADUATE EXPENSES for 1999–2000 ***Application fee:*** $20. ***Tuition:*** full-time $5600; part-time $700 per course. ***Required fees:*** full-time $30; $15 per term part-time. Full-time tuition and fees vary according to course load. Part-time tuition and fees vary according to course load. ***Payment plan:*** installment.

FRESHMAN FINANCIAL AID (Fall 1998) 3 applied for aid; of those 100% were deemed to have need. 100% of freshmen with need received aid; of those 100% had need fully met. *Average percent of need met:* 100% (excluding resources awarded to replace EFC). *Average financial aid package:* $3718 (excluding resources awarded to replace EFC).

UNDERGRADUATE FINANCIAL AID (Fall 1998) 54 applied for aid; of those 100% were deemed to have need. 100% of undergraduates with need received aid; of those 100% had need fully met. *Average percent of need met:* 100% (excluding resources awarded to replace EFC). *Average financial aid package:* $2815 (excluding resources awarded to replace EFC).

GIFT AID (NEED-BASED) ***Total amount:*** $637,363 (50% Federal, 35% institutional, 15% external sources). ***Scholarships, grants, and awards:*** Federal Pell, state, private, college/university gift aid from institutional funds.

GIFT AID (NON-NEED-BASED) ***Scholarships, grants, and awards by category:*** *Special Characteristics:* adult students, international students, married students. ***Tuition waivers:*** Full or partial for employees or children of employees, senior citizens.

LOANS ***Student loans:*** $31,320 (100% need-based). ***Programs:*** FFEL (Subsidized and Unsubsidized Stafford, PLUS).

APPLYING for FINANCIAL AID ***Required financial aid forms:*** FAFSA, institution's own form. ***Financial aid deadline:*** Continuous. ***Notification date:*** Continuous.

CONTACT Ms. Alexandra Suhoy, Financial Aid Counselor, Baltimore Hebrew University, 5800 Park Heights Avenue, Baltimore, MD 21215-3996, 410-578-6913 or toll-free 888-248-7420. *Fax:* 410-578-6940. *E-mail:* alexandra@bhu.edu

BAPTIST BIBLE COLLEGE

Springfield, MO

Tuition & fees: $2888 **Average undergraduate aid package: $6900**

ABOUT THE INSTITUTION Independent Baptist, coed. Awards: associate, bachelor's, and master's degrees. 8 undergraduate majors. Total enrollment: 968. Undergraduates: 916. Federal methodology is used as a basis for awarding need-based institutional aid.

UNDERGRADUATE EXPENSES for 1999–2000 ***Comprehensive fee:*** $6500 includes full-time tuition ($2478), mandatory fees ($410), and room and board ($3612). Full-time tuition and fees vary according to program. ***Part-time tuition:*** $105 per hour.

FRESHMAN FINANCIAL AID (Fall 1999, est.) *Average financial aid package:* $6900 (excluding resources awarded to replace EFC).

UNDERGRADUATE FINANCIAL AID (Fall 1999, est.) *Average financial aid package:* $6900 (excluding resources awarded to replace EFC).

Baptist Bible College (continued)

GIFT AID (NEED-BASED) ***Total amount:*** $837,350 ***Scholarships, grants, and awards:*** Federal Pell.

GIFT AID (NON-NEED-BASED) ***Total amount:*** $84,969 ***ROTC:*** Army cooperative.

LOANS ***Programs:*** Federal Direct (Subsidized and Unsubsidized Stafford, PLUS).

APPLYING for FINANCIAL AID ***Required financial aid form:*** FAFSA. ***Financial aid deadline:*** Continuous.

CONTACT Ms. Shirley Cutburth, Director of Financial Aid, Baptist Bible College, 628 East Kearney, Springfield, MO 65803-3498, 417-268-6034. *Fax:* 417-268-6694.

BAPTIST BIBLE COLLEGE OF INDIANAPOLIS

Indianapolis, IN

CONTACT Financial Aid Office, Baptist Bible College of Indianapolis, 601 North Shortridge Road, Indianapolis, IN 46219, 317-352-8736 or toll-free 800-273-2224.

BAPTIST BIBLE COLLEGE OF PENNSYLVANIA

Clarks Summit, PA

Tuition & fees: $8992 **Average undergraduate aid package: $5000**

ABOUT THE INSTITUTION Independent Baptist, coed. Awards: associate, bachelor's, master's, and doctoral degrees. 13 undergraduate majors. Total enrollment: 750. Undergraduates: 592. Federal methodology is used as a basis for awarding need-based institutional aid.

UNDERGRADUATE EXPENSES for 1999–2000 ***Application fee:*** $30. ***One-time required fee:*** $50. ***Comprehensive fee:*** $13,706 includes full-time tuition ($8128), mandatory fees ($864), and room and board ($4714). ***College room only:*** $1860. Full-time tuition and fees vary according to course load. Room and board charges vary according to board plan. ***Part-time tuition:*** $254 per semester hour. ***Part-time fees:*** $27 per semester hour. Part-time tuition and fees vary according to course load. ***Payment plan:*** installment.

FRESHMAN FINANCIAL AID (Fall 1999) *Average percent of need met:* 54% (excluding resources awarded to replace EFC). *Average financial aid package:* $6778 (excluding resources awarded to replace EFC).

UNDERGRADUATE FINANCIAL AID (Fall 1999) *Average percent of need met:* 44% (excluding resources awarded to replace EFC). *Average financial aid package:* $5000 (excluding resources awarded to replace EFC).

GIFT AID (NEED-BASED) ***Total amount:*** $774,543 ***Scholarships, grants, and awards:*** Federal Pell, state, college/university gift aid from institutional funds.

GIFT AID (NON-NEED-BASED) ***Total amount:*** $1,464,705 ***Scholarships, grants, and awards by category:*** *Academic Interests/Achievement:* education, general academic interests/achievements, religion/biblical studies. *Creative Arts/Performance:* music. *Special Achievements/Activities:* leadership, religious involvement. *Special Characteristics:* children and siblings of alumni, general special characteristics, married students, relatives of clergy, siblings of current students. ***Tuition waivers:*** Full or partial for employees or children of employees. ***ROTC:*** Army cooperative.

LOANS ***Programs:*** FFEL (Subsidized and Unsubsidized Stafford, PLUS), alternative loans.

WORK-STUDY ***State or other work-study/employment:*** Part-time jobs available.

APPLYING for FINANCIAL AID ***Required financial aid form:*** FAFSA. ***Financial aid deadline (priority):*** 5/1. ***Notification date:*** Continuous. Students must reply within 2 weeks of notification.

CONTACT Mr. Thomas Pollock, Director of Student Financial Services, Baptist Bible College of Pennsylvania, 538 Venard Road, Clarks Summit, PA 18411, 570-586-2400 Ext. 9205 or toll-free 800-451-7664. *Fax:* 570-586-1753. *E-mail:* tpollock@bbc.edu

BAPTIST MEMORIAL COLLEGE OF HEALTH SCIENCES

Memphis, TN

CONTACT Financial Aid Office, Baptist Memorial College of Health Sciences, 1003 Monroe Avenue, Memphis, TN 38104, 901-227-4330 or toll-free 800-796-7171.

BAPTIST MISSIONARY ASSOCIATION THEOLOGICAL SEMINARY

Jacksonville, TX

Tuition & fees: $2220 **Average undergraduate aid package: $1098**

ABOUT THE INSTITUTION Independent Baptist, coed, primarily men. Awards: associate, bachelor's, master's, and first professional degrees. 1 undergraduate major. Total enrollment: 50. Undergraduates: 27. Freshmen: 10. Federal methodology is used as a basis for awarding need-based institutional aid.

UNDERGRADUATE EXPENSES for 1999–2000 ***Application fee:*** $20. ***Tuition:*** full-time $2100; part-time $70 per semester hour. ***Required fees:*** full-time $120; $30 per term part-time. ***Payment plan:*** installment.

UNDERGRADUATE FINANCIAL AID (Fall 1998) 2 applied for aid; of those 100% were deemed to have need. 100% of undergraduates with need received aid. *Average percent of need met:* 50% (excluding resources awarded to replace EFC). *Average financial aid package:* $1098 (excluding resources awarded to replace EFC).

GIFT AID (NEED-BASED) ***Total amount:*** $17,722 (19% Federal, 81% institutional). ***Receiving aid:*** *All full-time undergraduates:* 67% (2). ***Scholarships, grants, and awards:*** Federal Pell, private.

GIFT AID (NON-NEED-BASED) ***Tuition waivers:*** Full or partial for employees or children of employees.

APPLYING for FINANCIAL AID ***Required financial aid forms:*** FAFSA, institution's own form. ***Financial aid deadline (priority):*** 8/1. ***Notification date:*** Continuous beginning 8/15.

CONTACT Dr. W. K. Benningfield, Dean/Registrar, Baptist Missionary Association Theological Seminary, 1530 East Pine Street, Jacksonville, TX 75766-5407, 903-586-2501. *Fax:* 903-586-0378. *E-mail:* bmatsem@flash.net

BARAT COLLEGE

Lake Forest, IL

Tuition & fees: $13,500 **Average undergraduate aid package: N/A**

ABOUT THE INSTITUTION Independent Roman Catholic, coed. Awards: bachelor's and master's degrees. 48 undergraduate majors. Total enrollment: 820. Undergraduates: 757. Freshmen: 127. Federal methodology is used as a basis for awarding need-based institutional aid.

UNDERGRADUATE EXPENSES for 1999–2000 ***Application fee:*** $20. ***Comprehensive fee:*** $18,750 includes full-time tuition ($13,500) and room and board ($5250). Full-time tuition and fees vary according to course load. ***Part-time tuition:*** $450 per credit hour. Part-time tuition and fees vary according to course load. ***Payment plan:*** deferred payment.

GIFT AID (NEED-BASED) ***Total amount:*** $1,429,539 (31% Federal, 69% state). ***Scholarships, grants, and awards:*** Federal Pell, FSEOG, state, private, college/university gift aid from institutional funds.

GIFT AID (NON-NEED-BASED) ***Scholarships, grants, and awards by category:*** *Academic Interests/Achievement:* biological sciences, general academic interests/achievements, physical sciences. *Creative Arts/Performance:* art/fine arts, dance, theater/drama. ***Tuition waivers:*** Full or partial for employees or children of employees.

LOANS ***Student loans:*** $2,371,715 (65% need-based, 35% non-need-based). ***Parent loans:*** $267,714 (100% need-based). ***Programs:*** FFEL (Subsidized and Unsubsidized Stafford, PLUS), Perkins, college/university.

WORK-STUDY ***Federal work-study:*** *Total amount:* $320,200; 171 jobs averaging $1872. ***State or other work-study/employment:*** *Total amount:* $158,300 (100% need-based). 82 part-time jobs averaging $1930.

ATHLETIC AWARDS *Total amount:* 208,920 (100% need-based).

APPLYING for FINANCIAL AID ***Required financial aid forms:*** FAFSA, institution's own form. ***Financial aid deadline (priority):*** 4/15. ***Notification date:*** Continuous. Students must reply within 4 weeks of notification.

CONTACT Timothy J. Carter, Director of Financial Aid, Barat College, 700 East Westleigh Road, Lake Forest, IL 60045-3297, 847-604-6278. *Fax:* 847-604-6300. *E-mail:* dtcarter@barat.edu

BARBER-SCOTIA COLLEGE

Concord, NC

Tuition & fees: $7866 **Average undergraduate aid package: $8741**

ABOUT THE INSTITUTION Independent religious, coed. Awards: bachelor's degrees. 16 undergraduate majors. Total enrollment: 480. Undergraduates: 480. Freshmen: 143. Both federal and institutional methodology are used as a basis for awarding need-based institutional aid.

UNDERGRADUATE EXPENSES for 1999–2000 ***Application fee:*** $15. ***Comprehensive fee:*** $11,366 includes full-time tuition ($7400), mandatory fees ($466), and room and board ($3500). ***College room only:*** $1800. Full-time tuition and fees vary according to course load. ***Part-time tuition:*** $310 per semester hour. ***Part-time fees:*** $44 per year part-time. Part-time tuition and fees vary according to course load. ***Payment plan:*** installment.

FRESHMAN FINANCIAL AID (Fall 1998) 193 applied for aid; of those 100% were deemed to have need. 100% of freshmen with need received aid; of those 84% had need fully met. *Average percent of need met:* 76% (excluding resources awarded to replace EFC). *Average financial aid package:* $8180 (excluding resources awarded to replace EFC).

UNDERGRADUATE FINANCIAL AID (Fall 1998) 451 applied for aid; of those 100% were deemed to have need. 100% of undergraduates with need received aid; of those 85% had need fully met. *Average percent of need met:* 76% (excluding resources awarded to replace EFC). *Average financial aid package:* $8741 (excluding resources awarded to replace EFC).

GIFT AID (NEED-BASED) ***Total amount:*** $1,783,917 (58% Federal, 10% state, 7% institutional, 25% external sources). ***Receiving aid:*** *Freshmen:* 51% (107); *all full-time undergraduates:* 56% (272). ***Average award:*** Freshmen: $7866; Undergraduates: $9788. ***Scholarships, grants, and awards:*** Federal Pell, FSEOG, state, private, college/university gift aid from institutional funds, United Negro College Fund.

GIFT AID (NON-NEED-BASED) ***Total amount:*** $422,190 (78% state, 22% institutional). ***Receiving aid:*** *Freshmen:* 49% (101); *Undergraduates:* 52% (253). ***Scholarships, grants, and awards by category:*** *Academic Interests/Achievement:* 12 awards ($12,000 total): business, communication, education, general academic interests/achievements, religion/biblical studies, social sciences. *Creative Arts/Performance:* music. *Special Achievements/Activities:* 2 awards ($22,000 total): cheerleading/drum major, leadership. *Special Characteristics:* 6 awards ($14,699 total): local/state students, religious affiliation. ***Tuition waivers:*** Full or partial for employees or children of employees. ***ROTC:*** Army cooperative, Air Force.

LOANS ***Student loans:*** $1,302,884 (72% need-based, 28% non-need-based). 72% of past graduating class borrowed through all loan programs. Average indebtedness per student: $12,125. ***Average need-based loan:*** Freshmen: $2500; Undergraduates: $4060. ***Parent loans:*** $419,476 (41% need-based, 59% non-need-based). ***Programs:*** Federal Direct (Subsidized and Unsubsidized Stafford, PLUS), FFEL (PLUS).

WORK-STUDY ***Federal work-study:*** *Total amount:* $125,310; 210 jobs averaging $520. ***State or other work-study/employment:*** *Total amount:* $4800 (100% non-need-based). 4 part-time jobs averaging $1200.

ATHLETIC AWARDS *Total amount:* 95,787 (100% non-need-based).

APPLYING for FINANCIAL AID ***Required financial aid forms:*** FAFSA, institution's own form, CSS Financial Aid PROFILE. ***Financial aid deadline (priority):*** 8/1. ***Notification date:*** Continuous beginning 8/24. Students must reply within 2 weeks of notification.

CONTACT Ms. Tangar Young, Financial Aid Assistant/Counselor, Barber-Scotia College, 145 Cabarrus Avenue, Concord, NC 28025-5187, 704-789-2909 or toll-free 800-610-0778. *Fax:* 704-789-2911. *E-mail:* tyoung@b-sc.edu

BARCLAY COLLEGE

Haviland, KS

Tuition & fees: $6250 **Average undergraduate aid package: $7500**

ABOUT THE INSTITUTION Independent religious, coed. Awards: associate and bachelor's degrees. 6 undergraduate majors. Total enrollment: 169. Undergraduates: 169. Freshmen: 23. Both federal and institutional methodology are used as a basis for awarding need-based institutional aid.

UNDERGRADUATE EXPENSES for 1999–2000 ***Application fee:*** $25. ***Comprehensive fee:*** $9350 includes full-time tuition ($5650), mandatory fees ($600), and room and board ($3100). ***College room only:*** $950. Room and board charges vary according to board plan. ***Part-time tuition:*** $230 per credit hour. ***Part-time fees:*** $35 per credit hour. Part-time tuition and fees vary according to course load. ***Payment plan:*** installment.

FRESHMAN FINANCIAL AID (Fall 1999, est.) 42 applied for aid; of those 83% were deemed to have need. 100% of freshmen with need received aid; of those 71% had need fully met. *Average percent of need met:* 75% (excluding resources awarded to replace EFC). *Average financial aid package:* $7500 (excluding resources awarded to replace EFC). 13% of all full-time freshmen had no need and received non-need-based aid.

UNDERGRADUATE FINANCIAL AID (Fall 1999, est.) 145 applied for aid; of those 79% were deemed to have need. 100% of undergraduates with need received aid; of those 61% had need fully met. *Average percent of need met:* 75% (excluding resources awarded to replace EFC). *Average financial aid package:* $7500 (excluding resources awarded to replace EFC). 15% of all full-time undergraduates had no need and received non-need-based aid.

GIFT AID (NEED-BASED) ***Total amount:*** $207,000 (80% Federal, 1% state, 19% institutional). ***Receiving aid:*** *Freshmen:* 67% (30); *all full-time undergraduates:* 45% (75). ***Average award:*** Freshmen: $1500; Undergraduates: $1500. ***Scholarships, grants, and awards:*** Federal Pell, FSEOG, state, private, college/university gift aid from institutional funds.

GIFT AID (NON-NEED-BASED) ***Total amount:*** $125,000 (68% institutional, 32% external sources). ***Receiving aid:*** *Freshmen:* 33% (15); *Undergraduates:* 55% (90). ***Scholarships, grants, and awards by category:*** *Academic Interests/Achievement:* general academic interests/achievements. *Creative Arts/Performance:* art/fine arts, music. *Special Achievements/Activities:* general special achievements/activities, leadership. *Special Characteristics:* children and siblings of alumni, children of faculty/staff, international students, local/state students, relatives of clergy, religious affiliation. ***Tuition waivers:*** Full or partial for employees or children of employees.

LOANS ***Student loans:*** $465,000 (72% need-based, 28% non-need-based). 70% of past graduating class borrowed through all loan programs. Average indebtedness per student: $10,000. ***Average need-based loan:*** Freshmen: $2625; Undergraduates: $3000. ***Parent loans:*** $95,000 (100% non-need-based). ***Programs:*** FFEL (Subsidized and Unsubsidized Stafford, PLUS).

WORK-STUDY ***Federal work-study:*** *Total amount:* $50,000; 50 jobs averaging $1000.

APPLYING for FINANCIAL AID ***Required financial aid form:*** FAFSA. ***Financial aid deadline (priority):*** 3/15. ***Notification date:*** 5/1. Students must reply by 8/1 or within 4 weeks of notification.

CONTACT Alecia Sampley, Financial Aid Director, Barclay College, 607 North Kingman, Haviland, KS 67059-0288, 800-862-0226. *Fax:* 316-862-5403.

BARD COLLEGE

Annandale-on-Hudson, NY

Tuition & fees: $24,000 **Average undergraduate aid package: $19,325**

ABOUT THE INSTITUTION Independent, coed. Awards: bachelor's, master's, and doctoral degrees. 86 undergraduate majors. Total enrollment: 1,427. Undergraduates: 1,233. Freshmen: 335. Both federal and institutional methodology are used as a basis for awarding need-based institutional aid.

UNDERGRADUATE EXPENSES for 1999–2000 ***Application fee:*** $40. ***Comprehensive fee:*** $31,220 includes full-time tuition ($23,480), mandatory fees ($520), and room and board ($7220). ***College room only:*** $3620. Room and board charges vary according to board plan. ***Part-time tuition:*** $734 per credit. ***Part-time fees:*** $160 per term part-time. Part-time tuition and fees vary according to course load. ***Payment plan:*** installment.

FRESHMAN FINANCIAL AID (Fall 1999, est.) 226 applied for aid; of those 88% were deemed to have need. 100% of freshmen with need received aid; of those 60% had need fully met. *Average percent of need met:* 85% (excluding resources awarded to replace EFC). *Average financial aid package:* $19,959 (excluding resources awarded to replace EFC). 6% of all full-time freshmen had no need and received non-need-based aid.

UNDERGRADUATE FINANCIAL AID (Fall 1999, est.) 812 applied for aid; of those 92% were deemed to have need. 100% of undergraduates with need received aid; of those 59% had need fully met. *Average percent of need met:* 85% (excluding resources awarded to replace EFC). *Average financial aid package:* $19,325 (excluding resources awarded to replace EFC). 4% of all full-time undergraduates had no need and received non-need-based aid.

GIFT AID (NEED-BASED) ***Total amount:*** $10,601,230 (7% Federal, 6% state, 85% institutional, 2% external sources). ***Receiving aid:*** *Freshmen:* 56% (197); *all full-time undergraduates:* 58% (715). ***Average award:*** Freshmen: $16,079; Undergraduates: $15,433. ***Scholarships, grants, and awards:*** Federal Pell, FSEOG, state, private, college/university gift aid from institutional funds.

GIFT AID (NON-NEED-BASED) ***Total amount:*** $596,081 (1% state, 97% institutional, 2% external sources). ***Scholarships, grants, and awards by category:*** *Academic Interests/Achievement:* 39 awards ($479,079 total): biological sciences, general academic interests/achievements, physical sciences. *Special Achievements/Activities:* 7 awards ($32,500 total): leadership. ***Tuition waivers:*** Full or partial for employees or children of employees.

LOANS ***Student loans:*** $2,954,696 (83% need-based, 17% non-need-based). 72% of past graduating class borrowed through all loan programs. Average indebtedness per student: $15,400. ***Average need-based loan:*** Freshmen: $3522; Undergraduates: $4144. ***Parent loans:*** $1,492,511 (80% need-based, 20% non-need-based). ***Programs:*** FFEL (Subsidized and Unsubsidized Stafford, PLUS), Perkins, college/university loans from institutional funds (for international students only).

WORK-STUDY ***Federal work-study:*** *Total amount:* $686,555; 471 jobs averaging $1500. ***State or other work-study/employment:*** *Total amount:* $206,980 (93% need-based, 7% non-need-based). 94 part-time jobs available.

APPLYING for FINANCIAL AID ***Required financial aid forms:*** FAFSA, CSS Financial Aid PROFILE, state aid form, noncustodial (divorced/separated) parent's statement, business/farm supplement. ***Financial aid deadline:*** 3/15 (priority: 2/15). ***Notification date:*** 4/1. Students must reply by 5/1 or within 2 weeks of notification.

CONTACT Mr. Gerald E. Kelly, Director of Financial Aid, Bard College, Annandale Road, Annandale-on-Hudson, NY 12504, 914-758-7525. *Fax:* 914-758-7336. *E-mail:* gkelly@bard.edu

BARNARD COLLEGE

New York, NY

Tuition & fees: $22,316 **Average undergraduate aid package: $21,706**

ABOUT THE INSTITUTION Independent, women only. Awards: bachelor's degrees. 51 undergraduate majors. Total university enrollment: 21,000. Total unit enrollment: 2,318. Undergraduates: 2,318. Freshmen: 558. Both federal and institutional methodology are used as a basis for awarding need-based institutional aid.

UNDERGRADUATE EXPENSES for 1999–2000 ***Application fee:*** $45. ***Comprehensive fee:*** $31,400 includes full-time tuition ($21,410), mandatory fees ($906), and room and board ($9084). ***College room only:*** $5632. Room and board charges vary according to board plan and housing facility. ***Part-time tuition:*** $714 per credit. ***Payment plans:*** tuition prepayment, installment, deferred payment.

FRESHMAN FINANCIAL AID (Fall 1999) 328 applied for aid; of those 76% were deemed to have need. 100% of freshmen with need received aid; of those 100% had need fully met. *Average percent of need met:* 100% (excluding resources awarded to replace EFC). *Average financial aid package:* $21,866 (excluding resources awarded to replace EFC). 3% of all full-time freshmen had no need and received non-need-based aid.

UNDERGRADUATE FINANCIAL AID (Fall 1999) 1,201 applied for aid; of those 87% were deemed to have need. 100% of undergraduates with need received aid; of those 100% had need fully met. *Average percent of need met:* 100% (excluding resources awarded to replace EFC). *Average financial aid package:* $21,706 (excluding resources awarded to replace EFC). 1% of all full-time undergraduates had no need and received non-need-based aid.

GIFT AID (NEED-BASED) ***Total amount:*** $17,296,421 (8% Federal, 8% state, 82% institutional, 2% external sources). ***Receiving aid:*** *Freshmen:* 42% (235); *all full-time undergraduates:* 43% (979). ***Average award:*** Freshmen: $19,407; Undergraduates: $17,610. ***Scholarships, grants, and awards:*** Federal Pell, FSEOG, state, private, college/university gift aid from institutional funds.

GIFT AID (NON-NEED-BASED) ***Total amount:*** $362,161 (1% state, 99% external sources). ***Tuition waivers:*** Full or partial for employees or children of employees.

LOANS ***Student loans:*** $3,218,808 (94% need-based, 6% non-need-based). 46% of past graduating class borrowed through all loan programs. Average indebtedness per student: $13,430. ***Average need-based loan:*** Freshmen: $2625; Undergraduates: $4050. ***Parent loans:*** $2,058,292 (100% non-need-based). ***Programs:*** FFEL (Subsidized and Unsubsidized Stafford, PLUS), Perkins, state, college/university.

WORK-STUDY ***Federal work-study:*** *Total amount:* $460,828; 480 jobs averaging $1020. ***State or other work-study/employment:*** *Total amount:* $836,183 (57% need-based, 43% non-need-based). 570 part-time jobs averaging $1470.

APPLYING for FINANCIAL AID ***Required financial aid forms:*** FAFSA, institution's own form, CSS Financial Aid PROFILE, state aid form, noncustodial (divorced/separated) parent's statement, business/farm supplement, parents' individual, corporate, and/or partnership federal income tax returns. ***Financial aid deadline:*** 2/1. ***Notification date:*** 4/1. Students must reply by 5/1.

CONTACT Ms. SuzanneClair Guard, Director of Financial Aid, Barnard College, 3009 Broadway, New York, NY 10027-6598, 212-854-2154. *Fax:* 212-531-1058. *E-mail:* sguard@barnard.columbia.edu

BARRY UNIVERSITY

Miami Shores, FL

Tuition & fees: $15,530 **Average undergraduate aid package: $14,430**

ABOUT THE INSTITUTION Independent Roman Catholic, coed. Awards: bachelor's, master's, doctoral, and first professional degrees and post-bachelor's, post-master's, and first-professional certificates. 58 undergraduate majors. Total enrollment: 7,909. Undergraduates: 5,468. Freshmen: 400. Federal methodology is used as a basis for awarding need-based institutional aid.

UNDERGRADUATE EXPENSES for 1999–2000 ***Application fee:*** $30. ***Comprehensive fee:*** $21,750 includes full-time tuition ($15,530) and room and board ($6220). Full-time tuition and fees vary according to location and program. Room and board charges vary according to board plan. ***Part-time tuition:*** $455 per credit. Part-time tuition and fees vary according to course load, location, and program. ***Payment plans:*** tuition prepayment, installment, deferred payment.

FRESHMAN FINANCIAL AID (Fall 1999, est.) 355 applied for aid; of those 75% were deemed to have need. 100% of freshmen with need received aid; of those 14% had need fully met. *Average percent of need met:* 95% (excluding resources awarded to replace EFC). *Average financial aid package:* $16,883 (excluding resources awarded to replace EFC). 31% of all full-time freshmen had no need and received non-need-based aid.

UNDERGRADUATE FINANCIAL AID (Fall 1999, est.) 2,235 applied for aid; of those 81% were deemed to have need. 100% of undergraduates with need received aid; of those 24% had need fully met. *Average percent of need met:* 85% (excluding resources awarded to replace EFC). *Average financial aid package:* $14,430 (excluding resources awarded to replace EFC). 20% of all full-time undergraduates had no need and received non-need-based aid.

GIFT AID (NEED-BASED) ***Total amount:*** $6,061,895 (45% Federal, 13% state, 42% institutional). ***Receiving aid:*** *Freshmen:* 60% (238); *all full-time undergraduates:* 54% (1,364). ***Average award:*** Freshmen: $5825; Undergraduates: $9335. ***Scholarships, grants, and awards:*** Federal Pell, FSEOG, state, private, college/university gift aid from institutional funds.

GIFT AID (NON-NEED-BASED) ***Total amount:*** $11,863,336 (1% Federal, 33% state, 65% institutional, 1% external sources). ***Receiving aid:*** *Freshmen:* 67% (266); *Undergraduates:* 71% (1,791). ***Scholarships, grants, and awards by category:*** *Academic Interests/Achievement:* general academic interests/achievements. *Creative Arts/Performance:* applied art and design, art/fine arts, theater/drama. *Special Achievements/Activities:* community service, general special achievements/activities, leadership, memberships, religious involvement. *Special Characteristics:* adult students, children and siblings of alumni, children of faculty/staff, general special characteristics, handicapped students, international students, members of minority groups, religious affiliation, siblings of current students. ***Tuition waivers:*** Full or partial for employees or children of employees. ***ROTC:*** Air Force cooperative.

LOANS ***Student loans:*** $12,458,898 (67% need-based, 33% non-need-based). 64% of past graduating class borrowed through all loan programs. Average indebtedness per student: $17,469. ***Average need-based loan:*** Freshmen: $2573; Undergraduates: $4228. ***Parent loans:*** $3,499,064 (100% non-need-based). ***Programs:*** FFEL (Subsidized and Unsubsidized Stafford, PLUS), Perkins, alternative loans.

WORK-STUDY ***Federal work-study:*** *Total amount:* $1,368,072; 447 jobs available.

ATHLETIC AWARDS *Total amount:* 1,307,260 (100% non-need-based).

APPLYING for FINANCIAL AID ***Required financial aid form:*** FAFSA. ***Financial aid deadline:*** Continuous. ***Notification date:*** Continuous. Students must reply within 2 weeks of notification.

CONTACT Mr. Dart Humeston, Director of Financial Aid, Barry University, 11300 Northeast Second Avenue, Miami Shores, FL 33161-6695, 305-899-3673 or toll-free 800-756-6000 (in-state), 800-695-2279 (out-of-state). *Fax:* 305-899-3104. *E-mail:* finaid@mail.barry.edu

BARTLESVILLE WESLEYAN COLLEGE

Bartlesville, OK

Tuition & fees: $9700 **Average undergraduate aid package: $6466**

ABOUT THE INSTITUTION Independent religious, coed. Awards: associate and bachelor's degrees. 37 undergraduate majors. Total enrollment: 603. Undergraduates: 603. Both federal and institutional methodology are used as a basis for awarding need-based institutional aid.

UNDERGRADUATE EXPENSES for 2000–2001 ***Application fee:*** $25. ***Comprehensive fee:*** $13,800 includes full-time tuition ($9200), mandatory fees ($500), and room and board ($4100). ***College room only:*** $2000. Room and board charges vary according to housing facility. ***Payment plans:*** installment, deferred payment.

FRESHMAN FINANCIAL AID (Fall 1999, est.) 65 applied for aid; of those 91% were deemed to have need. 100% of freshmen with need received aid; of those 17% had need fully met. *Average percent of need met:* 45% (excluding resources awarded to replace EFC). *Average financial aid package:* $7088 (excluding resources awarded to replace EFC). 14% of all full-time freshmen had no need and received non-need-based aid.

UNDERGRADUATE FINANCIAL AID (Fall 1999, est.) 615 applied for aid; of those 89% were deemed to have need. 100% of undergraduates with need received aid; of those 20% had need fully met. *Average percent of need met:* 55% (excluding resources awarded to replace EFC). *Average financial aid package:* $6466 (excluding resources awarded to replace EFC). 6% of all full-time undergraduates had no need and received non-need-based aid.

GIFT AID (NEED-BASED) ***Total amount:*** $743,518 (73% Federal, 10% state, 17% institutional). ***Receiving aid:*** *Freshmen:* 41% (30); *all full-time undergraduates:* 41% (283). ***Average award:*** Freshmen: $2100; Undergraduates: $2700. ***Scholarships, grants, and awards:*** Federal Pell, FSEOG, state, private, college/university gift aid from institutional funds.

GIFT AID (NON-NEED-BASED) ***Total amount:*** $872,966 (81% institutional, 19% external sources). ***Receiving aid:*** *Freshmen:* 62% (46); *Undergraduates:* 37% (251). ***Scholarships, grants, and awards by category:*** *Academic Interests/Achievement:* 177 awards ($292,200 total): biological sciences, computer science, education, general academic interests/achievements, religion/biblical studies. *Creative Arts/Performance:* 15 awards ($19,000 total): debating, music. *Special Achievements/Activities:* 191 awards ($88,414 total): religious involvement. *Special Characteristics:* 229 awards ($278,100 total): children and siblings of alumni, children of educators, children of faculty/staff, relatives of clergy, religious affiliation. ***Tuition waivers:*** Full or partial for employees or children of employees, senior citizens.

LOANS ***Student loans:*** $2,885,829 (100% need-based). 61% of past graduating class borrowed through all loan programs. ***Average need-based loan:*** Freshmen: $2625; Undergraduates: $4373. ***Parent loans:*** $562,647 (50% need-based, 50% non-need-based). ***Programs:*** FFEL (Subsidized and Unsubsidized Stafford, PLUS), college/university.

WORK-STUDY ***Federal work-study:*** *Total amount:* $175,129; 90 jobs averaging $1580. ***State or other work-study/employment:*** *Total amount:* $13,322 (100% need-based). 10 part-time jobs averaging $1794.

ATHLETIC AWARDS *Total amount:* 188,550 (100% non-need-based).

APPLYING for FINANCIAL AID ***Required financial aid forms:*** FAFSA, institution's own form, state aid form. ***Financial aid deadline (priority):*** 3/31. ***Notification date:*** Continuous beginning 5/1. Students must reply within 1 week of notification.

CONTACT Lee Kanakis, Director of Financial Aid, Bartlesville Wesleyan College, 2201 Silver Lake Road, Bartlesville, OK 74006, 918-335-6282 or toll-free 800-468-6292 (in-state). *Fax:* 918-335-6229. *E-mail:* oslcfinaid@bwc.edu

BARTON COLLEGE

Wilson, NC

Tuition & fees: $10,834 **Average undergraduate aid package: $9282**

ABOUT THE INSTITUTION Independent religious, coed. Awards: bachelor's degrees. 44 undergraduate majors. Total enrollment: 1,233. Undergraduates: 1,233. Freshmen: 285. Federal methodology is used as a basis for awarding need-based institutional aid.

UNDERGRADUATE EXPENSES for 1999–2000 ***Application fee:*** $25. ***Comprehensive fee:*** $14,726 includes full-time tuition ($10,030), mandatory fees ($804), and room and board ($3892). ***College room only:*** $1784. Full-time tuition and fees vary according to course load. Room and board charges vary according to board plan and housing facility. ***Part-time tuition:*** $206 per semester hour. Part-time tuition and fees vary according to course load and program. ***Payment plan:*** installment.

FRESHMAN FINANCIAL AID (Fall 1999) 250 applied for aid; of those 79% were deemed to have need. 95% of freshmen with need received aid; of those 68% had need fully met. *Average percent of need met:* 84% (excluding resources awarded to replace EFC). *Average financial aid package:* $8589 (excluding resources awarded to replace EFC). 19% of all full-time freshmen had no need and received non-need-based aid.

Barton College (continued)

UNDERGRADUATE FINANCIAL AID (Fall 1999) 805 applied for aid; of those 81% were deemed to have need. 89% of undergraduates with need received aid; of those 70% had need fully met. *Average percent of need met:* 82% (excluding resources awarded to replace EFC). *Average financial aid package:* $9282 (excluding resources awarded to replace EFC). 28% of all full-time undergraduates had no need and received non-need-based aid.

GIFT AID (NEED-BASED) ***Total amount:*** $1,759,458 (50% Federal, 43% state, 4% institutional, 3% external sources). ***Receiving aid:*** *Freshmen:* 54% (151); *all full-time undergraduates:* 50% (482). ***Average award:*** Freshmen: $1989; Undergraduates: $2258. ***Scholarships, grants, and awards:*** Federal Pell, FSEOG, state, private, college/university gift aid from institutional funds.

GIFT AID (NON-NEED-BASED) ***Total amount:*** $2,937,346 (35% state, 51% institutional, 14% external sources). ***Receiving aid:*** *Freshmen:* 49% (139); *Undergraduates:* 43% (413). ***Scholarships, grants, and awards by category:*** *Academic Interests/Achievement:* 447 awards ($795,526 total): biological sciences, business, communication, computer science, education, English, foreign languages, general academic interests/achievements, health fields, humanities, international studies, mathematics, physical sciences, religion/biblical studies, social sciences. *Creative Arts/Performance:* 4 awards ($3000 total): art/fine arts, music, theater/drama. *Special Achievements/Activities:* 480 awards ($665,579 total): general special achievements/activities, leadership, religious involvement. *Special Characteristics:* 140 awards ($399,507 total): children and siblings of alumni, children of faculty/staff, children of union members/company employees, ethnic background, handicapped students, international students, local/state students, members of minority groups, relatives of clergy, religious affiliation, siblings of current students, veterans. ***Tuition waivers:*** Full or partial for employees or children of employees, adult students.

LOANS ***Student loans:*** $3,743,757 (56% need-based, 44% non-need-based). 63% of past graduating class borrowed through all loan programs. Average indebtedness per student: $11,500. ***Average need-based loan:*** Freshmen: $2512; Undergraduates: $3800. ***Parent loans:*** $789,905 (100% non-need-based). ***Programs:*** FFEL (Subsidized and Unsubsidized Stafford, PLUS), Perkins, alternative loans.

WORK-STUDY ***Federal work-study:*** *Total amount:* $410,385; jobs available.

ATHLETIC AWARDS *Total amount:* 492,932 (100% non-need-based).

APPLYING for FINANCIAL AID ***Required financial aid form:*** FAFSA. ***Financial aid deadline (priority):*** 4/15. ***Notification date:*** Continuous. Students must reply within 2 weeks of notification.

CONTACT Ms. Bettie Westbrook, Director of Financial Aid, Barton College, Box 5000, Wilson, NC 27893, 252-399-6316 or toll-free 800-345-4973. *Fax:* 252-399-6572. *E-mail:* aid@barton.edu

BASSIST COLLEGE

Portland, OR

See The Art Institute of Portland

BASTYR UNIVERSITY

Kenmore, WA

Tuition & fees: $9825 **Average undergraduate aid package: N/A**

ABOUT THE INSTITUTION Independent, coed. Awards: bachelor's, master's, and first professional degrees. 5 undergraduate majors. Total enrollment: 900. Undergraduates: 164. Entering class: . Federal methodology is used as a basis for awarding need-based institutional aid.

UNDERGRADUATE EXPENSES for 1999–2000 ***Application fee:*** $60. ***One-time required fee:*** $300. ***Tuition:*** full-time $9345; part-time $192 per credit. ***Required fees:*** full-time $480; $15 per credit; $35 per term part-time. Full-time tuition and fees vary according to course load and program. Part-time tuition and fees vary according to course load and program.

UNDERGRADUATE FINANCIAL AID (Fall 1999, est.) 145 applied for aid; of those 100% were deemed to have need. 100% of undergraduates with need received aid. *Average percent of need met:* 50% (excluding resources awarded to replace EFC).

GIFT AID (NEED-BASED) ***Total amount:*** $395,924 (40% Federal, 54% state, 6% institutional). ***Receiving aid:*** *Entering class:* 50; *all full-time undergraduates:* 120. ***Scholarships, grants, and awards:*** Federal Pell, FSEOG, state, college/university gift aid from institutional funds.

GIFT AID (NON-NEED-BASED) ***Total amount:*** $7650 (20% institutional, 80% external sources). ***Scholarships, grants, and awards by category:*** *Academic Interests/Achievement:* health fields. ***Tuition waivers:*** Full or partial for employees or children of employees.

LOANS ***Student loans:*** $1,075,800 (100% need-based). 80% of past graduating class borrowed through all loan programs. ***Parent loans:*** $30,000 (100% need-based). ***Programs:*** FFEL (Subsidized and Unsubsidized Stafford, PLUS), Perkins.

WORK-STUDY ***Federal work-study:*** *Total amount:* $59,300; 39 jobs averaging $1500. ***State or other work-study/employment:*** *Total amount:* $28,500 (100% need-based). 20 part-time jobs averaging $1500.

APPLYING for FINANCIAL AID ***Required financial aid forms:*** FAFSA, institution's own form. ***Financial aid deadline (priority):*** 5/1. ***Notification date:*** Continuous beginning 6/15.

CONTACT Ms. Alex Campbell, Financial Aid Adviser, Bastyr University, 14500 Juanita Drive, NE, Kenmore, WA 98028, 425-602-3082. *Fax:* 425-602-3090. *E-mail:* finaid@bastyr.edu

BATES COLLEGE

Lewiston, ME

Comprehensive fee: $31,400 **Average undergraduate aid package: $20,487**

ABOUT THE INSTITUTION Independent, coed. Awards: bachelor's degrees. 34 undergraduate majors. Total enrollment: 1,706. Undergraduates: 1,706. Freshmen: 479. Both federal and institutional methodology are used as a basis for awarding need-based institutional aid.

UNDERGRADUATE EXPENSES for 1999–2000 ***Application fee:*** $50. ***Comprehensive fee:*** $31,400. ***Payment plan:*** installment.

FRESHMAN FINANCIAL AID (Fall 1999, est.) 271 applied for aid; of those 86% were deemed to have need. 99% of freshmen with need received aid; of those 100% had need fully met. *Average percent of need met:* 100% (excluding resources awarded to replace EFC). *Average financial aid package:* $21,805 (excluding resources awarded to replace EFC).

UNDERGRADUATE FINANCIAL AID (Fall 1999, est.) 844 applied for aid; of those 91% were deemed to have need. 96% of undergraduates with need received aid; of those 100% had need fully met. *Average percent of need met:* 100% (excluding resources awarded to replace EFC). *Average financial aid package:* $20,487 (excluding resources awarded to replace EFC).

GIFT AID (NEED-BASED) ***Total amount:*** $11,984,412 (4% Federal, 1% state, 91% institutional, 4% external sources). ***Receiving aid:*** *Freshmen:* 47% (224); *all full-time undergraduates:* 41% (693). ***Average award:*** Freshmen: $18,610; Undergraduates: $15,772. ***Scholarships, grants, and awards:*** Federal Pell, FSEOG, state, private, college/university gift aid from institutional funds.

GIFT AID (NON-NEED-BASED) ***Tuition waivers:*** Full or partial for employees or children of employees.

LOANS ***Student loans:*** $2,515,974 (100% need-based). Average indebtedness per student: $15,129. ***Average need-based loan:*** Freshmen: $2401; Undergraduates: $3494. ***Parent loans:*** $2,029,078 (100% non-need-based). ***Programs:*** FFEL (Subsidized and Unsubsidized Stafford, PLUS), Perkins, state, college/university.

WORK-STUDY ***Federal work-study:*** *Total amount:* $1,036,877; 639 jobs averaging $1615. ***State or other work-study/employment:*** *Total amount:* $83,000 (100% need-based). 52 part-time jobs averaging $1596.

APPLYING for FINANCIAL AID ***Required financial aid forms:*** FAFSA, CSS Financial Aid PROFILE, noncustodial (divorced/separated) parent's statement, business/farm supplement. ***Financial aid deadline:*** 1/15. ***Notification date:*** 4/8. Students must reply by 5/1.

CONTACT Mr. Leigh P. Campbell, Director of Financial Aid, Bates College, Lindholm House, 23 Campus Avenue, Lewiston, ME 04240-6028, 207-786-6060. *Fax:* 207-786-6025. *E-mail:* finaid@bates.edu

BAYAMÓN CENTRAL UNIVERSITY

Bayamón, PR

Tuition & fees: $3570 **Average undergraduate aid package: N/A**

ABOUT THE INSTITUTION Independent Roman Catholic, coed. Awards: associate, bachelor's, and master's degrees. 29 undergraduate majors. Total enrollment: 3,177. Undergraduates: 2,914. Freshmen: 507. Federal methodology is used as a basis for awarding need-based institutional aid.

UNDERGRADUATE EXPENSES for 1999–2000 ***Application fee:*** $15. ***Tuition:*** full-time $3330; part-time $110 per credit. ***Required fees:*** full-time $240; $140 per term part-time. Full-time tuition and fees vary according to program. Part-time tuition and fees vary according to program. ***Payment plan:*** deferred payment.

FRESHMAN FINANCIAL AID (Fall 1999, est.) 717 applied for aid; of those 98% were deemed to have need. 98% of freshmen with need received aid. *Average percent of need met:* 75% (excluding resources awarded to replace EFC).

UNDERGRADUATE FINANCIAL AID (Fall 1999, est.) 2,710 applied for aid; of those 98% were deemed to have need. 97% of undergraduates with need received aid. *Average percent of need met:* 75% (excluding resources awarded to replace EFC).

GIFT AID (NEED-BASED) ***Total amount:*** $7,622,182 (88% Federal, 8% state, 2% institutional, 2% external sources). ***Receiving aid:*** *Freshmen:* 86% (687); *all full-time undergraduates:* 89% (2,570). ***Average award:*** Freshmen: $4500; Undergraduates: $4500. ***Scholarships, grants, and awards:*** Federal Pell, FSEOG, state, college/university gift aid from institutional funds.

GIFT AID (NON-NEED-BASED) ***Tuition waivers:*** Full or partial for employees or children of employees. ***ROTC:*** Army cooperative, Air Force cooperative.

LOANS ***Student loans:*** $2,150,000 (88% need-based, 12% non-need-based). 5% of past graduating class borrowed through all loan programs. Average indebtedness per student: $7500. ***Average need-based loan:*** Freshmen: $2625; Undergraduates: $2625. ***Programs:*** Federal Direct (Subsidized and Unsubsidized Stafford).

WORK-STUDY ***Federal work-study:*** *Total amount:* $419,171; jobs available.

ATHLETIC AWARDS *Total amount:* 175,000 (100% need-based).

APPLYING for FINANCIAL AID ***Required financial aid forms:*** FAFSA, institution's own form, CSS Financial Aid PROFILE, commonwealth aid form. ***Financial aid deadline (priority):*** 4/15. ***Notification date:*** 7/15. Students must reply by 8/15.

CONTACT Mr. Henry Miranda Vázquez, Financial Aid Director, Bayamón Central University, PO Box 1725, Bayamón, PR 00960-1725, 787-786-3030 Ext. 2115. *Fax:* 787-785-4365. *E-mail:* hmiranda@ucb.edu.pr

BAYAMÓN TECHNOLOGICAL UNIVERSITY COLLEGE

Bayamón, PR

CONTACT Financial Aid Director, Bayamón Technological University College, 170 Carr 174 Parque Indust Minillas, Bayamon, PR 00959-1919, 787-786-2885 Ext. 2434.

BAYLOR UNIVERSITY

Waco, TX

Tuition & fees: $11,938 **Average undergraduate aid package: $8805**

ABOUT THE INSTITUTION Independent Baptist, coed. Awards: bachelor's, master's, doctoral, and first professional degrees. 117 undergraduate majors. Total enrollment: 13,334. Undergraduates: 11,472. Freshmen: 2,772. Federal methodology is used as a basis for awarding need-based institutional aid.

UNDERGRADUATE EXPENSES for 2000–2001 ***Application fee:*** $35. ***One-time required fee:*** $850. ***Comprehensive fee:*** $17,176 includes full-time tuition ($10,650), mandatory fees ($1288), and room and board ($5238). ***College room only:*** $2248. Room and board charges vary according to board plan and housing facility. ***Part-time tuition:*** $355 per semester hour. ***Part-time fees:*** $37 per semester hour; $1 per term part-time. ***Payment plans:*** guaranteed tuition, installment.

FRESHMAN FINANCIAL AID (Fall 1999) 2620 applied for aid; of those 50% were deemed to have need. 99% of freshmen with need received aid; of those 17% had need fully met. *Average percent of need met:* 65% (excluding resources awarded to replace EFC). *Average financial aid package:* $8143 (excluding resources awarded to replace EFC). 34% of all full-time freshmen had no need and received non-need-based aid.

UNDERGRADUATE FINANCIAL AID (Fall 1999) 8,739 applied for aid; of those 57% were deemed to have need. 98% of undergraduates with need received aid; of those 19% had need fully met. *Average percent of need met:* 69% (excluding resources awarded to replace EFC). *Average financial aid package:* $8805 (excluding resources awarded to replace EFC). 27% of all full-time undergraduates had no need and received non-need-based aid.

GIFT AID (NEED-BASED) ***Total amount:*** $19,676,634 (21% Federal, 30% state, 42% institutional, 7% external sources). ***Receiving aid:*** *Freshmen:* 47% (1,290); *all full-time undergraduates:* 42% (4,624). ***Average award:*** Freshmen: $4256; Undergraduates: $4359. ***Scholarships, grants, and awards:*** Federal Pell, FSEOG, state, private, college/university gift aid from institutional funds.

GIFT AID (NON-NEED-BASED) ***Total amount:*** $8,840,316 (82% institutional, 18% external sources). ***Receiving aid:*** *Freshmen:* 27% (759); *Undergraduates:* 19% (2,066). ***Scholarships, grants, and awards by category:*** *Academic Interests/Achievement:* 3,943 awards ($10,105,592 total): business, communication, computer science, education, engineering/technologies, English, foreign languages, general academic interests/achievements, health fields, home economics, humanities, international studies, mathematics, physical sciences, premedicine, religion/biblical studies, social sciences. *Creative Arts/Performance:* 414 awards ($898,853 total): art/fine arts, cinema/film/broadcasting, debating, journalism/publications, music, theater/drama. *Special Achievements/Activities:* 306 awards ($752,765 total): community service, leadership, religious involvement. *Special Characteristics:* 272 awards ($2,299,106 total): children of faculty/staff. ***Tuition waivers:*** Full or partial for employees or children of employees. ***ROTC:*** Air Force.

LOANS ***Student loans:*** $37,953,047 (61% need-based, 39% non-need-based). ***Average need-based loan:*** Freshmen: $2355; Undergraduates: $3243. ***Parent loans:*** $7,634,184 (27% need-based, 73% non-need-based). ***Programs:*** FFEL (Subsidized and Unsubsidized Stafford, PLUS), Perkins, Federal Nursing, state, college/university.

WORK-STUDY ***Federal work-study:*** *Total amount:* $7,480,724; jobs available. ***State or other work-study/employment:*** *Total amount:* $1,106,057 (12% need-based, 88% non-need-based). Part-time jobs available.

ATHLETIC AWARDS *Total amount:* 3,654,803 (32% need-based, 68% non-need-based).

APPLYING for FINANCIAL AID ***Required financial aid form:*** FAFSA. ***Financial aid deadline (priority):*** 3/1. ***Notification date:*** Continuous. Students must reply by 5/1 or within 2 weeks of notification.

CONTACT Office of Admission Services, Baylor University, PO Box 97056, Waco, TX 76798-7056, 254-710-3435 or toll-free 800-BAYLOR U. *Fax:* 254-710-3436. *E-mail:* admission_serv_office@baylor.edu

BAY PATH COLLEGE

Longmeadow, MA

Tuition & fees: $13,010 **Average undergraduate aid package: $10,047**

Bay Path College (continued)

ABOUT THE INSTITUTION Independent, women only. Awards: associate and bachelor's degrees. 21 undergraduate majors. Total enrollment: 656. Undergraduates: 656. Both federal and institutional methodology are used as a basis for awarding need-based institutional aid.

UNDERGRADUATE EXPENSES for 1999–2000 ***Application fee:*** $25. ***One-time required fee:*** $250. ***Comprehensive fee:*** $19,874 includes full-time tuition ($13,010) and room and board ($6864). Full-time tuition and fees vary according to course load. Room and board charges vary according to board plan. ***Part-time tuition:*** $350 per credit. Part-time tuition and fees vary according to course load. ***Payment plans:*** tuition prepayment, installment, deferred payment.

FRESHMAN FINANCIAL AID (Fall 1999) 73 applied for aid; of those 89% were deemed to have need. 100% of freshmen with need received aid; of those 8% had need fully met. *Average percent of need met:* 72% (excluding resources awarded to replace EFC). *Average financial aid package:* $10,171 (excluding resources awarded to replace EFC). 28% of all full-time freshmen had no need and received non-need-based aid.

UNDERGRADUATE FINANCIAL AID (Fall 1999) 344 applied for aid; of those 91% were deemed to have need. 100% of undergraduates with need received aid; of those 14% had need fully met. *Average percent of need met:* 75% (excluding resources awarded to replace EFC). *Average financial aid package:* $10,047 (excluding resources awarded to replace EFC). 19% of all full-time undergraduates had no need and received non-need-based aid.

GIFT AID (NEED-BASED) ***Total amount:*** $2,091,750 (19% Federal, 11% state, 68% institutional, 2% external sources). ***Receiving aid:*** *Freshmen:* 72% (65); *all full-time undergraduates:* 81% (313). ***Average award:*** Freshmen: $6718; Undergraduates: $6191. ***Scholarships, grants, and awards:*** Federal Pell, FSEOG, state, private, college/university gift aid from institutional funds.

GIFT AID (NON-NEED-BASED) ***Total amount:*** $538,425 (97% institutional, 3% external sources). ***Receiving aid:*** *Freshmen:* 3% (3); *Undergraduates:* 6% (23). ***Scholarships, grants, and awards by category:*** *Academic Interests/Achievement:* general academic interests/achievements. *Creative Arts/Performance:* dance, performing arts, theater/drama. *Special Achievements/Activities:* general special achievements/activities, memberships. *Special Characteristics:* adult students, children of faculty/staff, children of public servants, children with a deceased or disabled parent, general special characteristics, international students, out-of-state students, siblings of current students, twins. ***Tuition waivers:*** Full or partial for employees or children of employees. ***ROTC:*** Army cooperative, Air Force cooperative.

LOANS ***Student loans:*** $2,103,272 (78% need-based, 22% non-need-based). ***Average need-based loan:*** Freshmen: $3292; Undergraduates: $3871. ***Parent loans:*** $269,200 (50% need-based, 50% non-need-based). ***Programs:*** Federal Direct (Subsidized and Unsubsidized Stafford, PLUS), FFEL (Subsidized and Unsubsidized Stafford, PLUS), Perkins, state.

WORK-STUDY ***Federal work-study:*** *Total amount:* $88,843; 119 jobs averaging $747. ***State or other work-study/employment:*** *Total amount:* $36,626 (100% non-need-based). Part-time jobs available.

APPLYING for FINANCIAL AID ***Required financial aid forms:*** FAFSA, institution's own form, state aid form. ***Financial aid deadline (priority):*** 3/15. ***Notification date:*** Continuous. Students must reply within 2 weeks of notification.

CONTACT Phyllis Brand, Financial Aid Assistant, Bay Path College, 588 Longmeadow Street, Longmeadow, MA 01106-2292, 413-565-1261 or toll-free 800-782-7284. *Fax:* 413-565-1101. *E-mail:* pbrand@baypath.edu

BEACON COLLEGE

Columbus, GA

CONTACT Financial Aid Office, Beacon College, 1622 13th Avenue, Columbus, GA 31901, 706-323-5364.

BEAVER COLLEGE

Glenside, PA

Tuition & fees: $17,160 | **Average undergraduate aid package: $15,402**

ABOUT THE INSTITUTION Independent religious, coed. Awards: bachelor's, master's, and doctoral degrees. 50 undergraduate majors. Total enrollment: 2,765. Undergraduates: 1,635. Freshmen: 354. Federal methodology is used as a basis for awarding need-based institutional aid.

UNDERGRADUATE EXPENSES for 1999–2000 ***Application fee:*** $30. ***Comprehensive fee:*** $24,470 includes full-time tuition ($16,880), mandatory fees ($280), and room and board ($7310). Room and board charges vary according to board plan. ***Part-time tuition:*** $320 per credit. ***Payment plans:*** installment, deferred payment.

FRESHMAN FINANCIAL AID (Fall 1999) 316 applied for aid; of those 92% were deemed to have need. 99% of freshmen with need received aid; of those 14% had need fully met. *Average percent of need met:* 87% (excluding resources awarded to replace EFC). *Average financial aid package:* $16,339 (excluding resources awarded to replace EFC). 7% of all full-time freshmen had no need and received non-need-based aid.

UNDERGRADUATE FINANCIAL AID (Fall 1999) 1,191 applied for aid; of those 98% were deemed to have need. 95% of undergraduates with need received aid; of those 13% had need fully met. *Average percent of need met:* 82% (excluding resources awarded to replace EFC). *Average financial aid package:* $15,402 (excluding resources awarded to replace EFC). 6% of all full-time undergraduates had no need and received non-need-based aid.

GIFT AID (NEED-BASED) ***Total amount:*** $7,462,181 (16% Federal, 20% state, 58% institutional, 6% external sources). ***Receiving aid:*** *Freshmen:* 73% (233); *all full-time undergraduates:* 71% (904). ***Average award:*** Freshmen: $6360; Undergraduates: $5838. ***Scholarships, grants, and awards:*** Federal Pell, FSEOG, state, private, college/university gift aid from institutional funds.

GIFT AID (NON-NEED-BASED) ***Total amount:*** $4,315,845 (99% institutional, 1% external sources). ***Receiving aid:*** *Freshmen:* 78% (251); *Undergraduates:* 66% (837). ***Scholarships, grants, and awards by category:*** *Academic Interests/Achievement:* communication, English, general academic interests/achievements, mathematics. *Creative Arts/Performance:* art/fine arts. *Special Achievements/Activities:* community service, leadership. *Special Characteristics:* children and siblings of alumni, relatives of clergy, religious affiliation. ***Tuition waivers:*** Full or partial for employees or children of employees. ***ROTC:*** Army cooperative.

LOANS ***Student loans:*** $7,142,627 (52% need-based, 48% non-need-based). 60% of past graduating class borrowed through all loan programs. Average indebtedness per student: $17,125. ***Average need-based loan:*** Freshmen: $2160; Undergraduates: $2901. ***Parent loans:*** $901,290 (92% need-based, 8% non-need-based). ***Programs:*** FFEL (Subsidized and Unsubsidized Stafford, PLUS), Perkins, college/university.

WORK-STUDY ***Federal work-study:*** *Total amount:* $780,800; 707 jobs averaging $1104. ***State or other work-study/employment:*** *Total amount:* $50,425 (100% non-need-based). 47 part-time jobs averaging $1073.

APPLYING for FINANCIAL AID ***Required financial aid forms:*** FAFSA, institution's own form. ***Financial aid deadline (priority):*** 3/1. ***Notification date:*** Continuous. Students must reply by 5/1.

CONTACT Ms. Elizabeth Rihl Lewinsky, Director of Financial Aid, Beaver College, 450 South Easton Road, Glenside, PA 19038-3295, 215-572-2980 or toll-free 888-BEAVER3. *Fax:* 215-572-4049. *E-mail:* finaid@beaver.edu

BECKER COLLEGE

Worcester, MA

Tuition & fees: $11,710 | **Average undergraduate aid package: $6756**

ABOUT THE INSTITUTION Independent, coed. Awards: associate and bachelor's degrees (also includes Leicester, MA small town campus). 31

undergraduate majors. Total enrollment: 1,010. Undergraduates: 1,010. Freshmen: 420. Federal methodology is used as a basis for awarding need-based institutional aid.

UNDERGRADUATE EXPENSES for 1999–2000 ***Application fee:*** $25. ***Comprehensive fee:*** $17,540 includes full-time tuition ($11,490), mandatory fees ($220), and room and board ($5830). Full-time tuition and fees vary according to class time, course load, and program. ***Part-time tuition:*** $383 per credit. Part-time tuition and fees vary according to class time, course load, and program. ***Payment plan:*** installment.

FRESHMAN FINANCIAL AID (Fall 1999) 363 applied for aid; of those 90% were deemed to have need. 100% of freshmen with need received aid; of those 25% had need fully met. *Average percent of need met:* 66% (excluding resources awarded to replace EFC). *Average financial aid package:* $7407 (excluding resources awarded to replace EFC). 6% of all full-time freshmen had no need and received non-need-based aid.

UNDERGRADUATE FINANCIAL AID (Fall 1999) 787 applied for aid; of those 89% were deemed to have need. 100% of undergraduates with need received aid; of those 25% had need fully met. *Average percent of need met:* 61% (excluding resources awarded to replace EFC). *Average financial aid package:* $6756 (excluding resources awarded to replace EFC). 8% of all full-time undergraduates had no need and received non-need-based aid.

GIFT AID (NEED-BASED) ***Total amount:*** $3,166,349 (48% Federal, 10% state, 42% institutional). ***Receiving aid:*** *Freshmen:* 78% (304); *all full-time undergraduates:* 79% (658). ***Average award:*** Freshmen: $2310; Undergraduates: $2026. ***Scholarships, grants, and awards:*** Federal Pell, FSEOG, state, private, college/university gift aid from institutional funds.

GIFT AID (NON-NEED-BASED) ***Total amount:*** $292,996 (45% institutional, 55% external sources). ***Receiving aid:*** *Freshmen:* 20% (77); *Undergraduates:* 12% (104). ***Scholarships, grants, and awards by category:*** *Academic Interests/Achievement:* 5 awards ($6000 total): general academic interests/achievements. *Special Achievements/Activities:* 17 awards ($48,500 total): general special achievements/activities, leadership. *Special Characteristics:* 19 awards ($140,132 total): children of current students, children of faculty/staff, parents of current students, siblings of current students, spouses of current students, twins. ***Tuition waivers:*** Full or partial for employees or children of employees, senior citizens. ***ROTC:*** Army cooperative, Naval cooperative, Air Force cooperative.

LOANS ***Student loans:*** $4,041,963 (50% need-based, 50% non-need-based). 89% of past graduating class borrowed through all loan programs. Average indebtedness per student: $16,410. ***Average need-based loan:*** Freshmen: $1897; Undergraduates: $2688. ***Parent loans:*** $1,445,644 (100% non-need-based). ***Programs:*** FFEL (Subsidized and Unsubsidized Stafford, PLUS), Perkins, state.

WORK-STUDY ***Federal work-study:*** *Total amount:* $400,158; 422 jobs averaging $948.

APPLYING for FINANCIAL AID ***Required financial aid forms:*** FAFSA, institution's own form. ***Financial aid deadline (priority):*** 4/1. ***Notification date:*** Continuous. Students must reply within 2 weeks of notification.

CONTACT Ms. Lisa Flynn, Director of Financial Aid, Becker College, 61 Sever Street, PO Box 15071, Worcester, MA 01615-0071, 508-791-9241 Ext. 242 or toll-free 877-5BECKER Ext. 245. *Fax:* 508-890-1500. *E-mail:* flynn@go.becker.edu

BELHAVEN COLLEGE

Jackson, MS

Tuition & fees: $10,340 **Average undergraduate aid package: $10,875**

ABOUT THE INSTITUTION Independent Presbyterian, coed. Awards: bachelor's and master's degrees. 22 undergraduate majors. Total enrollment: 1,415. Undergraduates: 1,317. Freshmen: 147. Federal methodology is used as a basis for awarding need-based institutional aid.

UNDERGRADUATE EXPENSES for 1999–2000 ***Application fee:*** $25. ***One-time required fee:*** $30. ***Comprehensive fee:*** $14,190 includes full-time tuition ($9960), mandatory fees ($380), and room and board ($3850). Room and board charges vary according to housing facility. ***Part-time tuition:*** $267 per semester hour. ***Part-time fees:*** $50 per term part-time. Part-time tuition and fees vary according to course load. ***Payment plan:*** installment.

FRESHMAN FINANCIAL AID (Fall 1999) 147 applied for aid; of those 80% were deemed to have need. 100% of freshmen with need received aid; of those 11% had need fully met. *Average percent of need met:* 64% (excluding resources awarded to replace EFC). *Average financial aid package:* $10,218 (excluding resources awarded to replace EFC). 20% of all full-time freshmen had no need and received non-need-based aid.

UNDERGRADUATE FINANCIAL AID (Fall 1999) 954 applied for aid; of those 89% were deemed to have need. 100% of undergraduates with need received aid; of those 17% had need fully met. *Average percent of need met:* 66% (excluding resources awarded to replace EFC). *Average financial aid package:* $10,875 (excluding resources awarded to replace EFC). 14% of all full-time undergraduates had no need and received non-need-based aid.

GIFT AID (NEED-BASED) ***Total amount:*** $1,953,169 (66% Federal, 19% state, 2% institutional, 13% external sources). ***Receiving aid:*** *Freshmen:* 77% (113); *all full-time undergraduates:* 63% (732). ***Average award:*** Freshmen: $3058; Undergraduates: $2668. ***Scholarships, grants, and awards:*** Federal Pell, FSEOG, state, private, college/university gift aid from institutional funds.

GIFT AID (NON-NEED-BASED) ***Total amount:*** $1,725,019 (7% state, 92% institutional, 1% external sources). ***Receiving aid:*** *Freshmen:* 80% (117); *Undergraduates:* 50% (583). ***Scholarships, grants, and awards by category:*** *Academic Interests/Achievement:* general academic interests/achievements, religion/biblical studies. *Creative Arts/Performance:* applied art and design, art/fine arts, dance, music, performing arts, theater/drama. *Special Achievements/Activities:* cheerleading/drum major, junior miss, leadership. *Special Characteristics:* children of faculty/staff, international students, relatives of clergy. ***Tuition waivers:*** Full or partial for employees or children of employees, senior citizens.

LOANS ***Student loans:*** $6,397,596 (84% need-based, 16% non-need-based). 73% of past graduating class borrowed through all loan programs. Average indebtedness per student: $10,255. ***Average need-based loan:*** Freshmen: $2349; Undergraduates: $4401. ***Parent loans:*** $456,234 (73% need-based, 27% non-need-based). ***Programs:*** FFEL (Subsidized and Unsubsidized Stafford, PLUS), Perkins.

WORK-STUDY ***Federal work-study:*** *Total amount:* $182,810; 118 jobs averaging $1545.

ATHLETIC AWARDS *Total amount:* 789,928 (100% non-need-based).

APPLYING for FINANCIAL AID ***Required financial aid forms:*** FAFSA, state aid form. ***Financial aid deadline (priority):*** 4/1. ***Notification date:*** Continuous. Students must reply within 4 weeks of notification.

CONTACT Ms. Linda Phillips, Director of Financial Aid, Belhaven College, 1500 Peachtree Street, Jackson, MS 39202-1789, 601-968-5934 or toll-free 800-960-5940. *Fax:* 601-353-0701. *E-mail:* lphillips@belhaven.edu

BELLARMINE COLLEGE

Louisville, KY

Tuition & fees: $12,650 **Average undergraduate aid package: N/A**

ABOUT THE INSTITUTION Independent Roman Catholic, coed. Awards: bachelor's and master's degrees. 48 undergraduate majors. Total enrollment: 2,880. Undergraduates: 2,373. Freshmen: 329. Federal methodology is used as a basis for awarding need-based institutional aid.

UNDERGRADUATE EXPENSES for 1999–2000 ***Application fee:*** $25. ***Comprehensive fee:*** $16,590 includes full-time tuition ($12,480), mandatory fees ($170), and room and board ($3940). ***College room only:*** $2440. Room and board charges vary according to housing facility. ***Part-time tuition:*** $330 per credit. Part-time tuition and fees vary according to course load. ***Payment plans:*** installment, deferred payment.

FRESHMAN FINANCIAL AID (Fall 1999) 286 applied for aid; of those 73% were deemed to have need. 100% of freshmen with need received aid; of those 36% had need fully met. *Average percent of need met:* 83% (excluding resources awarded to replace EFC). *Average financial aid package:*

Bellarmine College (continued)

$11,469 (excluding resources awarded to replace EFC). 36% of all full-time freshmen had no need and received non-need-based aid.

GIFT AID (NEED-BASED) ***Total amount:*** $2,577,944 (21% Federal, 42% state, 37% institutional). ***Receiving aid:*** *Freshmen:* 64% (208). ***Average award:*** Freshmen: $7557. ***Scholarships, grants, and awards:*** Federal Pell, FSEOG, state, private, college/university gift aid from institutional funds.

GIFT AID (NON-NEED-BASED) ***Total amount:*** $4,191,280 (4% state, 93% institutional, 3% external sources). ***Receiving aid:*** *Freshmen:* 63% (205). ***Scholarships, grants, and awards by category:*** *Academic Interests/Achievement:* 762 awards ($2,648,399 total): biological sciences, business, education, general academic interests/achievements, health fields. *Creative Arts/Performance:* 46 awards ($35,250 total): art/fine arts, music. *Special Achievements/Activities:* 148 awards ($241,086 total): cheerleading/drum major, community service, general special achievements/activities, leadership, religious involvement. *Special Characteristics:* 192 awards ($436,279 total): adult students, children of faculty/staff, ethnic background, international students, local/state students, out-of-state students, previous college experience. ***Tuition waivers:*** Full or partial for employees or children of employees, senior citizens. ***ROTC:*** Army cooperative, Air Force cooperative.

LOANS ***Student loans:*** $4,082,845 (59% need-based, 41% non-need-based). 52% of past graduating class borrowed through all loan programs. Average indebtedness per student: $14,200. ***Average need-based loan:*** Freshmen: $2830. ***Parent loans:*** $464,707 (100% non-need-based). ***Programs:*** FFEL (Subsidized and Unsubsidized Stafford, PLUS), Perkins, college/university, alternative loans.

WORK-STUDY ***Federal work-study:*** *Total amount:* $326,113; 182 jobs averaging $1792.

ATHLETIC AWARDS *Total amount:* 786,960 (100% non-need-based).

APPLYING for FINANCIAL AID ***Required financial aid form:*** FAFSA. ***Financial aid deadline (priority):*** 3/1. ***Notification date:*** 4/1. Students must reply by 5/1 or within 2 weeks of notification.

CONTACT Mr. David R. Wuinee, Director of Financial Aid, Bellarmine College, 2001 Newburg Road, Louisville, KY 40205-0671, 502-452-8124 or toll-free 800-274-4723 Ext. 8131. *Fax:* 502-452-8002. *E-mail:* dwuinee@bellarmine.edu

BELLEVUE UNIVERSITY

Bellevue, NE

Tuition & fees: $4030 **Average undergraduate aid package: N/A**

ABOUT THE INSTITUTION Independent, coed. Awards: bachelor's and master's degrees. 21 undergraduate majors. Total enrollment: 3,035. Undergraduates: 2,486. Federal methodology is used as a basis for awarding need-based institutional aid.

UNDERGRADUATE EXPENSES for 2000–2001 ***Application fee:*** $25. ***Tuition:*** full-time $3960; part-time $132 per credit hour. ***Required fees:*** full-time $70; $35 per term part-time. Full-time tuition and fees vary according to program. ***Payment plans:*** installment, deferred payment.

FRESHMAN FINANCIAL AID (Fall 1999, est.) 78 applied for aid; of those 100% were deemed to have need. 100% of freshmen with need received aid; of those 100% had need fully met. *Average percent of need met:* 95% (excluding resources awarded to replace EFC). 18% of all full-time freshmen had no need and received non-need-based aid.

UNDERGRADUATE FINANCIAL AID (Fall 1999, est.) 1,178 applied for aid; of those 100% were deemed to have need. 100% of undergraduates with need received aid; of those 100% had need fully met. *Average percent of need met:* 95% (excluding resources awarded to replace EFC). 9% of all full-time undergraduates had no need and received non-need-based aid.

GIFT AID (NEED-BASED) ***Total amount:*** $1,499,650 (75% Federal, 20% state, 5% institutional). ***Receiving aid:*** *Freshmen:* 24% (23); *all full-time undergraduates:* 34% (541). ***Average award:*** Freshmen: $2760; Undergraduates: $2622. ***Scholarships, grants, and awards:*** Federal Pell, FSEOG, state, college/university gift aid from institutional funds.

GIFT AID (NON-NEED-BASED) ***Total amount:*** $318,392 (83% institutional, 17% external sources). ***Receiving aid:*** *Freshmen:* 14% (13); *Undergraduates:* 56% (880). ***Scholarships, grants, and awards by category:*** *Academic Interests/Achievement:* 121 awards ($100,524 total): business, general academic interests/achievements, humanities, mathematics, social sciences. *Creative Arts/Performance:* art/fine arts. *Special Achievements/Activities:* 12 awards ($5400 total): leadership. *Special Characteristics:* 156 awards ($99,779 total): general special characteristics, international students. ***Tuition waivers:*** Full or partial for employees or children of employees. ***ROTC:*** Army cooperative, Air Force cooperative.

LOANS ***Student loans:*** $11,943,257 (53% need-based, 47% non-need-based). ***Average need-based loan:*** Freshmen: $2536; Undergraduates: $7142. ***Parent loans:*** $255,107 (100% non-need-based). ***Programs:*** FFEL (Subsidized and Unsubsidized Stafford, PLUS).

WORK-STUDY ***Federal work-study:*** *Total amount:* $86,981; 47 jobs averaging $1851.

ATHLETIC AWARDS *Total amount:* 148,100 (100% non-need-based).

APPLYING for FINANCIAL AID ***Required financial aid forms:*** FAFSA, institution's own form. ***Financial aid deadline:*** Continuous. ***Notification date:*** Continuous beginning 4/1. Students must reply within 2 weeks of notification.

CONTACT Mr. Jon Dotterer, Director of Financial Aid, Bellevue University, 1000 Galvin Road South, Bellevue, NE 68005, 402-293-3762 or toll-free 800-756-7920. *Fax:* 402-293-2062.

BELLIN COLLEGE OF NURSING

Green Bay, WI

Tuition & fees: $9455 **Average undergraduate aid package: $10,030**

ABOUT THE INSTITUTION Independent, coed, primarily women. Awards: bachelor's degrees. 1 undergraduate major. Total enrollment: 160. Undergraduates: 160. Freshmen: 26. Federal methodology is used as a basis for awarding need-based institutional aid.

UNDERGRADUATE EXPENSES for 1999–2000 ***Application fee:*** $20. ***Tuition:*** full-time $9289; part-time $464 per credit. ***Required fees:*** full-time $166. Full-time tuition and fees vary according to student level. ***Payment plan:*** installment.

UNDERGRADUATE FINANCIAL AID (Fall 1999) 89 applied for aid; of those 88% were deemed to have need. 100% of undergraduates with need received aid; of those 24% had need fully met. *Average percent of need met:* 82% (excluding resources awarded to replace EFC). *Average financial aid package:* $10,030 (excluding resources awarded to replace EFC). 6% of all full-time undergraduates had no need and received non-need-based aid.

GIFT AID (NEED-BASED) ***Total amount:*** $412,335 (13% Federal, 12% state, 49% institutional, 26% external sources). ***Receiving aid:*** *All full-time undergraduates:* 54% (78). ***Average award:*** Undergraduates: $5286. ***Scholarships, grants, and awards:*** Federal Pell, FSEOG, state, private, college/university gift aid from institutional funds.

GIFT AID (NON-NEED-BASED) ***Total amount:*** $10,306 (49% institutional, 51% external sources). ***Receiving aid:*** *Undergraduates:* 2% (3). ***Scholarships, grants, and awards by category:*** *Academic Interests/Achievement:* 13 awards ($20,600 total): general academic interests/achievements. ***ROTC:*** Army cooperative.

LOANS ***Student loans:*** $664,031 (84% need-based, 16% non-need-based). 80% of past graduating class borrowed through all loan programs. Average indebtedness per student: $18,961. ***Average need-based loan:*** Undergraduates: $5200. ***Parent loans:*** $45,600 (64% need-based, 36% non-need-based). ***Programs:*** FFEL (Subsidized and Unsubsidized Stafford, PLUS), college/university.

WORK-STUDY ***Federal work-study:*** *Total amount:* $10,200; 7 jobs averaging $1457.

APPLYING for FINANCIAL AID ***Required financial aid form:*** FAFSA. ***Financial aid deadline (priority):*** 3/1. ***Notification date:*** 5/1. Students must reply within 2 weeks of notification.

CONTACT Ms. Lena C. Terry, Director of Financial Aid, Bellin College of Nursing, 725 South Webster Avenue, PO Box 23400, Green Bay, WI 54305-3400, 920-433-5801 or toll-free 800-236-8707 (in-state). *Fax:* 920-433-7416. *E-mail:* lcterry@bcon.edu

BELMONT ABBEY COLLEGE

Belmont, NC

Tuition & fees: $12,712 **Average undergraduate aid package: $14,000**

ABOUT THE INSTITUTION Independent Roman Catholic, coed. Awards: bachelor's degrees. 24 undergraduate majors. Total enrollment: 926. Undergraduates: 926. Freshmen: 199. Federal methodology is used as a basis for awarding need-based institutional aid.

UNDERGRADUATE EXPENSES for 2000–2001 ***Application fee:*** $25. ***Comprehensive fee:*** $19,240 includes full-time tuition ($12,116), mandatory fees ($596), and room and board ($6528). ***College room only:*** $3676. Full-time tuition and fees vary according to class time, course load, and student level. Room and board charges vary according to board plan and housing facility. ***Part-time tuition:*** $379 per credit hour. ***Part-time fees:*** $38 per credit hour. Part-time tuition and fees vary according to class time and course load. ***Payment plan:*** installment.

FRESHMAN FINANCIAL AID (Fall 1999, est.) 165 applied for aid; of those 85% were deemed to have need. 100% of freshmen with need received aid; of those 6% had need fully met. *Average percent of need met:* 74% (excluding resources awarded to replace EFC). *Average financial aid package:* $11,625 (excluding resources awarded to replace EFC). 11% of all full-time freshmen had no need and received non-need-based aid.

UNDERGRADUATE FINANCIAL AID (Fall 1999, est.) 617 applied for aid; of those 78% were deemed to have need. 100% of undergraduates with need received aid; of those 6% had need fully met. *Average percent of need met:* 72% (excluding resources awarded to replace EFC). *Average financial aid package:* $14,000 (excluding resources awarded to replace EFC). 13% of all full-time undergraduates had no need and received non-need-based aid.

GIFT AID (NEED-BASED) ***Total amount:*** $2,205,849 (25% Federal, 20% state, 55% institutional). ***Receiving aid:*** *Freshmen:* 61% (119); *all full-time undergraduates:* 52% (409). ***Average award:*** Freshmen: $6000; Undergraduates: $6500. ***Scholarships, grants, and awards:*** Federal Pell, FSEOG, state, private, college/university gift aid from institutional funds.

GIFT AID (NON-NEED-BASED) ***Total amount:*** $2,729,304 (27% state, 73% institutional). ***Receiving aid:*** *Freshmen:* 19% (37); *Undergraduates:* 13% (104). ***Scholarships, grants, and awards by category:*** *Academic Interests/Achievement:* 161 awards ($708,750 total): general academic interests/achievements. *Special Achievements/Activities:* 157 awards ($577,153 total): general special achievements/activities, leadership. *Special Characteristics:* 193 awards ($504,214 total): children of faculty/staff, international students, local/state students, religious affiliation, siblings of current students. ***Tuition waivers:*** Full or partial for employees or children of employees, senior citizens. ***ROTC:*** Army cooperative, Air Force cooperative.

LOANS ***Student loans:*** $1,187,474 (69% need-based, 31% non-need-based). 76% of past graduating class borrowed through all loan programs. Average indebtedness per student: $4000. ***Average need-based loan:*** Freshmen: $2625; Undergraduates: $4500. ***Parent loans:*** $403,162 (100% need-based). ***Programs:*** Federal Direct (Subsidized and Unsubsidized Stafford, PLUS), Perkins.

WORK-STUDY ***Federal work-study:*** *Total amount:* $275,000; 172 jobs averaging $1600.

ATHLETIC AWARDS *Total amount:* 501,549 (100% non-need-based).

APPLYING for FINANCIAL AID ***Required financial aid form:*** FAFSA. ***Financial aid deadline (priority):*** 4/1. ***Notification date:*** Continuous. Students must reply within 2 weeks of notification.

CONTACT Ms. Julie Hodge, Associate Director of Financial Aid, Belmont Abbey College, 100 Belmont Mt. Holly Road, Belmont, NC 28012-1802, 704-825-6718 or toll-free 888-BAC-0110. *Fax:* 704-825-6882. *E-mail:* hodge@crusader.bac.edu

BELMONT UNIVERSITY

Nashville, TN

Tuition & fees: $11,600 **Average undergraduate aid package: $11,764**

ABOUT THE INSTITUTION Independent Baptist, coed. Awards: bachelor's and master's degrees and post-bachelor's certificates. 74 undergraduate majors. Total enrollment: 3,026. Undergraduates: 2,521. Freshmen: 507. Federal methodology is used as a basis for awarding need-based institutional aid.

UNDERGRADUATE EXPENSES for 1999–2000 ***Application fee:*** $35. ***Comprehensive fee:*** $16,600 includes full-time tuition ($11,300), mandatory fees ($300), and room and board ($5000). ***College room only:*** $2390. Full-time tuition and fees vary according to class time and course load. Room and board charges vary according to board plan, housing facility, and location. ***Part-time tuition:*** $425 per semester hour. ***Part-time fees:*** $90 per term part-time. Part-time tuition and fees vary according to course load. ***Payment plans:*** installment, deferred payment.

FRESHMAN FINANCIAL AID (Fall 1999, est.) 403 applied for aid; of those 60% were deemed to have need. 100% of freshmen with need received aid; of those 32% had need fully met. *Average percent of need met:* 94% (excluding resources awarded to replace EFC). *Average financial aid package:* $10,913 (excluding resources awarded to replace EFC). 31% of all full-time freshmen had no need and received non-need-based aid.

UNDERGRADUATE FINANCIAL AID (Fall 1999, est.) 1,647 applied for aid; of those 65% were deemed to have need. 99% of undergraduates with need received aid; of those 29% had need fully met. *Average percent of need met:* 86% (excluding resources awarded to replace EFC). *Average financial aid package:* $11,764 (excluding resources awarded to replace EFC). 21% of all full-time undergraduates had no need and received non-need-based aid.

GIFT AID (NEED-BASED) ***Total amount:*** $3,691,279 (27% Federal, 6% state, 67% institutional). ***Receiving aid:*** *Freshmen:* 33% (158); *all full-time undergraduates:* 39% (821). ***Average award:*** Freshmen: $3841; Undergraduates: $3780. ***Scholarships, grants, and awards:*** Federal Pell, FSEOG, state, private, college/university gift aid from institutional funds.

GIFT AID (NON-NEED-BASED) ***Total amount:*** $2,521,190 (100% institutional). ***Receiving aid:*** *Freshmen:* 34% (159); *Undergraduates:* 25% (520). ***Scholarships, grants, and awards by category:*** *Academic Interests/Achievement:* general academic interests/achievements, religion/biblical studies. *Creative Arts/Performance:* music. *Special Characteristics:* children of faculty/staff, religious affiliation. ***Tuition waivers:*** Full or partial for employees or children of employees, senior citizens. ***ROTC:*** Army cooperative.

LOANS ***Student loans:*** $7,419,720 (97% need-based, 3% non-need-based). 62% of past graduating class borrowed through all loan programs. Average indebtedness per student: $20,469. ***Average need-based loan:*** Freshmen: $3699; Undergraduates: $5852. ***Parent loans:*** $8,362,840 (100% non-need-based). ***Programs:*** FFEL (Subsidized and Unsubsidized Stafford, PLUS), Perkins, college/university.

WORK-STUDY ***Federal work-study:*** *Total amount:* $694,179; 340 jobs averaging $2000.

ATHLETIC AWARDS *Total amount:* 1,514,550 (100% non-need-based).

APPLYING for FINANCIAL AID ***Required financial aid form:*** FAFSA. ***Financial aid deadline (priority):*** 3/1. ***Notification date:*** Continuous beginning 3/15. Students must reply within 2 weeks of notification.

CONTACT Mr. Clyde Walker, Director of Financial Aid, Belmont University, 1900 Belmont Boulevard, Nashville, TN 37212-3757, 615-460-6403 or toll-free 800-56E-NROL. *E-mail:* walkerc@mail.belmont.edu

BELOIT COLLEGE

Beloit, WI

Tuition & fees: $20,440 **Average undergraduate aid package: $16,256**

Beloit College (continued)

ABOUT THE INSTITUTION Independent, coed. Awards: bachelor's degrees. 56 undergraduate majors. Total enrollment: 1,223. Undergraduates: 1,223. Freshmen: 302. Both federal and institutional methodology are used as a basis for awarding need-based institutional aid.

UNDERGRADUATE EXPENSES for 1999–2000 ***Application fee:*** $25. ***Comprehensive fee:*** $25,068 includes full-time tuition ($20,220), mandatory fees ($220), and room and board ($4628). ***College room only:*** $2258. Room and board charges vary according to board plan and housing facility. ***Part-time tuition:*** $2530 per course. ***Payment plan:*** installment.

FRESHMAN FINANCIAL AID (Fall 1998) 259 applied for aid; of those 93% were deemed to have need. 100% of freshmen with need received aid; of those 100% had need fully met. *Average percent of need met:* 100% (excluding resources awarded to replace EFC). *Average financial aid package:* $15,879 (excluding resources awarded to replace EFC). 3% of all full-time freshmen had no need and received non-need-based aid.

UNDERGRADUATE FINANCIAL AID (Fall 1998) 985 applied for aid; of those 95% were deemed to have need. 100% of undergraduates with need received aid; of those 100% had need fully met. *Average percent of need met:* 100% (excluding resources awarded to replace EFC). *Average financial aid package:* $16,256 (excluding resources awarded to replace EFC). 5% of all full-time undergraduates had no need and received non-need-based aid.

GIFT AID (NEED-BASED) ***Total amount:*** $9,992,518 (7% Federal, 3% state, 87% institutional, 3% external sources). ***Receiving aid:*** *Freshmen:* 80% (239); *all full-time undergraduates:* 80% (912). ***Average award:*** Freshmen: $11,157; Undergraduates: $11,216. ***Scholarships, grants, and awards:*** Federal Pell, FSEOG, state, private, college/university gift aid from institutional funds.

GIFT AID (NON-NEED-BASED) ***Total amount:*** $445,000 (100% institutional). ***Scholarships, grants, and awards by category:*** *Academic Interests/Achievement:* general academic interests/achievements. *Creative Arts/Performance:* music. *Special Achievements/Activities:* community service, general special achievements/activities. *Special Characteristics:* members of minority groups, siblings of current students. ***Tuition waivers:*** Full or partial for employees or children of employees, adult students, senior citizens.

LOANS ***Student loans:*** $3,457,173 (73% need-based, 27% non-need-based). 75% of past graduating class borrowed through all loan programs. Average indebtedness per student: $12,896. ***Average need-based loan:*** Freshmen: $3379; Undergraduates: $3640. ***Parent loans:*** $659,500 (100% non-need-based). ***Programs:*** FFEL (Subsidized and Unsubsidized Stafford, PLUS), Perkins, college/university.

WORK-STUDY ***Federal work-study:*** *Total amount:* $767,252; jobs available. ***State or other work-study/employment:*** *Total amount:* $469,535 (67% need-based, 33% non-need-based). Part-time jobs available.

APPLYING for FINANCIAL AID ***Required financial aid forms:*** FAFSA, institution's own form, state aid form, noncustodial (divorced/separated) parent's statement. ***Financial aid deadline:*** 2/1. ***Notification date:*** Continuous. Students must reply by 5/1.

CONTACT Mr. John Urish, Director of Freshman Financial Aid, Beloit College, 700 College Street, Beloit, WI 53511-5596, 800-356-0751.

BEMIDJI STATE UNIVERSITY

Bemidji, MN

Tuition & fees (MN res): $3579 **Average undergraduate aid package: $5128**

ABOUT THE INSTITUTION State-supported, coed. Awards: associate, bachelor's, and master's degrees. 70 undergraduate majors. Total enrollment: 4,539. Undergraduates: 4,293. Freshmen: 616. Federal methodology is used as a basis for awarding need-based institutional aid.

UNDERGRADUATE EXPENSES for 1999–2000 ***Application fee:*** $20. ***Tuition, state resident:*** full-time $2970; part-time $100 per semester hour. ***Tuition, nonresident:*** full-time $5940; part-time $196 per semester hour. ***Required fees:*** full-time $609; $43 per semester hour. Full-time tuition and fees vary according to reciprocity agreements. Part-time tuition and fees vary according to course load and reciprocity agreements. ***College room and board:*** $3778; ***room only:*** $2048. Room and board charges vary according to board plan and housing facility. ***Payment plan:*** installment.

FRESHMAN FINANCIAL AID (Fall 1998) 515 applied for aid; of those 90% were deemed to have need. 93% of freshmen with need received aid; of those 90% had need fully met. *Average percent of need met:* 53% (excluding resources awarded to replace EFC). *Average financial aid package:* $4233 (excluding resources awarded to replace EFC). 5% of all full-time freshmen had no need and received non-need-based aid.

UNDERGRADUATE FINANCIAL AID (Fall 1998) 2,840 applied for aid; of those 92% were deemed to have need. 96% of undergraduates with need received aid; of those 85% had need fully met. *Average percent of need met:* 61% (excluding resources awarded to replace EFC). *Average financial aid package:* $5128 (excluding resources awarded to replace EFC). 4% of all full-time undergraduates had no need and received non-need-based aid.

GIFT AID (NEED-BASED) ***Total amount:*** $6,016,250 (59% Federal, 39% state, 1% institutional, 1% external sources). ***Receiving aid:*** *Freshmen:* 50% (285); *all full-time undergraduates:* 53% (1,759). ***Average award:*** Freshmen: $3175; Undergraduates: $3328. ***Scholarships, grants, and awards:*** Federal Pell, FSEOG, state, private, college/university gift aid from institutional funds.

GIFT AID (NON-NEED-BASED) ***Total amount:*** $1,867,412 (15% Federal, 22% state, 29% institutional, 34% external sources). ***Receiving aid:*** *Freshmen:* 24% (140); *Undergraduates:* 28% (946). ***Scholarships, grants, and awards by category:*** *Academic Interests/Achievement:* 445 awards ($493,483 total): general academic interests/achievements. *Creative Arts/Performance:* 14 awards ($4400 total): music, theater/drama. *Special Characteristics:* out-of-state students. ***Tuition waivers:*** Full or partial for employees or children of employees, senior citizens.

LOANS ***Student loans:*** $7,452,457 (57% need-based, 43% non-need-based). 68% of past graduating class borrowed through all loan programs. Average indebtedness per student: $12,670. ***Average need-based loan:*** Freshmen: $2006; Undergraduates: $2669. ***Parent loans:*** $94,658 (100% non-need-based). ***Programs:*** Federal Direct (Subsidized and Unsubsidized Stafford, PLUS), Perkins, state, Alaska Loans, Canadian Student Loans, Norwest Collegiate Loans, CitiAssist Loans.

WORK-STUDY ***Federal work-study:*** *Total amount:* $279,913; 256 jobs averaging $1093. ***State or other work-study/employment:*** *Total amount:* $359,967 (100% need-based). 359 part-time jobs available.

ATHLETIC AWARDS *Total amount:* 143,225 (100% non-need-based).

APPLYING for FINANCIAL AID ***Required financial aid forms:*** FAFSA, institution's own form. ***Financial aid deadline (priority):*** 5/15. ***Notification date:*** Continuous.

CONTACT Financial Aid Office, Bemidji State University, 1500 Birchmont Drive, NE, Bemidji, MN 56601-2699, 218-755-2034 or toll-free 800-475-2001 (in-state), 800-652-9747 (out-of-state). *Fax:* 218-755-4361. *E-mail:* financialaid@vax1.bemidji.msus.edu

BENEDICT COLLEGE

Columbia, SC

CONTACT Financial Aid Office, Benedict College, 1600 Harden Street, Columbia, SC 29204, 803-253-5105 or toll-free 800-868-6598 (in-state).

BENEDICTINE COLLEGE

Atchison, KS

Tuition & fees: $12,316 **Average undergraduate aid package: $12,960**

ABOUT THE INSTITUTION Independent Roman Catholic, coed. Awards: associate, bachelor's, and master's degrees. 44 undergraduate majors. Total enrollment: 1,434. Undergraduates: 1,390. Freshmen: 246. Federal methodology is used as a basis for awarding need-based institutional aid.

UNDERGRADUATE EXPENSES for 1999–2000 ***Application fee:*** $25. ***Comprehensive fee:*** $17,116 includes full-time tuition ($12,116), mandatory fees ($200), and room and board ($4800). ***College room only:*** $2140. Full-time tuition and fees vary according to course load and degree level. Room and board charges vary according to board plan and housing facility. ***Part-time tuition:*** $230 per credit hour. ***Part-time fees:*** $100 per term part-time. Part-time tuition and fees vary according to course load and degree level. ***Payment plan:*** installment.

FRESHMAN FINANCIAL AID (Fall 1999) 243 applied for aid; of those 83% were deemed to have need. 100% of freshmen with need received aid; of those 15% had need fully met. *Average percent of need met:* 80% (excluding resources awarded to replace EFC). *Average financial aid package:* $13,381 (excluding resources awarded to replace EFC). 9% of all full-time freshmen had no need and received non-need-based aid.

UNDERGRADUATE FINANCIAL AID (Fall 1999) 783 applied for aid; of those 77% were deemed to have need. 100% of undergraduates with need received aid; of those 22% had need fully met. *Average percent of need met:* 84% (excluding resources awarded to replace EFC). *Average financial aid package:* $12,960 (excluding resources awarded to replace EFC). 11% of all full-time undergraduates had no need and received non-need-based aid.

GIFT AID (NEED-BASED) ***Total amount:*** $1,317,192 (60% Federal, 40% state). ***Receiving aid:*** *Freshmen:* 75% (183); *all full-time undergraduates:* 65% (531). ***Average award:*** Freshmen: $2047; Undergraduates: $2345. ***Scholarships, grants, and awards:*** Federal Pell, FSEOG, state, college/university gift aid from institutional funds.

GIFT AID (NON-NEED-BASED) ***Total amount:*** $3,743,374 (96% institutional, 4% external sources). ***Receiving aid:*** *Freshmen:* 81% (198); *Undergraduates:* 72% (591). ***Scholarships, grants, and awards by category:*** *Academic Interests/Achievement:* general academic interests/achievements. *Creative Arts/Performance:* art/fine arts, journalism/publications, music, theater/drama. *Special Achievements/Activities:* general special achievements/activities. *Special Characteristics:* children of educators, children of faculty/staff, ethnic background, general special characteristics, international students, local/state students, members of minority groups, previous college experience, religious affiliation. ***Tuition waivers:*** Full or partial for employees or children of employees, senior citizens. ***ROTC:*** Army.

LOANS ***Student loans:*** $3,035,242 (77% need-based, 23% non-need-based). 79% of past graduating class borrowed through all loan programs. Average indebtedness per student: $15,539. ***Average need-based loan:*** Freshmen: $2299; Undergraduates: $2986. ***Parent loans:*** $321,552 (100% non-need-based). ***Programs:*** FFEL (Subsidized and Unsubsidized Stafford, PLUS), Perkins.

WORK-STUDY ***Federal work-study:*** *Total amount:* $516,514; 320 jobs averaging $1614. ***State or other work-study/employment:*** *Total amount:* $62,840 (100% non-need-based). 33 part-time jobs averaging $1904.

ATHLETIC AWARDS *Total amount:* 975,536 (100% non-need-based).

APPLYING for FINANCIAL AID ***Required financial aid forms:*** FAFSA, institution's own form, financial aid transcript (for transfers). ***Financial aid deadline:*** Continuous. ***Notification date:*** 3/15. Students must reply within 4 weeks of notification.

CONTACT Mr. Keith Jaloma, Director of Student Financial Aid, Benedictine College, 1020 North Second, Atchison, KS 66002-1499, 913-367-5340 Ext. 2484 or toll-free 800-467-5340. *Fax:* 913-367-3676. *E-mail:* kjaloma@benedictine.edu

BENEDICTINE UNIVERSITY

Lisle, IL

Tuition & fees: $14,060 **Average undergraduate aid package: N/A**

ABOUT THE INSTITUTION Independent Roman Catholic, coed. Awards: associate, bachelor's, master's, and doctoral degrees. 45 undergraduate majors. Total enrollment: 2,622. Undergraduates: 1,795. Freshmen: 260. Federal methodology is used as a basis for awarding need-based institutional aid.

UNDERGRADUATE EXPENSES for 1999–2000 ***Application fee:*** $30. ***Comprehensive fee:*** $19,240 includes full-time tuition ($13,700), mandatory fees ($360), and room and board ($5180). ***College room only:*** $2180. Full-time tuition and fees vary according to degree level. Room and board charges vary according to board plan and housing facility. ***Part-time tuition:*** $435 per semester hour. ***Part-time fees:*** $5 per semester hour. Part-time tuition and fees vary according to class time. ***Payment plans:*** installment, deferred payment.

GIFT AID (NEED-BASED) ***Scholarships, grants, and awards:*** Federal Pell, FSEOG, state, private, college/university gift aid from institutional funds.

GIFT AID (NON-NEED-BASED) ***Scholarships, grants, and awards by category:*** *Academic Interests/Achievement:* biological sciences, general academic interests/achievements, humanities, mathematics, physical sciences. *Creative Arts/Performance:* music. *Special Achievements/Activities:* general special achievements/activities. *Special Characteristics:* children and siblings of alumni, out-of-state students, previous college experience, siblings of current students. ***Tuition waivers:*** Full or partial for children of alumni, employees or children of employees. ***ROTC:*** Army cooperative.

LOANS ***Programs:*** FFEL (Subsidized and Unsubsidized Stafford, PLUS), Perkins, alternative loans.

WORK-STUDY Federal work-study jobs available. ***State or other work-study/employment:*** Part-time jobs available.

APPLYING for FINANCIAL AID ***Required financial aid forms:*** FAFSA, institution's own form, financial aid transcript (for transfers). ***Financial aid deadline:*** 6/30 (priority: 4/15). ***Notification date:*** Continuous. Students must reply within 2 weeks of notification.

CONTACT Diane Battistella, Director, Benedictine Central, Benedictine University, 5700 College Road, Lisle, IL 60532, 630-829-6415 or toll-free 800-829-6300. *E-mail:* dbattistella@ben.edu

BENNETT COLLEGE

Greensboro, NC

Tuition & fees: $8460 **Average undergraduate aid package: N/A**

ABOUT THE INSTITUTION Independent United Methodist, women only. Awards: bachelor's degrees. 25 undergraduate majors. Total enrollment: 640. Undergraduates: 640. Freshmen: 238. Federal methodology is used as a basis for awarding need-based institutional aid.

UNDERGRADUATE EXPENSES for 1999–2000 ***Application fee:*** $20. ***Comprehensive fee:*** $12,162 includes full-time tuition ($6720), mandatory fees ($1740), and room and board ($3702). ***College room only:*** $1784. ***Part-time tuition:*** $292 per semester hour. ***Payment plan:*** deferred payment.

GIFT AID (NEED-BASED) ***Scholarships, grants, and awards:*** Federal Pell, FSEOG, state, private, college/university gift aid from institutional funds, United Negro College Fund.

GIFT AID (NON-NEED-BASED) ***Scholarships, grants, and awards by category:*** *Academic Interests/Achievement:* general academic interests/achievements. *Special Characteristics:* children of faculty/staff, relatives of clergy, religious affiliation. ***Tuition waivers:*** Full or partial for employees or children of employees. ***ROTC:*** Army cooperative, Air Force cooperative.

LOANS ***Programs:*** Federal Direct (Subsidized and Unsubsidized Stafford, PLUS), Perkins.

WORK-STUDY Federal work-study jobs available.

APPLYING for FINANCIAL AID ***Required financial aid form:*** FAFSA. ***Financial aid deadline (priority):*** 3/1.

CONTACT Financial Aid Director, Bennett College, 900 East Washington Street, Greensboro, NC 27401, 336-370-8677.

BENNINGTON COLLEGE

Bennington, VT

Tuition & fees: $22,500 **Average undergraduate aid package: $17,610**

ABOUT THE INSTITUTION Independent, coed. Awards: bachelor's and master's degrees and post-bachelor's certificates. 57 undergraduate majors. Total enrollment: 571. Undergraduates: 447. Freshmen: 142. Federal methodology is used as a basis for awarding need-based institutional aid.

UNDERGRADUATE EXPENSES for 1999–2000 ***Application fee:*** $50. ***Comprehensive fee:*** $28,150 includes full-time tuition ($22,200), manda-

Bennington College (continued)

tory fees ($300), and room and board ($5650). ***College room only:*** $2950. ***Part-time tuition:*** $2775 per course. ***Payment plan:*** installment.

FRESHMAN FINANCIAL AID (Fall 1999) 111 applied for aid; of those 87% were deemed to have need. 100% of freshmen with need received aid; of those 6% had need fully met. *Average percent of need met:* 76% (excluding resources awarded to replace EFC). *Average financial aid package:* $17,125 (excluding resources awarded to replace EFC). 16% of all full-time freshmen had no need and received non-need-based aid.

UNDERGRADUATE FINANCIAL AID (Fall 1999) 367 applied for aid; of those 91% were deemed to have need. 100% of undergraduates with need received aid; of those 12% had need fully met. *Average percent of need met:* 77% (excluding resources awarded to replace EFC). *Average financial aid package:* $17,610 (excluding resources awarded to replace EFC). 12% of all full-time undergraduates had no need and received non-need-based aid.

GIFT AID (NEED-BASED) ***Total amount:*** $4,297,000 (10% Federal, 2% state, 85% institutional, 3% external sources). ***Receiving aid:*** *Freshmen:* 68% (96); *all full-time undergraduates:* 74% (329). ***Average award:*** Freshmen: $13,617; Undergraduates: $12,826. ***Scholarships, grants, and awards:*** Federal Pell, FSEOG, state, private, college/university gift aid from institutional funds.

GIFT AID (NON-NEED-BASED) ***Total amount:*** $340,000 (96% institutional, 4% external sources). ***Receiving aid:*** *Freshmen:* 3% (4); *Undergraduates:* 4% (16). ***Scholarships, grants, and awards by category:*** *Academic Interests/Achievement:* general academic interests/achievements. *Creative Arts/Performance:* general creative arts/performance. *Special Achievements/Activities:* general special achievements/activities. *Special Characteristics:* children of educators, children of faculty/staff, general special characteristics. ***Tuition waivers:*** Full or partial for employees or children of employees.

LOANS ***Student loans:*** $1,456,000 (88% need-based, 12% non-need-based). 88% of past graduating class borrowed through all loan programs. Average indebtedness per student: $19,300. ***Average need-based loan:*** Freshmen: $2680; Undergraduates: $3918. ***Parent loans:*** $909,000 (52% need-based, 48% non-need-based). ***Programs:*** FFEL (Subsidized and Unsubsidized Stafford, PLUS), college/university.

WORK-STUDY ***Federal work-study:*** *Total amount:* $246,000; 255 jobs averaging $1227. ***State or other work-study/employment:*** *Total amount:* $44,000 (100% need-based). 39 part-time jobs averaging $1119.

APPLYING for FINANCIAL AID ***Required financial aid forms:*** FAFSA, institution's own form, noncustodial (divorced/separated) parent's statement, parent and student income tax returns. ***Financial aid deadline (priority):*** 3/1. ***Notification date:*** Continuous. Students must reply by 5/1 or within 2 weeks of notification.

CONTACT Financial Aid Office, Bennington College, Bennington, VT 05201-9993, 802-440-4325 or toll-free 800-833-6845. *Fax:* 802-447-4269. *E-mail:* finaid@bennington.edu

BENTLEY COLLEGE

Waltham, MA

Tuition & fees: $18,910 **Average undergraduate aid package: $16,899**

ABOUT THE INSTITUTION Independent, coed. Awards: associate, bachelor's, and master's degrees. 16 undergraduate majors. Total enrollment: 5,709. Undergraduates: 4,209. Freshmen: 916. Both federal and institutional methodology are used as a basis for awarding need-based institutional aid.

UNDERGRADUATE EXPENSES for 2000–2001 ***Application fee:*** $35. ***Comprehensive fee:*** $27,510 includes full-time tuition ($18,795), mandatory fees ($115), and room and board ($8600). ***College room only:*** $4740. Room and board charges vary according to board plan and housing facility. Part-time tuition and fees vary according to class time. ***Payment plan:*** installment.

FRESHMAN FINANCIAL AID (Fall 1999) 647 applied for aid; of those 72% were deemed to have need. 100% of freshmen with need received aid; of those 35% had need fully met. *Average percent of need met:* 95% (excluding resources awarded to replace EFC). *Average financial aid package:* $16,579 (excluding resources awarded to replace EFC). 13% of all full-time freshmen had no need and received non-need-based aid.

UNDERGRADUATE FINANCIAL AID (Fall 1999) 2,260 applied for aid; of those 80% were deemed to have need. 98% of undergraduates with need received aid; of those 35% had need fully met. *Average percent of need met:* 96% (excluding resources awarded to replace EFC). *Average financial aid package:* $16,899 (excluding resources awarded to replace EFC). 9% of all full-time undergraduates had no need and received non-need-based aid.

GIFT AID (NEED-BASED) ***Total amount:*** $17,606,985 (9% Federal, 3% state, 88% institutional). ***Receiving aid:*** *Freshmen:* 51% (459); *all full-time undergraduates:* 48% (1,650). ***Average award:*** Freshmen: $10,864; Undergraduates: $9910. ***Scholarships, grants, and awards:*** Federal Pell, FSEOG, state, private, college/university gift aid from institutional funds.

GIFT AID (NON-NEED-BASED) ***Total amount:*** $3,380,882 (98% institutional, 2% external sources). ***Receiving aid:*** *Freshmen:* 5% (46); *Undergraduates:* 3% (117). ***Scholarships, grants, and awards by category:*** *Academic Interests/Achievement:* 1,513 awards ($10,926,790 total): general academic interests/achievements. *Special Achievements/Activities:* 30 awards ($147,500 total): community service. *Special Characteristics:* 37 awards ($629,070 total): members of minority groups. ***Tuition waivers:*** Full or partial for employees or children of employees. ***ROTC:*** Army cooperative.

LOANS ***Student loans:*** $10,911,157 (70% need-based, 30% non-need-based). 66% of past graduating class borrowed through all loan programs. Average indebtedness per student: $17,438. ***Average need-based loan:*** Freshmen: $3292; Undergraduates: $4275. ***Parent loans:*** $4,789,223 (9% need-based, 91% non-need-based). ***Programs:*** FFEL (Subsidized and Unsubsidized Stafford, PLUS), Perkins, state, college/university.

WORK-STUDY ***Federal work-study:*** *Total amount:* $2,127,302; 1,794 jobs available. ***State or other work-study/employment:*** *Total amount:* $987,805 (16% need-based, 84% non-need-based). Part-time jobs available.

APPLYING for FINANCIAL AID ***Required financial aid forms:*** FAFSA, CSS Financial Aid PROFILE, noncustodial (divorced/separated) parent's statement, business/farm supplement. ***Financial aid deadline:*** 2/1. ***Notification date:*** Continuous beginning 3/25.

CONTACT Ms. Donna Kendall, Director of Financial Assistance, Bentley College, 175 Forest Street, Waltham, MA 02452-4705, 781-891-3441 or toll-free 800-523-2354 (out-of-state).

BEREA COLLEGE

Berea, KY

Tuition & fees: $199 **Average undergraduate aid package: $19,042**

ABOUT THE INSTITUTION Independent, coed. Awards: bachelor's degrees. 51 undergraduate majors. Total enrollment: 1,522. Undergraduates: 1,522. Freshmen: 423. Federal methodology is used as a basis for awarding need-based institutional aid.

UNDERGRADUATE EXPENSES for 1999–2000 includes mandatory fees ($199) and room and board ($3686). Financial aid is provided to all students for tuition costs. ***Payment plan:*** deferred payment.

FRESHMAN FINANCIAL AID (Fall 1999) 423 applied for aid; of those 100% were deemed to have need. 100% of freshmen with need received aid. *Average percent of need met:* 91% (excluding resources awarded to replace EFC). *Average financial aid package:* $19,454 (excluding resources awarded to replace EFC).

UNDERGRADUATE FINANCIAL AID (Fall 1999) 1,511 applied for aid; of those 100% were deemed to have need. 100% of undergraduates with need received aid. *Average percent of need met:* 89% (excluding resources awarded to replace EFC). *Average financial aid package:* $19,042 (excluding resources awarded to replace EFC).

GIFT AID (NEED-BASED) ***Total amount:*** $26,808,641 (11% Federal, 4% state, 84% institutional, 1% external sources). ***Receiving aid:*** *Freshmen:* 100% (423); *all full-time undergraduates:* 100% (1,511). ***Average award:*** Freshmen: $18,551; Undergraduates: $17,698. ***Scholarships, grants, and awards:*** Federal Pell, FSEOG, state, private, college/university gift aid from institutional funds.

LOANS ***Student loans:*** $355,133 (72% need-based, 28% non-need-based). ***Average need-based loan:*** Freshmen: $441; Undergraduates: $1016. ***Programs:*** FFEL (Subsidized and Unsubsidized Stafford), Perkins, college/university.

WORK-STUDY ***Federal work-study:*** *Total amount:* $1,441,987; 1,235 jobs averaging $1172. ***State or other work-study/employment:*** *Total amount:* $334,155 (100% need-based). 276 part-time jobs averaging $1171.

APPLYING for FINANCIAL AID ***Required financial aid form:*** FAFSA. ***Financial aid deadline (priority):*** 2/1. ***Notification date:*** Continuous beginning 2/15. Students must reply by 5/1.

CONTACT Theresa Lowder, Financial Aid Counselor, Berea College, Labor and Financial Aid Office, CPO 2348, Berea, KY 40404, 606-985-3000 or toll-free 800-326-5948. *Fax:* 606-986-4506. *E-mail:* theresa_lowder@berea.edu

BERKLEE COLLEGE OF MUSIC

Boston, MA

Tuition & fees: $16,627 **Average undergraduate aid package: N/A**

ABOUT THE INSTITUTION Independent, coed. Awards: bachelor's degrees. 12 undergraduate majors. Total enrollment: 3,012. Undergraduates: 3,012. Freshmen: 509. Federal methodology is used as a basis for awarding need-based institutional aid.

UNDERGRADUATE EXPENSES for 2000–2001 ***Application fee:*** $65. ***One-time required fee:*** $250. ***Comprehensive fee:*** $25,517 includes full-time tuition ($16,590), mandatory fees ($37), and room and board ($8890). ***Payment plan:*** installment.

GIFT AID (NEED-BASED) ***Scholarships, grants, and awards:*** Federal Pell, FSEOG, state, private, college/university gift aid from institutional funds.

GIFT AID (NON-NEED-BASED) ***Scholarships, grants, and awards by category:*** *Creative Arts/Performance:* music. ***Tuition waivers:*** Full or partial for employees or children of employees.

LOANS ***Programs:*** Federal Direct (Subsidized and Unsubsidized Stafford, PLUS), Perkins, state.

WORK-STUDY Federal work-study jobs available.

APPLYING for FINANCIAL AID ***Required financial aid forms:*** FAFSA, institution's own form. ***Financial aid deadline (priority):*** 4/24. ***Notification date:*** Continuous. Students must reply within 2 weeks of notification.

CONTACT June A. Clooney, Associate Director of Financial Aid, Berklee College of Music, 1140 Boylston Street, Boston, MA 02215-3693, 617-747-2274 or toll-free 800-421-0084. *Fax:* 617-747-2065. *E-mail:* jclooney@berklee.edu

BERNARD M. BARUCH COLLEGE OF THE CITY UNIVERSITY OF NEW YORK

New York, NY

Tuition & fees (NY res): $3340 **Average undergraduate aid package: $4790**

ABOUT THE INSTITUTION State and locally supported, coed. Awards: bachelor's, master's, and doctoral degrees and post-master's certificates. 33 undergraduate majors. Total enrollment: 15,254. Undergraduates: 12,598. Freshmen: 1,165. Institutional methodology is used as a basis for awarding need-based institutional aid.

UNDERGRADUATE EXPENSES for 1999–2000 ***Application fee:*** $40. ***Tuition, state resident:*** full-time $3200; part-time $138 per credit. ***Tuition, nonresident:*** full-time $6800; part-time $228 per credit. ***Required fees:*** full-time $140; $38 per term. Full-time tuition and fees vary according to class time. Part-time tuition and fees vary according to class time. ***Payment plans:*** installment, deferred payment.

FRESHMAN FINANCIAL AID (Fall 1999, est.) 789 applied for aid; of those 94% were deemed to have need. 95% of freshmen with need received aid; of those 35% had need fully met. *Average percent of need met:* 68% (excluding resources awarded to replace EFC). *Average financial aid package:* $5412 (excluding resources awarded to replace EFC). 17% of all full-time freshmen had no need and received non-need-based aid.

UNDERGRADUATE FINANCIAL AID (Fall 1999, est.) 7,022 applied for aid; of those 91% were deemed to have need. 98% of undergraduates with need received aid; of those 41% had need fully met. *Average percent of need met:* 65% (excluding resources awarded to replace EFC). *Average financial aid package:* $4790 (excluding resources awarded to replace EFC). 6% of all full-time undergraduates had no need and received non-need-based aid.

GIFT AID (NEED-BASED) ***Total amount:*** $26,830,773 (42% Federal, 40% state, 7% institutional, 11% external sources). ***Receiving aid:*** *Freshmen:* 66% (620); *all full-time undergraduates:* 73% (5,900). ***Average award:*** Freshmen: $3920; Undergraduates: $3450. ***Scholarships, grants, and awards:*** Federal Pell, FSEOG, state, college/university gift aid from institutional funds.

GIFT AID (NON-NEED-BASED) ***Total amount:*** $2,839,800 (67% institutional, 33% external sources). ***Receiving aid:*** *Freshmen:* 73% (695); *Undergraduates:* 23% (1,845). ***Scholarships, grants, and awards by category:*** *Academic Interests/Achievement:* general academic interests/achievements. ***Tuition waivers:*** Full or partial for employees or children of employees, senior citizens.

LOANS ***Student loans:*** $7,250,053 (100% need-based). 10% of past graduating class borrowed through all loan programs. Average indebtedness per student: $8100. ***Average need-based loan:*** Freshmen: $2510; Undergraduates: $3650. ***Programs:*** Federal Direct (Subsidized and Unsubsidized Stafford, PLUS), Perkins.

WORK-STUDY ***Federal work-study:*** *Total amount:* $410,000; 520 jobs available. ***State or other work-study/employment:*** *Total amount:* $1,700,000 (47% need-based, 53% non-need-based). Part-time jobs available.

APPLYING for FINANCIAL AID ***Required financial aid forms:*** FAFSA, state aid form. ***Financial aid deadline:*** 4/30 (priority: 3/15). ***Notification date:*** Continuous. Students must reply by 6/1 or within 6 weeks of notification.

CONTACT Financial Aid Office, Bernard M. Baruch College of the City University of New York, 151 East 25th Street, Room 720, New York, NY 10010-5585, 212-802-2240. *Fax:* 212-802-2256. *E-mail:* financial_aid@baruch.cuny.edu

BERRY COLLEGE

Mount Berry, GA

Tuition & fees: $11,550 **Average undergraduate aid package: $11,100**

ABOUT THE INSTITUTION Independent interdenominational, coed. Awards: bachelor's and master's degrees. 69 undergraduate majors. Total enrollment: 2,086. Undergraduates: 1,896. Freshmen: 378. Federal methodology is used as a basis for awarding need-based institutional aid.

UNDERGRADUATE EXPENSES for 1999–2000 ***Application fee:*** $25. ***Comprehensive fee:*** $16,822 includes full-time tuition ($11,550) and room and board ($5272). ***College room only:*** $2892. Room and board charges vary according to board plan. ***Part-time tuition:*** $385 per semester hour. ***Payment plan:*** installment.

FRESHMAN FINANCIAL AID (Fall 1999, est.) 440 applied for aid; of those 55% were deemed to have need. 100% of freshmen with need received aid; of those 54% had need fully met. *Average percent of need met:* 96% (excluding resources awarded to replace EFC). *Average financial aid package:* $11,100 (excluding resources awarded to replace EFC). 41% of all full-time freshmen had no need and received non-need-based aid.

UNDERGRADUATE FINANCIAL AID (Fall 1999, est.) 1,860 applied for aid; of those 55% were deemed to have need. 100% of undergraduates with need received aid; of those 46% had need fully met. *Average percent of need met:* 96% (excluding resources awarded to replace EFC). *Average financial aid package:* $11,100 (excluding resources awarded to replace EFC). 42% of all full-time undergraduates had no need and received non-need-based aid.

GIFT AID (NEED-BASED) ***Total amount:*** $7,300,000 (11% Federal, 32% state, 53% institutional, 4% external sources). ***Receiving aid:*** *Freshmen:* 50% (220); *all full-time undergraduates:* 49% (910). ***Average award:*** Freshmen: $8800; Undergraduates: $8500. ***Scholarships, grants, and awards:*** Federal Pell, FSEOG, state, private, college/university gift aid from institutional funds.

Berry College (continued)

GIFT AID (NON-NEED-BASED) ***Total amount:*** $5,420,000 (1% Federal, 48% state, 44% institutional, 7% external sources). ***Receiving aid:*** *Freshmen:* 45% (200); *Undergraduates:* 45% (830). ***Scholarships, grants, and awards by category:*** *Academic Interests/Achievement:* 700 awards ($2,400,000 total): agriculture, communication, English, general academic interests/achievements, humanities, religion/biblical studies. *Creative Arts/Performance:* 150 awards ($250,000 total): art/fine arts, debating, journalism/publications, music, theater/drama. *Special Achievements/Activities:* 40 awards ($50,000 total): community service, religious involvement. *Special Characteristics:* 250 awards ($350,000 total): adult students, children of faculty/staff, ethnic background, local/state students, members of minority groups. ***Tuition waivers:*** Full or partial for employees or children of employees, adult students, senior citizens.

LOANS ***Student loans:*** $3,400,000 (65% need-based, 35% non-need-based). 48% of past graduating class borrowed through all loan programs. Average indebtedness per student: $11,266. ***Average need-based loan:*** Freshmen: $1800; Undergraduates: $3200. ***Parent loans:*** $900,000 (11% need-based, 89% non-need-based). ***Programs:*** FFEL (Subsidized and Unsubsidized Stafford, PLUS), Perkins, college/university.

WORK-STUDY ***Federal work-study:*** *Total amount:* $400,000; 235 jobs averaging $1800. ***State or other work-study/employment:*** *Total amount:* $2,400,000 (33% need-based, 67% non-need-based). 1,300 part-time jobs averaging $1850.

ATHLETIC AWARDS *Total amount:* 1,200,000 (33% need-based, 67% non-need-based).

APPLYING for FINANCIAL AID ***Required financial aid forms:*** FAFSA, institution's own form, state aid form. ***Financial aid deadline (priority):*** 4/1. ***Notification date:*** 4/15. Students must reply within 2 weeks of notification.

CONTACT Mr. William G. Fron, Director of Financial Aid, Berry College, 5007 Berry Station, Mount Berry, GA 30149-5007, 706-236-2276 or toll-free 800-237-7942. *Fax:* 706-290-2160. *E-mail:* wfron@berry.edu

BETHANY COLLEGE

Lindsborg, KS

Tuition & fees: $12,304 **Average undergraduate aid package: $7438**

ABOUT THE INSTITUTION Independent Lutheran, coed. Awards: bachelor's degrees. 38 undergraduate majors. Total enrollment: 587. Undergraduates: 587. Freshmen: 176. Federal methodology is used as a basis for awarding need-based institutional aid.

UNDERGRADUATE EXPENSES for 2000–2001 (est.) ***Application fee:*** $20. ***Comprehensive fee:*** $16,084 includes full-time tuition ($12,154), mandatory fees ($150), and room and board ($3780). ***College room only:*** $1660. Full-time tuition and fees vary according to location. Room and board charges vary according to board plan and housing facility. ***Part-time tuition:*** $195 per credit hour. Part-time tuition and fees vary according to course load. ***Payment plan:*** installment.

FRESHMAN FINANCIAL AID (Fall 1999) 164 applied for aid; of those 80% were deemed to have need. 100% of freshmen with need received aid; of those 39% had need fully met. *Average percent of need met:* 93% (excluding resources awarded to replace EFC). *Average financial aid package:* $6945 (excluding resources awarded to replace EFC). 17% of all full-time freshmen had no need and received non-need-based aid.

UNDERGRADUATE FINANCIAL AID (Fall 1999) 522 applied for aid; of those 82% were deemed to have need. 100% of undergraduates with need received aid; of those 49% had need fully met. *Average percent of need met:* 99% (excluding resources awarded to replace EFC). *Average financial aid package:* $7438 (excluding resources awarded to replace EFC). 16% of all full-time undergraduates had no need and received non-need-based aid.

GIFT AID (NEED-BASED) ***Total amount:*** $1,280,917 (39% Federal, 42% state, 19% institutional). ***Receiving aid:*** *Freshmen:* 63% (105); *all full-time undergraduates:* 63% (339). ***Average award:*** Freshmen: $4004; Undergraduates: $3839. ***Scholarships, grants, and awards:*** Federal Pell, FSEOG, state, private, college/university gift aid from institutional funds.

GIFT AID (NON-NEED-BASED) ***Total amount:*** $1,413,950 (93% institutional, 7% external sources). ***Receiving aid:*** *Freshmen:* 65% (108); *Undergraduates:* 60% (319). ***Scholarships, grants, and awards by category:*** *Academic Interests/Achievement:* 387 awards ($1,013,036 total): general academic interests/achievements. *Creative Arts/Performance:* 146 awards ($244,790 total): art/fine arts, music, theater/drama. *Special Achievements/Activities:* 20 awards ($5550 total): cheerleading/drum major. *Special Characteristics:* 8 awards ($8720 total): international students, relatives of clergy. ***Tuition waivers:*** Full or partial for employees or children of employees.

LOANS ***Student loans:*** $2,225,871 (71% need-based, 29% non-need-based). 82% of past graduating class borrowed through all loan programs. Average indebtedness per student: $15,296. ***Average need-based loan:*** Freshmen: $3705; Undergraduates: $4438. ***Parent loans:*** $336,921 (100% non-need-based). ***Programs:*** FFEL (Subsidized and Unsubsidized Stafford, PLUS), Perkins, college/university.

WORK-STUDY ***Federal work-study:*** *Total amount:* $150,000; 151 jobs averaging $1000. ***State or other work-study/employment:*** *Total amount:* $190,000 (100% non-need-based). Part-time jobs available.

ATHLETIC AWARDS *Total amount:* 635,524 (100% non-need-based).

APPLYING for FINANCIAL AID ***Required financial aid forms:*** FAFSA, institution's own form. ***Financial aid deadline (priority):*** 3/15. ***Notification date:*** Continuous. Students must reply within 3 weeks of notification.

CONTACT Ms. Brenda L. Meagher, Director of Financial Aid, Bethany College, 421 North First Street, Lindsborg, KS 67456-1897, 785-227-3311 Ext. 8248 or toll-free 800-826-2281. *Fax:* 785-227-2004. *E-mail:* meagherb@bethanylb.edu

BETHANY COLLEGE

Bethany, WV

Tuition & fees: $18,574 **Average undergraduate aid package: $16,302**

ABOUT THE INSTITUTION Independent religious, coed. Awards: bachelor's degrees. 36 undergraduate majors. Total enrollment: 718. Undergraduates: 718. Freshmen: 178. Both federal and institutional methodology are used as a basis for awarding need-based institutional aid.

UNDERGRADUATE EXPENSES for 1999–2000 ***Application fee:*** $25. ***Comprehensive fee:*** $24,696 includes full-time tuition ($18,230), mandatory fees ($344), and room and board ($6122). ***College room only:*** $2397. ***Part-time tuition:*** $686 per credit hour. ***Part-time fees:*** $344 per year part-time. ***Payment plan:*** installment.

FRESHMAN FINANCIAL AID (Fall 1999) 159 applied for aid; of those 94% were deemed to have need. 100% of freshmen with need received aid; of those 55% had need fully met. *Average percent of need met:* 91% (excluding resources awarded to replace EFC). *Average financial aid package:* $16,777 (excluding resources awarded to replace EFC). 8% of all full-time freshmen had no need and received non-need-based aid.

UNDERGRADUATE FINANCIAL AID (Fall 1999) 697 applied for aid; of those 89% were deemed to have need. 100% of undergraduates with need received aid; of those 46% had need fully met. *Average percent of need met:* 92% (excluding resources awarded to replace EFC). *Average financial aid package:* $16,302 (excluding resources awarded to replace EFC). 2% of all full-time undergraduates had no need and received non-need-based aid.

GIFT AID (NEED-BASED) ***Total amount:*** $5,422,746 (19% Federal, 3% state, 75% institutional, 3% external sources). ***Receiving aid:*** *Freshmen:* 86% (146); *all full-time undergraduates:* 64% (463). ***Scholarships, grants, and awards:*** Federal Pell, FSEOG, state, private, college/university gift aid from institutional funds.

GIFT AID (NON-NEED-BASED) ***Total amount:*** $3,823,975 (97% institutional, 3% external sources). ***Receiving aid:*** *Freshmen:* 81% (138); *Undergraduates:* 78% (561). ***Scholarships, grants, and awards by category:*** *Academic Interests/Achievement:* 327 awards ($2,299,421 total): general academic interests/achievements. *Creative Arts/Performance:* 4 awards ($7500 total): music. *Special Achievements/Activities:* 277 awards ($607,500 total): leadership, religious involvement. *Special Characteristics:* 178 awards ($809,554 total): children and siblings of alumni, children of faculty/staff, ethnic background, local/state students, relatives of clergy, religious affiliation. ***Tuition waivers:*** Full or partial for employees or children of employees.

LOANS ***Student loans:*** $2,593,466 (85% need-based, 15% non-need-based). 71% of past graduating class borrowed through all loan programs. Average indebtedness per student: $16,500. ***Average need-based loan:*** Freshmen: $4450; Undergraduates: $4700. ***Parent loans:*** $876,176 (100% need-based). ***Programs:*** Federal Direct (Subsidized and Unsubsidized Stafford, PLUS), Perkins, alternative loans.

WORK-STUDY ***Federal work-study:*** *Total amount:* $640,078; 483 jobs averaging $1325. ***State or other work-study/employment:*** *Total amount:* $68,080 (100% non-need-based). 170 part-time jobs averaging $400.

APPLYING for FINANCIAL AID ***Required financial aid forms:*** FAFSA, institution's own form. ***Financial aid deadline (priority):*** 3/1. ***Notification date:*** Continuous. Students must reply within 3 weeks of notification.

CONTACT Financial Aid Office, Bethany College, Bethany, WV 26032, 304-829-7141 or toll-free 800-922-7611 (out-of-state).

BETHANY COLLEGE OF THE ASSEMBLIES OF GOD

Scotts Valley, CA

Tuition & fees: $10,280 **Average undergraduate aid package: N/A**

ABOUT THE INSTITUTION Independent religious, coed. Awards: associate, bachelor's, and master's degrees. 18 undergraduate majors. Total enrollment: 553. Undergraduates: 511. Federal methodology is used as a basis for awarding need-based institutional aid.

UNDERGRADUATE EXPENSES for 1999–2000 ***Application fee:*** $35. ***Comprehensive fee:*** $14,860 includes full-time tuition ($9800), mandatory fees ($480), and room and board ($4580). ***College room only:*** $2080. Room and board charges vary according to board plan. ***Part-time tuition:*** $410 per credit hour. ***Part-time fees:*** $235 per term part-time.

UNDERGRADUATE FINANCIAL AID (Fall 1998) 529 applied for aid.

GIFT AID (NEED-BASED) ***Total amount:*** $1,923,373 (24% Federal, 29% state, 43% institutional, 4% external sources). ***Scholarships, grants, and awards:*** Federal Pell, FSEOG, state, private, college/university gift aid from institutional funds.

GIFT AID (NON-NEED-BASED) ***Scholarships, grants, and awards by category:*** *Academic Interests/Achievement:* 159 awards ($489,135 total): general academic interests/achievements. *Creative Arts/Performance:* 59 awards ($46,464 total): music, theater/drama. *Special Achievements/Activities:* 19 awards ($8500 total): cheerleading/drum major, leadership. *Special Characteristics:* 59 awards ($94,860 total): relatives of clergy.

LOANS ***Student loans:*** $2,672,689 (100% need-based). 67% of past graduating class borrowed through all loan programs. Average indebtedness per student: $13,664. ***Parent loans:*** $239,577 (100% need-based). ***Programs:*** FFEL (Subsidized and Unsubsidized Stafford, PLUS), Perkins.

WORK-STUDY ***Federal work-study:*** *Total amount:* $75,835; 75 jobs averaging $1013.

ATHLETIC AWARDS *Total amount:* 74,330 (100% need-based).

APPLYING for FINANCIAL AID ***Required financial aid forms:*** FAFSA, institution's own form. ***Financial aid deadline (priority):*** 3/2. ***Notification date:*** Continuous beginning 4/15. Students must reply within 2 weeks of notification.

CONTACT Deborah Snow, Financial Aid Director, Bethany College of the Assemblies of God, 800 Bethany Drive, Scotts Valley, CA 95066-2820, 831-438-3800 Ext. 1477 or toll-free 800-843-9410.

BETH BENJAMIN ACADEMY OF CONNECTICUT

Stamford, CT

CONTACT Financial Aid Office, Beth Benjamin Academy of Connecticut, 132 Prospect Street, Stamford, CT 06901-1202, 203-325-4351.

BETHEL COLLEGE

Mishawaka, IN

Tuition & fees: $11,950 **Average undergraduate aid package: $9514**

ABOUT THE INSTITUTION Independent religious, coed. Awards: associate, bachelor's, and master's degrees. 56 undergraduate majors. Total enrollment: 1,640. Undergraduates: 1,552. Freshmen: 277. Federal methodology is used as a basis for awarding need-based institutional aid.

UNDERGRADUATE EXPENSES for 1999–2000 ***Application fee:*** $25. ***One-time required fee:*** $350. ***Comprehensive fee:*** $15,900 includes full-time tuition ($11,950) and room and board ($3950). Room and board charges vary according to board plan and housing facility. ***Part-time tuition:*** $240 per hour. Part-time tuition and fees vary according to course load. ***Payment plan:*** installment.

FRESHMAN FINANCIAL AID (Fall 1999, est.) 252 applied for aid; of those 85% were deemed to have need. 100% of freshmen with need received aid; of those 2% had need fully met. *Average percent of need met:* 90% (excluding resources awarded to replace EFC). *Average financial aid package:* $5728 (excluding resources awarded to replace EFC). 8% of all full-time freshmen had no need and received non-need-based aid.

UNDERGRADUATE FINANCIAL AID (Fall 1999, est.) 1,015 applied for aid; of those 78% were deemed to have need. 100% of undergraduates with need received aid; of those 2% had need fully met. *Average percent of need met:* 90% (excluding resources awarded to replace EFC). *Average financial aid package:* $9514 (excluding resources awarded to replace EFC). 8% of all full-time undergraduates had no need and received non-need-based aid.

GIFT AID (NEED-BASED) ***Total amount:*** $4,122,449 (42% Federal, 58% state). ***Receiving aid:*** *Freshmen:* 56% (149); *all full-time undergraduates:* 50% (559). ***Average award:*** Freshmen: $3466; Undergraduates: $2590. ***Scholarships, grants, and awards:*** Federal Pell, FSEOG, state, private, college/university gift aid from institutional funds, Federal Nursing.

GIFT AID (NON-NEED-BASED) ***Total amount:*** $4,560,706 (1% state, 96% institutional, 3% external sources). ***Receiving aid:*** *Freshmen:* 79% (209); *Undergraduates:* 60% (677). ***Scholarships, grants, and awards by category:*** *Academic Interests/Achievement:* 484 awards ($1,554,766 total): biological sciences, business, communication, computer science, education, English, general academic interests/achievements, health fields, mathematics, physical sciences, religion/biblical studies, social sciences. *Creative Arts/Performance:* 72 awards ($138,050 total): art/fine arts, theater/drama. *Special Achievements/Activities:* 167 awards ($264,925 total): cheerleading/drum major, leadership. *Special Characteristics:* 670 awards ($1,864,158 total): adult students, children of faculty/staff, international students, relatives of clergy, religious affiliation, siblings of current students, spouses of current students. ***Tuition waivers:*** Full or partial for employees or children of employees, adult students. ***ROTC:*** Army cooperative, Air Force cooperative.

LOANS ***Student loans:*** $6,287,395 (100% need-based). 54% of past graduating class borrowed through all loan programs. Average indebtedness per student: $13,517. ***Average need-based loan:*** Freshmen: $2864; Undergraduates: $3299. ***Parent loans:*** $78,227 (100% non-need-based). ***Programs:*** FFEL (Subsidized and Unsubsidized Stafford, PLUS), Perkins, college/university.

WORK-STUDY ***Federal work-study:*** *Total amount:* $150,000; 150 jobs averaging $1000. ***State or other work-study/employment:*** *Total amount:* $350,000 (100% non-need-based). 175 part-time jobs averaging $2000.

ATHLETIC AWARDS *Total amount:* 743,045 (100% non-need-based).

APPLYING for FINANCIAL AID ***Required financial aid forms:*** FAFSA, institution's own form. ***Financial aid deadline (priority):*** 3/1. ***Notification date:*** Continuous. Students must reply within 2 weeks of notification.

CONTACT Mr. Guy A. Fisher, Director of Financial Aid, Bethel College, 1001 West McKinley Avenue, Mishawaka, IN 46545-5591, 219-257-3316 or toll-free 800-422-4101. *Fax:* 219-257-3326. *E-mail:* fisherg@bethel-in.edu

BETHEL COLLEGE
North Newton, KS

Tuition & fees: $11,800 **Average undergraduate aid package: $12,777**

ABOUT THE INSTITUTION Independent religious, coed. Awards: bachelor's degrees. 22 undergraduate majors. Total enrollment: 477. Undergraduates: 477. Freshmen: 120. Federal methodology is used as a basis for awarding need-based institutional aid.

UNDERGRADUATE EXPENSES for 2000–2001 ***Application fee:*** $20. ***Comprehensive fee:*** $16,500 includes full-time tuition ($11,700), mandatory fees ($100), and room and board ($4700). ***College room only:*** $2200. Full-time tuition and fees vary according to course load. Room and board charges vary according to board plan and housing facility. ***Part-time tuition:*** $430 per credit hour. Part-time tuition and fees vary according to course load. ***Payment plan:*** installment.

FRESHMAN FINANCIAL AID (Fall 1999, est.) 113 applied for aid; of those 83% were deemed to have need. 100% of freshmen with need received aid; of those 61% had need fully met. *Average percent of need met:* 98% (excluding resources awarded to replace EFC). *Average financial aid package:* $13,111 (excluding resources awarded to replace EFC). 20% of all full-time freshmen had no need and received non-need-based aid.

UNDERGRADUATE FINANCIAL AID (Fall 1999, est.) 354 applied for aid; of those 90% were deemed to have need. 100% of undergraduates with need received aid; of those 61% had need fully met. *Average percent of need met:* 97% (excluding resources awarded to replace EFC). *Average financial aid package:* $12,777 (excluding resources awarded to replace EFC). 17% of all full-time undergraduates had no need and received non-need-based aid.

GIFT AID (NEED-BASED) ***Total amount:*** $891,404 (33% Federal, 50% state, 17% institutional). ***Receiving aid:*** *Freshmen:* 69% (82); *all full-time undergraduates:* 63% (258). ***Average award:*** Freshmen: $4321; Undergraduates: $3672. ***Scholarships, grants, and awards:*** Federal Pell, FSEOG, state, college/university gift aid from institutional funds.

GIFT AID (NON-NEED-BASED) ***Total amount:*** $1,145,415 (90% institutional, 10% external sources). ***Receiving aid:*** *Freshmen:* 60% (71); *Undergraduates:* 58% (238). ***Scholarships, grants, and awards by category:*** *Academic Interests/Achievement:* 219 awards ($614,682 total): general academic interests/achievements. *Creative Arts/Performance:* 123 awards ($261,950 total): art/fine arts, music, theater/drama. *Special Characteristics:* 65 awards ($126,031 total): children and siblings of alumni, children of faculty/staff, international students, relatives of clergy. ***Tuition waivers:*** Full or partial for employees or children of employees, senior citizens.

LOANS ***Student loans:*** $1,577,892 (73% need-based, 27% non-need-based). 77% of past graduating class borrowed through all loan programs. Average indebtedness per student: $13,610. ***Average need-based loan:*** Freshmen: $3578; Undergraduates: $4495. ***Parent loans:*** $329,198 (100% non-need-based). ***Programs:*** FFEL (Subsidized and Unsubsidized Stafford, PLUS), Perkins.

WORK-STUDY ***Federal work-study:*** *Total amount:* $350,406; 157 jobs averaging $2231. ***State or other work-study/employment:*** *Total amount:* $12,000 (100% need-based). 8 part-time jobs averaging $1500.

ATHLETIC AWARDS *Total amount:* 334,035 (100% non-need-based).

APPLYING for FINANCIAL AID ***Required financial aid form:*** FAFSA. ***Financial aid deadline (priority):*** 3/1. ***Notification date:*** Continuous. Students must reply by 5/1 or within 2 weeks of notification.

CONTACT Mr. Tony Graber, Financial Aid Director, Bethel College, 300 East 27th Street, North Newton, KS 67117, 316-284-5232 or toll-free 800-522-1887. *Fax:* 316-284-5286. *E-mail:* tgraber@bethelks.edu

BETHEL COLLEGE
St. Paul, MN

Tuition & fees: $15,335 **Average undergraduate aid package: $12,726**

ABOUT THE INSTITUTION Independent religious, coed. Awards: associate, bachelor's, and master's degrees. 51 undergraduate majors. Total enrollment: 2,983. Undergraduates: 2,721. Freshmen: 519. Federal methodology is used as a basis for awarding need-based institutional aid.

UNDERGRADUATE EXPENSES for 1999–2000 ***Application fee:*** $25. ***Comprehensive fee:*** $20,745 includes full-time tuition ($15,300), mandatory fees ($35), and room and board ($5410). ***College room only:*** $3140. Room and board charges vary according to board plan. ***Part-time tuition:*** $580 per credit hour. Part-time tuition and fees vary according to course load. ***Payment plan:*** installment.

FRESHMAN FINANCIAL AID (Fall 1999, est.) 543 applied for aid; of those 70% were deemed to have need. 100% of freshmen with need received aid; of those 20% had need fully met. *Average percent of need met:* 86% (excluding resources awarded to replace EFC). *Average financial aid package:* $13,319 (excluding resources awarded to replace EFC). 25% of all full-time freshmen had no need and received non-need-based aid.

UNDERGRADUATE FINANCIAL AID (Fall 1999, est.) 2,085 applied for aid; of those 75% were deemed to have need. 100% of undergraduates with need received aid; of those 26% had need fully met. *Average percent of need met:* 83% (excluding resources awarded to replace EFC). *Average financial aid package:* $12,726 (excluding resources awarded to replace EFC). 19% of all full-time undergraduates had no need and received non-need-based aid.

GIFT AID (NEED-BASED) ***Total amount:*** $11,645,000 (11% Federal, 23% state, 63% institutional, 3% external sources). ***Receiving aid:*** *Freshmen:* 63% (379); *all full-time undergraduates:* 69% (1,556). ***Average award:*** Freshmen: $8345; Undergraduates: $7821. ***Scholarships, grants, and awards:*** Federal Pell, FSEOG, state, private, college/university gift aid from institutional funds.

GIFT AID (NON-NEED-BASED) ***Total amount:*** $1,695,000 (71% institutional, 29% external sources). ***Receiving aid:*** *Freshmen:* 4% (23); *Undergraduates:* 5% (105). ***Scholarships, grants, and awards by category:*** *Academic Interests/Achievement:* 1,060 awards ($2,770,000 total): general academic interests/achievements. *Creative Arts/Performance:* 54 awards ($54,000 total): art/fine arts, debating, music, theater/drama. *Special Achievements/Activities:* 900 awards ($900,000 total): community service, junior miss, leadership. *Special Characteristics:* 700 awards ($1,715,000 total): children and siblings of alumni, children of faculty/staff, ethnic background, international students, members of minority groups, out-of-state students, relatives of clergy, religious affiliation. ***Tuition waivers:*** Full or partial for employees or children of employees, senior citizens. ***ROTC:*** Army cooperative, Naval cooperative, Air Force cooperative.

LOANS ***Student loans:*** $6,166,000 (100% need-based). 73% of past graduating class borrowed through all loan programs. Average indebtedness per student: $16,903. ***Average need-based loan:*** Freshmen: $3713; Undergraduates: $4192. ***Programs:*** FFEL (Subsidized and Unsubsidized Stafford, PLUS), Perkins, state, alternative loans.

WORK-STUDY ***Federal work-study:*** *Total amount:* $360,000; 200 jobs averaging $1800. ***State or other work-study/employment:*** *Total amount:* $650,000 (100% need-based). 360 part-time jobs averaging $1805.

APPLYING for FINANCIAL AID ***Required financial aid forms:*** FAFSA, institution's own form. ***Financial aid deadline (priority):*** 4/15. ***Notification date:*** Continuous. Students must reply by 5/1 or within 3 weeks of notification.

CONTACT Mr. Daniel C. Nelson, Director of College Financial Planning, Bethel College, 3900 Bethel Drive, St. Paul, MN 55112-6999, 651-638-6241 or toll-free 800-255-8706 Ext. 6242. *Fax:* 651-635-1491. *E-mail:* dc-nelson@bethel.edu

BETHEL COLLEGE
McKenzie, TN

Tuition & fees: $7800 **Average undergraduate aid package: $8614**

ABOUT THE INSTITUTION Independent Cumberland Presbyterian, coed. Awards: bachelor's and master's degrees. 25 undergraduate majors. Total enrollment: 772. Undergraduates: 726. Freshmen: 147. Both federal and institutional methodology are used as a basis for awarding need-based institutional aid.

UNDERGRADUATE EXPENSES for 1999–2000 ***Application fee:*** $30. ***Comprehensive fee:*** $12,180 includes full-time tuition ($7550), mandatory fees ($250), and room and board ($4380). ***Part-time tuition:*** $225 per semester hour. ***Part-time fees:*** $10 per semester hour. Part-time tuition and fees vary according to course load. ***Payment plan:*** installment.

UNDERGRADUATE FINANCIAL AID (Fall 1999) 415 applied for aid; of those 63% were deemed to have need. 100% of undergraduates with need received aid; of those 23% had need fully met. *Average percent of need met:* 74% (excluding resources awarded to replace EFC). *Average financial aid package:* $8614 (excluding resources awarded to replace EFC). 30% of all full-time undergraduates had no need and received non-need-based aid.

GIFT AID (NEED-BASED) ***Total amount:*** $701,066 (68% Federal, 32% state). ***Receiving aid:*** *All full-time undergraduates:* 39% (201). ***Average award:*** Undergraduates: $1960. ***Scholarships, grants, and awards:*** Federal Pell, FSEOG, state, college/university gift aid from institutional funds.

GIFT AID (NON-NEED-BASED) ***Total amount:*** $1,529,111 (100% institutional). ***Receiving aid:*** *Undergraduates:* 51% (261). ***Scholarships, grants, and awards by category:*** *Academic Interests/Achievement:* general academic interests/achievements, religion/biblical studies. *Creative Arts/Performance:* music. *Special Characteristics:* children of faculty/staff, religious affiliation. ***Tuition waivers:*** Full or partial for employees or children of employees.

LOANS ***Student loans:*** $641,660 (69% need-based, 31% non-need-based). ***Average need-based loan:*** Undergraduates: $2391. ***Parent loans:*** $58,575 (100% non-need-based). ***Programs:*** FFEL (Subsidized and Unsubsidized Stafford, PLUS), Perkins, state loans (for Education majors).

WORK-STUDY ***Federal work-study:*** *Total amount:* $115,571; jobs available. ***State or other work-study/employment:*** *Total amount:* $41,847 (100% non-need-based). Part-time jobs available.

APPLYING for FINANCIAL AID ***Required financial aid forms:*** FAFSA, institution's own form. ***Financial aid deadline (priority):*** 2/15. ***Notification date:*** Continuous beginning 4/1. Students must reply within 3 weeks of notification.

CONTACT Ms. Laura Bateman, Director of Financial Aid, Bethel College, 325 Cherry Street, McKenzie, TN 38201, 901-352-4007. *Fax:* 901-352-4069.

BETHESDA CHRISTIAN UNIVERSITY

Anaheim, CA

CONTACT Financial Aid Office, Bethesda Christian University, 730 North Euclid Street, Anaheim, CA 92801, 714-517-1945.

BETH HAMEDRASH SHAAREI YOSHER INSTITUTE

Brooklyn, NY

CONTACT Financial Aid Office, Beth HaMedrash Shaarei Yosher Institute, 4102-10 16th Avenue, Brooklyn, NY 11204, 718-854-2290.

BETH HATALMUD RABBINICAL COLLEGE

Brooklyn, NY

CONTACT Financial Aid Office, Beth Hatalmud Rabbinical College, 2127 82nd Street, Brooklyn, NY 11204, 718-259-2525.

BETH MEDRASH GOVOHA

Lakewood, NJ

CONTACT Financial Aid Office, Beth Medrash Govoha, 617 Sixth Street, Lakewood, NJ 08701-2797, 732-367-1060.

BETHUNE-COOKMAN COLLEGE

Daytona Beach, FL

Tuition & fees: $8988 **Average undergraduate aid package: $9855**

ABOUT THE INSTITUTION Independent Methodist, coed. Awards: bachelor's degrees. 38 undergraduate majors. Total enrollment: 2,558. Undergraduates: 2,558. Freshmen: 698. Federal methodology is used as a basis for awarding need-based institutional aid.

UNDERGRADUATE EXPENSES for 2000–2001 (est.) ***Application fee:*** $25. ***Comprehensive fee:*** $14,522 includes full-time tuition ($8988) and room and board ($5534). ***Part-time tuition:*** $375 per credit hour.

FRESHMAN FINANCIAL AID (Fall 1998) 640 applied for aid; of those 95% were deemed to have need. 100% of freshmen with need received aid; of those 15% had need fully met. *Average percent of need met:* 65% (excluding resources awarded to replace EFC). *Average financial aid package:* $9465 (excluding resources awarded to replace EFC). 2% of all full-time freshmen had no need and received non-need-based aid.

UNDERGRADUATE FINANCIAL AID (Fall 1998) 2,242 applied for aid; of those 95% were deemed to have need. 100% of undergraduates with need received aid; of those 15% had need fully met. *Average percent of need met:* 71% (excluding resources awarded to replace EFC). *Average financial aid package:* $9855 (excluding resources awarded to replace EFC). 2% of all full-time undergraduates had no need and received non-need-based aid.

GIFT AID (NEED-BASED) ***Total amount:*** $9,312,544 (59% Federal, 11% state, 28% institutional, 2% external sources). ***Receiving aid:*** *Freshmen:* 89% (600); *all full-time undergraduates:* 89% (2,095). ***Average award:*** Freshmen: $5980; Undergraduates: $6235. ***Scholarships, grants, and awards:*** Federal Pell, FSEOG, state, private, college/university gift aid from institutional funds, United Negro College Fund, Federal Nursing.

GIFT AID (NON-NEED-BASED) ***Total amount:*** $3,043,100 (75% state, 25% institutional). ***Receiving aid:*** *Freshmen:* 53% (358); *Undergraduates:* 53% (1,249). ***Scholarships, grants, and awards by category:*** *Academic Interests/Achievement:* 145 awards ($909,500 total): education, general academic interests/achievements. *Creative Arts/Performance:* 332 awards ($1,568,000 total): music, performing arts. *Special Characteristics:* 4 awards ($3800 total): religious affiliation. ***Tuition waivers:*** Full or partial for employees or children of employees. ***ROTC:*** Army cooperative, Air Force cooperative.

LOANS ***Student loans:*** $9,339,939 (67% need-based, 33% non-need-based). 77% of past graduating class borrowed through all loan programs. Average indebtedness per student: $17,900. ***Average need-based loan:*** Freshmen: $2580; Undergraduates: $3315. ***Parent loans:*** $2,639,212 (100% non-need-based). ***Programs:*** Federal Direct (Subsidized and Unsubsidized Stafford, PLUS), Perkins.

WORK-STUDY ***Federal work-study:*** *Total amount:* $412,412; 286 jobs averaging $1400.

ATHLETIC AWARDS *Total amount:* 2,550,858 (100% non-need-based).

APPLYING for FINANCIAL AID ***Required financial aid form:*** FAFSA. ***Financial aid deadline (priority):*** 4/1.

CONTACT Mr. Joseph Coleman, Director of Financial Aid, Bethune-Cookman College, 640 Mary McLeod Bethune Boulevard, Daytona Beach, FL 32114-3099, 904-255-1401 Ext. 307 or toll-free 800-448-0228. *Fax:* 904-255-9284. *E-mail:* colemanj@cookman.edu

BEULAH HEIGHTS BIBLE COLLEGE

Atlanta, GA

Tuition & fees: $3200 **Average undergraduate aid package: N/A**

ABOUT THE INSTITUTION Independent Pentecostal, coed. Awards: associate and bachelor's degrees. 2 undergraduate majors. Total enrollment: 591. Undergraduates: 591. Freshmen: 117. Federal methodology is used as a basis for awarding need-based institutional aid.

UNDERGRADUATE EXPENSES for 1999–2000 ***Application fee:*** $20. ***Tuition:*** full-time $3120; part-time $130 per semester hour. ***Required fees:*** full-

Beulah Heights Bible College (continued)

time $80; $40 per term part-time. Full-time tuition and fees vary according to course load. ***Payment plans:*** installment, deferred payment.

FRESHMAN FINANCIAL AID (Fall 1999, est.) 20 applied for aid; of those 100% were deemed to have need. 100% of freshmen with need received aid. *Average percent of need met:* 80% (excluding resources awarded to replace EFC).

UNDERGRADUATE FINANCIAL AID (Fall 1999, est.) 138 applied for aid; of those 100% were deemed to have need. 100% of undergraduates with need received aid; of those 1% had need fully met. *Average percent of need met:* 80% (excluding resources awarded to replace EFC).

GIFT AID (NEED-BASED) ***Total amount:*** $366,435 (98% Federal, 2% external sources). ***Receiving aid:*** *Freshmen:* 56% (20); *all full-time undergraduates:* 49% (138). ***Average award:*** Freshmen: $3325; Undergraduates: $3325. ***Scholarships, grants, and awards:*** Federal Pell, FSEOG, private.

GIFT AID (NON-NEED-BASED) ***Total amount:*** $64,170 (100% institutional). ***Receiving aid:*** *Freshmen:* 8% (3); *Undergraduates:* 17% (47). ***Scholarships, grants, and awards by category:*** *Academic Interests/Achievement:* 8 awards ($8354 total): general academic interests/achievements. *Special Characteristics:* 17 awards ($55,816 total): adult students, general special characteristics, international students, married students. ***Tuition waivers:*** Full or partial for employees or children of employees.

LOANS ***Student loans:*** $883,581 (74% need-based, 26% non-need-based). Average indebtedness per student: $19,750. ***Average need-based loan:*** Freshmen: $2625; Undergraduates: $3500. ***Programs:*** FFEL (Subsidized and Unsubsidized Stafford, PLUS).

WORK-STUDY ***Federal work-study:*** *Total amount:* $20,762; 5 jobs averaging $3000.

APPLYING for FINANCIAL AID ***Required financial aid forms:*** FAFSA, institution's own form. ***Financial aid deadline (priority):*** 6/30. ***Notification date:*** 7/30. Students must reply within 2 weeks of notification.

CONTACT Ms. Patricia Banks, Financial Aid Director, Beulah Heights Bible College, 892 Berne Street, SE, Atlanta, GA 30316, 404-627-2681 or toll-free 888-777-BHBC. *Fax:* 404-627-0702.

BIOLA UNIVERSITY

La Mirada, CA

Tuition & fees: $15,914 **Average undergraduate aid package: $12,882**

ABOUT THE INSTITUTION Independent interdenominational, coed. Awards: bachelor's, master's, and doctoral degrees. 39 undergraduate majors. Total enrollment: 3,872. Undergraduates: 2,564. Freshmen: 565. Federal methodology is used as a basis for awarding need-based institutional aid.

UNDERGRADUATE EXPENSES for 1999–2000 ***Application fee:*** $45. ***Comprehensive fee:*** $21,053 includes full-time tuition ($15,914) and room and board ($5139). ***College room only:*** $2707. Full-time tuition and fees vary according to program. Room and board charges vary according to board plan and housing facility. ***Part-time tuition:*** $663 per unit. Part-time tuition and fees vary according to course load and program. ***Payment plan:*** installment.

FRESHMAN FINANCIAL AID (Fall 1999, est.) 438 applied for aid; of those 84% were deemed to have need. 100% of freshmen with need received aid; of those 18% had need fully met. *Average percent of need met:* 75% (excluding resources awarded to replace EFC). *Average financial aid package:* $12,324 (excluding resources awarded to replace EFC). 15% of all full-time freshmen had no need and received non-need-based aid.

UNDERGRADUATE FINANCIAL AID (Fall 1999, est.) 1,603 applied for aid; of those 86% were deemed to have need. 100% of undergraduates with need received aid; of those 18% had need fully met. *Average percent of need met:* 76% (excluding resources awarded to replace EFC). *Average financial aid package:* $12,882 (excluding resources awarded to replace EFC). 13% of all full-time undergraduates had no need and received non-need-based aid.

GIFT AID (NEED-BASED) ***Total amount:*** $11,638,974 (11% Federal, 36% state, 48% institutional, 5% external sources). ***Receiving aid:*** *Freshmen:* 53% (275); *all full-time undergraduates:* 52% (1,056). ***Average award:*** Freshmen: $8346; Undergraduates: $7695. ***Scholarships, grants, and awards:*** Federal Pell, FSEOG, state, private, college/university gift aid from institutional funds.

GIFT AID (NON-NEED-BASED) ***Total amount:*** $828,224 (82% institutional, 18% external sources). ***Receiving aid:*** *Freshmen:* 57% (294); *Undergraduates:* 48% (977). ***Scholarships, grants, and awards by category:*** *Academic Interests/Achievement:* 360 awards ($1,453,384 total): communication, general academic interests/achievements, health fields. *Creative Arts/Performance:* 120 awards ($306,205 total): art/fine arts, debating, journalism/publications, music, performing arts, theater/drama. *Special Achievements/Activities:* 136 awards ($305,569 total): community service. *Special Characteristics:* 282 awards ($420,997 total): adult students, children of faculty/staff, ethnic background, international students, relatives of clergy. ***Tuition waivers:*** Full or partial for employees or children of employees. ***ROTC:*** Army cooperative, Naval cooperative, Air Force cooperative.

LOANS ***Student loans:*** $8,329,640 (84% need-based, 16% non-need-based). 79% of past graduating class borrowed through all loan programs. Average indebtedness per student: $19,521. ***Average need-based loan:*** Freshmen: $2495; Undergraduates: $2996. ***Parent loans:*** $2,808,812 (56% need-based, 44% non-need-based). ***Programs:*** FFEL (Subsidized and Unsubsidized Stafford, PLUS), Perkins, Federal Nursing, college/university, alternative loans.

WORK-STUDY ***Federal work-study:*** *Total amount:* $338,700; 132 jobs averaging $2565.

ATHLETIC AWARDS *Total amount:* 519,400 (73% need-based, 27% non-need-based).

APPLYING for FINANCIAL AID ***Required financial aid forms:*** FAFSA, institution's own form, state aid form. ***Financial aid deadline (priority):*** 3/2. ***Notification date:*** Continuous beginning 3/15. Students must reply by 5/1.

CONTACT Financial Aid Office, Biola University, 13800 Biola Avenue, La Mirada, CA 90639-0001, 562-903-4742 or toll-free 800-652-4652. *E-mail:* finaid@biola.edu

BIRMINGHAM-SOUTHERN COLLEGE

Birmingham, AL

Tuition & fees: $15,498 **Average undergraduate aid package: $8521**

ABOUT THE INSTITUTION Independent Methodist, coed. Awards: bachelor's and master's degrees. 44 undergraduate majors. Total enrollment: 1,528. Undergraduates: 1,453. Freshmen: 337. Federal methodology is used as a basis for awarding need-based institutional aid.

UNDERGRADUATE EXPENSES for 1999–2000 ***Application fee:*** $25. ***Comprehensive fee:*** $20,958 includes full-time tuition ($15,170), mandatory fees ($328), and room and board ($5460). ***College room only:*** $2800. Full-time tuition and fees vary according to class time and course load. Room and board charges vary according to board plan and housing facility. ***Part-time tuition:*** $632 per credit. ***Part-time fees:*** $114 per term part-time. Part-time tuition and fees vary according to class time and course load. ***Payment plan:*** installment.

FRESHMAN FINANCIAL AID (Fall 1999) 213 applied for aid; of those 69% were deemed to have need. 100% of freshmen with need received aid; of those 95% had need fully met. *Average percent of need met:* 85% (excluding resources awarded to replace EFC). *Average financial aid package:* $9598 (excluding resources awarded to replace EFC). 50% of all full-time freshmen had no need and received non-need-based aid.

UNDERGRADUATE FINANCIAL AID (Fall 1999) 620 applied for aid; of those 74% were deemed to have need. 100% of undergraduates with need received aid; of those 96% had need fully met. *Average percent of need met:* 84% (excluding resources awarded to replace EFC). *Average financial aid package:* $8521 (excluding resources awarded to replace EFC). 44% of all full-time undergraduates had no need and received non-need-based aid.

GIFT AID (NEED-BASED) ***Total amount:*** $1,039,784 (34% Federal, 3% state, 63% institutional). ***Receiving aid:*** *Freshmen:* 26% (86); *all full-time*

undergraduates: 18% (249). ***Average award:*** Freshmen: $2152; Undergraduates: $3852. ***Scholarships, grants, and awards:*** Federal Pell, FSEOG, state, private, college/university gift aid from institutional funds.

GIFT AID (NON-NEED-BASED) ***Total amount:*** $6,841,750 (10% state, 86% institutional, 4% external sources). ***Receiving aid:*** *Freshmen:* 41% (138); *Undergraduates:* 30% (408). ***Scholarships, grants, and awards by category:*** *Academic Interests/Achievement:* 926 awards ($4,919,651 total): business, computer science, education, general academic interests/achievements, health fields, premedicine. *Creative Arts/Performance:* 49 awards ($230,800 total): art/fine arts, dance, music, performing arts, theater/drama. *Special Achievements/Activities:* 199 awards ($278,940 total): junior miss, memberships, religious involvement. *Special Characteristics:* 74 awards ($283,124 total): children and siblings of alumni, children of faculty/staff, relatives of clergy, religious affiliation. ***Tuition waivers:*** Full or partial for children of alumni, employees or children of employees. ***ROTC:*** Army cooperative, Air Force cooperative.

LOANS ***Student loans:*** $2,223,238 (60% need-based, 40% non-need-based). Average indebtedness per student: $13,226. ***Average need-based loan:*** Freshmen: $2825; Undergraduates: $3450. ***Parent loans:*** $195,293 (100% non-need-based). ***Programs:*** FFEL (Subsidized and Unsubsidized Stafford, PLUS), Perkins, college/university, CitiAssist Loans, alternative loans.

WORK-STUDY ***Federal work-study:*** *Total amount:* $263,724; 127 jobs averaging $2057. ***State or other work-study/employment:*** *Total amount:* $112,950 (100% non-need-based). 71 part-time jobs averaging $1530.

ATHLETIC AWARDS *Total amount:* 1,423,630 (100% non-need-based).

APPLYING for FINANCIAL AID ***Required financial aid form:*** FAFSA. ***Financial aid deadline (priority):*** 3/1. ***Notification date:*** Continuous. Students must reply within 2 weeks of notification.

CONTACT Financial Aid Office, Birmingham-Southern College, Box 549016, Birmingham, AL 35254, 205-226-4688 or toll-free 800-523-5793. *Fax:* 205-226-3082. *E-mail:* finaid@bsc.edu

BLACKBURN COLLEGE

Carlinville, IL

Tuition & fees: $8275 **Average undergraduate aid package: N/A**

ABOUT THE INSTITUTION Independent Presbyterian, coed. Awards: bachelor's degrees. 27 undergraduate majors. Total enrollment: 498. Undergraduates: 498. Federal methodology is used as a basis for awarding need-based institutional aid.

UNDERGRADUATE EXPENSES for 2000–2001 ***Comprehensive fee:*** $11,945 includes full-time tuition ($8190), mandatory fees ($85), and room and board ($3670). Full-time tuition and fees vary according to program. ***Part-time tuition:*** $334 per semester hour. ***Payment plan:*** installment.

GIFT AID (NEED-BASED) ***Scholarships, grants, and awards:*** Federal Pell, FSEOG, state, private, college/university gift aid from institutional funds.

GIFT AID (NON-NEED-BASED) ***Scholarships, grants, and awards by category:*** *Academic Interests/Achievement:* general academic interests/achievements. *Special Achievements/Activities:* general special achievements/activities. ***Tuition waivers:*** Full or partial for employees or children of employees.

LOANS ***Programs:*** FFEL (Subsidized and Unsubsidized Stafford, PLUS), Perkins, college/university.

APPLYING for FINANCIAL AID ***Required financial aid form:*** FAFSA. ***Financial aid deadline (priority):*** 4/1. ***Notification date:*** Continuous. Students must reply within 4 weeks of notification.

CONTACT Ms. Cheryl Gardner, Financial Aid Administrator, Blackburn College, 700 College Avenue, Carlinville, IL 62626-1498, 217-854-3231 Ext. 4227 or toll-free 800-233-3550. *Fax:* 217-854-3731. *E-mail:* cgard@mail.blackburn.edu

BLACK HILLS STATE UNIVERSITY

Spearfish, SD

Tuition & fees (SD res): $3363 **Average undergraduate aid package: N/A**

ABOUT THE INSTITUTION State-supported, coed. Awards: associate, bachelor's, and master's degrees and post-master's certificates. 42 undergraduate majors. Total enrollment: 3,785. Undergraduates: 3,485. Freshmen: 876. Federal methodology is used as a basis for awarding need-based institutional aid.

UNDERGRADUATE EXPENSES for 1999–2000 ***Application fee:*** $15. ***Tuition, state resident:*** full-time $1867; part-time $58 per credit. ***Tuition, nonresident:*** full-time $5941; part-time $186 per credit. ***Required fees:*** full-time $1496; $47 per credit. Full-time tuition and fees vary according to course load and reciprocity agreements. Part-time tuition and fees vary according to course load and reciprocity agreements. ***College room and board:*** $2785; ***room only:*** $1472. Room and board charges vary according to board plan. ***Payment plan:*** installment.

GIFT AID (NEED-BASED) ***Scholarships, grants, and awards:*** Federal Pell, FSEOG, state, private, college/university gift aid from institutional funds.

GIFT AID (NON-NEED-BASED) ***Scholarships, grants, and awards by category:*** *Academic Interests/Achievement:* biological sciences, business, communication, computer science, education, English, foreign languages, general academic interests/achievements, health fields, humanities, mathematics, military science, physical sciences, social sciences. *Creative Arts/Performance:* art/fine arts, music, theater/drama. ***Tuition waivers:*** Full or partial for employees or children of employees, senior citizens. ***ROTC:*** Army.

LOANS ***Programs:*** FFEL (Subsidized and Unsubsidized Stafford, PLUS), Perkins.

WORK-STUDY Federal work-study jobs available.

APPLYING for FINANCIAL AID ***Required financial aid form:*** FAFSA. ***Financial aid deadline (priority):*** 3/1. ***Notification date:*** 5/15. Students must reply within 2 weeks of notification.

CONTACT Ms. Deb Henriksen, Director of Financial Aid, Black Hills State University, 1200 University Street, Box 9502, Spearfish, SD 57799-9502, 605-642-6581 or toll-free 800-255-2478.

BLESSING-RIEMAN COLLEGE OF NURSING

Quincy, IL

Tuition & fees: $10,400 **Average undergraduate aid package: N/A**

ABOUT THE INSTITUTION Independent, coed, primarily women. Awards: bachelor's degrees. 1 undergraduate major. Total enrollment: 118. Undergraduates: 118. Freshmen: 19. Federal methodology is used as a basis for awarding need-based institutional aid.

UNDERGRADUATE EXPENSES for 1999–2000 ***Comprehensive fee:*** $14,970 includes full-time tuition ($10,100), mandatory fees ($300), and room and board ($4570). Full-time tuition and fees vary according to student level. Room and board charges vary according to student level. ***Part-time tuition:*** $280 per credit. College room and board for freshmen and sophomores is provided by Culver-Stockton College.

UNDERGRADUATE FINANCIAL AID (Fall 1999) 43 applied for aid; of those 100% were deemed to have need. 100% of undergraduates with need received aid; of those 5% had need fully met. *Average percent of need met:* 75% (excluding resources awarded to replace EFC).

GIFT AID (NEED-BASED) ***Total amount:*** $271,999 (7% Federal, 24% state, 58% institutional, 11% external sources). ***Receiving aid:*** *All full-time undergraduates:* 37% (16). ***Scholarships, grants, and awards:*** Federal Pell, state, private, college/university gift aid from institutional funds.

GIFT AID (NON-NEED-BASED) ***Receiving aid:*** *Undergraduates:* 100% (43). ***Tuition waivers:*** Full or partial for employees or children of employees.

LOANS ***Student loans:*** $134,711 (100% need-based). 70% of past graduating class borrowed through all loan programs. Average indebtedness per

Blessing-Rieman College of Nursing (continued)

student: $11,000. ***Parent loans:*** $4608 (100% need-based). ***Programs:*** FFEL (Subsidized and Unsubsidized Stafford, PLUS), Federal Nursing, college/university.

CONTACT Ms. Sara Brehm, Financial Aid Officer, Blessing-Rieman College of Nursing, Broadway at 11th Street, Quincy, IL 62301, 217-223-8400 Ext. 6993 or toll-free 800-877-9140. *Fax:* 217-223-1781. *E-mail:* sbrehm@blessinghospital.com

BLOOMFIELD COLLEGE

Bloomfield, NJ

Tuition & fees: $10,450 **Average undergraduate aid package: $9841**

ABOUT THE INSTITUTION Independent religious, coed. Awards: bachelor's degrees. 31 undergraduate majors. Total enrollment: 1,807. Undergraduates: 1,807. Freshmen: 249. Federal methodology is used as a basis for awarding need-based institutional aid.

UNDERGRADUATE EXPENSES for 1999–2000 ***Application fee:*** $25. ***Comprehensive fee:*** $15,600 includes full-time tuition ($10,300), mandatory fees ($150), and room and board ($5150). Full-time tuition and fees vary according to course load and program. Room and board charges vary according to board plan. ***Part-time tuition:*** $1040 per course. ***Part-time fees:*** $25 per term part-time. Part-time tuition and fees vary according to course load and program. ***Payment plans:*** installment, deferred payment.

FRESHMAN FINANCIAL AID (Fall 1999, est.) 246 applied for aid; of those 95% were deemed to have need. 98% of freshmen with need received aid; of those 3% had need fully met. *Average percent of need met:* 71% (excluding resources awarded to replace EFC). *Average financial aid package:* $10,885 (excluding resources awarded to replace EFC). 2% of all full-time freshmen had no need and received non-need-based aid.

UNDERGRADUATE FINANCIAL AID (Fall 1999, est.) 1,156 applied for aid; of those 96% were deemed to have need. 99% of undergraduates with need received aid; of those 5% had need fully met. *Average percent of need met:* 68% (excluding resources awarded to replace EFC). *Average financial aid package:* $9841 (excluding resources awarded to replace EFC). 3% of all full-time undergraduates had no need and received non-need-based aid.

GIFT AID (NEED-BASED) ***Total amount:*** $9,070,004 (27% Federal, 59% state, 14% institutional). ***Receiving aid:*** *Freshmen:* 85% (223); *all full-time undergraduates:* 85% (1,066). ***Average award:*** Freshmen: $8869; Undergraduates: $7777. ***Scholarships, grants, and awards:*** Federal Pell, FSEOG, state, private, college/university gift aid from institutional funds.

GIFT AID (NON-NEED-BASED) ***Total amount:*** $132,010 (8% state, 72% institutional, 20% external sources). ***Receiving aid:*** *Freshmen:* 6% (17); *Undergraduates:* 5% (63). ***Scholarships, grants, and awards by category:*** *Academic Interests/Achievement:* 41 awards ($90,459 total): general academic interests/achievements. *Special Characteristics:* 26 awards ($23,265 total): children and siblings of alumni, children of current students, handicapped students, relatives of clergy, siblings of current students, spouses of current students, twins. ***Tuition waivers:*** Full or partial for employees or children of employees, senior citizens. ***ROTC:*** Army cooperative.

LOANS ***Student loans:*** $2,329,056 (73% need-based, 27% non-need-based). 50% of past graduating class borrowed through all loan programs. Average indebtedness per student: $12,967. ***Average need-based loan:*** Freshmen: $2010; Undergraduates: $2590. ***Parent loans:*** $247,484 (100% non-need-based). ***Programs:*** FFEL (Subsidized and Unsubsidized Stafford, PLUS), state, college/university.

WORK-STUDY ***Federal work-study:*** *Total amount:* $184,788; 121 jobs averaging $1527. ***State or other work-study/employment:*** *Total amount:* $186,735 (100% non-need-based). 121 part-time jobs averaging $1543.

ATHLETIC AWARDS *Total amount:* 414,029 (100% non-need-based).

APPLYING for FINANCIAL AID ***Required financial aid forms:*** FAFSA, institution's own form. ***Financial aid deadline (priority):*** 6/1. ***Notification date:*** Continuous.

CONTACT Catherine M. Boscher-Murphy, Director of Financial Aid, Bloomfield College, 467 Franklin Street, Bloomfield, NJ 07003-9981, 973-748-9000 Ext. 212 or toll-free 800-848-4555. *Fax:* 973-743-3998. *E-mail:* catherine_boscher-murphy@bloomfield.edu

BLOOMSBURG UNIVERSITY OF PENNSYLVANIA

Bloomsburg, PA

Tuition & fees (PA res): $4455 **Average undergraduate aid package: $6872**

ABOUT THE INSTITUTION State-supported, coed. Awards: associate, bachelor's, and master's degrees. 50 undergraduate majors. Total enrollment: 7,567. Undergraduates: 6,878. Freshmen: 1,403. Federal methodology is used as a basis for awarding need-based institutional aid.

UNDERGRADUATE EXPENSES for 1999–2000 ***Application fee:*** $25. ***Tuition, state resident:*** full-time $3618; part-time $150 per credit. ***Tuition, nonresident:*** full-time $9046; part-time $377 per credit. ***Required fees:*** full-time $837; $28 per credit; $15 per term part-time. Full-time tuition and fees vary according to course load. Part-time tuition and fees vary according to course load. ***College room and board:*** $3784. Room and board charges vary according to board plan and housing facility.

FRESHMAN FINANCIAL AID (Fall 1999, est.) 1192 applied for aid; of those 80% were deemed to have need. 95% of freshmen with need received aid; of those 90% had need fully met. *Average percent of need met:* 65% (excluding resources awarded to replace EFC). *Average financial aid package:* $6643 (excluding resources awarded to replace EFC).

UNDERGRADUATE FINANCIAL AID (Fall 1999, est.) 4,962 applied for aid; of those 80% were deemed to have need. 95% of undergraduates with need received aid; of those 90% had need fully met. *Average percent of need met:* 65% (excluding resources awarded to replace EFC). *Average financial aid package:* $6872 (excluding resources awarded to replace EFC).

GIFT AID (NEED-BASED) ***Total amount:*** $8,037,871 (44% Federal, 52% state, 4% institutional). ***Receiving aid:*** *Freshmen:* 61% (856); *all full-time undergraduates:* 47% (2,888). ***Average award:*** Freshmen: $2910; Undergraduates: $2783. ***Scholarships, grants, and awards:*** Federal Pell, FSEOG, state, private, college/university gift aid from institutional funds.

GIFT AID (NON-NEED-BASED) ***Total amount:*** $1,348,539 (8% Federal, 3% state, 31% institutional, 58% external sources). ***Receiving aid:*** *Freshmen:* 17% (236); *Undergraduates:* 14% (855). ***Scholarships, grants, and awards by category:*** *Academic Interests/Achievement:* 260 awards ($211,575 total): biological sciences, business, communication, computer science, education, English, foreign languages, general academic interests/achievements, health fields, humanities, international studies, mathematics, physical sciences, religion/biblical studies, social sciences. *Special Characteristics:* 174 awards ($635,322 total): children of faculty/staff, international students. ***Tuition waivers:*** Full or partial for minority students, employees or children of employees. ***ROTC:*** Army, Air Force cooperative.

LOANS ***Student loans:*** $14,485,532 (64% need-based, 36% non-need-based). 88% of past graduating class borrowed through all loan programs. Average indebtedness per student: $13,300. ***Average need-based loan:*** Freshmen: $2391; Undergraduates: $3200. ***Parent loans:*** $2,436,745 (100% non-need-based). ***Programs:*** FFEL (Subsidized and Unsubsidized Stafford, PLUS), Perkins, state, college/university, alternative loans.

WORK-STUDY ***Federal work-study:*** *Total amount:* $697,605; 737 jobs averaging $947. ***State or other work-study/employment:*** *Total amount:* $1,345,318 (100% non-need-based). 1,044 part-time jobs averaging $1289.

ATHLETIC AWARDS *Total amount:* 372,446 (100% non-need-based).

APPLYING for FINANCIAL AID ***Required financial aid forms:*** FAFSA, state aid form. ***Financial aid deadline (priority):*** 3/15. ***Notification date:*** Continuous beginning 4/1.

CONTACT Mr. Thomas M. Lyons, Director of Financial Aid, Bloomsburg University of Pennsylvania, Ben Franklin Building, Room 19, 400 East 2nd Street, Bloomsburg, PA 17815-1905, 570-389-4279. *Fax:* 570-389-4795. *E-mail:* tlyons@bloomu.edu

BLUEFIELD COLLEGE

Bluefield, VA

Tuition & fees: $7280 **Average undergraduate aid package: N/A**

ABOUT THE INSTITUTION Independent Southern Baptist, coed. Awards: associate and bachelor's degrees. 33 undergraduate majors. Total enrollment: 1,035. Undergraduates: 1,035. Freshmen: 124. Federal methodology is used as a basis for awarding need-based institutional aid.

UNDERGRADUATE EXPENSES for 1999–2000 ***Application fee:*** $15. ***Comprehensive fee:*** $12,170 includes full-time tuition ($6900), mandatory fees ($380), and room and board ($4890). Room and board charges vary according to board plan. Part-time tuition and fees vary according to course load. ***Payment plans:*** tuition prepayment, installment.

GIFT AID (NEED-BASED) ***Scholarships, grants, and awards:*** Federal Pell, FSEOG, state, private, college/university gift aid from institutional funds.

GIFT AID (NON-NEED-BASED) ***Scholarships, grants, and awards by category:*** *Academic Interests/Achievement:* general academic interests/achievements. *Creative Arts/Performance:* art/fine arts, music, performing arts. *Special Achievements/Activities:* religious involvement. *Special Characteristics:* local/state students, members of minority groups, relatives of clergy. ***Tuition waivers:*** Full or partial for employees or children of employees, adult students, senior citizens.

LOANS ***Programs:*** FFEL (Subsidized and Unsubsidized Stafford, PLUS), alternative loans.

WORK-STUDY Federal work-study jobs available.

APPLYING for FINANCIAL AID ***Required financial aid forms:*** FAFSA, institution's own form, state aid form. ***Financial aid deadline (priority):*** 3/10. ***Notification date:*** 3/30. Students must reply within 2 weeks of notification.

CONTACT Ms. Eleanor Barnett, Director of Financial Aid, Bluefield College, 3000 College Drive, Bluefield, VA 24605, 540-326-4243 or toll-free 800-872-0175.

BLUEFIELD STATE COLLEGE

Bluefield, WV

Tuition & fees (WV res): $2178 **Average undergraduate aid package: $4500**

ABOUT THE INSTITUTION State-supported, coed. Awards: associate and bachelor's degrees. 28 undergraduate majors. Total enrollment: 2,339. Undergraduates: 2,339. Freshmen: 472. Federal methodology is used as a basis for awarding need-based institutional aid.

UNDERGRADUATE EXPENSES for 1999–2000 ***Tuition, state resident:*** full-time $2178; part-time $91 per credit hour. ***Tuition, nonresident:*** full-time $5290; part-time $222 per credit hour. Full-time tuition and fees vary according to program and reciprocity agreements. Part-time tuition and fees vary according to course load, program, and reciprocity agreements. ***Payment plan:*** deferred payment.

FRESHMAN FINANCIAL AID (Fall 1998) 300 applied for aid; of those 92% were deemed to have need. 100% of freshmen with need received aid; of those 22% had need fully met. *Average percent of need met:* 72% (excluding resources awarded to replace EFC). *Average financial aid package:* $4500 (excluding resources awarded to replace EFC). 15% of all full-time freshmen had no need and received non-need-based aid.

UNDERGRADUATE FINANCIAL AID (Fall 1998) 1,100 applied for aid; of those 55% were deemed to have need. 100% of undergraduates with need received aid; of those 20% had need fully met. *Average percent of need met:* 72% (excluding resources awarded to replace EFC). *Average financial aid package:* $4500 (excluding resources awarded to replace EFC). 14% of all full-time undergraduates had no need and received non-need-based aid.

GIFT AID (NEED-BASED) ***Total amount:*** $2,833,146 (82% Federal, 18% state). ***Receiving aid:*** *Freshmen:* 70% (275); *all full-time undergraduates:* 38% (600). ***Average award:*** Freshmen: $2900; Undergraduates: $2900. ***Scholarships, grants, and awards:*** Federal Pell, FSEOG, state, private, college/university gift aid from institutional funds.

GIFT AID (NON-NEED-BASED) ***Total amount:*** $330,422 (66% institutional, 34% external sources). ***Receiving aid:*** *Freshmen:* 10% (40); *Undergraduates:* 8% (120). ***Scholarships, grants, and awards by category:*** *Academic Interests/Achievement:* 385 awards ($207,392 total): engineering/technologies, general academic interests/achievements. *Creative Arts/Performance:* 10 awards ($5000 total): debating. *Special Achievements/Activities:* 10 awards ($5000 total): cheerleading/drum major, general special achievements/activities, junior miss, leadership. *Special Characteristics:* 2 awards ($1000 total): general special characteristics. ***Tuition waivers:*** Full or partial for senior citizens.

LOANS ***Student loans:*** $2,382,826 (69% need-based, 31% non-need-based). 50% of past graduating class borrowed through all loan programs. Average indebtedness per student: $6800. ***Average need-based loan:*** Freshmen: $2200; Undergraduates: $2200. ***Parent loans:*** $19,028 (100% non-need-based). ***Programs:*** Federal Direct (Subsidized and Unsubsidized Stafford, PLUS), Perkins.

WORK-STUDY ***Federal work-study:*** *Total amount:* $150,733; 106 jobs averaging $1422. ***State or other work-study/employment:*** *Total amount:* $263,548 (100% non-need-based). 172 part-time jobs averaging $1532.

ATHLETIC AWARDS *Total amount:* 92,343 (100% non-need-based).

APPLYING for FINANCIAL AID ***Required financial aid forms:*** FAFSA, institution's own form. ***Financial aid deadline (priority):*** 3/1. ***Notification date:*** 6/1.

CONTACT Mr. Tom Ilse, Director of Financial Aid, Bluefield State College, 219 Rock Street, Bluefield, WV 24701-2198, 304-327-4020 or toll-free 800-344-8892 Ext. 4065 (in-state), 800-654-7798 Ext. 4065 (out-of-state). *Fax:* 304-325-7747.

BLUE MOUNTAIN COLLEGE

Blue Mountain, MS

Tuition & fees: $5340 **Average undergraduate aid package: N/A**

ABOUT THE INSTITUTION Independent Southern Baptist, coed, primarily women. Awards: bachelor's degrees. 38 undergraduate majors. Total enrollment: 435. Undergraduates: 435. Freshmen: 50. Federal methodology is used as a basis for awarding need-based institutional aid.

UNDERGRADUATE EXPENSES for 1999–2000 ***Application fee:*** $10. ***Comprehensive fee:*** $8106 includes full-time tuition ($4980), mandatory fees ($360), and room and board ($2766). ***College room only:*** $966. Full-time tuition and fees vary according to course load. Room and board charges vary according to board plan and housing facility. ***Part-time tuition:*** $166 per semester hour. ***Part-time fees:*** $65 per term part-time. Part-time tuition and fees vary according to course load. ***Payment plan:*** installment.

FRESHMAN FINANCIAL AID (Fall 1998) 61 applied for aid; of those 90% were deemed to have need. 100% of freshmen with need received aid; of those 18% had need fully met. 7% of all full-time freshmen had no need and received non-need-based aid.

UNDERGRADUATE FINANCIAL AID (Fall 1998) 314 applied for aid; of those 83% were deemed to have need. 100% of undergraduates with need received aid; of those 19% had need fully met. 14% of all full-time undergraduates had no need and received non-need-based aid.

GIFT AID (NEED-BASED) ***Total amount:*** $922,381 (44% Federal, 29% state, 27% institutional). ***Receiving aid:*** *Freshmen:* 56% (38); *all full-time undergraduates:* 45% (165). ***Average award:*** Freshmen: $2016; Undergraduates: $1915. ***Scholarships, grants, and awards:*** Federal Pell, FSEOG, state, private, college/university gift aid from institutional funds.

GIFT AID (NON-NEED-BASED) ***Total amount:*** $112,283 (48% state, 52% institutional). ***Receiving aid:*** *Freshmen:* 65% (44); *Undergraduates:* 52% (190). ***Scholarships, grants, and awards by category:*** *Academic Interests/Achievement:* general academic interests/achievements. *Creative Arts/Performance:* music. *Special Achievements/Activities:* memberships, religious involvement. *Special Characteristics:* general special characteristics. ***Tuition waivers:*** Full or partial for employees or children of employees.

LOANS ***Student loans:*** $943,243 (83% need-based, 17% non-need-based). ***Average need-based loan:*** Freshmen: $2344; Undergraduates:

Blue Mountain College (continued)

$2079. ***Parent loans:*** $7100 (30% need-based, 70% non-need-based). ***Programs:*** FFEL (Subsidized and Unsubsidized Stafford, PLUS), Perkins.

WORK-STUDY ***Federal work-study:*** *Total amount:* $73,266; 59 jobs averaging $1400. ***State or other work-study/employment:*** *Total amount:* $50,399 (62% need-based, 38% non-need-based). 39 part-time jobs averaging $1400.

ATHLETIC AWARDS *Total amount:* 14,931 (67% need-based, 33% non-need-based).

APPLYING for FINANCIAL AID ***Required financial aid form:*** FAFSA. ***Financial aid deadline (priority):*** 5/1. ***Notification date:*** Continuous. Students must reply within 2 weeks of notification.

CONTACT Lynita J. Davis, Financial Aid Assistant, Blue Mountain College, PO Box 160, Blue Mountain, MS 38610-0160, 601-685-4771 Ext. 141 or toll-free 800-235-0136.

BLUFFTON COLLEGE

Bluffton, OH

Tuition & fees: $14,306 **Average undergraduate aid package: $12,395**

ABOUT THE INSTITUTION Independent Mennonite, coed. Awards: bachelor's and master's degrees. 55 undergraduate majors. Total enrollment: 1,014. Undergraduates: 999. Freshmen: 246. Both federal and institutional methodology are used as a basis for awarding need-based institutional aid.

UNDERGRADUATE EXPENSES for 2000–2001 (est.) ***Application fee:*** $20. ***Comprehensive fee:*** $19,428 includes full-time tuition ($14,056), mandatory fees ($250), and room and board ($5122). ***College room only:*** $2076. ***Part-time tuition:*** $414 per semester hour. ***Part-time fees:*** $125. Part-time tuition and fees vary according to course load. ***Payment plan:*** installment.

FRESHMAN FINANCIAL AID (Fall 1999) 235 applied for aid; of those 90% were deemed to have need. 100% of freshmen with need received aid; of those 86% had need fully met. *Average percent of need met:* 100% (excluding resources awarded to replace EFC). *Average financial aid package:* $13,232 (excluding resources awarded to replace EFC). 13% of all full-time freshmen had no need and received non-need-based aid.

UNDERGRADUATE FINANCIAL AID (Fall 1999) 687 applied for aid; of those 92% were deemed to have need. 100% of undergraduates with need received aid; of those 82% had need fully met. *Average percent of need met:* 100% (excluding resources awarded to replace EFC). *Average financial aid package:* $12,395 (excluding resources awarded to replace EFC). 19% of all full-time undergraduates had no need and received non-need-based aid.

GIFT AID (NEED-BASED) ***Total amount:*** $4,362,501 (11% Federal, 21% state, 58% institutional, 10% external sources). ***Receiving aid:*** *Freshmen:* 86% (212); *all full-time undergraduates:* 75% (624). ***Average award:*** Freshmen: $8801; Undergraduates: $6945. ***Scholarships, grants, and awards:*** Federal Pell, FSEOG, state, private, college/university gift aid from institutional funds.

GIFT AID (NON-NEED-BASED) ***Total amount:*** $781,481 (19% state, 49% institutional, 32% external sources). ***Receiving aid:*** *Freshmen:* 11% (26); *Undergraduates:* 7% (55). ***Scholarships, grants, and awards by category:*** *Academic Interests/Achievement:* 369 awards ($1,886,309 total): general academic interests/achievements. *Creative Arts/Performance:* 24 awards ($23,200 total): art/fine arts, music. *Special Achievements/Activities:* 96 awards ($238,039 total): leadership. *Special Characteristics:* 251 awards ($650,640 total): children of faculty/staff, international students, members of minority groups, out-of-state students, relatives of clergy, religious affiliation. ***Tuition waivers:*** Full or partial for employees or children of employees.

LOANS ***Student loans:*** $3,543,034 (94% need-based, 6% non-need-based). 78% of past graduating class borrowed through all loan programs. Average indebtedness per student: $16,587. ***Average need-based loan:*** Freshmen: $3521; Undergraduates: $4536. ***Parent loans:*** $959,767 (100% non-need-based). ***Programs:*** FFEL (Subsidized and Unsubsidized Stafford, PLUS), Perkins, state, alternative loans.

WORK-STUDY ***Federal work-study:*** *Total amount:* $614,300; 430 jobs averaging $1429. ***State or other work-study/employment:*** *Total amount:* $472,375 (56% need-based, 44% non-need-based). 325 part-time jobs averaging $1451.

APPLYING for FINANCIAL AID ***Required financial aid form:*** FAFSA. ***Financial aid deadline:*** 10/1 (priority: 5/1). ***Notification date:*** Continuous. Students must reply within 3 weeks of notification.

CONTACT Lawrence Matthews, Director of Financial Aid, Bluffton College, 280 West College Avenue, Bluffton, OH 45817-1196, 419-358-3266 or toll-free 800-488-3257. *Fax:* 419-358-3232. *E-mail:* matthewsl@bluffton.edu

BOISE BIBLE COLLEGE

Boise, ID

Tuition & fees: $4630 **Average undergraduate aid package: $6001**

ABOUT THE INSTITUTION Independent nondenominational, coed. Awards: associate and bachelor's degrees. 7 undergraduate majors. Total enrollment: 110. Undergraduates: 110. Freshmen: 26. Federal methodology is used as a basis for awarding need-based institutional aid.

UNDERGRADUATE EXPENSES for 1999–2000 ***Application fee:*** $25. ***Comprehensive fee:*** $8230 includes full-time tuition ($4560), mandatory fees ($70), and room and board ($3600). Room and board charges vary according to student level. ***Part-time tuition:*** $190 per semester hour. ***Part-time fees:*** $2 per semester hour. ***Payment plan:*** installment.

FRESHMAN FINANCIAL AID (Fall 1999, est.) 19 applied for aid; of those 89% were deemed to have need. 94% of freshmen with need received aid; of those 6% had need fully met. *Average percent of need met:* 46% (excluding resources awarded to replace EFC). *Average financial aid package:* $5485 (excluding resources awarded to replace EFC). 10% of all full-time freshmen had no need and received non-need-based aid.

UNDERGRADUATE FINANCIAL AID (Fall 1999, est.) 77 applied for aid; of those 73% were deemed to have need. 96% of undergraduates with need received aid; of those 6% had need fully met. *Average percent of need met:* 40% (excluding resources awarded to replace EFC). *Average financial aid package:* $6001 (excluding resources awarded to replace EFC). 3% of all full-time undergraduates had no need and received non-need-based aid.

GIFT AID (NEED-BASED) ***Total amount:*** $246,154 (36% Federal, 24% institutional, 40% external sources). ***Scholarships, grants, and awards:*** Federal Pell, FSEOG, private, college/university gift aid from institutional funds.

GIFT AID (NON-NEED-BASED) ***Total amount:*** $25,749 (40% institutional, 60% external sources). ***Receiving aid:*** *Freshmen:* 60% (12); *Undergraduates:* 21% (18). ***Scholarships, grants, and awards by category:*** *Academic Interests/Achievement:* 59 awards ($54,625 total): general academic interests/achievements, religion/biblical studies. *Creative Arts/Performance:* 12 awards ($20,815 total): music. *Special Achievements/Activities:* 10 awards ($5028 total): leadership, religious involvement. *Special Characteristics:* 22 awards ($19,196 total): children of faculty/staff, international students, relatives of clergy, spouses of current students. ***Tuition waivers:*** Full or partial for employees or children of employees.

LOANS ***Student loans:*** $205,176 (94% need-based, 6% non-need-based). 65% of past graduating class borrowed through all loan programs. ***Average need-based loan:*** Freshmen: $2155; Undergraduates: $3394. ***Parent loans:*** $4800 (100% need-based). ***Programs:*** FFEL (Subsidized and Unsubsidized Stafford, PLUS), Key Alternative Loans.

WORK-STUDY ***Federal work-study:*** *Total amount:* $6794; 5 jobs averaging $1359.

APPLYING for FINANCIAL AID ***Required financial aid forms:*** FAFSA, institution's own form. ***Financial aid deadline (priority):*** 5/1. ***Notification date:*** 7/1. Students must reply by 8/1.

CONTACT Mrs. Joyce Anderson, Financial Aid Director, Boise Bible College, 8695 Marigold Street, Boise, ID 83714-1220, 208-376-7731 Ext. 11 or toll-free 800-893-7755. *Fax:* 208-376-7743. *E-mail:* bbcfin@micron.net

BOISE STATE UNIVERSITY

Boise, ID

Tuition & fees (ID res): $2283 **Average undergraduate aid package: N/A**

ABOUT THE INSTITUTION State-supported, coed. Awards: associate, bachelor's, master's, and doctoral degrees. 91 undergraduate majors. Total enrollment: 16,215. Undergraduates: 14,576. Freshmen: 2,083. Federal methodology is used as a basis for awarding need-based institutional aid.

UNDERGRADUATE EXPENSES for 1999–2000 ***Application fee:*** $20. ***Tuition, state resident:*** full-time $0; part-time $115 per credit. ***Tuition, nonresident:*** full-time $5880; part-time $115 per credit. ***Required fees:*** full-time $2283. Part-time tuition and fees vary according to course load. ***College room and board:*** $3558. Room and board charges vary according to board plan and housing facility. ***Payment plan:*** deferred payment.

GIFT AID (NEED-BASED) ***Scholarships, grants, and awards:*** Federal Pell, FSEOG, state, private, college/university gift aid from institutional funds, Leveraged Educational Assistance Program (LEAP).

GIFT AID (NON-NEED-BASED) ***Scholarships, grants, and awards by category:*** *Academic Interests/Achievement:* biological sciences, business, communication, computer science, education, engineering/technologies, English, foreign languages, general academic interests/achievements, health fields, mathematics, military science, physical sciences, premedicine, social sciences. *Creative Arts/Performance:* art/fine arts, dance, debating, general creative arts/performance, journalism/publications, music, performing arts, theater/drama. *Special Achievements/Activities:* cheerleading/drum major, leadership, rodeo. *Special Characteristics:* ethnic background, first-generation college students, handicapped students, international students, local/state students, out-of-state students, veterans, veterans' children. ***Tuition waivers:*** Full or partial for employees or children of employees, senior citizens. ***ROTC:*** Army.

LOANS ***Programs:*** Federal Direct (Subsidized and Unsubsidized Stafford, PLUS), Perkins, Federal Nursing, college/university.

WORK-STUDY Federal work-study jobs available. ***State or other work-study/employment:*** Part-time jobs available.

APPLYING for FINANCIAL AID ***Required financial aid form:*** FAFSA. ***Financial aid deadline:*** 4/3 (priority: 3/1). ***Notification date:*** Continuous. Students must reply by 8/10.

CONTACT Mrs. Lois M. Kelly, Director of Financial Aid, Boise State University, Administration Building, Room 117, 1910 University Drive, Boise, ID 83725, 208-426-1664 or toll-free 800-632-6586 (in-state), 800-824-7017 (out-of-state). *E-mail:* faquest@boisestate.edu

BORICUA COLLEGE

New York, NY

Tuition & fees: $6600 **Average undergraduate aid package: $2650**

ABOUT THE INSTITUTION Independent, coed. Awards: associate, bachelor's, and master's degrees. 7 undergraduate majors. Total enrollment: 1,190. Undergraduates: 1,178. Freshmen: 324. Federal methodology is used as a basis for awarding need-based institutional aid.

UNDERGRADUATE EXPENSES for 1999–2000 ***Application fee:*** $20. ***Tuition:*** full-time $6600. ***Payment plan:*** deferred payment.

FRESHMAN FINANCIAL AID (Fall 1999, est.) *Average percent of need met:* 80% (excluding resources awarded to replace EFC). *Average financial aid package:* $3150 (excluding resources awarded to replace EFC).

UNDERGRADUATE FINANCIAL AID (Fall 1999, est.) *Average percent of need met:* 80% (excluding resources awarded to replace EFC). *Average financial aid package:* $2650 (excluding resources awarded to replace EFC).

GIFT AID (NEED-BASED) ***Total amount:*** $3,199,279 ***Scholarships, grants, and awards:*** Federal Pell, FSEOG, state, private, college/university gift aid from institutional funds.

GIFT AID (NON-NEED-BASED) ***Tuition waivers:*** Full or partial for employees or children of employees.

LOANS ***Programs:*** college/university.

WORK-STUDY Federal work-study jobs available.

APPLYING for FINANCIAL AID ***Required financial aid forms:*** FAFSA, institution's own form, CSS Financial Aid PROFILE, state aid form. ***Financial aid deadline (priority):*** 3/1. ***Notification date:*** Continuous. Students must reply within 2 weeks of notification.

CONTACT Ms. Rosalia Cruz, Financial Aid Administrator, Boricua College, 3755 Broadway, New York, NY 10032-1560, 212-694-1000 Ext. 611.

BOSTON ARCHITECTURAL CENTER

Boston, MA

Tuition & fees: $6330 **Average undergraduate aid package: N/A**

ABOUT THE INSTITUTION Independent, coed. Awards: bachelor's, master's, and first professional degrees. 2 undergraduate majors. Total enrollment: 975. Undergraduates: 795. Freshmen: 111. Both federal and institutional methodology are used as a basis for awarding need-based institutional aid.

UNDERGRADUATE EXPENSES for 1999–2000 ***Application fee:*** $50. ***Tuition:*** full-time $6245; part-time $508 per credit. ***Required fees:*** full-time $85. Part-time tuition and fees vary according to program. ***Payment plan:*** deferred payment.

GIFT AID (NEED-BASED) ***Scholarships, grants, and awards:*** Federal Pell, state.

GIFT AID (NON-NEED-BASED) ***Scholarships, grants, and awards by category:*** *Academic Interests/Achievement:* architecture.

LOANS ***Programs:*** FFEL (Subsidized and Unsubsidized Stafford, PLUS).

APPLYING for FINANCIAL AID ***Required financial aid forms:*** FAFSA, institution's own form. ***Financial aid deadline (priority):*** 6/1. ***Notification date:*** Continuous. Students must reply within 2 weeks of notification.

CONTACT Barbara Raguso, Financial Aid Counselor, Boston Architectural Center, 320 Newbury Street, Boston, MA 02115, 617-585-0125 or toll-free 877-585-0100. *Fax:* 617-585-0121.

BOSTON COLLEGE

Chestnut Hill, MA

Tuition & fees: $22,256 **Average undergraduate aid package: $19,036**

ABOUT THE INSTITUTION Independent Roman Catholic (Jesuit), coed. Awards: bachelor's, master's, doctoral, and first professional degrees and post-master's certificates (also offers continuing education program with significant enrollment not reflected in profile). 45 undergraduate majors. Total enrollment: 13,765. Undergraduates: 9,190. Freshmen: 2,284. Institutional methodology is used as a basis for awarding need-based institutional aid.

UNDERGRADUATE EXPENSES for 1999–2000 ***Application fee:*** $55. ***Comprehensive fee:*** $30,506 includes full-time tuition ($21,700), mandatory fees ($556), and room and board ($8250). ***College room only:*** $4620. Room and board charges vary according to housing facility. ***Payment plans:*** tuition prepayment, installment.

FRESHMAN FINANCIAL AID (Fall 1998) 1725 applied for aid; of those 61% were deemed to have need. 100% of freshmen with need received aid; of those 98% had need fully met. *Average percent of need met:* 98% (excluding resources awarded to replace EFC). *Average financial aid package:* $18,793 (excluding resources awarded to replace EFC).

UNDERGRADUATE FINANCIAL AID (Fall 1998) 5,618 applied for aid; of those 74% were deemed to have need. 100% of undergraduates with need received aid; of those 99% had need fully met. *Average percent of need met:* 99% (excluding resources awarded to replace EFC). *Average financial aid package:* $19,036 (excluding resources awarded to replace EFC).

GIFT AID (NEED-BASED) ***Total amount:*** $46,892,912 (8% Federal, 1% state, 91% institutional). ***Receiving aid:*** *Freshmen:* 39% (868); *all full-time undergraduates:* 40% (3,549). ***Average award:*** Freshmen: $13,934;

Boston College (continued)

Undergraduates: $13,213. ***Scholarships, grants, and awards:*** Federal Pell, FSEOG, state, private, college/university gift aid from institutional funds.

GIFT AID (NON-NEED-BASED) ***Total amount:*** $2,876,099 (32% institutional, 68% external sources). ***Scholarships, grants, and awards by category:*** *Academic Interests/Achievement:* general academic interests/achievements. *Special Characteristics:* children of faculty/staff. ***Tuition waivers:*** Full or partial for employees or children of employees. ***ROTC:*** Army cooperative, Naval cooperative, Air Force cooperative.

LOANS ***Student loans:*** $18,342,181 (100% need-based). Average indebtedness per student: $16,417. ***Average need-based loan:*** Freshmen: $3459; Undergraduates: $4423. ***Parent loans:*** $10,088,611 (100% non-need-based). ***Programs:*** FFEL (Subsidized and Unsubsidized Stafford, PLUS), Perkins, Federal Nursing, state.

WORK-STUDY ***Federal work-study:*** *Total amount:* $5,868,005; 4,147 jobs averaging $1415.

ATHLETIC AWARDS *Total amount:* 6,625,766 (100% non-need-based).

APPLYING for FINANCIAL AID ***Required financial aid forms:*** FAFSA, CSS Financial Aid PROFILE, noncustodial (divorced/separated) parent's statement, business/farm supplement. ***Financial aid deadline (priority):*** 2/1. ***Notification date:*** 4/1. Students must reply by 5/1.

CONTACT Mr. Bernie Pekala, Director of Financial Strategies, Boston College, 36 College Road, Chestnut Hill, MA 02467, 617-552-3300 or toll-free 800-360-2522. *Fax:* 617-552-0142. *E-mail:* pekala@bc.edu

BOSTON CONSERVATORY

Boston, MA

Tuition & fees: $18,135 **Average undergraduate aid package: $9212**

ABOUT THE INSTITUTION Independent, coed. Awards: bachelor's and master's degrees. 9 undergraduate majors. Total enrollment: 501. Undergraduates: 333. Freshmen: 102. Institutional methodology is used as a basis for awarding need-based institutional aid.

UNDERGRADUATE EXPENSES for 1999–2000 ***Application fee:*** $60. ***Comprehensive fee:*** $26,335 includes full-time tuition ($17,300), mandatory fees ($835), and room and board ($8200). Full-time tuition and fees vary according to course load, degree level, and program. ***Part-time tuition:*** $710 per credit. Part-time tuition and fees vary according to course load, degree level, and program.

FRESHMAN FINANCIAL AID (Fall 1998) 83 applied for aid; of those 61% were deemed to have need. 86% of freshmen with need received aid; of those 5% had need fully met. *Average percent of need met:* 50% (excluding resources awarded to replace EFC). *Average financial aid package:* $8583 (excluding resources awarded to replace EFC). 8% of all full-time freshmen had no need and received non-need-based aid.

UNDERGRADUATE FINANCIAL AID (Fall 1998) 288 applied for aid; of those 63% were deemed to have need. 94% of undergraduates with need received aid; of those 11% had need fully met. *Average percent of need met:* 50% (excluding resources awarded to replace EFC). *Average financial aid package:* $9212 (excluding resources awarded to replace EFC). 18% of all full-time undergraduates had no need and received non-need-based aid.

GIFT AID (NEED-BASED) ***Total amount:*** $239,465 (87% Federal, 13% state). ***Receiving aid:*** *Freshmen:* 17% (19); *all full-time undergraduates:* 20% (63). ***Scholarships, grants, and awards:*** Federal Pell, FSEOG, state, private.

GIFT AID (NON-NEED-BASED) ***Total amount:*** $982,410 (95% institutional, 5% external sources). ***Receiving aid:*** *Freshmen:* 32% (36); *Undergraduates:* 36% (115). ***Scholarships, grants, and awards by category:*** *Creative Arts/Performance:* dance, music, theater/drama.

LOANS ***Student loans:*** $750,000 (100% need-based). 72% of past graduating class borrowed through all loan programs. Average indebtedness per student: $15,000. ***Parent loans:*** $1,111,500 (100% non-need-based). ***Programs:*** FFEL (Subsidized and Unsubsidized Stafford, PLUS), state, college/university.

WORK-STUDY ***Federal work-study:*** *Total amount:* $53,000; 63 jobs averaging $840. ***State or other work-study/employment:*** *Total amount:* $30,000 (100% need-based). Part-time jobs available.

APPLYING for FINANCIAL AID ***Required financial aid forms:*** FAFSA, institution's own form. ***Financial aid deadline:*** 3/1. ***Notification date:*** 4/1. Students must reply by 5/1.

CONTACT Director of Financial Aid, Boston Conservatory, 8 The Fenway, Boston, MA 02215, 617-536-6340.

BOSTON UNIVERSITY

Boston, MA

Tuition & fees: $24,100 **Average undergraduate aid package: $21,654**

ABOUT THE INSTITUTION Independent, coed. Awards: bachelor's, master's, doctoral, and first professional degrees and post-master's certificates. 114 undergraduate majors. Total enrollment: 28,487. Undergraduates: 18,018. Freshmen: 4,225. Institutional methodology is used as a basis for awarding need-based institutional aid.

UNDERGRADUATE EXPENSES for 1999–2000 ***Application fee:*** $60. ***Comprehensive fee:*** $32,230 includes full-time tuition ($23,770), mandatory fees ($330), and room and board ($8130). ***College room only:*** $5020. Room and board charges vary according to board plan and housing facility. ***Part-time tuition:*** $743 per credit. ***Part-time fees:*** $40 per term part-time. ***Payment plans:*** tuition prepayment, installment.

FRESHMAN FINANCIAL AID (Fall 1999) 2558 applied for aid; of those 87% were deemed to have need. 100% of freshmen with need received aid; of those 66% had need fully met. *Average percent of need met:* 95% (excluding resources awarded to replace EFC). *Average financial aid package:* $21,214 (excluding resources awarded to replace EFC). 13% of all full-time freshmen had no need and received non-need-based aid.

UNDERGRADUATE FINANCIAL AID (Fall 1999) 7,920 applied for aid; of those 94% were deemed to have need. 99% of undergraduates with need received aid; of those 62% had need fully met. *Average percent of need met:* 93% (excluding resources awarded to replace EFC). *Average financial aid package:* $21,654 (excluding resources awarded to replace EFC). 11% of all full-time undergraduates had no need and received non-need-based aid.

GIFT AID (NEED-BASED) ***Total amount:*** $115,701,849 (7% Federal, 2% state, 87% institutional, 4% external sources). ***Receiving aid:*** *Freshmen:* 49% (2,090); *all full-time undergraduates:* 46% (6,978). ***Average award:*** Freshmen: $15,000; Undergraduates: $14,446. ***Scholarships, grants, and awards:*** Federal Pell, FSEOG, state, private, college/university gift aid from institutional funds.

GIFT AID (NON-NEED-BASED) ***Total amount:*** $17,984,453 (11% Federal, 76% institutional, 13% external sources). ***Receiving aid:*** *Freshmen:* 23% (981); *Undergraduates:* 14% (2,154). ***Scholarships, grants, and awards by category:*** *Academic Interests/Achievement:* 2,271 awards ($24,290,595 total): education, engineering/technologies, foreign languages, general academic interests/achievements. *Creative Arts/Performance:* 188 awards ($1,240,765 total): art/fine arts, music, theater/drama. *Special Achievements/Activities:* 145 awards ($1,457,020 total): general special achievements/activities, leadership, memberships. *Special Characteristics:* 602 awards ($6,392,768 total): children and siblings of alumni, local/state students, relatives of clergy, religious affiliation. ***Tuition waivers:*** Full or partial for employees or children of employees, senior citizens. ***ROTC:*** Army, Naval, Air Force.

LOANS ***Student loans:*** $40,205,773 (84% need-based, 16% non-need-based). 59% of past graduating class borrowed through all loan programs. Average indebtedness per student: $18,702. ***Average need-based loan:*** Freshmen: $3231; Undergraduates: $4251. ***Parent loans:*** $31,765,476 (33% need-based, 67% non-need-based). ***Programs:*** Federal Direct (Subsidized and Unsubsidized Stafford, PLUS), Perkins, state.

WORK-STUDY ***Federal work-study:*** *Total amount:* $8,925,560; 3,910 jobs averaging $2283. ***State or other work-study/employment:*** *Total amount:* $1,315,296 (54% need-based, 46% non-need-based). 179 part-time jobs averaging $7348.

ATHLETIC AWARDS *Total amount:* 6,288,405 (23% need-based, 77% non-need-based).

APPLYING for FINANCIAL AID ***Required financial aid forms:*** FAFSA, CSS Financial Aid PROFILE. ***Financial aid deadline (priority):*** 2/15. ***Notification date:*** Continuous beginning 3/15. Students must reply by 5/1 or within 2 weeks of notification.

CONTACT Ryan Williams, Director of Financial Assistance, Boston University, 881 Commonwealth Avenue, 5th Floor, Boston, MA 02215, 617-353-4176. *Fax:* 617-353-8200. *E-mail:* finaid@bu.edu

BOWDOIN COLLEGE

Brunswick, ME

Tuition & fees: $24,955 **Average undergraduate aid package: $19,647**

ABOUT THE INSTITUTION Independent, coed. Awards: bachelor's degrees. 37 undergraduate majors. Total enrollment: 1,608. Undergraduates: 1,608. Freshmen: 464. Institutional methodology is used as a basis for awarding need-based institutional aid.

UNDERGRADUATE EXPENSES for 1999–2000 ***Application fee:*** $55. ***Comprehensive fee:*** $31,475 includes full-time tuition ($24,435), mandatory fees ($520), and room and board ($6520). ***College room only:*** $2890. Room and board charges vary according to housing facility. ***Payment plan:*** installment.

FRESHMAN FINANCIAL AID (Fall 1998) 243 applied for aid; of those 65% were deemed to have need. 100% of freshmen with need received aid; of those 100% had need fully met. *Average percent of need met:* 100% (excluding resources awarded to replace EFC). *Average financial aid package:* $20,321 (excluding resources awarded to replace EFC).

UNDERGRADUATE FINANCIAL AID (Fall 1998) 856 applied for aid; of those 75% were deemed to have need. 100% of undergraduates with need received aid; of those 100% had need fully met. *Average percent of need met:* 100% (excluding resources awarded to replace EFC). *Average financial aid package:* $19,647 (excluding resources awarded to replace EFC).

GIFT AID (NEED-BASED) ***Total amount:*** $10,118,795 (7% Federal, 1% state, 88% institutional, 4% external sources). ***Receiving aid:*** *Freshmen:* 36% (156); *all full-time undergraduates:* 37% (641). ***Average award:*** Freshmen: $17,030; Undergraduates: $15,781. ***Scholarships, grants, and awards:*** Federal Pell, FSEOG, state, private, college/university gift aid from institutional funds.

GIFT AID (NON-NEED-BASED) ***Total amount:*** $312,046 (100% external sources). ***Tuition waivers:*** Full or partial for employees or children of employees.

LOANS ***Student loans:*** $3,367,330 (89% need-based, 11% non-need-based). 53% of past graduating class borrowed through all loan programs. Average indebtedness per student: $16,077. ***Average need-based loan:*** Freshmen: $2828; Undergraduates: $3063. ***Parent loans:*** $3,267,127 (100% non-need-based). ***Programs:*** FFEL (Subsidized and Unsubsidized Stafford, PLUS), Perkins, state, college/university.

WORK-STUDY ***Federal work-study:*** *Total amount:* $123,100; 127 jobs averaging $969. ***State or other work-study/employment:*** *Total amount:* $1,094,512 (52% need-based, 48% non-need-based). 930 part-time jobs averaging $1175.

APPLYING for FINANCIAL AID ***Required financial aid forms:*** FAFSA, institution's own form, CSS Financial Aid PROFILE, noncustodial (divorced/separated) parent's statement, business/farm supplement. ***Financial aid deadline (priority):*** 2/15. ***Notification date:*** 4/5. Students must reply by 5/1.

CONTACT Mr. Stephen Joyce, Director of Student Aid, Bowdoin College, 5300 College Station, Brunswick, ME 04011-8444, 207-725-3273. *Fax:* 207-725-3101. *E-mail:* sjoyce@bowdoin.edu

BOWIE STATE UNIVERSITY

Bowie, MD

Tuition & fees (MD res): $3664 **Average undergraduate aid package: $5957**

ABOUT THE INSTITUTION State-supported, coed. Awards: bachelor's and master's degrees. 33 undergraduate majors. Total enrollment: 4,770. Undergraduates: 3,114. Freshmen: 361. Federal methodology is used as a basis for awarding need-based institutional aid.

UNDERGRADUATE EXPENSES for 1999–2000 ***Application fee:*** $40. ***Tuition, state resident:*** full-time $2828; part-time $124 per credit. ***Tuition, nonresident:*** full-time $8145; part-time $341 per credit. ***Required fees:*** full-time $836; $122 per term part-time. Part-time tuition and fees vary according to course load. ***College room and board:*** $4012; ***room only:*** $2072. Room and board charges vary according to board plan and housing facility. ***Payment plan:*** deferred payment.

FRESHMAN FINANCIAL AID (Fall 1999) 287 applied for aid; of those 67% were deemed to have need. 98% of freshmen with need received aid; of those 22% had need fully met. *Average percent of need met:* 69% (excluding resources awarded to replace EFC). *Average financial aid package:* $5505 (excluding resources awarded to replace EFC). 8% of all full-time freshmen had no need and received non-need-based aid.

UNDERGRADUATE FINANCIAL AID (Fall 1999) 1,648 applied for aid; of those 71% were deemed to have need. 99% of undergraduates with need received aid; of those 23% had need fully met. *Average percent of need met:* 68% (excluding resources awarded to replace EFC). *Average financial aid package:* $5957 (excluding resources awarded to replace EFC). 7% of all full-time undergraduates had no need and received non-need-based aid.

GIFT AID (NEED-BASED) ***Total amount:*** $3,607,670 (63% Federal, 21% state, 16% institutional). ***Receiving aid:*** *Freshmen:* 22% (76); *all full-time undergraduates:* 18% (411). ***Average award:*** Freshmen: $1213; Undergraduates: $1226. ***Scholarships, grants, and awards:*** Federal Pell, FSEOG, state, private, college/university gift aid from institutional funds.

GIFT AID (NON-NEED-BASED) ***Total amount:*** $1,348,729 (15% state, 85% institutional). ***Receiving aid:*** *Freshmen:* 21% (72); *Undergraduates:* 9% (195). ***Scholarships, grants, and awards by category:*** *Academic Interests/Achievement:* biological sciences, business, communication, computer science, education, engineering/technologies, general academic interests/achievements, health fields, humanities, mathematics, military science, physical sciences, premedicine, social sciences. *Creative Arts/Performance:* applied art and design, art/fine arts, general creative arts/performance, music, performing arts, theater/drama. *Special Achievements/Activities:* community service, general special achievements/activities, leadership. *Special Characteristics:* first-generation college students, handicapped students, out-of-state students. ***Tuition waivers:*** Full or partial for employees or children of employees, senior citizens. ***ROTC:*** Army.

LOANS ***Student loans:*** $5,389,695 (72% need-based, 28% non-need-based). ***Parent loans:*** $302,000 (100% non-need-based). ***Programs:*** Federal Direct (Subsidized and Unsubsidized Stafford), FFEL (PLUS), Perkins.

WORK-STUDY Federal work-study jobs available.

ATHLETIC AWARDS *Total amount:* 193,481 (100% non-need-based).

APPLYING for FINANCIAL AID ***Required financial aid forms:*** FAFSA, institution's own form. ***Financial aid deadline (priority):*** 4/1. ***Notification date:*** Continuous beginning 4/15. Students must reply within 1 week of notification.

CONTACT Financial Aid Officer, Bowie State University, 14000 Jericho Park Road, Bowie, MD 20715, 301-464-6544. *Fax:* 301-464-7234.

BOWLING GREEN STATE UNIVERSITY

Bowling Green, OH

Tuition & fees (OH res): $4874 **Average undergraduate aid package: $5688**

ABOUT THE INSTITUTION State-supported, coed. Awards: bachelor's, master's, and doctoral degrees and post-master's certificates. 150 undergraduate majors. Total enrollment: 18,199. Undergraduates: 15,444. Freshmen: 3,534. Federal methodology is used as a basis for awarding need-based institutional aid.

UNDERGRADUATE EXPENSES for 1999–2000 ***Application fee:*** $35. ***Tuition, state resident:*** full-time $4058; part-time $200 per credit hour. ***Tuition, nonresident:*** full-time $9606; part-time $464 per credit hour. ***Required fees:*** full-time $816; $41 per credit hour. Part-time tuition and fees vary

Bowling Green State University (continued)

according to course load. ***College room and board:*** $5494. Room and board charges vary according to board plan and housing facility. ***Payment plan:*** installment.

FRESHMAN FINANCIAL AID (Fall 1999) 3066 applied for aid; of those 62% were deemed to have need. 98% of freshmen with need received aid; of those 30% had need fully met. *Average percent of need met:* 54% (excluding resources awarded to replace EFC). *Average financial aid package:* $5002 (excluding resources awarded to replace EFC). 5% of all full-time freshmen had no need and received non-need-based aid.

UNDERGRADUATE FINANCIAL AID (Fall 1999) 10,035 applied for aid; of those 69% were deemed to have need. 97% of undergraduates with need received aid; of those 31% had need fully met. *Average percent of need met:* 57% (excluding resources awarded to replace EFC). *Average financial aid package:* $5688 (excluding resources awarded to replace EFC). 5% of all full-time undergraduates had no need and received non-need-based aid.

GIFT AID (NEED-BASED) ***Total amount:*** $10,861,784 (62% Federal, 18% state, 20% institutional). ***Receiving aid:*** *Freshmen:* 17% (642); *all full-time undergraduates:* 19% (2,793). ***Average award:*** Freshmen: $2610; Undergraduates: $2697. ***Scholarships, grants, and awards:*** Federal Pell, FSEOG, state, private, college/university gift aid from institutional funds.

GIFT AID (NON-NEED-BASED) ***Total amount:*** $12,116,263 (1% Federal, 19% state, 51% institutional, 29% external sources). ***Receiving aid:*** *Freshmen:* 21% (768); *Undergraduates:* 15% (2,133). ***Scholarships, grants, and awards by category:*** *Academic Interests/Achievement:* biological sciences, business, communication, computer science, education, engineering/technologies, English, general academic interests/achievements, health fields, home economics, humanities, mathematics, military science, physical sciences, social sciences. *Creative Arts/Performance:* art/fine arts, cinema/film/broadcasting, creative writing, dance, debating, journalism/publications, music, performing arts, theater/drama. *Special Achievements/Activities:* general special achievements/activities, leadership. *Special Characteristics:* children and siblings of alumni, children of faculty/staff, general special characteristics, international students, members of minority groups. ***Tuition waivers:*** Full or partial for employees or children of employees, senior citizens. ***ROTC:*** Army, Air Force.

LOANS ***Student loans:*** $40,000,000 (62% need-based, 38% non-need-based). 55% of past graduating class borrowed through all loan programs. Average indebtedness per student: $15,000. ***Average need-based loan:*** Freshmen: $2581; Undergraduates: $3562. ***Parent loans:*** $9,073,045 (100% non-need-based). ***Programs:*** Federal Direct (Subsidized and Unsubsidized Stafford, PLUS), Perkins, Federal Nursing, state, college/university.

WORK-STUDY ***Federal work-study:*** *Total amount:* $1,250,161; 940 jobs available.

ATHLETIC AWARDS *Total amount:* 2,945,328 (100% non-need-based).

APPLYING for FINANCIAL AID ***Required financial aid form:*** FAFSA. ***Financial aid deadline:*** Continuous. ***Notification date:*** Continuous beginning 4/15. Students must reply within 3 weeks of notification.

CONTACT Office of Financial Aid, Bowling Green State University, 231 Administration Building, Bowling Green, OH 43403, 419-372-2651. *Fax:* 419-372-0404.

BRADLEY UNIVERSITY

Peoria, IL

Tuition & fees: $13,960 **Average undergraduate aid package: $11,112**

ABOUT THE INSTITUTION Independent, coed. Awards: bachelor's and master's degrees. 61 undergraduate majors. Total enrollment: 5,837. Undergraduates: 4,961. Freshmen: 1,079. Federal methodology is used as a basis for awarding need-based institutional aid.

UNDERGRADUATE EXPENSES for 1999–2000 ***Application fee:*** $35. ***Comprehensive fee:*** $19,260 includes full-time tuition ($13,880), mandatory fees ($80), and room and board ($5300). Room and board charges vary according to board plan. ***Part-time tuition:*** $377 per credit hour. Part-time tuition and fees vary according to course load. ***Payment plans:*** installment, deferred payment.

FRESHMAN FINANCIAL AID (Fall 1999) 702 applied for aid; of those 93% were deemed to have need. 100% of freshmen with need received aid; of those 70% had need fully met. *Average percent of need met:* 90% (excluding resources awarded to replace EFC). *Average financial aid package:* $11,210 (excluding resources awarded to replace EFC). 16% of all full-time freshmen had no need and received non-need-based aid.

UNDERGRADUATE FINANCIAL AID (Fall 1999) 3,414 applied for aid; of those 99% were deemed to have need. 100% of undergraduates with need received aid; of those 70% had need fully met. *Average percent of need met:* 90% (excluding resources awarded to replace EFC). *Average financial aid package:* $11,112 (excluding resources awarded to replace EFC). 11% of all full-time undergraduates had no need and received non-need-based aid.

GIFT AID (NEED-BASED) ***Total amount:*** $16,887,079 (11% Federal, 34% state, 55% institutional). ***Receiving aid:*** *Freshmen:* 59% (640); *all full-time undergraduates:* 69% (3,210). ***Average award:*** Freshmen: $8002; Undergraduates: $6903. ***Scholarships, grants, and awards:*** Federal Pell, FSEOG, state, private, college/university gift aid from institutional funds.

GIFT AID (NON-NEED-BASED) ***Total amount:*** $8,418,956 (2% state, 91% institutional, 7% external sources). ***Receiving aid:*** *Freshmen:* 20% (218); *Undergraduates:* 23% (1,079). ***Scholarships, grants, and awards by category:*** *Academic Interests/Achievement:* 2,510 awards ($13,030,500 total): general academic interests/achievements. *Creative Arts/Performance:* 215 awards ($201,650 total): art/fine arts, debating, music, theater/drama. *Special Achievements/Activities:* 30 awards ($30,000 total): community service, leadership. *Special Characteristics:* 387 awards ($2,161,607 total): children and siblings of alumni, children of faculty/staff, members of minority groups. ***Tuition waivers:*** Full or partial for employees or children of employees, senior citizens. ***ROTC:*** Army.

LOANS ***Student loans:*** $15,607,507 (65% need-based, 35% non-need-based). 77% of past graduating class borrowed through all loan programs. Average indebtedness per student: $15,350. ***Average need-based loan:*** Freshmen: $2640; Undergraduates: $4139. ***Parent loans:*** $3,505,155 (100% non-need-based). ***Programs:*** Federal Direct (Subsidized and Unsubsidized Stafford, PLUS), Perkins, Federal Nursing, college/university.

WORK-STUDY ***Federal work-study:*** *Total amount:* $820,442; 700 jobs averaging $1172.

ATHLETIC AWARDS *Total amount:* 1,492,164 (100% non-need-based).

APPLYING for FINANCIAL AID ***Required financial aid form:*** FAFSA. ***Financial aid deadline (priority):*** 3/1. ***Notification date:*** Continuous. Students must reply within 3 weeks of notification.

CONTACT Mr. David L. Pardieck, Director of Financial Assistance, Bradley University, 1501 West Bradley Avenue, Peoria, IL 61625-0002, 309-677-3089 or toll-free 800-447-6460. *E-mail:* dlp@bradley.edu

BRANDEIS UNIVERSITY

Waltham, MA

Tuition & fees: $25,174 **Average undergraduate aid package: $19,589**

ABOUT THE INSTITUTION Independent, coed. Awards: bachelor's, master's, and doctoral degrees and post-bachelor's certificates. 52 undergraduate majors. Total enrollment: 4,527. Undergraduates: 3,112. Freshmen: 794. Institutional methodology is used as a basis for awarding need-based institutional aid.

UNDERGRADUATE EXPENSES for 1999–2000 ***Application fee:*** $50. ***Comprehensive fee:*** $32,214 includes full-time tuition ($24,421), mandatory fees ($753), and room and board ($7040). Room and board charges vary according to board plan and housing facility. ***Payment plans:*** tuition prepayment, installment.

FRESHMAN FINANCIAL AID (Fall 1999, est.) 506 applied for aid; of those 79% were deemed to have need. 100% of freshmen with need received aid; of those 94% had need fully met. *Average percent of need met:* 94% (excluding resources awarded to replace EFC). *Average financial aid package:* $17,956 (excluding resources awarded to replace EFC). 15% of all full-time freshmen had no need and received non-need-based aid.

UNDERGRADUATE FINANCIAL AID (Fall 1999, est.) 1,789 applied for aid; of those 86% were deemed to have need. 100% of undergraduates with

need received aid; of those 92% had need fully met. *Average percent of need met:* 92% (excluding resources awarded to replace EFC). *Average financial aid package:* $19,589 (excluding resources awarded to replace EFC). 12% of all full-time undergraduates had no need and received non-need-based aid.

GIFT AID (NEED-BASED) ***Total amount:*** $20,523,299 (7% Federal, 3% state, 88% institutional, 2% external sources). ***Receiving aid:*** *Freshmen:* 50% (394); *all full-time undergraduates:* 48% (1,465). ***Average award:*** Freshmen: $13,454; Undergraduates: $13,491. ***Scholarships, grants, and awards:*** Federal Pell, FSEOG, state, private, college/university gift aid from institutional funds.

GIFT AID (NON-NEED-BASED) ***Total amount:*** $6,723,646 (97% institutional, 3% external sources). ***Receiving aid:*** *Freshmen:* 7% (57); *Undergraduates:* 4% (132). ***Scholarships, grants, and awards by category:*** *Academic Interests/Achievement:* 700 awards ($8,500,000 total): general academic interests/achievements. ***Tuition waivers:*** Full or partial for employees or children of employees. ***ROTC:*** Army cooperative, Air Force cooperative.

LOANS ***Student loans:*** $9,703,317 (75% need-based, 25% non-need-based). ***Average need-based loan:*** Freshmen: $3686; Undergraduates: $5048. ***Parent loans:*** $3,460,191 (33% need-based, 67% non-need-based). ***Programs:*** Federal Direct (Subsidized and Unsubsidized Stafford, PLUS), Perkins, state, college/university.

WORK-STUDY ***Federal work-study:*** *Total amount:* $1,496,042; jobs available. ***State or other work-study/employment:*** *Total amount:* $348,360 (34% need-based, 66% non-need-based). Part-time jobs available.

APPLYING for FINANCIAL AID ***Required financial aid forms:*** FAFSA, CSS Financial Aid PROFILE, noncustodial (divorced/separated) parent's statement, business/farm supplement. ***Financial aid deadline (priority):*** 1/31. ***Notification date:*** 4/1. Students must reply by 5/1.

CONTACT Peter Giumette, Director of Financial Aid, Brandeis University, 415 South Street, Kutz Hall 121, MS 027, Waltham, MA 02454-9110, 781-736-3700 or toll-free 800-622-0622 (out-of-state). *Fax:* 781-736-3719. *E-mail:* finaid@brandeis.edu

BRENAU UNIVERSITY

Gainesville, GA

Tuition & fees: $11,730 **Average undergraduate aid package: $11,907**

ABOUT THE INSTITUTION Independent, women only. Awards: bachelor's and master's degrees (also offers coed evening and weekend programs with significant enrollment not reflected in profile). 36 undergraduate majors. Total enrollment: 664. Undergraduates: 633. Freshmen: 131. Federal methodology is used as a basis for awarding need-based institutional aid.

UNDERGRADUATE EXPENSES for 1999–2000 ***Application fee:*** $30. ***Comprehensive fee:*** $18,606 includes full-time tuition ($11,730) and room and board ($6876). Full-time tuition and fees vary according to program. Room and board charges vary according to board plan. ***Part-time tuition:*** $391 per semester hour. Part-time tuition and fees vary according to program. ***Payment plan:*** installment.

FRESHMAN FINANCIAL AID (Fall 1999) 122 applied for aid; of those 64% were deemed to have need. 100% of freshmen with need received aid; of those 38% had need fully met. *Average percent of need met:* 91% (excluding resources awarded to replace EFC). *Average financial aid package:* $12,800 (excluding resources awarded to replace EFC). 33% of all full-time freshmen had no need and received non-need-based aid.

UNDERGRADUATE FINANCIAL AID (Fall 1999) 528 applied for aid; of those 70% were deemed to have need. 100% of undergraduates with need received aid; of those 33% had need fully met. *Average percent of need met:* 82% (excluding resources awarded to replace EFC). *Average financial aid package:* $11,907 (excluding resources awarded to replace EFC). 26% of all full-time undergraduates had no need and received non-need-based aid.

GIFT AID (NEED-BASED) ***Total amount:*** $3,278,105 (13% Federal, 25% state, 61% institutional, 1% external sources). ***Receiving aid:*** *Freshmen:* 59% (78); *all full-time undergraduates:* 62% (371). ***Average award:*** Freshmen: $10,863; Undergraduates: $8523. ***Scholarships, grants, and awards:*** Federal Pell, FSEOG, state, private, college/university gift aid from institutional funds.

GIFT AID (NON-NEED-BASED) ***Total amount:*** $1,012,025 (39% state, 60% institutional, 1% external sources). ***Receiving aid:*** *Freshmen:* 14% (18); *Undergraduates:* 9% (53). ***Scholarships, grants, and awards by category:*** *Academic Interests/Achievement:* 232 awards ($1,318,177 total): biological sciences, communication, education, general academic interests/achievements, health fields, humanities. *Creative Arts/Performance:* 79 awards ($156,050 total): applied art and design, art/fine arts, dance, music, theater/drama. *Special Characteristics:* 17 awards ($76,578 total): children of faculty/staff, ethnic background, general special characteristics. ***Tuition waivers:*** Full or partial for employees or children of employees.

LOANS ***Student loans:*** $1,680,316 (58% need-based, 42% non-need-based). 74% of past graduating class borrowed through all loan programs. Average indebtedness per student: $18,724. ***Average need-based loan:*** Freshmen: $2076; Undergraduates: $4192. ***Parent loans:*** $118,102 (100% non-need-based). ***Programs:*** FFEL (Subsidized and Unsubsidized Stafford, PLUS), Perkins, state.

WORK-STUDY ***Federal work-study:*** *Total amount:* $164,497; 118 jobs averaging $1394. ***State or other work-study/employment:*** *Total amount:* $29,966 (39% need-based, 61% non-need-based). 18 part-time jobs averaging $1665.

ATHLETIC AWARDS *Total amount:* 142,950 (22% need-based, 78% non-need-based).

APPLYING for FINANCIAL AID ***Required financial aid forms:*** FAFSA, state aid form. ***Financial aid deadline (priority):*** 5/1. ***Notification date:*** Continuous. Students must reply within 2 weeks of notification.

CONTACT Pam Barrett, Director of Financial Aid, Brenau University, One Centennial Circle, Gainesville, GA 30501-3697, 770-534-6152 or toll-free 800-252-5119 (out-of-state). *Fax:* 770-538-4306. *E-mail:* pbarrett@lib.brenau.edu

BRESCIA UNIVERSITY

Owensboro, KY

Tuition & fees: $9545 **Average undergraduate aid package: $8720**

ABOUT THE INSTITUTION Independent Roman Catholic, coed. Awards: associate, bachelor's, and master's degrees. 33 undergraduate majors. Total enrollment: 695. Undergraduates: 658. Freshmen: 92. Federal methodology is used as a basis for awarding need-based institutional aid.

UNDERGRADUATE EXPENSES for 2000–2001 ***Application fee:*** $25. ***Comprehensive fee:*** $13,785 includes full-time tuition ($9390), mandatory fees ($155), and room and board ($4240). Room and board charges vary according to board plan and housing facility. ***Part-time tuition:*** $315 per credit hour. ***Part-time fees:*** $40 per term part-time. Part-time tuition and fees vary according to course load. ***Payment plan:*** deferred payment.

FRESHMAN FINANCIAL AID (Fall 1999, est.) 82 applied for aid; of those 98% were deemed to have need. 100% of freshmen with need received aid; of those 25% had need fully met. *Average percent of need met:* 100% (excluding resources awarded to replace EFC). *Average financial aid package:* $8720 (excluding resources awarded to replace EFC). 9% of all full-time freshmen had no need and received non-need-based aid.

UNDERGRADUATE FINANCIAL AID (Fall 1999, est.) 390 applied for aid; of those 99% were deemed to have need. 100% of undergraduates with need received aid; of those 15% had need fully met. *Average percent of need met:* 100% (excluding resources awarded to replace EFC). *Average financial aid package:* $8720 (excluding resources awarded to replace EFC). 12% of all full-time undergraduates had no need and received non-need-based aid.

GIFT AID (NEED-BASED) ***Total amount:*** $2,753,760 (21% Federal, 25% state, 44% institutional, 10% external sources). ***Receiving aid:*** *Freshmen:* 46% (48); *all full-time undergraduates:* 49% (233). ***Average award:*** Freshmen: $5929; Undergraduates: $5571. ***Scholarships, grants, and awards:*** Federal Pell, FSEOG, state, private, college/university gift aid from institutional funds.

Brescia University (continued)

GIFT AID (NON-NEED-BASED) ***Total amount:*** $527,214 (5% state, 87% institutional, 8% external sources). ***Receiving aid:*** *Freshmen:* 19% (20); *Undergraduates:* 12% (59). ***Scholarships, grants, and awards by category:*** *Academic Interests/Achievement:* biological sciences, business, education, English, general academic interests/achievements, health fields, physical sciences, premedicine, social sciences. *Creative Arts/Performance:* art/fine arts, creative writing, music. *Special Characteristics:* children and siblings of alumni, children of faculty/staff, ethnic background, international students, members of minority groups. ***Tuition waivers:*** Full or partial for children of alumni, employees or children of employees, senior citizens.

LOANS ***Student loans:*** $2,300,251 (77% need-based, 23% non-need-based). 53% of past graduating class borrowed through all loan programs. ***Average need-based loan:*** Freshmen: $1036; Undergraduates: $3354. ***Parent loans:*** $525,475 (38% need-based, 62% non-need-based). ***Programs:*** FFEL (Subsidized and Unsubsidized Stafford, PLUS), Perkins, college/university.

WORK-STUDY ***Federal work-study:*** *Total amount:* $124,795; 84 jobs averaging $1236. ***State or other work-study/employment:*** *Total amount:* $68,822 (7% need-based, 93% non-need-based). Part-time jobs available.

ATHLETIC AWARDS *Total amount:* 494,941 (100% non-need-based).

APPLYING for FINANCIAL AID ***Required financial aid forms:*** FAFSA, institution's own form. ***Financial aid deadline (priority):*** 3/1. ***Notification date:*** Continuous. Students must reply within 2 weeks of notification.

CONTACT Ms. Vivian Rinaldo, Director of Financial Aid, Brescia University, 717 Frederica Street, Owensboro, KY 42301-3023, 270-686-4290 or toll-free 877-BRESCIA. *Fax:* 270-686-4266. *E-mail:* vivianp@brescia.edu

BREVARD COLLEGE

Brevard, NC

Tuition & fees: $12,310 **Average undergraduate aid package: $10,231**

ABOUT THE INSTITUTION Independent United Methodist, coed. Awards: associate and bachelor's degrees. 62 undergraduate majors. Total enrollment: 685. Undergraduates: 685. Freshmen: 204. Federal methodology is used as a basis for awarding need-based institutional aid.

UNDERGRADUATE EXPENSES for 1999–2000 ***Application fee:*** $20. ***Comprehensive fee:*** $17,130 includes full-time tuition ($11,480), mandatory fees ($830), and room and board ($4820). Room and board charges vary according to housing facility. ***Part-time tuition:*** $330 per semester hour. Part-time tuition and fees vary according to course load. ***Payment plan:*** installment.

FRESHMAN FINANCIAL AID (Fall 1999, est.) 133 applied for aid; of those 80% were deemed to have need. 100% of freshmen with need received aid; of those 34% had need fully met. *Average percent of need met:* 78% (excluding resources awarded to replace EFC). *Average financial aid package:* $10,355 (excluding resources awarded to replace EFC). 28% of all full-time freshmen had no need and received non-need-based aid.

UNDERGRADUATE FINANCIAL AID (Fall 1999, est.) 409 applied for aid; of those 88% were deemed to have need. 100% of undergraduates with need received aid; of those 32% had need fully met. *Average percent of need met:* 79% (excluding resources awarded to replace EFC). *Average financial aid package:* $10,231 (excluding resources awarded to replace EFC). 27% of all full-time undergraduates had no need and received non-need-based aid.

GIFT AID (NEED-BASED) ***Total amount:*** $1,521,720 (27% Federal, 18% state, 55% institutional). ***Receiving aid:*** *Freshmen:* 50% (99); *all full-time undergraduates:* 52% (326). ***Average award:*** Freshmen: $4340; Undergraduates: $4170. ***Scholarships, grants, and awards:*** Federal Pell, FSEOG, state, private, college/university gift aid from institutional funds.

GIFT AID (NON-NEED-BASED) ***Total amount:*** $1,619,300 (32% state, 62% institutional, 6% external sources). ***Receiving aid:*** *Freshmen:* 43% (86); *Undergraduates:* 48% (303). ***Scholarships, grants, and awards by category:*** *Academic Interests/Achievement:* 234 awards ($539,325 total): business, English, general academic interests/achievements, mathematics, physical sciences. *Creative Arts/Performance:* 121 awards ($196,977 total): art/fine arts, journalism/publications, music, theater/drama. *Special Achievements/Activities:* 49 awards ($48,850 total): community service, leadership. *Special Characteristics:* 309 awards ($913,481 total): children of faculty/staff, local/state students, relatives of clergy, religious affiliation. ***Tuition waivers:*** Full or partial for employees or children of employees.

LOANS ***Student loans:*** $1,257,075 (64% need-based, 36% non-need-based). 45% of past graduating class borrowed through all loan programs. Average indebtedness per student: $8618. ***Average need-based loan:*** Freshmen: $2556; Undergraduates: $2932. ***Parent loans:*** $545,290 (100% non-need-based). ***Programs:*** FFEL (Subsidized and Unsubsidized Stafford, PLUS), Perkins.

WORK-STUDY ***Federal work-study:*** *Total amount:* $67,750; jobs available. ***State or other work-study/employment:*** *Total amount:* $65,000 (100% non-need-based). 69 part-time jobs averaging $970.

ATHLETIC AWARDS *Total amount:* 613,250 (100% non-need-based).

APPLYING for FINANCIAL AID ***Required financial aid form:*** FAFSA. ***Financial aid deadline (priority):*** 4/15. ***Notification date:*** Continuous. Students must reply within 4 weeks of notification.

CONTACT Ms. Lisanne J. Masterson, Director, Financial Aid, Brevard College, 400 North Broad Street, Brevard, NC 28712, 828-884-8287 or toll-free 800-527-9090. *Fax:* 828-884-3790. *E-mail:* finaid@brevard.edu

BREWTON-PARKER COLLEGE

Mt. Vernon, GA

CONTACT Ms. Cecelia Hightower, Director of Financial Aid, Brewton-Parker College, Highway 280, Mt. Vernon, GA 30445-0197, 912-583-2241 or toll-free 800-342-1087.

BRIAR CLIFF COLLEGE

Sioux City, IA

Tuition & fees: $13,890 **Average undergraduate aid package: $13,650**

ABOUT THE INSTITUTION Independent Roman Catholic, coed. Awards: associate and bachelor's degrees. 41 undergraduate majors. Total enrollment: 1,001. Undergraduates: 1,001. Freshmen: 268. Federal methodology is used as a basis for awarding need-based institutional aid.

UNDERGRADUATE EXPENSES for 2000–2001 ***Application fee:*** $20. ***Comprehensive fee:*** $18,657 includes full-time tuition ($13,560), mandatory fees ($330), and room and board ($4767). ***College room only:*** $2361. Room and board charges vary according to board plan. ***Part-time tuition:*** $452 per credit hour. Part-time tuition and fees vary according to class time and course load. ***Payment plan:*** deferred payment.

FRESHMAN FINANCIAL AID (Fall 1998) 181 applied for aid; of those 92% were deemed to have need. 100% of freshmen with need received aid; of those 56% had need fully met. *Average percent of need met:* 89% (excluding resources awarded to replace EFC). *Average financial aid package:* $12,956 (excluding resources awarded to replace EFC).

UNDERGRADUATE FINANCIAL AID (Fall 1998) 676 applied for aid; of those 94% were deemed to have need. 100% of undergraduates with need received aid; of those 51% had need fully met. *Average percent of need met:* 92% (excluding resources awarded to replace EFC). *Average financial aid package:* $13,650 (excluding resources awarded to replace EFC). 1% of all full-time undergraduates had no need and received non-need-based aid.

GIFT AID (NEED-BASED) ***Total amount:*** $5,319,219 (13% Federal, 24% state, 63% institutional). ***Receiving aid:*** *Freshmen:* 61% (115); *all full-time undergraduates:* 60% (422). ***Scholarships, grants, and awards:*** Federal Pell, FSEOG, state, college/university gift aid from institutional funds.

GIFT AID (NON-NEED-BASED) ***Total amount:*** $75,000 (100% institutional). ***Receiving aid:*** *Freshmen:* 13% (24); *Undergraduates:* 43% (301). ***Scholarships, grants, and awards by category:*** *Academic Interests/Achievement:* biological sciences, business, communication, computer science, education, English, foreign languages, general academic interests/achievements, health fields, humanities, mathematics, physical sciences, religion/biblical studies, social sciences. *Creative Arts/Performance:* art/fine arts, music, theater/drama. *Special Achievements/Activities:* leadership, religious involvement. *Special Characteristics:* children and siblings of alumni, international students, members of minority groups. ***Tuition waivers:*** Full or partial for employees or children of employees, adult students, senior citizens.

LOANS ***Student loans:*** $1,864,242 (100% need-based). ***Parent loans:*** $179,974 (100% non-need-based). ***Programs:*** FFEL (Subsidized and Unsubsidized Stafford, PLUS), Perkins, college/university.

WORK-STUDY ***Federal work-study:*** *Total amount:* $556,617; 378 jobs averaging $1500. ***State or other work-study/employment:*** *Total amount:* $24,000 (100% need-based). Part-time jobs available.

ATHLETIC AWARDS *Total amount:* 547,588 (100% non-need-based).

APPLYING for FINANCIAL AID ***Required financial aid form:*** FAFSA. ***Financial aid deadline (priority):*** 3/15. ***Notification date:*** Continuous. Students must reply by 5/1 or within 2 weeks of notification.

CONTACT Financial Aid Office, Briar Cliff College, 3303 Rebecca Street, PO Box 2100, Sioux City, IA 51104-2100, 712-279-5440 or toll-free 800-662-3303. *Fax:* 712-279-5410.

BRIARCLIFFE COLLEGE

Bethpage, NY

Tuition & fees: $9070 **Average undergraduate aid package: N/A**

ABOUT THE INSTITUTION Proprietary, coed. Awards: associate and bachelor's degrees. 9 undergraduate majors. Total enrollment: 1,480. Undergraduates: 1,480. Freshmen: 525. Federal methodology is used as a basis for awarding need-based institutional aid.

UNDERGRADUATE EXPENSES for 1999–2000 ***Application fee:*** $25. ***Tuition:*** full-time $8700; part-time $290 per credit. ***Required fees:*** full-time $370; $18 per credit. ***Payment plans:*** installment, deferred payment.

GIFT AID (NEED-BASED) ***Total amount:*** $3,526,587 (35% Federal, 65% state). ***Scholarships, grants, and awards:*** Federal Pell, FSEOG, state, private, college/university gift aid from institutional funds.

GIFT AID (NON-NEED-BASED) ***Tuition waivers:*** Full or partial for employees or children of employees, senior citizens.

LOANS ***Student loans:*** $3,454,836 (100% need-based). ***Parent loans:*** $398,579 (100% need-based). ***Programs:*** FFEL (Subsidized and Unsubsidized Stafford, PLUS), state.

WORK-STUDY ***Federal work-study:*** *Total amount:* $84,525; 54 jobs averaging $1565.

ATHLETIC AWARDS *Total amount:* 416,102 (100% need-based).

APPLYING for FINANCIAL AID ***Required financial aid forms:*** FAFSA, institution's own form, state and federal income tax forms. ***Financial aid deadline:*** Continuous. ***Notification date:*** Continuous. Students must reply within 2 weeks of notification.

CONTACT Johanna Kelly, Financial Aid Director, Briarcliffe College, 1055 Stewart Avenue, Bethpage, NY 11714, 516-470-6000.

BRIDGEWATER COLLEGE

Bridgewater, VA

Tuition & fees: $14,970 **Average undergraduate aid package: $14,900**

ABOUT THE INSTITUTION Independent religious, coed. Awards: bachelor's degrees. 56 undergraduate majors. Total enrollment: 1,120. Undergraduates: 1,120. Freshmen: 324. Federal methodology is used as a basis for awarding need-based institutional aid.

UNDERGRADUATE EXPENSES for 2000–2001 ***Application fee:*** $30. ***Comprehensive fee:*** $21,940 includes full-time tuition ($14,470), mandatory fees ($500), and room and board ($6970). ***College room only:*** $3420. ***Payment plan:*** installment.

FRESHMAN FINANCIAL AID (Fall 1999) 285 applied for aid; of those 93% were deemed to have need. 100% of freshmen with need received aid; of those 42% had need fully met. *Average percent of need met:* 97% (excluding resources awarded to replace EFC). *Average financial aid package:* $14,804 (excluding resources awarded to replace EFC). 18% of all full-time freshmen had no need and received non-need-based aid.

UNDERGRADUATE FINANCIAL AID (Fall 1999) 887 applied for aid; of those 92% were deemed to have need. 100% of undergraduates with need received aid; of those 37% had need fully met. *Average percent of need met:* 96% (excluding resources awarded to replace EFC). *Average financial aid package:* $14,900 (excluding resources awarded to replace EFC). 24% of all full-time undergraduates had no need and received non-need-based aid.

GIFT AID (NEED-BASED) ***Total amount:*** $8,771,483 (8% Federal, 18% state, 72% institutional, 2% external sources). ***Receiving aid:*** *Freshmen:* 81% (264); *all full-time undergraduates:* 75% (812). ***Average award:*** Freshmen: $11,636; Undergraduates: $10,890. ***Scholarships, grants, and awards:*** Federal Pell, FSEOG, state, private, college/university gift aid from institutional funds.

GIFT AID (NON-NEED-BASED) ***Total amount:*** $2,124,761 (24% state, 75% institutional, 1% external sources). ***Receiving aid:*** *Freshmen:* 72% (233); *Undergraduates:* 59% (640). ***Scholarships, grants, and awards by category:*** *Academic Interests/Achievement:* 772 awards ($4,848,722 total): general academic interests/achievements. *Creative Arts/Performance:* 30 awards ($22,340 total): music. *Special Characteristics:* 253 awards ($542,750 total): ethnic background, religious affiliation, siblings of current students. ***Tuition waivers:*** Full or partial for employees or children of employees.

LOANS ***Student loans:*** $3,843,281 (75% need-based, 25% non-need-based). 77% of past graduating class borrowed through all loan programs. Average indebtedness per student: $17,630. ***Average need-based loan:*** Freshmen: $3760; Undergraduates: $4685. ***Parent loans:*** $1,184,284 (100% non-need-based). ***Programs:*** FFEL (Subsidized and Unsubsidized Stafford, PLUS), Perkins, college/university.

WORK-STUDY ***Federal work-study:*** *Total amount:* $340,849; 345 jobs averaging $988. ***State or other work-study/employment:*** *Total amount:* $30,828 (48% need-based, 52% non-need-based). 36 part-time jobs averaging $856.

APPLYING for FINANCIAL AID ***Required financial aid forms:*** FAFSA, state aid form. ***Financial aid deadline (priority):*** 3/1. ***Notification date:*** Continuous beginning 3/15. Students must reply within 2 weeks of notification.

CONTACT Mr. J. Vern Fairchilds Jr., Director of Financial Aid, Bridgewater College, College Box 27, Bridgewater, VA 22812-1599, 540-828-5376 or toll-free 800-759-8328. *Fax:* 540-828-5481. *E-mail:* vfairchi@bridgewater.edu

BRIDGEWATER STATE COLLEGE

Bridgewater, MA

Tuition & fees (MA res): $2123 **Average undergraduate aid package: $3470**

ABOUT THE INSTITUTION State-supported, coed. Awards: bachelor's and master's degrees and post-bachelor's and post-master's certificates. 60 undergraduate majors. Total enrollment: 8,955. Undergraduates: 7,155. Freshmen: 1,096. Federal methodology is used as a basis for awarding need-based institutional aid.

UNDERGRADUATE EXPENSES for 1999–2000 ***Application fee:*** $20; $40 for nonresidents. ***Tuition, state resident:*** full-time $1032; part-time $43 per semester hour. ***Tuition, nonresident:*** full-time $7050; part-time $294 per semester hour. ***Required fees:*** full-time $1091; $66 per semester hour; $12 per term part-time. ***College room and board:*** $4704; ***room only:*** $2684. Room and board charges vary according to board plan and housing facility. ***Payment plan:*** installment.

FRESHMAN FINANCIAL AID (Fall 1999) 753 applied for aid; of those 70% were deemed to have need. 83% of freshmen with need received aid; of those 34% had need fully met. *Average percent of need met:* 28% (excluding resources awarded to replace EFC). *Average financial aid package:* $3305 (excluding resources awarded to replace EFC). 14% of all full-time freshmen had no need and received non-need-based aid.

UNDERGRADUATE FINANCIAL AID (Fall 1999) 4,954 applied for aid; of those 73% were deemed to have need. 93% of undergraduates with need received aid; of those 69% had need fully met. *Average percent of need*

Bridgewater State College (continued)

met: 69% (excluding resources awarded to replace EFC). *Average financial aid package:* $3470 (excluding resources awarded to replace EFC). 14% of all full-time undergraduates had no need and received non-need-based aid.

GIFT AID (NEED-BASED) ***Total amount:*** $4,899,384 (51% Federal, 41% state, 8% institutional). ***Receiving aid:*** *Freshmen:* 37% (374); *all full-time undergraduates:* 33% (2,545). ***Average award:*** Freshmen: $2167; Undergraduates: $1786. ***Scholarships, grants, and awards:*** Federal Pell, FSEOG, state, private, college/university gift aid from institutional funds.

GIFT AID (NON-NEED-BASED) ***Total amount:*** $710,874 (52% state, 6% institutional, 42% external sources). ***Receiving aid:*** *Freshmen:* 9% (86); *Undergraduates:* 5% (383). ***Scholarships, grants, and awards by category:*** *Academic Interests/Achievement:* general academic interests/achievements. ***Tuition waivers:*** Full or partial for employees or children of employees. ***ROTC:*** Army cooperative, Air Force.

LOANS ***Student loans:*** $12,147,056 (55% need-based, 45% non-need-based). 41% of past graduating class borrowed through all loan programs. Average indebtedness per student: $8693. ***Average need-based loan:*** Freshmen: $2240; Undergraduates: $2056. ***Parent loans:*** $929,688 (100% non-need-based). ***Programs:*** Federal Direct (Subsidized and Unsubsidized Stafford, PLUS), Perkins, state.

WORK-STUDY ***Federal work-study:*** *Total amount:* $818,512; 471 jobs averaging $1729.

APPLYING for FINANCIAL AID ***Required financial aid form:*** FAFSA. ***Financial aid deadline (priority):*** 3/1. ***Notification date:*** 3/15.

CONTACT Office of Financial Aid, Bridgewater State College, Tillinghast Hall, Bridgewater, MA 02325-0001, 508-531-1341.

BRIGHAM YOUNG UNIVERSITY

Provo, UT

Tuition & fees: $2830 **Average undergraduate aid package: $3501**

ABOUT THE INSTITUTION Independent religious, coed. Awards: bachelor's, master's, doctoral, and first professional degrees. 104 undergraduate majors. Total enrollment: 32,731. Undergraduates: 30,037. Freshmen: 4,857. Both federal and institutional methodology are used as a basis for awarding need-based institutional aid.

UNDERGRADUATE EXPENSES for 1999–2000 ***Application fee:*** $25. ***Comprehensive fee:*** $7284 includes full-time tuition ($2830) and room and board ($4454). ***College room only:*** $1846. Full-time tuition and fees vary according to reciprocity agreements. Room and board charges vary according to board plan and housing facility. ***Part-time tuition:*** $145 per credit hour. Part-time tuition and fees vary according to course load and reciprocity agreements.

FRESHMAN FINANCIAL AID (Fall 1998) 2625 applied for aid; of those 55% were deemed to have need. 88% of freshmen with need received aid; of those 29% had need fully met. *Average percent of need met:* 26% (excluding resources awarded to replace EFC). *Average financial aid package:* $1938 (excluding resources awarded to replace EFC). 19% of all full-time freshmen had no need and received non-need-based aid.

UNDERGRADUATE FINANCIAL AID (Fall 1998) 22,021 applied for aid; of those 52% were deemed to have need. 93% of undergraduates with need received aid; of those 40% had need fully met. *Average percent of need met:* 37% (excluding resources awarded to replace EFC). *Average financial aid package:* $3501 (excluding resources awarded to replace EFC). 29% of all full-time undergraduates had no need and received non-need-based aid.

GIFT AID (NEED-BASED) ***Total amount:*** $19,193,067 (95% Federal, 5% institutional). ***Receiving aid:*** *Freshmen:* 14% (680); *all full-time undergraduates:* 27% (7,653). ***Average award:*** Freshmen: $1067; Undergraduates: $1488. ***Scholarships, grants, and awards:*** Federal Pell, state, private, college/university gift aid from institutional funds.

GIFT AID (NON-NEED-BASED) ***Total amount:*** $21,725,625 (83% institutional, 17% external sources). ***Receiving aid:*** *Freshmen:* 17% (837); *Undergraduates:* 18% (5,055). ***Scholarships, grants, and awards by category:*** *Academic Interests/Achievement:* agriculture, area/ethnic studies, biological sciences, business, communication, computer science, education, engineering/technologies, English, foreign languages, general academic interests/achievements, health fields, home economics, humanities, international studies, mathematics, military science, physical sciences, premedicine, religion/biblical studies, social sciences. *Creative Arts/Performance:* applied art and design, art/fine arts, cinema/film/broadcasting, creative writing, dance, journalism/publications, music, performing arts, theater/drama. *Special Achievements/Activities:* cheerleading/drum major, community service, general special achievements/activities, leadership, memberships, religious involvement. *Special Characteristics:* adult students, ethnic background, general special characteristics, handicapped students, international students, local/state students, members of minority groups, out-of-state students, religious affiliation. ***Tuition waivers:*** Full or partial for employees or children of employees. ***ROTC:*** Army, Air Force.

LOANS ***Student loans:*** $32,220,141 (75% need-based, 25% non-need-based). 50% of past graduating class borrowed through all loan programs. Average indebtedness per student: $11,350. ***Programs:*** FFEL (Subsidized and Unsubsidized Stafford, PLUS), college/university.

APPLYING for FINANCIAL AID ***Required financial aid form:*** FAFSA. ***Financial aid deadline:*** Continuous. ***Notification date:*** Continuous beginning 4/1.

CONTACT Norman B. Finlinson, Director of Financial Aid, Brigham Young University, A-41 Abraham Smoot Building, Provo, UT 84602-1009, 801-378-4104. *Fax:* 801-378-6226. *E-mail:* financial_aid@byu.edu

BRIGHAM YOUNG UNIVERSITY–HAWAII CAMPUS

Laie, HI

Tuition & fees: $2875 **Average undergraduate aid package: N/A**

ABOUT THE INSTITUTION Independent Latter-day Saints, coed. Awards: associate and bachelor's degrees and post-bachelor's certificates. 40 undergraduate majors. Total enrollment: 2,276. Undergraduates: 2,276. Freshmen: 407. Both federal and institutional methodology are used as a basis for awarding need-based institutional aid.

UNDERGRADUATE EXPENSES for 1999–2000 ***Application fee:*** $25. ***Comprehensive fee:*** $8000 includes full-time tuition ($2875) and room and board ($5125). ***College room only:*** $2050. Full-time tuition and fees vary according to program. Room and board charges vary according to board plan and housing facility. ***Part-time tuition:*** $155 per credit. Part-time tuition and fees vary according to program. Tuition for nonchurch members: $4325 full-time, $230 per credit part-time. ***Payment plan:*** installment.

GIFT AID (NEED-BASED) ***Scholarships, grants, and awards:*** Federal Pell, private, college/university gift aid from institutional funds.

GIFT AID (NON-NEED-BASED) ***Scholarships, grants, and awards by category:*** *Academic Interests/Achievement:* area/ethnic studies, biological sciences, business, communication, computer science, education, English, foreign languages, general academic interests/achievements, humanities, international studies, library science, mathematics, physical sciences, religion/biblical studies, social sciences. *Creative Arts/Performance:* art/fine arts, creative writing, journalism/publications, music, theater/drama. *Special Achievements/Activities:* cheerleading/drum major, community service, general special achievements/activities, junior miss, leadership, religious involvement. *Special Characteristics:* children of educators, children of faculty/staff, ethnic background, international students, religious affiliation. ***Tuition waivers:*** Full or partial for employees or children of employees. ***ROTC:*** Army cooperative, Naval cooperative, Air Force cooperative.

LOANS ***Programs:*** FFEL (Subsidized and Unsubsidized Stafford, PLUS), college/university.

WORK-STUDY ***State or other work-study/employment:*** Part-time jobs available.

APPLYING for FINANCIAL AID ***Required financial aid form:*** FAFSA. ***Financial aid deadline (priority):*** 4/30.

CONTACT Steve Bang, Director of Financial Aid, Brigham Young University–Hawaii Campus, 55-220 Kulanui Street, Laie, HI 96762, 808-293-3530. *Fax:* 808-293-3741. *E-mail:* bangs@byuh.edu

BROOKLYN COLLEGE OF THE CITY UNIVERSITY OF NEW YORK

Brooklyn, NY

CONTACT Financial Aid Office, Brooklyn College of the City University of New York, 2900 Bedford Avenue, Brooklyn, NY 11210-2889, 718-951-5051.

BROOKS INSTITUTE OF PHOTOGRAPHY

Santa Barbara, CA

Tuition & fees: $16,260 **Average undergraduate aid package: $11,000**

ABOUT THE INSTITUTION Proprietary, coed. Awards: bachelor's and master's degrees. 2 undergraduate majors. Total enrollment: 551. Undergraduates: 487. Freshmen: 36. Federal methodology is used as a basis for awarding need-based institutional aid.

UNDERGRADUATE EXPENSES for 1999–2000 ***Application fee:*** $35. ***Tuition:*** full-time $15,750. ***Required fees:*** full-time $510. ***Payment plans:*** installment, deferred payment.

FRESHMAN FINANCIAL AID (Fall 1999) *Average percent of need met:* 35% (excluding resources awarded to replace EFC). *Average financial aid package:* $7000 (excluding resources awarded to replace EFC).

UNDERGRADUATE FINANCIAL AID (Fall 1999) *Average percent of need met:* 40% (excluding resources awarded to replace EFC). *Average financial aid package:* $11,000 (excluding resources awarded to replace EFC).

GIFT AID (NEED-BASED) ***Total amount:*** $365,000 ***Scholarships, grants, and awards:*** Federal Pell, FSEOG, state, private.

GIFT AID (NON-NEED-BASED) ***Scholarships, grants, and awards by category:*** *Creative Arts/Performance:* applied art and design.

LOANS ***Programs:*** FFEL (Subsidized and Unsubsidized Stafford, PLUS), alternative loans.

WORK-STUDY Federal work-study jobs available.

APPLYING for FINANCIAL AID ***Required financial aid form:*** FAFSA. ***Financial aid deadline (priority):*** 3/2. ***Notification date:*** Continuous. Students must reply within 4 weeks of notification.

CONTACT Pam Hall, Financial Aid Assistant, Brooks Institute of Photography, 801 Alston Road, Santa Barbara, CA 93108, 805-966-3888 Ext. 3032. *Fax:* 805-966-2909.

BROWN UNIVERSITY

Providence, RI

Tuition & fees: $25,186 **Average undergraduate aid package: $20,655**

ABOUT THE INSTITUTION Independent, coed. Awards: bachelor's, master's, doctoral, and first professional degrees. 83 undergraduate majors. Total enrollment: 7,758. Undergraduates: 6,108. Freshmen: 1,388. Both federal and institutional methodology are used as a basis for awarding need-based institutional aid.

UNDERGRADUATE EXPENSES for 1999–2000 ***Application fee:*** $55. ***One-time required fee:*** $186. ***Comprehensive fee:*** $32,280 includes full-time tuition ($24,624), mandatory fees ($562), and room and board ($7094). ***College room only:*** $4370. Room and board charges vary according to board plan and housing facility. ***Part-time tuition:*** $3078 per course. ***Payment plans:*** tuition prepayment, installment, deferred payment.

FRESHMAN FINANCIAL AID (Fall 1999) 758 applied for aid; of those 74% were deemed to have need. 100% of freshmen with need received aid; of those 100% had need fully met. *Average percent of need met:* 100% (excluding resources awarded to replace EFC). *Average financial aid package:* $20,726 (excluding resources awarded to replace EFC). 8% of all full-time freshmen had no need and received non-need-based aid.

UNDERGRADUATE FINANCIAL AID (Fall 1999) 2,530 applied for aid; of those 92% were deemed to have need. 100% of undergraduates with need received aid; of those 100% had need fully met. *Average percent of need met:* 100% (excluding resources awarded to replace EFC). *Average financial aid package:* $20,655 (excluding resources awarded to replace EFC). 4% of all full-time undergraduates had no need and received non-need-based aid.

GIFT AID (NEED-BASED) ***Total amount:*** $32,843,150 (6% Federal, 89% institutional, 5% external sources). ***Receiving aid:*** *Freshmen:* 39% (539); *all full-time undergraduates:* 37% (2,158). ***Average award:*** Freshmen: $17,205; Undergraduates: $15,220. ***Scholarships, grants, and awards:*** Federal Pell, FSEOG, state, private, college/university gift aid from institutional funds.

GIFT AID (NON-NEED-BASED) ***Total amount:*** $414,117 (100% external sources). ***Receiving aid:*** *Freshmen:* 2% (28); *Undergraduates:* 2% (138). ***Tuition waivers:*** Full or partial for employees or children of employees. ***ROTC:*** Army cooperative.

LOANS ***Student loans:*** $12,120,777 (92% need-based, 8% non-need-based). 46% of past graduating class borrowed through all loan programs. Average indebtedness per student: $22,240. ***Average need-based loan:*** Freshmen: $3066; Undergraduates: $5106. ***Parent loans:*** $4,886,125 (100% non-need-based). ***Programs:*** Federal Direct (Subsidized and Unsubsidized Stafford, PLUS), Perkins, state, college/university.

WORK-STUDY ***Federal work-study:*** *Total amount:* $3,611,220; 2,030 jobs available. ***State or other work-study/employment:*** *Total amount:* $205,225 (100% need-based). Part-time jobs available.

APPLYING for FINANCIAL AID ***Required financial aid forms:*** FAFSA, institution's own form, CSS Financial Aid PROFILE, noncustodial (divorced/separated) parent's statement, business/farm supplement. ***Financial aid deadline:*** 3/1. ***Notification date:*** 4/1. Students must reply by 5/1.

CONTACT Mr. Paul Langhammer, Associate Director of Financial Aid, Brown University, 8 Fones Alley, Providence, RI 02912, 401-863-2721. *Fax:* 401-863-7575. *E-mail:* paul_langhammer@brown.edu

BRYAN COLLEGE

Dayton, TN

Tuition & fees: $11,200 **Average undergraduate aid package: $7457**

ABOUT THE INSTITUTION Independent interdenominational, coed. Awards: associate and bachelor's degrees. 27 undergraduate majors. Total enrollment: 521. Undergraduates: 521. Freshmen: 140. Both federal and institutional methodology are used as a basis for awarding need-based institutional aid.

UNDERGRADUATE EXPENSES for 1999–2000 ***Application fee:*** $20. ***Comprehensive fee:*** $15,200 includes full-time tuition ($11,200) and room and board ($4000). ***College room only:*** $1800. ***Part-time tuition:*** $450 per semester hour.

FRESHMAN FINANCIAL AID (Fall 1998) 147 applied for aid; of those 79% were deemed to have need. 100% of freshmen with need received aid; of those 16% had need fully met. *Average percent of need met:* 66% (excluding resources awarded to replace EFC). *Average financial aid package:* $7512 (excluding resources awarded to replace EFC). 19% of all full-time freshmen had no need and received non-need-based aid.

UNDERGRADUATE FINANCIAL AID (Fall 1998) 541 applied for aid; of those 78% were deemed to have need. 100% of undergraduates with need received aid; of those 15% had need fully met. *Average percent of need met:* 69% (excluding resources awarded to replace EFC). *Average financial aid package:* $7457 (excluding resources awarded to replace EFC). 20% of all full-time undergraduates had no need and received non-need-based aid.

GIFT AID (NEED-BASED) ***Total amount:*** $840,812 (57% Federal, 15% state, 28% institutional). ***Receiving aid:*** *Freshmen:* 52% (87); *all full-time undergraduates:* 49% (285). ***Average award:*** Freshmen: $2461; Undergraduates: $2309. ***Scholarships, grants, and awards:*** Federal Pell, FSEOG, state, private, college/university gift aid from institutional funds.

GIFT AID (NON-NEED-BASED) ***Total amount:*** $1,261,164 (1% state, 82% institutional, 17% external sources). ***Receiving aid:*** *Freshmen:* 62% (103);

Bryan College (continued)

Undergraduates: 61% (349). ***Scholarships, grants, and awards by category:*** *Academic Interests/Achievement:* 251 awards ($702,629 total): biological sciences, business, communication, education, English, foreign languages, general academic interests/achievements, humanities, mathematics, physical sciences, religion/biblical studies, social sciences. *Creative Arts/Performance:* 60 awards ($44,235 total): art/fine arts, journalism/publications, music, performing arts. *Special Achievements/Activities:* 61 awards ($72,690 total): cheerleading/drum major, community service, general special achievements/activities, leadership, religious involvement. *Special Characteristics:* 244 awards ($481,081 total): children and siblings of alumni, children of current students, children of faculty/staff, general special characteristics, handicapped students, international students, local/state students, relatives of clergy, religious affiliation, spouses of current students.

LOANS ***Student loans:*** $1,472,923 (72% need-based, 28% non-need-based). 84% of past graduating class borrowed through all loan programs. Average indebtedness per student: $10,952. ***Average need-based loan:*** Freshmen: $2531; Undergraduates: $3146. ***Parent loans:*** $429,495 (100% non-need-based). ***Programs:*** FFEL (Subsidized and Unsubsidized Stafford, PLUS), Perkins, state, college/university.

WORK-STUDY ***Federal work-study:*** *Total amount:* $143,246; 116 jobs averaging $1234. ***State or other work-study/employment:*** *Total amount:* $74,024 (100% non-need-based). 78 part-time jobs averaging $949.

ATHLETIC AWARDS *Total amount:* 303,823 (100% non-need-based).

APPLYING for FINANCIAL AID ***Required financial aid forms:*** FAFSA, institution's own form. ***Financial aid deadline (priority):*** 5/1. ***Notification date:*** Continuous. Students must reply within 1 week of notification.

CONTACT Anne Reed Rader, Director of Financial Aid, Bryan College, PO Box 7000, Dayton, TN 37321-7000, 423-775-7226 or toll-free 800-277-9522. *Fax:* 423-775-7330. *E-mail:* raderan@bryan.edu

BRYANT AND STRATTON COLLEGE

Cleveland, OH

Tuition & fees: $9024 **Average undergraduate aid package: $6200**

ABOUT THE INSTITUTION Proprietary, coed. Awards: associate and bachelor's degrees. 3 undergraduate majors. Total enrollment: 191. Undergraduates: 191. Freshmen: 49. Both federal and institutional methodology are used as a basis for awarding need-based institutional aid.

UNDERGRADUATE EXPENSES for 1999–2000 ***Application fee:*** $25. ***Tuition:*** full-time $9024; part-time $282 per semester hour. ***Payment plan:*** guaranteed tuition.

FRESHMAN FINANCIAL AID (Fall 1999, est.) 38 applied for aid; of those 95% were deemed to have need. 100% of freshmen with need received aid; of those 83% had need fully met. *Average percent of need met:* 76% (excluding resources awarded to replace EFC). *Average financial aid package:* $6200 (excluding resources awarded to replace EFC).

UNDERGRADUATE FINANCIAL AID (Fall 1999, est.) 110 applied for aid; of those 98% were deemed to have need. 90% of undergraduates with need received aid; of those 93% had need fully met. *Average percent of need met:* 89% (excluding resources awarded to replace EFC). *Average financial aid package:* $6200 (excluding resources awarded to replace EFC).

GIFT AID (NEED-BASED) ***Total amount:*** $439,783 (58% Federal, 42% state). ***Receiving aid:*** *Freshmen:* 52% (21); *all full-time undergraduates:* 71% (80). ***Average award:*** Freshmen: $1550; Undergraduates: $1500. ***Scholarships, grants, and awards:*** Federal Pell, FSEOG, state, private, college/university gift aid from institutional funds.

GIFT AID (NON-NEED-BASED) ***Total amount:*** $16,466 (53% institutional, 47% external sources). ***Scholarships, grants, and awards by category:*** *Academic Interests/Achievement:* general academic interests/achievements. ***Tuition waivers:*** Full or partial for employees or children of employees.

LOANS ***Student loans:*** $720,191 (57% need-based, 43% non-need-based). 93% of past graduating class borrowed through all loan programs. Average indebtedness per student: $12,000. ***Average need-based loan:*** Freshmen: $2625; Undergraduates: $3065. ***Parent loans:*** $108,568 (87% need-based, 13% non-need-based). ***Programs:*** FFEL (Subsidized and Unsubsidized Stafford, PLUS), Perkins.

WORK-STUDY ***Federal work-study:*** *Total amount:* $31,000; 8 jobs averaging $3000.

APPLYING for FINANCIAL AID ***Required financial aid forms:*** FAFSA, institution's own form. ***Financial aid deadline:*** Continuous. ***Notification date:*** Continuous.

CONTACT Financial Aid Supervisor, Bryant and Stratton College, 1700 East 13th Street, Cleveland, OH 44114-3203, 216-771-1700. *Fax:* 216-771-7787.

BRYANT COLLEGE

Smithfield, RI

Tuition & fees: $17,330 **Average undergraduate aid package: $12,519**

ABOUT THE INSTITUTION Independent, coed. Awards: associate, bachelor's, and master's degrees and post-master's certificates. 14 undergraduate majors. Total enrollment: 3,355. Undergraduates: 2,864. Freshmen: 652. Both federal and institutional methodology are used as a basis for awarding need-based institutional aid.

UNDERGRADUATE EXPENSES for 2000–2001 ***Application fee:*** $50. ***Comprehensive fee:*** $24,580 includes full-time tuition ($17,330) and room and board ($7250). ***College room only:*** $4250. Full-time tuition and fees vary according to course load and program. Room and board charges vary according to board plan and housing facility. ***Part-time tuition:*** $650 per course. Part-time tuition and fees vary according to course load and program. ***Payment plans:*** tuition prepayment, installment.

FRESHMAN FINANCIAL AID (Fall 1999, est.) 594 applied for aid; of those 75% were deemed to have need. 100% of freshmen with need received aid; of those 26% had need fully met. *Average percent of need met:* 80% (excluding resources awarded to replace EFC). *Average financial aid package:* $13,209 (excluding resources awarded to replace EFC). 18% of all full-time freshmen had no need and received non-need-based aid.

UNDERGRADUATE FINANCIAL AID (Fall 1999, est.) 2,254 applied for aid; of those 76% were deemed to have need. 100% of undergraduates with need received aid; of those 17% had need fully met. *Average percent of need met:* 79% (excluding resources awarded to replace EFC). *Average financial aid package:* $12,519 (excluding resources awarded to replace EFC). 18% of all full-time undergraduates had no need and received non-need-based aid.

GIFT AID (NEED-BASED) ***Total amount:*** $10,373,000 (10% Federal, 3% state, 86% institutional, 1% external sources). ***Receiving aid:*** *Freshmen:* 67% (429); *all full-time undergraduates:* 62% (1,542). ***Average award:*** Freshmen: $7380; Undergraduates: $6620. ***Scholarships, grants, and awards:*** Federal Pell, FSEOG, state, private, college/university gift aid from institutional funds.

GIFT AID (NON-NEED-BASED) ***Total amount:*** $2,387,667 (94% institutional, 6% external sources). ***Receiving aid:*** *Freshmen:* 14% (89); *Undergraduates:* 16% (386). ***Scholarships, grants, and awards by category:*** *Academic Interests/Achievement:* 672 awards ($3,608,684 total): general academic interests/achievements. *Special Achievements/Activities:* 593 awards ($1,765,500 total): leadership. *Special Characteristics:* 175 awards ($347,896 total): children and siblings of alumni, members of minority groups, siblings of current students. ***Tuition waivers:*** Full or partial for employees or children of employees. ***ROTC:*** Army.

LOANS ***Student loans:*** $10,328,046 (71% need-based, 29% non-need-based). 62% of past graduating class borrowed through all loan programs. Average indebtedness per student: $19,047. ***Average need-based loan:*** Freshmen: $3742; Undergraduates: $4391. ***Parent loans:*** $2,994,290 (33% need-based, 67% non-need-based). ***Programs:*** FFEL (Subsidized and Unsubsidized Stafford, PLUS), Perkins, state, college/university, alternative loans.

WORK-STUDY ***Federal work-study:*** *Total amount:* $244,458; 161 jobs averaging $1519. ***State or other work-study/employment:*** *Total amount:* $1,504,968 (100% need-based). 991 part-time jobs averaging $1519.

ATHLETIC AWARDS *Total amount:* 544,348 (41% need-based, 59% non-need-based).

APPLYING for FINANCIAL AID ***Required financial aid forms:*** FAFSA, CSS Financial Aid PROFILE. ***Financial aid deadline (priority):*** 12/1. ***Notification date:*** Continuous beginning 1/1.

CONTACT Mr. John Canning, Director of Financial Aid, Bryant College, Office of Financial Aid, 1150 Douglas Pike, Smithfield, RI 02917-1284, 401-232-6020 or toll-free 800-622-7001. *Fax:* 401-232-6319. *E-mail:* jcanning@bryant.edu

BRYN ATHYN COLLEGE OF THE NEW CHURCH

Bryn Athyn, PA

CONTACT Mr. Duane D. Hyatt, Business Manager, Bryn Athyn College of the New Church, PO Box 711, Bryn Athyn, PA 19009-0717, 215-938-2635. *Fax:* 215-938-2616. *E-mail:* ddhyatt@newchurch.edu

BRYN MAWR COLLEGE

Bryn Mawr, PA

Tuition & fees: $23,360 **Average undergraduate aid package: $20,802**

ABOUT THE INSTITUTION Independent, women only. Awards: bachelor's, master's, and doctoral degrees. 31 undergraduate majors. Total enrollment: 1,779. Undergraduates: 1,316. Freshmen: 321. Both federal and institutional methodology are used as a basis for awarding need-based institutional aid.

UNDERGRADUATE EXPENSES for 1999–2000 ***Application fee:*** $50. ***Comprehensive fee:*** $31,460 includes full-time tuition ($22,730), mandatory fees ($630), and room and board ($8100). Room and board charges vary according to board plan. ***Part-time tuition:*** $2850 per course. ***Payment plans:*** tuition prepayment, installment, deferred payment.

FRESHMAN FINANCIAL AID (Fall 1998) 224 applied for aid; of those 88% were deemed to have need. 100% of freshmen with need received aid; of those 100% had need fully met. *Average percent of need met:* 100% (excluding resources awarded to replace EFC). *Average financial aid package:* $21,246 (excluding resources awarded to replace EFC).

UNDERGRADUATE FINANCIAL AID (Fall 1998) 717 applied for aid; of those 95% were deemed to have need. 100% of undergraduates with need received aid; of those 100% had need fully met. *Average percent of need met:* 100% (excluding resources awarded to replace EFC). *Average financial aid package:* $20,802 (excluding resources awarded to replace EFC).

GIFT AID (NEED-BASED) ***Total amount:*** $10,631,209 (5% Federal, 2% state, 90% institutional, 3% external sources). ***Receiving aid:*** *Freshmen:* 57% (196); *all full-time undergraduates:* 55% (684). ***Average award:*** Freshmen: $17,665; Undergraduates: $15,542. ***Scholarships, grants, and awards:*** Federal Pell, FSEOG, state, private, college/university gift aid from institutional funds.

GIFT AID (NON-NEED-BASED) ***Tuition waivers:*** Full or partial for employees or children of employees, senior citizens. ***ROTC:*** Air Force cooperative.

LOANS ***Student loans:*** $2,643,211 (100% need-based). ***Average need-based loan:*** Freshmen: $2490; Undergraduates: $3818. ***Parent loans:*** $2,255,800 (100% non-need-based). ***Programs:*** FFEL (Subsidized and Unsubsidized Stafford, PLUS), Perkins, college/university, TERI Loans.

WORK-STUDY ***Federal work-study:*** *Total amount:* $859,584; 560 jobs averaging $1400. ***State or other work-study/employment:*** *Total amount:* $18,947 (100% need-based). Part-time jobs available.

APPLYING for FINANCIAL AID ***Required financial aid forms:*** FAFSA, institution's own form, CSS Financial Aid PROFILE, state aid form. ***Financial aid deadline:*** 1/15. ***Notification date:*** 4/1. Students must reply by 5/1.

CONTACT Jamie C. Hightower, Director of Financial Aid, Bryn Mawr College, 101 North Merion Avenue, Bryn Mawr, PA 19010-2899, 610-526-7922 or toll-free 800-BMC-1885 (out-of-state). *Fax:* 610-526-5249. *E-mail:* jhightow@brynmawr.edu

BUCKNELL UNIVERSITY

Lewisburg, PA

Tuition & fees: $22,881 **Average undergraduate aid package: $17,241**

ABOUT THE INSTITUTION Independent, coed. Awards: bachelor's and master's degrees. 49 undergraduate majors. Total enrollment: 3,560. Undergraduates: 3,403. Freshmen: 886. Both federal and institutional methodology are used as a basis for awarding need-based institutional aid.

UNDERGRADUATE EXPENSES for 1999–2000 ***Application fee:*** $50. ***Comprehensive fee:*** $28,350 includes full-time tuition ($22,740), mandatory fees ($141), and room and board ($5469). ***College room only:*** $2925. Room and board charges vary according to board plan and housing facility. ***Part-time tuition:*** $650 per credit. ***Payment plans:*** tuition prepayment, installment.

FRESHMAN FINANCIAL AID (Fall 1999, est.) 544 applied for aid; of those 82% were deemed to have need. 100% of freshmen with need received aid; of those 100% had need fully met. *Average percent of need met:* 100% (excluding resources awarded to replace EFC). *Average financial aid package:* $17,494 (excluding resources awarded to replace EFC).

UNDERGRADUATE FINANCIAL AID (Fall 1999, est.) 2,100 applied for aid; of those 86% were deemed to have need. 100% of undergraduates with need received aid; of those 100% had need fully met. *Average percent of need met:* 100% (excluding resources awarded to replace EFC). *Average financial aid package:* $17,241 (excluding resources awarded to replace EFC).

GIFT AID (NEED-BASED) ***Total amount:*** $25,134,000 (5% Federal, 5% state, 84% institutional, 6% external sources). ***Receiving aid:*** *Freshmen:* 40% (357); *all full-time undergraduates:* 43% (1,500). ***Average award:*** Freshmen: $16,857; Undergraduates: $16,423. ***Scholarships, grants, and awards:*** Federal Pell, FSEOG, state, private, college/university gift aid from institutional funds.

GIFT AID (NON-NEED-BASED) ***Tuition waivers:*** Full or partial for employees or children of employees. ***ROTC:*** Army.

LOANS ***Student loans:*** $7,100,000 (100% need-based). 60% of past graduating class borrowed through all loan programs. Average indebtedness per student: $15,500. ***Average need-based loan:*** Freshmen: $3073; Undergraduates: $2916. ***Parent loans:*** $4,250,000 (100% need-based). ***Programs:*** FFEL (Subsidized and Unsubsidized Stafford, PLUS), Perkins.

WORK-STUDY ***Federal work-study:*** *Total amount:* $525,000; 758 jobs averaging $700. ***State or other work-study/employment:*** *Total amount:* $2,800,000 (100% need-based). Part-time jobs available.

APPLYING for FINANCIAL AID ***Required financial aid forms:*** FAFSA, CSS Financial Aid PROFILE, noncustodial (divorced/separated) parent's statement, business/farm supplement. ***Financial aid deadline:*** 1/1. ***Notification date:*** 4/10. Students must reply by 5/1.

CONTACT Mr. Ronald T. Laszewski, Director of Financial Aid, Bucknell University, Office of Financial Aid, Lewisburg, PA 17837, 570-577-1331.

BUENA VISTA UNIVERSITY

Storm Lake, IA

Tuition & fees: $15,751 **Average undergraduate aid package: $16,257**

ABOUT THE INSTITUTION Independent religious, coed. Awards: bachelor's and master's degrees. 52 undergraduate majors. Total enrollment: 1,399. Undergraduates: 1,283. Freshmen: 325. Federal methodology is used as a basis for awarding need-based institutional aid.

UNDERGRADUATE EXPENSES for 1999–2000 ***Application fee:*** $25. ***Comprehensive fee:*** $20,258 includes full-time tuition ($15,751) and room and board ($4507). ***College room only:*** $2235. Room and board charges vary according to board plan, housing facility, and location. ***Part-time tuition:*** $546 per semester hour. Part-time tuition and fees vary according to course load. ***Payment plan:*** installment.

FRESHMAN FINANCIAL AID (Fall 1999, est.) 318 applied for aid; of those 94% were deemed to have need. 100% of freshmen with need received

Buena Vista University (continued)

aid; of those 17% had need fully met. *Average percent of need met:* 91% (excluding resources awarded to replace EFC). *Average financial aid package:* $16,295 (excluding resources awarded to replace EFC). 5% of all full-time freshmen had no need and received non-need-based aid.

UNDERGRADUATE FINANCIAL AID (Fall 1999, est.) 1,203 applied for aid; of those 95% were deemed to have need. 100% of undergraduates with need received aid; of those 38% had need fully met. *Average percent of need met:* 97% (excluding resources awarded to replace EFC). *Average financial aid package:* $16,257 (excluding resources awarded to replace EFC). 6% of all full-time undergraduates had no need and received non-need-based aid.

GIFT AID (NEED-BASED) ***Total amount:*** $11,632,972 (11% Federal, 26% state, 63% institutional). ***Receiving aid:*** *Freshmen:* 92% (298); *all full-time undergraduates:* 88% (1,129). ***Average award:*** Freshmen: $10,990; Undergraduates: $9808. ***Scholarships, grants, and awards:*** Federal Pell, FSEOG, state, private, college/university gift aid from institutional funds.

GIFT AID (NON-NEED-BASED) ***Total amount:*** $1,773,104 (1% state, 87% institutional, 12% external sources). ***Receiving aid:*** *Freshmen:* 59% (191); *Undergraduates:* 54% (692). ***Scholarships, grants, and awards by category:*** *Academic Interests/Achievement:* 160 awards ($768,760 total): biological sciences, computer science, education, general academic interests/achievements, humanities, mathematics. *Creative Arts/Performance:* 147 awards ($303,955 total): art/fine arts, music, theater/drama. *Special Achievements/Activities:* 395 awards ($1,770,275 total): general special achievements/activities, leadership. *Special Characteristics:* 312 awards ($737,372 total): international students, out-of-state students, religious affiliation, siblings of current students. ***Tuition waivers:*** Full or partial for employees or children of employees.

LOANS ***Student loans:*** $5,363,236 (81% need-based, 19% non-need-based). Average indebtedness per student: $15,960. ***Average need-based loan:*** Freshmen: $3418; Undergraduates: $4173. ***Programs:*** Federal Direct (Subsidized and Unsubsidized Stafford, PLUS), FFEL (Subsidized and Unsubsidized Stafford, PLUS), Perkins, college/university.

WORK-STUDY ***Federal work-study:*** *Total amount:* $589,607; jobs available. ***State or other work-study/employment:*** Part-time jobs available.

APPLYING for FINANCIAL AID ***Required financial aid form:*** FAFSA. ***Financial aid deadline (priority):*** 6/1. ***Notification date:*** Continuous. Students must reply within 2 weeks of notification.

CONTACT Mrs. Leanne Valentine, Director of Financial Aid, Buena Vista University, 610 West Fourth Street, Storm Lake, IA 50588, 712-749-2164 or toll-free 800-383-9600. *Fax:* 712-749-1451. *E-mail:* valentinel@bvu.edu

BURLINGTON COLLEGE

Burlington, VT

Tuition & fees: $9066 **Average undergraduate aid package: $7526**

ABOUT THE INSTITUTION Independent, coed. Awards: associate and bachelor's degrees. 10 undergraduate majors. Total enrollment: 205. Undergraduates: 205. Freshmen: 28. Federal methodology is used as a basis for awarding need-based institutional aid.

UNDERGRADUATE EXPENSES for 1999–2000 ***Application fee:*** $30. ***Tuition:*** full-time $8850; part-time $295 per credit. ***Required fees:*** full-time $216; $108 per term part-time. Full-time tuition and fees vary according to program. Part-time tuition and fees vary according to program. ***Payment plan:*** installment.

FRESHMAN FINANCIAL AID (Fall 1999) 9 applied for aid; of those 100% were deemed to have need. 100% of freshmen with need received aid; of those 11% had need fully met. *Average percent of need met:* 60% (excluding resources awarded to replace EFC). *Average financial aid package:* $7585 (excluding resources awarded to replace EFC).

UNDERGRADUATE FINANCIAL AID (Fall 1999) 63 applied for aid; of those 94% were deemed to have need. 100% of undergraduates with need received aid; of those 8% had need fully met. *Average percent of need met:* 67% (excluding resources awarded to replace EFC). *Average financial aid package:* $7526 (excluding resources awarded to replace EFC).

GIFT AID (NEED-BASED) ***Total amount:*** $322,262 (49% Federal, 40% state, 8% institutional, 3% external sources). ***Receiving aid:*** *Freshmen:* 67% (8); *all full-time undergraduates:* 48% (42). ***Average award:*** Freshmen: $3390; Undergraduates: $2811. ***Scholarships, grants, and awards:*** Federal Pell, FSEOG, state, private, college/university gift aid from institutional funds.

GIFT AID (NON-NEED-BASED) ***Scholarships, grants, and awards by category:*** *Special Achievements/Activities:* general special achievements/activities. ***Tuition waivers:*** Full or partial for employees or children of employees, senior citizens.

LOANS ***Student loans:*** $568,847 (86% need-based, 14% non-need-based). 85% of past graduating class borrowed through all loan programs. Average indebtedness per student: $16,508. ***Average need-based loan:*** Freshmen: $2695; Undergraduates: $4087. ***Parent loans:*** $30,616 (50% need-based, 50% non-need-based). ***Programs:*** FFEL (Subsidized and Unsubsidized Stafford, PLUS), Perkins.

WORK-STUDY ***Federal work-study:*** *Total amount:* $93,619; 57 jobs averaging $1725.

APPLYING for FINANCIAL AID ***Required financial aid form:*** FAFSA. ***Financial aid deadline:*** Continuous. ***Notification date:*** Continuous beginning 4/1. Students must reply within 3 weeks of notification.

CONTACT Ms. Yvonne Whitaker, Assistant Director, VSAC Financial Aid Services, Burlington College, PO Box 2000, Winooski, VT 05404, 802-654-3793 or toll-free 800-862-9616. *E-mail:* whitaker@vsac.org

BUTLER UNIVERSITY

Indianapolis, IN

Tuition & fees: $17,360 **Average undergraduate aid package: $12,212**

ABOUT THE INSTITUTION Independent, coed. Awards: associate, bachelor's, master's, and first professional degrees and post-bachelor's certificates. 51 undergraduate majors. Total enrollment: 4,147. Undergraduates: 3,294. Freshmen: 863. Federal methodology is used as a basis for awarding need-based institutional aid.

UNDERGRADUATE EXPENSES for 1999–2000 ***Application fee:*** $25. ***Comprehensive fee:*** $23,210 includes full-time tuition ($17,180), mandatory fees ($180), and room and board ($5850). Full-time tuition and fees vary according to program. Room and board charges vary according to board plan and housing facility. ***Part-time tuition:*** $720 per semester hour. Part-time tuition and fees vary according to program. ***Payment plans:*** tuition prepayment, installment.

FRESHMAN FINANCIAL AID (Fall 1998) 846 applied for aid; of those 69% were deemed to have need. 100% of freshmen with need received aid; of those 33% had need fully met. *Average percent of need met:* 86% (excluding resources awarded to replace EFC). *Average financial aid package:* $11,880 (excluding resources awarded to replace EFC). 29% of all full-time freshmen had no need and received non-need-based aid.

UNDERGRADUATE FINANCIAL AID (Fall 1998) 1,975 applied for aid; of those 87% were deemed to have need. 82% of undergraduates with need received aid; of those 29% had need fully met. *Average percent of need met:* 82% (excluding resources awarded to replace EFC). *Average financial aid package:* $12,212 (excluding resources awarded to replace EFC). 18% of all full-time undergraduates had no need and received non-need-based aid.

GIFT AID (NEED-BASED) ***Total amount:*** $17,638,322 (6% Federal, 16% state, 73% institutional, 5% external sources). ***Receiving aid:*** *Freshmen:* 64% (582); *all full-time undergraduates:* 41% (1,304). ***Scholarships, grants, and awards:*** Federal Pell, FSEOG, state, private, college/university gift aid from institutional funds.

GIFT AID (NON-NEED-BASED) ***Total amount:*** $5,586,501 (1% state, 93% institutional, 6% external sources). ***Receiving aid:*** *Freshmen:* 38% (344); *Undergraduates:* 19% (603). ***Scholarships, grants, and awards by category:*** *Academic Interests/Achievement:* biological sciences, business, communication, computer science, education, engineering/technologies, English, foreign languages, general academic interests/achievements, humanities, international studies, mathematics, physical sciences, social sciences. *Creative Arts/Performance:* art/fine arts, cinema/film/broadcasting, dance, music, theater/drama. ***Tuition waivers:*** Full or partial for employees or children of employees. ***ROTC:*** Army cooperative, Air Force cooperative.

LOANS ***Student loans:*** $9,026,231 (80% need-based, 20% non-need-based). 60% of past graduating class borrowed through all loan programs. Average indebtedness per student: $18,700. ***Parent loans:*** $2,026,823 (21% need-based, 79% non-need-based). ***Programs:*** FFEL (Subsidized and Unsubsidized Stafford, PLUS), Perkins.

WORK-STUDY ***Federal work-study:*** *Total amount:* $300,000; jobs available. ***State or other work-study/employment:*** *Total amount:* $1,250,000 (100% non-need-based). Part-time jobs available.

ATHLETIC AWARDS *Total amount:* 2,350,954 (23% need-based, 77% non-need-based).

APPLYING for FINANCIAL AID ***Required financial aid forms:*** FAFSA, institution's own form. ***Financial aid deadline (priority):*** 3/1. ***Notification date:*** 3/15. Students must reply within 3 weeks of notification.

CONTACT Ms. Kristine Butz, Associate Director of Financial Aid, Butler University, 4600 Sunset Avenue, Indianapolis, IN 46208-3485, 317-940-8200 or toll-free 888-940-8100. *Fax:* 317-940-8250. *E-mail:* butz@butler.edu

CABRINI COLLEGE

Radnor, PA

Tuition & fees: $16,000 **Average undergraduate aid package: N/A**

ABOUT THE INSTITUTION Independent Roman Catholic, coed. Awards: bachelor's and master's degrees. 38 undergraduate majors. Total enrollment: 2,002. Undergraduates: 1,620. Freshmen: 295. Both federal and institutional methodology are used as a basis for awarding need-based institutional aid.

UNDERGRADUATE EXPENSES for 1999–2000 ***Application fee:*** $25. ***Comprehensive fee:*** $23,200 includes full-time tuition ($15,250), mandatory fees ($750), and room and board ($7200). Full-time tuition and fees vary according to course load. Room and board charges vary according to housing facility. ***Part-time tuition:*** $290 per credit. ***Part-time fees:*** $45 per term part-time. Part-time tuition and fees vary according to course load. ***Payment plan:*** installment.

GIFT AID (NEED-BASED) ***Scholarships, grants, and awards:*** Federal Pell, FSEOG, state, private, college/university gift aid from institutional funds.

GIFT AID (NON-NEED-BASED) ***Scholarships, grants, and awards by category:*** *Academic Interests/Achievement:* general academic interests/achievements. *Special Achievements/Activities:* leadership. *Special Characteristics:* children and siblings of alumni, children of faculty/staff, siblings of current students, twins. ***Tuition waivers:*** Full or partial for children of alumni, employees or children of employees, senior citizens. ***ROTC:*** Army cooperative.

LOANS ***Programs:*** FFEL (Subsidized and Unsubsidized Stafford, PLUS), Perkins.

WORK-STUDY Federal work-study jobs available.

APPLYING for FINANCIAL AID ***Required financial aid form:*** FAFSA. ***Financial aid deadline (priority):*** 2/1. ***Notification date:*** Continuous. Students must reply within 2 weeks of notification.

CONTACT Ms. Christine Melton, Assistant Director of Financial Aid, Cabrini College, 610 King of Prussia Road, Grace Hall, Room 181, Radnor, PA 19087-3698, 610-902-8420 or toll-free 800-848-1003. *Fax:* 610-902-8426.

CALDWELL COLLEGE

Caldwell, NJ

Tuition & fees: $12,400 **Average undergraduate aid package: $7925**

ABOUT THE INSTITUTION Independent Roman Catholic, coed. Awards: bachelor's and master's degrees and post-master's certificates. 25 undergraduate majors. Total enrollment: 2,066. Undergraduates: 1,816. Freshmen: 271. Federal methodology is used as a basis for awarding need-based institutional aid.

UNDERGRADUATE EXPENSES for 1999–2000 ***Application fee:*** $40. ***Comprehensive fee:*** $18,300 includes full-time tuition ($12,400) and room and board ($5900). Full-time tuition and fees vary according to program. ***Part-time tuition:*** $319 per credit. Part-time tuition and fees vary according to course load and program. ***Payment plans:*** installment, deferred payment.

FRESHMAN FINANCIAL AID (Fall 1999, est.) 259 applied for aid; of those 88% were deemed to have need. 100% of freshmen with need received aid. *Average percent of need met:* 79% (excluding resources awarded to replace EFC). *Average financial aid package:* $8125 (excluding resources awarded to replace EFC). 16% of all full-time freshmen had no need and received non-need-based aid.

UNDERGRADUATE FINANCIAL AID (Fall 1999, est.) 823 applied for aid; of those 67% were deemed to have need. 100% of undergraduates with need received aid. *Average percent of need met:* 74% (excluding resources awarded to replace EFC). *Average financial aid package:* $7925 (excluding resources awarded to replace EFC). 26% of all full-time undergraduates had no need and received non-need-based aid.

GIFT AID (NEED-BASED) ***Total amount:*** $3,712,180 (20% Federal, 52% state, 21% institutional, 7% external sources). ***Receiving aid:*** *Freshmen:* 79% (227); *all full-time undergraduates:* 61% (549). ***Average award:*** Freshmen: $6735; Undergraduates: $6200. ***Scholarships, grants, and awards:*** Federal Pell, FSEOG, state, private, college/university gift aid from institutional funds.

GIFT AID (NON-NEED-BASED) ***Total amount:*** $1,043,108 (1% state, 99% institutional). ***Receiving aid:*** *Freshmen:* 49% (139); *Undergraduates:* 35% (321). ***Scholarships, grants, and awards by category:*** *Academic Interests/Achievement:* 244 awards ($1,516,108 total): general academic interests/achievements. *Creative Arts/Performance:* 39 awards ($24,500 total): art/fine arts, music. *Special Achievements/Activities:* 24 awards ($34,450 total): junior miss, leadership, religious involvement. *Special Characteristics:* 153 awards ($462,843 total): children and siblings of alumni, children of faculty/staff, international students, out-of-state students, religious affiliation, siblings of current students. ***Tuition waivers:*** Full or partial for employees or children of employees, senior citizens. ***ROTC:*** Army cooperative.

LOANS ***Student loans:*** $3,025,919 (63% need-based, 37% non-need-based). 64% of past graduating class borrowed through all loan programs. Average indebtedness per student: $11,350. ***Average need-based loan:*** Freshmen: $2625; Undergraduates: $3975. ***Parent loans:*** $438,019 (100% non-need-based). ***Programs:*** FFEL (Subsidized and Unsubsidized Stafford, PLUS), state, alternative loans.

WORK-STUDY ***Federal work-study:*** *Total amount:* $75,148; jobs available. ***State or other work-study/employment:*** *Total amount:* $62,000 (100% need-based). 12 part-time jobs averaging $5900.

ATHLETIC AWARDS *Total amount:* 174,070 (100% non-need-based).

APPLYING for FINANCIAL AID ***Required financial aid forms:*** FAFSA, institution's own form. ***Financial aid deadline (priority):*** 4/15. ***Notification date:*** Continuous. Students must reply within 2 weeks of notification.

CONTACT Ms. Lissa B. Anderson, Executive Director of Financial Aid, Caldwell College, 9 Ryerson Avenue, Caldwell, NJ 07006-6195, 973-618-3221 or toll-free 888-864-9516 (out-of-state).

CALIFORNIA BAPTIST UNIVERSITY

Riverside, CA

Tuition & fees: $10,682 **Average undergraduate aid package: $9100**

ABOUT THE INSTITUTION Independent Southern Baptist, coed. Awards: bachelor's and master's degrees. 21 undergraduate majors. Total enrollment: 2,058. Undergraduates: 1,618. Freshmen: 226. Federal methodology is used as a basis for awarding need-based institutional aid.

UNDERGRADUATE EXPENSES for 2000–2001 ***Application fee:*** $30. ***One-time required fee:*** $140. ***Comprehensive fee:*** $15,648 includes full-time tuition ($10,062), mandatory fees ($620), and room and board ($4966). ***College room only:*** $2250. Full-time tuition and fees vary according to program. Room and board charges vary according to board plan and

California Baptist University (continued)

housing facility. ***Part-time tuition:*** $387 per unit. ***Part-time fees:*** $50 per term part-time. Part-time tuition and fees vary according to course load. ***Payment plans:*** installment, deferred payment.

FRESHMAN FINANCIAL AID (Fall 1999, est.) 212 applied for aid; of those 100% were deemed to have need. 100% of freshmen with need received aid; of those 90% had need fully met. *Average percent of need met:* 90% (excluding resources awarded to replace EFC). *Average financial aid package:* $8600 (excluding resources awarded to replace EFC). 7% of all full-time freshmen had no need and received non-need-based aid.

UNDERGRADUATE FINANCIAL AID (Fall 1999, est.) 1,293 applied for aid; of those 99% were deemed to have need. 100% of undergraduates with need received aid; of those 90% had need fully met. *Average percent of need met:* 92% (excluding resources awarded to replace EFC). *Average financial aid package:* $9100 (excluding resources awarded to replace EFC). 8% of all full-time undergraduates had no need and received non-need-based aid.

GIFT AID (NEED-BASED) ***Total amount:*** $3,733,564 (39% Federal, 58% state, 3% institutional). ***Receiving aid:*** *Freshmen:* 56% (127); *all full-time undergraduates:* 55% (768). ***Average award:*** Freshmen: $5240; Undergraduates: $4925. ***Scholarships, grants, and awards:*** Federal Pell, FSEOG, state, private, college/university gift aid from institutional funds.

GIFT AID (NON-NEED-BASED) ***Total amount:*** $2,028,045 (100% institutional). ***Receiving aid:*** *Freshmen:* 75% (170); *Undergraduates:* 74% (1,024). ***Scholarships, grants, and awards by category:*** *Academic Interests/Achievement:* 320 awards ($794,652 total): business, general academic interests/achievements, religion/biblical studies. *Creative Arts/Performance:* 183 awards ($283,725 total): art/fine arts, music, theater/drama. *Special Characteristics:* 134 awards ($407,520 total): children of faculty/staff, relatives of clergy, siblings of current students, veterans. ***Tuition waivers:*** Full or partial for employees or children of employees. ***ROTC:*** Army cooperative, Air Force cooperative.

LOANS ***Student loans:*** $13,106,628 (49% need-based, 51% non-need-based). 96% of past graduating class borrowed through all loan programs. Average indebtedness per student: $15,800. ***Average need-based loan:*** Freshmen: $2330; Undergraduates: $4300. ***Parent loans:*** $186,095 (100% non-need-based). ***Programs:*** FFEL (Subsidized and Unsubsidized Stafford, PLUS), Perkins.

WORK-STUDY ***Federal work-study:*** *Total amount:* $110,000; 91 jobs averaging $1100.

ATHLETIC AWARDS *Total amount:* 1,039,976 (30% need-based, 70% non-need-based).

APPLYING for FINANCIAL AID ***Required financial aid forms:*** FAFSA, institution's own form. ***Financial aid deadline (priority):*** 3/2. ***Notification date:*** Continuous. Students must reply by 4/1 or within 2 weeks of notification.

CONTACT Mrs. Karen Sanders, Director of Financial Aid, California Baptist University, 8432 Magnolia Avenue, Riverside, CA 92504-3297, 909-343-4390 or toll-free 877-228-8866. *Fax:* 909-343-4518. *E-mail:* ksanders@calbaptist.edu

CALIFORNIA CHRISTIAN COLLEGE

Fresno, CA

CONTACT Financial Aid Office, California Christian College, 4881 East University Avenue, Fresno, CA 93703-3533, 559-251-4215.

CALIFORNIA COLLEGE FOR HEALTH SCIENCES

National City, CA

Tuition & fees: N/R — **Average undergraduate aid package: $5158**

ABOUT THE INSTITUTION Proprietary, coed. Awards: associate, bachelor's, and master's degrees (offers primarily external degree programs). 9 undergraduate majors. Total enrollment: 6,592. Federal methodology is used as a basis for awarding need-based institutional aid.

FRESHMAN FINANCIAL AID (Fall 1998) 44 applied for aid; of those 100% were deemed to have need. 100% of freshmen with need received aid. *Average percent of need met:* 85% (excluding resources awarded to replace EFC). *Average financial aid package:* $4664 (excluding resources awarded to replace EFC).

UNDERGRADUATE FINANCIAL AID (Fall 1998) 119 applied for aid; of those 100% were deemed to have need. 100% of undergraduates with need received aid. *Average percent of need met:* 76% (excluding resources awarded to replace EFC). *Average financial aid package:* $5158 (excluding resources awarded to replace EFC). 4% of all full-time undergraduates had no need and received non-need-based aid.

GIFT AID (NEED-BASED) ***Total amount:*** $125,895 (100% Federal). ***Receiving aid:*** *Freshmen:* 100% (44); *all full-time undergraduates:* 89% (114). ***Average award:*** Freshmen: $1763; Undergraduates: $1763. ***Scholarships, grants, and awards:*** Federal Pell.

GIFT AID (NON-NEED-BASED) ***Receiving aid:*** *Freshmen:* 100% (44); *Undergraduates:* 93% (119). ***Tuition waivers:*** Full or partial for employees or children of employees.

LOANS ***Student loans:*** $507,741 (44% need-based, 56% non-need-based). 91% of past graduating class borrowed through all loan programs. Average indebtedness per student: $14,125. ***Average need-based loan:*** Freshmen: $2526; Undergraduates: $3395. ***Parent loans:*** $25,789 (100% need-based). ***Programs:*** Federal Direct (Subsidized and Unsubsidized Stafford, PLUS), FFEL (Subsidized and Unsubsidized Stafford, PLUS).

APPLYING for FINANCIAL AID ***Required financial aid forms:*** FAFSA, institution's own form, income verification. ***Financial aid deadline (priority):*** 9/1. ***Notification date:*** Continuous. Students must reply within 2 weeks of notification.

CONTACT Gilda M. Maldonado, Financial Aid Director, California College for Health Sciences, 222 West 24th Street, National City, CA 91950-6605, 619-477-4800 Ext. 318 or toll-free 800-221-7374 (out-of-state). *Fax:* 619-477-5202. *E-mail:* gmaldona@cchs.edu

CALIFORNIA COLLEGE OF ARTS AND CRAFTS

San Francisco, CA

Tuition & fees: $18,368 — **Average undergraduate aid package: $13,089**

ABOUT THE INSTITUTION Independent, coed. Awards: bachelor's and master's degrees. 17 undergraduate majors. Total enrollment: 1,132. Undergraduates: 1,063. Freshmen: 99. Institutional methodology is used as a basis for awarding need-based institutional aid.

UNDERGRADUATE EXPENSES for 1999–2000 ***Application fee:*** $30. ***Comprehensive fee:*** $24,226 includes full-time tuition ($18,188), mandatory fees ($180), and room and board ($5858). ***College room only:*** $3500. Full-time tuition and fees vary according to course load. Room and board charges vary according to housing facility. ***Part-time tuition:*** $758 per unit. ***Part-time fees:*** $90 per term part-time. Part-time tuition and fees vary according to course load. ***Payment plans:*** installment, deferred payment.

FRESHMAN FINANCIAL AID (Fall 1999, est.) 87 applied for aid; of those 89% were deemed to have need. 100% of freshmen with need received aid. *Average percent of need met:* 63% (excluding resources awarded to replace EFC). *Average financial aid package:* $23,301 (excluding resources awarded to replace EFC). 7% of all full-time freshmen had no need and received non-need-based aid.

UNDERGRADUATE FINANCIAL AID (Fall 1999, est.) 622 applied for aid; of those 94% were deemed to have need. 100% of undergraduates with need received aid. *Average percent of need met:* 62% (excluding resources awarded to replace EFC). *Average financial aid package:* $13,089 (excluding resources awarded to replace EFC). 3% of all full-time undergraduates had no need and received non-need-based aid.

GIFT AID (NEED-BASED) ***Total amount:*** $6,077,516 (15% Federal, 27% state, 57% institutional, 1% external sources). ***Receiving aid:*** *Freshmen:* 66% (65); *all full-time undergraduates:* 61% (558). ***Average award:*** Freshmen: $8228; Undergraduates: $5384. ***Scholarships, grants, and awards:*** Federal Pell, FSEOG, state, private, college/university gift aid from institutional funds.

GIFT AID (NON-NEED-BASED) ***Total amount:*** $301,760 (100% institutional). ***Receiving aid:*** *Freshmen:* 46% (45); *Undergraduates:* 11% (104). ***Scholarships, grants, and awards by category:*** *Creative Arts/Performance:* applied art and design, art/fine arts, general creative arts/performance. *Special Characteristics:* ethnic background. ***Tuition waivers:*** Full or partial for employees or children of employees.

LOANS ***Student loans:*** $4,954,609 (58% need-based, 42% non-need-based). 62% of past graduating class borrowed through all loan programs. Average indebtedness per student: $22,500. ***Average need-based loan:*** Freshmen: $2679; Undergraduates: $4407. ***Parent loans:*** $511,522 (100% non-need-based). ***Programs:*** FFEL (Subsidized and Unsubsidized Stafford, PLUS), Perkins.

WORK-STUDY ***Federal work-study:*** *Total amount:* $236,146; 196 jobs averaging $1200. ***State or other work-study/employment:*** *Total amount:* $140,000 (100% non-need-based). 32 part-time jobs averaging $1037.

APPLYING for FINANCIAL AID ***Required financial aid forms:*** FAFSA, institution's own form, state aid form, financial aid transcript (for mid-year transfers only), student and parent federal tax returns. ***Financial aid deadline (priority):*** 3/2. ***Notification date:*** Continuous beginning 3/15. Students must reply within 2 weeks of notification.

CONTACT Alicia Hoey, Financial Aid Administrator, California College of Arts and Crafts, 1111 Eighth Street, San Francisco, CA 94107, 415-703-9528 or toll-free 800-447-1ART. *Fax:* 415-551-9261. *E-mail:* ahoey@ccac-art.edu

CALIFORNIA INSTITUTE OF INTEGRAL STUDIES

San Francisco, CA

Tuition & fees: $14,010 **Average undergraduate aid package: $5374**

ABOUT THE INSTITUTION Independent, coed. Awards: bachelor's, master's, and doctoral degrees. Federal methodology is used as a basis for awarding need-based institutional aid.

UNDERGRADUATE EXPENSES for 1999–2000 ***Tuition:*** full-time $13,740; part-time $370 per unit. ***Required fees:*** full-time $270. Full-time tuition and fees vary according to degree level. Part-time tuition and fees vary according to degree level. ***Payment plan:*** deferred payment.

UNDERGRADUATE FINANCIAL AID (Fall 1999) 37 applied for aid; of those 92% were deemed to have need. 100% of undergraduates with need received aid. *Average percent of need met:* 50% (excluding resources awarded to replace EFC). *Average financial aid package:* $5374 (excluding resources awarded to replace EFC). 4% of all full-time undergraduates had no need and received non-need-based aid.

GIFT AID (NEED-BASED) ***Total amount:*** $13,047 (100% Federal). ***Receiving aid:*** *All full-time undergraduates:* 27% (12). ***Average award:*** Undergraduates: $1087. ***Scholarships, grants, and awards:*** Federal Pell, state, private, college/university gift aid from institutional funds.

GIFT AID (NON-NEED-BASED) ***Total amount:*** $34,470 (10% state, 62% institutional, 28% external sources). ***Receiving aid:*** *Undergraduates:* 20% (9). ***Scholarships, grants, and awards by category:*** *Academic Interests/Achievement:* 4 awards ($18,320 total): general academic interests/achievements, humanities, social sciences. *Special Achievements/Activities:* 2 awards ($3100 total): community service, general special achievements/activities.

LOANS ***Student loans:*** $297,558 (45% need-based, 55% non-need-based). 80% of past graduating class borrowed through all loan programs. Average indebtedness per student: $15,000. ***Average need-based loan:*** Undergraduates: $3977. ***Parent loans:*** $5000 (100% non-need-based). ***Programs:*** FFEL (Subsidized and Unsubsidized Stafford, PLUS).

APPLYING for FINANCIAL AID ***Required financial aid forms:*** FAFSA, institution's own form. ***Financial aid deadline (priority):*** 6/15. ***Notification date:*** Continuous beginning 7/1. Students must reply within 4 weeks of notification.

CONTACT Samantha Kahn, Financial Aid Assistant, California Institute of Integral Studies, 1453 Mission Street, San Francisco, CA 94103, 415-575-6122. *Fax:* 415-575-1268. *E-mail:* finaid@ciis.edu

CALIFORNIA INSTITUTE OF TECHNOLOGY

Pasadena, CA

Tuition & fees: $19,959 **Average undergraduate aid package: $17,833**

ABOUT THE INSTITUTION Independent, coed. Awards: bachelor's, master's, and doctoral degrees. 32 undergraduate majors. Total enrollment: 1,889. Undergraduates: 907. Freshmen: 234. Both federal and institutional methodology are used as a basis for awarding need-based institutional aid.

UNDERGRADUATE EXPENSES for 2000–2001 ***Application fee:*** $40. ***Comprehensive fee:*** $26,139 includes full-time tuition ($19,743), mandatory fees ($216), and room and board ($6180). ***Payment plans:*** installment, deferred payment.

FRESHMAN FINANCIAL AID (Fall 1999) 187 applied for aid; of those 82% were deemed to have need. 100% of freshmen with need received aid; of those 100% had need fully met. *Average percent of need met:* 100% (excluding resources awarded to replace EFC). *Average financial aid package:* $17,842 (excluding resources awarded to replace EFC). 10% of all full-time freshmen had no need and received non-need-based aid.

UNDERGRADUATE FINANCIAL AID (Fall 1999) 712 applied for aid; of those 86% were deemed to have need. 100% of undergraduates with need received aid; of those 100% had need fully met. *Average percent of need met:* 100% (excluding resources awarded to replace EFC). *Average financial aid package:* $17,833 (excluding resources awarded to replace EFC). 4% of all full-time undergraduates had no need and received non-need-based aid.

GIFT AID (NEED-BASED) ***Total amount:*** $7,630,473 (10% Federal, 5% state, 85% institutional). ***Receiving aid:*** *Freshmen:* 58% (136); *all full-time undergraduates:* 59% (531). ***Average award:*** Freshmen: $16,618; Undergraduates: $16,020. ***Scholarships, grants, and awards:*** Federal Pell, FSEOG, state, private, college/university gift aid from institutional funds.

GIFT AID (NON-NEED-BASED) ***Total amount:*** $2,149,140 (6% state, 76% institutional, 18% external sources). ***Receiving aid:*** *Freshmen:* 6% (15); *Undergraduates:* 9% (79). ***Scholarships, grants, and awards by category:*** *Academic Interests/Achievement:* 116 awards ($1,624,688 total): general academic interests/achievements. ***Tuition waivers:*** Full or partial for employees or children of employees. ***ROTC:*** Army cooperative, Air Force cooperative.

LOANS ***Student loans:*** $1,614,714 (84% need-based, 16% non-need-based). 69% of past graduating class borrowed through all loan programs. Average indebtedness per student: $11,573. ***Average need-based loan:*** Freshmen: $3466; Undergraduates: $3376. ***Parent loans:*** $766,296 (100% non-need-based). ***Programs:*** Federal Direct (Subsidized and Unsubsidized Stafford, PLUS), Perkins, college/university.

WORK-STUDY ***Federal work-study:*** *Total amount:* $927,501; 417 jobs averaging $2224. ***State or other work-study/employment:*** *Total amount:* $112,836 (100% need-based). Part-time jobs available.

APPLYING for FINANCIAL AID ***Required financial aid forms:*** FAFSA, CSS Financial Aid PROFILE, business/farm supplement. ***Financial aid deadline (priority):*** 1/15. ***Notification date:*** 4/15. Students must reply by 5/1 or within 4 weeks of notification.

CONTACT David Levy, Director of Financial Aid, California Institute of Technology, Financial Aid Office, MC 12-63, Pasadena, CA 91125-0001, 626-395-6280 or toll-free 800-568-8324. *Fax:* 626-564-8136. *E-mail:* davidlevy@finaid.caltech.edu

CALIFORNIA INSTITUTE OF THE ARTS

Valencia, CA

Tuition & fees: $19,950 **Average undergraduate aid package: $17,674**

California Institute of the Arts (continued)

ABOUT THE INSTITUTION Independent, coed. Awards: bachelor's and master's degrees and post-bachelor's certificates. 14 undergraduate majors. Total enrollment: 1,224. Undergraduates: 804. Freshmen: 146. Federal methodology is used as a basis for awarding need-based institutional aid.

UNDERGRADUATE EXPENSES for 2000–2001 ***Application fee:*** $60. ***Comprehensive fee:*** $25,100 includes full-time tuition ($19,750), mandatory fees ($200), and room and board ($5150). ***College room only:*** $3000. Room and board charges vary according to housing facility.

FRESHMAN FINANCIAL AID (Fall 1999, est.) 111 applied for aid; of those 79% were deemed to have need. 99% of freshmen with need received aid; of those 2% had need fully met. *Average percent of need met:* 79% (excluding resources awarded to replace EFC). *Average financial aid package:* $15,072 (excluding resources awarded to replace EFC).

UNDERGRADUATE FINANCIAL AID (Fall 1999, est.) 612 applied for aid; of those 81% were deemed to have need. 100% of undergraduates with need received aid; of those 8% had need fully met. *Average percent of need met:* 82% (excluding resources awarded to replace EFC). *Average financial aid package:* $17,674 (excluding resources awarded to replace EFC).

GIFT AID (NEED-BASED) ***Total amount:*** $4,171,093 (16% Federal, 25% state, 57% institutional, 2% external sources). ***Receiving aid:*** *Freshmen:* 52% (76); *all full-time undergraduates:* 60% (468). ***Average award:*** Freshmen: $7295; Undergraduates: $8831. ***Scholarships, grants, and awards:*** Federal Pell, FSEOG, state, private, college/university gift aid from institutional funds.

GIFT AID (NON-NEED-BASED) ***Total amount:*** $270,291 (97% institutional, 3% external sources). ***Scholarships, grants, and awards by category:*** *Creative Arts/Performance:* applied art and design, art/fine arts, cinema/film/broadcasting, creative writing, dance, music, performing arts, theater/drama. *Special Characteristics:* children of educators, children of faculty/staff, ethnic background, members of minority groups. ***Tuition waivers:*** Full or partial for employees or children of employees.

LOANS ***Student loans:*** $3,172,965 (94% need-based, 6% non-need-based). 71% of past graduating class borrowed through all loan programs. Average indebtedness per student: $24,873. ***Average need-based loan:*** Freshmen: $3529; Undergraduates: $5196. ***Parent loans:*** $915,629 (69% need-based, 31% non-need-based). ***Programs:*** FFEL (Subsidized and Unsubsidized Stafford, PLUS), Perkins, college/university.

WORK-STUDY ***Federal work-study:*** *Total amount:* $374,736; 176 jobs averaging $2129. ***State or other work-study/employment:*** *Total amount:* $54,996 (100% need-based). 29 part-time jobs averaging $1896.

APPLYING for FINANCIAL AID ***Required financial aid form:*** FAFSA. ***Financial aid deadline (priority):*** 3/2. ***Notification date:*** Continuous beginning 4/15. Students must reply within 3 weeks of notification.

CONTACT Ms. Bobbi Heuer, Director of Financial Aid, California Institute of the Arts, 24700 McBean Parkway, Valencia, CA 91355-2340, 661-253-7869 or toll-free 800-292-ARTS (in-state), 800-545-ARTS (out-of-state). *Fax:* 661-287-3816.

CALIFORNIA LUTHERAN UNIVERSITY

Thousand Oaks, CA

Tuition & fees: $16,200 **Average undergraduate aid package: $12,175**

ABOUT THE INSTITUTION Independent Lutheran, coed. Awards: bachelor's and master's degrees. 48 undergraduate majors. Total enrollment: 2,753. Undergraduates: 1,750. Federal methodology is used as a basis for awarding need-based institutional aid.

UNDERGRADUATE EXPENSES for 1999–2000 ***Application fee:*** $45. ***Comprehensive fee:*** $22,440 includes full-time tuition ($16,020), mandatory fees ($180), and room and board ($6240). ***College room only:*** $3040. Room and board charges vary according to board plan. ***Part-time tuition:*** $535 per unit. ***Payment plan:*** installment.

FRESHMAN FINANCIAL AID (Fall 1999, est.) 288 applied for aid; of those 84% were deemed to have need. 98% of freshmen with need received aid. *Average financial aid package:* $13,982 (excluding resources awarded to replace EFC). 18% of all full-time freshmen had no need and received non-need-based aid.

UNDERGRADUATE FINANCIAL AID (Fall 1999, est.) 1,219 applied for aid; of those 87% were deemed to have need. 99% of undergraduates with need received aid. *Average financial aid package:* $12,175 (excluding resources awarded to replace EFC). 10% of all full-time undergraduates had no need and received non-need-based aid.

GIFT AID (NEED-BASED) ***Total amount:*** $7,006,870 (13% Federal, 21% state, 66% institutional). ***Receiving aid:*** *Freshmen:* 71% (224); *all full-time undergraduates:* 69% (1,034). ***Average award:*** Freshmen: $9486; Undergraduates: $7780. ***Scholarships, grants, and awards:*** Federal Pell, FSEOG, state, private, college/university gift aid from institutional funds.

GIFT AID (NON-NEED-BASED) ***Total amount:*** $4,697,758 (93% institutional, 7% external sources). ***Receiving aid:*** *Freshmen:* 56% (177); *Undergraduates:* 33% (497). ***Scholarships, grants, and awards by category:*** *Academic Interests/Achievement:* biological sciences, business, communication, computer science, education, English, foreign languages, general academic interests/achievements, mathematics, physical sciences, religion/biblical studies, social sciences. *Creative Arts/Performance:* art/fine arts, music, theater/drama. *Special Achievements/Activities:* leadership, religious involvement. *Special Characteristics:* adult students, children and siblings of alumni, children of faculty/staff, international students, relatives of clergy, religious affiliation. ***Tuition waivers:*** Full or partial for employees or children of employees. ***ROTC:*** Army cooperative, Air Force cooperative.

LOANS ***Student loans:*** $5,390,152 (66% need-based, 34% non-need-based). 60% of past graduating class borrowed through all loan programs. Average indebtedness per student: $14,500. ***Average need-based loan:*** Freshmen: $2493; Undergraduates: $3848. ***Parent loans:*** $1,127,366 (100% non-need-based). ***Programs:*** FFEL (Subsidized and Unsubsidized Stafford, PLUS), Perkins, college/university.

WORK-STUDY ***Federal work-study:*** *Total amount:* $209,712; jobs available. ***State or other work-study/employment:*** *Total amount:* $403,920 (9% need-based, 91% non-need-based). Part-time jobs available.

APPLYING for FINANCIAL AID ***Required financial aid form:*** FAFSA. ***Financial aid deadline (priority):*** 3/1. ***Notification date:*** 4/1. Students must reply by 5/1 or within 2 weeks of notification.

CONTACT Mrs. Betsy Kocher, Director of Student Financial Planning, California Lutheran University, 60 West Olsen Road, Thousand Oaks, CA 91360-2787, 805-493-3115 or toll-free 877-278-3678. *Fax:* 805-493-3114.

CALIFORNIA MARITIME ACADEMY

Vallejo, CA

Tuition & fees (area res): $3206 **Average undergraduate aid package: $8142**

ABOUT THE INSTITUTION State-supported, coed, primarily men. Awards: bachelor's degrees. 2 undergraduate majors. Total enrollment: 500. Undergraduates: 495. Federal methodology is used as a basis for awarding need-based institutional aid.

UNDERGRADUATE EXPENSES for 2000–2001 ***Application fee:*** $55. ***One-time required fee:*** $3700. ***Tuition, area resident:*** full-time $1428. ***Tuition, nonresident:*** full-time $7380. ***Required fees:*** full-time $1778. ***College room and board:*** $5750; ***room only:*** $2500. Room and board charges vary according to board plan and housing facility. ***Payment plan:*** installment.

FRESHMAN FINANCIAL AID (Fall 1999) 106 applied for aid; of those 76% were deemed to have need. 100% of freshmen with need received aid; of those 22% had need fully met. *Average percent of need met:* 67% (excluding resources awarded to replace EFC). *Average financial aid package:* $7532 (excluding resources awarded to replace EFC). 32% of all full-time freshmen had no need and received non-need-based aid.

UNDERGRADUATE FINANCIAL AID (Fall 1999) 340 applied for aid; of those 81% were deemed to have need. 100% of undergraduates with need received aid; of those 53% had need fully met. *Average percent of need met:* 82% (excluding resources awarded to replace EFC). *Average*

financial aid package: $8142 (excluding resources awarded to replace EFC). 25% of all full-time undergraduates had no need and received non-need-based aid.

GIFT AID (NEED-BASED) ***Total amount:*** $1,063,560 (48% Federal, 21% state, 31% external sources). ***Receiving aid:*** *Freshmen:* 49% (59); *all full-time undergraduates:* 61% (222). ***Average award:*** Freshmen: $3416; Undergraduates: $3798. ***Scholarships, grants, and awards:*** Federal Pell, FSEOG, state, private, college/university gift aid from institutional funds.

GIFT AID (NON-NEED-BASED) ***Total amount:*** $594,340 (2% state, 80% institutional, 18% external sources). ***Receiving aid:*** *Freshmen:* 3% (4); *Undergraduates:* 5% (17). ***Scholarships, grants, and awards by category:*** *Academic Interests/Achievement:* general academic interests/achievements. *Special Achievements/Activities:* community service, leadership. *Special Characteristics:* 134 awards ($474,168 total): first-generation college students, general special characteristics, local/state students, out-of-state students. ***ROTC:*** Naval cooperative.

LOANS ***Student loans:*** $1,647,522 (74% need-based, 26% non-need-based). 93% of past graduating class borrowed through all loan programs. Average indebtedness per student: $10,860. ***Average need-based loan:*** Freshmen: $4004; Undergraduates: $4261. ***Parent loans:*** $1,067,300 (22% need-based, 78% non-need-based). ***Programs:*** FFEL (Subsidized and Unsubsidized Stafford, PLUS), Perkins.

WORK-STUDY ***Federal work-study:*** *Total amount:* $25,825; 18 jobs averaging $1500.

APPLYING for FINANCIAL AID ***Required financial aid form:*** FAFSA. ***Financial aid deadline (priority):*** 3/2. ***Notification date:*** Continuous beginning 4/15. Students must reply by 6/30.

CONTACT Timothy P. Nolen, Financial Aid Manager, California Maritime Academy, 200 Maritime Academy Drive, Vallejo, CA 94590-0644, 707-654-1275 or toll-free 800-561-1945. *Fax:* 707-654-1007. *E-mail:* tnolen@csum.edu

CALIFORNIA NATIONAL UNIVERSITY FOR ADVANCED STUDIES

North Hills, CA

CONTACT Financial Aid Office, California National University for Advanced Studies, 16909 Parthenia Street, North Hills, CA 91343, 818-830-2411.

CALIFORNIA POLYTECHNIC STATE UNIVERSITY, SAN LUIS OBISPO

San Luis Obispo, CA

Tuition & fees (CA res): $2210 **Average undergraduate aid package: $6527**

ABOUT THE INSTITUTION State-supported, coed. Awards: bachelor's and master's degrees. 61 undergraduate majors. Total enrollment: 16,470. Undergraduates: 15,503. Freshmen: 2,716. Federal methodology is used as a basis for awarding need-based institutional aid.

UNDERGRADUATE EXPENSES for 1999–2000 ***Application fee:*** $55. ***Tuition, state resident:*** full-time $0. ***Tuition, nonresident:*** full-time $5904; part-time $164 per unit. ***Required fees:*** full-time $2210. Full-time tuition and fees vary according to course load. Part-time tuition and fees vary according to course load. ***College room and board:*** $5553; ***room only:*** $2781. Room and board charges vary according to board plan. ***Payment plan:*** installment.

FRESHMAN FINANCIAL AID (Fall 1999, est.) 2020 applied for aid; of those 57% were deemed to have need. 100% of freshmen with need received aid; of those 32% had need fully met. *Average percent of need met:* 74% (excluding resources awarded to replace EFC). *Average financial aid package:* $6234 (excluding resources awarded to replace EFC). 1% of all full-time freshmen had no need and received non-need-based aid.

UNDERGRADUATE FINANCIAL AID (Fall 1999, est.) 8,166 applied for aid; of those 78% were deemed to have need. 97% of undergraduates with need received aid; of those 35% had need fully met. *Average percent of need met:* 84% (excluding resources awarded to replace EFC). *Average financial aid package:* $6527 (excluding resources awarded to replace EFC). 14% of all full-time undergraduates had no need and received non-need-based aid.

GIFT AID (NEED-BASED) ***Total amount:*** $15,679,908 (51% Federal, 40% state, 7% institutional, 2% external sources). ***Receiving aid:*** *Freshmen:* 40% (1,067); *all full-time undergraduates:* 37% (5,276). ***Average award:*** Freshmen: $3395; Undergraduates: $3230. ***Scholarships, grants, and awards:*** Federal Pell, FSEOG, state, private, college/university gift aid from institutional funds.

GIFT AID (NON-NEED-BASED) ***Total amount:*** $2,130,200 (25% institutional, 75% external sources). ***Receiving aid:*** *Freshmen:* 13% (356); *Undergraduates:* 9% (1,234). ***Scholarships, grants, and awards by category:*** *Academic Interests/Achievement:* agriculture, architecture, biological sciences, business, communication, computer science, education, engineering/technologies, English, foreign languages, general academic interests/achievements, health fields, home economics, humanities, international studies, library science, mathematics, military science, physical sciences, social sciences. *Creative Arts/Performance:* applied art and design, art/fine arts, cinema/film/broadcasting, creative writing, dance, debating, general creative arts/performance, journalism/publications, music, performing arts, theater/drama. *Special Achievements/Activities:* community service, general special achievements/activities, leadership, rodeo. *Special Characteristics:* general special characteristics. ***Tuition waivers:*** Full or partial for employees or children of employees, senior citizens. ***ROTC:*** Army.

LOANS ***Student loans:*** $13,338,500 (17% need-based, 83% non-need-based). 68% of past graduating class borrowed through all loan programs. Average indebtedness per student: $17,340. ***Average need-based loan:*** Freshmen: $3200; Undergraduates: $4985. ***Parent loans:*** $3,131,625 (18% need-based, 82% non-need-based). ***Programs:*** FFEL (Subsidized and Unsubsidized Stafford, PLUS), Perkins, college/university.

WORK-STUDY ***Federal work-study:*** *Total amount:* $567,477; jobs available.

ATHLETIC AWARDS *Total amount:* 1,207,607 (100% need-based).

APPLYING for FINANCIAL AID ***Required financial aid forms:*** FAFSA, institution's own form. ***Financial aid deadline (priority):*** 3/2. ***Notification date:*** 4/15. Students must reply within 8 weeks of notification.

CONTACT Mary E. Spady, Associate Director of Financial Aid, California Polytechnic State University, San Luis Obispo, One Grand Avenue, San Luis Obispo, CA 93407, 805-756-5886. *Fax:* 805-756-7243. *E-mail:* mspady@calpoly.edu

CALIFORNIA STATE POLYTECHNIC UNIVERSITY, POMONA

Pomona, CA

Tuition & fees (CA res): $1875 **Average undergraduate aid package: $6889**

ABOUT THE INSTITUTION State-supported, coed. Awards: bachelor's and master's degrees. 86 undergraduate majors. Total enrollment: 18,021. Undergraduates: 16,086. Freshmen: 2,661. Federal methodology is used as a basis for awarding need-based institutional aid.

UNDERGRADUATE EXPENSES for 1999–2000 ***Application fee:*** $55. ***Tuition, state resident:*** full-time $0. ***Tuition, nonresident:*** full-time $7872; part-time $164 per unit. ***Required fees:*** full-time $1875; $389 per term part-time. Part-time tuition and fees vary according to course load. ***College room and board:*** $6278. Room and board charges vary according to board plan and housing facility. ***Payment plan:*** installment.

FRESHMAN FINANCIAL AID (Fall 1999) 1411 applied for aid; of those 77% were deemed to have need. 97% of freshmen with need received aid; of those 38% had need fully met. *Average percent of need met:* 83% (excluding resources awarded to replace EFC). *Average financial aid package:* $5642 (excluding resources awarded to replace EFC). 16% of all full-time freshmen had no need and received non-need-based aid.

UNDERGRADUATE FINANCIAL AID (Fall 1999) 7,441 applied for aid; of those 87% were deemed to have need. 99% of undergraduates with need received aid; of those 44% had need fully met. *Average percent of need met:* 92% (excluding resources awarded to replace EFC). *Average financial*

California State Polytechnic University, Pomona (continued)

aid package: $6889 (excluding resources awarded to replace EFC). 8% of all full-time undergraduates had no need and received non-need-based aid.

GIFT AID (NEED-BASED) ***Total amount:*** $24,047,499 (59% Federal, 39% state, 1% institutional, 1% external sources). ***Receiving aid:*** *Freshmen:* 42% (876); *all full-time undergraduates:* 42% (5,328). ***Average award:*** Freshmen: $4134; Undergraduates: $4016. ***Scholarships, grants, and awards:*** Federal Pell, FSEOG, state, private, college/university gift aid from institutional funds.

GIFT AID (NON-NEED-BASED) ***Total amount:*** $248,794 (47% Federal, 28% state, 13% institutional, 12% external sources). ***Receiving aid:*** *Freshmen:* 2% (36); *Undergraduates:* 1% (70). ***Scholarships, grants, and awards by category:*** *Academic Interests/Achievement:* agriculture, architecture, biological sciences, business, computer science, education, engineering/technologies, general academic interests/achievements, humanities, mathematics, physical sciences, social sciences. *Special Achievements/Activities:* hobbies/interests, leadership. *Special Characteristics:* children and siblings of alumni, children of current students, members of minority groups. ***Tuition waivers:*** Full or partial for employees or children of employees, senior citizens. ***ROTC:*** Army, Air Force cooperative.

LOANS ***Student loans:*** $33,448,711 (88% need-based, 12% non-need-based). Average indebtedness per student: $12,248. ***Average need-based loan:*** Freshmen: $2373; Undergraduates: $3492. ***Parent loans:*** $787,083 (56% need-based, 44% non-need-based). ***Programs:*** FFEL (Subsidized and Unsubsidized Stafford, PLUS), Perkins, college/university, alternative loans.

WORK-STUDY ***Federal work-study:*** *Total amount:* $881,200; 387 jobs averaging $2277.

ATHLETIC AWARDS *Total amount:* 109,635 (80% need-based, 20% non-need-based).

APPLYING for FINANCIAL AID ***Required financial aid form:*** FAFSA. ***Financial aid deadline (priority):*** 3/2. ***Notification date:*** Continuous beginning 4/1.

CONTACT Diana Brown, Assistant Director of Financial Aid, California State Polytechnic University, Pomona, 3801 West Temple Avenue, Pomona, CA 91768-2557, 909-869-3704. *Fax:* 909-869-4757. *E-mail:* dybrown@csupomona.edu

CALIFORNIA STATE UNIVERSITY, BAKERSFIELD

Bakersfield, CA

Tuition & fees (CA res): $1875 **Average undergraduate aid package: $5652**

ABOUT THE INSTITUTION State-supported, coed. Awards: bachelor's and master's degrees. 30 undergraduate majors. Total enrollment: 5,594. Undergraduates: 4,223. Federal methodology is used as a basis for awarding need-based institutional aid.

UNDERGRADUATE EXPENSES for 1999–2000 ***Application fee:*** $55. ***Tuition, state resident:*** full-time $0. ***Tuition, nonresident:*** full-time $7380; part-time $164 per unit. ***Required fees:*** full-time $1875; $415 per term part-time. ***College room and board:*** $4345. ***Payment plan:*** installment.

FRESHMAN FINANCIAL AID (Fall 1998) 380 applied for aid; of those 80% were deemed to have need. 97% of freshmen with need received aid; of those 13% had need fully met. *Average percent of need met:* 84% (excluding resources awarded to replace EFC). *Average financial aid package:* $5211 (excluding resources awarded to replace EFC). 5% of all full-time freshmen had no need and received non-need-based aid.

UNDERGRADUATE FINANCIAL AID (Fall 1998) 2,890 applied for aid; of those 86% were deemed to have need. 96% of undergraduates with need received aid; of those 26% had need fully met. *Average percent of need met:* 86% (excluding resources awarded to replace EFC). *Average financial aid package:* $5652 (excluding resources awarded to replace EFC). 3% of all full-time undergraduates had no need and received non-need-based aid.

GIFT AID (NEED-BASED) ***Total amount:*** $7,292,042 (58% Federal, 42% state). ***Receiving aid:*** *Freshmen:* 54% (263); *all full-time undergraduates:* 51% (2,070). ***Average award:*** Freshmen: $3964; Undergraduates: $3449. ***Scholarships, grants, and awards:*** Federal Pell, FSEOG, state, private, Federal Nursing.

GIFT AID (NON-NEED-BASED) ***Total amount:*** $427,623 (74% institutional, 26% external sources). ***Receiving aid:*** *Freshmen:* 16% (78); *Undergraduates:* 7% (301). ***Scholarships, grants, and awards by category:*** *Academic Interests/Achievement:* 255 awards ($194,178 total): agriculture, biological sciences, business, communication, education, engineering/technologies, general academic interests/achievements, health fields, international studies, physical sciences, social sciences. *Creative Arts/Performance:* 30 awards ($16,923 total): art/fine arts, music, theater/drama. *Special Achievements/Activities:* 7 awards ($12,262 total): community service, general special achievements/activities, leadership. *Special Characteristics:* 209 awards ($204,260 total): adult students, children of faculty/staff, first-generation college students, spouses of deceased or disabled public servants. ***Tuition waivers:*** Full or partial for employees or children of employees, senior citizens.

LOANS ***Student loans:*** $6,470,872 (82% need-based, 18% non-need-based). 57% of past graduating class borrowed through all loan programs. Average indebtedness per student: $8911. ***Average need-based loan:*** Freshmen: $2139; Undergraduates: $3293. ***Parent loans:*** $31,006 (100% non-need-based). ***Programs:*** Federal Direct (Subsidized and Unsubsidized Stafford, PLUS), Perkins, Federal Nursing, college/university.

WORK-STUDY ***Federal work-study:*** *Total amount:* $210,524; 159 jobs averaging $1324. ***State or other work-study/employment:*** *Total amount:* $23,167 (100% need-based). 25 part-time jobs averaging $927.

ATHLETIC AWARDS *Total amount:* 464,880 (100% non-need-based).

APPLYING for FINANCIAL AID ***Required financial aid form:*** FAFSA. ***Financial aid deadline (priority):*** 3/2. ***Notification date:*** 5/1. Students must reply within 3 weeks of notification.

CONTACT Mr. John Casdorph, Associate Director, Financial Aid, California State University, Bakersfield, 9001 Stockdale Highway, Bakersfield, CA 93311-1099, 661-664-3016 or toll-free 800-788-2782 (in-state). *Fax:* 661-665-6800.

CALIFORNIA STATE UNIVERSITY, CHICO

Chico, CA

Tuition & fees (CA res): $1994 **Average undergraduate aid package: N/A**

ABOUT THE INSTITUTION State-supported, coed. Awards: bachelor's and master's degrees and post-bachelor's certificates. 100 undergraduate majors. Total enrollment: 15,261. Undergraduates: 13,397. Freshmen: 2,052. Federal methodology is used as a basis for awarding need-based institutional aid.

UNDERGRADUATE EXPENSES for 1999–2000 ***Application fee:*** $55. ***Tuition, state resident:*** full-time $0. ***Tuition, nonresident:*** full-time $7380; part-time $246 per unit. ***Required fees:*** full-time $1994; $697 per term part-time. Full-time tuition and fees vary according to course load. Part-time tuition and fees vary according to course load. ***College room and board:*** $5860; ***room only:*** $3728. ***Payment plan:*** deferred payment.

GIFT AID (NEED-BASED) ***Total amount:*** $19,000,118 (61% Federal, 39% state). ***Scholarships, grants, and awards:*** Federal Pell, FSEOG, state, private, college/university gift aid from institutional funds, United Negro College Fund.

GIFT AID (NON-NEED-BASED) ***Total amount:*** $1,448,878 (1% Federal, 1% state, 44% institutional, 54% external sources). ***Scholarships, grants, and awards by category:*** *Academic Interests/Achievement:* agriculture, area/ethnic studies, biological sciences, business, communication, computer science, education, engineering/technologies, English, foreign languages, general academic interests/achievements, health fields, humanities, international studies, mathematics, physical sciences, social sciences. *Creative Arts/Performance:* applied art and design, art/fine arts, cinema/film/broadcasting, creative writing, dance, debating, general creative arts/performance, journalism/publications, music, performing arts, theater/drama. *Special Achievements/Activities:* community service, general special achievements/activities, hobbies/interests, leadership, memberships. *Special Characteristics:* adult students, children of faculty/staff, ethnic background, first-generation college students, handicapped students, international students, local/state students, married students, members of minority groups, out-of-state students. ***Tuition waivers:*** Full or partial for employees or children of employees, senior citizens.

LOANS ***Student loans:*** $34,871,644 (78% need-based, 22% non-need-based). ***Parent loans:*** $1,331,340 (100% non-need-based). ***Programs:*** Federal Direct (Subsidized and Unsubsidized Stafford, PLUS), Perkins, college/university.

WORK-STUDY ***Federal work-study:*** *Total amount:* $1,100,000; 367 jobs averaging $2889. ***State or other work-study/employment:*** *Total amount:* $133,028 (100% need-based). 90 part-time jobs averaging $1478.

APPLYING for FINANCIAL AID ***Required financial aid form:*** FAFSA. ***Financial aid deadline (priority):*** 3/2. ***Notification date:*** Continuous.

CONTACT Maudell Grant, Financial Aid Adviser, California State University, Chico, Financial Aid Office, Chico, CA 95929-0705, 530-898-6451 or toll-free 800-542-4426. *Fax:* 530-898-6883. *E-mail:* mgrant2@csuchico.edu

CALIFORNIA STATE UNIVERSITY, DOMINGUEZ HILLS

Carson, CA

Tuition & fees (CA res): $1730 **Average undergraduate aid package: $6173**

ABOUT THE INSTITUTION State-supported, coed. Awards: bachelor's and master's degrees. 71 undergraduate majors. Total enrollment: 12,524. Undergraduates: 7,683. Freshmen: 490. Federal methodology is used as a basis for awarding need-based institutional aid.

UNDERGRADUATE EXPENSES for 1999–2000 ***Application fee:*** $55. ***One-time required fee:*** $5. ***Tuition:*** part-time $246 per unit. ***Required fees:*** full-time $1730; $565 per term. Part-time tuition and fees vary according to course load. Room and board charges vary according to housing facility.

FRESHMAN FINANCIAL AID (Fall 1998) 454 applied for aid; of those 94% were deemed to have need. 97% of freshmen with need received aid; of those 49% had need fully met. *Average percent of need met:* 76% (excluding resources awarded to replace EFC). *Average financial aid package:* $5860 (excluding resources awarded to replace EFC). 3% of all full-time freshmen had no need and received non-need-based aid.

UNDERGRADUATE FINANCIAL AID (Fall 1998) 4,743 applied for aid; of those 93% were deemed to have need. 97% of undergraduates with need received aid; of those 67% had need fully met. *Average percent of need met:* 70% (excluding resources awarded to replace EFC). *Average financial aid package:* $6173 (excluding resources awarded to replace EFC). 4% of all full-time undergraduates had no need and received non-need-based aid.

GIFT AID (NEED-BASED) ***Total amount:*** $12,794,417 (60% Federal, 38% state, 1% institutional, 1% external sources). ***Receiving aid:*** *Freshmen:* 81% (390); *all full-time undergraduates:* 66% (3,684). ***Average award:*** Freshmen: $4127; Undergraduates: $3290. ***Scholarships, grants, and awards:*** Federal Pell, FSEOG, state, private, college/university gift aid from institutional funds.

GIFT AID (NON-NEED-BASED) ***Total amount:*** $111,559 (6% Federal, 44% institutional, 50% external sources). ***Receiving aid:*** *Freshmen:* 13% (62); *Undergraduates:* 8% (458). ***Scholarships, grants, and awards by category:*** *Academic Interests/Achievement:* 56 awards ($40,155 total): general academic interests/achievements. *Special Characteristics:* 13 awards ($9449 total): ethnic background, members of minority groups. ***Tuition waivers:*** Full or partial for employees or children of employees. ***ROTC:*** Army cooperative, Air Force cooperative.

LOANS ***Student loans:*** $12,342,038 (95% need-based, 5% non-need-based). Average indebtedness per student: $12,936. ***Average need-based loan:*** Freshmen: $2222; Undergraduates: $3882. ***Parent loans:*** $47,853 (100% need-based). ***Programs:*** Federal Direct (Subsidized and Unsubsidized Stafford, PLUS), Perkins, college/university.

WORK-STUDY ***Federal work-study:*** *Total amount:* $507,254; 256 jobs averaging $1981.

ATHLETIC AWARDS *Total amount:* 273,039 (54% need-based, 46% non-need-based).

APPLYING for FINANCIAL AID ***Required financial aid form:*** FAFSA. ***Financial aid deadline (priority):*** 3/2. ***Notification date:*** Continuous. Students must reply within 4 weeks of notification.

CONTACT Mr. James Woods, Director of Financial Aid, California State University, Dominguez Hills, 1000 East Victoria Street, Carson, CA 90747-0001, 310-243-3691. *E-mail:* jwoods@dhvx60.csudh.edu

CALIFORNIA STATE UNIVERSITY, FRESNO

Fresno, CA

Tuition & fees (CA res): $1746 **Average undergraduate aid package: $6065**

ABOUT THE INSTITUTION State-supported, coed. Awards: bachelor's, master's, and doctoral degrees. 87 undergraduate majors. Total enrollment: 18,325. Undergraduates: 14,767. Freshmen: 1,742. Federal methodology is used as a basis for awarding need-based institutional aid.

UNDERGRADUATE EXPENSES for 2000–2001 (est.) ***Application fee:*** $55. ***Tuition, state resident:*** full-time $0. ***Tuition, nonresident:*** full-time $9126; part-time $246 per unit. ***Required fees:*** full-time $1746; $573. ***College room and board:*** $5816. Room and board charges vary according to board plan and housing facility.

FRESHMAN FINANCIAL AID (Fall 1999, est.) 1360 applied for aid; of those 97% were deemed to have need. 86% of freshmen with need received aid; of those 56% had need fully met. *Average percent of need met:* 46% (excluding resources awarded to replace EFC). *Average financial aid package:* $5043 (excluding resources awarded to replace EFC). 5% of all full-time freshmen had no need and received non-need-based aid.

UNDERGRADUATE FINANCIAL AID (Fall 1999, est.) 8,407 applied for aid; of those 98% were deemed to have need. 91% of undergraduates with need received aid; of those 62% had need fully met. *Average percent of need met:* 67% (excluding resources awarded to replace EFC). *Average financial aid package:* $6065 (excluding resources awarded to replace EFC). 3% of all full-time undergraduates had no need and received non-need-based aid.

GIFT AID (NEED-BASED) ***Total amount:*** $24,305,884 (63% Federal, 37% state). ***Receiving aid:*** *Freshmen:* 54% (923); *all full-time undergraduates:* 57% (6,890). ***Average award:*** Freshmen: $4208; Undergraduates: $3708. ***Scholarships, grants, and awards:*** Federal Pell, FSEOG, state, private, college/university gift aid from institutional funds.

GIFT AID (NON-NEED-BASED) ***Total amount:*** $1,317,884 (71% institutional, 29% external sources). ***Receiving aid:*** *Freshmen:* 14% (234); *Undergraduates:* 15% (1,833). ***Scholarships, grants, and awards by category:*** *Academic Interests/Achievement:* agriculture, architecture, area/ethnic studies, biological sciences, business, communication, computer science, education, engineering/technologies, English, general academic interests/achievements, health fields, home economics, humanities, mathematics, physical sciences, premedicine, social sciences. *Creative Arts/Performance:* journalism/publications, music, theater/drama. *Special Achievements/Activities:* community service, general special achievements/activities, leadership. *Special Characteristics:* adult students, children and siblings of alumni, children of faculty/staff, handicapped students, local/state students, veterans, veterans' children. ***Tuition waivers:*** Full or partial for employees or children of employees, senior citizens. ***ROTC:*** Army, Air Force.

LOANS ***Student loans:*** $22,786,809 (72% need-based, 28% non-need-based). 55% of past graduating class borrowed through all loan programs. Average indebtedness per student: $13,557. ***Average need-based loan:*** Freshmen: $2336; Undergraduates: $3715. ***Parent loans:*** $224,540 (100% non-need-based). ***Programs:*** Federal Direct (Subsidized and Unsubsidized Stafford, PLUS), FFEL (Subsidized and Unsubsidized Stafford, PLUS), Perkins, Federal Nursing, college/university.

WORK-STUDY ***Federal work-study:*** *Total amount:* $922,306; 335 jobs available.

ATHLETIC AWARDS *Total amount:* 1,848,843 (100% non-need-based).

California State University, Fresno (continued)

APPLYING for FINANCIAL AID ***Required financial aid form:*** FAFSA. ***Financial aid deadline (priority):*** 3/1. ***Notification date:*** Continuous beginning 4/1. Students must reply within 3 weeks of notification.

CONTACT Financial Aid Office, California State University, Fresno, 5150 North Maple Avenue, JA 64, Fresno, CA 93704-8026, 559-278-2182. *Fax:* 559-278-4812.

CALIFORNIA STATE UNIVERSITY, FULLERTON

Fullerton, CA

Tuition & fees (CA res): $1809 **Average undergraduate aid package: $5464**

ABOUT THE INSTITUTION State-supported, coed. Awards: bachelor's and master's degrees. 90 undergraduate majors. Total enrollment: 27,167. Undergraduates: 22,449. Freshmen: 2,637. Federal methodology is used as a basis for awarding need-based institutional aid.

UNDERGRADUATE EXPENSES for 1999–2000 ***Application fee:*** $55. ***Tuition, state resident:*** full-time $0. ***Tuition, nonresident:*** full-time $7380; part-time $246 per unit. ***Required fees:*** full-time $1809; $604 per term part-time. ***College room and board: room only:*** $3672. ***Payment plan:*** installment.

FRESHMAN FINANCIAL AID (Fall 1999, est.) 1659 applied for aid; of those 73% were deemed to have need. 80% of freshmen with need received aid; of those 4% had need fully met. *Average percent of need met:* 67% (excluding resources awarded to replace EFC). *Average financial aid package:* $4692 (excluding resources awarded to replace EFC). 9% of all full-time freshmen had no need and received non-need-based aid.

UNDERGRADUATE FINANCIAL AID (Fall 1999, est.) 8,858 applied for aid; of those 83% were deemed to have need. 85% of undergraduates with need received aid; of those 2% had need fully met. *Average percent of need met:* 68% (excluding resources awarded to replace EFC). *Average financial aid package:* $5464 (excluding resources awarded to replace EFC). 6% of all full-time undergraduates had no need and received non-need-based aid.

GIFT AID (NEED-BASED) ***Total amount:*** $24,727,482 (60% Federal, 39% state, 1% external sources). ***Receiving aid:*** *Freshmen:* 34% (859); *all full-time undergraduates:* 33% (5,244). ***Average award:*** Freshmen: $4180; Undergraduates: $3664. ***Scholarships, grants, and awards:*** Federal Pell, FSEOG, state, private, college/university gift aid from institutional funds.

GIFT AID (NON-NEED-BASED) ***Total amount:*** $242,926 (40% institutional, 60% external sources). ***Scholarships, grants, and awards by category:*** *Academic Interests/Achievement:* business, communication, engineering/technologies, general academic interests/achievements, humanities, mathematics, military science, social sciences. *Creative Arts/Performance:* art/fine arts, music. *Special Achievements/Activities:* general special achievements/activities, leadership. ***Tuition waivers:*** Full or partial for minority students, employees or children of employees. ***ROTC:*** Army.

LOANS ***Student loans:*** $28,132,058 (70% need-based, 30% non-need-based). Average indebtedness per student: $11,554. ***Average need-based loan:*** Freshmen: $2279; Undergraduates: $3705. ***Parent loans:*** $386,981 (100% non-need-based). ***Programs:*** FFEL (Subsidized and Unsubsidized Stafford, PLUS), Perkins, college/university.

WORK-STUDY ***Federal work-study:*** *Total amount:* $1,319,976; 857 jobs averaging $1540.

ATHLETIC AWARDS *Total amount:* 764,820 (32% need-based, 68% non-need-based).

APPLYING for FINANCIAL AID ***Required financial aid form:*** FAFSA. ***Financial aid deadline:*** Continuous. ***Notification date:*** 3/1. Students must reply within 3 weeks of notification.

CONTACT Ms. Deborah S. McCracken, Director of Financial Aid, California State University, Fullerton, 800 North State College Boulevard, Fullerton, CA 92831-3599, 714-278-3128. *Fax:* 714-278-7090. *E-mail:* dmccracken@fullerton.edu

CALIFORNIA STATE UNIVERSITY, HAYWARD

Hayward, CA

Tuition & fees (CA res): $1683 **Average undergraduate aid package: $5743**

ABOUT THE INSTITUTION State-supported, coed. Awards: bachelor's and master's degrees and post-bachelor's and post-master's certificates. 91 undergraduate majors. Total enrollment: 12,667. Undergraduates: 9,364. Freshmen: 737. Federal methodology is used as a basis for awarding need-based institutional aid.

UNDERGRADUATE EXPENSES for 1999–2000 ***Application fee:*** $55. ***Tuition, state resident:*** full-time $0. ***Tuition, nonresident:*** full-time $7380; part-time $164 per unit. ***Required fees:*** full-time $1683; $361 per term part-time. Full-time tuition and fees vary according to course load. Part-time tuition and fees vary according to course load. ***College room and board: room only:*** $3100. ***Payment plan:*** installment.

FRESHMAN FINANCIAL AID (Fall 1998) 328 applied for aid; of those 92% were deemed to have need. 100% of freshmen with need received aid; of those 9% had need fully met. *Average percent of need met:* 62% (excluding resources awarded to replace EFC). *Average financial aid package:* $4624 (excluding resources awarded to replace EFC).

UNDERGRADUATE FINANCIAL AID (Fall 1998) 3,795 applied for aid; of those 95% were deemed to have need. 100% of undergraduates with need received aid; of those 10% had need fully met. *Average percent of need met:* 60% (excluding resources awarded to replace EFC). *Average financial aid package:* $5743 (excluding resources awarded to replace EFC).

GIFT AID (NEED-BASED) ***Total amount:*** $9,971,516 (63% Federal, 35% state, 2% institutional). ***Receiving aid:*** *Freshmen:* 17% (273); *all full-time undergraduates:* 31% (2,979). ***Average award:*** Freshmen: $3938; Undergraduates: $3347. ***Scholarships, grants, and awards:*** Federal Pell, FSEOG, state, private, college/university gift aid from institutional funds.

GIFT AID (NON-NEED-BASED) ***Scholarships, grants, and awards by category:*** *Academic Interests/Achievement:* general academic interests/achievements. *Creative Arts/Performance:* music. ***Tuition waivers:*** Full or partial for employees or children of employees, senior citizens.

LOANS ***Student loans:*** $12,618,484 (76% need-based, 24% non-need-based). ***Average need-based loan:*** Freshmen: $2513; Undergraduates: $3994. ***Parent loans:*** $139,133 (100% need-based). ***Programs:*** FFEL (Subsidized and Unsubsidized Stafford, PLUS), Perkins, college/university.

WORK-STUDY ***Federal work-study:*** *Total amount:* $504,483; 288 jobs averaging $1527.

APPLYING for FINANCIAL AID ***Required financial aid form:*** FAFSA. ***Financial aid deadline (priority):*** 3/2. ***Notification date:*** Continuous beginning 5/31. Students must reply within 3 weeks of notification.

CONTACT Office of Financial Aid, California State University, Hayward, 25800 Carlos Bee Boulevard, Hayward, CA 94542-3028, 510-885-3616. *Fax:* 510-885-4627. *E-mail:* finaid@csuhayward.edu

CALIFORNIA STATE UNIVERSITY, LONG BEACH

Long Beach, CA

Tuition & fees: N/R **Average undergraduate aid package: $6812**

ABOUT THE INSTITUTION State-supported, coed. Awards: bachelor's and master's degrees. 111 undergraduate majors. Total enrollment: 30,011. Undergraduates: 24,109. Freshmen: 3,476. Federal methodology is used as a basis for awarding need-based institutional aid.

UNDERGRADUATE EXPENSES for 1999–2000 ***Application fee:*** $55. ***Tuition, nonresident:*** full-time $7380; part-time $246 per unit. ***Required fees:*** full-time $1702; $551 per term part-time. Full-time tuition and fees vary according to program. Part-time tuition and fees vary according to course load and program. ***College room and board:*** $5400. Room and board charges vary according to board plan. ***Payment plan:*** installment.

FRESHMAN FINANCIAL AID (Fall 1999, est.) 2302 applied for aid; of those 74% were deemed to have need. 89% of freshmen with need received aid; of those 65% had need fully met. *Average percent of need met:* 72% (excluding resources awarded to replace EFC). *Average financial aid package:* $5525 (excluding resources awarded to replace EFC). 13% of all full-time freshmen had no need and received non-need-based aid.

UNDERGRADUATE FINANCIAL AID (Fall 1999, est.) 10,785 applied for aid; of those 86% were deemed to have need. 89% of undergraduates with need received aid; of those 54% had need fully met. *Average percent of need met:* 73% (excluding resources awarded to replace EFC). *Average financial aid package:* $6812 (excluding resources awarded to replace EFC). 15% of all full-time undergraduates had no need and received non-need-based aid.

GIFT AID (NEED-BASED) ***Total amount:*** $33,251,145 (56% Federal, 38% state, 5% institutional, 1% external sources). ***Receiving aid:*** *Freshmen:* 40% (1,333); *all full-time undergraduates:* 38% (7,042). ***Average award:*** Freshmen: $3497; Undergraduates: $3265. ***Scholarships, grants, and awards:*** Federal Pell, FSEOG, state, private, college/university gift aid from institutional funds.

GIFT AID (NON-NEED-BASED) ***Total amount:*** $33,750 (100% Federal). ***Receiving aid:*** *Freshmen:* 9; *Undergraduates:* 23. ***Scholarships, grants, and awards by category:*** *Academic Interests/Achievement:* general academic interests/achievements. *Creative Arts/Performance:* applied art and design, cinema/film/broadcasting, dance, music, performing arts, theater/drama. ***Tuition waivers:*** Full or partial for employees or children of employees, senior citizens. ***ROTC:*** Army.

LOANS ***Student loans:*** $40,785,522 (69% need-based, 31% non-need-based). 50% of past graduating class borrowed through all loan programs. ***Average need-based loan:*** Freshmen: $1500; Undergraduates: $3000. ***Parent loans:*** $597,561 (100% need-based). ***Programs:*** FFEL (Subsidized and Unsubsidized Stafford, PLUS), Perkins.

WORK-STUDY ***Federal work-study:*** *Total amount:* $1,597,719; 550 jobs available.

ATHLETIC AWARDS *Total amount:* 790,017 (100% non-need-based).

APPLYING for FINANCIAL AID ***Required financial aid form:*** FAFSA. ***Financial aid deadline (priority):*** 3/2. ***Notification date:*** 4/15. Students must reply within 3 weeks of notification.

CONTACT Office of Financial Aid, California State University, Long Beach, 1250 Bellflower Boulevard, Long Beach, CA 90840-0119, 562-985-1887.

CALIFORNIA STATE UNIVERSITY, LOS ANGELES

Los Angeles, CA

Tuition & fees (CA res): $1722 **Average undergraduate aid package: $6950**

ABOUT THE INSTITUTION State-supported, coed. Awards: bachelor's, master's, and doctoral degrees. 71 undergraduate majors. Total enrollment: 19,783. Undergraduates: 13,732. Freshmen: 1,246. Federal methodology is used as a basis for awarding need-based institutional aid.

UNDERGRADUATE EXPENSES for 1999–2000 ***Application fee:*** $55. ***Tuition, state resident:*** full-time $0. ***Tuition, nonresident:*** full-time $5904; part-time $164 per unit. ***Required fees:*** full-time $1722; $373 per term part-time. Part-time tuition and fees vary according to course load. ***College room and board: room only:*** $2979.

FRESHMAN FINANCIAL AID (Fall 1999) 984 applied for aid; of those 93% were deemed to have need. 96% of freshmen with need received aid. *Average percent of need met:* 86% (excluding resources awarded to replace EFC). *Average financial aid package:* $6114 (excluding resources awarded to replace EFC). 1% of all full-time freshmen had no need and received non-need-based aid.

UNDERGRADUATE FINANCIAL AID (Fall 1999) 7,460 applied for aid; of those 95% were deemed to have need. 95% of undergraduates with need received aid. *Average percent of need met:* 82% (excluding resources awarded to replace EFC). *Average financial aid package:* $6950 (excluding resources awarded to replace EFC). 1% of all full-time undergraduates had no need and received non-need-based aid.

GIFT AID (NEED-BASED) ***Total amount:*** $27,381,372 (57% Federal, 43% state). ***Receiving aid:*** *Freshmen:* 68% (845); *all full-time undergraduates:* 63% (6,211). ***Average award:*** Freshmen: $5005; Undergraduates: $4130. ***Scholarships, grants, and awards:*** Federal Pell, FSEOG, state, private, college/university gift aid from institutional funds.

GIFT AID (NON-NEED-BASED) ***Scholarships, grants, and awards by category:*** *Academic Interests/Achievement:* biological sciences, business, communication, computer science, education, engineering/technologies, English, foreign languages, general academic interests/achievements, health fields, mathematics, physical sciences, social sciences. *Creative Arts/Performance:* art/fine arts, general creative arts/performance, journalism/publications, music, theater/drama. *Special Achievements/Activities:* community service, general special achievements/activities. *Special Characteristics:* general special characteristics. ***Tuition waivers:*** Full or partial for employees or children of employees. ***ROTC:*** Army cooperative, Air Force cooperative.

LOANS ***Student loans:*** $9,641,567 (94% need-based, 6% non-need-based). ***Average need-based loan:*** Freshmen: $1897; Undergraduates: $1485. ***Parent loans:*** $114,153 (100% need-based). ***Programs:*** Federal Direct (Subsidized and Unsubsidized Stafford), FFEL (PLUS), Perkins, Federal Nursing.

WORK-STUDY ***Federal work-study:*** *Total amount:* $1,031,902; 302 jobs averaging $3417. ***State or other work-study/employment:*** *Total amount:* $77,240 (100% need-based). 23 part-time jobs averaging $3358.

ATHLETIC AWARDS *Total amount:* 297,665 (100% need-based).

APPLYING for FINANCIAL AID ***Required financial aid form:*** FAFSA. ***Financial aid deadline (priority):*** 3/2. ***Notification date:*** Continuous beginning 4/1.

CONTACT Vu T. Tran, Director of Financial Aid, California State University, Los Angeles, 5151 State University Drive, Los Angeles, CA 90032-8530, 323-343-3247. *E-mail:* vtran@cslanet.calstatela.edu

CALIFORNIA STATE UNIVERSITY, MONTEREY BAY

Seaside, CA

CONTACT Financial Aid Office, California State University, Monterey Bay, 100 Campus Center, Seaside, CA 93955-8001, 831-582-3330.

CALIFORNIA STATE UNIVERSITY, NORTHRIDGE

Northridge, CA

Tuition & fees (CA res): $1814 **Average undergraduate aid package: $7736**

ABOUT THE INSTITUTION State-supported, coed. Awards: bachelor's and master's degrees. 134 undergraduate majors. Total enrollment: 27,947. Undergraduates: 21,560. Federal methodology is used as a basis for awarding need-based institutional aid.

UNDERGRADUATE EXPENSES for 1999–2000 ***Application fee:*** $55. ***Tuition, state resident:*** full-time $0. ***Tuition, nonresident:*** full-time $7718; part-time $246 per unit. ***Required fees:*** full-time $1814; $607 per term part-time. ***College room and board:*** $5865; ***room only:*** $3540. Room and board charges vary according to housing facility.

FRESHMAN FINANCIAL AID (Fall 1999) 2075 applied for aid; of those 87% were deemed to have need. 97% of freshmen with need received aid; of those 25% had need fully met. *Average percent of need met:* 82% (excluding resources awarded to replace EFC). *Average financial aid package:* $7131 (excluding resources awarded to replace EFC). 6% of all full-time freshmen had no need and received non-need-based aid.

UNDERGRADUATE FINANCIAL AID (Fall 1999) 10,286 applied for aid; of those 90% were deemed to have need. 98% of undergraduates with need received aid; of those 35% had need fully met. *Average percent of need met:* 89% (excluding resources awarded to replace EFC). *Average financial aid package:* $7736 (excluding resources awarded to replace EFC). 5% of all full-time undergraduates had no need and received non-need-based aid.

California State University, Northridge (continued)

GIFT AID (NEED-BASED) ***Total amount:*** $34,885,322 (57% Federal, 41% state, 1% institutional, 1% external sources). ***Receiving aid:*** *Freshmen:* 61% (1,551); *all full-time undergraduates:* 49% (7,816). ***Average award:*** Freshmen: $4312; Undergraduates: $3866. ***Scholarships, grants, and awards:*** Federal Pell, FSEOG, state, private, college/university gift aid from institutional funds.

GIFT AID (NON-NEED-BASED) ***Total amount:*** $352,216 (55% institutional, 45% external sources). ***Scholarships, grants, and awards by category:*** *Academic Interests/Achievement:* business, computer science, education, engineering/technologies, general academic interests/achievements, social sciences. *Creative Arts/Performance:* journalism/publications, music. ***Tuition waivers:*** Full or partial for employees or children of employees, senior citizens. ***ROTC:*** Army cooperative, Air Force cooperative.

LOANS ***Student loans:*** $34,670,950 (89% need-based, 11% non-need-based). Average indebtedness per student: $12,147. ***Average need-based loan:*** Freshmen: $2027; Undergraduates: $4801. ***Parent loans:*** $686,958 (66% need-based, 34% non-need-based). ***Programs:*** FFEL (Subsidized and Unsubsidized Stafford, PLUS), Perkins, college/university.

WORK-STUDY ***Federal work-study:*** *Total amount:* $4,854,425; 2,622 jobs averaging $1851.

ATHLETIC AWARDS *Total amount:* 1,444,401 (36% need-based, 64% non-need-based).

APPLYING for FINANCIAL AID ***Required financial aid forms:*** FAFSA, state aid form. ***Financial aid deadline (priority):*** 3/2. ***Notification date:*** Continuous beginning 5/1.

CONTACT Financial Aid Office, California State University, Northridge, 18111 Nordhoff Street, Northridge, CA 91330-8307, 818-677-3000.

CALIFORNIA STATE UNIVERSITY, SACRAMENTO

Sacramento, CA

Tuition & fees (CA res): $1867 **Average undergraduate aid package: $6847**

ABOUT THE INSTITUTION State-supported, coed. Awards: bachelor's and master's degrees. 59 undergraduate majors. Total enrollment: 24,530. Undergraduates: 19,343. Freshmen: 1,836. Federal methodology is used as a basis for awarding need-based institutional aid.

UNDERGRADUATE EXPENSES for 2000–2001 ***Application fee:*** $55. ***Tuition, state resident:*** full-time $0. ***Tuition, nonresident:*** full-time $7380; part-time $246 per unit. ***Required fees:*** full-time $1867; $634 per term part-time. ***College room and board:*** $5510; ***room only:*** $3312. Room and board charges vary according to board plan. ***Payment plan:*** installment.

FRESHMAN FINANCIAL AID (Fall 1998) 761 applied for aid; of those 81% were deemed to have need. 94% of freshmen with need received aid; of those 16% had need fully met. *Average percent of need met:* 75% (excluding resources awarded to replace EFC). *Average financial aid package:* $6382 (excluding resources awarded to replace EFC). 7% of all full-time freshmen had no need and received non-need-based aid.

UNDERGRADUATE FINANCIAL AID (Fall 1998) 7,951 applied for aid; of those 89% were deemed to have need. 95% of undergraduates with need received aid; of those 20% had need fully met. *Average percent of need met:* 76% (excluding resources awarded to replace EFC). *Average financial aid package:* $6847 (excluding resources awarded to replace EFC). 4% of all full-time undergraduates had no need and received non-need-based aid.

GIFT AID (NEED-BASED) ***Total amount:*** $23,530,531 (57% Federal, 38% state, 2% institutional, 3% external sources). ***Receiving aid:*** *Freshmen:* 45% (512); *all full-time undergraduates:* 43% (5,625). ***Average award:*** Freshmen: $1588; Undergraduates: $1652. ***Scholarships, grants, and awards:*** Federal Pell, FSEOG, state, private, college/university gift aid from institutional funds, Federal Nursing.

GIFT AID (NON-NEED-BASED) ***Total amount:*** $600 (100% institutional). ***Scholarships, grants, and awards by category:*** *Academic Interests/Achievement:* general academic interests/achievements. *Creative Arts/Performance:* general creative arts/performance. *Special Achievements/Activities:* general special achievements/activities. *Special Characteristics:* general special characteristics. ***Tuition waivers:*** Full or partial for employees or children of employees, senior citizens. ***ROTC:*** Army cooperative, Air Force.

LOANS ***Student loans:*** $35,277,214 (67% need-based, 33% non-need-based). Average indebtedness per student: $15,529. ***Average need-based loan:*** Freshmen: $2138; Undergraduates: $3599. ***Parent loans:*** $2,026,714 (100% non-need-based). ***Programs:*** Federal Direct (Subsidized and Unsubsidized Stafford, PLUS), Perkins, Federal Nursing, state, college/university.

WORK-STUDY ***Federal work-study:*** *Total amount:* $1,249,516; jobs available. ***State or other work-study/employment:*** *Total amount:* $133,555 (100% need-based). Part-time jobs available.

ATHLETIC AWARDS *Total amount:* 1,364,861 (100% need-based).

APPLYING for FINANCIAL AID ***Required financial aid forms:*** FAFSA, institution's own form, state aid form. ***Financial aid deadline (priority):*** 3/2. ***Notification date:*** 5/1.

CONTACT Linda Joy Clemons, Financial Aid Director, California State University, Sacramento, 6000 J Street, Sacramento, CA 95819-6048, 916-278-6554. *Fax:* 916-278-6082. *E-mail:* ljclemons@csus.edu

CALIFORNIA STATE UNIVERSITY, SAN BERNARDINO

San Bernardino, CA

Tuition & fees: N/R **Average undergraduate aid package: $8763**

ABOUT THE INSTITUTION State-supported, coed. Awards: bachelor's and master's degrees. 55 undergraduate majors. Total enrollment: 13,280. Undergraduates: 9,471. Freshmen: 943. Federal methodology is used as a basis for awarding need-based institutional aid.

UNDERGRADUATE FINANCIAL AID (Fall 1998) 8,650 applied for aid; of those 100% were deemed to have need. 100% of undergraduates with need received aid; of those 100% had need fully met. *Average percent of need met:* 75% (excluding resources awarded to replace EFC). *Average financial aid package:* $8763 (excluding resources awarded to replace EFC).

GIFT AID (NEED-BASED) ***Total amount:*** $15,388,973 (64% Federal, 35% state, 1% institutional). ***Scholarships, grants, and awards:*** Federal Pell, FSEOG, state, college/university gift aid from institutional funds.

GIFT AID (NON-NEED-BASED) ***Total amount:*** $131,325 (100% institutional). ***Scholarships, grants, and awards by category:*** *Academic Interests/Achievement:* business, computer science, education, general academic interests/achievements, health fields, humanities, mathematics, military science. *Creative Arts/Performance:* general creative arts/performance, music, performing arts. *Special Characteristics:* children with a deceased or disabled parent, ethnic background, first-generation college students, local/state students. ***ROTC:*** Army, Air Force.

LOANS ***Student loans:*** $42,223,290 (99% need-based, 1% non-need-based). ***Average need-based loan:*** Undergraduates: $4025. ***Parent loans:*** $193,053 (100% non-need-based). ***Programs:*** Federal Direct (Subsidized and Unsubsidized Stafford), FFEL (PLUS), Perkins, college/university.

WORK-STUDY ***Federal work-study:*** *Total amount:* $922,235; 293 jobs available. ***State or other work-study/employment:*** *Total amount:* $232,370 (100% need-based). 69 part-time jobs averaging $3500.

ATHLETIC AWARDS *Total amount:* 203,939 (100% non-need-based).

APPLYING for FINANCIAL AID ***Required financial aid forms:*** FAFSA, state aid form. ***Financial aid deadline (priority):*** 3/2. ***Notification date:*** 5/1.

CONTACT Hank Kutak, Associate Director, Financial Aid, California State University, San Bernardino, 5500 University Parkway, San Bernardino, CA 92407-2397, 909-880-5222. *Fax:* 909-880-7024. *E-mail:* hkutak@csusb.edu

CALIFORNIA STATE UNIVERSITY, SAN MARCOS

San Marcos, CA

Tuition & fees (CA res): $1694 **Average undergraduate aid package: $4700**

ABOUT THE INSTITUTION State-supported, coed. Awards: bachelor's and master's degrees. 23 undergraduate majors. Total enrollment: 5,025. Undergraduates: 4,103. Freshmen: 362. Federal methodology is used as a basis for awarding need-based institutional aid.

UNDERGRADUATE EXPENSES for 1999–2000 ***Application fee:*** $55. ***One-time required fee:*** $5. ***Tuition, state resident:*** full-time $0. ***Tuition, nonresident:*** full-time $5904; part-time $246 per unit. ***Required fees:*** full-time $1694; $537 per term part-time. Part-time tuition and fees vary according to course load. ***College room and board: room only:*** $3924. Room and board charges vary according to housing facility.

UNDERGRADUATE FINANCIAL AID (Fall 1998) 1,970 applied for aid; of those 85% were deemed to have need. 96% of undergraduates with need received aid. *Average financial aid package:* $4700 (excluding resources awarded to replace EFC). 4% of all full-time undergraduates had no need and received non-need-based aid.

GIFT AID (NEED-BASED) ***Total amount:*** $4,352,490 (55% Federal, 39% state, 3% institutional, 3% external sources). ***Receiving aid:*** *All full-time undergraduates:* 33% (1,347). ***Average award:*** Undergraduates: $3231. ***Scholarships, grants, and awards:*** Federal Pell, FSEOG, state, private, college/university gift aid from institutional funds.

GIFT AID (NON-NEED-BASED) ***Total amount:*** $20,430 (100% state). ***Receiving aid:*** *Undergraduates:* 1% (30). ***Scholarships, grants, and awards by category:*** *Academic Interests/Achievement:* general academic interests/achievements, mathematics. ***Tuition waivers:*** Full or partial for employees or children of employees, senior citizens. ***ROTC:*** Air Force cooperative.

LOANS ***Student loans:*** $5,671,672 (66% need-based, 34% non-need-based). 49% of past graduating class borrowed through all loan programs. Average indebtedness per student: $11,293. ***Average need-based loan:*** Undergraduates: $3662. ***Parent loans:*** $118,300 (100% non-need-based). ***Programs:*** Federal Direct (Subsidized and Unsubsidized Stafford, PLUS), Perkins, college/university.

WORK-STUDY ***Federal work-study:*** *Total amount:* $162,417; 118 jobs averaging $1376. ***State or other work-study/employment:*** *Total amount:* $8409 (100% need-based). 14 part-time jobs averaging $601.

ATHLETIC AWARDS *Total amount:* 9624 (100% non-need-based).

APPLYING for FINANCIAL AID ***Required financial aid form:*** FAFSA. ***Financial aid deadline (priority):*** 3/2. ***Notification date:*** 4/15. Students must reply within 2 weeks of notification.

CONTACT Mr. Paul Phillips, Director of Financial Aid, California State University, San Marcos, Financial Aid Office, San Marcos, CA 92096-0001, 760-750-4851. *Fax:* 760-750-4030. *E-mail:* phillips@mailhost1.csusm.edu

CALIFORNIA STATE UNIVERSITY, STANISLAUS

Turlock, CA

Tuition & fees (CA res): $1877 **Average undergraduate aid package: $6279**

ABOUT THE INSTITUTION State-supported, coed. Awards: bachelor's and master's degrees. 38 undergraduate majors. Total enrollment: 6,489. Undergraduates: 5,048. Freshmen: 535. Federal methodology is used as a basis for awarding need-based institutional aid.

UNDERGRADUATE EXPENSES for 2000–2001 (est.) ***Application fee:*** $55. ***Tuition, state resident:*** full-time $0. ***Tuition, nonresident:*** full-time $9257. ***Required fees:*** full-time $1877; $518 per term part-time. ***College room and board:*** $6480; ***room only:*** $3541. Room and board charges vary according to board plan and housing facility.

FRESHMAN FINANCIAL AID (Fall 1999, est.) 465 applied for aid; of those 91% were deemed to have need. 95% of freshmen with need received aid; of those 32% had need fully met. *Average percent of need met:* 73% (excluding resources awarded to replace EFC). *Average financial aid package:* $5236 (excluding resources awarded to replace EFC). 3% of all full-time freshmen had no need and received non-need-based aid.

UNDERGRADUATE FINANCIAL AID (Fall 1999, est.) 2,475 applied for aid; of those 90% were deemed to have need. 99% of undergraduates with need received aid; of those 30% had need fully met. *Average percent of need met:* 79% (excluding resources awarded to replace EFC). *Average financial aid package:* $6279 (excluding resources awarded to replace EFC). 1% of all full-time undergraduates had no need and received non-need-based aid.

GIFT AID (NEED-BASED) ***Total amount:*** $7,440,033 (60% Federal, 39% state, 1% institutional). ***Receiving aid:*** *Freshmen:* 70% (362); *all full-time undergraduates:* 54% (2,160). ***Average award:*** Freshmen: $3926; Undergraduates: $3560. ***Scholarships, grants, and awards:*** Federal Pell, FSEOG, state, private, college/university gift aid from institutional funds.

GIFT AID (NON-NEED-BASED) ***Total amount:*** $733,945 (70% institutional, 30% external sources). ***Receiving aid:*** *Freshmen:* 2% (12); *Undergraduates:* 1% (59). ***Scholarships, grants, and awards by category:*** *Academic Interests/Achievement:* 32 awards ($24,000 total): biological sciences, business, communication, computer science, education, English, general academic interests/achievements, mathematics, physical sciences, social sciences. *Creative Arts/Performance:* 55 awards ($24,300 total): art/fine arts, music. *Special Achievements/Activities:* 31 awards ($43,000 total): leadership. *Special Characteristics:* 171 awards ($333,196 total): children of faculty/staff, first-generation college students, general special characteristics, local/state students, members of minority groups. ***Tuition waivers:*** Full or partial for senior citizens.

LOANS ***Student loans:*** $6,718,156 (100% need-based). Average indebtedness per student: $13,228. ***Average need-based loan:*** Freshmen: $2342; Undergraduates: $1543. ***Parent loans:*** $210,110 (100% need-based). ***Programs:*** FFEL (Subsidized and Unsubsidized Stafford, PLUS), Perkins, college/university.

WORK-STUDY ***Federal work-study:*** *Total amount:* $315,790; 159 jobs averaging $1850. ***State or other work-study/employment:*** *Total amount:* $57,065 (100% need-based). 34 part-time jobs averaging $1678.

ATHLETIC AWARDS *Total amount:* 106,100 (15% need-based, 85% non-need-based).

APPLYING for FINANCIAL AID ***Required financial aid forms:*** FAFSA, state aid form. ***Financial aid deadline (priority):*** 3/2. ***Notification date:*** Continuous beginning 5/1. Students must reply within 3 weeks of notification.

CONTACT Ms. Joan R. Hillery, Director of Financial Aid, California State University, Stanislaus, 801 West Monte Vista Avenue, Turlock, CA 95382, 209-667-3336 or toll-free 800-300-7420 (in-state). *Fax:* 209-667-3788. *E-mail:* jhillery@stan.csustan.edu

CALIFORNIA UNIVERSITY OF PENNSYLVANIA

California, PA

Tuition & fees (PA res): $4742 **Average undergraduate aid package: N/A**

ABOUT THE INSTITUTION State-supported, coed. Awards: associate, bachelor's, and master's degrees. 42 undergraduate majors. Total enrollment: 5,833. Undergraduates: 5,058. Freshmen: 984. Federal methodology is used as a basis for awarding need-based institutional aid.

UNDERGRADUATE EXPENSES for 1999–2000 ***Application fee:*** $25. ***Tuition, state resident:*** full-time $3618; part-time $150 per credit. ***Tuition, nonresident:*** full-time $9046; part-time $377 per credit. ***Required fees:*** full-time $1124; $180 per term part-time. Full-time tuition and fees vary according to location. Part-time tuition and fees vary according to location. ***College room and board:*** $4526. Room and board charges vary according to board plan. ***Payment plan:*** installment.

GIFT AID (NEED-BASED) ***Scholarships, grants, and awards:*** Federal Pell, FSEOG, state, college/university gift aid from institutional funds.

GIFT AID (NON-NEED-BASED) ***Scholarships, grants, and awards by category:*** *Academic Interests/Achievement:* general academic interests/

California University of Pennsylvania (continued)

achievements. *Creative Arts/Performance:* general creative arts/performance. *Special Characteristics:* ethnic background, international students, members of minority groups, veterans. ***Tuition waivers:*** Full or partial for employees or children of employees.

LOANS ***Programs:*** FFEL (Subsidized and Unsubsidized Stafford, PLUS), Perkins, college/university.

WORK-STUDY Federal work-study jobs available.

APPLYING for FINANCIAL AID ***Required financial aid form:*** FAFSA. ***Financial aid deadline (priority):*** 5/1. ***Notification date:*** Continuous. Students must reply within 2 weeks of notification.

CONTACT Financial Aid Office, California University of Pennsylvania, 250 University Avenue, California, PA 15419-1394, 724-938-4415.

CALUMET COLLEGE OF SAINT JOSEPH

Whiting, IN

Tuition & fees: $6750 **Average undergraduate aid package: N/A**

ABOUT THE INSTITUTION Independent Roman Catholic, coed. Awards: associate and bachelor's degrees. 23 undergraduate majors. Total enrollment: 1,004. Undergraduates: 1,004. Freshmen: 82. Both federal and institutional methodology are used as a basis for awarding need-based institutional aid.

UNDERGRADUATE EXPENSES for 1999–2000 ***Tuition:*** full-time $6750; part-time $225 per credit hour. ***Payment plan:*** installment.

GIFT AID (NEED-BASED) ***Total amount:*** $1,969,183 (49% Federal, 37% state, 14% institutional). ***Scholarships, grants, and awards:*** Federal Pell, FSEOG, state, private, college/university gift aid from institutional funds.

GIFT AID (NON-NEED-BASED) ***Total amount:*** $185,889 (100% institutional). ***Scholarships, grants, and awards by category:*** *Academic Interests/Achievement:* 47 awards ($69,426 total): general academic interests/achievements. *Special Achievements/Activities:* leadership. *Special Characteristics:* 157 awards ($213,087 total): adult students, children of faculty/staff, local/state students, previous college experience, religious affiliation. ***Tuition waivers:*** Full or partial for employees or children of employees, senior citizens.

LOANS ***Student loans:*** $14,691,789 (100% need-based). ***Parent loans:*** $7600 (100% need-based). ***Programs:*** FFEL (Subsidized and Unsubsidized Stafford, PLUS).

WORK-STUDY ***Federal work-study:*** *Total amount:* $51,536; 41 jobs averaging $2000.

APPLYING for FINANCIAL AID ***Required financial aid forms:*** FAFSA, institution's own form, CSS Financial Aid PROFILE. ***Financial aid deadline (priority):*** 3/1. ***Notification date:*** Continuous.

CONTACT Ms. Barbara Jerzyk, Director of Financial Aid, Calumet College of Saint Joseph, 2400 New York Avenue, Whiting, IN 46394-2195, 219-473-4219 or toll-free 877-700-9100. *E-mail:* bjerzyk@ccsj.edu

CALVARY BIBLE COLLEGE AND THEOLOGICAL SEMINARY

Kansas City, MO

ABOUT THE INSTITUTION Independent interdenominational, coed. Awards: associate, bachelor's, master's, and doctoral degrees. 24 undergraduate majors. Total enrollment: 280. Undergraduates: 229.

GIFT AID (NEED-BASED) ***Scholarships, grants, and awards:*** Federal Pell.

GIFT AID (NON-NEED-BASED) ***Scholarships, grants, and awards by category:*** *Academic Interests/Achievement:* education, general academic interests/achievements, religion/biblical studies. *Creative Arts/Performance:* general creative arts/performance. *Special Achievements/Activities:* general special achievements/activities, religious involvement. *Special Characteristics:* children of current students, parents of current students, relatives of clergy, siblings of current students, spouses of current students.

LOANS ***Programs:*** FFEL (Subsidized and Unsubsidized Stafford, PLUS).

APPLYING for FINANCIAL AID ***Required financial aid forms:*** FAFSA, institution's own form.

CONTACT Jim Long, Director of Financial Aid, Calvary Bible College and Theological Seminary, 15800 Calvary Road, Kansas City, MO 64147-1341, 816-322-5152 Ext. 1313 or toll-free 800-326-3960. *E-mail:* finaid@calvary.edu

CALVIN COLLEGE

Grand Rapids, MI

Tuition & fees: $14,040 **Average undergraduate aid package: $10,350**

ABOUT THE INSTITUTION Independent religious, coed. Awards: bachelor's and master's degrees and post-bachelor's certificates. 79 undergraduate majors. Total enrollment: 4,264. Undergraduates: 4,218. Freshmen: 1,061. Both federal and institutional methodology are used as a basis for awarding need-based institutional aid.

UNDERGRADUATE EXPENSES for 2000–2001 ***Application fee:*** $35. ***Comprehensive fee:*** $18,930 includes full-time tuition ($14,040) and room and board ($4890). ***College room only:*** $2100. Room and board charges vary according to board plan. ***Part-time tuition:*** $340 per credit hour. Part-time tuition and fees vary according to course load. ***Payment plans:*** tuition prepayment, installment.

FRESHMAN FINANCIAL AID (Fall 1999, est.) 847 applied for aid; of those 84% were deemed to have need. 100% of freshmen with need received aid; of those 35% had need fully met. *Average percent of need met:* 91% (excluding resources awarded to replace EFC). *Average financial aid package:* $10,250 (excluding resources awarded to replace EFC). 30% of all full-time freshmen had no need and received non-need-based aid.

UNDERGRADUATE FINANCIAL AID (Fall 1999, est.) 2,906 applied for aid; of those 89% were deemed to have need. 100% of undergraduates with need received aid; of those 33% had need fully met. *Average percent of need met:* 86% (excluding resources awarded to replace EFC). *Average financial aid package:* $10,350 (excluding resources awarded to replace EFC). 31% of all full-time undergraduates had no need and received non-need-based aid.

GIFT AID (NEED-BASED) ***Total amount:*** $17,948,000 (10% Federal, 17% state, 69% institutional, 4% external sources). ***Receiving aid:*** *Freshmen:* 67% (706); *all full-time undergraduates:* 63% (2,545). ***Average award:*** Freshmen: $7550; Undergraduates: $7000. ***Scholarships, grants, and awards:*** Federal Pell, FSEOG, state, private, college/university gift aid from institutional funds.

GIFT AID (NON-NEED-BASED) ***Total amount:*** $3,617,500 (94% institutional, 6% external sources). ***Receiving aid:*** *Freshmen:* 5% (55); *Undergraduates:* 2% (96). ***Scholarships, grants, and awards by category:*** *Academic Interests/Achievement:* 2,100 awards ($4,750,000 total): biological sciences, business, communication, education, engineering/technologies, English, general academic interests/achievements, health fields, humanities, international studies, physical sciences, premedicine, religion/biblical studies, social sciences. *Creative Arts/Performance:* 60 awards ($60,000 total): art/fine arts, music, performing arts, theater/drama. *Special Achievements/Activities:* 100 awards ($650,000 total): community service, religious involvement. *Special Characteristics:* 2,900 awards ($3,550,000 total): children and siblings of alumni, children of faculty/staff, children of union members/company employees, ethnic background, handicapped students, international students, members of minority groups, religious affiliation. ***Tuition waivers:*** Full or partial for employees or children of employees. ***ROTC:*** Army cooperative.

LOANS ***Student loans:*** $11,000,000 (79% need-based, 21% non-need-based). 69% of past graduating class borrowed through all loan programs. Average indebtedness per student: $16,000. ***Average need-based loan:*** Freshmen: $3300; Undergraduates: $4200. ***Parent loans:*** $725,000 (100% non-need-based). ***Programs:*** Federal Direct (Subsidized and Unsubsidized Stafford, PLUS), Perkins, state.

WORK-STUDY ***Federal work-study:*** *Total amount:* $750,000; 700 jobs averaging $1071. ***State or other work-study/employment:*** *Total amount:* $1,290,000 (47% need-based, 53% non-need-based). 1,020 part-time jobs averaging $1265.

APPLYING for FINANCIAL AID ***Required financial aid forms:*** FAFSA, institution's own form. ***Financial aid deadline (priority):*** 2/15. ***Notification date:*** Continuous beginning 3/20.

CONTACT Mr. Dave Brummel, Financial Aid Counselor, Calvin College, 3201 Burton Street, SE, Grand Rapids, MI 49546-4388, 616-957-6134 or toll-free 800-668-0122. *Fax:* 616-957-8513. *E-mail:* dlbrum@calvin.edu

CAMBRIDGE COLLEGE

Cambridge, MA

Tuition & fees: $7620 **Average undergraduate aid package: $5500**

ABOUT THE INSTITUTION Independent, coed. Awards: bachelor's and master's degrees. 1 undergraduate major. Total enrollment: 2,381. Undergraduates: 285. Federal methodology is used as a basis for awarding need-based institutional aid.

UNDERGRADUATE EXPENSES for 1999–2000 ***Application fee:*** $30. ***Tuition:*** full-time $7500; part-time $250 per credit hour. ***Required fees:*** full-time $120; $60 per term part-time.

FRESHMAN FINANCIAL AID (Fall 1998) *Average percent of need met:* 55% (excluding resources awarded to replace EFC). *Average financial aid package:* $5500 (excluding resources awarded to replace EFC).

UNDERGRADUATE FINANCIAL AID (Fall 1998) *Average percent of need met:* 80% (excluding resources awarded to replace EFC). *Average financial aid package:* $5500 (excluding resources awarded to replace EFC).

GIFT AID (NEED-BASED) ***Total amount:*** $187,172 ***Scholarships, grants, and awards:*** Federal Pell, FSEOG, state, private, college/university gift aid from institutional funds.

GIFT AID (NON-NEED-BASED) ***Scholarships, grants, and awards by category:*** *Academic Interests/Achievement:* education, general academic interests/achievements.

LOANS ***Programs:*** FFEL (Subsidized and Unsubsidized Stafford), Perkins, state.

WORK-STUDY Federal work-study jobs available.

APPLYING for FINANCIAL AID ***Required financial aid forms:*** FAFSA, institution's own form. ***Financial aid deadline:*** Continuous. ***Notification date:*** Continuous.

CONTACT Dr. Gerri Major, Director of Financial Aid, Cambridge College, 1000 Massachusetts Avenue, Cambridge, MA 02138, 617-868-1000 Ext. 137 or toll-free 800-877-4723. *E-mail:* gmajor@idea.cambridge.edu

CAMDEN COLLEGE OF ARTS AND SCIENCES

Camden, NJ

See Rutgers, The State University of New Jersey, Camden College of Arts and Sciences

CAMERON UNIVERSITY

Lawton, OK

Tuition & fees (OK res): $2050 **Average undergraduate aid package: $3825**

ABOUT THE INSTITUTION State-supported, coed. Awards: associate, bachelor's, and master's degrees. 58 undergraduate majors. Total enrollment: 5,099. Undergraduates: 4,493. Freshmen: 730. Federal methodology is used as a basis for awarding need-based institutional aid.

UNDERGRADUATE EXPENSES for 1999–2000 ***Application fee:*** $15. ***Tuition, state resident:*** full-time $2000; part-time $67 per semester hour. ***Tuition, nonresident:*** full-time $4790; part-time $160 per semester hour. ***Required fees:*** full-time $50; $50 per term part-time. Full-time tuition and fees vary according to course level, course load, degree level, and student level. Part-time tuition and fees vary according to course level, course load, degree level, and student level. ***College room and board:*** $2830. Room and board charges vary according to board plan. ***Payment plan:*** installment.

FRESHMAN FINANCIAL AID (Fall 1999, est.) 980 applied for aid; of those 56% were deemed to have need. 98% of freshmen with need received aid; of those 48% had need fully met. *Average percent of need met:* 95% (excluding resources awarded to replace EFC). *Average financial aid package:* $3600 (excluding resources awarded to replace EFC). 32% of all full-time freshmen had no need and received non-need-based aid.

UNDERGRADUATE FINANCIAL AID (Fall 1999, est.) 2,344 applied for aid; of those 56% were deemed to have need. 98% of undergraduates with need received aid; of those 48% had need fully met. *Average percent of need met:* 91% (excluding resources awarded to replace EFC). *Average financial aid package:* $3825 (excluding resources awarded to replace EFC). 36% of all full-time undergraduates had no need and received non-need-based aid.

GIFT AID (NEED-BASED) ***Total amount:*** $4,327,015 (82% Federal, 13% state, 1% institutional, 4% external sources). ***Receiving aid:*** *Freshmen:* 17% (193); *all full-time undergraduates:* 17% (463). ***Average award:*** Freshmen: $827; Undergraduates: $800. ***Scholarships, grants, and awards:*** Federal Pell, FSEOG, state, private, college/university gift aid from institutional funds.

GIFT AID (NON-NEED-BASED) ***Total amount:*** $1,047,780 (17% institutional, 83% external sources). ***Receiving aid:*** *Freshmen:* 14% (161); *Undergraduates:* 14% (386). ***Scholarships, grants, and awards by category:*** *Academic Interests/Achievement:* agriculture, biological sciences, business, communication, computer science, education, engineering/technologies, English, general academic interests/achievements, mathematics, military science, social sciences. *Creative Arts/Performance:* art/fine arts, creative writing, debating, journalism/publications, music, theater/drama. *Special Achievements/Activities:* leadership. *Special Characteristics:* members of minority groups. ***Tuition waivers:*** Full or partial for employees or children of employees, senior citizens. ***ROTC:*** Army.

LOANS ***Student loans:*** $3,878,903 (71% need-based, 29% non-need-based). 35% of past graduating class borrowed through all loan programs. Average indebtedness per student: $6300. ***Average need-based loan:*** Freshmen: $990; Undergraduates: $1615. ***Parent loans:*** $8384 (100% non-need-based). ***Programs:*** FFEL (Subsidized and Unsubsidized Stafford, PLUS).

WORK-STUDY ***Federal work-study:*** *Total amount:* $212,422; 93 jobs averaging $2284. ***State or other work-study/employment:*** *Total amount:* $312,515 (100% non-need-based). 362 part-time jobs averaging $863.

ATHLETIC AWARDS *Total amount:* 299,322 (100% non-need-based).

APPLYING for FINANCIAL AID ***Required financial aid form:*** FAFSA. ***Financial aid deadline:*** Continuous. ***Notification date:*** Continuous beginning 7/1.

CONTACT Mrs. Caryn Pacheco, Financial Aid Director, Cameron University, 2800 West Gore Boulevard, Lawton, OK 73505-6377, 580-581-2293 or toll-free 888-454-7600. *Fax:* 580-581-5514.

CAMPBELLSVILLE UNIVERSITY

Campbellsville, KY

Tuition & fees: $8240 **Average undergraduate aid package: $8798**

ABOUT THE INSTITUTION Independent religious, coed. Awards: associate, bachelor's, and master's degrees and post-bachelor's certificates. 47 undergraduate majors. Total enrollment: 1,608. Undergraduates: 1,548. Freshmen: 308. Federal methodology is used as a basis for awarding need-based institutional aid.

UNDERGRADUATE EXPENSES for 1999–2000 ***Application fee:*** $20. ***Comprehensive fee:*** $12,230 includes full-time tuition ($8000), mandatory fees ($240), and room and board ($3990). ***College room only:*** $1730. Room and board charges vary according to board plan and housing facility. ***Part-time tuition:*** $336 per credit. ***Part-time fees:*** $30 per term part-time. ***Payment plans:*** installment, deferred payment.

FRESHMAN FINANCIAL AID (Fall 1999, est.) *Average percent of need met:* 54% (excluding resources awarded to replace EFC). *Average financial aid package:* $7839 (excluding resources awarded to replace EFC).

Campbellsville University (continued)

UNDERGRADUATE FINANCIAL AID (Fall 1999, est.) *Average percent of need met:* 59% (excluding resources awarded to replace EFC). *Average financial aid package:* $8798 (excluding resources awarded to replace EFC).

GIFT AID (NEED-BASED) ***Total amount:*** $7,533,413 ***Scholarships, grants, and awards:*** Federal Pell, FSEOG, state.

GIFT AID (NON-NEED-BASED) ***Total amount:*** $222,680 ***Scholarships, grants, and awards by category:*** *Academic Interests/Achievement:* general academic interests/achievements. *Creative Arts/Performance:* art/fine arts, journalism/publications, music, theater/drama. *Special Achievements/Activities:* religious involvement. *Special Characteristics:* religious affiliation. ***Tuition waivers:*** Full or partial for minority students, employees or children of employees, senior citizens.

LOANS ***Programs:*** Federal Direct (Subsidized and Unsubsidized Stafford, PLUS), college/university.

WORK-STUDY Federal work-study jobs available. ***State or other work-study/employment:*** Part-time jobs available.

APPLYING for FINANCIAL AID ***Required financial aid form:*** FAFSA. ***Financial aid deadline (priority):*** 3/1. ***Notification date:*** Continuous beginning 3/15. Students must reply within 3 weeks of notification.

CONTACT Mr. Aaron Gabehart, Financial Aid Counselor, Campbellsville University, 1 University Drive, Campbellsville, KY 42718, 270-789-5305 or toll-free 800-264-6014. *Fax:* 270-789-5050.

CAMPBELL UNIVERSITY

Buies Creek, NC

Tuition & fees: $10,997 **Average undergraduate aid package: $10,952**

ABOUT THE INSTITUTION Independent Baptist, coed. Awards: associate, bachelor's, master's, doctoral, and first professional degrees. 59 undergraduate majors. Total enrollment: 3,265. Undergraduates: 2,201. Freshmen: 544. Federal methodology is used as a basis for awarding need-based institutional aid.

UNDERGRADUATE EXPENSES for 1999–2000 ***Application fee:*** $15. ***Comprehensive fee:*** $14,947 includes full-time tuition ($10,807), mandatory fees ($190), and room and board ($3950). Room and board charges vary according to board plan and housing facility. ***Part-time tuition:*** $180 per semester hour. ***Payment plan:*** installment.

FRESHMAN FINANCIAL AID (Fall 1999) 1247 applied for aid; of those 34% were deemed to have need. 100% of freshmen with need received aid; of those 84% had need fully met. *Average percent of need met:* 100% (excluding resources awarded to replace EFC). *Average financial aid package:* $15,117 (excluding resources awarded to replace EFC). 62% of all full-time freshmen had no need and received non-need-based aid.

UNDERGRADUATE FINANCIAL AID (Fall 1999) 3,507 applied for aid; of those 43% were deemed to have need. 100% of undergraduates with need received aid; of those 90% had need fully met. *Average percent of need met:* 100% (excluding resources awarded to replace EFC). *Average financial aid package:* $10,952 (excluding resources awarded to replace EFC). 52% of all full-time undergraduates had no need and received non-need-based aid.

GIFT AID (NEED-BASED) ***Total amount:*** $4,060,970 (38% Federal, 59% state, 3% institutional). ***Receiving aid:*** *Freshmen:* 24% (316); *all full-time undergraduates:* 32% (1,180). ***Average award:*** Freshmen: $2648; Undergraduates: $2536. ***Scholarships, grants, and awards:*** Federal Pell, FSEOG, state, private, college/university gift aid from institutional funds.

GIFT AID (NON-NEED-BASED) ***Total amount:*** $16,420,706 (2% Federal, 46% state, 39% institutional, 13% external sources). ***Receiving aid:*** *Freshmen:* 5% (59); *Undergraduates:* 7% (244). ***Scholarships, grants, and awards by category:*** *Academic Interests/Achievement:* general academic interests/achievements. *Creative Arts/Performance:* art/fine arts, creative writing, journalism/publications, music, theater/drama. *Special Achievements/Activities:* cheerleading/drum major, junior miss, religious involvement. *Special Characteristics:* children of faculty/staff, relatives of clergy. ***Tuition waivers:*** Full or partial for employees or children of employees. ***ROTC:*** Army.

LOANS ***Student loans:*** $12,876,536 (54% need-based, 46% non-need-based). 86% of past graduating class borrowed through all loan programs. Average indebtedness per student: $17,125. ***Average need-based loan:*** Freshmen: $2036; Undergraduates: $2737. ***Parent loans:*** $4,799,735 (21% need-based, 79% non-need-based). ***Programs:*** FFEL (Subsidized and Unsubsidized Stafford, PLUS), Perkins.

WORK-STUDY ***Federal work-study:*** *Total amount:* $1,143,629; 1,008 jobs averaging $1135. ***State or other work-study/employment:*** *Total amount:* $155,393 (100% non-need-based). 442 part-time jobs averaging $352.

ATHLETIC AWARDS *Total amount:* 1,490,995 (24% need-based, 76% non-need-based).

APPLYING for FINANCIAL AID ***Required financial aid form:*** FAFSA. ***Financial aid deadline (priority):*** 3/15. ***Notification date:*** 3/30. Students must reply within 2 weeks of notification.

CONTACT Office of Financial Aid, Campbell University, PO Box 36, Buies Creek, NC 27506, 910-893-1310 or toll-free 800-334-4111 (out-of-state).

CANISIUS COLLEGE

Buffalo, NY

Tuition & fees: $15,548 **Average undergraduate aid package: $16,910**

ABOUT THE INSTITUTION Independent Roman Catholic (Jesuit), coed. Awards: associate, bachelor's, and master's degrees. 55 undergraduate majors. Total enrollment: 4,739. Undergraduates: 3,329. Both federal and institutional methodology are used as a basis for awarding need-based institutional aid.

UNDERGRADUATE EXPENSES for 1999–2000 ***Application fee:*** $25. ***Comprehensive fee:*** $21,888 includes full-time tuition ($15,160), mandatory fees ($388), and room and board ($6340). ***College room only:*** $3360. Room and board charges vary according to board plan, housing facility, and student level. ***Part-time tuition:*** $433 per credit hour. ***Payment plans:*** installment, deferred payment.

FRESHMAN FINANCIAL AID (Fall 1999, est.) 731 applied for aid; of those 87% were deemed to have need. 100% of freshmen with need received aid. *Average financial aid package:* $14,274 (excluding resources awarded to replace EFC). 9% of all full-time freshmen had no need and received non-need-based aid.

UNDERGRADUATE FINANCIAL AID (Fall 1999, est.) 2,711 applied for aid; of those 82% were deemed to have need. 96% of undergraduates with need received aid. *Average financial aid package:* $16,910 (excluding resources awarded to replace EFC). 8% of all full-time undergraduates had no need and received non-need-based aid.

GIFT AID (NEED-BASED) ***Total amount:*** $19,887,069 (11% Federal, 16% state, 73% institutional). ***Receiving aid:*** *Freshmen:* 81% (603); *all full-time undergraduates:* 71% (2,041). ***Average award:*** Freshmen: $9374; Undergraduates: $9744. ***Scholarships, grants, and awards:*** Federal Pell, FSEOG, state, private, college/university gift aid from institutional funds, United Negro College Fund.

GIFT AID (NON-NEED-BASED) ***Total amount:*** $1,783,416 (16% Federal, 4% state, 60% institutional, 20% external sources). ***Receiving aid:*** *Freshmen:* 42% (312); *Undergraduates:* 21% (604). ***Scholarships, grants, and awards by category:*** *Academic Interests/Achievement:* 564 awards ($4,010,760 total): general academic interests/achievements. *Creative Arts/Performance:* 26 awards ($43,000 total): art/fine arts, music. *Special Achievements/Activities:* 135 awards ($213,500 total): community service, leadership, religious involvement. *Special Characteristics:* 417 awards ($1,874,998 total): children and siblings of alumni, children of educators, children of faculty/staff, international students, parents of current students, religious affiliation, siblings of current students, spouses of current students. ***Tuition waivers:*** Full or partial for employees or children of employees. ***ROTC:*** Army.

LOANS ***Student loans:*** $11,595,623 (64% need-based, 36% non-need-based). 73% of past graduating class borrowed through all loan programs. ***Average need-based loan:*** Freshmen: $3162; Undergraduates: $4753.

Parent loans: $1,644,529 (100% non-need-based). ***Programs:*** FFEL (Subsidized and Unsubsidized Stafford, PLUS), Perkins, college/university.

WORK-STUDY ***Federal work-study:*** *Total amount:* $780,499; 567 jobs averaging $1376. ***State or other work-study/employment:*** *Total amount:* $165,758 (100% non-need-based). Part-time jobs available.

ATHLETIC AWARDS *Total amount:* 1,309,441 (100% non-need-based).

APPLYING for FINANCIAL AID ***Required financial aid forms:*** FAFSA, institution's own form, state aid form. ***Financial aid deadline (priority):*** 2/1. ***Notification date:*** 4/1. Students must reply within 2 weeks of notification.

CONTACT Mr. Curtis Gaume, Director of Student Financial Aid, Canisius College, 2001 Main Street, Buffalo, NY 14208-1098, 716-888-2300 or toll-free 800-843-1517. *Fax:* 716-888-2377. *E-mail:* gaume@canisius.edu

CAPITAL UNIVERSITY

Columbus, OH

Tuition & fees: $16,000 **Average undergraduate aid package: $14,406**

ABOUT THE INSTITUTION Independent religious, coed. Awards: bachelor's, master's, and first professional degrees. 55 undergraduate majors. Total enrollment: 4,039. Undergraduates: 2,807. Freshmen: 542. Institutional methodology is used as a basis for awarding need-based institutional aid.

UNDERGRADUATE EXPENSES for 1999–2000 ***Application fee:*** $25. ***Comprehensive fee:*** $20,900 includes full-time tuition ($16,000) and room and board ($4900). Full-time tuition and fees vary according to program. Room and board charges vary according to board plan and housing facility. ***Part-time tuition:*** $534 per semester hour. ***Part-time fees:*** $25 per term part-time. ***Payment plan:*** installment.

FRESHMAN FINANCIAL AID (Fall 1999) 493 applied for aid; of those 89% were deemed to have need. 100% of freshmen with need received aid; of those 89% had need fully met. *Average financial aid package:* $13,666 (excluding resources awarded to replace EFC). 10% of all full-time freshmen had no need and received non-need-based aid.

UNDERGRADUATE FINANCIAL AID (Fall 1999) 1,671 applied for aid; of those 92% were deemed to have need. 100% of undergraduates with need received aid; of those 52% had need fully met. *Average financial aid package:* $14,406 (excluding resources awarded to replace EFC). 7% of all full-time undergraduates had no need and received non-need-based aid.

GIFT AID (NEED-BASED) ***Total amount:*** $5,164,763 (26% Federal, 17% state, 57% institutional). ***Receiving aid:*** *Freshmen:* 58% (307); *all full-time undergraduates:* 56% (1,090). ***Average award:*** Freshmen: $7112; Undergraduates: $7052. ***Scholarships, grants, and awards:*** Federal Pell, FSEOG, state, private, college/university gift aid from institutional funds.

GIFT AID (NON-NEED-BASED) ***Total amount:*** $10,588,340 (18% state, 75% institutional, 7% external sources). ***Receiving aid:*** *Freshmen:* 83% (441); *Undergraduates:* 78% (1,505). ***Scholarships, grants, and awards by category:*** *Academic Interests/Achievement:* general academic interests/achievements. *Creative Arts/Performance:* music. *Special Achievements/Activities:* hobbies/interests, leadership, religious involvement. *Special Characteristics:* children and siblings of alumni, children of faculty/staff, ethnic background, international students, members of minority groups, relatives of clergy, religious affiliation, siblings of current students. ***Tuition waivers:*** Full or partial for employees or children of employees, senior citizens. ***ROTC:*** Army.

LOANS ***Student loans:*** $9,203,900 (63% need-based, 37% non-need-based). 74% of past graduating class borrowed through all loan programs. Average indebtedness per student: $16,200. ***Average need-based loan:*** Freshmen: $3574; Undergraduates: $4268. ***Programs:*** FFEL (Subsidized and Unsubsidized Stafford, PLUS), Perkins, Federal Nursing, college/university.

WORK-STUDY ***Federal work-study:*** *Total amount:* $1,391,378; jobs available.

APPLYING for FINANCIAL AID ***Required financial aid form:*** FAFSA. ***Financial aid deadline (priority):*** 2/15. ***Notification date:*** Continuous beginning 4/1. Students must reply by 5/1 or within 2 weeks of notification.

CONTACT Office of Financial Aid, Capital University, 2199 East Main Street, Columbus, OH 43209-2394, 614-236-6511 or toll-free 800-289-6289. *Fax:* 614-236-6926. *E-mail:* finaid@capital.edu

CAPITOL COLLEGE

Laurel, MD

Tuition & fees: $12,308 **Average undergraduate aid package: $7600**

ABOUT THE INSTITUTION Independent, coed. Awards: associate, bachelor's, and master's degrees and post-bachelor's certificates. 7 undergraduate majors. Total enrollment: 830. Undergraduates: 719. Freshmen: 76. Federal methodology is used as a basis for awarding need-based institutional aid.

UNDERGRADUATE EXPENSES for 1999–2000 ***Application fee:*** $25. ***Tuition:*** full-time $11,808; part-time $447 per semester hour. ***Required fees:*** full-time $500; $10 per semester hour; $7 per term part-time. Part-time tuition and fees vary according to course load. ***Payment plans:*** guaranteed tuition, installment, deferred payment.

FRESHMAN FINANCIAL AID (Fall 1999, est.) 74 applied for aid; of those 95% were deemed to have need. 100% of freshmen with need received aid. *Average percent of need met:* 70% (excluding resources awarded to replace EFC). *Average financial aid package:* $7600 (excluding resources awarded to replace EFC). 3% of all full-time freshmen had no need and received non-need-based aid.

UNDERGRADUATE FINANCIAL AID (Fall 1999, est.) 693 applied for aid; of those 95% were deemed to have need. 100% of undergraduates with need received aid. *Average percent of need met:* 70% (excluding resources awarded to replace EFC). *Average financial aid package:* $7600 (excluding resources awarded to replace EFC). 1% of all full-time undergraduates had no need and received non-need-based aid.

GIFT AID (NEED-BASED) ***Total amount:*** $1,044,993 (33% Federal, 15% state, 52% institutional). ***Receiving aid:*** *Freshmen:* 95% (70); *all full-time undergraduates:* 79% (660). ***Scholarships, grants, and awards:*** Federal Pell, FSEOG, state, private, college/university gift aid from institutional funds.

GIFT AID (NON-NEED-BASED) ***Total amount:*** $130,974 (55% institutional, 45% external sources). ***Receiving aid:*** *Freshmen:* 41% (30); *Undergraduates:* 11% (91). ***Scholarships, grants, and awards by category:*** *Academic Interests/Achievement:* general academic interests/achievements. ***Tuition waivers:*** Full or partial for employees or children of employees. ***ROTC:*** Army cooperative, Naval cooperative, Air Force cooperative.

LOANS ***Student loans:*** $2,115,233 (100% need-based). 90% of past graduating class borrowed through all loan programs. Average indebtedness per student: $12,000. ***Average need-based loan:*** Freshmen: $3000; Undergraduates: $3500. ***Parent loans:*** $622,877 (100% need-based). ***Programs:*** FFEL (Subsidized and Unsubsidized Stafford, PLUS), Perkins, college/university.

WORK-STUDY ***Federal work-study:*** *Total amount:* $75,000; 34 jobs averaging $2200. ***State or other work-study/employment:*** *Total amount:* $60,000 (100% non-need-based). 15 part-time jobs averaging $4000.

APPLYING for FINANCIAL AID ***Required financial aid forms:*** FAFSA, institution's own form. ***Financial aid deadline (priority):*** 2/1. ***Notification date:*** Continuous beginning 5/15. Students must reply within 2 weeks of notification.

CONTACT James J. Marks, Director of Financial Aid, Capitol College, 11301 Springfield Road, Laurel, MD 20708-9759, 301-369-2800 Ext. 3039 or toll-free 800-950-1992. *Fax:* 301-953-3876. *E-mail:* jmarks@capitol-college.edu

CARDINAL STRITCH UNIVERSITY

Milwaukee, WI

Tuition & fees: $11,120 **Average undergraduate aid package: N/A**

ABOUT THE INSTITUTION Independent Roman Catholic, coed. Awards: associate, bachelor's, master's, and doctoral degrees. 39 undergraduate

Cardinal Stritch University (continued)

majors. Total enrollment: 5,658. Undergraduates: 2,955. Freshmen: 177. Both federal and institutional methodology are used as a basis for awarding need-based institutional aid.

UNDERGRADUATE EXPENSES for 1999–2000 ***Application fee:*** $20. ***One-time required fee:*** $20. ***Comprehensive fee:*** $15,600 includes full-time tuition ($11,000), mandatory fees ($120), and room and board ($4480). Full-time tuition and fees vary according to program. Room and board charges vary according to board plan. ***Part-time tuition:*** $344 per credit. ***Part-time fees:*** $42 per term part-time. Part-time tuition and fees vary according to course load and program. ***Payment plan:*** installment.

GIFT AID (NEED-BASED) ***Total amount:*** $5,706,348 (20% Federal, 14% state, 41% institutional, 25% external sources). ***Scholarships, grants, and awards:*** Federal Pell, FSEOG, state, private, college/university gift aid from institutional funds.

GIFT AID (NON-NEED-BASED) ***Scholarships, grants, and awards by category:*** *Academic Interests/Achievement:* general academic interests/achievements. *Creative Arts/Performance:* art/fine arts. *Special Achievements/Activities:* leadership. ***Tuition waivers:*** Full or partial for employees or children of employees.

LOANS ***Programs:*** Federal Direct (Subsidized and Unsubsidized Stafford, PLUS), FFEL (Subsidized and Unsubsidized Stafford, PLUS), Perkins, state, college/university.

WORK-STUDY Federal work-study jobs available.

APPLYING for FINANCIAL AID ***Required financial aid form:*** FAFSA. ***Financial aid deadline (priority):*** 4/1.

CONTACT Financial Aid Director, Cardinal Stritch University, 6801 North Yates Road, Milwaukee, WI 53217-3985, 414-410-4000 or toll-free 800-347-8822 Ext. 4040.

CARIBBEAN CENTER FOR ADVANCED STUDIES/MIAMI INSTITUTE OF PSYCHOLOGY

Miami, FL

See Carlos Albizu University

CARIBBEAN UNIVERSITY

Bayamón, PR

Tuition & fees: N/R **Average undergraduate aid package: N/A**

ABOUT THE INSTITUTION Independent, coed. Awards: associate, bachelor's, and master's degrees. 26 undergraduate majors. Federal methodology is used as a basis for awarding need-based institutional aid.

GIFT AID (NEED-BASED) ***Scholarships, grants, and awards:*** Federal Pell, FSEOG, state, Federal Nursing.

GIFT AID (NON-NEED-BASED) ***ROTC:*** Army cooperative.

LOANS ***Programs:*** Federal Direct (Subsidized Stafford), FFEL (Subsidized and Unsubsidized Stafford), Federal Nursing.

WORK-STUDY Federal work-study jobs available.

APPLYING for FINANCIAL AID ***Required financial aid forms:*** FAFSA, institution's own form, noncustodial (divorced/separated) parent's statement. ***Financial aid deadline:*** Continuous.

CONTACT Ruby Rivera, Student Aid Office Director, Caribbean University, Box 493, Bayamón, PR 00960-0493, 787-780-0070.

CARLETON COLLEGE

Northfield, MN

Tuition & fees: $23,469 **Average undergraduate aid package: $18,824**

ABOUT THE INSTITUTION Independent, coed. Awards: bachelor's degrees. 33 undergraduate majors. Total enrollment: 1,905. Undergraduates: 1,905. Freshmen: 510. Both federal and institutional methodology are used as a basis for awarding need-based institutional aid.

UNDERGRADUATE EXPENSES for 1999–2000 ***Application fee:*** $30. ***Comprehensive fee:*** $28,230 includes full-time tuition ($23,325), mandatory fees ($144), and room and board ($4761). ***College room only:*** $2067. Room and board charges vary according to board plan. ***Payment plans:*** tuition prepayment, installment.

FRESHMAN FINANCIAL AID (Fall 1999) 346 applied for aid; of those 71% were deemed to have need. 100% of freshmen with need received aid; of those 100% had need fully met. *Average percent of need met:* 100% (excluding resources awarded to replace EFC). *Average financial aid package:* $18,346 (excluding resources awarded to replace EFC). 24% of all full-time freshmen had no need and received non-need-based aid.

UNDERGRADUATE FINANCIAL AID (Fall 1999) 1,123 applied for aid; of those 85% were deemed to have need. 100% of undergraduates with need received aid; of those 100% had need fully met. *Average percent of need met:* 100% (excluding resources awarded to replace EFC). *Average financial aid package:* $18,824 (excluding resources awarded to replace EFC). 28% of all full-time undergraduates had no need and received non-need-based aid.

GIFT AID (NEED-BASED) ***Total amount:*** $12,716,309 (3% Federal, 4% state, 89% institutional, 4% external sources). ***Receiving aid:*** *Freshmen:* 47% (242); *all full-time undergraduates:* 50% (934). ***Average award:*** Freshmen: $14,101; Undergraduates: $13,740. ***Scholarships, grants, and awards:*** Federal Pell, FSEOG, state, private, college/university gift aid from institutional funds.

GIFT AID (NON-NEED-BASED) ***Total amount:*** $460,041 (4% Federal, 69% institutional, 27% external sources). ***Receiving aid:*** *Freshmen:* 23% (119); *Undergraduates:* 18% (336). ***Scholarships, grants, and awards by category:*** *Academic Interests/Achievement:* general academic interests/achievements. *Creative Arts/Performance:* music.

LOANS ***Student loans:*** $3,741,410 (87% need-based, 13% non-need-based). 56% of past graduating class borrowed through all loan programs. Average indebtedness per student: $14,720. ***Average need-based loan:*** Freshmen: $3237; Undergraduates: $4217. ***Parent loans:*** $1,070,896 (100% non-need-based). ***Programs:*** FFEL (Subsidized and Unsubsidized Stafford, PLUS), Perkins, state, college/university, Minnesota SELF Loan Program.

WORK-STUDY ***Federal work-study:*** *Total amount:* $594,507; 282 jobs averaging $2105. ***State or other work-study/employment:*** *Total amount:* $1,984,262 (69% need-based, 31% non-need-based). 1,059 part-time jobs averaging $1874.

APPLYING for FINANCIAL AID ***Required financial aid forms:*** FAFSA, CSS Financial Aid PROFILE, noncustodial (divorced/separated) parent's statement. ***Financial aid deadline:*** 2/1 (priority: 1/15). ***Notification date:*** 4/15. Students must reply by 5/1 or within 2 weeks of notification.

CONTACT Mr. Leonard M. Wenc, Director of Student Financial Services, Carleton College, One North College Street, Northfield, MN 55057-4001, 507-646-4254 or toll-free 800-995-2275. *Fax:* 507-646-4269.

CARLOS ALBIZU UNIVERSITY

Miami, FL

Tuition & fees: $6834 **Average undergraduate aid package: $4249**

ABOUT THE INSTITUTION Independent, coed, primarily women. Awards: bachelor's, master's, and doctoral degrees. 1 undergraduate major. Total enrollment: 617. Undergraduates: 69. Federal methodology is used as a basis for awarding need-based institutional aid.

UNDERGRADUATE EXPENSES for 1999–2000 ***Application fee:*** $25. ***Tuition:*** full-time $6300; part-time $210 per credit. ***Required fees:*** full-time $534; $178 per term part-time. ***Payment plan:*** installment.

UNDERGRADUATE FINANCIAL AID (Fall 1999, est.) 60 applied for aid; of those 80% were deemed to have need. 100% of undergraduates with need received aid; of those 4% had need fully met. *Average percent of need met:* 41% (excluding resources awarded to replace EFC). *Average*

financial aid package: $4249 (excluding resources awarded to replace EFC). 24% of all full-time undergraduates had no need and received non-need-based aid.

GIFT AID (NEED-BASED) ***Total amount:*** $67,059 (96% Federal, 4% state). ***Receiving aid:*** *All full-time undergraduates:* 40% (27). ***Average award:*** Undergraduates: $2484. ***Scholarships, grants, and awards:*** Federal Pell, FSEOG, state, college/university gift aid from institutional funds.

GIFT AID (NON-NEED-BASED) ***Total amount:*** $73,395 (100% institutional). ***Receiving aid:*** *Undergraduates:* 44% (30). ***Scholarships, grants, and awards by category:*** *Academic Interests/Achievement:* general academic interests/achievements. *Special Characteristics:* veterans. ***Tuition waivers:*** Full or partial for minority students, employees or children of employees.

LOANS ***Student loans:*** $127,711 (58% need-based, 42% non-need-based). ***Average need-based loan:*** Undergraduates: $2552. ***Programs:*** FFEL (Subsidized and Unsubsidized Stafford, PLUS).

WORK-STUDY ***Federal work-study:*** *Total amount:* $12,744; 4 jobs averaging $3186.

APPLYING for FINANCIAL AID ***Required financial aid forms:*** FAFSA, institution's own form.

CONTACT Carmen Freire, Senior Financial Aid Officer, Carlos Albizu University, 2173 Northwest 99th Avenue, Miami, FL 33172, 305-593-1223 Ext. 104 or toll-free 800-672-3246. *Fax:* 305-593-8902.

CARLOW COLLEGE

Pittsburgh, PA

Tuition & fees: $12,826 **Average undergraduate aid package: $11,045**

ABOUT THE INSTITUTION Independent Roman Catholic, coed, primarily women. Awards: bachelor's and master's degrees and post-bachelor's certificates. 33 undergraduate majors. Total enrollment: 2,113. Undergraduates: 1,767. Freshmen: 171. Both federal and institutional methodology are used as a basis for awarding need-based institutional aid.

UNDERGRADUATE EXPENSES for 1999–2000 ***Application fee:*** $20. ***Comprehensive fee:*** $17,902 includes full-time tuition ($12,450), mandatory fees ($376), and room and board ($5076). Full-time tuition and fees vary according to course load and program. Room and board charges vary according to board plan. ***Part-time tuition:*** $381 per credit. ***Part-time fees:*** $24 per credit. Part-time tuition and fees vary according to course load and program. ***Payment plans:*** installment, deferred payment.

FRESHMAN FINANCIAL AID (Fall 1998) 153 applied for aid; of those 92% were deemed to have need. 100% of freshmen with need received aid; of those 75% had need fully met. *Average percent of need met:* 95% (excluding resources awarded to replace EFC). *Average financial aid package:* $11,970 (excluding resources awarded to replace EFC). 4% of all full-time freshmen had no need and received non-need-based aid.

UNDERGRADUATE FINANCIAL AID (Fall 1998) 735 applied for aid; of those 92% were deemed to have need. 100% of undergraduates with need received aid; of those 75% had need fully met. *Average percent of need met:* 95% (excluding resources awarded to replace EFC). *Average financial aid package:* $11,045 (excluding resources awarded to replace EFC). 2% of all full-time undergraduates had no need and received non-need-based aid.

GIFT AID (NEED-BASED) ***Total amount:*** $4,222,227 (30% Federal, 33% state, 34% institutional, 3% external sources). ***Receiving aid:*** *Freshmen:* 82% (134); *all full-time undergraduates:* 71% (608). ***Average award:*** Freshmen: $5400; Undergraduates: $4100. ***Scholarships, grants, and awards:*** Federal Pell, FSEOG, state, private, college/university gift aid from institutional funds.

GIFT AID (NON-NEED-BASED) ***Total amount:*** $745,565 (88% institutional, 12% external sources). ***Receiving aid:*** *Freshmen:* 44% (71); *Undergraduates:* 39% (331). ***Scholarships, grants, and awards by category:*** *Academic Interests/Achievement:* 151 awards ($492,610 total): biological sciences, business, communication, computer science, education, English, general academic interests/achievements, humanities, mathematics, social sciences. *Creative Arts/Performance:* 7 awards ($15,300 total): art/fine arts, creative writing. *Special Achievements/Activities:* 33 awards ($74,677 total): leadership, religious involvement. *Special Characteristics:* 59 awards ($162,478 total): children of current students, children of educators, children of faculty/staff, international students, religious affiliation, siblings of current students, spouses of current students. ***Tuition waivers:*** Full or partial for employees or children of employees, adult students. ***ROTC:*** Army cooperative, Naval cooperative, Air Force cooperative.

LOANS ***Student loans:*** $5,548,045 (63% need-based, 37% non-need-based). 70% of past graduating class borrowed through all loan programs. Average indebtedness per student: $15,000. ***Average need-based loan:*** Freshmen: $3425; Undergraduates: $3610. ***Parent loans:*** $240,840 (100% non-need-based). ***Programs:*** FFEL (Subsidized and Unsubsidized Stafford, PLUS), Perkins, Federal Nursing, alternative loans.

WORK-STUDY ***Federal work-study:*** *Total amount:* $138,639; 227 jobs averaging $611.

ATHLETIC AWARDS *Total amount:* 113,100 (100% non-need-based).

APPLYING for FINANCIAL AID ***Required financial aid form:*** FAFSA. ***Financial aid deadline (priority):*** 4/3. ***Notification date:*** Continuous.

CONTACT Ms. Natalie Wilson, Director of Financial Aid, Carlow College, 3333 Fifth Avenue, Pittsburgh, PA 15213-3165, 412-578-6058 or toll-free 800-333-CARLOW. *E-mail:* finaid@carlow.edu

CARNEGIE MELLON UNIVERSITY

Pittsburgh, PA

Tuition & fees: $22,300 **Average undergraduate aid package: $15,789**

ABOUT THE INSTITUTION Independent, coed. Awards: bachelor's, master's, and doctoral degrees and post-bachelor's and post-master's certificates. 59 undergraduate majors. Total enrollment: 8,436. Undergraduates: 5,262. Freshmen: 1,254. Federal methodology is used as a basis for awarding need-based institutional aid.

UNDERGRADUATE EXPENSES for 1999–2000 ***Application fee:*** $50. ***Comprehensive fee:*** $29,110 includes full-time tuition ($22,100), mandatory fees ($200), and room and board ($6810). ***College room only:*** $4105. Room and board charges vary according to board plan, housing facility, and student level. ***Part-time tuition:*** $307 per unit. ***Payment plan:*** installment.

FRESHMAN FINANCIAL AID (Fall 1999) 951 applied for aid; of those 76% were deemed to have need. 100% of freshmen with need received aid; of those 36% had need fully met. *Average percent of need met:* 77% (excluding resources awarded to replace EFC). *Average financial aid package:* $15,710 (excluding resources awarded to replace EFC). 15% of all full-time freshmen had no need and received non-need-based aid.

UNDERGRADUATE FINANCIAL AID (Fall 1999) 3,189 applied for aid; of those 85% were deemed to have need. 100% of undergraduates with need received aid; of those 42% had need fully met. *Average percent of need met:* 78% (excluding resources awarded to replace EFC). *Average financial aid package:* $15,789 (excluding resources awarded to replace EFC). 15% of all full-time undergraduates had no need and received non-need-based aid.

GIFT AID (NEED-BASED) ***Total amount:*** $30,144,454 (8% Federal, 3% state, 85% institutional, 4% external sources). ***Receiving aid:*** *Freshmen:* 55% (707); *all full-time undergraduates:* 52% (2,582). ***Average award:*** Freshmen: $12,887; Undergraduates: $11,723. ***Scholarships, grants, and awards:*** Federal Pell, FSEOG, state, private, college/university gift aid from institutional funds.

GIFT AID (NON-NEED-BASED) ***Total amount:*** $10,617,839 (86% institutional, 14% external sources). ***Receiving aid:*** *Freshmen:* 20% (262); *Undergraduates:* 23% (1,137). ***Scholarships, grants, and awards by category:*** *Academic Interests/Achievement:* general academic interests/achievements. ***Tuition waivers:*** Full or partial for employees or children of employees. ***ROTC:*** Army, Naval, Air Force.

LOANS ***Student loans:*** $14,735,747 (94% need-based, 6% non-need-based). 56% of past graduating class borrowed through all loan programs. Average indebtedness per student: $17,880. ***Average need-based loan:*** Freshmen: $3886; Undergraduates: $4930. ***Parent loans:*** $5,174,087 (18% need-based, 82% non-need-based). ***Programs:*** FFEL (Subsidized and Unsubsidized Stafford, PLUS), Perkins.

Carnegie Mellon University (continued)

WORK-STUDY ***Federal work-study:*** *Total amount:* $3,515,951; 2,260 jobs available. ***State or other work-study/employment:*** *Total amount:* $167,783 (100% need-based). 1,250 part-time jobs available.

APPLYING for FINANCIAL AID ***Required financial aid forms:*** FAFSA, institution's own form, parent and student federal income tax returns, parents' W-2 forms. ***Financial aid deadline (priority):*** 2/15. ***Notification date:*** 4/1.

CONTACT Enrollment Services, Carnegie Mellon University, 5000 Forbes Avenue, Pittsburgh, PA 15213-3891, 412-268-8186. *Fax:* 412-268-8084. *E-mail:* thehub+@andrew.cmu.edu

CARROLL COLLEGE

Helena, MT

Tuition & fees: $11,778 **Average undergraduate aid package: $10,696**

ABOUT THE INSTITUTION Independent Roman Catholic, coed. Awards: associate and bachelor's degrees. 55 undergraduate majors. Total enrollment: 1,243. Undergraduates: 1,243. Freshmen: 245. Federal methodology is used as a basis for awarding need-based institutional aid.

UNDERGRADUATE EXPENSES for 1999–2000 ***Application fee:*** $25. ***Comprehensive fee:*** $16,494 includes full-time tuition ($11,778) and room and board ($4716). Room and board charges vary according to board plan, housing facility, and student level. ***Part-time tuition:*** $393 per semester hour. ***Payment plan:*** installment.

FRESHMAN FINANCIAL AID (Fall 1999) 220 applied for aid; of those 82% were deemed to have need. 100% of freshmen with need received aid; of those 24% had need fully met. *Average percent of need met:* 85% (excluding resources awarded to replace EFC). *Average financial aid package:* $11,090 (excluding resources awarded to replace EFC).

UNDERGRADUATE FINANCIAL AID (Fall 1999) 741 applied for aid; of those 86% were deemed to have need. 100% of undergraduates with need received aid; of those 21% had need fully met. *Average percent of need met:* 79% (excluding resources awarded to replace EFC). *Average financial aid package:* $10,696 (excluding resources awarded to replace EFC).

GIFT AID (NEED-BASED) ***Total amount:*** $3,374,478 (24% Federal, 69% institutional, 7% external sources). ***Receiving aid:*** *Freshmen:* 72% (177); *all full-time undergraduates:* 56% (599). ***Average award:*** Freshmen: $5548; Undergraduates: $5113. ***Scholarships, grants, and awards:*** Federal Pell, FSEOG, state, private, college/university gift aid from institutional funds.

GIFT AID (NON-NEED-BASED) ***Total amount:*** $1,137,432 (100% institutional). ***Receiving aid:*** *Freshmen:* 69% (170); *Undergraduates:* 49% (525). ***Scholarships, grants, and awards by category:*** *Academic Interests/Achievement:* general academic interests/achievements. *Creative Arts/Performance:* debating, music, theater/drama. *Special Achievements/Activities:* cheerleading/drum major, leadership, religious involvement. *Special Characteristics:* children and siblings of alumni, children of educators, children of faculty/staff, children of union members/company employees, international students, local/state students, siblings of current students, spouses of current students. ***Tuition waivers:*** Full or partial for employees or children of employees, senior citizens.

LOANS ***Student loans:*** $3,864,899 (77% need-based, 23% non-need-based). 70% of past graduating class borrowed through all loan programs. Average indebtedness per student: $21,364. ***Average need-based loan:*** Freshmen: $3666; Undergraduates: $4309. ***Parent loans:*** $398,065 (52% need-based, 48% non-need-based). ***Programs:*** FFEL (Subsidized and Unsubsidized Stafford, PLUS), Perkins.

WORK-STUDY ***Federal work-study:*** *Total amount:* $628,332; jobs available.

ATHLETIC AWARDS *Total amount:* 786,634 (45% need-based, 55% non-need-based).

APPLYING for FINANCIAL AID ***Required financial aid form:*** FAFSA. ***Financial aid deadline (priority):*** 3/1. ***Notification date:*** Continuous beginning 4/1. Students must reply within 4 weeks of notification.

CONTACT Financial Aid Office, Carroll College, 1601 North Benton Avenue, Helena, MT 59625-0002, 406-447-4300 or toll-free 800-99-ADMIT. *Fax:* 406-447-4533.

CARROLL COLLEGE

Waukesha, WI

Tuition & fees: $15,000 **Average undergraduate aid package: $13,219**

ABOUT THE INSTITUTION Independent Presbyterian, coed. Awards: bachelor's and master's degrees (master's degrees in education and physical therapy). 51 undergraduate majors. Total enrollment: 2,791. Undergraduates: 2,621. Freshmen: 504. Both federal and institutional methodology are used as a basis for awarding need-based institutional aid.

UNDERGRADUATE EXPENSES for 1999–2000 ***One-time required fee:*** $69. ***Comprehensive fee:*** $19,600 includes full-time tuition ($14,740), mandatory fees ($260), and room and board ($4600). ***College room only:*** $2470. Full-time tuition and fees vary according to program. Room and board charges vary according to board plan and housing facility. ***Part-time tuition:*** $185 per semester hour. Part-time tuition and fees vary according to course load and program. ***Payment plan:*** installment.

FRESHMAN FINANCIAL AID (Fall 1999, est.) 481 applied for aid; of those 73% were deemed to have need. 100% of freshmen with need received aid; of those 100% had need fully met. *Average percent of need met:* 100% (excluding resources awarded to replace EFC). *Average financial aid package:* $13,811 (excluding resources awarded to replace EFC). 27% of all full-time freshmen had no need and received non-need-based aid.

UNDERGRADUATE FINANCIAL AID (Fall 1999, est.) 1,789 applied for aid; of those 75% were deemed to have need. 100% of undergraduates with need received aid; of those 100% had need fully met. *Average percent of need met:* 100% (excluding resources awarded to replace EFC). *Average financial aid package:* $13,219 (excluding resources awarded to replace EFC). 23% of all full-time undergraduates had no need and received non-need-based aid.

GIFT AID (NEED-BASED) ***Total amount:*** $12,658,099 (9% Federal, 13% state, 74% institutional, 4% external sources). ***Receiving aid:*** *Freshmen:* 72% (351); *all full-time undergraduates:* 74% (1,342). ***Average award:*** Freshmen: $10,179; Undergraduates: $9050. ***Scholarships, grants, and awards:*** Federal Pell, FSEOG, state, private, college/university gift aid from institutional funds.

GIFT AID (NON-NEED-BASED) ***Total amount:*** $2,708,249 (3% state, 95% institutional, 2% external sources). ***Scholarships, grants, and awards by category:*** *Academic Interests/Achievement:* 1,252 awards ($4,915,830 total): biological sciences, computer science, general academic interests/achievements, health fields, humanities, mathematics, physical sciences, premedicine. *Creative Arts/Performance:* 150 awards ($268,750 total): journalism/publications, music, performing arts, theater/drama. *Special Achievements/Activities:* 25 awards ($120,500 total): junior miss, memberships. *Special Characteristics:* 225 awards ($555,225 total): children and siblings of alumni, children of current students, children of faculty/staff, international students, siblings of current students, spouses of current students. ***Tuition waivers:*** Full or partial for employees or children of employees.

LOANS ***Student loans:*** $7,340,794 (68% need-based, 32% non-need-based). 80% of past graduating class borrowed through all loan programs. Average indebtedness per student: $15,772. ***Average need-based loan:*** Freshmen: $2268; Undergraduates: $3186. ***Parent loans:*** $852,840 (88% need-based, 12% non-need-based). ***Programs:*** FFEL (Subsidized and Unsubsidized Stafford, PLUS), Perkins, college/university.

WORK-STUDY ***Federal work-study:*** *Total amount:* $636,667; 399 jobs averaging $1595. ***State or other work-study/employment:*** *Total amount:* $944,835 (100% non-need-based). 647 part-time jobs averaging $1460.

APPLYING for FINANCIAL AID ***Required financial aid form:*** FAFSA. ***Financial aid deadline:*** Continuous. ***Notification date:*** Continuous beginning 2/15. Students must reply by 5/1 or within 2 weeks of notification.

CONTACT Tim Opgenorth, Director of Financial Aid, Carroll College, 100 North East Avenue, Waukesha, WI 53186-5593, 262-524-7296 or toll-free 800-CARROLL. *Fax:* 262-524-7139. *E-mail:* topgen@ccadmin.cc.edu

CARSON-NEWMAN COLLEGE

Jefferson City, TN

Tuition & fees: $11,640 **Average undergraduate aid package: $10,643**

ABOUT THE INSTITUTION Independent Southern Baptist, coed. Awards: associate, bachelor's, and master's degrees. 68 undergraduate majors. Total enrollment: 2,205. Undergraduates: 1,946. Freshmen: 384. Federal methodology is used as a basis for awarding need-based institutional aid.

UNDERGRADUATE EXPENSES for 1999–2000 ***Application fee:*** $25. ***Comprehensive fee:*** $15,550 includes full-time tuition ($10,960), mandatory fees ($680), and room and board ($3910). ***College room only:*** $1560. Full-time tuition and fees vary according to class time. Room and board charges vary according to board plan. ***Part-time tuition:*** $450 per semester hour. ***Part-time fees:*** $200 per term part-time. Part-time tuition and fees vary according to class time. ***Payment plan:*** installment.

FRESHMAN FINANCIAL AID (Fall 1999, est.) 371 applied for aid; of those 76% were deemed to have need. 100% of freshmen with need received aid; of those 23% had need fully met. *Average percent of need met:* 82% (excluding resources awarded to replace EFC). *Average financial aid package:* $11,177 (excluding resources awarded to replace EFC). 21% of all full-time freshmen had no need and received non-need-based aid.

UNDERGRADUATE FINANCIAL AID (Fall 1999, est.) 1,708 applied for aid; of those 73% were deemed to have need. 100% of undergraduates with need received aid; of those 25% had need fully met. *Average percent of need met:* 80% (excluding resources awarded to replace EFC). *Average financial aid package:* $10,643 (excluding resources awarded to replace EFC). 24% of all full-time undergraduates had no need and received non-need-based aid.

GIFT AID (NEED-BASED) ***Total amount:*** $7,966,706 (21% Federal, 10% state, 65% institutional, 4% external sources). ***Receiving aid:*** *Freshmen:* 73% (279); *all full-time undergraduates:* 70% (1,235). ***Average award:*** Freshmen: $8110; Undergraduates: $7141. ***Scholarships, grants, and awards:*** Federal Pell, FSEOG, state, private, college/university gift aid from institutional funds.

GIFT AID (NON-NEED-BASED) ***Total amount:*** $1,731,925 (3% Federal, 3% state, 85% institutional, 9% external sources). ***Receiving aid:*** *Freshmen:* 11% (42); *Undergraduates:* 9% (151). ***Scholarships, grants, and awards by category:*** *Academic Interests/Achievement:* biological sciences, business, education, general academic interests/achievements, home economics, mathematics, military science, religion/biblical studies. *Creative Arts/Performance:* art/fine arts, debating, journalism/publications, music. *Special Achievements/Activities:* leadership, memberships. *Special Characteristics:* children and siblings of alumni, members of minority groups, relatives of clergy, siblings of current students. ***Tuition waivers:*** Full or partial for employees or children of employees, senior citizens. ***ROTC:*** Army, Air Force cooperative.

LOANS ***Student loans:*** $4,845,249 (93% need-based, 7% non-need-based). 65% of past graduating class borrowed through all loan programs. Average indebtedness per student: $14,591. ***Average need-based loan:*** Freshmen: $3292; Undergraduates: $3952. ***Parent loans:*** $1,018,826 (81% need-based, 19% non-need-based). ***Programs:*** FFEL (Subsidized and Unsubsidized Stafford, PLUS), Perkins, state, college/university, alternative loans.

WORK-STUDY ***Federal work-study:*** *Total amount:* $475,356; 353 jobs averaging $1347. ***State or other work-study/employment:*** *Total amount:* $359,182 (54% need-based, 46% non-need-based). 256 part-time jobs averaging $1403.

ATHLETIC AWARDS *Total amount:* 1,051,405 (81% need-based, 19% non-need-based).

APPLYING for FINANCIAL AID ***Required financial aid forms:*** FAFSA, institution's own form. ***Financial aid deadline (priority):*** 4/1. ***Notification date:*** Continuous. Students must reply within 2 weeks of notification.

CONTACT Mr. Don Elia, Director of Financial Aid, Carson-Newman College, 1646 Russell Avenue, Jefferson City, TN 37760, 800-478-9061 or toll-free 800-678-9061. *Fax:* 423-471-3502. *E-mail:* delia@cncadmnt.cn.edu

CARTHAGE COLLEGE

Kenosha, WI

Tuition & fees: $16,690 **Average undergraduate aid package: $14,384**

ABOUT THE INSTITUTION Independent religious, coed. Awards: bachelor's and master's degrees. 48 undergraduate majors. Total enrollment: 2,210. Undergraduates: 2,121. Freshmen: 436. Federal methodology is used as a basis for awarding need-based institutional aid.

UNDERGRADUATE EXPENSES for 1999–2000 ***Application fee:*** $25. ***Comprehensive fee:*** $21,500 includes full-time tuition ($16,690) and room and board ($4810). Room and board charges vary according to board plan. ***Part-time tuition:*** $250 per credit hour. Part-time tuition and fees vary according to class time. ***Payment plan:*** installment.

FRESHMAN FINANCIAL AID (Fall 1999, est.) *Average percent of need met:* 86% (excluding resources awarded to replace EFC). *Average financial aid package:* $13,941 (excluding resources awarded to replace EFC).

UNDERGRADUATE FINANCIAL AID (Fall 1999, est.) *Average percent of need met:* 93% (excluding resources awarded to replace EFC). *Average financial aid package:* $14,384 (excluding resources awarded to replace EFC).

GIFT AID (NEED-BASED) ***Total amount:*** $5,456,188 ***Scholarships, grants, and awards:*** Federal Pell, FSEOG, state, private, college/university gift aid from institutional funds.

GIFT AID (NON-NEED-BASED) ***Total amount:*** $7,785,747 ***Scholarships, grants, and awards by category:*** *Academic Interests/Achievement:* biological sciences, engineering/technologies, foreign languages, general academic interests/achievements, health fields, mathematics, physical sciences, premedicine. *Creative Arts/Performance:* art/fine arts, music, theater/drama. *Special Achievements/Activities:* general special achievements/activities, leadership, religious involvement. *Special Characteristics:* children and siblings of alumni, children of educators, children of public servants, local/state students, previous college experience, relatives of clergy, religious affiliation, siblings of current students. ***Tuition waivers:*** Full or partial for children of alumni, employees or children of employees. ***ROTC:*** Air Force cooperative.

LOANS ***Programs:*** FFEL (Subsidized and Unsubsidized Stafford, PLUS), Perkins, college/university, alternative loans.

WORK-STUDY Federal work-study jobs available. ***State or other work-study/employment:*** Part-time jobs available.

APPLYING for FINANCIAL AID ***Required financial aid form:*** FAFSA. ***Financial aid deadline (priority):*** 2/15. ***Notification date:*** Continuous beginning 3/1.

CONTACT Elise Albrecht, Director of Student Financial Planning, Carthage College, 2001 Alford Park Drive, Kenosha, WI 53140-1994, 262-551-6001 or toll-free 800-351-4058. *Fax:* 262-551-5762.

CASCADE COLLEGE

Portland, OR

Tuition & fees: $8590 **Average undergraduate aid package: N/A**

ABOUT THE INSTITUTION Independent religious, coed. Awards: bachelor's degrees. 6 undergraduate majors. Total enrollment: 310. Undergraduates: 310. Freshmen: 104. Federal methodology is used as a basis for awarding need-based institutional aid.

UNDERGRADUATE EXPENSES for 1999–2000 ***Application fee:*** $25. ***Comprehensive fee:*** $13,290 includes full-time tuition ($8390), mandatory fees ($200), and room and board ($4700). Full-time tuition and fees vary according to course load. Room and board charges vary according to board plan. ***Part-time tuition:*** $350 per semester hour.

GIFT AID (NEED-BASED) ***Scholarships, grants, and awards:*** Federal Pell, FSEOG.

GIFT AID (NON-NEED-BASED) ***Scholarships, grants, and awards by category:*** *Academic Interests/Achievement:* general academic interests/achievements. *Creative Arts/Performance:* music, theater/drama. *Special Characteristics:* children of faculty/staff, international students, siblings of

Cascade College (continued)

current students. ***Tuition waivers:*** Full or partial for employees or children of employees. ***ROTC:*** Army cooperative, Air Force cooperative.

LOANS ***Programs:*** FFEL (Subsidized and Unsubsidized Stafford, PLUS).

WORK-STUDY Federal work-study jobs available.

APPLYING for FINANCIAL AID ***Required financial aid form:*** FAFSA. ***Financial aid deadline:*** 8/1 (priority: 4/30).

CONTACT Ms. Kaelea Graul, Director of Student Financial Services, Cascade College, 9101 East Burnside Street, Portland, OR 97216-1515, 503-257-1218 or toll-free 800-550-7678.

CASE WESTERN RESERVE UNIVERSITY

Cleveland, OH

Tuition & fees: $20,260 **Average undergraduate aid package: $18,549**

ABOUT THE INSTITUTION Independent, coed. Awards: bachelor's, master's, doctoral, and first professional degrees. 58 undergraduate majors. Total enrollment: 9,300. Undergraduates: 3,380. Freshmen: 766. Both federal and institutional methodology are used as a basis for awarding need-based institutional aid.

UNDERGRADUATE EXPENSES for 2000–2001 ***Comprehensive fee:*** $26,075 includes full-time tuition ($20,100), mandatory fees ($160), and room and board ($5815). ***College room only:*** $3580. Room and board charges vary according to board plan and housing facility. ***Part-time tuition:*** $834 per credit. ***Part-time fees:*** $5 per credit. Part-time tuition and fees vary according to course load. ***Payment plans:*** tuition prepayment, installment.

FRESHMAN FINANCIAL AID (Fall 1999) 603 applied for aid; of those 81% were deemed to have need. 100% of freshmen with need received aid; of those 73% had need fully met. *Average percent of need met:* 95% (excluding resources awarded to replace EFC). *Average financial aid package:* $18,843 (excluding resources awarded to replace EFC). 28% of all full-time freshmen had no need and received non-need-based aid.

UNDERGRADUATE FINANCIAL AID (Fall 1999) 2,108 applied for aid; of those 84% were deemed to have need. 100% of undergraduates with need received aid; of those 73% had need fully met. *Average percent of need met:* 96% (excluding resources awarded to replace EFC). *Average financial aid package:* $18,549 (excluding resources awarded to replace EFC). 33% of all full-time undergraduates had no need and received non-need-based aid.

GIFT AID (NEED-BASED) ***Total amount:*** $23,172,115 (10% Federal, 9% state, 77% institutional, 4% external sources). ***Receiving aid:*** *Freshmen:* 63% (483); *all full-time undergraduates:* 59% (1,755). ***Average award:*** Freshmen: $13,355; Undergraduates: $12,334. ***Scholarships, grants, and awards:*** Federal Pell, FSEOG, state, private, college/university gift aid from institutional funds.

GIFT AID (NON-NEED-BASED) ***Total amount:*** $10,494,908 (1% Federal, 8% state, 87% institutional, 4% external sources). ***Receiving aid:*** *Freshmen:* 58% (442); *Undergraduates:* 52% (1,535). ***Scholarships, grants, and awards by category:*** *Academic Interests/Achievement:* 998 awards ($5,601,146 total): general academic interests/achievements. *Creative Arts/Performance:* 19 awards ($67,497 total): art/fine arts, creative writing, dance, music, theater/drama. *Special Achievements/Activities:* 74 awards ($108,235 total): leadership. *Special Characteristics:* 192 awards ($3,482,546 total): children of faculty/staff. ***Tuition waivers:*** Full or partial for employees or children of employees. ***ROTC:*** Army cooperative, Air Force cooperative.

LOANS ***Student loans:*** $10,678,871 (93% need-based, 7% non-need-based). 60% of past graduating class borrowed through all loan programs. Average indebtedness per student: $19,375. ***Average need-based loan:*** Freshmen: $4211; Undergraduates: $5295. ***Parent loans:*** $1,156,654 (31% need-based, 69% non-need-based). ***Programs:*** Federal Direct (Subsidized and Unsubsidized Stafford), FFEL (PLUS), Perkins, Federal Nursing, state, college/university.

WORK-STUDY ***Federal work-study:*** *Total amount:* $1,705,786; 766 jobs averaging $2225.

APPLYING for FINANCIAL AID ***Required financial aid forms:*** FAFSA, CSS Financial Aid PROFILE, noncustodial (divorced/separated) parent's statement, business/farm supplement, parent and student income tax returns and W-2 forms. ***Financial aid deadline:*** 4/15 (priority: 2/1). ***Notification date:*** Continuous. Students must reply by 5/1 or within 2 weeks of notification.

CONTACT Ms. Nancy Issa, Associate Director, Case Western Reserve University, 10900 Euclid Avenue, Cleveland, OH 44106-7049, 216-368-4530. *Fax:* 216-368-5054. *E-mail:* nxi@po.cwru.edu

CASTLETON STATE COLLEGE

Castleton, VT

Tuition & fees (VT res): $5030 **Average undergraduate aid package: N/A**

ABOUT THE INSTITUTION State-supported, coed. Awards: associate, bachelor's, and master's degrees and post-master's certificates. 42 undergraduate majors. Total enrollment: 1,691. Undergraduates: 1,579. Freshmen: 314. Federal methodology is used as a basis for awarding need-based institutional aid.

UNDERGRADUATE EXPENSES for 2000–2001 ***Application fee:*** $30. ***Tuition, state resident:*** full-time $4236; part-time $177 per credit. ***Tuition, nonresident:*** full-time $9924; part-time $414 per credit. ***Required fees:*** full-time $794. Full-time tuition and fees vary according to reciprocity agreements. Part-time tuition and fees vary according to course load and reciprocity agreements. ***College room and board:*** $5346; ***room only:*** $3156. Room and board charges vary according to board plan. ***Payment plan:*** installment.

FRESHMAN FINANCIAL AID (Fall 1998) 307 applied for aid; of those 86% were deemed to have need. 98% of freshmen with need received aid.

UNDERGRADUATE FINANCIAL AID (Fall 1998) 1,253 applied for aid; of those 89% were deemed to have need. 98% of undergraduates with need received aid.

GIFT AID (NEED-BASED) ***Total amount:*** $2,452,633 (59% Federal, 25% state, 8% institutional, 8% external sources). ***Scholarships, grants, and awards:*** Federal Pell, FSEOG, state, private, college/university gift aid from institutional funds.

GIFT AID (NON-NEED-BASED) ***Total amount:*** $62,690 (80% institutional, 20% external sources). ***Scholarships, grants, and awards by category:*** *Academic Interests/Achievement:* foreign languages, general academic interests/achievements. *Creative Arts/Performance:* applied art and design, art/fine arts, music. ***Tuition waivers:*** Full or partial for employees or children of employees, senior citizens.

LOANS ***Student loans:*** $5,463,124 (70% need-based, 30% non-need-based). ***Parent loans:*** $2,110,965 (82% need-based, 18% non-need-based). ***Programs:*** Federal Direct (Subsidized and Unsubsidized Stafford, PLUS), FFEL (Subsidized and Unsubsidized Stafford, PLUS), Perkins, Federal Nursing, college/university.

WORK-STUDY ***Federal work-study:*** *Total amount:* $426,379; 377 jobs averaging $1080. ***State or other work-study/employment:*** *Total amount:* $219,156 (100% non-need-based). 160 part-time jobs averaging $1300.

APPLYING for FINANCIAL AID ***Required financial aid forms:*** FAFSA, state aid form. ***Financial aid deadline (priority):*** 3/15. ***Notification date:*** Continuous. Students must reply within 2 weeks of notification.

CONTACT Mr. Kenneth G. Moulton, Director, Financial Aid, Castleton State College, Castleton, VT 05735, 802-468-1291 or toll-free 800-639-8521. *Fax:* 802-468-5237. *E-mail:* ken.moulton@castleton.edu

CATAWBA COLLEGE

Salisbury, NC

Tuition & fees: $12,600 **Average undergraduate aid package: N/A**

ABOUT THE INSTITUTION Independent religious, coed. Awards: bachelor's and master's degrees. 43 undergraduate majors. Total enrollment: 1,217. Undergraduates: 1,195. Freshmen: 276. Federal methodology is used as a basis for awarding need-based institutional aid.

UNDERGRADUATE EXPENSES for 1999–2000 ***Application fee:*** $25. ***One-time required fee:*** $275. ***Comprehensive fee:*** $17,440 includes full-time tuition ($12,600) and room and board ($4840). ***Part-time tuition:*** $390 per semester hour. ***Part-time fees:*** $30 per term part-time. ***Payment plan:*** installment.

FRESHMAN FINANCIAL AID (Fall 1998) 263 applied for aid; of those 85% were deemed to have need. 100% of freshmen with need received aid; of those 24% had need fully met. *Average financial aid package:* $8248 (excluding resources awarded to replace EFC).

UNDERGRADUATE FINANCIAL AID (Fall 1998) 1,186 applied for aid; of those 83% were deemed to have need. 99% of undergraduates with need received aid.

GIFT AID (NEED-BASED) ***Total amount:*** $1,158,377 (55% Federal, 44% state, 1% external sources). ***Receiving aid:*** *Freshmen:* 224; *all full-time undergraduates:* 979. ***Average award:*** Freshmen: $11,135; Undergraduates: $9220. ***Scholarships, grants, and awards:*** Federal Pell, FSEOG, state, private, college/university gift aid from institutional funds.

GIFT AID (NON-NEED-BASED) ***Total amount:*** $4,461,432 (19% state, 76% institutional, 5% external sources). ***Receiving aid:*** *Freshmen:* 224; *Undergraduates:* 979. ***Scholarships, grants, and awards by category:*** *Academic Interests/Achievement:* general academic interests/achievements. *Special Characteristics:* children of faculty/staff, religious affiliation. ***Tuition waivers:*** Full or partial for employees or children of employees. ***ROTC:*** Army cooperative.

LOANS ***Student loans:*** $3,257,620 (69% need-based, 31% non-need-based). 58% of past graduating class borrowed through all loan programs. ***Average need-based loan:*** Freshmen: $3993; Undergraduates: $3158. ***Parent loans:*** $920,658 (100% non-need-based). ***Programs:*** FFEL (Subsidized and Unsubsidized Stafford, PLUS), Perkins, college/university, TERI Loans, Nellie Mae Loans, Advantage Loans.

WORK-STUDY ***Federal work-study:*** *Total amount:* $350,778; 243 jobs averaging $1443. ***State or other work-study/employment:*** *Total amount:* $179,821 (100% non-need-based). 164 part-time jobs averaging $1096.

ATHLETIC AWARDS *Total amount:* 1,005,707 (100% non-need-based).

APPLYING for FINANCIAL AID ***Required financial aid form:*** FAFSA. ***Financial aid deadline (priority):*** 3/1. ***Notification date:*** Continuous.

CONTACT Judith K. Carter, Director of Scholarships and Financial Aid, Catawba College, 2300 West Innes Street, Salisbury, NC 28144-2488, 704-637-4416 or toll-free 800-CATAWBA. *Fax:* 704-637-4222. *E-mail:* jkcarter@catawba.edu

THE CATHOLIC UNIVERSITY OF AMERICA

Washington, DC

Tuition & fees: $18,972 **Average undergraduate aid package: $16,859**

ABOUT THE INSTITUTION Independent religious, coed. Awards: bachelor's, master's, doctoral, and first professional degrees and post-master's certificates. 70 undergraduate majors. Total enrollment: 5,597. Undergraduates: 2,557. Freshmen: 797. Federal methodology is used as a basis for awarding need-based institutional aid.

UNDERGRADUATE EXPENSES for 1999–2000 ***Application fee:*** $55. ***One-time required fee:*** $126. ***Comprehensive fee:*** $26,737 includes full-time tuition ($18,200), mandatory fees ($772), and room and board ($7765). ***College room only:*** $4285. Full-time tuition and fees vary according to program. Room and board charges vary according to board plan and housing facility. ***Part-time tuition:*** $700 per credit. ***Part-time fees:*** $194 per term part-time. ***Payment plans:*** installment, deferred payment.

FRESHMAN FINANCIAL AID (Fall 1999) 707 applied for aid; of those 72% were deemed to have need. 100% of freshmen with need received aid; of those 76% had need fully met. *Average percent of need met:* 89% (excluding resources awarded to replace EFC). *Average financial aid package:* $16,105 (excluding resources awarded to replace EFC). 25% of all full-time freshmen had no need and received non-need-based aid.

UNDERGRADUATE FINANCIAL AID (Fall 1999) 2,003 applied for aid; of those 71% were deemed to have need. 100% of undergraduates with need received aid; of those 65% had need fully met. *Average percent of need met:* 86% (excluding resources awarded to replace EFC). *Average financial aid package:* $16,859 (excluding resources awarded to replace EFC). 24% of all full-time undergraduates had no need and received non-need-based aid.

GIFT AID (NEED-BASED) ***Total amount:*** $14,152,513 (7% Federal, 91% institutional, 2% external sources). ***Receiving aid:*** *Freshmen:* 65% (496); *all full-time undergraduates:* 59% (1,354). ***Average award:*** Freshmen: $11,399; Undergraduates: $10,366. ***Scholarships, grants, and awards:*** Federal Pell, FSEOG, state, private, college/university gift aid from institutional funds, Federal Nursing.

GIFT AID (NON-NEED-BASED) ***Total amount:*** $4,699,566 (98% institutional, 2% external sources). ***Receiving aid:*** *Freshmen:* 12% (92); *Undergraduates:* 12% (265). ***Scholarships, grants, and awards by category:*** *Academic Interests/Achievement:* general academic interests/achievements. *Creative Arts/Performance:* music. *Special Characteristics:* children of faculty/staff, religious affiliation, siblings of current students. ***Tuition waivers:*** Full or partial for employees or children of employees. ***ROTC:*** Army cooperative, Naval cooperative, Air Force cooperative.

LOANS ***Student loans:*** $8,752,084 (90% need-based, 10% non-need-based). ***Average need-based loan:*** Freshmen: $4128; Undergraduates: $5748. ***Parent loans:*** $4,973,223 (83% need-based, 17% non-need-based). ***Programs:*** FFEL (Subsidized and Unsubsidized Stafford, PLUS), Perkins, Federal Nursing, college/university.

WORK-STUDY ***Federal work-study:*** *Total amount:* $882,810; jobs available. ***State or other work-study/employment:*** *Total amount:* $384,000 (69% need-based, 31% non-need-based). Part-time jobs available.

APPLYING for FINANCIAL AID ***Required financial aid forms:*** FAFSA, institution's own form. ***Financial aid deadline (priority):*** 2/1. ***Notification date:*** Continuous beginning 4/1. Students must reply by 5/1.

CONTACT Ms. Doris Torosian, Director of Financial Aid, The Catholic University of America, Cardinal Station, Washington, DC 20064, 202-319-5307 or toll-free 800-673-2772 (out-of-state). *Fax:* 202-319-6533.

CAZENOVIA COLLEGE

Cazenovia, NY

Tuition & fees: $12,140 **Average undergraduate aid package: N/A**

ABOUT THE INSTITUTION Independent, coed. Awards: associate and bachelor's degrees. 21 undergraduate majors. Total enrollment: 975. Undergraduates: 975. Freshmen: 292. Federal methodology is used as a basis for awarding need-based institutional aid.

UNDERGRADUATE EXPENSES for 1999–2000 ***Application fee:*** $25. ***Comprehensive fee:*** $18,068 includes full-time tuition ($11,640), mandatory fees ($500), and room and board ($5928). ***College room only:*** $3178. Room and board charges vary according to board plan. ***Part-time tuition:*** $297 per credit. Part-time tuition and fees vary according to class time and course load. ***Payment plan:*** installment.

GIFT AID (NEED-BASED) ***Scholarships, grants, and awards:*** Federal Pell, FSEOG, state, college/university gift aid from institutional funds.

GIFT AID (NON-NEED-BASED) ***Scholarships, grants, and awards by category:*** *Academic Interests/Achievement:* general academic interests/achievements. *Creative Arts/Performance:* general creative arts/performance. *Special Achievements/Activities:* general special achievements/activities. ***Tuition waivers:*** Full or partial for employees or children of employees. ***ROTC:*** Army cooperative.

LOANS ***Programs:*** Federal Direct (Subsidized and Unsubsidized Stafford, PLUS), college/university.

WORK-STUDY Federal work-study jobs available.

APPLYING for FINANCIAL AID ***Required financial aid forms:*** FAFSA, institution's own form. ***Financial aid deadline (priority):*** 3/15. ***Notification date:*** Continuous. Students must reply within 3 weeks of notification.

CONTACT Ms. Christine L. Mandel, Director of Financial Aid, Cazenovia College, 22 Sullivan Street, Cazenovia, NY 13035, 315-655-7208 or toll-free 800-654-3210. *Fax:* 315-655-4860.

CEDAR CREST COLLEGE

Allentown, PA

Tuition & fees: $17,110 **Average undergraduate aid package: $15,198**

ABOUT THE INSTITUTION Independent religious, women only. Awards: associate and bachelor's degrees. 57 undergraduate majors. Total enrollment: 1,679. Undergraduates: 1,679. Freshmen: 244. Federal methodology is used as a basis for awarding need-based institutional aid.

UNDERGRADUATE EXPENSES for 1999–2000 ***Application fee:*** $30. ***Comprehensive fee:*** $23,325 includes full-time tuition ($17,110) and room and board ($6215). ***College room only:*** $3348. Full-time tuition and fees vary according to course load. Room and board charges vary according to board plan. ***Part-time tuition:*** $487 per credit hour. Part-time tuition and fees vary according to class time. ***Payment plan:*** installment.

FRESHMAN FINANCIAL AID (Fall 1999) 230 applied for aid; of those 98% were deemed to have need. 100% of freshmen with need received aid; of those 31% had need fully met. *Average percent of need met:* 89% (excluding resources awarded to replace EFC). *Average financial aid package:* $16,708 (excluding resources awarded to replace EFC). 2% of all full-time freshmen had no need and received non-need-based aid.

UNDERGRADUATE FINANCIAL AID (Fall 1999) 790 applied for aid; of those 95% were deemed to have need. 100% of undergraduates with need received aid; of those 36% had need fully met. *Average percent of need met:* 88% (excluding resources awarded to replace EFC). *Average financial aid package:* $15,198 (excluding resources awarded to replace EFC). 3% of all full-time undergraduates had no need and received non-need-based aid.

GIFT AID (NEED-BASED) ***Total amount:*** $7,801,952 (12% Federal, 15% state, 70% institutional, 3% external sources). ***Receiving aid:*** *Freshmen:* 93% (225); *all full-time undergraduates:* 85% (736). ***Average award:*** Freshmen: $12,084; Undergraduates: $10,515. ***Scholarships, grants, and awards:*** Federal Pell, FSEOG, state, private, college/university gift aid from institutional funds.

GIFT AID (NON-NEED-BASED) ***Total amount:*** $704,610 (74% institutional, 26% external sources). ***Receiving aid:*** *Freshmen:* 5% (13); *Undergraduates:* 7% (62). ***Scholarships, grants, and awards by category:*** *Academic Interests/Achievement:* 362 awards ($1,695,285 total): general academic interests/achievements. *Creative Arts/Performance:* 46 awards ($66,000 total): art/fine arts, dance, performing arts, theater/drama. *Special Achievements/Activities:* 132 awards ($219,362 total): community service, general special achievements/activities, junior miss, leadership, memberships, religious involvement. *Special Characteristics:* 59 awards ($93,250 total): adult students, children and siblings of alumni, ethnic background, general special characteristics, previous college experience, relatives of clergy, religious affiliation, siblings of current students. ***Tuition waivers:*** Full or partial for employees or children of employees. ***ROTC:*** Army cooperative.

LOANS ***Student loans:*** $5,417,410 (78% need-based, 22% non-need-based). 68% of past graduating class borrowed through all loan programs. Average indebtedness per student: $19,095. ***Average need-based loan:*** Freshmen: $3356; Undergraduates: $4550. ***Parent loans:*** $713,086 (30% need-based, 70% non-need-based). ***Programs:*** FFEL (Subsidized and Unsubsidized Stafford, PLUS), Perkins, Federal Nursing, college/university.

WORK-STUDY ***Federal work-study:*** *Total amount:* $153,363; 114 jobs averaging $1500. ***State or other work-study/employment:*** *Total amount:* $407,987 (67% need-based, 33% non-need-based). 269 part-time jobs averaging $1500.

APPLYING for FINANCIAL AID ***Required financial aid forms:*** FAFSA, institution's own form. ***Financial aid deadline:*** Continuous. ***Notification date:*** Continuous beginning 10/1. Students must reply by 5/1.

CONTACT Ms. Donna M. Michel, Director of Financial Aid, Cedar Crest College, 100 College Drive, Allentown, PA 18104-6196, 610-740-3785 or toll-free 800-360-1222. *Fax:* 610-606-4653. *E-mail:* finaid@cedarcrest.edu

CEDARVILLE COLLEGE

Cedarville, OH

Tuition & fees: $10,740 **Average undergraduate aid package: $9452**

ABOUT THE INSTITUTION Independent Baptist, coed. Awards: associate and bachelor's degrees. 66 undergraduate majors. Total enrollment: 2,762. Undergraduates: 2,762. Freshmen: 722. Federal methodology is used as a basis for awarding need-based institutional aid.

UNDERGRADUATE EXPENSES for 1999–2000 ***Application fee:*** $30. ***Comprehensive fee:*** $15,528 includes full-time tuition ($10,608), mandatory fees ($132), and room and board ($4788). ***Part-time tuition:*** $221 per quarter hour. ***Part-time fees:*** $44 per term part-time. Part-time tuition and fees vary according to course load. ***Payment plan:*** installment.

FRESHMAN FINANCIAL AID (Fall 1998) 627 applied for aid; of those 83% were deemed to have need. 100% of freshmen with need received aid; of those 34% had need fully met. *Average percent of need met:* 28% (excluding resources awarded to replace EFC). *Average financial aid package:* $9203 (excluding resources awarded to replace EFC). 25% of all full-time freshmen had no need and received non-need-based aid.

UNDERGRADUATE FINANCIAL AID (Fall 1998) 1,815 applied for aid; of those 87% were deemed to have need. 100% of undergraduates with need received aid; of those 34% had need fully met. *Average percent of need met:* 40% (excluding resources awarded to replace EFC). *Average financial aid package:* $9452 (excluding resources awarded to replace EFC). 24% of all full-time undergraduates had no need and received non-need-based aid.

GIFT AID (NEED-BASED) ***Total amount:*** $2,131,776 (44% Federal, 13% state, 30% institutional, 13% external sources). ***Receiving aid:*** *Freshmen:* 26% (205); *all full-time undergraduates:* 31% (791). ***Average award:*** Freshmen: $915; Undergraduates: $1267. ***Scholarships, grants, and awards:*** Federal Pell, FSEOG, state, private, college/university gift aid from institutional funds.

GIFT AID (NON-NEED-BASED) ***Total amount:*** $4,472,296 (19% state, 52% institutional, 29% external sources). ***Receiving aid:*** *Freshmen:* 55% (440); *Undergraduates:* 39% (1,013). ***Scholarships, grants, and awards by category:*** *Academic Interests/Achievement:* 484 awards ($622,237 total): general academic interests/achievements. *Creative Arts/Performance:* 41 awards ($28,920 total): debating, music. *Special Achievements/Activities:* 269 awards ($319,862 total): leadership. *Special Characteristics:* 92 awards ($618,421 total): children of faculty/staff, general special characteristics, religious affiliation, veterans. ***Tuition waivers:*** Full or partial for employees or children of employees, senior citizens. ***ROTC:*** Army cooperative, Air Force cooperative.

LOANS ***Student loans:*** $7,473,022 (68% need-based, 32% non-need-based). 65% of past graduating class borrowed through all loan programs. Average indebtedness per student: $16,975. ***Average need-based loan:*** Freshmen: $2248; Undergraduates: $3443. ***Parent loans:*** $3,274,759 (100% non-need-based). ***Programs:*** FFEL (Subsidized and Unsubsidized Stafford, PLUS), Perkins, Federal Nursing, college/university.

WORK-STUDY ***Federal work-study:*** *Total amount:* $372,501; 174 jobs averaging $1223. ***State or other work-study/employment:*** *Total amount:* $1,251,680 (100% non-need-based). 1,061 part-time jobs averaging $1370.

ATHLETIC AWARDS *Total amount:* 288,890 (100% non-need-based).

APPLYING for FINANCIAL AID ***Required financial aid form:*** FAFSA. ***Financial aid deadline (priority):*** 3/1. ***Notification date:*** Continuous beginning 4/15. Students must reply within 4 weeks of notification.

CONTACT Mr. Fred Merritt, Director of Financial Aid, Cedarville College, Box 601, Cedarville, OH 45314-0601, 937-766-7866 or toll-free 800-CEDARVILLE. *E-mail:* merrittf@cedarville.edu

CENTENARY COLLEGE

Hackettstown, NJ

Tuition & fees: $14,340 **Average undergraduate aid package: $12,873**

ABOUT THE INSTITUTION Independent religious, coed. Awards: associate, bachelor's, and master's degrees and post-bachelor's certificates. 24 undergraduate majors. Total enrollment: 1,023. Undergraduates: 940. Freshmen: 142. Federal methodology is used as a basis for awarding need-based institutional aid.

UNDERGRADUATE EXPENSES for 1999–2000 ***Application fee:*** $25. ***Comprehensive fee:*** $20,490 includes full-time tuition ($13,800), mandatory fees ($540), and room and board ($6150). Full-time tuition and fees vary according to program. ***Part-time tuition:*** $268 per credit. ***Part-time fees:*** $20 per term part-time. Part-time tuition and fees vary according to course load and program. ***Payment plan:*** installment.

FRESHMAN FINANCIAL AID (Fall 1999, est.) 126 applied for aid; of those 91% were deemed to have need. 100% of freshmen with need received aid; of those 37% had need fully met. *Average percent of need met:* 81% (excluding resources awarded to replace EFC). *Average financial aid package:* $13,627 (excluding resources awarded to replace EFC). 21% of all full-time freshmen had no need and received non-need-based aid.

UNDERGRADUATE FINANCIAL AID (Fall 1999, est.) 450 applied for aid; of those 91% were deemed to have need. 100% of undergraduates with need received aid; of those 34% had need fully met. *Average percent of need met:* 81% (excluding resources awarded to replace EFC). *Average financial aid package:* $12,873 (excluding resources awarded to replace EFC). 25% of all full-time undergraduates had no need and received non-need-based aid.

GIFT AID (NEED-BASED) ***Total amount:*** $3,509,481 (16% Federal, 34% state, 43% institutional, 7% external sources). ***Receiving aid:*** *Freshmen:* 79% (114); *all full-time undergraduates:* 72% (393). ***Average award:*** Freshmen: $9904; Undergraduates: $8411. ***Scholarships, grants, and awards:*** Federal Pell, FSEOG, state, private, college/university gift aid from institutional funds.

GIFT AID (NON-NEED-BASED) ***Total amount:*** $623,393 (88% institutional, 12% external sources). ***Receiving aid:*** *Freshmen:* 1% (2); *Undergraduates:* 3% (14). ***Scholarships, grants, and awards by category:*** *Academic Interests/Achievement:* 275 awards ($840,000 total): general academic interests/achievements. *Special Achievements/Activities:* 161 awards ($455,000 total): leadership. *Special Characteristics:* 290 awards ($730,000 total): children and siblings of alumni, ethnic background, general special characteristics, local/state students, out-of-state students, previous college experience, religious affiliation, siblings of current students. ***Tuition waivers:*** Full or partial for employees or children of employees, senior citizens.

LOANS ***Student loans:*** $2,194,914 (82% need-based, 18% non-need-based). ***Average need-based loan:*** Freshmen: $3526; Undergraduates: $4311. ***Parent loans:*** $1,125,649 (34% need-based, 66% non-need-based). ***Programs:*** FFEL (Subsidized and Unsubsidized Stafford, PLUS), Perkins, state, NJ Class Loans.

WORK-STUDY ***Federal work-study:*** *Total amount:* $44,874; 40 jobs averaging $1200. ***State or other work-study/employment:*** *Total amount:* $86,044 (20% need-based, 80% non-need-based). 71 part-time jobs averaging $1200.

APPLYING for FINANCIAL AID ***Required financial aid forms:*** FAFSA, institution's own form. ***Financial aid deadline (priority):*** 4/15. ***Notification date:*** Continuous. Students must reply within 2 weeks of notification.

CONTACT Carol Strauss, Director of Financial Aid, Centenary College, 400 Jefferson Street, Hackettstown, NJ 07840-2100, 908-852-1400 Ext. 2207 or toll-free 800-236-8679. *Fax:* 908-813-2632. *E-mail:* straussc@centenarycollege.edu

CENTENARY COLLEGE OF LOUISIANA

Shreveport, LA

Tuition & fees: $14,600 **Average undergraduate aid package: $10,512**

ABOUT THE INSTITUTION Independent United Methodist, coed. Awards: bachelor's and master's degrees. 66 undergraduate majors. Total enrollment: 1,020. Undergraduates: 878. Freshmen: 269. Federal methodology is used as a basis for awarding need-based institutional aid.

UNDERGRADUATE EXPENSES for 2000–2001 (est.) ***Application fee:*** $30. ***Comprehensive fee:*** $19,100 includes full-time tuition ($14,200), mandatory fees ($400), and room and board ($4500). ***College room only:*** $2000. Full-time tuition and fees vary according to course load and student level. ***Part-time tuition:*** $473 per semester hour. ***Part-time fees:*** $30 per term part-time. ***Payment plans:*** guaranteed tuition, installment, deferred payment.

FRESHMAN FINANCIAL AID (Fall 1999) 260 applied for aid; of those 62% were deemed to have need. 100% of freshmen with need received aid; of those 35% had need fully met. *Average percent of need met:* 92% (excluding resources awarded to replace EFC). *Average financial aid package:* $12,066 (excluding resources awarded to replace EFC). 26% of all full-time freshmen had no need and received non-need-based aid.

UNDERGRADUATE FINANCIAL AID (Fall 1999) 655 applied for aid; of those 70% were deemed to have need. 100% of undergraduates with need received aid; of those 44% had need fully met. *Average percent of need met:* 84% (excluding resources awarded to replace EFC). *Average financial aid package:* $10,512 (excluding resources awarded to replace EFC). 23% of all full-time undergraduates had no need and received non-need-based aid.

GIFT AID (NEED-BASED) ***Total amount:*** $3,562,774 (12% Federal, 17% state, 69% institutional, 2% external sources). ***Receiving aid:*** *Freshmen:* 59% (160); *all full-time undergraduates:* 52% (449). ***Average award:*** Freshmen: $10,000; Undergraduates: $8158. ***Scholarships, grants, and awards:*** Federal Pell, FSEOG, state, private, college/university gift aid from institutional funds.

GIFT AID (NON-NEED-BASED) ***Total amount:*** $2,112,191 (13% state, 85% institutional, 2% external sources). ***Receiving aid:*** *Freshmen:* 12% (33); *Undergraduates:* 14% (122). ***Scholarships, grants, and awards by category:*** *Academic Interests/Achievement:* 465 awards ($2,649,559 total): biological sciences, business, communication, education, engineering/technologies, English, foreign languages, general academic interests/achievements, humanities, mathematics, physical sciences, premedicine, religion/biblical studies, social sciences. *Creative Arts/Performance:* 192 awards ($481,580 total): art/fine arts, dance, general creative arts/performance, music, theater/drama. *Special Achievements/Activities:* 63 awards ($112,225 total): community service, general special achievements/activities, leadership, religious involvement. *Special Characteristics:* 88 awards ($275,159 total): children of educators, children of faculty/staff, general special characteristics, international students, local/state students, members of minority groups, relatives of clergy, religious affiliation. ***Tuition waivers:*** Full or partial for employees or children of employees. ***ROTC:*** Army cooperative.

LOANS ***Student loans:*** $1,784,424 (57% need-based, 43% non-need-based). 43% of past graduating class borrowed through all loan programs. Average indebtedness per student: $16,500. ***Average need-based loan:*** Freshmen: $2860; Undergraduates: $3343. ***Parent loans:*** $493,316 (100% non-need-based). ***Programs:*** FFEL (Subsidized and Unsubsidized Stafford, PLUS), Perkins.

WORK-STUDY ***Federal work-study:*** *Total amount:* $248,403; 169 jobs averaging $1470. ***State or other work-study/employment:*** *Total amount:* $42,500 (100% non-need-based). 34 part-time jobs averaging $1250.

ATHLETIC AWARDS *Total amount:* 1,402,345 (36% need-based, 64% non-need-based).

APPLYING for FINANCIAL AID ***Required financial aid form:*** FAFSA. ***Financial aid deadline (priority):*** 2/15. ***Notification date:*** 3/15. Students must reply by 5/1.

CONTACT Ms. Mary Sue Rix, Director of Financial Aid, Centenary College of Louisiana, PO Box 41188, Shreveport, LA 71134-1188, 318-869-5137 or toll-free 800-234-4448. *Fax:* 318-869-5005. *E-mail:* msrix@centenary.edu

CENTER FOR CREATIVE STUDIES—COLLEGE OF ART AND DESIGN

Detroit, MI

Tuition & fees: $16,526 **Average undergraduate aid package: N/A**

Center for Creative Studies—College of Art and Design (continued)

ABOUT THE INSTITUTION Independent, coed. Awards: bachelor's degrees. 14 undergraduate majors. Total enrollment: 1,048. Undergraduates: 1,048. Freshmen: 166. Federal methodology is used as a basis for awarding need-based institutional aid.

UNDERGRADUATE EXPENSES for 2000–2001 ***Application fee:*** $35. ***Tuition:*** full-time $15,630; part-time $521 per credit hour. ***Required fees:*** full-time $896; $329 per term part-time. Part-time tuition and fees vary according to course load. Room and board charges vary according to housing facility. ***Payment plans:*** installment, deferred payment.

GIFT AID (NEED-BASED) ***Total amount:*** $2,495,119 (26% Federal, 46% state, 28% institutional). ***Scholarships, grants, and awards:*** Federal Pell, FSEOG, state, private, college/university gift aid from institutional funds.

GIFT AID (NON-NEED-BASED) ***Total amount:*** $2,237,826 (88% institutional, 12% external sources). ***Scholarships, grants, and awards by category:*** *Creative Arts/Performance:* applied art and design, art/fine arts. ***Tuition waivers:*** Full or partial for employees or children of employees.

LOANS ***Student loans:*** $3,865,410 (100% need-based). ***Parent loans:*** $613,772 (100% need-based). ***Programs:*** FFEL (Subsidized and Unsubsidized Stafford, PLUS), state, alternative loans.

WORK-STUDY ***Federal work-study:*** *Total amount:* $93,828; jobs available. ***State or other work-study/employment:*** *Total amount:* $144,658 (100% need-based). Part-time jobs available.

APPLYING for FINANCIAL AID ***Required financial aid form:*** FAFSA. ***Financial aid deadline (priority):*** 2/21. ***Notification date:*** Continuous beginning 3/15. Students must reply within 3 weeks of notification.

CONTACT Financial Aid Office, Center for Creative Studies—College of Art and Design, 201 East Kirby, Detroit, MI 48202-4034, 313-664-7495 or toll-free 800-952-ARTS. *Fax:* 313-872-1521. *E-mail:* finaid@ccscad.edu

CENTRAL BAPTIST COLLEGE

Conway, AR

ABOUT THE INSTITUTION Independent Baptist, coed. Awards: associate and bachelor's degrees. 10 undergraduate majors. Total enrollment: 321. Undergraduates: 321. Freshmen: 117.

GIFT AID (NEED-BASED) ***Scholarships, grants, and awards:*** Federal Pell, FSEOG, state, college/university gift aid from institutional funds.

GIFT AID (NON-NEED-BASED) ***Scholarships, grants, and awards by category:*** *Academic Interests/Achievement:* general academic interests/achievements. *Creative Arts/Performance:* journalism/publications, music. *Special Achievements/Activities:* religious involvement. *Special Characteristics:* adult students, general special characteristics, relatives of clergy.

LOANS ***Programs:*** FFEL (Subsidized and Unsubsidized Stafford, PLUS).

WORK-STUDY Federal work-study jobs available.

APPLYING for FINANCIAL AID ***Required financial aid form:*** FAFSA.

CONTACT Christi Bell, Financial Aid Director, Central Baptist College, 1501 College Avenue, Conway, AR 72032-6470, 800-205-6872 Ext. 104 or toll-free 800-205-6872. *Fax:* 501-329-2941. *E-mail:* cbell@admin.cbc.edu

CENTRAL BIBLE COLLEGE

Springfield, MO

Tuition & fees: $6260 **Average undergraduate aid package: $6389**

ABOUT THE INSTITUTION Independent religious, coed. Awards: associate and bachelor's degrees. 7 undergraduate majors. Total enrollment: 949. Undergraduates: 949. Freshmen: 172. Federal methodology is used as a basis for awarding need-based institutional aid.

UNDERGRADUATE EXPENSES for 2000–2001 ***Application fee:*** $75. ***Comprehensive fee:*** $9660 includes full-time tuition ($5760), mandatory fees ($500), and room and board ($3400). Full-time tuition and fees vary according to course load. Room and board charges vary according to housing facility. ***Part-time tuition:*** $230 per semester hour. ***Part-time fees:*** $180 per term part-time. Part-time tuition and fees vary according to course load. ***Payment plan:*** installment.

FRESHMAN FINANCIAL AID (Fall 1999, est.) 129 applied for aid; of those 91% were deemed to have need. 100% of freshmen with need received aid; of those 8% had need fully met. *Average percent of need met:* 57% (excluding resources awarded to replace EFC). *Average financial aid package:* $5510 (excluding resources awarded to replace EFC). 11% of all full-time freshmen had no need and received non-need-based aid.

UNDERGRADUATE FINANCIAL AID (Fall 1999, est.) 627 applied for aid; of those 92% were deemed to have need. 100% of undergraduates with need received aid; of those 15% had need fully met. *Average percent of need met:* 64% (excluding resources awarded to replace EFC). *Average financial aid package:* $6389 (excluding resources awarded to replace EFC). 10% of all full-time undergraduates had no need and received non-need-based aid.

GIFT AID (NEED-BASED) ***Total amount:*** $1,147,594 (77% Federal, 15% institutional, 8% external sources). ***Receiving aid:*** *Freshmen:* 71% (95); *all full-time undergraduates:* 71% (459). ***Average award:*** Freshmen: $2350; Undergraduates: $1932. ***Scholarships, grants, and awards:*** Federal Pell, FSEOG, college/university gift aid from institutional funds.

GIFT AID (NON-NEED-BASED) ***Total amount:*** $500 (100% external sources). ***Scholarships, grants, and awards by category:*** *Academic Interests/Achievement:* general academic interests/achievements. *Creative Arts/Performance:* art/fine arts, music, theater/drama. *Special Achievements/Activities:* community service, religious involvement. *Special Characteristics:* children of faculty/staff, ethnic background, relatives of clergy, religious affiliation, siblings of current students. ***Tuition waivers:*** Full or partial for employees or children of employees, senior citizens.

LOANS ***Student loans:*** $2,938,082 (87% need-based, 13% non-need-based). 88% of past graduating class borrowed through all loan programs. Average indebtedness per student: $10,330. ***Average need-based loan:*** Freshmen: $2846; Undergraduates: $4183. ***Parent loans:*** $103,615 (42% need-based, 58% non-need-based). ***Programs:*** FFEL (Subsidized and Unsubsidized Stafford, PLUS), Perkins, college/university.

WORK-STUDY ***Federal work-study:*** *Total amount:* $158,188; 131 jobs averaging $1244.

APPLYING for FINANCIAL AID ***Required financial aid form:*** FAFSA. ***Financial aid deadline (priority):*** 5/1. ***Notification date:*** Continuous beginning 5/15. Students must reply within 3 weeks of notification.

CONTACT Rick Woolverton, Director of Financial Aid, Central Bible College, 3000 North Grant, Springfield, MO 65803-1096, 417-833-2551 or toll-free 800-831-4222 Ext. 1184. *Fax:* 417-833-2168.

CENTRAL CHRISTIAN COLLEGE OF THE BIBLE

Moberly, MO

Tuition & fees: $4500 **Average undergraduate aid package: $4573**

ABOUT THE INSTITUTION Independent religious, coed. Awards: associate and bachelor's degrees. 8 undergraduate majors. Total enrollment: 150. Undergraduates: 150. Both federal and institutional methodology are used as a basis for awarding need-based institutional aid.

UNDERGRADUATE EXPENSES for 1999–2000 ***Application fee:*** $25. ***Comprehensive fee:*** $7100 includes full-time tuition ($4000), mandatory fees ($500), and room and board ($2600). Room and board charges vary according to board plan. ***Part-time tuition:*** $125 per credit. ***Part-time fees:*** $40 per term part-time. Part-time tuition and fees vary according to course load. ***Payment plan:*** deferred payment.

FRESHMAN FINANCIAL AID (Fall 1998) 34 applied for aid; of those 100% were deemed to have need. 94% of freshmen with need received aid. *Average percent of need met:* 52% (excluding resources awarded to replace EFC). *Average financial aid package:* $4799 (excluding resources awarded to replace EFC).

UNDERGRADUATE FINANCIAL AID (Fall 1998) 118 applied for aid; of those 97% were deemed to have need. 98% of undergraduates with need received aid. *Average percent of need met:* 52% (excluding resources awarded to replace EFC). *Average financial aid package:* $4573 (excluding resources awarded to replace EFC).

GIFT AID (NEED-BASED) ***Total amount:*** $280,499 (58% Federal, 20% institutional, 22% external sources). ***Receiving aid:*** *Freshmen:* 68% (23); *all full-time undergraduates:* 69% (81). ***Average award:*** Undergraduates: $1284. ***Scholarships, grants, and awards:*** Federal Pell, FSEOG, private, college/university gift aid from institutional funds.

GIFT AID (NON-NEED-BASED) ***Total amount:*** $76,057 (100% institutional). ***Receiving aid:*** *Freshmen:* 44% (15); *Undergraduates:* 42% (50). ***Scholarships, grants, and awards by category:*** *Academic Interests/Achievement:* 39 awards ($66,932 total): general academic interests/achievements. *Creative Arts/Performance:* 8 awards ($5875 total): music. *Special Achievements/Activities:* 3 awards ($3250 total): leadership, religious involvement. *Special Characteristics:* 15 awards ($7243 total): children and siblings of alumni, children of faculty/staff. ***Tuition waivers:*** Full or partial for children of alumni, employees or children of employees.

LOANS ***Student loans:*** $212,114 (87% need-based, 13% non-need-based). 60% of past graduating class borrowed through all loan programs. Average indebtedness per student: $9692. ***Average need-based loan:*** Freshmen: $10,808; Undergraduates: $3062. ***Programs:*** FFEL (Subsidized and Unsubsidized Stafford, PLUS).

WORK-STUDY ***Federal work-study:*** *Total amount:* $28,644; 24 jobs averaging $1193.

APPLYING for FINANCIAL AID ***Required financial aid form:*** institution's own form. ***Financial aid deadline:*** 3/15. ***Notification date:*** 4/15. Students must reply by 5/15 or within 2 weeks of notification.

CONTACT Veronica L. Hamblin, Financial Aid Director, Central Christian College of the Bible, 911 East Urbandale Drive, Moberly, MO 65270-1997, 660-263-3900 or toll-free 888-263-3900 (in-state). *Fax:* 660-263-3936. *E-mail:* vhamblin@cccb.edu

CENTRAL COLLEGE

Pella, IA

Tuition & fees: $14,186 **Average undergraduate aid package: $13,978**

ABOUT THE INSTITUTION Independent religious, coed. Awards: bachelor's degrees. 36 undergraduate majors. Total enrollment: 1,301. Undergraduates: 1,301. Freshmen: 404. Federal methodology is used as a basis for awarding need-based institutional aid.

UNDERGRADUATE EXPENSES for 1999–2000 ***Application fee:*** $25. ***Comprehensive fee:*** $19,130 includes full-time tuition ($14,070), mandatory fees ($116), and room and board ($4944). ***College room only:*** $2382. Room and board charges vary according to board plan. ***Part-time tuition:*** $488 per semester hour. ***Part-time fees:*** $116 per year part-time. Part-time tuition and fees vary according to course load. ***Payment plan:*** installment.

FRESHMAN FINANCIAL AID (Fall 1999) 375 applied for aid; of those 88% were deemed to have need. 100% of freshmen with need received aid; of those 28% had need fully met. *Average percent of need met:* 91% (excluding resources awarded to replace EFC). *Average financial aid package:* $14,349 (excluding resources awarded to replace EFC). 18% of all full-time freshmen had no need and received non-need-based aid.

UNDERGRADUATE FINANCIAL AID (Fall 1999) 1,154 applied for aid; of those 92% were deemed to have need. 100% of undergraduates with need received aid; of those 30% had need fully met. *Average percent of need met:* 90% (excluding resources awarded to replace EFC). *Average financial aid package:* $13,978 (excluding resources awarded to replace EFC). 19% of all full-time undergraduates had no need and received non-need-based aid.

GIFT AID (NEED-BASED) ***Total amount:*** $9,722,443 (9% Federal, 29% state, 59% institutional, 3% external sources). ***Receiving aid:*** *Freshmen:* 82% (331); *all full-time undergraduates:* 81% (1,053). ***Average award:*** Freshmen: $10,429; Undergraduates: $9513. ***Scholarships, grants, and awards:*** Federal Pell, FSEOG, state, private, college/university gift aid from institutional funds.

GIFT AID (NON-NEED-BASED) ***Total amount:*** $1,527,145 (1% state, 95% institutional, 4% external sources). ***Receiving aid:*** *Freshmen:* 15% (59); *Undergraduates:* 8% (108). ***Scholarships, grants, and awards by category:*** *Academic Interests/Achievement:* 2,182 awards ($5,926,133 total): biological sciences, business, communication, computer science, education, foreign languages, general academic interests/achievements, health fields, humanities, international studies, mathematics, physical sciences, religion/biblical studies. *Creative Arts/Performance:* 153 awards ($206,400 total): art/fine arts, music, theater/drama. *Special Achievements/Activities:* 22 awards ($59,500 total): community service, leadership, religious involvement. *Special Characteristics:* 901 awards ($1,090,772 total): children and siblings of alumni, children of faculty/staff, first-generation college students, general special characteristics, international students, local/state students, members of minority groups, out-of-state students, relatives of clergy, religious affiliation, siblings of current students. ***Tuition waivers:*** Full or partial for employees or children of employees.

LOANS ***Student loans:*** $4,235,859 (79% need-based, 21% non-need-based). 77% of past graduating class borrowed through all loan programs. Average indebtedness per student: $20,665. ***Average need-based loan:*** Freshmen: $2554; Undergraduates: $3181. ***Parent loans:*** $435,900 (100% non-need-based). ***Programs:*** Federal Direct (Subsidized and Unsubsidized Stafford, PLUS), Perkins, college/university, alternative loans.

WORK-STUDY ***Federal work-study:*** *Total amount:* $665,636; 628 jobs averaging $1060. ***State or other work-study/employment:*** *Total amount:* $683,555 (49% need-based, 51% non-need-based). 623 part-time jobs averaging $1097.

APPLYING for FINANCIAL AID ***Required financial aid form:*** FAFSA. ***Financial aid deadline (priority):*** 3/1. ***Notification date:*** Continuous beginning 3/10. Students must reply by 5/1 or within 2 weeks of notification.

CONTACT Ms. Jean Vander Wert, Director of Student Financial Planning, Central College, 812 University Street, Box 5800, Pella, IA 50219-1999, 515-628-5268 or toll-free 800-458-5503. *Fax:* 515-628-5316. *E-mail:* vanderwertj@central.edu

CENTRAL CONNECTICUT STATE UNIVERSITY

New Britain, CT

Tuition & fees (CT res): $3772 **Average undergraduate aid package: $7484**

ABOUT THE INSTITUTION State-supported, coed. Awards: bachelor's and master's degrees. 46 undergraduate majors. Total enrollment: 11,903. Undergraduates: 9,264. Federal methodology is used as a basis for awarding need-based institutional aid.

UNDERGRADUATE EXPENSES for 1999–2000 ***Application fee:*** $40. ***Tuition, state resident:*** full-time $2062; part-time $160 per credit hour. ***Tuition, nonresident:*** full-time $6674; part-time $160 per credit hour. ***Required fees:*** full-time $1710; $43 per term part-time. Full-time tuition and fees vary according to class time, course level, and reciprocity agreements. Part-time tuition and fees vary according to class time and course level. ***College room and board:*** $5652. Room and board charges vary according to board plan. ***Payment plans:*** installment, deferred payment.

FRESHMAN FINANCIAL AID (Fall 1998) 750 applied for aid; of those 80% were deemed to have need. 100% of freshmen with need received aid; of those 50% had need fully met. *Average percent of need met:* 80% (excluding resources awarded to replace EFC). *Average financial aid package:* $7484 (excluding resources awarded to replace EFC).

UNDERGRADUATE FINANCIAL AID (Fall 1998) 3,988 applied for aid; of those 90% were deemed to have need. 75% of undergraduates with need received aid; of those 46% had need fully met. *Average percent of need met:* 80% (excluding resources awarded to replace EFC). *Average financial aid package:* $7484 (excluding resources awarded to replace EFC).

GIFT AID (NEED-BASED) ***Total amount:*** $4,196,919 (68% Federal, 32% state). ***Receiving aid:*** *Freshmen:* 21% (282); *all full-time undergraduates:* 34% (2,000). ***Average award:*** Freshmen: $3742; Undergraduates: $3742. ***Scholarships, grants, and awards:*** Federal Pell, FSEOG, state, private, college/university gift aid from institutional funds.

Central Connecticut State University (continued)

GIFT AID (NON-NEED-BASED) ***Total amount:*** $2,606,039 (87% institutional, 13% external sources). ***Receiving aid:*** *Freshmen:* 14% (180); *Undergraduates:* 20% (1,200). ***Scholarships, grants, and awards by category:*** *Academic Interests/Achievement:* general academic interests/achievements. *Special Characteristics:* members of minority groups. ***Tuition waivers:*** Full or partial for employees or children of employees, senior citizens. ***ROTC:*** Army cooperative, Air Force cooperative.

LOANS ***Student loans:*** $13,533,790 (63% need-based, 37% non-need-based). 67% of past graduating class borrowed through all loan programs. Average indebtedness per student: $18,600. ***Average need-based loan:*** Freshmen: $2625; Undergraduates: $3875. ***Parent loans:*** $1,277,608 (100% non-need-based). ***Programs:*** Federal Direct (Subsidized and Unsubsidized Stafford, PLUS), Perkins.

WORK-STUDY ***Federal work-study:*** *Total amount:* $189,464; 226 jobs averaging $1000. ***State or other work-study/employment:*** *Total amount:* $59,808 (100% need-based). 42 part-time jobs averaging $1000.

ATHLETIC AWARDS *Total amount:* 1,087,496 (100% non-need-based).

APPLYING for FINANCIAL AID ***Required financial aid form:*** FAFSA. ***Financial aid deadline:*** 9/24 (priority: 4/22). ***Notification date:*** Continuous. Students must reply within 2 weeks of notification.

CONTACT Mrs. Elizabeth Mongillo, Financial Aid Counselor, Central Connecticut State University, 1615 Stanley Street, New Britain, CT 06050-4010, 860-832-2200 or toll-free 800-755-2278 (out-of-state). *Fax:* 860-832-1105. *E-mail:* finaid@ccsu.edu

CENTRAL METHODIST COLLEGE

Fayette, MO

Tuition & fees: $11,760 **Average undergraduate aid package: $11,207**

ABOUT THE INSTITUTION Independent Methodist, coed. Awards: associate, bachelor's, and master's degrees. 42 undergraduate majors. Total enrollment: 1,260. Undergraduates: 1,215. Freshmen: 236. Federal methodology is used as a basis for awarding need-based institutional aid.

UNDERGRADUATE EXPENSES for 2000–2001 ***Application fee:*** $20. ***Comprehensive fee:*** $16,090 includes full-time tuition ($11,390), mandatory fees ($370), and room and board ($4330). ***College room only:*** $1980. ***Part-time tuition:*** $470 per credit hour.

FRESHMAN FINANCIAL AID (Fall 1999, est.) 231 applied for aid; of those 85% were deemed to have need. 100% of freshmen with need received aid; of those 90% had need fully met. *Average percent of need met:* 80% (excluding resources awarded to replace EFC). *Average financial aid package:* $12,353 (excluding resources awarded to replace EFC). 12% of all full-time freshmen had no need and received non-need-based aid.

UNDERGRADUATE FINANCIAL AID (Fall 1999, est.) 1,018 applied for aid; of those 97% were deemed to have need. 100% of undergraduates with need received aid; of those 63% had need fully met. *Average percent of need met:* 85% (excluding resources awarded to replace EFC). *Average financial aid package:* $11,207 (excluding resources awarded to replace EFC). 5% of all full-time undergraduates had no need and received non-need-based aid.

GIFT AID (NEED-BASED) ***Total amount:*** $2,686,422 (42% Federal, 23% state, 35% institutional). ***Receiving aid:*** *Freshmen:* 85% (197); *all full-time undergraduates:* 77% (847). ***Average award:*** Freshmen: $2953; Undergraduates: $2828. ***Scholarships, grants, and awards:*** Federal Pell, FSEOG, state, private, college/university gift aid from institutional funds.

GIFT AID (NON-NEED-BASED) ***Total amount:*** $2,657,371 (3% state, 92% institutional, 5% external sources). ***Receiving aid:*** *Freshmen:* 85% (197); *Undergraduates:* 90% (984). ***Scholarships, grants, and awards by category:*** *Academic Interests/Achievement:* biological sciences, business, communication, computer science, education, English, foreign languages, general academic interests/achievements, health fields, humanities, mathematics, premedicine, social sciences. *Creative Arts/Performance:* debating, music, theater/drama. *Special Achievements/Activities:* cheerleading/drum major, leadership, religious involvement. *Special Characteristics:* children of faculty/staff, general special characteristics, international students, relatives of clergy, religious affiliation, siblings of current students, spouses of current students. ***ROTC:*** Army cooperative.

LOANS ***Student loans:*** $5,236,566 (69% need-based, 31% non-need-based). 90% of past graduating class borrowed through all loan programs. Average indebtedness per student: $16,252. ***Parent loans:*** $1,581,521 (100% non-need-based). ***Programs:*** FFEL (Subsidized and Unsubsidized Stafford, PLUS), Perkins.

WORK-STUDY ***Federal work-study:*** *Total amount:* $152,731; 163 jobs averaging $937. ***State or other work-study/employment:*** *Total amount:* $222,240 (48% need-based, 52% non-need-based). 183 part-time jobs averaging $1214.

ATHLETIC AWARDS *Total amount:* 863,569 (100% non-need-based).

APPLYING for FINANCIAL AID ***Required financial aid form:*** FAFSA. ***Financial aid deadline:*** Continuous. ***Notification date:*** Continuous beginning 2/1. Students must reply within 2 weeks of notification.

CONTACT Ms. Chris Forderhase, Director of Financial Assistance, Central Methodist College, 411 Central Methodist Square, Fayette, MO 65248-1198, 660-248-6245 Ext. 244 or toll-free 888-262-1854 (in-state). *Fax:* 660-248-6288.

CENTRAL MICHIGAN UNIVERSITY

Mount Pleasant, MI

Tuition & fees (MI res): $3630 **Average undergraduate aid package: $7121**

ABOUT THE INSTITUTION State-supported, coed. Awards: bachelor's, master's, and doctoral degrees and post-bachelor's and post-master's certificates. 104 undergraduate majors. Total enrollment: 26,321. Undergraduates: 17,866. Freshmen: 3,449. Federal methodology is used as a basis for awarding need-based institutional aid.

UNDERGRADUATE EXPENSES for 1999–2000 ***Application fee:*** $25. ***Tuition, state resident:*** full-time $3150; part-time $105 per credit. ***Tuition, nonresident:*** full-time $8175; part-time $272 per credit. ***Required fees:*** full-time $480; $90 per term part-time. ***College room and board:*** $4620; ***room only:*** $2310. Room and board charges vary according to board plan and housing facility.

FRESHMAN FINANCIAL AID (Fall 1999, est.) 2549 applied for aid; of those 71% were deemed to have need. 99% of freshmen with need received aid; of those 55% had need fully met. *Average percent of need met:* 95% (excluding resources awarded to replace EFC). *Average financial aid package:* $6581 (excluding resources awarded to replace EFC). 33% of all full-time freshmen had no need and received non-need-based aid.

UNDERGRADUATE FINANCIAL AID (Fall 1999, est.) 9,891 applied for aid; of those 76% were deemed to have need. 99% of undergraduates with need received aid; of those 60% had need fully met. *Average percent of need met:* 98% (excluding resources awarded to replace EFC). *Average financial aid package:* $7121 (excluding resources awarded to replace EFC). 29% of all full-time undergraduates had no need and received non-need-based aid.

GIFT AID (NEED-BASED) ***Total amount:*** $16,083,302 (54% Federal, 14% state, 27% institutional, 5% external sources). ***Receiving aid:*** *Freshmen:* 44% (1,497); *all full-time undergraduates:* 38% (5,492). ***Average award:*** Freshmen: $2743; Undergraduates: $2194. ***Scholarships, grants, and awards:*** Federal Pell, FSEOG, state, private, college/university gift aid from institutional funds.

GIFT AID (NON-NEED-BASED) ***Total amount:*** $4,706,458 (7% Federal, 2% state, 74% institutional, 17% external sources). ***Receiving aid:*** *Freshmen:* 4% (139); *Undergraduates:* 3% (407). ***Scholarships, grants, and awards by category:*** *Academic Interests/Achievement:* 3,647 awards ($5,082,789 total): biological sciences, foreign languages, general academic interests/achievements. *Creative Arts/Performance:* 137 awards ($142,930 total): cinema/film/broadcasting, music, theater/drama. *Special Achievements/Activities:* 82 awards ($99,540 total): leadership. *Special Characteristics:* 680 awards ($1,586,005 total): children of faculty/staff, international students, local/state students, members of minority groups, out-of-state students, veterans, veterans' children. ***Tuition waivers:*** Full or partial for employees or children of employees, senior citizens. ***ROTC:*** Army.

LOANS ***Student loans:*** $41,502,660 (67% need-based, 33% non-need-based). 64% of past graduating class borrowed through all loan programs. Average indebtedness per student: $16,757. ***Average need-based loan:*** Freshmen: $2219; Undergraduates: $3494. ***Parent loans:*** $5,863,054 (19% need-based, 81% non-need-based). ***Programs:*** Federal Direct (Subsidized and Unsubsidized Stafford, PLUS), Perkins, state, alternative loans.

WORK-STUDY ***Federal work-study:*** *Total amount:* $2,363,085; 1,268 jobs averaging $1864. ***State or other work-study/employment:*** *Total amount:* $6,882,312 (24% need-based, 76% non-need-based). 3,629 part-time jobs averaging $1896.

ATHLETIC AWARDS *Total amount:* 2,078,615 (28% need-based, 72% non-need-based).

APPLYING for FINANCIAL AID ***Required financial aid form:*** FAFSA. ***Financial aid deadline (priority):*** 2/21. ***Notification date:*** Continuous beginning 4/1. Students must reply within 4 weeks of notification.

CONTACT Ms. Terry Viau, Director of Scholarships and Financial Aid, Central Michigan University, WA 202, Mount Pleasant, MI 48859, 517-774-7424. *Fax:* 517-774-3634.

CENTRAL MISSOURI STATE UNIVERSITY

Warrensburg, MO

Tuition & fees (MO res): $2970 **Average undergraduate aid package: $7975**

ABOUT THE INSTITUTION State-supported, coed. Awards: associate, bachelor's, and master's degrees and post-master's certificates. 96 undergraduate majors. Total enrollment: 10,894. Undergraduates: 9,074. Freshmen: 1,412. Federal methodology is used as a basis for awarding need-based institutional aid.

UNDERGRADUATE EXPENSES for 1999–2000 ***Application fee:*** $25. ***Tuition, state resident:*** full-time $2970; part-time $99 per credit hour. ***Tuition, nonresident:*** full-time $5940; part-time $198 per credit hour. ***College room and board:*** $4104; ***room only:*** $2600. Room and board charges vary according to board plan and housing facility. ***Payment plans:*** installment, deferred payment.

FRESHMAN FINANCIAL AID (Fall 1999, est.) 1208 applied for aid; of those 60% were deemed to have need. 97% of freshmen with need received aid; of those 80% had need fully met. *Average percent of need met:* 69% (excluding resources awarded to replace EFC). *Average financial aid package:* $5750 (excluding resources awarded to replace EFC). 23% of all full-time freshmen had no need and received non-need-based aid.

UNDERGRADUATE FINANCIAL AID (Fall 1999, est.) 6,484 applied for aid; of those 60% were deemed to have need. 97% of undergraduates with need received aid; of those 78% had need fully met. *Average percent of need met:* 75% (excluding resources awarded to replace EFC). *Average financial aid package:* $7975 (excluding resources awarded to replace EFC). 23% of all full-time undergraduates had no need and received non-need-based aid.

GIFT AID (NEED-BASED) ***Total amount:*** $6,045,000 (97% Federal, 3% state). ***Receiving aid:*** *Freshmen:* 33% (440); *all full-time undergraduates:* 33% (2,340). ***Average award:*** Freshmen: $3250; Undergraduates: $2975. ***Scholarships, grants, and awards:*** Federal Pell, FSEOG, state, private, college/university gift aid from institutional funds.

GIFT AID (NON-NEED-BASED) ***Total amount:*** $6,340,000 (19% state, 60% institutional, 21% external sources). ***Receiving aid:*** *Freshmen:* 37% (489); *Undergraduates:* 25% (1,765). ***Scholarships, grants, and awards by category:*** *Academic Interests/Achievement:* 471 awards ($148,732 total): agriculture, biological sciences, business, communication, computer science, education, engineering/technologies, English, foreign languages, general academic interests/achievements, health fields, home economics, humanities, mathematics, military science, physical sciences, premedicine, religion/biblical studies, social sciences. *Creative Arts/Performance:* 436 awards ($129,441 total): applied art and design, art/fine arts, cinema/film/broadcasting, creative writing, debating, journalism/publications, music, performing arts, theater/drama. *Special Achievements/Activities:* 46 awards ($24,934 total): cheerleading/drum major, general special achievements/activities, leadership. *Special Characteristics:* 252 awards ($404,400 total): adult students, children and siblings of alumni, children of faculty/staff, ethnic background, first-generation college students, out-of-state students, previous college experience. ***Tuition waivers:*** Full or partial for children of alumni, employees or children of employees, senior citizens. ***ROTC:*** Army.

LOANS ***Student loans:*** $22,550,000 (65% need-based, 35% non-need-based). 55% of past graduating class borrowed through all loan programs. ***Average need-based loan:*** Freshmen: $2600; Undergraduates: $4500. ***Parent loans:*** $2,700,000 (100% non-need-based). ***Programs:*** Federal Direct (Subsidized and Unsubsidized Stafford, PLUS), Perkins, college/university.

WORK-STUDY ***Federal work-study:*** *Total amount:* $650,000; 500 jobs averaging $1300. ***State or other work-study/employment:*** *Total amount:* $2,200,000 (100% non-need-based). 1,467 part-time jobs averaging $1500.

ATHLETIC AWARDS *Total amount:* 890,000 (100% non-need-based).

APPLYING for FINANCIAL AID ***Required financial aid form:*** FAFSA. ***Financial aid deadline (priority):*** 3/1. ***Notification date:*** Continuous. Students must reply within 2 weeks of notification.

CONTACT Mr. Phil Shreves, Director of Financial Aid, Central Missouri State University, Office of Financial Aid, Administration Building 316, Warrensburg, MO 64093, 660-543-4040 or toll-free 800-956-0177 (in-state). *Fax:* 660-543-8080. *E-mail:* fedaid@cmsuvmb.cmsu.edu

CENTRAL STATE UNIVERSITY

Wilberforce, OH

Tuition & fees (OH res): $3443 **Average undergraduate aid package: N/A**

ABOUT THE INSTITUTION State-supported, coed. Awards: bachelor's and master's degrees. 46 undergraduate majors. Total enrollment: 1,026. Undergraduates: 998. Freshmen: 254. Federal methodology is used as a basis for awarding need-based institutional aid.

UNDERGRADUATE EXPENSES for 1999–2000 ***Application fee:*** $15. ***Tuition, state resident:*** full-time $3443; part-time $94 per quarter hour. ***Tuition, nonresident:*** full-time $7566; part-time $219 per quarter hour. ***College room and board:*** $4860; ***room only:*** $2499. ***Payment plan:*** installment.

GIFT AID (NEED-BASED) ***Scholarships, grants, and awards:*** Federal Pell, FSEOG, state, private, college/university gift aid from institutional funds.

GIFT AID (NON-NEED-BASED) ***Scholarships, grants, and awards by category:*** *Academic Interests/Achievement:* business, computer science, education, engineering/technologies, general academic interests/achievements, physical sciences. *Creative Arts/Performance:* music. *Special Characteristics:* children of faculty/staff, veterans, veterans' children. ***Tuition waivers:*** Full or partial for employees or children of employees. ***ROTC:*** Army.

LOANS ***Programs:*** FFEL (Subsidized and Unsubsidized Stafford, PLUS).

WORK-STUDY Federal work-study jobs available.

APPLYING for FINANCIAL AID ***Required financial aid form:*** FAFSA. ***Financial aid deadline (priority):*** 4/30. ***Notification date:*** Continuous. Students must reply within 2 weeks of notification.

CONTACT Financial Aid Counselor, Central State University, 1400 Brush Row Road, Wilberforce, OH 45384, 937-376-6011 or toll-free 800-388-CSU1 (in-state). *Fax:* 937-376-6530.

CENTRAL WASHINGTON UNIVERSITY

Ellensburg, WA

Tuition & fees (WA res): $3162 **Average undergraduate aid package: N/A**

ABOUT THE INSTITUTION State-supported, coed. Awards: bachelor's and master's degrees. 66 undergraduate majors. Total enrollment: 8,233. Undergraduates: 7,729. Freshmen: 1,080. Federal methodology is used as a basis for awarding need-based institutional aid.

UNDERGRADUATE EXPENSES for 2000–2001 (est.) ***Application fee:*** $40. ***Tuition, state resident:*** full-time $2838; part-time $95 per credit. ***Tuition, nonresident:*** full-time $10,089; part-time $336 per credit. ***Required fees:*** full-time $324; $6 per credit; $48 per term part-time. Full-time tuition and fees vary according to location. Part-time tuition and fees vary according

Central Washington University (continued)

to course load and location. ***College room and board:*** $4821. Room and board charges vary according to board plan and housing facility.

UNDERGRADUATE FINANCIAL AID (Fall 1998) 5,245 applied for aid; of those 100% were deemed to have need. 77% of undergraduates with need received aid; of those 22% had need fully met. *Average percent of need met:* 60% (excluding resources awarded to replace EFC). 16% of all full-time undergraduates had no need and received non-need-based aid.

GIFT AID (NEED-BASED) ***Total amount:*** $10,415,281 (44% Federal, 39% state, 11% institutional, 6% external sources). ***Receiving aid:*** *All full-time undergraduates:* 55% (4,044). ***Scholarships, grants, and awards:*** Federal Pell, FSEOG, state, private, college/university gift aid from institutional funds.

GIFT AID (NON-NEED-BASED) ***Total amount:*** $414,439 (84% institutional, 16% external sources). ***Scholarships, grants, and awards by category:*** *Academic Interests/Achievement:* education, English, general academic interests/achievements, mathematics, physical sciences, premedicine. *Creative Arts/Performance:* music, theater/drama. *Special Achievements/Activities:* hobbies/interests, memberships. *Special Characteristics:* adult students. ***Tuition waivers:*** Full or partial for employees or children of employees, senior citizens. ***ROTC:*** Army, Air Force.

LOANS ***Student loans:*** $25,087,573 (58% need-based, 42% non-need-based). Average indebtedness per student: $18,929. ***Average need-based loan:*** Undergraduates: $5500. ***Parent loans:*** $5,425,358 (100% non-need-based). ***Programs:*** Federal Direct (Subsidized and Unsubsidized Stafford, PLUS), Perkins.

WORK-STUDY ***Federal work-study:*** *Total amount:* $391,021; 130 jobs averaging $3000. ***State or other work-study/employment:*** *Total amount:* $474,811 (100% need-based). 158 part-time jobs averaging $3000.

ATHLETIC AWARDS *Total amount:* 210,248 (68% need-based, 32% non-need-based).

APPLYING for FINANCIAL AID ***Required financial aid form:*** FAFSA. ***Financial aid deadline (priority):*** 3/1. ***Notification date:*** Continuous beginning 3/15. Students must reply within 4 weeks of notification.

CONTACT Ms. Agnes Canedo, Director of Financial Aid, Central Washington University, 400 East 8th Avenue, Ellensburg, WA 98926-7495, 509-963-3049. *Fax:* 509-963-1788. *E-mail:* canedoa@cwu.edu

CENTRAL YESHIVA TOMCHEI TMIMIM-LUBAVITCH

Brooklyn, NY

CONTACT Rabbi Moshe M. Gluckowsky, Director of Financial Aid, Central Yeshiva Tomchei Tmimim-Lubavitch, 841-853 Ocean Parkway, Brooklyn, NY 11230, 718-859-2277.

CENTRE COLLEGE

Danville, KY

Comprehensive fee: $21,350 **Average undergraduate aid package: $15,120**

ABOUT THE INSTITUTION Independent religious, coed. Awards: bachelor's degrees. 31 undergraduate majors. Total enrollment: 1,022. Undergraduates: 1,022. Freshmen: 250. Both federal and institutional methodology are used as a basis for awarding need-based institutional aid.

UNDERGRADUATE EXPENSES for 1999–2000 ***Application fee:*** $30. ***Comprehensive fee:*** $21,350. Room and board charges vary according to board plan. ***Part-time tuition:*** $495 per semester hour. Part-time tuition and fees vary according to course load. ***Payment plan:*** installment.

FRESHMAN FINANCIAL AID (Fall 1999) 210 applied for aid; of those 80% were deemed to have need. 100% of freshmen with need received aid; of those 29% had need fully met. *Average percent of need met:* 100% (excluding resources awarded to replace EFC). *Average financial aid package:* $14,691 (excluding resources awarded to replace EFC). 28% of all full-time freshmen had no need and received non-need-based aid.

UNDERGRADUATE FINANCIAL AID (Fall 1999) 682 applied for aid; of those 87% were deemed to have need. 99% of undergraduates with need received aid; of those 37% had need fully met. *Average percent of need met:* 100% (excluding resources awarded to replace EFC). *Average financial aid package:* $15,120 (excluding resources awarded to replace EFC). 34% of all full-time undergraduates had no need and received non-need-based aid.

GIFT AID (NEED-BASED) ***Total amount:*** $5,868,620 (8% Federal, 12% state, 80% institutional). ***Receiving aid:*** *Freshmen:* 68% (169); *all full-time undergraduates:* 57% (579). ***Average award:*** Freshmen: $11,413; Undergraduates: $10,661. ***Scholarships, grants, and awards:*** Federal Pell, FSEOG, state, private, college/university gift aid from institutional funds.

GIFT AID (NON-NEED-BASED) ***Total amount:*** $2,250,623 (2% Federal, 4% state, 78% institutional, 16% external sources). ***Receiving aid:*** *Freshmen:* 27% (68); *Undergraduates:* 34% (344). ***Scholarships, grants, and awards by category:*** *Academic Interests/Achievement:* 585 awards ($2,693,050 total): general academic interests/achievements. *Special Characteristics:* 212 awards ($665,150 total): children and siblings of alumni, children of faculty/staff, local/state students, members of minority groups. ***Tuition waivers:*** Full or partial for children of alumni, employees or children of employees. ***ROTC:*** Army cooperative, Air Force cooperative.

LOANS ***Student loans:*** $2,110,075 (78% need-based, 22% non-need-based). 56% of past graduating class borrowed through all loan programs. Average indebtedness per student: $13,000. ***Average need-based loan:*** Freshmen: $3134; Undergraduates: $5634. ***Parent loans:*** $709,471 (100% non-need-based). ***Programs:*** FFEL (Subsidized and Unsubsidized Stafford, PLUS), Perkins, college/university.

WORK-STUDY ***Federal work-study:*** *Total amount:* $502,172; 392 jobs averaging $1281. ***State or other work-study/employment:*** *Total amount:* $73,450 (8% need-based, 92% non-need-based). Part-time jobs available.

APPLYING for FINANCIAL AID ***Required financial aid forms:*** FAFSA, institution's own form. ***Financial aid deadline:*** 3/1. ***Notification date:*** 4/1. Students must reply within 2 weeks of notification.

CONTACT Ms. Elaine Larson, Director of Student Financial Planning, Centre College, 600 West Walnut Street, Danville, KY 40422-1394, 606-238-5365 or toll-free 800-423-6236. *Fax:* 606-238-5373. *E-mail:* finaid@centre.edu

CHADRON STATE COLLEGE

Chadron, NE

Tuition & fees (NE res): $2263 **Average undergraduate aid package: N/A**

ABOUT THE INSTITUTION State-supported, coed. Awards: bachelor's and master's degrees. 31 undergraduate majors. Total enrollment: 2,768. Undergraduates: 2,483. Freshmen: 449. Federal methodology is used as a basis for awarding need-based institutional aid.

UNDERGRADUATE EXPENSES for 1999–2000 ***Application fee:*** $15. ***Tuition, state resident:*** full-time $1875; part-time $62 per semester hour. ***Tuition, nonresident:*** full-time $3750; part-time $125 per semester hour. ***Required fees:*** full-time $388; $11 per semester hour; $15 per term part-time. Full-time tuition and fees vary according to course load. Part-time tuition and fees vary according to course load. ***College room and board:*** $3300; ***room only:*** $1566. Room and board charges vary according to board plan and housing facility. ***Payment plan:*** installment.

GIFT AID (NEED-BASED) ***Total amount:*** $2,387,853 (82% Federal, 4% state, 14% external sources). ***Scholarships, grants, and awards:*** Federal Pell, FSEOG, state, private.

GIFT AID (NON-NEED-BASED) ***Scholarships, grants, and awards by category:*** *Academic Interests/Achievement:* general academic interests/achievements, health fields. *Creative Arts/Performance:* art/fine arts. *Special Achievements/Activities:* general special achievements/activities, rodeo. *Special Characteristics:* children of faculty/staff, general special characteristics, international students, local/state students, members of minority groups, out-of-state students, veterans, veterans' children. ***Tuition waivers:*** Full or partial for employees or children of employees, senior citizens.

LOANS ***Student loans:*** $3,309,497 (57% need-based, 43% non-need-based). Average indebtedness per student: $11,000. ***Parent loans:*** $305,807

(100% non-need-based). ***Programs:*** Federal Direct (Subsidized and Unsubsidized Stafford, PLUS), FFEL (Subsidized and Unsubsidized Stafford, PLUS), Perkins.

WORK-STUDY ***Federal work-study:*** *Total amount:* $444,709; jobs available.

APPLYING for FINANCIAL AID ***Required financial aid forms:*** FAFSA, institution's own form. ***Financial aid deadline (priority):*** 6/1. ***Notification date:*** Continuous. Students must reply within 2 weeks of notification.

CONTACT Ms. Sherry Douglas, Director of Financial Aid, Chadron State College, 1000 Main Street, Chadron, NE 69337, 308-432-6230 or toll-free 800-CHADRON (in-state). *Fax:* 308-432-6229. *E-mail:* sdouglas@csc1.csc.edu

CHAMINADE UNIVERSITY OF HONOLULU

Honolulu, HI

Tuition & fees: $11,700 **Average undergraduate aid package: $9261**

ABOUT THE INSTITUTION Independent Roman Catholic, coed. Awards: associate, bachelor's, and master's degrees. 23 undergraduate majors. Total enrollment: 2,740. Undergraduates: 2,029. Freshmen: 134. Federal methodology is used as a basis for awarding need-based institutional aid.

UNDERGRADUATE EXPENSES for 1999–2000 ***Application fee:*** $50. ***Comprehensive fee:*** $17,370 includes full-time tuition ($11,600), mandatory fees ($100), and room and board ($5670). ***College room only:*** $3100. Full-time tuition and fees vary according to class time. Room and board charges vary according to board plan and housing facility. ***Part-time tuition:*** $390 per credit hour. Part-time tuition and fees vary according to class time and course load. ***Payment plan:*** deferred payment.

FRESHMAN FINANCIAL AID (Fall 1998) 157 applied for aid; of those 90% were deemed to have need. 99% of freshmen with need received aid; of those 59% had need fully met. *Average percent of need met:* 52% (excluding resources awarded to replace EFC). *Average financial aid package:* $7419 (excluding resources awarded to replace EFC). 12% of all full-time freshmen had no need and received non-need-based aid.

UNDERGRADUATE FINANCIAL AID (Fall 1998) 804 applied for aid; of those 94% were deemed to have need. 100% of undergraduates with need received aid; of those 70% had need fully met. *Average percent of need met:* 73% (excluding resources awarded to replace EFC). *Average financial aid package:* $9261 (excluding resources awarded to replace EFC). 13% of all full-time undergraduates had no need and received non-need-based aid.

GIFT AID (NEED-BASED) ***Total amount:*** $1,120,379 (98% Federal, 2% state). ***Receiving aid:*** *Freshmen:* 65% (121); *all full-time undergraduates:* 50% (519). ***Average award:*** Freshmen: $5080; Undergraduates: $5359. ***Scholarships, grants, and awards:*** Federal Pell, FSEOG, state, private, college/university gift aid from institutional funds.

GIFT AID (NON-NEED-BASED) ***Total amount:*** $3,100,576 (71% institutional, 29% external sources). ***Receiving aid:*** *Freshmen:* 51% (95); *Undergraduates:* 59% (619). ***Scholarships, grants, and awards by category:*** *Academic Interests/Achievement:* biological sciences, business, communication, education, English, general academic interests/achievements, humanities, military science, social sciences. *Special Achievements/Activities:* community service, leadership, religious involvement. *Special Characteristics:* children and siblings of alumni, children of current students, children of faculty/staff, ethnic background, international students, local/state students, out-of-state students, parents of current students, previous college experience, religious affiliation, siblings of current students, spouses of current students, veterans. ***Tuition waivers:*** Full or partial for employees or children of employees. ***ROTC:*** Army cooperative, Air Force cooperative.

LOANS ***Student loans:*** $6,027,681 (58% need-based, 42% non-need-based). 31% of past graduating class borrowed through all loan programs. Average indebtedness per student: $21,805. ***Average need-based loan:*** Freshmen: $1958; Undergraduates: $3796. ***Parent loans:*** $881,966 (100% non-need-based). ***Programs:*** FFEL (Subsidized and Unsubsidized Stafford, PLUS), Perkins, CitiAssist Loans, Sallie Mae's Signature Education Loan Program, alternative loans.

WORK-STUDY ***Federal work-study:*** *Total amount:* $161,374; 248 jobs available.

ATHLETIC AWARDS *Total amount:* 444,116 (100% non-need-based).

APPLYING for FINANCIAL AID ***Required financial aid forms:*** FAFSA, institution's own form. ***Financial aid deadline (priority):*** 3/1. ***Notification date:*** Continuous. Students must reply within 3 weeks of notification.

CONTACT Mr. Eric Nemoto, Director of Financial Aid, Chaminade University of Honolulu, 3140 Waialae Avenue, Honolulu, HI 96816-1578, 808-735-4780 or toll-free 800-735-3733 (out-of-state). *Fax:* 808-739-8362. *E-mail:* enemoto@chaminade.edu

CHAMPLAIN COLLEGE

Burlington, VT

Tuition & fees: $10,585 **Average undergraduate aid package: $8532**

ABOUT THE INSTITUTION Independent, coed. Awards: associate and bachelor's degrees (the baccalaureate programs are part of the 2+2 curriculum). 26 undergraduate majors. Total enrollment: 2,440. Undergraduates: 2,440. Freshmen: 462. Both federal and institutional methodology are used as a basis for awarding need-based institutional aid.

UNDERGRADUATE EXPENSES for 1999–2000 ***Application fee:*** $35. ***Comprehensive fee:*** $18,035 includes full-time tuition ($10,485), mandatory fees ($100), and room and board ($7450). ***College room only:*** $4445. Room and board charges vary according to board plan. ***Part-time tuition:*** $318 per credit hour. ***Payment plan:*** installment.

FRESHMAN FINANCIAL AID (Fall 1999, est.) 437 applied for aid; of those 88% were deemed to have need. 100% of freshmen with need received aid; of those 13% had need fully met. *Average percent of need met:* 66% (excluding resources awarded to replace EFC). *Average financial aid package:* $8223 (excluding resources awarded to replace EFC). 14% of all full-time freshmen had no need and received non-need-based aid.

UNDERGRADUATE FINANCIAL AID (Fall 1999, est.) 1,077 applied for aid; of those 89% were deemed to have need. 100% of undergraduates with need received aid; of those 16% had need fully met. *Average percent of need met:* 69% (excluding resources awarded to replace EFC). *Average financial aid package:* $8532 (excluding resources awarded to replace EFC). 13% of all full-time undergraduates had no need and received non-need-based aid.

GIFT AID (NEED-BASED) ***Total amount:*** $4,163,587 (34% Federal, 36% state, 21% institutional, 9% external sources). ***Receiving aid:*** *Freshmen:* 66% (327); *all full-time undergraduates:* 67% (816). ***Average award:*** Freshmen: $4030; Undergraduates: $3922. ***Scholarships, grants, and awards:*** Federal Pell, FSEOG, state, private, college/university gift aid from institutional funds.

GIFT AID (NON-NEED-BASED) ***Total amount:*** $154,547 (9% state, 65% institutional, 26% external sources). ***Receiving aid:*** *Freshmen:* 2% (10); *Undergraduates:* 2% (22). ***Tuition waivers:*** Full or partial for employees or children of employees, senior citizens. ***ROTC:*** Army cooperative.

LOANS ***Student loans:*** $6,527,610 (82% need-based, 18% non-need-based). 92% of past graduating class borrowed through all loan programs. ***Average need-based loan:*** Freshmen: $3857; Undergraduates: $4273. ***Parent loans:*** $4,349,608 (40% need-based, 60% non-need-based). ***Programs:*** FFEL (Subsidized and Unsubsidized Stafford, PLUS), Perkins.

WORK-STUDY ***Federal work-study:*** *Total amount:* $374,960; jobs available.

ATHLETIC AWARDS *Total amount:* 173,552 (38% need-based, 62% non-need-based).

APPLYING for FINANCIAL AID ***Required financial aid forms:*** FAFSA, institution's own form, state aid form, noncustodial (divorced/separated) parent's statement. ***Financial aid deadline (priority):*** 5/1. ***Notification date:*** Continuous. Students must reply within 2 weeks of notification.

CONTACT David B. Myette, Director of Financial Aid, Champlain College, 163 South Willard Street, Burlington, VT 05401, 802-860-2730 or toll-free 800-570-5858. *Fax:* 802-860-2775. *E-mail:* myette@champlain.edu

CHAPMAN UNIVERSITY
Orange, CA

Tuition & fees: $20,994 **Average undergraduate aid package: $18,054**

ABOUT THE INSTITUTION Independent religious, coed. Awards: bachelor's, master's, and first professional degrees. 66 undergraduate majors. Total enrollment: 3,897. Undergraduates: 2,594. Freshmen: 562. Federal methodology is used as a basis for awarding need-based institutional aid.

UNDERGRADUATE EXPENSES for 2000–2001 (est.) ***Application fee:*** $30. ***Comprehensive fee:*** $28,614 includes full-time tuition ($20,724), mandatory fees ($270), and room and board ($7620). Room and board charges vary according to board plan and housing facility. ***Part-time tuition:*** $645 per credit. ***Part-time fees:*** $30 per term part-time. Part-time tuition and fees vary according to course load. ***Payment plans:*** tuition prepayment, installment, deferred payment.

FRESHMAN FINANCIAL AID (Fall 1998) 509 applied for aid; of those 77% were deemed to have need. 99% of freshmen with need received aid; of those 26% had need fully met. *Average percent of need met:* 83% (excluding resources awarded to replace EFC). *Average financial aid package:* $17,340 (excluding resources awarded to replace EFC). 14% of all full-time freshmen had no need and received non-need-based aid.

UNDERGRADUATE FINANCIAL AID (Fall 1998) 2,178 applied for aid; of those 82% were deemed to have need. 98% of undergraduates with need received aid; of those 25% had need fully met. *Average percent of need met:* 82% (excluding resources awarded to replace EFC). *Average financial aid package:* $18,054 (excluding resources awarded to replace EFC). 10% of all full-time undergraduates had no need and received non-need-based aid.

GIFT AID (NEED-BASED) ***Total amount:*** $21,724,648 (11% Federal, 13% state, 74% institutional, 2% external sources). ***Receiving aid:*** *Freshmen:* 75% (381); *all full-time undergraduates:* 70% (1,735). ***Average award:*** Freshmen: $13,284; Undergraduates: $11,908. ***Scholarships, grants, and awards:*** Federal Pell, FSEOG, state, college/university gift aid from institutional funds.

GIFT AID (NON-NEED-BASED) ***Total amount:*** $2,102,934 (98% institutional, 2% external sources). ***Scholarships, grants, and awards by category:*** *Academic Interests/Achievement:* 924 awards ($7,565,248 total): general academic interests/achievements, social sciences. *Creative Arts/Performance:* 95 awards ($917,831 total): art/fine arts, cinema/film/broadcasting, creative writing, dance, journalism/publications, music, theater/drama. *Special Achievements/Activities:* religious involvement. *Special Characteristics:* 118 awards ($173,000 total): children and siblings of alumni, relatives of clergy, religious affiliation. ***Tuition waivers:*** Full or partial for children of alumni, employees or children of employees. ***ROTC:*** Army cooperative, Air Force cooperative.

LOANS ***Student loans:*** $10,147,394 (96% need-based, 4% non-need-based). 59% of past graduating class borrowed through all loan programs. Average indebtedness per student: $18,893. ***Average need-based loan:*** Freshmen: $3629; Undergraduates: $5856. ***Parent loans:*** $3,301,896 (87% need-based, 13% non-need-based). ***Programs:*** FFEL (Subsidized and Unsubsidized Stafford, PLUS), Perkins, college/university.

WORK-STUDY ***Federal work-study:*** *Total amount:* $614,368; 474 jobs averaging $1296.

APPLYING for FINANCIAL AID ***Required financial aid forms:*** FAFSA, state aid form. ***Financial aid deadline (priority):*** 3/1. ***Notification date:*** 4/1. Students must reply within 3 weeks of notification.

CONTACT Gregory L. Ball, Director of Financial Aid, Chapman University, 333 North Glassell, Orange, CA 92866, 714-997-6741 or toll-free 888-CUAPPLY. *Fax:* 714-997-6743. *E-mail:* gball@chapman.edu

CHARLES R. DREW UNIVERSITY OF MEDICINE AND SCIENCE
Los Angeles, CA

Tuition & fees: $8400 **Average undergraduate aid package: N/A**

ABOUT THE INSTITUTION Independent, coed. Awards: associate, bachelor's, master's, and doctoral degrees. 7 undergraduate majors. Total enrollment: 653. Undergraduates: 232. Federal methodology is used as a basis for awarding need-based institutional aid.

UNDERGRADUATE EXPENSES for 1999–2000 ***Application fee:*** $35. ***One-time required fee:*** $100. ***Tuition:*** full-time $8400; part-time $200 per unit. Full-time tuition and fees vary according to course load.

GIFT AID (NEED-BASED) ***Scholarships, grants, and awards:*** Federal Pell, FSEOG, state, college/university gift aid from institutional funds.

LOANS ***Programs:*** FFEL (Subsidized and Unsubsidized Stafford, PLUS), Perkins, alternative loans.

WORK-STUDY Federal work-study jobs available.

APPLYING for FINANCIAL AID ***Required financial aid form:*** FAFSA. ***Financial aid deadline:*** 7/31 (priority: 5/2). ***Notification date:*** Continuous. Students must reply within 8 weeks of notification.

CONTACT Financial Aid Administrator, Charles R. Drew University of Medicine and Science, 1731 East 120th Street, Los Angeles, CA 90059, 323-563-4824. *Fax:* 323-569-0597.

CHARLESTON SOUTHERN UNIVERSITY
Charleston, SC

Tuition & fees: $10,410 **Average undergraduate aid package: $11,500**

ABOUT THE INSTITUTION Independent Baptist, coed. Awards: associate, bachelor's, and master's degrees. 42 undergraduate majors. Total enrollment: 2,594. Undergraduates: 2,359. Freshmen: 557. Federal methodology is used as a basis for awarding need-based institutional aid.

UNDERGRADUATE EXPENSES for 1999–2000 ***Application fee:*** $25. ***Comprehensive fee:*** $14,412 includes full-time tuition ($10,410) and room and board ($4002). Room and board charges vary according to housing facility. ***Part-time tuition:*** $170 per credit hour. Part-time tuition and fees vary according to course load.

FRESHMAN FINANCIAL AID (Fall 1999, est.) 813 applied for aid. *Average percent of need met:* 91% (excluding resources awarded to replace EFC). *Average financial aid package:* $11,500 (excluding resources awarded to replace EFC).

UNDERGRADUATE FINANCIAL AID (Fall 1999, est.) 1,665 applied for aid. *Average percent of need met:* 91% (excluding resources awarded to replace EFC). *Average financial aid package:* $11,500 (excluding resources awarded to replace EFC).

GIFT AID (NEED-BASED) ***Total amount:*** $4,182,952 (47% Federal, 52% state, 1% institutional). ***Scholarships, grants, and awards:*** Federal Pell, FSEOG, state, private, college/university gift aid from institutional funds.

GIFT AID (NON-NEED-BASED) ***Total amount:*** $3,423,905 (14% state, 78% institutional, 8% external sources). ***Scholarships, grants, and awards by category:*** *Academic Interests/Achievement:* 1,000 awards ($3,000,000 total): general academic interests/achievements. *Creative Arts/Performance:* 96 awards ($185,000 total): art/fine arts, music, performing arts. *Special Achievements/Activities:* $17,000 total: religious involvement. *Special Characteristics:* 210 awards ($459,500 total): adult students, children of faculty/staff, out-of-state students, relatives of clergy, religious affiliation. ***ROTC:*** Air Force.

LOANS ***Student loans:*** $9,748,429 (53% need-based, 47% non-need-based). Average indebtedness per student: $17,125. ***Parent loans:*** $1,449,881 (100% non-need-based). ***Programs:*** FFEL (Subsidized and Unsubsidized Stafford, PLUS), Perkins, state, college/university.

WORK-STUDY ***Federal work-study:*** *Total amount:* $828,098; 442 jobs averaging $1873.

ATHLETIC AWARDS *Total amount:* 1,419,902 (100% non-need-based).

APPLYING for FINANCIAL AID ***Required financial aid form:*** FAFSA. ***Financial aid deadline (priority):*** 4/15. ***Notification date:*** Continuous. Students must reply within 1 week of notification.

CONTACT Shannon K. Smith, Assistant Director of Financial Aid, Charleston Southern University, PO Box 118087, 9200 University Boulevard, Charleston, SC 29423-8087, 843-863-7050 or toll-free 800-947-7474. *Fax:* 843-863-7070.

CHARTER OAK STATE COLLEGE

New Britain, CT

ABOUT THE INSTITUTION State-supported, coed. Awards: associate and bachelor's degrees (offers only external degree programs). 1 undergraduate major. Total enrollment: 1,429. Undergraduates: 1,429.

GIFT AID (NEED-BASED) ***Scholarships, grants, and awards:*** college/university gift aid from institutional funds.

GIFT AID (NON-NEED-BASED) ***Scholarships, grants, and awards by category:*** *Academic Interests/Achievement:* general academic interests/achievements.

LOANS ***Programs:*** alternative loans.

APPLYING for FINANCIAL AID ***Required financial aid form:*** institution's own form.

CONTACT Mr. Paul Morganti, Convener, Financial Aid Committee, Charter Oak State College, 66 Cedar Street, Newington, CT 06111-2646, 860-666-4595 Ext. 25. *E-mail:* pmorganti@commnet.edu

CHATHAM COLLEGE

Pittsburgh, PA

Tuition & fees: $17,544 **Average undergraduate aid package: $17,247**

ABOUT THE INSTITUTION Independent, women only. Awards: bachelor's and master's degrees and post-bachelor's certificates. 37 undergraduate majors. Total enrollment: 1,009. Undergraduates: 580. Freshmen: 145. Both federal and institutional methodology are used as a basis for awarding need-based institutional aid.

UNDERGRADUATE EXPENSES for 1999–2000 ***Application fee:*** $25. ***Comprehensive fee:*** $23,664 includes full-time tuition ($17,388), mandatory fees ($156), and room and board ($6120). ***College room only:*** $3150. Room and board charges vary according to board plan. ***Part-time tuition:*** $423 per credit. ***Part-time fees:*** $39 per term part-time. ***Payment plan:*** installment.

FRESHMAN FINANCIAL AID (Fall 1999) 121 applied for aid; of those 90% were deemed to have need. 100% of freshmen with need received aid; of those 5% had need fully met. *Average percent of need met:* 65% (excluding resources awarded to replace EFC). *Average financial aid package:* $15,357 (excluding resources awarded to replace EFC). 5% of all full-time freshmen had no need and received non-need-based aid.

UNDERGRADUATE FINANCIAL AID (Fall 1999) 412 applied for aid; of those 92% were deemed to have need. 100% of undergraduates with need received aid; of those 2% had need fully met. *Average percent of need met:* 63% (excluding resources awarded to replace EFC). *Average financial aid package:* $17,247 (excluding resources awarded to replace EFC). 3% of all full-time undergraduates had no need and received non-need-based aid.

GIFT AID (NEED-BASED) ***Total amount:*** $4,319,181 (13% Federal, 13% state, 71% institutional, 3% external sources). ***Receiving aid:*** *Freshmen:* 63% (92); *all full-time undergraduates:* 72% (332). ***Average award:*** Freshmen: $7175; Undergraduates: $6238. ***Scholarships, grants, and awards:*** Federal Pell, FSEOG, state, private, college/university gift aid from institutional funds.

GIFT AID (NON-NEED-BASED) ***Total amount:*** $220,224 (100% institutional). ***Scholarships, grants, and awards by category:*** *Academic Interests/Achievement:* 408 awards ($2,094,107 total): general academic interests/achievements. *Creative Arts/Performance:* 3 awards ($9500 total): music, theater/drama. *Special Characteristics:* 72 awards ($203,119 total): children and siblings of alumni, children of faculty/staff, international students. ***Tuition waivers:*** Full or partial for employees or children of employees. ***ROTC:*** Army cooperative, Naval cooperative, Air Force cooperative.

LOANS ***Student loans:*** $2,076,630 (72% need-based, 28% non-need-based). 99% of past graduating class borrowed through all loan programs. Average indebtedness per student: $17,000. ***Average need-based loan:*** Freshmen: $2460; Undergraduates: $5163. ***Parent loans:*** $672,303 (76% need-based, 24% non-need-based). ***Programs:*** FFEL (Subsidized and Unsubsidized Stafford, PLUS), Perkins, alternative loans.

WORK-STUDY ***Federal work-study:*** *Total amount:* $534,400; 288 jobs averaging $1856.

APPLYING for FINANCIAL AID ***Required financial aid form:*** FAFSA. ***Financial aid deadline:*** 5/1. ***Notification date:*** Continuous. Students must reply within 2 weeks of notification.

CONTACT Lynn Jakub, Director of Financial Aid, Chatham College, Woodland Road, Pittsburgh, PA 15232-2826, 800-837-1610 Ext. 1777 or toll-free 800-837-1290. *Fax:* 412-365-1643.

CHESTNUT HILL COLLEGE

Philadelphia, PA

ABOUT THE INSTITUTION Independent Roman Catholic, women only. Awards: associate, bachelor's, master's, and doctoral degrees and post-bachelor's and post-master's certificates. 32 undergraduate majors. Total enrollment: 1,592. Undergraduates: 962. Freshmen: 117.

GIFT AID (NEED-BASED) ***Scholarships, grants, and awards:*** Federal Pell, FSEOG, state, private, college/university gift aid from institutional funds.

GIFT AID (NON-NEED-BASED) ***Scholarships, grants, and awards by category:*** *Academic Interests/Achievement:* biological sciences, general academic interests/achievements, humanities, physical sciences, premedicine. *Creative Arts/Performance:* art/fine arts. *Special Achievements/Activities:* junior miss. *Special Characteristics:* adult students, children of public servants, first-generation college students, international students, local/state students, out-of-state students, relatives of clergy.

LOANS ***Programs:*** FFEL (Subsidized and Unsubsidized Stafford, PLUS), Perkins.

WORK-STUDY ***Federal work-study:*** *Total amount:* $95,682; 106 jobs averaging $750.

APPLYING for FINANCIAL AID ***Required financial aid form:*** FAFSA.

CONTACT Mr. Michael Wisniewski, Director of Financial Aid, Chestnut Hill College, 9601 Germantown Avenue, Philadelphia, PA 19118-2693, 215-248-7101 or toll-free 800-248-0052 (out-of-state). *Fax:* 215-242-7714.

CHEYNEY UNIVERSITY OF PENNSYLVANIA

Cheyney, PA

Tuition & fees (PA res): $4173 **Average undergraduate aid package: $7100**

ABOUT THE INSTITUTION State-supported, coed. Awards: bachelor's and master's degrees. 31 undergraduate majors. Total enrollment: 1,821. Undergraduates: 1,140. Freshmen: 276. Federal methodology is used as a basis for awarding need-based institutional aid.

UNDERGRADUATE EXPENSES for 1999–2000 ***Application fee:*** $20. ***Tuition, state resident:*** full-time $3618; part-time $150 per credit hour. ***Tuition, nonresident:*** full-time $9046; part-time $377 per credit hour. ***Required fees:*** full-time $555; $139 per term part-time. Full-time tuition and fees vary according to reciprocity agreements. Part-time tuition and fees vary according to reciprocity agreements. ***College room and board:*** $4793; ***room only:*** $2410. Room and board charges vary according to board plan. ***Payment plan:*** deferred payment.

FRESHMAN FINANCIAL AID (Fall 1999, est.) 256 applied for aid; of those 90% were deemed to have need. 100% of freshmen with need received aid; of those 58% had need fully met. *Average percent of need met:* 82% (excluding resources awarded to replace EFC). *Average financial aid package:* $7400 (excluding resources awarded to replace EFC). 13% of all full-time freshmen had no need and received non-need-based aid.

UNDERGRADUATE FINANCIAL AID (Fall 1999, est.) 901 applied for aid; of those 88% were deemed to have need. 100% of undergraduates with need received aid; of those 35% had need fully met. *Average percent of need met:* 80% (excluding resources awarded to replace EFC). *Average financial aid package:* $7100 (excluding resources awarded to replace EFC). 7% of all full-time undergraduates had no need and received non-need-based aid.

GIFT AID (NEED-BASED) ***Total amount:*** $3,490,743 (72% Federal, 28% state). ***Receiving aid:*** *Freshmen:* 72% (200); *all full-time undergraduates:*

Cheyney University of Pennsylvania (continued)

61% (602). ***Average award:*** Freshmen: $5700; Undergraduates: $5400. ***Scholarships, grants, and awards:*** Federal Pell, FSEOG, state, private, college/university gift aid from institutional funds.

GIFT AID (NON-NEED-BASED) ***Total amount:*** $727,096 (88% institutional, 12% external sources). ***Receiving aid:*** *Freshmen:* 24% (67); *Undergraduates:* 25% (250). ***Scholarships, grants, and awards by category:*** *Academic Interests/Achievement:* 26 awards ($27,016 total): biological sciences, computer science, education, general academic interests/achievements, mathematics, premedicine. *Special Characteristics:* 6 awards ($8400 total): children of faculty/staff, ethnic background. ***Tuition waivers:*** Full or partial for employees or children of employees. ***ROTC:*** Army, Air Force cooperative.

LOANS ***Student loans:*** $5,942,770 (60% need-based, 40% non-need-based). 95% of past graduating class borrowed through all loan programs. Average indebtedness per student: $20,000. ***Average need-based loan:*** Freshmen: $2700; Undergraduates: $3900. ***Parent loans:*** $484,684 (100% non-need-based). ***Programs:*** Federal Direct (Subsidized and Unsubsidized Stafford, PLUS), FFEL (Subsidized and Unsubsidized Stafford, PLUS), Perkins.

WORK-STUDY ***Federal work-study:*** *Total amount:* $368,828; 352 jobs averaging $1047.

ATHLETIC AWARDS *Total amount:* 58,335 (100% non-need-based).

APPLYING for FINANCIAL AID ***Required financial aid form:*** FAFSA. ***Financial aid deadline (priority):*** 5/1. ***Notification date:*** Continuous. Students must reply within 2 weeks of notification.

CONTACT Mr. James Brown, Director of Financial Aid, Cheyney University of Pennsylvania, Cheyney and Creek Roads, Cheyney, PA 19319, 610-399-2302 or toll-free 800-CHEYNEY. *Fax:* 610-399-2411. *E-mail:* jbrown@cheyney.edu

CHICAGO STATE UNIVERSITY

Chicago, IL

Tuition & fees (IL res): $3151 **Average undergraduate aid package: N/A**

ABOUT THE INSTITUTION State-supported, coed. Awards: bachelor's and master's degrees. 63 undergraduate majors. Total enrollment: 7,580. Undergraduates: 5,585. Both federal and institutional methodology are used as a basis for awarding need-based institutional aid.

UNDERGRADUATE EXPENSES for 1999–2000 ***Application fee:*** $20. ***Tuition, state resident:*** full-time $3151; part-time $96 per credit hour. ***Tuition, nonresident:*** full-time $7735; part-time $286 per credit hour. ***Required fees:*** $141 per term part-time. ***College room and board:*** $5825. ***Payment plan:*** deferred payment.

GIFT AID (NEED-BASED) ***Scholarships, grants, and awards:*** Federal Pell, FSEOG, state, private, college/university gift aid from institutional funds, United Negro College Fund.

GIFT AID (NON-NEED-BASED) ***Scholarships, grants, and awards by category:*** *Academic Interests/Achievement:* general academic interests/achievements, physical sciences. *Creative Arts/Performance:* art/fine arts, journalism/publications, music. *Special Achievements/Activities:* leadership. ***Tuition waivers:*** Full or partial for employees or children of employees, senior citizens. ***ROTC:*** Army, Naval cooperative, Air Force cooperative.

LOANS ***Programs:*** FFEL (Subsidized and Unsubsidized Stafford, PLUS), state, college/university.

WORK-STUDY Federal work-study jobs available.

APPLYING for FINANCIAL AID ***Required financial aid form:*** FAFSA. ***Financial aid deadline (priority):*** 3/30. ***Notification date:*** Continuous beginning 4/15. Students must reply within 2 weeks of notification.

CONTACT Mr. Parvesh Singh, Director of Student Financial Aid, Chicago State University, 9501 South Martin Luther King Drive, Chicago, IL 60628, 773-995-2304.

CHOWAN COLLEGE

Murfreesboro, NC

Tuition & fees: $11,520 **Average undergraduate aid package: $12,203**

ABOUT THE INSTITUTION Independent Baptist, coed. Awards: associate and bachelor's degrees. 33 undergraduate majors. Total enrollment: 726. Undergraduates: 726. Freshmen: 254. Federal methodology is used as a basis for awarding need-based institutional aid.

UNDERGRADUATE EXPENSES for 1999–2000 ***Application fee:*** $20. ***Comprehensive fee:*** $16,120 includes full-time tuition ($11,470), mandatory fees ($50), and room and board ($4600). ***College room only:*** $2130. Room and board charges vary according to board plan. ***Part-time tuition:*** $260 per hour. Part-time tuition and fees vary according to course load and program. ***Payment plans:*** installment, deferred payment.

FRESHMAN FINANCIAL AID (Fall 1999) 240 applied for aid; of those 89% were deemed to have need. 100% of freshmen with need received aid; of those 32% had need fully met. *Average percent of need met:* 87% (excluding resources awarded to replace EFC). *Average financial aid package:* $11,765 (excluding resources awarded to replace EFC). 16% of all full-time freshmen had no need and received non-need-based aid.

UNDERGRADUATE FINANCIAL AID (Fall 1999) 634 applied for aid; of those 92% were deemed to have need. 100% of undergraduates with need received aid; of those 35% had need fully met. *Average percent of need met:* 89% (excluding resources awarded to replace EFC). *Average financial aid package:* $12,203 (excluding resources awarded to replace EFC). 16% of all full-time undergraduates had no need and received non-need-based aid.

GIFT AID (NEED-BASED) ***Total amount:*** $4,543,924 (20% Federal, 10% state, 68% institutional, 2% external sources). ***Receiving aid:*** *Freshmen:* 84% (214); *all full-time undergraduates:* 84% (583). ***Average award:*** Freshmen: $7813; Undergraduates: $7639. ***Scholarships, grants, and awards:*** Federal Pell, FSEOG, state, private, college/university gift aid from institutional funds.

GIFT AID (NON-NEED-BASED) ***Total amount:*** $711,200 (15% state, 80% institutional, 5% external sources). ***Receiving aid:*** *Freshmen:* 9% (22); *Undergraduates:* 7% (48). ***Scholarships, grants, and awards by category:*** *Academic Interests/Achievement:* 569 awards ($2,276,000 total): general academic interests/achievements. *Creative Arts/Performance:* 32 awards ($49,550 total): music. *Special Achievements/Activities:* 24 awards ($276,480 total): leadership. *Special Characteristics:* 222 awards ($434,629 total): children of faculty/staff, international students, local/state students, relatives of clergy, religious affiliation. ***Tuition waivers:*** Full or partial for employees or children of employees, senior citizens.

LOANS ***Student loans:*** $2,783,364 (85% need-based, 15% non-need-based). 74% of past graduating class borrowed through all loan programs. Average indebtedness per student: $17,056. ***Average need-based loan:*** Freshmen: $3407; Undergraduates: $3985. ***Parent loans:*** $987,837 (46% need-based, 54% non-need-based). ***Programs:*** FFEL (Subsidized and Unsubsidized Stafford, PLUS), Perkins.

WORK-STUDY ***Federal work-study:*** *Total amount:* $326,923; 327 jobs averaging $1000. ***State or other work-study/employment:*** *Total amount:* $56,158 (30% need-based, 70% non-need-based). 40 part-time jobs averaging $1432.

APPLYING for FINANCIAL AID ***Required financial aid form:*** FAFSA. ***Financial aid deadline (priority):*** 5/1. ***Notification date:*** Continuous. Students must reply within 2 weeks of notification.

CONTACT Mr. Clifton S. Collins, Director of Financial Aid, Chowan College, PO Box 1848, Murfreesboro, NC 27855, 252-398-1229 or toll-free 800-488-4101. *Fax:* 252-398-1190. *E-mail:* collic@chowan.edu

CHRISTENDOM COLLEGE

Front Royal, VA

Tuition & fees: $11,530 **Average undergraduate aid package: $9085**

ABOUT THE INSTITUTION Independent Roman Catholic, coed. Awards: associate, bachelor's, and master's degrees. 8 undergraduate majors.

Total enrollment: 344. Undergraduates: 259. Freshmen: 74. Institutional methodology is used as a basis for awarding need-based institutional aid.

UNDERGRADUATE EXPENSES for 2000–2001 ***Application fee:*** $25. ***Comprehensive fee:*** $16,100 includes full-time tuition ($11,300), mandatory fees ($230), and room and board ($4570). ***Part-time tuition:*** $495 per credit. ***Part-time fees:*** $115 per term part-time. ***Payment plans:*** tuition prepayment, installment.

FRESHMAN FINANCIAL AID (Fall 1999) 59 applied for aid; of those 71% were deemed to have need. 100% of freshmen with need received aid; of those 88% had need fully met. *Average percent of need met:* 90% (excluding resources awarded to replace EFC). *Average financial aid package:* $8617 (excluding resources awarded to replace EFC). 16% of all full-time freshmen had no need and received non-need-based aid.

UNDERGRADUATE FINANCIAL AID (Fall 1999) 160 applied for aid; of those 87% were deemed to have need. 100% of undergraduates with need received aid; of those 86% had need fully met. *Average percent of need met:* 90% (excluding resources awarded to replace EFC). *Average financial aid package:* $9085 (excluding resources awarded to replace EFC). 11% of all full-time undergraduates had no need and received non-need-based aid.

GIFT AID (NEED-BASED) ***Total amount:*** $469,639 (100% institutional). ***Receiving aid:*** *Freshmen:* 53% (39); *all full-time undergraduates:* 53% (133). ***Average award:*** Freshmen: $2815; Undergraduates: $3530. ***Scholarships, grants, and awards:*** private, college/university gift aid from institutional funds.

GIFT AID (NON-NEED-BASED) ***Total amount:*** $278,751 (93% institutional, 7% external sources). ***Receiving aid:*** *Freshmen:* 22% (16); *Undergraduates:* 14% (36). ***Scholarships, grants, and awards by category:*** *Academic Interests/Achievement:* 65 awards ($260,451 total): general academic interests/achievements. ***Tuition waivers:*** Full or partial for employees or children of employees.

LOANS ***Student loans:*** $411,350 (100% need-based). 59% of past graduating class borrowed through all loan programs. Average indebtedness per student: $8980. ***Average need-based loan:*** Freshmen: $3020; Undergraduates: $3215. ***Programs:*** college/university.

WORK-STUDY ***State or other work-study/employment:*** *Total amount:* $202,500 (100% need-based). 125 part-time jobs averaging $1620.

APPLYING for FINANCIAL AID ***Required financial aid form:*** institution's own form. ***Financial aid deadline (priority):*** 4/1. ***Notification date:*** Continuous. Students must reply within 4 weeks of notification.

CONTACT Mrs. Alisa Polk, Financial Aid Officer, Christendom College, 134 Christendom Drive, Front Royal, VA 22630-5103, 800-877-5456 Ext. 214 or toll-free 800-877-5456 Ext. 290. *Fax:* 540-636-1655. *E-mail:* christdm@shentel.net

CHRISTIAN BROTHERS UNIVERSITY

Memphis, TN

Tuition & fees: $13,490 **Average undergraduate aid package: N/A**

ABOUT THE INSTITUTION Independent Roman Catholic, coed. Awards: bachelor's and master's degrees. 40 undergraduate majors. Total enrollment: 1,992. Undergraduates: 1,598. Freshmen: 245. Both federal and institutional methodology are used as a basis for awarding need-based institutional aid.

UNDERGRADUATE EXPENSES for 1999–2000 ***Application fee:*** $25. ***Comprehensive fee:*** $17,440 includes full-time tuition ($13,140), mandatory fees ($350), and room and board ($3950). Room and board charges vary according to board plan and housing facility. ***Part-time tuition:*** $390 per semester hour. ***Part-time fees:*** $25 per term part-time. Part-time tuition and fees vary according to class time. ***Payment plans:*** installment, deferred payment.

GIFT AID (NEED-BASED) ***Total amount:*** $2,588,130 (35% Federal, 11% state, 54% institutional). ***Scholarships, grants, and awards:*** Federal Pell, FSEOG, state, private, college/university gift aid from institutional funds.

GIFT AID (NON-NEED-BASED) ***Total amount:*** $3,199,920 (1% state, 97% institutional, 2% external sources). ***Scholarships, grants, and awards by category:*** *Academic Interests/Achievement:* general academic interests/achievements. *Creative Arts/Performance:* general creative arts/performance, performing arts. *Special Achievements/Activities:* general special achievements/activities. *Special Characteristics:* general special characteristics. ***Tuition waivers:*** Full or partial for children of alumni, employees or children of employees. ***ROTC:*** Army cooperative, Naval cooperative, Air Force cooperative.

LOANS ***Student loans:*** $6,376,434 (51% need-based, 49% non-need-based). ***Parent loans:*** $381,849 (100% non-need-based). ***Programs:*** FFEL (Subsidized and Unsubsidized Stafford, PLUS), Perkins, college/university.

WORK-STUDY ***Federal work-study:*** *Total amount:* $180,000; 180 jobs averaging $1000. ***State or other work-study/employment:*** *Total amount:* $230,000 (100% non-need-based). Part-time jobs available.

ATHLETIC AWARDS *Total amount:* 473,000 (100% non-need-based).

APPLYING for FINANCIAL AID ***Required financial aid form:*** FAFSA. ***Financial aid deadline:*** Continuous. ***Notification date:*** Continuous. Students must reply within 2 weeks of notification.

CONTACT Mr. Jim Shannon, Student Financial Resources Director, Christian Brothers University, 650 East Parkway South, Memphis, TN 38104, 901-321-3305 or toll-free 800-288-7576.

CHRISTIAN HERITAGE COLLEGE

El Cajon, CA

Tuition & fees: $10,840 **Average undergraduate aid package: N/A**

ABOUT THE INSTITUTION Independent nondenominational, coed. Awards: bachelor's degrees. 27 undergraduate majors. Total enrollment: 648. Undergraduates: 648. Freshmen: 100. Institutional methodology is used as a basis for awarding need-based institutional aid.

UNDERGRADUATE EXPENSES for 1999–2000 ***Application fee:*** $25. ***Comprehensive fee:*** $15,565 includes full-time tuition ($10,840) and room and board ($4725). Full-time tuition and fees vary according to class time, course load, and program. Room and board charges vary according to housing facility. ***Part-time tuition:*** $365 per unit. Part-time tuition and fees vary according to class time, course load, and program. ***Payment plan:*** installment.

GIFT AID (NEED-BASED) ***Scholarships, grants, and awards:*** Federal Pell, FSEOG, state, private.

GIFT AID (NON-NEED-BASED) ***Scholarships, grants, and awards by category:*** *Academic Interests/Achievement:* general academic interests/achievements. *Creative Arts/Performance:* music. *Special Achievements/Activities:* leadership. *Special Characteristics:* children of faculty/staff, international students, out-of-state students, relatives of clergy. ***Tuition waivers:*** Full or partial for employees or children of employees. ***ROTC:*** Army cooperative, Air Force cooperative.

LOANS ***Programs:*** FFEL (Subsidized and Unsubsidized Stafford, PLUS).

WORK-STUDY Federal work-study jobs available.

APPLYING for FINANCIAL AID ***Required financial aid form:*** FAFSA. ***Financial aid deadline (priority):*** 3/2. ***Notification date:*** 4/1. Students must reply by 5/1 or within 3 weeks of notification.

CONTACT Office of Financial Aid, Christian Heritage College, 2100 Greenfield Drive, El Cajon, CA 92019, 619-441-2200 or toll-free 800-676-2242. *E-mail:* mkitsko@christianheritage.edu

CHRISTIAN LIFE COLLEGE

Mount Prospect, IL

CONTACT Financial Aid Office, Christian Life College, 400 East Gregory Street, Mount Prospect, IL 60056, 847-259-1840.

CHRISTOPHER NEWPORT UNIVERSITY

Newport News, VA

Tuition & fees (VA res): $3048 **Average undergraduate aid package: $4645**

Christopher Newport University (continued)

ABOUT THE INSTITUTION State-supported, coed. Awards: bachelor's and master's degrees. 55 undergraduate majors. Total enrollment: 5,164. Undergraduates: 4,978. Freshmen: 823. Federal methodology is used as a basis for awarding need-based institutional aid.

UNDERGRADUATE EXPENSES for 1999–2000 ***Application fee:*** $25. ***Tuition, state resident:*** full-time $1888; part-time $126 per semester hour. ***Tuition, nonresident:*** full-time $7656; part-time $366 per semester hour. ***Required fees:*** full-time $1160; $20 per term part-time. Full-time tuition and fees vary according to course load. Part-time tuition and fees vary according to course load. ***College room and board:*** $4950. ***Payment plan:*** installment.

FRESHMAN FINANCIAL AID (Fall 1998) 565 applied for aid; of those 83% were deemed to have need. 100% of freshmen with need received aid; of those 10% had need fully met. *Average percent of need met:* 66% (excluding resources awarded to replace EFC). *Average financial aid package:* $4645 (excluding resources awarded to replace EFC). 15% of all full-time freshmen had no need and received non-need-based aid.

UNDERGRADUATE FINANCIAL AID (Fall 1998) 2,690 applied for aid; of those 83% were deemed to have need. 100% of undergraduates with need received aid; of those 10% had need fully met. *Average percent of need met:* 66% (excluding resources awarded to replace EFC). *Average financial aid package:* $4645 (excluding resources awarded to replace EFC). 15% of all full-time undergraduates had no need and received non-need-based aid.

GIFT AID (NEED-BASED) ***Total amount:*** $4,246,731 (59% Federal, 39% state, 2% institutional). ***Receiving aid:*** *Freshmen:* 49% (341); *all full-time undergraduates:* 49% (1,626). ***Average award:*** Freshmen: $1938; Undergraduates: $1938. ***Scholarships, grants, and awards:*** Federal Pell, FSEOG, state, private, college/university gift aid from institutional funds.

GIFT AID (NON-NEED-BASED) ***Total amount:*** $558,333 (47% institutional, 53% external sources). ***Receiving aid:*** *Freshmen:* 12% (81); *Undergraduates:* 12% (384). ***Scholarships, grants, and awards by category:*** *Academic Interests/Achievement:* education, general academic interests/achievements, military science. *Creative Arts/Performance:* art/fine arts, music. *Special Achievements/Activities:* general special achievements/activities. ***Tuition waivers:*** Full or partial for employees or children of employees, senior citizens. ***ROTC:*** Army.

LOANS ***Student loans:*** $11,270,255 (61% need-based, 39% non-need-based). 59% of past graduating class borrowed through all loan programs. ***Average need-based loan:*** Freshmen: $1201; Undergraduates: $1201. ***Parent loans:*** $673,988 (100% non-need-based). ***Programs:*** FFEL (Subsidized and Unsubsidized Stafford, PLUS), Perkins, state, college/university, alternative loans.

WORK-STUDY ***Federal work-study:*** *Total amount:* $98,278; 156 jobs available. ***State or other work-study/employment:*** *Total amount:* $959,657 (100% non-need-based). 358 part-time jobs averaging $2680.

APPLYING for FINANCIAL AID ***Required financial aid form:*** FAFSA. ***Financial aid deadline (priority):*** 3/1. ***Notification date:*** Continuous beginning 4/1. Students must reply within 2 weeks of notification.

CONTACT Mrs. Marcia D. Boyd, Director of Financial Aid, Christopher Newport University, Financial Aid Office, 1 University Place, Newport News, VA 23606, 757-594-7227 or toll-free 800-333-4CNU. *Fax:* 757-594-7113.

CINCINNATI BIBLE COLLEGE AND SEMINARY

Cincinnati, OH

Tuition & fees: $6471 **Average undergraduate aid package: $6500**

ABOUT THE INSTITUTION Independent religious, coed. Awards: associate, bachelor's, and master's degrees. 12 undergraduate majors. Total enrollment: 868. Undergraduates: 619. Freshmen: 115. Federal methodology is used as a basis for awarding need-based institutional aid.

UNDERGRADUATE EXPENSES for 1999–2000 ***Application fee:*** $35. ***Comprehensive fee:*** $10,271 includes full-time tuition ($6171), mandatory fees ($300), and room and board ($3800). ***College room only:*** $1850. Room and board charges vary according to board plan. ***Part-time tuition:*** $187 per semester hour. ***Part-time fees:*** $12 per semester hour. ***Payment plans:*** installment, deferred payment.

FRESHMAN FINANCIAL AID (Fall 1998) 113 applied for aid; of those 88% were deemed to have need. 100% of freshmen with need received aid; of those 25% had need fully met. *Average percent of need met:* 85% (excluding resources awarded to replace EFC). *Average financial aid package:* $5000 (excluding resources awarded to replace EFC). 11% of all full-time freshmen had no need and received non-need-based aid.

UNDERGRADUATE FINANCIAL AID (Fall 1998) 414 applied for aid; of those 88% were deemed to have need. 100% of undergraduates with need received aid; of those 27% had need fully met. *Average percent of need met:* 85% (excluding resources awarded to replace EFC). *Average financial aid package:* $6500 (excluding resources awarded to replace EFC). 19% of all full-time undergraduates had no need and received non-need-based aid.

GIFT AID (NEED-BASED) ***Total amount:*** $888,369 (49% Federal, 23% state, 17% institutional, 11% external sources). ***Receiving aid:*** *Freshmen:* 64% (90); *all full-time undergraduates:* 64% (330). ***Average award:*** Freshmen: $1500; Undergraduates: $1500. ***Scholarships, grants, and awards:*** Federal Pell, FSEOG, state, college/university gift aid from institutional funds.

GIFT AID (NON-NEED-BASED) ***Total amount:*** $752,915 (34% state, 21% institutional, 45% external sources). ***Receiving aid:*** *Freshmen:* 53% (75); *Undergraduates:* 29% (150). ***Scholarships, grants, and awards by category:*** *Academic Interests/Achievement:* general academic interests/achievements, religion/biblical studies. *Creative Arts/Performance:* music. *Special Characteristics:* children of union members/company employees, international students, spouses of current students. ***Tuition waivers:*** Full or partial for employees or children of employees.

LOANS ***Student loans:*** $1,672,776 (75% need-based, 25% non-need-based). 68% of past graduating class borrowed through all loan programs. Average indebtedness per student: $14,589. ***Average need-based loan:*** Freshmen: $2500; Undergraduates: $4281. ***Parent loans:*** $277,224 (100% non-need-based). ***Programs:*** FFEL (Subsidized and Unsubsidized Stafford, PLUS), alternative loans.

WORK-STUDY ***Federal work-study:*** *Total amount:* $92,276; 100 jobs averaging $928.

APPLYING for FINANCIAL AID ***Required financial aid forms:*** FAFSA, institution's own form, state aid form. ***Financial aid deadline (priority):*** 3/15. ***Notification date:*** Continuous beginning 4/1. Students must reply within 2 weeks of notification.

CONTACT Ms. Carrie Derico, Financial Aid Coordinator, Cincinnati Bible College and Seminary, 2700 Glenway Avenue, Cincinnati, OH 45204-1799, 513-244-8450 or toll-free 800-949-4CBC. *Fax:* 513-244-8140. *E-mail:* financialaid@cincybible.edu

CIRCLEVILLE BIBLE COLLEGE

Circleville, OH

Tuition & fees: $6540 **Average undergraduate aid package: $8000**

ABOUT THE INSTITUTION Independent religious, coed. Awards: associate and bachelor's degrees. 11 undergraduate majors. Total enrollment: 212. Undergraduates: 212. Both federal and institutional methodology are used as a basis for awarding need-based institutional aid.

UNDERGRADUATE EXPENSES for 1999–2000 ***Application fee:*** $25. ***Comprehensive fee:*** $10,840 includes full-time tuition ($5850), mandatory fees ($690), and room and board ($4300). Full-time tuition and fees vary according to course load, program, and reciprocity agreements. ***Part-time tuition:*** $250 per semester hour. ***Part-time fees:*** $258 per term part-time. Part-time tuition and fees vary according to course load, program, and reciprocity agreements. ***Payment plan:*** installment.

FRESHMAN FINANCIAL AID (Fall 1998) 59 applied for aid; of those 97% were deemed to have need. 100% of freshmen with need received aid; of those 16% had need fully met. *Average percent of need met:* 75% (excluding resources awarded to replace EFC). *Average financial aid package:* $7200 (excluding resources awarded to replace EFC).

UNDERGRADUATE FINANCIAL AID (Fall 1998) 154 applied for aid; of those 98% were deemed to have need. 100% of undergraduates with need received aid; of those 31% had need fully met. *Average percent of need met:* 85% (excluding resources awarded to replace EFC). *Average financial aid package:* $8000 (excluding resources awarded to replace EFC).

GIFT AID (NEED-BASED) ***Total amount:*** $413,840 (60% Federal, 40% state). ***Receiving aid:*** *Freshmen:* 27% (16); *all full-time undergraduates:* 31% (48). ***Average award:*** Freshmen: $500; Undergraduates: $500. ***Scholarships, grants, and awards:*** Federal Pell, FSEOG, state, private, college/university gift aid from institutional funds.

GIFT AID (NON-NEED-BASED) ***Total amount:*** $178,230 (69% state, 16% institutional, 15% external sources). ***Receiving aid:*** *Freshmen:* 17% (10); *Undergraduates:* 16% (24). ***Scholarships, grants, and awards by category:*** *Academic Interests/Achievement:* 22 awards ($21,000 total): business, education, general academic interests/achievements, religion/biblical studies. *Creative Arts/Performance:* 2 awards ($1500 total): music. *Special Achievements/Activities:* 7 awards ($45,000 total): leadership. *Special Characteristics:* children of faculty/staff, international students, out-of-state students, relatives of clergy, religious affiliation, siblings of current students, veterans, veterans' children. ***Tuition waivers:*** Full or partial for employees or children of employees, senior citizens.

LOANS ***Student loans:*** $722,000 (100% need-based). 100% of past graduating class borrowed through all loan programs. Average indebtedness per student: $15,000. ***Parent loans:*** $50,000 (100% need-based). ***Programs:*** FFEL (Subsidized and Unsubsidized Stafford, PLUS), Perkins, college/university.

WORK-STUDY ***Federal work-study:*** *Total amount:* $56,500; 25 jobs averaging $500.

APPLYING for FINANCIAL AID ***Required financial aid forms:*** FAFSA, institution's own form, CSS Financial Aid PROFILE. ***Financial aid deadline (priority):*** 4/1. ***Notification date:*** 6/1.

CONTACT Mr. Rick Deckard, Financial Aid Officer, Circleville Bible College, 1476 Lancaster Pike, PO Box 458, Circleville, OH 43113-9487, 740-477-7774 or toll-free 800-701-0222. *Fax:* 740-477-7755. *E-mail:* cbcrdeckard@scioto.net

THE CITADEL, THE MILITARY COLLEGE OF SOUTH CAROLINA

Charleston, SC

Tuition & fees (SC res): $4258 **Average undergraduate aid package: $7406**

ABOUT THE INSTITUTION State-supported, coed, primarily men. Awards: bachelor's and master's degrees and post-master's certificates. 23 undergraduate majors. Total enrollment: 3,968. Undergraduates: 1,955. Freshmen: 517. Federal methodology is used as a basis for awarding need-based institutional aid.

UNDERGRADUATE EXPENSES for 1999–2000 ***Application fee:*** $35. ***Tuition, state resident:*** full-time $3396; part-time $132 per credit hour. ***Tuition, nonresident:*** full-time $8992; part-time $261 per credit hour. ***Required fees:*** full-time $862. ***College room and board:*** $4340. Deposit required to defray the cost of books, uniforms and supplies: $4300 for first-year students, $1310 for upperclassmen. ***Payment plan:*** installment.

FRESHMAN FINANCIAL AID (Fall 1999, est.) 382 applied for aid; of those 73% were deemed to have need. 97% of freshmen with need received aid; of those 23% had need fully met. *Average percent of need met:* 70% (excluding resources awarded to replace EFC). *Average financial aid package:* $6801 (excluding resources awarded to replace EFC). 22% of all full-time freshmen had no need and received non-need-based aid.

UNDERGRADUATE FINANCIAL AID (Fall 1999, est.) 1,036 applied for aid; of those 75% were deemed to have need. 98% of undergraduates with need received aid; of those 23% had need fully met. *Average percent of need met:* 77% (excluding resources awarded to replace EFC). *Average financial aid package:* $7406 (excluding resources awarded to replace EFC). 14% of all full-time undergraduates had no need and received non-need-based aid.

GIFT AID (NEED-BASED) ***Total amount:*** $740,665 (82% Federal, 18% state). ***Receiving aid:*** *Freshmen:* 40% (208); *all full-time undergraduates:* 29% (545). ***Average award:*** Freshmen: $6131; Undergraduates: $6383. ***Scholarships, grants, and awards:*** Federal Pell, FSEOG, state, private, college/university gift aid from institutional funds.

GIFT AID (NON-NEED-BASED) ***Total amount:*** $666,473 (81% state, 19% external sources). ***Receiving aid:*** *Freshmen:* 40% (208); *Undergraduates:* 30% (547). ***Scholarships, grants, and awards by category:*** *Academic Interests/Achievement:* biological sciences, engineering/technologies, general academic interests/achievements, military science. *Creative Arts/Performance:* journalism/publications, music. *Special Achievements/Activities:* leadership, religious involvement. *Special Characteristics:* children and siblings of alumni, children with a deceased or disabled parent, local/state students. ***Tuition waivers:*** Full or partial for senior citizens. ***ROTC:*** Army, Naval, Air Force.

LOANS ***Student loans:*** $3,137,256 (54% need-based, 46% non-need-based). 45% of past graduating class borrowed through all loan programs. Average indebtedness per student: $14,200. ***Average need-based loan:*** Freshmen: $2462; Undergraduates: $3123. ***Parent loans:*** $3,126,352 (100% non-need-based). ***Programs:*** Federal Direct (Subsidized and Unsubsidized Stafford, PLUS), Perkins, state, college/university.

WORK-STUDY ***Federal work-study:*** *Total amount:* $47,032; jobs available.

ATHLETIC AWARDS *Total amount:* 1,734,799 (100% non-need-based).

APPLYING for FINANCIAL AID ***Required financial aid form:*** FAFSA. ***Financial aid deadline (priority):*** 3/15. ***Notification date:*** 4/1. Students must reply within 2 weeks of notification.

CONTACT Lt. Col. Hank M. Fuller, Director of Financial Aid and Scholarships, The Citadel, The Military College of South Carolina, 171 Moultrie Street, Charleston, SC 29409, 843-953-5187 or toll-free 800-868-1842. *Fax:* 843-953-6759. *E-mail:* fullerh@citadel.edu

CITY COLLEGE OF THE CITY UNIVERSITY OF NEW YORK

New York, NY

Tuition & fees (NY res): $3309 **Average undergraduate aid package: N/A**

ABOUT THE INSTITUTION State and locally supported, coed. Awards: bachelor's, master's, and doctoral degrees. 57 undergraduate majors. Total enrollment: 10,993. Undergraduates: 8,349. Freshmen: 828. Both federal and institutional methodology are used as a basis for awarding need-based institutional aid.

UNDERGRADUATE EXPENSES for 1999–2000 ***Application fee:*** $40. ***Tuition, state resident:*** full-time $3200; part-time $135 per credit. ***Tuition, nonresident:*** full-time $6800; part-time $285 per credit. ***Required fees:*** full-time $109; $27 per term part-time. Full-time tuition and fees vary according to class time and program. Part-time tuition and fees vary according to class time and program. ***Payment plan:*** deferred payment.

GIFT AID (NEED-BASED) ***Scholarships, grants, and awards:*** Federal Pell, FSEOG, state, private, college/university gift aid from institutional funds.

GIFT AID (NON-NEED-BASED) ***Scholarships, grants, and awards by category:*** *Academic Interests/Achievement:* general academic interests/achievements. ***Tuition waivers:*** Full or partial for senior citizens. ***ROTC:*** Army cooperative, Air Force cooperative.

LOANS ***Programs:*** Federal Direct (Subsidized and Unsubsidized Stafford, PLUS), Perkins.

WORK-STUDY Federal work-study jobs available.

APPLYING for FINANCIAL AID ***Required financial aid forms:*** FAFSA, state aid form. ***Financial aid deadline (priority):*** 5/1. ***Notification date:*** Continuous beginning 6/1.

CONTACT Thelma Mason, Director of Financial Aid, City College of the City University of New York, 138th Street and Convent Avenue, Y Building, Room 120, New York, NY 10031, 212-650-5819.

CITY UNIVERSITY

Bellevue, WA

Tuition & fees: $6600 **Average undergraduate aid package: $4562**

ABOUT THE INSTITUTION Independent, coed. Awards: associate, bachelor's, and master's degrees and post-bachelor's certificates. 15 undergraduate majors. Total enrollment: 5,410. Undergraduates: 2,548. Entering class: . Federal methodology is used as a basis for awarding need-based institutional aid.

UNDERGRADUATE EXPENSES for 1999–2000 ***Application fee:*** $75. ***Tuition:*** full-time $6600; part-time $165 per credit. ***Payment plan:*** deferred payment.

UNDERGRADUATE FINANCIAL AID (Fall 1998) 299 applied for aid; of those 82% were deemed to have need. 100% of undergraduates with need received aid. *Average financial aid package:* $4562 (excluding resources awarded to replace EFC). 1% of all full-time undergraduates had no need and received non-need-based aid.

GIFT AID (NEED-BASED) ***Total amount:*** $280,107 (90% Federal, 10% institutional). ***Receiving aid:*** *Entering class:* 7% (5); *all full-time undergraduates:* 4% (127). ***Average award:*** Freshmen: $2573; Undergraduates: $2044. ***Scholarships, grants, and awards:*** Federal Pell, FSEOG, private, college/university gift aid from institutional funds.

GIFT AID (NON-NEED-BASED) ***Total amount:*** $11,135 (100% institutional). ***Receiving aid:*** *Undergraduates:* 1. ***Scholarships, grants, and awards by category:*** *Academic Interests/Achievement:* 2 awards ($11,135 total): general academic interests/achievements. ***Tuition waivers:*** Full or partial for employees or children of employees.

LOANS ***Student loans:*** $2,052,353 (93% need-based, 7% non-need-based). 15% of past graduating class borrowed through all loan programs. Average indebtedness per student: $16,609. ***Average need-based loan:*** Freshmen: $2310; Undergraduates: $3715. ***Programs:*** FFEL (Subsidized and Unsubsidized Stafford, PLUS).

WORK-STUDY ***Federal work-study:*** *Total amount:* $3880; jobs available.

APPLYING for FINANCIAL AID ***Required financial aid forms:*** FAFSA, institution's own form. ***Financial aid deadline:*** Continuous. ***Notification date:*** Continuous beginning 7/1.

CONTACT Ms. Jean L. Roberts, Director, Student Financial Services, City University, 335 116th Avenue SE, Bellevue, WA 98004, 425-637-1010 Ext. 4640 or toll-free 800-426-5596. *Fax:* 425-450-4663. *E-mail:* jroberts@cityu.edu

CLAFLIN UNIVERSITY

Orangeburg, SC

Tuition & fees: $7008 **Average undergraduate aid package: $11,650**

ABOUT THE INSTITUTION Independent United Methodist, coed. Awards: bachelor's degrees. 19 undergraduate majors. Total enrollment: 1,308. Undergraduates: 1,308. Federal methodology is used as a basis for awarding need-based institutional aid.

UNDERGRADUATE EXPENSES for 1999–2000 ***Application fee:*** $20. ***One-time required fee:*** $100. ***Comprehensive fee:*** $10,820 includes full-time tuition ($6978), mandatory fees ($30), and room and board ($3812). Room and board charges vary according to gender and housing facility. ***Part-time tuition:*** $225 per semester hour. ***Part-time fees:*** $15 per term part-time. ***Payment plans:*** installment, deferred payment.

FRESHMAN FINANCIAL AID (Fall 1999, est.) 317 applied for aid; of those 98% were deemed to have need. 100% of freshmen with need received aid. *Average percent of need met:* 73% (excluding resources awarded to replace EFC). *Average financial aid package:* $10,505 (excluding resources awarded to replace EFC).

UNDERGRADUATE FINANCIAL AID (Fall 1999, est.) 1,010 applied for aid; of those 97% were deemed to have need. 100% of undergraduates with need received aid. *Average percent of need met:* 81% (excluding resources awarded to replace EFC). *Average financial aid package:* $11,650 (excluding resources awarded to replace EFC).

GIFT AID (NEED-BASED) ***Total amount:*** $5,491,069 (46% Federal, 29% state, 20% institutional, 5% external sources). ***Average award:*** Freshmen: $5582; Undergraduates: $5424. ***Scholarships, grants, and awards:*** Federal Pell, FSEOG, state, private, college/university gift aid from institutional funds, United Negro College Fund.

GIFT AID (NON-NEED-BASED) ***Scholarships, grants, and awards by category:*** *Academic Interests/Achievement:* general academic interests/achievements. *Creative Arts/Performance:* applied art and design, art/fine arts, music. *Special Achievements/Activities:* cheerleading/drum major. *Special Characteristics:* children of faculty/staff, relatives of clergy, religious affiliation. ***Tuition waivers:*** Full or partial for employees or children of employees. ***ROTC:*** Army cooperative.

LOANS ***Student loans:*** $5,096,252 (100% need-based). 89% of past graduating class borrowed through all loan programs. Average indebtedness per student: $13,141. ***Average need-based loan:*** Freshmen: $4926; Undergraduates: $5676. ***Parent loans:*** $825,223 (100% need-based). ***Programs:*** Federal Direct (Subsidized and Unsubsidized Stafford, PLUS), FFEL (PLUS), Perkins, college/university.

WORK-STUDY ***Federal work-study:*** *Total amount:* $321,654; 257 jobs averaging $1294.

ATHLETIC AWARDS *Total amount:* 192,765 (100% need-based).

APPLYING for FINANCIAL AID ***Required financial aid forms:*** FAFSA, institution's own form. ***Financial aid deadline (priority):*** 4/15. ***Notification date:*** Continuous beginning 5/15. Students must reply within 2 weeks of notification.

CONTACT Ms. Yvonne C. Clarkson, Director of Student Financial Aid, Claflin University, Tingly Hall, Suite 2, 700 College Avenue NE, Orangeburg, SC 29115, 803-535-5331 or toll-free 800-922-1276 (in-state).

CLAREMONT MCKENNA COLLEGE

Claremont, CA

Tuition & fees: $20,760 **Average undergraduate aid package: $18,980**

ABOUT THE INSTITUTION Independent, coed. Awards: bachelor's degrees. 48 undergraduate majors. Total enrollment: 1,016. Undergraduates: 1,016. Freshmen: 252. Institutional methodology is used as a basis for awarding need-based institutional aid.

UNDERGRADUATE EXPENSES for 1999–2000 ***Application fee:*** $50. ***Comprehensive fee:*** $27,820 includes full-time tuition ($20,600), mandatory fees ($160), and room and board ($7060). Room and board charges vary according to board plan and housing facility. ***Part-time tuition:*** $3433 per course. ***Payment plan:*** installment.

FRESHMAN FINANCIAL AID (Fall 1999) 161 applied for aid; of those 78% were deemed to have need. 100% of freshmen with need received aid; of those 100% had need fully met. *Average percent of need met:* 100% (excluding resources awarded to replace EFC). *Average financial aid package:* $19,386 (excluding resources awarded to replace EFC). 14% of all full-time freshmen had no need and received non-need-based aid.

UNDERGRADUATE FINANCIAL AID (Fall 1999) 648 applied for aid; of those 90% were deemed to have need. 100% of undergraduates with need received aid; of those 100% had need fully met. *Average percent of need met:* 100% (excluding resources awarded to replace EFC). *Average financial aid package:* $18,980 (excluding resources awarded to replace EFC). 9% of all full-time undergraduates had no need and received non-need-based aid.

GIFT AID (NEED-BASED) ***Total amount:*** $9,011,649 (6% Federal, 15% state, 74% institutional, 5% external sources). ***Receiving aid:*** *Freshmen:* 49% (124); *all full-time undergraduates:* 56% (574). ***Average award:*** Freshmen: $16,233; Undergraduates: $15,879. ***Scholarships, grants, and awards:*** Federal Pell, FSEOG, state, private, college/university gift aid from institutional funds.

GIFT AID (NON-NEED-BASED) ***Total amount:*** $595,392 (61% institutional, 39% external sources). ***Receiving aid:*** *Freshmen:* 23% (57); *Undergraduates:* 19% (191). ***Scholarships, grants, and awards by category:*** *Academic Interests/Achievement:* general academic interests/achievements. *Special*

Characteristics: ethnic background. ***Tuition waivers:*** Full or partial for employees or children of employees. ***ROTC:*** Army, Naval cooperative, Air Force cooperative.

LOANS ***Student loans:*** $2,666,569 (48% need-based, 52% non-need-based). 59% of past graduating class borrowed through all loan programs. Average indebtedness per student: $16,266. ***Average need-based loan:*** Freshmen: $2803; Undergraduates: $2994. ***Parent loans:*** $729,831 (100% non-need-based). ***Programs:*** FFEL (Subsidized and Unsubsidized Stafford, PLUS), Perkins, college/university, alternative loans.

WORK-STUDY ***Federal work-study:*** *Total amount:* $339,650; 465 jobs averaging $1365. ***State or other work-study/employment:*** *Total amount:* $700,000 (100% non-need-based). Part-time jobs available.

APPLYING for FINANCIAL AID ***Required financial aid forms:*** FAFSA, CSS Financial Aid PROFILE. ***Financial aid deadline:*** 2/1. ***Notification date:*** 4/1. Students must reply by 5/1.

CONTACT Ms. Georgette R. DeVeres, Director of Financial Aid/Associate Dean of Admission, Claremont McKenna College, 890 Columbia Avenue, Claremont, CA 91711, 909-621-8356. *Fax:* 909-621-8516. *E-mail:* gdeveres@benson.mckenna.edu

CLARION UNIVERSITY OF PENNSYLVANIA

Clarion, PA

Tuition & fees (PA res): $4600 **Average undergraduate aid package: $8737**

ABOUT THE INSTITUTION State-supported, coed. Awards: associate, bachelor's, and master's degrees and post-master's certificates. 56 undergraduate majors. Total enrollment: 6,028. Undergraduates: 5,599. Freshmen: 1,352. Federal methodology is used as a basis for awarding need-based institutional aid.

UNDERGRADUATE EXPENSES for 1999–2000 ***Application fee:*** $25. ***Tuition, state resident:*** full-time $3618; part-time $150 per credit. ***Tuition, nonresident:*** full-time $5428; part-time $226 per credit. ***Required fees:*** full-time $982; $30 per credit; $70 per term part-time. Full-time tuition and fees vary according to course load and location. Part-time tuition and fees vary according to course load and location. ***College room and board:*** $3984; ***room only:*** $2300. Room and board charges vary according to board plan and housing facility. ***Payment plan:*** installment.

FRESHMAN FINANCIAL AID (Fall 1998) 1018 applied for aid; of those 90% were deemed to have need. 98% of freshmen with need received aid; of those 72% had need fully met. *Average percent of need met:* 93% (excluding resources awarded to replace EFC). *Average financial aid package:* $5814 (excluding resources awarded to replace EFC). 18% of all full-time freshmen had no need and received non-need-based aid.

UNDERGRADUATE FINANCIAL AID (Fall 1998) 4,326 applied for aid; of those 88% were deemed to have need. 100% of undergraduates with need received aid; of those 68% had need fully met. *Average percent of need met:* 95% (excluding resources awarded to replace EFC). *Average financial aid package:* $8737 (excluding resources awarded to replace EFC). 12% of all full-time undergraduates had no need and received non-need-based aid.

GIFT AID (NEED-BASED) ***Total amount:*** $8,404,755 (44% Federal, 53% state, 3% external sources). ***Receiving aid:*** *Freshmen:* 40% (452); *all full-time undergraduates:* 42% (1,916). ***Scholarships, grants, and awards:*** Federal Pell, FSEOG, state, private, Negro Emergency Education Drive.

GIFT AID (NON-NEED-BASED) ***Total amount:*** $236,400 (57% institutional, 43% external sources). ***Receiving aid:*** *Freshmen:* 26% (285); *Undergraduates:* 20% (918). ***Scholarships, grants, and awards by category:*** *Academic Interests/Achievement:* biological sciences, business, communication, computer science, education, English, foreign languages, general academic interests/achievements, humanities, international studies, library science, mathematics, physical sciences, premedicine, social sciences. *Creative Arts/Performance:* art/fine arts, performing arts, theater/drama. *Special Characteristics:* local/state students, members of minority groups. ***Tuition waivers:*** Full or partial for employees or children of employees, senior citizens.

LOANS ***Student loans:*** $14,692,975 (59% need-based, 41% non-need-based). 60% of past graduating class borrowed through all loan programs. Average indebtedness per student: $14,378. ***Parent loans:*** $1,787,709 (100% need-based). ***Programs:*** FFEL (Subsidized and Unsubsidized Stafford, PLUS), Perkins, college/university.

WORK-STUDY ***Federal work-study:*** *Total amount:* $425,000; 300 jobs averaging $1540. ***State or other work-study/employment:*** *Total amount:* $935,000 (100% non-need-based). 550 part-time jobs averaging $1540.

ATHLETIC AWARDS *Total amount:* 373,262 (100% non-need-based).

APPLYING for FINANCIAL AID ***Required financial aid forms:*** FAFSA, state aid form. ***Financial aid deadline (priority):*** 5/1. ***Notification date:*** Continuous.

CONTACT Ms. Mary Jo Phillips, Freshman Financial Aid Advisor, Clarion University of Pennsylvania, 104 Egbert Hall, Clarion, PA 16214-1232, 814-226-2315 or toll-free 800-672-7171 (in-state). *Fax:* 814-226-2520. *E-mail:* maphillips@mail.clarion.edu

CLARK ATLANTA UNIVERSITY

Atlanta, GA

Tuition & fees: $11,120 **Average undergraduate aid package: N/A**

ABOUT THE INSTITUTION Independent United Methodist, coed. Awards: bachelor's, master's, and doctoral degrees. 43 undergraduate majors. Total enrollment: 4,963. Undergraduates: 3,878. Freshmen: 715. Federal methodology is used as a basis for awarding need-based institutional aid.

UNDERGRADUATE EXPENSES for 2000–2001 ***Application fee:*** $35. ***Comprehensive fee:*** $17,094 includes full-time tuition ($10,720), mandatory fees ($400), and room and board ($5974). ***College room only:*** $3534. Room and board charges vary according to board plan and housing facility. ***Payment plan:*** deferred payment.

GIFT AID (NEED-BASED) ***Scholarships, grants, and awards:*** Federal Pell, FSEOG, state, private, college/university gift aid from institutional funds, United Negro College Fund.

GIFT AID (NON-NEED-BASED) ***Scholarships, grants, and awards by category:*** *Academic Interests/Achievement:* general academic interests/achievements. *Creative Arts/Performance:* music. *Special Achievements/Activities:* general special achievements/activities, leadership. *Special Characteristics:* general special characteristics. ***Tuition waivers:*** Full or partial for employees or children of employees. ***ROTC:*** Army, Naval.

LOANS ***Programs:*** FFEL (Subsidized and Unsubsidized Stafford, PLUS), Perkins.

WORK-STUDY Federal work-study jobs available.

APPLYING for FINANCIAL AID ***Required financial aid form:*** FAFSA. ***Financial aid deadline (priority):*** 3/1. ***Notification date:*** 5/1.

CONTACT Director of Financial Aid, Clark Atlanta University, 223 James P. Brawley Drive, Atlanta, GA 30314, 404-880-8111 or toll-free 800-688-3228.

CLARKE COLLEGE

Dubuque, IA

Tuition & fees: $13,586 **Average undergraduate aid package: $11,423**

ABOUT THE INSTITUTION Independent Roman Catholic, coed. Awards: associate, bachelor's, and master's degrees. 42 undergraduate majors. Total enrollment: 1,283. Undergraduates: 1,120. Freshmen: 188. Federal methodology is used as a basis for awarding need-based institutional aid.

UNDERGRADUATE EXPENSES for 1999–2000 ***Application fee:*** $25. ***Comprehensive fee:*** $18,668 includes full-time tuition ($13,196), mandatory fees ($390), and room and board ($5082). ***College room only:*** $2472. Full-time tuition and fees vary according to class time. Room and board charges vary according to board plan and housing facility. ***Part-time tuition:*** $315 per credit hour. ***Part-time fees:*** $5 per credit hour. Part-time tuition and fees vary according to class time. ***Payment plans:*** installment, deferred payment.

FRESHMAN FINANCIAL AID (Fall 1999) 173 applied for aid; of those 87% were deemed to have need. 100% of freshmen with need received aid; of those 32% had need fully met. *Average percent of need met:* 100%

Clarke College (continued)

(excluding resources awarded to replace EFC). *Average financial aid package:* $12,688 (excluding resources awarded to replace EFC). 20% of all full-time freshmen had no need and received non-need-based aid.

UNDERGRADUATE FINANCIAL AID (Fall 1999) 705 applied for aid; of those 89% were deemed to have need. 100% of undergraduates with need received aid; of those 24% had need fully met. *Average percent of need met:* 100% (excluding resources awarded to replace EFC). *Average financial aid package:* $11,423 (excluding resources awarded to replace EFC). 15% of all full-time undergraduates had no need and received non-need-based aid.

GIFT AID (NEED-BASED) ***Total amount:*** $4,621,128 (14% Federal, 25% state, 59% institutional, 2% external sources). ***Receiving aid:*** *Freshmen:* 78% (150); *all full-time undergraduates:* 74% (600). ***Average award:*** Freshmen: $9778; Undergraduates: $7710. ***Scholarships, grants, and awards:*** Federal Pell, FSEOG, state, private, college/university gift aid from institutional funds.

GIFT AID (NON-NEED-BASED) ***Total amount:*** $543,110 (93% institutional, 7% external sources). ***Receiving aid:*** *Freshmen:* 70% (136); *Undergraduates:* 56% (453). ***Scholarships, grants, and awards by category:*** *Academic Interests/Achievement:* computer science, education, foreign languages, general academic interests/achievements. *Creative Arts/Performance:* art/fine arts, music, theater/drama. *Special Achievements/Activities:* leadership. *Special Characteristics:* children and siblings of alumni, children of faculty/staff, international students, relatives of clergy, siblings of current students. ***Tuition waivers:*** Full or partial for children of alumni, employees or children of employees, adult students, senior citizens.

LOANS ***Student loans:*** $3,400,397 (70% need-based, 30% non-need-based). 70% of past graduating class borrowed through all loan programs. Average indebtedness per student: $16,838. ***Average need-based loan:*** Freshmen: $2801; Undergraduates: $3880. ***Parent loans:*** $281,632 (29% need-based, 71% non-need-based). ***Programs:*** FFEL (Subsidized and Unsubsidized Stafford, PLUS), Perkins, Federal Nursing, college/university, alternative loans.

WORK-STUDY ***Federal work-study:*** *Total amount:* $377,023; 268 jobs averaging $1404. ***State or other work-study/employment:*** *Total amount:* $136,535 (41% need-based, 59% non-need-based). 178 part-time jobs averaging $684.

APPLYING for FINANCIAL AID ***Required financial aid form:*** FAFSA. ***Financial aid deadline (priority):*** 4/15. ***Notification date:*** Continuous. Students must reply by 5/1 or within 2 weeks of notification.

CONTACT Mr. Michael Pope, Director of Financial Aid, Clarke College, 1550 Clarke Drive, Dubuque, IA 52001-3198, 319-588-6327 or toll-free 800-383-2345. *Fax:* 319-588-6789. *E-mail:* mpope@keller.clarke.edu

CLARKSON COLLEGE

Omaha, NE

Tuition & fees: $7176 **Average undergraduate aid package: N/A**

ABOUT THE INSTITUTION Independent religious, coed. Awards: associate, bachelor's, and master's degrees and post-master's certificates. 7 undergraduate majors. Total enrollment: 406. Undergraduates: 274. Freshmen: 29. Federal methodology is used as a basis for awarding need-based institutional aid.

UNDERGRADUATE EXPENSES for 1999–2000 ***Application fee:*** $15. ***Tuition:*** full-time $6768; part-time $282 per credit. ***Required fees:*** full-time $408; $17 per credit. Room and board charges vary according to housing facility and location. ***Payment plans:*** installment, deferred payment.

FRESHMAN FINANCIAL AID (Fall 1999, est.) 42 applied for aid; of those 81% were deemed to have need. 100% of freshmen with need received aid. 13% of all full-time freshmen had no need and received non-need-based aid.

UNDERGRADUATE FINANCIAL AID (Fall 1999, est.) 111 applied for aid; of those 76% were deemed to have need. 100% of undergraduates with need received aid. 18% of all full-time undergraduates had no need and received non-need-based aid.

GIFT AID (NEED-BASED) ***Total amount:*** $330,500 (48% Federal, 30% state, 22% institutional). ***Receiving aid:*** *Freshmen:* 46% (29); *all full-time undergraduates:* 49% (65). ***Average award:*** Freshmen: $3100; Undergraduates: $3600. ***Scholarships, grants, and awards:*** Federal Pell, FSEOG, state, private, college/university gift aid from institutional funds.

GIFT AID (NON-NEED-BASED) ***Total amount:*** $410,600 (98% institutional, 2% external sources). ***Receiving aid:*** *Freshmen:* 19% (12); *Undergraduates:* 23% (31). ***Scholarships, grants, and awards by category:*** *Academic Interests/Achievement:* business, general academic interests/achievements, health fields. *Special Characteristics:* children and siblings of alumni, children of faculty/staff, ethnic background, international students, veterans. ***Tuition waivers:*** Full or partial for minority students, employees or children of employees. ***ROTC:*** Army cooperative, Air Force cooperative.

LOANS ***Student loans:*** $1,900,000 (47% need-based, 53% non-need-based). 89% of past graduating class borrowed through all loan programs. ***Average need-based loan:*** Freshmen: $2000; Undergraduates: $2600. ***Parent loans:*** $100,000 (100% non-need-based). ***Programs:*** FFEL (Subsidized and Unsubsidized Stafford, PLUS), Federal Nursing, college/university.

WORK-STUDY ***Federal work-study:*** *Total amount:* $100,000; jobs available.

APPLYING for FINANCIAL AID ***Required financial aid forms:*** FAFSA, institution's own form. ***Financial aid deadline (priority):*** 4/1. ***Notification date:*** Continuous beginning 4/13. Students must reply within 3 weeks of notification.

CONTACT Jennifer Wurth, Director of Financial Aid, Clarkson College, 101 South 42nd Street, Omaha, NE 68131-2739, 402-552-2749 or toll-free 800-647-5500. *Fax:* 402-552-6165. *E-mail:* wurth@clrkcol.crhsnet.edu

CLARKSON UNIVERSITY

Potsdam, NY

Tuition & fees: $20,225 **Average undergraduate aid package: $14,647**

ABOUT THE INSTITUTION Independent, coed. Awards: bachelor's, master's, and doctoral degrees. 50 undergraduate majors. Total enrollment: 2,902. Undergraduates: 2,581. Freshmen: 707. Federal methodology is used as a basis for awarding need-based institutional aid.

UNDERGRADUATE EXPENSES for 1999–2000 ***Application fee:*** $30. ***Comprehensive fee:*** $27,709 includes full-time tuition ($19,825), mandatory fees ($400), and room and board ($7484). ***College room only:*** $3900. Full-time tuition and fees vary according to course load. Room and board charges vary according to housing facility. ***Part-time tuition:*** $661 per credit hour. ***Part-time fees:*** $105 per term part-time. Part-time tuition and fees vary according to course load. ***Payment plan:*** installment.

FRESHMAN FINANCIAL AID (Fall 1998) 560 applied for aid; of those 90% were deemed to have need. 100% of freshmen with need received aid; of those 26% had need fully met. *Average percent of need met:* 83% (excluding resources awarded to replace EFC). *Average financial aid package:* $14,980 (excluding resources awarded to replace EFC). 11% of all full-time freshmen had no need and received non-need-based aid.

UNDERGRADUATE FINANCIAL AID (Fall 1998) 2,061 applied for aid; of those 95% were deemed to have need. 100% of undergraduates with need received aid; of those 24% had need fully met. *Average percent of need met:* 87% (excluding resources awarded to replace EFC). *Average financial aid package:* $14,647 (excluding resources awarded to replace EFC). 4% of all full-time undergraduates had no need and received non-need-based aid.

GIFT AID (NEED-BASED) ***Total amount:*** $18,239,677 (10% Federal, 12% state, 77% institutional, 1% external sources). ***Receiving aid:*** *Freshmen:* 74% (453); *all full-time undergraduates:* 78% (1,857). ***Average award:*** Freshmen: $7859; Undergraduates: $9763. ***Scholarships, grants, and awards:*** Federal Pell, FSEOG, state, private, college/university gift aid from institutional funds.

GIFT AID (NON-NEED-BASED) ***Total amount:*** $7,076,583 (2% state, 73% institutional, 25% external sources). ***Receiving aid:*** *Freshmen:* 13% (81); *Undergraduates:* 18% (422). ***Scholarships, grants, and awards by category:*** *Academic Interests/Achievement:* biological sciences, business, computer science, engineering/technologies, general academic interests/

achievements, humanities, mathematics, military science, physical sciences. *Special Achievements/Activities:* 209 awards ($1,489,500 total): leadership. *Special Characteristics:* 1,481 awards ($3,735,447 total): children of faculty/staff, general special characteristics, international students, local/state students, members of minority groups. ***Tuition waivers:*** Full or partial for employees or children of employees. ***ROTC:*** Army, Air Force.

LOANS ***Student loans:*** $14,853,040 (83% need-based, 17% non-need-based). 80% of past graduating class borrowed through all loan programs. Average indebtedness per student: $18,110. ***Average need-based loan:*** Freshmen: $5300; Undergraduates: $6500. ***Parent loans:*** $2,963,686 (100% non-need-based). ***Programs:*** Federal Direct (Subsidized and Unsubsidized Stafford, PLUS), Perkins, college/university, Quick Loan Funds.

WORK-STUDY ***Federal work-study:*** *Total amount:* $496,824; 648 jobs averaging $767. ***State or other work-study/employment:*** *Total amount:* $300,755 (63% need-based, 37% non-need-based). 401 part-time jobs averaging $750.

ATHLETIC AWARDS *Total amount:* 497,856 (100% non-need-based).

APPLYING for FINANCIAL AID ***Required financial aid forms:*** FAFSA, institution's own form, state aid form. ***Financial aid deadline (priority):*** 3/1. ***Notification date:*** 3/23. Students must reply by 5/1 or within 2 weeks of notification.

CONTACT Suzanne E. Davis, Director for Financial Assistance, Clarkson University, Box 5615, Cubley-Reynolds, Potsdam, NY 13699-5615, 315-268-6413 or toll-free 800-527-6577. *E-mail:* daviss@agent.clarkson.edu

CLARK UNIVERSITY

Worcester, MA

Tuition & fees: $22,620 **Average undergraduate aid package: $18,138**

ABOUT THE INSTITUTION Independent, coed. Awards: bachelor's, master's, and doctoral degrees and post-bachelor's and post-master's certificates. 51 undergraduate majors. Total enrollment: 3,003. Undergraduates: 2,182. Freshmen: 481. Institutional methodology is used as a basis for awarding need-based institutional aid.

UNDERGRADUATE EXPENSES for 1999–2000 ***Application fee:*** $40. ***Comprehensive fee:*** $26,970 includes full-time tuition ($22,400), mandatory fees ($220), and room and board ($4350). ***College room only:*** $2650. Room and board charges vary according to board plan and housing facility. ***Part-time tuition:*** $2800 per course. ***Payment plans:*** tuition prepayment, installment.

FRESHMAN FINANCIAL AID (Fall 1999) 343 applied for aid; of those 90% were deemed to have need. 100% of freshmen with need received aid; of those 18% had need fully met. *Average percent of need met:* 82% (excluding resources awarded to replace EFC). *Average financial aid package:* $17,067 (excluding resources awarded to replace EFC). 17% of all full-time freshmen had no need and received non-need-based aid.

UNDERGRADUATE FINANCIAL AID (Fall 1999) 1,562 applied for aid; of those 77% were deemed to have need. 100% of undergraduates with need received aid. *Average percent of need met:* 87% (excluding resources awarded to replace EFC). *Average financial aid package:* $18,138 (excluding resources awarded to replace EFC). 19% of all full-time undergraduates had no need and received non-need-based aid.

GIFT AID (NEED-BASED) ***Total amount:*** $14,848,731 (11% Federal, 5% state, 82% institutional, 2% external sources). ***Receiving aid:*** *Freshmen:* 63% (303); *all full-time undergraduates:* 61% (1,183). ***Average award:*** Freshmen: $12,626; Undergraduates: $12,547. ***Scholarships, grants, and awards:*** Federal Pell, FSEOG, state, college/university gift aid from institutional funds.

GIFT AID (NON-NEED-BASED) ***Total amount:*** $2,697,010 (99% institutional, 1% external sources). ***Scholarships, grants, and awards by category:*** *Academic Interests/Achievement:* general academic interests/achievements. ***Tuition waivers:*** Full or partial for employees or children of employees. ***ROTC:*** Army cooperative, Air Force cooperative.

LOANS ***Student loans:*** $5,438,147 (79% need-based, 21% non-need-based). 64% of past graduating class borrowed through all loan programs. Average indebtedness per student: $17,224. ***Average need-based loan:*** Freshmen: $3428; Undergraduates: $4534. ***Programs:*** FFEL (Subsidized and Unsubsidized Stafford, PLUS), Perkins, state, college/university.

WORK-STUDY ***Federal work-study:*** *Total amount:* $1,230,400; 921 jobs averaging $1300.

APPLYING for FINANCIAL AID ***Required financial aid forms:*** FAFSA, CSS Financial Aid PROFILE. ***Financial aid deadline (priority):*** 2/1. ***Notification date:*** 3/31. Students must reply by 5/1 or within 2 weeks of notification.

CONTACT Ms. Becky L. Hiltunen, Director of Financial Assistance, Clark University, 950 Main Street, Worcester, MA 01610-1477, 508-793-7478 or toll-free 800-GO-CLARK (out-of-state). *Fax:* 508-793-8802. *E-mail:* finaid@clarku.edu

CLAYTON COLLEGE & STATE UNIVERSITY

Morrow, GA

Tuition & fees (GA res): $2702 **Average undergraduate aid package: N/A**

ABOUT THE INSTITUTION State-supported, coed. Awards: associate and bachelor's degrees. 79 undergraduate majors. Total enrollment: 4,447. Undergraduates: 4,447. Freshmen: 674. Federal methodology is used as a basis for awarding need-based institutional aid.

UNDERGRADUATE EXPENSES for 1999–2000 ***Application fee:*** $20. ***Tuition, state resident:*** full-time $1808; part-time $76 per hour. ***Tuition, nonresident:*** full-time $7232; part-time $302 per hour. ***Required fees:*** full-time $894; $447 per term part-time. Part-time tuition and fees vary according to program.

FRESHMAN FINANCIAL AID (Fall 1999, est.) 347 applied for aid; of those 60% were deemed to have need. 99% of freshmen with need received aid; of those 38% had need fully met. 25% of all full-time freshmen had no need and received non-need-based aid.

UNDERGRADUATE FINANCIAL AID (Fall 1999, est.) 1,325 applied for aid; of those 69% were deemed to have need. 97% of undergraduates with need received aid; of those 36% had need fully met. 20% of all full-time undergraduates had no need and received non-need-based aid.

GIFT AID (NEED-BASED) ***Total amount:*** $989,765 (100% Federal). ***Receiving aid:*** *Freshmen:* 18% (102); *all full-time undergraduates:* 28% (538). ***Scholarships, grants, and awards:*** Federal Pell, FSEOG, state.

GIFT AID (NON-NEED-BASED) ***Total amount:*** $1,558,476 (90% state, 7% institutional, 3% external sources). ***Receiving aid:*** *Freshmen:* 35% (194); *Undergraduates:* 24% (472). ***Scholarships, grants, and awards by category:*** *Academic Interests/Achievement:* 1,020 awards ($1,117,314 total): general academic interests/achievements. *Creative Arts/Performance:* 45 awards ($48,076 total): music. ***Tuition waivers:*** Full or partial for employees or children of employees, senior citizens. ***ROTC:*** Army cooperative.

LOANS ***Student loans:*** $2,532,842 (49% need-based, 51% non-need-based). ***Parent loans:*** $37,579 (100% non-need-based). ***Programs:*** FFEL (Subsidized and Unsubsidized Stafford, PLUS), Federal Nursing, state, college/university.

WORK-STUDY ***Federal work-study:*** *Total amount:* $36,322; 44 jobs averaging $826.

ATHLETIC AWARDS *Total amount:* 72,045 (100% non-need-based).

APPLYING for FINANCIAL AID ***Required financial aid forms:*** FAFSA, institution's own form. ***Financial aid deadline (priority):*** 4/1.

CONTACT Patricia Barton, Director of Financial Aid, Clayton College & State University, 5900 North Lee Street, Morrow, GA 30260, 770-961-3511. *Fax:* 770-961-2166. *E-mail:* financialaid@mail.clayton.edu

CLEAR CREEK BAPTIST BIBLE COLLEGE

Pineville, KY

Tuition & fees: $3170 **Average undergraduate aid package: $3597**

ABOUT THE INSTITUTION Independent Southern Baptist, coed, primarily men. Awards: associate and bachelor's degrees. 2 undergraduate majors.

Clear Creek Baptist Bible College (continued)

Total enrollment: 166. Undergraduates: 166. Freshmen: 15. Both federal and institutional methodology are used as a basis for awarding need-based institutional aid.

UNDERGRADUATE EXPENSES for 1999–2000 ***Application fee:*** $40. ***Comprehensive fee:*** $5910 includes full-time tuition ($2820), mandatory fees ($350), and room and board ($2740). Room and board charges vary according to housing facility. ***Part-time tuition:*** $160 per semester hour. ***Part-time fees:*** $110 per term part-time. Full-time tuition for nonchurch members: $3420. ***Payment plan:*** installment.

FRESHMAN FINANCIAL AID (Fall 1998) 10 applied for aid; of those 100% were deemed to have need. 100% of freshmen with need received aid. *Average percent of need met:* 36% (excluding resources awarded to replace EFC). *Average financial aid package:* $3329 (excluding resources awarded to replace EFC).

UNDERGRADUATE FINANCIAL AID (Fall 1998) 151 applied for aid; of those 100% were deemed to have need. 100% of undergraduates with need received aid. *Average percent of need met:* 54% (excluding resources awarded to replace EFC). *Average financial aid package:* $3597 (excluding resources awarded to replace EFC).

GIFT AID (NEED-BASED) ***Total amount:*** $528,997 (59% Federal, 17% institutional, 24% external sources). ***Receiving aid:*** *Freshmen:* 83% (10); *all full-time undergraduates:* 84% (139). ***Average award:*** Freshmen: $3329; Undergraduates: $3913. ***Scholarships, grants, and awards:*** Federal Pell, FSEOG, private, college/university gift aid from institutional funds.

GIFT AID (NON-NEED-BASED) ***Total amount:*** $29,752 (100% institutional). ***Receiving aid:*** *Freshmen:* 67% (8); *Undergraduates:* 30% (50). ***Scholarships, grants, and awards by category:*** *Academic Interests/Achievement:* 3 awards ($450 total): general academic interests/achievements. *Creative Arts/Performance:* music, theater/drama. *Special Achievements/Activities:* religious involvement.

WORK-STUDY ***Federal work-study:*** *Total amount:* $13,494; 51 jobs averaging $265.

APPLYING for FINANCIAL AID ***Required financial aid forms:*** FAFSA, institution's own form. ***Financial aid deadline (priority):*** 6/30. ***Notification date:*** 8/1.

CONTACT Mr. Sam Risner, Director of Financial Aid, Clear Creek Baptist Bible College, 300 Clear Creek Road, Pineville, KY 40977-9754, 606-337-3196 Ext. 142. *Fax:* 606-337-2372. *E-mail:* clearcreek@tcnet.net

CLEARWATER CHRISTIAN COLLEGE

Clearwater, FL

Tuition & fees: $8500 **Average undergraduate aid package: $5785**

ABOUT THE INSTITUTION Independent nondenominational, coed. Awards: associate and bachelor's degrees. 31 undergraduate majors. Total enrollment: 603. Undergraduates: 603. Freshmen: 191. Federal methodology is used as a basis for awarding need-based institutional aid.

UNDERGRADUATE EXPENSES for 1999–2000 ***Application fee:*** $25. ***Comprehensive fee:*** $12,198 includes full-time tuition ($8000), mandatory fees ($500), and room and board ($3698). Full-time tuition and fees vary according to course load and program. ***Part-time tuition:*** $330 per credit hour. ***Part-time fees:*** $125 per term part-time. Part-time tuition and fees vary according to course load and program. ***Payment plan:*** installment.

FRESHMAN FINANCIAL AID (Fall 1999, est.) 152 applied for aid; of those 100% were deemed to have need. 100% of freshmen with need received aid; of those 5% had need fully met. *Average percent of need met:* 48% (excluding resources awarded to replace EFC). *Average financial aid package:* $6621 (excluding resources awarded to replace EFC).

UNDERGRADUATE FINANCIAL AID (Fall 1999, est.) 537 applied for aid; of those 100% were deemed to have need. 100% of undergraduates with need received aid; of those 4% had need fully met. *Average percent of need met:* 33% (excluding resources awarded to replace EFC). *Average financial aid package:* $5785 (excluding resources awarded to replace EFC).

GIFT AID (NEED-BASED) ***Total amount:*** $693,899 (64% Federal, 20% state, 16% institutional). ***Receiving aid:*** *Freshmen:* 31% (51); *all full-time undergraduates:* 60% (372). ***Average award:*** Freshmen: $5582; Undergraduates: $1738. ***Scholarships, grants, and awards:*** Federal Pell, FSEOG, state, private, college/university gift aid from institutional funds.

GIFT AID (NON-NEED-BASED) ***Total amount:*** $1,555,275 (51% state, 42% institutional, 7% external sources). ***Receiving aid:*** *Freshmen:* 77% (129); *Undergraduates:* 72% (450). ***Scholarships, grants, and awards by category:*** *Academic Interests/Achievement:* business, education, general academic interests/achievements, mathematics, premedicine, religion/biblical studies. *Creative Arts/Performance:* music. *Special Characteristics:* children of educators, first-generation college students, local/state students. ***ROTC:*** Army cooperative, Air Force cooperative.

LOANS ***Student loans:*** $1,074,662 (73% need-based, 27% non-need-based). 48% of past graduating class borrowed through all loan programs. Average indebtedness per student: $13,051. ***Average need-based loan:*** Freshmen: $2374; Undergraduates: $3574. ***Parent loans:*** $219,088 (100% non-need-based). ***Programs:*** FFEL (Subsidized and Unsubsidized Stafford, PLUS), college/university, alternative loans.

WORK-STUDY ***Federal work-study:*** *Total amount:* $41,169; jobs available. ***State or other work-study/employment:*** *Total amount:* $19,800 (100% need-based). Part-time jobs available.

APPLYING for FINANCIAL AID ***Required financial aid form:*** FAFSA. ***Financial aid deadline (priority):*** 4/15. ***Notification date:*** Continuous. Students must reply within 2 weeks of notification.

CONTACT Ms. Ruth Strum, Director of Financial Aid, Clearwater Christian College, 3400 Gulf-to-Bay Boulevard, Clearwater, FL 33759-4595, 727-726-1153 Ext. 221 or toll-free 800-348-4463. *E-mail:* ruthstrum@clearwater.edu

CLEARY COLLEGE

Howell, MI

Tuition & fees: $7605 **Average undergraduate aid package: $2354**

ABOUT THE INSTITUTION Independent, coed. Awards: associate and bachelor's degrees. 10 undergraduate majors. Total enrollment: 642. Undergraduates: 642. Federal methodology is used as a basis for awarding need-based institutional aid.

UNDERGRADUATE EXPENSES for 1999–2000 ***Application fee:*** $25. ***Tuition:*** full-time $7605; part-time $169 per credit hour. ***Payment plans:*** installment, deferred payment.

UNDERGRADUATE FINANCIAL AID (Fall 1998) 242 applied for aid; of those 100% were deemed to have need. 100% of undergraduates with need received aid. *Average financial aid package:* $2354 (excluding resources awarded to replace EFC).

GIFT AID (NEED-BASED) ***Total amount:*** $706,986 (37% Federal, 43% state, 12% institutional, 8% external sources). ***Receiving aid:*** *All full-time undergraduates:* 31% (163). ***Average award:*** Undergraduates: $884. ***Scholarships, grants, and awards:*** Federal Pell, FSEOG, state, private, college/university gift aid from institutional funds.

GIFT AID (NON-NEED-BASED) ***Scholarships, grants, and awards by category:*** *Academic Interests/Achievement:* general academic interests/achievements. *Special Achievements/Activities:* community service, general special achievements/activities. *Special Characteristics:* children of faculty/staff. ***Tuition waivers:*** Full or partial for employees or children of employees, senior citizens. ***ROTC:*** Air Force cooperative.

LOANS ***Student loans:*** $1,713,403 (100% need-based). ***Average need-based loan:*** Undergraduates: $1470. ***Parent loans:*** $44,633 (100% need-based). ***Programs:*** FFEL (Subsidized and Unsubsidized Stafford, PLUS).

WORK-STUDY ***Federal work-study:*** *Total amount:* $9565; 5 jobs averaging $1913.

APPLYING for FINANCIAL AID ***Required financial aid forms:*** FAFSA, institution's own form. ***Financial aid deadline (priority):*** 3/1. ***Notification date:*** Continuous. Students must reply by 9/1.

CONTACT Vesta Smith-Campbell, Director of Financial Assistance, Cleary College, 3601 Plymouth Road, Ann Arbor, MI 48105, 800-686-1883 Ext. 3349 or toll-free 800-589-1979 Ext. 2249. *E-mail:* vscampbell@cleary.edu

CLEMSON UNIVERSITY

Clemson, SC

Tuition & fees (SC res): $3470 **Average undergraduate aid package: $7123**

ABOUT THE INSTITUTION State-supported, coed. Awards: bachelor's, master's, and doctoral degrees. 71 undergraduate majors. Total enrollment: 16,982. Undergraduates: 13,526. Freshmen: 2,891. Federal methodology is used as a basis for awarding need-based institutional aid.

UNDERGRADUATE EXPENSES for 1999–2000 ***Application fee:*** $40. ***Tuition, state resident:*** full-time $3280; part-time $138 per hour. ***Tuition, nonresident:*** full-time $9266; part-time $388 per hour. ***Required fees:*** full-time $190; $5 per term part-time. ***College room and board:*** $4122; ***room only:*** $2202. Room and board charges vary according to board plan and housing facility. ***Payment plans:*** installment, deferred payment.

FRESHMAN FINANCIAL AID (Fall 1999) 1810 applied for aid; of those 63% were deemed to have need. 97% of freshmen with need received aid; of those 52% had need fully met. *Average percent of need met:* 89% (excluding resources awarded to replace EFC). *Average financial aid package:* $7204 (excluding resources awarded to replace EFC). 41% of all full-time freshmen had no need and received non-need-based aid.

UNDERGRADUATE FINANCIAL AID (Fall 1999) 6,815 applied for aid; of those 72% were deemed to have need. 93% of undergraduates with need received aid; of those 40% had need fully met. *Average percent of need met:* 82% (excluding resources awarded to replace EFC). *Average financial aid package:* $7123 (excluding resources awarded to replace EFC). 29% of all full-time undergraduates had no need and received non-need-based aid.

GIFT AID (NEED-BASED) ***Total amount:*** $7,533,388 (55% Federal, 17% state, 17% institutional, 11% external sources). ***Receiving aid:*** *Freshmen:* 16% (452); *all full-time undergraduates:* 17% (2,260). ***Average award:*** Freshmen: $2756; Undergraduates: $2621. ***Scholarships, grants, and awards:*** Federal Pell, FSEOG, state, private, college/university gift aid from institutional funds, Federal Nursing.

GIFT AID (NON-NEED-BASED) ***Total amount:*** $14,478,155 (66% state, 20% institutional, 14% external sources). ***Receiving aid:*** *Freshmen:* 31% (893); *Undergraduates:* 17% (2,233). ***Scholarships, grants, and awards by category:*** *Academic Interests/Achievement:* agriculture, architecture, biological sciences, business, communication, computer science, education, engineering/technologies, English, foreign languages, general academic interests/achievements, health fields, humanities, international studies, mathematics, military science, physical sciences, premedicine, social sciences. *Special Characteristics:* children of faculty/staff, ethnic background, local/state students, members of minority groups. ***Tuition waivers:*** Full or partial for senior citizens. ***ROTC:*** Army, Air Force.

LOANS ***Student loans:*** $21,051,642 (58% need-based, 42% non-need-based). 46% of past graduating class borrowed through all loan programs. Average indebtedness per student: $13,987. ***Average need-based loan:*** Freshmen: $2606; Undergraduates: $3681. ***Parent loans:*** $3,434,000 (100% non-need-based). ***Programs:*** Federal Direct (PLUS), FFEL (Subsidized and Unsubsidized Stafford, PLUS), Perkins, state, college/university.

WORK-STUDY ***Federal work-study:*** *Total amount:* $1,460,765; 725 jobs averaging $2014.

ATHLETIC AWARDS *Total amount:* 2,403,130 (100% non-need-based).

APPLYING for FINANCIAL AID ***Required financial aid form:*** FAFSA. ***Financial aid deadline (priority):*** 4/1. ***Notification date:*** Continuous. Students must reply within 3 weeks of notification.

CONTACT Mr. Marvin G. Carmichael, Director of Financial Aid, Clemson University, G01 Sikes Hall, Clemson, SC 29634-5123, 864-656-2280. *Fax:* 864-656-1831. *E-mail:* finaid@clemson.edu

CLEVELAND COLLEGE OF JEWISH STUDIES

Beachwood, OH

Tuition & fees: $6015 **Average undergraduate aid package: N/A**

ABOUT THE INSTITUTION Independent, coed. Awards: bachelor's and master's degrees. 10 undergraduate majors. Total enrollment: 81. Undergraduates: 14. Freshmen: 1. Institutional methodology is used as a basis for awarding need-based institutional aid.

UNDERGRADUATE EXPENSES for 1999–2000 ***Application fee:*** $25. ***Tuition:*** full-time $6000; part-time $200 per credit. ***Required fees:*** full-time $15; $15 per year part-time. ***Payment plan:*** installment.

GIFT AID (NEED-BASED) ***Total amount:*** $2500 (100% institutional). ***Scholarships, grants, and awards:*** college/university gift aid from institutional funds.

GIFT AID (NON-NEED-BASED) ***Scholarships, grants, and awards by category:*** *Academic Interests/Achievement:* education, religion/biblical studies. ***Tuition waivers:*** Full or partial for employees or children of employees, senior citizens.

APPLYING for FINANCIAL AID ***Required financial aid form:*** institution's own form. ***Financial aid deadline:*** Continuous. ***Notification date:*** Continuous beginning 9/1. Students must reply within 2 weeks of notification.

CONTACT Ms. Linda Rosen, Director of Enrollment, Cleveland College of Jewish Studies, 26500 Shaker Boulevard, Beachwood, OH 44122-7116, 216-464-4050 Ext. 101 or toll-free 888-336-2257. *Fax:* 216-464-5827. *E-mail:* lrosen@ccjs.edu

CLEVELAND INSTITUTE OF ART

Cleveland, OH

Tuition & fees: $15,015 **Average undergraduate aid package: $11,636**

ABOUT THE INSTITUTION Independent, coed. Awards: bachelor's degrees. 13 undergraduate majors. Total enrollment: 525. Undergraduates: 525. Freshmen: 108. Federal methodology is used as a basis for awarding need-based institutional aid.

UNDERGRADUATE EXPENSES for 1999–2000 ***Application fee:*** $30. ***Comprehensive fee:*** $20,091 includes full-time tuition ($14,175), mandatory fees ($840), and room and board ($5076). ***College room only:*** $2956. ***Part-time tuition:*** $525 per credit. ***Part-time fees:*** $27 per credit. Part-time tuition and fees vary according to course load. ***Payment plan:*** installment.

FRESHMAN FINANCIAL AID (Fall 1999) 92 applied for aid; of those 85% were deemed to have need. 100% of freshmen with need received aid; of those 22% had need fully met. *Average percent of need met:* 71% (excluding resources awarded to replace EFC). *Average financial aid package:* $10,235 (excluding resources awarded to replace EFC). 27% of all full-time freshmen had no need and received non-need-based aid.

UNDERGRADUATE FINANCIAL AID (Fall 1999) 406 applied for aid; of those 89% were deemed to have need. 100% of undergraduates with need received aid; of those 27% had need fully met. *Average percent of need met:* 77% (excluding resources awarded to replace EFC). *Average financial aid package:* $11,636 (excluding resources awarded to replace EFC). 25% of all full-time undergraduates had no need and received non-need-based aid.

GIFT AID (NEED-BASED) ***Total amount:*** $2,123,200 (18% Federal, 22% state, 52% institutional, 8% external sources). ***Receiving aid:*** *Freshmen:* 73% (78); *all full-time undergraduates:* 74% (362). ***Average award:*** Freshmen: $5729; Undergraduates: $5786. ***Scholarships, grants, and awards:*** Federal Pell, FSEOG, state, private, college/university gift aid from institutional funds.

GIFT AID (NON-NEED-BASED) ***Total amount:*** $657,034 (9% state, 89% institutional, 2% external sources). ***Receiving aid:*** *Freshmen:* 8% (9); *Undergraduates:* 6% (31). ***Scholarships, grants, and awards by category:*** *Creative Arts/Performance:* art/fine arts. ***Tuition waivers:*** Full or partial for employees or children of employees.

Cleveland Institute of Art (continued)

LOANS ***Student loans:*** $2,165,280 (83% need-based, 17% non-need-based). 75% of past graduating class borrowed through all loan programs. Average indebtedness per student: $16,253. ***Average need-based loan:*** Freshmen: $3448; Undergraduates: $4801. ***Parent loans:*** $405,542 (44% need-based, 56% non-need-based). ***Programs:*** FFEL (Subsidized and Unsubsidized Stafford, PLUS), Perkins.

WORK-STUDY ***Federal work-study:*** *Total amount:* $389,149; 298 jobs averaging $1305.

APPLYING for FINANCIAL AID ***Required financial aid forms:*** FAFSA, institution's own form. ***Financial aid deadline (priority):*** 3/15. ***Notification date:*** Continuous beginning 3/16. Students must reply within 4 weeks of notification.

CONTACT Ms. Nancy Maldonado-Dillard, Director of Financial Aid, Cleveland Institute of Art, 11141 East Boulevard, Cleveland, OH 44106-1700, 216-421-7425 or toll-free 800-223-4700. *Fax:* 216-421-7438.

CLEVELAND INSTITUTE OF MUSIC

Cleveland, OH

Tuition & fees: $18,625 **Average undergraduate aid package: $14,283**

ABOUT THE INSTITUTION Independent, coed. Awards: bachelor's, master's, and doctoral degrees. 7 undergraduate majors. Total enrollment: 369. Undergraduates: 222. Freshmen: 52. Federal methodology is used as a basis for awarding need-based institutional aid.

UNDERGRADUATE EXPENSES for 1999–2000 ***Application fee:*** $70. ***One-time required fee:*** $500. ***Comprehensive fee:*** $24,215 includes full-time tuition ($17,875), mandatory fees ($750), and room and board ($5590). ***College room only:*** $3500. ***Part-time tuition:*** $800 per credit hour. ***Part-time fees:*** $750 per year part-time. ***Payment plan:*** installment.

FRESHMAN FINANCIAL AID (Fall 1999, est.) 36 applied for aid; of those 78% were deemed to have need. 100% of freshmen with need received aid; of those 32% had need fully met. *Average percent of need met:* 81% (excluding resources awarded to replace EFC). *Average financial aid package:* $13,409 (excluding resources awarded to replace EFC).

UNDERGRADUATE FINANCIAL AID (Fall 1999, est.) 173 applied for aid; of those 77% were deemed to have need. 100% of undergraduates with need received aid; of those 28% had need fully met. *Average percent of need met:* 80% (excluding resources awarded to replace EFC). *Average financial aid package:* $14,283 (excluding resources awarded to replace EFC). 35% of all full-time undergraduates had no need and received non-need-based aid.

GIFT AID (NEED-BASED) ***Total amount:*** $1,144,259 (8% Federal, 3% state, 86% institutional, 3% external sources). ***Receiving aid:*** *Freshmen:* 60% (28); *all full-time undergraduates:* 65% (134). ***Average award:*** Freshmen: $8797; Undergraduates: $8441. ***Scholarships, grants, and awards:*** Federal Pell, FSEOG, state, private, college/university gift aid from institutional funds.

GIFT AID (NON-NEED-BASED) ***Total amount:*** $547,454 (3% state, 91% institutional, 6% external sources). ***Receiving aid:*** *Freshmen:* 11% (5); *Undergraduates:* 8% (17). ***Scholarships, grants, and awards by category:*** *Creative Arts/Performance:* music. ***Tuition waivers:*** Full or partial for employees or children of employees. ***ROTC:*** Army cooperative, Air Force cooperative.

LOANS ***Student loans:*** $891,105 (79% need-based, 21% non-need-based). 75% of past graduating class borrowed through all loan programs. Average indebtedness per student: $12,053. ***Average need-based loan:*** Freshmen: $3736; Undergraduates: $4999. ***Parent loans:*** $128,540 (45% need-based, 55% non-need-based). ***Programs:*** Federal Direct (Subsidized and Unsubsidized Stafford, PLUS), Perkins, college/university.

WORK-STUDY ***Federal work-study:*** *Total amount:* $116,867; 67 jobs averaging $1744. ***State or other work-study/employment:*** *Total amount:* $34,900 (1% need-based, 99% non-need-based). 28 part-time jobs averaging $1246.

APPLYING for FINANCIAL AID ***Required financial aid forms:*** FAFSA, institution's own form, CSS Financial Aid PROFILE. ***Financial aid deadline:*** 2/15. ***Notification date:*** 4/1. Students must reply by 5/1 or within 2 weeks of notification.

CONTACT Ms. Carol E. Peffer, Director of Financial Aid, Cleveland Institute of Music, 11021 East Boulevard, Cleveland, OH 44106-1776, 216-791-5000 Ext. 262. *E-mail:* cxp21@po.cwru.edu

CLEVELAND STATE UNIVERSITY

Cleveland, OH

ABOUT THE INSTITUTION State-supported, coed. Awards: bachelor's, master's, doctoral, and first professional degrees. 63 undergraduate majors. Total enrollment: 15,683. Undergraduates: 10,457. Freshmen: 1,425.

GIFT AID (NEED-BASED) ***Scholarships, grants, and awards:*** Federal Pell, FSEOG, state, private, college/university gift aid from institutional funds.

GIFT AID (NON-NEED-BASED) ***Scholarships, grants, and awards by category:*** *Academic Interests/Achievement:* general academic interests/achievements. *Creative Arts/Performance:* art/fine arts, music, theater/drama. *Special Achievements/Activities:* general special achievements/activities. *Special Characteristics:* general special characteristics.

LOANS ***Programs:*** FFEL (Subsidized and Unsubsidized Stafford, PLUS), Perkins, state, college/university.

WORK-STUDY Federal work-study jobs available.

APPLYING for FINANCIAL AID ***Required financial aid form:*** FAFSA.

CONTACT Director of Financial Aid, Cleveland State University, 2344 Euclid Avenue #201, Cleveland, OH 44115-2407, 216-687-3765.

CLINCH VALLEY COLLEGE OF THE UNIVERSITY OF VIRGINIA

Wise, VA

See University of Virginia's College at Wise

COASTAL CAROLINA UNIVERSITY

Conway, SC

Tuition & fees (SC res): $3340 **Average undergraduate aid package: $6281**

ABOUT THE INSTITUTION State-supported, coed. Awards: bachelor's and master's degrees and post-bachelor's certificates. 25 undergraduate majors. Total enrollment: 4,615. Undergraduates: 4,370. Freshmen: 766. Federal methodology is used as a basis for awarding need-based institutional aid.

UNDERGRADUATE EXPENSES for 1999–2000 ***Application fee:*** $25. ***Tuition, state resident:*** full-time $3340; part-time $140 per semester hour. ***Tuition, nonresident:*** full-time $9280; part-time $385 per semester hour. ***Required fees:*** $35 per term part-time. Part-time tuition and fees vary according to course load. ***College room and board:*** $4970. Room and board charges vary according to board plan. ***Payment plans:*** installment, deferred payment.

FRESHMAN FINANCIAL AID (Fall 1998) 473 applied for aid; of those 86% were deemed to have need. 96% of freshmen with need received aid; of those 13% had need fully met. *Average percent of need met:* 53% (excluding resources awarded to replace EFC). *Average financial aid package:* $5305 (excluding resources awarded to replace EFC). 13% of all full-time freshmen had no need and received non-need-based aid.

UNDERGRADUATE FINANCIAL AID (Fall 1998) 1,875 applied for aid; of those 87% were deemed to have need. 97% of undergraduates with need received aid; of those 20% had need fully met. *Average percent of need met:* 62% (excluding resources awarded to replace EFC). *Average financial aid package:* $6281 (excluding resources awarded to replace EFC). 11% of all full-time undergraduates had no need and received non-need-based aid.

GIFT AID (NEED-BASED) ***Total amount:*** $2,523,242 (85% Federal, 15% state). ***Receiving aid:*** *Freshmen:* 21% (181); *all full-time undergraduates:*

22% (805). ***Average award:*** Freshmen: $2642; Undergraduates: $2602. ***Scholarships, grants, and awards:*** Federal Pell, FSEOG, state, private, college/university gift aid from institutional funds.

GIFT AID (NON-NEED-BASED) ***Total amount:*** $1,605,208 (37% state, 27% institutional, 36% external sources). ***Receiving aid:*** *Freshmen:* 6% (50); *Undergraduates:* 4% (127). ***Scholarships, grants, and awards by category:*** *Academic Interests/Achievement:* biological sciences, business, education, general academic interests/achievements, humanities, mathematics. *Creative Arts/Performance:* art/fine arts, music, theater/drama. *Special Characteristics:* first-generation college students, general special characteristics, international students, local/state students, out-of-state students, veterans' children. ***Tuition waivers:*** Full or partial for employees or children of employees, senior citizens.

LOANS ***Student loans:*** $8,609,122 (63% need-based, 37% non-need-based). Average indebtedness per student: $12,000. ***Average need-based loan:*** Freshmen: $4646; Undergraduates: $5836. ***Parent loans:*** $1,652,946 (100% non-need-based). ***Programs:*** FFEL (Subsidized and Unsubsidized Stafford, PLUS), Perkins, state.

WORK-STUDY ***Federal work-study:*** *Total amount:* $215,162; 110 jobs averaging $1956. ***State or other work-study/employment:*** *Total amount:* $546,772 (100% non-need-based). Part-time jobs available.

ATHLETIC AWARDS *Total amount:* 592,601 (100% non-need-based).

APPLYING for FINANCIAL AID ***Required financial aid form:*** FAFSA. ***Financial aid deadline (priority):*** 4/1. ***Notification date:*** Continuous.

CONTACT Glenn Hanson, Associate Director of Financial Aid, Coastal Carolina University, PO Box 261954, Conway, SC 29528-6054, 843-349-2325 or toll-free 800-277-7000. *Fax:* 843-349-2347. *E-mail:* glenn@coastal.edu

COE COLLEGE

Cedar Rapids, IA

Tuition & fees: $17,540 **Average undergraduate aid package: $18,048**

ABOUT THE INSTITUTION Independent religious, coed. Awards: bachelor's and master's degrees. 50 undergraduate majors. Total enrollment: 1,304. Undergraduates: 1,246. Freshmen: 328. Federal methodology is used as a basis for awarding need-based institutional aid.

UNDERGRADUATE EXPENSES for 1999–2000 ***Comprehensive fee:*** $22,560 includes full-time tuition ($17,390), mandatory fees ($150), and room and board ($5020). ***College room only:*** $2340. Room and board charges vary according to board plan. ***Part-time tuition:*** $880 per course. ***Payment plan:*** installment.

FRESHMAN FINANCIAL AID (Fall 1999, est.) 325 applied for aid; of those 88% were deemed to have need. 100% of freshmen with need received aid; of those 86% had need fully met. *Average percent of need met:* 96% (excluding resources awarded to replace EFC). *Average financial aid package:* $17,597 (excluding resources awarded to replace EFC). 9% of all full-time freshmen had no need and received non-need-based aid.

UNDERGRADUATE FINANCIAL AID (Fall 1999, est.) 1,080 applied for aid; of those 85% were deemed to have need. 100% of undergraduates with need received aid; of those 90% had need fully met. *Average percent of need met:* 95% (excluding resources awarded to replace EFC). *Average financial aid package:* $18,048 (excluding resources awarded to replace EFC). 14% of all full-time undergraduates had no need and received non-need-based aid.

GIFT AID (NEED-BASED) ***Total amount:*** $10,682,177 (8% Federal, 17% state, 72% institutional, 3% external sources). ***Receiving aid:*** *Freshmen:* 70% (230); *all full-time undergraduates:* 66% (737). ***Average award:*** Freshmen: $6996; Undergraduates: $6828. ***Scholarships, grants, and awards:*** Federal Pell, FSEOG, state, private, college/university gift aid from institutional funds.

GIFT AID (NON-NEED-BASED) ***Total amount:*** $1,410,238 (98% institutional, 2% external sources). ***Receiving aid:*** *Freshmen:* 76% (249); *Undergraduates:* 65% (730). ***Scholarships, grants, and awards by category:*** *Academic Interests/Achievement:* biological sciences, foreign languages, general academic interests/achievements, physical sciences, premedicine. *Creative Arts/Performance:* art/fine arts, creative writing, music, performing arts, theater/drama. *Special Achievements/Activities:* community service, leadership. *Special Characteristics:* children and siblings of alumni, international students, religious affiliation. ***Tuition waivers:*** Full or partial for children of alumni, employees or children of employees, adult students. ***ROTC:*** Army cooperative, Air Force cooperative.

LOANS ***Student loans:*** $4,902,173 (97% need-based, 3% non-need-based). 75% of past graduating class borrowed through all loan programs. Average indebtedness per student: $15,310. ***Average need-based loan:*** Freshmen: $4325; Undergraduates: $5143. ***Parent loans:*** $1,004,025 (89% need-based, 11% non-need-based). ***Programs:*** Federal Direct (Subsidized and Unsubsidized Stafford, PLUS), Perkins, college/university.

WORK-STUDY ***Federal work-study:*** *Total amount:* $416,400; 347 jobs averaging $1200. ***State or other work-study/employment:*** *Total amount:* $342,250 (23% need-based, 77% non-need-based). Part-time jobs available.

APPLYING for FINANCIAL AID ***Required financial aid form:*** FAFSA. ***Financial aid deadline (priority):*** 3/1. ***Notification date:*** Continuous. Students must reply by 5/1.

CONTACT Mr. Robert L. Baird, Director of Financial Aid/Associate Dean of Admissions, Coe College, 1220 1st Avenue, NE, Cedar Rapids, IA 52402-5070, 319-399-8540 or toll-free 877-225-5263. *Fax:* 319-399-8886. *E-mail:* rbaird@coe.edu

COGSWELL POLYTECHNICAL COLLEGE

Sunnyvale, CA

Tuition & fees: $8420 **Average undergraduate aid package: $3737**

ABOUT THE INSTITUTION Independent, coed. Awards: bachelor's degrees. 7 undergraduate majors. Total enrollment: 500. Undergraduates: 500. Freshmen: 30. Federal methodology is used as a basis for awarding need-based institutional aid.

UNDERGRADUATE EXPENSES for 2000–2001 ***Application fee:*** $50. ***Tuition:*** full-time $8400; part-time $350 per unit. ***Required fees:*** full-time $20; $10 per term part-time. Full-time tuition and fees vary according to course load. Part-time tuition and fees vary according to course load. ***Payment plan:*** deferred payment.

FRESHMAN FINANCIAL AID (Fall 1998) 13 applied for aid; of those 38% were deemed to have need. 100% of freshmen with need received aid. *Average percent of need met:* 31% (excluding resources awarded to replace EFC). *Average financial aid package:* $3448 (excluding resources awarded to replace EFC). 3% of all full-time freshmen had no need and received non-need-based aid.

UNDERGRADUATE FINANCIAL AID (Fall 1998) 114 applied for aid; of those 71% were deemed to have need. 100% of undergraduates with need received aid. *Average percent of need met:* 29% (excluding resources awarded to replace EFC). *Average financial aid package:* $3737 (excluding resources awarded to replace EFC). 14% of all full-time undergraduates had no need and received non-need-based aid.

GIFT AID (NEED-BASED) ***Total amount:*** $403,146 (54% Federal, 45% state, 1% institutional). ***Receiving aid:*** *Freshmen:* 15% (5); *all full-time undergraduates:* 32% (81). ***Average award:*** Freshmen: $2398; Undergraduates: $2111. ***Scholarships, grants, and awards:*** Federal Pell, FSEOG, state, private.

GIFT AID (NON-NEED-BASED) ***Receiving aid:*** *Freshmen:* 9% (3); *Undergraduates:* 2% (5). ***Scholarships, grants, and awards by category:*** *Academic Interests/Achievement:* computer science, engineering/technologies. ***Tuition waivers:*** Full or partial for employees or children of employees.

LOANS ***Student loans:*** $1,179,004 (53% need-based, 47% non-need-based). 32% of past graduating class borrowed through all loan programs. Average indebtedness per student: $22,345. ***Average need-based loan:*** Freshmen: $1050; Undergraduates: $1626. ***Parent loans:*** $277,645 (100% non-need-based). ***Programs:*** FFEL (Subsidized and Unsubsidized Stafford, PLUS).

WORK-STUDY ***Federal work-study:*** *Total amount:* $21,703; 10 jobs averaging $2000.

Cogswell Polytechnical College (continued)

APPLYING for FINANCIAL AID ***Required financial aid forms:*** FAFSA, institution's own form. ***Financial aid deadline:*** Continuous. ***Notification date:*** Continuous beginning 4/30. Students must reply within 4 weeks of notification.

CONTACT Guillermo Gaeta, Financial Aid Director, Cogswell Polytechnical College, 1175 Bordeaux Drive, Sunnyvale, CA 94089, 408-541-0100 Ext. 107 or toll-free 800-264-7955. *Fax:* 408-747-0765. *E-mail:* gsgaeta@cogswell.edu

COKER COLLEGE

Hartsville, SC

Tuition & fees: $14,552 **Average undergraduate aid package: $10,996**

ABOUT THE INSTITUTION Independent, coed. Awards: bachelor's degrees. 45 undergraduate majors. Total enrollment: 975. Undergraduates: 975. Federal methodology is used as a basis for awarding need-based institutional aid.

UNDERGRADUATE EXPENSES for 1999–2000 ***Application fee:*** $15. ***Comprehensive fee:*** $19,272 includes full-time tuition ($14,352), mandatory fees ($200), and room and board ($4720). ***College room only:*** $2670. Full-time tuition and fees vary according to location. Room and board charges vary according to housing facility. ***Part-time tuition:*** $598 per semester hour. ***Part-time fees:*** $2 per semester hour. Part-time tuition and fees vary according to location. ***Payment plan:*** installment.

FRESHMAN FINANCIAL AID (Fall 1999) 119 applied for aid; of those 91% were deemed to have need. 100% of freshmen with need received aid; of those 51% had need fully met. *Average percent of need met:* 94% (excluding resources awarded to replace EFC). *Average financial aid package:* $12,844 (excluding resources awarded to replace EFC). 9% of all full-time freshmen had no need and received non-need-based aid.

UNDERGRADUATE FINANCIAL AID (Fall 1999) 795 applied for aid; of those 93% were deemed to have need. 99% of undergraduates with need received aid; of those 35% had need fully met. *Average percent of need met:* 78% (excluding resources awarded to replace EFC). *Average financial aid package:* $10,996 (excluding resources awarded to replace EFC). 4% of all full-time undergraduates had no need and received non-need-based aid.

GIFT AID (NEED-BASED) ***Total amount:*** $3,001,822 (33% Federal, 47% state, 17% institutional, 3% external sources). ***Receiving aid:*** *Freshmen:* 79% (100); *all full-time undergraduates:* 73% (659). ***Average award:*** Freshmen: $3928; Undergraduates: $4222. ***Scholarships, grants, and awards:*** Federal Pell, FSEOG, state, private, college/university gift aid from institutional funds.

GIFT AID (NON-NEED-BASED) ***Total amount:*** $2,209,137 (5% Federal, 9% state, 82% institutional, 4% external sources). ***Receiving aid:*** *Freshmen:* 19% (24); *Undergraduates:* 11% (96). ***Scholarships, grants, and awards by category:*** *Academic Interests/Achievement:* general academic interests/achievements. *Creative Arts/Performance:* art/fine arts, dance, music, theater/drama. *Special Characteristics:* children and siblings of alumni. ***Tuition waivers:*** Full or partial for employees or children of employees, adult students.

LOANS ***Student loans:*** $3,919,220 (95% need-based, 5% non-need-based). 93% of past graduating class borrowed through all loan programs. Average indebtedness per student: $11,800. ***Average need-based loan:*** Freshmen: $3780; Undergraduates: $5173. ***Parent loans:*** $328,501 (100% non-need-based). ***Programs:*** FFEL (Subsidized and Unsubsidized Stafford, PLUS), Perkins.

WORK-STUDY ***Federal work-study:*** *Total amount:* $106,902; jobs available.

ATHLETIC AWARDS *Total amount:* 433,905 (100% non-need-based).

APPLYING for FINANCIAL AID ***Required financial aid form:*** FAFSA. ***Financial aid deadline (priority):*** 4/1. ***Notification date:*** Continuous. Students must reply within 3 weeks of notification.

CONTACT Mr. Hal Lewis, Director of Financial Aid, Coker College, 300 East College Avenue, Hartsville, SC 29550, 843-383-8055 or toll-free 800-950-1908. *Fax:* 843-383-8056.

COLBY COLLEGE

Waterville, ME

Comprehensive fee: $31,580 **Average undergraduate aid package: $20,100**

ABOUT THE INSTITUTION Independent, coed. Awards: bachelor's degrees. 35 undergraduate majors. Total enrollment: 1,764. Undergraduates: 1,764. Freshmen: 489. Both federal and institutional methodology are used as a basis for awarding need-based institutional aid.

UNDERGRADUATE EXPENSES for 1999–2000 ***Application fee:*** $50. ***Comprehensive fee:*** $31,580. ***Payment plan:*** installment.

FRESHMAN FINANCIAL AID (Fall 1999, est.) 254 applied for aid; of those 74% were deemed to have need. 100% of freshmen with need received aid; of those 100% had need fully met. *Average percent of need met:* 100% (excluding resources awarded to replace EFC). *Average financial aid package:* $19,100 (excluding resources awarded to replace EFC). 3% of all full-time freshmen had no need and received non-need-based aid.

UNDERGRADUATE FINANCIAL AID (Fall 1999, est.) 829 applied for aid; of those 77% were deemed to have need. 100% of undergraduates with need received aid; of those 100% had need fully met. *Average percent of need met:* 100% (excluding resources awarded to replace EFC). *Average financial aid package:* $20,100 (excluding resources awarded to replace EFC). 3% of all full-time undergraduates had no need and received non-need-based aid.

GIFT AID (NEED-BASED) ***Total amount:*** $9,717,100 (6% Federal, 1% state, 88% institutional, 5% external sources). ***Receiving aid:*** *Freshmen:* 34% (165); *all full-time undergraduates:* 32% (570). ***Average award:*** Freshmen: $21,000; Undergraduates: $21,700. ***Scholarships, grants, and awards:*** Federal Pell, FSEOG, state, private, college/university gift aid from institutional funds.

GIFT AID (NON-NEED-BASED) ***Tuition waivers:*** Full or partial for employees or children of employees, adult students, senior citizens. ***ROTC:*** Army cooperative.

LOANS ***Student loans:*** $3,170,900 (87% need-based, 13% non-need-based). 55% of past graduating class borrowed through all loan programs. Average indebtedness per student: $16,300. ***Average need-based loan:*** Freshmen: $4500; Undergraduates: $5500. ***Parent loans:*** $1,448,200 (100% non-need-based). ***Programs:*** Federal Direct (Subsidized and Unsubsidized Stafford, PLUS), Perkins, state, college/university.

WORK-STUDY ***Federal work-study:*** *Total amount:* $666,200; 438 jobs averaging $1500. ***State or other work-study/employment:*** *Total amount:* $20,400 (100% need-based). Part-time jobs available.

APPLYING for FINANCIAL AID ***Required financial aid forms:*** FAFSA, institution's own form, CSS Financial Aid PROFILE. ***Financial aid deadline:*** 2/1. ***Notification date:*** 4/1. Students must reply by 5/1.

CONTACT Ms. Lucia Whittelsey, Director of Financial Aid, Colby College, 4850 Mayflower Hill, Waterville, ME 04901-8848, 207-872-3168 or toll-free 800-723-3032. *Fax:* 207-872-3474. *E-mail:* lwwhitte@colby.edu

COLBY-SAWYER COLLEGE

New London, NH

Tuition & fees: $19,110 **Average undergraduate aid package: $14,280**

ABOUT THE INSTITUTION Independent, coed. Awards: associate and bachelor's degrees. 18 undergraduate majors. Total enrollment: 808. Undergraduates: 808. Freshmen: 236. Federal methodology is used as a basis for awarding need-based institutional aid.

UNDERGRADUATE EXPENSES for 2000–2001 ***Application fee:*** $40. ***Comprehensive fee:*** $26,350 includes full-time tuition ($18,960), mandatory fees ($150), and room and board ($7240). ***College room only:*** $3980. ***Part-time tuition:*** $630 per credit hour. ***Part-time fees:*** $75 per term part-time. Part-time tuition and fees vary according to course load. ***Payment plan:*** installment.

FRESHMAN FINANCIAL AID (Fall 1999, est.) 185 applied for aid; of those 86% were deemed to have need. 99% of freshmen with need received aid. *Average percent of need met:* 80% (excluding resources awarded to replace EFC). *Average financial aid package:* $13,000 (excluding resources awarded to replace EFC). 11% of all full-time freshmen had no need and received non-need-based aid.

UNDERGRADUATE FINANCIAL AID (Fall 1999, est.) 625 applied for aid; of those 88% were deemed to have need. 99% of undergraduates with need received aid. *Average percent of need met:* 80% (excluding resources awarded to replace EFC). *Average financial aid package:* $14,280 (excluding resources awarded to replace EFC). 7% of all full-time undergraduates had no need and received non-need-based aid.

GIFT AID (NEED-BASED) ***Receiving aid:*** *Freshmen:* 60% (142); *all full-time undergraduates:* 67% (508). ***Average award:*** Freshmen: $8500; Undergraduates: $8725. ***Scholarships, grants, and awards:*** Federal Pell, FSEOG, state, private, college/university gift aid from institutional funds.

GIFT AID (NON-NEED-BASED) ***Receiving aid:*** *Freshmen:* 14% (32); *Undergraduates:* 8% (64). ***Scholarships, grants, and awards by category:*** *Academic Interests/Achievement:* general academic interests/achievements. *Creative Arts/Performance:* art/fine arts, creative writing, music. *Special Achievements/Activities:* community service, leadership. *Special Characteristics:* children of faculty/staff. ***Tuition waivers:*** Full or partial for employees or children of employees. ***ROTC:*** Army cooperative, Air Force cooperative.

LOANS ***Student loans:*** 71% of past graduating class borrowed through all loan programs. Average indebtedness per student: $17,200. ***Programs:*** FFEL (Subsidized and Unsubsidized Stafford, PLUS), Perkins, college/university.

WORK-STUDY Federal work-study jobs available. ***State or other work-study/employment:*** Part-time jobs available.

APPLYING for FINANCIAL AID ***Required financial aid forms:*** FAFSA, institution's own form. ***Financial aid deadline (priority):*** 3/1. ***Notification date:*** Continuous beginning 3/25. Students must reply by 5/1 or within 3 weeks of notification.

CONTACT Ms. Jolene Greene Mitchell, Dean of Financial Aid, Colby-Sawyer College, 100 Main Street, New London, NH 03257-4648, 603-526-3717 or toll-free 800-272-1015. *Fax:* 603-526-3452. *E-mail:* jgmitche@colby-sawyer.edu

COLEGIO BIBLICO PENTECOSTAL

St. Just, PR

CONTACT Mr. Eric Ayala, Director of Financial Aid, Colegio Biblico Pentecostal, PO Box 901, St. Just, PR 00978-0901, 787-761-0640.

COLEGIO PENTECOSTAL MIZPA

Río Piedras, PR

CONTACT Financial Aid Office, Colegio Pentecostal Mizpa, Km. 0 Hm. 2, Bo. Caimito, Apartado 20966, Río Piedras, PR 00928-0966, 787-720-4476.

COLEGIO UNIVERSITARIO DEL ESTE

Carolina, PR

CONTACT Mr. Clotilde Santiago, Director of Financial Aid, Colegio Universitario del Este, Apartado 2010, Carolina, PR 00928, 787-257-7373 Ext. 3300.

COLEMAN COLLEGE

La Mesa, CA

Tuition & fees: N/R **Average undergraduate aid package: N/A**

ABOUT THE INSTITUTION Independent, coed. Awards: associate, bachelor's, and master's degrees. 5 undergraduate majors. Total enrollment: 1,060. Undergraduates: 1,044. Freshmen: 332. Both federal and institutional methodology are used as a basis for awarding need-based institutional aid.

UNDERGRADUATE EXPENSES for 1999–2000 ***Tuition:*** part-time $130 per unit. Tuition per degree: $13,260 for associate degree, $23,400 for bachelor's degree. ***Payment plans:*** guaranteed tuition, installment.

GIFT AID (NEED-BASED) ***Scholarships, grants, and awards:*** Federal Pell, FSEOG, state.

GIFT AID (NON-NEED-BASED) ***Scholarships, grants, and awards by category:*** *Academic Interests/Achievement:* general academic interests/achievements. *Special Characteristics:* children and siblings of alumni. ***Tuition waivers:*** Full or partial for employees or children of employees.

LOANS ***Programs:*** Federal Direct (Subsidized and Unsubsidized Stafford, PLUS), FFEL (Subsidized and Unsubsidized Stafford, PLUS).

WORK-STUDY Federal work-study jobs available.

APPLYING for FINANCIAL AID ***Required financial aid forms:*** FAFSA, institution's own form, state aid form. ***Financial aid deadline:*** Continuous. ***Notification date:*** Continuous.

CONTACT Financial Aid Office, Coleman College, 7380 Parkway Drive, La Mesa, CA 91942-1500, 619-465-3990. *Fax:* 619-465-0162. *E-mail:* faoffice@coleman.edu

COLGATE UNIVERSITY

Hamilton, NY

Tuition & fees: $24,750 **Average undergraduate aid package: $21,543**

ABOUT THE INSTITUTION Independent, coed. Awards: bachelor's and master's degrees. 52 undergraduate majors. Total enrollment: 2,876. Undergraduates: 2,868. Freshmen: 750. Institutional methodology is used as a basis for awarding need-based institutional aid.

UNDERGRADUATE EXPENSES for 1999–2000 ***Application fee:*** $50. ***Comprehensive fee:*** $31,080 includes full-time tuition ($24,575), mandatory fees ($175), and room and board ($6330). ***College room only:*** $3055. Full-time tuition and fees vary according to course load. Room and board charges vary according to board plan and housing facility. ***Part-time tuition:*** $3071 per course. Part-time tuition and fees vary according to course load. ***Payment plans:*** tuition prepayment, installment, deferred payment.

FRESHMAN FINANCIAL AID (Fall 1999, est.) 385 applied for aid; of those 87% were deemed to have need. 99% of freshmen with need received aid; of those 96% had need fully met. *Average percent of need met:* 96% (excluding resources awarded to replace EFC). *Average financial aid package:* $22,011 (excluding resources awarded to replace EFC).

UNDERGRADUATE FINANCIAL AID (Fall 1999, est.) 1,364 applied for aid; of those 89% were deemed to have need. 99% of undergraduates with need received aid; of those 74% had need fully met. *Average percent of need met:* 98% (excluding resources awarded to replace EFC). *Average financial aid package:* $21,543 (excluding resources awarded to replace EFC).

GIFT AID (NEED-BASED) ***Total amount:*** $21,672,617 (5% Federal, 3% state, 89% institutional, 3% external sources). ***Receiving aid:*** *Freshmen:* 41% (309); *all full-time undergraduates:* 55% (1,132). ***Average award:*** Freshmen: $19,942; Undergraduates: $18,622. ***Scholarships, grants, and awards:*** Federal Pell, FSEOG, state, college/university gift aid from institutional funds.

GIFT AID (NON-NEED-BASED) ***Tuition waivers:*** Full or partial for employees or children of employees. ***ROTC:*** Army cooperative.

LOANS ***Student loans:*** $3,531,345 (100% need-based). 40% of past graduating class borrowed through all loan programs. Average indebtedness per student: $12,777. ***Average need-based loan:*** Freshmen: $2283; Undergraduates: $3336. ***Parent loans:*** $4,364,361 (100% need-based). ***Programs:*** FFEL (Subsidized and Unsubsidized Stafford, PLUS), Perkins.

WORK-STUDY ***Federal work-study:*** *Total amount:* $1,090,150; 780 jobs averaging $1398.

APPLYING for FINANCIAL AID ***Required financial aid forms:*** FAFSA, CSS Financial Aid PROFILE, noncustodial (divorced/separated) parent's statement, business/farm supplement. ***Financial aid deadline:*** 2/1. ***Notification date:*** 4/1. Students must reply by 5/1 or within 2 weeks of notification.

Colgate University (continued)

CONTACT Susan Kazin, Director of First-year Student Aid, Colgate University, 13 Oak Drive, Hamilton, NY 13346-1386, 315-228-7431. *Fax:* 315-228-7989. *E-mail:* skazin@mail.colgate.edu

COLLEGE MISERICORDIA

Dallas, PA

Tuition & fees: $15,250 **Average undergraduate aid package: $12,709**

ABOUT THE INSTITUTION Independent Roman Catholic, coed. Awards: bachelor's and master's degrees. 30 undergraduate majors. Total enrollment: 1,663. Undergraduates: 1,506. Freshmen: 256. Federal methodology is used as a basis for awarding need-based institutional aid.

UNDERGRADUATE EXPENSES for 1999–2000 ***Application fee:*** $25. ***Comprehensive fee:*** $21,590 includes full-time tuition ($14,470), mandatory fees ($780), and room and board ($6340). ***College room only:*** $3470. Room and board charges vary according to board plan and housing facility. ***Part-time tuition:*** $362 per credit. ***Payment plans:*** installment, deferred payment.

FRESHMAN FINANCIAL AID (Fall 1998) 171 applied for aid; of those 93% were deemed to have need. 99% of freshmen with need received aid; of those 13% had need fully met. *Average percent of need met:* 82% (excluding resources awarded to replace EFC). *Average financial aid package:* $10,036 (excluding resources awarded to replace EFC). 7% of all full-time freshmen had no need and received non-need-based aid.

UNDERGRADUATE FINANCIAL AID (Fall 1998) 974 applied for aid; of those 92% were deemed to have need. 100% of undergraduates with need received aid; of those 30% had need fully met. *Average percent of need met:* 84% (excluding resources awarded to replace EFC). *Average financial aid package:* $12,709 (excluding resources awarded to replace EFC). 18% of all full-time undergraduates had no need and received non-need-based aid.

GIFT AID (NEED-BASED) ***Total amount:*** $3,885,017 (21% Federal, 31% state, 45% institutional, 3% external sources). ***Receiving aid:*** *Freshmen:* 76% (142); *all full-time undergraduates:* 72% (784). ***Average award:*** Freshmen: $5170; Undergraduates: $4541. ***Scholarships, grants, and awards:*** Federal Pell, FSEOG, state, private, college/university gift aid from institutional funds.

GIFT AID (NON-NEED-BASED) ***Total amount:*** $2,592,401 (100% institutional). ***Receiving aid:*** *Freshmen:* 53% (100); *Undergraduates:* 45% (491). ***Scholarships, grants, and awards by category:*** *Academic Interests/Achievement:* general academic interests/achievements, humanities. *Special Achievements/Activities:* general special achievements/activities. ***Tuition waivers:*** Full or partial for employees or children of employees. ***ROTC:*** Army cooperative, Air Force cooperative.

LOANS ***Student loans:*** $5,413,196 (69% need-based, 31% non-need-based). 92% of past graduating class borrowed through all loan programs. Average indebtedness per student: $16,900. ***Average need-based loan:*** Freshmen: $3039; Undergraduates: $4439. ***Parent loans:*** $1,179,291 (100% need-based). ***Programs:*** FFEL (Subsidized and Unsubsidized Stafford, PLUS), Perkins, Federal Nursing.

WORK-STUDY ***Federal work-study:*** *Total amount:* $244,648; jobs available. ***State or other work-study/employment:*** *Total amount:* $95,458 (100% need-based). Part-time jobs available.

APPLYING for FINANCIAL AID ***Required financial aid forms:*** FAFSA, institution's own form. ***Financial aid deadline (priority):*** 3/1. ***Notification date:*** 3/15. Students must reply within 2 weeks of notification.

CONTACT Margaret R. Charnick, Director of Financial Aid, College Misericordia, 301 Lake Street, Dallas, PA 18612-1098, 570-674-6313 or toll-free 800-852-7675. *E-mail:* admis@miseri.edu

COLLEGE OF AERONAUTICS

Flushing, NY

Tuition & fees: $8500 **Average undergraduate aid package: $8148**

ABOUT THE INSTITUTION Independent, coed, primarily men. Awards: associate and bachelor's degrees. 9 undergraduate majors. Total enrollment: 1,305. Undergraduates: 1,305. Freshmen: 320. Federal methodology is used as a basis for awarding need-based institutional aid.

UNDERGRADUATE EXPENSES for 1999–2000 ***Application fee:*** $25. ***Tuition:*** full-time $8250; part-time $275 per credit. ***Required fees:*** full-time $250; $125 per term part-time. Full-time tuition and fees vary according to program. ***Payment plan:*** installment.

FRESHMAN FINANCIAL AID (Fall 1998) 296 applied for aid; of those 93% were deemed to have need. 94% of freshmen with need received aid; of those 43% had need fully met. *Average percent of need met:* 50% (excluding resources awarded to replace EFC). *Average financial aid package:* $8148 (excluding resources awarded to replace EFC). 7% of all full-time freshmen had no need and received non-need-based aid.

UNDERGRADUATE FINANCIAL AID (Fall 1998) 865 applied for aid; of those 93% were deemed to have need. 93% of undergraduates with need received aid; of those 37% had need fully met. *Average percent of need met:* 50% (excluding resources awarded to replace EFC). *Average financial aid package:* $8148 (excluding resources awarded to replace EFC). 3% of all full-time undergraduates had no need and received non-need-based aid.

GIFT AID (NEED-BASED) ***Total amount:*** $4,407,438 (40% Federal, 46% state, 14% institutional). ***Receiving aid:*** *Freshmen:* 81% (258); *all full-time undergraduates:* 79% (741). ***Scholarships, grants, and awards:*** Federal Pell, FSEOG, state, private, college/university gift aid from institutional funds.

GIFT AID (NON-NEED-BASED) ***Total amount:*** $87,000 (94% institutional, 6% external sources). ***Receiving aid:*** *Freshmen:* 56% (179); *Undergraduates:* 52% (490). ***Scholarships, grants, and awards by category:*** *Academic Interests/Achievement:* general academic interests/achievements. ***ROTC:*** Army cooperative, Air Force cooperative.

LOANS ***Student loans:*** $1,988,550 (100% need-based). 92% of past graduating class borrowed through all loan programs. Average indebtedness per student: $18,000. ***Parent loans:*** $82,500 (100% need-based). ***Programs:*** FFEL (Subsidized and Unsubsidized Stafford, PLUS).

WORK-STUDY ***Federal work-study:*** *Total amount:* $101,721; 49 jobs averaging $2075.

APPLYING for FINANCIAL AID ***Required financial aid forms:*** FAFSA, state aid form. ***Financial aid deadline:*** Continuous. ***Notification date:*** Continuous. Students must reply within 2 weeks of notification.

CONTACT Christine Murad, Director of Financial Aid, College of Aeronautics, 86-01 23rd Avenue, LaGuardia Airport, Flushing, NY 11369, 718-429-6600 Ext. 141 or toll-free 800-776-2376 (in-state). *Fax:* 718-779-2231.

COLLEGE OF CHARLESTON

Charleston, SC

Tuition & fees (SC res): $3520 **Average undergraduate aid package: $5644**

ABOUT THE INSTITUTION State-supported, coed. Awards: bachelor's degrees (also offers graduate degree programs through University of Charleston, South Carolina). 38 undergraduate majors. Total enrollment: 11,624. Undergraduates: 9,713. Freshmen: 2,074. Federal methodology is used as a basis for awarding need-based institutional aid.

UNDERGRADUATE EXPENSES for 1999–2000 ***Application fee:*** $35. ***Tuition, state resident:*** full-time $3520; part-time $147 per semester hour. ***Tuition, nonresident:*** full-time $7210; part-time $300 per semester hour. ***Required fees:*** $15 per term part-time. Part-time tuition and fees vary according to course load. ***College room and board:*** $4070; ***room only:*** $2550. Room and board charges vary according to board plan. ***Payment plan:*** installment.

FRESHMAN FINANCIAL AID (Fall 1999) 1105 applied for aid; of those 68% were deemed to have need. 97% of freshmen with need received aid; of those 23% had need fully met. *Average percent of need met:* 66% (excluding resources awarded to replace EFC). *Average financial aid package:* $5068 (excluding resources awarded to replace EFC). 9% of all full-time freshmen had no need and received non-need-based aid.

UNDERGRADUATE FINANCIAL AID (Fall 1999) 4,212 applied for aid; of those 78% were deemed to have need. 96% of undergraduates with need received aid; of those 16% had need fully met. *Average percent of need met:* 64% (excluding resources awarded to replace EFC). *Average financial aid package:* $5644 (excluding resources awarded to replace EFC). 4% of all full-time undergraduates had no need and received non-need-based aid.

GIFT AID (NEED-BASED) ***Total amount:*** $4,177,656 (82% Federal, 18% state). ***Receiving aid:*** *Freshmen:* 27% (556); *all full-time undergraduates:* 25% (2,092). ***Average award:*** Freshmen: $4094; Undergraduates: $3474. ***Scholarships, grants, and awards:*** Federal Pell, FSEOG, state, private, college/university gift aid from institutional funds.

GIFT AID (NON-NEED-BASED) ***Total amount:*** $8,601,436 (47% state, 42% institutional, 11% external sources). ***Receiving aid:*** *Freshmen:* 2% (40); *Undergraduates:* 4% (342). ***Scholarships, grants, and awards by category:*** *Academic Interests/Achievement:* biological sciences, business, communication, computer science, education, engineering/technologies, English, foreign languages, general academic interests/achievements, health fields, humanities, physical sciences, premedicine, social sciences. *Creative Arts/Performance:* art/fine arts, music, performing arts, theater/drama. ***Tuition waivers:*** Full or partial for senior citizens. ***ROTC:*** Air Force cooperative.

LOANS ***Student loans:*** $17,901,964 (97% need-based, 3% non-need-based). 55% of past graduating class borrowed through all loan programs. Average indebtedness per student: $11,511. ***Average need-based loan:*** Freshmen: $3049; Undergraduates: $5261. ***Parent loans:*** $9,343,616 (100% non-need-based). ***Programs:*** Federal Direct (Subsidized and Unsubsidized Stafford, PLUS), Perkins.

WORK-STUDY ***Federal work-study:*** *Total amount:* $463,959; jobs available. ***State or other work-study/employment:*** *Total amount:* $1,378,145 (100% non-need-based). Part-time jobs available.

ATHLETIC AWARDS *Total amount:* 897,191 (100% non-need-based).

APPLYING for FINANCIAL AID ***Required financial aid form:*** FAFSA. ***Financial aid deadline (priority):*** 3/15. ***Notification date:*** Continuous beginning 4/10. Students must reply within 8 weeks of notification.

CONTACT Ms. Leslie Roberts, Counselor, College of Charleston, 66 George Street, Charleston, SC 29424-0002, 843-953-5540. *Fax:* 843-953-7192. *E-mail:* robertsl@cofc.edu

COLLEGE OF INSURANCE

New York, NY

Tuition & fees: $14,612 **Average undergraduate aid package: $17,397**

ABOUT THE INSTITUTION Independent, coed. Awards: associate, bachelor's, and master's degrees. 3 undergraduate majors. Total enrollment: 357. Undergraduates: 270. Freshmen: 13. Both federal and institutional methodology are used as a basis for awarding need-based institutional aid.

UNDERGRADUATE EXPENSES for 1999–2000 ***Application fee:*** $30. ***Comprehensive fee:*** $22,512 includes full-time tuition ($14,252), mandatory fees ($360), and room and board ($7900). Full-time tuition and fees vary according to program. Room and board charges vary according to board plan. ***Part-time tuition:*** $495 per credit. ***Part-time fees:*** $15 per credit. Part-time tuition and fees vary according to course load, degree level, and program. ***Payment plan:*** installment.

FRESHMAN FINANCIAL AID (Fall 1999, est.) 17 applied for aid; of those 82% were deemed to have need. 100% of freshmen with need received aid; of those 100% had need fully met. *Average percent of need met:* 99% (excluding resources awarded to replace EFC). *Average financial aid package:* $18,278 (excluding resources awarded to replace EFC). 22% of all full-time freshmen had no need and received non-need-based aid.

UNDERGRADUATE FINANCIAL AID (Fall 1999, est.) 60 applied for aid; of those 80% were deemed to have need. 100% of undergraduates with need received aid; of those 69% had need fully met. *Average percent of need met:* 94% (excluding resources awarded to replace EFC). *Average financial aid package:* $17,397 (excluding resources awarded to replace EFC). 21% of all full-time undergraduates had no need and received non-need-based aid.

GIFT AID (NEED-BASED) ***Total amount:*** $619,639 (13% Federal, 12% state, 63% institutional, 12% external sources). ***Receiving aid:*** *Freshmen:* 35% (8); *all full-time undergraduates:* 34% (41). ***Average award:*** Freshmen: $13,758; Undergraduates: $12,738. ***Scholarships, grants, and awards:*** Federal Pell, FSEOG, state, private, college/university gift aid from institutional funds, co-operative education tuition benefits.

GIFT AID (NON-NEED-BASED) ***Total amount:*** $457,540 (67% institutional, 33% external sources). ***Receiving aid:*** *Freshmen:* 35% (8); *Undergraduates:* 11% (14). ***Scholarships, grants, and awards by category:*** *Academic Interests/Achievement:* business, mathematics. *Special Characteristics:* children of faculty/staff, general special characteristics. ***Tuition waivers:*** Full or partial for employees or children of employees.

LOANS ***Student loans:*** $168,663 (70% need-based, 30% non-need-based). Average indebtedness per student: $16,435. ***Average need-based loan:*** Freshmen: $2062; Undergraduates: $3428. ***Parent loans:*** $31,665 (30% need-based, 70% non-need-based). ***Programs:*** FFEL (Subsidized and Unsubsidized Stafford, PLUS), Perkins, college/university.

WORK-STUDY ***Federal work-study:*** *Total amount:* $7940; 7 jobs averaging $1134. ***State or other work-study/employment:*** *Total amount:* $106,415 (19% need-based, 81% non-need-based). 33 part-time jobs averaging $3062.

APPLYING for FINANCIAL AID ***Required financial aid forms:*** FAFSA, institution's own form, state aid form (for NY residents). ***Financial aid deadline:*** Continuous. ***Notification date:*** Continuous. Students must reply by 8/30.

CONTACT Ms. Marjorie Melikian, Financial Aid Officer, College of Insurance, 101 Murray Street, New York, NY 10007-2165, 212-815-9222 or toll-free 800-356-5146. *Fax:* 212-964-3381. *E-mail:* financialaid@tci.edu

COLLEGE OF MOUNT ST. JOSEPH

Cincinnati, OH

Tuition & fees: $13,090 **Average undergraduate aid package: $11,000**

ABOUT THE INSTITUTION Independent Roman Catholic, coed. Awards: associate, bachelor's, and master's degrees. 38 undergraduate majors. Total enrollment: 2,096. Undergraduates: 1,941. Freshmen: 330. Federal methodology is used as a basis for awarding need-based institutional aid.

UNDERGRADUATE EXPENSES for 1999–2000 ***Application fee:*** $25. ***Comprehensive fee:*** $18,040 includes full-time tuition ($13,000), mandatory fees ($90), and room and board ($4950). Full-time tuition and fees vary according to course load and program. Room and board charges vary according to board plan and housing facility. ***Part-time tuition:*** $333 per semester hour. ***Part-time fees:*** $25 per term part-time. Part-time tuition and fees vary according to course load. ***Payment plan:*** installment.

FRESHMAN FINANCIAL AID (Fall 1998) 307 applied for aid; of those 71% were deemed to have need. 100% of freshmen with need received aid; of those 37% had need fully met. *Average percent of need met:* 95% (excluding resources awarded to replace EFC). *Average financial aid package:* $11,099 (excluding resources awarded to replace EFC). 23% of all full-time freshmen had no need and received non-need-based aid.

UNDERGRADUATE FINANCIAL AID (Fall 1998) 954 applied for aid; of those 71% were deemed to have need. 100% of undergraduates with need received aid; of those 37% had need fully met. *Average percent of need met:* 95% (excluding resources awarded to replace EFC). *Average financial aid package:* $11,000 (excluding resources awarded to replace EFC). 23% of all full-time undergraduates had no need and received non-need-based aid.

GIFT AID (NEED-BASED) ***Total amount:*** $6,038,113 (15% Federal, 22% state, 60% institutional, 3% external sources). ***Receiving aid:*** *Freshmen:* 70% (215); *all full-time undergraduates:* 56% (667). ***Average award:*** Freshmen: $7600; Undergraduates: $7600. ***Scholarships, grants, and awards:*** Federal Pell, FSEOG, state, private, college/university gift aid from institutional funds.

GIFT AID (NON-NEED-BASED) ***Total amount:*** $1,455,006 (6% Federal, 22% state, 68% institutional, 4% external sources). ***Receiving aid:*** *Freshmen:* 9% (28); *Undergraduates:* 7% (87). ***Scholarships, grants, and awards by category:*** *Academic Interests/Achievement:* 605 awards ($2,178,431 total): general academic interests/achievements. *Creative Arts/Performance:* 71 awards ($84,027 total): art/fine arts, music. *Special*

College of Mount St. Joseph (continued)

Achievements/Activities: 43 awards ($31,451 total): leadership. *Special Characteristics:* 52 awards ($49,451 total): adult students, children and siblings of alumni. ***Tuition waivers:*** Full or partial for employees or children of employees, senior citizens. ***ROTC:*** Army cooperative, Air Force cooperative.

LOANS ***Student loans:*** $6,247,915 (79% need-based, 21% non-need-based). 80% of past graduating class borrowed through all loan programs. Average indebtedness per student: $17,125. ***Average need-based loan:*** Freshmen: $3100; Undergraduates: $4700. ***Parent loans:*** $820,146 (30% need-based, 70% non-need-based). ***Programs:*** FFEL (Subsidized and Unsubsidized Stafford, PLUS), Perkins, Federal Nursing, state.

WORK-STUDY ***Federal work-study:*** *Total amount:* $138,950; 92 jobs averaging $1500. ***State or other work-study/employment:*** *Total amount:* $203,214 (55% need-based, 45% non-need-based). 135 part-time jobs averaging $1500.

APPLYING for FINANCIAL AID ***Required financial aid form:*** FAFSA. ***Financial aid deadline (priority):*** 3/1. ***Notification date:*** Continuous. Students must reply by 5/1 or within 4 weeks of notification.

CONTACT Ms. Kathryn Kelly, Director, Student Administrative Services, College of Mount St. Joseph, 5701 Delhi Road, Cincinnati, OH 45233-1670, 513-244-4418 or toll-free 800-654-9314. *Fax:* 513-244-4201. *E-mail:* kathy_kelly@mail.msj.edu

COLLEGE OF MOUNT SAINT VINCENT

Riverdale, NY

Tuition & fees: $15,070 **Average undergraduate aid package: $12,000**

ABOUT THE INSTITUTION Independent, coed. Awards: associate, bachelor's, and master's degrees and post-master's certificates. 38 undergraduate majors. Total enrollment: 1,480. Undergraduates: 1,255. Freshmen: 248. Federal methodology is used as a basis for awarding need-based institutional aid.

UNDERGRADUATE EXPENSES for 1999–2000 ***Application fee:*** $25. ***Comprehensive fee:*** $22,090 includes full-time tuition ($14,910), mandatory fees ($160), and room and board ($7020). ***Part-time tuition:*** $435 per credit. ***Part-time fees:*** $25 per term part-time. ***Payment plan:*** installment.

FRESHMAN FINANCIAL AID (Fall 1999, est.) *Average percent of need met:* 75% (excluding resources awarded to replace EFC). *Average financial aid package:* $13,300 (excluding resources awarded to replace EFC).

UNDERGRADUATE FINANCIAL AID (Fall 1999, est.) *Average percent of need met:* 75% (excluding resources awarded to replace EFC). *Average financial aid package:* $12,000 (excluding resources awarded to replace EFC).

GIFT AID (NEED-BASED) ***Total amount:*** $9,558,000 ***Scholarships, grants, and awards:*** Federal Pell, FSEOG, state, private, college/university gift aid from institutional funds.

GIFT AID (NON-NEED-BASED) ***Total amount:*** $2,000,000 ***Scholarships, grants, and awards by category:*** *Academic Interests/Achievement:* general academic interests/achievements. *Special Achievements/Activities:* leadership. *Special Characteristics:* children and siblings of alumni, children of faculty/staff, siblings of current students. ***Tuition waivers:*** Full or partial for employees or children of employees, senior citizens. ***ROTC:*** Army cooperative, Air Force cooperative.

LOANS ***Programs:*** FFEL (Subsidized and Unsubsidized Stafford, PLUS), Perkins, Federal Nursing.

WORK-STUDY Federal work-study jobs available.

APPLYING for FINANCIAL AID ***Required financial aid form:*** FAFSA. ***Financial aid deadline (priority):*** 3/1. ***Notification date:*** Continuous. Students must reply by 5/1 or within 2 weeks of notification.

CONTACT Ms. Monica Simotas, Director of Financial Aid, College of Mount Saint Vincent, 6301 Riverdale Avenue, Riverdale, NY 10471, 718-405-3289 or toll-free 800-665-CMSV.

THE COLLEGE OF NEW JERSEY

Ewing, NJ

Tuition & fees (NJ res): $5685 **Average undergraduate aid package: $6000**

ABOUT THE INSTITUTION State-supported, coed. Awards: bachelor's and master's degrees. 47 undergraduate majors. Total enrollment: 6,747. Undergraduates: 5,930. Freshmen: 1,209. Federal methodology is used as a basis for awarding need-based institutional aid.

UNDERGRADUATE EXPENSES for 1999–2000 ***Application fee:*** $50. ***Tuition, state resident:*** full-time $4445; part-time $151 per semester hour. ***Tuition, nonresident:*** full-time $7762; part-time $265 per semester hour. ***Required fees:*** full-time $1240; $41 per semester hour; $2 per term part-time. ***College room and board:*** $6330. Room and board charges vary according to board plan. ***Payment plans:*** installment, deferred payment.

FRESHMAN FINANCIAL AID (Fall 1998) 980 applied for aid; of those 90% were deemed to have need. 100% of freshmen with need received aid. *Average financial aid package:* $7000 (excluding resources awarded to replace EFC).

UNDERGRADUATE FINANCIAL AID (Fall 1998) 4,000 applied for aid; of those 98% were deemed to have need. 100% of undergraduates with need received aid. *Average financial aid package:* $6000 (excluding resources awarded to replace EFC).

GIFT AID (NEED-BASED) ***Scholarships, grants, and awards:*** Federal Pell, FSEOG, state, private, college/university gift aid from institutional funds, Federal Nursing.

GIFT AID (NON-NEED-BASED) ***Total amount:*** $13,465,132 (16% Federal, 33% state, 48% institutional, 3% external sources). ***Receiving aid:*** *Freshmen:* 58% (700); *Undergraduates:* 31% (1,700). ***Scholarships, grants, and awards by category:*** *Academic Interests/Achievement:* 1,500 awards ($5,800,000 total): engineering/technologies, general academic interests/achievements. *Creative Arts/Performance:* 20 awards ($20,000 total): music. *Special Characteristics:* 200 awards ($600,000 total): members of minority groups. ***Tuition waivers:*** Full or partial for employees or children of employees, senior citizens. ***ROTC:*** Army cooperative, Air Force cooperative.

LOANS ***Student loans:*** $11,200,000 (100% need-based). 60% of past graduating class borrowed through all loan programs. Average indebtedness per student: $13,000. ***Parent loans:*** $1,800,000 (100% need-based). ***Programs:*** Federal Direct (Subsidized and Unsubsidized Stafford, PLUS), Perkins, Federal Nursing, state, college/university.

WORK-STUDY ***Federal work-study:*** *Total amount:* $258,600; 281 jobs averaging $1200.

APPLYING for FINANCIAL AID ***Required financial aid form:*** FAFSA. ***Financial aid deadline:*** 6/1 (priority: 3/1). ***Notification date:*** Continuous. Students must reply within 2 weeks of notification.

CONTACT Director of Student Financial Assistance, The College of New Jersey, PO Box 7718, Ewing, NJ 08628, 609-771-3263 or toll-free 800-624-0967. *Fax:* 609-637-5154.

THE COLLEGE OF NEW ROCHELLE

New Rochelle, NY

Tuition & fees: $11,700 **Average undergraduate aid package: $11,878**

ABOUT THE INSTITUTION Independent, coed, primarily women. Awards: bachelor's and master's degrees. 37 undergraduate majors. Total enrollment: 7,221. Undergraduates: 5,512. Freshmen: 1,013. Federal methodology is used as a basis for awarding need-based institutional aid.

UNDERGRADUATE EXPENSES for 1999–2000 ***Application fee:*** $20. ***Comprehensive fee:*** $17,700 includes full-time tuition ($11,600), mandatory fees ($100), and room and board ($6000). Full-time tuition and fees vary according to course load and program. Room and board charges vary according to housing facility. ***Part-time tuition:*** $390 per credit. Part-time tuition and fees vary according to course load. ***Payment plans:*** tuition prepayment, installment.

UNDERGRADUATE FINANCIAL AID (Fall 1998) 748 applied for aid; of those 100% were deemed to have need. 100% of undergraduates with need received aid; of those 100% had need fully met. *Average percent of need met:* 100% (excluding resources awarded to replace EFC). *Average financial aid package:* $11,878 (excluding resources awarded to replace EFC).

GIFT AID (NEED-BASED) ***Total amount:*** $3,687,368 (34% Federal, 32% state, 34% institutional). ***Receiving aid:*** *All full-time undergraduates:* 536. ***Average award:*** Undergraduates: $6879. ***Scholarships, grants, and awards:*** Federal Pell, FSEOG, state, private, college/university gift aid from institutional funds, Federal Nursing.

GIFT AID (NON-NEED-BASED) ***Total amount:*** $1,432,057 (97% institutional, 3% external sources). ***Receiving aid:*** *Undergraduates:* 266. ***Scholarships, grants, and awards by category:*** *Academic Interests/Achievement:* area/ethnic studies, biological sciences, business, communication, education, English, foreign languages, general academic interests/achievements, health fields, humanities, mathematics, physical sciences, premedicine, religion/biblical studies, social sciences. *Creative Arts/Performance:* applied art and design, art/fine arts, cinema/film/broadcasting, creative writing, dance, debating, general creative arts/performance, journalism/publications, music, performing arts, theater/drama. *Special Achievements/Activities:* community service, general special achievements/activities, hobbies/interests, junior miss, leadership, memberships, religious involvement. *Special Characteristics:* children of current students, children of faculty/staff, general special characteristics, out-of-state students, parents of current students, previous college experience, siblings of current students, spouses of current students. ***Tuition waivers:*** Full or partial for employees or children of employees, senior citizens. ***ROTC:*** Army cooperative.

LOANS ***Student loans:*** $2,808,511 (100% need-based). ***Average need-based loan:*** Undergraduates: $4945. ***Parent loans:*** $312,489 (100% need-based). ***Programs:*** Federal Direct (Subsidized and Unsubsidized Stafford), FFEL (PLUS), Perkins, Federal Nursing.

WORK-STUDY ***Federal work-study:*** *Total amount:* $851,284; jobs available. ***State or other work-study/employment:*** *Total amount:* $82,500 (100% non-need-based). Part-time jobs available.

APPLYING for FINANCIAL AID ***Required financial aid forms:*** FAFSA, institution's own form, federal income tax form(s). ***Financial aid deadline:*** Continuous. ***Notification date:*** Continuous beginning 1/1.

CONTACT Dr. Ronald Pollack, Director of Financial Aid, The College of New Rochelle, 29 Castle Place, New Rochelle, NY 10805-2339, 914-654-5225 or toll-free 800-933-5923. *Fax:* 914-654-5554. *E-mail:* rpollack@cnr.edu

COLLEGE OF NOTRE DAME

Belmont, CA

ABOUT THE INSTITUTION Independent Roman Catholic, coed. Awards: bachelor's and master's degrees. 41 undergraduate majors. Total enrollment: 1,722. Undergraduates: 961.

GIFT AID (NEED-BASED) ***Scholarships, grants, and awards:*** Federal Pell, FSEOG, private, college/university gift aid from institutional funds.

GIFT AID (NON-NEED-BASED) ***Scholarships, grants, and awards by category:*** *Academic Interests/Achievement:* general academic interests/achievements. *Creative Arts/Performance:* music. *Special Achievements/Activities:* general special achievements/activities. *Special Characteristics:* children and siblings of alumni, general special characteristics.

LOANS ***Programs:*** FFEL (Subsidized and Unsubsidized Stafford, PLUS), Perkins, college/university.

WORK-STUDY Federal work-study jobs available.

APPLYING for FINANCIAL AID ***Required financial aid forms:*** FAFSA, institution's own form.

CONTACT Ms. Kathleen Kelly, Director of Financial Aid, College of Notre Dame, 1500 Ralston Avenue, Belmont, CA 94002, 650-508-3509 or toll-free 800-263-0545 (in-state).

COLLEGE OF NOTRE DAME OF MARYLAND

Baltimore, MD

Tuition & fees: $15,875 — **Average undergraduate aid package: $15,848**

ABOUT THE INSTITUTION Independent Roman Catholic, women only. Awards: bachelor's and master's degrees and post-bachelor's certificates. 33 undergraduate majors. Total enrollment: 3,139. Undergraduates: 2,037. Both federal and institutional methodology are used as a basis for awarding need-based institutional aid.

UNDERGRADUATE EXPENSES for 2000–2001 ***Application fee:*** $25. ***Comprehensive fee:*** $22,675 includes full-time tuition ($15,600), mandatory fees ($275), and room and board ($6800). ***Part-time tuition:*** $255 per credit. ***Part-time fees:*** $30 per term part-time. ***Payment plan:*** installment.

FRESHMAN FINANCIAL AID (Fall 1999) 111 applied for aid; of those 92% were deemed to have need. 100% of freshmen with need received aid; of those 76% had need fully met. *Average percent of need met:* 100% (excluding resources awarded to replace EFC). *Average financial aid package:* $15,957 (excluding resources awarded to replace EFC). 5% of all full-time freshmen had no need and received non-need-based aid.

UNDERGRADUATE FINANCIAL AID (Fall 1999) 453 applied for aid; of those 92% were deemed to have need. 100% of undergraduates with need received aid; of those 67% had need fully met. *Average percent of need met:* 100% (excluding resources awarded to replace EFC). *Average financial aid package:* $15,848 (excluding resources awarded to replace EFC). 7% of all full-time undergraduates had no need and received non-need-based aid.

GIFT AID (NEED-BASED) ***Total amount:*** $4,934,497 (12% Federal, 17% state, 69% institutional, 2% external sources). ***Receiving aid:*** *Freshmen:* 59% (86); *all full-time undergraduates:* 58% (349). ***Average award:*** Freshmen: $5999; Undergraduates: $5353. ***Scholarships, grants, and awards:*** Federal Pell, FSEOG, state, private, college/university gift aid from institutional funds.

GIFT AID (NON-NEED-BASED) ***Total amount:*** $309,255 (7% state, 89% institutional, 4% external sources). ***Receiving aid:*** *Freshmen:* 45% (66); *Undergraduates:* 36% (217). ***Scholarships, grants, and awards by category:*** *Academic Interests/Achievement:* 198 awards ($1,502,875 total): general academic interests/achievements. *Creative Arts/Performance:* 47 awards ($159,100 total): art/fine arts, general creative arts/performance. *Special Achievements/Activities:* 218 awards ($890,744 total): community service, leadership, memberships, religious involvement. *Special Characteristics:* 19 awards ($124,144 total): international students. ***Tuition waivers:*** Full or partial for employees or children of employees. ***ROTC:*** Army cooperative.

LOANS ***Student loans:*** $2,645,966 (88% need-based, 12% non-need-based). 62% of past graduating class borrowed through all loan programs. Average indebtedness per student: $17,000. ***Average need-based loan:*** Freshmen: $3233; Undergraduates: $4419. ***Parent loans:*** $549,345 (80% need-based, 20% non-need-based). ***Programs:*** FFEL (Subsidized and Unsubsidized Stafford, PLUS), Perkins.

WORK-STUDY ***Federal work-study:*** *Total amount:* $190,570; 275 jobs averaging $700.

APPLYING for FINANCIAL AID ***Required financial aid forms:*** FAFSA, institution's own form. ***Financial aid deadline (priority):*** 2/15. ***Notification date:*** Continuous beginning 3/15. Students must reply by 5/1.

CONTACT Ms. Teresa Drzewiecki, Director of Financial Aid, College of Notre Dame of Maryland, 4701 North Charles Street, Baltimore, MD 21210-2476, 410-532-5749 or toll-free 800-435-0200 (in-state), 800-435-0300 (out-of-state). *Fax:* 410-532-6287. *E-mail:* tdrzewie@ndm.edu

COLLEGE OF OUR LADY OF THE ELMS

Chicopee, MA

Tuition & fees: $14,720 — **Average undergraduate aid package: $11,892**

ABOUT THE INSTITUTION Independent Roman Catholic, coed, primarily women. Awards: bachelor's and master's degrees. 47 undergraduate majors. Total enrollment: 1,034. Undergraduates: 858. Freshmen: 334. Both federal and institutional methodology are used as a basis for awarding need-based institutional aid.

UNDERGRADUATE EXPENSES for 2000–2001 ***Application fee:*** $30. ***Comprehensive fee:*** $20,286 includes full-time tuition ($14,144), manda-

College of Our Lady of the Elms (continued)

tory fees ($576), and room and board ($5566). Room and board charges vary according to board plan. ***Part-time tuition:*** $310 per credit.

FRESHMAN FINANCIAL AID (Fall 1999) 106 applied for aid; of those 93% were deemed to have need. 100% of freshmen with need received aid; of those 28% had need fully met. *Average percent of need met:* 90% (excluding resources awarded to replace EFC). *Average financial aid package:* $11,585 (excluding resources awarded to replace EFC).

UNDERGRADUATE FINANCIAL AID (Fall 1999) 470 applied for aid; of those 94% were deemed to have need. 100% of undergraduates with need received aid; of those 25% had need fully met. *Average percent of need met:* 90% (excluding resources awarded to replace EFC). *Average financial aid package:* $11,892 (excluding resources awarded to replace EFC).

GIFT AID (NEED-BASED) ***Total amount:*** $2,801,356 (23% Federal, 16% state, 58% institutional, 3% external sources). ***Receiving aid:*** *Freshmen:* 80% (96); *all full-time undergraduates:* 87% (423). ***Average award:*** Freshmen: $6900; Undergraduates: $6007. ***Scholarships, grants, and awards:*** Federal Pell, FSEOG, state, private, college/university gift aid from institutional funds.

GIFT AID (NON-NEED-BASED) ***Total amount:*** $222,336 (1% Federal, 93% institutional, 6% external sources). ***Scholarships, grants, and awards by category:*** *Academic Interests/Achievement:* 27 awards ($187,336 total): general academic interests/achievements. *Special Characteristics:* 16 awards ($35,000 total): children of faculty/staff, general special characteristics, religious affiliation. ***Tuition waivers:*** Full or partial for employees or children of employees, senior citizens. ***ROTC:*** Army cooperative, Air Force cooperative.

LOANS ***Student loans:*** $3,607,809 (80% need-based, 20% non-need-based). 97% of past graduating class borrowed through all loan programs. Average indebtedness per student: $11,868. ***Average need-based loan:*** Freshmen: $4110; Undergraduates: $5527. ***Parent loans:*** $353,968 (48% need-based, 52% non-need-based). ***Programs:*** FFEL (Subsidized and Unsubsidized Stafford, PLUS), Perkins, state, alternative loans, MEFA Loans, Key Alternative Loans, Achiever Loans, PLATO Loans, CitiAssist Loans.

WORK-STUDY ***Federal work-study:*** *Total amount:* $131,115; 127 jobs averaging $1032. ***State or other work-study/employment:*** *Total amount:* $34,050 (85% need-based, 15% non-need-based). 9 part-time jobs averaging $3783.

APPLYING for FINANCIAL AID ***Required financial aid forms:*** FAFSA, institution's own form. ***Financial aid deadline (priority):*** 3/1. ***Notification date:*** Continuous. Students must reply by 5/1 or within 2 weeks of notification.

CONTACT Russell Stein, Assistant Director of Student Financial Aid Services, College of Our Lady of the Elms, 291 Springfield Street, Chicopee, MA 01013-2839, 413-594-2761 Ext. 303 or toll-free 800-255-ELMS. *Fax:* 413-594-2781. *E-mail:* steinr@elms.edu

COLLEGE OF SAINT BENEDICT

Saint Joseph, MN

Tuition & fees: $16,441 **Average undergraduate aid package: $14,488**

ABOUT THE INSTITUTION Independent Roman Catholic, women only. Awards: bachelor's degrees. 51 undergraduate majors. Total enrollment: 2,000. Undergraduates: 2,000. Freshmen: 515. Federal methodology is used as a basis for awarding need-based institutional aid.

UNDERGRADUATE EXPENSES for 1999–2000 ***Application fee:*** $25. ***Comprehensive fee:*** $21,481 includes full-time tuition ($16,195), mandatory fees ($246), and room and board ($5040). ***College room only:*** $2700. Room and board charges vary according to board plan and housing facility. ***Part-time tuition:*** $675 per credit. ***Part-time fees:*** $123 per term part-time. ***Payment plans:*** tuition prepayment, installment, deferred payment.

FRESHMAN FINANCIAL AID (Fall 1999, est.) 482 applied for aid; of those 78% were deemed to have need. 100% of freshmen with need received aid; of those 90% had need fully met. *Average percent of need met:* 91% (excluding resources awarded to replace EFC). *Average financial aid package:* $14,391 (excluding resources awarded to replace EFC). 19% of all full-time freshmen had no need and received non-need-based aid.

UNDERGRADUATE FINANCIAL AID (Fall 1999, est.) 1,611 applied for aid; of those 93% were deemed to have need. 100% of undergraduates with need received aid; of those 85% had need fully met. *Average percent of need met:* 91% (excluding resources awarded to replace EFC). *Average financial aid package:* $14,488 (excluding resources awarded to replace EFC). 11% of all full-time undergraduates had no need and received non-need-based aid.

GIFT AID (NEED-BASED) ***Total amount:*** $12,773,081 (9% Federal, 22% state, 64% institutional, 5% external sources). ***Receiving aid:*** *Freshmen:* 73% (376); *all full-time undergraduates:* 77% (1,505). ***Average award:*** Freshmen: $8634; Undergraduates: $8249. ***Scholarships, grants, and awards:*** Federal Pell, FSEOG, state, private, college/university gift aid from institutional funds.

GIFT AID (NON-NEED-BASED) ***Total amount:*** $2,151,532 (91% institutional, 9% external sources). ***Receiving aid:*** *Freshmen:* 32% (166); *Undergraduates:* 30% (586). ***Scholarships, grants, and awards by category:*** *Academic Interests/Achievement:* general academic interests/achievements. *Creative Arts/Performance:* 68 awards ($93,065 total): art/fine arts, music, theater/drama. *Special Achievements/Activities:* junior miss, memberships. *Special Characteristics:* ethnic background, international students. ***ROTC:*** Army cooperative.

LOANS ***Student loans:*** $7,024,856 (66% need-based, 34% non-need-based). 77% of past graduating class borrowed through all loan programs. Average indebtedness per student: $17,445. ***Average need-based loan:*** Freshmen: $4756; Undergraduates: $4994. ***Parent loans:*** $846,789 (100% non-need-based). ***Programs:*** FFEL (Subsidized and Unsubsidized Stafford, PLUS), Perkins, state, Minnesota SELF Loans, Norwest Collegiate Loans.

WORK-STUDY ***Federal work-study:*** *Total amount:* $1,119,182; 587 jobs averaging $1906. ***State or other work-study/employment:*** *Total amount:* $935,920 (43% need-based, 57% non-need-based). 448 part-time jobs averaging $2089.

APPLYING for FINANCIAL AID ***Required financial aid forms:*** FAFSA, institution's own form. ***Financial aid deadline (priority):*** 4/1. ***Notification date:*** Continuous. Students must reply by 5/1.

CONTACT Ms. Jane Haugen, Director of Financial Aid, College of Saint Benedict, 37 South College Avenue, Saint Joseph, MN 56374-2099, 320-363-5388 or toll-free 800-544-1489. *Fax:* 320-363-6099. *E-mail:* jhaugen@csbsju.edu

COLLEGE OF ST. CATHERINE

St. Paul, MN

Tuition & fees: $15,578 **Average undergraduate aid package: $16,277**

ABOUT THE INSTITUTION Independent Roman Catholic, women only. Awards: bachelor's and master's degrees and post-bachelor's certificates. 65 undergraduate majors. Total enrollment: 3,443. Undergraduates: 2,545. Freshmen: 282. Federal methodology is used as a basis for awarding need-based institutional aid.

UNDERGRADUATE EXPENSES for 1999–2000 ***Application fee:*** $20. ***Comprehensive fee:*** $20,128 includes full-time tuition ($15,456), mandatory fees ($122), and room and board ($4550). ***College room only:*** $2570. Full-time tuition and fees vary according to class time. Room and board charges vary according to board plan and housing facility. ***Part-time tuition:*** $483 per credit. ***Part-time fees:*** $61 per term part-time. Part-time tuition and fees vary according to class time. ***Payment plan:*** installment.

FRESHMAN FINANCIAL AID (Fall 1999) 230 applied for aid; of those 88% were deemed to have need. 100% of freshmen with need received aid; of those 61% had need fully met. *Average percent of need met:* 96% (excluding resources awarded to replace EFC). *Average financial aid package:* $17,479 (excluding resources awarded to replace EFC). 15% of all full-time freshmen had no need and received non-need-based aid.

UNDERGRADUATE FINANCIAL AID (Fall 1999) 1,199 applied for aid; of those 88% were deemed to have need. 100% of undergraduates with

need received aid; of those 56% had need fully met. *Average percent of need met:* 92% (excluding resources awarded to replace EFC). *Average financial aid package:* $16,277 (excluding resources awarded to replace EFC). 15% of all full-time undergraduates had no need and received non-need-based aid.

GIFT AID (NEED-BASED) ***Total amount:*** $6,579,754 (17% Federal, 30% state, 52% institutional, 1% external sources). ***Receiving aid:*** *Freshmen:* 68% (187); *all full-time undergraduates:* 68% (982). ***Average award:*** Freshmen: $6491; Undergraduates: $5563. ***Scholarships, grants, and awards:*** Federal Pell, FSEOG, state, private, college/university gift aid from institutional funds, Federal Nursing.

GIFT AID (NON-NEED-BASED) ***Total amount:*** $2,853,375 (1% Federal, 87% institutional, 12% external sources). ***Receiving aid:*** *Freshmen:* 58% (158); *Undergraduates:* 41% (599). ***Scholarships, grants, and awards by category:*** *Academic Interests/Achievement:* business, education, English, foreign languages, general academic interests/achievements, health fields, home economics, humanities, mathematics, physical sciences, premedicine, social sciences. *Creative Arts/Performance:* art/fine arts, music. *Special Achievements/Activities:* community service, general special achievements/ activities, leadership, memberships. *Special Characteristics:* adult students, children and siblings of alumni, children of educators, children of faculty/ staff, ethnic background, general special characteristics, international students, local/state students, out-of-state students, religious affiliation, siblings of current students. ***Tuition waivers:*** Full or partial for employees or children of employees, senior citizens. ***ROTC:*** Air Force cooperative.

LOANS ***Student loans:*** $8,687,801 (52% need-based, 48% non-need-based). 86% of past graduating class borrowed through all loan programs. Average indebtedness per student: $17,341. ***Average need-based loan:*** Freshmen: $2795; Undergraduates: $3885. ***Parent loans:*** $1,301,063 (100% non-need-based). ***Programs:*** FFEL (Subsidized and Unsubsidized Stafford, PLUS), Perkins, Federal Nursing, state, college/university.

WORK-STUDY ***Federal work-study:*** *Total amount:* $361,620; 500 jobs available. ***State or other work-study/employment:*** *Total amount:* $641,401 (81% need-based, 19% non-need-based). 250 part-time jobs available.

APPLYING for FINANCIAL AID ***Required financial aid forms:*** FAFSA, institution's own form. ***Financial aid deadline (priority):*** 4/1. ***Notification date:*** Continuous. Students must reply within 2 weeks of notification.

CONTACT Ms. Pamela Johnson, Director of Financial Aid, College of St. Catherine, Mail #F-11, 2004 Randolph Avenue, St. Paul, MN 55105-1789, 651-690-6540 or toll-free 800-945-4599 (in-state). *Fax:* 651-690-6558.

COLLEGE OF SAINT ELIZABETH

Morristown, NJ

Tuition & fees: $14,030 **Average undergraduate aid package: $16,470**

ABOUT THE INSTITUTION Independent Roman Catholic, women only. Awards: bachelor's and master's degrees and post-bachelor's certificates. 35 undergraduate majors. Total enrollment: 1,810. Undergraduates: 1,351. Freshmen: 135. Both federal and institutional methodology are used as a basis for awarding need-based institutional aid.

UNDERGRADUATE EXPENSES for 1999–2000 ***Application fee:*** $35. ***Comprehensive fee:*** $20,470 includes full-time tuition ($13,500), mandatory fees ($530), and room and board ($6440). ***Part-time tuition:*** $410 per semester hour. ***Part-time fees:*** $55 per course; $15 per term part-time. ***Payment plan:*** installment.

FRESHMAN FINANCIAL AID (Fall 1998) 137 applied for aid; of those 47% were deemed to have need. 100% of freshmen with need received aid; of those 12% had need fully met. *Average percent of need met:* 88% (excluding resources awarded to replace EFC). *Average financial aid package:* $17,752 (excluding resources awarded to replace EFC). 40% of all full-time freshmen had no need and received non-need-based aid.

UNDERGRADUATE FINANCIAL AID (Fall 1998) 554 applied for aid; of those 31% were deemed to have need. 100% of undergraduates with need received aid; of those 14% had need fully met. *Average percent of need met:* 86% (excluding resources awarded to replace EFC). *Average financial aid package:* $16,470 (excluding resources awarded to replace EFC). 39% of all full-time undergraduates had no need and received non-need-based aid.

GIFT AID (NEED-BASED) ***Total amount:*** $2,647,271 (17% Federal, 48% state, 35% institutional). ***Receiving aid:*** *Freshmen:* 44% (65); *all full-time undergraduates:* 29% (172). ***Average award:*** Freshmen: $15,890; Undergraduates: $14,269. ***Scholarships, grants, and awards:*** Federal Pell, FSEOG, state, private, college/university gift aid from institutional funds.

GIFT AID (NON-NEED-BASED) ***Total amount:*** $2,461,884 (2% state, 95% institutional, 3% external sources). ***Receiving aid:*** *Freshmen:* 22% (33); *Undergraduates:* 14% (82). ***Scholarships, grants, and awards by category:*** *Academic Interests/Achievement:* general academic interests/achievements. *Creative Arts/Performance:* art/fine arts. *Special Achievements/Activities:* junior miss. *Special Characteristics:* children and siblings of alumni, children of faculty/staff, children with a deceased or disabled parent, general special characteristics, handicapped students, international students, members of minority groups. ***Tuition waivers:*** Full or partial for employees or children of employees, senior citizens.

LOANS ***Student loans:*** $1,647,301 (51% need-based, 49% non-need-based). Average indebtedness per student: $14,261. ***Average need-based loan:*** Freshmen: $2933; Undergraduates: $3623. ***Parent loans:*** $344,394 (100% non-need-based). ***Programs:*** FFEL (Subsidized and Unsubsidized Stafford, PLUS), Perkins, state.

WORK-STUDY ***Federal work-study:*** *Total amount:* $25,243; 52 jobs averaging $485. ***State or other work-study/employment:*** *Total amount:* $34,288 (100% non-need-based). Part-time jobs available.

APPLYING for FINANCIAL AID ***Required financial aid form:*** FAFSA. ***Financial aid deadline (priority):*** 3/1. ***Notification date:*** Continuous. Students must reply by 5/1 or within 2 weeks of notification.

CONTACT Camille Green-Thomas, Director of Financial Aid, College of Saint Elizabeth, 2 Convent Road, Morristown, NJ 07960-6989, 973-290-4445 or toll-free 800-210-7900. *Fax:* 973-290-4421.

COLLEGE OF ST. FRANCIS

Joliet, IL

See University of St. Francis

COLLEGE OF ST. JOSEPH

Rutland, VT

Tuition & fees: $11,350 **Average undergraduate aid package: $9956**

ABOUT THE INSTITUTION Independent Roman Catholic, coed. Awards: associate, bachelor's, and master's degrees and post-bachelor's certificates. 20 undergraduate majors. Total enrollment: 534. Undergraduates: 385. Federal methodology is used as a basis for awarding need-based institutional aid.

UNDERGRADUATE EXPENSES for 1999–2000 ***Application fee:*** $25. ***Comprehensive fee:*** $17,400 includes full-time tuition ($11,250), mandatory fees ($100), and room and board ($6050). Full-time tuition and fees vary according to program. Room and board charges vary according to housing facility. ***Part-time tuition:*** $200 per credit. ***Part-time fees:*** $32 per term part-time. Part-time tuition and fees vary according to program. ***Payment plan:*** installment.

FRESHMAN FINANCIAL AID (Fall 1999) 38 applied for aid; of those 95% were deemed to have need. 100% of freshmen with need received aid; of those 6% had need fully met. *Average percent of need met:* 74% (excluding resources awarded to replace EFC). *Average financial aid package:* $10,723 (excluding resources awarded to replace EFC). 4% of all full-time freshmen had no need and received non-need-based aid.

UNDERGRADUATE FINANCIAL AID (Fall 1999) 177 applied for aid; of those 94% were deemed to have need. 100% of undergraduates with need received aid; of those 16% had need fully met. *Average percent of need met:* 72% (excluding resources awarded to replace EFC). *Average financial aid package:* $9956 (excluding resources awarded to replace EFC). 5% of all full-time undergraduates had no need and received non-need-based aid.

College of St. Joseph (continued)

GIFT AID (NEED-BASED) ***Total amount:*** $815,198 (33% Federal, 23% state, 39% institutional, 5% external sources). ***Receiving aid:*** *Freshmen:* 78% (36); *all full-time undergraduates:* 71% (155). ***Average award:*** Freshmen: $7431; Undergraduates: $5008. ***Scholarships, grants, and awards:*** Federal Pell, FSEOG, state, private, college/university gift aid from institutional funds.

GIFT AID (NON-NEED-BASED) ***Total amount:*** $16,332 (76% institutional, 24% external sources). ***Receiving aid:*** *Freshmen:* 2% (1); *Undergraduates:* 2% (4). ***Scholarships, grants, and awards by category:*** *Academic Interests/Achievement:* general academic interests/achievements. *Special Achievements/Activities:* community service, leadership. *Special Characteristics:* religious affiliation. ***Tuition waivers:*** Full or partial for employees or children of employees, senior citizens.

LOANS ***Student loans:*** $1,001,354 (89% need-based, 11% non-need-based). 80% of past graduating class borrowed through all loan programs. Average indebtedness per student: $14,585. ***Average need-based loan:*** Freshmen: $2333; Undergraduates: $4389. ***Parent loans:*** $235,156 (58% need-based, 42% non-need-based). ***Programs:*** FFEL (Subsidized and Unsubsidized Stafford, PLUS), Perkins.

WORK-STUDY ***Federal work-study:*** *Total amount:* $45,563; 60 jobs averaging $800. ***State or other work-study/employment:*** *Total amount:* $76,350 (67% need-based, 33% non-need-based). 82 part-time jobs averaging $925.

ATHLETIC AWARDS *Total amount:* 123,450 (93% need-based, 7% non-need-based).

APPLYING for FINANCIAL AID ***Required financial aid forms:*** FAFSA, institution's own form. ***Financial aid deadline:*** Continuous. ***Notification date:*** Continuous beginning 3/15. Students must reply within 2 weeks of notification.

CONTACT Ms. Renee Henry, Financial Aid Coordinator, College of St. Joseph, 71 Clement Road, Rutland, VT 05701-3899, 802-773-5900 Ext. 62. *Fax:* 802-773-5900 Ext. 3. *E-mail:* rhenry@csj.edu

COLLEGE OF SAINT MARY

Omaha, NE

Tuition & fees: $12,836 **Average undergraduate aid package: N/A**

ABOUT THE INSTITUTION Independent Roman Catholic, women only. Awards: associate and bachelor's degrees. 33 undergraduate majors. Total enrollment: 1,071. Undergraduates: 1,071. Freshmen: 118. Federal methodology is used as a basis for awarding need-based institutional aid.

UNDERGRADUATE EXPENSES for 1999–2000 ***Application fee:*** $20. ***One-time required fee:*** $25. ***Comprehensive fee:*** $17,434 includes full-time tuition ($12,428), mandatory fees ($408), and room and board ($4598). Room and board charges vary according to board plan and housing facility. ***Part-time tuition:*** $414 per credit hour. ***Part-time fees:*** $18 per credit hour. Part-time tuition and fees vary according to class time. ***Payment plans:*** installment, deferred payment.

GIFT AID (NEED-BASED) ***Scholarships, grants, and awards:*** Federal Pell, FSEOG, state.

GIFT AID (NON-NEED-BASED) ***Scholarships, grants, and awards by category:*** *Academic Interests/Achievement:* general academic interests/achievements. *Special Achievements/Activities:* leadership, religious involvement. *Special Characteristics:* out-of-state students. ***Tuition waivers:*** Full or partial for employees or children of employees, senior citizens. ***ROTC:*** Army cooperative, Air Force cooperative.

LOANS ***Programs:*** Federal Direct (Subsidized and Unsubsidized Stafford, PLUS), Perkins.

WORK-STUDY Federal work-study jobs available.

APPLYING for FINANCIAL AID ***Required financial aid form:*** FAFSA. ***Financial aid deadline (priority):*** 4/1. ***Notification date:*** Continuous.

CONTACT Judith Scherer-Connealy, Director of Financial Aid, College of Saint Mary, 1901 South 72nd Street, Omaha, NE 68124, 402-399-2415 or toll-free 800-926-5534.

THE COLLEGE OF SAINT ROSE

Albany, NY

Tuition & fees: $12,654 **Average undergraduate aid package: $10,225**

ABOUT THE INSTITUTION Independent, coed. Awards: bachelor's and master's degrees. 29 undergraduate majors. Total enrollment: 4,167. Undergraduates: 2,729. Freshmen: 406. Federal methodology is used as a basis for awarding need-based institutional aid.

UNDERGRADUATE EXPENSES for 1999–2000 ***Application fee:*** $30. ***Comprehensive fee:*** $19,012 includes full-time tuition ($12,434), mandatory fees ($220), and room and board ($6358). ***College room only:*** $2970. Full-time tuition and fees vary according to course load and program. Room and board charges vary according to board plan. ***Part-time tuition:*** $414 per credit. ***Part-time fees:*** $2 per credit; $15 per term part-time. Part-time tuition and fees vary according to class time.

FRESHMAN FINANCIAL AID (Fall 1999, est.) 389 applied for aid; of those 84% were deemed to have need. 100% of freshmen with need received aid; of those 20% had need fully met. *Average percent of need met:* 77% (excluding resources awarded to replace EFC). *Average financial aid package:* $10,468 (excluding resources awarded to replace EFC). 16% of all full-time freshmen had no need and received non-need-based aid.

UNDERGRADUATE FINANCIAL AID (Fall 1999, est.) 1,903 applied for aid; of those 88% were deemed to have need. 100% of undergraduates with need received aid; of those 19% had need fully met. *Average percent of need met:* 74% (excluding resources awarded to replace EFC). *Average financial aid package:* $10,225 (excluding resources awarded to replace EFC). 11% of all full-time undergraduates had no need and received non-need-based aid.

GIFT AID (NEED-BASED) ***Total amount:*** $8,509,858 (23% Federal, 33% state, 44% institutional). ***Receiving aid:*** *Freshmen:* 70% (280); *all full-time undergraduates:* 71% (1,455). ***Average award:*** Freshmen: $5595; Undergraduates: $5172. ***Scholarships, grants, and awards:*** Federal Pell, FSEOG, state, private, college/university gift aid from institutional funds.

GIFT AID (NON-NEED-BASED) ***Total amount:*** $3,807,574 (2% Federal, 1% state, 90% institutional, 7% external sources). ***Receiving aid:*** *Freshmen:* 48% (192); *Undergraduates:* 36% (730). ***Scholarships, grants, and awards by category:*** *Academic Interests/Achievement:* 567 awards ($2,239,688 total): business, education, engineering/technologies, English, foreign languages, general academic interests/achievements, mathematics, premedicine, social sciences. *Creative Arts/Performance:* 77 awards ($181,009 total): art/fine arts, music. *Special Achievements/Activities:* 5 awards ($5000 total): community service. *Special Characteristics:* 201 awards ($407,353 total): adult students, children and siblings of alumni, children of union members/company employees, ethnic background, general special characteristics, members of minority groups, siblings of current students, twins. ***Tuition waivers:*** Full or partial for employees or children of employees. ***ROTC:*** Army cooperative, Naval cooperative, Air Force cooperative.

LOANS ***Student loans:*** $17,852,125 (57% need-based, 43% non-need-based). 78% of past graduating class borrowed through all loan programs. Average indebtedness per student: $16,379. ***Average need-based loan:*** Freshmen: $2693; Undergraduates: $4016. ***Parent loans:*** $1,763,148 (100% need-based). ***Programs:*** FFEL (Subsidized and Unsubsidized Stafford, PLUS), Perkins, alternative loans.

WORK-STUDY ***Federal work-study:*** *Total amount:* $433,423; 429 jobs averaging $1022. ***State or other work-study/employment:*** *Total amount:* $99,000 (100% non-need-based). 100 part-time jobs averaging $1000.

ATHLETIC AWARDS *Total amount:* 668,567 (100% need-based).

APPLYING for FINANCIAL AID ***Required financial aid forms:*** FAFSA, state aid form. ***Financial aid deadline:*** 3/1. ***Notification date:*** Continuous beginning 3/15. Students must reply by 5/1 or within 2 weeks of notification.

CONTACT Christopher S. Moore, Director of Financial Aid, The College of Saint Rose, 432 Western Avenue, Albany, NY 12203-1419, 518-454-5168 or toll-free 800-637-8556. *Fax:* 518-454-2013. *E-mail:* finaid@mail.strose.edu

THE COLLEGE OF ST. SCHOLASTICA

Duluth, MN

Tuition & fees: $15,510 **Average undergraduate aid package: $11,602**

ABOUT THE INSTITUTION Independent religious, coed. Awards: bachelor's and master's degrees. 31 undergraduate majors. Total enrollment: 2,079. Undergraduates: 1,429. Freshmen: 300. Federal methodology is used as a basis for awarding need-based institutional aid.

UNDERGRADUATE EXPENSES for 1999–2000 ***Application fee:*** $25. ***Comprehensive fee:*** $20,270 includes full-time tuition ($15,420), mandatory fees ($90), and room and board ($4760). Room and board charges vary according to board plan and housing facility. ***Part-time tuition:*** $482 per credit. ***Part-time fees:*** $45 per term part-time. Part-time tuition and fees vary according to course load. ***Payment plan:*** installment.

FRESHMAN FINANCIAL AID (Fall 1999, est.) 297 applied for aid; of those 91% were deemed to have need. 100% of freshmen with need received aid; of those 57% had need fully met. *Average percent of need met:* 85% (excluding resources awarded to replace EFC). *Average financial aid package:* $12,129 (excluding resources awarded to replace EFC). 10% of all full-time freshmen had no need and received non-need-based aid.

UNDERGRADUATE FINANCIAL AID (Fall 1999, est.) 1,084 applied for aid; of those 90% were deemed to have need. 100% of undergraduates with need received aid; of those 51% had need fully met. *Average percent of need met:* 80% (excluding resources awarded to replace EFC). *Average financial aid package:* $11,602 (excluding resources awarded to replace EFC). 9% of all full-time undergraduates had no need and received non-need-based aid.

GIFT AID (NEED-BASED) ***Total amount:*** $5,653,224 (21% Federal, 38% state, 41% institutional). ***Receiving aid:*** *Freshmen:* 70% (236); *all full-time undergraduates:* 76% (938). ***Average award:*** Freshmen: $8598; Undergraduates: $7274. ***Scholarships, grants, and awards:*** Federal Pell, FSEOG, state, private, college/university gift aid from institutional funds, Federal Nursing.

GIFT AID (NON-NEED-BASED) ***Total amount:*** $4,393,971 (2% Federal, 85% institutional, 13% external sources). ***Receiving aid:*** *Freshmen:* 76% (255); *Undergraduates:* 73% (907). ***Scholarships, grants, and awards by category:*** *Academic Interests/Achievement:* general academic interests/achievements. *Creative Arts/Performance:* music. *Special Characteristics:* children and siblings of alumni, children of faculty/staff, international students, siblings of current students. ***Tuition waivers:*** Full or partial for employees or children of employees, senior citizens. ***ROTC:*** Army cooperative, Air Force cooperative.

LOANS ***Student loans:*** $6,235,509 (57% need-based, 43% non-need-based). 90% of past graduating class borrowed through all loan programs. Average indebtedness per student: $20,224. ***Average need-based loan:*** Freshmen: $2661; Undergraduates: $3627. ***Parent loans:*** $609,351 (100% non-need-based). ***Programs:*** FFEL (Subsidized and Unsubsidized Stafford, PLUS), Perkins, Federal Nursing, state, alternative loans.

WORK-STUDY ***Federal work-study:*** *Total amount:* $360,633; 215 jobs averaging $1700. ***State or other work-study/employment:*** *Total amount:* $376,703 (86% need-based, 14% non-need-based). 225 part-time jobs averaging $1700.

APPLYING for FINANCIAL AID ***Required financial aid forms:*** FAFSA, institution's own form, state aid form. ***Financial aid deadline (priority):*** 3/15. ***Notification date:*** Continuous. Students must reply within 2 weeks of notification.

CONTACT Mr. Jon P. Erickson, Director of Financial Aid, The College of St. Scholastica, 1200 Kenwood Avenue, Duluth, MN 55811-4199, 218-723-6725 or toll-free 800-447-5444. *Fax:* 218-723-6290.

COLLEGE OF SANTA FE

Santa Fe, NM

ABOUT THE INSTITUTION Independent, coed. Awards: associate, bachelor's, and master's degrees. 43 undergraduate majors. Total enrollment: 1,555. Undergraduates: 1,334. Freshmen: 486.

GIFT AID (NEED-BASED) ***Scholarships, grants, and awards:*** Federal Pell, FSEOG, state, private, college/university gift aid from institutional funds.

GIFT AID (NON-NEED-BASED) ***Scholarships, grants, and awards by category:*** *Academic Interests/Achievement:* business, education, general academic interests/achievements, humanities, physical sciences, social sciences. *Creative Arts/Performance:* art/fine arts, cinema/film/broadcasting, creative writing, music, performing arts, theater/drama. *Special Characteristics:* adult students, children of faculty/staff.

LOANS ***Programs:*** FFEL (Subsidized and Unsubsidized Stafford, PLUS), Perkins, college/university.

WORK-STUDY ***Federal work-study:*** *Total amount:* $329,260; 150 jobs averaging $2000. ***State or other work-study/employment:*** *Total amount:* $114,432 (100% need-based).

APPLYING for FINANCIAL AID ***Required financial aid forms:*** FAFSA, institution's own form, federal verification worksheet, income tax returns.

CONTACT Darlene Salazar, Associate Director of Financial Aid, College of Santa Fe, 1600 Saint Michael's Drive, Santa Fe, NM 87505-7634, 505-473-6459 or toll-free 800-456-2673. *Fax:* 505-473-6127.

COLLEGE OF STATEN ISLAND OF THE CITY UNIVERSITY OF NEW YORK

Staten Island, NY

Tuition & fees (NY res): $3316 **Average undergraduate aid package: N/A**

ABOUT THE INSTITUTION State and locally supported, coed. Awards: associate, bachelor's, and master's degrees and post-master's certificates. 55 undergraduate majors. Total enrollment: 11,370. Undergraduates: 10,130. Freshmen: 1,851. Federal methodology is used as a basis for awarding need-based institutional aid.

UNDERGRADUATE EXPENSES for 1999–2000 ***Application fee:*** $40. ***Tuition, state resident:*** full-time $3200; part-time $135 per semester hour. ***Tuition, nonresident:*** full-time $6800; part-time $285 per semester hour. ***Required fees:*** full-time $116; $32 per term part-time. ***Payment plan:*** deferred payment.

GIFT AID (NEED-BASED) ***Total amount:*** $8,045,693 (55% Federal, 45% state). ***Scholarships, grants, and awards:*** Federal Pell, FSEOG, state, private, college/university gift aid from institutional funds, Scholarships for Disadvantaged Students (SDS).

GIFT AID (NON-NEED-BASED) ***Total amount:*** $167,657 (100% external sources). ***Tuition waivers:*** Full or partial for employees or children of employees, senior citizens.

LOANS ***Student loans:*** $4,584,600 (100% need-based). ***Parent loans:*** $37,369 (100% non-need-based). ***Programs:*** Federal Direct (Subsidized and Unsubsidized Stafford, PLUS), Perkins.

WORK-STUDY ***Federal work-study:*** *Total amount:* $482,064; jobs available.

APPLYING for FINANCIAL AID ***Required financial aid forms:*** FAFSA, state aid form. ***Financial aid deadline:*** Continuous. ***Notification date:*** Continuous beginning 6/30.

CONTACT Alan Hoffner, Assistant Director, Financial Aid, College of Staten Island of the City University of New York, 2800 Victory Boulevard, Staten Island, NY 10314-6600, 718-982-2030. *Fax:* 718-982-2037. *E-mail:* hoffner@postbox.csi.cuny.edu

COLLEGE OF THE ATLANTIC

Bar Harbor, ME

Tuition & fees: $19,485 **Average undergraduate aid package: $15,771**

ABOUT THE INSTITUTION Independent, coed. Awards: bachelor's and master's degrees. 37 undergraduate majors. Total enrollment: 293. Undergraduates: 288. Freshmen: 73. Both federal and institutional methodology are used as a basis for awarding need-based institutional aid.

UNDERGRADUATE EXPENSES for 1999–2000 ***Application fee:*** $45. ***Comprehensive fee:*** $24,705 includes full-time tuition ($19,248), mandatory fees ($237), and room and board ($5220). ***College room only:***

College of the Atlantic (continued)

$3180. Room and board charges vary according to board plan. ***Part-time tuition:*** $2566 per term. ***Part-time fees:*** $79 per term part-time. ***Payment plan:*** installment.

FRESHMAN FINANCIAL AID (Fall 1999, est.) 57 applied for aid; of those 89% were deemed to have need. 100% of freshmen with need received aid; of those 84% had need fully met. *Average percent of need met:* 95% (excluding resources awarded to replace EFC). *Average financial aid package:* $17,408 (excluding resources awarded to replace EFC). 5% of all full-time freshmen had no need and received non-need-based aid.

UNDERGRADUATE FINANCIAL AID (Fall 1999, est.) 198 applied for aid; of those 91% were deemed to have need. 100% of undergraduates with need received aid; of those 48% had need fully met. *Average percent of need met:* 89% (excluding resources awarded to replace EFC). *Average financial aid package:* $15,771 (excluding resources awarded to replace EFC). 4% of all full-time undergraduates had no need and received non-need-based aid.

GIFT AID (NEED-BASED) ***Total amount:*** $2,067,058 (8% Federal, 2% state, 84% institutional, 6% external sources). ***Receiving aid:*** *Freshmen:* 66% (48); *all full-time undergraduates:* 62% (161). ***Average award:*** Freshmen: $11,828; Undergraduates: $9852. ***Scholarships, grants, and awards:*** Federal Pell, FSEOG, state, private, college/university gift aid from institutional funds.

GIFT AID (NON-NEED-BASED) ***Total amount:*** $29,700 (83% institutional, 17% external sources). ***Receiving aid:*** *Freshmen:* 12% (9); *Undergraduates:* 12% (31). ***Scholarships, grants, and awards by category:*** *Academic Interests/Achievement:* 47 awards ($225,111 total): general academic interests/achievements. ***Tuition waivers:*** Full or partial for employees or children of employees, adult students.

LOANS ***Student loans:*** $851,729 (95% need-based, 5% non-need-based). 69% of past graduating class borrowed through all loan programs. Average indebtedness per student: $13,887. ***Average need-based loan:*** Freshmen: $2964; Undergraduates: $4035. ***Parent loans:*** $219,405 (82% need-based, 18% non-need-based). ***Programs:*** FFEL (Subsidized and Unsubsidized Stafford, PLUS), Perkins.

WORK-STUDY ***Federal work-study:*** *Total amount:* $316,750; 153 jobs averaging $1922. ***State or other work-study/employment:*** *Total amount:* $2250 (100% need-based). 2 part-time jobs averaging $1125.

APPLYING for FINANCIAL AID ***Required financial aid forms:*** FAFSA, institution's own form, noncustodial (divorced/separated) parent's statement, financial aid transcript (for transfers). ***Financial aid deadline (priority):*** 2/15. ***Notification date:*** 4/1. Students must reply by 5/1 or within 2 weeks of notification.

CONTACT David Mahoney, Director of Financial Aid, College of the Atlantic, 105 Eden Street, Bar Harbor, ME 04609-1198, 207-288-5015 or toll-free 800-528-0025. *Fax:* 207-288-4126. *E-mail:* dmm@ecology.coa.edu

COLLEGE OF THE HOLY CROSS

Worcester, MA

Tuition & fees: $23,815 **Average undergraduate aid package: $17,236**

ABOUT THE INSTITUTION Independent Roman Catholic (Jesuit), coed. Awards: bachelor's degrees. 38 undergraduate majors. Total enrollment: 2,801. Undergraduates: 2,801. Freshmen: 722. Institutional methodology is used as a basis for awarding need-based institutional aid.

UNDERGRADUATE EXPENSES for 2000–2001 ***Application fee:*** $50. ***Comprehensive fee:*** $31,355 includes full-time tuition ($23,400), mandatory fees ($415), and room and board ($7540). ***College room only:*** $3770. Room and board charges vary according to board plan and housing facility. ***Payment plans:*** tuition prepayment, installment.

FRESHMAN FINANCIAL AID (Fall 1999) 463 applied for aid; of those 80% were deemed to have need. 100% of freshmen with need received aid; of those 100% had need fully met. *Average percent of need met:* 100% (excluding resources awarded to replace EFC). *Average financial aid package:* $16,724 (excluding resources awarded to replace EFC). 5% of all full-time freshmen had no need and received non-need-based aid.

UNDERGRADUATE FINANCIAL AID (Fall 1999) 1,631 applied for aid; of those 85% were deemed to have need. 100% of undergraduates with need received aid; of those 100% had need fully met. *Average percent of need met:* 100% (excluding resources awarded to replace EFC). *Average financial aid package:* $17,236 (excluding resources awarded to replace EFC). 6% of all full-time undergraduates had no need and received non-need-based aid.

GIFT AID (NEED-BASED) ***Total amount:*** $15,061,389 (6% Federal, 2% state, 74% institutional, 18% external sources). ***Receiving aid:*** *Freshmen:* 41% (301); *all full-time undergraduates:* 41% (1,131). ***Average award:*** Freshmen: $12,811; Undergraduates: $12,243. ***Scholarships, grants, and awards:*** Federal Pell, FSEOG, state, private, college/university gift aid from institutional funds.

GIFT AID (NON-NEED-BASED) ***Total amount:*** $1,463,959 (100% institutional). ***Scholarships, grants, and awards by category:*** *Academic Interests/Achievement:* 179 awards ($1,991,959 total): general academic interests/achievements, humanities, military science. *Creative Arts/Performance:* 1 award ($22,500 total): music. *Special Characteristics:* 24 awards ($539,730 total): children of faculty/staff. ***Tuition waivers:*** Full or partial for employees or children of employees. ***ROTC:*** Army cooperative, Naval, Air Force cooperative.

LOANS ***Student loans:*** $6,570,088 (81% need-based, 19% non-need-based). 62% of past graduating class borrowed through all loan programs. Average indebtedness per student: $16,430. ***Average need-based loan:*** Freshmen: $4576; Undergraduates: $5484. ***Parent loans:*** $6,815,871 (100% non-need-based). ***Programs:*** FFEL (Subsidized and Unsubsidized Stafford, PLUS), Perkins, college/university, MEFA Loans.

WORK-STUDY ***Federal work-study:*** *Total amount:* $1,338,068; 967 jobs averaging $1384.

ATHLETIC AWARDS *Total amount:* 3,116,783 (85% need-based, 15% non-need-based).

APPLYING for FINANCIAL AID ***Required financial aid forms:*** FAFSA, CSS Financial Aid PROFILE, noncustodial (divorced/separated) parent's statement, business/farm supplement. ***Financial aid deadline (priority):*** 2/1. ***Notification date:*** 4/1. Students must reply by 5/1.

CONTACT Lynne Myers, Director of Financial Aid, College of the Holy Cross, One College Street, Worcester, MA 01610-2395, 508-793-2265 or toll-free 800-442-2421. *Fax:* 508-793-2527.

COLLEGE OF THE OZARKS

Point Lookout, MO

Tuition & fees: $150 **Average undergraduate aid package: N/A**

ABOUT THE INSTITUTION Independent Presbyterian, coed. Awards: bachelor's degrees. 76 undergraduate majors. Total enrollment: 1,429. Undergraduates: 1,429. Freshmen: 270. Federal methodology is used as a basis for awarding need-based institutional aid.

UNDERGRADUATE EXPENSES for 2000–2001 (est.) includes mandatory fees ($150) and room and board ($2500). ***Part-time tuition:*** $125 per credit hour. ***Part-time fees:*** $75 per term part-time. Full-time students work 15 hours per week plus two 40-hour work weeks per year to defray the cost of tuition.

FRESHMAN FINANCIAL AID (Fall 1998) 467 applied for aid; of those 90% were deemed to have need. 100% of freshmen with need received aid; of those 26% had need fully met. *Average percent of need met:* 81% (excluding resources awarded to replace EFC). 10% of all full-time freshmen had no need and received non-need-based aid.

UNDERGRADUATE FINANCIAL AID (Fall 1998) 1,302 applied for aid; of those 90% were deemed to have need. 100% of undergraduates with need received aid; of those 36% had need fully met. *Average percent of need met:* 81% (excluding resources awarded to replace EFC). 10% of all full-time undergraduates had no need and received non-need-based aid.

GIFT AID (NEED-BASED) ***Total amount:*** $11,220,058 (15% Federal, 7% state, 78% institutional). ***Receiving aid:*** *Freshmen:* 64% (300); *all full-time undergraduates:* 69% (898). ***Average award:*** Freshmen: $6516; Undergraduates: $6516. ***Scholarships, grants, and awards:*** Federal Pell, FSEOG, state, private, college/university gift aid from institutional funds.

GIFT AID (NON-NEED-BASED) ***Total amount:*** $475,462 (5% state, 30% institutional, 65% external sources). ***Receiving aid:*** *Freshmen:* 26% (120); *Undergraduates:* 21% (274). ***Scholarships, grants, and awards by category:*** *Academic Interests/Achievement:* general academic interests/ achievements. ***ROTC:*** Army.

LOANS ***Student loans:*** $323,333 (100% non-need-based). ***Programs:*** alternative loans.

WORK-STUDY ***Federal work-study:*** *Total amount:* $684,932; jobs available. ***State or other work-study/employment:*** *Total amount:* $1,571,052 (90% need-based, 10% non-need-based). Part-time jobs available.

ATHLETIC AWARDS *Total amount:* 120,600 (100% non-need-based).

APPLYING for FINANCIAL AID ***Required financial aid form:*** FAFSA. ***Financial aid deadline (priority):*** 3/15. ***Notification date:*** 7/1.

CONTACT Samuel A. Ketcher, Director of Financial Aid, College of the Ozarks, PO Box 17, Point Lookout, MO 65726, 417-334-6411 Ext. 4290 or toll-free 800-222-0525. *Fax:* 417-335-2618. *E-mail:* ketcher@cofo.edu

COLLEGE OF THE SOUTHWEST

Hobbs, NM

Tuition & fees: $4640 **Average undergraduate aid package: $6415**

ABOUT THE INSTITUTION Independent, coed. Awards: bachelor's and master's degrees. 21 undergraduate majors. Total enrollment: 686. Undergraduates: 566. Freshmen: 33. Federal methodology is used as a basis for awarding need-based institutional aid.

UNDERGRADUATE EXPENSES for 1999–2000 ***Application fee:*** $25. ***Comprehensive fee:*** $8140 includes full-time tuition ($4500), mandatory fees ($140), and room and board ($3500). ***College room only:*** $1575. Room and board charges vary according to housing facility. ***Part-time tuition:*** $150 per semester hour. ***Part-time fees:*** $70 per term part-time. ***Payment plan:*** deferred payment.

FRESHMAN FINANCIAL AID (Fall 1999) 33 applied for aid; of those 55% were deemed to have need. 100% of freshmen with need received aid; of those 6% had need fully met. *Average percent of need met:* 51% (excluding resources awarded to replace EFC). *Average financial aid package:* $7268 (excluding resources awarded to replace EFC). 45% of all full-time freshmen had no need and received non-need-based aid.

UNDERGRADUATE FINANCIAL AID (Fall 1999) 340 applied for aid; of those 85% were deemed to have need. 98% of undergraduates with need received aid; of those 3% had need fully met. *Average percent of need met:* 47% (excluding resources awarded to replace EFC). *Average financial aid package:* $6415 (excluding resources awarded to replace EFC). 16% of all full-time undergraduates had no need and received non-need-based aid.

GIFT AID (NEED-BASED) ***Total amount:*** $1,053,818 (55% Federal, 45% state). ***Receiving aid:*** *Freshmen:* 55% (18); *all full-time undergraduates:* 70% (242). ***Average award:*** Freshmen: $2993; Undergraduates: $2831. ***Scholarships, grants, and awards:*** Federal Pell, FSEOG, state, private, college/university gift aid from institutional funds.

GIFT AID (NON-NEED-BASED) ***Total amount:*** $233,452 (58% institutional, 42% external sources). ***Receiving aid:*** *Freshmen:* 42% (14); *Undergraduates:* 17% (59). ***Scholarships, grants, and awards by category:*** *Academic Interests/Achievement:* 96 awards ($125,775 total): business, education, English, general academic interests/achievements, mathematics, social sciences. *Creative Arts/Performance:* 5 awards ($3000 total): music, theater/ drama. *Special Achievements/Activities:* general special achievements/ activities. ***Tuition waivers:*** Full or partial for employees or children of employees.

LOANS ***Student loans:*** $1,521,013 (62% need-based, 38% non-need-based). 65% of past graduating class borrowed through all loan programs. Average indebtedness per student: $11,687. ***Average need-based loan:*** Freshmen: $1476; Undergraduates: $4280. ***Parent loans:*** $11,300 (100% non-need-based). ***Programs:*** FFEL (Subsidized and Unsubsidized Stafford, PLUS), state.

WORK-STUDY ***Federal work-study:*** *Total amount:* $33,333; 21 jobs averaging $1388. ***State or other work-study/employment:*** *Total amount:* $95,505 (60% need-based, 40% non-need-based). 53 part-time jobs averaging $1425.

ATHLETIC AWARDS *Total amount:* 180,706 (100% non-need-based).

APPLYING for FINANCIAL AID ***Required financial aid form:*** institution's own form. ***Financial aid deadline (priority):*** 4/1. ***Notification date:*** 6/15. Students must reply within 2 weeks of notification.

CONTACT Mr. David L. Arnold, Director of Financial Aid, College of the Southwest, 6610 Lovington Highway, Hobbs, NM 88240-9129, 505-392-6561 Ext. 337 or toll-free 800-530-4400 Ext. 347. *Fax:* 505-392-6006. *E-mail:* darnold@csw.edu

COLLEGE OF VISUAL ARTS

St. Paul, MN

Tuition & fees: $11,020 **Average undergraduate aid package: $8120**

ABOUT THE INSTITUTION Independent, coed. Awards: bachelor's degrees. 6 undergraduate majors. Total enrollment: 278. Undergraduates: 278. Freshmen: 50. Federal methodology is used as a basis for awarding need-based institutional aid.

UNDERGRADUATE EXPENSES for 1999–2000 ***Application fee:*** $25. ***Tuition:*** full-time $10,910; part-time $455 per credit. ***Required fees:*** full-time $110. Part-time tuition and fees vary according to course load.

FRESHMAN FINANCIAL AID (Fall 1999, est.) 40 applied for aid; of those 92% were deemed to have need. 100% of freshmen with need received aid; of those 22% had need fully met. *Average percent of need met:* 80% (excluding resources awarded to replace EFC). *Average financial aid package:* $7748 (excluding resources awarded to replace EFC). 13% of all full-time freshmen had no need and received non-need-based aid.

UNDERGRADUATE FINANCIAL AID (Fall 1999, est.) 224 applied for aid; of those 72% were deemed to have need. 100% of undergraduates with need received aid; of those 19% had need fully met. *Average percent of need met:* 75% (excluding resources awarded to replace EFC). *Average financial aid package:* $8120 (excluding resources awarded to replace EFC). 9% of all full-time undergraduates had no need and received non-need-based aid.

GIFT AID (NEED-BASED) ***Total amount:*** $698,342 (27% Federal, 59% state, 14% institutional). ***Receiving aid:*** *Freshmen:* 47% (25); *all full-time undergraduates:* 45% (121). ***Average award:*** Freshmen: $4123; Undergraduates: $3758. ***Scholarships, grants, and awards:*** Federal Pell, FSEOG, state, private, college/university gift aid from institutional funds.

GIFT AID (NON-NEED-BASED) ***Total amount:*** $58,195 (80% institutional, 20% external sources). ***Receiving aid:*** *Freshmen:* 36% (19); *Undergraduates:* 33% (89). ***Scholarships, grants, and awards by category:*** *Creative Arts/Performance:* 25 awards ($46,295 total): art/fine arts. ***Tuition waivers:*** Full or partial for children of alumni, employees or children of employees.

LOANS ***Student loans:*** $1,422,606 (54% need-based, 46% non-need-based). 96% of past graduating class borrowed through all loan programs. Average indebtedness per student: $19,700. ***Average need-based loan:*** Freshmen: $2025; Undergraduates: $3819. ***Parent loans:*** $24,000 (50% need-based, 50% non-need-based). ***Programs:*** FFEL (Subsidized and Unsubsidized Stafford, PLUS), state, alternative loans.

WORK-STUDY ***Federal work-study:*** *Total amount:* $35,265; 24 jobs averaging $1500. ***State or other work-study/employment:*** *Total amount:* $77,303 (60% need-based, 40% non-need-based). 52 part-time jobs averaging $1500.

APPLYING for FINANCIAL AID ***Required financial aid forms:*** FAFSA, institution's own form. ***Financial aid deadline:*** Continuous. ***Notification date:*** Continuous beginning 1/1. Students must reply within 2 weeks of notification.

CONTACT Ms. Carolyn M. Chesebrough, Director of Financial Aid, College of Visual Arts, 344 Summit Avenue, St. Paul, MN 55102-2124, 651-224-3416 or toll-free 800-224-1536. *Fax:* 651-224-8854. *E-mail:* carolync@cva.edu

THE COLLEGE OF WEST VIRGINIA

Beckley, WV

Tuition & fees: $3840 **Average undergraduate aid package: $8124**

ABOUT THE INSTITUTION Independent, coed. Awards: associate, bachelor's, and master's degrees. 26 undergraduate majors. Total enrollment: 1,977. Undergraduates: 1,948. Freshmen: 226. Federal methodology is used as a basis for awarding need-based institutional aid.

UNDERGRADUATE EXPENSES for 1999–2000 ***Comprehensive fee:*** $8216 includes full-time tuition ($3240), mandatory fees ($600), and room and board ($4376). ***College room only:*** $2160. Full-time tuition and fees vary according to program. Room and board charges vary according to board plan. ***Part-time tuition:*** $135 per semester hour. ***Part-time fees:*** $25 per semester hour. Part-time tuition and fees vary according to program. ***Payment plan:*** installment.

FRESHMAN FINANCIAL AID (Fall 1999, est.) 263 applied for aid; of those 98% were deemed to have need. 100% of freshmen with need received aid; of those 8% had need fully met. *Average percent of need met:* 70% (excluding resources awarded to replace EFC). *Average financial aid package:* $7047 (excluding resources awarded to replace EFC). 2% of all full-time freshmen had no need and received non-need-based aid.

UNDERGRADUATE FINANCIAL AID (Fall 1999, est.) 1,031 applied for aid; of those 98% were deemed to have need. 100% of undergraduates with need received aid; of those 22% had need fully met. *Average percent of need met:* 75% (excluding resources awarded to replace EFC). *Average financial aid package:* $8124 (excluding resources awarded to replace EFC). 2% of all full-time undergraduates had no need and received non-need-based aid.

GIFT AID (NEED-BASED) ***Total amount:*** $3,231,222 (80% Federal, 16% state, 3% institutional, 1% external sources). ***Receiving aid:*** *Freshmen:* 92% (242); *all full-time undergraduates:* 85% (879). ***Average award:*** Freshmen: $3223; Undergraduates: $3060. ***Scholarships, grants, and awards:*** Federal Pell, FSEOG, state, private, college/university gift aid from institutional funds, Federal Nursing.

GIFT AID (NON-NEED-BASED) ***Total amount:*** $8825 (7% state, 93% institutional). ***Receiving aid:*** *Undergraduates:* 3. ***Scholarships, grants, and awards by category:*** *Academic Interests/Achievement:* business, computer science, education, general academic interests/achievements, health fields, humanities, social sciences. *Special Characteristics:* children and siblings of alumni, children of faculty/staff, children of union members/company employees, first-generation college students. ***Tuition waivers:*** Full or partial for employees or children of employees, adult students.

LOANS ***Student loans:*** $5,623,666 (91% need-based, 9% non-need-based). 89% of past graduating class borrowed through all loan programs. Average indebtedness per student: $11,423. ***Average need-based loan:*** Freshmen: $3123; Undergraduates: $4533. ***Parent loans:*** $111,698 (63% need-based, 37% non-need-based). ***Programs:*** FFEL (Subsidized and Unsubsidized Stafford, PLUS), alternative loans.

WORK-STUDY ***Federal work-study:*** *Total amount:* $150,000; 75 jobs averaging $2000.

ATHLETIC AWARDS *Total amount:* 70,944 (92% need-based, 8% non-need-based).

APPLYING for FINANCIAL AID ***Required financial aid forms:*** FAFSA, institution's own form. ***Financial aid deadline (priority):*** 3/1. ***Notification date:*** Continuous beginning 3/15. Students must reply within 2 weeks of notification.

CONTACT Mr. Roger H. Widmer, Director of Financial Aid, The College of West Virginia, PO Box AG, Beckley, WV 25802-2830, 304-253-7351 Ext. 1339 or toll-free 800-766-6067. *Fax:* 304-253-5072. *E-mail:* rwidmer@cwv.edu

THE COLLEGE OF WILLIAM AND MARY

Williamsburg, VA

Tuition & fees (VA res): $4610 **Average undergraduate aid package: $7965**

ABOUT THE INSTITUTION State-supported, coed. Awards: bachelor's, master's, doctoral, and first professional degrees. 43 undergraduate majors. Total enrollment: 7,553. Undergraduates: 5,552. Freshmen: 1,301. Federal methodology is used as a basis for awarding need-based institutional aid.

UNDERGRADUATE EXPENSES for 1999–2000 ***Application fee:*** $40. ***Tuition, state resident:*** full-time $4610; part-time $122 per credit hour. ***Tuition, nonresident:*** full-time $16,434; part-time $510 per credit hour. ***College room and board:*** $4897; ***room only:*** $2857. Room and board charges vary according to board plan and housing facility. ***Payment plan:*** installment.

FRESHMAN FINANCIAL AID (Fall 1999, est.) 786 applied for aid; of those 49% were deemed to have need. 99% of freshmen with need received aid; of those 38% had need fully met. *Average percent of need met:* 81% (excluding resources awarded to replace EFC). *Average financial aid package:* $7410 (excluding resources awarded to replace EFC). 37% of all full-time freshmen had no need and received non-need-based aid.

UNDERGRADUATE FINANCIAL AID (Fall 1999, est.) 2,638 applied for aid; of those 63% were deemed to have need. 99% of undergraduates with need received aid; of those 52% had need fully met. *Average percent of need met:* 89% (excluding resources awarded to replace EFC). *Average financial aid package:* $7965 (excluding resources awarded to replace EFC). 20% of all full-time undergraduates had no need and received non-need-based aid.

GIFT AID (NEED-BASED) ***Total amount:*** $7,164,000 (20% Federal, 25% state, 45% institutional, 10% external sources). ***Receiving aid:*** *Freshmen:* 24% (315); *all full-time undergraduates:* 26% (1,410). ***Average award:*** Freshmen: $5306; Undergraduates: $5080. ***Scholarships, grants, and awards:*** Federal Pell, FSEOG, state, private, college/university gift aid from institutional funds.

GIFT AID (NON-NEED-BASED) ***Total amount:*** $1,430,000 (6% state, 26% institutional, 68% external sources). ***Receiving aid:*** *Freshmen:* 2% (26); *Undergraduates:* 2% (89). ***Scholarships, grants, and awards by category:*** *Academic Interests/Achievement:* general academic interests/achievements. ***Tuition waivers:*** Full or partial for employees or children of employees, senior citizens. ***ROTC:*** Army.

LOANS ***Student loans:*** $9,000,000 (64% need-based, 36% non-need-based). ***Average need-based loan:*** Freshmen: $2652; Undergraduates: $3862. ***Parent loans:*** $5,175,000 (36% need-based, 64% non-need-based). ***Programs:*** FFEL (Subsidized and Unsubsidized Stafford, PLUS), Perkins.

WORK-STUDY ***Federal work-study:*** *Total amount:* $257,000; 261 jobs averaging $985.

ATHLETIC AWARDS *Total amount:* 3,008,000 (12% need-based, 88% non-need-based).

APPLYING for FINANCIAL AID ***Required financial aid form:*** FAFSA. ***Financial aid deadline:*** 3/15 (priority: 2/15). ***Notification date:*** 4/1. Students must reply by 5/1.

CONTACT Mr. Edward P. Irish, Director of Student Financial Aid, The College of William and Mary, Office of Student Financial Aid, PO Box 8795, Williamsburg, VA 23187-8795, 757-221-2420. *Fax:* 757-221-2515. *E-mail:* epiris@wm.edu

THE COLLEGE OF WOOSTER

Wooster, OH

Tuition & fees: $20,530 **Average undergraduate aid package: $17,365**

ABOUT THE INSTITUTION Independent religious, coed. Awards: bachelor's degrees. 52 undergraduate majors. Total enrollment: 1,709. Undergraduates: 1,709. Freshmen: 513. Both federal and institutional methodology are used as a basis for awarding need-based institutional aid.

UNDERGRADUATE EXPENSES for 1999–2000 ***Application fee:*** $35. ***Comprehensive fee:*** $25,950 includes full-time tuition ($20,530) and room and board ($5420). ***College room only:*** $2470. Full-time tuition and fees vary according to course load and reciprocity agreements. Part-time tuition and fees vary according to course load. ***Payment plan:*** installment.

FRESHMAN FINANCIAL AID (Fall 1999) 453 applied for aid; of those 77% were deemed to have need. 100% of freshmen with need received aid; of those 76% had need fully met. *Average percent of need met:* 100%

(excluding resources awarded to replace EFC). *Average financial aid package:* $17,780 (excluding resources awarded to replace EFC).

UNDERGRADUATE FINANCIAL AID (Fall 1999) 1,273 applied for aid; of those 87% were deemed to have need. 100% of undergraduates with need received aid; of those 75% had need fully met. *Average percent of need met:* 100% (excluding resources awarded to replace EFC). *Average financial aid package:* $17,365 (excluding resources awarded to replace EFC).

GIFT AID (NEED-BASED) ***Total amount:*** $14,591,496 (4% Federal, 6% state, 88% institutional, 2% external sources). ***Receiving aid:*** *Freshmen:* 350; *all full-time undergraduates:* 1,103. ***Average award:*** Freshmen: $14,515; Undergraduates: $13,870. ***Scholarships, grants, and awards:*** Federal Pell, FSEOG, state, private, college/university gift aid from institutional funds.

GIFT AID (NON-NEED-BASED) ***Total amount:*** $5,476,341 (7% state, 90% institutional, 3% external sources). ***Receiving aid:*** *Freshmen:* 54; *Undergraduates:* 140. ***Scholarships, grants, and awards by category:*** *Academic Interests/Achievement:* biological sciences, general academic interests/achievements, mathematics, physical sciences, social sciences. *Creative Arts/Performance:* dance, music, theater/drama. *Special Achievements/Activities:* community service, religious involvement. *Special Characteristics:* children of faculty/staff, handicapped students, international students, local/state students, members of minority groups. ***Tuition waivers:*** Full or partial for employees or children of employees.

LOANS ***Student loans:*** $4,176,272 (65% need-based, 35% non-need-based). 58% of past graduating class borrowed through all loan programs. Average indebtedness per student: $15,800. ***Average need-based loan:*** Freshmen: $3210; Undergraduates: $3815. ***Parent loans:*** $1,964,774 (10% need-based, 90% non-need-based). ***Programs:*** Federal Direct (Subsidized and Unsubsidized Stafford, PLUS), Perkins, college/university.

WORK-STUDY ***Federal work-study:*** *Total amount:* $726,191; 619 jobs averaging $1117. ***State or other work-study/employment:*** *Total amount:* $357,789 (61% need-based, 39% non-need-based). Part-time jobs available.

APPLYING for FINANCIAL AID ***Required financial aid forms:*** FAFSA, institution's own form, CSS Financial Aid PROFILE, noncustodial (divorced/separated) parent's statement. ***Financial aid deadline (priority):*** 2/15. ***Notification date:*** 4/1. Students must reply by 5/1.

CONTACT Office of Financial Aid, The College of Wooster, 1189 Beall Avenue, Wooster, OH 44691, 330-263-2317 or toll-free 800-877-9905. *E-mail:* financialaid@wooster.edu

COLORADO CHRISTIAN UNIVERSITY

Lakewood, CO

Tuition & fees: $10,790 **Average undergraduate aid package: $9274**

ABOUT THE INSTITUTION Independent interdenominational, coed. Awards: associate, bachelor's, and master's degrees. 36 undergraduate majors. Total enrollment: 2,026. Undergraduates: 1,786. Freshmen: 214. Federal methodology is used as a basis for awarding need-based institutional aid.

UNDERGRADUATE EXPENSES for 1999–2000 ***Application fee:*** $40. ***Comprehensive fee:*** $15,950 includes full-time tuition ($9960), mandatory fees ($830), and room and board ($5160). ***College room only:*** $2960. Room and board charges vary according to board plan. ***Part-time tuition:*** $415 per semester hour. Part-time tuition and fees vary according to program. ***Payment plan:*** installment.

FRESHMAN FINANCIAL AID (Fall 1999) 156 applied for aid; of those 78% were deemed to have need. 100% of freshmen with need received aid; of those 18% had need fully met. *Average percent of need met:* 64% (excluding resources awarded to replace EFC). *Average financial aid package:* $8424 (excluding resources awarded to replace EFC). 42% of all full-time freshmen had no need and received non-need-based aid.

UNDERGRADUATE FINANCIAL AID (Fall 1999) 661 applied for aid; of those 84% were deemed to have need. 100% of undergraduates with need received aid; of those 26% had need fully met. *Average percent of need met:* 72% (excluding resources awarded to replace EFC). *Average financial aid package:* $9274 (excluding resources awarded to replace EFC). 25% of all full-time undergraduates had no need and received non-need-based aid.

GIFT AID (NEED-BASED) ***Total amount:*** $2,389,551 (43% Federal, 43% institutional, 14% external sources). ***Receiving aid:*** *Freshmen:* 53% (112); *all full-time undergraduates:* 64% (475). ***Average award:*** Freshmen: $4954; Undergraduates: $4023. ***Scholarships, grants, and awards:*** Federal Pell, FSEOG, college/university gift aid from institutional funds.

GIFT AID (NON-NEED-BASED) ***Total amount:*** $425,012 (3% Federal, 64% institutional, 33% external sources). ***Receiving aid:*** *Freshmen:* 6% (13); *Undergraduates:* 7% (52). ***Scholarships, grants, and awards by category:*** *Academic Interests/Achievement:* business, general academic interests/achievements, humanities, religion/biblical studies. *Creative Arts/Performance:* art/fine arts, music, theater/drama. *Special Achievements/Activities:* community service, general special achievements/activities, leadership, religious involvement. *Special Characteristics:* children of educators, children of faculty/staff, religious affiliation. ***Tuition waivers:*** Full or partial for employees or children of employees. ***ROTC:*** Army cooperative, Air Force cooperative.

LOANS ***Student loans:*** $6,240,720 (73% need-based, 27% non-need-based). 86% of past graduating class borrowed through all loan programs. ***Average need-based loan:*** Freshmen: $3235; Undergraduates: $4885. ***Parent loans:*** $881,343 (46% need-based, 54% non-need-based). ***Programs:*** FFEL (Subsidized and Unsubsidized Stafford, PLUS), Perkins.

WORK-STUDY ***Federal work-study:*** *Total amount:* $171,532; jobs available. ***State or other work-study/employment:*** *Total amount:* $105,756 (31% need-based, 69% non-need-based). Part-time jobs available.

ATHLETIC AWARDS *Total amount:* 537,360 (52% need-based, 48% non-need-based).

APPLYING for FINANCIAL AID ***Required financial aid form:*** FAFSA. ***Financial aid deadline (priority):*** 3/15. ***Notification date:*** Continuous beginning 4/1. Students must reply by 5/1 or within 4 weeks of notification.

CONTACT Molly Burley, Acting Director of Financial Aid, Colorado Christian University, 180 South Garrison Street, Lakewood, CO 80226-7499, 303-963-3230 or toll-free 800-44-FAITH. *E-mail:* finaid@ccu.edu

THE COLORADO COLLEGE

Colorado Springs, CO

Tuition & fees: $21,822 **Average undergraduate aid package: $18,764**

ABOUT THE INSTITUTION Independent, coed. Awards: bachelor's and master's degrees (master's degree in education only). 35 undergraduate majors. Total enrollment: 1,964. Undergraduates: 1,941. Freshmen: 483. Institutional methodology is used as a basis for awarding need-based institutional aid.

UNDERGRADUATE EXPENSES for 1999–2000 ***Application fee:*** $40. ***Comprehensive fee:*** $27,390 includes full-time tuition ($21,822) and room and board ($5568). ***College room only:*** $2984. Room and board charges vary according to board plan. ***Payment plan:*** installment.

FRESHMAN FINANCIAL AID (Fall 1999) 258 applied for aid; of those 90% were deemed to have need. 100% of freshmen with need received aid; of those 39% had need fully met. *Average percent of need met:* 93% (excluding resources awarded to replace EFC). *Average financial aid package:* $18,894 (excluding resources awarded to replace EFC). 5% of all full-time freshmen had no need and received non-need-based aid.

UNDERGRADUATE FINANCIAL AID (Fall 1999) 923 applied for aid; of those 94% were deemed to have need. 100% of undergraduates with need received aid; of those 40% had need fully met. *Average percent of need met:* 93% (excluding resources awarded to replace EFC). *Average financial aid package:* $18,764 (excluding resources awarded to replace EFC). 8% of all full-time undergraduates had no need and received non-need-based aid.

GIFT AID (NEED-BASED) ***Total amount:*** $11,822,606 (8% Federal, 2% state, 87% institutional, 3% external sources). ***Receiving aid:*** *Freshmen:* 39% (214); *all full-time undergraduates:* 40% (787). ***Average award:***

The Colorado College (continued)

Freshmen: $16,267; Undergraduates: $15,463. ***Scholarships, grants, and awards:*** Federal Pell, FSEOG, state, private, college/university gift aid from institutional funds.

GIFT AID (NON-NEED-BASED) ***Total amount:*** $2,142,968 (3% state, 62% institutional, 35% external sources). ***Receiving aid:*** *Freshmen:* 3% (16); *Undergraduates:* 2% (33). ***Scholarships, grants, and awards by category:*** *Academic Interests/Achievement:* 60 awards ($581,000 total): general academic interests/achievements, physical sciences. *Special Characteristics:* international students. ***Tuition waivers:*** Full or partial for employees or children of employees. ***ROTC:*** Army cooperative.

LOANS ***Student loans:*** $3,706,541 (86% need-based, 14% non-need-based). Average indebtedness per student: $13,418. ***Average need-based loan:*** Freshmen: $3132; Undergraduates: $4151. ***Parent loans:*** $1,849,154 (28% need-based, 72% non-need-based). ***Programs:*** FFEL (Subsidized and Unsubsidized Stafford, PLUS), Perkins.

WORK-STUDY ***Federal work-study:*** *Total amount:* $431,522; 341 jobs averaging $1265. ***State or other work-study/employment:*** *Total amount:* $401,706 (65% need-based, 35% non-need-based). 314 part-time jobs averaging $1279.

ATHLETIC AWARDS *Total amount:* 842,199 (13% need-based, 87% non-need-based).

APPLYING for FINANCIAL AID ***Required financial aid forms:*** FAFSA, CSS Financial Aid PROFILE, noncustodial (divorced/separated) parent's statement. ***Financial aid deadline:*** 2/15. ***Notification date:*** 3/25. Students must reply by 5/1.

CONTACT Mr. James M. Swanson, Director of Financial Aid, The Colorado College, 14 East Cache La Poudre Street, Colorado Springs, CO 80903-3294, 719-389-6651 or toll-free 800-542-7214. *Fax:* 719-389-6173. *E-mail:* financialaid@coloradocollege.edu

THE COLORADO INSTITUTE OF ART

Denver, CO

See The Art Institute of Colorado

COLORADO SCHOOL OF MINES

Golden, CO

Tuition & fees (CO res): $5211 **Average undergraduate aid package: $10,195**

ABOUT THE INSTITUTION State-supported, coed. Awards: bachelor's, master's, and doctoral degrees. 17 undergraduate majors. Total enrollment: 3,202. Undergraduates: 2,473. Freshmen: 566. Both federal and institutional methodology are used as a basis for awarding need-based institutional aid.

UNDERGRADUATE EXPENSES for 1999–2000 ***Application fee:*** $25. ***Tuition, state resident:*** full-time $4616; part-time $154 per semester hour. ***Tuition, nonresident:*** full-time $14,716; part-time $491 per semester hour. ***Required fees:*** full-time $595. Part-time tuition and fees vary according to course load. ***College room and board:*** $4920. Room and board charges vary according to board plan and housing facility. ***Payment plan:*** installment.

FRESHMAN FINANCIAL AID (Fall 1998) 544 applied for aid; of those 86% were deemed to have need. 100% of freshmen with need received aid; of those 100% had need fully met. *Average percent of need met:* 100% (excluding resources awarded to replace EFC). *Average financial aid package:* $10,195 (excluding resources awarded to replace EFC). 8% of all full-time freshmen had no need and received non-need-based aid.

UNDERGRADUATE FINANCIAL AID (Fall 1998) 1,885 applied for aid; of those 86% were deemed to have need. 100% of undergraduates with need received aid; of those 100% had need fully met. *Average percent of need met:* 100% (excluding resources awarded to replace EFC). *Average financial aid package:* $10,195 (excluding resources awarded to replace EFC). 8% of all full-time undergraduates had no need and received non-need-based aid.

GIFT AID (NEED-BASED) ***Total amount:*** $4,222,386 (27% Federal, 12% state, 61% institutional). ***Receiving aid:*** *Freshmen:* 47% (315); *all full-time undergraduates:* 47% (1,091). ***Average award:*** Freshmen: $3870; Undergraduates: $3870. ***Scholarships, grants, and awards:*** Federal Pell, FSEOG, state, private, college/university gift aid from institutional funds.

GIFT AID (NON-NEED-BASED) ***Total amount:*** $2,707,516 (1% Federal, 1% state, 55% institutional, 43% external sources). ***Receiving aid:*** *Freshmen:* 32% (215); *Undergraduates:* 31% (714). ***Scholarships, grants, and awards by category:*** *Academic Interests/Achievement:* 300 awards ($847,303 total): business, computer science, engineering/technologies, general academic interests/achievements, mathematics, military science, physical sciences. *Creative Arts/Performance:* 25 awards ($40,000 total): music. *Special Characteristics:* 200 awards ($600,000 total): children and siblings of alumni, ethnic background, members of minority groups. ***ROTC:*** Army cooperative.

LOANS ***Student loans:*** $8,025,604 (74% need-based, 26% non-need-based). 69% of past graduating class borrowed through all loan programs. Average indebtedness per student: $17,500. ***Average need-based loan:*** Freshmen: $3580; Undergraduates: $3580. ***Parent loans:*** $1,036,337 (100% non-need-based). ***Programs:*** FFEL (Subsidized and Unsubsidized Stafford, PLUS), Perkins, college/university.

WORK-STUDY ***Federal work-study:*** *Total amount:* $183,767; 184 jobs averaging $1000. ***State or other work-study/employment:*** *Total amount:* $557,786 (34% need-based, 66% non-need-based). 560 part-time jobs averaging $1000.

ATHLETIC AWARDS *Total amount:* 797,267 (100% non-need-based).

APPLYING for FINANCIAL AID ***Required financial aid form:*** FAFSA. ***Financial aid deadline (priority):*** 3/1. ***Notification date:*** 4/1. Students must reply by 5/1 or within 2 weeks of notification.

CONTACT Mr. Roger A. Koester, Director of Financial Aid, Colorado School of Mines, 1500 Illinois Street, Golden, CO 80401-1887, 303-273-3207 or toll-free 800-446-9488 (out-of-state). *Fax:* 303-384-2252. *E-mail:* rkoester@mines.edu

COLORADO STATE UNIVERSITY

Fort Collins, CO

Tuition & fees (CO res): $3062 **Average undergraduate aid package: $6929**

ABOUT THE INSTITUTION State-supported, coed. Awards: bachelor's, master's, doctoral, and first professional degrees. 132 undergraduate majors. Total enrollment: 22,782. Undergraduates: 18,800. Freshmen: 3,137. Federal methodology is used as a basis for awarding need-based institutional aid.

UNDERGRADUATE EXPENSES for 1999–2000 ***Application fee:*** $30. ***Tuition, state resident:*** full-time $2340; part-time $130 per credit. ***Tuition, nonresident:*** full-time $10,026; part-time $557 per credit. ***Required fees:*** full-time $722; $130 per credit; $32 per term part-time. Full-time tuition and fees vary according to program. Part-time tuition and fees vary according to course load and program. ***College room and board:*** $5200. Room and board charges vary according to board plan and housing facility. ***Payment plan:*** installment.

FRESHMAN FINANCIAL AID (Fall 1998) 1803 applied for aid; of those 71% were deemed to have need. 99% of freshmen with need received aid; of those 37% had need fully met. *Average percent of need met:* 87% (excluding resources awarded to replace EFC). *Average financial aid package:* $5450 (excluding resources awarded to replace EFC). 24% of all full-time freshmen had no need and received non-need-based aid.

UNDERGRADUATE FINANCIAL AID (Fall 1998) 9,592 applied for aid; of those 78% were deemed to have need. 99% of undergraduates with need received aid; of those 43% had need fully met. *Average percent of need met:* 82% (excluding resources awarded to replace EFC). *Average financial aid package:* $6929 (excluding resources awarded to replace EFC). 20% of all full-time undergraduates had no need and received non-need-based aid.

GIFT AID (NEED-BASED) ***Total amount:*** $16,496,096 (49% Federal, 27% state, 15% institutional, 9% external sources). ***Receiving aid:*** *Freshmen:* 34% (1,015); *all full-time undergraduates:* 34% (5,602). ***Average award:***

Freshmen: $3652; Undergraduates: $3049. ***Scholarships, grants, and awards:*** Federal Pell, FSEOG, state, private, college/university gift aid from institutional funds.

GIFT AID (NON-NEED-BASED) ***Total amount:*** $3,679,699 (1% Federal, 11% state, 62% institutional, 26% external sources). ***Scholarships, grants, and awards by category:*** *Academic Interests/Achievement:* 5,080 awards ($6,694,833 total): general academic interests/achievements. *Creative Arts/Performance:* 244 awards ($190,250 total): art/fine arts, creative writing, dance, debating, music, theater/drama. *Special Achievements/Activities:* 486 awards ($1,177,589 total): general special achievements/activities. *Special Characteristics:* 260 awards ($655,997 total): first-generation college students. ***Tuition waivers:*** Full or partial for employees or children of employees. ***ROTC:*** Army, Air Force.

LOANS ***Student loans:*** $43,088,159 (83% need-based, 17% non-need-based). 64% of past graduating class borrowed through all loan programs. Average indebtedness per student: $14,253. ***Average need-based loan:*** Freshmen: $3154; Undergraduates: $5055. ***Parent loans:*** $12,001,582 (64% need-based, 36% non-need-based). ***Programs:*** Federal Direct (Subsidized and Unsubsidized Stafford, PLUS), Perkins.

WORK-STUDY ***Federal work-study:*** *Total amount:* $933,741; 717 jobs available. ***State or other work-study/employment:*** *Total amount:* $1,819,708 (75% need-based, 25% non-need-based). Part-time jobs available.

ATHLETIC AWARDS *Total amount:* 2,606,884 (40% need-based, 60% non-need-based).

APPLYING for FINANCIAL AID ***Required financial aid form:*** FAFSA. ***Financial aid deadline (priority):*** 3/1. ***Notification date:*** Continuous.

CONTACT Office of Student Financial Services, Colorado State University, Room 103 Administration Annex, Fort Collins, CO 80523, 970-491-6321. *E-mail:* sfservices@vines.colostate.edu

COLORADO TECHNICAL UNIVERSITY

Colorado Springs, CO

Tuition & fees: $6108 **Average undergraduate aid package: $3107**

ABOUT THE INSTITUTION Proprietary, coed. Awards: associate, bachelor's, master's, and doctoral degrees. 10 undergraduate majors. Total enrollment: 1,764. Undergraduates: 1,124. Freshmen: 358. Federal methodology is used as a basis for awarding need-based institutional aid.

UNDERGRADUATE EXPENSES for 1999–2000 ***Application fee:*** $50. ***One-time required fee:*** $100. ***Tuition:*** full-time $5940; part-time $165 per quarter hour. ***Required fees:*** full-time $168; $56 per term part-time. Part-time tuition and fees vary according to course load. ***Payment plan:*** installment.

FRESHMAN FINANCIAL AID (Fall 1998) 86 applied for aid; of those 73% were deemed to have need. 100% of freshmen with need received aid; of those 24% had need fully met. *Average percent of need met:* 64% (excluding resources awarded to replace EFC). *Average financial aid package:* $2160 (excluding resources awarded to replace EFC).

UNDERGRADUATE FINANCIAL AID (Fall 1998) 362 applied for aid; of those 79% were deemed to have need. 100% of undergraduates with need received aid; of those 29% had need fully met. *Average percent of need met:* 64% (excluding resources awarded to replace EFC). *Average financial aid package:* $3107 (excluding resources awarded to replace EFC).

GIFT AID (NEED-BASED) ***Total amount:*** $559,970 (73% Federal, 27% state). ***Receiving aid:*** *Freshmen:* 11% (18); *all full-time undergraduates:* 16% (99). ***Average award:*** Freshmen: $631; Undergraduates: $952. ***Scholarships, grants, and awards:*** Federal Pell, FSEOG, state, college/university gift aid from institutional funds.

GIFT AID (NON-NEED-BASED) ***Total amount:*** $235,119 (100% institutional). ***Scholarships, grants, and awards by category:*** *Academic Interests/Achievement:* general academic interests/achievements. ***Tuition waivers:*** Full or partial for employees or children of employees. ***ROTC:*** Army cooperative.

LOANS ***Student loans:*** $2,181,201 (64% need-based, 36% non-need-based). ***Parent loans:*** $54,893 (100% non-need-based). ***Programs:*** FFEL (Subsidized and Unsubsidized Stafford, PLUS), Perkins.

WORK-STUDY ***Federal work-study:*** *Total amount:* $50,530; jobs available.

APPLYING for FINANCIAL AID ***Required financial aid forms:*** FAFSA, institution's own form, state aid form. ***Financial aid deadline:*** Continuous. ***Notification date:*** Continuous.

CONTACT Financial Aid Manager, Colorado Technical University, 4435 North Chestnut Street, Colorado Springs, CO 80907-3896, 719-598-0200. *Fax:* 719-598-3740.

COLORADO TECHNICAL UNIVERSITY DENVER CAMPUS

Greenwood Village, CO

Tuition & fees: $6108 **Average undergraduate aid package: $2731**

ABOUT THE INSTITUTION Proprietary, coed. Awards: associate, bachelor's, master's, and doctoral degrees. 4 undergraduate majors. Total enrollment: 295. Undergraduates: 202. Freshmen: 2. Federal methodology is used as a basis for awarding need-based institutional aid.

UNDERGRADUATE EXPENSES for 1999–2000 ***Application fee:*** $50. ***Tuition:*** full-time $5940; part-time $165 per credit hour. ***Required fees:*** full-time $168; $56 per term part-time. Full-time tuition and fees vary according to course load. ***Payment plans:*** installment, deferred payment.

UNDERGRADUATE FINANCIAL AID (Fall 1998) 36 applied for aid; of those 44% were deemed to have need. 100% of undergraduates with need received aid; of those 25% had need fully met. *Average percent of need met:* 64% (excluding resources awarded to replace EFC). *Average financial aid package:* $2731 (excluding resources awarded to replace EFC). 5% of all full-time undergraduates had no need and received non-need-based aid.

GIFT AID (NEED-BASED) ***Total amount:*** $58,437 (84% Federal, 16% state). ***Receiving aid:*** *All full-time undergraduates:* 19% (12). ***Average award:*** Undergraduates: $913. ***Scholarships, grants, and awards:*** Federal Pell, FSEOG, state.

GIFT AID (NON-NEED-BASED) ***Total amount:*** $7870 (100% institutional).

LOANS ***Student loans:*** $341,975 (60% need-based, 40% non-need-based). 33% of past graduating class borrowed through all loan programs. Average indebtedness per student: $29,000. ***Average need-based loan:*** Undergraduates: $3195. ***Parent loans:*** $7309 (100% non-need-based). ***Programs:*** FFEL (Subsidized and Unsubsidized Stafford, PLUS), Perkins.

WORK-STUDY ***Federal work-study:*** *Total amount:* $1110; jobs available.

APPLYING for FINANCIAL AID ***Required financial aid form:*** FAFSA. ***Financial aid deadline:*** Continuous. ***Notification date:*** Continuous.

CONTACT LaTisha Garcia, Financial Aid Officer, Colorado Technical University Denver Campus, 5775 DTC Boulevard, Suite 100, Greenwood Village, CO 80111, 303-694-6600. *Fax:* 303-694-6673.

COLORADO TECHNICAL UNIVERSITY SIOUX FALLS CAMPUS

Sioux Falls, SD

CONTACT Financial Aid Office, Colorado Technical University Sioux Falls Campus, 3901 West 59th Street, Sioux Falls, SD 57108, 605-361-0200.

COLUMBIA COLLEGE

Columbia, MO

Tuition & fees: $9808 **Average undergraduate aid package: $6193**

ABOUT THE INSTITUTION Independent religious, coed. Awards: associate, bachelor's, and master's degrees. 41 undergraduate majors. Total enrollment: 8,002. Undergraduates: 7,865. Freshmen: 1,269. Federal methodology is used as a basis for awarding need-based institutional aid.

UNDERGRADUATE EXPENSES for 1999–2000 ***Application fee:*** $25. ***Comprehensive fee:*** $14,207 includes full-time tuition ($9808) and room and board ($4399). ***College room only:*** $2767. Full-time tuition and fees vary according to class time and course load. Room and board charges

Columbia College (continued)

vary according to board plan. ***Part-time tuition:*** $175 per credit hour. Part-time tuition and fees vary according to class time. ***Payment plan:*** deferred payment.

FRESHMAN FINANCIAL AID (Fall 1999) 437 applied for aid; of those 80% were deemed to have need. 80% of freshmen with need received aid; of those 13% had need fully met. *Average percent of need met:* 57% (excluding resources awarded to replace EFC). *Average financial aid package:* $6219 (excluding resources awarded to replace EFC). 5% of all full-time freshmen had no need and received non-need-based aid.

UNDERGRADUATE FINANCIAL AID (Fall 1999) 2,585 applied for aid; of those 78% were deemed to have need. 86% of undergraduates with need received aid; of those 18% had need fully met. *Average percent of need met:* 60% (excluding resources awarded to replace EFC). *Average financial aid package:* $6193 (excluding resources awarded to replace EFC). 7% of all full-time undergraduates had no need and received non-need-based aid.

GIFT AID (NEED-BASED) ***Total amount:*** $5,186,584 (90% Federal, 8% state, 2% institutional). ***Receiving aid:*** *Freshmen:* 40% (271); *all full-time undergraduates:* 37% (1,656). ***Average award:*** Freshmen: $4091; Undergraduates: $4517. ***Scholarships, grants, and awards:*** Federal Pell, FSEOG, state, private, college/university gift aid from institutional funds.

GIFT AID (NON-NEED-BASED) ***Total amount:*** $1,725,277 (3% state, 91% institutional, 6% external sources). ***Receiving aid:*** *Freshmen:* 22% (149); *Undergraduates:* 22% (969). ***Scholarships, grants, and awards by category:*** *Academic Interests/Achievement:* biological sciences, business, education, general academic interests/achievements, physical sciences, social sciences. *Creative Arts/Performance:* applied art and design, art/fine arts, music. *Special Achievements/Activities:* junior miss, leadership, memberships, religious involvement. *Special Characteristics:* children and siblings of alumni, children of current students, children of educators, children of faculty/staff, children of union members/company employees, children with a deceased or disabled parent, local/state students, parents of current students, religious affiliation, siblings of current students, veterans. ***Tuition waivers:*** Full or partial for children of alumni, employees or children of employees, senior citizens. ***ROTC:*** Army cooperative, Naval cooperative, Air Force cooperative.

LOANS ***Student loans:*** $7,822,994 (58% need-based, 42% non-need-based). Average indebtedness per student: $13,576. ***Average need-based loan:*** Freshmen: $3606; Undergraduates: $3447. ***Parent loans:*** $422,241 (100% non-need-based). ***Programs:*** Federal Direct (Subsidized and Unsubsidized Stafford, PLUS), Perkins.

WORK-STUDY ***Federal work-study:*** *Total amount:* $212,772; 147 jobs averaging $1438.

ATHLETIC AWARDS *Total amount:* 684,655 (100% non-need-based).

APPLYING for FINANCIAL AID ***Required financial aid forms:*** FAFSA, institution's own form. ***Financial aid deadline (priority):*** 3/1. ***Notification date:*** Continuous. Students must reply within 2 weeks of notification.

CONTACT Sharon Abernathy, Director of Financial Aid, Columbia College, 1001 Rogers Street, Columbia, MO 65216-0002, 573-875-7390 or toll-free 800-231-2391 Ext. 7366. *Fax:* 573-875-7452. *E-mail:* saabernathy@email.ccis.edu

COLUMBIA COLLEGE

New York, NY

Tuition & fees: $24,974 | **Average undergraduate aid package: $21,365**

ABOUT THE INSTITUTION Independent, coed. Awards: bachelor's degrees. 52 undergraduate majors. Total enrollment: 3,913. Undergraduates: 3,913. Freshmen: 964. Institutional methodology is used as a basis for awarding need-based institutional aid.

UNDERGRADUATE EXPENSES for 1999–2000 ***Application fee:*** $50. ***One-time required fee:*** $45. ***Comprehensive fee:*** $32,706 includes full-time tuition ($24,150), mandatory fees ($824), and room and board ($7732). ***Payment plans:*** tuition prepayment, installment.

FRESHMAN FINANCIAL AID (Fall 1999) 522 applied for aid; of those 85% were deemed to have need. 100% of freshmen with need received aid; of those 100% had need fully met. *Average percent of need met:* 100% (excluding resources awarded to replace EFC). *Average financial aid package:* $20,954 (excluding resources awarded to replace EFC).

UNDERGRADUATE FINANCIAL AID (Fall 1999) 1,839 applied for aid; of those 96% were deemed to have need. 100% of undergraduates with need received aid; of those 100% had need fully met. *Average percent of need met:* 100% (excluding resources awarded to replace EFC). *Average financial aid package:* $21,365 (excluding resources awarded to replace EFC).

GIFT AID (NEED-BASED) ***Total amount:*** $26,588,744 (9% Federal, 4% state, 82% institutional, 5% external sources). ***Receiving aid:*** *Freshmen:* 40% (385); *all full-time undergraduates:* 38% (1,477). ***Average award:*** Freshmen: $18,662; Undergraduates: $17,568. ***Scholarships, grants, and awards:*** Federal Pell, FSEOG, state, private, college/university gift aid from institutional funds.

GIFT AID (NON-NEED-BASED) ***Tuition waivers:*** Full or partial for employees or children of employees.

LOANS ***Student loans:*** $7,033,755 (100% need-based). 49% of past graduating class borrowed through all loan programs. ***Average need-based loan:*** Freshmen: $2970; Undergraduates: $4847. ***Parent loans:*** $7,460,301 (100% need-based). ***Programs:*** FFEL (Subsidized and Unsubsidized Stafford, PLUS), Perkins, alternative loans.

WORK-STUDY ***Federal work-study:*** *Total amount:* $3,319,016; jobs available.

APPLYING for FINANCIAL AID ***Required financial aid forms:*** FAFSA, institution's own form, CSS Financial Aid PROFILE, noncustodial (divorced/separated) parent's statement, business/farm supplement, parent and student income tax returns. ***Financial aid deadline:*** 2/10. ***Notification date:*** 4/1. Students must reply by 5/1 or within 4 weeks of notification.

CONTACT Student Financial Planning Office, Columbia College, 100 Hamilton Hall, 1130 Amsterdam Avenue, MC 2802, New York, NY 10027, 212-854-3711. *Fax:* 212-854-5353. *E-mail:* ugrad-finaid@columbia.edu

COLUMBIA COLLEGE

Caguas, PR

CONTACT Financial Aid Officer, Columbia College, Carr 183, Km 1.7, PO Box 8517, Caguas, PR 00726, 787-743-4041 Ext. 244 or toll-free 800-981-4877 Ext. 239 (in-state).

COLUMBIA COLLEGE

Columbia, SC

Tuition & fees: $15,060 | **Average undergraduate aid package: $14,347**

ABOUT THE INSTITUTION Independent United Methodist, women only. Awards: bachelor's and master's degrees. 48 undergraduate majors. Total enrollment: 1,375. Undergraduates: 1,237. Federal methodology is used as a basis for awarding need-based institutional aid.

UNDERGRADUATE EXPENSES for 2000–2001 ***Application fee:*** $20. ***Comprehensive fee:*** $20,050 includes full-time tuition ($14,760), mandatory fees ($300), and room and board ($4990). Room and board charges vary according to board plan. ***Part-time tuition:*** $395 per credit. ***Part-time fees:*** $150 per term. Part-time tuition and fees vary according to course load. ***Payment plan:*** installment.

FRESHMAN FINANCIAL AID (Fall 1999, est.) 259 applied for aid; of those 83% were deemed to have need. 100% of freshmen with need received aid; of those 31% had need fully met. *Average percent of need met:* 88% (excluding resources awarded to replace EFC). *Average financial aid package:* $15,209 (excluding resources awarded to replace EFC). 17% of all full-time freshmen had no need and received non-need-based aid.

UNDERGRADUATE FINANCIAL AID (Fall 1999, est.) 1,093 applied for aid; of those 90% were deemed to have need. 99% of undergraduates with need received aid; of those 25% had need fully met. *Average percent of need met:* 78% (excluding resources awarded to replace EFC). *Average*

financial aid package: $14,347 (excluding resources awarded to replace EFC). 11% of all full-time undergraduates had no need and received non-need-based aid.

GIFT AID (NEED-BASED) ***Total amount:*** $5,228,891 (22% Federal, 51% state, 27% institutional). ***Receiving aid:*** *Freshmen:* 83% (214); *all full-time undergraduates:* 88% (972). ***Average award:*** Freshmen: $8288; Undergraduates: $9001. ***Scholarships, grants, and awards:*** Federal Pell, FSEOG, state, private, college/university gift aid from institutional funds.

GIFT AID (NON-NEED-BASED) ***Total amount:*** $3,853,890 (18% state, 76% institutional, 6% external sources). ***Receiving aid:*** *Freshmen:* 79% (205); *Undergraduates:* 82% (904). ***Scholarships, grants, and awards by category:*** *Academic Interests/Achievement:* biological sciences, business, communication, education, English, foreign languages, general academic interests/achievements, humanities, mathematics, religion/biblical studies. *Creative Arts/Performance:* applied art and design, art/fine arts, dance, music. *Special Achievements/Activities:* leadership. *Special Characteristics:* children of faculty/staff, relatives of clergy. ***Tuition waivers:*** Full or partial for employees or children of employees. ***ROTC:*** Army cooperative.

LOANS ***Student loans:*** $6,743,843 (58% need-based, 42% non-need-based). ***Average need-based loan:*** Freshmen: $3786; Undergraduates: $4252. ***Parent loans:*** $1,023,369 (100% non-need-based). ***Programs:*** FFEL (Subsidized and Unsubsidized Stafford, PLUS), Perkins, state, SC Teacher Loans, United Methodist Student Loans.

WORK-STUDY ***Federal work-study:*** *Total amount:* $300,411; 287 jobs averaging $1047. ***State or other work-study/employment:*** *Total amount:* $187,162 (100% non-need-based). 187 part-time jobs averaging $1000.

ATHLETIC AWARDS *Total amount:* 57,500 (100% non-need-based).

APPLYING for FINANCIAL AID ***Required financial aid form:*** FAFSA. ***Financial aid deadline (priority):*** 4/1. ***Notification date:*** Continuous. Students must reply within 2 weeks of notification.

CONTACT Anita R. Kaminer, Director of Financial Aid, Columbia College, 1301 Columbia College Drive, Columbia, SC 29203-5998, 803-786-3644 or toll-free 800-277-1301. *Fax:* 803-786-3560.

COLUMBIA COLLEGE CHICAGO

Chicago, IL

Tuition & fees: $10,830 **Average undergraduate aid package: N/A**

ABOUT THE INSTITUTION Independent, coed. Awards: bachelor's and master's degrees. 32 undergraduate majors. Total enrollment: 8,848. Undergraduates: 8,346. Freshmen: 1,358. Both federal and institutional methodology are used as a basis for awarding need-based institutional aid.

UNDERGRADUATE EXPENSES for 1999–2000 ***Application fee:*** $25. ***One-time required fee:*** $35. ***Tuition:*** full-time $10,690; part-time $365 per semester hour. ***Required fees:*** full-time $140; $60 per term part-time. ***Payment plan:*** deferred payment.

GIFT AID (NEED-BASED) ***Scholarships, grants, and awards:*** Federal Pell, FSEOG, state, private, college/university gift aid from institutional funds.

GIFT AID (NON-NEED-BASED) ***Scholarships, grants, and awards by category:*** *Academic Interests/Achievement:* general academic interests/ achievements. *Creative Arts/Performance:* applied art and design, art/fine arts, cinema/film/broadcasting, creative writing, dance, journalism/ publications, performing arts, theater/drama. *Special Achievements/ Activities:* leadership. *Special Characteristics:* ethnic background, first-generation college students, handicapped students, members of minority groups. ***Tuition waivers:*** Full or partial for employees or children of employees.

LOANS ***Programs:*** Federal Direct (Subsidized and Unsubsidized Stafford, PLUS).

WORK-STUDY Federal work-study jobs available.

APPLYING for FINANCIAL AID ***Required financial aid forms:*** FAFSA, institution's own form. ***Financial aid deadline (priority):*** 1/1. ***Notification date:*** Continuous.

CONTACT Mr. John Olino, Director of Financial Aid, Columbia College Chicago, 600 South Michigan Avenue, Chicago, IL 60605-1997, 312-663-1600 Ext. 7473. *Fax:* 312-986-1091.

COLUMBIA COLLEGE–HOLLYWOOD

Tarzana, CA

Tuition & fees: $10,725 **Average undergraduate aid package: N/A**

ABOUT THE INSTITUTION Independent, coed. Awards: associate and bachelor's degrees. 5 undergraduate majors. Total enrollment: 144. Undergraduates: 144. Freshmen: 23.

UNDERGRADUATE EXPENSES for 1999–2000 ***Application fee:*** $50. ***One-time required fee:*** $75. ***Tuition:*** full-time $10,500; part-time $3000 per term. ***Required fees:*** full-time $225; $75 per term part-time. ***Payment plan:*** installment.

GIFT AID (NEED-BASED) ***Scholarships, grants, and awards:*** Federal Pell, FSEOG, state, private.

LOANS ***Programs:*** FFEL (Subsidized and Unsubsidized Stafford, PLUS).

WORK-STUDY Federal work-study jobs available.

APPLYING for FINANCIAL AID ***Required financial aid forms:*** FAFSA, institution's own form. ***Financial aid deadline (priority):*** 2/24.

CONTACT Rene Contreras, Financial Aid Administrator, Columbia College–Hollywood, 18618 Oxnard Street, Tarzana, CA 91356, 818-345-8414. *Fax:* 818-345-9053.

COLUMBIA COLLEGE OF NURSING

Milwaukee, WI

CONTACT Mr. Doug Cohen, Business Manager, Columbia College of Nursing, 2121 East Newport Avenue, Milwaukee, WI 53211-2952, 414-961-3887.

COLUMBIA INTERNATIONAL UNIVERSITY

Columbia, SC

Tuition & fees: $8630 **Average undergraduate aid package: N/A**

ABOUT THE INSTITUTION Independent nondenominational, coed. Awards: associate, bachelor's, master's, doctoral, and first professional degrees. 13 undergraduate majors. Total enrollment: 1,000. Undergraduates: 528. Freshmen: 131. Both federal and institutional methodology are used as a basis for awarding need-based institutional aid.

UNDERGRADUATE EXPENSES for 1999–2000 ***Application fee:*** $25. ***Comprehensive fee:*** $13,010 includes full-time tuition ($8470), mandatory fees ($160), and room and board ($4380). Full-time tuition and fees vary according to course load. Room and board charges vary according to board plan and housing facility. ***Part-time tuition:*** $355 per semester hour. Part-time tuition and fees vary according to course load. ***Payment plan:*** installment.

FRESHMAN FINANCIAL AID (Fall 1998) 57 applied for aid; of those 100% were deemed to have need. 100% of freshmen with need received aid. *Average percent of need met:* 50% (excluding resources awarded to replace EFC).

UNDERGRADUATE FINANCIAL AID (Fall 1998) 322 applied for aid; of those 100% were deemed to have need. 100% of undergraduates with need received aid; of those .3% had need fully met. *Average percent of need met:* 55% (excluding resources awarded to replace EFC).

GIFT AID (NEED-BASED) ***Total amount:*** $1,560,640 (23% Federal, 8% state, 68% institutional, 1% external sources). ***Receiving aid:*** *Freshmen:* 63% (47); *all full-time undergraduates:* 69% (271). ***Scholarships, grants, and awards:*** Federal Pell, FSEOG, state, private, college/university gift aid from institutional funds.

GIFT AID (NON-NEED-BASED) ***Total amount:*** $217,500 (23% state, 77% institutional). ***Receiving aid:*** *Freshmen:* 13% (10); *Undergraduates:* 18% (70). ***Scholarships, grants, and awards by category:*** *Academic Interests/ Achievement:* communication, education, English, general academic

Columbia International University (continued)

interests/achievements, humanities, international studies, religion/biblical studies. *Creative Arts/Performance:* music. *Special Achievements/Activities:* leadership. *Special Characteristics:* children and siblings of alumni, children of faculty/staff, ethnic background, general special characteristics, international students, married students, members of minority groups, relatives of clergy, religious affiliation, veterans. ***Tuition waivers:*** Full or partial for employees or children of employees.

LOANS ***Student loans:*** $2,176,733 (74% need-based, 26% non-need-based). 78% of past graduating class borrowed through all loan programs. ***Parent loans:*** $230,253 (100% non-need-based). ***Programs:*** FFEL (Subsidized and Unsubsidized Stafford, PLUS), college/university.

WORK-STUDY ***Federal work-study:*** *Total amount:* $106,589; 72 jobs averaging $2000.

APPLYING for FINANCIAL AID ***Required financial aid forms:*** FAFSA, institution's own form. ***Financial aid deadline (priority):*** 3/1. ***Notification date:*** 4/1.

CONTACT Mrs. Christy Brown, Financial Aid Counselor, Columbia International University, PO Box 3122, Columbia, SC 29230-3122, 803-754-4100 Ext. 3036 or toll-free 800-777-2227 Ext. 3024. *Fax:* 803-691-0739. *E-mail:* yesciu@ciu.edu

COLUMBIA UNION COLLEGE

Takoma Park, MD

Tuition & fees: $12,660 **Average undergraduate aid package: N/A**

ABOUT THE INSTITUTION Independent Seventh-day Adventist, coed. Awards: associate and bachelor's degrees. 29 undergraduate majors. Total enrollment: 964. Undergraduates: 964. Institutional methodology is used as a basis for awarding need-based institutional aid.

UNDERGRADUATE EXPENSES for 1999–2000 ***Application fee:*** $25. ***Comprehensive fee:*** $17,060 includes full-time tuition ($12,200), mandatory fees ($460), and room and board ($4400). ***Part-time tuition:*** $510 per semester hour. ***Part-time fees:*** $230 per term part-time. ***Payment plans:*** installment, deferred payment.

UNDERGRADUATE FINANCIAL AID (Fall 1998) 556 applied for aid.

GIFT AID (NEED-BASED) ***Total amount:*** $809,538 (72% Federal, 3% state, 25% institutional). ***Scholarships, grants, and awards:*** Federal Pell, FSEOG, state, private, college/university gift aid from institutional funds, Livingston Memorial Fund Scholarships, Kramer Scholarships.

GIFT AID (NON-NEED-BASED) ***Total amount:*** $1,232,635 (100% institutional). ***Scholarships, grants, and awards by category:*** *Academic Interests/Achievement:* general academic interests/achievements. *Creative Arts/Performance:* music. *Special Achievements/Activities:* leadership, memberships, religious involvement. *Special Characteristics:* local/state students. ***Tuition waivers:*** Full or partial for employees or children of employees, adult students, senior citizens.

LOANS ***Student loans:*** $3,559,581 (100% need-based). ***Programs:*** FFEL (Subsidized and Unsubsidized Stafford, PLUS), Perkins, PLATO Loans.

WORK-STUDY ***Federal work-study:*** *Total amount:* $78,395; jobs available.

ATHLETIC AWARDS *Total amount:* 539,193 (100% need-based).

APPLYING for FINANCIAL AID ***Required financial aid form:*** FAFSA.

CONTACT Ms. Brenda Billingy, Director, Financial Aid, Columbia Union College, 7600 Flower Avenue, Takoma Park, MD 20912, 301-891-4005 or toll-free 800-492-1715 (in-state), 800-835-4212 (out-of-state).

COLUMBIA UNIVERSITY, BARNARD COLLEGE

New York, NY

See Barnard College

COLUMBIA UNIVERSITY, COLUMBIA COLLEGE

New York, NY

See Columbia College

COLUMBIA UNIVERSITY, SCHOOL OF GENERAL STUDIES

New York, NY

Tuition & fees: $23,740 **Average undergraduate aid package: N/A**

ABOUT THE INSTITUTION Independent, coed. Awards: bachelor's degrees. 40 undergraduate majors. Total university enrollment: 19,000. Total unit enrollment: 1,145. Undergraduates: 1,145. Both federal and institutional methodology are used as a basis for awarding need-based institutional aid.

UNDERGRADUATE EXPENSES for 1999–2000 ***Application fee:*** $50. ***One-time required fee:*** $30. ***Comprehensive fee:*** $32,740 includes full-time tuition ($23,040), mandatory fees ($700), and room and board ($9000). Full-time tuition and fees vary according to course load. Room and board charges vary according to housing facility. ***Part-time tuition:*** $768 per credit. Part-time tuition and fees vary according to course load. ***Payment plans:*** tuition prepayment, deferred payment.

GIFT AID (NEED-BASED) ***Total amount:*** $1,773,935 (70% Federal, 29% state, 1% institutional). ***Scholarships, grants, and awards:*** Federal Pell, FSEOG, state, private, college/university gift aid from institutional funds.

GIFT AID (NON-NEED-BASED) ***Total amount:*** $2,325,348 (96% institutional, 4% external sources). ***Scholarships, grants, and awards by category:*** *Academic Interests/Achievement:* general academic interests/achievements. ***Tuition waivers:*** Full or partial for employees or children of employees.

LOANS ***Student loans:*** $6,409,538 (49% need-based, 51% non-need-based). ***Parent loans:*** $313,426 (100% non-need-based). ***Programs:*** FFEL (Subsidized and Unsubsidized Stafford, PLUS), Perkins, college/university.

WORK-STUDY ***Federal work-study:*** *Total amount:* $903,345; 457 jobs averaging $1975.

APPLYING for FINANCIAL AID ***Required financial aid forms:*** FAFSA, institution's own form. ***Financial aid deadline (priority):*** 7/1. ***Notification date:*** Continuous. Students must reply within 2 weeks of notification.

CONTACT Student Financial Planning, Columbia University, School of General Studies, 208 Kent Hall, New York, NY 10027, 212-854-7040 or toll-free 800-895-1169 (out-of-state).

COLUMBIA UNIVERSITY, THE FU FOUNDATION SCHOOL OF ENGINEERING AND APPLIED SCIENCE

New York, NY

Tuition & fees: $24,974 **Average undergraduate aid package: $22,438**

ABOUT THE INSTITUTION Independent, coed. Awards: bachelor's, master's, and doctoral degrees. 15 undergraduate majors. Total university enrollment: 21,000. Total unit enrollment: 1,248. Undergraduates: 1,248. Freshmen: 316. Institutional methodology is used as a basis for awarding need-based institutional aid.

UNDERGRADUATE EXPENSES for 1999–2000 ***Application fee:*** $50. ***One-time required fee:*** $45. ***Comprehensive fee:*** $32,706 includes full-time tuition ($24,150), mandatory fees ($824), and room and board ($7732). ***Payment plans:*** tuition prepayment, installment, deferred payment.

FRESHMAN FINANCIAL AID (Fall 1999) 210 applied for aid; of those 88% were deemed to have need. 100% of freshmen with need received aid; of those 100% had need fully met. *Average percent of need met:* 100% (excluding resources awarded to replace EFC). *Average financial aid package:* $21,208 (excluding resources awarded to replace EFC).

UNDERGRADUATE FINANCIAL AID (Fall 1999) 763 applied for aid; of those 93% were deemed to have need. 100% of undergraduates with need received aid; of those 100% had need fully met. *Average percent of need met:* 100% (excluding resources awarded to replace EFC). *Average financial aid package:* $22,438 (excluding resources awarded to replace EFC).

GIFT AID (NEED-BASED) ***Total amount:*** $11,332,550 (13% Federal, 7% state, 76% institutional, 4% external sources). ***Receiving aid:*** *Freshmen:* 48% (152); *all full-time undergraduates:* 50% (622). ***Average award:*** Freshmen: $19,080; Undergraduates: $17,915. ***Scholarships, grants, and awards:*** Federal Pell, FSEOG, state, private, college/university gift aid from institutional funds.

GIFT AID (NON-NEED-BASED) ***Tuition waivers:*** Full or partial for minority students, employees or children of employees.

LOANS ***Student loans:*** $3,075,606 (100% need-based). 53% of past graduating class borrowed through all loan programs. Average indebtedness per student: $16,449. ***Average need-based loan:*** Freshmen: $3369; Undergraduates: $4711. ***Parent loans:*** $1,753,596 (100% need-based). ***Programs:*** FFEL (Subsidized and Unsubsidized Stafford, PLUS), Perkins, alternative loans.

WORK-STUDY ***Federal work-study:*** *Total amount:* $1,421,539; jobs available.

APPLYING for FINANCIAL AID ***Required financial aid forms:*** FAFSA, institution's own form, CSS Financial Aid PROFILE, noncustodial (divorced/separated) parent's statement, business/farm supplement, parent and student income tax returns. ***Financial aid deadline:*** 2/10. ***Notification date:*** 4/1. Students must reply by 5/1 or within 4 weeks of notification.

CONTACT Student Financial Planning Office, Columbia University, The Fu Foundation School of Engineering and Applied Science, 100 Hamilton Hall, 1130 Amsterdam Avenue, MC 2802, New York, NY 10027, 212-854-3711. *Fax:* 212-854-5353. *E-mail:* ugrad-finaid@columbia.edu

COLUMBUS COLLEGE OF ART AND DESIGN
Columbus, OH

Tuition & fees: $13,440 **Average undergraduate aid package: N/A**

ABOUT THE INSTITUTION Independent, coed. Awards: bachelor's degrees. 16 undergraduate majors. Total enrollment: 1,542. Undergraduates: 1,542. Freshmen: 323. Federal methodology is used as a basis for awarding need-based institutional aid.

UNDERGRADUATE EXPENSES for 1999–2000 ***Application fee:*** $25. ***Comprehensive fee:*** $19,440 includes full-time tuition ($13,440) and room and board ($6000). ***Part-time tuition:*** $560 per semester hour. ***Part-time fees:*** $60 per term part-time. ***Payment plan:*** installment.

GIFT AID (NEED-BASED) ***Total amount:*** $8,939,396 (40% Federal, 4% state, 53% institutional, 3% external sources). ***Scholarships, grants, and awards:*** Federal Pell, FSEOG, state, private, college/university gift aid from institutional funds.

GIFT AID (NON-NEED-BASED) ***Total amount:*** $645,785 (100% state). ***Scholarships, grants, and awards by category:*** *Creative Arts/Performance:* art/fine arts. *Special Characteristics:* local/state students. ***Tuition waivers:*** Full or partial for employees or children of employees, senior citizens.

LOANS ***Student loans:*** $3,560,980 (100% need-based). ***Parent loans:*** $1,618,799 (100% need-based). ***Programs:*** FFEL (Subsidized and Unsubsidized Stafford, PLUS), Perkins, state.

WORK-STUDY ***Federal work-study:*** *Total amount:* $166,266; jobs available.

APPLYING for FINANCIAL AID ***Required financial aid forms:*** FAFSA, institution's own form. ***Financial aid deadline (priority):*** 4/3. ***Notification date:*** 4/30.

CONTACT Mrs. Anna Schofield, Director of Financial Aid, Columbus College of Art and Design, 107 North Ninth Street, Columbus, OH 43215-1758, 614-224-9101. *Fax:* 614-222-3218.

COLUMBUS STATE UNIVERSITY
Columbus, GA

Tuition & fees (GA res): $2444 **Average undergraduate aid package: N/A**

ABOUT THE INSTITUTION State-supported, coed. Awards: associate, bachelor's, and master's degrees. 58 undergraduate majors. Total enrollment: 4,911. Undergraduates: 4,278. Federal methodology is used as a basis for awarding need-based institutional aid.

UNDERGRADUATE EXPENSES for 1999–2000 ***Application fee:*** $20. ***Tuition, state resident:*** full-time $2126; part-time $76 per semester hour. ***Tuition, nonresident:*** full-time $7550; part-time $502 per semester hour. ***Required fees:*** full-time $318; $159 per term part-time. Part-time tuition and fees vary according to course load. ***College room and board:*** $3870. Room and board charges vary according to board plan, gender, and housing facility.

GIFT AID (NEED-BASED) ***Scholarships, grants, and awards:*** Federal Pell, FSEOG, state, private, college/university gift aid from institutional funds.

GIFT AID (NON-NEED-BASED) ***Scholarships, grants, and awards by category:*** *Academic Interests/Achievement:* general academic interests/achievements. *Creative Arts/Performance:* art/fine arts, music. ***Tuition waivers:*** Full or partial for employees or children of employees, senior citizens. ***ROTC:*** Army.

LOANS ***Programs:*** Federal Direct (Subsidized and Unsubsidized Stafford, PLUS), Perkins, college/university.

WORK-STUDY Federal work-study jobs available.

APPLYING for FINANCIAL AID ***Required financial aid form:*** FAFSA. ***Financial aid deadline (priority):*** 6/1. ***Notification date:*** 7/1. Students must reply within 4 weeks of notification.

CONTACT Mr. Al Pinckney, Director of Financial Aid, Columbus State University, 4225 University Avenue, Columbus, GA 31907-5645, 706-568-2036.

COMMONWEALTH INTERNATIONAL UNIVERSITY
Lakewood, CO

See Education America, Denver Campus

COMMUNITY HOSPITAL OF ROANOKE VALLEY–COLLEGE OF HEALTH SCIENCES
Roanoke, VA

Tuition & fees: $11,100 **Average undergraduate aid package: $12,822**

ABOUT THE INSTITUTION Independent, coed. Awards: associate and bachelor's degrees. 10 undergraduate majors. Total enrollment: 615. Undergraduates: 615. Freshmen: 40. Federal methodology is used as a basis for awarding need-based institutional aid.

UNDERGRADUATE EXPENSES for 1999–2000 ***Application fee:*** $25. ***Comprehensive fee:*** $15,260 includes full-time tuition ($11,100) and room and board ($4160). ***College room only:*** $2000. Full-time tuition and fees vary according to course level, course load, degree level, and program. Room and board charges vary according to board plan. ***Part-time tuition:*** $370 per credit hour. Part-time tuition and fees vary according to course level, course load, degree level, and program.

FRESHMAN FINANCIAL AID (Fall 1998) 47 applied for aid; of those 100% were deemed to have need. 100% of freshmen with need received aid; of those 17% had need fully met. *Average percent of need met:* 65% (excluding resources awarded to replace EFC). *Average financial aid package:* $10,782 (excluding resources awarded to replace EFC). 32% of all full-time freshmen had no need and received non-need-based aid.

UNDERGRADUATE FINANCIAL AID (Fall 1998) 325 applied for aid; of those 98% were deemed to have need. 100% of undergraduates with need received aid; of those 24% had need fully met. *Average percent of need met:* 73% (excluding resources awarded to replace EFC). *Average*

Community Hospital of Roanoke Valley–College of Health Sciences (continued)

financial aid package: $12,822 (excluding resources awarded to replace EFC). 8% of all full-time undergraduates had no need and received non-need-based aid.

GIFT AID (NEED-BASED) ***Total amount:*** $620,587 (60% Federal, 2% state, 12% institutional, 26% external sources). ***Receiving aid:*** *Freshmen:* 68% (47); *all full-time undergraduates:* 89% (310). ***Average award:*** Freshmen: $7163; Undergraduates: $6741. ***Scholarships, grants, and awards:*** Federal Pell, FSEOG, state, private, college/university gift aid from institutional funds.

GIFT AID (NON-NEED-BASED) ***Total amount:*** $3,010,925 (23% state, 77% institutional). ***Receiving aid:*** *Freshmen:* 4% (3); *Undergraduates:* 4% (15). ***Scholarships, grants, and awards by category:*** *Academic Interests/Achievement:* 15 awards ($15,000 total): health fields. *Special Characteristics:* local/state students. ***Tuition waivers:*** Full or partial for employees or children of employees.

LOANS ***Student loans:*** $2,533,153 (89% need-based, 11% non-need-based). 93% of past graduating class borrowed through all loan programs. Average indebtedness per student: $13,240. ***Average need-based loan:*** Freshmen: $3102; Undergraduates: $5738. ***Parent loans:*** $130,304 (52% need-based, 48% non-need-based). ***Programs:*** FFEL (Subsidized and Unsubsidized Stafford, PLUS), college/university.

WORK-STUDY ***Federal work-study:*** *Total amount:* $33,500; 24 jobs averaging $2400. ***State or other work-study/employment:*** *Total amount:* $15,000 (100% non-need-based). Part-time jobs available.

APPLYING for FINANCIAL AID ***Required financial aid forms:*** FAFSA, state aid form. ***Financial aid deadline (priority):*** 2/20. ***Notification date:*** Continuous beginning 4/15.

CONTACT Dr. Henry Tann, Associate Director of Financial Aid, Community Hospital of Roanoke Valley–College of Health Sciences, 920 South Jefferson Street, PO Box 13186, Roanoke, VA 24031-3186, 540-985-8483 or toll-free 888-985-8483. *Fax:* 540-985-9773. *E-mail:* htann@health.chs.edu

CONCEPTION SEMINARY COLLEGE

Conception, MO

Tuition & fees: $8650 **Average undergraduate aid package: $13,691**

ABOUT THE INSTITUTION Independent Roman Catholic, men only. Awards: bachelor's degrees. 1 undergraduate major. Total enrollment: 92. Undergraduates: 92. Freshmen: 9. Federal methodology is used as a basis for awarding need-based institutional aid.

UNDERGRADUATE EXPENSES for 2000–2001 ***Comprehensive fee:*** $13,718 includes full-time tuition ($8650) and room and board ($5068). ***College room only:*** $2078. Room and board charges vary according to board plan.

FRESHMAN FINANCIAL AID (Fall 1999) 11 applied for aid; of those 100% were deemed to have need. 100% of freshmen with need received aid; of those 55% had need fully met. *Average percent of need met:* 91% (excluding resources awarded to replace EFC). *Average financial aid package:* $13,543 (excluding resources awarded to replace EFC). 20% of all full-time freshmen had no need and received non-need-based aid.

UNDERGRADUATE FINANCIAL AID (Fall 1999) 59 applied for aid; of those 97% were deemed to have need. 100% of undergraduates with need received aid; of those 47% had need fully met. *Average percent of need met:* 92% (excluding resources awarded to replace EFC). *Average financial aid package:* $13,691 (excluding resources awarded to replace EFC). 34% of all full-time undergraduates had no need and received non-need-based aid.

GIFT AID (NEED-BASED) ***Total amount:*** $210,946 (52% Federal, 48% institutional). ***Receiving aid:*** *Freshmen:* 53% (8); *all full-time undergraduates:* 51% (46). ***Average award:*** Freshmen: $1000; Undergraduates: $1191. ***Scholarships, grants, and awards:*** Federal Pell, FSEOG, private, college/university gift aid from institutional funds.

GIFT AID (NON-NEED-BASED) ***Total amount:*** $695,613 (1% institutional, 99% external sources). ***Receiving aid:*** *Freshmen:* 20% (3); *Undergraduates:* 30% (27). ***Scholarships, grants, and awards by category:*** *Academic Interests/Achievement:* 12 awards ($6000 total): general academic interests/achievements, religion/biblical studies. *Special Characteristics:* 32 awards ($40,688 total): general special characteristics, religious affiliation.

LOANS ***Student loans:*** $129,562 (66% need-based, 34% non-need-based). Average indebtedness per student: $11,302. ***Average need-based loan:*** Freshmen: $2625; Undergraduates: $3215. ***Programs:*** FFEL (Subsidized and Unsubsidized Stafford, PLUS).

WORK-STUDY ***Federal work-study:*** *Total amount:* $20,197; 30 jobs averaging $673. ***State or other work-study/employment:*** *Total amount:* $17,754 (100% non-need-based). 29 part-time jobs averaging $612.

APPLYING for FINANCIAL AID ***Required financial aid form:*** FAFSA. ***Financial aid deadline:*** Continuous. ***Notification date:*** 8/1. Students must reply by 8/20.

CONTACT Br. Justin Hernandez, Director of Financial Aid, Conception Seminary College, PO Box 502, Conception, MO 64433-0502, 660-944-2851. *Fax:* 660-944-2829. *E-mail:* justin@conception.edu

CONCORD COLLEGE

Athens, WV

Tuition & fees (WV res): $2538 **Average undergraduate aid package: $4800**

ABOUT THE INSTITUTION State-supported, coed. Awards: associate and bachelor's degrees. 36 undergraduate majors. Total enrollment: 2,877. Undergraduates: 2,877. Freshmen: 632. Federal methodology is used as a basis for awarding need-based institutional aid.

UNDERGRADUATE EXPENSES for 1999–2000 ***One-time required fee:*** $40. ***Tuition, state resident:*** full-time $2538; part-time $106 per semester hour. ***Tuition, nonresident:*** full-time $5580; part-time $233 per semester hour. Full-time tuition and fees vary according to program. Part-time tuition and fees vary according to program. ***College room and board:*** $4018; ***room only:*** $1844. Room and board charges vary according to board plan and housing facility. ***Payment plans:*** installment, deferred payment.

FRESHMAN FINANCIAL AID (Fall 1999, est.) 552 applied for aid; of those 96% were deemed to have need. 85% of freshmen with need received aid; of those 72% had need fully met. *Average percent of need met:* 75% (excluding resources awarded to replace EFC). *Average financial aid package:* $4800 (excluding resources awarded to replace EFC).

UNDERGRADUATE FINANCIAL AID (Fall 1999, est.) 2,003 applied for aid; of those 96% were deemed to have need. 82% of undergraduates with need received aid; of those 74% had need fully met. *Average percent of need met:* 75% (excluding resources awarded to replace EFC). *Average financial aid package:* $4800 (excluding resources awarded to replace EFC).

GIFT AID (NEED-BASED) ***Total amount:*** $5,955,736 (50% Federal, 13% state, 30% institutional, 7% external sources). ***Receiving aid:*** *Freshmen:* 53% (326); *all full-time undergraduates:* 51% (1,204). ***Average award:*** Freshmen: $1200; Undergraduates: $1200. ***Scholarships, grants, and awards:*** Federal Pell, FSEOG, state, college/university gift aid from institutional funds.

GIFT AID (NON-NEED-BASED) ***Receiving aid:*** *Freshmen:* 55% (339); *Undergraduates:* 38% (907). ***Scholarships, grants, and awards by category:*** *Academic Interests/Achievement:* general academic interests/achievements. *Creative Arts/Performance:* art/fine arts, music, theater/drama. *Special Achievements/Activities:* community service. ***Tuition waivers:*** Full or partial for employees or children of employees.

LOANS ***Student loans:*** $4,480,377 (100% need-based). Average indebtedness per student: $10,000. ***Average need-based loan:*** Freshmen: $3500; Undergraduates: $3500. ***Parent loans:*** $324,014 (100% non-need-based). ***Programs:*** FFEL (Subsidized and Unsubsidized Stafford, PLUS), Perkins.

WORK-STUDY ***Federal work-study:*** *Total amount:* $191,344; jobs available. ***State or other work-study/employment:*** *Total amount:* $321,626 (100% non-need-based). Part-time jobs available.

ATHLETIC AWARDS *Total amount:* 275,428 (100% non-need-based).

APPLYING for FINANCIAL AID ***Required financial aid forms:*** FAFSA, institution's own form, verification worksheet. ***Financial aid deadline (priority):*** 4/15. ***Notification date:*** Continuous. Students must reply within 2 weeks of notification.

CONTACT Patricia Harmon, Financial Aid Director, Concord College, PO Box 1000, Athens, WV 24712-1000, 304-384-6075 or toll-free 888-384-5249 (out-of-state). *Fax:* 304-384-9044.

CONCORDIA COLLEGE

Selma, AL

Tuition & fees: $5642 **Average undergraduate aid package: $4356**

ABOUT THE INSTITUTION Independent Lutheran, coed. Awards: associate and bachelor's degrees. 5 undergraduate majors. Total enrollment: 546. Undergraduates: 546. Both federal and institutional methodology are used as a basis for awarding need-based institutional aid.

UNDERGRADUATE EXPENSES for 1999–2000 ***Application fee:*** $10. ***Comprehensive fee:*** $8542 includes full-time tuition ($5600), mandatory fees ($42), and room and board ($2900). ***College room only:*** $1500. Room and board charges vary according to board plan and housing facility. ***Part-time tuition:*** $195 per credit. ***Part-time fees:*** $21 per term part-time. ***Payment plan:*** installment.

FRESHMAN FINANCIAL AID (Fall 1998) 192 applied for aid; of those 85% were deemed to have need. 100% of freshmen with need received aid; of those 2% had need fully met. *Average percent of need met:* 23% (excluding resources awarded to replace EFC). *Average financial aid package:* $4356 (excluding resources awarded to replace EFC).

UNDERGRADUATE FINANCIAL AID (Fall 1998) 500 applied for aid; of those 94% were deemed to have need. 100% of undergraduates with need received aid; of those 1% had need fully met. *Average percent of need met:* 77% (excluding resources awarded to replace EFC). *Average financial aid package:* $4356 (excluding resources awarded to replace EFC).

GIFT AID (NEED-BASED) ***Total amount:*** $1,360,131 (87% Federal, 1% state, 12% institutional). ***Receiving aid:*** *Freshmen:* 13% (25); *all full-time undergraduates:* 15% (75). ***Scholarships, grants, and awards:*** Federal Pell, FSEOG, state, private.

GIFT AID (NON-NEED-BASED) ***Total amount:*** $258,792 (96% state, 4% institutional). ***Receiving aid:*** *Freshmen:* 11% (21); *Undergraduates:* 9% (43). ***Scholarships, grants, and awards by category:*** *Academic Interests/Achievement:* business, computer science, education, general academic interests/achievements, religion/biblical studies. *Creative Arts/Performance:* music. *Special Achievements/Activities:* cheerleading/drum major. ***Tuition waivers:*** Full or partial for employees or children of employees.

WORK-STUDY ***Federal work-study:*** *Total amount:* $49,201; jobs available. ***State or other work-study/employment:*** *Total amount:* $10,000 (100% need-based). Part-time jobs available.

ATHLETIC AWARDS *Total amount:* 50,784 (100% need-based).

APPLYING for FINANCIAL AID ***Required financial aid forms:*** FAFSA, institution's own form, state aid form. ***Financial aid deadline (priority):*** 4/15. ***Notification date:*** Continuous beginning 4/30. Students must reply within 2 weeks of notification.

CONTACT Tharsteen Bridges, Financial Aid Administrator, Concordia College, 1804 Green Street, Selma, AL 36701, 334-874-7143 Ext. 32.

CONCORDIA COLLEGE

Ann Arbor, MI

Tuition & fees: $13,800 **Average undergraduate aid package: $12,072**

ABOUT THE INSTITUTION Independent religious, coed. Awards: associate and bachelor's degrees. 28 undergraduate majors. Total enrollment: 573. Undergraduates: 573. Freshmen: 90. Federal methodology is used as a basis for awarding need-based institutional aid.

UNDERGRADUATE EXPENSES for 2000–2001 ***Application fee:*** $25. ***One-time required fee:*** $100. ***Comprehensive fee:*** $19,600 includes full-time tuition ($13,400), mandatory fees ($400), and room and board ($5800). Full-time tuition and fees vary according to class time and program. Room and board charges vary according to board plan and housing facility. ***Part-time tuition:*** $450 per credit hour. Part-time tuition and fees vary according to class time, course load, and program.

FRESHMAN FINANCIAL AID (Fall 1999, est.) 83 applied for aid; of those 92% were deemed to have need. 100% of freshmen with need received aid. *Average percent of need met:* 88% (excluding resources awarded to replace EFC). *Average financial aid package:* $12,087 (excluding resources awarded to replace EFC). 10% of all full-time freshmen had no need and received non-need-based aid.

UNDERGRADUATE FINANCIAL AID (Fall 1999, est.) 326 applied for aid; of those 91% were deemed to have need. 100% of undergraduates with need received aid. *Average percent of need met:* 90% (excluding resources awarded to replace EFC). *Average financial aid package:* $12,072 (excluding resources awarded to replace EFC). 9% of all full-time undergraduates had no need and received non-need-based aid.

GIFT AID (NEED-BASED) ***Total amount:*** $2,240,871 (12% Federal, 22% state, 53% institutional, 13% external sources). ***Scholarships, grants, and awards:*** Federal Pell, FSEOG, state, private, college/university gift aid from institutional funds.

GIFT AID (NON-NEED-BASED) ***Total amount:*** $422,338 (1% state, 74% institutional, 25% external sources). ***Scholarships, grants, and awards by category:*** *Academic Interests/Achievement:* general academic interests/achievements, religion/biblical studies. *Creative Arts/Performance:* art/fine arts, music, performing arts, theater/drama. *Special Achievements/Activities:* general special achievements/activities. *Special Characteristics:* children and siblings of alumni, relatives of clergy, religious affiliation. ***Tuition waivers:*** Full or partial for employees or children of employees. ***ROTC:*** Army cooperative, Air Force cooperative.

LOANS ***Student loans:*** $1,444,116 (74% need-based, 26% non-need-based). 69% of past graduating class borrowed through all loan programs. Average indebtedness per student: $20,026. ***Parent loans:*** $109,845 (29% need-based, 71% non-need-based). ***Programs:*** FFEL (Subsidized and Unsubsidized Stafford, PLUS), Perkins, state.

WORK-STUDY ***Federal work-study:*** *Total amount:* $72,250; jobs available. ***State or other work-study/employment:*** *Total amount:* $11,760 (100% need-based). Part-time jobs available.

ATHLETIC AWARDS *Total amount:* 244,800 (72% need-based, 28% non-need-based).

APPLYING for FINANCIAL AID ***Required financial aid forms:*** FAFSA, institution's own form. ***Financial aid deadline (priority):*** 5/1. ***Notification date:*** Continuous.

CONTACT Office of Financial Aid, Concordia College, 4090 Geddes Road, Ann Arbor, MI 48105-2797, 734-995-7408 or toll-free 800-253-0680. *Fax:* 734-995-4610.

CONCORDIA COLLEGE

Moorhead, MN

Tuition & fees: $14,020 **Average undergraduate aid package: $11,209**

ABOUT THE INSTITUTION Independent religious, coed. Awards: bachelor's degrees. 86 undergraduate majors. Total enrollment: 2,913. Undergraduates: 2,913. Freshmen: 797. Both federal and institutional methodology are used as a basis for awarding need-based institutional aid.

UNDERGRADUATE EXPENSES for 2000–2001 ***Application fee:*** $20. ***Comprehensive fee:*** $17,920 includes full-time tuition ($13,904), mandatory fees ($116), and room and board ($3900). ***College room only:*** $1700. Room and board charges vary according to board plan and housing facility. ***Part-time tuition:*** $2185 per course. ***Part-time fees:*** $116 per year part-time. Part-time tuition and fees vary according to course load. ***Payment plan:*** installment.

FRESHMAN FINANCIAL AID (Fall 1999, est.) 749 applied for aid; of those 84% were deemed to have need. 100% of freshmen with need received aid; of those 100% had need fully met. *Average percent of need met:* 100% (excluding resources awarded to replace EFC). *Average financial aid package:* $11,739 (excluding resources awarded to replace EFC).

Concordia College (continued)

UNDERGRADUATE FINANCIAL AID (Fall 1999, est.) 2,390 applied for aid; of those 87% were deemed to have need. 100% of undergraduates with need received aid; of those 100% had need fully met. *Average percent of need met:* 100% (excluding resources awarded to replace EFC). *Average financial aid package:* $11,209 (excluding resources awarded to replace EFC).

GIFT AID (NEED-BASED) ***Total amount:*** $10,621,993 (19% Federal, 30% state, 51% institutional). ***Receiving aid:*** *Freshmen:* 75% (627); *all full-time undergraduates:* 73% (2,089). ***Average award:*** Freshmen: $8044; Undergraduates: $7254. ***Scholarships, grants, and awards:*** Federal Pell, FSEOG, state, private, college/university gift aid from institutional funds.

GIFT AID (NON-NEED-BASED) ***Total amount:*** $1,389,601 (3% Federal, 87% institutional, 10% external sources). ***Receiving aid:*** *Freshmen:* 12% (100); *Undergraduates:* 12% (350). ***Scholarships, grants, and awards by category:*** *Academic Interests/Achievement:* 832 awards ($3,241,157 total): general academic interests/achievements. *Creative Arts/Performance:* 158 awards ($337,907 total): debating, music, theater/drama. *Special Characteristics:* 135 awards ($991,029 total): international students, members of minority groups. ***Tuition waivers:*** Full or partial for employees or children of employees. ***ROTC:*** Army cooperative, Air Force cooperative.

LOANS ***Student loans:*** $7,409,581 (88% need-based, 12% non-need-based). 81% of past graduating class borrowed through all loan programs. Average indebtedness per student: $18,135. ***Average need-based loan:*** Freshmen: $4200; Undergraduates: $4500. ***Parent loans:*** $195,985 (100% non-need-based). ***Programs:*** FFEL (Subsidized and Unsubsidized Stafford, PLUS), Perkins, state, college/university, alternative loans.

WORK-STUDY ***Federal work-study:*** *Total amount:* $846,769; 748 jobs averaging $1132. ***State or other work-study/employment:*** *Total amount:* $789,049 (79% need-based, 21% non-need-based). 588 part-time jobs available.

APPLYING for FINANCIAL AID ***Required financial aid forms:*** FAFSA, institution's own form. ***Financial aid deadline:*** Continuous. ***Notification date:*** Continuous beginning 2/1.

CONTACT Mr. Dale E. Thornton, Financial Aid Director, Concordia College, 901 South 8th Street, Moorhead, MN 56562, 218-299-3010 or toll-free 800-699-9897. *Fax:* 218-299-3947. *E-mail:* thornton@cord.edu

CONCORDIA COLLEGE

Bronxville, NY

Tuition & fees: $14,350 **Average undergraduate aid package: $11,600**

ABOUT THE INSTITUTION Independent Lutheran, coed. Awards: associate and bachelor's degrees. 23 undergraduate majors. Total enrollment: 574. Undergraduates: 574. Freshmen: 118. Federal methodology is used as a basis for awarding need-based institutional aid.

UNDERGRADUATE EXPENSES for 2000–2001 ***Application fee:*** $30. ***Comprehensive fee:*** $20,550 includes full-time tuition ($14,350) and room and board ($6200). ***College room only:*** $3100. Room and board charges vary according to board plan. ***Part-time tuition:*** $388 per credit hour. Part-time tuition and fees vary according to course load. ***Payment plan:*** installment.

UNDERGRADUATE FINANCIAL AID (Fall 1999) *Average financial aid package:* $11,600 (excluding resources awarded to replace EFC).

GIFT AID (NEED-BASED) ***Scholarships, grants, and awards:*** Federal Pell, FSEOG, state, private, college/university gift aid from institutional funds.

GIFT AID (NON-NEED-BASED) ***Scholarships, grants, and awards by category:*** *Academic Interests/Achievement:* education, general academic interests/achievements, religion/biblical studies, social sciences. *Creative Arts/Performance:* music. *Special Achievements/Activities:* community service. *Special Characteristics:* children of faculty/staff, relatives of clergy, religious affiliation. ***Tuition waivers:*** Full or partial for employees or children of employees, senior citizens.

LOANS ***Programs:*** FFEL (Subsidized and Unsubsidized Stafford, PLUS), college/university, alternative loans.

WORK-STUDY Federal work-study jobs available. ***State or other work-study/employment:*** Part-time jobs available.

APPLYING for FINANCIAL AID ***Required financial aid forms:*** FAFSA, state aid form, financial aid transcript (for transfers). ***Financial aid deadline (priority):*** 3/1. ***Notification date:*** Continuous. Students must reply within 3 weeks of notification.

CONTACT Mr. Ken Fick, Director of Financial Aid, Concordia College, 171 White Plains Road, Bronxville, NY 10708, 914-337-9300 Ext. 2146 or toll-free 800-YES-COLLEGE. *Fax:* 914-395-4500.

CONCORDIA UNIVERSITY

Irvine, CA

Tuition & fees: $15,700 **Average undergraduate aid package: $8000**

ABOUT THE INSTITUTION Independent religious, coed. Awards: bachelor's and master's degrees. 27 undergraduate majors. Total enrollment: 1,208. Undergraduates: 1,083. Freshmen: 193. Federal methodology is used as a basis for awarding need-based institutional aid.

UNDERGRADUATE EXPENSES for 2000–2001 ***Application fee:*** $40. ***Comprehensive fee:*** $20,990 includes full-time tuition ($15,700) and room and board ($5290). ***College room only:*** $3300. Room and board charges vary according to board plan. ***Part-time tuition:*** $480 per unit. ***Payment plan:*** installment.

FRESHMAN FINANCIAL AID (Fall 1999, est.) 170 applied for aid; of those 88% were deemed to have need. 100% of freshmen with need received aid; of those 47% had need fully met. *Average percent of need met:* 75% (excluding resources awarded to replace EFC). *Average financial aid package:* $8500 (excluding resources awarded to replace EFC). 25% of all full-time freshmen had no need and received non-need-based aid.

UNDERGRADUATE FINANCIAL AID (Fall 1999, est.) 584 applied for aid; of those 89% were deemed to have need. 100% of undergraduates with need received aid; of those 20% had need fully met. *Average percent of need met:* 70% (excluding resources awarded to replace EFC). *Average financial aid package:* $8000 (excluding resources awarded to replace EFC). 26% of all full-time undergraduates had no need and received non-need-based aid.

GIFT AID (NEED-BASED) ***Total amount:*** $3,295,770 (10% Federal, 9% state, 76% institutional, 5% external sources). ***Receiving aid:*** *Freshmen:* 68% (135); *all full-time undergraduates:* 71% (494). ***Average award:*** Freshmen: $6000; Undergraduates: $5000. ***Scholarships, grants, and awards:*** Federal Pell, FSEOG, state, private, college/university gift aid from institutional funds.

GIFT AID (NON-NEED-BASED) ***Total amount:*** $750,000 (93% institutional, 7% external sources). ***Receiving aid:*** *Freshmen:* 55% (110); *Undergraduates:* 54% (380). ***Scholarships, grants, and awards by category:*** *Academic Interests/Achievement:* education, general academic interests/achievements, religion/biblical studies. *Creative Arts/Performance:* 67 awards ($68,180 total): music, theater/drama. *Special Achievements/Activities:* 160 awards ($290,000 total): general special achievements/activities, religious involvement. *Special Characteristics:* 190 awards ($230,000 total): children of faculty/staff, ethnic background, first-generation college students, international students, members of minority groups, relatives of clergy, religious affiliation, siblings of current students. ***Tuition waivers:*** Full or partial for employees or children of employees.

LOANS ***Student loans:*** $6,000,000 (83% need-based, 17% non-need-based). 85% of past graduating class borrowed through all loan programs. Average indebtedness per student: $16,000. ***Average need-based loan:*** Freshmen: $2625; Undergraduates: $5500. ***Parent loans:*** $1,600,000 (38% need-based, 62% non-need-based). ***Programs:*** FFEL (Subsidized and Unsubsidized Stafford, PLUS).

WORK-STUDY ***Federal work-study:*** *Total amount:* $100,000; 50 jobs averaging $2000. ***State or other work-study/employment:*** *Total amount:* $600,000 (100% need-based). Part-time jobs available.

ATHLETIC AWARDS *Total amount:* 830,000 (60% need-based, 40% non-need-based).

APPLYING for FINANCIAL AID ***Required financial aid forms:*** FAFSA, institution's own form, state aid form. ***Financial aid deadline:*** 6/30 (priority: 3/2).

CONTACT Ms. Vernadean Herriford, Assistant Director of Financial Aid, Concordia University, 1530 Concordia West, Irvine, CA 92612-3299, 949-854-8002 Ext. 1173 or toll-free 800-229-1200. *Fax:* 949-854-6709. *E-mail:* herrifv@cui.edu

CONCORDIA UNIVERSITY

River Forest, IL

Tuition & fees: $13,860 **Average undergraduate aid package: $10,000**

ABOUT THE INSTITUTION Independent religious, coed. Awards: bachelor's and master's degrees. 54 undergraduate majors. Total enrollment: 1,885. Undergraduates: 1,280. Freshmen: 248. Federal methodology is used as a basis for awarding need-based institutional aid.

UNDERGRADUATE EXPENSES for 2000–2001 ***Application fee:*** $25. ***Comprehensive fee:*** $19,225 includes full-time tuition ($13,760), mandatory fees ($100), and room and board ($5365). ***Part-time tuition:*** $430 per semester hour. ***Payment plan:*** installment.

FRESHMAN FINANCIAL AID (Fall 1999) 216 applied for aid; of those 80% were deemed to have need. 97% of freshmen with need received aid; of those 78% had need fully met. *Average percent of need met:* 75% (excluding resources awarded to replace EFC). *Average financial aid package:* $12,000 (excluding resources awarded to replace EFC). 14% of all full-time freshmen had no need and received non-need-based aid.

UNDERGRADUATE FINANCIAL AID (Fall 1999) 973 applied for aid; of those 80% were deemed to have need. 97% of undergraduates with need received aid; of those 85% had need fully met. *Average percent of need met:* 75% (excluding resources awarded to replace EFC). *Average financial aid package:* $10,000 (excluding resources awarded to replace EFC). 13% of all full-time undergraduates had no need and received non-need-based aid.

GIFT AID (NEED-BASED) ***Total amount:*** $3,203,000 (17% Federal, 43% state, 26% institutional, 14% external sources). ***Receiving aid:*** *Freshmen:* 49% (123); *all full-time undergraduates:* 52% (559). ***Average award:*** Freshmen: $6500; Undergraduates: $5700. ***Scholarships, grants, and awards:*** Federal Pell, FSEOG, state, private, college/university gift aid from institutional funds.

GIFT AID (NON-NEED-BASED) ***Total amount:*** $4,073,600 (94% institutional, 6% external sources). ***Receiving aid:*** *Freshmen:* 37% (93); *Undergraduates:* 39% (422). ***Scholarships, grants, and awards by category:*** *Academic Interests/Achievement:* 500 awards ($2,999,000 total): biological sciences, business, communication, computer science, education, English, foreign languages, general academic interests/achievements, religion/biblical studies. *Creative Arts/Performance:* 10 awards ($14,000 total): art/fine arts, music. *Special Characteristics:* 611 awards ($1,091,000 total): children and siblings of alumni, children of faculty/staff, international students, out-of-state students, religious affiliation. ***Tuition waivers:*** Full or partial for employees or children of employees.

LOANS ***Student loans:*** $4,474,000 (57% need-based, 43% non-need-based). 85% of past graduating class borrowed through all loan programs. Average indebtedness per student: $14,400. ***Average need-based loan:*** Freshmen: $4300; Undergraduates: $3900. ***Parent loans:*** $500,000 (100% non-need-based). ***Programs:*** FFEL (Subsidized and Unsubsidized Stafford, PLUS), Perkins.

WORK-STUDY ***Federal work-study:*** *Total amount:* $84,000; 70 jobs averaging $1200. ***State or other work-study/employment:*** *Total amount:* $57,000 (100% non-need-based). 54 part-time jobs averaging $1055.

APPLYING for FINANCIAL AID ***Required financial aid forms:*** FAFSA, institution's own form. ***Financial aid deadline:*** 5/31 (priority: 4/15). ***Notification date:*** Continuous. Students must reply within 4 weeks of notification.

CONTACT Susan Herbert, Assistant Director of Student Financial Planning, Concordia University, 7400 Augusta Street, River Forest, IL 60305-1499, 708-209-3113 Ext. 3114 or toll-free 800-285-2668. *E-mail:* crffa@curf.edu

CONCORDIA UNIVERSITY

Seward, NE

Tuition & fees: $11,876 **Average undergraduate aid package: $13,165**

ABOUT THE INSTITUTION Independent religious, coed. Awards: bachelor's and master's degrees. 67 undergraduate majors. Total enrollment: 1,161. Undergraduates: 1,094. Freshmen: 262. Federal methodology is used as a basis for awarding need-based institutional aid.

UNDERGRADUATE EXPENSES for 1999–2000 ***Application fee:*** $15. ***Comprehensive fee:*** $15,814 includes full-time tuition ($11,876) and room and board ($3938). Room and board charges vary according to board plan. ***Part-time tuition:*** $361 per credit. Part-time tuition and fees vary according to course load. ***Payment plans:*** installment, deferred payment.

FRESHMAN FINANCIAL AID (Fall 1999, est.) 261 applied for aid; of those 95% were deemed to have need. 100% of freshmen with need received aid; of those 73% had need fully met. *Average percent of need met:* 87% (excluding resources awarded to replace EFC). *Average financial aid package:* $12,148 (excluding resources awarded to replace EFC). 5% of all full-time freshmen had no need and received non-need-based aid.

UNDERGRADUATE FINANCIAL AID (Fall 1999, est.) 1,078 applied for aid; of those 95% were deemed to have need. 100% of undergraduates with need received aid; of those 76% had need fully met. *Average percent of need met:* 88% (excluding resources awarded to replace EFC). *Average financial aid package:* $13,165 (excluding resources awarded to replace EFC). 5% of all full-time undergraduates had no need and received non-need-based aid.

GIFT AID (NEED-BASED) ***Total amount:*** $4,246,392 (18% Federal, 5% state, 67% institutional, 10% external sources). ***Receiving aid:*** *Freshmen:* 84% (219); *all full-time undergraduates:* 84% (910). ***Average award:*** Freshmen: $3865; Undergraduates: $3934. ***Scholarships, grants, and awards:*** Federal Pell, FSEOG, state, private, college/university gift aid from institutional funds.

GIFT AID (NON-NEED-BASED) ***Total amount:*** $2,511,218 (60% institutional, 40% external sources). ***Receiving aid:*** *Freshmen:* 48% (124); *Undergraduates:* 59% (638). ***Scholarships, grants, and awards by category:*** *Academic Interests/Achievement:* 905 awards ($1,918,781 total): biological sciences, business, communication, computer science, education, English, general academic interests/achievements, health fields, humanities, mathematics, physical sciences, premedicine, religion/biblical studies, social sciences. *Creative Arts/Performance:* 156 awards ($176,725 total): art/fine arts, music, theater/drama. *Special Characteristics:* 310 awards ($255,678 total): children and siblings of alumni, children of faculty/staff, international students, local/state students, members of minority groups. ***Tuition waivers:*** Full or partial for employees or children of employees.

LOANS ***Student loans:*** $4,649,536 (59% need-based, 41% non-need-based). ***Average need-based loan:*** Freshmen: $3590; Undergraduates: $3418. ***Parent loans:*** $6,019,816 (100% non-need-based). ***Programs:*** FFEL (Subsidized and Unsubsidized Stafford, PLUS), Perkins.

WORK-STUDY ***Federal work-study:*** *Total amount:* $110,061; 160 jobs available. ***State or other work-study/employment:*** *Total amount:* $15,250 (100% non-need-based). 18 part-time jobs averaging $847.

ATHLETIC AWARDS *Total amount:* 700,100 (100% non-need-based).

APPLYING for FINANCIAL AID ***Required financial aid forms:*** FAFSA, institution's own form. ***Financial aid deadline (priority):*** 3/1. ***Notification date:*** Continuous beginning 3/31. Students must reply within 4 weeks of notification.

CONTACT Mrs. Gloria F. Hennig, Director of Financial Aid, Concordia University, 800 North Columbia Avenue, Seward, NE 68434-1599, 402-643-7270 or toll-free 800-535-5494. *Fax:* 402-643-4073. *E-mail:* ghennig@seward.cune.edu

CONCORDIA UNIVERSITY

Portland, OR

Tuition & fees: $15,500 **Average undergraduate aid package: $12,000**

Concordia University (continued)

ABOUT THE INSTITUTION Independent religious, coed. Awards: associate, bachelor's, and master's degrees and post-bachelor's certificates. 31 undergraduate majors. Total enrollment: 992. Undergraduates: 910. Federal methodology is used as a basis for awarding need-based institutional aid.

UNDERGRADUATE EXPENSES for 2000–2001 (est.) ***Application fee:*** $20. ***Comprehensive fee:*** $19,320 includes full-time tuition ($15,500) and room and board ($3820). ***College room only:*** $1110. Full-time tuition and fees vary according to program. Room and board charges vary according to housing facility. ***Part-time tuition:*** $475 per credit. Part-time tuition and fees vary according to course load and program. ***Payment plan:*** installment.

FRESHMAN FINANCIAL AID (Fall 1999) 116 applied for aid; of those 85% were deemed to have need. 100% of freshmen with need received aid; of those 65% had need fully met. *Average percent of need met:* 85% (excluding resources awarded to replace EFC). *Average financial aid package:* $11,800 (excluding resources awarded to replace EFC). 19% of all full-time freshmen had no need and received non-need-based aid.

UNDERGRADUATE FINANCIAL AID (Fall 1999) 625 applied for aid; of those 79% were deemed to have need. 100% of undergraduates with need received aid; of those 65% had need fully met. *Average percent of need met:* 85% (excluding resources awarded to replace EFC). *Average financial aid package:* $12,000 (excluding resources awarded to replace EFC). 8% of all full-time undergraduates had no need and received non-need-based aid.

GIFT AID (NEED-BASED) ***Total amount:*** $3,696,000 (15% Federal, 5% state, 80% institutional). ***Receiving aid:*** *Freshmen:* 74% (99); *all full-time undergraduates:* 56% (415). ***Average award:*** Freshmen: $8700; Undergraduates: $7900. ***Scholarships, grants, and awards:*** Federal Pell, FSEOG, state, private, college/university gift aid from institutional funds.

GIFT AID (NON-NEED-BASED) ***Total amount:*** $353,000 (79% institutional, 21% external sources). ***Receiving aid:*** *Freshmen:* 39% (52); *Undergraduates:* 15% (113). ***Scholarships, grants, and awards by category:*** *Academic Interests/Achievement:* general academic interests/achievements. *Creative Arts/Performance:* music, theater/drama. *Special Achievements/Activities:* leadership, religious involvement. *Special Characteristics:* children of faculty/staff, relatives of clergy. ***Tuition waivers:*** Full or partial for employees or children of employees. ***ROTC:*** Air Force cooperative.

LOANS ***Student loans:*** $5,594,000 (53% need-based, 47% non-need-based). 65% of past graduating class borrowed through all loan programs. Average indebtedness per student: $10,500. ***Average need-based loan:*** Freshmen: $2600; Undergraduates: $5000. ***Parent loans:*** $2,409,000 (100% non-need-based). ***Programs:*** FFEL (Subsidized and Unsubsidized Stafford, PLUS), Perkins.

WORK-STUDY ***Federal work-study:*** *Total amount:* $86,000; 75 jobs averaging $1150. ***State or other work-study/employment:*** *Total amount:* $309,000 (100% non-need-based). 150 part-time jobs averaging $2050.

ATHLETIC AWARDS *Total amount:* 523,000 (100% non-need-based).

APPLYING for FINANCIAL AID ***Required financial aid form:*** FAFSA. ***Financial aid deadline:*** Continuous. ***Notification date:*** Continuous beginning 3/1. Students must reply by 5/1 or within 2 weeks of notification.

CONTACT Mr. James W. Cullen, Director of Financial Aid, Concordia University, 2811 Northeast Holman, Portland, OR 97211-6099, 503-493-6508 or toll-free 800-321-9371. *Fax:* 503-280-8661. *E-mail:* jcullen@cu-portland.edu

CONCORDIA UNIVERSITY AT AUSTIN

Austin, TX

Tuition & fees: $11,570 **Average undergraduate aid package: $10,258**

ABOUT THE INSTITUTION Independent religious, coed. Awards: associate, bachelor's, and master's degrees. 21 undergraduate majors. Total enrollment: 770. Undergraduates: 758. Freshmen: 156. Federal methodology is used as a basis for awarding need-based institutional aid.

UNDERGRADUATE EXPENSES for 1999–2000 ***Application fee:*** $25. ***Comprehensive fee:*** $16,770 includes full-time tuition ($11,500), mandatory fees ($70), and room and board ($5200). Room and board charges vary according to board plan and housing facility. ***Part-time tuition:*** $385 per semester hour.

FRESHMAN FINANCIAL AID (Fall 1999) 118 applied for aid; of those 75% were deemed to have need. 100% of freshmen with need received aid; of those 40% had need fully met. *Average percent of need met:* 85% (excluding resources awarded to replace EFC). *Average financial aid package:* $10,894 (excluding resources awarded to replace EFC). 22% of all full-time freshmen had no need and received non-need-based aid.

UNDERGRADUATE FINANCIAL AID (Fall 1999) 479 applied for aid; of those 75% were deemed to have need. 100% of undergraduates with need received aid; of those 50% had need fully met. *Average percent of need met:* 86% (excluding resources awarded to replace EFC). *Average financial aid package:* $10,258 (excluding resources awarded to replace EFC). 21% of all full-time undergraduates had no need and received non-need-based aid.

GIFT AID (NEED-BASED) ***Total amount:*** $1,618,055 (23% Federal, 36% state, 41% institutional). ***Receiving aid:*** *Freshmen:* 65% (88); *all full-time undergraduates:* 71% (357). ***Average award:*** Freshmen: $2706; Undergraduates: $2432. ***Scholarships, grants, and awards:*** Federal Pell, FSEOG, state, college/university gift aid from institutional funds.

GIFT AID (NON-NEED-BASED) ***Total amount:*** $873,545 (82% institutional, 18% external sources). ***Receiving aid:*** *Freshmen:* 56% (76); *Undergraduates:* 37% (184). ***Scholarships, grants, and awards by category:*** *Academic Interests/Achievement:* 50 awards ($316,615 total): general academic interests/achievements. *Creative Arts/Performance:* 17 awards ($29,750 total): music. *Special Achievements/Activities:* 122 awards ($364,245 total): leadership. *Special Characteristics:* 4 awards ($6500 total): general special characteristics, religious affiliation. ***Tuition waivers:*** Full or partial for employees or children of employees. ***ROTC:*** Army cooperative, Air Force cooperative.

LOANS ***Student loans:*** $1,648,846 (53% need-based, 47% non-need-based). 64% of past graduating class borrowed through all loan programs. Average indebtedness per student: $15,472. ***Average need-based loan:*** Freshmen: $2424; Undergraduates: $3705. ***Parent loans:*** $261,980 (100% non-need-based). ***Programs:*** FFEL (Subsidized and Unsubsidized Stafford, PLUS), state.

WORK-STUDY ***Federal work-study:*** *Total amount:* $92,967; 83 jobs averaging $1120.

APPLYING for FINANCIAL AID ***Required financial aid forms:*** FAFSA, institution's own form. ***Financial aid deadline (priority):*** 4/15. ***Notification date:*** Continuous. Students must reply within 2 weeks of notification.

CONTACT Ms. Pat M. Jost, Director of Financial Assistance, Concordia University at Austin, 3400 Interstate 35 North, Austin, TX 78705-2799, 512-452-7661 or toll-free 800-285-4252. *Fax:* 512-459-8517.

CONCORDIA UNIVERSITY AT ST. PAUL

St. Paul, MN

Tuition & fees: $14,752 **Average undergraduate aid package: $10,573**

ABOUT THE INSTITUTION Independent religious, coed. Awards: associate, bachelor's, and master's degrees. 37 undergraduate majors. Total enrollment: 1,711. Undergraduates: 1,504. Freshmen: 308. Federal methodology is used as a basis for awarding need-based institutional aid.

UNDERGRADUATE EXPENSES for 2000–2001 ***Application fee:*** $20. ***Comprehensive fee:*** $19,912 includes full-time tuition ($14,752) and room and board ($5160). ***Part-time tuition:*** $614 per semester hour. Part-time tuition and fees vary according to course load. ***Payment plan:*** installment.

FRESHMAN FINANCIAL AID (Fall 1999) 247 applied for aid; of those 84% were deemed to have need. 100% of freshmen with need received aid; of those 24% had need fully met. *Average percent of need met:* 86% (excluding resources awarded to replace EFC). *Average financial aid package:* $12,244 (excluding resources awarded to replace EFC). 15% of all full-time freshmen had no need and received non-need-based aid.

UNDERGRADUATE FINANCIAL AID (Fall 1999) 1,027 applied for aid; of those 87% were deemed to have need. 100% of undergraduates with

need received aid; of those 28% had need fully met. *Average percent of need met:* 81% (excluding resources awarded to replace EFC). *Average financial aid package:* $10,573 (excluding resources awarded to replace EFC). 11% of all full-time undergraduates had no need and received non-need-based aid.

GIFT AID (NEED-BASED) ***Total amount:*** $6,079,751 (11% Federal, 24% state, 53% institutional, 12% external sources). ***Receiving aid:*** *Freshmen:* 81% (208); *all full-time undergraduates:* 70% (876). ***Average award:*** Freshmen: $8833; Undergraduates: $6102. ***Scholarships, grants, and awards:*** Federal Pell, FSEOG, state, private, college/university gift aid from institutional funds.

GIFT AID (NON-NEED-BASED) ***Total amount:*** $545,702 (1% state, 78% institutional, 21% external sources). ***Receiving aid:*** *Freshmen:* 80% (207); *Undergraduates:* 43% (546). ***Scholarships, grants, and awards by category:*** *Academic Interests/Achievement:* general academic interests/achievements. *Creative Arts/Performance:* music. *Special Characteristics:* children of faculty/staff. ***Tuition waivers:*** Full or partial for employees or children of employees, senior citizens. ***ROTC:*** Army cooperative, Naval cooperative, Air Force cooperative.

LOANS ***Student loans:*** $5,416,394 (91% need-based, 9% non-need-based). Average indebtedness per student: $12,784. ***Average need-based loan:*** Freshmen: $2865; Undergraduates: $3568. ***Parent loans:*** $467,411 (91% need-based, 9% non-need-based). ***Programs:*** FFEL (Subsidized and Unsubsidized Stafford, PLUS), Perkins, state.

WORK-STUDY ***Federal work-study:*** *Total amount:* $542,904; jobs available. ***State or other work-study/employment:*** *Total amount:* $255,070 (96% need-based, 4% non-need-based). Part-time jobs available.

ATHLETIC AWARDS *Total amount:* 251,666 (77% need-based, 23% non-need-based).

APPLYING for FINANCIAL AID ***Required financial aid forms:*** FAFSA, institution's own form. ***Financial aid deadline:*** Continuous. ***Notification date:*** Continuous beginning 3/1. Students must reply within 3 weeks of notification.

CONTACT Diane Borchardt, Financial Aid Director, Concordia University at St. Paul, 275 North Syndicate Street, St. Paul, MN 55104-5494, 651-641-8209 or toll-free 800-333-4705. *Fax:* 651-641-8889. *E-mail:* borchardt@csp.edu

CONCORDIA UNIVERSITY WISCONSIN

Mequon, WI

Tuition & fees: $12,460 **Average undergraduate aid package: $10,790**

ABOUT THE INSTITUTION Independent religious, coed. Awards: bachelor's and master's degrees. 51 undergraduate majors. Total enrollment: 4,515. Undergraduates: 3,845. Freshmen: 277. Federal methodology is used as a basis for awarding need-based institutional aid.

UNDERGRADUATE EXPENSES for 1999–2000 ***Application fee:*** $25. ***Comprehensive fee:*** $16,660 includes full-time tuition ($12,400), mandatory fees ($60), and room and board ($4200). Full-time tuition and fees vary according to program. ***Part-time tuition:*** $520 per credit. Part-time tuition and fees vary according to class time and program. ***Payment plans:*** guaranteed tuition, installment, deferred payment.

FRESHMAN FINANCIAL AID (Fall 1999, est.) 330 applied for aid; of those 98% were deemed to have need. 100% of freshmen with need received aid; of those 71% had need fully met. *Average percent of need met:* 90% (excluding resources awarded to replace EFC). *Average financial aid package:* $11,506 (excluding resources awarded to replace EFC). 3% of all full-time freshmen had no need and received non-need-based aid.

UNDERGRADUATE FINANCIAL AID (Fall 1999, est.) 1,136 applied for aid; of those 96% were deemed to have need. 100% of undergraduates with need received aid; of those 70% had need fully met. *Average percent of need met:* 90% (excluding resources awarded to replace EFC). *Average financial aid package:* $10,790 (excluding resources awarded to replace EFC). 3% of all full-time undergraduates had no need and received non-need-based aid.

GIFT AID (NEED-BASED) ***Total amount:*** $7,136,952 (9% Federal, 11% state, 80% institutional). ***Receiving aid:*** *Freshmen:* 81% (273); *all full-time undergraduates:* 75% (891). ***Average award:*** Freshmen: $7110; Undergraduates: $6542. ***Scholarships, grants, and awards:*** Federal Pell, FSEOG, state, private, college/university gift aid from institutional funds.

GIFT AID (NON-NEED-BASED) ***Total amount:*** $2,188,216 (1% state, 69% institutional, 30% external sources). ***Receiving aid:*** *Freshmen:* 52% (174); *Undergraduates:* 50% (587). ***Scholarships, grants, and awards by category:*** *Academic Interests/Achievement:* 660 awards ($2,439,103 total): general academic interests/achievements. *Creative Arts/Performance:* 15 awards ($11,000 total): music, performing arts. *Special Achievements/Activities:* 93 awards ($124,000 total): leadership. *Special Characteristics:* 494 awards ($1,487,445 total): children of faculty/staff, out-of-state students, religious affiliation. ***Tuition waivers:*** Full or partial for employees or children of employees.

LOANS ***Student loans:*** $2,341,668 (68% need-based, 32% non-need-based). 60% of past graduating class borrowed through all loan programs. Average indebtedness per student: $15,247. ***Average need-based loan:*** Freshmen: $2185; Undergraduates: $3098. ***Parent loans:*** $381,299 (100% non-need-based). ***Programs:*** Federal Direct (Subsidized and Unsubsidized Stafford, PLUS).

WORK-STUDY ***Federal work-study:*** *Total amount:* $251,295; 200 jobs available. ***State or other work-study/employment:*** *Total amount:* $298,537 (100% non-need-based). Part-time jobs available.

APPLYING for FINANCIAL AID ***Required financial aid forms:*** FAFSA, institution's own form, federal income tax return. ***Financial aid deadline (priority):*** 5/1. ***Notification date:*** Continuous. Students must reply within 3 weeks of notification.

CONTACT Mr. R. Edward Schroeder, Director of Financial Aid, Concordia University Wisconsin, 12800 North Lake Shore Drive, Mequon, WI 53097-2402, 262-243-4347. *Fax:* 262-243-4351. *E-mail:* eschroed@cuw.edu

CONNECTICUT COLLEGE

New London, CT

Comprehensive fee: $30,595 **Average undergraduate aid package: $21,186**

ABOUT THE INSTITUTION Independent, coed. Awards: bachelor's and master's degrees. 45 undergraduate majors. Total enrollment: 1,820. Undergraduates: 1,764. Freshmen: 477. Both federal and institutional methodology are used as a basis for awarding need-based institutional aid.

UNDERGRADUATE EXPENSES for 1999–2000 ***Application fee:*** $50. ***Comprehensive fee:*** $30,595. ***Part-time tuition:*** $695 per course. Part-time tuition and fees vary according to program. ***Payment plan:*** installment.

FRESHMAN FINANCIAL AID (Fall 1999, est.) 285 applied for aid; of those 76% were deemed to have need. 100% of freshmen with need received aid; of those 100% had need fully met. *Average percent of need met:* 100% (excluding resources awarded to replace EFC). *Average financial aid package:* $20,158 (excluding resources awarded to replace EFC).

UNDERGRADUATE FINANCIAL AID (Fall 1999, est.) 904 applied for aid; of those 88% were deemed to have need. 100% of undergraduates with need received aid; of those 100% had need fully met. *Average percent of need met:* 100% (excluding resources awarded to replace EFC). *Average financial aid package:* $21,186 (excluding resources awarded to replace EFC).

GIFT AID (NEED-BASED) ***Total amount:*** $13,403,123 (7% Federal, 4% state, 85% institutional, 4% external sources). ***Receiving aid:*** *Freshmen:* 42% (202); *all full-time undergraduates:* 45% (780). ***Average award:*** Freshmen: $18,056; Undergraduates: $16,488. ***Scholarships, grants, and awards:*** Federal Pell, FSEOG, state, college/university gift aid from institutional funds.

GIFT AID (NON-NEED-BASED) ***Tuition waivers:*** Full or partial for employees or children of employees.

LOANS ***Student loans:*** $3,845,170 (85% need-based, 15% non-need-based). 51% of past graduating class borrowed through all loan programs. Average indebtedness per student: $17,280. ***Average need-based loan:*** Freshmen: $2821; Undergraduates: $4304. ***Parent loans:*** $2,624,768 (100% non-need-based). ***Programs:*** FFEL (Subsidized and Unsubsidized Stafford, PLUS), Perkins, college/university.

Connecticut College (continued)

WORK-STUDY ***Federal work-study:*** *Total amount:* $771,567; 756 jobs averaging $1021. ***State or other work-study/employment:*** *Total amount:* $22,250 (100% need-based). 12 part-time jobs averaging $1083.

APPLYING for FINANCIAL AID ***Required financial aid forms:*** FAFSA, CSS Financial Aid PROFILE, noncustodial (divorced/separated) parent's statement, business/farm supplement. ***Financial aid deadline:*** 1/15. ***Notification date:*** 4/1. Students must reply by 5/1 or within 2 weeks of notification.

CONTACT Ms. Elaine Solinga, Director of Financial Aid Services, Connecticut College, 270 Mohegan Avenue, New London, CT 06320-4196, 860-439-2200. *Fax:* 860-439-2159. *E-mail:* newaid@conncoll.edu

CONSERVATORY OF MUSIC OF PUERTO RICO

San Juan, PR

Tuition & fees: N/R **Average undergraduate aid package: N/A**

ABOUT THE INSTITUTION Commonwealth-supported, coed. Awards: bachelor's degrees. 6 undergraduate majors. Total enrollment: 242. Undergraduates: 242. Federal methodology is used as a basis for awarding need-based institutional aid.

GIFT AID (NEED-BASED) ***Scholarships, grants, and awards:*** Federal Pell, FSEOG, state, private, college/university gift aid from institutional funds.

GIFT AID (NON-NEED-BASED) ***Scholarships, grants, and awards by category:*** *Creative Arts/Performance:* music. ***ROTC:*** Army cooperative.

WORK-STUDY Federal work-study jobs available.

APPLYING for FINANCIAL AID ***Required financial aid forms:*** FAFSA, institution's own form.

CONTACT Mr. Jorge Medina, Director of Financial Aid, Conservatory of Music of Puerto Rico, 350 Rafael Lamar Street at FDR Avenue, San Juan, PR 00918, 787-751-0160 Ext. 235.

CONVERSE COLLEGE

Spartanburg, SC

Tuition & fees: $15,230 **Average undergraduate aid package: $13,770**

ABOUT THE INSTITUTION Independent, women only. Awards: bachelor's and master's degrees and post-master's certificates. 43 undergraduate majors. Total enrollment: 1,514. Undergraduates: 755. Freshmen: 173. Federal methodology is used as a basis for awarding need-based institutional aid.

UNDERGRADUATE EXPENSES for 1999–2000 ***Application fee:*** $35. ***Comprehensive fee:*** $19,875 includes full-time tuition ($15,230) and room and board ($4645). Full-time tuition and fees vary according to program. ***Part-time tuition:*** $490 per credit hour. Part-time tuition and fees vary according to program. ***Payment plan:*** installment.

FRESHMAN FINANCIAL AID (Fall 1999, est.) 171 applied for aid; of those 71% were deemed to have need. 100% of freshmen with need received aid; of those 50% had need fully met. *Average percent of need met:* 95% (excluding resources awarded to replace EFC). *Average financial aid package:* $15,335 (excluding resources awarded to replace EFC). 27% of all full-time freshmen had no need and received non-need-based aid.

UNDERGRADUATE FINANCIAL AID (Fall 1999, est.) 621 applied for aid; of those 74% were deemed to have need. 100% of undergraduates with need received aid; of those 55% had need fully met. *Average percent of need met:* 93% (excluding resources awarded to replace EFC). *Average financial aid package:* $13,770 (excluding resources awarded to replace EFC). 24% of all full-time undergraduates had no need and received non-need-based aid.

GIFT AID (NEED-BASED) ***Total amount:*** $4,554,615 (10% Federal, 22% state, 65% institutional, 3% external sources). ***Receiving aid:*** *Freshmen:* 67% (122); *all full-time undergraduates:* 70% (460). ***Average award:*** Freshmen: $12,388; Undergraduates: $10,189. ***Scholarships, grants, and awards:*** Federal Pell, FSEOG, state, private, college/university gift aid from institutional funds.

GIFT AID (NON-NEED-BASED) ***Total amount:*** $1,949,653 (23% state, 73% institutional, 4% external sources). ***Receiving aid:*** *Freshmen:* 20% (36); *Undergraduates:* 20% (132). ***Scholarships, grants, and awards by category:*** *Academic Interests/Achievement:* 529 awards ($3,327,850 total): general academic interests/achievements. *Creative Arts/Performance:* 109 awards ($322,080 total): applied art and design, creative writing, music, theater/drama. *Special Achievements/Activities:* 221 awards ($532,729 total): leadership. ***Tuition waivers:*** Full or partial for employees or children of employees, adult students, senior citizens. ***ROTC:*** Army cooperative.

LOANS ***Student loans:*** $2,628,407 (68% need-based, 32% non-need-based). 55% of past graduating class borrowed through all loan programs. Average indebtedness per student: $14,886. ***Average need-based loan:*** Freshmen: $3307; Undergraduates: $4278. ***Parent loans:*** $1,286,918 (12% need-based, 88% non-need-based). ***Programs:*** FFEL (Subsidized and Unsubsidized Stafford, PLUS), Perkins, state.

WORK-STUDY ***Federal work-study:*** *Total amount:* $242,040; 172 jobs averaging $1407. ***State or other work-study/employment:*** *Total amount:* $90,000 (100% non-need-based). 93 part-time jobs averaging $968.

ATHLETIC AWARDS *Total amount:* 210,130 (50% need-based, 50% non-need-based).

APPLYING for FINANCIAL AID ***Required financial aid form:*** FAFSA. ***Financial aid deadline:*** Continuous. ***Notification date:*** Continuous beginning 2/20. Students must reply by 5/1 or within 2 weeks of notification.

CONTACT Ms. Margaret P. Collins, Director of Financial Assistance, Converse College, 580 East Main Street, Spartanburg, SC 29302-0006, 864-596-9019 or toll-free 800-766-1125. *E-mail:* peggy.collins@converse.edu

COOK COLLEGE

New Brunswick, NJ

See Rutgers, The State University of New Jersey, Cook College

COOPER UNION FOR THE ADVANCEMENT OF SCIENCE AND ART

New York, NY

Tuition & fees: N/R **Average undergraduate aid package: N/A**

ABOUT THE INSTITUTION Independent, coed. Awards: bachelor's and master's degrees. 8 undergraduate majors. Total enrollment: 907. Undergraduates: 870. Freshmen: 186. Both federal and institutional methodology are used as a basis for awarding need-based institutional aid.

UNDERGRADUATE EXPENSES for 2000–2001 ***Application fee:*** $35. All students are awarded full-tuition scholarships. Living expenses subsidized by college-administered financial aid.

FRESHMAN FINANCIAL AID (Fall 1998) 108 applied for aid; of those 72% were deemed to have need. 100% of freshmen with need received aid; of those 96% had need fully met. *Average percent of need met:* 92% (excluding resources awarded to replace EFC). 60% of all full-time freshmen had no need and received non-need-based aid.

UNDERGRADUATE FINANCIAL AID (Fall 1998) 394 applied for aid; of those 87% were deemed to have need. 100% of undergraduates with need received aid; of those 84% had need fully met. *Average percent of need met:* 92% (excluding resources awarded to replace EFC). 62% of all full-time undergraduates had no need and received non-need-based aid.

GIFT AID (NEED-BASED) ***Total amount:*** $1,632,214 (30% Federal, 26% state, 33% institutional, 11% external sources). ***Receiving aid:*** *Freshmen:* 40% (78); *all full-time undergraduates:* 38% (341). ***Average award:*** Freshmen: $3150; Undergraduates: $3450. ***Scholarships, grants, and awards:*** Federal Pell, FSEOG, state, private, college/university gift aid from institutional funds.

GIFT AID (NON-NEED-BASED) ***Total amount:*** $6,900,124 (100% institutional). ***Receiving aid:*** *Freshmen:* 40% (78); *Undergraduates:* 38% (341).

LOANS ***Student loans:*** $905,648 (76% need-based, 24% non-need-based). ***Average need-based loan:*** Freshmen: $2100; Undergraduates:

$3350. ***Parent loans:*** $182,508 (100% non-need-based). ***Programs:*** FFEL (Subsidized and Unsubsidized Stafford, PLUS), Perkins, college/university.

WORK-STUDY ***Federal work-study:*** *Total amount:* $44,115; 54 jobs averaging $817. ***State or other work-study/employment:*** *Total amount:* $537,349 (5% need-based, 95% non-need-based). 308 part-time jobs averaging $1745.

APPLYING for FINANCIAL AID ***Required financial aid forms:*** FAFSA, CSS Financial Aid PROFILE. ***Financial aid deadline:*** 5/1 (priority: 4/15). ***Notification date:*** 6/1. Students must reply by 6/30 or within 2 weeks of notification.

CONTACT Ms. Mary Ruokonen, Director of Financial Aid, Cooper Union for the Advancement of Science and Art, 30 Cooper Square, New York, NY 10003-7120, 212-353-4130. *Fax:* 212-353-4343. *E-mail:* ruokon@cooper.edu

COPPIN STATE COLLEGE

Baltimore, MD

Tuition & fees (MD res): $3973 **Average undergraduate aid package: $5854**

ABOUT THE INSTITUTION State-supported, coed. Awards: bachelor's and master's degrees. 26 undergraduate majors. Total enrollment: 3,765. Undergraduates: 3,217. Federal methodology is used as a basis for awarding need-based institutional aid.

UNDERGRADUATE EXPENSES for 1999–2000 ***Application fee:*** $25. ***Tuition, state resident:*** full-time $3272; part-time $110 per credit hour. ***Tuition, nonresident:*** full-time $8164; part-time $262 per credit hour. ***Required fees:*** full-time $701; $18 per credit hour; $66 per term part-time. Part-time tuition and fees vary according to course load. ***College room and board:*** $5274; ***room only:*** $3380. Room and board charges vary according to housing facility. ***Payment plan:*** deferred payment.

FRESHMAN FINANCIAL AID (Fall 1999, est.) 434 applied for aid; of those 75% were deemed to have need. 96% of freshmen with need received aid; of those 11% had need fully met. *Average percent of need met:* 49% (excluding resources awarded to replace EFC). *Average financial aid package:* $4487 (excluding resources awarded to replace EFC). 9% of all full-time freshmen had no need and received non-need-based aid.

UNDERGRADUATE FINANCIAL AID (Fall 1999, est.) 1,941 applied for aid; of those 80% were deemed to have need. 98% of undergraduates with need received aid; of those 7% had need fully met. *Average percent of need met:* 56% (excluding resources awarded to replace EFC). *Average financial aid package:* $5854 (excluding resources awarded to replace EFC). 6% of all full-time undergraduates had no need and received non-need-based aid.

GIFT AID (NEED-BASED) ***Total amount:*** $4,327,958 (98% Federal, 1% state, 1% institutional). ***Receiving aid:*** *Freshmen:* 57% (250); *all full-time undergraduates:* 55% (1,225). ***Average award:*** Freshmen: $2727; Undergraduates: $3111. ***Scholarships, grants, and awards:*** Federal Pell, FSEOG, state, private, college/university gift aid from institutional funds.

GIFT AID (NON-NEED-BASED) ***Total amount:*** $291,463 (86% institutional, 14% external sources). ***Receiving aid:*** *Freshmen:* 21% (94); *Undergraduates:* 7% (158). ***Scholarships, grants, and awards by category:*** *Academic Interests/Achievement:* general academic interests/achievements. ***Tuition waivers:*** Full or partial for employees or children of employees. ***ROTC:*** Army.

LOANS ***Student loans:*** $5,618,110 (100% need-based). 65% of past graduating class borrowed through all loan programs. Average indebtedness per student: $12,000. ***Average need-based loan:*** Freshmen: $2727; Undergraduates: $3111. ***Parent loans:*** $2,302,347 (100% non-need-based). ***Programs:*** Federal Direct (Subsidized and Unsubsidized Stafford, PLUS), Perkins, state, college/university.

WORK-STUDY ***Federal work-study:*** *Total amount:* $286,277; 145 jobs available.

ATHLETIC AWARDS *Total amount:* 455,794 (100% non-need-based).

APPLYING for FINANCIAL AID ***Required financial aid forms:*** FAFSA, institution's own form, CSS Financial Aid PROFILE. ***Financial aid deadline:*** Continuous. ***Notification date:*** Continuous beginning 5/1. Students must reply within 2 weeks of notification.

CONTACT Fay Tayree, Associate Director, Financial Aid, Coppin State College, 2500 West North Avenue, Baltimore, MD 21216-3698, 410-383-5830 or toll-free 800-635-3674. *Fax:* 410-728-2979. *E-mail:* ftayree@coppin.edu

THE CORCORAN COLLEGE OF ART AND DESIGN

Washington, DC

Tuition & fees: $14,140 **Average undergraduate aid package: $7670**

ABOUT THE INSTITUTION Independent, coed. Awards: bachelor's degrees. 9 undergraduate majors. Total enrollment: 425. Undergraduates: 425. Freshmen: 44. Federal methodology is used as a basis for awarding need-based institutional aid.

UNDERGRADUATE EXPENSES for 1999–2000 ***Application fee:*** $30. ***Tuition:*** full-time $14,110; part-time $366 per credit. ***Required fees:*** full-time $30. Part-time tuition and fees vary according to course load. ***Payment plan:*** installment.

FRESHMAN FINANCIAL AID (Fall 1999, est.) 51 applied for aid; of those 76% were deemed to have need. 100% of freshmen with need received aid. *Average percent of need met:* 33% (excluding resources awarded to replace EFC). *Average financial aid package:* $6789 (excluding resources awarded to replace EFC). 24% of all full-time freshmen had no need and received non-need-based aid.

UNDERGRADUATE FINANCIAL AID (Fall 1999, est.) 222 applied for aid; of those 82% were deemed to have need. 100% of undergraduates with need received aid. *Average percent of need met:* 47% (excluding resources awarded to replace EFC). *Average financial aid package:* $7670 (excluding resources awarded to replace EFC). 18% of all full-time undergraduates had no need and received non-need-based aid.

GIFT AID (NEED-BASED) ***Total amount:*** $297,773 (75% Federal, 3% state, 22% institutional). ***Receiving aid:*** *Freshmen:* 57% (29); *all full-time undergraduates:* 62% (137). ***Average award:*** Freshmen: $2109; Undergraduates: $3246. ***Scholarships, grants, and awards:*** Federal Pell, FSEOG, state, college/university gift aid from institutional funds.

GIFT AID (NON-NEED-BASED) ***Receiving aid:*** *Freshmen:* 63% (32); *Undergraduates:* 53% (118). ***Scholarships, grants, and awards by category:*** *Academic Interests/Achievement:* 156 awards ($591,000 total): general academic interests/achievements. *Creative Arts/Performance:* 12 awards ($17,500 total): applied art and design, creative writing. *Special Achievements/Activities:* 47 awards ($64,547 total): general special achievements/activities. ***Tuition waivers:*** Full or partial for employees or children of employees.

LOANS ***Student loans:*** $1,230,239 (56% need-based, 44% non-need-based). 72% of past graduating class borrowed through all loan programs. ***Average need-based loan:*** Freshmen: $6523; Undergraduates: $8669. ***Parent loans:*** $645,792 (100% non-need-based). ***Programs:*** FFEL (Subsidized and Unsubsidized Stafford, PLUS), Perkins.

WORK-STUDY ***Federal work-study:*** *Total amount:* $50,723; 50 jobs averaging $1014.

APPLYING for FINANCIAL AID ***Required financial aid forms:*** FAFSA, institution's own form. ***Financial aid deadline (priority):*** 3/15. ***Notification date:*** Continuous beginning 4/1. Students must reply within 2 weeks of notification.

CONTACT Diane Morris, Financial Aid Director, The Corcoran College of Art and Design, 500 17th Street, NW, Washington, DC 20006-4804, 202-639-1816 or toll-free 888-CORCORAN (out-of-state). *Fax:* 202-737-6921. *E-mail:* dmorris@corcoran.org

CORNELL COLLEGE

Mount Vernon, IA

Tuition & fees: $18,995 **Average undergraduate aid package: $17,500**

Cornell College (continued)

ABOUT THE INSTITUTION Independent Methodist, coed. Awards: bachelor's degrees. 49 undergraduate majors. Total enrollment: 965. Undergraduates: 965. Freshmen: 269. Federal methodology is used as a basis for awarding need-based institutional aid.

UNDERGRADUATE EXPENSES for 1999–2000 ***Application fee:*** $25. ***Comprehensive fee:*** $24,135 includes full-time tuition ($18,835), mandatory fees ($160), and room and board ($5140). ***College room only:*** $2350. Full-time tuition and fees vary according to reciprocity agreements. Room and board charges vary according to board plan. ***Part-time tuition:*** $2355 per unit. Part-time tuition and fees vary according to course load and program. ***Payment plan:*** installment.

FRESHMAN FINANCIAL AID (Fall 1999, est.) 260 applied for aid; of those 83% were deemed to have need. 100% of freshmen with need received aid; of those 32% had need fully met. *Average percent of need met:* 90% (excluding resources awarded to replace EFC). *Average financial aid package:* $16,730 (excluding resources awarded to replace EFC). 16% of all full-time freshmen had no need and received non-need-based aid.

UNDERGRADUATE FINANCIAL AID (Fall 1999, est.) 922 applied for aid; of those 87% were deemed to have need. 100% of undergraduates with need received aid; of those 32% had need fully met. *Average percent of need met:* 85% (excluding resources awarded to replace EFC). *Average financial aid package:* $17,500 (excluding resources awarded to replace EFC). 13% of all full-time undergraduates had no need and received non-need-based aid.

GIFT AID (NEED-BASED) ***Total amount:*** $8,766,649 (7% Federal, 7% state, 85% institutional, 1% external sources). ***Receiving aid:*** *Freshmen:* 81% (217); *all full-time undergraduates:* 85% (802). ***Average award:*** Freshmen: $6260; Undergraduates: $5715. ***Scholarships, grants, and awards:*** Federal Pell, FSEOG, state, private, college/university gift aid from institutional funds.

GIFT AID (NON-NEED-BASED) ***Total amount:*** $2,200,779 (89% institutional, 11% external sources). ***Receiving aid:*** *Freshmen:* 78% (210); *Undergraduates:* 78% (734). ***Scholarships, grants, and awards by category:*** *Academic Interests/Achievement:* 645 awards ($4,774,875 total): general academic interests/achievements. *Creative Arts/Performance:* 89 awards ($259,045 total): art/fine arts, music, theater/drama. *Special Characteristics:* 12 awards ($179,995 total): children of educators, children of faculty/staff. ***Tuition waivers:*** Full or partial for employees or children of employees, adult students, senior citizens.

LOANS ***Student loans:*** $2,951,334 (81% need-based, 19% non-need-based). 87% of past graduating class borrowed through all loan programs. Average indebtedness per student: $18,025. ***Average need-based loan:*** Freshmen: $3400; Undergraduates: $4860. ***Parent loans:*** $410,252 (100% non-need-based). ***Programs:*** FFEL (Subsidized and Unsubsidized Stafford, PLUS), Perkins, college/university, United Methodist Student Loans.

WORK-STUDY ***Federal work-study:*** *Total amount:* $537,596; 570 jobs averaging $945. ***State or other work-study/employment:*** *Total amount:* $367,135 (35% need-based, 65% non-need-based). 400 part-time jobs available.

APPLYING for FINANCIAL AID ***Required financial aid forms:*** FAFSA, institution's own form. ***Financial aid deadline (priority):*** 3/1. ***Notification date:*** Continuous beginning 3/15. Students must reply by 5/1 or within 2 weeks of notification.

CONTACT Ms. Cindi P. Reints, Director of Financial Assistance, Cornell College, Wade House, 600 1st Street West, Mount Vernon, IA 52314-1098, 319-895-4216 or toll-free 800-747-1112. *Fax:* 319-895-4451. *E-mail:* creints@cornell-iowa.edu

CORNELL UNIVERSITY

Ithaca, NY

Tuition & fees: $23,848 **Average undergraduate aid package: $18,700**

ABOUT THE INSTITUTION Independent, coed. Awards: bachelor's, master's, doctoral, and first professional degrees. 156 undergraduate majors. Total enrollment: 19,021. Undergraduates: 13,669. Freshmen: 3,136. Institutional methodology is used as a basis for awarding need-based institutional aid.

UNDERGRADUATE EXPENSES for 1999–2000 ***Application fee:*** $65. ***Comprehensive fee:*** $31,675 includes full-time tuition ($23,760), mandatory fees ($88), and room and board ($7827). ***College room only:*** $4687. Room and board charges vary according to board plan and housing facility. ***Payment plans:*** tuition prepayment, installment.

FRESHMAN FINANCIAL AID (Fall 1999, est.) 2026 applied for aid; of those 77% were deemed to have need. 100% of freshmen with need received aid; of those 100% had need fully met. *Average percent of need met:* 100% (excluding resources awarded to replace EFC). *Average financial aid package:* $18,400 (excluding resources awarded to replace EFC).

UNDERGRADUATE FINANCIAL AID (Fall 1999, est.) 7,611 applied for aid; of those 88% were deemed to have need. 100% of undergraduates with need received aid; of those 100% had need fully met. *Average percent of need met:* 100% (excluding resources awarded to replace EFC). *Average financial aid package:* $18,700 (excluding resources awarded to replace EFC).

GIFT AID (NEED-BASED) ***Total amount:*** $80,372,000 (11% Federal, 8% state, 75% institutional, 6% external sources). ***Receiving aid:*** *Freshmen:* 43% (1,405); *all full-time undergraduates:* 44% (6,021). ***Average award:*** Freshmen: $14,900; Undergraduates: $13,500. ***Scholarships, grants, and awards:*** Federal Pell, FSEOG, state, private, college/university gift aid from institutional funds.

GIFT AID (NON-NEED-BASED) ***Tuition waivers:*** Full or partial for employees or children of employees. ***ROTC:*** Army, Naval, Air Force.

LOANS ***Student loans:*** $39,711,000 (100% need-based). 50% of past graduating class borrowed through all loan programs. Average indebtedness per student: $16,900. ***Average need-based loan:*** Freshmen: $5300; Undergraduates: $5900. ***Parent loans:*** $9,541,000 (100% need-based). ***Programs:*** Federal Direct (Subsidized and Unsubsidized Stafford, PLUS), Perkins, college/university, Key Bank Alternative Loans.

WORK-STUDY ***Federal work-study:*** *Total amount:* $10,289,000; 5,380 jobs averaging $1912.

APPLYING for FINANCIAL AID ***Required financial aid forms:*** FAFSA, CSS Financial Aid PROFILE, noncustodial (divorced/separated) parent's statement, business/farm supplement. ***Financial aid deadline:*** 2/14. ***Notification date:*** 4/3. Students must reply by 5/1 or within 2 weeks of notification.

CONTACT Mr. Thomas Keane, Director of Financial Aid, Cornell University, 203 Day Hall, Ithaca, NY 14853-2801, 607-255-5145. *Fax:* 607-255-0659.

CORNERSTONE UNIVERSITY

Grand Rapids, MI

Tuition & fees: $10,344 **Average undergraduate aid package: N/A**

ABOUT THE INSTITUTION Independent Baptist, coed. Awards: associate and bachelor's degrees. 38 undergraduate majors. Total enrollment: 1,508. Undergraduates: 1,508. Freshmen: 366. Both federal and institutional methodology are used as a basis for awarding need-based institutional aid.

UNDERGRADUATE EXPENSES for 1999–2000 ***Application fee:*** $25. ***Comprehensive fee:*** $15,056 includes full-time tuition ($9664), mandatory fees ($680), and room and board ($4712). ***College room only:*** $2160. ***Part-time tuition:*** $347 per credit hour. Part-time tuition and fees vary according to course load. ***Payment plan:*** installment.

FRESHMAN FINANCIAL AID (Fall 1999, est.) 335 applied for aid.

GIFT AID (NEED-BASED) ***Total amount:*** $4,600,000 (16% Federal, 41% state, 40% institutional, 3% external sources). ***Scholarships, grants, and awards:*** Federal Pell, FSEOG, state, private, college/university gift aid from institutional funds.

GIFT AID (NON-NEED-BASED) ***Total amount:*** $50,000 (80% institutional, 20% external sources). ***Scholarships, grants, and awards by category:*** *Academic Interests/Achievement:* general academic interests/achievements, religion/biblical studies. *Creative Arts/Performance:* music. *Special Achievements/Activities:* leadership, religious involvement. *Special Characteristics:* children of faculty/staff, children of union members/company employees, ethnic background, general special characteristics, international students, members of minority groups, out-of-state students. ***Tuition waivers:*** Full or partial for employees or children of employees. ***ROTC:*** Army cooperative.

LOANS ***Student loans:*** $4,973,053 (96% need-based, 4% non-need-based). ***Parent loans:*** $181,000 (94% need-based, 6% non-need-based). ***Programs:*** FFEL (Subsidized and Unsubsidized Stafford, PLUS), Perkins, state, college/university.

WORK-STUDY ***Federal work-study:*** *Total amount:* $134,000; jobs available. ***State or other work-study/employment:*** *Total amount:* $38,404 (100% need-based). Part-time jobs available.

ATHLETIC AWARDS *Total amount:* 426,000 (93% need-based, 7% non-need-based).

APPLYING for FINANCIAL AID ***Required financial aid form:*** FAFSA. ***Financial aid deadline (priority):*** 3/21. ***Notification date:*** Continuous. Students must reply within 2 weeks of notification.

CONTACT Mr. Geoff Marsh, Director of Student Financial Services, Cornerstone University, 1001 East Beltline Avenue, NE, Grand Rapids, MI 49525-5897, 616-222-1424 or toll-free 800-968-4722. *Fax:* 616-222-1400. *E-mail:* geoff_a_marsh@cornerstone.edu

CORNISH COLLEGE OF THE ARTS

Seattle, WA

Tuition & fees: $13,900 **Average undergraduate aid package: $12,061**

ABOUT THE INSTITUTION Independent, coed. Awards: bachelor's degrees. 10 undergraduate majors. Total enrollment: 659. Undergraduates: 659. Freshmen: 112. Federal methodology is used as a basis for awarding need-based institutional aid.

UNDERGRADUATE EXPENSES for 1999–2000 ***Application fee:*** $35. ***Tuition:*** full-time $13,700; part-time $575 per credit. ***Required fees:*** full-time $200; $100 per term part-time. Part-time tuition and fees vary according to program. ***Payment plan:*** installment.

FRESHMAN FINANCIAL AID (Fall 1999, est.) 83 applied for aid; of those 83% were deemed to have need. 100% of freshmen with need received aid; of those 13% had need fully met. *Average percent of need met:* 65% (excluding resources awarded to replace EFC). *Average financial aid package:* $10,025 (excluding resources awarded to replace EFC). 44% of all full-time freshmen had no need and received non-need-based aid.

UNDERGRADUATE FINANCIAL AID (Fall 1999, est.) 449 applied for aid; of those 87% were deemed to have need. 100% of undergraduates with need received aid; of those 21% had need fully met. *Average percent of need met:* 74% (excluding resources awarded to replace EFC). *Average financial aid package:* $12,061 (excluding resources awarded to replace EFC). 20% of all full-time undergraduates had no need and received non-need-based aid.

GIFT AID (NEED-BASED) ***Total amount:*** $1,888,264 (29% Federal, 16% state, 48% institutional, 7% external sources). ***Receiving aid:*** *Freshmen:* 51% (63); *all full-time undergraduates:* 73% (359). ***Average award:*** Freshmen: $4339; Undergraduates: $4818. ***Scholarships, grants, and awards:*** Federal Pell, FSEOG, state, private, college/university gift aid from institutional funds.

GIFT AID (NON-NEED-BASED) ***Total amount:*** $193,867 (85% institutional, 15% external sources). ***Receiving aid:*** *Freshmen:* 2% (3); *Undergraduates:* 2% (9). ***Scholarships, grants, and awards by category:*** *Academic Interests/Achievement:* general academic interests/achievements. *Creative Arts/Performance:* art/fine arts, dance, music, theater/drama. ***Tuition waivers:*** Full or partial for employees or children of employees.

LOANS ***Student loans:*** $2,651,801 (86% need-based, 14% non-need-based). 83% of past graduating class borrowed through all loan programs. Average indebtedness per student: $24,000. ***Average need-based loan:*** Freshmen: $4156; Undergraduates: $5652. ***Parent loans:*** $1,123,378 (51% need-based, 49% non-need-based). ***Programs:*** FFEL (Subsidized and Unsubsidized Stafford, PLUS), Perkins, college/university.

WORK-STUDY ***Federal work-study:*** *Total amount:* $631,353; 228 jobs averaging $2769.

APPLYING for FINANCIAL AID ***Required financial aid forms:*** FAFSA, institution's own form, state aid form. ***Financial aid deadline (priority):*** 2/1. ***Notification date:*** 4/15. Students must reply by 5/1 or within 2 weeks of notification.

CONTACT Office of Admissions and Financial Aid, Cornish College of the Arts, 710 East Roy Street, Seattle, WA 98102-4696, 206-726-5016 or toll-free 800-726-ARTS. *Fax:* 206-720-1011.

COVENANT COLLEGE

Lookout Mountain, GA

Tuition & fees: $15,960 **Average undergraduate aid package: $12,633**

ABOUT THE INSTITUTION Independent religious, coed. Awards: associate, bachelor's, and master's degrees (master's degree in education only). 20 undergraduate majors. Total enrollment: 1,116. Undergraduates: 1,049. Freshmen: 229. Federal methodology is used as a basis for awarding need-based institutional aid.

UNDERGRADUATE EXPENSES for 2000–2001 ***Application fee:*** $25. ***Comprehensive fee:*** $20,410 includes full-time tuition ($15,600), mandatory fees ($360), and room and board ($4450). Full-time tuition and fees vary according to program. Room and board charges vary according to board plan and housing facility. ***Part-time tuition:*** $650 per unit. Part-time tuition and fees vary according to program. ***Payment plan:*** installment.

FRESHMAN FINANCIAL AID (Fall 1999, est.) 223 applied for aid; of those 72% were deemed to have need. 100% of freshmen with need received aid; of those 19% had need fully met. *Average percent of need met:* 75% (excluding resources awarded to replace EFC). *Average financial aid package:* $11,580 (excluding resources awarded to replace EFC). 21% of all full-time freshmen had no need and received non-need-based aid.

UNDERGRADUATE FINANCIAL AID (Fall 1999, est.) 814 applied for aid; of those 73% were deemed to have need. 98% of undergraduates with need received aid; of those 25% had need fully met. *Average percent of need met:* 87% (excluding resources awarded to replace EFC). *Average financial aid package:* $12,633 (excluding resources awarded to replace EFC). 14% of all full-time undergraduates had no need and received non-need-based aid.

GIFT AID (NEED-BASED) ***Total amount:*** $4,600,254 (14% Federal, 6% state, 78% institutional, 2% external sources). ***Receiving aid:*** *Freshmen:* 62% (143); *all full-time undergraduates:* 62% (514). ***Average award:*** Freshmen: $5162; Undergraduates: $5091. ***Scholarships, grants, and awards:*** Federal Pell, FSEOG, state, private, college/university gift aid from institutional funds.

GIFT AID (NON-NEED-BASED) ***Total amount:*** $777,530 (1% Federal, 19% state, 77% institutional, 3% external sources). ***Receiving aid:*** *Freshmen:* 59% (134); *Undergraduates:* 57% (474). ***Scholarships, grants, and awards by category:*** *Academic Interests/Achievement:* 340 awards ($625,333 total): general academic interests/achievements. *Creative Arts/Performance:* 61 awards ($61,443 total): music. *Special Achievements/Activities:* 54 awards ($397,820 total): leadership. *Special Characteristics:* 491 awards ($1,255,105 total): children of faculty/staff, international students, members of minority groups, religious affiliation. ***Tuition waivers:*** Full or partial for employees or children of employees, senior citizens.

LOANS ***Student loans:*** $2,107,340 (95% need-based, 5% non-need-based). 56% of past graduating class borrowed through all loan programs. Average indebtedness per student: $17,214. ***Average need-based loan:*** Freshmen: $2011; Undergraduates: $4307. ***Parent loans:*** $522,976 (84% need-based, 16% non-need-based). ***Programs:*** FFEL (Subsidized and Unsubsidized Stafford, PLUS), Perkins, state, college/university.

WORK-STUDY ***Federal work-study:*** *Total amount:* $656,495; 345 jobs averaging $1903. ***State or other work-study/employment:*** *Total amount:* $20,726 (100% non-need-based). 15 part-time jobs averaging $1382.

ATHLETIC AWARDS *Total amount:* 288,800 (63% need-based, 37% non-need-based).

APPLYING for FINANCIAL AID ***Required financial aid forms:*** FAFSA, institution's own form, state aid form. ***Financial aid deadline (priority):*** 3/1. ***Notification date:*** 4/15. Students must reply within 3 weeks of notification.

Covenant College (continued)

CONTACT Mrs. Carolyn Hays, Student Financial Planning Coordinator, Covenant College, 14049 Scenic Highway, Lookout Mountain, GA 30750, 706-820-1560 Ext. 1150 or toll-free 888-451-2683 (in-state). *Fax:* 706-820-2820. *E-mail:* hays@covenant.edu

CREIGHTON UNIVERSITY

Omaha, NE

Tuition & fees: $14,132 **Average undergraduate aid package: $13,169**

ABOUT THE INSTITUTION Independent Roman Catholic (Jesuit), coed. Awards: associate, bachelor's, master's, doctoral, and first professional degrees. 49 undergraduate majors. Total enrollment: 6,325. Undergraduates: 3,976. Freshmen: 834. Federal methodology is used as a basis for awarding need-based institutional aid.

UNDERGRADUATE EXPENSES for 1999–2000 ***Application fee:*** $30. ***Comprehensive fee:*** $19,578 includes full-time tuition ($13,566), mandatory fees ($566), and room and board ($5446). ***College room only:*** $3222. Room and board charges vary according to board plan and housing facility. ***Part-time tuition:*** $424 per credit. ***Part-time fees:*** $30 per term part-time. Part-time tuition and fees vary according to course load. ***Payment plan:*** installment.

FRESHMAN FINANCIAL AID (Fall 1999) 628 applied for aid; of those 78% were deemed to have need. 100% of freshmen with need received aid; of those 50% had need fully met. *Average percent of need met:* 87% (excluding resources awarded to replace EFC). *Average financial aid package:* $12,581 (excluding resources awarded to replace EFC). 34% of all full-time freshmen had no need and received non-need-based aid.

UNDERGRADUATE FINANCIAL AID (Fall 1999) 1,410 applied for aid; of those 87% were deemed to have need. 99% of undergraduates with need received aid; of those 69% had need fully met. *Average percent of need met:* 89% (excluding resources awarded to replace EFC). *Average financial aid package:* $13,169 (excluding resources awarded to replace EFC). 15% of all full-time undergraduates had no need and received non-need-based aid.

GIFT AID (NEED-BASED) ***Total amount:*** $6,027,571 (32% Federal, 7% state, 54% institutional, 7% external sources). ***Receiving aid:*** *Freshmen:* 40% (342); *all full-time undergraduates:* 31% (1,059). ***Average award:*** Freshmen: $5674; Undergraduates: $5986. ***Scholarships, grants, and awards:*** Federal Pell, FSEOG, state, college/university gift aid from institutional funds.

GIFT AID (NON-NEED-BASED) ***Total amount:*** $7,066,068 (91% institutional, 9% external sources). ***Scholarships, grants, and awards by category:*** *Academic Interests/Achievement:* business, general academic interests/achievements, military science. *Creative Arts/Performance:* 8 awards ($55,000 total): art/fine arts, debating. *Special Characteristics:* children of faculty/staff, local/state students, members of minority groups, religious affiliation, siblings of current students. ***Tuition waivers:*** Full or partial for employees or children of employees, adult students. ***ROTC:*** Army, Air Force cooperative.

LOANS ***Student loans:*** $11,970,899 (65% need-based, 35% non-need-based). 55% of past graduating class borrowed through all loan programs. Average indebtedness per student: $19,441. ***Average need-based loan:*** Freshmen: $4000; Undergraduates: $6732. ***Parent loans:*** $2,388,085 (100% non-need-based). ***Programs:*** FFEL (Subsidized and Unsubsidized Stafford, PLUS), Perkins, Federal Nursing, college/university.

WORK-STUDY ***Federal work-study:*** *Total amount:* $962,727; 675 jobs available.

ATHLETIC AWARDS *Total amount:* 1,116,839 (100% non-need-based).

APPLYING for FINANCIAL AID ***Required financial aid forms:*** FAFSA, institution's own form. ***Financial aid deadline (priority):*** 5/15. ***Notification date:*** Continuous. Students must reply within 4 weeks of notification.

CONTACT Paula Kohles, Assistant Director of Financial Aid, Creighton University, 2500 California Plaza, Omaha, NE 68178, 402-280-2731 or toll-free 800-282-5835. *Fax:* 402-280-2895. *E-mail:* pkohles@creighton.edu

CRICHTON COLLEGE

Memphis, TN

Tuition & fees: $7152 **Average undergraduate aid package: $4162**

ABOUT THE INSTITUTION Independent, coed. Awards: bachelor's degrees. 17 undergraduate majors. Total enrollment: 896. Undergraduates: 896. Freshmen: 60. Federal methodology is used as a basis for awarding need-based institutional aid.

UNDERGRADUATE EXPENSES for 1999–2000 ***Application fee:*** $25. ***One-time required fee:*** $5. ***Tuition:*** full-time $7152; part-time $298 per semester hour. Full-time tuition and fees vary according to program. Part-time tuition and fees vary according to program.

FRESHMAN FINANCIAL AID (Fall 1998) 51 applied for aid; of those 80% were deemed to have need. 98% of freshmen with need received aid; of those 2% had need fully met. *Average percent of need met:* 39% (excluding resources awarded to replace EFC). *Average financial aid package:* $4854 (excluding resources awarded to replace EFC). 11% of all full-time freshmen had no need and received non-need-based aid.

UNDERGRADUATE FINANCIAL AID (Fall 1998) 662 applied for aid; of those 80% were deemed to have need. 98% of undergraduates with need received aid; of those 3% had need fully met. *Average percent of need met:* 35% (excluding resources awarded to replace EFC). *Average financial aid package:* $4162 (excluding resources awarded to replace EFC). 2% of all full-time undergraduates had no need and received non-need-based aid.

GIFT AID (NEED-BASED) ***Total amount:*** $721,744 (72% Federal, 28% state). ***Receiving aid:*** *Freshmen:* 41% (23); *all full-time undergraduates:* 41% (298). ***Average award:*** Freshmen: $2279; Undergraduates: $2894. ***Scholarships, grants, and awards:*** Federal Pell, FSEOG, state, private, college/university gift aid from institutional funds.

GIFT AID (NON-NEED-BASED) ***Total amount:*** $502,063 (1% state, 99% institutional). ***Receiving aid:*** *Freshmen:* 43% (24); *Undergraduates:* 43% (311). ***Scholarships, grants, and awards by category:*** *Academic Interests/Achievement:* 132 awards ($325,732 total): general academic interests/achievements. *Creative Arts/Performance:* 23 awards ($19,260 total): music, theater/drama. *Special Achievements/Activities:* 35 awards ($44,219 total): leadership. *Special Characteristics:* 96 awards ($182,932 total): children and siblings of alumni, general special characteristics, members of minority groups, relatives of clergy, religious affiliation. ***Tuition waivers:*** Full or partial for minority students, children of alumni, employees or children of employees, adult students.

LOANS ***Student loans:*** $3,200,594 (51% need-based, 49% non-need-based). 71% of past graduating class borrowed through all loan programs. Average indebtedness per student: $14,000. ***Average need-based loan:*** Freshmen: $2415; Undergraduates: $2331. ***Programs:*** Federal Direct (Subsidized and Unsubsidized Stafford), Perkins, college/university.

WORK-STUDY ***Federal work-study:*** *Total amount:* $97,753; 41 jobs averaging $2374.

APPLYING for FINANCIAL AID ***Required financial aid forms:*** FAFSA, institution's own form. ***Financial aid deadline (priority):*** 3/31. ***Notification date:*** Continuous. Students must reply within 2 weeks of notification.

CONTACT Mr. Rodney Fowler, Financial Aid Counselor, Crichton College, PO Box 757830, Memphis, TN 38175-7830, 901-367-9800 Ext. 3253 or toll-free 800-960-9777. *Fax:* 901-367-3866. *E-mail:* rodney@crichton.edu

THE CRISWELL COLLEGE

Dallas, TX

Tuition & fees: $3910 **Average undergraduate aid package: N/A**

ABOUT THE INSTITUTION Independent Baptist, coed. Awards: associate, bachelor's, master's, and first professional degrees. 5 undergraduate majors. Total enrollment: 451. Undergraduates: 336. Institutional methodology is used as a basis for awarding need-based institutional aid.

UNDERGRADUATE EXPENSES for 1999–2000 ***Application fee:*** $30. ***Tuition:*** full-time $3750; part-time $125 per credit hour. ***Required fees:*** full-time $160; $80 per term part-time. Part-time tuition and fees vary according to course load. ***Payment plan:*** installment.

GIFT AID (NEED-BASED) ***Scholarships, grants, and awards:*** private, college/university gift aid from institutional funds.

GIFT AID (NON-NEED-BASED) ***Scholarships, grants, and awards by category:*** *Academic Interests/Achievement:* general academic interests/achievements. *Special Achievements/Activities:* religious involvement. ***Tuition waivers:*** Full or partial for employees or children of employees.

LOANS ***Programs:*** college/university.

APPLYING for FINANCIAL AID ***Required financial aid form:*** institution's own form. ***Financial aid deadline (priority):*** 7/15. ***Notification date:*** Continuous. Students must reply within 6 weeks of notification.

CONTACT David Porter, Acting Director of Admissions and Enrollment Services, The Criswell College, 4010 Gaston Avenue, Dallas, TX 75246, 800-899-0012. *Fax:* 214-818-1310. *E-mail:* dporter@criswell.edu

CROWN COLLEGE

St. Bonifacius, MN

Tuition & fees: $10,570 **Average undergraduate aid package: $11,780**

ABOUT THE INSTITUTION Independent religious, coed. Awards: associate, bachelor's, and master's degrees. 28 undergraduate majors. Total enrollment: 800. Undergraduates: 794. Freshmen: 135. Federal methodology is used as a basis for awarding need-based institutional aid.

UNDERGRADUATE EXPENSES for 2000–2001 ***Application fee:*** $35. ***Comprehensive fee:*** $14,990 includes full-time tuition ($9840), mandatory fees ($730), and room and board ($4420). ***College room only:*** $2056. ***Part-time tuition:*** $328 per credit hour. ***Part-time fees:*** $192 per term part-time. Part-time tuition and fees vary according to course load. ***Payment plan:*** installment.

FRESHMAN FINANCIAL AID (Fall 1998) 127 applied for aid; of those 100% were deemed to have need. 100% of freshmen with need received aid; of those 74% had need fully met. *Average percent of need met:* 82% (excluding resources awarded to replace EFC). *Average financial aid package:* $11,273 (excluding resources awarded to replace EFC).

UNDERGRADUATE FINANCIAL AID (Fall 1998) 446 applied for aid; of those 100% were deemed to have need. 100% of undergraduates with need received aid; of those 47% had need fully met. *Average percent of need met:* 84% (excluding resources awarded to replace EFC). *Average financial aid package:* $11,780 (excluding resources awarded to replace EFC).

GIFT AID (NEED-BASED) ***Total amount:*** $1,918,555 (39% Federal, 42% state, 19% institutional). ***Receiving aid:*** *Freshmen:* 98% (125); *all full-time undergraduates:* 89% (403). ***Average award:*** Freshmen: $4235; Undergraduates: $3262. ***Scholarships, grants, and awards:*** Federal Pell, FSEOG, state, private, college/university gift aid from institutional funds.

GIFT AID (NON-NEED-BASED) ***Total amount:*** $535,373 (90% institutional, 10% external sources). ***Receiving aid:*** *Freshmen:* 79% (100); *Undergraduates:* 57% (261). ***Scholarships, grants, and awards by category:*** *Academic Interests/Achievement:* business, education, English, general academic interests/achievements, religion/biblical studies. *Creative Arts/Performance:* music. *Special Achievements/Activities:* leadership. *Special Characteristics:* children of educators, children of faculty/staff, relatives of clergy. ***Tuition waivers:*** Full or partial for employees or children of employees.

LOANS ***Student loans:*** $2,930,722 (100% need-based). 82% of past graduating class borrowed through all loan programs. Average indebtedness per student: $17,067. ***Parent loans:*** $189,146 (100% non-need-based). ***Programs:*** FFEL (Subsidized and Unsubsidized Stafford, PLUS), Perkins, state, SELF Loans, Wells Fargo Collegiate Loans, GAP Loans, Choice Loans.

WORK-STUDY ***Federal work-study:*** *Total amount:* $117,698; 121 jobs averaging $972. ***State or other work-study/employment:*** *Total amount:* $52,768 (77% need-based, 23% non-need-based). 72 part-time jobs averaging $733.

APPLYING for FINANCIAL AID ***Required financial aid forms:*** FAFSA, institution's own form. ***Financial aid deadline (priority):*** 8/1. ***Notification date:*** Continuous.

CONTACT Ms. Cheryl Wiebe, Director of Financial Aid, Crown College, 6425 County Road 30, St. Bonifacius, MN 55375-9002, 612-446-4175 or toll-free 800-68-CROWN. *Fax:* 612-446-4178. *E-mail:* wiebec@crown.edu

THE CULINARY INSTITUTE OF AMERICA

Hyde Park, NY

Tuition & fees: $15,605 **Average undergraduate aid package: $8325**

ABOUT THE INSTITUTION Independent, coed. Awards: associate and bachelor's degrees. 1 undergraduate major. Total enrollment: 2,120. Undergraduates: 2,120. Freshmen: 503. Federal methodology is used as a basis for awarding need-based institutional aid.

UNDERGRADUATE EXPENSES for 2000–2001 ***Application fee:*** $30. ***Comprehensive fee:*** $20,985 includes full-time tuition ($15,400), mandatory fees ($205), and room and board ($5380). Full-time tuition and fees vary according to course level, degree level, program, and student level. Room and board charges vary according to housing facility. ***Payment plan:*** installment.

UNDERGRADUATE FINANCIAL AID (Fall 1998) 1,900 applied for aid; of those 99% were deemed to have need. 100% of undergraduates with need received aid; of those 1% had need fully met. *Average percent of need met:* 50% (excluding resources awarded to replace EFC). *Average financial aid package:* $8325 (excluding resources awarded to replace EFC). .2% of all full-time undergraduates had no need and received non-need-based aid.

GIFT AID (NEED-BASED) ***Total amount:*** $7,375,220 (28% Federal, 13% state, 55% institutional, 4% external sources). ***Receiving aid:*** *All full-time undergraduates:* 66% (1,400). ***Average award:*** Undergraduates: $2000. ***Scholarships, grants, and awards:*** Federal Pell, FSEOG, state, private, college/university gift aid from institutional funds.

GIFT AID (NON-NEED-BASED) ***Total amount:*** $292,000 (79% Federal, 21% institutional). ***Receiving aid:*** *Undergraduates:* 1% (20). ***Scholarships, grants, and awards by category:*** *Creative Arts/Performance:* 8 awards ($28,500 total): general creative arts/performance. *Special Achievements/Activities:* 12 awards ($31,500 total): leadership. ***Tuition waivers:*** Full or partial for minority students, employees or children of employees.

LOANS ***Student loans:*** $13,610,306 (74% need-based, 26% non-need-based). 89% of past graduating class borrowed through all loan programs. Average indebtedness per student: $18,500. ***Average need-based loan:*** Undergraduates: $4280. ***Parent loans:*** $5,685,062 (100% non-need-based). ***Programs:*** FFEL (Subsidized and Unsubsidized Stafford, PLUS), Perkins, alternative loans.

WORK-STUDY ***Federal work-study:*** *Total amount:* $410,672; 760 jobs averaging $540.

APPLYING for FINANCIAL AID ***Required financial aid forms:*** FAFSA, institution's own form. ***Financial aid deadline:*** Continuous. ***Notification date:*** Continuous beginning 2/1. Students must reply within 2 weeks of notification.

CONTACT Patricia A. Arcuri, Director, Financial Aid, The Culinary Institute of America, 433 Albany Post Road, Hyde Park, NY 12538-1499, 914-451-1302 or toll-free 800-CULINARY. *Fax:* 914-451-1058. *E-mail:* p_arcuri@culinary.edu

CULVER-STOCKTON COLLEGE

Canton, MO

Tuition & fees: $10,650 **Average undergraduate aid package: $8318**

ABOUT THE INSTITUTION Independent religious, coed. Awards: bachelor's degrees. 30 undergraduate majors. Total enrollment: 870. Undergraduates: 870. Freshmen: 175. Federal methodology is used as a basis for awarding need-based institutional aid.

Culver-Stockton College (continued)

UNDERGRADUATE EXPENSES for 2000–2001 ***Application fee:*** $25. ***Comprehensive fee:*** $15,400 includes full-time tuition ($10,650) and room and board ($4750). ***Payment plan:*** installment.

FRESHMAN FINANCIAL AID (Fall 1999, est.) 159 applied for aid; of those 84% were deemed to have need. 100% of freshmen with need received aid; of those 41% had need fully met. *Average percent of need met:* 85% (excluding resources awarded to replace EFC). *Average financial aid package:* $8406 (excluding resources awarded to replace EFC). 17% of all full-time freshmen had no need and received non-need-based aid.

UNDERGRADUATE FINANCIAL AID (Fall 1999, est.) 659 applied for aid; of those 86% were deemed to have need. 100% of undergraduates with need received aid; of those 48% had need fully met. *Average percent of need met:* 85% (excluding resources awarded to replace EFC). *Average financial aid package:* $8318 (excluding resources awarded to replace EFC). 21% of all full-time undergraduates had no need and received non-need-based aid.

GIFT AID (NEED-BASED) ***Total amount:*** $3,186,714 (19% Federal, 9% state, 68% institutional, 4% external sources). ***Receiving aid:*** *Freshmen:* 77% (134); *all full-time undergraduates:* 69% (549). ***Average award:*** Freshmen: $5695; Undergraduates: $5609. ***Scholarships, grants, and awards:*** Federal Pell, FSEOG, state, private, college/university gift aid from institutional funds, National Benevolent Association of the Christian Church (Disciples of Christ) scholarships/grants.

GIFT AID (NON-NEED-BASED) ***Total amount:*** $839,668 (3% state, 87% institutional, 10% external sources). ***Receiving aid:*** *Freshmen:* 13% (22); *Undergraduates:* 16% (125). ***Scholarships, grants, and awards by category:*** *Academic Interests/Achievement:* 747 awards ($2,279,332 total): general academic interests/achievements. *Creative Arts/Performance:* 239 awards ($300,573 total): art/fine arts, debating, music, theater/drama. *Special Characteristics:* 205 awards ($272,511 total): children and siblings of alumni, local/state students, religious affiliation. ***Tuition waivers:*** Full or partial for children of alumni, employees or children of employees, adult students, senior citizens.

LOANS ***Student loans:*** $2,419,706 (63% need-based, 37% non-need-based). 94% of past graduating class borrowed through all loan programs. Average indebtedness per student: $8204. ***Average need-based loan:*** Freshmen: $2728; Undergraduates: $3184. ***Parent loans:*** $583,325 (20% need-based, 80% non-need-based). ***Programs:*** Federal Direct (Subsidized and Unsubsidized Stafford, PLUS), Perkins, state, college/university.

WORK-STUDY ***Federal work-study:*** *Total amount:* $118,125; 100 jobs averaging $1181. ***State or other work-study/employment:*** *Total amount:* $298,175 (62% need-based, 38% non-need-based). 298 part-time jobs averaging $1000.

ATHLETIC AWARDS *Total amount:* 608,788 (72% need-based, 28% non-need-based).

APPLYING for FINANCIAL AID ***Required financial aid form:*** FAFSA. ***Financial aid deadline:*** 6/15 (priority: 3/15). ***Notification date:*** Continuous. Students must reply within 2 weeks of notification.

CONTACT Ms. Carla D. Boren, Director of Student Financial Planning, Culver-Stockton College, 1 College Hill, Canton, MO 63435-1299, 217-231-6306 Ext. 6462 or toll-free 800-537-1883 (out-of-state). *Fax:* 217-231-6618. *E-mail:* cboren@culver.edu

CUMBERLAND COLLEGE

Williamsburg, KY

Tuition & fees: $9920 **Average undergraduate aid package: $10,631**

ABOUT THE INSTITUTION Independent Kentucky Baptist, coed. Awards: bachelor's and master's degrees. 45 undergraduate majors. Total enrollment: 1,662. Undergraduates: 1,540. Freshmen: 403. Federal methodology is used as a basis for awarding need-based institutional aid.

UNDERGRADUATE EXPENSES for 2000–2001 ***Application fee:*** $25. ***Comprehensive fee:*** $14,196 includes full-time tuition ($9698), mandatory fees ($222), and room and board ($4276). ***Part-time fees:*** $46 per term part-time. Part-time tuition and fees vary according to course load. ***Payment plan:*** installment.

FRESHMAN FINANCIAL AID (Fall 1999) 367 applied for aid; of those 90% were deemed to have need. 100% of freshmen with need received aid; of those 35% had need fully met. *Average percent of need met:* 90% (excluding resources awarded to replace EFC). *Average financial aid package:* $10,911 (excluding resources awarded to replace EFC). 15% of all full-time freshmen had no need and received non-need-based aid.

UNDERGRADUATE FINANCIAL AID (Fall 1999) 1,193 applied for aid; of those 90% were deemed to have need. 98% of undergraduates with need received aid; of those 34% had need fully met. *Average percent of need met:* 90% (excluding resources awarded to replace EFC). *Average financial aid package:* $10,631 (excluding resources awarded to replace EFC). 15% of all full-time undergraduates had no need and received non-need-based aid.

GIFT AID (NEED-BASED) ***Total amount:*** $4,095,627 (41% Federal, 32% state, 27% institutional). ***Receiving aid:*** *Freshmen:* 61% (244); *all full-time undergraduates:* 57% (779). ***Average award:*** Freshmen: $4786; Undergraduates: $5257. ***Scholarships, grants, and awards:*** Federal Pell, FSEOG, state, private, college/university gift aid from institutional funds.

GIFT AID (NON-NEED-BASED) ***Total amount:*** $3,562,303 (3% state, 89% institutional, 8% external sources). ***Receiving aid:*** *Freshmen:* 81% (325); *Undergraduates:* 74% (1,020). ***Scholarships, grants, and awards by category:*** *Academic Interests/Achievement:* 738 awards ($1,847,324 total): general academic interests/achievements. *Creative Arts/Performance:* 110 awards ($63,452 total): art/fine arts, music. *Special Achievements/Activities:* 232 awards ($426,450 total): cheerleading/drum major, community service, religious involvement. *Special Characteristics:* 282 awards ($358,687 total): children and siblings of alumni, children of faculty/staff, relatives of clergy, siblings of current students. ***Tuition waivers:*** Full or partial for employees or children of employees.

LOANS ***Student loans:*** $3,931,046 (70% need-based, 30% non-need-based). 74% of past graduating class borrowed through all loan programs. Average indebtedness per student: $14,469. ***Average need-based loan:*** Freshmen: $2435; Undergraduates: $3450. ***Parent loans:*** $497,100 (100% non-need-based). ***Programs:*** FFEL (Subsidized and Unsubsidized Stafford, PLUS), Perkins, college/university.

WORK-STUDY ***Federal work-study:*** *Total amount:* $751,471; 467 jobs averaging $1600. ***State or other work-study/employment:*** *Total amount:* $306,106 (100% need-based). 188 part-time jobs averaging $1600.

ATHLETIC AWARDS *Total amount:* 1,619,026 (100% non-need-based).

APPLYING for FINANCIAL AID ***Required financial aid form:*** FAFSA. ***Financial aid deadline (priority):*** 3/1. ***Notification date:*** Continuous beginning 4/1. Students must reply within 2 weeks of notification.

CONTACT Mr. Jack Stanfill, Director, Student Financial Planning, Cumberland College, 6190 College Station Drive, Williamsburg, KY 40769-1372, 606-549-2200 Ext. 4219 or toll-free 800-343-1609. *Fax:* 606-539-4515. *E-mail:* jackstan@cc.cumber.edu

CUMBERLAND UNIVERSITY

Lebanon, TN

Tuition & fees: $9900 **Average undergraduate aid package: N/A**

ABOUT THE INSTITUTION Independent, coed. Awards: associate, bachelor's, and master's degrees. 27 undergraduate majors. Total enrollment: 1,206. Undergraduates: 1,029. Freshmen: 269. Both federal and institutional methodology are used as a basis for awarding need-based institutional aid.

UNDERGRADUATE EXPENSES for 1999–2000 ***Application fee:*** $25. ***Comprehensive fee:*** $13,400 includes full-time tuition ($9850), mandatory fees ($50), and room and board ($3500). ***College room only:*** $1370. Room and board charges vary according to board plan and housing facility. ***Part-time tuition:*** $410 per semester hour. ***Part-time fees:*** $25 per term part-time. Part-time tuition and fees vary according to location. ***Payment plan:*** installment.

GIFT AID (NEED-BASED) ***Scholarships, grants, and awards:*** Federal Pell, FSEOG, state, private, college/university gift aid from institutional funds.

GIFT AID (NON-NEED-BASED) ***Scholarships, grants, and awards by category:*** *Academic Interests/Achievement:* general academic interests/

achievements. *Creative Arts/Performance:* art/fine arts, music, performing arts, theater/drama. *Special Achievements/Activities:* leadership. *Special Characteristics:* children of faculty/staff. ***Tuition waivers:*** Full or partial for employees or children of employees, senior citizens.

LOANS ***Programs:*** FFEL (Subsidized and Unsubsidized Stafford, PLUS), Perkins, alternative loans.

WORK-STUDY Federal work-study jobs available. ***State or other work-study/employment:*** Part-time jobs available.

APPLYING for FINANCIAL AID ***Required financial aid forms:*** FAFSA, institution's own form. ***Financial aid deadline (priority):*** 2/15. ***Notification date:*** Continuous beginning 5/1. Students must reply within 2 weeks of notification.

CONTACT Mr. Larry Vaughan, Director of Financial Aid, Cumberland University, One Cumberland Square, Lebanon, TN 37087-3554, 615-444-2562 Ext. 1222 or toll-free 800-467-0562 (out-of-state). *Fax:* 615-444-2569. *E-mail:* lvaughan@cumberland.edu

CURRY COLLEGE

Milton, MA

Tuition & fees: $17,300 **Average undergraduate aid package: $13,000**

ABOUT THE INSTITUTION Independent, coed. Awards: bachelor's and master's degrees. 27 undergraduate majors. Total enrollment: 2,424. Undergraduates: 2,305. Freshmen: 373. Both federal and institutional methodology are used as a basis for awarding need-based institutional aid.

UNDERGRADUATE EXPENSES for 1999–2000 ***Application fee:*** $40. ***Comprehensive fee:*** $24,010 includes full-time tuition ($16,500), mandatory fees ($800), and room and board ($6710). ***College room only:*** $3600. Room and board charges vary according to board plan. ***Part-time tuition:*** $550 per credit hour. ***Payment plan:*** installment.

FRESHMAN FINANCIAL AID (Fall 1999, est.) 350 applied for aid; of those 86% were deemed to have need. 100% of freshmen with need received aid. *Average percent of need met:* 75% (excluding resources awarded to replace EFC). *Average financial aid package:* $12,500 (excluding resources awarded to replace EFC).

UNDERGRADUATE FINANCIAL AID (Fall 1999, est.) 950 applied for aid; of those 84% were deemed to have need. 100% of undergraduates with need received aid. *Average percent of need met:* 65% (excluding resources awarded to replace EFC). *Average financial aid package:* $13,000 (excluding resources awarded to replace EFC).

GIFT AID (NEED-BASED) ***Total amount:*** $6,321,880 (13% Federal, 11% state, 74% institutional, 2% external sources). ***Receiving aid:*** *Freshmen:* 56% (280); *all full-time undergraduates:* 53% (650). ***Scholarships, grants, and awards:*** Federal Pell, FSEOG, state, private, college/university gift aid from institutional funds.

GIFT AID (NON-NEED-BASED) ***Tuition waivers:*** Full or partial for children of alumni, employees or children of employees, senior citizens. ***ROTC:*** Army cooperative.

LOANS ***Student loans:*** $2,820,386 (100% need-based). ***Parent loans:*** $1,505,652 (100% non-need-based). ***Programs:*** FFEL (Subsidized and Unsubsidized Stafford, PLUS), Perkins, state.

WORK-STUDY ***Federal work-study:*** *Total amount:* $234,567; 150 jobs averaging $1500. ***State or other work-study/employment:*** *Total amount:* $12,000 (100% need-based). Part-time jobs available.

APPLYING for FINANCIAL AID ***Required financial aid forms:*** FAFSA, institution's own form. ***Financial aid deadline (priority):*** 3/1. ***Notification date:*** Continuous. Students must reply by 5/1.

CONTACT Ms. Susan Hafner, Director of Financial Aid, Curry College, 1071 Blue Hill Avenue, Milton, MA 02186-9984, 617-333-2146 or toll-free 800-669-0686. *Fax:* 617-333-6860. *E-mail:* shafner@curry.edu

THE CURTIS INSTITUTE OF MUSIC

Philadelphia, PA

CONTACT Financial Aid Officer, The Curtis Institute of Music, 1726 Locust Street, Philadelphia, PA 19103-6107, 215-893-5252.

C.W. POST CAMPUS OF LONG ISLAND UNIVERSITY

Brookville, NY

See Long Island University, C.W. Post Campus

DAEMEN COLLEGE

Amherst, NY

Tuition & fees: $12,220 **Average undergraduate aid package: $8440**

ABOUT THE INSTITUTION Independent, coed. Awards: bachelor's and master's degrees and post-bachelor's and post-master's certificates. 35 undergraduate majors. Total enrollment: 1,740. Undergraduates: 1,630. Freshmen: 295. Federal methodology is used as a basis for awarding need-based institutional aid.

UNDERGRADUATE EXPENSES for 1999–2000 ***Application fee:*** $25. ***Comprehensive fee:*** $18,320 includes full-time tuition ($11,800), mandatory fees ($420), and room and board ($6100). Room and board charges vary according to board plan. ***Part-time tuition:*** $390 per credit. ***Part-time fees:*** $3 per credit; $68 per term part-time. Part-time tuition and fees vary according to course load. ***Payment plans:*** installment, deferred payment.

FRESHMAN FINANCIAL AID (Fall 1998) 336 applied for aid; of those 86% were deemed to have need. 100% of freshmen with need received aid; of those 13% had need fully met. *Average percent of need met:* 67% (excluding resources awarded to replace EFC). *Average financial aid package:* $8597 (excluding resources awarded to replace EFC). 10% of all full-time freshmen had no need and received non-need-based aid.

UNDERGRADUATE FINANCIAL AID (Fall 1998) 1,358 applied for aid; of those 87% were deemed to have need. 99% of undergraduates with need received aid; of those 12% had need fully met. *Average percent of need met:* 67% (excluding resources awarded to replace EFC). *Average financial aid package:* $8440 (excluding resources awarded to replace EFC). 7% of all full-time undergraduates had no need and received non-need-based aid.

GIFT AID (NEED-BASED) ***Total amount:*** $4,569,872 (24% Federal, 34% state, 42% institutional). ***Receiving aid:*** *Freshmen:* 75% (262); *all full-time undergraduates:* 75% (1,073). ***Average award:*** Freshmen: $4866; Undergraduates: $4034. ***Scholarships, grants, and awards:*** Federal Pell, FSEOG, state, private, college/university gift aid from institutional funds.

GIFT AID (NON-NEED-BASED) ***Total amount:*** $3,151,854 (2% Federal, 1% state, 90% institutional, 7% external sources). ***Receiving aid:*** *Freshmen:* 50% (176); *Undergraduates:* 39% (559). ***Scholarships, grants, and awards by category:*** *Academic Interests/Achievement:* 498 awards ($1,510,787 total): education, general academic interests/achievements, health fields. *Creative Arts/Performance:* 6 awards ($21,500 total): art/fine arts. *Special Characteristics:* 73 awards ($365,061 total): children and siblings of alumni, children of faculty/staff, general special characteristics, siblings of current students. ***Tuition waivers:*** Full or partial for children of alumni, employees or children of employees, senior citizens. ***ROTC:*** Army cooperative.

LOANS ***Student loans:*** $7,867,398 (14% need-based, 86% non-need-based). 95% of past graduating class borrowed through all loan programs. Average indebtedness per student: $19,500. ***Average need-based loan:*** Freshmen: $2833; Undergraduates: $3874. ***Parent loans:*** $936,677 (94% need-based, 6% non-need-based). ***Programs:*** FFEL (Subsidized and Unsubsidized Stafford, PLUS), Perkins, college/university, alternative loans.

WORK-STUDY ***Federal work-study:*** *Total amount:* $293,105; 308 jobs available.

Daemen College (continued)

ATHLETIC AWARDS *Total amount:* 359,987 (87% need-based, 13% non-need-based).

APPLYING for FINANCIAL AID ***Required financial aid forms:*** FAFSA, institution's own form, state aid form. ***Financial aid deadline (priority):*** 2/15. ***Notification date:*** Continuous beginning 3/1. Students must reply within 2 weeks of notification.

CONTACT Joyce Kish, Administrative Coordinator of Financial Aid, Daemen College, 4380 Main Street, Amherst, NY 14226-3592, 716-839-8254 or toll-free 800-462-7652. *Fax:* 716-839-8516. *E-mail:* jkish@daemen.edu

DAKOTA STATE UNIVERSITY

Madison, SD

Tuition & fees (SD res): $3588 **Average undergraduate aid package: $4873**

ABOUT THE INSTITUTION State-supported, coed. Awards: associate, bachelor's, and master's degrees. 32 undergraduate majors. Total enrollment: 1,920. Undergraduates: 1,517. Freshmen: 353. Federal methodology is used as a basis for awarding need-based institutional aid.

UNDERGRADUATE EXPENSES for 1999–2000 ***Application fee:*** $15. ***Tuition, state resident:*** full-time $3588; part-time $112 per credit hour. ***Tuition, nonresident:*** full-time $7661; part-time $239 per credit hour. ***College room and board:*** $2800. ***Payment plan:*** deferred payment.

UNDERGRADUATE FINANCIAL AID (Fall 1998) 1,043 applied for aid; of those 90% were deemed to have need. 100% of undergraduates with need received aid. *Average financial aid package:* $4873 (excluding resources awarded to replace EFC). 4% of all full-time undergraduates had no need and received non-need-based aid.

GIFT AID (NEED-BASED) ***Total amount:*** $986,492 (98% Federal, 2% institutional). ***Scholarships, grants, and awards:*** Federal Pell, FSEOG, state, private, college/university gift aid from institutional funds.

GIFT AID (NON-NEED-BASED) ***Total amount:*** $330,273 (4% state, 76% institutional, 20% external sources). ***Scholarships, grants, and awards by category:*** *Academic Interests/Achievement:* business, communication, computer science, education, English, general academic interests/achievements, mathematics. *Creative Arts/Performance:* music. *Special Achievements/Activities:* general special achievements/activities. ***Tuition waivers:*** Full or partial for employees or children of employees, senior citizens. ***ROTC:*** Air Force cooperative.

LOANS ***Student loans:*** $3,665,637 (95% need-based, 5% non-need-based). 90% of past graduating class borrowed through all loan programs. Average indebtedness per student: $13,840. ***Parent loans:*** $174,193 (20% need-based, 80% non-need-based). ***Programs:*** FFEL (Subsidized and Unsubsidized Stafford, PLUS), Perkins, alternative loans.

WORK-STUDY ***Federal work-study:*** *Total amount:* $287,245; 167 jobs averaging $1720. ***State or other work-study/employment:*** *Total amount:* $243,269 (100% non-need-based). 164 part-time jobs averaging $1483.

ATHLETIC AWARDS *Total amount:* 93,507 (100% non-need-based).

APPLYING for FINANCIAL AID ***Required financial aid form:*** FAFSA. ***Financial aid deadline (priority):*** 3/1. ***Notification date:*** 5/10. Students must reply within 2 weeks of notification.

CONTACT Ms. Rose M. Jamison, Financial Aid Director, Dakota State University, 103 Heston Hall, 820 North Washington, Madison, SD 57042-1799, 605-256-5152 or toll-free 888-DSU-9988. *Fax:* 605-256-5316. *E-mail:* dsuinfo@pluto.dsu.edu

DAKOTA WESLEYAN UNIVERSITY

Mitchell, SD

Tuition & fees: $9916 **Average undergraduate aid package: $10,201**

ABOUT THE INSTITUTION Independent United Methodist, coed. Awards: associate and bachelor's degrees. 35 undergraduate majors. Total enrollment: 715. Undergraduates: 700. Freshmen: 173. Federal methodology is used as a basis for awarding need-based institutional aid.

UNDERGRADUATE EXPENSES for 1999–2000 ***Application fee:*** $15. ***Comprehensive fee:*** $13,556 includes full-time tuition ($9916) and room and board ($3640). Full-time tuition and fees vary according to program. Room and board charges vary according to board plan. ***Part-time tuition:*** $202 per credit hour. Part-time tuition and fees vary according to course load and program. ***Payment plan:*** installment.

FRESHMAN FINANCIAL AID (Fall 1998) 157 applied for aid; of those 100% were deemed to have need. 100% of freshmen with need received aid; of those 31% had need fully met. *Average percent of need met:* 79% (excluding resources awarded to replace EFC). *Average financial aid package:* $10,201 (excluding resources awarded to replace EFC).

UNDERGRADUATE FINANCIAL AID (Fall 1998) 602 applied for aid; of those 100% were deemed to have need. 100% of undergraduates with need received aid; of those 41% had need fully met. *Average percent of need met:* 79% (excluding resources awarded to replace EFC). *Average financial aid package:* $10,201 (excluding resources awarded to replace EFC).

GIFT AID (NEED-BASED) ***Total amount:*** $2,401,129 (35% Federal, 61% institutional, 4% external sources). ***Receiving aid:*** *Freshmen:* 79% (133); *all full-time undergraduates:* 87% (533). ***Scholarships, grants, and awards:*** Federal Pell, FSEOG, private, college/university gift aid from institutional funds.

GIFT AID (NON-NEED-BASED) ***Total amount:*** $197,745 (87% institutional, 13% external sources). ***Receiving aid:*** *Freshmen:* 14% (24); *Undergraduates:* 13% (80). ***Scholarships, grants, and awards by category:*** *Academic Interests/Achievement:* biological sciences, business, education, English. *Creative Arts/Performance:* art/fine arts, debating, music, theater/drama. *Special Achievements/Activities:* leadership, religious involvement, rodeo. *Special Characteristics:* ethnic background, religious affiliation. ***Tuition waivers:*** Full or partial for employees or children of employees, senior citizens.

LOANS ***Student loans:*** $2,987,668 (95% need-based, 5% non-need-based). ***Parent loans:*** $166,503 (85% need-based, 15% non-need-based). ***Programs:*** FFEL (Subsidized and Unsubsidized Stafford, PLUS), Perkins, Methodist Loans (for members of Methodist Church).

WORK-STUDY ***Federal work-study:*** *Total amount:* $158,716; 116 jobs averaging $1182. ***State or other work-study/employment:*** *Total amount:* $167,194 (95% need-based, 5% non-need-based). Part-time jobs available.

ATHLETIC AWARDS *Total amount:* 358,087 (97% need-based, 3% non-need-based).

APPLYING for FINANCIAL AID ***Required financial aid forms:*** FAFSA, institution's own form. ***Financial aid deadline (priority):*** 3/1. ***Notification date:*** Continuous beginning 3/15.

CONTACT Wilma Hjellum, Manager of Student Financial Aid, Dakota Wesleyan University, 1200 West University Avenue, Mitchell, SD 57301-4398, 605-995-2656 or toll-free 800-333-8506. *E-mail:* wihjellu@dwu.edu

DALLAS BAPTIST UNIVERSITY

Dallas, TX

Tuition & fees: $8700 **Average undergraduate aid package: $8905**

ABOUT THE INSTITUTION Independent religious, coed. Awards: associate, bachelor's, and master's degrees. 37 undergraduate majors. Total enrollment: 3,921. Undergraduates: 3,150. Freshmen: 261. Federal methodology is used as a basis for awarding need-based institutional aid.

UNDERGRADUATE EXPENSES for 1999–2000 ***Application fee:*** $25. ***Comprehensive fee:*** $12,380 includes full-time tuition ($8700) and room and board ($3680). ***College room only:*** $1500. Room and board charges vary according to board plan. ***Part-time tuition:*** $290 per credit hour. ***Payment plan:*** installment.

FRESHMAN FINANCIAL AID (Fall 1998) 241 applied for aid; of those 68% were deemed to have need. 98% of freshmen with need received aid; of those 37% had need fully met. *Average percent of need met:* 66% (excluding resources awarded to replace EFC). *Average financial aid package:* $7554 (excluding resources awarded to replace EFC). 21% of all full-time freshmen had no need and received non-need-based aid.

UNDERGRADUATE FINANCIAL AID (Fall 1998) 1,183 applied for aid; of those 73% were deemed to have need. 98% of undergraduates with need received aid; of those 42% had need fully met. *Average percent of need met:* 72% (excluding resources awarded to replace EFC). *Average financial aid package:* $8905 (excluding resources awarded to replace EFC). 14% of all full-time undergraduates had no need and received non-need-based aid.

GIFT AID (NEED-BASED) ***Total amount:*** $1,820,220 (59% Federal, 39% state, 2% institutional). ***Receiving aid:*** *Freshmen:* 38% (96); *all full-time undergraduates:* 33% (502). ***Average award:*** Freshmen: $1884; Undergraduates: $1835. ***Scholarships, grants, and awards:*** Federal Pell, FSEOG, state, private, college/university gift aid from institutional funds.

GIFT AID (NON-NEED-BASED) ***Total amount:*** $2,733,644 (87% institutional, 13% external sources). ***Receiving aid:*** *Freshmen:* 54% (135); *Undergraduates:* 41% (619). ***Scholarships, grants, and awards by category:*** *Academic Interests/Achievement:* 508 awards ($798,463 total): education, general academic interests/achievements, mathematics, premedicine, religion/biblical studies. *Creative Arts/Performance:* 47 awards ($98,944 total): music. *Special Achievements/Activities:* 326 awards ($1,064,000 total): leadership, memberships. *Special Characteristics:* 337 awards ($623,815 total): children and siblings of alumni, children of faculty/staff, general special characteristics, relatives of clergy, religious affiliation. ***Tuition waivers:*** Full or partial for employees or children of employees. ***ROTC:*** Army cooperative, Air Force cooperative.

LOANS ***Student loans:*** $6,664,959 (50% need-based, 50% non-need-based). ***Average need-based loan:*** Freshmen: $2199; Undergraduates: $3033. ***Parent loans:*** $610,405 (100% non-need-based). ***Programs:*** FFEL (Subsidized and Unsubsidized Stafford, PLUS), Perkins, college/university.

WORK-STUDY ***Federal work-study:*** *Total amount:* $129,329; jobs available. ***State or other work-study/employment:*** *Total amount:* $9266 (100% need-based). Part-time jobs available.

ATHLETIC AWARDS *Total amount:* 353,207 (100% non-need-based).

APPLYING for FINANCIAL AID ***Required financial aid forms:*** FAFSA, institution's own form, CSS Financial Aid PROFILE. ***Financial aid deadline (priority):*** 3/15. ***Notification date:*** Continuous.

CONTACT Ms. Mari Notley, Director of Financial Aid, Dallas Baptist University, 3000 Mountain Creek Parkway, Dallas, TX 75211-9299, 214-333-5363 or toll-free 800-460-1328. *Fax:* 214-333-5586. *E-mail:* mari@dbu.edu

DALLAS CHRISTIAN COLLEGE

Dallas, TX

Tuition & fees: $5690 **Average undergraduate aid package: $4461**

ABOUT THE INSTITUTION Independent religious, coed. Awards: bachelor's degrees. 3 undergraduate majors. Total enrollment: 253. Undergraduates: 253. Freshmen: 41. Federal methodology is used as a basis for awarding need-based institutional aid.

UNDERGRADUATE EXPENSES for 1999–2000 ***Application fee:*** $20. ***Comprehensive fee:*** $9390 includes full-time tuition ($5440), mandatory fees ($250), and room and board ($3700). Full-time tuition and fees vary according to course load and program. ***Part-time tuition:*** $170 per semester hour. ***Part-time fees:*** $125 per term part-time. Part-time tuition and fees vary according to course load and program. ***Payment plan:*** installment.

FRESHMAN FINANCIAL AID (Fall 1999, est.) 34 applied for aid; of those 91% were deemed to have need. 100% of freshmen with need received aid. *Average financial aid package:* $4694 (excluding resources awarded to replace EFC). 9% of all full-time freshmen had no need and received non-need-based aid.

UNDERGRADUATE FINANCIAL AID (Fall 1999, est.) 142 applied for aid; of those 93% were deemed to have need. 100% of undergraduates with need received aid. *Average financial aid package:* $4461 (excluding resources awarded to replace EFC). 10% of all full-time undergraduates had no need and received non-need-based aid.

GIFT AID (NEED-BASED) ***Total amount:*** $220,000 (82% Federal, 18% institutional). ***Receiving aid:*** *Freshmen:* 38% (13); *all full-time undergraduates:* 21% (48). ***Scholarships, grants, and awards:*** Federal Pell, FSEOG, private, college/university gift aid from institutional funds.

GIFT AID (NON-NEED-BASED) ***Total amount:*** $310,000 (52% institutional, 48% external sources). ***Receiving aid:*** *Freshmen:* 15% (5); *Undergraduates:* 19% (43). ***Scholarships, grants, and awards by category:*** *Academic Interests/Achievement:* 30 awards ($77,000 total): education, general academic interests/achievements, religion/biblical studies. *Creative Arts/Performance:* 5 awards ($7000 total): music. *Special Achievements/Activities:* general special achievements/activities. *Special Characteristics:* 15 awards ($15,000 total): children and siblings of alumni, children of faculty/staff, religious affiliation. ***Tuition waivers:*** Full or partial for employees or children of employees.

LOANS ***Student loans:*** $700,000 (54% need-based, 46% non-need-based). 65% of past graduating class borrowed through all loan programs. ***Parent loans:*** $50,000 (100% non-need-based). ***Programs:*** FFEL (Subsidized and Unsubsidized Stafford, PLUS).

WORK-STUDY ***Federal work-study:*** *Total amount:* $56,000; 35 jobs averaging $1000.

APPLYING for FINANCIAL AID ***Required financial aid forms:*** FAFSA, institution's own form. ***Financial aid deadline (priority):*** 4/15. ***Notification date:*** Continuous beginning 5/10. Students must reply within 2 weeks of notification.

CONTACT Director, Student Financial Aid, Dallas Christian College, 2700 Christian Parkway, Dallas, TX 75234-7299, 972-241-3371 Ext. 142. *Fax:* 972-241-8021. *E-mail:* finaid@dallas.edu

DALTON STATE COLLEGE

Dalton, GA

Tuition & fees (GA res): $1318 **Average undergraduate aid package: N/A**

ABOUT THE INSTITUTION State-supported, coed. Awards: associate and bachelor's degrees. 53 undergraduate majors. Total enrollment: 3,051. Undergraduates: 3,051. Both federal and institutional methodology are used as a basis for awarding need-based institutional aid.

UNDERGRADUATE EXPENSES for 1999–2000 ***Tuition, state resident:*** full-time $1276; part-time $43 per credit hour. ***Tuition, nonresident:*** full-time $3702; part-time $123 per credit hour. ***Required fees:*** full-time $42; $2 per credit hour.

GIFT AID (NEED-BASED) ***Total amount:*** $3,418,974 (56% Federal, 38% state, 1% institutional, 5% external sources). ***Scholarships, grants, and awards:*** Federal Pell, FSEOG, state, private.

GIFT AID (NON-NEED-BASED) ***Scholarships, grants, and awards by category:*** *Academic Interests/Achievement:* business, health fields. ***Tuition waivers:*** Full or partial for senior citizens.

LOANS ***Programs:*** FFEL (Subsidized and Unsubsidized Stafford), Federal Nursing.

WORK-STUDY ***Federal work-study:*** *Total amount:* $82,639; jobs available. ***State or other work-study/employment:*** *Total amount:* $235,185 (100% need-based). Part-time jobs available.

APPLYING for FINANCIAL AID ***Required financial aid forms:*** FAFSA, institution's own form, state aid form, noncustodial (divorced/separated) parent's statement, financial aid transcript (for transfers), verification worksheet (for transfers). ***Financial aid deadline (priority):*** 7/1. ***Notification date:*** Continuous.

CONTACT Sylvia Graves, Director of Student Financial Aid, Dalton State College, 213 North College Drive, Dalton, GA 30720, 706-272-4542 or toll-free 800-829-4436. *Fax:* 706-272-2458.

DANA COLLEGE

Blair, NE

Tuition & fees: $12,700 **Average undergraduate aid package: $12,080**

ABOUT THE INSTITUTION Independent religious, coed. Awards: bachelor's degrees. 36 undergraduate majors. Total enrollment: 538. Undergraduates: 538. Freshmen: 148. Federal methodology is used as a basis for awarding need-based institutional aid.

Dana College (continued)

UNDERGRADUATE EXPENSES for 1999–2000 ***Application fee:*** $20. ***Comprehensive fee:*** $16,774 includes full-time tuition ($12,150), mandatory fees ($550), and room and board ($4074). ***College room only:*** $1600. Room and board charges vary according to board plan and housing facility. ***Part-time tuition:*** $390 per semester hour. ***Part-time fees:*** $30 per term part-time. Part-time tuition and fees vary according to course load.

FRESHMAN FINANCIAL AID (Fall 1999) 160 applied for aid; of those 88% were deemed to have need. 100% of freshmen with need received aid; of those 34% had need fully met. *Average percent of need met:* 90% (excluding resources awarded to replace EFC). *Average financial aid package:* $12,370 (excluding resources awarded to replace EFC). 10% of all full-time freshmen had no need and received non-need-based aid.

UNDERGRADUATE FINANCIAL AID (Fall 1999) 515 applied for aid; of those 84% were deemed to have need. 100% of undergraduates with need received aid; of those 33% had need fully met. *Average percent of need met:* 86% (excluding resources awarded to replace EFC). *Average financial aid package:* $12,080 (excluding resources awarded to replace EFC). 12% of all full-time undergraduates had no need and received non-need-based aid.

GIFT AID (NEED-BASED) ***Total amount:*** $1,280,733 (41% Federal, 10% state, 29% institutional, 20% external sources). ***Receiving aid:*** *Freshmen:* 58% (93); *all full-time undergraduates:* 53% (275). ***Average award:*** Freshmen: $4106; Undergraduates: $3819. ***Scholarships, grants, and awards:*** Federal Pell, FSEOG, state, private, college/university gift aid from institutional funds.

GIFT AID (NON-NEED-BASED) ***Total amount:*** $1,694,735 (100% institutional). ***Receiving aid:*** *Freshmen:* 75% (120); *Undergraduates:* 64% (332). ***Scholarships, grants, and awards by category:*** *Academic Interests/Achievement:* 237 awards ($871,262 total): communication, education, English, general academic interests/achievements, health fields, international studies, premedicine, religion/biblical studies, social sciences. *Creative Arts/Performance:* 113 awards ($249,088 total): applied art and design, art/fine arts, debating, music, theater/drama. *Special Achievements/Activities:* 181 awards ($240,000 total): general special achievements/activities, religious involvement. *Special Characteristics:* 332 awards ($711,857 total): children and siblings of alumni, children of faculty/staff, ethnic background, international students, local/state students, members of minority groups, out-of-state students, relatives of clergy, religious affiliation, siblings of current students, spouses of current students. ***Tuition waivers:*** Full or partial for employees or children of employees. ***ROTC:*** Army cooperative, Air Force cooperative.

LOANS ***Student loans:*** $2,247,625 (69% need-based, 31% non-need-based). 91% of past graduating class borrowed through all loan programs. Average indebtedness per student: $14,735. ***Average need-based loan:*** Freshmen: $3486; Undergraduates: $4100. ***Parent loans:*** $2,765,767 (9% need-based, 91% non-need-based). ***Programs:*** FFEL (Subsidized and Unsubsidized Stafford, PLUS), Perkins, college/university.

WORK-STUDY ***Federal work-study:*** *Total amount:* $97,000; 170 jobs averaging $600. ***State or other work-study/employment:*** *Total amount:* $85,474 (100% non-need-based). Part-time jobs available.

ATHLETIC AWARDS *Total amount:* 941,518 (100% non-need-based).

APPLYING for FINANCIAL AID ***Required financial aid forms:*** FAFSA, institution's own form. ***Financial aid deadline (priority):*** 4/1. ***Notification date:*** Continuous. Students must reply within 3 weeks of notification.

CONTACT Ms. Kris Weigelt, Financial Aid Counselor, Dana College, 2848 College Drive, Blair, NE 68008-1099, 402-426-7226 Ext. 7245 or toll-free 800-444-3262. *Fax:* 402-426-7225. *E-mail:* kweigelt@fs1.dana.edu

DANIEL WEBSTER COLLEGE

Nashua, NH

Tuition & fees: $15,650 **Average undergraduate aid package: $13,000**

ABOUT THE INSTITUTION Independent, coed. Awards: associate and bachelor's degrees. 15 undergraduate majors. Total enrollment: 1,043. Undergraduates: 1,043. Freshmen: 179. Federal methodology is used as a basis for awarding need-based institutional aid.

UNDERGRADUATE EXPENSES for 1999–2000 ***Application fee:*** $35. ***Comprehensive fee:*** $21,652 includes full-time tuition ($15,330), mandatory fees ($320), and room and board ($6002). ***College room only:*** $3116. Full-time tuition and fees vary according to class time and course load. Room and board charges vary according to board plan and housing facility. ***Part-time tuition:*** $638 per credit. ***Part-time fees:*** $200 per term part-time. Part-time tuition and fees vary according to class time. ***Payment plan:*** installment.

FRESHMAN FINANCIAL AID (Fall 1999) 166 applied for aid; of those 96% were deemed to have need. 100% of freshmen with need received aid. *Average percent of need met:* 80% (excluding resources awarded to replace EFC). *Average financial aid package:* $12,000 (excluding resources awarded to replace EFC). 3% of all full-time freshmen had no need and received non-need-based aid.

UNDERGRADUATE FINANCIAL AID (Fall 1999) 415 applied for aid; of those 94% were deemed to have need. 100% of undergraduates with need received aid. *Average percent of need met:* 80% (excluding resources awarded to replace EFC). *Average financial aid package:* $13,000 (excluding resources awarded to replace EFC). 2% of all full-time undergraduates had no need and received non-need-based aid.

GIFT AID (NEED-BASED) ***Total amount:*** $1,297,107 (26% Federal, 4% state, 64% institutional, 6% external sources). ***Receiving aid:*** *Freshmen:* 71% (127); *all full-time undergraduates:* 75% (330). ***Average award:*** Freshmen: $3500; Undergraduates: $3100. ***Scholarships, grants, and awards:*** Federal Pell, FSEOG, state, private, college/university gift aid from institutional funds.

GIFT AID (NON-NEED-BASED) ***Total amount:*** $1,264,410 (100% institutional). ***Receiving aid:*** *Freshmen:* 60% (108); *Undergraduates:* 58% (256). ***Scholarships, grants, and awards by category:*** *Academic Interests/Achievement:* 265 awards ($995,000 total): business, computer science, engineering/technologies, general academic interests/achievements. *Special Achievements/Activities:* 2 awards ($25,330 total): general special achievements/activities, leadership. ***Tuition waivers:*** Full or partial for employees or children of employees, senior citizens. ***ROTC:*** Army cooperative, Air Force cooperative.

LOANS ***Student loans:*** $3,455,009 (48% need-based, 52% non-need-based). 92% of past graduating class borrowed through all loan programs. Average indebtedness per student: $20,875. ***Average need-based loan:*** Freshmen: $2625; Undergraduates: $4531. ***Parent loans:*** $2,454,146 (100% non-need-based). ***Programs:*** Federal Direct (Subsidized and Unsubsidized Stafford, PLUS), Perkins, GATE Loans.

WORK-STUDY ***Federal work-study:*** *Total amount:* $77,773; 120 jobs averaging $700. ***State or other work-study/employment:*** *Total amount:* $70,000 (100% non-need-based). 70 part-time jobs averaging $1000.

APPLYING for FINANCIAL AID ***Required financial aid forms:*** FAFSA, institution's own form. ***Financial aid deadline (priority):*** 3/1. ***Notification date:*** Continuous beginning 4/1. Students must reply within 3 weeks of notification.

CONTACT Mary Ellen Severance, Director of Financial Assistance, Daniel Webster College, 20 University Drive, Nashua, NH 03063-1300, 603-577-6590 or toll-free 800-325-6876. *Fax:* 603-577-6001. *E-mail:* severance@dwc.edu

DARKEI NOAM RABBINICAL COLLEGE

Brooklyn, NY

CONTACT Ms. Rivi Horowitz, Director of Financial Aid, Darkei Noam Rabbinical College, 2822 Avenue J, Brooklyn, NY 11219, 718-338-6464.

DARTMOUTH COLLEGE

Hanover, NH

Tuition & fees: $24,884 **Average undergraduate aid package: $23,331**

ABOUT THE INSTITUTION Independent, coed. Awards: bachelor's, master's, doctoral, and first professional degrees. 51 undergraduate majors. Total enrollment: 5,344. Undergraduates: 4,057. Freshmen: 1,054. Both federal and institutional methodology are used as a basis for awarding need-based institutional aid.

UNDERGRADUATE EXPENSES for 1999–2000 ***Application fee:*** $60. ***One-time required fee:*** $90. ***Comprehensive fee:*** $31,274 includes full-time tuition ($24,624), mandatory fees ($260), and room and board ($6390). ***College room only:*** $4230. Room and board charges vary according to board plan and housing facility. ***Payment plans:*** tuition prepayment, installment.

FRESHMAN FINANCIAL AID (Fall 1999) 644 applied for aid; of those 78% were deemed to have need. 100% of freshmen with need received aid; of those 100% had need fully met. *Average percent of need met:* 100% (excluding resources awarded to replace EFC). *Average financial aid package:* $24,081 (excluding resources awarded to replace EFC). 11% of all full-time freshmen had no need and received non-need-based aid.

UNDERGRADUATE FINANCIAL AID (Fall 1999) 2,309 applied for aid; of those 84% were deemed to have need. 100% of undergraduates with need received aid; of those 100% had need fully met. *Average percent of need met:* 100% (excluding resources awarded to replace EFC). *Average financial aid package:* $23,331 (excluding resources awarded to replace EFC). 7% of all full-time undergraduates had no need and received non-need-based aid.

GIFT AID (NEED-BASED) ***Total amount:*** $29,434,366 (10% Federal, 90% institutional). ***Receiving aid:*** *Freshmen:* 42% (446); *all full-time undergraduates:* 43% (1,728). ***Average award:*** Freshmen: $21,551; Undergraduates: $17,909. ***Scholarships, grants, and awards:*** Federal Pell, FSEOG, state, college/university gift aid from institutional funds.

GIFT AID (NON-NEED-BASED) ***Total amount:*** $2,043,110 (100% external sources). ***ROTC:*** Army.

LOANS ***Student loans:*** $7,985,670 (88% need-based, 12% non-need-based). 53% of past graduating class borrowed through all loan programs. Average indebtedness per student: $14,818. ***Average need-based loan:*** Freshmen: $3114; Undergraduates: $4262. ***Parent loans:*** $8,898,095 (100% non-need-based). ***Programs:*** FFEL (Subsidized and Unsubsidized Stafford, PLUS), Perkins, college/university.

WORK-STUDY ***Federal work-study:*** *Total amount:* $2,588,052; jobs available. ***State or other work-study/employment:*** *Total amount:* $354,291 (100% need-based). Part-time jobs available.

APPLYING for FINANCIAL AID ***Required financial aid forms:*** FAFSA, CSS Financial Aid PROFILE, noncustodial (divorced/separated) parent's statement, business/farm supplement. ***Financial aid deadline:*** 2/1. ***Notification date:*** 4/15. Students must reply by 5/1.

CONTACT Ms. Virginia S. Hazen, Director of Financial Aid, Dartmouth College, 6024 McNutt Hall, Hanover, NH 03755, 603-646-2453. *Fax:* 603-646-1414. *E-mail:* v.hazen@dartmouth.edu

DAVENPORT COLLEGE OF BUSINESS

Grand Rapids, MI

ABOUT THE INSTITUTION Independent, coed. Awards: associate, bachelor's, and master's degrees. 15 undergraduate majors. Total enrollment: 2,278. Undergraduates: 2,214. Freshmen: 333.

GIFT AID (NEED-BASED) ***Scholarships, grants, and awards:*** Federal Pell, FSEOG, state, private, college/university gift aid from institutional funds.

GIFT AID (NON-NEED-BASED) ***Scholarships, grants, and awards by category:*** *Academic Interests/Achievement:* general academic interests/achievements.

LOANS ***Programs:*** FFEL (Subsidized and Unsubsidized Stafford, PLUS), Perkins, state.

WORK-STUDY Federal work-study jobs available.

APPLYING for FINANCIAL AID ***Required financial aid form:*** FAFSA.

CONTACT Mary Kay Bethune, Vice President for Financial Aid, Davenport College of Business, 415 East Fulton Street, Grand Rapids, MI 49503, 616-732-1130 or toll-free 800-632-9569 (out-of-state). *E-mail:* marykay@davenport.edu

DAVENPORT COLLEGE OF BUSINESS, KALAMAZOO CAMPUS

Kalamazoo, MI

Tuition & fees: $8895 **Average undergraduate aid package: N/A**

ABOUT THE INSTITUTION Independent, coed. Awards: associate and bachelor's degrees and post-bachelor's certificates. 13 undergraduate majors. Total enrollment: 1,284. Undergraduates: 1,284. Freshmen: 244. Federal methodology is used as a basis for awarding need-based institutional aid.

UNDERGRADUATE EXPENSES for 1999–2000 ***Application fee:*** $25. ***Tuition:*** full-time $8820; part-time $196 per credit hour. ***Required fees:*** full-time $75; $25 per term part-time. Part-time tuition and fees vary according to program. ***Payment plans:*** installment, deferred payment.

GIFT AID (NEED-BASED) ***Total amount:*** $2,453,720 (44% Federal, 44% state, 11% institutional, 1% external sources). ***Scholarships, grants, and awards:*** Federal Pell, FSEOG, state, private, college/university gift aid from institutional funds.

GIFT AID (NON-NEED-BASED) ***Tuition waivers:*** Full or partial for employees or children of employees.

LOANS ***Student loans:*** $3,145,519 (100% need-based). ***Parent loans:*** $64,881 (100% need-based). ***Programs:*** FFEL (Subsidized and Unsubsidized Stafford, PLUS), Perkins.

WORK-STUDY ***Federal work-study:*** *Total amount:* $84,094; jobs available. ***State or other work-study/employment:*** *Total amount:* $54,184 (100% need-based). Part-time jobs available.

APPLYING for FINANCIAL AID ***Required financial aid forms:*** FAFSA, institution's own form. ***Financial aid deadline (priority):*** 2/21. ***Notification date:*** Continuous beginning 5/1.

CONTACT Ms. Linda Reischer, Director of Financial Aid, Davenport College of Business, Kalamazoo Campus, 4123 West Main Street, Kalamazoo, MI 49006-2791, 616-382-2835 Ext. 3320 or toll-free 800-632-8928 Ext. 3308 (in-state). *Fax:* 616-382-3541. *E-mail:* kzlreischer@davenport.edu

DAVENPORT COLLEGE OF BUSINESS, LANSING CAMPUS

Lansing, MI

Tuition & fees: $8111 **Average undergraduate aid package: N/A**

ABOUT THE INSTITUTION Independent, coed. Awards: associate and bachelor's degrees. 10 undergraduate majors. Total enrollment: 1,223. Undergraduates: 1,223. Freshmen: 397. Federal methodology is used as a basis for awarding need-based institutional aid.

UNDERGRADUATE EXPENSES for 1999–2000 ***Application fee:*** $25. ***Tuition:*** full-time $8036; part-time $196 per credit hour. ***Required fees:*** full-time $75; $25 per term part-time. ***Payment plan:*** installment.

GIFT AID (NEED-BASED) ***Total amount:*** $2,507,103 (43% Federal, 48% state, 7% institutional, 2% external sources). ***Scholarships, grants, and awards:*** Federal Pell, FSEOG, state, private, college/university gift aid from institutional funds.

GIFT AID (NON-NEED-BASED) ***Scholarships, grants, and awards by category:*** *Academic Interests/Achievement:* 32 awards ($42,500 total): general academic interests/achievements. ***Tuition waivers:*** Full or partial for senior citizens. ***ROTC:*** Army cooperative.

LOANS ***Student loans:*** $2,350,928 (100% need-based). 61% of past graduating class borrowed through all loan programs. Average indebtedness per student: $3280. ***Parent loans:*** $60,489 (100% need-based). ***Programs:*** FFEL (Subsidized and Unsubsidized Stafford, PLUS), Perkins, state.

WORK-STUDY ***Federal work-study:*** *Total amount:* $67,689; jobs available. ***State or other work-study/employment:*** *Total amount:* $59,728 (100% need-based). Part-time jobs available.

Davenport College of Business, Lansing Campus (continued)

APPLYING for FINANCIAL AID ***Required financial aid form:*** FAFSA. ***Financial aid deadline (priority):*** 3/15. ***Notification date:*** Continuous beginning 4/1.

CONTACT Kevin Konen, Director of Financial Aid, Davenport College of Business, Lansing Campus, 220 East Kalamazoo Street, Lansing, MI 48933-2197, 517-484-2600 or toll-free 800-331-3306 (in-state). *Fax:* 517-484-1132. *E-mail:* lakkonen@davenport.edu

DAVID LIPSCOMB UNIVERSITY

Nashville, TN

Tuition & fees: $9689 **Average undergraduate aid package: N/A**

ABOUT THE INSTITUTION Independent religious, coed. Awards: bachelor's, master's, and first professional degrees. 64 undergraduate majors. Total enrollment: 2,504. Undergraduates: 2,317. Freshmen: 598. Federal methodology is used as a basis for awarding need-based institutional aid.

UNDERGRADUATE EXPENSES for 1999–2000 ***Application fee:*** $50. ***Comprehensive fee:*** $14,033 includes full-time tuition ($9345), mandatory fees ($344), and room and board ($4344). ***College room only:*** $2184. Full-time tuition and fees vary according to degree level and location. Room and board charges vary according to board plan, housing facility, and location. ***Part-time tuition:*** $312 per hour. ***Part-time fees:*** $10 per hour; $14. Part-time tuition and fees vary according to degree level and location. ***Payment plan:*** installment.

FRESHMAN FINANCIAL AID (Fall 1999, est.) 431 applied for aid; of those 81% were deemed to have need. 95% of freshmen with need received aid; of those 95% had need fully met. *Average percent of need met:* 100% (excluding resources awarded to replace EFC). 33% of all full-time freshmen had no need and received non-need-based aid.

UNDERGRADUATE FINANCIAL AID (Fall 1999, est.) 1,280 applied for aid; of those 81% were deemed to have need. 95% of undergraduates with need received aid; of those 98% had need fully met. *Average percent of need met:* 100% (excluding resources awarded to replace EFC). 29% of all full-time undergraduates had no need and received non-need-based aid.

GIFT AID (NEED-BASED) ***Total amount:*** $3,620,365 (20% Federal, 9% state, 70% institutional, 1% external sources). ***Receiving aid:*** *Freshmen:* 39% (232); *all full-time undergraduates:* 34% (690). ***Average award:*** Freshmen: $2900; Undergraduates: $2575. ***Scholarships, grants, and awards:*** Federal Pell, FSEOG, state, private, college/university gift aid from institutional funds.

GIFT AID (NON-NEED-BASED) ***Total amount:*** $2,539,358 (1% state, 95% institutional, 4% external sources). ***Scholarships, grants, and awards by category:*** *Academic Interests/Achievement:* 1,291 awards ($3,794,000 total): general academic interests/achievements. *Creative Arts/Performance:* 66 awards ($82,000 total): art/fine arts, journalism/publications, music, theater/drama. *Special Achievements/Activities:* 135 awards ($194,000 total): cheerleading/drum major, leadership, religious involvement. *Special Characteristics:* 174 awards ($622,000 total): adult students, children of educators, children of faculty/staff, children with a deceased or disabled parent, international students, members of minority groups, relatives of clergy. ***Tuition waivers:*** Full or partial for minority students, employees or children of employees. ***ROTC:*** Army cooperative, Air Force cooperative.

LOANS ***Student loans:*** $4,376,508 (63% need-based, 37% non-need-based). 67% of past graduating class borrowed through all loan programs. Average indebtedness per student: $13,750. ***Average need-based loan:*** Freshmen: $2825; Undergraduates: $4750. ***Programs:*** FFEL (Subsidized and Unsubsidized Stafford, PLUS), Perkins, state.

WORK-STUDY ***Federal work-study:*** *Total amount:* $120,101; 115 jobs averaging $1045.

ATHLETIC AWARDS *Total amount:* 803,268 (25% need-based, 75% non-need-based).

APPLYING for FINANCIAL AID ***Required financial aid form:*** FAFSA. ***Financial aid deadline (priority):*** 2/28. ***Notification date:*** Continuous. Students must reply by 5/1 or within 2 weeks of notification.

CONTACT Mr. R. Gerald Masterson, Assistant Vice President of Student Aid Services, David Lipscomb University, 3901 Granny White Pike, Nashville, TN 37204-3951, 615-269-1791 or toll-free 800-333-4358 Ext. 1776. *Fax:* 615-386-7640. *E-mail:* jerry.masterson@lipscomb.edu

DAVID N. MYERS COLLEGE

Cleveland, OH

Tuition & fees: $8760 **Average undergraduate aid package: N/A**

ABOUT THE INSTITUTION Independent, coed. Awards: associate and bachelor's degrees. 14 undergraduate majors. Total enrollment: 1,220. Undergraduates: 1,220. Freshmen: 93. Federal methodology is used as a basis for awarding need-based institutional aid.

UNDERGRADUATE EXPENSES for 2000–2001 (est.) ***Application fee:*** $25. ***Tuition:*** full-time $8760; part-time $292 per credit. ***Payment plans:*** installment, deferred payment.

FRESHMAN FINANCIAL AID (Fall 1998) 121 applied for aid; of those 93% were deemed to have need. 100% of freshmen with need received aid. 9% of all full-time freshmen had no need and received non-need-based aid.

UNDERGRADUATE FINANCIAL AID (Fall 1998) 584 applied for aid; of those 92% were deemed to have need. 96% of undergraduates with need received aid. 4% of all full-time undergraduates had no need and received non-need-based aid.

GIFT AID (NEED-BASED) ***Total amount:*** $1,934,427 (53% Federal, 44% state, 3% institutional). ***Receiving aid:*** *Freshmen:* 66% (85); *all full-time undergraduates:* 47% (400). ***Average award:*** Freshmen: $4250; Undergraduates: $4223. ***Scholarships, grants, and awards:*** Federal Pell, FSEOG, state, private, college/university gift aid from institutional funds.

GIFT AID (NON-NEED-BASED) ***Total amount:*** $1,400,194 (30% state, 66% institutional, 4% external sources). ***Receiving aid:*** *Freshmen:* 84% (108); *Undergraduates:* 51% (429). ***Scholarships, grants, and awards by category:*** *Academic Interests/Achievement:* business, general academic interests/achievements. *Special Characteristics:* children of faculty/staff, first-generation college students, public servants, veterans, veterans' children. ***Tuition waivers:*** Full or partial for employees or children of employees.

LOANS ***Student loans:*** $1,807,944 (69% need-based, 31% non-need-based). Average indebtedness per student: $15,906. ***Average need-based loan:*** Freshmen: $1691; Undergraduates: $3430. ***Parent loans:*** $15,816 (100% non-need-based). ***Programs:*** FFEL (Subsidized and Unsubsidized Stafford, PLUS), Perkins, college/university.

WORK-STUDY ***Federal work-study:*** *Total amount:* $53,630; 31 jobs averaging $1730.

APPLYING for FINANCIAL AID ***Required financial aid form:*** FAFSA. ***Financial aid deadline (priority):*** 4/30. ***Notification date:*** Continuous beginning 5/1. Students must reply within 2 weeks of notification.

CONTACT Ms. Sandra Bolton, Director of Financial Aid, David N. Myers College, 112 Prospect Avenue, Cleveland, OH 44115-1096, 216-696-9000 Ext. 818 or toll-free 800-424-3953. *Fax:* 216-696-6430. *E-mail:* sbolton@dnmyers.edu

DAVIDSON COLLEGE

Davidson, NC

Tuition & fees: $22,228 **Average undergraduate aid package: $13,889**

ABOUT THE INSTITUTION Independent Presbyterian, coed. Awards: bachelor's degrees. 21 undergraduate majors. Total enrollment: 1,652. Undergraduates: 1,652. Freshmen: 455. Institutional methodology is used as a basis for awarding need-based institutional aid.

UNDERGRADUATE EXPENSES for 1999–2000 ***Application fee:*** $50. ***Comprehensive fee:*** $28,568 includes full-time tuition ($22,014), mandatory fees ($214), and room and board ($6340). ***College room only:*** $3352. Room and board charges vary according to board plan and housing facility. ***Payment plan:*** installment.

FRESHMAN FINANCIAL AID (Fall 1998) 246 applied for aid; of those 66% were deemed to have need. 100% of freshmen with need received aid; of those 100% had need fully met. *Average percent of need met:* 100% (excluding resources awarded to replace EFC). *Average financial aid package:* $13,555 (excluding resources awarded to replace EFC). 20% of all full-time freshmen had no need and received non-need-based aid.

UNDERGRADUATE FINANCIAL AID (Fall 1998) 650 applied for aid; of those 81% were deemed to have need. 100% of undergraduates with need received aid; of those 98% had need fully met. *Average percent of need met:* 98% (excluding resources awarded to replace EFC). *Average financial aid package:* $13,889 (excluding resources awarded to replace EFC). 20% of all full-time undergraduates had no need and received non-need-based aid.

GIFT AID (NEED-BASED) ***Total amount:*** $7,054,381 (5% Federal, 6% state, 89% institutional). ***Receiving aid:*** *Freshmen:* 30% (141); *all full-time undergraduates:* 29% (482). ***Average award:*** Freshmen: $12,477; Undergraduates: $11,773. ***Scholarships, grants, and awards:*** Federal Pell, FSEOG, state, private, college/university gift aid from institutional funds, need-linked special talent scholarships.

GIFT AID (NON-NEED-BASED) ***Total amount:*** $3,378,946 (13% Federal, 9% state, 55% institutional, 23% external sources). ***Receiving aid:*** *Freshmen:* 5% (24); *Undergraduates:* 5% (78). ***Scholarships, grants, and awards by category:*** *Academic Interests/Achievement:* 198 awards ($1,141,664 total): biological sciences, education, foreign languages, general academic interests/achievements, mathematics, physical sciences, premedicine. *Creative Arts/Performance:* 35 awards ($177,500 total): art/fine arts, creative writing, music. *Special Achievements/Activities:* 36 awards ($450,435 total): community service, general special achievements/activities, leadership, religious involvement. *Special Characteristics:* 61 awards ($523,608 total): children of faculty/staff, ethnic background, members of minority groups, relatives of clergy. ***Tuition waivers:*** Full or partial for employees or children of employees. ***ROTC:*** Army, Air Force cooperative.

LOANS ***Student loans:*** $2,376,893 (54% need-based, 46% non-need-based). Average indebtedness per student: $14,011. ***Average need-based loan:*** Freshmen: $2302; Undergraduates: $3091. ***Parent loans:*** $1,845,115 (100% non-need-based). ***Programs:*** FFEL (Subsidized and Unsubsidized Stafford, PLUS), Perkins, alternative loans.

WORK-STUDY ***Federal work-study:*** *Total amount:* $254,283; 193 jobs averaging $1318. ***State or other work-study/employment:*** *Total amount:* $279,110 (80% need-based, 20% non-need-based). 220 part-time jobs averaging $1269.

ATHLETIC AWARDS *Total amount:* 1,054,565 (100% non-need-based).

APPLYING for FINANCIAL AID ***Required financial aid forms:*** FAFSA, CSS Financial Aid PROFILE, noncustodial (divorced/separated) parent's statement, business/farm supplement. ***Financial aid deadline (priority):*** 2/15. ***Notification date:*** 4/1. Students must reply by 5/1.

CONTACT Kathleen Stevenson-McNeely, Senior Associate Dean of Admission and Financial Aid, Davidson College, 413 North Main Street, PO Box 1539, Davidson, NC 28036, 704-892-2232 or toll-free 800-768-0380. *Fax:* 704-892-2845. *E-mail:* kastevensonmcneely@davidson.edu

DAVIS & ELKINS COLLEGE

Elkins, WV

Tuition & fees: $12,280 **Average undergraduate aid package: $11,082**

ABOUT THE INSTITUTION Independent Presbyterian, coed. Awards: associate and bachelor's degrees. 52 undergraduate majors. Total enrollment: 658. Undergraduates: 658. Freshmen: 163. Federal methodology is used as a basis for awarding need-based institutional aid.

UNDERGRADUATE EXPENSES for 1999–2000 ***Application fee:*** $25. ***Comprehensive fee:*** $17,610 includes full-time tuition ($12,080), mandatory fees ($200), and room and board ($5330). ***College room only:*** $2370. ***Part-time tuition:*** $485 per credit. ***Part-time fees:*** $50 per term part-time. Part-time tuition and fees vary according to course load. ***Payment plan:*** installment.

FRESHMAN FINANCIAL AID (Fall 1999, est.) 155 applied for aid; of those 97% were deemed to have need. 100% of freshmen with need received aid; of those 76% had need fully met. *Average percent of need met:* 95% (excluding resources awarded to replace EFC). *Average financial aid package:* $9659 (excluding resources awarded to replace EFC). 9% of all full-time freshmen had no need and received non-need-based aid.

UNDERGRADUATE FINANCIAL AID (Fall 1999, est.) 570 applied for aid; of those 90% were deemed to have need. 100% of undergraduates with need received aid; of those 80% had need fully met. *Average percent of need met:* 95% (excluding resources awarded to replace EFC). *Average financial aid package:* $11,082 (excluding resources awarded to replace EFC). 7% of all full-time undergraduates had no need and received non-need-based aid.

GIFT AID (NEED-BASED) ***Total amount:*** $1,963,807 (42% Federal, 13% state, 45% institutional). ***Receiving aid:*** *Freshmen:* 80% (135); *all full-time undergraduates:* 79% (462). ***Average award:*** Freshmen: $3863; Undergraduates: $4433. ***Scholarships, grants, and awards:*** Federal Pell, FSEOG, state, private, college/university gift aid from institutional funds.

GIFT AID (NON-NEED-BASED) ***Total amount:*** $1,269,337 (1% Federal, 5% state, 89% institutional, 5% external sources). ***Receiving aid:*** *Freshmen:* 31% (52); *Undergraduates:* 31% (180). ***Scholarships, grants, and awards by category:*** *Academic Interests/Achievement:* 375 awards ($972,553 total): biological sciences, engineering/technologies, general academic interests/achievements, health fields, physical sciences, religion/biblical studies. *Creative Arts/Performance:* 63 awards ($101,385 total): art/fine arts, music, performing arts, theater/drama. *Special Achievements/Activities:* 3 awards ($7000 total): leadership. *Special Characteristics:* 12 awards ($17,024 total): local/state students, religious affiliation. ***Tuition waivers:*** Full or partial for employees or children of employees.

LOANS ***Student loans:*** $2,118,064 (66% need-based, 34% non-need-based). 85% of past graduating class borrowed through all loan programs. Average indebtedness per student: $16,000. ***Average need-based loan:*** Freshmen: $1980; Undergraduates: $3009. ***Parent loans:*** $368,843 (100% non-need-based). ***Programs:*** FFEL (Subsidized and Unsubsidized Stafford, PLUS), Perkins, college/university.

WORK-STUDY ***Federal work-study:*** *Total amount:* $229,293; 168 jobs averaging $1365. ***State or other work-study/employment:*** *Total amount:* $147,634 (100% need-based). 122 part-time jobs averaging $1210.

ATHLETIC AWARDS *Total amount:* 394,592 (100% non-need-based).

APPLYING for FINANCIAL AID ***Required financial aid form:*** FAFSA. ***Financial aid deadline (priority):*** 3/1. ***Notification date:*** Continuous. Students must reply within 2 weeks of notification.

CONTACT Kevin D. Chenoweth, Director of Financial Planning, Davis & Elkins College, 100 Campus Drive, Elkins, WV 26241-3996, 304-637-1282 or toll-free 800-624-3157. *Fax:* 304-637-1413. *E-mail:* kdc@dne.edu

DEACONESS COLLEGE OF NURSING

St. Louis, MO

Tuition & fees: $8575 **Average undergraduate aid package: $6796**

ABOUT THE INSTITUTION Proprietary, coed. Awards: associate and bachelor's degrees. 1 undergraduate major. Total enrollment: 246. Undergraduates: 246. Freshmen: 39. Both federal and institutional methodology are used as a basis for awarding need-based institutional aid.

UNDERGRADUATE EXPENSES for 1999–2000 ***Application fee:*** $30. ***Comprehensive fee:*** $12,565 includes full-time tuition ($8500), mandatory fees ($75), and room and board ($3990). Room and board charges vary according to board plan and housing facility. ***Part-time tuition:*** $330 per credit. ***Part-time fees:*** $75 per term part-time. ***Payment plans:*** installment, deferred payment.

FRESHMAN FINANCIAL AID (Fall 1998) 37 applied for aid; of those 86% were deemed to have need. 100% of freshmen with need received aid; of those 22% had need fully met. *Average percent of need met:* 59% (excluding resources awarded to replace EFC). *Average financial aid package:* $6703 (excluding resources awarded to replace EFC). 20% of all full-time freshmen had no need and received non-need-based aid.

UNDERGRADUATE FINANCIAL AID (Fall 1998) 144 applied for aid; of those 91% were deemed to have need. 100% of undergraduates with need received aid; of those 17% had need fully met. *Average percent of*

Deaconess College of Nursing (continued)

need met: 60% (excluding resources awarded to replace EFC). *Average financial aid package:* $6796 (excluding resources awarded to replace EFC). 13% of all full-time undergraduates had no need and received non-need-based aid.

GIFT AID (NEED-BASED) ***Total amount:*** $381,392 (51% Federal, 18% state, 25% institutional, 6% external sources). ***Receiving aid:*** *Freshmen:* 57% (23); *all full-time undergraduates:* 50% (87). ***Average award:*** Freshmen: $2639; Undergraduates: $2973. ***Scholarships, grants, and awards:*** Federal Pell, FSEOG, college/university gift aid from institutional funds.

GIFT AID (NON-NEED-BASED) ***Total amount:*** $234,093 (78% institutional, 22% external sources). ***Receiving aid:*** *Freshmen:* 12% (5); *Undergraduates:* 28% (49). ***Scholarships, grants, and awards by category:*** *Academic Interests/Achievement:* 80 awards ($173,500 total): general academic interests/achievements, health fields. *Special Achievements/Activities:* 1 award ($8100 total): leadership.

LOANS ***Student loans:*** $1,101,250 (57% need-based, 43% non-need-based). 90% of past graduating class borrowed through all loan programs. ***Average need-based loan:*** Freshmen: $2254; Undergraduates: $3433. ***Parent loans:*** $163,876 (100% non-need-based). ***Programs:*** FFEL (Subsidized and Unsubsidized Stafford, PLUS).

WORK-STUDY ***Federal work-study:*** *Total amount:* $19,923; 15 jobs averaging $1328.

APPLYING for FINANCIAL AID ***Required financial aid forms:*** FAFSA, institution's own form. ***Financial aid deadline (priority):*** 4/1. ***Notification date:*** Continuous. Students must reply within 2 weeks of notification.

CONTACT Ms. Carrie Nelson, Student Financial Aid Counselor, Deaconess College of Nursing, 6150 Oakland Avenue, St. Louis, MO 63139-3215, 314-768-5604 or toll-free 800-942-4310. *E-mail:* carrie.nelson@tenethealth.com

DEFIANCE COLLEGE

Defiance, OH

Tuition & fees: $14,550 **Average undergraduate aid package: N/A**

ABOUT THE INSTITUTION Independent religious, coed. Awards: associate, bachelor's, and master's degrees. 44 undergraduate majors. Total enrollment: 1,040. Undergraduates: 833. Freshmen: 179. Federal methodology is used as a basis for awarding need-based institutional aid.

UNDERGRADUATE EXPENSES for 1999–2000 ***Application fee:*** $25. ***Comprehensive fee:*** $18,780 includes full-time tuition ($14,350), mandatory fees ($200), and room and board ($4230). ***Part-time tuition:*** $260 per semester hour. ***Part-time fees:*** $25 per term. ***Payment plan:*** installment.

FRESHMAN FINANCIAL AID (Fall 1998) 157 applied for aid; of those 88% were deemed to have need. 100% of freshmen with need received aid. 12% of all full-time freshmen had no need and received non-need-based aid.

UNDERGRADUATE FINANCIAL AID (Fall 1998) 572 applied for aid; of those 92% were deemed to have need. 100% of undergraduates with need received aid. 8% of all full-time undergraduates had no need and received non-need-based aid.

GIFT AID (NEED-BASED) ***Total amount:*** $1,482,481 (38% Federal, 11% state, 51% institutional). ***Scholarships, grants, and awards:*** Federal Pell, FSEOG, state, private, college/university gift aid from institutional funds.

GIFT AID (NON-NEED-BASED) ***Total amount:*** $2,892,915 (15% state, 81% institutional, 4% external sources). ***Scholarships, grants, and awards by category:*** *Academic Interests/Achievement:* biological sciences, business, communication, computer science, education, general academic interests/achievements, humanities, mathematics, physical sciences, premedicine, religion/biblical studies, social sciences. *Creative Arts/Performance:* music, theater/drama. *Special Achievements/Activities:* community service, general special achievements/activities, leadership, religious involvement. *Special Characteristics:* children of faculty/staff, children with a deceased or disabled parent, first-generation college students, general special characteristics, local/state students, members of minority groups, out-of-state students, previous college experience, relatives of clergy, religious affiliation. ***Tuition waivers:*** Full or partial for employees or children of employees, senior citizens.

LOANS ***Student loans:*** $3,492,758 (78% need-based, 22% non-need-based). 71% of past graduating class borrowed through all loan programs. Average indebtedness per student: $14,303. ***Parent loans:*** $523,951 (100% non-need-based). ***Programs:*** FFEL (Subsidized and Unsubsidized Stafford, PLUS), Perkins, alternative loans.

WORK-STUDY ***Federal work-study:*** *Total amount:* $55,236; 107 jobs averaging $516. ***State or other work-study/employment:*** *Total amount:* $165,501 (100% non-need-based). 216 part-time jobs averaging $766.

APPLYING for FINANCIAL AID ***Required financial aid form:*** FAFSA. ***Financial aid deadline (priority):*** 3/1. ***Notification date:*** Continuous. Students must reply within 3 weeks of notification.

CONTACT Ms. Amy Francis, Director of Financial Aid, Defiance College, 701 North Clinton Street, Defiance, OH 43512-1610, 419-784-4010 Ext. 376 or toll-free 800-520-4632 Ext. 2359.

DELAWARE STATE UNIVERSITY

Dover, DE

Tuition & fees (DE res): $3256 **Average undergraduate aid package: $5745**

ABOUT THE INSTITUTION State-supported, coed. Awards: bachelor's and master's degrees. 66 undergraduate majors. Total enrollment: 3,159. Undergraduates: 2,910. Freshmen: 684. Federal methodology is used as a basis for awarding need-based institutional aid.

UNDERGRADUATE EXPENSES for 1999–2000 ***Application fee:*** $10. ***Tuition, state resident:*** full-time $3096; part-time $129 per credit hour. ***Tuition, nonresident:*** full-time $7088; part-time $295 per credit hour. ***Required fees:*** full-time $160; $40 per term part-time. ***College room and board:*** $4880. Room and board charges vary according to housing facility. ***Payment plans:*** installment, deferred payment.

FRESHMAN FINANCIAL AID (Fall 1998) 513 applied for aid; of those 89% were deemed to have need. 98% of freshmen with need received aid; of those 37% had need fully met. *Average percent of need met:* 65% (excluding resources awarded to replace EFC). *Average financial aid package:* $5012 (excluding resources awarded to replace EFC).

UNDERGRADUATE FINANCIAL AID (Fall 1998) 1,855 applied for aid; of those 89% were deemed to have need. 98% of undergraduates with need received aid; of those 44% had need fully met. *Average percent of need met:* 73% (excluding resources awarded to replace EFC). *Average financial aid package:* $5745 (excluding resources awarded to replace EFC).

GIFT AID (NEED-BASED) ***Total amount:*** $5,834,260 (53% Federal, 4% state, 27% institutional, 16% external sources). ***Receiving aid:*** *Freshmen:* 54% (313); *all full-time undergraduates:* 49% (1,107). ***Scholarships, grants, and awards:*** Federal Pell, FSEOG, state, private, college/university gift aid from institutional funds.

GIFT AID (NON-NEED-BASED) ***Receiving aid:*** *Freshmen:* 29% (166); *Undergraduates:* 21% (483). ***Scholarships, grants, and awards by category:*** *Academic Interests/Achievement:* general academic interests/achievements. *Creative Arts/Performance:* music. *Special Characteristics:* out-of-state students. ***Tuition waivers:*** Full or partial for employees or children of employees, senior citizens. ***ROTC:*** Army, Air Force.

LOANS ***Student loans:*** $9,789,882 (100% need-based). ***Parent loans:*** $3,703,583 (100% need-based). ***Programs:*** FFEL (Subsidized and Unsubsidized Stafford, PLUS), Perkins, college/university.

WORK-STUDY ***Federal work-study:*** *Total amount:* $144,526; jobs available. ***State or other work-study/employment:*** *Total amount:* $73,947 (100% non-need-based). Part-time jobs available.

ATHLETIC AWARDS *Total amount:* 1,099,587 (100% need-based).

APPLYING for FINANCIAL AID ***Required financial aid form:*** FAFSA. ***Financial aid deadline (priority):*** 2/1. ***Notification date:*** Continuous beginning 3/1.

CONTACT Ms. Martha M. Hopkins, Associate Director of Financial Aid, Delaware State University, Grossley Hall, 1200 North DuPont Highway, Dover, DE 19901-2277, 302-857-7352.

DELAWARE VALLEY COLLEGE

Doylestown, PA

Tuition & fees: $15,687 **Average undergraduate aid package: $13,935**

ABOUT THE INSTITUTION Independent, coed. Awards: associate, bachelor's, and master's degrees. 26 undergraduate majors. Total enrollment: 1,916. Undergraduates: 1,890. Freshmen: 323. Federal methodology is used as a basis for awarding need-based institutional aid.

UNDERGRADUATE EXPENSES for 1999–2000 ***Application fee:*** $35. ***One-time required fee:*** $125. ***Comprehensive fee:*** $21,687 includes full-time tuition ($15,419), mandatory fees ($268), and room and board ($6000). ***College room only:*** $2687. Room and board charges vary according to board plan. ***Part-time tuition:*** $375 per credit. Part-time tuition and fees vary according to class time and student level. ***Payment plan:*** installment.

FRESHMAN FINANCIAL AID (Fall 1999) 280 applied for aid; of those 92% were deemed to have need. 100% of freshmen with need received aid; of those 42% had need fully met. *Average percent of need met:* 82% (excluding resources awarded to replace EFC). *Average financial aid package:* $14,235 (excluding resources awarded to replace EFC). 20% of all full-time freshmen had no need and received non-need-based aid.

UNDERGRADUATE FINANCIAL AID (Fall 1999) 1,173 applied for aid; of those 93% were deemed to have need. 100% of undergraduates with need received aid; of those 34% had need fully met. *Average percent of need met:* 76% (excluding resources awarded to replace EFC). *Average financial aid package:* $13,935 (excluding resources awarded to replace EFC). 18% of all full-time undergraduates had no need and received non-need-based aid.

GIFT AID (NEED-BASED) ***Total amount:*** $8,406,606 (11% Federal, 16% state, 71% institutional, 2% external sources). ***Receiving aid:*** *Freshmen:* 69% (226); *all full-time undergraduates:* 74% (1,003). ***Average award:*** Freshmen: $10,680; Undergraduates: $9367. ***Scholarships, grants, and awards:*** Federal Pell, FSEOG, state, private, college/university gift aid from institutional funds.

GIFT AID (NON-NEED-BASED) ***Total amount:*** $1,449,800 (89% institutional, 11% external sources). ***Receiving aid:*** *Freshmen:* 25% (82); *Undergraduates:* 21% (283). ***Scholarships, grants, and awards by category:*** *Academic Interests/Achievement:* 210 awards ($1,296,000 total): agriculture, biological sciences, business, computer science, education, English, general academic interests/achievements, mathematics, premedicine, social sciences. *Special Characteristics:* 6 awards ($91,800 total): children of educators, children of faculty/staff. ***Tuition waivers:*** Full or partial for employees or children of employees.

LOANS ***Student loans:*** $4,701,673 (73% need-based, 27% non-need-based). ***Average need-based loan:*** Freshmen: $2148; Undergraduates: $3092. ***Parent loans:*** $2,396,648 (43% need-based, 57% non-need-based). ***Programs:*** FFEL (Subsidized and Unsubsidized Stafford, PLUS), Perkins.

WORK-STUDY ***Federal work-study:*** *Total amount:* $210,000; 156 jobs averaging $1500. ***State or other work-study/employment:*** *Total amount:* $295,000 (78% need-based, 22% non-need-based). 201 part-time jobs averaging $1480.

APPLYING for FINANCIAL AID ***Required financial aid forms:*** FAFSA, state aid form. ***Financial aid deadline (priority):*** 4/1. ***Notification date:*** Continuous. Students must reply within 4 weeks of notification.

CONTACT Mr. Robert Sauer, Director of Student Financial Aid, Delaware Valley College, 700 East Butler Avenue, Doylestown, PA 18901-2697, 215-489-2297 or toll-free 800-2DELVAL (in-state). *Fax:* 215-489-4959. *E-mail:* sauerr@delvalcol.edu

DELTA STATE UNIVERSITY

Cleveland, MS

Tuition & fees (MS res): $2596 **Average undergraduate aid package: N/A**

ABOUT THE INSTITUTION State-supported, coed. Awards: bachelor's, master's, and doctoral degrees. 48 undergraduate majors. Total enrollment: 4,027. Undergraduates: 3,469. Freshmen: 465. Federal methodology is used as a basis for awarding need-based institutional aid.

UNDERGRADUATE EXPENSES for 1999–2000 ***Tuition, state resident:*** full-time $2596; part-time $91 per semester hour. ***Tuition, nonresident:*** full-time $5546; part-time $214 per semester hour. ***College room and board:*** $2730. ***Payment plan:*** installment.

FRESHMAN FINANCIAL AID (Fall 1999) 349 applied for aid.

UNDERGRADUATE FINANCIAL AID (Fall 1999) 2,367 applied for aid.

GIFT AID (NEED-BASED) ***Total amount:*** $3,344,495 (98% Federal, 2% state). ***Scholarships, grants, and awards:*** Federal Pell, FSEOG, state, private, college/university gift aid from institutional funds.

GIFT AID (NON-NEED-BASED) ***Total amount:*** $4,196,582 (49% state, 46% institutional, 5% external sources). ***Scholarships, grants, and awards by category:*** *Academic Interests/Achievement:* 522 awards ($432,573 total): biological sciences, general academic interests/achievements. *Creative Arts/Performance:* 256 awards ($391,018 total): art/fine arts, journalism/publications, music, performing arts. *Special Achievements/Activities:* 761 awards ($712,118 total): cheerleading/drum major, general special achievements/activities, leadership, memberships. *Special Characteristics:* 511 awards ($747,636 total): children and siblings of alumni, children of faculty/staff, general special characteristics, out-of-state students. ***Tuition waivers:*** Full or partial for children of alumni, employees or children of employees, senior citizens. ***ROTC:*** Air Force.

LOANS ***Student loans:*** $6,715,684 (70% need-based, 30% non-need-based). 75% of past graduating class borrowed through all loan programs. Average indebtedness per student: $12,900. ***Parent loans:*** $153,997 (100% non-need-based). ***Programs:*** FFEL (Subsidized and Unsubsidized Stafford, PLUS), Perkins, college/university.

WORK-STUDY ***Federal work-study:*** *Total amount:* $429,115; 305 jobs averaging $1450.

ATHLETIC AWARDS *Total amount:* 482,243 (100% non-need-based).

APPLYING for FINANCIAL AID ***Required financial aid forms:*** FAFSA, institution's own form. ***Financial aid deadline (priority):*** 5/1. ***Notification date:*** Continuous beginning 6/1. Students must reply within 4 weeks of notification.

CONTACT Ms. Ann Margaret Mullins, Director of Financial Aid, Delta State University, PO Box 3154, Cleveland, MS 38733-0001, 601-846-4670 or toll-free 800-468-6378. *Fax:* 601-846-4683. *E-mail:* amullins@dsu.deltast.edu

DENISON UNIVERSITY

Granville, OH

Tuition & fees: $22,210 **Average undergraduate aid package: $9772**

ABOUT THE INSTITUTION Independent, coed. Awards: bachelor's degrees. 38 undergraduate majors. Total enrollment: 2,089. Undergraduates: 2,089. Freshmen: 587. Federal methodology is used as a basis for awarding need-based institutional aid.

UNDERGRADUATE EXPENSES for 2000–2001 ***Application fee:*** $40. ***Comprehensive fee:*** $28,510 includes full-time tuition ($21,710), mandatory fees ($500), and room and board ($6300). Room and board charges vary according to housing facility. ***Part-time tuition:*** $678 per credit hour. Part-time tuition and fees vary according to course load. ***Payment plans:*** tuition prepayment, installment.

FRESHMAN FINANCIAL AID (Fall 1999, est.) 383 applied for aid; of those 81% were deemed to have need. 100% of freshmen with need received aid; of those 73% had need fully met. *Average percent of need met:* 97% (excluding resources awarded to replace EFC). *Average financial aid package:* $9069 (excluding resources awarded to replace EFC). 44% of all full-time freshmen had no need and received non-need-based aid.

UNDERGRADUATE FINANCIAL AID (Fall 1999, est.) 1,197 applied for aid; of those 84% were deemed to have need. 100% of undergraduates with need received aid; of those 72% had need fully met. *Average percent of need met:* 98% (excluding resources awarded to replace EFC). *Average*

Denison University (continued)

financial aid package: $9772 (excluding resources awarded to replace EFC). 49% of all full-time undergraduates had no need and received non-need-based aid.

GIFT AID (NEED-BASED) ***Total amount:*** $13,515,985 (4% Federal, 2% state, 94% institutional). ***Receiving aid:*** *Freshmen:* 43% (255); *all full-time undergraduates:* 41% (855). ***Average award:*** Freshmen: $11,025; Undergraduates: $11,417. ***Scholarships, grants, and awards:*** Federal Pell, FSEOG, state, private, college/university gift aid from institutional funds.

GIFT AID (NON-NEED-BASED) ***Total amount:*** $10,524,582 (1% Federal, 10% state, 84% institutional, 5% external sources). ***Receiving aid:*** *Freshmen:* 49% (289); *Undergraduates:* 45% (935). ***Scholarships, grants, and awards by category:*** *Academic Interests/Achievement:* biological sciences, communication, English, foreign languages, general academic interests/achievements, humanities, physical sciences. *Creative Arts/Performance:* art/fine arts, dance, music, theater/drama. *Special Achievements/Activities:* leadership. *Special Characteristics:* members of minority groups. ***Tuition waivers:*** Full or partial for employees or children of employees.

LOANS ***Student loans:*** $4,499,030 (62% need-based, 38% non-need-based). 55% of past graduating class borrowed through all loan programs. Average indebtedness per student: $14,021. ***Average need-based loan:*** Freshmen: $2642; Undergraduates: $3394. ***Parent loans:*** $1,391,687 (100% non-need-based). ***Programs:*** Federal Direct (Subsidized and Unsubsidized Stafford, PLUS), Perkins, college/university.

WORK-STUDY ***Federal work-study:*** *Total amount:* $959,837; 545 jobs averaging $1761. ***State or other work-study/employment:*** *Total amount:* $1,431,815 (100% non-need-based). 769 part-time jobs averaging $1862.

APPLYING for FINANCIAL AID ***Required financial aid form:*** FAFSA. ***Financial aid deadline (priority):*** 2/15. ***Notification date:*** 3/31. Students must reply by 5/1.

CONTACT Ms. Nancy Hoover, Director of Financial Aid, Denison University, PO Box M, Granville, OH 43023-0613, 740-587-6279 or toll-free 800-DENISON. *Fax:* 740-587-5706.

DENVER INSTITUTE OF TECHNOLOGY

Denver, CO

See Westwood College of Technology

DENVER TECHNICAL COLLEGE

Denver, CO

CONTACT Financial Aid Office, Denver Technical College, 925 South Niagara Street, Denver, CO 80224-1658, 303-329-3340. *Fax:* 303-321-3412.

DENVER TECHNICAL COLLEGE AT COLORADO SPRINGS

Colorado Springs, CO

CONTACT Financial Aid Office, Denver Technical College at Colorado Springs, 225 South Union Boulevard, Colorado Springs, CO 80910-3138, 719-632-3000.

DEPAUL UNIVERSITY

Chicago, IL

Tuition & fees: $14,700 **Average undergraduate aid package: $12,480**

ABOUT THE INSTITUTION Independent Roman Catholic, coed. Awards: bachelor's, master's, doctoral, and first professional degrees and post-bachelor's and post-master's certificates. 96 undergraduate majors. Total enrollment: 19,549. Undergraduates: 11,776. Freshmen: 1,750. Federal methodology is used as a basis for awarding need-based institutional aid.

UNDERGRADUATE EXPENSES for 1999–2000 ***Application fee:*** $25. ***Comprehensive fee:*** $21,000 includes full-time tuition ($14,670), mandatory fees ($30), and room and board ($6300). ***College room only:*** $4680. Full-time tuition and fees vary according to program. Room and board charges vary according to board plan and housing facility. ***Part-time tuition:*** $294 per quarter hour. ***Part-time fees:*** $10 per term part-time. Part-time tuition and fees vary according to program. ***Payment plans:*** installment, deferred payment.

FRESHMAN FINANCIAL AID (Fall 1998) 1457 applied for aid; of those 85% were deemed to have need. 100% of freshmen with need received aid. *Average percent of need met:* 65% (excluding resources awarded to replace EFC). *Average financial aid package:* $14,000 (excluding resources awarded to replace EFC). 10% of all full-time freshmen had no need and received non-need-based aid.

UNDERGRADUATE FINANCIAL AID (Fall 1998) 6,485 applied for aid; of those 90% were deemed to have need. 100% of undergraduates with need received aid. *Average percent of need met:* 67% (excluding resources awarded to replace EFC). *Average financial aid package:* $12,480 (excluding resources awarded to replace EFC). 7% of all full-time undergraduates had no need and received non-need-based aid.

GIFT AID (NEED-BASED) ***Total amount:*** $34,200,000 (17% Federal, 41% state, 42% institutional). ***Receiving aid:*** *Freshmen:* 62% (1,056); *all full-time undergraduates:* 61% (4,675). ***Average award:*** Freshmen: $9200; Undergraduates: $7475. ***Scholarships, grants, and awards:*** Federal Pell, FSEOG, state, private, college/university gift aid from institutional funds.

GIFT AID (NON-NEED-BASED) ***Total amount:*** $7,400,000 (91% institutional, 9% external sources). ***Receiving aid:*** *Freshmen:* 26% (448); *Undergraduates:* 24% (1,790). ***Scholarships, grants, and awards by category:*** *Academic Interests/Achievement:* biological sciences, business, computer science, education, general academic interests/achievements. *Creative Arts/Performance:* art/fine arts, debating, music, performing arts, theater/drama. *Special Achievements/Activities:* community service. *Special Characteristics:* children of faculty/staff. ***Tuition waivers:*** Full or partial for employees or children of employees. ***ROTC:*** Army.

LOANS ***Student loans:*** $33,000,000 (82% need-based, 18% non-need-based). 76% of past graduating class borrowed through all loan programs. Average indebtedness per student: $16,700. ***Average need-based loan:*** Freshmen: $3440; Undergraduates: $5250. ***Parent loans:*** $6,300,000 (100% non-need-based). ***Programs:*** Federal Direct (Subsidized and Unsubsidized Stafford, PLUS), Perkins.

WORK-STUDY ***Federal work-study:*** *Total amount:* $1,000,000; 649 jobs averaging $1540. ***State or other work-study/employment:*** *Total amount:* $3,700,000 (32% need-based, 68% non-need-based). 1,821 part-time jobs averaging $2032.

ATHLETIC AWARDS *Total amount:* 2,200,000 (100% non-need-based).

APPLYING for FINANCIAL AID ***Required financial aid form:*** FAFSA. ***Financial aid deadline:*** 5/1 (priority: 4/1). ***Notification date:*** Continuous. Students must reply within 4 weeks of notification.

CONTACT Christopher Rone, Financial Aid Officer, DePaul University, 1 East Jackson Boulevard, Suite 9000, Chicago, IL 60604-2287, 312-362-8091 or toll-free 800-4DE-PAUL (out-of-state). *Fax:* 312-362-8091.

DEPAUW UNIVERSITY

Greencastle, IN

Tuition & fees: $19,730 **Average undergraduate aid package: $17,960**

ABOUT THE INSTITUTION Independent religious, coed. Awards: bachelor's degrees. 41 undergraduate majors. Total enrollment: 2,216. Undergraduates: 2,216. Freshmen: 581. Both federal and institutional methodology are used as a basis for awarding need-based institutional aid.

UNDERGRADUATE EXPENSES for 1999–2000 ***Application fee:*** $40. ***Comprehensive fee:*** $25,810 includes full-time tuition ($19,420), mandatory fees ($310), and room and board ($6080). ***Part-time tuition:*** $607 per semester hour. ***Payment plans:*** tuition prepayment, installment, deferred payment.

FRESHMAN FINANCIAL AID (Fall 1999) 469 applied for aid; of those 77% were deemed to have need. 100% of freshmen with need received aid; of those 100% had need fully met. *Average percent of need met:* 100% (excluding resources awarded to replace EFC). *Average financial aid pack-*

age: $19,570 (excluding resources awarded to replace EFC). 38% of all full-time freshmen had no need and received non-need-based aid.

UNDERGRADUATE FINANCIAL AID (Fall 1999) 1,373 applied for aid; of those 84% were deemed to have need. 100% of undergraduates with need received aid; of those 100% had need fully met. *Average percent of need met:* 100% (excluding resources awarded to replace EFC). *Average financial aid package:* $17,960 (excluding resources awarded to replace EFC). 47% of all full-time undergraduates had no need and received non-need-based aid.

GIFT AID (NEED-BASED) ***Total amount:*** $14,714,967 (5% Federal, 10% state, 85% institutional). ***Receiving aid:*** *Freshmen:* 44% (258); *all full-time undergraduates:* 40% (867). ***Average award:*** Freshmen: $16,348; Undergraduates: $14,601. ***Scholarships, grants, and awards:*** Federal Pell, FSEOG, state, private, college/university gift aid from institutional funds.

GIFT AID (NON-NEED-BASED) ***Total amount:*** $9,452,466 (1% Federal, 88% institutional, 11% external sources). ***Receiving aid:*** *Freshmen:* 58% (335); *Undergraduates:* 45% (978). ***Scholarships, grants, and awards by category:*** *Academic Interests/Achievement:* 1,696 awards ($11,964,274 total): biological sciences, business, communication, computer science, general academic interests/achievements, humanities, mathematics, physical sciences. *Creative Arts/Performance:* 170 awards ($705,276 total): art/fine arts, cinema/film/broadcasting, debating, journalism/publications, music, theater/drama. *Special Achievements/Activities:* 101 awards ($1,032,115 total): community service, leadership. *Special Characteristics:* 310 awards ($1,619,244 total): children and siblings of alumni, children of faculty/staff, ethnic background, international students, members of minority groups, relatives of clergy, religious affiliation. ***Tuition waivers:*** Full or partial for employees or children of employees. ***ROTC:*** Army cooperative, Air Force cooperative.

LOANS ***Student loans:*** $3,341,865 (97% need-based, 3% non-need-based). 54% of past graduating class borrowed through all loan programs. Average indebtedness per student: $13,218. ***Average need-based loan:*** Freshmen: $2897; Undergraduates: $3172. ***Parent loans:*** $1,699,357 (61% need-based, 39% non-need-based). ***Programs:*** FFEL (Subsidized and Unsubsidized Stafford, PLUS), Perkins, college/university, alternative loans.

WORK-STUDY ***Federal work-study:*** *Total amount:* $1,043,404; jobs available. ***State or other work-study/employment:*** *Total amount:* $38,800 (49% need-based, 51% non-need-based). 732 part-time jobs available.

APPLYING for FINANCIAL AID ***Required financial aid forms:*** FAFSA, institution's own form. ***Financial aid deadline (priority):*** 2/15. ***Notification date:*** Continuous. Students must reply by 5/1.

CONTACT Joanne L. Haymaker, Associate Director of Financial Aid, DePauw University, 313 South Locust Street, Greencastle, IN 46135-0037, 765-658-4030 or toll-free 800-447-2495. *Fax:* 765-658-4177. *E-mail:* jhaymaker@depauw.edu

DESIGN INSTITUTE OF SAN DIEGO

San Diego, CA

Tuition & fees: $10,200 **Average undergraduate aid package: N/A**

ABOUT THE INSTITUTION Proprietary, coed. Awards: bachelor's degrees. 1 undergraduate major. Total enrollment: 261. Undergraduates: 261.

UNDERGRADUATE EXPENSES for 1999–2000 ***Application fee:*** $25. ***Tuition:*** full-time $10,200; part-time $425 per credit. ***Payment plan:*** installment.

GIFT AID (NEED-BASED) ***Scholarships, grants, and awards:*** Federal Pell, FSEOG, state.

LOANS ***Programs:*** Federal Direct (Subsidized and Unsubsidized Stafford).

WORK-STUDY Federal work-study jobs available.

APPLYING for FINANCIAL AID ***Required financial aid form:*** FAFSA. ***Financial aid deadline:*** Continuous.

CONTACT Ms. Jackie Brewer, Director of Financial Aid, Design Institute of San Diego, 8555 Commerce Avenue, San Diego, CA 92121, 858-566-1200 or toll-free 800-619-4DESIGN (out-of-state).

DETROIT COLLEGE OF BUSINESS

Dearborn, MI

Tuition & fees: $6768 **Average undergraduate aid package: $6786**

ABOUT THE INSTITUTION Independent, coed. Awards: associate, bachelor's, and master's degrees. 14 undergraduate majors. Total enrollment: 3,181. Undergraduates: 2,986. Freshmen: 339. Federal methodology is used as a basis for awarding need-based institutional aid.

UNDERGRADUATE EXPENSES for 1999–2000 ***Application fee:*** $20. ***Tuition:*** full-time $6768; part-time $188 per quarter hour. Full-time tuition and fees vary according to course load and location. Part-time tuition and fees vary according to course load and location. ***Payment plans:*** installment, deferred payment.

FRESHMAN FINANCIAL AID (Fall 1998) 386 applied for aid; of those 98% were deemed to have need. 99% of freshmen with need received aid; of those 9% had need fully met. *Average percent of need met:* 38% (excluding resources awarded to replace EFC). *Average financial aid package:* $6497 (excluding resources awarded to replace EFC). 6% of all full-time freshmen had no need and received non-need-based aid.

UNDERGRADUATE FINANCIAL AID (Fall 1998) 1,387 applied for aid; of those 98% were deemed to have need. 99% of undergraduates with need received aid; of those 7% had need fully met. *Average percent of need met:* 37% (excluding resources awarded to replace EFC). *Average financial aid package:* $6786 (excluding resources awarded to replace EFC). 6% of all full-time undergraduates had no need and received non-need-based aid.

GIFT AID (NEED-BASED) ***Total amount:*** $5,896,759 (46% Federal, 52% state, 1% institutional, 1% external sources). ***Receiving aid:*** *Freshmen:* 87% (372); *all full-time undergraduates:* 86% (1,332). ***Average award:*** Freshmen: $4760; Undergraduates: $4070. ***Scholarships, grants, and awards:*** Federal Pell, FSEOG, state, private, college/university gift aid from institutional funds.

GIFT AID (NON-NEED-BASED) ***Total amount:*** $613,784 (100% institutional). ***Receiving aid:*** *Freshmen:* 25% (108); *Undergraduates:* 22% (334). ***Scholarships, grants, and awards by category:*** *Academic Interests/Achievement:* 209 awards ($340,554 total): business, computer science, general academic interests/achievements. *Special Characteristics:* 239 awards ($211,071 total): adult students, children and siblings of alumni, children of faculty/staff, children of public servants, general special characteristics, local/state students. ***Tuition waivers:*** Full or partial for children of alumni, employees or children of employees.

LOANS ***Student loans:*** $6,362,914 (100% need-based). 48% of past graduating class borrowed through all loan programs. Average indebtedness per student: $5789. ***Average need-based loan:*** Freshmen: $2625; Undergraduates: $3859. ***Parent loans:*** $85,478 (100% non-need-based). ***Programs:*** FFEL (Subsidized and Unsubsidized Stafford, PLUS).

WORK-STUDY ***Federal work-study:*** *Total amount:* $94,200; 51 jobs averaging $1847. ***State or other work-study/employment:*** *Total amount:* $226,563 (98% need-based, 2% non-need-based). 79 part-time jobs averaging $2807.

APPLYING for FINANCIAL AID ***Required financial aid forms:*** FAFSA, institution's own form. ***Financial aid deadline (priority):*** 3/21. ***Notification date:*** Continuous beginning 5/1. Students must reply within 4 weeks of notification.

CONTACT Zena Skinner, Director of Financial Aid, Detroit College of Business, 4801 Oakman Boulevard, Dearborn, MI 48126-3799, 313-581-4400. *Fax:* 313-581-1985. *E-mail:* dbazskinner@dcb.edu

DETROIT COLLEGE OF BUSINESS–FLINT

Flint, MI

Tuition & fees: $5004 **Average undergraduate aid package: N/A**

ABOUT THE INSTITUTION Independent, coed. Awards: associate and bachelor's degrees. 9 undergraduate majors. Total enrollment: 957. Undergraduates: 946. Freshmen: 144. Federal methodology is used as a basis for awarding need-based institutional aid.

Detroit College of Business–Flint (continued)

UNDERGRADUATE EXPENSES for 1999–2000 ***Application fee:*** $20. ***Tuition:*** full-time $5004; part-time $139 per quarter hour. Full-time tuition and fees vary according to location. Part-time tuition and fees vary according to location. ***Payment plans:*** installment, deferred payment.

FRESHMAN FINANCIAL AID (Fall 1998) 139 applied for aid; of those 98% were deemed to have need. 99% of freshmen with need received aid; of those 9% had need fully met. *Average percent of need met:* 14% (excluding resources awarded to replace EFC). 7% of all full-time freshmen had no need and received non-need-based aid.

UNDERGRADUATE FINANCIAL AID (Fall 1998) 499 applied for aid; of those 98% were deemed to have need. 99% of undergraduates with need received aid; of those 7% had need fully met. *Average percent of need met:* 13% (excluding resources awarded to replace EFC). 6% of all full-time undergraduates had no need and received non-need-based aid.

GIFT AID (NEED-BASED) ***Total amount:*** $2,122,833 (46% Federal, 52% state, 1% institutional, 1% external sources). ***Receiving aid:*** *Freshmen:* 88% (134); *all full-time undergraduates:* 86% (480). ***Average award:*** Freshmen: $3046; Undergraduates: $3460. ***Scholarships, grants, and awards:*** Federal Pell, FSEOG, state, private, college/university gift aid from institutional funds.

GIFT AID (NON-NEED-BASED) ***Total amount:*** $141,170 (100% institutional). ***Receiving aid:*** *Freshmen:* 25% (39); *Undergraduates:* 22% (120). ***Scholarships, grants, and awards by category:*** *Academic Interests/Achievement:* business, general academic interests/achievements. *Special Characteristics:* adult students, children and siblings of alumni, children of public servants, general special characteristics, local/state students. ***Tuition waivers:*** Full or partial for children of alumni, employees or children of employees.

LOANS ***Student loans:*** $2,036,132 (100% need-based). 48% of past graduating class borrowed through all loan programs. Average indebtedness per student: $5789. ***Average need-based loan:*** Freshmen: $1500; Undergraduates: $1889. ***Parent loans:*** $30,772 (100% non-need-based). ***Programs:*** FFEL (Subsidized and Unsubsidized Stafford, PLUS).

WORK-STUDY ***Federal work-study:*** *Total amount:* $33,912; 51 jobs averaging $665. ***State or other work-study/employment:*** *Total amount:* $81,562 (98% need-based, 2% non-need-based). 79 part-time jobs averaging $1032.

APPLYING for FINANCIAL AID ***Required financial aid forms:*** FAFSA, institution's own form. ***Financial aid deadline (priority):*** 3/21. ***Notification date:*** Continuous beginning 5/1. Students must reply within 4 weeks of notification.

CONTACT Ms. Rita Miller, Director of Financial Aid, Detroit College of Business–Flint, 3488 North Jennings Road, Flint, MI 48504-1700, 810-789-2200 or toll-free 800-727-1443 (in-state). *Fax:* 810-789-2266. *E-mail:* flrmiller@dcb.edu

DETROIT COLLEGE OF BUSINESS, WARREN CAMPUS

Warren, MI

Tuition & fees: $6768 **Average undergraduate aid package: $6315**

ABOUT THE INSTITUTION Independent, coed. Awards: associate, bachelor's, and master's degrees. 12 undergraduate majors. Total enrollment: 2,088. Undergraduates: 2,019. Freshmen: 237. Federal methodology is used as a basis for awarding need-based institutional aid.

UNDERGRADUATE EXPENSES for 2000–2001 (est.) ***Application fee:*** $20. ***Tuition:*** full-time $6768. Full-time tuition and fees vary according to course load. Part-time tuition and fees vary according to course load. ***Payment plans:*** installment, deferred payment.

FRESHMAN FINANCIAL AID (Fall 1998) 255 applied for aid; of those 98% were deemed to have need. 99% of freshmen with need received aid; of those 9% had need fully met. *Average percent of need met:* 25% (excluding resources awarded to replace EFC). *Average financial aid package:* $6239 (excluding resources awarded to replace EFC). 8% of all full-time freshmen had no need and received non-need-based aid.

UNDERGRADUATE FINANCIAL AID (Fall 1998) 915 applied for aid; of those 98% were deemed to have need. 99% of undergraduates with need received aid; of those 7% had need fully met. *Average percent of need met:* 23% (excluding resources awarded to replace EFC). *Average financial aid package:* $6315 (excluding resources awarded to replace EFC). 6% of all full-time undergraduates had no need and received non-need-based aid.

GIFT AID (NEED-BASED) ***Total amount:*** $3,891,860 (46% Federal, 52% state, 1% institutional, 1% external sources). ***Receiving aid:*** *Freshmen:* 87% (245); *all full-time undergraduates:* 86% (879). ***Average award:*** Freshmen: $4225; Undergraduates: $4097. ***Scholarships, grants, and awards:*** Federal Pell, FSEOG, state, private, college/university gift aid from institutional funds.

GIFT AID (NON-NEED-BASED) ***Total amount:*** $405,097 (100% institutional). ***Receiving aid:*** *Freshmen:* 25% (71); *Undergraduates:* 22% (220). ***Scholarships, grants, and awards by category:*** *Academic Interests/Achievement:* 138 awards ($224,765 total): business, computer science, general academic interests/achievements. *Special Characteristics:* 157 awards ($139,307 total): adult students, children and siblings of alumni, children of public servants, general special characteristics, local/state students. ***Tuition waivers:*** Full or partial for children of alumni, employees or children of employees.

LOANS ***Student loans:*** $4,199,523 (100% need-based). 48% of past graduating class borrowed through all loan programs. Average indebtedness per student: $5789. ***Average need-based loan:*** Freshmen: $2625; Undergraduates: $3120. ***Parent loans:*** $56,415 (100% non-need-based). ***Programs:*** FFEL (Subsidized and Unsubsidized Stafford, PLUS).

WORK-STUDY ***Federal work-study:*** *Total amount:* $62,172; 34 jobs averaging $1829. ***State or other work-study/employment:*** *Total amount:* $149,532 (98% need-based, 2% non-need-based). 52 part-time jobs averaging $2875.

APPLYING for FINANCIAL AID ***Required financial aid forms:*** FAFSA, institution's own form. ***Financial aid deadline (priority):*** 3/21. ***Notification date:*** 5/1. Students must reply within 4 weeks of notification.

CONTACT Ms. Carol Agee, Director of Financial Aid, Detroit College of Business, Warren Campus, 27500 Dequindre Road, Warren, MI 48092-5209, 810-558-8700. *Fax:* 810-558-7528. *E-mail:* wcagee@dcb.edu

DEVRY INSTITUTE

North Brunswick, NJ

Tuition & fees: $7778 **Average undergraduate aid package: N/A**

ABOUT THE INSTITUTION Proprietary, coed. Awards: associate and bachelor's degrees. 4 undergraduate majors. Total enrollment: 3,640. Undergraduates: 3,640. Freshmen: 1,400. Both federal and institutional methodology are used as a basis for awarding need-based institutional aid.

UNDERGRADUATE EXPENSES for 1999–2000 ***Application fee:*** $25. ***Tuition:*** full-time $7778; part-time $290 per credit hour. Part-time tuition and fees vary according to class time and course load. ***Payment plan:*** deferred payment.

FRESHMAN FINANCIAL AID (Fall 1999) 1235 applied for aid; of those 94% were deemed to have need. 100% of freshmen with need received aid; of those 10% had need fully met. *Average percent of need met:* 61% (excluding resources awarded to replace EFC). 5% of all full-time freshmen had no need and received non-need-based aid.

UNDERGRADUATE FINANCIAL AID (Fall 1999) 2,837 applied for aid; of those 93% were deemed to have need. 100% of undergraduates with need received aid; of those 14% had need fully met. *Average percent of need met:* 65% (excluding resources awarded to replace EFC). 10% of all full-time undergraduates had no need and received non-need-based aid.

GIFT AID (NEED-BASED) ***Total amount:*** $9,325,285 (49% Federal, 45% state, 6% external sources). ***Receiving aid:*** *Freshmen:* 14% (802); *all full-time undergraduates:* 23% (1,693). ***Average award:*** Freshmen: $3316; Undergraduates: $2984. ***Scholarships, grants, and awards:*** Federal Pell, FSEOG.

GIFT AID (NON-NEED-BASED) ***Total amount:*** $77,188 (2% state, 98% external sources). ***Receiving aid:*** *Freshmen:* 2; *Undergraduates:* 4. ***Scholarships, grants, and awards by category:*** *Academic Interests/Achievement:* general academic interests/achievements. ***Tuition waivers:*** Full or partial for employees or children of employees.

LOANS ***Student loans:*** $29,733,062 (82% need-based, 18% non-need-based). 57% of past graduating class borrowed through all loan programs. Average indebtedness per student: $10,431. ***Average need-based loan:*** Freshmen: $4984; Undergraduates: $5851. ***Parent loans:*** $3,902,574 (53% need-based, 47% non-need-based). ***Programs:*** FFEL (Subsidized and Unsubsidized Stafford, PLUS), Perkins.

WORK-STUDY ***Federal work-study:*** *Total amount:* $330,011; jobs available.

APPLYING for FINANCIAL AID ***Required financial aid form:*** FAFSA. ***Financial aid deadline:*** Continuous. ***Notification date:*** Continuous.

CONTACT Albert Cama, Director of Financial Aid, DeVry Institute, 630 US Highway 1, North Brunswick, NJ 08902, 732-435-4880 or toll-free 800-333-3879.

DEVRY INSTITUTE OF TECHNOLOGY
Phoenix, AZ

Tuition & fees: $7778 **Average undergraduate aid package: $8234**

ABOUT THE INSTITUTION Proprietary, coed. Awards: associate and bachelor's degrees. 6 undergraduate majors. Total enrollment: 3,706. Undergraduates: 3,706. Freshmen: 1,069. Both federal and institutional methodology are used as a basis for awarding need-based institutional aid.

UNDERGRADUATE EXPENSES for 1999–2000 ***Application fee:*** $25. ***Tuition:*** full-time $7778; part-time $290 per credit hour. Part-time tuition and fees vary according to class time and course load. ***Payment plans:*** installment, deferred payment.

FRESHMAN FINANCIAL AID (Fall 1999) 1282 applied for aid; of those 94% were deemed to have need. 100% of freshmen with need received aid; of those 4% had need fully met. *Average percent of need met:* 44% (excluding resources awarded to replace EFC). *Average financial aid package:* $6204 (excluding resources awarded to replace EFC). 8% of all full-time freshmen had no need and received non-need-based aid.

UNDERGRADUATE FINANCIAL AID (Fall 1999) 3,846 applied for aid; of those 93% were deemed to have need. 100% of undergraduates with need received aid; of those 11% had need fully met. *Average percent of need met:* 54% (excluding resources awarded to replace EFC). *Average financial aid package:* $8234 (excluding resources awarded to replace EFC). 15% of all full-time undergraduates had no need and received non-need-based aid.

GIFT AID (NEED-BASED) ***Total amount:*** $5,627,003 (72% Federal, 7% institutional, 21% external sources). ***Receiving aid:*** *Freshmen:* 14% (528); *all full-time undergraduates:* 26% (1,694). ***Average award:*** Freshmen: $1097; Undergraduates: $1278. ***Scholarships, grants, and awards:*** Federal Pell, FSEOG, state.

GIFT AID (NON-NEED-BASED) ***Total amount:*** $143,368 (3% state, 28% institutional, 69% external sources). ***Receiving aid:*** *Freshmen:* 1; *Undergraduates:* 7. ***Scholarships, grants, and awards by category:*** *Academic Interests/Achievement:* business, computer science, engineering/technologies, general academic interests/achievements. ***Tuition waivers:*** Full or partial for employees or children of employees. ***ROTC:*** Air Force.

LOANS ***Student loans:*** $35,570,809 (84% need-based, 16% non-need-based). 67% of past graduating class borrowed through all loan programs. Average indebtedness per student: $13,147. ***Average need-based loan:*** Freshmen: $5052; Undergraduates: $6781. ***Parent loans:*** $4,897,207 (82% need-based, 18% non-need-based). ***Programs:*** FFEL (Subsidized and Unsubsidized Stafford, PLUS), Perkins, state.

WORK-STUDY Federal work-study jobs available.

APPLYING for FINANCIAL AID ***Required financial aid forms:*** FAFSA, state aid form. ***Financial aid deadline:*** Continuous. ***Notification date:*** Continuous.

CONTACT Margaret Burke, Financial Aid Officer, DeVry Institute of Technology, 2149 West Dunlap Avenue, Phoenix, AZ 85021-2995, 602-870-9222 or toll-free 800-528-0250 (out-of-state).

DEVRY INSTITUTE OF TECHNOLOGY
Fremont, CA

Tuition & fees: $8776 **Average undergraduate aid package: $9439**

ABOUT THE INSTITUTION Proprietary, coed. Awards: associate and bachelor's degrees. 6 undergraduate majors. Total enrollment: 1,417. Undergraduates: 1,417. Freshmen: 606. Both federal and institutional methodology are used as a basis for awarding need-based institutional aid.

UNDERGRADUATE EXPENSES for 1999–2000 ***Application fee:*** $25. ***Tuition:*** full-time $8776; part-time $325 per credit hour. Part-time tuition and fees vary according to class time and course load. ***Payment plans:*** installment, deferred payment.

FRESHMAN FINANCIAL AID (Fall 1999) 384 applied for aid; of those 93% were deemed to have need. 100% of freshmen with need received aid; of those 5% had need fully met. *Average percent of need met:* 50% (excluding resources awarded to replace EFC). *Average financial aid package:* $7892 (excluding resources awarded to replace EFC). 6% of all full-time freshmen had no need and received non-need-based aid.

UNDERGRADUATE FINANCIAL AID (Fall 1999) 1,153 applied for aid; of those 93% were deemed to have need. 100% of undergraduates with need received aid; of those 9% had need fully met. *Average percent of need met:* 56% (excluding resources awarded to replace EFC). *Average financial aid package:* $9439 (excluding resources awarded to replace EFC). 12% of all full-time undergraduates had no need and received non-need-based aid.

GIFT AID (NEED-BASED) ***Total amount:*** $2,394,328 (68% Federal, 25% state, 2% institutional, 5% external sources). ***Receiving aid:*** *Freshmen:* 9% (167); *all full-time undergraduates:* 20% (526). ***Average award:*** Freshmen: $1627; Undergraduates: $1771. ***Scholarships, grants, and awards:*** Federal Pell, FSEOG.

GIFT AID (NON-NEED-BASED) ***Total amount:*** $23,643 (16% state, 59% institutional, 25% external sources). ***Receiving aid:*** *Freshmen:* 2; *Undergraduates:* 4. ***Scholarships, grants, and awards by category:*** *Academic Interests/Achievement:* business, computer science, engineering/technologies, general academic interests/achievements. ***Tuition waivers:*** Full or partial for employees or children of employees.

LOANS ***Student loans:*** $13,433,000 (82% need-based, 18% non-need-based). 52% of past graduating class borrowed through all loan programs. Average indebtedness per student: $10,344. ***Average need-based loan:*** Freshmen: $6249; Undergraduates: $7504. ***Parent loans:*** $3,077,945 (79% need-based, 21% non-need-based). ***Programs:*** FFEL (Subsidized and Unsubsidized Stafford, PLUS), Perkins.

WORK-STUDY Federal work-study jobs available.

APPLYING for FINANCIAL AID ***Required financial aid form:*** FAFSA. ***Financial aid deadline:*** Continuous. ***Notification date:*** Continuous.

CONTACT Kim Kane, Director of Student Finance, DeVry Institute of Technology, 6600 Dumbarton Circle, Fremont, CA 94555, 510-574-1100 or toll-free 888-393-3879 (out-of-state). *Fax:* 510-742-0868.

DEVRY INSTITUTE OF TECHNOLOGY
Long Beach, CA

Tuition & fees: $7778 **Average undergraduate aid package: N/A**

ABOUT THE INSTITUTION Proprietary, coed. Awards: associate and bachelor's degrees. 7 undergraduate majors. Total enrollment: 2,627. Undergraduates: 2,627. Freshmen: 783. Both federal and institutional methodology are used as a basis for awarding need-based institutional aid.

UNDERGRADUATE EXPENSES for 1999–2000 ***Application fee:*** $25. ***Tuition:*** full-time $7778; part-time $290 per credit hour. Part-time tuition and fees vary according to class time and course load. ***Payment plan:*** installment.

DeVry Institute of Technology (continued)

FRESHMAN FINANCIAL AID (Fall 1999) 377 applied for aid; of those 96% were deemed to have need. 100% of freshmen with need received aid; of those 7% had need fully met. *Average percent of need met:* 56% (excluding resources awarded to replace EFC). 14% of all full-time freshmen had no need and received non-need-based aid.

UNDERGRADUATE FINANCIAL AID (Fall 1999) 1,720 applied for aid; of those 96% were deemed to have need. 100% of undergraduates with need received aid; of those 12% had need fully met. *Average percent of need met:* 62% (excluding resources awarded to replace EFC). 16% of all full-time undergraduates had no need and received non-need-based aid.

GIFT AID (NEED-BASED) ***Total amount:*** $4,928,774 (57% Federal, 34% state, 1% institutional, 8% external sources). ***Receiving aid:*** *Freshmen:* 51% (225); *all full-time undergraduates:* 50% (1,005). ***Average award:*** Freshmen: $2197; Undergraduates: $2537. ***Scholarships, grants, and awards:*** Federal Pell, FSEOG, state, private.

GIFT AID (NON-NEED-BASED) ***Total amount:*** $6831 (15% state, 85% institutional). ***Receiving aid:*** *Undergraduates:* 1. ***Scholarships, grants, and awards by category:*** *Academic Interests/Achievement:* business, computer science, engineering/technologies, general academic interests/achievements. ***Tuition waivers:*** Full or partial for employees or children of employees.

LOANS ***Student loans:*** $18,236,008 (88% need-based, 12% non-need-based). 97% of past graduating class borrowed through all loan programs. Average indebtedness per student: $15,493. ***Average need-based loan:*** Freshmen: $6257; Undergraduates: $7356. ***Parent loans:*** $2,091,358 (71% need-based, 29% non-need-based). ***Programs:*** FFEL (Subsidized and Unsubsidized Stafford, PLUS), Perkins, state, college/university.

WORK-STUDY ***Federal work-study:*** *Total amount:* $137,970; jobs available.

APPLYING for FINANCIAL AID ***Required financial aid forms:*** FAFSA, state aid form. ***Financial aid deadline:*** Continuous. ***Notification date:*** Continuous.

CONTACT Department of Financial Aid, DeVry Institute of Technology, 3880 Kilroy Airport Way, Long Beach, CA 90806, 562-427-0861 or toll-free 800-597-0444 (out-of-state).

DEVRY INSTITUTE OF TECHNOLOGY

Pomona, CA

Tuition & fees: $7778 **Average undergraduate aid package: N/A**

ABOUT THE INSTITUTION Proprietary, coed. Awards: associate and bachelor's degrees. 7 undergraduate majors. Total enrollment: 3,499. Undergraduates: 3,499. Freshmen: 934. Both federal and institutional methodology are used as a basis for awarding need-based institutional aid.

UNDERGRADUATE EXPENSES for 1999–2000 ***Application fee:*** $25. ***One-time required fee:*** $670. ***Tuition:*** full-time $7778; part-time $290 per credit hour. Part-time tuition and fees vary according to class time and course load. ***Payment plans:*** installment, deferred payment.

FRESHMAN FINANCIAL AID (Fall 1999) 494 applied for aid; of those 93% were deemed to have need. 100% of freshmen with need received aid; of those 8% had need fully met. *Average percent of need met:* 57% (excluding resources awarded to replace EFC). 16% of all full-time freshmen had no need and received non-need-based aid.

UNDERGRADUATE FINANCIAL AID (Fall 1999) 2,483 applied for aid; of those 95% were deemed to have need. 100% of undergraduates with need received aid; of those 11% had need fully met. *Average percent of need met:* 62% (excluding resources awarded to replace EFC). 16% of all full-time undergraduates had no need and received non-need-based aid.

GIFT AID (NEED-BASED) ***Total amount:*** $7,533,000 (56% Federal, 36% state, 1% institutional, 7% external sources). ***Receiving aid:*** *Freshmen:* 52% (285); *all full-time undergraduates:* 52% (1,473). ***Average award:*** Freshmen: $2090; Undergraduates: $2566. ***Scholarships, grants, and awards:*** Federal Pell, FSEOG, state, private.

GIFT AID (NON-NEED-BASED) ***Total amount:*** $7631 (79% state, 21% institutional). ***Receiving aid:*** *Freshmen:* 1; *Undergraduates:* 3. ***Scholarships, grants, and awards by category:*** *Academic Interests/Achievement:* business, computer science, engineering/technologies, general academic interests/achievements. ***Tuition waivers:*** Full or partial for employees or children of employees.

LOANS ***Student loans:*** $26,955,973 (88% need-based, 12% non-need-based). 97% of past graduating class borrowed through all loan programs. Average indebtedness per student: $16,431. ***Average need-based loan:*** Freshmen: $6547; Undergraduates: $7467. ***Parent loans:*** $3,436,730 (70% need-based, 30% non-need-based). ***Programs:*** FFEL (Subsidized and Unsubsidized Stafford, PLUS), Perkins, state.

WORK-STUDY ***Federal work-study:*** *Total amount:* $258,097; jobs available. ***State or other work-study/employment:*** *Total amount:* $2500 (100% need-based). Part-time jobs available.

APPLYING for FINANCIAL AID ***Required financial aid forms:*** FAFSA, state aid form. ***Financial aid deadline:*** Continuous. ***Notification date:*** Continuous.

CONTACT Ray Dominguez, Financial Aid Officer, DeVry Institute of Technology, 901 Corporate Center Drive, Pomona, CA 91768-2642, 909-622-8866 or toll-free 800-243-3660.

DEVRY INSTITUTE OF TECHNOLOGY

West Hills, CA

Tuition & fees: $7778 **Average undergraduate aid package: $7342**

ABOUT THE INSTITUTION Proprietary, coed. Awards: associate and bachelor's degrees. 6 undergraduate majors. Total enrollment: 367. Undergraduates: 367. Freshmen: 331. Both federal and institutional methodology are used as a basis for awarding need-based institutional aid.

UNDERGRADUATE EXPENSES for 1999–2000 ***Application fee:*** $25. ***Tuition:*** full-time 7778; part-time 290 per credit hour. Part-time tuition and fees vary according to class time and course load. ***Payment plan:*** installment.

FRESHMAN FINANCIAL AID (Fall 1999) 101 applied for aid; of those 88% were deemed to have need. 100% of freshmen with need received aid; of those 10% had need fully met. *Average percent of need met:* 62% (excluding resources awarded to replace EFC). *Average financial aid package:* $7347 (excluding resources awarded to replace EFC). 15% of all full-time freshmen had no need and received non-need-based aid.

UNDERGRADUATE FINANCIAL AID (Fall 1999) 221 applied for aid; of those 87% were deemed to have need. 100% of undergraduates with need received aid; of those 10% had need fully met. *Average percent of need met:* 63% (excluding resources awarded to replace EFC). *Average financial aid package:* $7342 (excluding resources awarded to replace EFC). 16% of all full-time undergraduates had no need and received non-need-based aid.

GIFT AID (NEED-BASED) ***Total amount:*** $406,938 (81% Federal, 12% state, 7% external sources). ***Receiving aid:*** *Freshmen:* 53% (56); *all full-time undergraduates:* 47% (107). ***Average award:*** Freshmen: $1917; Undergraduates: $1636. ***Scholarships, grants, and awards:*** Federal Pell, FSEOG, state.

GIFT AID (NON-NEED-BASED) ***Scholarships, grants, and awards by category:*** *Academic Interests/Achievement:* general academic interests/achievements. ***Tuition waivers:*** Full or partial for employees or children of employees.

LOANS ***Student loans:*** $1,947,438 (85% need-based, 15% non-need-based). 95% of past graduating class borrowed through all loan programs. Average indebtedness per student: $6125. ***Average need-based loan:*** Freshmen: $5430; Undergraduates: $5635. ***Parent loans:*** $282,700 (43% need-based, 57% non-need-based). ***Programs:*** FFEL (Subsidized and Unsubsidized Stafford, PLUS), Perkins.

WORK-STUDY ***Federal work-study:*** *Total amount:* $23,477; jobs available.

APPLYING for FINANCIAL AID ***Required financial aid form:*** FAFSA. ***Financial aid deadline:*** Continuous. ***Notification date:*** Continuous.

CONTACT Patricia Martinez, Assistant Director, Financial Aid, DeVry Institute of Technology, 22801 Roscoe Boulevard, West Hills, CA 91304, 818-932-3001. *Fax:* 818-932-3091.

DEVRY INSTITUTE OF TECHNOLOGY
Alpharetta, GA

Tuition & fees: $7778 **Average undergraduate aid package: N/A**

ABOUT THE INSTITUTION Proprietary, coed. Awards: associate and bachelor's degrees. 6 undergraduate majors. Total enrollment: 1,336. Undergraduates: 1,336. Freshmen: 367. Both federal and institutional methodology are used as a basis for awarding need-based institutional aid.

UNDERGRADUATE EXPENSES for 1999–2000 ***Application fee:*** $25. ***Tuition:*** full-time $7778; part-time $290 per credit hour. Part-time tuition and fees vary according to class time and course load. ***Payment plan:*** installment.

FRESHMAN FINANCIAL AID (Fall 1999) 261 applied for aid; of those 89% were deemed to have need. 100% of freshmen with need received aid; of those 15% had need fully met. *Average percent of need met:* 55% (excluding resources awarded to replace EFC). 15% of all full-time freshmen had no need and received non-need-based aid.

UNDERGRADUATE FINANCIAL AID (Fall 1999) 928 applied for aid; of those 90% were deemed to have need. 100% of undergraduates with need received aid; of those 20% had need fully met. *Average percent of need met:* 63% (excluding resources awarded to replace EFC). 24% of all full-time undergraduates had no need and received non-need-based aid.

GIFT AID (NEED-BASED) ***Total amount:*** $2,329,755 (39% Federal, 55% state, 5% institutional, 1% external sources). ***Receiving aid:*** *Freshmen:* 35% (195); *all full-time undergraduates:* 54% (686). ***Average award:*** Freshmen: $2568; Undergraduates: $2301. ***Scholarships, grants, and awards:*** Federal Pell, FSEOG, state, private, college/university gift aid from institutional funds.

GIFT AID (NON-NEED-BASED) ***Total amount:*** $309,447 (80% state, 16% institutional, 4% external sources). ***Receiving aid:*** *Freshmen:* 2% (12); *Undergraduates:* 2% (21). ***Scholarships, grants, and awards by category:*** *Academic Interests/Achievement:* business, computer science, engineering/technologies, general academic interests/achievements. ***Tuition waivers:*** Full or partial for employees or children of employees.

LOANS ***Student loans:*** $8,752,398 (84% need-based, 16% non-need-based). ***Average need-based loan:*** Freshmen: $5080; Undergraduates: $6743. ***Parent loans:*** $871,556 (68% need-based, 32% non-need-based). ***Programs:*** Federal Direct (Subsidized and Unsubsidized Stafford, PLUS), FFEL (Subsidized and Unsubsidized Stafford, PLUS), Perkins, state, college/university.

WORK-STUDY ***Federal work-study:*** *Total amount:* $108,089; jobs available.

APPLYING for FINANCIAL AID ***Required financial aid forms:*** FAFSA, state aid form. ***Financial aid deadline:*** Continuous. ***Notification date:*** Continuous.

CONTACT Robin Winston, Financial Aid Officer, DeVry Institute of Technology, 2555 Northwinds Parkway, Alpharetta, GA 30004, 770-521-4900.

DEVRY INSTITUTE OF TECHNOLOGY
Decatur, GA

Tuition & fees: $7778 **Average undergraduate aid package: N/A**

ABOUT THE INSTITUTION Proprietary, coed. Awards: associate and bachelor's degrees. 6 undergraduate majors. Total enrollment: 2,818. Undergraduates: 2,818. Freshmen: 887. Both federal and institutional methodology are used as a basis for awarding need-based institutional aid.

UNDERGRADUATE EXPENSES for 1999–2000 ***Application fee:*** $25. ***Tuition:*** full-time $7778; part-time $290 per credit hour. Part-time tuition and fees vary according to class time and course load. ***Payment plan:*** installment.

FRESHMAN FINANCIAL AID (Fall 1999) 655 applied for aid; of those 97% were deemed to have need. 100% of freshmen with need received aid; of those 9% had need fully met. *Average percent of need met:* 60% (excluding resources awarded to replace EFC). 11% of all full-time freshmen had no need and received non-need-based aid.

UNDERGRADUATE FINANCIAL AID (Fall 1999) 2,496 applied for aid; of those 96% were deemed to have need. 100% of undergraduates with need received aid; of those 14% had need fully met. *Average percent of need met:* 64% (excluding resources awarded to replace EFC). 17% of all full-time undergraduates had no need and received non-need-based aid.

GIFT AID (NEED-BASED) ***Total amount:*** $7,791,933 (50% Federal, 48% state, 1% institutional, 1% external sources). ***Receiving aid:*** *Freshmen:* 55% (557); *all full-time undergraduates:* 71% (2,085). ***Average award:*** Freshmen: $3279; Undergraduates: $2868. ***Scholarships, grants, and awards:*** Federal Pell, FSEOG, state, private, college/university gift aid from institutional funds.

GIFT AID (NON-NEED-BASED) ***Total amount:*** $342,621 (80% state, 5% institutional, 15% external sources). ***Receiving aid:*** *Freshmen:* 1% (14); *Undergraduates:* 1% (28). ***Scholarships, grants, and awards by category:*** *Academic Interests/Achievement:* business, computer science, engineering/technologies, general academic interests/achievements. ***Tuition waivers:*** Full or partial for employees or children of employees.

LOANS ***Student loans:*** $22,711,614 (90% need-based, 10% non-need-based). ***Average need-based loan:*** Freshmen: $5683; Undergraduates: $7163. ***Parent loans:*** $2,112,033 (77% need-based, 23% non-need-based). ***Programs:*** Federal Direct (Subsidized and Unsubsidized Stafford, PLUS), FFEL (Subsidized and Unsubsidized Stafford, PLUS), Perkins, state, college/university.

WORK-STUDY ***Federal work-study:*** *Total amount:* $1,058,868; jobs available.

APPLYING for FINANCIAL AID ***Required financial aid forms:*** FAFSA, state aid form. ***Financial aid deadline:*** Continuous. ***Notification date:*** Continuous.

CONTACT Robin Winston, Director of Financial Aid, DeVry Institute of Technology, 250 North Arcadia Avenue, Decatur, GA 30030-2198, 404-292-7900 or toll-free 800-221-4771 (out-of-state).

DEVRY INSTITUTE OF TECHNOLOGY
Addison, IL

Tuition & fees: $7778 **Average undergraduate aid package: $7278**

ABOUT THE INSTITUTION Proprietary, coed. Awards: associate and bachelor's degrees. 6 undergraduate majors. Total enrollment: 4,063. Undergraduates: 4,063. Freshmen: 835. Both federal and institutional methodology are used as a basis for awarding need-based institutional aid.

UNDERGRADUATE EXPENSES for 1999–2000 ***Application fee:*** $25. ***Tuition:*** full-time $7778; part-time $290 per credit hour. Part-time tuition and fees vary according to class time and course load. ***Payment plan:*** installment.

FRESHMAN FINANCIAL AID (Fall 1999) 991 applied for aid; of those 89% were deemed to have need. 100% of freshmen with need received aid; of those 8% had need fully met. *Average percent of need met:* 45% (excluding resources awarded to replace EFC). *Average financial aid package:* $5777 (excluding resources awarded to replace EFC). 11% of all full-time freshmen had no need and received non-need-based aid.

UNDERGRADUATE FINANCIAL AID (Fall 1999) 3,015 applied for aid; of those 88% were deemed to have need. 100% of undergraduates with need received aid; of those 16% had need fully met. *Average percent of need met:* 56% (excluding resources awarded to replace EFC). *Average financial aid package:* $7278 (excluding resources awarded to replace EFC). 20% of all full-time undergraduates had no need and received non-need-based aid.

GIFT AID (NEED-BASED) ***Total amount:*** $8,805,129 (39% Federal, 57% state, 1% institutional, 3% external sources). ***Receiving aid:*** *Freshmen:* 19% (536); *all full-time undergraduates:* 31% (1,568). ***Average award:*** Freshmen: $2360; Undergraduates: $2500. ***Scholarships, grants, and awards:*** Federal Pell, FSEOG, state, private.

GIFT AID (NON-NEED-BASED) ***Total amount:*** $205,752 (1% state, 45% institutional, 54% external sources). ***Receiving aid:*** *Freshmen:* 2; *Undergraduates:* 3. ***Scholarships, grants, and awards by category:***

DeVry Institute of Technology (continued)

Academic Interests/Achievement: business, computer science, engineering/technologies, general academic interests/achievements. ***Tuition waivers:*** Full or partial for employees or children of employees.

LOANS ***Student loans:*** $24,917,896 (72% need-based, 28% non-need-based). 77% of past graduating class borrowed through all loan programs. Average indebtedness per student: $11,095. ***Average need-based loan:*** Freshmen: $3320; Undergraduates: $4639. ***Parent loans:*** $3,420,067 (49% need-based, 51% non-need-based). ***Programs:*** Federal Direct (Subsidized and Unsubsidized Stafford, PLUS), FFEL (Subsidized and Unsubsidized Stafford, PLUS), Perkins, state.

WORK-STUDY ***Federal work-study:*** *Total amount:* $28,246; jobs available. ***State or other work-study/employment:*** *Total amount:* $439,787 (95% need-based, 5% non-need-based). Part-time jobs available.

APPLYING for FINANCIAL AID ***Required financial aid forms:*** FAFSA, state aid form. ***Financial aid deadline:*** Continuous. ***Notification date:*** Continuous.

CONTACT Kathy Facenda, Financial Aid Officer, DeVry Institute of Technology, 1221 North Swift Road, Addison, IL 60101-6106, 630-953-1300 or toll-free 800-346-5420 (out-of-state).

DEVRY INSTITUTE OF TECHNOLOGY

Chicago, IL

Tuition & fees: $7778 **Average undergraduate aid package: N/A**

ABOUT THE INSTITUTION Proprietary, coed. Awards: associate and bachelor's degrees. 5 undergraduate majors. Total enrollment: 4,001. Undergraduates: 4,001. Freshmen: 1,162. Both federal and institutional methodology are used as a basis for awarding need-based institutional aid.

UNDERGRADUATE EXPENSES for 1999–2000 ***Application fee:*** $25. ***Tuition:*** full-time $7778; part-time $290 per credit hour. Part-time tuition and fees vary according to class time and course load. ***Payment plan:*** installment.

FRESHMAN FINANCIAL AID (Fall 1999) 947 applied for aid; of those 99% were deemed to have need. 100% of freshmen with need received aid; of those 2% had need fully met. *Average percent of need met:* 38% (excluding resources awarded to replace EFC). 5% of all full-time freshmen had no need and received non-need-based aid.

UNDERGRADUATE FINANCIAL AID (Fall 1999) 3,472 applied for aid; of those 97% were deemed to have need. 100% of undergraduates with need received aid; of those 8% had need fully met. *Average percent of need met:* 53% (excluding resources awarded to replace EFC). 11% of all full-time undergraduates had no need and received non-need-based aid.

GIFT AID (NEED-BASED) ***Total amount:*** $17,017,956 (43% Federal, 56% state, 1% external sources). ***Receiving aid:*** *Freshmen:* 47% (833); *all full-time undergraduates:* 56% (2,743). ***Average award:*** Freshmen: $3928; Undergraduates: $4017. ***Scholarships, grants, and awards:*** Federal Pell, FSEOG, state, private, college/university gift aid from institutional funds.

GIFT AID (NON-NEED-BASED) ***Total amount:*** $10,313 (51% state, 17% institutional, 32% external sources). ***Receiving aid:*** *Undergraduates:* 1. ***Scholarships, grants, and awards by category:*** *Academic Interests/Achievement:* business, computer science, engineering/technologies, general academic interests/achievements. ***Tuition waivers:*** Full or partial for employees or children of employees.

LOANS ***Student loans:*** $24,055,474 (90% need-based, 10% non-need-based). 67% of past graduating class borrowed through all loan programs. Average indebtedness per student: $12,247. ***Average need-based loan:*** Freshmen: $2568; Undergraduates: $4845. ***Parent loans:*** $2,918,386 (73% need-based, 27% non-need-based). ***Programs:*** Federal Direct (Subsidized and Unsubsidized Stafford, PLUS), FFEL (Subsidized and Unsubsidized Stafford, PLUS), Perkins, state, college/university.

WORK-STUDY ***Federal work-study:*** *Total amount:* $663,408; jobs available.

APPLYING for FINANCIAL AID ***Required financial aid forms:*** FAFSA, state aid form. ***Financial aid deadline:*** Continuous. ***Notification date:*** Continuous.

CONTACT Carmilita Gee, Director of Financial Aid, DeVry Institute of Technology, 3300 North Campbell Avenue, Chicago, IL 60618-5994, 773-929-8500 or toll-free 800-383-3879 (out-of-state).

DEVRY INSTITUTE OF TECHNOLOGY

Kansas City, MO

Tuition & fees: $7778 **Average undergraduate aid package: N/A**

ABOUT THE INSTITUTION Proprietary, coed. Awards: associate and bachelor's degrees. 7 undergraduate majors. Total enrollment: 2,555. Undergraduates: 2,555. Freshmen: 499. Both federal and institutional methodology are used as a basis for awarding need-based institutional aid.

UNDERGRADUATE EXPENSES for 1999–2000 ***Application fee:*** $25. ***Tuition:*** full-time $7778; part-time $290 per credit hour. Part-time tuition and fees vary according to class time and course load. ***Payment plan:*** installment.

FRESHMAN FINANCIAL AID (Fall 1999) 449 applied for aid; of those 94% were deemed to have need. 100% of freshmen with need received aid; of those 6% had need fully met. *Average percent of need met:* 49% (excluding resources awarded to replace EFC). 12% of all full-time freshmen had no need and received non-need-based aid.

UNDERGRADUATE FINANCIAL AID (Fall 1999) 1,778 applied for aid; of those 94% were deemed to have need. 100% of undergraduates with need received aid; of those 15% had need fully met. *Average percent of need met:* 62% (excluding resources awarded to replace EFC). 20% of all full-time undergraduates had no need and received non-need-based aid.

GIFT AID (NEED-BASED) ***Total amount:*** $3,279,747 (67% Federal, 3% state, 8% institutional, 22% external sources). ***Receiving aid:*** *Freshmen:* 21% (239); *all full-time undergraduates:* 33% (824). ***Average award:*** Freshmen: $1556; Undergraduates: $1466. ***Scholarships, grants, and awards:*** Federal Pell, FSEOG, state, private.

GIFT AID (NON-NEED-BASED) ***Total amount:*** $443,718 (2% state, 29% institutional, 69% external sources). ***Receiving aid:*** *Freshmen:* 2; *Undergraduates:* 1% (14). ***Scholarships, grants, and awards by category:*** *Academic Interests/Achievement:* business, computer science, engineering/technologies, general academic interests/achievements. ***Tuition waivers:*** Full or partial for employees or children of employees.

LOANS ***Student loans:*** $20,989,326 (86% need-based, 14% non-need-based). 75% of past graduating class borrowed through all loan programs. ***Average need-based loan:*** Freshmen: $5310; Undergraduates: $7534. ***Parent loans:*** $2,403,190 (67% need-based, 33% non-need-based). ***Programs:*** FFEL (Subsidized and Unsubsidized Stafford, PLUS), Perkins.

WORK-STUDY ***Federal work-study:*** *Total amount:* $64,700; jobs available.

APPLYING for FINANCIAL AID ***Required financial aid form:*** FAFSA. ***Financial aid deadline:*** Continuous. ***Notification date:*** Continuous.

CONTACT Linda Bayless, Financial Aid Officer, DeVry Institute of Technology, 11224 Holmes Street, Kansas City, MO 64131-3698, 816-941-0430 or toll-free 800-821-3766 (out-of-state).

DEVRY INSTITUTE OF TECHNOLOGY

Long Island City, NY

Tuition & fees: $8776 **Average undergraduate aid package: $9259**

ABOUT THE INSTITUTION Proprietary, coed. Awards: associate and bachelor's degrees. 4 undergraduate majors. Total enrollment: 1,250. Undergraduates: 1,250. Freshmen: 785. Both federal and institutional methodology are used as a basis for awarding need-based institutional aid.

UNDERGRADUATE EXPENSES for 1999–2000 ***Application fee:*** $25. ***Tuition:*** full-time $8776; part-time $325 per credit hour. Part-time tuition and fees vary according to class time and course load. ***Payment plan:*** installment.

FRESHMAN FINANCIAL AID (Fall 1999) 656 applied for aid; of those 98% were deemed to have need. 100% of freshmen with need received aid; of those 5% had need fully met. *Average percent of need met:* 55% (excluding resources awarded to replace EFC). *Average financial aid package:*

$8644 (excluding resources awarded to replace EFC). 7% of all full-time freshmen had no need and received non-need-based aid.

UNDERGRADUATE FINANCIAL AID (Fall 1999) 1,329 applied for aid; of those 98% were deemed to have need. 100% of undergraduates with need received aid; of those 6% had need fully met. *Average percent of need met:* 57% (excluding resources awarded to replace EFC). *Average financial aid package:* $9259 (excluding resources awarded to replace EFC). 9% of all full-time undergraduates had no need and received non-need-based aid.

GIFT AID (NEED-BASED) ***Total amount:*** $5,969,718 (50% Federal, 45% state, 5% external sources). ***Receiving aid:*** *Freshmen:* 57% (524); *all full-time undergraduates:* 59% (997). ***Average award:*** Freshmen: $4189; Undergraduates: $3989. ***Scholarships, grants, and awards:*** Federal Pell, FSEOG, state.

GIFT AID (NON-NEED-BASED) ***Total amount:*** $6053 (100% external sources). ***Receiving aid:*** *Freshmen:* 2; *Undergraduates:* 3. ***Scholarships, grants, and awards by category:*** *Academic Interests/Achievement:* general academic interests/achievements. ***Tuition waivers:*** Full or partial for employees or children of employees.

LOANS ***Student loans:*** $10,602,139 (93% need-based, 7% non-need-based). 83% of past graduating class borrowed through all loan programs. ***Average need-based loan:*** Freshmen: $4455; Undergraduates: $5268. ***Parent loans:*** $1,219,215 (71% need-based, 29% non-need-based). ***Programs:*** FFEL (Subsidized and Unsubsidized Stafford, PLUS), Perkins.

WORK-STUDY ***Federal work-study:*** *Total amount:* $2500; jobs available.

APPLYING for FINANCIAL AID ***Required financial aid form:*** FAFSA. ***Financial aid deadline:*** Continuous. ***Notification date:*** Continuous.

CONTACT Betsy Scaria, Assistant Director, Student Finance, DeVry Institute of Technology, 30-20 Thomson Avenue, Long Island City, NY 11101, 718-361-0004 or toll-free 888-713-3879 (out-of-state). *Fax:* 718-392-7354.

DEVRY INSTITUTE OF TECHNOLOGY

Columbus, OH

Tuition & fees: $7778 **Average undergraduate aid package: $8152**

ABOUT THE INSTITUTION Proprietary, coed. Awards: associate and bachelor's degrees. 6 undergraduate majors. Total enrollment: 3,369. Undergraduates: 3,369. Freshmen: 925. Both federal and institutional methodology are used as a basis for awarding need-based institutional aid.

UNDERGRADUATE EXPENSES for 1999–2000 ***Application fee:*** $25. ***Tuition:*** full-time $7778; part-time $290 per credit hour. Part-time tuition and fees vary according to class time and course load. ***Payment plan:*** installment.

FRESHMAN FINANCIAL AID (Fall 1999) 1292 applied for aid; of those 95% were deemed to have need. 100% of freshmen with need received aid; of those 6% had need fully met. *Average percent of need met:* 43% (excluding resources awarded to replace EFC). *Average financial aid package:* $6215 (excluding resources awarded to replace EFC). 14% of all full-time freshmen had no need and received non-need-based aid.

UNDERGRADUATE FINANCIAL AID (Fall 1999) 3,494 applied for aid; of those 95% were deemed to have need. 100% of undergraduates with need received aid; of those 12% had need fully met. *Average percent of need met:* 55% (excluding resources awarded to replace EFC). *Average financial aid package:* $8152 (excluding resources awarded to replace EFC). 19% of all full-time undergraduates had no need and received non-need-based aid.

GIFT AID (NEED-BASED) ***Total amount:*** $8,671,838 (53% Federal, 24% state, 23% external sources). ***Receiving aid:*** *Freshmen:* 47% (804); *all full-time undergraduates:* 47% (1,912). ***Average award:*** Freshmen: $2006; Undergraduates: $2175. ***Scholarships, grants, and awards:*** Federal Pell, FSEOG, state, private.

GIFT AID (NON-NEED-BASED) ***Total amount:*** $149,815 (14% state, 1% institutional, 85% external sources). ***Receiving aid:*** *Freshmen:* 1% (9); *Undergraduates:* 1% (22). ***Scholarships, grants, and awards by category:*** *Academic Interests/Achievement:* business, computer science, engineering/technologies, general academic interests/achievements. ***Tuition waivers:*** Full or partial for employees or children of employees. ***ROTC:*** Army cooperative.

LOANS ***Student loans:*** $28,013,563 (89% need-based, 11% non-need-based). 89% of past graduating class borrowed through all loan programs. Average indebtedness per student: $11,451. ***Average need-based loan:*** Freshmen: $4134; Undergraduates: $5832. ***Parent loans:*** $4,373,385 (73% need-based, 27% non-need-based). ***Programs:*** Federal Direct (Subsidized and Unsubsidized Stafford, PLUS), FFEL (Subsidized and Unsubsidized Stafford, PLUS), Perkins, state, college/university.

WORK-STUDY ***Federal work-study:*** *Total amount:* $484,839; jobs available. ***State or other work-study/employment:*** *Total amount:* $30,080 (96% need-based, 4% non-need-based). Part-time jobs available.

APPLYING for FINANCIAL AID ***Required financial aid forms:*** FAFSA, state aid form. ***Financial aid deadline:*** Continuous. ***Notification date:*** Continuous.

CONTACT Cynthia Price, Financial Aid Officer, DeVry Institute of Technology, 1350 Alum Creek Drive, Columbus, OH 43209-2705, 614-253-7291 or toll-free 800-426-3916 (in-state), 800-426-3090 (out-of-state).

DEVRY INSTITUTE OF TECHNOLOGY

Irving, TX

Tuition & fees: $7778 **Average undergraduate aid package: N/A**

ABOUT THE INSTITUTION Proprietary, coed. Awards: associate and bachelor's degrees. 7 undergraduate majors. Total enrollment: 3,033. Undergraduates: 3,033. Freshmen: 945. Both federal and institutional methodology are used as a basis for awarding need-based institutional aid.

UNDERGRADUATE EXPENSES for 1999–2000 ***Application fee:*** $25. ***Tuition:*** full-time $7778; part-time $290 per credit hour. Part-time tuition and fees vary according to class time and course load. ***Payment plan:*** installment.

FRESHMAN FINANCIAL AID (Fall 1999) 984 applied for aid; of those 96% were deemed to have need. 100% of freshmen with need received aid; of those 6% had need fully met. *Average percent of need met:* 45% (excluding resources awarded to replace EFC). 13% of all full-time freshmen had no need and received non-need-based aid.

UNDERGRADUATE FINANCIAL AID (Fall 1999) 2,537 applied for aid; of those 95% were deemed to have need. 100% of undergraduates with need received aid; of those 14% had need fully met. *Average percent of need met:* 57% (excluding resources awarded to replace EFC). 18% of all full-time undergraduates had no need and received non-need-based aid.

GIFT AID (NEED-BASED) ***Total amount:*** $5,732,322 (68% Federal, 32% external sources). ***Receiving aid:*** *Freshmen:* 47% (621); *all full-time undergraduates:* 45% (1,425). ***Average award:*** Freshmen: $1759; Undergraduates: $1751. ***Scholarships, grants, and awards:*** Federal Pell, FSEOG, private.

GIFT AID (NON-NEED-BASED) ***Total amount:*** $183,701 (100% external sources). ***Receiving aid:*** *Freshmen:* 1; *Undergraduates:* 14. ***Scholarships, grants, and awards by category:*** *Academic Interests/Achievement:* business, computer science, engineering/technologies, general academic interests/achievements. ***Tuition waivers:*** Full or partial for employees or children of employees.

LOANS ***Student loans:*** $29,085,366 (84% need-based, 16% non-need-based). 89% of past graduating class borrowed through all loan programs. Average indebtedness per student: $12,939. ***Average need-based loan:*** Freshmen: $5102; Undergraduates: $6626. ***Parent loans:*** $4,938,714 (78% need-based, 22% non-need-based). ***Programs:*** FFEL (Subsidized and Unsubsidized Stafford, PLUS), Perkins, college/university.

WORK-STUDY ***Federal work-study:*** *Total amount:* $488,288; jobs available. ***State or other work-study/employment:*** *Total amount:* $2,384,312 (39% need-based, 61% non-need-based). Part-time jobs available.

APPLYING for FINANCIAL AID ***Required financial aid form:*** FAFSA. ***Financial aid deadline:*** Continuous. ***Notification date:*** Continuous.

DeVry Institute of Technology (continued)

CONTACT Nga Phan, Financial Aid Officer, DeVry Institute of Technology, 4800 Regent Boulevard, Irving, TX 75063-2440, 214-929-6777 or toll-free 800-443-3879 (in-state), 800-633-3879 (out-of-state).

DICKINSON COLLEGE

Carlisle, PA

Tuition & fees: $24,450 **Average undergraduate aid package: $20,228**

ABOUT THE INSTITUTION Independent, coed. Awards: bachelor's degrees. 42 undergraduate majors. Total enrollment: 2,067. Undergraduates: 2,067. Freshmen: 620. Both federal and institutional methodology are used as a basis for awarding need-based institutional aid.

UNDERGRADUATE EXPENSES for 2000–2001 ***Application fee:*** $40. ***One-time required fee:*** $25. ***Comprehensive fee:*** $30,900 includes full-time tuition ($24,050), mandatory fees ($400), and room and board ($6450). ***College room only:*** $3300. ***Payment plan:*** installment.

FRESHMAN FINANCIAL AID (Fall 1999) 519 applied for aid; of those 84% were deemed to have need. 100% of freshmen with need received aid; of those 39% had need fully met. *Average percent of need met:* 96% (excluding resources awarded to replace EFC). *Average financial aid package:* $19,318 (excluding resources awarded to replace EFC). 14% of all full-time freshmen had no need and received non-need-based aid.

UNDERGRADUATE FINANCIAL AID (Fall 1999) 1,521 applied for aid; of those 91% were deemed to have need. 100% of undergraduates with need received aid; of those 62% had need fully met. *Average percent of need met:* 94% (excluding resources awarded to replace EFC). *Average financial aid package:* $20,228 (excluding resources awarded to replace EFC). 9% of all full-time undergraduates had no need and received non-need-based aid.

GIFT AID (NEED-BASED) ***Total amount:*** $21,633,682 (4% Federal, 5% state, 89% institutional, 2% external sources). ***Receiving aid:*** *Freshmen:* 70% (431); *all full-time undergraduates:* 66% (1,357). ***Average award:*** Freshmen: $16,068; Undergraduates: $15,942. ***Scholarships, grants, and awards:*** Federal Pell, FSEOG, state, private, college/university gift aid from institutional funds.

GIFT AID (NON-NEED-BASED) ***Total amount:*** $2,990,761 (12% Federal, 1% state, 83% institutional, 4% external sources). ***Receiving aid:*** *Freshmen:* 13% (82); *Undergraduates:* 8% (173). ***Scholarships, grants, and awards by category:*** *Academic Interests/Achievement:* general academic interests/achievements, military science. *Creative Arts/Performance:* music. *Special Achievements/Activities:* general special achievements/activities. *Special Characteristics:* children of faculty/staff, general special characteristics, international students. ***Tuition waivers:*** Full or partial for employees or children of employees. ***ROTC:*** Army.

LOANS ***Student loans:*** $6,140,381 (76% need-based, 24% non-need-based). 70% of past graduating class borrowed through all loan programs. Average indebtedness per student: $17,752. ***Average need-based loan:*** Freshmen: $3166; Undergraduates: $4058. ***Parent loans:*** $2,584,687 (17% need-based, 83% non-need-based). ***Programs:*** FFEL (Subsidized and Unsubsidized Stafford, PLUS), Perkins, state, college/university.

WORK-STUDY ***Federal work-study:*** *Total amount:* $1,044,538; 784 jobs averaging $1332. ***State or other work-study/employment:*** *Total amount:* $205,120 (52% need-based, 48% non-need-based). 72 part-time jobs averaging $2850.

APPLYING for FINANCIAL AID ***Required financial aid forms:*** FAFSA, CSS Financial Aid PROFILE, noncustodial (divorced/separated) parent's statement, business/farm supplement. ***Financial aid deadline (priority):*** 2/1. ***Notification date:*** 3/20. Students must reply by 5/1 or within 2 weeks of notification.

CONTACT Judith B. Carter, Director of Financial Aid, Dickinson College, PO Box 1773, Carlisle, PA 17013-2896, 717-245-1308 or toll-free 800-644-1773. *Fax:* 717-245-1972. *E-mail:* finaid@dickinson.edu

DICKINSON STATE UNIVERSITY

Dickinson, ND

Tuition & fees (ND res): $2302 **Average undergraduate aid package: N/A**

ABOUT THE INSTITUTION State-supported, coed. Awards: associate and bachelor's degrees. 45 undergraduate majors. Total enrollment: 1,867. Undergraduates: 1,867. Freshmen: 399. Federal methodology is used as a basis for awarding need-based institutional aid.

UNDERGRADUATE EXPENSES for 1999–2000 ***Application fee:*** $25. ***Tuition, state resident:*** full-time $1906; part-time $79 per semester hour. ***Tuition, nonresident:*** full-time $5089; part-time $212 per semester hour. ***Required fees:*** full-time $396; $16 per semester hour. Full-time tuition and fees vary according to reciprocity agreements. Part-time tuition and fees vary according to reciprocity agreements. ***College room and board:*** $2610. Room and board charges vary according to board plan.

FRESHMAN FINANCIAL AID (Fall 1998) 305 applied for aid; of those 100% were deemed to have need. 100% of freshmen with need received aid.

UNDERGRADUATE FINANCIAL AID (Fall 1998) 1,747 applied for aid; of those 100% were deemed to have need. 100% of undergraduates with need received aid.

GIFT AID (NEED-BASED) ***Total amount:*** $1,595,505 (95% Federal, 5% state). ***Scholarships, grants, and awards:*** Federal Pell, FSEOG, state, college/university gift aid from institutional funds, National Guard tuition waivers.

GIFT AID (NON-NEED-BASED) ***Total amount:*** $380,731 (1% state, 59% institutional, 40% external sources). ***Scholarships, grants, and awards by category:*** *Academic Interests/Achievement:* general academic interests/achievements. *Special Achievements/Activities:* leadership, rodeo. *Special Characteristics:* ethnic background, general special characteristics, international students. ***Tuition waivers:*** Full or partial for minority students, senior citizens.

LOANS ***Student loans:*** $3,777,883 (81% need-based, 19% non-need-based). 81% of past graduating class borrowed through all loan programs. Average indebtedness per student: $8932. ***Parent loans:*** $123,098 (100% non-need-based). ***Programs:*** FFEL (Subsidized and Unsubsidized Stafford, PLUS), Perkins, Federal Nursing, state, college/university, Alaska Loans, Teacher Scholarship Loans, SELF Loans.

WORK-STUDY ***Federal work-study:*** *Total amount:* $185,570; 162 jobs averaging $1145. ***State or other work-study/employment:*** *Total amount:* $136,805 (100% non-need-based). 136 part-time jobs averaging $1006.

ATHLETIC AWARDS *Total amount:* 89,427 (100% non-need-based).

APPLYING for FINANCIAL AID ***Required financial aid form:*** FAFSA. ***Financial aid deadline (priority):*** 4/15. ***Notification date:*** 6/15. Students must reply within 2 weeks of notification.

CONTACT Ms. Sandy Klein, Director of Financial Aid, Dickinson State University, 291 Campus Drive, Dickinson, ND 58601-4896, 701-483-2371 or toll-free 800-279-4295. *Fax:* 701-483-2006. *E-mail:* sandy_klein@eagle.dsu.nodak.edu

DILLARD UNIVERSITY

New Orleans, LA

Tuition & fees: $9200 **Average undergraduate aid package: $14,254**

ABOUT THE INSTITUTION Independent interdenominational, coed. Awards: bachelor's degrees. 51 undergraduate majors. Total enrollment: 1,902. Undergraduates: 1,902. Freshmen: 638. Federal methodology is used as a basis for awarding need-based institutional aid.

UNDERGRADUATE EXPENSES for 2000–2001 ***Application fee:*** $10. ***Comprehensive fee:*** $14,000 includes full-time tuition ($9200) and room and board ($4800). ***College room only:*** $3875. Full-time tuition and fees vary according to program. ***Part-time tuition:*** $165 per credit hour. Part-time tuition and fees vary according to class time and program. ***Payment plan:*** installment.

FRESHMAN FINANCIAL AID (Fall 1999, est.) 613 applied for aid; of those 94% were deemed to have need. 100% of freshmen with need received aid; of those 100% had need fully met. *Average percent of need met:* 85% (excluding resources awarded to replace EFC). *Average financial aid package:* $13,646 (excluding resources awarded to replace EFC).

UNDERGRADUATE FINANCIAL AID (Fall 1999, est.) 1,888 applied for aid; of those 79% were deemed to have need. 96% of undergraduates with need received aid; of those 100% had need fully met. *Average percent of need met:* 85% (excluding resources awarded to replace EFC). *Average financial aid package:* $14,254 (excluding resources awarded to replace EFC).

GIFT AID (NEED-BASED) ***Total amount:*** $3,420,241 (99% Federal, 1% state). ***Scholarships, grants, and awards:*** Federal Pell, FSEOG, state, private, United Negro College Fund.

GIFT AID (NON-NEED-BASED) ***Total amount:*** $4,870,750 (1% state, 77% institutional, 22% external sources). ***Receiving aid:*** *Freshmen:* 21% (131); *Undergraduates:* 20% (387). ***Scholarships, grants, and awards by category:*** *Academic Interests/Achievement:* 1,778 awards ($3,331,726 total): general academic interests/achievements. *Creative Arts/Performance:* 64 awards ($125,075 total): music, performing arts, theater/drama. *Special Characteristics:* 56 awards ($245,403 total): children of faculty/staff, religious affiliation. ***ROTC:*** Army, Naval cooperative, Air Force cooperative.

LOANS ***Student loans:*** $8,939,246 (59% need-based, 41% non-need-based). 86% of past graduating class borrowed through all loan programs. Average indebtedness per student: $18,679. ***Average need-based loan:*** Freshmen: $2600; Undergraduates: $2814. ***Parent loans:*** $1,942,772 (100% non-need-based). ***Programs:*** FFEL (Subsidized and Unsubsidized Stafford, PLUS), Perkins, alternative loans.

WORK-STUDY ***Federal work-study:*** *Total amount:* $519,247; 203 jobs averaging $2340. ***State or other work-study/employment:*** *Total amount:* $519,282 (100% non-need-based). 230 part-time jobs averaging $2264.

ATHLETIC AWARDS *Total amount:* 383,820 (100% non-need-based).

APPLYING for FINANCIAL AID ***Required financial aid forms:*** FAFSA, institution's own form. ***Financial aid deadline (priority):*** 3/1. ***Notification date:*** Continuous beginning 3/15. Students must reply within 2 weeks of notification.

CONTACT Mrs. Cynthia Thornton, Director of Financial Aid, Dillard University, 2601 Gentilly Boulevard, New Orleans, LA 70122-3097, 504-286-4677. *Fax:* 504-283-5456. *E-mail:* cthornton@dillard.edu

DOANE COLLEGE

Crete, NE

Tuition & fees: $12,280 **Average undergraduate aid package: $11,161**

ABOUT THE INSTITUTION Independent religious, coed. Awards: bachelor's and master's degrees (nontraditional undergraduate programs and graduate programs offered at Lincoln campus). 40 undergraduate majors. Total enrollment: 2,163. Undergraduates: 1,608. Freshmen: 279. Federal methodology is used as a basis for awarding need-based institutional aid.

UNDERGRADUATE EXPENSES for 1999–2000 ***Application fee:*** $15. ***Comprehensive fee:*** $16,010 includes full-time tuition ($12,010), mandatory fees ($270), and room and board ($3730). Full-time tuition and fees vary according to location. Room and board charges vary according to board plan and location. ***Part-time tuition:*** $400 per credit. ***Part-time fees:*** $135 per term part-time. Part-time tuition and fees vary according to course load and location. ***Payment plan:*** installment.

FRESHMAN FINANCIAL AID (Fall 1999, est.) 274 applied for aid; of those 85% were deemed to have need. 100% of freshmen with need received aid; of those 38% had need fully met. *Average percent of need met:* 88% (excluding resources awarded to replace EFC). *Average financial aid package:* $11,833 (excluding resources awarded to replace EFC). 9% of all full-time freshmen had no need and received non-need-based aid.

UNDERGRADUATE FINANCIAL AID (Fall 1999, est.) 916 applied for aid; of those 87% were deemed to have need. 100% of undergraduates with need received aid; of those 32% had need fully met. *Average percent of need met:* 83% (excluding resources awarded to replace EFC). *Average financial aid package:* $11,161 (excluding resources awarded to replace EFC). 11% of all full-time undergraduates had no need and received non-need-based aid.

GIFT AID (NEED-BASED) ***Total amount:*** $4,187,149 (16% Federal, 6% state, 68% institutional, 10% external sources). ***Receiving aid:*** *Freshmen:* 70% (192); *all full-time undergraduates:* 69% (642). ***Scholarships, grants, and awards:*** Federal Pell, FSEOG, state, private, college/university gift aid from institutional funds.

GIFT AID (NON-NEED-BASED) ***Total amount:*** $442,117 (100% institutional). ***Scholarships, grants, and awards by category:*** *Academic Interests/Achievement:* biological sciences, business, communication, education, general academic interests/achievements, humanities, physical sciences, social sciences. *Creative Arts/Performance:* art/fine arts, music, theater/drama. *Special Achievements/Activities:* general special achievements/activities, leadership. *Special Characteristics:* religious affiliation, siblings of current students. ***Tuition waivers:*** Full or partial for employees or children of employees, senior citizens. ***ROTC:*** Army cooperative, Air Force cooperative.

LOANS ***Student loans:*** $2,844,542 (78% need-based, 22% non-need-based). 91% of past graduating class borrowed through all loan programs. Average indebtedness per student: $15,716. ***Average need-based loan:*** Freshmen: $2951; Undergraduates: $3707. ***Parent loans:*** $1,170,223 (100% non-need-based). ***Programs:*** FFEL (Subsidized and Unsubsidized Stafford, PLUS), Perkins.

WORK-STUDY ***Federal work-study:*** *Total amount:* $238,638; 446 jobs available. ***State or other work-study/employment:*** *Total amount:* $114,440 (100% non-need-based). 139 part-time jobs averaging $520.

ATHLETIC AWARDS *Total amount:* 791,422 (78% need-based, 22% non-need-based).

APPLYING for FINANCIAL AID ***Required financial aid form:*** institution's own form. ***Financial aid deadline (priority):*** 3/1. ***Notification date:*** Continuous beginning 3/6. Students must reply within 2 weeks of notification.

CONTACT Ms. Janet Dodson, Director of Financial Aid, Doane College, 1014 Boswell Avenue, Crete, NE 68333-2430, 402-826-8625 or toll-free 800-333-6263. *Fax:* 402-826-8600. *E-mail:* jdodson@doane.edu

DOMINICAN COLLEGE OF BLAUVELT

Orangeburg, NY

Tuition & fees: $12,370 **Average undergraduate aid package: N/A**

ABOUT THE INSTITUTION Independent, coed. Awards: associate, bachelor's, and master's degrees. 41 undergraduate majors. Total enrollment: 1,688. Undergraduates: 1,645. Freshmen: 135. Both federal and institutional methodology are used as a basis for awarding need-based institutional aid.

UNDERGRADUATE EXPENSES for 1999–2000 ***Application fee:*** $35. ***Comprehensive fee:*** $19,370 includes full-time tuition ($12,000), mandatory fees ($370), and room and board ($7000). Room and board charges vary according to board plan. ***Part-time tuition:*** $400 per credit. ***Part-time fees:*** $10 per credit. ***Payment plans:*** guaranteed tuition, installment.

GIFT AID (NEED-BASED) ***Scholarships, grants, and awards:*** Federal Pell, FSEOG, state, private, college/university gift aid from institutional funds.

GIFT AID (NON-NEED-BASED) ***Scholarships, grants, and awards by category:*** *Academic Interests/Achievement:* general academic interests/achievements. *Special Characteristics:* relatives of clergy. ***Tuition waivers:*** Full or partial for employees or children of employees, senior citizens. ***ROTC:*** Army cooperative.

LOANS ***Programs:*** FFEL (Subsidized and Unsubsidized Stafford, PLUS), Perkins, Federal Nursing.

WORK-STUDY Federal work-study jobs available.

APPLYING for FINANCIAL AID ***Required financial aid forms:*** FAFSA, institution's own form. ***Financial aid deadline (priority):*** 2/15. ***Notification date:*** Continuous beginning 3/1. Students must reply within 4 weeks of notification.

Dominican College of Blauvelt (continued)

CONTACT Ms. Eileen Felske, Director of Financial Aid, Dominican College of Blauvelt, 470 Western Highway, Orangeburg, NY 10962, 914-359-7800 Ext. 225. *Fax:* 914-359-2313.

DOMINICAN UNIVERSITY

River Forest, IL

Tuition & fees: $14,820 **Average undergraduate aid package: $11,539**

ABOUT THE INSTITUTION Independent Roman Catholic, coed. Awards: bachelor's and master's degrees. 47 undergraduate majors. Total enrollment: 2,360. Undergraduates: 1,147. Freshmen: 201. Federal methodology is used as a basis for awarding need-based institutional aid.

UNDERGRADUATE EXPENSES for 2000–2001 ***Application fee:*** $20. ***One-time required fee:*** $100. ***Comprehensive fee:*** $19,850 includes full-time tuition ($14,720), mandatory fees ($100), and room and board ($5030). Room and board charges vary according to board plan and housing facility. ***Part-time tuition:*** $490 per credit hour. Part-time tuition and fees vary according to program. ***Payment plan:*** installment.

FRESHMAN FINANCIAL AID (Fall 1998) 198 applied for aid. *Average percent of need met:* 90% (excluding resources awarded to replace EFC). *Average financial aid package:* $12,105 (excluding resources awarded to replace EFC). 18% of all full-time freshmen had no need and received non-need-based aid.

UNDERGRADUATE FINANCIAL AID (Fall 1998) 590 applied for aid. *Average percent of need met:* 90% (excluding resources awarded to replace EFC). *Average financial aid package:* $11,539 (excluding resources awarded to replace EFC). 13% of all full-time undergraduates had no need and received non-need-based aid.

GIFT AID (NEED-BASED) ***Total amount:*** $4,527,742 (13% Federal, 37% state, 49% institutional, 1% external sources). ***Scholarships, grants, and awards:*** Federal Pell, FSEOG, state, private, college/university gift aid from institutional funds.

GIFT AID (NON-NEED-BASED) ***Total amount:*** $489,584 (2% state, 94% institutional, 4% external sources). ***Scholarships, grants, and awards by category:*** *Academic Interests/Achievement:* 73 awards ($259,300 total): general academic interests/achievements. *Creative Arts/Performance:* 1 award ($3000 total): creative writing. *Special Achievements/Activities:* 112 awards ($98,500 total): religious involvement. *Special Characteristics:* 97 awards ($316,286 total): children and siblings of alumni, children of faculty/staff, international students, siblings of current students, spouses of current students, twins. ***Tuition waivers:*** Full or partial for children of alumni, employees or children of employees.

LOANS ***Student loans:*** $4,409,574 (55% need-based, 45% non-need-based). 76% of past graduating class borrowed through all loan programs. Average indebtedness per student: $12,013. ***Parent loans:*** $358,823 (100% non-need-based). ***Programs:*** FFEL (Subsidized and Unsubsidized Stafford, PLUS), Perkins.

WORK-STUDY ***Federal work-study:*** *Total amount:* $366,577; 202 jobs averaging $1815. ***State or other work-study/employment:*** *Total amount:* $143,880 (49% need-based, 51% non-need-based). 90 part-time jobs averaging $1602.

ATHLETIC AWARDS *Total amount:* 89,500 (83% need-based, 17% non-need-based).

APPLYING for FINANCIAL AID ***Required financial aid form:*** FAFSA. ***Financial aid deadline (priority):*** 6/1. ***Notification date:*** Continuous. Students must reply within 2 weeks of notification.

CONTACT Mr. Howard Florine, Director of Financial Aid, Dominican University, 7900 West Division, River Forest, IL 60305-1099, 708-524-6809 or toll-free 800-828-8475. *Fax:* 708-524-5990. *E-mail:* florineh@email.dom.edu

DOMINICAN UNIVERSITY OF CALIFORNIA

San Rafael, CA

Tuition & fees: $16,844 **Average undergraduate aid package: $16,216**

ABOUT THE INSTITUTION Independent religious, coed. Awards: bachelor's and master's degrees and post-bachelor's certificates. 21 undergraduate majors. Total enrollment: 1,431. Undergraduates: 984. Freshmen: 114. Federal methodology is used as a basis for awarding need-based institutional aid.

UNDERGRADUATE EXPENSES for 1999–2000 ***Application fee:*** $40. ***Comprehensive fee:*** $24,364 includes full-time tuition ($16,512), mandatory fees ($332), and room and board ($7520). Full-time tuition and fees vary according to program. Room and board charges vary according to board plan. ***Part-time tuition:*** $688 per unit. ***Part-time fees:*** $166 per term part-time. Part-time tuition and fees vary according to program. ***Payment plan:*** installment.

FRESHMAN FINANCIAL AID (Fall 1999) 105 applied for aid; of those 68% were deemed to have need. 100% of freshmen with need received aid; of those 24% had need fully met. *Average percent of need met:* 83% (excluding resources awarded to replace EFC). *Average financial aid package:* $17,018 (excluding resources awarded to replace EFC). 29% of all full-time freshmen had no need and received non-need-based aid.

UNDERGRADUATE FINANCIAL AID (Fall 1999) 438 applied for aid; of those 84% were deemed to have need. 100% of undergraduates with need received aid; of those 21% had need fully met. *Average percent of need met:* 78% (excluding resources awarded to replace EFC). *Average financial aid package:* $16,216 (excluding resources awarded to replace EFC). 11% of all full-time undergraduates had no need and received non-need-based aid.

GIFT AID (NEED-BASED) ***Total amount:*** $4,266,674 (16% Federal, 22% state, 60% institutional, 2% external sources). ***Receiving aid:*** *Freshmen:* 53% (58); *all full-time undergraduates:* 59% (344). ***Average award:*** Freshmen: $12,825; Undergraduates: $10,321. ***Scholarships, grants, and awards:*** Federal Pell, FSEOG, state, private, college/university gift aid from institutional funds.

GIFT AID (NON-NEED-BASED) ***Total amount:*** $547,953 (99% institutional, 1% external sources). ***Receiving aid:*** *Freshmen:* 12% (13); *Undergraduates:* 4% (22). ***Scholarships, grants, and awards by category:*** *Academic Interests/Achievement:* general academic interests/achievements. *Creative Arts/Performance:* music. *Special Achievements/Activities:* community service. *Special Characteristics:* children and siblings of alumni, members of minority groups. ***Tuition waivers:*** Full or partial for employees or children of employees. ***ROTC:*** Army cooperative, Air Force cooperative.

LOANS ***Student loans:*** $1,858,566 (100% need-based). ***Average need-based loan:*** Freshmen: $2863; Undergraduates: $4182. ***Parent loans:*** $2,396,964 (49% need-based, 51% non-need-based). ***Programs:*** FFEL (Subsidized and Unsubsidized Stafford, PLUS), Perkins, Federal Nursing.

WORK-STUDY ***Federal work-study:*** *Total amount:* $695,176; 314 jobs averaging $2229. ***State or other work-study/employment:*** *Total amount:* $179,774 (88% need-based, 12% non-need-based). 62 part-time jobs averaging $2956.

ATHLETIC AWARDS *Total amount:* 218,407 (32% need-based, 68% non-need-based).

APPLYING for FINANCIAL AID ***Required financial aid forms:*** FAFSA, institution's own form, state aid form. ***Financial aid deadline (priority):*** 3/2. ***Notification date:*** Continuous. Students must reply within 2 weeks of notification.

CONTACT Barbara Jenkins, Acting Director of Financial Aid, Dominican University of California, 50 Acacia Avenue, San Rafael, CA 94901-2298, 415-257-1302 or toll-free 888-323-6763. *Fax:* 415-458-3730. *E-mail:* jenkins@dominican.edu

DORDT COLLEGE

Sioux Center, IA

Tuition & fees: $12,650 **Average undergraduate aid package: $11,476**

ABOUT THE INSTITUTION Independent Christian Reformed, coed. Awards: associate, bachelor's, and master's degrees. 51 undergraduate majors. Total enrollment: 1,430. Undergraduates: 1,430. Freshmen: 349. Federal methodology is used as a basis for awarding need-based institutional aid.

UNDERGRADUATE EXPENSES for 1999–2000 ***Application fee:*** $25. ***Comprehensive fee:*** $16,250 includes full-time tuition ($12,500), mandatory fees ($150), and room and board ($3600). ***College room only:*** $1850. Room and board charges vary according to board plan and housing facility. ***Part-time tuition:*** $525 per credit hour. ***Part-time fees:*** $75 per term part-time. ***Payment plan:*** installment.

FRESHMAN FINANCIAL AID (Fall 1999, est.) 393 applied for aid; of those 90% were deemed to have need. 100% of freshmen with need received aid; of those 19% had need fully met. *Average percent of need met:* 77% (excluding resources awarded to replace EFC). *Average financial aid package:* $11,650 (excluding resources awarded to replace EFC). 14% of all full-time freshmen had no need and received non-need-based aid.

UNDERGRADUATE FINANCIAL AID (Fall 1999, est.) 1,289 applied for aid; of those 91% were deemed to have need. 100% of undergraduates with need received aid; of those 20% had need fully met. *Average percent of need met:* 76% (excluding resources awarded to replace EFC). *Average financial aid package:* $11,476 (excluding resources awarded to replace EFC). 15% of all full-time undergraduates had no need and received non-need-based aid.

GIFT AID (NEED-BASED) ***Total amount:*** $6,668,119 (15% Federal, 22% state, 56% institutional, 7% external sources). ***Receiving aid:*** *Freshmen:* 85% (353); *all full-time undergraduates:* 85% (1,173). ***Average award:*** Freshmen: $6828; Undergraduates: $6169. ***Scholarships, grants, and awards:*** Federal Pell, FSEOG, state, private, college/university gift aid from institutional funds.

GIFT AID (NON-NEED-BASED) ***Total amount:*** $499,367 (93% institutional, 7% external sources). ***Scholarships, grants, and awards by category:*** *Academic Interests/Achievement:* agriculture, business, communication, computer science, education, engineering/technologies, English, foreign languages, general academic interests/achievements, humanities, mathematics, physical sciences, premedicine, religion/biblical studies, social sciences. *Creative Arts/Performance:* journalism/publications, music, theater/drama. *Special Achievements/Activities:* general special achievements/activities, leadership. *Special Characteristics:* children and siblings of alumni, children of faculty/staff, general special characteristics, handicapped students, international students, local/state students, members of minority groups, out-of-state students, religious affiliation. ***Tuition waivers:*** Full or partial for children of alumni, employees or children of employees, senior citizens.

LOANS ***Student loans:*** $5,238,908 (92% need-based, 8% non-need-based). 90% of past graduating class borrowed through all loan programs. Average indebtedness per student: $14,271. ***Average need-based loan:*** Freshmen: $3774; Undergraduates: $4108. ***Parent loans:*** $299,171 (89% need-based, 11% non-need-based). ***Programs:*** FFEL (Subsidized and Unsubsidized Stafford, PLUS), Perkins, state, college/university.

WORK-STUDY ***Federal work-study:*** *Total amount:* $735,875; jobs available. ***State or other work-study/employment:*** *Total amount:* $634,469 (76% need-based, 24% non-need-based). Part-time jobs available.

ATHLETIC AWARDS *Total amount:* 210,625 (89% need-based, 11% non-need-based).

APPLYING for FINANCIAL AID ***Required financial aid forms:*** FAFSA, institution's own form. ***Financial aid deadline (priority):*** 4/1. ***Notification date:*** Continuous. Students must reply within 3 weeks of notification.

CONTACT Ms. Barbara Schaap, Coordinator of Scholarships, Dordt College, 498 4th Avenue NE, Sioux Center, IA 51250-1697, 712-722-6084 or toll-free 800-343-6738. *Fax:* 712-722-1967. *E-mail:* barb@dordt.edu

DOUGLASS COLLEGE

New Brunswick, NJ

See Rutgers, The State University of New Jersey, Douglass College

DOWLING COLLEGE

Oakdale, NY

Tuition & fees: $14,070 **Average undergraduate aid package: $11,847**

ABOUT THE INSTITUTION Independent, coed. Awards: bachelor's, master's, and doctoral degrees and post-master's certificates. 42 undergraduate majors. Total enrollment: 5,774. Undergraduates: 2,922. Freshmen: 339. Federal methodology is used as a basis for awarding need-based institutional aid.

UNDERGRADUATE EXPENSES for 1999–2000 ***Application fee:*** $25. ***Tuition:*** full-time $13,350; part-time $445 per credit hour. ***Required fees:*** full-time $720; $240 per term part-time. Full-time tuition and fees vary according to course load and degree level. Part-time tuition and fees vary according to course load and degree level. Room and board charges vary according to housing facility and location. ***Payment plans:*** guaranteed tuition, installment, deferred payment.

FRESHMAN FINANCIAL AID (Fall 1999, est.) 285 applied for aid; of those 85% were deemed to have need. 99% of freshmen with need received aid; of those 24% had need fully met. *Average percent of need met:* 75% (excluding resources awarded to replace EFC). *Average financial aid package:* $8505 (excluding resources awarded to replace EFC). 4% of all full-time freshmen had no need and received non-need-based aid.

UNDERGRADUATE FINANCIAL AID (Fall 1999, est.) 1,840 applied for aid; of those 91% were deemed to have need. 85% of undergraduates with need received aid; of those 28% had need fully met. *Average percent of need met:* 79% (excluding resources awarded to replace EFC). *Average financial aid package:* $11,847 (excluding resources awarded to replace EFC).

GIFT AID (NEED-BASED) ***Total amount:*** $6,043,331 (37% Federal, 30% state, 33% institutional). ***Receiving aid:*** *Freshmen:* 68% (229); *all full-time undergraduates:* 1,365. ***Average award:*** Freshmen: $4310; Undergraduates: $4238. ***Scholarships, grants, and awards:*** Federal Pell, FSEOG, state, private, college/university gift aid from institutional funds.

GIFT AID (NON-NEED-BASED) ***Total amount:*** $1,310,597 (2% state, 96% institutional, 2% external sources). ***Receiving aid:*** *Freshmen:* 19% (65); *Undergraduates:* 254. ***Scholarships, grants, and awards by category:*** *Academic Interests/Achievement:* business, education, general academic interests/achievements. *Special Achievements/Activities:* general special achievements/activities. *Special Characteristics:* children and siblings of alumni, children of educators, children of faculty/staff, children of public servants, children of union members/company employees, children of workers in trades, first-generation college students, general special characteristics, local/state students, public servants. ***Tuition waivers:*** Full or partial for minority students, children of alumni, employees or children of employees, adult students, senior citizens. ***ROTC:*** Army cooperative, Naval cooperative, Air Force cooperative.

LOANS ***Student loans:*** $10,600,646 (67% need-based, 33% non-need-based). 75% of past graduating class borrowed through all loan programs. Average indebtedness per student: $13,500. ***Average need-based loan:*** Freshmen: $2625; Undergraduates: $5500. ***Parent loans:*** $1,282,416 (52% need-based, 48% non-need-based). ***Programs:*** Federal Direct (Subsidized and Unsubsidized Stafford, PLUS), Perkins.

WORK-STUDY ***Federal work-study:*** *Total amount:* $401,323; 200 jobs averaging $2000. ***State or other work-study/employment:*** *Total amount:* $400,000 (100% non-need-based). 200 part-time jobs averaging $2000.

ATHLETIC AWARDS *Total amount:* 1,191,353 (59% need-based, 41% non-need-based).

APPLYING for FINANCIAL AID ***Required financial aid forms:*** FAFSA, institution's own form, state aid form. ***Financial aid deadline:*** Continuous. ***Notification date:*** Continuous beginning 3/15. Students must reply within 4 weeks of notification.

CONTACT Ms. Nancy Brewer, Director of Financial Aid, Dowling College, Idle Hour Boulevard, Oakdale, NY 11769-1999, 516-244-3036 or toll-free 800-DOWLING. *Fax:* 516-563-3827.

DRAKE UNIVERSITY

Des Moines, IA

Tuition & fees: $16,580 **Average undergraduate aid package: $14,149**

ABOUT THE INSTITUTION Independent, coed. Awards: bachelor's, master's, doctoral, and first professional degrees. 61 undergraduate majors. Total enrollment: 4,646. Undergraduates: 3,234. Freshmen: 676. Federal methodology is used as a basis for awarding need-based institutional aid.

UNDERGRADUATE EXPENSES for 1999–2000 ***Application fee:*** $25. ***Comprehensive fee:*** $21,450 includes full-time tuition ($16,480), mandatory fees ($100), and room and board ($4870). ***College room only:*** $2570. Full-time tuition and fees vary according to degree level and student level. Room and board charges vary according to board plan. ***Part-time tuition:*** $350 per semester hour. Part-time tuition and fees vary according to class time. ***Payment plans:*** tuition prepayment, installment.

FRESHMAN FINANCIAL AID (Fall 1999) 600 applied for aid; of those 78% were deemed to have need. 99% of freshmen with need received aid; of those 37% had need fully met. *Average percent of need met:* 90% (excluding resources awarded to replace EFC). *Average financial aid package:* $13,632 (excluding resources awarded to replace EFC). 36% of all full-time freshmen had no need and received non-need-based aid.

UNDERGRADUATE FINANCIAL AID (Fall 1999) 2,081 applied for aid; of those 85% were deemed to have need. 99% of undergraduates with need received aid; of those 32% had need fully met. *Average percent of need met:* 83% (excluding resources awarded to replace EFC). *Average financial aid package:* $14,149 (excluding resources awarded to replace EFC). 35% of all full-time undergraduates had no need and received non-need-based aid.

GIFT AID (NEED-BASED) ***Total amount:*** $16,587,683 (10% Federal, 12% state, 75% institutional, 3% external sources). ***Receiving aid:*** *Freshmen:* 60% (462); *all full-time undergraduates:* 59% (1,758). ***Average award:*** Freshmen: $10,167; Undergraduates: $9233. ***Scholarships, grants, and awards:*** Federal Pell, FSEOG, state, private, college/university gift aid from institutional funds.

GIFT AID (NON-NEED-BASED) ***Total amount:*** $7,364,748 (1% Federal, 95% institutional, 4% external sources). ***Receiving aid:*** *Freshmen:* 13% (99); *Undergraduates:* 8% (226). ***Scholarships, grants, and awards by category:*** *Academic Interests/Achievement:* 3,582 awards ($14,448,751 total): general academic interests/achievements. *Creative Arts/Performance:* 351 awards ($595,515 total): art/fine arts, music, theater/drama. *Special Characteristics:* 307 awards ($566,055 total): children and siblings of alumni, ethnic background, international students, members of minority groups. ***Tuition waivers:*** Full or partial for children of alumni, employees or children of employees, senior citizens. ***ROTC:*** Army, Air Force cooperative.

LOANS ***Student loans:*** $11,535,959 (65% need-based, 35% non-need-based). 68% of past graduating class borrowed through all loan programs. Average indebtedness per student: $19,630. ***Average need-based loan:*** Freshmen: $4113; Undergraduates: $5687. ***Parent loans:*** $1,627,084 (20% need-based, 80% non-need-based). ***Programs:*** FFEL (Subsidized and Unsubsidized Stafford, PLUS), Perkins, college/university.

WORK-STUDY ***Federal work-study:*** *Total amount:* $1,112,436; 685 jobs averaging $1624. ***State or other work-study/employment:*** *Total amount:* $905,824 (35% need-based, 65% non-need-based). Part-time jobs available.

ATHLETIC AWARDS *Total amount:* 1,529,923 (23% need-based, 77% non-need-based).

APPLYING for FINANCIAL AID ***Required financial aid form:*** FAFSA. ***Financial aid deadline (priority):*** 3/1. ***Notification date:*** Continuous beginning 3/18. Students must reply by 5/1 or within 3 weeks of notification.

CONTACT Office of Student Financial Planning, Drake University, 2507 University Avenue, Des Moines, IA 50311-4516, 800-44-DRAKE Ext. 2905 or toll-free 800-44DRAKE. *Fax:* 515-271-4042.

DREW UNIVERSITY

Madison, NJ

Tuition & fees: $23,008 **Average undergraduate aid package: $20,137**

ABOUT THE INSTITUTION Independent religious, coed. Awards: bachelor's, master's, doctoral, and first professional degrees and post-bachelor's certificates. 35 undergraduate majors. Total enrollment: 2,381. Undergraduates: 1,485. Freshmen: 407. Institutional methodology is used as a basis for awarding need-based institutional aid.

UNDERGRADUATE EXPENSES for 1999–2000 ***Application fee:*** $40. ***Comprehensive fee:*** $29,572 includes full-time tuition ($22,462), mandatory fees ($546), and room and board ($6564). Room and board charges vary according to board plan and housing facility. ***Part-time tuition:*** $936 per credit. ***Part-time fees:*** $23 per credit. ***Payment plans:*** tuition prepayment, installment.

UNDERGRADUATE FINANCIAL AID (Fall 1999, est.) 879 applied for aid; of those 82% were deemed to have need. 100% of undergraduates with need received aid; of those 52% had need fully met. *Average percent of need met:* 90% (excluding resources awarded to replace EFC). *Average financial aid package:* $20,137 (excluding resources awarded to replace EFC). 30% of all full-time undergraduates had no need and received non-need-based aid.

GIFT AID (NEED-BASED) ***Total amount:*** $10,028,927 (9% Federal, 16% state, 71% institutional, 4% external sources). ***Receiving aid:*** *All full-time undergraduates:* 51% (717). ***Average award:*** Undergraduates: $13,987. ***Scholarships, grants, and awards:*** Federal Pell, FSEOG, state, private, college/university gift aid from institutional funds.

GIFT AID (NON-NEED-BASED) ***Total amount:*** $4,324,668 (5% state, 90% institutional, 5% external sources). ***Receiving aid:*** *Undergraduates:* 7% (104). ***Scholarships, grants, and awards by category:*** *Academic Interests/Achievement:* general academic interests/achievements. *Creative Arts/Performance:* general creative arts/performance. ***Tuition waivers:*** Full or partial for employees or children of employees, senior citizens.

LOANS ***Student loans:*** $4,084,013 (86% need-based, 14% non-need-based). 61% of past graduating class borrowed through all loan programs. Average indebtedness per student: $12,880. ***Average need-based loan:*** Undergraduates: $5007. ***Programs:*** FFEL (Subsidized and Unsubsidized Stafford, PLUS), Perkins, state.

WORK-STUDY ***Federal work-study:*** *Total amount:* $952,445; jobs available.

APPLYING for FINANCIAL AID ***Required financial aid forms:*** FAFSA, CSS Financial Aid PROFILE. ***Financial aid deadline:*** 3/1. ***Notification date:*** 3/30. Students must reply by 5/1.

CONTACT Mrs. Joyce R. Farmer, Director of Financial Assistance, Drew University, 36 Madison Avenue, Madison, NJ 07940-1493, 973-408-3112.

DREXEL UNIVERSITY

Philadelphia, PA

Tuition & fees: $16,150 **Average undergraduate aid package: $13,622**

ABOUT THE INSTITUTION Independent, coed. Awards: bachelor's, master's, and doctoral degrees and post-master's certificates. 63 undergraduate majors. Total enrollment: 12,013. Undergraduates: 9,530. Freshmen: 1,941. Federal methodology is used as a basis for awarding need-based institutional aid.

UNDERGRADUATE EXPENSES for 1999–2000 ***Application fee:*** $35. ***One-time required fee:*** $125. ***Comprehensive fee:*** $23,992 includes full-time tuition ($15,240), mandatory fees ($910), and room and board ($7842). ***College room only:*** $4800. Full-time tuition and fees vary according to program and student level. Room and board charges vary according to housing facility. ***Part-time tuition:*** $386 per credit hour. ***Part-time fees:*** $67 per term part-time. Part-time tuition and fees vary according to class time. ***Payment plans:*** installment, deferred payment.

FRESHMAN FINANCIAL AID (Fall 1999) 1576 applied for aid; of those 88% were deemed to have need. 100% of freshmen with need received aid; of those 36% had need fully met. *Average percent of need met:* 80% (excluding resources awarded to replace EFC). *Average financial aid package:* $14,394 (excluding resources awarded to replace EFC). 10% of all full-time freshmen had no need and received non-need-based aid.

UNDERGRADUATE FINANCIAL AID (Fall 1999) 5,500 applied for aid; of those 90% were deemed to have need. 100% of undergraduates with need received aid; of those 31% had need fully met. *Average percent of* *need met:* 78% (excluding resources awarded to replace EFC). *Average financial aid package:* $13,622 (excluding resources awarded to replace EFC). 7% of all full-time undergraduates had no need and received non-need-based aid.

GIFT AID (NEED-BASED) ***Total amount:*** $44,104,857 (10% Federal, 11% state, 78% institutional, 1% external sources). ***Receiving aid:*** *Freshmen:* 69% (1,300); *all full-time undergraduates:* 59% (4,500). ***Average award:*** Freshmen: $7549; Undergraduates: $6811. ***Scholarships, grants, and awards:*** Federal Pell, FSEOG, state, private, college/university gift aid from institutional funds, United Negro College Fund.

GIFT AID (NON-NEED-BASED) ***Total amount:*** $4,859,202 (100% institutional). ***Receiving aid:*** *Freshmen:* 47% (883); *Undergraduates:* 33% (2,511). ***Scholarships, grants, and awards by category:*** *Academic Interests/Achievement:* general academic interests/achievements. *Creative Arts/Performance:* dance, music, performing arts, theater/drama. *Special Achievements/Activities:* cheerleading/drum major. *Special Characteristics:* children and siblings of alumni, siblings of current students, twins. ***Tuition waivers:*** Full or partial for employees or children of employees, senior citizens. ***ROTC:*** Army, Naval cooperative, Air Force cooperative.

LOANS ***Student loans:*** $27,482,133 (99% need-based, 1% non-need-based). ***Average need-based loan:*** Freshmen: $3074; Undergraduates: $3866. ***Parent loans:*** $3,700,731 (100% need-based). ***Programs:*** FFEL (Subsidized and Unsubsidized Stafford, PLUS), Perkins, college/university.

WORK-STUDY ***Federal work-study:*** *Total amount:* $2,580,406; jobs available.

ATHLETIC AWARDS *Total amount:* 2,408,020 (100% non-need-based).

APPLYING for FINANCIAL AID ***Required financial aid form:*** FAFSA. ***Financial aid deadline (priority):*** 2/15. ***Notification date:*** 4/1. Students must reply by 5/1.

CONTACT Ms. Jeanne Cavalieri, Director of Financial Aid, Drexel University, 3141 Chestnut Street, Philadelphia, PA 19104-2875, 215-895-2536 or toll-free 800-2-DREXEL (in-state). *Fax:* 215-895-5939.

DRURY UNIVERSITY

Springfield, MO

Tuition & fees: $10,695 **Average undergraduate aid package: $7983**

ABOUT THE INSTITUTION Independent, coed. Awards: bachelor's and master's degrees (also offers evening program with significant enrollment not reflected in profile). 41 undergraduate majors. Total enrollment: 1,760. Undergraduates: 1,431. Freshmen: 364. Federal methodology is used as a basis for awarding need-based institutional aid.

UNDERGRADUATE EXPENSES for 1999–2000 ***Application fee:*** $20. ***One-time required fee:*** $75. ***Comprehensive fee:*** $14,825 includes full-time tuition ($10,450), mandatory fees ($245), and room and board ($4130). Room and board charges vary according to board plan and housing facility. ***Part-time tuition:*** $346 per semester hour. ***Payment plans:*** tuition prepayment, installment, deferred payment.

FRESHMAN FINANCIAL AID (Fall 1999) 327 applied for aid; of those 93% were deemed to have need. 100% of freshmen with need received aid; of those 87% had need fully met. *Average percent of need met:* 82% (excluding resources awarded to replace EFC). *Average financial aid package:* $6998 (excluding resources awarded to replace EFC). 13% of all full-time freshmen had no need and received non-need-based aid.

UNDERGRADUATE FINANCIAL AID (Fall 1999) 1,244 applied for aid; of those 96% were deemed to have need. 100% of undergraduates with need received aid; of those 93% had need fully met. *Average percent of need met:* 84% (excluding resources awarded to replace EFC). *Average financial aid package:* $7983 (excluding resources awarded to replace EFC). 14% of all full-time undergraduates had no need and received non-need-based aid.

GIFT AID (NEED-BASED) ***Total amount:*** $6,693,093 (6% Federal, 9% state, 58% institutional, 27% external sources). ***Receiving aid:*** *Freshmen:* 83% (301); *all full-time undergraduates:* 85% (1,192). ***Average award:*** Freshmen: $5762; Undergraduates: $6828. ***Scholarships, grants, and awards:*** Federal Pell, FSEOG, state, private, college/university gift aid from institutional funds.

GIFT AID (NON-NEED-BASED) ***Total amount:*** $1,543,164 (21% state, 68% institutional, 11% external sources). ***Receiving aid:*** *Freshmen:* 78% (285); *Undergraduates:* 83% (1,172). ***Scholarships, grants, and awards by category:*** *Academic Interests/Achievement:* 1,401 awards ($2,967,840 total): architecture, biological sciences, business, communication, education, English, general academic interests/achievements, health fields, humanities, mathematics, physical sciences, premedicine, social sciences. *Creative Arts/Performance:* 156 awards ($105,177 total): art/fine arts, creative writing, music, theater/drama. *Special Achievements/Activities:* 746 awards ($283,180 total): cheerleading/drum major, leadership, religious involvement. *Special Characteristics:* 63 awards ($580,484 total): children and siblings of alumni, children of faculty/staff, relatives of clergy, religious affiliation. ***Tuition waivers:*** Full or partial for employees or children of employees, adult students, senior citizens. ***ROTC:*** Army cooperative.

LOANS ***Student loans:*** $4,263,060 (100% need-based). 58% of past graduating class borrowed through all loan programs. Average indebtedness per student: $12,800. ***Average need-based loan:*** Freshmen: $2240; Undergraduates: $4485. ***Parent loans:*** $412,782 (100% need-based). ***Programs:*** FFEL (Subsidized and Unsubsidized Stafford, PLUS), Perkins.

WORK-STUDY ***Federal work-study:*** *Total amount:* $253,840; jobs available. ***State or other work-study/employment:*** *Total amount:* $147,960 (100% non-need-based). Part-time jobs available.

ATHLETIC AWARDS *Total amount:* 811,592 (29% need-based, 71% non-need-based).

APPLYING for FINANCIAL AID ***Required financial aid forms:*** FAFSA, institution's own form. ***Financial aid deadline (priority):*** 3/15.

CONTACT Ms. Annette Avery, Director of Financial Aid, Drury University, 900 North Benton Avenue, Springfield, MO 65802-3791, 417-873-7312 or toll-free 800-922-2274 (in-state). *Fax:* 417-873-7529. *E-mail:* aavery@lib.drury.edu

DUKE UNIVERSITY

Durham, NC

Tuition & fees: $24,751 **Average undergraduate aid package: $19,056**

ABOUT THE INSTITUTION Independent religious, coed. Awards: bachelor's, master's, doctoral, and first professional degrees. 44 undergraduate majors. Total enrollment: 11,811. Undergraduates: 6,368. Freshmen: 1,630. Institutional methodology is used as a basis for awarding need-based institutional aid.

UNDERGRADUATE EXPENSES for 1999–2000 ***Application fee:*** $60. ***Comprehensive fee:*** $31,839 includes full-time tuition ($24,040), mandatory fees ($711), and room and board ($7088). ***College room only:*** $3788. Full-time tuition and fees vary according to program and student level. Room and board charges vary according to board plan and housing facility. ***Part-time tuition:*** $3005 per course. ***Part-time fees:*** $215 per term part-time. Part-time tuition and fees vary according to program and student level. ***Payment plans:*** tuition prepayment, installment, deferred payment.

FRESHMAN FINANCIAL AID (Fall 1999, est.) 831 applied for aid; of those 73% were deemed to have need. 100% of freshmen with need received aid; of those 100% had need fully met. *Average percent of need met:* 100% (excluding resources awarded to replace EFC). *Average financial aid package:* $18,566 (excluding resources awarded to replace EFC). 2% of all full-time freshmen had no need and received non-need-based aid.

UNDERGRADUATE FINANCIAL AID (Fall 1999, est.) 2,861 applied for aid; of those 82% were deemed to have need. 100% of undergraduates with need received aid; of those 100% had need fully met. *Average percent of need met:* 100% (excluding resources awarded to replace EFC). *Average financial aid package:* $19,056 (excluding resources awarded to replace EFC). 2% of all full-time undergraduates had no need and received non-need-based aid.

GIFT AID (NEED-BASED) ***Total amount:*** $31,962,069 (9% Federal, 5% state, 77% institutional, 9% external sources). ***Receiving aid:*** *Freshmen:* 33% (533); *all full-time undergraduates:* 33% (2,062). ***Average award:***

Duke University (continued)

Freshmen: $16,035; Undergraduates: $14,922. ***Scholarships, grants, and awards:*** Federal Pell, FSEOG, state, private, college/university gift aid from institutional funds.

GIFT AID (NON-NEED-BASED) ***Total amount:*** $2,991,533 (3% state, 91% institutional, 6% external sources). ***Receiving aid:*** *Freshmen:* 1% (12); *Undergraduates:* 1% (46). ***Scholarships, grants, and awards by category:*** *Academic Interests/Achievement:* 95 awards ($2,083,025 total): English, general academic interests/achievements, mathematics. *Creative Arts/Performance:* 25 awards ($54,038 total): creative writing, music, theater/drama. *Special Achievements/Activities:* 33 awards ($576,261 total): leadership. *Special Characteristics:* 38 awards ($542,027 total): children and siblings of alumni, children of faculty/staff, ethnic background, local/state students. ***Tuition waivers:*** Full or partial for employees or children of employees. ***ROTC:*** Army, Naval, Air Force.

LOANS ***Student loans:*** $10,849,811 (100% need-based). 36% of past graduating class borrowed through all loan programs. Average indebtedness per student: $16,098. ***Average need-based loan:*** Freshmen: $3007; Undergraduates: $4085. ***Parent loans:*** $6,134,076 (61% need-based, 39% non-need-based). ***Programs:*** FFEL (Subsidized and Unsubsidized Stafford, PLUS), Perkins, college/university, alternative loans.

WORK-STUDY ***Federal work-study:*** *Total amount:* $3,301,858; jobs available. ***State or other work-study/employment:*** *Total amount:* $234,748 (58% need-based, 42% non-need-based). Part-time jobs available.

ATHLETIC AWARDS *Total amount:* 8,968,969 (25% need-based, 75% non-need-based).

APPLYING for FINANCIAL AID ***Required financial aid forms:*** FAFSA, CSS Financial Aid PROFILE, noncustodial (divorced/separated) parent's statement, business/farm supplement, parent and student income tax returns. ***Financial aid deadline:*** 2/1. ***Notification date:*** 4/1. Students must reply by 5/1 or within 4 weeks of notification.

CONTACT Nerissa Rivera, Assistant Director of Financial Aid, Duke University, 2106 Campus Drive, Durham, NC 27708-0397, 919-684-6225. *Fax:* 919-660-9811.

DUQUESNE UNIVERSITY

Pittsburgh, PA

Tuition & fees: $15,588 **Average undergraduate aid package: $13,444**

ABOUT THE INSTITUTION Independent Roman Catholic, coed. Awards: bachelor's, master's, doctoral, and first professional degrees and post-bachelor's certificates. 67 undergraduate majors. Total enrollment: 9,742. Undergraduates: 5,537. Freshmen: 1,211. Federal methodology is used as a basis for awarding need-based institutional aid.

UNDERGRADUATE EXPENSES for 1999–2000 ***Application fee:*** $50. ***Comprehensive fee:*** $21,902 includes full-time tuition ($14,378), mandatory fees ($1210), and room and board ($6314). Full-time tuition and fees vary according to program. Room and board charges vary according to board plan. ***Part-time tuition:*** $485 per credit. ***Part-time fees:*** $46 per credit. Part-time tuition and fees vary according to program. ***Payment plans:*** installment, deferred payment.

FRESHMAN FINANCIAL AID (Fall 1999, est.) 1085 applied for aid; of those 76% were deemed to have need. 100% of freshmen with need received aid; of those 32% had need fully met. *Average percent of need met:* 88% (excluding resources awarded to replace EFC). *Average financial aid package:* $13,854 (excluding resources awarded to replace EFC). 15% of all full-time freshmen had no need and received non-need-based aid.

UNDERGRADUATE FINANCIAL AID (Fall 1999, est.) 4,632 applied for aid; of those 76% were deemed to have need. 99% of undergraduates with need received aid; of those 32% had need fully met. *Average percent of need met:* 81% (excluding resources awarded to replace EFC). *Average financial aid package:* $13,444 (excluding resources awarded to replace EFC). 15% of all full-time undergraduates had no need and received non-need-based aid.

GIFT AID (NEED-BASED) ***Total amount:*** $23,218,595 (10% Federal, 23% state, 62% institutional, 5% external sources). ***Receiving aid:*** *Freshmen:* 57% (690); *all full-time undergraduates:* 50% (2,731). ***Average award:*** Freshmen: $5958; Undergraduates: $5825. ***Scholarships, grants, and awards:*** Federal Pell, FSEOG, state, private, college/university gift aid from institutional funds.

GIFT AID (NON-NEED-BASED) ***Total amount:*** $6,442,621 (1% state, 94% institutional, 5% external sources). ***Receiving aid:*** *Freshmen:* 41% (493); *Undergraduates:* 32% (1,734). ***Scholarships, grants, and awards by category:*** *Academic Interests/Achievement:* 2,515 awards ($11,384,302 total): general academic interests/achievements. *Creative Arts/Performance:* 163 awards ($1,162,563 total): dance, music. *Special Characteristics:* 528 awards ($4,413,706 total): children of faculty/staff, international students, members of minority groups, relatives of clergy, religious affiliation. ***Tuition waivers:*** Full or partial for employees or children of employees, adult students, senior citizens. ***ROTC:*** Army cooperative, Air Force cooperative.

LOANS ***Student loans:*** $17,726,775 (94% need-based, 6% non-need-based). 69% of past graduating class borrowed through all loan programs. Average indebtedness per student: $17,842. ***Average need-based loan:*** Freshmen: $2781; Undergraduates: $4158. ***Parent loans:*** $10,482,889 (86% need-based, 14% non-need-based). ***Programs:*** FFEL (Subsidized and Unsubsidized Stafford, PLUS), Perkins, Federal Nursing, college/university, Health Professions Loans.

WORK-STUDY ***Federal work-study:*** *Total amount:* $1,500,000; 791 jobs available.

ATHLETIC AWARDS *Total amount:* 2,683,917 (48% need-based, 52% non-need-based).

APPLYING for FINANCIAL AID ***Required financial aid forms:*** FAFSA, institution's own form. ***Financial aid deadline:*** 5/1. ***Notification date:*** Continuous. Students must reply within 3 weeks of notification.

CONTACT Mr. Frank M. Dutkovich Jr., Director of Financial Aid, Duquesne University, 600 Forbes Avenue, Pittsburgh, PA 15282-0299, 412-396-6607 or toll-free 800-456-0590. *Fax:* 412-396-5284. *E-mail:* dutkovic@duq2.cc.duq.edu

D'YOUVILLE COLLEGE

Buffalo, NY

Tuition & fees: $11,250 **Average undergraduate aid package: $10,115**

ABOUT THE INSTITUTION Independent, coed. Awards: bachelor's and master's degrees and post-bachelor's and post-master's certificates. 26 undergraduate majors. Total enrollment: 2,140. Undergraduates: 1,081. Freshmen: 125. Federal methodology is used as a basis for awarding need-based institutional aid.

UNDERGRADUATE EXPENSES for 1999–2000 ***Application fee:*** $25. ***Comprehensive fee:*** $16,630 includes full-time tuition ($10,900), mandatory fees ($350), and room and board ($5380). ***Part-time tuition:*** $300 per credit. ***Part-time fees:*** $2 per credit; $115 per term part-time. Part-time tuition and fees vary according to course load. ***Payment plans:*** guaranteed tuition, installment, deferred payment.

FRESHMAN FINANCIAL AID (Fall 1999) 140 applied for aid; of those 88% were deemed to have need. 100% of freshmen with need received aid; of those 24% had need fully met. *Average percent of need met:* 83% (excluding resources awarded to replace EFC). *Average financial aid package:* $9257 (excluding resources awarded to replace EFC).

UNDERGRADUATE FINANCIAL AID (Fall 1999) 824 applied for aid; of those 88% were deemed to have need. 100% of undergraduates with need received aid; of those 37% had need fully met. *Average percent of need met:* 87% (excluding resources awarded to replace EFC). *Average financial aid package:* $10,115 (excluding resources awarded to replace EFC).

GIFT AID (NEED-BASED) ***Total amount:*** $3,324,385 (30% Federal, 38% state, 25% institutional, 7% external sources). ***Receiving aid:*** *Freshmen:* 69% (116); *all full-time undergraduates:* 68% (671). ***Average award:*** Freshmen: $5934; Undergraduates: $4806. ***Scholarships, grants, and awards:*** Federal Pell, FSEOG, state, private, college/university gift aid from institutional funds.

GIFT AID (NON-NEED-BASED) ***Total amount:*** $617,485 (100% institutional). ***Receiving aid:*** *Freshmen:* 5% (9); *Undergraduates:* 4% (36). ***Scholarships, grants, and awards by category:*** *Academic Interests/Achievement:*

300 awards ($617,485 total): biological sciences, business, education, English, general academic interests/achievements, health fields, humanities, international studies, premedicine, social sciences. ***Tuition waivers:*** Full or partial for minority students, children of alumni, employees or children of employees, adult students. ***ROTC:*** Army cooperative.

LOANS ***Student loans:*** $4,998,416 (100% need-based). ***Average need-based loan:*** Freshmen: $3111; Undergraduates: $5167. ***Parent loans:*** $415,136 (100% need-based). ***Programs:*** FFEL (Subsidized and Unsubsidized Stafford, PLUS), Perkins, Federal Nursing, college/university.

WORK-STUDY ***Federal work-study:*** *Total amount:* $124,154; 125 jobs averaging $1000. ***State or other work-study/employment:*** *Total amount:* $145,182 (100% need-based). 145 part-time jobs averaging $1000.

APPLYING for FINANCIAL AID ***Required financial aid form:*** FAFSA. ***Financial aid deadline (priority):*** 3/1. ***Notification date:*** 4/1. Students must reply within 3 weeks of notification.

CONTACT Ms. Lorraine A. Metz, Director of Financial Aid, D'Youville College, 320 Porter Avenue, Buffalo, NY 14201-1084, 716-881-7691 or toll-free 800-777-3921. *Fax:* 716-881-7790. *E-mail:* metzla@dyc.edu

EARLHAM COLLEGE

Richmond, IN

Tuition & fees: $20,256 **Average undergraduate aid package: $19,624**

ABOUT THE INSTITUTION Independent religious, coed. Awards: bachelor's degrees. 33 undergraduate majors. Total enrollment: 1,191. Undergraduates: 1,123. Freshmen: 296. Both federal and institutional methodology are used as a basis for awarding need-based institutional aid.

UNDERGRADUATE EXPENSES for 1999–2000 ***Application fee:*** $30. ***Comprehensive fee:*** $25,066 includes full-time tuition ($19,684), mandatory fees ($572), and room and board ($4810). ***College room only:*** $2304. Room and board charges vary according to board plan. ***Part-time tuition:*** $656 per semester hour. ***Payment plans:*** tuition prepayment, installment, deferred payment.

FRESHMAN FINANCIAL AID (Fall 1999, est.) 248 applied for aid; of those 90% were deemed to have need. 100% of freshmen with need received aid; of those 42% had need fully met. *Average percent of need met:* 94% (excluding resources awarded to replace EFC). *Average financial aid package:* $19,982 (excluding resources awarded to replace EFC). 5% of all full-time freshmen had no need and received non-need-based aid.

UNDERGRADUATE FINANCIAL AID (Fall 1999, est.) 813 applied for aid; of those 91% were deemed to have need. 100% of undergraduates with need received aid; of those 37% had need fully met. *Average percent of need met:* 94% (excluding resources awarded to replace EFC). *Average financial aid package:* $19,624 (excluding resources awarded to replace EFC). 3% of all full-time undergraduates had no need and received non-need-based aid.

GIFT AID (NEED-BASED) ***Total amount:*** $8,808,640 (10% Federal, 9% state, 81% institutional). ***Receiving aid:*** *Freshmen:* 72% (216); *all full-time undergraduates:* 65% (715). ***Average award:*** Freshmen: $11,401; Undergraduates: $11,594. ***Scholarships, grants, and awards:*** Federal Pell, FSEOG, state, private, college/university gift aid from institutional funds.

GIFT AID (NON-NEED-BASED) ***Total amount:*** $2,443,986 (80% institutional, 20% external sources). ***Receiving aid:*** *Freshmen:* 44% (132); *Undergraduates:* 31% (339). ***Scholarships, grants, and awards by category:*** *Academic Interests/Achievement:* 396 awards ($1,531,384 total): general academic interests/achievements, physical sciences. *Special Characteristics:* 112 awards ($272,555 total): religious affiliation. ***Tuition waivers:*** Full or partial for employees or children of employees.

LOANS ***Student loans:*** $3,100,233 (76% need-based, 24% non-need-based). 66% of past graduating class borrowed through all loan programs. Average indebtedness per student: $10,366. ***Average need-based loan:*** Freshmen: $3687; Undergraduates: $4155. ***Parent loans:*** $767,483 (100% non-need-based). ***Programs:*** Federal Direct (Subsidized and Unsubsidized Stafford, PLUS), Perkins, college/university.

WORK-STUDY ***Federal work-study:*** *Total amount:* $802,365; jobs available. ***State or other work-study/employment:*** *Total amount:* $75,167 (56% need-based, 44% non-need-based). Part-time jobs available.

APPLYING for FINANCIAL AID ***Required financial aid forms:*** FAFSA, institution's own form. ***Financial aid deadline (priority):*** 3/1. ***Notification date:*** 4/1.

CONTACT Mr. Robert W. Arnold, Director of Financial Aid, Earlham College, National Road West, Richmond, IN 47374-4095, 765-983-1217 or toll-free 800-327-5426. *Fax:* 765-983-1234.

EAST CAROLINA UNIVERSITY

Greenville, NC

Tuition & fees (NC res): $1998 **Average undergraduate aid package: N/A**

ABOUT THE INSTITUTION State-supported, coed. Awards: bachelor's, master's, doctoral, and first professional degrees and post-master's certificates. 84 undergraduate majors. Total enrollment: 18,811. Undergraduates: 15,246. Freshmen: 3,270. Federal methodology is used as a basis for awarding need-based institutional aid.

UNDERGRADUATE EXPENSES for 1999–2000 ***Application fee:*** $40. ***Tuition, state resident:*** full-time $992. ***Tuition, nonresident:*** full-time $8558. ***Required fees:*** full-time $1006. Part-time tuition and fees vary according to course load. ***College room and board:*** $4070; ***room only:*** $2050. Room and board charges vary according to board plan and housing facility. ***Payment plans:*** installment, deferred payment.

FRESHMAN FINANCIAL AID (Fall 1999) 2094 applied for aid; of those 60% were deemed to have need. 93% of freshmen with need received aid; of those 31% had need fully met. 17% of all full-time freshmen had no need and received non-need-based aid.

UNDERGRADUATE FINANCIAL AID (Fall 1999) 8,291 applied for aid; of those 50% were deemed to have need. 96% of undergraduates with need received aid; of those 43% had need fully met. 20% of all full-time undergraduates had no need and received non-need-based aid.

GIFT AID (NEED-BASED) ***Total amount:*** $10,025,019 (90% Federal, 3% state, 7% institutional). ***Receiving aid:*** *Freshmen:* 21% (672); *all full-time undergraduates:* 16% (2,184). ***Average award:*** Freshmen: $2184; Undergraduates: $2110. ***Scholarships, grants, and awards:*** Federal Pell, FSEOG, state, private, college/university gift aid from institutional funds.

GIFT AID (NON-NEED-BASED) ***Total amount:*** $5,470,626 (34% state, 44% institutional, 22% external sources). ***Receiving aid:*** *Freshmen:* 10% (314); *Undergraduates:* 6% (789). ***Scholarships, grants, and awards by category:*** *Academic Interests/Achievement:* biological sciences, business, education, general academic interests/achievements, health fields, home economics, humanities, military science. *Creative Arts/Performance:* applied art and design, art/fine arts, music. *Special Achievements/Activities:* leadership. *Special Characteristics:* adult students, children of faculty/staff, ethnic background, handicapped students, local/state students. ***Tuition waivers:*** Full or partial for employees or children of employees, senior citizens. ***ROTC:*** Army, Air Force.

LOANS ***Student loans:*** $26,571,526 (63% need-based, 37% non-need-based). 56% of past graduating class borrowed through all loan programs. Average indebtedness per student: $14,105. ***Average need-based loan:*** Freshmen: $2759; Undergraduates: $3339. ***Parent loans:*** $4,381,923 (100% non-need-based). ***Programs:*** FFEL (Subsidized and Unsubsidized Stafford, PLUS), Perkins, Federal Nursing.

WORK-STUDY ***Federal work-study:*** *Total amount:* $840,454; 500 jobs averaging $1600. ***State or other work-study/employment:*** *Total amount:* $459,360 (100% need-based). Part-time jobs available.

ATHLETIC AWARDS *Total amount:* 2,256,989 (100% non-need-based).

APPLYING for FINANCIAL AID ***Required financial aid form:*** FAFSA. ***Financial aid deadline (priority):*** 4/15. ***Notification date:*** Continuous. Students must reply within 3 weeks of notification.

CONTACT Ms. Rose Mary Stelma, Director of Financial Aid, East Carolina University, East 5th Street, Greenville, NC 27858-4353, 252-328-6610. *Fax:* 252-328-4347. *E-mail:* faques@mail.ecu.edu

EAST CENTRAL UNIVERSITY

Ada, OK

Tuition & fees (OK res): $1962 **Average undergraduate aid package: $3697**

ABOUT THE INSTITUTION State-supported, coed. Awards: bachelor's and master's degrees. 53 undergraduate majors. Total enrollment: 3,938. Undergraduates: 3,229. Freshmen: 1,119. Federal methodology is used as a basis for awarding need-based institutional aid.

UNDERGRADUATE EXPENSES for 1999–2000 ***One-time required fee:*** $21.50. ***Tuition, state resident:*** full-time $1919; part-time $64 per semester hour. ***Tuition, nonresident:*** full-time $4439; part-time $148 per semester hour. ***Required fees:*** full-time $43; $18 per term part-time. Full-time tuition and fees vary according to course level, course load, and student level. Part-time tuition and fees vary according to course level, course load, and student level. ***College room and board:*** $2226; ***room only:*** $726. Room and board charges vary according to board plan and housing facility.

FRESHMAN FINANCIAL AID (Fall 1999, est.) 593 applied for aid; of those 86% were deemed to have need. 98% of freshmen with need received aid; of those 37% had need fully met. *Average percent of need met:* 58% (excluding resources awarded to replace EFC). *Average financial aid package:* $2972 (excluding resources awarded to replace EFC). 5% of all full-time freshmen had no need and received non-need-based aid.

UNDERGRADUATE FINANCIAL AID (Fall 1999, est.) 1,735 applied for aid; of those 90% were deemed to have need. 98% of undergraduates with need received aid; of those 40% had need fully met. *Average percent of need met:* 61% (excluding resources awarded to replace EFC). *Average financial aid package:* $3697 (excluding resources awarded to replace EFC). 7% of all full-time undergraduates had no need and received non-need-based aid.

GIFT AID (NEED-BASED) ***Total amount:*** $4,893,069 (70% Federal, 30% state). ***Receiving aid:*** *Freshmen:* 44% (383); *all full-time undergraduates:* 47% (1,183). ***Average award:*** Freshmen: $2978; Undergraduates: $3013. ***Scholarships, grants, and awards:*** Federal Pell, FSEOG, state, private, college/university gift aid from institutional funds.

GIFT AID (NON-NEED-BASED) ***Total amount:*** $775,000 (45% institutional, 55% external sources). ***Receiving aid:*** *Freshmen:* 25% (216); *Undergraduates:* 24% (603). ***Scholarships, grants, and awards by category:*** *Academic Interests/Achievement:* communication, general academic interests/achievements, military science. *Creative Arts/Performance:* music, performing arts. *Special Achievements/Activities:* cheerleading/drum major. *Special Characteristics:* members of minority groups, veterans, veterans' children. ***Tuition waivers:*** Full or partial for employees or children of employees, senior citizens.

LOANS ***Student loans:*** $5,364,969 (79% need-based, 21% non-need-based). 60% of past graduating class borrowed through all loan programs. Average indebtedness per student: $11,865. ***Average need-based loan:*** Freshmen: $1162; Undergraduates: $1747. ***Parent loans:*** $60,922 (100% non-need-based). ***Programs:*** FFEL (Subsidized and Unsubsidized Stafford, PLUS), Perkins, college/university.

WORK-STUDY ***Federal work-study:*** *Total amount:* $413,130; 125 jobs averaging $3296. ***State or other work-study/employment:*** *Total amount:* $900,000 (100% non-need-based). 273 part-time jobs averaging $3296.

ATHLETIC AWARDS *Total amount:* 523,940 (100% non-need-based).

APPLYING for FINANCIAL AID ***Required financial aid forms:*** FAFSA, institution's own form. ***Financial aid deadline (priority):*** 3/1. ***Notification date:*** Continuous beginning 4/15. Students must reply within 2 weeks of notification.

CONTACT Beverly Wilcoxon, Director, Financial Aid, East Central University, 14th and Francis Streets, Ada, OK 74820-6899, 580-332-8000 Ext. 243. *Fax:* 580-436-5612. *E-mail:* bwilcoxn@mailclerk.ecok.edu

EASTERN COLLEGE

St. Davids, PA

ABOUT THE INSTITUTION Independent American Baptist, coed. Awards: associate, bachelor's, and master's degrees. 36 undergraduate majors. Total enrollment: 2,757. Undergraduates: 1,902. Freshmen: 381.

GIFT AID (NEED-BASED) ***Scholarships, grants, and awards:*** Federal Pell, FSEOG, state, private, college/university gift aid from institutional funds.

GIFT AID (NON-NEED-BASED) ***Scholarships, grants, and awards by category:*** *Academic Interests/Achievement:* general academic interests/achievements. *Creative Arts/Performance:* music. *Special Achievements/Activities:* leadership. *Special Characteristics:* relatives of clergy.

LOANS ***Programs:*** FFEL (Subsidized and Unsubsidized Stafford, PLUS), Perkins, state.

WORK-STUDY Federal work-study jobs available.

APPLYING for FINANCIAL AID ***Required financial aid forms:*** FAFSA, institution's own form, financial aid transcript (for transfers).

CONTACT Financial Aid Office, Eastern College, 1300 Eagle Road, St. Davids, PA 19087-3696, 610-341-5842 or toll-free 800-452-0996.

EASTERN CONNECTICUT STATE UNIVERSITY

Willimantic, CT

Tuition & fees (CT res): $4146 **Average undergraduate aid package: $5165**

ABOUT THE INSTITUTION State-supported, coed. Awards: associate, bachelor's, and master's degrees. 22 undergraduate majors. Total enrollment: 4,987. Undergraduates: 4,673. Freshmen: 932. Federal methodology is used as a basis for awarding need-based institutional aid.

UNDERGRADUATE EXPENSES for 1999–2000 ***Application fee:*** $40. ***Tuition, state resident:*** full-time $2142; part-time $149 per credit hour. ***Tuition, nonresident:*** full-time $6934; part-time $149 per credit hour. ***Required fees:*** full-time $2004; $40 per term part-time. Full-time tuition and fees vary according to reciprocity agreements. ***College room and board:*** $5850; ***room only:*** $3232. Room and board charges vary according to board plan and housing facility. ***Payment plans:*** installment, deferred payment.

FRESHMAN FINANCIAL AID (Fall 1999, est.) 759 applied for aid; of those 82% were deemed to have need. 79% of freshmen with need received aid; of those 75% had need fully met. *Average percent of need met:* 90% (excluding resources awarded to replace EFC). *Average financial aid package:* $4950 (excluding resources awarded to replace EFC). 13% of all full-time freshmen had no need and received non-need-based aid.

UNDERGRADUATE FINANCIAL AID (Fall 1999, est.) 3,050 applied for aid; of those 84% were deemed to have need. 79% of undergraduates with need received aid; of those 75% had need fully met. *Average percent of need met:* 90% (excluding resources awarded to replace EFC). *Average financial aid package:* $5165 (excluding resources awarded to replace EFC). 6% of all full-time undergraduates had no need and received non-need-based aid.

GIFT AID (NEED-BASED) ***Total amount:*** $2,248,987 (42% Federal, 17% state, 38% institutional, 3% external sources). ***Receiving aid:*** *Freshmen:* 43% (380); *all full-time undergraduates:* 44% (1,518). ***Average award:*** Freshmen: $4725; Undergraduates: $4430. ***Scholarships, grants, and awards:*** Federal Pell, FSEOG, state, private, college/university gift aid from institutional funds.

GIFT AID (NON-NEED-BASED) ***Total amount:*** $457,794 (16% Federal, 29% state, 31% institutional, 24% external sources). ***Receiving aid:*** *Freshmen:* 38% (336); *Undergraduates:* 40% (1,377). ***Scholarships, grants, and awards by category:*** *Academic Interests/Achievement:* 174 awards ($244,000 total): area/ethnic studies, biological sciences, business, communication, computer science, education, English, foreign languages, general academic interests/achievements, humanities, mathematics, physical sciences, social sciences. *Creative Arts/Performance:* 5 awards ($3000 total): music, theater/drama. *Special Achievements/Activities:* 16 awards ($21,000 total): community service, general special achievements/activities, leadership, memberships. *Special Characteristics:* 88 awards ($112,000 total): children of faculty/staff, children of union members/company employees, general special characteristics, international students, local/state students, members of minority groups, previous college experience, veterans. ***Tuition waivers:*** Full or partial for senior citizens. ***ROTC:*** Army cooperative, Air Force cooperative.

LOANS ***Student loans:*** $4,566,972 (54% need-based, 46% non-need-based). 60% of past graduating class borrowed through all loan programs. Average indebtedness per student: $10,200. ***Average need-based loan:*** Freshmen: $2600; Undergraduates: $3990. ***Parent loans:*** $509,257 (100% non-need-based). ***Programs:*** FFEL (Subsidized and Unsubsidized Stafford, PLUS), Perkins, state, college/university.

WORK-STUDY ***Federal work-study:*** *Total amount:* $129,480; 168 jobs averaging $771. ***State or other work-study/employment:*** *Total amount:* $70,072 (100% need-based). 94 part-time jobs averaging $746.

APPLYING for FINANCIAL AID ***Required financial aid forms:*** FAFSA, institution's own form. ***Financial aid deadline:*** 3/15. ***Notification date:*** Continuous. Students must reply within 3 weeks of notification.

CONTACT Neville Brown, Assistant to the Director of Financial Aid, Eastern Connecticut State University, 83 Windham Street, Willimantic, CT 06226-2295, 860-465-4428 or toll-free 877-353-3278. *Fax:* 860-465-4440. *E-mail:* brownn@ecsuc.ctstate.edu

EASTERN ILLINOIS UNIVERSITY

Charleston, IL

Tuition & fees (IL res): $3962 **Average undergraduate aid package: $6866**

ABOUT THE INSTITUTION State-supported, coed. Awards: bachelor's and master's degrees. 63 undergraduate majors. Total enrollment: 11,226. Undergraduates: 9,861. Freshmen: 1,495. Federal methodology is used as a basis for awarding need-based institutional aid.

UNDERGRADUATE EXPENSES for 2000–2001 ***Application fee:*** $25. ***Tuition, state resident:*** full-time $2910; part-time $97 per semester hour. ***Tuition, nonresident:*** full-time $8730; part-time $291 per semester hour. ***Required fees:*** full-time $1052; $44 per semester hour. Full-time tuition and fees vary according to course load. Part-time tuition and fees vary according to course load. ***College room and board:*** $4104. Room and board charges vary according to board plan. ***Payment plan:*** installment.

FRESHMAN FINANCIAL AID (Fall 1999) 1530 applied for aid; of those 77% were deemed to have need. 63% of freshmen with need received aid; of those 78% had need fully met. *Average percent of need met:* 19% (excluding resources awarded to replace EFC). *Average financial aid package:* $7024 (excluding resources awarded to replace EFC). 16% of all full-time freshmen had no need and received non-need-based aid.

UNDERGRADUATE FINANCIAL AID (Fall 1999) 6,874 applied for aid; of those 81% were deemed to have need. 77% of undergraduates with need received aid; of those 75% had need fully met. *Average percent of need met:* 21% (excluding resources awarded to replace EFC). *Average financial aid package:* $6866 (excluding resources awarded to replace EFC). 11% of all full-time undergraduates had no need and received non-need-based aid.

GIFT AID (NEED-BASED) ***Total amount:*** $11,313,889 (32% Federal, 54% state, 8% institutional, 6% external sources). ***Receiving aid:*** *Freshmen:* 24% (362); *all full-time undergraduates:* 23% (2,089). ***Average award:*** Freshmen: $2306; Undergraduates: $2205. ***Scholarships, grants, and awards:*** Federal Pell, FSEOG, state, college/university gift aid from institutional funds.

GIFT AID (NON-NEED-BASED) ***Total amount:*** $2,239,337 (2% Federal, 18% state, 55% institutional, 25% external sources). ***Receiving aid:*** *Freshmen:* 23% (361); *Undergraduates:* 19% (1,694). ***Scholarships, grants, and awards by category:*** *Academic Interests/Achievement:* education, general academic interests/achievements, mathematics, physical sciences. *Creative Arts/Performance:* debating, music, performing arts, theater/drama. *Special Achievements/Activities:* general special achievements/activities. ***Tuition waivers:*** Full or partial for employees or children of employees. ***ROTC:*** Army.

LOANS ***Student loans:*** $17,526,312 (76% need-based, 24% non-need-based). 54% of past graduating class borrowed through all loan programs. Average indebtedness per student: $12,211. ***Average need-based loan:*** Freshmen: $2153; Undergraduates: $2830. ***Parent loans:*** $1,206,600 (61% need-based, 39% non-need-based). ***Programs:*** Federal Direct (Subsidized and Unsubsidized Stafford, PLUS), Perkins.

WORK-STUDY ***Federal work-study:*** *Total amount:* $503,398; 417 jobs averaging $1207. ***State or other work-study/employment:*** *Total amount:* $12,815 (31% need-based, 69% non-need-based). Part-time jobs available.

ATHLETIC AWARDS *Total amount:* 1,444,397 (22% need-based, 78% non-need-based).

APPLYING for FINANCIAL AID ***Required financial aid forms:*** FAFSA, parent and student federal income tax returns, institutional verification forms. ***Financial aid deadline (priority):*** 4/15. ***Notification date:*** Continuous beginning 5/1. Students must reply within 2 weeks of notification.

CONTACT Ms. Betty Armstrong, Assistant Director of Financial Aid, Eastern Illinois University, 600 Lincoln Avenue, Charleston, IL 61920-3099, 217-581-7511 or toll-free 800-252-5711. *Fax:* 217-581-6422. *E-mail:* csbja@eiu.edu

EASTERN KENTUCKY UNIVERSITY

Richmond, KY

Tuition & fees (KY res): $2390 **Average undergraduate aid package: $7053**

ABOUT THE INSTITUTION State-supported, coed. Awards: associate, bachelor's, and master's degrees. 132 undergraduate majors. Total enrollment: 14,977. Undergraduates: 13,058. Freshmen: 2,157. Federal methodology is used as a basis for awarding need-based institutional aid.

UNDERGRADUATE EXPENSES for 1999–2000 ***Tuition, state resident:*** full-time $2390; part-time $100 per semester hour. ***Tuition, nonresident:*** full-time $6430; part-time $261 per semester hour. Part-time tuition and fees vary according to course load. ***College room and board:*** $3676; ***room only:*** $1356. Room and board charges vary according to board plan and housing facility. ***Payment plan:*** deferred payment.

FRESHMAN FINANCIAL AID (Fall 1999, est.) 1550 applied for aid; of those 76% were deemed to have need. 99% of freshmen with need received aid; of those 31% had need fully met. *Average percent of need met:* 81% (excluding resources awarded to replace EFC). *Average financial aid package:* $5711 (excluding resources awarded to replace EFC). 35% of all full-time freshmen had no need and received non-need-based aid.

UNDERGRADUATE FINANCIAL AID (Fall 1999, est.) 6,808 applied for aid; of those 84% were deemed to have need. 97% of undergraduates with need received aid; of those 38% had need fully met. *Average percent of need met:* 85% (excluding resources awarded to replace EFC). *Average financial aid package:* $7053 (excluding resources awarded to replace EFC). 20% of all full-time undergraduates had no need and received non-need-based aid.

GIFT AID (NEED-BASED) ***Total amount:*** $13,917,427 (76% Federal, 24% state). ***Receiving aid:*** *Freshmen:* 37% (764); *all full-time undergraduates:* 38% (3,878). ***Average award:*** Freshmen: $2983; Undergraduates: $3099. ***Scholarships, grants, and awards:*** Federal Pell, FSEOG, state, private, Federal Nursing.

GIFT AID (NON-NEED-BASED) ***Total amount:*** $4,535,420 (41% state, 49% institutional, 10% external sources). ***Receiving aid:*** *Freshmen:* 41% (838); *Undergraduates:* 20% (1,989). ***Scholarships, grants, and awards by category:*** *Academic Interests/Achievement:* general academic interests/achievements. *Creative Arts/Performance:* music. *Special Characteristics:* international students, out-of-state students. ***Tuition waivers:*** Full or partial for employees or children of employees. ***ROTC:*** Army, Air Force cooperative.

LOANS ***Student loans:*** $20,595,779 (67% need-based, 33% non-need-based). Average indebtedness per student: $13,804. ***Average need-based loan:*** Freshmen: $1991; Undergraduates: $2893. ***Parent loans:*** $919,095 (100% non-need-based). ***Programs:*** FFEL (Subsidized and Unsubsidized Stafford, PLUS), Perkins.

WORK-STUDY ***Federal work-study:*** *Total amount:* $968,265; jobs available. ***State or other work-study/employment:*** *Total amount:* $2,643,446 (100% non-need-based). Part-time jobs available.

ATHLETIC AWARDS *Total amount:* 1,536,382 (100% non-need-based).

Eastern Kentucky University (continued)

APPLYING for FINANCIAL AID ***Required financial aid forms:*** FAFSA, institution's own form. ***Financial aid deadline (priority):*** 4/1. ***Notification date:*** Continuous beginning 4/15.

CONTACT Mr. John Fish, Director of Student Financial Aid, Eastern Kentucky University, CPO 4-A, 521 Lancaster Avenue, Richmond, KY 40475-3101, 606-622-1754 or toll-free 800-262-7493 (in-state).

EASTERN MENNONITE UNIVERSITY

Harrisonburg, VA

Tuition & fees: $13,480 **Average undergraduate aid package: $12,247**

ABOUT THE INSTITUTION Independent Mennonite, coed. Awards: associate, bachelor's, master's, and first professional degrees and post-bachelor's and first-professional certificates. 55 undergraduate majors. Total enrollment: 1,349. Undergraduates: 1,099. Freshmen: 219. Federal methodology is used as a basis for awarding need-based institutional aid.

UNDERGRADUATE EXPENSES for 1999–2000 ***Application fee:*** $25. ***Comprehensive fee:*** $18,430 includes full-time tuition ($13,480) and room and board ($4950). ***College room only:*** $2500. Full-time tuition and fees vary according to program. Room and board charges vary according to board plan and housing facility. ***Part-time tuition:*** $565 per semester hour. Part-time tuition and fees vary according to program. ***Payment plan:*** installment.

FRESHMAN FINANCIAL AID (Fall 1999, est.) 213 applied for aid; of those 72% were deemed to have need. 100% of freshmen with need received aid; of those 27% had need fully met. *Average percent of need met:* 81% (excluding resources awarded to replace EFC). *Average financial aid package:* $11,789 (excluding resources awarded to replace EFC). 27% of all full-time freshmen had no need and received non-need-based aid.

UNDERGRADUATE FINANCIAL AID (Fall 1999, est.) 898 applied for aid; of those 71% were deemed to have need. 100% of undergraduates with need received aid; of those 29% had need fully met. *Average percent of need met:* 82% (excluding resources awarded to replace EFC). *Average financial aid package:* $12,247 (excluding resources awarded to replace EFC). 28% of all full-time undergraduates had no need and received non-need-based aid.

GIFT AID (NEED-BASED) ***Total amount:*** $3,933,941 (23% Federal, 17% state, 51% institutional, 9% external sources). ***Receiving aid:*** *Freshmen:* 72% (153); *all full-time undergraduates:* 67% (626). ***Average award:*** Freshmen: $7294; Undergraduates: $6454. ***Scholarships, grants, and awards:*** Federal Pell, FSEOG, state, private, college/university gift aid from institutional funds.

GIFT AID (NON-NEED-BASED) ***Total amount:*** $1,483,876 (14% state, 74% institutional, 12% external sources). ***Receiving aid:*** *Freshmen:* 6% (13); *Undergraduates:* 5% (47). ***Scholarships, grants, and awards by category:*** *Academic Interests/Achievement:* 716 awards ($1,845,590 total): biological sciences, business, education, English, foreign languages, general academic interests/achievements, humanities, mathematics, physical sciences, premedicine, religion/biblical studies, social sciences. *Creative Arts/Performance:* 14 awards ($14,300 total): art/fine arts, music. *Special Achievements/Activities:* 1 award ($450 total): religious involvement. *Special Characteristics:* 841 awards ($1,226,710 total): children and siblings of alumni, children of faculty/staff, ethnic background, general special characteristics, international students, religious affiliation. ***Tuition waivers:*** Full or partial for employees or children of employees.

LOANS ***Student loans:*** $3,340,239 (83% need-based, 17% non-need-based). 71% of past graduating class borrowed through all loan programs. Average indebtedness per student: $16,668. ***Average need-based loan:*** Freshmen: $4219; Undergraduates: $5446. ***Parent loans:*** $923,605 (81% need-based, 19% non-need-based). ***Programs:*** FFEL (Subsidized and Unsubsidized Stafford, PLUS), Perkins, Federal Nursing.

WORK-STUDY ***Federal work-study:*** *Total amount:* $569,548; 407 jobs averaging $1400. ***State or other work-study/employment:*** *Total amount:* $156,538 (90% need-based, 10% non-need-based). 100 part-time jobs averaging $1600.

APPLYING for FINANCIAL AID ***Required financial aid form:*** FAFSA. ***Financial aid deadline (priority):*** 3/15. ***Notification date:*** Continuous. Students must reply within 4 weeks of notification.

CONTACT Ms. Renee Leap, Assistant Director of Financial Aid, Eastern Mennonite University, 1200 Park Road, Harrisonburg, VA 22802-2462, 540-432-4137 or toll-free 800-368-2665. *Fax:* 540-432-4081. *E-mail:* leapr@emu.edu

EASTERN MICHIGAN UNIVERSITY

Ypsilanti, MI

Tuition & fees (MI res): $3754 **Average undergraduate aid package: $8300**

ABOUT THE INSTITUTION State-supported, coed. Awards: bachelor's, master's, and doctoral degrees and post-master's certificates. 128 undergraduate majors. Total enrollment: 22,956. Undergraduates: 18,043. Freshmen: 2,902. Federal methodology is used as a basis for awarding need-based institutional aid.

UNDERGRADUATE EXPENSES for 1999–2000 ***Application fee:*** $25. ***Tuition, state resident:*** full-time $3147; part-time $102 per credit hour. ***Tuition, nonresident:*** full-time $8215; part-time $265 per credit hour. ***Required fees:*** full-time $607; $17 per credit hour; $40 per term part-time. Full-time tuition and fees vary according to course level and reciprocity agreements. Part-time tuition and fees vary according to course level and reciprocity agreements. ***College room and board:*** $4842. Room and board charges vary according to board plan, housing facility, and location. ***Payment plan:*** installment.

FRESHMAN FINANCIAL AID (Fall 1999, est.) 2130 applied for aid; of those 69% were deemed to have need. 73% of freshmen with need received aid; of those 50% had need fully met. *Average percent of need met:* 67% (excluding resources awarded to replace EFC). *Average financial aid package:* $9829 (excluding resources awarded to replace EFC).

UNDERGRADUATE FINANCIAL AID (Fall 1999, est.) 9,048 applied for aid; of those 68% were deemed to have need. 56% of undergraduates with need received aid; of those 58% had need fully met. *Average percent of need met:* 85% (excluding resources awarded to replace EFC). *Average financial aid package:* $8300 (excluding resources awarded to replace EFC).

GIFT AID (NEED-BASED) ***Total amount:*** $9,735,453 (79% Federal, 12% state, 9% institutional). ***Receiving aid:*** *Freshmen:* 21% (761); *all full-time undergraduates:* 19% (2,343). ***Average award:*** Freshmen: $2905; Undergraduates: $2682. ***Scholarships, grants, and awards:*** Federal Pell, FSEOG, state, college/university gift aid from institutional funds, Nursing Disadvantaged Student Grants.

GIFT AID (NON-NEED-BASED) ***Total amount:*** $8,903,873 (73% institutional, 27% external sources). ***Receiving aid:*** *Freshmen:* 12% (418); *Undergraduates:* 15% (1,826). ***Scholarships, grants, and awards by category:*** *Academic Interests/Achievement:* 1,185 awards ($2,157,917 total): agriculture, architecture, biological sciences, business, communication, computer science, education, engineering/technologies, English, foreign languages, general academic interests/achievements, health fields, home economics, humanities, mathematics, physical sciences, religion/biblical studies, social sciences. *Creative Arts/Performance:* 128 awards ($64,000 total): applied art and design, art/fine arts, cinema/film/broadcasting, creative writing, dance, debating, general creative arts/performance, music, performing arts, theater/drama. *Special Achievements/Activities:* 506 awards ($254,000 total): leadership, religious involvement. *Special Characteristics:* 156 awards ($503,000 total): children and siblings of alumni, ethnic background, international students, members of minority groups, out-of-state students, religious affiliation. ***Tuition waivers:*** Full or partial for employees or children of employees. ***ROTC:*** Army, Naval cooperative, Air Force cooperative.

LOANS ***Student loans:*** $51,589,720 (51% need-based, 49% non-need-based). Average indebtedness per student: $11,719. ***Average need-based loan:*** Freshmen: $3568; Undergraduates: $4424. ***Parent loans:*** $4,081,184 (100% non-need-based). ***Programs:*** FFEL (Subsidized and Unsubsidized Stafford, PLUS), Perkins, state, college/university, alternative loans.

WORK-STUDY ***Federal work-study:*** *Total amount:* $1,295,367; jobs available. ***State or other work-study/employment:*** *Total amount:* $161,463 (100% need-based). Part-time jobs available.

ATHLETIC AWARDS *Total amount:* 2,678,698 (100% non-need-based).

APPLYING for FINANCIAL AID ***Required financial aid form:*** FAFSA. ***Financial aid deadline (priority):*** 3/15. ***Notification date:*** Continuous beginning 4/1. Students must reply within 3 weeks of notification.

CONTACT Ms. Bernice A. Lindke, Director of Financial Aid, Eastern Michigan University, 403 Pierce Hall, Ypsilanti, MI 48197, 734-487-0455 or toll-free 800-GO TO EMU. *Fax:* 734-487-1484. *E-mail:* financial.aid@emich.edu

EASTERN NAZARENE COLLEGE

Quincy, MA

Tuition & fees: $14,060 **Average undergraduate aid package: $9471**

ABOUT THE INSTITUTION Independent religious, coed. Awards: associate, bachelor's, and master's degrees. 62 undergraduate majors. Total enrollment: 1,558. Undergraduates: 1,341. Freshmen: 179. Federal methodology is used as a basis for awarding need-based institutional aid.

UNDERGRADUATE EXPENSES for 2000–2001 (est.) ***Application fee:*** $25. ***Comprehensive fee:*** $18,610 includes full-time tuition ($13,235), mandatory fees ($825), and room and board ($4550). Room and board charges vary according to board plan. ***Part-time tuition:*** $446 per credit. ***Part-time fees:*** $15 per term part-time. Part-time tuition and fees vary according to course load. ***Payment plan:*** installment.

FRESHMAN FINANCIAL AID (Fall 1999, est.) 179 applied for aid; of those 86% were deemed to have need. 100% of freshmen with need received aid; of those 13% had need fully met. *Average percent of need met:* 66% (excluding resources awarded to replace EFC). *Average financial aid package:* $9242 (excluding resources awarded to replace EFC). 14% of all full-time freshmen had no need and received non-need-based aid.

UNDERGRADUATE FINANCIAL AID (Fall 1999, est.) 622 applied for aid; of those 82% were deemed to have need. 100% of undergraduates with need received aid; of those 18% had need fully met. *Average percent of need met:* 68% (excluding resources awarded to replace EFC). *Average financial aid package:* $9471 (excluding resources awarded to replace EFC). 16% of all full-time undergraduates had no need and received non-need-based aid.

GIFT AID (NEED-BASED) ***Total amount:*** $2,770,806 (18% Federal, 8% state, 72% institutional, 2% external sources). ***Receiving aid:*** *Freshmen:* 82% (149); *all full-time undergraduates:* 74% (487). ***Average award:*** Freshmen: $4949; Undergraduates: $4464. ***Scholarships, grants, and awards:*** Federal Pell, FSEOG, state, private, college/university gift aid from institutional funds.

GIFT AID (NON-NEED-BASED) ***Total amount:*** $232,446 (95% institutional, 5% external sources). ***Receiving aid:*** *Freshmen:* 49% (88); *Undergraduates:* 38% (247). ***Scholarships, grants, and awards by category:*** *Academic Interests/Achievement:* $1,187,311 total: business, education, engineering/technologies, English, general academic interests/achievements, mathematics, physical sciences, premedicine, religion/biblical studies, social sciences. *Creative Arts/Performance:* $26,370 total: music, theater/drama. *Special Achievements/Activities:* $93,870 total: community service, leadership. *Special Characteristics:* $361,521 total: children and siblings of alumni, children of educators, ethnic background, international students, members of minority groups, relatives of clergy, religious affiliation, siblings of current students. ***Tuition waivers:*** Full or partial for employees or children of employees. ***ROTC:*** Army cooperative.

LOANS ***Student loans:*** $2,265,581 (96% need-based, 4% non-need-based). ***Average need-based loan:*** Freshmen: $2387; Undergraduates: $3786. ***Parent loans:*** $1,028,553 (96% need-based, 4% non-need-based). ***Programs:*** FFEL (Subsidized and Unsubsidized Stafford, PLUS), Perkins, state, alternative loans.

WORK-STUDY ***Federal work-study:*** *Total amount:* $267,164; 187 jobs averaging $1429.

APPLYING for FINANCIAL AID ***Required financial aid forms:*** FAFSA, institution's own form. ***Financial aid deadline (priority):*** 3/1. ***Notification date:*** Continuous beginning 3/15. Students must reply within 2 weeks of notification.

CONTACT Financial Aid Department, Eastern Nazarene College, 23 East Elm Avenue, Quincy, MA 02170, 617-745-3712 or toll-free 800-88-ENC88. *Fax:* 617-745-3929. *E-mail:* finaid@enc.edu

EASTERN NEW MEXICO UNIVERSITY

Portales, NM

Tuition & fees (NM res): $1830 **Average undergraduate aid package: $5861**

ABOUT THE INSTITUTION State-supported, coed. Awards: associate, bachelor's, and master's degrees. 55 undergraduate majors. Total enrollment: 3,562. Undergraduates: 3,012. Freshmen: 493. Federal methodology is used as a basis for awarding need-based institutional aid.

UNDERGRADUATE EXPENSES for 1999–2000 ***Tuition, state resident:*** full-time $1272; part-time $53 per credit hour. ***Tuition, nonresident:*** full-time $6156; part-time $256 per credit hour. ***Required fees:*** full-time $558; $23 per credit hour. ***College room and board:*** $3690; ***room only:*** $1890. Room and board charges vary according to board plan. ***Payment plan:*** installment.

FRESHMAN FINANCIAL AID (Fall 1998) 651 applied for aid; of those 100% were deemed to have need. 92% of freshmen with need received aid; of those 11% had need fully met. *Average percent of need met:* 51% (excluding resources awarded to replace EFC). *Average financial aid package:* $5038 (excluding resources awarded to replace EFC). 3% of all full-time freshmen had no need and received non-need-based aid.

UNDERGRADUATE FINANCIAL AID (Fall 1998) 2,603 applied for aid; of those 100% were deemed to have need. 93% of undergraduates with need received aid; of those 14% had need fully met. *Average percent of need met:* 55% (excluding resources awarded to replace EFC). *Average financial aid package:* $5861 (excluding resources awarded to replace EFC). 3% of all full-time undergraduates had no need and received non-need-based aid.

GIFT AID (NEED-BASED) ***Total amount:*** $4,747,087 (86% Federal, 14% state). ***Receiving aid:*** *Freshmen:* 64% (523); *all full-time undergraduates:* 65% (2,187). ***Average award:*** Freshmen: $2959; Undergraduates: $2918. ***Scholarships, grants, and awards:*** Federal Pell, FSEOG, state, private, college/university gift aid from institutional funds.

GIFT AID (NON-NEED-BASED) ***Total amount:*** $1,159,940 (28% institutional, 72% external sources). ***Receiving aid:*** *Freshmen:* 47% (389); *Undergraduates:* 45% (1,506). ***Scholarships, grants, and awards by category:*** *Academic Interests/Achievement:* agriculture, biological sciences, business, communication, computer science, education, engineering/technologies, English, foreign languages, general academic interests/achievements, health fields, home economics, humanities, mathematics, military science, physical sciences, premedicine, religion/biblical studies, social sciences. *Creative Arts/Performance:* applied art and design, art/fine arts, cinema/film/broadcasting, creative writing, dance, debating, general creative arts/performance, journalism/publications, music, performing arts, theater/drama. *Special Achievements/Activities:* community service, general special achievements/activities, hobbies/interests, leadership, memberships, rodeo. *Special Characteristics:* children and siblings of alumni, ethnic background, first-generation college students, general special characteristics, international students, members of minority groups, out-of-state students, veterans. ***Tuition waivers:*** Full or partial for employees or children of employees.

LOANS ***Student loans:*** $7,519,665 (82% need-based, 18% non-need-based). 61% of past graduating class borrowed through all loan programs. Average indebtedness per student: $16,511. ***Average need-based loan:*** Freshmen: $2622; Undergraduates: $3754. ***Parent loans:*** $73,754 (100% non-need-based). ***Programs:*** FFEL (Subsidized and Unsubsidized Stafford, PLUS), Perkins, state, college/university.

WORK-STUDY ***Federal work-study:*** *Total amount:* $1,204,524; 700 jobs averaging $1721. ***State or other work-study/employment:*** *Total amount:* $299,818 (75% need-based, 25% non-need-based). 212 part-time jobs averaging $1414.

Eastern New Mexico University (continued)

ATHLETIC AWARDS *Total amount:* 496,182 (100% non-need-based).

APPLYING for FINANCIAL AID ***Required financial aid form:*** FAFSA. ***Financial aid deadline (priority):*** 3/1. ***Notification date:*** 4/15. Students must reply within 2 weeks of notification.

CONTACT Ms. Phyllis Seefeld, Admissions Specialist, Eastern New Mexico University, Station 54, Portales, NM 88130, 505-562-2178 or toll-free 800-367-3668.

EASTERN OREGON UNIVERSITY

La Grande, OR

Tuition & fees: $3315 **Average undergraduate aid package: N/A**

ABOUT THE INSTITUTION State-supported, coed. Awards: associate, bachelor's, and master's degrees. 32 undergraduate majors. Total enrollment: 2,606. Undergraduates: 2,394. Freshmen: 380. Federal methodology is used as a basis for awarding need-based institutional aid.

UNDERGRADUATE EXPENSES for 1999–2000 ***Application fee:*** $50. ***One-time required fee:*** $75. ***Comprehensive fee:*** $7880 includes full-time tuition ($2316), mandatory fees ($999), and room and board ($4565). ***College room only:*** $3200. Full-time tuition and fees vary according to location. Room and board charges vary according to board plan and housing facility. ***Part-time tuition:*** $64 per credit. ***Part-time fees:*** $15 per credit; $85 per term part-time. Part-time tuition and fees vary according to course load and location. ***Payment plan:*** installment.

FRESHMAN FINANCIAL AID (Fall 1998) 285 applied for aid; of those 73% were deemed to have need. 100% of freshmen with need received aid.

UNDERGRADUATE FINANCIAL AID (Fall 1998) 1,511 applied for aid; of those 73% were deemed to have need. 100% of undergraduates with need received aid.

GIFT AID (NEED-BASED) ***Total amount:*** $2,619,566 (63% Federal, 15% state, 3% institutional, 19% external sources). ***Scholarships, grants, and awards:*** Federal Pell, FSEOG, state, private, college/university gift aid from institutional funds.

GIFT AID (NON-NEED-BASED) ***Scholarships, grants, and awards by category:*** *Academic Interests/Achievement:* agriculture, biological sciences, business, education, general academic interests/achievements, mathematics, physical sciences. *Creative Arts/Performance:* art/fine arts, music, theater/drama. *Special Achievements/Activities:* community service, leadership, rodeo. *Special Characteristics:* adult students, general special characteristics, international students, members of minority groups, out-of-state students. ***Tuition waivers:*** Full or partial for employees or children of employees.

LOANS ***Student loans:*** $5,459,394 (66% need-based, 34% non-need-based). ***Parent loans:*** $347,130 (100% non-need-based). ***Programs:*** FFEL (Subsidized and Unsubsidized Stafford, PLUS), Perkins.

WORK-STUDY ***Federal work-study:*** *Total amount:* $175,759; 95 jobs averaging $1850.

APPLYING for FINANCIAL AID ***Required financial aid forms:*** FAFSA, state aid form, institutional scholarship application forms. ***Financial aid deadline (priority):*** 1/1. ***Notification date:*** 3/1. Students must reply within 4 weeks of notification.

CONTACT Mr. Robert Clarke, Director of Financial Aid, Eastern Oregon University, 1410 L Avenue, La Grande, OR 97850-2899, 541-962-3393 or toll-free 800-452-8639. *Fax:* 541-962-3661. *E-mail:* rclarke@eou.edu

EASTERN WASHINGTON UNIVERSITY

Cheney, WA

Tuition & fees (WA res): $2907 **Average undergraduate aid package: $13,003**

ABOUT THE INSTITUTION State-supported, coed. Awards: bachelor's and master's degrees. 103 undergraduate majors. Total enrollment: 8,261. Undergraduates: 7,225. Freshmen: 1,079. Federal methodology is used as a basis for awarding need-based institutional aid.

UNDERGRADUATE EXPENSES for 1999–2000 ***Application fee:*** $35. ***Tuition, state resident:*** full-time $2700; part-time $90 per quarter hour. ***Tuition, nonresident:*** full-time $9594; part-time $320 per quarter hour. ***Required fees:*** full-time $207. Full-time tuition and fees vary according to reciprocity agreements. Part-time tuition and fees vary according to course load and reciprocity agreements. ***College room and board:*** $4399; ***room only:*** $2276. Room and board charges vary according to board plan and housing facility. ***Payment plan:*** installment.

FRESHMAN FINANCIAL AID (Fall 1998) 877 applied for aid; of those 79% were deemed to have need. 99% of freshmen with need received aid; of those 22% had need fully met. *Average percent of need met:* 40% (excluding resources awarded to replace EFC). *Average financial aid package:* $10,514 (excluding resources awarded to replace EFC). 9% of all full-time freshmen had no need and received non-need-based aid.

UNDERGRADUATE FINANCIAL AID (Fall 1998) 5,397 applied for aid; of those 62% were deemed to have need. 99% of undergraduates with need received aid; of those 20% had need fully met. *Average percent of need met:* 40% (excluding resources awarded to replace EFC). *Average financial aid package:* $13,003 (excluding resources awarded to replace EFC). 6% of all full-time undergraduates had no need and received non-need-based aid.

GIFT AID (NEED-BASED) ***Total amount:*** $12,104,210 (44% Federal, 43% state, 4% institutional, 9% external sources). ***Receiving aid:*** *Freshmen:* 50% (538); *all full-time undergraduates:* 39% (2,504). ***Average award:*** Freshmen: $3158; Undergraduates: $3633. ***Scholarships, grants, and awards:*** Federal Pell, FSEOG, state, private, college/university gift aid from institutional funds.

GIFT AID (NON-NEED-BASED) ***Total amount:*** $235,304 (33% institutional, 67% external sources). ***Receiving aid:*** *Freshmen:* 15% (163); *Undergraduates:* 5% (336). ***Scholarships, grants, and awards by category:*** *Academic Interests/Achievement:* 200 awards ($300,000 total): biological sciences, business, education, foreign languages, general academic interests/achievements, health fields, physical sciences, social sciences. *Creative Arts/Performance:* 38 awards ($37,000 total): art/fine arts, journalism/publications, music, theater/drama. *Special Characteristics:* 80 awards ($113,000 total): adult students, children and siblings of alumni, ethnic background, handicapped students, international students, out-of-state students. ***Tuition waivers:*** Full or partial for employees or children of employees. ***ROTC:*** Army.

LOANS ***Student loans:*** $26,882,507 (90% need-based, 10% non-need-based). 63% of past graduating class borrowed through all loan programs. Average indebtedness per student: $14,509. ***Average need-based loan:*** Freshmen: $1360; Undergraduates: $2369. ***Parent loans:*** $2,080,747 (63% need-based, 37% non-need-based). ***Programs:*** FFEL (Subsidized and Unsubsidized Stafford, PLUS), Perkins, college/university.

WORK-STUDY ***Federal work-study:*** *Total amount:* $725,723; 281 jobs averaging $2451. ***State or other work-study/employment:*** *Total amount:* $1,112,358 (67% need-based, 33% non-need-based). Part-time jobs available.

APPLYING for FINANCIAL AID ***Required financial aid form:*** FAFSA. ***Financial aid deadline (priority):*** 2/15. ***Notification date:*** Continuous beginning 4/1. Students must reply within 3 weeks of notification.

CONTACT Bruce DeFrates, Financial Aid Director, Eastern Washington University, 526 5th Street, Cheney, WA 99004-2431, 509-359-2314 or toll-free 888-740-1914 (out-of-state). *Fax:* 509-359-4330. *E-mail:* finaid@mail.ewu.edu

EASTMAN SCHOOL OF MUSIC

Rochester, NY

See University of Rochester

EAST STROUDSBURG UNIVERSITY OF PENNSYLVANIA

East Stroudsburg, PA

Tuition & fees (PA res): $4492 **Average undergraduate aid package: $4455**

ABOUT THE INSTITUTION State-supported, coed. Awards: associate, bachelor's, and master's degrees. 41 undergraduate majors. Total enrollment: 5,802. Undergraduates: 4,782. Freshmen: 859. Federal methodology is used as a basis for awarding need-based institutional aid.

UNDERGRADUATE EXPENSES for 1999–2000 ***Application fee:*** $25. ***Tuition, state resident:*** full-time $3618; part-time $150 per credit. ***Tuition, nonresident:*** full-time $9046; part-time $388 per credit. ***Required fees:*** full-time $874; $36 per credit. ***College room and board:*** $3938; ***room only:*** $2432. Room and board charges vary according to board plan and housing facility. ***Payment plan:*** installment.

FRESHMAN FINANCIAL AID (Fall 1999, est.) 1003 applied for aid; of those 71% were deemed to have need. 95% of freshmen with need received aid; of those 78% had need fully met. *Average percent of need met:* 88% (excluding resources awarded to replace EFC). *Average financial aid package:* $4123 (excluding resources awarded to replace EFC). 19% of all full-time freshmen had no need and received non-need-based aid.

UNDERGRADUATE FINANCIAL AID (Fall 1999, est.) 3,189 applied for aid; of those 73% were deemed to have need. 95% of undergraduates with need received aid; of those 81% had need fully met. *Average percent of need met:* 89% (excluding resources awarded to replace EFC). *Average financial aid package:* $4455 (excluding resources awarded to replace EFC). 20% of all full-time undergraduates had no need and received non-need-based aid.

GIFT AID (NEED-BASED) ***Total amount:*** $5,255,621 (48% Federal, 52% state). ***Receiving aid:*** *Freshmen:* 48% (504); *all full-time undergraduates:* 47% (1,633). ***Average award:*** Freshmen: $2661; Undergraduates: $2742. ***Scholarships, grants, and awards:*** Federal Pell, FSEOG, state, private, college/university gift aid from institutional funds.

GIFT AID (NON-NEED-BASED) ***Total amount:*** $453,203 (59% institutional, 41% external sources). ***Receiving aid:*** *Freshmen:* 2% (19); *Undergraduates:* 3% (112). ***Scholarships, grants, and awards by category:*** *Academic Interests/Achievement:* 224 awards ($164,117 total): biological sciences, business, communication, computer science, education, English, general academic interests/achievements, health fields, mathematics, physical sciences, social sciences. *Creative Arts/Performance:* 6 awards ($2050 total): applied art and design, music, theater/drama. *Special Achievements/Activities:* 19 awards ($4025 total): general special achievements/activities. *Special Characteristics:* 49 awards ($151,020 total): adult students, handicapped students, international students, members of minority groups. ***Tuition waivers:*** Full or partial for employees or children of employees, senior citizens. ***ROTC:*** Army cooperative, Air Force cooperative.

LOANS ***Student loans:*** $12,420,409 (51% need-based, 49% non-need-based). 67% of past graduating class borrowed through all loan programs. Average indebtedness per student: $14,139. ***Average need-based loan:*** Freshmen: $2720; Undergraduates: $3133. ***Parent loans:*** $1,941,592 (100% non-need-based). ***Programs:*** FFEL (Subsidized and Unsubsidized Stafford, PLUS), Perkins, alternative loans.

WORK-STUDY ***Federal work-study:*** *Total amount:* $433,145; 280 jobs averaging $1545. ***State or other work-study/employment:*** *Total amount:* $839,610 (100% non-need-based). 543 part-time jobs averaging $1545.

ATHLETIC AWARDS *Total amount:* 225,342 (100% non-need-based).

APPLYING for FINANCIAL AID ***Required financial aid form:*** FAFSA. ***Financial aid deadline:*** 3/1. ***Notification date:*** 4/1. Students must reply by 5/1.

CONTACT Georgia K. Prell, Director of Financial Aid, East Stroudsburg University of Pennsylvania, 200 Prospect Street, East Stroudsburg, PA 18301-2999, 570-422-3340 or toll-free 877-230-5547. *Fax:* 570-422-3056.

EAST TENNESSEE STATE UNIVERSITY

Johnson City, TN

Tuition & fees (TN res): $2532 **Average undergraduate aid package: $7082**

ABOUT THE INSTITUTION State-supported, coed. Awards: associate, bachelor's, master's, doctoral, and first professional degrees and post-master's certificates. 58 undergraduate majors. Total enrollment: 11,423. Undergraduates: 9,403. Freshmen: 1,511. Federal methodology is used as a basis for awarding need-based institutional aid.

UNDERGRADUATE EXPENSES for 1999–2000 ***Application fee:*** $15. ***Tuition, state resident:*** full-time $2020; part-time $90 per credit. ***Tuition, nonresident:*** full-time $7136; part-time $314 per credit. ***Required fees:*** full-time $512; $31 per credit; $4 per term part-time. ***College room and board:*** $3070; ***room only:*** $1750. Room and board charges vary according to board plan and housing facility. ***Payment plan:*** deferred payment.

FRESHMAN FINANCIAL AID (Fall 1998) 1401 applied for aid; of those 84% were deemed to have need. 73% of freshmen with need received aid; of those 37% had need fully met. *Average percent of need met:* 54% (excluding resources awarded to replace EFC). *Average financial aid package:* $4056 (excluding resources awarded to replace EFC). 22% of all full-time freshmen had no need and received non-need-based aid.

UNDERGRADUATE FINANCIAL AID (Fall 1998) 7,286 applied for aid; of those 78% were deemed to have need. 74% of undergraduates with need received aid; of those 42% had need fully met. *Average percent of need met:* 55% (excluding resources awarded to replace EFC). *Average financial aid package:* $7082 (excluding resources awarded to replace EFC). 27% of all full-time undergraduates had no need and received non-need-based aid.

GIFT AID (NEED-BASED) ***Total amount:*** $10,751,639 (88% Federal, 12% state). ***Receiving aid:*** *Freshmen:* 35% (520); *all full-time undergraduates:* 35% (2,706). ***Scholarships, grants, and awards:*** Federal Pell, FSEOG, state, private, Federal Nursing.

GIFT AID (NON-NEED-BASED) ***Total amount:*** $3,548,757 (84% institutional, 16% external sources). ***Receiving aid:*** *Freshmen:* 17% (249); *Undergraduates:* 14% (1,132). ***Scholarships, grants, and awards by category:*** *Academic Interests/Achievement:* biological sciences, business, computer science, education, engineering/technologies, English, general academic interests/achievements, health fields, mathematics, military science, social sciences. *Creative Arts/Performance:* art/fine arts, journalism/publications, music, theater/drama. *Special Achievements/Activities:* leadership, memberships. *Special Characteristics:* children of union members/company employees, members of minority groups. ***Tuition waivers:*** Full or partial for employees or children of employees, senior citizens. ***ROTC:*** Army.

LOANS ***Student loans:*** $6,123,011 (62% need-based, 38% non-need-based). ***Parent loans:*** $2,192,768 (100% non-need-based). ***Programs:*** FFEL (Subsidized and Unsubsidized Stafford, PLUS), Perkins, college/university.

WORK-STUDY ***Federal work-study:*** *Total amount:* $1,954,672; 1,350 jobs averaging $1448. ***State or other work-study/employment:*** *Total amount:* $360,826 (100% non-need-based). 344 part-time jobs averaging $1049.

ATHLETIC AWARDS *Total amount:* 1,520,081 (12% need-based, 88% non-need-based).

APPLYING for FINANCIAL AID ***Required financial aid form:*** FAFSA. ***Financial aid deadline (priority):*** 4/15. ***Notification date:*** Continuous. Students must reply within 3 weeks of notification.

CONTACT Cindy A. Johnson, Assistant Director, Financial Aid, East Tennessee State University, PO Box 70722, Johnson City, TN 37614, 423-439-4300 or toll-free 800-462-3878.

EAST TEXAS BAPTIST UNIVERSITY

Marshall, TX

Tuition & fees: $8450 **Average undergraduate aid package: $8246**

ABOUT THE INSTITUTION Independent Baptist, coed. Awards: associate and bachelor's degrees. 46 undergraduate majors. Total enrollment: 1,301. Undergraduates: 1,301. Freshmen: 307. Federal methodology is used as a basis for awarding need-based institutional aid.

UNDERGRADUATE EXPENSES for 2000–2001 ***Application fee:*** $25. ***Comprehensive fee:*** $11,652 includes full-time tuition ($7650), mandatory fees ($800), and room and board ($3202). ***College room only:*** $1350. Room and board charges vary according to board plan and housing facility. ***Part-time tuition:*** $255 per semester hour. ***Part-time fees:*** $35 per semester hour. ***Payment plan:*** installment.

East Texas Baptist University (continued)

FRESHMAN FINANCIAL AID (Fall 1999) 276 applied for aid; of those 92% were deemed to have need. 98% of freshmen with need received aid; of those 95% had need fully met. *Average percent of need met:* 86% (excluding resources awarded to replace EFC). *Average financial aid package:* $8433 (excluding resources awarded to replace EFC).

UNDERGRADUATE FINANCIAL AID (Fall 1999) 1,053 applied for aid; of those 98% were deemed to have need. 99% of undergraduates with need received aid; of those 95% had need fully met. *Average percent of need met:* 86% (excluding resources awarded to replace EFC). *Average financial aid package:* $8246 (excluding resources awarded to replace EFC).

GIFT AID (NEED-BASED) ***Total amount:*** $2,864,885 (37% Federal, 37% state, 19% institutional, 7% external sources). ***Receiving aid:*** *Freshmen:* 49% (142); *all full-time undergraduates:* 52% (565). ***Average award:*** Freshmen: $3524; Undergraduates: $2280. ***Scholarships, grants, and awards:*** Federal Pell, FSEOG, state, private, college/university gift aid from institutional funds.

GIFT AID (NON-NEED-BASED) ***Receiving aid:*** *Freshmen:* 37% (106); *Undergraduates:* 35% (379). ***Scholarships, grants, and awards by category:*** *Academic Interests/Achievement:* biological sciences, business, communication, computer science, education, English, foreign languages, general academic interests/achievements, health fields, mathematics, physical sciences, religion/biblical studies. *Creative Arts/Performance:* music, theater/drama. *Special Achievements/Activities:* cheerleading/drum major, general special achievements/activities, leadership, religious involvement. *Special Characteristics:* children and siblings of alumni, children of educators, children of faculty/staff, general special characteristics, international students, local/state students, previous college experience, religious affiliation, siblings of current students, twins. ***Tuition waivers:*** Full or partial for employees or children of employees.

LOANS ***Student loans:*** $2,550,844 (56% need-based, 44% non-need-based). 63% of past graduating class borrowed through all loan programs. Average indebtedness per student: $20,000. ***Average need-based loan:*** Freshmen: $1687; Undergraduates: $3155. ***Parent loans:*** $210,805 (100% non-need-based). ***Programs:*** FFEL (Subsidized and Unsubsidized Stafford, PLUS), Perkins, state, college/university.

WORK-STUDY ***Federal work-study:*** *Total amount:* $165,602; 96 jobs averaging $1648. ***State or other work-study/employment:*** *Total amount:* $290,156 (4% need-based, 96% non-need-based). Part-time jobs available.

APPLYING for FINANCIAL AID ***Required financial aid forms:*** FAFSA, institution's own form. ***Financial aid deadline (priority):*** 6/1. ***Notification date:*** Continuous. Students must reply within 3 weeks of notification.

CONTACT Ms. Pat Wilson, Director of Financial Aid, East Texas Baptist University, 1209 North Grove Street, Marshall, TX 75670-1498, 903-935-7963 Ext. 216 or toll-free 800-804-3828. *Fax:* 903-938-1705.

EAST-WEST UNIVERSITY

Chicago, IL

Tuition & fees: $8190 **Average undergraduate aid package: $7500**

ABOUT THE INSTITUTION Independent, coed. Awards: associate and bachelor's degrees. 17 undergraduate majors. Total enrollment: 760. Undergraduates: 760. Federal methodology is used as a basis for awarding need-based institutional aid.

UNDERGRADUATE EXPENSES for 1999–2000 ***Application fee:*** $30. ***Tuition:*** full-time $7800; part-time $265 per quarter hour. ***Required fees:*** full-time $390; $125 per term part-time. ***Payment plans:*** installment, deferred payment.

FRESHMAN FINANCIAL AID (Fall 1998) *Average percent of need met:* 90% (excluding resources awarded to replace EFC). *Average financial aid package:* $7500 (excluding resources awarded to replace EFC).

UNDERGRADUATE FINANCIAL AID (Fall 1998) *Average percent of need met:* 90% (excluding resources awarded to replace EFC). *Average financial aid package:* $7500 (excluding resources awarded to replace EFC).

GIFT AID (NEED-BASED) ***Total amount:*** $3,521,314 (37% Federal, 60% state, 3% institutional). ***Scholarships, grants, and awards:*** Federal Pell, FSEOG, state, college/university gift aid from institutional funds.

GIFT AID (NON-NEED-BASED) ***Scholarships, grants, and awards by category:*** *Academic Interests/Achievement:* general academic interests/achievements. ***Tuition waivers:*** Full or partial for employees or children of employees.

WORK-STUDY ***Federal work-study:*** *Total amount:* $38,820; 35 jobs available.

APPLYING for FINANCIAL AID ***Required financial aid form:*** FAFSA. ***Financial aid deadline (priority):*** 6/30.

CONTACT Office of Financial Aid, East-West University, 816 South Michigan Avenue, Chicago, IL 60605-2103, 312-939-0111.

ECKERD COLLEGE

St. Petersburg, FL

Tuition & fees: $18,220 **Average undergraduate aid package: $16,000**

ABOUT THE INSTITUTION Independent Presbyterian, coed. Awards: bachelor's degrees. 41 undergraduate majors. Total enrollment: 1,530. Undergraduates: 1,530. Freshmen: 403. Federal methodology is used as a basis for awarding need-based institutional aid.

UNDERGRADUATE EXPENSES for 1999–2000 ***Application fee:*** $25. ***Comprehensive fee:*** $23,180 includes full-time tuition ($18,025), mandatory fees ($195), and room and board ($4960). Room and board charges vary according to board plan and housing facility. ***Part-time tuition:*** $1925 per course. ***Payment plan:*** installment.

FRESHMAN FINANCIAL AID (Fall 1999, est.) 299 applied for aid; of those 83% were deemed to have need. 100% of freshmen with need received aid; of those 85% had need fully met. *Average percent of need met:* 85% (excluding resources awarded to replace EFC). *Average financial aid package:* $15,500 (excluding resources awarded to replace EFC).

UNDERGRADUATE FINANCIAL AID (Fall 1999, est.) 1,006 applied for aid; of those 87% were deemed to have need. 100% of undergraduates with need received aid; of those 85% had need fully met. *Average percent of need met:* 85% (excluding resources awarded to replace EFC). *Average financial aid package:* $16,000 (excluding resources awarded to replace EFC).

GIFT AID (NEED-BASED) ***Total amount:*** $7,385,600 (11% Federal, 2% state, 82% institutional, 5% external sources). ***Receiving aid:*** *Freshmen:* 62% (248); *all full-time undergraduates:* 57% (880). ***Scholarships, grants, and awards:*** Federal Pell, FSEOG, state, private, college/university gift aid from institutional funds.

GIFT AID (NON-NEED-BASED) ***Total amount:*** $5,531,000 (23% state, 73% institutional, 4% external sources). ***Receiving aid:*** *Freshmen:* 25% (99); *Undergraduates:* 23% (352). ***Scholarships, grants, and awards by category:*** *Academic Interests/Achievement:* general academic interests/achievements. *Creative Arts/Performance:* 50 awards ($250,000 total): art/fine arts, creative writing, music, theater/drama. *Special Achievements/Activities:* 25 awards ($125,000 total): community service, leadership. *Special Characteristics:* 140 awards ($729,000 total): children of faculty/staff, international students, local/state students, religious affiliation. ***Tuition waivers:*** Full or partial for employees or children of employees. ***ROTC:*** Army cooperative, Air Force cooperative.

LOANS ***Student loans:*** $4,237,000 (63% need-based, 37% non-need-based). 56% of past graduating class borrowed through all loan programs. Average indebtedness per student: $17,500. ***Parent loans:*** $1,440,000 (60% need-based, 40% non-need-based). ***Programs:*** FFEL (Subsidized and Unsubsidized Stafford, PLUS), Perkins, college/university.

WORK-STUDY ***Federal work-study:*** *Total amount:* $1,188,000; 635 jobs averaging $1800. ***State or other work-study/employment:*** *Total amount:* $109,100 (100% non-need-based). 85 part-time jobs averaging $1300.

ATHLETIC AWARDS *Total amount:* 1,150,000 (60% need-based, 40% non-need-based).

APPLYING for FINANCIAL AID ***Required financial aid form:*** FAFSA. ***Financial aid deadline (priority):*** 4/1. ***Notification date:*** Continuous. Students must reply by 5/1.

CONTACT Ms. Margaret Morris, Director of Financial Aid, Eckerd College, 4200 54th Avenue, South, St. Petersburg, FL 33711, 727-864-8334 or toll-free 800-456-9009. *Fax:* 727-866-2304. *E-mail:* morrismw@eckerd.edu

EDGEWOOD COLLEGE

Madison, WI

Tuition & fees: $11,650 **Average undergraduate aid package: $9940**

ABOUT THE INSTITUTION Independent Roman Catholic, coed. Awards: associate, bachelor's, and master's degrees. 41 undergraduate majors. Total enrollment: 1,938. Undergraduates: 1,430. Freshmen: 200. Federal methodology is used as a basis for awarding need-based institutional aid.

UNDERGRADUATE EXPENSES for 1999–2000 ***Application fee:*** $25. ***Comprehensive fee:*** $16,030 includes full-time tuition ($11,450), mandatory fees ($200), and room and board ($4380). ***College room only:*** $2196. Full-time tuition and fees vary according to program. Room and board charges vary according to board plan and housing facility. ***Part-time tuition:*** $340 per credit. ***Part-time fees:*** $55 per term part-time. Part-time tuition and fees vary according to course load and program. ***Payment plans:*** installment, deferred payment.

FRESHMAN FINANCIAL AID (Fall 1999, est.) 159 applied for aid; of those 72% were deemed to have need. 100% of freshmen with need received aid; of those 9% had need fully met. *Average percent of need met:* 61% (excluding resources awarded to replace EFC). *Average financial aid package:* $9776 (excluding resources awarded to replace EFC).

UNDERGRADUATE FINANCIAL AID (Fall 1999, est.) 626 applied for aid; of those 85% were deemed to have need. 100% of undergraduates with need received aid; of those 10% had need fully met. *Average percent of need met:* 58% (excluding resources awarded to replace EFC). *Average financial aid package:* $9940 (excluding resources awarded to replace EFC).

GIFT AID (NEED-BASED) ***Total amount:*** $2,954,977 (25% Federal, 25% state, 46% institutional, 4% external sources). ***Receiving aid:*** *Freshmen:* 60% (114); *all full-time undergraduates:* 56% (535). ***Average award:*** Freshmen: $6361; Undergraduates: $5870. ***Scholarships, grants, and awards:*** Federal Pell, FSEOG, state, private, college/university gift aid from institutional funds.

GIFT AID (NON-NEED-BASED) ***Total amount:*** $535,524 (86% institutional, 14% external sources). ***Receiving aid:*** *Freshmen:* 15% (28); *Undergraduates:* 42% (406). ***Scholarships, grants, and awards by category:*** *Academic Interests/Achievement:* general academic interests/achievements. *Creative Arts/Performance:* art/fine arts, creative writing, music, performing arts, theater/drama. *Special Achievements/Activities:* community service, hobbies/interests, leadership. *Special Characteristics:* first-generation college students, handicapped students, local/state students, members of minority groups, religious affiliation. ***Tuition waivers:*** Full or partial for employees or children of employees.

LOANS ***Student loans:*** $7,593,978 (72% need-based, 28% non-need-based). 61% of past graduating class borrowed through all loan programs. Average indebtedness per student: $18,318. ***Average need-based loan:*** Freshmen: $2625; Undergraduates: $4304. ***Parent loans:*** $444,960 (100% non-need-based). ***Programs:*** FFEL (Subsidized and Unsubsidized Stafford, PLUS), Perkins.

WORK-STUDY ***Federal work-study:*** *Total amount:* $87,293; jobs available. ***State or other work-study/employment:*** *Total amount:* $627,154 (58% need-based, 42% non-need-based). Part-time jobs available.

APPLYING for FINANCIAL AID ***Required financial aid forms:*** FAFSA, institution's own form. ***Financial aid deadline (priority):*** 3/15. ***Notification date:*** 3/30.

CONTACT Mr. Scott Flanagan, Dean of Admission and Financial Aid, Edgewood College, 855 Woodrow Street, Madison, WI 53711-1998, 608-663-2294 or toll-free 800-444-4861.

EDINBORO UNIVERSITY OF PENNSYLVANIA

Edinboro, PA

Tuition & fees (PA res): $4358 **Average undergraduate aid package: $5728**

ABOUT THE INSTITUTION State-supported, coed. Awards: associate, bachelor's, and master's degrees and post-bachelor's and post-master's certificates. 47 undergraduate majors. Total enrollment: 7,079. Undergraduates: 6,400. Freshmen: 1,372. Federal methodology is used as a basis for awarding need-based institutional aid.

UNDERGRADUATE EXPENSES for 1999–2000 ***Application fee:*** $25. ***Tuition, state resident:*** full-time $3618; part-time $150 per credit. ***Tuition, nonresident:*** full-time $5428; part-time $226 per credit. ***Required fees:*** full-time $740; $31 per credit. Part-time tuition and fees vary according to course load. ***College room and board:*** $3788; ***room only:*** $2108. Room and board charges vary according to board plan. ***Payment plan:*** installment.

FRESHMAN FINANCIAL AID (Fall 1999, est.) 1128 applied for aid; of those 95% were deemed to have need. 100% of freshmen with need received aid; of those 82% had need fully met. *Average percent of need met:* 90% (excluding resources awarded to replace EFC). *Average financial aid package:* $5728 (excluding resources awarded to replace EFC). 12% of all full-time freshmen had no need and received non-need-based aid.

UNDERGRADUATE FINANCIAL AID (Fall 1999, est.) 5,127 applied for aid; of those 95% were deemed to have need. 100% of undergraduates with need received aid; of those 80% had need fully met. *Average percent of need met:* 95% (excluding resources awarded to replace EFC). *Average financial aid package:* $5728 (excluding resources awarded to replace EFC). 12% of all full-time undergraduates had no need and received non-need-based aid.

GIFT AID (NEED-BASED) ***Total amount:*** $10,405,000 (44% Federal, 42% state, 4% institutional, 10% external sources). ***Receiving aid:*** *Freshmen:* 85% (1,073); *all full-time undergraduates:* 86% (4,857). ***Scholarships, grants, and awards:*** Federal Pell, FSEOG, state, private, college/university gift aid from institutional funds.

GIFT AID (NON-NEED-BASED) ***Total amount:*** $2,500,000 (16% Federal, 12% state, 20% institutional, 52% external sources). ***Receiving aid:*** *Freshmen:* 5% (65); *Undergraduates:* 4% (251). ***Scholarships, grants, and awards by category:*** *Academic Interests/Achievement:* 232 awards ($271,367 total): biological sciences, business, communication, computer science, education, engineering/technologies, English, foreign languages, general academic interests/achievements, health fields, humanities, mathematics, military science, physical sciences, premedicine, religion/biblical studies, social sciences. *Creative Arts/Performance:* 28 awards ($13,750 total): art/fine arts, cinema/film/broadcasting, journalism/publications, music. *Special Achievements/Activities:* general special achievements/activities. *Special Characteristics:* 876 awards ($2,322,698 total): adult students, children and siblings of alumni, children of faculty/staff, children of union members/company employees, children with a deceased or disabled parent, first-generation college students, general special characteristics, handicapped students, international students, local/state students, members of minority groups, out-of-state students, religious affiliation, veterans, veterans' children. ***Tuition waivers:*** Full or partial for employees or children of employees, senior citizens. ***ROTC:*** Army.

LOANS ***Student loans:*** $19,000,000 (63% need-based, 37% non-need-based). 85% of past graduating class borrowed through all loan programs. Average indebtedness per student: $17,500. ***Parent loans:*** $1,700,000 (100% non-need-based). ***Programs:*** FFEL (Subsidized and Unsubsidized Stafford, PLUS), Perkins, Federal Nursing, college/university.

WORK-STUDY ***Federal work-study:*** *Total amount:* $1,200,000; 532 jobs available. ***State or other work-study/employment:*** *Total amount:* $360,000 (50% need-based, 50% non-need-based). Part-time jobs available.

ATHLETIC AWARDS *Total amount:* 645,000 (67% need-based, 33% non-need-based).

APPLYING for FINANCIAL AID ***Required financial aid form:*** FAFSA. ***Financial aid deadline (priority):*** 3/15. ***Notification date:*** 3/31. Students must reply within 2 weeks of notification.

Edinboro University of Pennsylvania (continued)

CONTACT Mr. Kenneth Brandt, Director of Financial Aid, Edinboro University of Pennsylvania, Hamilton Hall, Edinboro, PA 16444, 814-732-5555 Ext. 266 or toll-free 888-846-2676 (in-state), 800-626-2203 (out-of-state). *Fax:* 814-732-2129. *E-mail:* brandt@edinboro.edu

EDUCATION AMERICA, DENVER CAMPUS

Lakewood, CO

CONTACT Financial Aid Office, Education America, Denver Campus, 11011 West 6th Avenue, Lakewood, CO 80215-0090, 303-445-0500 or toll-free 800-999-5181.

EDUCATION AMERICA, SOUTHEAST COLLEGE OF TECHNOLOGY, MOBILE CAMPUS

Mobile, AL

ABOUT THE INSTITUTION Independent.

GIFT AID (NEED-BASED) ***Scholarships, grants, and awards:*** Federal Pell, FSEOG.

GIFT AID (NON-NEED-BASED) ***Scholarships, grants, and awards by category:*** *Special Characteristics:* general special characteristics.

LOANS ***Programs:*** Federal Direct (Subsidized and Unsubsidized Stafford, PLUS).

APPLYING for FINANCIAL AID ***Required financial aid forms:*** FAFSA, institution's own form.

CONTACT Ms. Linda Calvanese, Financial Aid Director, Education America, Southeast College of Technology, Mobile Campus, 828 Downtowner Loop West, Mobile, AL 36609-5404, 334-343-8200 Ext. 212.

EDWARD WATERS COLLEGE

Jacksonville, FL

Tuition & fees: $6600 **Average undergraduate aid package: N/A**

ABOUT THE INSTITUTION Independent African Methodist Episcopal, coed. Awards: bachelor's degrees. 19 undergraduate majors. Total enrollment: 681. Undergraduates: 681. Federal methodology is used as a basis for awarding need-based institutional aid.

UNDERGRADUATE EXPENSES for 1999–2000 ***Application fee:*** $15. ***Comprehensive fee:*** $11,114 includes full-time tuition ($5520), mandatory fees ($1080), and room and board ($4514). ***Part-time tuition:*** $230 per semester hour. ***Part-time fees:*** $45 per semester hour.

GIFT AID (NEED-BASED) ***Scholarships, grants, and awards:*** Federal Pell, FSEOG, state, private, college/university gift aid from institutional funds, United Negro College Fund.

GIFT AID (NON-NEED-BASED) ***ROTC:*** Army cooperative.

LOANS ***Programs:*** FFEL (Subsidized and Unsubsidized Stafford, PLUS), state.

WORK-STUDY Federal work-study jobs available.

APPLYING for FINANCIAL AID ***Required financial aid form:*** FAFSA. ***Financial aid deadline (priority):*** 4/15. ***Notification date:*** 7/15. Students must reply within 2 weeks of notification.

CONTACT Ms. Lena Thompson, Director of Financial Aid, Edward Waters College, 1658 Kings Road, Jacksonville, FL 32209-6199, 904-366-2528.

ELECTRONIC DATA PROCESSING COLLEGE OF PUERTO RICO

San Juan, PR

CONTACT Mr. Angel Rivera, Financial Aid Director, Electronic Data Processing College of Puerto Rico, PO Box 192303, San Juan, PR 00919-2303, 787-765-3560 Ext. 4713. *Fax:* 787-765-2650.

ELIZABETH CITY STATE UNIVERSITY

Elizabeth City, NC

CONTACT Ms. Dorothy Riddick-Saunders, Interim Assistant Director of Financial Aid, Elizabeth City State University, 1704 Weeksville Road, Campus Box 914, Elizabeth City, NC 27909-7806, 252-335-3285 or toll-free 800-347-3278. *Fax:* 252-335-3716. *E-mail:* saundedr@alpha.ecsu.edu

ELIZABETHTOWN COLLEGE

Elizabethtown, PA

Tuition & fees: $18,220 **Average undergraduate aid package: $15,036**

ABOUT THE INSTITUTION Independent religious, coed. Awards: bachelor's degrees. 46 undergraduate majors. Total enrollment: 1,778. Undergraduates: 1,778. Freshmen: 504. Both federal and institutional methodology are used as a basis for awarding need-based institutional aid.

UNDERGRADUATE EXPENSES for 1999–2000 ***Application fee:*** $20. ***Comprehensive fee:*** $23,600 includes full-time tuition ($17,770), mandatory fees ($450), and room and board ($5380). ***College room only:*** $2680. Room and board charges vary according to board plan and housing facility. ***Part-time tuition:*** $480 per credit. ***Part-time fees:*** $40 per term part-time. Part-time tuition and fees vary according to class time, course load, and program. ***Payment plan:*** installment.

FRESHMAN FINANCIAL AID (Fall 1999) 421 applied for aid; of those 88% were deemed to have need. 100% of freshmen with need received aid; of those 22% had need fully met. *Average percent of need met:* 89% (excluding resources awarded to replace EFC). *Average financial aid package:* $15,187 (excluding resources awarded to replace EFC). 18% of all full-time freshmen had no need and received non-need-based aid.

UNDERGRADUATE FINANCIAL AID (Fall 1999) 1,305 applied for aid; of those 91% were deemed to have need. 100% of undergraduates with need received aid; of those 28% had need fully met. *Average percent of need met:* 90% (excluding resources awarded to replace EFC). *Average financial aid package:* $15,036 (excluding resources awarded to replace EFC). 17% of all full-time undergraduates had no need and received non-need-based aid.

GIFT AID (NEED-BASED) ***Total amount:*** $12,296,184 (5% Federal, 13% state, 79% institutional, 3% external sources). ***Receiving aid:*** *Freshmen:* 76% (371); *all full-time undergraduates:* 74% (1,179). ***Average award:*** Freshmen: $11,544; Undergraduates: $10,561. ***Scholarships, grants, and awards:*** Federal Pell, FSEOG, state, private, college/university gift aid from institutional funds.

GIFT AID (NON-NEED-BASED) ***Total amount:*** $1,872,090 (3% state, 87% institutional, 10% external sources). ***Receiving aid:*** *Freshmen:* 6% (30); *Undergraduates:* 6% (91). ***Scholarships, grants, and awards by category:*** *Academic Interests/Achievement:* 820 awards ($4,295,580 total): biological sciences, business, communication, computer science, education, engineering/technologies, English, foreign languages, general academic interests/achievements, health fields, humanities, international studies, mathematics, physical sciences, religion/biblical studies, social sciences. *Creative Arts/Performance:* 47 awards ($39,425 total): music. *Special Achievements/Activities:* 7 awards ($13,130 total): junior miss. *Special Characteristics:* 168 awards ($853,168 total): children of faculty/staff, international students, local/state students, members of minority groups, religious affiliation, siblings of current students. ***Tuition waivers:*** Full or partial for employees or children of employees.

LOANS ***Student loans:*** $5,781,997 (75% need-based, 25% non-need-based). 77% of past graduating class borrowed through all loan programs. Average indebtedness per student: $15,644. ***Average need-based loan:*** Freshmen: $2863; Undergraduates: $3716. ***Parent loans:*** $2,429,573 (23% need-based, 77% non-need-based). ***Programs:*** FFEL (Subsidized and Unsubsidized Stafford, PLUS), Perkins, state.

WORK-STUDY ***Federal work-study:*** *Total amount:* $875,202; 621 jobs averaging $1401. ***State or other work-study/employment:*** *Total amount:* $96,480 (22% need-based, 78% non-need-based). 37 part-time jobs averaging $2608.

APPLYING for FINANCIAL AID ***Required financial aid forms:*** FAFSA, institution's own form. ***Financial aid deadline (priority):*** 3/15. ***Notification date:*** Continuous. Students must reply by 5/1 or within 2 weeks of notification.

CONTACT Mr. M. Clarke Paine, Director of Financial Aid, Elizabethtown College, 1 Alpha Drive, Elizabethtown, PA 17022-2298, 717-361-1404. *Fax:* 717-361-1485. *E-mail:* painemc@etown.edu

ELMHURST COLLEGE

Elmhurst, IL

Tuition & fees: $13,900 **Average undergraduate aid package: $13,950**

ABOUT THE INSTITUTION Independent religious, coed. Awards: bachelor's and master's degrees. 67 undergraduate majors. Total enrollment: 2,802. Undergraduates: 2,678. Freshmen: 273. Federal methodology is used as a basis for awarding need-based institutional aid.

UNDERGRADUATE EXPENSES for 1999–2000 ***Application fee:*** $15. ***Comprehensive fee:*** $19,166 includes full-time tuition ($13,900) and room and board ($5266). ***College room only:*** $2866. Room and board charges vary according to board plan. ***Part-time tuition:*** $405 per credit hour. ***Payment plans:*** installment, deferred payment.

FRESHMAN FINANCIAL AID (Fall 1999) 263 applied for aid; of those 90% were deemed to have need. 100% of freshmen with need received aid; of those 81% had need fully met. *Average percent of need met:* 97% (excluding resources awarded to replace EFC). *Average financial aid package:* $13,832 (excluding resources awarded to replace EFC). 14% of all full-time freshmen had no need and received non-need-based aid.

UNDERGRADUATE FINANCIAL AID (Fall 1999) 1,522 applied for aid; of those 82% were deemed to have need. 100% of undergraduates with need received aid; of those 96% had need fully met. *Average percent of need met:* 97% (excluding resources awarded to replace EFC). *Average financial aid package:* $13,950 (excluding resources awarded to replace EFC). 6% of all full-time undergraduates had no need and received non-need-based aid.

GIFT AID (NEED-BASED) ***Total amount:*** $10,341,834 (10% Federal, 31% state, 59% institutional). ***Receiving aid:*** *Freshmen:* 75% (214); *all full-time undergraduates:* 67% (1,211). ***Average award:*** Freshmen: $9390; Undergraduates: $9237. ***Scholarships, grants, and awards:*** Federal Pell, FSEOG, state, private, college/university gift aid from institutional funds.

GIFT AID (NON-NEED-BASED) ***Total amount:*** $1,227,100 (4% state, 89% institutional, 7% external sources). ***Receiving aid:*** *Freshmen:* 33% (93); *Undergraduates:* 11% (204). ***Scholarships, grants, and awards by category:*** *Academic Interests/Achievement:* 346 awards ($1,748,280 total): biological sciences, business, communication, education, foreign languages, general academic interests/achievements, health fields, humanities, mathematics, physical sciences, religion/biblical studies, social sciences. *Creative Arts/Performance:* 41 awards ($51,500 total): music, theater/drama. *Special Characteristics:* 184 awards ($839,310 total): members of minority groups, religious affiliation. ***Tuition waivers:*** Full or partial for employees or children of employees, senior citizens. ***ROTC:*** Army cooperative, Air Force cooperative.

LOANS ***Student loans:*** $6,063,313 (60% need-based, 40% non-need-based). 70% of past graduating class borrowed through all loan programs. Average indebtedness per student: $12,850. ***Parent loans:*** $1,139,655 (100% non-need-based). ***Programs:*** Federal Direct (Subsidized and Unsubsidized Stafford, PLUS), Perkins, college/university.

WORK-STUDY ***Federal work-study:*** *Total amount:* $168,400; 174 jobs averaging $968. ***State or other work-study/employment:*** *Total amount:* $250,000 (100% non-need-based). 194 part-time jobs averaging $1288.

APPLYING for FINANCIAL AID ***Required financial aid forms:*** FAFSA, institution's own form. ***Financial aid deadline (priority):*** 4/15. ***Notification date:*** Continuous.

CONTACT Mr. Gary F. Rold, Director of Financial Aid, Elmhurst College, Goebel Hall 106A, 190 Prospect Avenue, Elmhurst, IL 60126-3296, 630-617-3079 or toll-free 800-697-1871 (out-of-state). *Fax:* 630-617-3245. *E-mail:* garyr@elmhurst.edu

ELMIRA COLLEGE

Elmira, NY

Tuition & fees: $22,540 **Average undergraduate aid package: $18,957**

ABOUT THE INSTITUTION Independent, coed. Awards: bachelor's and master's degrees. 69 undergraduate majors. Total enrollment: 2,058. Undergraduates: 1,640. Freshmen: 366. Institutional methodology is used as a basis for awarding need-based institutional aid.

UNDERGRADUATE EXPENSES for 2000–2001 (est.) ***Application fee:*** $40. ***Comprehensive fee:*** $29,820 includes full-time tuition ($21,960), mandatory fees ($580), and room and board ($7280). ***College room only:*** $4450. ***Part-time tuition:*** $240 per credit hour. ***Payment plans:*** tuition prepayment, installment.

FRESHMAN FINANCIAL AID (Fall 1999, est.) 255 applied for aid; of those 93% were deemed to have need. 100% of freshmen with need received aid; of those 31% had need fully met. *Average percent of need met:* 91% (excluding resources awarded to replace EFC). *Average financial aid package:* $19,012 (excluding resources awarded to replace EFC). 6% of all full-time freshmen had no need and received non-need-based aid.

UNDERGRADUATE FINANCIAL AID (Fall 1999, est.) 954 applied for aid; of those 94% were deemed to have need. 100% of undergraduates with need received aid; of those 31% had need fully met. *Average percent of need met:* 89% (excluding resources awarded to replace EFC). *Average financial aid package:* $18,957 (excluding resources awarded to replace EFC). 17% of all full-time undergraduates had no need and received non-need-based aid.

GIFT AID (NEED-BASED) ***Total amount:*** $10,853,081 (7% Federal, 7% state, 85% institutional, 1% external sources). ***Receiving aid:*** *Freshmen:* 78% (236); *all full-time undergraduates:* 75% (894). ***Average award:*** Freshmen: $13,555; Undergraduates: $12,606. ***Scholarships, grants, and awards:*** Federal Pell, FSEOG, state, private, college/university gift aid from institutional funds.

GIFT AID (NON-NEED-BASED) ***Total amount:*** $2,256,442 (2% state, 97% institutional, 1% external sources). ***Receiving aid:*** *Freshmen:* 10% (31); *Undergraduates:* 8% (90). ***Scholarships, grants, and awards by category:*** *Academic Interests/Achievement:* 521 awards ($5,434,671 total): general academic interests/achievements. *Special Achievements/Activities:* 220 awards ($548,750 total): leadership. *Special Characteristics:* 132 awards ($1,035,733 total): children of faculty/staff, international students, local/state students, previous college experience, siblings of current students. ***Tuition waivers:*** Full or partial for employees or children of employees. ***ROTC:*** Army cooperative, Air Force cooperative.

LOANS ***Student loans:*** $6,310,261 (78% need-based, 22% non-need-based). 64% of past graduating class borrowed through all loan programs. ***Average need-based loan:*** Freshmen: $4724; Undergraduates: $5717. ***Parent loans:*** $2,370,732 (32% need-based, 68% non-need-based). ***Programs:*** FFEL (Subsidized and Unsubsidized Stafford, PLUS), Perkins, college/university, GATE Loans, alternative loans.

WORK-STUDY ***Federal work-study:*** *Total amount:* $438,628; 337 jobs averaging $1300. ***State or other work-study/employment:*** *Total amount:* $357,487 (36% need-based, 64% non-need-based). 211 part-time jobs averaging $1690.

APPLYING for FINANCIAL AID ***Required financial aid forms:*** FAFSA, CSS Financial Aid PROFILE, state aid form. ***Financial aid deadline (priority):*** 2/1. ***Notification date:*** Continuous beginning 2/15. Students must reply by 5/1 or within 3 weeks of notification.

CONTACT Mrs. Kathleen L. Cohen, Dean of Financial Aid, Elmira College, Hamilton Hall, One Park Place, Elmira, NY 14901-2099, 607-735-1728 or toll-free 800-935-6472. *Fax:* 607-735-1718. *E-mail:* kcohen@elmira.edu

ELMS COLLEGE

Chicopee, MA

See College of Our Lady of the Elms

ELON COLLEGE

Elon College, NC

Tuition & fees: $12,896 **Average undergraduate aid package: $9365**

ABOUT THE INSTITUTION Independent religious, coed. Awards: bachelor's and master's degrees. 50 undergraduate majors. Total enrollment: 3,961. Undergraduates: 3,701. Freshmen: 1,000. Both federal and institutional methodology are used as a basis for awarding need-based institutional aid.

UNDERGRADUATE EXPENSES for 1999–2000 ***Application fee:*** $25. ***Comprehensive fee:*** $17,447 includes full-time tuition ($12,671), mandatory fees ($225), and room and board ($4551). Room and board charges vary according to board plan and housing facility. ***Part-time tuition:*** $257 per semester hour. Part-time tuition and fees vary according to course load. ***Payment plan:*** installment.

FRESHMAN FINANCIAL AID (Fall 1999, est.) 606 applied for aid; of those 67% were deemed to have need. 98% of freshmen with need received aid. *Average percent of need met:* 74% (excluding resources awarded to replace EFC). *Average financial aid package:* $8819 (excluding resources awarded to replace EFC). 31% of all full-time freshmen had no need and received non-need-based aid.

UNDERGRADUATE FINANCIAL AID (Fall 1999, est.) 1,842 applied for aid; of those 76% were deemed to have need. 99% of undergraduates with need received aid. *Average percent of need met:* 75% (excluding resources awarded to replace EFC). *Average financial aid package:* $9365 (excluding resources awarded to replace EFC). 23% of all full-time undergraduates had no need and received non-need-based aid.

GIFT AID (NEED-BASED) ***Total amount:*** $5,373,971 (17% Federal, 29% state, 50% institutional, 4% external sources). ***Receiving aid:*** *Freshmen:* 33% (326); *all full-time undergraduates:* 34% (1,193). ***Average award:*** Freshmen: $5080; Undergraduates: $5062. ***Scholarships, grants, and awards:*** Federal Pell, FSEOG, state, private, college/university gift aid from institutional funds.

GIFT AID (NON-NEED-BASED) ***Total amount:*** $2,192,988 (27% state, 66% institutional, 7% external sources). ***Receiving aid:*** *Freshmen:* 3% (33); *Undergraduates:* 2% (72). ***Scholarships, grants, and awards by category:*** *Academic Interests/Achievement:* 826 awards ($2,263,176 total): biological sciences, business, communication, computer science, education, engineering/technologies, general academic interests/achievements, mathematics, physical sciences, premedicine. *Creative Arts/Performance:* 109 awards ($98,325 total): art/fine arts, music, performing arts, theater/drama. *Special Achievements/Activities:* 54 awards ($81,750 total): leadership. *Special Characteristics:* children of faculty/staff, relatives of clergy. ***Tuition waivers:*** Full or partial for employees or children of employees. ***ROTC:*** Army.

LOANS ***Student loans:*** $6,168,150 (72% need-based, 28% non-need-based). 47% of past graduating class borrowed through all loan programs. Average indebtedness per student: $17,408. ***Average need-based loan:*** Freshmen: $2295; Undergraduates: $3204. ***Parent loans:*** $4,032,430 (100% non-need-based). ***Programs:*** FFEL (Subsidized and Unsubsidized Stafford, PLUS), Perkins, state, college/university, alternative loans.

WORK-STUDY ***Federal work-study:*** *Total amount:* $1,522,855; jobs available.

ATHLETIC AWARDS *Total amount:* 1,990,933 (38% need-based, 62% non-need-based).

APPLYING for FINANCIAL AID ***Required financial aid forms:*** FAFSA, institution's own form, CSS Financial Aid PROFILE. ***Financial aid deadline (priority):*** 2/15. ***Notification date:*** Continuous beginning 3/15. Students must reply within 2 weeks of notification.

CONTACT Mr. Joel T. Speckhard, Director of Financial Planning, Elon College, 2700 Campus Box, Elon College, NC 27244, 336-584-2478 or toll-free 800-334-8448. *Fax:* 336-586-6072. *E-mail:* joel.speckhard@elon.edu

EMBRY-RIDDLE AERONAUTICAL UNIVERSITY

Prescott, AZ

Tuition & fees: $11,020 **Average undergraduate aid package: $5198**

ABOUT THE INSTITUTION Independent, coed, primarily men. Awards: bachelor's degrees. 10 undergraduate majors. Total enrollment: 1,592. Undergraduates: 1,592. Freshmen: 313. Federal methodology is used as a basis for awarding need-based institutional aid.

UNDERGRADUATE EXPENSES for 2000–2001 ***Application fee:*** $30. ***Comprehensive fee:*** $15,446 includes full-time tuition ($10,700), mandatory fees ($320), and room and board ($4426). ***College room only:*** $2646. Full-time tuition and fees vary according to course load and program. Room and board charges vary according to board plan, housing facility, and location. Part-time tuition and fees vary according to course load and program.

FRESHMAN FINANCIAL AID (Fall 1998) 222 applied for aid; of those 77% were deemed to have need. 100% of freshmen with need received aid. *Average financial aid package:* $9463 (excluding resources awarded to replace EFC).

UNDERGRADUATE FINANCIAL AID (Fall 1998) 947 applied for aid; of those 87% were deemed to have need. 100% of undergraduates with need received aid. *Average financial aid package:* $5198 (excluding resources awarded to replace EFC).

GIFT AID (NEED-BASED) ***Total amount:*** $2,732,219 (35% Federal, 55% institutional, 10% external sources). ***Receiving aid:*** *Freshmen:* 40% (125); *all full-time undergraduates:* 38% (555). ***Average award:*** Freshmen: $3734; Undergraduates: $4480. ***Scholarships, grants, and awards:*** Federal Pell, FSEOG, state, private, college/university gift aid from institutional funds.

GIFT AID (NON-NEED-BASED) ***Scholarships, grants, and awards by category:*** *Academic Interests/Achievement:* 65 awards ($160,350 total): general academic interests/achievements. *Special Achievements/Activities:* 25 awards ($45,092 total): leadership. *Special Characteristics:* 105 awards ($459,300 total): children and siblings of alumni, children of faculty/staff. ***Tuition waivers:*** Full or partial for employees or children of employees. ***ROTC:*** Army, Air Force.

LOANS ***Student loans:*** $8,226,645 (100% need-based). 92% of past graduating class borrowed through all loan programs. Average indebtedness per student: $17,125. ***Average need-based loan:*** Freshmen: $2358; Undergraduates: $3926. ***Parent loans:*** $3,787,043 (100% need-based). ***Programs:*** Federal Direct (Subsidized and Unsubsidized Stafford, PLUS), Perkins, college/university, alternative loans.

WORK-STUDY ***Federal work-study:*** *Total amount:* $40,679; 41 jobs averaging $992. ***State or other work-study/employment:*** *Total amount:* $909,494 (100% need-based). Part-time jobs available.

ATHLETIC AWARDS *Total amount:* 194,100 (100% need-based).

APPLYING for FINANCIAL AID ***Required financial aid form:*** FAFSA. ***Financial aid deadline:*** 6/30 (priority: 4/15). ***Notification date:*** Continuous. Students must reply within 4 weeks of notification.

CONTACT Mr. Dan Lupin, Director of Financial Aid, Embry-Riddle Aeronautical University, 3200 Willow Creek Road, Prescott, AZ 86301-3720, 520-708-3765 or toll-free 800-888-3728. *E-mail:* lupind@erau.pr.edu

EMBRY-RIDDLE AERONAUTICAL UNIVERSITY

Daytona Beach, FL

Tuition & fees: $10,700 **Average undergraduate aid package: $10,679**

ABOUT THE INSTITUTION Independent, coed, primarily men. Awards: associate, bachelor's, and master's degrees. 16 undergraduate majors. Total enrollment: 4,909. Undergraduates: 4,637. Freshmen: 945. Federal methodology is used as a basis for awarding need-based institutional aid.

UNDERGRADUATE EXPENSES for 2000–2001 ***Application fee:*** $30. ***Comprehensive fee:*** $16,140 includes full-time tuition ($10,700) and

room and board ($5440). ***College room only:*** $3100. Full-time tuition and fees vary according to program and student level. Room and board charges vary according to board plan and housing facility. ***Part-time tuition:*** $605 per credit. Part-time tuition and fees vary according to program and student level. ***Payment plans:*** installment, deferred payment.

FRESHMAN FINANCIAL AID (Fall 1998) 742 applied for aid; of those 79% were deemed to have need. 100% of freshmen with need received aid. *Average financial aid package:* $10,723 (excluding resources awarded to replace EFC).

UNDERGRADUATE FINANCIAL AID (Fall 1998) 2,788 applied for aid; of those 87% were deemed to have need. 98% of undergraduates with need received aid. *Average financial aid package:* $10,679 (excluding resources awarded to replace EFC).

GIFT AID (NEED-BASED) ***Total amount:*** $8,081,433 (34% Federal, 20% state, 41% institutional, 5% external sources). ***Receiving aid:*** *Freshmen:* 48% (449); *all full-time undergraduates:* 41% (1,707). ***Average award:*** Freshmen: $3565; Undergraduates: $3650. ***Scholarships, grants, and awards:*** Federal Pell, FSEOG, state, private, college/university gift aid from institutional funds.

GIFT AID (NON-NEED-BASED) ***Receiving aid:*** *Freshmen:* 20% (186); *Undergraduates:* 15% (646). ***Scholarships, grants, and awards by category:*** *Academic Interests/Achievement:* 93 awards ($240,820 total): general academic interests/achievements. *Special Achievements/Activities:* 61 awards ($62,292 total): leadership. *Special Characteristics:* 130 awards ($529,000 total): children and siblings of alumni, children of faculty/staff. ***Tuition waivers:*** Full or partial for employees or children of employees. ***ROTC:*** Army, Air Force.

LOANS ***Student loans:*** $24,625,211 (100% need-based). 92% of past graduating class borrowed through all loan programs. Average indebtedness per student: $17,125. ***Average need-based loan:*** Freshmen: $2314; Undergraduates: $3841. ***Parent loans:*** $7,853,177 (100% need-based). ***Programs:*** Federal Direct (Subsidized and Unsubsidized Stafford, PLUS), Perkins, college/university, alternative loans.

WORK-STUDY ***Federal work-study:*** *Total amount:* $143,784; 171 jobs averaging $840. ***State or other work-study/employment:*** *Total amount:* $3,456,360 (100% need-based). Part-time jobs available.

ATHLETIC AWARDS *Total amount:* 443,702 (100% need-based).

APPLYING for FINANCIAL AID ***Required financial aid form:*** FAFSA. ***Financial aid deadline:*** 6/30 (priority: 4/15). ***Notification date:*** Continuous. Students must reply within 4 weeks of notification.

CONTACT Mr. Richard Ritzman, Director of Financial Aid, Embry-Riddle Aeronautical University, 600 South Clyde Morris Boulevard, Daytona Beach, FL 32114-3900, 800-943-6279 or toll-free 800-862-2416. *Fax:* 904-226-6307. *E-mail:* ritzmanr@cts.db.erau.edu

EMBRY-RIDDLE AERONAUTICAL UNIVERSITY, EXTENDED CAMPUS

Daytona Beach, FL

Tuition & fees: $1860 **Average undergraduate aid package: N/A**

ABOUT THE INSTITUTION Independent, coed, primarily men. Awards: associate, bachelor's, and master's degrees (programs offered at 100 military bases worldwide). 5 undergraduate majors. Total enrollment: 7,700. Undergraduates: 5,229. Freshmen: 74. Federal methodology is used as a basis for awarding need-based institutional aid.

UNDERGRADUATE EXPENSES for 1999–2000 ***Application fee:*** $30. ***Tuition:*** full-time $1860; part-time $155 per credit. Full-time tuition and fees vary according to location and program. Part-time tuition and fees vary according to location.

UNDERGRADUATE FINANCIAL AID (Fall 1998) 23 applied for aid; of those 78% were deemed to have need. 100% of undergraduates with need received aid.

GIFT AID (NEED-BASED) ***Total amount:*** $938,974 (82% Federal, 10% state, 7% institutional, 1% external sources). ***Receiving aid:*** *All full-time undergraduates:* 22% (17). ***Average award:*** Undergraduates: $2912. ***Scholarships, grants, and awards:*** Federal Pell, FSEOG, state, private, college/university gift aid from institutional funds.

GIFT AID (NON-NEED-BASED) ***Receiving aid:*** *Undergraduates:* 1% (1). ***Scholarships, grants, and awards by category:*** *Special Achievements/Activities:* 264 awards ($34,352 total): leadership. *Special Characteristics:* general special characteristics. ***Tuition waivers:*** Full or partial for employees or children of employees.

LOANS ***Student loans:*** $2,513,373 (100% need-based). 92% of past graduating class borrowed through all loan programs. Average indebtedness per student: $17,125. ***Average need-based loan:*** Undergraduates: $3059. ***Parent loans:*** $37,690 (100% need-based). ***Programs:*** Federal Direct (Subsidized and Unsubsidized Stafford, PLUS), Perkins, college/university.

APPLYING for FINANCIAL AID ***Required financial aid form:*** FAFSA. ***Financial aid deadline:*** 6/30 (priority: 4/15). ***Notification date:*** Continuous. Students must reply within 4 weeks of notification.

CONTACT Mr. Richard Ritzman, Director of Financial Aid, Embry-Riddle Aeronautical University, Extended Campus, 600 South Clyde Morris Boulevard, Daytona Beach, FL 32114-3900, 800-943-6279 or toll-free 800-862-2416 (out-of-state). *Fax:* 904-226-6307. *E-mail:* ritzmanr@cts.db.erau.edu

EMERSON COLLEGE

Boston, MA

Tuition & fees: $19,316 **Average undergraduate aid package: $12,600**

ABOUT THE INSTITUTION Independent, coed. Awards: bachelor's, master's, and doctoral degrees and first-professional certificates. 29 undergraduate majors. Total enrollment: 3,987. Undergraduates: 3,135. Freshmen: 652. Both federal and institutional methodology are used as a basis for awarding need-based institutional aid.

UNDERGRADUATE EXPENSES for 1999–2000 ***Application fee:*** $45. ***Comprehensive fee:*** $28,050 includes full-time tuition ($18,816), mandatory fees ($500), and room and board ($8734). ***College room only:*** $5200. Full-time tuition and fees vary according to course load and program. Room and board charges vary according to board plan. ***Part-time tuition:*** $588 per credit. ***Part-time fees:*** $196 per term part-time. Part-time tuition and fees vary according to course load and program. ***Payment plans:*** tuition prepayment, deferred payment.

FRESHMAN FINANCIAL AID (Fall 1999, est.) 512 applied for aid; of those 66% were deemed to have need. 100% of freshmen with need received aid; of those 70% had need fully met. *Average percent of need met:* 71% (excluding resources awarded to replace EFC). *Average financial aid package:* $14,900 (excluding resources awarded to replace EFC). 3% of all full-time freshmen had no need and received non-need-based aid.

UNDERGRADUATE FINANCIAL AID (Fall 1999, est.) 1,671 applied for aid; of those 84% were deemed to have need. 100% of undergraduates with need received aid; of those 62% had need fully met. *Average percent of need met:* 63% (excluding resources awarded to replace EFC). *Average financial aid package:* $12,600 (excluding resources awarded to replace EFC). 2% of all full-time undergraduates had no need and received non-need-based aid.

GIFT AID (NEED-BASED) ***Total amount:*** $10,119,135 (11% Federal, 5% state, 79% institutional, 5% external sources). ***Receiving aid:*** *Freshmen:* 46% (303); *all full-time undergraduates:* 40% (1,041). ***Average award:*** Freshmen: $10,600; Undergraduates: $9200. ***Scholarships, grants, and awards:*** Federal Pell, FSEOG, state, private, college/university gift aid from institutional funds.

GIFT AID (NON-NEED-BASED) ***Total amount:*** $2,032,580 (100% institutional). ***Receiving aid:*** *Freshmen:* 11% (70); *Undergraduates:* 12% (303). ***Scholarships, grants, and awards by category:*** *Academic Interests/Achievement:* 289 awards ($1,789,000 total): general academic interests/achievements. *Creative Arts/Performance:* 46 awards ($149,500 total): performing arts. ***Tuition waivers:*** Full or partial for employees or children of employees.

LOANS ***Student loans:*** $7,806,439 (100% need-based). 51% of past graduating class borrowed through all loan programs. Average indebted-

Emerson College (continued)

ness per student: $17,125. ***Average need-based loan:*** Freshmen: $3200; Undergraduates: $4300. ***Parent loans:*** $7,160,577 (100% non-need-based). ***Programs:*** Federal Direct (Subsidized and Unsubsidized Stafford, PLUS), Perkins, state.

WORK-STUDY ***Federal work-study:*** *Total amount:* $675,990; 406 jobs averaging $1665. ***State or other work-study/employment:*** *Total amount:* $687,126 (100% non-need-based). 430 part-time jobs averaging $1600.

APPLYING for FINANCIAL AID ***Required financial aid forms:*** FAFSA, institution's own form, CSS Financial Aid PROFILE, noncustodial (divorced/separated) parent's statement, business/farm supplement. ***Financial aid deadline (priority):*** 3/1. ***Notification date:*** 4/15. Students must reply within 2 weeks of notification.

CONTACT Daniel V. Pinch III, Director of Financial Assistance, Emerson College, 100 Beacon Street, Boston, MA 02116-1596, 617-824-8655. *Fax:* 617-824-8619. *E-mail:* dpinch@emerson.edu

EMMANUEL COLLEGE

Franklin Springs, GA

Tuition & fees: $7210 **Average undergraduate aid package: $6456**

ABOUT THE INSTITUTION Independent religious, coed. Awards: associate and bachelor's degrees. 16 undergraduate majors. Total enrollment: 837. Undergraduates: 837. Freshmen: 227. Federal methodology is used as a basis for awarding need-based institutional aid.

UNDERGRADUATE EXPENSES for 1999–2000 ***Application fee:*** $25. ***Comprehensive fee:*** $10,910 includes full-time tuition ($7130), mandatory fees ($80), and room and board ($3700). ***College room only:*** $1800. Room and board charges vary according to board plan. ***Part-time tuition:*** $240 per semester hour. ***Part-time fees:*** $15 per term part-time. ***Payment plan:*** installment.

FRESHMAN FINANCIAL AID (Fall 1999) 199 applied for aid; of those 69% were deemed to have need. 100% of freshmen with need received aid; of those 18% had need fully met. *Average percent of need met:* 69% (excluding resources awarded to replace EFC). *Average financial aid package:* $5879 (excluding resources awarded to replace EFC). 26% of all full-time freshmen had no need and received non-need-based aid.

UNDERGRADUATE FINANCIAL AID (Fall 1999) 746 applied for aid; of those 71% were deemed to have need. 99% of undergraduates with need received aid; of those 23% had need fully met. *Average percent of need met:* 73% (excluding resources awarded to replace EFC). *Average financial aid package:* $6456 (excluding resources awarded to replace EFC). 20% of all full-time undergraduates had no need and received non-need-based aid.

GIFT AID (NEED-BASED) ***Total amount:*** $654,056 (100% Federal). ***Receiving aid:*** *Freshmen:* 32% (65); *all full-time undergraduates:* 35% (266). ***Average award:*** Freshmen: $2312; Undergraduates: $2373. ***Scholarships, grants, and awards:*** Federal Pell, FSEOG.

GIFT AID (NON-NEED-BASED) ***Total amount:*** $2,060,826 (63% state, 29% institutional, 8% external sources). ***Receiving aid:*** *Freshmen:* 66% (133); *Undergraduates:* 64% (482). ***Scholarships, grants, and awards by category:*** *Academic Interests/Achievement:* 83 awards ($141,340 total): business, communication, education, English, general academic interests/achievements, religion/biblical studies. *Creative Arts/Performance:* 118 awards ($103,760 total): general creative arts/performance, music, theater/drama. *Special Achievements/Activities:* 28 awards ($28,200 total): general special achievements/activities, leadership, religious involvement. *Special Characteristics:* 455 awards ($375,851 total): adult students, children of faculty/staff, relatives of clergy, religious affiliation, siblings of current students. ***Tuition waivers:*** Full or partial for employees or children of employees, adult students, senior citizens.

LOANS ***Student loans:*** $1,797,220 (60% need-based, 40% non-need-based). 63% of past graduating class borrowed through all loan programs. Average indebtedness per student: $17,093. ***Average need-based loan:*** Freshmen: $1777; Undergraduates: $3345. ***Parent loans:*** $547,696 (100% non-need-based). ***Programs:*** FFEL (Subsidized and Unsubsidized Stafford, PLUS).

WORK-STUDY ***Federal work-study:*** *Total amount:* $143,905; 180 jobs averaging $800.

ATHLETIC AWARDS *Total amount:* 316,061 (100% non-need-based).

APPLYING for FINANCIAL AID ***Required financial aid forms:*** FAFSA, state aid form. ***Financial aid deadline:*** 5/15. ***Notification date:*** Continuous. Students must reply within 4 weeks of notification.

CONTACT Vince Welch, Director of Financial Aid, Emmanuel College, PO Box 129, Franklin Springs, GA 30639-0129, 706-245-7226 Ext. 2711 or toll-free 800-860-8800 (in-state). *Fax:* 706-245-4424.

EMMANUEL COLLEGE

Boston, MA

Tuition & fees: $16,612 **Average undergraduate aid package: $19,350**

ABOUT THE INSTITUTION Independent Roman Catholic, women only. Awards: bachelor's and master's degrees. 33 undergraduate majors. Total enrollment: 1,489. Undergraduates: 1,312. Freshmen: 144. Federal methodology is used as a basis for awarding need-based institutional aid.

UNDERGRADUATE EXPENSES for 2000–2001 ***Application fee:*** $40. ***Comprehensive fee:*** $24,002 includes full-time tuition ($16,112), mandatory fees ($500), and room and board ($7390). Part-time tuition and fees vary according to program. ***Payment plans:*** installment, deferred payment.

FRESHMAN FINANCIAL AID (Fall 1999) 112 applied for aid; of those 94% were deemed to have need. 100% of freshmen with need received aid; of those 10% had need fully met. *Average percent of need met:* 70% (excluding resources awarded to replace EFC). *Average financial aid package:* $20,458 (excluding resources awarded to replace EFC). 4% of all full-time freshmen had no need and received non-need-based aid.

UNDERGRADUATE FINANCIAL AID (Fall 1999) 366 applied for aid; of those 79% were deemed to have need. 100% of undergraduates with need received aid; of those 20% had need fully met. *Average percent of need met:* 68% (excluding resources awarded to replace EFC). *Average financial aid package:* $19,350 (excluding resources awarded to replace EFC). 1% of all full-time undergraduates had no need and received non-need-based aid.

GIFT AID (NEED-BASED) ***Total amount:*** $2,804,444 (17% Federal, 14% state, 69% institutional). ***Receiving aid:*** *Freshmen:* 71% (95); *all full-time undergraduates:* 36% (268). ***Average award:*** Freshmen: $9241; Undergraduates: $9577. ***Scholarships, grants, and awards:*** Federal Pell, FSEOG, state, private, college/university gift aid from institutional funds.

GIFT AID (NON-NEED-BASED) ***Total amount:*** $1,510,819 (93% institutional, 7% external sources). ***Receiving aid:*** *Freshmen:* 41% (55); *Undergraduates:* 20% (152). ***Scholarships, grants, and awards by category:*** *Academic Interests/Achievement:* 16 awards ($72,000 total): general academic interests/achievements. *Special Characteristics:* 26 awards ($131,480 total): children and siblings of alumni, children of educators, children of faculty/staff, international students, religious affiliation. ***Tuition waivers:*** Full or partial for employees or children of employees. ***ROTC:*** Army cooperative.

LOANS ***Student loans:*** $1,711,481 (84% need-based, 16% non-need-based). 80% of past graduating class borrowed through all loan programs. Average indebtedness per student: $19,349. ***Average need-based loan:*** Freshmen: $5173; Undergraduates: $5843. ***Parent loans:*** $514,224 (100% non-need-based). ***Programs:*** Federal Direct (Subsidized and Unsubsidized Stafford, PLUS), Perkins, state.

WORK-STUDY ***Federal work-study:*** *Total amount:* $504,743; 246 jobs averaging $2051.

APPLYING for FINANCIAL AID ***Required financial aid forms:*** FAFSA, institution's own form. ***Financial aid deadline (priority):*** 4/15. ***Notification date:*** Continuous. Students must reply within 2 weeks of notification.

CONTACT Anna Kelly, Director of Financial Aid, Emmanuel College, 400 The Fenway, Boston, MA 02115, 617-735-9725. *Fax:* 617-735-9877. *E-mail:* kelly@emmanuel.edu

EMMAUS BIBLE COLLEGE

Dubuque, IA

Tuition & fees: $5390 **Average undergraduate aid package: $3425**

ABOUT THE INSTITUTION Independent nondenominational, coed. Awards: associate and bachelor's degrees. 5 undergraduate majors. Total enrollment: 303. Undergraduates: 303. Freshmen: 83. Federal methodology is used as a basis for awarding need-based institutional aid.

UNDERGRADUATE EXPENSES for 1999–2000 ***Application fee:*** $10. ***Comprehensive fee:*** $8170 includes full-time tuition ($5260), mandatory fees ($130), and room and board ($2780). Full-time tuition and fees vary according to program. ***Part-time tuition:*** $120 per credit. Part-time tuition and fees vary according to course load. ***Payment plan:*** installment.

FRESHMAN FINANCIAL AID (Fall 1998) 78 applied for aid; of those 95% were deemed to have need. 95% of freshmen with need received aid; of those 4% had need fully met. *Average percent of need met:* 62% (excluding resources awarded to replace EFC). *Average financial aid package:* $2881 (excluding resources awarded to replace EFC).

UNDERGRADUATE FINANCIAL AID (Fall 1998) 268 applied for aid; of those 99% were deemed to have need. 98% of undergraduates with need received aid; of those 6% had need fully met. *Average percent of need met:* 72% (excluding resources awarded to replace EFC). *Average financial aid package:* $3425 (excluding resources awarded to replace EFC).

GIFT AID (NEED-BASED) ***Total amount:*** $565,300 (40% Federal, 27% institutional, 33% external sources). ***Receiving aid:*** *Freshmen:* 90% (70); *all full-time undergraduates:* 96% (258). ***Average award:*** Freshmen: $1805; Undergraduates: $2000. ***Scholarships, grants, and awards:*** Federal Pell, FSEOG, private, college/university gift aid from institutional funds.

GIFT AID (NON-NEED-BASED) ***Receiving aid:*** *Freshmen:* 58% (45); *Undergraduates:* 61% (163). ***Scholarships, grants, and awards by category:*** *Academic Interests/Achievement:* 39 awards ($7800 total): general academic interests/achievements. *Creative Arts/Performance:* 14 awards ($1400 total): music. *Special Achievements/Activities:* hobbies/interests, leadership, religious involvement. *Special Characteristics:* children of faculty/staff, general special characteristics, international students, out-of-state students, spouses of current students. ***Tuition waivers:*** Full or partial for employees or children of employees.

LOANS ***Student loans:*** $375,511 (100% need-based). 65% of past graduating class borrowed through all loan programs. Average indebtedness per student: $9400. ***Average need-based loan:*** Freshmen: $2433; Undergraduates: $2863. ***Parent loans:*** $25,489 (100% need-based). ***Programs:*** FFEL (Subsidized and Unsubsidized Stafford, PLUS), alternative loans.

APPLYING for FINANCIAL AID ***Required financial aid forms:*** FAFSA, institution's own form. ***Financial aid deadline (priority):*** 7/1. ***Notification date:*** Continuous.

CONTACT Miss Nancy Ferguson, Financial Aid Officer, Emmaus Bible College, 2570 Asbury Road, Dubuque, IA 52001-3097, 319-588-8000 Ext. 123 or toll-free 800-397-2425 Ext. 1. *Fax:* 319-588-1216. *E-mail:* financialaid@emmaus1.edu

EMORY & HENRY COLLEGE

Emory, VA

Tuition & fees: $13,150 **Average undergraduate aid package: $11,729**

ABOUT THE INSTITUTION Independent United Methodist, coed. Awards: bachelor's and master's degrees. 36 undergraduate majors. Total enrollment: 1,006. Undergraduates: 997. Freshmen: 277. Federal methodology is used as a basis for awarding need-based institutional aid.

UNDERGRADUATE EXPENSES for 2000–2001 ***Application fee:*** $25. ***Comprehensive fee:*** $18,472 includes full-time tuition ($12,950), mandatory fees ($200), and room and board ($5322). Full-time tuition and fees vary according to course load. Room and board charges vary according to board plan. ***Part-time tuition:*** $540 per semester hour. Part-time tuition and fees vary according to course load. ***Payment plan:*** installment.

FRESHMAN FINANCIAL AID (Fall 1999) 254 applied for aid; of those 83% were deemed to have need. 100% of freshmen with need received aid; of those 31% had need fully met. *Average percent of need met:* 91% (excluding resources awarded to replace EFC). *Average financial aid package:* $12,696 (excluding resources awarded to replace EFC). 21% of all full-time freshmen had no need and received non-need-based aid.

UNDERGRADUATE FINANCIAL AID (Fall 1999) 838 applied for aid; of those 86% were deemed to have need. 100% of undergraduates with need received aid; of those 29% had need fully met. *Average percent of need met:* 83% (excluding resources awarded to replace EFC). *Average financial aid package:* $11,729 (excluding resources awarded to replace EFC). 23% of all full-time undergraduates had no need and received non-need-based aid.

GIFT AID (NEED-BASED) ***Total amount:*** $5,777,548 (13% Federal, 25% state, 58% institutional, 4% external sources). ***Receiving aid:*** *Freshmen:* 76% (210); *all full-time undergraduates:* 71% (696). ***Average award:*** Freshmen: $9683; Undergraduates: $8301. ***Scholarships, grants, and awards:*** Federal Pell, FSEOG, state, private, college/university gift aid from institutional funds.

GIFT AID (NON-NEED-BASED) ***Total amount:*** $1,093,528 (40% state, 55% institutional, 5% external sources). ***Receiving aid:*** *Freshmen:* 58% (162); *Undergraduates:* 40% (396). ***Scholarships, grants, and awards by category:*** *Academic Interests/Achievement:* general academic interests/achievements. *Special Characteristics:* children of faculty/staff, relatives of clergy. ***Tuition waivers:*** Full or partial for employees or children of employees.

LOANS ***Student loans:*** $3,049,819 (93% need-based, 7% non-need-based). 73% of past graduating class borrowed through all loan programs. Average indebtedness per student: $18,000. ***Average need-based loan:*** Freshmen: $2778; Undergraduates: $3498. ***Parent loans:*** $1,895,646 (81% need-based, 19% non-need-based). ***Programs:*** Federal Direct (Subsidized and Unsubsidized Stafford, PLUS), Perkins.

WORK-STUDY ***Federal work-study:*** *Total amount:* $285,651; 250 jobs averaging $1200. ***State or other work-study/employment:*** *Total amount:* $42,221 (68% need-based, 32% non-need-based). Part-time jobs available.

APPLYING for FINANCIAL AID ***Required financial aid forms:*** FAFSA, institution's own form, state aid form. ***Financial aid deadline:*** 8/1 (priority: 4/1). ***Notification date:*** Continuous. Students must reply within 4 weeks of notification.

CONTACT Lois Williams, Acting Coordinator of Financial Aid, Emory & Henry College, PO Box 947, Emory, VA 24327-0947, 540-944-6115 or toll-free 800-848-5493. *Fax:* 540-944-6935. *E-mail:* lhwillia@ehc.edu

EMORY UNIVERSITY

Atlanta, GA

Tuition & fees: $23,130 **Average undergraduate aid package: $19,873**

ABOUT THE INSTITUTION Independent Methodist, coed. Awards: bachelor's, master's, doctoral, and first professional degrees (enrollment figures include Emory University, Oxford College; application data for main campus only). 52 undergraduate majors. Total enrollment: 11,294. Undergraduates: 6,215. Freshmen: 1,520. Institutional methodology is used as a basis for awarding need-based institutional aid.

UNDERGRADUATE EXPENSES for 1999–2000 ***Application fee:*** $40. ***Comprehensive fee:*** $30,880 includes full-time tuition ($22,870), mandatory fees ($260), and room and board ($7750). Room and board charges vary according to board plan, housing facility, and student level. ***Part-time tuition:*** $953 per semester hour. ***Part-time fees:*** $100 per term part-time. ***Payment plans:*** tuition prepayment, installment.

FRESHMAN FINANCIAL AID (Fall 1999) 563 applied for aid; of those 82% were deemed to have need. 100% of freshmen with need received aid; of those 95% had need fully met. *Average percent of need met:* 99% (excluding resources awarded to replace EFC). *Average financial aid package:* $19,203 (excluding resources awarded to replace EFC). 13% of all full-time freshmen had no need and received non-need-based aid.

UNDERGRADUATE FINANCIAL AID (Fall 1999) 2,209 applied for aid; of those 86% were deemed to have need. 100% of undergraduates with

Emory University (continued)

need received aid; of those 90% had need fully met. *Average percent of need met:* 99% (excluding resources awarded to replace EFC). *Average financial aid package:* $19,873 (excluding resources awarded to replace EFC). 17% of all full-time undergraduates had no need and received non-need-based aid.

GIFT AID (NEED-BASED) ***Total amount:*** $24,000,450 (5% Federal, 4% state, 90% institutional, 1% external sources). ***Receiving aid:*** *Freshmen:* 34% (404); *all full-time undergraduates:* 36% (1,722). ***Average award:*** Freshmen: $15,053; Undergraduates: $14,285. ***Scholarships, grants, and awards:*** Federal Pell, FSEOG, state, private, college/university gift aid from institutional funds.

GIFT AID (NON-NEED-BASED) ***Total amount:*** $6,820,114 (1% Federal, 30% state, 54% institutional, 15% external sources). ***Receiving aid:*** *Freshmen:* 18% (213); *Undergraduates:* 16% (756). ***Scholarships, grants, and awards by category:*** *Academic Interests/Achievement:* 400 awards ($4,817,271 total): general academic interests/achievements. *Creative Arts/Performance:* 4 awards ($91,480 total): debating, music, performing arts. *Special Characteristics:* 301 awards ($5,368,761 total): children of faculty/staff, relatives of clergy, religious affiliation. ***Tuition waivers:*** Full or partial for employees or children of employees. ***ROTC:*** Air Force cooperative.

LOANS ***Student loans:*** $10,187,450 (77% need-based, 23% non-need-based). 47% of past graduating class borrowed through all loan programs. Average indebtedness per student: $16,358. ***Average need-based loan:*** Freshmen: $3246; Undergraduates: $4885. ***Parent loans:*** $5,750,975 (100% non-need-based). ***Programs:*** FFEL (Subsidized and Unsubsidized Stafford, PLUS), Perkins, Federal Nursing, state, college/university.

WORK-STUDY ***Federal work-study:*** *Total amount:* $2,119,632; 1,325 jobs averaging $1600. ***State or other work-study/employment:*** *Total amount:* $516,137 (15% need-based, 85% non-need-based). 89 part-time jobs averaging $5799.

APPLYING for FINANCIAL AID ***Required financial aid forms:*** FAFSA, CSS Financial Aid PROFILE. ***Financial aid deadline:*** 4/1 (priority: 2/15). ***Notification date:*** 4/15. Students must reply within 4 weeks of notification.

CONTACT Julia Perreault, Director of Financial Aid, Emory University, 300 Boisfeuillet Jones Center, Atlanta, GA 30322-1100, 404-727-6039 or toll-free 800-727-6036. *Fax:* 404-727-6709. *E-mail:* finaid@emory.edu

EMPORIA STATE UNIVERSITY

Emporia, KS

Tuition & fees (KS res): $2086 **Average undergraduate aid package: $4929**

ABOUT THE INSTITUTION State-supported, coed. Awards: bachelor's, master's, and doctoral degrees. 39 undergraduate majors. Total enrollment: 5,610. Undergraduates: 4,162. Freshmen: 809. Federal methodology is used as a basis for awarding need-based institutional aid.

UNDERGRADUATE EXPENSES for 1999–2000 ***Application fee:*** $20. ***Tuition, state resident:*** full-time $1574; part-time $52 per credit hour. ***Tuition, nonresident:*** full-time $6040; part-time $201 per credit hour. ***Required fees:*** full-time $512; $29 per credit hour. ***College room and board:*** $3656; ***room only:*** $1780. Room and board charges vary according to board plan and housing facility. ***Payment plans:*** installment, deferred payment.

UNDERGRADUATE FINANCIAL AID (Fall 1999, est.) 3,083 applied for aid; of those 66% were deemed to have need. 100% of undergraduates with need received aid. *Average financial aid package:* $4929 (excluding resources awarded to replace EFC). 28% of all full-time undergraduates had no need and received non-need-based aid.

GIFT AID (NEED-BASED) ***Total amount:*** $3,225,987 (82% Federal, 14% state, 4% external sources). ***Receiving aid:*** *All full-time undergraduates:* 50% (1,807). ***Average award:*** Undergraduates: $2388. ***Scholarships, grants, and awards:*** Federal Pell, FSEOG, state, private, college/university gift aid from institutional funds, Jones Foundation Grants.

GIFT AID (NON-NEED-BASED) ***Total amount:*** $1,904,546 (2% Federal, 4% state, 65% institutional, 29% external sources). ***Receiving aid:*** *Undergraduates:* 39% (1,401). ***Scholarships, grants, and awards by category:*** *Academic Interests/Achievement:* 1,120 awards ($739,855 total): general academic interests/achievements. *Creative Arts/Performance:* 325 awards ($106,425 total): art/fine arts, debating, music, theater/drama. *Special Achievements/Activities:* 25 awards ($10,040 total): cheerleading/drum major, hobbies/interests, leadership. *Special Characteristics:* 280 awards ($116,740 total): children and siblings of alumni, children of faculty/staff, children of union members/company employees, ethnic background, general special characteristics, handicapped students, international students, local/state students, members of minority groups, out-of-state students, religious affiliation, veterans, veterans' children. ***Tuition waivers:*** Full or partial for employees or children of employees, senior citizens.

LOANS ***Student loans:*** $7,723,390 (62% need-based, 38% non-need-based). 56% of past graduating class borrowed through all loan programs. Average indebtedness per student: $12,827. ***Average need-based loan:*** Undergraduates: $3270. ***Parent loans:*** $257,286 (100% non-need-based). ***Programs:*** FFEL (Subsidized and Unsubsidized Stafford, PLUS), Perkins, college/university, Alaska Loans, alternative loans.

WORK-STUDY ***Federal work-study:*** *Total amount:* $542,461; 300 jobs averaging $1700. ***State or other work-study/employment:*** *Total amount:* $940,714 (1% need-based, 99% non-need-based). 500 part-time jobs averaging $2000.

ATHLETIC AWARDS *Total amount:* 628,221 (100% non-need-based).

APPLYING for FINANCIAL AID ***Required financial aid form:*** FAFSA. ***Financial aid deadline (priority):*** 3/15. ***Notification date:*** Continuous beginning 4/1. Students must reply within 2 weeks of notification.

CONTACT Mr. John Pappas, Associate Director of Financial Aid, Emporia State University, 1200 Commercial Street, Campus Box 4038, Emporia, KS 66801-5087, 316-341-5457 or toll-free 800-896-7544. *Fax:* 316-341-6088. *E-mail:* pappasjo@emporia.edu

ENDICOTT COLLEGE

Beverly, MA

Tuition & fees: $14,556 **Average undergraduate aid package: $11,170**

ABOUT THE INSTITUTION Independent, coed. Awards: associate, bachelor's, and master's degrees. 20 undergraduate majors. Total enrollment: 1,512. Undergraduates: 1,395. Freshmen: 407. Federal methodology is used as a basis for awarding need-based institutional aid.

UNDERGRADUATE EXPENSES for 1999–2000 ***Application fee:*** $25. ***Comprehensive fee:*** $21,966 includes full-time tuition ($14,000), mandatory fees ($556), and room and board ($7410). ***College room only:*** $5200. Room and board charges vary according to board plan and housing facility. ***Part-time tuition:*** $429 per credit. ***Part-time fees:*** $141 per term part-time. Part-time tuition and fees vary according to program. ***Payment plan:*** installment.

FRESHMAN FINANCIAL AID (Fall 1999) 319 applied for aid; of those 89% were deemed to have need. 100% of freshmen with need received aid; of those 6% had need fully met. *Average percent of need met:* 71% (excluding resources awarded to replace EFC). *Average financial aid package:* $11,160 (excluding resources awarded to replace EFC).

UNDERGRADUATE FINANCIAL AID (Fall 1999) 891 applied for aid; of those 88% were deemed to have need. 100% of undergraduates with need received aid; of those 11% had need fully met. *Average percent of need met:* 72% (excluding resources awarded to replace EFC). *Average financial aid package:* $11,170 (excluding resources awarded to replace EFC).

GIFT AID (NEED-BASED) ***Total amount:*** $4,749,126 (12% Federal, 6% state, 79% institutional, 3% external sources). ***Receiving aid:*** *Freshmen:* 279; *all full-time undergraduates:* 767. ***Average award:*** Freshmen: $6421; Undergraduates: $6006. ***Scholarships, grants, and awards:*** Federal Pell, FSEOG, state, private, college/university gift aid from institutional funds.

GIFT AID (NON-NEED-BASED) ***Total amount:*** $540,930 (97% institutional, 3% external sources). ***Receiving aid:*** *Freshmen:* 9; *Undergraduates:* 21. ***Scholarships, grants, and awards by category:*** *Academic Interests/Achievement:* 253 awards ($955,950 total): business, education, general academic interests/achievements, health fields. *Creative Arts/Performance:* 4 awards ($2000 total): art/fine arts. *Special Achievements/Activities:* 8

awards ($18,350 total): community service, general special achievements/activities, leadership. *Special Characteristics:* 49 awards ($29,900 total): children and siblings of alumni, children of educators, general special characteristics, local/state students. ***Tuition waivers:*** Full or partial for employees or children of employees, senior citizens.

LOANS ***Student loans:*** $3,920,880 (83% need-based, 17% non-need-based). 55% of past graduating class borrowed through all loan programs. Average indebtedness per student: $16,060. ***Average need-based loan:*** Freshmen: $4353; Undergraduates: $4867. ***Parent loans:*** $2,612,510 (47% need-based, 53% non-need-based). ***Programs:*** FFEL (Subsidized and Unsubsidized Stafford, PLUS), Perkins, state, college/university.

WORK-STUDY ***Federal work-study:*** *Total amount:* $109,824; 126 jobs averaging $872.

APPLYING for FINANCIAL AID ***Required financial aid forms:*** FAFSA, institution's own form, noncustodial (divorced/separated) parent's statement. ***Financial aid deadline (priority):*** 3/15. ***Notification date:*** Continuous. Students must reply within 2 weeks of notification.

CONTACT Ms. Marcia Toomey, Director of Financial Aid, Endicott College, 376 Hale Street, Beverly, MA 01915-2096, 978-232-2060 or toll-free 800-325-1114 (out-of-state). *Fax:* 978-232-2520. *E-mail:* mtoomey@endicott.edu

ERSKINE COLLEGE

Due West, SC

Tuition & fees: $15,229 **Average undergraduate aid package: $13,100**

ABOUT THE INSTITUTION Independent religious, coed. Awards: bachelor's degrees. 33 undergraduate majors. Total enrollment: 519. Undergraduates: 519. Freshmen: 159. Federal methodology is used as a basis for awarding need-based institutional aid.

UNDERGRADUATE EXPENSES for 1999–2000 ***Application fee:*** $15. ***Comprehensive fee:*** $19,998 includes full-time tuition ($14,269), mandatory fees ($960), and room and board ($4769). Room and board charges vary according to board plan and housing facility. ***Part-time tuition:*** $255 per semester hour. ***Payment plan:*** installment.

FRESHMAN FINANCIAL AID (Fall 1999) 149 applied for aid; of those 88% were deemed to have need. 100% of freshmen with need received aid; of those 63% had need fully met. *Average percent of need met:* 90% (excluding resources awarded to replace EFC). *Average financial aid package:* $14,325 (excluding resources awarded to replace EFC). 13% of all full-time freshmen had no need and received non-need-based aid.

UNDERGRADUATE FINANCIAL AID (Fall 1999) 482 applied for aid; of those 81% were deemed to have need. 99% of undergraduates with need received aid; of those 60% had need fully met. *Average percent of need met:* 92% (excluding resources awarded to replace EFC). *Average financial aid package:* $13,100 (excluding resources awarded to replace EFC). 21% of all full-time undergraduates had no need and received non-need-based aid.

GIFT AID (NEED-BASED) ***Total amount:*** $1,962,666 (21% Federal, 51% state, 28% institutional). ***Receiving aid:*** *Freshmen:* 81% (128); *all full-time undergraduates:* 71% (360). ***Scholarships, grants, and awards:*** Federal Pell, FSEOG, state, private, college/university gift aid from institutional funds.

GIFT AID (NON-NEED-BASED) ***Total amount:*** $2,881,552 (11% state, 81% institutional, 8% external sources). ***Receiving aid:*** *Freshmen:* 53% (83); *Undergraduates:* 51% (260). ***Scholarships, grants, and awards by category:*** *Academic Interests/Achievement:* general academic interests/achievements. *Creative Arts/Performance:* music, theater/drama. *Special Achievements/Activities:* general special achievements/activities, leadership, memberships. *Special Characteristics:* children and siblings of alumni, children of faculty/staff, children with a deceased or disabled parent, relatives of clergy, religious affiliation, siblings of current students. ***Tuition waivers:*** Full or partial for children of alumni, employees or children of employees.

LOANS ***Student loans:*** $654,087 (68% need-based, 32% non-need-based). 71% of past graduating class borrowed through all loan programs. Average indebtedness per student: $13,125. ***Parent loans:*** $254,742 (100% non-need-based). ***Programs:*** FFEL (Subsidized and Unsubsidized Stafford, PLUS), Perkins, state, college/university.

WORK-STUDY ***Federal work-study:*** *Total amount:* $100,361; 141 jobs averaging $800. ***State or other work-study/employment:*** *Total amount:* $21,750 (100% non-need-based). Part-time jobs available.

ATHLETIC AWARDS *Total amount:* 543,527 (100% non-need-based).

APPLYING for FINANCIAL AID ***Required financial aid forms:*** FAFSA, institution's own form, state aid form. ***Financial aid deadline:*** 6/30 (priority: 4/1). ***Notification date:*** Continuous.

CONTACT Rebecca Pressley, Director of Financial Aid, Erskine College, PO Box 337, Due West, SC 29639, 864-379-8832 or toll-free 800-241-8721. *Fax:* 864-379-2167. *E-mail:* pressley@erskine.edu

ESCUELA DE ARTES PLASTICAS DE PUERTO RICO

San Juan, PR

Tuition & fees: $4650 **Average undergraduate aid package: N/A**

ABOUT THE INSTITUTION Commonwealth-supported, coed. Awards: bachelor's degrees. 5 undergraduate majors. Total enrollment: 309. Undergraduates: 309. Freshmen: 72. Federal methodology is used as a basis for awarding need-based institutional aid.

UNDERGRADUATE EXPENSES for 1999–2000 ***Application fee:*** $20. ***Tuition:*** full-time $3150. ***Required fees:*** full-time $1500. ***Payment plan:*** deferred payment.

FRESHMAN FINANCIAL AID (Fall 1999, est.) 46 applied for aid; of those 100% were deemed to have need. 100% of freshmen with need received aid. *Average percent of need met:* 70% (excluding resources awarded to replace EFC).

UNDERGRADUATE FINANCIAL AID (Fall 1999, est.) 264 applied for aid; of those 100% were deemed to have need. 100% of undergraduates with need received aid. *Average percent of need met:* 85% (excluding resources awarded to replace EFC).

GIFT AID (NEED-BASED) ***Total amount:*** $831,293 (91% Federal, 6% state, 3% institutional). ***Scholarships, grants, and awards:*** Federal Pell, FSEOG, state, college/university gift aid from institutional funds.

GIFT AID (NON-NEED-BASED) ***Tuition waivers:*** Full or partial for employees or children of employees.

WORK-STUDY ***Federal work-study:*** *Total amount:* $12,736; 7 jobs averaging $1650.

APPLYING for FINANCIAL AID ***Required financial aid form:*** FAFSA. ***Financial aid deadline (priority):*** 7/11. ***Notification date:*** 8/30.

CONTACT Ms. Marion E. Muñoz, Financial Aid Administrator, Escuela de Artes Plasticas de Puerto Rico, PO Box 9021112, San Juan, PR 00902-1112, 787-725-8120 Ext. 231. *Fax:* 787-725-8111. *E-mail:* mmunoz@coqui.net

EUGENE BIBLE COLLEGE

Eugene, OR

Tuition & fees: $5913 **Average undergraduate aid package: $6000**

ABOUT THE INSTITUTION Independent religious, coed. Awards: bachelor's degrees. 6 undergraduate majors. Total enrollment: 210. Undergraduates: 210. Freshmen: 60. Both federal and institutional methodology are used as a basis for awarding need-based institutional aid.

UNDERGRADUATE EXPENSES for 1999–2000 ***Application fee:*** $30. ***Comprehensive fee:*** $9576 includes full-time tuition ($5325), mandatory fees ($588), and room and board ($3663). Room and board charges vary according to housing facility. ***Part-time tuition:*** $152 per credit. ***Part-time fees:*** $106 per term part-time. Part-time tuition and fees vary according to class time and course load. ***Payment plans:*** tuition prepayment, installment.

FRESHMAN FINANCIAL AID (Fall 1999, est.) 54 applied for aid; of those 87% were deemed to have need. 96% of freshmen with need received aid;

Eugene Bible College (continued)

of those 7% had need fully met. *Average percent of need met:* 70% (excluding resources awarded to replace EFC). *Average financial aid package:* $5000 (excluding resources awarded to replace EFC). 10% of all full-time freshmen had no need and received non-need-based aid.

UNDERGRADUATE FINANCIAL AID (Fall 1999, est.) 160 applied for aid; of those 89% were deemed to have need. 90% of undergraduates with need received aid; of those 5% had need fully met. *Average percent of need met:* 70% (excluding resources awarded to replace EFC). *Average financial aid package:* $6000 (excluding resources awarded to replace EFC). 7% of all full-time undergraduates had no need and received non-need-based aid.

GIFT AID (NEED-BASED) ***Total amount:*** $310,000 (66% Federal, 34% institutional). ***Receiving aid:*** *Freshmen:* 50% (30); *all full-time undergraduates:* 50% (87). ***Average award:*** Freshmen: $1800; Undergraduates: $2000. ***Scholarships, grants, and awards:*** Federal Pell, FSEOG, private, college/university gift aid from institutional funds.

GIFT AID (NON-NEED-BASED) ***Total amount:*** $53,000 (55% institutional, 45% external sources). ***Receiving aid:*** *Freshmen:* 15% (9); *Undergraduates:* 15% (26). ***Scholarships, grants, and awards by category:*** *Academic Interests/Achievement:* general academic interests/achievements, religion/biblical studies. *Creative Arts/Performance:* music. *Special Achievements/Activities:* community service, general special achievements/activities, hobbies/interests, leadership, religious involvement. *Special Characteristics:* general special characteristics, married students, relatives of clergy. ***Tuition waivers:*** Full or partial for employees or children of employees, senior citizens.

LOANS ***Student loans:*** $574,000 (96% need-based, 4% non-need-based). 85% of past graduating class borrowed through all loan programs. Average indebtedness per student: $17,500. ***Average need-based loan:*** Freshmen: $2000; Undergraduates: $3000. ***Parent loans:*** $100,000 (100% need-based). ***Programs:*** FFEL (Subsidized and Unsubsidized Stafford, PLUS), college/university, Key Alternative Loans, US Bank Signature Loans.

WORK-STUDY ***Federal work-study:*** *Total amount:* $15,000; 6 jobs averaging $1500. ***State or other work-study/employment:*** *Total amount:* $54,000 (74% need-based, 26% non-need-based). 25 part-time jobs averaging $2000.

APPLYING for FINANCIAL AID ***Required financial aid forms:*** FAFSA, institution's own form, CSS Financial Aid PROFILE. ***Financial aid deadline:*** 9/1 (priority: 3/1). ***Notification date:*** Continuous.

CONTACT Mr. Keith Mabus, Financial Aid Director, Eugene Bible College, 2155 Bailey Hill Road, Eugene, OR 97405-1194, 541-485-1780 Ext. 125 or toll-free 800-322-2638. *Fax:* 541-343-5801. *E-mail:* finaid@ebc.edu

EUGENE LANG COLLEGE, NEW SCHOOL UNIVERSITY

New York, NY

Tuition & fees: $19,915 **Average undergraduate aid package: $14,861**

ABOUT THE INSTITUTION Independent, coed. Awards: bachelor's degrees. 21 undergraduate majors. Total university enrollment: 7,700. Total unit enrollment: 520. Undergraduates: 520. Freshmen: 110. Federal methodology is used as a basis for awarding need-based institutional aid.

UNDERGRADUATE EXPENSES for 1999–2000 ***Application fee:*** $30. ***Comprehensive fee:*** $28,920 includes full-time tuition ($19,620), mandatory fees ($295), and room and board ($9005). ***College room only:*** $6485. Room and board charges vary according to board plan and housing facility. ***Part-time tuition:*** $720 per credit. ***Part-time fees:*** $58 per term part-time. Part-time tuition and fees vary according to course load. ***Payment plan:*** installment.

FRESHMAN FINANCIAL AID (Fall 1999, est.) 87 applied for aid; of those 99% were deemed to have need. 100% of freshmen with need received aid; of those 3% had need fully met. *Average percent of need met:* 68% (excluding resources awarded to replace EFC). *Average financial aid package:* $14,566 (excluding resources awarded to replace EFC). 10% of all full-time freshmen had no need and received non-need-based aid.

UNDERGRADUATE FINANCIAL AID (Fall 1999, est.) 388 applied for aid; of those 94% were deemed to have need. 100% of undergraduates with need received aid; of those 8% had need fully met. *Average percent of need met:* 69% (excluding resources awarded to replace EFC). *Average financial aid package:* $14,861 (excluding resources awarded to replace EFC). 4% of all full-time undergraduates had no need and received non-need-based aid.

GIFT AID (NEED-BASED) ***Total amount:*** $4,083,287 (8% Federal, 5% state, 85% institutional, 2% external sources). ***Receiving aid:*** *Freshmen:* 75% (83); *all full-time undergraduates:* 79% (358). ***Average award:*** Freshmen: $10,906; Undergraduates: $10,527. ***Scholarships, grants, and awards:*** Federal Pell, FSEOG, state, private, college/university gift aid from institutional funds.

GIFT AID (NON-NEED-BASED) ***Total amount:*** $25,062 (8% state, 92% institutional). ***Receiving aid:*** *Freshmen:* 3% (3); *Undergraduates:* 1% (6). ***Tuition waivers:*** Full or partial for employees or children of employees.

LOANS ***Student loans:*** $1,578,091 (96% need-based, 4% non-need-based). 65% of past graduating class borrowed through all loan programs. Average indebtedness per student: $17,125. ***Average need-based loan:*** Freshmen: $3125; Undergraduates: $4075. ***Parent loans:*** $520,041 (94% need-based, 6% non-need-based). ***Programs:*** FFEL (Subsidized and Unsubsidized Stafford, PLUS), Perkins, college/university.

WORK-STUDY ***Federal work-study:*** *Total amount:* $240,575; 150 jobs averaging $1760. ***State or other work-study/employment:*** *Total amount:* $36,000 (100% non-need-based). 18 part-time jobs averaging $2000.

APPLYING for FINANCIAL AID ***Required financial aid form:*** FAFSA. ***Financial aid deadline (priority):*** 3/1. ***Notification date:*** Continuous. Students must reply within 4 weeks of notification.

CONTACT Ms. Sandra Bembrey, Director of Financial Aid, Eugene Lang College, New School University, 66 Fifth Avenue, New York, NY 10011, 212-229-8930. *Fax:* 212-229-5919.

EUREKA COLLEGE

Eureka, IL

Tuition & fees: $15,450 **Average undergraduate aid package: $10,840**

ABOUT THE INSTITUTION Independent religious, coed. Awards: bachelor's degrees. 42 undergraduate majors. Total enrollment: 441. Undergraduates: 441. Both federal and institutional methodology are used as a basis for awarding need-based institutional aid.

UNDERGRADUATE EXPENSES for 1999–2000 ***Application fee:*** $15. ***Comprehensive fee:*** $20,310 includes full-time tuition ($15,200), mandatory fees ($250), and room and board ($4860). ***College room only:*** $2320. ***Part-time tuition:*** $485 per semester hour. ***Payment plan:*** installment.

FRESHMAN FINANCIAL AID (Fall 1999, est.) 136 applied for aid; of those 95% were deemed to have need. 100% of freshmen with need received aid; of those 84% had need fully met. *Average percent of need met:* 81% (excluding resources awarded to replace EFC). *Average financial aid package:* $11,921 (excluding resources awarded to replace EFC). 4% of all full-time freshmen had no need and received non-need-based aid.

UNDERGRADUATE FINANCIAL AID (Fall 1999, est.) 472 applied for aid; of those 95% were deemed to have need. 100% of undergraduates with need received aid; of those 84% had need fully met. *Average percent of need met:* 89% (excluding resources awarded to replace EFC). *Average financial aid package:* $10,840 (excluding resources awarded to replace EFC). 5% of all full-time undergraduates had no need and received non-need-based aid.

GIFT AID (NEED-BASED) ***Total amount:*** $4,386,569 (10% Federal, 31% state, 58% institutional, 1% external sources). ***Receiving aid:*** *Freshmen:* 91% (124); *all full-time undergraduates:* 81% (386). ***Average award:*** Freshmen: $8425; Undergraduates: $7815. ***Scholarships, grants, and awards:*** Federal Pell, FSEOG, state, private, college/university gift aid from institutional funds.

GIFT AID (NON-NEED-BASED) ***Total amount:*** $419,618 (2% state, 98% institutional). ***Receiving aid:*** *Freshmen:* 4% (5); *Undergraduates:* 13% (63). ***Scholarships, grants, and awards by category:*** *Academic Interests/*

Achievement: general academic interests/achievements, religion/biblical studies. *Creative Arts/Performance:* art/fine arts, performing arts. *Special Achievements/Activities:* leadership. *Special Characteristics:* religious affiliation. ***Tuition waivers:*** Full or partial for children of alumni, employees or children of employees.

LOANS ***Student loans:*** $1,752,158 (79% need-based, 21% non-need-based). 82% of past graduating class borrowed through all loan programs. Average indebtedness per student: $14,202. ***Average need-based loan:*** Freshmen: $2173; Undergraduates: $2717. ***Parent loans:*** $274,665 (100% non-need-based). ***Programs:*** FFEL (Subsidized and Unsubsidized Stafford, PLUS), Perkins, college/university, alternative loans.

WORK-STUDY ***Federal work-study:*** *Total amount:* $159,960; 244 jobs averaging $653.

APPLYING for FINANCIAL AID ***Required financial aid form:*** FAFSA. ***Financial aid deadline (priority):*** 3/1. ***Notification date:*** 5/1. Students must reply within 4 weeks of notification.

CONTACT Ms. Ellen Rigsby, Associate Director of Financial Aid, Eureka College, 300 East College Avenue, Eureka, IL 61530, 309-467-6311 or toll-free 888-4-EUREKA. *Fax:* 309-467-6576. *E-mail:* eraid@eureka.edu

EVANGEL UNIVERSITY

Springfield, MO

Tuition & fees: $9720 **Average undergraduate aid package: $8162**

ABOUT THE INSTITUTION Independent religious, coed. Awards: associate, bachelor's, and master's degrees. 47 undergraduate majors. Total enrollment: 1,564. Undergraduates: 1,525. Freshmen: 318. Federal methodology is used as a basis for awarding need-based institutional aid.

UNDERGRADUATE EXPENSES for 2000–2001 ***Application fee:*** $25. ***One-time required fee:*** $20. ***Comprehensive fee:*** $13,490 includes full-time tuition ($9250), mandatory fees ($470), and room and board ($3770). Full-time tuition and fees vary according to course load. Room and board charges vary according to board plan. ***Part-time tuition:*** $360 per credit hour. ***Payment plan:*** installment.

FRESHMAN FINANCIAL AID (Fall 1998) 301 applied for aid; of those 92% were deemed to have need. 100% of freshmen with need received aid; of those 13% had need fully met. *Average percent of need met:* 57% (excluding resources awarded to replace EFC). *Average financial aid package:* $7034 (excluding resources awarded to replace EFC). 44% of all full-time freshmen had no need and received non-need-based aid.

UNDERGRADUATE FINANCIAL AID (Fall 1998) 1,198 applied for aid; of those 92% were deemed to have need. 100% of undergraduates with need received aid; of those 15% had need fully met. *Average percent of need met:* 60% (excluding resources awarded to replace EFC). *Average financial aid package:* $8162 (excluding resources awarded to replace EFC). 33% of all full-time undergraduates had no need and received non-need-based aid.

GIFT AID (NEED-BASED) ***Total amount:*** $1,512,534 (94% Federal, 3% state, 3% institutional). ***Receiving aid:*** *Freshmen:* 36% (256); *all full-time undergraduates:* 61% (1,018). ***Average award:*** Freshmen: $3342; Undergraduates: $3399. ***Scholarships, grants, and awards:*** Federal Pell, FSEOG, state, college/university gift aid from institutional funds.

GIFT AID (NON-NEED-BASED) ***Total amount:*** $1,904,562 (76% institutional, 24% external sources). ***Receiving aid:*** *Freshmen:* 2% (13); *Undergraduates:* 2% (35). ***Scholarships, grants, and awards by category:*** *Academic Interests/Achievement:* 609 awards ($865,127 total): general academic interests/achievements. *Creative Arts/Performance:* 137 awards ($173,017 total): art/fine arts, debating, music. *Special Achievements/Activities:* 240 awards ($102,808 total): leadership. *Special Characteristics:* 106 awards ($610,235 total): children of faculty/staff. ***Tuition waivers:*** Full or partial for employees or children of employees. ***ROTC:*** Army.

LOANS ***Student loans:*** $5,949,877 (69% need-based, 31% non-need-based). 74% of past graduating class borrowed through all loan programs. Average indebtedness per student: $10,555. ***Average need-based loan:*** Freshmen: $3381; Undergraduates: $4415. ***Parent loans:*** $1,603,888 (100% non-need-based). ***Programs:*** FFEL (Subsidized and Unsubsidized Stafford, PLUS), Perkins, college/university.

WORK-STUDY ***Federal work-study:*** *Total amount:* $393,758; 305 jobs available. ***State or other work-study/employment:*** *Total amount:* $294,328 (42% need-based, 58% non-need-based). 192 part-time jobs averaging $1600.

ATHLETIC AWARDS *Total amount:* 794,232 (100% non-need-based).

APPLYING for FINANCIAL AID ***Required financial aid form:*** FAFSA. ***Financial aid deadline (priority):*** 4/1.

CONTACT Mrs. Kathy White, Financial Aid Director, Evangel University, 1111 North Glenstone, Springfield, MO 65802-2191, 417-865-2811 Ext. 7264 or toll-free 800-382-6435 (in-state). *E-mail:* whitek@evangel.edu

THE EVERGREEN STATE COLLEGE

Olympia, WA

Tuition & fees (WA res): $2898 **Average undergraduate aid package: $9472**

ABOUT THE INSTITUTION State-supported, coed. Awards: bachelor's and master's degrees. 91 undergraduate majors. Total enrollment: 4,102. Undergraduates: 3,855. Federal methodology is used as a basis for awarding need-based institutional aid.

UNDERGRADUATE EXPENSES for 1999–2000 ***Application fee:*** $35. ***Tuition, state resident:*** full-time $2757; part-time $92 per quarter hour. ***Tuition, nonresident:*** full-time $9759; part-time $325 per quarter hour. ***Required fees:*** full-time $141. ***College room and board:*** $4645. Room and board charges vary according to board plan and housing facility. ***Payment plan:*** installment.

FRESHMAN FINANCIAL AID (Fall 1998) 515 applied for aid; of those 85% were deemed to have need. 91% of freshmen with need received aid; of those 50% had need fully met. *Average percent of need met:* 89% (excluding resources awarded to replace EFC). *Average financial aid package:* $9197 (excluding resources awarded to replace EFC). 4% of all full-time freshmen had no need and received non-need-based aid.

UNDERGRADUATE FINANCIAL AID (Fall 1998) 2,273 applied for aid; of those 89% were deemed to have need. 91% of undergraduates with need received aid; of those 57% had need fully met. *Average percent of need met:* 89% (excluding resources awarded to replace EFC). *Average financial aid package:* $9472 (excluding resources awarded to replace EFC). 5% of all full-time undergraduates had no need and received non-need-based aid.

GIFT AID (NEED-BASED) ***Total amount:*** $4,087,749 (59% Federal, 29% state, 9% institutional, 3% external sources). ***Receiving aid:*** *Freshmen:* 38% (265); *all full-time undergraduates:* 47% (1,438). ***Average award:*** Freshmen: $3800; Undergraduates: $4300. ***Scholarships, grants, and awards:*** Federal Pell, FSEOG, state, private, college/university gift aid from institutional funds.

GIFT AID (NON-NEED-BASED) ***Total amount:*** $111,000 (18% state, 65% institutional, 17% external sources). ***Receiving aid:*** *Freshmen:* 4% (30); *Undergraduates:* 5% (140). ***Scholarships, grants, and awards by category:*** *Academic Interests/Achievement:* 2 awards ($2500 total): general academic interests/achievements. *Creative Arts/Performance:* 4 awards ($4000 total): applied art and design, art/fine arts, creative writing. *Special Achievements/Activities:* 1 award ($1000 total): community service. *Special Characteristics:* 49 awards ($105,138 total): adult students, members of minority groups.

LOANS ***Student loans:*** $9,820,143 (70% need-based, 30% non-need-based). Average indebtedness per student: $12,000. ***Average need-based loan:*** Freshmen: $2550; Undergraduates: $2500. ***Parent loans:*** $1,222,991 (100% non-need-based). ***Programs:*** FFEL (Subsidized and Unsubsidized Stafford, PLUS), Perkins, college/university.

WORK-STUDY ***Federal work-study:*** *Total amount:* $385,348; 255 jobs averaging $1511. ***State or other work-study/employment:*** *Total amount:* $361,800 (100% need-based). 150 part-time jobs averaging $2412.

APPLYING for FINANCIAL AID ***Required financial aid forms:*** FAFSA, institution's own form. ***Financial aid deadline (priority):*** 3/15. ***Notification date:*** Continuous beginning 4/15. Students must reply within 4 weeks of notification.

CONTACT Financial Aid Office, The Evergreen State College, Olympia, WA 98505, 360-866-6000 Ext. 6205. *Fax:* 360-866-6576.

FAIRFIELD UNIVERSITY

Fairfield, CT

Tuition & fees: $20,435 **Average undergraduate aid package: $14,460**

ABOUT THE INSTITUTION Independent Roman Catholic (Jesuit), coed. Awards: bachelor's and master's degrees and post-master's certificates. 32 undergraduate majors. Total enrollment: 5,127. Undergraduates: 4,064. Freshmen: 837. Federal methodology is used as a basis for awarding need-based institutional aid.

UNDERGRADUATE EXPENSES for 1999–2000 ***Application fee:*** $50. ***Comprehensive fee:*** $27,815 includes full-time tuition ($20,000), mandatory fees ($435), and room and board ($7380). Room and board charges vary according to board plan and housing facility. ***Part-time tuition:*** $310 per credit. ***Part-time fees:*** $25 per term part-time. Part-time tuition and fees vary according to course load. ***Payment plan:*** installment.

FRESHMAN FINANCIAL AID (Fall 1999) 586 applied for aid; of those 77% were deemed to have need. 97% of freshmen with need received aid; of those 22% had need fully met. *Average percent of need met:* 79% (excluding resources awarded to replace EFC). *Average financial aid package:* $14,013 (excluding resources awarded to replace EFC). 5% of all full-time freshmen had no need and received non-need-based aid.

UNDERGRADUATE FINANCIAL AID (Fall 1999) 1,985 applied for aid; of those 83% were deemed to have need. 98% of undergraduates with need received aid; of those 18% had need fully met. *Average percent of need met:* 77% (excluding resources awarded to replace EFC). *Average financial aid package:* $14,460 (excluding resources awarded to replace EFC). 5% of all full-time undergraduates had no need and received non-need-based aid.

GIFT AID (NEED-BASED) ***Total amount:*** $12,705,050 (6% Federal, 94% institutional). ***Receiving aid:*** *Freshmen:* 44% (371); *all full-time undergraduates:* 41% (1,331). ***Average award:*** Freshmen: $8646; Undergraduates: $8763. ***Scholarships, grants, and awards:*** Federal Pell, FSEOG, state, private, college/university gift aid from institutional funds.

GIFT AID (NON-NEED-BASED) ***Total amount:*** $2,721,056 (10% state, 77% institutional, 13% external sources). ***Receiving aid:*** *Freshmen:* 12% (98); *Undergraduates:* 8% (247). ***Scholarships, grants, and awards by category:*** *Academic Interests/Achievement:* 348 awards ($2,007,675 total): general academic interests/achievements. *Creative Arts/Performance:* 10 awards ($20,000 total): music, theater/drama. ***Tuition waivers:*** Full or partial for employees or children of employees. ***ROTC:*** Army cooperative.

LOANS ***Student loans:*** $10,241,187 (57% need-based, 43% non-need-based). 54% of past graduating class borrowed through all loan programs. Average indebtedness per student: $18,765. ***Average need-based loan:*** Freshmen: $2950; Undergraduates: $3609. ***Parent loans:*** $4,405,253 (100% non-need-based). ***Programs:*** FFEL (Subsidized and Unsubsidized Stafford, PLUS), Perkins, Federal Nursing, state, alternative loans.

WORK-STUDY ***Federal work-study:*** *Total amount:* $569,435; 406 jobs averaging $1369.

ATHLETIC AWARDS *Total amount:* 2,090,588 (100% non-need-based).

APPLYING for FINANCIAL AID ***Required financial aid forms:*** FAFSA, CSS Financial Aid PROFILE. ***Financial aid deadline (priority):*** 2/15. ***Notification date:*** 4/5. Students must reply by 5/1 or within 3 weeks of notification.

CONTACT Ms. Susan Kadir, Director of Financial Aid, Fairfield University, 1073 North Benson Road, Donnarumma Hall, Room 241, Fairfield, CT 06430-5195, 203-254-4125. *Fax:* 203-254-4008.

FAIRLEIGH DICKINSON UNIVERSITY, FLORHAM-MADISON CAMPUS

Madison, NJ

Tuition & fees: $15,593 **Average undergraduate aid package: $15,303**

ABOUT THE INSTITUTION Independent, coed. Awards: associate, bachelor's, and master's degrees and post-bachelor's and post-master's certificates. 39 undergraduate majors. Total enrollment: 3,351. Undergraduates: 2,433. Federal methodology is used as a basis for awarding need-based institutional aid.

UNDERGRADUATE EXPENSES for 1999–2000 ***Application fee:*** $35. ***Comprehensive fee:*** $22,193 includes full-time tuition ($14,732), mandatory fees ($861), and room and board ($6600). ***College room only:*** $3900. Room and board charges vary according to board plan and housing facility. ***Part-time tuition:*** $478 per credit. ***Part-time fees:*** $212 per term part-time. Part-time tuition and fees vary according to course load and program. ***Payment plans:*** installment, deferred payment.

FRESHMAN FINANCIAL AID (Fall 1999) 393 applied for aid; of those 84% were deemed to have need. 100% of freshmen with need received aid; of those 6% had need fully met. *Average percent of need met:* 84% (excluding resources awarded to replace EFC). *Average financial aid package:* $16,903 (excluding resources awarded to replace EFC). 24% of all full-time freshmen had no need and received non-need-based aid.

UNDERGRADUATE FINANCIAL AID (Fall 1999) 1,541 applied for aid; of those 88% were deemed to have need. 97% of undergraduates with need received aid; of those 6% had need fully met. *Average percent of need met:* 78% (excluding resources awarded to replace EFC). *Average financial aid package:* $15,303 (excluding resources awarded to replace EFC). 14% of all full-time undergraduates had no need and received non-need-based aid.

GIFT AID (NEED-BASED) ***Total amount:*** $10,854,003 (12% Federal, 26% state, 61% institutional, 1% external sources). ***Receiving aid:*** *Freshmen:* 55% (275); *all full-time undergraduates:* 57% (1,074). ***Average award:*** Freshmen: $7859; Undergraduates: $6989. ***Scholarships, grants, and awards:*** Federal Pell, FSEOG, state, private, college/university gift aid from institutional funds, Federal Nursing.

GIFT AID (NON-NEED-BASED) ***Total amount:*** $1,721,508 (1% state, 98% institutional, 1% external sources). ***Receiving aid:*** *Freshmen:* 66% (325); *Undergraduates:* 32% (602). ***Scholarships, grants, and awards by category:*** *Academic Interests/Achievement:* general academic interests/achievements. *Special Achievements/Activities:* leadership. *Special Characteristics:* children and siblings of alumni, international students, parents of current students, siblings of current students, spouses of current students. ***Tuition waivers:*** Full or partial for employees or children of employees, senior citizens.

LOANS ***Student loans:*** $5,327,054 (73% need-based, 27% non-need-based). Average indebtedness per student: $15,968. ***Average need-based loan:*** Freshmen: $1964; Undergraduates: $3785. ***Parent loans:*** $3,142,559 (85% need-based, 15% non-need-based). ***Programs:*** FFEL (Subsidized and Unsubsidized Stafford, PLUS), Perkins, Federal Nursing, state.

WORK-STUDY ***Federal work-study:*** *Total amount:* $482,021; 432 jobs averaging $1116.

APPLYING for FINANCIAL AID ***Required financial aid forms:*** FAFSA, institution's own form. ***Financial aid deadline (priority):*** 3/15. ***Notification date:*** Continuous. Students must reply by 5/1 or within 2 weeks of notification.

CONTACT Monique Gilbert, Associate Director of Financial Aid, Fairleigh Dickinson University, Florham-Madison Campus, 285 Madison Avenue, Madison, NJ 07940-1099, 973-443-8700 or toll-free 800-338-8803. *E-mail:* gilbert@mailbox.fdu.edu

FAIRLEIGH DICKINSON UNIVERSITY, TEANECK–HACKENSACK CAMPUS

Teaneck, NJ

Tuition & fees: $15,330 **Average undergraduate aid package: $15,776**

ABOUT THE INSTITUTION Independent, coed. Awards: associate, bachelor's, master's, and doctoral degrees and post-bachelor's, post-master's, and first-professional certificates. 58 undergraduate majors. Total enrollment: 5,597. Undergraduates: 3,823. Freshmen: 581. Federal methodology is used as a basis for awarding need-based institutional aid.

UNDERGRADUATE EXPENSES for 1999–2000 ***Application fee:*** $40. ***Comprehensive fee:*** $21,866 includes full-time tuition ($14,732), mandatory fees ($598), and room and board ($6536). ***College room only:***

$3908. Full-time tuition and fees vary according to degree level and program. Room and board charges vary according to board plan and housing facility. ***Part-time tuition:*** $478 per credit. ***Part-time fees:*** $106 per term part-time. Part-time tuition and fees vary according to program. ***Payment plans:*** installment, deferred payment.

FRESHMAN FINANCIAL AID (Fall 1999) 252 applied for aid; of those 90% were deemed to have need. 100% of freshmen with need received aid; of those 4% had need fully met. *Average percent of need met:* 77% (excluding resources awarded to replace EFC). *Average financial aid package:* $16,168 (excluding resources awarded to replace EFC). 17% of all full-time freshmen had no need and received non-need-based aid.

UNDERGRADUATE FINANCIAL AID (Fall 1999) 1,237 applied for aid; of those 92% were deemed to have need. 92% of undergraduates with need received aid; of those 5% had need fully met. *Average percent of need met:* 78% (excluding resources awarded to replace EFC). *Average financial aid package:* $15,776 (excluding resources awarded to replace EFC). 12% of all full-time undergraduates had no need and received non-need-based aid.

GIFT AID (NEED-BASED) ***Total amount:*** $9,789,781 (17% Federal, 31% state, 51% institutional, 1% external sources). ***Receiving aid:*** *Freshmen:* 58% (198); *all full-time undergraduates:* 59% (886). ***Average award:*** Freshmen: $8674; Undergraduates: $7824. ***Scholarships, grants, and awards:*** Federal Pell, FSEOG, state, private, college/university gift aid from institutional funds, Federal Nursing.

GIFT AID (NON-NEED-BASED) ***Total amount:*** $690,010 (1% state, 99% institutional). ***Receiving aid:*** *Freshmen:* 64% (219); *Undergraduates:* 35% (524). ***Scholarships, grants, and awards by category:*** *Academic Interests/Achievement:* general academic interests/achievements. *Special Achievements/Activities:* leadership. *Special Characteristics:* children and siblings of alumni, international students, parents of current students, siblings of current students, spouses of current students. ***Tuition waivers:*** Full or partial for employees or children of employees, senior citizens. ***ROTC:*** Army cooperative, Air Force cooperative.

LOANS ***Student loans:*** $4,672,273 (94% need-based, 6% non-need-based). Average indebtedness per student: $18,493. ***Average need-based loan:*** Freshmen: $1930; Undergraduates: $2345. ***Parent loans:*** $659,976 (88% need-based, 12% non-need-based). ***Programs:*** FFEL (Subsidized and Unsubsidized Stafford, PLUS), Perkins, Federal Nursing, state.

WORK-STUDY ***Federal work-study:*** *Total amount:* $404,435; 335 jobs averaging $1207.

ATHLETIC AWARDS *Total amount:* 1,398,150 (46% need-based, 54% non-need-based).

APPLYING for FINANCIAL AID ***Required financial aid forms:*** FAFSA, institution's own form. ***Financial aid deadline (priority):*** 3/15. ***Notification date:*** Continuous. Students must reply by 5/1 or within 2 weeks of notification.

CONTACT Theresa Coll, Campus Director of Financial Aid, Fairleigh Dickinson University, Teaneck–Hackensack Campus, 100 River Road, Teaneck, NJ 07666-1914, 201-692-2368 or toll-free 800-338-8803. *E-mail:* coll@es1serve.fdu.edu

FAIRMONT STATE COLLEGE

Fairmont, WV

Tuition & fees (WV res): $2244 **Average undergraduate aid package: $4090**

ABOUT THE INSTITUTION State-supported, coed. Awards: associate and bachelor's degrees. 60 undergraduate majors. Total enrollment: 6,645. Undergraduates: 6,645. Freshmen: 1,111. Federal methodology is used as a basis for awarding need-based institutional aid.

UNDERGRADUATE EXPENSES for 1999–2000 ***One-time required fee:*** $29. ***Tuition, state resident:*** full-time $2244; part-time $94 per credit. ***Tuition, nonresident:*** full-time $5228; part-time $218 per credit. Full-time tuition and fees vary according to program. Part-time tuition and fees vary according to program. ***College room and board:*** $3882; ***room only:*** $1786. Room and board charges vary according to board plan. ***Payment plans:*** installment, deferred payment.

FRESHMAN FINANCIAL AID (Fall 1998) 851 applied for aid; of those 93% were deemed to have need. 61% of freshmen with need received aid; of those 40% had need fully met. *Average percent of need met:* 62% (excluding resources awarded to replace EFC). *Average financial aid package:* $3558 (excluding resources awarded to replace EFC). 11% of all full-time freshmen had no need and received non-need-based aid.

UNDERGRADUATE FINANCIAL AID (Fall 1998) 2,983 applied for aid; of those 91% were deemed to have need. 89% of undergraduates with need received aid; of those 31% had need fully met. *Average percent of need met:* 71% (excluding resources awarded to replace EFC). *Average financial aid package:* $4090 (excluding resources awarded to replace EFC). 8% of all full-time undergraduates had no need and received non-need-based aid.

GIFT AID (NEED-BASED) ***Total amount:*** $7,236,585 (78% Federal, 17% state, 2% institutional, 3% external sources). ***Receiving aid:*** *Freshmen:* 33% (349); *all full-time undergraduates:* 43% (1,935). ***Average award:*** Freshmen: $1918; Undergraduates: $1953. ***Scholarships, grants, and awards:*** Federal Pell, FSEOG, state, private, college/university gift aid from institutional funds.

GIFT AID (NON-NEED-BASED) ***Total amount:*** $165,713 (25% state, 31% institutional, 44% external sources). ***Receiving aid:*** *Freshmen:* 7% (76); *Undergraduates:* 5% (215). ***Scholarships, grants, and awards by category:*** *Academic Interests/Achievement:* 65 awards ($85,000 total): business, education, engineering/technologies, foreign languages, general academic interests/achievements, health fields, humanities, mathematics, physical sciences, social sciences. *Creative Arts/Performance:* 59 awards ($59,200 total): art/fine arts, debating, music, theater/drama. *Special Characteristics:* 5 awards ($5800 total): general special characteristics. ***Tuition waivers:*** Full or partial for employees or children of employees. ***ROTC:*** Army, Air Force cooperative.

LOANS ***Student loans:*** $8,126,700 (77% need-based, 23% non-need-based). 54% of past graduating class borrowed through all loan programs. ***Average need-based loan:*** Freshmen: $1159; Undergraduates: $1870. ***Parent loans:*** $236,053 (27% need-based, 73% non-need-based). ***Programs:*** Federal Direct (Subsidized and Unsubsidized Stafford, PLUS), Perkins.

WORK-STUDY ***Federal work-study:*** *Total amount:* $321,089; 409 jobs averaging $888. ***State or other work-study/employment:*** *Total amount:* $478,076 (100% non-need-based). 400 part-time jobs averaging $1196.

ATHLETIC AWARDS *Total amount:* 174,525 (81% need-based, 19% non-need-based).

APPLYING for FINANCIAL AID ***Required financial aid form:*** FAFSA. ***Financial aid deadline (priority):*** 3/1. ***Notification date:*** Continuous beginning 4/15. Students must reply within 2 weeks of notification.

CONTACT Kaye C. Widney, Interim Director of Financial Aid, Fairmont State College, 1201 Locust Avenue, Fairmont, WV 26554, 304-367-4213 or toll-free 800-641-5678. *Fax:* 304-367-4584. *E-mail:* kwidney@mail.fscwv.edu

FAITH BAPTIST BIBLE COLLEGE AND THEOLOGICAL SEMINARY

Ankeny, IA

Tuition & fees: $7886 **Average undergraduate aid package: $4751**

ABOUT THE INSTITUTION Independent religious, coed. Awards: associate, bachelor's, master's, and first professional degrees. 9 undergraduate majors. Total enrollment: 436. Undergraduates: 364. Freshmen: 111. Federal methodology is used as a basis for awarding need-based institutional aid.

UNDERGRADUATE EXPENSES for 1999–2000 ***Application fee:*** $25. ***Comprehensive fee:*** $11,236 includes full-time tuition ($7086), mandatory fees ($800), and room and board ($3350). ***College room only:*** $1250. Full-time tuition and fees vary according to course load. ***Part-time tuition:*** $268 per semester hour. ***Part-time fees:*** $195 per term part-time. Part-time tuition and fees vary according to course load. ***Payment plan:*** installment.

FRESHMAN FINANCIAL AID (Fall 1999, est.) 100 applied for aid; of those 96% were deemed to have need. 90% of freshmen with need received aid.

Faith Baptist Bible College and Theological Seminary (continued)

Average percent of need met: 39% (excluding resources awarded to replace EFC). *Average financial aid package:* $5011 (excluding resources awarded to replace EFC). 14% of all full-time freshmen had no need and received non-need-based aid.

UNDERGRADUATE FINANCIAL AID (Fall 1999, est.) 295 applied for aid; of those 95% were deemed to have need. 91% of undergraduates with need received aid; of those 1% had need fully met. *Average percent of need met:* 46% (excluding resources awarded to replace EFC). *Average financial aid package:* $4751 (excluding resources awarded to replace EFC). 11% of all full-time undergraduates had no need and received non-need-based aid.

GIFT AID (NEED-BASED) ***Total amount:*** $677,321 (33% Federal, 60% state, 7% institutional). ***Receiving aid:*** *Freshmen:* 55% (71); *all full-time undergraduates:* 52% (186). ***Average award:*** Freshmen: $3710; Undergraduates: $3704. ***Scholarships, grants, and awards:*** Federal Pell, state, private, college/university gift aid from institutional funds.

GIFT AID (NON-NEED-BASED) ***Total amount:*** $307,863 (61% institutional, 39% external sources). ***Receiving aid:*** *Freshmen:* 47% (61); *Undergraduates:* 45% (161). ***Scholarships, grants, and awards by category:*** *Academic Interests/Achievement:* 49 awards ($10,100 total): general academic interests/achievements. *Creative Arts/Performance:* 2 awards ($978 total): music. *Special Achievements/Activities:* leadership. *Special Characteristics:* 53 awards ($121,126 total): children of faculty/staff, relatives of clergy, spouses of current students. ***Tuition waivers:*** Full or partial for employees or children of employees.

LOANS ***Student loans:*** $425,283 (82% need-based, 18% non-need-based). 45% of past graduating class borrowed through all loan programs. Average indebtedness per student: $12,979. ***Average need-based loan:*** Freshmen: $2625; Undergraduates: $3411. ***Parent loans:*** $54,750 (100% non-need-based). ***Programs:*** FFEL (Subsidized and Unsubsidized Stafford, PLUS).

APPLYING for FINANCIAL AID ***Required financial aid form:*** FAFSA. ***Financial aid deadline (priority):*** 5/1. ***Notification date:*** Continuous. Students must reply within 4 weeks of notification.

CONTACT Mr. Breck Appell, Director of Financial Assistance, Faith Baptist Bible College and Theological Seminary, 1900 Northwest 4th Street, Ankeny, IA 50021-2152, 515-964-0601 or toll-free 888-FAITH 4U. *Fax:* 515-964-1638. *E-mail:* fbbcfinaid@aol.com

FASHION INSTITUTE OF TECHNOLOGY

New York, NY

Tuition & fees (NY res): $3195 **Average undergraduate aid package: $5656**

ABOUT THE INSTITUTION State and locally supported, coed. Awards: associate, bachelor's, and master's degrees. 19 undergraduate majors. Total enrollment: 10,853. Undergraduates: 10,750. Freshmen: 1,103. Federal methodology is used as a basis for awarding need-based institutional aid.

UNDERGRADUATE EXPENSES for 1999–2000 ***Application fee:*** $30. ***Tuition, state resident:*** full-time $2985; part-time $125 per credit. ***Tuition, nonresident:*** full-time $7265; part-time $310 per credit. ***Required fees:*** full-time $210; $5 per term part-time. Full-time tuition and fees vary according to degree level and program. Part-time tuition and fees vary according to degree level and program. ***College room and board:*** $7339. Room and board charges vary according to board plan and housing facility. ***Payment plan:*** installment.

FRESHMAN FINANCIAL AID (Fall 1999, est.) 709 applied for aid; of those 85% were deemed to have need. 94% of freshmen with need received aid; of those 37% had need fully met. *Average percent of need met:* 77% (excluding resources awarded to replace EFC). *Average financial aid package:* $4921 (excluding resources awarded to replace EFC).

UNDERGRADUATE FINANCIAL AID (Fall 1999, est.) 3,194 applied for aid; of those 90% were deemed to have need. 92% of undergraduates with need received aid; of those 37% had need fully met. *Average percent of need met:* 75% (excluding resources awarded to replace EFC). *Average financial aid package:* $5656 (excluding resources awarded to replace EFC).

GIFT AID (NEED-BASED) ***Total amount:*** $8,886,763 (47% Federal, 31% state, 21% institutional, 1% external sources). ***Receiving aid:*** *Freshmen:* 49% (505); *all full-time undergraduates:* 41% (2,337). ***Average award:*** Freshmen: $3421; Undergraduates: $3289. ***Scholarships, grants, and awards:*** Federal Pell, FSEOG, state, private, college/university gift aid from institutional funds.

GIFT AID (NON-NEED-BASED) ***Tuition waivers:*** Full or partial for employees or children of employees.

LOANS ***Student loans:*** $8,071,614 (100% need-based). ***Average need-based loan:*** Freshmen: $3409; Undergraduates: $3760. ***Parent loans:*** $1,082,143 (100% need-based). ***Programs:*** FFEL (Subsidized and Unsubsidized Stafford, PLUS), Perkins, college/university, alternative loans.

WORK-STUDY ***Federal work-study:*** *Total amount:* $365,730; jobs available.

APPLYING for FINANCIAL AID ***Required financial aid forms:*** FAFSA, state aid form. ***Financial aid deadline (priority):*** 3/1. ***Notification date:*** Continuous beginning 4/15. Students must reply within 2 weeks of notification.

CONTACT Financial Aid Office, Fashion Institute of Technology, Seventh Avenue at 27th Street, New York, NY 10001-5992, 212-217-7684 or toll-free 800-GOTOFIT (out-of-state).

FAULKNER UNIVERSITY

Montgomery, AL

Tuition & fees: $7500 **Average undergraduate aid package: $6650**

ABOUT THE INSTITUTION Independent religious, coed. Awards: associate, bachelor's, master's, and first professional degrees. 49 undergraduate majors. Total enrollment: 2,645. Undergraduates: 2,232. Freshmen: 397. Federal methodology is used as a basis for awarding need-based institutional aid.

UNDERGRADUATE EXPENSES for 1999–2000 ***Application fee:*** $10. ***Comprehensive fee:*** $11,490 includes full-time tuition ($7500) and room and board ($3990). ***College room only:*** $1900. Full-time tuition and fees vary according to program. Room and board charges vary according to board plan and housing facility. ***Part-time tuition:*** $250 per semester hour. Part-time tuition and fees vary according to program. ***Payment plans:*** installment, deferred payment.

FRESHMAN FINANCIAL AID (Fall 1998) 279 applied for aid; of those 82% were deemed to have need. 100% of freshmen with need received aid; of those 6% had need fully met. *Average percent of need met:* 70% (excluding resources awarded to replace EFC). *Average financial aid package:* $4600 (excluding resources awarded to replace EFC). 6% of all full-time freshmen had no need and received non-need-based aid.

UNDERGRADUATE FINANCIAL AID (Fall 1998) 1,461 applied for aid; of those 82% were deemed to have need. 100% of undergraduates with need received aid; of those 4% had need fully met. *Average percent of need met:* 70% (excluding resources awarded to replace EFC). *Average financial aid package:* $6650 (excluding resources awarded to replace EFC). 4% of all full-time undergraduates had no need and received non-need-based aid.

GIFT AID (NEED-BASED) ***Total amount:*** $4,335,240 (56% Federal, 28% state, 13% institutional, 3% external sources). ***Receiving aid:*** *Freshmen:* 54% (163); *all full-time undergraduates:* 54% (863). ***Average award:*** Freshmen: $2150; Undergraduates: $2250. ***Scholarships, grants, and awards:*** Federal Pell, FSEOG, state, private, college/university gift aid from institutional funds.

GIFT AID (NON-NEED-BASED) ***Total amount:*** $97,600 (100% institutional). ***Receiving aid:*** *Freshmen:* 56% (171); *Undergraduates:* 53% (844). ***Scholarships, grants, and awards by category:*** *Academic Interests/Achievement:* 152 awards ($384,140 total): general academic interests/achievements, religion/biblical studies. *Creative Arts/Performance:* 44 awards ($21,138 total): journalism/publications, music, theater/drama. *Special Achievements/Activities:* 172 awards ($112,774 total): cheerleading/drum major, leadership, religious involvement. *Special Characteristics:* 60 awards ($44,300 total): adult students, children of faculty/staff, relatives of clergy, siblings of current students. ***Tuition waivers:*** Full or partial for employees or children of employees, adult students.

LOANS ***Student loans:*** $10,829,564 (100% need-based). 75% of past graduating class borrowed through all loan programs. Average indebtedness per student: $18,000. ***Average need-based loan:*** Freshmen: $2625; Undergraduates: $4500. ***Parent loans:*** $192,024 (100% need-based). ***Programs:*** FFEL (Subsidized and Unsubsidized Stafford, PLUS), Perkins.

WORK-STUDY ***Federal work-study:*** *Total amount:* $152,183; 139 jobs averaging $1095. ***State or other work-study/employment:*** *Total amount:* $1887 (100% need-based). 4 part-time jobs averaging $472.

ATHLETIC AWARDS *Total amount:* 412,787 (100% need-based).

APPLYING for FINANCIAL AID ***Required financial aid forms:*** FAFSA, institution's own form, state aid form. ***Financial aid deadline (priority):*** 5/1.

CONTACT William G. Jackson II, Director of Financial Aid, Faulkner University, 5345 Atlanta Highway, Montgomery, AL 36109-3398, 334-386-7195 or toll-free 800-879-9816. *Fax:* 334-386-7201.

FAYETTEVILLE STATE UNIVERSITY

Fayetteville, NC

Tuition & fees (NC res): $1702 **Average undergraduate aid package: N/A**

ABOUT THE INSTITUTION State-supported, coed. Awards: associate, bachelor's, master's, and doctoral degrees. 35 undergraduate majors. Federal methodology is used as a basis for awarding need-based institutional aid.

UNDERGRADUATE EXPENSES for 1999–2000 ***Application fee:*** $15. ***Tuition, state resident:*** full-time $962; part-time $241 per term. ***Tuition, nonresident:*** full-time $8232; part-time $2058 per term. ***Required fees:*** full-time $740; $186 per term part-time. Part-time tuition and fees vary according to course load. ***College room and board:*** $3800. ***Payment plan:*** installment.

GIFT AID (NEED-BASED) ***Scholarships, grants, and awards:*** Federal Pell, FSEOG, state, private, college/university gift aid from institutional funds.

GIFT AID (NON-NEED-BASED) ***Scholarships, grants, and awards by category:*** *Academic Interests/Achievement:* general academic interests/achievements. *Creative Arts/Performance:* music. *Special Characteristics:* local/state students. ***Tuition waivers:*** Full or partial for employees or children of employees, senior citizens. ***ROTC:*** Air Force.

LOANS ***Programs:*** Federal Direct (Subsidized and Unsubsidized Stafford, PLUS), Perkins, state, alternative loans.

WORK-STUDY Federal work-study jobs available.

APPLYING for FINANCIAL AID ***Required financial aid forms:*** FAFSA, institution's own form. ***Financial aid deadline:*** 4/1 (priority: 3/1).

CONTACT Office of Financial Aid, Fayetteville State University, 1200 Murchison Road, Fayetteville, NC 28301-4298, 910-486-1325 or toll-free 800-672-6667 (in-state), 800-222-2594 (out-of-state). *Fax:* 910-486-1423.

FELICIAN COLLEGE

Lodi, NJ

Tuition & fees: $11,060 **Average undergraduate aid package: $10,500**

ABOUT THE INSTITUTION Independent Roman Catholic, coed. Awards: associate, bachelor's, and master's degrees and post-bachelor's and post-master's certificates. 39 undergraduate majors. Total enrollment: 1,377. Undergraduates: 1,324. Freshmen: 241. Federal methodology is used as a basis for awarding need-based institutional aid.

UNDERGRADUATE EXPENSES for 1999–2000 ***Application fee:*** $25. ***Comprehensive fee:*** $16,730 includes full-time tuition ($10,560), mandatory fees ($500), and room and board ($5670). ***College room only:*** $2835. Full-time tuition and fees vary according to course load. ***Part-time tuition:*** $352 per semester hour. ***Part-time fees:*** $100 per term part-time. Part-time tuition and fees vary according to course load. ***Payment plans:*** installment, deferred payment.

FRESHMAN FINANCIAL AID (Fall 1998) 86 applied for aid; of those 62% were deemed to have need. 100% of freshmen with need received aid; of those 75% had need fully met. *Average percent of need met:* 62% (excluding resources awarded to replace EFC). *Average financial aid package:* $10,500 (excluding resources awarded to replace EFC). 62% of all full-time freshmen had no need and received non-need-based aid.

UNDERGRADUATE FINANCIAL AID (Fall 1998) 342 applied for aid; of those 62% were deemed to have need. 100% of undergraduates with need received aid; of those 57% had need fully met. *Average percent of need met:* 62% (excluding resources awarded to replace EFC). *Average financial aid package:* $10,500 (excluding resources awarded to replace EFC). 62% of all full-time undergraduates had no need and received non-need-based aid.

GIFT AID (NEED-BASED) ***Total amount:*** $2,428,324 (29% Federal, 63% state, 8% institutional). ***Scholarships, grants, and awards:*** Federal Pell, FSEOG, state, Federal Nursing.

GIFT AID (NON-NEED-BASED) ***Total amount:*** $6500 (100% state). ***Receiving aid:*** *Freshmen:* 24% (33); *Undergraduates:* 24% (131). ***Scholarships, grants, and awards by category:*** *Academic Interests/Achievement:* biological sciences, education, English, general academic interests/achievements, health fields, religion/biblical studies. ***Tuition waivers:*** Full or partial for employees or children of employees, senior citizens.

LOANS ***Student loans:*** $1,948,810 (58% need-based, 42% non-need-based). 62% of past graduating class borrowed through all loan programs. Average indebtedness per student: $18,000. ***Average need-based loan:*** Freshmen: $2625; Undergraduates: $5500. ***Parent loans:*** $98,736 (100% non-need-based). ***Programs:*** FFEL (Subsidized and Unsubsidized Stafford, PLUS), state, NJ Class Loans.

WORK-STUDY ***Federal work-study:*** *Total amount:* $93,526; 71 jobs averaging $1500.

ATHLETIC AWARDS *Total amount:* 407,754 (100% non-need-based).

APPLYING for FINANCIAL AID ***Required financial aid forms:*** FAFSA, institution's own form. ***Financial aid deadline (priority):*** 3/15. ***Notification date:*** Continuous.

CONTACT Norma Betz, Financial Aid Director, Felician College, 262 South Main Street, Lodi, NJ 07644-2198, 201-559-6040. *Fax:* 201-559-6118. *E-mail:* betzn@inet.felician.edu

FERRIS STATE UNIVERSITY

Big Rapids, MI

Tuition & fees (MI res): $4195 **Average undergraduate aid package: $7574**

ABOUT THE INSTITUTION State-supported, coed. Awards: associate, bachelor's, master's, and first professional degrees. 82 undergraduate majors. Total enrollment: 9,668. Undergraduates: 9,191. Freshmen: 2,142. Federal methodology is used as a basis for awarding need-based institutional aid.

UNDERGRADUATE EXPENSES for 1999–2000 ***Application fee:*** $20. ***Tuition, state resident:*** full-time $4118; part-time $172 per credit hour. ***Tuition, nonresident:*** full-time $8726; part-time $366 per credit hour. ***Required fees:*** full-time $77; $38 per term part-time. Full-time tuition and fees vary according to reciprocity agreements. Part-time tuition and fees vary according to course load and reciprocity agreements. ***College room and board:*** $5110. Room and board charges vary according to board plan and housing facility. ***Payment plans:*** installment, deferred payment.

FRESHMAN FINANCIAL AID (Fall 1999, est.) 1798 applied for aid; of those 98% were deemed to have need. 96% of freshmen with need received aid; of those 5% had need fully met. *Average percent of need met:* 75% (excluding resources awarded to replace EFC). *Average financial aid package:* $6237 (excluding resources awarded to replace EFC).

UNDERGRADUATE FINANCIAL AID (Fall 1999, est.) 5,662 applied for aid; of those 89% were deemed to have need. 96% of undergraduates with need received aid; of those 8% had need fully met. *Average percent of need met:* 81% (excluding resources awarded to replace EFC). *Average financial aid package:* $7574 (excluding resources awarded to replace EFC).

GIFT AID (NEED-BASED) ***Total amount:*** $11,381,238 (72% Federal, 19% state, 9% institutional). ***Receiving aid:*** *Freshmen:* 67% (1,417); *all full-time undergraduates:* 44% (3,175). ***Average award:*** Freshmen: $2494;

Ferris State University (continued)

Undergraduates: $3105. ***Scholarships, grants, and awards:*** Federal Pell, FSEOG, state, private, college/university gift aid from institutional funds.

GIFT AID (NON-NEED-BASED) ***Total amount:*** $4,406,680 (66% institutional, 34% external sources). ***Receiving aid:*** *Freshmen:* 10% (202); *Undergraduates:* 9% (620). ***Scholarships, grants, and awards by category:*** *Academic Interests/Achievement:* general academic interests/achievements. *Creative Arts/Performance:* debating, journalism/publications, music, theater/drama. *Special Characteristics:* children of faculty/staff. ***Tuition waivers:*** Full or partial for employees or children of employees. ***ROTC:*** Army cooperative.

LOANS ***Student loans:*** $30,676,930 (63% need-based, 37% non-need-based). 85% of past graduating class borrowed through all loan programs. Average indebtedness per student: $13,000. ***Average need-based loan:*** Freshmen: $1280; Undergraduates: $3400. ***Parent loans:*** $2,535,707 (100% non-need-based). ***Programs:*** Federal Direct (Subsidized and Unsubsidized Stafford, PLUS), Perkins, Federal Nursing, college/university.

WORK-STUDY ***Federal work-study:*** *Total amount:* $540,000; jobs available. ***State or other work-study/employment:*** *Total amount:* $1,452,376 (100% need-based). Part-time jobs available.

ATHLETIC AWARDS *Total amount:* 983,723 (100% non-need-based).

APPLYING for FINANCIAL AID ***Required financial aid form:*** FAFSA. ***Financial aid deadline (priority):*** 3/15. ***Notification date:*** Continuous.

CONTACT Mr. Dennis Batt, Associate Director of Financial Aid, Ferris State University, 420 Oak Street, Big Rapids, MI 49307-2020, 231-591-2110 or toll-free 800-433-7747. *E-mail:* battd@ferris.edu

FERRUM COLLEGE

Ferrum, VA

Tuition & fees: $10,990 **Average undergraduate aid package: $10,022**

ABOUT THE INSTITUTION Independent United Methodist, coed. Awards: bachelor's degrees. 34 undergraduate majors. Total enrollment: 945. Undergraduates: 945. Freshmen: 328. Federal methodology is used as a basis for awarding need-based institutional aid.

UNDERGRADUATE EXPENSES for 1999–2000 ***Application fee:*** $25. ***Comprehensive fee:*** $15,990 includes full-time tuition ($10,990) and room and board ($5000). ***Part-time tuition:*** $250 per credit hour. Part-time tuition and fees vary according to course load. ***Payment plan:*** installment.

FRESHMAN FINANCIAL AID (Fall 1999, est.) 276 applied for aid; of those 86% were deemed to have need. 100% of freshmen with need received aid; of those 58% had need fully met. *Average percent of need met:* 83% (excluding resources awarded to replace EFC). *Average financial aid package:* $10,084 (excluding resources awarded to replace EFC). 24% of all full-time freshmen had no need and received non-need-based aid.

UNDERGRADUATE FINANCIAL AID (Fall 1999, est.) 762 applied for aid; of those 91% were deemed to have need. 100% of undergraduates with need received aid; of those 56% had need fully met. *Average percent of need met:* 84% (excluding resources awarded to replace EFC). *Average financial aid package:* $10,022 (excluding resources awarded to replace EFC). 20% of all full-time undergraduates had no need and received non-need-based aid.

GIFT AID (NEED-BASED) ***Total amount:*** $4,323,956 (18% Federal, 34% state, 45% institutional, 3% external sources). ***Receiving aid:*** *Freshmen:* 73% (235); *all full-time undergraduates:* 76% (685). ***Average award:*** Freshmen: $6522; Undergraduates: $6473. ***Scholarships, grants, and awards:*** Federal Pell, FSEOG, state, private, college/university gift aid from institutional funds, Horatio Alger Scholarships.

GIFT AID (NON-NEED-BASED) ***Total amount:*** $572,315 (67% state, 33% institutional). ***Scholarships, grants, and awards by category:*** *Academic Interests/Achievement:* 378 awards ($851,600 total): general academic interests/achievements. *Creative Arts/Performance:* 33 awards ($39,000 total): music, performing arts, theater/drama. *Special Achievements/Activities:* 56 awards ($83,050 total): community service, general special achievements/activities. *Special Characteristics:* 468 awards ($752,918 total): children of educators, children of faculty/staff, general special characteristics, international students, local/state students, out-of-state students, relatives of clergy, religious affiliation, siblings of current students, veterans. ***Tuition waivers:*** Full or partial for employees or children of employees, senior citizens.

LOANS ***Student loans:*** $2,713,577 (95% need-based, 5% non-need-based). 86% of past graduating class borrowed through all loan programs. Average indebtedness per student: $17,093. ***Average need-based loan:*** Freshmen: $3654; Undergraduates: $4026. ***Parent loans:*** $2,053,275 (79% need-based, 21% non-need-based). ***Programs:*** FFEL (Subsidized and Unsubsidized Stafford, PLUS), Perkins, college/university.

WORK-STUDY ***Federal work-study:*** *Total amount:* $384,595; 272 jobs averaging $1425. ***State or other work-study/employment:*** *Total amount:* $110,000 (94% need-based, 6% non-need-based). 84 part-time jobs averaging $1310.

APPLYING for FINANCIAL AID ***Required financial aid forms:*** FAFSA, state aid form. ***Financial aid deadline (priority):*** 4/1. ***Notification date:*** Continuous.

CONTACT Mrs. Sheila M. Nelson-Hensley, Director of Financial Aid, Ferrum College, PO Box 1000, Spilman-Daniel House, Ferrum, VA 24088-9001, 540-365-4282 or toll-free 800-868-9797. *Fax:* 540-365-4266.

FINCH UNIVERSITY OF HEALTH SCIENCES/ THE CHICAGO MEDICAL SCHOOL

North Chicago, IL

Tuition & fees: $12,903 **Average undergraduate aid package: N/A**

ABOUT THE INSTITUTION Independent, coed. Awards: bachelor's, master's, doctoral, and first professional degrees. 2 undergraduate majors. Total enrollment: 1,372. Undergraduates: 28. Both federal and institutional methodology are used as a basis for awarding need-based institutional aid.

UNDERGRADUATE EXPENSES for 1999–2000 ***Application fee:*** $20. ***Tuition:*** full-time $12,903; part-time $359 per credit hour. Full-time tuition and fees vary according to program. Part-time tuition and fees vary according to program. ***Payment plan:*** installment.

GIFT AID (NEED-BASED) ***Scholarships, grants, and awards:*** Federal Pell, FSEOG, state, private, college/university gift aid from institutional funds.

GIFT AID (NON-NEED-BASED) ***Tuition waivers:*** Full or partial for employees or children of employees.

LOANS ***Programs:*** FFEL (Subsidized and Unsubsidized Stafford, PLUS), Perkins, state, college/university.

APPLYING for FINANCIAL AID ***Required financial aid forms:*** FAFSA, institution's own form. ***Financial aid deadline:*** 1/15. ***Notification date:*** Continuous beginning 7/1. Students must reply within 2 weeks of notification.

CONTACT Ms. Maryann DeCaire, Director of Financial Aid, Finch University of Health Sciences/The Chicago Medical School, 3333 Green Bay Road, North Chicago, IL 60064-3095, 847-578-3217. *Fax:* 847-578-3284.

FINLANDIA UNIVERSITY

Hancock, MI

Tuition & fees: $12,260 **Average undergraduate aid package: N/A**

ABOUT THE INSTITUTION Independent religious, coed. Awards: associate and bachelor's degrees. 14 undergraduate majors. Total enrollment: 363. Undergraduates: 363. Freshmen: 107. Federal methodology is used as a basis for awarding need-based institutional aid.

UNDERGRADUATE EXPENSES for 2000–2001 ***Application fee:*** $20. ***Comprehensive fee:*** $16,600 includes full-time tuition ($11,700), mandatory fees ($560), and room and board ($4340). ***College room only:*** $2340. ***Part-time tuition:*** $390 per credit. ***Part-time fees:*** $560 per year. Part-time tuition and fees vary according to course load. ***Payment plan:*** installment.

FRESHMAN FINANCIAL AID (Fall 1999, est.) 2% of all full-time freshmen had no need and received non-need-based aid.

UNDERGRADUATE FINANCIAL AID (Fall 1999, est.) 2% of all full-time undergraduates had no need and received non-need-based aid.

GIFT AID (NEED-BASED) ***Total amount:*** $1,741,937 (62% Federal, 36% state, 2% external sources). ***Scholarships, grants, and awards:*** Federal Pell, FSEOG, state, private, college/university gift aid from institutional funds.

GIFT AID (NON-NEED-BASED) ***Total amount:*** $324,888 (15% state, 85% institutional). ***Scholarships, grants, and awards by category:*** *Academic Interests/Achievement:* general academic interests/achievements. *Creative Arts/Performance:* art/fine arts, general creative arts/performance. *Special Achievements/Activities:* community service, general special achievements/activities, leadership, religious involvement. *Special Characteristics:* children of faculty/staff, first-generation college students, religious affiliation. ***Tuition waivers:*** Full or partial for employees or children of employees. ***ROTC:*** Army cooperative, Air Force cooperative.

LOANS ***Student loans:*** $1,436,069 (76% need-based, 24% non-need-based). 90% of past graduating class borrowed through all loan programs. ***Parent loans:*** $78,189 (100% need-based). ***Programs:*** FFEL (Subsidized and Unsubsidized Stafford, PLUS), Perkins, MI-Loan Program.

WORK-STUDY ***Federal work-study:*** *Total amount:* $145,055; jobs available. ***State or other work-study/employment:*** *Total amount:* $75,500 (98% need-based, 2% non-need-based). Part-time jobs available.

APPLYING for FINANCIAL AID ***Required financial aid forms:*** FAFSA, institution's own form. ***Financial aid deadline:*** 5/1 (priority: 2/15). ***Notification date:*** Continuous. Students must reply within 3 weeks of notification.

CONTACT Mary Ellen Hyttinen, Director of Financial Aid, Finlandia University, 601 Quincy Street, Hancock, MI 49930, 906-487-7240 or toll-free 800-682-7604. *Fax:* 906-487-7509. *E-mail:* finaid@ccisd.k12.mi.us

FISK UNIVERSITY

Nashville, TN

Tuition & fees: $8770 **Average undergraduate aid package: $12,500**

ABOUT THE INSTITUTION Independent religious, coed. Awards: bachelor's and master's degrees. 25 undergraduate majors. Total enrollment: 886. Undergraduates: 812. Freshmen: 262. Federal methodology is used as a basis for awarding need-based institutional aid.

UNDERGRADUATE EXPENSES for 1999–2000 ***Application fee:*** $25. ***Comprehensive fee:*** $13,700 includes full-time tuition ($8480), mandatory fees ($290), and room and board ($4930). ***Part-time tuition:*** $353 per credit hour. ***Part-time fees:*** $145 per term part-time. ***Payment plan:*** installment.

FRESHMAN FINANCIAL AID (Fall 1999, est.) 223 applied for aid; of those 95% were deemed to have need. 100% of freshmen with need received aid; of those 55% had need fully met. *Average percent of need met:* 75% (excluding resources awarded to replace EFC). *Average financial aid package:* $12,500 (excluding resources awarded to replace EFC). 10% of all full-time freshmen had no need and received non-need-based aid.

UNDERGRADUATE FINANCIAL AID (Fall 1999, est.) 754 applied for aid; of those 95% were deemed to have need. 100% of undergraduates with need received aid; of those 57% had need fully met. *Average percent of need met:* 75% (excluding resources awarded to replace EFC). *Average financial aid package:* $12,500 (excluding resources awarded to replace EFC). 9% of all full-time undergraduates had no need and received non-need-based aid.

GIFT AID (NEED-BASED) ***Total amount:*** $1,511,000 (81% Federal, 8% state, 11% external sources). ***Receiving aid:*** *Freshmen:* 58% (136); *all full-time undergraduates:* 63% (502). ***Average award:*** Freshmen: $3200; Undergraduates: $2000. ***Scholarships, grants, and awards:*** Federal Pell, FSEOG, state, private, college/university gift aid from institutional funds, United Negro College Fund.

GIFT AID (NON-NEED-BASED) ***Total amount:*** $1,894,649 (91% institutional, 9% external sources). ***Receiving aid:*** *Freshmen:* 42% (98); *Undergraduates:* 20% (155). ***Scholarships, grants, and awards by category:*** *Academic Interests/Achievement:* 137 awards ($749,199 total): general academic interests/achievements. *Special Characteristics:* 9 awards ($76,320 total): children of faculty/staff. ***Tuition waivers:*** Full or partial for employees or children of employees. ***ROTC:*** Army cooperative, Air Force cooperative.

LOANS ***Student loans:*** $4,488,000 (60% need-based, 40% non-need-based). 75% of past graduating class borrowed through all loan programs. Average indebtedness per student: $20,000. ***Average need-based loan:*** Freshmen: $2500; Undergraduates: $4000. ***Parent loans:*** $550,000 (100% need-based). ***Programs:*** Federal Direct (Subsidized and Unsubsidized Stafford, PLUS), Perkins.

WORK-STUDY ***Federal work-study:*** *Total amount:* $216,818; 190 jobs averaging $1150.

APPLYING for FINANCIAL AID ***Required financial aid form:*** FAFSA. ***Financial aid deadline (priority):*** 2/15. ***Notification date:*** Continuous beginning 4/15. Students must reply within 2 weeks of notification.

CONTACT Mark W. Adkins, Director of Financial Aid, Fisk University, 1000 17th Avenue North, Nashville, TN 37208-3051, 615-329-8585 or toll-free 800-443-FISK. *Fax:* 615-329-8774. *E-mail:* madkins@dubois.fisk.edu

FITCHBURG STATE COLLEGE

Fitchburg, MA

Tuition & fees (MA res): $3018 **Average undergraduate aid package: N/A**

ABOUT THE INSTITUTION State-supported, coed. Awards: bachelor's and master's degrees and post-master's certificates. 44 undergraduate majors. Total enrollment: 5,557. Undergraduates: 3,352. Freshmen: 401. Federal methodology is used as a basis for awarding need-based institutional aid.

UNDERGRADUATE EXPENSES for 1999–2000 ***Application fee:*** $10. ***Tuition, state resident:*** full-time $1090; part-time $45 per semester hour. ***Tuition, nonresident:*** full-time $7050; part-time $294 per semester hour. ***Required fees:*** full-time $1928; $80 per semester hour. Full-time tuition and fees vary according to class time, course load, and reciprocity agreements. Part-time tuition and fees vary according to class time, course load, and reciprocity agreements. ***College room and board:*** $4540. Room and board charges vary according to board plan and housing facility. ***Payment plan:*** installment.

GIFT AID (NEED-BASED) ***Total amount:*** $3,065,662 (52% Federal, 44% state, 4% institutional). ***Scholarships, grants, and awards:*** Federal Pell, FSEOG, state, private, college/university gift aid from institutional funds.

GIFT AID (NON-NEED-BASED) ***Total amount:*** $576,164 (57% institutional, 43% external sources). ***Scholarships, grants, and awards by category:*** *Academic Interests/Achievement:* biological sciences, business, communication, computer science, education, English, general academic interests/achievements, health fields, mathematics, social sciences. *Creative Arts/Performance:* performing arts. *Special Achievements/Activities:* general special achievements/activities, leadership. *Special Characteristics:* children and siblings of alumni. ***Tuition waivers:*** Full or partial for employees or children of employees, senior citizens.

LOANS ***Student loans:*** $6,256,025 (66% need-based, 34% non-need-based). ***Parent loans:*** $261,557 (100% non-need-based). ***Programs:*** Federal Direct (Subsidized and Unsubsidized Stafford, PLUS), Perkins, Federal Nursing, state.

WORK-STUDY ***Federal work-study:*** *Total amount:* $297,329; 336 jobs averaging $885. ***State or other work-study/employment:*** *Total amount:* $557,961 (100% non-need-based). Part-time jobs available.

APPLYING for FINANCIAL AID ***Required financial aid forms:*** FAFSA, institution's own form. ***Financial aid deadline (priority):*** 3/1. ***Notification date:*** Continuous beginning 4/1. Students must reply within 2 weeks of notification.

CONTACT Pamela McCafferty, Director of Financial Aid, Fitchburg State College, 160 Pearl Street, Fitchburg, MA 01420-2697, 978-665-3156 or toll-free 800-705-9692. *Fax:* 978-665-3559. *E-mail:* finaid@fsc.edu

FIVE TOWNS COLLEGE

Dix Hills, NY

Tuition & fees: $9620 **Average undergraduate aid package: $4500**

Five Towns College (continued)

ABOUT THE INSTITUTION Independent, coed. Awards: associate, bachelor's, and master's degrees. 19 undergraduate majors. Total enrollment: 848. Undergraduates: 803. Freshmen: 271. Federal methodology is used as a basis for awarding need-based institutional aid.

UNDERGRADUATE EXPENSES for 2000–2001 ***Application fee:*** $25. ***Tuition:*** full-time $9300; part-time $390 per credit. ***Required fees:*** full-time $320; $70 per term. Room and board charges vary according to board plan. ***Payment plans:*** installment, deferred payment.

FRESHMAN FINANCIAL AID (Fall 1998) 234 applied for aid; of those 98% were deemed to have need. 100% of freshmen with need received aid; of those 13% had need fully met. *Average percent of need met:* 45% (excluding resources awarded to replace EFC). *Average financial aid package:* $4000 (excluding resources awarded to replace EFC). 4% of all full-time freshmen had no need and received non-need-based aid.

UNDERGRADUATE FINANCIAL AID (Fall 1998) 610 applied for aid; of those 99% were deemed to have need. 100% of undergraduates with need received aid; of those 9% had need fully met. *Average percent of need met:* 50% (excluding resources awarded to replace EFC). *Average financial aid package:* $4500 (excluding resources awarded to replace EFC). 3% of all full-time undergraduates had no need and received non-need-based aid.

GIFT AID (NEED-BASED) ***Total amount:*** $2,077,455 (34% Federal, 51% state, 15% institutional). ***Receiving aid:*** *Freshmen:* 64% (168); *all full-time undergraduates:* 64% (450). ***Average award:*** Freshmen: $1500; Undergraduates: $1500. ***Scholarships, grants, and awards:*** Federal Pell, FSEOG, state, private, college/university gift aid from institutional funds.

GIFT AID (NON-NEED-BASED) ***Total amount:*** $110,866 (3% state, 92% institutional, 5% external sources). ***Receiving aid:*** *Freshmen:* 23% (62); *Undergraduates:* 23% (164). ***Scholarships, grants, and awards by category:*** *Academic Interests/Achievement:* 56 awards ($48,600 total): business, education, general academic interests/achievements. *Creative Arts/Performance:* 108 awards ($238,000 total): cinema/film/broadcasting, music, theater/drama. ***Tuition waivers:*** Full or partial for employees or children of employees, senior citizens.

LOANS ***Student loans:*** $1,324,145 (99% need-based, 1% non-need-based). 72% of past graduating class borrowed through all loan programs. Average indebtedness per student: $9000. ***Average need-based loan:*** Freshmen: $2625; Undergraduates: $4200. ***Parent loans:*** $1,410,208 (100% need-based). ***Programs:*** Federal Direct (Subsidized and Unsubsidized Stafford, PLUS).

WORK-STUDY ***Federal work-study:*** *Total amount:* $37,307; 44 jobs averaging $848.

APPLYING for FINANCIAL AID ***Required financial aid forms:*** FAFSA, institution's own form, state aid form. ***Financial aid deadline (priority):*** 4/30. ***Notification date:*** Continuous beginning 5/1.

CONTACT Ms. Mary Venezia, Financial Aid Administrator, Five Towns College, 305 North Service Road, Dix Hills, NY 11746-6055, 516-424-7000. *Fax:* 516-424-7006. *E-mail:* financialaid@ftc.edu

FLAGLER COLLEGE

St. Augustine, FL

Tuition & fees: $6130 **Average undergraduate aid package: $6743**

ABOUT THE INSTITUTION Independent, coed. Awards: bachelor's degrees. 23 undergraduate majors. Total enrollment: 1,736. Undergraduates: 1,736. Freshmen: 424. Federal methodology is used as a basis for awarding need-based institutional aid.

UNDERGRADUATE EXPENSES for 1999–2000 ***Application fee:*** $20. ***Comprehensive fee:*** $9930 includes full-time tuition ($6130) and room and board ($3800). ***Part-time tuition:*** $250 per credit hour.

FRESHMAN FINANCIAL AID (Fall 1999, est.) 373 applied for aid; of those 45% were deemed to have need. 98% of freshmen with need received aid; of those 15% had need fully met. *Average percent of need met:* 71% (excluding resources awarded to replace EFC). *Average financial aid package:* $6271 (excluding resources awarded to replace EFC). 46% of all full-time freshmen had no need and received non-need-based aid.

UNDERGRADUATE FINANCIAL AID (Fall 1999, est.) 1,468 applied for aid; of those 48% were deemed to have need. 99% of undergraduates with need received aid; of those 25% had need fully met. *Average percent of need met:* 74% (excluding resources awarded to replace EFC). *Average financial aid package:* $6743 (excluding resources awarded to replace EFC). 42% of all full-time undergraduates had no need and received non-need-based aid.

GIFT AID (NEED-BASED) ***Total amount:*** $2,437,000 (29% Federal, 62% state, 5% institutional, 4% external sources). ***Receiving aid:*** *Freshmen:* 25% (105); *all full-time undergraduates:* 26% (450). ***Average award:*** Freshmen: $2051; Undergraduates: $2156. ***Scholarships, grants, and awards:*** Federal Pell, FSEOG, state, private, college/university gift aid from institutional funds.

GIFT AID (NON-NEED-BASED) ***Total amount:*** $2,017,000 (82% state, 12% institutional, 6% external sources). ***Receiving aid:*** *Freshmen:* 30% (124); *Undergraduates:* 28% (482). ***Scholarships, grants, and awards by category:*** *Academic Interests/Achievement:* 80 awards ($220,000 total): business, communication, education, foreign languages, general academic interests/achievements, social sciences. *Special Achievements/Activities:* 5 awards ($4000 total): religious involvement. *Special Characteristics:* 10 awards ($27,000 total): children of faculty/staff, members of minority groups. ***Tuition waivers:*** Full or partial for employees or children of employees.

LOANS ***Student loans:*** $3,850,000 (74% need-based, 26% non-need-based). 60% of past graduating class borrowed through all loan programs. Average indebtedness per student: $13,763. ***Average need-based loan:*** Freshmen: $2423; Undergraduates: $3526. ***Parent loans:*** $535,000 (56% need-based, 44% non-need-based). ***Programs:*** Federal Direct (Subsidized and Unsubsidized Stafford, PLUS), Perkins.

WORK-STUDY ***Federal work-study:*** *Total amount:* $130,000; 230 jobs averaging $565. ***State or other work-study/employment:*** *Total amount:* $37,000 (32% need-based, 68% non-need-based). 80 part-time jobs averaging $462.

ATHLETIC AWARDS *Total amount:* 285,000 (22% need-based, 78% non-need-based).

APPLYING for FINANCIAL AID ***Required financial aid forms:*** FAFSA, institution's own form. ***Financial aid deadline:*** Continuous. ***Notification date:*** Continuous beginning 3/1. Students must reply within 2 weeks of notification.

CONTACT Mr. Chris Haffner, Assistant Director of Financial Aid, Flagler College, PO Box 1027, St. Augustine, FL 32085-1027, 904-829-6481 Ext. 225 or toll-free 800-304-4208. *Fax:* 904-826-0094.

FLORIDA AGRICULTURAL AND MECHANICAL UNIVERSITY

Tallahassee, FL

Tuition & fees (FL res): $2187 **Average undergraduate aid package: N/A**

ABOUT THE INSTITUTION State-supported, coed. Awards: associate, bachelor's, master's, doctoral, and first professional degrees. 71 undergraduate majors. Total enrollment: 12,082. Undergraduates: 10,691. Freshmen: 2,282. Federal methodology is used as a basis for awarding need-based institutional aid.

UNDERGRADUATE EXPENSES for 1999–2000 ***Application fee:*** $20. ***Tuition, state resident:*** full-time $2073; part-time $74 per semester hour. ***Tuition, nonresident:*** full-time $8596; part-time $307 per semester hour. ***Required fees:*** full-time $114. Full-time tuition and fees vary according to course load. Part-time tuition and fees vary according to course load. ***College room and board:*** $3942; ***room only:*** $2460. Room and board charges vary according to board plan and housing facility. ***Payment plans:*** tuition prepayment, deferred payment.

GIFT AID (NEED-BASED) ***Scholarships, grants, and awards:*** Federal Pell, FSEOG, state, private, college/university gift aid from institutional funds.

GIFT AID (NON-NEED-BASED) ***Scholarships, grants, and awards by category:*** *Academic Interests/Achievement:* agriculture, business, engineering/ technologies, general academic interests/achievements, health fields. *Creative Arts/Performance:* art/fine arts, general creative arts/performance, journalism/publications, music, theater/drama. *Special Achievements/ Activities:* general special achievements/activities. *Special Characteristics:* children with a deceased or disabled parent, ethnic background, general special characteristics, veterans' children. ***Tuition waivers:*** Full or partial for employees or children of employees, senior citizens. ***ROTC:*** Army, Naval, Air Force cooperative.

LOANS ***Programs:*** Federal Direct (Subsidized and Unsubsidized Stafford, PLUS), Perkins.

WORK-STUDY Federal work-study jobs available.

APPLYING for FINANCIAL AID ***Required financial aid form:*** FAFSA. ***Financial aid deadline (priority):*** 3/1. ***Notification date:*** Continuous.

CONTACT Saundra Inge, Acting Director of Student Financial Aid, Florida Agricultural and Mechanical University, Tallahassee, FL 32307-3200, 850-599-3730. *Fax:* 850-561-2730.

FLORIDA ATLANTIC UNIVERSITY

Boca Raton, FL

Tuition & fees (FL res): $2253 **Average undergraduate aid package: $5992**

ABOUT THE INSTITUTION State-supported, coed. Awards: associate, bachelor's, master's, and doctoral degrees. 59 undergraduate majors. Total enrollment: 20,126. Undergraduates: 16,470. Freshmen: 1,547. Federal methodology is used as a basis for awarding need-based institutional aid.

UNDERGRADUATE EXPENSES for 1999–2000 ***Application fee:*** $20. ***One-time required fee:*** $10. ***Tuition, state resident:*** full-time $2253; part-time $75 per semester hour. ***Tuition, nonresident:*** full-time $9242; part-time $308 per semester hour. Full-time tuition and fees vary according to course load. Part-time tuition and fees vary according to course load. ***College room and board:*** $4774; ***room only:*** $2721. Room and board charges vary according to board plan and housing facility. ***Payment plans:*** installment, deferred payment.

FRESHMAN FINANCIAL AID (Fall 1999, est.) 1029 applied for aid; of those 81% were deemed to have need. 98% of freshmen with need received aid; of those 15% had need fully met. *Average percent of need met:* 65% (excluding resources awarded to replace EFC). *Average financial aid package:* $5311 (excluding resources awarded to replace EFC). 5% of all full-time freshmen had no need and received non-need-based aid.

UNDERGRADUATE FINANCIAL AID (Fall 1999, est.) 3,825 applied for aid; of those 87% were deemed to have need. 98% of undergraduates with need received aid; of those 20% had need fully met. *Average percent of need met:* 66% (excluding resources awarded to replace EFC). *Average financial aid package:* $5992 (excluding resources awarded to replace EFC). 4% of all full-time undergraduates had no need and received non-need-based aid.

GIFT AID (NEED-BASED) ***Total amount:*** $16,100,290 (43% Federal, 26% state, 28% institutional, 3% external sources). ***Receiving aid:*** *Freshmen:* 33% (719); *all full-time undergraduates:* 35% (2,778). ***Average award:*** Freshmen: $3806; Undergraduates: $3553. ***Scholarships, grants, and awards:*** Federal Pell, FSEOG, state, private, college/university gift aid from institutional funds.

GIFT AID (NON-NEED-BASED) ***Scholarships, grants, and awards by category:*** *Academic Interests/Achievement:* business, engineering/ technologies, general academic interests/achievements, physical sciences, social sciences. ***Tuition waivers:*** Full or partial for employees or children of employees. ***ROTC:*** Army cooperative, Air Force cooperative.

LOANS ***Student loans:*** $19,009,565 (72% need-based, 28% non-need-based). ***Average need-based loan:*** Freshmen: $2442; Undergraduates: $4006. ***Parent loans:*** $1,087,466 (100% non-need-based). ***Programs:*** FFEL (Subsidized and Unsubsidized Stafford, PLUS), Perkins, college/ university.

WORK-STUDY ***Federal work-study:*** *Total amount:* $421,232; 170 jobs averaging $2477. ***State or other work-study/employment:*** *Total amount:* $860,300 (1% need-based, 99% non-need-based). 480 part-time jobs available.

ATHLETIC AWARDS *Total amount:* 645,925 (100% need-based).

APPLYING for FINANCIAL AID ***Required financial aid forms:*** FAFSA, financial aid transcript (for transfers). ***Financial aid deadline (priority):*** 3/1. ***Notification date:*** Continuous beginning 5/1. Students must reply within 2 weeks of notification.

CONTACT Director, Student Financial Aid, Florida Atlantic University, 777 Glades Road, Boca Raton, FL 33431-0991, 561-297-3000 or toll-free 800-299-4FAU.

FLORIDA BAPTIST THEOLOGICAL COLLEGE

Graceville, FL

Tuition & fees: $3960 **Average undergraduate aid package: $3000**

ABOUT THE INSTITUTION Independent Southern Baptist, coed. Awards: associate and bachelor's degrees. 10 undergraduate majors. Total enrollment: 510. Undergraduates: 510. Freshmen: 48. Federal methodology is used as a basis for awarding need-based institutional aid.

UNDERGRADUATE EXPENSES for 1999–2000 ***Application fee:*** $20. ***Comprehensive fee:*** $7110 includes full-time tuition ($3760), mandatory fees ($200), and room and board ($3150). Room and board charges vary according to board plan and housing facility. ***Part-time tuition:*** $120 per semester hour. ***Part-time fees:*** $100 per term part-time. ***Payment plan:*** deferred payment.

FRESHMAN FINANCIAL AID (Fall 1998) 50 applied for aid; of those 90% were deemed to have need. 96% of freshmen with need received aid; of those 47% had need fully met. *Average percent of need met:* 60% (excluding resources awarded to replace EFC). *Average financial aid package:* $2000 (excluding resources awarded to replace EFC). 20% of all full-time freshmen had no need and received non-need-based aid.

UNDERGRADUATE FINANCIAL AID (Fall 1998) 540 applied for aid; of those 96% were deemed to have need. 99% of undergraduates with need received aid; of those 78% had need fully met. *Average percent of need met:* 63% (excluding resources awarded to replace EFC). *Average financial aid package:* $3000 (excluding resources awarded to replace EFC). 13% of all full-time undergraduates had no need and received non-need-based aid.

GIFT AID (NEED-BASED) ***Total amount:*** $1,359,343 (51% Federal, 9% state, 28% institutional, 12% external sources). ***Scholarships, grants, and awards:*** Federal Pell, FSEOG, state, college/university gift aid from institutional funds.

GIFT AID (NON-NEED-BASED) ***Total amount:*** $41,673 (100% state). ***Receiving aid:*** *Freshmen:* 68% (38); *Undergraduates:* 18% (116). ***Scholarships, grants, and awards by category:*** *Academic Interests/Achievement:* religion/biblical studies. *Creative Arts/Performance:* music. *Special Characteristics:* religious affiliation. ***Tuition waivers:*** Full or partial for employees or children of employees.

LOANS ***Student loans:*** $620,756 (75% need-based, 25% non-need-based). Average indebtedness per student: $15,000. ***Average need-based loan:*** Freshmen: $2625; Undergraduates: $3500. ***Parent loans:*** $7861 (100% need-based). ***Programs:*** FFEL (Subsidized and Unsubsidized Stafford, PLUS), college/university.

WORK-STUDY ***Federal work-study:*** *Total amount:* $41,695; 23 jobs averaging $1600.

APPLYING for FINANCIAL AID ***Required financial aid forms:*** FAFSA, institution's own form. ***Financial aid deadline (priority):*** 4/1. ***Notification date:*** Continuous beginning 5/1. Students must reply within 3 weeks of notification.

CONTACT Angela Rathel, Director of Financial Aid, Florida Baptist Theological College, 5400 College Drive, Graceville, FL 32440-3306, 850-263-3261 Ext. 461 or toll-free 800-328-2660 Ext. 460. *Fax:* 850-263-7506. *E-mail:* finaid@fbtc.edu

FLORIDA CHRISTIAN COLLEGE

Kissimmee, FL

ABOUT THE INSTITUTION Independent religious, coed. Awards: associate and bachelor's degrees. 3 undergraduate majors. Total enrollment: 236. Undergraduates: 236. Freshmen: 45.

GIFT AID (NEED-BASED) ***Scholarships, grants, and awards:*** Federal Pell, FSEOG, state, private, college/university gift aid from institutional funds.

GIFT AID (NON-NEED-BASED) ***Scholarships, grants, and awards by category:*** *Academic Interests/Achievement:* religion/biblical studies. *Creative Arts/Performance:* music. *Special Characteristics:* children and siblings of alumni, children of faculty/staff, relatives of clergy, religious affiliation, spouses of current students.

LOANS ***Programs:*** FFEL (Subsidized and Unsubsidized Stafford, PLUS), college/university.

WORK-STUDY ***Federal work-study:*** *Total amount:* $30,165; 19 jobs averaging $700.

APPLYING for FINANCIAL AID ***Required financial aid forms:*** FAFSA, institution's own form.

CONTACT Ms. Sandra Peppard, Director of Student Financial Aid, Florida Christian College, 1011 Bill Beck Boulevard, Kissimmee, FL 34744-5301, 407-847-8966 Ext. 365. *Fax:* 407-847-3925. *E-mail:* sandi.peppard@fcc.edu

FLORIDA COLLEGE

Temple Terrace, FL

Tuition & fees: $7250 **Average undergraduate aid package: N/A**

ABOUT THE INSTITUTION Independent, coed. Awards: associate and bachelor's degrees. 3 undergraduate majors. Total enrollment: 530. Undergraduates: 530. Freshmen: 273. Both federal and institutional methodology are used as a basis for awarding need-based institutional aid.

UNDERGRADUATE EXPENSES for 1999–2000 ***Application fee:*** $25. ***Comprehensive fee:*** $12,790 includes full-time tuition ($7050), mandatory fees ($200), and room and board ($5540). ***College room only:*** $3200. Room and board charges vary according to housing facility. ***Part-time tuition:*** $315 per semester hour. ***Part-time fees:*** $75 per term part-time. ***Payment plan:*** installment.

GIFT AID (NEED-BASED) ***Scholarships, grants, and awards:*** Federal Pell, FSEOG, state, private, college/university gift aid from institutional funds.

GIFT AID (NON-NEED-BASED) ***Scholarships, grants, and awards by category:*** *Academic Interests/Achievement:* general academic interests/achievements. *Creative Arts/Performance:* debating, journalism/publications, music, theater/drama. *Special Characteristics:* children of educators, children of faculty/staff. ***Tuition waivers:*** Full or partial for employees or children of employees. ***ROTC:*** Army cooperative, Air Force cooperative.

LOANS ***Programs:*** FFEL (Subsidized and Unsubsidized Stafford, PLUS), Perkins.

APPLYING for FINANCIAL AID ***Required financial aid form:*** FAFSA. ***Financial aid deadline:*** 8/1 (priority: 4/1). ***Notification date:*** Continuous. Students must reply within 2 weeks of notification.

CONTACT Jessica Fannin, Financial Aid Officer, Florida College, 119 North Glen Arven Avenue, Temple Terrace, FL 33617-5578, 813-899-6774 or toll-free 800-326-7655.

FLORIDA GULF COAST UNIVERSITY

Fort Myers, FL

Tuition & fees (FL res): $2319 **Average undergraduate aid package: $6451**

ABOUT THE INSTITUTION State-supported, coed. Awards: bachelor's and master's degrees. 28 undergraduate majors. Total enrollment: 3,282. Undergraduates: 2,649. Freshmen: 263. Federal methodology is used as a basis for awarding need-based institutional aid.

UNDERGRADUATE EXPENSES for 1999–2000 ***Application fee:*** $20. ***One-time required fee:*** $10. ***Tuition, state resident:*** full-time $1990; part-time $66 per credit. ***Tuition, nonresident:*** full-time $8979; part-time $299 per credit. ***Required fees:*** full-time $329; $66 per credit. Full-time tuition and fees vary according to course load. Part-time tuition and fees vary according to course load. ***College room and board:*** $5326; ***room only:*** $3208. Room and board charges vary according to board plan.

FRESHMAN FINANCIAL AID (Fall 1998) 181 applied for aid; of those 45% were deemed to have need. 95% of freshmen with need received aid; of those 27% had need fully met. *Average percent of need met:* 79% (excluding resources awarded to replace EFC). *Average financial aid package:* $4833 (excluding resources awarded to replace EFC). 44% of all full-time freshmen had no need and received non-need-based aid.

UNDERGRADUATE FINANCIAL AID (Fall 1998) 816 applied for aid; of those 69% were deemed to have need. 97% of undergraduates with need received aid; of those 45% had need fully met. *Average percent of need met:* 88% (excluding resources awarded to replace EFC). *Average financial aid package:* $6451 (excluding resources awarded to replace EFC). 22% of all full-time undergraduates had no need and received non-need-based aid.

GIFT AID (NEED-BASED) ***Total amount:*** $1,696,619 (65% Federal, 9% state, 26% institutional). ***Receiving aid:*** *Freshmen:* 28% (64); *all full-time undergraduates:* 38% (431). ***Scholarships, grants, and awards:*** Federal Pell, FSEOG, state, private, college/university gift aid from institutional funds.

GIFT AID (NON-NEED-BASED) ***Total amount:*** $807,391 (48% state, 36% institutional, 16% external sources). ***Receiving aid:*** *Freshmen:* 17% (39); *Undergraduates:* 13% (147). ***Scholarships, grants, and awards by category:*** *Academic Interests/Achievement:* biological sciences, business, education, general academic interests/achievements, humanities, social sciences. *Creative Arts/Performance:* general creative arts/performance. *Special Achievements/Activities:* community service, general special achievements/activities, leadership, memberships. ***Tuition waivers:*** Full or partial for employees or children of employees, senior citizens.

LOANS ***Student loans:*** $4,743,810 (61% need-based, 39% non-need-based). ***Parent loans:*** $38,670 (100% non-need-based). ***Programs:*** FFEL (Subsidized and Unsubsidized Stafford, PLUS).

WORK-STUDY ***Federal work-study:*** *Total amount:* $1500; jobs available. ***State or other work-study/employment:*** *Total amount:* $97,519 (100% non-need-based). Part-time jobs available.

APPLYING for FINANCIAL AID ***Required financial aid form:*** FAFSA. ***Financial aid deadline (priority):*** 5/1. ***Notification date:*** Continuous. Students must reply within 2 weeks of notification.

CONTACT Venita Jones, Director, Student Financial Aid and Scholarships, Florida Gulf Coast University, 10501 FGCU Boulevard S, Fort Myers, FL 33965, 941-590-7920 or toll-free 800-590-3428. *Fax:* 941-590-7903. *E-mail:* faso@fgcu.edu

FLORIDA INSTITUTE OF TECHNOLOGY

Melbourne, FL

Tuition & fees: $17,300 **Average undergraduate aid package: $16,462**

ABOUT THE INSTITUTION Independent, coed. Awards: associate, bachelor's, master's, and doctoral degrees and post-bachelor's certificates. 35 undergraduate majors. Total enrollment: 4,178. Undergraduates: 1,933. Freshmen: 395. Federal methodology is used as a basis for awarding need-based institutional aid.

UNDERGRADUATE EXPENSES for 1999–2000 ***Application fee:*** $35. ***One-time required fee:*** $200. ***Comprehensive fee:*** $22,570 includes full-time tuition ($17,300) and room and board ($5270). ***College room only:*** $2270. Full-time tuition and fees vary according to program. Room and board charges vary according to board plan. ***Part-time tuition:*** $525 per credit hour. Part-time tuition and fees vary according to program. ***Payment plan:*** installment.

FRESHMAN FINANCIAL AID (Fall 1999) 344 applied for aid; of those 80% were deemed to have need. 100% of freshmen with need received aid; of those 20% had need fully met. *Average percent of need met:* 81% (exclud-

ing resources awarded to replace EFC). *Average financial aid package:* $16,621 (excluding resources awarded to replace EFC). 17% of all full-time freshmen had no need and received non-need-based aid.

UNDERGRADUATE FINANCIAL AID (Fall 1999) 1,382 applied for aid; of those 70% were deemed to have need. 99% of undergraduates with need received aid; of those 23% had need fully met. *Average percent of need met:* 80% (excluding resources awarded to replace EFC). *Average financial aid package:* $16,462 (excluding resources awarded to replace EFC). 22% of all full-time undergraduates had no need and received non-need-based aid.

GIFT AID (NEED-BASED) ***Total amount:*** $9,566,704 (17% Federal, 15% state, 66% institutional, 2% external sources). ***Receiving aid:*** *Freshmen:* 71% (275); *all full-time undergraduates:* 54% (956). ***Average award:*** Freshmen: $11,372; Undergraduates: $10,540. ***Scholarships, grants, and awards:*** Federal Pell, FSEOG, state, private, college/university gift aid from institutional funds.

GIFT AID (NON-NEED-BASED) ***Total amount:*** $3,134,616 (19% Federal, 11% state, 68% institutional, 2% external sources). ***Receiving aid:*** *Freshmen:* 60% (231); *Undergraduates:* 37% (666). ***Scholarships, grants, and awards by category:*** *Academic Interests/Achievement:* 1,073 awards ($5,055,197 total): biological sciences, business, communication, computer science, education, engineering/technologies, general academic interests/achievements, humanities, mathematics, military science, physical sciences, premedicine. *Special Characteristics:* 281 awards ($1,057,900 total): children and siblings of alumni, children of faculty/staff, local/state students. ***Tuition waivers:*** Full or partial for employees or children of employees, senior citizens. ***ROTC:*** Army.

LOANS ***Student loans:*** $6,759,198 (89% need-based, 11% non-need-based). 63% of past graduating class borrowed through all loan programs. Average indebtedness per student: $24,265. ***Average need-based loan:*** Freshmen: $3832; Undergraduates: $5074. ***Parent loans:*** $1,108,215 (88% need-based, 12% non-need-based). ***Programs:*** FFEL (Subsidized and Unsubsidized Stafford, PLUS), Perkins, college/university, alternative loans.

WORK-STUDY ***Federal work-study:*** *Total amount:* $834,100; 569 jobs averaging $1466.

ATHLETIC AWARDS *Total amount:* 635,807 (56% need-based, 44% non-need-based).

APPLYING for FINANCIAL AID ***Required financial aid form:*** FAFSA. ***Financial aid deadline (priority):*** 3/15. ***Notification date:*** Continuous. Students must reply by 5/1 or within 4 weeks of notification.

CONTACT Karen Lane, Financial Aid Office Manager, Florida Institute of Technology, 150 West University Boulevard, Melbourne, FL 32901-6975, 321-674-8070 or toll-free 800-348-4636 (in-state), 800-888-4348 (out-of-state). *Fax:* 321-724-2778. *E-mail:* klane@fit.edu

FLORIDA INTERNATIONAL UNIVERSITY

Miami, FL

Tuition & fees (FL res): $2326 **Average undergraduate aid package: N/A**

ABOUT THE INSTITUTION State-supported, coed. Awards: bachelor's, master's, and doctoral degrees. 79 undergraduate majors. Total enrollment: 31,293. Undergraduates: 25,709. Freshmen: 2,551. Federal methodology is used as a basis for awarding need-based institutional aid.

UNDERGRADUATE EXPENSES for 1999–2000 ***Application fee:*** $20. ***One-time required fee:*** $10. ***Tuition, state resident:*** full-time $2164; part-time $72 per credit hour. ***Tuition, nonresident:*** full-time $9153; part-time $305 per credit hour. ***Required fees:*** full-time $162; $81 per term part-time. Full-time tuition and fees vary according to course load. ***College room and board:*** $5206; ***room only:*** $3176. Room and board charges vary according to board plan and housing facility. ***Payment plan:*** tuition prepayment.

FRESHMAN FINANCIAL AID (Fall 1998) 1774 applied for aid; of those 83% were deemed to have need. 97% of freshmen with need received aid; of those 9% had need fully met.

UNDERGRADUATE FINANCIAL AID (Fall 1998) 8,386 applied for aid; of those 89% were deemed to have need. 93% of undergraduates with need received aid; of those 9% had need fully met.

GIFT AID (NEED-BASED) ***Total amount:*** $21,561,174 (62% Federal, 9% state, 28% institutional, 1% external sources). ***Receiving aid:*** *Freshmen:* 62% (1,238); *all full-time undergraduates:* 47% (6,172). ***Scholarships, grants, and awards:*** Federal Pell, FSEOG, state, private, college/university gift aid from institutional funds.

GIFT AID (NON-NEED-BASED) ***Total amount:*** $7,407,783 (3% Federal, 41% state, 14% institutional, 42% external sources). ***Receiving aid:*** *Freshmen:* 31% (624); *Undergraduates:* 13% (1,670). ***Scholarships, grants, and awards by category:*** *Academic Interests/Achievement:* architecture, biological sciences, business, communication, computer science, education, engineering/technologies, English, foreign languages, general academic interests/achievements, health fields, humanities, mathematics, physical sciences, social sciences. *Creative Arts/Performance:* dance, music, performing arts, theater/drama. *Special Characteristics:* 6,731 awards: members of minority groups. ***Tuition waivers:*** Full or partial for employees or children of employees, senior citizens. ***ROTC:*** Army, Air Force.

LOANS ***Student loans:*** $35,087,905 (79% need-based, 21% non-need-based). ***Parent loans:*** $556,312 (100% non-need-based). ***Programs:*** FFEL (Subsidized and Unsubsidized Stafford, PLUS), Perkins, college/university.

WORK-STUDY ***Federal work-study:*** *Total amount:* $645,114; 373 jobs averaging $1730. ***State or other work-study/employment:*** *Total amount:* $12,227 (100% need-based). 17 part-time jobs averaging $720.

ATHLETIC AWARDS *Total amount:* 1,131,659 (100% non-need-based).

APPLYING for FINANCIAL AID ***Required financial aid form:*** FAFSA. ***Financial aid deadline (priority):*** 3/1. ***Notification date:*** Continuous beginning 4/15.

CONTACT James C. McMillan, Associate Director, Financial Aid, Florida International University, University Park PC 125, Miami, FL 33199, 305-348-2489. *Fax:* 305-348-2346. *E-mail:* mcmillan@fiu.edu

FLORIDA MEMORIAL COLLEGE

Miami-Dade, FL

Tuition & fees: $7232 **Average undergraduate aid package: $11,300**

ABOUT THE INSTITUTION Independent religious, coed. Awards: bachelor's degrees. 22 undergraduate majors. Federal methodology is used as a basis for awarding need-based institutional aid.

UNDERGRADUATE EXPENSES for 1999–2000 ***Application fee:*** $15. ***Comprehensive fee:*** $10,468 includes full-time tuition ($6202), mandatory fees ($1030), and room and board ($3236). ***College room only:*** $1726. ***Part-time tuition:*** $258 per credit hour. ***Part-time fees:*** $258 per term part-time.

FRESHMAN FINANCIAL AID (Fall 1999, est.) 490 applied for aid; of those 90% were deemed to have need. 100% of freshmen with need received aid; of those 60% had need fully met. *Average percent of need met:* 86% (excluding resources awarded to replace EFC). *Average financial aid package:* $11,000 (excluding resources awarded to replace EFC). 10% of all full-time freshmen had no need and received non-need-based aid.

UNDERGRADUATE FINANCIAL AID (Fall 1999, est.) 1,695 applied for aid; of those 90% were deemed to have need. 100% of undergraduates with need received aid; of those 60% had need fully met. *Average percent of need met:* 88% (excluding resources awarded to replace EFC). *Average financial aid package:* $11,300 (excluding resources awarded to replace EFC). 10% of all full-time undergraduates had no need and received non-need-based aid.

GIFT AID (NEED-BASED) ***Total amount:*** $5,804,127 (66% Federal, 8% state, 22% institutional, 4% external sources). ***Receiving aid:*** *Freshmen:* 65% (331); *all full-time undergraduates:* 64% (1,144). ***Average award:*** Freshmen: $7000; Undergraduates: $7125. ***Scholarships, grants, and awards:*** Federal Pell, FSEOG, state, private, college/university gift aid from institutional funds, United Negro College Fund.

GIFT AID (NON-NEED-BASED) ***Total amount:*** $1,957,856 (100% state). ***Receiving aid:*** *Freshmen:* 69% (353); *Undergraduates:* 68% (1,220). ***Scholarships, grants, and awards by category:*** *Academic Interests/Achievement:* biological sciences, business, communication, computer science, education, English, foreign languages, general academic interests/achievements, health fields, humanities, mathematics, premedicine, religion/

Florida Memorial College (continued)

biblical studies, social sciences. *Creative Arts/Performance:* general creative arts/performance. *Special Achievements/Activities:* community service, leadership. *Special Characteristics:* general special characteristics. ***ROTC:*** Army, Air Force cooperative.

LOANS ***Student loans:*** $7,214,656 (64% need-based, 36% non-need-based). 40% of past graduating class borrowed through all loan programs. Average indebtedness per student: $10,000. ***Average need-based loan:*** Freshmen: $2625; Undergraduates: $3500. ***Parent loans:*** $360,509 (100% non-need-based). ***Programs:*** Federal Direct (Subsidized and Unsubsidized Stafford, PLUS).

WORK-STUDY ***Federal work-study:*** *Total amount:* $328,990; jobs available.

ATHLETIC AWARDS *Total amount:* 185,056 (100% need-based).

APPLYING for FINANCIAL AID ***Required financial aid form:*** FAFSA. ***Financial aid deadline (priority):*** 4/1. ***Notification date:*** Continuous. Students must reply within 6 weeks of notification.

CONTACT Brian Phillip, Director of Financial Aid, Florida Memorial College, 15800 Northwest 42nd Avenue, Miami, FL 33054, 305-626-3742 or toll-free 800-822-1362. *Fax:* 305-626-3106.

FLORIDA METROPOLITAN UNIVERSITY–FORT LAUDERDALE COLLEGE

Fort Lauderdale, FL

Tuition & fees: $6555 **Average undergraduate aid package: $7230**

ABOUT THE INSTITUTION Proprietary, coed. Awards: associate, bachelor's, and master's degrees. 9 undergraduate majors. Total enrollment: 697. Undergraduates: 650. Federal methodology is used as a basis for awarding need-based institutional aid.

UNDERGRADUATE EXPENSES for 1999–2000 ***Application fee:*** $25. ***Tuition:*** full-time $6480; part-time $190 per quarter hour. ***Required fees:*** full-time $75; $25 per term part-time. Full-time tuition and fees vary according to course load. ***Payment plan:*** installment.

FRESHMAN FINANCIAL AID (Fall 1999, est.) 192 applied for aid; of those 100% were deemed to have need. 100% of freshmen with need received aid; of those 100% had need fully met. *Average percent of need met:* 85% (excluding resources awarded to replace EFC). *Average financial aid package:* $7230 (excluding resources awarded to replace EFC).

UNDERGRADUATE FINANCIAL AID (Fall 1999, est.) 540 applied for aid; of those 100% were deemed to have need. 100% of undergraduates with need received aid; of those 100% had need fully met. *Average percent of need met:* 85% (excluding resources awarded to replace EFC). *Average financial aid package:* $7230 (excluding resources awarded to replace EFC).

GIFT AID (NEED-BASED) ***Total amount:*** $887,740 (76% Federal, 17% state, 7% institutional). ***Scholarships, grants, and awards:*** Federal Pell, FSEOG, state.

GIFT AID (NON-NEED-BASED) ***Scholarships, grants, and awards by category:*** *Academic Interests/Achievement:* 18 awards ($65,590 total): business, computer science.

LOANS ***Student loans:*** $3,898,260 (100% need-based). 90% of past graduating class borrowed through all loan programs. Average indebtedness per student: $21,085. ***Average need-based loan:*** Freshmen: $3500; Undergraduates: $3500. ***Parent loans:*** $324,000 (100% need-based). ***Programs:*** FFEL (Subsidized and Unsubsidized Stafford, PLUS).

WORK-STUDY ***Federal work-study:*** *Total amount:* $22,000; 4 jobs averaging $5500.

APPLYING for FINANCIAL AID ***Required financial aid form:*** FAFSA. ***Financial aid deadline:*** Continuous. ***Notification date:*** Continuous.

CONTACT Director of Student Finance, Florida Metropolitan University–Fort Lauderdale College, 1040 Bayview Drive, Fort Lauderdale, FL 33304-2522, 954-568-1600 Ext. 52 or toll-free 800-468-0168.

FLORIDA METROPOLITAN UNIVERSITY–ORLANDO COLLEGE, MELBOURNE

Melbourne, FL

Tuition & fees: $6555 **Average undergraduate aid package: N/A**

ABOUT THE INSTITUTION Proprietary, coed. Awards: associate, bachelor's, and master's degrees. 7 undergraduate majors. Total enrollment: 586. Undergraduates: 551. Federal methodology is used as a basis for awarding need-based institutional aid.

UNDERGRADUATE EXPENSES for 1999–2000 ***Application fee:*** $25. ***Tuition:*** full-time $6480; part-time $190 per quarter hour. ***Required fees:*** full-time $75; $25 per term part-time. Full-time tuition and fees vary according to course load and program. Part-time tuition and fees vary according to course load. ***Payment plans:*** guaranteed tuition, tuition prepayment, installment, deferred payment.

GIFT AID (NEED-BASED) ***Scholarships, grants, and awards:*** Federal Pell, FSEOG, state, private, college/university gift aid from institutional funds.

GIFT AID (NON-NEED-BASED) ***Tuition waivers:*** Full or partial for employees or children of employees.

LOANS ***Programs:*** Federal Direct (Subsidized and Unsubsidized Stafford, PLUS), college/university.

WORK-STUDY Federal work-study jobs available.

APPLYING for FINANCIAL AID ***Required financial aid forms:*** FAFSA, institution's own form, CSS Financial Aid PROFILE. ***Financial aid deadline:*** Continuous. ***Notification date:*** Continuous.

CONTACT Financial Aid Office, Florida Metropolitan University–Orlando College, Melbourne, 2401 North Harbor City Boulevard, Melbourne, FL 32935-6657, 407-253-2929 Ext. 19.

FLORIDA METROPOLITAN UNIVERSITY–ORLANDO COLLEGE, NORTH

Orlando, FL

Tuition & fees: $6555 **Average undergraduate aid package: N/A**

ABOUT THE INSTITUTION Proprietary, coed. Awards: associate, bachelor's, and master's degrees. 11 undergraduate majors. Total enrollment: 675. Undergraduates: 619. Freshmen: 86. Federal methodology is used as a basis for awarding need-based institutional aid.

UNDERGRADUATE EXPENSES for 1999–2000 ***Application fee:*** $50. ***Tuition:*** full-time $6480; part-time $190 per quarter hour. ***Required fees:*** full-time $75; $25 per term part-time. Full-time tuition and fees vary according to course load and program.

GIFT AID (NEED-BASED) ***Scholarships, grants, and awards:*** Federal Pell, FSEOG.

GIFT AID (NON-NEED-BASED) ***Scholarships, grants, and awards by category:*** *Special Characteristics:* children of faculty/staff. ***Tuition waivers:*** Full or partial for employees or children of employees.

LOANS ***Programs:*** FFEL (Subsidized and Unsubsidized Stafford, PLUS), Perkins.

WORK-STUDY Federal work-study jobs available.

APPLYING for FINANCIAL AID ***Required financial aid form:*** FAFSA. ***Financial aid deadline:*** Continuous.

CONTACT Ms. Linda Kaisrlik, Director of Student Finance, Florida Metropolitan University–Orlando College, North, 5421 Diplomat Circle, Orlando, FL 32810-5674, 407-628-5870 or toll-free 800-628-5870.

FLORIDA METROPOLITAN UNIVERSITY–ORLANDO COLLEGE, SOUTH

Orlando, FL

Tuition & fees: $4395 **Average undergraduate aid package: N/A**

ABOUT THE INSTITUTION Proprietary, coed. Awards: associate, bachelor's, and master's degrees. Total enrollment: 1,025. Undergraduates: 975.

UNDERGRADUATE EXPENSES for 1999–2000 ***Application fee:*** $50. ***Tuition:*** full-time $4320; part-time $190 per credit. ***Required fees:*** full-time $75; $25 per term part-time. Full-time tuition and fees vary according to course load.

GIFT AID (NEED-BASED) ***Scholarships, grants, and awards:*** Federal Pell, FSEOG, state.

LOANS ***Programs:*** FFEL (Subsidized and Unsubsidized Stafford, PLUS).

WORK-STUDY Federal work-study jobs available.

APPLYING for FINANCIAL AID ***Required financial aid form:*** FAFSA. ***Financial aid deadline:*** Continuous.

CONTACT Sherri Williams, Director of Financial Aid, Florida Metropolitan University–Orlando College, South, 2411 Sand Lake Road, Orlando, FL 32809, 407-851-2525.

FLORIDA METROPOLITAN UNIVERSITY–TAMPA COLLEGE

Tampa, FL

Tuition & fees: $6879 **Average undergraduate aid package: $6000**

ABOUT THE INSTITUTION Proprietary, coed. Awards: associate, bachelor's, and master's degrees. 10 undergraduate majors. Total enrollment: 986. Undergraduates: 895. Freshmen: 201. Federal methodology is used as a basis for awarding need-based institutional aid.

UNDERGRADUATE EXPENSES for 1999–2000 ***Application fee:*** $50. ***Tuition:*** full-time $6804; part-time $199 per quarter hour. ***Required fees:*** full-time $75; $25 per term part-time. Full-time tuition and fees vary according to course load and program. Part-time tuition and fees vary according to course level and program. ***Payment plans:*** guaranteed tuition, installment.

FRESHMAN FINANCIAL AID (Fall 1999, est.) 205 applied for aid; of those 100% were deemed to have need. 98% of freshmen with need received aid; of those 96% had need fully met. *Average percent of need met:* 75% (excluding resources awarded to replace EFC). *Average financial aid package:* $6000 (excluding resources awarded to replace EFC).

UNDERGRADUATE FINANCIAL AID (Fall 1999, est.) 733 applied for aid; of those 100% were deemed to have need. 99% of undergraduates with need received aid; of those 98% had need fully met. *Average percent of need met:* 75% (excluding resources awarded to replace EFC). *Average financial aid package:* $6000 (excluding resources awarded to replace EFC).

GIFT AID (NEED-BASED) ***Total amount:*** $1,500,000 (100% Federal). ***Receiving aid:*** *Freshmen:* 23% (60); *all full-time undergraduates:* 55% (500). ***Scholarships, grants, and awards:*** Federal Pell, FSEOG, state.

GIFT AID (NON-NEED-BASED) ***Total amount:*** $163,000 (92% state, 6% institutional, 2% external sources). ***Scholarships, grants, and awards by category:*** *Academic Interests/Achievement:* general academic interests/ achievements. ***Tuition waivers:*** Full or partial for employees or children of employees.

LOANS ***Student loans:*** $3,060,000 (98% need-based, 2% non-need-based). 82% of past graduating class borrowed through all loan programs. Average indebtedness per student: $12,000. ***Parent loans:*** $200,000 (100% need-based). ***Programs:*** FFEL (Subsidized and Unsubsidized Stafford, PLUS), college/university.

WORK-STUDY ***Federal work-study:*** *Total amount:* $80,000; jobs available.

APPLYING for FINANCIAL AID ***Required financial aid forms:*** FAFSA, institution's own form. ***Financial aid deadline:*** Continuous. ***Notification date:*** Continuous.

CONTACT Rod Kirkwood, Financial Aid Director, Florida Metropolitan University–Tampa College, 3319 West Hillsborough Avenue, Tampa, FL 33614, 813-879-6000 Ext. 145. *Fax:* 813-871-2483. *E-mail:* rkirkwood@ cci.edu

FLORIDA METROPOLITAN UNIVERSITY–TAMPA COLLEGE, BRANDON

Tampa, FL

Tuition & fees: $6555 **Average undergraduate aid package: N/A**

ABOUT THE INSTITUTION Proprietary, coed. Awards: associate, bachelor's, and master's degrees. 11 undergraduate majors. Total enrollment: 717. Undergraduates: 670. Freshmen: 116. Federal methodology is used as a basis for awarding need-based institutional aid.

UNDERGRADUATE EXPENSES for 1999–2000 ***Application fee:*** $50. ***Tuition:*** full-time $6480; part-time $190 per quarter hour. ***Required fees:*** full-time $75; $25 per term part-time. Full-time tuition and fees vary according to course load, degree level, and program. Part-time tuition and fees vary according to course load, degree level, and program. ***Payment plan:*** installment.

GIFT AID (NEED-BASED) ***Scholarships, grants, and awards:*** Federal Pell, FSEOG, state.

GIFT AID (NON-NEED-BASED) ***Scholarships, grants, and awards by category:*** *Academic Interests/Achievement:* general academic interests/ achievements. ***Tuition waivers:*** Full or partial for employees or children of employees.

LOANS ***Programs:*** FFEL (Subsidized and Unsubsidized Stafford, PLUS), PLATO Loans.

WORK-STUDY Federal work-study jobs available.

APPLYING for FINANCIAL AID ***Required financial aid form:*** FAFSA. ***Financial aid deadline:*** Continuous. ***Notification date:*** Continuous.

CONTACT Ed Stonko, Director of Financial Aid, Florida Metropolitan University–Tampa College, Brandon, 3924 Coconut Palm Drive, Tampa, FL 33619, 813-621-0041.

FLORIDA METROPOLITAN UNIVERSITY–TAMPA COLLEGE, LAKELAND

Lakeland, FL

Tuition & fees: $6555 **Average undergraduate aid package: N/A**

ABOUT THE INSTITUTION Proprietary, coed. Awards: associate, bachelor's, and master's degrees (bachelor's degree in business administration only). 9 undergraduate majors. Total enrollment: 536. Undergraduates: 505. Federal methodology is used as a basis for awarding need-based institutional aid.

UNDERGRADUATE EXPENSES for 1999–2000 ***Tuition:*** full-time $6480; part-time $190 per quarter hour. ***Required fees:*** full-time $75; $25 per term part-time. Full-time tuition and fees vary according to course load and program. Part-time tuition and fees vary according to course level and program. ***Payment plan:*** installment.

GIFT AID (NEED-BASED) ***Scholarships, grants, and awards:*** Federal Pell, FSEOG, state, college/university gift aid from institutional funds.

GIFT AID (NON-NEED-BASED) ***Scholarships, grants, and awards by category:*** *Academic Interests/Achievement:* business. ***Tuition waivers:*** Full or partial for employees or children of employees.

LOANS ***Programs:*** FFEL (Subsidized and Unsubsidized Stafford, PLUS), college/university.

WORK-STUDY Federal work-study jobs available.

APPLYING for FINANCIAL AID ***Required financial aid forms:*** FAFSA, institution's own form. ***Financial aid deadline:*** Continuous.

CONTACT Ann Mitchell, Director, Financial Aid, Florida Metropolitan University–Tampa College, Lakeland, 995 East Memorial Boulevard, Lakeland, FL 33801, 941-686-1444.

FLORIDA METROPOLITAN UNIVERSITY–TAMPA COLLEGE, PINELLAS

Clearwater, FL

ABOUT THE INSTITUTION Proprietary, coed. Awards: associate, bachelor's, and master's degrees. 6 undergraduate majors. Total enrollment: 884. Undergraduates: 720. Freshmen: 110.

GIFT AID (NEED-BASED) ***Scholarships, grants, and awards:*** Federal Pell, FSEOG, state, private.

GIFT AID (NON-NEED-BASED) ***Scholarships, grants, and awards by category:*** *Academic Interests/Achievement:* general academic interests/achievements.

LOANS ***Programs:*** FFEL (Subsidized and Unsubsidized Stafford, PLUS).

WORK-STUDY Federal work-study jobs available.

APPLYING for FINANCIAL AID ***Required financial aid form:*** FAFSA.

CONTACT Ms. Marcia Hutchinson, Director of Financial Aid, Florida Metropolitan University–Tampa College, Pinellas, 2471 North McMullen Booth Road, Suite 200, Clearwater, FL 33759, 727-725-2688 or toll-free 800-353-FMUS.

FLORIDA SOUTHERN COLLEGE

Lakeland, FL

Tuition & fees: $12,950 **Average undergraduate aid package: $12,111**

ABOUT THE INSTITUTION Independent religious, coed. Awards: bachelor's and master's degrees. 57 undergraduate majors. Total enrollment: 1,805. Undergraduates: 1,764. Freshmen: 425. Federal methodology is used as a basis for awarding need-based institutional aid.

UNDERGRADUATE EXPENSES for 2000–2001 ***Application fee:*** $30. ***Comprehensive fee:*** $18,500 includes full-time tuition ($12,750), mandatory fees ($200), and room and board ($5550). ***College room only:*** $2650. Room and board charges vary according to board plan and housing facility. ***Part-time tuition:*** $370 per semester hour. Part-time tuition and fees vary according to class time. ***Payment plan:*** installment.

FRESHMAN FINANCIAL AID (Fall 1999) 386 applied for aid; of those 78% were deemed to have need. 100% of freshmen with need received aid; of those 32% had need fully met. *Average percent of need met:* 80% (excluding resources awarded to replace EFC). *Average financial aid package:* $12,095 (excluding resources awarded to replace EFC). 19% of all full-time freshmen had no need and received non-need-based aid.

UNDERGRADUATE FINANCIAL AID (Fall 1999) 1,485 applied for aid; of those 79% were deemed to have need. 99% of undergraduates with need received aid; of those 32% had need fully met. *Average percent of need met:* 77% (excluding resources awarded to replace EFC). *Average financial aid package:* $12,111 (excluding resources awarded to replace EFC). 17% of all full-time undergraduates had no need and received non-need-based aid.

GIFT AID (NEED-BASED) ***Total amount:*** $9,498,746 (11% Federal, 30% state, 56% institutional, 3% external sources). ***Receiving aid:*** *Freshmen:* 70% (297); *all full-time undergraduates:* 68% (1,141). ***Average award:*** Freshmen: $9511; Undergraduates: $9042. ***Scholarships, grants, and awards:*** Federal Pell, FSEOG, state, private, college/university gift aid from institutional funds.

GIFT AID (NON-NEED-BASED) ***Total amount:*** $2,401,099 (39% state, 52% institutional, 9% external sources). ***Receiving aid:*** *Freshmen:* 41% (176); *Undergraduates:* 38% (644). ***Scholarships, grants, and awards by category:*** *Academic Interests/Achievement:* 850 awards ($3,158,779 total): agriculture, biological sciences, business, communication, general academic interests/achievements, physical sciences, religion/biblical studies, social sciences. *Creative Arts/Performance:* 260 awards ($335,700 total): art/fine arts, music, theater/drama. *Special Achievements/Activities:* 753 awards ($1,427,704 total): community service, general special achievements/activities, leadership. *Special Characteristics:* 1,117 awards ($2,128,666 total): children and siblings of alumni, children of faculty/staff, general special characteristics, local/state students, out-of-state students, relatives of clergy, siblings of current students. ***Tuition waivers:*** Full or partial for employees or children of employees. ***ROTC:*** Army.

LOANS ***Student loans:*** $3,787,649 (83% need-based, 17% non-need-based). 62% of past graduating class borrowed through all loan programs. Average indebtedness per student: $12,678. ***Average need-based loan:*** Freshmen: $3096; Undergraduates: $3871. ***Programs:*** FFEL (Subsidized and Unsubsidized Stafford, PLUS), Perkins.

WORK-STUDY ***Federal work-study:*** *Total amount:* $431,250; jobs available. ***State or other work-study/employment:*** *Total amount:* $314,650 (47% need-based, 53% non-need-based). Part-time jobs available.

ATHLETIC AWARDS *Total amount:* 980,722 (76% need-based, 24% non-need-based).

APPLYING for FINANCIAL AID ***Required financial aid forms:*** FAFSA, institution's own form. ***Financial aid deadline:*** 8/1 (priority: 4/1). ***Notification date:*** Continuous. Students must reply within 2 weeks of notification.

CONTACT Ms. Tasha Newman, Financial Aid Counselor, Florida Southern College, 111 Lake Hollingsworth Drive, Lakeland, FL 33801-5698, 941-680-3944 or toll-free 800-274-4131. *Fax:* 941-680-4567. *E-mail:* tnewman@flsouthern.edu

FLORIDA STATE UNIVERSITY

Tallahassee, FL

Tuition & fees (FL res): $2196 **Average undergraduate aid package: $3127**

ABOUT THE INSTITUTION State-supported, coed. Awards: associate, bachelor's, master's, doctoral, and first professional degrees and post-bachelor's and post-master's certificates. 149 undergraduate majors. Total enrollment: 32,878. Undergraduates: 25,965. Freshmen: 4,937. Federal methodology is used as a basis for awarding need-based institutional aid.

UNDERGRADUATE EXPENSES for 1999–2000 ***Application fee:*** $20. ***Tuition, state resident:*** full-time $2196; part-time $73 per semester hour. ***Tuition, nonresident:*** full-time $9184; part-time $306 per semester hour. Full-time tuition and fees vary according to location. Part-time tuition and fees vary according to location. ***College room and board:*** $4952; ***room only:*** $2694. Room and board charges vary according to board plan and housing facility. ***Payment plans:*** tuition prepayment, installment.

FRESHMAN FINANCIAL AID (Fall 1999) 3953 applied for aid; of those 43% were deemed to have need. 88% of freshmen with need received aid; of those 5% had need fully met. *Average percent of need met:* 21% (excluding resources awarded to replace EFC). *Average financial aid package:* $2946 (excluding resources awarded to replace EFC). 38% of all full-time freshmen had no need and received non-need-based aid.

UNDERGRADUATE FINANCIAL AID (Fall 1999) 13,662 applied for aid; of those 69% were deemed to have need. 88% of undergraduates with need received aid; of those 3% had need fully met. *Average percent of need met:* 29% (excluding resources awarded to replace EFC). *Average financial aid package:* $3127 (excluding resources awarded to replace EFC). 32% of all full-time undergraduates had no need and received non-need-based aid.

GIFT AID (NEED-BASED) ***Total amount:*** $23,417,111 (57% Federal, 12% state, 30% institutional, 1% external sources). ***Receiving aid:*** *Freshmen:* 27% (1,317); *all full-time undergraduates:* 33% (7,255). ***Average award:*** Freshmen: $2056; Undergraduates: $2932. ***Scholarships, grants, and awards:*** Federal Pell, FSEOG, state, private, college/university gift aid from institutional funds.

GIFT AID (NON-NEED-BASED) ***Total amount:*** $15,519,759 (57% state, 41% institutional, 2% external sources). ***Receiving aid:*** *Freshmen:* 16% (763); *Undergraduates:* 19% (4,256). ***Scholarships, grants, and awards by category:*** *Academic Interests/Achievement:* general academic interests/achievements. *Creative Arts/Performance:* music. *Special Characteristics:* local/state students. ***Tuition waivers:*** Full or partial for employees or children of employees, senior citizens. ***ROTC:*** Army, Naval cooperative, Air Force.

LOANS ***Student loans:*** $32,441,353 (84% need-based, 16% non-need-based). 67% of past graduating class borrowed through all loan programs. Average indebtedness per student: $15,458. ***Average need-based loan:***

Freshmen: $2382; Undergraduates: $3006. ***Parent loans:*** $7,303,985 (100% non-need-based). ***Programs:*** FFEL (Subsidized and Unsubsidized Stafford, PLUS), Perkins, college/university.

WORK-STUDY ***Federal work-study:*** *Total amount:* $748,725; 421 jobs averaging $1778. ***State or other work-study/employment:*** *Total amount:* $28,755 (100% need-based). 18 part-time jobs averaging $1598.

ATHLETIC AWARDS *Total amount:* 1,521,173 (100% non-need-based).

APPLYING for FINANCIAL AID ***Required financial aid form:*** FAFSA. ***Financial aid deadline (priority):*** 2/15. ***Notification date:*** Continuous beginning 3/15. Students must reply within 2 weeks of notification.

CONTACT Darryl Marshall, Director of Financial Aid, Florida State University, University Center A4400, Tallahassee, FL 32306-2430, 850-644-5716. *Fax:* 850-644-6404. *E-mail:* finaid@admin.fsu.edu

FONTBONNE COLLEGE

St. Louis, MO

Tuition & fees: $11,343 **Average undergraduate aid package: $8500**

ABOUT THE INSTITUTION Independent Roman Catholic, coed. Awards: bachelor's and master's degrees. 41 undergraduate majors. Total enrollment: 2,076. Undergraduates: 1,362. Freshmen: 146. Federal methodology is used as a basis for awarding need-based institutional aid.

UNDERGRADUATE EXPENSES for 1999–2000 ***Application fee:*** $20. ***Comprehensive fee:*** $16,193 includes full-time tuition ($11,183), mandatory fees ($160), and room and board ($4850). Full-time tuition and fees vary according to class time, program, and reciprocity agreements. Room and board charges vary according to board plan and housing facility. ***Part-time tuition:*** $346 per hour. ***Part-time fees:*** $7 per hour. Part-time tuition and fees vary according to class time, course load, program, and reciprocity agreements. ***Payment plans:*** installment, deferred payment.

FRESHMAN FINANCIAL AID (Fall 1998) 139 applied for aid; of those 77% were deemed to have need. 100% of freshmen with need received aid; of those 43% had need fully met. *Average percent of need met:* 76% (excluding resources awarded to replace EFC). *Average financial aid package:* $8500 (excluding resources awarded to replace EFC). 22% of all full-time freshmen had no need and received non-need-based aid.

UNDERGRADUATE FINANCIAL AID (Fall 1998) 801 applied for aid; of those 67% were deemed to have need. 100% of undergraduates with need received aid; of those 25% had need fully met. *Average percent of need met:* 76% (excluding resources awarded to replace EFC). *Average financial aid package:* $8500 (excluding resources awarded to replace EFC). 31% of all full-time undergraduates had no need and received non-need-based aid.

GIFT AID (NEED-BASED) ***Total amount:*** $2,055,888 (24% Federal, 15% state, 61% institutional). ***Receiving aid:*** *Freshmen:* 72% (107); *all full-time undergraduates:* 64% (537). ***Scholarships, grants, and awards:*** Federal Pell, FSEOG, state, private, college/university gift aid from institutional funds.

GIFT AID (NON-NEED-BASED) ***Total amount:*** $1,604,814 (3% state, 93% institutional, 4% external sources). ***Receiving aid:*** *Freshmen:* 39% (58); *Undergraduates:* 27% (226). ***Scholarships, grants, and awards by category:*** *Academic Interests/Achievement:* computer science, English, general academic interests/achievements. *Creative Arts/Performance:* art/fine arts, creative writing, theater/drama. *Special Achievements/Activities:* community service, general special achievements/activities, leadership. *Special Characteristics:* religious affiliation, siblings of current students. ***Tuition waivers:*** Full or partial for employees or children of employees, senior citizens. ***ROTC:*** Army cooperative.

LOANS ***Student loans:*** $2,091,103 (82% need-based, 18% non-need-based). ***Parent loans:*** $145,330 (100% non-need-based). ***Programs:*** FFEL (Subsidized and Unsubsidized Stafford, PLUS), Perkins, CitiAssist Loans.

WORK-STUDY ***Federal work-study:*** *Total amount:* $233,050; jobs available. ***State or other work-study/employment:*** *Total amount:* $94,775 (100% non-need-based). Part-time jobs available.

APPLYING for FINANCIAL AID ***Required financial aid forms:*** FAFSA, institution's own form. ***Financial aid deadline:*** 7/1 (priority: 4/1). ***Notification date:*** Continuous. Students must reply within 3 weeks of notification.

CONTACT Ms. Nicole Moore, Director of Financial Aid, Fontbonne College, 6800 Wydown Boulevard, St. Louis, MO 63105-3098, 314-889-1414. *E-mail:* nmoore@fontbonne.edu

FORDHAM UNIVERSITY

New York, NY

Tuition & fees: $19,660 **Average undergraduate aid package: $16,351**

ABOUT THE INSTITUTION Independent Roman Catholic (Jesuit), coed. Awards: bachelor's, master's, doctoral, and first professional degrees (branch locations: an 85-acre campus at Rose Hill and an 8-acre campus at Lincoln Center). 82 undergraduate majors. Total enrollment: 13,551. Undergraduates: 6,578. Freshmen: 1,584. Both federal and institutional methodology are used as a basis for awarding need-based institutional aid.

UNDERGRADUATE EXPENSES for 1999–2000 ***Application fee:*** $50. ***Comprehensive fee:*** $26,140 includes full-time tuition ($19,200), mandatory fees ($460), and room and board ($6480). ***College room only:*** $3580. Room and board charges vary according to housing facility. ***Part-time tuition:*** $640 per credit. ***Part-time fees:*** $230 per term part-time. Part-time tuition and fees vary according to class time and location. ***Payment plans:*** tuition prepayment, installment.

FRESHMAN FINANCIAL AID (Fall 1998) 1293 applied for aid; of those 88% were deemed to have need. 99% of freshmen with need received aid; of those 15% had need fully met. *Average percent of need met:* 75% (excluding resources awarded to replace EFC). *Average financial aid package:* $16,570 (excluding resources awarded to replace EFC). 10% of all full-time freshmen had no need and received non-need-based aid.

UNDERGRADUATE FINANCIAL AID (Fall 1998) 4,257 applied for aid; of those 93% were deemed to have need. 99% of undergraduates with need received aid; of those 18% had need fully met. *Average percent of need met:* 75% (excluding resources awarded to replace EFC). *Average financial aid package:* $16,351 (excluding resources awarded to replace EFC). 7% of all full-time undergraduates had no need and received non-need-based aid.

GIFT AID (NEED-BASED) ***Total amount:*** $39,235,568 (10% Federal, 13% state, 76% institutional, 1% external sources). ***Receiving aid:*** *Freshmen:* 69% (1,063); *all full-time undergraduates:* 69% (3,677). ***Average award:*** Freshmen: $11,689; Undergraduates: $10,652. ***Scholarships, grants, and awards:*** Federal Pell, FSEOG, state, private, college/university gift aid from institutional funds.

GIFT AID (NON-NEED-BASED) ***Total amount:*** $2,445,981 (89% institutional, 11% external sources). ***Receiving aid:*** *Freshmen:* 3% (53); *Undergraduates:* 3% (170). ***Scholarships, grants, and awards by category:*** *Academic Interests/Achievement:* communication, foreign languages, general academic interests/achievements. *Creative Arts/Performance:* music. *Special Achievements/Activities:* general special achievements/activities. *Special Characteristics:* children and siblings of alumni, children of faculty/staff, children of union members/company employees, children with a deceased or disabled parent, handicapped students, veterans, veterans' children. ***Tuition waivers:*** Full or partial for employees or children of employees. ***ROTC:*** Army, Naval cooperative, Air Force cooperative.

LOANS ***Student loans:*** $16,893,189 (85% need-based, 15% non-need-based). 68% of past graduating class borrowed through all loan programs. Average indebtedness per student: $15,379. ***Average need-based loan:*** Freshmen: $2820; Undergraduates: $4120. ***Parent loans:*** $5,799,638 (39% need-based, 61% non-need-based). ***Programs:*** FFEL (Subsidized and Unsubsidized Stafford, PLUS), Perkins.

WORK-STUDY ***Federal work-study:*** *Total amount:* $2,290,968; 1,133 jobs averaging $2022. ***State or other work-study/employment:*** *Total amount:* $546,012 (67% need-based, 33% non-need-based). Part-time jobs available.

ATHLETIC AWARDS *Total amount:* 3,089,712 (69% need-based, 31% non-need-based).

APPLYING for FINANCIAL AID ***Required financial aid forms:*** FAFSA, institution's own form, CSS Financial Aid PROFILE, state aid form, noncustodial (divorced/separated) parent's statement, business/farm

Fordham University (continued)

supplement. ***Financial aid deadline (priority):*** 2/1. ***Notification date:*** 4/1. Students must reply by 5/1 or within 2 weeks of notification.

CONTACT Calvin Brian Ghanoo, Senior Assistant Director of Financial Aid, Fordham University, 441 East Fordham Road, Thebaud Hall, New York, NY 10458, 718-817-3800 or toll-free 800-FORDHAM. *E-mail:* fa_financialaid@murray.fordham.edu

FORT HAYS STATE UNIVERSITY

Hays, KS

Tuition & fees (KS res): $2063 Average undergraduate aid package: N/A

ABOUT THE INSTITUTION State-supported, coed. Awards: associate, bachelor's, and master's degrees. 55 undergraduate majors. Total enrollment: 5,533. Undergraduates: 4,414. Federal methodology is used as a basis for awarding need-based institutional aid.

UNDERGRADUATE EXPENSES for 1999–2000 ***Application fee:*** $20. ***Tuition, state resident:*** full-time $2063; part-time $69 per credit hour. ***Tuition, nonresident:*** full-time $6531; part-time $218 per credit hour. Full-time tuition and fees vary according to course load, location, and reciprocity agreements. Part-time tuition and fees vary according to course load and location. ***College room and board:*** $3770; ***room only:*** $1915. Room and board charges vary according to board plan, housing facility, and student level. ***Payment plan:*** installment.

GIFT AID (NEED-BASED) ***Scholarships, grants, and awards:*** Federal Pell, FSEOG, state, private, college/university gift aid from institutional funds.

GIFT AID (NON-NEED-BASED) ***Scholarships, grants, and awards by category:*** *Academic Interests/Achievement:* agriculture, biological sciences, business, communication, computer science, education, engineering/technologies, English, foreign languages, general academic interests/achievements, health fields, humanities, international studies, library science, mathematics, physical sciences, premedicine, social sciences. *Creative Arts/Performance:* applied art and design, art/fine arts, cinema/film/broadcasting, creative writing, debating, journalism/publications, music, performing arts, theater/drama. *Special Achievements/Activities:* cheerleading/drum major, rodeo. *Special Characteristics:* adult students, members of minority groups. ***Tuition waivers:*** Full or partial for senior citizens.

LOANS ***Programs:*** FFEL (Subsidized and Unsubsidized Stafford, PLUS), Perkins, state.

WORK-STUDY Federal work-study jobs available. ***State or other work-study/employment:*** Part-time jobs available.

APPLYING for FINANCIAL AID ***Required financial aid forms:*** FAFSA, institution's own form. ***Financial aid deadline (priority):*** 3/15. ***Notification date:*** Continuous beginning 4/15. Students must reply within 8 weeks of notification.

CONTACT Craig Karlin, Director of Financial Assistance, Fort Hays State University, Custer Hall, Room 306, 600 Park Street, Hays, KS 67601, 785-628-4408 or toll-free 800-432-0248. *Fax:* 785-628-4014. *E-mail:* ckarlin@fhsu.edu

FORT LEWIS COLLEGE

Durango, CO

Tuition & fees (CO res): $2219 Average undergraduate aid package: $4550

ABOUT THE INSTITUTION State-supported, coed. Awards: bachelor's degrees. 54 undergraduate majors. Total enrollment: 4,357. Undergraduates: 4,357. Federal methodology is used as a basis for awarding need-based institutional aid.

UNDERGRADUATE EXPENSES for 1999–2000 ***Application fee:*** $20. ***One-time required fee:*** $45. ***Tuition, state resident:*** full-time $1676; part-time $102 per credit hour. ***Tuition, nonresident:*** full-time $8128; part-time $506 per credit hour. ***Required fees:*** full-time $543; $51 per term part-time. Full-time tuition and fees vary according to reciprocity agreements. Part-time tuition and fees vary according to course load. ***College room and board:*** $4452; ***room only:*** $2270. Room and board charges vary according to board plan and housing facility.

FRESHMAN FINANCIAL AID (Fall 1998) 985 applied for aid; of those 58% were deemed to have need. 98% of freshmen with need received aid; of those 37% had need fully met. *Average percent of need met:* 77% (excluding resources awarded to replace EFC). *Average financial aid package:* $4685 (excluding resources awarded to replace EFC). 11% of all full-time freshmen had no need and received non-need-based aid.

UNDERGRADUATE FINANCIAL AID (Fall 1998) 2,780 applied for aid; of those 68% were deemed to have need. 100% of undergraduates with need received aid; of those 80% had need fully met. *Average percent of need met:* 75% (excluding resources awarded to replace EFC). *Average financial aid package:* $4550 (excluding resources awarded to replace EFC). 9% of all full-time undergraduates had no need and received non-need-based aid.

GIFT AID (NEED-BASED) ***Total amount:*** $4,049,300 (56% Federal, 14% state, 30% external sources). ***Receiving aid:*** *Freshmen:* 25% (393); *all full-time undergraduates:* 40% (1,556). ***Average award:*** Freshmen: $2510; Undergraduates: $2666. ***Scholarships, grants, and awards:*** Federal Pell, FSEOG, state, private, college/university gift aid from institutional funds.

GIFT AID (NON-NEED-BASED) ***Total amount:*** $1,150,901 (49% institutional, 51% external sources). ***Receiving aid:*** *Freshmen:* 14% (227); *Undergraduates:* 10% (402). ***Scholarships, grants, and awards by category:*** *Academic Interests/Achievement:* 40 awards ($22,100 total): biological sciences, business, communication, computer science, education, engineering/technologies, English, foreign languages, general academic interests/achievements, humanities, mathematics, physical sciences, social sciences. *Creative Arts/Performance:* 10 awards ($5250 total): art/fine arts, music, performing arts, theater/drama. *Special Achievements/Activities:* 7 awards ($4125 total): general special achievements/activities. *Special Characteristics:* 288 awards ($376,142 total): ethnic background, first-generation college students, local/state students, members of minority groups, out-of-state students. ***Tuition waivers:*** Full or partial for minority students, employees or children of employees.

LOANS ***Student loans:*** $6,539,657 (98% need-based, 2% non-need-based). Average indebtedness per student: $13,432. ***Average need-based loan:*** Freshmen: $2110; Undergraduates: $3520. ***Parent loans:*** $1,055,149 (100% non-need-based). ***Programs:*** FFEL (Subsidized and Unsubsidized Stafford, PLUS), Perkins, college/university.

WORK-STUDY ***Federal work-study:*** *Total amount:* $207,119; 149 jobs averaging $1390. ***State or other work-study/employment:*** *Total amount:* $657,905 (35% need-based, 65% non-need-based). 522 part-time jobs averaging $1046.

ATHLETIC AWARDS *Total amount:* 199,406 (100% non-need-based).

APPLYING for FINANCIAL AID ***Required financial aid form:*** FAFSA. ***Financial aid deadline (priority):*** 2/15. ***Notification date:*** Continuous beginning 3/23. Students must reply within 2 weeks of notification.

CONTACT Mr. Rick Willis, Director of Financial Aid, Fort Lewis College, 1000 Rim Drive, Durango, CO 81301-3999, 970-247-7142 Ext. 7464. *E-mail:* willis_r@fortlewis.edu

FORT VALLEY STATE UNIVERSITY

Fort Valley, GA

Tuition & fees (GA res): $2294 Average undergraduate aid package: N/A

ABOUT THE INSTITUTION State-supported, coed. Awards: associate, bachelor's, master's, doctoral, and first professional degrees. 34 undergraduate majors. Total enrollment: 2,656. Undergraduates: 2,332. Freshmen: 422. Federal methodology is used as a basis for awarding need-based institutional aid.

UNDERGRADUATE EXPENSES for 1999–2000 ***Application fee:*** $20. ***Tuition, state resident:*** full-time $1808; part-time $76 per credit. ***Tuition, nonresident:*** full-time $7232; part-time $302 per credit. ***Required fees:*** full-time $486; $243 per term part-time. Full-time tuition and fees vary according to course load. Part-time tuition and fees vary according to course load. ***College room and board:*** $3432; ***room only:*** $1700. Room and board charges vary according to board plan.

GIFT AID (NEED-BASED) ***Total amount:*** $5,432,697 (86% Federal, 10% state, 3% institutional, 1% external sources). ***Scholarships, grants, and awards:*** Federal Pell, FSEOG, state, private, college/university gift aid from institutional funds.

GIFT AID (NON-NEED-BASED) ***Scholarships, grants, and awards by category:*** *Academic Interests/Achievement:* agriculture, business, general academic interests/achievements, home economics, military science, premedicine, social sciences. *Creative Arts/Performance:* journalism/publications, music. *Special Achievements/Activities:* general special achievements/activities. *Special Characteristics:* handicapped students, international students, local/state students, members of minority groups, out-of-state students. ***Tuition waivers:*** Full or partial for employees or children of employees, senior citizens. ***ROTC:*** Army.

LOANS ***Student loans:*** $12,120,456 (100% need-based). ***Parent loans:*** $98,422 (100% need-based). ***Programs:*** Federal Direct (Subsidized and Unsubsidized Stafford, PLUS), FFEL (Subsidized and Unsubsidized Stafford, PLUS), Perkins, state, college/university.

WORK-STUDY ***Federal work-study:*** *Total amount:* $639,793; jobs available.

ATHLETIC AWARDS *Total amount:* 325,352 (100% need-based).

APPLYING for FINANCIAL AID ***Required financial aid forms:*** FAFSA, institution's own form. ***Financial aid deadline (priority):*** 4/15. ***Notification date:*** Continuous. Students must reply within 2 weeks of notification.

CONTACT Beatricia M. King, Financial Aid Director, Fort Valley State University, PO Box 4129, Fort Valley, GA 31030-3298, 912-825-6182 or toll-free 800-248-7343. *Fax:* 912-825-6976. *E-mail:* kingb@mail.fvsu.edu

FRAMINGHAM STATE COLLEGE

Framingham, MA

Tuition & fees (MA res): $2830 **Average undergraduate aid package: $5025**

ABOUT THE INSTITUTION State-supported, coed. Awards: bachelor's and master's degrees and post-bachelor's certificates. 83 undergraduate majors. Total enrollment: 5,697. Undergraduates: 4,296. Freshmen: 625. Federal methodology is used as a basis for awarding need-based institutional aid.

UNDERGRADUATE EXPENSES for 2000–2001 (est.) ***Application fee:*** $10. ***One-time required fee:*** $86. ***Tuition, state resident:*** full-time $1030; part-time $182 per course. ***Tuition, nonresident:*** full-time $7050; part-time $1175 per course. ***Required fees:*** full-time $1800; $86 per credit hour. Full-time tuition and fees vary according to class time and student level. Part-time tuition and fees vary according to class time, course load, and student level. ***College room and board:*** $4154. Room and board charges vary according to board plan. ***Payment plan:*** installment.

FRESHMAN FINANCIAL AID (Fall 1998) 484 applied for aid; of those 70% were deemed to have need. 100% of freshmen with need received aid; of those 33% had need fully met. *Average percent of need met:* 90% (excluding resources awarded to replace EFC). *Average financial aid package:* $4805 (excluding resources awarded to replace EFC). 14% of all full-time freshmen had no need and received non-need-based aid.

UNDERGRADUATE FINANCIAL AID (Fall 1998) 1,802 applied for aid; of those 73% were deemed to have need. 100% of undergraduates with need received aid; of those 53% had need fully met. *Average percent of need met:* 93% (excluding resources awarded to replace EFC). *Average financial aid package:* $5025 (excluding resources awarded to replace EFC). 12% of all full-time undergraduates had no need and received non-need-based aid.

GIFT AID (NEED-BASED) ***Total amount:*** $2,500,363 (47% Federal, 44% state, 5% institutional, 4% external sources). ***Receiving aid:*** *Freshmen:* 40% (245); *all full-time undergraduates:* 28% (868). ***Average award:*** Freshmen: $1941; Undergraduates: $1832. ***Scholarships, grants, and awards:*** Federal Pell, FSEOG, state, private, college/university gift aid from institutional funds.

GIFT AID (NON-NEED-BASED) ***Total amount:*** $148,938 (37% state, 33% institutional, 30% external sources). ***Receiving aid:*** *Freshmen:* 3; *Undergraduates:* 12. ***Scholarships, grants, and awards by category:*** *Academic Interests/Achievement:* biological sciences, education, general academic interests/achievements, home economics, physical sciences. *Special Characteristics:* children of faculty/staff, children of public servants, children of union members/company employees, local/state students, veterans. ***Tuition waivers:*** Full or partial for employees or children of employees, senior citizens. ***ROTC:*** Army cooperative.

LOANS ***Student loans:*** $7,361,805 (57% need-based, 43% non-need-based). 66% of past graduating class borrowed through all loan programs. Average indebtedness per student: $12,339. ***Average need-based loan:*** Freshmen: $2576; Undergraduates: $3058. ***Parent loans:*** $255,542 (16% need-based, 84% non-need-based). ***Programs:*** FFEL (Subsidized and Unsubsidized Stafford, PLUS), Perkins, state.

WORK-STUDY ***Federal work-study:*** *Total amount:* $180,357; 150 jobs averaging $1200.

APPLYING for FINANCIAL AID ***Required financial aid form:*** FAFSA. ***Financial aid deadline (priority):*** 3/1. ***Notification date:*** 4/15. Students must reply within 2 weeks of notification.

CONTACT Ms. Susan Lanzillo, Director of Financial Aid, Framingham State College, 100 State Street, Framingham, MA 01701-9101, 508-626-4534. *Fax:* 508-626-4598. *E-mail:* sgillespie@frc.mass.edu

FRANCISCAN UNIVERSITY OF STEUBENVILLE

Steubenville, OH

Tuition & fees: $12,270 **Average undergraduate aid package: $9134**

ABOUT THE INSTITUTION Independent Roman Catholic, coed. Awards: associate, bachelor's, and master's degrees. 30 undergraduate majors. Total enrollment: 2,150. Undergraduates: 1,694. Freshmen: 321. Federal methodology is used as a basis for awarding need-based institutional aid.

UNDERGRADUATE EXPENSES for 1999–2000 ***Application fee:*** $20. ***Comprehensive fee:*** $17,240 includes full-time tuition ($11,990), mandatory fees ($280), and room and board ($4970). Room and board charges vary according to board plan. ***Part-time tuition:*** $400 per credit. ***Part-time fees:*** $10 per credit. Part-time tuition and fees vary according to class time. ***Payment plan:*** installment.

FRESHMAN FINANCIAL AID (Fall 1999, est.) 287 applied for aid; of those 93% were deemed to have need. 94% of freshmen with need received aid; of those 20% had need fully met. *Average percent of need met:* 70% (excluding resources awarded to replace EFC). *Average financial aid package:* $7188 (excluding resources awarded to replace EFC).

UNDERGRADUATE FINANCIAL AID (Fall 1999, est.) 1,392 applied for aid; of those 92% were deemed to have need. 97% of undergraduates with need received aid; of those 23% had need fully met. *Average percent of need met:* 80% (excluding resources awarded to replace EFC). *Average financial aid package:* $9134 (excluding resources awarded to replace EFC).

GIFT AID (NEED-BASED) ***Total amount:*** $4,934,755 (25% Federal, 10% state, 60% institutional, 5% external sources). ***Receiving aid:*** *Freshmen:* 70% (220); *all full-time undergraduates:* 77% (1,191). ***Average award:*** Freshmen: $2594; Undergraduates: $2659. ***Scholarships, grants, and awards:*** Federal Pell, FSEOG, state, private, college/university gift aid from institutional funds.

GIFT AID (NON-NEED-BASED) ***Total amount:*** $592,549 (20% state, 66% institutional, 14% external sources). ***Receiving aid:*** *Freshmen:* 43% (136); *Undergraduates:* 31% (476). ***Scholarships, grants, and awards by category:*** *Academic Interests/Achievement:* 416 awards ($866,830 total): general academic interests/achievements. *Special Achievements/Activities:* 22 awards ($91,266 total): religious involvement. *Special Characteristics:* 413 awards ($941,348 total): children of faculty/staff, international students, local/state students, religious affiliation, siblings of current students. ***Tuition waivers:*** Full or partial for employees or children of employees.

LOANS ***Student loans:*** $8,440,962 (89% need-based, 11% non-need-based). 83% of past graduating class borrowed through all loan programs. Average indebtedness per student: $19,692. ***Average need-based loan:***

Franciscan University of Steubenville (continued)

Freshmen: $2527; Undergraduates: $3812. ***Parent loans:*** $633,469 (73% need-based, 27% non-need-based). ***Programs:*** FFEL (Subsidized and Unsubsidized Stafford, PLUS), Perkins, GATE Loans.

WORK-STUDY ***Federal work-study:*** *Total amount:* $227,610; 287 jobs averaging $772. ***State or other work-study/employment:*** *Total amount:* $622,390 (100% need-based). 526 part-time jobs averaging $1183.

APPLYING for FINANCIAL AID ***Required financial aid forms:*** FAFSA, institution's own form. ***Financial aid deadline (priority):*** 3/15. ***Notification date:*** Continuous.

CONTACT Enrollment Services Office, Franciscan University of Steubenville, 1235 University Boulevard, Steubenville, OH 43952-6701, 740-283-6226 or toll-free 800-783-6220.

FRANCIS MARION UNIVERSITY

Florence, SC

Tuition & fees (SC res): $3470 **Average undergraduate aid package: N/A**

ABOUT THE INSTITUTION State-supported, coed. Awards: bachelor's and master's degrees. 35 undergraduate majors. Total enrollment: 3,814. Undergraduates: 2,923. Federal methodology is used as a basis for awarding need-based institutional aid.

UNDERGRADUATE EXPENSES for 1999–2000 ***Application fee:*** $25. ***Tuition, state resident:*** full-time $3260; part-time $163 per credit hour. ***Tuition, nonresident:*** full-time $6520; part-time $326 per credit hour. ***Required fees:*** full-time $210; $6 per credit hour; $30 per term part-time. Full-time tuition and fees vary according to course load. Part-time tuition and fees vary according to course load. ***College room and board:*** $3550. Room and board charges vary according to board plan and housing facility.

GIFT AID (NEED-BASED) ***Total amount:*** $3,250,000 (62% Federal, 38% state). ***Scholarships, grants, and awards:*** Federal Pell, FSEOG, state, private.

GIFT AID (NON-NEED-BASED) ***Total amount:*** $1,335,500 (5% Federal, 1% state, 68% institutional, 26% external sources). ***Scholarships, grants, and awards by category:*** *Academic Interests/Achievement:* biological sciences, business, education, English, general academic interests/achievements, health fields, humanities, mathematics, premedicine, social sciences. *Creative Arts/Performance:* art/fine arts, music, theater/drama. *Special Achievements/Activities:* cheerleading/drum major. *Special Characteristics:* adult students, children and siblings of alumni, children of faculty/staff, handicapped students, international students, out-of-state students, spouses of deceased or disabled public servants, veterans, veterans' children. ***Tuition waivers:*** Full or partial for employees or children of employees, senior citizens.

LOANS ***Student loans:*** $7,650,000 (61% need-based, 39% non-need-based). Average indebtedness per student: $14,855. ***Parent loans:*** $500,000 (100% non-need-based). ***Programs:*** FFEL (Subsidized and Unsubsidized Stafford, PLUS), Perkins, state.

WORK-STUDY ***Federal work-study:*** *Total amount:* $161,685; jobs available. ***State or other work-study/employment:*** *Total amount:* $504,631 (100% non-need-based). Part-time jobs available.

ATHLETIC AWARDS *Total amount:* 460,000 (100% non-need-based).

APPLYING for FINANCIAL AID ***Required financial aid forms:*** FAFSA, institution's own form. ***Financial aid deadline (priority):*** 3/1. ***Notification date:*** 4/1.

CONTACT Director of Financial Assistance, Francis Marion University, Box 100547, Florence, SC 29501-0547, 843-661-1190 or toll-free 800-368-7551.

FRANKLIN AND MARSHALL COLLEGE

Lancaster, PA

Tuition & fees: $23,720 **Average undergraduate aid package: $17,860**

ABOUT THE INSTITUTION Independent, coed. Awards: bachelor's degrees. 30 undergraduate majors. Total enrollment: 1,864. Undergraduates: 1,864. Freshmen: 516. Both federal and institutional methodology are used as a basis for awarding need-based institutional aid.

UNDERGRADUATE EXPENSES for 1999–2000 ***Application fee:*** $50. ***Comprehensive fee:*** $29,450 includes full-time tuition ($23,720) and room and board ($5730). ***College room only:*** $3686. Full-time tuition and fees vary according to reciprocity agreements. Room and board charges vary according to board plan and housing facility. ***Part-time tuition:*** $2965 per course. Part-time tuition and fees vary according to course load. ***Payment plan:*** installment.

FRESHMAN FINANCIAL AID (Fall 1999) 307 applied for aid; of those 83% were deemed to have need. 100% of freshmen with need received aid; of those 100% had need fully met. *Average percent of need met:* 100% (excluding resources awarded to replace EFC). *Average financial aid package:* $16,971 (excluding resources awarded to replace EFC). 11% of all full-time freshmen had no need and received non-need-based aid.

UNDERGRADUATE FINANCIAL AID (Fall 1999) 1,093 applied for aid; of those 88% were deemed to have need. 100% of undergraduates with need received aid; of those 100% had need fully met. *Average percent of need met:* 100% (excluding resources awarded to replace EFC). *Average financial aid package:* $17,860 (excluding resources awarded to replace EFC). 11% of all full-time undergraduates had no need and received non-need-based aid.

GIFT AID (NEED-BASED) ***Total amount:*** $11,879,440 (5% Federal, 5% state, 90% institutional). ***Receiving aid:*** *Freshmen:* 45% (234); *all full-time undergraduates:* 46% (876). ***Average award:*** Freshmen: $13,778; Undergraduates: $13,718. ***Scholarships, grants, and awards:*** Federal Pell, FSEOG, state, private, college/university gift aid from institutional funds.

GIFT AID (NON-NEED-BASED) ***Total amount:*** $1,833,333 (78% institutional, 22% external sources). ***Receiving aid:*** *Freshmen:* 16% (82); *Undergraduates:* 11% (209). ***Scholarships, grants, and awards by category:*** *Academic Interests/Achievement:* 433 awards ($2,757,630 total): general academic interests/achievements. *Special Achievements/Activities:* 11 awards ($44,000 total): community service. *Special Characteristics:* 43 awards ($180,064 total): local/state students. ***Tuition waivers:*** Full or partial for employees or children of employees.

LOANS ***Student loans:*** $4,382,426 (79% need-based, 21% non-need-based). 51% of past graduating class borrowed through all loan programs. Average indebtedness per student: $15,982. ***Average need-based loan:*** Freshmen: $2950; Undergraduates: $4117. ***Parent loans:*** $2,493,912 (100% non-need-based). ***Programs:*** FFEL (Subsidized and Unsubsidized Stafford, PLUS), Perkins, college/university loans from institutional funds (for international students only).

WORK-STUDY ***Federal work-study:*** *Total amount:* $725,155; 541 jobs averaging $1340. ***State or other work-study/employment:*** *Total amount:* $462,785 (25% need-based, 75% non-need-based). Part-time jobs available.

APPLYING for FINANCIAL AID ***Required financial aid forms:*** FAFSA, CSS Financial Aid PROFILE, state aid form. ***Financial aid deadline:*** 2/1. ***Notification date:*** 4/1. Students must reply by 5/1.

CONTACT Mr. Christopher K. Hanlon, Director of Student Aid, Franklin and Marshall College, PO Box 3003, Lancaster, PA 17604-3003, 717-291-3991. *Fax:* 717-291-4389. *E-mail:* c_hanlon@admin.fandm.edu

FRANKLIN COLLEGE OF INDIANA

Franklin, IN

Tuition & fees: $13,635 **Average undergraduate aid package: $13,333**

ABOUT THE INSTITUTION Independent religious, coed. Awards: bachelor's degrees. 32 undergraduate majors. Total enrollment: 953. Undergraduates: 953. Freshmen: 248. Federal methodology is used as a basis for awarding need-based institutional aid.

UNDERGRADUATE EXPENSES for 1999–2000 ***Application fee:*** $15. ***One-time required fee:*** $135. ***Comprehensive fee:*** $17,795 includes full-time tuition ($13,500), mandatory fees ($135), and room and board ($4160). ***College room only:*** $2300. Room and board charges vary according to board plan and housing facility. ***Part-time tuition:*** $180 per credit. ***Part-time fees:*** $5 per credit. Part-time tuition and fees vary according to course load. ***Payment plan:*** installment.

FRESHMAN FINANCIAL AID (Fall 1999) 244 applied for aid; of those 84% were deemed to have need. 100% of freshmen with need received aid; of those 83% had need fully met. *Average percent of need met:* 98% (excluding resources awarded to replace EFC). *Average financial aid package:* $12,916 (excluding resources awarded to replace EFC). 15% of all full-time freshmen had no need and received non-need-based aid.

UNDERGRADUATE FINANCIAL AID (Fall 1999) 890 applied for aid; of those 84% were deemed to have need. 100% of undergraduates with need received aid; of those 89% had need fully met. *Average percent of need met:* 98% (excluding resources awarded to replace EFC). *Average financial aid package:* $13,333 (excluding resources awarded to replace EFC). 13% of all full-time undergraduates had no need and received non-need-based aid.

GIFT AID (NEED-BASED) ***Total amount:*** $5,779,589 (9% Federal, 30% state, 58% institutional, 3% external sources). ***Receiving aid:*** *Freshmen:* 83% (206); *all full-time undergraduates:* 82% (747). ***Average award:*** Freshmen: $9126; Undergraduates: $9309. ***Scholarships, grants, and awards:*** Federal Pell, FSEOG, state, private, college/university gift aid from institutional funds.

GIFT AID (NON-NEED-BASED) ***Total amount:*** $1,242,519 (4% state, 91% institutional, 5% external sources). ***Receiving aid:*** *Freshmen:* 75% (186); *Undergraduates:* 70% (640). ***Scholarships, grants, and awards by category:*** *Academic Interests/Achievement:* 659 awards ($2,921,738 total): general academic interests/achievements, mathematics. *Creative Arts/Performance:* 49 awards ($275,000 total): journalism/publications, music, performing arts, theater/drama. *Special Characteristics:* 37 awards ($56,010 total): children and siblings of alumni, children of faculty/staff, local/state students, religious affiliation. ***Tuition waivers:*** Full or partial for employees or children of employees, senior citizens. ***ROTC:*** Army cooperative.

LOANS ***Student loans:*** $3,048,457 (67% need-based, 33% non-need-based). 75% of past graduating class borrowed through all loan programs. Average indebtedness per student: $16,050. ***Average need-based loan:*** Freshmen: $2975; Undergraduates: $3200. ***Parent loans:*** $846,531 (100% non-need-based). ***Programs:*** FFEL (Subsidized and Unsubsidized Stafford, PLUS), Perkins.

WORK-STUDY ***Federal work-study:*** *Total amount:* $121,851; jobs available. ***State or other work-study/employment:*** *Total amount:* $68,302 (71% need-based, 29% non-need-based). Part-time jobs available.

APPLYING for FINANCIAL AID ***Required financial aid form:*** FAFSA. ***Financial aid deadline (priority):*** 3/1. ***Notification date:*** Continuous beginning 3/15. Students must reply by 5/1 or within 3 weeks of notification.

CONTACT Dr. Charles R. Carothers, Director of Financial Aid, Franklin College of Indiana, 501 East Monroe Street, Franklin, IN 46131-2598, 317-738-8075 or toll-free 800-852-0232. *Fax:* 317-738-8072. *E-mail:* ccarothers@franklincollege.edu

FRANKLIN PIERCE COLLEGE

Rindge, NH

Tuition & fees: $17,990 **Average undergraduate aid package: $14,769**

ABOUT THE INSTITUTION Independent, coed. Awards: associate, bachelor's, and master's degrees (profile does not reflect significant enrollment at 6 continuing education sites; master's degree is only offered at these sites). 50 undergraduate majors. Total enrollment: 1,383. Undergraduates: 1,383. Freshmen: 436. Federal methodology is used as a basis for awarding need-based institutional aid.

UNDERGRADUATE EXPENSES for 1999–2000 ***Comprehensive fee:*** $24,040 includes full-time tuition ($17,250), mandatory fees ($740), and room and board ($6050). ***College room only:*** $3300. ***Part-time tuition:*** $575 per credit. ***Payment plan:*** installment.

FRESHMAN FINANCIAL AID (Fall 1999, est.) 402 applied for aid; of those 97% were deemed to have need. 100% of freshmen with need received aid; of those 15% had need fully met. *Average percent of need met:* 85% (excluding resources awarded to replace EFC). *Average financial aid package:* $14,379 (excluding resources awarded to replace EFC). 7% of all full-time freshmen had no need and received non-need-based aid.

UNDERGRADUATE FINANCIAL AID (Fall 1999, est.) 1,307 applied for aid; of those 95% were deemed to have need. 100% of undergraduates with need received aid; of those 7% had need fully met. *Average percent of need met:* 85% (excluding resources awarded to replace EFC). *Average financial aid package:* $14,769 (excluding resources awarded to replace EFC). 4% of all full-time undergraduates had no need and received non-need-based aid.

GIFT AID (NEED-BASED) ***Total amount:*** $10,860,598 (10% Federal, 1% state, 87% institutional, 2% external sources). ***Receiving aid:*** *Freshmen:* 91% (390); *all full-time undergraduates:* 92% (1,240). ***Average award:*** Freshmen: $9946; Undergraduates: $9826. ***Scholarships, grants, and awards:*** Federal Pell, FSEOG, state, private, college/university gift aid from institutional funds.

GIFT AID (NON-NEED-BASED) ***Total amount:*** $445,550 (9% state, 88% institutional, 3% external sources). ***Receiving aid:*** *Freshmen:* 7% (30); *Undergraduates:* 6% (80). ***Scholarships, grants, and awards by category:*** *Academic Interests/Achievement:* 1,197 awards ($6,061,449 total): communication, general academic interests/achievements. *Creative Arts/Performance:* 4 awards ($8000 total): performing arts. *Special Characteristics:* 101 awards ($729,494 total): adult students, children of faculty/staff, international students, local/state students, out-of-state students, siblings of current students. ***Tuition waivers:*** Full or partial for employees or children of employees, senior citizens. ***ROTC:*** Air Force cooperative.

LOANS ***Student loans:*** $6,900,000 (81% need-based, 19% non-need-based). 95% of past graduating class borrowed through all loan programs. Average indebtedness per student: $18,000. ***Average need-based loan:*** Freshmen: $4000; Undergraduates: $4516. ***Parent loans:*** $3,700,000 (59% need-based, 41% non-need-based). ***Programs:*** FFEL (Subsidized and Unsubsidized Stafford, PLUS), Perkins, state, alternative loans.

WORK-STUDY ***Federal work-study:*** *Total amount:* $300,000; 187 jobs averaging $1600. ***State or other work-study/employment:*** *Total amount:* $300,000 (77% need-based, 23% non-need-based). 354 part-time jobs averaging $847.

ATHLETIC AWARDS *Total amount:* 764,690 (98% need-based, 2% non-need-based).

APPLYING for FINANCIAL AID ***Required financial aid form:*** FAFSA. ***Financial aid deadline:*** Continuous. ***Notification date:*** Continuous beginning 2/15. Students must reply within 4 weeks of notification.

CONTACT Mr. Bruce Palmer, Director of Financial Aid/Associate Dean of Enrollment Services, Franklin Pierce College, College Road, PO Box 60, Rindge, NH 03461-0060, 603-899-4180 or toll-free 800-437-0048. *Fax:* 603-899-4372. *E-mail:* palmerb@fpc.edu

FRANKLIN UNIVERSITY

Columbus, OH

Tuition & fees: $5531 **Average undergraduate aid package: N/A**

ABOUT THE INSTITUTION Independent, coed. Awards: associate, bachelor's, and master's degrees. 13 undergraduate majors. Total enrollment: 4,473. Undergraduates: 3,812. Freshmen: 128. Both federal and institutional methodology are used as a basis for awarding need-based institutional aid.

UNDERGRADUATE EXPENSES for 1999–2000 ***One-time required fee:*** $25. ***Tuition:*** full-time $5456; part-time $176 per credit hour. ***Required fees:*** full-time $75; $25 per term part-time. Full-time tuition and fees vary according to course load and program. Part-time tuition and fees vary according to program. ***Payment plans:*** installment, deferred payment.

FRESHMAN FINANCIAL AID (Fall 1999) 33 applied for aid; of those 73% were deemed to have need. 83% of freshmen with need received aid. 14% of all full-time freshmen had no need and received non-need-based aid.

UNDERGRADUATE FINANCIAL AID (Fall 1999) 619 applied for aid; of those 79% were deemed to have need. 96% of undergraduates with need received aid. 10% of all full-time undergraduates had no need and received non-need-based aid.

Franklin University (continued)

GIFT AID (NEED-BASED) ***Total amount:*** $1,554,026 (53% Federal, 38% state, 6% institutional, 3% external sources). ***Receiving aid:*** *Freshmen:* 24% (15); *all full-time undergraduates:* 26% (294). ***Average award:*** Freshmen: $4045; Undergraduates: $3496. ***Scholarships, grants, and awards:*** Federal Pell, FSEOG, state, private, college/university gift aid from institutional funds.

GIFT AID (NON-NEED-BASED) ***Total amount:*** $959,822 (90% state, 6% institutional, 4% external sources). ***Receiving aid:*** *Freshmen:* 25% (16); *Undergraduates:* 34% (387). ***Scholarships, grants, and awards by category:*** *Academic Interests/Achievement:* general academic interests/achievements. *Special Achievements/Activities:* leadership. *Special Characteristics:* members of minority groups. ***Tuition waivers:*** Full or partial for employees or children of employees. ***ROTC:*** Army cooperative, Air Force cooperative.

LOANS ***Student loans:*** $7,320,093 (46% need-based, 54% non-need-based). ***Average need-based loan:*** Freshmen: $2214; Undergraduates: $4330. ***Parent loans:*** $575,914 (100% need-based). ***Programs:*** FFEL (Subsidized and Unsubsidized Stafford, PLUS), college/university.

WORK-STUDY ***Federal work-study:*** *Total amount:* $367,541; jobs available.

APPLYING for FINANCIAL AID ***Required financial aid forms:*** FAFSA, institution's own form. ***Financial aid deadline (priority):*** 6/30. ***Notification date:*** Continuous. Students must reply within 2 weeks of notification.

CONTACT Ms. Amy Jackson, Financial Aid Assistant, Franklin University, 201 South Grant Avenue, Columbus, OH 43215-5399, 614-341-6245 or toll-free 877-341-6300. *Fax:* 614-220-8931. *E-mail:* finaid@franklin.edu

FREED-HARDEMAN UNIVERSITY

Henderson, TN

CONTACT Doris Maness, Director of Financial Aid, Freed-Hardeman University, 158 East Main Street, Henderson, TN 38340-2399, 901-989-6662 or toll-free 800-630-3480. *Fax:* 901-989-6775. *E-mail:* dmaness@fhu.edu

FREE WILL BAPTIST BIBLE COLLEGE

Nashville, TN

Tuition & fees: $6442 **Average undergraduate aid package: N/A**

ABOUT THE INSTITUTION Independent Free Will Baptist, coed. Awards: associate and bachelor's degrees. 13 undergraduate majors. Total enrollment: 334. Undergraduates: 334. Federal methodology is used as a basis for awarding need-based institutional aid.

UNDERGRADUATE EXPENSES for 1999–2000 ***Application fee:*** $25. ***Comprehensive fee:*** $10,120 includes full-time tuition ($6040), mandatory fees ($402), and room and board ($3678). ***College room only:*** $1418. ***Part-time tuition:*** $189 per semester hour. ***Part-time fees:*** $100 per term part-time. Part-time tuition and fees vary according to course load. ***Payment plans:*** installment, deferred payment.

FRESHMAN FINANCIAL AID (Fall 1999) 77 applied for aid; of those 95% were deemed to have need. 97% of freshmen with need received aid.

UNDERGRADUATE FINANCIAL AID (Fall 1999) 315 applied for aid; of those 74% were deemed to have need. 88% of undergraduates with need received aid.

GIFT AID (NEED-BASED) ***Total amount:*** $358,361 (66% Federal, 7% state, 11% institutional, 16% external sources). ***Receiving aid:*** *Freshmen:* 36% (28); *all full-time undergraduates:* 21% (69). ***Scholarships, grants, and awards:*** Federal Pell, FSEOG, state, private, college/university gift aid from institutional funds.

GIFT AID (NON-NEED-BASED) ***Total amount:*** $4000 (100% institutional). ***Scholarships, grants, and awards by category:*** *Academic Interests/Achievement:* general academic interests/achievements. *Creative Arts/Performance:* creative writing, music. *Special Characteristics:* children and siblings of alumni. ***Tuition waivers:*** Full or partial for employees or children of employees. ***ROTC:*** Army cooperative, Air Force cooperative.

LOANS ***Parent loans:*** $90,834 (100% non-need-based). ***Programs:*** FFEL (Subsidized and Unsubsidized Stafford, PLUS), college/university.

WORK-STUDY Federal work-study jobs available.

APPLYING for FINANCIAL AID ***Required financial aid forms:*** FAFSA, institution's own form. ***Financial aid deadline (priority):*** 4/15. ***Notification date:*** Continuous beginning 7/1. Students must reply within 2 weeks of notification.

CONTACT Director of Financial Aid, Free Will Baptist Bible College, 3606 West End Avenue, Nashville, TN 37205-2498, 615-383-1340 Ext. 2250 or toll-free 800-763-9222.

FRESNO PACIFIC UNIVERSITY

Fresno, CA

Tuition & fees: $14,248 **Average undergraduate aid package: $15,556**

ABOUT THE INSTITUTION Independent religious, coed. Awards: associate, bachelor's, and master's degrees. 42 undergraduate majors. Total enrollment: 1,677. Undergraduates: 875. Freshmen: 168. Federal methodology is used as a basis for awarding need-based institutional aid.

UNDERGRADUATE EXPENSES for 2000–2001 ***Application fee:*** $30. ***Comprehensive fee:*** $18,668 includes full-time tuition ($13,950), mandatory fees ($298), and room and board ($4420). ***College room only:*** $2000. Room and board charges vary according to board plan and housing facility. ***Part-time tuition:*** $495 per unit. ***Part-time fees:*** $89 per term part-time. ***Payment plan:*** installment.

FRESHMAN FINANCIAL AID (Fall 1999) 158 applied for aid; of those 87% were deemed to have need. 100% of freshmen with need received aid; of those 46% had need fully met. *Average percent of need met:* 99% (excluding resources awarded to replace EFC). *Average financial aid package:* $16,464 (excluding resources awarded to replace EFC). 11% of all full-time freshmen had no need and received non-need-based aid.

UNDERGRADUATE FINANCIAL AID (Fall 1999) 696 applied for aid; of those 84% were deemed to have need. 99% of undergraduates with need received aid; of those 45% had need fully met. *Average percent of need met:* 99% (excluding resources awarded to replace EFC). *Average financial aid package:* $15,556 (excluding resources awarded to replace EFC). 16% of all full-time undergraduates had no need and received non-need-based aid.

GIFT AID (NEED-BASED) ***Total amount:*** $6,281,019 (16% Federal, 48% state, 34% institutional, 2% external sources). ***Receiving aid:*** *Freshmen:* 65% (106); *all full-time undergraduates:* 54% (436). ***Average award:*** Freshmen: $10,082; Undergraduates: $8664. ***Scholarships, grants, and awards:*** Federal Pell, FSEOG, state, college/university gift aid from institutional funds.

GIFT AID (NON-NEED-BASED) ***Total amount:*** $572,920 (94% institutional, 6% external sources). ***Receiving aid:*** *Freshmen:* 85% (137); *Undergraduates:* 71% (570). ***Scholarships, grants, and awards by category:*** *Academic Interests/Achievement:* 82 awards ($120,934 total): general academic interests/achievements. *Creative Arts/Performance:* 177 awards ($169,345 total): art/fine arts, music, theater/drama. *Special Achievements/Activities:* 144 awards ($71,312 total): community service, leadership. *Special Characteristics:* international students, relatives of clergy, religious affiliation. ***Tuition waivers:*** Full or partial for employees or children of employees, senior citizens.

LOANS ***Student loans:*** $3,885,357 (100% need-based). ***Average need-based loan:*** Freshmen: $2374; Undergraduates: $2535. ***Parent loans:*** $748,511 (100% need-based). ***Programs:*** FFEL (Subsidized and Unsubsidized Stafford, PLUS), Perkins, college/university.

WORK-STUDY ***Federal work-study:*** *Total amount:* $611,390; 366 jobs averaging $1670.

ATHLETIC AWARDS *Total amount:* 500,975 (63% need-based, 37% non-need-based).

APPLYING for FINANCIAL AID ***Required financial aid forms:*** FAFSA, institution's own form. ***Financial aid deadline (priority):*** 3/2. ***Notification date:*** Continuous beginning 4/1. Students must reply by 6/15 or within 3 weeks of notification.

CONTACT Financial Aid Office, Fresno Pacific University, 1717 South Chestnut Avenue, Fresno, CA 93702-4709, 559-453-2041 or toll-free 800-660-6089 (in-state). *Fax:* 559-453-2007.

FRIENDS UNIVERSITY

Wichita, KS

Tuition & fees: $11,010 **Average undergraduate aid package: $9223**

ABOUT THE INSTITUTION Independent, coed. Awards: associate, bachelor's, and master's degrees. 59 undergraduate majors. Total enrollment: 3,245. Undergraduates: 2,614. Federal methodology is used as a basis for awarding need-based institutional aid.

UNDERGRADUATE EXPENSES for 1999–2000 ***Application fee:*** $15. ***Comprehensive fee:*** $14,430 includes full-time tuition ($10,920), mandatory fees ($90), and room and board ($3420). Full-time tuition and fees vary according to course load. Room and board charges vary according to student level. ***Part-time tuition:*** $364 per semester hour. ***Part-time fees:*** $3 per semester hour. Part-time tuition and fees vary according to course load. ***Payment plan:*** installment.

FRESHMAN FINANCIAL AID (Fall 1998) 233 applied for aid; of those 94% were deemed to have need. 100% of freshmen with need received aid; of those 14% had need fully met. *Average percent of need met:* 63% (excluding resources awarded to replace EFC). *Average financial aid package:* $8329 (excluding resources awarded to replace EFC). 37% of all full-time freshmen had no need and received non-need-based aid.

UNDERGRADUATE FINANCIAL AID (Fall 1998) 1,476 applied for aid; of those 96% were deemed to have need. 100% of undergraduates with need received aid; of those 17% had need fully met. *Average percent of need met:* 63% (excluding resources awarded to replace EFC). *Average financial aid package:* $9223 (excluding resources awarded to replace EFC). 17% of all full-time undergraduates had no need and received non-need-based aid.

GIFT AID (NEED-BASED) ***Total amount:*** $4,080,446 (29% Federal, 18% state, 43% institutional, 10% external sources). ***Receiving aid:*** *Freshmen:* 55% (191); *all full-time undergraduates:* 46% (1,066). ***Average award:*** Freshmen: $4103; Undergraduates: $2704. ***Scholarships, grants, and awards:*** Federal Pell, FSEOG, state, college/university gift aid from institutional funds.

GIFT AID (NON-NEED-BASED) ***Total amount:*** $529,174 (81% institutional, 19% external sources). ***Receiving aid:*** *Freshmen:* 4% (14); *Undergraduates:* 3% (61). ***Scholarships, grants, and awards by category:*** *Academic Interests/Achievement:* 963 awards ($1,397,012 total): biological sciences, business, communication, computer science, education, English, foreign languages, general academic interests/achievements, health fields, humanities, mathematics, physical sciences, premedicine, religion/biblical studies, social sciences. *Creative Arts/Performance:* 252 awards ($190,812 total): applied art and design, art/fine arts, dance, music, performing arts, theater/drama. *Special Achievements/Activities:* 94 awards ($46,000 total): leadership. *Special Characteristics:* 52 awards ($37,858 total): children and siblings of alumni, international students, relatives of clergy, religious affiliation. ***Tuition waivers:*** Full or partial for employees or children of employees, senior citizens.

LOANS ***Student loans:*** $15,386,098 (87% need-based, 13% non-need-based). 93% of past graduating class borrowed through all loan programs. Average indebtedness per student: $10,132. ***Average need-based loan:*** Freshmen: $4100; Undergraduates: $6402. ***Parent loans:*** $286,506 (52% need-based, 48% non-need-based). ***Programs:*** FFEL (Subsidized and Unsubsidized Stafford, PLUS), Perkins, college/university.

WORK-STUDY ***Federal work-study:*** *Total amount:* $162,617; 148 jobs averaging $1098. ***State or other work-study/employment:*** *Total amount:* $134,363 (8% need-based, 92% non-need-based). 90 part-time jobs averaging $1492.

ATHLETIC AWARDS *Total amount:* 347,612 (100% need-based).

APPLYING for FINANCIAL AID ***Required financial aid forms:*** FAFSA, institution's own form. ***Financial aid deadline (priority):*** 4/1. ***Notification date:*** Continuous. Students must reply within 2 weeks of notification.

CONTACT Myra Pfannenstiel, Director of Financial Aid, Friends University, 2100 University Street, Wichita, KS 67213, 316-295-5590 or toll-free 800-577-2233. *Fax:* 316-295-5703. *E-mail:* pfannem@friends.edu

FROSTBURG STATE UNIVERSITY

Frostburg, MD

Tuition & fees (MD res): $4132 **Average undergraduate aid package: $4583**

ABOUT THE INSTITUTION State-supported, coed. Awards: bachelor's and master's degrees. 44 undergraduate majors. Total enrollment: 5,198. Undergraduates: 4,313. Freshmen: 937. Both federal and institutional methodology are used as a basis for awarding need-based institutional aid.

UNDERGRADUATE EXPENSES for 2000–2001 ***Application fee:*** $30. ***Tuition, state resident:*** full-time $3342; part-time $138 per credit hour. ***Tuition, nonresident:*** full-time $8492; part-time $244 per credit hour. ***Required fees:*** full-time $790; $33 per credit hour; $9 per term part-time. Full-time tuition and fees vary according to course load and program. Part-time tuition and fees vary according to course load and program. ***College room and board:*** $5214; ***room only:*** $2650. Room and board charges vary according to board plan and housing facility. ***Payment plans:*** installment, deferred payment.

FRESHMAN FINANCIAL AID (Fall 1998) 720 applied for aid; of those 71% were deemed to have need. 97% of freshmen with need received aid; of those 24% had need fully met. *Average percent of need met:* 55% (excluding resources awarded to replace EFC). *Average financial aid package:* $3798 (excluding resources awarded to replace EFC). 18% of all full-time freshmen had no need and received non-need-based aid.

UNDERGRADUATE FINANCIAL AID (Fall 1998) 2,797 applied for aid; of those 76% were deemed to have need. 98% of undergraduates with need received aid; of those 12% had need fully met. *Average percent of need met:* 76% (excluding resources awarded to replace EFC). *Average financial aid package:* $4583 (excluding resources awarded to replace EFC). 14% of all full-time undergraduates had no need and received non-need-based aid.

GIFT AID (NEED-BASED) ***Total amount:*** $4,319,297 (55% Federal, 39% state, 6% external sources). ***Receiving aid:*** *Freshmen:* 40% (378); *all full-time undergraduates:* 38% (1,556). ***Average award:*** Freshmen: $1555; Undergraduates: $1450. ***Scholarships, grants, and awards:*** Federal Pell, FSEOG, state, private, college/university gift aid from institutional funds.

GIFT AID (NON-NEED-BASED) ***Total amount:*** $1,212,537 (18% state, 61% institutional, 21% external sources). ***Receiving aid:*** *Freshmen:* 9% (90); *Undergraduates:* 7% (286). ***Scholarships, grants, and awards by category:*** *Academic Interests/Achievement:* biological sciences, business, communication, education, English, foreign languages, general academic interests/achievements, international studies, mathematics, physical sciences, social sciences. *Creative Arts/Performance:* art/fine arts, music, theater/drama. *Special Achievements/Activities:* community service, hobbies/interests, leadership. *Special Characteristics:* adult students, children and siblings of alumni, children of union members/company employees, handicapped students, local/state students, out-of-state students, veterans, veterans' children. ***Tuition waivers:*** Full or partial for employees or children of employees, senior citizens.

LOANS ***Student loans:*** $9,670,995 (65% need-based, 35% non-need-based). 62% of past graduating class borrowed through all loan programs. Average indebtedness per student: $13,103. ***Average need-based loan:*** Freshmen: $2061; Undergraduates: $2728. ***Parent loans:*** $3,069,299 (100% non-need-based). ***Programs:*** FFEL (Subsidized and Unsubsidized Stafford, PLUS), Perkins, college/university.

WORK-STUDY ***Federal work-study:*** *Total amount:* $261,103; 292 jobs averaging $895. ***State or other work-study/employment:*** *Total amount:* $349,957 (100% non-need-based). Part-time jobs available.

APPLYING for FINANCIAL AID ***Required financial aid form:*** FAFSA. ***Financial aid deadline:*** 3/1 (priority: 2/15). ***Notification date:*** 3/15. Students must reply within 3 weeks of notification.

Frostburg State University (continued)

CONTACT Mrs. Marjorie Robison, Director of Financial Aid, Frostburg State University, 101 Braddock Road, Frostburg, MD 21532-1099, 301-687-4301. *Fax:* 301-687-3029. *E-mail:* mrobison@frostburg.umd.edu

FURMAN UNIVERSITY

Greenville, SC

Tuition & fees: $18,266 **Average undergraduate aid package: $14,200**

ABOUT THE INSTITUTION Independent, coed. Awards: bachelor's and master's degrees. 44 undergraduate majors. Total enrollment: 3,453. Undergraduates: 2,840. Freshmen: 684. Both federal and institutional methodology are used as a basis for awarding need-based institutional aid.

UNDERGRADUATE EXPENSES for 1999–2000 ***Application fee:*** $40. ***Comprehensive fee:*** $23,114 includes full-time tuition ($17,888), mandatory fees ($378), and room and board ($4848). ***College room only:*** $2584. Room and board charges vary according to board plan and housing facility. ***Part-time tuition:*** $559 per credit hour. ***Part-time fees:*** $200 per term part-time. Part-time tuition and fees vary according to course load. ***Payment plan:*** installment.

FRESHMAN FINANCIAL AID (Fall 1999, est.) 581 applied for aid; of those 60% were deemed to have need. 100% of freshmen with need received aid; of those 85% had need fully met. *Average percent of need met:* 88% (excluding resources awarded to replace EFC). *Average financial aid package:* $12,630 (excluding resources awarded to replace EFC). 7% of all full-time freshmen had no need and received non-need-based aid.

UNDERGRADUATE FINANCIAL AID (Fall 1999, est.) 2,368 applied for aid; of those 55% were deemed to have need. 100% of undergraduates with need received aid; of those 85% had need fully met. *Average percent of need met:* 85% (excluding resources awarded to replace EFC). *Average financial aid package:* $14,200 (excluding resources awarded to replace EFC). 9% of all full-time undergraduates had no need and received non-need-based aid.

GIFT AID (NEED-BASED) ***Total amount:*** $7,126,702 (11% Federal, 28% state, 59% institutional, 2% external sources). ***Receiving aid:*** *Freshmen:* 45% (307); *all full-time undergraduates:* 42% (1,107). ***Average award:*** Freshmen: $8600; Undergraduates: $9400. ***Scholarships, grants, and awards:*** Federal Pell, FSEOG, state, private, college/university gift aid from institutional funds.

GIFT AID (NON-NEED-BASED) ***Total amount:*** $9,088,799 (1% Federal, 16% state, 68% institutional, 15% external sources). ***Receiving aid:*** *Freshmen:* 4% (29); *Undergraduates:* 4% (117). ***Scholarships, grants, and awards by category:*** *Academic Interests/Achievement:* 1,679 awards ($5,730,639 total): biological sciences, business, computer science, education, engineering/technologies, English, general academic interests/achievements, health fields, humanities, mathematics, military science, physical sciences, religion/biblical studies, social sciences. *Creative Arts/Performance:* 245 awards ($538,050 total): art/fine arts, creative writing, music, theater/drama. *Special Achievements/Activities:* 47 awards ($100,420 total): religious involvement. *Special Characteristics:* 67 awards ($188,931 total): relatives of clergy, religious affiliation. ***Tuition waivers:*** Full or partial for employees or children of employees. ***ROTC:*** Army.

LOANS ***Student loans:*** $4,101,952 (65% need-based, 35% non-need-based). 52% of past graduating class borrowed through all loan programs. Average indebtedness per student: $11,750. ***Average need-based loan:*** Freshmen: $116; Undergraduates: $289. ***Parent loans:*** $1,414,000 (100% non-need-based). ***Programs:*** FFEL (Subsidized and Unsubsidized Stafford, PLUS), Perkins, college/university, alternative loans, TERI Loans.

WORK-STUDY ***Federal work-study:*** *Total amount:* $320,063; jobs available. ***State or other work-study/employment:*** *Total amount:* $360,500 (100% non-need-based). 425 part-time jobs averaging $848.

ATHLETIC AWARDS *Total amount:* 3,383,000 (100% non-need-based).

APPLYING for FINANCIAL AID ***Required financial aid forms:*** FAFSA, institution's own form. ***Financial aid deadline (priority):*** 2/1. ***Notification date:*** 3/15. Students must reply by 5/1.

CONTACT Martin Carney, Director of Financial Aid, Furman University, 3300 Poinsett Highway, Greenville, SC 29613, 864-294-2204. *Fax:* 864-294-3127.

GALLAUDET UNIVERSITY

Washington, DC

Tuition & fees: $7180 **Average undergraduate aid package: N/A**

ABOUT THE INSTITUTION Independent, coed. Awards: bachelor's, master's, and doctoral degrees (all undergraduate programs open primarily to hearing-impaired). 52 undergraduate majors. Total enrollment: 1,661. Undergraduates: 1,244. Freshmen: 253. Both federal and institutional methodology are used as a basis for awarding need-based institutional aid.

UNDERGRADUATE EXPENSES for 1999–2000 ***Application fee:*** $35. ***One-time required fee:*** $10. ***Comprehensive fee:*** $14,310 includes full-time tuition ($6870), mandatory fees ($310), and room and board ($7130). ***College room only:*** $4070. Room and board charges vary according to board plan. ***Part-time tuition:*** $344 per credit hour. ***Payment plan:*** installment.

GIFT AID (NEED-BASED) ***Scholarships, grants, and awards:*** Federal Pell, FSEOG, state, college/university gift aid from institutional funds.

GIFT AID (NON-NEED-BASED) ***Scholarships, grants, and awards by category:*** *Academic Interests/Achievement:* general academic interests/achievements. *Special Characteristics:* children of educators, children of faculty/staff, handicapped students, international students. ***Tuition waivers:*** Full or partial for employees or children of employees.

LOANS ***Programs:*** FFEL (Subsidized and Unsubsidized Stafford, PLUS), Perkins.

WORK-STUDY Federal work-study jobs available. ***State or other work-study/employment:*** Part-time jobs available.

APPLYING for FINANCIAL AID ***Required financial aid forms:*** FAFSA, institution's own form. ***Financial aid deadline (priority):*** 8/15. ***Notification date:*** Continuous. Students must reply within 4 weeks of notification.

CONTACT Mrs. Nancy C. Goodman, Director of Financial Aid, Gallaudet University, 800 Florida Avenue, NE, Washington, DC 20002-3695, 202-651-5290 or toll-free 800-995-0550 (out-of-state). *Fax:* 202-651-5740.

GANNON UNIVERSITY

Erie, PA

Tuition & fees: $13,408 **Average undergraduate aid package: $11,950**

ABOUT THE INSTITUTION Independent Roman Catholic, coed. Awards: associate, bachelor's, master's, and doctoral degrees. 59 undergraduate majors. Total enrollment: 3,292. Undergraduates: 2,490. Freshmen: 520. Federal methodology is used as a basis for awarding need-based institutional aid.

UNDERGRADUATE EXPENSES for 1999–2000 ***Application fee:*** $25. ***Comprehensive fee:*** $18,848 includes full-time tuition ($13,020), mandatory fees ($388), and room and board ($5440). ***College room only:*** $3020. Full-time tuition and fees vary according to class time and program. Room and board charges vary according to housing facility. ***Part-time tuition:*** $405 per credit. ***Part-time fees:*** $12 per credit. Part-time tuition and fees vary according to class time and program. ***Payment plan:*** installment.

FRESHMAN FINANCIAL AID (Fall 1999, est.) 496 applied for aid; of those 84% were deemed to have need. 100% of freshmen with need received aid; of those 43% had need fully met. *Average percent of need met:* 70% (excluding resources awarded to replace EFC). *Average financial aid package:* $13,270 (excluding resources awarded to replace EFC). 16% of all full-time freshmen had no need and received non-need-based aid.

UNDERGRADUATE FINANCIAL AID (Fall 1999, est.) 2,016 applied for aid; of those 91% were deemed to have need. 100% of undergraduates with need received aid; of those 42% had need fully met. *Average percent of need met:* 80% (excluding resources awarded to replace EFC). *Average*

financial aid package: $11,950 (excluding resources awarded to replace EFC). 10% of all full-time undergraduates had no need and received non-need-based aid.

GIFT AID (NEED-BASED) ***Total amount:*** $7,228,036 (24% Federal, 35% state, 41% institutional). ***Receiving aid:*** *Freshmen:* 83% (419); *all full-time undergraduates:* 87% (1,834). ***Average award:*** Freshmen: $9070; Undergraduates: $9070. ***Scholarships, grants, and awards:*** Federal Pell, FSEOG, state, private, college/university gift aid from institutional funds.

GIFT AID (NON-NEED-BASED) ***Total amount:*** $6,644,602 (88% institutional, 12% external sources). ***Receiving aid:*** *Freshmen:* 41% (207); *Undergraduates:* 45% (958). ***Scholarships, grants, and awards by category:*** *Academic Interests/Achievement:* 728 awards ($2,042,700 total): biological sciences, business, education, engineering/technologies, English, foreign languages, general academic interests/achievements, international studies, mathematics, premedicine, religion/biblical studies. *Creative Arts/Performance:* 49 awards ($87,000 total): music, theater/drama. *Special Achievements/Activities:* 777 awards ($1,432,767 total): community service, leadership. *Special Characteristics:* 20 awards ($50,000 total): adult students, ethnic background, international students, members of minority groups, religious affiliation. ***Tuition waivers:*** Full or partial for employees or children of employees, senior citizens. ***ROTC:*** Army.

LOANS ***Student loans:*** $10,794,229 (59% need-based, 41% non-need-based). 90% of past graduating class borrowed through all loan programs. Average indebtedness per student: $19,005. ***Average need-based loan:*** Freshmen: $2500; Undergraduates: $4200. ***Parent loans:*** $1,096,676 (100% non-need-based). ***Programs:*** FFEL (Subsidized and Unsubsidized Stafford, PLUS), Perkins, Federal Nursing.

WORK-STUDY ***Federal work-study:*** *Total amount:* $573,333; 536 jobs averaging $1131. ***State or other work-study/employment:*** *Total amount:* $300,000 (100% non-need-based). 321 part-time jobs averaging $1025.

ATHLETIC AWARDS *Total amount:* 1,066,648 (100% non-need-based).

APPLYING for FINANCIAL AID ***Required financial aid forms:*** FAFSA, institution's own form. ***Financial aid deadline (priority):*** 3/15. ***Notification date:*** Continuous. Students must reply within 4 weeks of notification.

CONTACT Mr. James Treiber, Director of Financial Aid, Gannon University, University Square, Erie, PA 16541, 814-871-7337 or toll-free 800-GANNONU. *Fax:* 814-871-5803. *E-mail:* treiber001@gannon.edu

GARDNER-WEBB UNIVERSITY

Boiling Springs, NC

Tuition & fees: $11,660 **Average undergraduate aid package: $9576**

ABOUT THE INSTITUTION Independent Baptist, coed. Awards: associate, bachelor's, and master's degrees. 41 undergraduate majors. Total enrollment: 3,042. Undergraduates: 2,411. Freshmen: 407. Both federal and institutional methodology are used as a basis for awarding need-based institutional aid.

UNDERGRADUATE EXPENSES for 1999–2000 ***Application fee:*** $25. ***Comprehensive fee:*** $16,420 includes full-time tuition ($11,660) and room and board ($4760). ***College room only:*** $2320. Room and board charges vary according to board plan and housing facility. ***Part-time tuition:*** $240 per credit hour. Part-time tuition and fees vary according to course load.

FRESHMAN FINANCIAL AID (Fall 1998) 347 applied for aid; of those 81% were deemed to have need. 100% of freshmen with need received aid; of those 46% had need fully met. *Average percent of need met:* 90% (excluding resources awarded to replace EFC). *Average financial aid package:* $10,454 (excluding resources awarded to replace EFC).

UNDERGRADUATE FINANCIAL AID (Fall 1998) 941 applied for aid; of those 87% were deemed to have need. 100% of undergraduates with need received aid; of those 45% had need fully met. *Average percent of need met:* 81% (excluding resources awarded to replace EFC). *Average financial aid package:* $9576 (excluding resources awarded to replace EFC).

GIFT AID (NEED-BASED) ***Total amount:*** $7,845,875 (18% Federal, 30% state, 43% institutional, 9% external sources). ***Receiving aid:*** *Freshmen:* 69% (279); *all full-time undergraduates:* 41% (805). ***Average award:*** Freshmen: $7296; Undergraduates: $9519. ***Scholarships, grants, and awards:*** Federal Pell, FSEOG, state, private, college/university gift aid from institutional funds.

GIFT AID (NON-NEED-BASED) ***Total amount:*** $1,392,994 (52% state, 39% institutional, 9% external sources). ***Receiving aid:*** *Freshmen:* 31% (126); *Undergraduates:* 17% (337). ***Scholarships, grants, and awards by category:*** *Academic Interests/Achievement:* 686 awards ($2,077,905 total): biological sciences, business, communication, computer science, education, English, foreign languages, general academic interests/achievements, health fields, humanities, mathematics, physical sciences, premedicine, religion/biblical studies, social sciences. *Creative Arts/Performance:* 26 awards ($57,550 total): music, theater/drama. *Special Achievements/Activities:* 376 awards ($299,230 total): cheerleading/drum major, religious involvement. *Special Characteristics:* 1,513 awards ($2,558,942 total): children of faculty/staff, handicapped students, local/state students, members of minority groups, out-of-state students, relatives of clergy.

LOANS ***Student loans:*** $6,268,255 (85% need-based, 15% non-need-based). 62% of past graduating class borrowed through all loan programs. ***Average need-based loan:*** Freshmen: $2860; Undergraduates: $6596. ***Parent loans:*** $935,805 (46% need-based, 54% non-need-based). ***Programs:*** FFEL (Subsidized and Unsubsidized Stafford, PLUS), Perkins, Federal Nursing, state, college/university.

WORK-STUDY ***Federal work-study:*** *Total amount:* $230,044; 146 jobs averaging $1576. ***State or other work-study/employment:*** *Total amount:* $786,533 (61% need-based, 39% non-need-based). 511 part-time jobs averaging $1538.

ATHLETIC AWARDS *Total amount:* 1,172,299 (73% need-based, 27% non-need-based).

APPLYING for FINANCIAL AID ***Required financial aid forms:*** FAFSA, institution's own form, state aid form. ***Financial aid deadline:*** Continuous. ***Notification date:*** Continuous beginning 3/20. Students must reply within 4 weeks of notification.

CONTACT Ms. Cindy Wallace, Assistant Director, Financial Planning, Gardner-Webb University, PO Box 955, Boiling Springs, NC 28017, 704-406-4494 or toll-free 800-253-6472. *Fax:* 704-406-4102. *E-mail:* cwallace@gardner-webb.edu

GENEVA COLLEGE

Beaver Falls, PA

Tuition & fees: $12,650 **Average undergraduate aid package: $9000**

ABOUT THE INSTITUTION Independent religious, coed. Awards: associate, bachelor's, and master's degrees. 35 undergraduate majors. Total enrollment: 2,127. Undergraduates: 1,877. Freshmen: 348. Federal methodology is used as a basis for awarding need-based institutional aid.

UNDERGRADUATE EXPENSES for 1999–2000 ***Application fee:*** $25. ***Comprehensive fee:*** $17,602 includes full-time tuition ($12,350), mandatory fees ($300), and room and board ($4952). ***College room only:*** $2476. Full-time tuition and fees vary according to course load and reciprocity agreements. Room and board charges vary according to board plan. ***Part-time tuition:*** $390 per credit. ***Part-time fees:*** $50 per term part-time. Part-time tuition and fees vary according to course load and reciprocity agreements. ***Payment plan:*** installment.

FRESHMAN FINANCIAL AID (Fall 1999) 320 applied for aid; of those 94% were deemed to have need. 100% of freshmen with need received aid; of those 95% had need fully met. *Average percent of need met:* 75% (excluding resources awarded to replace EFC). *Average financial aid package:* $9000 (excluding resources awarded to replace EFC). 4% of all full-time freshmen had no need and received non-need-based aid.

UNDERGRADUATE FINANCIAL AID (Fall 1999) 1,150 applied for aid; of those 93% were deemed to have need. 100% of undergraduates with need received aid; of those 84% had need fully met. *Average percent of need met:* 75% (excluding resources awarded to replace EFC). *Average financial aid package:* $9000 (excluding resources awarded to replace EFC). 2% of all full-time undergraduates had no need and received non-need-based aid.

Geneva College (continued)

GIFT AID (NEED-BASED) ***Total amount:*** $6,037,439 (25% Federal, 36% state, 39% institutional). ***Receiving aid:*** *Freshmen:* 82% (290); *all full-time undergraduates:* 81% (1,022). ***Scholarships, grants, and awards:*** Federal Pell, FSEOG, state, private, college/university gift aid from institutional funds.

GIFT AID (NON-NEED-BASED) ***Total amount:*** $1,985,489 (91% institutional, 9% external sources). ***Receiving aid:*** *Freshmen:* 56% (200); *Undergraduates:* 59% (743). ***Scholarships, grants, and awards by category:*** *Academic Interests/Achievement:* engineering/technologies, general academic interests/achievements. *Creative Arts/Performance:* music. *Special Characteristics:* children of faculty/staff, relatives of clergy, religious affiliation. ***Tuition waivers:*** Full or partial for employees or children of employees. ***ROTC:*** Army cooperative.

LOANS ***Student loans:*** $8,328,612 (45% need-based, 55% non-need-based). 90% of past graduating class borrowed through all loan programs. Average indebtedness per student: $20,000. ***Programs:*** Federal Direct (Subsidized and Unsubsidized Stafford, PLUS), Perkins.

WORK-STUDY ***Federal work-study:*** *Total amount:* $210,000; 205 jobs averaging $1000.

ATHLETIC AWARDS *Total amount:* 866,518 (100% non-need-based).

APPLYING for FINANCIAL AID ***Required financial aid form:*** FAFSA. ***Financial aid deadline (priority):*** 4/15. ***Notification date:*** Continuous. Students must reply within 4 weeks of notification.

CONTACT Mr. Steve Bell, Director of Financial Aid, Geneva College, 3200 College Avenue, Beaver Falls, PA 15010-3599, 800-847-8255. *Fax:* 724-847-6776. *E-mail:* financialaid@geneva.edu

GEORGE FOX UNIVERSITY

Newberg, OR

Tuition & fees: $17,610 **Average undergraduate aid package: $14,792**

ABOUT THE INSTITUTION Independent Friends, coed. Awards: bachelor's, master's, doctoral, and first professional degrees. 48 undergraduate majors. Total enrollment: 2,414. Undergraduates: 1,677. Freshmen: 287. Federal methodology is used as a basis for awarding need-based institutional aid.

UNDERGRADUATE EXPENSES for 2000–2001 ***Application fee:*** $40. ***Comprehensive fee:*** $23,160 includes full-time tuition ($17,300), mandatory fees ($310), and room and board ($5550). ***College room only:*** $2830. Full-time tuition and fees vary according to program. Room and board charges vary according to housing facility. ***Part-time tuition:*** $535 per semester hour. ***Part-time fees:*** $100 per term. Part-time tuition and fees vary according to course load. ***Payment plan:*** installment.

FRESHMAN FINANCIAL AID (Fall 1999, est.) 270 applied for aid; of those 83% were deemed to have need. 100% of freshmen with need received aid; of those 47% had need fully met. *Average percent of need met:* 84% (excluding resources awarded to replace EFC). *Average financial aid package:* $15,561 (excluding resources awarded to replace EFC). 16% of all full-time freshmen had no need and received non-need-based aid.

UNDERGRADUATE FINANCIAL AID (Fall 1999, est.) 1,288 applied for aid; of those 84% were deemed to have need. 99% of undergraduates with need received aid; of those 46% had need fully met. *Average percent of need met:* 84% (excluding resources awarded to replace EFC). *Average financial aid package:* $14,792 (excluding resources awarded to replace EFC). 14% of all full-time undergraduates had no need and received non-need-based aid.

GIFT AID (NEED-BASED) ***Total amount:*** $8,498,076 (9% Federal, 8% state, 74% institutional, 9% external sources). ***Receiving aid:*** *Freshmen:* 77% (223); *all full-time undergraduates:* 79% (1,075). ***Average award:*** Freshmen: $10,240; Undergraduates: $9044. ***Scholarships, grants, and awards:*** Federal Pell, FSEOG, state, private, college/university gift aid from institutional funds.

GIFT AID (NON-NEED-BASED) ***Total amount:*** $1,922,717 (71% institutional, 29% external sources). ***Receiving aid:*** *Freshmen:* 7% (21); *Undergraduates:* 7% (99). ***Scholarships, grants, and awards by category:*** *Academic Interests/Achievement:* biological sciences, education, general academic interests/achievements, mathematics, physical sciences, religion/biblical studies. *Creative Arts/Performance:* debating, music, theater/drama. *Special Achievements/Activities:* leadership, religious involvement. *Special Characteristics:* children and siblings of alumni, ethnic background, international students, members of minority groups, out-of-state students, relatives of clergy, religious affiliation. ***Tuition waivers:*** Full or partial for minority students, employees or children of employees, senior citizens. ***ROTC:*** Air Force cooperative.

LOANS ***Student loans:*** $4,809,131 (87% need-based, 13% non-need-based). 83% of past graduating class borrowed through all loan programs. Average indebtedness per student: $15,708. ***Average need-based loan:*** Freshmen: $4302; Undergraduates: $4677. ***Parent loans:*** $2,119,820 (42% need-based, 58% non-need-based). ***Programs:*** Federal Direct (Subsidized and Unsubsidized Stafford, PLUS), Perkins, Alaska Loans.

WORK-STUDY ***Federal work-study:*** *Total amount:* $1,143,297; 840 jobs averaging $1895.

APPLYING for FINANCIAL AID ***Required financial aid forms:*** FAFSA, state aid form. ***Financial aid deadline (priority):*** 3/1. ***Notification date:*** 4/1.

CONTACT Mr. Kevin Multop, Associate Director of Financial Aid, George Fox University, 414 North Meridian, Newberg, OR 97132-2697, 503-538-8383 or toll-free 800-765-4369. *Fax:* 503-554-3880. *E-mail:* kmultop@georgefox.edu

GEORGE MASON UNIVERSITY

Fairfax, VA

Tuition & fees (VA res): $3756 **Average undergraduate aid package: $6049**

ABOUT THE INSTITUTION State-supported, coed. Awards: bachelor's, master's, doctoral, and first professional degrees and post-bachelor's certificates. 60 undergraduate majors. Total enrollment: 24,180. Undergraduates: 15,262. Freshmen: 2,130. Federal methodology is used as a basis for awarding need-based institutional aid.

UNDERGRADUATE EXPENSES for 1999–2000 ***Application fee:*** $30. ***One-time required fee:*** $100. ***Tuition, state resident:*** full-time $3756; part-time $156 per credit hour. ***Tuition, nonresident:*** full-time $12,516; part-time $522 per credit hour. Full-time tuition and fees vary according to course load. Part-time tuition and fees vary according to course load. ***College room and board:*** $5298; ***room only:*** $3300. Room and board charges vary according to board plan and housing facility. ***Payment plans:*** installment, deferred payment.

FRESHMAN FINANCIAL AID (Fall 1999, est.) 1552 applied for aid; of those 65% were deemed to have need. 82% of freshmen with need received aid; of those 54% had need fully met. *Average percent of need met:* 55% (excluding resources awarded to replace EFC). *Average financial aid package:* $5720 (excluding resources awarded to replace EFC). 12% of all full-time freshmen had no need and received non-need-based aid.

UNDERGRADUATE FINANCIAL AID (Fall 1999, est.) 8,821 applied for aid; of those 72% were deemed to have need. 83% of undergraduates with need received aid; of those 51% had need fully met. *Average percent of need met:* 59% (excluding resources awarded to replace EFC). *Average financial aid package:* $6049 (excluding resources awarded to replace EFC). 11% of all full-time undergraduates had no need and received non-need-based aid.

GIFT AID (NEED-BASED) ***Total amount:*** $12,044,015 (53% Federal, 44% state, 3% institutional). ***Receiving aid:*** *Freshmen:* 29% (598); *all full-time undergraduates:* 33% (3,503). ***Average award:*** Freshmen: $3731; Undergraduates: $3311. ***Scholarships, grants, and awards:*** Federal Pell, FSEOG, state, private, college/university gift aid from institutional funds.

GIFT AID (NON-NEED-BASED) ***Total amount:*** $1,868,103 (45% institutional, 55% external sources). ***Receiving aid:*** *Freshmen:* 14% (284); *Undergraduates:* 7% (733). ***Scholarships, grants, and awards by category:*** *Academic Interests/Achievement:* general academic interests/achievements. ***Tuition waivers:*** Full or partial for employees or children of employees, senior citizens. ***ROTC:*** Army, Air Force cooperative.

LOANS ***Student loans:*** $25,708,971 (74% need-based, 26% non-need-based). 55% of past graduating class borrowed through all loan programs. Average indebtedness per student: $13,826. ***Average need-based loan:***

Freshmen: $2566; Undergraduates: $3569. ***Parent loans:*** $3,909,614 (16% need-based, 84% non-need-based). ***Programs:*** Federal Direct (Subsidized and Unsubsidized Stafford, PLUS), Perkins.

WORK-STUDY ***Federal work-study:*** *Total amount:* $1,312,549; jobs available.

ATHLETIC AWARDS *Total amount:* 1,912,904 (100% non-need-based).

APPLYING for FINANCIAL AID ***Required financial aid form:*** FAFSA. ***Financial aid deadline (priority):*** 3/1. ***Notification date:*** Continuous beginning 4/1. Students must reply within 3 weeks of notification.

CONTACT Office of Student Financial Aid, George Mason University, Mail Stop 3B5, Fairfax, VA 22030-4444, 703-993-2353.

GEORGETOWN COLLEGE

Georgetown, KY

Tuition & fees: $12,390 **Average undergraduate aid package: $11,821**

ABOUT THE INSTITUTION Independent religious, coed. Awards: bachelor's and master's degrees. 45 undergraduate majors. Total enrollment: 1,672. Undergraduates: 1,338. Freshmen: 340. Federal methodology is used as a basis for awarding need-based institutional aid.

UNDERGRADUATE EXPENSES for 2000–2001 ***Application fee:*** $25. ***Comprehensive fee:*** $16,990 includes full-time tuition ($12,150), mandatory fees ($240), and room and board ($4600). ***College room only:*** $2220. Room and board charges vary according to board plan, housing facility, and location. ***Part-time tuition:*** $470 per semester hour. ***Part-time fees:*** $15 per term. Part-time tuition and fees vary according to course load. ***Payment plan:*** deferred payment.

FRESHMAN FINANCIAL AID (Fall 1999, est.) 293 applied for aid; of those 71% were deemed to have need. 100% of freshmen with need received aid; of those 35% had need fully met. *Average percent of need met:* 94% (excluding resources awarded to replace EFC). *Average financial aid package:* $11,619 (excluding resources awarded to replace EFC). 34% of all full-time freshmen had no need and received non-need-based aid.

UNDERGRADUATE FINANCIAL AID (Fall 1999, est.) 1,014 applied for aid; of those 74% were deemed to have need. 100% of undergraduates with need received aid; of those 38% had need fully met. *Average percent of need met:* 93% (excluding resources awarded to replace EFC). *Average financial aid package:* $11,821 (excluding resources awarded to replace EFC). 35% of all full-time undergraduates had no need and received non-need-based aid.

GIFT AID (NEED-BASED) ***Total amount:*** $6,088,983 (12% Federal, 17% state, 64% institutional, 7% external sources). ***Receiving aid:*** *Freshmen:* 61% (206); *all full-time undergraduates:* 56% (725). ***Average award:*** Freshmen: $5993; Undergraduates: $6034. ***Scholarships, grants, and awards:*** Federal Pell, FSEOG, state, private, college/university gift aid from institutional funds.

GIFT AID (NON-NEED-BASED) ***Total amount:*** $2,532,718 (6% state, 86% institutional, 8% external sources). ***Receiving aid:*** *Freshmen:* 41% (138); *Undergraduates:* 36% (467). ***Scholarships, grants, and awards by category:*** *Academic Interests/Achievement:* general academic interests/achievements. *Creative Arts/Performance:* art/fine arts, music, performing arts, theater/drama. *Special Achievements/Activities:* religious involvement. *Special Characteristics:* children of faculty/staff, relatives of clergy, religious affiliation. ***Tuition waivers:*** Full or partial for employees or children of employees. ***ROTC:*** Army, Air Force cooperative.

LOANS ***Student loans:*** $3,032,910 (63% need-based, 37% non-need-based). 61% of past graduating class borrowed through all loan programs. Average indebtedness per student: $14,393. ***Average need-based loan:*** Freshmen: $2574; Undergraduates: $3393. ***Parent loans:*** $474,630 (100% non-need-based). ***Programs:*** FFEL (Subsidized and Unsubsidized Stafford, PLUS), Perkins, college/university.

WORK-STUDY ***Federal work-study:*** *Total amount:* $180,000; jobs available. ***State or other work-study/employment:*** *Total amount:* $263,340 (100% non-need-based). Part-time jobs available.

ATHLETIC AWARDS *Total amount:* 630,971 (49% need-based, 51% non-need-based).

APPLYING for FINANCIAL AID ***Required financial aid form:*** FAFSA. ***Financial aid deadline (priority):*** 2/15. ***Notification date:*** 4/1. Students must reply by 5/1 or within 4 weeks of notification.

CONTACT Ms. Anne Leigh Bisese, Director of Financial Planning, Georgetown College, 400 East College Street, Georgetown, KY 40324-1696, 502-863-8027 or toll-free 800-788-9985. *Fax:* 502-868-8884.

GEORGETOWN UNIVERSITY

Washington, DC

Tuition & fees: $23,295 **Average undergraduate aid package: $19,048**

ABOUT THE INSTITUTION Independent Roman Catholic (Jesuit), coed. Awards: bachelor's, master's, doctoral, and first professional degrees. 38 undergraduate majors. Total enrollment: 12,498. Undergraduates: 6,361. Freshmen: 1,498. Both federal and institutional methodology are used as a basis for awarding need-based institutional aid.

UNDERGRADUATE EXPENSES for 1999–2000 ***Application fee:*** $50. ***Comprehensive fee:*** $31,988 includes full-time tuition ($23,088), mandatory fees ($207), and room and board ($8693). ***College room only:*** $5605. Room and board charges vary according to board plan and housing facility. ***Part-time tuition:*** $962 per credit hour. Part-time tuition and fees vary according to course load. ***Payment plans:*** installment, deferred payment.

FRESHMAN FINANCIAL AID (Fall 1999, est.) 832 applied for aid; of those 77% were deemed to have need. 100% of freshmen with need received aid; of those 100% had need fully met. *Average percent of need met:* 100% (excluding resources awarded to replace EFC). *Average financial aid package:* $18,895 (excluding resources awarded to replace EFC). 6% of all full-time freshmen had no need and received non-need-based aid.

UNDERGRADUATE FINANCIAL AID (Fall 1999, est.) 2,852 applied for aid; of those 86% were deemed to have need. 100% of undergraduates with need received aid; of those 100% had need fully met. *Average percent of need met:* 100% (excluding resources awarded to replace EFC). *Average financial aid package:* $19,048 (excluding resources awarded to replace EFC). 5% of all full-time undergraduates had no need and received non-need-based aid.

GIFT AID (NEED-BASED) ***Total amount:*** $33,715,000 (9% Federal, 86% institutional, 5% external sources). ***Receiving aid:*** *Freshmen:* 42% (616); *all full-time undergraduates:* 32% (2,066). ***Average award:*** Freshmen: $14,271; Undergraduates: $12,555. ***Scholarships, grants, and awards:*** Federal Pell, FSEOG, state, private, college/university gift aid from institutional funds.

GIFT AID (NON-NEED-BASED) ***Total amount:*** $1,900,000 (56% Federal, 5% institutional, 39% external sources). ***Receiving aid:*** *Freshmen:* 7; *Undergraduates:* 16. ***Scholarships, grants, and awards by category:*** *Special Characteristics:* children of faculty/staff. ***Tuition waivers:*** Full or partial for employees or children of employees. ***ROTC:*** Army, Naval cooperative, Air Force cooperative.

LOANS ***Student loans:*** $14,800,000 (80% need-based, 20% non-need-based). 50% of past graduating class borrowed through all loan programs. Average indebtedness per student: $19,016. ***Average need-based loan:*** Freshmen: $2231; Undergraduates: $4048. ***Parent loans:*** $10,000,000 (100% non-need-based). ***Programs:*** FFEL (Subsidized and Unsubsidized Stafford, PLUS), Perkins, Federal Nursing, district, alternative loans.

WORK-STUDY ***Federal work-study:*** *Total amount:* $5,600,000; 2,150 jobs averaging $2600.

ATHLETIC AWARDS *Total amount:* 2,700,000 (26% need-based, 74% non-need-based).

APPLYING for FINANCIAL AID ***Required financial aid forms:*** FAFSA, CSS Financial Aid PROFILE, noncustodial (divorced/separated) parent's statement, business/farm supplement. ***Financial aid deadline (priority):*** 2/1. ***Notification date:*** 4/1. Students must reply by 5/1 or within 2 weeks of notification.

CONTACT Ms. Patricia A. McWade, Dean of Student Financial Services, Georgetown University, 37th and O Street, NW, Box 1252, Washington, DC 20057, 202-687-4547. *Fax:* 202-687-6542. *E-mail:* mcwadep@gunet.georgetown.edu

THE GEORGE WASHINGTON UNIVERSITY

Washington, DC

Tuition & fees: $23,375 **Average undergraduate aid package: $20,900**

ABOUT THE INSTITUTION Independent, coed. Awards: associate, bachelor's, master's, doctoral, and first professional degrees and post-bachelor's and post-master's certificates. 79 undergraduate majors. Total enrollment: 20,346. Undergraduates: 8,695. Freshmen: 2,120. Both federal and institutional methodology are used as a basis for awarding need-based institutional aid.

UNDERGRADUATE EXPENSES for 1999–2000 ***Application fee:*** $60. ***Comprehensive fee:*** $31,585 includes full-time tuition ($22,340), mandatory fees ($1035), and room and board ($8210). ***College room only:*** $5510. Room and board charges vary according to board plan and housing facility. ***Part-time tuition:*** $722 per credit hour. ***Part-time fees:*** $34 per credit hour. ***Payment plans:*** installment, deferred payment.

FRESHMAN FINANCIAL AID (Fall 1998) 1179 applied for aid; of those 67% were deemed to have need. 99% of freshmen with need received aid; of those 76% had need fully met. *Average percent of need met:* 94% (excluding resources awarded to replace EFC). *Average financial aid package:* $21,700 (excluding resources awarded to replace EFC). 20% of all full-time freshmen had no need and received non-need-based aid.

UNDERGRADUATE FINANCIAL AID (Fall 1998) 3,708 applied for aid; of those 74% were deemed to have need. 99% of undergraduates with need received aid; of those 71% had need fully met. *Average percent of need met:* 92% (excluding resources awarded to replace EFC). *Average financial aid package:* $20,900 (excluding resources awarded to replace EFC). 19% of all full-time undergraduates had no need and received non-need-based aid.

GIFT AID (NEED-BASED) ***Total amount:*** $32,508,497 (8% Federal, 92% institutional). ***Receiving aid:*** *Freshmen:* 43% (767); *all full-time undergraduates:* 40% (2,668). ***Average award:*** Freshmen: $12,500; Undergraduates: $11,750. ***Scholarships, grants, and awards:*** Federal Pell, FSEOG, state, college/university gift aid from institutional funds.

GIFT AID (NON-NEED-BASED) ***Total amount:*** $10,964,209 (100% institutional). ***Receiving aid:*** *Freshmen:* 4% (78); *Undergraduates:* 3% (182). ***Scholarships, grants, and awards by category:*** *Academic Interests/Achievement:* engineering/technologies, general academic interests/achievements, mathematics. *Creative Arts/Performance:* debating, music, performing arts, theater/drama. *Special Achievements/Activities:* leadership. *Special Characteristics:* children of faculty/staff, international students, local/state students, siblings of current students. ***Tuition waivers:*** Full or partial for employees or children of employees. ***ROTC:*** Army cooperative, Naval, Air Force cooperative.

LOANS ***Student loans:*** $18,308,419 (62% need-based, 38% non-need-based). 52% of past graduating class borrowed through all loan programs. Average indebtedness per student: $18,953. ***Average need-based loan:*** Freshmen: $3000; Undergraduates: $4100. ***Parent loans:*** $10,041,549 (11% need-based, 89% non-need-based). ***Programs:*** FFEL (Subsidized and Unsubsidized Stafford, PLUS), Perkins.

WORK-STUDY ***Federal work-study:*** *Total amount:* $2,779,372; 936 jobs averaging $2970. ***State or other work-study/employment:*** *Total amount:* $13,211 (48% need-based, 52% non-need-based). 8 part-time jobs averaging $1651.

ATHLETIC AWARDS *Total amount:* 3,068,149 (3% need-based, 97% non-need-based).

APPLYING for FINANCIAL AID ***Required financial aid forms:*** FAFSA, CSS Financial Aid PROFILE. ***Financial aid deadline (priority):*** 2/1. ***Notification date:*** 3/20. Students must reply by 5/1 or within 2 weeks of notification.

CONTACT Mr. Daniel E. Small, Director, Student Financial Assistance, The George Washington University, 2121 I Street, NW, 3rd Floor, Washington, DC 20052, 202-994-6620 or toll-free 800-447-3765. *Fax:* 202-994-0906.

GEORGIA BAPTIST COLLEGE OF NURSING

Atlanta, GA

Tuition & fees: $1508 **Average undergraduate aid package: $7600**

ABOUT THE INSTITUTION Independent Baptist, coed, primarily women. Awards: bachelor's degrees. 1 undergraduate major. Total enrollment: 337. Undergraduates: 337. Freshmen: 29. Federal methodology is used as a basis for awarding need-based institutional aid.

UNDERGRADUATE EXPENSES for 1999–2000 ***Application fee:*** $35. ***Tuition:*** full-time $1024; part-time $318 per semester hour. ***Required fees:*** full-time $484; $240 per term part-time. Full-time tuition and fees vary according to course level and course load. ***Payment plans:*** installment, deferred payment.

FRESHMAN FINANCIAL AID (Fall 1998) 32 applied for aid; of those 72% were deemed to have need. 100% of freshmen with need received aid. *Average percent of need met:* 65% (excluding resources awarded to replace EFC). *Average financial aid package:* $9125 (excluding resources awarded to replace EFC). 28% of all full-time freshmen had no need and received non-need-based aid.

UNDERGRADUATE FINANCIAL AID (Fall 1998) 330 applied for aid; of those 82% were deemed to have need. 100% of undergraduates with need received aid. *Average percent of need met:* 52% (excluding resources awarded to replace EFC). *Average financial aid package:* $7600 (excluding resources awarded to replace EFC). 14% of all full-time undergraduates had no need and received non-need-based aid.

GIFT AID (NEED-BASED) ***Total amount:*** $208,101 (100% Federal). ***Receiving aid:*** *Freshmen:* 72% (23); *all full-time undergraduates:* 69% (229). ***Average award:*** Freshmen: $2500; Undergraduates: $3500. ***Scholarships, grants, and awards:*** Federal Pell, FSEOG, state, private, college/university gift aid from institutional funds.

GIFT AID (NON-NEED-BASED) ***Total amount:*** $1,035,153 (59% state, 35% institutional, 6% external sources). ***Receiving aid:*** *Freshmen:* 72% (23); *Undergraduates:* 69% (228). ***Scholarships, grants, and awards by category:*** *Academic Interests/Achievement:* general academic interests/achievements, health fields. *Special Achievements/Activities:* religious involvement. *Special Characteristics:* 123 awards ($196,943 total): children and siblings of alumni, relatives of clergy, religious affiliation.

LOANS ***Student loans:*** $1,288,232 (66% need-based, 34% non-need-based). 79% of past graduating class borrowed through all loan programs. Average indebtedness per student: $13,653. ***Average need-based loan:*** Freshmen: $2625; Undergraduates: $6237. ***Parent loans:*** $35,463 (100% non-need-based). ***Programs:*** FFEL (Subsidized and Unsubsidized Stafford, PLUS), state.

APPLYING for FINANCIAL AID ***Required financial aid forms:*** FAFSA, institution's own form, state aid form. ***Financial aid deadline:*** Continuous. ***Notification date:*** Continuous. Students must reply within 4 weeks of notification.

CONTACT Ms. Ann F. McQuay, Director of Financial Aid, Georgia Baptist College of Nursing, 274 Boulevard, NE, Atlanta, GA 30312, 404-265-4801 or toll-free 800-551-8835 (in-state). *Fax:* 404-265-6759.

GEORGIA COLLEGE AND STATE UNIVERSITY

Milledgeville, GA

Tuition & fees (GA res): $2214 **Average undergraduate aid package: N/A**

ABOUT THE INSTITUTION State-supported, coed. Awards: bachelor's and master's degrees and post-master's certificates. 39 undergraduate majors. Total enrollment: 5,026. Undergraduates: 3,947. Freshmen: 760. Federal methodology is used as a basis for awarding need-based institutional aid.

UNDERGRADUATE EXPENSES for 1999–2000 ***Application fee:*** $25. ***Tuition, state resident:*** full-time $1808; part-time $76 per semester hour. ***Tuition, nonresident:*** full-time $7232; part-time $302 per semester hour. ***Required fees:*** full-time $406; $203 per term part-time. Part-time tuition and fees vary according to course load. ***College room and board:*** $4170; ***room only:*** $2210. Room and board charges vary according to board plan and housing facility.

FRESHMAN FINANCIAL AID (Fall 1998) 702 applied for aid; of those 38% were deemed to have need. 98% of freshmen with need received aid. 5% of all full-time freshmen had no need and received non-need-based aid.

UNDERGRADUATE FINANCIAL AID (Fall 1998) 2,889 applied for aid; of those 42% were deemed to have need. 95% of undergraduates with need received aid. 2% of all full-time undergraduates had no need and received non-need-based aid.

GIFT AID (NEED-BASED) ***Total amount:*** $2,293,071 (100% Federal). ***Receiving aid:*** *Freshmen:* 12% (89); *all full-time undergraduates:* 13% (450). ***Scholarships, grants, and awards:*** Federal Pell, FSEOG, state, private, college/university gift aid from institutional funds.

GIFT AID (NON-NEED-BASED) ***Total amount:*** $3,537,444 (85% state, 9% institutional, 6% external sources). ***Receiving aid:*** *Freshmen:* 34% (252); *Undergraduates:* 26% (876). ***Scholarships, grants, and awards by category:*** *Academic Interests/Achievement:* business, general academic interests/achievements, health fields, international studies. *Creative Arts/Performance:* debating, journalism/publications, music, theater/drama. *Special Achievements/Activities:* cheerleading/drum major, community service, general special achievements/activities. *Special Characteristics:* children of faculty/staff, international students, members of minority groups, out-of-state students. ***Tuition waivers:*** Full or partial for senior citizens. ***ROTC:*** Army.

LOANS ***Student loans:*** $8,065,206 (64% need-based, 36% non-need-based). Average indebtedness per student: $13,206. ***Parent loans:*** $407,715 (100% non-need-based). ***Programs:*** Federal Direct (Subsidized and Unsubsidized Stafford, PLUS), Perkins, college/university.

WORK-STUDY ***Federal work-study:*** *Total amount:* $213,357; jobs available.

ATHLETIC AWARDS *Total amount:* 267,081 (100% non-need-based).

APPLYING for FINANCIAL AID ***Required financial aid forms:*** FAFSA, institutional scholarship application form. ***Financial aid deadline (priority):*** 3/1. ***Notification date:*** Continuous beginning 3/15. Students must reply within 2 weeks of notification.

CONTACT Mrs. Cathy Crawley, Associate Director of Financial Aid, Georgia College and State University, Campus Box 30, Milledgeville, GA 31061, 912-445-5149 or toll-free 800-342-0471 (in-state). *Fax:* 912-445-0729. *E-mail:* ccrawley@mail.gcsu.edu

GEORGIA INSTITUTE OF TECHNOLOGY

Atlanta, GA

Tuition & fees (GA res): $3108 **Average undergraduate aid package: $5890**

ABOUT THE INSTITUTION State-supported, coed. Awards: bachelor's, master's, and doctoral degrees. 27 undergraduate majors. Total enrollment: 14,074. Undergraduates: 10,256. Freshmen: 2,320. Federal methodology is used as a basis for awarding need-based institutional aid.

UNDERGRADUATE EXPENSES for 1999–2000 ***Application fee:*** $50. ***Tuition, state resident:*** full-time $2414; part-time $101 per semester hour. ***Tuition, nonresident:*** full-time $9656; part-time $403 per semester hour. ***Required fees:*** full-time $694; $36 per term part-time. Part-time tuition and fees vary according to course load. ***College room and board:*** $5118; ***room only:*** $2800. Room and board charges vary according to board plan and housing facility.

FRESHMAN FINANCIAL AID (Fall 1999) 1972 applied for aid; of those 43% were deemed to have need. 97% of freshmen with need received aid; of those 38% had need fully met. *Average percent of need met:* 74% (excluding resources awarded to replace EFC). *Average financial aid package:* $6226 (excluding resources awarded to replace EFC). 44% of all full-time freshmen had no need and received non-need-based aid.

UNDERGRADUATE FINANCIAL AID (Fall 1999) 7,449 applied for aid; of those 43% were deemed to have need. 96% of undergraduates with need received aid; of those 40% had need fully met. *Average percent of need met:* 72% (excluding resources awarded to replace EFC). *Average financial aid package:* $5890 (excluding resources awarded to replace EFC). 36% of all full-time undergraduates had no need and received non-need-based aid.

GIFT AID (NEED-BASED) ***Total amount:*** $10,998,458 (27% Federal, 37% state, 25% institutional, 11% external sources). ***Receiving aid:*** *Freshmen:* 28% (654); *all full-time undergraduates:* 23% (2,182). ***Average award:*** Freshmen: $3776; Undergraduates: $3331. ***Scholarships, grants, and awards:*** Federal Pell, FSEOG, state, private, college/university gift aid from institutional funds.

GIFT AID (NON-NEED-BASED) ***Total amount:*** $16,424,913 (1% Federal, 55% state, 30% institutional, 14% external sources). ***Receiving aid:*** *Freshmen:* 12% (274); *Undergraduates:* 8% (723). ***Scholarships, grants, and awards by category:*** *Academic Interests/Achievement:* 1,448 awards ($2,467,680 total): general academic interests/achievements. *Special Achievements/Activities:* 263 awards ($453,967 total): leadership. *Special Characteristics:* 80 awards ($127,117 total): children of faculty/staff, ethnic background, general special characteristics, members of minority groups. ***ROTC:*** Army, Naval, Air Force.

LOANS ***Student loans:*** $16,011,292 (74% need-based, 26% non-need-based). ***Average need-based loan:*** Freshmen: $3006; Undergraduates: $3792. ***Parent loans:*** $8,135,679 (58% need-based, 42% non-need-based). ***Programs:*** FFEL (Subsidized and Unsubsidized Stafford, PLUS), Perkins, college/university.

WORK-STUDY ***Federal work-study:*** *Total amount:* $402,203; 200 jobs averaging $2400.

ATHLETIC AWARDS *Total amount:* 3,036,411 (28% need-based, 72% non-need-based).

APPLYING for FINANCIAL AID ***Required financial aid forms:*** FAFSA, institution's own form. ***Financial aid deadline (priority):*** 3/1. ***Notification date:*** 4/1.

CONTACT Mr. Jerry McTier, Director of Student Financial Planning and Services, Georgia Institute of Technology, 225 North Avenue, NW, Atlanta, GA 30332-0460, 404-894-4160. *Fax:* 404-894-7412.

GEORGIAN COURT COLLEGE

Lakewood, NJ

Tuition & fees: $12,334 **Average undergraduate aid package: $10,656**

ABOUT THE INSTITUTION Independent Roman Catholic, women only. Awards: bachelor's and master's degrees. 27 undergraduate majors. Total enrollment: 2,420. Undergraduates: 1,582. Freshmen: 142. Federal methodology is used as a basis for awarding need-based institutional aid.

UNDERGRADUATE EXPENSES for 1999–2000 ***Application fee:*** $30. ***Comprehensive fee:*** $16,334 includes full-time tuition ($12,134), mandatory fees ($200), and room and board ($4000). Room and board charges vary according to board plan and housing facility. ***Part-time tuition:*** $337 per credit. ***Part-time fees:*** $48 per term part-time. ***Payment plans:*** installment, deferred payment.

FRESHMAN FINANCIAL AID (Fall 1998) 65 applied for aid; of those 85% were deemed to have need. 98% of freshmen with need received aid; of those 74% had need fully met. *Average percent of need met:* 87% (excluding resources awarded to replace EFC). *Average financial aid package:* $11,867 (excluding resources awarded to replace EFC). 12% of all full-time freshmen had no need and received non-need-based aid.

UNDERGRADUATE FINANCIAL AID (Fall 1998) 814 applied for aid; of those 79% were deemed to have need. 99% of undergraduates with need received aid; of those 37% had need fully met. *Average percent of need met:* 80% (excluding resources awarded to replace EFC). *Average financial aid package:* $10,656 (excluding resources awarded to replace EFC). 5% of all full-time undergraduates had no need and received non-need-based aid.

GIFT AID (NEED-BASED) ***Total amount:*** $3,591,985 (20% Federal, 60% state, 20% institutional). ***Receiving aid:*** *Freshmen:* 70% (51); *all full-time undergraduates:* 52% (498). ***Scholarships, grants, and awards:*** Federal Pell, FSEOG, state, private, college/university gift aid from institutional funds.

Georgian Court College (continued)

GIFT AID (NON-NEED-BASED) ***Total amount:*** $1,808,268 (1% state, 99% institutional). ***Receiving aid:*** *Freshmen:* 60% (44); *Undergraduates:* 40% (382). ***Scholarships, grants, and awards by category:*** *Academic Interests/Achievement:* biological sciences, foreign languages, general academic interests/achievements, mathematics, physical sciences. *Creative Arts/Performance:* art/fine arts. *Special Achievements/Activities:* general special achievements/activities, junior miss. *Special Characteristics:* children and siblings of alumni, religious affiliation, siblings of current students, spouses of current students, veterans. ***Tuition waivers:*** Full or partial for employees or children of employees, senior citizens.

LOANS ***Student loans:*** $3,309,718 (100% need-based). 76% of past graduating class borrowed through all loan programs. Average indebtedness per student: $14,047. ***Parent loans:*** $141,134 (100% need-based). ***Programs:*** FFEL (Subsidized and Unsubsidized Stafford, PLUS), Perkins, state.

WORK-STUDY ***Federal work-study:*** *Total amount:* $88,384; jobs available. ***State or other work-study/employment:*** *Total amount:* $167,259 (100% need-based). Part-time jobs available.

ATHLETIC AWARDS *Total amount:* 300,730 (100% non-need-based).

APPLYING for FINANCIAL AID ***Required financial aid forms:*** FAFSA, institution's own form. ***Financial aid deadline:*** Continuous. ***Notification date:*** Continuous beginning 3/1. Students must reply within 2 weeks of notification.

CONTACT Susan Barschow, Director of Financial Aid, Georgian Court College, 900 Lakewood Avenue, Lakewood, NJ 08701-2697, 732-364-2200 Ext. 258 or toll-free 800-458-8422.

GEORGIA SOUTHERN UNIVERSITY

Statesboro, GA

Tuition & fees (GA res): $2432 **Average undergraduate aid package: $5306**

ABOUT THE INSTITUTION State-supported, coed. Awards: bachelor's, master's, and doctoral degrees and post-master's certificates. 76 undergraduate majors. Total enrollment: 14,476. Undergraduates: 12,909. Freshmen: 3,291. Federal methodology is used as a basis for awarding need-based institutional aid.

UNDERGRADUATE EXPENSES for 1999–2000 ***Application fee:*** $20. ***One-time required fee:*** $50. ***Tuition, state resident:*** full-time $1808; part-time $76 per semester hour. ***Tuition, nonresident:*** full-time $7232; part-time $302 per semester hour. ***Required fees:*** full-time $624; $312 per term part-time. Part-time tuition and fees vary according to course load. ***College room and board:*** $4284; ***room only:*** $2040. Room and board charges vary according to board plan and housing facility.

FRESHMAN FINANCIAL AID (Fall 1998) 2781 applied for aid; of those 64% were deemed to have need. 100% of freshmen with need received aid; of those 26% had need fully met. *Average percent of need met:* 73% (excluding resources awarded to replace EFC). *Average financial aid package:* $4452 (excluding resources awarded to replace EFC). 8% of all full-time freshmen had no need and received non-need-based aid.

UNDERGRADUATE FINANCIAL AID (Fall 1998) 8,694 applied for aid; of those 68% were deemed to have need. 100% of undergraduates with need received aid; of those 25% had need fully met. *Average percent of need met:* 78% (excluding resources awarded to replace EFC). *Average financial aid package:* $5306 (excluding resources awarded to replace EFC). 4% of all full-time undergraduates had no need and received non-need-based aid.

GIFT AID (NEED-BASED) ***Total amount:*** $17,381,375 (50% Federal, 50% state). ***Receiving aid:*** *Freshmen:* 56% (1,605); *all full-time undergraduates:* 43% (4,757). ***Average award:*** Freshmen: $2206; Undergraduates: $1953. ***Scholarships, grants, and awards:*** Federal Pell, FSEOG, state, private, college/university gift aid from institutional funds.

GIFT AID (NON-NEED-BASED) ***Total amount:*** $1,797,683 (33% state, 36% institutional, 31% external sources). ***Receiving aid:*** *Freshmen:* 10% (296); *Undergraduates:* 6% (665). ***Scholarships, grants, and awards by category:*** *Academic Interests/Achievement:* 490 awards ($579,906 total): biological sciences, business, education, engineering/technologies, foreign languages, general academic interests/achievements, health fields, military science. *Creative Arts/Performance:* 61 awards ($55,400 total): art/fine arts, music. *Special Achievements/Activities:* 6 awards ($2500 total): memberships. *Special Characteristics:* 10 awards ($12,250 total): handicapped students, local/state students. ***Tuition waivers:*** Full or partial for senior citizens. ***ROTC:*** Army.

LOANS ***Student loans:*** $32,974,862 (59% need-based, 41% non-need-based). 76% of past graduating class borrowed through all loan programs. Average indebtedness per student: $13,021. ***Average need-based loan:*** Freshmen: $1725; Undergraduates: $2723. ***Parent loans:*** $2,213,621 (100% non-need-based). ***Programs:*** Federal Direct (Subsidized and Unsubsidized Stafford, PLUS), Perkins, Service-Cancelable State Direct Student Loans.

WORK-STUDY ***Federal work-study:*** *Total amount:* $540,358; 442 jobs averaging $1223. ***State or other work-study/employment:*** *Total amount:* $1,248,363 (100% non-need-based). 1,337 part-time jobs averaging $934.

ATHLETIC AWARDS *Total amount:* 1,217,382 (100% non-need-based).

APPLYING for FINANCIAL AID ***Required financial aid form:*** FAFSA. ***Financial aid deadline (priority):*** 3/17. ***Notification date:*** 5/15.

CONTACT Ms. Connie Murphey, Director of Financial Aid, Georgia Southern University, Box 8065, Statesboro, GA 30460-8065, 912-681-5413. *Fax:* 912-681-0081.

GEORGIA SOUTHWESTERN STATE UNIVERSITY

Americus, GA

Tuition & fees (GA res): $2312 **Average undergraduate aid package: N/A**

ABOUT THE INSTITUTION State-supported, coed. Awards: associate, bachelor's, and master's degrees and post-master's certificates. 59 undergraduate majors. Total enrollment: 2,569. Undergraduates: 2,067. Freshmen: 284. Federal methodology is used as a basis for awarding need-based institutional aid.

UNDERGRADUATE EXPENSES for 1999–2000 ***Application fee:*** $20. ***Tuition, state resident:*** full-time $1808; part-time $76 per semester hour. ***Tuition, nonresident:*** full-time $7232; part-time $302 per semester hour. ***Required fees:*** full-time $504; $252 per term part-time. Part-time tuition and fees vary according to course load. ***College room and board:*** $3484; ***room only:*** $1700. Room and board charges vary according to board plan and housing facility.

FRESHMAN FINANCIAL AID (Fall 1999) 200 applied for aid; of those 82% were deemed to have need. 100% of freshmen with need received aid; of those 53% had need fully met. *Average percent of need met:* 100% (excluding resources awarded to replace EFC). 38% of all full-time freshmen had no need and received non-need-based aid.

UNDERGRADUATE FINANCIAL AID (Fall 1999) 1,807 applied for aid; of those 61% were deemed to have need. 100% of undergraduates with need received aid; of those 71% had need fully met. *Average percent of need met:* 100% (excluding resources awarded to replace EFC). 47% of all full-time undergraduates had no need and received non-need-based aid.

GIFT AID (NEED-BASED) ***Total amount:*** $4,870,978 (76% Federal, 24% state). ***Receiving aid:*** *Freshmen:* 33% (86); *all full-time undergraduates:* 48% (983). ***Average award:*** Freshmen: $2500; Undergraduates: $2500. ***Scholarships, grants, and awards:*** Federal Pell, FSEOG, state, private, college/university gift aid from institutional funds.

GIFT AID (NON-NEED-BASED) ***Total amount:*** $95,011 (100% institutional). ***Receiving aid:*** *Freshmen:* 11% (28); *Undergraduates:* 4% (89). ***Scholarships, grants, and awards by category:*** *Academic Interests/Achievement:* 37 awards ($86,500 total): general academic interests/achievements. *Creative Arts/Performance:* 53 awards ($22,810 total): art/fine arts, music. *Special Achievements/Activities:* 41 awards ($71,887 total): leadership. *Special Characteristics:* local/state students. ***Tuition waivers:*** Full or partial for senior citizens.

LOANS ***Student loans:*** $4,444,433 (66% need-based, 34% non-need-based). 60% of past graduating class borrowed through all loan programs.

Average indebtedness per student: $20,000. ***Parent loans:*** $77,433 (100% non-need-based). ***Programs:*** FFEL (Subsidized and Unsubsidized Stafford, PLUS), Perkins, state, college/university.

WORK-STUDY ***Federal work-study:*** *Total amount:* $110,000; 221 jobs available. ***State or other work-study/employment:*** *Total amount:* $156,834 (100% non-need-based). 89 part-time jobs averaging $1648.

ATHLETIC AWARDS *Total amount:* 227,643 (100% non-need-based).

APPLYING for FINANCIAL AID ***Required financial aid forms:*** FAFSA, institution's own form. ***Financial aid deadline (priority):*** 4/1. ***Notification date:*** Continuous beginning 5/1. Students must reply within 8 weeks of notification.

CONTACT Ms. Freida Jones, Director of Financial Aid, Georgia Southwestern State University, 800 Wheatley Street, Americus, GA 31709-4693, 912-928-1378 or toll-free 800-338-0082. *Fax:* 912-931-2061.

GEORGIA STATE UNIVERSITY

Atlanta, GA

Tuition & fees (GA res): $2886 **Average undergraduate aid package: N/A**

ABOUT THE INSTITUTION State-supported, coed. Awards: bachelor's, master's, doctoral, and first professional degrees and post-master's certificates. 54 undergraduate majors. Total enrollment: 23,410. Undergraduates: 16,309. Freshmen: 1,875. Federal methodology is used as a basis for awarding need-based institutional aid.

UNDERGRADUATE EXPENSES for 1999–2000 ***Application fee:*** $25. ***Tuition, state resident:*** full-time $2414; part-time $101 per credit. ***Tuition, nonresident:*** full-time $9656; part-time $403 per credit. ***Required fees:*** full-time $472; $236 per term part-time. Full-time tuition and fees vary according to course load and program. Part-time tuition and fees vary according to course load and program. ***College room and board: room only:*** $4190.

FRESHMAN FINANCIAL AID (Fall 1999) 1610 applied for aid; of those 98% were deemed to have need. 100% of freshmen with need received aid.

UNDERGRADUATE FINANCIAL AID (Fall 1999) 7,227 applied for aid; of those 91% were deemed to have need. 100% of undergraduates with need received aid.

GIFT AID (NEED-BASED) ***Total amount:*** $8,114,851 (99% Federal, 1% institutional). ***Scholarships, grants, and awards:*** Federal Pell, FSEOG, state, private, college/university gift aid from institutional funds.

GIFT AID (NON-NEED-BASED) ***Total amount:*** $9,258,014 (91% state, 6% institutional, 3% external sources). ***Receiving aid:*** *Freshmen:* 82% (1,378); *Undergraduates:* 36% (3,418). ***Scholarships, grants, and awards by category:*** *Academic Interests/Achievement:* area/ethnic studies, biological sciences, business, communication, computer science, education, general academic interests/achievements, health fields, international studies, mathematics, physical sciences, social sciences. *Creative Arts/Performance:* applied art and design, art/fine arts, journalism/publications, music, performing arts, theater/drama. *Special Achievements/Activities:* community service, leadership, memberships. ***Tuition waivers:*** Full or partial for senior citizens. ***ROTC:*** Army, Naval cooperative.

LOANS ***Student loans:*** $35,781,607 (59% need-based, 41% non-need-based). ***Parent loans:*** $558,282 (100% non-need-based). ***Programs:*** Federal Direct (Subsidized and Unsubsidized Stafford, PLUS), Perkins, state, college/university.

WORK-STUDY ***Federal work-study:*** *Total amount:* $1,595,786; 784 jobs averaging $2035.

ATHLETIC AWARDS *Total amount:* 1,079,399 (100% non-need-based).

APPLYING for FINANCIAL AID ***Required financial aid form:*** FAFSA. ***Financial aid deadline (priority):*** 4/1. ***Notification date:*** Continuous beginning 5/1. Students must reply within 2 weeks of notification.

CONTACT Gwyndolyn L. Francis, Director, Financial Aid, Georgia State University, 122 Sparks Hall, Atlanta, GA 30303, 404-651-2227 or toll-free 404-651-2365 (in-state).

GETTYSBURG COLLEGE

Gettysburg, PA

Tuition & fees: $24,032 **Average undergraduate aid package: $19,800**

ABOUT THE INSTITUTION Independent religious, coed. Awards: bachelor's degrees. 58 undergraduate majors. Total enrollment: 2,182. Undergraduates: 2,182. Freshmen: 689. Both federal and institutional methodology are used as a basis for awarding need-based institutional aid.

UNDERGRADUATE EXPENSES for 1999–2000 ***Application fee:*** $45. ***Comprehensive fee:*** $29,676 includes full-time tuition ($23,922), mandatory fees ($110), and room and board ($5644). ***College room only:*** $3012. Room and board charges vary according to board plan and housing facility. ***Part-time tuition:*** $2658 per course. ***Payment plan:*** installment.

FRESHMAN FINANCIAL AID (Fall 1998) 420 applied for aid; of those 90% were deemed to have need. 97% of freshmen with need received aid; of those 100% had need fully met. *Average percent of need met:* 100% (excluding resources awarded to replace EFC). *Average financial aid package:* $19,800 (excluding resources awarded to replace EFC). 4% of all full-time freshmen had no need and received non-need-based aid.

UNDERGRADUATE FINANCIAL AID (Fall 1998) 1,389 applied for aid; of those 93% were deemed to have need. 99% of undergraduates with need received aid; of those 98% had need fully met. *Average percent of need met:* 100% (excluding resources awarded to replace EFC). *Average financial aid package:* $19,800 (excluding resources awarded to replace EFC). 2% of all full-time undergraduates had no need and received non-need-based aid.

GIFT AID (NEED-BASED) ***Total amount:*** $17,939,547 (3% Federal, 4% state, 93% institutional). ***Receiving aid:*** *Freshmen:* 53% (370); *all full-time undergraduates:* 55% (1,264). ***Average award:*** Freshmen: $15,300; Undergraduates: $14,800. ***Scholarships, grants, and awards:*** Federal Pell, FSEOG, state, private, college/university gift aid from institutional funds.

GIFT AID (NON-NEED-BASED) ***Total amount:*** $2,368,620 (82% institutional, 18% external sources). ***Receiving aid:*** *Freshmen:* 13% (91); *Undergraduates:* 13% (291). ***Scholarships, grants, and awards by category:*** *Academic Interests/Achievement:* general academic interests/achievements.

LOANS ***Student loans:*** $5,673,730 (85% need-based, 15% non-need-based). 75% of past graduating class borrowed through all loan programs. Average indebtedness per student: $13,900. ***Average need-based loan:*** Freshmen: $3000; Undergraduates: $3500. ***Parent loans:*** $3,105,180 (100% non-need-based). ***Programs:*** FFEL (Subsidized and Unsubsidized Stafford, PLUS), Perkins, college/university.

WORK-STUDY ***Federal work-study:*** *Total amount:* $411,315; jobs available. ***State or other work-study/employment:*** *Total amount:* $506,245 (3% need-based, 97% non-need-based). Part-time jobs available.

APPLYING for FINANCIAL AID ***Required financial aid forms:*** FAFSA, CSS Financial Aid PROFILE, noncustodial (divorced/separated) parent's statement, business/farm supplement. ***Financial aid deadline:*** 3/15 (priority: 2/15). ***Notification date:*** 3/30. Students must reply by 5/1.

CONTACT Mr. Ronald L. Shunk, Director of Financial Aid, Gettysburg College, Eisenhower House, Gettysburg, PA 17325-1411, 717-337-6611 or toll-free 800-431-0803. *Fax:* 717-337-6145.

GLENVILLE STATE COLLEGE

Glenville, WV

Tuition & fees (WV res): $2208 **Average undergraduate aid package: $5885**

ABOUT THE INSTITUTION State-supported, coed. Awards: associate and bachelor's degrees. 35 undergraduate majors. Total enrollment: 2,260. Undergraduates: 2,260. Federal methodology is used as a basis for awarding need-based institutional aid.

UNDERGRADUATE EXPENSES for 1999–2000 ***Tuition, state resident:*** full-time $2208; part-time $92 per credit hour. ***Tuition, nonresident:***

Glenville State College (continued)

full-time $5208; part-time $217 per credit hour. ***College room and board:*** $3710. Room and board charges vary according to board plan and housing facility. ***Payment plan:*** installment.

FRESHMAN FINANCIAL AID (Fall 1999, est.) 370 applied for aid; of those 88% were deemed to have need. 95% of freshmen with need received aid; of those 29% had need fully met. *Average percent of need met:* 65% (excluding resources awarded to replace EFC). *Average financial aid package:* $5638 (excluding resources awarded to replace EFC). 4% of all full-time freshmen had no need and received non-need-based aid.

UNDERGRADUATE FINANCIAL AID (Fall 1999, est.) 1,297 applied for aid; of those 96% were deemed to have need. 96% of undergraduates with need received aid; of those 49% had need fully met. *Average percent of need met:* 78% (excluding resources awarded to replace EFC). *Average financial aid package:* $5885 (excluding resources awarded to replace EFC). 3% of all full-time undergraduates had no need and received non-need-based aid.

GIFT AID (NEED-BASED) ***Total amount:*** $3,197,967 (78% Federal, 22% state). ***Receiving aid:*** *Freshmen:* 58% (275); *all full-time undergraduates:* 59% (1,003). ***Average award:*** Freshmen: $3245; Undergraduates: $3572. ***Scholarships, grants, and awards:*** Federal Pell, FSEOG, state.

GIFT AID (NON-NEED-BASED) ***Total amount:*** $322,232 (4% state, 55% institutional, 41% external sources). ***Receiving aid:*** *Freshmen:* 13% (63); *Undergraduates:* 7% (119). ***Scholarships, grants, and awards by category:*** *Academic Interests/Achievement:* 138 awards ($229,182 total): general academic interests/achievements. *Creative Arts/Performance:* 20 awards ($29,742 total): art/fine arts, music. *Special Characteristics:* 2 awards ($2000 total): first-generation college students, veterans' children.

LOANS ***Student loans:*** $3,325,970 (77% need-based, 23% non-need-based). 48% of past graduating class borrowed through all loan programs. Average indebtedness per student: $12,116. ***Average need-based loan:*** Freshmen: $2100; Undergraduates: $2651. ***Parent loans:*** $94,036 (100% non-need-based). ***Programs:*** Federal Direct (Subsidized and Unsubsidized Stafford, PLUS), Perkins.

WORK-STUDY ***Federal work-study:*** *Total amount:* $151,479; 207 jobs averaging $731. ***State or other work-study/employment:*** *Total amount:* $335,000 (100% non-need-based). 350 part-time jobs averaging $957.

ATHLETIC AWARDS *Total amount:* 246,792 (100% non-need-based).

APPLYING for FINANCIAL AID ***Required financial aid form:*** FAFSA. ***Financial aid deadline (priority):*** 3/1. ***Notification date:*** Continuous beginning 4/15. Students must reply within 3 weeks of notification.

CONTACT Ms. Karen Lay, Financial Aid Administrator, Glenville State College, 200 High Street, Glenville, WV 26351-1200, 304-462-4103 or toll-free 800-924-2010 (in-state). *Fax:* 304-462-4407. *E-mail:* lay@wvngsc.wvnet.edu

GLOBAL UNIVERSITY OF THE ASSEMBLIES OF GOD

Springfield, MO

CONTACT Financial Aid Office, Global University of the Assemblies of God, 1211 South Glenstone Avenue, Springfield, MO 65804, 417-862-9533 or toll-free 800-443-1083.

GMI ENGINEERING & MANAGEMENT INSTITUTE

Flint, MI

See Kettering University

GODDARD COLLEGE

Plainfield, VT

Tuition & fees: $15,470 **Average undergraduate aid package: $17,100**

ABOUT THE INSTITUTION Independent, coed. Awards: bachelor's and master's degrees. 52 undergraduate majors. Total enrollment: 562. Undergraduates: 348. Freshmen: 37. Federal methodology is used as a basis for awarding need-based institutional aid.

UNDERGRADUATE EXPENSES for 1999–2000 ***Application fee:*** $40. ***Comprehensive fee:*** $20,758 includes full-time tuition ($15,218), mandatory fees ($252), and room and board ($5288). ***College room only:*** $2318. ***Payment plan:*** installment.

FRESHMAN FINANCIAL AID (Fall 1999, est.) 31 applied for aid; of those 58% were deemed to have need. 100% of freshmen with need received aid. *Average percent of need met:* 74% (excluding resources awarded to replace EFC). *Average financial aid package:* $18,100 (excluding resources awarded to replace EFC). 42% of all full-time freshmen had no need and received non-need-based aid.

UNDERGRADUATE FINANCIAL AID (Fall 1999, est.) 220 applied for aid; of those 70% were deemed to have need. 100% of undergraduates with need received aid. *Average percent of need met:* 77% (excluding resources awarded to replace EFC). *Average financial aid package:* $17,100 (excluding resources awarded to replace EFC). 30% of all full-time undergraduates had no need and received non-need-based aid.

GIFT AID (NEED-BASED) ***Total amount:*** $1,232,095 (27% Federal, 6% state, 67% institutional). ***Receiving aid:*** *Freshmen:* 58% (18); *all full-time undergraduates:* 70% (155). ***Average award:*** Freshmen: $11,200; Undergraduates: $8700. ***Scholarships, grants, and awards:*** Federal Pell, FSEOG, state, private, college/university gift aid from institutional funds.

GIFT AID (NON-NEED-BASED) ***Total amount:*** $465,875 (82% institutional, 18% external sources). ***Receiving aid:*** *Freshmen:* 58% (18); *Undergraduates:* 70% (155). ***Scholarships, grants, and awards by category:*** *Creative Arts/Performance:* general creative arts/performance. *Special Achievements/Activities:* community service, general special achievements/activities. *Special Characteristics:* 15 awards ($5000 total): local/state students. ***Tuition waivers:*** Full or partial for employees or children of employees.

LOANS ***Student loans:*** $1,076,548 (100% need-based). 87% of past graduating class borrowed through all loan programs. Average indebtedness per student: $17,125. ***Average need-based loan:*** Freshmen: $2625; Undergraduates: $5500. ***Parent loans:*** $310,900 (100% need-based). ***Programs:*** FFEL (Subsidized and Unsubsidized Stafford, PLUS), Perkins, college/university.

WORK-STUDY ***Federal work-study:*** *Total amount:* $194,515; 130 jobs averaging $1496.

APPLYING for FINANCIAL AID ***Required financial aid form:*** FAFSA. ***Financial aid deadline (priority):*** 3/1. ***Notification date:*** Continuous beginning 4/1. Students must reply within 2 weeks of notification.

CONTACT Ceil Rathburn, Director of Financial Aid, Goddard College, 123 Pitkin Road, Plainfield, VT 05667, 802-454-8311 Ext. 324 or toll-free 800-468-4888 Ext. 307. *Fax:* 802-454-1029. *E-mail:* finaid@earth.goddard.edu

GOD'S BIBLE SCHOOL AND COLLEGE

Cincinnati, OH

CONTACT Financial Aid Director, God's Bible School and College, 1810 Young Street, Cincinnati, OH 45210-1599, 513-721-7944 Ext. 205 or toll-free 800-486-4637.

GOLDEN GATE UNIVERSITY

San Francisco, CA

Tuition & fees: $8592 **Average undergraduate aid package: N/A**

ABOUT THE INSTITUTION Independent, coed. Awards: associate, bachelor's, master's, doctoral, and first professional degrees. 16 undergraduate majors. Total enrollment: 5,379. Undergraduates: 1,302. Freshmen: 19. Federal methodology is used as a basis for awarding need-based institutional aid.

UNDERGRADUATE EXPENSES for 1999–2000 ***Application fee:*** $55. ***Tuition:*** full-time $8592; part-time $1074 per course. Full-time tuition and fees vary according to course level, location, and program. Part-time tuition and fees vary according to course level, location, and program. ***Payment plan:*** installment.

GIFT AID (NEED-BASED) ***Scholarships, grants, and awards:*** Federal Pell, FSEOG, state, private, college/university gift aid from institutional funds.

GIFT AID (NON-NEED-BASED) ***Scholarships, grants, and awards by category:*** *Academic Interests/Achievement:* general academic interests/ achievements. *Special Achievements/Activities:* leadership. *Special Characteristics:* members of minority groups. ***Tuition waivers:*** Full or partial for employees or children of employees.

LOANS ***Programs:*** FFEL (Subsidized and Unsubsidized Stafford, PLUS), Perkins, college/university.

WORK-STUDY Federal work-study jobs available.

APPLYING for FINANCIAL AID ***Required financial aid form:*** FAFSA. ***Financial aid deadline:*** Continuous. ***Notification date:*** Continuous beginning 4/1. Students must reply within 3 weeks of notification.

CONTACT Mr. David Gin, Director of Student Financial Services, Golden Gate University, 536 Mission Street, San Francisco, CA 94105-2968, 415-442-7065 or toll-free 800-448-4968. *Fax:* 415-442-7807. *E-mail:* dgin@ggu.edu

GOLDEY-BEACOM COLLEGE

Wilmington, DE

Tuition & fees: $9398 **Average undergraduate aid package: N/A**

ABOUT THE INSTITUTION Independent, coed. Awards: associate, bachelor's, and master's degrees. 7 undergraduate majors. Total enrollment: 1,397. Undergraduates: 1,248. Freshmen: 330. Federal methodology is used as a basis for awarding need-based institutional aid.

UNDERGRADUATE EXPENSES for 2000–2001 ***Application fee:*** $30. ***Tuition:*** full-time $9248; part-time $272 per credit. ***Required fees:*** full-time $150; $5 per credit. ***Payment plans:*** installment, deferred payment.

FRESHMAN FINANCIAL AID (Fall 1999) 161 applied for aid; of those 100% were deemed to have need.

UNDERGRADUATE FINANCIAL AID (Fall 1999) 523 applied for aid; of those 95% were deemed to have need.

GIFT AID (NEED-BASED) ***Total amount:*** $794,722 (44% Federal, 7% state, 49% institutional). ***Scholarships, grants, and awards:*** Federal Pell, FSEOG, state, private, college/university gift aid from institutional funds.

GIFT AID (NON-NEED-BASED) ***Scholarships, grants, and awards by category:*** *Academic Interests/Achievement:* business. ***Tuition waivers:*** Full or partial for employees or children of employees.

LOANS ***Student loans:*** $1,778,216 (75% need-based, 25% non-need-based). ***Parent loans:*** $329,547 (100% non-need-based). ***Programs:*** FFEL (Subsidized and Unsubsidized Stafford, PLUS), Perkins.

WORK-STUDY ***Federal work-study:*** *Total amount:* $45,000; jobs available.

ATHLETIC AWARDS *Total amount:* 126,170 (100% non-need-based).

APPLYING for FINANCIAL AID ***Required financial aid form:*** FAFSA. ***Financial aid deadline (priority):*** 4/1. ***Notification date:*** Continuous. Students must reply within 2 weeks of notification.

CONTACT Jane H. Lysle, Dean, Financial Aid and Academic Support, Goldey-Beacom College, 4701 Limestone Road, Wilmington, DE 19808-1999, 302-998-8814 Ext. 265 or toll-free 800-833-4877. *Fax:* 302-998-8631. *E-mail:* lyslej@goldey.gbc.edu

GONZAGA UNIVERSITY

Spokane, WA

Tuition & fees: $16,860 **Average undergraduate aid package: $11,510**

ABOUT THE INSTITUTION Independent Roman Catholic, coed. Awards: bachelor's, master's, doctoral, and first professional degrees and post-master's certificates. 51 undergraduate majors. Total enrollment: 4,171. Undergraduates: 2,747. Freshmen: 682. Federal methodology is used as a basis for awarding need-based institutional aid.

UNDERGRADUATE EXPENSES for 1999–2000 ***Application fee:*** $40. ***Comprehensive fee:*** $22,210 includes full-time tuition ($16,710), mandatory fees ($150), and room and board ($5350). Full-time tuition and fees vary according to course load, degree level, location, program, and reciprocity agreements. Room and board charges vary according to board plan and housing facility. ***Part-time tuition:*** $480 per credit hour. ***Part-time fees:*** $25 per term part-time. Part-time tuition and fees vary according to course load, degree level, location, program, and reciprocity agreements. ***Payment plans:*** installment, deferred payment.

FRESHMAN FINANCIAL AID (Fall 1998) 569 applied for aid; of those 85% were deemed to have need. 100% of freshmen with need received aid; of those 7% had need fully met. *Average percent of need met:* 66% (excluding resources awarded to replace EFC). *Average financial aid package:* $11,055 (excluding resources awarded to replace EFC). 25% of all full-time freshmen had no need and received non-need-based aid.

UNDERGRADUATE FINANCIAL AID (Fall 1998) 1,771 applied for aid; of those 88% were deemed to have need. 100% of undergraduates with need received aid; of those 7% had need fully met. *Average percent of need met:* 69% (excluding resources awarded to replace EFC). *Average financial aid package:* $11,510 (excluding resources awarded to replace EFC). 27% of all full-time undergraduates had no need and received non-need-based aid.

GIFT AID (NEED-BASED) ***Total amount:*** $9,416,381 (18% Federal, 8% state, 68% institutional, 6% external sources). ***Receiving aid:*** *Freshmen:* 71% (472); *all full-time undergraduates:* 67% (1,485). ***Average award:*** Freshmen: $8261; Undergraduates: $7821. ***Scholarships, grants, and awards:*** Federal Pell, FSEOG, state, private, college/university gift aid from institutional funds, Federal Nursing.

GIFT AID (NON-NEED-BASED) ***Total amount:*** $4,525,554 (97% institutional, 3% external sources). ***Receiving aid:*** *Freshmen:* 42% (281); *Undergraduates:* 33% (743). ***Scholarships, grants, and awards by category:*** *Academic Interests/Achievement:* 77 awards ($125,983 total): business, engineering/ technologies. *Creative Arts/Performance:* 60 awards ($92,693 total): debating, music. *Special Characteristics:* 286 awards ($1,203,570 total): children and siblings of alumni, members of minority groups, siblings of current students. ***Tuition waivers:*** Full or partial for employees or children of employees, senior citizens. ***ROTC:*** Army.

LOANS ***Student loans:*** $10,657,892 (69% need-based, 31% non-need-based). 80% of past graduating class borrowed through all loan programs. Average indebtedness per student: $19,731. ***Average need-based loan:*** Freshmen: $4488; Undergraduates: $5219. ***Parent loans:*** $2,118,557 (100% non-need-based). ***Programs:*** FFEL (Subsidized and Unsubsidized Stafford, PLUS), Perkins, Federal Nursing, college/university.

WORK-STUDY ***Federal work-study:*** *Total amount:* $840,610; 438 jobs averaging $1998. ***State or other work-study/employment:*** *Total amount:* $856,799 (100% need-based). Part-time jobs available.

ATHLETIC AWARDS *Total amount:* 1,396,688 (100% non-need-based).

APPLYING for FINANCIAL AID ***Required financial aid form:*** FAFSA. ***Financial aid deadline (priority):*** 2/1. ***Notification date:*** 3/15. Students must reply by 5/1 or within 3 weeks of notification.

CONTACT Cori Reeves, Assistant Director for Financial Aid, Gonzaga University, 502 East Boone Avenue, Spokane, WA 99258-0072, 509-323-6582 Ext. 6586 or toll-free 800-322-2584 Ext. 6572. *Fax:* 509-323-5816. *E-mail:* reeves@gu.gonzaga.edu

GORDON COLLEGE

Wenham, MA

Tuition & fees: $16,420 **Average undergraduate aid package: $13,675**

ABOUT THE INSTITUTION Independent nondenominational, coed. Awards: bachelor's and master's degrees. 36 undergraduate majors. Total enrollment: 1,549. Undergraduates: 1,488. Freshmen: 385. Both federal and institutional methodology are used as a basis for awarding need-based institutional aid.

UNDERGRADUATE EXPENSES for 1999–2000 ***Application fee:*** $40. ***Comprehensive fee:*** $21,470 includes full-time tuition ($15,740), mandatory fees ($680), and room and board ($5050). ***College room only:***

Gordon College (continued)

$3400. Room and board charges vary according to board plan and housing facility. ***Part-time tuition:*** $4320 per term. ***Part-time fees:*** $170 per term part-time. Part-time tuition and fees vary according to course load. ***Payment plans:*** tuition prepayment, installment.

FRESHMAN FINANCIAL AID (Fall 1999) 329 applied for aid; of those 83% were deemed to have need. 100% of freshmen with need received aid; of those 62% had need fully met. *Average percent of need met:* 84% (excluding resources awarded to replace EFC). *Average financial aid package:* $12,885 (excluding resources awarded to replace EFC). 27% of all full-time freshmen had no need and received non-need-based aid.

UNDERGRADUATE FINANCIAL AID (Fall 1999) 1,207 applied for aid; of those 92% were deemed to have need. 100% of undergraduates with need received aid; of those 20% had need fully met. *Average percent of need met:* 83% (excluding resources awarded to replace EFC). *Average financial aid package:* $13,675 (excluding resources awarded to replace EFC). 24% of all full-time undergraduates had no need and received non-need-based aid.

GIFT AID (NEED-BASED) ***Total amount:*** $8,833,135 (10% Federal, 4% state, 81% institutional, 5% external sources). ***Receiving aid:*** *Freshmen:* 61% (235); *all full-time undergraduates:* 72% (1,067). ***Average award:*** Freshmen: $9138; Undergraduates: $7925. ***Scholarships, grants, and awards:*** Federal Pell, FSEOG, state, private, college/university gift aid from institutional funds.

GIFT AID (NON-NEED-BASED) ***Total amount:*** $1,974,251 (98% institutional, 2% external sources). ***Receiving aid:*** *Freshmen:* 10% (40); *Undergraduates:* 5% (70). ***Scholarships, grants, and awards by category:*** *Academic Interests/Achievement:* general academic interests/achievements. *Creative Arts/Performance:* 39 awards ($77,500 total): music. *Special Achievements/Activities:* 74 awards ($688,000 total): leadership. *Special Characteristics:* children and siblings of alumni, relatives of clergy. ***Tuition waivers:*** Full or partial for employees or children of employees. ***ROTC:*** Army cooperative, Air Force cooperative.

LOANS ***Student loans:*** $6,982,369 (75% need-based, 25% non-need-based). 67% of past graduating class borrowed through all loan programs. Average indebtedness per student: $10,429. ***Average need-based loan:*** Freshmen: $2840; Undergraduates: $4722. ***Parent loans:*** $1,148,663 (100% non-need-based). ***Programs:*** FFEL (Subsidized and Unsubsidized Stafford, PLUS), Perkins, state, college/university.

WORK-STUDY ***Federal work-study:*** *Total amount:* $1,339,460; 850 jobs averaging $1527. ***State or other work-study/employment:*** *Total amount:* $18,300 (100% need-based). 13 part-time jobs averaging $1407.

APPLYING for FINANCIAL AID ***Required financial aid forms:*** FAFSA, CSS Financial Aid PROFILE, state aid form, parent and student income tax returns and W-2 forms. ***Financial aid deadline (priority):*** 3/1. ***Notification date:*** 4/15. Students must reply by 5/1 or within 2 weeks of notification.

CONTACT Mr. Keith D. Conant, Director of Financial Aid, Gordon College, 255 Grapevine Road, Wenham, MA 01984-1899, 978-927-2300 Ext. 4035 or toll-free 800-343-1379. *Fax:* 978-524-3722. *E-mail:* kconant@hope.gordon.edu

GOSHEN COLLEGE

Goshen, IN

Tuition & fees: $13,140 **Average undergraduate aid package: $12,974**

ABOUT THE INSTITUTION Independent Mennonite, coed. Awards: bachelor's degrees. 50 undergraduate majors. Total enrollment: 1,084. Undergraduates: 1,084. Freshmen: 226. Both federal and institutional methodology are used as a basis for awarding need-based institutional aid.

UNDERGRADUATE EXPENSES for 2000–2001 (est.) ***Application fee:*** $25. ***Comprehensive fee:*** $17,780 includes full-time tuition ($12,870), mandatory fees ($270), and room and board ($4640). ***College room only:*** $2350. Room and board charges vary according to board plan and student level. Part-time tuition and fees vary according to course load.

FRESHMAN FINANCIAL AID (Fall 1999) 221 applied for aid; of those 69% were deemed to have need. 100% of freshmen with need received aid; of those 46% had need fully met. *Average percent of need met:* 94% (excluding resources awarded to replace EFC). *Average financial aid package:* $12,683 (excluding resources awarded to replace EFC). 26% of all full-time freshmen had no need and received non-need-based aid.

UNDERGRADUATE FINANCIAL AID (Fall 1999) 873 applied for aid; of those 67% were deemed to have need. 100% of undergraduates with need received aid; of those 45% had need fully met. *Average percent of need met:* 92% (excluding resources awarded to replace EFC). *Average financial aid package:* $12,974 (excluding resources awarded to replace EFC). 26% of all full-time undergraduates had no need and received non-need-based aid.

GIFT AID (NEED-BASED) ***Total amount:*** $4,754,290 (10% Federal, 18% state, 61% institutional, 11% external sources). ***Receiving aid:*** *Freshmen:* 69% (153); *all full-time undergraduates:* 66% (583). ***Average award:*** Freshmen: $8280; Undergraduates: $7418. ***Scholarships, grants, and awards:*** Federal Pell, FSEOG, state, private, college/university gift aid from institutional funds.

GIFT AID (NON-NEED-BASED) ***Total amount:*** $1,077,419 (1% Federal, 74% institutional, 25% external sources). ***Receiving aid:*** *Freshmen:* 63% (140); *Undergraduates:* 54% (480). ***Scholarships, grants, and awards by category:*** *Academic Interests/Achievement:* business, communication, education, general academic interests/achievements. *Creative Arts/Performance:* music. *Special Characteristics:* children and siblings of alumni, ethnic background, first-generation college students, general special characteristics, international students, siblings of current students. ***Tuition waivers:*** Full or partial for employees or children of employees.

LOANS ***Student loans:*** $2,815,411 (73% need-based, 27% non-need-based). 66% of past graduating class borrowed through all loan programs. Average indebtedness per student: $12,552. ***Average need-based loan:*** Freshmen: $3291; Undergraduates: $4418. ***Parent loans:*** $528,919 (100% non-need-based). ***Programs:*** Federal Direct (Subsidized and Unsubsidized Stafford, PLUS), Perkins, Federal Nursing, college/university.

WORK-STUDY ***Federal work-study:*** *Total amount:* $500,881; 434 jobs averaging $1154. ***State or other work-study/employment:*** *Total amount:* $25,401 (10% need-based, 90% non-need-based). 15 part-time jobs averaging $1693.

ATHLETIC AWARDS *Total amount:* 195,415 (84% need-based, 16% non-need-based).

APPLYING for FINANCIAL AID ***Required financial aid form:*** FAFSA. ***Financial aid deadline (priority):*** 3/1. ***Notification date:*** Continuous beginning 3/15. Students must reply by 5/1 or within 2 weeks of notification.

CONTACT Mr. Galen Graber, Director of Student Financial Aid, Goshen College, 1700 South Main, Goshen, IN 46526-4794, 219-535-7525 or toll-free 800-348-7422. *Fax:* 219-535-7654. *E-mail:* galen@goshen.edu

GOUCHER COLLEGE

Baltimore, MD

Tuition & fees: $20,485 **Average undergraduate aid package: $15,700**

ABOUT THE INSTITUTION Independent, coed. Awards: bachelor's and master's degrees. 28 undergraduate majors. Total enrollment: 1,706. Undergraduates: 1,137. Freshmen: 303. Both federal and institutional methodology are used as a basis for awarding need-based institutional aid.

UNDERGRADUATE EXPENSES for 1999–2000 ***Application fee:*** $40. ***Comprehensive fee:*** $27,865 includes full-time tuition ($20,200), mandatory fees ($285), and room and board ($7380). ***College room only:*** $4910. Room and board charges vary according to board plan. ***Part-time tuition:*** $710 per semester hour. ***Payment plan:*** installment.

FRESHMAN FINANCIAL AID (Fall 1998) 295 applied for aid; of those 99% were deemed to have need. 92% of freshmen with need received aid. *Average percent of need met:* 100% (excluding resources awarded to replace EFC). *Average financial aid package:* $15,700 (excluding resources awarded to replace EFC). 2% of all full-time freshmen had no need and received non-need-based aid.

UNDERGRADUATE FINANCIAL AID (Fall 1998) 707 applied for aid; of those 99% were deemed to have need. 93% of undergraduates with need received aid. *Average percent of need met:* 100% (excluding resources awarded to replace EFC). *Average financial aid package:* $15,700 (excluding resources awarded to replace EFC). 2% of all full-time undergraduates had no need and received non-need-based aid.

GIFT AID (NEED-BASED) ***Total amount:*** $4,746,767 (14% Federal, 11% state, 75% institutional). ***Receiving aid:*** *Freshmen:* 78% (264); *all full-time undergraduates:* 58% (641). ***Average award:*** Freshmen: $11,000; Undergraduates: $11,000. ***Scholarships, grants, and awards:*** Federal Pell, FSEOG, state, private, college/university gift aid from institutional funds.

GIFT AID (NON-NEED-BASED) ***Total amount:*** $6,445,382 (2% state, 97% institutional, 1% external sources). ***Receiving aid:*** *Freshmen:* 38% (129); *Undergraduates:* 30% (334). ***Scholarships, grants, and awards by category:*** *Academic Interests/Achievement:* biological sciences, business, general academic interests/achievements, physical sciences, social sciences. *Creative Arts/Performance:* art/fine arts, dance, music, theater/drama. ***Tuition waivers:*** Full or partial for employees or children of employees, adult students.

LOANS ***Student loans:*** $2,830,818 (78% need-based, 22% non-need-based). 89% of past graduating class borrowed through all loan programs. Average indebtedness per student: $6928. ***Average need-based loan:*** Freshmen: $2189; Undergraduates: $3786. ***Parent loans:*** $1,246,195 (100% non-need-based). ***Programs:*** FFEL (Subsidized and Unsubsidized Stafford, PLUS), Perkins, college/university.

WORK-STUDY ***Federal work-study:*** *Total amount:* $672,442; 553 jobs averaging $1158.

APPLYING for FINANCIAL AID ***Required financial aid forms:*** FAFSA, institution's own form, CSS Financial Aid PROFILE, state aid form, noncustodial (divorced/separated) parent's statement, business/farm supplement. ***Financial aid deadline (priority):*** 2/15. ***Notification date:*** 4/1. Students must reply by 5/1 or within 2 weeks of notification.

CONTACT Sharon Hassan, Director of Student Financial Aid, Goucher College, 1021 Dulaney Valley Road, Baltimore, MD 21204-2794, 410-337-6141 or toll-free 800-GOUCHER. *Fax:* 410-337-6504.

GOVERNORS STATE UNIVERSITY

University Park, IL

Tuition & fees (IL res): $2398 **Average undergraduate aid package: N/A**

ABOUT THE INSTITUTION State-supported, coed. Awards: bachelor's and master's degrees. 33 undergraduate majors. Total enrollment: 5,900. Undergraduates: 3,024. Federal methodology is used as a basis for awarding need-based institutional aid.

UNDERGRADUATE EXPENSES for 1999–2000 ***One-time required fee:*** $10. ***Tuition, state resident:*** full-time $2208; part-time $92 per credit hour. ***Tuition, nonresident:*** full-time $6624; part-time $276 per credit hour. ***Required fees:*** full-time $190; $95 per term part-time. Full-time tuition and fees vary according to location. Part-time tuition and fees vary according to course load and location. ***Payment plans:*** installment, deferred payment.

GIFT AID (NEED-BASED) ***Scholarships, grants, and awards:*** Federal Pell, FSEOG, state, private, college/university gift aid from institutional funds.

GIFT AID (NON-NEED-BASED) ***Scholarships, grants, and awards by category:*** *Academic Interests/Achievement:* biological sciences, business, communication, education, English, health fields, mathematics, physical sciences, social sciences. *Creative Arts/Performance:* general creative arts/performance. *Special Achievements/Activities:* general special achievements/activities. *Special Characteristics:* children of educators, children of public servants, members of minority groups, veterans. ***Tuition waivers:*** Full or partial for employees or children of employees, senior citizens. ***ROTC:*** Army cooperative, Air Force cooperative.

LOANS ***Programs:*** Federal Direct (Subsidized and Unsubsidized Stafford), Perkins.

WORK-STUDY Federal work-study jobs available. ***State or other work-study/employment:*** Part-time jobs available.

APPLYING for FINANCIAL AID ***Required financial aid forms:*** FAFSA, institution's own form. ***Financial aid deadline (priority):*** 5/1. ***Notification date:*** Continuous.

CONTACT Office of Financial Aid, Governors State University, One University Parkway, University Park, IL 60466-0975, 708-534-5000.

GRACE BIBLE COLLEGE

Grand Rapids, MI

Tuition & fees: $7100 **Average undergraduate aid package: $6928**

ABOUT THE INSTITUTION Independent religious, coed. Awards: associate and bachelor's degrees. 14 undergraduate majors. Total enrollment: 146. Undergraduates: 146. Freshmen: 42. Federal methodology is used as a basis for awarding need-based institutional aid.

UNDERGRADUATE EXPENSES for 1999–2000 ***Comprehensive fee:*** $11,250 includes full-time tuition ($6800), mandatory fees ($300), and room and board ($4150). ***College room only:*** $1800. Room and board charges vary according to housing facility. ***Part-time tuition:*** $285 per semester hour. Part-time tuition and fees vary according to course load. ***Payment plan:*** installment.

FRESHMAN FINANCIAL AID (Fall 1998) 28 applied for aid; of those 93% were deemed to have need. 100% of freshmen with need received aid; of those 8% had need fully met. *Average percent of need met:* 57% (excluding resources awarded to replace EFC). *Average financial aid package:* $5297 (excluding resources awarded to replace EFC). 21% of all full-time freshmen had no need and received non-need-based aid.

UNDERGRADUATE FINANCIAL AID (Fall 1998) 99 applied for aid; of those 94% were deemed to have need. 100% of undergraduates with need received aid; of those 9% had need fully met. *Average percent of need met:* 68% (excluding resources awarded to replace EFC). *Average financial aid package:* $6928 (excluding resources awarded to replace EFC). 18% of all full-time undergraduates had no need and received non-need-based aid.

GIFT AID (NEED-BASED) ***Total amount:*** $473,477 (27% Federal, 30% state, 40% institutional, 3% external sources). ***Receiving aid:*** *Freshmen:* 79% (26); *all full-time undergraduates:* 82% (93). ***Average award:*** Freshmen: $4026; Undergraduates: $3667. ***Scholarships, grants, and awards:*** Federal Pell, FSEOG, state, private, college/university gift aid from institutional funds.

GIFT AID (NON-NEED-BASED) ***Total amount:*** $36,135 (73% institutional, 27% external sources). ***Receiving aid:*** *Freshmen:* 76% (25); *Undergraduates:* 78% (89). ***Scholarships, grants, and awards by category:*** *Academic Interests/Achievement:* 63 awards ($27,669 total): general academic interests/achievements. *Creative Arts/Performance:* 18 awards ($16,958 total): music. *Special Characteristics:* 7 awards ($1625 total): general special characteristics. ***Tuition waivers:*** Full or partial for employees or children of employees, senior citizens.

LOANS ***Student loans:*** $334,775 (74% need-based, 26% non-need-based). 65% of past graduating class borrowed through all loan programs. Average indebtedness per student: $15,632. ***Average need-based loan:*** Freshmen: $1440; Undergraduates: $2792. ***Parent loans:*** $68,722 (100% need-based). ***Programs:*** FFEL (Subsidized and Unsubsidized Stafford, PLUS), state.

WORK-STUDY ***Federal work-study:*** *Total amount:* $29,465; 33 jobs averaging $893. ***State or other work-study/employment:*** *Total amount:* $7875 (100% need-based). 15 part-time jobs averaging $525.

APPLYING for FINANCIAL AID ***Required financial aid form:*** FAFSA. ***Financial aid deadline (priority):*** 2/15.

CONTACT Mrs. Marlene DeVries, Director of Financial Aid, Grace Bible College, 1011 Aldon Street, SW, PO Box 910, Grand Rapids, MI 49509-1921, 616-538-2330 or toll-free 800-968-1887. *Fax:* 616-538-0599.

GRACE COLLEGE

Winona Lake, IN

Tuition & fees: $10,500 **Average undergraduate aid package: $10,490**

ABOUT THE INSTITUTION Independent religious, coed. Awards: associate, bachelor's, and master's degrees. 36 undergraduate majors. Total enroll-

Grace College (continued)

ment: 1,045. Undergraduates: 923. Freshmen: 210. Federal methodology is used as a basis for awarding need-based institutional aid.

UNDERGRADUATE EXPENSES for 1999–2000 ***Application fee:*** $20. ***Comprehensive fee:*** $15,100 includes full-time tuition ($10,500) and room and board ($4600). ***College room only:*** $2200. Room and board charges vary according to board plan and housing facility. ***Part-time tuition:*** $3750 per term. Part-time tuition and fees vary according to course load. ***Payment plan:*** installment.

FRESHMAN FINANCIAL AID (Fall 1999) 158 applied for aid; of those 84% were deemed to have need. 100% of freshmen with need received aid; of those 45% had need fully met. *Average percent of need met:* 88% (excluding resources awarded to replace EFC). *Average financial aid package:* $10,224 (excluding resources awarded to replace EFC). 22% of all full-time freshmen had no need and received non-need-based aid.

UNDERGRADUATE FINANCIAL AID (Fall 1999) 643 applied for aid; of those 89% were deemed to have need. 100% of undergraduates with need received aid; of those 45% had need fully met. *Average percent of need met:* 90% (excluding resources awarded to replace EFC). *Average financial aid package:* $10,490 (excluding resources awarded to replace EFC). 22% of all full-time undergraduates had no need and received non-need-based aid.

GIFT AID (NEED-BASED) ***Total amount:*** $3,203,875 (17% Federal, 24% state, 46% institutional, 13% external sources). ***Receiving aid:*** *Freshmen:* 74% (128); *all full-time undergraduates:* 75% (558). ***Average award:*** Freshmen: $6060; Undergraduates: $5801. ***Scholarships, grants, and awards:*** Federal Pell, FSEOG, state, college/university gift aid from institutional funds.

GIFT AID (NON-NEED-BASED) ***Total amount:*** $917,061 (2% state, 65% institutional, 33% external sources). ***Receiving aid:*** *Freshmen:* 9% (15); *Undergraduates:* 9% (64). ***Scholarships, grants, and awards by category:*** *Academic Interests/Achievement:* general academic interests/achievements. *Creative Arts/Performance:* art/fine arts, music, theater/drama. *Special Characteristics:* children of faculty/staff, relatives of clergy. ***Tuition waivers:*** Full or partial for employees or children of employees.

LOANS ***Student loans:*** $3,354,080 (76% need-based, 24% non-need-based). 72% of past graduating class borrowed through all loan programs. Average indebtedness per student: $11,985. ***Average need-based loan:*** Freshmen: $3778; Undergraduates: $4321. ***Parent loans:*** $375,825 (26% need-based, 74% non-need-based). ***Programs:*** FFEL (Subsidized and Unsubsidized Stafford, PLUS), Perkins.

WORK-STUDY ***Federal work-study:*** *Total amount:* $167,668; jobs available.

ATHLETIC AWARDS *Total amount:* 320,170 (55% need-based, 45% non-need-based).

APPLYING for FINANCIAL AID ***Required financial aid form:*** FAFSA. ***Financial aid deadline (priority):*** 3/1. ***Notification date:*** Continuous beginning 3/15.

CONTACT Office of Student Financial Aid Services, Grace College, 200 Seminary Drive, Winona Lake, IN 46590-1294, 800-544-7223 or toll-free 800-54-GRACE (in-state), 800-54 GRACE (out-of-state). *Fax:* 219-372-5144.

GRACELAND COLLEGE

Lamoni, IA

Tuition & fees: $11,810 **Average undergraduate aid package: $13,429**

ABOUT THE INSTITUTION Independent Reorganized Latter Day Saints, coed. Awards: bachelor's and master's degrees. 48 undergraduate majors. Total enrollment: 3,345. Undergraduates: 3,252. Freshmen: 307. Federal methodology is used as a basis for awarding need-based institutional aid.

UNDERGRADUATE EXPENSES for 1999–2000 ***Application fee:*** $30. ***One-time required fee:*** $100. ***Comprehensive fee:*** $15,640 includes full-time tuition ($11,700), mandatory fees ($110), and room and board ($3830). ***College room only:*** $1430. Full-time tuition and fees vary according to course load. Room and board charges vary according to board plan, housing facility, and location. ***Part-time tuition:*** $365 per semester hour. ***Part-time fees:*** $55 per term part-time. Part-time tuition and fees vary according to location. ***Payment plan:*** installment.

FRESHMAN FINANCIAL AID (Fall 1999) 242 applied for aid; of those 89% were deemed to have need. 100% of freshmen with need received aid; of those 53% had need fully met. *Average percent of need met:* 93% (excluding resources awarded to replace EFC). *Average financial aid package:* $14,770 (excluding resources awarded to replace EFC). 14% of all full-time freshmen had no need and received non-need-based aid.

UNDERGRADUATE FINANCIAL AID (Fall 1999) 1,018 applied for aid; of those 90% were deemed to have need. 100% of undergraduates with need received aid; of those 52% had need fully met. *Average percent of need met:* 91% (excluding resources awarded to replace EFC). *Average financial aid package:* $13,429 (excluding resources awarded to replace EFC). 15% of all full-time undergraduates had no need and received non-need-based aid.

GIFT AID (NEED-BASED) ***Total amount:*** $2,952,903 (40% Federal, 27% state, 33% institutional). ***Receiving aid:*** *Freshmen:* 64% (172); *all full-time undergraduates:* 56% (700). ***Average award:*** Freshmen: $4455; Undergraduates: $4021. ***Scholarships, grants, and awards:*** Federal Pell, FSEOG, state, college/university gift aid from institutional funds.

GIFT AID (NON-NEED-BASED) ***Total amount:*** $5,719,618 (1% state, 87% institutional, 12% external sources). ***Receiving aid:*** *Freshmen:* 74% (198); *Undergraduates:* 60% (750). ***Scholarships, grants, and awards by category:*** *Academic Interests/Achievement:* 512 awards ($1,164,616 total): general academic interests/achievements. *Creative Arts/Performance:* 313 awards ($498,318 total): applied art and design, creative writing, debating, music, theater/drama. *Special Achievements/Activities:* 246 awards ($249,664 total): leadership, religious involvement. *Special Characteristics:* 725 awards ($1,816,175 total): children of faculty/staff, children of public servants, general special characteristics, international students, local/state students, members of minority groups, religious affiliation. ***Tuition waivers:*** Full or partial for employees or children of employees, senior citizens.

LOANS ***Student loans:*** $4,892,190 (66% need-based, 34% non-need-based). 73% of past graduating class borrowed through all loan programs. Average indebtedness per student: $15,649. ***Average need-based loan:*** Freshmen: $3840; Undergraduates: $4535. ***Parent loans:*** $337,936 (100% non-need-based). ***Programs:*** Federal Direct (Subsidized and Unsubsidized Stafford, PLUS), Perkins, college/university.

WORK-STUDY ***Federal work-study:*** *Total amount:* $315,182; jobs available. ***State or other work-study/employment:*** *Total amount:* $880,091 (38% need-based, 62% non-need-based). Part-time jobs available.

ATHLETIC AWARDS *Total amount:* 1,534,520 (100% non-need-based).

APPLYING for FINANCIAL AID ***Required financial aid form:*** FAFSA. ***Financial aid deadline:*** Continuous. ***Notification date:*** Continuous beginning 3/1. Students must reply within 3 weeks of notification.

CONTACT Ms. Nancy Wolff, Director of Financial Aid, Graceland College, 700 College Avenue, Lamoni, IA 50140, 515-784-5140 or toll-free 800-346-9208. *Fax:* 515-784-5488. *E-mail:* wolff@graceland.edu

GRACE UNIVERSITY

Omaha, NE

Tuition & fees: $7964 **Average undergraduate aid package: $5298**

ABOUT THE INSTITUTION Independent interdenominational, coed. Awards: associate, bachelor's, and master's degrees. 31 undergraduate majors. Total enrollment: 533. Undergraduates: 448. Freshmen: 90. Federal methodology is used as a basis for awarding need-based institutional aid.

UNDERGRADUATE EXPENSES for 1999–2000 ***Application fee:*** $25. ***Comprehensive fee:*** $11,364 includes full-time tuition ($7440), mandatory fees ($524), and room and board ($3400). Room and board charges vary according to board plan and housing facility. ***Part-time tuition:*** $248 per credit hour. ***Part-time fees:*** $122 per term part-time. Part-time tuition and fees vary according to course load. ***Payment plan:*** deferred payment.

FRESHMAN FINANCIAL AID (Fall 1999, est.) 102 applied for aid; of those 92% were deemed to have need. 100% of freshmen with need received aid; of those 16% had need fully met. *Average percent of need met:* 66%

(excluding resources awarded to replace EFC). *Average financial aid package:* $3627 (excluding resources awarded to replace EFC). 8% of all full-time freshmen had no need and received non-need-based aid.

UNDERGRADUATE FINANCIAL AID (Fall 1999, est.) 325 applied for aid; of those 88% were deemed to have need. 100% of undergraduates with need received aid; of those 15% had need fully met. *Average percent of need met:* 67% (excluding resources awarded to replace EFC). *Average financial aid package:* $5298 (excluding resources awarded to replace EFC). 10% of all full-time undergraduates had no need and received non-need-based aid.

GIFT AID (NEED-BASED) ***Total amount:*** $825,840 (40% Federal, 12% state, 43% institutional, 5% external sources). ***Receiving aid:*** *Freshmen:* 92% (94); *all full-time undergraduates:* 88% (286). ***Average award:*** Freshmen: $1968; Undergraduates: $1968. ***Scholarships, grants, and awards:*** Federal Pell, FSEOG, state, college/university gift aid from institutional funds.

GIFT AID (NON-NEED-BASED) ***Total amount:*** $87,545 (60% institutional, 40% external sources). ***Receiving aid:*** *Freshmen:* 20% (20); *Undergraduates:* 19% (62). ***Scholarships, grants, and awards by category:*** *Academic Interests/Achievement:* 35 awards ($29,050 total): business, general academic interests/achievements, health fields, international studies, religion/biblical studies. *Creative Arts/Performance:* 7 awards ($5700 total): cinema/film/broadcasting, music. *Special Achievements/Activities:* 40 awards ($76,750 total): leadership, religious involvement. *Special Characteristics:* 84 awards ($91,292 total): adult students, children and siblings of alumni, children of faculty/staff, general special characteristics, relatives of clergy, religious affiliation, siblings of current students, spouses of current students. ***Tuition waivers:*** Full or partial for children of alumni, employees or children of employees, senior citizens.

LOANS ***Student loans:*** $1,083,345 (66% need-based, 34% non-need-based). 50% of past graduating class borrowed through all loan programs. Average indebtedness per student: $11,000. ***Average need-based loan:*** Freshmen: $2376; Undergraduates: $4047. ***Parent loans:*** $359,167 (39% need-based, 61% non-need-based). ***Programs:*** FFEL (Subsidized and Unsubsidized Stafford, PLUS).

WORK-STUDY Federal work-study jobs available.

APPLYING for FINANCIAL AID ***Required financial aid form:*** FAFSA. ***Financial aid deadline (priority):*** 2/1. ***Notification date:*** 4/15. Students must reply within 2 weeks of notification.

CONTACT Office of Financial Aid, Grace University, 1311 South Ninth Street, Omaha, NE 68108-3629, 402-449-2810 or toll-free 800-383-1422. *E-mail:* gufinaid@graceu.edu

GRAMBLING STATE UNIVERSITY

Grambling, LA

Tuition & fees (LA res): $2301 **Average undergraduate aid package: N/A**

ABOUT THE INSTITUTION State-supported, coed. Awards: associate, bachelor's, master's, and doctoral degrees. 73 undergraduate majors. Total enrollment: 5,070. Undergraduates: 4,649. Federal methodology is used as a basis for awarding need-based institutional aid.

UNDERGRADUATE EXPENSES for 1999–2000 ***Application fee:*** $10. ***Tuition, state resident:*** full-time $2301; part-time $708 per term. ***Tuition, nonresident:*** full-time $7651; part-time $2,046 per term. Part-time tuition and fees vary according to course load. ***College room and board:*** $2636. ***Payment plan:*** installment.

FRESHMAN FINANCIAL AID (Fall 1998) 1132 applied for aid; of those 75% were deemed to have need. 97% of freshmen with need received aid. *Average percent of need met:* 76% (excluding resources awarded to replace EFC). 23% of all full-time freshmen had no need and received non-need-based aid.

UNDERGRADUATE FINANCIAL AID (Fall 1998) 5,233 applied for aid; of those 86% were deemed to have need. 83% of undergraduates with need received aid. *Average percent of need met:* 80% (excluding resources awarded to replace EFC). 14% of all full-time undergraduates had no need and received non-need-based aid.

GIFT AID (NEED-BASED) ***Total amount:*** $9,073,490 (100% Federal). ***Receiving aid:*** *Freshmen:* 58% (680); *all full-time undergraduates:* 50% (2,661). ***Average award:*** Freshmen: $3650; Undergraduates: $4125. ***Scholarships, grants, and awards:*** Federal Pell, FSEOG, state, private, college/university gift aid from institutional funds.

GIFT AID (NON-NEED-BASED) ***Total amount:*** $2,989,666 (31% state, 53% institutional, 16% external sources). ***Receiving aid:*** *Freshmen:* 32% (377); *Undergraduates:* 54% (2,908). ***Scholarships, grants, and awards by category:*** *Academic Interests/Achievement:* 401 awards ($1,343,127 total): biological sciences, business, communication, computer science, education, English, general academic interests/achievements, health fields, mathematics, military science, physical sciences, premedicine, social sciences. *Creative Arts/Performance:* 30 awards ($39,700 total): dance, music, theater/drama. *Special Achievements/Activities:* 216 awards ($213,684 total): cheerleading/drum major, leadership. *Special Characteristics:* 460 awards ($1,969,465 total): children and siblings of alumni, children of faculty/staff, ethnic background, international students, local/state students, members of minority groups, out-of-state students, veterans, veterans' children. ***Tuition waivers:*** Full or partial for employees or children of employees, senior citizens. ***ROTC:*** Army, Air Force.

LOANS ***Student loans:*** $24,302,341 (62% need-based, 38% non-need-based). 95% of past graduating class borrowed through all loan programs. Average indebtedness per student: $18,350. ***Average need-based loan:*** Freshmen: $924; Undergraduates: $3560. ***Parent loans:*** $993,685 (100% non-need-based). ***Programs:*** FFEL (Subsidized and Unsubsidized Stafford, PLUS), Perkins, college/university.

WORK-STUDY ***Federal work-study:*** *Total amount:* $699,912; 881 jobs available. ***State or other work-study/employment:*** *Total amount:* $451,837 (100% non-need-based). 510 part-time jobs available.

ATHLETIC AWARDS *Total amount:* 817,500 (100% non-need-based).

APPLYING for FINANCIAL AID ***Required financial aid forms:*** FAFSA, institution's own form. ***Financial aid deadline (priority):*** 1/6. ***Notification date:*** Continuous. Students must reply within 2 weeks of notification.

CONTACT Mrs. Anne Rugege, Assistant Director, Student Financial Aid, Grambling State University, PO Box 629, Grambling, LA 71245, 318-274-6415. *Fax:* 318-274-3358. *E-mail:* rugegea@martin.gram.edu

GRAND CANYON UNIVERSITY

Phoenix, AZ

Tuition & fees: $8380 **Average undergraduate aid package: $8068**

ABOUT THE INSTITUTION Independent Southern Baptist, coed. Awards: bachelor's and master's degrees. 55 undergraduate majors. Total enrollment: 2,991. Undergraduates: 1,534. Freshmen: 242. Federal methodology is used as a basis for awarding need-based institutional aid.

UNDERGRADUATE EXPENSES for 1999–2000 ***Application fee:*** $25. ***Comprehensive fee:*** $12,626 includes full-time tuition ($7680), mandatory fees ($700), and room and board ($4246). Full-time tuition and fees vary according to course load. Room and board charges vary according to board plan and housing facility. ***Part-time tuition:*** $320 per semester hour. ***Part-time fees:*** $6 per semester hour. Part-time tuition and fees vary according to course load. ***Payment plan:*** installment.

FRESHMAN FINANCIAL AID (Fall 1998) 215 applied for aid; of those 71% were deemed to have need. 98% of freshmen with need received aid; of those 11% had need fully met. *Average percent of need met:* 68% (excluding resources awarded to replace EFC). *Average financial aid package:* $7987 (excluding resources awarded to replace EFC). 24% of all full-time freshmen had no need and received non-need-based aid.

UNDERGRADUATE FINANCIAL AID (Fall 1998) 1,118 applied for aid; of those 68% were deemed to have need. 98% of undergraduates with need received aid; of those 11% had need fully met. *Average percent of need met:* 64% (excluding resources awarded to replace EFC). *Average financial aid package:* $8068 (excluding resources awarded to replace EFC). 24% of all full-time undergraduates had no need and received non-need-based aid.

GIFT AID (NEED-BASED) ***Total amount:*** $1,068,775 (98% Federal, 2% state). ***Receiving aid:*** *Freshmen:* 27% (65); *all full-time undergraduates:*

Grand Canyon University (continued)

27% (341). ***Average award:*** Freshmen: $6584; Undergraduates: $7270. ***Scholarships, grants, and awards:*** Federal Pell, FSEOG, state, private, college/university gift aid from institutional funds, Bureau of Indian Affairs Grants.

GIFT AID (NON-NEED-BASED) ***Total amount:*** $2,785,375 (1% Federal, 2% state, 77% institutional, 20% external sources). ***Receiving aid:*** *Freshmen:* 55% (132); *Undergraduates:* 45% (555). ***Scholarships, grants, and awards by category:*** *Academic Interests/Achievement:* biological sciences, business, communication, education, English, general academic interests/achievements, health fields, humanities, mathematics, military science, physical sciences, premedicine, religion/biblical studies, social sciences. *Creative Arts/Performance:* applied art and design, art/fine arts, music, performing arts, theater/drama. *Special Achievements/Activities:* leadership, memberships. *Special Characteristics:* children and siblings of alumni, children of faculty/staff, ethnic background, members of minority groups, out-of-state students, relatives of clergy, religious affiliation. ***Tuition waivers:*** Full or partial for employees or children of employees. ***ROTC:*** Army, Air Force cooperative.

LOANS ***Student loans:*** $3,037,619 (100% need-based). 79% of past graduating class borrowed through all loan programs. ***Average need-based loan:*** Freshmen: $2846; Undergraduates: $4097. ***Parent loans:*** $852,545 (100% non-need-based). ***Programs:*** FFEL (Subsidized and Unsubsidized Stafford, PLUS), Perkins, state, alternative loans.

WORK-STUDY ***Federal work-study:*** *Total amount:* $315,546; 180 jobs averaging $1810.

ATHLETIC AWARDS *Total amount:* 651,443 (100% non-need-based).

APPLYING for FINANCIAL AID ***Required financial aid form:*** FAFSA. ***Financial aid deadline:*** Continuous. ***Notification date:*** Continuous beginning 3/15.

CONTACT Director of Financial Aid, Grand Canyon University, 3300 West Camelback Road, PO Box 11097, Phoenix, AZ 85017-3030, 800-800-9776 Ext. 2885 or toll-free 800-800-9776 (in-state). *Fax:* 602-589-2044.

GRAND VALLEY STATE UNIVERSITY

Allendale, MI

Tuition & fees (MI res): $4108 **Average undergraduate aid package: $5518**

ABOUT THE INSTITUTION State-supported, coed. Awards: bachelor's and master's degrees and post-master's certificates. 117 undergraduate majors. Total enrollment: 17,452. Undergraduates: 14,229. Freshmen: 2,572. Federal methodology is used as a basis for awarding need-based institutional aid.

UNDERGRADUATE EXPENSES for 1999–2000 ***Application fee:*** $20. ***Tuition, state resident:*** full-time $4048; part-time $179 per semester hour. ***Tuition, nonresident:*** full-time $8830; part-time $378 per semester hour. ***Required fees:*** full-time $60. Full-time tuition and fees vary according to student level. Part-time tuition and fees vary according to student level. ***College room and board:*** $4910. Room and board charges vary according to board plan and housing facility. ***Payment plans:*** installment, deferred payment.

FRESHMAN FINANCIAL AID (Fall 1998) 2030 applied for aid; of those 72% were deemed to have need. 98% of freshmen with need received aid; of those 100% had need fully met. *Average percent of need met:* 100% (excluding resources awarded to replace EFC). *Average financial aid package:* $5674 (excluding resources awarded to replace EFC). 20% of all full-time freshmen had no need and received non-need-based aid.

UNDERGRADUATE FINANCIAL AID (Fall 1998) 7,779 applied for aid; of those 77% were deemed to have need. 96% of undergraduates with need received aid; of those 93% had need fully met. *Average percent of need met:* 93% (excluding resources awarded to replace EFC). *Average financial aid package:* $5518 (excluding resources awarded to replace EFC). 12% of all full-time undergraduates had no need and received non-need-based aid.

GIFT AID (NEED-BASED) ***Total amount:*** $11,966,928 (53% Federal, 19% state, 28% institutional). ***Receiving aid:*** *Freshmen:* 51% (1,274); *all full-time undergraduates:* 31% (3,360). ***Average award:*** Freshmen: $3300; Undergraduates: $2460. ***Scholarships, grants, and awards:*** Federal Pell, FSEOG, state, private, college/university gift aid from institutional funds, Federal Nursing.

GIFT AID (NON-NEED-BASED) ***Total amount:*** $4,693,548 (1% state, 71% institutional, 28% external sources). ***Receiving aid:*** *Freshmen:* 21% (532); *Undergraduates:* 7% (793). ***Scholarships, grants, and awards by category:*** *Academic Interests/Achievement:* general academic interests/achievements. *Creative Arts/Performance:* art/fine arts, music, theater/drama. *Special Characteristics:* children of faculty/staff, children of union members/company employees, handicapped students, local/state students, members of minority groups, out-of-state students. ***Tuition waivers:*** Full or partial for employees or children of employees.

LOANS ***Student loans:*** $27,679,462 (59% need-based, 41% non-need-based). 65% of past graduating class borrowed through all loan programs. Average indebtedness per student: $11,600. ***Average need-based loan:*** Freshmen: $2154; Undergraduates: $2860. ***Parent loans:*** $1,086,580 (100% non-need-based). ***Programs:*** Federal Direct (Subsidized and Unsubsidized Stafford, PLUS), Perkins, Federal Nursing, state.

WORK-STUDY ***Federal work-study:*** *Total amount:* $1,092,805; jobs available. ***State or other work-study/employment:*** *Total amount:* $3,805,910 (8% need-based, 92% non-need-based). Part-time jobs available.

ATHLETIC AWARDS *Total amount:* 897,635 (100% non-need-based).

APPLYING for FINANCIAL AID ***Required financial aid form:*** FAFSA. ***Financial aid deadline (priority):*** 2/15. ***Notification date:*** 4/1. Students must reply within 3 weeks of notification.

CONTACT Mr. Ken Fridsma, Director of Financial Aid, Grand Valley State University, 100 Student Services Building, Allendale, MI 49401-9403, 616-895-3234 or toll-free 800-748-0246. *Fax:* 616-895-3180. *E-mail:* fridsmak@gvsu.edu

GRAND VIEW COLLEGE

Des Moines, IA

Tuition & fees: $12,520 **Average undergraduate aid package: $11,240**

ABOUT THE INSTITUTION Independent religious, coed. Awards: associate and bachelor's degrees. 35 undergraduate majors. Total enrollment: 1,419. Undergraduates: 1,419. Freshmen: 226. Federal methodology is used as a basis for awarding need-based institutional aid.

UNDERGRADUATE EXPENSES for 1999–2000 ***Comprehensive fee:*** $16,352 includes full-time tuition ($12,430), mandatory fees ($90), and room and board ($3832). Room and board charges vary according to board plan, housing facility, and student level. ***Part-time tuition:*** $380 per credit. Part-time tuition and fees vary according to class time. ***Payment plans:*** installment, deferred payment.

FRESHMAN FINANCIAL AID (Fall 1999) 144 applied for aid; of those 91% were deemed to have need. 100% of freshmen with need received aid; of those 31% had need fully met. *Average percent of need met:* 84% (excluding resources awarded to replace EFC). *Average financial aid package:* $11,687 (excluding resources awarded to replace EFC). 19% of all full-time freshmen had no need and received non-need-based aid.

UNDERGRADUATE FINANCIAL AID (Fall 1999) 745 applied for aid; of those 92% were deemed to have need. 100% of undergraduates with need received aid; of those 44% had need fully met. *Average percent of need met:* 87% (excluding resources awarded to replace EFC). *Average financial aid package:* $11,240 (excluding resources awarded to replace EFC). 29% of all full-time undergraduates had no need and received non-need-based aid.

GIFT AID (NEED-BASED) ***Total amount:*** $5,526,968 (16% Federal, 37% state, 42% institutional, 5% external sources). ***Receiving aid:*** *Freshmen:* 81% (131); *all full-time undergraduates:* 70% (677). ***Average award:*** Freshmen: $8422; Undergraduates: $6939. ***Scholarships, grants, and awards:*** Federal Pell, FSEOG, state, private, college/university gift aid from institutional funds.

GIFT AID (NON-NEED-BASED) ***Total amount:*** $579,336 (1% state, 90% institutional, 9% external sources). ***Receiving aid:*** *Freshmen:* 5% (8); *Undergraduates:* 6% (53). ***Scholarships, grants, and awards by category:*** *Academic Interests/Achievement:* 289 awards ($1,117,967 total): general academic interests/achievements. *Creative Arts/Performance:* 58 awards ($32,550 total): art/fine arts, music, theater/drama. *Special Characteristics:* 27 awards ($143,134 total): children of faculty/staff. ***Tuition waivers:*** Full or partial for employees or children of employees, senior citizens. ***ROTC:*** Army cooperative, Air Force cooperative.

LOANS ***Student loans:*** $5,033,697 (75% need-based, 25% non-need-based). 90% of past graduating class borrowed through all loan programs. Average indebtedness per student: $10,762. ***Average need-based loan:*** Freshmen: $2709; Undergraduates: $3984. ***Parent loans:*** $470,989 (30% need-based, 70% non-need-based). ***Programs:*** FFEL (Subsidized and Unsubsidized Stafford, PLUS), Perkins.

WORK-STUDY ***Federal work-study:*** *Total amount:* $100,000; jobs available. ***State or other work-study/employment:*** *Total amount:* $275,328 (93% need-based, 7% non-need-based). Part-time jobs available.

ATHLETIC AWARDS *Total amount:* 332,274 (57% need-based, 43% non-need-based).

APPLYING for FINANCIAL AID ***Required financial aid form:*** FAFSA. ***Financial aid deadline (priority):*** 3/1. ***Notification date:*** Continuous beginning 3/15. Students must reply by 5/1 or within 2 weeks of notification.

CONTACT Financial Aid Office, Grand View College, 1200 Grandview Avenue, Des Moines, IA 50316-1599, 515-263-2820 or toll-free 800-444-6083.

GRATZ COLLEGE

Melrose Park, PA

CONTACT Mr. James Glick, Controller, Gratz College, Old York Road and Melrose Avenue, Melrose Park, PA 19027, 215-635-7300 or toll-free 800-475-4635 Ext. 140.

GREAT LAKES CHRISTIAN COLLEGE

Lansing, MI

CONTACT Financial Aid Officer, Great Lakes Christian College, 6211 West Willow Highway, Lansing, MI 48917-1299, 517-321-0242 or toll-free 800-YES-GLCC.

GREEN MOUNTAIN COLLEGE

Poultney, VT

Tuition & fees: $17,200 **Average undergraduate aid package: N/A**

ABOUT THE INSTITUTION Independent religious, coed. Awards: bachelor's degrees. 23 undergraduate majors. Total enrollment: 641. Undergraduates: 641. Freshmen: 196. Federal methodology is used as a basis for awarding need-based institutional aid.

UNDERGRADUATE EXPENSES for 1999–2000 ***Application fee:*** $30. ***Comprehensive fee:*** $21,500 includes full-time tuition ($17,000), mandatory fees ($200), and room and board ($4300). ***Part-time tuition:*** $567 per credit. ***Part-time fees:*** $100 per term part-time. Part-time tuition and fees vary according to course load. ***Payment plan:*** installment.

FRESHMAN FINANCIAL AID (Fall 1999, est.) *Average percent of need met:* 85% (excluding resources awarded to replace EFC). *Average financial aid package:* $15,500 (excluding resources awarded to replace EFC).

GIFT AID (NEED-BASED) ***Total amount:*** $651,420 ***Scholarships, grants, and awards:*** Federal Pell, FSEOG, state, private, college/university gift aid from institutional funds.

GIFT AID (NON-NEED-BASED) ***Total amount:*** $1,779,127 ***Scholarships, grants, and awards by category:*** *Academic Interests/Achievement:* English, general academic interests/achievements. *Creative Arts/Performance:* art/fine arts, creative writing, music, theater/drama. *Special Achievements/Activities:* community service, leadership, religious involvement. *Special Characteristics:* children of faculty/staff, local/state students, siblings of current students. ***Tuition waivers:*** Full or partial for employees or children of employees. ***ROTC:*** Army cooperative, Naval cooperative, Air Force cooperative.

LOANS ***Programs:*** FFEL (Subsidized and Unsubsidized Stafford, PLUS), Perkins.

WORK-STUDY Federal work-study jobs available.

APPLYING for FINANCIAL AID ***Required financial aid form:*** FAFSA. ***Financial aid deadline:*** Continuous.

CONTACT Dino Koff, Director of Financial Aid, Green Mountain College, One College Circle, Poultney, VT 05764-1199, 802-287-8210 or toll-free 800-776-6675 (out-of-state). *Fax:* 802-287-8099.

GREENSBORO COLLEGE

Greensboro, NC

Tuition & fees: $11,700 **Average undergraduate aid package: $6942**

ABOUT THE INSTITUTION Independent United Methodist, coed. Awards: bachelor's degrees. 42 undergraduate majors. Total enrollment: 991. Undergraduates: 991. Freshmen: 229. Federal methodology is used as a basis for awarding need-based institutional aid.

UNDERGRADUATE EXPENSES for 1999–2000 ***Application fee:*** $35. ***Comprehensive fee:*** $16,600 includes full-time tuition ($11,500), mandatory fees ($200), and room and board ($4900). Full-time tuition and fees vary according to course load. Room and board charges vary according to housing facility. ***Part-time tuition:*** $275 per semester hour. Part-time tuition and fees vary according to course load. ***Payment plan:*** installment.

FRESHMAN FINANCIAL AID (Fall 1999, est.) 211 applied for aid; of those 75% were deemed to have need. 100% of freshmen with need received aid; of those 27% had need fully met. *Average percent of need met:* 76% (excluding resources awarded to replace EFC). *Average financial aid package:* $8900 (excluding resources awarded to replace EFC). 21% of all full-time freshmen had no need and received non-need-based aid.

UNDERGRADUATE FINANCIAL AID (Fall 1999, est.) 771 applied for aid; of those 86% were deemed to have need. 99% of undergraduates with need received aid; of those 56% had need fully met. *Average percent of need met:* 84% (excluding resources awarded to replace EFC). *Average financial aid package:* $6942 (excluding resources awarded to replace EFC). 14% of all full-time undergraduates had no need and received non-need-based aid.

GIFT AID (NEED-BASED) ***Total amount:*** $1,042,552 (51% Federal, 22% state, 12% institutional, 15% external sources). ***Receiving aid:*** *Freshmen:* 40% (90); *all full-time undergraduates:* 63% (516). ***Average award:*** Freshmen: $2415; Undergraduates: $1700. ***Scholarships, grants, and awards:*** Federal Pell, FSEOG, state, private, college/university gift aid from institutional funds.

GIFT AID (NON-NEED-BASED) ***Total amount:*** $2,826,251 (24% state, 76% institutional). ***Receiving aid:*** *Freshmen:* 58% (130); *Undergraduates:* 69% (567). ***Scholarships, grants, and awards by category:*** *Academic Interests/Achievement:* 305 awards ($840,677 total): general academic interests/achievements. *Creative Arts/Performance:* 59 awards ($160,270 total): art/fine arts, music, theater/drama. *Special Achievements/Activities:* 70 awards ($62,285 total): community service, leadership, religious involvement. *Special Characteristics:* 122 awards ($226,911 total): adult students, children and siblings of alumni, children of faculty/staff, international students, relatives of clergy, religious affiliation, siblings of current students, veterans. ***Tuition waivers:*** Full or partial for employees or children of employees. ***ROTC:*** Army cooperative, Air Force cooperative.

LOANS ***Student loans:*** $3,070,727 (52% need-based, 48% non-need-based). 61% of past graduating class borrowed through all loan programs. Average indebtedness per student: $12,229. ***Average need-based loan:*** Freshmen: $2962; Undergraduates: $3893. ***Parent loans:*** $740,846 (71% need-based, 29% non-need-based). ***Programs:*** FFEL (Subsidized and Unsubsidized Stafford, PLUS), Perkins, college/university.

WORK-STUDY ***Federal work-study:*** *Total amount:* $230,009; 199 jobs available. ***State or other work-study/employment:*** *Total amount:* $23,300 (100% non-need-based). Part-time jobs available.

APPLYING for FINANCIAL AID ***Required financial aid forms:*** FAFSA, state aid form. ***Financial aid deadline (priority):*** 3/15. ***Notification date:*** Continuous. Students must reply within 2 weeks of notification.

Greensboro College (continued)

CONTACT Mr. Ron Elmore, Director of Financial Aid, Greensboro College, 815 West Market Street, Greensboro, NC 27401-1875, 910-272-7102 Ext. 339 or toll-free 800-346-8226. *Fax:* 910-271-6634. *E-mail:* relmore@gborocollege.edu

GREENVILLE COLLEGE

Greenville, IL

Tuition & fees: $12,586 **Average undergraduate aid package: $12,608**

ABOUT THE INSTITUTION Independent Free Methodist, coed. Awards: bachelor's and master's degrees. 56 undergraduate majors. Total enrollment: 1,081. Undergraduates: 1,049. Freshmen: 215. Federal methodology is used as a basis for awarding need-based institutional aid.

UNDERGRADUATE EXPENSES for 1999–2000 ***Application fee:*** $25. ***Comprehensive fee:*** $17,436 includes full-time tuition ($12,576), mandatory fees ($10), and room and board ($4850). ***College room only:*** $2290. ***Part-time tuition:*** $370 per credit hour. ***Payment plan:*** installment.

FRESHMAN FINANCIAL AID (Fall 1999, est.) 192 applied for aid; of those 89% were deemed to have need. 100% of freshmen with need received aid; of those 25% had need fully met. *Average percent of need met:* 91% (excluding resources awarded to replace EFC). *Average financial aid package:* $12,895 (excluding resources awarded to replace EFC). 38% of all full-time freshmen had no need and received non-need-based aid.

UNDERGRADUATE FINANCIAL AID (Fall 1999, est.) 754 applied for aid; of those 91% were deemed to have need. 100% of undergraduates with need received aid; of those 31% had need fully met. *Average percent of need met:* 89% (excluding resources awarded to replace EFC). *Average financial aid package:* $12,608 (excluding resources awarded to replace EFC). 18% of all full-time undergraduates had no need and received non-need-based aid.

GIFT AID (NEED-BASED) ***Total amount:*** $5,806,779 (13% Federal, 24% state, 60% institutional, 3% external sources). ***Receiving aid:*** *Freshmen:* 62% (171); *all full-time undergraduates:* 82% (687). ***Average award:*** Freshmen: $9168; Undergraduates: $8387. ***Scholarships, grants, and awards:*** Federal Pell, FSEOG, state, private, college/university gift aid from institutional funds.

GIFT AID (NON-NEED-BASED) ***Total amount:*** $857,185 (1% Federal, 2% state, 91% institutional, 6% external sources). ***Receiving aid:*** *Freshmen:* 5% (14); *Undergraduates:* 7% (57). ***Scholarships, grants, and awards by category:*** *Academic Interests/Achievement:* 407 awards ($1,566,000 total): biological sciences, business, education, engineering/technologies, general academic interests/achievements, mathematics, religion/biblical studies. *Creative Arts/Performance:* 110 awards ($135,250 total): applied art and design, art/fine arts, music, performing arts. *Special Achievements/Activities:* 120 awards ($165,000 total): leadership. *Special Characteristics:* 614 awards ($1,211,000 total): children and siblings of alumni, children of faculty/staff, international students, local/state students, out-of-state students, relatives of clergy, religious affiliation, siblings of current students. ***Tuition waivers:*** Full or partial for children of alumni, employees or children of employees, senior citizens.

LOANS ***Student loans:*** $3,139,552 (80% need-based, 20% non-need-based). 82% of past graduating class borrowed through all loan programs. ***Average need-based loan:*** Freshmen: $3031; Undergraduates: $3625. ***Parent loans:*** $563,374 (19% need-based, 81% non-need-based). ***Programs:*** Federal Direct (Subsidized and Unsubsidized Stafford, PLUS), Perkins, college/university.

WORK-STUDY ***Federal work-study:*** *Total amount:* $411,215; 338 jobs averaging $940. ***State or other work-study/employment:*** *Total amount:* $10,000 (100% non-need-based). Part-time jobs available.

APPLYING for FINANCIAL AID ***Required financial aid form:*** FAFSA. ***Financial aid deadline:*** Continuous. ***Notification date:*** Continuous beginning 3/23. Students must reply within 3 weeks of notification.

CONTACT Mr. Karl Somerville, Director of Student Financial Services, Greenville College, PO Box 159, Greenville, IL 62246-9913, 618-664-2800 Ext. 4420 or toll-free 800-248-2288 (in-state), 800-345-4440 (out-of-state). *Fax:* 618-664-9841. *E-mail:* ksomerville@greenville.edu

GRINNELL COLLEGE

Grinnell, IA

Tuition & fees: $19,460 **Average undergraduate aid package: $17,122**

ABOUT THE INSTITUTION Independent, coed. Awards: bachelor's degrees. 33 undergraduate majors. Total enrollment: 1,335. Undergraduates: 1,335. Freshmen: 325. Institutional methodology is used as a basis for awarding need-based institutional aid.

UNDERGRADUATE EXPENSES for 1999–2000 ***Application fee:*** $30. ***Comprehensive fee:*** $25,060 includes full-time tuition ($18,990), mandatory fees ($470), and room and board ($5600). ***College room only:*** $2610. Room and board charges vary according to board plan. ***Payment plans:*** tuition prepayment, installment.

FRESHMAN FINANCIAL AID (Fall 1999, est.) 304 applied for aid; of those 70% were deemed to have need. 100% of freshmen with need received aid; of those 100% had need fully met. *Average percent of need met:* 100% (excluding resources awarded to replace EFC). *Average financial aid package:* $17,528 (excluding resources awarded to replace EFC). 26% of all full-time freshmen had no need and received non-need-based aid.

UNDERGRADUATE FINANCIAL AID (Fall 1999, est.) 1,241 applied for aid; of those 67% were deemed to have need. 100% of undergraduates with need received aid; of those 100% had need fully met. *Average percent of need met:* 100% (excluding resources awarded to replace EFC). *Average financial aid package:* $17,122 (excluding resources awarded to replace EFC). 27% of all full-time undergraduates had no need and received non-need-based aid.

GIFT AID (NEED-BASED) ***Total amount:*** $11,020,404 (4% Federal, 3% state, 90% institutional, 3% external sources). ***Receiving aid:*** *Freshmen:* 66% (213); *all full-time undergraduates:* 59% (833). ***Average award:*** Freshmen: $14,322; Undergraduates: $13,372. ***Scholarships, grants, and awards:*** Federal Pell, FSEOG, state, college/university gift aid from institutional funds.

GIFT AID (NON-NEED-BASED) ***Total amount:*** $2,511,556 (1% Federal, 89% institutional, 10% external sources). ***Receiving aid:*** *Freshmen:* 8% (27); *Undergraduates:* 3% (48). ***Scholarships, grants, and awards by category:*** *Academic Interests/Achievement:* 535 awards ($3,408,575 total): general academic interests/achievements. ***Tuition waivers:*** Full or partial for employees or children of employees.

LOANS ***Student loans:*** $2,083,678 (100% need-based). 59% of past graduating class borrowed through all loan programs. Average indebtedness per student: $12,148. ***Average need-based loan:*** Freshmen: $3651; Undergraduates: $3427. ***Programs:*** FFEL (Subsidized and Unsubsidized Stafford, PLUS), Perkins, college/university.

WORK-STUDY ***Federal work-study:*** *Total amount:* $498,045; 383 jobs averaging $1300. ***State or other work-study/employment:*** *Total amount:* $397,044 (45% need-based, 55% non-need-based). 297 part-time jobs averaging $1337.

APPLYING for FINANCIAL AID ***Required financial aid forms:*** FAFSA, institution's own form, noncustodial (divorced/separated) parent's statement. ***Financial aid deadline:*** 2/1. ***Notification date:*** 4/1. Students must reply by 5/1.

CONTACT Mr. Arnold Woods, Director of Student Financial Aid, Grinnell College, Mears Cottage, Third Floor, Grinnell, IA 50112-0805, 515-269-3250 or toll-free 800-247-0113. *Fax:* 515-269-4937. *E-mail:* woods@grinnell.edu

GROVE CITY COLLEGE

Grove City, PA

Tuition & fees: $7506 **Average undergraduate aid package: $3310**

ABOUT THE INSTITUTION Independent Presbyterian, coed. Awards: bachelor's and master's degrees. 40 undergraduate majors. Total enrollment: 2,324. Undergraduates: 2,313. Freshmen: 587. Both federal and institutional methodology are used as a basis for awarding need-based institutional aid.

UNDERGRADUATE EXPENSES for 1999–2000 ***Application fee:*** $30. ***Comprehensive fee:*** $11,554 includes full-time tuition ($7506) and room and board ($4048). Full-time tuition and fees vary according to course load and program. ***Part-time tuition:*** $240 per credit hour.

FRESHMAN FINANCIAL AID (Fall 1999, est.) 405 applied for aid; of those 51% were deemed to have need. 93% of freshmen with need received aid; of those 26% had need fully met. *Average percent of need met:* 84% (excluding resources awarded to replace EFC). *Average financial aid package:* $3320 (excluding resources awarded to replace EFC). 42% of all full-time freshmen had no need and received non-need-based aid.

UNDERGRADUATE FINANCIAL AID (Fall 1999, est.) 1,824 applied for aid; of those 37% were deemed to have need. 96% of undergraduates with need received aid; of those 31% had need fully met. *Average percent of need met:* 77% (excluding resources awarded to replace EFC). *Average financial aid package:* $3310 (excluding resources awarded to replace EFC). 28% of all full-time undergraduates had no need and received non-need-based aid.

GIFT AID (NEED-BASED) ***Total amount:*** $2,295,527 (42% state, 57% institutional, 1% external sources). ***Receiving aid:*** *Freshmen:* 30% (176); *all full-time undergraduates:* 24% (551). ***Scholarships, grants, and awards:*** state, private, college/university gift aid from institutional funds.

GIFT AID (NON-NEED-BASED) ***Total amount:*** $1,301,049 (47% institutional, 53% external sources). ***Receiving aid:*** *Freshmen:* 19% (110); *Undergraduates:* 12% (272). ***Scholarships, grants, and awards by category:*** *Academic Interests/Achievement:* 231 awards ($549,822 total): biological sciences, business, communication, engineering/technologies, foreign languages, general academic interests/achievements, physical sciences. *Creative Arts/Performance:* 4 awards ($4000 total): creative writing, music. *Special Achievements/Activities:* 15 awards ($39,950 total): general special achievements/activities, leadership, memberships, religious involvement. *Special Characteristics:* 41 awards ($246,286 total): children of faculty/staff, members of minority groups, out-of-state students, veterans. ***Tuition waivers:*** Full or partial for employees or children of employees.

LOANS ***Student loans:*** $5,212,458 (21% need-based, 79% non-need-based). 51% of past graduating class borrowed through all loan programs. Average indebtedness per student: $11,383. ***Average need-based loan:*** Freshmen: $1857; Undergraduates: $3655. ***Programs:*** state, college/university.

WORK-STUDY ***State or other work-study/employment:*** *Total amount:* $126,294 (20% need-based, 80% non-need-based). Part-time jobs available.

APPLYING for FINANCIAL AID ***Required financial aid form:*** institution's own form. ***Financial aid deadline:*** 4/15. ***Notification date:*** 6/10.

CONTACT Patty Peterson, Director of Financial Aid, Grove City College, 100 Campus Drive, Grove City, PA 16127-2104, 724-458-2163. *Fax:* 724-458-3368.

GUILFORD COLLEGE

Greensboro, NC

Tuition & fees: $16,970 **Average undergraduate aid package: $14,420**

ABOUT THE INSTITUTION Independent religious, coed. Awards: bachelor's degrees. 43 undergraduate majors. Total enrollment: 1,245. Undergraduates: 1,245. Freshmen: 223. Federal methodology is used as a basis for awarding need-based institutional aid.

UNDERGRADUATE EXPENSES for 2000–2001 ***Application fee:*** $25. ***Comprehensive fee:*** $22,580 includes full-time tuition ($16,400), mandatory fees ($570), and room and board ($5610). ***College room only:*** $2960. Room and board charges vary according to board plan and housing facility. ***Part-time tuition:*** $497 per credit. ***Part-time fees:*** $15 per term part-time. Part-time tuition and fees vary according to course load. ***Payment plan:*** installment.

FRESHMAN FINANCIAL AID (Fall 1999, est.) 195 applied for aid; of those 62% were deemed to have need. 100% of freshmen with need received aid; of those 85% had need fully met. *Average percent of need met:* 92% (excluding resources awarded to replace EFC). *Average financial aid package:* $14,742 (excluding resources awarded to replace EFC). 17% of all full-time freshmen had no need and received non-need-based aid.

UNDERGRADUATE FINANCIAL AID (Fall 1999, est.) 817 applied for aid; of those 62% were deemed to have need. 100% of undergraduates with need received aid; of those 78% had need fully met. *Average percent of need met:* 93% (excluding resources awarded to replace EFC). *Average financial aid package:* $14,420 (excluding resources awarded to replace EFC). 24% of all full-time undergraduates had no need and received non-need-based aid.

GIFT AID (NEED-BASED) ***Total amount:*** $4,915,123 (10% Federal, 10% state, 80% institutional). ***Receiving aid:*** *Freshmen:* 54% (120); *all full-time undergraduates:* 55% (504). ***Average award:*** Freshmen: $2948; Undergraduates: $4486. ***Scholarships, grants, and awards:*** Federal Pell, FSEOG, state, private, college/university gift aid from institutional funds.

GIFT AID (NON-NEED-BASED) ***Total amount:*** $2,135,783 (6% state, 94% institutional). ***Receiving aid:*** *Freshmen:* 43% (96); *Undergraduates:* 36% (336). ***Scholarships, grants, and awards by category:*** *Academic Interests/Achievement:* biological sciences, education, general academic interests/achievements, mathematics. *Creative Arts/Performance:* art/fine arts, music. *Special Achievements/Activities:* community service, general special achievements/activities, religious involvement. *Special Characteristics:* adult students, children of faculty/staff, ethnic background, general special characteristics, members of minority groups, religious affiliation. ***Tuition waivers:*** Full or partial for employees or children of employees. ***ROTC:*** Army cooperative, Air Force cooperative.

LOANS ***Student loans:*** $2,223,107 (87% need-based, 13% non-need-based). Average indebtedness per student: $14,260. ***Average need-based loan:*** Freshmen: $3426; Undergraduates: $4513. ***Parent loans:*** $701,864 (100% non-need-based). ***Programs:*** FFEL (Subsidized and Unsubsidized Stafford, PLUS), Perkins, college/university.

WORK-STUDY ***Federal work-study:*** *Total amount:* $170,025; 145 jobs averaging $1172. ***State or other work-study/employment:*** *Total amount:* $196,771 (54% need-based, 46% non-need-based). 181 part-time jobs averaging $1085.

APPLYING for FINANCIAL AID ***Required financial aid forms:*** FAFSA, institution's own form, noncustodial (divorced/separated) parent's statement, business/farm supplement. ***Financial aid deadline (priority):*** 3/1. ***Notification date:*** Continuous. Students must reply by 5/1 or within 4 weeks of notification.

CONTACT Mr. Anthony E. Gurley, Director of Student Financial Assistance and Planning, Guilford College, 5800 West Friendly Avenue, Greensboro, NC 27410-4173, 336-316-2142 or toll-free 800-992-7759. *Fax:* 336-316-2954. *E-mail:* agurley@guilford.edu

GUSTAVUS ADOLPHUS COLLEGE

St. Peter, MN

Tuition & fees: $17,430 **Average undergraduate aid package: $13,459**

ABOUT THE INSTITUTION Independent religious, coed. Awards: bachelor's degrees. 63 undergraduate majors. Total enrollment: 2,543. Undergraduates: 2,543. Freshmen: 654. Federal methodology is used as a basis for awarding need-based institutional aid.

UNDERGRADUATE EXPENSES for 1999–2000 ***Application fee:*** $25. ***Comprehensive fee:*** $21,750 includes full-time tuition ($17,200), mandatory fees ($230), and room and board ($4320). ***College room only:*** $2050. Full-time tuition and fees vary according to student level. Room and board charges vary according to board plan, housing facility, and student level. ***Part-time tuition:*** $1875 per course. ***Part-time fees:*** $165 per year part-time. ***Payment plans:*** tuition prepayment, installment.

FRESHMAN FINANCIAL AID (Fall 1999, est.) 533 applied for aid; of those 77% were deemed to have need. 100% of freshmen with need received aid. *Average percent of need met:* 90% (excluding resources awarded to replace EFC). *Average financial aid package:* $16,290 (excluding resources awarded to replace EFC). 36% of all full-time freshmen had no need and received non-need-based aid.

UNDERGRADUATE FINANCIAL AID (Fall 1999, est.) 1,983 applied for aid; of those 82% were deemed to have need. 100% of undergraduates with need received aid. *Average percent of need met:* 90% (excluding resources

Gustavus Adolphus College (continued)

awarded to replace EFC). *Average financial aid package:* $13,459 (excluding resources awarded to replace EFC). 26% of all full-time undergraduates had no need and received non-need-based aid.

GIFT AID (NEED-BASED) ***Total amount:*** $14,795,297 (8% Federal, 18% state, 68% institutional, 6% external sources). ***Receiving aid:*** *Freshmen:* 62% (405); *all full-time undergraduates:* 63% (1,578). ***Average award:*** Freshmen: $10,618; Undergraduates: $8806. ***Scholarships, grants, and awards:*** Federal Pell, FSEOG, state, private, college/university gift aid from institutional funds, Federal Nursing.

GIFT AID (NON-NEED-BASED) ***Total amount:*** $2,881,463 (1% Federal, 87% institutional, 12% external sources). ***Receiving aid:*** *Freshmen:* 32% (210); *Undergraduates:* 22% (547). ***Scholarships, grants, and awards by category:*** *Academic Interests/Achievement:* 479 awards ($1,829,642 total): general academic interests/achievements. *Creative Arts/Performance:* 113 awards ($118,800 total): music, theater/drama. *Special Achievements/Activities:* 138 awards ($206,679 total): community service. *Special Characteristics:* 88 awards ($190,250 total): children and siblings of alumni. ***Tuition waivers:*** Full or partial for employees or children of employees, senior citizens. ***ROTC:*** Army cooperative.

LOANS ***Student loans:*** $7,858,994 (83% need-based, 17% non-need-based). 68% of past graduating class borrowed through all loan programs. Average indebtedness per student: $16,952. ***Average need-based loan:*** Freshmen: $4413; Undergraduates: $4000. ***Parent loans:*** $1,011,677 (73% need-based, 27% non-need-based). ***Programs:*** Federal Direct (Subsidized and Unsubsidized Stafford, PLUS), Perkins, Federal Nursing, state, college/university.

WORK-STUDY ***Federal work-study:*** *Total amount:* $1,073,990; 712 jobs averaging $1508. ***State or other work-study/employment:*** *Total amount:* $1,439,700 (75% need-based, 25% non-need-based). 921 part-time jobs averaging $1556.

APPLYING for FINANCIAL AID ***Required financial aid forms:*** FAFSA, institution's own form, noncustodial (divorced/separated) parent's statement. ***Financial aid deadline (priority):*** 2/15. ***Notification date:*** Continuous beginning 3/1. Students must reply by 5/1 or within 2 weeks of notification.

CONTACT Mr. Kirk Carlson, Assistant Director of Financial Aid, Gustavus Adolphus College, 800 West College Avenue, St. Peter, MN 56082-1498, 507-933-7691 or toll-free 800-GUSTAVU(S). *E-mail:* kcarlson@gustavus.edu

GWYNEDD-MERCY COLLEGE

Gwynedd Valley, PA

Tuition & fees: $13,540 **Average undergraduate aid package: $12,720**

ABOUT THE INSTITUTION Independent Roman Catholic, coed. Awards: associate, bachelor's, and master's degrees and post-bachelor's and post-master's certificates. 39 undergraduate majors. Total enrollment: 1,686. Undergraduates: 1,395. Freshmen: 152. Federal methodology is used as a basis for awarding need-based institutional aid.

UNDERGRADUATE EXPENSES for 1999–2000 ***Application fee:*** $25. ***Comprehensive fee:*** $20,040 includes full-time tuition ($13,500), mandatory fees ($40), and room and board ($6500). Full-time tuition and fees vary according to program. Room and board charges vary according to board plan. ***Part-time tuition:*** $290 per credit. ***Part-time fees:*** $2 per credit; $25 per term part-time. Part-time tuition and fees vary according to program. ***Payment plan:*** installment.

FRESHMAN FINANCIAL AID (Fall 1999, est.) 141 applied for aid; of those 90% were deemed to have need. 97% of freshmen with need received aid; of those 70% had need fully met. *Average percent of need met:* 85% (excluding resources awarded to replace EFC). *Average financial aid package:* $13,507 (excluding resources awarded to replace EFC). 14% of all full-time freshmen had no need and received non-need-based aid.

UNDERGRADUATE FINANCIAL AID (Fall 1999, est.) 530 applied for aid; of those 97% were deemed to have need. 99% of undergraduates with need received aid; of those 70% had need fully met. *Average percent of need met:* 80% (excluding resources awarded to replace EFC). *Average financial aid package:* $12,720 (excluding resources awarded to replace EFC). 9% of all full-time undergraduates had no need and received non-need-based aid.

GIFT AID (NEED-BASED) ***Total amount:*** $4,170,891 (13% Federal, 20% state, 66% institutional, 1% external sources). ***Receiving aid:*** *Freshmen:* 84% (123); *all full-time undergraduates:* 68% (493). ***Average award:*** Freshmen: $8066; Undergraduates: $6491. ***Scholarships, grants, and awards:*** Federal Pell, FSEOG, state, private, college/university gift aid from institutional funds, Scholarships for Disadvantaged Students (SDS).

GIFT AID (NON-NEED-BASED) ***Total amount:*** $704,801 (98% institutional, 2% external sources). ***Receiving aid:*** *Freshmen:* 31% (46); *Undergraduates:* 24% (175). ***Scholarships, grants, and awards by category:*** *Academic Interests/Achievement:* 178 awards ($957,150 total): biological sciences, business, communication, computer science, education, English, general academic interests/achievements, health fields, humanities, mathematics, premedicine, social sciences. *Special Achievements/Activities:* 79 awards ($156,250 total): community service, general special achievements/activities, leadership. *Special Characteristics:* 1 award ($1000 total): children and siblings of alumni. ***Tuition waivers:*** Full or partial for employees or children of employees.

LOANS ***Student loans:*** $3,257,810 (58% need-based, 42% non-need-based). Average indebtedness per student: $14,282. ***Average need-based loan:*** Freshmen: $2911; Undergraduates: $3236. ***Parent loans:*** $299,415 (30% need-based, 70% non-need-based). ***Programs:*** FFEL (Subsidized and Unsubsidized Stafford, PLUS), Perkins, Federal Nursing, alternative loans.

WORK-STUDY ***Federal work-study:*** *Total amount:* $238,625; 190 jobs averaging $1255. ***State or other work-study/employment:*** *Total amount:* $2500 (100% need-based). Part-time jobs available.

APPLYING for FINANCIAL AID ***Required financial aid forms:*** FAFSA, institution's own form, state aid form, federal income tax form(s). ***Financial aid deadline (priority):*** 3/15. ***Notification date:*** Continuous. Students must reply by 5/1 or within 4 weeks of notification.

CONTACT Sr. Barbara A. Kaufmann, Director, Student Financial Aid, Gwynedd-Mercy College, PO Box 901, Gwynedd Valley, PA 19437-0901, 215-641-5570 or toll-free 800-DIAL-GMC (in-state). *Fax:* 215-542-4604.

HAMILTON COLLEGE

Clinton, NY

Tuition & fees: $25,050 **Average undergraduate aid package: $19,490**

ABOUT THE INSTITUTION Independent, coed. Awards: bachelor's degrees. 44 undergraduate majors. Total enrollment: 1,740. Undergraduates: 1,740. Freshmen: 500. Both federal and institutional methodology are used as a basis for awarding need-based institutional aid.

UNDERGRADUATE EXPENSES for 1999–2000 ***Application fee:*** $50. ***Comprehensive fee:*** $31,250 includes full-time tuition ($25,000), mandatory fees ($50), and room and board ($6200). Room and board charges vary according to board plan. ***Part-time tuition:*** $2400 per unit. ***Payment plans:*** installment, deferred payment.

FRESHMAN FINANCIAL AID (Fall 1999, est.) 326 applied for aid; of those 76% were deemed to have need. 100% of freshmen with need received aid; of those 100% had need fully met. *Average percent of need met:* 99% (excluding resources awarded to replace EFC). *Average financial aid package:* $19,925 (excluding resources awarded to replace EFC). 2% of all full-time freshmen had no need and received non-need-based aid.

UNDERGRADUATE FINANCIAL AID (Fall 1999, est.) 1,314 applied for aid; of those 74% were deemed to have need. 100% of undergraduates with need received aid; of those 100% had need fully met. *Average percent of need met:* 99% (excluding resources awarded to replace EFC). *Average financial aid package:* $19,490 (excluding resources awarded to replace EFC). 1% of all full-time undergraduates had no need and received non-need-based aid.

GIFT AID (NEED-BASED) ***Total amount:*** $15,506,494 (5% Federal, 5% state, 88% institutional, 2% external sources). ***Receiving aid:*** *Freshmen:* 49% (243); *all full-time undergraduates:* 55% (950). ***Average award:***

Freshmen: $17,054; Undergraduates: $15,920. ***Scholarships, grants, and awards:*** Federal Pell, FSEOG, state, private, college/university gift aid from institutional funds.

GIFT AID (NON-NEED-BASED) ***Total amount:*** $188,769 (4% state, 42% institutional, 54% external sources). ***Receiving aid:*** *Freshmen:* 1% (3); *Undergraduates:* 8. ***Scholarships, grants, and awards by category:*** *Academic Interests/Achievement:* general academic interests/achievements. ***Tuition waivers:*** Full or partial for employees or children of employees, adult students. ***ROTC:*** Army cooperative, Air Force cooperative.

LOANS ***Student loans:*** $2,720,468 (99% need-based, 1% non-need-based). 74% of past graduating class borrowed through all loan programs. Average indebtedness per student: $16,776. ***Average need-based loan:*** Freshmen: $1921; Undergraduates: $2778. ***Programs:*** FFEL (Subsidized and Unsubsidized Stafford, PLUS), Perkins, college/university.

WORK-STUDY ***Federal work-study:*** *Total amount:* $771,537; jobs available.

APPLYING for FINANCIAL AID ***Required financial aid forms:*** FAFSA, CSS Financial Aid PROFILE, noncustodial (divorced/separated) parent's statement, business/farm supplement. ***Financial aid deadline:*** 2/1. ***Notification date:*** 4/1. Students must reply by 5/1 or within 2 weeks of notification.

CONTACT Mr. Kevin Michaelsen, Associate Director of Financial Aid, Hamilton College, 198 College Hill Road, Clinton, NY 13323-1218, 315-859-4434 or toll-free 800-843-2655. *Fax:* 315-859-4457. *E-mail:* kmichael@hamilton.edu

HAMILTON TECHNICAL COLLEGE

Davenport, IA

Tuition & fees: $5850 **Average undergraduate aid package: N/A**

ABOUT THE INSTITUTION Proprietary, coed. Awards: associate and bachelor's degrees. 2 undergraduate majors. Total enrollment: 400. Undergraduates: 400.

UNDERGRADUATE EXPENSES for 1999–2000 ***Application fee:*** $25. ***Tuition:*** full-time $5850. ***Payment plans:*** guaranteed tuition, installment.

GIFT AID (NEED-BASED) ***Scholarships, grants, and awards:*** Federal Pell.

LOANS ***Programs:*** Federal Direct (Subsidized and Unsubsidized Stafford, PLUS).

APPLYING for FINANCIAL AID ***Required financial aid form:*** FAFSA. ***Financial aid deadline (priority):*** 6/30. ***Notification date:*** Continuous.

CONTACT Ms. Lisa Boyd, Director of Financial Aid, Hamilton Technical College, 1011 East 53rd Street, Davenport, IA 52807-2653, 319-386-3570 Ext. 33. *Fax:* 319-386-6756.

HAMLINE UNIVERSITY

St. Paul, MN

Tuition & fees: $15,798 **Average undergraduate aid package: $15,205**

ABOUT THE INSTITUTION Independent religious, coed. Awards: bachelor's, master's, doctoral, and first professional degrees. 58 undergraduate majors. Total enrollment: 3,111. Undergraduates: 1,833. Freshmen: 421. Both federal and institutional methodology are used as a basis for awarding need-based institutional aid.

UNDERGRADUATE EXPENSES for 1999–2000 ***Comprehensive fee:*** $21,089 includes full-time tuition ($15,574), mandatory fees ($224), and room and board ($5291). ***College room only:*** $2728. Room and board charges vary according to board plan. ***Part-time tuition:*** $1947 per course. ***Part-time fees:*** $112 per term part-time. Part-time tuition and fees vary according to course load. ***Payment plan:*** installment.

FRESHMAN FINANCIAL AID (Fall 1999, est.) 419 applied for aid; of those 78% were deemed to have need. 100% of freshmen with need received aid; of those 17% had need fully met. *Average percent of need met:* 72% (excluding resources awarded to replace EFC). *Average financial aid package:* $15,507 (excluding resources awarded to replace EFC). 15% of all full-time freshmen had no need and received non-need-based aid.

UNDERGRADUATE FINANCIAL AID (Fall 1999, est.) 1,397 applied for aid; of those 83% were deemed to have need. 100% of undergraduates with need received aid; of those 22% had need fully met. *Average percent of need met:* 73% (excluding resources awarded to replace EFC). *Average financial aid package:* $15,205 (excluding resources awarded to replace EFC). 14% of all full-time undergraduates had no need and received non-need-based aid.

GIFT AID (NEED-BASED) ***Total amount:*** $11,687,725 (2% Federal, 20% state, 73% institutional, 5% external sources). ***Receiving aid:*** *Freshmen:* 78% (328); *all full-time undergraduates:* 75% (1,152). ***Average award:*** Freshmen: $10,205; Undergraduates: $9390. ***Scholarships, grants, and awards:*** Federal Pell, FSEOG, state, private, college/university gift aid from institutional funds.

GIFT AID (NON-NEED-BASED) ***Total amount:*** $804,723 (98% institutional, 2% external sources). ***Receiving aid:*** *Undergraduates:* 3. ***Scholarships, grants, and awards by category:*** *Academic Interests/Achievement:* biological sciences, general academic interests/achievements. *Creative Arts/Performance:* creative writing. *Special Achievements/Activities:* religious involvement. *Special Characteristics:* children of faculty/staff, local/state students, out-of-state students, relatives of clergy. ***Tuition waivers:*** Full or partial for employees or children of employees. ***ROTC:*** Air Force cooperative.

LOANS ***Student loans:*** $3,053,531 (51% need-based, 49% non-need-based). 78% of past graduating class borrowed through all loan programs. Average indebtedness per student: $18,887. ***Average need-based loan:*** Freshmen: $561; Undergraduates: $1010. ***Parent loans:*** $455,648 (100% non-need-based). ***Programs:*** Federal Direct (Subsidized and Unsubsidized Stafford, PLUS), FFEL (Subsidized and Unsubsidized Stafford, PLUS), Perkins, state, United Methodist Student Loans, SELF Loans.

WORK-STUDY ***Federal work-study:*** *Total amount:* $1,025,251; 546 jobs averaging $1878. ***State or other work-study/employment:*** *Total amount:* $544,232 (47% need-based, 53% non-need-based). Part-time jobs available.

APPLYING for FINANCIAL AID ***Required financial aid forms:*** FAFSA, institution's own form. ***Financial aid deadline (priority):*** 5/1. ***Notification date:*** Continuous.

CONTACT Ms. Cheryl Anderson-Dooley, Associate Director, Financial Aid, Hamline University, 1536 Hewitt Avenue, MS C1915, St. Paul, MN 55104, 651-523-2280 or toll-free 800-753-9753. *Fax:* 651-523-2585. *E-mail:* cdooley@gw.hamline.edu

HAMPDEN-SYDNEY COLLEGE

Hampden-Sydney, VA

Tuition & fees: $16,531 **Average undergraduate aid package: $12,638**

ABOUT THE INSTITUTION Independent Presbyterian, men only. Awards: bachelor's degrees. 24 undergraduate majors. Total enrollment: 996. Undergraduates: 996. Freshmen: 307. Both federal and institutional methodology are used as a basis for awarding need-based institutional aid.

UNDERGRADUATE EXPENSES for 1999–2000 ***Application fee:*** $30. ***Comprehensive fee:*** $22,429 includes full-time tuition ($16,048), mandatory fees ($483), and room and board ($5898). ***College room only:*** $2464. Room and board charges vary according to housing facility. ***Part-time tuition:*** $536 per semester hour. ***Payment plan:*** installment.

FRESHMAN FINANCIAL AID (Fall 1999, est.) 219 applied for aid; of those 74% were deemed to have need. 100% of freshmen with need received aid; of those 45% had need fully met. *Average percent of need met:* 83% (excluding resources awarded to replace EFC). *Average financial aid package:* $12,396 (excluding resources awarded to replace EFC).

UNDERGRADUATE FINANCIAL AID (Fall 1999, est.) 643 applied for aid; of those 78% were deemed to have need. 100% of undergraduates with need received aid; of those 47% had need fully met. *Average percent of need met:* 87% (excluding resources awarded to replace EFC). *Average financial aid package:* $12,638 (excluding resources awarded to replace EFC).

GIFT AID (NEED-BASED) ***Total amount:*** $4,603,076 (6% Federal, 17% state, 75% institutional, 2% external sources). ***Receiving aid:*** *Freshmen:* 58% (161); *all full-time undergraduates:* 57% (500). ***Average award:***

Hampden-Sydney College (continued)

Freshmen: $9274; Undergraduates: $9145. ***Scholarships, grants, and awards:*** Federal Pell, FSEOG, state, private, college/university gift aid from institutional funds.

GIFT AID (NON-NEED-BASED) ***Total amount:*** $2,176,847 (38% state, 57% institutional, 5% external sources). ***Receiving aid:*** *Freshmen:* 13% (37); *Undergraduates:* 12% (106). ***Scholarships, grants, and awards by category:*** *Academic Interests/Achievement:* 265 awards ($1,697,683 total): general academic interests/achievements, religion/biblical studies. *Special Characteristics:* 10 awards ($141,580 total): children of faculty/staff. ***Tuition waivers:*** Full or partial for employees or children of employees. ***ROTC:*** Army cooperative.

LOANS ***Student loans:*** $3,373,067 (46% need-based, 54% non-need-based). 79% of past graduating class borrowed through all loan programs. Average indebtedness per student: $10,400. ***Average need-based loan:*** Freshmen: $2634; Undergraduates: $3097. ***Parent loans:*** $4,547,402 (16% need-based, 84% non-need-based). ***Programs:*** FFEL (Subsidized and Unsubsidized Stafford, PLUS), Perkins, college/university.

WORK-STUDY ***Federal work-study:*** *Total amount:* $198,990; 140 jobs averaging $1400.

APPLYING for FINANCIAL AID ***Required financial aid forms:*** FAFSA, CSS Financial Aid PROFILE. ***Financial aid deadline (priority):*** 3/1. ***Notification date:*** Continuous. Students must reply by 5/1 or within 2 weeks of notification.

CONTACT Mrs. Lynn Clements, Financial Aid Counselor, Hampden-Sydney College, PO Box 726, Hampden-Sydney, VA 23943-0667, 804-223-6119 or toll-free 800-755-0733. *Fax:* 804-223-6075.

HAMPSHIRE COLLEGE

Amherst, MA

Tuition & fees: $25,400 **Average undergraduate aid package: $21,500**

ABOUT THE INSTITUTION Independent, coed. Awards: bachelor's degrees. 130 undergraduate majors. Total enrollment: 1,172. Undergraduates: 1,172. Freshmen: 295. Institutional methodology is used as a basis for awarding need-based institutional aid.

UNDERGRADUATE EXPENSES for 1999–2000 ***Application fee:*** $50. ***One-time required fee:*** $90. ***Comprehensive fee:*** $32,022 includes full-time tuition ($24,984), mandatory fees ($416), and room and board ($6622). ***College room only:*** $4209. Room and board charges vary according to board plan.

FRESHMAN FINANCIAL AID (Fall 1999, est.) 295 applied for aid. *Average percent of need met:* 100% (excluding resources awarded to replace EFC). *Average financial aid package:* $19,925 (excluding resources awarded to replace EFC). 14% of all full-time freshmen had no need and received non-need-based aid.

UNDERGRADUATE FINANCIAL AID (Fall 1999, est.) 729 applied for aid. *Average percent of need met:* 100% (excluding resources awarded to replace EFC). *Average financial aid package:* $21,500 (excluding resources awarded to replace EFC). 12% of all full-time undergraduates had no need and received non-need-based aid.

GIFT AID (NEED-BASED) ***Total amount:*** $9,839,855 (9% Federal, 1% state, 90% institutional). ***Scholarships, grants, and awards:*** Federal Pell, FSEOG, state, private, college/university gift aid from institutional funds.

GIFT AID (NON-NEED-BASED) ***Total amount:*** $228,185 (36% institutional, 64% external sources). ***Scholarships, grants, and awards by category:*** *Academic Interests/Achievement:* general academic interests/achievements, international studies, social sciences. *Special Achievements/Activities:* community service, leadership. *Special Characteristics:* children of faculty/staff. ***Tuition waivers:*** Full or partial for employees or children of employees.

LOANS ***Student loans:*** $1,906,320 (87% need-based, 13% non-need-based). 60% of past graduating class borrowed through all loan programs. Average indebtedness per student: $16,000. ***Parent loans:*** $2,485,600 (100% non-need-based). ***Programs:*** Federal Direct (Subsidized and Unsubsidized Stafford), FFEL (PLUS).

WORK-STUDY ***Federal work-study:*** *Total amount:* $896,740; 463 jobs averaging $2000. ***State or other work-study/employment:*** *Total amount:* $742,800 (39% need-based, 61% non-need-based). 223 part-time jobs available.

APPLYING for FINANCIAL AID ***Required financial aid forms:*** FAFSA, institution's own form, CSS Financial Aid PROFILE, noncustodial (divorced/separated) parent's statement, business/farm supplement. ***Financial aid deadline (priority):*** 2/1. ***Notification date:*** 4/1. Students must reply by 5/1 or within 2 weeks of notification.

CONTACT Ms. Kathleen Methot, Director of Financial Aid, Hampshire College, 893 West Street, Amherst, MA 01002, 413-559-5484. *Fax:* 413-559-5585. *E-mail:* finaid@hampshire.edu

HAMPTON UNIVERSITY

Hampton, VA

Tuition & fees: $10,580 **Average undergraduate aid package: N/A**

ABOUT THE INSTITUTION Independent, coed. Awards: associate, bachelor's, master's, and doctoral degrees and post-master's certificates. 80 undergraduate majors. Total enrollment: 5,824. Undergraduates: 5,435. Freshmen: 1,376. Federal methodology is used as a basis for awarding need-based institutional aid.

UNDERGRADUATE EXPENSES for 1999–2000 ***Application fee:*** $25. ***Comprehensive fee:*** $15,334 includes full-time tuition ($9490), mandatory fees ($1090), and room and board ($4754). Full-time tuition and fees vary according to program. Room and board charges vary according to housing facility. ***Part-time tuition:*** $230 per hour. ***Part-time fees:*** $545 per term part-time. Part-time tuition and fees vary according to program. ***Payment plan:*** installment.

GIFT AID (NEED-BASED) ***Scholarships, grants, and awards:*** Federal Pell, FSEOG, state, private.

GIFT AID (NON-NEED-BASED) ***Scholarships, grants, and awards by category:*** *Academic Interests/Achievement:* general academic interests/achievements. *Creative Arts/Performance:* music. *Special Characteristics:* international students, members of minority groups. ***Tuition waivers:*** Full or partial for employees or children of employees. ***ROTC:*** Army, Naval.

LOANS ***Programs:*** Federal Direct (Subsidized and Unsubsidized Stafford, PLUS), Perkins, college/university.

WORK-STUDY Federal work-study jobs available.

APPLYING for FINANCIAL AID ***Required financial aid form:*** FAFSA. ***Financial aid deadline:*** 3/1.

CONTACT Director of Financial Aid, Hampton University, Hampton, VA 23668, 757-727-5332 or toll-free 800-624-3328.

HANNIBAL-LAGRANGE COLLEGE

Hannibal, MO

Tuition & fees: $8440 **Average undergraduate aid package: N/A**

ABOUT THE INSTITUTION Independent Southern Baptist, coed. Awards: associate and bachelor's degrees. 44 undergraduate majors. Total enrollment: 1,139. Undergraduates: 1,139. Freshmen: 128. Federal methodology is used as a basis for awarding need-based institutional aid.

UNDERGRADUATE EXPENSES for 1999–2000 ***Application fee:*** $25. ***Comprehensive fee:*** $11,666 includes full-time tuition ($8160), mandatory fees ($280), and room and board ($3226). Full-time tuition and fees vary according to program. Room and board charges vary according to board plan and housing facility. ***Part-time tuition:*** $272 per credit hour. ***Part-time fees:*** $55 per term part-time. Part-time tuition and fees vary according to course load and program. ***Payment plan:*** deferred payment.

GIFT AID (NEED-BASED) ***Total amount:*** $890,172 (71% Federal, 29% state). ***Scholarships, grants, and awards:*** Federal Pell, FSEOG, state, private.

GIFT AID (NON-NEED-BASED) ***Total amount:*** $1,079,287 (87% institutional, 13% external sources). ***Scholarships, grants, and awards by category:*** *Academic Interests/Achievement:* 474 awards: general academic interests/

achievements, religion/biblical studies. *Creative Arts/Performance:* 104 awards ($96,953 total): art/fine arts, journalism/publications, music, performing arts, theater/drama. *Special Characteristics:* 191 awards ($165,810 total): children of faculty/staff, public servants, relatives of clergy, religious affiliation. ***Tuition waivers:*** Full or partial for employees or children of employees, senior citizens.

LOANS ***Student loans:*** $2,249,658 (100% need-based). 70% of past graduating class borrowed through all loan programs. Average indebtedness per student: $14,563. ***Parent loans:*** $385,928 (100% need-based). ***Programs:*** FFEL (Subsidized and Unsubsidized Stafford, PLUS), Perkins, state, college/university.

WORK-STUDY ***Federal work-study:*** *Total amount:* $66,723; 110 jobs averaging $607.

ATHLETIC AWARDS *Total amount:* 342,240 (100% need-based).

APPLYING for FINANCIAL AID ***Required financial aid form:*** institution's own form. ***Financial aid deadline:*** Continuous. ***Notification date:*** Continuous beginning 1/1.

CONTACT Amy Blackwell, Director, Financial Aid, Hannibal-LaGrange College, 2800 Palmyra Road, Hannibal, MO 63401-1940, 573-221-3675 Ext. 279 or toll-free 800-HLG-1119. *Fax:* 573-221-6594.

HANOVER COLLEGE

Hanover, IN

Tuition & fees: $11,045 **Average undergraduate aid package: $10,287**

ABOUT THE INSTITUTION Independent Presbyterian, coed. Awards: bachelor's degrees. 30 undergraduate majors. Total enrollment: 1,123. Undergraduates: 1,123. Freshmen: 342. Federal methodology is used as a basis for awarding need-based institutional aid.

UNDERGRADUATE EXPENSES for 1999–2000 ***Application fee:*** $25. ***One-time required fee:*** $50. ***Comprehensive fee:*** $15,700 includes full-time tuition ($10,700), mandatory fees ($345), and room and board ($4655). ***College room only:*** $2150. Room and board charges vary according to housing facility. ***Part-time tuition:*** $1190 per unit. ***Payment plan:*** installment.

FRESHMAN FINANCIAL AID (Fall 1999) 280 applied for aid; of those 73% were deemed to have need. 100% of freshmen with need received aid; of those 50% had need fully met. *Average percent of need met:* 94% (excluding resources awarded to replace EFC). *Average financial aid package:* $10,084 (excluding resources awarded to replace EFC). 40% of all full-time freshmen had no need and received non-need-based aid.

UNDERGRADUATE FINANCIAL AID (Fall 1999) 762 applied for aid; of those 74% were deemed to have need. 100% of undergraduates with need received aid; of those 41% had need fully met. *Average percent of need met:* 94% (excluding resources awarded to replace EFC). *Average financial aid package:* $10,287 (excluding resources awarded to replace EFC). 38% of all full-time undergraduates had no need and received non-need-based aid.

GIFT AID (NEED-BASED) ***Total amount:*** $2,495,747 (10% Federal, 40% state, 50% institutional). ***Receiving aid:*** *Freshmen:* 60% (205); *all full-time undergraduates:* 49% (545). ***Average award:*** Freshmen: $7807; Undergraduates: $7157. ***Scholarships, grants, and awards:*** Federal Pell, state, private, college/university gift aid from institutional funds.

GIFT AID (NON-NEED-BASED) ***Total amount:*** $3,276,567 (1% state, 91% institutional, 8% external sources). ***Receiving aid:*** *Freshmen:* 11% (38); *Undergraduates:* 6% (71). ***Scholarships, grants, and awards by category:*** *Academic Interests/Achievement:* 335 awards ($2,122,670 total): general academic interests/achievements. *Creative Arts/Performance:* 45 awards ($85,500 total): music. *Special Characteristics:* 83 awards ($461,825 total): children of faculty/staff, international students, members of minority groups, religious affiliation. ***Tuition waivers:*** Full or partial for employees or children of employees, senior citizens.

LOANS ***Student loans:*** $2,027,448 (71% need-based, 29% non-need-based). 46% of past graduating class borrowed through all loan programs. Average indebtedness per student: $11,735. ***Average need-based loan:*** Freshmen: $1741; Undergraduates: $2929. ***Parent loans:*** $760,071 (100% non-need-based). ***Programs:*** FFEL (Subsidized and Unsubsidized Stafford, PLUS).

APPLYING for FINANCIAL AID ***Required financial aid form:*** FAFSA. ***Financial aid deadline:*** 3/1. ***Notification date:*** 3/30.

CONTACT Dennis R. Thomas, Director of Financial Aid, Hanover College, PO Box 108, Hanover, IN 47243-0108, 812-866-7030 or toll-free 800-213-2178. *Fax:* 812-866-7098. *E-mail:* thomasdr@hanover.edu

HARDING UNIVERSITY

Searcy, AR

Tuition & fees: $8472 **Average undergraduate aid package: $8349**

ABOUT THE INSTITUTION Independent religious, coed. Awards: bachelor's and master's degrees. 74 undergraduate majors. Total enrollment: 3,976. Undergraduates: 3,752. Freshmen: 940. Federal methodology is used as a basis for awarding need-based institutional aid.

UNDERGRADUATE EXPENSES for 1999–2000 ***Application fee:*** $25. ***Comprehensive fee:*** $12,722 includes full-time tuition ($8272), mandatory fees ($200), and room and board ($4250). ***College room only:*** $1998. Room and board charges vary according to board plan and housing facility. ***Part-time tuition:*** $258 per semester hour. ***Part-time fees:*** $10 per semester hour. Part-time tuition and fees vary according to course load. ***Payment plans:*** tuition prepayment, installment.

FRESHMAN FINANCIAL AID (Fall 1999) 714 applied for aid; of those 80% were deemed to have need. 100% of freshmen with need received aid; of those 75% had need fully met. *Average percent of need met:* 75% (excluding resources awarded to replace EFC). *Average financial aid package:* $7832 (excluding resources awarded to replace EFC). 33% of all full-time freshmen had no need and received non-need-based aid.

UNDERGRADUATE FINANCIAL AID (Fall 1999) 2,764 applied for aid; of those 79% were deemed to have need. 100% of undergraduates with need received aid; of those 75% had need fully met. *Average percent of need met:* 75% (excluding resources awarded to replace EFC). *Average financial aid package:* $8349 (excluding resources awarded to replace EFC). 31% of all full-time undergraduates had no need and received non-need-based aid.

GIFT AID (NEED-BASED) ***Total amount:*** $6,468,390 (40% Federal, 12% state, 40% institutional, 8% external sources). ***Receiving aid:*** *Freshmen:* 55% (512); *all full-time undergraduates:* 51% (1,866). ***Average award:*** Freshmen: $3687; Undergraduates: $3466. ***Scholarships, grants, and awards:*** Federal Pell, FSEOG, state, private, college/university gift aid from institutional funds.

GIFT AID (NON-NEED-BASED) ***Total amount:*** $4,457,312 (11% state, 82% institutional, 7% external sources). ***Receiving aid:*** *Freshmen:* 1% (5); *Undergraduates:* 1% (19). ***Scholarships, grants, and awards by category:*** *Academic Interests/Achievement:* 1,579 awards ($3,431,927 total): general academic interests/achievements. *Creative Arts/Performance:* 109 awards ($107,331 total): music. *Special Achievements/Activities:* 135 awards ($197,968 total): cheerleading/drum major, religious involvement. *Special Characteristics:* 165 awards ($1,252,471 total): children with a deceased or disabled parent, international students, siblings of current students. ***Tuition waivers:*** Full or partial for employees or children of employees, senior citizens. ***ROTC:*** Army cooperative.

LOANS ***Student loans:*** $11,505,026 (83% need-based, 17% non-need-based). 63% of past graduating class borrowed through all loan programs. Average indebtedness per student: $22,420. ***Average need-based loan:*** Freshmen: $2398; Undergraduates: $3534. ***Parent loans:*** $4,070,735 (47% need-based, 53% non-need-based). ***Programs:*** FFEL (Subsidized and Unsubsidized Stafford, PLUS), Perkins, Federal Nursing, state, college/university.

WORK-STUDY ***Federal work-study:*** *Total amount:* $520,071; 708 jobs averaging $735. ***State or other work-study/employment:*** *Total amount:* $862,063 (45% need-based, 55% non-need-based). 1,408 part-time jobs averaging $612.

ATHLETIC AWARDS *Total amount:* 1,168,452 (41% need-based, 59% non-need-based).

Harding University (continued)

APPLYING for FINANCIAL AID ***Required financial aid forms:*** FAFSA, institution's own form. ***Financial aid deadline:*** Continuous. ***Notification date:*** Continuous beginning 2/15. Students must reply within 2 weeks of notification.

CONTACT Mr. Zearl D. Watson, Director of Student Financial Services, Harding University, Box 12282, Searcy, AR 72149-0001, 501-279-4257 or toll-free 800-477-4407. *Fax:* 501-279-4129. *E-mail:* watson@harding.edu

HARDIN-SIMMONS UNIVERSITY

Abilene, TX

Tuition & fees: $9330 **Average undergraduate aid package: $10,773**

ABOUT THE INSTITUTION Independent Baptist, coed. Awards: bachelor's, master's, and first professional degrees. 69 undergraduate majors. Total enrollment: 2,291. Undergraduates: 1,924. Freshmen: 365. Federal methodology is used as a basis for awarding need-based institutional aid.

UNDERGRADUATE EXPENSES for 1999–2000 ***Application fee:*** $25. ***Comprehensive fee:*** $12,666 includes full-time tuition ($8700), mandatory fees ($630), and room and board ($3336). ***College room only:*** $1730. Full-time tuition and fees vary according to program. Room and board charges vary according to board plan and housing facility. ***Part-time tuition:*** $290 per semester hour. Part-time tuition and fees vary according to course load and program. ***Payment plans:*** guaranteed tuition, installment, deferred payment.

FRESHMAN FINANCIAL AID (Fall 1998) 395 applied for aid; of those 73% were deemed to have need. 100% of freshmen with need received aid. *Average financial aid package:* $8258 (excluding resources awarded to replace EFC). 14% of all full-time freshmen had no need and received non-need-based aid.

UNDERGRADUATE FINANCIAL AID (Fall 1998) 1,462 applied for aid; of those 84% were deemed to have need. 100% of undergraduates with need received aid; of those 1% had need fully met. *Average percent of need met:* 1% (excluding resources awarded to replace EFC). *Average financial aid package:* $10,773 (excluding resources awarded to replace EFC). 10% of all full-time undergraduates had no need and received non-need-based aid.

GIFT AID (NEED-BASED) ***Total amount:*** $6,633,118 (21% Federal, 23% state, 49% institutional, 7% external sources). ***Receiving aid:*** *Freshmen:* 54% (221); *all full-time undergraduates:* 55% (954). ***Average award:*** Freshmen: $2822; Undergraduates: $2940. ***Scholarships, grants, and awards:*** Federal Pell, FSEOG, state, private, college/university gift aid from institutional funds.

GIFT AID (NON-NEED-BASED) ***Receiving aid:*** *Freshmen:* 54% (222); *Undergraduates:* 48% (839). ***Scholarships, grants, and awards by category:*** *Academic Interests/Achievement:* 1,123 awards ($1,739,605 total): biological sciences, business, communication, education, English, general academic interests/achievements, mathematics, premedicine, religion/biblical studies, social sciences. *Creative Arts/Performance:* 118 awards ($117,357 total): art/fine arts, music, theater/drama. *Special Achievements/Activities:* 100 awards ($123,265 total): general special achievements/activities, junior miss, leadership. *Special Characteristics:* 471 awards ($692,343 total): children of faculty/staff, ethnic background, general special characteristics, public servants, religious affiliation. ***Tuition waivers:*** Full or partial for employees or children of employees.

LOANS ***Student loans:*** $8,819,815 (48% need-based, 52% non-need-based). 84% of past graduating class borrowed through all loan programs. Average indebtedness per student: $12,080. ***Average need-based loan:*** Freshmen: $2548; Undergraduates: $3919. ***Parent loans:*** $560,460 (100% non-need-based). ***Programs:*** FFEL (Subsidized and Unsubsidized Stafford, PLUS), Perkins, state, college/university.

WORK-STUDY ***Federal work-study:*** *Total amount:* $223,722; 286 jobs averaging $782. ***State or other work-study/employment:*** *Total amount:* $567,853 (4% need-based, 96% non-need-based). 598 part-time jobs averaging $949.

APPLYING for FINANCIAL AID ***Required financial aid forms:*** FAFSA, institution's own form. ***Financial aid deadline (priority):*** 3/15. ***Notification date:*** Continuous.

CONTACT Travis Seekins, Assistant Director of Enrollment Services, Hardin-Simmons University, PO Box 16050, Abilene, TX 79698-6050, 915-670-1206 or toll-free 800-568-2692. *Fax:* 915-671-2115. *E-mail:* seekins@hsutx.edu

HARRINGTON INSTITUTE OF INTERIOR DESIGN

Chicago, IL

Tuition & fees: $11,086 **Average undergraduate aid package: $3936**

ABOUT THE INSTITUTION Proprietary, coed. Awards: associate and bachelor's degrees. 1 undergraduate major. Total enrollment: 512. Undergraduates: 512. Freshmen: 37. Federal methodology is used as a basis for awarding need-based institutional aid.

UNDERGRADUATE EXPENSES for 1999–2000 ***Application fee:*** $50. ***Tuition:*** full-time $11,036; part-time $2586 per term. ***Required fees:*** full-time $50; $25 per term part-time. ***Payment plan:*** installment.

UNDERGRADUATE FINANCIAL AID (Fall 1999, est.) 125 applied for aid; of those 82% were deemed to have need. 100% of undergraduates with need received aid. *Average percent of need met:* 33% (excluding resources awarded to replace EFC). *Average financial aid package:* $3936 (excluding resources awarded to replace EFC).

GIFT AID (NEED-BASED) ***Total amount:*** $150,000 (100% Federal). ***Receiving aid:*** *All full-time undergraduates:* 16% (39). ***Average award:*** Undergraduates: $2106. ***Scholarships, grants, and awards:*** Federal Pell.

GIFT AID (NON-NEED-BASED) ***Total amount:*** $8500 (41% institutional, 59% external sources).

LOANS ***Student loans:*** $2,005,000 (100% need-based). 49% of past graduating class borrowed through all loan programs. Average indebtedness per student: $20,714. ***Average need-based loan:*** Undergraduates: $5834. ***Parent loans:*** $480,000 (100% need-based). ***Programs:*** FFEL (Subsidized and Unsubsidized Stafford, PLUS), EXCEL Loans.

APPLYING for FINANCIAL AID ***Required financial aid forms:*** FAFSA, Stafford Student Loan form. ***Financial aid deadline (priority):*** 5/1. ***Notification date:*** Continuous. Students must reply within 2 weeks of notification.

CONTACT Ms. Renee Darosky, Director of Financial Aid, Harrington Institute of Interior Design, 410 South Michigan Avenue, Chicago, IL 60605-1496, 312-939-4975 or toll-free 877-939-4975 (out-of-state). *Fax:* 312-939-8005. *E-mail:* financialaid@interiordesign.edu

HARRIS-STOWE STATE COLLEGE

St. Louis, MO

Tuition & fees (MO res): $2064 **Average undergraduate aid package: N/A**

ABOUT THE INSTITUTION State-supported, coed. Awards: bachelor's degrees. 11 undergraduate majors. Total enrollment: 1,735. Undergraduates: 1,735. Freshmen: 181. Federal methodology is used as a basis for awarding need-based institutional aid.

UNDERGRADUATE EXPENSES for 1999–2000 ***One-time required fee:*** $15. ***Tuition, state resident:*** full-time $2064; part-time $86 per credit hour. ***Tuition, nonresident:*** full-time $4056; part-time $169 per credit hour. Full-time tuition and fees vary according to course load. ***Payment plan:*** installment.

FRESHMAN FINANCIAL AID (Fall 1998) 52 applied for aid; of those 73% were deemed to have need. 100% of freshmen with need received aid; of those 29% had need fully met. *Average percent of need met:* 68% (excluding resources awarded to replace EFC). 11% of all full-time freshmen had no need and received non-need-based aid.

UNDERGRADUATE FINANCIAL AID (Fall 1998) 546 applied for aid; of those 97% were deemed to have need. 100% of undergraduates with need received aid; of those 18% had need fully met. *Average percent of*

need met: 87% (excluding resources awarded to replace EFC). 8% of all full-time undergraduates had no need and received non-need-based aid.

GIFT AID (NEED-BASED) ***Total amount:*** $1,840,813 (96% Federal, 3% state, 1% institutional). ***Receiving aid:*** *Freshmen:* 26% (26); *all full-time undergraduates:* 57% (430). ***Average award:*** Freshmen: $1902; Undergraduates: $2844. ***Scholarships, grants, and awards:*** Federal Pell, FSEOG, state, private, college/university gift aid from institutional funds.

GIFT AID (NON-NEED-BASED) ***Total amount:*** $341,044 (7% state, 93% institutional). ***Receiving aid:*** *Freshmen:* 11% (11); *Undergraduates:* 15% (111). ***Scholarships, grants, and awards by category:*** *Academic Interests/Achievement:* general academic interests/achievements. *Creative Arts/Performance:* 20 awards: music, theater/drama. ***Tuition waivers:*** Full or partial for employees or children of employees. ***ROTC:*** Air Force cooperative.

LOANS ***Student loans:*** $2,565,795 (79% need-based, 21% non-need-based). 68% of past graduating class borrowed through all loan programs. Average indebtedness per student: $14,562. ***Average need-based loan:*** Freshmen: $2161; Undergraduates: $3934. ***Programs:*** FFEL (Subsidized and Unsubsidized Stafford, PLUS), Perkins, college/university.

WORK-STUDY ***Federal work-study:*** *Total amount:* $122,723; 158 jobs averaging $776. ***State or other work-study/employment:*** *Total amount:* $113,897 (11% need-based, 89% non-need-based). Part-time jobs available.

ATHLETIC AWARDS *Total amount:* 133,328 (100% non-need-based).

APPLYING for FINANCIAL AID ***Required financial aid forms:*** FAFSA, institution's own form. ***Financial aid deadline (priority):*** 4/1. ***Notification date:*** Continuous. Students must reply within 3 weeks of notification.

CONTACT Joye Freeman, Director of Financial Aid, Harris-Stowe State College, 3026 Laclede Avenue, St. Louis, MO 63103-2136, 314-340-3502. *Fax:* 314-340-3503. *E-mail:* freemanj@mail1.hssc.edu

HARTWICK COLLEGE

Oneonta, NY

Tuition & fees: $23,800 **Average undergraduate aid package: N/A**

ABOUT THE INSTITUTION Independent, coed. Awards: bachelor's degrees. 32 undergraduate majors. Total enrollment: 1,450. Undergraduates: 1,450. Freshmen: 396. Both federal and institutional methodology are used as a basis for awarding need-based institutional aid.

UNDERGRADUATE EXPENSES for 1999–2000 ***Application fee:*** $35. ***Comprehensive fee:*** $30,140 includes full-time tuition ($23,475), mandatory fees ($325), and room and board ($6340). ***College room only:*** $3175. Room and board charges vary according to board plan and housing facility. ***Part-time tuition:*** $2638 per course. ***Payment plan:*** installment.

GIFT AID (NEED-BASED) ***Scholarships, grants, and awards:*** Federal Pell, FSEOG, state, private, college/university gift aid from institutional funds.

GIFT AID (NON-NEED-BASED) ***Scholarships, grants, and awards by category:*** *Academic Interests/Achievement:* general academic interests/achievements. *Special Achievements/Activities:* general special achievements/activities. *Special Characteristics:* children and siblings of alumni, children of faculty/staff, siblings of current students. ***Tuition waivers:*** Full or partial for employees or children of employees.

LOANS ***Programs:*** FFEL (Subsidized and Unsubsidized Stafford, PLUS), Perkins, college/university.

WORK-STUDY Federal work-study jobs available.

APPLYING for FINANCIAL AID ***Required financial aid forms:*** FAFSA, institution's own form. ***Financial aid deadline:*** 2/1. ***Notification date:*** 4/1. Students must reply by 5/1 or within 2 weeks of notification.

CONTACT Financial Aid Department, Hartwick College, West Street, Oneonta, NY 13820, 607-431-4130 or toll-free 888-HARTWICK (out-of-state).

HARVARD UNIVERSITY

Cambridge, MA

Tuition & fees: $24,407 **Average undergraduate aid package: $22,010**

ABOUT THE INSTITUTION Independent, coed. Awards: bachelor's, master's, doctoral, and first professional degrees. 141 undergraduate majors. Total enrollment: 17,606. Undergraduates: 6,684. Both federal and institutional methodology are used as a basis for awarding need-based institutional aid.

UNDERGRADUATE EXPENSES for 1999–2000 ***Application fee:*** $60. ***Comprehensive fee:*** $32,164 includes full-time tuition ($22,054), mandatory fees ($2353), and room and board ($7757). ***College room only:*** $4072. ***Payment plans:*** tuition prepayment, installment.

FRESHMAN FINANCIAL AID (Fall 1998) 984 applied for aid; of those 86% were deemed to have need. 100% of freshmen with need received aid; of those 100% had need fully met. *Average percent of need met:* 100% (excluding resources awarded to replace EFC). *Average financial aid package:* $21,390 (excluding resources awarded to replace EFC). 26% of all full-time freshmen had no need and received non-need-based aid.

UNDERGRADUATE FINANCIAL AID (Fall 1998) 3,562 applied for aid; of those 94% were deemed to have need. 100% of undergraduates with need received aid; of those 100% had need fully met. *Average percent of need met:* 100% (excluding resources awarded to replace EFC). *Average financial aid package:* $22,010 (excluding resources awarded to replace EFC). 18% of all full-time undergraduates had no need and received non-need-based aid.

GIFT AID (NEED-BASED) ***Total amount:*** $58,725,867 (8% Federal, 85% institutional, 7% external sources). ***Receiving aid:*** *Freshmen:* 50% (824); *all full-time undergraduates:* 49% (3,259). ***Average award:*** Freshmen: $18,828; Undergraduates: $18,022. ***Scholarships, grants, and awards:*** Federal Pell, FSEOG, state, private, college/university gift aid from institutional funds.

GIFT AID (NON-NEED-BASED) ***Total amount:*** $4,418,331 (27% Federal, 73% external sources). ***ROTC:*** Army cooperative, Naval cooperative, Air Force cooperative.

LOANS ***Student loans:*** $16,127,349 (67% need-based, 33% non-need-based). 58% of past graduating class borrowed through all loan programs. Average indebtedness per student: $14,744. ***Average need-based loan:*** Freshmen: $2556; Undergraduates: $3409. ***Parent loans:*** $9,110,744 (100% non-need-based). ***Programs:*** Federal Direct (Subsidized and Unsubsidized Stafford, PLUS), Perkins, state, college/university.

WORK-STUDY ***Federal work-study:*** *Total amount:* $1,671,000; 1,065 jobs averaging $1560. ***State or other work-study/employment:*** *Total amount:* $6,491,956 (33% need-based, 67% non-need-based). Part-time jobs available.

APPLYING for FINANCIAL AID ***Required financial aid forms:*** FAFSA, CSS Financial Aid PROFILE, tax returns. ***Financial aid deadline (priority):*** 2/1. ***Notification date:*** 4/1. Students must reply by 5/1 or within 2 weeks of notification.

CONTACT Financial Aid Office, Harvard University, 312 Byerly Hall, 8 Garden Street, Cambridge, MA 02138, 617-495-1581. *Fax:* 617-496-0256.

HARVEY MUDD COLLEGE

Claremont, CA

Tuition & fees: $22,083 **Average undergraduate aid package: $17,616**

ABOUT THE INSTITUTION Independent, coed. Awards: bachelor's and master's degrees. 6 undergraduate majors. Total enrollment: 709. Undergraduates: 703. Freshmen: 170. Both federal and institutional methodology are used as a basis for awarding need-based institutional aid.

UNDERGRADUATE EXPENSES for 1999–2000 ***Application fee:*** $50. ***Comprehensive fee:*** $30,100 includes full-time tuition ($21,584), mandatory fees ($499), and room and board ($8017). ***College room only:*** $4077. Room and board charges vary according to board plan. ***Part-time tuition:*** $674 per credit hour. ***Part-time fees:*** $499 per year part-time. ***Payment plan:*** installment.

FRESHMAN FINANCIAL AID (Fall 1999) 134 applied for aid; of those 78% were deemed to have need. 100% of freshmen with need received aid; of those 100% had need fully met. *Average percent of need met:* 100% (excluding resources awarded to replace EFC). *Average financial aid pack-*

Harvey Mudd College (continued)

age: $17,939 (excluding resources awarded to replace EFC). 29% of all full-time freshmen had no need and received non-need-based aid.

UNDERGRADUATE FINANCIAL AID (Fall 1999) 476 applied for aid; of those 87% were deemed to have need. 100% of undergraduates with need received aid; of those 100% had need fully met. *Average percent of need met:* 100% (excluding resources awarded to replace EFC). *Average financial aid package:* $17,616 (excluding resources awarded to replace EFC). 22% of all full-time undergraduates had no need and received non-need-based aid.

GIFT AID (NEED-BASED) ***Total amount:*** $4,550,207 (7% Federal, 13% state, 80% institutional). ***Receiving aid:*** *Freshmen:* 61% (103); *all full-time undergraduates:* 55% (381). ***Average award:*** Freshmen: $13,953; Undergraduates: $13,140. ***Scholarships, grants, and awards:*** Federal Pell, FSEOG, state, private, college/university gift aid from institutional funds.

GIFT AID (NON-NEED-BASED) ***Total amount:*** $960,160 (7% state, 38% institutional, 55% external sources). ***Receiving aid:*** *Freshmen:* 11% (19); *Undergraduates:* 7% (51). ***Scholarships, grants, and awards by category:*** *Academic Interests/Achievement:* 237 awards ($689,000 total): general academic interests/achievements. ***Tuition waivers:*** Full or partial for employees or children of employees. ***ROTC:*** Army cooperative, Air Force.

LOANS ***Student loans:*** $2,459,039 (72% need-based, 28% non-need-based). 65% of past graduating class borrowed through all loan programs. Average indebtedness per student: $17,544. ***Average need-based loan:*** Freshmen: $3132; Undergraduates: $4636. ***Parent loans:*** $1,820,193 (100% non-need-based). ***Programs:*** FFEL (Subsidized and Unsubsidized Stafford, PLUS), Perkins, college/university, alternative loans.

WORK-STUDY ***Federal work-study:*** *Total amount:* $491,219; 310 jobs averaging $1585. ***State or other work-study/employment:*** *Total amount:* $3928 (100% need-based). 4 part-time jobs averaging $982.

APPLYING for FINANCIAL AID ***Required financial aid forms:*** FAFSA, CSS Financial Aid PROFILE, state aid form, noncustodial (divorced/separated) parent's statement, business/farm supplement. ***Financial aid deadline:*** 2/1. ***Notification date:*** 4/1. Students must reply by 5/1 or within 2 weeks of notification.

CONTACT Office of Financial Aid, Harvey Mudd College, 301 East 12th Street, Claremont, CA 91711-5994, 909-621-8055. *Fax:* 909-607-7046. *E-mail:* financial_aid@hmc.edu

HASTINGS COLLEGE

Hastings, NE

Tuition & fees: $12,916 | **Average undergraduate aid package: $10,292**

ABOUT THE INSTITUTION Independent Presbyterian, coed. Awards: bachelor's and master's degrees. 72 undergraduate majors. Total enrollment: 1,148. Undergraduates: 1,118. Freshmen: 288. Federal methodology is used as a basis for awarding need-based institutional aid.

UNDERGRADUATE EXPENSES for 2000–2001 ***Application fee:*** $20. ***Comprehensive fee:*** $16,982 includes full-time tuition ($12,396), mandatory fees ($520), and room and board ($4066). ***College room only:*** $1714. Full-time tuition and fees vary according to degree level and program. Room and board charges vary according to board plan. Part-time tuition and fees vary according to course load, degree level, and program. ***Payment plans:*** installment, deferred payment.

FRESHMAN FINANCIAL AID (Fall 1999) 292 applied for aid; of those 72% were deemed to have need. 99% of freshmen with need received aid; of those 20% had need fully met. *Average percent of need met:* 77% (excluding resources awarded to replace EFC). *Average financial aid package:* $10,472 (excluding resources awarded to replace EFC). 14% of all full-time freshmen had no need and received non-need-based aid.

UNDERGRADUATE FINANCIAL AID (Fall 1999) 1,092 applied for aid; of those 73% were deemed to have need. 100% of undergraduates with need received aid; of those 23% had need fully met. *Average percent of need met:* 77% (excluding resources awarded to replace EFC). *Average financial aid package:* $10,292 (excluding resources awarded to replace EFC). 16% of all full-time undergraduates had no need and received non-need-based aid.

GIFT AID (NEED-BASED) ***Total amount:*** $3,956,967 (21% Federal, 5% state, 69% institutional, 5% external sources). ***Receiving aid:*** *Freshmen:* 71% (208); *all full-time undergraduates:* 73% (795). ***Scholarships, grants, and awards:*** Federal Pell, FSEOG, state, private, college/university gift aid from institutional funds.

GIFT AID (NON-NEED-BASED) ***Total amount:*** $1,174,369 (93% institutional, 7% external sources). ***Receiving aid:*** *Freshmen:* 70% (204); *Undergraduates:* 67% (729). ***Scholarships, grants, and awards by category:*** *Academic Interests/Achievement:* general academic interests/achievements. *Creative Arts/Performance:* art/fine arts, debating, music, performing arts, theater/drama. *Special Achievements/Activities:* cheerleading/drum major. *Special Characteristics:* adult students, children of educators, children of faculty/staff, relatives of clergy, religious affiliation, siblings of current students. ***Tuition waivers:*** Full or partial for employees or children of employees, adult students.

LOANS ***Student loans:*** $3,635,671 (78% need-based, 22% non-need-based). 85% of past graduating class borrowed through all loan programs. Average indebtedness per student: $15,778. ***Average need-based loan:*** Freshmen: $3391; Undergraduates: $4711. ***Parent loans:*** $922,940 (100% non-need-based). ***Programs:*** FFEL (Subsidized and Unsubsidized Stafford, PLUS), Perkins, college/university.

WORK-STUDY ***Federal work-study:*** *Total amount:* $89,368; jobs available. ***State or other work-study/employment:*** *Total amount:* $429,305 (100% non-need-based). Part-time jobs available.

ATHLETIC AWARDS *Total amount:* 1,704,617 (70% need-based, 30% non-need-based).

APPLYING for FINANCIAL AID ***Required financial aid forms:*** FAFSA, institution's own form. ***Financial aid deadline:*** 9/1 (priority: 5/1). ***Notification date:*** Continuous. Students must reply within 2 weeks of notification.

CONTACT Mr. Ian Roberts, Director, Financial Aid, Hastings College, 7th and Turner, Hastings, NE 68901, 402-461-7455 or toll-free 800-532-7642. *Fax:* 402-461-7490. *E-mail:* iroberts@hastings.edu

HAVERFORD COLLEGE

Haverford, PA

Tuition & fees: $23,780 | **Average undergraduate aid package: $19,984**

ABOUT THE INSTITUTION Independent, coed. Awards: bachelor's degrees. 44 undergraduate majors. Total enrollment: 1,118. Undergraduates: 1,118. Freshmen: 302. Both federal and institutional methodology are used as a basis for awarding need-based institutional aid.

UNDERGRADUATE EXPENSES for 1999–2000 ***Application fee:*** $50. ***Comprehensive fee:*** $31,400 includes full-time tuition ($23,556), mandatory fees ($224), and room and board ($7620). ***College room only:*** $4210. Room and board charges vary according to board plan. ***Payment plan:*** installment.

FRESHMAN FINANCIAL AID (Fall 1999, est.) 159 applied for aid; of those 72% were deemed to have need. 100% of freshmen with need received aid; of those 100% had need fully met. *Average percent of need met:* 100% (excluding resources awarded to replace EFC). *Average financial aid package:* $20,998 (excluding resources awarded to replace EFC).

UNDERGRADUATE FINANCIAL AID (Fall 1999, est.) 552 applied for aid; of those 88% were deemed to have need. 100% of undergraduates with need received aid; of those 100% had need fully met. *Average percent of need met:* 100% (excluding resources awarded to replace EFC). *Average financial aid package:* $19,984 (excluding resources awarded to replace EFC).

GIFT AID (NEED-BASED) ***Total amount:*** $7,759,210 (6% Federal, 3% state, 87% institutional, 4% external sources). ***Receiving aid:*** *Freshmen:* 34% (103); *all full-time undergraduates:* 39% (437). ***Average award:*** Freshmen: $17,492; Undergraduates: $15,703. ***Scholarships, grants, and awards:*** Federal Pell, FSEOG, state, private, college/university gift aid from institutional funds.

GIFT AID (NON-NEED-BASED) ***Tuition waivers:*** Full or partial for employees or children of employees.

LOANS ***Student loans:*** $1,702,936 (91% need-based, 9% non-need-based). 43% of past graduating class borrowed through all loan programs. Average indebtedness per student: $13,821. ***Average need-based loan:*** Freshmen: $2207; Undergraduates: $2969. ***Parent loans:*** $1,084,401 (100% non-need-based). ***Programs:*** FFEL (Subsidized and Unsubsidized Stafford, PLUS), Perkins.

WORK-STUDY ***Federal work-study:*** *Total amount:* $242,478; 231 jobs averaging $1049. ***State or other work-study/employment:*** *Total amount:* $433,136 (50% need-based, 50% non-need-based). 412 part-time jobs averaging $1049.

APPLYING for FINANCIAL AID ***Required financial aid forms:*** FAFSA, CSS Financial Aid PROFILE, state aid form, noncustodial (divorced/separated) parent's statement, business/farm supplement. ***Financial aid deadline:*** 1/31. ***Notification date:*** 4/15. Students must reply by 5/1.

CONTACT Mr. David J. Hoy, Director of Financial Aid Office, Haverford College, 370 Lancaster Avenue, Haverford, PA 19041-1392, 610-896-1350. *Fax:* 610-896-1338. *E-mail:* finaid@haverford.edu

HAWAII PACIFIC UNIVERSITY

Honolulu, HI

Tuition & fees: $8460 **Average undergraduate aid package: $10,794**

ABOUT THE INSTITUTION Independent, coed. Awards: associate, bachelor's, and master's degrees and post-bachelor's certificates. 45 undergraduate majors. Total enrollment: 8,064. Undergraduates: 6,914. Freshmen: 464. Federal methodology is used as a basis for awarding need-based institutional aid.

UNDERGRADUATE EXPENSES for 1999–2000 ***Application fee:*** $50. ***Comprehensive fee:*** $16,580 includes full-time tuition ($8460) and room and board ($8120). Full-time tuition and fees vary according to program and student level. Room and board charges vary according to housing facility. ***Part-time tuition:*** $155 per credit. Part-time tuition and fees vary according to course load. ***Payment plan:*** installment.

FRESHMAN FINANCIAL AID (Fall 1999, est.) 204 applied for aid; of those 76% were deemed to have need. 98% of freshmen with need received aid; of those 37% had need fully met. *Average percent of need met:* 78% (excluding resources awarded to replace EFC). *Average financial aid package:* $12,108 (excluding resources awarded to replace EFC). 9% of all full-time freshmen had no need and received non-need-based aid.

UNDERGRADUATE FINANCIAL AID (Fall 1999, est.) 1,743 applied for aid; of those 68% were deemed to have need. 99% of undergraduates with need received aid; of those 33% had need fully met. *Average percent of need met:* 77% (excluding resources awarded to replace EFC). *Average financial aid package:* $10,794 (excluding resources awarded to replace EFC). 10% of all full-time undergraduates had no need and received non-need-based aid.

GIFT AID (NEED-BASED) ***Total amount:*** $3,277,573 (76% Federal, 24% external sources). ***Receiving aid:*** *Freshmen:* 24% (99); *all full-time undergraduates:* 23% (903). ***Average award:*** Freshmen: $3366; Undergraduates: $3096. ***Scholarships, grants, and awards:*** Federal Pell, FSEOG, state, private, college/university gift aid from institutional funds.

GIFT AID (NON-NEED-BASED) ***Total amount:*** $2,127,486 (88% institutional, 12% external sources). ***Receiving aid:*** *Freshmen:* 14% (60); *Undergraduates:* 16% (610). ***Scholarships, grants, and awards by category:*** *Academic Interests/Achievement:* 246 awards ($1,187,046 total): general academic interests/achievements. *Creative Arts/Performance:* 60 awards ($494,100 total): dance, music. *Special Achievements/Activities:* 108 awards ($570,747 total): cheerleading/drum major, general special achievements/activities, hobbies/interests, junior miss, memberships. *Special Characteristics:* 102 awards ($308,410 total): children of faculty/staff, ethnic background, general special characteristics, international students, relatives of clergy, religious affiliation. ***Tuition waivers:*** Full or partial for employees or children of employees. ***ROTC:*** Army cooperative, Air Force cooperative.

LOANS ***Student loans:*** $12,160,076 (55% need-based, 45% non-need-based). Average indebtedness per student: $15,600. ***Average need-based loan:*** Freshmen: $3977; Undergraduates: $5452. ***Programs:*** FFEL (Subsidized and Unsubsidized Stafford, PLUS), Perkins, Federal Nursing.

WORK-STUDY ***Federal work-study:*** *Total amount:* $375,000; 125 jobs averaging $3000.

ATHLETIC AWARDS *Total amount:* 947,144 (100% non-need-based).

APPLYING for FINANCIAL AID ***Required financial aid form:*** FAFSA. ***Financial aid deadline (priority):*** 3/1. ***Notification date:*** Continuous beginning 4/1. Students must reply within 4 weeks of notification.

CONTACT Director of Financial Aid, Hawaii Pacific University, 1164 Bishop Street, Suite 201, Honolulu, HI 96813-2785, 808-544-0253 or toll-free 800-669-4724 (out-of-state). *Fax:* 808-544-1136.

HEBREW COLLEGE

Brookline, MA

ABOUT THE INSTITUTION Independent Jewish, coed. Awards: bachelor's and master's degrees. 2 undergraduate majors.

GIFT AID (NEED-BASED) ***Scholarships, grants, and awards:*** college/university gift aid from institutional funds.

GIFT AID (NON-NEED-BASED) ***Scholarships, grants, and awards by category:*** *Academic Interests/Achievement:* education.

LOANS ***Programs:*** Federal Direct (Subsidized and Unsubsidized Stafford).

APPLYING for FINANCIAL AID ***Required financial aid forms:*** FAFSA, institution's own form.

CONTACT Ms. Norma Frankel, Registrar, Hebrew College, 43 Hawes Street, Brookline, MA 02146-5495, 617-278-4944 or toll-free 800-866-4814. *Fax:* 617-264-9264. *E-mail:* nfrankel@lynx.neu.edu

HEBREW THEOLOGICAL COLLEGE

Skokie, IL

CONTACT Ms. Rhoda Morris, Financial Aid Administrator, Hebrew Theological College, 7135 Carpenter Road, Skokie, IL 60077-3263, 847-982-2500. *Fax:* 847-674-6381.

HEIDELBERG COLLEGE

Tiffin, OH

Tuition & fees: $16,672 **Average undergraduate aid package: $14,909**

ABOUT THE INSTITUTION Independent religious, coed. Awards: bachelor's and master's degrees. 44 undergraduate majors. Total enrollment: 1,581. Undergraduates: 1,360. Freshmen: 326. Federal methodology is used as a basis for awarding need-based institutional aid.

UNDERGRADUATE EXPENSES for 1999–2000 ***Application fee:*** $25. ***Comprehensive fee:*** $21,936 includes full-time tuition ($16,422), mandatory fees ($250), and room and board ($5264). ***College room only:*** $2392. Room and board charges vary according to housing facility. ***Part-time tuition:*** $380 per semester hour. ***Part-time fees:*** $50 per term part-time. Part-time tuition and fees vary according to location. ***Payment plans:*** installment, deferred payment.

FRESHMAN FINANCIAL AID (Fall 1999, est.) 263 applied for aid; of those 93% were deemed to have need. 100% of freshmen with need received aid; of those 19% had need fully met. *Average percent of need met:* 86% (excluding resources awarded to replace EFC). *Average financial aid package:* $14,643 (excluding resources awarded to replace EFC). 10% of all full-time freshmen had no need and received non-need-based aid.

UNDERGRADUATE FINANCIAL AID (Fall 1999, est.) 898 applied for aid; of those 93% were deemed to have need. 100% of undergraduates with need received aid; of those 24% had need fully met. *Average percent of need met:* 89% (excluding resources awarded to replace EFC). *Average financial aid package:* $14,909 (excluding resources awarded to replace EFC). 15% of all full-time undergraduates had no need and received non-need-based aid.

GIFT AID (NEED-BASED) ***Total amount:*** $9,269,956 (9% Federal, 14% state, 75% institutional, 2% external sources). ***Receiving aid:*** *Freshmen:* 90% (244); *all full-time undergraduates:* 85% (838). ***Average award:***

Heidelberg College (continued)

Freshmen: $11,412; Undergraduates: $10,949. ***Scholarships, grants, and awards:*** Federal Pell, FSEOG, state, private, college/university gift aid from institutional funds.

GIFT AID (NON-NEED-BASED) ***Total amount:*** $1,080,148 (18% state, 75% institutional, 7% external sources). ***Receiving aid:*** *Freshmen:* 9% (24); *Undergraduates:* 8% (75). ***Scholarships, grants, and awards by category:*** *Academic Interests/Achievement:* 378 awards ($1,666,500 total): general academic interests/achievements, mathematics, physical sciences. *Creative Arts/Performance:* 61 awards ($100,700 total): music. *Special Characteristics:* 232 awards ($213,087 total): local/state students, religious affiliation. ***Tuition waivers:*** Full or partial for employees or children of employees.

LOANS ***Student loans:*** $3,960,030 (85% need-based, 15% non-need-based). 78% of past graduating class borrowed through all loan programs. Average indebtedness per student: $18,725. ***Average need-based loan:*** Freshmen: $2739; Undergraduates: $3556. ***Parent loans:*** $804,106 (32% need-based, 68% non-need-based). ***Programs:*** FFEL (Subsidized and Unsubsidized Stafford, PLUS), Perkins.

WORK-STUDY ***Federal work-study:*** *Total amount:* $297,550; 327 jobs averaging $910. ***State or other work-study/employment:*** *Total amount:* $173,316 (49% need-based, 51% non-need-based). 155 part-time jobs averaging $1115.

APPLYING for FINANCIAL AID ***Required financial aid form:*** FAFSA. ***Financial aid deadline (priority):*** 3/1. ***Notification date:*** Continuous beginning 3/15. Students must reply within 2 weeks of notification.

CONTACT Ms. Juli L. Weininger, Director of Financial Aid, Heidelberg College, 310 East Market Street, Tiffin, OH 44883-2462, 419-448-2293 or toll-free 800-434-3352. *Fax:* 419-448-2124.

HELLENIC COLLEGE

Brookline, MA

Tuition & fees: $8615 **Average undergraduate aid package: $8000**

ABOUT THE INSTITUTION Independent Greek Orthodox, coed. Awards: bachelor's degrees. 5 undergraduate majors. Total enrollment: 51. Undergraduates: 51. Freshmen: 5. Both federal and institutional methodology are used as a basis for awarding need-based institutional aid.

UNDERGRADUATE EXPENSES for 1999–2000 ***Application fee:*** $35. ***One-time required fee:*** $50. ***Comprehensive fee:*** $15,215 includes full-time tuition ($8400), mandatory fees ($215), and room and board ($6600). Room and board charges vary according to housing facility. ***Part-time tuition:*** $350 per credit. ***Part-time fees:*** $50 per term part-time.

FRESHMAN FINANCIAL AID (Fall 1998) 2 applied for aid; of those 100% were deemed to have need. 100% of freshmen with need received aid; of those 50% had need fully met. *Average percent of need met:* 75% (excluding resources awarded to replace EFC). *Average financial aid package:* $6000 (excluding resources awarded to replace EFC).

UNDERGRADUATE FINANCIAL AID (Fall 1998) 18 applied for aid; of those 100% were deemed to have need. 100% of undergraduates with need received aid; of those 83% had need fully met. *Average percent of need met:* 75% (excluding resources awarded to replace EFC). *Average financial aid package:* $8000 (excluding resources awarded to replace EFC).

GIFT AID (NEED-BASED) ***Total amount:*** $101,487 (41% Federal, 44% institutional, 15% external sources). ***Receiving aid:*** *Freshmen:* 100% (2); *all full-time undergraduates:* 36% (18). ***Average award:*** Freshmen: $2100; Undergraduates: $2100. ***Scholarships, grants, and awards:*** Federal Pell, FSEOG, state, private, college/university gift aid from institutional funds.

GIFT AID (NON-NEED-BASED) ***Total amount:*** $21,000 (100% institutional). ***Receiving aid:*** *Freshmen:* 100% (2); *Undergraduates:* 36% (18). ***Scholarships, grants, and awards by category:*** *Academic Interests/Achievement:* general academic interests/achievements, religion/biblical studies. *Special Achievements/Activities:* leadership, religious involvement. *Special Characteristics:* children and siblings of alumni, children of faculty/staff, religious affiliation. ***Tuition waivers:*** Full or partial for minority students, children of alumni, employees or children of employees.

LOANS ***Student loans:*** $57,400 (100% need-based). Average indebtedness per student: $15,000. ***Parent loans:*** $8000 (100% need-based). ***Programs:*** FFEL (Subsidized and Unsubsidized Stafford, PLUS), state.

WORK-STUDY ***Federal work-study:*** *Total amount:* $12,800; 8 jobs averaging $1000.

APPLYING for FINANCIAL AID ***Required financial aid forms:*** FAFSA, institution's own form. ***Financial aid deadline (priority):*** 5/1. ***Notification date:*** Continuous beginning 6/1. Students must reply within 2 weeks of notification.

CONTACT Ms. Alexandra McInnis, Director of Financial Aid, Hellenic College, 50 Goddard Avenue, Brookline, MA 02146-7496, 617-731-3500. *Fax:* 617-850-1460. *E-mail:* amcinnis@hchc.edu

HENDERSON STATE UNIVERSITY

Arkadelphia, AR

Tuition & fees (AR res): $2488 **Average undergraduate aid package: $5426**

ABOUT THE INSTITUTION State-supported, coed. Awards: associate, bachelor's, and master's degrees. 34 undergraduate majors. Total enrollment: 3,500. Undergraduates: 3,114. Freshmen: 568. Federal methodology is used as a basis for awarding need-based institutional aid.

UNDERGRADUATE EXPENSES for 1999–2000 ***One-time required fee:*** $20. ***Tuition, state resident:*** full-time $2280; part-time $95 per semester hour. ***Tuition, nonresident:*** full-time $4560; part-time $190 per semester hour. ***Required fees:*** full-time $208; $2 per semester hour; $50 per term part-time. Full-time tuition and fees vary according to course load. Part-time tuition and fees vary according to course load. ***College room and board:*** $2976. Room and board charges vary according to board plan and housing facility.

FRESHMAN FINANCIAL AID (Fall 1998) 521 applied for aid; of those 71% were deemed to have need. 96% of freshmen with need received aid; of those 26% had need fully met. *Average percent of need met:* 61% (excluding resources awarded to replace EFC). *Average financial aid package:* $3722 (excluding resources awarded to replace EFC). 17% of all full-time freshmen had no need and received non-need-based aid.

UNDERGRADUATE FINANCIAL AID (Fall 1998) 2,327 applied for aid; of those 61% were deemed to have need. 94% of undergraduates with need received aid; of those 28% had need fully met. *Average percent of need met:* 72% (excluding resources awarded to replace EFC). *Average financial aid package:* $5426 (excluding resources awarded to replace EFC). 16% of all full-time undergraduates had no need and received non-need-based aid.

GIFT AID (NEED-BASED) ***Total amount:*** $3,259,962 (94% Federal, 6% state). ***Receiving aid:*** *Freshmen:* 41% (229); *all full-time undergraduates:* 43% (1,148). ***Average award:*** Freshmen: $4200; Undergraduates: $4200. ***Scholarships, grants, and awards:*** Federal Pell, FSEOG, state, private, college/university gift aid from institutional funds.

GIFT AID (NON-NEED-BASED) ***Total amount:*** $2,220,453 (99% institutional, 1% external sources). ***Receiving aid:*** *Freshmen:* 41% (228); *Undergraduates:* 18% (474). ***Scholarships, grants, and awards by category:*** *Academic Interests/Achievement:* biological sciences, general academic interests/achievements. *Creative Arts/Performance:* cinema/film/broadcasting, debating, journalism/publications, music, theater/drama. *Special Achievements/Activities:* leadership. *Special Characteristics:* children of faculty/staff, international students, out-of-state students. ***Tuition waivers:*** Full or partial for employees or children of employees, senior citizens.

LOANS ***Student loans:*** $6,544,415 (68% need-based, 32% non-need-based). Average indebtedness per student: $13,000. ***Average need-based loan:*** Freshmen: $2162; Undergraduates: $3590. ***Parent loans:*** $220,873 (100% non-need-based). ***Programs:*** FFEL (Subsidized and Unsubsidized Stafford, PLUS), Perkins.

WORK-STUDY ***Federal work-study:*** *Total amount:* $393,593; jobs available. ***State or other work-study/employment:*** *Total amount:* $127,166 (100% non-need-based). Part-time jobs available.

ATHLETIC AWARDS *Total amount:* 594,000 (100% non-need-based).

APPLYING for FINANCIAL AID ***Required financial aid form:*** FAFSA. ***Financial aid deadline:*** 6/1. ***Notification date:*** Continuous. Students must reply within 2 weeks of notification.

CONTACT Ms. Jo Holland, Director of Financial Aid, Henderson State University, Box 7812, Arkadelphia, AR 71999-0001, 870-230-5094 or toll-free 800-228-7333. *Fax:* 870-230-5144. *E-mail:* hollanj@oaks.hsu.edu

HENDRIX COLLEGE

Conway, AR

Tuition & fees: $11,615 **Average undergraduate aid package: $11,601**

ABOUT THE INSTITUTION Independent United Methodist, coed. Awards: bachelor's degrees. 26 undergraduate majors. Total enrollment: 1,147. Undergraduates: 1,143. Freshmen: 369. Both federal and institutional methodology are used as a basis for awarding need-based institutional aid.

UNDERGRADUATE EXPENSES for 1999–2000 ***Application fee:*** $25. ***Comprehensive fee:*** $16,030 includes full-time tuition ($11,440), mandatory fees ($175), and room and board ($4415). Room and board charges vary according to housing facility. ***Part-time tuition:*** $1270 per course. ***Part-time fees:*** $15 per term part-time. Additional part-time mandatory fees per term: $55 for fall term, $35 for winter and spring terms. ***Payment plan:*** installment.

FRESHMAN FINANCIAL AID (Fall 1999) 331 applied for aid; of those 55% were deemed to have need. 100% of freshmen with need received aid; of those 59% had need fully met. *Average percent of need met:* 91% (excluding resources awarded to replace EFC). *Average financial aid package:* $12,598 (excluding resources awarded to replace EFC). 18% of all full-time freshmen had no need and received non-need-based aid.

UNDERGRADUATE FINANCIAL AID (Fall 1999) 1,074 applied for aid; of those 55% were deemed to have need. 100% of undergraduates with need received aid; of those 53% had need fully met. *Average percent of need met:* 89% (excluding resources awarded to replace EFC). *Average financial aid package:* $11,601 (excluding resources awarded to replace EFC). 13% of all full-time undergraduates had no need and received non-need-based aid.

GIFT AID (NEED-BASED) ***Total amount:*** $1,157,146 (53% Federal, 6% state, 41% institutional). ***Receiving aid:*** *Freshmen:* 36% (119); *all full-time undergraduates:* 30% (327). ***Average award:*** Freshmen: $3100; Undergraduates: $3467. ***Scholarships, grants, and awards:*** Federal Pell, FSEOG, state, private, college/university gift aid from institutional funds.

GIFT AID (NON-NEED-BASED) ***Total amount:*** $5,878,476 (1% Federal, 38% state, 55% institutional, 6% external sources). ***Receiving aid:*** *Freshmen:* 53% (176); *Undergraduates:* 51% (547). ***Scholarships, grants, and awards by category:*** *Academic Interests/Achievement:* 774 awards ($2,834,073 total): general academic interests/achievements. *Creative Arts/Performance:* 64 awards ($33,501 total): art/fine arts, music, theater/drama. *Special Achievements/Activities:* 106 awards ($135,554 total): leadership, religious involvement. *Special Characteristics:* 80 awards ($435,010 total): children of faculty/staff, international students, members of minority groups, previous college experience, relatives of clergy. ***Tuition waivers:*** Full or partial for employees or children of employees. ***ROTC:*** Army cooperative.

LOANS ***Student loans:*** $2,532,863 (66% need-based, 34% non-need-based). 66% of past graduating class borrowed through all loan programs. ***Average need-based loan:*** Freshmen: $2739; Undergraduates: $3846. ***Parent loans:*** $716,532 (100% non-need-based). ***Programs:*** FFEL (Subsidized and Unsubsidized Stafford, PLUS), Perkins.

WORK-STUDY ***Federal work-study:*** *Total amount:* $429,336; 310 jobs averaging $1375. ***State or other work-study/employment:*** *Total amount:* $234,874 (100% non-need-based). 151 part-time jobs averaging $1575.

APPLYING for FINANCIAL AID ***Required financial aid forms:*** FAFSA, institution's own form, state aid form. ***Financial aid deadline (priority):*** 2/16. ***Notification date:*** Continuous. Students must reply within 4 weeks of notification.

CONTACT Ms. Gina Fox, Director of Financial Aid, Hendrix College, 1600 Washington Avenue, Conway, AR 72032, 501-450-1368 or toll-free 800-277-9017. *Fax:* 501-450-3871. *E-mail:* student_aid@hendrix.edu

HENRY COGSWELL COLLEGE

Everett, WA

Tuition & fees: $10,800 **Average undergraduate aid package: $3708**

ABOUT THE INSTITUTION Independent, coed, primarily men. Awards: bachelor's degrees. 5 undergraduate majors. Total enrollment: 252. Undergraduates: 252. Freshmen: 65. Federal methodology is used as a basis for awarding need-based institutional aid.

UNDERGRADUATE EXPENSES for 1999–2000 ***Application fee:*** $50. ***Tuition:*** full-time $10,800; part-time $450 per credit. ***Payment plans:*** guaranteed tuition, installment, deferred payment.

FRESHMAN FINANCIAL AID (Fall 1998) 12 applied for aid; of those 92% were deemed to have need. 100% of freshmen with need received aid. *Average percent of need met:* 19% (excluding resources awarded to replace EFC). *Average financial aid package:* $2818 (excluding resources awarded to replace EFC). 1% of all full-time freshmen had no need and received non-need-based aid.

UNDERGRADUATE FINANCIAL AID (Fall 1998) 35 applied for aid; of those 94% were deemed to have need. 100% of undergraduates with need received aid. *Average percent of need met:* 15% (excluding resources awarded to replace EFC). *Average financial aid package:* $3708 (excluding resources awarded to replace EFC). 1% of all full-time undergraduates had no need and received non-need-based aid.

GIFT AID (NEED-BASED) ***Total amount:*** $88,589 (32% Federal, 68% institutional). ***Receiving aid:*** *Freshmen:* 2% (2); *all full-time undergraduates:* 4% (10). ***Average award:*** Freshmen: $3450; Undergraduates: $2195. ***Scholarships, grants, and awards:*** Federal Pell, FSEOG, private, college/university gift aid from institutional funds.

GIFT AID (NON-NEED-BASED) ***Total amount:*** $3500 (100% external sources). ***Scholarships, grants, and awards by category:*** *Academic Interests/Achievement:* 28 awards ($60,362 total): general academic interests/achievements. ***Tuition waivers:*** Full or partial for employees or children of employees.

LOANS ***Student loans:*** $211,745 (49% need-based, 51% non-need-based). 20% of past graduating class borrowed through all loan programs. Average indebtedness per student: $16,432. ***Average need-based loan:*** Freshmen: $2081; Undergraduates: $3556. ***Parent loans:*** $58,345 (100% non-need-based). ***Programs:*** FFEL (Subsidized and Unsubsidized Stafford, PLUS).

WORK-STUDY ***Federal work-study:*** *Total amount:* $2033; 5 jobs averaging $542.

APPLYING for FINANCIAL AID ***Required financial aid forms:*** FAFSA, institution's own form. ***Financial aid deadline:*** Continuous. ***Notification date:*** Continuous beginning 1/1. Students must reply within 15 weeks of notification.

CONTACT Kelley Campbell, Financial Aid Director, Henry Cogswell College, 2802 Wetmore Avenue, Suite 100, Everett, WA 98201, 425-258-3351. *Fax:* 425-257-0405. *E-mail:* kc@henrycogswell.edu

HERITAGE BIBLE COLLEGE

Dunn, NC

Tuition & fees: $4000 **Average undergraduate aid package: $3125**

ABOUT THE INSTITUTION Independent Pentecostal Free Will Baptist, coed. Awards: associate and bachelor's degrees. 1 undergraduate major. Total enrollment: 86. Undergraduates: 86. Freshmen: 31. Federal methodology is used as a basis for awarding need-based institutional aid.

UNDERGRADUATE EXPENSES for 1999–2000 ***Application fee:*** $20. ***Comprehensive fee:*** $6236 includes full-time tuition ($3600), mandatory fees ($400), and room and board ($2236). ***College room only:*** $1320. Full-time tuition and fees vary according to course load. Room and board charges vary according to board plan and housing facility. ***Part-time***

Heritage Bible College (continued)

tuition: $120 per credit hour. ***Part-time fees:*** $100 per term part-time. Part-time tuition and fees vary according to course load. ***Payment plans:*** installment, deferred payment.

FRESHMAN FINANCIAL AID (Fall 1998) 13 applied for aid; of those 100% were deemed to have need. 100% of freshmen with need received aid. *Average financial aid package:* $3167 (excluding resources awarded to replace EFC).

UNDERGRADUATE FINANCIAL AID (Fall 1998) 37 applied for aid; of those 100% were deemed to have need. 95% of undergraduates with need received aid. *Average financial aid package:* $3125 (excluding resources awarded to replace EFC).

GIFT AID (NEED-BASED) ***Total amount:*** $92,726 (88% Federal, 12% institutional). ***Receiving aid:*** *Freshmen:* 29% (6); *all full-time undergraduates:* 33% (16). ***Average award:*** Freshmen: $3042; Undergraduates: $333. ***Scholarships, grants, and awards:*** Federal Pell, FSEOG, private, college/university gift aid from institutional funds.

LOANS ***Student loans:*** $55,478 (100% need-based). 55% of past graduating class borrowed through all loan programs. Average indebtedness per student: $15,152. ***Average need-based loan:*** Freshmen: $1875; Undergraduates: $1662. ***Programs:*** FFEL (Subsidized and Unsubsidized Stafford, PLUS).

WORK-STUDY ***Federal work-study:*** *Total amount:* $5558; 5 jobs averaging $5558.

APPLYING for FINANCIAL AID ***Required financial aid forms:*** FAFSA, institution's own form, verification documents. ***Financial aid deadline (priority):*** 5/20. ***Notification date:*** Continuous beginning 5/25. Students must reply within 4 weeks of notification.

CONTACT Mrs. Nell Register, Director of Financial Aid, Heritage Bible College, Box 1628, Dunn, NC 28335, 910-892-3178. *Fax:* 910-892-1809. *E-mail:* hbchead@intrstar.net

HERITAGE COLLEGE

Toppenish, WA

Tuition & fees: $5190 **Average undergraduate aid package: $6635**

ABOUT THE INSTITUTION Independent, coed. Awards: associate, bachelor's, and master's degrees. 25 undergraduate majors. Total enrollment: 1,152. Undergraduates: 665. Freshmen: 30. Federal methodology is used as a basis for awarding need-based institutional aid.

UNDERGRADUATE EXPENSES for 1999–2000 ***One-time required fee:*** $30. ***Tuition:*** full-time $5160; part-time $215 per credit hour. ***Required fees:*** full-time $30. ***Payment plans:*** installment, deferred payment.

FRESHMAN FINANCIAL AID (Fall 1999) 95 applied for aid; of those 100% were deemed to have need. 100% of freshmen with need received aid; of those 3% had need fully met. *Average percent of need met:* 37% (excluding resources awarded to replace EFC). *Average financial aid package:* $4336 (excluding resources awarded to replace EFC). 1% of all full-time freshmen had no need and received non-need-based aid.

UNDERGRADUATE FINANCIAL AID (Fall 1999) 520 applied for aid; of those 99% were deemed to have need. 100% of undergraduates with need received aid; of those 16% had need fully met. *Average percent of need met:* 54% (excluding resources awarded to replace EFC). *Average financial aid package:* $6635 (excluding resources awarded to replace EFC). 4% of all full-time undergraduates had no need and received non-need-based aid.

GIFT AID (NEED-BASED) ***Total amount:*** $2,511,408 (56% Federal, 27% state, 14% institutional, 3% external sources). ***Receiving aid:*** *Freshmen:* 64% (94); *all full-time undergraduates:* 65% (469). ***Average award:*** Freshmen: $3386; Undergraduates: $3933. ***Scholarships, grants, and awards:*** Federal Pell, FSEOG, state, private, college/university gift aid from institutional funds.

GIFT AID (NON-NEED-BASED) ***Total amount:*** $1722 (30% institutional, 70% external sources). ***Receiving aid:*** *Undergraduates:* 2. ***Scholarships, grants, and awards by category:*** *Academic Interests/Achievement:* biological sciences, business, communication, computer science, education, general academic interests/achievements, physical sciences, social sciences. ***Tuition waivers:*** Full or partial for employees or children of employees, senior citizens.

LOANS ***Student loans:*** $1,317,624 (90% need-based, 10% non-need-based). 37% of past graduating class borrowed through all loan programs. Average indebtedness per student: $4092. ***Average need-based loan:*** Freshmen: $369; Undergraduates: $1657. ***Parent loans:*** $5224 (100% non-need-based). ***Programs:*** FFEL (Subsidized and Unsubsidized Stafford, PLUS), Perkins, college/university.

WORK-STUDY ***Federal work-study:*** *Total amount:* $541,253; 218 jobs averaging $2486. ***State or other work-study/employment:*** *Total amount:* $164,061 (99% need-based, 1% non-need-based). 43 part-time jobs averaging $3646.

APPLYING for FINANCIAL AID ***Required financial aid forms:*** FAFSA, institution's own form. ***Financial aid deadline (priority):*** 2/10. ***Notification date:*** Continuous beginning 2/15. Students must reply within 2 weeks of notification.

CONTACT Ms. Becky Cochran, Coordinator of Student Grants, Heritage College, 3240 Fort Road, Toppenish, WA 98948-9599, 509-865-8500 or toll-free 509-865-8508. *Fax:* 509-865-4469. *E-mail:* cochran_b@heritage.edu

HIGH POINT UNIVERSITY

High Point, NC

Tuition & fees: $12,440 **Average undergraduate aid package: N/A**

ABOUT THE INSTITUTION Independent United Methodist, coed. Awards: bachelor's and master's degrees. 49 undergraduate majors. Total enrollment: 2,831. Undergraduates: 2,658. Freshmen: 507. Both federal and institutional methodology are used as a basis for awarding need-based institutional aid.

UNDERGRADUATE EXPENSES for 2000–2001 ***Application fee:*** $25. ***Comprehensive fee:*** $18,210 includes full-time tuition ($11,260), mandatory fees ($1180), and room and board ($5770). ***College room only:*** $2480. Full-time tuition and fees vary according to class time. Room and board charges vary according to board plan. ***Part-time tuition:*** $193 per semester hour.

GIFT AID (NEED-BASED) ***Scholarships, grants, and awards:*** Federal Pell, FSEOG, state, private, college/university gift aid from institutional funds.

GIFT AID (NON-NEED-BASED) ***Scholarships, grants, and awards by category:*** *Academic Interests/Achievement:* biological sciences, business, education, English, foreign languages, general academic interests/achievements, humanities, international studies, mathematics, physical sciences, premedicine, religion/biblical studies. *Creative Arts/Performance:* music. *Special Characteristics:* relatives of clergy. ***Tuition waivers:*** Full or partial for employees or children of employees. ***ROTC:*** Army cooperative, Air Force cooperative.

LOANS ***Programs:*** Federal Direct (Subsidized and Unsubsidized Stafford, PLUS), Perkins.

WORK-STUDY Federal work-study jobs available.

APPLYING for FINANCIAL AID ***Required financial aid forms:*** FAFSA, state aid form. ***Financial aid deadline (priority):*** 3/1. ***Notification date:*** Continuous. Students must reply by 5/1 or within 3 weeks of notification.

CONTACT Office of Financial Aid, High Point University, Box 3232, University Station, Montlieu Avenue, High Point, NC 27262, 336-841-9124 or toll-free 800-345-6993. *Fax:* 336-841-5123.

HILBERT COLLEGE

Hamburg, NY

Tuition & fees: $10,800 **Average undergraduate aid package: $6738**

ABOUT THE INSTITUTION Independent, coed. Awards: associate and bachelor's degrees. 11 undergraduate majors. Total enrollment: 842.

Undergraduates: 842. Freshmen: 114. Both federal and institutional methodology are used as a basis for awarding need-based institutional aid.

UNDERGRADUATE EXPENSES for 1999–2000 ***Application fee:*** $20. ***Comprehensive fee:*** $15,340 includes full-time tuition ($10,250), mandatory fees ($550), and room and board ($4540). ***College room only:*** $1790. Room and board charges vary according to board plan and housing facility. ***Part-time tuition:*** $267 per credit. ***Part-time fees:*** $12 per credit; $5 per term part-time. ***Payment plans:*** installment, deferred payment.

FRESHMAN FINANCIAL AID (Fall 1999, est.) 108 applied for aid; of those 98% were deemed to have need. 94% of freshmen with need received aid; of those 12% had need fully met. *Average percent of need met:* 85% (excluding resources awarded to replace EFC). *Average financial aid package:* $6944 (excluding resources awarded to replace EFC). 2% of all full-time freshmen had no need and received non-need-based aid.

UNDERGRADUATE FINANCIAL AID (Fall 1999, est.) 566 applied for aid; of those 98% were deemed to have need. 93% of undergraduates with need received aid; of those 14% had need fully met. *Average percent of need met:* 82% (excluding resources awarded to replace EFC). *Average financial aid package:* $6738 (excluding resources awarded to replace EFC). 2% of all full-time undergraduates had no need and received non-need-based aid.

GIFT AID (NEED-BASED) ***Total amount:*** $3,086,006 (26% Federal, 31% state, 43% institutional). ***Receiving aid:*** *Freshmen:* 91% (98); *all full-time undergraduates:* 86% (489). ***Average award:*** Freshmen: $4419; Undergraduates: $3748. ***Scholarships, grants, and awards:*** Federal Pell, FSEOG, state, private, college/university gift aid from institutional funds.

GIFT AID (NON-NEED-BASED) ***Total amount:*** $944,899 (100% institutional). ***Receiving aid:*** *Freshmen:* 50% (54); *Undergraduates:* 51% (291). ***Scholarships, grants, and awards by category:*** *Academic Interests/Achievement:* general academic interests/achievements. *Special Achievements/Activities:* leadership. *Special Characteristics:* children of educators, members of minority groups. ***Tuition waivers:*** Full or partial for employees or children of employees, senior citizens.

LOANS ***Student loans:*** $3,212,594 (55% need-based, 45% non-need-based). ***Average need-based loan:*** Freshmen: $2493; Undergraduates: $3548. ***Parent loans:*** $110,789 (100% non-need-based). ***Programs:*** FFEL (Subsidized and Unsubsidized Stafford, PLUS), Perkins, alternative loans.

WORK-STUDY ***Federal work-study:*** *Total amount:* $75,700; 48 jobs averaging $1577.

APPLYING for FINANCIAL AID ***Required financial aid form:*** FAFSA. ***Financial aid deadline:*** 5/1 (priority: 3/1). ***Notification date:*** Continuous. Students must reply within 2 weeks of notification.

CONTACT Ms. Leigh M. Fiorenzo, Director of Financial Aid, Hilbert College, 5200 South Park Avenue, Hamburg, NY 14075-1597, 716-649-7900 Ext. 249. *Fax:* 716-649-1152.

HILLSDALE COLLEGE

Hillsdale, MI

Tuition & fees: $13,460 **Average undergraduate aid package: $13,524**

ABOUT THE INSTITUTION Independent, coed. Awards: bachelor's degrees. 38 undergraduate majors. Total enrollment: 1,167. Undergraduates: 1,167. Freshmen: 323. Both federal and institutional methodology are used as a basis for awarding need-based institutional aid.

UNDERGRADUATE EXPENSES for 1999–2000 ***Application fee:*** $15. ***Comprehensive fee:*** $19,090 includes full-time tuition ($13,220), mandatory fees ($240), and room and board ($5630). ***College room only:*** $2630. Room and board charges vary according to board plan. ***Part-time tuition:*** $520 per semester hour. Part-time tuition and fees vary according to course load. ***Payment plan:*** installment.

FRESHMAN FINANCIAL AID (Fall 1998) 328 applied for aid; of those 58% were deemed to have need. 100% of freshmen with need received aid; of those 29% had need fully met. *Average percent of need met:* 77% (excluding resources awarded to replace EFC). *Average financial aid package:* $10,090 (excluding resources awarded to replace EFC). 20% of all full-time freshmen had no need and received non-need-based aid.

UNDERGRADUATE FINANCIAL AID (Fall 1998) 1,024 applied for aid; of those 61% were deemed to have need. 100% of undergraduates with need received aid; of those 27% had need fully met. *Average percent of need met:* 76% (excluding resources awarded to replace EFC). *Average financial aid package:* $13,524 (excluding resources awarded to replace EFC). 24% of all full-time undergraduates had no need and received non-need-based aid.

GIFT AID (NEED-BASED) ***Total amount:*** $4,671,585 (13% state, 85% institutional, 2% external sources). ***Scholarships, grants, and awards:*** state, private, college/university gift aid from institutional funds.

GIFT AID (NON-NEED-BASED) ***Total amount:*** $1,491,813 (98% institutional, 2% external sources). ***Receiving aid:*** *Freshmen:* 28% (98); *Undergraduates:* 35% (408). ***Scholarships, grants, and awards by category:*** *Academic Interests/Achievement:* 675 awards ($1,945,040 total): biological sciences, business, education, English, foreign languages, general academic interests/achievements, health fields, humanities, international studies, mathematics, physical sciences, premedicine, religion/biblical studies. *Creative Arts/Performance:* 55 awards ($86,000 total): art/fine arts, music. *Special Achievements/Activities:* 245 awards ($943,712 total): community service, general special achievements/activities, leadership. *Special Characteristics:* 46 awards ($341,040 total): children of faculty/staff, international students. ***Tuition waivers:*** Full or partial for employees or children of employees. ***ROTC:*** Army cooperative, Naval cooperative, Air Force cooperative.

LOANS ***Student loans:*** $2,333,198 (89% need-based, 11% non-need-based). 60% of past graduating class borrowed through all loan programs. Average indebtedness per student: $13,385. ***Programs:*** state, college/university, alternative loans.

WORK-STUDY ***State or other work-study/employment:*** 625 part-time jobs available.

ATHLETIC AWARDS *Total amount:* 1,502,513 (39% need-based, 61% non-need-based).

APPLYING for FINANCIAL AID ***Required financial aid forms:*** institution's own form, CSS Financial Aid PROFILE, FAFSA (for state aid only). ***Financial aid deadline (priority):*** 3/15. ***Notification date:*** Continuous. Students must reply by 5/1 or within 4 weeks of notification.

CONTACT Mrs. Connie Bricker, Director of Student Financial Aid, Hillsdale College, 33 East College Street, Hillsdale, MI 49242-1298, 517-437-7341. *Fax:* 517-437-3923. *E-mail:* connie.bricker@ac.hillsdale.edu

HILLSDALE FREE WILL BAPTIST COLLEGE

Moore, OK

Tuition & fees: $5840 **Average undergraduate aid package: N/A**

ABOUT THE INSTITUTION Independent Free Will Baptist, coed. Awards: associate and bachelor's degrees. 16 undergraduate majors. Total enrollment: 247. Undergraduates: 247. Freshmen: 62. Federal methodology is used as a basis for awarding need-based institutional aid.

UNDERGRADUATE EXPENSES for 1999–2000 ***Application fee:*** $20. ***One-time required fee:*** $20. ***Comprehensive fee:*** $9790 includes full-time tuition ($5250), mandatory fees ($590), and room and board ($3950). ***College room only:*** $1700. Full-time tuition and fees vary according to course load. Room and board charges vary according to board plan and housing facility. ***Part-time tuition:*** $175 per credit hour. ***Part-time fees:*** $130 per term part-time. Part-time tuition and fees vary according to course load. ***Payment plan:*** deferred payment.

GIFT AID (NEED-BASED) ***Scholarships, grants, and awards:*** Federal Pell, FSEOG, state, private, college/university gift aid from institutional funds, Bureau of Indian Affairs Grants.

GIFT AID (NON-NEED-BASED) ***Scholarships, grants, and awards by category:*** *Academic Interests/Achievement:* business, education, English, general academic interests/achievements, mathematics, religion/biblical studies. *Creative Arts/Performance:* music, performing arts. *Special Achievements/Activities:* community service, religious involvement. *Special Characteristics:* adult students, children and siblings of alumni, relatives

Hillsdale Free Will Baptist College (continued)

of clergy, religious affiliation, siblings of current students, spouses of current students. ***Tuition waivers:*** Full or partial for children of alumni, employees or children of employees, adult students, senior citizens.

LOANS ***Programs:*** FFEL (Subsidized and Unsubsidized Stafford, PLUS), Perkins, state, alternative loans.

WORK-STUDY ***State or other work-study/employment:*** Part-time jobs available.

APPLYING for FINANCIAL AID ***Required financial aid form:*** FAFSA. ***Financial aid deadline:*** Continuous. ***Notification date:*** Continuous beginning 6/1. Students must reply within 2 weeks of notification.

CONTACT Ms. Pamela Thompson, Director of Admissions and Financial Aid, Hillsdale Free Will Baptist College, PO Box 7208, Moore, OK 73153-1208, 405-912-9006. *Fax:* 405-912-9050. *E-mail:* pamthompson@hc.edu

HIRAM COLLEGE

Hiram, OH

Tuition & fees: $17,710 **Average undergraduate aid package: $16,738**

ABOUT THE INSTITUTION Independent religious, coed. Awards: bachelor's degrees. 35 undergraduate majors. Total enrollment: 1,204. Undergraduates: 1,204. Freshmen: 286. Both federal and institutional methodology are used as a basis for awarding need-based institutional aid.

UNDERGRADUATE EXPENSES for 1999–2000 ***Application fee:*** $25. ***Comprehensive fee:*** $23,734 includes full-time tuition ($17,230), mandatory fees ($480), and room and board ($6024). ***College room only:*** $2724. Room and board charges vary according to board plan and housing facility. ***Part-time tuition:*** $575 per credit hour. ***Part-time fees:*** $30 per term part-time. Part-time tuition and fees vary according to class time. ***Payment plan:*** installment.

FRESHMAN FINANCIAL AID (Fall 1999) 280 applied for aid; of those 94% were deemed to have need. 99% of freshmen with need received aid; of those 70% had need fully met. *Average percent of need met:* 85% (excluding resources awarded to replace EFC). *Average financial aid package:* $16,588 (excluding resources awarded to replace EFC).

UNDERGRADUATE FINANCIAL AID (Fall 1999) 821 applied for aid; of those 93% were deemed to have need. 99% of undergraduates with need received aid; of those 70% had need fully met. *Average percent of need met:* 85% (excluding resources awarded to replace EFC). *Average financial aid package:* $16,738 (excluding resources awarded to replace EFC).

GIFT AID (NEED-BASED) ***Total amount:*** $5,017,233 (19% Federal, 11% state, 69% institutional, 1% external sources). ***Receiving aid:*** *Freshmen:* 74% (222); *all full-time undergraduates:* 74% (653). ***Average award:*** Freshmen: $9642; Undergraduates: $9032. ***Scholarships, grants, and awards:*** Federal Pell, FSEOG, state, private, college/university gift aid from institutional funds.

GIFT AID (NON-NEED-BASED) ***Total amount:*** $3,926,521 (19% state, 81% institutional). ***Receiving aid:*** *Freshmen:* 81% (246); *Undergraduates:* 80% (705). ***Scholarships, grants, and awards by category:*** *Academic Interests/Achievement:* 478 awards ($2,371,620 total): general academic interests/achievements, physical sciences, religion/biblical studies, social sciences. *Creative Arts/Performance:* 41 awards ($50,320 total): music. *Special Achievements/Activities:* 15 awards ($165,000 total): leadership. *Special Characteristics:* 131 awards ($342,500 total): children and siblings of alumni, members of minority groups, religious affiliation. ***Tuition waivers:*** Full or partial for employees or children of employees.

LOANS ***Student loans:*** $4,378,971 (78% need-based, 22% non-need-based). 82% of past graduating class borrowed through all loan programs. Average indebtedness per student: $17,125. ***Average need-based loan:*** Freshmen: $2625; Undergraduates: $4833. ***Parent loans:*** $907,945 (100% non-need-based). ***Programs:*** FFEL (Subsidized and Unsubsidized Stafford, PLUS), Perkins, state, college/university.

WORK-STUDY ***Federal work-study:*** *Total amount:* $1,022,997; 703 jobs averaging $1443. ***State or other work-study/employment:*** *Total amount:* $100,000 (100% non-need-based). 62 part-time jobs averaging $1600.

APPLYING for FINANCIAL AID ***Required financial aid form:*** FAFSA. ***Financial aid deadline (priority):*** 2/15. ***Notification date:*** 3/15. Students must reply by 5/1 or within 2 weeks of notification.

CONTACT Robert L. Ritz, Director of Financial Aid, Hiram College, Box 67, Hiram, OH 44234-0067, 330-569-5107 or toll-free 800-362-5280. *Fax:* 330-569-5499.

HOBART AND WILLIAM SMITH COLLEGES

Geneva, NY

Tuition & fees: $24,342 **Average undergraduate aid package: $21,368**

ABOUT THE INSTITUTION Independent, coed. Awards: bachelor's degrees. 49 undergraduate majors. Total enrollment: 1,830. Undergraduates: 1,830. Freshmen: 503. Both federal and institutional methodology are used as a basis for awarding need-based institutional aid.

UNDERGRADUATE EXPENSES for 1999–2000 ***Application fee:*** $45. ***Comprehensive fee:*** $31,224 includes full-time tuition ($23,865), mandatory fees ($477), and room and board ($6882). ***College room only:*** $3507. Room and board charges vary according to board plan and housing facility. ***Part-time tuition:*** $2652 per course. Part-time tuition and fees vary according to course load. ***Payment plans:*** tuition prepayment, installment, deferred payment.

FRESHMAN FINANCIAL AID (Fall 1998) 346 applied for aid; of those 97% were deemed to have need. 100% of freshmen with need received aid; of those 24% had need fully met. *Average percent of need met:* 90% (excluding resources awarded to replace EFC). *Average financial aid package:* $21,008 (excluding resources awarded to replace EFC). 13% of all full-time freshmen had no need and received non-need-based aid.

UNDERGRADUATE FINANCIAL AID (Fall 1998) 1,263 applied for aid; of those 96% were deemed to have need. 100% of undergraduates with need received aid; of those 22% had need fully met. *Average percent of need met:* 89% (excluding resources awarded to replace EFC). *Average financial aid package:* $21,368 (excluding resources awarded to replace EFC). 13% of all full-time undergraduates had no need and received non-need-based aid.

GIFT AID (NEED-BASED) ***Total amount:*** $20,050,302 (6% Federal, 8% state, 84% institutional, 2% external sources). ***Receiving aid:*** *Freshmen:* 87% (331); *all full-time undergraduates:* 86% (1,191). ***Average award:*** Freshmen: $17,766; Undergraduates: $16,805. ***Scholarships, grants, and awards:*** Federal Pell, FSEOG, state, private, college/university gift aid from institutional funds.

GIFT AID (NON-NEED-BASED) ***Total amount:*** $760,498 (1% state, 94% institutional, 5% external sources). ***Receiving aid:*** *Freshmen:* 5% (19); *Undergraduates:* 3% (40). ***Scholarships, grants, and awards by category:*** *Academic Interests/Achievement:* 16 awards ($130,841 total): general academic interests/achievements. *Creative Arts/Performance:* 3 awards ($15,000 total): art/fine arts, creative writing, dance, music, performing arts. *Special Achievements/Activities:* 14 awards ($81,750 total): leadership. ***Tuition waivers:*** Full or partial for employees or children of employees.

LOANS ***Student loans:*** $4,985,448 (88% need-based, 12% non-need-based). 72% of past graduating class borrowed through all loan programs. Average indebtedness per student: $15,338. ***Average need-based loan:*** Freshmen: $2286; Undergraduates: $3620. ***Parent loans:*** $2,959,404 (29% need-based, 71% non-need-based). ***Programs:*** FFEL (Subsidized and Unsubsidized Stafford, PLUS), Perkins.

WORK-STUDY ***Federal work-study:*** *Total amount:* $953,132; 1,023 jobs averaging $931. ***State or other work-study/employment:*** *Total amount:* $333,955 (56% need-based, 44% non-need-based). Part-time jobs available.

APPLYING for FINANCIAL AID ***Required financial aid forms:*** FAFSA, CSS Financial Aid PROFILE, state aid form, noncustodial (divorced/separated) parent's statement, business/farm supplement. ***Financial aid deadline:*** 3/15 (priority: 2/15). ***Notification date:*** 4/1. Students must reply by 5/1 or within 3 weeks of notification.

CONTACT Samantha Veeder, Director of Financial Aid, Hobart and William Smith Colleges, Geneva, NY 14456-3397, 315-781-3316 or toll-free 800-245-0100. *E-mail:* finaid@hws.edu

HOBE SOUND BIBLE COLLEGE

Hobe Sound, FL

Tuition & fees: $4080 **Average undergraduate aid package: $3520**

ABOUT THE INSTITUTION Independent nondenominational, coed. Awards: associate and bachelor's degrees. 8 undergraduate majors. Total enrollment: 150. Undergraduates: 150. Freshmen: 42. Both federal and institutional methodology are used as a basis for awarding need-based institutional aid.

UNDERGRADUATE EXPENSES for 1999–2000 ***Application fee:*** $25. ***Comprehensive fee:*** $7090 includes full-time tuition ($3940), mandatory fees ($140), and room and board ($3010). Room and board charges vary according to housing facility. ***Part-time tuition:*** $155 per semester hour. ***Payment plan:*** installment.

FRESHMAN FINANCIAL AID (Fall 1999, est.) 33 applied for aid; of those 91% were deemed to have need. 100% of freshmen with need received aid; of those 77% had need fully met. *Average percent of need met:* 77% (excluding resources awarded to replace EFC). *Average financial aid package:* $3865 (excluding resources awarded to replace EFC).

UNDERGRADUATE FINANCIAL AID (Fall 1999, est.) 110 applied for aid; of those 84% were deemed to have need. 100% of undergraduates with need received aid; of those 37% had need fully met. *Average percent of need met:* 84% (excluding resources awarded to replace EFC). *Average financial aid package:* $3520 (excluding resources awarded to replace EFC).

GIFT AID (NEED-BASED) ***Total amount:*** $162,700 (61% Federal, 9% state, 28% institutional, 2% external sources). ***Receiving aid:*** *Freshmen:* 64% (27); *all full-time undergraduates:* 27% (38). ***Average award:*** Freshmen: $2150; Undergraduates: $1987. ***Scholarships, grants, and awards:*** Federal Pell, FSEOG, state, college/university gift aid from institutional funds.

GIFT AID (NON-NEED-BASED) ***Receiving aid:*** *Freshmen:* 26% (11); *Undergraduates:* 11% (15). ***Scholarships, grants, and awards by category:*** *Academic Interests/Achievement:* 16 awards ($12,000 total): general academic interests/achievements. ***Tuition waivers:*** Full or partial for employees or children of employees.

LOANS ***Student loans:*** $50,000 (100% need-based). Average indebtedness per student: $11,000. ***Programs:*** FFEL (Subsidized and Unsubsidized Stafford, PLUS).

WORK-STUDY ***Federal work-study:*** *Total amount:* $6800; 4 jobs averaging $1875. ***State or other work-study/employment:*** *Total amount:* $96,000 (100% need-based). 30 part-time jobs averaging $3200.

APPLYING for FINANCIAL AID ***Required financial aid form:*** FAFSA. ***Financial aid deadline (priority):*** 9/1. ***Notification date:*** Continuous.

CONTACT Phillip Gray, Director of Financial Aid, Hobe Sound Bible College, PO Box 1065, Hobe Sound, FL 33475-1065, 561-546-5534 Ext. 1007 or toll-free 800-881-5534. *Fax:* 561-545-1422. *E-mail:* hsbcfinaid@aol.com

HOFSTRA UNIVERSITY

Hempstead, NY

Tuition & fees: $14,512 **Average undergraduate aid package: $7839**

ABOUT THE INSTITUTION Independent, coed. Awards: associate, bachelor's, master's, doctoral, and first professional degrees and post-bachelor's certificates. 74 undergraduate majors. Total enrollment: 13,141. Undergraduates: 9,300. Freshmen: 1,906. Federal methodology is used as a basis for awarding need-based institutional aid.

UNDERGRADUATE EXPENSES for 1999–2000 ***Application fee:*** $40. ***Comprehensive fee:*** $21,572 includes full-time tuition ($13,750), mandatory fees ($762), and room and board ($7060). ***College room only:*** $4670. Room and board charges vary according to board plan and housing facility. ***Part-time tuition:*** $452 per semester hour. ***Part-time fees:*** $112 per term part-time. Part-time tuition and fees vary according to course load. ***Payment plans:*** installment, deferred payment.

FRESHMAN FINANCIAL AID (Fall 1999, est.) 1541 applied for aid; of those 94% were deemed to have need. 100% of freshmen with need received aid. *Average financial aid package:* $11,362 (excluding resources awarded to replace EFC). 4% of all full-time freshmen had no need and received non-need-based aid.

UNDERGRADUATE FINANCIAL AID (Fall 1999, est.) 6,185 applied for aid; of those 91% were deemed to have need. 100% of undergraduates with need received aid. *Average financial aid package:* $7839 (excluding resources awarded to replace EFC). 3% of all full-time undergraduates had no need and received non-need-based aid.

GIFT AID (NEED-BASED) ***Total amount:*** $14,818,521 (41% Federal, 59% institutional). ***Receiving aid:*** *Freshmen:* 60% (1,118); *all full-time undergraduates:* 50% (3,950). ***Average award:*** Freshmen: $4244; Undergraduates: $3006. ***Scholarships, grants, and awards:*** Federal Pell, FSEOG, state, private, college/university gift aid from institutional funds.

GIFT AID (NON-NEED-BASED) ***Total amount:*** $13,221,751 (2% Federal, 57% state, 36% institutional, 5% external sources). ***Receiving aid:*** *Freshmen:* 49% (922); *Undergraduates:* 48% (3,808). ***Scholarships, grants, and awards by category:*** *Academic Interests/Achievement:* communication, general academic interests/achievements. *Creative Arts/Performance:* 130 awards ($218,350 total): art/fine arts, dance, music, theater/drama. *Special Achievements/Activities:* 21 awards ($15,300 total): leadership. *Special Characteristics:* general special characteristics. ***Tuition waivers:*** Full or partial for employees or children of employees, senior citizens. ***ROTC:*** Army.

LOANS ***Student loans:*** $15,930,582 (52% need-based, 48% non-need-based). ***Average need-based loan:*** Freshmen: $2434; Undergraduates: $3814. ***Parent loans:*** $4,795,361 (100% non-need-based). ***Programs:*** FFEL (Subsidized and Unsubsidized Stafford, PLUS), Perkins, college/university.

WORK-STUDY ***Federal work-study:*** *Total amount:* $1,199,232; 561 jobs averaging $2138. ***State or other work-study/employment:*** *Total amount:* $162,283 (100% need-based). 51 part-time jobs averaging $3182.

ATHLETIC AWARDS *Total amount:* 4,108,308 (100% non-need-based).

APPLYING for FINANCIAL AID ***Required financial aid forms:*** FAFSA, state aid form. ***Financial aid deadline (priority):*** 2/15. ***Notification date:*** Continuous beginning 3/1. Students must reply by 5/1 or within 4 weeks of notification.

CONTACT Mr. Mark Davis, Executive Director of Information Systems for Enrollment Services, Hofstra University, 126 Hofstra University, Hempstead, NY 11549, 516-463-6526 or toll-free 800-HOFSTRA. *Fax:* 516-463-4936. *E-mail:* fnamvd@office.hofstra.edu

HOLLINS UNIVERSITY

Roanoke, VA

Tuition & fees: $16,710 **Average undergraduate aid package: $14,846**

ABOUT THE INSTITUTION Independent, women only. Awards: bachelor's and master's degrees and post-master's certificates. 29 undergraduate majors. Total enrollment: 1,084. Undergraduates: 826. Freshmen: 238. Federal methodology is used as a basis for awarding need-based institutional aid.

UNDERGRADUATE EXPENSES for 1999–2000 ***Application fee:*** $25. ***Comprehensive fee:*** $22,835 includes full-time tuition ($16,460), mandatory fees ($250), and room and board ($6125). ***College room only:*** $3640. ***Part-time tuition:*** $514 per credit. ***Part-time fees:*** $125 per year part-time. ***Payment plans:*** tuition prepayment, installment.

FRESHMAN FINANCIAL AID (Fall 1999) 208 applied for aid; of those 76% were deemed to have need. 100% of freshmen with need received aid; of those 42% had need fully met. *Average percent of need met:* 90% (excluding resources awarded to replace EFC). *Average financial aid package:* $14,604 (excluding resources awarded to replace EFC). 26% of all full-time freshmen had no need and received non-need-based aid.

UNDERGRADUATE FINANCIAL AID (Fall 1999) 500 applied for aid; of those 86% were deemed to have need. 100% of undergraduates with need received aid; of those 32% had need fully met. *Average percent of need met:* 89% (excluding resources awarded to replace EFC). *Average*

Hollins University (continued)

financial aid package: $14,846 (excluding resources awarded to replace EFC). 18% of all full-time undergraduates had no need and received non-need-based aid.

GIFT AID (NEED-BASED) ***Total amount:*** $4,951,303 (10% Federal, 11% state, 77% institutional, 2% external sources). ***Receiving aid:*** *Freshmen:* 66% (158); *all full-time undergraduates:* 53% (380). ***Average award:*** Freshmen: $9800; Undergraduates: $6009. ***Scholarships, grants, and awards:*** Federal Pell, FSEOG, state, private, college/university gift aid from institutional funds.

GIFT AID (NON-NEED-BASED) ***Total amount:*** $1,477,320 (9% state, 91% institutional). ***Receiving aid:*** *Freshmen:* 53% (125); *Undergraduates:* 48% (341). ***Scholarships, grants, and awards by category:*** *Academic Interests/Achievement:* 339 awards ($1,779,500 total): general academic interests/achievements. *Creative Arts/Performance:* 21 awards ($64,723 total): art/fine arts, creative writing, dance, music. *Special Achievements/Activities:* 19 awards ($19,050 total): community service, general special achievements/activities, leadership. *Special Characteristics:* 234 awards ($302,437 total): children and siblings of alumni, local/state students. ***Tuition waivers:*** Full or partial for employees or children of employees.

LOANS ***Student loans:*** $2,449,926 (57% need-based, 43% non-need-based). 56% of past graduating class borrowed through all loan programs. Average indebtedness per student: $14,809. ***Average need-based loan:*** Freshmen: $3740; Undergraduates: $4133. ***Parent loans:*** $850,406 (83% need-based, 17% non-need-based). ***Programs:*** Federal Direct (Subsidized and Unsubsidized Stafford, PLUS), Perkins, Key Alternative Loans, PLATO Loans, CitiAssist Loans, GATE Loans.

WORK-STUDY ***Federal work-study:*** *Total amount:* $524,393; 306 jobs averaging $1713. ***State or other work-study/employment:*** *Total amount:* $76,950 (100% non-need-based). 38 part-time jobs averaging $2025.

APPLYING for FINANCIAL AID ***Required financial aid forms:*** FAFSA, state aid form. ***Financial aid deadline:*** 2/15 (priority: 2/1). ***Notification date:*** 3/15. Students must reply by 5/1.

CONTACT Mrs. Rebecca R. Eckstein, Director of Financial Aid, Hollins University, PO Box 9718, Roanoke, VA 24020-1688, 540-362-6332 or toll-free 800-456-9595. *Fax:* 540-362-6093. *E-mail:* reckstein@hollins.edu

HOLY APOSTLES COLLEGE AND SEMINARY

Cromwell, CT

Tuition & fees: $5630 **Average undergraduate aid package: $9500**

ABOUT THE INSTITUTION Independent Roman Catholic, coed. Awards: associate, bachelor's, master's, and first professional degrees. 6 undergraduate majors. Total enrollment: 169. Undergraduates: 13. Freshmen: 4. Federal methodology is used as a basis for awarding need-based institutional aid.

UNDERGRADUATE EXPENSES for 1999–2000 ***Application fee:*** $50. ***Comprehensive fee:*** $11,560 includes full-time tuition ($5550), mandatory fees ($80), and room and board ($5930). Full-time tuition and fees vary according to program. ***Part-time tuition:*** $185 per credit hour. Part-time tuition and fees vary according to program. ***Payment plan:*** installment.

UNDERGRADUATE FINANCIAL AID (Fall 1998) 3 applied for aid; of those 100% were deemed to have need. 100% of undergraduates with need received aid. *Average percent of need met:* 50% (excluding resources awarded to replace EFC). *Average financial aid package:* $9500 (excluding resources awarded to replace EFC).

GIFT AID (NEED-BASED) ***Total amount:*** $10,000 (70% Federal, 30% external sources). ***Receiving aid:*** *All full-time undergraduates:* 33% (1). ***Average award:*** Undergraduates: $700. ***Scholarships, grants, and awards:*** Federal Pell, FSEOG, state, private.

GIFT AID (NON-NEED-BASED) ***Tuition waivers:*** Full or partial for employees or children of employees.

LOANS ***Student loans:*** $17,575 (100% need-based). 30% of past graduating class borrowed through all loan programs. ***Average need-based loan:*** Undergraduates: $2500. ***Programs:*** FFEL (Subsidized and Unsubsidized Stafford, PLUS).

APPLYING for FINANCIAL AID ***Required financial aid forms:*** FAFSA, institution's own form. ***Financial aid deadline:*** Continuous. ***Notification date:*** 6/30. Students must reply within 4 weeks of notification.

CONTACT Ms. Marilyn Mancarella, Financial Aid Counselor, Holy Apostles College and Seminary, 33 Prospect Hill Road, Cromwell, CT 06416-2005, 860-632-3020 or toll-free 800-330-7272. *Fax:* 860-632-3049. *E-mail:* marmac7@juno.com

HOLY FAMILY COLLEGE

Philadelphia, PA

Tuition & fees: $11,860 **Average undergraduate aid package: $8632**

ABOUT THE INSTITUTION Independent Roman Catholic, coed. Awards: associate, bachelor's, and master's degrees and post-bachelor's certificates. 44 undergraduate majors. Total enrollment: 2,590. Undergraduates: 1,927. Freshmen: 248. Federal methodology is used as a basis for awarding need-based institutional aid.

UNDERGRADUATE EXPENSES for 1999–2000 ***Application fee:*** $25. ***Tuition:*** full-time $11,500; part-time $260 per credit. ***Required fees:*** full-time $360; $50 per term part-time. Full-time tuition and fees vary according to course load and program. Part-time tuition and fees vary according to program. ***Payment plans:*** installment, deferred payment.

FRESHMAN FINANCIAL AID (Fall 1999, est.) 208 applied for aid; of those 86% were deemed to have need. 100% of freshmen with need received aid. *Average percent of need met:* 63% (excluding resources awarded to replace EFC). *Average financial aid package:* $9460 (excluding resources awarded to replace EFC). 12% of all full-time freshmen had no need and received non-need-based aid.

UNDERGRADUATE FINANCIAL AID (Fall 1999, est.) 952 applied for aid; of those 95% were deemed to have need. 100% of undergraduates with need received aid. *Average percent of need met:* 69% (excluding resources awarded to replace EFC). *Average financial aid package:* $8632 (excluding resources awarded to replace EFC).

GIFT AID (NEED-BASED) ***Total amount:*** $3,452,335 (26% Federal, 43% state, 31% institutional). ***Receiving aid:*** *Freshmen:* 72% (163); *all full-time undergraduates:* 73% (768). ***Average award:*** Freshmen: $3151. ***Scholarships, grants, and awards:*** Federal Pell, FSEOG, state, private, college/university gift aid from institutional funds.

GIFT AID (NON-NEED-BASED) ***Total amount:*** $973,921 (91% institutional, 9% external sources). ***Receiving aid:*** *Freshmen:* 12% (28). ***Scholarships, grants, and awards by category:*** *Academic Interests/Achievement:* 501 awards ($1,108,575 total): general academic interests/achievements. ***Tuition waivers:*** Full or partial for employees or children of employees.

LOANS ***Student loans:*** $5,039,494 (71% need-based, 29% non-need-based). 50% of past graduating class borrowed through all loan programs. Average indebtedness per student: $17,125. ***Parent loans:*** $299,743 (100% non-need-based). ***Programs:*** FFEL (Subsidized and Unsubsidized Stafford, PLUS), Perkins, Federal Nursing, college/university.

WORK-STUDY ***Federal work-study:*** *Total amount:* $231,386; 237 jobs averaging $976. ***State or other work-study/employment:*** *Total amount:* $40,889 (100% need-based). 51 part-time jobs averaging $802.

ATHLETIC AWARDS *Total amount:* 372,236 (100% non-need-based).

APPLYING for FINANCIAL AID ***Required financial aid forms:*** FAFSA, institution's own form. ***Financial aid deadline (priority):*** 2/1. ***Notification date:*** Continuous beginning 4/1. Students must reply within 2 weeks of notification.

CONTACT Financial Aid Office, Holy Family College, Grant and Frankford Avenues, Philadelphia, PA 19114-2094, 215-637-5538 or toll-free 800-637-1191. *Fax:* 215-599-1694.

HOLY NAMES COLLEGE

Oakland, CA

Tuition & fees: $15,070 **Average undergraduate aid package: $16,000**

ABOUT THE INSTITUTION Independent Roman Catholic, coed, primarily women. Awards: bachelor's and master's degrees and post-bachelor's certificates. 11 undergraduate majors. Total enrollment: 934. Undergraduates: 596. Freshmen: 57. Federal methodology is used as a basis for awarding need-based institutional aid.

UNDERGRADUATE EXPENSES for 2000–2001 ***Application fee:*** $35. ***Comprehensive fee:*** $21,470 includes full-time tuition ($14,950), mandatory fees ($120), and room and board ($6400). Full-time tuition and fees vary according to course load. Room and board charges vary according to housing facility. ***Part-time tuition:*** $295 per unit. ***Part-time fees:*** $60 per term part-time. Part-time tuition and fees vary according to class time and location. ***Payment plans:*** installment, deferred payment.

FRESHMAN FINANCIAL AID (Fall 1999) 40 applied for aid; of those 90% were deemed to have need. 100% of freshmen with need received aid; of those 3% had need fully met. *Average percent of need met:* 75% (excluding resources awarded to replace EFC). *Average financial aid package:* $16,000 (excluding resources awarded to replace EFC).

UNDERGRADUATE FINANCIAL AID (Fall 1999) 187 applied for aid; of those 90% were deemed to have need. 100% of undergraduates with need received aid; of those 4% had need fully met. *Average percent of need met:* 75% (excluding resources awarded to replace EFC). *Average financial aid package:* $16,000 (excluding resources awarded to replace EFC).

GIFT AID (NEED-BASED) ***Total amount:*** $1,428,368 (24% Federal, 32% state, 44% institutional). ***Receiving aid:*** *Freshmen:* 79% (34); *all full-time undergraduates:* 81% (167). ***Average award:*** Freshmen: $8000; Undergraduates: $7200. ***Scholarships, grants, and awards:*** Federal Pell, FSEOG, state, private, college/university gift aid from institutional funds.

GIFT AID (NON-NEED-BASED) ***Total amount:*** $314,150 (97% institutional, 3% external sources). ***Receiving aid:*** *Freshmen:* 16% (7); *Undergraduates:* 14% (28). ***Scholarships, grants, and awards by category:*** *Academic Interests/Achievement:* 22 awards ($64,380 total): general academic interests/achievements. *Creative Arts/Performance:* 10 awards ($49,250 total): music. *Special Achievements/Activities:* 27 awards ($193,753 total): community service, leadership. *Special Characteristics:* 15 awards ($76,150 total): religious affiliation. ***Tuition waivers:*** Full or partial for employees or children of employees. ***ROTC:*** Army cooperative, Air Force cooperative.

LOANS ***Student loans:*** $572,185 (73% need-based, 27% non-need-based). 63% of past graduating class borrowed through all loan programs. Average indebtedness per student: $16,324. ***Average need-based loan:*** Freshmen: $3125; Undergraduates: $4775. ***Parent loans:*** $121,950 (100% non-need-based). ***Programs:*** FFEL (Subsidized and Unsubsidized Stafford, PLUS), Perkins, alternative loans.

WORK-STUDY ***Federal work-study:*** *Total amount:* $80,000; 51 jobs averaging $1570.

ATHLETIC AWARDS *Total amount:* 454,373 (100% non-need-based).

APPLYING for FINANCIAL AID ***Required financial aid form:*** FAFSA. ***Financial aid deadline (priority):*** 3/2. ***Notification date:*** Continuous beginning 4/1. Students must reply by 5/1 or within 2 weeks of notification.

CONTACT Kara I. Moore, Director of Financial Aid, Holy Names College, 3500 Mountain Boulevard, Oakland, CA 94619-1699, 510-436-1327 or toll-free 800-430-1321. *Fax:* 510-436-1666. *E-mail:* moorek@hnc.edu

HOOD COLLEGE

Frederick, MD

Tuition & fees: $17,600 **Average undergraduate aid package: $18,873**

ABOUT THE INSTITUTION Independent religious, women only. Awards: bachelor's and master's degrees (also offers adult program with significant enrollment not reflected in profile). 30 undergraduate majors. Total enrollment: 1,776. Undergraduates: 894. Freshmen: 169. Federal methodology is used as a basis for awarding need-based institutional aid.

UNDERGRADUATE EXPENSES for 1999–2000 ***Application fee:*** $35. ***Comprehensive fee:*** $24,500 includes full-time tuition ($17,275), mandatory fees ($325), and room and board ($6900). ***College room only:*** $3600. Room and board charges vary according to board plan. ***Part-time tuition:*** $500 per credit. ***Part-time fees:*** $100 per term part-time. Part-time tuition and fees vary according to course load. ***Payment plans:*** tuition prepayment, installment, deferred payment.

FRESHMAN FINANCIAL AID (Fall 1999, est.) 127 applied for aid; of those 91% were deemed to have need. 100% of freshmen with need received aid; of those 91% had need fully met. *Average percent of need met:* 90% (excluding resources awarded to replace EFC). *Average financial aid package:* $18,771 (excluding resources awarded to replace EFC). 23% of all full-time freshmen had no need and received non-need-based aid.

UNDERGRADUATE FINANCIAL AID (Fall 1999, est.) 482 applied for aid; of those 89% were deemed to have need. 100% of undergraduates with need received aid; of those 91% had need fully met. *Average percent of need met:* 91% (excluding resources awarded to replace EFC). *Average financial aid package:* $18,873 (excluding resources awarded to replace EFC). 26% of all full-time undergraduates had no need and received non-need-based aid.

GIFT AID (NEED-BASED) ***Total amount:*** $5,888,751 (8% Federal, 10% state, 75% institutional, 7% external sources). ***Receiving aid:*** *Freshmen:* 68% (115); *all full-time undergraduates:* 69% (419). ***Average award:*** Freshmen: $14,118; Undergraduates: $13,487. ***Scholarships, grants, and awards:*** Federal Pell, FSEOG, state, private, college/university gift aid from institutional funds.

GIFT AID (NON-NEED-BASED) ***Total amount:*** $1,749,880 (2% state, 93% institutional, 5% external sources). ***Scholarships, grants, and awards by category:*** *Academic Interests/Achievement:* general academic interests/achievements. *Creative Arts/Performance:* creative writing. *Special Achievements/Activities:* leadership, memberships. ***Tuition waivers:*** Full or partial for employees or children of employees, senior citizens. ***ROTC:*** Army cooperative.

LOANS ***Student loans:*** $2,595,492 (87% need-based, 13% non-need-based). 62% of past graduating class borrowed through all loan programs. Average indebtedness per student: $12,255. ***Average need-based loan:*** Freshmen: $3425; Undergraduates: $5003. ***Parent loans:*** $658,027 (85% need-based, 15% non-need-based). ***Programs:*** Federal Direct (Subsidized and Unsubsidized Stafford, PLUS), Perkins.

WORK-STUDY ***Federal work-study:*** *Total amount:* $312,300; 180 jobs averaging $1735. ***State or other work-study/employment:*** *Total amount:* $400,625 (63% need-based, 37% non-need-based). 235 part-time jobs averaging $1704.

APPLYING for FINANCIAL AID ***Required financial aid form:*** FAFSA. ***Financial aid deadline:*** 2/15. ***Notification date:*** Continuous. Students must reply by 5/1 or within 3 weeks of notification.

CONTACT Ms. Linda J. Weippert, Director of Financial Aid, Hood College, 401 Rosemont Avenue, Frederick, MD 21701-8575, 301-696-3411 or toll-free 800-922-1599. *E-mail:* weippert@hood.edu

HOPE COLLEGE

Holland, MI

Tuition & fees: $16,024 **Average undergraduate aid package: $14,227**

ABOUT THE INSTITUTION Independent religious, coed. Awards: bachelor's degrees. 43 undergraduate majors. Total enrollment: 2,943. Undergraduates: 2,943. Freshmen: 755. Institutional methodology is used as a basis for awarding need-based institutional aid.

UNDERGRADUATE EXPENSES for 1999–2000 ***Application fee:*** $25. ***Comprehensive fee:*** $21,054 includes full-time tuition ($15,934), mandatory fees ($90), and room and board ($5030). ***College room only:*** $2294. Room and board charges vary according to board plan and housing facility. Part-time tuition and fees vary according to course load. ***Payment plan:*** installment.

FRESHMAN FINANCIAL AID (Fall 1999) 605 applied for aid; of those 68% were deemed to have need. 100% of freshmen with need received aid; of those 49% had need fully met. *Average percent of need met:* 95% (excluding resources awarded to replace EFC). *Average financial aid package:* $14,215 (excluding resources awarded to replace EFC). 26% of all full-time freshmen had no need and received non-need-based aid.

Hope College (continued)

UNDERGRADUATE FINANCIAL AID (Fall 1999) 1,918 applied for aid; of those 73% were deemed to have need. 100% of undergraduates with need received aid; of those 61% had need fully met. *Average percent of need met:* 96% (excluding resources awarded to replace EFC). *Average financial aid package:* $14,227 (excluding resources awarded to replace EFC). 27% of all full-time undergraduates had no need and received non-need-based aid.

GIFT AID (NEED-BASED) ***Total amount:*** $11,661,448 (8% Federal, 24% state, 68% institutional). ***Receiving aid:*** *Freshmen:* 50% (380); *all full-time undergraduates:* 47% (1,300). ***Average award:*** Freshmen: $10,219; Undergraduates: $9605. ***Scholarships, grants, and awards:*** Federal Pell, FSEOG, state, private, college/university gift aid from institutional funds.

GIFT AID (NON-NEED-BASED) ***Total amount:*** $5,756,716 (1% Federal, 87% institutional, 12% external sources). ***Receiving aid:*** *Freshmen:* 41% (307); *Undergraduates:* 33% (913). ***Scholarships, grants, and awards by category:*** *Academic Interests/Achievement:* 1,597 awards ($8,125,606 total): general academic interests/achievements. *Creative Arts/Performance:* 110 awards ($273,050 total): art/fine arts, dance, music, performing arts, theater/drama. ***Tuition waivers:*** Full or partial for employees or children of employees.

LOANS ***Student loans:*** $7,414,267 (64% need-based, 36% non-need-based). 62% of past graduating class borrowed through all loan programs. Average indebtedness per student: $16,259. ***Average need-based loan:*** Freshmen: $3174; Undergraduates: $3975. ***Parent loans:*** $1,141,189 (100% non-need-based). ***Programs:*** Federal Direct (Subsidized and Unsubsidized Stafford, PLUS), Perkins, state, MI-Loan Program.

WORK-STUDY ***Federal work-study:*** *Total amount:* $302,768; 202 jobs averaging $1500. ***State or other work-study/employment:*** *Total amount:* $1,205,656 (61% need-based, 39% non-need-based). 804 part-time jobs averaging $1500.

APPLYING for FINANCIAL AID ***Required financial aid forms:*** FAFSA, CSS Financial Aid PROFILE. ***Financial aid deadline (priority):*** 2/15. ***Notification date:*** Continuous beginning 3/16.

CONTACT Ms. Phyllis Hooyman, Director of Financial Aid, Hope College, 141 East 12th Street, PO Box 9000, Holland, MI 49422-9000, 616-395-7765 or toll-free 800-968-7850. *Fax:* 616-395-7160. *E-mail:* hooyman@hope.edu

HOPE INTERNATIONAL UNIVERSITY

Fullerton, CA

Tuition & fees: $11,220 **Average undergraduate aid package: N/A**

ABOUT THE INSTITUTION Independent religious, coed. Awards: associate, bachelor's, and master's degrees. 19 undergraduate majors. Total enrollment: 971. Undergraduates: 793. Freshmen: 112. Federal methodology is used as a basis for awarding need-based institutional aid.

UNDERGRADUATE EXPENSES for 1999–2000 ***Application fee:*** $30. ***One-time required fee:*** $200. ***Comprehensive fee:*** $15,720 includes full-time tuition ($10,980), mandatory fees ($240), and room and board ($4500). Room and board charges vary according to board plan and housing facility. ***Part-time tuition:*** $407 per unit. ***Part-time fees:*** $240 per year part-time. Part-time tuition and fees vary according to course load. ***Payment plan:*** installment.

GIFT AID (NEED-BASED) ***Scholarships, grants, and awards:*** Federal Pell, FSEOG, state, private, college/university gift aid from institutional funds.

GIFT AID (NON-NEED-BASED) ***Scholarships, grants, and awards by category:*** *Academic Interests/Achievement:* general academic interests/achievements. *Creative Arts/Performance:* music. *Special Achievements/Activities:* leadership, religious involvement. *Special Characteristics:* children and siblings of alumni, children of faculty/staff, international students, local/state students, relatives of clergy, siblings of current students, spouses of current students, veterans, veterans' children. ***Tuition waivers:*** Full or partial for employees or children of employees, senior citizens.

LOANS ***Programs:*** FFEL (Subsidized and Unsubsidized Stafford, PLUS), Perkins, college/university.

WORK-STUDY Federal work-study jobs available.

APPLYING for FINANCIAL AID ***Required financial aid forms:*** FAFSA, institution's own form. ***Financial aid deadline (priority):*** 3/2. ***Notification date:*** Continuous. Students must reply within 3 weeks of notification.

CONTACT Mr. Mai Bui, Director of Financial Aid, Hope International University, 2500 East Nutwood Avenue, Fullerton, CA 92831, 714-879-3901 or toll-free 800-762-1294 Ext. 2235. *Fax:* 714-526-0231.

HOUGHTON COLLEGE

Houghton, NY

Tuition & fees: $15,140 **Average undergraduate aid package: $12,340**

ABOUT THE INSTITUTION Independent Wesleyan, coed. Awards: associate and bachelor's degrees. 49 undergraduate majors. Total enrollment: 1,380. Undergraduates: 1,380. Freshmen: 294. Both federal and institutional methodology are used as a basis for awarding need-based institutional aid.

UNDERGRADUATE EXPENSES for 2000–2001 (est.) ***Application fee:*** $25. ***Comprehensive fee:*** $20,540 includes full-time tuition ($15,140) and room and board ($5400). ***College room only:*** $2700. Full-time tuition and fees vary according to course load and program. Room and board charges vary according to board plan and housing facility. ***Part-time tuition:*** $630 per hour. Part-time tuition and fees vary according to course load. ***Payment plan:*** installment.

FRESHMAN FINANCIAL AID (Fall 1998) 288 applied for aid; of those 88% were deemed to have need. 100% of freshmen with need received aid; of those 22% had need fully met. *Average percent of need met:* 83% (excluding resources awarded to replace EFC). *Average financial aid package:* $10,118 (excluding resources awarded to replace EFC). 11% of all full-time freshmen had no need and received non-need-based aid.

UNDERGRADUATE FINANCIAL AID (Fall 1998) 969 applied for aid; of those 95% were deemed to have need. 100% of undergraduates with need received aid; of those 20% had need fully met. *Average percent of need met:* 76% (excluding resources awarded to replace EFC). *Average financial aid package:* $12,340 (excluding resources awarded to replace EFC). 8% of all full-time undergraduates had no need and received non-need-based aid.

GIFT AID (NEED-BASED) ***Total amount:*** $3,721,796 (23% Federal, 28% state, 40% institutional, 9% external sources). ***Receiving aid:*** *Freshmen:* 76% (233); *all full-time undergraduates:* 77% (902). ***Average award:*** Freshmen: $4143; Undergraduates: $3950. ***Scholarships, grants, and awards:*** Federal Pell, FSEOG, state, private, college/university gift aid from institutional funds.

GIFT AID (NON-NEED-BASED) ***Total amount:*** $1,638,500 (3% state, 97% institutional). ***Receiving aid:*** *Freshmen:* 66% (202); *Undergraduates:* 56% (662). ***Scholarships, grants, and awards by category:*** *Academic Interests/Achievement:* 553 awards ($1,361,025 total): general academic interests/achievements. *Creative Arts/Performance:* 75 awards ($82,875 total): art/fine arts, music. *Special Achievements/Activities:* 17 awards ($102,300 total): religious involvement. *Special Characteristics:* 305 awards ($341,675 total): parents of current students, relatives of clergy, religious affiliation, siblings of current students. ***Tuition waivers:*** Full or partial for employees or children of employees, senior citizens. ***ROTC:*** Army cooperative.

LOANS ***Student loans:*** $4,834,712 (69% need-based, 31% non-need-based). 75% of past graduating class borrowed through all loan programs. Average indebtedness per student: $16,850. ***Average need-based loan:*** Freshmen: $3105; Undergraduates: $4088. ***Parent loans:*** $888,005 (100% non-need-based). ***Programs:*** FFEL (Subsidized and Unsubsidized Stafford, PLUS), Perkins, college/university, alternative loans.

WORK-STUDY ***Federal work-study:*** *Total amount:* $484,201; 682 jobs averaging $710. ***State or other work-study/employment:*** *Total amount:* $183,750 (100% non-need-based). 194 part-time jobs averaging $947.

ATHLETIC AWARDS *Total amount:* 378,148 (100% non-need-based).

APPLYING for FINANCIAL AID ***Required financial aid forms:*** FAFSA, institution's own form, state aid form. ***Financial aid deadline (priority):*** 3/1. ***Notification date:*** Continuous beginning 3/15. Students must reply within 4 weeks of notification.

CONTACT Mr. Troy Martin, Director of Financial Aid, Houghton College, One Willard Avenue, Houghton, NY 14744, 716-567-9328 or toll-free 800-777-2556. *Fax:* 716-567-9610. *E-mail:* tmartin@houghton.edu

HOUSTON BAPTIST UNIVERSITY

Houston, TX

Tuition & fees: $10,828 **Average undergraduate aid package: N/A**

ABOUT THE INSTITUTION Independent Baptist, coed. Awards: associate, bachelor's, and master's degrees. 52 undergraduate majors. Total enrollment: 2,362. Undergraduates: 1,779. Freshmen: 599. Federal methodology is used as a basis for awarding need-based institutional aid.

UNDERGRADUATE EXPENSES for 2000–2001 ***Application fee:*** $25. ***Comprehensive fee:*** $14,728 includes full-time tuition ($10,048), mandatory fees ($780), and room and board ($3900). Full-time tuition and fees vary according to course load and student level. Room and board charges vary according to board plan. ***Part-time tuition:*** $298 per credit hour. ***Part-time fees:*** $240 per term part-time. Part-time tuition and fees vary according to course load and student level. ***Payment plans:*** guaranteed tuition, installment, deferred payment.

GIFT AID (NEED-BASED) ***Scholarships, grants, and awards:*** Federal Pell, FSEOG, state.

GIFT AID (NON-NEED-BASED) ***Scholarships, grants, and awards by category:*** *Academic Interests/Achievement:* general academic interests/achievements, health fields, religion/biblical studies. *Creative Arts/Performance:* art/fine arts, music. *Special Achievements/Activities:* general special achievements/activities. *Special Characteristics:* general special characteristics. ***Tuition waivers:*** Full or partial for employees or children of employees, senior citizens. ***ROTC:*** Army cooperative, Naval cooperative.

LOANS ***Programs:*** Federal Direct (Subsidized and Unsubsidized Stafford, PLUS).

WORK-STUDY Federal work-study jobs available.

APPLYING for FINANCIAL AID ***Required financial aid forms:*** FAFSA, institution's own form. ***Financial aid deadline (priority):*** 2/15. ***Notification date:*** 5/1. Students must reply within 4 weeks of notification.

CONTACT Sherry Byrd, Director of Financial Aid, Houston Baptist University, 7502 Fondren Road, Houston, TX 77074-3298, 281-649-3204 or toll-free 800-969-3210. *Fax:* 281-649-3474.

HOWARD PAYNE UNIVERSITY

Brownwood, TX

Tuition & fees: $9000 **Average undergraduate aid package: N/A**

ABOUT THE INSTITUTION Independent Southern Baptist, coed. Awards: bachelor's degrees. 64 undergraduate majors. Total enrollment: 1,496. Undergraduates: 1,496. Freshmen: 364. Federal methodology is used as a basis for awarding need-based institutional aid.

UNDERGRADUATE EXPENSES for 1999–2000 ***Application fee:*** $25. ***Comprehensive fee:*** $12,830 includes full-time tuition ($8400), mandatory fees ($600), and room and board ($3830). ***College room only:*** $1720. Full-time tuition and fees vary according to course load. Room and board charges vary according to board plan, gender, and housing facility. ***Part-time tuition:*** $175 per semester hour. ***Part-time fees:*** $100 per term part-time. ***Payment plan:*** installment.

GIFT AID (NEED-BASED) ***Total amount:*** $2,353,829 (55% Federal, 45% state). ***Scholarships, grants, and awards:*** Federal Pell, FSEOG, state, college/university gift aid from institutional funds.

GIFT AID (NON-NEED-BASED) ***Total amount:*** $2,831,547 (87% institutional, 13% external sources). ***Scholarships, grants, and awards by category:*** *Academic Interests/Achievement:* biological sciences, business, communication, education, general academic interests/achievements, mathematics, religion/biblical studies, social sciences. *Creative Arts/Performance:* art/fine arts, cinema/film/broadcasting, music, theater/drama. *Special Achievements/Activities:* community service, leadership, religious involvement. *Special Characteristics:* children and siblings of alumni, children of faculty/staff, relatives of clergy, religious affiliation. ***Tuition waivers:*** Full or partial for employees or children of employees, senior citizens. ***ROTC:*** Army cooperative.

LOANS ***Student loans:*** $4,214,650 (58% need-based, 42% non-need-based). 65% of past graduating class borrowed through all loan programs. ***Parent loans:*** $504,697 (100% non-need-based). ***Programs:*** FFEL (Subsidized and Unsubsidized Stafford, PLUS), Perkins, state.

WORK-STUDY ***Federal work-study:*** *Total amount:* $133,420; 167 jobs averaging $800. ***State or other work-study/employment:*** *Total amount:* $142,113 (9% need-based, 91% non-need-based). 110 part-time jobs averaging $1000.

APPLYING for FINANCIAL AID ***Required financial aid forms:*** FAFSA, institution's own form. ***Financial aid deadline (priority):*** 3/15. ***Notification date:*** Continuous. Students must reply within 3 weeks of notification.

CONTACT Mrs. Glenda Huff, Director of Student Aid, Howard Payne University, HPU Station, Box 825, Brownwood, TX 76801-2794, 915-649-8015 or toll-free 800-880-4478. *Fax:* 915-649-8901. *E-mail:* financial-aid@hputx.edu

HOWARD UNIVERSITY

Washington, DC

CONTACT Director of Admissions and Student Financial Services, Howard University, 2400 Sixth Street, NW, Washington, DC 20059-0002, 202-806-2705 or toll-free 800-HOWARD-U (out-of-state).

HUMBOLDT STATE UNIVERSITY

Arcata, CA

Tuition & fees (CA res): $1861 **Average undergraduate aid package: $6794**

ABOUT THE INSTITUTION State-supported, coed. Awards: bachelor's and master's degrees. 75 undergraduate majors. Total enrollment: 7,545. Undergraduates: 6,570. Freshmen: 760. Federal methodology is used as a basis for awarding need-based institutional aid.

UNDERGRADUATE EXPENSES for 2000–2001 (est.) ***Application fee:*** $55. ***Tuition, state resident:*** full-time $0. ***Tuition, nonresident:*** full-time $5904. ***Required fees:*** full-time $1861; $629 per term part-time. ***College room and board:*** $5845; ***room only:*** $3366. Room and board charges vary according to board plan and housing facility. ***Payment plan:*** installment.

FRESHMAN FINANCIAL AID (Fall 1999) 562 applied for aid; of those 73% were deemed to have need. 90% of freshmen with need received aid; of those 3% had need fully met. *Average percent of need met:* 69% (excluding resources awarded to replace EFC). *Average financial aid package:* $6038 (excluding resources awarded to replace EFC).

UNDERGRADUATE FINANCIAL AID (Fall 1999) 3,900 applied for aid; of those 96% were deemed to have need. 83% of undergraduates with need received aid; of those 21% had need fully met. *Average percent of need met:* 80% (excluding resources awarded to replace EFC). *Average financial aid package:* $6794 (excluding resources awarded to replace EFC).

GIFT AID (NEED-BASED) ***Total amount:*** $11,823,635 (56% Federal, 38% state, 3% institutional, 3% external sources). ***Receiving aid:*** *Freshmen:* 42% (317); *all full-time undergraduates:* 40% (2,725). ***Average award:*** Freshmen: $4225; Undergraduates: $3594. ***Scholarships, grants, and awards:*** Federal Pell, FSEOG, state, private, college/university gift aid from institutional funds.

GIFT AID (NON-NEED-BASED) ***Tuition waivers:*** Full or partial for employees or children of employees, senior citizens.

LOANS ***Student loans:*** $11,400,000 (83% need-based, 17% non-need-based). 50% of past graduating class borrowed through all loan programs. Average indebtedness per student: $14,000. ***Average need-based loan:*** Freshmen: $2419; Undergraduates: $3742. ***Parent loans:*** $910,000 (100% non-need-based). ***Programs:*** Federal Direct (Subsidized and Unsubsidized Stafford, PLUS), Perkins.

WORK-STUDY ***Federal work-study:*** *Total amount:* $750,000; jobs available. ***State or other work-study/employment:*** *Total amount:* $160,000 (100% need-based). Part-time jobs available.

Humboldt State University (continued)

ATHLETIC AWARDS *Total amount:* 74,000 (100% need-based).

APPLYING for FINANCIAL AID ***Required financial aid form:*** FAFSA. ***Financial aid deadline (priority):*** 3/2. ***Notification date:*** Continuous beginning 3/10. Students must reply within 6 weeks of notification.

CONTACT Ms. Elizabeth Mikles, Financial Aid Associate Director, Humboldt State University, 1 Harpst Street, Arcata, CA 95521-8299, 707-826-4321. *Fax:* 707-826-5360. *E-mail:* mikles@humboldt.edu

HUMPHREYS COLLEGE

Stockton, CA

Tuition & fees: $6804 **Average undergraduate aid package: $3500**

ABOUT THE INSTITUTION Independent, coed. Awards: associate, bachelor's, and first professional degrees. 13 undergraduate majors. Total enrollment: 721. Undergraduates: 597. Federal methodology is used as a basis for awarding need-based institutional aid.

UNDERGRADUATE EXPENSES for 1999–2000 ***Application fee:*** $20. ***Tuition:*** full-time $6804; part-time $162 per unit. Part-time tuition and fees vary according to course load. ***Payment plans:*** tuition prepayment, installment.

UNDERGRADUATE FINANCIAL AID (Fall 1999, est.) 271 applied for aid. *Average percent of need met:* 100% (excluding resources awarded to replace EFC). *Average financial aid package:* $3500 (excluding resources awarded to replace EFC).

GIFT AID (NEED-BASED) ***Total amount:*** $1,148,811 (67% Federal, 30% state, 2% institutional, 1% external sources). ***Scholarships, grants, and awards:*** Federal Pell, FSEOG, state, private, college/university gift aid from institutional funds.

GIFT AID (NON-NEED-BASED) ***Scholarships, grants, and awards by category:*** *Academic Interests/Achievement:* business, computer science, general academic interests/achievements. *Special Achievements/Activities:* community service. *Special Characteristics:* ethnic background, members of minority groups. ***Tuition waivers:*** Full or partial for employees or children of employees.

LOANS ***Student loans:*** $3,063,948 (60% need-based, 40% non-need-based). ***Parent loans:*** $68,000 (100% non-need-based). ***Programs:*** FFEL (Subsidized and Unsubsidized Stafford, PLUS).

WORK-STUDY ***Federal work-study:*** *Total amount:* $59,690; jobs available.

APPLYING for FINANCIAL AID ***Required financial aid form:*** FAFSA. ***Financial aid deadline (priority):*** 1/1. ***Notification date:*** Continuous. Students must reply by 6/30.

CONTACT Ms. Rita Franco, Financial Aid Adviser, Humphreys College, 6650 Inglewood Avenue, Stockton, CA 95207-3896, 209-478-0800 Ext. 124.

HUNTER COLLEGE OF THE CITY UNIVERSITY OF NEW YORK

New York, NY

Tuition & fees (NY res): $3333 **Average undergraduate aid package: $4491**

ABOUT THE INSTITUTION State and locally supported, coed. Awards: bachelor's and master's degrees. 54 undergraduate majors. Total enrollment: 20,001. Undergraduates: 15,568. Freshmen: 1,920. Federal methodology is used as a basis for awarding need-based institutional aid.

UNDERGRADUATE EXPENSES for 1999–2000 ***Application fee:*** $40. ***Tuition, state resident:*** full-time $3200; part-time $135 per credit. ***Tuition, nonresident:*** full-time $6800; part-time $285 per credit. ***Required fees:*** full-time $133; $49 per term part-time. Room and board charges vary according to housing facility. ***Payment plan:*** deferred payment.

FRESHMAN FINANCIAL AID (Fall 1999, est.) *Average financial aid package:* $4061 (excluding resources awarded to replace EFC).

UNDERGRADUATE FINANCIAL AID (Fall 1999, est.) *Average financial aid package:* $4491 (excluding resources awarded to replace EFC).

GIFT AID (NEED-BASED) ***Total amount:*** $21,684,722 (56% Federal, 44% state). ***Scholarships, grants, and awards:*** Federal Pell, FSEOG, state, private, college/university gift aid from institutional funds.

GIFT AID (NON-NEED-BASED) ***Total amount:*** $1,545,549 (24% state, 76% external sources). ***Scholarships, grants, and awards by category:*** *Academic Interests/Achievement:* general academic interests/achievements. ***Tuition waivers:*** Full or partial for senior citizens.

LOANS ***Student loans:*** $8,553,267 (78% need-based, 22% non-need-based). 40% of past graduating class borrowed through all loan programs. Average indebtedness per student: $7200. ***Parent loans:*** $206,864 (100% need-based). ***Programs:*** Federal Direct (Subsidized and Unsubsidized Stafford, PLUS), Perkins.

WORK-STUDY ***Federal work-study:*** *Total amount:* $1,315,738; jobs available.

APPLYING for FINANCIAL AID ***Required financial aid forms:*** FAFSA, state aid form. ***Financial aid deadline (priority):*** 4/1. ***Notification date:*** Continuous.

CONTACT Kevin McGowan, Director, Financial Aid, Hunter College of the City University of New York, 695 Park Avenue, New York, NY 10021-5085, 212-772-4820.

HUNTINGDON COLLEGE

Montgomery, AL

Tuition & fees: $11,910 **Average undergraduate aid package: $10,541**

ABOUT THE INSTITUTION Independent United Methodist, coed. Awards: associate and bachelor's degrees. 59 undergraduate majors. Total enrollment: 705. Undergraduates: 705. Freshmen: 163. Federal methodology is used as a basis for awarding need-based institutional aid.

UNDERGRADUATE EXPENSES for 2000–2001 ***Application fee:*** $25. ***Comprehensive fee:*** $17,650 includes full-time tuition ($11,000), mandatory fees ($910), and room and board ($5740). Full-time tuition and fees vary according to class time and reciprocity agreements. Room and board charges vary according to housing facility. ***Part-time tuition:*** $390 per semester hour. Part-time tuition and fees vary according to class time and course load. ***Payment plan:*** deferred payment.

FRESHMAN FINANCIAL AID (Fall 1999, est.) 147 applied for aid; of those 68% were deemed to have need. 100% of freshmen with need received aid; of those 35% had need fully met. *Average percent of need met:* 88% (excluding resources awarded to replace EFC). *Average financial aid package:* $9615 (excluding resources awarded to replace EFC). 31% of all full-time freshmen had no need and received non-need-based aid.

UNDERGRADUATE FINANCIAL AID (Fall 1999, est.) 502 applied for aid; of those 80% were deemed to have need. 100% of undergraduates with need received aid; of those 53% had need fully met. *Average percent of need met:* 92% (excluding resources awarded to replace EFC). *Average financial aid package:* $10,541 (excluding resources awarded to replace EFC). 24% of all full-time undergraduates had no need and received non-need-based aid.

GIFT AID (NEED-BASED) ***Total amount:*** $1,669,106 (27% Federal, 72% institutional, 1% external sources). ***Receiving aid:*** *Freshmen:* 59% (95); *all full-time undergraduates:* 61% (380). ***Average award:*** Freshmen: $6363; Undergraduates: $6762. ***Scholarships, grants, and awards:*** Federal Pell, FSEOG, state, private, college/university gift aid from institutional funds.

GIFT AID (NON-NEED-BASED) ***Total amount:*** $2,464,204 (13% state, 83% institutional, 4% external sources). ***Receiving aid:*** *Freshmen:* 38% (62); *Undergraduates:* 35% (219). ***Scholarships, grants, and awards by category:*** *Academic Interests/Achievement:* 285 awards ($1,549,300 total): general academic interests/achievements. *Creative Arts/Performance:* 70 awards ($63,548 total): applied art and design, dance, music, theater/drama. *Special Achievements/Activities:* 121 awards ($245,084 total): junior miss, leadership. *Special Characteristics:* 129 awards ($231,356 total): international students, relatives of clergy, religious affiliation. ***Tuition waivers:*** Full or partial for employees or children of employees. ***ROTC:*** Army cooperative, Air Force cooperative.

LOANS ***Student loans:*** $1,360,541 (57% need-based, 43% non-need-based). 58% of past graduating class borrowed through all loan programs.

Average indebtedness per student: $15,262. ***Average need-based loan:*** Freshmen: $2589; Undergraduates: $3189. ***Parent loans:*** $402,152 (100% non-need-based). ***Programs:*** FFEL (Subsidized and Unsubsidized Stafford, PLUS), Perkins.

WORK-STUDY ***Federal work-study:*** *Total amount:* $116,450; 137 jobs averaging $850.

ATHLETIC AWARDS *Total amount:* 141,750 (100% non-need-based).

APPLYING for FINANCIAL AID ***Required financial aid forms:*** FAFSA, institution's own form. ***Financial aid deadline (priority):*** 4/15. ***Notification date:*** Continuous. Students must reply by 5/1 or within 4 weeks of notification.

CONTACT Mr. Thomas G. Dismukes Jr., Director of Student Financial Aid, Huntingdon College, 1500 East Fairview Avenue, Montgomery, AL 36106-2148, 334-833-4519 or toll-free 800-763-0313. *Fax:* 334-833-4347. *E-mail:* tommyd@huntingdon.edu

HUNTINGTON COLLEGE

Huntington, IN

Tuition & fees: $14,230 — **Average undergraduate aid package: $11,164**

ABOUT THE INSTITUTION Independent religious, coed. Awards: bachelor's and master's degrees and post-bachelor's certificates. 42 undergraduate majors. Total enrollment: 904. Undergraduates: 857. Freshmen: 222. Both federal and institutional methodology are used as a basis for awarding need-based institutional aid.

UNDERGRADUATE EXPENSES for 2000–2001 ***Application fee:*** $15. ***Comprehensive fee:*** $19,420 includes full-time tuition ($13,540), mandatory fees ($690), and room and board ($5190). ***College room only:*** $2350. ***Part-time tuition:*** $430 per semester hour. Part-time tuition and fees vary according to course load. ***Payment plans:*** guaranteed tuition, installment.

FRESHMAN FINANCIAL AID (Fall 1999) 217 applied for aid; of those 71% were deemed to have need. 100% of freshmen with need received aid; of those 99% had need fully met. *Average percent of need met:* 99% (excluding resources awarded to replace EFC). *Average financial aid package:* $11,470 (excluding resources awarded to replace EFC). 26% of all full-time freshmen had no need and received non-need-based aid.

UNDERGRADUATE FINANCIAL AID (Fall 1999) 713 applied for aid; of those 75% were deemed to have need. 100% of undergraduates with need received aid; of those 98% had need fully met. *Average percent of need met:* 97% (excluding resources awarded to replace EFC). *Average financial aid package:* $11,164 (excluding resources awarded to replace EFC). 22% of all full-time undergraduates had no need and received non-need-based aid.

GIFT AID (NEED-BASED) ***Total amount:*** $2,748,370 (16% Federal, 32% state, 46% institutional, 6% external sources). ***Receiving aid:*** *Freshmen:* 64% (142); *all full-time undergraduates:* 65% (489). ***Average award:*** Freshmen: $7195; Undergraduates: $6462. ***Scholarships, grants, and awards:*** Federal Pell, FSEOG, state, private, college/university gift aid from institutional funds.

GIFT AID (NON-NEED-BASED) ***Total amount:*** $649,360 (91% institutional, 9% external sources). ***Receiving aid:*** *Freshmen:* 28% (63); *Undergraduates:* 23% (174). ***Scholarships, grants, and awards by category:*** *Academic Interests/Achievement:* general academic interests/achievements. *Creative Arts/Performance:* art/fine arts, journalism/publications, music, theater/drama. *Special Characteristics:* children and siblings of alumni, children of current students, children of faculty/staff, international students, parents of current students, relatives of clergy, religious affiliation, siblings of current students, spouses of current students. ***Tuition waivers:*** Full or partial for minority students, children of alumni, employees or children of employees, adult students, senior citizens.

LOANS ***Student loans:*** $2,326,230 (79% need-based, 21% non-need-based). 66% of past graduating class borrowed through all loan programs. Average indebtedness per student: $18,125. ***Average need-based loan:*** Freshmen: $3145; Undergraduates: $4161. ***Parent loans:*** $454,870 (50% need-based, 50% non-need-based). ***Programs:*** FFEL (Subsidized and Unsubsidized Stafford, PLUS), Perkins.

WORK-STUDY ***Federal work-study:*** *Total amount:* $217,600; 136 jobs averaging $1600.

ATHLETIC AWARDS *Total amount:* 395,213 (42% need-based, 58% non-need-based).

APPLYING for FINANCIAL AID ***Required financial aid forms:*** FAFSA, institution's own form. ***Financial aid deadline (priority):*** 3/1. ***Notification date:*** Continuous beginning 3/15. Students must reply by 5/1.

CONTACT Candy Smith, Financial Aid Assistant, Huntington College, 2303 College Avenue, Huntington, IN 46750-1299, 219-359-4015 or toll-free 800-642-6493. *Fax:* 219-358-3699. *E-mail:* csmith@huntington.edu

HURON UNIVERSITY

Huron, SD

Tuition & fees: $7500 — **Average undergraduate aid package: $2683**

ABOUT THE INSTITUTION Proprietary, coed. Awards: associate and bachelor's degrees. 13 undergraduate majors. Total enrollment: 566. Undergraduates: 544. Freshmen: 129. Institutional methodology is used as a basis for awarding need-based institutional aid.

UNDERGRADUATE EXPENSES for 2000–2001 (est.) ***Application fee:*** $35. ***Comprehensive fee:*** $11,400 includes full-time tuition ($7200), mandatory fees ($300), and room and board ($3900). ***College room only:*** $1950. Room and board charges vary according to board plan and housing facility. ***Part-time tuition:*** $200 per quarter hour. ***Part-time fees:*** $100 per term part-time. ***Payment plans:*** guaranteed tuition, tuition prepayment, installment, deferred payment.

FRESHMAN FINANCIAL AID (Fall 1998) 115 applied for aid; of those 91% were deemed to have need. 96% of freshmen with need received aid; of those 18% had need fully met. *Average percent of need met:* 48% (excluding resources awarded to replace EFC). *Average financial aid package:* $2099 (excluding resources awarded to replace EFC). 8% of all full-time freshmen had no need and received non-need-based aid.

UNDERGRADUATE FINANCIAL AID (Fall 1998) 423 applied for aid; of those 92% were deemed to have need. 99% of undergraduates with need received aid; of those 37% had need fully met. *Average percent of need met:* 52% (excluding resources awarded to replace EFC). *Average financial aid package:* $2683 (excluding resources awarded to replace EFC). 7% of all full-time undergraduates had no need and received non-need-based aid.

GIFT AID (NEED-BASED) ***Total amount:*** $669,148 (100% Federal). ***Receiving aid:*** *Freshmen:* 48% (58); *all full-time undergraduates:* 52% (227). ***Average award:*** Freshmen: $796; Undergraduates: $873. ***Scholarships, grants, and awards:*** Federal Pell, FSEOG, college/university gift aid from institutional funds.

GIFT AID (NON-NEED-BASED) ***Total amount:*** $616,978 (80% institutional, 20% external sources). ***Receiving aid:*** *Freshmen:* 69% (84); *Undergraduates:* 79% (345). ***Scholarships, grants, and awards by category:*** *Academic Interests/Achievement:* general academic interests/achievements. *Creative Arts/Performance:* music. *Special Achievements/Activities:* cheerleading/drum major. ***Tuition waivers:*** Full or partial for children of alumni, employees or children of employees.

LOANS ***Student loans:*** $2,055,272 (64% need-based, 36% non-need-based). ***Average need-based loan:*** Freshmen: $877; Undergraduates: $1247. ***Parent loans:*** $242,772 (100% non-need-based). ***Programs:*** FFEL (Subsidized and Unsubsidized Stafford, PLUS), Perkins.

WORK-STUDY ***Federal work-study:*** *Total amount:* $50,645; jobs available.

ATHLETIC AWARDS *Total amount:* 1,324,692 (100% non-need-based).

APPLYING for FINANCIAL AID ***Required financial aid form:*** FAFSA. ***Financial aid deadline:*** Continuous. ***Notification date:*** Continuous.

CONTACT Mrs. Mary Heidrick, Director of Financial Aid, Huron University, 333 9th Street SW, Huron, SD 57350-2798, 605-352-8721 or toll-free 800-710-7159.

HUSSON COLLEGE

Bangor, ME

Tuition & fees: $9310 **Average undergraduate aid package: $9410**

ABOUT THE INSTITUTION Independent, coed. Awards: associate, bachelor's, and master's degrees and post-bachelor's and post-master's certificates. 30 undergraduate majors. Total enrollment: 1,955. Undergraduates: 1,613. Freshmen: 183. Federal methodology is used as a basis for awarding need-based institutional aid.

UNDERGRADUATE EXPENSES for 1999–2000 ***Application fee:*** $25. ***Comprehensive fee:*** $14,300 includes full-time tuition ($9210), mandatory fees ($100), and room and board ($4990). Full-time tuition and fees vary according to class time. ***Part-time tuition:*** $307 per semester hour. Part-time tuition and fees vary according to class time and course load. ***Payment plans:*** tuition prepayment, installment.

FRESHMAN FINANCIAL AID (Fall 1998) *Average percent of need met:* 86% (excluding resources awarded to replace EFC). *Average financial aid package:* $10,650 (excluding resources awarded to replace EFC).

UNDERGRADUATE FINANCIAL AID (Fall 1998) 1,184 applied for aid; of those 100% were deemed to have need. 100% of undergraduates with need received aid. *Average percent of need met:* 86% (excluding resources awarded to replace EFC). *Average financial aid package:* $9410 (excluding resources awarded to replace EFC). 1% of all full-time undergraduates had no need and received non-need-based aid.

GIFT AID (NEED-BASED) ***Total amount:*** $2,883,450 (31% Federal, 12% state, 55% institutional, 2% external sources). ***Receiving aid:*** *All full-time undergraduates:* 39% (876). ***Average award:*** Undergraduates: $5910. ***Scholarships, grants, and awards:*** Federal Pell, FSEOG, state, private, college/university gift aid from institutional funds.

GIFT AID (NON-NEED-BASED) ***Total amount:*** $156,000 (100% external sources). ***Receiving aid:*** *Undergraduates:* 25% (565). ***Scholarships, grants, and awards by category:*** *Academic Interests/Achievement:* business, computer science, education, general academic interests/achievements, health fields. *Special Achievements/Activities:* general special achievements/activities, leadership. *Special Characteristics:* 59 awards ($173,185 total): children of union members/company employees. ***Tuition waivers:*** Full or partial for employees or children of employees, senior citizens. ***ROTC:*** Army cooperative, Naval cooperative.

LOANS ***Student loans:*** $5,302,031 (92% need-based, 8% non-need-based). 96% of past graduating class borrowed through all loan programs. Average indebtedness per student: $17,125. ***Average need-based loan:*** Undergraduates: $4282. ***Parent loans:*** $373,432 (100% non-need-based). ***Programs:*** FFEL (Subsidized and Unsubsidized Stafford, PLUS), Perkins, alternative loans.

WORK-STUDY ***Federal work-study:*** *Total amount:* $270,099; jobs available. ***State or other work-study/employment:*** *Total amount:* $20,000 (100% non-need-based). Part-time jobs available.

APPLYING for FINANCIAL AID ***Required financial aid forms:*** FAFSA, state aid form. ***Financial aid deadline (priority):*** 4/1. ***Notification date:*** Continuous. Students must reply by 5/1 or within 2 weeks of notification.

CONTACT Director of Financial Aid, Husson College, One College Circle, Bangor, ME 04401, 207-941-7156 or toll-free 800-4-HUSSON. *Fax:* 207-941-7988.

HUSTON-TILLOTSON COLLEGE

Austin, TX

Tuition & fees: $6350 **Average undergraduate aid package: $9852**

ABOUT THE INSTITUTION Independent interdenominational, coed. Awards: bachelor's degrees. 22 undergraduate majors. Total enrollment: 547. Undergraduates: 547. Freshmen: 118. Federal methodology is used as a basis for awarding need-based institutional aid.

UNDERGRADUATE EXPENSES for 1999–2000 ***Application fee:*** $25. ***Comprehensive fee:*** $11,032 includes full-time tuition ($6350) and room and board ($4682). Room and board charges vary according to housing facility. ***Part-time tuition:*** $175 per credit hour. ***Part-time fees:*** $225 per term part-time. Part-time tuition and fees vary according to course load. ***Payment plan:*** installment.

FRESHMAN FINANCIAL AID (Fall 1999, est.) *Average percent of need met:* 60% (excluding resources awarded to replace EFC). *Average financial aid package:* $8456 (excluding resources awarded to replace EFC).

UNDERGRADUATE FINANCIAL AID (Fall 1999, est.) *Average percent of need met:* 68% (excluding resources awarded to replace EFC). *Average financial aid package:* $9852 (excluding resources awarded to replace EFC).

GIFT AID (NEED-BASED) ***Total amount:*** $1,341,818 ***Scholarships, grants, and awards:*** Federal Pell, FSEOG, state, private, college/university gift aid from institutional funds.

GIFT AID (NON-NEED-BASED) ***Total amount:*** $96,353 ***Scholarships, grants, and awards by category:*** *Academic Interests/Achievement:* general academic interests/achievements. *Creative Arts/Performance:* music. *Special Characteristics:* general special characteristics. ***Tuition waivers:*** Full or partial for employees or children of employees.

LOANS ***Programs:*** FFEL (Subsidized and Unsubsidized Stafford, PLUS), alternative loans.

WORK-STUDY Federal work-study jobs available. ***State or other work-study/employment:*** Part-time jobs available.

APPLYING for FINANCIAL AID ***Required financial aid forms:*** FAFSA, institution's own form. ***Financial aid deadline (priority):*** 3/15. ***Notification date:*** Continuous. Students must reply within 2 weeks of notification.

CONTACT Sara L. Jackson, Director of Financial Aid, Huston-Tillotson College, 900 Chicon Street, Austin, TX 78702, 512-505-3030.

IDAHO STATE UNIVERSITY

Pocatello, ID

Tuition & fees (ID res): $2398 **Average undergraduate aid package: $9030**

ABOUT THE INSTITUTION State-supported, coed. Awards: associate, bachelor's, master's, doctoral, and first professional degrees and post-bachelor's and post-master's certificates. 83 undergraduate majors. Total enrollment: 12,666. Undergraduates: 10,403. Freshmen: 1,613. Federal methodology is used as a basis for awarding need-based institutional aid.

UNDERGRADUATE EXPENSES for 1999–2000 ***Application fee:*** $20. ***Tuition, state resident:*** full-time $0. ***Tuition, nonresident:*** full-time $6240; part-time $90 per credit. ***Required fees:*** full-time $2398; $119 per credit. Full-time tuition and fees vary according to reciprocity agreements. Part-time tuition and fees vary according to reciprocity agreements. ***College room and board:*** $3780; ***room only:*** $1640. Room and board charges vary according to board plan and housing facility. ***Payment plan:*** deferred payment.

FRESHMAN FINANCIAL AID (Fall 1998) 801 applied for aid; of those 96% were deemed to have need. 100% of freshmen with need received aid; of those 97% had need fully met. *Average percent of need met:* 80% (excluding resources awarded to replace EFC). *Average financial aid package:* $8127 (excluding resources awarded to replace EFC).

UNDERGRADUATE FINANCIAL AID (Fall 1998) 3,494 applied for aid; of those 95% were deemed to have need. 100% of undergraduates with need received aid; of those 97% had need fully met. *Average percent of need met:* 80% (excluding resources awarded to replace EFC). *Average financial aid package:* $9030 (excluding resources awarded to replace EFC).

GIFT AID (NEED-BASED) ***Total amount:*** $11,456,219 (95% Federal, 1% state, 4% external sources). ***Receiving aid:*** *Freshmen:* 23% (301); *all full-time undergraduates:* 29% (2,090). ***Average award:*** Freshmen: $2267; Undergraduates: $2519. ***Scholarships, grants, and awards:*** Federal Pell, FSEOG, state, private.

GIFT AID (NON-NEED-BASED) ***Total amount:*** $6,946,663 (5% Federal, 4% state, 32% institutional, 59% external sources). ***Receiving aid:*** *Freshmen:* 41% (549); *Undergraduates:* 33% (2,389). ***Scholarships, grants, and awards by category:*** *Academic Interests/Achievement:* 1,582 awards ($1,819,412 total): biological sciences, business, communication, computer science, education, engineering/technologies, English, foreign languages, general academic interests/achievements, health fields, home economics, humanities, international studies, mathematics, physical sciences, premedicine, religion/biblical studies, social sciences. *Creative Arts/Performance:* 174 awards ($59,747 total): art/fine arts, debating, music, performing arts, theater/drama. *Special Achievements/Activities:* 156 awards ($45,093 total): general special achievements/activities, junior miss, leadership, memberships, rodeo. *Special Characteristics:* 135 awards ($167,717 total): children and siblings of alumni, children of faculty/staff, first-generation college students, handicapped students, local/state students, members of minority groups, out-of-state students. ***Tuition waivers:*** Full or partial for employees or children of employees, senior citizens. ***ROTC:*** Army cooperative.

LOANS ***Student loans:*** $43,031,744 (58% need-based, 42% non-need-based). Average indebtedness per student: $17,657. ***Average need-based loan:*** Freshmen: $5339; Undergraduates: $5339. ***Parent loans:*** $334,021 (100% non-need-based). ***Programs:*** Federal Direct (Subsidized and Unsubsidized Stafford, PLUS), Perkins.

WORK-STUDY ***Federal work-study:*** *Total amount:* $827,204; 822 jobs averaging $1006. ***State or other work-study/employment:*** *Total amount:* $4,440,567 (10% need-based, 90% non-need-based). 2,205 part-time jobs averaging $2014.

ATHLETIC AWARDS *Total amount:* 1,818,242 (100% non-need-based).

APPLYING for FINANCIAL AID ***Required financial aid form:*** FAFSA. ***Financial aid deadline (priority):*** 3/15. ***Notification date:*** 5/1.

CONTACT Mr. Doug Severs, Director of Financial Aid, Idaho State University, Campus Box 8077, Pocatello, ID 83209, 208-236-2981. *Fax:* 208-236-4755. *E-mail:* sevedoug@isu.edu

ILLINOIS COLLEGE

Jacksonville, IL

Tuition & fees: $10,200 **Average undergraduate aid package: $10,043**

ABOUT THE INSTITUTION Independent interdenominational, coed. Awards: bachelor's degrees. 41 undergraduate majors. Total enrollment: 899. Undergraduates: 899. Freshmen: 240. Federal methodology is used as a basis for awarding need-based institutional aid.

UNDERGRADUATE EXPENSES for 1999–2000 ***Application fee:*** $10. ***Comprehensive fee:*** $14,700 includes full-time tuition ($10,200) and room and board ($4500). ***Part-time tuition:*** $425 per credit. ***Payment plans:*** installment, deferred payment.

FRESHMAN FINANCIAL AID (Fall 1998) 235 applied for aid; of those 81% were deemed to have need. 100% of freshmen with need received aid; of those 58% had need fully met. *Average percent of need met:* 97% (excluding resources awarded to replace EFC). *Average financial aid package:* $10,473 (excluding resources awarded to replace EFC). 16% of all full-time freshmen had no need and received non-need-based aid.

UNDERGRADUATE FINANCIAL AID (Fall 1998) 751 applied for aid; of those 87% were deemed to have need. 100% of undergraduates with need received aid; of those 59% had need fully met. *Average percent of need met:* 91% (excluding resources awarded to replace EFC). *Average financial aid package:* $10,043 (excluding resources awarded to replace EFC). 24% of all full-time undergraduates had no need and received non-need-based aid.

GIFT AID (NEED-BASED) ***Total amount:*** $3,285,782 (16% Federal, 55% state, 29% institutional). ***Receiving aid:*** *Freshmen:* 70% (169); *all full-time undergraduates:* 68% (600). ***Average award:*** Freshmen: $5372; Undergraduates: $5332. ***Scholarships, grants, and awards:*** Federal Pell, FSEOG, state, private, college/university gift aid from institutional funds.

GIFT AID (NON-NEED-BASED) ***Total amount:*** $1,467,245 (2% state, 79% institutional, 19% external sources). ***Receiving aid:*** *Freshmen:* 39% (94); *Undergraduates:* 38% (335). ***Scholarships, grants, and awards by category:*** *Academic Interests/Achievement:* general academic interests/achievements. *Creative Arts/Performance:* art/fine arts, debating, music. *Special Characteristics:* children of educators, children of faculty/staff, local/state students, members of minority groups, previous college experience. ***Tuition waivers:*** Full or partial for employees or children of employees.

LOANS ***Student loans:*** $2,905,863 (73% need-based, 27% non-need-based). 80% of past graduating class borrowed through all loan programs. Average indebtedness per student: $12,801. ***Average need-based loan:*** Freshmen: $3204; Undergraduates: $3695. ***Parent loans:*** $395,238 (100% non-need-based). ***Programs:*** FFEL (Subsidized and Unsubsidized Stafford, PLUS), Perkins.

WORK-STUDY ***Federal work-study:*** *Total amount:* $408,759; jobs available.

APPLYING for FINANCIAL AID ***Required financial aid form:*** FAFSA. ***Financial aid deadline (priority):*** 4/15. ***Notification date:*** Continuous. Students must reply within 2 weeks of notification.

CONTACT Kate Taylor, Director of Financial Aid, Illinois College, 1101 West College Avenue, Jacksonville, IL 62650-2299, 217-245-3035 or toll-free 888-595-3030. *Fax:* 217-245-3034. *E-mail:* finaid@hilltop.ic.edu

THE ILLINOIS INSTITUTE OF ART

Chicago, IL

Tuition & fees: $11,904 **Average undergraduate aid package: N/A**

ABOUT THE INSTITUTION Proprietary, coed. Awards: associate and bachelor's degrees. 5 undergraduate majors. Total enrollment: 805. Undergraduates: 805. Federal methodology is used as a basis for awarding need-based institutional aid.

UNDERGRADUATE EXPENSES for 1999–2000 ***Application fee:*** $50. ***One-time required fee:*** $50. ***Tuition:*** full-time $11,904; part-time $248 per credit. ***Payment plans:*** tuition prepayment, installment, deferred payment.

GIFT AID (NEED-BASED) ***Total amount:*** $457,987 (52% Federal, 48% external sources). ***Scholarships, grants, and awards:*** Federal Pell, FSEOG, college/university gift aid from institutional funds.

GIFT AID (NON-NEED-BASED) ***Scholarships, grants, and awards by category:*** *Academic Interests/Achievement:* general academic interests/achievements. *Creative Arts/Performance:* general creative arts/performance. ***Tuition waivers:*** Full or partial for employees or children of employees.

LOANS ***Student loans:*** $2,412,626 (53% need-based, 47% non-need-based). 77% of past graduating class borrowed through all loan programs. Average indebtedness per student: $15,800. ***Programs:*** FFEL (Subsidized and Unsubsidized Stafford, PLUS).

WORK-STUDY ***Federal work-study:*** *Total amount:* $13,870; jobs available.

APPLYING for FINANCIAL AID ***Required financial aid form:*** FAFSA. ***Financial aid deadline:*** Continuous.

CONTACT Mr. Joseph Payne, Director of Student Financial Services, The Illinois Institute of Art, 1000 Plaza Drive, Schaumburg, IL 60173, 800-314-3450 or toll-free 800-351-3450 Ext. 132.

THE ILLINOIS INSTITUTE OF ART AT SCHAUMBURG

Schaumberg, IL

CONTACT Financial Aid Office, The Illinois Institute of Art at Schaumburg, 1000 Plaza Drive, Schaumberg, IL 60173, 847-619-3450 or toll-free 800-314-3450.

ILLINOIS INSTITUTE OF TECHNOLOGY

Chicago, IL

Tuition & fees: $17,600 **Average undergraduate aid package: $18,080**

ABOUT THE INSTITUTION Independent, coed. Awards: bachelor's, master's, doctoral, and first professional degrees and post-bachelor's certificates. 21 undergraduate majors. Total enrollment: 6,062. Undergraduates: 1,706. Freshmen: 278. Federal methodology is used as a basis for awarding need-based institutional aid.

Illinois Institute of Technology (continued)

UNDERGRADUATE EXPENSES for 1999–2000 ***Application fee:*** $30. ***Comprehensive fee:*** $22,850 includes full-time tuition ($17,500), mandatory fees ($100), and room and board ($5250). ***College room only:*** $2350. Room and board charges vary according to board plan. ***Part-time tuition:*** $550 per semester hour. ***Part-time fees:*** $2 per semester hour. ***Payment plan:*** installment.

FRESHMAN FINANCIAL AID (Fall 1999, est.) 209 applied for aid; of those 91% were deemed to have need. 100% of freshmen with need received aid. *Average percent of need met:* 93% (excluding resources awarded to replace EFC). *Average financial aid package:* $20,600 (excluding resources awarded to replace EFC). 16% of all full-time freshmen had no need and received non-need-based aid.

UNDERGRADUATE FINANCIAL AID (Fall 1999, est.) 839 applied for aid; of those 85% were deemed to have need. 100% of undergraduates with need received aid. *Average percent of need met:* 97% (excluding resources awarded to replace EFC). *Average financial aid package:* $18,080 (excluding resources awarded to replace EFC). 13% of all full-time undergraduates had no need and received non-need-based aid.

GIFT AID (NEED-BASED) ***Total amount:*** $4,334,446 (22% Federal, 35% state, 43% institutional). ***Receiving aid:*** *Freshmen:* 35% (98); *all full-time undergraduates:* 22% (275). ***Average award:*** Freshmen: $6221; Undergraduates: $4699. ***Scholarships, grants, and awards:*** Federal Pell, FSEOG, state, private, college/university gift aid from institutional funds.

GIFT AID (NON-NEED-BASED) ***Total amount:*** $9,863,105 (9% Federal, 89% institutional, 2% external sources). ***Receiving aid:*** *Freshmen:* 16% (45); *Undergraduates:* 16% (203). ***Scholarships, grants, and awards by category:*** *Academic Interests/Achievement:* architecture, biological sciences, computer science, engineering/technologies, general academic interests/achievements, mathematics, physical sciences, premedicine, social sciences. *Special Achievements/Activities:* community service, general special achievements/activities, leadership, memberships. *Special Characteristics:* children and siblings of alumni, children of faculty/staff, ethnic background, general special characteristics, international students, local/state students, members of minority groups, out-of-state students, previous college experience, siblings of current students, spouses of current students. ***Tuition waivers:*** Full or partial for employees or children of employees. ***ROTC:*** Army, Naval, Air Force.

LOANS ***Student loans:*** $3,734,102 (71% need-based, 29% non-need-based). 74% of past graduating class borrowed through all loan programs. Average indebtedness per student: $19,138. ***Average need-based loan:*** Freshmen: $2033; Undergraduates: $3125. ***Parent loans:*** $1,421,579 (100% non-need-based). ***Programs:*** FFEL (Subsidized and Unsubsidized Stafford, PLUS), Perkins, college/university.

WORK-STUDY ***Federal work-study:*** *Total amount:* $640,130; 372 jobs averaging $1721.

ATHLETIC AWARDS *Total amount:* 382,639 (100% non-need-based).

APPLYING for FINANCIAL AID ***Required financial aid form:*** FAFSA. ***Financial aid deadline:*** Continuous. ***Notification date:*** 5/1. Students must reply within 2 weeks of notification.

CONTACT David Jeitner, Associate Director of Admissions, Illinois Institute of Technology, 10 West 33rd Street, Chicago, IL 60616, 312-567-6978 or toll-free 800-448-2329 (out-of-state).

ILLINOIS STATE UNIVERSITY

Normal, IL

Tuition & fees (IL res): $4340 **Average undergraduate aid package: $7120**

ABOUT THE INSTITUTION State-supported, coed. Awards: bachelor's, master's, and doctoral degrees and post-master's certificates. 53 undergraduate majors. Total enrollment: 20,470. Undergraduates: 17,705. Freshmen: 3,080. Federal methodology is used as a basis for awarding need-based institutional aid.

UNDERGRADUATE EXPENSES for 1999–2000 ***Tuition, state resident:*** full-time $3219; part-time $107 per credit. ***Tuition, nonresident:*** full-time $9657; part-time $322 per credit. ***Required fees:*** full-time $1121; $39 per credit. Full-time tuition and fees vary according to course load. Part-time tuition and fees vary according to course load. ***College room and board:*** $4238; ***room only:*** $2247. Room and board charges vary according to board plan. ***Payment plan:*** installment.

FRESHMAN FINANCIAL AID (Fall 1999) 2325 applied for aid; of those 57% were deemed to have need. 94% of freshmen with need received aid; of those 36% had need fully met. *Average percent of need met:* 82% (excluding resources awarded to replace EFC). *Average financial aid package:* $5911 (excluding resources awarded to replace EFC). 8% of all full-time freshmen had no need and received non-need-based aid.

UNDERGRADUATE FINANCIAL AID (Fall 1999) 11,092 applied for aid; of those 70% were deemed to have need. 96% of undergraduates with need received aid; of those 40% had need fully met. *Average percent of need met:* 82% (excluding resources awarded to replace EFC). *Average financial aid package:* $7120 (excluding resources awarded to replace EFC). 6% of all full-time undergraduates had no need and received non-need-based aid.

GIFT AID (NEED-BASED) ***Total amount:*** $26,941,164 (33% Federal, 64% state, 1% institutional, 2% external sources). ***Receiving aid:*** *Freshmen:* 27% (822); *all full-time undergraduates:* 30% (4,890). ***Average award:*** Freshmen: $4894; Undergraduates: $5240. ***Scholarships, grants, and awards:*** Federal Pell, FSEOG, state, private, college/university gift aid from institutional funds.

GIFT AID (NON-NEED-BASED) ***Total amount:*** $3,448,044 (17% Federal, 53% state, 11% institutional, 19% external sources). ***Receiving aid:*** *Freshmen:* 10% (321); *Undergraduates:* 8% (1,256). ***Scholarships, grants, and awards by category:*** *Academic Interests/Achievement:* agriculture, biological sciences, business, communication, computer science, education, engineering/technologies, English, foreign languages, general academic interests/achievements, health fields, home economics, humanities, international studies, library science, mathematics, military science, physical sciences, premedicine, social sciences. *Creative Arts/Performance:* applied art and design, art/fine arts, cinema/film/broadcasting, creative writing, debating, general creative arts/performance, music, performing arts, theater/drama. *Special Achievements/Activities:* community service, general special achievements/activities, hobbies/interests, leadership. *Special Characteristics:* children of faculty/staff, children of union members/company employees, children with a deceased or disabled parent, first-generation college students, general special characteristics, handicapped students, local/state students, members of minority groups, previous college experience, veterans, veterans' children. ***Tuition waivers:*** Full or partial for minority students, employees or children of employees, senior citizens. ***ROTC:*** Army.

LOANS ***Student loans:*** $37,114,601 (68% need-based, 32% non-need-based). 84% of past graduating class borrowed through all loan programs. Average indebtedness per student: $9283. ***Average need-based loan:*** Freshmen: $2350; Undergraduates: $3797. ***Parent loans:*** $6,636,317 (100% non-need-based). ***Programs:*** Federal Direct (Subsidized and Unsubsidized Stafford, PLUS), Perkins, college/university.

WORK-STUDY ***Federal work-study:*** *Total amount:* $2,234,706; 1,148 jobs averaging $1947. ***State or other work-study/employment:*** *Total amount:* $877,619 (11% need-based, 89% non-need-based). Part-time jobs available.

ATHLETIC AWARDS *Total amount:* 1,837,111 (25% need-based, 75% non-need-based).

APPLYING for FINANCIAL AID ***Required financial aid form:*** FAFSA. ***Financial aid deadline (priority):*** 3/1. ***Notification date:*** Continuous beginning 4/1.

CONTACT Mr. David Krueger, Acting Assistant Director of Financial Aid, Illinois State University, Campus Box 2320, Normal, IL 61790-2320, 309-438-2231 or toll-free 800-366-2478 (in-state). *E-mail:* askfao@ilstu.edu

ILLINOIS WESLEYAN UNIVERSITY

Bloomington, IL

Tuition & fees: $20,410 **Average undergraduate aid package: $15,664**

ABOUT THE INSTITUTION Independent, coed. Awards: bachelor's degrees. 50 undergraduate majors. Total enrollment: 2,091. Undergraduates: 2,091. Freshmen: 553. Both federal and institutional methodology are used as a basis for awarding need-based institutional aid.

UNDERGRADUATE EXPENSES for 2000–2001 ***Comprehensive fee:*** $25,560 includes full-time tuition ($20,284), mandatory fees ($126), and room and board ($5150). ***College room only:*** $3030. ***Payment plan:*** installment.

FRESHMAN FINANCIAL AID (Fall 1999, est.) 378 applied for aid; of those 96% were deemed to have need. 100% of freshmen with need received aid; of those 78% had need fully met. *Average percent of need met:* 99% (excluding resources awarded to replace EFC). *Average financial aid package:* $15,033 (excluding resources awarded to replace EFC). 25% of all full-time freshmen had no need and received non-need-based aid.

UNDERGRADUATE FINANCIAL AID (Fall 1999, est.) 1,458 applied for aid; of those 89% were deemed to have need. 100% of undergraduates with need received aid; of those 86% had need fully met. *Average percent of need met:* 99% (excluding resources awarded to replace EFC). *Average financial aid package:* $15,664 (excluding resources awarded to replace EFC). 26% of all full-time undergraduates had no need and received non-need-based aid.

GIFT AID (NEED-BASED) ***Total amount:*** $13,659,014 (5% Federal, 25% state, 66% institutional, 4% external sources). ***Receiving aid:*** *Freshmen:* 66% (363); *all full-time undergraduates:* 63% (1,302). ***Average award:*** Freshmen: $11,554; Undergraduates: $10,491. ***Scholarships, grants, and awards:*** Federal Pell, FSEOG, state, private, college/university gift aid from institutional funds.

GIFT AID (NON-NEED-BASED) ***Total amount:*** $3,736,360 (1% state, 93% institutional, 6% external sources). ***Receiving aid:*** *Freshmen:* 6% (34); *Undergraduates:* 3% (56). ***Scholarships, grants, and awards by category:*** *Academic Interests/Achievement:* 383 awards ($2,098,125 total): general academic interests/achievements. *Creative Arts/Performance:* 116 awards ($652,125 total): art/fine arts, music, theater/drama. *Special Achievements/Activities:* 43 awards ($179,020 total): community service, general special achievements/activities, hobbies/interests, leadership. *Special Characteristics:* 40 awards ($518,014 total): international students. ***Tuition waivers:*** Full or partial for employees or children of employees. ***ROTC:*** Army cooperative.

LOANS ***Student loans:*** $6,056,265 (87% need-based, 13% non-need-based). 78% of past graduating class borrowed through all loan programs. Average indebtedness per student: $16,258. ***Average need-based loan:*** Freshmen: $3244; Undergraduates: $4546. ***Parent loans:*** $918,081 (100% non-need-based). ***Programs:*** FFEL (Subsidized and Unsubsidized Stafford, PLUS), Perkins, Federal Nursing, college/university.

WORK-STUDY ***Federal work-study:*** *Total amount:* $445,528; 250 jobs averaging $1780. ***State or other work-study/employment:*** *Total amount:* $1,135,723 (90% need-based, 10% non-need-based). 692 part-time jobs averaging $1641.

APPLYING for FINANCIAL AID ***Required financial aid forms:*** FAFSA, institution's own form, CSS Financial Aid PROFILE, business/farm supplement. ***Financial aid deadline:*** 3/1. ***Notification date:*** Continuous. Students must reply within 4 weeks of notification.

CONTACT Mr. Lynn Nichelson, Director of Financial Aid, Illinois Wesleyan University, 1312 North Park Street, PO Box 2900, Bloomington, IL 61702-2900, 309-556-3096 or toll-free 800-332-2498. *Fax:* 309-556-3411. *E-mail:* lnichels@titan.iwu.edu

IMMACULATA COLLEGE

Immaculata, PA

Tuition & fees: $13,400 **Average undergraduate aid package: $13,689**

ABOUT THE INSTITUTION Independent Roman Catholic, women only. Awards: associate, bachelor's, master's, and doctoral degrees. 53 undergraduate majors. Total enrollment: 3,005. Undergraduates: 2,360. Freshmen: 121. Federal methodology is used as a basis for awarding need-based institutional aid.

UNDERGRADUATE EXPENSES for 1999–2000 ***Application fee:*** $25. ***Comprehensive fee:*** $19,900 includes full-time tuition ($13,100), mandatory fees ($300), and room and board ($6500). ***College room only:*** $3450. ***Part-time tuition:*** $255 per credit. ***Payment plan:*** installment.

FRESHMAN FINANCIAL AID (Fall 1999) 120 applied for aid; of those 80% were deemed to have need. 100% of freshmen with need received aid; of those 27% had need fully met. *Average percent of need met:* 53% (excluding resources awarded to replace EFC). *Average financial aid package:* $11,723 (excluding resources awarded to replace EFC). 8% of all full-time freshmen had no need and received non-need-based aid.

UNDERGRADUATE FINANCIAL AID (Fall 1999) 388 applied for aid; of those 76% were deemed to have need. 100% of undergraduates with need received aid; of those 27% had need fully met. *Average percent of need met:* 48% (excluding resources awarded to replace EFC). *Average financial aid package:* $13,689 (excluding resources awarded to replace EFC). 7% of all full-time undergraduates had no need and received non-need-based aid.

GIFT AID (NEED-BASED) ***Total amount:*** $1,278,935 (18% Federal, 25% state, 47% institutional, 10% external sources). ***Receiving aid:*** *Freshmen:* 66% (79); *all full-time undergraduates:* 53% (211). ***Average award:*** Freshmen: $2577; Undergraduates: $2040. ***Scholarships, grants, and awards:*** Federal Pell, FSEOG, state, private, college/university gift aid from institutional funds.

GIFT AID (NON-NEED-BASED) ***Total amount:*** $2,317,414 (100% institutional). ***Receiving aid:*** *Freshmen:* 80% (96); *Undergraduates:* 75% (296). ***Scholarships, grants, and awards by category:*** *Academic Interests/Achievement:* general academic interests/achievements. *Creative Arts/Performance:* music. *Special Achievements/Activities:* community service, leadership, memberships, religious involvement. *Special Characteristics:* children of faculty/staff, relatives of clergy, siblings of current students. ***Tuition waivers:*** Full or partial for employees or children of employees, senior citizens.

LOANS ***Student loans:*** $1,334,884 (100% need-based). 90% of past graduating class borrowed through all loan programs. Average indebtedness per student: $17,125. ***Average need-based loan:*** Freshmen: $2625; Undergraduates: $4833. ***Parent loans:*** $547,134 (100% non-need-based). ***Programs:*** FFEL (Subsidized and Unsubsidized Stafford, PLUS), Perkins.

WORK-STUDY ***Federal work-study:*** *Total amount:* $152,350; 165 jobs averaging $938. ***State or other work-study/employment:*** *Total amount:* $90,550 (100% non-need-based). Part-time jobs available.

APPLYING for FINANCIAL AID ***Required financial aid form:*** FAFSA. ***Financial aid deadline:*** Continuous. ***Notification date:*** Continuous beginning 3/15.

CONTACT Mr. Ken Rasp, Dean, Enrollment Services, Immaculata College, 1145 King Road, Box 500, Immaculata, PA 19345-0500, 610-647-4400 or toll-free 877-428-6328. *Fax:* 610-251-1668.

INDIANA INSTITUTE OF TECHNOLOGY

Fort Wayne, IN

Tuition & fees: $12,300 **Average undergraduate aid package: $9125**

ABOUT THE INSTITUTION Independent, coed. Awards: associate, bachelor's, and master's degrees. 15 undergraduate majors. Total enrollment: 1,931. Undergraduates: 1,931. Freshmen: 304. Federal methodology is used as a basis for awarding need-based institutional aid.

UNDERGRADUATE EXPENSES for 1999–2000 ***Application fee:*** $25. ***Comprehensive fee:*** $16,864 includes full-time tuition ($12,300) and room and board ($4564). Full-time tuition and fees vary according to course load. Room and board charges vary according to housing facility and student level. ***Part-time tuition:*** $2968 per term. Part-time tuition and fees vary according to class time and course load. ***Payment plan:*** deferred payment.

FRESHMAN FINANCIAL AID (Fall 1999, est.) 148 applied for aid; of those 93% were deemed to have need. 100% of freshmen with need received aid; of those 8% had need fully met. *Average percent of need met:* 63% (excluding resources awarded to replace EFC). *Average financial aid package:* $9998 (excluding resources awarded to replace EFC).

UNDERGRADUATE FINANCIAL AID (Fall 1999, est.) 529 applied for aid; of those 91% were deemed to have need. 100% of undergraduates with need received aid; of those 17% had need fully met. *Average percent of*

Indiana Institute of Technology (continued)

need met: 70% (excluding resources awarded to replace EFC). *Average financial aid package:* $9125 (excluding resources awarded to replace EFC).

GIFT AID (NEED-BASED) ***Total amount:*** $3,497,359 (16% Federal, 18% state, 57% institutional, 9% external sources). ***Receiving aid:*** *Freshmen:* 135; *all full-time undergraduates:* 445. ***Average award:*** Freshmen: $7164; Undergraduates: $6789. ***Scholarships, grants, and awards:*** Federal Pell, FSEOG, state, private, college/university gift aid from institutional funds.

GIFT AID (NON-NEED-BASED) ***Total amount:*** $89,601 (16% institutional, 84% external sources). ***Receiving aid:*** *Freshmen:* 9; *Undergraduates:* 37. ***Scholarships, grants, and awards by category:*** *Academic Interests/Achievement:* business, computer science, engineering/technologies, general academic interests/achievements. *Special Characteristics:* children of faculty/staff, local/state students, out-of-state students, siblings of current students. ***Tuition waivers:*** Full or partial for employees or children of employees.

LOANS ***Student loans:*** $2,458,772 (73% need-based, 27% non-need-based). Average indebtedness per student: $16,500. ***Average need-based loan:*** Freshmen: $2827; Undergraduates: $3035. ***Parent loans:*** $394,056 (58% need-based, 42% non-need-based). ***Programs:*** FFEL (Subsidized and Unsubsidized Stafford, PLUS), Perkins.

WORK-STUDY ***Federal work-study:*** *Total amount:* $64,372; jobs available. ***State or other work-study/employment:*** *Total amount:* $94,194 (89% need-based, 11% non-need-based). Part-time jobs available.

ATHLETIC AWARDS *Total amount:* 611,045 (83% need-based, 17% non-need-based).

APPLYING for FINANCIAL AID ***Required financial aid forms:*** FAFSA, institution's own form. ***Financial aid deadline (priority):*** 3/1. ***Notification date:*** Continuous. Students must reply within 2 weeks of notification.

CONTACT Ms. Teresa M. Vasquez, Director of Financial Aid, Indiana Institute of Technology, 1600 East Washington Boulevard, Fort Wayne, IN 46803-1297, 800-937-2448 Ext. 2208 or toll-free 800-937-2448 (in-state), 888-666-TECH (out-of-state). *Fax:* 219-422-1578. *E-mail:* vasquez@indtech.edu

INDIANA STATE UNIVERSITY

Terre Haute, IN

Tuition & fees (IN res): $3426 **Average undergraduate aid package: $5573**

ABOUT THE INSTITUTION State-supported, coed. Awards: associate, bachelor's, master's, doctoral, and first professional degrees. 149 undergraduate majors. Total enrollment: 10,985. Undergraduates: 9,334. Freshmen: 2,075. Federal methodology is used as a basis for awarding need-based institutional aid.

UNDERGRADUATE EXPENSES for 1999–2000 ***Application fee:*** $20. ***Tuition, state resident:*** full-time $3426; part-time $123 per credit hour. ***Tuition, nonresident:*** full-time $8554; part-time $300 per credit hour. Full-time tuition and fees vary according to course load. Part-time tuition and fees vary according to course load. ***College room and board:*** $4434. Room and board charges vary according to board plan and housing facility. ***Payment plans:*** installment, deferred payment.

FRESHMAN FINANCIAL AID (Fall 1999) 1545 applied for aid; of those 73% were deemed to have need. 98% of freshmen with need received aid; of those 16% had need fully met. *Average percent of need met:* 70% (excluding resources awarded to replace EFC). *Average financial aid package:* $4460 (excluding resources awarded to replace EFC). 7% of all full-time freshmen had no need and received non-need-based aid.

UNDERGRADUATE FINANCIAL AID (Fall 1999) 5,162 applied for aid; of those 81% were deemed to have need. 93% of undergraduates with need received aid; of those 26% had need fully met. *Average percent of need met:* 73% (excluding resources awarded to replace EFC). *Average financial aid package:* $5573 (excluding resources awarded to replace EFC). 4% of all full-time undergraduates had no need and received non-need-based aid.

GIFT AID (NEED-BASED) ***Total amount:*** $10,147,725 (55% Federal, 45% state). ***Receiving aid:*** *Freshmen:* 35% (671); *all full-time undergraduates:* 33% (2,433). ***Average award:*** Freshmen: $3405; Undergraduates: $3311. ***Scholarships, grants, and awards:*** Federal Pell, FSEOG, state, private, college/university gift aid from institutional funds.

GIFT AID (NON-NEED-BASED) ***Total amount:*** $4,929,309 (15% state, 65% institutional, 20% external sources). ***Receiving aid:*** *Freshmen:* 19% (358); *Undergraduates:* 14% (1,073). ***Scholarships, grants, and awards by category:*** *Academic Interests/Achievement:* general academic interests/achievements. *Creative Arts/Performance:* art/fine arts, performing arts. *Special Characteristics:* children and siblings of alumni, children of faculty/staff, children with a deceased or disabled parent, members of minority groups, veterans' children. ***Tuition waivers:*** Full or partial for employees or children of employees. ***ROTC:*** Army, Air Force.

LOANS ***Student loans:*** $17,690,638 (98% need-based, 2% non-need-based). 43% of past graduating class borrowed through all loan programs. Average indebtedness per student: $4129. ***Average need-based loan:*** Freshmen: $2811; Undergraduates: $4204. ***Parent loans:*** $2,344,809 (100% non-need-based). ***Programs:*** Federal Direct (Subsidized and Unsubsidized Stafford, PLUS), Perkins, college/university.

WORK-STUDY ***Federal work-study:*** *Total amount:* $443,450; 417 jobs averaging $1053. ***State or other work-study/employment:*** *Total amount:* $7060 (100% need-based). 5 part-time jobs averaging $1412.

ATHLETIC AWARDS *Total amount:* 1,702,283 (100% non-need-based).

APPLYING for FINANCIAL AID ***Required financial aid form:*** FAFSA. ***Financial aid deadline (priority):*** 3/1. ***Notification date:*** Continuous beginning 4/15.

CONTACT Ms. Kathleen White, Associate Director, Client Services, Indiana State University, Tirey Hall, Room 150, Terre Haute, IN 47809-1401, 812-237-7711 or toll-free 800-742-0891. *Fax:* 812-237-4330.

INDIANA UNIVERSITY BLOOMINGTON

Bloomington, IN

Tuition & fees (IN res): $4212 **Average undergraduate aid package: $6335**

ABOUT THE INSTITUTION State-supported, coed. Awards: associate, bachelor's, master's, doctoral, and first professional degrees. 140 undergraduate majors. Total enrollment: 36,201. Undergraduates: 28,511. Freshmen: 6,583. Federal methodology is used as a basis for awarding need-based institutional aid.

UNDERGRADUATE EXPENSES for 1999–2000 ***Application fee:*** $40. ***Tuition, state resident:*** full-time $3752. ***Tuition, nonresident:*** full-time $12,460. ***Required fees:*** full-time $460. Part-time tuition and fees vary according to course load. ***College room and board:*** $5492; ***room only:*** $2892. Room and board charges vary according to board plan and housing facility. ***Payment plan:*** deferred payment.

FRESHMAN FINANCIAL AID (Fall 1999, est.) 4382 applied for aid; of those 60% were deemed to have need. 95% of freshmen with need received aid; of those 20% had need fully met. *Average percent of need met:* 69% (excluding resources awarded to replace EFC). *Average financial aid package:* $6085 (excluding resources awarded to replace EFC). 27% of all full-time freshmen had no need and received non-need-based aid.

UNDERGRADUATE FINANCIAL AID (Fall 1999, est.) 14,604 applied for aid; of those 67% were deemed to have need. 96% of undergraduates with need received aid; of those 21% had need fully met. *Average percent of need met:* 71% (excluding resources awarded to replace EFC). *Average financial aid package:* $6335 (excluding resources awarded to replace EFC). 21% of all full-time undergraduates had no need and received non-need-based aid.

GIFT AID (NEED-BASED) ***Total amount:*** $21,199,745 (44% Federal, 41% state, 15% institutional). ***Receiving aid:*** *Freshmen:* 23% (1,471); *all full-time undergraduates:* 21% (5,378). ***Average award:*** Freshmen: $4215; Undergraduates: $3803. ***Scholarships, grants, and awards:*** Federal Pell, FSEOG, state, private, college/university gift aid from institutional funds.

GIFT AID (NON-NEED-BASED) ***Total amount:*** $17,437,692 (2% state, 84% institutional, 14% external sources). ***Receiving aid:*** *Freshmen:* 17% (1,124); *Undergraduates:* 12% (3,083). ***Scholarships, grants, and awards by category:*** *Academic Interests/Achievement:* general academic interests/achievements. *Creative Arts/Performance:* general creative arts/performance.

Special Achievements/Activities: general special achievements/activities. *Special Characteristics:* general special characteristics. ***Tuition waivers:*** Full or partial for employees or children of employees. ***ROTC:*** Army, Air Force.

LOANS ***Student loans:*** $49,944,309 (60% need-based, 40% non-need-based). ***Average need-based loan:*** Freshmen: $2957; Undergraduates: $3776. ***Parent loans:*** $18,989,927 (100% non-need-based). ***Programs:*** Federal Direct (Subsidized and Unsubsidized Stafford, PLUS), Perkins, Federal Nursing, college/university.

WORK-STUDY ***Federal work-study:*** *Total amount:* $2,069,000; 1,390 jobs averaging $1488.

ATHLETIC AWARDS *Total amount:* 2,264,540 (100% non-need-based).

APPLYING for FINANCIAL AID ***Required financial aid forms:*** FAFSA, institution's own form. ***Financial aid deadline (priority):*** 3/1. ***Notification date:*** Continuous beginning 5/1.

CONTACT Automated Client Inquiry System, Indiana University Bloomington, Franklin Hall, Room 208, Bloomington, IN 47405, 812-855-RSVP. *Fax:* 812-856-RSVP. *E-mail:* rsvposfa@indiana.edu

INDIANA UNIVERSITY EAST

Richmond, IN

Tuition & fees (IN res): $3104 Average undergraduate aid package: $6115

ABOUT THE INSTITUTION State-supported, coed. Awards: associate and bachelor's degrees. 21 undergraduate majors. Total enrollment: 2,254. Undergraduates: 2,215. Freshmen: 420. Federal methodology is used as a basis for awarding need-based institutional aid.

UNDERGRADUATE EXPENSES for 1999–2000 ***Application fee:*** $25. ***Tuition, state resident:*** full-time $2922; part-time $97 per credit hour. ***Tuition, nonresident:*** full-time $7692; part-time $256 per credit hour. ***Required fees:*** full-time $182. Full-time tuition and fees vary according to course load. Part-time tuition and fees vary according to course load. ***Payment plan:*** deferred payment.

FRESHMAN FINANCIAL AID (Fall 1999, est.) 226 applied for aid; of those 75% were deemed to have need. 94% of freshmen with need received aid; of those 29% had need fully met. *Average percent of need met:* 71% (excluding resources awarded to replace EFC). *Average financial aid package:* $5257 (excluding resources awarded to replace EFC). 12% of all full-time freshmen had no need and received non-need-based aid.

UNDERGRADUATE FINANCIAL AID (Fall 1999, est.) 836 applied for aid; of those 82% were deemed to have need. 96% of undergraduates with need received aid; of those 21% had need fully met. *Average percent of need met:* 69% (excluding resources awarded to replace EFC). *Average financial aid package:* $6115 (excluding resources awarded to replace EFC). 9% of all full-time undergraduates had no need and received non-need-based aid.

GIFT AID (NEED-BASED) ***Total amount:*** $2,359,705 (62% Federal, 36% state, 2% institutional). ***Receiving aid:*** *Freshmen:* 51% (127); *all full-time undergraduates:* 53% (523). ***Average award:*** Freshmen: $3017; Undergraduates: $3298. ***Scholarships, grants, and awards:*** Federal Pell, FSEOG, state, private, college/university gift aid from institutional funds.

GIFT AID (NON-NEED-BASED) ***Total amount:*** $444,157 (14% Federal, 25% state, 35% institutional, 26% external sources). ***Receiving aid:*** *Freshmen:* 20% (49); *Undergraduates:* 22% (219). ***Scholarships, grants, and awards by category:*** *Academic Interests/Achievement:* general academic interests/achievements. *Creative Arts/Performance:* general creative arts/performance. *Special Achievements/Activities:* general special achievements/activities. *Special Characteristics:* general special characteristics. ***Tuition waivers:*** Full or partial for employees or children of employees.

LOANS ***Student loans:*** $2,863,433 (58% need-based, 42% non-need-based). ***Average need-based loan:*** Freshmen: $2043; Undergraduates: $2688. ***Parent loans:*** $21,890 (100% non-need-based). ***Programs:*** FFEL (Subsidized and Unsubsidized Stafford, PLUS), Perkins, Federal Nursing, college/university.

WORK-STUDY ***Federal work-study:*** *Total amount:* $1,535,091; 428 jobs averaging $3587.

APPLYING for FINANCIAL AID ***Required financial aid forms:*** FAFSA, institution's own form. ***Financial aid deadline (priority):*** 3/1. ***Notification date:*** Continuous beginning 5/1.

CONTACT Pat Lemmons, Financial Aid Director, Indiana University East, 2325 Chester Boulevard, Whitewater Hall, Richmond, IN 47374-1289, 765-973-8231 or toll-free 800-959-3278. *Fax:* 765-973-8388. *E-mail:* plemmons@indiana.edu

INDIANA UNIVERSITY KOKOMO

Kokomo, IN

Tuition & fees (IN res): $3104 Average undergraduate aid package: $4437

ABOUT THE INSTITUTION State-supported, coed. Awards: associate, bachelor's, and master's degrees. 17 undergraduate majors. Total enrollment: 2,634. Undergraduates: 2,326. Freshmen: 434. Federal methodology is used as a basis for awarding need-based institutional aid.

UNDERGRADUATE EXPENSES for 1999–2000 ***Application fee:*** $30. ***Tuition, state resident:*** full-time $2922; part-time $97 per credit hour. ***Tuition, nonresident:*** full-time $7692; part-time $256 per credit hour. ***Required fees:*** full-time $182. Full-time tuition and fees vary according to course load. Part-time tuition and fees vary according to course load.

FRESHMAN FINANCIAL AID (Fall 1999, est.) 184 applied for aid; of those 57% were deemed to have need. 93% of freshmen with need received aid; of those 11% had need fully met. *Average percent of need met:* 63% (excluding resources awarded to replace EFC). *Average financial aid package:* $3691 (excluding resources awarded to replace EFC). 25% of all full-time freshmen had no need and received non-need-based aid.

UNDERGRADUATE FINANCIAL AID (Fall 1999, est.) 641 applied for aid; of those 68% were deemed to have need. 96% of undergraduates with need received aid; of those 13% had need fully met. *Average percent of need met:* 63% (excluding resources awarded to replace EFC). *Average financial aid package:* $4437 (excluding resources awarded to replace EFC). 17% of all full-time undergraduates had no need and received non-need-based aid.

GIFT AID (NEED-BASED) ***Total amount:*** $1,415,222 (57% Federal, 38% state, 5% institutional). ***Receiving aid:*** *Freshmen:* 24% (70); *all full-time undergraduates:* 28% (295). ***Average award:*** Freshmen: $3298; Undergraduates: $3517. ***Scholarships, grants, and awards:*** Federal Pell, FSEOG, state, private, college/university gift aid from institutional funds.

GIFT AID (NON-NEED-BASED) ***Total amount:*** $463,983 (29% Federal, 49% institutional, 22% external sources). ***Receiving aid:*** *Freshmen:* 13% (38); *Undergraduates:* 12% (126). ***Scholarships, grants, and awards by category:*** *Academic Interests/Achievement:* general academic interests/achievements. *Creative Arts/Performance:* general creative arts/performance. *Special Achievements/Activities:* general special achievements/activities. *Special Characteristics:* general special characteristics. ***Tuition waivers:*** Full or partial for employees or children of employees. ***ROTC:*** Army cooperative.

LOANS ***Student loans:*** $1,560,871 (58% need-based, 42% non-need-based). ***Average need-based loan:*** Freshmen: $2069; Undergraduates: $2845. ***Parent loans:*** $28,886 (100% non-need-based). ***Programs:*** FFEL (Subsidized and Unsubsidized Stafford, PLUS), Perkins, Federal Nursing, college/university.

WORK-STUDY ***Federal work-study:*** *Total amount:* $67,675; 47 jobs averaging $1440.

APPLYING for FINANCIAL AID ***Required financial aid forms:*** FAFSA, institution's own form. ***Financial aid deadline (priority):*** 3/1. ***Notification date:*** Continuous beginning 5/1.

CONTACT Julie Chism, Counselor, Indiana University Kokomo, 2300 South Washington Street, PO Box 9003, Kelley Student Center, Room 201H, Kokomo, IN 46904-9003, 765-455-9431 or toll-free 888-875-4485. *E-mail:* jchism@iukfs1.iuk.indiana.edu

INDIANA UNIVERSITY NORTHWEST

Gary, IN

Tuition & fees (IN res): $3128 **Average undergraduate aid package: $5105**

ABOUT THE INSTITUTION State-supported, coed. Awards: associate, bachelor's, and master's degrees. 44 undergraduate majors. Total enrollment: 4,748. Undergraduates: 4,170. Freshmen: 680. Federal methodology is used as a basis for awarding need-based institutional aid.

UNDERGRADUATE EXPENSES for 1999–2000 ***Application fee:*** $25. ***Tuition, state resident:*** full-time $2922; part-time $97 per credit hour. ***Tuition, nonresident:*** full-time $7692; part-time $256 per credit hour. ***Required fees:*** full-time $206. Full-time tuition and fees vary according to course load. Part-time tuition and fees vary according to course load. ***Payment plans:*** installment, deferred payment.

FRESHMAN FINANCIAL AID (Fall 1999, est.) 328 applied for aid; of those 77% were deemed to have need. 95% of freshmen with need received aid; of those 11% had need fully met. *Average percent of need met:* 60% (excluding resources awarded to replace EFC). *Average financial aid package:* $4362 (excluding resources awarded to replace EFC). 13% of all full-time freshmen had no need and received non-need-based aid.

UNDERGRADUATE FINANCIAL AID (Fall 1999, est.) 1,443 applied for aid; of those 81% were deemed to have need. 97% of undergraduates with need received aid; of those 14% had need fully met. *Average percent of need met:* 64% (excluding resources awarded to replace EFC). *Average financial aid package:* $5105 (excluding resources awarded to replace EFC). 13% of all full-time undergraduates had no need and received non-need-based aid.

GIFT AID (NEED-BASED) ***Total amount:*** $4,204,367 (67% Federal, 33% state). ***Receiving aid:*** *Freshmen:* 35% (188); *all full-time undergraduates:* 40% (885). ***Average award:*** Freshmen: $3298; Undergraduates: $3517. ***Scholarships, grants, and awards:*** Federal Pell, FSEOG, state, private, college/university gift aid from institutional funds, Federal Nursing.

GIFT AID (NON-NEED-BASED) ***Total amount:*** $442,071 (22% Federal, 59% institutional, 19% external sources). ***Receiving aid:*** *Freshmen:* 6% (30); *Undergraduates:* 6% (130). ***Scholarships, grants, and awards by category:*** *Academic Interests/Achievement:* general academic interests/achievements. *Creative Arts/Performance:* general creative arts/performance. *Special Achievements/Activities:* general special achievements/activities. *Special Characteristics:* general special characteristics. ***Tuition waivers:*** Full or partial for employees or children of employees, senior citizens. ***ROTC:*** Army.

LOANS ***Student loans:*** $3,880,070 (64% need-based, 36% non-need-based). ***Average need-based loan:*** Freshmen: $2167; Undergraduates: $2731. ***Parent loans:*** $31,836 (100% non-need-based). ***Programs:*** FFEL (Subsidized and Unsubsidized Stafford, PLUS), Perkins, college/university.

WORK-STUDY ***Federal work-study:*** *Total amount:* $539,601; 208 jobs averaging $2594.

APPLYING for FINANCIAL AID ***Required financial aid forms:*** FAFSA, institution's own form. ***Financial aid deadline (priority):*** 3/1. ***Notification date:*** Continuous beginning 5/1.

CONTACT James Frybort, Counselor, Indiana University Northwest, 3400 Broadway, Hawthorn Hall, Room 101, Gary, IN 46408-1197, 219-980-6881 or toll-free 800-437-5409. *Fax:* 219-981-4219. *E-mail:* jfrybort@iunhaw1.iun.indiana.edu

INDIANA UNIVERSITY OF PENNSYLVANIA

Indiana, PA

Tuition & fees (PA res): $4397 **Average undergraduate aid package: $6483**

ABOUT THE INSTITUTION State-supported, coed. Awards: associate, bachelor's, master's, and doctoral degrees. 78 undergraduate majors. Total enrollment: 13,442. Undergraduates: 11,892. Freshmen: 2,575. Both federal and institutional methodology are used as a basis for awarding need-based institutional aid.

UNDERGRADUATE EXPENSES for 1999–2000 ***Application fee:*** $30. ***Tuition, state resident:*** full-time $3618; part-time $150 per semester hour. ***Tuition, nonresident:*** full-time $9046; part-time $377 per semester hour. ***Required fees:*** full-time $779; $186 per term part-time. Full-time tuition and fees vary according to course load and location. Part-time tuition and fees vary according to course load and location. ***College room and board:*** $3782; ***room only:*** $2100. Room and board charges vary according to board plan and housing facility. ***Payment plans:*** installment, deferred payment.

FRESHMAN FINANCIAL AID (Fall 1998) 2204 applied for aid; of those 97% were deemed to have need. 95% of freshmen with need received aid; of those 53% had need fully met. *Average percent of need met:* 84% (excluding resources awarded to replace EFC). *Average financial aid package:* $6006 (excluding resources awarded to replace EFC). 4% of all full-time freshmen had no need and received non-need-based aid.

UNDERGRADUATE FINANCIAL AID (Fall 1998) 9,370 applied for aid; of those 95% were deemed to have need. 95% of undergraduates with need received aid; of those 53% had need fully met. *Average percent of need met:* 92% (excluding resources awarded to replace EFC). *Average financial aid package:* $6483 (excluding resources awarded to replace EFC). 14% of all full-time undergraduates had no need and received non-need-based aid.

GIFT AID (NEED-BASED) ***Total amount:*** $18,802,414 (51% Federal, 49% state). ***Receiving aid:*** *Freshmen:* 46% (1,189); *all full-time undergraduates:* 57% (6,170). ***Average award:*** Freshmen: $3135; Undergraduates: $3190. ***Scholarships, grants, and awards:*** Federal Pell, FSEOG, state, private, college/university gift aid from institutional funds.

GIFT AID (NON-NEED-BASED) ***Total amount:*** $2,485,687 (50% institutional, 50% external sources). ***Receiving aid:*** *Freshmen:* 16% (406); *Undergraduates:* 12% (1,345). ***Scholarships, grants, and awards by category:*** *Academic Interests/Achievement:* area/ethnic studies, biological sciences, business, communication, computer science, education, engineering/technologies, English, foreign languages, general academic interests/achievements, health fields, home economics, humanities, international studies, mathematics, physical sciences, premedicine, social sciences. *Creative Arts/Performance:* applied art and design, art/fine arts, dance, general creative arts/performance, journalism/publications, music, performing arts, theater/drama. *Special Achievements/Activities:* community service, general special achievements/activities, hobbies/interests, leadership. *Special Characteristics:* adult students, ethnic background. ***Tuition waivers:*** Full or partial for minority students, employees or children of employees. ***ROTC:*** Army.

LOANS ***Student loans:*** $39,428,086 (69% need-based, 31% non-need-based). 60% of past graduating class borrowed through all loan programs. Average indebtedness per student: $10,000. ***Average need-based loan:*** Freshmen: $3080; Undergraduates: $3920. ***Parent loans:*** $3,406,028 (100% non-need-based). ***Programs:*** FFEL (Subsidized and Unsubsidized Stafford, PLUS), Perkins.

WORK-STUDY ***Federal work-study:*** *Total amount:* $1,955,888; 1,867 jobs available. ***State or other work-study/employment:*** *Total amount:* $4,104,164 (100% non-need-based). Part-time jobs available.

ATHLETIC AWARDS *Total amount:* 533,751 (100% non-need-based).

APPLYING for FINANCIAL AID ***Required financial aid forms:*** FAFSA, state aid form. ***Financial aid deadline:*** 4/15. ***Notification date:*** Continuous beginning 6/1.

CONTACT Mr. Frederick A. Joseph, Director of Financial Aid, Indiana University of Pennsylvania, 308 Pratt Hall, Indiana, PA 15705, 724-357-2218 or toll-free 800-442-6830. *Fax:* 724-357-4079. *E-mail:* fajoseph@grove.iup.edu

INDIANA UNIVERSITY–PURDUE UNIVERSITY FORT WAYNE

Fort Wayne, IN

Tuition & fees (IN res): $2827 **Average undergraduate aid package: N/A**

ABOUT THE INSTITUTION State-supported, coed. Awards: associate, bachelor's, and master's degrees and post-bachelor's certificates. 73

undergraduate majors. Total enrollment: 10,556. Undergraduates: 9,733. Freshmen: 1,604. Federal methodology is used as a basis for awarding need-based institutional aid.

UNDERGRADUATE EXPENSES for 1999–2000 ***Application fee:*** $30. ***Tuition, state resident:*** full-time $2551; part-time $106 per semester hour. ***Tuition, nonresident:*** full-time $6252; part-time $260 per semester hour. ***Required fees:*** full-time $276; $12 per semester hour. Full-time tuition and fees vary according to course load. Part-time tuition and fees vary according to course load. ***Payment plans:*** installment, deferred payment.

FRESHMAN FINANCIAL AID (Fall 1998) 602 applied for aid; of those 72% were deemed to have need. 94% of freshmen with need received aid; of those 27% had need fully met. *Average percent of need met:* 67% (excluding resources awarded to replace EFC).

UNDERGRADUATE FINANCIAL AID (Fall 1998) 2,408 applied for aid; of those 76% were deemed to have need. 95% of undergraduates with need received aid; of those 40% had need fully met. *Average percent of need met:* 83% (excluding resources awarded to replace EFC).

GIFT AID (NEED-BASED) ***Total amount:*** $7,000,451 (48% Federal, 30% state, 5% institutional, 17% external sources). ***Receiving aid:*** *Freshmen:* 30% (276); *all full-time undergraduates:* 29% (1,121). ***Scholarships, grants, and awards:*** Federal Pell, FSEOG, state, private.

GIFT AID (NON-NEED-BASED) ***Receiving aid:*** *Freshmen:* 3% (26); *Undergraduates:* 2% (94). ***Scholarships, grants, and awards by category:*** *Academic Interests/Achievement:* biological sciences, business, communication, computer science, education, engineering/technologies, English, foreign languages, general academic interests/achievements, health fields, humanities, mathematics, physical sciences, premedicine, social sciences. *Creative Arts/Performance:* art/fine arts, music, theater/drama. *Special Characteristics:* children and siblings of alumni, children of faculty/staff, children with a deceased or disabled parent, handicapped students, local/state students, spouses of deceased or disabled public servants. ***Tuition waivers:*** Full or partial for employees or children of employees, senior citizens.

LOANS ***Student loans:*** $12,732,296 (53% need-based, 47% non-need-based). 40% of past graduating class borrowed through all loan programs. Average indebtedness per student: $8088. ***Parent loans:*** $88,526 (100% need-based). ***Programs:*** FFEL (Subsidized and Unsubsidized Stafford, PLUS), Perkins, Federal Nursing.

WORK-STUDY ***Federal work-study:*** *Total amount:* $200,943; jobs available.

ATHLETIC AWARDS *Total amount:* 273,235 (60% need-based, 40% non-need-based).

APPLYING for FINANCIAL AID ***Required financial aid form:*** FAFSA. ***Financial aid deadline (priority):*** 3/1. ***Notification date:*** 4/30. Students must reply within 4 weeks of notification.

CONTACT Mr. Robert M. Zellers, Director of Financial Aid, Indiana University–Purdue University Fort Wayne, 2101 East Coliseum Boulevard, Fort Wayne, IN 46805-1499, 219-481-6130. *E-mail:* zellers@ipfw.edu

INDIANA UNIVERSITY–PURDUE UNIVERSITY INDIANAPOLIS

Indianapolis, IN

Tuition & fees (IN res): $3713 **Average undergraduate aid package: $5754**

ABOUT THE INSTITUTION State-supported, coed. Awards: associate, bachelor's, master's, doctoral, and first professional degrees. 76 undergraduate majors. Total enrollment: 27,587. Undergraduates: 20,416. Freshmen: 3,455. Federal methodology is used as a basis for awarding need-based institutional aid.

UNDERGRADUATE EXPENSES for 1999–2000 ***Application fee:*** $35. ***Tuition, state resident:*** full-time $3432; part-time $114 per credit hour. ***Tuition, nonresident:*** full-time $10,680; part-time $356 per credit hour. ***Required fees:*** full-time $281. Full-time tuition and fees vary according to course load. Part-time tuition and fees vary according to course load. ***College room and board:*** $3450; ***room only:*** $1850. Room and board charges vary according to board plan and housing facility. ***Payment plans:*** installment, deferred payment.

FRESHMAN FINANCIAL AID (Fall 1999, est.) 1797 applied for aid; of those 79% were deemed to have need. 91% of freshmen with need received aid; of those 7% had need fully met. *Average percent of need met:* 52% (excluding resources awarded to replace EFC). *Average financial aid package:* $4561 (excluding resources awarded to replace EFC). 11% of all full-time freshmen had no need and received non-need-based aid.

UNDERGRADUATE FINANCIAL AID (Fall 1999, est.) 7,716 applied for aid; of those 85% were deemed to have need. 94% of undergraduates with need received aid; of those 8% had need fully met. *Average percent of need met:* 57% (excluding resources awarded to replace EFC). *Average financial aid package:* $5754 (excluding resources awarded to replace EFC). 9% of all full-time undergraduates had no need and received non-need-based aid.

GIFT AID (NEED-BASED) ***Total amount:*** $19,206,077 (50% Federal, 45% state, 5% institutional). ***Receiving aid:*** *Freshmen:* 37% (958); *all full-time undergraduates:* 38% (4,338). ***Average award:*** Freshmen: $3625; Undergraduates: $3663. ***Scholarships, grants, and awards:*** Federal Pell, FSEOG, state, private, college/university gift aid from institutional funds.

GIFT AID (NON-NEED-BASED) ***Total amount:*** $4,352,214 (21% Federal, 6% state, 47% institutional, 26% external sources). ***Receiving aid:*** *Freshmen:* 13% (333); *Undergraduates:* 11% (1,217). ***Scholarships, grants, and awards by category:*** *Academic Interests/Achievement:* general academic interests/achievements. *Creative Arts/Performance:* general creative arts/performance. *Special Achievements/Activities:* general special achievements/activities. *Special Characteristics:* general special characteristics. ***Tuition waivers:*** Full or partial for employees or children of employees. ***ROTC:*** Army, Air Force cooperative.

LOANS ***Student loans:*** $29,123,100 (66% need-based, 34% non-need-based). ***Average need-based loan:*** Freshmen: $2333; Undergraduates: $3365. ***Parent loans:*** $974,493 (100% non-need-based). ***Programs:*** FFEL (Subsidized and Unsubsidized Stafford, PLUS), Perkins, Federal Nursing, college/university.

WORK-STUDY ***Federal work-study:*** *Total amount:* $3,080,394; 948 jobs averaging $3249.

ATHLETIC AWARDS *Total amount:* 569,767 (100% non-need-based).

APPLYING for FINANCIAL AID ***Required financial aid forms:*** FAFSA, institution's own form. ***Financial aid deadline (priority):*** 3/1. ***Notification date:*** Continuous beginning 5/1.

CONTACT Office of Scholarships and Financial Aid, Indiana University–Purdue University Indianapolis, 425 North University Boulevard, Cavanaugh Hall, Room 103, Indianapolis, IN 46202-5145, 317-278-FAST. *Fax:* 317-274-5930.

INDIANA UNIVERSITY SOUTH BEND

South Bend, IN

Tuition & fees (IN res): $3197 **Average undergraduate aid package: $4887**

ABOUT THE INSTITUTION State-supported, coed. Awards: associate, bachelor's, and master's degrees and post-bachelor's certificates. 53 undergraduate majors. Total enrollment: 7,070. Undergraduates: 5,702. Freshmen: 870. Federal methodology is used as a basis for awarding need-based institutional aid.

UNDERGRADUATE EXPENSES for 1999–2000 ***Application fee:*** $40. ***Tuition, state resident:*** full-time $2975; part-time $99 per credit hour. ***Tuition, nonresident:*** full-time $8259; part-time $275 per credit hour. ***Required fees:*** full-time $222. Full-time tuition and fees vary according to course load. Part-time tuition and fees vary according to course load. ***Payment plans:*** installment, deferred payment.

FRESHMAN FINANCIAL AID (Fall 1999, est.) 444 applied for aid; of those 76% were deemed to have need. 87% of freshmen with need received aid; of those 9% had need fully met. *Average percent of need met:* 59% (excluding resources awarded to replace EFC). *Average financial aid package:* $4259 (excluding resources awarded to replace EFC). 10% of all full-time freshmen had no need and received non-need-based aid.

UNDERGRADUATE FINANCIAL AID (Fall 1999, est.) 1,872 applied for aid; of those 82% were deemed to have need. 91% of undergraduates with need received aid; of those 12% had need fully met. *Average percent of*

Indiana University South Bend (continued)

need met: 62% (excluding resources awarded to replace EFC). *Average financial aid package:* $4887 (excluding resources awarded to replace EFC). 8% of all full-time undergraduates had no need and received non-need-based aid.

GIFT AID (NEED-BASED) ***Total amount:*** $3,456,155 (59% Federal, 41% state). ***Receiving aid:*** *Freshmen:* 31% (197); *all full-time undergraduates:* 30% (848). ***Average award:*** Freshmen: $3311; Undergraduates: $3174. ***Scholarships, grants, and awards:*** Federal Pell, FSEOG, state, private, college/university gift aid from institutional funds.

GIFT AID (NON-NEED-BASED) ***Total amount:*** $1,328,385 (14% Federal, 11% state, 50% institutional, 25% external sources). ***Receiving aid:*** *Freshmen:* 11% (72); *Undergraduates:* 11% (307). ***Scholarships, grants, and awards by category:*** *Academic Interests/Achievement:* general academic interests/achievements. *Creative Arts/Performance:* general creative arts/performance. *Special Achievements/Activities:* general special achievements/activities. *Special Characteristics:* general special characteristics. ***Tuition waivers:*** Full or partial for employees or children of employees. ***ROTC:*** Army cooperative, Naval cooperative, Air Force cooperative.

LOANS ***Student loans:*** $5,302,217 (68% need-based, 32% non-need-based). ***Average need-based loan:*** Freshmen: $2247; Undergraduates: $3096. ***Parent loans:*** $73,214 (100% non-need-based). ***Programs:*** Federal Direct (Subsidized and Unsubsidized Stafford, PLUS), Perkins, Federal Nursing, college/university.

WORK-STUDY ***Federal work-study:*** *Total amount:* $385,623; 160 jobs averaging $2410.

ATHLETIC AWARDS *Total amount:* 74,708 (100% non-need-based).

APPLYING for FINANCIAL AID ***Required financial aid forms:*** FAFSA, institution's own form. ***Financial aid deadline (priority):*** 3/1. ***Notification date:*** Continuous beginning 5/1.

CONTACT Cyndi Lang, Financial Aid Administrator, Indiana University South Bend, 1700 Mishawaka Avenue, PO Box 7111, South Bend, IN 46634-7111, 219-237-4490. *Fax:* 219-237-4834. *E-mail:* clang@iusb.edu

INDIANA UNIVERSITY SOUTHEAST

New Albany, IN

Tuition & fees (IN res): $3092 **Average undergraduate aid package: $4449**

ABOUT THE INSTITUTION State-supported, coed. Awards: associate, bachelor's, and master's degrees. 37 undergraduate majors. Total enrollment: 6,115. Undergraduates: 5,440. Freshmen: 956. Federal methodology is used as a basis for awarding need-based institutional aid.

UNDERGRADUATE EXPENSES for 1999–2000 ***Application fee:*** $29. ***Tuition, state resident:*** full-time $2922; part-time $97 per credit hour. ***Tuition, nonresident:*** full-time $7692; part-time $256 per credit hour. ***Required fees:*** full-time $170. Full-time tuition and fees vary according to course load. Part-time tuition and fees vary according to course load.

FRESHMAN FINANCIAL AID (Fall 1999, est.) 577 applied for aid; of those 60% were deemed to have need. 95% of freshmen with need received aid; of those 11% had need fully met. *Average percent of need met:* 60% (excluding resources awarded to replace EFC). *Average financial aid package:* $3857 (excluding resources awarded to replace EFC). 17% of all full-time freshmen had no need and received non-need-based aid.

UNDERGRADUATE FINANCIAL AID (Fall 1999, est.) 1,861 applied for aid; of those 70% were deemed to have need. 96% of undergraduates with need received aid; of those 13% had need fully met. *Average percent of need met:* 61% (excluding resources awarded to replace EFC). *Average financial aid package:* $4449 (excluding resources awarded to replace EFC). 13% of all full-time undergraduates had no need and received non-need-based aid.

GIFT AID (NEED-BASED) ***Total amount:*** $3,510,439 (62% Federal, 33% state, 5% institutional). ***Receiving aid:*** *Freshmen:* 31% (223); *all full-time undergraduates:* 32% (897). ***Average award:*** Freshmen: $3374; Undergraduates: $3236. ***Scholarships, grants, and awards:*** Federal Pell, FSEOG, state, private, college/university gift aid from institutional funds.

GIFT AID (NON-NEED-BASED) ***Total amount:*** $914,650 (18% Federal, 1% state, 64% institutional, 17% external sources). ***Receiving aid:*** *Freshmen:* 17% (123); *Undergraduates:* 15% (412). ***Scholarships, grants, and awards by category:*** *Academic Interests/Achievement:* general academic interests/achievements. *Creative Arts/Performance:* general creative arts/performance. *Special Achievements/Activities:* general special achievements/activities. *Special Characteristics:* general special characteristics. ***Tuition waivers:*** Full or partial for employees or children of employees. ***ROTC:*** Army cooperative, Air Force cooperative.

LOANS ***Student loans:*** $4,145,289 (65% need-based, 35% non-need-based). ***Average need-based loan:*** Freshmen: $2177; Undergraduates: $2853. ***Parent loans:*** $53,771 (100% non-need-based). ***Programs:*** FFEL (Subsidized and Unsubsidized Stafford, PLUS), Perkins, Federal Nursing, college/university.

WORK-STUDY ***Federal work-study:*** *Total amount:* $173,212; 115 jobs averaging $1506.

ATHLETIC AWARDS *Total amount:* 52,608 (100% non-need-based).

APPLYING for FINANCIAL AID ***Required financial aid forms:*** FAFSA, institution's own form. ***Financial aid deadline (priority):*** 3/1. ***Notification date:*** Continuous beginning 5/1.

CONTACT Patrick Mrozowski, Director of Financial Aid, Indiana University Southeast, LB-002, New Albany, IN 47150, 812-941-2246 or toll-free 800-852-8835. *E-mail:* pmrozows@iusmail.ius.indiana.edu

INDIANA WESLEYAN UNIVERSITY

Marion, IN

Tuition & fees: $11,760 **Average undergraduate aid package: N/A**

ABOUT THE INSTITUTION Independent Wesleyan, coed. Awards: associate, bachelor's, and master's degrees (also offers adult program with significant enrollment not reflected in profile). 60 undergraduate majors. Total enrollment: 6,899. Undergraduates: 4,898. Freshmen: 822. Federal methodology is used as a basis for awarding need-based institutional aid.

UNDERGRADUATE EXPENSES for 1999–2000 ***Application fee:*** $25. ***Comprehensive fee:*** $16,340 includes full-time tuition ($11,760) and room and board ($4580). ***College room only:*** $1990. Room and board charges vary according to board plan. ***Part-time tuition:*** $250 per credit hour. Part-time tuition and fees vary according to course load. ***Payment plan:*** installment.

GIFT AID (NEED-BASED) ***Scholarships, grants, and awards:*** Federal Pell, FSEOG, state, private, college/university gift aid from institutional funds.

GIFT AID (NON-NEED-BASED) ***Scholarships, grants, and awards by category:*** *Academic Interests/Achievement:* general academic interests/achievements. *Creative Arts/Performance:* art/fine arts, music. *Special Characteristics:* children and siblings of alumni, relatives of clergy, religious affiliation, siblings of current students. ***Tuition waivers:*** Full or partial for employees or children of employees.

LOANS ***Programs:*** FFEL (Subsidized and Unsubsidized Stafford, PLUS), Perkins, college/university.

WORK-STUDY Federal work-study jobs available. ***State or other work-study/employment:*** Part-time jobs available.

APPLYING for FINANCIAL AID ***Required financial aid form:*** FAFSA. ***Financial aid deadline (priority):*** 3/1.

CONTACT Financial Aid Office, Indiana Wesleyan University, 4201 South Washington Street, Marion, IN 46953-4999, 765-677-2116 or toll-free 800-332-6901. *Fax:* 765-677-2809.

INSTITUTE FOR CHRISTIAN STUDIES

Austin, TX

Tuition & fees: $1560 **Average undergraduate aid package: N/A**

ABOUT THE INSTITUTION Independent religious, coed. Awards: bachelor's degrees. 1 undergraduate major. Total enrollment: 56. Undergraduates: 56. Federal methodology is used as a basis for awarding need-based institutional aid.

UNDERGRADUATE EXPENSES for 1999–2000 ***Tuition:*** full-time $1560; part-time $195 per course. ***Payment plan:*** installment.

UNDERGRADUATE FINANCIAL AID (Fall 1998) 14 applied for aid; of those 71% were deemed to have need. 100% of undergraduates with need received aid; of those 100% had need fully met. *Average percent of need met:* 100% (excluding resources awarded to replace EFC). 4% of all full-time undergraduates had no need and received non-need-based aid.

GIFT AID (NEED-BASED) ***Total amount:*** $28,645 (70% Federal, 30% institutional). ***Receiving aid:*** *All full-time undergraduates:* 38% (10). ***Scholarships, grants, and awards:*** Federal Pell, college/university gift aid from institutional funds.

GIFT AID (NON-NEED-BASED) ***Total amount:*** $1200 (100% Federal). ***Scholarships, grants, and awards by category:*** *Academic Interests/Achievement:* religion/biblical studies.

LOANS ***Student loans:*** $34,938 (100% need-based). 20% of past graduating class borrowed through all loan programs. Average indebtedness per student: $5500. ***Programs:*** FFEL (Subsidized and Unsubsidized Stafford, PLUS), college/university.

WORK-STUDY ***Federal work-study:*** *Total amount:* $6500; 5 jobs averaging $1200. ***State or other work-study/employment:*** *Total amount:* $4525 (100% need-based). Part-time jobs available.

APPLYING for FINANCIAL AID ***Required financial aid forms:*** FAFSA, institution's own form. ***Financial aid deadline (priority):*** 4/15.

CONTACT David Arthur, Financial Aid Officer, Institute for Christian Studies, 1909 University Avenue, Austin, TX 78705-5610, 512-476-2772 Ext. 204 or toll-free 800-ICS-AUSTIN (in-state). *Fax:* 512-476-3919. *E-mail:* darthur@mail.ics.edu

INSTITUTE OF COMPUTER TECHNOLOGY

Los Angeles, CA

Tuition & fees: N/R **Average undergraduate aid package: N/A**

ABOUT THE INSTITUTION Proprietary, coed. Awards: associate and bachelor's degrees. 3 undergraduate majors. Total enrollment: 231. Undergraduates: 231. Federal methodology is used as a basis for awarding need-based institutional aid.

GIFT AID (NEED-BASED) ***Scholarships, grants, and awards:*** Federal Pell, FSEOG, state.

GIFT AID (NON-NEED-BASED) ***Scholarships, grants, and awards by category:*** *Academic Interests/Achievement:* general academic interests/achievements.

LOANS ***Programs:*** FFEL (Subsidized and Unsubsidized Stafford, PLUS), college/university.

APPLYING for FINANCIAL AID ***Required financial aid form:*** FAFSA. ***Financial aid deadline:*** Continuous.

CONTACT Office of Financial Aid, Institute of Computer Technology, 3200 Wilshire Boulevard, Los Angeles, CA 90010, 213-381-3333. *Fax:* 213-383-9369.

INTER AMERICAN UNIVERSITY OF PUERTO RICO, AGUADILLA CAMPUS

Aguadilla, PR

CONTACT Mr. Juan Gonzalez, Director of Financial Aid, Inter American University of Puerto Rico, Aguadilla Campus, PO Box 20000, Aguadilla, PR 00605, 787-891-0925 Ext. 2108. *Fax:* 787-882-3020.

INTER AMERICAN UNIVERSITY OF PUERTO RICO, ARECIBO CAMPUS

Arecibo, PR

Tuition & fees: $2940 **Average undergraduate aid package: N/A**

ABOUT THE INSTITUTION Independent, coed. Awards: associate, bachelor's, and master's degrees. 17 undergraduate majors. Total enrollment: 3,623. Undergraduates: 3,603. Freshmen: 463. Federal methodology is used as a basis for awarding need-based institutional aid.

UNDERGRADUATE EXPENSES for 1999–2000 ***Application fee:*** $19. ***Tuition:*** full-time $2640; part-time $110 per credit hour. ***Required fees:*** full-time $300; $150 per term part-time. ***Payment plan:*** guaranteed tuition.

GIFT AID (NEED-BASED) ***Scholarships, grants, and awards:*** Federal Pell, FSEOG, private, college/university gift aid from institutional funds.

GIFT AID (NON-NEED-BASED) ***Tuition waivers:*** Full or partial for employees or children of employees. ***ROTC:*** Army cooperative.

LOANS ***Programs:*** Federal Direct (Subsidized and Unsubsidized Stafford, PLUS), Perkins.

APPLYING for FINANCIAL AID ***Required financial aid forms:*** FAFSA, institution's own form.

CONTACT Financial Aid Director, Inter American University of Puerto Rico, Arecibo Campus, PO Box 4050, Arecibo, PR 00614-4050, 787-878-5475 Ext. 2275.

INTER AMERICAN UNIVERSITY OF PUERTO RICO, BARRANQUITAS CAMPUS

Barranquitas, PR

Tuition & fees: N/R **Average undergraduate aid package: N/A**

ABOUT THE INSTITUTION Independent, coed. Awards: associate and bachelor's degrees. 8 undergraduate majors. Total enrollment: 1,710. Undergraduates: 1,710. Federal methodology is used as a basis for awarding need-based institutional aid.

FRESHMAN FINANCIAL AID (Fall 1998) 396 applied for aid; of those 100% were deemed to have need. 78% of freshmen with need received aid.

UNDERGRADUATE FINANCIAL AID (Fall 1998) 1,154 applied for aid; of those 100% were deemed to have need. 80% of undergraduates with need received aid.

GIFT AID (NEED-BASED) ***Total amount:*** $2,674,319 (86% Federal, 9% state, 5% institutional). ***Receiving aid:*** *Freshmen:* 54% (215); *all full-time undergraduates:* 60% (698). ***Scholarships, grants, and awards:*** Federal Pell, FSEOG, state, private, college/university gift aid from institutional funds.

GIFT AID (NON-NEED-BASED) ***Scholarships, grants, and awards by category:*** *Special Characteristics:* adult students, veterans. ***Tuition waivers:*** Full or partial for minority students. ***ROTC:*** Army cooperative.

LOANS ***Student loans:*** $978,300 (100% need-based). ***Programs:*** Federal Direct (Subsidized Stafford), Perkins.

WORK-STUDY ***Federal work-study:*** *Total amount:* $189,137; 315 jobs available.

APPLYING for FINANCIAL AID ***Required financial aid forms:*** FAFSA, institution's own form. ***Financial aid deadline (priority):*** 4/30.

CONTACT Mr. Eduardo Fontánez Colón, Financial Aid Officer, Inter American University of Puerto Rico, Barranquitas Campus, Box 517, Barranquitas, PR 00794, 787-857-3600 Ext. 2049. *Fax:* 787-857-2244.

INTER AMERICAN UNIVERSITY OF PUERTO RICO, BAYAMÓN CAMPUS

Bayamón, PR

CONTACT Financial Aid Office, Inter American University of Puerto Rico, Bayamón Campus, 500 Road 830, Bayamon, PR 00957, 787-279-1912 Ext. 2025.

INTER AMERICAN UNIVERSITY OF PUERTO RICO, FAJARDO CAMPUS

Fajardo, PR

CONTACT Financial Aid Director, Inter American University of Puerto Rico, Fajardo Campus, Call Box 700003, Fajardo, PR 00738-7003, 787-863-2390 Ext. 2208.

INTER AMERICAN UNIVERSITY OF PUERTO RICO, GUAYAMA CAMPUS

Guayama, PR

Tuition & fees: $3700 **Average undergraduate aid package: N/A**

ABOUT THE INSTITUTION Independent, coed. Awards: associate and bachelor's degrees. 15 undergraduate majors. Total enrollment: 1,246. Undergraduates: 1,246. Federal methodology is used as a basis for awarding need-based institutional aid.

UNDERGRADUATE EXPENSES for 1999–2000 ***Tuition:*** full-time $3300; part-time $110 per credit. ***Required fees:*** full-time $400; $100 per term part-time. ***Payment plan:*** deferred payment.

GIFT AID (NEED-BASED) ***Total amount:*** $5,206,373 (83% Federal, 7% state, 10% institutional). ***Scholarships, grants, and awards:*** Federal Pell, FSEOG, state, college/university gift aid from institutional funds, Federal Nursing.

GIFT AID (NON-NEED-BASED) ***Tuition waivers:*** Full or partial for employees or children of employees. ***ROTC:*** Army cooperative.

LOANS ***Student loans:*** $2,253,191 (100% need-based). 80% of past graduating class borrowed through all loan programs. ***Programs:*** Federal Direct (Subsidized and Unsubsidized Stafford, PLUS), Perkins, Federal Nursing.

WORK-STUDY ***Federal work-study:*** *Total amount:* $175,767; 643 jobs averaging $300.

ATHLETIC AWARDS *Total amount:* 10,136 (100% need-based).

APPLYING for FINANCIAL AID ***Required financial aid form:*** FAFSA. ***Financial aid deadline:*** Continuous. ***Notification date:*** Continuous beginning 7/1. Students must reply within 5 weeks of notification.

CONTACT Sr. Jose A. Vechini, Director of Financial Aid Office, Inter American University of Puerto Rico, Guayama Campus, Call Box 10004, Guyama, PR 00785, 787-864-2222 Ext. 2206. *Fax:* 787-864-8232. *E-mail:* javechi@inter.edu

INTER AMERICAN UNIVERSITY OF PUERTO RICO, METROPOLITAN CAMPUS

San Juan, PR

CONTACT Office of Financial Aid, Inter American University of Puerto Rico, Metropolitan Campus, PO Box 1293, Hato Rey, PR 00919, 787-758-2891.

INTER AMERICAN UNIVERSITY OF PUERTO RICO, PONCE CAMPUS

Mercedita, PR

CONTACT Financial Aid Officer, Inter American University of Puerto Rico, Ponce Campus, Street #1, Km. 123.2, Mercedita, PR 00715-2201, 787-284-1912 Ext. 2015.

INTER AMERICAN UNIVERSITY OF PUERTO RICO, SAN GERMÁN CAMPUS

San Germán, PR

Tuition & fees: $3996 **Average undergraduate aid package: $1592**

ABOUT THE INSTITUTION Independent, coed. Awards: associate, bachelor's, and master's degrees. 60 undergraduate majors. Total enrollment: 5,425. Undergraduates: 4,619. Both federal and institutional methodology are used as a basis for awarding need-based institutional aid.

UNDERGRADUATE EXPENSES for 1999–2000 ***Comprehensive fee:*** $6196 includes full-time tuition ($3630), mandatory fees ($366), and room and board ($2200). ***College room only:*** $900. Room and board charges vary according to housing facility. ***Part-time tuition:*** $110 per credit. ***Part-time fees:*** $183 per term part-time. ***Payment plan:*** deferred payment.

FRESHMAN FINANCIAL AID (Fall 1998) 882 applied for aid; of those 87% were deemed to have need. 99% of freshmen with need received aid. *Average percent of need met:* 28% (excluding resources awarded to replace EFC). *Average financial aid package:* $1491 (excluding resources awarded to replace EFC).

UNDERGRADUATE FINANCIAL AID (Fall 1998) 3,992 applied for aid; of those 89% were deemed to have need. 100% of undergraduates with need received aid; of those 1% had need fully met. *Average percent of need met:* 36% (excluding resources awarded to replace EFC). *Average financial aid package:* $1592 (excluding resources awarded to replace EFC).

GIFT AID (NEED-BASED) ***Total amount:*** $12,533,721 (88% Federal, 6% state, 6% institutional). ***Receiving aid:*** *Freshmen:* 75% (761); *all full-time undergraduates:* 81% (3,520). ***Scholarships, grants, and awards:*** Federal Pell, FSEOG, state, college/university gift aid from institutional funds.

GIFT AID (NON-NEED-BASED) ***Receiving aid:*** *Freshmen:* 2% (19); *Undergraduates:* 3% (122). ***Scholarships, grants, and awards by category:*** *Academic Interests/Achievement:* general academic interests/achievements. ***Tuition waivers:*** Full or partial for employees or children of employees. ***ROTC:*** Army cooperative, Naval cooperative, Air Force cooperative.

LOANS ***Student loans:*** $7,622,164 (100% need-based). ***Programs:*** Federal Direct (Subsidized and Unsubsidized Stafford, PLUS), Perkins.

WORK-STUDY ***Federal work-study:*** *Total amount:* $487,756; jobs available.

APPLYING for FINANCIAL AID ***Required financial aid forms:*** FAFSA, institution's own form. ***Financial aid deadline (priority):*** 4/26. ***Notification date:*** Continuous beginning 6/15.

CONTACT Ms. María I. Lugo, Financial Aid Director, Inter American University of Puerto Rico, San Germán Campus, PO Box 5100, San Germán, PR 00683-5008, 787-264-1912 Ext. 7252. *Fax:* 787-892-6350.

INTERIOR DESIGNERS INSTITUTE

Newport Beach, CA

CONTACT Office of Financial Aid, Interior Designers Institute, 1061 Camelback Road, Newport Beach, CA 92660, 714-675-4451.

INTERNATIONAL ACADEMY OF DESIGN

Tampa, FL

Tuition & fees: $10,260 **Average undergraduate aid package: N/A**

ABOUT THE INSTITUTION Proprietary, coed. Awards: associate and bachelor's degrees. 6 undergraduate majors. Total enrollment: 900. Undergraduates: 900. Freshmen: 153. Federal methodology is used as a basis for awarding need-based institutional aid.

UNDERGRADUATE EXPENSES for 1999–2000 ***Application fee:*** $100. ***Tuition:*** full-time $10,260; part-time $285 per credit. ***Payment plans:*** guaranteed tuition, installment, deferred payment.

GIFT AID (NEED-BASED) ***Scholarships, grants, and awards:*** Federal Pell, FSEOG, state, college/university gift aid from institutional funds.

GIFT AID (NON-NEED-BASED) ***Scholarships, grants, and awards by category:*** *Academic Interests/Achievement:* general academic interests/achievements. *Creative Arts/Performance:* applied art and design. ***Tuition waivers:*** Full or partial for employees or children of employees.

LOANS ***Programs:*** FFEL (Subsidized and Unsubsidized Stafford, PLUS), alternative loans.

WORK-STUDY Federal work-study jobs available.

APPLYING for FINANCIAL AID ***Required financial aid forms:*** FAFSA, institution's own form. ***Financial aid deadline:*** Continuous. ***Notification date:*** Continuous. Students must reply within 2 weeks of notification.

CONTACT Director of Financial Services, International Academy of Design, 5225 Memorial Highway, Tampa, FL 33634-7350, 813-881-0007 or toll-free 800-ACADEMY.

INTERNATIONAL ACADEMY OF MERCHANDISING & DESIGN, LTD.

Chicago, IL

Tuition & fees: $10,692 **Average undergraduate aid package: N/A**

ABOUT THE INSTITUTION Proprietary, coed. Awards: associate and bachelor's degrees. 6 undergraduate majors. Total enrollment: 1,383. Undergraduates: 1,383. Freshmen: 494. Federal methodology is used as a basis for awarding need-based institutional aid.

UNDERGRADUATE EXPENSES for 1999–2000 ***Application fee:*** $50. ***Tuition:*** full-time $10,692; part-time $799 per course. Full-time tuition and fees vary according to program. Part-time tuition and fees vary according to program. ***Payment plans:*** installment, deferred payment.

GIFT AID (NEED-BASED) ***Scholarships, grants, and awards:*** Federal Pell, FSEOG, private.

GIFT AID (NON-NEED-BASED) ***Tuition waivers:*** Full or partial for employees or children of employees.

APPLYING for FINANCIAL AID ***Required financial aid form:*** FAFSA.

CONTACT Financial Aid Department, International Academy of Merchandising & Design, Ltd., 1 North State Street, Chicago, IL 60602, 312-980-9200 or toll-free 877-ACADEMY (out-of-state). *Fax:* 312-541-3929.

INTERNATIONAL BAPTIST COLLEGE

Tempe, AZ

Tuition & fees: $4350 **Average undergraduate aid package: N/A**

ABOUT THE INSTITUTION Independent Baptist, coed. Awards: associate, bachelor's, master's, and doctoral degrees. 3 undergraduate majors. Total enrollment: 65. Undergraduates: 53. Institutional methodology is used as a basis for awarding need-based institutional aid.

UNDERGRADUATE EXPENSES for 1999–2000 ***Application fee:*** $25. ***Comprehensive fee:*** $7350 includes full-time tuition ($4000), mandatory fees ($350), and room and board ($3000). ***Part-time tuition:*** $150 per semester hour. ***Part-time fees:*** $8 per semester hour.

GIFT AID (NEED-BASED) ***Scholarships, grants, and awards:*** private, college/university gift aid from institutional funds.

GIFT AID (NON-NEED-BASED) ***Scholarships, grants, and awards by category:*** *Academic Interests/Achievement:* general academic interests/achievements.

APPLYING for FINANCIAL AID ***Required financial aid form:*** institution's own form. ***Financial aid deadline:*** Continuous.

CONTACT Mr. Jerry Petreau, President, International Baptist College, 2150 East Southern Avenue, Tempe, AZ 85282, 480-838-7070 or toll-free 800-422-4858. *Fax:* 480-838-5432.

INTERNATIONAL BIBLE COLLEGE

Florence, AL

Tuition & fees: $5492 **Average undergraduate aid package: N/A**

ABOUT THE INSTITUTION Independent religious, coed. Awards: associate and bachelor's degrees. 1 undergraduate major. Total enrollment: 146. Undergraduates: 146. Freshmen: 16. Federal methodology is used as a basis for awarding need-based institutional aid.

UNDERGRADUATE EXPENSES for 1999–2000 ***Tuition:*** full-time $5012; part-time $179 per semester hour. ***Required fees:*** full-time $480; $20 per semester hour. ***Payment plans:*** installment, deferred payment.

GIFT AID (NEED-BASED) ***Scholarships, grants, and awards:*** Federal Pell, FSEOG, college/university gift aid from institutional funds.

GIFT AID (NON-NEED-BASED) ***Scholarships, grants, and awards by category:*** *Academic Interests/Achievement:* general academic interests/achievements. ***Tuition waivers:*** Full or partial for employees or children of employees.

LOANS ***Programs:*** FFEL (Subsidized and Unsubsidized Stafford).

WORK-STUDY Federal work-study jobs available.

APPLYING for FINANCIAL AID ***Required financial aid forms:*** FAFSA, federal income tax form(s). ***Financial aid deadline (priority):*** 6/1. ***Notification date:*** Continuous beginning 7/15.

CONTACT Ms. Angie Horton, Financial Aid Counselor, International Bible College, PO Box IBC, Florence, AL 35630, 800-367-3565. *E-mail:* ahorton@i-b-c.edu

INTERNATIONAL COLLEGE

Naples, FL

Tuition & fees: $6870 **Average undergraduate aid package: $7000**

ABOUT THE INSTITUTION Independent, coed. Awards: associate, bachelor's, and master's degrees. 7 undergraduate majors. Total enrollment: 796. Undergraduates: 782. Freshmen: 65. Federal methodology is used as a basis for awarding need-based institutional aid.

UNDERGRADUATE EXPENSES for 1999–2000 ***Application fee:*** $20. ***Tuition:*** full-time $6600; part-time $275 per credit. ***Required fees:*** full-time $270; $135 per term part-time. ***Payment plan:*** installment.

FRESHMAN FINANCIAL AID (Fall 1999, est.) 52 applied for aid; of those 92% were deemed to have need. 100% of freshmen with need received aid; of those 88% had need fully met. *Average percent of need met:* 50% (excluding resources awarded to replace EFC). *Average financial aid package:* $7000 (excluding resources awarded to replace EFC).

UNDERGRADUATE FINANCIAL AID (Fall 1999, est.) 625 applied for aid; of those 98% were deemed to have need. 100% of undergraduates with need received aid; of those 96% had need fully met. *Average percent of need met:* 50% (excluding resources awarded to replace EFC). *Average financial aid package:* $7000 (excluding resources awarded to replace EFC).

GIFT AID (NEED-BASED) ***Total amount:*** $1,290,000 (93% Federal, 7% state). ***Receiving aid:*** *Freshmen:* 49% (30); *all full-time undergraduates:* 65% (450). ***Average award:*** Freshmen: $3000; Undergraduates: $3000. ***Scholarships, grants, and awards:*** Federal Pell, FSEOG, state, private, college/university gift aid from institutional funds.

GIFT AID (NON-NEED-BASED) ***Total amount:*** $1,225,000 (90% state, 4% institutional, 6% external sources). ***Receiving aid:*** *Freshmen:* 41% (25); *Undergraduates:* 36% (250). ***Scholarships, grants, and awards by category:*** *Special Achievements/Activities:* 60 awards ($50,000 total): general special achievements/activities. ***Tuition waivers:*** Full or partial for employees or children of employees.

LOANS ***Student loans:*** $6,000,000 (67% need-based, 33% non-need-based). Average indebtedness per student: $20,000. ***Average need-based loan:*** Freshmen: $3500; Undergraduates: $3500. ***Parent loans:*** $20,000 (100% non-need-based). ***Programs:*** FFEL (Subsidized and Unsubsidized Stafford, PLUS).

WORK-STUDY ***Federal work-study:*** *Total amount:* $64,000; jobs available.

APPLYING for FINANCIAL AID ***Required financial aid form:*** FAFSA. ***Financial aid deadline:*** Continuous. ***Notification date:*** Continuous.

CONTACT Mr. Joe Gilchrist, Director of Financial Aid, International College, 2654 East Tamiami Trail, Naples, FL 34112, 941-774-4700 or toll-free 800-466-8017. *Fax:* 941-774-4593. *E-mail:* joegil@naples.net

INTERNATIONAL COLLEGE AND GRADUATE SCHOOL
Honolulu, HI

CONTACT Mr. Jon Rawlings, Executive Vice President, International College and Graduate School, 20 Dowsett Avenue, Honolulu, HI 96817, 808-595-4247.

INTERNATIONAL FINE ARTS COLLEGE
Miami, FL

CONTACT Ms. Karen Vidal, Director of Financial Aid and Residences, International Fine Arts College, 1737 North Bayshore Drive, Miami, FL 33132-1121, 305-373-4684 or toll-free 800-225-9023.

INTERNATIONAL UNIVERSITY
Englewood, CO

See Jones International University

IONA COLLEGE
New Rochelle, NY

Tuition & fees: $15,070 **Average undergraduate aid package: $14,955**

ABOUT THE INSTITUTION Independent religious, coed. Awards: associate, bachelor's, and master's degrees. 62 undergraduate majors. Total enrollment: 4,544. Undergraduates: 3,474. Freshmen: 844. Federal methodology is used as a basis for awarding need-based institutional aid.

UNDERGRADUATE EXPENSES for 1999–2000 ***Application fee:*** $25. ***One-time required fee:*** $25. ***Comprehensive fee:*** $23,500 includes full-time tuition ($14,700), mandatory fees ($370), and room and board ($8430). Full-time tuition and fees vary according to class time. ***Part-time tuition:*** $490 per credit. ***Part-time fees:*** $185 per term part-time. Part-time tuition and fees vary according to class time and course load. ***Payment plans:*** installment, deferred payment.

FRESHMAN FINANCIAL AID (Fall 1999, est.) 691 applied for aid; of those 90% were deemed to have need. 100% of freshmen with need received aid; of those 63% had need fully met. *Average percent of need met:* 92% (excluding resources awarded to replace EFC). *Average financial aid package:* $15,488 (excluding resources awarded to replace EFC). 22% of all full-time freshmen had no need and received non-need-based aid.

UNDERGRADUATE FINANCIAL AID (Fall 1999, est.) 2,354 applied for aid; of those 89% were deemed to have need. 99% of undergraduates with need received aid; of those 65% had need fully met. *Average percent of need met:* 91% (excluding resources awarded to replace EFC). *Average financial aid package:* $14,955 (excluding resources awarded to replace EFC). 23% of all full-time undergraduates had no need and received non-need-based aid.

GIFT AID (NEED-BASED) ***Total amount:*** $7,628,661 (31% Federal, 41% state, 26% institutional, 2% external sources). ***Receiving aid:*** *Freshmen:* 77% (616); *all full-time undergraduates:* 72% (1,966). ***Average award:*** Freshmen: $9244; Undergraduates: $8651. ***Scholarships, grants, and awards:*** Federal Pell, FSEOG, state, private, college/university gift aid from institutional funds.

GIFT AID (NON-NEED-BASED) ***Total amount:*** $11,627,530 (100% institutional). ***Receiving aid:*** *Freshmen:* 53% (424); *Undergraduates:* 9% (244). ***Scholarships, grants, and awards by category:*** *Academic Interests/Achievement:* 2,058 awards ($10,536,570 total): general academic interests/achievements. *Creative Arts/Performance:* 18 awards ($95,550 total): music. *Special Characteristics:* 207 awards ($243,000 total): children and siblings of alumni, siblings of current students. ***Tuition waivers:*** Full or partial for employees or children of employees, senior citizens. ***ROTC:*** Army cooperative.

LOANS ***Student loans:*** $10,019,114 (61% need-based, 39% non-need-based). 64% of past graduating class borrowed through all loan programs. Average indebtedness per student: $16,086. ***Average need-based loan:*** Freshmen: $7405; Undergraduates: $7654. ***Parent loans:*** $2,761,963 (100% non-need-based). ***Programs:*** FFEL (Subsidized and Unsubsidized Stafford, PLUS), Perkins, alternative loans.

WORK-STUDY ***Federal work-study:*** *Total amount:* $477,509; jobs available. ***State or other work-study/employment:*** *Total amount:* $293,400 (100% non-need-based). Part-time jobs available.

ATHLETIC AWARDS *Total amount:* 1,445,592 (100% non-need-based).

APPLYING for FINANCIAL AID ***Required financial aid forms:*** FAFSA, institution's own form. ***Financial aid deadline:*** Continuous. ***Notification date:*** Continuous beginning 12/20. Students must reply by 5/1 or within 2 weeks of notification.

CONTACT Mary Grant, Director, Student Financial Services, Iona College, 715 North Avenue, New Rochelle, NY 10801-1890, 914-633-2676. *Fax:* 914-633-2486. *E-mail:* mgrant@iona.edu

IOWA STATE UNIVERSITY OF SCIENCE AND TECHNOLOGY
Ames, IA

Tuition & fees (IA res): $3132 **Average undergraduate aid package: $6032**

ABOUT THE INSTITUTION State-supported, coed. Awards: bachelor's, master's, doctoral, and first professional degrees and post-master's certificates. 120 undergraduate majors. Total enrollment: 26,110. Undergraduates: 21,503. Freshmen: 4,085. Federal methodology is used as a basis for awarding need-based institutional aid.

UNDERGRADUATE EXPENSES for 2000–2001 ***Application fee:*** $20. ***Tuition, state resident:*** full-time $2906; part-time $122 per semester hour. ***Tuition, nonresident:*** full-time $9748; part-time $407 per semester hour. ***Required fees:*** full-time $226. Full-time tuition and fees vary according to class time and program. Part-time tuition and fees vary according to class time, course load, and program. ***College room and board:*** $4171; ***room only:*** $2267. Room and board charges vary according to board plan and housing facility. ***Payment plans:*** installment, deferred payment.

FRESHMAN FINANCIAL AID (Fall 1998) 3446 applied for aid; of those 69% were deemed to have need. 100% of freshmen with need received aid; of those 18% had need fully met. *Average percent of need met:* 100% (excluding resources awarded to replace EFC). *Average financial aid package:* $5283 (excluding resources awarded to replace EFC). 28% of all full-time freshmen had no need and received non-need-based aid.

UNDERGRADUATE FINANCIAL AID (Fall 1998) 16,239 applied for aid; of those 72% were deemed to have need. 100% of undergraduates with need received aid; of those 26% had need fully met. *Average percent of need met:* 100% (excluding resources awarded to replace EFC). *Average financial aid package:* $6032 (excluding resources awarded to replace EFC). 21% of all full-time undergraduates had no need and received non-need-based aid.

GIFT AID (NEED-BASED) ***Total amount:*** $22,866,414 (47% Federal, 5% state, 31% institutional, 17% external sources). ***Receiving aid:*** *Freshmen:* 43% (1,626); *all full-time undergraduates:* 37% (7,897). ***Average award:*** Freshmen: $2430; Undergraduates: $3061. ***Scholarships, grants, and awards:*** Federal Pell, FSEOG, state, private, college/university gift aid from institutional funds.

GIFT AID (NON-NEED-BASED) ***Total amount:*** $9,790,000 (5% Federal, 3% state, 54% institutional, 38% external sources). ***Receiving aid:*** *Freshmen:* 8% (315); *Undergraduates:* 13% (2,832). ***Scholarships, grants, and awards by category:*** *Academic Interests/Achievement:* agriculture, architecture, area/ethnic studies, biological sciences, business, communication, computer science, education, engineering/technologies, English, foreign languages, general academic interests/achievements, health fields, home economics, humanities, international studies, library science, mathematics, physical sciences, premedicine, social sciences. *Creative Arts/Performance:* music. *Special Achievements/Activities:* community service, leadership. *Special Characteristics:* adult students, ethnic background, first-generation college students, international students, members of minority groups, out-of-state students. ***ROTC:*** Army, Naval, Air Force.

LOANS ***Student loans:*** $76,076,683 (64% need-based, 36% non-need-based). 68% of past graduating class borrowed through all loan programs.

Average indebtedness per student: $16,836. ***Average need-based loan:*** Freshmen: $2924; Undergraduates: $3817. ***Parent loans:*** $4,171,521 (23% need-based, 77% non-need-based). ***Programs:*** Federal Direct (Subsidized and Unsubsidized Stafford, PLUS), Perkins, college/university, alternative loans.

WORK-STUDY ***Federal work-study:*** *Total amount:* $2,636,333; 1,399 jobs averaging $1884. ***State or other work-study/employment:*** *Total amount:* $1,025,240 (4% need-based, 96% non-need-based). 544 part-time jobs averaging $1885.

ATHLETIC AWARDS *Total amount:* 3,252,045 (31% need-based, 69% non-need-based).

APPLYING for FINANCIAL AID ***Required financial aid form:*** FAFSA. ***Financial aid deadline (priority):*** 3/1. ***Notification date:*** Continuous beginning 4/1. Students must reply within 2 weeks of notification.

CONTACT Mr. Earl E. Dowling, Director of Financial Aid, Iowa State University of Science and Technology, 12 Beardshear Hall, Ames, IA 50011, 515-294-2223 or toll-free 800-262-3810. *Fax:* 515-294-2592. *E-mail:* eedowli@iastate.edu

IOWA WESLEYAN COLLEGE

Mount Pleasant, IA

Tuition & fees: $12,700 **Average undergraduate aid package: $13,478**

ABOUT THE INSTITUTION Independent United Methodist, coed. Awards: bachelor's degrees. 44 undergraduate majors. Total enrollment: 785. Undergraduates: 785. Freshmen: 114. Federal methodology is used as a basis for awarding need-based institutional aid.

UNDERGRADUATE EXPENSES for 1999–2000 ***Application fee:*** $15. ***Comprehensive fee:*** $17,070 includes full-time tuition ($12,700) and room and board ($4370). ***College room only:*** $1850. Room and board charges vary according to board plan and housing facility. ***Part-time tuition:*** $300 per credit hour. Part-time tuition and fees vary according to class time. ***Payment plans:*** installment, deferred payment.

FRESHMAN FINANCIAL AID (Fall 1999, est.) 106 applied for aid; of those 97% were deemed to have need. 100% of freshmen with need received aid; of those 28% had need fully met. *Average percent of need met:* 89% (excluding resources awarded to replace EFC). *Average financial aid package:* $13,218 (excluding resources awarded to replace EFC). 7% of all full-time freshmen had no need and received non-need-based aid.

UNDERGRADUATE FINANCIAL AID (Fall 1999, est.) 452 applied for aid; of those 96% were deemed to have need. 100% of undergraduates with need received aid; of those 28% had need fully met. *Average percent of need met:* 90% (excluding resources awarded to replace EFC). *Average financial aid package:* $13,478 (excluding resources awarded to replace EFC). 8% of all full-time undergraduates had no need and received non-need-based aid.

GIFT AID (NEED-BASED) ***Total amount:*** $3,281,778 (18% Federal, 31% state, 48% institutional, 3% external sources). ***Receiving aid:*** *Freshmen:* 89% (103); *all full-time undergraduates:* 87% (433). ***Average award:*** Freshmen: $9480; Undergraduates: $9237. ***Scholarships, grants, and awards:*** Federal Pell, FSEOG, state, private, college/university gift aid from institutional funds.

GIFT AID (NON-NEED-BASED) ***Total amount:*** $247,187 (96% institutional, 4% external sources). ***Receiving aid:*** *Freshmen:* 11% (13); *Undergraduates:* 14% (68). ***Scholarships, grants, and awards by category:*** *Academic Interests/Achievement:* 69 awards ($33,100 total): biological sciences, communication, general academic interests/achievements. *Creative Arts/Performance:* 20 awards ($60,200 total): art/fine arts, music. *Special Achievements/Activities:* cheerleading/drum major. *Special Characteristics:* 88 awards ($195,687 total): children of faculty/staff, international students, members of minority groups, relatives of clergy, religious affiliation. ***Tuition waivers:*** Full or partial for employees or children of employees.

LOANS ***Student loans:*** $2,233,091 (68% need-based, 32% non-need-based). 68% of past graduating class borrowed through all loan programs. Average indebtedness per student: $14,752. ***Average need-based loan:*** Freshmen: $2590; Undergraduates: $4182. ***Parent loans:*** $150,000 (60% need-based, 40% non-need-based). ***Programs:*** FFEL (Subsidized and Unsubsidized Stafford, PLUS), Perkins, alternative loans.

WORK-STUDY ***Federal work-study:*** *Total amount:* $120,000; 170 jobs available. ***State or other work-study/employment:*** *Total amount:* $40,000 (28% need-based, 72% non-need-based). 30 part-time jobs averaging $1333.

ATHLETIC AWARDS *Total amount:* 690,036 (91% need-based, 9% non-need-based).

APPLYING for FINANCIAL AID ***Required financial aid form:*** FAFSA. ***Financial aid deadline (priority):*** 4/1. ***Notification date:*** Continuous. Students must reply within 3 weeks of notification.

CONTACT Ms. Marsha Boender, Director of Enrollment Management, Iowa Wesleyan College, 601 North Main Street, Mount Pleasant, IA 52641-1398, 319-385-6242 or toll-free 800-582-2383. *Fax:* 319-385-6296. *E-mail:* mboender@iwc.edu

ITHACA COLLEGE

Ithaca, NY

Tuition & fees: $18,410 **Average undergraduate aid package: $16,634**

ABOUT THE INSTITUTION Independent, coed. Awards: bachelor's and master's degrees. 100 undergraduate majors. Total enrollment: 5,960. Undergraduates: 5,702. Freshmen: 1,589. Both federal and institutional methodology are used as a basis for awarding need-based institutional aid.

UNDERGRADUATE EXPENSES for 1999–2000 ***Application fee:*** $45. ***Comprehensive fee:*** $26,366 includes full-time tuition ($18,410) and room and board ($7956). ***College room only:*** $3980. Room and board charges vary according to housing facility. ***Part-time tuition:*** $575 per credit. ***Part-time fees:*** $15 per term part-time. ***Payment plan:*** installment.

FRESHMAN FINANCIAL AID (Fall 1999) 1260 applied for aid; of those 84% were deemed to have need. 100% of freshmen with need received aid; of those 39% had need fully met. *Average percent of need met:* 84% (excluding resources awarded to replace EFC). *Average financial aid package:* $16,682 (excluding resources awarded to replace EFC). 5% of all full-time freshmen had no need and received non-need-based aid.

UNDERGRADUATE FINANCIAL AID (Fall 1999) 4,164 applied for aid; of those 90% were deemed to have need. 99% of undergraduates with need received aid; of those 39% had need fully met. *Average percent of need met:* 84% (excluding resources awarded to replace EFC). *Average financial aid package:* $16,634 (excluding resources awarded to replace EFC). 3% of all full-time undergraduates had no need and received non-need-based aid.

GIFT AID (NEED-BASED) ***Total amount:*** $37,572,675 (6% Federal, 8% state, 84% institutional, 2% external sources). ***Receiving aid:*** *Freshmen:* 65% (1,025); *all full-time undergraduates:* 64% (3,535). ***Average award:*** Freshmen: $11,659; Undergraduates: $10,686. ***Scholarships, grants, and awards:*** Federal Pell, FSEOG, state, private, college/university gift aid from institutional funds.

GIFT AID (NON-NEED-BASED) ***Total amount:*** $4,284,613 (2% Federal, 88% institutional, 10% external sources). ***Receiving aid:*** *Freshmen:* 13% (210); *Undergraduates:* 13% (730). ***Scholarships, grants, and awards by category:*** *Academic Interests/Achievement:* 1,522 awards ($7,478,250 total): general academic interests/achievements. *Creative Arts/Performance:* 17 awards ($164,410 total): music, theater/drama. *Special Achievements/Activities:* 36 awards ($216,000 total): leadership. *Special Characteristics:* 164 awards ($161,500 total): siblings of current students. ***Tuition waivers:*** Full or partial for employees or children of employees. ***ROTC:*** Army cooperative, Air Force cooperative.

LOANS ***Student loans:*** $16,821,187 (87% need-based, 13% non-need-based). 75% of past graduating class borrowed through all loan programs. Average indebtedness per student: $16,673. ***Average need-based loan:*** Freshmen: $3317; Undergraduates: $4342. ***Parent loans:*** $6,438,767 (29% need-based, 71% non-need-based). ***Programs:*** FFEL (Subsidized and Unsubsidized Stafford, PLUS), Perkins, college/university.

Ithaca College (continued)

WORK-STUDY ***Federal work-study:*** *Total amount:* $1,108,485; 1,215 jobs averaging $911. ***State or other work-study/employment:*** *Total amount:* $5,476,270 (72% need-based, 28% non-need-based). 3,728 part-time jobs averaging $1469.

APPLYING for FINANCIAL AID ***Required financial aid forms:*** FAFSA, CSS/Financial Aid PROFILE (for Early Decision applicants only). ***Financial aid deadline (priority):*** 2/1. ***Notification date:*** Continuous beginning 3/15.

CONTACT Mr. Larry Chambers, Director of Financial Aid, Ithaca College, 350 Egbert Hall, Ithaca, NY 14850-7130, 800-429-4275 or toll-free 800-429-4274. *Fax:* 607-274-1895. *E-mail:* finaid@ithaca.edu

JACKSON STATE UNIVERSITY

Jackson, MS

CONTACT Mr. Gene Blakley, Director of Financial Aid, Jackson State University, 1400 J.R. Lynch Street, PO Box 17065, Jackson, MS 39217, 601-968-2227 or toll-free 800-682-5390 (in-state), 800-848-6817 (out-of-state). *E-mail:* gblakley@ccaix.jsums.edu

JACKSONVILLE STATE UNIVERSITY

Jacksonville, AL

Tuition & fees (AL res): $2440 **Average undergraduate aid package: N/A**

ABOUT THE INSTITUTION State-supported, coed. Awards: bachelor's and master's degrees. 58 undergraduate majors. Total enrollment: 7,928. Undergraduates: 6,640. Freshmen: 1,069. Federal methodology is used as a basis for awarding need-based institutional aid.

UNDERGRADUATE EXPENSES for 1999–2000 ***Application fee:*** $20. ***One-time required fee:*** $10. ***Tuition, state resident:*** full-time $2440; part-time $102 per semester hour. ***Tuition, nonresident:*** full-time $4880; part-time $204 per semester hour. Full-time tuition and fees vary according to course load and reciprocity agreements. Part-time tuition and fees vary according to course load and reciprocity agreements. ***College room and board:*** $3080; ***room only:*** $1150. Room and board charges vary according to board plan and housing facility.

GIFT AID (NEED-BASED) ***Total amount:*** $5,314,863 (98% Federal, 2% state). ***Scholarships, grants, and awards:*** Federal Pell, FSEOG, state, private, college/university gift aid from institutional funds, Federal Nursing.

GIFT AID (NON-NEED-BASED) ***Total amount:*** $4,450,500 (48% institutional, 52% external sources). ***Scholarships, grants, and awards by category:*** *Academic Interests/Achievement:* 200 awards ($450,000 total): biological sciences, business, communication, computer science, education, English, general academic interests/achievements, health fields, home economics, humanities, mathematics, military science, physical sciences, social sciences. *Creative Arts/Performance:* 150 awards ($300,000 total): art/fine arts, journalism/publications, music, theater/drama. *Special Achievements/Activities:* 70 awards ($150,000 total): cheerleading/drum major, general special achievements/activities, leadership. ***Tuition waivers:*** Full or partial for employees or children of employees, senior citizens. ***ROTC:*** Army.

LOANS ***Student loans:*** $16,724,082 (98% need-based, 2% non-need-based). Average indebtedness per student: $12,000. ***Parent loans:*** $254,301 (100% non-need-based). ***Programs:*** Federal Direct (Subsidized and Unsubsidized Stafford, PLUS), college/university.

WORK-STUDY ***Federal work-study:*** *Total amount:* $467,359; jobs available. ***State or other work-study/employment:*** *Total amount:* $1,071,357 (100% non-need-based). Part-time jobs available.

ATHLETIC AWARDS *Total amount:* 750,000 (100% non-need-based).

APPLYING for FINANCIAL AID ***Required financial aid forms:*** FAFSA, institution's own form. ***Financial aid deadline (priority):*** 3/15. ***Notification date:*** Continuous beginning 5/15. Students must reply within 2 weeks of notification.

CONTACT Mr. Larry Smith, Director of Financial Aid, Jacksonville State University, 400 Pelham Road North, Jacksonville, AL 36265-9982, 256-782-5006 or toll-free 800-231-5291. *Fax:* 256-782-5476. *E-mail:* lsmith@jsucc.jsu.edu

JACKSONVILLE UNIVERSITY

Jacksonville, FL

Tuition & fees: $14,950 **Average undergraduate aid package: $13,358**

ABOUT THE INSTITUTION Independent, coed. Awards: bachelor's and master's degrees. 60 undergraduate majors. Total enrollment: 2,093. Undergraduates: 1,832. Freshmen: 315. Federal methodology is used as a basis for awarding need-based institutional aid.

UNDERGRADUATE EXPENSES for 1999–2000 ***Application fee:*** $30. ***Comprehensive fee:*** $20,160 includes full-time tuition ($14,390), mandatory fees ($560), and room and board ($5210). ***College room only:*** $2430. Room and board charges vary according to board plan and housing facility. ***Payment plan:*** installment.

FRESHMAN FINANCIAL AID (Fall 1999) 269 applied for aid; of those 72% were deemed to have need. 100% of freshmen with need received aid; of those 38% had need fully met. *Average percent of need met:* 82% (excluding resources awarded to replace EFC). *Average financial aid package:* $14,144 (excluding resources awarded to replace EFC). 17% of all full-time freshmen had no need and received non-need-based aid.

UNDERGRADUATE FINANCIAL AID (Fall 1999) 1,238 applied for aid; of those 72% were deemed to have need. 100% of undergraduates with need received aid; of those 41% had need fully met. *Average percent of need met:* 83% (excluding resources awarded to replace EFC). *Average financial aid package:* $13,358 (excluding resources awarded to replace EFC). 18% of all full-time undergraduates had no need and received non-need-based aid.

GIFT AID (NEED-BASED) ***Total amount:*** $8,461,886 (22% Federal, 22% state, 55% institutional, 1% external sources). ***Receiving aid:*** *Freshmen:* 50% (154); *all full-time undergraduates:* 46% (686). ***Average award:*** Freshmen: $11,011; Undergraduates: $9963. ***Scholarships, grants, and awards:*** Federal Pell, FSEOG, state, private, college/university gift aid from institutional funds.

GIFT AID (NON-NEED-BASED) ***Total amount:*** $2,256,462 (30% Federal, 19% state, 51% institutional). ***Receiving aid:*** *Freshmen:* 52% (161); *Undergraduates:* 52% (787). ***Scholarships, grants, and awards by category:*** *Academic Interests/Achievement:* business, general academic interests/achievements, physical sciences. *Creative Arts/Performance:* art/fine arts, dance, music, theater/drama. *Special Achievements/Activities:* community service, general special achievements/activities, leadership. *Special Characteristics:* children of current students, children of faculty/staff, siblings of current students, spouses of current students. ***Tuition waivers:*** Full or partial for employees or children of employees. ***ROTC:*** Naval.

LOANS ***Student loans:*** $5,384,968 (58% need-based, 42% non-need-based). ***Average need-based loan:*** Freshmen: $3852; Undergraduates: $3118. ***Parent loans:*** $1,281,523 (97% need-based, 3% non-need-based). ***Programs:*** FFEL (Subsidized and Unsubsidized Stafford, PLUS), Perkins, college/university.

WORK-STUDY ***Federal work-study:*** *Total amount:* $235,150; jobs available.

ATHLETIC AWARDS *Total amount:* 2,013,866 (37% need-based, 63% non-need-based).

APPLYING for FINANCIAL AID ***Required financial aid forms:*** FAFSA, W-2 forms, federal income tax form(s). ***Financial aid deadline (priority):*** 3/15. ***Notification date:*** Continuous. Students must reply by 5/1 or within 2 weeks of notification.

CONTACT Mrs. Catherine Huntress, Director of Student Financial Assistance, Jacksonville University, 2800 University Boulevard North, Jacksonville, FL 32211, 904-745-7060 or toll-free 800-225-2027. *Fax:* 904-745-7148. *E-mail:* chuntres@ju.edu

JAMES MADISON UNIVERSITY

Harrisonburg, VA

Tuition & fees (VA res): $3926 **Average undergraduate aid package: $5036**

ABOUT THE INSTITUTION State-supported, coed. Awards: bachelor's, master's, and doctoral degrees (also offers specialist in education degree). 51 undergraduate majors. Total enrollment: 15,223. Undergraduates: 14,156. Freshmen: 3,039. Federal methodology is used as a basis for awarding need-based institutional aid.

UNDERGRADUATE EXPENSES for 1999–2000 ***Application fee:*** $30. ***Tuition, state resident:*** full-time $3926; part-time $1085 per term. ***Tuition, nonresident:*** full-time $9532; part-time $2770 per term. Part-time tuition and fees vary according to course load. ***College room and board:*** $5182; ***room only:*** $2788. ***Payment plan:*** installment.

FRESHMAN FINANCIAL AID (Fall 1998) 1867 applied for aid; of those 61% were deemed to have need. 89% of freshmen with need received aid; of those 14% had need fully met. *Average percent of need met:* 74% (excluding resources awarded to replace EFC). *Average financial aid package:* $4522 (excluding resources awarded to replace EFC). 18% of all full-time freshmen had no need and received non-need-based aid.

UNDERGRADUATE FINANCIAL AID (Fall 1998) 6,152 applied for aid; of those 68% were deemed to have need. 92% of undergraduates with need received aid; of those 21% had need fully met. *Average percent of need met:* 74% (excluding resources awarded to replace EFC). *Average financial aid package:* $5036 (excluding resources awarded to replace EFC). 16% of all full-time undergraduates had no need and received non-need-based aid.

GIFT AID (NEED-BASED) ***Total amount:*** $7,452,036 (36% Federal, 44% state, 5% institutional, 15% external sources). ***Receiving aid:*** *Freshmen:* 21% (631); *all full-time undergraduates:* 18% (2,251). ***Average award:*** Freshmen: $3452; Undergraduates: $3179. ***Scholarships, grants, and awards:*** Federal Pell, FSEOG, state, private, college/university gift aid from institutional funds.

GIFT AID (NON-NEED-BASED) ***Total amount:*** $1,666,251 (14% Federal, 3% state, 16% institutional, 67% external sources). ***Receiving aid:*** *Freshmen:* 2% (56); *Undergraduates:* 1% (173). ***Scholarships, grants, and awards by category:*** *Academic Interests/Achievement:* architecture, biological sciences, business, computer science, education, engineering/technologies, English, general academic interests/achievements, health fields, humanities, international studies, mathematics, military science, physical sciences, premedicine, religion/biblical studies, social sciences. *Creative Arts/Performance:* art/fine arts, dance, journalism/publications, music, theater/drama. *Special Achievements/Activities:* cheerleading/drum major, general special achievements/activities, leadership. *Special Characteristics:* children and siblings of alumni, children of faculty/staff, members of minority groups, siblings of current students. ***Tuition waivers:*** Full or partial for employees or children of employees, senior citizens. ***ROTC:*** Army.

LOANS ***Student loans:*** $20,158,645 (73% need-based, 27% non-need-based). 40% of past graduating class borrowed through all loan programs. Average indebtedness per student: $12,000. ***Average need-based loan:*** Freshmen: $2636; Undergraduates: $3476. ***Parent loans:*** $7,172,600 (57% need-based, 43% non-need-based). ***Programs:*** FFEL (Subsidized and Unsubsidized Stafford, PLUS), Perkins, college/university.

WORK-STUDY ***Federal work-study:*** *Total amount:* $285,032; jobs available.

ATHLETIC AWARDS *Total amount:* 2,752,865 (28% need-based, 72% non-need-based).

APPLYING for FINANCIAL AID ***Required financial aid form:*** FAFSA. ***Financial aid deadline:*** 2/15. ***Notification date:*** 4/15. Students must reply within 2 weeks of notification.

CONTACT Lisa Tumer, Director of Financial Aid and Scholarships, James Madison University, Sonner Hall MSC 0102, Harrisonburg, VA 22807, 540-568-7820.

JAMESTOWN COLLEGE

Jamestown, ND

Tuition & fees: $7550 **Average undergraduate aid package: $8632**

ABOUT THE INSTITUTION Independent Presbyterian, coed. Awards: bachelor's degrees. 26 undergraduate majors. Total enrollment: 1,131. Undergraduates: 1,131. Freshmen: 301. Both federal and institutional methodology are used as a basis for awarding need-based institutional aid.

UNDERGRADUATE EXPENSES for 2000–2001 ***Application fee:*** $20. ***Comprehensive fee:*** $10,850 includes full-time tuition ($7550) and room and board ($3300). ***College room only:*** $1480. Room and board charges vary according to board plan and housing facility. ***Part-time tuition:*** $230 per credit hour. Part-time tuition and fees vary according to course load. ***Payment plan:*** installment.

FRESHMAN FINANCIAL AID (Fall 1999) 285 applied for aid; of those 74% were deemed to have need. 100% of freshmen with need received aid; of those 35% had need fully met. *Average percent of need met:* 82% (excluding resources awarded to replace EFC). *Average financial aid package:* $7475 (excluding resources awarded to replace EFC). 26% of all full-time freshmen had no need and received non-need-based aid.

UNDERGRADUATE FINANCIAL AID (Fall 1999) 1,047 applied for aid; of those 77% were deemed to have need. 100% of undergraduates with need received aid; of those 36% had need fully met. *Average percent of need met:* 84% (excluding resources awarded to replace EFC). *Average financial aid package:* $8632 (excluding resources awarded to replace EFC). 24% of all full-time undergraduates had no need and received non-need-based aid.

GIFT AID (NEED-BASED) ***Total amount:*** $3,455,244 (31% Federal, 4% state, 60% institutional, 5% external sources). ***Receiving aid:*** *Freshmen:* 74% (210); *all full-time undergraduates:* 76% (802). ***Average award:*** Freshmen: $4265; Undergraduates: $4531. ***Scholarships, grants, and awards:*** Federal Pell, FSEOG, state, private, college/university gift aid from institutional funds.

GIFT AID (NON-NEED-BASED) ***Total amount:*** $924,810 (1% state, 91% institutional, 8% external sources). ***Receiving aid:*** *Freshmen:* 10% (28); *Undergraduates:* 7% (74). ***Scholarships, grants, and awards by category:*** *Academic Interests/Achievement:* 251 awards ($840,949 total): general academic interests/achievements. *Special Characteristics:* 47 awards ($188,734 total): children of faculty/staff. ***Tuition waivers:*** Full or partial for employees or children of employees.

LOANS ***Student loans:*** $4,405,891 (73% need-based, 27% non-need-based). 85% of past graduating class borrowed through all loan programs. Average indebtedness per student: $15,000. ***Average need-based loan:*** Freshmen: $2963; Undergraduates: $3876. ***Parent loans:*** $112,300 (42% need-based, 58% non-need-based). ***Programs:*** FFEL (Subsidized and Unsubsidized Stafford, PLUS), Perkins, Federal Nursing, college/university, alternative loans.

WORK-STUDY ***Federal work-study:*** *Total amount:* $177,199; 298 jobs averaging $727. ***State or other work-study/employment:*** *Total amount:* $129,350 (3% need-based, 97% non-need-based). 164 part-time jobs averaging $766.

ATHLETIC AWARDS *Total amount:* 296,513 (63% need-based, 37% non-need-based).

APPLYING for FINANCIAL AID ***Required financial aid forms:*** FAFSA, institution's own form. ***Financial aid deadline:*** Continuous. ***Notification date:*** Continuous beginning 10/1. Students must reply within 4 weeks of notification.

CONTACT Mary Reed, Director of Financial Aid, Jamestown College, 6085 College Lane, Jamestown, ND 58405, 701-252-3467 or toll-free 800-336-2554. *Fax:* 701-253-4318. *E-mail:* mreed@jc.edu

JARVIS CHRISTIAN COLLEGE

Hawkins, TX

Tuition & fees: $5200 **Average undergraduate aid package: $8670**

Jarvis Christian College (continued)

ABOUT THE INSTITUTION Independent religious, coed. Awards: bachelor's degrees. 23 undergraduate majors. Total enrollment: 519. Undergraduates: 519. Freshmen: 115. Federal methodology is used as a basis for awarding need-based institutional aid.

UNDERGRADUATE EXPENSES for 1999–2000 ***Application fee:*** $25. ***Comprehensive fee:*** $8950 includes full-time tuition ($5200) and room and board ($3750). ***College room only:*** $1610. ***Part-time tuition:*** $173 per semester hour. ***Payment plans:*** tuition prepayment, deferred payment.

FRESHMAN FINANCIAL AID (Fall 1999) 115 applied for aid; of those 97% were deemed to have need. 100% of freshmen with need received aid; of those 75% had need fully met. *Average percent of need met:* 90% (excluding resources awarded to replace EFC). *Average financial aid package:* $8235 (excluding resources awarded to replace EFC). 3% of all full-time freshmen had no need and received non-need-based aid.

UNDERGRADUATE FINANCIAL AID (Fall 1999) 505 applied for aid; of those 98% were deemed to have need. 100% of undergraduates with need received aid; of those 64% had need fully met. *Average percent of need met:* 85% (excluding resources awarded to replace EFC). *Average financial aid package:* $8670 (excluding resources awarded to replace EFC). 2% of all full-time undergraduates had no need and received non-need-based aid.

GIFT AID (NEED-BASED) ***Total amount:*** $1,988,526 (63% Federal, 35% state, 2% external sources). ***Receiving aid:*** *Freshmen:* 83% (96); *all full-time undergraduates:* 81% (420). ***Average award:*** Freshmen: $6175; Undergraduates: $5751. ***Scholarships, grants, and awards:*** Federal Pell, FSEOG, state, private, college/university gift aid from institutional funds, United Negro College Fund.

GIFT AID (NON-NEED-BASED) ***Total amount:*** $389,988 (92% institutional, 8% external sources). ***Receiving aid:*** *Freshmen:* 30% (34); *Undergraduates:* 37% (191). ***Scholarships, grants, and awards by category:*** *Academic Interests/Achievement:* education, general academic interests/achievements. *Special Characteristics:* religious affiliation. ***Tuition waivers:*** Full or partial for employees or children of employees.

LOANS ***Student loans:*** $1,433,745 (80% need-based, 20% non-need-based). ***Average need-based loan:*** Freshmen: $2625; Undergraduates: $3850. ***Parent loans:*** $60,373 (100% non-need-based). ***Programs:*** FFEL (Subsidized and Unsubsidized Stafford, PLUS), Perkins.

WORK-STUDY ***Federal work-study:*** *Total amount:* $239,610; 197 jobs averaging $1440. ***State or other work-study/employment:*** *Total amount:* $5760 (100% need-based). 6 part-time jobs averaging $1440.

ATHLETIC AWARDS *Total amount:* 246,327 (100% non-need-based).

APPLYING for FINANCIAL AID ***Required financial aid forms:*** FAFSA, institution's own form. ***Financial aid deadline (priority):*** 4/1. ***Notification date:*** Continuous beginning 5/1. Students must reply within 2 weeks of notification.

CONTACT Mr. Eric King, Assistant Director of Financial Aid, Jarvis Christian College, PO Drawer 1470, Hawkins, TX 75765-9989, 903-769-5743 or toll-free 800-292-9517. *Fax:* 903-769-4842.

JERSEY CITY STATE COLLEGE

Jersey City, NJ

See New Jersey City University

JEWISH HOSPITAL COLLEGE OF NURSING AND ALLIED HEALTH

St. Louis, MO

Tuition & fees: $10,034 **Average undergraduate aid package: $8000**

ABOUT THE INSTITUTION Independent, coed, primarily women. Awards: associate, bachelor's, and master's degrees and post-bachelor's and post-master's certificates. 3 undergraduate majors. Total enrollment: 479. Undergraduates: 388. Freshmen: 9. Federal methodology is used as a basis for awarding need-based institutional aid.

UNDERGRADUATE EXPENSES for 1999–2000 ***Application fee:*** $25. ***Tuition:*** full-time $9834; part-time $298 per credit hour. ***Required fees:*** full-time $200; $35 per term part-time. Full-time tuition and fees vary according to program. Part-time tuition and fees vary according to course load and program. Room and board charges vary according to housing facility. ***Payment plans:*** installment, deferred payment.

FRESHMAN FINANCIAL AID (Fall 1999, est.) *Average financial aid package:* $8000 (excluding resources awarded to replace EFC).

UNDERGRADUATE FINANCIAL AID (Fall 1999, est.) *Average financial aid package:* $8000 (excluding resources awarded to replace EFC).

GIFT AID (NEED-BASED) ***Total amount:*** $306,998 (48% Federal, 11% state, 34% institutional, 7% external sources). ***Scholarships, grants, and awards:*** Federal Pell, FSEOG, state, private, college/university gift aid from institutional funds.

GIFT AID (NON-NEED-BASED) ***Total amount:*** $79,075 (100% institutional). ***Scholarships, grants, and awards by category:*** *Academic Interests/Achievement:* 15 awards ($76,000 total): general academic interests/achievements.

LOANS ***Student loans:*** $1,263,378 (51% need-based, 49% non-need-based). Average indebtedness per student: $10,000. ***Parent loans:*** $25,000 (100% non-need-based). ***Programs:*** FFEL (Subsidized and Unsubsidized Stafford, PLUS), state, college/university.

WORK-STUDY ***Federal work-study:*** *Total amount:* $21,885; 8 jobs averaging $2735.

APPLYING for FINANCIAL AID ***Required financial aid forms:*** FAFSA, institution's own form. ***Financial aid deadline (priority):*** 4/1. ***Notification date:*** Continuous beginning 6/1. Students must reply within 2 weeks of notification.

CONTACT Regina Blackshear, Financial Aid Officer, Jewish Hospital College of Nursing and Allied Health, 306 South Kingshighway, St. Louis, MO 63110-1091, 314-454-7770 or toll-free 800-832-9009 (in-state).

JEWISH THEOLOGICAL SEMINARY OF AMERICA

New York, NY

Tuition & fees: $8720 **Average undergraduate aid package: N/A**

ABOUT THE INSTITUTION Independent Jewish, coed. Awards: bachelor's, master's, and doctoral degrees (double bachelor's degree with Barnard College, Columbia University). 8 undergraduate majors. Total enrollment: 574. Undergraduates: 175. Freshmen: 48. Both federal and institutional methodology are used as a basis for awarding need-based institutional aid.

UNDERGRADUATE EXPENSES for 1999–2000 ***Application fee:*** $60. ***Tuition:*** full-time $8320; part-time $445 per credit. ***Required fees:*** full-time $400; $200 per term part-time. Full-time tuition and fees vary according to program. Part-time tuition and fees vary according to program. Room and board charges vary according to housing facility. ***Payment plan:*** installment.

FRESHMAN FINANCIAL AID (Fall 1999, est.) 26 applied for aid; of those 77% were deemed to have need. 100% of freshmen with need received aid; of those 75% had need fully met. *Average percent of need met:* 100% (excluding resources awarded to replace EFC). 26% of all full-time freshmen had no need and received non-need-based aid.

UNDERGRADUATE FINANCIAL AID (Fall 1999, est.) 97 applied for aid; of those 94% were deemed to have need. 100% of undergraduates with need received aid; of those 89% had need fully met. *Average percent of need met:* 75% (excluding resources awarded to replace EFC). 21% of all full-time undergraduates had no need and received non-need-based aid.

GIFT AID (NEED-BASED) ***Total amount:*** $1,360,016 (1% state, 99% institutional). ***Receiving aid:*** *Freshmen:* 43% (20); *all full-time undergraduates:* 51% (91). ***Scholarships, grants, and awards:*** Federal Pell, state, private, college/university gift aid from institutional funds.

GIFT AID (NON-NEED-BASED) ***Total amount:*** $331,420 (100% institutional). ***Receiving aid:*** *Freshmen:* 43% (20); *Undergraduates:* 39% (70). ***Scholarships, grants, and awards by category:*** *Academic Interests/Achievement:*

general academic interests/achievements. ***Tuition waivers:*** Full or partial for employees or children of employees, senior citizens.

LOANS ***Student loans:*** $300,749 (96% need-based, 4% non-need-based). 69% of past graduating class borrowed through all loan programs. Average indebtedness per student: $12,325. ***Parent loans:*** $203,990 (100% need-based). ***Programs:*** FFEL (Subsidized and Unsubsidized Stafford, PLUS).

APPLYING for FINANCIAL AID ***Required financial aid forms:*** FAFSA, institution's own form, CSS Financial Aid PROFILE, noncustodial (divorced/separated) parent's statement. ***Financial aid deadline:*** 3/1. ***Notification date:*** Continuous beginning 4/1. Students must reply within 8 weeks of notification.

CONTACT Financial Aid Office, Jewish Theological Seminary of America, 3080 Broadway, New York, NY 10027-4649, 212-678-8000 Ext. 8007. *Fax:* 212-678-8002. *E-mail:* financialaid@jtsa.edu

JOHN BROWN UNIVERSITY

Siloam Springs, AR

Tuition & fees: $11,492 **Average undergraduate aid package: $9323**

ABOUT THE INSTITUTION Independent interdenominational, coed. Awards: associate, bachelor's, and master's degrees. 59 undergraduate majors. Total enrollment: 1,517. Undergraduates: 1,421. Freshmen: 271. Federal methodology is used as a basis for awarding need-based institutional aid.

UNDERGRADUATE EXPENSES for 2000–2001 ***Application fee:*** $25. ***Comprehensive fee:*** $15,970 includes full-time tuition ($11,022), mandatory fees ($470), and room and board ($4478). Room and board charges vary according to board plan and housing facility. Part-time tuition and fees vary according to course load and program. ***Payment plan:*** installment.

FRESHMAN FINANCIAL AID (Fall 1999) 211 applied for aid; of those 85% were deemed to have need. 100% of freshmen with need received aid; of those 22% had need fully met. *Average percent of need met:* 80% (excluding resources awarded to replace EFC). *Average financial aid package:* $10,060 (excluding resources awarded to replace EFC). 21% of all full-time freshmen had no need and received non-need-based aid.

UNDERGRADUATE FINANCIAL AID (Fall 1999) 806 applied for aid; of those 89% were deemed to have need. 100% of undergraduates with need received aid; of those 11% had need fully met. *Average percent of need met:* 60% (excluding resources awarded to replace EFC). *Average financial aid package:* $9323 (excluding resources awarded to replace EFC). 15% of all full-time undergraduates had no need and received non-need-based aid.

GIFT AID (NEED-BASED) ***Total amount:*** $3,818,853 (18% Federal, 13% state, 60% institutional, 9% external sources). ***Receiving aid:*** *Freshmen:* 59% (173); *all full-time undergraduates:* 48% (634). ***Average award:*** Freshmen: $6575; Undergraduates: $5522. ***Scholarships, grants, and awards:*** Federal Pell, FSEOG, state, private, college/university gift aid from institutional funds.

GIFT AID (NON-NEED-BASED) ***Total amount:*** $512,270 (16% state, 79% institutional, 5% external sources). ***Receiving aid:*** *Freshmen:* 10% (30); *Undergraduates:* 5% (65). ***Scholarships, grants, and awards by category:*** *Academic Interests/Achievement:* 533 awards ($1,252,040 total): general academic interests/achievements. *Creative Arts/Performance:* 68 awards ($78,173 total): journalism/publications, music. *Special Achievements/Activities:* 420 awards ($578,475 total): cheerleading/drum major, leadership. *Special Characteristics:* 287 awards ($588,756 total): children and siblings of alumni, children of educators, children of faculty/staff, ethnic background, international students, members of minority groups, relatives of clergy, siblings of current students. ***Tuition waivers:*** Full or partial for minority students, employees or children of employees, adult students, senior citizens. ***ROTC:*** Army cooperative.

LOANS ***Student loans:*** $2,946,637 (86% need-based, 14% non-need-based). 62% of past graduating class borrowed through all loan programs. Average indebtedness per student: $12,260. ***Average need-based loan:*** Freshmen: $3815; Undergraduates: $4762. ***Parent loans:*** $695,732 (40% need-based, 60% non-need-based). ***Programs:*** FFEL (Subsidized and Unsubsidized Stafford, PLUS), Perkins, state, alternative loans.

WORK-STUDY ***Federal work-study:*** *Total amount:* $257,870; 175 jobs averaging $1540. ***State or other work-study/employment:*** *Total amount:* $410,385 (76% need-based, 24% non-need-based). 300 part-time jobs averaging $1540.

ATHLETIC AWARDS *Total amount:* 641,220 (37% need-based, 63% non-need-based).

APPLYING for FINANCIAL AID ***Required financial aid form:*** FAFSA. ***Financial aid deadline (priority):*** 3/1. ***Notification date:*** Continuous. Students must reply within 4 weeks of notification.

CONTACT Ms. Judy Blank, Assistant Director of Student Financial Aid, John Brown University, 2000 West University, Siloam Springs, AR 72761-2121, 501-524-7115 or toll-free 877-JBU-INFO. *Fax:* 501-524-4196. *E-mail:* finaid@adm.jbu.edu

JOHN CARROLL UNIVERSITY

University Heights, OH

Tuition & fees: $16,384 **Average undergraduate aid package: $13,230**

ABOUT THE INSTITUTION Independent Roman Catholic (Jesuit), coed. Awards: bachelor's and master's degrees. 49 undergraduate majors. Total enrollment: 4,389. Undergraduates: 3,527. Freshmen: 834. Federal methodology is used as a basis for awarding need-based institutional aid.

UNDERGRADUATE EXPENSES for 2000–2001 ***Application fee:*** $25. ***Comprehensive fee:*** $22,512 includes full-time tuition ($16,334), mandatory fees ($50), and room and board ($6128). ***College room only:*** $3310. Room and board charges vary according to board plan. ***Part-time tuition:*** $492 per credit hour. Part-time tuition and fees vary according to course load. ***Payment plan:*** installment.

FRESHMAN FINANCIAL AID (Fall 1999) 746 applied for aid; of those 80% were deemed to have need. 100% of freshmen with need received aid; of those 43% had need fully met. *Average percent of need met:* 94% (excluding resources awarded to replace EFC). *Average financial aid package:* $13,942 (excluding resources awarded to replace EFC). 24% of all full-time freshmen had no need and received non-need-based aid.

UNDERGRADUATE FINANCIAL AID (Fall 1999) 2,622 applied for aid; of those 81% were deemed to have need. 100% of undergraduates with need received aid; of those 47% had need fully met. *Average percent of need met:* 88% (excluding resources awarded to replace EFC). *Average financial aid package:* $13,230 (excluding resources awarded to replace EFC). 25% of all full-time undergraduates had no need and received non-need-based aid.

GIFT AID (NEED-BASED) ***Total amount:*** $14,933,872 (10% Federal, 6% state, 82% institutional, 2% external sources). ***Receiving aid:*** *Freshmen:* 69% (572); *all full-time undergraduates:* 62% (2,035). ***Average award:*** Freshmen: $7159; Undergraduates: $6671. ***Scholarships, grants, and awards:*** Federal Pell, FSEOG, state, private, college/university gift aid from institutional funds, American Values Scholarships.

GIFT AID (NON-NEED-BASED) ***Total amount:*** $7,221,445 (5% Federal, 36% state, 55% institutional, 4% external sources). ***Receiving aid:*** *Freshmen:* 66% (549); *Undergraduates:* 58% (1,895). ***Scholarships, grants, and awards by category:*** *Academic Interests/Achievement:* biological sciences, foreign languages, general academic interests/achievements, mathematics, military science, physical sciences. *Special Achievements/Activities:* community service, leadership. *Special Characteristics:* children of faculty/staff. ***Tuition waivers:*** Full or partial for employees or children of employees. ***ROTC:*** Army.

LOANS ***Student loans:*** $11,707,000 (60% need-based, 40% non-need-based). 85% of past graduating class borrowed through all loan programs. Average indebtedness per student: $12,695. ***Average need-based loan:*** Freshmen: $3332; Undergraduates: $3975. ***Parent loans:*** $2,991,185 (100% non-need-based). ***Programs:*** FFEL (Subsidized and Unsubsidized Stafford, PLUS), Perkins, state, college/university.

WORK-STUDY ***Federal work-study:*** *Total amount:* $678,995; 416 jobs averaging $1632. ***State or other work-study/employment:*** *Total amount:* $684,223 (84% need-based, 16% non-need-based). 419 part-time jobs averaging $1633.

John Carroll University (continued)

APPLYING for FINANCIAL AID ***Required financial aid form:*** FAFSA. ***Financial aid deadline (priority):*** 3/1. ***Notification date:*** Continuous. Students must reply by 5/1 or within 4 weeks of notification.

CONTACT Financial Aid Counselor, John Carroll University, 20700 North Park Boulevard, University Heights, OH 44118-4581, 216-397-4248. *Fax:* 216-397-3098. *E-mail:* jcuofa@jcu.edu

JOHN F. KENNEDY UNIVERSITY

Orinda, CA

Tuition & fees: $10,251 **Average undergraduate aid package: N/A**

ABOUT THE INSTITUTION Independent, coed. Awards: bachelor's, master's, doctoral, and first professional degrees and post-bachelor's and post-master's certificates. 6 undergraduate majors. Total enrollment: 1,641. Undergraduates: 249. Federal methodology is used as a basis for awarding need-based institutional aid.

UNDERGRADUATE EXPENSES for 1999–2000 ***Application fee:*** $50. ***Tuition:*** full-time $10,215; part-time $227 per quarter hour. ***Required fees:*** full-time $36; $9 per term part-time.

UNDERGRADUATE FINANCIAL AID (Fall 1999) 200 applied for aid.

GIFT AID (NEED-BASED) ***Total amount:*** $158,968 (55% Federal, 45% state). ***Scholarships, grants, and awards:*** Federal Pell, FSEOG, state, college/university gift aid from institutional funds.

GIFT AID (NON-NEED-BASED) ***Tuition waivers:*** Full or partial for employees or children of employees.

LOANS ***Student loans:*** $1,800,000 (100% need-based). ***Programs:*** FFEL (Subsidized and Unsubsidized Stafford), Perkins, college/university.

APPLYING for FINANCIAL AID ***Required financial aid forms:*** FAFSA, institution's own form. ***Financial aid deadline (priority):*** 3/2. ***Notification date:*** Continuous.

CONTACT Mindy Bergeron, Director of Financial Aid, John F. Kennedy University, 12 Altarinda Road, Orinda, CA 94563-2689, 925-258-2385. *Fax:* 925-258-2266. *E-mail:* bergeron@jfku.edu

JOHN JAY COLLEGE OF CRIMINAL JUSTICE OF THE CITY UNIVERSITY OF NEW YORK

New York, NY

Tuition & fees (NY res): $3312 **Average undergraduate aid package: $4800**

ABOUT THE INSTITUTION State and locally supported, coed. Awards: associate, bachelor's, and master's degrees. 12 undergraduate majors. Total enrollment: 10,476. Undergraduates: 9,335. Freshmen: 1,407. Federal methodology is used as a basis for awarding need-based institutional aid.

UNDERGRADUATE EXPENSES for 2000–2001 ***Application fee:*** $40. ***Tuition, state resident:*** full-time $3200; part-time $135 per credit. ***Tuition, nonresident:*** full-time $6800; part-time $285 per credit. ***Required fees:*** full-time $112; $46 per term part-time. Full-time tuition and fees vary according to course level and course load. Part-time tuition and fees vary according to course level.

FRESHMAN FINANCIAL AID (Fall 1998) 1308 applied for aid; of those 100% were deemed to have need. 80% of freshmen with need received aid. *Average percent of need met:* 75% (excluding resources awarded to replace EFC). *Average financial aid package:* $4800 (excluding resources awarded to replace EFC).

UNDERGRADUATE FINANCIAL AID (Fall 1998) 6,600 applied for aid; of those 98% were deemed to have need. 80% of undergraduates with need received aid. *Average percent of need met:* 75% (excluding resources awarded to replace EFC). *Average financial aid package:* $4800 (excluding resources awarded to replace EFC).

GIFT AID (NEED-BASED) ***Total amount:*** $25,288,649 (52% Federal, 48% state). ***Scholarships, grants, and awards:*** Federal Pell, FSEOG, state, college/university gift aid from institutional funds.

GIFT AID (NON-NEED-BASED) ***Total amount:*** $1,755,950 (45% Federal, 53% state, 2% external sources). ***Scholarships, grants, and awards by category:*** *Academic Interests/Achievement:* general academic interests/achievements. ***ROTC:*** Naval cooperative, Air Force cooperative.

LOANS ***Student loans:*** $7,787,667 (82% need-based, 18% non-need-based). 50% of past graduating class borrowed through all loan programs. Average indebtedness per student: $10,000. ***Average need-based loan:*** Freshmen: $2400; Undergraduates: $2400. ***Parent loans:*** $144,872 (100% non-need-based). ***Programs:*** Federal Direct (Subsidized and Unsubsidized Stafford, PLUS), Perkins.

WORK-STUDY ***Federal work-study:*** *Total amount:* $408,340; 387 jobs averaging $1055. ***State or other work-study/employment:*** *Total amount:* $1,900,000 (100% non-need-based). 190 part-time jobs averaging $10,000.

APPLYING for FINANCIAL AID ***Required financial aid form:*** FAFSA. ***Financial aid deadline (priority):*** 6/1. ***Notification date:*** Continuous beginning 7/15. Students must reply within 2 weeks of notification.

CONTACT Mr. John H. Emmons, Director of Financial Aid, John Jay College of Criminal Justice of the City University of New York, 445 West 59th Street, New York, NY 10019-1093, 212-237-8150. *E-mail:* jemmons@jjay.cuny.edu

JOHNS HOPKINS UNIVERSITY

Baltimore, MD

Tuition & fees: $23,660 **Average undergraduate aid package: $22,436**

ABOUT THE INSTITUTION Independent, coed. Awards: bachelor's, master's, and doctoral degrees. 56 undergraduate majors. Total enrollment: 5,293. Undergraduates: 3,924. Freshmen: 1,018. Both federal and institutional methodology are used as a basis for awarding need-based institutional aid.

UNDERGRADUATE EXPENSES for 1999–2000 ***Application fee:*** $55. ***One-time required fee:*** $500. ***Comprehensive fee:*** $31,530 includes full-time tuition ($23,660) and room and board ($7870). ***College room only:*** $4500. Room and board charges vary according to board plan and housing facility. ***Part-time tuition:*** $790 per credit. ***Payment plans:*** tuition prepayment, installment.

FRESHMAN FINANCIAL AID (Fall 1999) 666 applied for aid; of those 76% were deemed to have need. 100% of freshmen with need received aid; of those 83% had need fully met. *Average percent of need met:* 95% (excluding resources awarded to replace EFC). *Average financial aid package:* $19,735 (excluding resources awarded to replace EFC). 7% of all full-time freshmen had no need and received non-need-based aid.

UNDERGRADUATE FINANCIAL AID (Fall 1999) 2,030 applied for aid; of those 92% were deemed to have need. 90% of undergraduates with need received aid; of those 81% had need fully met. *Average percent of need met:* 95% (excluding resources awarded to replace EFC). *Average financial aid package:* $22,436 (excluding resources awarded to replace EFC). 5% of all full-time undergraduates had no need and received non-need-based aid.

GIFT AID (NEED-BASED) ***Total amount:*** $23,792,609 (7% Federal, 2% state, 87% institutional, 4% external sources). ***Receiving aid:*** *Freshmen:* 40% (403); *all full-time undergraduates:* 29% (1,143). ***Average award:*** Freshmen: $18,166; Undergraduates: $16,183. ***Scholarships, grants, and awards:*** Federal Pell, FSEOG, state, private, college/university gift aid from institutional funds.

GIFT AID (NON-NEED-BASED) ***Total amount:*** $3,179,645 (26% Federal, 10% state, 57% institutional, 7% external sources). ***Receiving aid:*** *Freshmen:* 20% (204); *Undergraduates:* 19% (745). ***Scholarships, grants, and awards by category:*** *Academic Interests/Achievement:* general academic interests/achievements. *Special Characteristics:* children of faculty/staff. ***Tuition waivers:*** Full or partial for employees or children of employees. ***ROTC:*** Army, Air Force cooperative.

LOANS ***Student loans:*** $8,327,913 (85% need-based, 15% non-need-based). 55% of past graduating class borrowed through all loan programs. Average indebtedness per student: $16,100. ***Average need-based loan:***

Freshmen: $2360; Undergraduates: $4388. ***Parent loans:*** $5,231,342 (100% non-need-based). ***Programs:*** Federal Direct (Subsidized and Unsubsidized Stafford), FFEL (PLUS), Perkins, college/university.

WORK-STUDY ***Federal work-study:*** *Total amount:* $2,629,268; jobs available.

ATHLETIC AWARDS *Total amount:* 445,912 (100% non-need-based).

APPLYING for FINANCIAL AID ***Required financial aid forms:*** FAFSA, institution's own form, state aid form, noncustodial (divorced/separated) parent's statement, business/farm supplement, federal income tax form(s). ***Financial aid deadline:*** 2/15 (priority: 2/1). ***Notification date:*** 4/1. Students must reply by 5/1 or within 4 weeks of notification.

CONTACT Ms. Ellen Frishberg, Director of Student Financial Services, Johns Hopkins University, 146 Garland Hall, Baltimore, MD 21218, 410-516-8028.

JOHNSON & WALES UNIVERSITY

North Miami, FL

Tuition & fees: N/R **Average undergraduate aid package: $11,831**

ABOUT THE INSTITUTION Independent, coed. Awards: associate and bachelor's degrees. 11 undergraduate majors. Total enrollment: 1,156. Undergraduates: 1,156. Freshmen: 371. Both federal and institutional methodology are used as a basis for awarding need-based institutional aid.

FRESHMAN FINANCIAL AID (Fall 1999) 455 applied for aid; of those 94% were deemed to have need. 99% of freshmen with need received aid; of those 17% had need fully met. *Average percent of need met:* 60% (excluding resources awarded to replace EFC). *Average financial aid package:* $11,648 (excluding resources awarded to replace EFC). 2% of all full-time freshmen had no need and received non-need-based aid.

UNDERGRADUATE FINANCIAL AID (Fall 1999) 1,166 applied for aid; of those 93% were deemed to have need. 99% of undergraduates with need received aid; of those 19% had need fully met. *Average percent of need met:* 62% (excluding resources awarded to replace EFC). *Average financial aid package:* $11,831 (excluding resources awarded to replace EFC). 3% of all full-time undergraduates had no need and received non-need-based aid.

GIFT AID (NEED-BASED) ***Total amount:*** $3,357,472 (57% Federal, 3% state, 40% institutional). ***Receiving aid:*** *Freshmen:* 70% (358); *all full-time undergraduates:* 64% (873). ***Average award:*** Freshmen: $2791; Undergraduates: $2303. ***Scholarships, grants, and awards:*** Federal Pell, FSEOG, state, college/university gift aid from institutional funds.

GIFT AID (NON-NEED-BASED) ***Total amount:*** $1,795,620 (6% Federal, 1% state, 74% institutional, 19% external sources). ***Receiving aid:*** *Freshmen:* 43% (219); *Undergraduates:* 44% (593). ***Scholarships, grants, and awards by category:*** *Academic Interests/Achievement:* business, general academic interests/achievements. *Special Achievements/Activities:* general special achievements/activities, leadership, memberships. *Special Characteristics:* children of current students, children of faculty/staff, previous college experience, siblings of current students, spouses of current students. ***Tuition waivers:*** Full or partial for employees or children of employees.

LOANS ***Student loans:*** $7,640,228 (76% need-based, 24% non-need-based). 86% of past graduating class borrowed through all loan programs. Average indebtedness per student: $11,155. ***Average need-based loan:*** Freshmen: $2538; Undergraduates: $3966. ***Parent loans:*** $2,046,303 (100% non-need-based). ***Programs:*** FFEL (Subsidized and Unsubsidized Stafford, PLUS), Perkins, college/university.

WORK-STUDY ***Federal work-study:*** *Total amount:* $536,885; 307 jobs averaging $1749.

APPLYING for FINANCIAL AID ***Required financial aid form:*** FAFSA. ***Financial aid deadline:*** Continuous. ***Notification date:*** Continuous beginning 3/1. Students must reply within 2 weeks of notification.

CONTACT Ms. Lynn Robinson, Director of Financial Aid, Johnson & Wales University, 8 Abbott Park Place, Providence, RI 02903-3703, 401-598-4648 or toll-free 800-232-2433. *Fax:* 401-598-1040. *E-mail:* admissions@jwu.edu

JOHNSON & WALES UNIVERSITY

Providence, RI

Tuition & fees: $13,845 **Average undergraduate aid package: $10,407**

ABOUT THE INSTITUTION Independent, coed. Awards: associate, bachelor's, master's, and doctoral degrees (branch locations: Charleston, SC; Vail, CO; Denver, CO; North Miami, FL; Norfolk, VA; Worcester, MA; Gothenberg, Sweden). 47 undergraduate majors. Total enrollment: 8,811. Undergraduates: 8,236. Freshmen: 2,300. Both federal and institutional methodology are used as a basis for awarding need-based institutional aid.

UNDERGRADUATE EXPENSES for 2000–2001 ***Comprehensive fee:*** $19,815 includes full-time tuition ($13,275), mandatory fees ($570), and room and board ($5970). Full-time tuition and fees vary according to program. Room and board charges vary according to housing facility. Part-time tuition and fees vary according to program. ***Payment plans:*** guaranteed tuition, installment.

FRESHMAN FINANCIAL AID (Fall 1999) 1892 applied for aid; of those 90% were deemed to have need. 99% of freshmen with need received aid; of those 32% had need fully met. *Average percent of need met:* 60% (excluding resources awarded to replace EFC). *Average financial aid package:* $10,688 (excluding resources awarded to replace EFC). 5% of all full-time freshmen had no need and received non-need-based aid.

UNDERGRADUATE FINANCIAL AID (Fall 1999) 5,235 applied for aid; of those 88% were deemed to have need. 99% of undergraduates with need received aid; of those 33% had need fully met. *Average percent of need met:* 63% (excluding resources awarded to replace EFC). *Average financial aid package:* $10,407 (excluding resources awarded to replace EFC). 4% of all full-time undergraduates had no need and received non-need-based aid.

GIFT AID (NEED-BASED) ***Total amount:*** $11,137,245 (46% Federal, 3% state, 51% institutional). ***Receiving aid:*** *Freshmen:* 64% (1,413); *all full-time undergraduates:* 51% (3,500). ***Average award:*** Freshmen: $2044; Undergraduates: $2284. ***Scholarships, grants, and awards:*** Federal Pell, FSEOG, state, college/university gift aid from institutional funds.

GIFT AID (NON-NEED-BASED) ***Total amount:*** $7,607,607 (1% Federal, 4% state, 70% institutional, 25% external sources). ***Receiving aid:*** *Freshmen:* 39% (863); *Undergraduates:* 36% (2,456). ***Scholarships, grants, and awards by category:*** *Academic Interests/Achievement:* business, general academic interests/achievements, international studies. *Special Achievements/Activities:* general special achievements/activities, leadership, memberships. *Special Characteristics:* children of current students, children of faculty/staff, previous college experience, siblings of current students, spouses of current students. ***Tuition waivers:*** Full or partial for employees or children of employees. ***ROTC:*** Army cooperative.

LOANS ***Student loans:*** $32,558,628 (69% need-based, 31% non-need-based). 92% of past graduating class borrowed through all loan programs. Average indebtedness per student: $13,431. ***Average need-based loan:*** Freshmen: $2538; Undergraduates: $4056. ***Parent loans:*** $11,043,627 (100% non-need-based). ***Programs:*** FFEL (Subsidized and Unsubsidized Stafford, PLUS), Perkins, college/university.

WORK-STUDY ***Federal work-study:*** *Total amount:* $3,062,952; 1,742 jobs averaging $1758. ***State or other work-study/employment:*** *Total amount:* $44,265 (100% need-based). Part-time jobs available.

APPLYING for FINANCIAL AID ***Required financial aid form:*** FAFSA. ***Financial aid deadline:*** Continuous. ***Notification date:*** Continuous beginning 3/1. Students must reply within 2 weeks of notification.

CONTACT Ms. Lynn Robinson, Director of Financial Aid, Johnson & Wales University, 8 Abbott Park Place, Providence, RI 02903-3703, 401-598-4648 or toll-free 800-342-5598 (out-of-state). *Fax:* 401-598-1040. *E-mail:* admissions@jwu.edu

JOHNSON & WALES UNIVERSITY

Charleston, SC

Tuition & fees: N/R **Average undergraduate aid package: $9028**

Johnson & Wales University (continued)

ABOUT THE INSTITUTION Independent, coed. Awards: associate and bachelor's degrees. 3 undergraduate majors. Total enrollment: 1,450. Undergraduates: 1,450. Freshmen: 364. Both federal and institutional methodology are used as a basis for awarding need-based institutional aid.

FRESHMAN FINANCIAL AID (Fall 1999) 266 applied for aid; of those 91% were deemed to have need. 99% of freshmen with need received aid; of those 24% had need fully met. *Average percent of need met:* 57% (excluding resources awarded to replace EFC). *Average financial aid package:* $10,313 (excluding resources awarded to replace EFC). 4% of all full-time freshmen had no need and received non-need-based aid.

UNDERGRADUATE FINANCIAL AID (Fall 1999) 1,086 applied for aid; of those 87% were deemed to have need. 99% of undergraduates with need received aid; of those 27% had need fully met. *Average percent of need met:* 56% (excluding resources awarded to replace EFC). *Average financial aid package:* $9028 (excluding resources awarded to replace EFC). 4% of all full-time undergraduates had no need and received non-need-based aid.

GIFT AID (NEED-BASED) ***Total amount:*** $2,653,519 (69% Federal, 31% institutional). ***Receiving aid:*** *Freshmen:* 59% (178); *all full-time undergraduates:* 46% (658). ***Average award:*** Freshmen: $1539; Undergraduates: $1709. ***Scholarships, grants, and awards:*** Federal Pell, FSEOG, state, college/university gift aid from institutional funds.

GIFT AID (NON-NEED-BASED) ***Total amount:*** $1,302,049 (7% Federal, 9% state, 55% institutional, 29% external sources). ***Receiving aid:*** *Freshmen:* 43% (130); *Undergraduates:* 31% (450). ***Scholarships, grants, and awards by category:*** *Academic Interests/Achievement:* general academic interests/achievements. *Special Achievements/Activities:* general special achievements/activities, leadership, memberships. *Special Characteristics:* children of current students, children of faculty/staff, previous college experience, siblings of current students, spouses of current students. ***Tuition waivers:*** Full or partial for employees or children of employees.

LOANS ***Student loans:*** $5,149,534 (60% need-based, 40% non-need-based). 99% of past graduating class borrowed through all loan programs. Average indebtedness per student: $11,562. ***Average need-based loan:*** Freshmen: $2609; Undergraduates: $3582. ***Parent loans:*** $2,172,393 (100% non-need-based). ***Programs:*** FFEL (Subsidized and Unsubsidized Stafford, PLUS), Perkins, college/university.

WORK-STUDY ***Federal work-study:*** *Total amount:* $420,262; 232 jobs averaging $1811.

APPLYING for FINANCIAL AID ***Required financial aid form:*** FAFSA. ***Financial aid deadline:*** Continuous. ***Notification date:*** Continuous beginning 3/1. Students must reply within 2 weeks of notification.

CONTACT Ms. Lynn Robinson, Director of Financial Aid, Johnson & Wales University, 8 Abbott Park Place, Providence, RI 02903-3703, 401-598-4648 or toll-free 800-868-1522 (out-of-state). *Fax:* 401-598-1040. *E-mail:* admissions@jwu.edu

JOHNSON BIBLE COLLEGE

Knoxville, TN

Tuition & fees: $5280 **Average undergraduate aid package: $3433**

ABOUT THE INSTITUTION Independent religious, coed. Awards: associate, bachelor's, and master's degrees. 14 undergraduate majors. Total enrollment: 575. Undergraduates: 486. Freshmen: 106. Both federal and institutional methodology are used as a basis for awarding need-based institutional aid.

UNDERGRADUATE EXPENSES for 2000–2001 ***Application fee:*** $35. ***Comprehensive fee:*** $8650 includes full-time tuition ($4740), mandatory fees ($540), and room and board ($3370). Room and board charges vary according to housing facility. ***Part-time tuition:*** $198 per semester hour. ***Part-time fees:*** $17 per semester hour. Part-time tuition and fees vary according to course load. ***Payment plan:*** installment.

FRESHMAN FINANCIAL AID (Fall 1999, est.) 145 applied for aid; of those 100% were deemed to have need. 100% of freshmen with need received aid. *Average percent of need met:* 47% (excluding resources awarded to replace EFC). *Average financial aid package:* $2988 (excluding resources awarded to replace EFC).

UNDERGRADUATE FINANCIAL AID (Fall 1999, est.) 432 applied for aid; of those 100% were deemed to have need. 100% of undergraduates with need received aid. *Average percent of need met:* 55% (excluding resources awarded to replace EFC). *Average financial aid package:* $3433 (excluding resources awarded to replace EFC).

GIFT AID (NEED-BASED) ***Total amount:*** $633,208 (76% Federal, 13% state, 11% institutional). ***Receiving aid:*** *Freshmen:* 48% (70); *all full-time undergraduates:* 50% (217). ***Average award:*** Freshmen: $973; Undergraduates: $1334. ***Scholarships, grants, and awards:*** Federal Pell, FSEOG, state, college/university gift aid from institutional funds.

GIFT AID (NON-NEED-BASED) ***Total amount:*** $1,426,170 (58% institutional, 42% external sources). ***Receiving aid:*** *Freshmen:* 88% (129); *Undergraduates:* 85% (370). ***Scholarships, grants, and awards by category:*** *Academic Interests/Achievement:* general academic interests/achievements. *Special Achievements/Activities:* community service, general special achievements/activities, leadership, religious involvement. *Special Characteristics:* children of current students, children of faculty/staff, ethnic background, general special characteristics, international students, married students, members of minority groups, parents of current students, relatives of clergy, religious affiliation, siblings of current students, spouses of current students. ***Tuition waivers:*** Full or partial for employees or children of employees.

LOANS ***Student loans:*** $1,260,118 (100% need-based). 63% of past graduating class borrowed through all loan programs. Average indebtedness per student: $11,980. ***Average need-based loan:*** Freshmen: $563; Undergraduates: $716. ***Parent loans:*** $167,036 (50% need-based, 50% non-need-based). ***Programs:*** FFEL (Subsidized and Unsubsidized Stafford, PLUS), college/university.

WORK-STUDY ***Federal work-study:*** *Total amount:* $163,672; jobs available. ***State or other work-study/employment:*** *Total amount:* $292,728 (100% need-based). Part-time jobs available.

APPLYING for FINANCIAL AID ***Required financial aid forms:*** FAFSA, institution's own form. ***Financial aid deadline:*** Continuous. ***Notification date:*** Continuous. Students must reply within 2 weeks of notification.

CONTACT Mrs. Janette Overton, Financial Aid Director, Johnson Bible College, 7900 Johnson Drive, Knoxville, TN 37998-0001, 423-251-2303 or toll-free 800-827-2122. *Fax:* 423-251-2337.

JOHNSON C. SMITH UNIVERSITY

Charlotte, NC

Tuition & fees: $9974 **Average undergraduate aid package: $6200**

ABOUT THE INSTITUTION Independent, coed. Awards: bachelor's degrees. 31 undergraduate majors. Total enrollment: 1,591. Undergraduates: 1,591. Freshmen: 595. Federal methodology is used as a basis for awarding need-based institutional aid.

UNDERGRADUATE EXPENSES for 1999–2000 ***Application fee:*** $25. ***Comprehensive fee:*** $13,849 includes full-time tuition ($8857), mandatory fees ($1117), and room and board ($3875). ***College room only:*** $2202. Room and board charges vary according to board plan, housing facility, and location. ***Part-time tuition:*** $192 per semester hour. ***Part-time fees:*** $61 per term part-time. Part-time tuition and fees vary according to course load. ***Payment plan:*** installment.

FRESHMAN FINANCIAL AID (Fall 1999, est.) 480 applied for aid; of those 96% were deemed to have need. 100% of freshmen with need received aid; of those 1% had need fully met. *Average percent of need met:* 90% (excluding resources awarded to replace EFC). *Average financial aid package:* $4500 (excluding resources awarded to replace EFC). 12% of all full-time freshmen had no need and received non-need-based aid.

UNDERGRADUATE FINANCIAL AID (Fall 1999, est.) 1,335 applied for aid; of those 99% were deemed to have need. 100% of undergraduates with need received aid; of those 2% had need fully met. *Average percent of need met:* 90% (excluding resources awarded to replace EFC). *Average*

financial aid package: $6200 (excluding resources awarded to replace EFC). 13% of all full-time undergraduates had no need and received non-need-based aid.

GIFT AID (NEED-BASED) ***Total amount:*** $3,800,000 (66% Federal, 9% state, 24% institutional, 1% external sources). ***Receiving aid:*** *Freshmen:* 29% (175); *all full-time undergraduates:* 21% (320). ***Average award:*** Freshmen: $1500; Undergraduates: $2000. ***Scholarships, grants, and awards:*** Federal Pell, FSEOG, state, private, college/university gift aid from institutional funds, United Negro College Fund.

GIFT AID (NON-NEED-BASED) ***Total amount:*** $651,000 (77% state, 23% external sources). ***Receiving aid:*** *Freshmen:* 50% (300); *Undergraduates:* 60% (920). ***Scholarships, grants, and awards by category:*** *Academic Interests/Achievement:* general academic interests/achievements. *Creative Arts/Performance:* music. *Special Achievements/Activities:* community service, general special achievements/activities, leadership. ***Tuition waivers:*** Full or partial for employees or children of employees. ***ROTC:*** Army, Air Force.

LOANS ***Student loans:*** $6,522,000 (62% need-based, 38% non-need-based). 85% of past graduating class borrowed through all loan programs. Average indebtedness per student: $22,000. ***Parent loans:*** $3,365,000 (96% need-based, 4% non-need-based). ***Programs:*** Federal Direct (Subsidized and Unsubsidized Stafford, PLUS), Perkins, college/university.

WORK-STUDY ***Federal work-study:*** *Total amount:* $400,000; 400 jobs averaging $1000.

ATHLETIC AWARDS *Total amount:* 780,000 (100% non-need-based).

APPLYING for FINANCIAL AID ***Required financial aid form:*** FAFSA. ***Financial aid deadline (priority):*** 4/1. ***Notification date:*** Continuous. Students must reply within 2 weeks of notification.

CONTACT Ms. Cynthia Anderson, Director of Financial Aid, Johnson C. Smith University, 100 Beatties Ford Road, Charlotte, NC 28216, 704-378-1034 or toll-free 800-782-7303. *Fax:* 704-378-1292.

JOHNSON STATE COLLEGE

Johnson, VT

Tuition & fees (VT res): $5009 **Average undergraduate aid package: $7634**

ABOUT THE INSTITUTION State-supported, coed. Awards: associate, bachelor's, and master's degrees. 57 undergraduate majors. Total enrollment: 1,541. Undergraduates: 1,398. Freshmen: 234. Federal methodology is used as a basis for awarding need-based institutional aid.

UNDERGRADUATE EXPENSES for 1999–2000 ***Application fee:*** $30. ***Tuition, state resident:*** full-time $4092; part-time $171 per credit. ***Tuition, nonresident:*** full-time $9588; part-time $400 per credit. ***Required fees:*** full-time $917; $16 per credit; $98 per term part-time. Full-time tuition and fees vary according to reciprocity agreements. Part-time tuition and fees vary according to course load and reciprocity agreements. ***College room and board:*** $5298; ***room only:*** $3108. Room and board charges vary according to board plan and housing facility. ***Payment plans:*** installment, deferred payment.

FRESHMAN FINANCIAL AID (Fall 1999) 204 applied for aid; of those 82% were deemed to have need. 100% of freshmen with need received aid; of those 39% had need fully met. *Average percent of need met:* 79% (excluding resources awarded to replace EFC). *Average financial aid package:* $7538 (excluding resources awarded to replace EFC). 16% of all full-time freshmen had no need and received non-need-based aid.

UNDERGRADUATE FINANCIAL AID (Fall 1999) 876 applied for aid; of those 84% were deemed to have need. 100% of undergraduates with need received aid; of those 24% had need fully met. *Average percent of need met:* 79% (excluding resources awarded to replace EFC). *Average financial aid package:* $7634 (excluding resources awarded to replace EFC). 13% of all full-time undergraduates had no need and received non-need-based aid.

GIFT AID (NEED-BASED) ***Total amount:*** $2,495,240 (49% Federal, 22% state, 21% institutional, 8% external sources). ***Receiving aid:*** *Freshmen:* 53% (124); *all full-time undergraduates:* 61% (643). ***Average award:*** Freshmen: $3018; Undergraduates: $3572. ***Scholarships, grants, and awards:*** Federal Pell, FSEOG, state, private, college/university gift aid from institutional funds.

GIFT AID (NON-NEED-BASED) ***Total amount:*** $96,865 (94% institutional, 6% external sources). ***Receiving aid:*** *Freshmen:* 48% (111); *Undergraduates:* 18% (193). ***Scholarships, grants, and awards by category:*** *Academic Interests/Achievement:* 93 awards ($107,800 total): business, education, general academic interests/achievements, mathematics. *Creative Arts/Performance:* 13 awards ($6450 total): art/fine arts, dance, music, performing arts, theater/drama. *Special Achievements/Activities:* 116 awards ($154,203 total): community service, general special achievements/activities, leadership, memberships. *Special Characteristics:* 80 awards ($62,200 total): general special characteristics, international students, local/state students, members of minority groups. ***Tuition waivers:*** Full or partial for employees or children of employees, senior citizens. ***ROTC:*** Army cooperative.

LOANS ***Student loans:*** $3,435,174 (88% need-based, 12% non-need-based). Average indebtedness per student: $16,910. ***Average need-based loan:*** Freshmen: $2584; Undergraduates: $3316. ***Parent loans:*** $1,670,799 (67% need-based, 33% non-need-based). ***Programs:*** Federal Direct (Subsidized and Unsubsidized Stafford, PLUS), Perkins.

WORK-STUDY ***Federal work-study:*** *Total amount:* $592,007; 406 jobs averaging $1458.

APPLYING for FINANCIAL AID ***Required financial aid form:*** FAFSA. ***Financial aid deadline (priority):*** 3/1. ***Notification date:*** Continuous beginning 4/1. Students must reply within 3 weeks of notification.

CONTACT Ms. Kimberly Goodell, Financial Aid Officer, Johnson State College, 337 College Hill, Johnson, VT 05656-9405, 800-635-2356. *Fax:* 802-635-1463. *E-mail:* goodellk@badger.jsc.vsc.edu

JOHN WESLEY COLLEGE

High Point, NC

Tuition & fees: $5556 **Average undergraduate aid package: N/A**

ABOUT THE INSTITUTION Independent interdenominational, coed. Awards: associate and bachelor's degrees. 10 undergraduate majors. Total enrollment: 154. Undergraduates: 154. Freshmen: 10. Federal methodology is used as a basis for awarding need-based institutional aid.

UNDERGRADUATE EXPENSES for 1999–2000 ***Application fee:*** $30. ***Tuition:*** full-time $5336; part-time $220 per semester hour. ***Required fees:*** full-time $220; $110 per term part-time. Part-time tuition and fees vary according to course load. Room and board charges vary according to housing facility. ***Payment plan:*** installment.

FRESHMAN FINANCIAL AID (Fall 1998) 14 applied for aid; of those 100% were deemed to have need. 100% of freshmen with need received aid; of those 7% had need fully met. *Average percent of need met:* 55% (excluding resources awarded to replace EFC). 5% of all full-time freshmen had no need and received non-need-based aid.

UNDERGRADUATE FINANCIAL AID (Fall 1998) 79 applied for aid; of those 100% were deemed to have need. 100% of undergraduates with need received aid; of those 19% had need fully met. *Average percent of need met:* 80% (excluding resources awarded to replace EFC). 11% of all full-time undergraduates had no need and received non-need-based aid.

GIFT AID (NEED-BASED) ***Total amount:*** $137,777 (72% Federal, 28% institutional). ***Receiving aid:*** *Freshmen:* 52% (11); *all full-time undergraduates:* 37% (57). ***Average award:*** Freshmen: $1925. ***Scholarships, grants, and awards:*** Federal Pell, FSEOG, private, college/university gift aid from institutional funds.

GIFT AID (NON-NEED-BASED) ***Total amount:*** $56,668 (100% external sources). ***Receiving aid:*** *Freshmen:* 5% (1); *Undergraduates:* 13% (20). ***Scholarships, grants, and awards by category:*** *Academic Interests/Achievement:* education, general academic interests/achievements, religion/biblical studies. *Special Achievements/Activities:* religious involvement. *Special Characteristics:* 20 awards ($24,100 total): children of faculty/staff, general special characteristics, married students, spouses of current students. ***Tuition waivers:*** Full or partial for employees or children of employees.

John Wesley College (continued)

LOANS ***Student loans:*** $320,259 (100% need-based). 80% of past graduating class borrowed through all loan programs. ***Average need-based loan:*** Freshmen: $2450; Undergraduates: $2100. ***Programs:*** Federal Direct (Subsidized and Unsubsidized Stafford, PLUS), FFEL (Subsidized and Unsubsidized Stafford, PLUS).

WORK-STUDY ***Federal work-study:*** *Total amount:* $23,773; 9 jobs averaging $2500.

APPLYING for FINANCIAL AID ***Required financial aid forms:*** FAFSA, institution's own form. ***Financial aid deadline (priority):*** 8/1. ***Notification date:*** Continuous.

CONTACT Mr. Ronald Adams, Director of Financial Aid, John Wesley College, 2314 North Centennial Street, High Point, NC 27265-3197, 336-889-2262. *Fax:* 336-889-2261. *E-mail:* radams@johnwesley.edu

JONES COLLEGE

Jacksonville, FL

CONTACT Mrs. Denise Wendle, Director of Financial Aid, Jones College, 5353 Arlington Expressway, Jacksonville, FL 32211-5540, 904-743-1122. *Fax:* 904-743-4446. *E-mail:* dwendle@jones.edu

JONES INTERNATIONAL UNIVERSITY

Englewood, CO

Tuition & fees: $3750 **Average undergraduate aid package: N/A**

ABOUT THE INSTITUTION Independent, coed. Awards: bachelor's and master's degrees. 1 undergraduate major. Total enrollment: 114. Undergraduates: 18.

UNDERGRADUATE EXPENSES for 1999–2000 ***Application fee:*** $75. ***Tuition:*** full-time $3600; part-time $600 per course. ***Required fees:*** full-time $150; $25 per course. ***Payment plan:*** guaranteed tuition.

GIFT AID (NEED-BASED) ***Scholarships, grants, and awards:*** Sallie Mae CASHE Scholarships.

LOANS ***Programs:*** Sallie Mae Loans, PLATO Loans.

CONTACT Gloria Brown, Admissions Coordinator, Jones International University, 9697 East Mineral Avenue, Englewood, CO 80112, 303-784-8048 or toll-free 800-811-5663. *Fax:* 303-784-8547. *E-mail:* gbrown@international.edu

JUDSON COLLEGE

Marion, AL

Tuition & fees: $7640 **Average undergraduate aid package: $8764**

ABOUT THE INSTITUTION Independent Baptist, women only. Awards: bachelor's degrees. 26 undergraduate majors. Total enrollment: 308. Undergraduates: 308. Freshmen: 79. Federal methodology is used as a basis for awarding need-based institutional aid.

UNDERGRADUATE EXPENSES for 2000–2001 (est.) ***Application fee:*** $25. ***One-time required fee:*** $195. ***Comprehensive fee:*** $12,240 includes full-time tuition ($7400), mandatory fees ($240), and room and board ($4600). Full-time tuition and fees vary according to course load. ***Part-time tuition:*** $216 per semester hour. ***Part-time fees:*** $75 per term. Part-time tuition and fees vary according to course load. ***Payment plan:*** installment.

FRESHMAN FINANCIAL AID (Fall 1999) 79 applied for aid; of those 82% were deemed to have need. 100% of freshmen with need received aid; of those 29% had need fully met. *Average percent of need met:* 85% (excluding resources awarded to replace EFC). *Average financial aid package:* $9008 (excluding resources awarded to replace EFC). 18% of all full-time freshmen had no need and received non-need-based aid.

UNDERGRADUATE FINANCIAL AID (Fall 1999) 254 applied for aid; of those 68% were deemed to have need. 100% of undergraduates with need received aid; of those 19% had need fully met. *Average percent of need met:* 86% (excluding resources awarded to replace EFC). *Average financial aid package:* $8764 (excluding resources awarded to replace EFC). 20% of all full-time undergraduates had no need and received non-need-based aid.

GIFT AID (NEED-BASED) ***Total amount:*** $1,056,581 (22% Federal, 13% state, 58% institutional, 7% external sources). ***Receiving aid:*** *Freshmen:* 82% (65); *all full-time undergraduates:* 66% (172). ***Average award:*** Freshmen: $6249; Undergraduates: $5757. ***Scholarships, grants, and awards:*** Federal Pell, FSEOG, state, private, college/university gift aid from institutional funds.

GIFT AID (NON-NEED-BASED) ***Total amount:*** $345,340 (13% state, 77% institutional, 10% external sources). ***Receiving aid:*** *Freshmen:* 11% (9); *Undergraduates:* 9% (23). ***Scholarships, grants, and awards by category:*** *Academic Interests/Achievement:* 73 awards ($256,950 total): general academic interests/achievements. *Creative Arts/Performance:* 13 awards ($19,300 total): art/fine arts, music. *Special Achievements/Activities:* 82 awards ($112,800 total): general special achievements/activities, junior miss. *Special Characteristics:* 64 awards ($66,234 total): children of educators, children of faculty/staff, relatives of clergy, religious affiliation. ***Tuition waivers:*** Full or partial for employees or children of employees. ***ROTC:*** Army cooperative.

LOANS ***Student loans:*** $563,883 (67% need-based, 33% non-need-based). 58% of past graduating class borrowed through all loan programs. Average indebtedness per student: $12,085. ***Average need-based loan:*** Freshmen: $2538; Undergraduates: $2746. ***Parent loans:*** $83,112 (100% non-need-based). ***Programs:*** FFEL (Subsidized and Unsubsidized Stafford, PLUS), Perkins, college/university.

WORK-STUDY ***Federal work-study:*** *Total amount:* $60,364; 60 jobs averaging $1010. ***State or other work-study/employment:*** *Total amount:* $139,434 (83% need-based, 17% non-need-based). 98 part-time jobs averaging $1100.

ATHLETIC AWARDS *Total amount:* 34,350 (48% need-based, 52% non-need-based).

APPLYING for FINANCIAL AID ***Required financial aid forms:*** FAFSA, institution's own form, state aid form. ***Financial aid deadline (priority):*** 3/1. ***Notification date:*** Continuous. Students must reply within 2 weeks of notification.

CONTACT Mrs. Doris A. Wilson, Director of Financial Aid, Judson College, PO Box 120, Marion, AL 36756, 334-683-5157 or toll-free 800-447-9472. *Fax:* 334-683-5158. *E-mail:* dwilson@future.judson.edu

JUDSON COLLEGE

Elgin, IL

Tuition & fees: $13,890 **Average undergraduate aid package: $10,092**

ABOUT THE INSTITUTION Independent Baptist, coed. Awards: bachelor's degrees. 48 undergraduate majors. Total enrollment: 1,100. Undergraduates: 1,100. Freshmen: 223. Both federal and institutional methodology are used as a basis for awarding need-based institutional aid.

UNDERGRADUATE EXPENSES for 1999–2000 ***Application fee:*** $30. ***Comprehensive fee:*** $19,250 includes full-time tuition ($13,340), mandatory fees ($550), and room and board ($5360). ***Part-time tuition:*** $460 per semester hour. Part-time tuition and fees vary according to course load. ***Payment plan:*** installment.

FRESHMAN FINANCIAL AID (Fall 1999, est.) 206 applied for aid; of those 82% were deemed to have need. 100% of freshmen with need received aid; of those 21% had need fully met. *Average percent of need met:* 88% (excluding resources awarded to replace EFC). *Average financial aid package:* $11,884 (excluding resources awarded to replace EFC). 13% of all full-time freshmen had no need and received non-need-based aid.

UNDERGRADUATE FINANCIAL AID (Fall 1999, est.) 760 applied for aid; of those 89% were deemed to have need. 100% of undergraduates with need received aid; of those 9% had need fully met. *Average percent of need met:* 85% (excluding resources awarded to replace EFC). *Average financial aid package:* $10,092 (excluding resources awarded to replace EFC). 11% of all full-time undergraduates had no need and received non-need-based aid.

GIFT AID (NEED-BASED) ***Total amount:*** $5,354,342 (7% Federal, 28% state, 62% institutional, 3% external sources). ***Receiving aid:*** *Freshmen:* 78% (163); *all full-time undergraduates:* 79% (651). ***Average award:*** Freshmen: $8707; Undergraduates: $6000. ***Scholarships, grants, and awards:*** Federal Pell, FSEOG, state, private, college/university gift aid from institutional funds.

GIFT AID (NON-NEED-BASED) ***Total amount:*** $591,874 (83% institutional, 17% external sources). ***Receiving aid:*** *Freshmen:* 54% (113); *Undergraduates:* 59% (489). ***Scholarships, grants, and awards by category:*** *Academic Interests/Achievement:* architecture, general academic interests/achievements. *Creative Arts/Performance:* art/fine arts, journalism/publications, music, performing arts, theater/drama. *Special Achievements/Activities:* cheerleading/drum major, leadership. *Special Characteristics:* children and siblings of alumni, children of faculty/staff, international students, local/state students, out-of-state students, religious affiliation, siblings of current students. ***Tuition waivers:*** Full or partial for employees or children of employees, senior citizens. ***ROTC:*** Army cooperative.

LOANS ***Student loans:*** $3,535,900 (67% need-based, 33% non-need-based). ***Average need-based loan:*** Freshmen: $3097; Undergraduates: $3598. ***Parent loans:*** $647,095 (100% non-need-based). ***Programs:*** Federal Direct (Subsidized and Unsubsidized Stafford), Perkins.

WORK-STUDY ***Federal work-study:*** *Total amount:* $110,000; jobs available. ***State or other work-study/employment:*** *Total amount:* $300,000 (67% need-based, 33% non-need-based). Part-time jobs available.

ATHLETIC AWARDS *Total amount:* 552,638 (72% need-based, 28% non-need-based).

APPLYING for FINANCIAL AID ***Required financial aid forms:*** FAFSA, institution's own form. ***Financial aid deadline (priority):*** 5/1. ***Notification date:*** Continuous. Students must reply within 3 weeks of notification.

CONTACT Mr. David M. Vollman, Financial Aid Specialist, Judson College, 1151 North State Street, Elgin, IL 60123-1498, 847-695-2500 Ext. 2331 or toll-free 800-879-5376. *Fax:* 847-695-0216.

THE JUILLIARD SCHOOL

New York, NY

Tuition & fees: $16,600 **Average undergraduate aid package: $15,188**

ABOUT THE INSTITUTION Independent, coed. Awards: bachelor's, master's, and doctoral degrees. 7 undergraduate majors. Total enrollment: 961. Undergraduates: 665. Freshmen: 94. Federal methodology is used as a basis for awarding need-based institutional aid.

UNDERGRADUATE EXPENSES for 1999–2000 ***Application fee:*** $100. ***Comprehensive fee:*** $23,450 includes full-time tuition ($16,000), mandatory fees ($600), and room and board ($6850). Room and board charges vary according to housing facility. ***Payment plan:*** installment.

FRESHMAN FINANCIAL AID (Fall 1999) 107 applied for aid; of those 82% were deemed to have need. 100% of freshmen with need received aid; of those 14% had need fully met. *Average percent of need met:* 73% (excluding resources awarded to replace EFC). *Average financial aid package:* $15,186 (excluding resources awarded to replace EFC). 6% of all full-time freshmen had no need and received non-need-based aid.

UNDERGRADUATE FINANCIAL AID (Fall 1999) 420 applied for aid; of those 83% were deemed to have need. 100% of undergraduates with need received aid; of those 9% had need fully met. *Average percent of need met:* 71% (excluding resources awarded to replace EFC). *Average financial aid package:* $15,188 (excluding resources awarded to replace EFC). 7% of all full-time undergraduates had no need and received non-need-based aid.

GIFT AID (NEED-BASED) ***Total amount:*** $4,046,891 (10% Federal, 2% state, 86% institutional, 2% external sources). ***Receiving aid:*** *Freshmen:* 60% (75); *all full-time undergraduates:* 73% (330). ***Average award:*** Freshmen: $13,639; Undergraduates: $12,021. ***Scholarships, grants, and awards:*** Federal Pell, FSEOG, state, private, college/university gift aid from institutional funds.

GIFT AID (NON-NEED-BASED) ***Total amount:*** $219,000 (97% institutional, 3% external sources). ***Scholarships, grants, and awards by category:*** *Creative Arts/Performance:* dance, music, performing arts, theater/drama. *Special Achievements/Activities:* general special achievements/activities. *Special Characteristics:* general special characteristics. ***Tuition waivers:*** Full or partial for employees or children of employees.

LOANS ***Student loans:*** $1,392,294 (94% need-based, 6% non-need-based). 68% of past graduating class borrowed through all loan programs. Average indebtedness per student: $17,298. ***Average need-based loan:*** Freshmen: $2441; Undergraduates: $3980. ***Parent loans:*** $451,930 (61% need-based, 39% non-need-based). ***Programs:*** Federal Direct (Subsidized and Unsubsidized Stafford, PLUS), Perkins, college/university.

WORK-STUDY ***Federal work-study:*** *Total amount:* $173,630; 232 jobs averaging $1168. ***State or other work-study/employment:*** *Total amount:* $39,500 (100% non-need-based). Part-time jobs available.

APPLYING for FINANCIAL AID ***Required financial aid forms:*** FAFSA, institution's own form, state aid form, tax returns, salary documentation. ***Financial aid deadline (priority):*** 3/1. ***Notification date:*** 4/1. Students must reply within 2 weeks of notification.

CONTACT Mary Gray, Director of Admissions, The Juilliard School, 60 Lincoln Center Plaza, New York, NY 10023-6588, 212-799-5000 Ext. 223. *Fax:* 212-724-0263.

JUNIATA COLLEGE

Huntingdon, PA

Tuition & fees: $19,360 **Average undergraduate aid package: $16,697**

ABOUT THE INSTITUTION Independent religious, coed. Awards: bachelor's degrees. 67 undergraduate majors. Total enrollment: 1,268. Undergraduates: 1,268. Freshmen: 327. Both federal and institutional methodology are used as a basis for awarding need-based institutional aid.

UNDERGRADUATE EXPENSES for 2000–2001 ***Application fee:*** $30. ***Comprehensive fee:*** $24,650 includes full-time tuition ($18,940), mandatory fees ($420), and room and board ($5290). ***College room only:*** $2770. ***Payment plan:*** installment.

FRESHMAN FINANCIAL AID (Fall 1999) 277 applied for aid; of those 89% were deemed to have need. 100% of freshmen with need received aid; of those 53% had need fully met. *Average percent of need met:* 94% (excluding resources awarded to replace EFC). *Average financial aid package:* $16,280 (excluding resources awarded to replace EFC).

UNDERGRADUATE FINANCIAL AID (Fall 1999) 1,072 applied for aid; of those 91% were deemed to have need. 100% of undergraduates with need received aid; of those 54% had need fully met. *Average percent of need met:* 97% (excluding resources awarded to replace EFC). *Average financial aid package:* $16,697 (excluding resources awarded to replace EFC).

GIFT AID (NEED-BASED) ***Total amount:*** $11,301,021 (7% Federal, 14% state, 77% institutional, 2% external sources). ***Receiving aid:*** *Freshmen:* 76% (246); *all full-time undergraduates:* 81% (967). ***Average award:*** Freshmen: $11,685; Undergraduates: $11,098. ***Scholarships, grants, and awards:*** Federal Pell, FSEOG, state, private, college/university gift aid from institutional funds.

GIFT AID (NON-NEED-BASED) ***Total amount:*** $2,136,484 (1% Federal, 98% institutional, 1% external sources). ***Receiving aid:*** *Freshmen:* 63% (205); *Undergraduates:* 72% (857). ***Scholarships, grants, and awards by category:*** *Academic Interests/Achievement:* biological sciences, business, communication, computer science, education, English, foreign languages, general academic interests/achievements, health fields, humanities, international studies, mathematics, physical sciences, premedicine, social sciences. *Creative Arts/Performance:* music, performing arts. *Special Achievements/Activities:* community service, general special achievements/activities, leadership. *Special Characteristics:* adult students, children and siblings of alumni, children of faculty/staff, ethnic background, international students, local/state students. ***Tuition waivers:*** Full or partial for employees or children of employees, adult students.

LOANS ***Student loans:*** $4,517,159 (93% need-based, 7% non-need-based). 78% of past graduating class borrowed through all loan programs. Average indebtedness per student: $16,395. ***Average need-based loan:***

Juniata College (continued)

Freshmen: $3131; Undergraduates: $4067. ***Parent loans:*** $1,336,793 (92% need-based, 8% non-need-based). ***Programs:*** FFEL (Subsidized and Unsubsidized Stafford, PLUS), Perkins.

WORK-STUDY ***Federal work-study:*** *Total amount:* $626,390; 506 jobs averaging $1236. ***State or other work-study/employment:*** *Total amount:* $857,899 (63% need-based, 37% non-need-based). 606 part-time jobs averaging $1421.

APPLYING for FINANCIAL AID ***Required financial aid forms:*** FAFSA, CSS Financial Aid PROFILE. ***Financial aid deadline (priority):*** 3/1. ***Notification date:*** Continuous. Students must reply within 2 weeks of notification.

CONTACT Mr. Randall S. Rennell, Director of Student Financial Planning, Juniata College, 1700 Moore Street, Huntingdon, PA 16652-2119, 814-641-3142 or toll-free 877-JUNIATA. *Fax:* 814-641-3100. *E-mail:* rennelr@juniata.edu

KALAMAZOO COLLEGE

Kalamazoo, MI

Tuition & fees: $19,188 **Average undergraduate aid package: $15,408**

ABOUT THE INSTITUTION Independent religious, coed. Awards: bachelor's degrees. 24 undergraduate majors. Total enrollment: 1,367. Undergraduates: 1,367. Freshmen: 370. Both federal and institutional methodology are used as a basis for awarding need-based institutional aid.

UNDERGRADUATE EXPENSES for 1999–2000 ***Application fee:*** $35. ***One-time required fee:*** $70. ***Comprehensive fee:*** $24,975 includes full-time tuition ($19,188) and room and board ($5787). ***College room only:*** $2865. Room and board charges vary according to board plan and housing facility. Part-time tuition and fees vary according to course load. ***Payment plans:*** installment, deferred payment.

FRESHMAN FINANCIAL AID (Fall 1999) 283 applied for aid; of those 61% were deemed to have need. 100% of freshmen with need received aid; of those 88% had need fully met. *Average percent of need met:* 98% (excluding resources awarded to replace EFC). *Average financial aid package:* $15,625 (excluding resources awarded to replace EFC). 53% of all full-time freshmen had no need and received non-need-based aid.

UNDERGRADUATE FINANCIAL AID (Fall 1999) 883 applied for aid; of those 83% were deemed to have need. 100% of undergraduates with need received aid; of those 82% had need fully met. *Average financial aid package:* $15,408 (excluding resources awarded to replace EFC). 36% of all full-time undergraduates had no need and received non-need-based aid.

GIFT AID (NEED-BASED) ***Total amount:*** $8,012,106 (6% Federal, 14% state, 80% institutional). ***Receiving aid:*** *Freshmen:* 47% (173); *all full-time undergraduates:* 52% (685). ***Average award:*** Freshmen: $11,148; Undergraduates: $10,072. ***Scholarships, grants, and awards:*** Federal Pell, FSEOG, state, private, college/university gift aid from institutional funds.

GIFT AID (NON-NEED-BASED) ***Total amount:*** $5,440,430 (1% Federal, 74% institutional, 25% external sources). ***Receiving aid:*** *Freshmen:* 11% (40); *Undergraduates:* 9% (120). ***Scholarships, grants, and awards by category:*** *Academic Interests/Achievement:* biological sciences, English, foreign languages, general academic interests/achievements, mathematics, physical sciences, social sciences. *Creative Arts/Performance:* art/fine arts, cinema/film/broadcasting, music, theater/drama. *Special Achievements/Activities:* general special achievements/activities. *Special Characteristics:* children of faculty/staff, international students, members of minority groups. ***Tuition waivers:*** Full or partial for employees or children of employees. ***ROTC:*** Army cooperative.

LOANS ***Student loans:*** $3,543,517 (68% need-based, 32% non-need-based). Average indebtedness per student: $17,100. ***Average need-based loan:*** Freshmen: $3300; Undergraduates: $4090. ***Parent loans:*** $862,426 (100% non-need-based). ***Programs:*** Federal Direct (Subsidized and Unsubsidized Stafford, PLUS), Perkins, state.

WORK-STUDY ***Federal work-study:*** *Total amount:* $569,000; 375 jobs averaging $1580.

APPLYING for FINANCIAL AID ***Required financial aid forms:*** FAFSA, institution's own form. ***Financial aid deadline (priority):*** 2/15. ***Notification date:*** 3/31. Students must reply by 5/1.

CONTACT Mr. Craig Schmidt, Assistant Director of Financial Aid, Kalamazoo College, 1200 Academy Street, Kalamazoo, MI 49006-3295, 616-337-7192 or toll-free 800-253-3602. *Fax:* 616-337-7390.

KANSAS CITY ART INSTITUTE

Kansas City, MO

Tuition & fees: $19,010 **Average undergraduate aid package: $13,241**

ABOUT THE INSTITUTION Independent, coed. Awards: bachelor's degrees. 9 undergraduate majors. Total enrollment: 550. Undergraduates: 550. Freshmen: 128. Federal methodology is used as a basis for awarding need-based institutional aid.

UNDERGRADUATE EXPENSES for 2000–2001 ***Application fee:*** $25. ***Comprehensive fee:*** $24,510 includes full-time tuition ($18,218), mandatory fees ($792), and room and board ($5500). Room and board charges vary according to board plan and housing facility. ***Part-time tuition:*** $700 per credit hour.

FRESHMAN FINANCIAL AID (Fall 1999, est.) 94 applied for aid; of those 82% were deemed to have need. 100% of freshmen with need received aid; of those 18% had need fully met. *Average percent of need met:* 67% (excluding resources awarded to replace EFC). *Average financial aid package:* $12,827 (excluding resources awarded to replace EFC). 20% of all full-time freshmen had no need and received non-need-based aid.

UNDERGRADUATE FINANCIAL AID (Fall 1999, est.) 413 applied for aid; of those 86% were deemed to have need. 100% of undergraduates with need received aid; of those 19% had need fully met. *Average percent of need met:* 71% (excluding resources awarded to replace EFC). *Average financial aid package:* $13,241 (excluding resources awarded to replace EFC). 34% of all full-time undergraduates had no need and received non-need-based aid.

GIFT AID (NEED-BASED) ***Total amount:*** $2,567,549 (13% Federal, 4% state, 80% institutional, 3% external sources). ***Receiving aid:*** *Freshmen:* 80% (77); *all full-time undergraduates:* 66% (355). ***Average award:*** Freshmen: $7960; Undergraduates: $6973. ***Scholarships, grants, and awards:*** Federal Pell, FSEOG, state, college/university gift aid from institutional funds.

GIFT AID (NON-NEED-BASED) ***Total amount:*** $1,081,132 (1% state, 93% institutional, 6% external sources). ***Receiving aid:*** *Freshmen:* 9% (9); *Undergraduates:* 5% (26). ***Scholarships, grants, and awards by category:*** *Creative Arts/Performance:* 295 awards ($2,262,060 total): art/fine arts. ***Tuition waivers:*** Full or partial for employees or children of employees.

LOANS ***Student loans:*** $2,667,697 (84% need-based, 16% non-need-based). 76% of past graduating class borrowed through all loan programs. Average indebtedness per student: $17,125. ***Average need-based loan:*** Freshmen: $4506; Undergraduates: $5949. ***Parent loans:*** $1,510,351 (43% need-based, 57% non-need-based). ***Programs:*** FFEL (Subsidized and Unsubsidized Stafford, PLUS), Perkins, alternative loans.

WORK-STUDY ***Federal work-study:*** *Total amount:* $117,892; 163 jobs averaging $1000.

APPLYING for FINANCIAL AID ***Required financial aid form:*** FAFSA. ***Financial aid deadline (priority):*** 2/15. ***Notification date:*** 3/31. Students must reply within 2 weeks of notification.

CONTACT Ms. Teresa Potts, Director of Financial Aid, Kansas City Art Institute, 4415 Warwick Boulevard, Kansas City, MO 64111-1874, 816-802-3448 or toll-free 800-522-5224. *Fax:* 816-802-3453. *E-mail:* tpotts@kcai.edu

KANSAS NEWMAN COLLEGE

Wichita, KS

See Newman University

KANSAS STATE UNIVERSITY

Manhattan, KS

Tuition & fees (KS res): $2592 **Average undergraduate aid package: $7615**

ABOUT THE INSTITUTION State-supported, coed. Awards: associate, bachelor's, master's, doctoral, and first professional degrees. 91 undergraduate majors. Total enrollment: 21,543. Undergraduates: 17,903. Freshmen: 3,504. Federal methodology is used as a basis for awarding need-based institutional aid.

UNDERGRADUATE EXPENSES for 1999–2000 ***Application fee:*** $20. ***Tuition, state resident:*** full-time $2090; part-time $70 per semester hour. ***Tuition, nonresident:*** full-time $8693; part-time $290 per semester hour. ***Required fees:*** full-time $502; $17 per semester hour; $47 per term part-time. Full-time tuition and fees vary according to degree level and location. Part-time tuition and fees vary according to degree level and location. ***College room and board:*** $3950. ***Payment plans:*** installment, deferred payment.

FRESHMAN FINANCIAL AID (Fall 1998) 3293 applied for aid; of those 71% were deemed to have need. 90% of freshmen with need received aid; of those 14% had need fully met. *Average percent of need met:* 61% (excluding resources awarded to replace EFC). *Average financial aid package:* $4801 (excluding resources awarded to replace EFC). 8% of all full-time freshmen had no need and received non-need-based aid.

UNDERGRADUATE FINANCIAL AID (Fall 1998) 14,658 applied for aid; of those 65% were deemed to have need. 91% of undergraduates with need received aid; of those 21% had need fully met. *Average percent of need met:* 68% (excluding resources awarded to replace EFC). *Average financial aid package:* $7615 (excluding resources awarded to replace EFC). 8% of all full-time undergraduates had no need and received non-need-based aid.

GIFT AID (NEED-BASED) ***Total amount:*** $12,259,185 (77% Federal, 23% state). ***Receiving aid:*** *Freshmen:* 24% (850); *all full-time undergraduates:* 25% (4,557). ***Average award:*** Freshmen: $3216; Undergraduates: $6515. ***Scholarships, grants, and awards:*** Federal Pell, FSEOG, state.

GIFT AID (NON-NEED-BASED) ***Total amount:*** $11,218,591 (62% institutional, 38% external sources). ***Receiving aid:*** *Freshmen:* 27% (946); *Undergraduates:* 13% (2,413). ***Scholarships, grants, and awards by category:*** *Academic Interests/Achievement:* agriculture, architecture, biological sciences, business, communication, computer science, education, engineering/technologies, English, foreign languages, general academic interests/achievements, health fields, home economics, humanities, mathematics, military science, physical sciences, premedicine, social sciences. *Creative Arts/Performance:* art/fine arts, debating, music, theater/drama. *Special Achievements/Activities:* general special achievements/activities, leadership. ***ROTC:*** Army, Air Force.

LOANS ***Student loans:*** $39,716,582 (100% need-based). Average indebtedness per student: $15,927. ***Average need-based loan:*** Freshmen: $1554; Undergraduates: $4165. ***Programs:*** Federal Direct (Subsidized and Unsubsidized Stafford), FFEL (PLUS), Perkins, college/university.

WORK-STUDY ***Federal work-study:*** *Total amount:* $2,172,817; jobs available.

APPLYING for FINANCIAL AID ***Required financial aid form:*** FAFSA. ***Financial aid deadline (priority):*** 3/1. ***Notification date:*** 4/1. Students must reply within 2 weeks of notification.

CONTACT Mr. Larry Moeder, Director of Student Financial Assistance, Kansas State University, 104 Fairchild Hall, Manhattan, KS 66506, 785-532-6420 or toll-free 800-432-8270 (in-state). *E-mail:* larrym@ksu.edu

KANSAS WESLEYAN UNIVERSITY

Salina, KS

Tuition & fees: $11,000 **Average undergraduate aid package: $10,970**

ABOUT THE INSTITUTION Independent United Methodist, coed. Awards: associate, bachelor's, and master's degrees. 40 undergraduate majors. Total enrollment: 735. Undergraduates: 684. Freshmen: 116. Federal methodology is used as a basis for awarding need-based institutional aid.

UNDERGRADUATE EXPENSES for 1999–2000 ***Application fee:*** $15. ***Comprehensive fee:*** $15,000 includes full-time tuition ($11,000) and room and board ($4000). ***Part-time tuition:*** $160 per credit. Part-time tuition and fees vary according to course load. ***Payment plan:*** installment.

FRESHMAN FINANCIAL AID (Fall 1999, est.) 97 applied for aid; of those 90% were deemed to have need. 100% of freshmen with need received aid; of those 100% had need fully met. *Average percent of need met:* 100% (excluding resources awarded to replace EFC). *Average financial aid package:* $10,851 (excluding resources awarded to replace EFC). 10% of all full-time freshmen had no need and received non-need-based aid.

UNDERGRADUATE FINANCIAL AID (Fall 1999, est.) 463 applied for aid; of those 89% were deemed to have need. 100% of undergraduates with need received aid; of those 100% had need fully met. *Average percent of need met:* 100% (excluding resources awarded to replace EFC). *Average financial aid package:* $10,970 (excluding resources awarded to replace EFC). 11% of all full-time undergraduates had no need and received non-need-based aid.

GIFT AID (NEED-BASED) ***Total amount:*** $1,313,000 (50% Federal, 42% state, 8% institutional). ***Receiving aid:*** *Freshmen:* 89% (87); *all full-time undergraduates:* 88% (413). ***Average award:*** Freshmen: $4043; Undergraduates: $4323. ***Scholarships, grants, and awards:*** Federal Pell, FSEOG, state, private, college/university gift aid from institutional funds.

GIFT AID (NON-NEED-BASED) ***Total amount:*** $1,180,000 (80% institutional, 20% external sources). ***Receiving aid:*** *Freshmen:* 89% (87); *Undergraduates:* 88% (413). ***Scholarships, grants, and awards by category:*** *Academic Interests/Achievement:* 248 awards ($750,000 total): biological sciences, business, communication, computer science, education, English, foreign languages, general academic interests/achievements, mathematics, physical sciences, premedicine, religion/biblical studies, social sciences. *Creative Arts/Performance:* 24 awards ($35,150 total): dance, music, theater/drama. *Special Achievements/Activities:* 12 awards ($16,000 total): cheerleading/drum major. *Special Characteristics:* 35 awards ($83,100 total): children and siblings of alumni, children of faculty/staff, siblings of current students, twins. ***Tuition waivers:*** Full or partial for children of alumni, employees or children of employees, senior citizens.

LOANS ***Student loans:*** $2,473,000 (68% need-based, 32% non-need-based). 87% of past graduating class borrowed through all loan programs. Average indebtedness per student: $10,911. ***Average need-based loan:*** Freshmen: $2966; Undergraduates: $3194. ***Parent loans:*** $380,000 (100% non-need-based). ***Programs:*** Federal Direct (Subsidized and Unsubsidized Stafford, PLUS), Perkins.

WORK-STUDY ***Federal work-study:*** *Total amount:* $75,000; 100 jobs averaging $750. ***State or other work-study/employment:*** *Total amount:* $47,600 (100% non-need-based). Part-time jobs available.

ATHLETIC AWARDS *Total amount:* 708,700 (97% need-based, 3% non-need-based).

APPLYING for FINANCIAL AID ***Required financial aid form:*** FAFSA. ***Financial aid deadline (priority):*** 3/15. ***Notification date:*** Continuous. Students must reply within 2 weeks of notification.

CONTACT Mrs. Glenna Alexander, Director of Financial Assistance, Kansas Wesleyan University, 100 East Claflin, Salina, KS 67401-6196, 785-827-5541 Ext. 1130 or toll-free 800-874-1154 Ext. 1285. *Fax:* 785-827-0927. *E-mail:* kglennaa@acck.edu

KEAN UNIVERSITY

Union, NJ

Tuition & fees (NJ res): $4384 **Average undergraduate aid package: $3762**

ABOUT THE INSTITUTION State-supported, coed. Awards: bachelor's and master's degrees and post-bachelor's and post-master's certificates. 43 undergraduate majors. Total enrollment: 11,199. Undergraduates: 9,228. Freshmen: 1,036. Federal methodology is used as a basis for awarding need-based institutional aid.

UNDERGRADUATE EXPENSES for 1999–2000 ***Application fee:*** $35. ***Tuition, state resident:*** full-time $3373; part-time $113 per hour. ***Tuition, nonresident:*** full-time $5070; part-time $170 per hour. ***Required fees:*** full-time $1011; $31 per hour. ***College room and board: room only:***

Kean University (continued)

$4330. Room and board charges vary according to board plan and housing facility. ***Payment plans:*** installment, deferred payment.

FRESHMAN FINANCIAL AID (Fall 1998) 854 applied for aid; of those 74% were deemed to have need. 96% of freshmen with need received aid; of those 19% had need fully met. *Average percent of need met:* 61% (excluding resources awarded to replace EFC). *Average financial aid package:* $3878 (excluding resources awarded to replace EFC). 13% of all full-time freshmen had no need and received non-need-based aid.

UNDERGRADUATE FINANCIAL AID (Fall 1998) 4,083 applied for aid; of those 82% were deemed to have need. 95% of undergraduates with need received aid; of those 21% had need fully met. *Average percent of need met:* 69% (excluding resources awarded to replace EFC). *Average financial aid package:* $3762 (excluding resources awarded to replace EFC). 8% of all full-time undergraduates had no need and received non-need-based aid.

GIFT AID (NEED-BASED) ***Total amount:*** $9,474,501 (55% Federal, 45% state). ***Receiving aid:*** *Freshmen:* 44% (490); *all full-time undergraduates:* 43% (2,575). ***Average award:*** Freshmen: $3714; Undergraduates: $3616. ***Scholarships, grants, and awards:*** Federal Pell, FSEOG, state, private, college/university gift aid from institutional funds.

GIFT AID (NON-NEED-BASED) ***Total amount:*** $668,242 (10% state, 80% institutional, 10% external sources). ***Receiving aid:*** *Freshmen:* 22% (246); *Undergraduates:* 33% (1,986). ***Scholarships, grants, and awards by category:*** *Academic Interests/Achievement:* business, education, general academic interests/achievements, health fields, humanities. *Special Achievements/Activities:* community service, leadership. ***Tuition waivers:*** Full or partial for employees or children of employees, senior citizens. ***ROTC:*** Air Force cooperative.

LOANS ***Student loans:*** $13,730,742 (63% need-based, 37% non-need-based). ***Average need-based loan:*** Freshmen: $2463; Undergraduates: $3256. ***Parent loans:*** $873,145 (100% non-need-based). ***Programs:*** Federal Direct (Subsidized and Unsubsidized Stafford, PLUS), FFEL (Subsidized and Unsubsidized Stafford, PLUS), Perkins, state, college/university.

WORK-STUDY ***Federal work-study:*** *Total amount:* $269,767; jobs available. ***State or other work-study/employment:*** *Total amount:* $87,002 (100% non-need-based). Part-time jobs available.

APPLYING for FINANCIAL AID ***Required financial aid form:*** FAFSA. ***Financial aid deadline (priority):*** 3/15. ***Notification date:*** Continuous beginning 4/15. Students must reply within 2 weeks of notification.

CONTACT Mr. Burt Batty, Director of Financial Aid, Kean University, 1000 Morris Avenue, Union, NJ 07083, 908-527-2050. *Fax:* 908-289-4150.

KEENE STATE COLLEGE

Keene, NH

Tuition & fees (NH res): $5046 **Average undergraduate aid package: $6923**

ABOUT THE INSTITUTION State-supported, coed. Awards: associate, bachelor's, and master's degrees and post-bachelor's and post-master's certificates. 53 undergraduate majors. Total enrollment: 4,452. Undergraduates: 4,233. Freshmen: 1,019. Federal methodology is used as a basis for awarding need-based institutional aid.

UNDERGRADUATE EXPENSES for 1999–2000 ***Application fee:*** $25; $35 for nonresidents. ***Tuition, state resident:*** full-time $3830; part-time $164 per credit. ***Tuition, nonresident:*** full-time $9140; part-time $460 per credit. ***Required fees:*** full-time $1216; $48 per credit; $10 per term part-time. Part-time tuition and fees vary according to course load. ***College room and board:*** $4938; ***room only:*** $3358. Room and board charges vary according to board plan and housing facility. ***Payment plan:*** installment.

FRESHMAN FINANCIAL AID (Fall 1998) 646 applied for aid; of those 78% were deemed to have need. 98% of freshmen with need received aid; of those 39% had need fully met. *Average percent of need met:* 74% (excluding resources awarded to replace EFC). *Average financial aid package:* $6955 (excluding resources awarded to replace EFC). 17% of all full-time freshmen had no need and received non-need-based aid.

UNDERGRADUATE FINANCIAL AID (Fall 1998) 2,560 applied for aid; of those 80% were deemed to have need. 98% of undergraduates with need received aid; of those 43% had need fully met. *Average percent of need met:* 80% (excluding resources awarded to replace EFC). *Average financial aid package:* $6923 (excluding resources awarded to replace EFC). 16% of all full-time undergraduates had no need and received non-need-based aid.

GIFT AID (NEED-BASED) ***Total amount:*** $4,399,456 (42% Federal, 8% state, 50% institutional). ***Receiving aid:*** *Freshmen:* 45% (352); *all full-time undergraduates:* 35% (1,226). ***Average award:*** Freshmen: $3506; Undergraduates: $3331. ***Scholarships, grants, and awards:*** Federal Pell, FSEOG, state, private, college/university gift aid from institutional funds.

GIFT AID (NON-NEED-BASED) ***Total amount:*** $1,129,091 (1% state, 61% institutional, 38% external sources). ***Receiving aid:*** *Freshmen:* 25% (193); *Undergraduates:* 14% (478). ***Scholarships, grants, and awards by category:*** *Academic Interests/Achievement:* general academic interests/achievements. *Creative Arts/Performance:* art/fine arts, music, theater/drama. ***Tuition waivers:*** Full or partial for employees or children of employees. ***ROTC:*** Army cooperative, Air Force cooperative.

LOANS ***Student loans:*** $11,422,636 (65% need-based, 35% non-need-based). 69% of past graduating class borrowed through all loan programs. Average indebtedness per student: $16,439. ***Average need-based loan:*** Freshmen: $2833; Undergraduates: $3678. ***Parent loans:*** $2,375,031 (100% non-need-based). ***Programs:*** FFEL (Subsidized and Unsubsidized Stafford, PLUS), Perkins, state, college/university.

WORK-STUDY ***Federal work-study:*** *Total amount:* $556,494; jobs available. ***State or other work-study/employment:*** *Total amount:* $300,762 (100% need-based). Part-time jobs available.

APPLYING for FINANCIAL AID ***Required financial aid forms:*** FAFSA, noncustodial (divorced/separated) parent's statement, business/farm supplement, verification documents, income tax return. ***Financial aid deadline (priority):*** 3/1. ***Notification date:*** 5/15. Students must reply within 2 weeks of notification.

CONTACT Ms. Patricia Blodgett, Director of Student Financial Management, Keene State College, 229 Main Street, Keene, NH 03435-2606, 603-358-2280 or toll-free 800-572-1909. *Fax:* 603-358-2767. *E-mail:* pblodget@keene.edu

KEHILATH YAKOV RABBINICAL SEMINARY

Brooklyn, NY

CONTACT Financial Aid Office, Kehilath Yakov Rabbinical Seminary, 206 Wilson Street, Brooklyn, NY 11211-7207, 718-963-1212.

KENDALL COLLEGE

Evanston, IL

Tuition & fees: $11,600 **Average undergraduate aid package: N/A**

ABOUT THE INSTITUTION Independent United Methodist, coed. Awards: associate and bachelor's degrees. 16 undergraduate majors. Total enrollment: 545. Undergraduates: 545. Both federal and institutional methodology are used as a basis for awarding need-based institutional aid.

UNDERGRADUATE EXPENSES for 2000–2001 (est.) ***Application fee:*** $30. ***Comprehensive fee:*** $16,600 includes full-time tuition ($11,500), mandatory fees ($100), and room and board ($5000). Full-time tuition and fees vary according to program. Room and board charges vary according to housing facility. ***Part-time tuition:*** $348 per credit. ***Part-time fees:*** $50 per term part-time. Part-time tuition and fees vary according to program. ***Payment plan:*** installment.

GIFT AID (NEED-BASED) ***Scholarships, grants, and awards:*** Federal Pell, state, private, college/university gift aid from institutional funds.

GIFT AID (NON-NEED-BASED) ***Scholarships, grants, and awards by category:*** *Academic Interests/Achievement:* general academic interests/achievements. *Special Achievements/Activities:* general special achievements/activities, leadership. *Special Characteristics:* children of faculty/staff, international students, members of minority groups. ***Tuition waivers:*** Full or partial for employees or children of employees.

LOANS ***Programs:*** FFEL (Subsidized and Unsubsidized Stafford, PLUS), Perkins, TERI Loans, Key Alternative Loans, EXCEL Loans.

WORK-STUDY Federal work-study jobs available.

APPLYING for FINANCIAL AID ***Required financial aid form:*** FAFSA. ***Financial aid deadline:*** 3/15.

CONTACT Nichole Tortorello, Assistant Director of Financial Aid, Kendall College, 2408 Orrington Avenue, Evanston, IL 60201, 847-866-1300 Ext. 1347.

KENDALL COLLEGE OF ART AND DESIGN

Grand Rapids, MI

Tuition & fees: $10,860 **Average undergraduate aid package: $7885**

ABOUT THE INSTITUTION Independent, coed. Awards: bachelor's degrees. 6 undergraduate majors. Total enrollment: 653. Undergraduates: 653. Freshmen: 122. Federal methodology is used as a basis for awarding need-based institutional aid.

UNDERGRADUATE EXPENSES for 1999–2000 ***Application fee:*** $35. ***Tuition:*** full-time $10,500; part-time $350 per credit. ***Required fees:*** full-time $360; $130 per term part-time. Full-time tuition and fees vary according to course load. Part-time tuition and fees vary according to course load. ***Payment plans:*** tuition prepayment, installment, deferred payment.

FRESHMAN FINANCIAL AID (Fall 1999, est.) 168 applied for aid; of those 77% were deemed to have need. 100% of freshmen with need received aid; of those 7% had need fully met. *Average percent of need met:* 60% (excluding resources awarded to replace EFC). *Average financial aid package:* $7253 (excluding resources awarded to replace EFC). 10% of all full-time freshmen had no need and received non-need-based aid.

UNDERGRADUATE FINANCIAL AID (Fall 1999, est.) 431 applied for aid; of those 77% were deemed to have need. 100% of undergraduates with need received aid; of those 12% had need fully met. *Average percent of need met:* 62% (excluding resources awarded to replace EFC). *Average financial aid package:* $7885 (excluding resources awarded to replace EFC). 7% of all full-time undergraduates had no need and received non-need-based aid.

GIFT AID (NEED-BASED) ***Total amount:*** $1,460,920 (32% Federal, 57% state, 11% institutional). ***Receiving aid:*** *Freshmen:* 65% (120); *all full-time undergraduates:* 64% (303). ***Average award:*** Freshmen: $3672; Undergraduates: $3651. ***Scholarships, grants, and awards:*** Federal Pell, FSEOG, state, private, college/university gift aid from institutional funds.

GIFT AID (NON-NEED-BASED) ***Total amount:*** $643,159 (90% institutional, 10% external sources). ***Receiving aid:*** *Freshmen:* 27% (50); *Undergraduates:* 30% (143). ***Scholarships, grants, and awards by category:*** *Creative Arts/Performance:* 242 awards ($580,470 total): applied art and design, art/fine arts. ***Tuition waivers:*** Full or partial for employees or children of employees.

LOANS ***Student loans:*** $2,031,713 (60% need-based, 40% non-need-based). 59% of past graduating class borrowed through all loan programs. Average indebtedness per student: $18,861. ***Average need-based loan:*** Freshmen: $2870; Undergraduates: $3504. ***Parent loans:*** $264,205 (100% non-need-based). ***Programs:*** FFEL (Subsidized and Unsubsidized Stafford, PLUS), Perkins, state, alternative loans.

WORK-STUDY ***Federal work-study:*** *Total amount:* $65,066; 32 jobs averaging $2033.

APPLYING for FINANCIAL AID ***Required financial aid form:*** FAFSA. ***Financial aid deadline (priority):*** 2/15. ***Notification date:*** 4/15. Students must reply within 4 weeks of notification.

CONTACT Ms. Sandy K. Britton, Director of Student Business Affairs, Kendall College of Art and Design, 111 Division Avenue North, Grand Rapids, MI 49503, 800-676-2787 Ext. 113 or toll-free 800-676-2787. *Fax:* 616-831-9689. *E-mail:* brittons@kcad.edu

KENNESAW STATE UNIVERSITY

Kennesaw, GA

Tuition & fees (GA res): $2306 **Average undergraduate aid package: N/A**

ABOUT THE INSTITUTION State-supported, coed. Awards: bachelor's and master's degrees. 44 undergraduate majors. Total enrollment: 13,148. Undergraduates: 11,664. Freshmen: 1,974. Federal methodology is used as a basis for awarding need-based institutional aid.

UNDERGRADUATE EXPENSES for 1999–2000 ***Application fee:*** $20. ***Tuition, state resident:*** full-time $1808; part-time $76 per credit hour. ***Tuition, nonresident:*** full-time $7232; part-time $302 per credit hour. ***Required fees:*** full-time $498; $249 per term part-time. Part-time tuition and fees vary according to course load. ***Payment plan:*** deferred payment.

FRESHMAN FINANCIAL AID (Fall 1998) 642 applied for aid; of those 48% were deemed to have need. 100% of freshmen with need received aid; of those 64% had need fully met.

UNDERGRADUATE FINANCIAL AID (Fall 1998) 4,277 applied for aid; of those 62% were deemed to have need. 99% of undergraduates with need received aid; of those 66% had need fully met.

GIFT AID (NEED-BASED) ***Total amount:*** $4,056,793 (99% Federal, 1% institutional). ***Receiving aid:*** *Freshmen:* 16% (118); *all full-time undergraduates:* 20% (1,304). ***Scholarships, grants, and awards:*** Federal Pell, FSEOG, state, private, college/university gift aid from institutional funds, Georgia HOPE Scholarships.

GIFT AID (NON-NEED-BASED) ***Total amount:*** $5,920,242 (95% state, 2% institutional, 3% external sources). ***Receiving aid:*** *Freshmen:* 38% (290); *Undergraduates:* 32% (2,070). ***Scholarships, grants, and awards by category:*** *Academic Interests/Achievement:* biological sciences, business, education, English, general academic interests/achievements, health fields, international studies, mathematics, physical sciences, premedicine, social sciences. *Creative Arts/Performance:* art/fine arts, music, performing arts. *Special Achievements/Activities:* community service. *Special Characteristics:* children and siblings of alumni, children of workers in trades, general special characteristics, local/state students, members of minority groups. ***Tuition waivers:*** Full or partial for employees or children of employees, senior citizens. ***ROTC:*** Army, Air Force cooperative.

LOANS ***Student loans:*** $18,553,944 (64% need-based, 36% non-need-based). ***Parent loans:*** $69,022 (100% non-need-based). ***Programs:*** FFEL (Subsidized and Unsubsidized Stafford, PLUS), Perkins, state, college/university.

WORK-STUDY ***Federal work-study:*** *Total amount:* $68,251; jobs available.

ATHLETIC AWARDS *Total amount:* 187,736 (100% non-need-based).

APPLYING for FINANCIAL AID ***Required financial aid form:*** FAFSA. ***Financial aid deadline (priority):*** 4/1.

CONTACT Office of Student Financial Aid, Kennesaw State University, 1000 Chastain Road, Kennesaw, GA 30144-5591, 770-423-6074. *Fax:* 770-423-6708. *E-mail:* finaid@ksumail.kennesaw.edu

KENT STATE UNIVERSITY

Kent, OH

Tuition & fees (OH res): $6016 **Average undergraduate aid package: $5604**

ABOUT THE INSTITUTION State-supported, coed. Awards: associate, bachelor's, master's, and doctoral degrees. 145 undergraduate majors. Total enrollment: 21,653. Undergraduates: 17,275. Freshmen: 3,820. Federal methodology is used as a basis for awarding need-based institutional aid.

UNDERGRADUATE EXPENSES for 1999–2000 ***Application fee:*** $30. ***Tuition, state resident:*** full-time $5014; part-time $228 per hour. ***Tuition, nonresident:*** full-time $9918; part-time $451 per hour. ***Required fees:*** full-time $1002. Full-time tuition and fees vary according to course load and program. Part-time tuition and fees vary according to course load and program. ***College room and board:*** $4530. Room and board charges vary according to board plan and housing facility. ***Payment plan:*** installment.

FRESHMAN FINANCIAL AID (Fall 1999, est.) 3974 applied for aid; of those 81% were deemed to have need. 100% of freshmen with need

Kent State University (continued)

received aid; of those 17% had need fully met. *Average percent of need met:* 72% (excluding resources awarded to replace EFC). *Average financial aid package:* $5055 (excluding resources awarded to replace EFC). 14% of all full-time freshmen had no need and received non-need-based aid.

UNDERGRADUATE FINANCIAL AID (Fall 1999, est.) 11,854 applied for aid; of those 84% were deemed to have need. 100% of undergraduates with need received aid; of those 21% had need fully met. *Average percent of need met:* 73% (excluding resources awarded to replace EFC). *Average financial aid package:* $5604 (excluding resources awarded to replace EFC). 10% of all full-time undergraduates had no need and received non-need-based aid.

GIFT AID (NEED-BASED) ***Total amount:*** $25,791,006 (58% Federal, 24% state, 14% institutional, 4% external sources). ***Receiving aid:*** *Freshmen:* 44% (2,468); *all full-time undergraduates:* 38% (7,105). ***Average award:*** Freshmen: $3085; Undergraduates: $3298. ***Scholarships, grants, and awards:*** Federal Pell, FSEOG, state, private, college/university gift aid from institutional funds.

GIFT AID (NON-NEED-BASED) ***Total amount:*** $4,527,091 (2% Federal, 30% state, 52% institutional, 16% external sources). ***Receiving aid:*** *Freshmen:* 8% (430); *Undergraduates:* 4% (715). ***Scholarships, grants, and awards by category:*** *Academic Interests/Achievement:* architecture, area/ethnic studies, biological sciences, business, communication, education, English, general academic interests/achievements, health fields, international studies, library science, mathematics, military science, physical sciences, social sciences. *Creative Arts/Performance:* art/fine arts, journalism/publications, music, theater/drama. *Special Achievements/Activities:* community service, general special achievements/activities, leadership. *Special Characteristics:* adult students, children and siblings of alumni, children of faculty/staff, children of union members/company employees, children with a deceased or disabled parent, ethnic background, handicapped students, international students, members of minority groups, out-of-state students. ***Tuition waivers:*** Full or partial for employees or children of employees. ***ROTC:*** Army, Air Force.

LOANS ***Student loans:*** $91,891,083 (82% need-based, 18% non-need-based). 62% of past graduating class borrowed through all loan programs. Average indebtedness per student: $16,666. ***Average need-based loan:*** Freshmen: $2894; Undergraduates: $3560. ***Parent loans:*** $35,376,434 (11% need-based, 89% non-need-based). ***Programs:*** Federal Direct (Subsidized and Unsubsidized Stafford, PLUS), Perkins, Federal Nursing, state, college/university, alternative loans.

WORK-STUDY ***Federal work-study:*** *Total amount:* $1,640,479; 783 jobs averaging $2095.

ATHLETIC AWARDS *Total amount:* 2,653,190 (38% need-based, 62% non-need-based).

APPLYING for FINANCIAL AID ***Required financial aid forms:*** FAFSA, University Scholarship Application form. ***Financial aid deadline (priority):*** 3/1. ***Notification date:*** 3/15. Students must reply within 2 weeks of notification.

CONTACT Constance Dubick, Associate Director, Student Financial Aid, Kent State University, 103 Michael Schwartz Center, PO Box 5190, Kent, OH 44242-0001, 330-672-2972 Ext. 18 or toll-free 800-988-KENT. *Fax:* 330-672-4014. *E-mail:* constance@sfa.kent.edu

KENTUCKY CHRISTIAN COLLEGE

Grayson, KY

Tuition & fees: $6880 **Average undergraduate aid package: $8404**

ABOUT THE INSTITUTION Independent religious, coed. Awards: associate and bachelor's degrees. 13 undergraduate majors. Total enrollment: 564. Undergraduates: 564. Freshmen: 157. Federal methodology is used as a basis for awarding need-based institutional aid.

UNDERGRADUATE EXPENSES for 1999–2000 ***Application fee:*** $25. ***Comprehensive fee:*** $10,794 includes full-time tuition ($6880) and room and board ($3914). Room and board charges vary according to board plan. ***Part-time tuition:*** $215 per credit hour. ***Payment plans:*** tuition prepayment, installment.

FRESHMAN FINANCIAL AID (Fall 1999, est.) 149 applied for aid; of those 81% were deemed to have need. 98% of freshmen with need received aid; of those 15% had need fully met. *Average percent of need met:* 48% (excluding resources awarded to replace EFC). *Average financial aid package:* $7479 (excluding resources awarded to replace EFC). 16% of all full-time freshmen had no need and received non-need-based aid.

UNDERGRADUATE FINANCIAL AID (Fall 1999, est.) 517 applied for aid; of those 78% were deemed to have need. 98% of undergraduates with need received aid; of those 20% had need fully met. *Average percent of need met:* 55% (excluding resources awarded to replace EFC). *Average financial aid package:* $8404 (excluding resources awarded to replace EFC). 17% of all full-time undergraduates had no need and received non-need-based aid.

GIFT AID (NEED-BASED) ***Total amount:*** $646,595 (71% Federal, 24% state, 5% institutional). ***Receiving aid:*** *Freshmen:* 43% (66); *all full-time undergraduates:* 40% (215). ***Average award:*** Freshmen: $2864; Undergraduates: $2939. ***Scholarships, grants, and awards:*** Federal Pell, FSEOG, state, private, college/university gift aid from institutional funds.

GIFT AID (NON-NEED-BASED) ***Total amount:*** $1,160,812 (2% state, 61% institutional, 37% external sources). ***Receiving aid:*** *Freshmen:* 74% (115); *Undergraduates:* 69% (370). ***Scholarships, grants, and awards by category:*** *Academic Interests/Achievement:* 123 awards ($332,808 total): business, education, general academic interests/achievements, religion/biblical studies. *Creative Arts/Performance:* 33 awards ($112,985 total): debating, music, performing arts, theater/drama. *Special Achievements/Activities:* 24 awards ($12,688 total): community service, general special achievements/activities, leadership, religious involvement. *Special Characteristics:* 95 awards ($252,396 total): children and siblings of alumni, children of faculty/staff, general special characteristics, members of minority groups, out-of-state students, religious affiliation. ***Tuition waivers:*** Full or partial for minority students, employees or children of employees.

LOANS ***Student loans:*** $1,811,161 (67% need-based, 33% non-need-based). 70% of past graduating class borrowed through all loan programs. Average indebtedness per student: $17,119. ***Average need-based loan:*** Freshmen: $2583; Undergraduates: $3526. ***Parent loans:*** $403,282 (100% non-need-based). ***Programs:*** FFEL (Subsidized and Unsubsidized Stafford, PLUS), Perkins.

WORK-STUDY ***Federal work-study:*** *Total amount:* $371,141; 254 jobs averaging $1461. ***State or other work-study/employment:*** *Total amount:* $66,700 (100% non-need-based). 39 part-time jobs averaging $1710.

APPLYING for FINANCIAL AID ***Required financial aid forms:*** FAFSA, institution's own form. ***Financial aid deadline (priority):*** 4/1. ***Notification date:*** Continuous beginning 5/1. Students must reply within 2 weeks of notification.

CONTACT Mrs. Jennie M. Bender, Director of Financial Aid, Kentucky Christian College, 100 Academic Parkway, Grayson, KY 41143-2205, 606-474-3226 or toll-free 800-522-3181. *Fax:* 606-474-3155. *E-mail:* jbender@email.kcc.edu

KENTUCKY MOUNTAIN BIBLE COLLEGE

Vancleve, KY

Tuition & fees: $4170 **Average undergraduate aid package: N/A**

ABOUT THE INSTITUTION Independent interdenominational, coed. Awards: associate and bachelor's degrees. 6 undergraduate majors. Total enrollment: 80. Undergraduates: 80. Freshmen: 15. Both federal and institutional methodology are used as a basis for awarding need-based institutional aid.

UNDERGRADUATE EXPENSES for 2000–2001 ***Application fee:*** $25. ***Comprehensive fee:*** $6970 includes full-time tuition ($3750), mandatory fees ($420), and room and board ($2800). ***College room only:*** $750. Full-time tuition and fees vary according to course load. Room and board charges vary according to housing facility. ***Part-time tuition:*** $125 per credit. ***Part-time fees:*** $88 per term part-time. Part-time tuition and fees vary according to course load. ***Payment plan:*** installment.

GIFT AID (NEED-BASED) ***Scholarships, grants, and awards:*** Federal Pell, FSEOG, state, private, college/university gift aid from institutional funds.

GIFT AID (NON-NEED-BASED) ***Scholarships, grants, and awards by category:*** *Academic Interests/Achievement:* general academic interests/achievements. *Creative Arts/Performance:* music. *Special Characteristics:* children of faculty/staff. ***Tuition waivers:*** Full or partial for employees or children of employees.

LOANS ***Programs:*** FFEL (Subsidized and Unsubsidized Stafford), college/university.

WORK-STUDY Federal work-study jobs available.

APPLYING for FINANCIAL AID ***Required financial aid form:*** FAFSA. ***Financial aid deadline:*** 8/31 (priority: 3/31). ***Notification date:*** Continuous.

CONTACT Mrs. Jewel MacGregor, Director of Financial Aid, Kentucky Mountain Bible College, 855 Highway 541, Vancleve, KY 41385, 606-666-5000 or toll-free 800-879-KMBC.

KENTUCKY STATE UNIVERSITY

Frankfort, KY

ABOUT THE INSTITUTION State-related, coed. Awards: associate, bachelor's, and master's degrees (Louisville). 32 undergraduate majors. Total enrollment: 2,393. Undergraduates: 2,277. Freshmen: 373.

GIFT AID (NEED-BASED) ***Scholarships, grants, and awards:*** Federal Pell, FSEOG, state, private.

GIFT AID (NON-NEED-BASED) ***Scholarships, grants, and awards by category:*** *Academic Interests/Achievement:* general academic interests/achievements. *Creative Arts/Performance:* music. *Special Characteristics:* adult students, children with a deceased or disabled parent, handicapped students.

LOANS ***Programs:*** Federal Direct (Subsidized and Unsubsidized Stafford, PLUS), Perkins, state.

WORK-STUDY ***Federal work-study:*** *Total amount:* $400,000; 1,000 jobs available.

APPLYING for FINANCIAL AID ***Required financial aid forms:*** FAFSA, institution's own form, CSS Financial Aid PROFILE, state aid form, noncustodial (divorced/separated) parent's statement, business/farm supplement.

CONTACT Office of Financial Aid, Kentucky State University, East Main Street, Frankfort, KY 40601, 502-227-5960 or toll-free 800-633-9415 (in-state), 800-325-1716 (out-of-state).

KENTUCKY WESLEYAN COLLEGE

Owensboro, KY

Tuition & fees: $10,020 **Average undergraduate aid package: $12,250**

ABOUT THE INSTITUTION Independent Methodist, coed. Awards: bachelor's degrees. 35 undergraduate majors. Total enrollment: 747. Undergraduates: 747. Freshmen: 194. Federal methodology is used as a basis for awarding need-based institutional aid.

UNDERGRADUATE EXPENSES for 1999–2000 ***Application fee:*** $20. ***Comprehensive fee:*** $14,790 includes full-time tuition ($10,020) and room and board ($4770). ***College room only:*** $2190. Full-time tuition and fees vary according to course load. ***Part-time tuition:*** $310 per semester hour. ***Part-time fees:*** $50 per term part-time. Part-time tuition and fees vary according to course load. ***Payment plans:*** installment, deferred payment.

FRESHMAN FINANCIAL AID (Fall 1999, est.) 231 applied for aid; of those 81% were deemed to have need. 100% of freshmen with need received aid; of those 54% had need fully met. *Average percent of need met:* 83% (excluding resources awarded to replace EFC). *Average financial aid package:* $13,725 (excluding resources awarded to replace EFC). 11% of all full-time freshmen had no need and received non-need-based aid.

UNDERGRADUATE FINANCIAL AID (Fall 1999, est.) 674 applied for aid; of those 85% were deemed to have need. 100% of undergraduates with need received aid; of those 85% had need fully met. *Average percent of need met:* 77% (excluding resources awarded to replace EFC). *Average financial aid package:* $12,250 (excluding resources awarded to replace EFC). 12% of all full-time undergraduates had no need and received non-need-based aid.

GIFT AID (NEED-BASED) ***Total amount:*** $4,682,991 (13% Federal, 15% state, 70% institutional, 2% external sources). ***Receiving aid:*** *Freshmen:* 76% (187); *all full-time undergraduates:* 83% (572). ***Average award:*** Freshmen: $7245; Undergraduates: $7460. ***Scholarships, grants, and awards:*** Federal Pell, FSEOG, state, private, college/university gift aid from institutional funds.

GIFT AID (NON-NEED-BASED) ***Total amount:*** $144,203 (50% state, 50% external sources). ***Receiving aid:*** *Freshmen:* 53% (130); *Undergraduates:* 75% (515). ***Scholarships, grants, and awards by category:*** *Academic Interests/Achievement:* $1,588,965 total: general academic interests/achievements. *Creative Arts/Performance:* 13 awards ($36,800 total): art/fine arts, music, theater/drama. *Special Achievements/Activities:* 88 awards ($236,040 total): junior miss, leadership. *Special Characteristics:* 53 awards ($257,600 total): children and siblings of alumni, children of faculty/staff, children of union members/company employees, general special characteristics, out-of-state students, relatives of clergy, religious affiliation, siblings of current students. ***Tuition waivers:*** Full or partial for children of alumni, employees or children of employees, senior citizens.

LOANS ***Student loans:*** $2,063,557 (64% need-based, 36% non-need-based). 63% of past graduating class borrowed through all loan programs. Average indebtedness per student: $12,000. ***Average need-based loan:*** Freshmen: $2000; Undergraduates: $4100. ***Parent loans:*** $170,092 (94% need-based, 6% non-need-based). ***Programs:*** FFEL (Subsidized and Unsubsidized Stafford, PLUS), Perkins, state, college/university, United Methodist Higher Education Foundation Loans, Bagby Loans, alternative loans.

WORK-STUDY ***Federal work-study:*** *Total amount:* $144,149; 188 jobs averaging $767. ***State or other work-study/employment:*** *Total amount:* $3415 (100% need-based). 4 part-time jobs averaging $854.

ATHLETIC AWARDS *Total amount:* 686,068 (97% need-based, 3% non-need-based).

APPLYING for FINANCIAL AID ***Required financial aid forms:*** FAFSA, institution's own form. ***Financial aid deadline (priority):*** 3/1. ***Notification date:*** Continuous beginning 3/15. Students must reply within 3 weeks of notification.

CONTACT Ms. Gerry Covert, Director of Financial Aid, Kentucky Wesleyan College, 3000 Frederica Street, Owensboro, KY 42301, 270-926-3111 Ext. 5115 or toll-free 800-999-0592 (in-state), 270-999-0592 (out-of-state). *Fax:* 270-926-3196. *E-mail:* gcovert@kwc.edu

KENYON COLLEGE

Gambier, OH

Tuition & fees: $24,590 **Average undergraduate aid package: $18,626**

ABOUT THE INSTITUTION Independent, coed. Awards: bachelor's degrees. 41 undergraduate majors. Total enrollment: 1,588. Undergraduates: 1,588. Freshmen: 459. Both federal and institutional methodology are used as a basis for awarding need-based institutional aid.

UNDERGRADUATE EXPENSES for 1999–2000 ***Application fee:*** $45. ***Comprehensive fee:*** $28,750 includes full-time tuition ($23,900), mandatory fees ($690), and room and board ($4160). ***College room only:*** $1820. Room and board charges vary according to housing facility. ***Payment plan:*** installment.

FRESHMAN FINANCIAL AID (Fall 1998) 297 applied for aid; of those 65% were deemed to have need. 99% of freshmen with need received aid; of those 61% had need fully met. *Average percent of need met:* 95% (excluding resources awarded to replace EFC). *Average financial aid package:* $17,391 (excluding resources awarded to replace EFC). 10% of all full-time freshmen had no need and received non-need-based aid.

UNDERGRADUATE FINANCIAL AID (Fall 1998) 1,050 applied for aid; of those 65% were deemed to have need. 98% of undergraduates with need received aid; of those 70% had need fully met. *Average percent of need met:* 96% (excluding resources awarded to replace EFC). *Average financial*

Kenyon College (continued)

aid package: $18,626 (excluding resources awarded to replace EFC). 6% of all full-time undergraduates had no need and received non-need-based aid.

GIFT AID (NEED-BASED) ***Total amount:*** $11,403,234 (4% Federal, 2% state, 86% institutional, 8% external sources). ***Receiving aid:*** *Freshmen:* 40% (183); *all full-time undergraduates:* 41% (637). ***Average award:*** Freshmen: $12,735; Undergraduates: $13,017. ***Scholarships, grants, and awards:*** Federal Pell, FSEOG, state, private, college/university gift aid from institutional funds.

GIFT AID (NON-NEED-BASED) ***Total amount:*** $1,122,375 (11% state, 81% institutional, 8% external sources). ***Receiving aid:*** *Freshmen:* 15% (66); *Undergraduates:* 13% (196). ***Scholarships, grants, and awards by category:*** *Academic Interests/Achievement:* 329 awards ($2,028,136 total): general academic interests/achievements. *Special Characteristics:* 36 awards ($465,160 total): ethnic background. ***Tuition waivers:*** Full or partial for employees or children of employees.

LOANS ***Student loans:*** $3,273,918 (61% need-based, 39% non-need-based). Average indebtedness per student: $16,650. ***Average need-based loan:*** Freshmen: $4111; Undergraduates: $5115. ***Parent loans:*** $1,594,354 (32% need-based, 68% non-need-based). ***Programs:*** FFEL (Subsidized and Unsubsidized Stafford, PLUS), Perkins, college/university.

WORK-STUDY ***Federal work-study:*** *Total amount:* $293,784; 311 jobs averaging $918. ***State or other work-study/employment:*** *Total amount:* $138,953 (100% need-based). 495 part-time jobs averaging $765.

APPLYING for FINANCIAL AID ***Required financial aid forms:*** FAFSA, CSS Financial Aid PROFILE. ***Financial aid deadline:*** 2/15. ***Notification date:*** 4/1. Students must reply by 5/1.

CONTACT Mr. Craig Daugherty, Director of Financial Aid, Kenyon College, Stephens Hall, Gambier, OH 43022-9623, 740-427-5430 or toll-free 800-848-2468. *Fax:* 740-427-5240. *E-mail:* daugherty@kenyon.edu

KETTERING UNIVERSITY

Flint, MI

Tuition & fees: $14,775 **Average undergraduate aid package: $5465**

ABOUT THE INSTITUTION Independent, coed. Awards: bachelor's and master's degrees. 19 undergraduate majors. Total enrollment: 3,166. Undergraduates: 2,553. Freshmen: 525. Federal methodology is used as a basis for awarding need-based institutional aid.

UNDERGRADUATE EXPENSES for 1999–2000 ***Application fee:*** $25. ***Comprehensive fee:*** $18,795 includes full-time tuition ($14,640), mandatory fees ($135), and room and board ($4020). ***College room only:*** $2540. Room and board charges vary according to student level. ***Payment plan:*** installment.

FRESHMAN FINANCIAL AID (Fall 1999, est.) 497 applied for aid; of those 93% were deemed to have need. 100% of freshmen with need received aid; of those 18% had need fully met. *Average percent of need met:* 80% (excluding resources awarded to replace EFC). *Average financial aid package:* $8168 (excluding resources awarded to replace EFC). 5% of all full-time freshmen had no need and received non-need-based aid.

UNDERGRADUATE FINANCIAL AID (Fall 1999, est.) 2,478 applied for aid; of those 89% were deemed to have need. 100% of undergraduates with need received aid; of those 39% had need fully met. *Average percent of need met:* 76% (excluding resources awarded to replace EFC). *Average financial aid package:* $5465 (excluding resources awarded to replace EFC). 7% of all full-time undergraduates had no need and received non-need-based aid.

GIFT AID (NEED-BASED) ***Total amount:*** $4,349,760 (28% Federal, 47% state, 22% institutional, 3% external sources). ***Receiving aid:*** *Freshmen:* 83% (434); *all full-time undergraduates:* 53% (1,347). ***Average award:*** Freshmen: $6273. ***Scholarships, grants, and awards:*** Federal Pell, FSEOG, state, private, college/university gift aid from institutional funds.

GIFT AID (NON-NEED-BASED) ***Total amount:*** $2,045,008 (90% institutional, 10% external sources). ***Receiving aid:*** *Freshmen:* 83% (435); *Undergraduates:* 18% (460). ***Scholarships, grants, and awards by category:*** *Academic Interests/Achievement:* business, computer science, engineering/technologies, general academic interests/achievements, mathematics, physical sciences. *Special Achievements/Activities:* general special achievements/activities, memberships. *Special Characteristics:* local/state students. ***Tuition waivers:*** Full or partial for employees or children of employees.

LOANS ***Student loans:*** $16,534,771 (52% need-based, 48% non-need-based). Average indebtedness per student: $30,000. ***Average need-based loan:*** Freshmen: $1875; Undergraduates: $2695. ***Parent loans:*** $1,798,349 (60% need-based, 40% non-need-based). ***Programs:*** Federal Direct (Subsidized and Unsubsidized Stafford, PLUS), state, alternative loans.

WORK-STUDY ***Federal work-study:*** *Total amount:* $211,050; 450 jobs averaging $469. ***State or other work-study/employment:*** *Total amount:* $21,111,951 (99% need-based, 1% non-need-based). Part-time jobs available.

APPLYING for FINANCIAL AID ***Required financial aid form:*** FAFSA. ***Financial aid deadline (priority):*** 2/14. ***Notification date:*** Continuous beginning 2/15. Students must reply within 2 weeks of notification.

CONTACT Melissa Ruterbusch, Director, Financial Aid, Kettering University, 1700 West Third Avenue, Flint, MI 48504-4898, 800-955-4464 Ext. 7859 or toll-free 800-955-4464 Ext. 7865 (in-state), 800-955-4464 (out-of-state). *Fax:* 810-762-9807. *E-mail:* finaid@kettering.edu

KEUKA COLLEGE

Keuka Park, NY

Tuition & fees: $13,085 **Average undergraduate aid package: $9521**

ABOUT THE INSTITUTION Independent religious, coed. Awards: bachelor's degrees. 26 undergraduate majors. Total enrollment: 895. Undergraduates: 895. Freshmen: 270. Federal methodology is used as a basis for awarding need-based institutional aid.

UNDERGRADUATE EXPENSES for 1999–2000 ***Application fee:*** $30. ***Comprehensive fee:*** $19,455 includes full-time tuition ($12,730), mandatory fees ($355), and room and board ($6370). Full-time tuition and fees vary according to program. Room and board charges vary according to board plan and housing facility. ***Part-time tuition:*** $425 per credit hour. Part-time tuition and fees vary according to program. ***Payment plan:*** installment.

FRESHMAN FINANCIAL AID (Fall 1998) 227 applied for aid; of those 100% were deemed to have need. 100% of freshmen with need received aid. *Average percent of need met:* 82% (excluding resources awarded to replace EFC). *Average financial aid package:* $12,400 (excluding resources awarded to replace EFC).

UNDERGRADUATE FINANCIAL AID (Fall 1998) 872 applied for aid; of those 92% were deemed to have need. 100% of undergraduates with need received aid. *Average percent of need met:* 82% (excluding resources awarded to replace EFC). *Average financial aid package:* $9521 (excluding resources awarded to replace EFC).

GIFT AID (NEED-BASED) ***Total amount:*** $5,076,784 (14% Federal, 24% state, 59% institutional, 3% external sources). ***Scholarships, grants, and awards:*** Federal Pell, FSEOG, state, private, college/university gift aid from institutional funds.

GIFT AID (NON-NEED-BASED) ***Tuition waivers:*** Full or partial for employees or children of employees.

LOANS ***Student loans:*** $3,956,960 (100% need-based). ***Parent loans:*** $599,263 (80% need-based, 20% non-need-based). ***Programs:*** FFEL (Subsidized and Unsubsidized Stafford, PLUS), Perkins.

WORK-STUDY ***Federal work-study:*** *Total amount:* $477,986; 543 jobs averaging $880.

APPLYING for FINANCIAL AID ***Required financial aid forms:*** FAFSA, institution's own form. ***Financial aid deadline (priority):*** 3/15. ***Notification date:*** Continuous. Students must reply within 2 weeks of notification.

CONTACT Jennifer Bates, Director of Financial Aid, Keuka College, Financial Aid Office, Keuka Park, NY 14478-0098, 315-536-4411 Ext. 5232 or toll-free 800-33-KEUKA. *Fax:* 315-536-5327. *E-mail:* jbates@mail.keuka.edu

KING COLLEGE

Bristol, TN

Tuition & fees: $10,750 **Average undergraduate aid package: $11,005**

ABOUT THE INSTITUTION Independent religious, coed. Awards: bachelor's degrees. 43 undergraduate majors. Total enrollment: 587. Undergraduates: 587. Freshmen: 133. Federal methodology is used as a basis for awarding need-based institutional aid.

UNDERGRADUATE EXPENSES for 1999–2000 ***Application fee:*** $20. ***Comprehensive fee:*** $14,600 includes full-time tuition ($10,030), mandatory fees ($720), and room and board ($3850). ***College room only:*** $1900. ***Part-time tuition:*** $285 per semester hour. ***Part-time fees:*** $70 per term part-time. Part-time tuition and fees vary according to course load and program. ***Payment plans:*** guaranteed tuition, tuition prepayment, installment.

FRESHMAN FINANCIAL AID (Fall 1999) 144 applied for aid; of those 69% were deemed to have need. 100% of freshmen with need received aid; of those 17% had need fully met. *Average percent of need met:* 77% (excluding resources awarded to replace EFC). *Average financial aid package:* $10,626 (excluding resources awarded to replace EFC). 31% of all full-time freshmen had no need and received non-need-based aid.

UNDERGRADUATE FINANCIAL AID (Fall 1999) 490 applied for aid; of those 72% were deemed to have need. 100% of undergraduates with need received aid; of those 16% had need fully met. *Average percent of need met:* 77% (excluding resources awarded to replace EFC). *Average financial aid package:* $11,005 (excluding resources awarded to replace EFC). 28% of all full-time undergraduates had no need and received non-need-based aid.

GIFT AID (NEED-BASED) ***Total amount:*** $2,441,790 (19% Federal, 7% state, 66% institutional, 8% external sources). ***Receiving aid:*** *Freshmen:* 69% (99); *all full-time undergraduates:* 72% (351). ***Average award:*** Freshmen: $8355; Undergraduates: $7930. ***Scholarships, grants, and awards:*** Federal Pell, FSEOG, state, private, college/university gift aid from institutional funds.

GIFT AID (NON-NEED-BASED) ***Total amount:*** $584,159 (85% institutional, 15% external sources). ***Receiving aid:*** *Freshmen:* 7% (10); *Undergraduates:* 4% (21). ***Scholarships, grants, and awards by category:*** *Academic Interests/Achievement:* 233 awards ($1,047,870 total): general academic interests/achievements. *Creative Arts/Performance:* 19 awards ($19,000 total): music, performing arts, theater/drama. *Special Achievements/Activities:* 30 awards ($102,500 total): cheerleading/drum major, community service. *Special Characteristics:* 25 awards ($192,540 total): children of faculty/staff, members of minority groups, relatives of clergy. ***Tuition waivers:*** Full or partial for employees or children of employees. ***ROTC:*** Army cooperative.

LOANS ***Student loans:*** $1,173,886 (87% need-based, 13% non-need-based). 74% of past graduating class borrowed through all loan programs. Average indebtedness per student: $14,636. ***Average need-based loan:*** Freshmen: $2158; Undergraduates: $2797. ***Parent loans:*** $111,599 (31% need-based, 69% non-need-based). ***Programs:*** FFEL (Subsidized and Unsubsidized Stafford, PLUS), Perkins, college/university.

WORK-STUDY ***Federal work-study:*** *Total amount:* $98,906; 82 jobs averaging $1074. ***State or other work-study/employment:*** *Total amount:* $3780 (100% non-need-based). Part-time jobs available.

ATHLETIC AWARDS *Total amount:* 617,598 (51% need-based, 49% non-need-based).

APPLYING for FINANCIAL AID ***Required financial aid forms:*** FAFSA, institution's own form. ***Financial aid deadline (priority):*** 3/1. ***Notification date:*** Continuous beginning 3/15. Students must reply within 2 weeks of notification.

CONTACT Mrs. Mildred B. Greeson, Director of Financial Aid, King College, 1350 King College Road, Bristol, TN 37620-2699, 423-652-4725 or toll-free 800-362-0014. *Fax:* 423-652-4727. *E-mail:* mbgreeson@king.edu

KING'S COLLEGE

Wilkes-Barre, PA

Tuition & fees: $15,910 **Average undergraduate aid package: $12,439**

ABOUT THE INSTITUTION Independent Roman Catholic, coed. Awards: associate, bachelor's, and master's degrees. 42 undergraduate majors. Total enrollment: 2,217. Undergraduates: 2,091. Freshmen: 428. Federal methodology is used as a basis for awarding need-based institutional aid.

UNDERGRADUATE EXPENSES for 1999–2000 ***Application fee:*** $30. ***Comprehensive fee:*** $22,530 includes full-time tuition ($15,240), mandatory fees ($670), and room and board ($6620). ***College room only:*** $3130. Room and board charges vary according to board plan and housing facility. ***Part-time tuition:*** $374 per credit hour. ***Payment plans:*** installment, deferred payment.

FRESHMAN FINANCIAL AID (Fall 1999, est.) 395 applied for aid; of those 88% were deemed to have need. 99% of freshmen with need received aid; of those 22% had need fully met. *Average percent of need met:* 86% (excluding resources awarded to replace EFC). *Average financial aid package:* $13,799 (excluding resources awarded to replace EFC). 18% of all full-time freshmen had no need and received non-need-based aid.

UNDERGRADUATE FINANCIAL AID (Fall 1999, est.) 1,498 applied for aid; of those 89% were deemed to have need. 100% of undergraduates with need received aid; of those 30% had need fully met. *Average percent of need met:* 80% (excluding resources awarded to replace EFC). *Average financial aid package:* $12,439 (excluding resources awarded to replace EFC). 19% of all full-time undergraduates had no need and received non-need-based aid.

GIFT AID (NEED-BASED) ***Total amount:*** $11,412,366 (8% Federal, 18% state, 72% institutional, 2% external sources). ***Receiving aid:*** *Freshmen:* 81% (344); *all full-time undergraduates:* 77% (1,327). ***Average award:*** Freshmen: $10,066; Undergraduates: $10,738. ***Scholarships, grants, and awards:*** Federal Pell, FSEOG, state, private, college/university gift aid from institutional funds.

GIFT AID (NON-NEED-BASED) ***Total amount:*** $2,014,993 (4% Federal, 95% institutional, 1% external sources). ***Receiving aid:*** *Freshmen:* 24% (103); *Undergraduates:* 32% (557). ***Scholarships, grants, and awards by category:*** *Academic Interests/Achievement:* biological sciences, business, communication, computer science, education, English, foreign languages, general academic interests/achievements, health fields, humanities, mathematics, physical sciences, premedicine, religion/biblical studies, social sciences. *Creative Arts/Performance:* debating. *Special Achievements/Activities:* community service, general special achievements/activities, leadership. *Special Characteristics:* children of faculty/staff, international students, relatives of clergy, siblings of current students. ***Tuition waivers:*** Full or partial for employees or children of employees, senior citizens. ***ROTC:*** Army, Air Force cooperative.

LOANS ***Student loans:*** $6,770,176 (92% need-based, 8% non-need-based). 74% of past graduating class borrowed through all loan programs. Average indebtedness per student: $15,500. ***Average need-based loan:*** Freshmen: $2959; Undergraduates: $4285. ***Parent loans:*** $1,481,057 (90% need-based, 10% non-need-based). ***Programs:*** FFEL (Subsidized and Unsubsidized Stafford, PLUS), Perkins, state.

WORK-STUDY ***Federal work-study:*** *Total amount:* $334,678; jobs available. ***State or other work-study/employment:*** *Total amount:* $148,783 (64% need-based, 36% non-need-based). Part-time jobs available.

APPLYING for FINANCIAL AID ***Required financial aid forms:*** FAFSA, institution's own form, state aid form. ***Financial aid deadline (priority):*** 3/1. ***Notification date:*** Continuous. Students must reply within 3 weeks of notification.

CONTACT Mr. Henry L. Chance, Director of Financial Aid, King's College, 133 North River Street, Wilkes-Barre, PA 18711-0801, 570-208-5868 or toll-free 888-KINGSPA. *Fax:* 570-208-6015. *E-mail:* hlchance@kings.edu

KNOX COLLEGE

Galesburg, IL

Tuition & fees: $21,174 **Average undergraduate aid package: $17,686**

ABOUT THE INSTITUTION Independent, coed. Awards: bachelor's degrees. 33 undergraduate majors. Total enrollment: 1,220. Undergraduates: 1,220. Freshmen: 300. Both federal and institutional methodology are used as a basis for awarding need-based institutional aid.

UNDERGRADUATE EXPENSES for 2000–2001 ***Application fee:*** $35. ***Comprehensive fee:*** $26,610 includes full-time tuition ($20,940), mandatory fees ($234), and room and board ($5436). ***College room only:*** $2418. Room and board charges vary according to board plan and housing facility. ***Payment plans:*** tuition prepayment, installment.

FRESHMAN FINANCIAL AID (Fall 1999, est.) 263 applied for aid; of those 89% were deemed to have need. 100% of freshmen with need received aid; of those 100% had need fully met. *Average percent of need met:* 100% (excluding resources awarded to replace EFC). *Average financial aid package:* $18,657 (excluding resources awarded to replace EFC). 16% of all full-time freshmen had no need and received non-need-based aid.

UNDERGRADUATE FINANCIAL AID (Fall 1999, est.) 966 applied for aid; of those 92% were deemed to have need. 100% of undergraduates with need received aid; of those 100% had need fully met. *Average percent of need met:* 100% (excluding resources awarded to replace EFC). *Average financial aid package:* $17,686 (excluding resources awarded to replace EFC). 17% of all full-time undergraduates had no need and received non-need-based aid.

GIFT AID (NEED-BASED) ***Total amount:*** $12,146,574 (5% Federal, 11% state, 81% institutional, 3% external sources). ***Receiving aid:*** *Freshmen:* 78% (235); *all full-time undergraduates:* 76% (892). ***Average award:*** Freshmen: $14,863; Undergraduates: $13,617. ***Scholarships, grants, and awards:*** Federal Pell, FSEOG, state, private, college/university gift aid from institutional funds.

GIFT AID (NON-NEED-BASED) ***Total amount:*** $1,707,764 (1% state, 93% institutional, 6% external sources). ***Receiving aid:*** *Freshmen:* 6% (17); *Undergraduates:* 5% (59). ***Scholarships, grants, and awards by category:*** *Academic Interests/Achievement:* general academic interests/achievements, mathematics. *Creative Arts/Performance:* art/fine arts, creative writing, music, theater/drama. *Special Achievements/Activities:* community service. ***Tuition waivers:*** Full or partial for employees or children of employees.

LOANS ***Student loans:*** $3,338,854 (81% need-based, 19% non-need-based). 79% of past graduating class borrowed through all loan programs. Average indebtedness per student: $15,715. ***Average need-based loan:*** Freshmen: $3391; Undergraduates: $4311. ***Parent loans:*** $1,032,133 (100% non-need-based). ***Programs:*** Federal Direct (Subsidized and Unsubsidized Stafford, PLUS), Perkins, college/university.

WORK-STUDY ***Federal work-study:*** *Total amount:* $725,096; 876 jobs averaging $828. ***State or other work-study/employment:*** *Total amount:* $196,164 (100% need-based). 131 part-time jobs averaging $1497.

APPLYING for FINANCIAL AID ***Required financial aid forms:*** FAFSA, institution's own form, income tax returns. ***Financial aid deadline (priority):*** 3/1. ***Notification date:*** 4/15. Students must reply by 5/1 or within 2 weeks of notification.

CONTACT Ms. Teresa K. Jackson, Director of Financial Aid, Knox College, 2 East South Street, Galesburg, IL 61401, 309-341-7130 or toll-free 800-678-KNOX. *Fax:* 309-341-7070. *E-mail:* tjackson@knox.edu

KOL YAAKOV TORAH CENTER

Monsey, NY

CONTACT Office of Financial Aid, Kol Yaakov Torah Center, 29 West Maple Avenue, Monsey, NY 10952-2954, 914-425-3863.

KUTZTOWN UNIVERSITY OF PENNSYLVANIA

Kutztown, PA

Tuition & fees (PA res): $4448 **Average undergraduate aid package: $5072**

ABOUT THE INSTITUTION State-supported, coed. Awards: bachelor's and master's degrees. 56 undergraduate majors. Total enrollment: 8,069. Undergraduates: 7,059. Freshmen: 1,554. Federal methodology is used as a basis for awarding need-based institutional aid.

UNDERGRADUATE EXPENSES for 1999–2000 ***Application fee:*** $30. ***One-time required fee:*** $48. ***Tuition, state resident:*** full-time $3618; part-time $150 per credit. ***Tuition, nonresident:*** full-time $9046; part-time $377 per credit. ***Required fees:*** full-time $830; $35 per credit. Part-time tuition and fees vary according to course load. ***College room and board:*** $4082; ***room only:*** $2820. Room and board charges vary according to board plan. ***Payment plans:*** tuition prepayment, installment, deferred payment.

FRESHMAN FINANCIAL AID (Fall 1998) 1175 applied for aid; of those 70% were deemed to have need. 100% of freshmen with need received aid; of those 63% had need fully met. *Average percent of need met:* 59% (excluding resources awarded to replace EFC). *Average financial aid package:* $4001 (excluding resources awarded to replace EFC). 16% of all full-time freshmen had no need and received non-need-based aid.

UNDERGRADUATE FINANCIAL AID (Fall 1998) 4,703 applied for aid; of those 74% were deemed to have need. 100% of undergraduates with need received aid; of those 63% had need fully met. *Average percent of need met:* 67% (excluding resources awarded to replace EFC). *Average financial aid package:* $5072 (excluding resources awarded to replace EFC). 15% of all full-time undergraduates had no need and received non-need-based aid.

GIFT AID (NEED-BASED) ***Total amount:*** $6,499,165 (42% Federal, 51% state, 3% institutional, 4% external sources). ***Receiving aid:*** *Freshmen:* 42% (603); *all full-time undergraduates:* 39% (2,515). ***Average award:*** Freshmen: $2621; Undergraduates: $2672. ***Scholarships, grants, and awards:*** Federal Pell, FSEOG, state, private, college/university gift aid from institutional funds.

GIFT AID (NON-NEED-BASED) ***Total amount:*** $450,286 (10% Federal, 32% state, 17% institutional, 41% external sources). ***Receiving aid:*** *Freshmen:* 2% (34); *Undergraduates:* 6% (385). ***Scholarships, grants, and awards by category:*** *Academic Interests/Achievement:* general academic interests/achievements. *Creative Arts/Performance:* applied art and design, music. *Special Achievements/Activities:* general special achievements/activities. *Special Characteristics:* 80 awards ($223,136 total): children of faculty/staff. ***Tuition waivers:*** Full or partial for employees or children of employees. ***ROTC:*** Army cooperative, Air Force cooperative.

LOANS ***Student loans:*** $14,166,988 (67% need-based, 33% non-need-based). 69% of past graduating class borrowed through all loan programs. Average indebtedness per student: $12,817. ***Average need-based loan:*** Freshmen: $2303; Undergraduates: $3063. ***Parent loans:*** $2,331,292 (28% need-based, 72% non-need-based). ***Programs:*** FFEL (Subsidized and Unsubsidized Stafford, PLUS), Perkins.

WORK-STUDY ***Federal work-study:*** *Total amount:* $276,872; 284 jobs averaging $975. ***State or other work-study/employment:*** *Total amount:* $738,062 (17% need-based, 83% non-need-based). 1,351 part-time jobs averaging $546.

ATHLETIC AWARDS *Total amount:* 266,517 (54% need-based, 46% non-need-based).

APPLYING for FINANCIAL AID ***Required financial aid form:*** FAFSA. ***Financial aid deadline (priority):*** 2/15. ***Notification date:*** 3/30.

CONTACT Ms. Anita Faust, Director of Financial Aid, Kutztown University of Pennsylvania, 218 Stratton Administration Center, Kutztown, PA 19530-0730, 610-683-4077 or toll-free 877-628-1915. *Fax:* 610-683-1380. *E-mail:* faust@kutztown.edu

LABORATORY INSTITUTE OF MERCHANDISING

New York, NY

Tuition & fees: $12,950 **Average undergraduate aid package: $10,000**

ABOUT THE INSTITUTION Proprietary, coed, primarily women. Awards: associate and bachelor's degrees. 2 undergraduate majors. Total enrollment: 267. Undergraduates: 267. Freshmen: 79. Federal methodology is used as a basis for awarding need-based institutional aid.

UNDERGRADUATE EXPENSES for 2000–2001 ***Application fee:*** $35. ***Tuition:*** full-time $12,800; part-time $390 per credit. ***Required fees:*** full-time $150; $75 per term part-time. ***Payment plan:*** installment.

FRESHMAN FINANCIAL AID (Fall 1999, est.) 60 applied for aid; of those 93% were deemed to have need. 100% of freshmen with need received aid. *Average percent of need met:* 85% (excluding resources awarded to replace EFC). *Average financial aid package:* $11,000 (excluding resources awarded to replace EFC). 6% of all full-time freshmen had no need and received non-need-based aid.

UNDERGRADUATE FINANCIAL AID (Fall 1999, est.) 218 applied for aid; of those 96% were deemed to have need. 100% of undergraduates with need received aid. *Average percent of need met:* 85% (excluding resources awarded to replace EFC). *Average financial aid package:* $10,000 (excluding resources awarded to replace EFC). 3% of all full-time undergraduates had no need and received non-need-based aid.

GIFT AID (NEED-BASED) ***Total amount:*** $450,443 (52% Federal, 35% state, 13% institutional). ***Receiving aid:*** *Freshmen:* 42% (33); *all full-time undergraduates:* 42% (113). ***Average award:*** Freshmen: $1000; Undergraduates: $1000. ***Scholarships, grants, and awards:*** Federal Pell, FSEOG, state, college/university gift aid from institutional funds.

GIFT AID (NON-NEED-BASED) ***Total amount:*** $143,575 (100% institutional). ***Receiving aid:*** *Freshmen:* 36% (28); *Undergraduates:* 28% (75). ***Scholarships, grants, and awards by category:*** *Academic Interests/Achievement:* 72 awards ($143,575 total): general academic interests/achievements. *Special Achievements/Activities:* 1 award: general special achievements/activities, memberships. *Special Characteristics:* local/state students.

LOANS ***Student loans:*** $657,840 (94% need-based, 6% non-need-based). 60% of past graduating class borrowed through all loan programs. Average indebtedness per student: $14,000. ***Average need-based loan:*** Freshmen: $2625; Undergraduates: $3500. ***Parent loans:*** $219,700 (83% need-based, 17% non-need-based). ***Programs:*** Federal Direct (Subsidized and Unsubsidized Stafford, PLUS), Perkins.

APPLYING for FINANCIAL AID ***Required financial aid forms:*** FAFSA, institution's own form. ***Financial aid deadline:*** Continuous. ***Notification date:*** Continuous beginning 2/15. Students must reply within 2 weeks of notification.

CONTACT Mrs. Linda G. Gayton, Director of Financial Aid, Laboratory Institute of Merchandising, 12 East 53rd Street, New York, NY 10022-5268, 212-752-1530 Ext. 26 or toll-free 800-677-1323. *Fax:* 212-832-6708.

LAFAYETTE COLLEGE

Easton, PA

Tuition & fees: $22,929 **Average undergraduate aid package: $19,556**

ABOUT THE INSTITUTION Independent religious, coed. Awards: bachelor's degrees. 34 undergraduate majors. Total enrollment: 2,283. Undergraduates: 2,283. Freshmen: 582. Institutional methodology is used as a basis for awarding need-based institutional aid.

UNDERGRADUATE EXPENSES for 1999–2000 ***Application fee:*** $50. ***Comprehensive fee:*** $30,035 includes full-time tuition ($22,844), mandatory fees ($85), and room and board ($7106). ***College room only:*** $3900. Room and board charges vary according to board plan. ***Part-time tuition:*** $990 per course. ***Payment plans:*** tuition prepayment, deferred payment.

FRESHMAN FINANCIAL AID (Fall 1999) 404 applied for aid; of those 77% were deemed to have need. 100% of freshmen with need received aid; of those 97% had need fully met. *Average percent of need met:* 97% (excluding resources awarded to replace EFC). *Average financial aid package:* $20,195 (excluding resources awarded to replace EFC). 3% of all full-time freshmen had no need and received non-need-based aid.

UNDERGRADUATE FINANCIAL AID (Fall 1999) 1,282 applied for aid; of those 80% were deemed to have need. 100% of undergraduates with need received aid; of those 94% had need fully met. *Average percent of need met:* 95% (excluding resources awarded to replace EFC). *Average financial aid package:* $19,556 (excluding resources awarded to replace EFC). 3% of all full-time undergraduates had no need and received non-need-based aid.

GIFT AID (NEED-BASED) ***Total amount:*** $15,746,606 (4% Federal, 4% state, 90% institutional, 2% external sources). ***Receiving aid:*** *Freshmen:* 53% (309); *all full-time undergraduates:* 46% (999). ***Average award:*** Freshmen: $16,341; Undergraduates: $14,812. ***Scholarships, grants, and awards:*** Federal Pell, FSEOG, state, private, college/university gift aid from institutional funds.

GIFT AID (NON-NEED-BASED) ***Total amount:*** $1,162,873 (85% institutional, 15% external sources). ***Receiving aid:*** *Freshmen:* 4% (25); *Undergraduates:* 4% (80). ***Scholarships, grants, and awards by category:*** *Academic Interests/Achievement:* 105 awards ($817,264 total): general academic interests/achievements. ***Tuition waivers:*** Full or partial for employees or children of employees. ***ROTC:*** Army cooperative.

LOANS ***Student loans:*** $4,111,188 (73% need-based, 27% non-need-based). 50% of past graduating class borrowed through all loan programs. Average indebtedness per student: $13,875. ***Average need-based loan:*** Freshmen: $2732; Undergraduates: $3752. ***Parent loans:*** $4,858,253 (3% need-based, 97% non-need-based). ***Programs:*** FFEL (Subsidized and Unsubsidized Stafford, PLUS), Perkins, state, college/university, Parent loans (HELP).

WORK-STUDY ***Federal work-study:*** *Total amount:* $203,570; 199 jobs averaging $1023. ***State or other work-study/employment:*** *Total amount:* $549,214 (85% need-based, 15% non-need-based). 138 part-time jobs averaging $3980.

APPLYING for FINANCIAL AID ***Required financial aid forms:*** FAFSA, CSS Financial Aid PROFILE, noncustodial (divorced/separated) parent's statement, business/farm supplement, parent and student income tax returns (with all schedules and W-2 forms). ***Financial aid deadline:*** 2/1. ***Notification date:*** 4/1. Students must reply by 5/1.

CONTACT Arlina B. DeNardo, Director of Student Financial Aid, Lafayette College, 107 Markle Hall, Easton, PA 18042-1777, 610-330-5055. *Fax:* 610-330-5355. *E-mail:* denardoa@lafayette.edu

LAGRANGE COLLEGE

LaGrange, GA

Tuition & fees: $11,001 **Average undergraduate aid package: $16,831**

ABOUT THE INSTITUTION Independent United Methodist, coed. Awards: associate, bachelor's, and master's degrees. 38 undergraduate majors. Total enrollment: 996. Undergraduates: 951. Freshmen: 186. Federal methodology is used as a basis for awarding need-based institutional aid.

UNDERGRADUATE EXPENSES for 1999–2000 ***Application fee:*** $20. ***Comprehensive fee:*** $15,657 includes full-time tuition ($10,761), mandatory fees ($240), and room and board ($4656). Full-time tuition and fees vary according to location. ***Part-time tuition:*** $211 per quarter hour. ***Part-time fees:*** $80 per term part-time. Part-time tuition and fees vary according to location. ***Payment plan:*** installment.

FRESHMAN FINANCIAL AID (Fall 1999) 160 applied for aid; of those 72% were deemed to have need. 99% of freshmen with need received aid; of those 36% had need fully met. *Average percent of need met:* 79% (excluding resources awarded to replace EFC). *Average financial aid package:* $10,728 (excluding resources awarded to replace EFC). 27% of all full-time freshmen had no need and received non-need-based aid.

UNDERGRADUATE FINANCIAL AID (Fall 1999) 655 applied for aid; of those 80% were deemed to have need. 100% of undergraduates with need received aid; of those 46% had need fully met. *Average percent of need met:* 85% (excluding resources awarded to replace EFC). *Average*

LaGrange College (continued)

financial aid package: $16,831 (excluding resources awarded to replace EFC). 17% of all full-time undergraduates had no need and received non-need-based aid.

GIFT AID (NEED-BASED) ***Total amount:*** $3,288,475 (19% Federal, 27% state, 48% institutional, 6% external sources). ***Receiving aid:*** *Freshmen:* 66% (114); *all full-time undergraduates:* 68% (524). ***Average award:*** Freshmen: $8603; Undergraduates: $7515. ***Scholarships, grants, and awards:*** Federal Pell, FSEOG, state, private, college/university gift aid from institutional funds.

GIFT AID (NON-NEED-BASED) ***Total amount:*** $1,456,914 (1% Federal, 40% state, 50% institutional, 9% external sources). ***Receiving aid:*** *Freshmen:* 27% (47); *Undergraduates:* 27% (211). ***Scholarships, grants, and awards by category:*** *Academic Interests/Achievement:* 250 awards ($776,849 total): English, general academic interests/achievements, mathematics, physical sciences, religion/biblical studies, social sciences. *Creative Arts/Performance:* 21 awards ($25,150 total): art/fine arts, music, theater/drama. *Special Achievements/Activities:* 35 awards ($43,468 total): community service, leadership, religious involvement. *Special Characteristics:* 11 awards ($15,500 total): relatives of clergy. ***Tuition waivers:*** Full or partial for employees or children of employees.

LOANS ***Student loans:*** $2,372,789 (81% need-based, 19% non-need-based). Average indebtedness per student: $16,000. ***Average need-based loan:*** Freshmen: $2564; Undergraduates: $3240. ***Parent loans:*** $398,709 (100% non-need-based). ***Programs:*** FFEL (Subsidized and Unsubsidized Stafford, PLUS), Perkins.

WORK-STUDY ***Federal work-study:*** *Total amount:* $72,328; 58 jobs averaging $1292. ***State or other work-study/employment:*** *Total amount:* $247,361 (38% need-based, 62% non-need-based). 196 part-time jobs averaging $1262.

APPLYING for FINANCIAL AID ***Required financial aid forms:*** FAFSA, institution's own form, state aid form. ***Financial aid deadline (priority):*** 5/1. ***Notification date:*** Continuous. Students must reply by 8/15 or within 2 weeks of notification.

CONTACT Sylvia Smith, Director of Financial Aid, LaGrange College, 601 Broad Street, LaGrange, GA 30240-2999, 706-812-7241 or toll-free 800-593-2885.

LAKE ERIE COLLEGE

Painesville, OH

Tuition & fees: $15,140 **Average undergraduate aid package: N/A**

ABOUT THE INSTITUTION Independent, coed. Awards: bachelor's and master's degrees. 29 undergraduate majors. Total enrollment: 725. Undergraduates: 509. Federal methodology is used as a basis for awarding need-based institutional aid.

UNDERGRADUATE EXPENSES for 1999–2000 ***Application fee:*** $25. ***Comprehensive fee:*** $20,400 includes full-time tuition ($14,280), mandatory fees ($860), and room and board ($5260). ***College room only:*** $2820. Room and board charges vary according to board plan. ***Payment plan:*** installment.

FRESHMAN FINANCIAL AID (Fall 1998) 64 applied for aid. *Average percent of need met:* 92% (excluding resources awarded to replace EFC).

UNDERGRADUATE FINANCIAL AID (Fall 1998) 300 applied for aid. *Average percent of need met:* 85% (excluding resources awarded to replace EFC).

GIFT AID (NEED-BASED) ***Total amount:*** $1,236,996 (24% Federal, 14% state, 49% institutional, 13% external sources). ***Scholarships, grants, and awards:*** Federal Pell, FSEOG, state, private, college/university gift aid from institutional funds.

GIFT AID (NON-NEED-BASED) ***Total amount:*** $799,007 (28% state, 72% institutional). ***Scholarships, grants, and awards by category:*** *Academic Interests/Achievement:* biological sciences, general academic interests/achievements. *Creative Arts/Performance:* art/fine arts, general creative arts/performance, performing arts. *Special Achievements/Activities:* hobbies/interests. *Special Characteristics:* children of faculty/staff. ***Tuition waivers:*** Full or partial for employees or children of employees, senior citizens.

LOANS ***Student loans:*** $1,885,498 (61% need-based, 39% non-need-based). ***Parent loans:*** $295,164 (100% non-need-based). ***Programs:*** FFEL (Subsidized and Unsubsidized Stafford, PLUS), Perkins, state, college/university.

WORK-STUDY ***Federal work-study:*** *Total amount:* $21,084; 14 jobs averaging $1506. ***State or other work-study/employment:*** *Total amount:* $126,367 (100% non-need-based). 119 part-time jobs averaging $1062.

APPLYING for FINANCIAL AID ***Required financial aid form:*** FAFSA. ***Financial aid deadline:*** Continuous. ***Notification date:*** Continuous beginning 1/15. Students must reply by 5/1 or within 2 weeks of notification.

CONTACT Financial Aid Office, Lake Erie College, 391 West Washington Street, Painesville, OH 44077-3389, 440-639-7815 or toll-free 800-916-0904. *Fax:* 440-352-3533.

LAKE FOREST COLLEGE

Lake Forest, IL

Tuition & fees: $21,190 **Average undergraduate aid package: $17,152**

ABOUT THE INSTITUTION Independent, coed. Awards: bachelor's and master's degrees. 36 undergraduate majors. Total enrollment: 1,254. Undergraduates: 1,241. Freshmen: 341. Both federal and institutional methodology are used as a basis for awarding need-based institutional aid.

UNDERGRADUATE EXPENSES for 2000–2001 ***Application fee:*** $35. ***Comprehensive fee:*** $26,190 includes full-time tuition ($20,900), mandatory fees ($290), and room and board ($5000). ***College room only:*** $2740. Room and board charges vary according to housing facility. ***Part-time tuition:*** $2610 per course. ***Payment plan:*** installment.

FRESHMAN FINANCIAL AID (Fall 1999, est.) 298 applied for aid; of those 91% were deemed to have need. 100% of freshmen with need received aid; of those 100% had need fully met. *Average percent of need met:* 100% (excluding resources awarded to replace EFC). *Average financial aid package:* $16,465 (excluding resources awarded to replace EFC). 10% of all full-time freshmen had no need and received non-need-based aid.

UNDERGRADUATE FINANCIAL AID (Fall 1999, est.) 1,049 applied for aid; of those 88% were deemed to have need. 100% of undergraduates with need received aid; of those 100% had need fully met. *Average percent of need met:* 100% (excluding resources awarded to replace EFC). *Average financial aid package:* $17,152 (excluding resources awarded to replace EFC). 10% of all full-time undergraduates had no need and received non-need-based aid.

GIFT AID (NEED-BASED) ***Total amount:*** $12,827,182 (7% Federal, 9% state, 82% institutional, 2% external sources). ***Receiving aid:*** *Freshmen:* 79% (271); *all full-time undergraduates:* 74% (919). ***Average award:*** Freshmen: $12,462; Undergraduates: $12,739. ***Scholarships, grants, and awards:*** Federal Pell, FSEOG, state, private, college/university gift aid from institutional funds.

GIFT AID (NON-NEED-BASED) ***Total amount:*** $1,611,610 (1% state, 98% institutional, 1% external sources). ***Scholarships, grants, and awards by category:*** *Academic Interests/Achievement:* 122 awards ($1,059,550 total): general academic interests/achievements. *Creative Arts/Performance:* 28 awards ($100,500 total): art/fine arts, music, theater/drama. *Special Achievements/Activities:* 21 awards ($77,000 total): leadership. *Special Characteristics:* 9 awards ($91,080 total): children and siblings of alumni, previous college experience. ***Tuition waivers:*** Full or partial for employees or children of employees.

LOANS ***Student loans:*** $3,035,305 (93% need-based, 7% non-need-based). 63% of past graduating class borrowed through all loan programs. Average indebtedness per student: $14,604. ***Average need-based loan:*** Freshmen: $2883; Undergraduates: $3442. ***Parent loans:*** $735,543 (81% need-based, 19% non-need-based). ***Programs:*** FFEL (Subsidized and Unsubsidized Stafford, PLUS), Perkins, state, college/university.

WORK-STUDY ***Federal work-study:*** *Total amount:* $633,875; 429 jobs averaging $1478.

APPLYING for FINANCIAL AID ***Required financial aid forms:*** FAFSA, federal income tax return. ***Financial aid deadline (priority):*** 3/1. ***Notification date:*** 3/15. Students must reply by 5/1.

CONTACT Mr. Jerry Cebrzynski, Director of Financial Aid, Lake Forest College, 555 North Sheridan Road, Lake Forest, IL 60045-2399, 847-234-3100 or toll-free 800-828-4751. *Fax:* 847-735-6271. *E-mail:* cebrzynski@lfc.edu

LAKELAND COLLEGE

Sheboygan, WI

Tuition & fees: $12,480 **Average undergraduate aid package: $10,004**

ABOUT THE INSTITUTION Independent religious, coed. Awards: bachelor's and master's degrees. 46 undergraduate majors. Total enrollment: 3,482. Undergraduates: 3,328. Freshmen: 179. Federal methodology is used as a basis for awarding need-based institutional aid.

UNDERGRADUATE EXPENSES for 1999–2000 ***Application fee:*** $20. ***Comprehensive fee:*** $17,160 includes full-time tuition ($11,980), mandatory fees ($500), and room and board ($4680). ***College room only:*** $2260. Full-time tuition and fees vary according to location. Room and board charges vary according to board plan and housing facility. ***Part-time tuition:*** $1140 per course. Part-time tuition and fees vary according to class time and location. ***Payment plan:*** installment.

FRESHMAN FINANCIAL AID (Fall 1999, est.) 188 applied for aid; of those 87% were deemed to have need. 100% of freshmen with need received aid; of those 30% had need fully met. *Average percent of need met:* 84% (excluding resources awarded to replace EFC). *Average financial aid package:* $10,323 (excluding resources awarded to replace EFC). 48% of all full-time freshmen had no need and received non-need-based aid.

UNDERGRADUATE FINANCIAL AID (Fall 1999, est.) 840 applied for aid; of those 90% were deemed to have need. 100% of undergraduates with need received aid; of those 55% had need fully met. *Average percent of need met:* 90% (excluding resources awarded to replace EFC). *Average financial aid package:* $10,004 (excluding resources awarded to replace EFC). 34% of all full-time undergraduates had no need and received non-need-based aid.

GIFT AID (NEED-BASED) ***Total amount:*** $4,624,095 (22% Federal, 16% state, 60% institutional, 2% external sources). ***Receiving aid:*** *Freshmen:* 43% (162); *all full-time undergraduates:* 62% (708). ***Average award:*** Freshmen: $7080; Undergraduates: $5977. ***Scholarships, grants, and awards:*** Federal Pell, FSEOG, state, private, college/university gift aid from institutional funds.

GIFT AID (NON-NEED-BASED) ***Total amount:*** $880,210 (2% state, 90% institutional, 8% external sources). ***Receiving aid:*** *Freshmen:* 3% (11); *Undergraduates:* 6% (63). ***Scholarships, grants, and awards by category:*** *Academic Interests/Achievement:* business, engineering/technologies, English, general academic interests/achievements. *Creative Arts/Performance:* journalism/publications, music, performing arts. *Special Achievements/Activities:* community service, leadership, religious involvement. *Special Characteristics:* religious affiliation, siblings of current students. ***Tuition waivers:*** Full or partial for employees or children of employees, senior citizens.

LOANS ***Student loans:*** $6,045,008 (62% need-based, 38% non-need-based). 75% of past graduating class borrowed through all loan programs. Average indebtedness per student: $10,301. ***Average need-based loan:*** Freshmen: $2583; Undergraduates: $3603. ***Parent loans:*** $270,391 (36% need-based, 64% non-need-based). ***Programs:*** FFEL (Subsidized and Unsubsidized Stafford, PLUS), Perkins.

WORK-STUDY ***Federal work-study:*** *Total amount:* $308,228; jobs available. ***State or other work-study/employment:*** *Total amount:* $137,759 (9% need-based, 91% non-need-based). Part-time jobs available.

APPLYING for FINANCIAL AID ***Required financial aid forms:*** FAFSA, institution's own form. ***Financial aid deadline (priority):*** 5/1. ***Notification date:*** Continuous. Students must reply within 2 weeks of notification.

CONTACT Mr. Don Seymour, Director of Financial Aid, Lakeland College, PO Box 359, Sheboygan, WI 53082-0359, 920-565-1214 or toll-free 800-242-3347 (in-state). *Fax:* 920-565-1206.

LAKE SUPERIOR STATE UNIVERSITY

Sault Sainte Marie, MI

Tuition & fees (MI res): $4034 **Average undergraduate aid package: $3382**

ABOUT THE INSTITUTION State-supported, coed. Awards: associate, bachelor's, and master's degrees. 73 undergraduate majors. Total enrollment: 3,197. Undergraduates: 3,117. Freshmen: 520. Both federal and institutional methodology are used as a basis for awarding need-based institutional aid.

UNDERGRADUATE EXPENSES for 1999–2000 ***Application fee:*** $25. ***Tuition, state resident:*** full-time $3838; part-time $160 per semester hour. ***Tuition, nonresident:*** full-time $7542; part-time $314 per semester hour. ***Required fees:*** full-time $196; $98 per term part-time. Full-time tuition and fees vary according to reciprocity agreements. Part-time tuition and fees vary according to reciprocity agreements. ***College room and board:*** $4930; ***room only:*** $4273. Room and board charges vary according to board plan.

FRESHMAN FINANCIAL AID (Fall 1999) 416 applied for aid; of those 100% were deemed to have need. 100% of freshmen with need received aid. *Average financial aid package:* $3550 (excluding resources awarded to replace EFC).

UNDERGRADUATE FINANCIAL AID (Fall 1999) 1,951 applied for aid; of those 100% were deemed to have need. 100% of undergraduates with need received aid. *Average financial aid package:* $3382 (excluding resources awarded to replace EFC).

GIFT AID (NEED-BASED) ***Total amount:*** $4,261,026 (40% Federal, 14% state, 30% institutional, 16% external sources). ***Receiving aid:*** *Freshmen:* 33% (174); *all full-time undergraduates:* 33% (810). ***Average award:*** Freshmen: $2585; Undergraduates: $2420. ***Scholarships, grants, and awards:*** Federal Pell, FSEOG, state, private, college/university gift aid from institutional funds, Federal Nursing, third party payments.

GIFT AID (NON-NEED-BASED) ***Receiving aid:*** *Freshmen:* 47% (244); *Undergraduates:* 36% (870). ***Scholarships, grants, and awards by category:*** *Academic Interests/Achievement:* general academic interests/achievements. *Creative Arts/Performance:* general creative arts/performance. *Special Achievements/Activities:* general special achievements/activities. *Special Characteristics:* general special characteristics. ***Tuition waivers:*** Full or partial for minority students, children of alumni, employees or children of employees, senior citizens.

LOANS ***Student loans:*** $7,016,826 (100% need-based). ***Average need-based loan:*** Freshmen: $2498; Undergraduates: $3086. ***Parent loans:*** $1,030,532 (100% need-based). ***Programs:*** Federal Direct (Subsidized and Unsubsidized Stafford, PLUS), Perkins, Federal Nursing, state.

WORK-STUDY ***Federal work-study:*** *Total amount:* $223,300; jobs available. ***State or other work-study/employment:*** *Total amount:* $122,749 (100% need-based). Part-time jobs available.

ATHLETIC AWARDS *Total amount:* 570,957 (100% need-based).

APPLYING for FINANCIAL AID ***Required financial aid form:*** FAFSA. ***Financial aid deadline:*** Continuous. ***Notification date:*** Continuous. Students must reply within 3 weeks of notification.

CONTACT Mrs. Deborah J. Faust, Director of Financial Aid, Lake Superior State University, 650 West Easterday Avenue, Sault Sainte Marie, MI 49783-1699, 906-635-2678 or toll-free 888-800-LSSU Ext. 2231.

LAKEVIEW COLLEGE OF NURSING

Danville, IL

Tuition & fees: $7440 **Average undergraduate aid package: N/A**

ABOUT THE INSTITUTION Independent, coed, primarily women. Awards: bachelor's degrees. 1 undergraduate major. Total enrollment: 78. Undergraduates: 78. Federal methodology is used as a basis for awarding need-based institutional aid.

Lakeview College of Nursing (continued)

UNDERGRADUATE EXPENSES for 1999–2000 ***Application fee:*** $50. ***One-time required fee:*** $120. ***Tuition:*** full-time $7440; part-time $240 per credit hour. Full-time tuition and fees vary according to course load. ***Payment plans:*** installment, deferred payment.

UNDERGRADUATE FINANCIAL AID (Fall 1998) 22 applied for aid; of those 95% were deemed to have need. 100% of undergraduates with need received aid.

GIFT AID (NEED-BASED) ***Total amount:*** $254,424 (29% Federal, 45% state, 22% institutional, 4% external sources). ***Receiving aid:*** *All full-time undergraduates:* 84% (21). ***Scholarships, grants, and awards:*** Federal Pell, state, private, college/university gift aid from institutional funds.

GIFT AID (NON-NEED-BASED) ***Total amount:*** $29,753 (38% institutional, 62% external sources). ***Receiving aid:*** *Undergraduates:* 28% (7). ***Scholarships, grants, and awards by category:*** *Academic Interests/Achievement:* health fields.

LOANS ***Student loans:*** $152,801 (58% need-based, 42% non-need-based). 52% of past graduating class borrowed through all loan programs. ***Programs:*** FFEL (Subsidized and Unsubsidized Stafford, PLUS), college/university.

APPLYING for FINANCIAL AID ***Required financial aid forms:*** FAFSA, institution's own form. ***Financial aid deadline (priority):*** 4/15. ***Notification date:*** Continuous.

CONTACT Ms. Sandra J. Brooks, Financial Aid Officer, Lakeview College of Nursing, 812 North Logan, Danville, IL 61832, 217-443-5238. *Fax:* 217-431-4015. *E-mail:* lcn4@soltec.net

LAMAR UNIVERSITY

Beaumont, TX

Tuition & fees (TX res): $2161 **Average undergraduate aid package: $1175**

ABOUT THE INSTITUTION State-supported, coed. Awards: associate, bachelor's, master's, and doctoral degrees. 102 undergraduate majors. Total enrollment: 8,149. Undergraduates: 7,382. Federal methodology is used as a basis for awarding need-based institutional aid.

UNDERGRADUATE EXPENSES for 1999–2000 ***Tuition, state resident:*** full-time $1584; part-time $396 per term. ***Tuition, nonresident:*** full-time $7104; part-time $1776 per term. ***Required fees:*** full-time $577; $204 per term part-time. Part-time tuition and fees vary according to course load. ***College room and board:*** $3516. Room and board charges vary according to board plan and housing facility. ***Payment plan:*** installment.

FRESHMAN FINANCIAL AID (Fall 1999, est.) 997 applied for aid; of those 87% were deemed to have need. 100% of freshmen with need received aid. *Average percent of need met:* 14% (excluding resources awarded to replace EFC). *Average financial aid package:* $1222 (excluding resources awarded to replace EFC). 44% of all full-time freshmen had no need and received non-need-based aid.

UNDERGRADUATE FINANCIAL AID (Fall 1999, est.) 3,183 applied for aid; of those 87% were deemed to have need. 81% of undergraduates with need received aid; of those 3% had need fully met. *Average percent of need met:* 11% (excluding resources awarded to replace EFC). *Average financial aid package:* $1175 (excluding resources awarded to replace EFC). 27% of all full-time undergraduates had no need and received non-need-based aid.

GIFT AID (NEED-BASED) ***Total amount:*** $6,887,000 (80% Federal, 17% state, 3% institutional). ***Receiving aid:*** *Freshmen:* 30% (502); *all full-time undergraduates:* 40% (1,681). ***Scholarships, grants, and awards:*** Federal Pell, FSEOG, state.

GIFT AID (NON-NEED-BASED) ***Total amount:*** $975,000 (51% institutional, 49% external sources). ***Receiving aid:*** *Freshmen:* 15% (251); *Undergraduates:* 21% (871). ***Scholarships, grants, and awards by category:*** *Academic Interests/Achievement:* general academic interests/achievements. *Creative Arts/Performance:* general creative arts/performance. *Special Achievements/Activities:* general special achievements/activities. ***Tuition waivers:*** Full or partial for senior citizens.

LOANS ***Student loans:*** $14,000,000 (100% need-based). 14% of past graduating class borrowed through all loan programs. Average indebtedness per student: $8800. ***Parent loans:*** $160,000 (100% need-based). ***Programs:*** FFEL (Subsidized and Unsubsidized Stafford, PLUS), Perkins, college/university.

WORK-STUDY ***Federal work-study:*** *Total amount:* $225,000; jobs available. ***State or other work-study/employment:*** *Total amount:* $10,500 (100% need-based). Part-time jobs available.

APPLYING for FINANCIAL AID ***Required financial aid forms:*** FAFSA, institution's own form. ***Financial aid deadline (priority):*** 4/1. ***Notification date:*** Continuous beginning 5/1.

CONTACT Financial Aid Department, Lamar University, PO Box 10042, Beaumont, TX 77710, 409-880-8450. *Fax:* 409-880-8934.

LAMBUTH UNIVERSITY

Jackson, TN

Tuition & fees: $7918 **Average undergraduate aid package: $5912**

ABOUT THE INSTITUTION Independent United Methodist, coed. Awards: bachelor's degrees. 51 undergraduate majors. Total enrollment: 975. Undergraduates: 975. Freshmen: 224. Federal methodology is used as a basis for awarding need-based institutional aid.

UNDERGRADUATE EXPENSES for 1999–2000 ***Application fee:*** $25. ***Comprehensive fee:*** $12,138 includes full-time tuition ($7818), mandatory fees ($100), and room and board ($4220). ***College room only:*** $1900. Room and board charges vary according to board plan and housing facility. ***Part-time tuition:*** $260 per credit hour. ***Part-time fees:*** $50 per term part-time. Part-time tuition and fees vary according to class time and course load. ***Payment plans:*** installment, deferred payment.

FRESHMAN FINANCIAL AID (Fall 1999, est.) 224 applied for aid; of those 58% were deemed to have need. 100% of freshmen with need received aid; of those 47% had need fully met. *Average percent of need met:* 76% (excluding resources awarded to replace EFC). *Average financial aid package:* $7568 (excluding resources awarded to replace EFC). 31% of all full-time freshmen had no need and received non-need-based aid.

UNDERGRADUATE FINANCIAL AID (Fall 1999, est.) 987 applied for aid; of those 55% were deemed to have need. 100% of undergraduates with need received aid; of those 38% had need fully met. *Average percent of need met:* 57% (excluding resources awarded to replace EFC). *Average financial aid package:* $5912 (excluding resources awarded to replace EFC). 26% of all full-time undergraduates had no need and received non-need-based aid.

GIFT AID (NEED-BASED) ***Total amount:*** $1,524,170 (41% Federal, 25% state, 34% institutional). ***Receiving aid:*** *Freshmen:* 58% (129); *all full-time undergraduates:* 54% (532). ***Average award:*** Freshmen: $5427; Undergraduates: $3278. ***Scholarships, grants, and awards:*** Federal Pell, FSEOG, state, private, college/university gift aid from institutional funds.

GIFT AID (NON-NEED-BASED) ***Total amount:*** $1,270,973 (8% state, 83% institutional, 9% external sources). ***Receiving aid:*** *Freshmen:* 3% (7); *Undergraduates:* 2% (22). ***Scholarships, grants, and awards by category:*** *Academic Interests/Achievement:* $1,846,000 total: general academic interests/achievements. *Creative Arts/Performance:* $60,000 total: dance, music, theater/drama. *Special Achievements/Activities:* $6000 total: cheerleading/drum major. *Special Characteristics:* $110,636 total: adult students, children of faculty/staff, relatives of clergy, religious affiliation. ***Tuition waivers:*** Full or partial for employees or children of employees, adult students, senior citizens.

LOANS ***Student loans:*** $2,209,697 (64% need-based, 36% non-need-based). 70% of past graduating class borrowed through all loan programs. Average indebtedness per student: $11,000. ***Average need-based loan:*** Freshmen: $2883; Undergraduates: $3512. ***Parent loans:*** $281,835 (100% non-need-based). ***Programs:*** FFEL (Subsidized and Unsubsidized Stafford, PLUS), Perkins, United Methodist Student Loans.

WORK-STUDY ***Federal work-study:*** *Total amount:* $124,124; 118 jobs averaging $1052. ***State or other work-study/employment:*** *Total amount:* $69,400 (100% non-need-based). 61 part-time jobs averaging $1138.

ATHLETIC AWARDS *Total amount:* 383,436 (100% non-need-based).

APPLYING for FINANCIAL AID ***Required financial aid form:*** FAFSA. ***Financial aid deadline (priority):*** 2/15. ***Notification date:*** Continuous. Students must reply within 4 weeks of notification.

CONTACT Ms. Lisa A. Warmath, Director of Scholarships and Financial Aid, Lambuth University, 705 Lambuth Boulevard, Jackson, TN 38301, 901-425-3331 or toll-free 800-526-2884. *Fax:* 901-425-3496. *E-mail:* warmath@lambuth.edu

LANCASTER BIBLE COLLEGE

Lancaster, PA

Tuition & fees: $9430 **Average undergraduate aid package: $7053**

ABOUT THE INSTITUTION Independent nondenominational, coed. Awards: associate, bachelor's, and master's degrees. 3 undergraduate majors. Total enrollment: 704. Undergraduates: 652. Freshmen: 107. Federal methodology is used as a basis for awarding need-based institutional aid.

UNDERGRADUATE EXPENSES for 1999–2000 ***Application fee:*** $15. ***Comprehensive fee:*** $13,730 includes full-time tuition ($9100), mandatory fees ($330), and room and board ($4300). ***College room only:*** $1800. Full-time tuition and fees vary according to program. Room and board charges vary according to board plan. ***Part-time tuition:*** $305 per credit hour. ***Part-time fees:*** $11 per credit hour. Part-time tuition and fees vary according to program. ***Payment plan:*** installment.

FRESHMAN FINANCIAL AID (Fall 1999, est.) 97 applied for aid; of those 92% were deemed to have need. 99% of freshmen with need received aid; of those 10% had need fully met. *Average percent of need met:* 38% (excluding resources awarded to replace EFC). *Average financial aid package:* $7054 (excluding resources awarded to replace EFC). 8% of all full-time freshmen had no need and received non-need-based aid.

UNDERGRADUATE FINANCIAL AID (Fall 1999, est.) 388 applied for aid; of those 95% were deemed to have need. 98% of undergraduates with need received aid; of those 7% had need fully met. *Average percent of need met:* 43% (excluding resources awarded to replace EFC). *Average financial aid package:* $7053 (excluding resources awarded to replace EFC). 3% of all full-time undergraduates had no need and received non-need-based aid.

GIFT AID (NEED-BASED) ***Total amount:*** $1,453,620 (25% Federal, 35% state, 38% institutional, 2% external sources). ***Receiving aid:*** *Freshmen:* 67% (71); *all full-time undergraduates:* 62% (294). ***Average award:*** Freshmen: $4351; Undergraduates: $4139. ***Scholarships, grants, and awards:*** Federal Pell, FSEOG, state, private, college/university gift aid from institutional funds, Office of Vocational Rehabilitation, Blindness and Visual Services Awards.

GIFT AID (NON-NEED-BASED) ***Total amount:*** $465,790 (81% institutional, 19% external sources). ***Receiving aid:*** *Freshmen:* 61% (65); *Undergraduates:* 40% (191). ***Scholarships, grants, and awards by category:*** *Academic Interests/Achievement:* 74 awards ($48,700 total): general academic interests/achievements. *Creative Arts/Performance:* 9 awards ($5500 total): music. *Special Achievements/Activities:* 70 awards ($56,600 total): leadership, religious involvement. *Special Characteristics:* 218 awards ($714,553 total): adult students, children and siblings of alumni, children of faculty/staff, international students, married students, relatives of clergy, religious affiliation, siblings of current students, spouses of current students. ***Tuition waivers:*** Full or partial for children of alumni, employees or children of employees, adult students, senior citizens.

LOANS ***Student loans:*** $1,477,626 (75% need-based, 25% non-need-based). Average indebtedness per student: $13,071. ***Average need-based loan:*** Freshmen: $2632; Undergraduates: $3198. ***Parent loans:*** $89,800 (100% non-need-based). ***Programs:*** FFEL (Subsidized and Unsubsidized Stafford, PLUS), Perkins, state, alternative loans.

WORK-STUDY ***Federal work-study:*** *Total amount:* $104,829; 102 jobs averaging $1200.

APPLYING for FINANCIAL AID ***Required financial aid forms:*** FAFSA, state aid form. ***Financial aid deadline (priority):*** 5/1. ***Notification date:*** Continuous. Students must reply within 2 weeks of notification.

CONTACT Karen Fox, Director of Financial Aid, Lancaster Bible College, PO Box 3403, Lancaster, PA 17608-3403, 717-560-8254 or toll-free 888-CALL LBC. *Fax:* 717-560-8214. *E-mail:* kfox@lbc.edu

LANDER UNIVERSITY

Greenwood, SC

Tuition & fees (SC res): $3820 **Average undergraduate aid package: $5310**

ABOUT THE INSTITUTION State-supported, coed. Awards: bachelor's and master's degrees. 35 undergraduate majors. Total enrollment: 2,883. Undergraduates: 2,471. Freshmen: 497. Federal methodology is used as a basis for awarding need-based institutional aid.

UNDERGRADUATE EXPENSES for 1999–2000 ***Application fee:*** $25. ***Tuition, state resident:*** full-time $3770. ***Tuition, nonresident:*** full-time $8668. ***Required fees:*** full-time $50. ***College room and board:*** $3855. Room and board charges vary according to board plan and housing facility. ***Payment plan:*** installment.

FRESHMAN FINANCIAL AID (Fall 1998) 295 applied for aid; of those 65% were deemed to have need. 70% of freshmen with need received aid; of those 60% had need fully met. *Average percent of need met:* 60% (excluding resources awarded to replace EFC). *Average financial aid package:* $4430 (excluding resources awarded to replace EFC). 36% of all full-time freshmen had no need and received non-need-based aid.

UNDERGRADUATE FINANCIAL AID (Fall 1998) 1,566 applied for aid; of those 60% were deemed to have need. 88% of undergraduates with need received aid; of those 59% had need fully met. *Average percent of need met:* 63% (excluding resources awarded to replace EFC). *Average financial aid package:* $5310 (excluding resources awarded to replace EFC). 20% of all full-time undergraduates had no need and received non-need-based aid.

GIFT AID (NEED-BASED) ***Total amount:*** $2,550,928 (64% Federal, 16% state, 18% institutional, 2% external sources). ***Receiving aid:*** *Freshmen:* 21% (101); *all full-time undergraduates:* 30% (645). ***Average award:*** Freshmen: $1750; Undergraduates: $1880. ***Scholarships, grants, and awards:*** Federal Pell, FSEOG, state, private, college/university gift aid from institutional funds, Federal Nursing.

GIFT AID (NON-NEED-BASED) ***Total amount:*** $989,139 (83% state, 1% institutional, 16% external sources). ***Receiving aid:*** *Freshmen:* 8% (40); *Undergraduates:* 14% (290). ***Scholarships, grants, and awards by category:*** *Academic Interests/Achievement:* 330 awards ($320,000 total): biological sciences, business, computer science, education, engineering/technologies, English, foreign languages, general academic interests/achievements, health fields, humanities, mathematics, physical sciences. *Creative Arts/Performance:* 47 awards ($16,000 total): art/fine arts, music, theater/drama. *Special Achievements/Activities:* 13 awards ($7000 total): leadership. *Special Characteristics:* 32 awards ($41,000 total): members of minority groups, out-of-state students. ***Tuition waivers:*** Full or partial for senior citizens. ***ROTC:*** Army.

LOANS ***Student loans:*** $5,878,301 (64% need-based, 36% non-need-based). Average indebtedness per student: $16,450. ***Average need-based loan:*** Freshmen: $2030; Undergraduates: $3880. ***Parent loans:*** $603,058 (100% non-need-based). ***Programs:*** FFEL (Subsidized and Unsubsidized Stafford, PLUS), Perkins, college/university.

WORK-STUDY ***Federal work-study:*** *Total amount:* $160,000; 139 jobs averaging $1315. ***State or other work-study/employment:*** *Total amount:* $431,000 (100% non-need-based). 220 part-time jobs averaging $1960.

ATHLETIC AWARDS *Total amount:* 329,108 (100% non-need-based).

APPLYING for FINANCIAL AID ***Required financial aid form:*** FAFSA. ***Financial aid deadline:*** Continuous. ***Notification date:*** Continuous beginning 4/1.

CONTACT Ian M. Hubbard, Director of Financial Aid, Lander University, 320 Stanley Avenue, Greenwood, SC 29649-2099, 864-388-8340 or toll-free 888-452-6337. *Fax:* 864-388-8890. *E-mail:* mhubbard@lander.edu

LANE COLLEGE
Jackson, TN

Tuition & fees: $6150 **Average undergraduate aid package: N/A**

ABOUT THE INSTITUTION Independent religious, coed. Awards: bachelor's degrees. 19 undergraduate majors. Total enrollment: 666. Undergraduates: 666. Freshmen: 202. Federal methodology is used as a basis for awarding need-based institutional aid.

UNDERGRADUATE EXPENSES for 1999–2000 ***Comprehensive fee:*** $9950 includes full-time tuition ($5600), mandatory fees ($550), and room and board ($3800). Full-time tuition and fees vary according to course load. ***Part-time tuition:*** $250 per semester hour. Part-time tuition and fees vary according to course load. ***Payment plans:*** installment, deferred payment.

GIFT AID (NEED-BASED) ***Scholarships, grants, and awards:*** Federal Pell, FSEOG, state, private, college/university gift aid from institutional funds, United Negro College Fund.

GIFT AID (NON-NEED-BASED) ***Scholarships, grants, and awards by category:*** *Academic Interests/Achievement:* general academic interests/achievements. ***Tuition waivers:*** Full or partial for employees or children of employees.

LOANS ***Programs:*** Federal Direct (Subsidized and Unsubsidized Stafford, PLUS).

WORK-STUDY Federal work-study jobs available.

APPLYING for FINANCIAL AID ***Required financial aid form:*** FAFSA. ***Financial aid deadline (priority):*** 3/31.

CONTACT Financial Aid Office, Lane College, 545 Lane Avenue, Jackson, TN 38301, 901-426-7536 or toll-free 800-960-7533. *Fax:* 901-426-7652.

LANGSTON UNIVERSITY
Langston, OK

Tuition & fees (OK res): $1704 **Average undergraduate aid package: N/A**

ABOUT THE INSTITUTION State-supported, coed. Awards: associate, bachelor's, and master's degrees. 56 undergraduate majors. Total enrollment: 3,926. Undergraduates: 3,880. Freshmen: 508. Federal methodology is used as a basis for awarding need-based institutional aid.

UNDERGRADUATE EXPENSES for 1999–2000 ***Tuition, state resident:*** full-time $1176; part-time $49 per credit hour. ***Tuition, nonresident:*** full-time $3192; part-time $133 per credit hour. ***Required fees:*** full-time $528; $15 per credit hour; $4 per term part-time. Full-time tuition and fees vary according to course level. Part-time tuition and fees vary according to course level. ***College room and board:*** $2944.

GIFT AID (NEED-BASED) ***Scholarships, grants, and awards:*** Federal Pell, FSEOG, state.

GIFT AID (NON-NEED-BASED) ***Scholarships, grants, and awards by category:*** *Academic Interests/Achievement:* agriculture, business, education, general academic interests/achievements, health fields. *Creative Arts/Performance:* music. *Special Achievements/Activities:* leadership. ***ROTC:*** Army cooperative.

LOANS ***Programs:*** Federal Direct (Subsidized and Unsubsidized Stafford, PLUS), FFEL (Subsidized and Unsubsidized Stafford, PLUS).

WORK-STUDY Federal work-study jobs available.

APPLYING for FINANCIAL AID ***Required financial aid form:*** FAFSA. ***Financial aid deadline (priority):*** 3/15. ***Notification date:*** 6/30.

CONTACT Office of Financial Aid, Langston University, PO Box 668, Langston, OK 73050, 405-466-3282.

LA ROCHE COLLEGE
Pittsburgh, PA

Tuition & fees: $11,450 **Average undergraduate aid package: N/A**

ABOUT THE INSTITUTION Independent religious, coed. Awards: bachelor's and master's degrees. 36 undergraduate majors. Total enrollment: 1,623. Undergraduates: 1,380. Freshmen: 308. Federal methodology is used as a basis for awarding need-based institutional aid.

UNDERGRADUATE EXPENSES for 1999–2000 ***Application fee:*** $25. ***Comprehensive fee:*** $15,580 includes full-time tuition ($11,100), mandatory fees ($350), and room and board ($4130). ***College room only:*** $3760. Full-time tuition and fees vary according to program. ***Part-time tuition:*** $400 per credit hour. ***Part-time fees:*** $6 per credit hour; $54 per term part-time. Part-time tuition and fees vary according to program. ***Payment plan:*** installment.

GIFT AID (NEED-BASED) ***Scholarships, grants, and awards:*** Federal Pell, FSEOG, state, college/university gift aid from institutional funds.

GIFT AID (NON-NEED-BASED) ***Scholarships, grants, and awards by category:*** *Academic Interests/Achievement:* computer science, English, foreign languages, general academic interests/achievements. *Creative Arts/Performance:* applied art and design. *Special Achievements/Activities:* community service. *Special Characteristics:* adult students, members of minority groups. ***Tuition waivers:*** Full or partial for employees or children of employees, senior citizens. ***ROTC:*** Army cooperative, Air Force cooperative.

LOANS ***Programs:*** FFEL (Subsidized and Unsubsidized Stafford, PLUS), Perkins.

WORK-STUDY Federal work-study jobs available.

APPLYING for FINANCIAL AID ***Required financial aid forms:*** FAFSA, institution's own form. ***Financial aid deadline (priority):*** 5/1. ***Notification date:*** Continuous. Students must reply within 2 weeks of notification.

CONTACT Ms. Janet R. McLaughlin, Director of Financial Aid, La Roche College, 9000 Babcock Boulevard, Pittsburgh, PA 15237-5898, 412-536-1121 or toll-free 800-838-4LRC. *Fax:* 412-536-1072. *E-mail:* mclaugj1@laroche.edu

LA SALLE UNIVERSITY
Philadelphia, PA

Tuition & fees: $17,260 **Average undergraduate aid package: $13,261**

ABOUT THE INSTITUTION Independent Roman Catholic, coed. Awards: associate, bachelor's, master's, and doctoral degrees. 72 undergraduate majors. Total enrollment: 5,630. Undergraduates: 3,980. Freshmen: 727. Both federal and institutional methodology are used as a basis for awarding need-based institutional aid.

UNDERGRADUATE EXPENSES for 1999–2000 ***Application fee:*** $35. ***Comprehensive fee:*** $23,862 includes full-time tuition ($16,880), mandatory fees ($380), and room and board ($6602). ***College room only:*** $3632. Full-time tuition and fees vary according to program. Room and board charges vary according to board plan, housing facility, and location. ***Part-time tuition:*** $315 per credit hour. ***Part-time fees:*** $10 per course; $20 per term part-time. Part-time tuition and fees vary according to class time and course load. ***Payment plans:*** installment, deferred payment.

FRESHMAN FINANCIAL AID (Fall 1999, est.) 777 applied for aid; of those 85% were deemed to have need. 100% of freshmen with need received aid; of those 22% had need fully met. *Average percent of need met:* 80% (excluding resources awarded to replace EFC). *Average financial aid package:* $13,745 (excluding resources awarded to replace EFC). 12% of all full-time freshmen had no need and received non-need-based aid.

UNDERGRADUATE FINANCIAL AID (Fall 1999, est.) 2,761 applied for aid; of those 81% were deemed to have need. 100% of undergraduates with need received aid; of those 20% had need fully met. *Average percent of need met:* 79% (excluding resources awarded to replace EFC). *Average financial aid package:* $13,261 (excluding resources awarded to replace EFC). 14% of all full-time undergraduates had no need and received non-need-based aid.

GIFT AID (NEED-BASED) ***Total amount:*** $12,006,369 (12% Federal, 19% state, 69% institutional). ***Receiving aid:*** *Freshmen:* 70% (564); *all full-time undergraduates:* 60% (1,848). ***Average award:*** Freshmen: $6842; Undergraduates: $6425. ***Scholarships, grants, and awards:*** Federal Pell, FSEOG, state, private, college/university gift aid from institutional funds.

GIFT AID (NON-NEED-BASED) ***Total amount:*** $15,413,057 (98% institutional, 2% external sources). ***Receiving aid:*** *Freshmen:* 62% (498); *Undergraduates:* 48% (1,480). ***Scholarships, grants, and awards by category:*** *Academic Interests/Achievement:* 1,840 awards ($12,069,171 total): general academic interests/achievements. *Special Achievements/Activities:* 20 awards ($172,360 total): community service. *Special Characteristics:* 53 awards ($809,333 total): children of faculty/staff, members of minority groups. ***Tuition waivers:*** Full or partial for employees or children of employees. ***ROTC:*** Army cooperative, Air Force cooperative.

LOANS ***Student loans:*** $9,567,167 (70% need-based, 30% non-need-based). 59% of past graduating class borrowed through all loan programs. Average indebtedness per student: $17,000. ***Average need-based loan:*** Freshmen: $2511; Undergraduates: $3745. ***Parent loans:*** $2,969,503 (100% non-need-based). ***Programs:*** FFEL (Subsidized and Unsubsidized Stafford, PLUS), Perkins.

WORK-STUDY ***Federal work-study:*** *Total amount:* $616,175; 340 jobs averaging $1812.

ATHLETIC AWARDS *Total amount:* 1,869,446 (100% non-need-based).

APPLYING for FINANCIAL AID ***Required financial aid form:*** FAFSA. ***Financial aid deadline (priority):*** 3/15.

CONTACT Michael Wisniewski, Director of Financial Aid, La Salle University, 1900 West Olney Avenue, Philadelphia, PA 19141-1199, 215-951-1070 or toll-free 800-328-1910.

LASELL COLLEGE

Newton, MA

Tuition & fees: $14,900 **Average undergraduate aid package: $15,967**

ABOUT THE INSTITUTION Independent, coed. Awards: associate and bachelor's degrees. 28 undergraduate majors. Total enrollment: 706. Undergraduates: 706. Freshmen: 276. Both federal and institutional methodology are used as a basis for awarding need-based institutional aid.

UNDERGRADUATE EXPENSES for 1999–2000 ***Application fee:*** $25. ***One-time required fee:*** $400. ***Comprehensive fee:*** $22,400 includes full-time tuition ($14,300), mandatory fees ($600), and room and board ($7500). Full-time tuition and fees vary according to program. ***Part-time tuition:*** $475 per semester hour. ***Part-time fees:*** $150 per term part-time. Part-time tuition and fees vary according to course load and program. One-time mandatory fee for part-time students: $200. ***Payment plan:*** installment.

FRESHMAN FINANCIAL AID (Fall 1999) 254 applied for aid; of those 89% were deemed to have need. 100% of freshmen with need received aid; of those 12% had need fully met. *Average percent of need met:* 82% (excluding resources awarded to replace EFC). *Average financial aid package:* $15,816 (excluding resources awarded to replace EFC). 11% of all full-time freshmen had no need and received non-need-based aid.

UNDERGRADUATE FINANCIAL AID (Fall 1999) 633 applied for aid; of those 91% were deemed to have need. 100% of undergraduates with need received aid; of those 16% had need fully met. *Average percent of need met:* 84% (excluding resources awarded to replace EFC). *Average financial aid package:* $15,967 (excluding resources awarded to replace EFC). 9% of all full-time undergraduates had no need and received non-need-based aid.

GIFT AID (NEED-BASED) ***Total amount:*** $6,016,700 (11% Federal, 6% state, 80% institutional, 3% external sources). ***Receiving aid:*** *Freshmen:* 82% (227); *all full-time undergraduates:* 84% (579). ***Average award:*** Freshmen: $11,133; Undergraduates: $10,337. ***Scholarships, grants, and awards:*** Federal Pell, FSEOG, state, private, college/university gift aid from institutional funds.

GIFT AID (NON-NEED-BASED) ***Total amount:*** $393,856 (95% institutional, 5% external sources). ***Receiving aid:*** *Freshmen:* 6% (17); *Undergraduates:* 4% (26). ***Scholarships, grants, and awards by category:*** *Academic Interests/Achievement:* general academic interests/achievements. *Special Achievements/Activities:* community service, general special achievements/activities, leadership. *Special Characteristics:* children and siblings of alumni, children of current students, children of faculty/staff, siblings of current students, twins. ***Tuition waivers:*** Full or partial for children of alumni, employees or children of employees.

LOANS ***Student loans:*** $2,973,571 (88% need-based, 12% non-need-based). 95% of past graduating class borrowed through all loan programs. Average indebtedness per student: $17,209. ***Average need-based loan:*** Freshmen: $3777; Undergraduates: $4766. ***Parent loans:*** $1,667,184 (50% need-based, 50% non-need-based). ***Programs:*** FFEL (Subsidized and Unsubsidized Stafford, PLUS), Perkins, state.

WORK-STUDY ***Federal work-study:*** *Total amount:* $501,514; 484 jobs available.

APPLYING for FINANCIAL AID ***Required financial aid forms:*** FAFSA, CSS Financial Aid PROFILE. ***Financial aid deadline (priority):*** 4/1. ***Notification date:*** Continuous. Students must reply within 4 weeks of notification.

CONTACT Mr. Daniel T. Barkowitz, Director of Student Financial Planning, Lasell College, 1844 Commonwealth Avenue, Newton, MA 02166-2709, 617-243-2227 or toll-free 888-LASELL-4. *Fax:* 617-243-2326. *E-mail:* finaid@lasell.edu

LA SIERRA UNIVERSITY

Riverside, CA

CONTACT Ms. B. Marilyn Dietel, Director of Financial Aid, La Sierra University, 4700 Pierce Street, Riverside, CA 92515, 909-785-2175 or toll-free 800-874-5587. *Fax:* 909-785-2942. *E-mail:* finaid@lasierra.edu

LAWRENCE TECHNOLOGICAL UNIVERSITY

Southfield, MI

Tuition & fees: $10,340 **Average undergraduate aid package: N/A**

ABOUT THE INSTITUTION Independent, coed. Awards: associate, bachelor's, and master's degrees. 23 undergraduate majors. Total enrollment: 3,837. Undergraduates: 2,942. Federal methodology is used as a basis for awarding need-based institutional aid.

UNDERGRADUATE EXPENSES for 1999–2000 ***Application fee:*** $30. ***Tuition:*** full-time $10,140; part-time $330 per credit hour. ***Required fees:*** full-time $200; $100 per term part-time. Full-time tuition and fees vary according to program and student level. Part-time tuition and fees vary according to program and student level. Room and board charges vary according to housing facility. ***Payment plan:*** installment.

FRESHMAN FINANCIAL AID (Fall 1999, est.) 488 applied for aid; of those 90% were deemed to have need. 92% of freshmen with need received aid; of those 15% had need fully met. *Average percent of need met:* 96% (excluding resources awarded to replace EFC). 6% of all full-time freshmen had no need and received non-need-based aid.

UNDERGRADUATE FINANCIAL AID (Fall 1999, est.) 1,191 applied for aid; of those 89% were deemed to have need. 91% of undergraduates with need received aid; of those 14% had need fully met. *Average percent of need met:* 95% (excluding resources awarded to replace EFC). 8% of all full-time undergraduates had no need and received non-need-based aid.

GIFT AID (NEED-BASED) ***Total amount:*** $2,796,246 (33% Federal, 65% state, 2% external sources). ***Receiving aid:*** *Freshmen:* 56% (302); *all full-time undergraduates:* 60% (798). ***Average award:*** Freshmen: $7250; Undergraduates: $6850. ***Scholarships, grants, and awards:*** Federal Pell, FSEOG, state, private, college/university gift aid from institutional funds.

GIFT AID (NON-NEED-BASED) ***Total amount:*** $2,679,866 (100% institutional). ***Receiving aid:*** *Freshmen:* 40% (215); *Undergraduates:* 38% (509). ***Scholarships, grants, and awards by category:*** *Academic Interests/Achievement:* 627 awards ($2,986,645 total): architecture, business, computer science, education, engineering/technologies, general academic interests/achievements, humanities, mathematics, physical sciences. *Special Achievements/Activities:* 1 award ($10,100 total): general special achievements/activities, hobbies/interests. *Special Characteristics:* 11 awards ($76,624 total): children of faculty/staff. ***Tuition waivers:*** Full or partial for employees or children of employees. ***ROTC:*** Army cooperative, Air Force cooperative.

LOANS ***Student loans:*** $6,660,598 (100% need-based). 53% of past graduating class borrowed through all loan programs. Average indebted-

Lawrence Technological University (continued)

ness per student: $15,400. ***Average need-based loan:*** Freshmen: $2625; Undergraduates: $5500. ***Parent loans:*** $956,565 (100% need-based). ***Programs:*** Federal Direct (Subsidized and Unsubsidized Stafford, PLUS), Perkins, college/university.

WORK-STUDY ***Federal work-study:*** *Total amount:* $89,037; 80 jobs averaging $1266. ***State or other work-study/employment:*** *Total amount:* $36,803 (100% need-based). 30 part-time jobs averaging $1224.

APPLYING for FINANCIAL AID ***Required financial aid form:*** FAFSA. ***Financial aid deadline (priority):*** 8/1. ***Notification date:*** Continuous. Students must reply within 3 weeks of notification.

CONTACT Mr. Paul F. Kinder, Director of Financial Aid, Lawrence Technological University, 21000 West Ten Mile Road, Southfield, MI 48075-1058, 248-204-2126 or toll-free 800-225-5588. *Fax:* 248-204-2124. *E-mail:* paul@ltu.edu

LAWRENCE UNIVERSITY

Appleton, WI

Tuition & fees: $21,012 **Average undergraduate aid package: $19,124**

ABOUT THE INSTITUTION Independent, coed. Awards: bachelor's degrees. 42 undergraduate majors. Total enrollment: 1,246. Undergraduates: 1,246. Freshmen: 327. Both federal and institutional methodology are used as a basis for awarding need-based institutional aid.

UNDERGRADUATE EXPENSES for 1999–2000 ***Application fee:*** $30. ***Comprehensive fee:*** $25,709 includes full-time tuition ($20,880), mandatory fees ($132), and room and board ($4697). ***College room only:*** $2085. Room and board charges vary according to board plan. ***Payment plan:*** installment.

FRESHMAN FINANCIAL AID (Fall 1999) 270 applied for aid; of those 84% were deemed to have need. 100% of freshmen with need received aid; of those 83% had need fully met. *Average percent of need met:* 100% (excluding resources awarded to replace EFC). *Average financial aid package:* $18,345 (excluding resources awarded to replace EFC). 22% of all full-time freshmen had no need and received non-need-based aid.

UNDERGRADUATE FINANCIAL AID (Fall 1999) 952 applied for aid; of those 87% were deemed to have need. 100% of undergraduates with need received aid; of those 84% had need fully met. *Average percent of need met:* 100% (excluding resources awarded to replace EFC). *Average financial aid package:* $19,124 (excluding resources awarded to replace EFC). 21% of all full-time undergraduates had no need and received non-need-based aid.

GIFT AID (NEED-BASED) ***Total amount:*** $10,962,644 (6% Federal, 6% state, 85% institutional, 3% external sources). ***Receiving aid:*** *Freshmen:* 68% (225); *all full-time undergraduates:* 68% (820). ***Average award:*** Freshmen: $13,387; Undergraduates: $13,425. ***Scholarships, grants, and awards:*** Federal Pell, FSEOG, state, private, college/university gift aid from institutional funds.

GIFT AID (NON-NEED-BASED) ***Total amount:*** $1,993,883 (1% Federal, 93% institutional, 6% external sources). ***Receiving aid:*** *Freshmen:* 4% (14); *Undergraduates:* 4% (49). ***Scholarships, grants, and awards by category:*** *Academic Interests/Achievement:* general academic interests/achievements. *Creative Arts/Performance:* music. *Special Characteristics:* international students, local/state students, members of minority groups. ***Tuition waivers:*** Full or partial for employees or children of employees.

LOANS ***Student loans:*** $3,586,524 (86% need-based, 14% non-need-based). 81% of past graduating class borrowed through all loan programs. Average indebtedness per student: $17,727. ***Average need-based loan:*** Freshmen: $3780; Undergraduates: $4488. ***Parent loans:*** $832,762 (100% non-need-based). ***Programs:*** Federal Direct (Subsidized and Unsubsidized Stafford, PLUS), Perkins, college/university.

WORK-STUDY ***Federal work-study:*** *Total amount:* $1,219,748; 622 jobs averaging $1961. ***State or other work-study/employment:*** *Total amount:* $347,806 (100% non-need-based). 164 part-time jobs averaging $2147.

APPLYING for FINANCIAL AID ***Required financial aid forms:*** FAFSA, institution's own form. ***Financial aid deadline (priority):*** 3/1. ***Notification date:*** Continuous beginning 3/15. Students must reply by 5/1.

CONTACT Ms. Cheryl Schaffer, Director of Financial Aid, Lawrence University, PO Box 599, Appleton, WI 54912-0599, 920-832-6583 or toll-free 800-227-0982. *Fax:* 920-832-6782. *E-mail:* cheryl.a.schaffer@lawrence.edu

LEBANON VALLEY COLLEGE

Annville, PA

Tuition & fees: $17,260 **Average undergraduate aid package: $13,762**

ABOUT THE INSTITUTION Independent United Methodist, coed. Awards: associate, bachelor's, and master's degrees (offers master of business administration degree on a part-time basis only). 35 undergraduate majors. Total enrollment: 2,033. Undergraduates: 1,773. Freshmen: 407. Both federal and institutional methodology are used as a basis for awarding need-based institutional aid.

UNDERGRADUATE EXPENSES for 1999–2000 ***Application fee:*** $25. ***Comprehensive fee:*** $22,750 includes full-time tuition ($16,730), mandatory fees ($530), and room and board ($5490). ***College room only:*** $2670. Room and board charges vary according to board plan and housing facility. ***Part-time tuition:*** $322 per credit. ***Part-time fees:*** $25 per term part-time. Part-time tuition and fees vary according to class time.

FRESHMAN FINANCIAL AID (Fall 1999) 362 applied for aid; of those 88% were deemed to have need. 100% of freshmen with need received aid; of those 32% had need fully met. *Average percent of need met:* 87% (excluding resources awarded to replace EFC). *Average financial aid package:* $13,761 (excluding resources awarded to replace EFC). 18% of all full-time freshmen had no need and received non-need-based aid.

UNDERGRADUATE FINANCIAL AID (Fall 1999) 1,155 applied for aid; of those 91% were deemed to have need. 100% of undergraduates with need received aid; of those 35% had need fully met. *Average percent of need met:* 87% (excluding resources awarded to replace EFC). *Average financial aid package:* $13,762 (excluding resources awarded to replace EFC). 15% of all full-time undergraduates had no need and received non-need-based aid.

GIFT AID (NEED-BASED) ***Total amount:*** $10,132,489 (4% Federal, 18% state, 74% institutional, 4% external sources). ***Receiving aid:*** *Freshmen:* 79% (320); *all full-time undergraduates:* 79% (1,053). ***Average award:*** Freshmen: $9349; Undergraduates: $9357. ***Scholarships, grants, and awards:*** Federal Pell, FSEOG, state, private, college/university gift aid from institutional funds.

GIFT AID (NON-NEED-BASED) ***Total amount:*** $1,526,160 (97% institutional, 3% external sources). ***Receiving aid:*** *Freshmen:* 63% (257); *Undergraduates:* 59% (786). ***Scholarships, grants, and awards by category:*** *Academic Interests/Achievement:* 960 awards ($6,393,169 total): biological sciences, general academic interests/achievements. *Creative Arts/Performance:* 27 awards ($27,000 total): music. *Special Achievements/Activities:* 15 awards ($7500 total): general special achievements/activities. *Special Characteristics:* 93 awards ($227,985 total): children and siblings of alumni, ethnic background, handicapped students. ***Tuition waivers:*** Full or partial for employees or children of employees. ***ROTC:*** Army cooperative.

LOANS ***Student loans:*** $5,758,369 (58% need-based, 42% non-need-based). 82% of past graduating class borrowed through all loan programs. Average indebtedness per student: $17,462. ***Average need-based loan:*** Freshmen: $3399; Undergraduates: $3639. ***Parent loans:*** $2,349,977 (94% need-based, 6% non-need-based). ***Programs:*** Federal Direct (Subsidized and Unsubsidized Stafford, PLUS), Perkins, college/university, alternative loans.

WORK-STUDY ***Federal work-study:*** *Total amount:* $589,690; 502 jobs averaging $1175.

APPLYING for FINANCIAL AID ***Required financial aid forms:*** FAFSA, institution's own form. ***Financial aid deadline (priority):*** 3/1. ***Notification date:*** Continuous. Students must reply by 5/1 or within 2 weeks of notification.

CONTACT Ms. Karin Right-Nolan, Director of Financial Aid, Lebanon Valley College, 101 North College Avenue, Annville, PA 17003-0501, 800-445-6181. *Fax:* 717-867-6026. *E-mail:* right@lvc.edu

LEE COLLEGE AT THE UNIVERSITY OF JUDAISM

Bel Air, CA

See University of Judaism

LEES-MCRAE COLLEGE

Banner Elk, NC

Tuition & fees: $11,200 **Average undergraduate aid package: N/A**

ABOUT THE INSTITUTION Independent religious, coed. Awards: bachelor's degrees. 32 undergraduate majors. Total enrollment: 643. Undergraduates: 643. Freshmen: 183. Federal methodology is used as a basis for awarding need-based institutional aid.

UNDERGRADUATE EXPENSES for 2000–2001 ***Application fee:*** $15. ***Comprehensive fee:*** $15,300 includes full-time tuition ($11,200) and room and board ($4100). ***College room only:*** $1890. ***Part-time tuition:*** $340 per credit hour. ***Payment plan:*** installment.

GIFT AID (NEED-BASED) ***Scholarships, grants, and awards:*** Federal Pell, FSEOG, state, private, college/university gift aid from institutional funds.

GIFT AID (NON-NEED-BASED) ***Scholarships, grants, and awards by category:*** *Academic Interests/Achievement:* general academic interests/achievements. *Creative Arts/Performance:* dance, journalism/publications, performing arts, theater/drama. *Special Achievements/Activities:* cheerleading/drum major, general special achievements/activities, leadership. *Special Characteristics:* children of educators, children of faculty/staff, children with a deceased or disabled parent, international students, local/state students, previous college experience, relatives of clergy, religious affiliation, veterans. ***Tuition waivers:*** Full or partial for employees or children of employees. ***ROTC:*** Army cooperative.

LOANS ***Programs:*** FFEL (Subsidized and Unsubsidized Stafford, PLUS), Perkins.

WORK-STUDY Federal work-study jobs available.

APPLYING for FINANCIAL AID ***Required financial aid form:*** FAFSA. ***Financial aid deadline (priority):*** 3/15. ***Notification date:*** 4/15. Students must reply within 4 weeks of notification.

CONTACT Lester McKenzie, Director of Financial Aid, Lees-McRae College, PO Box 128, Banner Elk, NC 28604-0128, 828-898-5241 or toll-free 800-280-4562. *E-mail:* mckenzie@lmc.edu

LEE UNIVERSITY

Cleveland, TN

Tuition & fees: $6862 **Average undergraduate aid package: $6644**

ABOUT THE INSTITUTION Independent religious, coed. Awards: bachelor's and master's degrees. 35 undergraduate majors. Total enrollment: 3,259. Undergraduates: 3,155. Freshmen: 618. Federal methodology is used as a basis for awarding need-based institutional aid.

UNDERGRADUATE EXPENSES for 2000–2001 ***Application fee:*** $25. ***Comprehensive fee:*** $10,882 includes full-time tuition ($6700), mandatory fees ($162), and room and board ($4020). ***College room only:*** $1990. Full-time tuition and fees vary according to program. Room and board charges vary according to board plan and housing facility. ***Part-time tuition:*** $280 per semester hour. ***Part-time fees:*** $10 per term part-time. Part-time tuition and fees vary according to program. ***Payment plan:*** deferred payment.

FRESHMAN FINANCIAL AID (Fall 1998) 531 applied for aid; of those 81% were deemed to have need. 100% of freshmen with need received aid; of those 22% had need fully met. *Average percent of need met:* 62% (excluding resources awarded to replace EFC). *Average financial aid package:* $5589 (excluding resources awarded to replace EFC).

UNDERGRADUATE FINANCIAL AID (Fall 1998) 2,000 applied for aid; of those 87% were deemed to have need. 100% of undergraduates with need received aid; of those 16% had need fully met. *Average percent of need met:* 61% (excluding resources awarded to replace EFC). *Average financial aid package:* $6644 (excluding resources awarded to replace EFC).

GIFT AID (NEED-BASED) ***Total amount:*** $4,910,806 (49% Federal, 6% state, 42% institutional, 3% external sources). ***Receiving aid:*** *Freshmen:* 56% (341); *all full-time undergraduates:* 46% (1,347). ***Average award:*** Freshmen: $3057; Undergraduates: $2748. ***Scholarships, grants, and awards:*** Federal Pell, FSEOG, state, private, college/university gift aid from institutional funds.

GIFT AID (NON-NEED-BASED) ***Total amount:*** $1,068,713 (2% state, 88% institutional, 10% external sources). ***Receiving aid:*** *Freshmen:* 6% (38); *Undergraduates:* 3% (78). ***Scholarships, grants, and awards by category:*** *Academic Interests/Achievement:* biological sciences, business, communication, education, English, general academic interests/achievements, health fields, humanities, mathematics, physical sciences, premedicine, religion/biblical studies, social sciences. *Creative Arts/Performance:* cinema/film/broadcasting, journalism/publications, music, performing arts, theater/drama. *Special Achievements/Activities:* general special achievements/activities, leadership. *Special Characteristics:* children of current students, children of faculty/staff, parents of current students, siblings of current students, spouses of current students. ***Tuition waivers:*** Full or partial for employees or children of employees.

LOANS ***Student loans:*** $8,518,579 (81% need-based, 19% non-need-based). 75% of past graduating class borrowed through all loan programs. Average indebtedness per student: $10,982. ***Average need-based loan:*** Freshmen: $2442; Undergraduates: $3739. ***Parent loans:*** $2,138,654 (45% need-based, 55% non-need-based). ***Programs:*** FFEL (Subsidized and Unsubsidized Stafford, PLUS), Perkins, college/university, Signature Loans.

WORK-STUDY ***Federal work-study:*** *Total amount:* $278,035; 291 jobs averaging $955.

ATHLETIC AWARDS *Total amount:* 585,193 (100% non-need-based).

APPLYING for FINANCIAL AID ***Required financial aid forms:*** FAFSA, institution's own form. ***Financial aid deadline (priority):*** 4/15. ***Notification date:*** Continuous. Students must reply within 3 weeks of notification.

CONTACT Mr. Michael Ellis, Director of Financial Aid, Lee University, 1120 North Ocoee Street, PO Box 3450, Cleveland, TN 37320-3450, 423-614-8300 or toll-free 800-LEE-9930. *Fax:* 423-614-8308. *E-mail:* finaid@leeuniversity.edu

LEHIGH UNIVERSITY

Bethlehem, PA

Tuition & fees: $23,150 **Average undergraduate aid package: $18,100**

ABOUT THE INSTITUTION Independent, coed. Awards: bachelor's, master's, and doctoral degrees and post-master's certificates. 56 undergraduate majors. Total enrollment: 6,359. Undergraduates: 4,605. Freshmen: 1,078. Both federal and institutional methodology are used as a basis for awarding need-based institutional aid.

UNDERGRADUATE EXPENSES for 1999–2000 ***Application fee:*** $50. ***Comprehensive fee:*** $29,780 includes full-time tuition ($23,150) and room and board ($6630). ***College room only:*** $3680. Full-time tuition and fees vary according to program. Room and board charges vary according to board plan and housing facility. ***Part-time tuition:*** $965 per credit hour. Part-time tuition and fees vary according to program. ***Payment plans:*** tuition prepayment, installment, deferred payment.

FRESHMAN FINANCIAL AID (Fall 1999, est.) 732 applied for aid; of those 80% were deemed to have need. 89% of freshmen with need received aid; of those 100% had need fully met. *Average percent of need met:* 95% (excluding resources awarded to replace EFC). *Average financial aid package:* $19,650 (excluding resources awarded to replace EFC). 4% of all full-time freshmen had no need and received non-need-based aid.

UNDERGRADUATE FINANCIAL AID (Fall 1999, est.) 2,672 applied for aid; of those 88% were deemed to have need. 97% of undergraduates with need received aid; of those 100% had need fully met. *Average percent of*

Lehigh University (continued)

need met: 95% (excluding resources awarded to replace EFC). *Average financial aid package:* $18,100 (excluding resources awarded to replace EFC). 4% of all full-time undergraduates had no need and received non-need-based aid.

GIFT AID (NEED-BASED) ***Total amount:*** $34,780,812 (5% Federal, 4% state, 89% institutional, 2% external sources). ***Receiving aid:*** *Freshmen:* 49% (524); *all full-time undergraduates:* 50% (2,271). ***Average award:*** Freshmen: $14,787; Undergraduates: $13,676. ***Scholarships, grants, and awards:*** Federal Pell, FSEOG, state, private, college/university gift aid from institutional funds.

GIFT AID (NON-NEED-BASED) ***Total amount:*** $2,417,088 (2% Federal, 62% institutional, 36% external sources). ***Receiving aid:*** *Undergraduates:* 8% (372). ***Scholarships, grants, and awards by category:*** *Academic Interests/Achievement:* 300 awards ($2,030,000 total): general academic interests/achievements. *Creative Arts/Performance:* 18 awards ($45,000 total): general creative arts/performance, music, performing arts, theater/drama. *Special Characteristics:* 400 awards ($2,428,667 total): children of faculty/staff. ***Tuition waivers:*** Full or partial for employees or children of employees, senior citizens. ***ROTC:*** Army.

LOANS ***Student loans:*** $12,715,000 (84% need-based, 16% non-need-based). Average indebtedness per student: $15,178. ***Parent loans:*** $5000 (100% non-need-based). ***Programs:*** FFEL (Subsidized and Unsubsidized Stafford, PLUS), Perkins, college/university.

WORK-STUDY ***Federal work-study:*** *Total amount:* $980,000; 974 jobs averaging $1335. ***State or other work-study/employment:*** *Total amount:* $470,000 (7% need-based, 93% non-need-based). Part-time jobs available.

ATHLETIC AWARDS *Total amount:* 491,400 (28% need-based, 72% non-need-based).

APPLYING for FINANCIAL AID ***Required financial aid forms:*** FAFSA, CSS Financial Aid PROFILE, noncustodial (divorced/separated) parent's statement, business/farm supplement. ***Financial aid deadline:*** 2/1 (priority: 1/15). ***Notification date:*** 4/1. Students must reply by 5/1 or within 2 weeks of notification.

CONTACT William E. Stanford, Director, Financial Aid, Lehigh University, 218 West Packer Avenue, Bethlehem, PA 18015-3094, 610-758-3181. *Fax:* 610-758-6211. *E-mail:* wes2@lehigh.edu

LEHMAN COLLEGE OF THE CITY UNIVERSITY OF NEW YORK

Bronx, NY

Tuition & fees (NY res): $3320 **Average undergraduate aid package: $5300**

ABOUT THE INSTITUTION State and locally supported, coed. Awards: bachelor's and master's degrees. 50 undergraduate majors. Total enrollment: 9,074. Undergraduates: 7,228. Federal methodology is used as a basis for awarding need-based institutional aid.

UNDERGRADUATE EXPENSES for 2000–2001 ***Application fee:*** $40. ***Tuition, state resident:*** full-time $3200; part-time $135 per credit. ***Tuition, nonresident:*** full-time $6800; part-time $285 per credit. ***Required fees:*** full-time $120; $40 per term part-time. Full-time tuition and fees vary according to course load and program. Part-time tuition and fees vary according to course load and program. ***Payment plan:*** installment.

FRESHMAN FINANCIAL AID (Fall 1999, est.) 506 applied for aid; of those 100% were deemed to have need. 100% of freshmen with need received aid. *Average percent of need met:* 76% (excluding resources awarded to replace EFC). *Average financial aid package:* $4800 (excluding resources awarded to replace EFC).

UNDERGRADUATE FINANCIAL AID (Fall 1999, est.) 3,900 applied for aid; of those 95% were deemed to have need. 100% of undergraduates with need received aid. *Average percent of need met:* 72% (excluding resources awarded to replace EFC). *Average financial aid package:* $5300 (excluding resources awarded to replace EFC).

GIFT AID (NEED-BASED) ***Total amount:*** $11,492,080 (70% Federal, 30% state). ***Receiving aid:*** *Freshmen:* 74% (474); *all full-time undergraduates:* 83% (3,505). ***Average award:*** Freshmen: $4100; Undergraduates: $3800. ***Scholarships, grants, and awards:*** Federal Pell, FSEOG, state.

GIFT AID (NON-NEED-BASED) ***Tuition waivers:*** Full or partial for senior citizens. ***ROTC:*** Army cooperative.

LOANS ***Student loans:*** $2,314,579 (100% need-based). 37% of past graduating class borrowed through all loan programs. Average indebtedness per student: $7200. ***Average need-based loan:*** Freshmen: $2300; Undergraduates: $3400. ***Programs:*** Federal Direct (Subsidized and Unsubsidized Stafford, PLUS), Perkins.

WORK-STUDY ***Federal work-study:*** *Total amount:* $837,355; 1,228 jobs available.

APPLYING for FINANCIAL AID ***Required financial aid forms:*** FAFSA, state aid form. ***Financial aid deadline:*** Continuous. ***Notification date:*** Continuous beginning 6/1.

CONTACT David Martinez, Director of Financial Aid, Lehman College of the City University of New York, 250 Bedford Park Boulevard West, Bronx, NY 10468-1589, 718-960-8545 or toll-free 877-Lehman1 (out-of-state). *Fax:* 718-960-8328. *E-mail:* aidlc@cunyvm.cuny.edu

LE MOYNE COLLEGE

Syracuse, NY

Tuition & fees: $14,980 **Average undergraduate aid package: $12,578**

ABOUT THE INSTITUTION Independent Roman Catholic (Jesuit), coed. Awards: bachelor's and master's degrees and post-bachelor's certificates. 36 undergraduate majors. Total enrollment: 3,116. Undergraduates: 2,387. Freshmen: 473. Both federal and institutional methodology are used as a basis for awarding need-based institutional aid.

UNDERGRADUATE EXPENSES for 1999–2000 ***Application fee:*** $35. ***Comprehensive fee:*** $21,300 includes full-time tuition ($14,580), mandatory fees ($400), and room and board ($6320). ***College room only:*** $3860. Room and board charges vary according to board plan and housing facility. ***Part-time tuition:*** $329 per credit hour. Part-time tuition and fees vary according to class time. ***Payment plans:*** installment, deferred payment.

FRESHMAN FINANCIAL AID (Fall 1999) 428 applied for aid; of those 84% were deemed to have need. 100% of freshmen with need received aid; of those 85% had need fully met. *Average percent of need met:* 85% (excluding resources awarded to replace EFC). *Average financial aid package:* $11,900 (excluding resources awarded to replace EFC). 14% of all full-time freshmen had no need and received non-need-based aid.

UNDERGRADUATE FINANCIAL AID (Fall 1999) 1,791 applied for aid; of those 95% were deemed to have need. 100% of undergraduates with need received aid; of those 91% had need fully met. *Average percent of need met:* 85% (excluding resources awarded to replace EFC). *Average financial aid package:* $12,578 (excluding resources awarded to replace EFC). 4% of all full-time undergraduates had no need and received non-need-based aid.

GIFT AID (NEED-BASED) ***Total amount:*** $14,346,527 (11% Federal, 22% state, 65% institutional, 2% external sources). ***Receiving aid:*** *Freshmen:* 74% (352); *all full-time undergraduates:* 81% (1,615). ***Average award:*** Freshmen: $9000; Undergraduates: $9100. ***Scholarships, grants, and awards:*** Federal Pell, FSEOG, state, private, college/university gift aid from institutional funds.

GIFT AID (NON-NEED-BASED) ***Total amount:*** $541,736 (9% state, 76% institutional, 15% external sources). ***Receiving aid:*** *Freshmen:* 14% (64); *Undergraduates:* 4% (78). ***Scholarships, grants, and awards by category:*** *Academic Interests/Achievement:* general academic interests/achievements. *Special Achievements/Activities:* leadership. *Special Characteristics:* children and siblings of alumni, members of minority groups. ***Tuition waivers:*** Full or partial for employees or children of employees. ***ROTC:*** Army cooperative, Air Force cooperative.

LOANS ***Student loans:*** $9,078,114 (71% need-based, 29% non-need-based). 95% of past graduating class borrowed through all loan programs. Average indebtedness per student: $16,000. ***Average need-based loan:***

Freshmen: $2904; Undergraduates: $3994. ***Parent loans:*** $2,287,554 (15% need-based, 85% non-need-based). ***Programs:*** FFEL (Subsidized and Unsubsidized Stafford, PLUS), Perkins.

WORK-STUDY ***Federal work-study:*** *Total amount:* $559,000; jobs available.

ATHLETIC AWARDS *Total amount:* 839,380 (85% need-based, 15% non-need-based).

APPLYING for FINANCIAL AID ***Required financial aid forms:*** FAFSA, institution's own form. ***Financial aid deadline (priority):*** 2/1. ***Notification date:*** 3/15. Students must reply by 5/1 or within 2 weeks of notification.

CONTACT Mr. William Cheetham, Director of Financial Aid, Le Moyne College, Financial Aid Office, Syracuse, NY 13214-1399, 315-445-4400 or toll-free 800-333-4733. *Fax:* 315-445-4182. *E-mail:* cheethwc@oak.lemoyne.edu

LEMOYNE-OWEN COLLEGE

Memphis, TN

Tuition & fees: $6900 **Average undergraduate aid package: $7513**

ABOUT THE INSTITUTION Independent religious, coed. Awards: bachelor's and master's degrees. 21 undergraduate majors. Total enrollment: 1,013. Undergraduates: 974. Freshmen: 320. Federal methodology is used as a basis for awarding need-based institutional aid.

UNDERGRADUATE EXPENSES for 1999–2000 ***Application fee:*** $25. ***Comprehensive fee:*** $10,950 includes full-time tuition ($6900) and room and board ($4050). ***College room only:*** $2100. Room and board charges vary according to housing facility. ***Part-time tuition:*** $288 per credit hour. ***Payment plans:*** tuition prepayment, installment, deferred payment.

FRESHMAN FINANCIAL AID (Fall 1998) 133 applied for aid; of those 95% were deemed to have need. 100% of freshmen with need received aid; of those 1% had need fully met. *Average percent of need met:* 59% (excluding resources awarded to replace EFC). *Average financial aid package:* $7014 (excluding resources awarded to replace EFC). 5% of all full-time freshmen had no need and received non-need-based aid.

UNDERGRADUATE FINANCIAL AID (Fall 1998) 965 applied for aid; of those 92% were deemed to have need. 100% of undergraduates with need received aid; of those 3% had need fully met. *Average percent of need met:* 63% (excluding resources awarded to replace EFC). *Average financial aid package:* $7513 (excluding resources awarded to replace EFC). 6% of all full-time undergraduates had no need and received non-need-based aid.

GIFT AID (NEED-BASED) ***Total amount:*** $3,398,117 (53% Federal, 15% state, 24% institutional, 8% external sources). ***Receiving aid:*** *Freshmen:* 89% (118); *all full-time undergraduates:* 89% (860). ***Average award:*** Freshmen: $2100; Undergraduates: $3107. ***Scholarships, grants, and awards:*** Federal Pell, FSEOG, state, private, college/university gift aid from institutional funds, United Negro College Fund.

GIFT AID (NON-NEED-BASED) ***Total amount:*** $198,578 (77% institutional, 23% external sources). ***Receiving aid:*** *Freshmen:* 4% (5); *Undergraduates:* 1% (5). ***Scholarships, grants, and awards by category:*** *Academic Interests/Achievement:* 44 awards ($194,078 total): general academic interests/achievements. *Creative Arts/Performance:* 2 awards ($6700 total): music. *Special Characteristics:* 36 awards ($45,864 total): children of educators, children of faculty/staff, handicapped students, international students, spouses of current students. ***Tuition waivers:*** Full or partial for employees or children of employees. ***ROTC:*** Army cooperative, Air Force cooperative.

LOANS ***Student loans:*** $3,191,572 (97% need-based, 3% non-need-based). 80% of past graduating class borrowed through all loan programs. Average indebtedness per student: $10,500. ***Average need-based loan:*** Freshmen: $2625; Undergraduates: $3500. ***Parent loans:*** $103,719 (93% need-based, 7% non-need-based). ***Programs:*** Federal Direct (Subsidized and Unsubsidized Stafford, PLUS), Perkins.

WORK-STUDY ***Federal work-study:*** *Total amount:* $278,918; 300 jobs averaging $1000. ***State or other work-study/employment:*** *Total amount:* $24,000 (100% non-need-based). 20 part-time jobs averaging $1200.

ATHLETIC AWARDS *Total amount:* 352,406 (79% need-based, 21% non-need-based).

APPLYING for FINANCIAL AID ***Required financial aid forms:*** FAFSA, institution's own form. ***Financial aid deadline:*** Continuous. ***Notification date:*** Continuous beginning 5/1. Students must reply within 2 weeks of notification.

CONTACT Regina Venson, Director, Student Financial Services, LeMoyne-Owen College, 807 Walker Avenue, Memphis, TN 38126-6595, 901-774-9090 or toll-free 800-737-7778 (in-state). *Fax:* 901-942-6244. *E-mail:* regina_venson@nile.lemoyne-owen.edu

LENOIR-RHYNE COLLEGE

Hickory, NC

ABOUT THE INSTITUTION Independent Lutheran, coed. Awards: bachelor's and master's degrees. 54 undergraduate majors. Total enrollment: 1,483. Undergraduates: 1,353.

GIFT AID (NEED-BASED) ***Scholarships, grants, and awards:*** Federal Pell, FSEOG, state, college/university gift aid from institutional funds.

GIFT AID (NON-NEED-BASED) ***Scholarships, grants, and awards by category:*** *Academic Interests/Achievement:* general academic interests/achievements. *Creative Arts/Performance:* music, performing arts, theater/drama. *Special Achievements/Activities:* community service, leadership. *Special Characteristics:* children and siblings of alumni, children of faculty/staff, local/state students, relatives of clergy, religious affiliation, siblings of current students.

LOANS ***Programs:*** Federal Direct (Subsidized and Unsubsidized Stafford, PLUS), Perkins.

WORK-STUDY Federal work-study jobs available.

APPLYING for FINANCIAL AID ***Required financial aid forms:*** FAFSA, institution's own form, state aid form.

CONTACT Daniel G. Klock, Director of Financial Planning, Lenoir-Rhyne College, PO Box 7419, Hickory, NC 28603, 828-328-7304 or toll-free 800-277-5721. *Fax:* 828-328-7039. *E-mail:* klockd@lrc.edu

LESLEY COLLEGE

Cambridge, MA

Tuition & fees: $15,600 **Average undergraduate aid package: $11,200**

ABOUT THE INSTITUTION Independent, women only. Awards: associate, bachelor's, master's, and doctoral degrees and post-master's certificates. 12 undergraduate majors. Total enrollment: 5,508. Undergraduates: 571. Both federal and institutional methodology are used as a basis for awarding need-based institutional aid.

UNDERGRADUATE EXPENSES for 1999–2000 ***Application fee:*** $35. ***Comprehensive fee:*** $22,800 includes full-time tuition ($15,450), mandatory fees ($150), and room and board ($7200). Full-time tuition and fees vary according to course load. ***Part-time tuition:*** $454 per credit. ***Payment plan:*** installment.

FRESHMAN FINANCIAL AID (Fall 1999, est.) 164 applied for aid; of those 91% were deemed to have need. 100% of freshmen with need received aid; of those 7% had need fully met. *Average percent of need met:* 94% (excluding resources awarded to replace EFC). *Average financial aid package:* $12,285 (excluding resources awarded to replace EFC). 14% of all full-time freshmen had no need and received non-need-based aid.

UNDERGRADUATE FINANCIAL AID (Fall 1999, est.) 441 applied for aid; of those 87% were deemed to have need. 100% of undergraduates with need received aid; of those 5% had need fully met. *Average percent of need met:* 93% (excluding resources awarded to replace EFC). *Average financial aid package:* $11,200 (excluding resources awarded to replace EFC). 6% of all full-time undergraduates had no need and received non-need-based aid.

GIFT AID (NEED-BASED) ***Total amount:*** $3,011,043 (16% Federal, 8% state, 70% institutional, 6% external sources). ***Receiving aid:*** *Freshmen:* 81% (149); *all full-time undergraduates:* 71% (384). ***Scholarships, grants, and awards:*** Federal Pell, FSEOG, state, college/university gift aid from institutional funds.

Lesley College (continued)

GIFT AID (NON-NEED-BASED) ***Total amount:*** $1,264,417 (100% institutional). ***Receiving aid:*** *Freshmen:* 22% (40); *Undergraduates:* 15% (81). ***Scholarships, grants, and awards by category:*** *Academic Interests/Achievement:* 47 awards ($253,000 total): education, general academic interests/achievements. *Special Achievements/Activities:* 53 awards ($263,500 total): community service, general special achievements/activities, leadership. *Special Characteristics:* 54 awards ($659,745 total): ethnic background, local/state students, members of minority groups. ***Tuition waivers:*** Full or partial for employees or children of employees.

LOANS ***Student loans:*** $1,765,551 (78% need-based, 22% non-need-based). 79% of past graduating class borrowed through all loan programs. Average indebtedness per student: $13,378. ***Average need-based loan:*** Freshmen: $3582; Undergraduates: $4155. ***Parent loans:*** $900,000 (100% non-need-based). ***Programs:*** FFEL (Subsidized and Unsubsidized Stafford, PLUS), Perkins, state.

WORK-STUDY ***Federal work-study:*** *Total amount:* $217,274; 113 jobs averaging $1922.

APPLYING for FINANCIAL AID ***Required financial aid forms:*** FAFSA, institution's own form, parent and student federal income tax returns. ***Financial aid deadline (priority):*** 2/1. ***Notification date:*** Continuous beginning 3/15. Students must reply by 5/1 or within 3 weeks of notification.

CONTACT Paul Henderson, Director, Financial Aid, Lesley College, 29 Everett Street, Cambridge, MA 02138-2790, 617-349-8710 or toll-free 800-999-1959 Ext. 8800. *Fax:* 617-349-8717.

LESTER L. COX COLLEGE OF NURSING AND HEALTH SCIENCES

Springfield, MO

CONTACT Financial Aid Office, Lester L. Cox College of Nursing and Health Sciences, 1423 North Jefferson, Springfield, MO 65802, 417-269-3401.

LETOURNEAU UNIVERSITY

Longview, TX

Tuition & fees: $12,240 **Average undergraduate aid package: $11,748**

ABOUT THE INSTITUTION Independent nondenominational, coed. Awards: associate, bachelor's, and master's degrees. 37 undergraduate majors. Total enrollment: 2,805. Undergraduates: 2,523. Freshmen: 263. Federal methodology is used as a basis for awarding need-based institutional aid.

UNDERGRADUATE EXPENSES for 2000–2001 ***Application fee:*** $25. ***One-time required fee:*** $75. ***Comprehensive fee:*** $17,490 includes full-time tuition ($12,090), mandatory fees ($150), and room and board ($5250). Room and board charges vary according to board plan. Part-time tuition and fees vary according to course load. ***Payment plan:*** installment.

FRESHMAN FINANCIAL AID (Fall 1999, est.) 249 applied for aid; of those 96% were deemed to have need. 100% of freshmen with need received aid; of those 25% had need fully met. *Average percent of need met:* 86% (excluding resources awarded to replace EFC). *Average financial aid package:* $10,646 (excluding resources awarded to replace EFC). 7% of all full-time freshmen had no need and received non-need-based aid.

UNDERGRADUATE FINANCIAL AID (Fall 1999, est.) 1,748 applied for aid; of those 90% were deemed to have need. 100% of undergraduates with need received aid; of those 13% had need fully met. *Average percent of need met:* 84% (excluding resources awarded to replace EFC). *Average financial aid package:* $11,748 (excluding resources awarded to replace EFC). 16% of all full-time undergraduates had no need and received non-need-based aid.

GIFT AID (NEED-BASED) ***Total amount:*** $3,628,491 (31% Federal, 22% state, 47% institutional). ***Receiving aid:*** *Freshmen:* 73% (191); *all full-time undergraduates:* 58% (1,416). ***Average award:*** Freshmen: $2276; Undergraduates: $2100. ***Scholarships, grants, and awards:*** Federal Pell, FSEOG, state, private, college/university gift aid from institutional funds.

GIFT AID (NON-NEED-BASED) ***Total amount:*** $2,249,071 (74% institutional, 26% external sources). ***Receiving aid:*** *Freshmen:* 71% (186); *Undergraduates:* 19% (472). ***Scholarships, grants, and awards by category:*** *Academic Interests/Achievement:* 469 awards ($1,067,124 total): general academic interests/achievements. *Creative Arts/Performance:* 28 awards ($25,405 total): journalism/publications, music. *Special Characteristics:* 186 awards ($539,612 total): children of faculty/staff, international students, local/state students, relatives of clergy, spouses of current students. ***Tuition waivers:*** Full or partial for employees or children of employees.

LOANS ***Student loans:*** $6,788,793 (52% need-based, 48% non-need-based). 72% of past graduating class borrowed through all loan programs. Average indebtedness per student: $17,263. ***Average need-based loan:*** Freshmen: $2865; Undergraduates: $3969. ***Parent loans:*** $744,208 (100% non-need-based). ***Programs:*** FFEL (Subsidized and Unsubsidized Stafford, PLUS), Perkins.

WORK-STUDY ***Federal work-study:*** *Total amount:* $161,982; 323 jobs available. ***State or other work-study/employment:*** *Total amount:* $13,253 (100% need-based). Part-time jobs available.

APPLYING for FINANCIAL AID ***Required financial aid forms:*** FAFSA, institution's own form. ***Financial aid deadline (priority):*** 2/15. ***Notification date:*** Continuous beginning 3/1. Students must reply within 3 weeks of notification.

CONTACT Ms. Delinda Hall, Director of Financial Aid, LeTourneau University, PO Box 7001, Longview, TX 75607-7001, 903-233-3430 or toll-free 800-759-8811. *Fax:* 903-233-3411. *E-mail:* halll@letu.edu

LEWIS & CLARK COLLEGE

Portland, OR

Tuition & fees: $21,520 **Average undergraduate aid package: $19,060**

ABOUT THE INSTITUTION Independent, coed. Awards: bachelor's, master's, and first professional degrees. 32 undergraduate majors. Total enrollment: 3,203. Undergraduates: 1,742. Freshmen: 512. Both federal and institutional methodology are used as a basis for awarding need-based institutional aid.

UNDERGRADUATE EXPENSES for 2000–2001 ***Application fee:*** $45. ***Comprehensive fee:*** $27,620 includes full-time tuition ($21,520) and room and board ($6100). ***College room only:*** $3280. Room and board charges vary according to board plan and student level. ***Part-time tuition:*** $1070 per semester hour. ***Part-time fees:*** $10 per semester hour. Part-time tuition and fees vary according to course load. ***Payment plan:*** installment.

FRESHMAN FINANCIAL AID (Fall 1999) 369 applied for aid; of those 86% were deemed to have need. 99% of freshmen with need received aid; of those 26% had need fully met. *Average percent of need met:* 86% (excluding resources awarded to replace EFC). *Average financial aid package:* $19,670 (excluding resources awarded to replace EFC). 17% of all full-time freshmen had no need and received non-need-based aid.

UNDERGRADUATE FINANCIAL AID (Fall 1999) 1,056 applied for aid; of those 90% were deemed to have need. 100% of undergraduates with need received aid; of those 50% had need fully met. *Average percent of need met:* 84% (excluding resources awarded to replace EFC). *Average financial aid package:* $19,060 (excluding resources awarded to replace EFC). 12% of all full-time undergraduates had no need and received non-need-based aid.

GIFT AID (NEED-BASED) ***Total amount:*** $11,297,716 (9% Federal, 3% state, 82% institutional, 6% external sources). ***Receiving aid:*** *Freshmen:* 60% (310); *all full-time undergraduates:* 53% (921). ***Average award:*** Freshmen: $13,292; Undergraduates: $11,457. ***Scholarships, grants, and awards:*** Federal Pell, FSEOG, state, private, college/university gift aid from institutional funds.

GIFT AID (NON-NEED-BASED) ***Total amount:*** $1,128,269 (2% Federal, 92% institutional, 6% external sources). ***Receiving aid:*** *Freshmen:* 26% (132); *Undergraduates:* 20% (350). ***Scholarships, grants, and awards by category:*** *Academic Interests/Achievement:* communication, general academic interests/achievements. *Creative Arts/Performance:* debating, music. *Special Achievements/Activities:* community service. ***Tuition waivers:*** Full or partial for employees or children of employees.

LOANS ***Student loans:*** $5,319,333 (93% need-based, 7% non-need-based). ***Average need-based loan:*** Freshmen: $2136; Undergraduates: $4563. ***Parent loans:*** $1,769,263 (75% need-based, 25% non-need-based). ***Programs:*** FFEL (Subsidized and Unsubsidized Stafford, PLUS), Perkins, state.

WORK-STUDY ***Federal work-study:*** *Total amount:* $1,105,764; jobs available.

APPLYING for FINANCIAL AID ***Required financial aid form:*** FAFSA. ***Financial aid deadline (priority):*** 3/1. ***Notification date:*** 4/1. Students must reply by 5/1 or within 2 weeks of notification.

CONTACT Glendi Gaddis, Director of Student Financial Services, Lewis & Clark College, Campus Box 56, Templeton Student Center, Portland, OR 97219-7899, 503-768-7090 or toll-free 800-444-4111. *E-mail:* sfs@lclark.edu

LEWIS-CLARK STATE COLLEGE

Lewiston, ID

Tuition & fees (ID res): $2204 **Average undergraduate aid package: $5562**

ABOUT THE INSTITUTION State-supported, coed. Awards: associate and bachelor's degrees. 51 undergraduate majors. Total enrollment: 3,151. Undergraduates: 3,151. Freshmen: 486. Federal methodology is used as a basis for awarding need-based institutional aid.

UNDERGRADUATE EXPENSES for 1999–2000 ***Application fee:*** $20. ***Tuition, state resident:*** full-time $0; part-time $102 per credit. ***Tuition, nonresident:*** full-time $5272; part-time $102 per credit. ***Required fees:*** full-time $2204. ***College room and board:*** $3500. Room and board charges vary according to board plan and housing facility. ***Payment plan:*** deferred payment.

FRESHMAN FINANCIAL AID (Fall 1998) 304 applied for aid; of those 85% were deemed to have need. 85% of freshmen with need received aid; of those 100% had need fully met. *Average percent of need met:* 100% (excluding resources awarded to replace EFC). *Average financial aid package:* $3336 (excluding resources awarded to replace EFC). 15% of all full-time freshmen had no need and received non-need-based aid.

UNDERGRADUATE FINANCIAL AID (Fall 1998) 1,561 applied for aid; of those 84% were deemed to have need. 92% of undergraduates with need received aid; of those 100% had need fully met. *Average percent of need met:* 100% (excluding resources awarded to replace EFC). *Average financial aid package:* $5562 (excluding resources awarded to replace EFC). 11% of all full-time undergraduates had no need and received non-need-based aid.

GIFT AID (NEED-BASED) ***Total amount:*** $2,463,439 (86% Federal, 2% state, 5% institutional, 7% external sources). ***Receiving aid:*** *Freshmen:* 34% (153); *all full-time undergraduates:* 35% (893). ***Average award:*** Freshmen: $1574; Undergraduates: $2550. ***Scholarships, grants, and awards:*** Federal Pell, FSEOG, state, private, college/university gift aid from institutional funds.

GIFT AID (NON-NEED-BASED) ***Total amount:*** $221,535 (55% institutional, 45% external sources). ***Receiving aid:*** *Freshmen:* 15% (67); *Undergraduates:* 13% (319). ***Scholarships, grants, and awards by category:*** *Academic Interests/Achievement:* 294 awards ($389,520 total): education, general academic interests/achievements, health fields, mathematics. *Creative Arts/Performance:* 18 awards ($20,790 total): art/fine arts, creative writing, music. *Special Achievements/Activities:* 38 awards ($9699 total): junior miss, leadership, rodeo. *Special Characteristics:* 48 awards ($172,354 total): ethnic background, first-generation college students, members of minority groups, out-of-state students. ***Tuition waivers:*** Full or partial for employees or children of employees, senior citizens. ***ROTC:*** Army, Naval cooperative, Air Force.

LOANS ***Student loans:*** $5,506,195 (66% need-based, 34% non-need-based). ***Average need-based loan:*** Freshmen: $2309; Undergraduates: $3307. ***Parent loans:*** $393,693 (100% non-need-based). ***Programs:*** Federal Direct (Subsidized and Unsubsidized Stafford), FFEL (PLUS), Perkins, Federal Nursing, college/university.

WORK-STUDY ***Federal work-study:*** *Total amount:* $163,492; 131 jobs averaging $1248. ***State or other work-study/employment:*** *Total amount:* $103,045 (91% need-based, 9% non-need-based). 77 part-time jobs averaging $1220.

ATHLETIC AWARDS *Total amount:* 401,543 (100% non-need-based).

APPLYING for FINANCIAL AID ***Required financial aid form:*** FAFSA. ***Financial aid deadline (priority):*** 3/1. ***Notification date:*** Continuous beginning 3/13. Students must reply within 3 weeks of notification.

CONTACT Ms. Laura Hughes, Director of Financial Aid, Lewis-Clark State College, 500 8th Avenue, Lewiston, ID 83501-2698, 208-799-2224 or toll-free 800-933-LCSC Ext. 2210. *Fax:* 208-799-2063. *E-mail:* lhughes@lcsc.edu

LEWIS UNIVERSITY

Romeoville, IL

Tuition & fees: $12,810 **Average undergraduate aid package: $12,039**

ABOUT THE INSTITUTION Independent religious, coed. Awards: associate, bachelor's, and master's degrees and post-master's certificates. 53 undergraduate majors. Total enrollment: 4,108. Undergraduates: 3,228. Freshmen: 432. Federal methodology is used as a basis for awarding need-based institutional aid.

UNDERGRADUATE EXPENSES for 1999–2000 ***Application fee:*** $30. ***Comprehensive fee:*** $18,540 includes full-time tuition ($12,810) and room and board ($5730). Full-time tuition and fees vary according to course load. Room and board charges vary according to board plan and housing facility. ***Part-time tuition:*** $427 per credit hour. Part-time tuition and fees vary according to course load. ***Payment plan:*** installment.

FRESHMAN FINANCIAL AID (Fall 1999, est.) 418 applied for aid; of those 74% were deemed to have need. 100% of freshmen with need received aid; of those 30% had need fully met. *Average percent of need met:* 92% (excluding resources awarded to replace EFC). *Average financial aid package:* $13,087 (excluding resources awarded to replace EFC). 7% of all full-time freshmen had no need and received non-need-based aid.

UNDERGRADUATE FINANCIAL AID (Fall 1999, est.) 1,916 applied for aid; of those 79% were deemed to have need. 90% of undergraduates with need received aid; of those 28% had need fully met. *Average percent of need met:* 83% (excluding resources awarded to replace EFC). *Average financial aid package:* $12,039 (excluding resources awarded to replace EFC). 9% of all full-time undergraduates had no need and received non-need-based aid.

GIFT AID (NEED-BASED) ***Total amount:*** $6,720,183 (20% Federal, 62% state, 18% institutional). ***Receiving aid:*** *Freshmen:* 62% (267); *all full-time undergraduates:* 59% (1,199). ***Average award:*** Freshmen: $7930; Undergraduates: $8423. ***Scholarships, grants, and awards:*** Federal Pell, FSEOG, state, private, college/university gift aid from institutional funds.

GIFT AID (NON-NEED-BASED) ***Total amount:*** $5,538,440 (2% Federal, 1% state, 94% institutional, 3% external sources). ***Receiving aid:*** *Freshmen:* 34% (146); *Undergraduates:* 30% (608). ***Scholarships, grants, and awards by category:*** *Academic Interests/Achievement:* general academic interests/achievements. *Creative Arts/Performance:* dance, theater/drama. *Special Achievements/Activities:* community service, general special achievements/activities. *Special Characteristics:* children and siblings of alumni. ***Tuition waivers:*** Full or partial for children of alumni, employees or children of employees. ***ROTC:*** Army, Air Force cooperative.

LOANS ***Student loans:*** $7,707,119 (61% need-based, 39% non-need-based). ***Average need-based loan:*** Freshmen: $2428; Undergraduates: $3623. ***Parent loans:*** $889,939 (100% non-need-based). ***Programs:*** FFEL (Subsidized and Unsubsidized Stafford, PLUS), Perkins.

WORK-STUDY ***Federal work-study:*** *Total amount:* $398,414; jobs available. ***State or other work-study/employment:*** *Total amount:* $415,586 (100% non-need-based). Part-time jobs available.

ATHLETIC AWARDS *Total amount:* 1,458,737 (100% non-need-based).

APPLYING for FINANCIAL AID ***Required financial aid form:*** FAFSA. ***Financial aid deadline (priority):*** 5/1. ***Notification date:*** Continuous.

Lewis University (continued)

CONTACT Ms. Janeen Decharinte, Director of Financial Aid, Lewis University, Route 53, Romeoville, IL 60446, 815-836-5262 or toll-free 800-897-9000. *Fax:* 815-836-5135. *E-mail:* decharja@lewisu.edu

LIBERTY UNIVERSITY

Lynchburg, VA

Tuition & fees: $8750 **Average undergraduate aid package: N/A**

ABOUT THE INSTITUTION Independent nondenominational, coed. Awards: associate, bachelor's, master's, doctoral, and first professional degrees (also offers external degree program with significant enrollment not reflected in profile). 34 undergraduate majors. Total enrollment: 6,679. Undergraduates: 5,942. Freshmen: 1,118. Federal methodology is used as a basis for awarding need-based institutional aid.

UNDERGRADUATE EXPENSES for 2000–2001 ***Application fee:*** $35. ***Comprehensive fee:*** $13,550 includes full-time tuition ($8550), mandatory fees ($200), and room and board ($4800). Full-time tuition and fees vary according to course load. ***Part-time tuition:*** $285 per semester hour. ***Part-time fees:*** $50 per term part-time. Part-time tuition and fees vary according to course load. ***Payment plan:*** installment.

GIFT AID (NEED-BASED) ***Total amount:*** $3,664,544 (91% Federal, 1% state, 8% institutional). ***Scholarships, grants, and awards:*** Federal Pell, FSEOG, state, private, college/university gift aid from institutional funds.

GIFT AID (NON-NEED-BASED) ***Total amount:*** $15,515,564 (18% state, 82% institutional). ***Scholarships, grants, and awards by category:*** *Academic Interests/Achievement:* general academic interests/achievements. *Creative Arts/Performance:* 135 awards ($253,210 total): debating, journalism/publications, music, performing arts. *Special Achievements/Activities:* 497 awards ($1,675,874 total): cheerleading/drum major, general special achievements/activities, leadership, religious involvement. *Special Characteristics:* international students, relatives of clergy, religious affiliation. ***Tuition waivers:*** Full or partial for employees or children of employees.

LOANS ***Student loans:*** $13,116,922 (69% need-based, 31% non-need-based). Average indebtedness per student: $13,562. ***Parent loans:*** $2,277,022 (100% non-need-based). ***Programs:*** FFEL (Subsidized and Unsubsidized Stafford, PLUS).

WORK-STUDY ***Federal work-study:*** *Total amount:* $260,671; jobs available.

ATHLETIC AWARDS *Total amount:* 1,846,332 (100% non-need-based).

APPLYING for FINANCIAL AID ***Required financial aid form:*** FAFSA. ***Financial aid deadline (priority):*** 4/15. ***Notification date:*** Continuous. Students must reply within 3 weeks of notification.

CONTACT Rhonda Allbeck, Director, Financial Aid Office, Liberty University, 1971 University Boulevard, Lynchburg, VA 24502, 804-582-2288 or toll-free 800-543-5317. *Fax:* 804-582-2053. *E-mail:* rfallbeck@liberty.edu

LIFE BIBLE COLLEGE

San Dimas, CA

Tuition & fees: $5625 **Average undergraduate aid package: $5205**

ABOUT THE INSTITUTION Independent religious, coed. Awards: associate and bachelor's degrees. 3 undergraduate majors. Total enrollment: 501. Undergraduates: 501. Freshmen: 79. Both federal and institutional methodology are used as a basis for awarding need-based institutional aid.

UNDERGRADUATE EXPENSES for 2000–2001 ***Application fee:*** $35. ***Comprehensive fee:*** $8725 includes full-time tuition ($5375), mandatory fees ($250), and room and board ($3100). ***Part-time tuition:*** $175 per semester hour. Part-time tuition and fees vary according to course load. ***Payment plan:*** installment.

FRESHMAN FINANCIAL AID (Fall 1998) 67 applied for aid; of those 99% were deemed to have need. 94% of freshmen with need received aid; of those 6% had need fully met. *Average percent of need met:* 35% (excluding resources awarded to replace EFC). *Average financial aid package:* $4076 (excluding resources awarded to replace EFC). 4% of all full-time freshmen had no need and received non-need-based aid.

UNDERGRADUATE FINANCIAL AID (Fall 1998) 380 applied for aid; of those 99% were deemed to have need. 99% of undergraduates with need received aid; of those 12% had need fully met. *Average percent of need met:* 44% (excluding resources awarded to replace EFC). *Average financial aid package:* $5205 (excluding resources awarded to replace EFC). 4% of all full-time undergraduates had no need and received non-need-based aid.

GIFT AID (NEED-BASED) ***Total amount:*** $628,549 (51% Federal, 31% state, 15% institutional, 3% external sources). ***Receiving aid:*** *Freshmen:* 72% (50); *all full-time undergraduates:* 85% (333). ***Average award:*** Freshmen: $1746; Undergraduates: $2130. ***Scholarships, grants, and awards:*** Federal Pell, FSEOG, state, private, college/university gift aid from institutional funds.

GIFT AID (NON-NEED-BASED) ***Total amount:*** $124,232 (65% institutional, 35% external sources). ***Receiving aid:*** *Freshmen:* 23% (16); *Undergraduates:* 10% (40). ***Scholarships, grants, and awards by category:*** *Special Characteristics:* 86 awards ($112,928 total): children and siblings of alumni, children of faculty/staff, relatives of clergy, spouses of current students. ***Tuition waivers:*** Full or partial for employees or children of employees.

LOANS ***Student loans:*** $514,190 (100% need-based). 29% of past graduating class borrowed through all loan programs. Average indebtedness per student: $5218. ***Average need-based loan:*** Freshmen: $2291; Undergraduates: $3092. ***Parent loans:*** $62,571 (100% need-based). ***Programs:*** FFEL (Subsidized and Unsubsidized Stafford, PLUS).

WORK-STUDY ***Federal work-study:*** *Total amount:* $13,172; 13 jobs averaging $1013.

APPLYING for FINANCIAL AID ***Required financial aid forms:*** FAFSA, institution's own form, state aid form. ***Financial aid deadline (priority):*** 7/15. ***Notification date:*** Continuous beginning 8/1. Students must reply by 8/15.

CONTACT Mr. Roy Pattillo, Director of Financial Aid, LIFE Bible College, 1100 Covina Boulevard, San Dimas, CA 91773-3298, 909-599-5433 Ext. 322 or toll-free 800-356-0001. *Fax:* 909-599-6690. *E-mail:* roypatt@lifebible.edu

LIFE UNIVERSITY

Marietta, GA

Tuition & fees: N/R **Average undergraduate aid package: N/A**

ABOUT THE INSTITUTION Independent, coed. Federal methodology is used as a basis for awarding need-based institutional aid.

FRESHMAN FINANCIAL AID (Fall 1999) 154 applied for aid; of those 86% were deemed to have need. 88% of freshmen with need received aid; of those 24% had need fully met. *Average percent of need met:* 24% (excluding resources awarded to replace EFC). 11% of all full-time freshmen had no need and received non-need-based aid.

UNDERGRADUATE FINANCIAL AID (Fall 1999) 415 applied for aid; of those 89% were deemed to have need. 92% of undergraduates with need received aid; of those 25% had need fully met. *Average percent of need met:* 25% (excluding resources awarded to replace EFC). 9% of all full-time undergraduates had no need and received non-need-based aid.

GIFT AID (NEED-BASED) ***Total amount:*** $594,685 (100% Federal). ***Receiving aid:*** *Freshmen:* 28% (59); *all full-time undergraduates:* 28% (155). ***Average award:*** Freshmen: $2757; Undergraduates: $2907. ***Scholarships, grants, and awards:*** Federal Pell, FSEOG, state, private, college/university gift aid from institutional funds.

GIFT AID (NON-NEED-BASED) ***Total amount:*** $482,268 (56% state, 44% institutional). ***Receiving aid:*** *Freshmen:* 31% (67); *Undergraduates:* 25% (139). ***Scholarships, grants, and awards by category:*** *Academic Interests/Achievement:* 5 awards ($25,988 total): general academic interests/achievements. *Special Achievements/Activities:* 6 awards ($35,726 total): general special achievements/activities. *Special Characteristics:* 49 awards ($203,837 total): children and siblings of alumni, ethnic background, international students.

LOANS ***Student loans:*** $2,168,707 (53% need-based, 47% non-need-based). 60% of past graduating class borrowed through all loan programs. Average indebtedness per student: $11,327. ***Average need-based loan:***

Freshmen: $2725; Undergraduates: $3898. ***Parent loans:*** $1,275,260 (100% non-need-based). ***Programs:*** FFEL (Subsidized and Unsubsidized Stafford, PLUS), Perkins, college/university, alternative loans.

WORK-STUDY ***Federal work-study:*** *Total amount:* $79,566; 44 jobs averaging $1808.

ATHLETIC AWARDS *Total amount:* 283,820 (100% non-need-based).

APPLYING for FINANCIAL AID ***Required financial aid forms:*** FAFSA, institution's own form. ***Financial aid deadline (priority):*** 3/1. ***Notification date:*** Continuous beginning 5/1.

CONTACT David M. Haygood, Director of Financial Aid, Life University, 1269 Barclay Circle, Marietta, GA 30060, 770-426-2915. *Fax:* 770-425-6261. *E-mail:* dhaygood@life.edu

LIMESTONE COLLEGE

Gaffney, SC

Tuition & fees: $10,100 **Average undergraduate aid package: $5659**

ABOUT THE INSTITUTION Independent, coed. Awards: associate and bachelor's degrees. 35 undergraduate majors. Total enrollment: 1,994. Undergraduates: 1,994. Freshmen: 475. Federal methodology is used as a basis for awarding need-based institutional aid.

UNDERGRADUATE EXPENSES for 2000–2001 ***Application fee:*** $25. ***Comprehensive fee:*** $14,900 includes full-time tuition ($10,100) and room and board ($4800). ***College room only:*** $2400. Full-time tuition and fees vary according to class time, course load, and program. ***Part-time tuition:*** $421 per semester hour. Part-time tuition and fees vary according to class time and program. ***Payment plan:*** installment.

FRESHMAN FINANCIAL AID (Fall 1998) 165 applied for aid; of those 90% were deemed to have need. 100% of freshmen with need received aid; of those 23% had need fully met. *Average percent of need met:* 62% (excluding resources awarded to replace EFC). *Average financial aid package:* $6312 (excluding resources awarded to replace EFC). 12% of all full-time freshmen had no need and received non-need-based aid.

UNDERGRADUATE FINANCIAL AID (Fall 1998) 924 applied for aid; of those 91% were deemed to have need. 100% of undergraduates with need received aid; of those 21% had need fully met. *Average percent of need met:* 58% (excluding resources awarded to replace EFC). *Average financial aid package:* $5659 (excluding resources awarded to replace EFC). 16% of all full-time undergraduates had no need and received non-need-based aid.

GIFT AID (NEED-BASED) ***Total amount:*** $2,274,919 (35% Federal, 29% state, 32% institutional, 4% external sources). ***Receiving aid:*** *Freshmen:* 30% (140); *all full-time undergraduates:* 47% (751). ***Average award:*** Freshmen: $3891; Undergraduates: $2835. ***Scholarships, grants, and awards:*** Federal Pell, FSEOG, state, private, college/university gift aid from institutional funds.

GIFT AID (NON-NEED-BASED) ***Total amount:*** $248,347 (13% state, 76% institutional, 11% external sources). ***Receiving aid:*** *Freshmen:* 3% (14); *Undergraduates:* 3% (48). ***Scholarships, grants, and awards by category:*** *Academic Interests/Achievement:* 135 awards ($142,935 total): biological sciences, business, communication, computer science, education, English, general academic interests/achievements, humanities, mathematics, religion/biblical studies, social sciences. *Creative Arts/Performance:* 53 awards ($80,750 total): art/fine arts, music, performing arts, theater/drama. *Special Achievements/Activities:* 27 awards ($15,473 total): cheerleading/drum major, leadership, religious involvement. *Special Characteristics:* 387 awards ($425,121 total): children and siblings of alumni, children of faculty/staff, general special characteristics, local/state students, out-of-state students, siblings of current students. ***Tuition waivers:*** Full or partial for employees or children of employees. ***ROTC:*** Army cooperative.

LOANS ***Student loans:*** $2,928,766 (80% need-based, 20% non-need-based). 47% of past graduating class borrowed through all loan programs. Average indebtedness per student: $6339. ***Average need-based loan:*** Freshmen: $2106; Undergraduates: $2715. ***Parent loans:*** $297,612 (47% need-based, 53% non-need-based). ***Programs:*** FFEL (Subsidized and Unsubsidized Stafford, PLUS), Perkins.

WORK-STUDY ***Federal work-study:*** *Total amount:* $91,987; 82 jobs averaging $1122. ***State or other work-study/employment:*** *Total amount:* $27,944 (12% need-based, 88% non-need-based). 24 part-time jobs averaging $1164.

ATHLETIC AWARDS *Total amount:* 172,950 (94% need-based, 6% non-need-based).

APPLYING for FINANCIAL AID ***Required financial aid form:*** FAFSA. ***Financial aid deadline (priority):*** 5/1. ***Notification date:*** Continuous. Students must reply within 2 weeks of notification.

CONTACT Ms. Virginia Hickey, Director of Financial Aid, Limestone College, 1115 College Drive, Gaffney, SC 29340-3798, 864-489-7151 Ext. 597 or toll-free 800-795-7151 Ext. 554 (in-state), 800-795-7151 Ext. 553 (out-of-state). *Fax:* 864-487-8706.

LINCOLN CHRISTIAN COLLEGE

Lincoln, IL

Tuition & fees: $6708 **Average undergraduate aid package: N/A**

ABOUT THE INSTITUTION Independent religious, coed. Awards: associate and bachelor's degrees. 13 undergraduate majors. Total enrollment: 625. Undergraduates: 625. Freshmen: 129. Federal methodology is used as a basis for awarding need-based institutional aid.

UNDERGRADUATE EXPENSES for 1999–2000 ***Application fee:*** $20. ***Comprehensive fee:*** $10,608 includes full-time tuition ($5824), mandatory fees ($884), and room and board ($3900). ***College room only:*** $1790. Room and board charges vary according to board plan. ***Part-time tuition:*** $182 per semester hour. ***Part-time fees:*** $12 per hour; $250. Part-time tuition and fees vary according to course load. ***Payment plans:*** installment, deferred payment.

GIFT AID (NEED-BASED) ***Scholarships, grants, and awards:*** Federal Pell, FSEOG, state.

GIFT AID (NON-NEED-BASED) ***Scholarships, grants, and awards by category:*** *Academic Interests/Achievement:* general academic interests/achievements. ***Tuition waivers:*** Full or partial for employees or children of employees.

LOANS ***Programs:*** FFEL (Subsidized and Unsubsidized Stafford, PLUS), Perkins.

WORK-STUDY Federal work-study jobs available. ***State or other work-study/employment:*** Part-time jobs available.

APPLYING for FINANCIAL AID ***Required financial aid form:*** FAFSA. ***Financial aid deadline (priority):*** 2/1. ***Notification date:*** Continuous beginning 4/1. Students must reply within 2 weeks of notification.

CONTACT Mr. Jack A. Getchel, Director of Financial Aid, Lincoln Christian College, 100 Campus View Drive, Lincoln, IL 62656, 217-732-3168 Ext. 2226 or toll-free 888-522-5228. *Fax:* 217-732-5914. *E-mail:* jgetchel@lccs.edu

LINCOLN MEMORIAL UNIVERSITY

Harrogate, TN

Tuition & fees: $9600 **Average undergraduate aid package: $7201**

ABOUT THE INSTITUTION Independent, coed. Awards: associate, bachelor's, and master's degrees and post-master's certificates. 35 undergraduate majors. Total enrollment: 1,701. Undergraduates: 875. Freshmen: 142. Federal methodology is used as a basis for awarding need-based institutional aid.

UNDERGRADUATE EXPENSES for 2000–2001 ***Application fee:*** $25. ***Comprehensive fee:*** $13,500 includes full-time tuition ($9600) and room and board ($3900). ***College room only:*** $1680. Room and board charges vary according to board plan and housing facility. ***Part-time tuition:*** $400 per semester hour. ***Payment plans:*** installment, deferred payment.

FRESHMAN FINANCIAL AID (Fall 1998) 201 applied for aid; of those 84% were deemed to have need. 100% of freshmen with need received aid; of those 69% had need fully met. *Average percent of need met:* 95% (excluding resources awarded to replace EFC). *Average financial aid package:*

Lincoln Memorial University (continued)

$7490 (excluding resources awarded to replace EFC). 12% of all full-time freshmen had no need and received non-need-based aid.

UNDERGRADUATE FINANCIAL AID (Fall 1998) 671 applied for aid; of those 84% were deemed to have need. 100% of undergraduates with need received aid; of those 90% had need fully met. *Average percent of need met:* 90% (excluding resources awarded to replace EFC). *Average financial aid package:* $7201 (excluding resources awarded to replace EFC). 10% of all full-time undergraduates had no need and received non-need-based aid.

GIFT AID (NEED-BASED) ***Total amount:*** $1,839,344 (55% Federal, 17% state, 28% institutional). ***Receiving aid:*** *Freshmen:* 45% (110); *all full-time undergraduates:* 45% (366). ***Average award:*** Freshmen: $4870; Undergraduates: $4700. ***Scholarships, grants, and awards:*** Federal Pell, FSEOG, state, private, college/university gift aid from institutional funds.

GIFT AID (NON-NEED-BASED) ***Total amount:*** $1,413,982 (81% institutional, 19% external sources). ***Receiving aid:*** *Freshmen:* 13% (33); *Undergraduates:* 41% (333). ***Scholarships, grants, and awards by category:*** *Academic Interests/Achievement:* 316 awards ($1,078,838 total): general academic interests/achievements. *Creative Arts/Performance:* 20 awards ($16,000 total): music. *Special Achievements/Activities:* 10 awards ($2215 total): cheerleading/drum major. *Special Characteristics:* 20 awards ($126,126 total): children of faculty/staff. ***Tuition waivers:*** Full or partial for employees or children of employees, senior citizens.

LOANS ***Student loans:*** $2,990,273 (60% need-based, 40% non-need-based). 80% of past graduating class borrowed through all loan programs. Average indebtedness per student: $11,200. ***Average need-based loan:*** Freshmen: $2625; Undergraduates: $3300. ***Parent loans:*** $99,797 (100% non-need-based). ***Programs:*** FFEL (Subsidized and Unsubsidized Stafford, PLUS), Perkins.

WORK-STUDY ***Federal work-study:*** *Total amount:* $172,960; 138 jobs averaging $1250.

ATHLETIC AWARDS *Total amount:* 872,700 (100% non-need-based).

APPLYING for FINANCIAL AID ***Required financial aid form:*** FAFSA. ***Financial aid deadline (priority):*** 4/1. ***Notification date:*** Continuous beginning 4/15. Students must reply within 2 weeks of notification.

CONTACT Christy Graham, Director of Financial Aid, Lincoln Memorial University, Cumberland Gap Parkway, Harrogate, TN 37752-1901, 423-869-6336 or toll-free 800-325-0900. *Fax:* 423-869-4825.

LINCOLN UNIVERSITY

Jefferson City, MO

Tuition & fees (MO res): $2368 **Average undergraduate aid package: $8625**

ABOUT THE INSTITUTION State-supported, coed. Awards: associate, bachelor's, and master's degrees. 40 undergraduate majors. Total enrollment: 3,347. Undergraduates: 3,088. Federal methodology is used as a basis for awarding need-based institutional aid.

UNDERGRADUATE EXPENSES for 1999–2000 ***Application fee:*** $17. ***One-time required fee:*** $142. ***Tuition, state resident:*** full-time $2208; part-time $92 per credit hour. ***Tuition, nonresident:*** full-time $4416; part-time $184 per credit hour. ***Required fees:*** full-time $160; $5 per credit hour; $20 per term part-time. ***College room and board:*** $3790; ***room only:*** $1850. ***Payment plan:*** deferred payment.

FRESHMAN FINANCIAL AID (Fall 1999, est.) 825 applied for aid; of those 82% were deemed to have need. 80% of freshmen with need received aid; of those 70% had need fully met. *Average percent of need met:* 80% (excluding resources awarded to replace EFC). *Average financial aid package:* $5750 (excluding resources awarded to replace EFC). 34% of all full-time freshmen had no need and received non-need-based aid.

UNDERGRADUATE FINANCIAL AID (Fall 1999, est.) 3,329 applied for aid; of those 88% were deemed to have need. 72% of undergraduates with need received aid; of those 85% had need fully met. *Average percent of need met:* 85% (excluding resources awarded to replace EFC). *Average financial aid package:* $8625 (excluding resources awarded to replace EFC). 30% of all full-time undergraduates had no need and received non-need-based aid.

GIFT AID (NEED-BASED) ***Total amount:*** $2,387,371 (93% Federal, 7% state). ***Receiving aid:*** *Freshmen:* 40% (415); *all full-time undergraduates:* 43% (1,782). ***Average award:*** Freshmen: $4229; Undergraduates: $4229. ***Scholarships, grants, and awards:*** Federal Pell, FSEOG, state, private, college/university gift aid from institutional funds, United Negro College Fund.

GIFT AID (NON-NEED-BASED) ***Total amount:*** $1,060,830 (2% state, 60% institutional, 38% external sources). ***Receiving aid:*** *Freshmen:* 14% (146); *Undergraduates:* 14% (589). ***Scholarships, grants, and awards by category:*** *Academic Interests/Achievement:* 161 awards ($616,194 total): agriculture, biological sciences, education, general academic interests/achievements, military science, physical sciences, religion/biblical studies. *Creative Arts/Performance:* 52 awards ($71,036 total): art/fine arts, journalism/publications, music, theater/drama. *Special Achievements/Activities:* 1 award ($2000 total): memberships. *Special Characteristics:* 51 awards ($56,947 total): children of faculty/staff, general special characteristics, local/state students, veterans. ***Tuition waivers:*** Full or partial for employees or children of employees, senior citizens. ***ROTC:*** Army.

LOANS ***Student loans:*** $5,504,622 (71% need-based, 29% non-need-based). 86% of past graduating class borrowed through all loan programs. Average indebtedness per student: $17,125. ***Average need-based loan:*** Freshmen: $2625; Undergraduates: $5500. ***Parent loans:*** $133,781 (100% non-need-based). ***Programs:*** FFEL (Subsidized and Unsubsidized Stafford, PLUS), state.

WORK-STUDY ***Federal work-study:*** *Total amount:* $264,538; jobs available.

ATHLETIC AWARDS *Total amount:* 482,520 (100% non-need-based).

APPLYING for FINANCIAL AID ***Required financial aid form:*** FAFSA. ***Financial aid deadline (priority):*** 3/31. ***Notification date:*** Continuous beginning 6/1. Students must reply within 2 weeks of notification.

CONTACT Mr. Alfred Robinson, Acting Associate Director of Financial Aid, Lincoln University, 820 Chestnut Street, Jefferson City, MO 65102-0029, 573-681-6156 or toll-free 800-521-5052. *Fax:* 573-681-5871.

LINCOLN UNIVERSITY

Lincoln University, PA

Tuition & fees (PA res): $5208 **Average undergraduate aid package: N/A**

ABOUT THE INSTITUTION State-related, coed. Awards: bachelor's and master's degrees. 47 undergraduate majors. Total enrollment: 2,008. Undergraduates: 1,454. Freshmen: 358. Federal methodology is used as a basis for awarding need-based institutional aid.

UNDERGRADUATE EXPENSES for 1999–2000 ***Application fee:*** $20. ***One-time required fee:*** $105. ***Tuition, state resident:*** full-time $3748; part-time $156 per credit hour. ***Tuition, nonresident:*** full-time $6256; part-time $277 per credit hour. ***Required fees:*** full-time $1460; $62 per credit hour. Full-time tuition and fees vary according to course load. ***College room and board:*** $5034; ***room only:*** $2756. Room and board charges vary according to board plan. ***Payment plans:*** installment, deferred payment.

GIFT AID (NEED-BASED) ***Scholarships, grants, and awards:*** Federal Pell, FSEOG, state, college/university gift aid from institutional funds.

GIFT AID (NON-NEED-BASED) ***Scholarships, grants, and awards by category:*** *Academic Interests/Achievement:* biological sciences, business, communication, computer science, education, general academic interests/achievements, humanities, mathematics, physical sciences. *Creative Arts/Performance:* music. ***Tuition waivers:*** Full or partial for employees or children of employees. ***ROTC:*** Army cooperative, Air Force cooperative.

LOANS ***Programs:*** FFEL (Subsidized and Unsubsidized Stafford, PLUS), Perkins.

WORK-STUDY Federal work-study jobs available.

APPLYING for FINANCIAL AID ***Required financial aid form:*** FAFSA. ***Financial aid deadline:*** 3/15.

CONTACT Lloyd Asparagus, Director of Financial Aid, Lincoln University, Lincoln Hall, Lincoln University, PA 19352, 610-932-8300 or toll-free 800-215-4858.

LINDENWOOD UNIVERSITY

St. Charles, MO

CONTACT Dr. David R. Williams, Dean of the College, Lindenwood University, 209 South Kingshighway, St. Charles, MO 63301-1695, 314-949-4902. *Fax:* 314-949-4910.

LINDSEY WILSON COLLEGE

Columbia, KY

ABOUT THE INSTITUTION Independent United Methodist, coed. Awards: associate, bachelor's, and master's degrees. 26 undergraduate majors. Total enrollment: 1,415. Undergraduates: 1,366.

GIFT AID (NEED-BASED) ***Scholarships, grants, and awards:*** Federal Pell, FSEOG, state, private, college/university gift aid from institutional funds.

GIFT AID (NON-NEED-BASED) ***Scholarships, grants, and awards by category:*** *Academic Interests/Achievement:* general academic interests/achievements. *Creative Arts/Performance:* art/fine arts, music. *Special Achievements/Activities:* junior miss, leadership, religious involvement. *Special Characteristics:* children of faculty/staff, international students, relatives of clergy, religious affiliation.

LOANS ***Programs:*** FFEL (Subsidized and Unsubsidized Stafford, PLUS), Perkins, college/university.

WORK-STUDY Federal work-study jobs available.

APPLYING for FINANCIAL AID ***Required financial aid forms:*** FAFSA, institution's own form.

CONTACT Ms. Marilyn D. Radford, Assistant Director of Student Financial Services, Lindsey Wilson College, 210 Lindsey Wilson Street, Columbia, KY 42728-1298, 502-384-8022 or toll-free 800-264-0138. *Fax:* 502-384-8200. *E-mail:* radfordm@lindsey.edu

LINFIELD COLLEGE

McMinnville, OR

Tuition & fees: $17,720 **Average undergraduate aid package: $14,800**

ABOUT THE INSTITUTION Independent American Baptist, coed. Awards: bachelor's degrees. 32 undergraduate majors. Total enrollment: 1,550. Undergraduates: 1,550. Freshmen: 399. Federal methodology is used as a basis for awarding need-based institutional aid.

UNDERGRADUATE EXPENSES for 1999–2000 ***Application fee:*** $40. ***One-time required fee:*** $300. ***Comprehensive fee:*** $23,020 includes full-time tuition ($17,590), mandatory fees ($130), and room and board ($5300). ***College room only:*** $2560. Room and board charges vary according to housing facility. ***Part-time tuition:*** $550 per credit hour. ***Part-time fees:*** $40 per term part-time. Part-time tuition and fees vary according to course load. ***Payment plan:*** installment.

FRESHMAN FINANCIAL AID (Fall 1999) 382 applied for aid; of those 72% were deemed to have need. 100% of freshmen with need received aid; of those 56% had need fully met. *Average percent of need met:* 83% (excluding resources awarded to replace EFC). *Average financial aid package:* $14,200 (excluding resources awarded to replace EFC). 26% of all full-time freshmen had no need and received non-need-based aid.

UNDERGRADUATE FINANCIAL AID (Fall 1999) 1,485 applied for aid; of those 73% were deemed to have need. 100% of undergraduates with need received aid; of those 63% had need fully met. *Average percent of need met:* 87% (excluding resources awarded to replace EFC). *Average financial aid package:* $14,800 (excluding resources awarded to replace EFC). 18% of all full-time undergraduates had no need and received non-need-based aid.

GIFT AID (NEED-BASED) ***Total amount:*** $8,963,469 (10% Federal, 4% state, 78% institutional, 8% external sources). ***Receiving aid:*** *Freshmen:* 69% (274); *all full-time undergraduates:* 72% (1,084). ***Average award:*** Freshmen: $8995; Undergraduates: $8584. ***Scholarships, grants, and awards:*** Federal Pell, FSEOG, state, private, college/university gift aid from institutional funds.

GIFT AID (NON-NEED-BASED) ***Total amount:*** $2,398,350 (93% institutional, 7% external sources). ***Receiving aid:*** *Freshmen:* 26% (103); *Undergraduates:* 25% (378). ***Scholarships, grants, and awards by category:*** *Academic Interests/Achievement:* general academic interests/achievements. *Creative Arts/Performance:* debating, music. *Special Achievements/Activities:* leadership. *Special Characteristics:* children of faculty/staff. ***Tuition waivers:*** Full or partial for employees or children of employees, senior citizens. ***ROTC:*** Air Force cooperative.

LOANS ***Student loans:*** $6,351,299 (57% need-based, 43% non-need-based). 68% of past graduating class borrowed through all loan programs. Average indebtedness per student: $17,600. ***Average need-based loan:*** Freshmen: $3755; Undergraduates: $4766. ***Parent loans:*** $1,771,198 (100% non-need-based). ***Programs:*** FFEL (Subsidized and Unsubsidized Stafford, PLUS), Perkins, alternative loans.

WORK-STUDY ***Federal work-study:*** *Total amount:* $1,168,929; 753 jobs averaging $1575. ***State or other work-study/employment:*** *Total amount:* $615,587 (100% non-need-based). 414 part-time jobs averaging $1487.

APPLYING for FINANCIAL AID ***Required financial aid form:*** FAFSA. ***Financial aid deadline (priority):*** 2/1. ***Notification date:*** 3/25. Students must reply by 5/1.

CONTACT Dan Preston, Director of Financial Aid, Linfield College, 900 Southeast Baker Street, McMinnville, OR 97128-6894, 503-434-2225 or toll-free 800-640-2287. *Fax:* 503-434-2486. *E-mail:* dpreston@linfield.edu

LIPSCOMB UNIVERSITY

Nashville, TN

See David Lipscomb University

LIST COLLEGE OF JEWISH STUDIES

New York, NY

See Jewish Theological Seminary of America

LIVINGSTON COLLEGE

Piscataway, NJ

See Rutgers, The State University of New Jersey, Livingston College

LIVINGSTONE COLLEGE

Salisbury, NC

CONTACT Ethelene Huey, Financial Aid Director, Livingstone College, 701 West Monroe Street, Salisbury, NC 28144-5298, 704-638-5711 or toll-free 800-835-3435. *Fax:* 704-638-5560.

LOCK HAVEN UNIVERSITY OF PENNSYLVANIA

Lock Haven, PA

Tuition & fees (PA res): $4244 **Average undergraduate aid package: $5414**

ABOUT THE INSTITUTION State-supported, coed. Awards: associate, bachelor's, and master's degrees. 68 undergraduate majors. Total enrollment: 3,857. Undergraduates: 3,740. Freshmen: 941. Federal methodology is used as a basis for awarding need-based institutional aid.

UNDERGRADUATE EXPENSES for 1999–2000 ***Application fee:*** $25. ***Tuition, state resident:*** full-time $3618; part-time $150 per semester hour. ***Tuition, nonresident:*** full-time $7046; part-time $294 per semester hour. ***Required fees:*** full-time $626; $17 per semester hour; $36 per term part-time.

Lock Haven University of Pennsylvania (continued)

Part-time tuition and fees vary according to course load. ***College room and board:*** $4136. Room and board charges vary according to board plan. ***Payment plan:*** installment.

FRESHMAN FINANCIAL AID (Fall 1999, est.) 843 applied for aid; of those 85% were deemed to have need. 100% of freshmen with need received aid; of those 45% had need fully met. *Average percent of need met:* 75% (excluding resources awarded to replace EFC). *Average financial aid package:* $3969 (excluding resources awarded to replace EFC). 14% of all full-time freshmen had no need and received non-need-based aid.

UNDERGRADUATE FINANCIAL AID (Fall 1999, est.) 2,960 applied for aid; of those 71% were deemed to have need. 100% of undergraduates with need received aid; of those 52% had need fully met. *Average percent of need met:* 76% (excluding resources awarded to replace EFC). *Average financial aid package:* $5414 (excluding resources awarded to replace EFC). 18% of all full-time undergraduates had no need and received non-need-based aid.

GIFT AID (NEED-BASED) ***Total amount:*** $5,071,608 (47% Federal, 52% state, 1% external sources). ***Receiving aid:*** *Freshmen:* 53% (466); *all full-time undergraduates:* 35% (1,303). ***Average award:*** Freshmen: $3575; Undergraduates: $3575. ***Scholarships, grants, and awards:*** Federal Pell, FSEOG, state, private, college/university gift aid from institutional funds.

GIFT AID (NON-NEED-BASED) ***Total amount:*** $580,346 (8% Federal, 14% state, 42% institutional, 36% external sources). ***Receiving aid:*** *Freshmen:* 18% (160); *Undergraduates:* 12% (435). ***Scholarships, grants, and awards by category:*** *Academic Interests/Achievement:* biological sciences, communication, education, English, foreign languages, general academic interests/achievements, international studies, library science, mathematics, physical sciences, social sciences. *Creative Arts/Performance:* art/fine arts, journalism/publications, music. *Special Achievements/Activities:* leadership, memberships. *Special Characteristics:* handicapped students, local/state students, members of minority groups, previous college experience. ***Tuition waivers:*** Full or partial for minority students, employees or children of employees. ***ROTC:*** Army.

LOANS ***Student loans:*** $11,381,236 (56% need-based, 44% non-need-based). 74% of past graduating class borrowed through all loan programs. Average indebtedness per student: $16,472. ***Average need-based loan:*** Freshmen: $2500; Undergraduates: $4863. ***Parent loans:*** $1,334,226 (100% non-need-based). ***Programs:*** FFEL (Subsidized and Unsubsidized Stafford, PLUS), Perkins, college/university.

WORK-STUDY ***Federal work-study:*** *Total amount:* $256,470; 202 jobs averaging $1296. ***State or other work-study/employment:*** *Total amount:* $675,375 (100% non-need-based). 1,098 part-time jobs averaging $615.

ATHLETIC AWARDS *Total amount:* 393,124 (100% non-need-based).

APPLYING for FINANCIAL AID ***Required financial aid forms:*** FAFSA, institution's own form. ***Financial aid deadline (priority):*** 3/15. ***Notification date:*** Continuous beginning 4/1. Students must reply by 5/1 or within 2 weeks of notification.

CONTACT Dr. William A. Irwin, Director, Financial Aid Office, Lock Haven University of Pennsylvania, Russell Hall, Lock Haven, PA 17745-2390, 877-405-3057 or toll-free 800-332-8900 (in-state), 800-233-8978 (out-of-state). *Fax:* 570-893-2918.

LOGAN UNIVERSITY OF CHIROPRACTIC

Chesterfield, MO

Tuition & fees: $9360 **Average undergraduate aid package: N/A**

ABOUT THE INSTITUTION Independent, coed. Awards: first professional degrees. 1 undergraduate major. Total enrollment: 954. Undergraduates: 74. Federal methodology is used as a basis for awarding need-based institutional aid.

UNDERGRADUATE EXPENSES for 1999–2000 ***Application fee:*** $35. ***Tuition:*** full-time $9190; part-time $95 per credit hour. ***Required fees:*** full-time $170; $35 per term part-time. ***Payment plan:*** installment.

GIFT AID (NEED-BASED) ***Total amount:*** $90,000 (89% Federal, 11% state). ***Scholarships, grants, and awards:*** Federal Pell, FSEOG, state, private, college/university gift aid from institutional funds.

GIFT AID (NON-NEED-BASED) ***Total amount:*** $100,650 (50% state, 40% institutional, 10% external sources). ***Scholarships, grants, and awards by category:*** *Academic Interests/Achievement:* 65 awards ($40,650 total): general academic interests/achievements. *Special Characteristics:* 1 award ($9430 total): children of faculty/staff. ***Tuition waivers:*** Full or partial for employees or children of employees.

LOANS ***Student loans:*** $23,500,000 (100% need-based). ***Parent loans:*** $40,000 (100% non-need-based). ***Programs:*** FFEL (Subsidized and Unsubsidized Stafford, PLUS), Perkins, state, college/university.

WORK-STUDY ***Federal work-study:*** *Total amount:* $350,000; 130 jobs averaging $2693.

APPLYING for FINANCIAL AID ***Required financial aid forms:*** FAFSA, institution's own form. ***Financial aid deadline:*** Continuous. ***Notification date:*** Continuous beginning 5/15.

CONTACT Elizabeth A. Lowry, Director of Financial Aid, Logan University of Chiropractic, 1851 Schoettler Road, PO Box 1065, Chesterfield, MO 63006-1065, 314-227-2100 Ext. 149 or toll-free 800-782-3344. *Fax:* 314-207-2425.

LOMA LINDA UNIVERSITY

Loma Linda, CA

Tuition & fees: $14,220 **Average undergraduate aid package: $14,023**

ABOUT THE INSTITUTION Independent Seventh-day Adventist, coed. Awards: associate, bachelor's, master's, doctoral, and first professional degrees and post-bachelor's and post-master's certificates. 14 undergraduate majors. Total enrollment: 3,583. Undergraduates: 1,272. Federal methodology is used as a basis for awarding need-based institutional aid.

UNDERGRADUATE EXPENSES for 1999–2000 ***Application fee:*** $50. ***Tuition:*** full-time $14,220. Full-time tuition and fees vary according to course load, degree level, and program. Part-time tuition and fees vary according to course load, degree level, and program. Room and board charges vary according to housing facility. Part-time tuition per unit: $395 for 1 to 6 units, $237 for 7 to 11 units.

UNDERGRADUATE FINANCIAL AID (Fall 1998) 706 applied for aid; of those 93% were deemed to have need. 99% of undergraduates with need received aid; of those 25% had need fully met. *Average percent of need met:* 83% (excluding resources awarded to replace EFC). *Average financial aid package:* $14,023 (excluding resources awarded to replace EFC). .2% of all full-time undergraduates had no need and received non-need-based aid.

GIFT AID (NEED-BASED) ***Total amount:*** $2,665,617 (54% Federal, 34% state, 4% institutional, 8% external sources). ***Receiving aid:*** *All full-time undergraduates:* 45% (383). ***Average award:*** Undergraduates: $3009. ***Scholarships, grants, and awards:*** Federal Pell, FSEOG, state, private, college/university gift aid from institutional funds, Federal Nursing.

GIFT AID (NON-NEED-BASED) ***Total amount:*** $124,811 (100% external sources). ***Receiving aid:*** *Undergraduates:* 4% (36).

LOANS ***Student loans:*** 77% of past graduating class borrowed through all loan programs. ***Average need-based loan:*** Undergraduates: $4687. ***Programs:*** FFEL (Subsidized and Unsubsidized Stafford, PLUS), Perkins, college/university.

WORK-STUDY Federal work-study jobs available.

APPLYING for FINANCIAL AID ***Required financial aid forms:*** FAFSA, institution's own form. ***Financial aid deadline (priority):*** 3/2. ***Notification date:*** Continuous.

CONTACT Barbara Peterson, Acting Director of Financial Aid, Loma Linda University, 11139 Anderson Street, Loma Linda, CA 92350, 909-558-4509. *Fax:* 909-558-4879. *E-mail:* finaid@univ.llu.edu

LONG ISLAND UNIVERSITY, BRENTWOOD CAMPUS

Brentwood, NY

CONTACT Financial Aid Office, Long Island University, Brentwood Campus, 100 Second Avenue, Brentwood, NY 11717, 631-273-5112.

LONG ISLAND UNIVERSITY, BROOKLYN CAMPUS

Brooklyn, NY

Tuition & fees: $15,450 **Average undergraduate aid package: $13,709**

ABOUT THE INSTITUTION Independent, coed. Awards: associate, bachelor's, master's, doctoral, and first professional degrees and post-bachelor's certificates. 58 undergraduate majors. Total enrollment: 8,025. Undergraduates: 5,974. Freshmen: 1,124. Both federal and institutional methodology are used as a basis for awarding need-based institutional aid.

UNDERGRADUATE EXPENSES for 1999–2000 ***Application fee:*** $30. ***Comprehensive fee:*** $20,550 includes full-time tuition ($14,750), mandatory fees ($700), and room and board ($5100). ***College room only:*** $4300. Room and board charges vary according to board plan. ***Part-time tuition:*** $487 per credit. Part-time tuition and fees vary according to course load.

FRESHMAN FINANCIAL AID (Fall 1999, est.) 1062 applied for aid; of those 97% were deemed to have need. 100% of freshmen with need received aid; of those 51% had need fully met. *Average percent of need met:* 74% (excluding resources awarded to replace EFC). *Average financial aid package:* $11,205 (excluding resources awarded to replace EFC). 5% of all full-time freshmen had no need and received non-need-based aid.

UNDERGRADUATE FINANCIAL AID (Fall 1999, est.) 4,266 applied for aid; of those 97% were deemed to have need. 100% of undergraduates with need received aid; of those 51% had need fully met. *Average percent of need met:* 84% (excluding resources awarded to replace EFC). *Average financial aid package:* $13,709 (excluding resources awarded to replace EFC). 4% of all full-time undergraduates had no need and received non-need-based aid.

GIFT AID (NEED-BASED) ***Total amount:*** $37,839,525 (41% Federal, 35% state, 23% institutional, 1% external sources). ***Receiving aid:*** *Freshmen:* 86% (937); *all full-time undergraduates:* 86% (3,765). ***Average award:*** Freshmen: $9199; Undergraduates: $10,578. ***Scholarships, grants, and awards:*** Federal Pell, FSEOG, state, private, college/university gift aid from institutional funds, Scholarships for Disadvantaged Students (Nursing and Pharmacy).

GIFT AID (NON-NEED-BASED) ***Total amount:*** $1,728,765 (97% institutional, 3% external sources). ***Receiving aid:*** *Freshmen:* 36% (391); *Undergraduates:* 36% (1,572). ***Scholarships, grants, and awards by category:*** *Academic Interests/Achievement:* 662 awards ($2,947,223 total): general academic interests/achievements, health fields. *Creative Arts/Performance:* 67 awards ($368,420 total): art/fine arts, cinema/film/broadcasting, dance, music. *Special Achievements/Activities:* 98 awards ($407,117 total): cheerleading/drum major, leadership. *Special Characteristics:* 3,504 awards ($5,099,131 total): children and siblings of alumni, children of faculty/staff, ethnic background, first-generation college students, general special characteristics, international students. ***Tuition waivers:*** Full or partial for employees or children of employees, senior citizens.

LOANS ***Student loans:*** $35,293,967 (79% need-based, 21% non-need-based). 90% of past graduating class borrowed through all loan programs. Average indebtedness per student: $19,380. ***Average need-based loan:*** Freshmen: $4312; Undergraduates: $8534. ***Parent loans:*** $5,397,636 (100% non-need-based). ***Programs:*** Federal Direct (Subsidized and Unsubsidized Stafford, PLUS), Perkins, Federal Health Professions Student Loans, alternative loans.

WORK-STUDY ***Federal work-study:*** *Total amount:* $1,172,034; jobs available.

ATHLETIC AWARDS *Total amount:* 2,079,026 (92% need-based, 8% non-need-based).

APPLYING for FINANCIAL AID ***Required financial aid forms:*** FAFSA, CSS Financial Aid PROFILE. ***Financial aid deadline:*** Continuous. ***Notification date:*** Continuous beginning 4/1. Students must reply by 11/6.

CONTACT Ms. Rose Iannicelli, Dean of Financial Aid, Long Island University, Brooklyn Campus, 1 University Plaza, Brooklyn, NY 11201-8423, 718-488-1037 or toll-free 800-LIU-PLAN (in-state).

LONG ISLAND UNIVERSITY, C.W. POST CAMPUS

Brookville, NY

Tuition & fees: N/R **Average undergraduate aid package: N/A**

ABOUT THE INSTITUTION Independent, coed. Awards: associate, bachelor's, master's, and doctoral degrees. 77 undergraduate majors. Total enrollment: 9,281. Undergraduates: 5,748. Freshmen: 725. Both federal and institutional methodology are used as a basis for awarding need-based institutional aid.

GIFT AID (NEED-BASED) ***Scholarships, grants, and awards:*** Federal Pell, FSEOG, state, private, college/university gift aid from institutional funds.

GIFT AID (NON-NEED-BASED) ***Scholarships, grants, and awards by category:*** *Academic Interests/Achievement:* general academic interests/achievements. *Creative Arts/Performance:* art/fine arts, cinema/film/broadcasting, dance, music, theater/drama. *Special Characteristics:* adult students, children of faculty/staff, international students. ***Tuition waivers:*** Full or partial for employees or children of employees, senior citizens. ***ROTC:*** Army cooperative, Air Force cooperative.

LOANS ***Programs:*** Federal Direct (Subsidized and Unsubsidized Stafford, PLUS), Perkins.

WORK-STUDY Federal work-study jobs available. ***State or other work-study/employment:*** Part-time jobs available.

APPLYING for FINANCIAL AID ***Required financial aid forms:*** FAFSA, CSS Financial Aid PROFILE. ***Financial aid deadline:*** 5/15 (priority: 3/15). ***Notification date:*** Continuous. Students must reply within 2 weeks of notification.

CONTACT Ms. Michele Siskind, Senior Associate Director of Financial Aid, Long Island University, C.W. Post Campus, 720 Northern Boulevard, Brookville, NY 11548-1300, 516-299-3216 or toll-free 800-LIU-PLAN. *E-mail:* michele.siskind@liunet.edu

LONG ISLAND UNIVERSITY, SOUTHAMPTON COLLEGE

Southampton, NY

Tuition & fees: $16,120 **Average undergraduate aid package: $12,874**

ABOUT THE INSTITUTION Independent, coed. Awards: bachelor's and master's degrees. 29 undergraduate majors. Total enrollment: 2,879. Undergraduates: 2,649. Freshmen: 335. Federal methodology is used as a basis for awarding need-based institutional aid.

UNDERGRADUATE EXPENSES for 1999–2000 ***Application fee:*** $30. ***Comprehensive fee:*** $23,910 includes full-time tuition ($15,340), mandatory fees ($780), and room and board ($7790). ***College room only:*** $4200. Full-time tuition and fees vary according to location. Room and board charges vary according to board plan and housing facility. ***Part-time tuition:*** $478 per credit hour. ***Part-time fees:*** $185 per term part-time. Part-time tuition and fees vary according to course load and location. ***Payment plans:*** installment, deferred payment.

FRESHMAN FINANCIAL AID (Fall 1999) 299 applied for aid; of those 87% were deemed to have need. 96% of freshmen with need received aid. 7% of all full-time freshmen had no need and received non-need-based aid.

UNDERGRADUATE FINANCIAL AID (Fall 1999) 1,287 applied for aid; of those 84% were deemed to have need. 93% of undergraduates with need received aid. *Average financial aid package:* $12,874 (excluding resources awarded to replace EFC). 10% of all full-time undergraduates had no need and received non-need-based aid.

Long Island University, Southampton College (continued)

GIFT AID (NEED-BASED) ***Total amount:*** $5,478,421 (27% Federal, 17% state, 56% institutional). ***Receiving aid:*** *Freshmen:* 69% (231); *all full-time undergraduates:* 65% (863). ***Average award:*** Undergraduates: $7211. ***Scholarships, grants, and awards:*** Federal Pell, FSEOG, state, private, college/university gift aid from institutional funds.

GIFT AID (NON-NEED-BASED) ***Total amount:*** $3,962,431 (97% institutional, 3% external sources). ***Receiving aid:*** *Freshmen:* 70% (234); *Undergraduates:* 61% (811). ***Scholarships, grants, and awards by category:*** *Academic Interests/Achievement:* 627 awards ($1,130,868 total): business, education, general academic interests/achievements, humanities, physical sciences, social sciences. *Creative Arts/Performance:* 62 awards ($191,900 total): art/fine arts, creative writing. *Special Characteristics:* 49 awards ($160,352 total): children and siblings of alumni, children of faculty/staff, ethnic background, local/state students, siblings of current students. ***Tuition waivers:*** Full or partial for children of alumni, employees or children of employees, senior citizens.

LOANS ***Student loans:*** $3,325,981 (78% need-based, 22% non-need-based). Average indebtedness per student: $15,235. ***Average need-based loan:*** Undergraduates: $2752. ***Parent loans:*** $1,734,886 (100% non-need-based). ***Programs:*** Federal Direct (Subsidized and Unsubsidized Stafford, PLUS), Perkins, college/university.

WORK-STUDY ***Federal work-study:*** *Total amount:* $356,775; 287 jobs averaging $1200.

ATHLETIC AWARDS *Total amount:* 626,906 (100% non-need-based).

APPLYING for FINANCIAL AID ***Required financial aid forms:*** FAFSA, institution's own form, state aid form. ***Financial aid deadline:*** Continuous. ***Notification date:*** Continuous beginning 3/1. Students must reply by 5/1 or within 4 weeks of notification.

CONTACT Ms. Susan M. Taylor, Director of Financial Aid, Long Island University, Southampton College, 239 Montauk Highway, Southampton, NY 11968-4198, 631-287-8283 or toll-free 800-LIU PLAN Ext. 2. *Fax:* 631-287-8125.

LONGWOOD COLLEGE

Farmville, VA

Tuition & fees (VA res): $3924 **Average undergraduate aid package: $6420**

ABOUT THE INSTITUTION State-supported, coed. Awards: bachelor's and master's degrees. 78 undergraduate majors. Total enrollment: 3,709. Undergraduates: 3,208. Freshmen: 816. Federal methodology is used as a basis for awarding need-based institutional aid.

UNDERGRADUATE EXPENSES for 1999–2000 ***Application fee:*** $25. ***Tuition, state resident:*** full-time $2020; part-time $84 per credit hour. ***Tuition, nonresident:*** full-time $7466; part-time $311 per credit hour. ***Required fees:*** full-time $1904; $31 per credit hour. ***College room and board:*** $4620; ***room only:*** $2710. Room and board charges vary according to board plan. ***Payment plan:*** installment.

FRESHMAN FINANCIAL AID (Fall 1999) 556 applied for aid; of those 69% were deemed to have need. 100% of freshmen with need received aid; of those 26% had need fully met. *Average percent of need met:* 76% (excluding resources awarded to replace EFC). *Average financial aid package:* $5934 (excluding resources awarded to replace EFC). 14% of all full-time freshmen had no need and received non-need-based aid.

UNDERGRADUATE FINANCIAL AID (Fall 1999) 1,910 applied for aid; of those 71% were deemed to have need. 100% of undergraduates with need received aid; of those 39% had need fully met. *Average percent of need met:* 83% (excluding resources awarded to replace EFC). *Average financial aid package:* $6420 (excluding resources awarded to replace EFC). 17% of all full-time undergraduates had no need and received non-need-based aid.

GIFT AID (NEED-BASED) ***Total amount:*** $4,021,033 (32% Federal, 47% state, 16% institutional, 5% external sources). ***Receiving aid:*** *Freshmen:* 44% (344); *all full-time undergraduates:* 41% (1,218). ***Average award:*** Freshmen: $2851; Undergraduates: $2800. ***Scholarships, grants, and awards:*** Federal Pell, FSEOG, state, private, college/university gift aid from institutional funds.

GIFT AID (NON-NEED-BASED) ***Total amount:*** $739,883 (4% state, 69% institutional, 27% external sources). ***Receiving aid:*** *Freshmen:* 4% (30); *Undergraduates:* 4% (131). ***Scholarships, grants, and awards by category:*** *Academic Interests/Achievement:* 233 awards ($279,682 total): business, computer science, education, English, general academic interests/achievements, humanities, mathematics. *Creative Arts/Performance:* 27 awards ($14,802 total): art/fine arts, music, theater/drama. *Special Achievements/Activities:* 14 awards ($13,600 total): memberships. *Special Characteristics:* 39 awards ($84,331 total): children and siblings of alumni, general special characteristics, local/state students. ***Tuition waivers:*** Full or partial for employees or children of employees, senior citizens. ***ROTC:*** Army.

LOANS ***Student loans:*** $8,533,067 (62% need-based, 38% non-need-based). 92% of past graduating class borrowed through all loan programs. Average indebtedness per student: $14,197. ***Average need-based loan:*** Freshmen: $2563; Undergraduates: $3212. ***Parent loans:*** $2,883,085 (16% need-based, 84% non-need-based). ***Programs:*** FFEL (Subsidized and Unsubsidized Stafford, PLUS), Perkins, college/university.

WORK-STUDY ***Federal work-study:*** *Total amount:* $586,994; 418 jobs averaging $1404. ***State or other work-study/employment:*** *Total amount:* $707,624 (100% non-need-based). 433 part-time jobs averaging $1634.

ATHLETIC AWARDS *Total amount:* 443,146 (25% need-based, 75% non-need-based).

APPLYING for FINANCIAL AID ***Required financial aid form:*** FAFSA. ***Financial aid deadline (priority):*** 3/1. ***Notification date:*** Continuous beginning 4/1. Students must reply within 2 weeks of notification.

CONTACT Mr. Jeff Scofield, Director of Financial Aid, Longwood College, 201 High Street, Farmville, VA 23909-1898, 804-395-2077 or toll-free 800-281-4677. *Fax:* 804-395-2829. *E-mail:* jscofiel@longwood.lwc.edu

LORAS COLLEGE

Dubuque, IA

Tuition & fees: $15,350 **Average undergraduate aid package: $14,108**

ABOUT THE INSTITUTION Independent Roman Catholic, coed. Awards: associate, bachelor's, and master's degrees. 60 undergraduate majors. Total enrollment: 1,683. Undergraduates: 1,551. Freshmen: 376. Federal methodology is used as a basis for awarding need-based institutional aid.

UNDERGRADUATE EXPENSES for 2000–2001 (est.) ***Application fee:*** $25. ***Comprehensive fee:*** $21,154 includes full-time tuition ($15,190), mandatory fees ($160), and room and board ($5804). ***College room only:*** $2902. Room and board charges vary according to board plan and housing facility. ***Part-time tuition:*** $344 per credit. ***Payment plan:*** installment.

FRESHMAN FINANCIAL AID (Fall 1999, est.) 420 applied for aid; of those 94% were deemed to have need. 99% of freshmen with need received aid; of those 33% had need fully met. *Average percent of need met:* 90% (excluding resources awarded to replace EFC). *Average financial aid package:* $15,389 (excluding resources awarded to replace EFC). 11% of all full-time freshmen had no need and received non-need-based aid.

UNDERGRADUATE FINANCIAL AID (Fall 1999, est.) 1,400 applied for aid; of those 98% were deemed to have need. 100% of undergraduates with need received aid; of those 33% had need fully met. *Average percent of need met:* 93% (excluding resources awarded to replace EFC). *Average financial aid package:* $14,108 (excluding resources awarded to replace EFC). 4% of all full-time undergraduates had no need and received non-need-based aid.

GIFT AID (NEED-BASED) ***Total amount:*** $7,604,398 (11% Federal, 26% state, 63% institutional). ***Receiving aid:*** *Freshmen:* 77% (339); *all full-time undergraduates:* 69% (986). ***Average award:*** Freshmen: $4264; Undergraduates: $4935. ***Scholarships, grants, and awards:*** Federal Pell, FSEOG, state, college/university gift aid from institutional funds.

GIFT AID (NON-NEED-BASED) ***Total amount:*** $4,150,438 (1% state, 97% institutional, 2% external sources). ***Receiving aid:*** *Freshmen:* 33% (148); *Undergraduates:* 36% (520). ***Scholarships, grants, and awards by category:*** *Academic Interests/Achievement:* engineering/technologies, general academic interests/achievements, physical sciences. *Creative Arts/*

Performance: 20 awards: music. *Special Achievements/Activities:* community service, memberships, religious involvement. *Special Characteristics:* children and siblings of alumni, siblings of current students. ***Tuition waivers:*** Full or partial for children of alumni, employees or children of employees, senior citizens.

LOANS ***Student loans:*** $5,418,570 (70% need-based, 30% non-need-based). 74% of past graduating class borrowed through all loan programs. Average indebtedness per student: $14,728. ***Average need-based loan:*** Freshmen: $3521; Undergraduates: $4025. ***Parent loans:*** $551,441 (100% non-need-based). ***Programs:*** FFEL (Subsidized and Unsubsidized Stafford, PLUS), Perkins, college/university.

WORK-STUDY ***Federal work-study:*** *Total amount:* $267,383; 236 jobs averaging $1133. ***State or other work-study/employment:*** *Total amount:* $168,537 (27% need-based, 73% non-need-based). 110 part-time jobs averaging $1532.

APPLYING for FINANCIAL AID ***Required financial aid form:*** FAFSA. ***Financial aid deadline (priority):*** 4/15. ***Notification date:*** Continuous. Students must reply within 3 weeks of notification.

CONTACT Ms. Julie A. Dunn, Director of Financial Planning, Loras College, 1450 Alta Vista Street, Dubuque, IA 52004-0178, 319-588-7136 or toll-free 800-245-6727. *Fax:* 319-588-7119. *E-mail:* jdunn@loras.edu

LOUISE SALINGER ACADEMY OF FASHION

San Francisco, CA

See Art Institutes International at San Francisco

LOUISIANA COLLEGE

Pineville, LA

Tuition & fees: $7413 **Average undergraduate aid package: N/A**

ABOUT THE INSTITUTION Independent Southern Baptist, coed. Awards: associate and bachelor's degrees. 64 undergraduate majors. Total enrollment: 979. Undergraduates: 979. Freshmen: 269. Federal methodology is used as a basis for awarding need-based institutional aid.

UNDERGRADUATE EXPENSES for 1999–2000 ***Application fee:*** $25. ***Comprehensive fee:*** $10,573 includes full-time tuition ($6912), mandatory fees ($501), and room and board ($3160). ***College room only:*** $1400. Full-time tuition and fees vary according to program. Room and board charges vary according to board plan and housing facility. ***Part-time tuition:*** $216 per credit hour. Part-time tuition and fees vary according to course load and program.

GIFT AID (NEED-BASED) ***Scholarships, grants, and awards:*** Federal Pell, FSEOG, state, private.

GIFT AID (NON-NEED-BASED) ***Scholarships, grants, and awards by category:*** *Academic Interests/Achievement:* business, general academic interests/achievements, health fields, religion/biblical studies. *Creative Arts/Performance:* music, performing arts, theater/drama. *Special Achievements/Activities:* leadership. *Special Characteristics:* children of faculty/staff. ***Tuition waivers:*** Full or partial for employees or children of employees, senior citizens.

LOANS ***Programs:*** FFEL (Subsidized and Unsubsidized Stafford, PLUS), college/university.

WORK-STUDY Federal work-study jobs available.

APPLYING for FINANCIAL AID ***Required financial aid forms:*** FAFSA, institution's own form. ***Financial aid deadline (priority):*** 3/31. ***Notification date:*** 4/30. Students must reply within 2 weeks of notification.

CONTACT Kristi Speir, Financial Aid Director, Louisiana College, 1140 College Drive, Pineville, LA 71359-0001, 318-487-7386 or toll-free 800-487-1906. *Fax:* 318-487-7449.

LOUISIANA STATE UNIVERSITY AND AGRICULTURAL AND MECHANICAL COLLEGE

Baton Rouge, LA

Tuition & fees (LA res): $2881 **Average undergraduate aid package: $5876**

ABOUT THE INSTITUTION State-supported, coed. Awards: bachelor's, master's, doctoral, and first professional degrees and post-master's certificates. 68 undergraduate majors. Total enrollment: 30,966. Undergraduates: 25,911. Freshmen: 5,187. Federal methodology is used as a basis for awarding need-based institutional aid.

UNDERGRADUATE EXPENSES for 1999–2000 ***Application fee:*** $25. ***Tuition, state resident:*** full-time $2301; part-time $495 per term. ***Tuition, nonresident:*** full-time $6501; part-time $1385 per term. ***Required fees:*** full-time $580. ***College room and board:*** $4220; ***room only:*** $2300. Room and board charges vary according to board plan and housing facility. ***Payment plan:*** deferred payment.

FRESHMAN FINANCIAL AID (Fall 1998) 4277 applied for aid; of those 46% were deemed to have need. 99% of freshmen with need received aid; of those 49% had need fully met. *Average percent of need met:* 73% (excluding resources awarded to replace EFC). *Average financial aid package:* $4952 (excluding resources awarded to replace EFC). 52% of all full-time freshmen had no need and received non-need-based aid.

UNDERGRADUATE FINANCIAL AID (Fall 1998) 14,267 applied for aid; of those 56% were deemed to have need. 97% of undergraduates with need received aid; of those 62% had need fully met. *Average percent of need met:* 73% (excluding resources awarded to replace EFC). *Average financial aid package:* $5876 (excluding resources awarded to replace EFC). 43% of all full-time undergraduates had no need and received non-need-based aid.

GIFT AID (NEED-BASED) ***Total amount:*** $11,097,293 (96% Federal, 2% state, 2% institutional). ***Receiving aid:*** *Freshmen:* 19% (906); *all full-time undergraduates:* 22% (4,655). ***Average award:*** Freshmen: $2163; Undergraduates: $2239. ***Scholarships, grants, and awards:*** Federal Pell, FSEOG, state, private, college/university gift aid from institutional funds.

GIFT AID (NON-NEED-BASED) ***Total amount:*** $33,813,315 (1% Federal, 70% state, 25% institutional, 4% external sources). ***Receiving aid:*** *Freshmen:* 37% (1,762); *Undergraduates:* 21% (4,481). ***Scholarships, grants, and awards by category:*** *Academic Interests/Achievement:* agriculture, architecture, biological sciences, business, communication, computer science, education, engineering/technologies, English, foreign languages, general academic interests/achievements, home economics, humanities, mathematics, military science, physical sciences, premedicine. *Creative Arts/Performance:* applied art and design, art/fine arts, journalism/publications, music, performing arts, theater/drama. *Special Achievements/Activities:* leadership. *Special Characteristics:* children and siblings of alumni, children with a deceased or disabled parent, general special characteristics. ***Tuition waivers:*** Full or partial for children of alumni, employees or children of employees, senior citizens. ***ROTC:*** Army, Naval cooperative, Air Force.

LOANS ***Student loans:*** $36,506,462 (56% need-based, 44% non-need-based). 49% of past graduating class borrowed through all loan programs. Average indebtedness per student: $17,093. ***Average need-based loan:*** Freshmen: $2192; Undergraduates: $3545. ***Parent loans:*** $4,773,526 (100% non-need-based). ***Programs:*** FFEL (Subsidized and Unsubsidized Stafford, PLUS), Perkins.

WORK-STUDY ***Federal work-study:*** *Total amount:* $1,233,501; 942 jobs averaging $1309. ***State or other work-study/employment:*** *Total amount:* $11,678,950 (100% non-need-based). 6,131 part-time jobs averaging $1913.

ATHLETIC AWARDS *Total amount:* 3,232,434 (100% non-need-based).

APPLYING for FINANCIAL AID ***Required financial aid form:*** FAFSA. ***Financial aid deadline (priority):*** 4/1. ***Notification date:*** Continuous. Students must reply within 3 weeks of notification.

Louisiana State University and Agricultural and Mechanical College (continued)

CONTACT Judith Vidrine, Associate Director of Financial Aid, Louisiana State University and Agricultural and Mechanical College, LSU 202 Himes Hall, Baton Rouge, LA 70803-3103, 225-388-3103. *Fax:* 225-388-6300. *E-mail:* jvidri1@lsu.edu

LOUISIANA STATE UNIVERSITY HEALTH SCIENCES CENTER

New Orleans, LA

CONTACT Financial Aid Office, Louisiana State University Health Sciences Center, 433 Bolivar Street, New Orleans, LA 70112-2223, 504-568-4808.

LOUISIANA STATE UNIVERSITY IN SHREVEPORT

Shreveport, LA

Tuition & fees (LA res): $2200 **Average undergraduate aid package: N/A**

ABOUT THE INSTITUTION State-supported, coed. Awards: bachelor's and master's degrees. 34 undergraduate majors. Total enrollment: 4,239. Undergraduates: 3,553. Freshmen: 501. Federal methodology Is used as a basis for awarding need-based institutional aid.

UNDERGRADUATE EXPENSES for 1999–2000 ***Application fee:*** $10. ***Tuition, state resident:*** full-time $1950; part-time $225 per course. ***Tuition, nonresident:*** full-time $6110; part-time $715 per course. ***Required fees:*** full-time $250; $5 per credit hour; $65 per term part-time. Full-time tuition and fees vary according to course load. Part-time tuition and fees vary according to course load and location. ***College room and board: room only:*** $4032. Room and board charges vary according to housing facility. ***Payment plan:*** deferred payment.

GIFT AID (NEED-BASED) ***Scholarships, grants, and awards:*** Federal Pell, FSEOG, state, private.

GIFT AID (NON-NEED-BASED) ***Scholarships, grants, and awards by category:*** *Academic Interests/Achievement:* biological sciences, business, computer science, education, English, general academic interests/achievements, premedicine. ***Tuition waivers:*** Full or partial for employees or children of employees, senior citizens. ***ROTC:*** Army.

LOANS ***Programs:*** FFEL (Subsidized and Unsubsidized Stafford, PLUS).

WORK-STUDY Federal work-study jobs available. ***State or other work-study/employment:*** Part-time jobs available.

APPLYING for FINANCIAL AID ***Required financial aid form:*** FAFSA. ***Financial aid deadline (priority):*** 4/1. ***Notification date:*** Continuous. Students must reply by 6/1.

CONTACT Office of Student Financial Aid, Louisiana State University in Shreveport, One University Place, Shreveport, LA 71115-2399, 318-797-5363 or toll-free 800-229-5957 (in-state). *Fax:* 318-797-5366.

LOUISIANA TECH UNIVERSITY

Ruston, LA

Tuition & fees (LA res): $2549 **Average undergraduate aid package: $5675**

ABOUT THE INSTITUTION State-supported, coed. Awards: associate, bachelor's, master's, and doctoral degrees. 68 undergraduate majors. Total enrollment: 10,036. Undergraduates: 8,735. Federal methodology is used as a basis for awarding need-based institutional aid.

UNDERGRADUATE EXPENSES for 1999–2000 ***Application fee:*** $20. ***Tuition, state resident:*** full-time $2379; part-time $546 per term. ***Tuition, nonresident:*** full-time $6759; part-time $1366 per term. ***Required fees:*** full-time $170; $5 per credit hour. Full-time tuition and fees vary according to program. Part-time tuition and fees vary according to course load and program. ***College room and board:*** $3120. Room and board charges vary according to board plan and housing facility.

FRESHMAN FINANCIAL AID (Fall 1999) 1063 applied for aid; of those 65% were deemed to have need. 100% of freshmen with need received aid; of those 19% had need fully met. *Average percent of need met:* 69% (excluding resources awarded to replace EFC). *Average financial aid package:* $4983 (excluding resources awarded to replace EFC). 26% of all full-time freshmen had no need and received non-need-based aid.

UNDERGRADUATE FINANCIAL AID (Fall 1999) 3,633 applied for aid; of those 73% were deemed to have need. 100% of undergraduates with need received aid; of those 13% had need fully met. *Average percent of need met:* 66% (excluding resources awarded to replace EFC). *Average financial aid package:* $5675 (excluding resources awarded to replace EFC).

GIFT AID (NEED-BASED) ***Total amount:*** $8,977,359 (53% Federal, 31% state, 11% institutional, 5% external sources). ***Receiving aid:*** *Freshmen:* 49% (640); *all full-time undergraduates:* 2,270. ***Average award:*** Freshmen: $3686; Undergraduates: $3864. ***Scholarships, grants, and awards:*** Federal Pell, FSEOG, state, private, college/university gift aid from institutional funds.

GIFT AID (NON-NEED-BASED) ***Total amount:*** $3,250,995 (67% state, 22% institutional, 11% external sources). ***Receiving aid:*** *Freshmen:* 10% (126); *Undergraduates:* 339. ***Scholarships, grants, and awards by category:*** *Academic Interests/Achievement:* agriculture, architecture, business, computer science, education, engineering/technologies, general academic interests/achievements, health fields, home economics, humanities, physical sciences. *Creative Arts/Performance:* debating, journalism/publications, music, performing arts, theater/drama. *Special Achievements/Activities:* cheerleading/drum major. *Special Characteristics:* children of faculty/staff, children with a deceased or disabled parent, out-of-state students, public servants, spouses of deceased or disabled public servants. ***Tuition waivers:*** Full or partial for children of alumni, employees or children of employees, senior citizens. ***ROTC:*** Army cooperative, Air Force.

LOANS ***Student loans:*** $15,882,803 (71% need-based, 29% non-need-based). 82% of past graduating class borrowed through all loan programs. ***Average need-based loan:*** Freshmen: $1855; Undergraduates: $2910. ***Parent loans:*** $1,925,303 (30% need-based, 70% non-need-based). ***Programs:*** FFEL (Subsidized and Unsubsidized Stafford, PLUS), Perkins, Federal Nursing.

WORK-STUDY ***Federal work-study:*** *Total amount:* $616,127; 328 jobs averaging $1903. ***State or other work-study/employment:*** 1,066 part-time jobs available.

ATHLETIC AWARDS *Total amount:* 829,522 (88% need-based, 12% non-need-based).

APPLYING for FINANCIAL AID ***Required financial aid forms:*** FAFSA, institution's own form. ***Financial aid deadline (priority):*** 4/15. ***Notification date:*** Continuous beginning 5/15. Students must reply within 2 weeks of notification.

CONTACT Financial Aid Office, Louisiana Tech University, PO Box 7925, Ruston, LA 71272, 318-257-2641 or toll-free 800-LATECH1. *Fax:* 318-257-2628. *E-mail:* techaid@ltfa.latech.edu

LOURDES COLLEGE

Sylvania, OH

Tuition & fees: $9368 **Average undergraduate aid package: $10,226**

ABOUT THE INSTITUTION Independent Roman Catholic, coed. Awards: associate and bachelor's degrees. 23 undergraduate majors. Total enrollment: 1,258. Undergraduates: 1,258. Freshmen: 81. Federal methodology is used as a basis for awarding need-based institutional aid.

UNDERGRADUATE EXPENSES for 1999–2000 ***Application fee:*** $30. ***Tuition:*** full-time $8768; part-time $274 per credit hour. ***Required fees:*** full-time $600; $25 per credit hour. Full-time tuition and fees vary according to course load and program. Part-time tuition and fees vary according to course load and program. ***Payment plans:*** installment, deferred payment.

FRESHMAN FINANCIAL AID (Fall 1998) 33 applied for aid; of those 91% were deemed to have need. 97% of freshmen with need received aid. *Average percent of need met:* 53% (excluding resources awarded to replace EFC). *Average financial aid package:* $7899 (excluding resources awarded to replace EFC). 6% of all full-time freshmen had no need and received non-need-based aid.

UNDERGRADUATE FINANCIAL AID (Fall 1998) 422 applied for aid; of those 86% were deemed to have need. 100% of undergraduates with need received aid; of those 9% had need fully met. *Average percent of need met:* 53% (excluding resources awarded to replace EFC). *Average financial aid package:* $10,226 (excluding resources awarded to replace EFC). 6% of all full-time undergraduates had no need and received non-need-based aid.

GIFT AID (NEED-BASED) ***Total amount:*** $1,537,111 (57% Federal, 35% state, 6% institutional, 2% external sources). ***Receiving aid:*** *Freshmen:* 72% (26); *all full-time undergraduates:* 72% (314). ***Average award:*** Freshmen: $3276; Undergraduates: $3927. ***Scholarships, grants, and awards:*** Federal Pell, FSEOG, state, private, college/university gift aid from institutional funds.

GIFT AID (NON-NEED-BASED) ***Total amount:*** $619,142 (48% state, 46% institutional, 6% external sources). ***Receiving aid:*** *Freshmen:* 81% (29); *Undergraduates:* 76% (332). ***Scholarships, grants, and awards by category:*** *Academic Interests/Achievement:* general academic interests/achievements. *Creative Arts/Performance:* art/fine arts, music. *Special Achievements/Activities:* general special achievements/activities. *Special Characteristics:* children and siblings of alumni, children of faculty/staff, international students, local/state students, members of minority groups. ***Tuition waivers:*** Full or partial for employees or children of employees, senior citizens. ***ROTC:*** Army cooperative.

LOANS ***Student loans:*** $3,903,833 (54% need-based, 46% non-need-based). ***Average need-based loan:*** Freshmen: $2207; Undergraduates: $4106. ***Parent loans:*** $44,107 (100% non-need-based). ***Programs:*** FFEL (Subsidized and Unsubsidized Stafford, PLUS), Perkins, state, college/university.

WORK-STUDY ***Federal work-study:*** *Total amount:* $59,057; jobs available.

APPLYING for FINANCIAL AID ***Required financial aid forms:*** FAFSA, institution's own form. ***Financial aid deadline (priority):*** 3/1. ***Notification date:*** Continuous beginning 5/1. Students must reply within 2 weeks of notification.

CONTACT Ms. Pamela Curavo, Director of Financial Aid, Lourdes College, 6832 Convent Boulevard, Sylvania, OH 43560-2898, 419-885-3211 or toll-free 800-878-3210. *Fax:* 419-882-3987. *E-mail:* pcuravo@lourdes.edu

LOYOLA COLLEGE IN MARYLAND

Baltimore, MD

Tuition & fees: $18,830 **Average undergraduate aid package: $13,625**

ABOUT THE INSTITUTION Independent Roman Catholic (Jesuit), coed. Awards: bachelor's, master's, and doctoral degrees and post-bachelor's and post-master's certificates. 32 undergraduate majors. Total enrollment: 6,263. Undergraduates: 3,377. Freshmen: 940. Institutional methodology is used as a basis for awarding need-based institutional aid.

UNDERGRADUATE EXPENSES for 2000–2001 ***Application fee:*** $30. ***Comprehensive fee:*** $26,430 includes full-time tuition ($18,310), mandatory fees ($520), and room and board ($7600). Full-time tuition and fees vary according to student level. Room and board charges vary according to board plan and housing facility. ***Part-time tuition:*** $365 per credit. ***Part-time fees:*** $25 per term part-time. ***Payment plan:*** guaranteed tuition.

FRESHMAN FINANCIAL AID (Fall 1999) 662 applied for aid; of those 69% were deemed to have need. 100% of freshmen with need received aid; of those 93% had need fully met. *Average percent of need met:* 97% (excluding resources awarded to replace EFC). *Average financial aid package:* $14,020 (excluding resources awarded to replace EFC). 15% of all full-time freshmen had no need and received non-need-based aid.

UNDERGRADUATE FINANCIAL AID (Fall 1999) 1,991 applied for aid; of those 72% were deemed to have need. 94% of undergraduates with need received aid; of those 97% had need fully met. *Average percent of need met:* 98% (excluding resources awarded to replace EFC). *Average financial aid package:* $13,625 (excluding resources awarded to replace EFC). 16% of all full-time undergraduates had no need and received non-need-based aid.

GIFT AID (NEED-BASED) ***Total amount:*** $12,815,500 (7% Federal, 6% state, 84% institutional, 3% external sources). ***Receiving aid:*** *Freshmen:* 34% (323); *all full-time undergraduates:* 32% (1,013). ***Average award:*** Freshmen: $10,285; Undergraduates: $8030. ***Scholarships, grants, and awards:*** Federal Pell, FSEOG, state, private, college/university gift aid from institutional funds.

GIFT AID (NON-NEED-BASED) ***Total amount:*** $2,642,900 (6% Federal, 6% state, 77% institutional, 11% external sources). ***Receiving aid:*** *Freshmen:* 24% (221); *Undergraduates:* 20% (642). ***Scholarships, grants, and awards by category:*** *Academic Interests/Achievement:* general academic interests/achievements. *Special Characteristics:* local/state students, members of minority groups. ***Tuition waivers:*** Full or partial for employees or children of employees. ***ROTC:*** Army, Air Force cooperative.

LOANS ***Student loans:*** $7,465,000 (74% need-based, 26% non-need-based). 65% of past graduating class borrowed through all loan programs. Average indebtedness per student: $15,020. ***Average need-based loan:*** Freshmen: $1985; Undergraduates: $3845. ***Parent loans:*** $6,334,300 (100% non-need-based). ***Programs:*** Federal Direct (Subsidized and Unsubsidized Stafford, PLUS), Perkins.

WORK-STUDY ***Federal work-study:*** *Total amount:* $656,300; 377 jobs averaging $1750. ***State or other work-study/employment:*** *Total amount:* $450,300 (56% need-based, 44% non-need-based). 57 part-time jobs available.

ATHLETIC AWARDS *Total amount:* 2,277,800 (27% need-based, 73% non-need-based).

APPLYING for FINANCIAL AID ***Required financial aid forms:*** FAFSA, CSS Financial Aid PROFILE, noncustodial (divorced/separated) parent's statement, business/farm supplement. ***Financial aid deadline:*** 2/1. ***Notification date:*** 4/10. Students must reply by 5/1.

CONTACT Mr. Mark L. Lindenmeyer, Director of Financial Aid, Loyola College in Maryland, 4501 North Charles Street, Baltimore, MD 21210-2699, 410-617-2576 or toll-free 800-221-9107 Ext. 2252 (in-state). *Fax:* 410-617-5149. *E-mail:* lindenmeyer@loyola.edu

LOYOLA MARYMOUNT UNIVERSITY

Los Angeles, CA

Tuition & fees: $19,225 **Average undergraduate aid package: $18,241**

ABOUT THE INSTITUTION Independent Roman Catholic, coed. Awards: bachelor's, master's, and first professional degrees. 39 undergraduate majors. Total enrollment: 7,305. Undergraduates: 4,727. Freshmen: 1,024. Institutional methodology is used as a basis for awarding need-based institutional aid.

UNDERGRADUATE EXPENSES for 2000–2001 ***Application fee:*** $40. ***Comprehensive fee:*** $26,833 includes full-time tuition ($19,100), mandatory fees ($125), and room and board ($7608). ***College room only:*** $4328. Full-time tuition and fees vary according to course load. Room and board charges vary according to board plan and housing facility. ***Part-time tuition:*** $795 per unit. ***Part-time fees:*** $2 per unit; $14 per term part-time. Part-time tuition and fees vary according to course load. ***Payment plan:*** installment.

FRESHMAN FINANCIAL AID (Fall 1999, est.) 772 applied for aid; of those 92% were deemed to have need. 100% of freshmen with need received aid; of those 28% had need fully met. *Average percent of need met:* 97% (excluding resources awarded to replace EFC). *Average financial aid package:* $18,484 (excluding resources awarded to replace EFC). 7% of all full-time freshmen had no need and received non-need-based aid.

UNDERGRADUATE FINANCIAL AID (Fall 1999, est.) 3,227 applied for aid; of those 83% were deemed to have need. 94% of undergraduates with need received aid; of those 39% had need fully met. *Average percent of need met:* 96% (excluding resources awarded to replace EFC). *Average financial aid package:* $18,241 (excluding resources awarded to replace EFC). 6% of all full-time undergraduates had no need and received non-need-based aid.

Loyola Marymount University (continued)

GIFT AID (NEED-BASED) ***Total amount:*** $24,555,672 (20% Federal, 27% state, 53% institutional). ***Receiving aid:*** *Freshmen:* 54% (549); *all full-time undergraduates:* 50% (2,221). ***Average award:*** Freshmen: $12,743; Undergraduates: $12,978. ***Scholarships, grants, and awards:*** Federal Pell, FSEOG, state, private, college/university gift aid from institutional funds.

GIFT AID (NON-NEED-BASED) ***Total amount:*** $1,524,000 (84% institutional, 16% external sources). ***Receiving aid:*** *Freshmen:* 3% (34); *Undergraduates:* 4% (191). ***Scholarships, grants, and awards by category:*** *Academic Interests/Achievement:* general academic interests/achievements. *Creative Arts/Performance:* debating, music. *Special Achievements/Activities:* community service, religious involvement. *Special Characteristics:* children of faculty/staff. ***Tuition waivers:*** Full or partial for employees or children of employees. ***ROTC:*** Army cooperative, Naval cooperative, Air Force.

LOANS ***Student loans:*** $18,960,559 (66% need-based, 34% non-need-based). 68% of past graduating class borrowed through all loan programs. Average indebtedness per student: $18,426. ***Average need-based loan:*** Freshmen: $2740; Undergraduates: $2120. ***Parent loans:*** $7,920,000 (100% non-need-based). ***Programs:*** FFEL (Subsidized and Unsubsidized Stafford, PLUS), Perkins, college/university.

WORK-STUDY ***Federal work-study:*** *Total amount:* $4,710,425; jobs available. ***State or other work-study/employment:*** *Total amount:* $2,297,675 (100% non-need-based). Part-time jobs available.

ATHLETIC AWARDS *Total amount:* 2,652,169 (100% non-need-based).

APPLYING for FINANCIAL AID ***Required financial aid forms:*** FAFSA, CSS Financial Aid PROFILE. ***Financial aid deadline (priority):*** 2/15. ***Notification date:*** Continuous beginning 3/15. Students must reply within 2 weeks of notification.

CONTACT Ms. Darlene Wilson, Financial Aid Counselor, Loyola Marymount University, 7900 Loyola Boulevard, Los Angeles, CA 90045-8350, 310-338-2753 or toll-free 800-LMU-INFO. *E-mail:* dwilson@lmumail.lmu.edu

LOYOLA UNIVERSITY CHICAGO

Chicago, IL

Tuition & fees: $18,310 **Average undergraduate aid package: $17,834**

ABOUT THE INSTITUTION Independent Roman Catholic (Jesuit), coed. Awards: bachelor's, master's, doctoral, and first professional degrees (also offers adult part-time program with significant enrollment not reflected in profile). 45 undergraduate majors. Total enrollment: 13,359. Undergraduates: 7,596. Freshmen: 1,067. Federal methodology is used as a basis for awarding need-based institutional aid.

UNDERGRADUATE EXPENSES for 1999–2000 ***Application fee:*** $25. ***Comprehensive fee:*** $25,316 includes full-time tuition ($17,750), mandatory fees ($560), and room and board ($7006). ***College room only:*** $5206. Room and board charges vary according to board plan and housing facility. ***Part-time tuition:*** $350 per semester hour. ***Part-time fees:*** $57 per term part-time. Part-time tuition and fees vary according to course load. ***Payment plan:*** installment.

FRESHMAN FINANCIAL AID (Fall 1999) 936 applied for aid; of those 82% were deemed to have need. 99% of freshmen with need received aid; of those 31% had need fully met. *Average percent of need met:* 87% (excluding resources awarded to replace EFC). *Average financial aid package:* $17,876 (excluding resources awarded to replace EFC). 13% of all full-time freshmen had no need and received non-need-based aid.

UNDERGRADUATE FINANCIAL AID (Fall 1999) 4,641 applied for aid; of those 81% were deemed to have need. 99% of undergraduates with need received aid; of those 40% had need fully met. *Average percent of need met:* 87% (excluding resources awarded to replace EFC). *Average financial aid package:* $17,834 (excluding resources awarded to replace EFC). 13% of all full-time undergraduates had no need and received non-need-based aid.

GIFT AID (NEED-BASED) ***Total amount:*** $35,984,229 (11% Federal, 24% state, 63% institutional, 2% external sources). ***Receiving aid:*** *Freshmen:* 70% (745); *all full-time undergraduates:* 61% (3,499). ***Average award:*** Freshmen: $13,060; Undergraduates: $11,510. ***Scholarships, grants, and awards:*** Federal Pell, FSEOG, state, private, college/university gift aid from institutional funds.

GIFT AID (NON-NEED-BASED) ***Total amount:*** $5,743,615 (1% state, 95% institutional, 4% external sources). ***Receiving aid:*** *Freshmen:* 8% (83); *Undergraduates:* 6% (334). ***Scholarships, grants, and awards by category:*** *Academic Interests/Achievement:* 50 awards ($100,000 total): area/ethnic studies, biological sciences, business, communication, computer science, education, English, foreign languages, general academic interests/achievements, health fields, humanities, international studies, mathematics, physical sciences, premedicine, social sciences. *Creative Arts/Performance:* 50 awards ($100,000 total): art/fine arts, debating, journalism/publications, music, theater/drama. *Special Achievements/Activities:* 25 awards ($75,000 total): community service, general special achievements/activities, leadership, memberships. *Special Characteristics:* 10 awards ($20,000 total): adult students, ethnic background, general special characteristics, religious affiliation, veterans. ***Tuition waivers:*** Full or partial for employees or children of employees. ***ROTC:*** Army cooperative, Naval cooperative, Air Force cooperative.

LOANS ***Student loans:*** $20,020,262 (71% need-based, 29% non-need-based). 64% of past graduating class borrowed through all loan programs. Average indebtedness per student: $18,300. ***Average need-based loan:*** Freshmen: $2860; Undergraduates: $4270. ***Parent loans:*** $3,421,059 (25% need-based, 75% non-need-based). ***Programs:*** FFEL (Subsidized and Unsubsidized Stafford, PLUS), Perkins, Federal Nursing, state, college/university, alternative loans.

WORK-STUDY ***Federal work-study:*** *Total amount:* $3,245,299; 2,100 jobs averaging $2020.

ATHLETIC AWARDS *Total amount:* 1,925,873 (52% need-based, 48% non-need-based).

APPLYING for FINANCIAL AID ***Required financial aid form:*** FAFSA. ***Financial aid deadline (priority):*** 3/1. ***Notification date:*** Continuous beginning 3/2. Students must reply within 3 weeks of notification.

CONTACT Mr. Terry Richards, Director of Financial Aid, Loyola University Chicago, 6525 North Sheridan Road, Granada Centre 360, Chicago, IL 60626, 773-508-3155 or toll-free 800-262-2373. *Fax:* 773-508-3397. *E-mail:* tricha@luc.edu

LOYOLA UNIVERSITY NEW ORLEANS

New Orleans, LA

Tuition & fees: $15,481 **Average undergraduate aid package: $13,122**

ABOUT THE INSTITUTION Independent Roman Catholic (Jesuit), coed. Awards: bachelor's, master's, and first professional degrees. 50 undergraduate majors. Total enrollment: 5,008. Undergraduates: 3,478. Freshmen: 814. Federal methodology is used as a basis for awarding need-based institutional aid.

UNDERGRADUATE EXPENSES for 2000–2001 ***Application fee:*** $20. ***Comprehensive fee:*** $21,597 includes full-time tuition ($14,989), mandatory fees ($492), and room and board ($6116). ***College room only:*** $3638. Room and board charges vary according to board plan and housing facility. ***Part-time tuition:*** $530 per credit hour. ***Payment plan:*** installment.

FRESHMAN FINANCIAL AID (Fall 1999) 624 applied for aid; of those 75% were deemed to have need. 100% of freshmen with need received aid; of those 43% had need fully met. *Average percent of need met:* 96% (excluding resources awarded to replace EFC). *Average financial aid package:* $13,633 (excluding resources awarded to replace EFC). 19% of all full-time freshmen had no need and received non-need-based aid.

UNDERGRADUATE FINANCIAL AID (Fall 1999) 1,936 applied for aid; of those 81% were deemed to have need. 99% of undergraduates with need received aid; of those 35% had need fully met. *Average percent of need met:* 86% (excluding resources awarded to replace EFC). *Average financial aid package:* $13,122 (excluding resources awarded to replace EFC). 13% of all full-time undergraduates had no need and received non-need-based aid.

GIFT AID (NEED-BASED) ***Total amount:*** $5,024,380 (31% Federal, 69% institutional). ***Receiving aid:*** *Freshmen:* 36% (283); *all full-time undergraduates:* 40% (1,090). ***Average award:*** Freshmen: $3749; Undergraduates: $4521. ***Scholarships, grants, and awards:*** Federal Pell, FSEOG, college/university gift aid from institutional funds.

GIFT AID (NON-NEED-BASED) ***Total amount:*** $16,035,398 (11% state, 86% institutional, 3% external sources). ***Receiving aid:*** *Freshmen:* 54% (434); *Undergraduates:* 43% (1,168). ***Scholarships, grants, and awards by category:*** *Academic Interests/Achievement:* business, general academic interests/achievements, social sciences. *Creative Arts/Performance:* art/fine arts, music, theater/drama. *Special Characteristics:* children of faculty/staff. ***Tuition waivers:*** Full or partial for employees or children of employees, senior citizens. ***ROTC:*** Army cooperative, Naval cooperative, Air Force cooperative.

LOANS ***Student loans:*** $6,185,958 (71% need-based, 29% non-need-based). 54% of past graduating class borrowed through all loan programs. Average indebtedness per student: $15,887. ***Average need-based loan:*** Freshmen: $2532; Undergraduates: $3958. ***Parent loans:*** $1,696,778 (100% non-need-based). ***Programs:*** Federal Direct (Subsidized and Unsubsidized Stafford, PLUS), Perkins.

WORK-STUDY ***Federal work-study:*** *Total amount:* $1,005,009; 540 jobs averaging $1841.

APPLYING for FINANCIAL AID ***Required financial aid form:*** FAFSA. ***Financial aid deadline (priority):*** 5/1. ***Notification date:*** Continuous. Students must reply within 4 weeks of notification.

CONTACT Wallace P. Boudet III, Director of Scholarships and Financial Aid, Loyola University New Orleans, 6363 Saint Charles Avenue, Box 206, New Orleans, LA 70118-6195, 504-865-3231 or toll-free 800-4-LOYOLA. *Fax:* 504-865-3233. *E-mail:* finaid@loyno.edu

LUBBOCK CHRISTIAN UNIVERSITY

Lubbock, TX

Tuition & fees: $9316 **Average undergraduate aid package: $10,924**

ABOUT THE INSTITUTION Independent religious, coed. Awards: bachelor's and master's degrees. 32 undergraduate majors. Total enrollment: 1,461. Undergraduates: 1,368. Freshmen: 352. Federal methodology is used as a basis for awarding need-based institutional aid.

UNDERGRADUATE EXPENSES for 1999–2000 ***Application fee:*** $20. ***Comprehensive fee:*** $13,016 includes full-time tuition ($8760), mandatory fees ($556), and room and board ($3700). Full-time tuition and fees vary according to program. Room and board charges vary according to board plan and housing facility. ***Part-time tuition:*** $129 per credit hour. ***Part-time fees:*** $148 per term part-time. Part-time tuition and fees vary according to course load and program. ***Payment plans:*** tuition prepayment, installment.

FRESHMAN FINANCIAL AID (Fall 1999) 249 applied for aid; of those 85% were deemed to have need. 100% of freshmen with need received aid; of those 42% had need fully met. *Average percent of need met:* 87% (excluding resources awarded to replace EFC). *Average financial aid package:* $10,314 (excluding resources awarded to replace EFC). 28% of all full-time freshmen had no need and received non-need-based aid.

UNDERGRADUATE FINANCIAL AID (Fall 1999) 847 applied for aid; of those 88% were deemed to have need. 100% of undergraduates with need received aid; of those 42% had need fully met. *Average percent of need met:* 90% (excluding resources awarded to replace EFC). *Average financial aid package:* $10,924 (excluding resources awarded to replace EFC). 34% of all full-time undergraduates had no need and received non-need-based aid.

GIFT AID (NEED-BASED) ***Total amount:*** $4,113,584 (28% Federal, 28% state, 37% institutional, 7% external sources). ***Receiving aid:*** *Freshmen:* 72% (211); *all full-time undergraduates:* 63% (709). ***Average award:*** Freshmen: $6239; Undergraduates: $5391. ***Scholarships, grants, and awards:*** Federal Pell, FSEOG, state, private, college/university gift aid from institutional funds.

GIFT AID (NON-NEED-BASED) ***Total amount:*** $635,652 (1% Federal, 89% institutional, 10% external sources). ***Receiving aid:*** *Freshmen:* 8% (24); *Undergraduates:* 5% (55). ***Scholarships, grants, and awards by category:*** *Academic Interests/Achievement:* agriculture, business, communication, computer science, education, English, foreign languages, general academic interests/achievements, humanities, physical sciences, religion/biblical studies, social sciences. *Creative Arts/Performance:* art/fine arts, journalism/publications, music, performing arts, theater/drama. *Special Achievements/Activities:* cheerleading/drum major, leadership. *Special Characteristics:* general special characteristics. ***ROTC:*** Army cooperative, Naval cooperative, Air Force cooperative.

LOANS ***Student loans:*** $6,521,599 (77% need-based, 23% non-need-based). ***Average need-based loan:*** Freshmen: $3239; Undergraduates: $4912. ***Parent loans:*** $1,774,788 (33% need-based, 67% non-need-based). ***Programs:*** FFEL (Subsidized and Unsubsidized Stafford, PLUS), Perkins.

WORK-STUDY ***Federal work-study:*** *Total amount:* $590,583; jobs available. ***State or other work-study/employment:*** Part-time jobs available.

ATHLETIC AWARDS *Total amount:* 633,274 (39% need-based, 61% non-need-based).

APPLYING for FINANCIAL AID ***Required financial aid forms:*** FAFSA, institution's own form. ***Financial aid deadline (priority):*** 6/15. ***Notification date:*** Continuous. Students must reply within 2 weeks of notification.

CONTACT Tia Clary, Financial Aid Director, Lubbock Christian University, 5601 19th Street, Lubbock, TX 79407, 806-796-8800 Ext. 267 or toll-free 800-933-7601 Ext. 260. *Fax:* 806-796-8925. *E-mail:* tia.clary@lcu.edu

LUTHERAN BIBLE INSTITTUE OF SEATTLE

Issaquah, WA

See Trinity Lutheran College

LUTHERAN COLLEGE OF HEALTH PROFESSIONS

Fort Wayne, IN

See University of Saint Francis

LUTHER COLLEGE

Decorah, IA

Tuition & fees: $17,290 **Average undergraduate aid package: $14,316**

ABOUT THE INSTITUTION Independent religious, coed. Awards: bachelor's degrees. 96 undergraduate majors. Total enrollment: 2,550. Undergraduates: 2,550. Freshmen: 608. Federal methodology is used as a basis for awarding need-based institutional aid.

UNDERGRADUATE EXPENSES for 1999–2000 ***Application fee:*** $25. ***Comprehensive fee:*** $21,100 includes full-time tuition ($17,290) and room and board ($3810). ***College room only:*** $1980. Full-time tuition and fees vary according to course load. ***Part-time tuition:*** $618 per semester hour. Part-time tuition and fees vary according to course load. ***Payment plan:*** installment.

FRESHMAN FINANCIAL AID (Fall 1999, est.) 534 applied for aid; of those 78% were deemed to have need. 100% of freshmen with need received aid; of those 33% had need fully met. *Average percent of need met:* 89% (excluding resources awarded to replace EFC). *Average financial aid package:* $14,054 (excluding resources awarded to replace EFC). 23% of all full-time freshmen had no need and received non-need-based aid.

UNDERGRADUATE FINANCIAL AID (Fall 1999, est.) 1,873 applied for aid; of those 87% were deemed to have need. 100% of undergraduates with need received aid; of those 29% had need fully met. *Average percent of need met:* 88% (excluding resources awarded to replace EFC). *Average financial aid package:* $14,316 (excluding resources awarded to replace EFC). 22% of all full-time undergraduates had no need and received non-need-based aid.

GIFT AID (NEED-BASED) ***Total amount:*** $14,968,783 (9% Federal, 13% state, 72% institutional, 6% external sources). ***Receiving aid:*** *Freshmen:*

Luther College (continued)

68% (415); *all full-time undergraduates:* 65% (1,622). ***Average award:*** Freshmen: $7163; Undergraduates: $6910. ***Scholarships, grants, and awards:*** Federal Pell, FSEOG, state, private, college/university gift aid from institutional funds.

GIFT AID (NON-NEED-BASED) ***Total amount:*** $4,460,906 (1% Federal, 1% state, 90% institutional, 8% external sources). ***Receiving aid:*** *Freshmen:* 50% (302); *Undergraduates:* 41% (1,024). ***Scholarships, grants, and awards by category:*** *Academic Interests/Achievement:* 1,200 awards ($6,361,500 total): general academic interests/achievements. *Creative Arts/Performance:* 633 awards ($616,360 total): music. *Special Characteristics:* 395 awards ($165,100 total): religious affiliation. ***Tuition waivers:*** Full or partial for employees or children of employees.

LOANS ***Student loans:*** $8,072,488 (81% need-based, 19% non-need-based). 69% of past graduating class borrowed through all loan programs. Average indebtedness per student: $16,942. ***Average need-based loan:*** Freshmen: $3102; Undergraduates: $3956. ***Parent loans:*** $1,721,519 (100% non-need-based). ***Programs:*** Federal Direct (Subsidized and Unsubsidized Stafford, PLUS), Perkins, college/university.

WORK-STUDY ***Federal work-study:*** *Total amount:* $948,950; 638 jobs averaging $1487. ***State or other work-study/employment:*** *Total amount:* $1,647,831 (28% need-based, 72% non-need-based). 1,100 part-time jobs averaging $1463.

APPLYING for FINANCIAL AID ***Required financial aid forms:*** FAFSA, institution's own form. ***Financial aid deadline (priority):*** 3/1. ***Notification date:*** Continuous beginning 4/1. Students must reply by 5/1 or within 4 weeks of notification.

CONTACT Ms. Janice Cordell, Director of Student Financial Planning, Luther College, 700 College Drive, Decorah, IA 52101-1045, 319-387-1018 or toll-free 800-458-8437. *Fax:* 319-387-2159. *E-mail:* cordellj@luther.edu

LUTHER RICE BIBLE COLLEGE AND SEMINARY

Lithonia, GA

CONTACT Dr. Dennis Vines, Director of Financial Aid, Luther Rice Bible College and Seminary, 3038 Evans Mill Road, Lithonia, GA 30038-2418, 770-484-1204 or toll-free 800-442-1577.

LYCOMING COLLEGE

Williamsport, PA

Tuition & fees: $17,600 — **Average undergraduate aid package: $14,323**

ABOUT THE INSTITUTION Independent United Methodist, coed. Awards: bachelor's degrees. 49 undergraduate majors. Total enrollment: 1,534. Undergraduates: 1,534. Freshmen: 394. Federal methodology is used as a basis for awarding need-based institutional aid.

UNDERGRADUATE EXPENSES for 1999–2000 ***Application fee:*** $25. ***Comprehensive fee:*** $22,560 includes full-time tuition ($17,520), mandatory fees ($80), and room and board ($4960). ***Part-time tuition:*** $548 per credit. ***Payment plan:*** installment.

FRESHMAN FINANCIAL AID (Fall 1999) 378 applied for aid; of those 90% were deemed to have need. 100% of freshmen with need received aid; of those 24% had need fully met. *Average percent of need met:* 78% (excluding resources awarded to replace EFC). *Average financial aid package:* $13,605 (excluding resources awarded to replace EFC). 7% of all full-time freshmen had no need and received non-need-based aid.

UNDERGRADUATE FINANCIAL AID (Fall 1999) 1,340 applied for aid; of those 88% were deemed to have need. 100% of undergraduates with need received aid; of those 27% had need fully met. *Average percent of need met:* 82% (excluding resources awarded to replace EFC). *Average financial aid package:* $14,323 (excluding resources awarded to replace EFC). 7% of all full-time undergraduates had no need and received non-need-based aid.

GIFT AID (NEED-BASED) ***Total amount:*** $13,001,461 (7% Federal, 14% state, 76% institutional, 3% external sources). ***Receiving aid:*** *Freshmen:* 86% (339); *all full-time undergraduates:* 84% (1,172). ***Average award:*** Freshmen: $11,374; Undergraduates: $10,996. ***Scholarships, grants, and awards:*** Federal Pell, FSEOG, state, private, college/university gift aid from institutional funds.

GIFT AID (NON-NEED-BASED) ***Total amount:*** $939,288 (100% institutional). ***Receiving aid:*** *Freshmen:* 12% (49); *Undergraduates:* 6% (78). ***Scholarships, grants, and awards by category:*** *Academic Interests/Achievement:* 597 awards ($4,027,234 total): biological sciences, business, communication, computer science, education, English, foreign languages, general academic interests/achievements, health fields, humanities, international studies, mathematics, physical sciences, premedicine, religion/biblical studies, social sciences. *Creative Arts/Performance:* 159 awards ($264,700 total): art/fine arts, creative writing, music, theater/drama. *Special Achievements/Activities:* 4 awards ($10,000 total): leadership. *Special Characteristics:* 46 awards ($616,763 total): children of educators, children of faculty/staff, relatives of clergy. ***Tuition waivers:*** Full or partial for employees or children of employees. ***ROTC:*** Army cooperative.

LOANS ***Student loans:*** $5,597,451 (72% need-based, 28% non-need-based). 94% of past graduating class borrowed through all loan programs. Average indebtedness per student: $14,900. ***Average need-based loan:*** Freshmen: $3006; Undergraduates: $3992. ***Parent loans:*** $2,030,128 (100% need-based). ***Programs:*** FFEL (Subsidized and Unsubsidized Stafford, PLUS), Perkins, college/university.

WORK-STUDY ***Federal work-study:*** *Total amount:* $294,493; 537 jobs averaging $607. ***State or other work-study/employment:*** *Total amount:* $215,000 (100% non-need-based). Part-time jobs available.

APPLYING for FINANCIAL AID ***Required financial aid forms:*** FAFSA, institution's own form. ***Financial aid deadline (priority):*** 4/15. ***Notification date:*** Continuous. Students must reply by 5/1 or within 4 weeks of notification.

CONTACT Mr. Benjamin H. Comfort III, Director of Financial Aid, Lycoming College, 700 College Place, Long Hall, Williamsport, PA 17701-5192, 570-321-4040 or toll-free 800-345-3920. *Fax:* 570-321-4337. *E-mail:* comfort@lycoming.edu

LYME ACADEMY OF FINE ARTS

Old Lyme, CT

Tuition & fees: $10,550 — **Average undergraduate aid package: N/A**

ABOUT THE INSTITUTION Independent, coed. Awards: bachelor's degrees. 3 undergraduate majors. Total enrollment: 171. Undergraduates: 171. Freshmen: 8. Both federal and institutional methodology are used as a basis for awarding need-based institutional aid.

UNDERGRADUATE EXPENSES for 1999–2000 ***Application fee:*** $35. ***Tuition:*** full-time $10,500; part-time $438 per credit. ***Required fees:*** full-time $50; $45 per term part-time. ***Payment plan:*** installment.

FRESHMAN FINANCIAL AID (Fall 1999) 8 applied for aid; of those 100% were deemed to have need. 100% of freshmen with need received aid.

UNDERGRADUATE FINANCIAL AID (Fall 1999) 48 applied for aid; of those 100% were deemed to have need. 100% of undergraduates with need received aid.

GIFT AID (NEED-BASED) ***Total amount:*** $145,423 (21% Federal, 49% state, 30% external sources). ***Scholarships, grants, and awards:*** Federal Pell, FSEOG, state, private, college/university gift aid from institutional funds.

GIFT AID (NON-NEED-BASED) ***Total amount:*** $48,150 (100% institutional). ***Scholarships, grants, and awards by category:*** *Creative Arts/Performance:* 29 awards ($48,150 total): art/fine arts. ***Tuition waivers:*** Full or partial for employees or children of employees.

LOANS ***Student loans:*** $128,414 (100% need-based). ***Parent loans:*** $46,900 (100% need-based). ***Programs:*** FFEL (Subsidized and Unsubsidized Stafford, PLUS), Nellie Mae Loans, EXCEL Loans, TERI Loans, Connecticut Student Loan Foundation FFELP loans, alternative loans.

WORK-STUDY ***Federal work-study:*** *Total amount:* $5699; 3 jobs averaging $1900. ***State or other work-study/employment:*** *Total amount:* $3600 (100% need-based). 8 part-time jobs averaging $450.

APPLYING for FINANCIAL AID ***Required financial aid forms:*** institution's own form, CSS Financial Aid PROFILE. ***Financial aid deadline:*** 3/15. ***Notification date:*** Continuous beginning 4/15. Students must reply within 2 weeks of notification.

CONTACT Mr. Jim Falconer, Financial Aid Officer, Lyme Academy of Fine Arts, 84 Lyme Street, Old Lyme, CT 06371, 860-434-5232 Ext. 121. *Fax:* 860-434-8725. *E-mail:* jfalconer@lymeacademy.edu

LYNCHBURG COLLEGE

Lynchburg, VA

Tuition & fees: $18,105 **Average undergraduate aid package: $13,127**

ABOUT THE INSTITUTION Independent religious, coed. Awards: bachelor's and master's degrees. 46 undergraduate majors. Total enrollment: 2,025. Undergraduates: 1,721. Freshmen: 474. Federal methodology is used as a basis for awarding need-based institutional aid.

UNDERGRADUATE EXPENSES for 2000–2001 ***Application fee:*** $30. ***Comprehensive fee:*** $22,505 includes full-time tuition ($17,980), mandatory fees ($125), and room and board ($4400). ***College room only:*** $2600. Room and board charges vary according to board plan. ***Part-time tuition:*** $280 per credit hour. Part-time tuition and fees vary according to course load. ***Payment plan:*** installment.

FRESHMAN FINANCIAL AID (Fall 1999, est.) 364 applied for aid; of those 79% were deemed to have need. 100% of freshmen with need received aid; of those 29% had need fully met. *Average percent of need met:* 90% (excluding resources awarded to replace EFC). *Average financial aid package:* $13,556 (excluding resources awarded to replace EFC). 36% of all full-time freshmen had no need and received non-need-based aid.

UNDERGRADUATE FINANCIAL AID (Fall 1999, est.) 1,127 applied for aid; of those 85% were deemed to have need. 100% of undergraduates with need received aid; of those 34% had need fully met. *Average percent of need met:* 89% (excluding resources awarded to replace EFC). *Average financial aid package:* $13,127 (excluding resources awarded to replace EFC). 33% of all full-time undergraduates had no need and received non-need-based aid.

GIFT AID (NEED-BASED) ***Total amount:*** $8,551,375 (9% Federal, 17% state, 70% institutional, 4% external sources). ***Receiving aid:*** *Freshmen:* 60% (289); *all full-time undergraduates:* 61% (945). ***Average award:*** Freshmen: $13,656; Undergraduates: $13,339. ***Scholarships, grants, and awards:*** Federal Pell, FSEOG, state, college/university gift aid from institutional funds.

GIFT AID (NON-NEED-BASED) ***Total amount:*** $3,963,454 (21% state, 79% institutional). ***Receiving aid:*** *Freshmen:* 14% (66); *Undergraduates:* 10% (155). ***Scholarships, grants, and awards by category:*** *Academic Interests/Achievement:* 1,092 awards ($6,354,000 total): general academic interests/achievements. *Special Characteristics:* 15 awards ($158,097 total): children of faculty/staff. ***Tuition waivers:*** Full or partial for employees or children of employees, adult students, senior citizens.

LOANS ***Student loans:*** $5,142,117 (59% need-based, 41% non-need-based). 71% of past graduating class borrowed through all loan programs. Average indebtedness per student: $17,992. ***Average need-based loan:*** Freshmen: $2712; Undergraduates: $3720. ***Parent loans:*** $1,941,065 (55% need-based, 45% non-need-based). ***Programs:*** FFEL (Subsidized and Unsubsidized Stafford, PLUS), Perkins.

WORK-STUDY ***Federal work-study:*** *Total amount:* $212,737; 369 jobs averaging $1187. ***State or other work-study/employment:*** *Total amount:* $511,440 (44% need-based, 56% non-need-based). 257 part-time jobs averaging $1114.

APPLYING for FINANCIAL AID ***Required financial aid form:*** FAFSA. ***Financial aid deadline (priority):*** 3/1. ***Notification date:*** Continuous beginning 3/15. Students must reply by 5/1.

CONTACT Sarah Snow, Coordinator of Financial Aid, Lynchburg College, 1501 Lakeside Drive, Lynchburg, VA 24501-3199, 804-544-8228 or toll-free 800-426-8101. *Fax:* 804-544-8653. *E-mail:* snow_s@mail.lynchburg.edu

LYNDON STATE COLLEGE

Lyndonville, VT

Tuition & fees (VT res): $4864 **Average undergraduate aid package: $12,563**

ABOUT THE INSTITUTION State-supported, coed. Awards: associate, bachelor's, and master's degrees. 31 undergraduate majors. Total enrollment: 1,239. Undergraduates: 1,138. Freshmen: 276. Federal methodology is used as a basis for awarding need-based institutional aid.

UNDERGRADUATE EXPENSES for 1999–2000 ***Application fee:*** $30. ***One-time required fee:*** $150. ***Tuition, state resident:*** full-time $4092; part-time $171 per credit hour. ***Tuition, nonresident:*** full-time $9588; part-time $400 per credit hour. ***Required fees:*** full-time $772; $32 per credit hour. Full-time tuition and fees vary according to reciprocity agreements. Part-time tuition and fees vary according to reciprocity agreements. ***College room and board:*** $5298. Room and board charges vary according to board plan and housing facility.

FRESHMAN FINANCIAL AID (Fall 1999) 249 applied for aid; of those 85% were deemed to have need. 100% of freshmen with need received aid; of those 22% had need fully met. *Average percent of need met:* 86% (excluding resources awarded to replace EFC). *Average financial aid package:* $10,989 (excluding resources awarded to replace EFC). 8% of all full-time freshmen had no need and received non-need-based aid.

UNDERGRADUATE FINANCIAL AID (Fall 1999) 839 applied for aid; of those 87% were deemed to have need. 100% of undergraduates with need received aid; of those 11% had need fully met. *Average percent of need met:* 87% (excluding resources awarded to replace EFC). *Average financial aid package:* $12,563 (excluding resources awarded to replace EFC). 14% of all full-time undergraduates had no need and received non-need-based aid.

GIFT AID (NEED-BASED) ***Total amount:*** $2,365,044 (43% Federal, 23% state, 25% institutional, 9% external sources). ***Receiving aid:*** *Freshmen:* 41% (112); *all full-time undergraduates:* 39% (389). ***Average award:*** Freshmen: $1705; Undergraduates: $1583. ***Scholarships, grants, and awards:*** Federal Pell, FSEOG, state, private, college/university gift aid from institutional funds, Child-Care Grant Program, faculty/staff awards.

GIFT AID (NON-NEED-BASED) ***Total amount:*** $33,080 (100% external sources). ***Receiving aid:*** *Freshmen:* 17% (45); *Undergraduates:* 6% (60). ***Scholarships, grants, and awards by category:*** *Academic Interests/Achievement:* business, education, general academic interests/achievements, humanities. *Special Achievements/Activities:* community service, leadership. *Special Characteristics:* adult students, children of faculty/staff, siblings of current students. ***Tuition waivers:*** Full or partial for employees or children of employees, senior citizens. ***ROTC:*** Air Force.

LOANS ***Student loans:*** $3,550,620 (96% need-based, 4% non-need-based). ***Average need-based loan:*** Freshmen: $3116; Undergraduates: $4186. ***Parent loans:*** $2,609,314 (74% need-based, 26% non-need-based). ***Programs:*** Federal Direct (Subsidized and Unsubsidized Stafford, PLUS), Perkins.

WORK-STUDY ***Federal work-study:*** *Total amount:* $251,813; 223 jobs averaging $1129.

APPLYING for FINANCIAL AID ***Required financial aid form:*** FAFSA. ***Financial aid deadline (priority):*** 2/11. ***Notification date:*** Continuous beginning 4/1. Students must reply within 2 weeks of notification.

CONTACT Ms. Terry Van Zile, Assistant Director of Financial Aid, Lyndon State College, 1001 College Road, Lyndonville, VT 05851, 802-626-6217 or toll-free 800-225-1998 (in-state). *E-mail:* vanzilet@mail.lsc.vsc.edu

LYNN UNIVERSITY

Boca Raton, FL

Tuition & fees: $19,250 **Average undergraduate aid package: $14,829**

Lynn University (continued)

ABOUT THE INSTITUTION Independent, coed. Awards: associate, bachelor's, master's, and doctoral degrees. 39 undergraduate majors. Total enrollment: 1,949. Undergraduates: 1,761. Federal methodology is used as a basis for awarding need-based institutional aid.

UNDERGRADUATE EXPENSES for 2000–2001 ***Application fee:*** $25. ***Comprehensive fee:*** $26,050 includes full-time tuition ($18,500), mandatory fees ($750), and room and board ($6800). Part-time tuition and fees vary according to class time. ***Payment plans:*** installment, deferred payment.

FRESHMAN FINANCIAL AID (Fall 1999, est.) 212 applied for aid; of those 75% were deemed to have need. 100% of freshmen with need received aid; of those 35% had need fully met. *Average percent of need met:* 74% (excluding resources awarded to replace EFC). *Average financial aid package:* $13,206 (excluding resources awarded to replace EFC). 10% of all full-time freshmen had no need and received non-need-based aid.

UNDERGRADUATE FINANCIAL AID (Fall 1999, est.) 870 applied for aid; of those 87% were deemed to have need. 100% of undergraduates with need received aid; of those 14% had need fully met. *Average percent of need met:* 66% (excluding resources awarded to replace EFC). *Average financial aid package:* $14,829 (excluding resources awarded to replace EFC). 13% of all full-time undergraduates had no need and received non-need-based aid.

GIFT AID (NEED-BASED) ***Total amount:*** $4,647,185 (26% Federal, 12% state, 56% institutional, 6% external sources). ***Receiving aid:*** *Freshmen:* 41% (160); *all full-time undergraduates:* 49% (715). ***Average award:*** Freshmen: $9750; Undergraduates: $5200. ***Scholarships, grants, and awards:*** Federal Pell, FSEOG, state, private, college/university gift aid from institutional funds.

GIFT AID (NON-NEED-BASED) ***Total amount:*** $3,670,777 (11% state, 74% institutional, 15% external sources). ***Receiving aid:*** *Freshmen:* 16% (60); *Undergraduates:* 14% (201). ***Scholarships, grants, and awards by category:*** *Academic Interests/Achievement:* business, general academic interests/achievements, health fields, premedicine. *Creative Arts/Performance:* cinema/film/broadcasting, music. *Special Achievements/Activities:* community service, general special achievements/activities. *Special Characteristics:* children of faculty/staff, siblings of current students. ***Tuition waivers:*** Full or partial for employees or children of employees.

LOANS ***Student loans:*** $3,449,433 (77% need-based, 23% non-need-based). Average indebtedness per student: $14,200. ***Average need-based loan:*** Freshmen: $2713; Undergraduates: $3850. ***Parent loans:*** $1,631,697 (100% non-need-based). ***Programs:*** FFEL (Subsidized and Unsubsidized Stafford, PLUS), Perkins, state, college/university.

WORK-STUDY ***Federal work-study:*** *Total amount:* $124,604; jobs available. ***State or other work-study/employment:*** *Total amount:* $184,453 (26% need-based, 74% non-need-based). Part-time jobs available.

ATHLETIC AWARDS *Total amount:* 1,612,533 (100% non-need-based).

APPLYING for FINANCIAL AID ***Required financial aid form:*** FAFSA. ***Financial aid deadline (priority):*** 3/1. ***Notification date:*** Continuous. Students must reply within 2 weeks of notification.

CONTACT Ms. Barrie Tripp, New Student Financial Services Counselor/Associate Director, Financial Aid, Lynn University, 3601 North Military Trail, Boca Raton, FL 33431-5598, 561-237-7814 or toll-free 800-544-8035 (out-of-state). *Fax:* 561-237-7815. *E-mail:* btripp@lynn.edu

LYON COLLEGE

Batesville, AR

Tuition & fees: $10,622 **Average undergraduate aid package: $11,633**

ABOUT THE INSTITUTION Independent Presbyterian, coed. Awards: bachelor's degrees. 17 undergraduate majors. Total enrollment: 462. Undergraduates: 462. Freshmen: 145. Federal methodology is used as a basis for awarding need-based institutional aid.

UNDERGRADUATE EXPENSES for 1999–2000 ***Application fee:*** $25. ***One-time required fee:*** $200. ***Comprehensive fee:*** $15,325 includes full-time tuition ($10,272), mandatory fees ($350), and room and board ($4703). ***College room only:*** $1935. ***Part-time tuition:*** $82 per credit hour. Part-time tuition and fees vary according to course load. ***Payment plan:*** installment.

FRESHMAN FINANCIAL AID (Fall 1999, est.) 107 applied for aid; of those 86% were deemed to have need. 100% of freshmen with need received aid; of those 60% had need fully met. *Average percent of need met:* 94% (excluding resources awarded to replace EFC). *Average financial aid package:* $11,526 (excluding resources awarded to replace EFC). 9% of all full-time freshmen had no need and received non-need-based aid.

UNDERGRADUATE FINANCIAL AID (Fall 1999, est.) 291 applied for aid; of those 88% were deemed to have need. 100% of undergraduates with need received aid; of those 65% had need fully met. *Average percent of need met:* 95% (excluding resources awarded to replace EFC). *Average financial aid package:* $11,633 (excluding resources awarded to replace EFC). 12% of all full-time undergraduates had no need and received non-need-based aid.

GIFT AID (NEED-BASED) ***Total amount:*** $2,132,050 (17% Federal, 17% state, 62% institutional, 4% external sources). ***Receiving aid:*** *Freshmen:* 65% (92); *all full-time undergraduates:* 61% (255). ***Average award:*** Freshmen: $9550; Undergraduates: $8934. ***Scholarships, grants, and awards:*** Federal Pell, FSEOG, state, private, college/university gift aid from institutional funds.

GIFT AID (NON-NEED-BASED) ***Total amount:*** $1,324,587 (1% Federal, 21% state, 74% institutional, 4% external sources). ***Receiving aid:*** *Freshmen:* 16% (23); *Undergraduates:* 14% (60). ***Scholarships, grants, and awards by category:*** *Academic Interests/Achievement:* 258 awards ($1,578,723 total): general academic interests/achievements. *Creative Arts/Performance:* 17 awards ($44,772 total): art/fine arts, dance, performing arts, theater/drama. *Special Achievements/Activities:* 41 awards ($111,750 total): leadership. *Special Characteristics:* 46 awards ($231,700 total): children and siblings of alumni, ethnic background, first-generation college students, international students, local/state students, religious affiliation. ***Tuition waivers:*** Full or partial for employees or children of employees.

LOANS ***Student loans:*** $891,539 (62% need-based, 38% non-need-based). 57% of past graduating class borrowed through all loan programs. Average indebtedness per student: $13,610. ***Average need-based loan:*** Freshmen: $1355; Undergraduates: $2179. ***Parent loans:*** $106,223 (12% need-based, 88% non-need-based). ***Programs:*** FFEL (Subsidized and Unsubsidized Stafford, PLUS), Perkins, college/university.

WORK-STUDY ***Federal work-study:*** *Total amount:* $104,949; 88 jobs averaging $1394. ***State or other work-study/employment:*** *Total amount:* $103,475 (27% need-based, 73% non-need-based). 81 part-time jobs averaging $1277.

ATHLETIC AWARDS *Total amount:* 499,636 (29% need-based, 71% non-need-based).

APPLYING for FINANCIAL AID ***Required financial aid form:*** FAFSA. ***Financial aid deadline (priority):*** 2/15. ***Notification date:*** Continuous beginning 3/1.

CONTACT Ms. Debra Hintz, Associate Dean of Financial Aid, Lyon College, 2300 Highland Road, Batesville, AR 72501, 870-793-9813 or toll-free 800-423-2542. *Fax:* 870-793-1791.

MACALESTER COLLEGE

St. Paul, MN

Tuition & fees: $20,688 **Average undergraduate aid package: $16,006**

ABOUT THE INSTITUTION Independent Presbyterian, coed. Awards: bachelor's degrees. 39 undergraduate majors. Total enrollment: 1,835. Undergraduates: 1,835. Freshmen: 460. Institutional methodology is used as a basis for awarding need-based institutional aid.

UNDERGRADUATE EXPENSES for 1999–2000 ***Application fee:*** $40. ***Comprehensive fee:*** $26,448 includes full-time tuition ($20,560), mandatory fees ($128), and room and board ($5760). ***College room only:*** $2990. ***Part-time tuition:*** $645 per semester hour. ***Payment plan:*** installment.

FRESHMAN FINANCIAL AID (Fall 1999, est.) 385 applied for aid. *Average percent of need met:* 100% (excluding resources awarded to replace EFC).

Average financial aid package: $16,295 (excluding resources awarded to replace EFC). 6% of all full-time freshmen had no need and received non-need-based aid.

UNDERGRADUATE FINANCIAL AID (Fall 1999, est.) 1,374 applied for aid. *Average percent of need met:* 100% (excluding resources awarded to replace EFC). *Average financial aid package:* $16,006 (excluding resources awarded to replace EFC). 9% of all full-time undergraduates had no need and received non-need-based aid.

GIFT AID (NEED-BASED) ***Total amount:*** $16,276,315 (4% Federal, 5% state, 88% institutional, 3% external sources). ***Scholarships, grants, and awards:*** Federal Pell, FSEOG, state, private, college/university gift aid from institutional funds.

GIFT AID (NON-NEED-BASED) ***Total amount:*** $711,889 (87% institutional, 13% external sources). ***Scholarships, grants, and awards by category:*** *Academic Interests/Achievement:* general academic interests/achievements. ***Tuition waivers:*** Full or partial for employees or children of employees. ***ROTC:*** Naval cooperative, Air Force cooperative.

LOANS ***Student loans:*** $4,389,979 (65% need-based, 35% non-need-based). 58% of past graduating class borrowed through all loan programs. Average indebtedness per student: $14,350. ***Parent loans:*** $592,102 (100% non-need-based). ***Programs:*** FFEL (Subsidized and Unsubsidized Stafford, PLUS), Perkins, state, college/university.

WORK-STUDY ***Federal work-study:*** *Total amount:* $503,928; 272 jobs averaging $1853. ***State or other work-study/employment:*** *Total amount:* $1,580,306 (94% need-based, 6% non-need-based). 817 part-time jobs available.

APPLYING for FINANCIAL AID ***Required financial aid forms:*** FAFSA, CSS Financial Aid PROFILE, noncustodial (divorced/separated) parent's statement, business/farm supplement, W-2 forms, federal income tax form(s). ***Financial aid deadline (priority):*** 2/8. ***Notification date:*** 3/27. Students must reply by 5/1.

CONTACT Jenae Schmidt, Financial Aid Assistant, Macalester College, 1600 Grand Avenue, St. Paul, MN 55105, 651-696-6214 or toll-free 800-231-7974. *Fax:* 651-696-6724. *E-mail:* finaid@macalester.edu

MACHZIKEI HADATH RABBINICAL COLLEGE

Brooklyn, NY

CONTACT Rabbi Baruch Rozmarin, Director of Financial Aid, Machzikei Hadath Rabbinical College, 5407 16th Avenue, Brooklyn, NY 11204-1805, 718-854-8777.

MACMURRAY COLLEGE

Jacksonville, IL

Tuition & fees: $12,375 **Average undergraduate aid package: $13,376**

ABOUT THE INSTITUTION Independent United Methodist, coed. Awards: associate and bachelor's degrees. 38 undergraduate majors. Total enrollment: 692. Undergraduates: 692. Freshmen: 186. Federal methodology is used as a basis for awarding need-based institutional aid.

UNDERGRADUATE EXPENSES for 1999–2000 ***Application fee:*** $20. ***Comprehensive fee:*** $16,805 includes full-time tuition ($12,300), mandatory fees ($75), and room and board ($4430). ***College room only:*** $1860. ***Part-time tuition:*** $375 per credit hour. ***Payment plan:*** installment.

FRESHMAN FINANCIAL AID (Fall 1999) 186 applied for aid; of those 97% were deemed to have need. 100% of freshmen with need received aid; of those 20% had need fully met. *Average percent of need met:* 73% (excluding resources awarded to replace EFC). *Average financial aid package:* $14,336 (excluding resources awarded to replace EFC). 3% of all full-time freshmen had no need and received non-need-based aid.

UNDERGRADUATE FINANCIAL AID (Fall 1999) 594 applied for aid; of those 96% were deemed to have need. 100% of undergraduates with need received aid; of those 43% had need fully met. *Average percent of need met:* 71% (excluding resources awarded to replace EFC). *Average financial aid package:* $13,376 (excluding resources awarded to replace EFC). 3% of all full-time undergraduates had no need and received non-need-based aid.

GIFT AID (NEED-BASED) ***Total amount:*** $4,577,609 (16% Federal, 34% state, 47% institutional, 3% external sources). ***Receiving aid:*** *Freshmen:* 95% (180); *all full-time undergraduates:* 89% (573). ***Average award:*** Freshmen: $9875; Undergraduates: $12,185. ***Scholarships, grants, and awards:*** Federal Pell, FSEOG, state, private, college/university gift aid from institutional funds.

GIFT AID (NON-NEED-BASED) ***Total amount:*** $409,235 (5% state, 87% institutional, 8% external sources). ***Receiving aid:*** *Freshmen:* 3% (6); *Undergraduates:* 3% (21). ***Scholarships, grants, and awards by category:*** *Academic Interests/Achievement:* 293 awards ($763,150 total): biological sciences, English, foreign languages, general academic interests/achievements, health fields, physical sciences, religion/biblical studies, social sciences. *Creative Arts/Performance:* 16 awards ($29,172 total): art/fine arts, music. *Special Achievements/Activities:* 13 awards ($26,505 total): leadership, religious involvement. *Special Characteristics:* 50 awards ($80,560 total): children and siblings of alumni, children of faculty/staff, international students, out-of-state students, previous college experience, religious affiliation, siblings of current students. ***Tuition waivers:*** Full or partial for children of alumni, employees or children of employees, senior citizens.

LOANS ***Student loans:*** $3,117,901 (76% need-based, 24% non-need-based). 94% of past graduating class borrowed through all loan programs. Average indebtedness per student: $17,242. ***Average need-based loan:*** Freshmen: $4214; Undergraduates: $4577. ***Parent loans:*** $372,694 (79% need-based, 21% non-need-based). ***Programs:*** FFEL (Subsidized and Unsubsidized Stafford, PLUS), Perkins, college/university.

WORK-STUDY ***Federal work-study:*** *Total amount:* $126,897; 157 jobs averaging $808. ***State or other work-study/employment:*** *Total amount:* $261,327 (94% need-based, 6% non-need-based). 214 part-time jobs averaging $1221.

APPLYING for FINANCIAL AID ***Required financial aid form:*** FAFSA. ***Financial aid deadline (priority):*** 5/31. ***Notification date:*** Continuous.

CONTACT Rhonda I. Cors, Associate Director of Financial Aid, MacMurray College, 447 East College, Jacksonville, IL 62650, 217-479-7041 or toll-free 800-252-7485 (in-state). *Fax:* 217-245-0405. *E-mail:* rhonda@mac.edu

MACON STATE COLLEGE

Macon, GA

Tuition & fees (GA res): $1322 **Average undergraduate aid package: N/A**

ABOUT THE INSTITUTION State-supported, coed. Awards: associate and bachelor's degrees. 53 undergraduate majors. Total enrollment: 3,558. Undergraduates: 3,558. Freshmen: 607. Federal methodology is used as a basis for awarding need-based institutional aid.

UNDERGRADUATE EXPENSES for 1999–2000 ***Application fee:*** $10. ***Tuition, state resident:*** full-time $1234; part-time $52 per credit hour. ***Tuition, nonresident:*** full-time $3085; part-time $207 per credit hour. ***Required fees:*** full-time $88; $44 per term part-time. Full-time tuition and fees vary according to course level, degree level, and student level. Part-time tuition and fees vary according to course level, course load, degree level, and student level.

GIFT AID (NEED-BASED) ***Scholarships, grants, and awards:*** Federal Pell, FSEOG, state, college/university gift aid from institutional funds, Georgia HOPE Scholarships.

GIFT AID (NON-NEED-BASED) ***Tuition waivers:*** Full or partial for senior citizens.

LOANS ***Programs:*** FFEL (Subsidized and Unsubsidized Stafford, PLUS).

WORK-STUDY Federal work-study jobs available. ***State or other work-study/employment:*** Part-time jobs available.

APPLYING for FINANCIAL AID ***Required financial aid forms:*** FAFSA, institution's own form. ***Financial aid deadline (priority):*** 4/1.

CONTACT Office of Financial Aid, Macon State College, 100 College Station Drive, Macon, GA 31206, 912-471-2717 or toll-free 800-272-7619.

MADONNA UNIVERSITY

Livonia, MI

Tuition & fees: $6610 **Average undergraduate aid package: N/A**

ABOUT THE INSTITUTION Independent Roman Catholic, coed. Awards: associate, bachelor's, and master's degrees. 65 undergraduate majors. Total enrollment: 3,929. Undergraduates: 3,206. Freshmen: 246. Federal methodology is used as a basis for awarding need-based institutional aid.

UNDERGRADUATE EXPENSES for 1999–2000 ***Comprehensive fee:*** $11,286 includes full-time tuition ($6510), mandatory fees ($100), and room and board ($4676). ***College room only:*** $2526. Full-time tuition and fees vary according to course load and program. Room and board charges vary according to board plan. ***Part-time tuition:*** $217 per semester hour. ***Part-time fees:*** $50 per term part-time. Part-time tuition and fees vary according to course load and program. ***Payment plan:*** deferred payment.

GIFT AID (NEED-BASED) ***Scholarships, grants, and awards:*** Federal Pell, FSEOG, state, private, college/university gift aid from institutional funds.

GIFT AID (NON-NEED-BASED) ***Scholarships, grants, and awards by category:*** *Academic Interests/Achievement:* business, communication, computer science, education, general academic interests/achievements, humanities. ***Tuition waivers:*** Full or partial for employees or children of employees.

LOANS ***Programs:*** Federal Direct (Subsidized and Unsubsidized Stafford, PLUS), FFEL (Subsidized and Unsubsidized Stafford, PLUS), Perkins.

WORK-STUDY Federal work-study jobs available.

APPLYING for FINANCIAL AID ***Required financial aid form:*** FAFSA. ***Financial aid deadline (priority):*** 3/1. ***Notification date:*** 6/1.

CONTACT Financial Aid Secretary, Madonna University, 36600 Schoolcraft Road, Livonia, MI 48150-1173, 734-432-5663 or toll-free 800-852-4951.

MAGDALEN COLLEGE

Warner, NH

CONTACT Financial Aid Office, Magdalen College, 511 Kearsarge Mountain Road, Warner, NH 03278, 603-456-2656.

MAGNOLIA BIBLE COLLEGE

Kosciusko, MS

Tuition & fees: $4540 **Average undergraduate aid package: $4072**

ABOUT THE INSTITUTION Independent religious, coed, primarily men. Awards: bachelor's degrees. 1 undergraduate major. Total enrollment: 51. Undergraduates: 51. Freshmen: 1. Federal methodology is used as a basis for awarding need-based institutional aid.

UNDERGRADUATE EXPENSES for 1999–2000 ***Comprehensive fee:*** $6284 includes full-time tuition ($4500), mandatory fees ($40), and room and board ($1744). ***College room only:*** $1000. Room and board charges vary according to housing facility. ***Part-time tuition:*** $150 per semester hour. ***Part-time fees:*** $20 per term part-time. ***Payment plan:*** deferred payment.

FRESHMAN FINANCIAL AID (Fall 1999) 2 applied for aid; of those 100% were deemed to have need. 100% of freshmen with need received aid. *Average percent of need met:* 70% (excluding resources awarded to replace EFC). *Average financial aid package:* $2175 (excluding resources awarded to replace EFC).

UNDERGRADUATE FINANCIAL AID (Fall 1999) 22 applied for aid; of those 73% were deemed to have need. 100% of undergraduates with need received aid; of those 6% had need fully met. *Average percent of need met:* 53% (excluding resources awarded to replace EFC). *Average financial aid package:* $4072 (excluding resources awarded to replace EFC).

GIFT AID (NEED-BASED) ***Total amount:*** $55,402 (73% Federal, 2% state, 25% institutional). ***Receiving aid:*** *Freshmen:* 100% (2); *all full-time undergraduates:* 44% (11). ***Average award:*** Freshmen: $1775; Undergraduates: $3579. ***Scholarships, grants, and awards:*** Federal Pell, FSEOG, state, college/university gift aid from institutional funds.

GIFT AID (NON-NEED-BASED) ***Total amount:*** $23,138 (1% state, 99% institutional). ***Receiving aid:*** *Undergraduates:* 44% (11). ***Scholarships, grants, and awards by category:*** *Academic Interests/Achievement:* 8 awards ($23,013 total): general academic interests/achievements. *Creative Arts/Performance:* 1 award ($3600 total): music. *Special Characteristics:* 2 awards ($818 total): general special characteristics, spouses of current students. ***Tuition waivers:*** Full or partial for employees or children of employees.

LOANS ***Student loans:*** $5100 (31% need-based, 69% non-need-based). 33% of past graduating class borrowed through all loan programs. Average indebtedness per student: $5258. ***Average need-based loan:*** Freshmen: $800; Undergraduates: $800. ***Programs:*** FFEL (Subsidized and Unsubsidized Stafford, PLUS).

WORK-STUDY ***Federal work-study:*** *Total amount:* $6211; 4 jobs averaging $1553. ***State or other work-study/employment:*** *Total amount:* $1751 (100% non-need-based). 1 part-time job averaging $1751.

APPLYING for FINANCIAL AID ***Required financial aid form:*** FAFSA. ***Financial aid deadline (priority):*** 8/1. ***Notification date:*** Continuous. Students must reply within 4 weeks of notification.

CONTACT Mr. Allen Coker, Admissions Counselor, Magnolia Bible College, PO Box 1109, Kosciusko, MS 39090-1109, 601-289-2896 Ext. 106 or toll-free 800-748-8655 (in-state). *Fax:* 601-289-1850.

MAHARISHI UNIVERSITY OF MANAGEMENT

Fairfield, IA

Tuition & fees: $15,630 **Average undergraduate aid package: $19,495**

ABOUT THE INSTITUTION Independent, coed. Awards: associate, bachelor's, master's, and doctoral degrees. 45 undergraduate majors. Total enrollment: 1,291. Undergraduates: 977. Freshmen: 68. Federal methodology is used as a basis for awarding need-based institutional aid.

UNDERGRADUATE EXPENSES for 2000–2001 ***Application fee:*** $25. ***Comprehensive fee:*** $20,830 includes full-time tuition ($15,200), mandatory fees ($430), and room and board ($5200). ***College room only:*** $2720. Full-time tuition and fees vary according to program. Room and board charges vary according to housing facility. ***Part-time tuition:*** $3800 per term. Part-time tuition and fees vary according to program. ***Payment plan:*** installment.

FRESHMAN FINANCIAL AID (Fall 1999, est.) 77 applied for aid; of those 90% were deemed to have need. 100% of freshmen with need received aid; of those 26% had need fully met. *Average percent of need met:* 82% (excluding resources awarded to replace EFC). *Average financial aid package:* $16,746 (excluding resources awarded to replace EFC). 9% of all full-time freshmen had no need and received non-need-based aid.

UNDERGRADUATE FINANCIAL AID (Fall 1999, est.) 190 applied for aid; of those 95% were deemed to have need. 100% of undergraduates with need received aid; of those 37% had need fully met. *Average percent of need met:* 84% (excluding resources awarded to replace EFC). *Average financial aid package:* $19,495 (excluding resources awarded to replace EFC). 5% of all full-time undergraduates had no need and received non-need-based aid.

GIFT AID (NEED-BASED) ***Total amount:*** $2,284,211 (16% Federal, 7% state, 77% institutional). ***Receiving aid:*** *Freshmen:* 88% (69); *all full-time undergraduates:* 93% (180). ***Average award:*** Freshmen: $11,043; Undergraduates: $11,652. ***Scholarships, grants, and awards:*** Federal Pell, FSEOG, state, private, college/university gift aid from institutional funds.

GIFT AID (NON-NEED-BASED) ***Total amount:*** $176,593 (99% institutional, 1% external sources). ***Receiving aid:*** *Freshmen:* 6% (5); *Undergraduates:* 6% (12). ***Scholarships, grants, and awards by category:*** *Academic Interests/Achievement:* 17 awards ($56,682 total): engineering/technologies, general academic interests/achievements. *Creative Arts/Performance:* 8 awards ($8450 total): creative writing, general creative arts/performance, music. *Special Achievements/Activities:* 16 awards ($9881 total): leadership. *Special Characteristics:* 108 awards ($715,925 total): children and siblings of alumni, children of faculty/staff, ethnic background, international students, local/state students, veterans, veterans' children. ***Tuition waivers:*** Full or partial for children of alumni, employees or children of employees, senior citizens.

LOANS ***Student loans:*** $1,017,200 (91% need-based, 9% non-need-based). 69% of past graduating class borrowed through all loan programs. Average indebtedness per student: $16,454. ***Average need-based loan:*** Freshmen: $3917; Undergraduates: $5975. ***Programs:*** FFEL (Subsidized and Unsubsidized Stafford, PLUS), Perkins, college/university, alternative loans.

WORK-STUDY ***Federal work-study:*** *Total amount:* $112,418; 83 jobs averaging $1354. ***State or other work-study/employment:*** *Total amount:* $130,012 (100% need-based). 55 part-time jobs averaging $2363.

APPLYING for FINANCIAL AID ***Required financial aid form:*** FAFSA. ***Financial aid deadline (priority):*** 4/15. ***Notification date:*** Continuous. Students must reply by 5/30 or within 4 weeks of notification.

CONTACT Mr. Bill Christensen, Associate Director of Financial Aid, Maharishi University of Management, 1000 North 4th Street, DB 1127, Fairfield, IA 52557-1127, 515-472-1156. *Fax:* 515-472-1133. *E-mail:* finaid@mum.edu

MAINE COLLEGE OF ART

Portland, ME

Tuition & fees: $16,718 **Average undergraduate aid package: $13,135**

ABOUT THE INSTITUTION Independent, coed. Awards: bachelor's and master's degrees. 7 undergraduate majors. Total enrollment: 408. Undergraduates: 382. Freshmen: 86. Both federal and institutional methodology are used as a basis for awarding need-based institutional aid.

UNDERGRADUATE EXPENSES for 1999–2000 ***Application fee:*** $40. ***One-time required fee:*** $22. ***Comprehensive fee:*** $23,107 includes full-time tuition ($16,530), mandatory fees ($188), and room and board ($6389). ***College room only:*** $3965. Room and board charges vary according to housing facility. ***Part-time tuition:*** $689 per credit hour. ***Payment plans:*** installment, deferred payment.

FRESHMAN FINANCIAL AID (Fall 1999) 78 applied for aid; of those 94% were deemed to have need. 100% of freshmen with need received aid; of those 8% had need fully met. *Average percent of need met:* 59% (excluding resources awarded to replace EFC). *Average financial aid package:* $11,183 (excluding resources awarded to replace EFC). 34% of all full-time freshmen had no need and received non-need-based aid.

UNDERGRADUATE FINANCIAL AID (Fall 1999) 270 applied for aid; of those 93% were deemed to have need. 100% of undergraduates with need received aid; of those 14% had need fully met. *Average percent of need met:* 67% (excluding resources awarded to replace EFC). *Average financial aid package:* $13,135 (excluding resources awarded to replace EFC). 18% of all full-time undergraduates had no need and received non-need-based aid.

GIFT AID (NEED-BASED) ***Total amount:*** $2,025,454 (16% Federal, 4% state, 76% institutional, 4% external sources). ***Receiving aid:*** *Freshmen:* 66% (73); *all full-time undergraduates:* 82% (250). ***Average award:*** Freshmen: $7076; Undergraduates: $7280. ***Scholarships, grants, and awards:*** Federal Pell, FSEOG, state, private, college/university gift aid from institutional funds.

GIFT AID (NON-NEED-BASED) ***Total amount:*** $224,565 (100% institutional). ***Receiving aid:*** *Freshmen:* 5% (5); *Undergraduates:* 3% (10). ***Scholarships, grants, and awards by category:*** *Creative Arts/Performance:* 112 awards ($537,443 total): art/fine arts. *Special Characteristics:* 3 awards ($8000 total): international students.

LOANS ***Student loans:*** $2,093,548 (86% need-based, 14% non-need-based). 73% of past graduating class borrowed through all loan programs. ***Average need-based loan:*** Freshmen: $3987; Undergraduates: $5430. ***Parent loans:*** $519,466 (61% need-based, 39% non-need-based). ***Programs:*** FFEL (Subsidized and Unsubsidized Stafford, PLUS), Perkins, alternative loans.

WORK-STUDY ***Federal work-study:*** *Total amount:* $107,377; 74 jobs averaging $1451.

APPLYING for FINANCIAL AID ***Required financial aid form:*** FAFSA. ***Financial aid deadline (priority):*** 3/1. ***Notification date:*** Continuous beginning 3/15. Students must reply within 2 weeks of notification.

CONTACT Michelle A. Leclerc, Director of Financial Aid, Maine College of Art, 97 Spring Street, Portland, ME 04101-3987, 207-772-3052 or toll-free 800-639-4808. *Fax:* 207-772-5069. *E-mail:* mleclerc@meca.edu

MAINE MARITIME ACADEMY

Castine, ME

Tuition & fees (ME res): $5092 **Average undergraduate aid package: $8431**

ABOUT THE INSTITUTION State-supported, coed. Awards: associate, bachelor's, and master's degrees and post-bachelor's certificates. 12 undergraduate majors. Total enrollment: 696. Undergraduates: 680. Freshmen: 152. Federal methodology is used as a basis for awarding need-based institutional aid.

UNDERGRADUATE EXPENSES for 1999–2000 ***Application fee:*** $15. ***Tuition, state resident:*** full-time $4462; part-time $153 per credit hour. ***Tuition, nonresident:*** full-time $8270; part-time $274 per credit hour. ***Required fees:*** full-time $630; $315 per term part-time. Full-time tuition and fees vary according to course load, reciprocity agreements, and student level. Part-time tuition and fees vary according to program. ***College room and board:*** $5022. Room and board charges vary according to board plan. ***Payment plan:*** installment.

FRESHMAN FINANCIAL AID (Fall 1999, est.) 137 applied for aid; of those 92% were deemed to have need. 100% of freshmen with need received aid; of those 22% had need fully met. *Average percent of need met:* 75% (excluding resources awarded to replace EFC). *Average financial aid package:* $8018 (excluding resources awarded to replace EFC). 26% of all full-time freshmen had no need and received non-need-based aid.

UNDERGRADUATE FINANCIAL AID (Fall 1999, est.) 540 applied for aid; of those 95% were deemed to have need. 100% of undergraduates with need received aid; of those 32% had need fully met. *Average percent of need met:* 83% (excluding resources awarded to replace EFC). *Average financial aid package:* $8431 (excluding resources awarded to replace EFC). 25% of all full-time undergraduates had no need and received non-need-based aid.

GIFT AID (NEED-BASED) ***Total amount:*** $1,508,961 (50% Federal, 12% state, 30% institutional, 8% external sources). ***Receiving aid:*** *Freshmen:* 63% (125); *all full-time undergraduates:* 68% (464). ***Average award:*** Freshmen: $3803; Undergraduates: $3354. ***Scholarships, grants, and awards:*** Federal Pell, FSEOG, state, private, college/university gift aid from institutional funds.

GIFT AID (NON-NEED-BASED) ***Total amount:*** $156,755 (48% Federal, 28% institutional, 24% external sources). ***Receiving aid:*** *Freshmen:* 6% (11); *Undergraduates:* 5% (34). ***Scholarships, grants, and awards by category:*** *Academic Interests/Achievement:* 38 awards ($78,500 total): biological sciences, engineering/technologies, general academic interests/achievements. *Special Characteristics:* 18 awards ($39,324 total): children of faculty/staff, local/state students, out-of-state students. ***Tuition waivers:*** Full or partial for employees or children of employees. ***ROTC:*** Naval.

LOANS ***Student loans:*** $2,990,159 (73% need-based, 27% non-need-based). 86% of past graduating class borrowed through all loan programs. Average indebtedness per student: $13,358. ***Average need-based loan:*** Freshmen: $3736; Undergraduates: $4699. ***Parent loans:*** $318,294 (21% need-based, 79% non-need-based). ***Programs:*** FFEL (Subsidized and Unsubsidized Stafford, PLUS), Perkins, state, college/university.

WORK-STUDY ***Federal work-study:*** *Total amount:* $169,966; jobs available.

APPLYING for FINANCIAL AID ***Required financial aid forms:*** FAFSA, institution's own form. ***Financial aid deadline (priority):*** 4/15. ***Notification date:*** Continuous. Students must reply within 3 weeks of notification.

CONTACT Ms. Holly Bayle, Assistant Director of Financial Aid, Maine Maritime Academy, Pleasant Street, Castine, ME 04420, 207-326-2205 or toll-free 800-464-6565 (in-state), 800-227-8465 (out-of-state). *Fax:* 207-326-2515.

MALONE COLLEGE

Canton, OH

Tuition & fees: $12,380 **Average undergraduate aid package: $10,082**

ABOUT THE INSTITUTION Independent religious, coed. Awards: bachelor's and master's degrees and post-bachelor's certificates. 43 undergraduate majors. Total enrollment: 2,193. Undergraduates: 1,949. Freshmen: 409. Federal methodology is used as a basis for awarding need-based institutional aid.

UNDERGRADUATE EXPENSES for 1999–2000 ***Application fee:*** $20. ***Comprehensive fee:*** $17,630 includes full-time tuition ($12,150), mandatory fees ($230), and room and board ($5250). ***College room only:*** $2940. Room and board charges vary according to board plan. ***Part-time tuition:*** $305 per semester hour. ***Part-time fees:*** $58 per term part-time. Part-time tuition and fees vary according to course load. ***Payment plan:*** installment.

FRESHMAN FINANCIAL AID (Fall 1999) 405 applied for aid; of those 86% were deemed to have need. 100% of freshmen with need received aid; of those 82% had need fully met. *Average percent of need met:* 85% (excluding resources awarded to replace EFC). *Average financial aid package:* $11,257 (excluding resources awarded to replace EFC). 11% of all full-time freshmen had no need and received non-need-based aid.

UNDERGRADUATE FINANCIAL AID (Fall 1999) 1,598 applied for aid; of those 77% were deemed to have need. 100% of undergraduates with need received aid; of those 82% had need fully met. *Average percent of need met:* 84% (excluding resources awarded to replace EFC). *Average financial aid package:* $10,082 (excluding resources awarded to replace EFC). 21% of all full-time undergraduates had no need and received non-need-based aid.

GIFT AID (NEED-BASED) ***Total amount:*** $6,960,527 (16% Federal, 27% state, 52% institutional, 5% external sources). ***Receiving aid:*** *Freshmen:* 86% (348); *all full-time undergraduates:* 71% (1,220). ***Average award:*** Freshmen: $8077; Undergraduates: $6631. ***Scholarships, grants, and awards:*** Federal Pell, FSEOG, state, private, college/university gift aid from institutional funds.

GIFT AID (NON-NEED-BASED) ***Total amount:*** $1,189,462 (30% state, 67% institutional, 3% external sources). ***Receiving aid:*** *Freshmen:* 84% (341); *Undergraduates:* 68% (1,183). ***Scholarships, grants, and awards by category:*** *Academic Interests/Achievement:* 755 awards ($3,040,706 total): biological sciences, business, communication, computer science, education, English, foreign languages, general academic interests/achievements, health fields, humanities, international studies, mathematics, physical sciences, premedicine, religion/biblical studies, social sciences. *Creative Arts/Performance:* 104 awards ($113,375 total): debating, journalism/publications, music, theater/drama. *Special Achievements/Activities:* 63 awards ($144,195 total): community service, junior miss, leadership, religious involvement. *Special Characteristics:* 334 awards ($391,501 total): children and siblings of alumni, children of faculty/staff, international students, parents of current students, relatives of clergy, religious affiliation, siblings of current students, spouses of current students. ***Tuition waivers:*** Full or partial for employees or children of employees, senior citizens.

LOANS ***Student loans:*** $5,272,271 (88% need-based, 12% non-need-based). 68% of past graduating class borrowed through all loan programs. Average indebtedness per student: $15,114. ***Average need-based loan:*** Freshmen: $2375; Undergraduates: $2855. ***Parent loans:*** $1,041,425 (86% need-based, 14% non-need-based). ***Programs:*** FFEL (Subsidized and Unsubsidized Stafford, PLUS), Perkins, college/university.

WORK-STUDY ***Federal work-study:*** *Total amount:* $571,798; 379 jobs averaging $1516. ***State or other work-study/employment:*** *Total amount:* $184,720 (76% need-based, 24% non-need-based). Part-time jobs available.

ATHLETIC AWARDS *Total amount:* 1,341,717 (69% need-based, 31% non-need-based).

APPLYING for FINANCIAL AID ***Required financial aid forms:*** FAFSA, institution's own form. ***Financial aid deadline (priority):*** 3/1. ***Notification date:*** Continuous. Students must reply within 2 weeks of notification.

CONTACT Ms. Patricia L. Little, Director of Financial Aid, Malone College, 515 25th Street, NW, Canton, OH 44709-3897, 330-471-8162 or toll-free 800-521-1146. *Fax:* 330-471-8478. *E-mail:* plittle@malone.edu

MANCHESTER COLLEGE

North Manchester, IN

Tuition & fees: $13,930 **Average undergraduate aid package: $15,220**

ABOUT THE INSTITUTION Independent religious, coed. Awards: associate, bachelor's, and master's degrees. 59 undergraduate majors. Total enrollment: 1,081. Undergraduates: 1,065. Freshmen: 329. Federal methodology is used as a basis for awarding need-based institutional aid.

UNDERGRADUATE EXPENSES for 1999–2000 ***Application fee:*** $20. ***Comprehensive fee:*** $19,040 includes full-time tuition ($13,930) and room and board ($5110). Room and board charges vary according to board plan and housing facility. ***Part-time tuition:*** $460 per semester hour. ***Payment plans:*** installment, deferred payment.

FRESHMAN FINANCIAL AID (Fall 1999) 322 applied for aid; of those 75% were deemed to have need. 100% of freshmen with need received aid; of those 80% had need fully met. *Average percent of need met:* 98% (excluding resources awarded to replace EFC). *Average financial aid package:* $15,556 (excluding resources awarded to replace EFC). 17% of all full-time freshmen had no need and received non-need-based aid.

UNDERGRADUATE FINANCIAL AID (Fall 1999) 1,046 applied for aid; of those 76% were deemed to have need. 100% of undergraduates with need received aid; of those 82% had need fully met. *Average percent of need met:* 97% (excluding resources awarded to replace EFC). *Average financial aid package:* $15,220 (excluding resources awarded to replace EFC). 16% of all full-time undergraduates had no need and received non-need-based aid.

GIFT AID (NEED-BASED) ***Total amount:*** $8,146,667 (11% Federal, 30% state, 55% institutional, 4% external sources). ***Receiving aid:*** *Freshmen:* 74% (243); *all full-time undergraduates:* 73% (800). ***Average award:*** Freshmen: $11,382; Undergraduates: $10,222. ***Scholarships, grants, and awards:*** Federal Pell, FSEOG, state, private, college/university gift aid from institutional funds.

GIFT AID (NON-NEED-BASED) ***Total amount:*** $1,423,730 (1% Federal, 4% state, 89% institutional, 6% external sources). ***Receiving aid:*** *Freshmen:* 64% (209); *Undergraduates:* 61% (670). ***Scholarships, grants, and awards by category:*** *Academic Interests/Achievement:* business, English, foreign languages, general academic interests/achievements, religion/biblical studies. *Creative Arts/Performance:* art/fine arts, cinema/film/broadcasting, journalism/publications, music, performing arts, theater/drama. *Special Achievements/Activities:* community service, memberships. *Special Characteristics:* children and siblings of alumni, ethnic background, international students, members of minority groups, previous college experience, religious affiliation. ***Tuition waivers:*** Full or partial for employees or children of employees.

LOANS ***Student loans:*** $3,024,613 (89% need-based, 11% non-need-based). 84% of past graduating class borrowed through all loan programs. Average indebtedness per student: $13,370. ***Average need-based loan:*** Freshmen: $2867; Undergraduates: $4033. ***Parent loans:*** $292,078 (62% need-based, 38% non-need-based). ***Programs:*** FFEL (Subsidized and Unsubsidized Stafford, PLUS), Perkins, college/university.

WORK-STUDY ***Federal work-study:*** *Total amount:* $148,450; 125 jobs averaging $1200. ***State or other work-study/employment:*** *Total amount:* $1,632,225 (74% need-based, 26% non-need-based). Part-time jobs available.

APPLYING for FINANCIAL AID ***Required financial aid form:*** FAFSA. ***Financial aid deadline:*** Continuous. ***Notification date:*** Continuous beginning 2/15. Students must reply by 5/1 or within 2 weeks of notification.

CONTACT Ms. Gina Voelz, Director of Financial Aid, Manchester College, 604 East College Avenue, North Manchester, IN 46962-1225, 219-982-5066 or toll-free 800-852-3648. *Fax:* 219-982-6868. *E-mail:* glvoelz@manchester.edu

MANHATTAN CHRISTIAN COLLEGE
Manhattan, KS

Tuition & fees: $6870 **Average undergraduate aid package: $5278**

ABOUT THE INSTITUTION Independent religious, coed. Awards: associate and bachelor's degrees. 9 undergraduate majors. Total enrollment: 400. Undergraduates: 400. Freshmen: 108. Federal methodology is used as a basis for awarding need-based institutional aid.

UNDERGRADUATE EXPENSES for 2000–2001 ***Application fee:*** $25. ***One-time required fee:*** $30. ***Comprehensive fee:*** $10,480 includes full-time tuition ($6870) and room and board ($3610). Room and board charges vary according to board plan. ***Part-time tuition:*** $160 per hour. Part-time tuition and fees vary according to course load. ***Payment plan:*** installment.

FRESHMAN FINANCIAL AID (Fall 1998) 72 applied for aid; of those 89% were deemed to have need. 100% of freshmen with need received aid; of those 20% had need fully met. *Average percent of need met:* 76% (excluding resources awarded to replace EFC). *Average financial aid package:* $5841 (excluding resources awarded to replace EFC). 10% of all full-time freshmen had no need and received non-need-based aid.

UNDERGRADUATE FINANCIAL AID (Fall 1998) 347 applied for aid; of those 95% were deemed to have need. 100% of undergraduates with need received aid; of those 16% had need fully met. *Average percent of need met:* 42% (excluding resources awarded to replace EFC). *Average financial aid package:* $5278 (excluding resources awarded to replace EFC). 4% of all full-time undergraduates had no need and received non-need-based aid.

GIFT AID (NEED-BASED) ***Total amount:*** $328,913 (95% Federal, 5% state). ***Receiving aid:*** *Freshmen:* 37% (29); *all full-time undergraduates:* 44% (158). ***Average award:*** Freshmen: $2359; Undergraduates: $1926. ***Scholarships, grants, and awards:*** Federal Pell, FSEOG, state, private, college/university gift aid from institutional funds.

GIFT AID (NON-NEED-BASED) ***Total amount:*** $667,717 (66% institutional, 34% external sources). ***Receiving aid:*** *Freshmen:* 78% (61); *Undergraduates:* 64% (234). ***Scholarships, grants, and awards by category:*** *Academic Interests/Achievement:* 221 awards: general academic interests/achievements, religion/biblical studies. *Creative Arts/Performance:* 13 awards ($6500 total): music. *Special Achievements/Activities:* 25 awards ($28,299 total): leadership. *Special Characteristics:* children of faculty/staff. ***Tuition waivers:*** Full or partial for employees or children of employees, senior citizens.

LOANS ***Student loans:*** $976,538 (77% need-based, 23% non-need-based). 65% of past graduating class borrowed through all loan programs. ***Average need-based loan:*** Freshmen: $2495; Undergraduates: $2999. ***Parent loans:*** $49,591 (81% need-based, 19% non-need-based). ***Programs:*** FFEL (Subsidized and Unsubsidized Stafford, PLUS), Perkins.

WORK-STUDY ***Federal work-study:*** *Total amount:* $74,671; 66 jobs averaging $1131.

APPLYING for FINANCIAL AID ***Required financial aid form:*** FAFSA. ***Financial aid deadline (priority):*** 4/1. ***Notification date:*** Continuous. Students must reply within 2 weeks of notification.

CONTACT Mrs. Margaret Carlisle, Director of Financial Aid, Manhattan Christian College, 1415 Anderson Avenue, Manhattan, KS 66502-4081, 785-539-3571 or toll-free 877-246-4622. *E-mail:* carlisle@mccks.edu

MANHATTAN COLLEGE
Riverdale, NY

Tuition & fees: $15,810 **Average undergraduate aid package: $12,198**

ABOUT THE INSTITUTION Independent religious, coed. Awards: bachelor's and master's degrees. 60 undergraduate majors. Total enrollment: 3,087. Undergraduates: 2,703. Freshmen: 647. Both federal and institutional methodology are used as a basis for awarding need-based institutional aid.

UNDERGRADUATE EXPENSES for 1999–2000 ***Application fee:*** $35. ***One-time required fee:*** $200. ***Comprehensive fee:*** $23,260 includes full-time tuition ($15,500), mandatory fees ($310), and room and board ($7450). Full-time tuition and fees vary according to program. Room and board charges vary according to board plan. ***Part-time tuition:*** $425 per credit hour. ***Part-time fees:*** $100 per term part-time. ***Payment plan:*** installment.

FRESHMAN FINANCIAL AID (Fall 1999, est.) 546 applied for aid; of those 80% were deemed to have need. 98% of freshmen with need received aid; of those 1% had need fully met. *Average percent of need met:* 88% (excluding resources awarded to replace EFC). *Average financial aid package:* $11,743 (excluding resources awarded to replace EFC). 8% of all full-time freshmen had no need and received non-need-based aid.

UNDERGRADUATE FINANCIAL AID (Fall 1999, est.) 2,040 applied for aid; of those 78% were deemed to have need. 99% of undergraduates with need received aid; of those 1% had need fully met. *Average percent of need met:* 79% (excluding resources awarded to replace EFC). *Average financial aid package:* $12,198 (excluding resources awarded to replace EFC). 13% of all full-time undergraduates had no need and received non-need-based aid.

GIFT AID (NEED-BASED) ***Total amount:*** $11,596,896 (16% Federal, 18% state, 64% institutional, 2% external sources). ***Receiving aid:*** *Freshmen:* 59% (381); *all full-time undergraduates:* 59% (1,426). ***Average award:*** Freshmen: $6952; Undergraduates: $6946. ***Scholarships, grants, and awards:*** Federal Pell, FSEOG, state, private, college/university gift aid from institutional funds.

GIFT AID (NON-NEED-BASED) ***Total amount:*** $3,195,900 (1% state, 99% institutional). ***Receiving aid:*** *Freshmen:* 21% (136); *Undergraduates:* 17% (412). ***Scholarships, grants, and awards by category:*** *Academic Interests/Achievement:* biological sciences, business, computer science, foreign languages, general academic interests/achievements, mathematics, military science. *Creative Arts/Performance:* music. *Special Achievements/Activities:* community service, leadership. *Special Characteristics:* children of faculty/staff. ***Tuition waivers:*** Full or partial for employees or children of employees. ***ROTC:*** Army cooperative, Air Force.

LOANS ***Student loans:*** $8,983,182 (74% need-based, 26% non-need-based). ***Average need-based loan:*** Freshmen: $2625; Undergraduates: $3907. ***Parent loans:*** $1,573,266 (100% non-need-based). ***Programs:*** Federal Direct (Subsidized and Unsubsidized Stafford, PLUS), FFEL (Subsidized and Unsubsidized Stafford, PLUS), Perkins.

WORK-STUDY ***Federal work-study:*** *Total amount:* $420,000; jobs available. ***State or other work-study/employment:*** *Total amount:* $321,862 (100% non-need-based). Part-time jobs available.

ATHLETIC AWARDS *Total amount:* 2,025,000 (100% non-need-based).

APPLYING for FINANCIAL AID ***Required financial aid forms:*** FAFSA, institution's own form, state aid form. ***Financial aid deadline (priority):*** 3/1. ***Notification date:*** 4/1. Students must reply by 5/1.

CONTACT Office of Student Financial Services, Manhattan College, 4513 Manhattan College Parkway, Riverdale, NY 10471, 718-862-7100 or toll-free 800-622-9235 (in-state). *Fax:* 718-862-8027. *E-mail:* finaid@manhattan.edu

MANHATTAN SCHOOL OF MUSIC
New York, NY

Tuition & fees: $19,580 **Average undergraduate aid package: $15,915**

ABOUT THE INSTITUTION Independent, coed. Awards: bachelor's, master's, and doctoral degrees and post-bachelor's and post-master's certificates. 6 undergraduate majors. Total enrollment: 818. Undergraduates: 391. Freshmen: 84. Both federal and institutional methodology are used as a basis for awarding need-based institutional aid.

UNDERGRADUATE EXPENSES for 1999–2000 ***Application fee:*** $90. ***Tuition:*** full-time $19,000. ***Required fees:*** full-time $580. ***Payment plan:*** installment.

FRESHMAN FINANCIAL AID (Fall 1998) 81 applied for aid; of those 94% were deemed to have need. 80% of freshmen with need received aid; of those 5% had need fully met. *Average percent of need met:* 60% (excluding resources awarded to replace EFC). *Average financial aid package:* $17,081 (excluding resources awarded to replace EFC). 5% of all full-time freshmen had no need and received non-need-based aid.

Manhattan School of Music (continued)

UNDERGRADUATE FINANCIAL AID (Fall 1998) 242 applied for aid; of those 96% were deemed to have need. 94% of undergraduates with need received aid; of those 3% had need fully met. *Average percent of need met:* 60% (excluding resources awarded to replace EFC). *Average financial aid package:* $15,915 (excluding resources awarded to replace EFC). 5% of all full-time undergraduates had no need and received non-need-based aid.

GIFT AID (NEED-BASED) ***Total amount:*** $2,079,047 (14% Federal, 8% state, 72% institutional, 6% external sources). ***Receiving aid:*** *Freshmen:* 44% (40); *all full-time undergraduates:* 43% (168). ***Average award:*** Freshmen: $10,685; Undergraduates: $8844. ***Scholarships, grants, and awards:*** Federal Pell, FSEOG, state, private, college/university gift aid from institutional funds.

GIFT AID (NON-NEED-BASED) ***Total amount:*** $51,270 (100% institutional). ***Receiving aid:*** *Freshmen:* 5% (5); *Undergraduates:* 5% (21). ***Scholarships, grants, and awards by category:*** *Creative Arts/Performance:* music. ***Tuition waivers:*** Full or partial for employees or children of employees.

LOANS ***Student loans:*** $1,002,679 (97% need-based, 3% non-need-based). 60% of past graduating class borrowed through all loan programs. Average indebtedness per student: $17,125. ***Average need-based loan:*** Freshmen: $2075; Undergraduates: $3684. ***Parent loans:*** $1,142,288 (73% need-based, 27% non-need-based). ***Programs:*** FFEL (Subsidized and Unsubsidized Stafford, PLUS).

WORK-STUDY ***Federal work-study:*** *Total amount:* $61,592; 105 jobs averaging $1187. ***State or other work-study/employment:*** Part-time jobs available.

APPLYING for FINANCIAL AID ***Required financial aid forms:*** FAFSA, institution's own form, CSS Financial Aid PROFILE, noncustodial (divorced/separated) parent's statement, verification worksheet. ***Financial aid deadline (priority):*** 3/15. ***Notification date:*** 4/1. Students must reply by 5/1 or within 2 weeks of notification.

CONTACT Ms. Amy Anderson, Director of Financial Aid, Manhattan School of Music, 120 Claremont Avenue, New York, NY 10027-4698, 212-749-2802 Ext. 449. *Fax:* 212-749-5471. *E-mail:* aanderson@msmnyc.edu

MANHATTANVILLE COLLEGE

Purchase, NY

Tuition & fees: $19,620 **Average undergraduate aid package: $18,668**

ABOUT THE INSTITUTION Independent, coed. Awards: bachelor's and master's degrees. 47 undergraduate majors. Total enrollment: 2,396. Undergraduates: 1,509. Federal methodology is used as a basis for awarding need-based institutional aid.

UNDERGRADUATE EXPENSES for 2000–2001 ***Application fee:*** $40. ***Comprehensive fee:*** $27,620 includes full-time tuition ($18,860), mandatory fees ($760), and room and board ($8000). Part-time tuition and fees vary according to program. ***Payment plans:*** installment, deferred payment.

FRESHMAN FINANCIAL AID (Fall 1999, est.) 387 applied for aid; of those 84% were deemed to have need. 100% of freshmen with need received aid; of those 20% had need fully met. *Average percent of need met:* 91% (excluding resources awarded to replace EFC). *Average financial aid package:* $18,974 (excluding resources awarded to replace EFC). 11% of all full-time freshmen had no need and received non-need-based aid.

UNDERGRADUATE FINANCIAL AID (Fall 1999, est.) 1,016 applied for aid; of those 92% were deemed to have need. 100% of undergraduates with need received aid; of those 48% had need fully met. *Average percent of need met:* 91% (excluding resources awarded to replace EFC). *Average financial aid package:* $18,668 (excluding resources awarded to replace EFC). 14% of all full-time undergraduates had no need and received non-need-based aid.

GIFT AID (NEED-BASED) ***Total amount:*** $6,769,819 (14% Federal, 19% state, 67% institutional). ***Scholarships, grants, and awards:*** Federal Pell, FSEOG, state, private, college/university gift aid from institutional funds.

GIFT AID (NON-NEED-BASED) ***Total amount:*** $7,490,068 (99% institutional, 1% external sources). ***Receiving aid:*** *Freshmen:* 51% (198); *Undergraduates:* 58% (754). ***Scholarships, grants, and awards by category:*** *Academic Interests/Achievement:* general academic interests/achievements. *Special Achievements/Activities:* community service. ***Tuition waivers:*** Full or partial for employees or children of employees, senior citizens.

LOANS ***Student loans:*** $4,572,705 (61% need-based, 39% non-need-based). 64% of past graduating class borrowed through all loan programs. ***Average need-based loan:*** Freshmen: $2910; Undergraduates: $3814. ***Parent loans:*** $912,993 (100% non-need-based). ***Programs:*** FFEL (Subsidized and Unsubsidized Stafford, PLUS), Perkins.

WORK-STUDY ***Federal work-study:*** *Total amount:* $151,010; 248 jobs averaging $717. ***State or other work-study/employment:*** *Total amount:* $76,579 (100% need-based). Part-time jobs available.

APPLYING for FINANCIAL AID ***Required financial aid forms:*** FAFSA, state aid form. ***Financial aid deadline (priority):*** 4/15. ***Notification date:*** Continuous. Students must reply by 5/1 or within 2 weeks of notification.

CONTACT Maria A. Barlaam, Director of Financial Aid, Manhattanville College, 2900 Purchase Street, Purchase, NY 10577-2132, 914-323-5357 or toll-free 800-328-4553. *Fax:* 914-323-5382. *E-mail:* barlaamm@mville.edu

MANKATO STATE UNIVERSITY

Mankato, MN

See Minnesota State University, Mankato

MANNES COLLEGE OF MUSIC, NEW SCHOOL UNIVERSITY

New York, NY

Tuition & fees: $18,000 **Average undergraduate aid package: $9528**

ABOUT THE INSTITUTION Independent, coed. Awards: bachelor's and master's degrees and post-master's certificates. 7 undergraduate majors. Total university enrollment: 7,179. Total unit enrollment: 323. Undergraduates: 160. Freshmen: 28. Federal methodology is used as a basis for awarding need-based institutional aid.

UNDERGRADUATE EXPENSES for 1999–2000 ***Application fee:*** $100. ***Tuition:*** full-time $18,000. ***Payment plan:*** installment.

FRESHMAN FINANCIAL AID (Fall 1999, est.) 59 applied for aid; of those 97% were deemed to have need. 100% of freshmen with need received aid; of those 11% had need fully met. *Average percent of need met:* 49% (excluding resources awarded to replace EFC). *Average financial aid package:* $10,808 (excluding resources awarded to replace EFC). 6% of all full-time freshmen had no need and received non-need-based aid.

UNDERGRADUATE FINANCIAL AID (Fall 1999, est.) 297 applied for aid; of those 98% were deemed to have need. 100% of undergraduates with need received aid; of those 12% had need fully met. *Average percent of need met:* 52% (excluding resources awarded to replace EFC). *Average financial aid package:* $9528 (excluding resources awarded to replace EFC). 5% of all full-time undergraduates had no need and received non-need-based aid.

GIFT AID (NEED-BASED) ***Total amount:*** $1,969,245 (11% Federal, 5% state, 84% institutional). ***Receiving aid:*** *Freshmen:* 82% (55); *all full-time undergraduates:* 84% (290). ***Average award:*** Freshmen: $5500; Undergraduates: $5075. ***Scholarships, grants, and awards:*** Federal Pell, FSEOG, state, private, college/university gift aid from institutional funds.

GIFT AID (NON-NEED-BASED) ***Receiving aid:*** *Freshmen:* 25% (17); *Undergraduates:* 27% (93). ***Tuition waivers:*** Full or partial for employees or children of employees.

LOANS ***Student loans:*** $943,310 (59% need-based, 41% non-need-based). 74% of past graduating class borrowed through all loan programs. Average indebtedness per student: $18,380. ***Average need-based loan:*** Freshmen: $3980; Undergraduates: $4450. ***Parent loans:*** $373,515 (36% need-based, 64% non-need-based). ***Programs:*** FFEL (Subsidized and Unsubsidized Stafford, PLUS), Perkins, college/university.

WORK-STUDY ***Federal work-study:*** *Total amount:* $41,081; 14 jobs averaging $2040.

APPLYING for FINANCIAL AID ***Required financial aid form:*** FAFSA. ***Financial aid deadline (priority):*** 3/1. ***Notification date:*** 6/1. Students must reply within 4 weeks of notification.

CONTACT Mr. Ramon Verdejo, Assistant Director of Financial Aid, Mannes College of Music, New School University, 150 West 85th Street, New York, NY 10024-4402, 212-580-0210 Ext. 248 or toll-free 800-292-3040 (out-of-state). *Fax:* 212-580-1738. *E-mail:* verdejor@newschool.edu

MANSFIELD UNIVERSITY OF PENNSYLVANIA

Mansfield, PA

Tuition & fees (PA res): $4560 **Average undergraduate aid package: $1920**

ABOUT THE INSTITUTION State-supported, coed. Awards: associate, bachelor's, and master's degrees and post-bachelor's certificates. 91 undergraduate majors. Total enrollment: 3,063. Undergraduates: 2,913. Freshmen: 632. Federal methodology is used as a basis for awarding need-based institutional aid.

UNDERGRADUATE EXPENSES for 1999–2000 ***Application fee:*** $25. ***Tuition, state resident:*** full-time $3618; part-time $150 per credit. ***Tuition, nonresident:*** full-time $9046; part-time $377 per credit. ***Required fees:*** full-time $942; $15 per credit; $43 per term part-time. Full-time tuition and fees vary according to reciprocity agreements. Part-time tuition and fees vary according to course load and reciprocity agreements. ***College room and board:*** $3852. Room and board charges vary according to board plan. ***Payment plans:*** installment, deferred payment.

FRESHMAN FINANCIAL AID (Fall 1998) 754 applied for aid; of those 97% were deemed to have need. 90% of freshmen with need received aid; of those 14% had need fully met. *Average financial aid package:* $1559 (excluding resources awarded to replace EFC).

UNDERGRADUATE FINANCIAL AID (Fall 1998) 1,923 applied for aid; of those 91% were deemed to have need. 89% of undergraduates with need received aid; of those 14% had need fully met. *Average financial aid package:* $1920 (excluding resources awarded to replace EFC).

GIFT AID (NEED-BASED) ***Total amount:*** $4,026,697 (52% Federal, 47% state, 1% institutional). ***Scholarships, grants, and awards:*** Federal Pell, FSEOG, state, private, college/university gift aid from institutional funds.

GIFT AID (NON-NEED-BASED) ***Total amount:*** $532,826 (17% state, 36% institutional, 47% external sources). ***Receiving aid:*** *Freshmen:* 70% (562); *Undergraduates:* 59% (1,326). ***Scholarships, grants, and awards by category:*** *Academic Interests/Achievement:* 75 awards ($75,000 total): biological sciences, communication, education, general academic interests/achievements, health fields, mathematics, physical sciences. *Creative Arts/Performance:* 14 awards ($13,000 total): art/fine arts, journalism/publications, music. *Special Characteristics:* 26 awards ($83,200 total): local/state students, members of minority groups. ***Tuition waivers:*** Full or partial for employees or children of employees, senior citizens.

LOANS ***Student loans:*** $6,860,838 (67% need-based, 33% non-need-based). 64% of past graduating class borrowed through all loan programs. Average indebtedness per student: $20,862. ***Parent loans:*** $497,636 (100% non-need-based). ***Programs:*** FFEL (Subsidized and Unsubsidized Stafford, PLUS), Perkins, alternative loans.

WORK-STUDY ***Federal work-study:*** *Total amount:* $399,573; 268 jobs averaging $1490. ***State or other work-study/employment:*** *Total amount:* $288,447 (100% non-need-based). 256 part-time jobs averaging $1084.

ATHLETIC AWARDS *Total amount:* 85,646 (100% non-need-based).

APPLYING for FINANCIAL AID ***Required financial aid forms:*** FAFSA, institution's own form. ***Financial aid deadline (priority):*** 5/1. ***Notification date:*** Continuous. Students must reply within 4 weeks of notification.

CONTACT Ms. Darcie Stephens, Director of Financial Aid, Mansfield University of Pennsylvania, 109 South Hall, Mansfield, PA 16933, 570-662-4129 or toll-free 800-577-6826. *Fax:* 570-662-4136. *E-mail:* dstephen@mnsfld.edu

MAPLE SPRINGS BAPTIST BIBLE COLLEGE AND SEMINARY

Capitol Heights, MD

ABOUT THE INSTITUTION Independent Baptist. Awards: associate, bachelor's, master's, and doctoral degrees. 1 undergraduate major. Total enrollment: 151. Undergraduates: 89. Freshmen: 20.

GIFT AID (NEED-BASED) ***Scholarships, grants, and awards:*** private.

GIFT AID (NON-NEED-BASED) ***Scholarships, grants, and awards by category:*** *Academic Interests/Achievement:* religion/biblical studies. *Special Characteristics:* general special characteristics.

APPLYING for FINANCIAL AID ***Required financial aid form:*** institution's own form.

CONTACT Ms. Fannie B. Thompson, Director of Business Affairs, Maple Springs Baptist Bible College and Seminary, 4130 Belt Road, Capitol Heights, MD 20743, 301-736-3631. *Fax:* 301-735-6507.

MARANATHA BAPTIST BIBLE COLLEGE

Watertown, WI

Tuition & fees: $6370 **Average undergraduate aid package: $5104**

ABOUT THE INSTITUTION Independent Baptist, coed. Awards: associate, bachelor's, and master's degrees. 19 undergraduate majors. Total enrollment: 746. Undergraduates: 715. Freshmen: 219. Federal methodology is used as a basis for awarding need-based institutional aid.

UNDERGRADUATE EXPENSES for 1999–2000 ***Application fee:*** $25. ***Comprehensive fee:*** $10,170 includes full-time tuition ($5760), mandatory fees ($610), and room and board ($3800). ***Part-time tuition:*** $180 per semester hour. ***Part-time fees:*** $6 per semester hour; $125 per term part-time. ***Payment plan:*** installment.

FRESHMAN FINANCIAL AID (Fall 1998) 171 applied for aid; of those 95% were deemed to have need. 88% of freshmen with need received aid; of those 6% had need fully met. *Average percent of need met:* 55% (excluding resources awarded to replace EFC). *Average financial aid package:* $5525 (excluding resources awarded to replace EFC). 2% of all full-time freshmen had no need and received non-need-based aid.

UNDERGRADUATE FINANCIAL AID (Fall 1998) 589 applied for aid; of those 79% were deemed to have need. 92% of undergraduates with need received aid; of those 8% had need fully met. *Average percent of need met:* 53% (excluding resources awarded to replace EFC). *Average financial aid package:* $5104 (excluding resources awarded to replace EFC). 3% of all full-time undergraduates had no need and received non-need-based aid.

GIFT AID (NEED-BASED) ***Total amount:*** $1,007,656 (51% Federal, 17% state, 16% institutional, 16% external sources). ***Receiving aid:*** *Freshmen:* 64% (138); *all full-time undergraduates:* 55% (386). ***Average award:*** Freshmen: $2679; Undergraduates: $2627. ***Scholarships, grants, and awards:*** Federal Pell, state, private, college/university gift aid from institutional funds.

GIFT AID (NON-NEED-BASED) ***Total amount:*** $19,156 (50% state, 50% institutional). ***Receiving aid:*** *Freshmen:* 1% (2); *Undergraduates:* 1% (8). ***Scholarships, grants, and awards by category:*** *Academic Interests/Achievement:* 17 awards ($12,750 total): general academic interests/achievements. *Special Characteristics:* 102 awards ($120,250 total): children and siblings of alumni, children of educators, general special characteristics, relatives of clergy, religious affiliation. ***Tuition waivers:*** Full or partial for children of alumni, employees or children of employees. ***ROTC:*** Air Force cooperative.

LOANS ***Student loans:*** $1,200,384 (90% need-based, 10% non-need-based). 61% of past graduating class borrowed through all loan programs. Average indebtedness per student: $10,829. ***Average need-based loan:*** Freshmen: $2478; Undergraduates: $1790. ***Parent loans:*** $129,530 (100% need-based). ***Programs:*** FFEL (Subsidized and Unsubsidized Stafford, PLUS).

WORK-STUDY ***State or other work-study/employment:*** *Total amount:* $361,160 (100% need-based). 370 part-time jobs averaging $976.

Maranatha Baptist Bible College (continued)

APPLYING for FINANCIAL AID ***Required financial aid form:*** FAFSA. ***Financial aid deadline (priority):*** 3/1. ***Notification date:*** Continuous. Students must reply within 2 weeks of notification.

CONTACT Mr. Bob Mercer, Financial Aid Administrator, Maranatha Baptist Bible College, 745 West Main Street, Watertown, WI 53094, 920-206-2318 or toll-free 800-622-2947. *Fax:* 920-261-9109.

MARIAN COLLEGE

Indianapolis, IN

Tuition & fees: $14,416 **Average undergraduate aid package: $12,255**

ABOUT THE INSTITUTION Independent Roman Catholic, coed. Awards: associate and bachelor's degrees. 39 undergraduate majors. Total enrollment: 1,318. Undergraduates: 1,318. Freshmen: 265. Federal methodology is used as a basis for awarding need-based institutional aid.

UNDERGRADUATE EXPENSES for 1999–2000 ***Application fee:*** $20. ***Comprehensive fee:*** $19,292 includes full-time tuition ($14,012), mandatory fees ($404), and room and board ($4876). Room and board charges vary according to board plan and housing facility. ***Part-time tuition:*** $600 per credit hour. ***Part-time fees:*** $128 per term part-time. Part-time tuition and fees vary according to class time and course load. ***Payment plans:*** installment, deferred payment.

FRESHMAN FINANCIAL AID (Fall 1999) 243 applied for aid; of those 86% were deemed to have need. 100% of freshmen with need received aid; of those 53% had need fully met. *Average percent of need met:* 100% (excluding resources awarded to replace EFC). *Average financial aid package:* $15,039 (excluding resources awarded to replace EFC). 3% of all full-time freshmen had no need and received non-need-based aid.

UNDERGRADUATE FINANCIAL AID (Fall 1999) 859 applied for aid; of those 84% were deemed to have need. 100% of undergraduates with need received aid; of those 42% had need fully met. *Average percent of need met:* 85% (excluding resources awarded to replace EFC). *Average financial aid package:* $12,255 (excluding resources awarded to replace EFC). 8% of all full-time undergraduates had no need and received non-need-based aid.

GIFT AID (NEED-BASED) ***Total amount:*** $4,497,634 (17% Federal, 43% state, 40% institutional). ***Receiving aid:*** *Freshmen:* 80% (200); *all full-time undergraduates:* 73% (632). ***Average award:*** Freshmen: $7145; Undergraduates: $5544. ***Scholarships, grants, and awards:*** Federal Pell, FSEOG, state, private, college/university gift aid from institutional funds.

GIFT AID (NON-NEED-BASED) ***Total amount:*** $2,648,319 (87% institutional, 13% external sources). ***Receiving aid:*** *Freshmen:* 49% (124); *Undergraduates:* 50% (433). ***Scholarships, grants, and awards by category:*** *Academic Interests/Achievement:* 333 awards ($1,800,000 total): general academic interests/achievements. *Creative Arts/Performance:* 10 awards ($35,000 total): applied art and design, art/fine arts, music, performing arts, theater/drama. *Special Achievements/Activities:* 110 awards ($110,000 total): community service, religious involvement. *Special Characteristics:* 270 awards ($760,000 total): adult students, children and siblings of alumni, children of faculty/staff, international students, members of minority groups, religious affiliation, siblings of current students, spouses of current students. ***Tuition waivers:*** Full or partial for children of alumni, employees or children of employees, senior citizens. ***ROTC:*** Army cooperative, Air Force cooperative.

LOANS ***Student loans:*** $3,705,833 (55% need-based, 45% non-need-based). 80% of past graduating class borrowed through all loan programs. Average indebtedness per student: $15,674. ***Average need-based loan:*** Freshmen: $2704; Undergraduates: $3100. ***Parent loans:*** $356,639 (100% non-need-based). ***Programs:*** FFEL (Subsidized and Unsubsidized Stafford, PLUS), Perkins.

WORK-STUDY ***Federal work-study:*** *Total amount:* $126,550; jobs available. ***State or other work-study/employment:*** *Total amount:* $118,431 (30% need-based, 70% non-need-based). Part-time jobs available.

ATHLETIC AWARDS *Total amount:* 595,804 (100% non-need-based).

APPLYING for FINANCIAL AID ***Required financial aid forms:*** FAFSA, institution's own form, financial aid transcript (for transfers). ***Financial aid deadline (priority):*** 3/1. ***Notification date:*** Continuous.

CONTACT Mr. John E. Shelton, Assistant Dean of Financial Aid, Marian College, 3200 Cold Spring Road, Indianapolis, IN 46222-1997, 317-955-6040 or toll-free 800-772-7264 (in-state). *Fax:* 317-955-6424. *E-mail:* jshelton@marian.edu

MARIAN COLLEGE OF FOND DU LAC

Fond du Lac, WI

Tuition & fees: $12,256 **Average undergraduate aid package: $10,635**

ABOUT THE INSTITUTION Independent Roman Catholic, coed. Awards: bachelor's and master's degrees. 42 undergraduate majors. Total enrollment: 2,378. Undergraduates: 1,571. Freshmen: 227. Federal methodology is used as a basis for awarding need-based institutional aid.

UNDERGRADUATE EXPENSES for 1999–2000 ***Application fee:*** $15. ***Comprehensive fee:*** $16,620 includes full-time tuition ($11,966), mandatory fees ($290), and room and board ($4364). ***College room only:*** $2036. Room and board charges vary according to board plan, housing facility, and location. ***Part-time tuition:*** $255 per credit. ***Part-time fees:*** $290 per year part-time. Part-time tuition and fees vary according to class time, course load, and program. ***Payment plan:*** installment.

FRESHMAN FINANCIAL AID (Fall 1999) 231 applied for aid; of those 85% were deemed to have need. 98% of freshmen with need received aid; of those 57% had need fully met. *Average percent of need met:* 90% (excluding resources awarded to replace EFC). *Average financial aid package:* $11,188 (excluding resources awarded to replace EFC). 13% of all full-time freshmen had no need and received non-need-based aid.

UNDERGRADUATE FINANCIAL AID (Fall 1999) 922 applied for aid; of those 81% were deemed to have need. 99% of undergraduates with need received aid; of those 78% had need fully met. *Average percent of need met:* 85% (excluding resources awarded to replace EFC). *Average financial aid package:* $10,635 (excluding resources awarded to replace EFC). 16% of all full-time undergraduates had no need and received non-need-based aid.

GIFT AID (NEED-BASED) ***Total amount:*** $5,015,392 (15% Federal, 18% state, 65% institutional, 2% external sources). ***Receiving aid:*** *Freshmen:* 62% (157); *all full-time undergraduates:* 62% (605). ***Average award:*** Freshmen: $10,229; Undergraduates: $8290. ***Scholarships, grants, and awards:*** Federal Pell, FSEOG, state, private, college/university gift aid from institutional funds, endowed scholarships.

GIFT AID (NON-NEED-BASED) ***Total amount:*** $748,187 (2% Federal, 96% institutional, 2% external sources). ***Receiving aid:*** *Freshmen:* 76% (193); *Undergraduates:* 58% (562). ***Scholarships, grants, and awards by category:*** *Academic Interests/Achievement:* 751 awards ($2,794,450 total): general academic interests/achievements. *Creative Arts/Performance:* 39 awards ($42,100 total): music. *Special Characteristics:* 72 awards ($169,024 total): children of faculty/staff, children with a deceased or disabled parent, general special characteristics, siblings of current students. ***Tuition waivers:*** Full or partial for employees or children of employees, senior citizens. ***ROTC:*** Army.

LOANS ***Student loans:*** $4,456,262 (87% need-based, 13% non-need-based). 85% of past graduating class borrowed through all loan programs. Average indebtedness per student: $14,500. ***Average need-based loan:*** Freshmen: $2610; Undergraduates: $6015. ***Parent loans:*** $582,598 (43% need-based, 57% non-need-based). ***Programs:*** FFEL (Subsidized and Unsubsidized Stafford, PLUS), Perkins, Federal Nursing.

WORK-STUDY ***Federal work-study:*** *Total amount:* $93,459; 85 jobs averaging $1100. ***State or other work-study/employment:*** *Total amount:* $153,188 (100% non-need-based). Part-time jobs available.

APPLYING for FINANCIAL AID ***Required financial aid forms:*** FAFSA, institution's own form. ***Financial aid deadline (priority):*** 3/1. ***Notification date:*** Continuous. Students must reply within 3 weeks of notification.

CONTACT Ms. Debra E. McKinney, Director of Financial Aid, Marian College of Fond du Lac, 45 South National Avenue, Fond du Lac, WI 54935-4699, 920-923-7614 or toll-free 800-2-MARIAN (in-state). *Fax:* 920-923-8767.

MARIETTA COLLEGE

Marietta, OH

Tuition & fees: $17,510 **Average undergraduate aid package: $15,800**

ABOUT THE INSTITUTION Independent, coed. Awards: associate, bachelor's, and master's degrees. 48 undergraduate majors. Total enrollment: 1,214. Undergraduates: 1,153. Freshmen: 302. Federal methodology is used as a basis for awarding need-based institutional aid.

UNDERGRADUATE EXPENSES for 1999–2000 ***Application fee:*** $25. ***Comprehensive fee:*** $22,480 includes full-time tuition ($17,310), mandatory fees ($200), and room and board ($4970). ***College room only:*** $2680. ***Part-time tuition:*** $575 per credit hour. Part-time tuition and fees vary according to class time. ***Payment plan:*** installment.

FRESHMAN FINANCIAL AID (Fall 1999) 265 applied for aid; of those 93% were deemed to have need. 100% of freshmen with need received aid; of those 5% had need fully met. *Average percent of need met:* 92% (excluding resources awarded to replace EFC). *Average financial aid package:* $15,910 (excluding resources awarded to replace EFC). 10% of all full-time freshmen had no need and received non-need-based aid.

UNDERGRADUATE FINANCIAL AID (Fall 1999) 874 applied for aid; of those 93% were deemed to have need. 100% of undergraduates with need received aid; of those 11% had need fully met. *Average percent of need met:* 91% (excluding resources awarded to replace EFC). *Average financial aid package:* $15,800 (excluding resources awarded to replace EFC). 10% of all full-time undergraduates had no need and received non-need-based aid.

GIFT AID (NEED-BASED) ***Total amount:*** $5,316,626 (14% Federal, 6% state, 80% institutional). ***Receiving aid:*** *Freshmen:* 58% (175); *all full-time undergraduates:* 61% (635). ***Average award:*** Freshmen: $8133; Undergraduates: $7194. ***Scholarships, grants, and awards:*** Federal Pell, FSEOG, state, private, college/university gift aid from institutional funds.

GIFT AID (NON-NEED-BASED) ***Total amount:*** $3,529,273 (16% state, 78% institutional, 6% external sources). ***Receiving aid:*** *Freshmen:* 67% (203); *Undergraduates:* 63% (650). ***Scholarships, grants, and awards by category:*** *Academic Interests/Achievement:* 470 awards ($2,737,000 total): general academic interests/achievements. *Creative Arts/Performance:* 35 awards ($91,500 total): art/fine arts. *Special Achievements/Activities:* 4 awards ($12,000 total): general special achievements/activities. *Special Characteristics:* 57 awards ($136,250 total): children and siblings of alumni, siblings of current students. ***Tuition waivers:*** Full or partial for employees or children of employees.

LOANS ***Student loans:*** $3,111,670 (83% need-based, 17% non-need-based). 72% of past graduating class borrowed through all loan programs. Average indebtedness per student: $16,077. ***Average need-based loan:*** Freshmen: $3080; Undergraduates: $5305. ***Parent loans:*** $1,550,561 (100% non-need-based). ***Programs:*** Federal Direct (Subsidized and Unsubsidized Stafford, PLUS), FFEL (Subsidized and Unsubsidized Stafford, PLUS), Perkins, state.

WORK-STUDY ***Federal work-study:*** *Total amount:* $710,000; 650 jobs averaging $1092.

APPLYING for FINANCIAL AID ***Required financial aid form:*** FAFSA. ***Financial aid deadline (priority):*** 3/1. ***Notification date:*** 3/15. Students must reply within 2 weeks of notification.

CONTACT Mr. James T. Begany, Director of Student Financial Services, Marietta College, 215 Fifth Street, Marietta, OH 45750-4000, 740-376-4712 or toll-free 800-331-7896. *Fax:* 740-376-4990. *E-mail:* finaid@marietta.edu

MARIST COLLEGE

Poughkeepsie, NY

Tuition & fees: $14,754 **Average undergraduate aid package: $10,593**

ABOUT THE INSTITUTION Independent, coed. Awards: bachelor's and master's degrees. 47 undergraduate majors. Total enrollment: 5,010. Undergraduates: 4,428. Freshmen: 1,124. Federal methodology is used as a basis for awarding need-based institutional aid.

UNDERGRADUATE EXPENSES for 1999–2000 ***Application fee:*** $35. ***One-time required fee:*** $25. ***Comprehensive fee:*** $22,172 includes full-time tuition ($14,374), mandatory fees ($380), and room and board ($7418). ***College room only:*** $4624. Room and board charges vary according to board plan and housing facility. ***Part-time tuition:*** $335 per credit. ***Part-time fees:*** $60 per term part-time. ***Payment plan:*** installment.

FRESHMAN FINANCIAL AID (Fall 1999) 1075 applied for aid; of those 79% were deemed to have need. 81% of freshmen with need received aid; of those 17% had need fully met. *Average percent of need met:* 74% (excluding resources awarded to replace EFC). *Average financial aid package:* $11,966 (excluding resources awarded to replace EFC). 16% of all full-time freshmen had no need and received non-need-based aid.

UNDERGRADUATE FINANCIAL AID (Fall 1999) 3,060 applied for aid; of those 82% were deemed to have need. 90% of undergraduates with need received aid; of those 12% had need fully met. *Average percent of need met:* 72% (excluding resources awarded to replace EFC). *Average financial aid package:* $10,593 (excluding resources awarded to replace EFC). 16% of all full-time undergraduates had no need and received non-need-based aid.

GIFT AID (NEED-BASED) ***Total amount:*** $12,153,871 (15% Federal, 15% state, 70% institutional). ***Receiving aid:*** *Freshmen:* 47% (510); *all full-time undergraduates:* 39% (1,478). ***Average award:*** Freshmen: $8815; Undergraduates: $7241. ***Scholarships, grants, and awards:*** Federal Pell, FSEOG, state, private, college/university gift aid from institutional funds.

GIFT AID (NON-NEED-BASED) ***Total amount:*** $1,997,825 (13% state, 87% institutional). ***Receiving aid:*** *Freshmen:* 28% (300); *Undergraduates:* 22% (827). ***Scholarships, grants, and awards by category:*** *Academic Interests/Achievement:* general academic interests/achievements. *Creative Arts/Performance:* debating, music. *Special Achievements/Activities:* general special achievements/activities. ***Tuition waivers:*** Full or partial for employees or children of employees.

LOANS ***Student loans:*** $16,040,564 (77% need-based, 23% non-need-based). 83% of past graduating class borrowed through all loan programs. Average indebtedness per student: $16,350. ***Average need-based loan:*** Freshmen: $2210; Undergraduates: $4311. ***Parent loans:*** $3,959,436 (72% need-based, 28% non-need-based). ***Programs:*** FFEL (Subsidized and Unsubsidized Stafford, PLUS), Perkins, alternative loans, Key Alternative Loans, CitiAssist Loans, TERI Loans, Signature Loans, EXCEL Loans.

WORK-STUDY ***Federal work-study:*** *Total amount:* $270,805; jobs available. ***State or other work-study/employment:*** Part-time jobs available.

APPLYING for FINANCIAL AID ***Required financial aid forms:*** FAFSA, institution's own form. ***Financial aid deadline (priority):*** 2/15. ***Notification date:*** Continuous beginning 3/15. Students must reply by 5/1 or within 2 weeks of notification.

CONTACT Joseph R. Weglarz, Director of Financial Aid, Marist College, 290 North Road, Poughkeepsie, NY 12601, 914-575-3230 or toll-free 800-436-5483. *E-mail:* joseph.weglarz@marist.edu

MARLBORO COLLEGE

Marlboro, VT

Tuition & fees: $19,560 **Average undergraduate aid package: $19,450**

ABOUT THE INSTITUTION Independent, coed. Awards: bachelor's and master's degrees. 80 undergraduate majors. Total enrollment: 290. Undergraduates: 290. Freshmen: 93. Both federal and institutional methodology are used as a basis for awarding need-based institutional aid.

UNDERGRADUATE EXPENSES for 2000–2001 ***Application fee:*** $30. ***Comprehensive fee:*** $26,310 includes full-time tuition ($18,800), mandatory fees ($760), and room and board ($6750). ***College room only:*** $3300. ***Part-time tuition:*** $630 per credit. ***Part-time fees:*** $165 per term part-time.

FRESHMAN FINANCIAL AID (Fall 1999) 81 applied for aid; of those 94% were deemed to have need. 100% of freshmen with need received aid; of those 38% had need fully met. *Average percent of need met:* 90% (excluding resources awarded to replace EFC). *Average financial aid package:* $19,307 (excluding resources awarded to replace EFC).

Marlboro College (continued)

UNDERGRADUATE FINANCIAL AID (Fall 1999) 228 applied for aid; of those 92% were deemed to have need. 100% of undergraduates with need received aid; of those 26% had need fully met. *Average percent of need met:* 89% (excluding resources awarded to replace EFC). *Average financial aid package:* $19,450 (excluding resources awarded to replace EFC). 4% of all full-time undergraduates had no need and received non-need-based aid.

GIFT AID (NEED-BASED) ***Total amount:*** $2,301,656 (12% Federal, 4% state, 80% institutional, 4% external sources). ***Receiving aid:*** *Freshmen:* 82% (76); *all full-time undergraduates:* 72% (199). ***Average award:*** Freshmen: $12,534; Undergraduates: $11,569. ***Scholarships, grants, and awards:*** Federal Pell, FSEOG, state, private, college/university gift aid from institutional funds.

GIFT AID (NON-NEED-BASED) ***Total amount:*** $38,873 (77% institutional, 23% external sources). ***Receiving aid:*** *Freshmen:* 1% (1); *Undergraduates:* 1% (2). ***Scholarships, grants, and awards by category:*** *Academic Interests/Achievement:* 38 awards ($169,500 total): general academic interests/achievements. *Special Characteristics:* 4 awards ($2500 total): children and siblings of alumni.

LOANS ***Student loans:*** $1,074,488 (76% need-based, 24% non-need-based). 82% of past graduating class borrowed through all loan programs. Average indebtedness per student: $15,906. ***Average need-based loan:*** Freshmen: $2619; Undergraduates: $3712. ***Parent loans:*** $865,808 (34% need-based, 66% non-need-based). ***Programs:*** FFEL (Subsidized and Unsubsidized Stafford, PLUS).

WORK-STUDY ***Federal work-study:*** *Total amount:* $338,373; 182 jobs averaging $1859. ***State or other work-study/employment:*** *Total amount:* $42,760 (80% need-based, 20% non-need-based). 5 part-time jobs averaging $1672.

APPLYING for FINANCIAL AID ***Required financial aid forms:*** FAFSA, CSS Financial Aid PROFILE, state aid form, noncustodial (divorced/separated) parent's statement. ***Financial aid deadline (priority):*** 3/1. ***Notification date:*** 4/1. Students must reply by 5/1 or within 2 weeks of notification.

CONTACT Cathy Pollard, Associate Director of Financial Aid/Work-Study Coordinator, Marlboro College, South Road, PO Box A, Marlboro, VT 05344, 802-258-9312 or toll-free 800-343-0049 (out-of-state). *Fax:* 802-258-9300. *E-mail:* finaid@marlboro.edu

MARQUETTE UNIVERSITY

Milwaukee, WI

Tuition & fees: $17,336 **Average undergraduate aid package: $15,461**

ABOUT THE INSTITUTION Independent Roman Catholic (Jesuit), coed. Awards: associate, bachelor's, master's, doctoral, and first professional degrees. 74 undergraduate majors. Total enrollment: 10,780. Undergraduates: 7,437. Freshmen: 1,718. Federal methodology is used as a basis for awarding need-based institutional aid.

UNDERGRADUATE EXPENSES for 1999–2000 ***Application fee:*** $30. ***Comprehensive fee:*** $23,422 includes full-time tuition ($17,080), mandatory fees ($256), and room and board ($6086). Full-time tuition and fees vary according to program and student level. Room and board charges vary according to board plan and housing facility. ***Part-time tuition:*** $350 per credit. Part-time tuition and fees vary according to program. ***Payment plans:*** tuition prepayment, installment.

FRESHMAN FINANCIAL AID (Fall 1999, est.) 1372 applied for aid; of those 80% were deemed to have need. 100% of freshmen with need received aid; of those 68% had need fully met. *Average percent of need met:* 90% (excluding resources awarded to replace EFC). *Average financial aid package:* $15,777 (excluding resources awarded to replace EFC). 15% of all full-time freshmen had no need and received non-need-based aid.

UNDERGRADUATE FINANCIAL AID (Fall 1999, est.) 4,700 applied for aid; of those 86% were deemed to have need. 100% of undergraduates with need received aid; of those 42% had need fully met. *Average percent of need met:* 87% (excluding resources awarded to replace EFC). *Average financial aid package:* $15,461 (excluding resources awarded to replace EFC). 9% of all full-time undergraduates had no need and received non-need-based aid.

GIFT AID (NEED-BASED) ***Total amount:*** $33,916,174 (7% Federal, 8% state, 79% institutional, 6% external sources). ***Receiving aid:*** *Freshmen:* 63% (1,088); *all full-time undergraduates:* 58% (3,931). ***Average award:*** Freshmen: $9762; Undergraduates: $9232. ***Scholarships, grants, and awards:*** Federal Pell, FSEOG, state, private, college/university gift aid from institutional funds.

GIFT AID (NON-NEED-BASED) ***Total amount:*** $4,653,269 (2% state, 87% institutional, 11% external sources). ***Receiving aid:*** *Freshmen:* 5% (83); *Undergraduates:* 3% (191). ***Scholarships, grants, and awards by category:*** *Academic Interests/Achievement:* biological sciences, business, communication, engineering/technologies, foreign languages, general academic interests/achievements, health fields, mathematics. *Creative Arts/Performance:* theater/drama. ***Tuition waivers:*** Full or partial for employees or children of employees, senior citizens. ***ROTC:*** Army, Naval, Air Force.

LOANS ***Student loans:*** $22,712,897 (78% need-based, 22% non-need-based). 51% of past graduating class borrowed through all loan programs. ***Average need-based loan:*** Freshmen: $4101; Undergraduates: $5094. ***Parent loans:*** $8,315,676 (25% need-based, 75% non-need-based). ***Programs:*** Federal Direct (Subsidized and Unsubsidized Stafford, PLUS), Perkins, Federal Nursing, college/university.

WORK-STUDY ***Federal work-study:*** *Total amount:* $1,200,000; jobs available. ***State or other work-study/employment:*** *Total amount:* $3,400,000 (100% non-need-based). Part-time jobs available.

ATHLETIC AWARDS *Total amount:* 559,347 (70% need-based, 30% non-need-based).

APPLYING for FINANCIAL AID ***Required financial aid form:*** FAFSA. ***Financial aid deadline:*** Continuous. ***Notification date:*** 3/15. Students must reply by 5/1 or within 2 weeks of notification.

CONTACT Daniel L. Goyette, Director of Financial Aid, Marquette University, Office of Student Financial Aid, 1212 Building, Room 415, PO Box 1881, Milwaukee, WI 53201-1881, 414-288-7390 or toll-free 800-222-6544. *Fax:* 414-288-1718. *E-mail:* financialaid@marquette.edu

MARSHALL UNIVERSITY

Huntington, WV

Tuition & fees (WV res): $2886 **Average undergraduate aid package: $5358**

ABOUT THE INSTITUTION State-supported, coed. Awards: associate, bachelor's, master's, doctoral, and first professional degrees and post-master's certificates. 87 undergraduate majors. Total enrollment: 13,369. Undergraduates: 9,424. Freshmen: 1,847. Federal methodology is used as a basis for awarding need-based institutional aid.

UNDERGRADUATE EXPENSES for 1999–2000 ***Application fee:*** $15; $30 for nonresidents. ***Tuition, state resident:*** full-time $2440; part-time $83 per semester hour. ***Tuition, nonresident:*** full-time $6512; part-time $253 per semester hour. ***Required fees:*** full-time $446; $19 per semester hour. Full-time tuition and fees vary according to program and reciprocity agreements. Part-time tuition and fees vary according to program and reciprocity agreements. ***College room and board:*** $4652; ***room only:*** $2432. Room and board charges vary according to board plan and housing facility. ***Payment plans:*** installment, deferred payment.

FRESHMAN FINANCIAL AID (Fall 1999) 1178 applied for aid; of those 76% were deemed to have need. 99% of freshmen with need received aid; of those 28% had need fully met. *Average percent of need met:* 63% (excluding resources awarded to replace EFC). *Average financial aid package:* $5205 (excluding resources awarded to replace EFC). 25% of all full-time freshmen had no need and received non-need-based aid.

UNDERGRADUATE FINANCIAL AID (Fall 1999) 5,170 applied for aid; of those 79% were deemed to have need. 98% of undergraduates with need received aid; of those 40% had need fully met. *Average percent of need met:* 69% (excluding resources awarded to replace EFC). *Average financial aid package:* $5358 (excluding resources awarded to replace EFC). 14% of all full-time undergraduates had no need and received non-need-based aid.

GIFT AID (NEED-BASED) ***Total amount:*** $10,807,695 (71% Federal, 29% state). ***Receiving aid:*** *Freshmen:* 42% (663); *all full-time undergraduates:* 36% (2,931). ***Average award:*** Freshmen: $3223; Undergraduates: $3059. ***Scholarships, grants, and awards:*** Federal Pell, FSEOG, state, private, college/university gift aid from institutional funds.

GIFT AID (NON-NEED-BASED) ***Total amount:*** $3,778,477 (67% institutional, 33% external sources). ***Receiving aid:*** *Freshmen:* 33% (521); *Undergraduates:* 14% (1,123). ***Scholarships, grants, and awards by category:*** *Academic Interests/Achievement:* general academic interests/achievements. *Special Characteristics:* veterans' children. ***ROTC:*** Army.

LOANS ***Student loans:*** $17,951,599 (99% need-based, 1% non-need-based). 54% of past graduating class borrowed through all loan programs. Average indebtedness per student: $13,020. ***Average need-based loan:*** Freshmen: $3055; Undergraduates: $4129. ***Parent loans:*** $1,514,920 (100% non-need-based). ***Programs:*** Federal Direct (Subsidized and Unsubsidized Stafford, PLUS), Perkins, state, college/university.

WORK-STUDY ***Federal work-study:*** *Total amount:* $585,136; jobs available. ***State or other work-study/employment:*** *Total amount:* $233,956 (100% non-need-based). Part-time jobs available.

ATHLETIC AWARDS *Total amount:* 2,024,580 (100% non-need-based).

APPLYING for FINANCIAL AID ***Required financial aid form:*** FAFSA. ***Financial aid deadline (priority):*** 3/1. ***Notification date:*** 5/1. Students must reply within 2 weeks of notification.

CONTACT Ms. Nadine A. Hamrick, Associate Director, Student Financial Aid, Marshall University, 400 Hal Greer Boulevard, Huntington, WV 25755-3300, 304-696-2277 or toll-free 800-642-3499 (in-state). *Fax:* 304-696-3242. *E-mail:* hamrick@marshall.edu

MARS HILL COLLEGE

Mars Hill, NC

Tuition & fees: $11,600 **Average undergraduate aid package: N/A**

ABOUT THE INSTITUTION Independent Baptist, coed. Awards: bachelor's degrees. 61 undergraduate majors. Total enrollment: 1,224. Undergraduates: 1,224. Freshmen: 347. Federal methodology is used as a basis for awarding need-based institutional aid.

UNDERGRADUATE EXPENSES for 1999–2000 ***Application fee:*** $25. ***Comprehensive fee:*** $15,900 includes full-time tuition ($10,800), mandatory fees ($800), and room and board ($4300). ***College room only:*** $2200. Full-time tuition and fees vary according to course load. Room and board charges vary according to board plan and housing facility. ***Part-time tuition:*** $345 per credit. Part-time tuition and fees vary according to course load. ***Payment plan:*** installment.

GIFT AID (NEED-BASED) ***Total amount:*** $2,365,843 (42% Federal, 31% state, 21% institutional, 6% external sources). ***Scholarships, grants, and awards:*** Federal Pell, FSEOG, state, private, college/university gift aid from institutional funds.

GIFT AID (NON-NEED-BASED) ***Total amount:*** $3,000,357 (39% state, 61% institutional). ***Scholarships, grants, and awards by category:*** *Academic Interests/Achievement:* general academic interests/achievements. *Creative Arts/Performance:* dance, music, theater/drama. *Special Achievements/Activities:* cheerleading/drum major. ***Tuition waivers:*** Full or partial for employees or children of employees.

LOANS ***Student loans:*** $3,114,395 (75% need-based, 25% non-need-based). ***Parent loans:*** $1,065,389 (100% non-need-based). ***Programs:*** FFEL (Subsidized and Unsubsidized Stafford, PLUS), Perkins, college/university.

WORK-STUDY ***Federal work-study:*** *Total amount:* $478,860; 343 jobs averaging $1500. ***State or other work-study/employment:*** *Total amount:* $99,196 (100% non-need-based). 51 part-time jobs averaging $1300.

ATHLETIC AWARDS *Total amount:* 766,144 (100% non-need-based).

APPLYING for FINANCIAL AID ***Required financial aid forms:*** FAFSA, state aid form. ***Financial aid deadline (priority):*** 4/15. ***Notification date:*** Continuous. Students must reply within 2 weeks of notification.

CONTACT Mr. Scott Miller, Director of Financial Aid, Mars Hill College, 124 Cascade Street, Mars Hill, NC 28754, 828-689-1123 or toll-free 800-543-1514. *Fax:* 828-689-1300. *E-mail:* smiller@mhc.edu

MARTIN LUTHER COLLEGE

New Ulm, MN

Tuition & fees: $5145 **Average undergraduate aid package: $4013**

ABOUT THE INSTITUTION Independent religious, coed. Awards: bachelor's degrees. 6 undergraduate majors. Total enrollment: 912. Undergraduates: 912. Freshmen: 242. Federal methodology is used as a basis for awarding need-based institutional aid.

UNDERGRADUATE EXPENSES for 2000–2001 ***Application fee:*** $25. ***Comprehensive fee:*** $7485 includes full-time tuition ($4610), mandatory fees ($535), and room and board ($2340). ***College room only:*** $600. ***Part-time tuition:*** $125 per semester hour. ***Part-time fees:*** $65 per term part-time. ***Payment plan:*** installment.

FRESHMAN FINANCIAL AID (Fall 1998) 217 applied for aid; of those 96% were deemed to have need. 97% of freshmen with need received aid; of those 96% had need fully met. *Average percent of need met:* 95% (excluding resources awarded to replace EFC). *Average financial aid package:* $4013 (excluding resources awarded to replace EFC). 7% of all full-time freshmen had no need and received non-need-based aid.

UNDERGRADUATE FINANCIAL AID (Fall 1998) 826 applied for aid; of those 96% were deemed to have need. 99% of undergraduates with need received aid; of those 84% had need fully met. *Average percent of need met:* 95% (excluding resources awarded to replace EFC). *Average financial aid package:* $4013 (excluding resources awarded to replace EFC). 6% of all full-time undergraduates had no need and received non-need-based aid.

GIFT AID (NEED-BASED) ***Total amount:*** $1,638,013 (31% Federal, 13% state, 51% institutional, 5% external sources). ***Receiving aid:*** *Freshmen:* 81% (182); *all full-time undergraduates:* 84% (715). ***Average award:*** Freshmen: $2291; Undergraduates: $2291. ***Scholarships, grants, and awards:*** Federal Pell, FSEOG, state, private, college/university gift aid from institutional funds.

GIFT AID (NON-NEED-BASED) ***Total amount:*** $648,808 (51% institutional, 49% external sources). ***Receiving aid:*** *Freshmen:* 24% (55); *Undergraduates:* 25% (209). ***Scholarships, grants, and awards by category:*** *Academic Interests/Achievement:* 215 awards ($106,900 total): general academic interests/achievements. *Creative Arts/Performance:* 8 awards ($2200 total): music. *Special Achievements/Activities:* 15 awards ($11,940 total): general special achievements/activities.

LOANS ***Student loans:*** $981,928 (71% need-based, 29% non-need-based). 62% of past graduating class borrowed through all loan programs. Average indebtedness per student: $8694. ***Average need-based loan:*** Freshmen: $2424; Undergraduates: $2424. ***Parent loans:*** $39,719 (100% non-need-based). ***Programs:*** FFEL (Subsidized and Unsubsidized Stafford, PLUS), Perkins, state, college/university.

WORK-STUDY ***Federal work-study:*** *Total amount:* $42,652; 49 jobs averaging $871. ***State or other work-study/employment:*** *Total amount:* $5890 (100% need-based). 7 part-time jobs averaging $841.

APPLYING for FINANCIAL AID ***Required financial aid forms:*** FAFSA, institution's own form. ***Financial aid deadline:*** 5/1. ***Notification date:*** Continuous. Students must reply within 2 weeks of notification.

CONTACT Mr. Daniel Hosbach, Associate Director of Financial Aid, Martin Luther College, 1995 Luther Court, New Ulm, MN 56073-3965, 507-354-8221 Ext. 221. *Fax:* 507-354-8225. *E-mail:* hosbacdj@mlc-wels.edu

MARTIN METHODIST COLLEGE

Pulaski, TN

Tuition & fees: $8520 **Average undergraduate aid package: $5610**

ABOUT THE INSTITUTION Independent United Methodist, coed. Awards: associate and bachelor's degrees. 64 undergraduate majors. Total enroll-

Martin Methodist College (continued)

ment: 550. Undergraduates: 550. Freshmen: 132. Federal methodology is used as a basis for awarding need-based institutional aid.

UNDERGRADUATE EXPENSES for 1999–2000 ***Application fee:*** $25. ***Comprehensive fee:*** $11,920 includes full-time tuition ($8500), mandatory fees ($20), and room and board ($3400). Room and board charges vary according to housing facility. ***Part-time tuition:*** $355 per hour. Part-time tuition and fees vary according to class time. ***Payment plan:*** installment.

FRESHMAN FINANCIAL AID (Fall 1998) 141 applied for aid; of those 72% were deemed to have need. 100% of freshmen with need received aid; of those 75% had need fully met. *Average percent of need met:* 89% (excluding resources awarded to replace EFC). *Average financial aid package:* $6514 (excluding resources awarded to replace EFC). 10% of all full-time freshmen had no need and received non-need-based aid.

UNDERGRADUATE FINANCIAL AID (Fall 1998) 467 applied for aid; of those 75% were deemed to have need. 100% of undergraduates with need received aid; of those 58% had need fully met. *Average percent of need met:* 85% (excluding resources awarded to replace EFC). *Average financial aid package:* $5610 (excluding resources awarded to replace EFC). 14% of all full-time undergraduates had no need and received non-need-based aid.

GIFT AID (NEED-BASED) ***Total amount:*** $1,089,871 (45% Federal, 23% state, 27% institutional, 5% external sources). ***Receiving aid:*** *Freshmen:* 49% (91); *all full-time undergraduates:* 36% (196). ***Average award:*** Freshmen: $3560; Undergraduates: $3390. ***Scholarships, grants, and awards:*** Federal Pell, FSEOG, state, private, college/university gift aid from institutional funds.

GIFT AID (NON-NEED-BASED) ***Total amount:*** $96,300 (60% institutional, 40% external sources). ***Receiving aid:*** *Freshmen:* 21% (39); *Undergraduates:* 20% (111). ***Scholarships, grants, and awards by category:*** *Academic Interests/Achievement:* 86 awards ($106,210 total): general academic interests/achievements. *Creative Arts/Performance:* 43 awards ($56,530 total): art/fine arts, music, theater/drama. *Special Achievements/Activities:* 9 awards ($9000 total): cheerleading/drum major. *Special Characteristics:* 196 awards ($191,788 total): local/state students, religious affiliation. ***Tuition waivers:*** Full or partial for employees or children of employees.

LOANS ***Student loans:*** $954,647 (75% need-based, 25% non-need-based). 62% of past graduating class borrowed through all loan programs. Average indebtedness per student: $7985. ***Average need-based loan:*** Freshmen: $1310; Undergraduates: $2750. ***Parent loans:*** $26,350 (100% non-need-based). ***Programs:*** FFEL (Subsidized and Unsubsidized Stafford, PLUS).

WORK-STUDY ***Federal work-study:*** *Total amount:* $41,037; 51 jobs averaging $805. ***State or other work-study/employment:*** *Total amount:* $67,376 (44% need-based, 56% non-need-based). 72 part-time jobs averaging $935.

ATHLETIC AWARDS *Total amount:* 684,494 (59% need-based, 41% non-need-based).

APPLYING for FINANCIAL AID ***Required financial aid forms:*** FAFSA, institution's own form. ***Financial aid deadline (priority):*** 2/1. ***Notification date:*** 3/1. Students must reply within 4 weeks of notification.

CONTACT Ms. Anita Beecham, Financial Aid Assistant, Martin Methodist College, 433 West Madison Street, Pulaski, TN 38478-2716, 931-363-9808 or toll-free 800-467-1273. *Fax:* 931-363-9818.

MARTIN UNIVERSITY

Indianapolis, IN

Tuition & fees: $6720 **Average undergraduate aid package: N/A**

ABOUT THE INSTITUTION Independent, coed. Awards: bachelor's and master's degrees. 28 undergraduate majors. Total enrollment: 556. Undergraduates: 481. Freshmen: 41. Federal methodology is used as a basis for awarding need-based institutional aid.

UNDERGRADUATE EXPENSES for 1999–2000 ***Application fee:*** $25. ***Tuition:*** full-time $6600; part-time $275 per credit. ***Required fees:*** full-time $120; $60 per term part-time. ***Payment plans:*** installment, deferred payment.

FRESHMAN FINANCIAL AID (Fall 1999, est.) 175 applied for aid; of those 86% were deemed to have need. 100% of freshmen with need received aid. *Average percent of need met:* 40% (excluding resources awarded to replace EFC). 14% of all full-time freshmen had no need and received non-need-based aid.

UNDERGRADUATE FINANCIAL AID (Fall 1999, est.) 300 applied for aid; of those 83% were deemed to have need. 100% of undergraduates with need received aid. *Average percent of need met:* 65% (excluding resources awarded to replace EFC). 11% of all full-time undergraduates had no need and received non-need-based aid.

GIFT AID (NEED-BASED) ***Total amount:*** $1,100,000 (55% Federal, 45% state). ***Receiving aid:*** *Freshmen:* 77% (135); *all full-time undergraduates:* 46% (220). ***Scholarships, grants, and awards:*** Federal Pell, FSEOG, state, private, college/university gift aid from institutional funds.

GIFT AID (NON-NEED-BASED) ***Receiving aid:*** *Freshmen:* 86% (150); *Undergraduates:* 53% (250). ***Scholarships, grants, and awards by category:*** *Creative Arts/Performance:* music. ***Tuition waivers:*** Full or partial for employees or children of employees.

LOANS ***Student loans:*** $1,000,000 (80% need-based, 20% non-need-based). 80% of past graduating class borrowed through all loan programs. Average indebtedness per student: $20,000. ***Programs:*** FFEL (Subsidized and Unsubsidized Stafford, PLUS).

WORK-STUDY ***Federal work-study:*** *Total amount:* $47,000; jobs available.

APPLYING for FINANCIAL AID ***Required financial aid form:*** FAFSA. ***Financial aid deadline (priority):*** 3/1. ***Notification date:*** Continuous.

CONTACT Financial Aid Office, Martin University, 2171 Avondale Place, PO Box 18567, Indianapolis, IN 46218-3867, 317-543-3258. *Fax:* 317-543-4790.

MARY BALDWIN COLLEGE

Staunton, VA

Tuition & fees: $14,645 **Average undergraduate aid package: $14,459**

ABOUT THE INSTITUTION Independent religious, coed, primarily women. Awards: bachelor's and master's degrees. 39 undergraduate majors. Total enrollment: 1,556. Undergraduates: 1,478. Freshmen: 295. Federal methodology is used as a basis for awarding need-based institutional aid.

UNDERGRADUATE EXPENSES for 1999–2000 ***Application fee:*** $25. ***Comprehensive fee:*** $22,095 includes full-time tuition ($14,475), mandatory fees ($170), and room and board ($7450). Room and board charges vary according to housing facility. ***Part-time tuition:*** $290 per semester hour. ***Payment plan:*** installment.

FRESHMAN FINANCIAL AID (Fall 1998) 276 applied for aid; of those 89% were deemed to have need. 100% of freshmen with need received aid; of those 20% had need fully met. *Average percent of need met:* 88% (excluding resources awarded to replace EFC). *Average financial aid package:* $15,168 (excluding resources awarded to replace EFC). 19% of all full-time freshmen had no need and received non-need-based aid.

UNDERGRADUATE FINANCIAL AID (Fall 1998) 847 applied for aid; of those 92% were deemed to have need. 100% of undergraduates with need received aid; of those 28% had need fully met. *Average percent of need met:* 91% (excluding resources awarded to replace EFC). *Average financial aid package:* $14,459 (excluding resources awarded to replace EFC). 23% of all full-time undergraduates had no need and received non-need-based aid.

GIFT AID (NEED-BASED) ***Total amount:*** $6,816,325 (14% Federal, 26% state, 58% institutional, 2% external sources). ***Receiving aid:*** *Freshmen:* 72% (243); *all full-time undergraduates:* 70% (758). ***Scholarships, grants, and awards:*** Federal Pell, FSEOG, state, private, college/university gift aid from institutional funds.

GIFT AID (NON-NEED-BASED) ***Total amount:*** $1,869,189 (9% Federal, 32% state, 59% institutional). ***Receiving aid:*** *Freshmen:* 7% (24); *Undergraduates:* 5% (55). ***Scholarships, grants, and awards by category:***

Academic Interests/Achievement: general academic interests/achievements. *Special Achievements/Activities:* leadership. *Special Characteristics:* children of educators, children of faculty/staff. ***Tuition waivers:*** Full or partial for employees or children of employees. ***ROTC:*** Army, Naval, Air Force.

LOANS ***Student loans:*** $5,184,086 (93% need-based, 7% non-need-based). ***Parent loans:*** $1,695,123 (87% need-based, 13% non-need-based). ***Programs:*** FFEL (Subsidized and Unsubsidized Stafford, PLUS), Perkins, college/university.

WORK-STUDY ***Federal work-study:*** *Total amount:* $379,250; 301 jobs averaging $1300. ***State or other work-study/employment:*** *Total amount:* $116,279 (8% need-based, 92% non-need-based). Part-time jobs available.

APPLYING for FINANCIAL AID ***Required financial aid form:*** FAFSA. ***Financial aid deadline:*** 5/15. ***Notification date:*** Continuous.

CONTACT Jacqui Elliott-Wonderly, Associate Dean of Admissions/Director of Financial Aid, Mary Baldwin College, Financial Aid Office, Staunton, VA 24401, 540-887-7022 or toll-free 800-468-2262. *Fax:* 540-887-7229. *E-mail:* jelliott@mbc.edu

MARYCREST INTERNATIONAL UNIVERSITY

Davenport, IA

Tuition & fees: $12,760 **Average undergraduate aid package: N/A**

ABOUT THE INSTITUTION Independent, coed. Awards: associate, bachelor's, and master's degrees. 28 undergraduate majors. Total enrollment: 771. Undergraduates: 357. Freshmen: 45. Federal methodology is used as a basis for awarding need-based institutional aid.

UNDERGRADUATE EXPENSES for 1999–2000 ***Application fee:*** $25. ***Comprehensive fee:*** $17,600 includes full-time tuition ($12,400), mandatory fees ($360), and room and board ($4840). ***College room only:*** $1900. Room and board charges vary according to housing facility. ***Part-time tuition:*** $415 per credit hour. ***Part-time fees:*** $12 per credit hour. Part-time tuition and fees vary according to class time and location. ***Payment plans:*** installment, deferred payment.

GIFT AID (NEED-BASED) ***Scholarships, grants, and awards:*** Federal Pell, FSEOG, state, private, college/university gift aid from institutional funds.

GIFT AID (NON-NEED-BASED) ***Scholarships, grants, and awards by category:*** *Academic Interests/Achievement:* biological sciences, business, communication, computer science, education, English, general academic interests/achievements, health fields, humanities, international studies, social sciences. *Creative Arts/Performance:* art/fine arts, creative writing, journalism/publications. *Special Achievements/Activities:* community service, leadership, religious involvement. *Special Characteristics:* children and siblings of alumni, children of educators, ethnic background, general special characteristics, international students, members of minority groups, out-of-state students. ***Tuition waivers:*** Full or partial for employees or children of employees.

LOANS ***Programs:*** FFEL (Subsidized and Unsubsidized Stafford, PLUS), Perkins, alternative loans.

WORK-STUDY Federal work-study jobs available.

APPLYING for FINANCIAL AID ***Required financial aid form:*** FAFSA. ***Financial aid deadline (priority):*** 4/1. ***Notification date:*** Continuous. Students must reply within 2 weeks of notification.

CONTACT Linda VanHese, Director of Financial Aid, Marycrest International University, 1607 West 12th Street, Davenport, IA 52804-4096, 319-327-9625 or toll-free 800-728-9705 Ext. 2225. *Fax:* 319-327-9606. *E-mail:* lvanhese@mcrest.edu

MARYGROVE COLLEGE

Detroit, MI

CONTACT Mr. Donald Hurt, Director of Financial Aid, Marygrove College, 8425 West McNichols Road, Detroit, MI 48221-2599, 313-862-8000 Ext. 436.

MARYLAND INSTITUTE, COLLEGE OF ART

Baltimore, MD

Tuition & fees: $18,710 **Average undergraduate aid package: N/A**

ABOUT THE INSTITUTION Independent, coed. Awards: bachelor's and master's degrees and post-bachelor's certificates. 14 undergraduate majors. Total enrollment: 1,254. Undergraduates: 1,115. Freshmen: 305. Both federal and institutional methodology are used as a basis for awarding need-based institutional aid.

UNDERGRADUATE EXPENSES for 1999–2000 ***Application fee:*** $45. ***Tuition:*** full-time $18,460; part-time $770 per credit. ***Required fees:*** full-time $250; $125 per term part-time. Room and board charges vary according to board plan and housing facility. ***Payment plan:*** installment.

GIFT AID (NEED-BASED) ***Scholarships, grants, and awards:*** Federal Pell, FSEOG, state, private, college/university gift aid from institutional funds.

GIFT AID (NON-NEED-BASED) ***Scholarships, grants, and awards by category:*** *Academic Interests/Achievement:* general academic interests/achievements. *Creative Arts/Performance:* applied art and design, art/fine arts. *Special Characteristics:* children of faculty/staff, international students, local/state students, religious affiliation. ***Tuition waivers:*** Full or partial for employees or children of employees. ***ROTC:*** Army cooperative.

LOANS ***Programs:*** Perkins.

WORK-STUDY Federal work-study jobs available.

APPLYING for FINANCIAL AID ***Required financial aid forms:*** FAFSA, institution's own form. ***Financial aid deadline (priority):*** 3/1. ***Notification date:*** 4/15. Students must reply by 5/1 or within 2 weeks of notification.

CONTACT Ms. Diane Prengaman, Associate Vice President for Financial Aid, Maryland Institute, College of Art, 1300 Mount Royal Avenue, Baltimore, MD 21217, 410-225-2285. *E-mail:* dprengam@mica.edu

MARYLHURST UNIVERSITY

Marylhurst, OR

CONTACT Financial Aid Office, Marylhurst University, PO Box 261, Marylhurst, OR 97036-0261, 503-636-8141 or toll-free 800-634-9982 Ext. 3317 (out-of-state).

MARYMOUNT COLLEGE

Tarrytown, NY

Tuition & fees: $15,130 **Average undergraduate aid package: N/A**

ABOUT THE INSTITUTION Independent, women only. Awards: associate and bachelor's degrees. 66 undergraduate majors. Total enrollment: 898. Undergraduates: 898. Freshmen: 166. Federal methodology is used as a basis for awarding need-based institutional aid.

UNDERGRADUATE EXPENSES for 2000–2001 ***Application fee:*** $30. ***Comprehensive fee:*** $22,930 includes full-time tuition ($14,700), mandatory fees ($430), and room and board ($7800). ***Part-time tuition:*** $475 per semester hour. ***Part-time fees:*** $108 per term part-time. Part-time tuition and fees vary according to class time and course load. ***Payment plans:*** installment, deferred payment.

GIFT AID (NEED-BASED) ***Total amount:*** $3,013,450 (53% Federal, 41% state, 5% institutional, 1% external sources). ***Scholarships, grants, and awards:*** Federal Pell, FSEOG, state, private, college/university gift aid from institutional funds.

GIFT AID (NON-NEED-BASED) ***Total amount:*** $9142 (67% state, 33% external sources). ***Scholarships, grants, and awards by category:*** *Academic Interests/Achievement:* general academic interests/achievements. *Creative Arts/Performance:* art/fine arts. *Special Achievements/Activities:* community service, leadership. *Special Characteristics:* general special characteristics. ***Tuition waivers:*** Full or partial for employees or children of employees.

Marymount College (continued)

LOANS ***Student loans:*** $3,967,360 (86% need-based, 14% non-need-based). ***Parent loans:*** $779,636 (100% need-based). ***Programs:*** Federal Direct (Subsidized and Unsubsidized Stafford, PLUS), Perkins, alternative loans.

WORK-STUDY ***Federal work-study:*** *Total amount:* $313,919; jobs available. ***State or other work-study/employment:*** *Total amount:* $7200 (56% need-based, 44% non-need-based). Part-time jobs available.

APPLYING for FINANCIAL AID ***Required financial aid forms:*** FAFSA, state aid form. ***Financial aid deadline:*** 5/1 (priority: 2/15). ***Notification date:*** Continuous. Students must reply within 2 weeks of notification.

CONTACT Ms. Dianne S. Pepitone, Director of Financial Assistance, Marymount College, 100 Marymount Avenue, Tarrytown, NY 10591-3796, 914-332-8345 or toll-free 800-724-4312. *Fax:* 914-631-8586.

MARYMOUNT MANHATTAN COLLEGE

New York, NY

Tuition & fees: $13,605 **Average undergraduate aid package: $12,504**

ABOUT THE INSTITUTION Independent, coed. Awards: bachelor's degrees. 20 undergraduate majors. Total enrollment: 2,455. Undergraduates: 2,455. Freshmen: 528. Federal methodology is used as a basis for awarding need-based institutional aid.

UNDERGRADUATE EXPENSES for 1999–2000 ***Application fee:*** $50. ***Tuition:*** full-time $13,050; part-time $365 per credit. ***Required fees:*** full-time $555; $210 per term part-time. Room and board charges vary according to housing facility. ***Payment plan:*** installment.

FRESHMAN FINANCIAL AID (Fall 1999, est.) 501 applied for aid; of those 85% were deemed to have need. 100% of freshmen with need received aid; of those 21% had need fully met. *Average percent of need met:* 85% (excluding resources awarded to replace EFC). *Average financial aid package:* $12,418 (excluding resources awarded to replace EFC). 14% of all full-time freshmen had no need and received non-need-based aid.

UNDERGRADUATE FINANCIAL AID (Fall 1999, est.) 1,250 applied for aid; of those 86% were deemed to have need. 100% of undergraduates with need received aid; of those 19% had need fully met. *Average percent of need met:* 85% (excluding resources awarded to replace EFC). *Average financial aid package:* $12,504 (excluding resources awarded to replace EFC). 12% of all full-time undergraduates had no need and received non-need-based aid.

GIFT AID (NEED-BASED) ***Total amount:*** $9,105,957 (20% Federal, 16% state, 64% institutional). ***Receiving aid:*** *Freshmen:* 72% (384); *all full-time undergraduates:* 64% (1,025). ***Average award:*** Freshmen: $10,493; Undergraduates: $8894. ***Scholarships, grants, and awards:*** Federal Pell, FSEOG, state, private, college/university gift aid from institutional funds.

GIFT AID (NON-NEED-BASED) ***Total amount:*** $738,182 (78% institutional, 22% external sources). ***Receiving aid:*** *Freshmen:* 52% (276); *Undergraduates:* 37% (600). ***Scholarships, grants, and awards by category:*** *Academic Interests/Achievement:* general academic interests/achievements. *Creative Arts/Performance:* art/fine arts, dance, theater/drama. *Special Achievements/Activities:* leadership. *Special Characteristics:* children and siblings of alumni, international students. ***Tuition waivers:*** Full or partial for employees or children of employees, senior citizens.

LOANS ***Student loans:*** $5,154,144 (93% need-based, 7% non-need-based). 67% of past graduating class borrowed through all loan programs. ***Average need-based loan:*** Freshmen: $2612; Undergraduates: $3384. ***Parent loans:*** $7,708,620 (74% need-based, 26% non-need-based). ***Programs:*** FFEL (Subsidized and Unsubsidized Stafford, PLUS).

WORK-STUDY ***Federal work-study:*** *Total amount:* $204,054; 136 jobs averaging $1286.

APPLYING for FINANCIAL AID ***Required financial aid form:*** FAFSA. ***Financial aid deadline (priority):*** 2/15. ***Notification date:*** Continuous beginning 3/1. Students must reply within 4 weeks of notification.

CONTACT Director of Financial Aid, Marymount Manhattan College, 221 East 71st Street, New York, NY 10021-4597, 212-517-0480 or toll-free 800-MARYMOUNT (out-of-state).

MARYMOUNT UNIVERSITY

Arlington, VA

Tuition & fees: $13,870 **Average undergraduate aid package: N/A**

ABOUT THE INSTITUTION Independent religious, coed. Awards: associate, bachelor's, and master's degrees. 37 undergraduate majors. Total enrollment: 3,427. Undergraduates: 1,969. Freshmen: 265. Both federal and institutional methodology are used as a basis for awarding need-based institutional aid.

UNDERGRADUATE EXPENSES for 1999–2000 ***Application fee:*** $35. ***Comprehensive fee:*** $20,030 includes full-time tuition ($13,750), mandatory fees ($120), and room and board ($6160). ***Part-time tuition:*** $450 per credit hour. ***Part-time fees:*** $5 per credit hour. ***Payment plans:*** installment, deferred payment.

GIFT AID (NEED-BASED) ***Scholarships, grants, and awards:*** Federal Pell, FSEOG, state, college/university gift aid from institutional funds, Federal Nursing.

GIFT AID (NON-NEED-BASED) ***Scholarships, grants, and awards by category:*** *Academic Interests/Achievement:* biological sciences, business, communication, computer science, English, general academic interests/achievements, health fields, humanities, mathematics, social sciences. *Special Achievements/Activities:* general special achievements/activities, leadership. *Special Characteristics:* children and siblings of alumni, children of faculty/staff, siblings of current students. ***Tuition waivers:*** Full or partial for children of alumni, employees or children of employees, senior citizens. ***ROTC:*** Army cooperative.

LOANS ***Programs:*** Federal Direct (Subsidized and Unsubsidized Stafford, PLUS), Perkins, Federal Nursing.

WORK-STUDY Federal work-study jobs available.

APPLYING for FINANCIAL AID ***Required financial aid forms:*** FAFSA, institution's own form, state aid form. ***Financial aid deadline (priority):*** 3/1. ***Notification date:*** Continuous beginning 3/15. Students must reply within 2 weeks of notification.

CONTACT Ms. Debbie A. Raines, Director of Financial Aid, Marymount University, 2807 North Glebe Road, Arlington, VA 22207-4299, 703-284-1530 or toll-free 800-548-7638. *Fax:* 703-522-0349.

MARYVILLE COLLEGE

Maryville, TN

Tuition & fees: $16,025 **Average undergraduate aid package: $15,168**

ABOUT THE INSTITUTION Independent Presbyterian, coed. Awards: bachelor's degrees. 51 undergraduate majors. Total enrollment: 1,001. Undergraduates: 1,001. Freshmen: 313. Federal methodology is used as a basis for awarding need-based institutional aid.

UNDERGRADUATE EXPENSES for 1999–2000 ***Application fee:*** $25. ***Comprehensive fee:*** $21,105 includes full-time tuition ($15,600), mandatory fees ($425), and room and board ($5080). ***College room only:*** $2400. Room and board charges vary according to board plan and housing facility. ***Part-time tuition:*** $650 per semester hour. ***Part-time fees:*** $425 per year part-time. ***Payment plans:*** installment, deferred payment.

FRESHMAN FINANCIAL AID (Fall 1999, est.) 310 applied for aid; of those 83% were deemed to have need. 100% of freshmen with need received aid; of those 22% had need fully met. *Average percent of need met:* 100% (excluding resources awarded to replace EFC). *Average financial aid package:* $15,895 (excluding resources awarded to replace EFC). 17% of all full-time freshmen had no need and received non-need-based aid.

UNDERGRADUATE FINANCIAL AID (Fall 1999, est.) 962 applied for aid; of those 84% were deemed to have need. 100% of undergraduates with need received aid; of those 22% had need fully met. *Average percent of need met:* 100% (excluding resources awarded to replace EFC). *Average financial aid package:* $15,168 (excluding resources awarded to replace EFC). 16% of all full-time undergraduates had no need and received non-need-based aid.

GIFT AID (NEED-BASED) ***Total amount:*** $8,355,559 (10% Federal, 5% state, 85% institutional). ***Receiving aid:*** *Freshmen:* 82% (257); *all full-time undergraduates:* 83% (807). ***Average award:*** Freshmen: $11,022; Undergraduates: $10,263. ***Scholarships, grants, and awards:*** Federal Pell, FSEOG, state, private, college/university gift aid from institutional funds.

GIFT AID (NON-NEED-BASED) ***Total amount:*** $1,995,662 (87% institutional, 13% external sources). ***Receiving aid:*** *Freshmen:* 11% (35); *Undergraduates:* 12% (113). ***Scholarships, grants, and awards by category:*** *Academic Interests/Achievement:* 968 awards ($5,132,381 total): general academic interests/achievements. *Creative Arts/Performance:* 118 awards ($252,300 total): art/fine arts, music, theater/drama. *Special Achievements/Activities:* 87 awards ($170,314 total): community service, leadership. *Special Characteristics:* 98 awards ($159,950 total): local/state students, members of minority groups, relatives of clergy, religious affiliation. ***Tuition waivers:*** Full or partial for employees or children of employees.

LOANS ***Student loans:*** $3,627,494 (76% need-based, 24% non-need-based). 81% of past graduating class borrowed through all loan programs. Average indebtedness per student: $16,397. ***Average need-based loan:*** Freshmen: $3810; Undergraduates: $3363. ***Parent loans:*** $411,146 (100% non-need-based). ***Programs:*** FFEL (Subsidized and Unsubsidized Stafford, PLUS), Perkins, state, college/university.

WORK-STUDY ***Federal work-study:*** *Total amount:* $361,889; 307 jobs averaging $1179. ***State or other work-study/employment:*** *Total amount:* $572,394 (100% non-need-based). 416 part-time jobs averaging $1376.

APPLYING for FINANCIAL AID ***Required financial aid form:*** FAFSA. ***Financial aid deadline (priority):*** 3/1. ***Notification date:*** Continuous beginning 3/15. Students must reply within 4 weeks of notification.

CONTACT Dick Smelser, Director of Financial Aid, Maryville College, 502 East Lamar Alexander Parkway, Maryville, TN 37804-5907, 865-981-8100 or toll-free 800-597-2687. *Fax:* 865-981-8010. *E-mail:* smelser@maryvillecollege.edu

MARYVILLE UNIVERSITY OF SAINT LOUIS

St. Louis, MO

Tuition & fees: $12,280 **Average undergraduate aid package: $10,279**

ABOUT THE INSTITUTION Independent, coed. Awards: bachelor's and master's degrees. 44 undergraduate majors. Total enrollment: 3,060. Undergraduates: 2,530. Freshmen: 221. Both federal and institutional methodology are used as a basis for awarding need-based institutional aid.

UNDERGRADUATE EXPENSES for 1999–2000 ***Application fee:*** $20. ***Comprehensive fee:*** $17,680 includes full-time tuition ($12,160), mandatory fees ($120), and room and board ($5400). ***Part-time tuition:*** $347 per credit hour. ***Part-time fees:*** $30 per term part-time. Part-time tuition and fees vary according to class time. ***Payment plans:*** installment, deferred payment.

FRESHMAN FINANCIAL AID (Fall 1999, est.) 164 applied for aid; of those 79% were deemed to have need. 100% of freshmen with need received aid; of those 15% had need fully met. *Average percent of need met:* 89% (excluding resources awarded to replace EFC). *Average financial aid package:* $10,992 (excluding resources awarded to replace EFC). 18% of all full-time freshmen had no need and received non-need-based aid.

UNDERGRADUATE FINANCIAL AID (Fall 1999, est.) 1,108 applied for aid; of those 76% were deemed to have need. 97% of undergraduates with need received aid; of those 15% had need fully met. *Average percent of need met:* 68% (excluding resources awarded to replace EFC). *Average financial aid package:* $10,279 (excluding resources awarded to replace EFC). 20% of all full-time undergraduates had no need and received non-need-based aid.

GIFT AID (NEED-BASED) ***Total amount:*** $5,422,099 (13% Federal, 10% state, 77% institutional). ***Receiving aid:*** *Freshmen:* 65% (129); *all full-time undergraduates:* 61% (820). ***Average award:*** Freshmen: $8776; Undergraduates: $6211. ***Scholarships, grants, and awards:*** Federal Pell, FSEOG, state, private, college/university gift aid from institutional funds.

GIFT AID (NON-NEED-BASED) ***Total amount:*** $817,773 (12% state, 68% institutional, 20% external sources). ***Receiving aid:*** *Freshmen:* 43% (86); *Undergraduates:* 31% (424). ***Scholarships, grants, and awards by category:*** *Academic Interests/Achievement:* education, general academic interests/achievements. *Creative Arts/Performance:* applied art and design, art/fine arts. *Special Achievements/Activities:* community service, general special achievements/activities, leadership. *Special Characteristics:* children of current students, members of minority groups, parents of current students, religious affiliation, siblings of current students, spouses of current students, twins. ***Tuition waivers:*** Full or partial for employees or children of employees, senior citizens. ***ROTC:*** Army cooperative.

LOANS ***Student loans:*** $5,759,694 (63% need-based, 37% non-need-based). Average indebtedness per student: $11,751. ***Average need-based loan:*** Freshmen: $2713; Undergraduates: $3650. ***Parent loans:*** $909,895 (100% non-need-based). ***Programs:*** Federal Direct (Subsidized and Unsubsidized Stafford, PLUS), Perkins, Sallie Mae Signature Loans, Keybank Loans, TERI Loans, Norwest Collegiate Loans, CitiAssist Loans.

WORK-STUDY ***Federal work-study:*** *Total amount:* $195,900; 132 jobs averaging $1484. ***State or other work-study/employment:*** *Total amount:* $227,496 (100% non-need-based). 126 part-time jobs averaging $1805.

APPLYING for FINANCIAL AID ***Required financial aid forms:*** FAFSA, institution's own form. ***Financial aid deadline (priority):*** 4/1. ***Notification date:*** Continuous. Students must reply by 5/1 or within 2 weeks of notification.

CONTACT Ms. Martha Harbaugh, Director of Financial Aid, Maryville University of Saint Louis, 13550 Conway Road, St. Louis, MO 63141-7299, 314-529-9360 or toll-free 800-627-9855. *Fax:* 314-529-9199. *E-mail:* fin_aid@maryville.edu

MARY WASHINGTON COLLEGE

Fredericksburg, VA

Tuition & fees (VA res): $3204 **Average undergraduate aid package: $4690**

ABOUT THE INSTITUTION State-supported, coed. Awards: bachelor's and master's degrees. 40 undergraduate majors. Total enrollment: 4,000. Undergraduates: 3,965. Freshmen: 837. Federal methodology is used as a basis for awarding need-based institutional aid.

UNDERGRADUATE EXPENSES for 1999–2000 ***Application fee:*** $35. ***Tuition, state resident:*** full-time $1550; part-time $101 per credit hour. ***Tuition, nonresident:*** full-time $7980; part-time $320 per credit hour. ***Required fees:*** full-time $1654. Part-time tuition and fees vary according to course load. ***College room and board:*** $5298; ***room only:*** $2994. Room and board charges vary according to board plan. ***Payment plan:*** installment.

FRESHMAN FINANCIAL AID (Fall 1999, est.) 626 applied for aid; of those 63% were deemed to have need. 95% of freshmen with need received aid; of those 5% had need fully met. *Average percent of need met:* 65% (excluding resources awarded to replace EFC). *Average financial aid package:* $4510 (excluding resources awarded to replace EFC). 20% of all full-time freshmen had no need and received non-need-based aid.

UNDERGRADUATE FINANCIAL AID (Fall 1999, est.) 2,356 applied for aid; of those 65% were deemed to have need. 95% of undergraduates with need received aid; of those 5% had need fully met. *Average percent of need met:* 54% (excluding resources awarded to replace EFC). *Average financial aid package:* $4690 (excluding resources awarded to replace EFC). 11% of all full-time undergraduates had no need and received non-need-based aid.

GIFT AID (NEED-BASED) ***Total amount:*** $1,984,991 (38% Federal, 46% state, 16% institutional). ***Receiving aid:*** *Freshmen:* 36% (299); *all full-time undergraduates:* 36% (1,163). ***Average award:*** Freshmen: $2175; Undergraduates: $2605. ***Scholarships, grants, and awards:*** Federal Pell, FSEOG, state, college/university gift aid from institutional funds.

GIFT AID (NON-NEED-BASED) ***Total amount:*** $841,016 (52% institutional, 48% external sources). ***Receiving aid:*** *Freshmen:* 8% (64); *Undergraduates:* 9% (291). ***Scholarships, grants, and awards by category:*** *Academic Interests/Achievement:* business, computer science, education, English, foreign languages, general academic interests/achievements, mathematics, physical sciences, social sciences. *Creative Arts/Performance;* art/fine

Mary Washington College (continued)

arts, dance, journalism/publications, music, theater/drama. *Special Characteristics:* adult students, children and siblings of alumni, children of faculty/staff, local/state students, members of minority groups. ***Tuition waivers:*** Full or partial for minority students.

LOANS ***Student loans:*** $5,322,887 (59% need-based, 41% non-need-based). 77% of past graduating class borrowed through all loan programs. Average indebtedness per student: $11,000. ***Average need-based loan:*** Freshmen: $2386; Undergraduates: $4376. ***Parent loans:*** $2,040,275 (100% non-need-based). ***Programs:*** FFEL (Subsidized and Unsubsidized Stafford, PLUS), Perkins.

WORK-STUDY ***Federal work-study:*** *Total amount:* $54,543; 71 jobs averaging $800. ***State or other work-study/employment:*** *Total amount:* $1,019,647 (100% non-need-based). 1,350 part-time jobs available.

APPLYING for FINANCIAL AID ***Required financial aid form:*** FAFSA. ***Financial aid deadline:*** 3/1. ***Notification date:*** 4/15. Students must reply by 5/1 or within 2 weeks of notification.

CONTACT Mr. Robert U. MacDonald, Senior Associate Dean for Financial Aid, Mary Washington College, 1301 College Avenue, Fredericksburg, VA 22401-5358, 540-654-2468 or toll-free 800-468-5614. *E-mail:* rmacdona@mwc.edu

MARYWOOD UNIVERSITY

Scranton, PA

Tuition & fees: $15,623 **Average undergraduate aid package: $13,000**

ABOUT THE INSTITUTION Independent Roman Catholic, coed. Awards: associate, bachelor's, master's, and doctoral degrees and post-bachelor's and post-master's certificates. 55 undergraduate majors. Total enrollment: 2,903. Undergraduates: 1,633. Freshmen: 289. Federal methodology is used as a basis for awarding need-based institutional aid.

UNDERGRADUATE EXPENSES for 1999–2000 ***Application fee:*** $20. ***Comprehensive fee:*** $22,163 includes full-time tuition ($15,008), mandatory fees ($615), and room and board ($6540). ***College room only:*** $3430. Room and board charges vary according to board plan and housing facility. ***Part-time tuition:*** $469 per credit. ***Part-time fees:*** $115 per term part-time. Part-time tuition and fees vary according to course load. ***Payment plans:*** installment, deferred payment.

FRESHMAN FINANCIAL AID (Fall 1998) 278 applied for aid; of those 77% were deemed to have need. 100% of freshmen with need received aid. *Average percent of need met:* 75% (excluding resources awarded to replace EFC). *Average financial aid package:* $12,205 (excluding resources awarded to replace EFC). 23% of all full-time freshmen had no need and received non-need-based aid.

UNDERGRADUATE FINANCIAL AID (Fall 1998) 1,331 applied for aid; of those 85% were deemed to have need. 100% of undergraduates with need received aid. *Average percent of need met:* 86% (excluding resources awarded to replace EFC). *Average financial aid package:* $13,000 (excluding resources awarded to replace EFC). 18% of all full-time undergraduates had no need and received non-need-based aid.

GIFT AID (NEED-BASED) ***Total amount:*** $8,817,134 (18% Federal, 19% state, 60% institutional, 3% external sources). ***Receiving aid:*** *Freshmen:* 76% (213); *all full-time undergraduates:* 81% (1,128). ***Scholarships, grants, and awards:*** Federal Pell, FSEOG, state, private, college/university gift aid from institutional funds.

GIFT AID (NON-NEED-BASED) ***Total amount:*** $1,945,318 (96% institutional, 4% external sources). ***Receiving aid:*** *Freshmen:* 76% (213); *Undergraduates:* 81% (1,128). ***Scholarships, grants, and awards by category:*** *Academic Interests/Achievement:* general academic interests/achievements. *Creative Arts/Performance:* art/fine arts, cinema/film/broadcasting, music, performing arts, theater/drama. *Special Achievements/Activities:* community service, leadership. *Special Characteristics:* adult students, children of current students, ethnic background, international students, local/state students, religious affiliation, siblings of current students, spouses of current students. ***Tuition waivers:*** Full or partial for employees or children of employees, senior citizens. ***ROTC:*** Army cooperative, Air Force cooperative.

LOANS ***Student loans:*** $6,168,674 (62% need-based, 38% non-need-based). 79% of past graduating class borrowed through all loan programs. Average indebtedness per student: $19,170. ***Average need-based loan:*** Freshmen: $2625; Undergraduates: $4075. ***Parent loans:*** $353,600 (100% non-need-based). ***Programs:*** FFEL (Subsidized and Unsubsidized Stafford, PLUS), Perkins, state, alternative loans.

WORK-STUDY ***Federal work-study:*** *Total amount:* $212,179; 212 jobs averaging $1000. ***State or other work-study/employment:*** *Total amount:* $218,639 (100% non-need-based). Part-time jobs available.

APPLYING for FINANCIAL AID ***Required financial aid forms:*** FAFSA, institution's own form. ***Financial aid deadline:*** Continuous. ***Notification date:*** Continuous beginning 3/1. Students must reply by 5/1 or within 3 weeks of notification.

CONTACT Mr. Stanley F. Skrutski, Director of Financial Aid, Marywood University, 2300 Adams Avenue, Scranton, PA 18509-1598, 570-348-6225 or toll-free 800-346-5014 (in-state), 800-340-6014 (out-of-state). *Fax:* 570-961-4739. *E-mail:* bfin01.mis@mis.marywood.edu

MASON GROSS SCHOOL OF THE ARTS

New Brunswick, NJ

See Rutgers, The State University of New Jersey, Mason Gross School of the Arts

MASSACHUSETTS COLLEGE OF ART

Boston, MA

Tuition & fees (MA res): $3808 **Average undergraduate aid package: $8440**

ABOUT THE INSTITUTION State-supported, coed. Awards: bachelor's and master's degrees and post-bachelor's certificates. 16 undergraduate majors. Total enrollment: 2,371. Undergraduates: 2,266. Freshmen: 250. Federal methodology is used as a basis for awarding need-based institutional aid.

UNDERGRADUATE EXPENSES for 1999–2000 ***Application fee:*** $25; $65 for nonresidents. ***Tuition, state resident:*** full-time $1140; part-time $142 per course. ***Tuition, nonresident:*** full-time $8000; part-time $1000 per course. ***Required fees:*** full-time $2668; $935 per term part-time. Full-time tuition and fees vary according to reciprocity agreements. Part-time tuition and fees vary according to class time, course load, and reciprocity agreements. ***College room and board:*** $7164. Room and board charges vary according to housing facility. ***Payment plan:*** installment.

FRESHMAN FINANCIAL AID (Fall 1999) 188 applied for aid; of those 87% were deemed to have need. 100% of freshmen with need received aid; of those 53% had need fully met. *Average percent of need met:* 85% (excluding resources awarded to replace EFC). *Average financial aid package:* $7780 (excluding resources awarded to replace EFC). 11% of all full-time freshmen had no need and received non-need-based aid.

UNDERGRADUATE FINANCIAL AID (Fall 1999) 874 applied for aid; of those 92% were deemed to have need. 100% of undergraduates with need received aid; of those 62% had need fully met. *Average percent of need met:* 83% (excluding resources awarded to replace EFC). *Average financial aid package:* $8440 (excluding resources awarded to replace EFC). 9% of all full-time undergraduates had no need and received non-need-based aid.

GIFT AID (NEED-BASED) ***Total amount:*** $1,039,277 (41% Federal, 31% state, 9% institutional, 19% external sources). ***Receiving aid:*** *Freshmen:* 39% (98); *all full-time undergraduates:* 41% (513). ***Average award:*** Freshmen: $2880; Undergraduates: $2666. ***Scholarships, grants, and awards:*** Federal Pell, FSEOG, state, private, college/university gift aid from institutional funds.

GIFT AID (NON-NEED-BASED) ***Total amount:*** $53,269 (47% institutional, 53% external sources). ***Receiving aid:*** *Freshmen:* 22% (55); *Undergraduates:* 10% (129). ***Scholarships, grants, and awards by category:*** *Academic Interests/Achievement:* general academic interests/achievements. *Creative Arts/Performance:* applied art and design, art/fine arts. *Special Achievements/Activities:* community service, general special achievements/activities.

Special Characteristics: children of faculty/staff, children of union members/company employees. ***Tuition waivers:*** Full or partial for employees or children of employees, senior citizens.

LOANS ***Student loans:*** $2,056,847 (75% need-based, 25% non-need-based). 61% of past graduating class borrowed through all loan programs. Average indebtedness per student: $16,760. ***Average need-based loan:*** Freshmen: $2634; Undergraduates: $4050. ***Parent loans:*** $1,253,235 (67% need-based, 33% non-need-based). ***Programs:*** Federal Direct (Subsidized and Unsubsidized Stafford, PLUS), FFEL (Subsidized and Unsubsidized Stafford, PLUS), Perkins, state, college/university, alternative loans.

WORK-STUDY ***Federal work-study:*** *Total amount:* $120,187; 100 jobs averaging $800.

APPLYING for FINANCIAL AID ***Required financial aid form:*** FAFSA. ***Financial aid deadline (priority):*** 3/15. ***Notification date:*** Continuous. Students must reply within 3 weeks of notification.

CONTACT Ms. Laura M. Hofeldt, Assistant Director of Financial Aid, Massachusetts College of Art, 621 Huntington Avenue, Boston, MA 02115-5882, 617-232-1555. *Fax:* 617-566-4034. *E-mail:* lhofeldt@massart.edu

MASSACHUSETTS COLLEGE OF LIBERAL ARTS

North Adams, MA

Tuition & fees (MA res): $3357 **Average undergraduate aid package: $6217**

ABOUT THE INSTITUTION State-supported, coed. Awards: bachelor's and master's degrees and post-bachelor's certificates. 37 undergraduate majors. Total enrollment: 1,520. Undergraduates: 1,392. Freshmen: 225. Federal methodology is used as a basis for awarding need-based institutional aid.

UNDERGRADUATE EXPENSES for 2000–2001 ***Application fee:*** $10. ***Tuition, area resident:*** part-time $370 per credit. ***Tuition, state resident:*** full-time $1090. ***Tuition, nonresident:*** full-time $7050. ***Required fees:*** full-time $2267. Full-time tuition and fees vary according to reciprocity agreements. Part-time tuition and fees vary according to reciprocity agreements. ***College room and board:*** $4290; ***room only:*** $2748. Room and board charges vary according to board plan and housing facility. ***Payment plan:*** installment.

FRESHMAN FINANCIAL AID (Fall 1999) 212 applied for aid; of those 78% were deemed to have need. 94% of freshmen with need received aid; of those 40% had need fully met. *Average percent of need met:* 71% (excluding resources awarded to replace EFC). *Average financial aid package:* $6020 (excluding resources awarded to replace EFC). 19% of all full-time freshmen had no need and received non-need-based aid.

UNDERGRADUATE FINANCIAL AID (Fall 1999) 893 applied for aid; of those 82% were deemed to have need. 94% of undergraduates with need received aid; of those 42% had need fully met. *Average percent of need met:* 75% (excluding resources awarded to replace EFC). *Average financial aid package:* $6217 (excluding resources awarded to replace EFC). 13% of all full-time undergraduates had no need and received non-need-based aid.

GIFT AID (NEED-BASED) ***Total amount:*** $2,073,389 (44% Federal, 28% state, 24% institutional, 4% external sources). ***Receiving aid:*** *Freshmen:* 52% (114); *all full-time undergraduates:* 48% (523). ***Average award:*** Freshmen: $3441; Undergraduates: $3366. ***Scholarships, grants, and awards:*** Federal Pell, FSEOG, state, private, college/university gift aid from institutional funds.

GIFT AID (NON-NEED-BASED) ***Total amount:*** $87,348 (100% external sources). ***Receiving aid:*** *Freshmen:* 54% (120); *Undergraduates:* 26% (286). ***Scholarships, grants, and awards by category:*** *Academic Interests/Achievement:* 190 awards ($301,345 total): biological sciences, business, communication, computer science, education, English, general academic interests/achievements, health fields, humanities, mathematics, physical sciences, social sciences. *Creative Arts/Performance:* 16 awards ($14,900 total): applied art and design, art/fine arts, cinema/film/broadcasting, journalism/publications, music, performing arts, theater/drama. *Special Achievements/Activities:* general special achievements/activities, leadership, memberships. *Special Characteristics:* first-generation college students, handicapped students, local/state students, out-of-state students. ***Tuition waivers:*** Full or partial for employees or children of employees, senior citizens.

LOANS ***Student loans:*** $3,166,576 (72% need-based, 28% non-need-based). 83% of past graduating class borrowed through all loan programs. Average indebtedness per student: $15,524. ***Average need-based loan:*** Freshmen: $2663; Undergraduates: $3375. ***Parent loans:*** $509,176 (16% need-based, 84% non-need-based). ***Programs:*** FFEL (Subsidized and Unsubsidized Stafford, PLUS), Perkins, state.

WORK-STUDY ***Federal work-study:*** *Total amount:* $270,770; 207 jobs averaging $1308. ***State or other work-study/employment:*** *Total amount:* $675,423 (100% non-need-based). 171 part-time jobs averaging $3950.

APPLYING for FINANCIAL AID ***Required financial aid forms:*** FAFSA, institution's own form. ***Financial aid deadline (priority):*** 4/1. ***Notification date:*** 4/15. Students must reply within 2 weeks of notification.

CONTACT Elizabeth M. Petri, Director of Financial Aid, Massachusetts College of Liberal Arts, 375 Church Street, North Adams, MA 01247, 413-662-5219 or toll-free 800-292-6632 (in-state). *Fax:* 413-662-5010. *E-mail:* epetri@mcla.mass.edu

MASSACHUSETTS COLLEGE OF PHARMACY AND HEALTH SCIENCES

Boston, MA

Tuition & fees: $17,320 **Average undergraduate aid package: $14,774**

ABOUT THE INSTITUTION Independent, coed. Awards: bachelor's, master's, doctoral, and first professional degrees and first-professional certificates (bachelor of science in nursing program for registered nurses only). 6 undergraduate majors. Total enrollment: 2,002. Undergraduates: 939. Freshmen: 10. Federal methodology is used as a basis for awarding need-based institutional aid.

UNDERGRADUATE EXPENSES for 1999–2000 ***Application fee:*** $60. ***Comprehensive fee:*** $25,220 includes full-time tuition ($16,900), mandatory fees ($420), and room and board ($7900). Full-time tuition and fees vary according to course level and program. ***Part-time tuition:*** $487 per semester hour. ***Part-time fees:*** $210 per term part-time. Part-time tuition and fees vary according to course level and program. ***Payment plan:*** installment.

FRESHMAN FINANCIAL AID (Fall 1999, est.) 88 applied for aid; of those 93% were deemed to have need. 100% of freshmen with need received aid; of those 13% had need fully met. *Average percent of need met:* 78% (excluding resources awarded to replace EFC). *Average financial aid package:* $15,601 (excluding resources awarded to replace EFC). 7% of all full-time freshmen had no need and received non-need-based aid.

UNDERGRADUATE FINANCIAL AID (Fall 1999, est.) 976 applied for aid; of those 95% were deemed to have need. 100% of undergraduates with need received aid; of those 16% had need fully met. *Average percent of need met:* 67% (excluding resources awarded to replace EFC). *Average financial aid package:* $14,774 (excluding resources awarded to replace EFC). 4% of all full-time undergraduates had no need and received non-need-based aid.

GIFT AID (NEED-BASED) ***Total amount:*** $4,485,409 (29% Federal, 12% state, 55% institutional, 4% external sources). ***Receiving aid:*** *Freshmen:* 78% (81); *all full-time undergraduates:* 71% (852). ***Average award:*** Freshmen: $7470; Undergraduates: $4089. ***Scholarships, grants, and awards:*** Federal Pell, FSEOG, state, private, college/university gift aid from institutional funds.

GIFT AID (NON-NEED-BASED) ***Total amount:*** $240,708 (100% institutional). ***Receiving aid:*** *Freshmen:* 17% (18); *Undergraduates:* 6% (69). ***Scholarships, grants, and awards by category:*** *Academic Interests/Achievement:* general academic interests/achievements. ***Tuition waivers:*** Full or partial for employees or children of employees. ***ROTC:*** Army cooperative, Naval cooperative, Air Force cooperative.

LOANS ***Student loans:*** $11,969,954 (92% need-based, 8% non-need-based). 99% of past graduating class borrowed through all loan programs. Average indebtedness per student: $23,372. ***Average need-based loan:*** Freshmen: $7074; Undergraduates: $10,477. ***Parent loans:*** $691,305 (70%

Massachusetts College of Pharmacy and Health Sciences (continued)

need-based, 30% non-need-based). ***Programs:*** FFEL (Subsidized and Unsubsidized Stafford, PLUS), Perkins, college/university.

WORK-STUDY ***Federal work-study:*** *Total amount:* $203,471; 118 jobs averaging $1724.

APPLYING for FINANCIAL AID ***Required financial aid forms:*** FAFSA, institution's own form. ***Financial aid deadline (priority):*** 3/15. ***Notification date:*** Continuous. Students must reply by 5/1 or within 2 weeks of notification.

CONTACT Ms. Martha Magee, Associate Director of Financial Aid, Massachusetts College of Pharmacy and Health Sciences, 179 Longwood Avenue, Boston, MA 02115-5896, 617-732-2864 or toll-free 800-225-5506 (out-of-state). *Fax:* 617-732-2801. *E-mail:* mmagee@mcp.edu

MASSACHUSETTS INSTITUTE OF TECHNOLOGY

Cambridge, MA

Tuition & fees: $25,000 **Average undergraduate aid package: $23,445**

ABOUT THE INSTITUTION Independent, coed. Awards: bachelor's, master's, and doctoral degrees. 62 undergraduate majors. Total enrollment: 9,972. Undergraduates: 4,300. Freshmen: 1,048. Both federal and institutional methodology are used as a basis for awarding need-based institutional aid.

UNDERGRADUATE EXPENSES for 1999–2000 ***Application fee:*** $55. ***Comprehensive fee:*** $31,900 includes full-time tuition ($25,000) and room and board ($6900). Room and board charges vary according to board plan and housing facility. ***Payment plan:*** deferred payment.

FRESHMAN FINANCIAL AID (Fall 1998) 806 applied for aid; of those 74% were deemed to have need. 100% of freshmen with need received aid; of those 100% had need fully met. *Average percent of need met:* 100% (excluding resources awarded to replace EFC). *Average financial aid package:* $23,365 (excluding resources awarded to replace EFC).

UNDERGRADUATE FINANCIAL AID (Fall 1998) 2,687 applied for aid; of those 83% were deemed to have need. 100% of undergraduates with need received aid; of those 100% had need fully met. *Average percent of need met:* 100% (excluding resources awarded to replace EFC). *Average financial aid package:* $23,445 (excluding resources awarded to replace EFC).

GIFT AID (NEED-BASED) ***Total amount:*** $36,862,749 (11% Federal, 2% state, 53% institutional, 34% external sources). ***Receiving aid:*** *Freshmen:* 50% (524); *all full-time undergraduates:* 53% (2,018). ***Average award:*** Freshmen: $16,470; Undergraduates: $16,566. ***Scholarships, grants, and awards:*** Federal Pell, FSEOG, state, private, college/university gift aid from institutional funds.

GIFT AID (NON-NEED-BASED) ***Receiving aid:*** *Freshmen:* 29% (306); *Undergraduates:* 21% (785). ***Tuition waivers:*** Full or partial for employees or children of employees. ***ROTC:*** Army, Naval, Air Force.

LOANS ***Student loans:*** $13,044,408 (100% need-based). 56% of past graduating class borrowed through all loan programs. ***Average need-based loan:*** Freshmen: $4964; Undergraduates: $5286. ***Parent loans:*** $6,556,423 (100% need-based). ***Programs:*** Federal Direct (Subsidized and Unsubsidized Stafford), FFEL (PLUS), Perkins, state, college/university.

WORK-STUDY ***Federal work-study:*** *Total amount:* $3,429,033; 1,329 jobs averaging $2580.

APPLYING for FINANCIAL AID ***Required financial aid forms:*** FAFSA, institution's own form, CSS Financial Aid PROFILE. ***Financial aid deadline (priority):*** 1/11. ***Notification date:*** 3/10. Students must reply by 5/1 or within 2 weeks of notification.

CONTACT Student Financial Aid Office, Massachusetts Institute of Technology, 77 Massachusetts Avenue, Room 11-320, Cambridge, MA 02139-4307, 617-253-4971. *Fax:* 617-258-8301. *E-mail:* finaid@mit.edu

MASSACHUSETTS MARITIME ACADEMY

Buzzards Bay, MA

Tuition & fees (MA res): $2873 **Average undergraduate aid package: $6706**

ABOUT THE INSTITUTION State-supported, coed. Awards: bachelor's degrees. 8 undergraduate majors. Total enrollment: 800. Undergraduates: 800. Freshmen: 181. Federal methodology is used as a basis for awarding need-based institutional aid.

UNDERGRADUATE EXPENSES for 2000–2001 ***Application fee:*** $10; $40 for nonresidents. ***One-time required fee:*** $1450. ***Tuition, state resident:*** full-time $1090. ***Tuition, nonresident:*** full-time $9170. ***Required fees:*** full-time $1783. Full-time tuition and fees vary according to reciprocity agreements. ***College room and board:*** $4560; ***room only:*** $2260.

FRESHMAN FINANCIAL AID (Fall 1998) 173 applied for aid; of those 67% were deemed to have need. 98% of freshmen with need received aid; of those 35% had need fully met. *Average percent of need met:* 81% (excluding resources awarded to replace EFC). *Average financial aid package:* $6593 (excluding resources awarded to replace EFC). 7% of all full-time freshmen had no need and received non-need-based aid.

UNDERGRADUATE FINANCIAL AID (Fall 1998) 571 applied for aid; of those 71% were deemed to have need. 96% of undergraduates with need received aid; of those 59% had need fully met. *Average percent of need met:* 87% (excluding resources awarded to replace EFC). *Average financial aid package:* $6706 (excluding resources awarded to replace EFC). 5% of all full-time undergraduates had no need and received non-need-based aid.

GIFT AID (NEED-BASED) ***Total amount:*** $1,094,806 (39% Federal, 24% state, 34% institutional, 3% external sources). ***Receiving aid:*** *Freshmen:* 37% (87); *all full-time undergraduates:* 46% (298). ***Scholarships, grants, and awards:*** Federal Pell, FSEOG, state, private, college/university gift aid from institutional funds.

GIFT AID (NON-NEED-BASED) ***Total amount:*** $56,817 (10% state, 79% institutional, 11% external sources). ***Receiving aid:*** *Freshmen:* 4% (9); *Undergraduates:* 4% (25). ***Scholarships, grants, and awards by category:*** *Academic Interests/Achievement:* general academic interests/achievements. ***Tuition waivers:*** Full or partial for employees or children of employees. ***ROTC:*** Army cooperative.

LOANS ***Student loans:*** $1,418,411 (82% need-based, 18% non-need-based). ***Parent loans:*** $341,938 (22% need-based, 78% non-need-based). ***Programs:*** Federal Direct (Subsidized and Unsubsidized Stafford, PLUS), Perkins, state.

WORK-STUDY ***Federal work-study:*** *Total amount:* $178,524; jobs available.

APPLYING for FINANCIAL AID ***Required financial aid forms:*** FAFSA, institution's own form. ***Financial aid deadline (priority):*** 3/15. ***Notification date:*** Continuous beginning 3/30.

CONTACT Mr. Michael Cuff, Director of Financial Aid, Massachusetts Maritime Academy, 101 Academy Drive, Buzzards Bay, MA 02532-3400, 508-830-5087 or toll-free 800-544-3411. *Fax:* 508-830-5077.

THE MASTER'S COLLEGE AND SEMINARY

Santa Clarita, CA

Tuition & fees: $13,400 **Average undergraduate aid package: $12,250**

ABOUT THE INSTITUTION Independent nondenominational, coed. Awards: bachelor's, master's, and first professional degrees. 45 undergraduate majors. Total enrollment: 1,295. Undergraduates: 969. Freshmen: 192. Federal methodology is used as a basis for awarding need-based institutional aid.

UNDERGRADUATE EXPENSES for 1999–2000 ***Application fee:*** $35. ***Comprehensive fee:*** $18,700 includes full-time tuition ($13,200), mandatory fees ($200), and room and board ($5300). ***College room only:*** $3000. Full-time tuition and fees vary according to course load. Room and board charges vary according to board plan. ***Part-time tuition:*** $550 per unit. ***Part-time fees:*** $100 per term part-time. Part-time tuition and fees vary according to course load. ***Payment plans:*** installment, deferred payment.

FRESHMAN FINANCIAL AID (Fall 1999, est.) 189 applied for aid; of those 81% were deemed to have need. 100% of freshmen with need received aid; of those 17% had need fully met. *Average percent of need met:* 73% (excluding resources awarded to replace EFC). *Average financial aid package:* $11,769 (excluding resources awarded to replace EFC). 5% of all full-time freshmen had no need and received non-need-based aid.

UNDERGRADUATE FINANCIAL AID (Fall 1999, est.) 702 applied for aid; of those 88% were deemed to have need. 100% of undergraduates with need received aid; of those 24% had need fully met. *Average percent of need met:* 78% (excluding resources awarded to replace EFC). *Average financial aid package:* $12,250 (excluding resources awarded to replace EFC). 8% of all full-time undergraduates had no need and received non-need-based aid.

GIFT AID (NEED-BASED) ***Total amount:*** $3,180,123 (21% Federal, 57% state, 22% institutional). ***Receiving aid:*** *Freshmen:* 48% (145); *all full-time undergraduates:* 61% (574). ***Average award:*** Freshmen: $7918; Undergraduates: $7615. ***Scholarships, grants, and awards:*** Federal Pell, FSEOG, state, private, college/university gift aid from institutional funds.

GIFT AID (NON-NEED-BASED) ***Total amount:*** $1,863,730 (92% institutional, 8% external sources). ***Receiving aid:*** *Freshmen:* 2% (6); *Undergraduates:* 4% (37). ***Scholarships, grants, and awards by category:*** *Academic Interests/Achievement:* biological sciences, business, education, general academic interests/achievements, mathematics, physical sciences, religion/biblical studies, social sciences. *Creative Arts/Performance:* music. *Special Achievements/Activities:* community service, general special achievements/activities, leadership. *Special Characteristics:* children of faculty/staff, general special characteristics, international students. ***Tuition waivers:*** Full or partial for employees or children of employees.

LOANS ***Student loans:*** $2,880,640 (67% need-based, 33% non-need-based). 63% of past graduating class borrowed through all loan programs. Average indebtedness per student: $14,204. ***Average need-based loan:*** Freshmen: $2772; Undergraduates: $3898. ***Parent loans:*** $972,582 (100% non-need-based). ***Programs:*** FFEL (Subsidized and Unsubsidized Stafford, PLUS), Perkins.

WORK-STUDY ***Federal work-study:*** *Total amount:* $76,252; 45 jobs averaging $2666. ***State or other work-study/employment:*** *Total amount:* $637,898 (100% need-based). Part-time jobs available.

ATHLETIC AWARDS *Total amount:* 597,445 (100% non-need-based).

APPLYING for FINANCIAL AID ***Required financial aid forms:*** FAFSA, institution's own form, state aid form. ***Financial aid deadline (priority):*** 3/2. ***Notification date:*** Continuous beginning 3/17. Students must reply within 2 weeks of notification.

CONTACT Ms. Sharon Shook, Director of Financial Aid, The Master's College and Seminary, 21726 West Placerita Canyon Road, Santa Clarita, CA 91321-1200, 661-259-3540 or toll-free 800-568-6248. *E-mail:* sshook@masters.edu

MAYO SCHOOL OF HEALTH-RELATED SCIENCES

Rochester, MN

Tuition & fees: N/R **Average undergraduate aid package: $11,100**

ABOUT THE INSTITUTION Independent, coed. Awards: associate, bachelor's, and master's degrees and post-bachelor's certificates. 4 undergraduate majors. Federal methodology is used as a basis for awarding need-based institutional aid.

UNDERGRADUATE FINANCIAL AID (Fall 1999) 32 applied for aid; of those 100% were deemed to have need. 94% of undergraduates with need received aid; of those 3% had need fully met. *Average percent of need met:* 75% (excluding resources awarded to replace EFC). *Average financial aid package:* $11,100 (excluding resources awarded to replace EFC). 2% of all full-time undergraduates had no need and received non-need-based aid.

GIFT AID (NEED-BASED) ***Total amount:*** $61,281 (41% Federal, 5% state, 47% institutional, 7% external sources). ***Receiving aid:*** *All full-time undergraduates:* 28% (15). ***Average award:*** Undergraduates: $4071. ***Scholarships, grants, and awards:*** Federal Pell, state, private, college/university gift aid from institutional funds.

GIFT AID (NON-NEED-BASED) ***Total amount:*** $3000 (100% external sources). ***Receiving aid:*** *Undergraduates:* 4% (2).

LOANS ***Student loans:*** $256,313 (100% need-based). 67% of past graduating class borrowed through all loan programs. Average indebtedness per student: $15,760. ***Average need-based loan:*** Undergraduates: $7600. ***Parent loans:*** $15,356 (100% need-based). ***Programs:*** FFEL (Subsidized and Unsubsidized Stafford, PLUS), state, college/university.

APPLYING for FINANCIAL AID ***Required financial aid forms:*** FAFSA, institution's own form. ***Financial aid deadline:*** Continuous. ***Notification date:*** Continuous beginning 5/15. Students must reply within 2 weeks of notification.

CONTACT Sandra Putnam, Assistant Financial Aid Director, Mayo School of Health-Related Sciences, 200 First Street, SW, Rochester, MN 55905, 507-284-4839 or toll-free 800-626-9041. *Fax:* 507-266-5298. *E-mail:* putnam.sandra@mayo.edu

MAYVILLE STATE UNIVERSITY

Mayville, ND

Tuition & fees (ND res): $3106 **Average undergraduate aid package: $5394**

ABOUT THE INSTITUTION State-supported, coed. Awards: associate and bachelor's degrees. 28 undergraduate majors. Total enrollment: 851. Undergraduates: 851. Freshmen: 158. Federal methodology is used as a basis for awarding need-based institutional aid.

UNDERGRADUATE EXPENSES for 1999–2000 ***Application fee:*** $25. ***Tuition, state resident:*** full-time $1906; part-time $79 per credit hour. ***Tuition, nonresident:*** full-time $5089; part-time $212 per credit hour. ***Required fees:*** full-time $1200; $50 per credit hour. Full-time tuition and fees vary according to reciprocity agreements. Part-time tuition and fees vary according to reciprocity agreements. ***College room and board:*** $3042; ***room only:*** $1214. Room and board charges vary according to board plan and housing facility.

FRESHMAN FINANCIAL AID (Fall 1998) 146 applied for aid; of those 62% were deemed to have need. 94% of freshmen with need received aid. *Average percent of need met:* 68% (excluding resources awarded to replace EFC). *Average financial aid package:* $4721 (excluding resources awarded to replace EFC). 17% of all full-time freshmen had no need and received non-need-based aid.

UNDERGRADUATE FINANCIAL AID (Fall 1998) 467 applied for aid; of those 76% were deemed to have need. 97% of undergraduates with need received aid. *Average percent of need met:* 87% (excluding resources awarded to replace EFC). *Average financial aid package:* $5394 (excluding resources awarded to replace EFC). 14% of all full-time undergraduates had no need and received non-need-based aid.

GIFT AID (NEED-BASED) ***Total amount:*** $681,374 (83% Federal, 6% state, 5% institutional, 6% external sources). ***Receiving aid:*** *Freshmen:* 38% (67); *all full-time undergraduates:* 44% (268). ***Average award:*** Freshmen: $2320; Undergraduates: $1546. ***Scholarships, grants, and awards:*** Federal Pell, FSEOG, state.

GIFT AID (NON-NEED-BASED) ***Total amount:*** $28,275 (15% Federal, 21% state, 3% institutional, 61% external sources). ***Receiving aid:*** *Freshmen:* 12% (21); *Undergraduates:* 8% (49). ***Scholarships, grants, and awards by category:*** *Academic Interests/Achievement:* biological sciences, business, education, English, general academic interests/achievements, library science, mathematics, physical sciences. *Special Characteristics:* children of union members/company employees, international students, local/state students, members of minority groups. ***Tuition waivers:*** Full or partial for minority students, senior citizens. ***ROTC:*** Army cooperative.

LOANS ***Student loans:*** $1,626,675 (82% need-based, 18% non-need-based). 64% of past graduating class borrowed through all loan programs. Average indebtedness per student: $15,468. ***Average need-based loan:*** Freshmen: $2517; Undergraduates: $3617. ***Parent loans:*** $46,535 (37%

Mayville State University (continued)

need-based, 63% non-need-based). ***Programs:*** FFEL (Subsidized and Unsubsidized Stafford, PLUS), Perkins, college/university.

WORK-STUDY ***Federal work-study:*** *Total amount:* $96,831; jobs available. ***State or other work-study/employment:*** *Total amount:* $172,271 (100% non-need-based). Part-time jobs available.

ATHLETIC AWARDS *Total amount:* 119,679 (61% need-based, 39% non-need-based).

APPLYING for FINANCIAL AID ***Required financial aid form:*** FAFSA. ***Financial aid deadline (priority):*** 4/15. ***Notification date:*** Continuous. Students must reply within 2 weeks of notification.

CONTACT Ms. Shirley Hanson, Assistant Director, Student Financial Aid, Mayville State University, 330 3rd Street NE, Mayville, ND 58257-1299, 701-786-4767 or toll-free 800-437-4104.

THE MCGREGOR SCHOOL OF ANTIOCH UNIVERSITY

Yellow Springs, OH

Tuition & fees: $10,176 **Average undergraduate aid package: $6500**

ABOUT THE INSTITUTION Independent, coed. Awards: bachelor's and master's degrees. 6 undergraduate majors. Total enrollment: 740. Undergraduates: 172. Both federal and institutional methodology are used as a basis for awarding need-based institutional aid.

UNDERGRADUATE EXPENSES for 1999–2000 ***Application fee:*** $45. ***Tuition:*** full-time $10,176; part-time $212 per credit. Full-time tuition and fees vary according to course load. Part-time tuition and fees vary according to course load. ***Payment plan:*** installment.

UNDERGRADUATE FINANCIAL AID (Fall 1998) 213 applied for aid; of those 87% were deemed to have need. 100% of undergraduates with need received aid. *Average percent of need met:* 25% (excluding resources awarded to replace EFC). *Average financial aid package:* $6500 (excluding resources awarded to replace EFC). 2% of all full-time undergraduates had no need and received non-need-based aid.

GIFT AID (NEED-BASED) ***Total amount:*** $129,941 (68% Federal, 32% state). ***Receiving aid:*** *All full-time undergraduates:* 33% (129). ***Average award:*** Undergraduates: $1632. ***Scholarships, grants, and awards:*** Federal Pell, FSEOG, state.

GIFT AID (NON-NEED-BASED) ***Total amount:*** $34,650 (100% state). ***Receiving aid:*** *Undergraduates:* 16% (63). ***Tuition waivers:*** Full or partial for employees or children of employees.

LOANS ***Student loans:*** $759,551 (54% need-based, 46% non-need-based). 54% of past graduating class borrowed through all loan programs. Average indebtedness per student: $18,000. ***Average need-based loan:*** Undergraduates: $5000. ***Programs:*** FFEL (Subsidized and Unsubsidized Stafford, PLUS), Perkins.

WORK-STUDY ***Federal work-study:*** *Total amount:* $1550; 1 job averaging $1550.

APPLYING for FINANCIAL AID ***Required financial aid forms:*** FAFSA, institution's own form. ***Financial aid deadline:*** Continuous. ***Notification date:*** Continuous beginning 3/1.

CONTACT Kathy John, Director of Financial Aid, The McGregor School of Antioch University, 800 Livermore Street, Yellow Springs, OH 45387-1609, 937-767-6321 Ext. 6778. *Fax:* 937-767-6499. *E-mail:* kjohn@mcgregor.edu

MCKENDREE COLLEGE

Lebanon, IL

Tuition & fees: $11,250 **Average undergraduate aid package: $10,369**

ABOUT THE INSTITUTION Independent religious, coed. Awards: bachelor's degrees. 45 undergraduate majors. Total enrollment: 2,061. Undergraduates: 2,061. Freshmen: 256. Federal methodology is used as a basis for awarding need-based institutional aid.

UNDERGRADUATE EXPENSES for 1999–2000 ***Comprehensive fee:*** $15,500 includes full-time tuition ($11,250) and room and board ($4250). Full-time tuition and fees vary according to class time, course load, and location. Room and board charges vary according to board plan and housing facility. ***Part-time tuition:*** $375 per credit hour. Part-time tuition and fees vary according to class time, course load, and location. ***Payment plan:*** installment.

FRESHMAN FINANCIAL AID (Fall 1999, est.) 221 applied for aid; of those 79% were deemed to have need. 100% of freshmen with need received aid; of those 79% had need fully met. *Average percent of need met:* 100% (excluding resources awarded to replace EFC). *Average financial aid package:* $10,585 (excluding resources awarded to replace EFC). 27% of all full-time freshmen had no need and received non-need-based aid.

UNDERGRADUATE FINANCIAL AID (Fall 1999, est.) 1,143 applied for aid; of those 88% were deemed to have need. 100% of undergraduates with need received aid; of those 66% had need fully met. *Average percent of need met:* 87% (excluding resources awarded to replace EFC). *Average financial aid package:* $10,369 (excluding resources awarded to replace EFC). 20% of all full-time undergraduates had no need and received non-need-based aid.

GIFT AID (NEED-BASED) ***Total amount:*** $5,285,471 (34% Federal, 50% state, 16% institutional). ***Receiving aid:*** *Freshmen:* 67% (159); *all full-time undergraduates:* 69% (867). ***Average award:*** Freshmen: $7093; Undergraduates: $7787. ***Scholarships, grants, and awards:*** Federal Pell, FSEOG, state, private, college/university gift aid from institutional funds.

GIFT AID (NON-NEED-BASED) ***Total amount:*** $3,387,615 (1% state, 91% institutional, 8% external sources). ***Receiving aid:*** *Freshmen:* 64% (154); *Undergraduates:* 62% (778). ***Scholarships, grants, and awards by category:*** *Academic Interests/Achievement:* 659 awards ($2,623,846 total): biological sciences, business, general academic interests/achievements, mathematics, physical sciences, religion/biblical studies. *Creative Arts/Performance:* music. *Special Achievements/Activities:* 32 awards ($94,239 total): cheerleading/drum major, community service, leadership. *Special Characteristics:* 133 awards ($323,981 total): children of faculty/staff, general special characteristics, out-of-state students, religious affiliation. ***Tuition waivers:*** Full or partial for employees or children of employees. ***ROTC:*** Army cooperative, Air Force cooperative.

LOANS ***Student loans:*** $4,829,416 (44% need-based, 56% non-need-based). Average indebtedness per student: $11,434. ***Average need-based loan:*** Freshmen: $1973; Undergraduates: $3143. ***Parent loans:*** $933,783 (100% non-need-based). ***Programs:*** FFEL (Subsidized and Unsubsidized Stafford, PLUS), Perkins.

WORK-STUDY ***Federal work-study:*** *Total amount:* $934,396; 507 jobs averaging $1824.

ATHLETIC AWARDS *Total amount:* 1,368,877 (100% non-need-based).

APPLYING for FINANCIAL AID ***Required financial aid forms:*** FAFSA, institution's own form. ***Financial aid deadline (priority):*** 5/31. ***Notification date:*** Continuous.

CONTACT Dr. Robert J. Clement, Director of Financial Aid, McKendree College, 701 College Road, Lebanon, IL 62254-1299, 618-537-6828 or toll-free 800-232-7228 Ext. 6831. *Fax:* 618-537-6530. *E-mail:* rclement@atlas.mckendree.edu

MCMURRY UNIVERSITY

Abilene, TX

Tuition & fees: $9695 **Average undergraduate aid package: $9226**

ABOUT THE INSTITUTION Independent United Methodist, coed. Awards: bachelor's degrees. 59 undergraduate majors. Total enrollment: 1,339. Undergraduates: 1,339. Freshmen: 306. Federal methodology is used as a basis for awarding need-based institutional aid.

UNDERGRADUATE EXPENSES for 1999–2000 ***Application fee:*** $20. ***Comprehensive fee:*** $13,939 includes full-time tuition ($8670), mandatory fees ($1025), and room and board ($4244). ***College room only:*** $1990. Full-time tuition and fees vary according to course load. Room and board charges vary according to board plan. ***Part-time tuition:*** $289 per semester hour. ***Part-time fees:*** $32 per semester hour. Part-time tuition and fees vary according to course load. ***Payment plans:*** guaranteed tuition, installment.

FRESHMAN FINANCIAL AID (Fall 1998) 258 applied for aid; of those 85% were deemed to have need. 100% of freshmen with need received aid; of those 11% had need fully met. *Average percent of need met:* 73% (excluding resources awarded to replace EFC). *Average financial aid package:* $8892 (excluding resources awarded to replace EFC). 13% of all full-time freshmen had no need and received non-need-based aid.

UNDERGRADUATE FINANCIAL AID (Fall 1998) 1,039 applied for aid; of those 86% were deemed to have need. 99% of undergraduates with need received aid; of those 7% had need fully met. *Average percent of need met:* 76% (excluding resources awarded to replace EFC). *Average financial aid package:* $9226 (excluding resources awarded to replace EFC). 14% of all full-time undergraduates had no need and received non-need-based aid.

GIFT AID (NEED-BASED) ***Total amount:*** $4,242,666 (35% Federal, 28% state, 33% institutional, 4% external sources). ***Receiving aid:*** *Freshmen:* 69% (183); *all full-time undergraduates:* 69% (773). ***Average award:*** Freshmen: $5869; Undergraduates: $5218. ***Scholarships, grants, and awards:*** Federal Pell, FSEOG, state, private, college/university gift aid from institutional funds.

GIFT AID (NON-NEED-BASED) ***Total amount:*** $1,058,687 (93% institutional, 7% external sources). ***Receiving aid:*** *Freshmen:* 63% (168); *Undergraduates:* 55% (612). ***Scholarships, grants, and awards by category:*** *Academic Interests/Achievement:* general academic interests/achievements, religion/biblical studies. *Creative Arts/Performance:* art/fine arts, music, theater/drama. *Special Achievements/Activities:* general special achievements/activities, junior miss. *Special Characteristics:* children of faculty/staff, international students, local/state students, previous college experience, relatives of clergy, religious affiliation, veterans. ***Tuition waivers:*** Full or partial for employees or children of employees. ***ROTC:*** Air Force cooperative.

LOANS ***Student loans:*** $4,973,260 (90% need-based, 10% non-need-based). 62% of past graduating class borrowed through all loan programs. Average indebtedness per student: $14,250. ***Average need-based loan:*** Freshmen: $2488; Undergraduates: $3528. ***Parent loans:*** $496,024 (86% need-based, 14% non-need-based). ***Programs:*** FFEL (Subsidized and Unsubsidized Stafford, PLUS), Perkins, state, Jones Nursing Loans, Ralston Nursing Loans.

WORK-STUDY ***Federal work-study:*** *Total amount:* $267,133; 288 jobs averaging $928. ***State or other work-study/employment:*** *Total amount:* $72,253 (52% need-based, 48% non-need-based). 102 part-time jobs averaging $708.

APPLYING for FINANCIAL AID ***Required financial aid forms:*** FAFSA, institution's own form. ***Financial aid deadline (priority):*** 3/15. ***Notification date:*** Continuous. Students must reply within 3 weeks of notification.

CONTACT Ms. Kathyrn Martin, Director of Financial Aid, McMurry University, Box 908, McMurry Station, Abilene, TX 79697, 915-793-4713 or toll-free 800-477-0077. *Fax:* 915-793-4718. *E-mail:* martink@mcmurryadm.mcm.edu

MCNEESE STATE UNIVERSITY

Lake Charles, LA

Tuition & fees (LA res): $2113 **Average undergraduate aid package: $3693**

ABOUT THE INSTITUTION State-supported, coed. Awards: associate, bachelor's, and master's degrees. 53 undergraduate majors. Total enrollment: 7,879. Undergraduates: 6,865. Freshmen: 1,332. Federal methodology is used as a basis for awarding need-based institutional aid.

UNDERGRADUATE EXPENSES for 1999–2000 ***Application fee:*** $10. ***Tuition, state resident:*** full-time $1650; part-time $412 per course. ***Tuition, nonresident:*** full-time $7520; part-time $1,710 per course. ***Required fees:*** full-time $463; $176 per term part-time. Full-time tuition and fees vary according to course load. Part-time tuition and fees vary according to course load. ***College room and board:*** $2328; ***room only:*** $1110. Room and board charges vary according to board plan and housing facility. ***Payment plan:*** installment.

FRESHMAN FINANCIAL AID (Fall 1999, est.) 3263 applied for aid; of those 99% were deemed to have need. 95% of freshmen with need received aid; of those 52% had need fully met. *Average percent of need met:* 38% (excluding resources awarded to replace EFC). *Average financial aid package:* $3167 (excluding resources awarded to replace EFC). 2% of all full-time freshmen had no need and received non-need-based aid.

UNDERGRADUATE FINANCIAL AID (Fall 1999, est.) 8,223 applied for aid; of those 74% were deemed to have need. 85% of undergraduates with need received aid; of those 70% had need fully met. *Average percent of need met:* 46% (excluding resources awarded to replace EFC). *Average financial aid package:* $3693 (excluding resources awarded to replace EFC). 3% of all full-time undergraduates had no need and received non-need-based aid.

GIFT AID (NEED-BASED) ***Total amount:*** $5,441,194 (99% Federal, 1% state). ***Receiving aid:*** *Freshmen:* 30% (1,045); *all full-time undergraduates:* 28% (2,396). ***Average award:*** Freshmen: $1737; Undergraduates: $1872. ***Scholarships, grants, and awards:*** Federal Pell, FSEOG, state, private, college/university gift aid from institutional funds.

GIFT AID (NON-NEED-BASED) ***Scholarships, grants, and awards by category:*** *Academic Interests/Achievement:* agriculture, biological sciences, business, communication, computer science, education, engineering/technologies, English, foreign languages, general academic interests/achievements, health fields, home economics, humanities, library science, mathematics, physical sciences, premedicine, social sciences. *Creative Arts/Performance:* art/fine arts, debating, music, theater/drama. *Special Achievements/Activities:* cheerleading/drum major, community service, general special achievements/activities, hobbies/interests, leadership, memberships, rodeo. *Special Characteristics:* adult students, children and siblings of alumni, children of faculty/staff, children of workers in trades, children with a deceased or disabled parent, ethnic background, first-generation college students, general special characteristics, international students, local/state students, members of minority groups, out-of-state students, religious affiliation, veterans, veterans' children. ***Tuition waivers:*** Full or partial for employees or children of employees, senior citizens.

LOANS ***Student loans:*** $9,248,846 (71% need-based, 29% non-need-based). ***Average need-based loan:*** Freshmen: $2123; Undergraduates: $2972. ***Parent loans:*** $61,891 (100% non-need-based). ***Programs:*** FFEL (Subsidized and Unsubsidized Stafford, PLUS), Perkins, college/university.

WORK-STUDY ***Federal work-study:*** *Total amount:* $398,343; jobs available. ***State or other work-study/employment:*** *Total amount:* $202,863 (100% non-need-based). 435 part-time jobs available.

APPLYING for FINANCIAL AID ***Required financial aid forms:*** FAFSA, institution's own form. ***Financial aid deadline (priority):*** 5/1. ***Notification date:*** 6/15. Students must reply within 2 weeks of notification.

CONTACT Ms. Taina J. Savoit, Director of Financial Aid, McNeese State University, PO Box 93260, Lake Charles, LA 70609-3260, 318-475-5065 or toll-free 800-622-3352.

MCP HAHNEMANN UNIVERSITY

Philadelphia, PA

Tuition & fees: $10,225 **Average undergraduate aid package: N/A**

ABOUT THE INSTITUTION Independent, coed. Awards: associate, bachelor's, master's, doctoral, and first professional degrees and post-bachelor's and post-master's certificates. 14 undergraduate majors. Total enrollment: 2,784. Undergraduates: 723. Freshmen: 28. Federal methodology is used as a basis for awarding need-based institutional aid.

UNDERGRADUATE EXPENSES for 1999–2000 ***Application fee:*** $35. ***Comprehensive fee:*** $18,751 includes full-time tuition ($10,100), mandatory fees ($125), and room and board ($8526). ***College room only:*** $4926. Full-time tuition and fees vary according to program. Room and board charges vary according to housing facility. ***Part-time tuition:*** $460 per credit. ***Part-time fees:*** $32 per term part-time. Part-time tuition and fees vary according to course load and program. ***Payment plan:*** installment.

GIFT AID (NEED-BASED) ***Scholarships, grants, and awards:*** Federal Pell, FSEOG, state, private, college/university gift aid from institutional funds, Federal Nursing.

MCP Hahnemann University (continued)

GIFT AID (NON-NEED-BASED) ***Tuition waivers:*** Full or partial for employees or children of employees.

LOANS ***Programs:*** Federal Direct (Subsidized and Unsubsidized Stafford, PLUS), Perkins, state, college/university, Signature Loans.

WORK-STUDY Federal work-study jobs available.

APPLYING for FINANCIAL AID ***Required financial aid form:*** FAFSA. ***Financial aid deadline (priority):*** 5/1.

CONTACT James Iannuzzi, Director, Financial Aid, MCP Hahnemann University, New College Building, 245 North 15th Street, Philadelphia, PA 19102-1192, 215-762-7734 or toll-free 800-2-DREXEL Ext. 6333.

MCPHERSON COLLEGE

McPherson, KS

Tuition & fees: $11,700 **Average undergraduate aid package: $12,152**

ABOUT THE INSTITUTION Independent religious, coed. Awards: associate and bachelor's degrees. 42 undergraduate majors. Total enrollment: 494. Undergraduates: 494. Freshmen: 129. Federal methodology is used as a basis for awarding need-based institutional aid.

UNDERGRADUATE EXPENSES for 2000–2001 ***Application fee:*** $25. ***Comprehensive fee:*** $16,600 includes full-time tuition ($11,500), mandatory fees ($200), and room and board ($4900). Room and board charges vary according to board plan and housing facility. Part-time tuition and fees vary according to course load.

FRESHMAN FINANCIAL AID (Fall 1999) 117 applied for aid; of those 88% were deemed to have need. 100% of freshmen with need received aid; of those 18% had need fully met. *Average percent of need met:* 82% (excluding resources awarded to replace EFC). *Average financial aid package:* $11,134 (excluding resources awarded to replace EFC). 16% of all full-time freshmen had no need and received non-need-based aid.

UNDERGRADUATE FINANCIAL AID (Fall 1999) 386 applied for aid; of those 91% were deemed to have need. 100% of undergraduates with need received aid; of those 20% had need fully met. *Average percent of need met:* 84% (excluding resources awarded to replace EFC). *Average financial aid package:* $12,152 (excluding resources awarded to replace EFC). 15% of all full-time undergraduates had no need and received non-need-based aid.

GIFT AID (NEED-BASED) ***Total amount:*** $974,074 (52% Federal, 26% state, 22% institutional). ***Receiving aid:*** *Freshmen:* 72% (89); *all full-time undergraduates:* 65% (274). ***Average award:*** Freshmen: $3357; Undergraduates: $3427. ***Scholarships, grants, and awards:*** Federal Pell, FSEOG, state, private, college/university gift aid from institutional funds.

GIFT AID (NON-NEED-BASED) ***Total amount:*** $1,638,556 (93% institutional, 7% external sources). ***Receiving aid:*** *Freshmen:* 77% (95); *Undergraduates:* 77% (325). ***Scholarships, grants, and awards by category:*** *Academic Interests/Achievement:* 416 awards ($1,424,099 total): general academic interests/achievements. ***Tuition waivers:*** Full or partial for employees or children of employees, senior citizens.

LOANS ***Student loans:*** $2,012,742 (73% need-based, 27% non-need-based). 86% of past graduating class borrowed through all loan programs. Average indebtedness per student: $19,075. ***Average need-based loan:*** Freshmen: $2990; Undergraduates: $4157. ***Parent loans:*** $395,240 (100% non-need-based). ***Programs:*** FFEL (Subsidized and Unsubsidized Stafford, PLUS), Perkins.

WORK-STUDY ***Federal work-study:*** *Total amount:* $427,941; 216 jobs averaging $1980.

APPLYING for FINANCIAL AID ***Required financial aid form:*** FAFSA. ***Financial aid deadline (priority):*** 3/1. ***Notification date:*** Continuous beginning 3/15. Students must reply within 4 weeks of notification.

CONTACT Mr. Fred Schmidt, Director of Financial Aid and Admissions, McPherson College, PO Box 1402, McPherson, KS 67460-1402, 316-241-0731 Ext. 1270 or toll-free 800-365-7402 Ext. 1270. *Fax:* 316-241-8443. *E-mail:* schmidtf@mcpherson.edu

MEDAILLE COLLEGE

Buffalo, NY

Tuition & fees: $11,450 **Average undergraduate aid package: N/A**

ABOUT THE INSTITUTION Independent, coed. Awards: associate, bachelor's, and master's degrees. 24 undergraduate majors. Total enrollment: 1,415. Undergraduates: 1,302. Freshmen: 179. Federal methodology is used as a basis for awarding need-based institutional aid.

UNDERGRADUATE EXPENSES for 1999–2000 ***Application fee:*** $25. ***Comprehensive fee:*** $16,750 includes full-time tuition ($11,190), mandatory fees ($260), and room and board ($5300). Full-time tuition and fees vary according to location. Room and board charges vary according to board plan and housing facility. ***Part-time tuition:*** $373 per credit hour. ***Part-time fees:*** $78 per term part-time. Part-time tuition and fees vary according to course load. ***Payment plan:*** installment.

GIFT AID (NEED-BASED) ***Scholarships, grants, and awards:*** Federal Pell, FSEOG, state, college/university gift aid from institutional funds.

GIFT AID (NON-NEED-BASED) ***Scholarships, grants, and awards by category:*** *Academic Interests/Achievement:* general academic interests/achievements. *Special Characteristics:* adult students. ***Tuition waivers:*** Full or partial for employees or children of employees, adult students, senior citizens. ***ROTC:*** Army cooperative.

LOANS ***Programs:*** FFEL (Subsidized and Unsubsidized Stafford, PLUS).

WORK-STUDY Federal work-study jobs available.

APPLYING for FINANCIAL AID ***Required financial aid forms:*** FAFSA, institution's own form, state aid form. ***Financial aid deadline:*** Continuous. ***Notification date:*** Continuous beginning 4/1. Students must reply within 2 weeks of notification.

CONTACT Ms. Jacqueline Matheny, Director of Enrollment Management and Admissions, Medaille College, 18 Agassiz Circle, Buffalo, NY 14214-2695, 716-884-3281 or toll-free 800-292-1582 (in-state). *Fax:* 716-884-0291.

MEDCENTER ONE COLLEGE OF NURSING

Bismarck, ND

Tuition & fees: $3236 **Average undergraduate aid package: N/A**

ABOUT THE INSTITUTION Independent, coed, primarily women. Awards: bachelor's degrees. 1 undergraduate major. Total enrollment: 82. Undergraduates: 82. Federal methodology is used as a basis for awarding need-based institutional aid.

UNDERGRADUATE EXPENSES for 1999–2000 ***Application fee:*** $40. ***Tuition:*** full-time $2956; part-time $123 per credit. ***Required fees:*** full-time $280; $5 per credit; $80. Part-time tuition and fees vary according to course load. Room and board charges vary according to housing facility.

UNDERGRADUATE FINANCIAL AID (Fall 1999, est.) 73 applied for aid; of those 100% were deemed to have need. 100% of undergraduates with need received aid; of those 59% had need fully met. *Average percent of need met:* 94% (excluding resources awarded to replace EFC).

GIFT AID (NEED-BASED) ***Total amount:*** $101,638 (77% Federal, 7% state, 12% institutional, 4% external sources). ***Receiving aid:*** *All full-time undergraduates:* 35% (29). ***Average award:*** Undergraduates: $3140. ***Scholarships, grants, and awards:*** Federal Pell, FSEOG, state, private, college/university gift aid from institutional funds.

GIFT AID (NON-NEED-BASED) ***Total amount:*** $20,050 (57% institutional, 43% external sources). ***Receiving aid:*** *Undergraduates:* 6% (5). ***Scholarships, grants, and awards by category:*** *Academic Interests/Achievement:* 13 awards ($7700 total): health fields. *Special Achievements/Activities:* 7 awards ($7000 total): general special achievements/activities. *Special Characteristics:* 3 awards ($5350 total): general special characteristics, local/state students.

LOANS ***Student loans:*** $354,527 (59% need-based, 41% non-need-based). 81% of past graduating class borrowed through all loan programs.

Average need-based loan: Undergraduates: $3419. ***Programs:*** FFEL (Subsidized and Unsubsidized Stafford, PLUS), Perkins, Federal Nursing, college/university.

WORK-STUDY ***Federal work-study:*** *Total amount:* $6900; 6 jobs averaging $1100.

APPLYING for FINANCIAL AID ***Required financial aid forms:*** FAFSA, state aid form. ***Financial aid deadline (priority):*** 5/1. ***Notification date:*** 6/15. Students must reply within 2 weeks of notification.

CONTACT Ms. Janell Thomas, Financial Aid Director, Medcenter One College of Nursing, 512 North 7th Street, Bismarck, ND 58501-4494, 701-323-6270. *Fax:* 701-323-6967. *E-mail:* jthomas@mohs.org

MEDGAR EVERS COLLEGE OF THE CITY UNIVERSITY OF NEW YORK

Brooklyn, NY

Tuition & fees (NY res): $3282 **Average undergraduate aid package: N/A**

ABOUT THE INSTITUTION State and locally supported, coed. Awards: associate and bachelor's degrees. 16 undergraduate majors. Total enrollment: 5,057. Undergraduates: 5,057. Freshmen: 717. Federal methodology is used as a basis for awarding need-based institutional aid.

UNDERGRADUATE EXPENSES for 1999–2000 ***Application fee:*** $40. ***Tuition, state resident:*** full-time $3200; part-time $135 per credit. ***Tuition, nonresident:*** full-time $6800; part-time $285 per credit. ***Required fees:*** full-time $82; $41 per term part-time.

GIFT AID (NEED-BASED) ***Scholarships, grants, and awards:*** Federal Pell, FSEOG, state, private, college/university gift aid from institutional funds.

GIFT AID (NON-NEED-BASED) ***Scholarships, grants, and awards by category:*** *Academic Interests/Achievement:* general academic interests/achievements.

LOANS ***Programs:*** Federal Direct (Subsidized and Unsubsidized Stafford, PLUS), Perkins.

WORK-STUDY Federal work-study jobs available.

APPLYING for FINANCIAL AID ***Required financial aid forms:*** FAFSA, University Financial Aid Information Supplemental Request (FASIR). ***Financial aid deadline (priority):*** 6/1. ***Notification date:*** Continuous beginning 9/1.

CONTACT Ms. Louise Martin, Director of Financial Aid, Medgar Evers College of the City University of New York, 1150 Carroll Street, Room 225, Brooklyn, NY 11225, 718-270-6038.

MEDICAL COLLEGE OF GEORGIA

Augusta, GA

Tuition & fees (GA res): $2700 **Average undergraduate aid package: $7795**

ABOUT THE INSTITUTION State-supported, coed. Awards: bachelor's, master's, doctoral, and first professional degrees. 10 undergraduate majors. Total enrollment: 1,974. Undergraduates: 625. Federal methodology is used as a basis for awarding need-based institutional aid.

UNDERGRADUATE EXPENSES for 1999–2000 ***Application fee:*** $25. ***Tuition, state resident:*** full-time $2414; part-time $101 per semester hour. ***Tuition, nonresident:*** full-time $9656; part-time $403 per semester hour. ***Required fees:*** full-time $286; $143 per term part-time. Part-time tuition and fees vary according to course load. ***College room and board: room only:*** $1302. Room and board charges vary according to housing facility.

UNDERGRADUATE FINANCIAL AID (Fall 1999, est.) 525 applied for aid; of those 92% were deemed to have need. 100% of undergraduates with need received aid; of those 84% had need fully met. *Average percent of need met:* 71% (excluding resources awarded to replace EFC). *Average financial aid package:* $7795 (excluding resources awarded to replace EFC). 16% of all full-time undergraduates had no need and received non-need-based aid.

GIFT AID (NEED-BASED) ***Total amount:*** $554,237 (61% Federal, 19% institutional, 20% external sources). ***Receiving aid:*** *All full-time undergraduates:* 34% (238). ***Average award:*** Undergraduates: $2246. ***Scholarships, grants, and awards:*** Federal Pell, FSEOG, state, private, college/university gift aid from institutional funds, Federal Nursing.

GIFT AID (NON-NEED-BASED) ***Total amount:*** $620,297 (100% state). ***Receiving aid:*** *Undergraduates:* 32% (228). ***Scholarships, grants, and awards by category:*** *Academic Interests/Achievement:* general academic interests/achievements. ***Tuition waivers:*** Full or partial for senior citizens.

LOANS ***Student loans:*** $2,404,031 (58% need-based, 42% non-need-based). 53% of past graduating class borrowed through all loan programs. Average indebtedness per student: $13,186. ***Average need-based loan:*** Undergraduates: $5405. ***Parent loans:*** $96,058 (100% non-need-based). ***Programs:*** FFEL (Subsidized and Unsubsidized Stafford, PLUS), Perkins, Federal Nursing, state, college/university.

WORK-STUDY ***Federal work-study:*** *Total amount:* $27,372; 24 jobs averaging $1140.

APPLYING for FINANCIAL AID ***Required financial aid forms:*** FAFSA, institution's own form, financial aid transcript (for mid-year transfers). ***Financial aid deadline (priority):*** 3/31. ***Notification date:*** Continuous beginning 4/1. Students must reply within 2 weeks of notification.

CONTACT Ms. Sandra D. Fowler, Director of Student Financial Aid, Medical College of Georgia, Room 2013 Kelly Building-Administration, 1120 Fifteenth Street, Augusta, GA 30912-7320, 706-721-4901. *Fax:* 706-721-9407.

MEDICAL UNIVERSITY OF SOUTH CAROLINA

Charleston, SC

Tuition & fees (SC res): $4626 **Average undergraduate aid package: N/A**

ABOUT THE INSTITUTION State-supported, coed. Awards: bachelor's, master's, doctoral, and first professional degrees and post-bachelor's and post-master's certificates. 4 undergraduate majors. Total enrollment: 2,383. Undergraduates: 422. Federal methodology is used as a basis for awarding need-based institutional aid.

UNDERGRADUATE EXPENSES for 1999–2000 ***Application fee:*** $55. ***One-time required fee:*** $160. ***Tuition, state resident:*** full-time $4450; part-time $197 per hour. ***Tuition, nonresident:*** full-time $12,974; part-time $588 per hour. ***Required fees:*** full-time $176; $408 per term part-time. Full-time tuition and fees vary according to program. Part-time tuition and fees vary according to program. ***Payment plan:*** installment.

GIFT AID (NEED-BASED) ***Scholarships, grants, and awards:*** Federal Pell, FSEOG, state, private, college/university gift aid from institutional funds, Federal Nursing, Scholarships for Disadvantaged Students (SDS).

GIFT AID (NON-NEED-BASED) ***Scholarships, grants, and awards by category:*** *Academic Interests/Achievement:* general academic interests/achievements. ***Tuition waivers:*** Full or partial for employees or children of employees, senior citizens.

LOANS ***Programs:*** FFEL (Subsidized and Unsubsidized Stafford, PLUS), Perkins, Federal Nursing, state, Health Professions Loans, Loans for Disadvantaged Students program, Primary Care Loans, alternative loans, TERI Loans.

WORK-STUDY Federal work-study jobs available.

APPLYING for FINANCIAL AID ***Required financial aid forms:*** FAFSA, institution's own form, income tax forms. ***Financial aid deadline (priority):*** 3/15.

CONTACT William H. Vandiver, Associate Director for Financial Aid Services, Medical University of South Carolina, 45 Courtenay Drive, PO Box 250176, Charleston, SC 29425, 843-792-2536. *Fax:* 843-792-2535. *E-mail:* vandivew@musc.edu

MEMPHIS COLLEGE OF ART

Memphis, TN

Tuition & fees: $11,990 **Average undergraduate aid package: $5600**

Memphis College of Art (continued)

ABOUT THE INSTITUTION Independent, coed. Awards: bachelor's and master's degrees. 16 undergraduate majors. Total enrollment: 290. Undergraduates: 236. Both federal and institutional methodology are used as a basis for awarding need-based institutional aid.

UNDERGRADUATE EXPENSES for 1999–2000 ***Application fee:*** $25. ***Tuition:*** full-time $11,940; part-time $500 per credit hour. ***Required fees:*** full-time $50; $25 per term part-time. Part-time tuition and fees vary according to course load. Room and board charges vary according to housing facility. ***Payment plans:*** installment, deferred payment.

FRESHMAN FINANCIAL AID (Fall 1999, est.) 35 applied for aid; of those 86% were deemed to have need. 100% of freshmen with need received aid; of those 83% had need fully met. *Average percent of need met:* 92% (excluding resources awarded to replace EFC). *Average financial aid package:* $5100 (excluding resources awarded to replace EFC). 38% of all full-time freshmen had no need and received non-need-based aid.

UNDERGRADUATE FINANCIAL AID (Fall 1999, est.) 163 applied for aid; of those 85% were deemed to have need. 100% of undergraduates with need received aid; of those 65% had need fully met. *Average percent of need met:* 80% (excluding resources awarded to replace EFC). *Average financial aid package:* $5600 (excluding resources awarded to replace EFC). 34% of all full-time undergraduates had no need and received non-need-based aid.

GIFT AID (NEED-BASED) ***Total amount:*** $273,753 (81% Federal, 16% state, 3% institutional). ***Receiving aid:*** *Freshmen:* 8% (4); *all full-time undergraduates:* 5% (11). ***Average award:*** Freshmen: $3000; Undergraduates: $3000. ***Scholarships, grants, and awards:*** Federal Pell, FSEOG, state, private.

GIFT AID (NON-NEED-BASED) ***Total amount:*** $482,328 (94% institutional, 6% external sources). ***Receiving aid:*** *Freshmen:* 62% (30); *Undergraduates:* 59% (139). ***Scholarships, grants, and awards by category:*** *Academic Interests/Achievement:* general academic interests/achievements. *Creative Arts/Performance:* applied art and design, art/fine arts. ***Tuition waivers:*** Full or partial for employees or children of employees.

LOANS ***Student loans:*** $830,118 (62% need-based, 38% non-need-based). 88% of past graduating class borrowed through all loan programs. Average indebtedness per student: $16,500. ***Average need-based loan:*** Freshmen: $2625; Undergraduates: $5500. ***Parent loans:*** $429,469 (100% non-need-based). ***Programs:*** FFEL (Subsidized and Unsubsidized Stafford, PLUS), Perkins, college/university.

WORK-STUDY ***Federal work-study:*** *Total amount:* $36,538; jobs available. ***State or other work-study/employment:*** *Total amount:* $90,388 (100% non-need-based). Part-time jobs available.

APPLYING for FINANCIAL AID ***Required financial aid forms:*** FAFSA, institution's own form. ***Financial aid deadline (priority):*** 3/1. ***Notification date:*** Continuous.

CONTACT Cindy Stanley, Director of Financial Aid, Memphis College of Art, 1930 Poplar Avenue, Memphis, TN 38104-2764, 901-272-5136 or toll-free 800-727-1088. *Fax:* 901-272-5158. *E-mail:* cstanley@mca.edu

MENLO COLLEGE
Atherton, CA

Tuition & fees: $16,800 **Average undergraduate aid package: $14,482**

ABOUT THE INSTITUTION Independent, coed. Awards: bachelor's degrees. 3 undergraduate majors. Total enrollment: 626. Undergraduates: 626. Freshmen: 128. Federal methodology is used as a basis for awarding need-based institutional aid.

UNDERGRADUATE EXPENSES for 1999–2000 ***Application fee:*** $40. ***One-time required fee:*** $300. ***Comprehensive fee:*** $23,600 includes full-time tuition ($16,800) and room and board ($6800). Room and board charges vary according to housing facility. ***Part-time tuition:*** $700 per unit. Part-time tuition and fees vary according to course load. ***Payment plan:*** installment.

FRESHMAN FINANCIAL AID (Fall 1999) 81 applied for aid; of those 91% were deemed to have need. 100% of freshmen with need received aid; of those 22% had need fully met. *Average percent of need met:* 74% (excluding resources awarded to replace EFC). *Average financial aid package:* $12,937 (excluding resources awarded to replace EFC). 47% of all full-time freshmen had no need and received non-need-based aid.

UNDERGRADUATE FINANCIAL AID (Fall 1999) 278 applied for aid; of those 91% were deemed to have need. 100% of undergraduates with need received aid; of those 28% had need fully met. *Average percent of need met:* 80% (excluding resources awarded to replace EFC). *Average financial aid package:* $14,482 (excluding resources awarded to replace EFC). 45% of all full-time undergraduates had no need and received non-need-based aid.

GIFT AID (NEED-BASED) ***Total amount:*** $2,828,773 (13% Federal, 10% state, 72% institutional, 5% external sources). ***Receiving aid:*** *Freshmen:* 53% (74); *all full-time undergraduates:* 53% (244). ***Average award:*** Freshmen: $10,423; Undergraduates: $10,580. ***Scholarships, grants, and awards:*** Federal Pell, FSEOG, state, college/university gift aid from institutional funds.

GIFT AID (NON-NEED-BASED) ***Total amount:*** $944,347 (96% institutional, 4% external sources). ***Receiving aid:*** *Freshmen:* 4% (6); *Undergraduates:* 4% (19). ***Scholarships, grants, and awards by category:*** *Academic Interests/Achievement:* 180 awards ($1,456,750 total): general academic interests/achievements. *Special Achievements/Activities:* 82 awards ($254,931 total): leadership. ***Tuition waivers:*** Full or partial for employees or children of employees. ***ROTC:*** Army cooperative.

LOANS ***Student loans:*** $1,811,948 (77% need-based, 23% non-need-based). 73% of past graduating class borrowed through all loan programs. ***Average need-based loan:*** Freshmen: $2427; Undergraduates: $3785. ***Parent loans:*** $583,046 (46% need-based, 54% non-need-based). ***Programs:*** FFEL (Subsidized and Unsubsidized Stafford, PLUS).

WORK-STUDY ***Federal work-study:*** *Total amount:* $32,562; 45 jobs averaging $849.

APPLYING for FINANCIAL AID ***Required financial aid form:*** FAFSA. ***Financial aid deadline:*** Continuous. ***Notification date:*** Continuous beginning 2/1.

CONTACT Leslie Wills, Financial Aid Officer, Menlo College, 1000 El Camino Real, Atherton, CA 94027-4301, 650-688-3880 or toll-free 800-556-3656.

MENNONITE COLLEGE OF NURSING
Normal, IL

See Illinois State University

MERCER UNIVERSITY
Macon, GA

Tuition & fees: $16,290 **Average undergraduate aid package: $14,026**

ABOUT THE INSTITUTION Independent Baptist, coed. Awards: bachelor's, master's, doctoral, and first professional degrees and post-bachelor's and post-master's certificates. 55 undergraduate majors. Total enrollment: 6,745. Undergraduates: 4,092. Freshmen: 754. Federal methodology is used as a basis for awarding need-based institutional aid.

UNDERGRADUATE EXPENSES for 1999–2000 ***Application fee:*** $25. ***Comprehensive fee:*** $21,670 includes full-time tuition ($16,290) and room and board ($5380). ***College room only:*** $2600. Full-time tuition and fees vary according to course load, location, and program. Room and board charges vary according to board plan and housing facility. ***Part-time tuition:*** $544 per credit hour. Part-time tuition and fees vary according to course load, location, and program. ***Payment plan:*** installment.

FRESHMAN FINANCIAL AID (Fall 1999, est.) 628 applied for aid; of those 81% were deemed to have need. 100% of freshmen with need received aid; of those 81% had need fully met. *Average percent of need met:* 88% (excluding resources awarded to replace EFC). *Average financial aid package:* $15,820 (excluding resources awarded to replace EFC). 25% of all full-time freshmen had no need and received non-need-based aid.

UNDERGRADUATE FINANCIAL AID (Fall 1999, est.) 2,703 applied for aid; of those 79% were deemed to have need. 100% of undergraduates with

need received aid; of those 87% had need fully met. *Average percent of need met:* 83% (excluding resources awarded to replace EFC). *Average financial aid package:* $14,026 (excluding resources awarded to replace EFC). 29% of all full-time undergraduates had no need and received non-need-based aid.

GIFT AID (NEED-BASED) ***Total amount:*** $16,806,340 (16% Federal, 25% state, 53% institutional, 6% external sources). ***Receiving aid:*** *Freshmen:* 72% (508); *all full-time undergraduates:* 65% (2,124). ***Average award:*** Freshmen: $10,522; Undergraduates: $8087. ***Scholarships, grants, and awards:*** Federal Pell, FSEOG, state, private, college/university gift aid from institutional funds.

GIFT AID (NON-NEED-BASED) ***Total amount:*** $7,122,936 (27% state, 68% institutional, 5% external sources). ***Receiving aid:*** *Freshmen:* 21% (151); *Undergraduates:* 14% (454). ***Scholarships, grants, and awards by category:*** *Academic Interests/Achievement:* 1,573 awards ($7,944,646 total): biological sciences, education, English, general academic interests/achievements, international studies, military science, religion/biblical studies. *Creative Arts/Performance:* 110 awards ($212,634 total): art/fine arts, debating, music, theater/drama. *Special Achievements/Activities:* 9 awards ($45,533 total): community service, general special achievements/activities, junior miss, memberships. *Special Characteristics:* 1,862 awards ($6,228,209 total): adult students, children of faculty/staff, children of public servants, children of union members/company employees, general special characteristics, international students, local/state students, members of minority groups, relatives of clergy, religious affiliation, siblings of current students. ***Tuition waivers:*** Full or partial for employees or children of employees. ***ROTC:*** Army cooperative.

LOANS ***Student loans:*** $12,229,877 (76% need-based, 24% non-need-based). 66% of past graduating class borrowed through all loan programs. Average indebtedness per student: $12,833. ***Average need-based loan:*** Freshmen: $2805; Undergraduates: $3974. ***Parent loans:*** $1,445,074 (26% need-based, 74% non-need-based). ***Programs:*** Federal Direct (Subsidized and Unsubsidized Stafford, PLUS), Perkins, college/university.

WORK-STUDY ***Federal work-study:*** *Total amount:* $707,476; 407 jobs averaging $1738.

ATHLETIC AWARDS *Total amount:* 1,694,858 (33% need-based, 67% non-need-based).

APPLYING for FINANCIAL AID ***Required financial aid forms:*** FAFSA, institution's own form, state aid form. ***Financial aid deadline (priority):*** 4/1. ***Notification date:*** Continuous. Students must reply within 2 weeks of notification.

CONTACT Ms. Carol Williams, University Director of Financial Aid, Mercer University, 1400 Coleman Avenue, Macon, GA 31207-0003, 912-301-2670 or toll-free 800-342-0841 (in-state), 800-637-2378 (out-of-state). *Fax:* 912-301-2671. *E-mail:* williams_ck@mercer.edu

MERCY COLLEGE

Dobbs Ferry, NY

Tuition & fees: $7950 **Average undergraduate aid package: N/A**

ABOUT THE INSTITUTION Independent, coed. Awards: associate, bachelor's, and master's degrees. 52 undergraduate majors. Total enrollment: 13,434. Undergraduates: 5,756. Freshmen: 1,146. Federal methodology is used as a basis for awarding need-based institutional aid.

UNDERGRADUATE EXPENSES for 1999–2000 ***Application fee:*** $35. ***Comprehensive fee:*** $15,450 includes full-time tuition ($7950) and room and board ($7500). Full-time tuition and fees vary according to course load and degree level. Room and board charges vary according to board plan and housing facility. ***Part-time tuition:*** $335 per credit. ***Payment plans:*** installment, deferred payment.

GIFT AID (NEED-BASED) ***Scholarships, grants, and awards:*** Federal Pell, FSEOG, state, college/university gift aid from institutional funds.

GIFT AID (NON-NEED-BASED) ***Scholarships, grants, and awards by category:*** *Academic Interests/Achievement:* general academic interests/achievements. ***Tuition waivers:*** Full or partial for children of alumni, employees or children of employees, senior citizens. ***ROTC:*** Air Force cooperative.

LOANS ***Programs:*** Federal Direct (Subsidized and Unsubsidized Stafford, PLUS).

WORK-STUDY Federal work-study jobs available.

APPLYING for FINANCIAL AID ***Required financial aid form:*** FAFSA. ***Financial aid deadline (priority):*** 2/1.

CONTACT Lorene Chapman, Director of Financial Aid, Mercy College, 555 Broadway, Dobbs Ferry, NY 10522, 800-MERCY-NY. *E-mail:* chapman@mercynet.edu

MERCY COLLEGE OF HEALTH SCIENCES

Des Moines, IA

CONTACT Financial Aid Office, Mercy College of Health Sciences, 928 Sixth Avenue, Des Moines, IA 50309-1239, 515-643-3180 or toll-free 800-637-2994.

MERCYHURST COLLEGE

Erie, PA

Tuition & fees: $14,190 **Average undergraduate aid package: $8300**

ABOUT THE INSTITUTION Independent Roman Catholic, coed. Awards: associate, bachelor's, and master's degrees and post-bachelor's certificates. 93 undergraduate majors. Total enrollment: 2,998. Undergraduates: 2,832. Freshmen: 668. Federal methodology is used as a basis for awarding need-based institutional aid.

UNDERGRADUATE EXPENSES for 2000–2001 ***Application fee:*** $30. ***Comprehensive fee:*** $19,296 includes full-time tuition ($13,290), mandatory fees ($900), and room and board ($5106). Room and board charges vary according to board plan and housing facility. ***Part-time tuition:*** $443 per credit. ***Part-time fees:*** $300 per term part-time. Part-time tuition and fees vary according to course load and location. ***Payment plan:*** installment.

FRESHMAN FINANCIAL AID (Fall 1999, est.) 887 applied for aid; of those 86% were deemed to have need. 91% of freshmen with need received aid; of those 76% had need fully met. *Average percent of need met:* 89% (excluding resources awarded to replace EFC). *Average financial aid package:* $6036 (excluding resources awarded to replace EFC). 7% of all full-time freshmen had no need and received non-need-based aid.

UNDERGRADUATE FINANCIAL AID (Fall 1999, est.) 2,066 applied for aid; of those 84% were deemed to have need. 87% of undergraduates with need received aid; of those 46% had need fully met. *Average percent of need met:* 83% (excluding resources awarded to replace EFC). *Average financial aid package:* $8300 (excluding resources awarded to replace EFC). 9% of all full-time undergraduates had no need and received non-need-based aid.

GIFT AID (NEED-BASED) ***Total amount:*** $7,169,575 (29% Federal, 42% state, 23% institutional, 6% external sources). ***Receiving aid:*** *Freshmen:* 65% (623); *all full-time undergraduates:* 59% (1,358). ***Average award:*** Freshmen: $2650; Undergraduates: $2549. ***Scholarships, grants, and awards:*** Federal Pell, FSEOG, state, private, college/university gift aid from institutional funds.

GIFT AID (NON-NEED-BASED) ***Total amount:*** $2,113,157 (100% institutional). ***Receiving aid:*** *Freshmen:* 49% (475); *Undergraduates:* 44% (1,011). ***Scholarships, grants, and awards by category:*** *Academic Interests/Achievement:* 523 awards ($1,599,966 total): general academic interests/achievements. *Creative Arts/Performance:* 125 awards ($477,729 total): art/fine arts, dance, music. *Special Achievements/Activities:* 810 awards ($1,623,727 total): community service, general special achievements/activities, leadership, religious involvement. *Special Characteristics:* 136 awards ($1,500,000 total): children of faculty/staff, local/state students, members of minority groups, siblings of current students. ***Tuition waivers:*** Full or partial for employees or children of employees. ***ROTC:*** Army cooperative.

LOANS ***Student loans:*** $11,488,096 (74% need-based, 26% non-need-based). 81% of past graduating class borrowed through all loan programs. Average indebtedness per student: $16,781. ***Average need-based loan:***

Mercyhurst College (continued)

Freshmen: $2650; Undergraduates: $4641. ***Parent loans:*** $2,247,436 (100% need-based). ***Programs:*** FFEL (Subsidized and Unsubsidized Stafford, PLUS), Perkins, college/university.

WORK-STUDY ***Federal work-study:*** *Total amount:* $227,962; jobs available. ***State or other work-study/employment:*** *Total amount:* $929,971 (60% need-based, 40% non-need-based). Part-time jobs available.

ATHLETIC AWARDS *Total amount:* 2,449,935 (100% non-need-based).

APPLYING for FINANCIAL AID ***Required financial aid forms:*** FAFSA, institution's own form. ***Financial aid deadline (priority):*** 3/1. ***Notification date:*** Continuous. Students must reply by 5/1.

CONTACT Mrs. Sheila W. Richter, Director of Financial Aid, Mercyhurst College, 501 East 38th Street, Erie, PA 16546, 814-824-2288 Ext. 2287 or toll-free 800-825-1926. *Fax:* 814-824-2438. *E-mail:* srichter@mercyhurst.edu

MEREDITH COLLEGE

Raleigh, NC

Tuition & fees: $9840 **Average undergraduate aid package: $8649**

ABOUT THE INSTITUTION Independent religious, women only. Awards: bachelor's and master's degrees and post-bachelor's certificates. 57 undergraduate majors. Total enrollment: 2,643. Undergraduates: 2,457. Freshmen: 460. Both federal and institutional methodology are used as a basis for awarding need-based institutional aid.

UNDERGRADUATE EXPENSES for 2000–2001 ***Application fee:*** $35. ***Comprehensive fee:*** $14,100 includes full-time tuition ($9840) and room and board ($4260). ***Part-time tuition:*** $295 per semester hour. ***Payment plan:*** installment.

FRESHMAN FINANCIAL AID (Fall 1999) 329 applied for aid; of those 71% were deemed to have need. 100% of freshmen with need received aid; of those 36% had need fully met. *Average percent of need met:* 86% (excluding resources awarded to replace EFC). *Average financial aid package:* $8054 (excluding resources awarded to replace EFC). 49% of all full-time freshmen had no need and received non-need-based aid.

UNDERGRADUATE FINANCIAL AID (Fall 1999) 1,107 applied for aid; of those 77% were deemed to have need. 100% of undergraduates with need received aid; of those 34% had need fully met. *Average percent of need met:* 84% (excluding resources awarded to replace EFC). *Average financial aid package:* $8649 (excluding resources awarded to replace EFC). 33% of all full-time undergraduates had no need and received non-need-based aid.

GIFT AID (NEED-BASED) ***Total amount:*** $4,895,336 (16% Federal, 63% state, 17% institutional, 4% external sources). ***Receiving aid:*** *Freshmen:* 51% (230); *all full-time undergraduates:* 46% (824). ***Average award:*** Freshmen: $6149; Undergraduates: $5378. ***Scholarships, grants, and awards:*** Federal Pell, FSEOG, state, private, college/university gift aid from institutional funds.

GIFT AID (NON-NEED-BASED) ***Total amount:*** $1,827,509 (55% state, 39% institutional, 6% external sources). ***Receiving aid:*** *Freshmen:* 10% (45); *Undergraduates:* 5% (97). ***Scholarships, grants, and awards by category:*** *Academic Interests/Achievement:* education, English, general academic interests/achievements, mathematics. *Creative Arts/Performance:* applied art and design, art/fine arts, music. *Special Achievements/Activities:* leadership. *Special Characteristics:* local/state students. ***Tuition waivers:*** Full or partial for employees or children of employees. ***ROTC:*** Army cooperative, Air Force cooperative.

LOANS ***Student loans:*** $5,419,112 (64% need-based, 36% non-need-based). 58% of past graduating class borrowed through all loan programs. ***Average need-based loan:*** Freshmen: $1520; Undergraduates: $3031. ***Parent loans:*** $1,200,406 (100% non-need-based). ***Programs:*** FFEL (Subsidized and Unsubsidized Stafford, PLUS), Perkins.

WORK-STUDY ***Federal work-study:*** *Total amount:* $203,566; 170 jobs averaging $1197. ***State or other work-study/employment:*** *Total amount:* $18,749 (100% non-need-based). 15 part-time jobs averaging $1249.

APPLYING for FINANCIAL AID ***Required financial aid forms:*** FAFSA, institution's own form. ***Financial aid deadline (priority):*** 2/15. ***Notification date:*** 4/1. Students must reply by 5/1 or within 4 weeks of notification.

CONTACT Mr. William Cox, Director of Financial Assistance, Meredith College, 3800 Hillsborough Street, Raleigh, NC 27607-5298, 919-760-8565 or toll-free 800-MEREDITH. *E-mail:* coxw@meredith.edu

MERRIMACK COLLEGE

North Andover, MA

Tuition & fees: $15,710 **Average undergraduate aid package: $13,800**

ABOUT THE INSTITUTION Independent Roman Catholic, coed. Awards: associate, bachelor's, and master's degrees. 48 undergraduate majors. Total enrollment: 2,677. Undergraduates: 2,677. Freshmen: 787. Both federal and institutional methodology are used as a basis for awarding need-based institutional aid.

UNDERGRADUATE EXPENSES for 1999–2000 ***Application fee:*** $40. ***Comprehensive fee:*** $23,210 includes full-time tuition ($15,710) and room and board ($7500). ***College room only:*** $4200. Room and board charges vary according to board plan and housing facility. ***Part-time tuition:*** $580 per credit. Part-time tuition and fees vary according to class time. ***Payment plans:*** installment, deferred payment.

FRESHMAN FINANCIAL AID (Fall 1999, est.) 465 applied for aid; of those 97% were deemed to have need. 97% of freshmen with need received aid; of those 72% had need fully met. *Average percent of need met:* 80% (excluding resources awarded to replace EFC). *Average financial aid package:* $13,360 (excluding resources awarded to replace EFC). 3% of all full-time freshmen had no need and received non-need-based aid.

UNDERGRADUATE FINANCIAL AID (Fall 1999, est.) 1,830 applied for aid; of those 98% were deemed to have need. 99% of undergraduates with need received aid; of those 64% had need fully met. *Average percent of need met:* 70% (excluding resources awarded to replace EFC). *Average financial aid package:* $13,800 (excluding resources awarded to replace EFC). 3% of all full-time undergraduates had no need and received non-need-based aid.

GIFT AID (NEED-BASED) ***Total amount:*** $11,373,316 (7% Federal, 7% state, 86% institutional). ***Receiving aid:*** *Freshmen:* 80% (437); *all full-time undergraduates:* 80% (1,722). ***Average award:*** Freshmen: $8235; Undergraduates: $5800. ***Scholarships, grants, and awards:*** Federal Pell, FSEOG, state, private, college/university gift aid from institutional funds.

GIFT AID (NON-NEED-BASED) ***Total amount:*** $1,405,702 (84% institutional, 16% external sources). ***Receiving aid:*** *Freshmen:* 4% (20); *Undergraduates:* 11% (235). ***Scholarships, grants, and awards by category:*** *Academic Interests/Achievement:* 25 awards ($150,000 total): general academic interests/achievements. *Creative Arts/Performance:* 2 awards ($23,565 total): art/fine arts, theater/drama. *Special Achievements/Activities:* 32 awards ($320,000 total): leadership. *Special Characteristics:* 50 awards ($455,325 total): children and siblings of alumni, children of faculty/staff, relatives of clergy, siblings of current students. ***Tuition waivers:*** Full or partial for employees or children of employees, senior citizens. ***ROTC:*** Air Force cooperative.

LOANS ***Student loans:*** $6,163,505 (78% need-based, 22% non-need-based). 80% of past graduating class borrowed through all loan programs. ***Average need-based loan:*** Freshmen: $4125; Undergraduates: $7000. ***Parent loans:*** $2,669,094 (100% non-need-based). ***Programs:*** Federal Direct (Subsidized and Unsubsidized Stafford, PLUS), Perkins, state, college/university, MEFA Loans, alternative loans.

WORK-STUDY ***Federal work-study:*** *Total amount:* $160,000; jobs available. ***State or other work-study/employment:*** *Total amount:* $170,000 (100% need-based). 200 part-time jobs averaging $1000.

ATHLETIC AWARDS *Total amount:* 1,100,000 (100% non-need-based).

APPLYING for FINANCIAL AID ***Required financial aid forms:*** FAFSA, CSS Financial Aid PROFILE, noncustodial (divorced/separated) parent's statement, business/farm supplement. ***Financial aid deadline:*** 2/15. ***Notification date:*** Continuous beginning 3/1. Students must reply by 5/1 or within 2 weeks of notification.

CONTACT Penny King, Associate Director of Financial Aid, Merrimack College, 315 Turnpike Street, North Andover, MA 01845, 978-837-5186. *Fax:* 978-837-5067. *E-mail:* pking@merrimack.edu

MESA STATE COLLEGE

Grand Junction, CO

Tuition & fees (CO res): $2123 **Average undergraduate aid package: $6007**

ABOUT THE INSTITUTION State-supported, coed. Awards: associate, bachelor's, and master's degrees. 67 undergraduate majors. Total enrollment: 4,892. Undergraduates: 4,852. Freshmen: 1,044. Federal methodology is used as a basis for awarding need-based institutional aid.

UNDERGRADUATE EXPENSES for 1999–2000 ***Application fee:*** $30. ***Tuition, state resident:*** full-time $1577; part-time $79 per credit hour. ***Tuition, nonresident:*** full-time $5966; part-time $298 per credit hour. ***Required fees:*** full-time $546; $26 per credit hour. Full-time tuition and fees vary according to course load. ***College room and board:*** $5048; ***room only:*** $2438. Room and board charges vary according to board plan and housing facility.

FRESHMAN FINANCIAL AID (Fall 1999, est.) 706 applied for aid; of those 91% were deemed to have need. 100% of freshmen with need received aid; of those 75% had need fully met. *Average percent of need met:* 77% (excluding resources awarded to replace EFC). *Average financial aid package:* $6007 (excluding resources awarded to replace EFC).

UNDERGRADUATE FINANCIAL AID (Fall 1999, est.) 2,619 applied for aid; of those 91% were deemed to have need. 100% of undergraduates with need received aid; of those 75% had need fully met. *Average percent of need met:* 79% (excluding resources awarded to replace EFC). *Average financial aid package:* $6007 (excluding resources awarded to replace EFC).

GIFT AID (NEED-BASED) ***Total amount:*** $5,179,049 (78% Federal, 22% state). ***Receiving aid:*** *Freshmen:* 42% (385); *all full-time undergraduates:* 37% (1,430). ***Average award:*** Freshmen: $2356; Undergraduates: $2356. ***Scholarships, grants, and awards:*** Federal Pell, FSEOG, state, private, college/university gift aid from institutional funds.

GIFT AID (NON-NEED-BASED) ***Total amount:*** $1,844,558 (16% state, 32% institutional, 52% external sources). ***Receiving aid:*** *Freshmen:* 32% (289); *Undergraduates:* 31% (1,205). ***Scholarships, grants, and awards by category:*** *Academic Interests/Achievement:* biological sciences, business, communication, computer science, education, engineering/technologies, English, general academic interests/achievements, health fields, humanities, mathematics, physical sciences, social sciences. *Creative Arts/Performance:* art/fine arts, creative writing, journalism/publications, music, theater/drama. *Special Achievements/Activities:* general special achievements/activities, hobbies/interests. *Special Characteristics:* first-generation college students, local/state students, members of minority groups, out-of-state students. ***Tuition waivers:*** Full or partial for employees or children of employees, senior citizens.

LOANS ***Student loans:*** $7,367,910 (72% need-based, 28% non-need-based). 53% of past graduating class borrowed through all loan programs. Average indebtedness per student: $13,600. ***Average need-based loan:*** Freshmen: $2443; Undergraduates: $2443. ***Parent loans:*** $474,978 (100% non-need-based). ***Programs:*** FFEL (Subsidized and Unsubsidized Stafford, PLUS), Perkins.

WORK-STUDY ***Federal work-study:*** *Total amount:* $342,903; 201 jobs averaging $1706. ***State or other work-study/employment:*** *Total amount:* $1,287,562 (57% need-based, 43% non-need-based). Part-time jobs available.

ATHLETIC AWARDS *Total amount:* 450,669 (100% non-need-based).

APPLYING for FINANCIAL AID ***Required financial aid form:*** FAFSA. ***Financial aid deadline (priority):*** 3/1. ***Notification date:*** Continuous beginning 4/1. Students must reply within 5 weeks of notification.

CONTACT Ms. Sylvia M. Jones, Director of Financial Aid, Mesa State College, PO Box 2647, Grand Junction, CO 81502-2647, 970-248-1396 or toll-free 800-982-MESA. *Fax:* 970-248-1191. *E-mail:* sjones@mesastate.edu

MESIVTA OF EASTERN PARKWAY RABBINICAL SEMINARY

Brooklyn, NY

CONTACT Rabbi Joseph Halberstadt, Dean, Mesivta of Eastern Parkway Rabbinical Seminary, 510 Dahill Road, Brooklyn, NY 11218-5559, 718-438-1002.

MESIVTA TIFERETH JERUSALEM OF AMERICA

New York, NY

CONTACT Rabbi Dickstein, Director of Financial Aid, Mesivta Tifereth Jerusalem of America, 141 East Broadway, New York, NY 10002-6301, 212-964-2830.

MESIVTA TORAH VODAATH RABBINICAL SEMINARY

Brooklyn, NY

CONTACT Mrs. Kayla Goldring, Director of Financial Aid, Mesivta Torah Vodaath Rabbinical Seminary, 425 East Ninth Street, Brooklyn, NY 11218-5209, 718-941-8000.

MESSENGER COLLEGE

Joplin, MO

Tuition & fees: $3430 **Average undergraduate aid package: N/A**

ABOUT THE INSTITUTION Independent Pentecostal, coed. Awards: associate and bachelor's degrees. 4 undergraduate majors. Total enrollment: 98. Undergraduates: 98. Freshmen: 31. Federal methodology is used as a basis for awarding need-based institutional aid.

UNDERGRADUATE EXPENSES for 1999–2000 ***Application fee:*** $10. ***Comprehensive fee:*** $6370 includes full-time tuition ($3150), mandatory fees ($280), and room and board ($2940). ***Part-time tuition:*** $105 per credit. ***Part-time fees:*** $7 per credit. ***Payment plan:*** installment.

GIFT AID (NEED-BASED) ***Scholarships, grants, and awards:*** Federal Pell, FSEOG, private.

GIFT AID (NON-NEED-BASED) ***Scholarships, grants, and awards by category:*** *Academic Interests/Achievement:* education, general academic interests/achievements, religion/biblical studies. *Special Achievements/Activities:* religious involvement. *Special Characteristics:* religious affiliation. ***Tuition waivers:*** Full or partial for employees or children of employees.

LOANS ***Programs:*** FFEL (Subsidized and Unsubsidized Stafford, PLUS).

WORK-STUDY Federal work-study jobs available.

APPLYING for FINANCIAL AID ***Required financial aid forms:*** FAFSA, institution's own form. ***Financial aid deadline:*** Continuous.

CONTACT Sharon Shackelford, Financial Aid Officer, Messenger College, 300 East 50th Street, Joplin, MO 64804, 417-624-7070 Ext. 308. *Fax:* 417-624-5070. *E-mail:* mc@pcg.org

MESSIAH COLLEGE

Grantham, PA

Tuition & fees: $15,096 **Average undergraduate aid package: $11,909**

ABOUT THE INSTITUTION Independent interdenominational, coed. Awards: bachelor's degrees. 58 undergraduate majors. Total enrollment: 2,735. Undergraduates: 2,735. Freshmen: 678. Federal methodology is used as a basis for awarding need-based institutional aid.

UNDERGRADUATE EXPENSES for 1999–2000 ***Application fee:*** $30. ***Comprehensive fee:*** $20,676 includes full-time tuition ($15,000), mandatory fees ($96), and room and board ($5580). ***College room only:*** $2850.

Messiah College (continued)

Room and board charges vary according to board plan. ***Part-time tuition:*** $625 per credit. ***Part-time fees:*** $4 per credit. ***Payment plan:*** installment.

FRESHMAN FINANCIAL AID (Fall 1999) 589 applied for aid; of those 84% were deemed to have need. 100% of freshmen with need received aid; of those 14% had need fully met. *Average percent of need met:* 74% (excluding resources awarded to replace EFC). *Average financial aid package:* $11,726 (excluding resources awarded to replace EFC). 23% of all full-time freshmen had no need and received non-need-based aid.

UNDERGRADUATE FINANCIAL AID (Fall 1999) 2,142 applied for aid; of those 90% were deemed to have need. 100% of undergraduates with need received aid; of those 18% had need fully met. *Average percent of need met:* 75% (excluding resources awarded to replace EFC). *Average financial aid package:* $11,909 (excluding resources awarded to replace EFC). 21% of all full-time undergraduates had no need and received non-need-based aid.

GIFT AID (NEED-BASED) ***Total amount:*** $9,744,535 (14% Federal, 18% state, 68% institutional). ***Receiving aid:*** *Freshmen:* 66% (450); *all full-time undergraduates:* 66% (1,746). ***Average award:*** Freshmen: $7407; Undergraduates: $6468. ***Scholarships, grants, and awards:*** Federal Pell, FSEOG, state, private, college/university gift aid from institutional funds.

GIFT AID (NON-NEED-BASED) ***Total amount:*** $5,521,403 (1% Federal, 88% institutional, 11% external sources). ***Receiving aid:*** *Freshmen:* 65% (444); *Undergraduates:* 52% (1,373). ***Scholarships, grants, and awards by category:*** *Academic Interests/Achievement:* general academic interests/achievements. *Creative Arts/Performance:* art/fine arts, music. *Special Achievements/Activities:* leadership. *Special Characteristics:* adult students, children and siblings of alumni, children of current students, children of educators, children of faculty/staff, ethnic background, international students, married students, members of minority groups, parents of current students, relatives of clergy, religious affiliation, siblings of current students, spouses of current students. ***Tuition waivers:*** Full or partial for minority students, children of alumni, employees or children of employees, adult students, senior citizens.

LOANS ***Student loans:*** $9,648,808 (71% need-based, 29% non-need-based). 62% of past graduating class borrowed through all loan programs. Average indebtedness per student: $16,999. ***Average need-based loan:*** Freshmen: $2381; Undergraduates: $3522. ***Parent loans:*** $2,641,212 (100% non-need-based). ***Programs:*** Federal Direct (Subsidized and Unsubsidized Stafford, PLUS), Perkins, Federal Nursing.

WORK-STUDY ***Federal work-study:*** *Total amount:* $1,261,991; 777 jobs averaging $1624. ***State or other work-study/employment:*** *Total amount:* $1,127,867 (100% non-need-based). 549 part-time jobs averaging $2054.

APPLYING for FINANCIAL AID ***Required financial aid form:*** FAFSA. ***Financial aid deadline (priority):*** 4/1. ***Notification date:*** Continuous. Students must reply within 4 weeks of notification.

CONTACT Mr. Michael Strite, Assistant Director of Financial Aid, Messiah College, One College Avenue, Grantham, PA 17027, 717-691-6007 or toll-free 800-382-1349 (in-state), 800-233-4220 (out-of-state). *Fax:* 717-796-5374. *E-mail:* mstrite@messiah.edu

METHODIST COLLEGE

Fayetteville, NC

Tuition & fees: $12,704 **Average undergraduate aid package: $10,800**

ABOUT THE INSTITUTION Independent United Methodist, coed. Awards: associate and bachelor's degrees. 54 undergraduate majors. Total enrollment: 1,940. Undergraduates: 1,940. Freshmen: 775. Federal methodology is used as a basis for awarding need-based institutional aid.

UNDERGRADUATE EXPENSES for 1999–2000 ***Application fee:*** $25. ***Comprehensive fee:*** $17,534 includes full-time tuition ($12,600), mandatory fees ($104), and room and board ($4830). ***College room only:*** $2330. Full-time tuition and fees vary according to program. Room and board charges vary according to board plan and housing facility. ***Part-time tuition:*** $420 per semester hour. Part-time tuition and fees vary according to program. ***Payment plans:*** installment, deferred payment.

FRESHMAN FINANCIAL AID (Fall 1998) 540 applied for aid; of those 85% were deemed to have need. 98% of freshmen with need received aid. *Average percent of need met:* 80% (excluding resources awarded to replace EFC). *Average financial aid package:* $9625 (excluding resources awarded to replace EFC). 15% of all full-time freshmen had no need and received non-need-based aid.

UNDERGRADUATE FINANCIAL AID (Fall 1998) 1,409 applied for aid; of those 94% were deemed to have need. 93% of undergraduates with need received aid. *Average percent of need met:* 84% (excluding resources awarded to replace EFC). *Average financial aid package:* $10,800 (excluding resources awarded to replace EFC). 8% of all full-time undergraduates had no need and received non-need-based aid.

GIFT AID (NEED-BASED) ***Total amount:*** $5,430,668 (34% Federal, 18% state, 48% institutional). ***Receiving aid:*** *Freshmen:* 78% (437); *all full-time undergraduates:* 59% (946). ***Average award:*** Freshmen: $6500; Undergraduates: $7200. ***Scholarships, grants, and awards:*** Federal Pell, FSEOG, state, private, college/university gift aid from institutional funds.

GIFT AID (NON-NEED-BASED) ***Total amount:*** $4,208,464 (38% state, 58% institutional, 4% external sources). ***Receiving aid:*** *Freshmen:* 71% (400); *Undergraduates:* 58% (934). ***Scholarships, grants, and awards by category:*** *Academic Interests/Achievement:* 315 awards ($1,110,677 total): general academic interests/achievements. *Creative Arts/Performance:* 56 awards ($58,300 total): dance, debating, music, theater/drama. *Special Characteristics:* 44 awards ($282,803 total): children of faculty/staff. ***Tuition waivers:*** Full or partial for employees or children of employees, senior citizens. ***ROTC:*** Army, Air Force cooperative.

LOANS ***Student loans:*** $6,163,241 (58% need-based, 42% non-need-based). 78% of past graduating class borrowed through all loan programs. Average indebtedness per student: $17,944. ***Average need-based loan:*** Freshmen: $2625; Undergraduates: $4500. ***Parent loans:*** $1,491,648 (90% need-based, 10% non-need-based). ***Programs:*** FFEL (Subsidized and Unsubsidized Stafford, PLUS), Perkins, college/university.

WORK-STUDY ***Federal work-study:*** *Total amount:* $949,389; 791 jobs averaging $1200. ***State or other work-study/employment:*** *Total amount:* $420,000 (100% non-need-based). 350 part-time jobs averaging $1200.

APPLYING for FINANCIAL AID ***Required financial aid form:*** FAFSA. ***Financial aid deadline (priority):*** 5/1. ***Notification date:*** Continuous. Students must reply within 2 weeks of notification.

CONTACT Bonnie J. Adamson, Director of Financial Aid, Methodist College, 5400 Ramsey Street, Fayetteville, NC 28311-1420, 910-630-7192 or toll-free 800-488-7110 Ext. 7027. *Fax:* 910-630-7285. *E-mail:* adamson@methodist.edu

METROPOLITAN COLLEGE OF COURT REPORTING

Phoenix, AZ

Tuition & fees: N/R **Average undergraduate aid package: $5400**

ABOUT THE INSTITUTION Proprietary, coed. Awards: associate and bachelor's degrees. Total enrollment: 102. Undergraduates: 102. Freshmen: 26. Federal methodology is used as a basis for awarding need-based institutional aid.

FRESHMAN FINANCIAL AID (Fall 1998) 13 applied for aid; of those 100% were deemed to have need. 100% of freshmen with need received aid; of those 100% had need fully met. *Average percent of need met:* 90% (excluding resources awarded to replace EFC). *Average financial aid package:* $5400 (excluding resources awarded to replace EFC).

UNDERGRADUATE FINANCIAL AID (Fall 1998) 82 applied for aid; of those 100% were deemed to have need. 100% of undergraduates with need received aid; of those 98% had need fully met. *Average percent of need met:* 90% (excluding resources awarded to replace EFC). *Average financial aid package:* $5400 (excluding resources awarded to replace EFC).

GIFT AID (NEED-BASED) ***Total amount:*** $7700 (22% state, 78% institutional). ***Scholarships, grants, and awards:*** Federal Pell, state.

LOANS ***Student loans:*** $320,000 (100% need-based). ***Parent loans:*** $12,000 (100% need-based). ***Programs:*** FFEL (Subsidized and Unsubsidized Stafford, PLUS).

APPLYING for FINANCIAL AID ***Required financial aid forms:*** FAFSA, institution's own form. ***Financial aid deadline:*** Continuous. ***Notification date:*** Continuous.

CONTACT Mr. Tom Kildow, Financial Aid Director, Metropolitan College of Court Reporting, 4610 East Elwood Street, #12, Phoenix, AZ 85040, 602-955-5900. *Fax:* 602-894-8999.

METROPOLITAN COLLEGE OF COURT REPORTING

Albuquerque, NM

Tuition & fees: N/R **Average undergraduate aid package: N/A**

ABOUT THE INSTITUTION Proprietary, coed. Both federal and institutional methodology are used as a basis for awarding need-based institutional aid.

GIFT AID (NEED-BASED) ***Scholarships, grants, and awards:*** Federal Pell, private.

GIFT AID (NON-NEED-BASED) ***Scholarships, grants, and awards by category:*** *Special Characteristics:* local/state students, married students, veterans.

LOANS ***Student loans:*** 90% of past graduating class borrowed through all loan programs. ***Programs:*** Federal Direct (Subsidized and Unsubsidized Stafford, PLUS), FFEL (Subsidized and Unsubsidized Stafford, PLUS).

APPLYING for FINANCIAL AID ***Required financial aid form:*** FAFSA. ***Financial aid deadline:*** Continuous.

CONTACT Melissa J. Sandoval-Griego, Director of Financial Aid, Metropolitan College of Court Reporting, 1717 Louisiana Boulevard NE, Suite 207, Albuquerque, NM 87110-7027, 505-888-3400. *Fax:* 505-254-3738.

METROPOLITAN STATE COLLEGE OF DENVER

Denver, CO

Tuition & fees (CO res): $2112 **Average undergraduate aid package: $6299**

ABOUT THE INSTITUTION State-supported, coed. Awards: bachelor's degrees. 48 undergraduate majors. Total enrollment: 17,716. Undergraduates: 17,716. Freshmen: 1,807. Federal methodology is used as a basis for awarding need-based institutional aid.

UNDERGRADUATE EXPENSES for 1999–2000 ***Application fee:*** $25. ***Tuition, state resident:*** full-time $1718; part-time $72 per semester hour. ***Tuition, nonresident:*** full-time $7039; part-time $293 per semester hour. ***Required fees:*** full-time $394; $103 per term part-time. Full-time tuition and fees vary according to course load and location. Part-time tuition and fees vary according to course load and location. ***Payment plan:*** deferred payment.

FRESHMAN FINANCIAL AID (Fall 1998) 3547 applied for aid. *Average percent of need met:* 60% (excluding resources awarded to replace EFC). *Average financial aid package:* $5924 (excluding resources awarded to replace EFC).

UNDERGRADUATE FINANCIAL AID (Fall 1998) 12,021 applied for aid. *Average percent of need met:* 60% (excluding resources awarded to replace EFC). *Average financial aid package:* $6299 (excluding resources awarded to replace EFC). 7% of all full-time undergraduates had no need and received non-need-based aid.

GIFT AID (NEED-BASED) ***Total amount:*** $11,566,635 (70% Federal, 30% state). ***Scholarships, grants, and awards:*** Federal Pell, FSEOG, state, private, college/university gift aid from institutional funds.

GIFT AID (NON-NEED-BASED) ***Total amount:*** $2,575,645 (44% state, 41% institutional, 15% external sources). ***Scholarships, grants, and awards by category:*** *Academic Interests/Achievement:* general academic interests/achievements. *Creative Arts/Performance:* general creative arts/performance, music. *Special Achievements/Activities:* general special achievements/activities. ***Tuition waivers:*** Full or partial for senior citizens. ***ROTC:*** Air Force cooperative.

LOANS ***Student loans:*** $32,953,789 (61% need-based, 39% non-need-based). Average indebtedness per student: $23,000. ***Parent loans:*** $280,555 (100% need-based). ***Programs:*** FFEL (Subsidized and Unsubsidized Stafford, PLUS), Perkins.

WORK-STUDY ***Federal work-study:*** *Total amount:* $522,116; 226 jobs averaging $2310. ***State or other work-study/employment:*** *Total amount:* $1,699,147 (100% need-based). 705 part-time jobs averaging $2427.

APPLYING for FINANCIAL AID ***Required financial aid form:*** FAFSA. ***Financial aid deadline (priority):*** 2/15. ***Notification date:*** 5/1. Students must reply within 2 weeks of notification.

CONTACT Office of Financial Aid, Metropolitan State College of Denver, PO Box 173362, Denver, CO 80217-3362, 303-575-5880.

METROPOLITAN STATE UNIVERSITY

St. Paul, MN

Tuition & fees (MN res): $2269 **Average undergraduate aid package: N/A**

ABOUT THE INSTITUTION State-supported, coed. Awards: bachelor's and master's degrees (offers primarily part-time evening degree programs). 24 undergraduate majors. Total enrollment: 4,894. Undergraduates: 4,653. Federal methodology is used as a basis for awarding need-based institutional aid.

UNDERGRADUATE EXPENSES for 1999–2000 ***Application fee:*** $20. ***Tuition, state resident:*** full-time $2117; part-time $8820 per credit. ***Tuition, nonresident:*** full-time $4679; part-time $195 per credit. ***Required fees:*** full-time $152; $6 per credit. Full-time tuition and fees vary according to course load.

GIFT AID (NEED-BASED) ***Scholarships, grants, and awards:*** Federal Pell, FSEOG, state, private, college/university gift aid from institutional funds.

GIFT AID (NON-NEED-BASED) ***Scholarships, grants, and awards by category:*** *Academic Interests/Achievement:* general academic interests/achievements. ***Tuition waivers:*** Full or partial for employees or children of employees, senior citizens.

LOANS ***Programs:*** FFEL (Subsidized and Unsubsidized Stafford, PLUS), state.

WORK-STUDY Federal work-study jobs available.

APPLYING for FINANCIAL AID ***Required financial aid forms:*** FAFSA, institution's own form, federal income tax form(s), financial aid transcript (for transfers). ***Financial aid deadline (priority):*** 6/1. ***Notification date:*** Continuous beginning 6/15. Students must reply within 2 weeks of notification.

CONTACT Mr. R. D. Cleaveland, Director, Financial Aid, Metropolitan State University, Founder's Hall, Room 105, 700 East 7th Street, St. Paul, MN 55106-5000, 651-772-7670. *E-mail:* jim.cleaveland@metrostate.edu

MIAMI UNIVERSITY

Oxford, OH

Tuition & fees (OH res): $6112 **Average undergraduate aid package: $5889**

ABOUT THE INSTITUTION State-related, coed. Awards: bachelor's, master's, and doctoral degrees and post-master's certificates. 102 undergraduate majors. Total enrollment: 16,575. Undergraduates: 15,288. Freshmen: 3,605. Federal methodology is used as a basis for awarding need-based institutional aid.

UNDERGRADUATE EXPENSES for 1999–2000 ***Application fee:*** $35. ***Tuition, state resident:*** full-time $5052; part-time $210 per credit hour. ***Tuition, nonresident:*** full-time $11,706; part-time $488 per credit hour. ***Required fees:*** full-time $1060; $44 per credit hour; $18 per term part-time. Full-time tuition and fees vary according to course load. Part-time tuition and fees vary according to course load. ***College room and board:*** $5330; ***room only:*** $2530. Room and board charges vary according to board plan and housing facility. ***Payment plan:*** installment.

Miami University (continued)

FRESHMAN FINANCIAL AID (Fall 1999) 3162 applied for aid; of those 49% were deemed to have need. 99% of freshmen with need received aid; of those 25% had need fully met. *Average percent of need met:* 75% (excluding resources awarded to replace EFC). *Average financial aid package:* $5603 (excluding resources awarded to replace EFC). 46% of all full-time freshmen had no need and received non-need-based aid.

UNDERGRADUATE FINANCIAL AID (Fall 1999) 9,484 applied for aid; of those 59% were deemed to have need. 99% of undergraduates with need received aid; of those 25% had need fully met. *Average percent of need met:* 74% (excluding resources awarded to replace EFC). *Average financial aid package:* $5889 (excluding resources awarded to replace EFC). 25% of all full-time undergraduates had no need and received non-need-based aid.

GIFT AID (NEED-BASED) ***Total amount:*** $9,909,424 (52% Federal, 12% state, 36% institutional). ***Receiving aid:*** *Freshmen:* 20% (727); *all full-time undergraduates:* 17% (2,505). ***Average award:*** Freshmen: $3414; Undergraduates: $3600. ***Scholarships, grants, and awards:*** Federal Pell, FSEOG, state, private, college/university gift aid from institutional funds.

GIFT AID (NON-NEED-BASED) ***Total amount:*** $9,952,497 (15% state, 56% institutional, 29% external sources). ***Receiving aid:*** *Freshmen:* 25% (899); *Undergraduates:* 10% (1,452). ***Scholarships, grants, and awards by category:*** *Academic Interests/Achievement:* architecture, education, engineering/technologies, general academic interests/achievements. *Creative Arts/Performance:* art/fine arts, music, theater/drama. *Special Achievements/Activities:* general special achievements/activities. *Special Characteristics:* children of faculty/staff, local/state students, members of minority groups, out-of-state students. ***Tuition waivers:*** Full or partial for employees or children of employees. ***ROTC:*** Army cooperative, Naval, Air Force.

LOANS ***Student loans:*** $33,736,259 (54% need-based, 46% non-need-based). 69% of past graduating class borrowed through all loan programs. Average indebtedness per student: $16,710. ***Average need-based loan:*** Freshmen: $2545; Undergraduates: $3485. ***Parent loans:*** $7,094,389 (100% non-need-based). ***Programs:*** Federal Direct (Subsidized and Unsubsidized Stafford, PLUS), Perkins, Federal Nursing, state, college/university, alternative loans.

WORK-STUDY ***Federal work-study:*** *Total amount:* $1,654,865; 1,102 jobs averaging $1598.

ATHLETIC AWARDS *Total amount:* 3,324,051 (2% need-based, 98% non-need-based).

APPLYING for FINANCIAL AID ***Required financial aid form:*** FAFSA. ***Financial aid deadline (priority):*** 2/15. ***Notification date:*** 3/31. Students must reply by 5/1 or within 3 weeks of notification.

CONTACT Office of Student Financial Aid, Miami University, Campus Avenue Building, Oxford, OH 45056-3427, 513-529-8734. *E-mail:* financialaid@muohio.edu

MICHIGAN CHRISTIAN COLLEGE

Rochester Hills, MI

See Rochester College

MICHIGAN STATE UNIVERSITY

East Lansing, MI

Tuition & fees (MI res): $5590 **Average undergraduate aid package: $7142**

ABOUT THE INSTITUTION State-supported, coed. Awards: bachelor's, master's, doctoral, and first professional degrees. 137 undergraduate majors. Total enrollment: 43,038. Undergraduates: 33,966. Freshmen: 6,716. Federal methodology is used as a basis for awarding need-based institutional aid.

UNDERGRADUATE EXPENSES for 1999–2000 ***Application fee:*** $30. ***Tuition, state resident:*** full-time $5004; part-time $147 per semester hour. ***Tuition, nonresident:*** full-time $12,406; part-time $394 per semester hour. ***Required fees:*** full-time $586; $241 per term part-time. Full-time tuition and fees vary according to program and student level. Part-time tuition and fees vary according to course load, program, and student level. ***College room and board:*** $4298; ***room only:*** $1860. Room and board charges vary according to board plan and housing facility. ***Payment plans:*** guaranteed tuition, deferred payment.

FRESHMAN FINANCIAL AID (Fall 1999, est.) 4414 applied for aid; of those 63% were deemed to have need. 99% of freshmen with need received aid; of those 50% had need fully met. *Average percent of need met:* 87% (excluding resources awarded to replace EFC). *Average financial aid package:* $6766 (excluding resources awarded to replace EFC). 19% of all full-time freshmen had no need and received non-need-based aid.

UNDERGRADUATE FINANCIAL AID (Fall 1999, est.) 16,732 applied for aid; of those 71% were deemed to have need. 99% of undergraduates with need received aid; of those 56% had need fully met. *Average percent of need met:* 88% (excluding resources awarded to replace EFC). *Average financial aid package:* $7142 (excluding resources awarded to replace EFC). 14% of all full-time undergraduates had no need and received non-need-based aid.

GIFT AID (NEED-BASED) ***Total amount:*** $54,831,988 (24% Federal, 27% state, 39% institutional, 10% external sources). ***Receiving aid:*** *Freshmen:* 33% (2,157); *all full-time undergraduates:* 29% (8,505). ***Average award:*** Freshmen: $3204; Undergraduates: $2878. ***Scholarships, grants, and awards:*** Federal Pell, FSEOG, state, private, college/university gift aid from institutional funds.

GIFT AID (NON-NEED-BASED) ***Total amount:*** $180,750 (100% Federal). ***Receiving aid:*** *Freshmen:* 8; *Undergraduates:* 43. ***Scholarships, grants, and awards by category:*** *Academic Interests/Achievement:* agriculture, architecture, biological sciences, business, computer science, education, engineering/technologies, general academic interests/achievements, military science, social sciences. *Creative Arts/Performance:* creative writing, debating, journalism/publications, music, performing arts, theater/drama. *Special Achievements/Activities:* community service, hobbies/interests, junior miss, leadership, memberships, religious involvement. *Special Characteristics:* children and siblings of alumni, children of faculty/staff, children of union members/company employees, ethnic background, first-generation college students, members of minority groups, out-of-state students, public servants, religious affiliation, spouses of deceased or disabled public servants, veterans, veterans' children. ***Tuition waivers:*** Full or partial for employees or children of employees. ***ROTC:*** Army, Air Force.

LOANS ***Student loans:*** $68,303,926 (63% need-based, 37% non-need-based). 70% of past graduating class borrowed through all loan programs. Average indebtedness per student: $17,875. ***Average need-based loan:*** Freshmen: $2107; Undergraduates: $4008. ***Parent loans:*** $2,174,205 (100% need-based). ***Programs:*** Federal Direct (Subsidized and Unsubsidized Stafford, PLUS), Perkins, state, college/university.

WORK-STUDY ***Federal work-study:*** *Total amount:* $5,308,750; 2,504 jobs averaging $2120. ***State or other work-study/employment:*** *Total amount:* $3,428,068 (100% need-based). 2,729 part-time jobs averaging $1256.

ATHLETIC AWARDS *Total amount:* 4,626,222 (28% need-based, 72% non-need-based).

APPLYING for FINANCIAL AID ***Required financial aid form:*** FAFSA. ***Financial aid deadline:*** 6/30 (priority: 2/21). ***Notification date:*** Continuous.

CONTACT Keith Williams, Financial Aid Officer, Michigan State University, 252 Student Services Building, East Lansing, MI 48824-1113, 517-353-5940. *E-mail:* willi398@msu.edu

MICHIGAN TECHNOLOGICAL UNIVERSITY

Houghton, MI

Tuition & fees (MI res): $4491 **Average undergraduate aid package: $6397**

ABOUT THE INSTITUTION State-supported, coed. Awards: associate, bachelor's, master's, and doctoral degrees. 60 undergraduate majors. Total enrollment: 6,321. Undergraduates: 5,661. Freshmen: 1,155. Federal methodology is used as a basis for awarding need-based institutional aid.

UNDERGRADUATE EXPENSES for 1999–2000 ***Application fee:*** $30. ***Tuition, state resident:*** full-time $4365; part-time $122 per credit hour. ***Tuition, nonresident:*** full-time $10,578; part-time $294 per credit hour. ***Required fees:*** full-time $126; $42 per term part-time. Full-time tuition and fees vary according to student level. Part-time tuition and fees vary according to course load and student level. ***College room and board:*** $4726. Room and board charges vary according to board plan and housing facility. ***Payment plan:*** installment.

FRESHMAN FINANCIAL AID (Fall 1999, est.) 1155 applied for aid; of those 54% were deemed to have need. 100% of freshmen with need received aid; of those 45% had need fully met. *Average percent of need met:* 84% (excluding resources awarded to replace EFC). *Average financial aid package:* $6072 (excluding resources awarded to replace EFC). 40% of all full-time freshmen had no need and received non-need-based aid.

UNDERGRADUATE FINANCIAL AID (Fall 1999, est.) 5,474 applied for aid; of those 47% were deemed to have need. 100% of undergraduates with need received aid; of those 47% had need fully met. *Average percent of need met:* 79% (excluding resources awarded to replace EFC). *Average financial aid package:* $6397 (excluding resources awarded to replace EFC). 36% of all full-time undergraduates had no need and received non-need-based aid.

GIFT AID (NEED-BASED) ***Total amount:*** $10,327,415 (21% Federal, 10% state, 57% institutional, 12% external sources). ***Receiving aid:*** *Freshmen:* 50% (583); *all full-time undergraduates:* 42% (2,303). ***Average award:*** Freshmen: $3876; Undergraduates: $3938. ***Scholarships, grants, and awards:*** Federal Pell, FSEOG, state, private, college/university gift aid from institutional funds.

GIFT AID (NON-NEED-BASED) ***Total amount:*** $6,297,443 (70% institutional, 30% external sources). ***Receiving aid:*** *Freshmen:* 27% (309); *Undergraduates:* 22% (1,198). ***Scholarships, grants, and awards by category:*** *Academic Interests/Achievement:* 2,409 awards ($6,308,946 total): biological sciences, business, communication, computer science, engineering/technologies, general academic interests/achievements, humanities, mathematics, physical sciences, premedicine, social sciences. *Special Achievements/Activities:* 37 awards ($9731 total): leadership. *Special Characteristics:* 603 awards ($3,325,356 total): children and siblings of alumni, children of faculty/staff, ethnic background, general special characteristics, international students, local/state students, members of minority groups, out-of-state students, previous college experience. ***Tuition waivers:*** Full or partial for children of alumni, employees or children of employees, senior citizens. ***ROTC:*** Army, Air Force.

LOANS ***Student loans:*** $12,081,217 (54% need-based, 46% non-need-based). 79% of past graduating class borrowed through all loan programs. Average indebtedness per student: $6397. ***Average need-based loan:*** Freshmen: $2996; Undergraduates: $3601. ***Parent loans:*** $1,582,671 (67% need-based, 33% non-need-based). ***Programs:*** Federal Direct (Subsidized and Unsubsidized Stafford, PLUS), Perkins, state, college/university, alternative loans.

WORK-STUDY ***Federal work-study:*** *Total amount:* $336,012; 258 jobs averaging $1357. ***State or other work-study/employment:*** *Total amount:* $3,432,852 (3% need-based, 97% non-need-based). 2,412 part-time jobs averaging $1432.

ATHLETIC AWARDS *Total amount:* 947,958 (23% need-based, 77% non-need-based).

APPLYING for FINANCIAL AID ***Required financial aid form:*** FAFSA. ***Financial aid deadline (priority):*** 2/21. ***Notification date:*** Continuous. Students must reply within 4 weeks of notification.

CONTACT Adrene Remali, System Administrator, Michigan Technological University, 1400 Townsend Drive, Houghton, MI 49931-1295, 906-487-3222. *Fax:* 906-487-3343. *E-mail:* adrene@mtu.edu

MID-AMERICA BIBLE COLLEGE

Oklahoma City, OK

Tuition & fees: $5552 **Average undergraduate aid package: $4500**

ABOUT THE INSTITUTION Independent religious, coed. Awards: associate and bachelor's degrees. 15 undergraduate majors. Total enrollment: 577. Undergraduates: 577. Freshmen: 88. Federal methodology is used as a basis for awarding need-based institutional aid.

UNDERGRADUATE EXPENSES for 1999–2000 ***Application fee:*** $20. ***Comprehensive fee:*** $8748 includes full-time tuition ($5016), mandatory fees ($536), and room and board ($3196). ***College room only:*** $1598. ***Part-time tuition:*** $209 per semester hour. ***Payment plan:*** installment.

UNDERGRADUATE FINANCIAL AID (Fall 1999) 581 applied for aid; of those 100% were deemed to have need. 100% of undergraduates with need received aid. *Average percent of need met:* 75% (excluding resources awarded to replace EFC). *Average financial aid package:* $4500 (excluding resources awarded to replace EFC). 1% of all full-time undergraduates had no need and received non-need-based aid.

GIFT AID (NEED-BASED) ***Total amount:*** $528,833 (94% Federal, 6% state). ***Scholarships, grants, and awards:*** Federal Pell, FSEOG, state, college/university gift aid from institutional funds.

GIFT AID (NON-NEED-BASED) ***Total amount:*** $1,205,848 (83% institutional, 17% external sources). ***Receiving aid:*** *Undergraduates:* 34% (213). ***Scholarships, grants, and awards by category:*** *Academic Interests/Achievement:* business, education, English, general academic interests/achievements, religion/biblical studies. *Creative Arts/Performance:* music. *Special Achievements/Activities:* community service, general special achievements/activities, leadership, memberships, religious involvement. *Special Characteristics:* children of faculty/staff, general special characteristics, international students, members of minority groups, religious affiliation, spouses of current students. ***Tuition waivers:*** Full or partial for employees or children of employees.

LOANS ***Student loans:*** $1,998,427 (69% need-based, 31% non-need-based). ***Average need-based loan:*** Undergraduates: $3400. ***Parent loans:*** $14,021 (100% non-need-based). ***Programs:*** Federal Direct (Subsidized and Unsubsidized Stafford, PLUS), FFEL (Subsidized and Unsubsidized Stafford, PLUS), Perkins, college/university.

WORK-STUDY ***Federal work-study:*** *Total amount:* $80,104; jobs available. ***State or other work-study/employment:*** *Total amount:* $27,386 (100% need-based). Part-time jobs available.

APPLYING for FINANCIAL AID ***Required financial aid form:*** FAFSA. ***Financial aid deadline (priority):*** 5/1. ***Notification date:*** 6/1.

CONTACT Mr. Derry Ebert, Director of Financial Aid, Mid-America Bible College, 3500 Southwest 119th Street, Oklahoma City, OK 73170-4504, 405-691-3800. *Fax:* 405-692-3165. *E-mail:* finaid@mabc.edu

MIDAMERICA NAZARENE UNIVERSITY

Olathe, KS

Tuition & fees: $10,474 **Average undergraduate aid package: N/A**

ABOUT THE INSTITUTION Independent religious, coed. Awards: associate, bachelor's, and master's degrees. 42 undergraduate majors. Total enrollment: 1,559. Undergraduates: 1,173. Freshmen: 222. Federal methodology is used as a basis for awarding need-based institutional aid.

UNDERGRADUATE EXPENSES for 1999–2000 ***Application fee:*** $15. ***Comprehensive fee:*** $15,534 includes full-time tuition ($9580), mandatory fees ($894), and room and board ($5060). Full-time tuition and fees vary according to course load. Room and board charges vary according to board plan and housing facility. ***Part-time tuition:*** $320 per semester hour. ***Part-time fees:*** $319 per term part-time. Part-time tuition and fees vary according to course load. ***Payment plan:*** installment.

GIFT AID (NEED-BASED) ***Scholarships, grants, and awards:*** Federal Pell, FSEOG, state, private, college/university gift aid from institutional funds.

GIFT AID (NON-NEED-BASED) ***Scholarships, grants, and awards by category:*** *Academic Interests/Achievement:* agriculture, general academic interests/achievements, health fields. *Creative Arts/Performance:* cinema/film/broadcasting, music. *Special Achievements/Activities:* cheerleading/drum major, leadership. *Special Characteristics:* children of faculty/staff, general special characteristics, relatives of clergy, religious affiliation. ***Tuition waivers:*** Full or partial for employees or children of employees, senior citizens. ***ROTC:*** Army cooperative, Air Force cooperative.

LOANS ***Programs:*** FFEL (Subsidized and Unsubsidized Stafford, PLUS), Perkins.

WORK-STUDY Federal work-study jobs available.

MidAmerica Nazarene University (continued)

APPLYING for FINANCIAL AID ***Required financial aid forms:*** FAFSA, federal income tax return. ***Financial aid deadline (priority):*** 3/1. ***Notification date:*** Continuous beginning 4/1. Students must reply within 2 weeks of notification.

CONTACT Ms. Sharon Williams, Director of Student Financial Services, MidAmerica Nazarene University, 2030 East College Way, Olathe, KS 66062-1899, 913-782-3750 Ext. 228 or toll-free 800-800-8887. *E-mail:* swilliam@mnu.edu

MID-CONTINENT COLLEGE

Mayfield, KY

Tuition & fees: $2960 **Average undergraduate aid package: $4565**

ABOUT THE INSTITUTION Independent Southern Baptist, coed. Awards: bachelor's degrees. 7 undergraduate majors. Total enrollment: 245. Undergraduates: 245. Freshmen: 43. Federal methodology is used as a basis for awarding need-based institutional aid.

UNDERGRADUATE EXPENSES for 1999–2000 ***Application fee:*** $10. ***Comprehensive fee:*** $5948 includes full-time tuition ($2640), mandatory fees ($320), and room and board ($2988). ***College room only:*** $1412. Full-time tuition and fees vary according to course load and program. Room and board charges vary according to board plan. ***Part-time tuition:*** $110 per semester hour. ***Part-time fees:*** $12 per semester hour; $45 per term part-time. Part-time tuition and fees vary according to course load and program.

FRESHMAN FINANCIAL AID (Fall 1999, est.) 36 applied for aid; of those 61% were deemed to have need. 100% of freshmen with need received aid. *Average percent of need met:* 51% (excluding resources awarded to replace EFC). *Average financial aid package:* $5257 (excluding resources awarded to replace EFC). 5% of all full-time freshmen had no need and received non-need-based aid.

UNDERGRADUATE FINANCIAL AID (Fall 1999, est.) 164 applied for aid; of those 68% were deemed to have need. 100% of undergraduates with need received aid. *Average percent of need met:* 51% (excluding resources awarded to replace EFC). *Average financial aid package:* $4565 (excluding resources awarded to replace EFC). 2% of all full-time undergraduates had no need and received non-need-based aid.

GIFT AID (NEED-BASED) ***Total amount:*** $433,142 (59% Federal, 35% state, 3% institutional, 3% external sources). ***Receiving aid:*** *Freshmen:* 58% (22); *all full-time undergraduates:* 64% (109). ***Average award:*** Freshmen: $5257; Undergraduates: $4682. ***Scholarships, grants, and awards:*** Federal Pell, FSEOG, state, private, college/university gift aid from institutional funds.

GIFT AID (NON-NEED-BASED) ***Scholarships, grants, and awards by category:*** *Academic Interests/Achievement:* 16 awards ($13,430 total): education, general academic interests/achievements, religion/biblical studies. *Special Characteristics:* 8 awards ($6875 total): children and siblings of alumni, children of union members/company employees, married students, relatives of clergy. ***Tuition waivers:*** Full or partial for employees or children of employees.

LOANS ***Student loans:*** $236,110 (100% need-based). 37% of past graduating class borrowed through all loan programs. Average indebtedness per student: $9960. ***Average need-based loan:*** Freshmen: $2615; Undergraduates: $3460. ***Programs:*** FFEL (Subsidized and Unsubsidized Stafford, PLUS).

WORK-STUDY ***Federal work-study:*** *Total amount:* $15,642; 5 jobs averaging $2472. ***State or other work-study/employment:*** *Total amount:* $43,507 (100% non-need-based). 22 part-time jobs available.

ATHLETIC AWARDS *Total amount:* 25,937 (100% need-based).

APPLYING for FINANCIAL AID ***Required financial aid forms:*** FAFSA, institution's own form. ***Financial aid deadline (priority):*** 4/1. ***Notification date:*** Continuous.

CONTACT Doug Cook, Director of Financial Aid, Mid-Continent College, 99 Powell Road East, Mayfield, KY 42066, 502-247-8521 Ext. 20 or toll-free 800-232-4662. *Fax:* 502-247-3115. *E-mail:* dcook@midcontinent.edu

MIDDLEBURY COLLEGE

Middlebury, VT

Comprehensive fee: $31,790 **Average undergraduate aid package: $23,538**

ABOUT THE INSTITUTION Independent, coed. Awards: bachelor's, master's, and doctoral degrees. 58 undergraduate majors. Total enrollment: 2,270. Undergraduates: 2,265. Freshmen: 524. Both federal and institutional methodology are used as a basis for awarding need-based institutional aid.

UNDERGRADUATE EXPENSES for 1999–2000 ***Application fee:*** $55. ***Comprehensive fee:*** $31,790. ***Payment plans:*** tuition prepayment, installment.

FRESHMAN FINANCIAL AID (Fall 1999, est.) 289 applied for aid; of those 76% were deemed to have need. 100% of freshmen with need received aid; of those 100% had need fully met. *Average percent of need met:* 100% (excluding resources awarded to replace EFC). *Average financial aid package:* $23,354 (excluding resources awarded to replace EFC).

UNDERGRADUATE FINANCIAL AID (Fall 1999, est.) 951 applied for aid; of those 85% were deemed to have need. 100% of undergraduates with need received aid; of those 100% had need fully met. *Average percent of need met:* 100% (excluding resources awarded to replace EFC). *Average financial aid package:* $23,538 (excluding resources awarded to replace EFC).

GIFT AID (NEED-BASED) ***Total amount:*** $13,713,948 (5% Federal, 1% state, 92% institutional, 2% external sources). ***Receiving aid:*** *Freshmen:* 40% (208); *all full-time undergraduates:* 34% (761). ***Average award:*** Freshmen: $18,736; Undergraduates: $18,020. ***Scholarships, grants, and awards:*** Federal Pell, FSEOG, state, private, college/university gift aid from institutional funds.

GIFT AID (NON-NEED-BASED) ***Tuition waivers:*** Full or partial for children of alumni, employees or children of employees.

LOANS ***Student loans:*** $4,770,629 (83% need-based, 17% non-need-based). 50% of past graduating class borrowed through all loan programs. Average indebtedness per student: $18,731. ***Average need-based loan:*** Freshmen: $4291; Undergraduates: $4958. ***Parent loans:*** $2,614,960 (100% non-need-based). ***Programs:*** Federal Direct (Subsidized and Unsubsidized Stafford, PLUS), Perkins, college/university.

WORK-STUDY ***Federal work-study:*** *Total amount:* $1,112,363; 587 jobs averaging $1895. ***State or other work-study/employment:*** *Total amount:* $240,651 (100% need-based). 133 part-time jobs averaging $1810.

APPLYING for FINANCIAL AID ***Required financial aid forms:*** FAFSA, CSS Financial Aid PROFILE, noncustodial (divorced/separated) parent's statement, business/farm supplement, federal income tax return. ***Financial aid deadline (priority):*** 12/31. ***Notification date:*** 4/1. Students must reply by 5/1.

CONTACT Gail Rothman, Financial Aid Assistant, Middlebury College, The Emma Willard House, Middlebury, VT 05753-6002, 802-443-5158. *Fax:* 802-443-2065. *E-mail:* financialaid@middlebury.edu

MIDDLE TENNESSEE STATE UNIVERSITY

Murfreesboro, TN

Tuition & fees (TN res): $2516 **Average undergraduate aid package: $4450**

ABOUT THE INSTITUTION State-supported, coed. Awards: associate, bachelor's, master's, and doctoral degrees and post-master's certificates. 58 undergraduate majors. Total enrollment: 18,993. Undergraduates: 17,037. Freshmen: 2,612. Federal methodology is used as a basis for awarding need-based institutional aid.

UNDERGRADUATE EXPENSES for 1999–2000 ***Application fee:*** $15. ***Tuition, state resident:*** full-time $2020; part-time $90 per semester hour. ***Tuition, nonresident:*** full-time $7136; part-time $314 per semester hour. ***Required fees:*** full-time $496; $17 per semester hour; $25 per term part-time. Part-time tuition and fees vary according to course load. ***College room***

and board: $3096; ***room only:*** $1920. Room and board charges vary according to board plan and housing facility. ***Payment plan:*** deferred payment.

FRESHMAN FINANCIAL AID (Fall 1998) 1066 applied for aid; of those 67% were deemed to have need. 95% of freshmen with need received aid; of those 28% had need fully met. *Average percent of need met:* 80% (excluding resources awarded to replace EFC). *Average financial aid package:* $3894 (excluding resources awarded to replace EFC). 5% of all full-time freshmen had no need and received non-need-based aid.

UNDERGRADUATE FINANCIAL AID (Fall 1998) 7,986 applied for aid; of those 65% were deemed to have need. 96% of undergraduates with need received aid; of those 41% had need fully met. *Average percent of need met:* 78% (excluding resources awarded to replace EFC). *Average financial aid package:* $4450 (excluding resources awarded to replace EFC). 7% of all full-time undergraduates had no need and received non-need-based aid.

GIFT AID (NEED-BASED) ***Total amount:*** $10,946,507 (80% Federal, 13% state, 7% external sources). ***Receiving aid:*** *Freshmen:* 15% (381); *all full-time undergraduates:* 21% (2,888). ***Average award:*** Freshmen: $1922; Undergraduates: $2196. ***Scholarships, grants, and awards:*** Federal Pell, FSEOG, state, private, college/university gift aid from institutional funds.

GIFT AID (NON-NEED-BASED) ***Total amount:*** $3,842,663 (99% institutional, 1% external sources). ***Receiving aid:*** *Freshmen:* 4% (113); *Undergraduates:* 5% (730). ***Scholarships, grants, and awards by category:*** *Academic Interests/Achievement:* 2,001 awards ($3,162,672 total): agriculture, biological sciences, business, communication, computer science, education, English, foreign languages, general academic interests/achievements, health fields, home economics, humanities, international studies, mathematics, military science, physical sciences, premedicine, social sciences. *Creative Arts/Performance:* 499 awards ($189,710 total): dance, music. *Special Achievements/Activities:* 70 awards ($157,106 total): cheerleading/drum major, general special achievements/activities, leadership. *Special Characteristics:* 505 awards ($1,023,713 total): adult students, members of minority groups. ***Tuition waivers:*** Full or partial for employees or children of employees, senior citizens. ***ROTC:*** Army, Air Force cooperative.

LOANS ***Student loans:*** $36,993,869 (99% need-based, 1% non-need-based). Average indebtedness per student: $17,372. ***Average need-based loan:*** Freshmen: $996; Undergraduates: $1690. ***Parent loans:*** $1,419,849 (100% non-need-based). ***Programs:*** FFEL (Subsidized and Unsubsidized Stafford, PLUS), Perkins, college/university.

WORK-STUDY ***Federal work-study:*** *Total amount:* $979,829; 459 jobs averaging $2135.

ATHLETIC AWARDS *Total amount:* 1,812,662 (100% non-need-based).

APPLYING for FINANCIAL AID ***Required financial aid form:*** FAFSA. ***Financial aid deadline (priority):*** 5/15. ***Notification date:*** Continuous. Students must reply within 2 weeks of notification.

CONTACT David Hutton, Financial Aid Director, Middle Tennessee State University, 218 Cope Administration Building, Murfreesboro, TN 37132, 615-898-2830. *Fax:* 615-898-5167. *E-mail:* financialaid@mtsu.edu

MIDLAND LUTHERAN COLLEGE

Fremont, NE

Tuition & fees: $13,320 **Average undergraduate aid package: $12,381**

ABOUT THE INSTITUTION Independent Lutheran, coed. Awards: associate and bachelor's degrees. 57 undergraduate majors. Total enrollment: 1,036. Undergraduates: 1,036. Freshmen: 272. Both federal and institutional methodology are used as a basis for awarding need-based institutional aid.

UNDERGRADUATE EXPENSES for 1999–2000 ***Application fee:*** $30. ***Comprehensive fee:*** $16,930 includes full-time tuition ($13,320) and room and board ($3610). ***College room only:*** $1530. Full-time tuition and fees vary according to course load. Room and board charges vary according to board plan. ***Part-time tuition:*** $330 per credit hour. Part-time tuition and fees vary according to course load. ***Payment plan:*** installment.

FRESHMAN FINANCIAL AID (Fall 1999) 269 applied for aid; of those 85% were deemed to have need. 100% of freshmen with need received aid; of those 25% had need fully met. *Average percent of need met:* 91% (excluding resources awarded to replace EFC). *Average financial aid package:* $12,419 (excluding resources awarded to replace EFC).

UNDERGRADUATE FINANCIAL AID (Fall 1999) 911 applied for aid; of those 85% were deemed to have need. 100% of undergraduates with need received aid; of those 44% had need fully met. *Average percent of need met:* 96% (excluding resources awarded to replace EFC). *Average financial aid package:* $12,381 (excluding resources awarded to replace EFC).

GIFT AID (NEED-BASED) ***Total amount:*** $1,972,907 (46% Federal, 13% state, 41% institutional). ***Receiving aid:*** *Freshmen:* 229; *all full-time undergraduates:* 778. ***Average award:*** Freshmen: $8247; Undergraduates: $7765. ***Scholarships, grants, and awards:*** Federal Pell, FSEOG, state, private, college/university gift aid from institutional funds.

GIFT AID (NON-NEED-BASED) ***Total amount:*** $128,050 (22% institutional, 78% external sources). ***Scholarships, grants, and awards by category:*** *Academic Interests/Achievement:* general academic interests/achievements. *Creative Arts/Performance:* art/fine arts, debating, journalism/publications, music, theater/drama. *Special Achievements/Activities:* community service, general special achievements/activities, leadership, religious involvement. *Special Characteristics:* handicapped students, international students, members of minority groups, religious affiliation, siblings of current students. ***Tuition waivers:*** Full or partial for employees or children of employees, senior citizens.

LOANS ***Student loans:*** $3,866,231 (76% need-based, 24% non-need-based). 82% of past graduating class borrowed through all loan programs. Average indebtedness per student: $18,491. ***Average need-based loan:*** Freshmen: $3599; Undergraduates: $3641. ***Parent loans:*** $495,680 (100% non-need-based). ***Programs:*** FFEL (Subsidized and Unsubsidized Stafford, PLUS), Perkins, college/university.

WORK-STUDY ***Federal work-study:*** *Total amount:* $210,057; 210 jobs averaging $1000. ***State or other work-study/employment:*** *Total amount:* $172,960 (100% non-need-based). 118 part-time jobs averaging $1465.

ATHLETIC AWARDS *Total amount:* 1,579,510 (86% need-based, 14% non-need-based).

APPLYING for FINANCIAL AID ***Required financial aid forms:*** FAFSA, institution's own form. ***Financial aid deadline:*** Continuous. ***Notification date:*** Continuous beginning 3/1. Students must reply within 4 weeks of notification.

CONTACT Mr. Douglas G. Watson, Director of Financial Aid, Midland Lutheran College, 900 North Clarkson Street, Fremont, NE 68025-4200, 402-721-5480 Ext. 6521 or toll-free 800-642-8382 Ext. 6500. *Fax:* 402-721-0250. *E-mail:* watson@admin.mlc.edu

MIDWAY COLLEGE

Midway, KY

Tuition & fees: $9122 **Average undergraduate aid package: $9287**

ABOUT THE INSTITUTION Independent religious, women only. Awards: associate and bachelor's degrees. 17 undergraduate majors. Total enrollment: 816. Undergraduates: 816. Freshmen: 128. Federal methodology is used as a basis for awarding need-based institutional aid.

UNDERGRADUATE EXPENSES for 1999–2000 ***Application fee:*** $15. ***Comprehensive fee:*** $13,972 includes full-time tuition ($9062), mandatory fees ($60), and room and board ($4850). ***College room only:*** $2275. Full-time tuition and fees vary according to program. Room and board charges vary according to board plan. ***Part-time tuition:*** $302 per semester hour. ***Part-time fees:*** $2 per semester hour. Part-time tuition and fees vary according to class time and course load. ***Payment plan:*** installment.

FRESHMAN FINANCIAL AID (Fall 1999) 115 applied for aid; of those 93% were deemed to have need. 100% of freshmen with need received aid; of those 31% had need fully met. *Average percent of need met:* 69% (excluding resources awarded to replace EFC). *Average financial aid package:* $8908 (excluding resources awarded to replace EFC). 2% of all full-time freshmen had no need and received non-need-based aid.

UNDERGRADUATE FINANCIAL AID (Fall 1999) 407 applied for aid; of those 90% were deemed to have need. 100% of undergraduates with

Midway College (continued)

need received aid; of those 31% had need fully met. *Average percent of need met:* 69% (excluding resources awarded to replace EFC). *Average financial aid package:* $9287 (excluding resources awarded to replace EFC). 4% of all full-time undergraduates had no need and received non-need-based aid.

GIFT AID (NEED-BASED) ***Total amount:*** $2,011,711 (32% Federal, 30% state, 35% institutional, 3% external sources). ***Receiving aid:*** *Freshmen:* 62% (105); *all full-time undergraduates:* 72% (363). ***Average award:*** Freshmen: $8271; Undergraduates: $8643. ***Scholarships, grants, and awards:*** Federal Pell, FSEOG, state, private, college/university gift aid from institutional funds.

GIFT AID (NON-NEED-BASED) ***Total amount:*** $133,199 (84% institutional, 16% external sources). ***Receiving aid:*** *Freshmen:* 19% (32); *Undergraduates:* 20% (101). ***Scholarships, grants, and awards by category:*** *Academic Interests/Achievement:* general academic interests/achievements. *Creative Arts/Performance:* art/fine arts, music. *Special Achievements/Activities:* junior miss, religious involvement. *Special Characteristics:* children and siblings of alumni, children of faculty/staff, members of minority groups, relatives of clergy, religious affiliation. ***Tuition waivers:*** Full or partial for employees or children of employees, senior citizens. ***ROTC:*** Army cooperative.

LOANS ***Student loans:*** $2,567,386 (72% need-based, 28% non-need-based). 59% of past graduating class borrowed through all loan programs. Average indebtedness per student: $15,946. ***Average need-based loan:*** Freshmen: $2465; Undergraduates: $3675. ***Parent loans:*** $232,873 (9% need-based, 91% non-need-based). ***Programs:*** FFEL (Subsidized and Unsubsidized Stafford, PLUS), Perkins, college/university.

WORK-STUDY ***Federal work-study:*** *Total amount:* $140,798; 136 jobs averaging $1035. ***State or other work-study/employment:*** *Total amount:* $15,890 (100% non-need-based). 13 part-time jobs averaging $1222.

ATHLETIC AWARDS *Total amount:* 223,044 (64% need-based, 36% non-need-based).

APPLYING for FINANCIAL AID ***Required financial aid forms:*** FAFSA, institution's own form. ***Financial aid deadline (priority):*** 3/15. ***Notification date:*** Continuous. Students must reply within 4 weeks of notification.

CONTACT Chrarisse Gillet, Director of Financial Aid, Midway College, 512 East Stephens Street, Midway, KY 40347-1120, 606-846-5410 or toll-free 800-755-0031. *Fax:* 606-846-5751. *E-mail:* cgillet@midway.edu

MIDWESTERN STATE UNIVERSITY

Wichita Falls, TX

Tuition & fees (TX res): $2426 **Average undergraduate aid package: N/A**

ABOUT THE INSTITUTION State-supported, coed. Awards: associate, bachelor's, and master's degrees. 50 undergraduate majors. Total enrollment: 5,765. Undergraduates: 5,090. Freshmen: 850. Federal methodology is used as a basis for awarding need-based institutional aid.

UNDERGRADUATE EXPENSES for 1999–2000 ***Tuition, state resident:*** full-time $1860; part-time $62 per credit hour. ***Tuition, nonresident:*** full-time $8340; part-time $278 per credit hour. ***Required fees:*** full-time $566; $17 per credit hour; $58 per term part-time. Full-time tuition and fees vary according to course load. Part-time tuition and fees vary according to course load. ***College room and board:*** $3728; ***room only:*** $1894. Room and board charges vary according to board plan and housing facility. ***Payment plan:*** installment.

GIFT AID (NEED-BASED) ***Total amount:*** $3,167,254 (75% Federal, 25% state). ***Scholarships, grants, and awards:*** Federal Pell, FSEOG, state, college/university gift aid from institutional funds.

GIFT AID (NON-NEED-BASED) ***Total amount:*** $2,020,042 (61% institutional, 39% external sources). ***Scholarships, grants, and awards by category:*** *Academic Interests/Achievement:* general academic interests/achievements. *Creative Arts/Performance:* creative writing, general creative arts/performance, journalism/publications, music, theater/drama. *Special Achievements/Activities:* cheerleading/drum major, general special achievements/activities, leadership, memberships. *Special Characteristics:* general special characteristics. ***Tuition waivers:*** Full or partial for employees or children of employees.

LOANS ***Student loans:*** $5,798,927 (66% need-based, 34% non-need-based). ***Parent loans:*** $159,378 (100% non-need-based). ***Programs:*** FFEL (Subsidized and Unsubsidized Stafford, PLUS), Perkins, state, college/university.

WORK-STUDY ***Federal work-study:*** *Total amount:* $119,789; 90 jobs averaging $1331. ***State or other work-study/employment:*** *Total amount:* $16,093 (100% need-based). 12 part-time jobs averaging $1341.

ATHLETIC AWARDS *Total amount:* 416,791 (100% non-need-based).

APPLYING for FINANCIAL AID ***Required financial aid forms:*** FAFSA, institution's own form. ***Financial aid deadline (priority):*** 6/1. ***Notification date:*** Continuous. Students must reply within 2 weeks of notification.

CONTACT Ms. Kathy Pennartz, Director of Financial Aid, Midwestern State University, 3410 Taft Boulevard, Wichita Falls, TX 76308-2096, 940-397-4214 or toll-free 800-842-1922 (in-state).

MILES COLLEGE

Birmingham, AL

Tuition & fees: $4630 **Average undergraduate aid package: N/A**

ABOUT THE INSTITUTION Independent Christian Methodist Episcopal, coed. Awards: bachelor's degrees. 15 undergraduate majors. Total enrollment: 1,390. Undergraduates: 1,390. Federal methodology is used as a basis for awarding need-based institutional aid.

UNDERGRADUATE EXPENSES for 1999–2000 ***Application fee:*** $25. ***Comprehensive fee:*** $7570 includes full-time tuition ($4280), mandatory fees ($350), and room and board ($2940). Room and board charges vary according to housing facility. ***Part-time tuition:*** $180 per semester hour.

GIFT AID (NEED-BASED) ***Scholarships, grants, and awards:*** Federal Pell, FSEOG, state, private, college/university gift aid from institutional funds, United Negro College Fund.

GIFT AID (NON-NEED-BASED) ***Scholarships, grants, and awards by category:*** *Academic Interests/Achievement:* general academic interests/achievements. *Creative Arts/Performance:* general creative arts/performance. *Special Achievements/Activities:* general special achievements/activities. *Special Characteristics:* general special characteristics, handicapped students. ***ROTC:*** Army cooperative, Air Force cooperative.

LOANS ***Programs:*** Federal Direct (Subsidized and Unsubsidized Stafford, PLUS), Perkins.

WORK-STUDY Federal work-study jobs available.

APPLYING for FINANCIAL AID ***Required financial aid form:*** FAFSA. ***Financial aid deadline (priority):*** 4/15. ***Notification date:*** 5/31. Students must reply within 2 weeks of notification.

CONTACT P. N. Lanier, Coordinator, Financial Aid, Miles College, PO Box 3800, Birmingham, AL 35208, 205-929-1665. *Fax:* 205-929-1668.

MILLERSVILLE UNIVERSITY OF PENNSYLVANIA

Millersville, PA

Tuition & fees (PA res): $4595 **Average undergraduate aid package: $6000**

ABOUT THE INSTITUTION State-supported, coed. Awards: associate, bachelor's, and master's degrees and post-bachelor's and post-master's certificates. 76 undergraduate majors. Total enrollment: 7,307. Undergraduates: 6,401. Freshmen: 1,284. Federal methodology is used as a basis for awarding need-based institutional aid.

UNDERGRADUATE EXPENSES for 1999–2000 ***Application fee:*** $25. ***Tuition, state resident:*** full-time $3618; part-time $150 per credit. ***Tuition, nonresident:*** full-time $9046; part-time $377 per credit. ***Required fees:*** full-time $977; $41 per credit. Part-time tuition and fees vary according to course load. ***College room and board:*** $4730. Room and board charges vary according to board plan. ***Payment plan:*** installment.

FRESHMAN FINANCIAL AID (Fall 1999, est.) 1090 applied for aid; of those 66% were deemed to have need. 94% of freshmen with need received aid. *Average financial aid package:* $5900 (excluding resources awarded to replace EFC). 2% of all full-time freshmen had no need and received non-need-based aid.

UNDERGRADUATE FINANCIAL AID (Fall 1999, est.) 4,984 applied for aid; of those 54% were deemed to have need. 76% of undergraduates with need received aid. *Average financial aid package:* $6000 (excluding resources awarded to replace EFC). 2% of all full-time undergraduates had no need and received non-need-based aid.

GIFT AID (NEED-BASED) ***Total amount:*** $5,621,200 (39% Federal, 59% state, 1% institutional, 1% external sources). ***Receiving aid:*** *Freshmen:* 45% (552); *all full-time undergraduates:* 30% (1,640). ***Average award:*** Freshmen: $1650; Undergraduates: $1650. ***Scholarships, grants, and awards:*** Federal Pell, FSEOG, state, private, college/university gift aid from institutional funds.

GIFT AID (NON-NEED-BASED) ***Total amount:*** $3,507,800 (18% institutional, 82% external sources). ***Scholarships, grants, and awards by category:*** *Academic Interests/Achievement:* general academic interests/achievements. *Special Characteristics:* children of union members/company employees. ***Tuition waivers:*** Full or partial for employees or children of employees, senior citizens.

LOANS ***Student loans:*** $16,948,000 (56% need-based, 44% non-need-based). 59% of past graduating class borrowed through all loan programs. Average indebtedness per student: $12,507. ***Average need-based loan:*** Freshmen: $2800; Undergraduates: $2800. ***Parent loans:*** $1,569,600 (100% non-need-based). ***Programs:*** FFEL (Subsidized and Unsubsidized Stafford, PLUS), Perkins, college/university.

WORK-STUDY ***Federal work-study:*** *Total amount:* $329,800; jobs available.

ATHLETIC AWARDS *Total amount:* 282,000 (100% non-need-based).

APPLYING for FINANCIAL AID ***Required financial aid form:*** FAFSA. ***Financial aid deadline:*** 3/15. ***Notification date:*** 6/1. Students must reply within 2 weeks of notification.

CONTACT Mr. Dwight G. Horsey, Director of Financial Aid, Millersville University of Pennsylvania, PO Box 1002, Millersville, PA 17551-0302, 717-872-3026 or toll-free 800-MU-ADMIT (out-of-state). *Fax:* 717-871-2248. *E-mail:* dwight.horsey@millersv.edu

MILLIGAN COLLEGE

Milligan College, TN

Tuition & fees: $11,480 **Average undergraduate aid package: $9896**

ABOUT THE INSTITUTION Independent Christian, coed. Awards: bachelor's and master's degrees. 50 undergraduate majors. Total enrollment: 914. Undergraduates: 796. Freshmen: 214. Federal methodology is used as a basis for awarding need-based institutional aid.

UNDERGRADUATE EXPENSES for 1999–2000 ***Application fee:*** $30. ***Comprehensive fee:*** $15,480 includes full-time tuition ($11,100), mandatory fees ($380), and room and board ($4000). ***College room only:*** $1900. Full-time tuition and fees vary according to class time. Room and board charges vary according to board plan and housing facility. ***Part-time tuition:*** $460 per hour. ***Part-time fees:*** $95 per term part-time. Part-time tuition and fees vary according to class time and course load. ***Payment plan:*** installment.

FRESHMAN FINANCIAL AID (Fall 1998) 179 applied for aid; of those 85% were deemed to have need. 100% of freshmen with need received aid; of those 39% had need fully met. *Average percent of need met:* 23% (excluding resources awarded to replace EFC). *Average financial aid package:* $9163 (excluding resources awarded to replace EFC). 14% of all full-time freshmen had no need and received non-need-based aid.

UNDERGRADUATE FINANCIAL AID (Fall 1998) 742 applied for aid; of those 96% were deemed to have need. 100% of undergraduates with need received aid; of those 16% had need fully met. *Average percent of need met:* 43% (excluding resources awarded to replace EFC). *Average financial aid package:* $9896 (excluding resources awarded to replace EFC). 7% of all full-time undergraduates had no need and received non-need-based aid.

GIFT AID (NEED-BASED) ***Total amount:*** $838,994 (56% Federal, 7% state, 29% institutional, 8% external sources). ***Receiving aid:*** *Freshmen:* 46% (98); *all full-time undergraduates:* 51% (393). ***Average award:*** Freshmen: $2965; Undergraduates: $2693. ***Scholarships, grants, and awards:*** Federal Pell, FSEOG, state, college/university gift aid from institutional funds.

GIFT AID (NON-NEED-BASED) ***Total amount:*** $1,912,342 (82% institutional, 18% external sources). ***Receiving aid:*** *Freshmen:* 71% (152); *Undergraduates:* 81% (630). ***Scholarships, grants, and awards by category:*** *Academic Interests/Achievement:* communication, English, general academic interests/achievements, health fields, religion/biblical studies. *Creative Arts/Performance:* art/fine arts, music, theater/drama. *Special Achievements/Activities:* general special achievements/activities. *Special Characteristics:* children of faculty/staff. ***Tuition waivers:*** Full or partial for employees or children of employees. ***ROTC:*** Army cooperative.

LOANS ***Student loans:*** $4,207,575 (55% need-based, 45% non-need-based). 70% of past graduating class borrowed through all loan programs. Average indebtedness per student: $19,275. ***Average need-based loan:*** Freshmen: $2858; Undergraduates: $3328. ***Parent loans:*** $638,640 (100% non-need-based). ***Programs:*** FFEL (Subsidized and Unsubsidized Stafford, PLUS), Perkins, Wells Fargo Collegiate Loans, Signature Loans.

WORK-STUDY ***Federal work-study:*** *Total amount:* $177,744; 140 jobs averaging $1270. ***State or other work-study/employment:*** *Total amount:* $341,062 (100% non-need-based). 290 part-time jobs averaging $1176.

ATHLETIC AWARDS *Total amount:* 1,946,560 (100% non-need-based).

APPLYING for FINANCIAL AID ***Required financial aid forms:*** FAFSA, institution's own form. ***Financial aid deadline (priority):*** 3/1. ***Notification date:*** Continuous beginning 3/15. Students must reply within 2 weeks of notification.

CONTACT Mrs. Nancy M. Beverly, Director of Financial Aid, Milligan College, PO Box 250, Milligan College, TN 37682, 423-461-8949 or toll-free 800-262-8337 (in-state). *Fax:* 423-461-8755. *E-mail:* nmbeverly@milligan.edu

MILLIKIN UNIVERSITY

Decatur, IL

Tuition & fees: $16,008 **Average undergraduate aid package: $14,497**

ABOUT THE INSTITUTION Independent religious, coed. Awards: bachelor's degrees. 51 undergraduate majors. Total enrollment: 2,272. Undergraduates: 2,272. Freshmen: 595. Both federal and institutional methodology are used as a basis for awarding need-based institutional aid.

UNDERGRADUATE EXPENSES for 1999–2000 ***Comprehensive fee:*** $21,601 includes full-time tuition ($15,808), mandatory fees ($200), and room and board ($5593). ***College room only:*** $2938. Full-time tuition and fees vary according to course load. Room and board charges vary according to board plan and housing facility. ***Part-time tuition:*** $450 per credit. ***Payment plan:*** installment.

FRESHMAN FINANCIAL AID (Fall 1999) 579 applied for aid; of those 83% were deemed to have need. 99% of freshmen with need received aid; of those 73% had need fully met. *Average percent of need met:* 92% (excluding resources awarded to replace EFC). *Average financial aid package:* $14,935 (excluding resources awarded to replace EFC). 19% of all full-time freshmen had no need and received non-need-based aid.

UNDERGRADUATE FINANCIAL AID (Fall 1999) 2,109 applied for aid; of those 83% were deemed to have need. 99% of undergraduates with need received aid; of those 73% had need fully met. *Average percent of need met:* 89% (excluding resources awarded to replace EFC). *Average financial aid package:* $14,497 (excluding resources awarded to replace EFC). 19% of all full-time undergraduates had no need and received non-need-based aid.

GIFT AID (NEED-BASED) ***Total amount:*** $18,095,657 (8% Federal, 28% state, 61% institutional, 3% external sources). ***Receiving aid:*** *Freshmen:* 73% (435); *all full-time undergraduates:* 73% (1,581). ***Average award:*** Freshmen: $10,000; Undergraduates: $8300. ***Scholarships, grants, and awards:*** Federal Pell, FSEOG, state, private, college/university gift aid from institutional funds.

Millikin University (continued)

GIFT AID (NON-NEED-BASED) ***Total amount:*** $2,495,834 (2% state, 98% institutional). ***Receiving aid:*** *Freshmen:* 19% (111); *Undergraduates:* 18% (398). ***Scholarships, grants, and awards by category:*** *Academic Interests/Achievement:* general academic interests/achievements. *Creative Arts/Performance:* art/fine arts, dance, music, theater/drama. *Special Achievements/Activities:* community service. *Special Characteristics:* children of union members/company employees, ethnic background, international students, relatives of clergy, religious affiliation. ***Tuition waivers:*** Full or partial for employees or children of employees.

LOANS ***Student loans:*** $6,406,136 (82% need-based, 18% non-need-based). 89% of past graduating class borrowed through all loan programs. Average indebtedness per student: $14,468. ***Parent loans:*** $720,319 (100% need-based). ***Programs:*** FFEL (Subsidized and Unsubsidized Stafford, PLUS), Perkins, college/university, alternative loans.

WORK-STUDY ***Federal work-study:*** *Total amount:* $1,355,618; 814 jobs averaging $1665.

APPLYING for FINANCIAL AID ***Required financial aid forms:*** FAFSA, institution's own form. ***Financial aid deadline:*** 6/1 (priority: 4/1). ***Notification date:*** Continuous. Students must reply within 2 weeks of notification.

CONTACT Ms. Jeanne Puckett, Director of Financial Aid, Millikin University, 1184 West Main Street, Decatur, IL 62522-2084, 217-424-6343 or toll-free 800-373-7733. *Fax:* 217-425-4669. *E-mail:* jpuckett@mail.millikin.edu

MILLSAPS COLLEGE

Jackson, MS

Tuition & fees: $15,029 **Average undergraduate aid package: $15,692**

ABOUT THE INSTITUTION Independent United Methodist, coed. Awards: bachelor's and master's degrees. 26 undergraduate majors. Total enrollment: 1,314. Undergraduates: 1,191. Freshmen: 284. Federal methodology is used as a basis for awarding need-based institutional aid.

UNDERGRADUATE EXPENSES for 1999–2000 ***Application fee:*** $25. ***Comprehensive fee:*** $21,135 includes full-time tuition ($14,190), mandatory fees ($839), and room and board ($6106). ***College room only:*** $3684. Room and board charges vary according to housing facility. Part-time tuition and fees vary according to course load. ***Payment plan:*** installment.

FRESHMAN FINANCIAL AID (Fall 1999) 282 applied for aid; of those 64% were deemed to have need. 100% of freshmen with need received aid; of those 48% had need fully met. *Average percent of need met:* 94% (excluding resources awarded to replace EFC). *Average financial aid package:* $16,527 (excluding resources awarded to replace EFC). 34% of all full-time freshmen had no need and received non-need-based aid.

UNDERGRADUATE FINANCIAL AID (Fall 1999) 1,081 applied for aid; of those 62% were deemed to have need. 100% of undergraduates with need received aid; of those 47% had need fully met. *Average percent of need met:* 90% (excluding resources awarded to replace EFC). *Average financial aid package:* $15,692 (excluding resources awarded to replace EFC). 35% of all full-time undergraduates had no need and received non-need-based aid.

GIFT AID (NEED-BASED) ***Total amount:*** $7,348,219 (12% Federal, 3% state, 85% institutional). ***Receiving aid:*** *Freshmen:* 63% (180); *all full-time undergraduates:* 60% (672). ***Average award:*** Freshmen: $11,952; Undergraduates: $10,908. ***Scholarships, grants, and awards:*** Federal Pell, FSEOG, state, private, college/university gift aid from institutional funds, foundation, civic group, and church-sponsored scholarships/grants.

GIFT AID (NON-NEED-BASED) ***Total amount:*** $4,372,395 (9% state, 84% institutional, 7% external sources). ***Receiving aid:*** *Freshmen:* 16% (46); *Undergraduates:* 14% (161). ***Scholarships, grants, and awards by category:*** *Academic Interests/Achievement:* 1,359 awards ($9,332,017 total): business, general academic interests/achievements. *Creative Arts/Performance:* 17 awards ($33,500 total): art/fine arts, music, theater/drama. *Special Characteristics:* 129 awards ($445,988 total): adult students, children of faculty/staff, ethnic background, members of minority groups, relatives of clergy, religious affiliation. ***Tuition waivers:*** Full or partial for employees or children of employees. ***ROTC:*** Army cooperative.

LOANS ***Student loans:*** $3,319,882 (67% need-based, 33% non-need-based). 61% of past graduating class borrowed through all loan programs. Average indebtedness per student: $18,743. ***Average need-based loan:*** Freshmen: $3310; Undergraduates: $4171. ***Parent loans:*** $424,182 (8% need-based, 92% non-need-based). ***Programs:*** FFEL (Subsidized and Unsubsidized Stafford, PLUS), Perkins, college/university.

WORK-STUDY ***Federal work-study:*** *Total amount:* $296,812; 268 jobs averaging $1105. ***State or other work-study/employment:*** *Total amount:* $111,160 (17% need-based, 83% non-need-based). 63 part-time jobs averaging $1764.

APPLYING for FINANCIAL AID ***Required financial aid forms:*** FAFSA, institution's own form, state aid form. ***Financial aid deadline:*** Continuous. ***Notification date:*** Continuous beginning 3/10. Students must reply by 5/1 or within 2 weeks of notification.

CONTACT Ann Hendrick, Director of Student Aid and Financial Planning, Millsaps College, 1701 North State Street, Jackson, MS 39210-0001, 601-974-1220 or toll-free 800-352-1050. *Fax:* 601-974-1224.

MILLS COLLEGE

Oakland, CA

Tuition & fees: $17,852 **Average undergraduate aid package: $18,246**

ABOUT THE INSTITUTION Independent, women only. Awards: bachelor's, master's, and doctoral degrees. 39 undergraduate majors. Total enrollment: 1,122. Undergraduates: 727. Freshmen: 116. Both federal and institutional methodology are used as a basis for awarding need-based institutional aid.

UNDERGRADUATE EXPENSES for 1999–2000 ***Application fee:*** $40. ***Comprehensive fee:*** $25,148 includes full-time tuition ($17,250), mandatory fees ($602), and room and board ($7296). Room and board charges vary according to board plan and housing facility. ***Part-time tuition:*** $2690 per course. ***Part-time fees:*** $301 per term part-time. ***Payment plan:*** installment.

FRESHMAN FINANCIAL AID (Fall 1999, est.) 107 applied for aid; of those 94% were deemed to have need. 100% of freshmen with need received aid; of those 57% had need fully met. *Average percent of need met:* 97% (excluding resources awarded to replace EFC). *Average financial aid package:* $19,395 (excluding resources awarded to replace EFC). 10% of all full-time freshmen had no need and received non-need-based aid.

UNDERGRADUATE FINANCIAL AID (Fall 1999, est.) 606 applied for aid; of those 94% were deemed to have need. 99% of undergraduates with need received aid; of those 41% had need fully met. *Average percent of need met:* 87% (excluding resources awarded to replace EFC). *Average financial aid package:* $18,246 (excluding resources awarded to replace EFC). 11% of all full-time undergraduates had no need and received non-need-based aid.

GIFT AID (NEED-BASED) ***Total amount:*** $7,175,289 (9% Federal, 25% state, 64% institutional, 2% external sources). ***Receiving aid:*** *Freshmen:* 81% (98); *all full-time undergraduates:* 74% (550). ***Average award:*** Freshmen: $14,145; Undergraduates: $13,046. ***Scholarships, grants, and awards:*** Federal Pell, FSEOG, state, private, college/university gift aid from institutional funds.

GIFT AID (NON-NEED-BASED) ***Total amount:*** $282,790 (1% Federal, 97% institutional, 2% external sources). ***Scholarships, grants, and awards by category:*** *Academic Interests/Achievement:* biological sciences, computer science, general academic interests/achievements, mathematics, physical sciences, premedicine. *Creative Arts/Performance:* art/fine arts, music. *Special Characteristics:* children of faculty/staff. ***Tuition waivers:*** Full or partial for employees or children of employees. ***ROTC:*** Army cooperative.

LOANS ***Student loans:*** $2,912,311 (96% need-based, 4% non-need-based). 78% of past graduating class borrowed through all loan programs. Average indebtedness per student: $17,083. ***Average need-based loan:*** Freshmen: $3782; Undergraduates: $4549. ***Parent loans:*** $366,486 (85% need-based, 15% non-need-based). ***Programs:*** FFEL (Subsidized and Unsubsidized Stafford, PLUS), Perkins, college/university.

WORK-STUDY ***Federal work-study:*** *Total amount:* $436,239; 208 jobs averaging $2108. ***State or other work-study/employment:*** *Total amount:* $372,358 (75% need-based, 25% non-need-based). 188 part-time jobs averaging $1998.

APPLYING for FINANCIAL AID ***Required financial aid forms:*** FAFSA, institution's own form, state aid form, noncustodial (divorced/separated) parent's statement. ***Financial aid deadline (priority):*** 2/15. ***Notification date:*** 4/1. Students must reply by 5/1.

CONTACT The M Center/Financial Aid, Mills College, 5000 MacArthur Boulevard, Oakland, CA 94613, 510-430-2000 or toll-free 800-87-MILLS. *E-mail:* mcenter-finaid@mills.edu

MILWAUKEE INSTITUTE OF ART AND DESIGN

Milwaukee, WI

Tuition & fees: $15,080 **Average undergraduate aid package: $13,210**

ABOUT THE INSTITUTION Independent, coed. Awards: bachelor's degrees. 9 undergraduate majors. Total enrollment: 625. Undergraduates: 625. Freshmen: 139. Federal methodology is used as a basis for awarding need-based institutional aid.

UNDERGRADUATE EXPENSES for 1999–2000 ***Application fee:*** $25. ***Comprehensive fee:*** $21,538 includes full-time tuition ($14,950), mandatory fees ($130), and room and board ($6458). Full-time tuition and fees vary according to student level. Room and board charges vary according to board plan. ***Part-time tuition:*** $500 per credit. ***Part-time fees:*** $65 per term part-time. Part-time tuition and fees vary according to course load. ***Payment plan:*** deferred payment.

FRESHMAN FINANCIAL AID (Fall 1998) 124 applied for aid; of those 92% were deemed to have need. 100% of freshmen with need received aid; of those 27% had need fully met. *Average percent of need met:* 72% (excluding resources awarded to replace EFC). *Average financial aid package:* $13,425 (excluding resources awarded to replace EFC). 26% of all full-time freshmen had no need and received non-need-based aid.

UNDERGRADUATE FINANCIAL AID (Fall 1998) 435 applied for aid; of those 94% were deemed to have need. 100% of undergraduates with need received aid; of those 26% had need fully met. *Average percent of need met:* 73% (excluding resources awarded to replace EFC). *Average financial aid package:* $13,210 (excluding resources awarded to replace EFC). 13% of all full-time undergraduates had no need and received non-need-based aid.

GIFT AID (NEED-BASED) ***Total amount:*** $2,676,075 (15% Federal, 16% state, 69% institutional). ***Receiving aid:*** *Freshmen:* 74% (114); *all full-time undergraduates:* 86% (403). ***Average award:*** Freshmen: $7161; Undergraduates: $6682. ***Scholarships, grants, and awards:*** Federal Pell, FSEOG, state, private, college/university gift aid from institutional funds.

GIFT AID (NON-NEED-BASED) ***Total amount:*** $358,481 (74% institutional, 26% external sources). ***Receiving aid:*** *Freshmen:* 4% (6); *Undergraduates:* 5% (21). ***Scholarships, grants, and awards by category:*** *Academic Interests/Achievement:* general academic interests/achievements. *Creative Arts/Performance:* applied art and design, art/fine arts. *Special Characteristics:* children of faculty/staff, ethnic background, local/state students, members of minority groups. ***Tuition waivers:*** Full or partial for employees or children of employees.

LOANS ***Student loans:*** $3,276,630 (80% need-based, 20% non-need-based). 96% of past graduating class borrowed through all loan programs. Average indebtedness per student: $21,053. ***Average need-based loan:*** Freshmen: $5200; Undergraduates: $6017. ***Parent loans:*** $325,030 (100% non-need-based). ***Programs:*** FFEL (Subsidized and Unsubsidized Stafford, PLUS), college/university, Norwest Collegiate Loans, Signature Loans.

WORK-STUDY ***Federal work-study:*** *Total amount:* $86,000; 70 jobs averaging $1142.

APPLYING for FINANCIAL AID ***Required financial aid form:*** FAFSA. ***Financial aid deadline:*** 3/1. ***Notification date:*** 4/1. Students must reply by 5/1 or within 4 weeks of notification.

CONTACT Mr. Lloyd Mueller, Director of Financial Aid, Milwaukee Institute of Art and Design, 273 East Erie Street, Milwaukee, WI 53202-6003, 414-291-3272 or toll-free 888-749-MIAD. *Fax:* 414-291-8077. *E-mail:* llmuelle@miad.edu

MILWAUKEE SCHOOL OF ENGINEERING

Milwaukee, WI

Tuition & fees: $19,845 **Average undergraduate aid package: $12,400**

ABOUT THE INSTITUTION Independent, coed, primarily men. Awards: associate, bachelor's, and master's degrees. 13 undergraduate majors. Total enrollment: 2,711. Undergraduates: 2,343. Freshmen: 511. Federal methodology is used as a basis for awarding need-based institutional aid.

UNDERGRADUATE EXPENSES for 2000–2001 ***Application fee:*** $25. ***One-time required fee:*** $1140. ***Comprehensive fee:*** $24,555 includes full-time tuition ($19,845) and room and board ($4710). ***College room only:*** $2850. Full-time tuition and fees vary according to student level. Room and board charges vary according to board plan and housing facility. ***Part-time tuition:*** $345 per quarter hour. Part-time tuition and fees vary according to course load. ***Payment plan:*** installment.

FRESHMAN FINANCIAL AID (Fall 1998) 403 applied for aid; of those 97% were deemed to have need. 100% of freshmen with need received aid; of those 10% had need fully met. *Average percent of need met:* 75% (excluding resources awarded to replace EFC). *Average financial aid package:* $13,400 (excluding resources awarded to replace EFC). 6% of all full-time freshmen had no need and received non-need-based aid.

UNDERGRADUATE FINANCIAL AID (Fall 1998) 1,536 applied for aid; of those 99% were deemed to have need. 100% of undergraduates with need received aid; of those 13% had need fully met. *Average percent of need met:* 85% (excluding resources awarded to replace EFC). *Average financial aid package:* $12,400 (excluding resources awarded to replace EFC). 8% of all full-time undergraduates had no need and received non-need-based aid.

GIFT AID (NEED-BASED) ***Total amount:*** $7,553,658 (12% Federal, 16% state, 72% institutional). ***Receiving aid:*** *Freshmen:* 86% (385); *all full-time undergraduates:* 86% (1,466). ***Scholarships, grants, and awards:*** Federal Pell, FSEOG, state, private, college/university gift aid from institutional funds.

GIFT AID (NON-NEED-BASED) ***Total amount:*** $698,273 (56% institutional, 44% external sources). ***Receiving aid:*** *Freshmen:* 5% (21); *Undergraduates:* 4% (62). ***Scholarships, grants, and awards by category:*** *Academic Interests/Achievement:* business, communication, computer science, engineering/technologies, general academic interests/achievements, health fields. *Special Characteristics:* children and siblings of alumni, children of faculty/staff. ***Tuition waivers:*** Full or partial for employees or children of employees. ***ROTC:*** Army cooperative, Air Force cooperative.

LOANS ***Student loans:*** $6,554,672 (84% need-based, 16% non-need-based). 85% of past graduating class borrowed through all loan programs. Average indebtedness per student: $21,500. ***Programs:*** FFEL (Subsidized and Unsubsidized Stafford, PLUS), Perkins, college/university.

WORK-STUDY ***Federal work-study:*** *Total amount:* $297,667; 141 jobs averaging $2079. ***State or other work-study/employment:*** 100 part-time jobs averaging $2340.

APPLYING for FINANCIAL AID ***Required financial aid form:*** FAFSA. ***Financial aid deadline (priority):*** 3/15. ***Notification date:*** Continuous beginning 4/1. Students must reply within 4 weeks of notification.

CONTACT Mr. Louis LaSota, Director, Financial Aid, Milwaukee School of Engineering, 1025 North Broadway Street, Milwaukee, WI 53202-3109, 414-277-7222 or toll-free 800-332-6763. *Fax:* 414-277-6952. *E-mail:* lasota@msoe.edu

MINNEAPOLIS COLLEGE OF ART AND DESIGN

Minneapolis, MN

Tuition & fees: $18,190 **Average undergraduate aid package: $12,081**

Minneapolis College of Art and Design (continued)

ABOUT THE INSTITUTION Independent, coed. Awards: bachelor's and master's degrees and post-bachelor's certificates. 12 undergraduate majors. Total enrollment: 602. Undergraduates: 577. Freshmen: 87. Federal methodology is used as a basis for awarding need-based institutional aid.

UNDERGRADUATE EXPENSES for 1999–2000 ***Application fee:*** $35. ***Tuition:*** full-time $17,910; part-time $597 per credit. ***Required fees:*** full-time $280; $40 per term part-time. Room and board charges vary according to housing facility. ***Payment plan:*** installment.

FRESHMAN FINANCIAL AID (Fall 1999) 138 applied for aid; of those 88% were deemed to have need. 100% of freshmen with need received aid; of those 45% had need fully met. *Average percent of need met:* 66% (excluding resources awarded to replace EFC). *Average financial aid package:* $10,034 (excluding resources awarded to replace EFC).

UNDERGRADUATE FINANCIAL AID (Fall 1999) 479 applied for aid; of those 90% were deemed to have need. 100% of undergraduates with need received aid; of those 42% had need fully met. *Average percent of need met:* 75% (excluding resources awarded to replace EFC). *Average financial aid package:* $12,081 (excluding resources awarded to replace EFC).

GIFT AID (NEED-BASED) ***Total amount:*** $2,230,093 (18% Federal, 21% state, 61% institutional). ***Receiving aid:*** *Freshmen:* 104; *all full-time undergraduates:* 367. ***Average award:*** Freshmen: $4997; Undergraduates: $5198. ***Scholarships, grants, and awards:*** Federal Pell, FSEOG, state, private, college/university gift aid from institutional funds.

GIFT AID (NON-NEED-BASED) ***Total amount:*** $337,653 (100% institutional). ***Receiving aid:*** *Freshmen:* 27; *Undergraduates:* 81. ***Scholarships, grants, and awards by category:*** *Creative Arts/Performance:* 89 awards ($337,653 total): applied art and design, art/fine arts, general creative arts/performance. ***Tuition waivers:*** Full or partial for children of alumni, employees or children of employees.

LOANS ***Student loans:*** $4,010,924 (68% need-based, 32% non-need-based). 90% of past graduating class borrowed through all loan programs. Average indebtedness per student: $22,250. ***Average need-based loan:*** Freshmen: $2674; Undergraduates: $7114. ***Parent loans:*** $364,449 (100% non-need-based). ***Programs:*** FFEL (Subsidized and Unsubsidized Stafford, PLUS), Perkins, state, college/university.

WORK-STUDY ***Federal work-study:*** *Total amount:* $52,275; 30 jobs averaging $1800. ***State or other work-study/employment:*** *Total amount:* $190,000 (100% need-based). 110 part-time jobs averaging $1800.

APPLYING for FINANCIAL AID ***Required financial aid form:*** FAFSA. ***Financial aid deadline:*** Continuous. ***Notification date:*** 4/1. Students must reply within 2 weeks of notification.

CONTACT Ms. Susan Neppl, Director of Enrollment and Student Financial Services, Minneapolis College of Art and Design, 2501 Stevens Avenue South, Minneapolis, MN 55404-4347, 612-874-3762 or toll-free 800-874-6223. *Fax:* 612-874-3701.

MINNESOTA BIBLE COLLEGE

Rochester, MN

Tuition & fees: $6056 **Average undergraduate aid package: N/A**

ABOUT THE INSTITUTION Independent religious, coed. Awards: associate and bachelor's degrees. 5 undergraduate majors. Total enrollment: 114. Undergraduates: 114. Freshmen: 16. Federal methodology is used as a basis for awarding need-based institutional aid.

UNDERGRADUATE EXPENSES for 1999–2000 ***Application fee:*** $30. ***Tuition:*** full-time $5746; part-time $169 per semester hour. ***Required fees:*** full-time $310. Room and board charges vary according to housing facility. ***Payment plan:*** installment.

FRESHMAN FINANCIAL AID (Fall 1999, est.) 16 applied for aid; of those 81% were deemed to have need. 100% of freshmen with need received aid; of those 77% had need fully met. *Average percent of need met:* 93% (excluding resources awarded to replace EFC). 24% of all full-time freshmen had no need and received non-need-based aid.

UNDERGRADUATE FINANCIAL AID (Fall 1999, est.) 81 applied for aid; of those 88% were deemed to have need. 100% of undergraduates with need received aid; of those 62% had need fully met. *Average percent of need met:* 84% (excluding resources awarded to replace EFC). 14% of all full-time undergraduates had no need and received non-need-based aid.

GIFT AID (NEED-BASED) ***Total amount:*** $222,014 (48% Federal, 32% state, 15% institutional, 5% external sources). ***Receiving aid:*** *Freshmen:* 76% (13); *all full-time undergraduates:* 72% (71). ***Average award:*** Freshmen: $8394; Undergraduates: $7271. ***Scholarships, grants, and awards:*** Federal Pell, FSEOG, state, private, college/university gift aid from institutional funds.

GIFT AID (NON-NEED-BASED) ***Total amount:*** $12,205 (45% institutional, 55% external sources). ***Receiving aid:*** *Freshmen:* 18% (3); *Undergraduates:* 14% (14). ***Scholarships, grants, and awards by category:*** *Academic Interests/Achievement:* 54 awards ($55,242 total): general academic interests/achievements, religion/biblical studies. *Creative Arts/Performance:* 2 awards ($1000 total): art/fine arts, music. *Special Achievements/Activities:* 12 awards ($5304 total): general special achievements/activities, leadership, religious involvement. *Special Characteristics:* 27 awards ($48,276 total): children of current students, children of educators, children of faculty/staff, general special characteristics, international students, parents of current students, religious affiliation, siblings of current students, spouses of current students. ***Tuition waivers:*** Full or partial for employees or children of employees, senior citizens.

LOANS ***Student loans:*** $291,891 (76% need-based, 24% non-need-based). 66% of past graduating class borrowed through all loan programs. Average indebtedness per student: $18,558. ***Average need-based loan:*** Freshmen: $4125; Undergraduates: $3882. ***Parent loans:*** $5044 (100% non-need-based). ***Programs:*** FFEL (Subsidized and Unsubsidized Stafford, PLUS), state, college/university.

WORK-STUDY ***Federal work-study:*** *Total amount:* $8687; 11 jobs averaging $789. ***State or other work-study/employment:*** *Total amount:* $21,044 (17% need-based, 83% non-need-based). 4 part-time jobs averaging $917.

APPLYING for FINANCIAL AID ***Required financial aid forms:*** FAFSA, institution's own form. ***Financial aid deadline (priority):*** 6/1. ***Notification date:*** Continuous beginning 7/1. Students must reply within 2 weeks of notification.

CONTACT Kimber Schletty, Director of Financial Aid, Minnesota Bible College, 920 Mayowood Road SW, Rochester, MN 55902-2275, 507-288-4563 or toll-free 800-456-7651. *Fax:* 507-288-9046. *E-mail:* kschletty@mnbc.edu

MINNESOTA STATE UNIVERSITY, MANKATO

Mankato, MN

Tuition & fees (MN res): $3492 **Average undergraduate aid package: N/A**

ABOUT THE INSTITUTION State-supported, coed. Awards: associate, bachelor's, and master's degrees and post-master's certificates. 124 undergraduate majors. Total enrollment: 12,085. Undergraduates: 10,442. Freshmen: 2,038. Federal methodology is used as a basis for awarding need-based institutional aid.

UNDERGRADUATE EXPENSES for 1999–2000 ***Application fee:*** $20. ***Tuition, state resident:*** full-time $2996; part-time $104 per credit. ***Tuition, nonresident:*** full-time $5796; part-time $220 per credit. ***Required fees:*** full-time $496; $21 per credit. Full-time tuition and fees vary according to course load and reciprocity agreements. Part-time tuition and fees vary according to course load and reciprocity agreements. ***College room and board:*** $5348; ***room only:*** $2004. Room and board charges vary according to board plan. ***Payment plan:*** installment.

GIFT AID (NEED-BASED) ***Scholarships, grants, and awards:*** Federal Pell, FSEOG, state, private, college/university gift aid from institutional funds.

GIFT AID (NON-NEED-BASED) ***Scholarships, grants, and awards by category:*** *Academic Interests/Achievement:* business, computer science, engineering/technologies, general academic interests/achievements, mathematics, physical sciences. *Creative Arts/Performance:* applied art and design, art/fine arts, creative writing, debating, music, theater/drama. *Special Achievements/Activities:* leadership. *Special Characteristics:* children of union members/company employees, local/state students, out-of-state students. ***Tuition waivers:*** Full or partial for employees or children of employees, senior citizens. ***ROTC:*** Army.

LOANS ***Programs:*** FFEL (Subsidized and Unsubsidized Stafford, PLUS), Perkins, SELF Loans.

WORK-STUDY Federal work-study jobs available. ***State or other work-study/employment:*** Part-time jobs available.

APPLYING for FINANCIAL AID ***Required financial aid form:*** FAFSA.

CONTACT Office of Financial Aid, Minnesota State University, Mankato, 109 Wigley Administration Center, Mankato, MN 56001, 507-389-1185 or toll-free 800-722-0544.

MINNESOTA STATE UNIVERSITY MOORHEAD

Moorhead, MN

Tuition & fees (MN res): $3179 **Average undergraduate aid package: $4557**

ABOUT THE INSTITUTION State-supported, coed. Awards: associate, bachelor's, and master's degrees and post-master's certificates. 85 undergraduate majors. Total enrollment: 7,059. Undergraduates: 6,729. Freshmen: 1,158. Federal methodology is used as a basis for awarding need-based institutional aid.

UNDERGRADUATE EXPENSES for 1999–2000 ***Application fee:*** $20. ***Tuition, state resident:*** full-time $2729; part-time $85 per credit. ***Tuition, nonresident:*** full-time $6118; part-time $191 per credit. ***Required fees:*** full-time $450; $19 per credit. Full-time tuition and fees vary according to reciprocity agreements. Part-time tuition and fees vary according to reciprocity agreements. ***College room and board:*** $3264; ***room only:*** $1978. Room and board charges vary according to board plan. ***Payment plan:*** deferred payment.

FRESHMAN FINANCIAL AID (Fall 1999) 1163 applied for aid; of those 94% were deemed to have need. 97% of freshmen with need received aid; of those 8% had need fully met. *Average percent of need met:* 44% (excluding resources awarded to replace EFC). *Average financial aid package:* $3925 (excluding resources awarded to replace EFC). 4% of all full-time freshmen had no need and received non-need-based aid.

UNDERGRADUATE FINANCIAL AID (Fall 1999) 4,670 applied for aid; of those 93% were deemed to have need. 96% of undergraduates with need received aid; of those 10% had need fully met. *Average percent of need met:* 50% (excluding resources awarded to replace EFC). *Average financial aid package:* $4557 (excluding resources awarded to replace EFC). 4% of all full-time undergraduates had no need and received non-need-based aid.

GIFT AID (NEED-BASED) ***Total amount:*** $5,006,952 (62% Federal, 36% state, 2% external sources). ***Receiving aid:*** *Freshmen:* 38% (520); *all full-time undergraduates:* 37% (2,126). ***Average award:*** Freshmen: $2534; Undergraduates: $2430. ***Scholarships, grants, and awards:*** Federal Pell, FSEOG, state, private, college/university gift aid from institutional funds.

GIFT AID (NON-NEED-BASED) ***Total amount:*** $1,351,845 (3% state, 94% institutional, 3% external sources). ***Receiving aid:*** *Freshmen:* 46% (631); *Undergraduates:* 49% (2,806). ***Scholarships, grants, and awards by category:*** *Academic Interests/Achievement:* general academic interests/achievements. *Creative Arts/Performance:* art/fine arts, music, theater/drama. *Special Achievements/Activities:* community service, general special achievements/activities. *Special Characteristics:* members of minority groups. ***Tuition waivers:*** Full or partial for employees or children of employees, senior citizens. ***ROTC:*** Army cooperative, Air Force cooperative.

LOANS ***Student loans:*** $18,202,569 (47% need-based, 53% non-need-based). 70% of past graduating class borrowed through all loan programs. Average indebtedness per student: $13,100. ***Average need-based loan:*** Freshmen: $2297; Undergraduates: $2840. ***Parent loans:*** $175,773 (100% non-need-based). ***Programs:*** Federal Direct (Subsidized and Unsubsidized Stafford, PLUS), Perkins, state.

WORK-STUDY ***Federal work-study:*** *Total amount:* $514,045; 328 jobs averaging $1567. ***State or other work-study/employment:*** *Total amount:* $2,085,372 (25% need-based, 75% non-need-based). Part-time jobs available.

ATHLETIC AWARDS *Total amount:* 165,950 (100% non-need-based).

APPLYING for FINANCIAL AID ***Required financial aid form:*** FAFSA. ***Financial aid deadline (priority):*** 3/1. ***Notification date:*** 6/15. Students must reply within 2 weeks of notification.

CONTACT Ms. Carolyn Zehren, Acting Director of Financial Aid, Minnesota State University Moorhead, 1104 7th Avenue South, Moorhead, MN 56563-0002, 218-236-2251 or toll-free 800-593-7246. *E-mail:* zehren@mhd1.moorhead.msus.edu

MINOT STATE UNIVERSITY

Minot, ND

Tuition & fees (ND res): $2331 **Average undergraduate aid package: $7782**

ABOUT THE INSTITUTION State-supported, coed. Awards: bachelor's and master's degrees. 46 undergraduate majors. Total enrollment: 3,155. Undergraduates: 2,982. Freshmen: 525. Federal methodology is used as a basis for awarding need-based institutional aid.

UNDERGRADUATE EXPENSES for 1999–2000 ***Application fee:*** $25. ***Tuition, state resident:*** full-time $2050; part-time $97 per semester hour. ***Tuition, nonresident:*** full-time $5474; part-time $240 per semester hour. ***Required fees:*** full-time $281. Full-time tuition and fees vary according to program and reciprocity agreements. Part-time tuition and fees vary according to course load, program, and reciprocity agreements. ***College room and board:*** $2724; ***room only:*** $1021. Room and board charges vary according to board plan, housing facility, and student level.

UNDERGRADUATE FINANCIAL AID (Fall 1999, est.) 2,909 applied for aid; of those 88% were deemed to have need. 100% of undergraduates with need received aid. *Average percent of need met:* 100% (excluding resources awarded to replace EFC). *Average financial aid package:* $7782 (excluding resources awarded to replace EFC).

GIFT AID (NEED-BASED) ***Total amount:*** $2,882,515 (92% Federal, 6% state, 2% institutional). ***Scholarships, grants, and awards:*** Federal Pell, FSEOG, state, college/university gift aid from institutional funds, Federal Nursing.

GIFT AID (NON-NEED-BASED) ***Total amount:*** $2,623,837 (3% Federal, 2% state, 9% institutional, 86% external sources). ***Scholarships, grants, and awards by category:*** *Academic Interests/Achievement:* business, communication, computer science, education, English, general academic interests/achievements, health fields, humanities, mathematics, social sciences. *Creative Arts/Performance:* music, theater/drama. *Special Characteristics:* ethnic background, international students, local/state students, members of minority groups, veterans, veterans' children. ***Tuition waivers:*** Full or partial for minority students.

LOANS ***Student loans:*** $7,505,870 (73% need-based, 27% non-need-based). 84% of past graduating class borrowed through all loan programs. Average indebtedness per student: $11,884. ***Parent loans:*** $85,059 (100% non-need-based). ***Programs:*** FFEL (Subsidized and Unsubsidized Stafford, PLUS), Perkins, Federal Nursing, college/university.

WORK-STUDY ***Federal work-study:*** *Total amount:* $205,105; 170 jobs averaging $1450.

ATHLETIC AWARDS *Total amount:* 98,628 (100% non-need-based).

APPLYING for FINANCIAL AID ***Required financial aid form:*** FAFSA. ***Financial aid deadline (priority):*** 4/15. ***Notification date:*** Continuous beginning 6/1. Students must reply within 2 weeks of notification.

CONTACT Mr. Dale Gehring, Director of Financial Aid, Minot State University, 500 University Avenue, West, Minot, ND 58707-0002, 701-858-3862 or toll-free 800-777-0750. *Fax:* 701-839-6933. *E-mail:* gehringd@warp6.cs.misu.nodak.edu

MIRRER YESHIVA

Brooklyn, NY

CONTACT Financial Aid Office, Mirrer Yeshiva, 1795 Ocean Parkway, Brooklyn, NY 11223-2010, 718-645-0536.

MISSISSIPPI COLLEGE

Clinton, MS

Tuition & fees: $9614 **Average undergraduate aid package: $12,369**

ABOUT THE INSTITUTION Independent Southern Baptist, coed. Awards: bachelor's, master's, and first professional degrees and post-master's certificates. 53 undergraduate majors. Total enrollment: 3,560. Undergraduates: 2,522. Freshmen: 405. Federal methodology is used as a basis for awarding need-based institutional aid.

UNDERGRADUATE EXPENSES for 2000–2001 ***Application fee:*** $25. ***Comprehensive fee:*** $13,790 includes full-time tuition ($9090), mandatory fees ($524), and room and board ($4176). ***College room only:*** $1980. Full-time tuition and fees vary according to course load. Room and board charges vary according to board plan and housing facility. ***Part-time tuition:*** $303 per credit hour. ***Part-time fees:*** $75 per term part-time. Part-time tuition and fees vary according to course load. ***Payment plans:*** installment, deferred payment.

FRESHMAN FINANCIAL AID (Fall 1999, est.) 391 applied for aid; of those 47% were deemed to have need. 99% of freshmen with need received aid; of those 45% had need fully met. *Average percent of need met:* 49% (excluding resources awarded to replace EFC). *Average financial aid package:* $10,424 (excluding resources awarded to replace EFC). 52% of all full-time freshmen had no need and received non-need-based aid.

UNDERGRADUATE FINANCIAL AID (Fall 1999, est.) 1,990 applied for aid; of those 54% were deemed to have need. 99% of undergraduates with need received aid; of those 43% had need fully met. *Average percent of need met:* 51% (excluding resources awarded to replace EFC). *Average financial aid package:* $12,369 (excluding resources awarded to replace EFC). 44% of all full-time undergraduates had no need and received non-need-based aid.

GIFT AID (NEED-BASED) ***Total amount:*** $6,069,667 (27% Federal, 11% state, 61% institutional, 1% external sources). ***Receiving aid:*** *Freshmen:* 17% (66); *all full-time undergraduates:* 23% (466). ***Average award:*** Freshmen: $2891; Undergraduates: $2685. ***Scholarships, grants, and awards:*** Federal Pell, FSEOG, state, private, college/university gift aid from institutional funds.

GIFT AID (NON-NEED-BASED) ***Total amount:*** $10,766,379 (11% state, 87% institutional, 2% external sources). ***Receiving aid:*** *Freshmen:* 44% (175); *Undergraduates:* 45% (931). ***Scholarships, grants, and awards by category:*** *Academic Interests/Achievement:* $7,335,784 total: biological sciences, communication, education, general academic interests/achievements, health fields, humanities, mathematics, physical sciences, religion/biblical studies. *Creative Arts/Performance:* $426,263 total: applied art and design, art/fine arts, music. *Special Achievements/Activities:* $167,220 total: general special achievements/activities. *Special Characteristics:* $1,439,709 total: children of faculty/staff, general special characteristics, members of minority groups, relatives of clergy. ***Tuition waivers:*** Full or partial for employees or children of employees. ***ROTC:*** Army cooperative.

LOANS ***Student loans:*** $7,316,195 (83% need-based, 17% non-need-based). Average indebtedness per student: $22,588. ***Average need-based loan:*** Freshmen: $2711; Undergraduates: $4201. ***Parent loans:*** $366,909 (100% non-need-based). ***Programs:*** FFEL (Subsidized and Unsubsidized Stafford, PLUS), Perkins, Federal Nursing, college/university.

WORK-STUDY ***Federal work-study:*** *Total amount:* $295,157; jobs available.

APPLYING for FINANCIAL AID ***Required financial aid form:*** FAFSA. ***Financial aid deadline (priority):*** 3/1. ***Notification date:*** Continuous beginning 4/15.

CONTACT Mary Givhan, Director of Financial Aid, Mississippi College, PO Box 4035, Clinton, MS 39058, 601-925-3319 or toll-free 800-738-1236. *E-mail:* givhan@mc.edu

MISSISSIPPI STATE UNIVERSITY

Mississippi State, MS

Tuition & fees (MS res): $3329 **Average undergraduate aid package: $5440**

ABOUT THE INSTITUTION State-supported, coed. Awards: bachelor's, master's, doctoral, and first professional degrees and post-master's certificates. 70 undergraduate majors. Total enrollment: 16,076. Undergraduates: 12,879. Freshmen: 2,024. Federal methodology is used as a basis for awarding need-based institutional aid.

UNDERGRADUATE EXPENSES for 1999–2000 ***Application fee:*** $25 for nonresidents. ***Tuition, state resident:*** full-time $3017; part-time $126 per credit hour. ***Tuition, nonresident:*** full-time $6119; part-time $255 per credit hour. ***Required fees:*** full-time $312. Full-time tuition and fees vary according to location. Part-time tuition and fees vary according to course load and location. ***College room and board:*** $3690; ***room only:*** $1800. Room and board charges vary according to board plan and housing facility.

FRESHMAN FINANCIAL AID (Fall 1998) 1702 applied for aid; of those 74% were deemed to have need. 91% of freshmen with need received aid; of those 17% had need fully met. *Average percent of need met:* 61% (excluding resources awarded to replace EFC). *Average financial aid package:* $3903 (excluding resources awarded to replace EFC). 30% of all full-time freshmen had no need and received non-need-based aid.

UNDERGRADUATE FINANCIAL AID (Fall 1998) 10,384 applied for aid; of those 75% were deemed to have need. 89% of undergraduates with need received aid; of those 35% had need fully met. *Average percent of need met:* 67% (excluding resources awarded to replace EFC). *Average financial aid package:* $5440 (excluding resources awarded to replace EFC). 21% of all full-time undergraduates had no need and received non-need-based aid.

GIFT AID (NEED-BASED) ***Total amount:*** $15,544,748 (53% Federal, 15% state, 21% institutional, 11% external sources). ***Receiving aid:*** *Freshmen:* 59% (1,083); *all full-time undergraduates:* 51% (6,108). ***Average award:*** Freshmen: $2461; Undergraduates: $2385. ***Scholarships, grants, and awards:*** Federal Pell, FSEOG, state, private, college/university gift aid from institutional funds.

GIFT AID (NON-NEED-BASED) ***Total amount:*** $4,742,478 (42% state, 51% institutional, 7% external sources). ***Receiving aid:*** *Freshmen:* 10% (181); *Undergraduates:* 5% (654). ***Scholarships, grants, and awards by category:*** *Academic Interests/Achievement:* agriculture, architecture, area/ethnic studies, biological sciences, business, communication, computer science, education, engineering/technologies, English, foreign languages, general academic interests/achievements, health fields, home economics, humanities, international studies, library science, mathematics, military science, physical sciences, premedicine, religion/biblical studies, social sciences. *Creative Arts/Performance:* applied art and design, art/fine arts, cinema/film/broadcasting, creative writing, dance, debating, general creative arts/performance, journalism/publications, music, performing arts, theater/drama. *Special Achievements/Activities:* cheerleading/drum major, general special achievements/activities, leadership, memberships. *Special Characteristics:* adult students, children and siblings of alumni, children of educators, children of faculty/staff, children of public servants, first-generation college students, handicapped students, local/state students, out-of-state students, previous college experience, spouses of deceased or disabled public servants. ***Tuition waivers:*** Full or partial for children of alumni, employees or children of employees, senior citizens. ***ROTC:*** Army, Air Force.

LOANS ***Student loans:*** $29,796,832 (90% need-based, 10% non-need-based). Average indebtedness per student: $17,712. ***Average need-based loan:*** Freshmen: $2397; Undergraduates: $3254. ***Parent loans:*** $3,801,366 (26% need-based, 74% non-need-based). ***Programs:*** FFEL (Subsidized and Unsubsidized Stafford, PLUS), Perkins, state, college/university.

WORK-STUDY ***Federal work-study:*** *Total amount:* $2,431,681; 1,004 jobs averaging $2422.

ATHLETIC AWARDS *Total amount:* 1,687,297 (100% non-need-based).

APPLYING for FINANCIAL AID ***Required financial aid forms:*** FAFSA, state aid form. ***Financial aid deadline (priority):*** 4/1. ***Notification date:*** Continuous. Students must reply within 3 weeks of notification.

CONTACT Mr. Bruce Crain, Director of Financial Aid, Mississippi State University, PO Box 6035, Mississippi State, MS 39762, 601-325-3990.

MISSISSIPPI UNIVERSITY FOR WOMEN

Columbus, MS

Tuition & fees (MS res): $2556 **Average undergraduate aid package: N/A**

ABOUT THE INSTITUTION State-supported, coed. Awards: associate, bachelor's, and master's degrees. 39 undergraduate majors. Total enrollment: 3,314. Undergraduates: 3,180. Freshmen: 332. Federal methodology is used as a basis for awarding need-based institutional aid.

UNDERGRADUATE EXPENSES for 1999–2000 ***Application fee:*** $25 for nonresidents. ***Tuition, state resident:*** full-time $2556; part-time $106 per semester hour. ***Tuition, nonresident:*** full-time $5546; part-time $231 per semester hour. ***College room and board:*** $2590; ***room only:*** $1260. Room and board charges vary according to board plan. ***Payment plans:*** installment, deferred payment.

GIFT AID (NEED-BASED) ***Scholarships, grants, and awards:*** Federal Pell, FSEOG, state.

GIFT AID (NON-NEED-BASED) ***Scholarships, grants, and awards by category:*** *Academic Interests/Achievement:* general academic interests/achievements. *Creative Arts/Performance:* art/fine arts, dance, journalism/publications, music, performing arts, theater/drama. *Special Achievements/Activities:* junior miss. *Special Characteristics:* adult students, children and siblings of alumni, children of faculty/staff, ethnic background, international students, members of minority groups, out-of-state students. ***Tuition waivers:*** Full or partial for minority students, children of alumni, employees or children of employees, adult students. ***ROTC:*** Army cooperative, Air Force cooperative.

LOANS ***Programs:*** FFEL (Subsidized and Unsubsidized Stafford, PLUS), Perkins.

WORK-STUDY Federal work-study jobs available.

APPLYING for FINANCIAL AID ***Required financial aid forms:*** FAFSA, state aid form. ***Financial aid deadline (priority):*** 4/15. ***Notification date:*** Continuous. Students must reply within 2 weeks of notification.

CONTACT Mr. W. G. Wyckoff, Director of Financial Aid, Mississippi University for Women, Box W-1614, Columbus, MS 39701-4044, 662-329-7114 or toll-free 877-GO 2 THE W. *Fax:* 662-241-7481. *E-mail:* bwyckoff@muw.edu

MISSISSIPPI VALLEY STATE UNIVERSITY

Itta Bena, MS

Tuition & fees (MS res): $2346 **Average undergraduate aid package: $8493**

ABOUT THE INSTITUTION State-supported, coed. Awards: bachelor's and master's degrees. 28 undergraduate majors. Total enrollment: 2,509. Undergraduates: 2,212. Freshmen: 560. Federal methodology is used as a basis for awarding need-based institutional aid.

UNDERGRADUATE EXPENSES for 1999–2000 ***Tuition, state resident:*** full-time $2126; part-time $110 per semester hour. ***Tuition, nonresident:*** full-time $4871; part-time $121 per semester hour. ***Required fees:*** full-time $220. Full-time tuition and fees vary according to course load. Part-time tuition and fees vary according to course load. ***College room and board:*** $2844. ***Payment plan:*** installment.

FRESHMAN FINANCIAL AID (Fall 1999) 429 applied for aid; of those 100% were deemed to have need. 100% of freshmen with need received aid; of those 96% had need fully met. *Average percent of need met:* 80% (excluding resources awarded to replace EFC). *Average financial aid package:* $8493 (excluding resources awarded to replace EFC). 14% of all full-time freshmen had no need and received non-need-based aid.

UNDERGRADUATE FINANCIAL AID (Fall 1999) 1,602 applied for aid; of those 100% were deemed to have need. 100% of undergraduates with need received aid; of those 96% had need fully met. *Average percent of need met:* 80% (excluding resources awarded to replace EFC). *Average financial aid package:* $8493 (excluding resources awarded to replace EFC). 16% of all full-time undergraduates had no need and received non-need-based aid.

GIFT AID (NEED-BASED) ***Total amount:*** $5,853,548 (99% Federal, 1% institutional). ***Receiving aid:*** *Freshmen:* 68% (343); *all full-time undergraduates:* 67% (1,280). ***Average award:*** Freshmen: $3525; Undergraduates: $3525. ***Scholarships, grants, and awards:*** Federal Pell, FSEOG, state, private, college/university gift aid from institutional funds.

GIFT AID (NON-NEED-BASED) ***Total amount:*** $1,751,597 (8% Federal, 28% state, 59% institutional, 5% external sources). ***Receiving aid:*** *Freshmen:* 26% (132); *Undergraduates:* 26% (496). ***Scholarships, grants, and awards by category:*** *Academic Interests/Achievement:* general academic interests/achievements. *Creative Arts/Performance:* art/fine arts, journalism/publications, music. *Special Characteristics:* members of minority groups. ***Tuition waivers:*** Full or partial for children of alumni, employees or children of employees. ***ROTC:*** Army, Air Force.

LOANS ***Student loans:*** $9,747,071 (100% need-based). ***Average need-based loan:*** Freshmen: $4280; Undergraduates: $4280. ***Parent loans:*** $537,345 (100% non-need-based). ***Programs:*** Federal Direct (Unsubsidized Stafford, PLUS).

WORK-STUDY ***Federal work-study:*** *Total amount:* $454,999; jobs available. ***State or other work-study/employment:*** *Total amount:* $23,901 (100% need-based). Part-time jobs available.

ATHLETIC AWARDS *Total amount:* 608,684 (100% non-need-based).

APPLYING for FINANCIAL AID ***Required financial aid forms:*** FAFSA, institution's own form. ***Financial aid deadline (priority):*** 4/1. ***Notification date:*** 7/15.

CONTACT Mr. Darrell G. Boyd, Director of Student Financial Aid, Mississippi Valley State University, 14000 Highway 82W #7268, Itta Bena, MS 38941-1400, 601-254-3335 or toll-free 800-844-6885 (in-state). *Fax:* 601-254-7900. *E-mail:* dboyd@fielding.mvsu.edu

MISSOURI BAPTIST COLLEGE

St. Louis, MO

Tuition & fees: $9408 **Average undergraduate aid package: $4925**

ABOUT THE INSTITUTION Independent Southern Baptist, coed. Awards: associate and bachelor's degrees (also offers some graduate courses). 31 undergraduate majors. Total enrollment: 2,974. Undergraduates: 2,963. Both federal and institutional methodology are used as a basis for awarding need-based institutional aid.

UNDERGRADUATE EXPENSES for 1999–2000 ***Application fee:*** $25. ***Comprehensive fee:*** $13,888 includes full-time tuition ($9090), mandatory fees ($318), and room and board ($4480). Full-time tuition and fees vary according to course load, location, and program. ***Part-time tuition:*** $320 per credit hour. ***Part-time fees:*** $4 per credit hour; $15 per term part-time. Part-time tuition and fees vary according to course load and location. ***Payment plan:*** installment.

UNDERGRADUATE FINANCIAL AID (Fall 1998) 1,080 applied for aid; of those 100% were deemed to have need. 100% of undergraduates with need received aid; of those 1% had need fully met. *Average percent of need met:* 36% (excluding resources awarded to replace EFC). *Average financial aid package:* $4925 (excluding resources awarded to replace EFC).

GIFT AID (NEED-BASED) ***Total amount:*** $994,791 (49% Federal, 14% state, 37% institutional). ***Receiving aid:*** *All full-time undergraduates:* 660. ***Average award:*** Undergraduates: $3920. ***Scholarships, grants, and awards:*** Federal Pell, FSEOG, state, private, college/university gift aid from institutional funds.

GIFT AID (NON-NEED-BASED) ***Total amount:*** $1,203,711 (5% state, 84% institutional, 11% external sources). ***Receiving aid:*** *Undergraduates:* 160. ***Scholarships, grants, and awards by category:*** *Academic Interests/Achievement:* 410 awards ($973,173 total): general academic interests/achievements, religion/biblical studies. *Creative Arts/Performance:* 42 awards ($40,860 total): music. *Special Achievements/Activities:* 7 awards ($5375

Missouri Baptist College (continued)

total): cheerleading/drum major, religious involvement. *Special Characteristics:* 397 awards ($497,553 total): children and siblings of alumni, children of current students, children of faculty/staff, parents of current students, public servants, relatives of clergy, religious affiliation, siblings of current students. ***Tuition waivers:*** Full or partial for children of alumni, employees or children of employees, senior citizens. ***ROTC:*** Army cooperative.

LOANS ***Student loans:*** $2,447,624 (100% need-based). ***Average need-based loan:*** Undergraduates: $3557. ***Parent loans:*** $88,663 (100% need-based). ***Programs:*** FFEL (Subsidized and Unsubsidized Stafford, PLUS).

WORK-STUDY ***Federal work-study:*** *Total amount:* $56,685; 50 jobs averaging $1134. ***State or other work-study/employment:*** *Total amount:* $190,316 (100% non-need-based). 50 part-time jobs averaging $3806.

ATHLETIC AWARDS *Total amount:* 893,244 (100% non-need-based).

APPLYING for FINANCIAL AID ***Required financial aid forms:*** FAFSA, institution's own form. ***Financial aid deadline:*** 11/15. ***Notification date:*** Continuous. Students must reply within 2 weeks of notification.

CONTACT Bob Miller, Director of Financial Aid, Missouri Baptist College, 1 College Park Drive, St. Louis, MO 63141-8698, 314-434-1115 Ext. 4151 or toll-free 877-434-1115 Ext. 2290. *Fax:* 314-434-7596. *E-mail:* millerb@mobap.edu

MISSOURI SOUTHERN STATE COLLEGE

Joplin, MO

Tuition & fees (MO res): $2496 **Average undergraduate aid package: $3354**

ABOUT THE INSTITUTION State-supported, coed. Awards: associate and bachelor's degrees. 61 undergraduate majors. Total enrollment: 5,651. Undergraduates: 5,651. Freshmen: 950. Federal methodology is used as a basis for awarding need-based institutional aid.

UNDERGRADUATE EXPENSES for 2000–2001 ***Application fee:*** $15. ***One-time required fee:*** $15. ***Tuition, state resident:*** full-time $2370; part-time $79 per credit. ***Tuition, nonresident:*** full-time $4740; part-time $158 per credit. ***Required fees:*** full-time $126; $43 per term part-time. Full-time tuition and fees vary according to course load. ***College room and board:*** $3610; ***room only:*** $2410. Room and board charges vary according to housing facility. ***Payment plan:*** deferred payment.

FRESHMAN FINANCIAL AID (Fall 1999, est.) 813 applied for aid; of those 84% were deemed to have need. 100% of freshmen with need received aid; of those 7% had need fully met. *Average percent of need met:* 85% (excluding resources awarded to replace EFC). *Average financial aid package:* $3667 (excluding resources awarded to replace EFC).

UNDERGRADUATE FINANCIAL AID (Fall 1999, est.) 3,761 applied for aid; of those 76% were deemed to have need. 100% of undergraduates with need received aid; of those 7% had need fully met. *Average percent of need met:* 82% (excluding resources awarded to replace EFC). *Average financial aid package:* $3354 (excluding resources awarded to replace EFC).

GIFT AID (NEED-BASED) ***Total amount:*** $3,638,844 (94% Federal, 6% state). ***Receiving aid:*** *Freshmen:* 53% (429); *all full-time undergraduates:* 40% (1,510). ***Average award:*** Freshmen: $1836; Undergraduates: $1986. ***Scholarships, grants, and awards:*** Federal Pell, FSEOG, state.

GIFT AID (NON-NEED-BASED) ***Total amount:*** $2,175,668 (13% state, 47% institutional, 40% external sources). ***Receiving aid:*** *Freshmen:* 42% (342); *Undergraduates:* 26% (986). ***Scholarships, grants, and awards by category:*** *Academic Interests/Achievement:* 625 awards ($1,005,353 total): general academic interests/achievements. *Creative Arts/Performance:* 188 awards ($148,814 total): art/fine arts, debating, journalism/publications, music, theater/drama. *Special Achievements/Activities:* 32 awards ($20,859 total): general special achievements/activities. *Special Characteristics:* 97 awards ($78,777 total): children of faculty/staff. ***Tuition waivers:*** Full or partial for employees or children of employees, senior citizens.

LOANS ***Student loans:*** $7,322,238 (100% need-based). 54% of past graduating class borrowed through all loan programs. Average indebtedness per student: $11,571. ***Average need-based loan:*** Freshmen: $1703; Undergraduates: $2949. ***Parent loans:*** $83,651 (100% non-need-based). ***Programs:*** Federal Direct (Subsidized and Unsubsidized Stafford, PLUS), Perkins, state.

WORK-STUDY ***Federal work-study:*** *Total amount:* $217,843; 146 jobs averaging $1492. ***State or other work-study/employment:*** *Total amount:* $540,177 (100% non-need-based). 408 part-time jobs averaging $1324.

ATHLETIC AWARDS *Total amount:* 596,034 (100% non-need-based).

APPLYING for FINANCIAL AID ***Required financial aid form:*** FAFSA. ***Financial aid deadline (priority):*** 2/15. ***Notification date:*** Continuous. Students must reply within 2 weeks of notification.

CONTACT Mr. James E. Gilbert, Director of Financial Aid, Missouri Southern State College, 3950 East Newman Road, Joplin, MO 64801-1595, 417-625-9325 or toll-free 800-606-MSSC. *Fax:* 417-625-3121. *E-mail:* gilbert-j@mail.mssc.edu

MISSOURI TECH

St. Louis, MO

Tuition & fees: $8850 **Average undergraduate aid package: N/A**

ABOUT THE INSTITUTION Proprietary, coed. Awards: associate and bachelor's degrees. 4 undergraduate majors. Total enrollment: 229. Undergraduates: 229. Both federal and institutional methodology are used as a basis for awarding need-based institutional aid.

UNDERGRADUATE EXPENSES for 1999–2000 ***Tuition:*** full-time $8850; part-time $295 per credit hour. Full-time tuition and fees vary according to course load. Part-time tuition and fees vary according to course load.

GIFT AID (NEED-BASED) ***Scholarships, grants, and awards:*** Federal Pell, private, college/university gift aid from institutional funds.

GIFT AID (NON-NEED-BASED) ***Scholarships, grants, and awards by category:*** *Academic Interests/Achievement:* general academic interests/achievements.

LOANS ***Programs:*** FFEL (Subsidized and Unsubsidized Stafford, PLUS), college/university.

APPLYING for FINANCIAL AID ***Required financial aid forms:*** FAFSA, institution's own form. ***Financial aid deadline:*** Continuous. ***Notification date:*** Continuous.

CONTACT Ms. Elizabeth Voyles, Director of Financial Aid, Missouri Tech, 1167 Corporate Lake Drive, St. Louis, MO 63132-1716, 314-569-3600 or toll-free 800-230-3600 (out-of-state). *Fax:* 314-569-1167.

MISSOURI VALLEY COLLEGE

Marshall, MO

Tuition & fees: $11,900 **Average undergraduate aid package: N/A**

ABOUT THE INSTITUTION Independent religious, coed. Awards: associate and bachelor's degrees. 36 undergraduate majors. Total enrollment: 1,569. Undergraduates: 1,569. Freshmen: 474. Federal methodology is used as a basis for awarding need-based institutional aid.

UNDERGRADUATE EXPENSES for 2000–2001 ***Application fee:*** $10. ***Comprehensive fee:*** $16,900 includes full-time tuition ($11,500), mandatory fees ($400), and room and board ($5000). ***Payment plan:*** installment.

GIFT AID (NEED-BASED) ***Total amount:*** $9,477,425 (17% Federal, 6% state, 77% institutional). ***Scholarships, grants, and awards:*** Federal Pell, FSEOG, state, private, college/university gift aid from institutional funds.

GIFT AID (NON-NEED-BASED) ***Total amount:*** $1,465,675 (87% institutional, 13% external sources). ***Scholarships, grants, and awards by category:*** *Special Achievements/Activities:* general special achievements/activities. ***Tuition waivers:*** Full or partial for children of alumni, employees or children of employees, senior citizens.

LOANS ***Student loans:*** $3,836,352 (100% need-based). 84% of past graduating class borrowed through all loan programs. Average indebtedness per student: $15,300. ***Parent loans:*** $192,182 (100% need-based). ***Programs:*** FFEL (Subsidized and Unsubsidized Stafford, PLUS), Perkins.

WORK-STUDY ***Federal work-study:*** *Total amount:* $183,448; 136 jobs averaging $1349. ***State or other work-study/employment:*** *Total amount:* $1,045,665 (87% need-based, 13% non-need-based). 975 part-time jobs averaging $1084.

APPLYING for FINANCIAL AID ***Required financial aid form:*** FAFSA. ***Financial aid deadline:*** 9/15 (priority: 3/20). ***Notification date:*** Continuous. Students must reply within 4 weeks of notification.

CONTACT Bette Gorrell, Director of Financial Aid, Missouri Valley College, 500 East College, Marshall, MO 65340-3197, 660-831-4176.

MISSOURI WESTERN STATE COLLEGE

St. Joseph, MO

Tuition & fees (MO res): $2774 **Average undergraduate aid package: N/A**

ABOUT THE INSTITUTION State-supported, coed. Awards: associate and bachelor's degrees. 38 undergraduate majors. Total enrollment: 5,157. Undergraduates: 5,157. Freshmen: 1,060. Federal methodology is used as a basis for awarding need-based institutional aid.

UNDERGRADUATE EXPENSES for 1999–2000 ***Application fee:*** $15. ***One-time required fee:*** $15. ***Tuition, state resident:*** full-time $2622; part-time $96 per hour. ***Tuition, nonresident:*** full-time $4830; part-time $171 per hour. ***Required fees:*** full-time $152; $5 per hour; $10 per term part-time. ***College room and board:*** $3600. Room and board charges vary according to board plan and housing facility. ***Payment plans:*** installment, deferred payment.

FRESHMAN FINANCIAL AID (Fall 1998) *Average financial aid package:* $3566 (excluding resources awarded to replace EFC).

GIFT AID (NEED-BASED) ***Total amount:*** $5,628,839 (71% Federal, 3% state, 17% institutional, 9% external sources). ***Scholarships, grants, and awards:*** Federal Pell, FSEOG, state, private, college/university gift aid from institutional funds.

GIFT AID (NON-NEED-BASED) ***Total amount:*** $544,693 (23% state, 77% institutional). ***Scholarships, grants, and awards by category:*** *Academic Interests/Achievement:* biological sciences, business, communication, computer science, education, engineering/technologies, English, general academic interests/achievements, health fields, humanities, mathematics, military science, physical sciences, social sciences. *Creative Arts/Performance:* art/fine arts, dance, music. *Special Achievements/Activities:* cheerleading/drum major, community service, general special achievements/activities, leadership. *Special Characteristics:* children of faculty/staff, members of minority groups, out-of-state students. ***Tuition waivers:*** Full or partial for employees or children of employees, senior citizens. ***ROTC:*** Army.

LOANS ***Student loans:*** $9,838,277 (66% need-based, 34% non-need-based). 68% of past graduating class borrowed through all loan programs. Average indebtedness per student: $15,150. ***Parent loans:*** $250,728 (100% need-based). ***Programs:*** FFEL (Subsidized and Unsubsidized Stafford, PLUS), Perkins, college/university.

WORK-STUDY ***Federal work-study:*** *Total amount:* $290,482; 307 jobs available. ***State or other work-study/employment:*** *Total amount:* $1,239,740 (100% need-based). 537 part-time jobs available.

ATHLETIC AWARDS *Total amount:* 565,335 (100% need-based).

APPLYING for FINANCIAL AID ***Required financial aid forms:*** FAFSA, institution's own form, state aid form. ***Financial aid deadline (priority):*** 3/1. ***Notification date:*** Continuous beginning 3/2. Students must reply within 3 weeks of notification.

CONTACT Robert Berger, Director of Financial Aid, Missouri Western State College, 4525 Downs Drive, St. Joseph, MO 64507-2294, 816-271-4361 or toll-free 800-662-7041 Ext. 60. *Fax:* 816-271-5833.

MOLLOY COLLEGE

Rockville Centre, NY

ABOUT THE INSTITUTION Independent, coed. Awards: associate, bachelor's, and master's degrees and post-master's certificates. 44 undergraduate majors. Total enrollment: 2,347. Undergraduates: 1,920. Freshmen: 225.

GIFT AID (NEED-BASED) ***Scholarships, grants, and awards:*** Federal Pell, FSEOG, state, private, college/university gift aid from institutional funds.

GIFT AID (NON-NEED-BASED) ***Scholarships, grants, and awards by category:*** *Academic Interests/Achievement:* general academic interests/achievements. *Creative Arts/Performance:* art/fine arts, music, performing arts. *Special Characteristics:* ethnic background, siblings of current students.

LOANS ***Programs:*** FFEL (Subsidized and Unsubsidized Stafford, PLUS), Perkins, Federal Nursing.

WORK-STUDY Federal work-study jobs available.

APPLYING for FINANCIAL AID ***Required financial aid forms:*** FAFSA, institution's own form, CSS Financial Aid PROFILE.

CONTACT Financial Aid Office, Molloy College, 1000 Hempstead Avenue, PO Box 5002, Rockville Centre, NY 11571-5002, 516-678-5000 or toll-free 888-4MOLLOY.

MONMOUTH COLLEGE

Monmouth, IL

Tuition & fees: $15,720 **Average undergraduate aid package: N/A**

ABOUT THE INSTITUTION Independent religious, coed. Awards: bachelor's degrees. 37 undergraduate majors. Total enrollment: 1,057. Undergraduates: 1,057. Freshmen: 274. Federal methodology is used as a basis for awarding need-based institutional aid.

UNDERGRADUATE EXPENSES for 1999–2000 ***Comprehensive fee:*** $20,130 includes full-time tuition ($15,720) and room and board ($4410). ***College room only:*** $2410. Room and board charges vary according to board plan and housing facility. ***Part-time tuition:*** $655 per semester hour. ***Payment plan:*** installment.

GIFT AID (NEED-BASED) ***Scholarships, grants, and awards:*** Federal Pell, FSEOG, state, private, college/university gift aid from institutional funds.

GIFT AID (NON-NEED-BASED) ***Scholarships, grants, and awards by category:*** *Academic Interests/Achievement:* general academic interests/achievements. *Creative Arts/Performance:* art/fine arts, music, theater/drama. ***Tuition waivers:*** Full or partial for employees or children of employees. ***ROTC:*** Army cooperative.

LOANS ***Programs:*** FFEL (Subsidized and Unsubsidized Stafford, PLUS), Perkins.

WORK-STUDY Federal work-study jobs available.

APPLYING for FINANCIAL AID ***Required financial aid form:*** FAFSA. ***Financial aid deadline (priority):*** 4/15. ***Notification date:*** Continuous.

CONTACT Ms. Jayne Whiteside, Director of Financial Aid, Monmouth College, 700 East Broadway, Monmouth, IL 61462-1998, 309-457-2129 or toll-free 800-747-2687. *Fax:* 309-457-2152.

MONMOUTH UNIVERSITY

West Long Branch, NJ

Tuition & fees: $15,686 **Average undergraduate aid package: $11,181**

ABOUT THE INSTITUTION Independent, coed. Awards: associate, bachelor's, and master's degrees and post-master's certificates. 33 undergraduate majors. Total enrollment: 5,425. Undergraduates: 4,004. Freshmen: 836. Federal methodology is used as a basis for awarding need-based institutional aid.

UNDERGRADUATE EXPENSES for 1999–2000 ***Application fee:*** $35. ***Comprehensive fee:*** $22,162 includes full-time tuition ($15,138), mandatory fees ($548), and room and board ($6476). ***College room only:*** $3376. Room and board charges vary according to board plan and housing facility. ***Part-time tuition:*** $438 per credit. ***Part-time fees:*** $137 per term part-time. ***Payment plan:*** installment.

FRESHMAN FINANCIAL AID (Fall 1998) 701 applied for aid; of those 88% were deemed to have need. 98% of freshmen with need received aid; of those 13% had need fully met. *Average percent of need met:* 39% (excluding resources awarded to replace EFC). *Average financial aid package:* $10,242 (excluding resources awarded to replace EFC). 20% of all full-time freshmen had no need and received non-need-based aid.

Monmouth University (continued)

UNDERGRADUATE FINANCIAL AID (Fall 1998) 2,488 applied for aid; of those 90% were deemed to have need. 99% of undergraduates with need received aid; of those 7% had need fully met. *Average percent of need met:* 42% (excluding resources awarded to replace EFC). *Average financial aid package:* $11,181 (excluding resources awarded to replace EFC). 27% of all full-time undergraduates had no need and received non-need-based aid.

GIFT AID (NEED-BASED) ***Total amount:*** $7,056,824 (28% Federal, 66% state, 3% institutional, 3% external sources). ***Receiving aid:*** *Freshmen:* 40% (333); *all full-time undergraduates:* 37% (1,259). ***Average award:*** Freshmen: $6450; Undergraduates: $6250. ***Scholarships, grants, and awards:*** Federal Pell, FSEOG, state, private, college/university gift aid from institutional funds.

GIFT AID (NON-NEED-BASED) ***Total amount:*** $8,902,898 (97% institutional, 3% external sources). ***Receiving aid:*** *Freshmen:* 59% (491); *Undergraduates:* 55% (1,861). ***Scholarships, grants, and awards by category:*** *Academic Interests/Achievement:* general academic interests/achievements. *Special Characteristics:* adult students, children and siblings of alumni, children of faculty/staff, general special characteristics, international students, out-of-state students. ***Tuition waivers:*** Full or partial for employees or children of employees, senior citizens.

LOANS ***Student loans:*** $9,745,740 (70% need-based, 30% non-need-based). 45% of past graduating class borrowed through all loan programs. Average indebtedness per student: $18,750. ***Average need-based loan:*** Freshmen: $2842; Undergraduates: $4100. ***Parent loans:*** $7,446,965 (100% non-need-based). ***Programs:*** Federal Direct (Subsidized and Unsubsidized Stafford, PLUS), Perkins, state, college/university.

WORK-STUDY ***Federal work-study:*** *Total amount:* $216,227; jobs available.

ATHLETIC AWARDS *Total amount:* 1,359,315 (100% non-need-based).

APPLYING for FINANCIAL AID ***Required financial aid form:*** FAFSA. ***Financial aid deadline:*** Continuous. ***Notification date:*** Continuous beginning 2/1. Students must reply within 2 weeks of notification.

CONTACT Financial Aid Office, Monmouth University, 400 Cedar Avenue, West Long Branch, NJ 07764-1898, 732-571-3463 or toll-free 800-543-9671 (out-of-state).

MONTANA STATE UNIVERSITY–BILLINGS

Billings, MT

Tuition & fees (MT res): $2922 **Average undergraduate aid package: $4877**

ABOUT THE INSTITUTION State-supported, coed. Awards: associate, bachelor's, and master's degrees. 48 undergraduate majors. Total enrollment: 4,279. Undergraduates: 3,873. Freshmen: 777. Federal methodology is used as a basis for awarding need-based institutional aid.

UNDERGRADUATE EXPENSES for 1999–2000 ***Application fee:*** $30. ***One-time required fee:*** $5. ***Tuition, state resident:*** full-time $2922; part-time $696 per term. ***Tuition, nonresident:*** full-time $7885; part-time $1,841 per term. Full-time tuition and fees vary according to course load and reciprocity agreements. Part-time tuition and fees vary according to course load and reciprocity agreements. ***College room and board:*** $4200. Room and board charges vary according to board plan and housing facility. ***Payment plan:*** installment.

FRESHMAN FINANCIAL AID (Fall 1999, est.) 538 applied for aid; of those 87% were deemed to have need. 94% of freshmen with need received aid; of those 18% had need fully met. *Average percent of need met:* 67% (excluding resources awarded to replace EFC). *Average financial aid package:* $4100 (excluding resources awarded to replace EFC). 13% of all full-time freshmen had no need and received non-need-based aid.

UNDERGRADUATE FINANCIAL AID (Fall 1999, est.) 2,277 applied for aid; of those 88% were deemed to have need. 95% of undergraduates with need received aid; of those 22% had need fully met. *Average percent of need met:* 71% (excluding resources awarded to replace EFC). *Average financial aid package:* $4877 (excluding resources awarded to replace EFC). 11% of all full-time undergraduates had no need and received non-need-based aid.

GIFT AID (NEED-BASED) ***Receiving aid:*** *Freshmen:* 47% (316); *all full-time undergraduates:* 49% (1,460). ***Average award:*** Freshmen: $2124; Undergraduates: $2299. ***Scholarships, grants, and awards:*** Federal Pell, FSEOG, state, private, college/university gift aid from institutional funds.

GIFT AID (NON-NEED-BASED) ***Receiving aid:*** *Freshmen:* 20% (130); *Undergraduates:* 13% (378). ***Scholarships, grants, and awards by category:*** *Academic Interests/Achievement:* biological sciences, business, communication, education, English, general academic interests/achievements, humanities, mathematics, social sciences. *Creative Arts/Performance:* art/fine arts, music, theater/drama. *Special Achievements/Activities:* general special achievements/activities. *Special Characteristics:* children and siblings of alumni, children of faculty/staff, children of union members/company employees, ethnic background, local/state students, out-of-state students. ***Tuition waivers:*** Full or partial for employees or children of employees, senior citizens.

LOANS ***Student loans:*** Average indebtedness per student: $13,555. ***Average need-based loan:*** Freshmen: $2289; Undergraduates: $3199. ***Programs:*** FFEL (Subsidized and Unsubsidized Stafford, PLUS), Perkins, college/university.

WORK-STUDY Federal work-study jobs available. ***State or other work-study/employment:*** Part-time jobs available.

APPLYING for FINANCIAL AID ***Required financial aid form:*** FAFSA. ***Financial aid deadline (priority):*** 3/1. ***Notification date:*** 5/1. Students must reply within 3 weeks of notification.

CONTACT Director of Financial Aid, Montana State University–Billings, 1500 North 30th Street, Billings, MT 59101, 406-657-2188 or toll-free 800-565-6782. *E-mail:* mhawkins@msubillings.edu

MONTANA STATE UNIVERSITY–BOZEMAN

Bozeman, MT

Tuition & fees (MT res): $2965 **Average undergraduate aid package: $6141**

ABOUT THE INSTITUTION State-supported, coed. Awards: bachelor's, master's, and doctoral degrees. 48 undergraduate majors. Total enrollment: 11,658. Undergraduates: 10,458. Freshmen: 2,015. Federal methodology is used as a basis for awarding need-based institutional aid.

UNDERGRADUATE EXPENSES for 1999–2000 ***Application fee:*** $30. ***Tuition, state resident:*** full-time $2965; part-time $91 per credit. ***Tuition, nonresident:*** full-time $8715; part-time $327 per credit. Full-time tuition and fees vary according to course load and reciprocity agreements. Part-time tuition and fees vary according to course load and reciprocity agreements. ***College room and board:*** $4650. Room and board charges vary according to board plan and housing facility. ***Payment plans:*** installment, deferred payment.

FRESHMAN FINANCIAL AID (Fall 1999, est.) 1313 applied for aid; of those 75% were deemed to have need. 96% of freshmen with need received aid; of those 34% had need fully met. *Average percent of need met:* 82% (excluding resources awarded to replace EFC). *Average financial aid package:* $5841 (excluding resources awarded to replace EFC). 22% of all full-time freshmen had no need and received non-need-based aid.

UNDERGRADUATE FINANCIAL AID (Fall 1999, est.) 5,652 applied for aid; of those 82% were deemed to have need. 97% of undergraduates with need received aid; of those 40% had need fully met. *Average percent of need met:* 82% (excluding resources awarded to replace EFC). *Average financial aid package:* $6141 (excluding resources awarded to replace EFC). 16% of all full-time undergraduates had no need and received non-need-based aid.

GIFT AID (NEED-BASED) ***Total amount:*** $9,205,504 (70% Federal, 6% state, 11% institutional, 13% external sources). ***Receiving aid:*** *Freshmen:* 37% (707); *all full-time undergraduates:* 38% (3,407). ***Average award:*** Freshmen: $2509; Undergraduates: $2552. ***Scholarships, grants, and awards:*** Federal Pell, FSEOG, state, private, college/university gift aid from institutional funds, Federal Nursing.

GIFT AID (NON-NEED-BASED) ***Total amount:*** $1,736,563 (42% institutional, 58% external sources). ***Receiving aid:*** *Freshmen:* 4% (71); *Undergraduates:* 2% (177). ***Scholarships, grants, and awards by category:*** *Academic Interests/Achievement:* agriculture, architecture, area/ethnic studies, biological sciences, business, communication, computer science, education, engineering/technologies, English, foreign languages, general academic interests/achievements, health fields, home economics, humanities, mathematics, military science, physical sciences, social sciences. *Creative Arts/Performance:* art/fine arts, cinema/film/broadcasting, dance, music, theater/drama. ***Tuition waivers:*** Full or partial for minority students, employees or children of employees, senior citizens. ***ROTC:*** Army, Air Force.

LOANS ***Student loans:*** $28,233,299 (74% need-based, 26% non-need-based). 70% of past graduating class borrowed through all loan programs. Average indebtedness per student: $17,000. ***Average need-based loan:*** Freshmen: $3815; Undergraduates: $4283. ***Parent loans:*** $2,783,199 (17% need-based, 83% non-need-based). ***Programs:*** Federal Direct (Subsidized and Unsubsidized Stafford, PLUS), Perkins, Federal Nursing, college/university, Freeborn Loans.

WORK-STUDY ***Federal work-study:*** *Total amount:* $2,268,252; jobs available. ***State or other work-study/employment:*** *Total amount:* $53,975 (90% need-based, 10% non-need-based). Part-time jobs available.

ATHLETIC AWARDS *Total amount:* 1,924,775 (22% need-based, 78% non-need-based).

APPLYING for FINANCIAL AID ***Required financial aid form:*** FAFSA. ***Financial aid deadline (priority):*** 3/1. ***Notification date:*** Continuous beginning 4/1. Students must reply within 3 weeks of notification.

CONTACT Mr. James R. Craig, Director of Financial Aid Services, Montana State University–Bozeman, PO Box 174160, Bozeman, MT 59717-4160, 406-994-2845 or toll-free 888-MSU-CATS. *Fax:* 406-994-6962. *E-mail:* finaid@montana.edu

MONTANA STATE UNIVERSITY–NORTHERN

Havre, MT

Tuition & fees (MT res): $2691 **Average undergraduate aid package: N/A**

ABOUT THE INSTITUTION State-supported, coed. Awards: associate, bachelor's, and master's degrees. 29 undergraduate majors. Total enrollment: 1,704. Undergraduates: 1,487. Freshmen: 290. Federal methodology is used as a basis for awarding need-based institutional aid.

UNDERGRADUATE EXPENSES for 1999–2000 ***Application fee:*** $30. ***Tuition, state resident:*** full-time $2691; part-time $101 per credit. ***Tuition, nonresident:*** full-time $7857; part-time $286 per credit. Full-time tuition and fees vary according to course load, location, and reciprocity agreements. Part-time tuition and fees vary according to course load, location, and reciprocity agreements. ***College room and board:*** $3800. ***Payment plan:*** deferred payment.

GIFT AID (NEED-BASED) ***Scholarships, grants, and awards:*** Federal Pell, FSEOG, state, private, college/university gift aid from institutional funds.

GIFT AID (NON-NEED-BASED) ***Scholarships, grants, and awards by category:*** *Academic Interests/Achievement:* general academic interests/achievements. *Creative Arts/Performance:* art/fine arts. *Special Achievements/Activities:* community service, general special achievements/activities, hobbies/interests, memberships, rodeo. *Special Characteristics:* adult students, children and siblings of alumni, general special characteristics, international students, members of minority groups, out-of-state students, veterans. ***Tuition waivers:*** Full or partial for minority students, employees or children of employees, senior citizens.

LOANS ***Programs:*** FFEL (Subsidized and Unsubsidized Stafford, PLUS), Perkins, Federal Nursing, college/university, alternative loans.

WORK-STUDY Federal work-study jobs available. ***State or other work-study/employment:*** Part-time jobs available.

APPLYING for FINANCIAL AID ***Required financial aid form:*** FAFSA. ***Financial aid deadline (priority):*** 3/1.

CONTACT Office of Financial Aid, Montana State University–Northern, PO Box 7751, Havre, MT 59501, 406-265-3787 or toll-free 800-662-6132 (in-state).

MONTANA TECH OF THE UNIVERSITY OF MONTANA

Butte, MT

Tuition & fees (MT res): $2865 **Average undergraduate aid package: $6000**

ABOUT THE INSTITUTION State-supported, coed. Awards: associate, bachelor's, and master's degrees. 54 undergraduate majors. Total enrollment: 2,450. Undergraduates: 2,355. Freshmen: 378. Federal methodology is used as a basis for awarding need-based institutional aid.

UNDERGRADUATE EXPENSES for 1999–2000 ***Application fee:*** $30. ***Tuition, state resident:*** full-time $2865; part-time $711 per term. ***Tuition, nonresident:*** full-time $8162; part-time $2,035 per term. Full-time tuition and fees vary according to course level, course load, degree level, reciprocity agreements, and student level. Part-time tuition and fees vary according to course level, course load, degree level, reciprocity agreements, and student level. ***College room and board:*** $4090. Room and board charges vary according to housing facility. ***Payment plan:*** deferred payment.

FRESHMAN FINANCIAL AID (Fall 1999, est.) 200 applied for aid; of those 75% were deemed to have need. 93% of freshmen with need received aid; of those 50% had need fully met. *Average percent of need met:* 50% (excluding resources awarded to replace EFC). *Average financial aid package:* $4500 (excluding resources awarded to replace EFC). 9% of all full-time freshmen had no need and received non-need-based aid.

UNDERGRADUATE FINANCIAL AID (Fall 1999, est.) 1,500 applied for aid; of those 87% were deemed to have need. 92% of undergraduates with need received aid; of those 58% had need fully met. *Average percent of need met:* 60% (excluding resources awarded to replace EFC). *Average financial aid package:* $6000 (excluding resources awarded to replace EFC). 5% of all full-time undergraduates had no need and received non-need-based aid.

GIFT AID (NEED-BASED) ***Total amount:*** $1,790,000 (84% Federal, 8% state, 6% institutional, 2% external sources). ***Receiving aid:*** *Freshmen:* 29% (100); *all full-time undergraduates:* 47% (900). ***Average award:*** Freshmen: $1000; Undergraduates: $1000. ***Scholarships, grants, and awards:*** Federal Pell, FSEOG, state, private, college/university gift aid from institutional funds.

GIFT AID (NON-NEED-BASED) ***Total amount:*** $1,190,000 (71% institutional, 29% external sources). ***Receiving aid:*** *Freshmen:* 9% (30); *Undergraduates:* 5% (100). ***Scholarships, grants, and awards by category:*** *Academic Interests/Achievement:* business, computer science, engineering/technologies, general academic interests/achievements, health fields, mathematics, physical sciences. *Special Achievements/Activities:* general special achievements/activities. *Special Characteristics:* general special characteristics. ***Tuition waivers:*** Full or partial for minority students, employees or children of employees, senior citizens.

LOANS ***Student loans:*** $7,000,000 (71% need-based, 29% non-need-based). 70% of past graduating class borrowed through all loan programs. Average indebtedness per student: $11,500. ***Average need-based loan:*** Freshmen: $2500; Undergraduates: $5000. ***Parent loans:*** $50,000 (100% need-based). ***Programs:*** FFEL (Subsidized and Unsubsidized Stafford, PLUS), Perkins.

WORK-STUDY ***Federal work-study:*** *Total amount:* $175,000; 200 jobs available. ***State or other work-study/employment:*** *Total amount:* $125,000 (100% need-based). 75 part-time jobs averaging $1800.

ATHLETIC AWARDS *Total amount:* 250,000 (100% non-need-based).

APPLYING for FINANCIAL AID ***Required financial aid forms:*** FAFSA, institution's own form. ***Financial aid deadline (priority):*** 3/1. ***Notification date:*** Continuous beginning 4/15. Students must reply within 3 weeks of notification.

CONTACT Mike Richardson, Director of Financial Aid, Montana Tech of The University of Montana, West Park Street, Butte, MT 59701-8997, 406-496-4212 or toll-free 800-445-TECH Ext. 1. *Fax:* 406-496-4710.

NTCLAIR STATE UNIVERSITY

Upper Montclair, NJ

& fees (NJ res): $4320 **Average undergraduate aid package: $7191**

ABOUT THE INSTITUTION State-supported, coed. Awards: bachelor's, master's, and doctoral degrees. 78 undergraduate majors. Total enrollment: 12,757. Undergraduates: 9,742. Federal methodology is used as a basis for awarding need-based institutional aid.

UNDERGRADUATE EXPENSES for 1999–2000 ***Application fee:*** $40. ***Tuition, state resident:*** full-time $3365; part-time $105 per credit. ***Tuition, nonresident:*** full-time $5280; part-time $165 per credit. ***Required fees:*** full-time $955; $30 per credit. ***College room and board:*** $6212; ***room only:*** $4160. Room and board charges vary according to board plan and housing facility. ***Payment plan:*** installment.

FRESHMAN FINANCIAL AID (Fall 1998) 864 applied for aid; of those 79% were deemed to have need. 95% of freshmen with need received aid; of those 38% had need fully met. *Average percent of need met:* 70% (excluding resources awarded to replace EFC). *Average financial aid package:* $7197 (excluding resources awarded to replace EFC). 17% of all full-time freshmen had no need and received non-need-based aid.

UNDERGRADUATE FINANCIAL AID (Fall 1998) 4,529 applied for aid; of those 82% were deemed to have need. 97% of undergraduates with need received aid; of those 36% had need fully met. *Average percent of need met:* 67% (excluding resources awarded to replace EFC). *Average financial aid package:* $7191 (excluding resources awarded to replace EFC). 12% of all full-time undergraduates had no need and received non-need-based aid.

GIFT AID (NEED-BASED) ***Total amount:*** $11,239,425 (50% Federal, 50% state). ***Receiving aid:*** *Freshmen:* 6% (61); *all full-time undergraduates:* 4% (259). ***Average award:*** Freshmen: $1697; Undergraduates: $1255. ***Scholarships, grants, and awards:*** Federal Pell, FSEOG, state, college/university gift aid from institutional funds.

GIFT AID (NON-NEED-BASED) ***Total amount:*** $1,459,211 (35% state, 31% institutional, 34% external sources). ***Receiving aid:*** *Freshmen:* 7% (73); *Undergraduates:* 4% (317). ***Scholarships, grants, and awards by category:*** *Academic Interests/Achievement:* 320 awards ($980,231 total): general academic interests/achievements. ***Tuition waivers:*** Full or partial for employees or children of employees, senior citizens.

LOANS ***Student loans:*** $16,942,532 (62% need-based, 38% non-need-based). Average indebtedness per student: $11,198. ***Average need-based loan:*** Freshmen: $2368; Undergraduates: $3447. ***Parent loans:*** $4,573,366 (100% non-need-based). ***Programs:*** Federal Direct (Subsidized and Unsubsidized Stafford, PLUS), Perkins.

WORK-STUDY ***Federal work-study:*** *Total amount:* $388,706; 391 jobs averaging $994. ***State or other work-study/employment:*** *Total amount:* $1,166,177 (100% non-need-based). 592 part-time jobs averaging $1970.

APPLYING for FINANCIAL AID ***Required financial aid form:*** FAFSA. ***Financial aid deadline (priority):*** 3/1. ***Notification date:*** Continuous beginning 4/1. Students must reply within 2 weeks of notification.

CONTACT Bryan J. Terry, Director of Financial Aid, Montclair State University, Valley Road and Normal Avenue, Upper Montclair, NJ 07043-9987, 973-655-7022 or toll-free 800-331-9205. *Fax:* 973-655-7712. *E-mail:* terryb@donne.montclair.edu

MONTEREY INSTITUTE OF INTERNATIONAL STUDIES

Monterey, CA

Tuition & fees: $19,500 **Average undergraduate aid package: N/A**

ABOUT THE INSTITUTION Independent, coed. Awards: bachelor's and master's degrees. 1 undergraduate major. Total enrollment: 655. Undergraduates: 20. Federal methodology is used as a basis for awarding need-based institutional aid.

UNDERGRADUATE EXPENSES for 2000–2001 ***Application fee:*** $50. ***Tuition:*** full-time $19,500; part-time $820 per credit. ***Payment plan:*** installment.

UNDERGRADUATE FINANCIAL AID (Fall 1998) 19 applied for aid; of those 100% were deemed to have need. 100% of undergraduates with need received aid; of those 89% had need fully met. *Average percent of need met:* 99% (excluding resources awarded to replace EFC).

GIFT AID (NEED-BASED) ***Total amount:*** $158,252 (24% Federal, 13% state, 59% institutional, 4% external sources). ***Receiving aid:*** *All full-time undergraduates:* 82% (18). ***Scholarships, grants, and awards:*** Federal Pell, FSEOG, state, private, college/university gift aid from institutional funds.

GIFT AID (NON-NEED-BASED) ***Total amount:*** $9100 (100% institutional). ***Receiving aid:*** *Undergraduates:* 9% (2). ***Scholarships, grants, and awards by category:*** *Academic Interests/Achievement:* international studies. ***Tuition waivers:*** Full or partial for employees or children of employees.

LOANS ***Student loans:*** $140,000 (100% need-based). ***Programs:*** Federal Direct (Subsidized and Unsubsidized Stafford), Perkins.

WORK-STUDY ***Federal work-study:*** *Total amount:* $36,000; jobs available. ***State or other work-study/employment:*** *Total amount:* $22,000 (100% non-need-based). Part-time jobs available.

APPLYING for FINANCIAL AID ***Required financial aid form:*** FAFSA. ***Financial aid deadline (priority):*** 3/15. ***Notification date:*** Continuous beginning 3/20. Students must reply by 5/1 or within 6 weeks of notification.

CONTACT Mr. Michael E. Benson, Director of Financial Aid, Monterey Institute of International Studies, 425 Van Buren Street, Monterey, CA 93940, 831-647-4119 or toll-free 800-824-7235 (in-state). *Fax:* 831-647-4199. *E-mail:* mbenson@miis.edu

MONTREAT COLLEGE

Montreat, NC

Tuition & fees: $10,862 **Average undergraduate aid package: $9446**

ABOUT THE INSTITUTION Independent Presbyterian, coed. Awards: associate, bachelor's, and master's degrees. 36 undergraduate majors. Total enrollment: 1,054. Undergraduates: 992. Federal methodology is used as a basis for awarding need-based institutional aid.

UNDERGRADUATE EXPENSES for 1999–2000 ***Application fee:*** $15. ***Comprehensive fee:*** $15,274 includes full-time tuition ($10,862) and room and board ($4412). ***Part-time tuition:*** $240 per semester hour. ***Payment plan:*** installment.

FRESHMAN FINANCIAL AID (Fall 1998) 119 applied for aid; of those 76% were deemed to have need. 99% of freshmen with need received aid. *Average financial aid package:* $9227 (excluding resources awarded to replace EFC). 16% of all full-time freshmen had no need and received non-need-based aid.

UNDERGRADUATE FINANCIAL AID (Fall 1998) 1,117 applied for aid; of those 73% were deemed to have need. 100% of undergraduates with need received aid. *Average financial aid package:* $9446 (excluding resources awarded to replace EFC). 26% of all full-time undergraduates had no need and received non-need-based aid.

GIFT AID (NEED-BASED) ***Total amount:*** $3,296,563 (19% Federal, 44% state, 16% institutional, 21% external sources). ***Receiving aid:*** *Freshmen:* 61% (89); *all full-time undergraduates:* 66% (759). ***Average award:*** Freshmen: $4327; Undergraduates: $4343. ***Scholarships, grants, and awards:*** Federal Pell, FSEOG, state, private, college/university gift aid from institutional funds.

GIFT AID (NON-NEED-BASED) ***Total amount:*** $613,944 (47% state, 22% institutional, 31% external sources). ***Scholarships, grants, and awards by category:*** *Academic Interests/Achievement:* 106 awards ($219,085 total): general academic interests/achievements. *Creative Arts/Performance:* 27 awards ($19,099 total): art/fine arts, music, theater/drama. *Special Characteristics:* 20 awards ($118,956 total): children of faculty/staff, international students, local/state students, relatives of clergy. ***Tuition waivers:*** Full or partial for employees or children of employees, senior citizens.

LOANS ***Student loans:*** $4,254,262 (90% need-based, 10% non-need-based). 86% of past graduating class borrowed through all loan programs. Average indebtedness per student: $16,274. ***Average need-based loan:***

Freshmen: $3164; Undergraduates: $5651. ***Parent loans:*** $153,223 (84% need-based, 16% non-need-based). ***Programs:*** FFEL (Subsidized and Unsubsidized Stafford, PLUS), Perkins.

WORK-STUDY ***Federal work-study:*** *Total amount:* $24,489; 22 jobs averaging $1113. ***State or other work-study/employment:*** *Total amount:* $93,424 (91% need-based, 9% non-need-based). 84 part-time jobs averaging $1112.

ATHLETIC AWARDS *Total amount:* 363,274 (85% need-based, 15% non-need-based).

APPLYING for FINANCIAL AID ***Required financial aid forms:*** FAFSA, institution's own form, state aid form (for NC residents). ***Financial aid deadline (priority):*** 5/15. ***Notification date:*** Continuous. Students must reply within 2 weeks of notification.

CONTACT Ms. Wanda M. Olson, Director of Financial Aid, Montreat College, PO Box 1267, Montreat, NC 28757-1267, 828-669-8012 Ext. 3795 or toll-free 800-622-6968 (in-state). *Fax:* 828-669-0120. *E-mail:* wolson@montreat.edu

MONTSERRAT COLLEGE OF ART

Beverly, MA

Tuition & fees: $12,950 **Average undergraduate aid package: $8536**

ABOUT THE INSTITUTION Independent, coed. Awards: bachelor's degrees and post-bachelor's certificates. 8 undergraduate majors. Total enrollment: 386. Undergraduates: 386. Freshmen: 106. Federal methodology is used as a basis for awarding need-based institutional aid.

UNDERGRADUATE EXPENSES for 1999–2000 ***Application fee:*** $40. ***Tuition:*** full-time $12,550; part-time $418 per credit. ***Required fees:*** full-time $400; $48 per course. Full-time tuition and fees vary according to course load. Part-time tuition and fees vary according to course load. Room and board charges vary according to housing facility. ***Payment plan:*** installment.

FRESHMAN FINANCIAL AID (Fall 1999, est.) 83 applied for aid; of those 87% were deemed to have need. 100% of freshmen with need received aid; of those 3% had need fully met. *Average percent of need met:* 52% (excluding resources awarded to replace EFC). *Average financial aid package:* $7787 (excluding resources awarded to replace EFC). 37% of all full-time freshmen had no need and received non-need-based aid.

UNDERGRADUATE FINANCIAL AID (Fall 1999, est.) 253 applied for aid; of those 87% were deemed to have need. 100% of undergraduates with need received aid; of those 9% had need fully met. *Average percent of need met:* 60% (excluding resources awarded to replace EFC). *Average financial aid package:* $8536 (excluding resources awarded to replace EFC). 24% of all full-time undergraduates had no need and received non-need-based aid.

GIFT AID (NEED-BASED) ***Total amount:*** $705,487 (32% Federal, 13% state, 45% institutional, 10% external sources). ***Receiving aid:*** *Freshmen:* 48% (55); *all full-time undergraduates:* 56% (162). ***Average award:*** Freshmen: $3097; Undergraduates: $3163. ***Scholarships, grants, and awards:*** Federal Pell, FSEOG, state, private, college/university gift aid from institutional funds.

GIFT AID (NON-NEED-BASED) ***Total amount:*** $33,050 (86% institutional, 14% external sources). ***Scholarships, grants, and awards by category:*** *Creative Arts/Performance:* 47 awards ($127,429 total): applied art and design, art/fine arts. *Special Characteristics:* 2 awards ($1200 total): siblings of current students. ***Tuition waivers:*** Full or partial for employees or children of employees.

LOANS ***Student loans:*** $1,535,366 (79% need-based, 21% non-need-based). 95% of past graduating class borrowed through all loan programs. Average indebtedness per student: $11,000. ***Average need-based loan:*** Freshmen: $4447; Undergraduates: $5219. ***Parent loans:*** $610,964 (54% need-based, 46% non-need-based). ***Programs:*** FFEL (Subsidized and Unsubsidized Stafford, PLUS), state, alternative loans.

WORK-STUDY ***Federal work-study:*** *Total amount:* $33,484; 34 jobs averaging $984.

APPLYING for FINANCIAL AID ***Required financial aid form:*** FAFSA. ***Financial aid deadline (priority):*** 3/1. ***Notification date:*** Continuous beginning 4/15. Students must reply within 2 weeks of notification.

CONTACT Ms. Ellen Kayser, Director of Financial Aid, Montserrat College of Art, 23 Essex Street, PO Box 26, Beverly, MA 01915, 978-922-8222 or toll-free 800-836-0487. *Fax:* 978-922-4268. *E-mail:* ekayser@montserrat.edu

MOODY BIBLE INSTITUTE

Chicago, IL

Tuition & fees: $1225 **Average undergraduate aid package: $1146**

ABOUT THE INSTITUTION Independent nondenominational, coed. Awards: bachelor's, master's, and first professional degrees. 9 undergraduate majors. Total enrollment: 1,458. Undergraduates: 1,335. Freshmen: 210. Institutional methodology is used as a basis for awarding need-based institutional aid.

UNDERGRADUATE EXPENSES for 1999–2000 ***Application fee:*** $35. includes mandatory fees ($1225) and room and board ($4770). Room and board charges vary according to housing facility. ***Part-time fees:*** $630 per term part-time. ***Payment plan:*** installment.

FRESHMAN FINANCIAL AID (Fall 1999, est.) 20 applied for aid; of those 100% were deemed to have need. 100% of freshmen with need received aid. *Average percent of need met:* 75% (excluding resources awarded to replace EFC). *Average financial aid package:* $2250 (excluding resources awarded to replace EFC).

UNDERGRADUATE FINANCIAL AID (Fall 1999, est.) 400 applied for aid; of those 98% were deemed to have need. 100% of undergraduates with need received aid. *Average percent of need met:* 70% (excluding resources awarded to replace EFC). *Average financial aid package:* $1146 (excluding resources awarded to replace EFC). 7% of all full-time undergraduates had no need and received non-need-based aid.

GIFT AID (NEED-BASED) ***Total amount:*** $390,964 (100% institutional). ***Receiving aid:*** *All full-time undergraduates:* 24% (302). ***Average award:*** Undergraduates: $1131. ***Scholarships, grants, and awards:*** private, college/university gift aid from institutional funds.

GIFT AID (NON-NEED-BASED) ***Total amount:*** $124,260 (100% institutional). ***Receiving aid:*** *Freshmen:* 10% (20); *Undergraduates:* 2% (20). ***Scholarships, grants, and awards by category:*** *Academic Interests/Achievement:* 38 awards ($41,430 total): general academic interests/achievements. *Special Achievements/Activities:* 32 awards ($22,300 total): leadership. *Special Characteristics:* 20 awards ($44,250 total): members of minority groups. ***Tuition waivers:*** Full or partial for employees or children of employees.

LOANS ***Student loans:*** 5% of past graduating class borrowed through all loan programs. Average indebtedness per student: $10,000. ***Programs:*** alternative loans.

APPLYING for FINANCIAL AID ***Required financial aid form:*** institution's own form. ***Financial aid deadline:*** Continuous. ***Notification date:*** Continuous beginning 7/1. Students must reply by 8/15.

CONTACT Jennifer Dietrich, Student Grants Coordinator, Moody Bible Institute, 820 North LaSalle Boulevard, Chicago, IL 60610-3284, 312-329-4178 or toll-free 800-967-4MBI. *Fax:* 312-329-4197. *E-mail:* jdietric@moody.edu

MOORE COLLEGE OF ART AND DESIGN

Philadelphia, PA

Tuition & fees: $16,025 **Average undergraduate aid package: $13,345**

ABOUT THE INSTITUTION Independent, women only. Awards: bachelor's degrees. 14 undergraduate majors. Total enrollment: 495. Undergraduates: 495. Freshmen: 81. Federal methodology is used as a basis for awarding need-based institutional aid.

UNDERGRADUATE EXPENSES for 1999–2000 ***Application fee:*** $35. ***Comprehensive fee:*** $22,175 includes full-time tuition ($15,475), mandatory fees ($550), and room and board ($6150). ***Part-time tuition:*** $645 per credit. ***Part-time fees:*** $275 per term part-time. ***Payment plan:*** installment.

FRESHMAN FINANCIAL AID (Fall 1999, est.) 73 applied for aid; of those 89% were deemed to have need. 100% of freshmen with need received aid; of those 8% had need fully met. *Average percent of need met:* 69%

Moore College of Art and Design (continued)

(excluding resources awarded to replace EFC). *Average financial aid package:* $12,664 (excluding resources awarded to replace EFC). 19% of all full-time freshmen had no need and received non-need-based aid.

UNDERGRADUATE FINANCIAL AID (Fall 1999, est.) 334 applied for aid; of those 92% were deemed to have need. 100% of undergraduates with need received aid; of those 10% had need fully met. *Average percent of need met:* 70% (excluding resources awarded to replace EFC). *Average financial aid package:* $13,345 (excluding resources awarded to replace EFC). 25% of all full-time undergraduates had no need and received non-need-based aid.

GIFT AID (NEED-BASED) ***Total amount:*** $2,897,455 (16% Federal, 11% state, 72% institutional, 1% external sources). ***Receiving aid:*** *Freshmen:* 81% (65); *all full-time undergraduates:* 75% (308). ***Average award:*** Freshmen: $3590; Undergraduates: $3810. ***Scholarships, grants, and awards:*** Federal Pell, FSEOG, state, private, college/university gift aid from institutional funds.

GIFT AID (NON-NEED-BASED) ***Total amount:*** $281,276 (100% institutional). ***Receiving aid:*** *Freshmen:* 6% (5); *Undergraduates:* 1% (6). ***Scholarships, grants, and awards by category:*** *Academic Interests/Achievement:* general academic interests/achievements. *Creative Arts/Performance:* art/fine arts. ***Tuition waivers:*** Full or partial for employees or children of employees.

LOANS ***Student loans:*** $2,274,764 (100% need-based). 79% of past graduating class borrowed through all loan programs. Average indebtedness per student: $25,000. ***Average need-based loan:*** Freshmen: $2625; Undergraduates: $4615. ***Parent loans:*** $596,052 (100% need-based). ***Programs:*** FFEL (Subsidized and Unsubsidized Stafford, PLUS), Perkins.

WORK-STUDY ***Federal work-study:*** *Total amount:* $124,244; 87 jobs averaging $1428. ***State or other work-study/employment:*** *Total amount:* $11,717 (100% need-based). Part-time jobs available.

APPLYING for FINANCIAL AID ***Required financial aid form:*** FAFSA. ***Financial aid deadline (priority):*** 3/1. ***Notification date:*** Continuous. Students must reply within 2 weeks of notification.

CONTACT Rochelle Iannuzzi, Director of Financial Aid, Moore College of Art and Design, 20th and the Parkway, Philadelphia, PA 19103-1179, 215-568-4515 Ext. 4042 or toll-free 800-523-2025. *Fax:* 215-568-8017. *E-mail:* riannuzzi@moore.edu

MOORHEAD STATE UNIVERSITY

Moorhead, MN

See Minnesota State University Moorhead

MORAVIAN COLLEGE

Bethlehem, PA

Tuition & fees: $18,575 **Average undergraduate aid package: $15,040**

ABOUT THE INSTITUTION Independent religious, coed. Awards: bachelor's, master's, and first professional degrees. 40 undergraduate majors. Total enrollment: 1,782. Undergraduates: 1,703. Freshmen: 318. Both federal and institutional methodology are used as a basis for awarding need-based institutional aid.

UNDERGRADUATE EXPENSES for 1999–2000 ***Application fee:*** $30. ***Comprehensive fee:*** $24,495 includes full-time tuition ($18,245), mandatory fees ($330), and room and board ($5920). ***College room only:*** $3220. Room and board charges vary according to board plan and housing facility. ***Part-time tuition:*** $507 per credit. ***Part-time fees:*** $75 per term part-time. Part-time tuition and fees vary according to class time. ***Payment plan:*** installment.

FRESHMAN FINANCIAL AID (Fall 1999, est.) 295 applied for aid; of those 88% were deemed to have need. 100% of freshmen with need received aid; of those 23% had need fully met. *Average percent of need met:* 84% (excluding resources awarded to replace EFC). *Average financial aid package:* $14,898 (excluding resources awarded to replace EFC). 14% of all full-time freshmen had no need and received non-need-based aid.

UNDERGRADUATE FINANCIAL AID (Fall 1999, est.) 1,093 applied for aid; of those 90% were deemed to have need. 100% of undergraduates with need received aid; of those 29% had need fully met. *Average percent of need met:* 84% (excluding resources awarded to replace EFC). *Average financial aid package:* $15,040 (excluding resources awarded to replace EFC). 15% of all full-time undergraduates had no need and received non-need-based aid.

GIFT AID (NEED-BASED) ***Total amount:*** $9,329,279 (7% Federal, 13% state, 78% institutional, 2% external sources). ***Receiving aid:*** *Freshmen:* 81% (258); *all full-time undergraduates:* 82% (983). ***Average award:*** Freshmen: $10,561; Undergraduates: $9824. ***Scholarships, grants, and awards:*** Federal Pell, FSEOG, state, private, college/university gift aid from institutional funds.

GIFT AID (NON-NEED-BASED) ***Total amount:*** $1,063,175 (2% state, 86% institutional, 12% external sources). ***Receiving aid:*** *Freshmen:* 8% (25); *Undergraduates:* 7% (88). ***Scholarships, grants, and awards by category:*** *Academic Interests/Achievement:* foreign languages, general academic interests/achievements, physical sciences. *Creative Arts/Performance:* music. *Special Achievements/Activities:* religious involvement. *Special Characteristics:* adult students, children and siblings of alumni, children of educators, children of faculty/staff, ethnic background, international students, relatives of clergy, religious affiliation. ***Tuition waivers:*** Full or partial for employees or children of employees. ***ROTC:*** Army cooperative.

LOANS ***Student loans:*** $5,988,951 (74% need-based, 26% non-need-based). ***Average need-based loan:*** Freshmen: $3347; Undergraduates: $4434. ***Parent loans:*** $1,611,989 (37% need-based, 63% non-need-based). ***Programs:*** FFEL (Subsidized and Unsubsidized Stafford, PLUS), Perkins.

WORK-STUDY ***Federal work-study:*** *Total amount:* $756,567; jobs available. ***State or other work-study/employment:*** *Total amount:* $325,500 (6% need-based, 94% non-need-based). Part-time jobs available.

APPLYING for FINANCIAL AID ***Required financial aid forms:*** FAFSA, CSS Financial Aid PROFILE, state aid form, noncustodial (divorced/separated) parent's statement, business/farm supplement. ***Financial aid deadline (priority):*** 2/15. ***Notification date:*** 4/15. Students must reply by 5/1 or within 2 weeks of notification.

CONTACT Mr. Stephen C. Cassel, Director of Financial Aid, Moravian College, 1200 Main Street, Bethlehem, PA 18018-6650, 610-861-1330. *Fax:* 610-861-1346. *E-mail:* mescc01@moravian.edu

MOREHEAD STATE UNIVERSITY

Morehead, KY

Tuition & fees (KY res): $2440 **Average undergraduate aid package: $5252**

ABOUT THE INSTITUTION State-supported, coed. Awards: associate, bachelor's, and master's degrees and post-master's certificates. 56 undergraduate majors. Total enrollment: 8,160. Undergraduates: 6,638. Freshmen: 1,372. Federal methodology is used as a basis for awarding need-based institutional aid.

UNDERGRADUATE EXPENSES for 1999–2000 ***Tuition, state resident:*** full-time $2440; part-time $102 per credit hour. ***Tuition, nonresident:*** full-time $6480; part-time $270 per credit hour. ***College room and board:*** $3300. Room and board charges vary according to board plan and housing facility. ***Payment plans:*** installment, deferred payment.

FRESHMAN FINANCIAL AID (Fall 1999) 1137 applied for aid; of those 78% were deemed to have need. 100% of freshmen with need received aid; of those 32% had need fully met. *Average percent of need met:* 88% (excluding resources awarded to replace EFC). *Average financial aid package:* $4722 (excluding resources awarded to replace EFC). 28% of all full-time freshmen had no need and received non-need-based aid.

UNDERGRADUATE FINANCIAL AID (Fall 1999) 4,771 applied for aid; of those 84% were deemed to have need. 99% of undergraduates with need received aid; of those 42% had need fully met. *Average percent of need met:* 90% (excluding resources awarded to replace EFC). *Average financial aid package:* $5252 (excluding resources awarded to replace EFC). 22% of all full-time undergraduates had no need and received non-need-based aid.

GIFT AID (NEED-BASED) ***Total amount:*** $9,164,760 (78% Federal, 22% state). ***Receiving aid:*** *Freshmen:* 46% (616); *all full-time undergraduates:* 53% (2,949). ***Average award:*** Freshmen: $3015; Undergraduates: $3085. ***Scholarships, grants, and awards:*** Federal Pell, FSEOG, state, private, college/university gift aid from institutional funds.

GIFT AID (NON-NEED-BASED) ***Total amount:*** $4,190,150 (11% state, 73% institutional, 16% external sources). ***Receiving aid:*** *Freshmen:* 51% (672); *Undergraduates:* 25% (1,385). ***Scholarships, grants, and awards by category:*** *Academic Interests/Achievement:* 1,347 awards ($2,026,514 total): agriculture, business, general academic interests/achievements, physical sciences. *Creative Arts/Performance:* 109 awards ($78,300 total): art/fine arts, cinema/film/broadcasting, journalism/publications, music, theater/drama. *Special Achievements/Activities:* 251 awards ($171,670 total): cheerleading/drum major, leadership. *Special Characteristics:* 652 awards ($671,476 total): adult students, children and siblings of alumni, local/state students, members of minority groups, out-of-state students. ***Tuition waivers:*** Full or partial for employees or children of employees, senior citizens. ***ROTC:*** Army.

LOANS ***Student loans:*** $9,732,301 (57% need-based, 43% non-need-based). 59% of past graduating class borrowed through all loan programs. Average indebtedness per student: $13,230. ***Average need-based loan:*** Freshmen: $2046; Undergraduates: $2514. ***Parent loans:*** $464,797 (100% non-need-based). ***Programs:*** Federal Direct (Subsidized and Unsubsidized Stafford, PLUS), Perkins, college/university.

WORK-STUDY ***Federal work-study:*** *Total amount:* $1,135,105; 820 jobs averaging $1402. ***State or other work-study/employment:*** *Total amount:* $529,350 (100% non-need-based). 606 part-time jobs available.

ATHLETIC AWARDS *Total amount:* 633,995 (100% non-need-based).

APPLYING for FINANCIAL AID ***Required financial aid forms:*** FAFSA, institution's own form, financial aid transcript (for transfers). ***Financial aid deadline (priority):*** 3/15. ***Notification date:*** Continuous.

CONTACT Mr. Tim P. Rhodes, Director of Financial Aid and Admissions, Morehead State University, 305 Howell-McDowell Administration Building, Morehead, KY 40351, 606-783-2011 or toll-free 800-585-6781. *Fax:* 606-783-2293. *E-mail:* t.rhodes@morehead-st.edu

MOREHOUSE COLLEGE

Atlanta, GA

ABOUT THE INSTITUTION Independent, men only. Awards: bachelor's degrees. 33 undergraduate majors. Total enrollment: 3,012. Undergraduates: 3,012. Freshmen: 748.

GIFT AID (NEED-BASED) ***Scholarships, grants, and awards:*** Federal Pell, FSEOG, state, United Negro College Fund.

GIFT AID (NON-NEED-BASED) ***Scholarships, grants, and awards by category:*** *Academic Interests/Achievement:* business, general academic interests/achievements, military science. *Creative Arts/Performance:* music. *Special Achievements/Activities:* community service, leadership, religious involvement. *Special Characteristics:* children of faculty/staff.

LOANS ***Programs:*** Federal Direct (Subsidized and Unsubsidized Stafford, PLUS), Perkins, Resource Loans.

WORK-STUDY Federal work-study jobs available.

APPLYING for FINANCIAL AID ***Required financial aid forms:*** FAFSA, state aid form.

CONTACT James A. Stotts, Acting Director of Financial Aid, Morehouse College, 830 Westview Drive, SW, Atlanta, GA 30314, 404-215-2638 or toll-free 800-851-1254. *Fax:* 404-215-2711. *E-mail:* jstotts@morehouse.edu

MORGAN STATE UNIVERSITY

Baltimore, MD

Tuition & fees (MD res): $3874 **Average undergraduate aid package: N/A**

ABOUT THE INSTITUTION State-supported, coed. Awards: bachelor's, master's, and doctoral degrees. 56 undergraduate majors. Total enrollment: 6,299. Undergraduates: 5,805. Both federal and institutional methodology are used as a basis for awarding need-based institutional aid.

UNDERGRADUATE EXPENSES for 1999–2000 ***Application fee:*** $25. ***Tuition, state resident:*** full-time $2906; part-time $131 per semester hour. ***Tuition, nonresident:*** full-time $8490; part-time $295 per semester hour. ***Required fees:*** full-time $968; $175 per term part-time. ***College room and board:*** $5718; ***room only:*** $3150. Room and board charges vary according to board plan and housing facility. ***Payment plans:*** installment, deferred payment.

GIFT AID (NEED-BASED) ***Scholarships, grants, and awards:*** Federal Pell, FSEOG, state, private, college/university gift aid from institutional funds.

GIFT AID (NON-NEED-BASED) ***Scholarships, grants, and awards by category:*** *Academic Interests/Achievement:* general academic interests/achievements. ***Tuition waivers:*** Full or partial for employees or children of employees, senior citizens. ***ROTC:*** Army.

LOANS ***Programs:*** Federal Direct (Subsidized and Unsubsidized Stafford, PLUS), Perkins.

WORK-STUDY Federal work-study jobs available. ***State or other work-study/employment:*** Part-time jobs available.

APPLYING for FINANCIAL AID ***Required financial aid forms:*** FAFSA, institution's own form, federal income tax form(s), financial aid transcript (for transfers). ***Financial aid deadline (priority):*** 4/1.

CONTACT Director of Financial Aid, Morgan State University, 1700 East Cold Spring Lane, Baltimore, MD 21251, 443-885-3170 or toll-free 800-332-6674.

MORNINGSIDE COLLEGE

Sioux City, IA

Tuition & fees: $13,146 **Average undergraduate aid package: $13,415**

ABOUT THE INSTITUTION Independent United Methodist, coed. Awards: bachelor's and master's degrees. 52 undergraduate majors. Total enrollment: 1,153. Undergraduates: 1,021. Freshmen: 164. Federal methodology is used as a basis for awarding need-based institutional aid.

UNDERGRADUATE EXPENSES for 1999–2000 ***Application fee:*** $15. ***Comprehensive fee:*** $17,782 includes full-time tuition ($12,800), mandatory fees ($346), and room and board ($4636). ***College room only:*** $2460. Room and board charges vary according to board plan and housing facility. ***Part-time tuition:*** $420 per semester hour. Part-time tuition and fees vary according to course load. ***Payment plan:*** installment.

FRESHMAN FINANCIAL AID (Fall 1999, est.) 163 applied for aid; of those 93% were deemed to have need. 100% of freshmen with need received aid; of those 64% had need fully met. *Average percent of need met:* 89% (excluding resources awarded to replace EFC). *Average financial aid package:* $13,740 (excluding resources awarded to replace EFC). 9% of all full-time freshmen had no need and received non-need-based aid.

UNDERGRADUATE FINANCIAL AID (Fall 1999, est.) 792 applied for aid; of those 93% were deemed to have need. 99% of undergraduates with need received aid; of those 59% had need fully met. *Average percent of need met:* 90% (excluding resources awarded to replace EFC). *Average financial aid package:* $13,415 (excluding resources awarded to replace EFC). 12% of all full-time undergraduates had no need and received non-need-based aid.

GIFT AID (NEED-BASED) ***Total amount:*** $3,688,850 (20% Federal, 46% state, 34% institutional). ***Receiving aid:*** *Freshmen:* 80% (137); *all full-time undergraduates:* 71% (628). ***Average award:*** Freshmen: $5948; Undergraduates: $4872. ***Scholarships, grants, and awards:*** Federal Pell, FSEOG, state, private, college/university gift aid from institutional funds.

GIFT AID (NON-NEED-BASED) ***Total amount:*** $2,905,169 (91% institutional, 9% external sources). ***Receiving aid:*** *Freshmen:* 82% (140); *Undergraduates:* 72% (635). ***Scholarships, grants, and awards by category:*** *Academic Interests/Achievement:* 506 awards ($1,480,380 total): biological sciences, business, communication, education, English, general academic interests/achievements, humanities, mathematics, premedicine, religion/biblical studies, social sciences. *Creative Arts/Performance:* 116 awards ($221,213 total): art/fine arts, cinema/film/broadcasting, journalism/publications, music, theater/drama. *Special Characteristics:* 697 awards

Morningside College (continued)

($861,533 total): adult students, children and siblings of alumni, children of faculty/staff, first-generation college students, international students, local/state students, relatives of clergy, religious affiliation. ***Tuition waivers:*** Full or partial for children of alumni, employees or children of employees, senior citizens.

LOANS ***Student loans:*** $3,723,254 (59% need-based, 41% non-need-based). 56% of past graduating class borrowed through all loan programs. Average indebtedness per student: $15,028. ***Average need-based loan:*** Freshmen: $2046; Undergraduates: $2946. ***Parent loans:*** $163,669 (100% non-need-based). ***Programs:*** FFEL (Subsidized and Unsubsidized Stafford, PLUS), Perkins, state, college/university, partnership loan (through Iowa Student Loan Liquidity Corporation).

WORK-STUDY ***Federal work-study:*** *Total amount:* $348,961; 353 jobs available. ***State or other work-study/employment:*** *Total amount:* $190,757 (14% need-based, 86% non-need-based). 150 part-time jobs averaging $1500.

ATHLETIC AWARDS *Total amount:* 1,340,892 (100% non-need-based).

APPLYING for FINANCIAL AID ***Required financial aid form:*** FAFSA. ***Financial aid deadline (priority):*** 3/1. ***Notification date:*** Continuous beginning 3/31. Students must reply within 2 weeks of notification.

CONTACT Karen K. Gagnon, Director of Student Financial Planning, Morningside College, 1501 Morningside Avenue, Sioux City, IA 51106, 712-274-5159 or toll-free 800-831-0806. *Fax:* 712-274-5101. *E-mail:* kkg001@alpha.morningside.edu

MORRIS BROWN COLLEGE

Atlanta, GA

CONTACT Student Financial Aid Director/Dean, Enrollment Management, Morris Brown College, 643 Martin Luther King Jr. Drive, NW, Atlanta, GA 30314-4140, 404-220-0270 Ext. 706.

MORRIS COLLEGE

Sumter, SC

ABOUT THE INSTITUTION Independent religious, coed. Awards: bachelor's degrees. 20 undergraduate majors. Total enrollment: 907. Undergraduates: 907. Freshmen: 264.

GIFT AID (NEED-BASED) ***Scholarships, grants, and awards:*** Federal Pell, FSEOG, state, private, college/university gift aid from institutional funds, United Negro College Fund.

GIFT AID (NON-NEED-BASED) ***Scholarships, grants, and awards by category:*** *Academic Interests/Achievement:* biological sciences, business, education, general academic interests/achievements, mathematics. *Creative Arts/Performance:* creative writing, music, performing arts.

LOANS ***Programs:*** Federal Direct (Subsidized and Unsubsidized Stafford, PLUS), Perkins.

WORK-STUDY Federal work-study jobs available.

APPLYING for FINANCIAL AID ***Required financial aid forms:*** FAFSA, institution's own form.

CONTACT Ms. Sandra S. Gibson, Director of Financial Aid, Morris College, 100 West College Street, Sumter, SC 29150-3599, 803-934-3238 or toll-free 888-775-1345. *Fax:* 803-773-3687.

MORRISON UNIVERSITY

Reno, NV

Tuition & fees: $5580	Average undergraduate aid package: N/A

ABOUT THE INSTITUTION Proprietary, coed. Awards: associate, bachelor's, and master's degrees. 9 undergraduate majors. Total enrollment: 150. Undergraduates: 150. Federal methodology is used as a basis for awarding need-based institutional aid.

UNDERGRADUATE EXPENSES for 1999–2000 ***Application fee:*** $25. ***One-time required fee:*** $75. ***Tuition:*** full-time $5580; part-time $155 per credit. Full-time tuition and fees vary according to degree level. ***Payment plans:*** guaranteed tuition, installment.

FRESHMAN FINANCIAL AID (Fall 1998) 22 applied for aid; of those 100% were deemed to have need. 100% of freshmen with need received aid; of those 82% had need fully met. *Average percent of need met:* 82% (excluding resources awarded to replace EFC).

UNDERGRADUATE FINANCIAL AID (Fall 1998) 129 applied for aid; of those 98% were deemed to have need. 100% of undergraduates with need received aid; of those 33% had need fully met. *Average percent of need met:* 71% (excluding resources awarded to replace EFC).

GIFT AID (NEED-BASED) ***Total amount:*** $123,172 (93% Federal, 7% institutional). ***Receiving aid:*** *Freshmen:* 38% (14); *all full-time undergraduates:* 39% (59). ***Scholarships, grants, and awards:*** Federal Pell, state.

GIFT AID (NON-NEED-BASED) ***Scholarships, grants, and awards by category:*** *Academic Interests/Achievement:* business. *Special Characteristics:* general special characteristics. ***Tuition waivers:*** Full or partial for employees or children of employees.

LOANS ***Student loans:*** $1,064,015 (53% need-based, 47% non-need-based). 58% of past graduating class borrowed through all loan programs. ***Parent loans:*** $25,572 (100% non-need-based). ***Programs:*** alternative loans.

APPLYING for FINANCIAL AID ***Required financial aid form:*** FAFSA. ***Financial aid deadline:*** Continuous. ***Notification date:*** Continuous.

CONTACT Linda M. Kuchenbecker, Director of Financial Aid, Morrison University, 140 Washington Street, Reno, NV 89503-5600, 775-323-4145 or toll-free 800-369-6144.

MOUNT ALOYSIUS COLLEGE

Cresson, PA

Tuition & fees: $10,980	Average undergraduate aid package: $4650

ABOUT THE INSTITUTION Independent Roman Catholic, coed. Awards: associate and bachelor's degrees. 24 undergraduate majors. Total enrollment: 1,221. Undergraduates: 1,221. Freshmen: 163. Federal methodology is used as a basis for awarding need-based institutional aid.

UNDERGRADUATE EXPENSES for 2000–2001 ***Application fee:*** $25. ***Comprehensive fee:*** $15,810 includes full-time tuition ($10,780), mandatory fees ($200), and room and board ($4830). ***College room only:*** $2140. Full-time tuition and fees vary according to program. Room and board charges vary according to board plan and housing facility. ***Part-time tuition:*** $385 per credit. ***Part-time fees:*** $50 per term part-time. Part-time tuition and fees vary according to class time, course level, course load, program, and student level.

FRESHMAN FINANCIAL AID (Fall 1999, est.) 164 applied for aid; of those 98% were deemed to have need. 100% of freshmen with need received aid. *Average percent of need met:* 80% (excluding resources awarded to replace EFC). *Average financial aid package:* $4650 (excluding resources awarded to replace EFC).

UNDERGRADUATE FINANCIAL AID (Fall 1999, est.) 789 applied for aid; of those 99% were deemed to have need. 100% of undergraduates with need received aid. *Average percent of need met:* 75% (excluding resources awarded to replace EFC). *Average financial aid package:* $4650 (excluding resources awarded to replace EFC).

GIFT AID (NEED-BASED) ***Total amount:*** $3,180,361 (31% Federal, 45% state, 23% institutional, 1% external sources). ***Receiving aid:*** *Freshmen:* 98% (161); *all full-time undergraduates:* 97% (779). ***Average award:*** Freshmen: $2000; Undergraduates: $1000. ***Scholarships, grants, and awards:*** Federal Pell, FSEOG, state, private, college/university gift aid from institutional funds.

GIFT AID (NON-NEED-BASED) ***Total amount:*** $26,000 (100% institutional). ***Receiving aid:*** *Freshmen:* 2% (3); *Undergraduates:* 1% (10). ***Scholarships, grants, and awards by category:*** *Academic Interests/Achievement:* 281 awards ($595,951 total): general academic interests/achievements. *Creative Arts/Performance:* 10 awards ($31,500 total): music. ***Tuition waivers:*** Full or partial for employees or children of employees.

LOANS ***Student loans:*** $3,789,755 (100% need-based). 88% of past graduating class borrowed through all loan programs. Average indebtedness per student: $17,000. ***Parent loans:*** $421,682 (100% need-based). ***Programs:*** FFEL (Subsidized and Unsubsidized Stafford, PLUS), Perkins, Federal Nursing, alternative loans.

WORK-STUDY ***Federal work-study:*** *Total amount:* $208,826; 159 jobs averaging $1313.

ATHLETIC AWARDS *Total amount:* 119,702 (100% need-based).

APPLYING for FINANCIAL AID ***Required financial aid forms:*** FAFSA, state aid form. ***Financial aid deadline:*** 5/1 (priority: 2/15). ***Notification date:*** Continuous. Students must reply within 4 weeks of notification.

CONTACT Ms. Stacy L. Klinehans, Director of Financial Aid, Mount Aloysius College, 7373 Admiral Peary Highway, Cresson, PA 16630-1900, 814-886-6357 or toll-free 888-823-2220. *Fax:* 814-886-2978. *E-mail:* sklinehans@mtaloy.edu

MOUNT ANGEL SEMINARY

Saint Benedict, OR

Tuition & fees: $8850 **Average undergraduate aid package: N/A**

ABOUT THE INSTITUTION Independent Roman Catholic, men only. Awards: bachelor's, master's, and first professional degrees (only candidates for the priesthood are admitted). 3 undergraduate majors. Federal methodology is used as a basis for awarding need-based institutional aid.

UNDERGRADUATE EXPENSES for 1999–2000 ***Application fee:*** $25. ***Comprehensive fee:*** $13,750 includes full-time tuition ($8850) and room and board ($4900). ***Part-time tuition:*** $330 per credit hour.

GIFT AID (NEED-BASED) ***Scholarships, grants, and awards:*** Federal Pell, state.

GIFT AID (NON-NEED-BASED) ***Scholarships, grants, and awards by category:*** *Academic Interests/Achievement:* general academic interests/achievements. *Special Achievements/Activities:* community service. *Special Characteristics:* adult students, members of minority groups, out-of-state students.

LOANS ***Programs:*** FFEL (Subsidized and Unsubsidized Stafford).

APPLYING for FINANCIAL AID ***Required financial aid form:*** FAFSA. ***Financial aid deadline (priority):*** 6/15.

CONTACT Dorene Preis, Director of Student Financial Aid, Mount Angel Seminary, Saint Benedict, OR 97373, 503-845-3951. *Fax:* 503-845-3126.

MOUNT CARMEL COLLEGE OF NURSING

Columbus, OH

ABOUT THE INSTITUTION Independent. Awards: bachelor's degrees.

GIFT AID (NEED-BASED) ***Scholarships, grants, and awards:*** Federal Pell, FSEOG, state, private, college/university gift aid from institutional funds.

GIFT AID (NON-NEED-BASED) ***Scholarships, grants, and awards by category:*** *Academic Interests/Achievement:* general academic interests/achievements. *Special Achievements/Activities:* community service. *Special Characteristics:* members of minority groups.

LOANS ***Programs:*** FFEL (Subsidized and Unsubsidized Stafford, PLUS), Perkins, Federal Nursing, state, college/university.

APPLYING for FINANCIAL AID ***Required financial aid forms:*** FAFSA, institution's own form.

CONTACT Financial Aid Office, Mount Carmel College of Nursing, 127 South Davis Avenue, Columbus, OH 43222, 614-234-5800.

MOUNT HOLYOKE COLLEGE

South Hadley, MA

Tuition & fees: $24,354 **Average undergraduate aid package: $20,966**

ABOUT THE INSTITUTION Independent, women only. Awards: bachelor's degrees. 48 undergraduate majors. Total enrollment: 1,982. Undergraduates: 1,979. Freshmen: 554. Both federal and institutional methodology are used as a basis for awarding need-based institutional aid.

UNDERGRADUATE EXPENSES for 1999–2000 ***Application fee:*** $55. ***Comprehensive fee:*** $31,464 includes full-time tuition ($24,200), mandatory fees ($154), and room and board ($7110). ***College room only:*** $3480. ***Part-time tuition:*** $755 per credit hour. ***Part-time fees:*** $154 per year part-time. ***Payment plans:*** tuition prepayment, installment.

FRESHMAN FINANCIAL AID (Fall 1999, est.) 418 applied for aid; of those 87% were deemed to have need. 100% of freshmen with need received aid; of those 100% had need fully met. *Average percent of need met:* 100% (excluding resources awarded to replace EFC). *Average financial aid package:* $20,942 (excluding resources awarded to replace EFC).

UNDERGRADUATE FINANCIAL AID (Fall 1999, est.) 1,552 applied for aid; of those 94% were deemed to have need. 100% of undergraduates with need received aid; of those 100% had need fully met. *Average percent of need met:* 100% (excluding resources awarded to replace EFC). *Average financial aid package:* $20,966 (excluding resources awarded to replace EFC).

GIFT AID (NEED-BASED) ***Total amount:*** $23,746,761 (6% Federal, 1% state, 91% institutional, 2% external sources). ***Receiving aid:*** *Freshmen:* 65% (359); *all full-time undergraduates:* 69% (1,398). ***Average award:*** Freshmen: $17,786; Undergraduates: $16,947. ***Scholarships, grants, and awards:*** Federal Pell, FSEOG, state, private, college/university gift aid from institutional funds.

GIFT AID (NON-NEED-BASED) ***Tuition waivers:*** Full or partial for employees or children of employees. ***ROTC:*** Army cooperative, Air Force cooperative.

LOANS ***Student loans:*** $5,995,105 (100% need-based). 73% of past graduating class borrowed through all loan programs. Average indebtedness per student: $15,000. ***Average need-based loan:*** Freshmen: $3050; Undergraduates: $4290. ***Parent loans:*** $3,419,080 (100% non-need-based). ***Programs:*** Federal Direct (Subsidized and Unsubsidized Stafford, PLUS), Perkins, state, college/university.

WORK-STUDY ***Federal work-study:*** *Total amount:* $1,138,723; 750 jobs averaging $1500. ***State or other work-study/employment:*** *Total amount:* $761,134 (100% need-based). 500 part-time jobs averaging $1500.

APPLYING for FINANCIAL AID ***Required financial aid forms:*** FAFSA, CSS Financial Aid PROFILE, noncustodial (divorced/separated) parent's statement, business/farm supplement. ***Financial aid deadline:*** 2/15. ***Notification date:*** 4/1. Students must reply by 5/1.

CONTACT Ms. Jill Cashman, Director of Financial Assistance, Mount Holyoke College, 50 College Street, South Hadley, MA 01075-1492, 413-538-2291. *Fax:* 413-538-2512. *E-mail:* jcashman@mtholyoke.edu

MOUNT IDA COLLEGE

Newton Centre, MA

Tuition & fees: $15,830 **Average undergraduate aid package: N/A**

ABOUT THE INSTITUTION Independent, coed. Awards: associate and bachelor's degrees. 40 undergraduate majors. Total enrollment: 1,471. Undergraduates: 1,471. Freshmen: 542.

UNDERGRADUATE EXPENSES for 2000–2001 ***Application fee:*** $25. ***Comprehensive fee:*** $24,780 includes full-time tuition ($15,300), mandatory fees ($530), and room and board ($8950). ***Part-time tuition:*** $1050 per course. Part-time tuition and fees vary according to course load. ***Payment plan:*** installment.

GIFT AID (NEED-BASED) ***Scholarships, grants, and awards:*** Federal Pell, FSEOG, state, private, college/university gift aid from institutional funds.

GIFT AID (NON-NEED-BASED) ***Tuition waivers:*** Full or partial for employees or children of employees.

LOANS ***Programs:*** Federal Direct (Subsidized and Unsubsidized Stafford, PLUS), state.

WORK-STUDY ***Federal work-study:*** 450 jobs averaging $1000. ***State or other work-study/employment:*** 50 part-time jobs averaging $1000.

APPLYING for FINANCIAL AID ***Required financial aid forms:*** FAFSA, institution's own form. ***Financial aid deadline (priority):*** 6/1. ***Notification date:*** Continuous. Students must reply within 4 weeks of notification.

Mount Ida College (continued)

CONTACT Office of Financial Aid, Mount Ida College, 777 Dedham Street, Newton Centre, MA 02459-3310, 617-928-4785.

MOUNT MARTY COLLEGE

Yankton, SD

Tuition & fees: $10,128 **Average undergraduate aid package: $10,284**

ABOUT THE INSTITUTION Independent Roman Catholic, coed. Awards: associate, bachelor's, and master's degrees. 31 undergraduate majors. Total enrollment: 1,013. Undergraduates: 949. Freshmen: 150. Federal methodology is used as a basis for awarding need-based institutional aid.

UNDERGRADUATE EXPENSES for 1999–2000 ***Application fee:*** $35. ***Comprehensive fee:*** $14,148 includes full-time tuition ($9248), mandatory fees ($880), and room and board ($4020). ***Part-time tuition:*** $160 per credit. ***Part-time fees:*** $50 per term part-time. Part-time tuition and fees vary according to course load. ***Payment plans:*** guaranteed tuition, installment.

FRESHMAN FINANCIAL AID (Fall 1999) 93 applied for aid; of those 88% were deemed to have need. 98% of freshmen with need received aid; of those 21% had need fully met. *Average percent of need met:* 86% (excluding resources awarded to replace EFC). *Average financial aid package:* $10,575 (excluding resources awarded to replace EFC). 11% of all full-time freshmen had no need and received non-need-based aid.

UNDERGRADUATE FINANCIAL AID (Fall 1999) 398 applied for aid; of those 84% were deemed to have need. 99% of undergraduates with need received aid; of those 32% had need fully met. *Average percent of need met:* 86% (excluding resources awarded to replace EFC). *Average financial aid package:* $10,284 (excluding resources awarded to replace EFC). 13% of all full-time undergraduates had no need and received non-need-based aid.

GIFT AID (NEED-BASED) ***Total amount:*** $1,633,509 (35% Federal, 58% institutional, 7% external sources). ***Receiving aid:*** *Freshmen:* 86% (80); *all full-time undergraduates:* 83% (333). ***Average award:*** Freshmen: $5243; Undergraduates: $4649. ***Scholarships, grants, and awards:*** Federal Pell, FSEOG, state, private, college/university gift aid from institutional funds.

GIFT AID (NON-NEED-BASED) ***Total amount:*** $174,668 (94% institutional, 6% external sources). ***Receiving aid:*** *Freshmen:* 74% (69); *Undergraduates:* 74% (297). ***Scholarships, grants, and awards by category:*** *Academic Interests/Achievement:* 350 awards ($511,256 total): general academic interests/achievements. *Creative Arts/Performance:* 54 awards ($24,725 total): creative writing, music, theater/drama. *Special Achievements/Activities:* 138 awards ($170,900 total): leadership, memberships, religious involvement. *Special Characteristics:* 35 awards ($109,521 total): children of current students, children of faculty/staff, international students, parents of current students, religious affiliation, siblings of current students, spouses of current students. ***Tuition waivers:*** Full or partial for employees or children of employees. ***ROTC:*** Army cooperative.

LOANS ***Student loans:*** $1,873,050 (77% need-based, 23% non-need-based). 78% of past graduating class borrowed through all loan programs. Average indebtedness per student: $17,285. ***Average need-based loan:*** Freshmen: $3533; Undergraduates: $4206. ***Parent loans:*** $192,917 (4% need-based, 96% non-need-based). ***Programs:*** FFEL (Subsidized and Unsubsidized Stafford, PLUS), Perkins, Federal Nursing.

WORK-STUDY ***Federal work-study:*** *Total amount:* $252,811; 208 jobs averaging $1215. ***State or other work-study/employment:*** *Total amount:* $63,413 (2% need-based, 98% non-need-based). 61 part-time jobs averaging $1023.

ATHLETIC AWARDS *Total amount:* 270,488 (27% need-based, 73% non-need-based).

APPLYING for FINANCIAL AID ***Required financial aid forms:*** FAFSA, institution's own form. ***Financial aid deadline (priority):*** 3/1. ***Notification date:*** Continuous beginning 3/15. Students must reply within 2 weeks of notification.

CONTACT Mr. Ken Kocer, Director of Financial Assistance, Mount Marty College, 1105 West 8th Street, Yankton, SD 57078-3724, 605-668-1589 or toll-free 800-658-4552. *Fax:* 605-668-1607. *E-mail:* kkocer@mtmc.edu

MOUNT MARY COLLEGE

Milwaukee, WI

Tuition & fees: $12,270 **Average undergraduate aid package: $10,005**

ABOUT THE INSTITUTION Independent Roman Catholic, women only. Awards: bachelor's and master's degrees. 41 undergraduate majors. Total enrollment: 1,257. Undergraduates: 1,105. Freshmen: 110. Federal methodology is used as a basis for awarding need-based institutional aid.

UNDERGRADUATE EXPENSES for 1999–2000 ***Application fee:*** $25. ***Comprehensive fee:*** $16,460 includes full-time tuition ($12,120), mandatory fees ($150), and room and board ($4190). Room and board charges vary according to board plan and housing facility. ***Part-time tuition:*** $365 per credit. ***Part-time fees:*** $40 per term part-time. Part-time tuition and fees vary according to course load. ***Payment plan:*** installment.

FRESHMAN FINANCIAL AID (Fall 1999, est.) 93 applied for aid; of those 90% were deemed to have need. 100% of freshmen with need received aid; of those 27% had need fully met. *Average percent of need met:* 76% (excluding resources awarded to replace EFC). *Average financial aid package:* $9710 (excluding resources awarded to replace EFC). 8% of all full-time freshmen had no need and received non-need-based aid.

UNDERGRADUATE FINANCIAL AID (Fall 1999, est.) 498 applied for aid; of those 90% were deemed to have need. 100% of undergraduates with need received aid; of those 28% had need fully met. *Average percent of need met:* 78% (excluding resources awarded to replace EFC). *Average financial aid package:* $10,005 (excluding resources awarded to replace EFC). 9% of all full-time undergraduates had no need and received non-need-based aid.

GIFT AID (NEED-BASED) ***Total amount:*** $2,219,278 (26% Federal, 23% state, 48% institutional, 3% external sources). ***Receiving aid:*** *Freshmen:* 61% (82); *all full-time undergraduates:* 68% (386). ***Average award:*** Freshmen: $5750; Undergraduates: $4333. ***Scholarships, grants, and awards:*** Federal Pell, FSEOG, state, private, college/university gift aid from institutional funds, Metropolitan Milwaukee Association of Commerce Awards.

GIFT AID (NON-NEED-BASED) ***Total amount:*** $314,364 (1% state, 97% institutional, 2% external sources). ***Receiving aid:*** *Freshmen:* 7% (9); *Undergraduates:* 3% (16). ***Scholarships, grants, and awards by category:*** *Academic Interests/Achievement:* 90 awards ($600,381 total): business, communication, education, English, general academic interests/achievements, home economics, humanities, mathematics, physical sciences, social sciences. *Creative Arts/Performance:* 6 awards ($4450 total): applied art and design, art/fine arts, music. *Special Achievements/Activities:* 42 awards ($71,200 total): general special achievements/activities, leadership. *Special Characteristics:* 31 awards ($91,128 total): children of faculty/staff, international students, parents of current students, siblings of current students. ***Tuition waivers:*** Full or partial for employees or children of employees, senior citizens. ***ROTC:*** Army cooperative.

LOANS ***Student loans:*** $3,862,020 (79% need-based, 21% non-need-based). 71% of past graduating class borrowed through all loan programs. ***Average need-based loan:*** Freshmen: $3099; Undergraduates: $5202. ***Parent loans:*** $499,518 (42% need-based, 58% non-need-based). ***Programs:*** FFEL (Subsidized and Unsubsidized Stafford, PLUS), Perkins, state.

WORK-STUDY ***Federal work-study:*** *Total amount:* $64,999; 79 jobs averaging $823. ***State or other work-study/employment:*** *Total amount:* $85,955 (100% non-need-based). 127 part-time jobs averaging $677.

APPLYING for FINANCIAL AID ***Required financial aid form:*** FAFSA. ***Financial aid deadline (priority):*** 3/1. ***Notification date:*** Continuous. Students must reply within 2 weeks of notification.

CONTACT Debra Duff, Associate Director of Financial Aid, Mount Mary College, 2900 North Menomonee River Parkway, Milwaukee, WI 53222-4597, 414-256-1258. *Fax:* 414-256-0180. *E-mail:* duffd@mtmary.edu

MOUNT MERCY COLLEGE

Cedar Rapids, IA

Tuition & fees: $13,850 **Average undergraduate aid package: $12,412**

ABOUT THE INSTITUTION Independent Roman Catholic, coed. Awards: bachelor's degrees. 36 undergraduate majors. Total enrollment: 1,291. Undergraduates: 1,291. Freshmen: 186. Federal methodology is used as a basis for awarding need-based institutional aid.

UNDERGRADUATE EXPENSES for 2000–2001 ***Application fee:*** $20. ***Comprehensive fee:*** $18,450 includes full-time tuition ($13,850) and room and board ($4600). ***College room only:*** $1870. Full-time tuition and fees vary according to course load. Room and board charges vary according to board plan. ***Part-time tuition:*** $385 per credit hour. Part-time tuition and fees vary according to course load. ***Payment plan:*** installment.

FRESHMAN FINANCIAL AID (Fall 1999) 173 applied for aid; of those 91% were deemed to have need. 100% of freshmen with need received aid; of those 41% had need fully met. *Average percent of need met:* 87% (excluding resources awarded to replace EFC). *Average financial aid package:* $12,631 (excluding resources awarded to replace EFC). 13% of all full-time freshmen had no need and received non-need-based aid.

UNDERGRADUATE FINANCIAL AID (Fall 1999) 725 applied for aid; of those 92% were deemed to have need. 100% of undergraduates with need received aid; of those 40% had need fully met. *Average percent of need met:* 86% (excluding resources awarded to replace EFC). *Average financial aid package:* $12,412 (excluding resources awarded to replace EFC). 19% of all full-time undergraduates had no need and received non-need-based aid.

GIFT AID (NEED-BASED) ***Total amount:*** $2,619,547 (22% Federal, 71% state, 7% institutional). ***Receiving aid:*** *Freshmen:* 66% (119); *all full-time undergraduates:* 38% (315). ***Average award:*** Freshmen: $3437; Undergraduates: $3988. ***Scholarships, grants, and awards:*** Federal Pell, FSEOG, state, college/university gift aid from institutional funds.

GIFT AID (NON-NEED-BASED) ***Total amount:*** $4,386,324 (98% institutional, 2% external sources). ***Receiving aid:*** *Freshmen:* 87% (158); *Undergraduates:* 62% (513). ***Scholarships, grants, and awards by category:*** *Academic Interests/Achievement:* 901 awards ($3,215,233 total): general academic interests/achievements. *Creative Arts/Performance:* 108 awards ($76,287 total): art/fine arts, music, theater/drama. *Special Achievements/Activities:* 188 awards ($268,881 total): leadership. ***Tuition waivers:*** Full or partial for employees or children of employees.

LOANS ***Student loans:*** $4,351,945 (74% need-based, 26% non-need-based). 84% of past graduating class borrowed through all loan programs. Average indebtedness per student: $16,382. ***Average need-based loan:*** Freshmen: $2664; Undergraduates: $3736. ***Parent loans:*** $156,623 (41% need-based, 59% non-need-based). ***Programs:*** Federal Direct (Subsidized and Unsubsidized Stafford, PLUS), Perkins, Federal Nursing, state, college/university.

WORK-STUDY ***Federal work-study:*** *Total amount:* $231,927; 220 jobs averaging $1100. ***State or other work-study/employment:*** *Total amount:* $198,536 (49% need-based, 51% non-need-based). 127 part-time jobs averaging $1200.

APPLYING for FINANCIAL AID ***Required financial aid form:*** FAFSA. ***Financial aid deadline (priority):*** 3/1. ***Notification date:*** Continuous beginning 3/15.

CONTACT Lois M. Mulbrook, Director of Financial Aid, Mount Mercy College, 1330 Elmhurst Drive, NE, Cedar Rapids, IA 52402-4797, 319-368-6467 or toll-free 800-248-4504. *Fax:* 319-364-3546. *E-mail:* lmmulbro@mmc.mtmercy.edu

MOUNT OLIVE COLLEGE

Mount Olive, NC

Tuition & fees: $9210 **Average undergraduate aid package: $6627**

ABOUT THE INSTITUTION Independent Free Will Baptist, coed. Awards: associate and bachelor's degrees. 20 undergraduate majors. Total enrollment: 1,822. Undergraduates: 1,822. Freshmen: 149. Federal methodology is used as a basis for awarding need-based institutional aid.

UNDERGRADUATE EXPENSES for 2000–2001 ***Application fee:*** $20. ***Comprehensive fee:*** $13,210 includes full-time tuition ($9100), mandatory fees ($110), and room and board ($4000). ***College room only:*** $1850. Full-time tuition and fees vary according to location. Room and board charges vary according to board plan and housing facility. ***Part-time tuition:*** $210 per semester hour. Part-time tuition and fees vary according to course load and location. ***Payment plan:*** installment.

FRESHMAN FINANCIAL AID (Fall 1999) 127 applied for aid; of those 87% were deemed to have need. 100% of freshmen with need received aid; of those 30% had need fully met. *Average percent of need met:* 76% (excluding resources awarded to replace EFC). *Average financial aid package:* $7119 (excluding resources awarded to replace EFC). 19% of all full-time freshmen had no need and received non-need-based aid.

UNDERGRADUATE FINANCIAL AID (Fall 1999) 986 applied for aid; of those 90% were deemed to have need. 100% of undergraduates with need received aid; of those 27% had need fully met. *Average percent of need met:* 71% (excluding resources awarded to replace EFC). *Average financial aid package:* $6627 (excluding resources awarded to replace EFC). 12% of all full-time undergraduates had no need and received non-need-based aid.

GIFT AID (NEED-BASED) ***Total amount:*** $3,721,041 (22% Federal, 52% state, 18% institutional, 8% external sources). ***Receiving aid:*** *Freshmen:* 49% (111); *all full-time undergraduates:* 40% (887). ***Average award:*** Freshmen: $5806; Undergraduates: $4463. ***Scholarships, grants, and awards:*** Federal Pell, FSEOG, state, private, college/university gift aid from institutional funds.

GIFT AID (NON-NEED-BASED) ***Total amount:*** $1,551,048 (48% state, 24% institutional, 28% external sources). ***Receiving aid:*** *Freshmen:* 11% (24); *Undergraduates:* 3% (68). ***Scholarships, grants, and awards by category:*** *Academic Interests/Achievement:* 93 awards ($284,022 total): general academic interests/achievements, mathematics. *Creative Arts/Performance:* 64 awards ($97,450 total): art/fine arts, music. *Special Achievements/Activities:* 121 awards ($232,063 total): leadership. *Special Characteristics:* 77 awards ($186,288 total): children of faculty/staff, religious affiliation. ***Tuition waivers:*** Full or partial for employees or children of employees, senior citizens.

LOANS ***Student loans:*** $2,552,539 (65% need-based, 35% non-need-based). 36% of past graduating class borrowed through all loan programs. Average indebtedness per student: $7453. ***Average need-based loan:*** Freshmen: $1860; Undergraduates: $3003. ***Parent loans:*** $59,194 (25% need-based, 75% non-need-based). ***Programs:*** FFEL (Subsidized and Unsubsidized Stafford, PLUS), Perkins, alternative loans.

WORK-STUDY ***Federal work-study:*** *Total amount:* $49,402; 101 jobs averaging $489.

ATHLETIC AWARDS *Total amount:* 468,657 (100% need-based).

APPLYING for FINANCIAL AID ***Required financial aid forms:*** FAFSA, institution's own form, state aid form. ***Financial aid deadline (priority):*** 3/1. ***Notification date:*** Continuous beginning 3/15. Students must reply within 2 weeks of notification.

CONTACT Ms. Diane H. Graham, Assistant Director of Financial Aid, Mount Olive College, 634 Henderson Street, Mount Olive, NC 28365, 919-658-2502 Ext. 3004 or toll-free 800-653-0854 (in-state). *Fax:* 919-658-7180.

MOUNT ST. CLARE COLLEGE

Clinton, IA

Tuition & fees: $12,800 **Average undergraduate aid package: $10,316**

ABOUT THE INSTITUTION Independent Roman Catholic, coed. Awards: associate and bachelor's degrees. 24 undergraduate majors. Total enrollment: 669. Undergraduates: 590. Freshmen: 117. Federal methodology is used as a basis for awarding need-based institutional aid.

UNDERGRADUATE EXPENSES for 1999–2000 ***Application fee:*** $20. ***One-time required fee:*** $20. ***Comprehensive fee:*** $17,160 includes full-time tuition ($12,580), mandatory fees ($220), and room and board ($4360).

Mount St. Clare College (continued)

College room only: $1990. Room and board charges vary according to board plan and housing facility. ***Part-time tuition:*** $367 per credit hour. ***Part-time fees:*** $8 per credit hour. Part-time tuition and fees vary according to course load. ***Payment plan:*** installment.

FRESHMAN FINANCIAL AID (Fall 1999) 112 applied for aid; of those 94% were deemed to have need. 100% of freshmen with need received aid; of those 39% had need fully met. *Average percent of need met:* 90% (excluding resources awarded to replace EFC). *Average financial aid package:* $10,674 (excluding resources awarded to replace EFC). 6% of all full-time freshmen had no need and received non-need-based aid.

UNDERGRADUATE FINANCIAL AID (Fall 1999) 469 applied for aid; of those 91% were deemed to have need. 100% of undergraduates with need received aid; of those 45% had need fully met. *Average percent of need met:* 93% (excluding resources awarded to replace EFC). *Average financial aid package:* $10,316 (excluding resources awarded to replace EFC). 8% of all full-time undergraduates had no need and received non-need-based aid.

GIFT AID (NEED-BASED) ***Total amount:*** $2,799,633 (16% Federal, 24% state, 59% institutional, 1% external sources). ***Receiving aid:*** *Freshmen:* 91% (105); *all full-time undergraduates:* 86% (429). ***Average award:*** Freshmen: $9122; Undergraduates: $7782. ***Scholarships, grants, and awards:*** Federal Pell, FSEOG, state, private, college/university gift aid from institutional funds.

GIFT AID (NON-NEED-BASED) ***Scholarships, grants, and awards by category:*** *Academic Interests/Achievement:* 212 awards ($637,386 total): biological sciences, business, communication, computer science, education, English, foreign languages, general academic interests/achievements, health fields, humanities, mathematics, physical sciences, premedicine, social sciences. *Creative Arts/Performance:* 44 awards ($72,131 total): art/fine arts, journalism/publications, music. *Special Achievements/Activities:* 41 awards ($33,785 total): community service, leadership, memberships, religious involvement. *Special Characteristics:* 60 awards ($88,983 total): children and siblings of alumni, children of current students, children of faculty/staff, international students, local/state students, parents of current students, relatives of clergy, siblings of current students, spouses of current students, twins. ***Tuition waivers:*** Full or partial for children of alumni, employees or children of employees, senior citizens.

LOANS ***Student loans:*** $1,897,045 (100% need-based). 81% of past graduating class borrowed through all loan programs. Average indebtedness per student: $13,219. ***Average need-based loan:*** Freshmen: $2298; Undergraduates: $3418. ***Parent loans:*** $957,648 (100% need-based). ***Programs:*** FFEL (Subsidized and Unsubsidized Stafford, PLUS), Perkins, state.

WORK-STUDY ***Federal work-study:*** *Total amount:* $118,000; 96 jobs averaging $1229. ***State or other work-study/employment:*** *Total amount:* $48,895 (100% need-based). 41 part-time jobs averaging $1193.

ATHLETIC AWARDS *Total amount:* 901,969 (100% need-based).

APPLYING for FINANCIAL AID ***Required financial aid form:*** FAFSA. ***Financial aid deadline:*** 6/1 (priority: 3/1). ***Notification date:*** Continuous. Students must reply within 3 weeks of notification.

CONTACT Lisa Kramer, Director of Financial Aid, Mount St. Clare College, 400 North Bluff Boulevard, PO Box 2967, Clinton, IA 52733-2967, 319-242-4023 Ext. 1243 or toll-free 800-242-4153 Ext. 3400. *Fax:* 319-242-8684.

MOUNT SAINT MARY COLLEGE

Newburgh, NY

Tuition & fees: $11,470 **Average undergraduate aid package: $8200**

ABOUT THE INSTITUTION Independent, coed. Awards: bachelor's and master's degrees. 32 undergraduate majors. Total enrollment: 2,019. Undergraduates: 1,598. Both federal and institutional methodology are used as a basis for awarding need-based institutional aid.

UNDERGRADUATE EXPENSES for 1999–2000 ***Application fee:*** $25. ***One-time required fee:*** $15. ***Comprehensive fee:*** $17,170 includes full-time tuition ($11,100), mandatory fees ($370), and room and board ($5700). Room and board charges vary according to board plan and student level. ***Part-time tuition:*** $370 per credit hour. ***Part-time fees:*** $15 per term part-time. ***Payment plan:*** installment.

FRESHMAN FINANCIAL AID (Fall 1999, est.) *Average percent of need met:* 75% (excluding resources awarded to replace EFC). *Average financial aid package:* $7800 (excluding resources awarded to replace EFC).

UNDERGRADUATE FINANCIAL AID (Fall 1999, est.) *Average percent of need met:* 78% (excluding resources awarded to replace EFC). *Average financial aid package:* $8200 (excluding resources awarded to replace EFC).

GIFT AID (NEED-BASED) ***Total amount:*** $3,377,585 (30% Federal, 42% state, 26% institutional, 2% external sources). ***Scholarships, grants, and awards:*** Federal Pell, FSEOG, state, private, college/university gift aid from institutional funds.

GIFT AID (NON-NEED-BASED) ***Total amount:*** $994,750 (100% institutional). ***Scholarships, grants, and awards by category:*** *Academic Interests/Achievement:* 269 awards ($994,750 total): general academic interests/achievements. *Special Characteristics:* 76 awards ($304,962 total): children of faculty/staff. ***Tuition waivers:*** Full or partial for employees or children of employees. ***ROTC:*** Army cooperative.

LOANS ***Student loans:*** $5,588,808 (57% need-based, 43% non-need-based). 65% of past graduating class borrowed through all loan programs. Average indebtedness per student: $14,500. ***Parent loans:*** $1,209,291 (100% need-based). ***Programs:*** FFEL (Subsidized and Unsubsidized Stafford, PLUS), Perkins, Federal Nursing.

WORK-STUDY ***Federal work-study:*** *Total amount:* $133,783; 150 jobs averaging $1000. ***State or other work-study/employment:*** *Total amount:* $70,250 (100% need-based). 54 part-time jobs averaging $1500.

APPLYING for FINANCIAL AID ***Required financial aid forms:*** FAFSA, institution's own form. ***Financial aid deadline (priority):*** 3/15. ***Notification date:*** Continuous beginning 4/1. Students must reply within 2 weeks of notification.

CONTACT Susan F. Twomey, Director of Financial Aid, Mount Saint Mary College, 330 Powell Avenue, Newburgh, NY 12550-3494, 914-569-3298 or toll-free 888-937-6762. *E-mail:* twomey@msmc.edu

MOUNT ST. MARY'S COLLEGE

Los Angeles, CA

Tuition & fees: $17,328 **Average undergraduate aid package: N/A**

ABOUT THE INSTITUTION Independent Roman Catholic, coed, primarily women. Awards: associate, bachelor's, and master's degrees. 40 undergraduate majors. Total enrollment: 2,066. Undergraduates: 1,753. Freshmen: 320. Federal methodology is used as a basis for awarding need-based institutional aid.

UNDERGRADUATE EXPENSES for 1999–2000 ***Application fee:*** $35. ***Comprehensive fee:*** $23,962 includes full-time tuition ($16,776), mandatory fees ($552), and room and board ($6634). Full-time tuition and fees vary according to program. Room and board charges vary according to housing facility. ***Part-time tuition:*** $722 per unit. ***Part-time fees:*** $56 per term part-time. Part-time tuition and fees vary according to program. ***Payment plan:*** deferred payment.

GIFT AID (NEED-BASED) ***Scholarships, grants, and awards:*** Federal Pell, FSEOG, state, private, college/university gift aid from institutional funds.

GIFT AID (NON-NEED-BASED) ***Scholarships, grants, and awards by category:*** *Academic Interests/Achievement:* education, general academic interests/achievements. *Special Achievements/Activities:* community service, leadership. *Special Characteristics:* children and siblings of alumni. ***Tuition waivers:*** Full or partial for employees or children of employees. ***ROTC:*** Army cooperative, Naval cooperative, Air Force cooperative.

LOANS ***Programs:*** FFEL (Subsidized and Unsubsidized Stafford, PLUS), Federal Nursing, college/university.

WORK-STUDY Federal work-study jobs available. ***State or other work-study/employment:*** Part-time jobs available.

APPLYING for FINANCIAL AID ***Required financial aid form:*** FAFSA. ***Financial aid deadline:*** Continuous.

CONTACT Mr. Jim Whitaker, Financial Aid Director, Mount St. Mary's College, 12001 Chalon Road, Los Angeles, CA 90049, 310-954-4190 or toll-free 800-999-9893.

MOUNT SAINT MARY'S COLLEGE AND SEMINARY

Emmitsburg, MD

Tuition & fees: $16,720 **Average undergraduate aid package: $12,856**

ABOUT THE INSTITUTION Independent Roman Catholic, coed. Awards: bachelor's, master's, and first professional degrees. 31 undergraduate majors. Total enrollment: 1,730. Undergraduates: 1,354. Freshmen: 369. Both federal and institutional methodology are used as a basis for awarding need-based institutional aid.

UNDERGRADUATE EXPENSES for 1999–2000 ***Application fee:*** $25. ***Comprehensive fee:*** $23,370 includes full-time tuition ($16,520), mandatory fees ($200), and room and board ($6650). ***College room only:*** $3325. Room and board charges vary according to board plan. ***Part-time tuition:*** $550 per credit. ***Part-time fees:*** $5 per credit. Part-time tuition and fees vary according to course load. ***Payment plans:*** tuition prepayment, installment.

FRESHMAN FINANCIAL AID (Fall 1999) 309 applied for aid; of those 78% were deemed to have need. 100% of freshmen with need received aid; of those 32% had need fully met. *Average percent of need met:* 82% (excluding resources awarded to replace EFC). *Average financial aid package:* $12,808 (excluding resources awarded to replace EFC). 34% of all full-time freshmen had no need and received non-need-based aid.

UNDERGRADUATE FINANCIAL AID (Fall 1999) 1,005 applied for aid; of those 86% were deemed to have need. 100% of undergraduates with need received aid; of those 32% had need fully met. *Average percent of need met:* 76% (excluding resources awarded to replace EFC). *Average financial aid package:* $12,856 (excluding resources awarded to replace EFC). 23% of all full-time undergraduates had no need and received non-need-based aid.

GIFT AID (NEED-BASED) ***Total amount:*** $7,260,077 (6% Federal, 9% state, 83% institutional, 2% external sources). ***Receiving aid:*** *Freshmen:* 65% (240); *all full-time undergraduates:* 68% (854). ***Average award:*** Freshmen: $8650; Undergraduates: $8945. ***Scholarships, grants, and awards:*** Federal Pell, FSEOG, state, private, college/university gift aid from institutional funds.

GIFT AID (NON-NEED-BASED) ***Total amount:*** $2,441,430 (3% Federal, 2% state, 93% institutional, 2% external sources). ***Receiving aid:*** *Freshmen:* 14% (50); *Undergraduates:* 9% (110). ***Scholarships, grants, and awards by category:*** *Academic Interests/Achievement:* general academic interests/achievements. *Special Characteristics:* members of minority groups, siblings of current students. ***Tuition waivers:*** Full or partial for employees or children of employees. ***ROTC:*** Army cooperative.

LOANS ***Student loans:*** $4,359,906 (63% need-based, 37% non-need-based). 56% of past graduating class borrowed through all loan programs. Average indebtedness per student: $15,463. ***Average need-based loan:*** Freshmen: $3010; Undergraduates: $3875. ***Parent loans:*** $2,070,696 (37% need-based, 63% non-need-based). ***Programs:*** FFEL (Subsidized and Unsubsidized Stafford, PLUS), Perkins, state.

WORK-STUDY ***Federal work-study:*** *Total amount:* $155,525; 119 jobs averaging $1310. ***State or other work-study/employment:*** *Total amount:* $315,449 (38% need-based, 62% non-need-based). 221 part-time jobs averaging $1425.

ATHLETIC AWARDS *Total amount:* 1,300,357 (38% need-based, 62% non-need-based).

APPLYING for FINANCIAL AID ***Required financial aid forms:*** FAFSA, CSS Financial Aid PROFILE. ***Financial aid deadline:*** 3/15 (priority: 2/15). ***Notification date:*** Continuous. Students must reply by 5/1.

CONTACT Mr. Joseph Paul Zanella, Director of Financial Aid, Mount Saint Mary's College and Seminary, 16300 Old Emmitsburg Road, Emmitsburg, MD 21727-7799, 301-447-5207 or toll-free 800-448-4347. *Fax:* 301-447-5755.

MOUNT SENARIO COLLEGE

Ladysmith, WI

Tuition & fees: $12,250 **Average undergraduate aid package: $10,598**

ABOUT THE INSTITUTION Independent, coed. Awards: associate and bachelor's degrees. 24 undergraduate majors. Total enrollment: 930. Undergraduates: 930. Freshmen: 99. Federal methodology is used as a basis for awarding need-based institutional aid.

UNDERGRADUATE EXPENSES for 2000–2001 ***Application fee:*** $10. ***Comprehensive fee:*** $16,990 includes full-time tuition ($12,250) and room and board ($4740). ***College room only:*** $2150. Full-time tuition and fees vary according to course load. ***Part-time tuition:*** $525 per credit. Part-time tuition and fees vary according to course load. ***Payment plan:*** installment.

FRESHMAN FINANCIAL AID (Fall 1999, est.) 96 applied for aid; of those 100% were deemed to have need. 100% of freshmen with need received aid. *Average financial aid package:* $10,816 (excluding resources awarded to replace EFC).

UNDERGRADUATE FINANCIAL AID (Fall 1999, est.) 413 applied for aid; of those 100% were deemed to have need. 100% of undergraduates with need received aid. *Average financial aid package:* $10,598 (excluding resources awarded to replace EFC).

GIFT AID (NEED-BASED) ***Total amount:*** $3,177,894 (23% Federal, 19% state, 58% institutional). ***Receiving aid:*** *Freshmen:* 96% (93); *all full-time undergraduates:* 77% (339). ***Average award:*** Freshmen: $7684; Undergraduates: $7540. ***Scholarships, grants, and awards:*** Federal Pell, FSEOG, state, private, college/university gift aid from institutional funds.

GIFT AID (NON-NEED-BASED) ***Scholarships, grants, and awards by category:*** *Academic Interests/Achievement:* general academic interests/achievements. *Creative Arts/Performance:* art/fine arts. *Special Achievements/Activities:* cheerleading/drum major. *Special Characteristics:* children and siblings of alumni, children of faculty/staff, international students, local/state students, previous college experience, siblings of current students. ***Tuition waivers:*** Full or partial for employees or children of employees.

LOANS ***Student loans:*** $1,774,738 (100% need-based). ***Average need-based loan:*** Freshmen: $4052; Undergraduates: $4024. ***Parent loans:*** $138,152 (100% need-based). ***Programs:*** FFEL (Subsidized and Unsubsidized Stafford, PLUS), Perkins, alternative loans.

WORK-STUDY ***Federal work-study:*** *Total amount:* $99,004; jobs available. ***State or other work-study/employment:*** *Total amount:* $93,872 (100% need-based). Part-time jobs available.

APPLYING for FINANCIAL AID ***Required financial aid form:*** FAFSA. ***Financial aid deadline (priority):*** 5/15. ***Notification date:*** Continuous. Students must reply within 2 weeks of notification.

CONTACT Ms. Pam Vacho, Director of Financial Aid, Mount Senario College, 1500 College Avenue, Ladysmith, WI 54848-2128, 715-532-5511 Ext. 1116 or toll-free 800-281-6514 (out-of-state). *Fax:* 715-532-7690. *E-mail:* pvacho@mscfs.edu

MT. SIERRA COLLEGE

Monrovia, CA

CONTACT Financial Aid Office, Mt. Sierra College, 101 East Huntington Drive, Monrovia, CA 91016, 626-873-2144.

MOUNT UNION COLLEGE

Alliance, OH

Tuition & fees: $14,880 **Average undergraduate aid package: $12,720**

ABOUT THE INSTITUTION Independent United Methodist, coed. Awards: bachelor's degrees. 41 undergraduate majors. Total enrollment: 2,277. Undergraduates: 2,277. Freshmen: 661. Federal methodology is used as a basis for awarding need-based institutional aid.

UNDERGRADUATE EXPENSES for 1999–2000 ***Application fee:*** $2. ***Comprehensive fee:*** $19,250 includes full-time tuition ($14,080), manda-

Mount Union College (continued)

tory fees ($800), and room and board ($4370). ***College room only:*** $1750. Room and board charges vary according to housing facility. ***Part-time tuition:*** $595 per semester hour. ***Payment plans:*** tuition prepayment, installment.

FRESHMAN FINANCIAL AID (Fall 1999, est.) 539 applied for aid; of those 93% were deemed to have need. 100% of freshmen with need received aid; of those 35% had need fully met. *Average percent of need met:* 86% (excluding resources awarded to replace EFC). *Average financial aid package:* $12,672 (excluding resources awarded to replace EFC). 13% of all full-time freshmen had no need and received non-need-based aid.

UNDERGRADUATE FINANCIAL AID (Fall 1999, est.) 1,613 applied for aid; of those 94% were deemed to have need. 100% of undergraduates with need received aid; of those 39% had need fully met. *Average percent of need met:* 87% (excluding resources awarded to replace EFC). *Average financial aid package:* $12,720 (excluding resources awarded to replace EFC). 15% of all full-time undergraduates had no need and received non-need-based aid.

GIFT AID (NEED-BASED) ***Total amount:*** $14,275,277 (7% Federal, 16% state, 74% institutional, 3% external sources). ***Receiving aid:*** *Freshmen:* 78% (499); *all full-time undergraduates:* 73% (1,506). ***Average award:*** Freshmen: $9347; Undergraduates: $8856. ***Scholarships, grants, and awards:*** Federal Pell, FSEOG, state, private, college/university gift aid from institutional funds.

GIFT AID (NON-NEED-BASED) ***Total amount:*** $1,803,865 (24% state, 67% institutional, 9% external sources). ***Receiving aid:*** *Freshmen:* 38% (241); *Undergraduates:* 35% (729). ***Scholarships, grants, and awards by category:*** *Academic Interests/Achievement:* 771 awards ($3,873,443 total): general academic interests/achievements. *Creative Arts/Performance:* 166 awards ($401,750 total): art/fine arts, cinema/film/broadcasting, debating, journalism/publications, music, theater/drama. *Special Characteristics:* 141 awards ($874,374 total): children and siblings of alumni, children of faculty/staff, international students, relatives of clergy. ***Tuition waivers:*** Full or partial for children of alumni, employees or children of employees, adult students, senior citizens. ***ROTC:*** Army cooperative, Air Force cooperative.

LOANS ***Student loans:*** $7,149,023 (76% need-based, 24% non-need-based). 64% of past graduating class borrowed through all loan programs. Average indebtedness per student: $15,601. ***Average need-based loan:*** Freshmen: $2612; Undergraduates: $3194. ***Parent loans:*** $7290 (51% need-based, 49% non-need-based). ***Programs:*** FFEL (Subsidized and Unsubsidized Stafford, PLUS), Perkins, alternative loans.

WORK-STUDY ***Federal work-study:*** *Total amount:* $986,346; 1,012 jobs available. ***State or other work-study/employment:*** *Total amount:* $288,695 (40% need-based, 60% non-need-based). 225 part-time jobs averaging $1275.

APPLYING for FINANCIAL AID ***Required financial aid forms:*** FAFSA, institution's own form. ***Financial aid deadline:*** Continuous. ***Notification date:*** Continuous beginning 3/15. Students must reply within 4 weeks of notification.

CONTACT Mrs. Sandra S. Pittenger, Director of Student Financial Services, Mount Union College, 1972 Clark Avenue, Alliance, OH 44601-3993, 330-823-2674 or toll-free 800-334-6682 (in-state), 800-992-6682 (out-of-state). *Fax:* 330-821-3457.

MOUNT VERNON COLLEGE

Washington, DC

See The George Washington University

MOUNT VERNON NAZARENE COLLEGE

Mount Vernon, OH

Tuition & fees: $11,926 **Average undergraduate aid package: $5823**

ABOUT THE INSTITUTION Independent Nazarene, coed. Awards: associate, bachelor's, and master's degrees. 59 undergraduate majors. Total enrollment: 1,916. Undergraduates: 1,843. Freshmen: 396. Federal methodology is used as a basis for awarding need-based institutional aid.

UNDERGRADUATE EXPENSES for 2000–2001 ***Application fee:*** $25. ***Comprehensive fee:*** $16,129 includes full-time tuition ($11,468), mandatory fees ($458), and room and board ($4203). ***College room only:*** $2385. ***Part-time tuition:*** $410 per credit hour. ***Part-time fees:*** $14 per credit hour. ***Payment plan:*** installment.

FRESHMAN FINANCIAL AID (Fall 1999, est.) 375 applied for aid; of those 87% were deemed to have need. 100% of freshmen with need received aid; of those 10% had need fully met. *Average percent of need met:* 87% (excluding resources awarded to replace EFC). *Average financial aid package:* $5914 (excluding resources awarded to replace EFC). 13% of all full-time freshmen had no need and received non-need-based aid.

UNDERGRADUATE FINANCIAL AID (Fall 1999, est.) 1,595 applied for aid; of those 69% were deemed to have need. 100% of undergraduates with need received aid; of those 13% had need fully met. *Average percent of need met:* 85% (excluding resources awarded to replace EFC). *Average financial aid package:* $5823 (excluding resources awarded to replace EFC). 17% of all full-time undergraduates had no need and received non-need-based aid.

GIFT AID (NEED-BASED) ***Total amount:*** $2,876,411 (32% Federal, 14% state, 12% institutional, 42% external sources). ***Receiving aid:*** *Freshmen:* 67% (250); *all full-time undergraduates:* 48% (839). ***Average award:*** Freshmen: $2867; Undergraduates: $3325. ***Scholarships, grants, and awards:*** Federal Pell, FSEOG, state, private, college/university gift aid from institutional funds.

GIFT AID (NON-NEED-BASED) ***Total amount:*** $3,010,465 (47% state, 53% institutional). ***Receiving aid:*** *Freshmen:* 76% (286); *Undergraduates:* 52% (920). ***Scholarships, grants, and awards by category:*** *Academic Interests/Achievement:* 521 awards ($1,003,144 total): business, computer science, education, general academic interests/achievements, health fields, home economics, religion/biblical studies. *Creative Arts/Performance:* 17 awards ($9900 total): music. *Special Achievements/Activities:* 48 awards ($40,050 total): general special achievements/activities, junior miss, religious involvement. *Special Characteristics:* 634 awards ($949,468 total): children of faculty/staff, international students, local/state students, relatives of clergy, religious affiliation, siblings of current students, spouses of current students, veterans, veterans' children. ***Tuition waivers:*** Full or partial for employees or children of employees.

LOANS ***Student loans:*** $7,357,465 (66% need-based, 34% non-need-based). 83% of past graduating class borrowed through all loan programs. Average indebtedness per student: $16,253. ***Average need-based loan:*** Freshmen: $3682; Undergraduates: $4773. ***Parent loans:*** $2,151,555 (100% need-based). ***Programs:*** FFEL (Subsidized and Unsubsidized Stafford, PLUS), Perkins, college/university.

WORK-STUDY ***Federal work-study:*** *Total amount:* $242,384; 181 jobs available. ***State or other work-study/employment:*** *Total amount:* $417,022 (96% need-based, 4% non-need-based). 265 part-time jobs averaging $1574.

ATHLETIC AWARDS *Total amount:* 274,410 (17% need-based, 83% non-need-based).

APPLYING for FINANCIAL AID ***Required financial aid forms:*** FAFSA, institution's own form. ***Financial aid deadline (priority):*** 3/13. ***Notification date:*** Continuous beginning 3/15. Students must reply within 4 weeks of notification.

CONTACT Mrs. Joanne E. Bowman, Director of Student Financial Planning, Mount Vernon Nazarene College, 800 Martinsburg Road, Mount Vernon, OH 43050-9500, 740-397-6862 Ext. 4520 or toll-free 800-782-2435. *Fax:* 740-393-0511.

MUHLENBERG COLLEGE

Allentown, PA

Tuition & fees: $20,085 **Average undergraduate aid package: $14,559**

ABOUT THE INSTITUTION Independent religious, coed. Awards: bachelor's degrees. 45 undergraduate majors. Total enrollment: 2,443. Undergraduates: 2,443. Freshmen: 552. Institutional methodology is used as a basis for awarding need-based institutional aid.

UNDERGRADUATE EXPENSES for 1999–2000 ***Application fee:*** $40. ***Comprehensive fee:*** $25,475 includes full-time tuition ($19,910), mandatory fees ($175), and room and board ($5390). ***College room only:*** $2795. Room and board charges vary according to board plan, housing facility, and location. ***Part-time tuition:*** $1405 per course. ***Part-time fees:*** $88 per term part-time. ***Payment plans:*** tuition prepayment, installment.

FRESHMAN FINANCIAL AID (Fall 1999) 391 applied for aid; of those 78% were deemed to have need. 100% of freshmen with need received aid; of those 95% had need fully met. *Average percent of need met:* 97% (excluding resources awarded to replace EFC). *Average financial aid package:* $13,899 (excluding resources awarded to replace EFC). 29% of all full-time freshmen had no need and received non-need-based aid.

UNDERGRADUATE FINANCIAL AID (Fall 1999) 1,153 applied for aid; of those 83% were deemed to have need. 100% of undergraduates with need received aid; of those 98% had need fully met. *Average percent of need met:* 97% (excluding resources awarded to replace EFC). *Average financial aid package:* $14,559 (excluding resources awarded to replace EFC). 22% of all full-time undergraduates had no need and received non-need-based aid.

GIFT AID (NEED-BASED) ***Total amount:*** $10,216,738 (5% Federal, 6% state, 88% institutional, 1% external sources). ***Receiving aid:*** *Freshmen:* 53% (293); *all full-time undergraduates:* 45% (928). ***Average award:*** Freshmen: $10,291; Undergraduates: $10,791. ***Scholarships, grants, and awards:*** Federal Pell, FSEOG, state, private, college/university gift aid from institutional funds.

GIFT AID (NON-NEED-BASED) ***Total amount:*** $2,757,666 (2% state, 93% institutional, 5% external sources). ***Receiving aid:*** *Freshmen:* 8% (44); *Undergraduates:* 7% (148). ***Scholarships, grants, and awards by category:*** *Academic Interests/Achievement:* general academic interests/achievements. *Creative Arts/Performance:* dance, music, performing arts, theater/drama. *Special Achievements/Activities:* leadership, memberships. *Special Characteristics:* relatives of clergy. ***Tuition waivers:*** Full or partial for employees or children of employees. ***ROTC:*** Army cooperative.

LOANS ***Student loans:*** $5,957,725 (56% need-based, 44% non-need-based). ***Average need-based loan:*** Freshmen: $3203; Undergraduates: $3408. ***Parent loans:*** $1,757,297 (16% need-based, 84% non-need-based). ***Programs:*** FFEL (Subsidized and Unsubsidized Stafford, PLUS), Perkins, college/university.

WORK-STUDY ***Federal work-study:*** *Total amount:* $264,375; 212 jobs available. ***State or other work-study/employment:*** *Total amount:* $215,825 (37% need-based, 63% non-need-based). 175 part-time jobs averaging $1250.

APPLYING for FINANCIAL AID ***Required financial aid forms:*** FAFSA, institution's own form, CSS Financial Aid PROFILE, noncustodial (divorced/separated) parent's statement, business/farm supplement, parent and student federal income tax returns. ***Financial aid deadline:*** 2/15. ***Notification date:*** 4/1. Students must reply by 5/1.

CONTACT Mr. Greg Mitton, Director of Financial Aid, Muhlenberg College, 2400 Chew Street, Allentown, PA 18104-5586, 484-664-3175. *Fax:* 484-664-3234. *E-mail:* mitton@muhlenberg.edu

MULTNOMAH BIBLE COLLEGE AND BIBLICAL SEMINARY

Portland, OR

Tuition & fees: $8600 **Average undergraduate aid package: $7090**

ABOUT THE INSTITUTION Independent interdenominational, coed. Awards: bachelor's, master's, and first professional degrees. 12 undergraduate majors. Total enrollment: 775. Undergraduates: 545. Freshmen: 101. Federal methodology is used as a basis for awarding need-based institutional aid.

UNDERGRADUATE EXPENSES for 1999–2000 ***Application fee:*** $40. ***Comprehensive fee:*** $12,320 includes full-time tuition ($8600) and room and board ($3720). ***College room only:*** $1930. Room and board charges vary according to board plan and housing facility. ***Part-time tuition:*** $360 per semester hour. Part-time tuition and fees vary according to course load. ***Payment plan:*** installment.

FRESHMAN FINANCIAL AID (Fall 1998) 86 applied for aid; of those 86% were deemed to have need. 100% of freshmen with need received aid; of those 14% had need fully met. *Average percent of need met:* 65% (excluding resources awarded to replace EFC). *Average financial aid package:* $6590 (excluding resources awarded to replace EFC). 23% of all full-time freshmen had no need and received non-need-based aid.

UNDERGRADUATE FINANCIAL AID (Fall 1998) 450 applied for aid; of those 90% were deemed to have need. 100% of undergraduates with need received aid; of those 18% had need fully met. *Average percent of need met:* 69% (excluding resources awarded to replace EFC). *Average financial aid package:* $7090 (excluding resources awarded to replace EFC). 16% of all full-time undergraduates had no need and received non-need-based aid.

GIFT AID (NEED-BASED) ***Total amount:*** $1,261,285 (38% Federal, 45% institutional, 17% external sources). ***Receiving aid:*** *Freshmen:* 74% (71); *all full-time undergraduates:* 77% (375). ***Average award:*** Freshmen: $3514; Undergraduates: $3036. ***Scholarships, grants, and awards:*** Federal Pell, FSEOG, private, college/university gift aid from institutional funds.

GIFT AID (NON-NEED-BASED) ***Total amount:*** $181,054 (36% institutional, 64% external sources). ***Receiving aid:*** *Freshmen:* 2% (2); *Undergraduates:* 2% (10). ***Scholarships, grants, and awards by category:*** *Academic Interests/Achievement:* communication, general academic interests/achievements, religion/biblical studies. *Special Characteristics:* children of current students, international students, religious affiliation, siblings of current students. ***Tuition waivers:*** Full or partial for employees or children of employees.

LOANS ***Student loans:*** $1,924,839 (86% need-based, 14% non-need-based). 88% of past graduating class borrowed through all loan programs. ***Average need-based loan:*** Freshmen: $2676; Undergraduates: $3801. ***Parent loans:*** $734,535 (53% need-based, 47% non-need-based). ***Programs:*** FFEL (Subsidized and Unsubsidized Stafford, PLUS).

WORK-STUDY ***Federal work-study:*** *Total amount:* $144,125; 80 jobs averaging $1400.

APPLYING for FINANCIAL AID ***Required financial aid forms:*** FAFSA, institution's own form. ***Financial aid deadline (priority):*** 3/15. ***Notification date:*** Continuous beginning 4/15. Students must reply within 3 weeks of notification.

CONTACT Mr. David Allen, Director of Financial Aid, Multnomah Bible College and Biblical Seminary, 8435 Northeast Glisan Street, Portland, OR 97220-5898, 503-251-5335 or toll-free 800-275-4672. *Fax:* 503-254-1268.

MURRAY STATE UNIVERSITY

Murray, KY

Tuition & fees: N/R **Average undergraduate aid package: $4570**

ABOUT THE INSTITUTION State-supported, coed. Awards: associate, bachelor's, and master's degrees. 85 undergraduate majors. Total enrollment: 8,903. Undergraduates: 7,288. Freshmen: 1,206. Federal methodology is used as a basis for awarding need-based institutional aid.

UNDERGRADUATE EXPENSES for 2000–2001 ***Application fee:*** $20. ***Tuition, state resident:*** part-time $111 per credit hour. ***Tuition, nonresident:*** full-time $2256; part-time $292 per credit hour. ***Required fees:*** full-time $350; $90 per term part-time. Full-time tuition and fees vary according to reciprocity agreements. Part-time tuition and fees vary according to course load and reciprocity agreements. ***College room and board:*** $3570; ***room only:*** $1750. ***Payment plans:*** installment, deferred payment.

FRESHMAN FINANCIAL AID (Fall 1998) 1019 applied for aid; of those 60% were deemed to have need. 94% of freshmen with need received aid; of those 97% had need fully met. *Average percent of need met:* 95% (excluding resources awarded to replace EFC). *Average financial aid package:* $4570 (excluding resources awarded to replace EFC). 41% of all full-time freshmen had no need and received non-need-based aid.

Murray State University (continued)

UNDERGRADUATE FINANCIAL AID (Fall 1998) 5,112 applied for aid; of those 60% were deemed to have need. 92% of undergraduates with need received aid; of those 98% had need fully met. *Average percent of need met:* 90% (excluding resources awarded to replace EFC). *Average financial aid package:* $4570 (excluding resources awarded to replace EFC). 33% of all full-time undergraduates had no need and received non-need-based aid.

GIFT AID (NEED-BASED) ***Total amount:*** $6,268,462 (79% Federal, 21% state). ***Receiving aid:*** *Freshmen:* 29% (370); *all full-time undergraduates:* 30% (1,910). ***Average award:*** Freshmen: $2135; Undergraduates: $2135. ***Scholarships, grants, and awards:*** Federal Pell, FSEOG, state, private, college/university gift aid from institutional funds.

GIFT AID (NON-NEED-BASED) ***Total amount:*** $3,634,538 (76% institutional, 24% external sources). ***Receiving aid:*** *Freshmen:* 24% (310); *Undergraduates:* 21% (1,360). ***Scholarships, grants, and awards by category:*** *Academic Interests/Achievement:* 1,084 awards ($1,957,193 total): agriculture, biological sciences, business, communication, computer science, education, English, foreign languages, general academic interests/achievements, health fields, home economics, mathematics, physical sciences, premedicine, social sciences. *Creative Arts/Performance:* 130 awards ($60,963 total): applied art and design, art/fine arts, creative writing, dance, debating, general creative arts/performance, journalism/publications, music, theater/drama. *Special Achievements/Activities:* 62 awards ($107,870 total): general special achievements/activities, junior miss, leadership, rodeo. *Special Characteristics:* 415 awards ($641,023 total): adult students, children and siblings of alumni, children of faculty/staff, general special characteristics, handicapped students, international students, local/state students, members of minority groups. ***Tuition waivers:*** Full or partial for children of alumni, employees or children of employees, senior citizens. ***ROTC:*** Army cooperative.

LOANS ***Student loans:*** $15,890,718 (66% need-based, 34% non-need-based). Average indebtedness per student: $14,375. ***Average need-based loan:*** Freshmen: $1840; Undergraduates: $1840. ***Parent loans:*** $697,091 (100% non-need-based). ***Programs:*** FFEL (Subsidized and Unsubsidized Stafford, PLUS), Perkins, Federal Nursing, college/university.

WORK-STUDY ***Federal work-study:*** *Total amount:* $560,102; 408 jobs averaging $1373. ***State or other work-study/employment:*** *Total amount:* $3,192,723 (100% non-need-based). 2,055 part-time jobs averaging $1554.

ATHLETIC AWARDS *Total amount:* 1,395,243 (100% non-need-based).

APPLYING for FINANCIAL AID ***Required financial aid forms:*** FAFSA, institution's own form, financial aid transcript (for transfers). ***Financial aid deadline (priority):*** 4/1. ***Notification date:*** Continuous beginning 4/15.

CONTACT Charles Vinson, Director of Student Financial Aid, Murray State University, B2 Sparks Hall, Murray, KY 42071-0009, 270-762-2546 or toll-free 800-272-4678. *Fax:* 270-762-3116. *E-mail:* charles.vinson@murraystate.edu

MUSICIANS INSTITUTE

Hollywood, CA

Tuition & fees: $12,000 — **Average undergraduate aid package: N/A**

ABOUT THE INSTITUTION Proprietary, coed. Awards: associate and bachelor's degrees. 1 undergraduate major. Federal methodology is used as a basis for awarding need-based institutional aid.

UNDERGRADUATE EXPENSES for 1999–2000 ***Application fee:*** $100. ***Tuition:*** full-time $12,000; part-time $200 per credit.

GIFT AID (NEED-BASED) ***Scholarships, grants, and awards:*** Federal Pell, FSEOG, state.

LOANS ***Programs:*** FFEL (Subsidized and Unsubsidized Stafford, PLUS).

WORK-STUDY Federal work-study jobs available.

APPLYING for FINANCIAL AID ***Required financial aid forms:*** FAFSA, institution's own form. ***Financial aid deadline:*** Continuous. ***Notification date:*** Continuous beginning 6/1. Students must reply within 4 weeks of notification.

CONTACT Director of Financial Aid, Musicians Institute, 1655 North McCadden Place, Hollywood, CA 90028, 323-462-1384 or toll-free 800-255-PLAY.

MUSKINGUM COLLEGE

New Concord, OH

Tuition & fees: $12,665 — **Average undergraduate aid package: $11,954**

ABOUT THE INSTITUTION Independent religious, coed. Awards: bachelor's and master's degrees. 54 undergraduate majors. Total enrollment: 1,871. Undergraduates: 1,562. Freshmen: 421. Federal methodology is used as a basis for awarding need-based institutional aid.

UNDERGRADUATE EXPENSES for 2000–2001 ***One-time required fee:*** 125. ***Comprehensive fee:*** 17,765 includes full-time tuition (12,250), mandatory fees (415), and room and board (5100). ***College room only:*** 2500. Room and board charges vary according to board plan and housing facility. ***Part-time tuition:*** 220 per hour. Part-time tuition and fees vary according to course load. ***Payment plan:*** installment.

FRESHMAN FINANCIAL AID (Fall 1999, est.) 366 applied for aid; of those 86% were deemed to have need. 100% of freshmen with need received aid; of those 46% had need fully met. *Average percent of need met:* 95% (excluding resources awarded to replace EFC). *Average financial aid package:* $11,937 (excluding resources awarded to replace EFC). 21% of all full-time freshmen had no need and received non-need-based aid.

UNDERGRADUATE FINANCIAL AID (Fall 1999, est.) 1,198 applied for aid; of those 90% were deemed to have need. 100% of undergraduates with need received aid; of those 50% had need fully met. *Average percent of need met:* 87% (excluding resources awarded to replace EFC). *Average financial aid package:* $11,954 (excluding resources awarded to replace EFC). 24% of all full-time undergraduates had no need and received non-need-based aid.

GIFT AID (NEED-BASED) ***Total amount:*** $8,561,300 (9% Federal, 20% state, 66% institutional, 5% external sources). ***Receiving aid:*** *Freshmen:* 75% (316); *all full-time undergraduates:* 73% (1,077). ***Average award:*** Freshmen: $8852; Undergraduates: $8226. ***Scholarships, grants, and awards:*** Federal Pell, FSEOG, state, private, college/university gift aid from institutional funds.

GIFT AID (NON-NEED-BASED) ***Total amount:*** $1,325,200 (20% state, 75% institutional, 5% external sources). ***Receiving aid:*** *Freshmen:* 74% (312); *Undergraduates:* 73% (1,069). ***Scholarships, grants, and awards by category:*** *Academic Interests/Achievement:* 560 awards ($2,266,150 total): biological sciences, computer science, general academic interests/achievements, mathematics, physical sciences, premedicine. *Creative Arts/Performance:* 200 awards ($237,950 total): art/fine arts, cinema/film/broadcasting, debating, music, theater/drama. *Special Characteristics:* 1,171 awards ($819,540 total): children and siblings of alumni, local/state students, members of minority groups, religious affiliation, siblings of current students. ***Tuition waivers:*** Full or partial for employees or children of employees, senior citizens.

LOANS ***Student loans:*** $4,372,700 (79% need-based, 21% non-need-based). 79% of past graduating class borrowed through all loan programs. Average indebtedness per student: $14,872. ***Average need-based loan:*** Freshmen: $3155; Undergraduates: $3837. ***Parent loans:*** $1,334,800 (100% non-need-based). ***Programs:*** FFEL (Subsidized and Unsubsidized Stafford, PLUS), Perkins, college/university.

WORK-STUDY ***Federal work-study:*** *Total amount:* $166,000; 208 jobs averaging $800. ***State or other work-study/employment:*** *Total amount:* $264,000 (67% need-based, 33% non-need-based). 330 part-time jobs averaging $800.

APPLYING for FINANCIAL AID ***Required financial aid form:*** FAFSA. ***Financial aid deadline (priority):*** 3/15. ***Notification date:*** 3/20. Students must reply by 5/1.

CONTACT Mr. Jeff Zellers, Dean of Enrollment, Muskingum College, 163 Stormont Street, New Concord, OH 43762, 740-826-8139 or toll-free 800-752-6082. *Fax:* 740-826-8100. *E-mail:* jzellers@muskingum.edu

NAES COLLEGE

Chicago, IL

Tuition & fees: $5140 **Average undergraduate aid package: N/A**

ABOUT THE INSTITUTION Independent, coed. Awards: bachelor's degrees. 1 undergraduate major. Total enrollment: 70. Undergraduates: 70. Freshmen: 1. Federal methodology is used as a basis for awarding need-based institutional aid.

UNDERGRADUATE EXPENSES for 1999–2000 ***Tuition:*** full-time $5000; part-time $208 per credit. ***Required fees:*** full-time $140; $70 per term part-time. ***Payment plan:*** tuition prepayment.

GIFT AID (NEED-BASED) ***Scholarships, grants, and awards:*** Federal Pell, FSEOG, state, private, tribal scholarships.

WORK-STUDY Federal work-study jobs available.

APPLYING for FINANCIAL AID ***Required financial aid form:*** FAFSA. ***Financial aid deadline:*** Continuous. ***Notification date:*** 9/15.

CONTACT Mr. Timothy Murphy, Financial Aid Officer, NAES College, 2838 West Peterson Avenue, Chicago, IL 60659-3813, 773-761-5000. *Fax:* 773-761-3808.

NAROPA UNIVERSITY

Boulder, CO

Tuition & fees: $12,867 **Average undergraduate aid package: N/A**

ABOUT THE INSTITUTION Independent, coed. Awards: bachelor's and master's degrees and post-master's certificates. 15 undergraduate majors. Total enrollment: 986. Undergraduates: 397. Freshmen: 93. Federal methodology is used as a basis for awarding need-based institutional aid.

UNDERGRADUATE EXPENSES for 1999–2000 ***Application fee:*** $35. ***Tuition:*** full-time $12,300; part-time $410 per semester hour. ***Required fees:*** full-time $567; $284 per term part-time. Full-time tuition and fees vary according to course load. Part-time tuition and fees vary according to course load. ***Payment plans:*** tuition prepayment, installment, deferred payment.

FRESHMAN FINANCIAL AID (Fall 1999, est.) 22 applied for aid; of those 91% were deemed to have need. 100% of freshmen with need received aid; of those 20% had need fully met. *Average percent of need met:* 81% (excluding resources awarded to replace EFC). 6% of all full-time freshmen had no need and received non-need-based aid.

UNDERGRADUATE FINANCIAL AID (Fall 1999, est.) 204 applied for aid; of those 94% were deemed to have need. 100% of undergraduates with need received aid; of those 11% had need fully met. *Average percent of need met:* 86% (excluding resources awarded to replace EFC). 4% of all full-time undergraduates had no need and received non-need-based aid.

GIFT AID (NEED-BASED) ***Total amount:*** $1,065,201 (30% Federal, 68% institutional, 2% external sources). ***Receiving aid:*** *Freshmen:* 42% (13); *all full-time undergraduates:* 51% (154). ***Average award:*** Freshmen: $5517; Undergraduates: $6734. ***Scholarships, grants, and awards:*** Federal Pell, FSEOG, private, college/university gift aid from institutional funds.

GIFT AID (NON-NEED-BASED) ***Total amount:*** $7760 (100% external sources). ***Tuition waivers:*** Full or partial for employees or children of employees.

LOANS ***Student loans:*** $1,879,604 (96% need-based, 4% non-need-based). 67% of past graduating class borrowed through all loan programs. Average indebtedness per student: $19,816. ***Average need-based loan:*** Freshmen: $4495; Undergraduates: $8590. ***Parent loans:*** $1,538,697 (58% need-based, 42% non-need-based). ***Programs:*** FFEL (Subsidized and Unsubsidized Stafford, PLUS), Perkins.

WORK-STUDY ***Federal work-study:*** *Total amount:* $603,598; 140 jobs averaging $4311. ***State or other work-study/employment:*** *Total amount:* $58,550 (100% need-based). 13 part-time jobs averaging $4504.

APPLYING for FINANCIAL AID ***Required financial aid form:*** FAFSA. ***Financial aid deadline (priority):*** 3/1. ***Notification date:*** Continuous beginning 4/1.

CONTACT Financial Aid Office, Naropa University, 2130 Arapahoe Avenue, Boulder, CO 80302-6697, 303-546-3534 or toll-free 800-772-0410 (out-of-state). *Fax:* 303-442-0792. *E-mail:* finaid@naropa.edu

NATIONAL AMERICAN UNIVERSITY

Colorado Springs, CO

ABOUT THE INSTITUTION Proprietary, coed. Awards: associate and bachelor's degrees. 5 undergraduate majors. Total enrollment: 350. Undergraduates: 350.

GIFT AID (NEED-BASED) ***Scholarships, grants, and awards:*** Federal Pell, FSEOG, state, private.

GIFT AID (NON-NEED-BASED) ***Scholarships, grants, and awards by category:*** *Academic Interests/Achievement:* general academic interests/achievements.

LOANS ***Programs:*** Federal Direct (Subsidized and Unsubsidized Stafford, PLUS), FFEL (Subsidized and Unsubsidized Stafford, PLUS), Perkins.

WORK-STUDY Federal work-study jobs available.

APPLYING for FINANCIAL AID ***Required financial aid forms:*** FAFSA, institution's own form.

CONTACT Financial Aid Coordinator, National American University, 2577 North Chelton Road, Colorado Springs, CO 80909, 719-471-4205 or toll-free 888-471-4781.

NATIONAL AMERICAN UNIVERSITY

Denver, CO

CONTACT Cheryl Schunneman, Director of Financial Aid, National American University, 321 Kansas City Street, Rapid City, SD 57701, 605-394-4800.

NATIONAL AMERICAN UNIVERSITY

Kansas City, MO

CONTACT Mary Anderson, Coordinator of Financial Aid, National American University, 4200 Blue Ridge, Kansas City, MO 64133, 816-353-4554. *Fax:* 816-353-1176.

NATIONAL AMERICAN UNIVERSITY

Albuquerque, NM

CONTACT Ms. Cheryl Schunneman, Director of Financial Aid, National American University, 321 Kansas City Street, Rapid City, SD 57701, 605-394-4800 or toll-free 800-843-8892.

NATIONAL AMERICAN UNIVERSITY

Rapid City, SD

CONTACT Financial Aid Director, National American University, 321 Kansas City Street, Rapid City, SD 57709-1780, 605-394-4800 or toll-free 800-843-8892.

NATIONAL AMERICAN UNIVERSITY–ST. PAUL CAMPUS

St. Paul, MN

CONTACT Sue Nelson, Financial Aid Coordinator, National American University–St. Paul Campus, 1380 Energy Lane, Suite 13, St. Paul, MN 55108-9952, 612-644-1265. *Fax:* 612-644-0690.

NATIONAL AMERICAN UNIVERSITY–SIOUX FALLS BRANCH

Sioux Falls, SD

CONTACT Ms. Jan Hegemeyer, Coordinator of Financial Aid, National American University–Sioux Falls Branch, 2801 South Kiwanis, #100, Sioux Falls, SD 57105-4293, 605-334-5430.

THE NATIONAL COLLEGE OF CHIROPRACTIC

Lombard, IL

Tuition & fees: $17,203 **Average undergraduate aid package: N/A**

ABOUT THE INSTITUTION Independent, coed. Awards: first professional degrees and first-professional certificates. 1 undergraduate major. Total enrollment: 770. Federal methodology is used as a basis for awarding need-based institutional aid.

UNDERGRADUATE EXPENSES for 1999–2000 ***Application fee:*** $55. ***Tuition:*** full-time $16,875. ***Required fees:*** full-time $328. Full-time tuition and fees vary according to course load. Room and board charges vary according to housing facility.

GIFT AID (NEED-BASED) ***Scholarships, grants, and awards:*** state, college/university gift aid from institutional funds.

LOANS ***Student loans:*** $20,500 (100% need-based). ***Programs:*** FFEL (Subsidized and Unsubsidized Stafford), Perkins.

WORK-STUDY ***Federal work-study:*** *Total amount:* $1000; jobs available.

APPLYING for FINANCIAL AID ***Required financial aid forms:*** FAFSA, institution's own form, income tax forms. ***Financial aid deadline:*** Continuous.

CONTACT Ms. Cheryl Jordan, Director of Financial Aid, The National College of Chiropractic, 200 East Roosevelt Road, Lombard, IL 60148-4583, 630-889-6515 or toll-free 800-826-6285.

THE NATIONAL HISPANIC UNIVERSITY

San Jose, CA

Tuition & fees: $3100 **Average undergraduate aid package: N/A**

ABOUT THE INSTITUTION Independent, coed. Awards: associate and bachelor's degrees and post-bachelor's certificates. 5 undergraduate majors. Total enrollment: 190. Undergraduates: 190. Federal methodology is used as a basis for awarding need-based institutional aid.

UNDERGRADUATE EXPENSES for 1999–2000 ***Application fee:*** $50. ***Tuition:*** full-time $3000; part-time $125 per unit. ***Required fees:*** full-time $100; $50 per term part-time.

GIFT AID (NEED-BASED) ***Scholarships, grants, and awards:*** Federal Pell, FSEOG, state, private, college/university gift aid from institutional funds.

LOANS ***Programs:*** FFEL (Subsidized and Unsubsidized Stafford, PLUS).

WORK-STUDY Federal work-study jobs available.

APPLYING for FINANCIAL AID ***Required financial aid form:*** FAFSA. ***Financial aid deadline:*** Continuous.

CONTACT Roehl Galang, Financial Aid Administrator, The National Hispanic University, 14271 Story Road, San Jose, CA 95127-3823, 408-273-2708. *Fax:* 408-254-1369.

NATIONAL-LOUIS UNIVERSITY

Evanston, IL

Tuition & fees: $13,095 **Average undergraduate aid package: N/A**

ABOUT THE INSTITUTION Independent, coed. Awards: bachelor's, master's, and doctoral degrees and post-bachelor's and post-master's certificates. 26 undergraduate majors. Total enrollment: 7,577. Undergraduates: 3,586. Freshmen: 209. Federal methodology is used as a basis for awarding need-based institutional aid.

UNDERGRADUATE EXPENSES for 1999–2000 ***Application fee:*** $25. ***Tuition:*** full-time $13,095; part-time $291 per quarter hour. Full-time tuition and fees vary according to location and program. Part-time tuition and fees vary according to location and program. Room and board charges vary according to board plan. ***Payment plans:*** installment, deferred payment.

GIFT AID (NEED-BASED) ***Scholarships, grants, and awards:*** Federal Pell, FSEOG, state, private, college/university gift aid from institutional funds.

GIFT AID (NON-NEED-BASED) ***Scholarships, grants, and awards by category:*** *Academic Interests/Achievement:* general academic interests/achievements. *Creative Arts/Performance:* theater/drama. *Special Achievements/Activities:* community service, leadership. ***Tuition waivers:*** Full or partial for employees or children of employees.

LOANS ***Programs:*** FFEL (Subsidized and Unsubsidized Stafford, PLUS), Perkins.

WORK-STUDY Federal work-study jobs available.

APPLYING for FINANCIAL AID ***Required financial aid forms:*** FAFSA, institution's own form. ***Financial aid deadline (priority):*** 4/15. ***Notification date:*** Continuous beginning 5/15. Students must reply within 2 weeks of notification.

CONTACT Director of Financial Aid, National-Louis University, 2840 Sheridan Road, Evanston, IL 60201-1796, 847-475-1100 or toll-free 888-NLU-TODAY Ext. 5151 (in-state), 800-443-5522 Ext. 5151 (out-of-state).

NATIONAL UNIVERSITY

La Jolla, CA

Tuition & fees: $7485 **Average undergraduate aid package: N/A**

ABOUT THE INSTITUTION Independent, coed. Awards: associate, bachelor's, and master's degrees and post-bachelor's certificates. 22 undergraduate majors. Total enrollment: 17,064. Undergraduates: 5,071. Freshmen: 1,245. Federal methodology is used as a basis for awarding need-based institutional aid.

UNDERGRADUATE EXPENSES for 1999–2000 ***Application fee:*** $60. ***Tuition:*** full-time $7425; part-time $825 per course. ***Required fees:*** full-time $60; $60 per year part-time. Full-time tuition and fees vary according to course load. Part-time tuition and fees vary according to course load.

GIFT AID (NEED-BASED) ***Total amount:*** $4,507,245 (64% Federal, 36% state). ***Scholarships, grants, and awards:*** Federal Pell, FSEOG, state, private, college/university gift aid from institutional funds.

GIFT AID (NON-NEED-BASED) ***Scholarships, grants, and awards by category:*** *Academic Interests/Achievement:* general academic interests/achievements. *Special Achievements/Activities:* leadership. ***ROTC:*** Army cooperative, Air Force cooperative.

LOANS ***Student loans:*** $37,626,468 (52% need-based, 48% non-need-based). 70% of past graduating class borrowed through all loan programs. ***Parent loans:*** $240,156 (100% non-need-based). ***Programs:*** Federal Direct (Subsidized and Unsubsidized Stafford), FFEL (Subsidized and Unsubsidized Stafford, PLUS), Perkins, college/university.

APPLYING for FINANCIAL AID ***Required financial aid forms:*** FAFSA, institution's own form. ***Financial aid deadline:*** Continuous. ***Notification date:*** Continuous beginning 6/1.

CONTACT Valerie Ryan, Financial Aid Officer, National University, 11255 North Torrey Pines Road, La Jolla, CA 92037-1011, 619-642-8513 or toll-free 800-628-8648. *Fax:* 619-642-8720. *E-mail:* vryan@nu.edu

NAZARENE BIBLE COLLEGE

Colorado Springs, CO

Tuition & fees: $5760 **Average undergraduate aid package: N/A**

ABOUT THE INSTITUTION Independent religious, coed. Awards: associate and bachelor's degrees. 6 undergraduate majors. Total enrollment: 462. Undergraduates: 462. Freshmen: 41. Federal methodology is used as a basis for awarding need-based institutional aid.

UNDERGRADUATE EXPENSES for 1999–2000 ***Application fee:*** $20. ***Tuition:*** full-time $5550; part-time $110 per quarter hour. ***Required fees:*** full-time $210; $10 per term part-time.

FRESHMAN FINANCIAL AID (Fall 1998) 18 applied for aid; of those 94% were deemed to have need. 100% of freshmen with need received aid.

UNDERGRADUATE FINANCIAL AID (Fall 1998) 167 applied for aid; of those 95% were deemed to have need. 100% of undergraduates with need received aid.

GIFT AID (NEED-BASED) ***Total amount:*** $565,756 (76% Federal, 16% institutional, 8% external sources). ***Receiving aid:*** *Freshmen:* 75% (15); *all full-time undergraduates:* 41% (83). ***Scholarships, grants, and awards:*** Federal Pell, FSEOG, college/university gift aid from institutional funds.

GIFT AID (NON-NEED-BASED) ***Total amount:*** $1300 (100% institutional). ***Receiving aid:*** *Freshmen:* 50% (10); *Undergraduates:* 6% (13). ***Tuition waivers:*** Full or partial for employees or children of employees.

LOANS ***Student loans:*** $849,409 (74% need-based, 26% non-need-based). 75% of past graduating class borrowed through all loan programs. ***Programs:*** FFEL (Subsidized and Unsubsidized Stafford, PLUS), Perkins, college/university.

WORK-STUDY ***Federal work-study:*** *Total amount:* $17,622; 12 jobs averaging $2500.

APPLYING for FINANCIAL AID ***Required financial aid form:*** FAFSA. ***Financial aid deadline:*** Continuous. ***Notification date:*** Continuous beginning 2/1.

CONTACT Mr. Malcolm Britton, Director of Financial Aid, Nazarene Bible College, 1111 Academy Park Loop, Colorado Springs, CO 80910-3717, 719-596-5110 Ext. 118 or toll-free 800-873-3873 (out-of-state). *Fax:* 719-550-9437. *E-mail:* mbritton@nbc.edu

NAZARENE INDIAN BIBLE COLLEGE

Albuquerque, NM

Tuition & fees: $4020 **Average undergraduate aid package: $3074**

ABOUT THE INSTITUTION Independent religious, coed. Awards: associate and bachelor's degrees. 4 undergraduate majors. Total enrollment: 37. Undergraduates: 37. Freshmen: 8. Institutional methodology is used as a basis for awarding need-based institutional aid.

UNDERGRADUATE EXPENSES for 1999–2000 ***Comprehensive fee:*** $5595 includes full-time tuition ($3960), mandatory fees ($60), and room and board ($1575).

FRESHMAN FINANCIAL AID (Fall 1999, est.) 4 applied for aid; of those 100% were deemed to have need. 100% of freshmen with need received aid; of those 25% had need fully met. *Average percent of need met:* 85% (excluding resources awarded to replace EFC). *Average financial aid package:* $3074 (excluding resources awarded to replace EFC).

UNDERGRADUATE FINANCIAL AID (Fall 1999, est.) 29 applied for aid; of those 100% were deemed to have need. 97% of undergraduates with need received aid; of those 64% had need fully met. *Average percent of need met:* 85% (excluding resources awarded to replace EFC). *Average financial aid package:* $3074 (excluding resources awarded to replace EFC).

GIFT AID (NEED-BASED) ***Total amount:*** $118,198 (67% Federal, 8% institutional, 25% external sources). ***Receiving aid:*** *Freshmen:* 100% (4); *all full-time undergraduates:* 90% (26). ***Average award:*** Freshmen: $3125; Undergraduates: $3125. ***Scholarships, grants, and awards:*** Federal Pell, private, college/university gift aid from institutional funds, tribal awards.

GIFT AID (NON-NEED-BASED) ***Scholarships, grants, and awards by category:*** *Academic Interests/Achievement:* general academic interests/achievements, religion/biblical studies. *Special Characteristics:* ethnic background, veterans. ***Tuition waivers:*** Full or partial for employees or children of employees.

LOANS ***Student loans:*** $72,133 (100% need-based). 75% of past graduating class borrowed through all loan programs. ***Average need-based loan:*** Freshmen: $3796; Undergraduates: $3796. ***Programs:*** Federal Direct (Subsidized and Unsubsidized Stafford), FFEL (Subsidized Stafford), college/university.

APPLYING for FINANCIAL AID ***Required financial aid forms:*** FAFSA, institution's own form. ***Financial aid deadline:*** Continuous. ***Notification date:*** Continuous beginning 9/8.

CONTACT Mary E. Jimenez, Director of Financial Aid, Nazarene Indian Bible College, 2315 Markham Road, SW, Albuquerque, NM 87105, 505-877-0240 or toll-free 888-877-NIBC. *Fax:* 505-877-6214. *E-mail:* nibc1@aol.com

NAZARETH COLLEGE OF ROCHESTER

Rochester, NY

Tuition & fees: $14,046 **Average undergraduate aid package: $13,245**

ABOUT THE INSTITUTION Independent, coed. Awards: bachelor's and master's degrees. 67 undergraduate majors. Total enrollment: 2,874. Undergraduates: 1,793. Freshmen: 332. Both federal and institutional methodology are used as a basis for awarding need-based institutional aid.

UNDERGRADUATE EXPENSES for 1999–2000 ***Application fee:*** $40. ***Comprehensive fee:*** $20,422 includes full-time tuition ($13,620), mandatory fees ($426), and room and board ($6376). ***College room only:*** $3660. Full-time tuition and fees vary according to course load. Room and board charges vary according to board plan and housing facility. ***Part-time tuition:*** $378 per credit hour. ***Part-time fees:*** $20 per term part-time. ***Payment plan:*** installment.

FRESHMAN FINANCIAL AID (Fall 1999) 312 applied for aid; of those 86% were deemed to have need. 100% of freshmen with need received aid. *Average percent of need met:* 85% (excluding resources awarded to replace EFC). *Average financial aid package:* $12,186 (excluding resources awarded to replace EFC). 13% of all full-time freshmen had no need and received non-need-based aid.

UNDERGRADUATE FINANCIAL AID (Fall 1999) 1,332 applied for aid; of those 90% were deemed to have need. 100% of undergraduates with need received aid. *Average percent of need met:* 85% (excluding resources awarded to replace EFC). *Average financial aid package:* $13,245 (excluding resources awarded to replace EFC). 11% of all full-time undergraduates had no need and received non-need-based aid.

GIFT AID (NEED-BASED) ***Total amount:*** $8,762,527 (12% Federal, 21% state, 64% institutional, 3% external sources). ***Receiving aid:*** *Freshmen:* 80% (266); *all full-time undergraduates:* 78% (1,186). ***Average award:*** Freshmen: $8525; Undergraduates: $7523. ***Scholarships, grants, and awards:*** Federal Pell, FSEOG, state, private, college/university gift aid from institutional funds.

GIFT AID (NON-NEED-BASED) ***Total amount:*** $341,494 (3% state, 87% institutional, 10% external sources). ***Receiving aid:*** *Freshmen:* 5% (17); *Undergraduates:* 4% (61). ***Scholarships, grants, and awards by category:*** *Academic Interests/Achievement:* 264 awards ($1,306,793 total): general academic interests/achievements. *Creative Arts/Performance:* 51 awards ($90,106 total): art/fine arts, music, theater/drama. *Special Characteristics:* 93 awards ($338,204 total): children and siblings of alumni, children of faculty/staff, siblings of current students. ***Tuition waivers:*** Full or partial for employees or children of employees. ***ROTC:*** Air Force cooperative.

LOANS ***Student loans:*** $7,526,304 (67% need-based, 33% non-need-based). 76% of past graduating class borrowed through all loan programs. Average indebtedness per student: $18,095. ***Average need-based loan:*** Freshmen: $2899; Undergraduates: $4611. ***Parent loans:*** $1,322,937 (100% non-need-based). ***Programs:*** FFEL (Subsidized and Unsubsidized Stafford, PLUS), Perkins.

WORK-STUDY ***Federal work-study:*** *Total amount:* $761,068; 600 jobs averaging $1268.

APPLYING for FINANCIAL AID ***Required financial aid forms:*** FAFSA, institution's own form. ***Financial aid deadline (priority):*** 2/15. ***Notification date:*** 3/15. Students must reply by 5/1 or within 2 weeks of notification.

CONTACT Dr. Bruce C. Woolley, Director of Financial Aid, Nazareth College of Rochester, 4245 East Avenue, Rochester, NY 14618-3790, 716-389-2310 or toll-free 800-462-3944 (in-state). *Fax:* 716-389-2317. *E-mail:* bcwoolle@naz.edu

NEBRASKA CHRISTIAN COLLEGE

Norfolk, NE

Tuition & fees: $4930 **Average undergraduate aid package: N/A**

Nebraska Christian College (continued)

ABOUT THE INSTITUTION Independent religious, coed. Awards: associate and bachelor's degrees. 10 undergraduate majors. Total enrollment: 130. Undergraduates: 130. Both federal and institutional methodology are used as a basis for awarding need-based institutional aid.

UNDERGRADUATE EXPENSES for 1999–2000 ***Comprehensive fee:*** $7890 includes full-time tuition ($4500), mandatory fees ($430), and room and board ($2960). ***College room only:*** $1350. ***Part-time tuition:*** $150 per credit hour. ***Part-time fees:*** $108 per term part-time. Part-time tuition and fees vary according to course load.

FRESHMAN FINANCIAL AID (Fall 1999, est.) 43 applied for aid; of those 100% were deemed to have need. 100% of freshmen with need received aid.

UNDERGRADUATE FINANCIAL AID (Fall 1999, est.) 67 applied for aid; of those 100% were deemed to have need. 100% of undergraduates with need received aid.

GIFT AID (NEED-BASED) ***Total amount:*** $359,830 (40% Federal, 7% state, 37% institutional, 16% external sources). ***Receiving aid:*** *Freshmen:* 100% (43); *all full-time undergraduates:* 96% (67). ***Scholarships, grants, and awards:*** Federal Pell, FSEOG, state, private, college/university gift aid from institutional funds.

GIFT AID (NON-NEED-BASED) ***Scholarships, grants, and awards by category:*** *Academic Interests/Achievement:* 83 awards ($105,000 total): general academic interests/achievements. *Creative Arts/Performance:* 10 awards ($5260 total): general creative arts/performance, music. *Special Characteristics:* 15 awards ($12,300 total): children of educators, children of faculty/staff, international students, relatives of clergy, spouses of current students. ***Tuition waivers:*** Full or partial for employees or children of employees.

LOANS ***Student loans:*** $231,300 (100% need-based). 60% of past graduating class borrowed through all loan programs. ***Average need-based loan:*** Freshmen: $2300; Undergraduates: $3400. ***Parent loans:*** $17,500 (100% need-based). ***Programs:*** FFEL (Subsidized and Unsubsidized Stafford, PLUS).

WORK-STUDY ***Federal work-study:*** *Total amount:* $15,700; 7 jobs averaging $2200.

APPLYING for FINANCIAL AID ***Required financial aid forms:*** FAFSA, institution's own form. ***Financial aid deadline:*** Continuous. ***Notification date:*** Continuous beginning 4/1. Students must reply within 2 weeks of notification.

CONTACT Linda Bigbee, Director of Financial Aid, Nebraska Christian College, 1800 Syracuse, Norfolk, NE 68701-2458, 402-379-5017. *Fax:* 402-379-5100. *E-mail:* lbigbee@nechristian.edu

NEBRASKA METHODIST COLLEGE OF NURSING AND ALLIED HEALTH

Omaha, NE

Tuition & fees: $8700 **Average undergraduate aid package: $8325**

ABOUT THE INSTITUTION Independent religious, coed, primarily women. Awards: associate, bachelor's, and master's degrees. 5 undergraduate majors. Total enrollment: 411. Undergraduates: 387. Freshmen: 39. Federal methodology is used as a basis for awarding need-based institutional aid.

UNDERGRADUATE EXPENSES for 1999–2000 ***Application fee:*** $25. ***Tuition:*** full-time $8160; part-time $272 per credit hour. ***Required fees:*** full-time $540; $18 per credit hour. Room and board charges vary according to housing facility and location. ***Payment plan:*** installment.

FRESHMAN FINANCIAL AID (Fall 1999) 22 applied for aid; of those 86% were deemed to have need. 100% of freshmen with need received aid; of those 21% had need fully met. *Average percent of need met:* 74% (excluding resources awarded to replace EFC). *Average financial aid package:* $7022 (excluding resources awarded to replace EFC). 28% of all full-time freshmen had no need and received non-need-based aid.

UNDERGRADUATE FINANCIAL AID (Fall 1999) 156 applied for aid; of those 83% were deemed to have need. 100% of undergraduates with need received aid; of those 45% had need fully met. *Average percent of need met:* 84% (excluding resources awarded to replace EFC). *Average financial aid package:* $8325 (excluding resources awarded to replace EFC). 25% of all full-time undergraduates had no need and received non-need-based aid.

GIFT AID (NEED-BASED) ***Total amount:*** $750,020 (35% Federal, 9% state, 44% institutional, 12% external sources). ***Receiving aid:*** *Freshmen:* 66% (19); *all full-time undergraduates:* 64% (113). ***Average award:*** Freshmen: $4613; Undergraduates: $3667. ***Scholarships, grants, and awards:*** Federal Pell, FSEOG, state, private, college/university gift aid from institutional funds.

GIFT AID (NON-NEED-BASED) ***Total amount:*** $194,311 (82% institutional, 18% external sources). ***Receiving aid:*** *Freshmen:* 7% (2); *Undergraduates:* 6% (11). ***Scholarships, grants, and awards by category:*** *Academic Interests/Achievement:* general academic interests/achievements. ***ROTC:*** Army cooperative.

LOANS ***Student loans:*** $1,600,216 (72% need-based, 28% non-need-based). 82% of past graduating class borrowed through all loan programs. ***Average need-based loan:*** Freshmen: $2409; Undergraduates: $4658. ***Parent loans:*** $23,500 (100% non-need-based). ***Programs:*** FFEL (Subsidized and Unsubsidized Stafford, PLUS), Perkins, Federal Nursing, college/university, alternative loans.

WORK-STUDY ***State or other work-study/employment:*** *Total amount:* $1600 (100% non-need-based). 1 part-time job averaging $1600.

APPLYING for FINANCIAL AID ***Required financial aid forms:*** FAFSA, institution's own form. ***Financial aid deadline (priority):*** 5/1. ***Notification date:*** Continuous. Students must reply within 3 weeks of notification.

CONTACT Ms. Brenda Boyd, Financial Aid Coordinator, Nebraska Methodist College of Nursing and Allied Health, 8501 West Dodge Road, Omaha, NE 68114-3426, 402-354-4874 or toll-free 800-335-5510. *Fax:* 402-354-8893. *E-mail:* bboyd@nmhs.org

NEBRASKA WESLEYAN UNIVERSITY

Lincoln, NE

Tuition & fees: $12,826 **Average undergraduate aid package: $9748**

ABOUT THE INSTITUTION Independent United Methodist, coed. Awards: bachelor's degrees. 39 undergraduate majors. Total enrollment: 1,675. Undergraduates: 1,675. Freshmen: 359. Federal methodology is used as a basis for awarding need-based institutional aid.

UNDERGRADUATE EXPENSES for 1999–2000 ***Application fee:*** $20. ***One-time required fee:*** $80. ***Comprehensive fee:*** $16,800 includes full-time tuition ($12,584), mandatory fees ($242), and room and board ($3974). Room and board charges vary according to board plan. ***Part-time tuition:*** $475 per hour. Part-time tuition and fees vary according to class time and course load. ***Payment plan:*** installment.

FRESHMAN FINANCIAL AID (Fall 1999, est.) 289 applied for aid; of those 89% were deemed to have need. 100% of freshmen with need received aid; of those 18% had need fully met. *Average percent of need met:* 72% (excluding resources awarded to replace EFC). *Average financial aid package:* $9695 (excluding resources awarded to replace EFC). 25% of all full-time freshmen had no need and received non-need-based aid.

UNDERGRADUATE FINANCIAL AID (Fall 1999, est.) 1,181 applied for aid; of those 89% were deemed to have need. 100% of undergraduates with need received aid; of those 19% had need fully met. *Average percent of need met:* 73% (excluding resources awarded to replace EFC). *Average financial aid package:* $9748 (excluding resources awarded to replace EFC). 20% of all full-time undergraduates had no need and received non-need-based aid.

GIFT AID (NEED-BASED) ***Total amount:*** $6,178,071 (16% Federal, 3% state, 78% institutional, 3% external sources). ***Receiving aid:*** *Freshmen:* 71% (256); *all full-time undergraduates:* 64% (1,031). ***Average award:*** Freshmen: $6528; Undergraduates: $5977. ***Scholarships, grants, and awards:*** Federal Pell, FSEOG, state, private, college/university gift aid from institutional funds.

GIFT AID (NON-NEED-BASED) ***Total amount:*** $770,388 (94% institutional, 6% external sources). ***Receiving aid:*** *Freshmen:* 1% (3); *Undergraduates:* 1% (13). ***Scholarships, grants, and awards by category:*** *Academic*

Interests/Achievement: general academic interests/achievements. *Creative Arts/Performance:* art/fine arts, music, theater/drama. *Special Characteristics:* relatives of clergy, siblings of current students. ***Tuition waivers:*** Full or partial for employees or children of employees, adult students, senior citizens. ***ROTC:*** Army cooperative, Air Force cooperative.

LOANS ***Student loans:*** $4,602,901 (85% need-based, 15% non-need-based). ***Average need-based loan:*** Freshmen: $3414; Undergraduates: $4113. ***Parent loans:*** $950,392 (17% need-based, 83% non-need-based). ***Programs:*** FFEL (Subsidized and Unsubsidized Stafford, PLUS), Perkins.

WORK-STUDY ***Federal work-study:*** *Total amount:* $191,000; jobs available. ***State or other work-study/employment:*** *Total amount:* $409,000 (51% need-based, 49% non-need-based). Part-time jobs available.

APPLYING for FINANCIAL AID ***Required financial aid form:*** FAFSA. ***Financial aid deadline:*** 3/1. ***Notification date:*** Continuous. Students must reply within 4 weeks of notification.

CONTACT Mr. Claire Fredstrom, Director of Financial Aid, Nebraska Wesleyan University, 5000 Saint Paul Avenue, Lincoln, NE 68504, 402-465-2167 or toll-free 800-541-3818. *Fax:* 402-465-2179. *E-mail:* cdf@nebrwesleyan.edu

NER ISRAEL RABBINICAL COLLEGE

Baltimore, MD

CONTACT Mr. Moshe Pelberg, Financial Aid Administrator, Ner Israel Rabbinical College, 400 Mount Wilson Lane, Baltimore, MD 21208, 410-484-7200.

NEUMANN COLLEGE

Aston, PA

Tuition & fees: $13,920 **Average undergraduate aid package: N/A**

ABOUT THE INSTITUTION Independent Roman Catholic, coed. Awards: associate, bachelor's, and master's degrees. 16 undergraduate majors. Total enrollment: 1,625. Undergraduates: 1,445. Freshmen: 379. Federal methodology is used as a basis for awarding need-based institutional aid.

UNDERGRADUATE EXPENSES for 1999–2000 ***Application fee:*** $35. ***Comprehensive fee:*** $20,420 includes full-time tuition ($13,350), mandatory fees ($570), and room and board ($6500). ***College room only:*** $3600. Full-time tuition and fees vary according to program. ***Part-time tuition:*** $320 per credit. Part-time tuition and fees vary according to program. ***Payment plans:*** installment, deferred payment.

GIFT AID (NEED-BASED) ***Scholarships, grants, and awards:*** Federal Pell, FSEOG, state, college/university gift aid from institutional funds.

GIFT AID (NON-NEED-BASED) ***Scholarships, grants, and awards by category:*** *Academic Interests/Achievement:* general academic interests/achievements. *Special Characteristics:* children of faculty/staff. ***Tuition waivers:*** Full or partial for employees or children of employees. ***ROTC:*** Army cooperative.

LOANS ***Programs:*** FFEL (Subsidized and Unsubsidized Stafford, PLUS), Federal Nursing.

WORK-STUDY Federal work-study jobs available.

APPLYING for FINANCIAL AID ***Required financial aid form:*** FAFSA. ***Financial aid deadline:*** Continuous.

CONTACT Office of Admissions and Financial Aid, Neumann College, One Neumann Drive, Aston, PA 19014-1298, 610-459-0905 or toll-free 800-963-8626.

NEWARK COLLEGE OF ARTS AND SCIENCES

Newark, NJ

See Rutgers, The State University of New Jersey, Newark College of Arts and Sciences

NEWBERRY COLLEGE

Newberry, SC

Tuition & fees: $13,952 **Average undergraduate aid package: N/A**

ABOUT THE INSTITUTION Independent Lutheran, coed. Awards: bachelor's degrees. 40 undergraduate majors. Total enrollment: 750. Undergraduates: 750. Freshmen: 179. Federal methodology is used as a basis for awarding need-based institutional aid.

UNDERGRADUATE EXPENSES for 1999–2000 ***Application fee:*** $30. ***One-time required fee:*** $100. ***Comprehensive fee:*** $17,952 includes full-time tuition ($13,602), mandatory fees ($350), and room and board ($4000). ***College room only:*** $1730. Room and board charges vary according to board plan and housing facility. ***Part-time tuition:*** $185 per semester hour. ***Part-time fees:*** $30 per term part-time. ***Payment plan:*** installment.

GIFT AID (NEED-BASED) ***Scholarships, grants, and awards:*** Federal Pell, FSEOG, state, private, college/university gift aid from institutional funds.

GIFT AID (NON-NEED-BASED) ***Scholarships, grants, and awards by category:*** *Academic Interests/Achievement:* biological sciences, business, communication, education, foreign languages, general academic interests/achievements. *Creative Arts/Performance:* music, theater/drama. *Special Characteristics:* children of faculty/staff, local/state students, relatives of clergy, religious affiliation. ***Tuition waivers:*** Full or partial for employees or children of employees. ***ROTC:*** Army.

LOANS ***Programs:*** Federal Direct (Subsidized and Unsubsidized Stafford, PLUS), FFEL (Subsidized and Unsubsidized Stafford, PLUS), Perkins, state, college/university.

WORK-STUDY Federal work-study jobs available.

APPLYING for FINANCIAL AID ***Required financial aid form:*** FAFSA. ***Financial aid deadline (priority):*** 3/15. ***Notification date:*** Continuous. Students must reply within 2 weeks of notification.

CONTACT Ms. Cathryn Flaherty, Director of Financial Aid, Newberry College, 2100 College Street, Newberry, SC 29108, 803-321-5120 or toll-free 800-845-4955 Ext. 5127. *Fax:* 803-321-5627.

NEW COLLEGE OF CALIFORNIA

San Francisco, CA

CONTACT Director of Student Financial Aid, New College of California, 50 Fell Street, San Francisco, CA 94102-5206, 415-241-1300 Ext. 338 or toll-free 888-437-3460.

NEW COLLEGE OF THE UNIVERSITY OF SOUTH FLORIDA

Sarasota, FL

Tuition & fees (FL res): $2492 **Average undergraduate aid package: $9962**

ABOUT THE INSTITUTION State-supported, coed. Awards: bachelor's degrees. 31 undergraduate majors. Total enrollment: 617. Undergraduates: 617. Freshmen: 128. Federal methodology is used as a basis for awarding need-based institutional aid.

UNDERGRADUATE EXPENSES for 1999–2000 ***Application fee:*** $20. ***Tuition, state resident:*** full-time $2492. ***Tuition, nonresident:*** full-time $10,878. Full-time tuition and fees vary according to student level. ***College room and board:*** $4663. Room and board charges vary according to board plan and housing facility. ***Payment plans:*** tuition prepayment, installment.

FRESHMAN FINANCIAL AID (Fall 1999) 88 applied for aid; of those 62% were deemed to have need. 100% of freshmen with need received aid; of those 60% had need fully met. *Average percent of need met:* 100% (excluding resources awarded to replace EFC). *Average financial aid package:* $9945 (excluding resources awarded to replace EFC). 26% of all full-time freshmen had no need and received non-need-based aid.

UNDERGRADUATE FINANCIAL AID (Fall 1999) 308 applied for aid; of those 74% were deemed to have need. 98% of undergraduates with need received aid; of those 59% had need fully met. *Average percent of need*

New College of the University of South Florida (continued)

met: 100% (excluding resources awarded to replace EFC). *Average financial aid package:* $9962 (excluding resources awarded to replace EFC). 12% of all full-time undergraduates had no need and received non-need-based aid.

GIFT AID (NEED-BASED) ***Total amount:*** $352,635 (66% Federal, 34% institutional). ***Receiving aid:*** *Freshmen:* 18% (23); *all full-time undergraduates:* 27% (169). ***Average award:*** Freshmen: $2871; Undergraduates: $2430. ***Scholarships, grants, and awards:*** Federal Pell, FSEOG, state, college/university gift aid from institutional funds.

GIFT AID (NON-NEED-BASED) ***Total amount:*** $2,055,060 (1% Federal, 45% state, 50% institutional, 4% external sources). ***Receiving aid:*** *Freshmen:* 43% (55); *Undergraduates:* 28% (174). ***Scholarships, grants, and awards by category:*** *Academic Interests/Achievement:* general academic interests/achievements. ***ROTC:*** Army cooperative, Air Force cooperative.

LOANS ***Student loans:*** $855,045 (59% need-based, 41% non-need-based). 38% of past graduating class borrowed through all loan programs. Average indebtedness per student: $15,800. ***Average need-based loan:*** Freshmen: $1364; Undergraduates: $2316. ***Parent loans:*** $61,912 (100% non-need-based). ***Programs:*** FFEL (Subsidized and Unsubsidized Stafford, PLUS), Perkins, college/university.

WORK-STUDY ***Federal work-study:*** *Total amount:* $145,961; jobs available.

APPLYING for FINANCIAL AID ***Required financial aid form:*** FAFSA. ***Financial aid deadline (priority):*** 3/1. ***Notification date:*** Continuous. Students must reply by 5/1 or within 2 weeks of notification.

CONTACT Ramona Arnold, Financial Aid Coordinator, New College of the University of South Florida, 5700 North Tamiami Trail, Sarasota, FL 34243-2197, 941-359-4255. *E-mail:* finaid@sar.usf.edu

NEW ENGLAND COLLEGE

Henniker, NH

Tuition & fees: $18,097 **Average undergraduate aid package: $16,651**

ABOUT THE INSTITUTION Independent, coed. Awards: bachelor's and master's degrees. 38 undergraduate majors. Total enrollment: 758. Undergraduates: 708. Freshmen: 213. Federal methodology is used as a basis for awarding need-based institutional aid.

UNDERGRADUATE EXPENSES for 1999–2000 ***Application fee:*** $30. ***Comprehensive fee:*** $24,311 includes full-time tuition ($17,674), mandatory fees ($423), and room and board ($6214). Room and board charges vary according to board plan. ***Part-time tuition:*** $737 per credit. ***Part-time fees:*** $110 per term part-time. Part-time tuition and fees vary according to course load. ***Payment plan:*** installment.

FRESHMAN FINANCIAL AID (Fall 1999, est.) 171 applied for aid; of those 100% were deemed to have need. 100% of freshmen with need received aid. *Average percent of need met:* 85% (excluding resources awarded to replace EFC). *Average financial aid package:* $15,068 (excluding resources awarded to replace EFC). 17% of all full-time freshmen had no need and received non-need-based aid.

UNDERGRADUATE FINANCIAL AID (Fall 1999, est.) 422 applied for aid; of those 100% were deemed to have need. 100% of undergraduates with need received aid. *Average percent of need met:* 84% (excluding resources awarded to replace EFC). *Average financial aid package:* $16,651 (excluding resources awarded to replace EFC). 8% of all full-time undergraduates had no need and received non-need-based aid.

GIFT AID (NEED-BASED) ***Total amount:*** $4,433,381 (16% Federal, 1% state, 81% institutional, 2% external sources). ***Receiving aid:*** *Freshmen:* 80% (164); *all full-time undergraduates:* 63% (406). ***Average award:*** Freshmen: $10,953; Undergraduates: $9255. ***Scholarships, grants, and awards:*** Federal Pell, FSEOG, state, private, college/university gift aid from institutional funds.

GIFT AID (NON-NEED-BASED) ***Total amount:*** $445,493 (100% institutional). ***Receiving aid:*** *Freshmen:* 37% (76); *Undergraduates:* 39% (249). ***Scholarships, grants, and awards by category:*** *Academic Interests/Achievement:* general academic interests/achievements. *Creative Arts/Performance:* 3 awards ($4500 total): art/fine arts. *Special Achievements/Activities:* 66 awards ($99,750 total): community service, leadership. *Special Characteristics:* children of educators, children of faculty/staff, local/state students, siblings of current students. ***Tuition waivers:*** Full or partial for employees or children of employees. ***ROTC:*** Army cooperative.

LOANS ***Student loans:*** $2,437,516 (100% need-based). 80% of past graduating class borrowed through all loan programs. Average indebtedness per student: $14,750. ***Average need-based loan:*** Freshmen: $5975; Undergraduates: $7214. ***Parent loans:*** $1,129,232 (100% need-based). ***Programs:*** FFEL (Subsidized and Unsubsidized Stafford, PLUS), Perkins.

WORK-STUDY ***Federal work-study:*** *Total amount:* $383,947; 247 jobs averaging $1500. ***State or other work-study/employment:*** *Total amount:* $21,000 (100% need-based). Part-time jobs available.

APPLYING for FINANCIAL AID ***Required financial aid forms:*** FAFSA, institution's own form. ***Financial aid deadline (priority):*** 3/1. ***Notification date:*** 3/15. Students must reply by 5/1 or within 2 weeks of notification.

CONTACT Nancy E. Welch, Director of Financial Aid, New England College, 7 Main Street, Henniker, NH 03242-3293, 603-428-2284 or toll-free 800-521-7642 (out-of-state). *Fax:* 603-428-2266. *E-mail:* nw@nec1.nec.edu

NEW ENGLAND CONSERVATORY OF MUSIC

Boston, MA

Tuition & fees: $19,800 **Average undergraduate aid package: $14,957**

ABOUT THE INSTITUTION Independent, coed. Awards: bachelor's, master's, and doctoral degrees. 7 undergraduate majors. Total enrollment: 768. Undergraduates: 398. Freshmen: 84. Federal methodology is used as a basis for awarding need-based institutional aid.

UNDERGRADUATE EXPENSES for 1999–2000 ***Application fee:*** $75. ***Comprehensive fee:*** $28,400 includes full-time tuition ($19,650), mandatory fees ($150), and room and board ($8600). Full-time tuition and fees vary according to program. Room and board charges vary according to housing facility. ***Part-time tuition:*** $635 per credit hour. ***Part-time fees:*** $150 per year part-time. Part-time tuition and fees vary according to program. Tuition for studio instruction: $4915 per term.

FRESHMAN FINANCIAL AID (Fall 1999, est.) 54 applied for aid; of those 89% were deemed to have need. 98% of freshmen with need received aid; of those 21% had need fully met. *Average percent of need met:* 67% (excluding resources awarded to replace EFC). *Average financial aid package:* $14,808 (excluding resources awarded to replace EFC). 4% of all full-time freshmen had no need and received non-need-based aid.

UNDERGRADUATE FINANCIAL AID (Fall 1999, est.) 294 applied for aid; of those 86% were deemed to have need. 93% of undergraduates with need received aid; of those 17% had need fully met. *Average percent of need met:* 67% (excluding resources awarded to replace EFC). *Average financial aid package:* $14,957 (excluding resources awarded to replace EFC). 7% of all full-time undergraduates had no need and received non-need-based aid.

GIFT AID (NEED-BASED) ***Total amount:*** $2,246,074 (14% Federal, 3% state, 79% institutional, 4% external sources). ***Receiving aid:*** *Freshmen:* 54% (45); *all full-time undergraduates:* 55% (214). ***Average award:*** Freshmen: $10,639; Undergraduates: $10,079. ***Scholarships, grants, and awards:*** Federal Pell, FSEOG, state, private, college/university gift aid from institutional funds.

GIFT AID (NON-NEED-BASED) ***Total amount:*** $128,765 (100% institutional). ***Receiving aid:*** *Freshmen:* 4% (3); *Undergraduates:* 1% (3). ***Scholarships, grants, and awards by category:*** *Creative Arts/Performance:* 28 awards ($128,765 total): music, theater/drama.

LOANS ***Student loans:*** $1,160,071 (77% need-based, 23% non-need-based). 85% of past graduating class borrowed through all loan programs. Average indebtedness per student: $19,000. ***Average need-based loan:*** Freshmen: $3691; Undergraduates: $4546. ***Parent loans:*** $667,828 (100% non-need-based). ***Programs:*** FFEL (Subsidized and Unsubsidized Stafford, PLUS), Perkins, state.

WORK-STUDY ***Federal work-study:*** *Total amount:* $259,276; 166 jobs averaging $1562.

APPLYING for FINANCIAL AID ***Required financial aid forms:*** FAFSA, institution's own form. ***Financial aid deadline (priority):*** 2/2. ***Notification date:*** Continuous beginning 4/1. Students must reply by 5/1 or within 2 weeks of notification.

CONTACT Jill D'Amico, Director of Financial Aid, New England Conservatory of Music, 290 Huntington Avenue, Boston, MA 02115-5000, 617-585-1110. *Fax:* 617-585-1115. *E-mail:* jdamico@newenglandconservatory.edu

NEW ENGLAND INSTITUTE OF APPLIED ARTS AND SCIENCES

Newton Centre, MA

See Mount Ida College

THE NEW ENGLAND SCHOOL OF ART AND DESIGN AT SUFFOLK UNIVERSITY

Boston, MA

See Suffolk University

NEW HAMPSHIRE COLLEGE

Manchester, NH

Tuition & fees: $15,848 **Average undergraduate aid package: N/A**

ABOUT THE INSTITUTION Independent, coed. Awards: associate, bachelor's, master's, and doctoral degrees. 32 undergraduate majors. Total enrollment: 5,580. Undergraduates: 4,058. Freshmen: 933. Federal methodology is used as a basis for awarding need-based institutional aid.

UNDERGRADUATE EXPENSES for 2000–2001 ***Comprehensive fee:*** $22,638 includes full-time tuition ($15,598), mandatory fees ($250), and room and board ($6790). ***College room only:*** $4750. Full-time tuition and fees vary according to class time. Room and board charges vary according to board plan and housing facility. ***Part-time tuition:*** $650 per credit. Part-time tuition and fees vary according to class time. ***Payment plans:*** installment, deferred payment.

GIFT AID (NEED-BASED) ***Scholarships, grants, and awards:*** Federal Pell, FSEOG, state, college/university gift aid from institutional funds.

GIFT AID (NON-NEED-BASED) ***Scholarships, grants, and awards by category:*** *Academic Interests/Achievement:* general academic interests/achievements. *Special Achievements/Activities:* leadership, memberships. *Special Characteristics:* children of faculty/staff, general special characteristics, local/state students, siblings of current students. ***Tuition waivers:*** Full or partial for employees or children of employees, senior citizens. ***ROTC:*** Army cooperative, Air Force cooperative.

LOANS ***Programs:*** FFEL (Subsidized and Unsubsidized Stafford, PLUS), Perkins.

WORK-STUDY Federal work-study jobs available.

APPLYING for FINANCIAL AID ***Required financial aid form:*** FAFSA. ***Financial aid deadline (priority):*** 3/15. ***Notification date:*** Continuous. Students must reply within 3 weeks of notification.

CONTACT Director of Financial Aid, New Hampshire College, 2500 North River Road, Manchester, NH 03106, 603-645-9645 or toll-free 800-NHC-4YOU.

NEW JERSEY CITY UNIVERSITY

Jersey City, NJ

ABOUT THE INSTITUTION State-supported, coed. Awards: bachelor's and master's degrees. 27 undergraduate majors. Total enrollment: 8,024. Undergraduates: 5,783. Freshmen: 857.

GIFT AID (NEED-BASED) ***Scholarships, grants, and awards:*** Federal Pell, FSEOG, state, college/university gift aid from institutional funds.

GIFT AID (NON-NEED-BASED) ***Scholarships, grants, and awards by category:*** *Academic Interests/Achievement:* biological sciences, business, communication, education, general academic interests/achievements, mathematics. *Creative Arts/Performance:* art/fine arts, dance, music.

LOANS ***Programs:*** FFEL (Subsidized and Unsubsidized Stafford, PLUS), Perkins, state.

WORK-STUDY Federal work-study jobs available.

APPLYING for FINANCIAL AID ***Required financial aid form:*** FAFSA.

CONTACT Financial Aid Office, New Jersey City University, 2039 Kennedy Boulevard, Jersey City, NJ 07305-1957, 201-200-3173 or toll-free 800-441-NJCU. *Fax:* 201-200-3181.

NEW JERSEY INSTITUTE OF TECHNOLOGY

Newark, NJ

Tuition & fees (NJ res): $6480 **Average undergraduate aid package: $8817**

ABOUT THE INSTITUTION State-supported, coed. Awards: bachelor's, master's, and doctoral degrees. 34 undergraduate majors. Total enrollment: 8,261. Undergraduates: 5,270. Freshmen: 681. Both federal and institutional methodology are used as a basis for awarding need-based institutional aid.

UNDERGRADUATE EXPENSES for 1999–2000 ***Application fee:*** $35. ***Tuition, state resident:*** full-time $5508; part-time $206 per credit. ***Tuition, nonresident:*** full-time $9852; part-time $424 per credit. ***Required fees:*** full-time $972; $41 per credit. Full-time tuition and fees vary according to degree level. Part-time tuition and fees vary according to degree level. ***College room and board:*** $7050. Room and board charges vary according to board plan and housing facility. ***Payment plans:*** installment, deferred payment.

FRESHMAN FINANCIAL AID (Fall 1998) 526 applied for aid; of those 77% were deemed to have need. 100% of freshmen with need received aid; of those 43% had need fully met. *Average percent of need met:* 85% (excluding resources awarded to replace EFC). *Average financial aid package:* $8874 (excluding resources awarded to replace EFC). 19% of all full-time freshmen had no need and received non-need-based aid.

UNDERGRADUATE FINANCIAL AID (Fall 1998) 2,681 applied for aid; of those 80% were deemed to have need. 100% of undergraduates with need received aid; of those 41% had need fully met. *Average percent of need met:* 84% (excluding resources awarded to replace EFC). *Average financial aid package:* $8817 (excluding resources awarded to replace EFC). 11% of all full-time undergraduates had no need and received non-need-based aid.

GIFT AID (NEED-BASED) ***Total amount:*** $8,457,680 (34% Federal, 60% state, 6% institutional). ***Receiving aid:*** *Freshmen:* 51% (286); *all full-time undergraduates:* 49% (1,667). ***Scholarships, grants, and awards:*** Federal Pell, FSEOG, state, private, college/university gift aid from institutional funds.

GIFT AID (NON-NEED-BASED) ***Total amount:*** $4,319,255 (13% state, 68% institutional, 19% external sources). ***Receiving aid:*** *Freshmen:* 29% (164); *Undergraduates:* 32% (1,107). ***Scholarships, grants, and awards by category:*** *Academic Interests/Achievement:* architecture, general academic interests/achievements. *Special Characteristics:* out-of-state students. ***Tuition waivers:*** Full or partial for employees or children of employees. ***ROTC:*** Air Force.

LOANS ***Student loans:*** $7,795,445 (97% need-based, 3% non-need-based). ***Parent loans:*** $516,956 (100% non-need-based). ***Programs:*** Federal Direct (Subsidized and Unsubsidized Stafford, PLUS), Perkins, state.

WORK-STUDY ***Federal work-study:*** *Total amount:* $1,529,775; 897 jobs averaging $1705. ***State or other work-study/employment:*** Part-time jobs available.

ATHLETIC AWARDS *Total amount:* 176,000 (100% non-need-based).

APPLYING for FINANCIAL AID ***Required financial aid form:*** FAFSA. ***Financial aid deadline:*** 5/15 (priority: 3/15). ***Notification date:*** Continuous. Students must reply within 2 weeks of notification.

CONTACT Ms. Kathy Bialk, Director of Financial Aid, New Jersey Institute of Technology, University Heights, Newark, NJ 07102, 973-596-3478 or toll-free 800-925-NJIT. *Fax:* 973-802-1854. *E-mail:* kathy.j.bialk@njit.edu

NEWMAN UNIVERSITY

Wichita, KS

Tuition & fees: $10,268 **Average undergraduate aid package: $8872**

ABOUT THE INSTITUTION Independent Roman Catholic, coed. Awards: associate, bachelor's, and master's degrees. 31 undergraduate majors. Total enrollment: 1,938. Undergraduates: 1,524. Freshmen: 159. Federal methodology is used as a basis for awarding need-based institutional aid.

UNDERGRADUATE EXPENSES for 2000–2001 ***Application fee:*** $15. ***Comprehensive fee:*** $14,218 includes full-time tuition ($10,148), mandatory fees ($120), and room and board ($3950). ***College room only:*** $1850. Full-time tuition and fees vary according to class time. Room and board charges vary according to housing facility. ***Part-time tuition:*** $337 per semester hour. ***Part-time fees:*** $5 per semester hour. Part-time tuition and fees vary according to class time. ***Payment plans:*** installment, deferred payment.

FRESHMAN FINANCIAL AID (Fall 1998) 108 applied for aid; of those 82% were deemed to have need. 100% of freshmen with need received aid; of those 45% had need fully met. *Average percent of need met:* 88% (excluding resources awarded to replace EFC). *Average financial aid package:* $9425 (excluding resources awarded to replace EFC). 5% of all full-time freshmen had no need and received non-need-based aid.

UNDERGRADUATE FINANCIAL AID (Fall 1998) 799 applied for aid; of those 80% were deemed to have need. 100% of undergraduates with need received aid; of those 32% had need fully met. *Average percent of need met:* 68% (excluding resources awarded to replace EFC). *Average financial aid package:* $8872 (excluding resources awarded to replace EFC). 10% of all full-time undergraduates had no need and received non-need-based aid.

GIFT AID (NEED-BASED) ***Total amount:*** $1,602,273 (54% Federal, 46% state). ***Receiving aid:*** *Freshmen:* 65% (71); *all full-time undergraduates:* 57% (480). ***Scholarships, grants, and awards:*** Federal Pell, FSEOG, state, private, college/university gift aid from institutional funds.

GIFT AID (NON-NEED-BASED) ***Total amount:*** $2,094,416 (84% institutional, 16% external sources). ***Receiving aid:*** *Freshmen:* 80% (88); *Undergraduates:* 67% (570). ***Scholarships, grants, and awards by category:*** *Academic Interests/Achievement:* general academic interests/achievements. *Creative Arts/Performance:* debating, music, theater/drama. *Special Achievements/Activities:* community service, leadership, memberships, religious involvement. *Special Characteristics:* children and siblings of alumni, ethnic background, international students, out-of-state students, previous college experience, religious affiliation, siblings of current students. ***Tuition waivers:*** Full or partial for minority students, children of alumni, employees or children of employees.

LOANS ***Student loans:*** $5,338,877 (56% need-based, 44% non-need-based). 66% of past graduating class borrowed through all loan programs. ***Parent loans:*** $117,664 (100% non-need-based). ***Programs:*** FFEL (Subsidized and Unsubsidized Stafford, PLUS), Perkins.

WORK-STUDY ***Federal work-study:*** *Total amount:* $80,432; 170 jobs averaging $473. ***State or other work-study/employment:*** *Total amount:* $70,869 (100% non-need-based). 74 part-time jobs averaging $958.

ATHLETIC AWARDS *Total amount:* 492,225 (100% non-need-based).

APPLYING for FINANCIAL AID ***Required financial aid forms:*** FAFSA, institution's own form. ***Financial aid deadline (priority):*** 3/1. ***Notification date:*** Continuous.

CONTACT Todd Martin, Financial Aid Counselor, Newman University, 3100 McCormick Avenue, Wichita, KS 67213, 316-942-4291 Ext. 103 or toll-free 877-NEWMANU. *Fax:* 316-942-4483. *E-mail:* martint@newmanu.edu

NEW MEXICO HIGHLANDS UNIVERSITY

Las Vegas, NM

Tuition & fees (NM res): $1866 **Average undergraduate aid package: N/A**

ABOUT THE INSTITUTION State-supported, coed. Awards: associate, bachelor's, and master's degrees. 44 undergraduate majors. Total enrollment: 3,199. Undergraduates: 1,945. Federal methodology is used as a basis for awarding need-based institutional aid.

UNDERGRADUATE EXPENSES for 1999–2000 ***Application fee:*** $15. ***One-time required fee:*** $5. ***Tuition, state resident:*** full-time $1866; part-time $78 per semester hour. ***Tuition, nonresident:*** full-time $7578; part-time $316 per semester hour. Full-time tuition and fees vary according to degree level. Part-time tuition and fees vary according to course load and degree level. ***College room and board:*** $2730. Room and board charges vary according to board plan and housing facility. ***Payment plan:*** deferred payment.

GIFT AID (NEED-BASED) ***Scholarships, grants, and awards:*** Federal Pell, FSEOG, state, private, college/university gift aid from institutional funds.

GIFT AID (NON-NEED-BASED) ***Scholarships, grants, and awards by category:*** *Academic Interests/Achievement:* general academic interests/achievements. *Creative Arts/Performance:* art/fine arts, music, theater/drama. ***Tuition waivers:*** Full or partial for employees or children of employees, senior citizens.

LOANS ***Programs:*** Federal Direct (Subsidized and Unsubsidized Stafford, PLUS), FFEL (Subsidized and Unsubsidized Stafford, PLUS), Perkins, state.

WORK-STUDY Federal work-study jobs available.

APPLYING for FINANCIAL AID ***Required financial aid form:*** FAFSA. ***Financial aid deadline (priority):*** 3/1. ***Notification date:*** Continuous beginning 5/15. Students must reply within 2 weeks of notification.

CONTACT Eileen Sedillo, Associate Director of Financial Aid, New Mexico Highlands University, PO Box 9000, Las Vegas, NM 87701, 505-454-3430 or toll-free 800-338-6648 (in-state). *Fax:* 505-454-3398. *E-mail:* sedillo_e@nmhu.edu

NEW MEXICO INSTITUTE OF MINING AND TECHNOLOGY

Socorro, NM

Tuition & fees (NM res): $2328 **Average undergraduate aid package: $7979**

ABOUT THE INSTITUTION State-supported, coed. Awards: associate, bachelor's, master's, and doctoral degrees. 36 undergraduate majors. Total enrollment: 1,513. Undergraduates: 1,218. Freshmen: 249. Federal methodology is used as a basis for awarding need-based institutional aid.

UNDERGRADUATE EXPENSES for 1999–2000 ***Application fee:*** $15. ***One-time required fee:*** $16. ***Tuition, state resident:*** full-time $1600; part-time $67 per credit hour. ***Tuition, nonresident:*** full-time $6600; part-time $275 per credit hour. ***Required fees:*** full-time $728; $22 per credit hour; $27 per term part-time. Part-time tuition and fees vary according to course load. ***College room and board:*** $3584. Room and board charges vary according to board plan and housing facility. ***Payment plan:*** deferred payment.

FRESHMAN FINANCIAL AID (Fall 1998) 198 applied for aid; of those 48% were deemed to have need. 100% of freshmen with need received aid; of those 90% had need fully met. *Average percent of need met:* 90% (excluding resources awarded to replace EFC). *Average financial aid package:* $7405 (excluding resources awarded to replace EFC). 52% of all full-time freshmen had no need and received non-need-based aid.

UNDERGRADUATE FINANCIAL AID (Fall 1998) 657 applied for aid; of those 78% were deemed to have need. 100% of undergraduates with need received aid; of those 90% had need fully met. *Average percent of need met:* 90% (excluding resources awarded to replace EFC). *Average financial aid package:* $7979 (excluding resources awarded to replace EFC). 32% of all full-time undergraduates had no need and received non-need-based aid.

GIFT AID (NEED-BASED) ***Total amount:*** $1,381,078 (73% Federal, 25% state, 2% external sources). ***Receiving aid:*** *Freshmen:* 39% (77); *all full-time undergraduates:* 42% (402). ***Average award:*** Freshmen: $3162;

Undergraduates: $3261. ***Scholarships, grants, and awards:*** Federal Pell, FSEOG, state, private, New Mexico Scholar Program, Legislative Endowment Scholarships.

GIFT AID (NON-NEED-BASED) ***Total amount:*** $1,897,243 (13% state, 72% institutional, 15% external sources). ***Receiving aid:*** *Freshmen:* 43% (85); *Undergraduates:* 37% (351). ***Scholarships, grants, and awards by category:*** *Academic Interests/Achievement:* communication, engineering/technologies, general academic interests/achievements, physical sciences. *Special Characteristics:* children of faculty/staff. ***Tuition waivers:*** Full or partial for employees or children of employees, senior citizens.

LOANS ***Student loans:*** $1,421,347 (100% need-based). 48% of past graduating class borrowed through all loan programs. Average indebtedness per student: $14,500. ***Average need-based loan:*** Freshmen: $2180; Undergraduates: $3626. ***Parent loans:*** $40,681 (100% non-need-based). ***Programs:*** Federal Direct (Subsidized and Unsubsidized Stafford, PLUS), Perkins, state, college/university.

WORK-STUDY ***Federal work-study:*** *Total amount:* $394,686; 226 jobs averaging $1750. ***State or other work-study/employment:*** *Total amount:* $185,139 (53% need-based, 47% non-need-based). Part-time jobs available.

APPLYING for FINANCIAL AID ***Required financial aid forms:*** FAFSA, institution's own form. ***Financial aid deadline (priority):*** 3/1. ***Notification date:*** Continuous beginning 4/1. Students must reply by 5/31 or within 2 weeks of notification.

CONTACT Ms. Ann Hansen, Director of Financial Aid, New Mexico Institute of Mining and Technology, 801 Leroy Place, Socorro, NM 87801, 505-835-5333 or toll-free 800-428-TECH. *Fax:* 505-835-5959. *E-mail:* ahansen@admin.nmt.edu

NEW MEXICO STATE UNIVERSITY

Las Cruces, NM

ABOUT THE INSTITUTION State-supported, coed. Awards: associate, bachelor's, master's, and doctoral degrees and post-master's certificates. 85 undergraduate majors. Total enrollment: 15,449. Undergraduates: 12,831. Freshmen: 2,266.

GIFT AID (NEED-BASED) ***Scholarships, grants, and awards:*** Federal Pell, FSEOG, state, private, college/university gift aid from institutional funds.

GIFT AID (NON-NEED-BASED) ***Scholarships, grants, and awards by category:*** *Academic Interests/Achievement:* agriculture, biological sciences, business, communication, computer science, education, engineering/technologies, English, foreign languages, general academic interests/achievements, health fields, home economics, humanities, mathematics, military science, physical sciences, social sciences. *Creative Arts/Performance:* applied art and design, art/fine arts, general creative arts/performance, journalism/publications, music, performing arts, theater/drama. *Special Achievements/Activities:* leadership, rodeo. *Special Characteristics:* adult students, children and siblings of alumni, children of faculty/staff, local/state students, married students, members of minority groups, out-of-state students, previous college experience, spouses of current students, veterans' children.

LOANS ***Programs:*** FFEL (Subsidized and Unsubsidized Stafford, PLUS), Perkins.

WORK-STUDY Federal work-study jobs available.

APPLYING for FINANCIAL AID ***Required financial aid forms:*** FAFSA, institution's own form.

CONTACT Ms. Lydia Bruner, Director of Financial Aid, New Mexico State University, Box 30001, Department 5100, Las Cruces, NM 88003-8001, 505-646-4105 or toll-free 800-662-6678. *Fax:* 505-646-7381. *E-mail:* lbruner@nmsu.edu

NEW ORLEANS BAPTIST THEOLOGICAL SEMINARY

New Orleans, LA

ABOUT THE INSTITUTION Independent Southern Baptist, coed. Awards: associate, bachelor's, master's, doctoral, and first professional degrees. 1 undergraduate major. Total enrollment: 1,736. Undergraduates: 634. Freshmen: 124.

GIFT AID (NEED-BASED) ***Scholarships, grants, and awards:*** private.

LOANS ***Programs:*** college/university.

APPLYING for FINANCIAL AID ***Required financial aid form:*** institution's own form.

CONTACT Financial Aid Office, New Orleans Baptist Theological Seminary, 3939 Gentilly Boulevard, New Orleans, LA 70126-4858, 504-282-4455 Ext. 3348 or toll-free 800-662-8701.

NEW SCHOOL BACHELOR OF ARTS, NEW SCHOOL UNIVERSITY

New York, NY

Tuition & fees: $13,068 | **Average undergraduate aid package: $9743**

ABOUT THE INSTITUTION Independent, coed. Awards: bachelor's, master's, and doctoral degrees. 1 undergraduate major. Total enrollment: 1,236. Undergraduates: 733. Entering class: 1. Federal methodology is used as a basis for awarding need-based institutional aid.

UNDERGRADUATE EXPENSES for 1999–2000 ***Application fee:*** $30. ***Tuition:*** full-time $12,672; part-time $528 per credit. ***Required fees:*** full-time $396; $108 per term part-time. Room and board charges vary according to housing facility. ***Payment plan:*** installment.

UNDERGRADUATE FINANCIAL AID (Fall 1999, est.) 115 applied for aid; of those 97% were deemed to have need. 100% of undergraduates with need received aid. *Average percent of need met:* 70% (excluding resources awarded to replace EFC). *Average financial aid package:* $9743 (excluding resources awarded to replace EFC).

GIFT AID (NEED-BASED) ***Total amount:*** $1,073,220 (19% Federal, 11% state, 68% institutional, 2% external sources). ***Receiving aid:*** *All full-time undergraduates:* 61% (102). ***Average award:*** Undergraduates: $3693. ***Scholarships, grants, and awards:*** Federal Pell, FSEOG, state, private, college/university gift aid from institutional funds.

GIFT AID (NON-NEED-BASED) ***Total amount:*** $5009 (100% institutional). ***Receiving aid:*** *Undergraduates:* 1% (2). ***Scholarships, grants, and awards by category:*** *Academic Interests/Achievement:* 3 awards ($5009 total): general academic interests/achievements. ***Tuition waivers:*** Full or partial for employees or children of employees.

LOANS ***Student loans:*** $1,569,925 (100% need-based). 80% of past graduating class borrowed through all loan programs. Average indebtedness per student: $14,500. ***Average need-based loan:*** Undergraduates: $3931. ***Parent loans:*** $45,500 (100% need-based). ***Programs:*** FFEL (Subsidized and Unsubsidized Stafford, PLUS), Perkins, state, college/university, alternative loans.

WORK-STUDY ***Federal work-study:*** *Total amount:* $37,000; 20 jobs averaging $1850.

APPLYING for FINANCIAL AID ***Required financial aid form:*** FAFSA. ***Financial aid deadline (priority):*** 3/1. ***Notification date:*** 6/1. Students must reply within 4 weeks of notification.

CONTACT Lisa Shaheen, Financial Aid Counselor/Student Employment Coordinator, New School Bachelor of Arts, New School University, 66 Fifth Avenue, New York, NY 10011, 212-229-8930. *Fax:* 212-229-5919. *E-mail:* shaheenl@newschool.edu

NEWSCHOOL OF ARCHITECTURE

San Diego, CA

Tuition & fees: $15,909 | **Average undergraduate aid package: N/A**

Newschool of Architecture (continued)

ABOUT THE INSTITUTION Proprietary, coed. Awards: associate, bachelor's, master's, and first professional degrees. 6 undergraduate majors. Total enrollment: 130. Federal methodology is used as a basis for awarding need-based institutional aid.

UNDERGRADUATE EXPENSES for 1999–2000 ***Application fee:*** $25. ***Comprehensive fee:*** $21,909 includes full-time tuition ($15,750), mandatory fees ($159), and room and board ($6000). Full-time tuition and fees vary according to course load. ***Part-time tuition:*** $350 per quarter hour. ***Part-time fees:*** $53 per term part-time. ***Payment plans:*** tuition prepayment, installment, deferred payment.

GIFT AID (NEED-BASED) ***Scholarships, grants, and awards:*** Federal Pell, FSEOG, state.

GIFT AID (NON-NEED-BASED) ***Scholarships, grants, and awards by category:*** *Academic Interests/Achievement:* architecture, general academic interests/achievements. ***Tuition waivers:*** Full or partial for employees or children of employees.

LOANS ***Programs:*** FFEL (Subsidized and Unsubsidized Stafford, PLUS).

WORK-STUDY Federal work-study jobs available.

APPLYING for FINANCIAL AID ***Required financial aid forms:*** FAFSA, institution's own form. ***Financial aid deadline:*** Continuous. ***Notification date:*** Continuous beginning 7/1. Students must reply within 4 weeks of notification.

CONTACT Ms. Pamela B. Palermo, Director of Financial Aid, Newschool of Architecture, 1249 F Street, San Diego, CA 92101-6634, 619-235-4100 Ext. 103. *Fax:* 619-235-4651. *E-mail:* financialaid@newschoolarch.edu

NEW SCHOOL UNIVERSITY, EUGENE LANG COLLEGE

New York, NY

See Eugene Lang College, New School University

NEW SCHOOL UNIVERSITY, MANNES COLLEGE OF MUSIC

New York, NY

See Mannes College of Music, New School University

NEW SCHOOL UNIVERSITY, PARSONS SCHOOL OF DESIGN

New York, NY

See Parsons School of Design, New School University

NEW YORK INSTITUTE OF TECHNOLOGY

Old Westbury, NY

Tuition & fees: $11,990 **Average undergraduate aid package: N/A**

ABOUT THE INSTITUTION Independent, coed. Awards: associate, bachelor's, master's, and first professional degrees and post-bachelor's certificates. 77 undergraduate majors. Total enrollment: 9,292. Undergraduates: 5,750. Freshmen: 785. Federal methodology is used as a basis for awarding need-based institutional aid.

UNDERGRADUATE EXPENSES for 1999–2000 ***Application fee:*** $50. ***Comprehensive fee:*** $18,500 includes full-time tuition ($11,990) and room and board ($6510). ***College room only:*** $3480. Full-time tuition and fees vary according to program. Room and board charges vary according to board plan and housing facility. ***Part-time tuition:*** $370 per credit. ***Part-time fees:*** $90 per term part-time. Part-time tuition and fees vary according to course load and program. ***Payment plan:*** installment.

FRESHMAN FINANCIAL AID (Fall 1998) 1096 applied for aid; of those 87% were deemed to have need. 71% of freshmen with need received aid.

UNDERGRADUATE FINANCIAL AID (Fall 1998) 2,975 applied for aid; of those 91% were deemed to have need. 90% of undergraduates with need received aid.

GIFT AID (NEED-BASED) ***Total amount:*** $11,275,941 (40% Federal, 41% state, 19% institutional). ***Receiving aid:*** *Freshmen:* 45% (624); *all full-time undergraduates:* 57% (2,263). ***Scholarships, grants, and awards:*** Federal Pell, FSEOG, state, private, college/university gift aid from institutional funds.

GIFT AID (NON-NEED-BASED) ***Total amount:*** $6,273,879 (97% institutional, 3% external sources). ***Receiving aid:*** *Freshmen:* 18% (258); *Undergraduates:* 40% (1,564). ***Scholarships, grants, and awards by category:*** *Academic Interests/Achievement:* general academic interests/achievements. *Special Characteristics:* children of educators, children of faculty/staff, children of public servants, local/state students, previous college experience, public servants, spouses of deceased or disabled public servants, veterans. ***Tuition waivers:*** Full or partial for employees or children of employees, senior citizens. ***ROTC:*** Air Force.

LOANS ***Student loans:*** $14,164,920 (64% need-based, 36% non-need-based). 75% of past graduating class borrowed through all loan programs. Average indebtedness per student: $17,125. ***Parent loans:*** $1,644,872 (100% non-need-based). ***Programs:*** FFEL (Subsidized and Unsubsidized Stafford, PLUS), Perkins, Federal Nursing, alternative loans.

WORK-STUDY ***Federal work-study:*** *Total amount:* $306,526; jobs available.

ATHLETIC AWARDS *Total amount:* 1,243,369 (100% non-need-based).

APPLYING for FINANCIAL AID ***Required financial aid forms:*** FAFSA, CSS Financial Aid PROFILE. ***Financial aid deadline (priority):*** 2/15. ***Notification date:*** Continuous. Students must reply by 5/1 or within 2 weeks of notification.

CONTACT James Newell, Director, Financial Aid Office, New York Institute of Technology, PO Box 8000, Old Westbury, NY 11568-8000, 516-686-7680 or toll-free 800-345-NYIT. *Fax:* 516-686-7997.

NEW YORK SCHOOL OF INTERIOR DESIGN

New York, NY

Tuition & fees: $16,070 **Average undergraduate aid package: $5500**

ABOUT THE INSTITUTION Independent, coed. Awards: associate, bachelor's, and master's degrees. 1 undergraduate major. Total enrollment: 706. Undergraduates: 694. Freshmen: 199. Federal methodology is used as a basis for awarding need-based institutional aid.

UNDERGRADUATE EXPENSES for 2000–2001 ***Application fee:*** $50. ***Tuition:*** full-time $16,000; part-time $500 per credit. ***Required fees:*** full-time $70; $35 per term part-time. Full-time tuition and fees vary according to course load. Part-time tuition and fees vary according to course load. ***Payment plans:*** installment, deferred payment.

FRESHMAN FINANCIAL AID (Fall 1999) 14 applied for aid; of those 79% were deemed to have need. 100% of freshmen with need received aid. *Average percent of need met:* 60% (excluding resources awarded to replace EFC). *Average financial aid package:* $5000 (excluding resources awarded to replace EFC).

UNDERGRADUATE FINANCIAL AID (Fall 1999) 51 applied for aid; of those 84% were deemed to have need. 100% of undergraduates with need received aid. *Average percent of need met:* 60% (excluding resources awarded to replace EFC). *Average financial aid package:* $5500 (excluding resources awarded to replace EFC).

GIFT AID (NEED-BASED) ***Total amount:*** $275,505 (33% Federal, 36% state, 31% institutional). ***Receiving aid:*** *Freshmen:* 44% (11); *all full-time undergraduates:* 34% (43). ***Average award:*** Freshmen: $5000; Undergraduates: $5500. ***Scholarships, grants, and awards:*** Federal Pell, FSEOG, state, college/university gift aid from institutional funds.

GIFT AID (NON-NEED-BASED) ***Tuition waivers:*** Full or partial for employees or children of employees.

LOANS ***Student loans:*** $508,086 (100% need-based). 25% of past graduating class borrowed through all loan programs. Average indebtedness per student: $7500. ***Parent loans:*** $19,080 (100% need-based). ***Programs:*** FFEL (Subsidized and Unsubsidized Stafford, PLUS).

WORK-STUDY ***Federal work-study:*** *Total amount:* $31,979; 15 jobs averaging $3000.

APPLYING for FINANCIAL AID ***Required financial aid forms:*** FAFSA, institution's own form. ***Financial aid deadline (priority):*** 5/1. ***Notification date:*** 8/1. Students must reply within 2 weeks of notification.

CONTACT Jeff Namian, Director of Financial Aid, New York School of Interior Design, 170 East 70th Street, New York, NY 10021-5110, 212-472-1500 Ext. 207 or toll-free 800-336-9743. *Fax:* 212-472-3800. *E-mail:* jeff@nysid.edu

NEW YORK STATE COLLEGE OF CERAMICS

Alfred, NY

See Alfred University

NEW YORK UNIVERSITY

New York, NY

Tuition & fees: $23,456 **Average undergraduate aid package: $15,999**

ABOUT THE INSTITUTION Independent, coed. Awards: associate, bachelor's, master's, doctoral, and first professional degrees and post-master's certificates. 140 undergraduate majors. Total enrollment: 37,132. Undergraduates: 18,204. Freshmen: 3,642. Both federal and institutional methodology are used as a basis for awarding need-based institutional aid.

UNDERGRADUATE EXPENSES for 1999–2000 ***Application fee:*** $50. ***Comprehensive fee:*** $32,316 includes full-time tuition ($23,456) and room and board ($8860). Full-time tuition and fees vary according to program. Room and board charges vary according to board plan and housing facility. ***Part-time tuition:*** $644 per credit. Part-time tuition and fees vary according to program. ***Payment plans:*** tuition prepayment, installment, deferred payment.

FRESHMAN FINANCIAL AID (Fall 1999) 2772 applied for aid; of those 81% were deemed to have need. 100% of freshmen with need received aid. *Average percent of need met:* 75% (excluding resources awarded to replace EFC). *Average financial aid package:* $16,534 (excluding resources awarded to replace EFC). 17% of all full-time freshmen had no need and received non-need-based aid.

UNDERGRADUATE FINANCIAL AID (Fall 1999) 10,545 applied for aid; of those 88% were deemed to have need. 99% of undergraduates with need received aid. *Average percent of need met:* 73% (excluding resources awarded to replace EFC). *Average financial aid package:* $15,999 (excluding resources awarded to replace EFC). 14% of all full-time undergraduates had no need and received non-need-based aid.

GIFT AID (NEED-BASED) ***Total amount:*** $88,001,155 (11% Federal, 12% state, 73% institutional, 4% external sources). ***Receiving aid:*** *Freshmen:* 59% (2,104); *all full-time undergraduates:* 53% (8,522). ***Average award:*** Freshmen: $10,769; Undergraduates: $9811. ***Scholarships, grants, and awards:*** Federal Pell, FSEOG, state, private, college/university gift aid from institutional funds, Federal Nursing.

GIFT AID (NON-NEED-BASED) ***Total amount:*** $11,353,449 (81% institutional, 19% external sources). ***Scholarships, grants, and awards by category:*** *Academic Interests/Achievement:* 1,822 awards ($9,225,546 total): general academic interests/achievements. ***Tuition waivers:*** Full or partial for employees or children of employees. ***ROTC:*** Army cooperative, Air Force cooperative.

LOANS ***Student loans:*** $55,734,522 (92% need-based, 8% non-need-based). 63% of past graduating class borrowed through all loan programs. Average indebtedness per student: $17,985. ***Average need-based loan:*** Freshmen: $3985; Undergraduates: $4766. ***Parent loans:*** $31,700,272 (100% need-based). ***Programs:*** FFEL (Subsidized and Unsubsidized Stafford, PLUS), Perkins, Federal Nursing, state, college/university.

WORK-STUDY ***Federal work-study:*** *Total amount:* $5,500,000; 2,900 jobs averaging $1900.

APPLYING for FINANCIAL AID ***Required financial aid forms:*** FAFSA, state aid form. ***Financial aid deadline (priority):*** 2/15. ***Notification date:*** 4/1.

CONTACT Financial Aid Office, New York University, 25 West Fourth Street, New York, NY 10012-1199, 212-998-4444. *Fax:* 212-995-4661. *E-mail:* financial.aid@nyu.edu

NIAGARA UNIVERSITY

Niagara Falls, NY

Tuition & fees: $13,940 **Average undergraduate aid package: $14,720**

ABOUT THE INSTITUTION Independent religious, coed. Awards: associate, bachelor's, and master's degrees and post-master's certificates. 52 undergraduate majors. Total enrollment: 2,940. Undergraduates: 2,357. Freshmen: 580. Federal methodology is used as a basis for awarding need-based institutional aid.

UNDERGRADUATE EXPENSES for 1999–2000 ***Application fee:*** $30. ***One-time required fee:*** $100. ***Comprehensive fee:*** $20,270 includes full-time tuition ($13,400), mandatory fees ($540), and room and board ($6330). Room and board charges vary according to board plan. ***Part-time tuition:*** $406 per credit hour. ***Part-time fees:*** $10 per term part-time. Part-time tuition and fees vary according to program. ***Payment plans:*** installment, deferred payment.

FRESHMAN FINANCIAL AID (Fall 1999) 560 applied for aid; of those 97% were deemed to have need. 100% of freshmen with need received aid; of those 18% had need fully met. *Average percent of need met:* 75% (excluding resources awarded to replace EFC). *Average financial aid package:* $13,074 (excluding resources awarded to replace EFC). 6% of all full-time freshmen had no need and received non-need-based aid.

UNDERGRADUATE FINANCIAL AID (Fall 1999) 2,010 applied for aid; of those 93% were deemed to have need. 100% of undergraduates with need received aid; of those 20% had need fully met. *Average percent of need met:* 77% (excluding resources awarded to replace EFC). *Average financial aid package:* $14,720 (excluding resources awarded to replace EFC). 8% of all full-time undergraduates had no need and received non-need-based aid.

GIFT AID (NEED-BASED) ***Total amount:*** $13,059,343 (12% Federal, 18% state, 68% institutional, 2% external sources). ***Receiving aid:*** *Freshmen:* 87% (502); *all full-time undergraduates:* 85% (1,834). ***Average award:*** Freshmen: $7957; Undergraduates: $8106. ***Scholarships, grants, and awards:*** Federal Pell, FSEOG, state, private, college/university gift aid from institutional funds.

GIFT AID (NON-NEED-BASED) ***Total amount:*** $3,020,498 (1% Federal, 1% state, 98% institutional). ***Receiving aid:*** *Freshmen:* 4% (21); *Undergraduates:* 3% (75). ***Scholarships, grants, and awards by category:*** *Academic Interests/Achievement:* 1,799 awards ($9,215,416 total): general academic interests/achievements. *Creative Arts/Performance:* 29 awards ($91,407 total): theater/drama. *Special Achievements/Activities:* 10 awards ($20,000 total): community service. *Special Characteristics:* 83 awards ($685,268 total): children of faculty/staff, relatives of clergy. ***Tuition waivers:*** Full or partial for employees or children of employees. ***ROTC:*** Army.

LOANS ***Student loans:*** $7,649,676 (66% need-based, 34% non-need-based). 78% of past graduating class borrowed through all loan programs. Average indebtedness per student: $12,743. ***Average need-based loan:*** Freshmen: $3403; Undergraduates: $3980. ***Parent loans:*** $2,340,200 (87% need-based, 13% non-need-based). ***Programs:*** FFEL (Subsidized and Unsubsidized Stafford, PLUS), Perkins, Federal Nursing, college/university.

WORK-STUDY ***Federal work-study:*** *Total amount:* $1,023,747; jobs available. ***State or other work-study/employment:*** *Total amount:* $100,224 (100% non-need-based). 38 part-time jobs averaging $2658.

ATHLETIC AWARDS *Total amount:* 1,447,397 (95% need-based, 5% non-need-based).

APPLYING for FINANCIAL AID ***Required financial aid forms:*** FAFSA, state aid form. ***Financial aid deadline (priority):*** 2/15. ***Notification date:*** Continuous beginning 3/15. Students must reply within 3 weeks of notification.

CONTACT Mrs. Maureen E. Salfi, Director of Financial Aid, Niagara University, Financial Aid Office, Niagara University, NY 14109, 716-286-8686 or toll-free 800-462-2111. *Fax:* 716-286-8678. *E-mail:* finaid@niagara.edu

NICHOLLS STATE UNIVERSITY

Thibodaux, LA

CONTACT Financial Aid Department, Nicholls State University, 906 East First Street, Thibodaux, LA 70310, 504-448-4048 or toll-free 877-NICHOLLS (in-state), 877-NICHOLS (out-of-state). *Fax:* 504-448-4929.

NICHOLS COLLEGE

Dudley, MA

Tuition & fees: $14,550 **Average undergraduate aid package: $11,448**

ABOUT THE INSTITUTION Independent, coed. Awards: associate, bachelor's, and master's degrees. 14 undergraduate majors. Total enrollment: 1,431. Undergraduates: 1,175. Freshmen: 225. Federal methodology is used as a basis for awarding need-based institutional aid.

UNDERGRADUATE EXPENSES for 1999–2000 ***Application fee:*** $25. ***Comprehensive fee:*** $21,090 includes full-time tuition ($14,200), mandatory fees ($350), and room and board ($6540). ***College room only:*** $3220. Full-time tuition and fees vary according to course load. Room and board charges vary according to housing facility. ***Part-time tuition:*** $474 per credit. Part-time tuition and fees vary according to class time, course load, and location. ***Payment plan:*** installment.

FRESHMAN FINANCIAL AID (Fall 1999, est.) 234 applied for aid; of those 78% were deemed to have need. 100% of freshmen with need received aid; of those 35% had need fully met. *Average percent of need met:* 76% (excluding resources awarded to replace EFC). *Average financial aid package:* $11,576 (excluding resources awarded to replace EFC).

UNDERGRADUATE FINANCIAL AID (Fall 1999, est.) 624 applied for aid; of those 81% were deemed to have need. 100% of undergraduates with need received aid; of those 41% had need fully met. *Average percent of need met:* 79% (excluding resources awarded to replace EFC). *Average financial aid package:* $11,448 (excluding resources awarded to replace EFC).

GIFT AID (NEED-BASED) ***Total amount:*** $3,314,170 (11% Federal, 9% state, 77% institutional, 3% external sources). ***Receiving aid:*** *Freshmen:* 182; *all full-time undergraduates:* 495. ***Average award:*** Freshmen: $7029; Undergraduates: $6477. ***Scholarships, grants, and awards:*** Federal Pell, FSEOG, state, private, college/university gift aid from institutional funds.

GIFT AID (NON-NEED-BASED) ***Total amount:*** $756,681 (92% institutional, 8% external sources). ***Receiving aid:*** *Freshmen:* 18; *Undergraduates:* 51. ***Scholarships, grants, and awards by category:*** *Academic Interests/Achievement:* general academic interests/achievements. *Special Achievements/Activities:* general special achievements/activities. *Special Characteristics:* 25 awards ($106,139 total): children of faculty/staff, children of union members/company employees, siblings of current students. ***Tuition waivers:*** Full or partial for employees or children of employees. ***ROTC:*** Army.

LOANS ***Student loans:*** $2,873,160 (75% need-based, 25% non-need-based). 91% of past graduating class borrowed through all loan programs. Average indebtedness per student: $18,799. ***Average need-based loan:*** Freshmen: $4050; Undergraduates: $4551. ***Parent loans:*** $1,300,237 (40% need-based, 60% non-need-based). ***Programs:*** FFEL (Subsidized and Unsubsidized Stafford, PLUS), state.

WORK-STUDY ***Federal work-study:*** *Total amount:* $213,634; 217 jobs available.

APPLYING for FINANCIAL AID ***Required financial aid form:*** FAFSA. ***Financial aid deadline (priority):*** 3/1. ***Notification date:*** Continuous beginning 4/1. Students must reply by 6/1 or within 3 weeks of notification.

CONTACT Ms. Diane L. Gillespie, Director of Financial Aid, Nichols College, PO Box 5000, Dudley, MA 01571, 508-943-2055 Ext. 2276 or toll-free 800-470-3379. *Fax:* 508-943-9885.

NORFOLK STATE UNIVERSITY

Norfolk, VA

Tuition & fees (VA res): $2708 **Average undergraduate aid package: $7410**

ABOUT THE INSTITUTION State-supported, coed. Awards: associate, bachelor's, master's, and doctoral degrees. 48 undergraduate majors. Total enrollment: 6,987. Undergraduates: 6,139. Freshmen: 1,166. Federal methodology is used as a basis for awarding need-based institutional aid.

UNDERGRADUATE EXPENSES for 1999–2000 ***Application fee:*** $25. ***One-time required fee:*** $35. ***Tuition, state resident:*** full-time $2708; part-time $45 per credit. ***Tuition, nonresident:*** full-time $7172; part-time $230 per credit. ***Required fees:*** $6 per credit; $53 per term part-time. ***College room and board:*** $5494; ***room only:*** $3552. Room and board charges vary according to board plan and housing facility.

FRESHMAN FINANCIAL AID (Fall 1999, est.) 90% of freshmen with need received aid; of those 35% had need fully met. *Average percent of need met:* 85% (excluding resources awarded to replace EFC). *Average financial aid package:* $5900 (excluding resources awarded to replace EFC).

UNDERGRADUATE FINANCIAL AID (Fall 1999, est.) 95% of undergraduates with need received aid; of those 25% had need fully met. *Average percent of need met:* 65% (excluding resources awarded to replace EFC). *Average financial aid package:* $7410 (excluding resources awarded to replace EFC).

GIFT AID (NEED-BASED) ***Total amount:*** $11,681,073 (66% Federal, 34% state). ***Receiving aid:*** *Freshmen:* 582; *all full-time undergraduates:* 3,002. ***Average award:*** Freshmen: $5925; Undergraduates: $4785. ***Scholarships, grants, and awards:*** Federal Pell, FSEOG, state, private, college/university gift aid from institutional funds.

GIFT AID (NON-NEED-BASED) ***Total amount:*** $2,123,850 (81% institutional, 19% external sources). ***Receiving aid:*** *Freshmen:* 420; *Undergraduates:* 2,169. ***Scholarships, grants, and awards by category:*** *Academic Interests/Achievement:* biological sciences, computer science, general academic interests/achievements, mathematics. *Creative Arts/Performance:* music, performing arts. *Special Achievements/Activities:* general special achievements/activities. ***ROTC:*** Army, Naval.

LOANS ***Student loans:*** $21,063,711 (72% need-based, 28% non-need-based). 85% of past graduating class borrowed through all loan programs. Average indebtedness per student: $17,000. ***Average need-based loan:*** Freshmen: $2625; Undergraduates: $3500. ***Parent loans:*** $2,116,311 (100% non-need-based). ***Programs:*** Federal Direct (Subsidized and Unsubsidized Stafford), FFEL (PLUS), Perkins, state.

WORK-STUDY ***Federal work-study:*** *Total amount:* $571,276; 350 jobs averaging $1632. ***State or other work-study/employment:*** *Total amount:* $300,000 (100% need-based). 250 part-time jobs averaging $1200.

ATHLETIC AWARDS *Total amount:* 2,655,672 (100% non-need-based).

APPLYING for FINANCIAL AID ***Required financial aid form:*** FAFSA. ***Financial aid deadline (priority):*** 3/15. ***Notification date:*** Continuous beginning 6/1. Students must reply within 2 weeks of notification.

CONTACT Mrs. Estherine Harding, Director of Financial Aid, Norfolk State University, 700 Park Avenue, Norfolk, VA 23504-3907, 757-823-8381.

NORTH ADAMS STATE COLLEGE

North Adams, MA

See Massachusetts College of Liberal Arts

NORTH CAROLINA AGRICULTURAL AND TECHNICAL STATE UNIVERSITY

Greensboro, NC

Tuition & fees (NC res): $1889 **Average undergraduate aid package: $8643**

ABOUT THE INSTITUTION State-supported, coed. Awards: bachelor's, master's, and doctoral degrees. 60 undergraduate majors. Total enrollment: 7,603. Undergraduates: 6,684. Freshmen: 1,538. Federal methodology is used as a basis for awarding need-based institutional aid.

UNDERGRADUATE EXPENSES for 1999–2000 ***Application fee:*** $35. ***Tuition, state resident:*** full-time $962; part-time $241 per term. ***Tuition, nonresident:*** full-time $8232; part-time $2058 per term. ***Required fees:*** full-time $927; $304 per term part-time. Part-time tuition and fees vary according to course load. ***College room and board:*** $4010. Room and board charges vary according to board plan. ***Payment plan:*** deferred payment.

FRESHMAN FINANCIAL AID (Fall 1998) 1312 applied for aid; of those 93% were deemed to have need. 99% of freshmen with need received aid; of those 24% had need fully met. *Average percent of need met:* 36% (excluding resources awarded to replace EFC). *Average financial aid package:* $5719 (excluding resources awarded to replace EFC). 11% of all full-time freshmen had no need and received non-need-based aid.

UNDERGRADUATE FINANCIAL AID (Fall 1998) 4,643 applied for aid; of those 98% were deemed to have need. 97% of undergraduates with need received aid; of those 30% had need fully met. *Average percent of need met:* 39% (excluding resources awarded to replace EFC). *Average financial aid package:* $8643 (excluding resources awarded to replace EFC). 13% of all full-time undergraduates had no need and received non-need-based aid.

GIFT AID (NEED-BASED) ***Total amount:*** $7,431,474 (87% Federal, 13% state). ***Receiving aid:*** *Freshmen:* 67% (973); *all full-time undergraduates:* 56% (3,257). ***Average award:*** Freshmen: $2804; Undergraduates: $2636. ***Scholarships, grants, and awards:*** Federal Pell, FSEOG, state, private, college/university gift aid from institutional funds, United Negro College Fund, Federal Nursing.

GIFT AID (NON-NEED-BASED) ***Total amount:*** $5,098,246 (29% state, 31% institutional, 40% external sources). ***Receiving aid:*** *Freshmen:* 29% (426); *Undergraduates:* 20% (1,198). ***Scholarships, grants, and awards by category:*** *Academic Interests/Achievement:* military science. *Creative Arts/Performance:* music, theater/drama. *Special Characteristics:* ethnic background, handicapped students, members of minority groups. ***ROTC:*** Army, Air Force.

LOANS ***Student loans:*** $15,676,196 (69% need-based, 31% non-need-based). ***Average need-based loan:*** Freshmen: $2521; Undergraduates: $3477. ***Parent loans:*** $2,054,341 (100% non-need-based). ***Programs:*** Federal Direct (Subsidized and Unsubsidized Stafford, PLUS), Perkins, alternative loans.

WORK-STUDY ***Federal work-study:*** *Total amount:* $589,813; jobs available. ***State or other work-study/employment:*** *Total amount:* $492,792 (100% non-need-based). Part-time jobs available.

ATHLETIC AWARDS *Total amount:* 964,330 (100% non-need-based).

APPLYING for FINANCIAL AID ***Required financial aid form:*** FAFSA. ***Financial aid deadline (priority):*** 3/15. ***Notification date:*** Continuous beginning 4/1. Students must reply within 2 weeks of notification.

CONTACT Mrs. Sherri Avent, Director of Student Financial Aid, North Carolina Agricultural and Technical State University, Dowdy Building, Greensboro, NC 27411, 336-334-7973 or toll-free 800-443-8964 (in-state). *Fax:* 336-334-7954.

NORTH CAROLINA CENTRAL UNIVERSITY

Durham, NC

Tuition & fees (NC res): $1887 **Average undergraduate aid package: $6301**

ABOUT THE INSTITUTION State-supported, coed. Awards: bachelor's, master's, and first professional degrees. 48 undergraduate majors. Total enrollment: 5,595. Undergraduates: 4,036. Freshmen: 653. Federal methodology is used as a basis for awarding need-based institutional aid.

UNDERGRADUATE EXPENSES for 1999–2000 ***Application fee:*** $30. ***Tuition, state resident:*** full-time $962. ***Tuition, nonresident:*** full-time $8232. ***Required fees:*** full-time $925. Part-time tuition and fees vary according to course load. ***College room and board:*** $3904; ***room only:*** $2250.

FRESHMAN FINANCIAL AID (Fall 1998) 621 applied for aid; of those 85% were deemed to have need. 100% of freshmen with need received aid; of those 33% had need fully met. *Average percent of need met:* 76% (excluding resources awarded to replace EFC). *Average financial aid package:* $5447 (excluding resources awarded to replace EFC). 14% of all full-time freshmen had no need and received non-need-based aid.

UNDERGRADUATE FINANCIAL AID (Fall 1998) 2,897 applied for aid; of those 87% were deemed to have need. 100% of undergraduates with need received aid; of those 28% had need fully met. *Average percent of need met:* 74% (excluding resources awarded to replace EFC). *Average financial aid package:* $6301 (excluding resources awarded to replace EFC). 12% of all full-time undergraduates had no need and received non-need-based aid.

GIFT AID (NEED-BASED) ***Total amount:*** $6,229,378 (88% Federal, 12% state). ***Receiving aid:*** *Freshmen:* 59% (396); *all full-time undergraduates:* 58% (1,859). ***Average award:*** Freshmen: $2719; Undergraduates: $2712. ***Scholarships, grants, and awards:*** Federal Pell, FSEOG, state, private, college/university gift aid from institutional funds.

GIFT AID (NON-NEED-BASED) ***Total amount:*** $4,296,615 (5% Federal, 29% state, 50% institutional, 16% external sources). ***Receiving aid:*** *Freshmen:* 44% (296); *Undergraduates:* 41% (1,318). ***Scholarships, grants, and awards by category:*** *Academic Interests/Achievement:* biological sciences, general academic interests/achievements, physical sciences, social sciences. *Creative Arts/Performance:* theater/drama. *Special Characteristics:* general special characteristics. ***Tuition waivers:*** Full or partial for employees or children of employees. ***ROTC:*** Army cooperative, Naval cooperative, Air Force cooperative.

LOANS ***Student loans:*** $27,749,569 (59% need-based, 41% non-need-based). ***Average need-based loan:*** Freshmen: $2423; Undergraduates: $3594. ***Parent loans:*** $1,862,748 (100% non-need-based). ***Programs:*** Federal Direct (Subsidized and Unsubsidized Stafford, PLUS), Perkins.

WORK-STUDY ***Federal work-study:*** *Total amount:* $419,520; 350 jobs averaging $1200. ***State or other work-study/employment:*** *Total amount:* $298,584 (100% non-need-based). 150 part-time jobs averaging $2000.

ATHLETIC AWARDS *Total amount:* 336,699 (100% non-need-based).

APPLYING for FINANCIAL AID ***Required financial aid form:*** FAFSA. ***Financial aid deadline (priority):*** 4/1. ***Notification date:*** Continuous beginning 4/30. Students must reply within 2 weeks of notification.

CONTACT Sharon J. Oliver, Assistant Vice Chancellor for Scholarships and Student Aid, North Carolina Central University, 106 Student Services Building, Durham, NC 27707-3129, 919-530-7412.

NORTH CAROLINA SCHOOL OF THE ARTS

Winston-Salem, NC

Tuition & fees (NC res): $2517 **Average undergraduate aid package: $6476**

ABOUT THE INSTITUTION State-supported, coed. Awards: bachelor's and master's degrees. 7 undergraduate majors. Total enrollment: 794. Undergraduates: 727. Freshmen: 176. Federal methodology is used as a basis for awarding need-based institutional aid.

UNDERGRADUATE EXPENSES for 1999–2000 ***Application fee:*** $35. ***Tuition, state resident:*** full-time $1497. ***Tuition, nonresident:*** full-time $10,125. ***Required fees:*** full-time $1020. Full-time tuition and fees vary according to program. Part-time tuition and fees vary according to course load. ***College room and board:*** $4462; ***room only:*** $2315. Room and board charges vary according to board plan and housing facility.

FRESHMAN FINANCIAL AID (Fall 1998) 135 applied for aid; of those 75% were deemed to have need. 100% of freshmen with need received aid; of those 1% had need fully met. *Average percent of need met:* 53% (excluding resources awarded to replace EFC). *Average financial aid package:* $5183 (excluding resources awarded to replace EFC). 20% of all full-time freshmen had no need and received non-need-based aid.

UNDERGRADUATE FINANCIAL AID (Fall 1998) 426 applied for aid; of those 80% were deemed to have need. 100% of undergraduates with need received aid; of those 8% had need fully met. *Average percent of need met:* 61% (excluding resources awarded to replace EFC). *Average financial aid package:* $6476 (excluding resources awarded to replace EFC). 13% of all full-time undergraduates had no need and received non-need-based aid.

GIFT AID (NEED-BASED) ***Total amount:*** $1,023,322 (37% Federal, 7% state, 52% institutional, 4% external sources). ***Receiving aid:*** *Freshmen:* 49% (83); *all full-time undergraduates:* 43% (295). ***Average award:*** Freshmen: $3465; Undergraduates: $3535. ***Scholarships, grants, and awards:*** Federal Pell, FSEOG, state, private, college/university gift aid from institutional funds.

North Carolina School of the Arts (continued)

GIFT AID (NON-NEED-BASED) ***Total amount:*** $95,558 (54% state, 28% institutional, 18% external sources). ***Receiving aid:*** *Freshmen:* 4% (6); *Undergraduates:* 1% (8). ***Scholarships, grants, and awards by category:*** *Creative Arts/Performance:* applied art and design, cinema/film/broadcasting, dance, music, performing arts, theater/drama.

LOANS ***Student loans:*** $1,851,518 (68% need-based, 32% non-need-based). 61% of past graduating class borrowed through all loan programs. Average indebtedness per student: $16,300. ***Average need-based loan:*** Freshmen: $2510; Undergraduates: $4081. ***Parent loans:*** $578,145 (100% non-need-based). ***Programs:*** Federal Direct (Subsidized and Unsubsidized Stafford, PLUS), Perkins.

WORK-STUDY ***Federal work-study:*** *Total amount:* $46,499; 126 jobs averaging $369.

APPLYING for FINANCIAL AID ***Required financial aid form:*** FAFSA. ***Financial aid deadline (priority):*** 3/1. ***Notification date:*** 4/15. Students must reply within 2 weeks of notification.

CONTACT Jane C. Kamiab, Director of Financial Aid, North Carolina School of the Arts, 1533 South Main Street, Winston-Salem, NC 27127, 336-770-3297. *Fax:* 336-770-1489.

NORTH CAROLINA STATE UNIVERSITY

Raleigh, NC

Tuition & fees (NC res): $2514 **Average undergraduate aid package: $5661**

ABOUT THE INSTITUTION State-supported, coed. Awards: associate, bachelor's, master's, doctoral, and first professional degrees and first-professional certificates. 87 undergraduate majors. Total enrollment: 28,011. Undergraduates: 21,684. Freshmen: 3,666. Both federal and institutional methodology are used as a basis for awarding need-based institutional aid.

UNDERGRADUATE EXPENSES for 1999–2000 ***Application fee:*** $55. ***Tuition, state resident:*** full-time $1528; part-time $667 per term. ***Tuition, nonresident:*** full-time $11,580; part-time $2959 per term. ***Required fees:*** full-time $986. Full-time tuition and fees vary according to program. Part-time tuition and fees vary according to course load and program. ***College room and board:*** $4560; ***room only:*** $2370. Room and board charges vary according to board plan and housing facility.

FRESHMAN FINANCIAL AID (Fall 1999) 2501 applied for aid; of those 61% were deemed to have need. 98% of freshmen with need received aid; of those 23% had need fully met. *Average percent of need met:* 82% (excluding resources awarded to replace EFC). *Average financial aid package:* $6314 (excluding resources awarded to replace EFC). 18% of all full-time freshmen had no need and received non-need-based aid.

UNDERGRADUATE FINANCIAL AID (Fall 1999) 12,389 applied for aid; of those 65% were deemed to have need. 96% of undergraduates with need received aid; of those 23% had need fully met. *Average percent of need met:* 84% (excluding resources awarded to replace EFC). *Average financial aid package:* $5661 (excluding resources awarded to replace EFC). 13% of all full-time undergraduates had no need and received non-need-based aid.

GIFT AID (NEED-BASED) ***Total amount:*** $13,532,400 (49% Federal, 3% state, 48% institutional). ***Receiving aid:*** *Freshmen:* 41% (1,472); *all full-time undergraduates:* 36% (7,490). ***Average award:*** Freshmen: $3791; Undergraduates: $3120. ***Scholarships, grants, and awards:*** Federal Pell, FSEOG, state, private, college/university gift aid from institutional funds.

GIFT AID (NON-NEED-BASED) ***Total amount:*** $8,782,024 (4% state, 53% institutional, 43% external sources). ***Receiving aid:*** *Freshmen:* 11% (398); *Undergraduates:* 7% (1,539). ***Scholarships, grants, and awards by category:*** *Academic Interests/Achievement:* agriculture, biological sciences, business, education, engineering/technologies, general academic interests/achievements, humanities, mathematics, physical sciences, social sciences. ***Tuition waivers:*** Full or partial for senior citizens. ***ROTC:*** Army, Naval, Air Force.

LOANS ***Student loans:*** $31,349,585 (55% need-based, 45% non-need-based). 36% of past graduating class borrowed through all loan programs. Average indebtedness per student: $14,801. ***Average need-based loan:*** Freshmen: $1786; Undergraduates: $2418. ***Parent loans:*** $4,522,565 (100% non-need-based). ***Programs:*** FFEL (Subsidized and Unsubsidized Stafford, PLUS), Perkins, state, college/university.

WORK-STUDY ***Federal work-study:*** *Total amount:* $533,142; 784 jobs available. ***State or other work-study/employment:*** *Total amount:* $598,898 (100% non-need-based). Part-time jobs available.

ATHLETIC AWARDS *Total amount:* 3,894,984 (100% non-need-based).

APPLYING for FINANCIAL AID ***Required financial aid forms:*** FAFSA, institution's own form. ***Financial aid deadline (priority):*** 3/1. ***Notification date:*** Continuous beginning 3/15. Students must reply by 5/1 or within 2 weeks of notification.

CONTACT Ms. Julia Rice Mallette, Director of Financial Aid, North Carolina State University, 2005 Harris Hall, Box 7302, Raleigh, NC 27695-7302, 919-515-2334. *E-mail:* julie_rice@ncsu.edu

NORTH CAROLINA WESLEYAN COLLEGE

Rocky Mount, NC

Tuition & fees: $8556 **Average undergraduate aid package: $9579**

ABOUT THE INSTITUTION Independent religious, coed. Awards: bachelor's degrees (also offers adult part-time degree program with significant enrollment not reflected in profile). 26 undergraduate majors. Total enrollment: 2,024. Undergraduates: 2,024. Freshmen: 216. Federal methodology is used as a basis for awarding need-based institutional aid.

UNDERGRADUATE EXPENSES for 1999–2000 ***Application fee:*** $25. ***Comprehensive fee:*** $14,528 includes full-time tuition ($7724), mandatory fees ($832), and room and board ($5972). ***College room only:*** $3088. Room and board charges vary according to board plan and housing facility. ***Part-time tuition:*** $167 per credit. ***Part-time fees:*** $4 per credit; $69 per term part-time. Part-time tuition and fees vary according to course load. ***Payment plan:*** installment.

FRESHMAN FINANCIAL AID (Fall 1999, est.) 182 applied for aid; of those 89% were deemed to have need. 100% of freshmen with need received aid. *Average percent of need met:* 78% (excluding resources awarded to replace EFC). *Average financial aid package:* $9325 (excluding resources awarded to replace EFC). 19% of all full-time freshmen had no need and received non-need-based aid.

UNDERGRADUATE FINANCIAL AID (Fall 1999, est.) 624 applied for aid; of those 89% were deemed to have need. 100% of undergraduates with need received aid. *Average percent of need met:* 73% (excluding resources awarded to replace EFC). *Average financial aid package:* $9579 (excluding resources awarded to replace EFC). 21% of all full-time undergraduates had no need and received non-need-based aid.

GIFT AID (NEED-BASED) ***Total amount:*** $1,848,270 (43% Federal, 42% state, 15% institutional). ***Receiving aid:*** *Freshmen:* 69% (139); *all full-time undergraduates:* 68% (478). ***Average award:*** Freshmen: $5200; Undergraduates: $5079. ***Scholarships, grants, and awards:*** Federal Pell, FSEOG, state, private, college/university gift aid from institutional funds.

GIFT AID (NON-NEED-BASED) ***Total amount:*** $1,909,099 (30% state, 59% institutional, 11% external sources). ***Receiving aid:*** *Freshmen:* 75% (151); *Undergraduates:* 74% (516). ***Scholarships, grants, and awards by category:*** *Academic Interests/Achievement:* general academic interests/achievements. ***Tuition waivers:*** Full or partial for employees or children of employees, senior citizens.

LOANS ***Student loans:*** $2,895,358 (55% need-based, 45% non-need-based). 63% of past graduating class borrowed through all loan programs. Average indebtedness per student: $11,250. ***Average need-based loan:*** Freshmen: $2625; Undergraduates: $3500. ***Parent loans:*** $864,375 (100% non-need-based). ***Programs:*** Federal Direct (Subsidized Stafford), FFEL (Subsidized and Unsubsidized Stafford, PLUS), Perkins.

WORK-STUDY ***Federal work-study:*** *Total amount:* $185,567; 201 jobs averaging $923. ***State or other work-study/employment:*** *Total amount:* $121,920 (100% non-need-based). Part-time jobs available.

APPLYING for FINANCIAL AID ***Required financial aid form:*** FAFSA. ***Financial aid deadline (priority):*** 4/15. ***Notification date:*** Continuous. Students must reply within 4 weeks of notification.

CONTACT Ms. Tara Keeter, Director of Financial Aid, North Carolina Wesleyan College, 3400 North Wesleyan Boulevard, Rocky Mount, NC 27804, 252-985-5291 or toll-free 800-488-6292.

NORTH CENTRAL COLLEGE

Naperville, IL

Tuition & fees: $15,216 **Average undergraduate aid package: $13,316**

ABOUT THE INSTITUTION Independent United Methodist, coed. Awards: bachelor's and master's degrees. 61 undergraduate majors. Total enrollment: 2,545. Undergraduates: 2,179. Freshmen: 402. Federal methodology is used as a basis for awarding need-based institutional aid.

UNDERGRADUATE EXPENSES for 1999–2000 ***Application fee:*** $25. ***Comprehensive fee:*** $20,466 includes full-time tuition ($15,096), mandatory fees ($120), and room and board ($5250). ***Part-time tuition:*** $441 per credit. Part-time tuition and fees vary according to course load and program. ***Payment plan:*** installment.

FRESHMAN FINANCIAL AID (Fall 1999, est.) 338 applied for aid; of those 85% were deemed to have need. 100% of freshmen with need received aid; of those 39% had need fully met. *Average percent of need met:* 92% (excluding resources awarded to replace EFC). *Average financial aid package:* $14,033 (excluding resources awarded to replace EFC). 15% of all full-time freshmen had no need and received non-need-based aid.

UNDERGRADUATE FINANCIAL AID (Fall 1999, est.) 1,286 applied for aid; of those 86% were deemed to have need. 100% of undergraduates with need received aid; of those 43% had need fully met. *Average percent of need met:* 88% (excluding resources awarded to replace EFC). *Average financial aid package:* $13,316 (excluding resources awarded to replace EFC). 16% of all full-time undergraduates had no need and received non-need-based aid.

GIFT AID (NEED-BASED) ***Total amount:*** $12,851,017 (5% Federal, 21% state, 72% institutional, 2% external sources). ***Receiving aid:*** *Freshmen:* 70% (282); *all full-time undergraduates:* 54% (952). ***Average award:*** Freshmen: $10,591; Undergraduates: $8630. ***Scholarships, grants, and awards:*** Federal Pell, FSEOG, state, private, college/university gift aid from institutional funds.

GIFT AID (NON-NEED-BASED) ***Total amount:*** $262,956 (88% institutional, 12% external sources). ***Receiving aid:*** *Freshmen:* 20% (82); *Undergraduates:* 17% (302). ***Scholarships, grants, and awards by category:*** *Academic Interests/Achievement:* 699 awards ($3,509,419 total): education, general academic interests/achievements, international studies. *Creative Arts/Performance:* 178 awards ($205,160 total): art/fine arts, cinema/film/broadcasting, debating, music, theater/drama. *Special Achievements/Activities:* 53 awards ($63,250 total): religious involvement. *Special Characteristics:* 76 awards ($572,971 total): adult students, children of faculty/staff, relatives of clergy. ***Tuition waivers:*** Full or partial for employees or children of employees, senior citizens. ***ROTC:*** Army cooperative, Naval cooperative, Air Force cooperative.

LOANS ***Student loans:*** $5,972,129 (82% need-based, 18% non-need-based). 63% of past graduating class borrowed through all loan programs. Average indebtedness per student: $14,061. ***Average need-based loan:*** Freshmen: $1857; Undergraduates: $3556. ***Parent loans:*** $379,977 (23% need-based, 77% non-need-based). ***Programs:*** FFEL (Subsidized and Unsubsidized Stafford, PLUS), Perkins, state, college/university.

WORK-STUDY ***Federal work-study:*** *Total amount:* $125,666; 179 jobs averaging $702. ***State or other work-study/employment:*** *Total amount:* $737,301 (95% need-based, 5% non-need-based). Part-time jobs available.

APPLYING for FINANCIAL AID ***Required financial aid forms:*** FAFSA, institution's own form, federal income tax forms (student and parent). ***Financial aid deadline:*** Continuous. ***Notification date:*** Continuous beginning 3/1. Students must reply within 4 weeks of notification.

CONTACT Ms. Katherine A. Edmunds, Director of Financial Aid, North Central College, 30 North Brainard Street, PO Box 3063, Naperville, IL 60566-7063, 630-637-5600 or toll-free 800-411-1861. *Fax:* 630-637-5608. *E-mail:* kae@noctrl.edu

NORTH CENTRAL UNIVERSITY

Minneapolis, MN

ABOUT THE INSTITUTION Independent religious, coed. Awards: associate and bachelor's degrees. 27 undergraduate majors. Total enrollment: 1,172. Undergraduates: 1,172. Freshmen: 270.

GIFT AID (NEED-BASED) ***Scholarships, grants, and awards:*** Federal Pell, FSEOG, state, private, college/university gift aid from institutional funds.

GIFT AID (NON-NEED-BASED) ***Scholarships, grants, and awards by category:*** *Academic Interests/Achievement:* general academic interests/achievements. *Creative Arts/Performance:* art/fine arts, music, theater/drama. *Special Achievements/Activities:* community service, general special achievements/activities, leadership, memberships, religious involvement. *Special Characteristics:* adult students, children of current students, children of faculty/staff, general special characteristics, international students, married students, relatives of clergy, religious affiliation, siblings of current students, spouses of current students.

LOANS ***Programs:*** FFEL (Subsidized and Unsubsidized Stafford, PLUS), Perkins, state.

WORK-STUDY Federal work-study jobs available.

APPLYING for FINANCIAL AID ***Required financial aid form:*** FAFSA.

CONTACT Mrs. Donna Jager, Director of Financial Aid, North Central University, 910 Elliot Avenue, Minneapolis, MN 55404-1322, 612-343-4488 or toll-free 800-289-6222. *Fax:* 612-343-4778.

NORTH DAKOTA STATE UNIVERSITY

Fargo, ND

Tuition & fees (ND res): $2886 **Average undergraduate aid package: $4926**

ABOUT THE INSTITUTION State-supported, coed. Awards: bachelor's, master's, doctoral, and first professional degrees. 108 undergraduate majors. Total enrollment: 9,638. Undergraduates: 8,761. Freshmen: 1,709. Federal methodology is used as a basis for awarding need-based institutional aid.

UNDERGRADUATE EXPENSES for 1999–2000 ***Application fee:*** $25. ***One-time required fee:*** $45. ***Tuition, state resident:*** full-time $2480; part-time $103 per credit. ***Tuition, nonresident:*** full-time $6622; part-time $276 per credit. ***Required fees:*** full-time $406; $17 per credit. Full-time tuition and fees vary according to course load, program, and reciprocity agreements. Part-time tuition and fees vary according to course load, program, and reciprocity agreements. ***College room and board:*** $3408; ***room only:*** $1264. Room and board charges vary according to board plan and housing facility. ***Payment plan:*** installment.

FRESHMAN FINANCIAL AID (Fall 1999, est.) 1497 applied for aid; of those 79% were deemed to have need. 99% of freshmen with need received aid; of those 56% had need fully met. *Average percent of need met:* 22% (excluding resources awarded to replace EFC). *Average financial aid package:* $4635 (excluding resources awarded to replace EFC). 23% of all full-time freshmen had no need and received non-need-based aid.

UNDERGRADUATE FINANCIAL AID (Fall 1999, est.) 5,347 applied for aid; of those 80% were deemed to have need. 99% of undergraduates with need received aid; of those 54% had need fully met. *Average percent of need met:* 30% (excluding resources awarded to replace EFC). *Average financial aid package:* $4926 (excluding resources awarded to replace EFC). 17% of all full-time undergraduates had no need and received non-need-based aid.

GIFT AID (NEED-BASED) ***Total amount:*** $7,222,497 (67% Federal, 8% state, 19% institutional, 6% external sources). ***Receiving aid:*** *Freshmen:* 54% (851); *all full-time undergraduates:* 36% (2,740). ***Average award:*** Freshmen: $2921; Undergraduates: $2396. ***Scholarships, grants, and awards:*** Federal Pell, FSEOG, state, private, college/university gift aid from institutional funds, diversity waivers.

GIFT AID (NON-NEED-BASED) ***Total amount:*** $1,027,424 (10% state, 72% institutional, 18% external sources). ***Receiving aid:*** *Freshmen:* 14% (229); *Undergraduates:* 9% (678). ***Scholarships, grants, and awards by category:*** *Academic Interests/Achievement:* 697 awards ($1,262,359 total):

North Dakota State University (continued)

agriculture, architecture, biological sciences, business, communication, computer science, education, engineering/technologies, English, foreign languages, general academic interests/achievements, health fields, home economics, humanities, international studies, mathematics, military science, physical sciences, premedicine, social sciences. *Creative Arts/Performance:* 48 awards ($50,881 total): art/fine arts, debating, music, theater/drama. *Special Characteristics:* ethnic background, general special characteristics, international students, local/state students, members of minority groups, previous college experience, veterans, veterans' children. ***Tuition waivers:*** Full or partial for minority students, employees or children of employees, senior citizens. ***ROTC:*** Army, Air Force.

LOANS ***Student loans:*** $20,817,145 (85% need-based, 15% non-need-based). 56% of past graduating class borrowed through all loan programs. Average indebtedness per student: $18,624. ***Average need-based loan:*** Freshmen: $2769; Undergraduates: $3695. ***Parent loans:*** $499,982 (65% need-based, 35% non-need-based). ***Programs:*** FFEL (Subsidized and Unsubsidized Stafford, PLUS), Perkins, Federal Nursing, state, college/university, alternative loans.

WORK-STUDY ***Federal work-study:*** *Total amount:* $1,273,976; 1,052 jobs available.

ATHLETIC AWARDS *Total amount:* 681,960 (50% need-based, 50% non-need-based).

APPLYING for FINANCIAL AID ***Required financial aid form:*** FAFSA. ***Financial aid deadline (priority):*** 4/15. ***Notification date:*** Continuous.

CONTACT Mr. Bob Neas, Director of Financial Aid, North Dakota State University, PO Box 5315, Fargo, ND 58105, 701-231-7533 or toll-free 800-488-NDSU. *Fax:* 701-231-6126. *E-mail:* rneas@gwmail.nodak.edu

NORTHEASTERN ILLINOIS UNIVERSITY

Chicago, IL

Tuition & fees (IL res): $2890 **Average undergraduate aid package: N/A**

ABOUT THE INSTITUTION State-supported, coed. Awards: bachelor's and master's degrees. 36 undergraduate majors. Total enrollment: 10,937. Undergraduates: 8,205. Freshmen: 1,012. Federal methodology is used as a basis for awarding need-based institutional aid.

UNDERGRADUATE EXPENSES for 1999–2000 ***Tuition, state resident:*** full-time $2576; part-time $94 per credit hour. ***Tuition, nonresident:*** full-time $7100; part-time $283 per credit hour. ***Required fees:*** full-time $314; $13 per credit hour. Full-time tuition and fees vary according to course load. Part-time tuition and fees vary according to course load. ***Payment plan:*** deferred payment.

GIFT AID (NEED-BASED) ***Scholarships, grants, and awards:*** Federal Pell, FSEOG, state, private, college/university gift aid from institutional funds, Bureau of Indian Affairs Grants.

GIFT AID (NON-NEED-BASED) ***Scholarships, grants, and awards by category:*** *Academic Interests/Achievement:* education, general academic interests/achievements. *Creative Arts/Performance:* applied art and design, art/fine arts, dance, music, performing arts, theater/drama. *Special Achievements/Activities:* general special achievements/activities, leadership. *Special Characteristics:* children of faculty/staff, general special characteristics, members of minority groups. ***Tuition waivers:*** Full or partial for employees or children of employees, senior citizens. ***ROTC:*** Army cooperative, Naval cooperative, Air Force cooperative.

LOANS ***Programs:*** FFEL (Subsidized and Unsubsidized Stafford, PLUS), Perkins, college/university.

WORK-STUDY Federal work-study jobs available. ***State or other work-study/employment:*** Part-time jobs available.

APPLYING for FINANCIAL AID ***Required financial aid forms:*** FAFSA, institution's own form. ***Financial aid deadline (priority):*** 3/1.

CONTACT Financial Aid Office, Northeastern Illinois University, 5500 North St. Louis Avenue, Chicago, IL 60625, 773-794-2900.

NORTHEASTERN STATE UNIVERSITY

Tahlequah, OK

Tuition & fees (OK res): $1865 **Average undergraduate aid package: $4108**

ABOUT THE INSTITUTION State-supported, coed. Awards: bachelor's, master's, and doctoral degrees. 68 undergraduate majors. Total enrollment: 8,462. Undergraduates: 7,254. Federal methodology is used as a basis for awarding need-based institutional aid.

UNDERGRADUATE EXPENSES for 1999–2000 ***Tuition, state resident:*** full-time $1470; part-time $49 per semester hour. ***Tuition, nonresident:*** full-time $3990; part-time $133 per semester hour. ***Required fees:*** full-time $395; $13 per semester hour. Full-time tuition and fees vary according to course level, course load, location, and student level. Part-time tuition and fees vary according to course level, course load, and student level. ***College room and board:*** $2610. Room and board charges vary according to board plan and housing facility.

FRESHMAN FINANCIAL AID (Fall 1998) 774 applied for aid; of those 82% were deemed to have need. 98% of freshmen with need received aid; of those 60% had need fully met. *Average percent of need met:* 57% (excluding resources awarded to replace EFC). *Average financial aid package:* $3903 (excluding resources awarded to replace EFC). 18% of all full-time freshmen had no need and received non-need-based aid.

UNDERGRADUATE FINANCIAL AID (Fall 1998) 4,837 applied for aid; of those 82% were deemed to have need. 98% of undergraduates with need received aid; of those 60% had need fully met. *Average percent of need met:* 60% (excluding resources awarded to replace EFC). *Average financial aid package:* $4108 (excluding resources awarded to replace EFC). 15% of all full-time undergraduates had no need and received non-need-based aid.

GIFT AID (NEED-BASED) ***Total amount:*** $10,948,715 (67% Federal, 23% state, 10% external sources). ***Receiving aid:*** *Freshmen:* 60% (543); *all full-time undergraduates:* 60% (3,396). ***Average award:*** Freshmen: $2690; Undergraduates: $2562. ***Scholarships, grants, and awards:*** Federal Pell, FSEOG, state, private, college/university gift aid from institutional funds.

GIFT AID (NON-NEED-BASED) ***Total amount:*** $765,591 (84% state, 16% external sources). ***Receiving aid:*** *Freshmen:* 10% (94); *Undergraduates:* 10% (586). ***Scholarships, grants, and awards by category:*** *Academic Interests/Achievement:* biological sciences, business, communication, computer science, education, English, foreign languages, general academic interests/achievements, health fields, home economics, humanities, library science, mathematics, physical sciences, premedicine, social sciences. *Creative Arts/Performance:* applied art and design, art/fine arts, dance, debating, journalism/publications, music, performing arts, theater/drama. *Special Achievements/Activities:* cheerleading/drum major, general special achievements/activities, hobbies/interests, junior miss.

LOANS ***Student loans:*** $19,719,577 (100% need-based). ***Average need-based loan:*** Freshmen: $2634; Undergraduates: $2927. ***Parent loans:*** $626,171 (100% non-need-based). ***Programs:*** FFEL (Subsidized and Unsubsidized Stafford, PLUS), Perkins, college/university.

WORK-STUDY ***Federal work-study:*** *Total amount:* $708,647; jobs available. ***State or other work-study/employment:*** *Total amount:* $1,377,299 (100% non-need-based). Part-time jobs available.

ATHLETIC AWARDS *Total amount:* 600,225 (60% need-based, 40% non-need-based).

APPLYING for FINANCIAL AID ***Required financial aid forms:*** FAFSA, institution's own form. ***Financial aid deadline (priority):*** 3/1. ***Notification date:*** Continuous beginning 4/1. Students must reply within 2 weeks of notification.

CONTACT Dr. William McFarland, Director, Office of Student Financial Services, Northeastern State University, 600 North Grand, Tahlequah, OK 74464-2399, 918-456-5511 or toll-free 800-722-9614 (in-state). *E-mail:* mcfarlaw@cherokee.nsuok.edu

NORTHEASTERN UNIVERSITY

Boston, MA

Tuition & fees: $18,867 **Average undergraduate aid package: $11,653**

ABOUT THE INSTITUTION Independent, coed. Awards: associate, bachelor's, master's, doctoral, and first professional degrees and post-master's certificates. 99 undergraduate majors. Total enrollment: 16,628. Undergraduates: 12,300. Freshmen: 2,395. Federal methodology is used as a basis for awarding need-based institutional aid.

UNDERGRADUATE EXPENSES for 1999–2000 ***Application fee:*** $45. ***Comprehensive fee:*** $27,477 includes full-time tuition ($18,675), mandatory fees ($192), and room and board ($8610). ***College room only:*** $4485. Full-time tuition and fees vary according to class time and student level. Room and board charges vary according to board plan and housing facility. Part-time tuition and fees vary according to class time and program. ***Payment plans:*** installment, deferred payment.

FRESHMAN FINANCIAL AID (Fall 1998) 2234 applied for aid; of those 92% were deemed to have need. 100% of freshmen with need received aid. *Average percent of need met:* 63% (excluding resources awarded to replace EFC). *Average financial aid package:* $13,190 (excluding resources awarded to replace EFC). 1% of all full-time freshmen had no need and received non-need-based aid.

UNDERGRADUATE FINANCIAL AID (Fall 1998) 8,817 applied for aid; of those 98% were deemed to have need. 100% of undergraduates with need received aid. *Average percent of need met:* 62% (excluding resources awarded to replace EFC). *Average financial aid package:* $11,653 (excluding resources awarded to replace EFC). 1% of all full-time undergraduates had no need and received non-need-based aid.

GIFT AID (NEED-BASED) ***Total amount:*** $46,028,670 (19% Federal, 10% state, 71% institutional). ***Receiving aid:*** *Freshmen:* 68% (1,922); *all full-time undergraduates:* 47% (5,813). ***Scholarships, grants, and awards:*** Federal Pell, FSEOG, state, private, college/university gift aid from institutional funds, Federal Nursing.

GIFT AID (NON-NEED-BASED) ***Total amount:*** $8,566,563 (100% institutional). ***Receiving aid:*** *Freshmen:* 6% (182); *Undergraduates:* 5% (568). ***Scholarships, grants, and awards by category:*** *Academic Interests/Achievement:* general academic interests/achievements. *Special Characteristics:* children of faculty/staff. ***Tuition waivers:*** Full or partial for employees or children of employees, senior citizens. ***ROTC:*** Army, Naval cooperative, Air Force cooperative.

LOANS ***Student loans:*** $43,418,677 (90% need-based, 10% non-need-based). ***Programs:*** FFEL (Subsidized and Unsubsidized Stafford, PLUS), Perkins, Federal Nursing, state, college/university, MassPlan Loans, TERI Loans, Signature Loans, Massachusetts No-Interest Loans (NIL).

WORK-STUDY ***Federal work-study:*** *Total amount:* $5,732,070; 3,605 jobs averaging $1590.

ATHLETIC AWARDS *Total amount:* 4,442,077 (100% non-need-based).

APPLYING for FINANCIAL AID ***Required financial aid forms:*** FAFSA, CSS Financial Aid PROFILE. ***Financial aid deadline (priority):*** 2/15. ***Notification date:*** Continuous beginning 3/15. Students must reply by 5/1.

CONTACT Ms. Marilyn Molnar, Director of Student Financial Services, Northeastern University, PO Box 75, Boston, MA 02117, 617-373-3190. *Fax:* 617-373-8735. *E-mail:* m.molnar@nunet.neu.edu

NORTHEAST LOUISIANA UNIVERSITY

Monroe, LA

See University of Louisiana at Monroe

NORTHERN ARIZONA UNIVERSITY

Flagstaff, AZ

Tuition & fees (AZ res): $2262 **Average undergraduate aid package: $8222**

ABOUT THE INSTITUTION State-supported, coed. Awards: bachelor's, master's, and doctoral degrees. 113 undergraduate majors. Total enrollment: 19,980. Undergraduates: 13,946. Freshmen: 2,249. Federal methodology is used as a basis for awarding need-based institutional aid.

UNDERGRADUATE EXPENSES for 1999–2000 ***Application fee:*** $40. ***Tuition, state resident:*** full-time $2188; part-time $115 per semester hour. ***Tuition, nonresident:*** full-time $8304; part-time $346 per semester hour. ***Required fees:*** full-time $74; $37 per term part-time. Part-time tuition and fees vary according to course load. ***College room and board:*** $3682; ***room only:*** $1832. Room and board charges vary according to board plan and housing facility.

FRESHMAN FINANCIAL AID (Fall 1998) 1747 applied for aid; of those 57% were deemed to have need. 96% of freshmen with need received aid; of those 28% had need fully met. *Average percent of need met:* 65% (excluding resources awarded to replace EFC). *Average financial aid package:* $5987 (excluding resources awarded to replace EFC). 23% of all full-time freshmen had no need and received non-need-based aid.

UNDERGRADUATE FINANCIAL AID (Fall 1998) 10,010 applied for aid; of those 63% were deemed to have need. 98% of undergraduates with need received aid; of those 39% had need fully met. *Average percent of need met:* 65% (excluding resources awarded to replace EFC). *Average financial aid package:* $8222 (excluding resources awarded to replace EFC). 15% of all full-time undergraduates had no need and received non-need-based aid.

GIFT AID (NEED-BASED) ***Total amount:*** $17,275,646 (61% Federal, 1% state, 27% institutional, 11% external sources). ***Receiving aid:*** *Freshmen:* 25% (553); *all full-time undergraduates:* 34% (4,219). ***Average award:*** Freshmen: $2812; Undergraduates: $3167. ***Scholarships, grants, and awards:*** Federal Pell, FSEOG, state, private, college/university gift aid from institutional funds.

GIFT AID (NON-NEED-BASED) ***Total amount:*** $2,454,034 (16% Federal, 57% institutional, 27% external sources). ***Receiving aid:*** *Freshmen:* 24% (549); *Undergraduates:* 18% (2,191). ***Scholarships, grants, and awards by category:*** *Academic Interests/Achievement:* 149 awards ($138,248 total): biological sciences, business, communication, engineering/technologies, English, general academic interests/achievements, health fields, humanities, mathematics, military science, physical sciences, social sciences. *Creative Arts/Performance:* 321 awards ($742,363 total): art/fine arts, cinema/film/broadcasting, debating, journalism/publications, music, performing arts, theater/drama. *Special Characteristics:* 2,035 awards ($3,606,734 total): children and siblings of alumni, children of educators, handicapped students, international students, local/state students, out-of-state students. ***Tuition waivers:*** Full or partial for employees or children of employees. ***ROTC:*** Army, Air Force.

LOANS ***Student loans:*** $32,240,040 (88% need-based, 12% non-need-based). 59% of past graduating class borrowed through all loan programs. Average indebtedness per student: $16,396. ***Average need-based loan:*** Freshmen: $3626; Undergraduates: $5461. ***Parent loans:*** $2,466,447 (66% need-based, 34% non-need-based). ***Programs:*** Federal Direct (Subsidized and Unsubsidized Stafford, PLUS), Perkins, Federal Nursing, college/university.

WORK-STUDY ***Federal work-study:*** *Total amount:* $846,916; 593 jobs averaging $1428.

ATHLETIC AWARDS *Total amount:* 677,292 (43% need-based, 57% non-need-based).

APPLYING for FINANCIAL AID ***Required financial aid form:*** FAFSA. ***Financial aid deadline (priority):*** 2/14. ***Notification date:*** Continuous.

CONTACT Mr. Thurburn H. Barker Jr., Senior Management Analyst, Northern Arizona University, Box 4108, Flagstaff, AZ 86011, 520-523-5699 or toll-free 888-MORE-NAU. *Fax:* 520-523-1551. *E-mail:* thurburn.barker@nau.edu

NORTHERN ILLINOIS UNIVERSITY

De Kalb, IL

Tuition & fees (IL res): $4099 **Average undergraduate aid package: N/A**

ABOUT THE INSTITUTION State-supported, coed. Awards: bachelor's, master's, doctoral, and first professional degrees. 58 undergraduate majors.

Northern Illinois University (continued)

Total enrollment: 22,843. Undergraduates: 16,893. Freshmen: 2,951. Federal methodology is used as a basis for awarding need-based institutional aid.

UNDERGRADUATE EXPENSES for 1999–2000 ***Tuition, state resident:*** full-time $3060; part-time $113 per credit hour. ***Tuition, nonresident:*** full-time $6120; part-time $226 per credit hour. ***Required fees:*** full-time $1039; $43 per credit hour. Full-time tuition and fees vary according to course load. Part-time tuition and fees vary according to course load. ***College room and board:*** $4400. Room and board charges vary according to board plan and housing facility. ***Payment plan:*** installment.

GIFT AID (NEED-BASED) ***Scholarships, grants, and awards:*** Federal Pell, FSEOG, state, private, college/university gift aid from institutional funds.

GIFT AID (NON-NEED-BASED) ***Scholarships, grants, and awards by category:*** *Academic Interests/Achievement:* general academic interests/achievements. *Creative Arts/Performance:* art/fine arts, music, performing arts, theater/drama. *Special Characteristics:* children of faculty/staff, international students, members of minority groups, veterans. ***Tuition waivers:*** Full or partial for minority students, employees or children of employees. ***ROTC:*** Army, Air Force cooperative.

LOANS ***Programs:*** FFEL (Subsidized and Unsubsidized Stafford, PLUS), Perkins, college/university.

WORK-STUDY Federal work-study jobs available. ***State or other work-study/employment:*** Part-time jobs available.

APPLYING for FINANCIAL AID ***Required financial aid forms:*** FAFSA, institution's own form. ***Financial aid deadline (priority):*** 3/1.

CONTACT Ms. Kathleen D. Brunson, Director of Student Financial Aid, Northern Illinois University, Swen Parson Hall, Room 245, DeKalb, IL 60115, 815-753-1300 or toll-free 800-892-3050 (in-state). *Fax:* 815-753-9475.

NORTHERN KENTUCKY UNIVERSITY

Highland Heights, KY

Tuition & fees (KY res): $2442 **Average undergraduate aid package: $4632**

ABOUT THE INSTITUTION State-supported, coed. Awards: associate, bachelor's, master's, and first professional degrees and post-master's certificates. 73 undergraduate majors. Total enrollment: 11,823. Undergraduates: 10,644. Freshmen: 1,873. Federal methodology is used as a basis for awarding need-based institutional aid.

UNDERGRADUATE EXPENSES for 1999–2000 ***Application fee:*** $25. ***Tuition, state resident:*** full-time $2100; part-time $89 per semester hour. ***Tuition, nonresident:*** full-time $6140; part-time $257 per semester hour. ***Required fees:*** full-time $342; $14 per semester hour. Full-time tuition and fees vary according to course load. Part-time tuition and fees vary according to course load. ***College room and board:*** $3654; ***room only:*** $3326. Room and board charges vary according to board plan and housing facility. ***Payment plan:*** installment.

FRESHMAN FINANCIAL AID (Fall 1998) 1565 applied for aid; of those 99% were deemed to have need. 72% of freshmen with need received aid. *Average percent of need met:* 90% (excluding resources awarded to replace EFC). *Average financial aid package:* $3835 (excluding resources awarded to replace EFC). 12% of all full-time freshmen had no need and received non-need-based aid.

UNDERGRADUATE FINANCIAL AID (Fall 1998) 6,098 applied for aid; of those 96% were deemed to have need. 85% of undergraduates with need received aid. *Average percent of need met:* 85% (excluding resources awarded to replace EFC). *Average financial aid package:* $4632 (excluding resources awarded to replace EFC). 3% of all full-time undergraduates had no need and received non-need-based aid.

GIFT AID (NEED-BASED) ***Total amount:*** $5,370,314 (82% Federal, 18% state). ***Receiving aid:*** *Freshmen:* 38% (663); *all full-time undergraduates:* 30% (3,061). ***Average award:*** Freshmen: $2900; Undergraduates: $2900. ***Scholarships, grants, and awards:*** Federal Pell, FSEOG, state, private.

GIFT AID (NON-NEED-BASED) ***Total amount:*** $2,001,447 (74% institutional, 26% external sources). ***Receiving aid:*** *Freshmen:* 26% (456); *Undergraduates:* 6% (556). ***Scholarships, grants, and awards by category:*** *Academic Interests/Achievement:* 281 awards ($620,498 total): general academic interests/achievements. *Creative Arts/Performance:* 91 awards ($76,085 total): art/fine arts. *Special Characteristics:* 185 awards ($283,463 total): members of minority groups, out-of-state students, spouses of deceased or disabled public servants, veterans' children. ***Tuition waivers:*** Full or partial for employees or children of employees, senior citizens. ***ROTC:*** Army cooperative, Air Force cooperative.

LOANS ***Student loans:*** $23,165,705 (100% need-based). 40% of past graduating class borrowed through all loan programs. Average indebtedness per student: $20,400. ***Average need-based loan:*** Freshmen: $2625; Undergraduates: $5130. ***Parent loans:*** $950,793 (100% non-need-based). ***Programs:*** FFEL (Subsidized and Unsubsidized Stafford, PLUS), Perkins, alternative loans.

WORK-STUDY ***Federal work-study:*** *Total amount:* $407,501; 295 jobs available. ***State or other work-study/employment:*** *Total amount:* $1,058,640 (100% non-need-based). Part-time jobs available.

ATHLETIC AWARDS *Total amount:* 378,336 (100% non-need-based).

APPLYING for FINANCIAL AID ***Required financial aid form:*** FAFSA. ***Financial aid deadline (priority):*** 3/1. ***Notification date:*** 6/1. Students must reply within 3 weeks of notification.

CONTACT Mr. Robert F. Sprague, Director of Student Financial Assistance, Northern Kentucky University, 412 Administrative Center, Nunn Drive, Highland Heights, KY 41099-7101, 606-572-5144 or toll-free 800-637-9948. *Fax:* 606-572-6997. *E-mail:* spraguer@nku.edu

NORTHERN MICHIGAN UNIVERSITY

Marquette, MI

Tuition & fees (MI res): $3146 **Average undergraduate aid package: $5100**

ABOUT THE INSTITUTION State-supported, coed. Awards: associate, bachelor's, and master's degrees. 110 undergraduate majors. Total enrollment: 8,092. Undergraduates: 7,254. Federal methodology is used as a basis for awarding need-based institutional aid.

UNDERGRADUATE EXPENSES for 1999–2000 ***Application fee:*** $25. ***Tuition, state resident:*** full-time $2772; part-time $116 per credit hour. ***Tuition, nonresident:*** full-time $5208; part-time $217 per credit hour. ***Required fees:*** full-time $374; $115 per term part-time. Part-time tuition and fees vary according to course load. ***College room and board:*** $4640; ***room only:*** $2242. Room and board charges vary according to housing facility. ***Payment plan:*** installment.

UNDERGRADUATE FINANCIAL AID (Fall 1999, est.) *Average financial aid package:* $5100 (excluding resources awarded to replace EFC).

GIFT AID (NEED-BASED) ***Scholarships, grants, and awards:*** Federal Pell, FSEOG, state, college/university gift aid from institutional funds.

GIFT AID (NON-NEED-BASED) ***Scholarships, grants, and awards by category:*** *Academic Interests/Achievement:* business, engineering/technologies, general academic interests/achievements, health fields, military science, premedicine. *Creative Arts/Performance:* applied art and design, music, theater/drama. *Special Achievements/Activities:* leadership. *Special Characteristics:* adult students, children of union members/company employees, members of minority groups, out-of-state students. ***Tuition waivers:*** Full or partial for children of alumni, employees or children of employees, senior citizens. ***ROTC:*** Army.

LOANS ***Programs:*** Federal Direct (Subsidized and Unsubsidized Stafford, PLUS), Perkins.

WORK-STUDY Federal work-study jobs available. ***State or other work-study/employment:*** Part-time jobs available.

APPLYING for FINANCIAL AID ***Required financial aid form:*** FAFSA. ***Financial aid deadline (priority):*** 2/1. ***Notification date:*** 5/1.

CONTACT Shirley J. Niemi, Director of Financial Aid, Northern Michigan University, 1401 Presque Isle Avenue, Marquette, MI 49855, 906-227-2327 or toll-free 800-682-9797 Ext. 1 (in-state), 800-682-9797 (out-of-state). *Fax:* 906-227-2312. *E-mail:* sniemi@nmu.edu

NORTHERN STATE UNIVERSITY

Aberdeen, SD

CONTACT Ms. Sharon Kienow, Director of Financial Assistance, Northern State University, 1200 South Jay Street, Aberdeen, SD 57401-7198, 605-626-2640. *Fax:* 605-626-3022. *E-mail:* kienows@wolf.northern.edu

NORTH GEORGIA COLLEGE & STATE UNIVERSITY

Dahlonega, GA

Tuition & fees (GA res): $2210 **Average undergraduate aid package: N/A**

ABOUT THE INSTITUTION State-supported, coed. Awards: associate, bachelor's, and master's degrees. 36 undergraduate majors. Total enrollment: 3,525. Undergraduates: 3,144. Freshmen: 644. Federal methodology is used as a basis for awarding need-based institutional aid.

UNDERGRADUATE EXPENSES for 1999–2000 ***Application fee:*** $25. ***Tuition, state resident:*** full-time $1808; part-time $76 per semester hour. ***Tuition, nonresident:*** full-time $7232; part-time $302 per semester hour. ***Required fees:*** full-time $402; $201 per term part-time. Part-time tuition and fees vary according to course load. ***College room and board:*** $3526; ***room only:*** $1728. Room and board charges vary according to board plan and housing facility.

GIFT AID (NEED-BASED) ***Total amount:*** $1,109,279 (97% Federal, 3% institutional). ***Scholarships, grants, and awards:*** Federal Pell, FSEOG, state, private, college/university gift aid from institutional funds.

GIFT AID (NON-NEED-BASED) ***Total amount:*** $3,707,077 (2% Federal, 87% state, 5% institutional, 6% external sources). ***Scholarships, grants, and awards by category:*** *Academic Interests/Achievement:* general academic interests/achievements, military science. *Creative Arts/Performance:* applied art and design, general creative arts/performance, music. *Special Achievements/Activities:* cheerleading/drum major, leadership. *Special Characteristics:* general special characteristics. ***Tuition waivers:*** Full or partial for employees or children of employees, senior citizens. ***ROTC:*** Army.

LOANS ***Student loans:*** $3,347,128 (43% need-based, 57% non-need-based). ***Parent loans:*** $29,987 (100% non-need-based). ***Programs:*** FFEL (Subsidized and Unsubsidized Stafford, PLUS), Perkins, college/university.

WORK-STUDY ***Federal work-study:*** *Total amount:* $137,697; 99 jobs averaging $1391. ***State or other work-study/employment:*** *Total amount:* $464,290 (100% non-need-based). Part-time jobs available.

ATHLETIC AWARDS *Total amount:* 188,179 (100% non-need-based).

APPLYING for FINANCIAL AID ***Required financial aid forms:*** FAFSA, institution's own form. ***Financial aid deadline (priority):*** 4/15. ***Notification date:*** Continuous beginning 5/15. Students must reply within 3 weeks of notification.

CONTACT Ms. Deborah Barbone, Director of Financial Aid, North Georgia College & State University, 110 Barnes Hall, Dahlonega, GA 30597-1001, 706-864-1412 or toll-free 800-498-9581. *Fax:* 706-864-1667. *E-mail:* finaid@ngcsu.edu

NORTH GREENVILLE COLLEGE

Tigerville, SC

Tuition & fees: $7650 **Average undergraduate aid package: $8100**

ABOUT THE INSTITUTION Independent Southern Baptist, coed. Awards: associate and bachelor's degrees. 24 undergraduate majors. Total enrollment: 1,220. Undergraduates: 1,220. Freshmen: 348. Federal methodology is used as a basis for awarding need-based institutional aid.

UNDERGRADUATE EXPENSES for 1999–2000 ***Application fee:*** $20. ***Comprehensive fee:*** $12,150 includes full-time tuition ($7550), mandatory fees ($100), and room and board ($4500). ***Part-time tuition:*** $175 per hour. ***Part-time fees:*** $50 per term part-time. Part-time tuition and fees vary according to course load. ***Payment plan:*** installment.

FRESHMAN FINANCIAL AID (Fall 1999) 456 applied for aid; of those 100% were deemed to have need. 100% of freshmen with need received aid; of those 85% had need fully met. *Average percent of need met:* 90% (excluding resources awarded to replace EFC). *Average financial aid package:* $8100 (excluding resources awarded to replace EFC).

UNDERGRADUATE FINANCIAL AID (Fall 1999) 1,170 applied for aid; of those 100% were deemed to have need. 100% of undergraduates with need received aid; of those 85% had need fully met. *Average percent of need met:* 90% (excluding resources awarded to replace EFC). *Average financial aid package:* $8100 (excluding resources awarded to replace EFC).

GIFT AID (NEED-BASED) ***Total amount:*** $5,371,788 (19% Federal, 26% state, 48% institutional, 7% external sources). ***Receiving aid:*** *Freshmen:* 77% (364); *all full-time undergraduates:* 77% (936). ***Average award:*** Freshmen: $328; Undergraduates: $328. ***Scholarships, grants, and awards:*** Federal Pell, FSEOG, state, private, college/university gift aid from institutional funds.

GIFT AID (NON-NEED-BASED) ***Scholarships, grants, and awards by category:*** *Academic Interests/Achievement:* education, general academic interests/achievements, military science, religion/biblical studies. *Creative Arts/Performance:* art/fine arts, journalism/publications, music, theater/drama. *Special Achievements/Activities:* cheerleading/drum major, junior miss, religious involvement. *Special Characteristics:* children of faculty/staff, siblings of current students. ***Tuition waivers:*** Full or partial for employees or children of employees. ***ROTC:*** Army cooperative.

LOANS ***Student loans:*** $2,537,818 (65% need-based, 35% non-need-based). ***Average need-based loan:*** Freshmen: $1538; Undergraduates: $1538. ***Parent loans:*** $418,387 (100% need-based). ***Programs:*** FFEL (Subsidized and Unsubsidized Stafford, PLUS), Perkins, state, college/university.

WORK-STUDY ***Federal work-study:*** *Total amount:* $131,900; 132 jobs averaging $1000. ***State or other work-study/employment:*** *Total amount:* $109,600 (100% need-based). 110 part-time jobs averaging $1000.

ATHLETIC AWARDS *Total amount:* 418,000 (100% need-based).

APPLYING for FINANCIAL AID ***Required financial aid form:*** FAFSA. ***Financial aid deadline (priority):*** 6/30. ***Notification date:*** Continuous.

CONTACT Ms. Shirley Eskew, Assistant Director of Financial Aid, North Greenville College, PO Box 1892, Tigerville, SC 29688-1892, 864-977-7057 or toll-free 800-468-6642. *Fax:* 864-977-7177.

NORTHLAND COLLEGE

Ashland, WI

Tuition & fees: $14,675 **Average undergraduate aid package: $12,185**

ABOUT THE INSTITUTION Independent religious, coed. Awards: bachelor's degrees. 55 undergraduate majors. Total enrollment: 782. Undergraduates: 782. Freshmen: 203. Both federal and institutional methodology are used as a basis for awarding need-based institutional aid.

UNDERGRADUATE EXPENSES for 2000–2001 ***Comprehensive fee:*** $19,145 includes full-time tuition ($14,415), mandatory fees ($260), and room and board ($4470). ***College room only:*** $1860. Room and board charges vary according to board plan and housing facility. ***Payment plans:*** tuition prepayment, installment.

FRESHMAN FINANCIAL AID (Fall 1998) 151 applied for aid; of those 90% were deemed to have need. 100% of freshmen with need received aid; of those 14% had need fully met. *Average percent of need met:* 83% (excluding resources awarded to replace EFC). *Average financial aid package:* $12,085 (excluding resources awarded to replace EFC). 3% of all full-time freshmen had no need and received non-need-based aid.

UNDERGRADUATE FINANCIAL AID (Fall 1998) 763 applied for aid; of those 87% were deemed to have need. 100% of undergraduates with need received aid; of those 17% had need fully met. *Average percent of need met:* 84% (excluding resources awarded to replace EFC). *Average financial aid package:* $12,185 (excluding resources awarded to replace EFC). 4% of all full-time undergraduates had no need and received non-need-based aid.

Northland College (continued)

GIFT AID (NEED-BASED) ***Total amount:*** $4,166,587 (23% Federal, 11% state, 64% institutional, 2% external sources). ***Receiving aid:*** *Freshmen:* 76% (134); *all full-time undergraduates:* 81% (636). ***Scholarships, grants, and awards:*** Federal Pell, FSEOG, state, private, college/university gift aid from institutional funds, Bureau of Indian Affairs Grants.

GIFT AID (NON-NEED-BASED) ***Total amount:*** $219,617 (13% state, 82% institutional, 5% external sources). ***Receiving aid:*** *Freshmen:* 3% (5); *Undergraduates:* 3% (23). ***Scholarships, grants, and awards by category:*** *Academic Interests/Achievement:* general academic interests/achievements. *Creative Arts/Performance:* music. *Special Achievements/Activities:* leadership. *Special Characteristics:* ethnic background. ***Tuition waivers:*** Full or partial for employees or children of employees.

LOANS ***Student loans:*** $3,340,622 (87% need-based, 13% non-need-based). ***Parent loans:*** $742,137 (33% need-based, 67% non-need-based). ***Programs:*** Federal Direct (Subsidized and Unsubsidized Stafford, PLUS), Perkins.

WORK-STUDY ***Federal work-study:*** *Total amount:* $754,901; jobs available. ***State or other work-study/employment:*** *Total amount:* $263,378 (42% need-based, 58% non-need-based). Part-time jobs available.

ATHLETIC AWARDS *Total amount:* 49,898 (64% need-based, 36% non-need-based).

APPLYING for FINANCIAL AID ***Required financial aid forms:*** FAFSA, institution's own form. ***Financial aid deadline (priority):*** 4/15. ***Notification date:*** Continuous. Students must reply by 5/1 or within 4 weeks of notification.

CONTACT Ms. Susan Bradford, Assistant Director of Financial Aid, Northland College, 1411 Ellis Avenue, Ashland, WI 54806, 715-682-1255 or toll-free 800-753-1840 (in-state).

NORTH PARK UNIVERSITY

Chicago, IL

ABOUT THE INSTITUTION Independent religious, coed. Awards: bachelor's, master's, doctoral, and first professional degrees. 56 undergraduate majors. Total enrollment: 2,154. Undergraduates: 1,619. Freshmen: 487.

GIFT AID (NEED-BASED) ***Scholarships, grants, and awards:*** Federal Pell, FSEOG, state, private, college/university gift aid from institutional funds.

GIFT AID (NON-NEED-BASED) ***Scholarships, grants, and awards by category:*** *Academic Interests/Achievement:* general academic interests/achievements. *Creative Arts/Performance:* art/fine arts, music, theater/drama. *Special Achievements/Activities:* community service.

LOANS ***Programs:*** FFEL (Subsidized and Unsubsidized Stafford, PLUS), Perkins.

WORK-STUDY Federal work-study jobs available.

APPLYING for FINANCIAL AID ***Required financial aid form:*** FAFSA.

CONTACT Dr. Lucy Shaker, Director of Financial Aid, North Park University, 3225 West Foster Avenue, Chicago, IL 60625-4895, 773-244-5526 or toll-free 800-888-NPC8. *Fax:* 773-244-4953.

NORTHWEST CHRISTIAN COLLEGE

Eugene, OR

Tuition & fees: $13,905 **Average undergraduate aid package: N/A**

ABOUT THE INSTITUTION Independent interdenominational, coed. Awards: associate, bachelor's, and master's degrees. 20 undergraduate majors. Total enrollment: 431. Undergraduates: 418. Freshmen: 69. Federal methodology is used as a basis for awarding need-based institutional aid.

UNDERGRADUATE EXPENSES for 2000–2001 ***Application fee:*** $25. ***Comprehensive fee:*** $19,062 includes full-time tuition ($13,905) and room and board ($5157). ***College room only:*** $2130. Room and board charges vary according to board plan and housing facility. ***Part-time tuition:*** $309 per credit. ***Payment plans:*** installment, deferred payment.

FRESHMAN FINANCIAL AID (Fall 1999, est.) 67 applied for aid; of those 94% were deemed to have need. 100% of freshmen with need received aid; of those 14% had need fully met. *Average percent of need met:* 79% (excluding resources awarded to replace EFC). *Average financial aid package:* $13,157 (excluding resources awarded to replace EFC). 6% of all full-time freshmen had no need and received non-need-based aid.

GIFT AID (NEED-BASED) ***Total amount:*** $1,048,330 (43% Federal, 17% state, 25% institutional, 15% external sources). ***Receiving aid:*** *Freshmen:* 91% (63). ***Average award:*** Freshmen: $4480. ***Scholarships, grants, and awards:*** Federal Pell, FSEOG, state, private, college/university gift aid from institutional funds.

GIFT AID (NON-NEED-BASED) ***Total amount:*** $578,884 (100% institutional). ***Receiving aid:*** *Freshmen:* 12% (8). ***Scholarships, grants, and awards by category:*** *Academic Interests/Achievement:* general academic interests/achievements. *Creative Arts/Performance:* general creative arts/performance, music. *Special Achievements/Activities:* general special achievements/activities, leadership, religious involvement. *Special Characteristics:* children of faculty/staff, relatives of clergy, religious affiliation. ***Tuition waivers:*** Full or partial for employees or children of employees. ***ROTC:*** Army cooperative.

LOANS ***Student loans:*** $2,180,089 (60% need-based, 40% non-need-based). 84% of past graduating class borrowed through all loan programs. Average indebtedness per student: $18,687. ***Parent loans:*** $86,631 (100% need-based). ***Programs:*** FFEL (Subsidized and Unsubsidized Stafford, PLUS), Perkins.

WORK-STUDY ***Federal work-study:*** *Total amount:* $71,865; 28 jobs averaging $2550. ***State or other work-study/employment:*** *Total amount:* $356,184 (100% need-based). 140 part-time jobs averaging $2550.

ATHLETIC AWARDS *Total amount:* 55,000 (100% non-need-based).

APPLYING for FINANCIAL AID ***Required financial aid forms:*** FAFSA, institution's own form. ***Financial aid deadline (priority):*** 3/1. ***Notification date:*** Continuous beginning 3/15. Students must reply within 3 weeks of notification.

CONTACT Jocelyn Hubbs, Financial Aid Counselor, Northwest Christian College, 828 East 11th Avenue, Eugene, OR 97401-3727, 541-684-7218 or toll-free 877-463-6622. *Fax:* 541-684-7323.

NORTHWEST COLLEGE

Kirkland, WA

Tuition & fees: $9870 **Average undergraduate aid package: $9996**

ABOUT THE INSTITUTION Independent religious, coed. Awards: associate and bachelor's degrees. 34 undergraduate majors. Total enrollment: 972. Undergraduates: 972. Freshmen: 210. Federal methodology is used as a basis for awarding need-based institutional aid.

UNDERGRADUATE EXPENSES for 1999–2000 ***Application fee:*** $30. ***Comprehensive fee:*** $14,900 includes full-time tuition ($9672), mandatory fees ($198), and room and board ($5030). Room and board charges vary according to board plan. ***Part-time tuition:*** $403 per credit hour. ***Part-time fees:*** $21 per credit hour. ***Payment plans:*** installment, deferred payment.

FRESHMAN FINANCIAL AID (Fall 1999, est.) 173 applied for aid; of those 87% were deemed to have need. 100% of freshmen with need received aid; of those 31% had need fully met. *Average percent of need met:* 81% (excluding resources awarded to replace EFC). *Average financial aid package:* $10,743 (excluding resources awarded to replace EFC). 25% of all full-time freshmen had no need and received non-need-based aid.

UNDERGRADUATE FINANCIAL AID (Fall 1999, est.) 653 applied for aid; of those 89% were deemed to have need. 100% of undergraduates with need received aid; of those 34% had need fully met. *Average percent of need met:* 79% (excluding resources awarded to replace EFC). *Average financial aid package:* $9996 (excluding resources awarded to replace EFC). 27% of all full-time undergraduates had no need and received non-need-based aid.

GIFT AID (NEED-BASED) ***Total amount:*** $2,616,163 (22% Federal, 9% state, 58% institutional, 11% external sources). ***Receiving aid:*** *Freshmen:* 73% (147); *all full-time undergraduates:* 58% (525). ***Average award:***

Freshmen: $6576; Undergraduates: $4842. ***Scholarships, grants, and awards:*** Federal Pell, FSEOG, state, private, college/university gift aid from institutional funds.

GIFT AID (NON-NEED-BASED) ***Total amount:*** $210,873 (3% state, 76% institutional, 21% external sources). ***Receiving aid:*** *Freshmen:* 8% (16); *Undergraduates:* 5% (41). ***Scholarships, grants, and awards by category:*** *Academic Interests/Achievement:* 137 awards ($204,375 total): education, general academic interests/achievements, religion/biblical studies. *Creative Arts/Performance:* 32 awards ($201,548 total): art/fine arts, creative writing, debating, journalism/publications, music, theater/drama. *Special Achievements/Activities:* 150 awards ($217,603 total): leadership, religious involvement. *Special Characteristics:* 242 awards ($643,365 total): children of current students, children of faculty/staff, general special characteristics, international students, married students, parents of current students, relatives of clergy, religious affiliation, siblings of current students, spouses of current students. ***Tuition waivers:*** Full or partial for employees or children of employees, senior citizens.

LOANS ***Student loans:*** $3,418,658 (76% need-based, 24% non-need-based). 94% of past graduating class borrowed through all loan programs. Average indebtedness per student: $10,722. ***Average need-based loan:*** Freshmen: $3153; Undergraduates: $4441. ***Parent loans:*** $3,099,828 (94% need-based, 6% non-need-based). ***Programs:*** FFEL (Subsidized and Unsubsidized Stafford, PLUS), Perkins, alternative loans.

WORK-STUDY ***Federal work-study:*** *Total amount:* $130,177; 58 jobs averaging $2244. ***State or other work-study/employment:*** *Total amount:* $200,250 (90% need-based, 10% non-need-based). 46 part-time jobs averaging $3906.

ATHLETIC AWARDS *Total amount:* 340,423 (73% need-based, 27% non-need-based).

APPLYING for FINANCIAL AID ***Required financial aid forms:*** FAFSA, institution's own form. ***Financial aid deadline (priority):*** 3/1. ***Notification date:*** 4/15. Students must reply within 4 weeks of notification.

CONTACT Ms. Lana J. Walter, Director of Financial Aid, Northwest College, PO Box 579, Kirkland, WA 98083-0579, 425-889-5336 or toll-free 800-669-3781. *Fax:* 425-827-0148. *E-mail:* lana.walter@ncag.edu

NORTHWEST COLLEGE OF ART

Poulsbo, WA

Tuition & fees: $8200 — **Average undergraduate aid package: N/A**

ABOUT THE INSTITUTION Proprietary, coed. Awards: bachelor's degrees. 2 undergraduate majors. Total enrollment: 83. Undergraduates: 83. Freshmen: 25. Federal methodology is used as a basis for awarding need-based institutional aid.

UNDERGRADUATE EXPENSES for 1999–2000 ***Application fee:*** $50. ***Tuition:*** full-time $8000; part-time $330 per credit. ***Required fees:*** full-time $200; $100 per term part-time. Part-time tuition and fees vary according to course load. ***Payment plan:*** installment.

GIFT AID (NEED-BASED) ***Scholarships, grants, and awards:*** Federal Pell, state, private, college/university gift aid from institutional funds.

GIFT AID (NON-NEED-BASED) ***Scholarships, grants, and awards by category:*** *Creative Arts/Performance:* applied art and design, art/fine arts. ***Tuition waivers:*** Full or partial for employees or children of employees.

LOANS ***Programs:*** FFEL (Subsidized and Unsubsidized Stafford, PLUS).

APPLYING for FINANCIAL AID ***Required financial aid form:*** FAFSA. ***Financial aid deadline:*** Continuous.

CONTACT Director of Financial Aid, Northwest College of Art, 16464 State Highway 305, Poulsbo, WA 98370, 360-779-9993 or toll-free 800-769-ARTS.

NORTHWESTERN COLLEGE

Orange City, IA

Tuition & fees: $12,270 — **Average undergraduate aid package: $13,471**

ABOUT THE INSTITUTION Independent religious, coed. Awards: associate and bachelor's degrees. 35 undergraduate majors. Total enrollment: 1,219. Undergraduates: 1,219. Freshmen: 366. Federal methodology is used as a basis for awarding need-based institutional aid.

UNDERGRADUATE EXPENSES for 1999–2000 ***Application fee:*** $25. ***Comprehensive fee:*** $15,770 includes full-time tuition ($12,270) and room and board ($3500). ***College room only:*** $1500. ***Part-time tuition:*** $385 per credit hour. Part-time tuition and fees vary according to course load. ***Payment plan:*** installment.

FRESHMAN FINANCIAL AID (Fall 1999) 345 applied for aid; of those 85% were deemed to have need. 100% of freshmen with need received aid; of those 86% had need fully met. *Average percent of need met:* 92% (excluding resources awarded to replace EFC). *Average financial aid package:* $13,608 (excluding resources awarded to replace EFC). 5% of all full-time freshmen had no need and received non-need-based aid.

UNDERGRADUATE FINANCIAL AID (Fall 1999) 1,119 applied for aid; of those 84% were deemed to have need. 100% of undergraduates with need received aid; of those 87% had need fully met. *Average percent of need met:* 92% (excluding resources awarded to replace EFC). *Average financial aid package:* $13,471 (excluding resources awarded to replace EFC). 5% of all full-time undergraduates had no need and received non-need-based aid.

GIFT AID (NEED-BASED) ***Total amount:*** $7,726,715 (14% Federal, 25% state, 61% institutional). ***Receiving aid:*** *Freshmen:* 80% (292); *all full-time undergraduates:* 80% (941). ***Average award:*** Freshmen: $7212; Undergraduates: $10,401. ***Scholarships, grants, and awards:*** Federal Pell, FSEOG, state, private, college/university gift aid from institutional funds.

GIFT AID (NON-NEED-BASED) ***Total amount:*** $456,777 (6% state, 55% institutional, 39% external sources). ***Receiving aid:*** *Freshmen:* 20% (73); *Undergraduates:* 51% (602). ***Scholarships, grants, and awards by category:*** *Academic Interests/Achievement:* 690 awards ($2,181,389 total): biological sciences, business, communication, computer science, education, engineering/technologies, English, foreign languages, general academic interests/achievements, health fields, humanities, mathematics, physical sciences, premedicine, religion/biblical studies, social sciences. *Creative Arts/Performance:* 219 awards ($213,803 total): art/fine arts, journalism/publications, music, theater/drama. *Special Characteristics:* 592 awards ($690,505 total): adult students, children and siblings of alumni, children of faculty/staff, international students, religious affiliation, siblings of current students. ***Tuition waivers:*** Full or partial for employees or children of employees.

LOANS ***Student loans:*** $3,961,537 (76% need-based, 24% non-need-based). 82% of past graduating class borrowed through all loan programs. Average indebtedness per student: $10,140. ***Average need-based loan:*** Freshmen: $3500; Undergraduates: $5500. ***Parent loans:*** $278,287 (100% non-need-based). ***Programs:*** FFEL (Subsidized and Unsubsidized Stafford, PLUS), Perkins, college/university, alternative loans.

WORK-STUDY ***Federal work-study:*** *Total amount:* $339,360; 387 jobs averaging $800. ***State or other work-study/employment:*** *Total amount:* $218,885 (11% need-based, 89% non-need-based). 217 part-time jobs averaging $800.

ATHLETIC AWARDS *Total amount:* 568,075 (62% need-based, 38% non-need-based).

APPLYING for FINANCIAL AID ***Required financial aid forms:*** FAFSA, institution's own form. ***Financial aid deadline (priority):*** 4/1. ***Notification date:*** Continuous. Students must reply within 3 weeks of notification.

CONTACT Mrs. Carol Bogaard, Director of Financial Aid, Northwestern College, 101 Seventh Street, SW, Orange City, IA 51041-1996, 712-737-7131 or toll-free 800-747-4757. *Fax:* 712-737-7164.

NORTHWESTERN COLLEGE

St. Paul, MN

Tuition & fees: $14,982 — **Average undergraduate aid package: N/A**

ABOUT THE INSTITUTION Independent nondenominational, coed. Awards: associate and bachelor's degrees. 47 undergraduate majors. Total enroll-

Northwestern College (continued)

ment: 1,744. Undergraduates: 1,744. Freshmen: 404. Federal methodology is used as a basis for awarding need-based institutional aid.

UNDERGRADUATE EXPENSES for 2000–2001 ***Application fee:*** $20. ***Comprehensive fee:*** $19,430 includes full-time tuition ($14,982) and room and board ($4448). ***College room only:*** $2566. Full-time tuition and fees vary according to course load and program. Room and board charges vary according to board plan. ***Part-time tuition:*** $625 per credit. Part-time tuition and fees vary according to program. ***Payment plan:*** installment.

FRESHMAN FINANCIAL AID (Fall 1999) 406 applied for aid; of those 90% were deemed to have need. 100% of freshmen with need received aid. 6% of all full-time freshmen had no need and received non-need-based aid.

UNDERGRADUATE FINANCIAL AID (Fall 1999) 1,139 applied for aid; of those 93% were deemed to have need. 100% of undergraduates with need received aid. 6% of all full-time undergraduates had no need and received non-need-based aid.

GIFT AID (NEED-BASED) ***Total amount:*** $6,712,828 (18% Federal, 30% state, 52% institutional). ***Receiving aid:*** *Freshmen:* 57% (276); *all full-time undergraduates:* 72% (948). ***Scholarships, grants, and awards:*** Federal Pell, FSEOG, state, private, college/university gift aid from institutional funds.

GIFT AID (NON-NEED-BASED) ***Total amount:*** $2,935,664 (1% state, 85% institutional, 14% external sources). ***Receiving aid:*** *Freshmen:* 47% (225); *Undergraduates:* 66% (881). ***Scholarships, grants, and awards by category:*** *Academic Interests/Achievement:* 1,116 awards ($1,877,627 total): general academic interests/achievements. *Creative Arts/Performance:* 118 awards ($94,000 total): music. *Special Achievements/Activities:* leadership. *Special Characteristics:* 378 awards ($1,089,000 total): children of faculty/staff, relatives of clergy, siblings of current students. ***Tuition waivers:*** Full or partial for employees or children of employees, senior citizens. ***ROTC:*** Army cooperative, Air Force cooperative.

LOANS ***Student loans:*** $4,396,290 (80% need-based, 20% non-need-based). 77% of past graduating class borrowed through all loan programs. Average indebtedness per student: $16,000. ***Parent loans:*** $1,362,720 (100% non-need-based). ***Programs:*** FFEL (Subsidized and Unsubsidized Stafford, PLUS), Perkins, state.

WORK-STUDY ***Federal work-study:*** *Total amount:* $254,646; 185 jobs averaging $1375. ***State or other work-study/employment:*** *Total amount:* $218,716 (100% need-based). 149 part-time jobs averaging $1354.

APPLYING for FINANCIAL AID ***Required financial aid forms:*** FAFSA, institution's own form. ***Financial aid deadline (priority):*** 3/1. ***Notification date:*** Continuous.

CONTACT Mr. Richard L. Blatchley, Director of Financial Aid, Northwestern College, 3003 Snelling Avenue North, St. Paul, MN 55113-1598, 651-631-5321 or toll-free 800-827-6827. *Fax:* 651-628-3332. *E-mail:* rlb@nwc.edu

NORTHWESTERN OKLAHOMA STATE UNIVERSITY

Alva, OK

Tuition & fees (OK res): $1987 **Average undergraduate aid package: $6200**

ABOUT THE INSTITUTION State-supported, coed. Awards: bachelor's and master's degrees. 38 undergraduate majors. Total enrollment: 1,970. Undergraduates: 1,647. Freshmen: 320. Federal methodology is used as a basis for awarding need-based institutional aid.

UNDERGRADUATE EXPENSES for 1999–2000 ***Application fee:*** $15. ***Tuition, state resident:*** full-time $1957; part-time $61 per credit hour. ***Tuition, nonresident:*** full-time $4645; part-time $145 per credit hour. ***Required fees:*** full-time $30; $15 per term part-time. Full-time tuition and fees vary according to course load, location, and student level. Part-time tuition and fees vary according to course load, location, and student level. ***College room and board:*** $2316. Room and board charges vary according to board plan.

FRESHMAN FINANCIAL AID (Fall 1998) 230 applied for aid; of those 83% were deemed to have need. 96% of freshmen with need received aid; of those 54% had need fully met. *Average percent of need met:* 90% (excluding resources awarded to replace EFC). *Average financial aid package:* $5800 (excluding resources awarded to replace EFC). 21% of all full-time freshmen had no need and received non-need-based aid.

UNDERGRADUATE FINANCIAL AID (Fall 1998) 843 applied for aid; of those 94% were deemed to have need. 96% of undergraduates with need received aid; of those 59% had need fully met. *Average percent of need met:* 85% (excluding resources awarded to replace EFC). *Average financial aid package:* $6200 (excluding resources awarded to replace EFC). 10% of all full-time undergraduates had no need and received non-need-based aid.

GIFT AID (NEED-BASED) ***Total amount:*** $1,514,149 (87% Federal, 13% state). ***Receiving aid:*** *Freshmen:* 62% (160); *all full-time undergraduates:* 65% (680). ***Average award:*** Freshmen: $4150; Undergraduates: $4150. ***Scholarships, grants, and awards:*** Federal Pell, FSEOG, state, college/university gift aid from institutional funds.

GIFT AID (NON-NEED-BASED) ***Total amount:*** $889,100 (44% institutional, 56% external sources). ***Receiving aid:*** *Freshmen:* 35% (90); *Undergraduates:* 20% (210). ***Scholarships, grants, and awards by category:*** *Academic Interests/Achievement:* 280 awards ($364,000 total): agriculture, biological sciences, business, communication, computer science, education, English, foreign languages, general academic interests/achievements, humanities, library science, mathematics, premedicine, social sciences. *Creative Arts/Performance:* 115 awards ($136,500 total): general creative arts/performance, music, theater/drama. *Special Achievements/Activities:* 25 awards ($35,000 total): cheerleading/drum major, memberships, rodeo. ***Tuition waivers:*** Full or partial for employees or children of employees, senior citizens.

LOANS ***Student loans:*** $1,965,783 (53% need-based, 47% non-need-based). 50% of past graduating class borrowed through all loan programs. Average indebtedness per student: $9000. ***Average need-based loan:*** Freshmen: $2625; Undergraduates: $4000. ***Parent loans:*** $41,585 (100% need-based). ***Programs:*** FFEL (Subsidized and Unsubsidized Stafford, PLUS), Perkins.

WORK-STUDY ***Federal work-study:*** *Total amount:* $132,621; 130 jobs averaging $1020. ***State or other work-study/employment:*** *Total amount:* $109,785 (100% non-need-based). 120 part-time jobs averaging $915.

ATHLETIC AWARDS *Total amount:* 230,000 (100% non-need-based).

APPLYING for FINANCIAL AID ***Required financial aid form:*** FAFSA. ***Financial aid deadline (priority):*** 3/1. ***Notification date:*** Continuous beginning 6/1. Students must reply by 8/15.

CONTACT Mr. David Pecha, Director of Financial Aid, Northwestern Oklahoma State University, 709 Oklahoma Boulevard, Alva, OK 73717-2799, 580-327-1700 Ext. 8542. *Fax:* 580-327-8674. *E-mail:* dmpecha@ranger1.nwalva.edu

NORTHWESTERN POLYTECHNIC UNIVERSITY

Fremont, CA

CONTACT Financial Aid Office, Northwestern Polytechnic University, 117 Fourier Avenue, Fremont, CA 94539-7482, 510-657-5911.

NORTHWESTERN STATE UNIVERSITY OF LOUISIANA

Natchitoches, LA

Tuition & fees (LA res): $2327 **Average undergraduate aid package: N/A**

ABOUT THE INSTITUTION State-supported, coed. Awards: associate, bachelor's, master's, and doctoral degrees. 47 undergraduate majors. Total enrollment: 9,005. Undergraduates: 8,040. Freshmen: 1,813. Federal methodology is used as a basis for awarding need-based institutional aid.

UNDERGRADUATE EXPENSES for 1999–2000 ***Application fee:*** $15. ***Tuition, state resident:*** full-time $2030. ***Tuition, nonresident:*** full-time $7256. ***Required fees:*** full-time $297. Part-time tuition and fees vary according to course load. ***College room and board:*** $2596; ***room only:*** $1300. Room and board charges vary according to board plan and housing facility. ***Payment plan:*** installment.

GIFT AID (NEED-BASED) ***Scholarships, grants, and awards:*** Federal Pell, FSEOG.

GIFT AID (NON-NEED-BASED) ***Scholarships, grants, and awards by category:*** *Academic Interests/Achievement:* general academic interests/achievements. *Creative Arts/Performance:* dance, debating, music, theater/drama. *Special Achievements/Activities:* cheerleading/drum major, leadership. *Special Characteristics:* adult students, children and siblings of alumni. ***Tuition waivers:*** Full or partial for children of alumni, employees or children of employees. ***ROTC:*** Army.

LOANS ***Programs:*** FFEL (Subsidized and Unsubsidized Stafford, PLUS), Perkins.

WORK-STUDY Federal work-study jobs available.

APPLYING for FINANCIAL AID ***Required financial aid form:*** FAFSA. ***Financial aid deadline (priority):*** 5/3. ***Notification date:*** Continuous.

CONTACT Kenn Posey, Director of Student Financial Aid, Northwestern State University of Louisiana, 350 Sam Sibley Drive, Natchitoches, LA 71497, 318-357-5961 or toll-free 800-426-3754 (in-state), 800-327-1903 (out-of-state).

NORTHWESTERN UNIVERSITY

Evanston, IL

Tuition & fees: $23,562 **Average undergraduate aid package: $19,985**

ABOUT THE INSTITUTION Independent, coed. Awards: bachelor's, master's, doctoral, and first professional degrees. 66 undergraduate majors. Total enrollment: 15,406. Undergraduates: 7,842. Freshmen: 1,952. Both federal and institutional methodology are used as a basis for awarding need-based institutional aid.

UNDERGRADUATE EXPENSES for 1999–2000 ***Application fee:*** $55. ***Comprehensive fee:*** $30,532 includes full-time tuition ($23,496), mandatory fees ($66), and room and board ($6970). Room and board charges vary according to board plan and housing facility. ***Part-time tuition:*** $2788 per course. ***Payment plan:*** installment.

FRESHMAN FINANCIAL AID (Fall 1999, est.) 1281 applied for aid; of those 69% were deemed to have need. 100% of freshmen with need received aid; of those 100% had need fully met. *Average percent of need met:* 100% (excluding resources awarded to replace EFC). *Average financial aid package:* $20,455 (excluding resources awarded to replace EFC). 11% of all full-time freshmen had no need and received non-need-based aid.

UNDERGRADUATE FINANCIAL AID (Fall 1999, est.) 4,173 applied for aid; of those 89% were deemed to have need. 100% of undergraduates with need received aid; of those 100% had need fully met. *Average percent of need met:* 100% (excluding resources awarded to replace EFC). *Average financial aid package:* $19,985 (excluding resources awarded to replace EFC). 7% of all full-time undergraduates had no need and received non-need-based aid.

GIFT AID (NEED-BASED) ***Total amount:*** $48,742,145 (8% Federal, 5% state, 81% institutional, 6% external sources). ***Receiving aid:*** *Freshmen:* 43% (837); *all full-time undergraduates:* 45% (3,470). ***Average award:*** Freshmen: $15,851; Undergraduates: $14,047. ***Scholarships, grants, and awards:*** Federal Pell, FSEOG, state, private, college/university gift aid from institutional funds.

GIFT AID (NON-NEED-BASED) ***Total amount:*** $1,183,775 (100% external sources). ***Tuition waivers:*** Full or partial for employees or children of employees. ***ROTC:*** Army cooperative, Naval, Air Force cooperative.

LOANS ***Student loans:*** $14,659,195 (84% need-based, 16% non-need-based). 49% of past graduating class borrowed through all loan programs. Average indebtedness per student: $13,222. ***Average need-based loan:*** Freshmen: $2735; Undergraduates: $3600. ***Parent loans:*** $13,790,613 (100% non-need-based). ***Programs:*** FFEL (Subsidized and Unsubsidized Stafford, PLUS), Perkins, college/university.

WORK-STUDY ***Federal work-study:*** *Total amount:* $3,400,000; 2,100 jobs averaging $1600. ***State or other work-study/employment:*** *Total amount:* $2,156,580 (100% need-based). Part-time jobs available.

ATHLETIC AWARDS *Total amount:* 6,586,131 (100% non-need-based).

APPLYING for FINANCIAL AID ***Required financial aid forms:*** FAFSA, CSS Financial Aid PROFILE, noncustodial (divorced/separated) parent's statement, business/farm supplement. ***Financial aid deadline (priority):*** 2/1. ***Notification date:*** 4/15. Students must reply by 5/1 or within 2 weeks of notification.

CONTACT Mr. Allen Lentino, Associate Director of Admission and Financial Aid, Northwestern University, 1801 Hinman Avenue, Evanston, IL 60208, 847-491-8443.

NORTHWEST MISSOURI STATE UNIVERSITY

Maryville, MO

Tuition & fees (MO res): $3330 **Average undergraduate aid package: $4744**

ABOUT THE INSTITUTION State-supported, coed. Awards: bachelor's and master's degrees. 117 undergraduate majors. Total enrollment: 6,462. Undergraduates: 5,313. Freshmen: 1,214. Federal methodology is used as a basis for awarding need-based institutional aid.

UNDERGRADUATE EXPENSES for 2000–2001 ***Application fee:*** $15. ***Tuition, state resident:*** full-time $3210; part-time $107 per credit hour. ***Tuition, nonresident:*** full-time $5468; part-time $182 per credit hour. ***Required fees:*** full-time $120; $4 per credit hour. ***College room and board:*** $4150. Room and board charges vary according to housing facility. ***Payment plan:*** installment.

FRESHMAN FINANCIAL AID (Fall 1999, est.) 915 applied for aid; of those 74% were deemed to have need. 99% of freshmen with need received aid; of those 4% had need fully met. *Average percent of need met:* 54% (excluding resources awarded to replace EFC). *Average financial aid package:* $4160 (excluding resources awarded to replace EFC). 10% of all full-time freshmen had no need and received non-need-based aid.

UNDERGRADUATE FINANCIAL AID (Fall 1999, est.) 3,287 applied for aid; of those 78% were deemed to have need. 98% of undergraduates with need received aid; of those 6% had need fully met. *Average percent of need met:* 53% (excluding resources awarded to replace EFC). *Average financial aid package:* $4744 (excluding resources awarded to replace EFC). 7% of all full-time undergraduates had no need and received non-need-based aid.

GIFT AID (NEED-BASED) ***Total amount:*** $5,209,770 (50% Federal, 3% state, 32% institutional, 15% external sources). ***Receiving aid:*** *Freshmen:* 29% (347); *all full-time undergraduates:* 26% (1,268). ***Average award:*** Freshmen: $1944; Undergraduates: $2022. ***Scholarships, grants, and awards:*** Federal Pell, FSEOG, state, private, college/university gift aid from institutional funds.

GIFT AID (NON-NEED-BASED) ***Total amount:*** $2,065,918 (73% institutional, 27% external sources). ***Receiving aid:*** *Freshmen:* 46% (557); *Undergraduates:* 26% (1,256). ***Scholarships, grants, and awards by category:*** *Academic Interests/Achievement:* 1,584 awards ($1,842,305 total): agriculture, biological sciences, business, communication, computer science, education, English, foreign languages, general academic interests/achievements, health fields, home economics, humanities, mathematics, physical sciences, social sciences. *Creative Arts/Performance:* 163 awards ($145,980 total): art/fine arts, debating, journalism/publications, music, theater/drama. *Special Achievements/Activities:* 121 awards ($52,384 total): cheerleading/drum major, general special achievements/activities, leadership, memberships. *Special Characteristics:* 177 awards ($140,143 total): children and siblings of alumni, general special characteristics, members of minority groups. ***Tuition waivers:*** Full or partial for employees or children of employees, senior citizens.

LOANS ***Student loans:*** $12,319,626 (64% need-based, 36% non-need-based). 52% of past graduating class borrowed through all loan programs. Average indebtedness per student: $13,493. ***Average need-based loan:***

Northwest Missouri State University (continued)

Freshmen: $2454; Undergraduates: $3398. ***Parent loans:*** $3,499,882 (100% non-need-based). ***Programs:*** Federal Direct (Subsidized and Unsubsidized Stafford, PLUS), Perkins, college/university.

WORK-STUDY ***Federal work-study:*** *Total amount:* $526,604; 345 jobs averaging $1526. ***State or other work-study/employment:*** *Total amount:* $291,447 (100% non-need-based). Part-time jobs available.

ATHLETIC AWARDS *Total amount:* 606,410 (42% need-based, 58% non-need-based).

APPLYING for FINANCIAL AID ***Required financial aid form:*** FAFSA. ***Financial aid deadline (priority):*** 3/1. ***Notification date:*** 4/15. Students must reply within 3 weeks of notification.

CONTACT Director of Financial Assistance, Northwest Missouri State University, 800 University Drive, Maryville, MO 64468-6001, 660-562-1363 or toll-free 800-633-1175.

NORTHWEST NAZARENE UNIVERSITY

Nampa, ID

Tuition & fees: $13,500 **Average undergraduate aid package: $9759**

ABOUT THE INSTITUTION Independent religious, coed. Awards: bachelor's and master's degrees. 58 undergraduate majors. Total enrollment: 1,843. Undergraduates: 1,114. Freshmen: 310. Federal methodology is used as a basis for awarding need-based institutional aid.

UNDERGRADUATE EXPENSES for 2000–2001 ***Application fee:*** $20. ***Comprehensive fee:*** $17,520 includes full-time tuition ($12,990), mandatory fees ($510), and room and board ($4020). Room and board charges vary according to board plan and student level. Part-time tuition and fees vary according to course load. ***Payment plans:*** tuition prepayment, installment.

FRESHMAN FINANCIAL AID (Fall 1999) 300 applied for aid; of those 88% were deemed to have need. 100% of freshmen with need received aid; of those 22% had need fully met. *Average percent of need met:* 72% (excluding resources awarded to replace EFC). *Average financial aid package:* $9654 (excluding resources awarded to replace EFC). 11% of all full-time freshmen had no need and received non-need-based aid.

UNDERGRADUATE FINANCIAL AID (Fall 1999) 1,024 applied for aid; of those 93% were deemed to have need. 98% of undergraduates with need received aid; of those 21% had need fully met. *Average percent of need met:* 69% (excluding resources awarded to replace EFC). *Average financial aid package:* $9759 (excluding resources awarded to replace EFC). 8% of all full-time undergraduates had no need and received non-need-based aid.

GIFT AID (NEED-BASED) ***Total amount:*** $4,876,850 (16% Federal, 64% institutional, 20% external sources). ***Receiving aid:*** *Freshmen:* 87% (262); *all full-time undergraduates:* 86% (895). ***Average award:*** Freshmen: $6267; Undergraduates: $5996. ***Scholarships, grants, and awards:*** Federal Pell, FSEOG, state, private, college/university gift aid from institutional funds.

GIFT AID (NON-NEED-BASED) ***Total amount:*** $359,104 (91% institutional, 9% external sources). ***Receiving aid:*** *Freshmen:* 10% (31); *Undergraduates:* 6% (67). ***Scholarships, grants, and awards by category:*** *Academic Interests/Achievement:* 13 awards ($8220 total): biological sciences, business, computer science, education, English, general academic interests/achievements, health fields, mathematics, military science, physical sciences, premedicine, religion/biblical studies, social sciences. *Creative Arts/Performance:* 1 award ($500 total): art/fine arts, debating, general creative arts/performance, journalism/publications, music, performing arts, theater/drama. *Special Achievements/Activities:* 2 awards ($600 total): cheerleading/drum major, general special achievements/activities, leadership, religious involvement. *Special Characteristics:* 11 awards ($10,020 total): children and siblings of alumni, children of educators, ethnic background, international students, members of minority groups, out-of-state students, relatives of clergy, religious affiliation, veterans. ***Tuition waivers:*** Full or partial for employees or children of employees. ***ROTC:*** Army.

LOANS ***Student loans:*** $4,237,123 (94% need-based, 6% non-need-based). 76% of past graduating class borrowed through all loan programs. Average indebtedness per student: $19,545. ***Average need-based loan:*** Freshmen: $4329; Undergraduates: $5808. ***Parent loans:*** $1,457,931 (92% need-based, 8% non-need-based). ***Programs:*** FFEL (Subsidized and Unsubsidized Stafford, PLUS), Perkins, college/university.

WORK-STUDY ***Federal work-study:*** *Total amount:* $412,325; 299 jobs averaging $1372.

ATHLETIC AWARDS *Total amount:* 574,358 (90% need-based, 10% non-need-based).

APPLYING for FINANCIAL AID ***Required financial aid forms:*** FAFSA, institution's own form. ***Financial aid deadline (priority):*** 3/1. ***Notification date:*** Continuous beginning 4/1. Students must reply within 3 weeks of notification.

CONTACT Mr. Wes Maggard, Director of Financial Aid, Northwest Nazarene University, 623 Holly Street, Nampa, ID 83686, 208-467-8774 or toll-free 877-NNU-4YOU. *Fax:* 208-467-8645. *E-mail:* mwmaggard@nnu.edu

NORTHWOOD UNIVERSITY

Midland, MI

Tuition & fees: $11,625 **Average undergraduate aid package: N/A**

ABOUT THE INSTITUTION Independent, coed. Awards: associate, bachelor's, and master's degrees. 12 undergraduate majors. Total enrollment: 3,373. Undergraduates: 3,190. Freshmen: 463. Federal methodology is used as a basis for awarding need-based institutional aid.

UNDERGRADUATE EXPENSES for 1999–2000 ***Application fee:*** $15. ***Comprehensive fee:*** $16,833 includes full-time tuition ($11,325), mandatory fees ($300), and room and board ($5208). Room and board charges vary according to board plan. ***Part-time tuition:*** $235 per credit hour. Part-time tuition and fees vary according to course load. ***Payment plan:*** installment.

FRESHMAN FINANCIAL AID (Fall 1998) 415 applied for aid; of those 87% were deemed to have need. 100% of freshmen with need received aid; of those 21% had need fully met. *Average percent of need met:* 95% (excluding resources awarded to replace EFC). 21% of all full-time freshmen had no need and received non-need-based aid.

UNDERGRADUATE FINANCIAL AID (Fall 1998) 971 applied for aid; of those 90% were deemed to have need. 100% of undergraduates with need received aid; of those 24% had need fully met. *Average percent of need met:* 96% (excluding resources awarded to replace EFC). 27% of all full-time undergraduates had no need and received non-need-based aid.

GIFT AID (NEED-BASED) ***Total amount:*** $4,809,509 (19% Federal, 31% state, 50% institutional). ***Receiving aid:*** *Freshmen:* 51% (311); *all full-time undergraduates:* 50% (695). ***Scholarships, grants, and awards:*** Federal Pell, FSEOG, state, private, college/university gift aid from institutional funds.

GIFT AID (NON-NEED-BASED) ***Total amount:*** $3,459,458 (100% institutional). ***Receiving aid:*** *Freshmen:* 37% (224); *Undergraduates:* 40% (557). ***Scholarships, grants, and awards by category:*** *Academic Interests/Achievement:* business, general academic interests/achievements. *Special Characteristics:* children and siblings of alumni, children of faculty/staff, siblings of current students. ***Tuition waivers:*** Full or partial for children of alumni, employees or children of employees.

LOANS ***Student loans:*** $3,326,160 (66% need-based, 34% non-need-based). ***Parent loans:*** $866,491 (100% need-based). ***Programs:*** FFEL (Subsidized and Unsubsidized Stafford, PLUS), state.

WORK-STUDY ***Federal work-study:*** *Total amount:* $114,693; jobs available. ***State or other work-study/employment:*** *Total amount:* $228,151 (100% need-based). Part-time jobs available.

ATHLETIC AWARDS *Total amount:* 1,749,045 (34% need-based, 66% non-need-based).

APPLYING for FINANCIAL AID ***Required financial aid form:*** FAFSA. ***Financial aid deadline:*** Continuous. ***Notification date:*** Continuous beginning 4/1.

CONTACT William L. Healy, Director of Financial Aid, Northwood University, 3225 Cook Road, Midland, MI 48640-2398, 517-837-4230 or toll-free 800-457-7878. *E-mail:* healyw@northwood.edu

NORTHWOOD UNIVERSITY, FLORIDA CAMPUS

West Palm Beach, FL

Tuition & fees: $11,625 **Average undergraduate aid package: $13,515**

ABOUT THE INSTITUTION Independent, coed. Awards: associate and bachelor's degrees. 9 undergraduate majors. Total enrollment: 975. Undergraduates: 975. Freshmen: 191. Federal methodology is used as a basis for awarding need-based institutional aid.

UNDERGRADUATE EXPENSES for 1999–2000 ***Application fee:*** $15. ***Comprehensive fee:*** $17,858 includes full-time tuition ($11,325), mandatory fees ($300), and room and board ($6233). Room and board charges vary according to board plan. ***Part-time tuition:*** $235 per credit hour. Part-time tuition and fees vary according to course load. ***Payment plan:*** installment.

FRESHMAN FINANCIAL AID (Fall 1998) 116 applied for aid; of those 90% were deemed to have need. 99% of freshmen with need received aid. *Average financial aid package:* $13,229 (excluding resources awarded to replace EFC). 16% of all full-time freshmen had no need and received non-need-based aid.

UNDERGRADUATE FINANCIAL AID (Fall 1998) 266 applied for aid; of those 88% were deemed to have need. 100% of undergraduates with need received aid. *Average percent of need met:* 89% (excluding resources awarded to replace EFC). *Average financial aid package:* $13,515 (excluding resources awarded to replace EFC). 20% of all full-time undergraduates had no need and received non-need-based aid.

GIFT AID (NEED-BASED) ***Total amount:*** $1,006,502 (34% Federal, 66% institutional). ***Receiving aid:*** *Freshmen:* 36% (82); *all full-time undergraduates:* 35% (182). ***Average award:*** Freshmen: $5563; Undergraduates: $5332. ***Scholarships, grants, and awards:*** Federal Pell, FSEOG, state, private, college/university gift aid from institutional funds.

GIFT AID (NON-NEED-BASED) ***Total amount:*** $549,079 (6% state, 90% institutional, 4% external sources). ***Receiving aid:*** *Freshmen:* 26% (59); *Undergraduates:* 25% (132). ***Scholarships, grants, and awards by category:*** *Academic Interests/Achievement:* business, general academic interests/achievements. *Special Achievements/Activities:* memberships. *Special Characteristics:* children and siblings of alumni, children of faculty/staff, children of union members/company employees, local/state students, siblings of current students. ***Tuition waivers:*** Full or partial for children of alumni, employees or children of employees.

LOANS ***Student loans:*** $971,626 (68% need-based, 32% non-need-based). 41% of past graduating class borrowed through all loan programs. Average indebtedness per student: $13,378. ***Average need-based loan:*** Undergraduates: $3338. ***Parent loans:*** $366,200 (100% non-need-based). ***Programs:*** FFEL (Subsidized and Unsubsidized Stafford, PLUS).

WORK-STUDY ***Federal work-study:*** *Total amount:* $81,000; 45 jobs averaging $1800. ***State or other work-study/employment:*** *Total amount:* $48,000 (100% need-based). 27 part-time jobs averaging $1800.

ATHLETIC AWARDS *Total amount:* 271,605 (100% non-need-based).

APPLYING for FINANCIAL AID ***Required financial aid form:*** FAFSA. ***Financial aid deadline (priority):*** 4/1. ***Notification date:*** Continuous. Students must reply within 2 weeks of notification.

CONTACT Ms. Joan Begin, Director of Financial Aid, Northwood University, Florida Campus, 2600 North Military Trail, West Palm Beach, FL 33409-2999, 561-478-5590 or toll-free 800-458-8325. *Fax:* 561-478-5535.

NORTHWOOD UNIVERSITY, TEXAS CAMPUS

Cedar Hill, TX

Tuition & fees: $11,625 **Average undergraduate aid package: $9982**

ABOUT THE INSTITUTION Independent, coed. Awards: associate and bachelor's degrees. 11 undergraduate majors. Total enrollment: 1,007. Undergraduates: 1,007. Freshmen: 212. Both federal and institutional methodology are used as a basis for awarding need-based institutional aid.

UNDERGRADUATE EXPENSES for 1999–2000 ***Application fee:*** $15. ***Comprehensive fee:*** $16,771 includes full-time tuition ($11,325), mandatory fees ($300), and room and board ($5146). Room and board charges vary according to board plan. ***Part-time tuition:*** $235 per credit hour. Part-time tuition and fees vary according to course load. ***Payment plan:*** installment.

FRESHMAN FINANCIAL AID (Fall 1998) 181 applied for aid; of those 91% were deemed to have need. 100% of freshmen with need received aid; of those 34% had need fully met. *Average percent of need met:* 34% (excluding resources awarded to replace EFC). *Average financial aid package:* $9486 (excluding resources awarded to replace EFC).

UNDERGRADUATE FINANCIAL AID (Fall 1998) 369 applied for aid; of those 92% were deemed to have need. 100% of undergraduates with need received aid; of those 32% had need fully met. *Average percent of need met:* 32% (excluding resources awarded to replace EFC). *Average financial aid package:* $9982 (excluding resources awarded to replace EFC).

GIFT AID (NEED-BASED) ***Total amount:*** $1,274,585 (37% Federal, 63% institutional). ***Receiving aid:*** *Freshmen:* 63% (138); *all full-time undergraduates:* 63% (291). ***Average award:*** Freshmen: $4455; Undergraduates: $4317. ***Scholarships, grants, and awards:*** Federal Pell, FSEOG, private, college/university gift aid from institutional funds.

GIFT AID (NON-NEED-BASED) ***Total amount:*** $1,142,201 (97% institutional, 3% external sources). ***Receiving aid:*** *Freshmen:* 65% (143); *Undergraduates:* 63% (290). ***Scholarships, grants, and awards by category:*** *Academic Interests/Achievement:* business, general academic interests/achievements. *Special Achievements/Activities:* general special achievements/activities, memberships. *Special Characteristics:* children and siblings of alumni, children of faculty/staff, general special characteristics, local/state students, siblings of current students. ***Tuition waivers:*** Full or partial for children of alumni, employees or children of employees.

LOANS ***Student loans:*** $1,457,649 (65% need-based, 35% non-need-based). Average indebtedness per student: $17,125. ***Average need-based loan:*** Freshmen: $2625; Undergraduates: $3360. ***Parent loans:*** $286,105 (100% non-need-based). ***Programs:*** FFEL (Subsidized and Unsubsidized Stafford, PLUS), alternative loans.

WORK-STUDY ***Federal work-study:*** *Total amount:* $50,400; 28 jobs averaging $1800.

ATHLETIC AWARDS *Total amount:* 425,460 (100% non-need-based).

APPLYING for FINANCIAL AID ***Required financial aid form:*** FAFSA. ***Financial aid deadline:*** Continuous. ***Notification date:*** Continuous beginning 3/1.

CONTACT Cynthia S. Butler, Director of Financial Aid, Northwood University, Texas Campus, PO Box 58, 1114 West FM 1382, Cedar Hill, TX 75106-0058, 972-293-5430 Ext. 5479 or toll-free 800-927-9663. *Fax:* 972-291-3824. *E-mail:* butlerc@northwood.edu

NORWICH UNIVERSITY

Northfield, VT

Tuition & fees: $15,156 **Average undergraduate aid package: N/A**

ABOUT THE INSTITUTION Independent, coed. Awards: bachelor's and master's degrees and post-master's certificates. 29 undergraduate majors. Total enrollment: 2,706. Undergraduates: 2,183. Freshmen: 492. Both federal and institutional methodology are used as a basis for awarding need-based institutional aid.

UNDERGRADUATE EXPENSES for 1999–2000 ***Application fee:*** $35. ***Comprehensive fee:*** $20,874 includes full-time tuition ($15,000), mandatory fees ($156), and room and board ($5718). Full-time tuition and fees vary according to degree level, location, and program. Room and board charges vary according to board plan and location. ***Part-time tuition:*** $425 per credit hour. ***Part-time fees:*** $25 per term part-time. Part-time tuition and fees vary according to course load, degree level, location, and program. ***Payment plan:*** installment.

Norwich University (continued)

GIFT AID (NEED-BASED) ***Scholarships, grants, and awards:*** Federal Pell, FSEOG, state, private, college/university gift aid from institutional funds.

GIFT AID (NON-NEED-BASED) ***Scholarships, grants, and awards by category:*** *Academic Interests/Achievement:* general academic interests/achievements. *Special Achievements/Activities:* community service, leadership. *Special Characteristics:* general special characteristics. ***Tuition waivers:*** Full or partial for employees or children of employees. ***ROTC:*** Army, Naval, Air Force.

LOANS ***Programs:*** FFEL (Subsidized and Unsubsidized Stafford, PLUS), Perkins, college/university.

WORK-STUDY Federal work-study jobs available.

APPLYING for FINANCIAL AID ***Required financial aid forms:*** FAFSA, CSS Financial Aid PROFILE. ***Financial aid deadline (priority):*** 3/1. ***Notification date:*** Continuous.

CONTACT Director of Student Financial Planning, Norwich University, 158 Harmon Drive, Northfield, VT 05663, 802-485-2015 or toll-free 800-468-6679 (in-state).

NOTRE DAME COLLEGE

Manchester, NH

Tuition & fees: $14,378 **Average undergraduate aid package: N/A**

ABOUT THE INSTITUTION Independent Roman Catholic, coed. Awards: associate, bachelor's, and master's degrees. 22 undergraduate majors. Total enrollment: 1,216. Undergraduates: 685. Freshmen: 136. Federal methodology is used as a basis for awarding need-based institutional aid.

UNDERGRADUATE EXPENSES for 1999–2000 ***Application fee:*** $25. ***Comprehensive fee:*** $20,091 includes full-time tuition ($14,098), mandatory fees ($280), and room and board ($5713). ***College room only:*** $2715. Full-time tuition and fees vary according to course load and program. Room and board charges vary according to housing facility. ***Part-time tuition:*** $220 per credit. Part-time tuition and fees vary according to class time and course load. ***Payment plan:*** installment.

GIFT AID (NEED-BASED) ***Scholarships, grants, and awards:*** Federal Pell, FSEOG, state, private, college/university gift aid from institutional funds.

GIFT AID (NON-NEED-BASED) ***Scholarships, grants, and awards by category:*** *Academic Interests/Achievement:* general academic interests/achievements. *Special Characteristics:* children and siblings of alumni, siblings of current students. ***Tuition waivers:*** Full or partial for children of alumni, employees or children of employees. ***ROTC:*** Air Force cooperative.

LOANS ***Programs:*** FFEL (Subsidized and Unsubsidized Stafford, PLUS), Perkins.

WORK-STUDY Federal work-study jobs available.

APPLYING for FINANCIAL AID ***Required financial aid form:*** FAFSA. ***Financial aid deadline (priority):*** 3/15. ***Notification date:*** Continuous.

CONTACT Sue Bienvenue, Director of Financial Aid, Notre Dame College, 2321 Elm Street, Manchester, NH 03104-2299, 603-669-4298 or toll-free 800-754-0405. *Fax:* 603-644-8316.

NOTRE DAME COLLEGE OF OHIO

South Euclid, OH

Tuition & fees: $13,618 **Average undergraduate aid package: $11,044**

ABOUT THE INSTITUTION Independent Roman Catholic, women only. Awards: associate, bachelor's, and master's degrees. 33 undergraduate majors. Total enrollment: 726. Undergraduates: 651. Freshmen: 52. Federal methodology is used as a basis for awarding need-based institutional aid.

UNDERGRADUATE EXPENSES for 1999–2000 ***Application fee:*** $30. ***Comprehensive fee:*** $18,866 includes full-time tuition ($13,418), mandatory fees ($200), and room and board ($5248). ***College room only:*** $2624. Full-time tuition and fees vary according to class time. Room and board charges vary according to board plan. ***Part-time tuition:*** $338 per credit. Part-time tuition and fees vary according to class time. ***Payment plan:*** installment.

FRESHMAN FINANCIAL AID (Fall 1999, est.) 35 applied for aid; of those 97% were deemed to have need. 100% of freshmen with need received aid. *Average percent of need met:* 90% (excluding resources awarded to replace EFC). *Average financial aid package:* $12,847 (excluding resources awarded to replace EFC).

UNDERGRADUATE FINANCIAL AID (Fall 1999, est.) 220 applied for aid; of those 100% were deemed to have need. 100% of undergraduates with need received aid. *Average percent of need met:* 90% (excluding resources awarded to replace EFC). *Average financial aid package:* $11,044 (excluding resources awarded to replace EFC).

GIFT AID (NEED-BASED) ***Total amount:*** $741,626 (29% Federal, 19% state, 46% institutional, 6% external sources). ***Receiving aid:*** *Freshmen:* 89% (34); *all full-time undergraduates:* 98% (219). ***Average award:*** Freshmen: $9533; Undergraduates: $7266. ***Scholarships, grants, and awards:*** Federal Pell, FSEOG, state, private, college/university gift aid from institutional funds.

GIFT AID (NON-NEED-BASED) ***Total amount:*** $1,176,291 (17% state, 83% institutional). ***Receiving aid:*** *Freshmen:* 71% (27); *Undergraduates:* 70% (156). ***Scholarships, grants, and awards by category:*** *Academic Interests/Achievement:* general academic interests/achievements. *Special Characteristics:* children and siblings of alumni, children of faculty/staff, relatives of clergy, siblings of current students, twins. ***Tuition waivers:*** Full or partial for employees or children of employees.

LOANS ***Student loans:*** $777,339 (100% need-based). 90% of past graduating class borrowed through all loan programs. Average indebtedness per student: $15,649. ***Average need-based loan:*** Freshmen: $2625; Undergraduates: $2522. ***Parent loans:*** $23,821 (100% non-need-based). ***Programs:*** FFEL (Subsidized and Unsubsidized Stafford, PLUS), Perkins, state, alternative loans.

WORK-STUDY ***Federal work-study:*** *Total amount:* $30,000; 17 jobs averaging $1500. ***State or other work-study/employment:*** *Total amount:* $56,247 (100% need-based). Part-time jobs available.

ATHLETIC AWARDS *Total amount:* 23,550 (100% non-need-based).

APPLYING for FINANCIAL AID ***Required financial aid form:*** FAFSA. ***Financial aid deadline:*** 4/1. ***Notification date:*** Continuous. Students must reply within 2 weeks of notification.

CONTACT Ms. Mary E. McCrystal, Financial Aid Director, Notre Dame College of Ohio, 4545 College Road, South Euclid, OH 44121-4293, 216-381-1680 Ext. 263 or toll-free 800-NDC-1680 Ext. 355. *Fax:* 216-381-3802. *E-mail:* mmccrystal@ndc.edu

NOVA SOUTHEASTERN UNIVERSITY

Fort Lauderdale, FL

Tuition & fees: $11,800 **Average undergraduate aid package: $14,062**

ABOUT THE INSTITUTION Independent, coed. Awards: bachelor's, master's, doctoral, and first professional degrees and first-professional certificates. 20 undergraduate majors. Total enrollment: 17,810. Undergraduates: 4,218. Freshmen: 280. Federal methodology is used as a basis for awarding need-based institutional aid.

UNDERGRADUATE EXPENSES for 1999–2000 ***Application fee:*** $25. ***Comprehensive fee:*** $18,190 includes full-time tuition ($11,600), mandatory fees ($200), and room and board ($6390). Room and board charges vary according to board plan and housing facility. ***Part-time tuition:*** $387 per credit. ***Part-time fees:*** $25 per term part-time. ***Payment plan:*** installment.

FRESHMAN FINANCIAL AID (Fall 1999, est.) 216 applied for aid; of those 86% were deemed to have need. 99% of freshmen with need received aid; of those 2% had need fully met. *Average percent of need met:* 34% (excluding resources awarded to replace EFC). *Average financial aid package:* $15,510 (excluding resources awarded to replace EFC). 7% of all full-time freshmen had no need and received non-need-based aid.

UNDERGRADUATE FINANCIAL AID (Fall 1999, est.) 2,534 applied for aid; of those 75% were deemed to have need. 99% of undergraduates with need received aid; of those 3% had need fully met. *Average percent of need met:* 32% (excluding resources awarded to replace EFC). *Average*

financial aid package: $14,062 (excluding resources awarded to replace EFC). 4% of all full-time undergraduates had no need and received non-need-based aid.

GIFT AID (NEED-BASED) ***Total amount:*** $9,022,283 (42% Federal, 27% state, 31% institutional). ***Receiving aid:*** *Freshmen:* 70% (161); *all full-time undergraduates:* 53% (1,366). ***Average award:*** Freshmen: $5283; Undergraduates: $4782. ***Scholarships, grants, and awards:*** Federal Pell, FSEOG, state, private, college/university gift aid from institutional funds.

GIFT AID (NON-NEED-BASED) ***Total amount:*** $6,333,552 (54% state, 46% institutional). ***Receiving aid:*** *Freshmen:* 70% (160); *Undergraduates:* 61% (1,574). ***Scholarships, grants, and awards by category:*** *Academic Interests/Achievement:* 647 awards ($2,670,450 total): general academic interests/achievements. *Special Characteristics:* 14 awards ($93,284 total): children of faculty/staff. ***Tuition waivers:*** Full or partial for employees or children of employees.

LOANS ***Student loans:*** $25,310,778 (53% need-based, 47% non-need-based). ***Average need-based loan:*** Freshmen: $4165; Undergraduates: $6704. ***Parent loans:*** $323,483 (100% non-need-based). ***Programs:*** FFEL (Subsidized and Unsubsidized Stafford, PLUS), Perkins, college/university.

WORK-STUDY ***Federal work-study:*** *Total amount:* $3,990,988; 822 jobs averaging $4855. ***State or other work-study/employment:*** *Total amount:* $706,272 (100% need-based). 224 part-time jobs averaging $3153.

ATHLETIC AWARDS *Total amount:* 543,000 (100% non-need-based).

APPLYING for FINANCIAL AID ***Required financial aid forms:*** FAFSA, institution's own form. ***Financial aid deadline (priority):*** 4/1. ***Notification date:*** Continuous. Students must reply within 4 weeks of notification.

CONTACT Grace Salas, Assistant Director of Student Financial Aid, Nova Southeastern University, 3301 College Avenue, Fort Lauderdale, FL 33314, 954-262-7448 or toll-free 800-541-6682. *Fax:* 954-262-3967. *E-mail:* salas@nsu.nova.edu

NYACK COLLEGE

Nyack, NY

Tuition & fees: $12,740 **Average undergraduate aid package: $13,073**

ABOUT THE INSTITUTION Independent religious, coed. Awards: associate, bachelor's, master's, and first professional degrees and post-bachelor's certificates. 28 undergraduate majors. Total enrollment: 1,814. Undergraduates: 1,424. Freshmen: 330. Both federal and institutional methodology are used as a basis for awarding need-based institutional aid.

UNDERGRADUATE EXPENSES for 2000–2001 ***Application fee:*** $15. ***Comprehensive fee:*** $18,540 includes full-time tuition ($11,990), mandatory fees ($750), and room and board ($5800). Full-time tuition and fees vary according to location and program. Room and board charges vary according to housing facility. ***Part-time tuition:*** $500 per credit hour. ***Part-time fees:*** $170 per term. Part-time tuition and fees vary according to course load, location, and program. ***Payment plan:*** installment.

FRESHMAN FINANCIAL AID (Fall 1999) 296 applied for aid; of those 95% were deemed to have need. 100% of freshmen with need received aid; of those 19% had need fully met. *Average percent of need met:* 73% (excluding resources awarded to replace EFC). *Average financial aid package:* $12,502 (excluding resources awarded to replace EFC). 35% of all full-time freshmen had no need and received non-need-based aid.

UNDERGRADUATE FINANCIAL AID (Fall 1999) 1,155 applied for aid; of those 94% were deemed to have need. 100% of undergraduates with need received aid; of those 20% had need fully met. *Average percent of need met:* 71% (excluding resources awarded to replace EFC). *Average financial aid package:* $13,073 (excluding resources awarded to replace EFC). 19% of all full-time undergraduates had no need and received non-need-based aid.

GIFT AID (NEED-BASED) ***Total amount:*** $5,987,069 (27% Federal, 25% state, 47% institutional, 1% external sources). ***Receiving aid:*** *Freshmen:* 65% (281); *all full-time undergraduates:* 74% (989). ***Average award:*** Freshmen: $8363; Undergraduates: $7740. ***Scholarships, grants, and awards:*** Federal Pell, FSEOG, state, private, college/university gift aid from institutional funds.

GIFT AID (NON-NEED-BASED) ***Total amount:*** $424,170 (2% state, 82% institutional, 16% external sources). ***Receiving aid:*** *Freshmen:* 3% (14); *Undergraduates:* 3% (41). ***Scholarships, grants, and awards by category:*** *Academic Interests/Achievement:* 536 awards ($855,825 total): general academic interests/achievements. *Creative Arts/Performance:* 33 awards ($93,440 total): journalism/publications, music, performing arts, theater/drama. *Special Achievements/Activities:* 11 awards ($13,250 total): general special achievements/activities, leadership, religious involvement. *Special Characteristics:* 366 awards ($885,141 total): children and siblings of alumni, children of current students, children of faculty/staff, first-generation college students, international students, out-of-state students, relatives of clergy, religious affiliation. ***Tuition waivers:*** Full or partial for employees or children of employees.

LOANS ***Student loans:*** $6,938,832 (87% need-based, 13% non-need-based). 67% of past graduating class borrowed through all loan programs. Average indebtedness per student: $17,000. ***Average need-based loan:*** Freshmen: $3438; Undergraduates: $4758. ***Parent loans:*** $607,927 (60% need-based, 40% non-need-based). ***Programs:*** FFEL (Subsidized and Unsubsidized Stafford, PLUS), Perkins.

WORK-STUDY ***Federal work-study:*** *Total amount:* $182,000; 182 jobs averaging $1000. ***State or other work-study/employment:*** *Total amount:* $77,450 (98% need-based, 2% non-need-based). 36 part-time jobs averaging $2151.

ATHLETIC AWARDS *Total amount:* 796,387 (74% need-based, 26% non-need-based).

APPLYING for FINANCIAL AID ***Required financial aid form:*** FAFSA. ***Financial aid deadline (priority):*** 3/1. ***Notification date:*** Continuous. Students must reply by 7/1 or within 4 weeks of notification.

CONTACT Financial Aid Office, Nyack College, 1 South Boulevard, Nyack, NY 10960-3698, 914-358-1710 Ext. 151 or toll-free 800-33-NYACK. *Fax:* 914-358-7016.

OAK HILLS CHRISTIAN COLLEGE

Bemidji, MN

Tuition & fees: $8590 **Average undergraduate aid package: N/A**

ABOUT THE INSTITUTION Independent interdenominational, coed. Awards: associate and bachelor's degrees. 8 undergraduate majors. Total enrollment: 155. Undergraduates: 155. Freshmen: 33. Federal methodology is used as a basis for awarding need-based institutional aid.

UNDERGRADUATE EXPENSES for 1999–2000 ***Application fee:*** $20. ***Comprehensive fee:*** $11,690 includes full-time tuition ($7970), mandatory fees ($620), and room and board ($3100). ***College room only:*** $1480. Full-time tuition and fees vary according to course load. Room and board charges vary according to housing facility. ***Part-time tuition:*** $250 per semester hour. ***Part-time fees:*** $310 per term part-time. Part-time tuition and fees vary according to course load. ***Payment plan:*** installment.

GIFT AID (NEED-BASED) ***Scholarships, grants, and awards:*** Federal Pell, FSEOG, state, private, college/university gift aid from institutional funds.

GIFT AID (NON-NEED-BASED) ***Scholarships, grants, and awards by category:*** *Academic Interests/Achievement:* general academic interests/achievements. *Special Characteristics:* children of faculty/staff, international students, out-of-state students, siblings of current students, spouses of current students. ***Tuition waivers:*** Full or partial for employees or children of employees.

LOANS ***Programs:*** FFEL (Subsidized and Unsubsidized Stafford, PLUS), state, alternative loans, SELF Loans.

APPLYING for FINANCIAL AID ***Required financial aid forms:*** FAFSA, institution's own form. ***Financial aid deadline:*** Continuous. ***Notification date:*** Continuous.

CONTACT Mr. Daniel Hovestol, Financial Aid Director, Oak Hills Christian College, 1600 Oak Hills Road, SW, Bemidji, MN 56601-8832, 218-751-8670 Ext. 220 or toll-free 888-751-8670 Ext. 285. *Fax:* 218-751-8825. *E-mail:* ohfinaid@northernnet.com

OAKLAND CITY UNIVERSITY

Oakland City, IN

Tuition & fees: $10,096 **Average undergraduate aid package: N/A**

ABOUT THE INSTITUTION Independent General Baptist, coed. Awards: associate, bachelor's, master's, doctoral, and first professional degrees. 51 undergraduate majors. Total enrollment: 1,444. Undergraduates: 1,258. Federal methodology is used as a basis for awarding need-based institutional aid.

UNDERGRADUATE EXPENSES for 1999–2000 ***Application fee:*** $25. ***Comprehensive fee:*** $13,826 includes full-time tuition ($9900), mandatory fees ($196), and room and board ($3730). ***College room only:*** $1200. Full-time tuition and fees vary according to location and program. Room and board charges vary according to housing facility. ***Part-time tuition:*** $330 per credit hour. ***Part-time fees:*** $63 per term part-time. Part-time tuition and fees vary according to location and program. ***Payment plans:*** installment, deferred payment.

GIFT AID (NEED-BASED) ***Scholarships, grants, and awards:*** Federal Pell, FSEOG, state, private, college/university gift aid from institutional funds.

GIFT AID (NON-NEED-BASED) ***Scholarships, grants, and awards by category:*** *Academic Interests/Achievement:* general academic interests/achievements. *Creative Arts/Performance:* art/fine arts, music, theater/drama. *Special Achievements/Activities:* religious involvement. *Special Characteristics:* religious affiliation. ***Tuition waivers:*** Full or partial for minority students, employees or children of employees.

LOANS ***Programs:*** FFEL (Subsidized and Unsubsidized Stafford, PLUS), Perkins.

WORK-STUDY Federal work-study jobs available.

APPLYING for FINANCIAL AID ***Required financial aid form:*** FAFSA. ***Financial aid deadline (priority):*** 3/1. ***Notification date:*** Continuous beginning 4/15.

CONTACT Mrs. Caren K. Richeson, Director of Financial Aid, Oakland City University, 143 North Lucretia Street, Oakland City, IN 47660-1099, 800-737-5125. *Fax:* 812-749-1438.

OAKLAND UNIVERSITY

Rochester, MI

Tuition & fees (MI res): $4292 **Average undergraduate aid package: $5750**

ABOUT THE INSTITUTION State-supported, coed. Awards: bachelor's, master's, and doctoral degrees and post-bachelor's and post-master's certificates. 70 undergraduate majors. Total enrollment: 14,664. Undergraduates: 11,624. Freshmen: 1,813. Federal methodology is used as a basis for awarding need-based institutional aid.

UNDERGRADUATE EXPENSES for 1999–2000 ***Application fee:*** $25. ***Tuition, state resident:*** full-time $3864; part-time $119 per credit hour. ***Tuition, nonresident:*** full-time $11,258; part-time $350 per credit hour. ***Required fees:*** full-time $428; $214 per term part-time. Full-time tuition and fees vary according to program and student level. Part-time tuition and fees vary according to program and student level. ***College room and board:*** $4715. Room and board charges vary according to housing facility. ***Payment plans:*** installment, deferred payment.

FRESHMAN FINANCIAL AID (Fall 1999, est.) 1250 applied for aid; of those 65% were deemed to have need. 100% of freshmen with need received aid; of those 33% had need fully met. *Average percent of need met:* 90% (excluding resources awarded to replace EFC). *Average financial aid package:* $5460 (excluding resources awarded to replace EFC). 33% of all full-time freshmen had no need and received non-need-based aid.

UNDERGRADUATE FINANCIAL AID (Fall 1999, est.) 3,850 applied for aid; of those 78% were deemed to have need. 100% of undergraduates with need received aid; of those 24% had need fully met. *Average percent of need met:* 90% (excluding resources awarded to replace EFC). *Average financial aid package:* $5750 (excluding resources awarded to replace EFC). 20% of all full-time undergraduates had no need and received non-need-based aid.

GIFT AID (NEED-BASED) ***Total amount:*** $6,617,500 (52% Federal, 10% state, 35% institutional, 3% external sources). ***Receiving aid:*** *Freshmen:* 27% (465); *all full-time undergraduates:* 23% (1,735). ***Average award:*** Freshmen: $3050; Undergraduates: $2775. ***Scholarships, grants, and awards:*** Federal Pell, FSEOG, state, college/university gift aid from institutional funds.

GIFT AID (NON-NEED-BASED) ***Total amount:*** $2,096,000 (1% state, 83% institutional, 16% external sources). ***Receiving aid:*** *Freshmen:* 13% (225); *Undergraduates:* 7% (545). ***Scholarships, grants, and awards by category:*** *Academic Interests/Achievement:* 850 awards ($1,650,000 total): biological sciences, engineering/technologies, general academic interests/achievements. *Creative Arts/Performance:* 70 awards ($90,000 total): music, performing arts. *Special Achievements/Activities:* 75 awards ($85,000 total): leadership. *Special Characteristics:* 95 awards ($645,000 total): children of union members/company employees, out-of-state students. ***Tuition waivers:*** Full or partial for employees or children of employees.

LOANS ***Student loans:*** $13,650,000 (58% need-based, 42% non-need-based). ***Average need-based loan:*** Freshmen: $2250; Undergraduates: $3300. ***Parent loans:*** $750,000 (17% need-based, 83% non-need-based). ***Programs:*** Federal Direct (Subsidized and Unsubsidized Stafford, PLUS), Perkins.

WORK-STUDY ***Federal work-study:*** *Total amount:* $1,576,000; 630 jobs averaging $2500. ***State or other work-study/employment:*** *Total amount:* $155,000 (100% need-based). 105 part-time jobs averaging $1475.

ATHLETIC AWARDS *Total amount:* 953,000 (11% need-based, 89% non-need-based).

APPLYING for FINANCIAL AID ***Required financial aid forms:*** FAFSA, institution's own form. ***Financial aid deadline (priority):*** 4/1. ***Notification date:*** Continuous. Students must reply within 2 weeks of notification.

CONTACT Mr. Robert E. Johnson, Associate Vice President for Enrollment Management, Oakland University, 101 North Foundation Hall, Rochester, MI 48309-4401, 248-370-3360 or toll-free 800-OAK-UNIV. *E-mail:* rejohnso@oakland.edu

OAKWOOD COLLEGE

Huntsville, AL

Tuition & fees: $9058 **Average undergraduate aid package: N/A**

ABOUT THE INSTITUTION Independent Seventh-day Adventist, coed. Awards: associate and bachelor's degrees. 41 undergraduate majors. Total enrollment: 1,736. Undergraduates: 1,736. Freshmen: 407. Federal methodology is used as a basis for awarding need-based institutional aid.

UNDERGRADUATE EXPENSES for 2000–2001 ***Application fee:*** $20. ***Comprehensive fee:*** $14,350 includes full-time tuition ($8820), mandatory fees ($238), and room and board ($5292). Room and board charges vary according to board plan and housing facility. ***Part-time tuition:*** $350 per credit hour. ***Part-time fees:*** $119 per term part-time. Part-time tuition and fees vary according to course load. ***Payment plan:*** installment.

GIFT AID (NEED-BASED) ***Scholarships, grants, and awards:*** Federal Pell, FSEOG, private, college/university gift aid from institutional funds, Lettie Pate Whitehead Foundation Scholarships.

GIFT AID (NON-NEED-BASED) ***Scholarships, grants, and awards by category:*** *Academic Interests/Achievement:* general academic interests/achievements. *Special Characteristics:* general special characteristics. ***Tuition waivers:*** Full or partial for employees or children of employees.

LOANS ***Programs:*** FFEL (Subsidized and Unsubsidized Stafford, PLUS), alternative loans.

APPLYING for FINANCIAL AID ***Required financial aid forms:*** FAFSA, verification worksheet. ***Financial aid deadline (priority):*** 3/31. ***Notification date:*** Continuous beginning 5/1.

CONTACT Financial Aid Director, Oakwood College, 7000 Adventist Boulevard, Huntsville, AL 35896, 256-726-7210 or toll-free 800-824-5312 (in-state).

OBERLIN COLLEGE

Oberlin, OH

Tuition & fees: $24,264 **Average undergraduate aid package: $22,215**

ABOUT THE INSTITUTION Independent, coed. Awards: bachelor's and master's degrees. 53 undergraduate majors. Total enrollment: 2,967. Undergraduates: 2,951. Freshmen: 727. Institutional methodology is used as a basis for awarding need-based institutional aid.

UNDERGRADUATE EXPENSES for 1999–2000 ***Application fee:*** $30. ***Comprehensive fee:*** $30,442 includes full-time tuition ($24,096), mandatory fees ($168), and room and board ($6178). ***College room only:*** $3200. Room and board charges vary according to housing facility. ***Part-time tuition:*** $1004 per credit hour. ***Part-time fees:*** $84 per term part-time. ***Payment plan:*** installment.

FRESHMAN FINANCIAL AID (Fall 1998) 524 applied for aid; of those 81% were deemed to have need. 100% of freshmen with need received aid; of those 100% had need fully met. *Average percent of need met:* 100% (excluding resources awarded to replace EFC). *Average financial aid package:* $21,919 (excluding resources awarded to replace EFC).

UNDERGRADUATE FINANCIAL AID (Fall 1998) 2,069 applied for aid; of those 81% were deemed to have need. 100% of undergraduates with need received aid; of those 100% had need fully met. *Average percent of need met:* 100% (excluding resources awarded to replace EFC). *Average financial aid package:* $22,215 (excluding resources awarded to replace EFC).

GIFT AID (NEED-BASED) ***Total amount:*** $26,724,993 (5% Federal, 1% state, 92% institutional, 2% external sources). ***Receiving aid:*** *Freshmen:* 53% (382); *all full-time undergraduates:* 55% (1,561). ***Scholarships, grants, and awards:*** Federal Pell, FSEOG, state, private, college/university gift aid from institutional funds.

GIFT AID (NON-NEED-BASED) ***Total amount:*** $2,229,132 (1% Federal, 4% state, 83% institutional, 12% external sources). ***Scholarships, grants, and awards by category:*** *Academic Interests/Achievement:* 318 awards ($1,344,382 total): general academic interests/achievements. *Creative Arts/Performance:* 356 awards ($2,678,812 total): music. ***Tuition waivers:*** Full or partial for employees or children of employees.

LOANS ***Student loans:*** $5,374,806 (100% need-based). 53% of past graduating class borrowed through all loan programs. Average indebtedness per student: $13,926. ***Parent loans:*** $1,927,649 (89% need-based, 11% non-need-based). ***Programs:*** FFEL (Subsidized and Unsubsidized Stafford, PLUS), Perkins, college/university.

WORK-STUDY ***Federal work-study:*** *Total amount:* $1,808,751; 1,539 jobs available.

APPLYING for FINANCIAL AID ***Required financial aid forms:*** FAFSA, CSS Financial Aid PROFILE, noncustodial (divorced/separated) parent's statement. ***Financial aid deadline (priority):*** 2/15. ***Notification date:*** 4/1. Students must reply by 5/1 or within 2 weeks of notification.

CONTACT Office of Financial Aid, Oberlin College, 52 West Lorain Street, Oberlin, OH 44074, 800-693-3173 or toll-free 800-622-OBIE. *Fax:* 440-775-8249. *E-mail:* financial.aid@oberlin.edu

OCCIDENTAL COLLEGE

Los Angeles, CA

Tuition & fees: $23,850 **Average undergraduate aid package: $23,869**

ABOUT THE INSTITUTION Independent, coed. Awards: bachelor's and master's degrees. 31 undergraduate majors. Total enrollment: 1,603. Undergraduates: 1,570. Freshmen: 411. Both federal and institutional methodology are used as a basis for awarding need-based institutional aid.

UNDERGRADUATE EXPENSES for 2000–2001 (est.) ***Application fee:*** $50. ***Comprehensive fee:*** $30,730 includes full-time tuition ($23,532), mandatory fees ($318), and room and board ($6880). ***College room only:*** $2924. Room and board charges vary according to board plan and housing facility. ***Part-time tuition:*** $980 per unit. ***Payment plans:*** tuition prepayment, installment.

FRESHMAN FINANCIAL AID (Fall 1999, est.) 311 applied for aid; of those 72% were deemed to have need. 100% of freshmen with need received aid; of those 100% had need fully met. *Average percent of need met:* 100% (excluding resources awarded to replace EFC). *Average financial aid package:* $23,507 (excluding resources awarded to replace EFC). 20% of all full-time freshmen had no need and received non-need-based aid.

UNDERGRADUATE FINANCIAL AID (Fall 1999, est.) 1,314 applied for aid; of those 75% were deemed to have need. 94% of undergraduates with need received aid; of those 98% had need fully met. *Average percent of need met:* 95% (excluding resources awarded to replace EFC). *Average financial aid package:* $23,869 (excluding resources awarded to replace EFC). 21% of all full-time undergraduates had no need and received non-need-based aid.

GIFT AID (NEED-BASED) ***Total amount:*** $15,113,067 (8% Federal, 18% state, 72% institutional, 2% external sources). ***Receiving aid:*** *Freshmen:* 48% (198); *all full-time undergraduates:* 50% (777). ***Average award:*** Freshmen: $11,254; Undergraduates: $10,298. ***Scholarships, grants, and awards:*** Federal Pell, FSEOG, state, private, college/university gift aid from institutional funds.

GIFT AID (NON-NEED-BASED) ***Total amount:*** $2,030,030 (97% institutional, 3% external sources). ***Receiving aid:*** *Freshmen:* 25% (101); *Undergraduates:* 22% (347). ***Scholarships, grants, and awards by category:*** *Academic Interests/Achievement:* general academic interests/achievements. *Creative Arts/Performance:* 1 award ($1000 total): music. *Special Achievements/Activities:* general special achievements/activities. ***Tuition waivers:*** Full or partial for employees or children of employees. ***ROTC:*** Army cooperative, Naval cooperative, Air Force cooperative.

LOANS ***Student loans:*** $6,725,750 (89% need-based, 11% non-need-based). 70% of past graduating class borrowed through all loan programs. Average indebtedness per student: $14,049. ***Average need-based loan:*** Freshmen: $3731; Undergraduates: $5845. ***Parent loans:*** $1,551,146 (100% non-need-based). ***Programs:*** FFEL (Subsidized and Unsubsidized Stafford, PLUS), Perkins, college/university.

WORK-STUDY ***Federal work-study:*** *Total amount:* $1,592,839; 700 jobs averaging $2272. ***State or other work-study/employment:*** *Total amount:* $241,554 (100% need-based). 116 part-time jobs averaging $2082.

APPLYING for FINANCIAL AID ***Required financial aid forms:*** FAFSA, CSS Financial Aid PROFILE, state aid form, noncustodial (divorced/separated) parent's statement, business/farm supplement, parent and student income tax and W-2 forms. ***Financial aid deadline (priority):*** 2/1. ***Notification date:*** 4/1. Students must reply by 5/1 or within 2 weeks of notification.

CONTACT Maureen McRae Levy, Director of Financial Aid, Occidental College, 1600 Campus Road, Los Angeles, CA 90041, 323-259-2548 or toll-free 800-825-5262. *Fax:* 323-341-4961. *E-mail:* finaid@oxy.edu

OGLALA LAKOTA COLLEGE

Kyle, SD

Tuition & fees: N/R **Average undergraduate aid package: N/A**

ABOUT THE INSTITUTION State and locally supported, coed. Awards: associate, bachelor's, and master's degrees. 23 undergraduate majors. Federal methodology is used as a basis for awarding need-based institutional aid.

GIFT AID (NEED-BASED) ***Scholarships, grants, and awards:*** Federal Pell, FSEOG, state, private, college/university gift aid from institutional funds.

GIFT AID (NON-NEED-BASED) ***Scholarships, grants, and awards by category:*** *Academic Interests/Achievement:* business, education, health fields, social sciences. ***Tuition waivers:*** Full or partial for employees or children of employees.

WORK-STUDY Federal work-study jobs available.

APPLYING for FINANCIAL AID ***Required financial aid form:*** FAFSA. ***Financial aid deadline (priority):*** 8/21. ***Notification date:*** Continuous beginning 10/21.

Oglala Lakota College (continued)

CONTACT Christy Red Hair, Financial Aid Director, Oglala Lakota College, PO Box 490, Kyle, SD 57752-0490, 605-455-2321 Ext. 245.

OGLETHORPE UNIVERSITY

Atlanta, GA

Tuition & fees: $17,700 **Average undergraduate aid package: $16,493**

ABOUT THE INSTITUTION Independent, coed. Awards: bachelor's and master's degrees. 31 undergraduate majors. Total enrollment: 1,288. Undergraduates: 1,178. Freshmen: 198. Federal methodology is used as a basis for awarding need-based institutional aid.

UNDERGRADUATE EXPENSES for 1999–2000 ***Application fee:*** $30. ***Comprehensive fee:*** $23,000 includes full-time tuition ($17,500), mandatory fees ($200), and room and board ($5300). Room and board charges vary according to board plan and housing facility. ***Part-time tuition:*** $850 per course. Part-time tuition and fees vary according to class time. ***Payment plans:*** tuition prepayment, installment.

FRESHMAN FINANCIAL AID (Fall 1998) 203 applied for aid; of those 78% were deemed to have need. 100% of freshmen with need received aid; of those 42% had need fully met. *Average percent of need met:* 89% (excluding resources awarded to replace EFC). *Average financial aid package:* $16,108 (excluding resources awarded to replace EFC). 23% of all full-time freshmen had no need and received non-need-based aid.

UNDERGRADUATE FINANCIAL AID (Fall 1998) 691 applied for aid; of those 70% were deemed to have need. 100% of undergraduates with need received aid; of those 34% had need fully met. *Average percent of need met:* 87% (excluding resources awarded to replace EFC). *Average financial aid package:* $16,493 (excluding resources awarded to replace EFC). 25% of all full-time undergraduates had no need and received non-need-based aid.

GIFT AID (NEED-BASED) ***Total amount:*** $5,083,470 (8% Federal, 11% state, 79% institutional, 2% external sources). ***Receiving aid:*** *Freshmen:* 69% (148); *all full-time undergraduates:* 55% (462). ***Scholarships, grants, and awards:*** Federal Pell, FSEOG, state, private, college/university gift aid from institutional funds.

GIFT AID (NON-NEED-BASED) ***Total amount:*** $2,833,500 (20% state, 74% institutional, 6% external sources). ***Receiving aid:*** *Freshmen:* 49% (106); *Undergraduates:* 44% (370). ***Scholarships, grants, and awards by category:*** *Academic Interests/Achievement:* general academic interests/achievements. *Creative Arts/Performance:* journalism/publications, music, performing arts, theater/drama. *Special Achievements/Activities:* community service, religious involvement. *Special Characteristics:* children of faculty/staff, siblings of current students. ***Tuition waivers:*** Full or partial for employees or children of employees.

LOANS ***Student loans:*** $1,733,049 (89% need-based, 11% non-need-based). ***Parent loans:*** $1,030,443 (29% need-based, 71% non-need-based). ***Programs:*** Federal Direct (Subsidized and Unsubsidized Stafford, PLUS), FFEL (Subsidized and Unsubsidized Stafford, PLUS), Perkins.

WORK-STUDY ***Federal work-study:*** *Total amount:* $405,199; jobs available. ***State or other work-study/employment:*** *Total amount:* $107,258 (71% need-based, 29% non-need-based). Part-time jobs available.

APPLYING for FINANCIAL AID ***Required financial aid forms:*** FAFSA, institution's own form, state aid form. ***Financial aid deadline:*** Continuous. ***Notification date:*** Continuous. Students must reply by 5/1 or within 4 weeks of notification.

CONTACT Mr. Patrick Bonones, Director of Financial Aid, Oglethorpe University, 4484 Peachtree Road, NE, Atlanta, GA 30319-2797, 404-364-8356 or toll-free 800-428-4484. *Fax:* 404-364-8500. *E-mail:* pbonones@facstaff.oglethorpe.edu

OHIO DOMINICAN COLLEGE

Columbus, OH

Tuition & fees: $10,250 **Average undergraduate aid package: N/A**

ABOUT THE INSTITUTION Independent Roman Catholic, coed. Awards: associate and bachelor's degrees. 38 undergraduate majors. Total enrollment: 2,135. Undergraduates: 2,135. Freshmen: 213. Federal methodology is used as a basis for awarding need-based institutional aid.

UNDERGRADUATE EXPENSES for 1999–2000 ***Comprehensive fee:*** $15,320 includes full-time tuition ($10,250) and room and board ($5070). Room and board charges vary according to housing facility. ***Part-time tuition:*** $321 per credit hour. ***Payment plan:*** installment.

GIFT AID (NEED-BASED) ***Scholarships, grants, and awards:*** Federal Pell, FSEOG, state, private, college/university gift aid from institutional funds.

GIFT AID (NON-NEED-BASED) ***Scholarships, grants, and awards by category:*** *Academic Interests/Achievement:* general academic interests/achievements. *Special Achievements/Activities:* leadership. ***Tuition waivers:*** Full or partial for employees or children of employees, senior citizens. ***ROTC:*** Army cooperative, Air Force cooperative.

LOANS ***Programs:*** FFEL (Subsidized and Unsubsidized Stafford, PLUS), Perkins.

WORK-STUDY Federal work-study jobs available.

APPLYING for FINANCIAL AID ***Required financial aid form:*** FAFSA. ***Financial aid deadline (priority):*** 4/1. ***Notification date:*** Continuous. Students must reply within 2 weeks of notification.

CONTACT Ms. Cynthia A. Hahn, Director of Financial Aid, Ohio Dominican College, 1216 Sunbury Road, Columbus, OH 43219, 614-251-4640 or toll-free 800-854-2670. *Fax:* 614-251-4456. *E-mail:* fin-aid@odc.edu

OHIO NORTHERN UNIVERSITY

Ada, OH

Tuition & fees: $21,435 **Average undergraduate aid package: $17,640**

ABOUT THE INSTITUTION Independent United Methodist, coed. Awards: bachelor's and first professional degrees. 52 undergraduate majors. Total enrollment: 3,159. Undergraduates: 2,381. Freshmen: 622. Federal methodology is used as a basis for awarding need-based institutional aid.

UNDERGRADUATE EXPENSES for 2000–2001 ***Application fee:*** $30. ***Comprehensive fee:*** $26,700 includes full-time tuition ($21,435) and room and board ($5265). ***College room only:*** $2310. Full-time tuition and fees vary according to program. Room and board charges vary according to board plan. ***Part-time tuition:*** $573 per quarter hour. Part-time tuition and fees vary according to program. ***Payment plan:*** installment.

FRESHMAN FINANCIAL AID (Fall 1999) 682 applied for aid; of those 98% were deemed to have need. 100% of freshmen with need received aid; of those 27% had need fully met. *Average percent of need met:* 92% (excluding resources awarded to replace EFC). *Average financial aid package:* $19,655 (excluding resources awarded to replace EFC). 9% of all full-time freshmen had no need and received non-need-based aid.

UNDERGRADUATE FINANCIAL AID (Fall 1999) 2,588 applied for aid; of those 90% were deemed to have need. 100% of undergraduates with need received aid; of those 25% had need fully met. *Average percent of need met:* 89% (excluding resources awarded to replace EFC). *Average financial aid package:* $17,640 (excluding resources awarded to replace EFC). 15% of all full-time undergraduates had no need and received non-need-based aid.

GIFT AID (NEED-BASED) ***Total amount:*** $26,677,738 (7% Federal, 11% state, 80% institutional, 2% external sources). ***Receiving aid:*** *Freshmen:* 89% (665); *all full-time undergraduates:* 81% (2,340). ***Average award:*** Freshmen: $14,348; Undergraduates: $11,819. ***Scholarships, grants, and awards:*** Federal Pell, FSEOG, state, private, college/university gift aid from institutional funds.

GIFT AID (NON-NEED-BASED) ***Total amount:*** $7,515,653 (1% Federal, 9% state, 78% institutional, 12% external sources). ***Receiving aid:*** *Freshmen:* 68% (512); *Undergraduates:* 65% (1,872). ***Scholarships, grants, and awards by category:*** *Academic Interests/Achievement:* 1,667 awards ($10,335,157 total): biological sciences, business, communication, computer science, education, engineering/technologies, English, foreign languages, general academic interests/achievements, health fields, humanities, international studies, mathematics, physical sciences, premedicine, religion/biblical studies, social sciences. *Creative Arts/Performance:* 130 awards

($632,336 total): art/fine arts, dance, music, performing arts, theater/drama. *Special Achievements/Activities:* 344 awards ($2,079,479 total): junior miss. *Special Characteristics:* 326 awards ($2,012,338 total): children of faculty/staff, relatives of clergy, religious affiliation, siblings of current students. ***Tuition waivers:*** Full or partial for employees or children of employees. ***ROTC:*** Army cooperative, Air Force cooperative.

LOANS ***Student loans:*** $15,010,178 (61% need-based, 39% non-need-based). 85% of past graduating class borrowed through all loan programs. Average indebtedness per student: $16,400. ***Average need-based loan:*** Freshmen: $3681; Undergraduates: $4205. ***Parent loans:*** $1,841,278 (20% need-based, 80% non-need-based). ***Programs:*** FFEL (Subsidized and Unsubsidized Stafford, PLUS), Perkins, state, college/university.

WORK-STUDY ***Federal work-study:*** *Total amount:* $822,793; jobs available. ***State or other work-study/employment:*** *Total amount:* $2,120,592 (92% need-based, 8% non-need-based). Part-time jobs available.

APPLYING for FINANCIAL AID ***Required financial aid forms:*** FAFSA, institution's own form. ***Financial aid deadline:*** 6/1 (priority: 4/15). ***Notification date:*** Continuous. Students must reply within 2 weeks of notification.

CONTACT Mr. Wendell Schick, Director of Financial Aid, Ohio Northern University, 525 South Main Street, Ada, OH 45810-1599, 419-772-2272. *Fax:* 419-772-2313. *E-mail:* w-schick@onu.edu

THE OHIO STATE UNIVERSITY

Columbus, OH

Tuition & fees (OH res): $4137 **Average undergraduate aid package: $7043**

ABOUT THE INSTITUTION State-supported, coed. Awards: bachelor's, master's, doctoral, and first professional degrees and post-master's certificates. 208 undergraduate majors. Total enrollment: 48,003. Undergraduates: 36,092. Freshmen: 6,119. Federal methodology is used as a basis for awarding need-based institutional aid.

UNDERGRADUATE EXPENSES for 1999–2000 ***Application fee:*** $30. ***Tuition, state resident:*** full-time $3780. ***Tuition, nonresident:*** full-time $11,730. ***Required fees:*** full-time $357. Part-time tuition and fees vary according to course load. ***College room and board:*** $5328. Room and board charges vary according to board plan and housing facility. ***Payment plan:*** installment.

FRESHMAN FINANCIAL AID (Fall 1999, est.) 4373 applied for aid; of those 68% were deemed to have need. 100% of freshmen with need received aid; of those 27% had need fully met. *Average percent of need met:* 73% (excluding resources awarded to replace EFC). *Average financial aid package:* $6533 (excluding resources awarded to replace EFC). 20% of all full-time freshmen had no need and received non-need-based aid.

UNDERGRADUATE FINANCIAL AID (Fall 1999, est.) 18,612 applied for aid; of those 77% were deemed to have need. 100% of undergraduates with need received aid; of those 29% had need fully met. *Average percent of need met:* 74% (excluding resources awarded to replace EFC). *Average financial aid package:* $7043 (excluding resources awarded to replace EFC). 8% of all full-time undergraduates had no need and received non-need-based aid.

GIFT AID (NEED-BASED) ***Total amount:*** $27,376,670 (55% Federal, 19% state, 25% institutional, 1% external sources). ***Receiving aid:*** *Freshmen:* 26% (1,518); *all full-time undergraduates:* 24% (7,454). ***Average award:*** Freshmen: $3252; Undergraduates: $3380. ***Scholarships, grants, and awards:*** Federal Pell, FSEOG, state, private, college/university gift aid from institutional funds, United Negro College Fund.

GIFT AID (NON-NEED-BASED) ***Total amount:*** $33,358,308 (4% Federal, 12% state, 67% institutional, 17% external sources). ***Receiving aid:*** *Freshmen:* 40% (2,399); *Undergraduates:* 20% (6,331). ***Scholarships, grants, and awards by category:*** *Academic Interests/Achievement:* agriculture, architecture, area/ethnic studies, biological sciences, business, communication, computer science, education, engineering/technologies, English, foreign languages, general academic interests/achievements, health fields, home economics, humanities, international studies, mathematics, military science, physical sciences, premedicine, social sciences. *Creative Arts/Performance:* creative writing, dance, journalism/publications, music, performing arts, theater/drama. *Special Achievements/Activities:* cheerleading/drum major, hobbies/interests, leadership, memberships. *Special Characteristics:* adult students, children and siblings of alumni, children of faculty/staff, children of public servants, children of union members/company employees, children of workers in trades, children with a deceased or disabled parent, ethnic background, handicapped students, members of minority groups, out-of-state students, previous college experience. ***Tuition waivers:*** Full or partial for employees or children of employees, senior citizens. ***ROTC:*** Army, Naval, Air Force.

LOANS ***Student loans:*** $89,768,978 (60% need-based, 40% non-need-based). 50% of past graduating class borrowed through all loan programs. Average indebtedness per student: $11,800. ***Average need-based loan:*** Freshmen: $2976; Undergraduates: $4021. ***Parent loans:*** $20,314,034 (100% non-need-based). ***Programs:*** Federal Direct (Subsidized and Unsubsidized Stafford, PLUS), Perkins, Federal Nursing, college/university.

WORK-STUDY ***Federal work-study:*** *Total amount:* $7,138,633; 2,737 jobs averaging $2608.

ATHLETIC AWARDS *Total amount:* 5,985,677 (100% non-need-based).

APPLYING for FINANCIAL AID ***Required financial aid form:*** FAFSA. ***Financial aid deadline (priority):*** 2/15. ***Notification date:*** 4/1. Students must reply by 5/1 or within 4 weeks of notification.

CONTACT Ms. Tally Hart, Director of Student Financial Aid, The Ohio State University, 517 Lincoln Tower, 1800 Cannon Drive, Columbus, OH 43210-1230, 614-292-0300. *Fax:* 614-292-7527. *E-mail:* finaid@fa.adm.ohio-state.edu

OHIO UNIVERSITY

Athens, OH

Tuition & fees (OH res): $4800 **Average undergraduate aid package: $6528**

ABOUT THE INSTITUTION State-supported, coed. Awards: associate, bachelor's, master's, doctoral, and first professional degrees. 172 undergraduate majors. Total enrollment: 19,638. Undergraduates: 16,554. Freshmen: 3,448. Federal methodology is used as a basis for awarding need-based institutional aid.

UNDERGRADUATE EXPENSES for 1999–2000 ***Application fee:*** $30. ***Tuition, state resident:*** full-time $4800; part-time $154 per quarter hour. ***Tuition, nonresident:*** full-time $10,101; part-time $329 per quarter hour. ***College room and board:*** $5484; ***room only:*** $2697. Room and board charges vary according to board plan. ***Payment plan:*** installment.

FRESHMAN FINANCIAL AID (Fall 1999, est.) 3044 applied for aid; of those 53% were deemed to have need. 97% of freshmen with need received aid; of those 45% had need fully met. *Average percent of need met:* 79% (excluding resources awarded to replace EFC). *Average financial aid package:* $6007 (excluding resources awarded to replace EFC). 19% of all full-time freshmen had no need and received non-need-based aid.

UNDERGRADUATE FINANCIAL AID (Fall 1999, est.) 10,490 applied for aid; of those 65% were deemed to have need. 98% of undergraduates with need received aid; of those 42% had need fully met. *Average percent of need met:* 80% (excluding resources awarded to replace EFC). *Average financial aid package:* $6528 (excluding resources awarded to replace EFC). 15% of all full-time undergraduates had no need and received non-need-based aid.

GIFT AID (NEED-BASED) ***Total amount:*** $8,232,237 (75% Federal, 20% state, 5% institutional). ***Receiving aid:*** *Freshmen:* 16% (567); *all full-time undergraduates:* 17% (2,754). ***Average award:*** Freshmen: $2799; Undergraduates: $2914. ***Scholarships, grants, and awards:*** Federal Pell, FSEOG, state, private, college/university gift aid from institutional funds.

GIFT AID (NON-NEED-BASED) ***Total amount:*** $9,628,137 (7% state, 69% institutional, 24% external sources). ***Receiving aid:*** *Freshmen:* 31% (1,069); *Undergraduates:* 16% (2,609). ***Scholarships, grants, and awards by category:*** *Academic Interests/Achievement:* area/ethnic studies, biological sciences, business, communication, computer science, education, engineering/technologies, English, foreign languages, general academic interests/achievements, health fields, home economics, humanities, international studies, mathematics, military science, physical sciences, premedicine, social sciences. *Creative Arts/Performance:* applied art and design, art/fine arts, cinema/film/broadcasting, dance, debating, journalism/publications, music, performing arts, theater/drama. *Special Characteristics:* children of

Ohio University (continued)

faculty/staff, members of minority groups. ***Tuition waivers:*** Full or partial for employees or children of employees. ***ROTC:*** Army, Air Force.

LOANS ***Student loans:*** $35,106,208 (61% need-based, 39% non-need-based). 58% of past graduating class borrowed through all loan programs. Average indebtedness per student: $13,850. ***Average need-based loan:*** Freshmen: $2537; Undergraduates: $3663. ***Parent loans:*** $20,612,867 (100% non-need-based). ***Programs:*** Federal Direct (Subsidized and Unsubsidized Stafford, PLUS), Perkins, college/university.

WORK-STUDY ***Federal work-study:*** *Total amount:* $1,606,280; jobs available. ***State or other work-study/employment:*** *Total amount:* $531,697 (100% non-need-based). Part-time jobs available.

ATHLETIC AWARDS *Total amount:* 2,859,738 (100% non-need-based).

APPLYING for FINANCIAL AID ***Required financial aid form:*** FAFSA. ***Financial aid deadline (priority):*** 3/15. ***Notification date:*** 4/1.

CONTACT Ms. Sondra Williams, Director of Financial Aid, Ohio University, 020 Chubb Hall, Athens, OH 45701-2979, 740-593-4141. *Fax:* 740-593-0560. *E-mail:* willias1@ohio.edu

OHIO UNIVERSITY–CHILLICOTHE

Chillicothe, OH

Tuition & fees (OH res): $3192 **Average undergraduate aid package: $6512**

ABOUT THE INSTITUTION State-supported, coed. Awards: associate and bachelor's degrees (offers first 2 years of most bachelor's degree programs available at the main campus in Athens; also offers several bachelor's degree programs that can be completed at this campus and several programs exclusive to this campus; also offers some graduate programs). 14 undergraduate majors. Total enrollment: 1,628. Undergraduates: 1,509. Federal methodology is used as a basis for awarding need-based institutional aid.

UNDERGRADUATE EXPENSES for 1999–2000 ***Application fee:*** $20. ***Tuition, state resident:*** full-time $3192; part-time $97 per credit hour. ***Tuition, nonresident:*** full-time $7803; part-time $250 per credit hour. ***Payment plan:*** installment.

FRESHMAN FINANCIAL AID (Fall 1999, est.) 199 applied for aid; of those 79% were deemed to have need. 98% of freshmen with need received aid; of those 41% had need fully met. *Average percent of need met:* 75% (excluding resources awarded to replace EFC). *Average financial aid package:* $5519 (excluding resources awarded to replace EFC). 9% of all full-time freshmen had no need and received non-need-based aid.

UNDERGRADUATE FINANCIAL AID (Fall 1999, est.) 551 applied for aid; of those 85% were deemed to have need. 99% of undergraduates with need received aid; of those 34% had need fully met. *Average percent of need met:* 77% (excluding resources awarded to replace EFC). *Average financial aid package:* $6512 (excluding resources awarded to replace EFC). 9% of all full-time undergraduates had no need and received non-need-based aid.

GIFT AID (NEED-BASED) ***Total amount:*** $1,082,354 (82% Federal, 16% state, 2% institutional). ***Receiving aid:*** *Freshmen:* 23% (94); *all full-time undergraduates:* 38% (314). ***Average award:*** Freshmen: $2691; Undergraduates: $3055. ***Scholarships, grants, and awards:*** Federal Pell, FSEOG, state, college/university gift aid from institutional funds.

GIFT AID (NON-NEED-BASED) ***Total amount:*** $266,231 (8% state, 67% institutional, 25% external sources). ***Receiving aid:*** *Freshmen:* 11% (47); *Undergraduates:* 9% (76). ***Scholarships, grants, and awards by category:*** *Academic Interests/Achievement:* general academic interests/achievements. *Creative Arts/Performance:* applied art and design, art/fine arts. *Special Characteristics:* local/state students, members of minority groups. ***Tuition waivers:*** Full or partial for employees or children of employees, senior citizens. ***ROTC:*** Army, Air Force cooperative.

LOANS ***Student loans:*** $2,539,216 (57% need-based, 43% non-need-based). ***Average need-based loan:*** Freshmen: $2434; Undergraduates: $3149. ***Parent loans:*** $501,251 (100% non-need-based). ***Programs:*** Federal Direct (Subsidized and Unsubsidized Stafford, PLUS), college/university.

WORK-STUDY ***Federal work-study:*** *Total amount:* $37,575; jobs available.

APPLYING for FINANCIAL AID ***Required financial aid form:*** FAFSA. ***Financial aid deadline (priority):*** 3/15.

CONTACT Ms. Sondra Williams, Director of Financial Aid, Ohio University–Chillicothe, 020 Chubb Hall, Athens, OH 45701, 740-593-4141 or toll-free 877-462-6824 (in-state). *Fax:* 740-593-0560. *E-mail:* willias1@ohio.edu

OHIO UNIVERSITY–EASTERN

St. Clairsville, OH

Tuition & fees (OH res): $2128 **Average undergraduate aid package: $5712**

ABOUT THE INSTITUTION State-supported, coed. Awards: associate and bachelor's degrees (also offers some graduate courses). 77 undergraduate majors. Federal methodology is used as a basis for awarding need-based institutional aid.

UNDERGRADUATE EXPENSES for 1999–2000 ***Application fee:*** $15. ***Tuition, state resident:*** full-time $2128; part-time $97 per credit hour. ***Tuition, nonresident:*** full-time $8276; part-time $250 per credit hour.

FRESHMAN FINANCIAL AID (Fall 1999, est.) 151 applied for aid; of those 83% were deemed to have need. 99% of freshmen with need received aid; of those 34% had need fully met. *Average percent of need met:* 71% (excluding resources awarded to replace EFC). *Average financial aid package:* $4817 (excluding resources awarded to replace EFC). 9% of all full-time freshmen had no need and received non-need-based aid.

UNDERGRADUATE FINANCIAL AID (Fall 1999, est.) 472 applied for aid; of those 88% were deemed to have need. 97% of undergraduates with need received aid; of those 27% had need fully met. *Average percent of need met:* 71% (excluding resources awarded to replace EFC). *Average financial aid package:* $5712 (excluding resources awarded to replace EFC). 8% of all full-time undergraduates had no need and received non-need-based aid.

GIFT AID (NEED-BASED) ***Total amount:*** $854,533 (81% Federal, 16% state, 3% institutional). ***Receiving aid:*** *Freshmen:* 24% (66); *all full-time undergraduates:* 43% (264). ***Average award:*** Freshmen: $3325; Undergraduates: $3068. ***Scholarships, grants, and awards:*** Federal Pell, FSEOG, state, private, college/university gift aid from institutional funds.

GIFT AID (NON-NEED-BASED) ***Total amount:*** $173,235 (6% state, 66% institutional, 28% external sources). ***Receiving aid:*** *Freshmen:* 18% (49); *Undergraduates:* 14% (84). ***Scholarships, grants, and awards by category:*** *Academic Interests/Achievement:* area/ethnic studies, biological sciences, business, communication, computer science, education, engineering/technologies, English, foreign languages, general academic interests/achievements, health fields, home economics, humanities, international studies, mathematics, military science, physical sciences, premedicine, social sciences. *Creative Arts/Performance:* applied art and design, art/fine arts, cinema/film/broadcasting, dance, debating, journalism/publications, music, performing arts, theater/drama. *Special Characteristics:* children of faculty/staff, members of minority groups.

LOANS ***Student loans:*** $1,697,046 (67% need-based, 33% non-need-based). ***Average need-based loan:*** Freshmen: $2322; Undergraduates: $3465. ***Parent loans:*** $379,503 (100% non-need-based). ***Programs:*** Federal Direct (Subsidized and Unsubsidized Stafford, PLUS), Perkins, college/university.

WORK-STUDY ***Federal work-study:*** *Total amount:* $44,625; jobs available.

APPLYING for FINANCIAL AID ***Required financial aid form:*** FAFSA. ***Financial aid deadline (priority):*** 3/15. ***Notification date:*** 4/1.

CONTACT Ms. Sondra Williams, Director of Financial Aid, Ohio University–Eastern, 020 Chubb Hall, Athens, OH 45701-2979, 740-593-4141 or toll-free 800-648-3331 (in-state). *Fax:* 740-593-0560. *E-mail:* willias1@ohio.edu

OHIO UNIVERSITY–LANCASTER

Lancaster, OH

Tuition & fees (OH res): $2128 **Average undergraduate aid package: $5632**

ABOUT THE INSTITUTION State-supported, coed. Awards: associate, bachelor's, and master's degrees. 20 undergraduate majors. Federal methodology is used as a basis for awarding need-based institutional aid.

UNDERGRADUATE EXPENSES for 1999–2000 ***Application fee:*** $15. ***Tuition, state resident:*** full-time $2128; part-time $97 per quarter hour. ***Tuition, nonresident:*** full-time $8276; part-time $250 per quarter hour.

FRESHMAN FINANCIAL AID (Fall 1999, est.) 224 applied for aid; of those 70% were deemed to have need. 95% of freshmen with need received aid; of those 30% had need fully met. *Average percent of need met:* 69% (excluding resources awarded to replace EFC). *Average financial aid package:* $5310 (excluding resources awarded to replace EFC). 14% of all full-time freshmen had no need and received non-need-based aid.

UNDERGRADUATE FINANCIAL AID (Fall 1999, est.) 513 applied for aid; of those 78% were deemed to have need. 96% of undergraduates with need received aid; of those 28% had need fully met. *Average percent of need met:* 71% (excluding resources awarded to replace EFC). *Average financial aid package:* $5632 (excluding resources awarded to replace EFC). 13% of all full-time undergraduates had no need and received non-need-based aid.

GIFT AID (NEED-BASED) ***Total amount:*** $786,413 (82% Federal, 16% state, 2% institutional). ***Receiving aid:*** *Freshmen:* 22% (93); *all full-time undergraduates:* 32% (237). ***Average award:*** Freshmen: $2834; Undergraduates: $2893. ***Scholarships, grants, and awards:*** Federal Pell, FSEOG, state, private, college/university gift aid from institutional funds.

GIFT AID (NON-NEED-BASED) ***Total amount:*** $303,202 (2% state, 74% institutional, 24% external sources). ***Receiving aid:*** *Freshmen:* 12% (50); *Undergraduates:* 11% (84). ***Scholarships, grants, and awards by category:*** *Academic Interests/Achievement:* area/ethnic studies, biological sciences, business, communication, computer science, education, engineering/technologies, English, foreign languages, general academic interests/achievements, health fields, home economics, humanities, international studies, mathematics, military science, physical sciences, premedicine, social sciences. *Creative Arts/Performance:* applied art and design, art/fine arts, cinema/film/broadcasting, dance, debating, journalism/publications, music, performing arts, theater/drama. *Special Characteristics:* children of faculty/staff, members of minority groups. ***ROTC:*** Army cooperative, Air Force cooperative.

LOANS ***Student loans:*** $2,012,454 (55% need-based, 45% non-need-based). ***Average need-based loan:*** Freshmen: $2446; Undergraduates: $3069. ***Parent loans:*** $451,215 (100% non-need-based). ***Programs:*** Federal Direct (Subsidized and Unsubsidized Stafford, PLUS), Perkins, college/university.

WORK-STUDY ***Federal work-study:*** *Total amount:* $33,638; jobs available.

ATHLETIC AWARDS *Total amount:* 458,559 (100% non-need-based).

APPLYING for FINANCIAL AID ***Required financial aid form:*** FAFSA. ***Financial aid deadline (priority):*** 3/15. ***Notification date:*** 4/1.

CONTACT Ms. Sondra Williams, Director of Financial Aid, Ohio University–Lancaster, 020 Chubb Hall, Athens, OH 45701-2979, 740-593-4141 or toll-free 888-446-4468. *Fax:* 740-593-0560. *E-mail:* willias1@ohio.edu

OHIO UNIVERSITY–ZANESVILLE

Zanesville, OH

Tuition & fees (OH res): $2128 **Average undergraduate aid package: $5737**

ABOUT THE INSTITUTION State-supported, coed. Awards: associate, bachelor's, and master's degrees (offers first 2 years of most bachelor's degree programs available at the main campus in Athens; also offers several bachelor's degree programs that can be completed at this campus; also offers some graduate courses). 9 undergraduate majors. Total enrollment: 1,222. Undergraduates: 1,178. Freshmen: 262. Federal methodology is used as a basis for awarding need-based institutional aid.

UNDERGRADUATE EXPENSES for 1999–2000 ***Application fee:*** $20. ***Tuition, state resident:*** full-time $2128; part-time $97 per quarter hour. ***Tuition, nonresident:*** full-time $8276; part-time $250 per quarter hour.

FRESHMAN FINANCIAL AID (Fall 1999, est.) 195 applied for aid; of those 83% were deemed to have need. 98% of freshmen with need received aid; of those 38% had need fully met. *Average percent of need met:* 73% (excluding resources awarded to replace EFC). *Average financial aid package:* $5217 (excluding resources awarded to replace EFC). 9% of all full-time freshmen had no need and received non-need-based aid.

UNDERGRADUATE FINANCIAL AID (Fall 1999, est.) 494 applied for aid; of those 86% were deemed to have need. 97% of undergraduates with need received aid; of those 34% had need fully met. *Average percent of need met:* 73% (excluding resources awarded to replace EFC). *Average financial aid package:* $5737 (excluding resources awarded to replace EFC). 8% of all full-time undergraduates had no need and received non-need-based aid.

GIFT AID (NEED-BASED) ***Total amount:*** $888,830 (79% Federal, 18% state, 3% institutional). ***Receiving aid:*** *Freshmen:* 27% (94); *all full-time undergraduates:* 37% (261). ***Average award:*** Freshmen: $2659; Undergraduates: $2906. ***Scholarships, grants, and awards:*** Federal Pell, FSEOG, state, private, college/university gift aid from institutional funds.

GIFT AID (NON-NEED-BASED) ***Total amount:*** $404,021 (4% state, 73% institutional, 23% external sources). ***Receiving aid:*** *Freshmen:* 22% (74); *Undergraduates:* 18% (127). ***Scholarships, grants, and awards by category:*** *Academic Interests/Achievement:* general academic interests/achievements. *Special Characteristics:* general special characteristics. ***Tuition waivers:*** Full or partial for employees or children of employees, senior citizens.

LOANS ***Student loans:*** $1,873,055 (62% need-based, 38% non-need-based). ***Average need-based loan:*** Freshmen: $2525; Undergraduates: $3164. ***Parent loans:*** $390,063 (100% non-need-based). ***Programs:*** college/university.

WORK-STUDY ***Federal work-study:*** *Total amount:* $27,065; jobs available.

APPLYING for FINANCIAL AID ***Required financial aid form:*** FAFSA. ***Financial aid deadline (priority):*** 4/1.

CONTACT Ms. Sondra Williams, Director of Financial Aid, Ohio University–Zanesville, 020 Chubb Hall, Athens, OH 45701, 740-593-4141. *Fax:* 740-593-0560. *E-mail:* willias1@ohio.edu

OHIO VALLEY COLLEGE

Parkersburg, WV

Tuition & fees: $7528 **Average undergraduate aid package: $8251**

ABOUT THE INSTITUTION Independent religious, coed. Awards: associate and bachelor's degrees. 19 undergraduate majors. Total enrollment: 407. Undergraduates: 407. Freshmen: 88. Federal methodology is used as a basis for awarding need-based institutional aid.

UNDERGRADUATE EXPENSES for 1999–2000 ***Application fee:*** $20. ***One-time required fee:*** $37. ***Comprehensive fee:*** $11,528 includes full-time tuition ($6860), mandatory fees ($668), and room and board ($4000). Full-time tuition and fees vary according to course load. Room and board charges vary according to board plan. ***Part-time tuition:*** $215 per credit hour. Part-time tuition and fees vary according to course load. ***Payment plan:*** installment.

FRESHMAN FINANCIAL AID (Fall 1998) 101 applied for aid; of those 86% were deemed to have need. 100% of freshmen with need received aid; of those 11% had need fully met. *Average percent of need met:* 70% (excluding resources awarded to replace EFC). *Average financial aid package:* $6613 (excluding resources awarded to replace EFC). 3% of all full-time freshmen had no need and received non-need-based aid.

UNDERGRADUATE FINANCIAL AID (Fall 1998) 380 applied for aid; of those 91% were deemed to have need. 100% of undergraduates with need received aid; of those 12% had need fully met. *Average percent of need met:* 70% (excluding resources awarded to replace EFC). *Average financial aid package:* $8251 (excluding resources awarded to replace EFC). 6% of all full-time undergraduates had no need and received non-need-based aid.

GIFT AID (NEED-BASED) ***Total amount:*** $514,001 (91% Federal, 9% state). ***Receiving aid:*** *Freshmen:* 64% (72); *all full-time undergraduates:* 49% (215). ***Average award:*** Freshmen: $3488; Undergraduates: $4301. ***Scholarships, grants, and awards:*** Federal Pell, FSEOG, state, private, college/university gift aid from institutional funds.

Ohio Valley College (continued)

GIFT AID (NON-NEED-BASED) ***Total amount:*** $361,714 (85% institutional, 15% external sources). ***Receiving aid:*** *Freshmen:* 49% (55); *Undergraduates:* 44% (190). ***Scholarships, grants, and awards by category:*** *Academic Interests/Achievement:* business, education, English, general academic interests/achievements, religion/biblical studies. *Creative Arts/Performance:* general creative arts/performance, music, performing arts. *Special Achievements/Activities:* general special achievements/activities, leadership. *Special Characteristics:* children of faculty/staff, general special characteristics, religious affiliation. ***Tuition waivers:*** Full or partial for employees or children of employees, senior citizens. ***ROTC:*** Air Force cooperative.

LOANS ***Student loans:*** $1,579,044 (100% need-based). 80% of past graduating class borrowed through all loan programs. Average indebtedness per student: $17,780. ***Average need-based loan:*** Freshmen: $3125; Undergraduates: $3950. ***Parent loans:*** $303,500 (100% non-need-based). ***Programs:*** FFEL (Subsidized and Unsubsidized Stafford, PLUS), Perkins.

WORK-STUDY ***Federal work-study:*** *Total amount:* $106,676; jobs available. ***State or other work-study/employment:*** *Total amount:* $28,242 (100% non-need-based). Part-time jobs available.

ATHLETIC AWARDS *Total amount:* 179,862 (100% non-need-based).

APPLYING for FINANCIAL AID ***Required financial aid form:*** FAFSA. ***Financial aid deadline (priority):*** 3/1. ***Notification date:*** Continuous beginning 4/1. Students must reply within 2 weeks of notification.

CONTACT Debbie S. Clark, Director of Financial Aid, Ohio Valley College, 4501 College Parkway, Parkersburg, WV 26101-8100, 304-485-7384 Ext. 124 or toll-free 800-678-6780 (out-of-state). *Fax:* 304-485-3106. *E-mail:* dsclark@ovc.edu

OHIO WESLEYAN UNIVERSITY

Delaware, OH

Tuition & fees: $20,940 **Average undergraduate aid package: $19,785**

ABOUT THE INSTITUTION Independent United Methodist, coed. Awards: bachelor's degrees. 63 undergraduate majors. Total enrollment: 1,930. Undergraduates: 1,930. Freshmen: 524. Federal methodology is used as a basis for awarding need-based institutional aid.

UNDERGRADUATE EXPENSES for 1999–2000 ***Application fee:*** $35. ***Comprehensive fee:*** $27,500 includes full-time tuition ($20,940) and room and board ($6560). ***College room only:*** $3330. Room and board charges vary according to board plan and location. ***Part-time tuition:*** $2280 per course. ***Payment plan:*** installment.

FRESHMAN FINANCIAL AID (Fall 1999) 362 applied for aid; of those 86% were deemed to have need. 100% of freshmen with need received aid; of those 42% had need fully met. *Average percent of need met:* 99% (excluding resources awarded to replace EFC). *Average financial aid package:* $19,922 (excluding resources awarded to replace EFC). 39% of all full-time freshmen had no need and received non-need-based aid.

UNDERGRADUATE FINANCIAL AID (Fall 1999) 1,700 applied for aid; of those 65% were deemed to have need. 100% of undergraduates with need received aid; of those 41% had need fully met. *Average percent of need met:* 98% (excluding resources awarded to replace EFC). *Average financial aid package:* $19,785 (excluding resources awarded to replace EFC). 40% of all full-time undergraduates had no need and received non-need-based aid.

GIFT AID (NEED-BASED) ***Total amount:*** $9,490,335 (11% Federal, 2% state, 87% institutional). ***Receiving aid:*** *Freshmen:* 48% (249); *all full-time undergraduates:* 49% (931). ***Average award:*** Freshmen: $7605; Undergraduates: $8306. ***Scholarships, grants, and awards:*** Federal Pell, FSEOG, state, private, college/university gift aid from institutional funds.

GIFT AID (NON-NEED-BASED) ***Total amount:*** $14,559,448 (8% state, 85% institutional, 7% external sources). ***Receiving aid:*** *Freshmen:* 58% (304); *Undergraduates:* 54% (1,020). ***Scholarships, grants, and awards by category:*** *Academic Interests/Achievement:* general academic interests/achievements, humanities, mathematics, physical sciences, premedicine. *Creative Arts/Performance:* art/fine arts, music, theater/drama. *Special Achievements/Activities:* community service, religious involvement. *Special Characteristics:* children and siblings of alumni, children of faculty/staff, international students, local/state students, members of minority groups, out-of-state students, relatives of clergy, religious affiliation. ***Tuition waivers:*** Full or partial for children of alumni, employees or children of employees, senior citizens. ***ROTC:*** Army cooperative.

LOANS ***Student loans:*** $6,549,236 (61% need-based, 39% non-need-based). 69% of past graduating class borrowed through all loan programs. Average indebtedness per student: $19,253. ***Average need-based loan:*** Freshmen: $4367; Undergraduates: $4716. ***Parent loans:*** $1,148,398 (100% non-need-based). ***Programs:*** Federal Direct (Subsidized and Unsubsidized Stafford, PLUS), Perkins, state, college/university, alternative loans.

WORK-STUDY ***Federal work-study:*** *Total amount:* $928,028; 751 jobs averaging $1236. ***State or other work-study/employment:*** *Total amount:* $66,000 (100% non-need-based). 47 part-time jobs averaging $1404.

APPLYING for FINANCIAL AID ***Required financial aid forms:*** FAFSA, institution's own form. ***Financial aid deadline (priority):*** 3/15. ***Notification date:*** Continuous. Students must reply within 2 weeks of notification.

CONTACT Mr. Gregory W. Matthews, Director of Financial Aid, Ohio Wesleyan University, 61 South Sandusky Street, Delaware, OH 43015, 740-368-3050 or toll-free 800-922-8953. *Fax:* 740-368-3066. *E-mail:* owfinaid@cc.owu.edu

OHR HAMEIR THEOLOGICAL SEMINARY

Peekskill, NY

CONTACT Financial Aid Office, Ohr Hameir Theological Seminary, Furnace Woods Road, Peekskill, NY 10566, 914-736-1500.

OHR SOMAYACH/JOSEPH TANENBAUM EDUCATIONAL CENTER

Monsey, NY

Tuition & fees: N/R **Average undergraduate aid package: N/A**

ABOUT THE INSTITUTION Independent Jewish, men only. 1 undergraduate major.

APPLYING for FINANCIAL AID ***Financial aid deadline (priority):*** 7/31. ***Notification date:*** Continuous.

CONTACT Financial Aid Office, Ohr Somayach/Joseph Tanenbaum Educational Center, PO Box 334244, Route 306, Monsey, NY 10952-0334, 914-425-1370.

OKLAHOMA BAPTIST UNIVERSITY

Shawnee, OK

Tuition & fees: $9440 **Average undergraduate aid package: N/A**

ABOUT THE INSTITUTION Independent Southern Baptist, coed. Awards: bachelor's and master's degrees. 100 undergraduate majors. Total enrollment: 2,123. Undergraduates: 2,098. Federal methodology is used as a basis for awarding need-based institutional aid.

UNDERGRADUATE EXPENSES for 2000–2001 ***Application fee:*** $25. ***Comprehensive fee:*** $12,857 includes full-time tuition ($8800), mandatory fees ($640), and room and board ($3417). ***College room only:*** $1600. Full-time tuition and fees vary according to course load. Room and board charges vary according to board plan and housing facility. ***Part-time tuition:*** $260 per credit hour. ***Part-time fees:*** $320 per year part-time. Part-time tuition and fees vary according to course load. ***Payment plan:*** installment.

GIFT AID (NEED-BASED) ***Scholarships, grants, and awards:*** Federal Pell, FSEOG, state.

GIFT AID (NON-NEED-BASED) ***Scholarships, grants, and awards by category:*** *Academic Interests/Achievement:* general academic interests/achievements, religion/biblical studies. *Creative Arts/Performance:* art/fine arts, music, performing arts. *Special Achievements/Activities:* leadership, religious involvement. *Special Characteristics:* children and siblings of alumni, children of faculty/staff, general special characteristics, local/state students, out-of-state students, relatives of clergy, religious affiliation. ***Tuition waivers:*** Full or partial for employees or children of employees, senior citizens. ***ROTC:*** Air Force cooperative.

LOANS ***Programs:*** FFEL (Subsidized and Unsubsidized Stafford, PLUS), Perkins.

WORK-STUDY ***State or other work-study/employment:*** Part-time jobs available.

APPLYING for FINANCIAL AID ***Required financial aid form:*** FAFSA. ***Financial aid deadline (priority):*** 3/1. ***Notification date:*** Continuous. Students must reply by 5/1.

CONTACT Student Financial Services, Oklahoma Baptist University, 500 West University, Shawnee, OK 74804, 405-878-2016 or toll-free 800-654-3285.

OKLAHOMA CHRISTIAN UNIVERSITY OF SCIENCE AND ARTS

Oklahoma City, OK

Tuition & fees: $9590 **Average undergraduate aid package: $8750**

ABOUT THE INSTITUTION Independent religious, coed. Awards: bachelor's and master's degrees. 58 undergraduate majors. Total enrollment: 1,734. Undergraduates: 1,701. Federal methodology is used as a basis for awarding need-based institutional aid.

UNDERGRADUATE EXPENSES for 1999–2000 ***Application fee:*** $25. ***Comprehensive fee:*** $13,690 includes full-time tuition ($8850), mandatory fees ($740), and room and board ($4100). ***Part-time tuition:*** $370 per semester hour. ***Part-time fees:*** $250 per term part-time. ***Payment plan:*** tuition prepayment.

FRESHMAN FINANCIAL AID (Fall 1999) 407 applied for aid; of those 60% were deemed to have need. 100% of freshmen with need received aid. *Average percent of need met:* 83% (excluding resources awarded to replace EFC). *Average financial aid package:* $9400 (excluding resources awarded to replace EFC).

UNDERGRADUATE FINANCIAL AID (Fall 1999) 1,594 applied for aid; of those 72% were deemed to have need. 100% of undergraduates with need received aid. *Average percent of need met:* 83% (excluding resources awarded to replace EFC). *Average financial aid package:* $8750 (excluding resources awarded to replace EFC).

GIFT AID (NEED-BASED) ***Total amount:*** $2,875,000 (44% Federal, 3% state, 31% institutional, 22% external sources). ***Receiving aid:*** *Freshmen:* 210; *all full-time undergraduates:* 840. ***Average award:*** Freshmen: $2650; Undergraduates: $2200. ***Scholarships, grants, and awards:*** Federal Pell, FSEOG, state, private, college/university gift aid from institutional funds.

GIFT AID (NON-NEED-BASED) ***Total amount:*** $3,740,000 (100% institutional). ***Receiving aid:*** *Freshmen:* 223; *Undergraduates:* 996. ***Scholarships, grants, and awards by category:*** *Academic Interests/Achievement:* business, communication, computer science, education, engineering/technologies, general academic interests/achievements, mathematics, physical sciences, premedicine, religion/biblical studies. *Creative Arts/Performance:* art/fine arts, journalism/publications, music, performing arts, theater/drama. *Special Achievements/Activities:* leadership, religious involvement. *Special Characteristics:* children and siblings of alumni, children of current students, children of educators, children of faculty/staff, general special characteristics, international students, parents of current students, siblings of current students, spouses of current students. ***Tuition waivers:*** Full or partial for employees or children of employees. ***ROTC:*** Army cooperative, Air Force cooperative.

LOANS ***Student loans:*** $4,732,000 (70% need-based, 30% non-need-based). 63% of past graduating class borrowed through all loan programs. Average indebtedness per student: $17,200. ***Average need-based loan:*** Freshmen: $3625; Undergraduates: $4250. ***Parent loans:*** $2,200,000 (100% non-need-based). ***Programs:*** FFEL (Subsidized and Unsubsidized Stafford, PLUS), Perkins.

WORK-STUDY ***Federal work-study:*** *Total amount:* $300,000; 230 jobs averaging $1500.

ATHLETIC AWARDS *Total amount:* 1,228,000 (100% non-need-based).

APPLYING for FINANCIAL AID ***Required financial aid forms:*** FAFSA, institution's own form. ***Financial aid deadline (priority):*** 3/15. ***Notification date:*** Continuous beginning 4/1. Students must reply within 4 weeks of notification.

CONTACT Andy Carpenter, Student Financial Aid Director, Oklahoma Christian University of Science and Arts, Box 11000, Oklahoma City, OK 73136-1100, 405-425-5190 or toll-free 800-877-5010 (in-state). *Fax:* 405-425-5197.

OKLAHOMA CITY UNIVERSITY

Oklahoma City, OK

Tuition & fees: $9558 **Average undergraduate aid package: $9956**

ABOUT THE INSTITUTION Independent United Methodist, coed. Awards: bachelor's, master's, and first professional degrees. 70 undergraduate majors. Total enrollment: 4,143. Undergraduates: 2,100. Freshmen: 346. Federal methodology is used as a basis for awarding need-based institutional aid.

UNDERGRADUATE EXPENSES for 1999–2000 ***Application fee:*** $20. ***Comprehensive fee:*** $18,358 includes full-time tuition ($9320), mandatory fees ($238), and room and board ($8800). ***College room only:*** $2920. Full-time tuition and fees vary according to program. Room and board charges vary according to board plan and housing facility. ***Part-time tuition:*** $315 per semester hour. ***Part-time fees:*** $2 per semester hour; $55 per term part-time. Part-time tuition and fees vary according to program. ***Payment plans:*** installment, deferred payment.

FRESHMAN FINANCIAL AID (Fall 1998) 298 applied for aid; of those 43% were deemed to have need. 100% of freshmen with need received aid. *Average financial aid package:* $9406 (excluding resources awarded to replace EFC).

UNDERGRADUATE FINANCIAL AID (Fall 1998) 1,220 applied for aid; of those 46% were deemed to have need. 100% of undergraduates with need received aid. *Average financial aid package:* $9956 (excluding resources awarded to replace EFC).

GIFT AID (NEED-BASED) ***Total amount:*** $1,719,370 (54% Federal, 10% state, 31% institutional, 5% external sources). ***Receiving aid:*** *Freshmen:* 36% (111); *all full-time undergraduates:* 28% (445). ***Average award:*** Freshmen: $2537; Undergraduates: $2942. ***Scholarships, grants, and awards:*** Federal Pell, FSEOG, state, private, college/university gift aid from institutional funds.

GIFT AID (NON-NEED-BASED) ***Total amount:*** $4,494,778 (95% institutional, 5% external sources). ***Receiving aid:*** *Freshmen:* 36% (113); *Undergraduates:* 23% (363). ***Scholarships, grants, and awards by category:*** *Academic Interests/Achievement:* business, communication, education, general academic interests/achievements, religion/biblical studies. *Creative Arts/Performance:* dance, music, performing arts. *Special Achievements/Activities:* cheerleading/drum major, general special achievements/activities, junior miss, leadership, religious involvement. *Special Characteristics:* children of faculty/staff, relatives of clergy. ***Tuition waivers:*** Full or partial for employees or children of employees. ***ROTC:*** Army cooperative, Air Force cooperative.

LOANS ***Student loans:*** $4,130,770 (56% need-based, 44% non-need-based). 52% of past graduating class borrowed through all loan programs. Average indebtedness per student: $17,563. ***Average need-based loan:*** Freshmen: $2963; Undergraduates: $3855. ***Parent loans:*** $862,253 (100% non-need-based). ***Programs:*** FFEL (Subsidized and Unsubsidized Stafford, PLUS), Perkins, college/university.

WORK-STUDY ***Federal work-study:*** *Total amount:* $387,099; 258 jobs averaging $1500. ***State or other work-study/employment:*** *Total amount:* $194,178 (100% non-need-based). 131 part-time jobs averaging $1406.

ATHLETIC AWARDS *Total amount:* 1,055,847 (100% non-need-based).

APPLYING for FINANCIAL AID ***Required financial aid forms:*** FAFSA, institution's own form. ***Financial aid deadline:*** Continuous. ***Notification date:*** 4/15.

CONTACT Financial Aid Office, Oklahoma City University, 2501 North Blackwelder, Oklahoma City, OK 73106-1402, 405-521-5211 or toll-free 800-633-7242 (in-state). *Fax:* 405-521-5466.

OKLAHOMA PANHANDLE STATE UNIVERSITY

Goodwell, OK

Tuition & fees (OK res): $1960 **Average undergraduate aid package: N/A**

ABOUT THE INSTITUTION State-supported, coed. Awards: associate and bachelor's degrees. 32 undergraduate majors. Total enrollment: 1,133. Undergraduates: 1,133. Freshmen: 220. Both federal and institutional methodology are used as a basis for awarding need-based institutional aid.

UNDERGRADUATE EXPENSES for 1999–2000 ***Tuition, state resident:*** full-time $1910; part-time $49 per credit hour. ***Tuition, nonresident:*** full-time $4130; part-time $133 per credit hour. ***Required fees:*** full-time $50; $12 per credit hour; $33 per term part-time. Full-time tuition and fees vary according to student level. Part-time tuition and fees vary according to course load and student level. ***College room and board:*** $2368; ***room only:*** $770. Room and board charges vary according to board plan and housing facility.

GIFT AID (NEED-BASED) ***Scholarships, grants, and awards:*** Federal Pell, FSEOG, state, private, college/university gift aid from institutional funds.

GIFT AID (NON-NEED-BASED) ***Scholarships, grants, and awards by category:*** *Academic Interests/Achievement:* agriculture, education, English, general academic interests/achievements, mathematics. *Creative Arts/Performance:* cinema/film/broadcasting, debating, music, theater/drama. *Special Achievements/Activities:* cheerleading/drum major, general special achievements/activities, rodeo. *Special Characteristics:* children of faculty/staff, general special characteristics, local/state students, out-of-state students, veterans, veterans' children. ***Tuition waivers:*** Full or partial for employees or children of employees.

LOANS ***Programs:*** FFEL (Subsidized and Unsubsidized Stafford, PLUS), Perkins.

WORK-STUDY Federal work-study jobs available. ***State or other work-study/employment:*** Part-time jobs available.

APPLYING for FINANCIAL AID ***Required financial aid form:*** FAFSA. ***Financial aid deadline (priority):*** 1/1. ***Notification date:*** Continuous.

CONTACT Ms. Mary Ellen Riley, Director of Financial Aid, Oklahoma Panhandle State University, PO Box 430, Goodwell, OK 73939-0430, 580-349-2611 Ext. 324 or toll-free 800-664-6778. *E-mail:* mriley@opsu.edu

OKLAHOMA STATE UNIVERSITY

Stillwater, OK

Tuition & fees (OK res): $2458 **Average undergraduate aid package: $7292**

ABOUT THE INSTITUTION State-supported, coed. Awards: bachelor's, master's, doctoral, and first professional degrees. 118 undergraduate majors. Total enrollment: 21,087. Undergraduates: 16,203. Freshmen: 2,929. Federal methodology is used as a basis for awarding need-based institutional aid.

UNDERGRADUATE EXPENSES for 1999–2000 ***Application fee:*** $25. ***Tuition, state resident:*** full-time $1830; part-time $61 per credit hour. ***Tuition, nonresident:*** full-time $5910; part-time $197 per credit hour. ***Required fees:*** full-time $628; $17 per credit hour; $53 per term part-time. Full-time tuition and fees vary according to course level, program, and reciprocity agreements. Part-time tuition and fees vary according to course level, course load, program, and reciprocity agreements. ***College room and board:*** $4536; ***room only:*** $2064. Room and board charges vary according to board plan and housing facility. ***Payment plans:*** installment, deferred payment.

FRESHMAN FINANCIAL AID (Fall 1998) 2054 applied for aid; of those 57% were deemed to have need. 98% of freshmen with need received aid; of those 26% had need fully met. *Average percent of need met:* 75% (excluding resources awarded to replace EFC). *Average financial aid package:* $6198 (excluding resources awarded to replace EFC). 37% of all full-time freshmen had no need and received non-need-based aid.

UNDERGRADUATE FINANCIAL AID (Fall 1998) 10,080 applied for aid; of those 67% were deemed to have need. 99% of undergraduates with need received aid; of those 36% had need fully met. *Average percent of need met:* 80% (excluding resources awarded to replace EFC). *Average financial aid package:* $7292 (excluding resources awarded to replace EFC). 26% of all full-time undergraduates had no need and received non-need-based aid.

GIFT AID (NEED-BASED) ***Total amount:*** $15,169,222 (62% Federal, 20% state, 11% institutional, 7% external sources). ***Receiving aid:*** *Freshmen:* 32% (800); *all full-time undergraduates:* 33% (4,675). ***Average award:*** Freshmen: $2637; Undergraduates: $2670. ***Scholarships, grants, and awards:*** Federal Pell, FSEOG, state, private, college/university gift aid from institutional funds.

GIFT AID (NON-NEED-BASED) ***Total amount:*** $5,217,146 (6% Federal, 25% state, 42% institutional, 27% external sources). ***Receiving aid:*** *Freshmen:* 33% (847); *Undergraduates:* 22% (3,044). ***Scholarships, grants, and awards by category:*** *Academic Interests/Achievement:* agriculture, architecture, area/ethnic studies, biological sciences, business, communication, computer science, education, engineering/technologies, English, foreign languages, general academic interests/achievements, home economics, humanities, international studies, mathematics, military science, physical sciences, premedicine, social sciences. *Creative Arts/Performance:* music. *Special Achievements/Activities:* cheerleading/drum major, community service, leadership. *Special Characteristics:* adult students, children and siblings of alumni, members of minority groups, out-of-state students. ***Tuition waivers:*** Full or partial for minority students, children of alumni. ***ROTC:*** Army, Air Force.

LOANS ***Student loans:*** $34,753,935 (84% need-based, 16% non-need-based). Average indebtedness per student: $14,113. ***Average need-based loan:*** Freshmen: $2471; Undergraduates: $3699. ***Parent loans:*** $7,987,722 (58% need-based, 42% non-need-based). ***Programs:*** Federal Direct (Subsidized and Unsubsidized Stafford, PLUS), Perkins, college/university.

WORK-STUDY ***Federal work-study:*** *Total amount:* $1,341,305; 760 jobs averaging $1400. ***State or other work-study/employment:*** *Total amount:* $6,141,909 (100% non-need-based). Part-time jobs available.

ATHLETIC AWARDS *Total amount:* 2,479,422 (38% need-based, 62% non-need-based).

APPLYING for FINANCIAL AID ***Required financial aid form:*** FAFSA. ***Financial aid deadline:*** Continuous. ***Notification date:*** Continuous beginning 3/15. Students must reply within 2 weeks of notification.

CONTACT Office of Student Financial Aid, Oklahoma State University, 101 Hanner Hall, Stillwater, OK 74078, 405-744-6604 or toll-free 800-233-5019 (in-state), 800-852-1255 (out-of-state). *Fax:* 405-744-5285. *E-mail:* finaid@okway.okstate.edu

OLD DOMINION UNIVERSITY

Norfolk, VA

Tuition & fees (VA res): $3796 **Average undergraduate aid package: $6550**

ABOUT THE INSTITUTION State-supported, coed. Awards: bachelor's, master's, and doctoral degrees and post-master's certificates. 43 undergraduate majors. Total enrollment: 18,873. Undergraduates: 13,065. Freshmen: 1,578. Federal methodology is used as a basis for awarding need-based institutional aid.

UNDERGRADUATE EXPENSES for 1999–2000 ***Application fee:*** $30. ***Tuition, state resident:*** full-time $2184; part-time $73 per semester hour. ***Tuition, nonresident:*** full-time $9774; part-time $326 per semester hour. ***Required fees:*** full-time $1612; $49 per semester hour. Full-time tuition and fees vary according to course level and location. Part-time tuition and fees vary according to course level and location. ***College room and board:*** $5114; ***room only:*** $3100. Room and board charges vary according to board plan and housing facility. ***Payment plans:*** installment, deferred payment.

FRESHMAN FINANCIAL AID (Fall 1999) 1352 applied for aid; of those 70% were deemed to have need. 99% of freshmen with need received aid; of those 40% had need fully met. *Average percent of need met:* 66% (excluding resources awarded to replace EFC). *Average financial aid pack-*

age: $6685 (excluding resources awarded to replace EFC). 19% of all full-time freshmen had no need and received non-need-based aid.

UNDERGRADUATE FINANCIAL AID (Fall 1999) 6,688 applied for aid; of those 74% were deemed to have need. 98% of undergraduates with need received aid; of those 41% had need fully met. *Average percent of need met:* 72% (excluding resources awarded to replace EFC). *Average financial aid package:* $6550 (excluding resources awarded to replace EFC). 14% of all full-time undergraduates had no need and received non-need-based aid.

GIFT AID (NEED-BASED) ***Total amount:*** $13,680,499 (49% Federal, 46% state, 4% institutional, 1% external sources). ***Receiving aid:*** *Freshmen:* 44% (686); *all full-time undergraduates:* 42% (3,560). ***Average award:*** Freshmen: $3662; Undergraduates: $3426. ***Scholarships, grants, and awards:*** Federal Pell, FSEOG, state, private, college/university gift aid from institutional funds.

GIFT AID (NON-NEED-BASED) ***Total amount:*** $3,628,541 (2% state, 75% institutional, 23% external sources). ***Receiving aid:*** *Freshmen:* 22% (338); *Undergraduates:* 10% (871). ***Scholarships, grants, and awards by category:*** *Academic Interests/Achievement:* 1,304 awards ($2,282,642 total): biological sciences, business, engineering/technologies, English, general academic interests/achievements, health fields, humanities, military science, physical sciences. *Creative Arts/Performance:* 48 awards ($33,552 total): art/fine arts, dance, music, performing arts, theater/drama. *Special Achievements/Activities:* 40 awards ($50,874 total): cheerleading/drum major, community service, leadership, memberships. *Special Characteristics:* 43 awards ($185,552 total): children of faculty/staff, handicapped students, international students, local/state students, members of minority groups, previous college experience, veterans' children. ***Tuition waivers:*** Full or partial for employees or children of employees, senior citizens. ***ROTC:*** Army, Naval.

LOANS ***Student loans:*** $27,534,189 (61% need-based, 39% non-need-based). 80% of past graduating class borrowed through all loan programs. Average indebtedness per student: $16,500. ***Average need-based loan:*** Freshmen: $2383; Undergraduates: $3521. ***Parent loans:*** $2,078,247 (100% non-need-based). ***Programs:*** Federal Direct (Subsidized and Unsubsidized Stafford, PLUS), Perkins.

WORK-STUDY ***Federal work-study:*** *Total amount:* $3,083,404; 1,474 jobs averaging $2092.

ATHLETIC AWARDS *Total amount:* 1,458,057 (100% non-need-based).

APPLYING for FINANCIAL AID ***Required financial aid form:*** FAFSA. ***Financial aid deadline (priority):*** 2/15. ***Notification date:*** Continuous beginning 4/1. Students must reply within 2 weeks of notification.

CONTACT Betty Diamond, Director of Student Financial Aid, Old Dominion University, 121 Rollins Hall, Norfolk, VA 23529-0052, 757-683-3689 or toll-free 800-348-7926. *Fax:* 757-683-3450. *E-mail:* bdiamond@odu.edu

OLIVET COLLEGE

Olivet, MI

Tuition & fees: $13,158 **Average undergraduate aid package: N/A**

ABOUT THE INSTITUTION Independent religious, coed. Awards: bachelor's and master's degrees. 40 undergraduate majors. Total enrollment: 918. Undergraduates: 870.

UNDERGRADUATE EXPENSES for 1999–2000 ***Application fee:*** $25. ***Comprehensive fee:*** $17,410 includes full-time tuition ($12,948), mandatory fees ($210), and room and board ($4252). ***College room only:*** $2264. Room and board charges vary according to board plan and housing facility. ***Part-time tuition:*** $460 per semester hour. ***Part-time fees:*** $105 per term part-time. Part-time tuition and fees vary according to course load. ***Payment plan:*** installment.

GIFT AID (NEED-BASED) ***Scholarships, grants, and awards:*** Federal Pell, FSEOG, state, private, college/university gift aid from institutional funds.

GIFT AID (NON-NEED-BASED) ***Scholarships, grants, and awards by category:*** *Academic Interests/Achievement:* general academic interests/achievements. *Creative Arts/Performance:* music. *Special Achievements/Activities:* community service, leadership. ***Tuition waivers:*** Full or partial for employees or children of employees.

LOANS ***Programs:*** Federal Direct (Subsidized and Unsubsidized Stafford, PLUS), Perkins, state.

WORK-STUDY Federal work-study jobs available. ***State or other work-study/employment:*** Part-time jobs available.

APPLYING for FINANCIAL AID ***Required financial aid form:*** FAFSA. ***Financial aid deadline:*** Continuous.

CONTACT Mr. Bernie McConnell, Director of Admissions, Olivet College, 320 South Main Street, Olivet, MI 49076-9701, 800-456-7189. *Fax:* 616-749-3821. *E-mail:* bmcconnell@olivetnet.edu

OLIVET NAZARENE UNIVERSITY

Bourbonnais, IL

Tuition & fees: $12,728 **Average undergraduate aid package: $12,323**

ABOUT THE INSTITUTION Independent religious, coed. Awards: bachelor's and master's degrees. 76 undergraduate majors. Total enrollment: 2,498. Undergraduates: 1,850. Freshmen: 411. Federal methodology is used as a basis for awarding need-based institutional aid.

UNDERGRADUATE EXPENSES for 2000–2001 ***Comprehensive fee:*** $17,424 includes full-time tuition ($11,928), mandatory fees ($800), and room and board ($4696). Full-time tuition and fees vary according to course load. Room and board charges vary according to board plan. ***Part-time tuition:*** $480 per hour. ***Part-time fees:*** $10 per term. Part-time tuition and fees vary according to course load. ***Payment plan:*** installment.

FRESHMAN FINANCIAL AID (Fall 1999) 370 applied for aid; of those 91% were deemed to have need. 99% of freshmen with need received aid; of those 24% had need fully met. *Average percent of need met:* 93% (excluding resources awarded to replace EFC). *Average financial aid package:* $13,179 (excluding resources awarded to replace EFC). 15% of all full-time freshmen had no need and received non-need-based aid.

UNDERGRADUATE FINANCIAL AID (Fall 1999) 1,359 applied for aid; of those 86% were deemed to have need. 100% of undergraduates with need received aid; of those 26% had need fully met. *Average percent of need met:* 92% (excluding resources awarded to replace EFC). *Average financial aid package:* $12,323 (excluding resources awarded to replace EFC). 21% of all full-time undergraduates had no need and received non-need-based aid.

GIFT AID (NEED-BASED) ***Total amount:*** $8,494,272 (14% Federal, 27% state, 59% institutional). ***Receiving aid:*** *Freshmen:* 48% (193); *all full-time undergraduates:* 45% (697). ***Average award:*** Freshmen: $4529; Undergraduates: $4870. ***Scholarships, grants, and awards:*** Federal Pell, FSEOG, state, private, college/university gift aid from institutional funds.

GIFT AID (NON-NEED-BASED) ***Total amount:*** $765,801 (7% Federal, 10% state, 83% external sources). ***Receiving aid:*** *Freshmen:* 75% (305); *Undergraduates:* 65% (1,017). ***Scholarships, grants, and awards by category:*** *Academic Interests/Achievement:* general academic interests/achievements. *Creative Arts/Performance:* art/fine arts, music. *Special Achievements/Activities:* religious involvement. *Special Characteristics:* children of current students, children of faculty/staff, general special characteristics, international students, parents of current students, relatives of clergy, religious affiliation, siblings of current students, spouses of current students. ***Tuition waivers:*** Full or partial for employees or children of employees. ***ROTC:*** Army cooperative.

LOANS ***Student loans:*** $5,361,216 (66% need-based, 34% non-need-based). 79% of past graduating class borrowed through all loan programs. Average indebtedness per student: $15,300. ***Average need-based loan:*** Freshmen: $3816; Undergraduates: $4037. ***Parent loans:*** $1,447,591 (100% non-need-based). ***Programs:*** FFEL (Subsidized and Unsubsidized Stafford, PLUS), Perkins.

WORK-STUDY ***Federal work-study:*** *Total amount:* $207,626; 410 jobs averaging $984. ***State or other work-study/employment:*** *Total amount:* $441,694 (100% non-need-based). Part-time jobs available.

ATHLETIC AWARDS *Total amount:* 1,012,873 (100% non-need-based).

APPLYING for FINANCIAL AID ***Required financial aid forms:*** FAFSA, institution's own form. ***Financial aid deadline (priority):*** 3/1. ***Notification date:*** Continuous.

Olivet Nazarene University (continued)

CONTACT Mr. Greg Bruner, Assistant Director of Financial Aid, Olivet Nazarene University, Box 6007, Bourbonnais, IL 60914, 815-939-5249 or toll-free 800-648-1463. *Fax:* 815-939-5074. *E-mail:* gbruner@olivet.edu

O'MORE COLLEGE OF DESIGN

Franklin, TN

Tuition & fees: $8505 **Average undergraduate aid package: N/A**

ABOUT THE INSTITUTION Independent, coed. Awards: bachelor's degrees. 4 undergraduate majors. Total enrollment: 145. Undergraduates: 145. Federal methodology is used as a basis for awarding need-based institutional aid.

UNDERGRADUATE EXPENSES for 1999–2000 ***Application fee:*** $25. ***Tuition:*** full-time $8500; part-time $375 per semester hour. ***Required fees:*** full-time $5; $5 per year part-time. ***Payment plans:*** installment, deferred payment.

GIFT AID (NEED-BASED) ***Scholarships, grants, and awards:*** Federal Pell, college/university gift aid from institutional funds.

GIFT AID (NON-NEED-BASED) ***Scholarships, grants, and awards by category:*** *Academic Interests/Achievement:* general academic interests/achievements.

LOANS ***Programs:*** FFEL (Subsidized and Unsubsidized Stafford, PLUS).

APPLYING for FINANCIAL AID ***Required financial aid forms:*** FAFSA, institution's own form. ***Financial aid deadline (priority):*** 5/1.

CONTACT Office of Financial Aid, O'More College of Design, 423 South Margin Street, Franklin, TN 37064-2816, 615-794-4254 Ext. 30.

ORAL ROBERTS UNIVERSITY

Tulsa, OK

Tuition & fees: $11,650 **Average undergraduate aid package: $11,612**

ABOUT THE INSTITUTION Independent interdenominational, coed. Awards: bachelor's, master's, and doctoral degrees. 66 undergraduate majors. Total enrollment: 3,552. Undergraduates: 3,064. Freshmen: 780. Federal methodology is used as a basis for awarding need-based institutional aid.

UNDERGRADUATE EXPENSES for 2000–2001 ***Application fee:*** $35. ***Comprehensive fee:*** $16,726 includes full-time tuition ($11,300), mandatory fees ($350), and room and board ($5076). Room and board charges vary according to board plan. ***Part-time tuition:*** $475 per credit hour. ***Part-time fees:*** $85 per term part-time. ***Payment plan:*** installment.

FRESHMAN FINANCIAL AID (Fall 1999, est.) 601 applied for aid; of those 89% were deemed to have need. 100% of freshmen with need received aid; of those 55% had need fully met. *Average percent of need met:* 100% (excluding resources awarded to replace EFC). *Average financial aid package:* $11,895 (excluding resources awarded to replace EFC). 24% of all full-time freshmen had no need and received non-need-based aid.

UNDERGRADUATE FINANCIAL AID (Fall 1999, est.) 2,107 applied for aid; of those 91% were deemed to have need. 100% of undergraduates with need received aid; of those 45% had need fully met. *Average percent of need met:* 92% (excluding resources awarded to replace EFC). *Average financial aid package:* $11,612 (excluding resources awarded to replace EFC). 23% of all full-time undergraduates had no need and received non-need-based aid.

GIFT AID (NEED-BASED) ***Total amount:*** $10,491,774 (26% Federal, 1% state, 67% institutional, 6% external sources). ***Receiving aid:*** *Freshmen:* 69% (518); *all full-time undergraduates:* 63% (1,790). ***Average award:*** Freshmen: $6930; Undergraduates: $6224. ***Scholarships, grants, and awards:*** Federal Pell, FSEOG, state, private, college/university gift aid from institutional funds.

GIFT AID (NON-NEED-BASED) ***Total amount:*** $3,749,155 (2% state, 91% institutional, 7% external sources). ***Receiving aid:*** *Freshmen:* 25% (188); *Undergraduates:* 26% (748). ***Scholarships, grants, and awards by category:*** *Academic Interests/Achievement:* 1,478 awards ($6,198,365 total): biological sciences, business, communication, education, engineering/technologies, general academic interests/achievements, health fields, religion/biblical studies. *Creative Arts/Performance:* 275 awards ($537,158 total): applied art and design, art/fine arts, cinema/film/broadcasting, journalism/publications, music. *Special Achievements/Activities:* 255 awards ($1,301,387 total): cheerleading/drum major, community service, general special achievements/activities, leadership, memberships, religious involvement. *Special Characteristics:* 1,412 awards ($2,235,131 total): children and siblings of alumni, children of faculty/staff, general special characteristics, international students, relatives of clergy, siblings of current students. ***Tuition waivers:*** Full or partial for children of alumni, employees or children of employees.

LOANS ***Student loans:*** $15,205,194 (71% need-based, 29% non-need-based). 79% of past graduating class borrowed through all loan programs. Average indebtedness per student: $25,223. ***Average need-based loan:*** Freshmen: $4933; Undergraduates: $5584. ***Parent loans:*** $4,669,785 (100% non-need-based). ***Programs:*** FFEL (Subsidized and Unsubsidized Stafford, PLUS), Perkins, state, college/university, alternative loans.

WORK-STUDY ***Federal work-study:*** *Total amount:* $503,067; 503 jobs averaging $1000. ***State or other work-study/employment:*** *Total amount:* $1,250,000 (100% non-need-based). 500 part-time jobs available.

ATHLETIC AWARDS *Total amount:* 2,052,137 (29% need-based, 71% non-need-based).

APPLYING for FINANCIAL AID ***Required financial aid form:*** FAFSA. ***Financial aid deadline (priority):*** 3/15. ***Notification date:*** Continuous. Students must reply within 3 weeks of notification.

CONTACT Stephen Thannickal, Director of Financial Aid, Oral Roberts University, PO Box 700540, Tulsa, OK 74170, 918-495-7088 or toll-free 800-678-8876. *Fax:* 918-495-6803. *E-mail:* finaid@oru.edu

OREGON COLLEGE OF ART AND CRAFT

Portland, OR

Tuition & fees: $11,710 **Average undergraduate aid package: $10,286**

ABOUT THE INSTITUTION Independent, coed. Awards: bachelor's degrees and post-bachelor's certificates. 1 undergraduate major. Total enrollment: 95. Undergraduates: 95. Freshmen: 2. Federal methodology is used as a basis for awarding need-based institutional aid.

UNDERGRADUATE EXPENSES for 2000–2001 ***Application fee:*** $30. ***Tuition:*** full-time $11,520; part-time $500 per credit hour. ***Required fees:*** full-time $190; $95 per term part-time. Full-time tuition and fees vary according to course load. ***Payment plan:*** installment.

FRESHMAN FINANCIAL AID (Fall 1999, est.) 2 applied for aid; of those 100% were deemed to have need. 100% of freshmen with need received aid. *Average percent of need met:* 51% (excluding resources awarded to replace EFC). *Average financial aid package:* $8792 (excluding resources awarded to replace EFC).

UNDERGRADUATE FINANCIAL AID (Fall 1999, est.) 27 applied for aid; of those 100% were deemed to have need. 100% of undergraduates with need received aid; of those 4% had need fully met. *Average percent of need met:* 45% (excluding resources awarded to replace EFC). *Average financial aid package:* $10,286 (excluding resources awarded to replace EFC).

GIFT AID (NEED-BASED) ***Total amount:*** $58,022 (67% Federal, 24% state, 9% institutional). ***Receiving aid:*** *Freshmen:* 100% (2); *all full-time undergraduates:* 49% (21). ***Average award:*** Freshmen: $2168; Undergraduates: $4024. ***Scholarships, grants, and awards:*** Federal Pell, FSEOG, state, college/university gift aid from institutional funds.

GIFT AID (NON-NEED-BASED) ***Total amount:*** $14,500 (69% institutional, 31% external sources). ***Receiving aid:*** *Undergraduates:* 9% (4). ***Scholarships, grants, and awards by category:*** *Creative Arts/Performance:* 2 awards ($10,000 total): art/fine arts.

LOANS ***Student loans:*** $355,125 (100% need-based). 69% of past graduating class borrowed through all loan programs. Average indebtedness per student: $17,207. ***Average need-based loan:*** Freshmen: $2625; Undergraduates: $9389. ***Programs:*** FFEL (Subsidized and Unsubsidized Stafford, PLUS).

WORK-STUDY ***Federal work-study:*** *Total amount:* $10,000; 5 jobs averaging $2000. ***State or other work-study/employment:*** *Total amount:* $52,000 (100% need-based). Part-time jobs available.

APPLYING for FINANCIAL AID ***Required financial aid form:*** FAFSA. ***Financial aid deadline (priority):*** 2/1. ***Notification date:*** Continuous beginning 3/15. Students must reply within 2 weeks of notification.

CONTACT Mr. Paul Krull, Director of Financial Aid, Oregon College of Art and Craft, 8245 Southwest Barnes Road, Portland, OR 97225, 503-297-5544 Ext. 131 or toll-free 800-390-0632. *Fax:* 503-297-3155.

OREGON HEALTH SCIENCES UNIVERSITY

Portland, OR

Tuition & fees (OR res): $5747 **Average undergraduate aid package: $9640**

ABOUT THE INSTITUTION State-related, coed. Awards: bachelor's, master's, doctoral, and first professional degrees and post-bachelor's, post-master's, and first-professional certificates. 5 undergraduate majors. Total enrollment: 1,849. Undergraduates: 657. Federal methodology is used as a basis for awarding need-based institutional aid.

UNDERGRADUATE EXPENSES for 1999–2000 ***Application fee:*** $60. ***Tuition, state resident:*** full-time $4647; part-time $109 per credit hour. ***Tuition, nonresident:*** full-time $11,873; part-time $272 per credit hour. ***Required fees:*** full-time $1100; $176 per term part-time. Full-time tuition and fees vary according to location, program, and student level. ***College room and board: room only:*** $2070. ***Payment plan:*** deferred payment.

UNDERGRADUATE FINANCIAL AID (Fall 1999, est.) 403 applied for aid; of those 96% were deemed to have need. 99% of undergraduates with need received aid; of those 1% had need fully met. *Average percent of need met:* 53% (excluding resources awarded to replace EFC). *Average financial aid package:* $9640 (excluding resources awarded to replace EFC). 4% of all full-time undergraduates had no need and received non-need-based aid.

GIFT AID (NEED-BASED) ***Total amount:*** $698,772 (71% Federal, 16% state, 12% institutional, 1% external sources). ***Receiving aid:*** *All full-time undergraduates:* 34% (163). ***Average award:*** Undergraduates: $3360. ***Scholarships, grants, and awards:*** Federal Pell, FSEOG, state, private, college/university gift aid from institutional funds.

GIFT AID (NON-NEED-BASED) ***Total amount:*** $403,809 (3% institutional, 97% external sources). ***Receiving aid:*** *Undergraduates:* 18% (85). ***Scholarships, grants, and awards by category:*** *Academic Interests/Achievement:* health fields. *Special Characteristics:* ethnic background. ***Tuition waivers:*** Full or partial for employees or children of employees. ***ROTC:*** Army cooperative.

LOANS ***Student loans:*** $5,666,899 (49% need-based, 51% non-need-based). 68% of past graduating class borrowed through all loan programs. ***Average need-based loan:*** Undergraduates: $6839. ***Parent loans:*** $322,523 (100% non-need-based). ***Programs:*** Federal Direct (Subsidized and Unsubsidized Stafford, PLUS), Perkins, Federal Nursing, state, college/university.

WORK-STUDY ***Federal work-study:*** *Total amount:* $116,667; 58 jobs averaging $2000.

APPLYING for FINANCIAL AID ***Required financial aid forms:*** FAFSA, institution's own form. ***Financial aid deadline (priority):*** 3/1. ***Notification date:*** 6/1. Students must reply within 4 weeks of notification.

CONTACT Ms. Rebecca L. Cady, Associate Director of Financial Aid, Oregon Health Sciences University, 3181 SW Sam Jackson Park Road, L-109, Portland, OR 97201-3098, 503-494-7800. *Fax:* 503-494-4629. *E-mail:* finaid@ohsu.edu

OREGON INSTITUTE OF TECHNOLOGY

Klamath Falls, OR

Tuition & fees (OR res): $3378 **Average undergraduate aid package: N/A**

ABOUT THE INSTITUTION State-supported, coed. Awards: associate, bachelor's, and master's degrees. 22 undergraduate majors. Total enrollment: 2,795. Undergraduates: 2,792. Freshmen: 324. Federal methodology is used as a basis for awarding need-based institutional aid.

UNDERGRADUATE EXPENSES for 1999–2000 ***Application fee:*** $50. ***One-time required fee:*** $25. ***Tuition, state resident:*** full-time $2592; part-time $72 per credit. ***Tuition, nonresident:*** full-time $10,650; part-time $72 per credit. ***Required fees:*** full-time $786; $97 per term part-time. Full-time tuition and fees vary according to course load. Part-time tuition and fees vary according to course load. ***College room and board:*** $4866. Room and board charges vary according to board plan. ***Payment plans:*** installment, deferred payment.

GIFT AID (NEED-BASED) ***Total amount:*** $3,258,941 (70% Federal, 26% state, 4% external sources). ***Scholarships, grants, and awards:*** Federal Pell, FSEOG, state, private, college/university gift aid from institutional funds.

GIFT AID (NON-NEED-BASED) ***Total amount:*** $419,141 (39% institutional, 61% external sources). ***Scholarships, grants, and awards by category:*** *Academic Interests/Achievement:* general academic interests/achievements. *Special Characteristics:* ethnic background, members of minority groups. ***Tuition waivers:*** Full or partial for employees or children of employees, senior citizens. ***ROTC:*** Army.

LOANS ***Student loans:*** $7,221,540 (100% need-based). Average indebtedness per student: $17,000. ***Parent loans:*** $555,313 (100% non-need-based). ***Programs:*** FFEL (Subsidized and Unsubsidized Stafford, PLUS), Perkins, college/university.

WORK-STUDY ***Federal work-study:*** *Total amount:* $239,507; 235 jobs averaging $1020.

ATHLETIC AWARDS *Total amount:* 109,253 (52% need-based, 48% non-need-based).

APPLYING for FINANCIAL AID ***Required financial aid form:*** FAFSA. ***Financial aid deadline:*** 3/1. ***Notification date:*** 4/15. Students must reply within 3 weeks of notification.

CONTACT Judy Saling, Financial Aid Director, Oregon Institute of Technology, 3201 Campus Drive, Klamath Falls, OR 97601-8801, 541-885-1280 or toll-free 800-422-2017 (in-state), 800-343-6653 (out-of-state). *Fax:* 541-885-1024.

OREGON STATE UNIVERSITY

Corvallis, OR

Tuition & fees (OR res): $3549 **Average undergraduate aid package: N/A**

ABOUT THE INSTITUTION State-supported, coed. Awards: bachelor's, master's, doctoral, and first professional degrees. 121 undergraduate majors. Total enrollment: 16,091. Undergraduates: 12,783. Freshmen: 2,846. Federal methodology is used as a basis for awarding need-based institutional aid.

UNDERGRADUATE EXPENSES for 1999–2000 ***Application fee:*** $50. ***One-time required fee:*** $50. ***Tuition, state resident:*** full-time $3549; part-time $75 per credit. ***Tuition, nonresident:*** full-time $12,393; part-time $321 per credit. Part-time tuition and fees vary according to course load. ***College room and board:*** $5394. Room and board charges vary according to board plan and housing facility. ***Payment plan:*** deferred payment.

GIFT AID (NEED-BASED) ***Total amount:*** $14,852,548 (52% Federal, 20% state, 28% institutional). ***Scholarships, grants, and awards:*** Federal Pell, FSEOG, state, private, college/university gift aid from institutional funds.

GIFT AID (NON-NEED-BASED) ***Total amount:*** $1,656,104 (4% state, 96% institutional). ***Scholarships, grants, and awards by category:*** *Academic Interests/Achievement:* general academic interests/achievements. *Creative Arts/Performance:* music. *Special Achievements/Activities:* general special achievements/activities. *Special Characteristics:* general special characteristics. ***ROTC:*** Army, Naval, Air Force.

LOANS ***Student loans:*** $47,404,981 (80% need-based, 20% non-need-based). ***Parent loans:*** $12,528,265 (29% need-based, 71% non-need-based). ***Programs:*** Federal Direct (Subsidized and Unsubsidized Stafford, PLUS), Perkins, college/university.

WORK-STUDY ***Federal work-study:*** *Total amount:* $2,689,520; jobs available.

Oregon State University (continued)

APPLYING for FINANCIAL AID ***Required financial aid form:*** FAFSA. ***Financial aid deadline (priority):*** 2/1. ***Notification date:*** 4/1. Students must reply within 4 weeks of notification.

CONTACT Financial Aid Office, Oregon State University, 218 Kerr Administration Building, Corvallis, OR 97331-2120, 541-737-2241 or toll-free 800-291-4192 (in-state).

OTIS COLLEGE OF ART AND DESIGN

Los Angeles, CA

Tuition & fees: $19,294 **Average undergraduate aid package: $6900**

ABOUT THE INSTITUTION Independent, coed. Awards: bachelor's and master's degrees. 10 undergraduate majors. Total enrollment: 834. Undergraduates: 811. Freshmen: 121. Institutional methodology is used as a basis for awarding need-based institutional aid.

UNDERGRADUATE EXPENSES for 2000–2001 ***Application fee:*** $50. ***Tuition:*** full-time $18,894; part-time $630 per credit. ***Required fees:*** full-time $400. ***Payment plan:*** installment.

FRESHMAN FINANCIAL AID (Fall 1999, est.) 160 applied for aid; of those 94% were deemed to have need. 100% of freshmen with need received aid. *Average percent of need met:* 72% (excluding resources awarded to replace EFC). *Average financial aid package:* $6800 (excluding resources awarded to replace EFC). 7% of all full-time freshmen had no need and received non-need-based aid.

UNDERGRADUATE FINANCIAL AID (Fall 1999, est.) 633 applied for aid; of those 96% were deemed to have need. 100% of undergraduates with need received aid. *Average percent of need met:* 72% (excluding resources awarded to replace EFC). *Average financial aid package:* $6900 (excluding resources awarded to replace EFC). 3% of all full-time undergraduates had no need and received non-need-based aid.

GIFT AID (NEED-BASED) ***Total amount:*** $4,900,000 (18% Federal, 22% state, 60% institutional). ***Receiving aid:*** *Freshmen:* 68% (139); *all full-time undergraduates:* 73% (595). ***Average award:*** Freshmen: $4400; Undergraduates: $4800. ***Scholarships, grants, and awards:*** Federal Pell, FSEOG, state, private, college/university gift aid from institutional funds.

GIFT AID (NON-NEED-BASED) ***Total amount:*** $40,000 (100% institutional). ***Receiving aid:*** *Freshmen:* 5% (11); *Undergraduates:* 2% (19). ***Scholarships, grants, and awards by category:*** *Creative Arts/Performance:* applied art and design, art/fine arts. ***Tuition waivers:*** Full or partial for employees or children of employees.

LOANS ***Student loans:*** $1,438,000 (90% need-based, 10% non-need-based). 78% of past graduating class borrowed through all loan programs. ***Average need-based loan:*** Freshmen: $2000; Undergraduates: $4000. ***Parent loans:*** $500,000 (90% need-based, 10% non-need-based). ***Programs:*** FFEL (Subsidized and Unsubsidized Stafford, PLUS), Perkins.

WORK-STUDY ***Federal work-study:*** *Total amount:* $130,000; 120 jobs averaging $1000. ***State or other work-study/employment:*** *Total amount:* $30,000 (83% need-based, 17% non-need-based). 10 part-time jobs averaging $1000.

APPLYING for FINANCIAL AID ***Required financial aid forms:*** FAFSA, institution's own form. ***Financial aid deadline (priority):*** 2/15. ***Notification date:*** Continuous beginning 3/15. Students must reply within 2 weeks of notification.

CONTACT Ms. Robin Bailey-Chen, Director of Financial Aid, Otis College of Art and Design, 9045 Lincoln Boulevard, Los Angeles, CA 90045-9785, 310-665-6880 or toll-free 800-527-OTIS. *E-mail:* otisaid@otisart.edu

OTTAWA UNIVERSITY

Ottawa, KS

Tuition & fees: $10,250 **Average undergraduate aid package: $5974**

ABOUT THE INSTITUTION Independent American Baptist, coed. Awards: bachelor's and master's degrees (also offers adult, international and on-line education programs with significant enrollment not reflected in profile). 19 undergraduate majors. Total enrollment: 474. Undergraduates: 474. Freshmen: 136. Federal methodology is used as a basis for awarding need-based institutional aid.

UNDERGRADUATE EXPENSES for 1999–2000 ***Application fee:*** $15. ***Comprehensive fee:*** $14,470 includes full-time tuition ($10,040), mandatory fees ($210), and room and board ($4220). ***College room only:*** $2000. Full-time tuition and fees vary according to course load. Room and board charges vary according to board plan and housing facility. ***Part-time tuition:*** $335 per credit hour. ***Part-time fees:*** $55 per term part-time. Part-time tuition and fees vary according to course load. ***Payment plans:*** installment, deferred payment.

FRESHMAN FINANCIAL AID (Fall 1999, est.) 127 applied for aid; of those 99% were deemed to have need. 94% of freshmen with need received aid. *Average percent of need met:* 80% (excluding resources awarded to replace EFC). *Average financial aid package:* $5735 (excluding resources awarded to replace EFC).

UNDERGRADUATE FINANCIAL AID (Fall 1999, est.) 462 applied for aid; of those 100% were deemed to have need. 96% of undergraduates with need received aid. *Average percent of need met:* 80% (excluding resources awarded to replace EFC). *Average financial aid package:* $5974 (excluding resources awarded to replace EFC).

GIFT AID (NEED-BASED) ***Total amount:*** $833,955 (65% Federal, 35% state). ***Receiving aid:*** *Freshmen:* 51% (67); *all full-time undergraduates:* 49% (233). ***Average award:*** Freshmen: $3015; Undergraduates: $2918. ***Scholarships, grants, and awards:*** Federal Pell, FSEOG, state, private, college/university gift aid from institutional funds.

GIFT AID (NON-NEED-BASED) ***Total amount:*** $1,707,834 (96% institutional, 4% external sources). ***Scholarships, grants, and awards by category:*** *Academic Interests/Achievement:* biological sciences, business, communication, education, English, foreign languages, general academic interests/achievements, health fields, humanities, international studies, mathematics, physical sciences, premedicine, religion/biblical studies, social sciences. *Creative Arts/Performance:* art/fine arts, music, theater/drama. *Special Achievements/Activities:* cheerleading/drum major, general special achievements/activities, junior miss, religious involvement. *Special Characteristics:* children and siblings of alumni, children of faculty/staff, local/state students, religious affiliation. ***Tuition waivers:*** Full or partial for employees or children of employees, senior citizens.

LOANS ***Student loans:*** $1,288,118 (86% need-based, 14% non-need-based). 70% of past graduating class borrowed through all loan programs. Average indebtedness per student: $14,000. ***Average need-based loan:*** Undergraduates: $3949. ***Parent loans:*** $98,756 (100% non-need-based). ***Programs:*** FFEL (Subsidized and Unsubsidized Stafford, PLUS), Perkins.

WORK-STUDY ***Federal work-study:*** *Total amount:* $169,834; 179 jobs averaging $949. ***State or other work-study/employment:*** *Total amount:* $74,897 (100% non-need-based). 82 part-time jobs averaging $913.

ATHLETIC AWARDS *Total amount:* 414,419 (100% non-need-based).

APPLYING for FINANCIAL AID ***Required financial aid forms:*** FAFSA, institution's own form. ***Financial aid deadline (priority):*** 3/15. ***Notification date:*** Continuous. Students must reply within 4 weeks of notification.

CONTACT Mr. Mike Weatherred, Associate Director of Financial Aid, Ottawa University, 1001 South Cedar, Box 3, Ottawa, KS 66067-3399, 785-242-5200 Ext. 5460 or toll-free 800-755-5200. *E-mail:* finaid@ottawa.edu

OTTERBEIN COLLEGE

Westerville, OH

Tuition & fees: $16,260 **Average undergraduate aid package: N/A**

ABOUT THE INSTITUTION Independent United Methodist, coed. Awards: bachelor's and master's degrees. 63 undergraduate majors. Total enrollment: 3,001. Undergraduates: 2,587. Freshmen: 518.

UNDERGRADUATE EXPENSES for 1999–2000 ***Application fee:*** $20. ***Comprehensive fee:*** $21,381 includes full-time tuition ($16,260) and room and board ($5121). ***College room only:*** $2262. Room and board charges vary according to housing facility. ***Part-time tuition:*** $195 per credit hour. ***Payment plan:*** installment.

GIFT AID (NEED-BASED) ***Scholarships, grants, and awards:*** Federal Pell, FSEOG, state, private, college/university gift aid from institutional funds.

GIFT AID (NON-NEED-BASED) ***Scholarships, grants, and awards by category:*** *Academic Interests/Achievement:* general academic interests/achievements. *Creative Arts/Performance:* art/fine arts, music, theater/drama. *Special Achievements/Activities:* community service, leadership. *Special Characteristics:* children and siblings of alumni, children of faculty/staff, general special characteristics, international students, members of minority groups, previous college experience, relatives of clergy, siblings of current students. ***Tuition waivers:*** Full or partial for employees or children of employees. ***ROTC:*** Army cooperative, Air Force cooperative.

LOANS ***Programs:*** FFEL (Subsidized and Unsubsidized Stafford, PLUS), Perkins, Federal Nursing, college/university.

WORK-STUDY Federal work-study jobs available.

APPLYING for FINANCIAL AID ***Required financial aid form:*** FAFSA. ***Financial aid deadline (priority):*** 4/1. ***Notification date:*** Continuous.

CONTACT Mr. Thomas V. Yarnell, Director of Financial Aid, Otterbein College, One Otterbein College, Westerville, OH 43081-2006, 614-823-1502 or toll-free 800-488-8144. *Fax:* 614-823-1200.

OUACHITA BAPTIST UNIVERSITY

Arkadelphia, AR

Tuition & fees: $9010 **Average undergraduate aid package: $10,614**

ABOUT THE INSTITUTION Independent Baptist, coed. Awards: associate and bachelor's degrees. 47 undergraduate majors. Total enrollment: 1,638. Undergraduates: 1,638. Freshmen: 448. Federal methodology is used as a basis for awarding need-based institutional aid.

UNDERGRADUATE EXPENSES for 1999–2000 ***Application fee:*** $25. ***Comprehensive fee:*** $12,460 includes full-time tuition ($8850), mandatory fees ($160), and room and board ($3450). Room and board charges vary according to board plan and housing facility. ***Part-time tuition:*** $260 per semester hour. ***Payment plan:*** installment.

FRESHMAN FINANCIAL AID (Fall 1999, est.) 434 applied for aid; of those 56% were deemed to have need. 92% of freshmen with need received aid; of those 25% had need fully met. *Average percent of need met:* 80% (excluding resources awarded to replace EFC). *Average financial aid package:* $10,152 (excluding resources awarded to replace EFC). 45% of all full-time freshmen had no need and received non-need-based aid.

UNDERGRADUATE FINANCIAL AID (Fall 1999, est.) 1,148 applied for aid; of those 71% were deemed to have need. 93% of undergraduates with need received aid; of those 25% had need fully met. *Average percent of need met:* 75% (excluding resources awarded to replace EFC). *Average financial aid package:* $10,614 (excluding resources awarded to replace EFC). 38% of all full-time undergraduates had no need and received non-need-based aid.

GIFT AID (NEED-BASED) ***Total amount:*** $4,626,573 (18% Federal, 15% state, 58% institutional, 9% external sources). ***Receiving aid:*** *Freshmen:* 50% (224); *all full-time undergraduates:* 48% (741). ***Average award:*** Freshmen: $8636; Undergraduates: $7839. ***Scholarships, grants, and awards:*** Federal Pell, FSEOG, state, private, college/university gift aid from institutional funds.

GIFT AID (NON-NEED-BASED) ***Total amount:*** $2,199,356 (18% state, 71% institutional, 11% external sources). ***Receiving aid:*** *Freshmen:* 38% (169); *Undergraduates:* 44% (675). ***Scholarships, grants, and awards by category:*** *Academic Interests/Achievement:* 373 awards ($560,000 total): area/ethnic studies, biological sciences, business, communication, computer science, education, engineering/technologies, English, foreign languages, general academic interests/achievements, health fields, home economics, humanities, international studies, mathematics, physical sciences, premedicine, religion/biblical studies, social sciences. *Creative Arts/Performance:* 167 awards ($500,992 total): art/fine arts, journalism/publications, music, performing arts, theater/drama. *Special Achievements/Activities:* 808 awards ($2,425,630 total): community service, general special achievements/activities, leadership, religious involvement. *Special Characteristics:* 238 awards ($1,187,852 total): children of faculty/staff, international students, relatives of clergy, religious affiliation. ***Tuition waivers:*** Full or partial for employees or children of employees. ***ROTC:*** Army cooperative.

LOANS ***Student loans:*** $2,881,020 (60% need-based, 40% non-need-based). Average indebtedness per student: $13,865. ***Average need-based loan:*** Freshmen: $2175; Undergraduates: $2699. ***Parent loans:*** $448,837 (64% need-based, 36% non-need-based). ***Programs:*** FFEL (Subsidized and Unsubsidized Stafford, PLUS), Perkins, college/university.

WORK-STUDY ***Federal work-study:*** *Total amount:* $714,447; 476 jobs averaging $1500. ***State or other work-study/employment:*** *Total amount:* $463,722 (100% non-need-based). 331 part-time jobs averaging $1400.

ATHLETIC AWARDS *Total amount:* 1,043,911 (64% need-based, 36% non-need-based).

APPLYING for FINANCIAL AID ***Required financial aid forms:*** FAFSA, institution's own form. ***Financial aid deadline:*** 6/1 (priority: 2/15). ***Notification date:*** Continuous.

CONTACT Mrs. Susan Hurst, Director of Financial Aid, Ouachita Baptist University, Box 3774, Arkadelphia, AR 71998-0001, 870-245-5570 or toll-free 800-342-5628 (in-state). *Fax:* 870-245-5318. *E-mail:* hursts@alpha.obu.edu

OUR LADY OF HOLY CROSS COLLEGE

New Orleans, LA

Tuition & fees: $5950 **Average undergraduate aid package: N/A**

ABOUT THE INSTITUTION Independent Roman Catholic, coed. Awards: associate, bachelor's, and master's degrees and post-bachelor's certificates. 22 undergraduate majors. Total enrollment: 1,243. Undergraduates: 1,086. Freshmen: 146. Federal methodology is used as a basis for awarding need-based institutional aid.

UNDERGRADUATE EXPENSES for 1999–2000 ***Application fee:*** $15. ***Tuition:*** full-time $5700; part-time $190 per semester hour. ***Required fees:*** full-time $250; $125 per term part-time. ***Payment plan:*** installment.

GIFT AID (NEED-BASED) ***Total amount:*** $1,091,754 (100% Federal). ***Scholarships, grants, and awards:*** Federal Pell, FSEOG, state, private, college/university gift aid from institutional funds, Federal Nursing.

GIFT AID (NON-NEED-BASED) ***Total amount:*** $142,829 (45% state, 47% institutional, 8% external sources). ***Scholarships, grants, and awards by category:*** *Academic Interests/Achievement:* 36 awards ($77,893 total): general academic interests/achievements. *Special Characteristics:* 73 awards ($175,736 total): children of faculty/staff, general special characteristics, relatives of clergy, religious affiliation. ***Tuition waivers:*** Full or partial for employees or children of employees. ***ROTC:*** Army cooperative, Naval cooperative, Air Force cooperative.

LOANS ***Student loans:*** $3,896,737 (64% need-based, 36% non-need-based). 70% of past graduating class borrowed through all loan programs. Average indebtedness per student: $18,500. ***Parent loans:*** $93,950 (100% non-need-based). ***Programs:*** FFEL (Subsidized and Unsubsidized Stafford, PLUS).

WORK-STUDY ***Federal work-study:*** *Total amount:* $53,811; 31 jobs averaging $1736.

APPLYING for FINANCIAL AID ***Required financial aid forms:*** FAFSA, institution's own form, Federal Stafford Loan application and information sheet. ***Financial aid deadline (priority):*** 4/15. ***Notification date:*** 5/15. Students must reply within 2 weeks of notification.

CONTACT Mrs. Johnell S. Armer, Acting Director of Financial Aid, Our Lady of Holy Cross College, 4123 Woodland Drive, New Orleans, LA 70131-7399, 504-394-7744 or toll-free 800-259-7744 Ext. 175. *Fax:* 504-391-2421.

OUR LADY OF THE LAKE UNIVERSITY OF SAN ANTONIO

San Antonio, TX

Tuition & fees: $11,408 **Average undergraduate aid package: $12,060**

Our Lady of the Lake University of San Antonio (continued)

ABOUT THE INSTITUTION Independent Roman Catholic, coed. Awards: bachelor's, master's, and doctoral degrees. 38 undergraduate majors. Total enrollment: 3,564. Undergraduates: 2,330. Freshmen: 308. Federal methodology is used as a basis for awarding need-based institutional aid.

UNDERGRADUATE EXPENSES for 1999–2000 ***Application fee:*** $25. ***Comprehensive fee:*** $15,760 includes full-time tuition ($11,150), mandatory fees ($258), and room and board ($4352). ***College room only:*** $2412. Room and board charges vary according to board plan and housing facility. ***Part-time tuition:*** $362 per credit hour. ***Part-time fees:*** $4 per credit hour; $38 per term part-time. ***Payment plan:*** installment.

FRESHMAN FINANCIAL AID (Fall 1999, est.) 306 applied for aid; of those 94% were deemed to have need. 100% of freshmen with need received aid. *Average financial aid package:* $12,467 (excluding resources awarded to replace EFC). 4% of all full-time freshmen had no need and received non-need-based aid.

UNDERGRADUATE FINANCIAL AID (Fall 1999, est.) 1,250 applied for aid; of those 96% were deemed to have need. 100% of undergraduates with need received aid. *Average financial aid package:* $12,060 (excluding resources awarded to replace EFC). 5% of all full-time undergraduates had no need and received non-need-based aid.

GIFT AID (NEED-BASED) ***Total amount:*** $4,885,722 (47% Federal, 48% state, 5% institutional). ***Receiving aid:*** *Freshmen:* 83% (256); *all full-time undergraduates:* 76% (1,024). ***Average award:*** Freshmen: $4889; Undergraduates: $3735. ***Scholarships, grants, and awards:*** Federal Pell, FSEOG, state, private, college/university gift aid from institutional funds.

GIFT AID (NON-NEED-BASED) ***Total amount:*** $4,224,995 (94% institutional, 6% external sources). ***Receiving aid:*** *Freshmen:* 92% (284); *Undergraduates:* 80% (1,077). ***Scholarships, grants, and awards by category:*** *Academic Interests/Achievement:* general academic interests/achievements. *Creative Arts/Performance:* art/fine arts, music. *Special Characteristics:* children of faculty/staff. ***Tuition waivers:*** Full or partial for employees or children of employees. ***ROTC:*** Army cooperative, Air Force cooperative.

LOANS ***Student loans:*** $7,927,600 (63% need-based, 37% non-need-based). 84% of past graduating class borrowed through all loan programs. Average indebtedness per student: $16,649. ***Average need-based loan:*** Freshmen: $2815; Undergraduates: $3607. ***Parent loans:*** $670,380 (100% non-need-based). ***Programs:*** FFEL (Subsidized and Unsubsidized Stafford, PLUS), Perkins, state, alternative loans.

WORK-STUDY ***Federal work-study:*** *Total amount:* $640,922; jobs available. ***State or other work-study/employment:*** *Total amount:* $324,750 (100% need-based). Part-time jobs available.

APPLYING for FINANCIAL AID ***Required financial aid form:*** FAFSA. ***Financial aid deadline:*** Continuous. ***Notification date:*** Continuous beginning 2/15. Students must reply within 3 weeks of notification.

CONTACT Ms. Terri McKinney, Director of Financial Aid, Our Lady of the Lake University of San Antonio, 411 Southwest 24th Street, San Antonio, TX 78207-4689, 210-434-6711 Ext. 320 or toll-free 800-436-6558. *Fax:* 210-431-3958. *E-mail:* mckit@lake.ollusa.edu

OZARK CHRISTIAN COLLEGE

Joplin, MO

Tuition & fees: $5325 **Average undergraduate aid package: N/A**

ABOUT THE INSTITUTION Independent Christian, coed. Awards: associate and bachelor's degrees. 7 undergraduate majors. Total enrollment: 697. Undergraduates: 697. Federal methodology is used as a basis for awarding need-based institutional aid.

UNDERGRADUATE EXPENSES for 2000–2001 ***Application fee:*** $30. ***Comprehensive fee:*** $8805 includes full-time tuition ($4640), mandatory fees ($685), and room and board ($3480). ***College room only:*** $1590. Room and board charges vary according to board plan. ***Part-time tuition:*** $145 per credit. ***Payment plans:*** installment, deferred payment.

GIFT AID (NEED-BASED) ***Total amount:*** $566,119 (89% Federal, 11% institutional). ***Scholarships, grants, and awards:*** Federal Pell, FSEOG, private, college/university gift aid from institutional funds.

GIFT AID (NON-NEED-BASED) ***Total amount:*** $766,927 (57% institutional, 43% external sources). ***Scholarships, grants, and awards by category:*** *Academic Interests/Achievement:* education, general academic interests/achievements, religion/biblical studies. *Creative Arts/Performance:* music, theater/drama. *Special Achievements/Activities:* religious involvement. *Special Characteristics:* children of faculty/staff, international students, religious affiliation, spouses of current students. ***Tuition waivers:*** Full or partial for employees or children of employees, senior citizens.

LOANS ***Student loans:*** $787,933 (100% need-based). ***Parent loans:*** $71,730 (100% need-based). ***Programs:*** FFEL (Subsidized and Unsubsidized Stafford, PLUS), college/university.

WORK-STUDY ***Federal work-study:*** *Total amount:* $33,445; 32 jobs averaging $1045.

APPLYING for FINANCIAL AID ***Required financial aid forms:*** FAFSA, institution's own form. ***Financial aid deadline:*** 4/1. ***Notification date:*** Continuous. Students must reply within 6 weeks of notification.

CONTACT Kristen Peterson, Application Processor, Ozark Christian College, 1111 North Main Street, Joplin, MO 64801-4804, 417-624-2518 Ext. 2017 or toll-free 800-299-4622. *Fax:* 417-624-0090. *E-mail:* finaid@occ.edu

PACE UNIVERSITY, NEW YORK CITY CAMPUS

New York, NY

ABOUT THE INSTITUTION Independent, coed. Awards: associate, bachelor's, master's, and doctoral degrees and post-bachelor's and post-master's certificates. 60 undergraduate majors. Total enrollment: 7,971. Undergraduates: 5,869. Freshmen: 1,137.

GIFT AID (NEED-BASED) ***Scholarships, grants, and awards:*** Federal Pell, FSEOG, state, private, college/university gift aid from institutional funds.

GIFT AID (NON-NEED-BASED) ***Scholarships, grants, and awards by category:*** *Academic Interests/Achievement:* business, education, English, foreign languages, general academic interests/achievements, health fields, social sciences. *Creative Arts/Performance:* debating. *Special Achievements/Activities:* community service, general special achievements/activities, leadership.

LOANS ***Programs:*** Federal Direct (Subsidized and Unsubsidized Stafford, PLUS), Perkins, Federal Nursing.

WORK-STUDY Federal work-study jobs available.

APPLYING for FINANCIAL AID ***Required financial aid forms:*** FAFSA, state aid form.

CONTACT Ms. Regina K. Robinson, University Director of Financial Aid, Pace University, New York City Campus, 1 Pace Plaza, New York, NY 10038, 212-346-1300 or toll-free 800-874-7223. *Fax:* 212-346-1750. *E-mail:* rrobinson@pace.edu

PACE UNIVERSITY, PLEASANTVILLE/BRIARCLIFF CAMPUS

Pleasantville, NY

CONTACT Financial Aid Office, Pace University, Pleasantville/Briarcliff Campus, 861 Bedford Road, Pleasantville, NY 10570, 914-773-3200 or toll-free 800-874-7223.

PACIFIC LUTHERAN UNIVERSITY

Tacoma, WA

Tuition & fees: $16,224 **Average undergraduate aid package: $14,990**

ABOUT THE INSTITUTION Independent religious, coed. Awards: bachelor's and master's degrees. 63 undergraduate majors. Total enrollment: 3,602. Undergraduates: 3,302. Freshmen: 568. Federal methodology is used as a basis for awarding need-based institutional aid.

UNDERGRADUATE EXPENSES for 1999–2000 ***Application fee:*** $35. ***Comprehensive fee:*** $21,262 includes full-time tuition ($16,224) and

room and board ($5038). ***College room only:*** $2472. Room and board charges vary according to board plan. ***Part-time tuition:*** $507 per semester hour. ***Payment plan:*** installment.

FRESHMAN FINANCIAL AID (Fall 1999, est.) 494 applied for aid; of those 84% were deemed to have need. 98% of freshmen with need received aid; of those 43% had need fully met. *Average percent of need met:* 92% (excluding resources awarded to replace EFC). *Average financial aid package:* $14,649 (excluding resources awarded to replace EFC). 15% of all full-time freshmen had no need and received non-need-based aid.

UNDERGRADUATE FINANCIAL AID (Fall 1999, est.) 2,355 applied for aid; of those 88% were deemed to have need. 98% of undergraduates with need received aid; of those 35% had need fully met. *Average percent of need met:* 90% (excluding resources awarded to replace EFC). *Average financial aid package:* $14,990 (excluding resources awarded to replace EFC). 17% of all full-time undergraduates had no need and received non-need-based aid.

GIFT AID (NEED-BASED) ***Total amount:*** $12,899,127 (15% Federal, 12% state, 68% institutional, 5% external sources). ***Receiving aid:*** *Freshmen:* 67% (379); *all full-time undergraduates:* 65% (1,947). ***Average award:*** Freshmen: $6754; Undergraduates: $6972. ***Scholarships, grants, and awards:*** Federal Pell, FSEOG, state, private, college/university gift aid from institutional funds, Federal Nursing.

GIFT AID (NON-NEED-BASED) ***Total amount:*** $9,346,429 (1% Federal, 95% institutional, 4% external sources). ***Receiving aid:*** *Freshmen:* 50% (279); *Undergraduates:* 29% (861). ***Scholarships, grants, and awards by category:*** *Academic Interests/Achievement:* 1,193 awards ($5,022,856 total): general academic interests/achievements. *Special Achievements/Activities:* 73 awards ($100,000 total): leadership. *Special Characteristics:* 555 awards ($1,547,121 total): children and siblings of alumni, children of educators, children of faculty/staff, international students, previous college experience, relatives of clergy. ***Tuition waivers:*** Full or partial for employees or children of employees, senior citizens. ***ROTC:*** Army.

LOANS ***Student loans:*** $14,364,943 (86% need-based, 14% non-need-based). 83% of past graduating class borrowed through all loan programs. Average indebtedness per student: $19,267. ***Average need-based loan:*** Freshmen: $3650; Undergraduates: $5871. ***Parent loans:*** $2,160,371 (16% need-based, 84% non-need-based). ***Programs:*** FFEL (Subsidized and Unsubsidized Stafford, PLUS), Perkins, Federal Nursing, state, college/university.

WORK-STUDY ***Federal work-study:*** *Total amount:* $2,635,960; 1,124 jobs averaging $2345. ***State or other work-study/employment:*** *Total amount:* $2,703,613 (33% need-based, 67% non-need-based). 900 part-time jobs averaging $3004.

APPLYING for FINANCIAL AID ***Required financial aid form:*** FAFSA. ***Financial aid deadline (priority):*** 3/1. ***Notification date:*** 4/7. Students must reply by 5/1 or within 4 weeks of notification.

CONTACT Ms. Joan Riley, Associate Director, Systems, Pacific Lutheran University, Tacoma, WA 98447, 253-535-7168 or toll-free 800-274-6758. *Fax:* 253-535-5136. *E-mail:* rileyjo@plu.edu

PACIFIC NORTHWEST COLLEGE OF ART

Portland, OR

Tuition & fees: $13,200 **Average undergraduate aid package: $9895**

ABOUT THE INSTITUTION Independent, coed. Awards: bachelor's degrees. 9 undergraduate majors. Total enrollment: 317. Undergraduates: 317. Freshmen: 39. Federal methodology is used as a basis for awarding need-based institutional aid.

UNDERGRADUATE EXPENSES for 2000–2001 ***Application fee:*** $30. ***One-time required fee:*** $5. ***Tuition:*** full-time $12,420; part-time $535 per semester hour. ***Required fees:*** full-time $780; $12 per term part-time. ***Payment plan:*** installment.

FRESHMAN FINANCIAL AID (Fall 1999, est.) 42 applied for aid; of those 93% were deemed to have need. 100% of freshmen with need received aid. *Average financial aid package:* $9856 (excluding resources awarded to replace EFC).

UNDERGRADUATE FINANCIAL AID (Fall 1999, est.) 204 applied for aid; of those 88% were deemed to have need. 100% of undergraduates with need received aid. *Average financial aid package:* $9895 (excluding resources awarded to replace EFC). 2% of all full-time undergraduates had no need and received non-need-based aid.

GIFT AID (NEED-BASED) ***Total amount:*** $753,470 (38% Federal, 17% state, 45% institutional). ***Receiving aid:*** *Freshmen:* 93% (39); *all full-time undergraduates:* 68% (175). ***Average award:*** Freshmen: $3180; Undergraduates: $3792. ***Scholarships, grants, and awards:*** Federal Pell, FSEOG, state, private, college/university gift aid from institutional funds.

GIFT AID (NON-NEED-BASED) ***Total amount:*** $91,472 (99% institutional, 1% external sources). ***Receiving aid:*** *Freshmen:* 2% (1); *Undergraduates:* 3% (9). ***Scholarships, grants, and awards by category:*** *Creative Arts/Performance:* art/fine arts. ***Tuition waivers:*** Full or partial for employees or children of employees.

LOANS ***Student loans:*** $1,128,231 (57% need-based, 43% non-need-based). ***Average need-based loan:*** Freshmen: $2625; Undergraduates: $4241. ***Parent loans:*** $215,392 (90% need-based, 10% non-need-based). ***Programs:*** FFEL (Subsidized and Unsubsidized Stafford, PLUS), college/university, Sallie Mae Signature Loans.

WORK-STUDY ***Federal work-study:*** *Total amount:* $27,667; 23 jobs averaging $1200. ***State or other work-study/employment:*** *Total amount:* $25,000 (100% need-based). 21 part-time jobs averaging $1200.

APPLYING for FINANCIAL AID ***Required financial aid form:*** FAFSA. ***Financial aid deadline (priority):*** 3/1. ***Notification date:*** Continuous beginning 3/15. Students must reply by 5/1 or within 2 weeks of notification.

CONTACT Ms. Regina Broich, Assistant Director of Financial Aid, Pacific Northwest College of Art, 1241 Northwest Johnson Street, Portland, OR 97209, 503-821-8976 or toll-free 800-818-PNCA. *Fax:* 503-821-8978. *E-mail:* regina@pnca.edu

PACIFIC OAKS COLLEGE

Pasadena, CA

Tuition & fees: $12,060 **Average undergraduate aid package: N/A**

ABOUT THE INSTITUTION Independent, coed, primarily women. Awards: bachelor's and master's degrees and post-master's certificates. 7 undergraduate majors. Total enrollment: 833. Undergraduates: 253. Both federal and institutional methodology are used as a basis for awarding need-based institutional aid.

UNDERGRADUATE EXPENSES for 1999–2000 ***Application fee:*** $55. ***Tuition:*** full-time $12,000; part-time $500 per unit. ***Required fees:*** full-time $60; $30 per term part-time. Full-time tuition and fees vary according to program. ***Payment plan:*** installment.

GIFT AID (NEED-BASED) ***Total amount:*** $349,503 (27% Federal, 48% state, 21% institutional, 4% external sources). ***Scholarships, grants, and awards:*** Federal Pell, FSEOG, state, private, college/university gift aid from institutional funds.

GIFT AID (NON-NEED-BASED) ***Tuition waivers:*** Full or partial for employees or children of employees.

LOANS ***Student loans:*** $1,235,176 (65% need-based, 35% non-need-based). 65% of past graduating class borrowed through all loan programs. Average indebtedness per student: $20,000. ***Parent loans:*** $13,585 (100% need-based). ***Programs:*** FFEL (Subsidized and Unsubsidized Stafford, PLUS), Perkins.

WORK-STUDY ***Federal work-study:*** *Total amount:* $15,255; jobs available.

APPLYING for FINANCIAL AID ***Required financial aid forms:*** FAFSA, institution's own form, state aid form, financial aid transcript (for transfers). ***Financial aid deadline (priority):*** 4/15. ***Notification date:*** Continuous. Students must reply within 4 weeks of notification.

CONTACT Heather Vaughan, Financial Aid Office Technician, Pacific Oaks College, 5 Westmoreland Place, Pasadena, CA 91103, 626-397-1350 or toll-free 800-684-0900. *Fax:* 626-577-6144. *E-mail:* financial@pacificoaks.edu

PACIFIC UNION COLLEGE

Angwin, CA

Tuition & fees: $14,475 **Average undergraduate aid package: $12,498**

ABOUT THE INSTITUTION Independent Seventh-day Adventist, coed. Awards: associate, bachelor's, and master's degrees. 88 undergraduate majors. Total enrollment: 1,625. Undergraduates: 1,623. Freshmen: 378. Both federal and institutional methodology are used as a basis for awarding need-based institutional aid.

UNDERGRADUATE EXPENSES for 1999–2000 ***Application fee:*** $30. ***Comprehensive fee:*** $18,900 includes full-time tuition ($14,475) and room and board ($4425). ***College room only:*** $2655. ***Part-time tuition:*** $418 per credit. ***Payment plans:*** guaranteed tuition, installment, deferred payment.

FRESHMAN FINANCIAL AID (Fall 1999, est.) 356 applied for aid; of those 98% were deemed to have need. 100% of freshmen with need received aid; of those 25% had need fully met. *Average percent of need met:* 72% (excluding resources awarded to replace EFC). *Average financial aid package:* $11,840 (excluding resources awarded to replace EFC). 3% of all full-time freshmen had no need and received non-need-based aid.

UNDERGRADUATE FINANCIAL AID (Fall 1999, est.) 1,194 applied for aid; of those 99% were deemed to have need. 100% of undergraduates with need received aid; of those 28% had need fully met. *Average percent of need met:* 76% (excluding resources awarded to replace EFC). *Average financial aid package:* $12,498 (excluding resources awarded to replace EFC). 17% of all full-time undergraduates had no need and received non-need-based aid.

GIFT AID (NEED-BASED) ***Total amount:*** $8,251,893 (21% Federal, 28% state, 49% institutional, 2% external sources). ***Receiving aid:*** *Freshmen:* 95% (349); *all full-time undergraduates:* 77% (1,107). ***Average award:*** Freshmen: $8523; Undergraduates: $6942. ***Scholarships, grants, and awards:*** Federal Pell, FSEOG, state, private, college/university gift aid from institutional funds.

GIFT AID (NON-NEED-BASED) ***Total amount:*** $3,319,702 (98% institutional, 2% external sources). ***Receiving aid:*** *Freshmen:* 2% (8); *Undergraduates:* 1% (21). ***Scholarships, grants, and awards by category:*** *Academic Interests/Achievement:* general academic interests/achievements. *Special Achievements/Activities:* general special achievements/activities, leadership, religious involvement. *Special Characteristics:* general special characteristics, international students, members of minority groups. ***Tuition waivers:*** Full or partial for employees or children of employees, senior citizens.

LOANS ***Student loans:*** $6,831,618 (100% need-based). Average indebtedness per student: $11,870. ***Average need-based loan:*** Freshmen: $3311; Undergraduates: $5556. ***Parent loans:*** $274,632 (100% need-based). ***Programs:*** FFEL (Subsidized and Unsubsidized Stafford, PLUS), Perkins, state, college/university.

WORK-STUDY Federal work-study jobs available.

APPLYING for FINANCIAL AID ***Required financial aid forms:*** FAFSA, institution's own form, CSS Financial Aid PROFILE, state aid form. ***Financial aid deadline (priority):*** 3/2. ***Notification date:*** Continuous beginning 5/1. Students must reply within 2 weeks of notification.

CONTACT Glen Bobst Jr., Director of Student Financial Services, Pacific Union College, Student Financial Services, One Angwin Avenue, Angwin, CA 94508, 707-965-7200 or toll-free 800-862-7080. *Fax:* 707-965-7615. *E-mail:* student_finance@puc.edu

PACIFIC UNIVERSITY

Forest Grove, OR

Tuition & fees: $17,800 **Average undergraduate aid package: $15,832**

ABOUT THE INSTITUTION Independent, coed. Awards: bachelor's, master's, doctoral, and first professional degrees. 48 undergraduate majors. Total enrollment: 2,064. Undergraduates: 1,072. Freshmen: 292. Federal methodology is used as a basis for awarding need-based institutional aid.

UNDERGRADUATE EXPENSES for 2000–2001 (est.) ***Application fee:*** $30. ***One-time required fee:*** $750. ***Comprehensive fee:*** $22,703 includes full-time tuition ($17,300), mandatory fees ($500), and room and board ($4903). ***College room only:*** $2360. Full-time tuition and fees vary according to program. Room and board charges vary according to board plan and housing facility. ***Part-time tuition:*** $577 per semester hour. Part-time tuition and fees vary according to course load and program. ***Payment plans:*** installment, deferred payment.

FRESHMAN FINANCIAL AID (Fall 1999, est.) 258 applied for aid; of those 92% were deemed to have need. 100% of freshmen with need received aid; of those 34% had need fully met. *Average percent of need met:* 95% (excluding resources awarded to replace EFC). *Average financial aid package:* $15,957 (excluding resources awarded to replace EFC). 15% of all full-time freshmen had no need and received non-need-based aid.

UNDERGRADUATE FINANCIAL AID (Fall 1999, est.) 782 applied for aid; of those 97% were deemed to have need. 100% of undergraduates with need received aid; of those 34% had need fully met. *Average percent of need met:* 94% (excluding resources awarded to replace EFC). *Average financial aid package:* $15,832 (excluding resources awarded to replace EFC). 14% of all full-time undergraduates had no need and received non-need-based aid.

GIFT AID (NEED-BASED) ***Total amount:*** $7,343,604 (10% Federal, 4% state, 80% institutional, 6% external sources). ***Receiving aid:*** *Freshmen:* 80% (235); *all full-time undergraduates:* 76% (755). ***Average award:*** Freshmen: $10,934; Undergraduates: $9698. ***Scholarships, grants, and awards:*** Federal Pell, FSEOG, state, private, college/university gift aid from institutional funds.

GIFT AID (NON-NEED-BASED) ***Total amount:*** $1,123,952 (1% state, 92% institutional, 7% external sources). ***Receiving aid:*** *Freshmen:* 11% (31); *Undergraduates:* 7% (74). ***Scholarships, grants, and awards by category:*** *Academic Interests/Achievement:* 614 awards ($4,224,125 total): general academic interests/achievements. *Creative Arts/Performance:* 47 awards ($85,900 total): debating, music, theater/drama. *Special Characteristics:* 33 awards ($466,180 total): children and siblings of alumni, children of faculty/staff, international students, relatives of clergy. ***Tuition waivers:*** Full or partial for employees or children of employees. ***ROTC:*** Army cooperative, Air Force cooperative.

LOANS ***Student loans:*** $4,922,563 (74% need-based, 26% non-need-based). 90% of past graduating class borrowed through all loan programs. Average indebtedness per student: $18,500. ***Average need-based loan:*** Freshmen: $3903; Undergraduates: $4745. ***Parent loans:*** $547,892 (29% need-based, 71% non-need-based). ***Programs:*** Federal Direct (Subsidized and Unsubsidized Stafford, PLUS), Perkins, CitiAssist Loans.

WORK-STUDY ***Federal work-study:*** *Total amount:* $994,246; 598 jobs averaging $1663. ***State or other work-study/employment:*** *Total amount:* $259,657 (28% need-based, 72% non-need-based). 159 part-time jobs averaging $1633.

APPLYING for FINANCIAL AID ***Required financial aid form:*** FAFSA. ***Financial aid deadline:*** Continuous. ***Notification date:*** Continuous beginning 3/10. Students must reply by 5/1 or within 2 weeks of notification.

CONTACT Mr. G. Michael Johnson, Director of Financial Aid, Pacific University, 2043 College Way, Forest Grove, OR 97116-1797, 503-359-2222 or toll-free 800-677-6712. *Fax:* 503-359-2950. *E-mail:* johnsong@pacificu.edu

PAIER COLLEGE OF ART, INC.

Hamden, CT

Tuition & fees: $10,835 **Average undergraduate aid package: $5741**

ABOUT THE INSTITUTION Proprietary, coed. Awards: associate and bachelor's degrees. 8 undergraduate majors. Total enrollment: 276. Undergraduates: 276. Freshmen: 63. Federal methodology is used as a basis for awarding need-based institutional aid.

UNDERGRADUATE EXPENSES for 1999–2000 ***Application fee:*** $25. ***Tuition:*** full-time $10,500; part-time $335 per semester hour. ***Required fees:*** full-time $335; $33 per term part-time. Full-time tuition and fees vary according to course load, degree level, and program. Part-time tuition and fees vary according to course load, degree level, and program. ***Payment plan:*** installment.

FRESHMAN FINANCIAL AID (Fall 1999) 25 applied for aid; of those 76% were deemed to have need. 100% of freshmen with need received aid. *Average percent of need met:* 58% (excluding resources awarded to replace EFC). *Average financial aid package:* $4892 (excluding resources awarded to replace EFC). 9% of all full-time freshmen had no need and received non-need-based aid.

UNDERGRADUATE FINANCIAL AID (Fall 1999) 90 applied for aid; of those 89% were deemed to have need. 98% of undergraduates with need received aid. *Average percent of need met:* 63% (excluding resources awarded to replace EFC). *Average financial aid package:* $5741 (excluding resources awarded to replace EFC). 5% of all full-time undergraduates had no need and received non-need-based aid.

GIFT AID (NEED-BASED) ***Total amount:*** $315,158 (20% Federal, 78% state, 2% institutional). ***Receiving aid:*** *Freshmen:* 40% (18); *all full-time undergraduates:* 49% (77). ***Average award:*** Freshmen: $2830; Undergraduates: $2889. ***Scholarships, grants, and awards:*** Federal Pell, FSEOG, state, private, college/university gift aid from institutional funds, Connecticut Independent College Student Grants.

GIFT AID (NON-NEED-BASED) ***Tuition waivers:*** Full or partial for employees or children of employees, senior citizens.

LOANS ***Student loans:*** $434,571 (71% need-based, 29% non-need-based). 49% of past graduating class borrowed through all loan programs. Average indebtedness per student: $20,044. ***Average need-based loan:*** Freshmen: $2062; Undergraduates: $2852. ***Parent loans:*** $68,154 (100% non-need-based). ***Programs:*** FFEL (Subsidized and Unsubsidized Stafford, PLUS), Perkins.

APPLYING for FINANCIAL AID ***Required financial aid form:*** FAFSA. ***Financial aid deadline (priority):*** 4/15. ***Notification date:*** Continuous beginning 6/1. Students must reply within 3 weeks of notification.

CONTACT Mr. John DeRose, Director of Financial Aid, Paier College of Art, Inc., 20 Gorham Avenue, Hamden, CT 06514-3902, 203-287-3034.

PAINE COLLEGE

Augusta, GA

Tuition & fees: $7528 **Average undergraduate aid package: $7126**

ABOUT THE INSTITUTION Independent Methodist, coed. Awards: bachelor's degrees. 18 undergraduate majors. Total enrollment: 858. Undergraduates: 858. Freshmen: 198. Both federal and institutional methodology are used as a basis for awarding need-based institutional aid.

UNDERGRADUATE EXPENSES for 1999–2000 ***Application fee:*** $10. ***Comprehensive fee:*** $10,814 includes full-time tuition ($7068), mandatory fees ($460), and room and board ($3286). ***College room only:*** $1352. Full-time tuition and fees vary according to course load and reciprocity agreements. Room and board charges vary according to housing facility. ***Part-time tuition:*** $295 per semester hour. ***Part-time fees:*** $230 per term part-time. Part-time tuition and fees vary according to course load, location, and reciprocity agreements. ***Payment plan:*** installment.

FRESHMAN FINANCIAL AID (Fall 1999) 100% of freshmen with need received aid; of those 11% had need fully met. *Average percent of need met:* 60% (excluding resources awarded to replace EFC). *Average financial aid package:* $7151 (excluding resources awarded to replace EFC).

UNDERGRADUATE FINANCIAL AID (Fall 1999) 100% of undergraduates with need received aid; of those 7% had need fully met. *Average percent of need met:* 59% (excluding resources awarded to replace EFC). *Average financial aid package:* $7126 (excluding resources awarded to replace EFC).

GIFT AID (NEED-BASED) ***Total amount:*** $3,364,953 (50% Federal, 27% state, 14% institutional, 9% external sources). ***Receiving aid:*** *Freshmen:* 150; *all full-time undergraduates:* 749. ***Average award:*** Freshmen: $4785; Undergraduates: $4398. ***Scholarships, grants, and awards:*** Federal Pell, FSEOG, state, private, college/university gift aid from institutional funds, United Negro College Fund.

GIFT AID (NON-NEED-BASED) ***Total amount:*** $211,774 (50% state, 38% institutional, 12% external sources). ***Receiving aid:*** *Freshmen:* 14; *Undergraduates:* 37. ***Scholarships, grants, and awards by category:*** *Academic Interests/Achievement:* business, communication, computer science, education, English, general academic interests/achievements, humanities, mathematics, military science, physical sciences, premedicine. *Creative Arts/Performance:* music. *Special Characteristics:* children and siblings of alumni, children of faculty/staff, local/state students, religious affiliation, siblings of current students. ***Tuition waivers:*** Full or partial for children of alumni, employees or children of employees. ***ROTC:*** Army cooperative.

LOANS ***Student loans:*** $2,910,563 (92% need-based, 8% non-need-based). 71% of past graduating class borrowed through all loan programs. Average indebtedness per student: $19,750. ***Average need-based loan:*** Freshmen: $2219; Undergraduates: $2784. ***Parent loans:*** $565,341 (74% need-based, 26% non-need-based). ***Programs:*** Federal Direct (Subsidized and Unsubsidized Stafford, PLUS), Perkins.

WORK-STUDY ***Federal work-study:*** *Total amount:* $330,212; jobs available. ***State or other work-study/employment:*** *Total amount:* $84,715 (90% need-based, 10% non-need-based). Part-time jobs available.

ATHLETIC AWARDS *Total amount:* 173,783 (100% need-based).

APPLYING for FINANCIAL AID ***Required financial aid forms:*** FAFSA, institution's own form, CSS Financial Aid PROFILE, state aid form. ***Financial aid deadline:*** 5/30 (priority: 4/15).

CONTACT Ms. Gerri Bogan, Director of Financial Aid, Paine College, 1235 15th Street, Augusta, GA 30901, 706-821-8262 or toll-free 800-476-7703.

PALM BEACH ATLANTIC COLLEGE

West Palm Beach, FL

Tuition & fees: $11,120 **Average undergraduate aid package: $10,152**

ABOUT THE INSTITUTION Independent nondenominational, coed. Awards: associate, bachelor's, and master's degrees. 31 undergraduate majors. Total enrollment: 2,163. Undergraduates: 1,838. Freshmen: 389. Federal methodology is used as a basis for awarding need-based institutional aid.

UNDERGRADUATE EXPENSES for 1999–2000 ***Application fee:*** $25. ***Comprehensive fee:*** $15,590 includes full-time tuition ($11,040), mandatory fees ($80), and room and board ($4470). ***College room only:*** $2200. Full-time tuition and fees vary according to class time. Room and board charges vary according to board plan and housing facility. Part-time tuition and fees vary according to class time and course load. ***Payment plan:*** installment.

FRESHMAN FINANCIAL AID (Fall 1999) 520 applied for aid; of those 66% were deemed to have need. 100% of freshmen with need received aid; of those 37% had need fully met. *Average percent of need met:* 85% (excluding resources awarded to replace EFC). *Average financial aid package:* $8902 (excluding resources awarded to replace EFC). 31% of all full-time freshmen had no need and received non-need-based aid.

UNDERGRADUATE FINANCIAL AID (Fall 1999) 1,346 applied for aid; of those 44% were deemed to have need. 100% of undergraduates with need received aid; of those 63% had need fully met. *Average percent of need met:* 85% (excluding resources awarded to replace EFC). *Average financial aid package:* $10,152 (excluding resources awarded to replace EFC). 50% of all full-time undergraduates had no need and received non-need-based aid.

GIFT AID (NEED-BASED) ***Total amount:*** $2,679,770 (46% Federal, 9% state, 45% institutional). ***Receiving aid:*** *Freshmen:* 59% (342); *all full-time undergraduates:* 28% (420). ***Average award:*** Freshmen: $2400; Undergraduates: $2650. ***Scholarships, grants, and awards:*** Federal Pell, FSEOG, state, private, college/university gift aid from institutional funds.

GIFT AID (NON-NEED-BASED) ***Total amount:*** $5,470,153 (1% Federal, 42% state, 56% institutional, 1% external sources). ***Receiving aid:*** *Freshmen:* 59% (342); *Undergraduates:* 39% (587). ***Scholarships, grants, and awards by category:*** *Academic Interests/Achievement:* general academic interests/achievements. *Creative Arts/Performance:* debating, music, theater/drama. *Special Achievements/Activities:* leadership, religious involvement. *Special Characteristics:* children of current students, relatives of clergy,

Palm Beach Atlantic College (continued)

siblings of current students, spouses of current students. ***Tuition waivers:*** Full or partial for employees or children of employees, senior citizens.

LOANS ***Student loans:*** $6,599,987 (62% need-based, 38% non-need-based). 74% of past graduating class borrowed through all loan programs. Average indebtedness per student: $16,600. ***Average need-based loan:*** Freshmen: $2470; Undergraduates: $3690. ***Parent loans:*** $792,216 (100% non-need-based). ***Programs:*** FFEL (Subsidized and Unsubsidized Stafford, PLUS), Perkins, college/university.

WORK-STUDY ***Federal work-study:*** *Total amount:* $180,415; jobs available.

ATHLETIC AWARDS *Total amount:* 265,525 (100% non-need-based).

APPLYING for FINANCIAL AID ***Required financial aid forms:*** FAFSA, institution's own form, state aid form. ***Financial aid deadline:*** Continuous. ***Notification date:*** Continuous beginning 3/1.

CONTACT Ms. Kathy Fruge, Director of Student Financial Planning, Palm Beach Atlantic College, PO Box 24708, West Palm Beach, FL 33416, 561-803-2126 or toll-free 800-238-3998. *E-mail:* frugek@pbac.edu

PALMER COLLEGE OF CHIROPRACTIC

Davenport, IA

Tuition & fees: $15,705 **Average undergraduate aid package: N/A**

ABOUT THE INSTITUTION Independent, coed. Awards: associate, bachelor's, master's, and first professional degrees. 2 undergraduate majors. Total enrollment: 1,728. Undergraduates: 40. Freshmen: 6. Federal methodology is used as a basis for awarding need-based institutional aid.

UNDERGRADUATE EXPENSES for 1999–2000 ***Application fee:*** $25. ***One-time required fee:*** $150. ***Tuition:*** full-time $15,645; part-time $200 per credit hour. ***Required fees:*** full-time $60; $20 per term part-time. Full-time tuition and fees vary according to degree level. Part-time tuition and fees vary according to degree level. ***Payment plan:*** deferred payment.

GIFT AID (NEED-BASED) ***Scholarships, grants, and awards:*** Federal Pell, FSEOG, state, private, college/university gift aid from institutional funds.

GIFT AID (NON-NEED-BASED) ***Scholarships, grants, and awards by category:*** *Academic Interests/Achievement:* biological sciences, general academic interests/achievements, health fields. *Special Achievements/Activities:* community service, junior miss, leadership. *Special Characteristics:* international students, members of minority groups, out-of-state students. ***Tuition waivers:*** Full or partial for employees or children of employees.

LOANS ***Programs:*** FFEL (Subsidized and Unsubsidized Stafford, PLUS), Perkins, Alaska Student Loan Program.

WORK-STUDY Federal work-study jobs available.

APPLYING for FINANCIAL AID ***Required financial aid form:*** FAFSA. ***Financial aid deadline:*** Continuous. ***Notification date:*** Continuous.

CONTACT Financial Planning Office, Palmer College of Chiropractic, 1000 Brady Street, Davenport, IA 52803, 319-884-5889 or toll-free 800-722-3648. *Fax:* 319-884-5414.

PARK UNIVERSITY

Parkville, MO

Tuition & fees: $4770 **Average undergraduate aid package: $6377**

ABOUT THE INSTITUTION Independent religious, coed. Awards: associate, bachelor's, and master's degrees. 30 undergraduate majors. Total enrollment: 1,224. Undergraduates: 1,122. Freshmen: 145. Federal methodology is used as a basis for awarding need-based institutional aid.

UNDERGRADUATE EXPENSES for 1999–2000 ***Application fee:*** $25. ***Comprehensive fee:*** $9560 includes full-time tuition ($4770) and room and board ($4790). Room and board charges vary according to housing facility. ***Part-time tuition:*** $159 per credit hour. ***Payment plan:*** installment.

FRESHMAN FINANCIAL AID (Fall 1999) 91 applied for aid; of those 66% were deemed to have need. 100% of freshmen with need received aid; of those 42% had need fully met. *Average percent of need met:* 23% (excluding resources awarded to replace EFC). *Average financial aid package:* $6449 (excluding resources awarded to replace EFC). 23% of all full-time freshmen had no need and received non-need-based aid.

UNDERGRADUATE FINANCIAL AID (Fall 1999) 668 applied for aid; of those 75% were deemed to have need. 99% of undergraduates with need received aid; of those 40% had need fully met. *Average percent of need met:* 21% (excluding resources awarded to replace EFC). *Average financial aid package:* $6377 (excluding resources awarded to replace EFC). 15% of all full-time undergraduates had no need and received non-need-based aid.

GIFT AID (NEED-BASED) ***Receiving aid:*** *Freshmen:* 31% (33); *all full-time undergraduates:* 27% (234). ***Average award:*** Freshmen: $2310; Undergraduates: $2106. ***Scholarships, grants, and awards:*** Federal Pell, FSEOG, state, private, college/university gift aid from institutional funds.

GIFT AID (NON-NEED-BASED) ***Receiving aid:*** *Freshmen:* 49% (52); *Undergraduates:* 46% (396). ***Scholarships, grants, and awards by category:*** *Academic Interests/Achievement:* general academic interests/achievements. *Creative Arts/Performance:* art/fine arts, theater/drama. *Special Achievements/Activities:* cheerleading/drum major. *Special Characteristics:* children of faculty/staff, religious affiliation, siblings of current students. ***Tuition waivers:*** Full or partial for employees or children of employees, senior citizens. ***ROTC:*** Army.

LOANS ***Student loans:*** 82% of past graduating class borrowed through all loan programs. Average indebtedness per student: $10,500. ***Average need-based loan:*** Freshmen: $3256; Undergraduates: $3438. ***Programs:*** FFEL (Subsidized and Unsubsidized Stafford, PLUS), Perkins, college/university.

WORK-STUDY Federal work-study jobs available.

APPLYING for FINANCIAL AID ***Required financial aid forms:*** FAFSA, institution's own form. ***Financial aid deadline (priority):*** 4/1. ***Notification date:*** Continuous. Students must reply within 2 weeks of notification.

CONTACT Ms. Cathy Colapietro, Associate Director of Student Financial Services, Park University, 8700 NW River Park Drive, Parkville, MO 64152, 816-741-2000 Ext. 6728 or toll-free 800-745-7275. *Fax:* 816-741-9668.

PARSONS SCHOOL OF DESIGN, NEW SCHOOL UNIVERSITY

New York, NY

Tuition & fees: $21,780 **Average undergraduate aid package: $13,782**

ABOUT THE INSTITUTION Independent, coed. Awards: associate, bachelor's, and master's degrees. 12 undergraduate majors. Total university enrollment: 7,700. Total unit enrollment: 2,716. Undergraduates: 2,397. Freshmen: 371. Federal methodology is used as a basis for awarding need-based institutional aid.

UNDERGRADUATE EXPENSES for 2000–2001 ***Application fee:*** $40. ***Tuition:*** full-time $21,550; part-time $734 per credit. ***Required fees:*** full-time $230. Part-time tuition and fees vary according to program. Room and board charges vary according to board plan. ***Payment plan:*** installment.

FRESHMAN FINANCIAL AID (Fall 1999, est.) 329 applied for aid; of those 85% were deemed to have need. 100% of freshmen with need received aid; of those 12% had need fully met. *Average percent of need met:* 66% (excluding resources awarded to replace EFC). *Average financial aid package:* $11,628 (excluding resources awarded to replace EFC). 23% of all full-time freshmen had no need and received non-need-based aid.

UNDERGRADUATE FINANCIAL AID (Fall 1999, est.) 1,482 applied for aid; of those 86% were deemed to have need. 100% of undergraduates with need received aid; of those 12% had need fully met. *Average percent of need met:* 65% (excluding resources awarded to replace EFC). *Average financial aid package:* $13,782 (excluding resources awarded to replace EFC). 15% of all full-time undergraduates had no need and received non-need-based aid.

GIFT AID (NEED-BASED) ***Total amount:*** $12,368,040 (16% Federal, 10% state, 73% institutional, 1% external sources). ***Receiving aid:*** *Freshmen:* 77% (280); *all full-time undergraduates:* 60% (1,270). ***Average award:***

Freshmen: $6503; Undergraduates: $7154. ***Scholarships, grants, and awards:*** Federal Pell, FSEOG, state, private, college/university gift aid from institutional funds.

GIFT AID (NON-NEED-BASED) ***Total amount:*** $315,342 (10% Federal, 6% state, 46% institutional, 38% external sources). ***Receiving aid:*** *Freshmen:* 4% (15); *Undergraduates:* 2% (48). ***Scholarships, grants, and awards by category:*** *Creative Arts/Performance:* 48 awards ($145,200 total): general creative arts/performance. ***Tuition waivers:*** Full or partial for employees or children of employees.

LOANS ***Student loans:*** $10,945,119 (52% need-based, 48% non-need-based). 70% of past graduating class borrowed through all loan programs. Average indebtedness per student: $27,125. ***Average need-based loan:*** Freshmen: $3625; Undergraduates: $5281. ***Parent loans:*** $2,576,207 (100% non-need-based). ***Programs:*** FFEL (Subsidized and Unsubsidized Stafford, PLUS), Perkins, college/university.

WORK-STUDY ***Federal work-study:*** *Total amount:* $308,000; 154 jobs averaging $2000. ***State or other work-study/employment:*** *Total amount:* $261,000 (100% non-need-based). 75 part-time jobs averaging $3480.

APPLYING for FINANCIAL AID ***Required financial aid form:*** FAFSA. ***Financial aid deadline (priority):*** 3/1. ***Notification date:*** Continuous. Students must reply within 4 weeks of notification.

CONTACT Sandra Bembry, Director of Financial Aid, Parsons School of Design, New School University, 66 Fifth Avenue, New York, NY 10011, 212-229-8930 or toll-free 800-252-0852. *Fax:* 212-229-5919.

PATTEN COLLEGE

Oakland, CA

ABOUT THE INSTITUTION Independent interdenominational, coed. Awards: associate, bachelor's, and master's degrees and post-bachelor's certificates. 7 undergraduate majors. Total enrollment: 635. Undergraduates: 635. Freshmen: 27.

GIFT AID (NEED-BASED) ***Scholarships, grants, and awards:*** Federal Pell, FSEOG, state, private, college/university gift aid from institutional funds.

GIFT AID (NON-NEED-BASED) ***Scholarships, grants, and awards by category:*** *Academic Interests/Achievement:* religion/biblical studies. *Special Achievements/Activities:* leadership, religious involvement. *Special Characteristics:* religious affiliation.

LOANS ***Programs:*** FFEL (Subsidized and Unsubsidized Stafford, PLUS), Perkins.

WORK-STUDY Federal work-study jobs available.

APPLYING for FINANCIAL AID ***Required financial aid forms:*** FAFSA, institution's own form, state aid form.

CONTACT Mr. Robert A. Olivera, Dean of Enrollment Services, Patten College, 2433 Coolidge Avenue, Oakland, CA 94601-2699, 510-261-8500 Ext. 783. *Fax:* 510-534-8969. *E-mail:* oliverob@patten.edu

PAUL QUINN COLLEGE

Dallas, TX

Tuition & fees: $5670 **Average undergraduate aid package: N/A**

ABOUT THE INSTITUTION Independent African Methodist Episcopal, coed. Awards: bachelor's degrees. 18 undergraduate majors. Federal methodology is used as a basis for awarding need-based institutional aid.

UNDERGRADUATE EXPENSES for 1999–2000 ***Application fee:*** $15. ***Comprehensive fee:*** $9470 includes full-time tuition ($5100), mandatory fees ($570), and room and board ($3800). ***College room only:*** $1400. ***Part-time tuition:*** $170 per semester hour. ***Part-time fees:*** $285 per term part-time. Part-time tuition and fees vary according to course load. ***Payment plan:*** installment.

GIFT AID (NEED-BASED) ***Scholarships, grants, and awards:*** Federal Pell, FSEOG, state, private, college/university gift aid from institutional funds, United Negro College Fund.

GIFT AID (NON-NEED-BASED) ***Scholarships, grants, and awards by category:*** *Academic Interests/Achievement:* general academic interests/achievements. *Creative Arts/Performance:* music, performing arts. *Special Achievements/Activities:* community service, general special achievements/activities, religious involvement. *Special Characteristics:* adult students, children of educators, children of faculty/staff, first-generation college students, local/state students, married students, out-of-state students, previous college experience, spouses of current students, twins, veterans.

LOANS ***Programs:*** FFEL (Subsidized and Unsubsidized Stafford, PLUS), alternative loans.

WORK-STUDY Federal work-study jobs available. ***State or other work-study/employment:*** Part-time jobs available.

APPLYING for FINANCIAL AID ***Required financial aid forms:*** FAFSA, institution's own form. ***Financial aid deadline:*** 4/1. ***Notification date:*** 5/31. Students must reply by 6/1 or within 2 weeks of notification.

CONTACT Director of Financial Aid, Paul Quinn College, 3837 Simpson Stuart Road, Dallas, TX 75241, 214-302-3530 or toll-free 800-237-2648.

PEABODY CONSERVATORY OF MUSIC OF THE JOHNS HOPKINS UNIVERSITY

Baltimore, MD

Tuition & fees: $21,975 **Average undergraduate aid package: $16,145**

ABOUT THE INSTITUTION Independent, coed. Awards: bachelor's, master's, and doctoral degrees. 7 undergraduate majors. Total enrollment: 654. Undergraduates: 352. Freshmen: 86. Federal methodology is used as a basis for awarding need-based institutional aid.

UNDERGRADUATE EXPENSES for 1999–2000 ***Application fee:*** $50. ***One-time required fee:*** $500. ***Comprehensive fee:*** $30,035 includes full-time tuition ($21,700), mandatory fees ($275), and room and board ($8060). Room and board charges vary according to board plan and housing facility. ***Part-time tuition:*** $620 per semester hour. Part-time tuition and fees vary according to course load.

FRESHMAN FINANCIAL AID (Fall 1999, est.) 80 applied for aid; of those 85% were deemed to have need. 100% of freshmen with need received aid; of those 15% had need fully met. *Average percent of need met:* 66% (excluding resources awarded to replace EFC). *Average financial aid package:* $13,219 (excluding resources awarded to replace EFC). 20% of all full-time freshmen had no need and received non-need-based aid.

UNDERGRADUATE FINANCIAL AID (Fall 1999, est.) 221 applied for aid; of those 88% were deemed to have need. 99% of undergraduates with need received aid; of those 20% had need fully met. *Average percent of need met:* 71% (excluding resources awarded to replace EFC). *Average financial aid package:* $16,145 (excluding resources awarded to replace EFC). 25% of all full-time undergraduates had no need and received non-need-based aid.

GIFT AID (NEED-BASED) ***Total amount:*** $1,183,700 (15% Federal, 6% state, 79% institutional). ***Receiving aid:*** *Freshmen:* 55% (60); *all full-time undergraduates:* 53% (179). ***Average award:*** Freshmen: $4521; Undergraduates: $5010. ***Scholarships, grants, and awards:*** Federal Pell, FSEOG, state, private, college/university gift aid from institutional funds.

GIFT AID (NON-NEED-BASED) ***Total amount:*** $1,020,212 (4% state, 91% institutional, 5% external sources). ***Receiving aid:*** *Freshmen:* 39% (42); *Undergraduates:* 35% (119). ***Scholarships, grants, and awards by category:*** *Creative Arts/Performance:* 169 awards ($864,300 total): music. ***Tuition waivers:*** Full or partial for employees or children of employees.

LOANS ***Student loans:*** $975,841 (47% need-based, 53% non-need-based). 66% of past graduating class borrowed through all loan programs. ***Average need-based loan:*** Freshmen: $3988; Undergraduates: $4773. ***Parent loans:*** $574,500 (100% non-need-based). ***Programs:*** Federal Direct (Subsidized and Unsubsidized Stafford), FFEL (PLUS), Perkins, college/university.

WORK-STUDY ***Federal work-study:*** *Total amount:* $82,158; 83 jobs averaging $990. ***State or other work-study/employment:*** *Total amount:* $53,213 (100% non-need-based). 110 part-time jobs averaging $484.

APPLYING for FINANCIAL AID ***Required financial aid forms:*** FAFSA, institution's own form. ***Financial aid deadline (priority):*** 2/1. ***Notification date:*** 4/1. Students must reply within 2 weeks of notification.

Peabody Conservatory of Music of The Johns Hopkins University (continued)

CONTACT Doris Rohr, Financial Aid Officer, Peabody Conservatory of Music of The Johns Hopkins University, 1 East Mount Vernon Place, Baltimore, MD 21202-2397, 410-659-8171 or toll-free 800-368-2521 (out-of-state). *Fax:* 410-659-8102. *E-mail:* drohr@peabody.jhu.edu

PEACE COLLEGE

Raleigh, NC

Tuition & fees: $9927 **Average undergraduate aid package: $8320**

ABOUT THE INSTITUTION Independent religious, women only. Awards: associate and bachelor's degrees. 11 undergraduate majors. Total enrollment: 572. Undergraduates: 572. Freshmen: 171. Federal methodology is used as a basis for awarding need-based institutional aid.

UNDERGRADUATE EXPENSES for 2000–2001 ***Application fee:*** $25. ***Comprehensive fee:*** $14,927 includes full-time tuition ($9727), mandatory fees ($200), and room and board ($5000). ***Part-time tuition:*** $300 per semester hour. ***Payment plan:*** installment.

UNDERGRADUATE FINANCIAL AID (Fall 1998) 334 applied for aid; of those 82% were deemed to have need. 100% of undergraduates with need received aid. *Average percent of need met:* 85% (excluding resources awarded to replace EFC). *Average financial aid package:* $8320 (excluding resources awarded to replace EFC). 20% of all full-time undergraduates had no need and received non-need-based aid.

GIFT AID (NEED-BASED) ***Total amount:*** $1,507,055 (16% Federal, 49% state, 27% institutional, 8% external sources). ***Receiving aid:*** *All full-time undergraduates:* 47% (274). ***Scholarships, grants, and awards:*** Federal Pell, FSEOG, state, private, college/university gift aid from institutional funds, Federal Nursing, North Carolina State Contractual Scholarships.

GIFT AID (NON-NEED-BASED) ***Total amount:*** $810,941 (45% state, 48% institutional, 7% external sources). ***Receiving aid:*** *Undergraduates:* 27% (155). ***Scholarships, grants, and awards by category:*** *Academic Interests/Achievement:* biological sciences, business, communication, general academic interests/achievements. *Creative Arts/Performance:* applied art and design, art/fine arts, general creative arts/performance, music, theater/drama. *Special Achievements/Activities:* general special achievements/activities, junior miss, leadership, religious involvement. *Special Characteristics:* children and siblings of alumni, children of faculty/staff, out-of-state students, relatives of clergy, religious affiliation. ***Tuition waivers:*** Full or partial for employees or children of employees. ***ROTC:*** Army cooperative, Naval cooperative, Air Force cooperative.

LOANS ***Student loans:*** $798,202 (86% need-based, 14% non-need-based). ***Parent loans:*** $351,813 (64% need-based, 36% non-need-based). ***Programs:*** FFEL (Subsidized and Unsubsidized Stafford, PLUS).

WORK-STUDY ***Federal work-study:*** *Total amount:* $28,995; 68 jobs averaging $426. ***State or other work-study/employment:*** *Total amount:* $120,067 (43% need-based, 57% non-need-based). Part-time jobs available.

APPLYING for FINANCIAL AID ***Required financial aid forms:*** FAFSA, institution's own form. ***Financial aid deadline (priority):*** 4/1. ***Notification date:*** Continuous. Students must reply within 2 weeks of notification.

CONTACT Ms. Amy Coats, Director of Financial Aid, Peace College, 15 East Peace Street, Raleigh, NC 27604, 919-508-2249 or toll-free 800-PEACE-47. *Fax:* 919-508-2326. *E-mail:* acoats@peace.edu

PEIRCE COLLEGE

Philadelphia, PA

Tuition & fees: $8220 **Average undergraduate aid package: $3500**

ABOUT THE INSTITUTION Independent, coed, primarily women. Awards: associate and bachelor's degrees and post-bachelor's certificates. 15 undergraduate majors. Total enrollment: 2,334. Undergraduates: 2,334. Freshmen: 362. Both federal and institutional methodology are used as a basis for awarding need-based institutional aid.

UNDERGRADUATE EXPENSES for 1999–2000 ***Application fee:*** $20. ***Tuition:*** full-time $7980; part-time $266 per credit. ***Required fees:*** full-time $240; $60 per term part-time. ***Payment plan:*** deferred payment.

FRESHMAN FINANCIAL AID (Fall 1999) 222 applied for aid; of those 72% were deemed to have need. 100% of freshmen with need received aid; of those 19% had need fully met. *Average percent of need met:* 60% (excluding resources awarded to replace EFC). *Average financial aid package:* $4000 (excluding resources awarded to replace EFC). 28% of all full-time freshmen had no need and received non-need-based aid.

UNDERGRADUATE FINANCIAL AID (Fall 1999) 700 applied for aid; of those 79% were deemed to have need. 100% of undergraduates with need received aid; of those 23% had need fully met. *Average percent of need met:* 45% (excluding resources awarded to replace EFC). *Average financial aid package:* $3500 (excluding resources awarded to replace EFC). 13% of all full-time undergraduates had no need and received non-need-based aid.

GIFT AID (NEED-BASED) ***Total amount:*** $3,295,566 (61% Federal, 33% state, 6% institutional). ***Receiving aid:*** *Freshmen:* 18% (40); *all full-time undergraduates:* 30% (275). ***Average award:*** Freshmen: $1500; Undergraduates: $1000. ***Scholarships, grants, and awards:*** Federal Pell, FSEOG, state, private, college/university gift aid from institutional funds.

GIFT AID (NON-NEED-BASED) ***Total amount:*** $337,693 (100% institutional). ***Receiving aid:*** *Freshmen:* 23% (50); *Undergraduates:* 33% (300). ***Scholarships, grants, and awards by category:*** *Academic Interests/Achievement:* 70 awards ($250,000 total): general academic interests/achievements. *Special Achievements/Activities:* 10 awards ($40,000 total): community service, leadership, memberships. *Special Characteristics:* 30 awards ($258,077 total): children of public servants, general special characteristics, local/state students, out-of-state students, previous college experience. ***Tuition waivers:*** Full or partial for children of alumni, employees or children of employees.

LOANS ***Student loans:*** $3,369,903 (65% need-based, 35% non-need-based). 75% of past graduating class borrowed through all loan programs. Average indebtedness per student: $12,500. ***Average need-based loan:*** Freshmen: $4000; Undergraduates: $4000. ***Parent loans:*** $98,316 (100% need-based). ***Programs:*** FFEL (Subsidized and Unsubsidized Stafford, PLUS), Perkins, college/university.

WORK-STUDY ***Federal work-study:*** *Total amount:* $108,000; 108 jobs averaging $1000.

APPLYING for FINANCIAL AID ***Required financial aid forms:*** FAFSA, institution's own form. ***Financial aid deadline (priority):*** 2/15. ***Notification date:*** 4/15. Students must reply within 3 weeks of notification.

CONTACT Lisa A. Gargiulo, Registration Supervisor, Peirce College, 1420 Pine Street, Philadelphia, PA 19102, 215-545-6400 or toll-free 888-467-3472 Ext. 214. *Fax:* 215-893-4347. *E-mail:* lagargiulo@peirce.edu

PENNSYLVANIA COLLEGE OF OPTOMETRY

Elkins Park, PA

CONTACT Susan Keenan, Associate Director of Financial Aid, Pennsylvania College of Optometry, 1200 West Godfrey Avenue, Philadelphia, PA 19141, 215-276-6000 or toll-free 800-824-6262 (out-of-state).

PENNSYLVANIA SCHOOL OF ART & DESIGN

Lancaster, PA

Tuition & fees: $9290 **Average undergraduate aid package: N/A**

ABOUT THE INSTITUTION Independent, coed. Awards: bachelor's degrees. 2 undergraduate majors. Total enrollment: 168. Undergraduates: 168. Freshmen: 63.

UNDERGRADUATE EXPENSES for 1999–2000 ***Application fee:*** $35. ***Tuition:*** full-time $8940; part-time $298 per credit. ***Required fees:*** full-time $350; $110 per term part-time. Full-time tuition and fees vary according to course load and program. Part-time tuition and fees vary according to course load and program. ***Payment plan:*** installment.

GIFT AID (NEED-BASED) ***Scholarships, grants, and awards:*** Federal Pell, FSEOG, state.

GIFT AID (NON-NEED-BASED) ***Tuition waivers:*** Full or partial for employees or children of employees.

LOANS ***Programs:*** FFEL (Subsidized and Unsubsidized Stafford, PLUS).

WORK-STUDY Federal work-study jobs available.

APPLYING for FINANCIAL AID ***Required financial aid forms:*** FAFSA, state aid form. ***Financial aid deadline (priority):*** 8/1. ***Notification date:*** Continuous. Students must reply within 2 weeks of notification.

CONTACT Financial Aid Office, Pennsylvania School of Art & Design, 204 North Prince Street, PO Box 59, Lancaster, PA 17608-0059, 717-396-7833. *Fax:* 717-396-1339.

PENNSYLVANIA STATE UNIVERSITY ABINGTON COLLEGE

Abington, PA

Tuition & fees (PA res): $6312 **Average undergraduate aid package: N/A**

ABOUT THE INSTITUTION State-related, coed. Awards: associate and bachelor's degrees. 12 undergraduate majors. Total enrollment: 3,220. Undergraduates: 3,219. Freshmen: 807. Federal methodology is used as a basis for awarding need-based institutional aid.

UNDERGRADUATE EXPENSES for 1999–2000 ***Application fee:*** $50. ***Tuition, state resident:*** full-time $6058; part-time $243 per credit. ***Tuition, nonresident:*** full-time $9418; part-time $393 per credit. ***Required fees:*** full-time $254; $43 per credit. Full-time tuition and fees vary according to course level, location, program, and student level. Part-time tuition and fees vary according to course level, course load, location, program, and student level. ***Payment plan:*** deferred payment.

GIFT AID (NEED-BASED) ***Scholarships, grants, and awards:*** Federal Pell, FSEOG, state, private, college/university gift aid from institutional funds.

GIFT AID (NON-NEED-BASED) ***Tuition waivers:*** Full or partial for employees or children of employees, senior citizens. ***ROTC:*** Army, Air Force cooperative.

LOANS ***Programs:*** FFEL (Subsidized and Unsubsidized Stafford, PLUS), Perkins, college/university.

WORK-STUDY Federal work-study jobs available. ***State or other work-study/employment:*** Part-time jobs available.

APPLYING for FINANCIAL AID ***Required financial aid form:*** FAFSA. ***Financial aid deadline:*** Continuous. ***Notification date:*** Continuous beginning 3/1.

CONTACT Ms. Karen Jacobs-Hakim, Financial Aid Counselor, Pennsylvania State University Abington College, 106 Sutherland Building, Abington, PA 19001, 215-881-7348. *Fax:* 215-881-7317. *E-mail:* kxj10@psu.edu

PENNSYLVANIA STATE UNIVERSITY ALTOONA COLLEGE

Altoona, PA

Tuition & fees (PA res): $6332 **Average undergraduate aid package: N/A**

ABOUT THE INSTITUTION State-related, coed. Awards: associate and bachelor's degrees. 16 undergraduate majors. Total enrollment: 3,869. Undergraduates: 3,842. Freshmen: 1,310. Federal methodology is used as a basis for awarding need-based institutional aid.

UNDERGRADUATE EXPENSES for 1999–2000 ***Application fee:*** $50. ***Tuition, state resident:*** full-time $6058; part-time $243 per credit. ***Tuition, nonresident:*** full-time $9418; part-time $393 per credit. ***Required fees:*** full-time $274; $46 per credit. Full-time tuition and fees vary according to course level, location, program, and student level. Part-time tuition and fees vary according to course level, course load, location, program, and student level. ***College room and board:*** $4690; ***room only:*** $2280. Room and board charges vary according to board plan and housing facility. ***Payment plan:*** deferred payment.

GIFT AID (NEED-BASED) ***Scholarships, grants, and awards:*** Federal Pell, FSEOG, state, private, college/university gift aid from institutional funds.

GIFT AID (NON-NEED-BASED) ***Tuition waivers:*** Full or partial for employees or children of employees, senior citizens. ***ROTC:*** Army.

LOANS ***Programs:*** FFEL (Subsidized and Unsubsidized Stafford, PLUS), Perkins, college/university.

WORK-STUDY Federal work-study jobs available. ***State or other work-study/employment:*** Part-time jobs available.

APPLYING for FINANCIAL AID ***Required financial aid form:*** FAFSA. ***Financial aid deadline:*** Continuous. ***Notification date:*** Continuous beginning 3/1.

CONTACT Mr. David Pearlman, Assistant Director of Student Affairs, Pennsylvania State University Altoona College, 101 Smith Building, Altoona, PA 16601-3760, 814-949-5055 or toll-free 800-848-9843. *Fax:* 814-949-5536. *E-mail:* dpp1@psu.edu

PENNSYLVANIA STATE UNIVERSITY AT ERIE, THE BEHREND COLLEGE

Erie, PA

Tuition & fees (PA res): $6436 **Average undergraduate aid package: N/A**

ABOUT THE INSTITUTION State-related, coed. Awards: associate, bachelor's, and master's degrees. 26 undergraduate majors. Total enrollment: 3,648. Undergraduates: 3,501. Freshmen: 848. Federal methodology is used as a basis for awarding need-based institutional aid.

UNDERGRADUATE EXPENSES for 1999–2000 ***Application fee:*** $50. ***Tuition, state resident:*** full-time $6162; part-time $258 per credit. ***Tuition, nonresident:*** full-time $11,836; part-time $493 per credit. ***Required fees:*** full-time $274; $46 per credit. Full-time tuition and fees vary according to course level, location, program, and student level. Part-time tuition and fees vary according to course level, course load, location, program, and student level. ***College room and board:*** $4690; ***room only:*** $2280. Room and board charges vary according to board plan and housing facility. ***Payment plan:*** deferred payment.

GIFT AID (NEED-BASED) ***Scholarships, grants, and awards:*** Federal Pell, FSEOG, state, private, college/university gift aid from institutional funds.

GIFT AID (NON-NEED-BASED) ***Tuition waivers:*** Full or partial for employees or children of employees, senior citizens.

LOANS ***Programs:*** FFEL (Subsidized and Unsubsidized Stafford, PLUS), Perkins, college/university.

WORK-STUDY Federal work-study jobs available. ***State or other work-study/employment:*** Part-time jobs available.

APPLYING for FINANCIAL AID ***Required financial aid form:*** FAFSA. ***Financial aid deadline:*** Continuous. ***Notification date:*** Continuous beginning 3/1.

CONTACT Ms. Jane Brady, Assistant Director of Admissions and Graduate Admissions, Pennsylvania State University at Erie, The Behrend College, 200 Glenhill Farmhouse, Erie, PA 16563, 814-898-6162. *Fax:* 814-898-6044. *E-mail:* jub9@psu.edu

PENNSYLVANIA STATE UNIVERSITY BERKS CAMPUS OF THE BERKS–LEHIGH VALLEY COLLEGE

Reading, PA

Tuition & fees (PA res): $6332 **Average undergraduate aid package: N/A**

ABOUT THE INSTITUTION State-related, coed. Awards: associate and bachelor's degrees. 12 undergraduate majors. Total enrollment: 2,067. Undergraduates: 2,049. Freshmen: 762. Federal methodology is used as a basis for awarding need-based institutional aid.

UNDERGRADUATE EXPENSES for 1999–2000 ***Application fee:*** $50. ***Tuition, state resident:*** full-time $6058; part-time $243 per credit. ***Tuition, nonresident:*** full-time $9418; part-time $393 per credit. ***Required fees:*** full-time $274; $46 per credit. Full-time tuition and fees vary according to course level, location, program, and student level. Part-time tuition and fees vary according to course level, course load, location, program, and

Pennsylvania State University Berks Campus of the Berks–Lehigh Valley College (continued)

student level. ***College room and board:*** $4690; ***room only:*** $2280. Room and board charges vary according to board plan and housing facility. ***Payment plan:*** deferred payment.

GIFT AID (NEED-BASED) ***Scholarships, grants, and awards:*** Federal Pell, FSEOG, state, private, college/university gift aid from institutional funds.

GIFT AID (NON-NEED-BASED) ***Tuition waivers:*** Full or partial for employees or children of employees, senior citizens. ***ROTC:*** Army.

LOANS ***Programs:*** FFEL (Subsidized and Unsubsidized Stafford, PLUS), Perkins, college/university.

WORK-STUDY Federal work-study jobs available. ***State or other work-study/employment:*** Part-time jobs available.

APPLYING for FINANCIAL AID ***Required financial aid form:*** FAFSA. ***Financial aid deadline:*** Continuous. ***Notification date:*** Continuous beginning 3/1.

CONTACT Ms. Joetta Bradica, Campus Aid Representative, Pennsylvania State University Berks Campus of the Berks–Lehigh Valley College, PO Box 7009, Tulperhocken Road, Reading, PA 19610-6009, 610-396-6070. *Fax:* 610-396-6077. *E-mail:* jrb27@psu.edu

PENNSYLVANIA STATE UNIVERSITY HARRISBURG CAMPUS OF THE CAPITAL COLLEGE

Middletown, PA

Tuition & fees (PA res): $6416 **Average undergraduate aid package: N/A**

ABOUT THE INSTITUTION State-related, coed. Awards: bachelor's, master's, and doctoral degrees. 26 undergraduate majors. Total enrollment: 3,238. Undergraduates: 1,878. Freshmen: 2. Federal methodology is used as a basis for awarding need-based institutional aid.

UNDERGRADUATE EXPENSES for 1999–2000 ***Application fee:*** $50. ***Tuition, state resident:*** full-time $6162; part-time $258 per credit. ***Tuition, nonresident:*** full-time $11,836; part-time $493 per credit. ***Required fees:*** full-time $254; $43 per credit. Full-time tuition and fees vary according to course level, location, program, and student level. Part-time tuition and fees vary according to course level, course load, location, program, and student level. ***College room and board:*** $4690; ***room only:*** $2280. Room and board charges vary according to board plan and housing facility. ***Payment plan:*** deferred payment.

GIFT AID (NEED-BASED) ***Scholarships, grants, and awards:*** Federal Pell, FSEOG, state, private, college/university gift aid from institutional funds.

GIFT AID (NON-NEED-BASED) ***Tuition waivers:*** Full or partial for employees or children of employees, senior citizens. ***ROTC:*** Army cooperative.

LOANS ***Programs:*** FFEL (Subsidized and Unsubsidized Stafford, PLUS), Perkins, college/university.

WORK-STUDY Federal work-study jobs available. ***State or other work-study/employment:*** Part-time jobs available.

APPLYING for FINANCIAL AID ***Required financial aid form:*** FAFSA. ***Financial aid deadline:*** Continuous. ***Notification date:*** Continuous beginning 3/1.

CONTACT Ms. Carolyn Julian, Student Aid Adviser, Pennsylvania State University Harrisburg Campus of the Capital College, W112 Olmstead, Middletown, PA 17057-4898, 717-948-6307 or toll-free 800-222-2056 (in-state). *Fax:* 717-948-6008. *E-mail:* czb3@psu.edu

PENNSYLVANIA STATE UNIVERSITY LEHIGH VALLEY CAMPUS OF THE BERKS-LEHIGH VALLEY COLLEGE

Fogelsville, PA

Tuition & fees (PA res): $6242 **Average undergraduate aid package: N/A**

ABOUT THE INSTITUTION State-related, coed. Awards: associate and bachelor's degrees. 5 undergraduate majors. Total enrollment: 671. Undergraduates: 639. Freshmen: 211. Federal methodology is used as a basis for awarding need-based institutional aid.

UNDERGRADUATE EXPENSES for 1999–2000 ***Application fee:*** $50. ***Tuition, state resident:*** full-time $5968; part-time $241 per credit. ***Tuition, nonresident:*** full-time $9244; part-time $386 per credit. ***Required fees:*** full-time $274; $46 per credit. Full-time tuition and fees vary according to course level, location, program, and student level. Part-time tuition and fees vary according to course level, course load, location, program, and student level. College housing is available through Berks campus only. ***Payment plan:*** deferred payment.

GIFT AID (NEED-BASED) ***Scholarships, grants, and awards:*** Federal Pell, FSEOG, state, private, college/university gift aid from institutional funds.

GIFT AID (NON-NEED-BASED) ***Tuition waivers:*** Full or partial for employees or children of employees, senior citizens.

LOANS ***Programs:*** FFEL (Subsidized and Unsubsidized Stafford, PLUS), Perkins, college/university.

WORK-STUDY Federal work-study jobs available. ***State or other work-study/employment:*** Part-time jobs available.

APPLYING for FINANCIAL AID ***Required financial aid form:*** FAFSA. ***Financial aid deadline:*** Continuous. ***Notification date:*** Continuous beginning 3/1.

CONTACT Ms. Joan Willertz, Financial Aid Coordinator, Pennsylvania State University Lehigh Valley Campus of the Berks-Lehigh Valley College, 163 Academic Building, Fogelsville, PA 18051, 610-285-5033. *Fax:* 610-285-5220. *E-mail:* jcw4@psu.edu

PENNSYLVANIA STATE UNIVERSITY SCHUYLKILL CAMPUS OF THE CAPITAL COLLEGE

Schuylkill Haven, PA

Tuition & fees (PA res): $6222 **Average undergraduate aid package: N/A**

ABOUT THE INSTITUTION State-related, coed. Awards: associate and bachelor's degrees (bachelor's degree programs completed at the Harrisburg campus). 13 undergraduate majors. Total enrollment: 1,015. Undergraduates: 993. Freshmen: 265. Federal methodology is used as a basis for awarding need-based institutional aid.

UNDERGRADUATE EXPENSES for 1999–2000 ***Application fee:*** $50. ***Tuition, state resident:*** full-time $5968; part-time $241 per credit. ***Tuition, nonresident:*** full-time $9244; part-time $386 per credit. ***Required fees:*** full-time $254; $43 per credit. Full-time tuition and fees vary according to course level, location, program, and student level. Part-time tuition and fees vary according to course level, course load, location, program, and student level. ***College room and board:*** $4690; ***room only:*** $2280. Room and board charges vary according to board plan and housing facility. ***Payment plan:*** deferred payment.

GIFT AID (NEED-BASED) ***Scholarships, grants, and awards:*** Federal Pell, FSEOG, state, private, college/university gift aid from institutional funds.

GIFT AID (NON-NEED-BASED) ***Tuition waivers:*** Full or partial for employees or children of employees, senior citizens. ***ROTC:*** Army.

LOANS ***Programs:*** FFEL (Subsidized and Unsubsidized Stafford, PLUS), Perkins, college/university.

WORK-STUDY Federal work-study jobs available. ***State or other work-study/employment:*** Part-time jobs available.

APPLYING for FINANCIAL AID ***Required financial aid form:*** FAFSA. ***Financial aid deadline:*** Continuous. ***Notification date:*** Continuous beginning 3/1.

CONTACT Karen Pothering, Student Aid Advisor, Pennsylvania State University Schuylkill Campus of the Capital College, 200 University Drive, Schuylkill Haven, PA 17972-2208, 570-385-6244. *Fax:* 570-385-3672. *E-mail:* krp1@psu.edu

PENNSYLVANIA STATE UNIVERSITY UNIVERSITY PARK CAMPUS

State College, PA

Tuition & fees (PA res): $6436 **Average undergraduate aid package: $8114**

ABOUT THE INSTITUTION State-related, coed. Awards: associate, bachelor's, master's, and doctoral degrees. 133 undergraduate majors. Total enrollment: 40,658. Undergraduates: 34,505. Freshmen: 5,069. Federal methodology is used as a basis for awarding need-based institutional aid.

UNDERGRADUATE EXPENSES for 1999–2000 ***Application fee:*** $50. ***Tuition, state resident:*** full-time $6162; part-time $258 per credit. ***Tuition, nonresident:*** full-time $13,278; part-time $554 per credit. ***Required fees:*** full-time $274; $46 per credit. Full-time tuition and fees vary according to course level, course load, location, program, and student level. Part-time tuition and fees vary according to course level, course load, location, program, and student level. ***College room and board:*** $4690; ***room only:*** $2280. Room and board charges vary according to board plan. ***Payment plan:*** deferred payment.

FRESHMAN FINANCIAL AID (Fall 1998) 9607 applied for aid; of those 82% were deemed to have need. 94% of freshmen with need received aid; of those 6% had need fully met. *Average percent of need met:* 64% (excluding resources awarded to replace EFC). *Average financial aid package:* $6985 (excluding resources awarded to replace EFC). 14% of all full-time freshmen had no need and received non-need-based aid.

UNDERGRADUATE FINANCIAL AID (Fall 1998) 37,981 applied for aid; of those 87% were deemed to have need. 96% of undergraduates with need received aid; of those 7% had need fully met. *Average percent of need met:* 69% (excluding resources awarded to replace EFC). *Average financial aid package:* $8114 (excluding resources awarded to replace EFC). 13% of all full-time undergraduates had no need and received non-need-based aid.

GIFT AID (NEED-BASED) ***Total amount:*** $88,424,437 (43% Federal, 44% state, 13% institutional). ***Receiving aid:*** *Freshmen:* 45% (5,370); *all full-time undergraduates:* 41% (22,069). ***Average award:*** Freshmen: $3023; Undergraduates: $3024. ***Scholarships, grants, and awards:*** Federal Pell, FSEOG, state, private, college/university gift aid from institutional funds.

GIFT AID (NON-NEED-BASED) ***Total amount:*** $19,234,128 (59% institutional, 41% external sources). ***Receiving aid:*** *Freshmen:* 19% (2,276); *Undergraduates:* 17% (9,258). ***Tuition waivers:*** Full or partial for employees or children of employees, senior citizens. ***ROTC:*** Army, Naval, Air Force.

LOANS ***Student loans:*** $142,369,343 (67% need-based, 33% non-need-based). 64% of past graduating class borrowed through all loan programs. Average indebtedness per student: $17,125. ***Average need-based loan:*** Freshmen: $2486; Undergraduates: $3532. ***Parent loans:*** $29,643,537 (100% non-need-based). ***Programs:*** FFEL (Subsidized and Unsubsidized Stafford, PLUS), Perkins, college/university.

WORK-STUDY ***Federal work-study:*** *Total amount:* $3,815,241; 3,312 jobs averaging $1190. ***State or other work-study/employment:*** *Total amount:* $1,580,025 (100% need-based). 20 part-time jobs averaging $760.

ATHLETIC AWARDS *Total amount:* 5,321,029 (100% non-need-based).

APPLYING for FINANCIAL AID ***Required financial aid form:*** FAFSA. ***Financial aid deadline:*** Continuous. ***Notification date:*** Continuous beginning 3/1.

CONTACT Ms. Anna Griswold, Assistant Vice Provost for Student Financial Aid, Pennsylvania State University University Park Campus, 314 Shields Building, University Park, PA 16802, 814-865-6301. *Fax:* 814-863-0322. *E-mail:* amg5@psu.edu

PEPPERDINE UNIVERSITY

Malibu, CA

Tuition & fees: $23,070 **Average undergraduate aid package: N/A**

ABOUT THE INSTITUTION Independent religious, coed. Awards: bachelor's, master's, doctoral, and first professional degrees (the university is organized into five colleges: Seaver, the School of Law, the School of Business and Management, the School of Public Policy, and the Graduate School of Education and Psychology. Seaver College is the undergraduate, residential, liberal arts school of the University and is committed to providing education of outstanding academic quality with particular attention to Christian values). 43 undergraduate majors. Total enrollment: 7,885. Undergraduates: 3,230. Federal methodology is used as a basis for awarding need-based institutional aid.

UNDERGRADUATE EXPENSES for 1999–2000 ***Application fee:*** $55. ***Comprehensive fee:*** $30,080 includes full-time tuition ($23,000), mandatory fees ($70), and room and board ($7010). ***College room only:*** $4440. Room and board charges vary according to housing facility. ***Part-time tuition:*** $720 per unit. ***Payment plans:*** tuition prepayment, installment, deferred payment.

GIFT AID (NEED-BASED) ***Scholarships, grants, and awards:*** Federal Pell, FSEOG, state, private, college/university gift aid from institutional funds.

GIFT AID (NON-NEED-BASED) ***Scholarships, grants, and awards by category:*** *Academic Interests/Achievement:* biological sciences, business, communication, education, general academic interests/achievements, humanities, international studies, religion/biblical studies, social sciences. *Creative Arts/Performance:* art/fine arts, debating, journalism/publications, music, performing arts, theater/drama. ***Tuition waivers:*** Full or partial for employees or children of employees. ***ROTC:*** Army cooperative, Naval cooperative, Air Force cooperative.

LOANS ***Programs:*** FFEL (Subsidized and Unsubsidized Stafford, PLUS), Perkins, state, college/university, GATE Loans, EXCEL Loans, Signature Loans.

WORK-STUDY Federal work-study jobs available.

APPLYING for FINANCIAL AID ***Required financial aid forms:*** FAFSA, institution's own form, state aid form, W-2 forms, federal income tax form(s), financial aid transcript (for transfers). ***Financial aid deadline:*** 4/1 (priority: 1/15). ***Notification date:*** 4/15. Students must reply by 5/1.

CONTACT Ms. Edna Powell, Director of Financial Assistance, Pepperdine University, 24255 Pacific Coast Highway, Malibu, CA 90263-0001, 310-456-4301.

PERU STATE COLLEGE

Peru, NE

ABOUT THE INSTITUTION State-supported, coed. Awards: bachelor's and master's degrees. 49 undergraduate majors. Total enrollment: 1,664. Undergraduates: 1,454. Freshmen: 193.

GIFT AID (NEED-BASED) ***Scholarships, grants, and awards:*** Federal Pell, FSEOG, state, college/university gift aid from institutional funds.

GIFT AID (NON-NEED-BASED) ***Scholarships, grants, and awards by category:*** *Academic Interests/Achievement:* biological sciences, business, computer science, education, English, general academic interests/achievements, humanities, mathematics, physical sciences, premedicine, social sciences. *Creative Arts/Performance:* art/fine arts, music, theater/drama. *Special Achievements/Activities:* leadership, memberships.

LOANS ***Programs:*** FFEL (Subsidized and Unsubsidized Stafford, PLUS), Perkins, college/university.

WORK-STUDY Federal work-study jobs available.

APPLYING for FINANCIAL AID ***Required financial aid forms:*** FAFSA, institution's own form.

CONTACT Financial Aid Office, Peru State College, PO Box 10, Peru, NE 68421, 402-872-3815 or toll-free 800-742-4412 (in-state).

PFEIFFER UNIVERSITY

Misenheimer, NC

Tuition & fees: $10,844 **Average undergraduate aid package: $7369**

ABOUT THE INSTITUTION Independent United Methodist, coed. Awards: bachelor's and master's degrees. 33 undergraduate majors. Total enrollment: 1,612. Undergraduates: 969. Freshmen: 159. Federal methodology is used as a basis for awarding need-based institutional aid.

Pfeiffer University (continued)

UNDERGRADUATE EXPENSES for 1999–2000 ***Application fee:*** $25. ***Comprehensive fee:*** $15,211 includes full-time tuition ($10,844) and room and board ($4367). ***College room only:*** $2270. Full-time tuition and fees vary according to course load. Room and board charges vary according to board plan and housing facility. ***Part-time tuition:*** $249 per semester hour. ***Payment plans:*** installment, deferred payment.

FRESHMAN FINANCIAL AID (Fall 1999, est.) 147 applied for aid; of those 90% were deemed to have need. 100% of freshmen with need received aid; of those 26% had need fully met. *Average percent of need met:* 80% (excluding resources awarded to replace EFC). *Average financial aid package:* $5830 (excluding resources awarded to replace EFC). 13% of all full-time freshmen had no need and received non-need-based aid.

UNDERGRADUATE FINANCIAL AID (Fall 1999, est.) 705 applied for aid; of those 91% were deemed to have need. 100% of undergraduates with need received aid; of those 28% had need fully met. *Average percent of need met:* 83% (excluding resources awarded to replace EFC). *Average financial aid package:* $7369 (excluding resources awarded to replace EFC). 6% of all full-time undergraduates had no need and received non-need-based aid.

GIFT AID (NEED-BASED) ***Total amount:*** $2,494,269 (27% Federal, 25% state, 44% institutional, 4% external sources). ***Receiving aid:*** *Freshmen:* 79% (127); *all full-time undergraduates:* 77% (627). ***Average award:*** Freshmen: $3885; Undergraduates: $4645. ***Scholarships, grants, and awards:*** Federal Pell, FSEOG, state, private, United Methodist Board of Higher Education and Ministry Scholarships.

GIFT AID (NON-NEED-BASED) ***Total amount:*** $1,770,592 (1% Federal, 55% state, 43% institutional, 1% external sources). ***Receiving aid:*** *Freshmen:* 8% (13); *Undergraduates:* 6% (50). ***Scholarships, grants, and awards by category:*** *Academic Interests/Achievement:* general academic interests/achievements, international studies. *Creative Arts/Performance:* music. ***Tuition waivers:*** Full or partial for employees or children of employees. ***ROTC:*** Army cooperative.

LOANS ***Student loans:*** $4,555,997 (59% need-based, 41% non-need-based). ***Average need-based loan:*** Freshmen: $1683; Undergraduates: $2530. ***Parent loans:*** $758,528 (100% non-need-based). ***Programs:*** FFEL (Subsidized and Unsubsidized Stafford, PLUS), Perkins, United Methodist Board of Higher Education and Ministry Loans.

WORK-STUDY ***Federal work-study:*** *Total amount:* $254,872; jobs available.

ATHLETIC AWARDS *Total amount:* 642,390 (100% non-need-based).

APPLYING for FINANCIAL AID ***Required financial aid form:*** FAFSA. ***Financial aid deadline (priority):*** 3/15. ***Notification date:*** Continuous beginning 4/15. Students must reply within 2 weeks of notification.

CONTACT Financial Aid Office, Pfeiffer University, PO Box 960, Misenheimer, NC 28109, 704-463-1360 or toll-free 800-338-2060. *Fax:* 704-463-1363.

PHILADELPHIA COLLEGE OF BIBLE

Langhorne, PA

Tuition & fees: $10,355 **Average undergraduate aid package: $7108**

ABOUT THE INSTITUTION Independent nondenominational, coed. Awards: associate, bachelor's, and master's degrees. 11 undergraduate majors. Total enrollment: 1,434. Undergraduates: 1,073. Freshmen: 196. Federal methodology is used as a basis for awarding need-based institutional aid.

UNDERGRADUATE EXPENSES for 2000–2001 ***Application fee:*** $25. ***Comprehensive fee:*** $15,428 includes full-time tuition ($10,070), mandatory fees ($285), and room and board ($5073). ***College room only:*** $2395. Full-time tuition and fees vary according to course load, location, and program. Room and board charges vary according to board plan, housing facility, and location. ***Part-time tuition:*** $303 per credit. ***Part-time fees:*** $6 per credit. Part-time tuition and fees vary according to course load, location, and program. ***Payment plan:*** installment.

FRESHMAN FINANCIAL AID (Fall 1999) 165 applied for aid; of those 87% were deemed to have need. 100% of freshmen with need received aid; of those 16% had need fully met. *Average percent of need met:* 58% (excluding resources awarded to replace EFC). *Average financial aid package:* $6705 (excluding resources awarded to replace EFC). 11% of all full-time freshmen had no need and received non-need-based aid.

UNDERGRADUATE FINANCIAL AID (Fall 1999) 625 applied for aid; of those 87% were deemed to have need. 100% of undergraduates with need received aid; of those 17% had need fully met. *Average percent of need met:* 60% (excluding resources awarded to replace EFC). *Average financial aid package:* $7108 (excluding resources awarded to replace EFC). 29% of all full-time undergraduates had no need and received non-need-based aid.

GIFT AID (NEED-BASED) ***Total amount:*** $2,506,835 (22% Federal, 17% state, 55% institutional, 6% external sources). ***Receiving aid:*** *Freshmen:* 72% (138); *all full-time undergraduates:* 57% (520). ***Average award:*** Freshmen: $5055; Undergraduates: $4612. ***Scholarships, grants, and awards:*** Federal Pell, FSEOG, state, private, college/university gift aid from institutional funds.

GIFT AID (NON-NEED-BASED) ***Total amount:*** $687,627 (1% Federal, 1% state, 90% institutional, 8% external sources). ***Receiving aid:*** *Freshmen:* 7% (13); *Undergraduates:* 4% (39). ***Scholarships, grants, and awards by category:*** *Academic Interests/Achievement:* 261 awards ($379,480 total): general academic interests/achievements. *Creative Arts/Performance:* 59 awards ($66,550 total): music. *Special Achievements/Activities:* 566 awards ($540,900 total): general special achievements/activities, leadership, religious involvement. *Special Characteristics:* 268 awards ($1,067,515 total): children and siblings of alumni, children of faculty/staff, international students, relatives of clergy, siblings of current students. ***Tuition waivers:*** Full or partial for children of alumni, employees or children of employees.

LOANS ***Student loans:*** $1,635,137 (81% need-based, 19% non-need-based). 67% of past graduating class borrowed through all loan programs. Average indebtedness per student: $12,170. ***Average need-based loan:*** Freshmen: $1500; Undergraduates: $2283. ***Parent loans:*** $379,837 (50% need-based, 50% non-need-based). ***Programs:*** FFEL (Subsidized and Unsubsidized Stafford, PLUS).

WORK-STUDY ***Federal work-study:*** *Total amount:* $116,422; 75 jobs averaging $1000.

APPLYING for FINANCIAL AID ***Required financial aid form:*** FAFSA. ***Financial aid deadline (priority):*** 5/1. ***Notification date:*** Continuous. Students must reply within 2 weeks of notification.

CONTACT Mr. Travis S. Roy, Director of Financial Aid, Philadelphia College of Bible, 200 Manor Avenue, Langhorne, PA 19047-2990, 215-702-4246 or toll-free 800-876-5800 (out-of-state). *E-mail:* troy@pcb.edu

PHILADELPHIA COLLEGE OF PHARMACY AND SCIENCE

Philadelphia, PA

See University of the Sciences in Philadelphia

PHILADELPHIA COLLEGE OF TEXTILES AND SCIENCE

Philadelphia, PA

See Philadelphia University

PHILADELPHIA UNIVERSITY

Philadelphia, PA

Tuition & fees: $14,738 **Average undergraduate aid package: $11,935**

ABOUT THE INSTITUTION Independent, coed. Awards: bachelor's and master's degrees. 28 undergraduate majors. Total enrollment: 3,401. Undergraduates: 2,805. Freshmen: 623. Federal methodology is used as a basis for awarding need-based institutional aid.

UNDERGRADUATE EXPENSES for 1999–2000 ***Application fee:*** $35. ***Comprehensive fee:*** $21,314 includes full-time tuition ($14,692), mandatory fees ($46), and room and board ($6576). ***College room only:*** $3202.

Full-time tuition and fees vary according to program. Room and board charges vary according to board plan and housing facility. ***Part-time tuition:*** $474 per credit. Part-time tuition and fees vary according to class time and program. ***Payment plans:*** installment, deferred payment.

FRESHMAN FINANCIAL AID (Fall 1999) 515 applied for aid; of those 85% were deemed to have need. 100% of freshmen with need received aid; of those 15% had need fully met. *Average percent of need met:* 77% (excluding resources awarded to replace EFC). *Average financial aid package:* $12,627 (excluding resources awarded to replace EFC). 27% of all full-time freshmen had no need and received non-need-based aid.

UNDERGRADUATE FINANCIAL AID (Fall 1999) 1,706 applied for aid; of those 87% were deemed to have need. 100% of undergraduates with need received aid; of those 14% had need fully met. *Average percent of need met:* 73% (excluding resources awarded to replace EFC). *Average financial aid package:* $11,935 (excluding resources awarded to replace EFC). 24% of all full-time undergraduates had no need and received non-need-based aid.

GIFT AID (NEED-BASED) ***Total amount:*** $11,167,628 (13% Federal, 14% state, 72% institutional, 1% external sources). ***Receiving aid:*** *Freshmen:* 71% (435); *all full-time undergraduates:* 67% (1,449). ***Average award:*** Freshmen: $8347; Undergraduates: $7229. ***Scholarships, grants, and awards:*** Federal Pell, FSEOG, state, college/university gift aid from institutional funds.

GIFT AID (NON-NEED-BASED) ***Total amount:*** $1,056,443 (95% institutional, 5% external sources). ***Receiving aid:*** *Freshmen:* 7% (44); *Undergraduates:* 6% (132). ***Scholarships, grants, and awards by category:*** *Academic Interests/Achievement:* 1,706 awards ($7,218,162 total): general academic interests/achievements. ***Tuition waivers:*** Full or partial for employees or children of employees.

LOANS ***Student loans:*** $8,338,230 (76% need-based, 24% non-need-based). 64% of past graduating class borrowed through all loan programs. Average indebtedness per student: $19,630. ***Average need-based loan:*** Freshmen: $3496; Undergraduates: $4191. ***Parent loans:*** $3,048,145 (29% need-based, 71% non-need-based). ***Programs:*** FFEL (Subsidized and Unsubsidized Stafford, PLUS), Perkins, alternative loans.

WORK-STUDY ***Federal work-study:*** *Total amount:* $1,169,750; 665 jobs averaging $1800.

ATHLETIC AWARDS *Total amount:* 810,909 (31% need-based, 69% non-need-based).

APPLYING for FINANCIAL AID ***Required financial aid form:*** FAFSA. ***Financial aid deadline:*** 4/15. ***Notification date:*** Continuous. Students must reply within 3 weeks of notification.

CONTACT Ms. Lisa J. Cooper, Director of Financial Aid, Philadelphia University, Schoolhouse Lane and Henry Avenue, Philadelphia, PA 19144-5497, 215-951-2940. *Fax:* 215-951-2907.

PHILANDER SMITH COLLEGE

Little Rock, AR

Tuition & fees: $3808 **Average undergraduate aid package: N/A**

ABOUT THE INSTITUTION Independent United Methodist, coed. Awards: bachelor's degrees. 20 undergraduate majors. Total enrollment: 932. Undergraduates: 932. Freshmen: 170. Federal methodology is used as a basis for awarding need-based institutional aid.

UNDERGRADUATE EXPENSES for 1999–2000 ***Application fee:*** $10. ***Comprehensive fee:*** $6554 includes full-time tuition ($3616), mandatory fees ($192), and room and board ($2746). ***College room only:*** $1334. Full-time tuition and fees vary according to class time, course load, location, and program. ***Part-time tuition:*** $140 per credit. ***Part-time fees:*** $5 per credit. Part-time tuition and fees vary according to class time and course load. ***Payment plans:*** installment, deferred payment.

GIFT AID (NEED-BASED) ***Scholarships, grants, and awards:*** Federal Pell, FSEOG, state, private, college/university gift aid from institutional funds.

GIFT AID (NON-NEED-BASED) ***Scholarships, grants, and awards by category:*** *Academic Interests/Achievement:* general academic interests/achievements. *Creative Arts/Performance:* music. ***Tuition waivers:*** Full or partial for employees or children of employees. ***ROTC:*** Army cooperative.

LOANS ***Programs:*** Federal Direct (Subsidized and Unsubsidized Stafford, PLUS), Perkins, state.

WORK-STUDY Federal work-study jobs available.

APPLYING for FINANCIAL AID ***Required financial aid forms:*** FAFSA, institution's own form. ***Financial aid deadline (priority):*** 4/15. ***Notification date:*** Continuous. Students must reply within 2 weeks of notification.

CONTACT Director of Financial Aid, Philander Smith College, 812 West 13th Street, Little Rock, AR 72202-3799, 501-370-5350 or toll-free 800-446-6772.

PIEDMONT BAPTIST COLLEGE

Winston-Salem, NC

Tuition & fees: $5750 **Average undergraduate aid package: $1200**

ABOUT THE INSTITUTION Independent Baptist, coed. Awards: associate, bachelor's, and master's degrees. 14 undergraduate majors. Total enrollment: 320. Undergraduates: 300. Freshmen: 50. Federal methodology is used as a basis for awarding need-based institutional aid.

UNDERGRADUATE EXPENSES for 1999–2000 ***Application fee:*** $30. ***Comprehensive fee:*** $9150 includes full-time tuition ($5270), mandatory fees ($480), and room and board ($3400). Full-time tuition and fees vary according to course load. ***Part-time tuition:*** $215 per credit hour. ***Part-time fees:*** $140 per term part-time. Part-time tuition and fees vary according to course load. ***Payment plan:*** installment.

FRESHMAN FINANCIAL AID (Fall 1998) 65 applied for aid; of those 100% were deemed to have need. 100% of freshmen with need received aid. *Average percent of need met:* 30% (excluding resources awarded to replace EFC). *Average financial aid package:* $1500 (excluding resources awarded to replace EFC).

UNDERGRADUATE FINANCIAL AID (Fall 1998) 153 applied for aid; of those 100% were deemed to have need. 100% of undergraduates with need received aid. *Average percent of need met:* 20% (excluding resources awarded to replace EFC). *Average financial aid package:* $1200 (excluding resources awarded to replace EFC).

GIFT AID (NEED-BASED) ***Total amount:*** $702,190 (45% Federal, 52% institutional, 3% external sources). ***Receiving aid:*** *Freshmen:* 73% (65); *all full-time undergraduates:* 62% (153). ***Scholarships, grants, and awards:*** Federal Pell, FSEOG, college/university gift aid from institutional funds.

GIFT AID (NON-NEED-BASED) ***Receiving aid:*** *Freshmen:* 4% (4); *Undergraduates:* 11% (26). ***Scholarships, grants, and awards by category:*** *Academic Interests/Achievement:* general academic interests/achievements. *Special Characteristics:* children of faculty/staff, relatives of clergy, spouses of current students, veterans. ***Tuition waivers:*** Full or partial for children of alumni, employees or children of employees, adult students.

LOANS ***Student loans:*** $489,936 (100% need-based). 85% of past graduating class borrowed through all loan programs. Average indebtedness per student: $15,000. ***Parent loans:*** $31,296 (100% need-based). ***Programs:*** FFEL (Subsidized and Unsubsidized Stafford, PLUS).

WORK-STUDY ***Federal work-study:*** *Total amount:* $23,990; 18 jobs available.

APPLYING for FINANCIAL AID ***Required financial aid forms:*** FAFSA, institution's own form. ***Financial aid deadline (priority):*** 6/1. ***Notification date:*** 8/1. Students must reply within 3 weeks of notification.

CONTACT Nancy Minton, Director of Financial Aid, Piedmont Baptist College, 716 Franklin Street, Winston-Salem, NC 27101-5197, 336-725-8344 Ext. 2322 or toll-free 800-937-5097. *Fax:* 336-725-5522. *E-mail:* mintonn@pbc.edu

PIEDMONT COLLEGE

Demorest, GA

Tuition & fees: $9500 **Average undergraduate aid package: $8042**

ABOUT THE INSTITUTION Independent religious, coed. Awards: bachelor's and master's degrees. 41 undergraduate majors. Total enrollment: 1,742.

Piedmont College (continued)

Undergraduates: 1,042. Freshmen: 236. Both federal and institutional methodology are used as a basis for awarding need-based institutional aid.

UNDERGRADUATE EXPENSES for 2000–2001 ***Application fee:*** $20. ***Comprehensive fee:*** $13,900 includes full-time tuition ($9500) and room and board ($4400). ***College room only:*** $2250. Full-time tuition and fees vary according to program. Room and board charges vary according to board plan and housing facility. ***Part-time tuition:*** $396 per credit hour. Part-time tuition and fees vary according to program. ***Payment plan:*** installment.

FRESHMAN FINANCIAL AID (Fall 1999, est.) 149 applied for aid; of those 90% were deemed to have need. 100% of freshmen with need received aid; of those 84% had need fully met. *Average percent of need met:* 85% (excluding resources awarded to replace EFC). *Average financial aid package:* $7621 (excluding resources awarded to replace EFC). 10% of all full-time freshmen had no need and received non-need-based aid.

UNDERGRADUATE FINANCIAL AID (Fall 1999, est.) 867 applied for aid; of those 90% were deemed to have need. 90% of undergraduates with need received aid; of those 50% had need fully met. *Average percent of need met:* 89% (excluding resources awarded to replace EFC). *Average financial aid package:* $8042 (excluding resources awarded to replace EFC). 9% of all full-time undergraduates had no need and received non-need-based aid.

GIFT AID (NEED-BASED) ***Total amount:*** $1,223,532 (62% Federal, 38% institutional). ***Receiving aid:*** *Freshmen:* 81% (120); *all full-time undergraduates:* 49% (421). ***Average award:*** Freshmen: $2310; Undergraduates: $2721. ***Scholarships, grants, and awards:*** Federal Pell, FSEOG, state, private, college/university gift aid from institutional funds.

GIFT AID (NON-NEED-BASED) ***Total amount:*** $3,631,180 (48% state, 51% institutional, 1% external sources). ***Receiving aid:*** *Freshmen:* 83% (123); *Undergraduates:* 73% (631). ***Scholarships, grants, and awards by category:*** *Academic Interests/Achievement:* 489 awards ($388,554 total): biological sciences, education, English, foreign languages, general academic interests/achievements, health fields, humanities, mathematics, premedicine, religion/biblical studies. *Creative Arts/Performance:* 54 awards ($44,400 total): art/fine arts, music, theater/drama. *Special Achievements/Activities:* 168 awards ($449,900 total): leadership. *Special Characteristics:* 46 awards ($316,948 total): adult students, children of faculty/staff, international students, out-of-state students. ***Tuition waivers:*** Full or partial for employees or children of employees. ***ROTC:*** Army cooperative, Air Force cooperative.

LOANS ***Student loans:*** $3,357,624 (67% need-based, 33% non-need-based). 67% of past graduating class borrowed through all loan programs. Average indebtedness per student: $13,048. ***Average need-based loan:*** Freshmen: $1602; Undergraduates: $5110. ***Parent loans:*** $230,144 (100% non-need-based). ***Programs:*** Federal Direct (Subsidized and Unsubsidized Stafford, PLUS).

WORK-STUDY ***Federal work-study:*** *Total amount:* $106,178; 48 jobs averaging $2212. ***State or other work-study/employment:*** *Total amount:* $173,821 (35% need-based, 65% non-need-based). 140 part-time jobs averaging $1241.

APPLYING for FINANCIAL AID ***Required financial aid forms:*** FAFSA, institution's own form, state aid form. ***Financial aid deadline (priority):*** 5/1. ***Notification date:*** 6/15. Students must reply within 2 weeks of notification.

CONTACT Mrs. Kim Lovell, Director of Financial Aid, Piedmont College, PO Box 10, Demorest, GA 30535-0010, 706-778-3000 Ext. 1191 or toll-free 800-277-7020. *Fax:* 706-776-2811. *E-mail:* klovell@piedmont.edu

PIKEVILLE COLLEGE

Pikeville, KY

Tuition & fees: $7800 **Average undergraduate aid package: $8500**

ABOUT THE INSTITUTION Independent religious, coed. Awards: associate, bachelor's, and first professional degrees. 27 undergraduate majors. Total enrollment: 953. Undergraduates: 773. Freshmen: 207. Both federal and institutional methodology are used as a basis for awarding need-based institutional aid.

UNDERGRADUATE EXPENSES for 2000–2001 ***Comprehensive fee:*** $11,140 includes full-time tuition ($7800) and room and board ($3340). ***Part-time tuition:*** $310 per semester hour. ***Payment plan:*** installment.

FRESHMAN FINANCIAL AID (Fall 1999) 207 applied for aid; of those 94% were deemed to have need. 100% of freshmen with need received aid; of those 59% had need fully met. *Average percent of need met:* 94% (excluding resources awarded to replace EFC). *Average financial aid package:* $8500 (excluding resources awarded to replace EFC). 6% of all full-time freshmen had no need and received non-need-based aid.

UNDERGRADUATE FINANCIAL AID (Fall 1999) 723 applied for aid; of those 94% were deemed to have need. 100% of undergraduates with need received aid; of those 76% had need fully met. *Average percent of need met:* 94% (excluding resources awarded to replace EFC). *Average financial aid package:* $8500 (excluding resources awarded to replace EFC). 4% of all full-time undergraduates had no need and received non-need-based aid.

GIFT AID (NEED-BASED) ***Total amount:*** $2,449,337 (48% Federal, 39% state, 13% external sources). ***Receiving aid:*** *Freshmen:* 83% (172); *all full-time undergraduates:* 72% (524). ***Average award:*** Freshmen: $3200; Undergraduates: $3200. ***Scholarships, grants, and awards:*** Federal Pell, FSEOG, state, private, college/university gift aid from institutional funds.

GIFT AID (NON-NEED-BASED) ***Total amount:*** $1,671,749 (5% state, 90% institutional, 5% external sources). ***Receiving aid:*** *Freshmen:* 84% (174); *Undergraduates:* 82% (591). ***Scholarships, grants, and awards by category:*** *Academic Interests/Achievement:* 586 awards ($1,507,913 total): general academic interests/achievements. *Creative Arts/Performance:* 59 awards ($56,535 total): music. *Special Achievements/Activities:* 1 award ($1000 total): community service. *Special Characteristics:* 1 award ($2500 total): members of minority groups. ***Tuition waivers:*** Full or partial for employees or children of employees, senior citizens.

LOANS ***Student loans:*** $1,311,450 (70% need-based, 30% non-need-based). 63% of past graduating class borrowed through all loan programs. Average indebtedness per student: $12,000. ***Average need-based loan:*** Freshmen: $3000; Undergraduates: $3000. ***Parent loans:*** $12,332 (100% non-need-based). ***Programs:*** FFEL (Subsidized and Unsubsidized Stafford, PLUS), Perkins, college/university.

WORK-STUDY ***Federal work-study:*** *Total amount:* $274,066; 211 jobs averaging $1200. ***State or other work-study/employment:*** *Total amount:* $11,600 (14% need-based, 86% non-need-based). 5 part-time jobs averaging $2300.

ATHLETIC AWARDS *Total amount:* 493,218 (100% non-need-based).

APPLYING for FINANCIAL AID ***Required financial aid forms:*** FAFSA, statement of educational purpose, registration status. ***Financial aid deadline (priority):*** 3/15. ***Notification date:*** Continuous. Students must reply within 2 weeks of notification.

CONTACT Mrs. Zelena O'Sullivan, Director of Student Financial Services, Pikeville College, 214 Sycamore Street, Pikeville, KY 41501, 606-432-9382. *Fax:* 606-432-9328.

PINE MANOR COLLEGE

Chestnut Hill, MA

Tuition & fees: $11,440 **Average undergraduate aid package: $14,492**

ABOUT THE INSTITUTION Independent, women only. Awards: associate, bachelor's, and master's degrees. 37 undergraduate majors. Total enrollment: 329. Undergraduates: 329. Freshmen: 98. Both federal and institutional methodology are used as a basis for awarding need-based institutional aid.

UNDERGRADUATE EXPENSES for 1999–2000 ***Application fee:*** $25. ***Comprehensive fee:*** $18,600 includes full-time tuition ($11,440) and room and board ($7160). ***College room only:*** $3580. Room and board charges vary according to housing facility. ***Part-time tuition:*** $210 per credit. ***Payment plans:*** tuition prepayment, installment.

FRESHMAN FINANCIAL AID (Fall 1999) 72 applied for aid; of those 90% were deemed to have need. 100% of freshmen with need received aid; of those 40% had need fully met. *Average percent of need met:* 93% (excluding resources awarded to replace EFC). *Average financial aid package:* $14,360 (excluding resources awarded to replace EFC). 2% of all full-time freshmen had no need and received non-need-based aid.

UNDERGRADUATE FINANCIAL AID (Fall 1999) 217 applied for aid; of those 94% were deemed to have need. 100% of undergraduates with need received aid; of those 41% had need fully met. *Average percent of need met:* 93% (excluding resources awarded to replace EFC). *Average financial aid package:* $14,492 (excluding resources awarded to replace EFC). 3% of all full-time undergraduates had no need and received non-need-based aid.

GIFT AID (NEED-BASED) ***Total amount:*** $2,086,670 (12% Federal, 6% state, 80% institutional, 2% external sources). ***Receiving aid:*** *Freshmen:* 66% (65); *all full-time undergraduates:* 63% (205). ***Average award:*** Freshmen: $9866; Undergraduates: $10,105. ***Scholarships, grants, and awards:*** Federal Pell, FSEOG, state, private, college/university gift aid from institutional funds.

GIFT AID (NON-NEED-BASED) ***Total amount:*** $47,723 (99% institutional, 1% external sources). ***Receiving aid:*** *Freshmen:* 13% (13); *Undergraduates:* 26% (83). ***Scholarships, grants, and awards by category:*** *Academic Interests/Achievement:* biological sciences, education, general academic interests/achievements, health fields. *Special Achievements/Activities:* general special achievements/activities, leadership. *Special Characteristics:* children and siblings of alumni, ethnic background, international students, local/state students, members of minority groups, siblings of current students. ***Tuition waivers:*** Full or partial for children of alumni, employees or children of employees, adult students.

LOANS ***Student loans:*** $975,207 (77% need-based, 23% non-need-based). 71% of past graduating class borrowed through all loan programs. Average indebtedness per student: $15,229. ***Average need-based loan:*** Freshmen: $2680; Undergraduates: $3582. ***Parent loans:*** $160,471 (31% need-based, 69% non-need-based). ***Programs:*** FFEL (Subsidized and Unsubsidized Stafford, PLUS), state.

WORK-STUDY ***Federal work-study:*** *Total amount:* $165,012; 139 jobs averaging $1402.

APPLYING for FINANCIAL AID ***Required financial aid forms:*** FAFSA, CSS Financial Aid PROFILE. ***Financial aid deadline (priority):*** 3/1. ***Notification date:*** Continuous. Students must reply within 2 weeks of notification.

CONTACT Ms. Linda Schoendorf, Director of Financial Aid, Pine Manor College, 400 Heath Street, Chestnut Hill, MA 02167, 617-731-7129 or toll-free 800-762-1357. *Fax:* 617-731-7199. *E-mail:* schoendl@pmc.edu

PITTSBURG STATE UNIVERSITY
Pittsburg, KS

Tuition & fees (KS res): $2142 | **Average undergraduate aid package: $5553**

ABOUT THE INSTITUTION State-supported, coed. Awards: associate, bachelor's, and master's degrees. 88 undergraduate majors. Total enrollment: 6,289. Undergraduates: 5,211. Federal methodology is used as a basis for awarding need-based institutional aid.

UNDERGRADUATE EXPENSES for 1999–2000 ***Application fee:*** $20. ***Tuition, state resident:*** full-time $2142; part-time $78 per semester hour. ***Tuition, nonresident:*** full-time $6608; part-time $227 per semester hour. ***College room and board:*** $3715. Room and board charges vary according to board plan. ***Payment plan:*** installment.

FRESHMAN FINANCIAL AID (Fall 1999, est.) 618 applied for aid; of those 78% were deemed to have need. 94% of freshmen with need received aid; of those 11% had need fully met. *Average percent of need met:* 72% (excluding resources awarded to replace EFC). *Average financial aid package:* $4635 (excluding resources awarded to replace EFC). 26% of all full-time freshmen had no need and received non-need-based aid.

UNDERGRADUATE FINANCIAL AID (Fall 1999, est.) 2,962 applied for aid; of those 84% were deemed to have need. 95% of undergraduates with need received aid; of those 13% had need fully met. *Average percent of need met:* 78% (excluding resources awarded to replace EFC). *Average financial aid package:* $5553 (excluding resources awarded t EFC). 20% of all full-time undergraduates had no need and non-need-based aid.

GIFT AID (NEED-BASED) ***Total amount:*** $5,276,970 (62% Fe state, 12% institutional, 17% external sources). ***Receiving aid:*** 33% (313); *all full-time undergraduates:* 32% (1,502). ***Avera*** Freshmen: $2246; Undergraduates: $2394. ***Scholarships, gi awards:*** Federal Pell, FSEOG, state, private, college/university g institutional funds.

GIFT AID (NON-NEED-BASED) ***Total amount:*** $1,081,269 (1% institutional, 38% external sources). ***Receiving aid:*** *Freshmen Undergraduates:* 4% (167). ***Scholarships, grants, and awards l*** *Academic Interests/Achievement:* 1,029 awards ($1,159,323 to cal sciences, business, communication, computer science, engineering/technologies, English, foreign languages, gener interests/achievements, health fields, home economics, n military science, physical sciences, social sciences. *Cr Performance:* 163 awards ($121,492 total): music. *Special Ch* general special characteristics. ***Tuition waivers:*** Full or partial f or children of employees. ***ROTC:*** Army.

LOANS ***Student loans:*** $10,616,667 (77% need-based, 23 based). 72% of past graduating class borrowed through all lc Average indebtedness per student: $10,433. ***Average nee*** Freshmen: $2622; Undergraduates: $3714. ***Parent loans:*** $! need-based, 67% non-need-based). ***Programs:*** FFEL (Si Unsubsidized Stafford, PLUS), Perkins, Federal Nursing, coll

WORK-STUDY ***Federal work-study:*** *Total amount:* $433, averaging $2406. ***State or other work-study/employment:*** $1,042,335 (16% need-based, 84% non-need-based). 682 averaging $1529.

ATHLETIC AWARDS *Total amount:* 571,758 (44% need-ba need-based).

APPLYING for FINANCIAL AID ***Required financial ai Financial aid deadline (priority):*** 3/1. ***Notification date:*** C ning 4/1. Students must reply within 2 weeks of notifica

CONTACT Joanna McCormick, Director, Student Finar Pittsburg State University, 1701 South Broadway, Pitts 5880, 316-235-4237 or toll-free 800-854-7488 Ext. 2. *Fa E-mail:* jmccormi@pittstate.edu

PITZER COLLEGE
Claremont, CA

Tuition & fees: $24,096 | **Average undergraduate a**

ABOUT THE INSTITUTION Independent, coed. Awards: 40 undergraduate majors. Total enrollment: 930. Ur Freshmen: 246. Both federal and institutional method basis for awarding need-based institutional aid.

UNDERGRADUATE EXPENSES for 1999–2000 ***Ap Comprehensive fee:*** $30,386 includes full-time tuitio tory fees ($2576), and room and board ($6290). $4124. Full-time tuition and fees vary according to cc board charges vary according to board plan. ***Part-ti*** course. ***Part-time fees:*** $298 per course; $96 per time tuition and fees vary according to course l installment, deferred payment.

FRESHMAN FINANCIAL AID (Fall 1999, est.) 143 a 80% were deemed to have need. 99% of freshmen of those 100% had need fully met. *Average perce* (excluding resources awarded to replace EFC). *Ave age:* $21,942 (excluding resources awarded to r full-time freshmen had no need and received non

UNDERGRADUATE FINANCIAL AID (Fall 1999, e of those 92% were deemed to have need. 100% need received aid; of those 100% had need fully *need met:* 100% (excluding resources awarded

'itzer College (continued)

'inancial aid package: $22,648 (excluding resources awarded to replace FC). 2% of all full-time undergraduates had no need and received non-eed-based aid.

IFT AID (NEED-BASED) ***Total amount:*** $7,732,934 (10% Federal, 16% tate, 72% institutional, 2% external sources). ***Receiving aid:*** *Freshmen:* 6% (112); *all full-time undergraduates:* 51% (434). ***Average award:*** 'eshmen: $18,676; Undergraduates: $15,613. ***Scholarships, grants, and wards:*** Federal Pell, FSEOG, state, private, college/university gift aid from stitutional funds.

'FT AID (NON-NEED-BASED) ***Total amount:*** $210,000 (100% institutional). ***eceiving aid:*** *Freshmen:* 2% (6); *Undergraduates:* 2% (21). ***Scholar-ips, grants, and awards by category:*** *Academic Interests/Achievement:* neral academic interests/achievements. *Special Achievements/Activities:* mmunity service, leadership. ***Tuition waivers:*** Full or partial for employees children of employees.

ANS ***Student loans:*** $2,429,057 (96% need-based, 4% non-need-sed). 60% of past graduating class borrowed through all loan programs. erage indebtedness per student: $20,530. ***Average need-based loan:*** shmen: $3284; Undergraduates: $4999. ***Parent loans:*** $801,789 (100% 1-need-based). ***Programs:*** FFEL (Subsidized and Unsubsidized Stafford, JS), Perkins, college/university.

RK-STUDY ***Federal work-study:*** *Total amount:* $959,563; 385 jobs raging $2492.

'LYING for FINANCIAL AID ***Required financial aid forms:*** FAFSA, CSS ncial Aid PROFILE, state aid form, noncustodial (divorced/separated) ent's statement, business/farm supplement. ***Financial aid deadline:*** ***Notification date:*** 4/1. Students must reply by 5/1.

ITACT Ms. Abigail W. Parsons, Associate Vice President, Admission Financial Aid, Pitzer College, 1050 North Mills Avenue, Claremont, CA 11-6101, 909-621-8208 or toll-free 800-748-9371. *Fax:* 909-607-5. *E-mail:* abby_parsons@pitzer.edu

PLATTSBURGH STATE UNIVERSITY OF NEW YORK

Plattsburgh, NY

& fees (NY res): $3957 **Average undergraduate aid package: $6701**

T THE INSTITUTION State-supported, coed. Awards: bachelor's and r's degrees and post-master's certificates. 46 undergraduate majors. enrollment: 6,015. Undergraduates: 5,326. Freshmen: 887. Federal odology is used as a basis for awarding need-based institutional aid.

RGRADUATE EXPENSES for 1999–2000 ***Application fee:*** $30. ***Tuition, resident:*** full-time $3400; part-time $137 per credit hour. ***Tuition, sident:*** full-time $8300; part-time $346 per credit hour. ***Required*** full-time $557; $19 per credit hour. Part-time tuition and fees vary ling to course load. ***College room and board:*** $4850; ***room only:*** . Room and board charges vary according to board plan. ***Payment*** installment, deferred payment.

MAN FINANCIAL AID (Fall 1998) 861 applied for aid; of those 75% eemed to have need. 98% of freshmen with need received aid; of 5% had need fully met. *Average percent of need met:* 69% (exclud-sources awarded to replace EFC). *Average financial aid package:* (excluding resources awarded to replace EFC). 25% of all full-time en had no need and received non-need-based aid.

GRADUATE FINANCIAL AID (Fall 1998) 4,120 applied for aid; of 76% were deemed to have need. 100% of undergraduates with ceived aid; of those 77% had need fully met. *Average percent of et:* 71% (excluding resources awarded to replace EFC). *Average l aid package:* $6701 (excluding resources awarded to replace 6% of all full-time undergraduates had no need and received d-based aid.

D (NEED-BASED) ***Total amount:*** $8,570,831 (45% Federal, 49% % institutional, 2% external sources). ***Receiving aid:*** *Freshmen:* 58); *all full-time undergraduates:* 52% (2,512). ***Average award:*** n: $1029; Undergraduates: $782. ***Scholarships, grants, and awards:*** Federal Pell, FSEOG, state, private, college/university gift aid from institutional funds, Scholarships for Disadvantaged Students (SDS), Empire State Minority Honors Scholarships.

GIFT AID (NON-NEED-BASED) ***Total amount:*** $399,708 (5% state, 64% institutional, 31% external sources). ***Receiving aid:*** *Freshmen:* 14% (128); *Undergraduates:* 5% (251). ***Scholarships, grants, and awards by category:*** *Academic Interests/Achievement:* area/ethnic studies, biological sciences, business, communication, computer science, education, engineering/technologies, English, general academic interests/achievements, health fields, home economics, humanities, international studies, mathematics, physical sciences, premedicine, social sciences. *Creative Arts/Performance:* art/fine arts, music. *Special Achievements/Activities:* community service, general special achievements/activities, leadership. *Special Characteristics:* international students, members of minority groups, out-of-state students. ***Tuition waivers:*** Full or partial for employees or children of employees, senior citizens.

LOANS ***Student loans:*** $18,767,618 (61% need-based, 39% non-need-based). 73% of past graduating class borrowed through all loan programs. Average indebtedness per student: $15,474. ***Average need-based loan:*** Freshmen: $2553; Undergraduates: $4819. ***Parent loans:*** $2,467,631 (100% non-need-based). ***Programs:*** Federal Direct (Subsidized and Unsubsidized Stafford, PLUS), Perkins, Federal Nursing, alternative loans.

WORK-STUDY ***Federal work-study:*** *Total amount:* $418,259; jobs available. ***State or other work-study/employment:*** *Total amount:* $893,274 (100% non-need-based). Part-time jobs available.

APPLYING for FINANCIAL AID ***Required financial aid forms:*** FAFSA, state aid form. ***Financial aid deadline (priority):*** 3/1. ***Notification date:*** Continuous beginning 4/1. Students must reply by 5/1 or within 3 weeks of notification.

CONTACT Ms. Laura J. Dominy, Financial Aid Director, Plattsburgh State University of New York, 101 Broad Street, Kehoe Administration Building 406, Plattsburgh, NY 12901, 518-564-2072 or toll-free 800-388-6473 (in-state). *E-mail:* dominylj@plattsburgh.edu

PLYMOUTH STATE COLLEGE

Plymouth, NH

Tuition & fees (NH res): $5032 **Average undergraduate aid package: $7226**

ABOUT THE INSTITUTION State-supported, coed. Awards: associate, bachelor's, and master's degrees and post-bachelor's and post-master's certificates. 79 undergraduate majors. Total enrollment: 3,897. Undergraduates: 3,417. Freshmen: 783. Federal methodology is used as a basis for awarding need-based institutional aid.

UNDERGRADUATE EXPENSES for 1999–2000 ***Application fee:*** $30. ***Tuition, state resident:*** full-time $3830; part-time $164 per credit hour. ***Tuition, nonresident:*** full-time $9140; part-time $457 per credit hour. ***Required fees:*** full-time $1202; $56 per credit hour. Full-time tuition and fees vary according to reciprocity agreements. Part-time tuition and fees vary according to course load. ***College room and board:*** $5030; ***room only:*** $3354. Room and board charges vary according to board plan and housing facility. ***Payment plan:*** installment.

FRESHMAN FINANCIAL AID (Fall 1999) 613 applied for aid; of those 80% were deemed to have need. 100% of freshmen with need received aid; of those 10% had need fully met. *Average percent of need met:* 81% (excluding resources awarded to replace EFC). *Average financial aid package:* $7480 (excluding resources awarded to replace EFC). 3% of all full-time freshmen had no need and received non-need-based aid.

UNDERGRADUATE FINANCIAL AID (Fall 1999) 2,388 applied for aid; of those 81% were deemed to have need. 100% of undergraduates with need received aid; of those 17% had need fully met. *Average percent of need met:* 79% (excluding resources awarded to replace EFC). *Average financial aid package:* $7226 (excluding resources awarded to replace EFC). 3% of all full-time undergraduates had no need and received non-need-based aid.

GIFT AID (NEED-BASED) ***Total amount:*** $4,251,875 (43% Federal, 7% state, 50% institutional). ***Receiving aid:*** *Freshmen:* 48% (372); *all full-time undergraduates:* 41% (1,290). ***Average award:*** Freshmen: $3551;

Undergraduates: $3081. ***Scholarships, grants, and awards:*** Federal Pell, FSEOG, state, private, college/university gift aid from institutional funds.

GIFT AID (NON-NEED-BASED) ***Total amount:*** $508,336 (19% institutional, 81% external sources). ***Receiving aid:*** *Freshmen:* 11% (83); *Undergraduates:* 7% (204). ***Scholarships, grants, and awards by category:*** *Academic Interests/Achievement:* 98 awards ($129,500 total): general academic interests/achievements. *Creative Arts/Performance:* 11 awards ($20,000 total): creative writing, dance, music, theater/drama. *Special Characteristics:* 9 awards ($41,130 total): children of faculty/staff, international students. ***Tuition waivers:*** Full or partial for employees or children of employees, senior citizens. ***ROTC:*** Army cooperative, Air Force cooperative.

LOANS ***Student loans:*** $10,103,809 (70% need-based, 30% non-need-based). 60% of past graduating class borrowed through all loan programs. Average indebtedness per student: $16,343. ***Average need-based loan:*** Freshmen: $2927; Undergraduates: $3895. ***Parent loans:*** $2,922,283 (100% non-need-based). ***Programs:*** FFEL (Subsidized and Unsubsidized Stafford, PLUS), Perkins.

WORK-STUDY ***Federal work-study:*** *Total amount:* $1,929,592; 1,079 jobs averaging $1789.

APPLYING for FINANCIAL AID ***Required financial aid form:*** FAFSA. ***Financial aid deadline (priority):*** 3/1. ***Notification date:*** Continuous.

CONTACT Mr. Robert A. Tuveson, Director of Financial Aid, Plymouth State College, 17 High Street, MSC #18, Plymouth, NH 03264-1595, 603-535-2338 or toll-free 800-842-6900. *Fax:* 603-535-2627. *E-mail:* rtuveson@mail.plymouth.edu

POINT LOMA NAZARENE UNIVERSITY

San Diego, CA

Tuition & fees: $13,626 **Average undergraduate aid package: $11,493**

ABOUT THE INSTITUTION Independent Nazarene, coed. Awards: bachelor's and master's degrees and post-bachelor's and post-master's certificates. 43 undergraduate majors. Total enrollment: 2,711. Undergraduates: 2,350. Freshmen: 554. Federal methodology is used as a basis for awarding need-based institutional aid.

UNDERGRADUATE EXPENSES for 1999–2000 ***Application fee:*** $20. ***Comprehensive fee:*** $19,106 includes full-time tuition ($13,186), mandatory fees ($440), and room and board ($5480). Full-time tuition and fees vary according to course load. Room and board charges vary according to board plan. ***Part-time tuition:*** $549 per unit. ***Part-time fees:*** $15 per unit. Part-time tuition and fees vary according to course load and student level. ***Payment plan:*** installment.

FRESHMAN FINANCIAL AID (Fall 1998) 515 applied for aid; of those 71% were deemed to have need. 100% of freshmen with need received aid; of those 24% had need fully met. *Average percent of need met:* 71% (excluding resources awarded to replace EFC). *Average financial aid package:* $9860 (excluding resources awarded to replace EFC). 25% of all full-time freshmen had no need and received non-need-based aid.

UNDERGRADUATE FINANCIAL AID (Fall 1998) 1,922 applied for aid; of those 74% were deemed to have need. 100% of undergraduates with need received aid; of those 25% had need fully met. *Average percent of need met:* 76% (excluding resources awarded to replace EFC). *Average financial aid package:* $11,493 (excluding resources awarded to replace EFC). 22% of all full-time undergraduates had no need and received non-need-based aid.

GIFT AID (NEED-BASED) ***Total amount:*** $4,599,091 (45% Federal, 55% state). ***Receiving aid:*** *Freshmen:* 53% (286); *all full-time undergraduates:* 54% (1,158). ***Average award:*** Freshmen: $6268; Undergraduates: $7428. ***Scholarships, grants, and awards:*** Federal Pell, FSEOG, state, private, college/university gift aid from institutional funds.

GIFT AID (NON-NEED-BASED) ***Total amount:*** $7,349,340 (1% state, 95% institutional, 4% external sources). ***Receiving aid:*** *Freshmen:* 67% (360); *Undergraduates:* 63% (1,346). ***Scholarships, grants, and awards by category:*** *Academic Interests/Achievement:* biological sciences, business, communication, education, engineering/technologies, general academic interests/achievements, health fields, home economics, humanities, mathematics, religion/biblical studies, social sciences. *Creative Arts/Performance:* art/fine arts, debating, music, theater/drama. *Special Characteristics:* children and siblings of alumni, children of faculty/staff, local/state students, relatives of clergy, religious affiliation, siblings of current students. ***Tuition waivers:*** Full or partial for employees or children of employees, senior citizens. ***ROTC:*** Army cooperative, Naval cooperative, Air Force cooperative.

LOANS ***Student loans:*** $6,953,453 (62% need-based, 38% non-need-based). ***Average need-based loan:*** Freshmen: $2629; Undergraduates: $4041. ***Parent loans:*** $2,763,255 (100% non-need-based). ***Programs:*** FFEL (Subsidized and Unsubsidized Stafford, PLUS), Perkins, Federal Nursing, state, college/university.

WORK-STUDY ***Federal work-study:*** *Total amount:* $715,675; 450 jobs averaging $1590.

ATHLETIC AWARDS *Total amount:* 718,117 (100% non-need-based).

APPLYING for FINANCIAL AID ***Required financial aid forms:*** FAFSA, institution's own form. ***Financial aid deadline (priority):*** 3/15. ***Notification date:*** 5/30. Students must reply within 4 weeks of notification.

CONTACT Ms. Susan R. Tornquist, Director, Financial Aid, Point Loma Nazarene University, 3900 Lomaland Drive, San Diego, CA 92106, 619-849-2296. *Fax:* 619-849-7017.

POINT PARK COLLEGE

Pittsburgh, PA

Tuition & fees: $12,454 **Average undergraduate aid package: $8553**

ABOUT THE INSTITUTION Independent, coed. Awards: associate, bachelor's, and master's degrees and post-bachelor's and post-master's certificates. 45 undergraduate majors. Total enrollment: 2,619. Undergraduates: 2,417. Freshmen: 282. Federal methodology is used as a basis for awarding need-based institutional aid.

UNDERGRADUATE EXPENSES for 1999–2000 ***Application fee:*** $20. ***Comprehensive fee:*** $17,788 includes full-time tuition ($12,054), mandatory fees ($400), and room and board ($5334). ***College room only:*** $2550. Full-time tuition and fees vary according to course load. Room and board charges vary according to board plan. ***Part-time tuition:*** $321 per credit. ***Part-time fees:*** $6 per credit. Part-time tuition and fees vary according to course load. ***Payment plans:*** installment, deferred payment.

FRESHMAN FINANCIAL AID (Fall 1998) 309 applied for aid; of those 78% were deemed to have need. 100% of freshmen with need received aid; of those 12% had need fully met. *Average percent of need met:* 75% (excluding resources awarded to replace EFC). *Average financial aid package:* $8553 (excluding resources awarded to replace EFC). 21% of all full-time freshmen had no need and received non-need-based aid.

UNDERGRADUATE FINANCIAL AID (Fall 1998) 1,463 applied for aid; of those 78% were deemed to have need. 100% of undergraduates with need received aid; of those 8% had need fully met. *Average percent of need met:* 75% (excluding resources awarded to replace EFC). *Average financial aid package:* $8553 (excluding resources awarded to replace EFC). 21% of all full-time undergraduates had no need and received non-need-based aid.

GIFT AID (NEED-BASED) ***Total amount:*** $4,438,188 (32% Federal, 38% state, 27% institutional, 3% external sources). ***Receiving aid:*** *Freshmen:* 78% (241); *all full-time undergraduates:* 78% (1,138). ***Average award:*** Freshmen: $6415; Undergraduates: $6942. ***Scholarships, grants, and awards:*** Federal Pell, FSEOG, state, private, college/university gift aid from institutional funds.

GIFT AID (NON-NEED-BASED) ***Total amount:*** $2,439,656 (100% institutional). ***Receiving aid:*** *Freshmen:* 56% (174); *Undergraduates:* 57% (829). ***Scholarships, grants, and awards by category:*** *Academic Interests/Achievement:* 391 awards ($937,280 total): general academic interests/achievements. *Creative Arts/Performance:* 233 awards ($311,210 total): dance, journalism/publications, performing arts, theater/drama. *Special Achievements/Activities:* 100 awards ($138,570 total): community service. *Special Characteristics:* 94 awards ($59,596 total): children and siblings of alumni, siblings of current students. ***Tuition waivers:*** Full or partial for employees or children of employees, senior citizens. ***ROTC:*** Army cooperative, Air Force cooperative.

Point Park College (continued)

LOANS ***Student loans:*** $9,277,832 (61% need-based, 39% non-need-based). 84% of past graduating class borrowed through all loan programs. ***Average need-based loan:*** Freshmen: $3125; Undergraduates: $3256. ***Parent loans:*** $743,826 (100% non-need-based). ***Programs:*** FFEL (Subsidized and Unsubsidized Stafford, PLUS), Perkins, college/university.

WORK-STUDY ***Federal work-study:*** *Total amount:* $287,288; 278 jobs averaging $1033.

ATHLETIC AWARDS *Total amount:* 438,227 (100% non-need-based).

APPLYING for FINANCIAL AID ***Required financial aid form:*** FAFSA. ***Financial aid deadline:*** Continuous. ***Notification date:*** Continuous beginning 2/15. Students must reply by 5/1.

CONTACT Sandra M. Cronin, Director of Financial Aid, Point Park College, 201 Wood Street, Pittsburgh, PA 15222-1984, 412-392-3930 or toll-free 800-321-0129. *E-mail:* scronin@ppc.edu

POLYTECHNIC UNIVERSITY, BROOKLYN CAMPUS

Brooklyn, NY

Tuition & fees: $20,810 **Average undergraduate aid package: $17,554**

ABOUT THE INSTITUTION Independent, coed. Awards: bachelor's, master's, and doctoral degrees (most information given is for both Brooklyn and Farmingdale campuses). 17 undergraduate majors. Total enrollment: 3,420. Undergraduates: 1,807. Freshmen: 468. Federal methodology is used as a basis for awarding need-based institutional aid.

UNDERGRADUATE EXPENSES for 1999–2000 ***Application fee:*** $40. ***Comprehensive fee:*** $26,280 includes full-time tuition ($20,210), mandatory fees ($600), and room and board ($5470). Full-time tuition and fees vary according to course load. Room and board charges vary according to board plan. ***Part-time tuition:*** $640 per credit. ***Part-time fees:*** $200 per term part-time. Part-time tuition and fees vary according to course load. College room and board is available through Long Island University. ***Payment plans:*** tuition prepayment, deferred payment.

FRESHMAN FINANCIAL AID (Fall 1998) 301 applied for aid; of those 83% were deemed to have need. 100% of freshmen with need received aid; of those 90% had need fully met. *Average percent of need met:* 84% (excluding resources awarded to replace EFC). *Average financial aid package:* $16,980 (excluding resources awarded to replace EFC).

UNDERGRADUATE FINANCIAL AID (Fall 1998) 1,144 applied for aid; of those 87% were deemed to have need. 100% of undergraduates with need received aid; of those 58% had need fully met. *Average percent of need met:* 81% (excluding resources awarded to replace EFC). *Average financial aid package:* $17,554 (excluding resources awarded to replace EFC).

GIFT AID (NEED-BASED) ***Total amount:*** $6,497,226 (38% Federal, 44% state, 18% institutional). ***Receiving aid:*** *Freshmen:* 77% (242); *all full-time undergraduates:* 81% (957). ***Average award:*** Freshmen: $6179; Undergraduates: $6341. ***Scholarships, grants, and awards:*** Federal Pell, FSEOG, state, private, college/university gift aid from institutional funds.

GIFT AID (NON-NEED-BASED) ***Total amount:*** $8,074,011 (1% state, 97% institutional, 2% external sources). ***Receiving aid:*** *Freshmen:* 61% (192); *Undergraduates:* 59% (696). ***Scholarships, grants, and awards by category:*** *Academic Interests/Achievement:* computer science, engineering/technologies, general academic interests/achievements. ***Tuition waivers:*** Full or partial for minority students, employees or children of employees. ***ROTC:*** Air Force cooperative.

LOANS ***Student loans:*** $3,662,263 (83% need-based, 17% non-need-based). 53% of past graduating class borrowed through all loan programs. Average indebtedness per student: $19,341. ***Average need-based loan:*** Freshmen: $3191; Undergraduates: $3769. ***Parent loans:*** $367,058 (100% non-need-based). ***Programs:*** FFEL (Subsidized and Unsubsidized Stafford, PLUS), Perkins, college/university, alternative loans.

WORK-STUDY ***Federal work-study:*** *Total amount:* $895,460; jobs available.

APPLYING for FINANCIAL AID ***Required financial aid forms:*** FAFSA, institution's own form. ***Financial aid deadline:*** Continuous. ***Notification date:*** Continuous beginning 3/15. Students must reply within 2 weeks of notification.

CONTACT Office of Financial Aid Services, Polytechnic University, Brooklyn Campus, 333 Jay Street, Brooklyn, NY 11201-2990, 718-260-3300 or toll-free 800-POLYTECH. *Fax:* 718-260-3052.

POLYTECHNIC UNIVERSITY OF PUERTO RICO

Hato Rey, PR

Tuition & fees: $4485 **Average undergraduate aid package: N/A**

ABOUT THE INSTITUTION Independent, coed. Awards: bachelor's and master's degrees. 9 undergraduate majors. Total enrollment: 5,005. Undergraduates: 4,560. Freshmen: 658. Federal methodology is used as a basis for awarding need-based institutional aid.

UNDERGRADUATE EXPENSES for 1999–2000 ***Application fee:*** $30. ***One-time required fee:*** $10. ***Tuition:*** full-time $4200; part-time $115 per credit hour. ***Required fees:*** full-time $285; $95 per credit hour. Full-time tuition and fees vary according to program. Part-time tuition and fees vary according to program. ***Payment plan:*** deferred payment.

GIFT AID (NEED-BASED) ***Scholarships, grants, and awards:*** Federal Pell, FSEOG, state, college/university gift aid from institutional funds.

GIFT AID (NON-NEED-BASED) ***Scholarships, grants, and awards by category:*** *Academic Interests/Achievement:* architecture, engineering/technologies. ***Tuition waivers:*** Full or partial for employees or children of employees. ***ROTC:*** Army cooperative.

LOANS ***Programs:*** FFEL (Subsidized and Unsubsidized Stafford, PLUS).

WORK-STUDY Federal work-study jobs available.

APPLYING for FINANCIAL AID ***Required financial aid forms:*** FAFSA, institution's own form.

CONTACT Carmen Rivera, Director of Financial Aid, Polytechnic University of Puerto Rico, 377 Ponce de Leon Avenue, Hato Rey, PR 00919, 787-754-8000 Ext. 253. *Fax:* 787-766-1163.

POMONA COLLEGE

Claremont, CA

Tuition & fees: $23,170 **Average undergraduate aid package: $22,032**

ABOUT THE INSTITUTION Independent, coed. Awards: bachelor's degrees. 54 undergraduate majors. Total enrollment: 1,549. Undergraduates: 1,549. Freshmen: 390. Both federal and institutional methodology are used as a basis for awarding need-based institutional aid.

UNDERGRADUATE EXPENSES for 1999–2000 ***Application fee:*** $55. ***Comprehensive fee:*** $30,920 includes full-time tuition ($22,940), mandatory fees ($230), and room and board ($7750). Room and board charges vary according to board plan. ***Part-time tuition:*** $3830 per course. ***Payment plan:*** installment.

FRESHMAN FINANCIAL AID (Fall 1999) 235 applied for aid; of those 81% were deemed to have need. 100% of freshmen with need received aid; of those 100% had need fully met. *Average percent of need met:* 100% (excluding resources awarded to replace EFC). *Average financial aid package:* $21,310 (excluding resources awarded to replace EFC).

UNDERGRADUATE FINANCIAL AID (Fall 1999) 940 applied for aid; of those 89% were deemed to have need. 100% of undergraduates with need received aid; of those 100% had need fully met. *Average percent of need met:* 100% (excluding resources awarded to replace EFC). *Average financial aid package:* $22,032 (excluding resources awarded to replace EFC).

GIFT AID (NEED-BASED) ***Total amount:*** $14,407,000 (5% Federal, 9% state, 83% institutional, 3% external sources). ***Receiving aid:*** *Freshmen:* 49% (190); *all full-time undergraduates:* 54% (840). ***Average award:***

Freshmen: $16,530; Undergraduates: $17,150. ***Scholarships, grants, and awards:*** Federal Pell, FSEOG, state, private, college/university gift aid from institutional funds.

GIFT AID (NON-NEED-BASED) ***Tuition waivers:*** Full or partial for employees or children of employees.

LOANS ***Student loans:*** $2,700,000 (100% need-based). 63% of past graduating class borrowed through all loan programs. Average indebtedness per student: $15,800. ***Average need-based loan:*** Freshmen: $3500; Undergraduates: $3500. ***Programs:*** FFEL (Subsidized and Unsubsidized Stafford, PLUS), Perkins, college/university.

WORK-STUDY ***Federal work-study:*** *Total amount:* $400,000; 216 jobs averaging $1852. ***State or other work-study/employment:*** *Total amount:* $1,000,000 (100% need-based). 538 part-time jobs averaging $1859.

APPLYING for FINANCIAL AID ***Required financial aid forms:*** FAFSA, CSS Financial Aid PROFILE, state aid form, noncustodial (divorced/separated) parent's statement, business/farm supplement. ***Financial aid deadline:*** 2/1. ***Notification date:*** 4/10. Students must reply by 5/1.

CONTACT Ms. Colleen MacDonald, Assistant Director of Financial Aid, Pomona College, 550 North College Avenue, Room 117, Claremont, CA 91711, 909-621-8205. *Fax:* 909-607-7941. *E-mail:* colleenm@pomadm.pomona.edu

PONTIFICAL CATHOLIC UNIVERSITY OF PUERTO RICO

Ponce, PR

Tuition & fees: N/R **Average undergraduate aid package: $4961**

ABOUT THE INSTITUTION Independent Roman Catholic, coed. Awards: associate, bachelor's, master's, doctoral, and first professional degrees (branch locations: Arecibo, Guayama, Mayagüez). 50 undergraduate majors. Total enrollment: 7,851. Undergraduates: 6,207. Freshmen: 1,228. Federal methodology is used as a basis for awarding need-based institutional aid.

UNDERGRADUATE EXPENSES for 1999–2000 ***Application fee:*** $15.

FRESHMAN FINANCIAL AID (Fall 1999, est.) 1791 applied for aid; of those 90% were deemed to have need. 90% of freshmen with need received aid; of those 15% had need fully met. *Average percent of need met:* 63% (excluding resources awarded to replace EFC). *Average financial aid package:* $4961 (excluding resources awarded to replace EFC). 7% of all full-time freshmen had no need and received non-need-based aid.

UNDERGRADUATE FINANCIAL AID (Fall 1999, est.) 8,196 applied for aid; of those 90% were deemed to have need. 90% of undergraduates with need received aid; of those 15% had need fully met. *Average percent of need met:* 63% (excluding resources awarded to replace EFC). *Average financial aid package:* $4961 (excluding resources awarded to replace EFC). 2% of all full-time undergraduates had no need and received non-need-based aid.

GIFT AID (NEED-BASED) ***Total amount:*** $22,234,903 (91% Federal, 9% state). ***Receiving aid:*** *Freshmen:* 62% (1,161); *all full-time undergraduates:* 62% (5,311). ***Scholarships, grants, and awards:*** Federal Pell, FSEOG, state, private, college/university gift aid from institutional funds, Federal Nursing Grants (for disadvantaged students).

GIFT AID (NON-NEED-BASED) ***Receiving aid:*** *Freshmen:* 12% (218); *Undergraduates:* 12% (996). ***Scholarships, grants, and awards by category:*** *Academic Interests/Achievement:* general academic interests/achievements. *Creative Arts/Performance:* music, performing arts, theater/drama. *Special Characteristics:* children of faculty/staff, first-generation college students, spouses of current students, veterans, veterans' children. ***Tuition waivers:*** Full or partial for employees or children of employees. ***ROTC:*** Army cooperative.

LOANS ***Student loans:*** $18,623,457 (100% need-based). ***Parent loans:*** $4000 (100% need-based). ***Programs:*** Federal Direct (Subsidized and Unsubsidized Stafford, PLUS), FFEL (Subsidized and Unsubsidized Stafford), Perkins.

WORK-STUDY ***Federal work-study:*** *Total amount:* $1,454,254; 1,850 jobs available. ***State or other work-study/employment:*** *Total amount:* $650,000 (38% need-based, 62% non-need-based). 198 part-time jobs available.

APPLYING for FINANCIAL AID ***Required financial aid forms:*** FAFSA, institution's own form, noncustodial (divorced/separated) parent's statement. ***Financial aid deadline (priority):*** 5/14. ***Notification date:*** 7/15. Students must reply within 4 weeks of notification.

CONTACT Mrs. Margie Alustiza, Director, Financial Aid, Pontifical Catholic University of Puerto Rico, 2250 Las Americas Avenue, Suite 549, Ponce, PR 00717-0777, 787-841-2000 Ext. 1054 or toll-free 800-981-5040. *Fax:* 787-840-4295. *E-mail:* malustiza@pucpr.edu

PONTIFICAL COLLEGE JOSEPHINUM

Columbus, OH

Tuition & fees: $7590 **Average undergraduate aid package: $8500**

ABOUT THE INSTITUTION Independent Roman Catholic, coed, primarily men. Awards: bachelor's and master's degrees. 7 undergraduate majors. Federal methodology is used as a basis for awarding need-based institutional aid.

UNDERGRADUATE EXPENSES for 1999–2000 ***Application fee:*** $25. ***Comprehensive fee:*** $12,530 includes full-time tuition ($7590) and room and board ($4940). ***College room only:*** $2470. ***Part-time tuition:*** $317 per credit hour. ***Payment plans:*** installment, deferred payment.

FRESHMAN FINANCIAL AID (Fall 1999, est.) 9 applied for aid; of those 67% were deemed to have need. 100% of freshmen with need received aid.

UNDERGRADUATE FINANCIAL AID (Fall 1999, est.) 33 applied for aid; of those 61% were deemed to have need. 100% of undergraduates with need received aid; of those 15% had need fully met. *Average percent of need met:* 66% (excluding resources awarded to replace EFC). *Average financial aid package:* $8500 (excluding resources awarded to replace EFC). 21% of all full-time undergraduates had no need and received non-need-based aid.

GIFT AID (NEED-BASED) ***Total amount:*** $124,540 (34% Federal, 12% state, 54% institutional). ***Receiving aid:*** *Freshmen:* 67% (6); *all full-time undergraduates:* 61% (20). ***Average award:*** Undergraduates: $5000. ***Scholarships, grants, and awards:*** Federal Pell, FSEOG, state, private, college/university gift aid from institutional funds.

GIFT AID (NON-NEED-BASED) ***Total amount:*** $259,620 (8% state, 47% institutional, 45% external sources). ***Receiving aid:*** *Freshmen:* 67% (6); *Undergraduates:* 61% (20). ***Scholarships, grants, and awards by category:*** *Special Characteristics:* local/state students.

LOANS ***Student loans:*** $17,513 (100% need-based). 60% of past graduating class borrowed through all loan programs. Average indebtedness per student: $15,000. ***Average need-based loan:*** Undergraduates: $4700. ***Programs:*** FFEL (Subsidized and Unsubsidized Stafford, PLUS), Perkins.

WORK-STUDY ***Federal work-study:*** *Total amount:* $8405; jobs available.

APPLYING for FINANCIAL AID ***Required financial aid forms:*** FAFSA, institution's own form. ***Financial aid deadline (priority):*** 5/15. ***Notification date:*** Continuous. Students must reply within 2 weeks of notification.

CONTACT Mrs. Linda Bryant, Director of Financial Aid, Pontifical College Josephinum, 7625 North High Street, Columbus, OH 43235-1498, 614-885-5585 Ext. 446. *Fax:* 614-885-2307. *E-mail:* lbryant@pcj.edu

PORTLAND STATE UNIVERSITY

Portland, OR

Tuition & fees (OR res): $3468 **Average undergraduate aid package: $6229**

ABOUT THE INSTITUTION State-supported, coed. Awards: bachelor's, master's, and doctoral degrees and post-bachelor's certificates. 62 undergraduate majors. Total enrollment: 18,184. Undergraduates: 12,696. Freshmen: 1,005. Federal methodology is used as a basis for awarding need-based institutional aid.

UNDERGRADUATE EXPENSES for 1999–2000 ***Application fee:*** $50. ***Tuition, state resident:*** full-time $2694; part-time $673 per term. ***Tuition, nonresident:*** full-time $10,887; part-time $2723 per term. ***Required fees:*** full-time $774; $214 per term part-time. Full-time tuition and fees vary

Portland State University (continued)

according to student level. Part-time tuition and fees vary according to course level and course load. ***College room and board:*** $6150; ***room only:*** $4050. Room and board charges vary according to board plan and housing facility. ***Payment plans:*** installment, deferred payment.

FRESHMAN FINANCIAL AID (Fall 1998) *Average percent of need met:* 53% (excluding resources awarded to replace EFC). *Average financial aid package:* $4354 (excluding resources awarded to replace EFC). 9% of all full-time freshmen had no need and received non-need-based aid.

UNDERGRADUATE FINANCIAL AID (Fall 1998) *Average percent of need met:* 64% (excluding resources awarded to replace EFC). *Average financial aid package:* $6229 (excluding resources awarded to replace EFC). 5% of all full-time undergraduates had no need and received non-need-based aid.

GIFT AID (NEED-BASED) ***Total amount:*** $8,321,770 (80% Federal, 20% state). ***Scholarships, grants, and awards:*** Federal Pell, FSEOG, state, private, college/university gift aid from institutional funds.

GIFT AID (NON-NEED-BASED) ***Total amount:*** $1,361,104 (11% institutional, 89% external sources). ***Scholarships, grants, and awards by category:*** *Academic Interests/Achievement:* business, engineering/technologies, foreign languages, general academic interests/achievements, humanities, physical sciences. *Creative Arts/Performance:* art/fine arts, music, theater/drama. *Special Achievements/Activities:* community service, memberships. ***Tuition waivers:*** Full or partial for minority students, employees or children of employees, senior citizens. ***ROTC:*** Army, Air Force cooperative.

LOANS ***Student loans:*** $27,977,382 (59% need-based, 41% non-need-based). ***Parent loans:*** $1,709,514 (100% non-need-based). ***Programs:*** Federal Direct (Subsidized and Unsubsidized Stafford, PLUS), Perkins.

WORK-STUDY ***Federal work-study:*** *Total amount:* $1,845,995; jobs available.

ATHLETIC AWARDS *Total amount:* 1,469,033 (100% non-need-based).

APPLYING for FINANCIAL AID ***Required financial aid form:*** FAFSA. ***Financial aid deadline:*** Continuous. ***Notification date:*** Continuous. Students must reply within 4 weeks of notification.

CONTACT Mr. Samuel Collie, Director of Student Financial Aid, Portland State University, PO Box 751, Portland, OR 97207-0751, 503-725-5448 or toll-free 800-547-8887. *Fax:* 503-725-4882. *E-mail:* collies@pdx.edu

POTOMAC COLLEGE

Washington, DC

Tuition & fees: N/R | **Average undergraduate aid package: N/A**

ABOUT THE INSTITUTION Proprietary, coed. Awards: bachelor's degrees. 2 undergraduate majors. Federal methodology is used as a basis for awarding need-based institutional aid.

GIFT AID (NEED-BASED) ***Scholarships, grants, and awards:*** Federal Pell.

GIFT AID (NON-NEED-BASED) ***Tuition waivers:*** Full or partial for employees or children of employees.

LOANS ***Programs:*** FFEL (Subsidized and Unsubsidized Stafford).

APPLYING for FINANCIAL AID ***Required financial aid forms:*** FAFSA, institution's own form, personal data sheet. ***Financial aid deadline:*** Continuous. ***Notification date:*** Continuous. Students must reply within 4 weeks of notification.

CONTACT Financial Aid Counselor, Potomac College, 4000 Chesapeake Street NW, Washington, DC 20016, 202-686-0876 or toll-free 888-686-0876. *Fax:* 202-686-0818.

PRACTICAL BIBLE COLLEGE

Bible School Park, NY

Tuition & fees: $6370 | **Average undergraduate aid package: $4630**

ABOUT THE INSTITUTION Independent nondenominational, coed. Awards: associate and bachelor's degrees. 1 undergraduate major. Total enrollment: 225. Undergraduates: 225. Freshmen: 48. Federal methodology is used as a basis for awarding need-based institutional aid.

UNDERGRADUATE EXPENSES for 1999–2000 ***Application fee:*** $25. ***Comprehensive fee:*** $10,170 includes full-time tuition ($5800), mandatory fees ($570), and room and board ($3800). Room and board charges vary according to housing facility. ***Part-time tuition:*** $245 per credit. ***Part-time fees:*** $215 per term part-time. Part-time tuition and fees vary according to class time and course load. ***Payment plan:*** installment.

FRESHMAN FINANCIAL AID (Fall 1999, est.) 53 applied for aid; of those 70% were deemed to have need. 86% of freshmen with need received aid; of those 9% had need fully met. *Average percent of need met:* 40% (excluding resources awarded to replace EFC). *Average financial aid package:* $3020 (excluding resources awarded to replace EFC). 17% of all full-time freshmen had no need and received non-need-based aid.

UNDERGRADUATE FINANCIAL AID (Fall 1999, est.) 185 applied for aid; of those 88% were deemed to have need. 96% of undergraduates with need received aid; of those 12% had need fully met. *Average percent of need met:* 35% (excluding resources awarded to replace EFC). *Average financial aid package:* $4630 (excluding resources awarded to replace EFC). 9% of all full-time undergraduates had no need and received non-need-based aid.

GIFT AID (NEED-BASED) ***Total amount:*** $635,977 (50% Federal, 31% state, 19% institutional). ***Receiving aid:*** *Freshmen:* 53% (31); *all full-time undergraduates:* 62% (120). ***Average award:*** Freshmen: $2348; Undergraduates: $4220. ***Scholarships, grants, and awards:*** Federal Pell, FSEOG, state, private, college/university gift aid from institutional funds.

GIFT AID (NON-NEED-BASED) ***Total amount:*** $89,410 (77% institutional, 23% external sources). ***Receiving aid:*** *Freshmen:* 16% (9); *Undergraduates:* 18% (36). ***Scholarships, grants, and awards by category:*** *Academic Interests/Achievement:* general academic interests/achievements, religion/biblical studies. *Creative Arts/Performance:* music. *Special Achievements/Activities:* leadership. *Special Characteristics:* children and siblings of alumni, children of educators, children of faculty/staff, general special characteristics, international students, married students, relatives of clergy, siblings of current students, spouses of current students. ***Tuition waivers:*** Full or partial for children of alumni, employees or children of employees.

LOANS ***Student loans:*** $285,845 (100% need-based). 19% of past graduating class borrowed through all loan programs. Average indebtedness per student: $4804. ***Average need-based loan:*** Freshmen: $3854; Undergraduates: $4617. ***Parent loans:*** $51,384 (100% need-based). ***Programs:*** FFEL (Subsidized and Unsubsidized Stafford, PLUS), college/university.

WORK-STUDY ***Federal work-study:*** *Total amount:* $112,560; 68 jobs averaging $1655.

APPLYING for FINANCIAL AID ***Required financial aid forms:*** FAFSA, state aid form. ***Financial aid deadline (priority):*** 7/15. ***Notification date:*** 8/15. Students must reply within 2 weeks of notification.

CONTACT Ms. Karen S. Francis, Financial Aid Director, Practical Bible College, PO Box 601, Bible School Park, NY 13737-0601, 607-729-1581 Ext. 401 or toll-free 800-331-4137 Ext. 406. *Fax:* 607-729-2962. *E-mail:* pbcfa@practical.edu

PRAIRIE VIEW A&M UNIVERSITY

Prairie View, TX

Tuition & fees: N/R | **Average undergraduate aid package: $6600**

ABOUT THE INSTITUTION State-supported, coed. Awards: bachelor's and master's degrees. 41 undergraduate majors. Total enrollment: 6,271. Undergraduates: 4,963. Freshmen: 1,094. Federal methodology is used as a basis for awarding need-based institutional aid.

FRESHMAN FINANCIAL AID (Fall 1999) 988 applied for aid; of those 87% were deemed to have need. 100% of freshmen with need received aid. *Average percent of need met:* 75% (excluding resources awarded to replace EFC). *Average financial aid package:* $6100 (excluding resources awarded to replace EFC). 7% of all full-time freshmen had no need and received non-need-based aid.

UNDERGRADUATE FINANCIAL AID (Fall 1999) 4,811 applied for aid; of those 94% were deemed to have need. 100% of undergraduates with

need received aid. *Average percent of need met:* 75% (excluding resources awarded to replace EFC). *Average financial aid package:* $6600 (excluding resources awarded to replace EFC). 5% of all full-time undergraduates had no need and received non-need-based aid.

GIFT AID (NEED-BASED) ***Total amount:*** $9,374,820 (80% Federal, 6% state, 13% institutional, 1% external sources). ***Receiving aid:*** *Freshmen:* 66% (753); *all full-time undergraduates:* 86% (4,280). ***Average award:*** Freshmen: $3325; Undergraduates: $3325. ***Scholarships, grants, and awards:*** Federal Pell, FSEOG, state, private, college/university gift aid from institutional funds.

GIFT AID (NON-NEED-BASED) ***Total amount:*** $608,505 (97% institutional, 3% external sources). ***Receiving aid:*** *Freshmen:* 24% (275); *Undergraduates:* 24% (1,195). ***Scholarships, grants, and awards by category:*** *Academic Interests/Achievement:* 211 awards ($311,000 total): agriculture, architecture, education, general academic interests/achievements, premedicine. *Creative Arts/Performance:* 10 awards ($20,000 total): art/fine arts, music, performing arts. *Special Characteristics:* ethnic background. ***Tuition waivers:*** Full or partial for minority students, employees or children of employees. ***ROTC:*** Army, Naval.

LOANS ***Student loans:*** $15,581,892 (72% need-based, 28% non-need-based). ***Average need-based loan:*** Freshmen: $2625; Undergraduates: $4000. ***Parent loans:*** $547,759 (61% need-based, 39% non-need-based). ***Programs:*** Federal Direct (Subsidized and Unsubsidized Stafford, PLUS), FFEL (Subsidized and Unsubsidized Stafford, PLUS), Perkins, state.

WORK-STUDY ***Federal work-study:*** *Total amount:* $1,289,448; 558 jobs averaging $2311. ***State or other work-study/employment:*** *Total amount:* $249,600 (10% need-based, 90% non-need-based). 375 part-time jobs averaging $601.

ATHLETIC AWARDS *Total amount:* 167,777 (47% need-based, 53% non-need-based).

APPLYING for FINANCIAL AID ***Required financial aid forms:*** FAFSA, institution's own form, CSS Financial Aid PROFILE. ***Financial aid deadline (priority):*** 4/1. ***Notification date:*** 6/1. Students must reply within 2 weeks of notification.

CONTACT Mr. A. D. James Jr., Executive Director, Student Financial Services, Prairie View A&M University, PO Box 2967, Prairie View, TX 77446-2967, 409-857-2423. *Fax:* 409-857-2425. *E-mail:* ad_james@pvamu.edu

PRATT INSTITUTE

Brooklyn, NY

Tuition & fees: $20,084 | **Average undergraduate aid package: $12,590**

ABOUT THE INSTITUTION Independent, coed. Awards: associate, bachelor's, and master's degrees. 22 undergraduate majors. Total enrollment: 4,148. Undergraduates: 2,752. Freshmen: 644. Federal methodology is used as a basis for awarding need-based institutional aid.

UNDERGRADUATE EXPENSES for 2000–2001 ***Application fee:*** $35. ***Comprehensive fee:*** $27,884 includes full-time tuition ($19,524), mandatory fees ($560), and room and board ($7800). ***College room only:*** $4700. ***Part-time tuition:*** $620 per credit. ***Part-time fees:*** $167 per term part-time. ***Payment plans:*** installment, deferred payment.

FRESHMAN FINANCIAL AID (Fall 1999) 521 applied for aid; of those 91% were deemed to have need. 100% of freshmen with need received aid. *Average percent of need met:* 63% (excluding resources awarded to replace EFC). *Average financial aid package:* $12,215 (excluding resources awarded to replace EFC). 8% of all full-time freshmen had no need and received non-need-based aid.

UNDERGRADUATE FINANCIAL AID (Fall 1999) 1,921 applied for aid; of those 91% were deemed to have need. 100% of undergraduates with need received aid. *Average percent of need met:* 60% (excluding resources awarded to replace EFC). *Average financial aid package:* $12,590 (excluding resources awarded to replace EFC). 8% of all full-time undergraduates had no need and received non-need-based aid.

GIFT AID (NEED-BASED) ***Total amount:*** $15,716,940 (12% Federal, 8% state, 78% institutional, 2% external sources). ***Receiving aid:*** *Freshmen:* 63% (382); *all full-time undergraduates:* 63% (1,551). ***Average award:*** Freshmen: $5595; Undergraduates: $6120. ***Scholarships, grants, and awards:*** Federal Pell, FSEOG, state, college/university gift aid from institutional funds.

GIFT AID (NON-NEED-BASED) ***Total amount:*** $1,011,888 (95% institutional, 5% external sources). ***Receiving aid:*** *Freshmen:* 68% (414); *Undergraduates:* 57% (1,391). ***Scholarships, grants, and awards by category:*** *Academic Interests/Achievement:* architecture. *Creative Arts/Performance:* applied art and design. ***Tuition waivers:*** Full or partial for employees or children of employees. ***ROTC:*** Army cooperative.

LOANS ***Student loans:*** $6,574,168 (100% need-based). ***Average need-based loan:*** Freshmen: $3170; Undergraduates: $4955. ***Parent loans:*** $6,931,303 (100% need-based). ***Programs:*** FFEL (Subsidized and Unsubsidized Stafford, PLUS), Perkins, college/university.

WORK-STUDY ***Federal work-study:*** *Total amount:* $431,636; 370 jobs averaging $1167.

APPLYING for FINANCIAL AID ***Required financial aid forms:*** FAFSA, institution's own form. ***Financial aid deadline (priority):*** 2/1. ***Notification date:*** Continuous beginning 4/15.

CONTACT Karen Price-Scott, Director of Financial Aid, Pratt Institute, 200 Willoughby Avenue, Brooklyn, NY 11205-3899, 718-636-3519 or toll-free 800-331-0834. *Fax:* 718-636-3739. *E-mail:* kpricesc@pratt.edu

PRESBYTERIAN COLLEGE

Clinton, SC

Tuition & fees: $16,524 | **Average undergraduate aid package: $15,331**

ABOUT THE INSTITUTION Independent Presbyterian, coed. Awards: bachelor's degrees. 31 undergraduate majors. Total enrollment: 1,119. Undergraduates: 1,119. Freshmen: 333. Federal methodology is used as a basis for awarding need-based institutional aid.

UNDERGRADUATE EXPENSES for 1999–2000 ***Application fee:*** $30. ***Comprehensive fee:*** $21,174 includes full-time tuition ($15,122), mandatory fees ($1402), and room and board ($4650). ***College room only:*** $2196. Room and board charges vary according to board plan. ***Part-time tuition:*** $630 per semester hour. ***Part-time fees:*** $8 per semester hour; $15 per term part-time. ***Payment plans:*** tuition prepayment, installment.

FRESHMAN FINANCIAL AID (Fall 1999, est.) 328 applied for aid; of those 68% were deemed to have need. 100% of freshmen with need received aid; of those 17% had need fully met. *Average financial aid package:* $15,684 (excluding resources awarded to replace EFC). 30% of all full-time freshmen had no need and received non-need-based aid.

UNDERGRADUATE FINANCIAL AID (Fall 1999, est.) 1,014 applied for aid; of those 66% were deemed to have need. 100% of undergraduates with need received aid; of those 17% had need fully met. *Average financial aid package:* $15,331 (excluding resources awarded to replace EFC). 31% of all full-time undergraduates had no need and received non-need-based aid.

GIFT AID (NEED-BASED) ***Total amount:*** $5,052,761 (8% Federal, 31% state, 61% institutional). ***Receiving aid:*** *Freshmen:* 66% (224); *all full-time undergraduates:* 63% (672). ***Average award:*** Freshmen: $14,430; Undergraduates: $13,160. ***Scholarships, grants, and awards:*** Federal Pell, FSEOG, state, private, college/university gift aid from institutional funds.

GIFT AID (NON-NEED-BASED) ***Total amount:*** $4,977,753 (10% state, 86% institutional, 4% external sources). ***Receiving aid:*** *Freshmen:* 31% (104); *Undergraduates:* 32% (342). ***Scholarships, grants, and awards by category:*** *Academic Interests/Achievement:* general academic interests/achievements. *Creative Arts/Performance:* music. *Special Achievements/Activities:* leadership, religious involvement. *Special Characteristics:* children of faculty/staff, relatives of clergy, religious affiliation. ***Tuition waivers:*** Full or partial for employees or children of employees, senior citizens. ***ROTC:*** Army.

LOANS ***Student loans:*** $2,349,008 (42% need-based, 58% non-need-based). 73% of past graduating class borrowed through all loan programs. Average indebtedness per student: $13,113. ***Average need-based loan:***

Presbyterian College (continued)

Freshmen: $2404; Undergraduates: $3117. ***Parent loans:*** $297,669 (100% non-need-based). ***Programs:*** FFEL (Subsidized and Unsubsidized Stafford, PLUS), Perkins, college/university.

WORK-STUDY ***Federal work-study:*** *Total amount:* $158,659; jobs available. ***State or other work-study/employment:*** *Total amount:* $135,865 (100% non-need-based). Part-time jobs available.

ATHLETIC AWARDS *Total amount:* 1,163,716 (100% non-need-based).

APPLYING for FINANCIAL AID ***Required financial aid forms:*** FAFSA, institution's own form. ***Financial aid deadline (priority):*** 3/1. ***Notification date:*** Continuous. Students must reply within 3 weeks of notification.

CONTACT Ms. Judi Gillespie, Director of Financial Aid, Presbyterian College, 503 South Broad Street, Clinton, SC 29325, 864-833-8287 or toll-free 800-476-7272. *Fax:* 864-833-8481. *E-mail:* jgillesp@admin.presby.edu

PRESCOTT COLLEGE

Prescott, AZ

Tuition & fees: $13,450 **Average undergraduate aid package: $5095**

ABOUT THE INSTITUTION Independent, coed. Awards: bachelor's and master's degrees. 49 undergraduate majors. Total enrollment: 748. Undergraduates: 662. Freshmen: 40. Federal methodology is used as a basis for awarding need-based institutional aid.

UNDERGRADUATE EXPENSES for 1999–2000 ***Application fee:*** $45. ***Tuition:*** full-time $12,350; part-time $2100 per term. ***Required fees:*** full-time $1100; $110 per year part-time. Full-time tuition and fees vary according to course load and program. Part-time tuition and fees vary according to course load and program. ***Payment plan:*** installment.

FRESHMAN FINANCIAL AID (Fall 1998) 33 applied for aid; of those 100% were deemed to have need. 100% of freshmen with need received aid. *Average percent of need met:* 19% (excluding resources awarded to replace EFC). *Average financial aid package:* $3996 (excluding resources awarded to replace EFC). 12% of all full-time freshmen had no need and received non-need-based aid.

UNDERGRADUATE FINANCIAL AID (Fall 1998) 571 applied for aid; of those 100% were deemed to have need. 100% of undergraduates with need received aid. *Average percent of need met:* 22% (excluding resources awarded to replace EFC). *Average financial aid package:* $5095 (excluding resources awarded to replace EFC). 4% of all full-time undergraduates had no need and received non-need-based aid.

GIFT AID (NEED-BASED) ***Total amount:*** $912,989 (70% Federal, 3% state, 27% institutional). ***Receiving aid:*** *Freshmen:* 22% (9); *all full-time undergraduates:* 56% (461). ***Average award:*** Freshmen: $3031; Undergraduates: $2654. ***Scholarships, grants, and awards:*** Federal Pell, FSEOG, state, private, college/university gift aid from institutional funds.

GIFT AID (NON-NEED-BASED) ***Total amount:*** $260,788 (1% institutional, 99% external sources). ***Receiving aid:*** *Freshmen:* 60% (24); *Undergraduates:* 18% (150). ***Scholarships, grants, and awards by category:*** *Academic Interests/Achievement:* 5 awards ($2500 total): biological sciences. ***Tuition waivers:*** Full or partial for employees or children of employees.

LOANS ***Student loans:*** $4,498,625 (100% need-based). Average indebtedness per student: $16,787. ***Average need-based loan:*** Freshmen: $2451; Undergraduates: $3666. ***Parent loans:*** $734,436 (100% need-based). ***Programs:*** FFEL (Subsidized and Unsubsidized Stafford, PLUS), Perkins.

WORK-STUDY ***Federal work-study:*** *Total amount:* $102,204; 125 jobs averaging $818. ***State or other work-study/employment:*** *Total amount:* $7448 (100% need-based). 8 part-time jobs averaging $931.

APPLYING for FINANCIAL AID ***Required financial aid forms:*** FAFSA, institution's own form. ***Financial aid deadline:*** Continuous. ***Notification date:*** Continuous. Students must reply within 2 weeks of notification.

CONTACT Donna Endresen, Director of Financial Aid, Prescott College, 220 Grove Avenue, Prescott, AZ 86301-2990, 520-778-2090 Ext. 1201 or toll-free 800-628-6364 (out-of-state). *Fax:* 520-776-5225. *E-mail:* finaid@prescott.edu

PRESENTATION COLLEGE

Aberdeen, SD

Tuition & fees: $7762 **Average undergraduate aid package: $5616**

ABOUT THE INSTITUTION Independent Roman Catholic, coed. Awards: associate and bachelor's degrees. 19 undergraduate majors. Total enrollment: 471. Undergraduates: 471. Freshmen: 76. Both federal and institutional methodology are used as a basis for awarding need-based institutional aid.

UNDERGRADUATE EXPENSES for 1999–2000 ***Application fee:*** $15. ***Comprehensive fee:*** $11,162 includes full-time tuition ($7502), mandatory fees ($260), and room and board ($3400). Full-time tuition and fees vary according to program. Room and board charges vary according to board plan and housing facility. ***Part-time tuition:*** $286 per credit. ***Part-time fees:*** $130 per term part-time. Part-time tuition and fees vary according to course load and program. ***Payment plan:*** installment.

UNDERGRADUATE FINANCIAL AID (Fall 1999) 391 applied for aid; of those 100% were deemed to have need. 100% of undergraduates with need received aid; of those 40% had need fully met. *Average percent of need met:* 87% (excluding resources awarded to replace EFC). *Average financial aid package:* $5616 (excluding resources awarded to replace EFC).

GIFT AID (NEED-BASED) ***Total amount:*** $933,362 (56% Federal, 41% institutional, 3% external sources). ***Receiving aid:*** *All full-time undergraduates:* 46% (209). ***Average award:*** Undergraduates: $1497. ***Scholarships, grants, and awards:*** Federal Pell, FSEOG, private, college/university gift aid from institutional funds.

GIFT AID (NON-NEED-BASED) ***Receiving aid:*** *Undergraduates:* 39% (177). ***Scholarships, grants, and awards by category:*** *Academic Interests/Achievement:* 142 awards ($131,001 total): business, communication, computer science, general academic interests/achievements, health fields, religion/biblical studies, social sciences. *Special Characteristics:* 11 awards ($80,000 total): children and siblings of alumni, children of current students, children of faculty/staff, parents of current students, siblings of current students, spouses of current students. ***Tuition waivers:*** Full or partial for employees or children of employees, senior citizens.

LOANS ***Student loans:*** $1,778,624 (64% need-based, 36% non-need-based). ***Average need-based loan:*** Undergraduates: $1728. ***Parent loans:*** $144,903 (100% need-based). ***Programs:*** FFEL (Subsidized and Unsubsidized Stafford, PLUS), Perkins, college/university.

WORK-STUDY ***Federal work-study:*** *Total amount:* $48,500; 51 jobs averaging $1000. ***State or other work-study/employment:*** *Total amount:* $22,500 (100% need-based). 24 part-time jobs averaging $1000.

ATHLETIC AWARDS *Total amount:* 46,750 (100% non-need-based).

APPLYING for FINANCIAL AID ***Required financial aid form:*** FAFSA. ***Financial aid deadline (priority):*** 4/1. ***Notification date:*** 4/15. Students must reply within 2 weeks of notification.

CONTACT Ms. Valerie Weisser, Director of Financial Aid, Presentation College, 1500 North Main Street, Aberdeen, SD 57401-1299, 605-229-8427 or toll-free 800-247-6499 (in-state), 800-437-6060 (out-of-state).

PRINCETON UNIVERSITY

Princeton, NJ

Tuition & fees: $24,630 **Average undergraduate aid package: $21,800**

ABOUT THE INSTITUTION Independent, coed. Awards: bachelor's, master's, and doctoral degrees. 33 undergraduate majors. Total enrollment: 6,440. Undergraduates: 4,672. Freshmen: 1,148. Both federal and institutional methodology are used as a basis for awarding need-based institutional aid.

UNDERGRADUATE EXPENSES for 1999–2000 ***Application fee:*** $60. ***Comprehensive fee:*** $31,599 includes full-time tuition ($24,630) and room and board ($6969). ***College room only:*** $3262. ***Payment plans:*** installment, deferred payment.

FRESHMAN FINANCIAL AID (Fall 1999, est.) 638 applied for aid; of those 75% were deemed to have need. 100% of freshmen with need received aid; of those 100% had need fully met. *Average percent of need met:* 100% (excluding resources awarded to replace EFC). *Average financial aid package:* $22,300 (excluding resources awarded to replace EFC).

UNDERGRADUATE FINANCIAL AID (Fall 1999, est.) 2,220 applied for aid; of those 82% were deemed to have need. 100% of undergraduates with need received aid; of those 100% had need fully met. *Average percent of need met:* 100% (excluding resources awarded to replace EFC). *Average financial aid package:* $21,800 (excluding resources awarded to replace EFC).

GIFT AID (NEED-BASED) ***Total amount:*** $31,427,000 (6% Federal, 2% state, 86% institutional, 6% external sources). ***Receiving aid:*** *Freshmen:* 41% (475); *all full-time undergraduates:* 39% (1,758). ***Average award:*** Freshmen: $19,600; Undergraduates: $17,800. ***Scholarships, grants, and awards:*** Federal Pell, FSEOG, state, private, college/university gift aid from institutional funds.

GIFT AID (NON-NEED-BASED) ***Tuition waivers:*** Full or partial for employees or children of employees. ***ROTC:*** Army, Air Force cooperative.

LOANS ***Student loans:*** $5,000,000 (100% need-based). Average indebtedness per student: $15,500. ***Average need-based loan:*** Freshmen: $2650; Undergraduates: $3420. ***Parent loans:*** $8,200,000 (100% non-need-based). ***Programs:*** FFEL (Subsidized and Unsubsidized Stafford, PLUS), Perkins, college/university.

WORK-STUDY ***Federal work-study:*** *Total amount:* $1,200,000; 1,290 jobs averaging $930. ***State or other work-study/employment:*** *Total amount:* $800,000 (100% need-based). 1,000 part-time jobs averaging $800.

APPLYING for FINANCIAL AID ***Required financial aid forms:*** FAFSA, institution's own form, CSS Financial Aid PROFILE. ***Financial aid deadline (priority):*** 2/1. ***Notification date:*** 4/1. Students must reply by 5/1.

CONTACT Mr. Don Betterton, Director of Financial Aid, Princeton University, Box 591, Princeton, NJ 08544-1019, 609-258-3330.

PRINCIPIA COLLEGE

Elsah, IL

Tuition & fees: $15,984 **Average undergraduate aid package: $11,257**

ABOUT THE INSTITUTION Independent Christian Science, coed. Awards: bachelor's degrees. 30 undergraduate majors. Total enrollment: 548. Undergraduates: 548. Freshmen: 127. Institutional methodology is used as a basis for awarding need-based institutional aid.

UNDERGRADUATE EXPENSES for 2000–2001 ***Application fee:*** $35. ***Comprehensive fee:*** $21,768 includes full-time tuition ($15,714), mandatory fees ($270), and room and board ($5784). ***College room only:*** $2808. ***Part-time tuition:*** $1746 per course. ***Payment plan:*** installment.

FRESHMAN FINANCIAL AID (Fall 1999) 94 applied for aid; of those 94% were deemed to have need. 100% of freshmen with need received aid; of those 90% had need fully met. *Average percent of need met:* 90% (excluding resources awarded to replace EFC). *Average financial aid package:* $10,909 (excluding resources awarded to replace EFC). 35% of all full-time freshmen had no need and received non-need-based aid.

UNDERGRADUATE FINANCIAL AID (Fall 1999) 361 applied for aid; of those 96% were deemed to have need. 100% of undergraduates with need received aid; of those 90% had need fully met. *Average percent of need met:* 90% (excluding resources awarded to replace EFC). *Average financial aid package:* $11,257 (excluding resources awarded to replace EFC). 34% of all full-time undergraduates had no need and received non-need-based aid.

GIFT AID (NEED-BASED) ***Total amount:*** $3,646,904 (100% institutional). ***Receiving aid:*** *Freshmen:* 65% (88); *all full-time undergraduates:* 66% (347). ***Average award:*** Freshmen: $8039; Undergraduates: $8522. ***Scholarships, grants, and awards:*** college/university gift aid from institutional funds.

GIFT AID (NON-NEED-BASED) ***Total amount:*** $645,668 (100% institutional). ***Receiving aid:*** *Freshmen:* 28% (38); *Undergraduates:* 19% (102). ***Scholarships, grants, and awards by category:*** *Academic Interests/Achievement:* 94 awards ($631,335 total): general academic interests/achievements. *Special Characteristics:* 15 awards ($37,500 total): children and siblings of alumni. ***Tuition waivers:*** Full or partial for employees or children of employees.

LOANS ***Student loans:*** $948,288 (100% need-based). 70% of past graduating class borrowed through all loan programs. Average indebtedness per student: $8764. ***Average need-based loan:*** Freshmen: $3280; Undergraduates: $3262. ***Programs:*** college/university.

WORK-STUDY ***State or other work-study/employment:*** *Total amount:* $261,000 (100% need-based). 174 part-time jobs averaging $1500.

APPLYING for FINANCIAL AID ***Required financial aid forms:*** institution's own form, CSS Financial Aid PROFILE. ***Financial aid deadline:*** Continuous. ***Notification date:*** Continuous beginning 12/1.

CONTACT Mr. Brooks F. Benjamin, Director of Financial Aid, Principia College, 1 Maybeck Place, Elsah, IL 62028-9799, 618-374-5186 or toll-free 800-277-4648 Ext. 2802. *Fax:* 618-374-5906.

PROVIDENCE COLLEGE

Providence, RI

Tuition & fees: $17,945 **Average undergraduate aid package: $14,350**

ABOUT THE INSTITUTION Independent Roman Catholic, coed. Awards: associate, bachelor's, and master's degrees. 40 undergraduate majors. Total enrollment: 5,442. Undergraduates: 4,505. Freshmen: 978. Both federal and institutional methodology are used as a basis for awarding need-based institutional aid.

UNDERGRADUATE EXPENSES for 1999–2000 ***Application fee:*** $50. ***Comprehensive fee:*** $25,300 includes full-time tuition ($17,640), mandatory fees ($305), and room and board ($7355). ***College room only:*** $3645. Room and board charges vary according to board plan, housing facility, and student level. ***Part-time tuition:*** $180 per credit. Part-time tuition and fees vary according to course load. ***Payment plan:*** installment.

FRESHMAN FINANCIAL AID (Fall 1999, est.) 714 applied for aid; of those 79% were deemed to have need. 100% of freshmen with need received aid; of those 25% had need fully met. *Average percent of need met:* 75% (excluding resources awarded to replace EFC). *Average financial aid package:* $13,175 (excluding resources awarded to replace EFC). 11% of all full-time freshmen had no need and received non-need-based aid.

UNDERGRADUATE FINANCIAL AID (Fall 1999, est.) 2,636 applied for aid; of those 85% were deemed to have need. 100% of undergraduates with need received aid; of those 25% had need fully met. *Average percent of need met:* 85% (excluding resources awarded to replace EFC). *Average financial aid package:* $14,350 (excluding resources awarded to replace EFC). 11% of all full-time undergraduates had no need and received non-need-based aid.

GIFT AID (NEED-BASED) ***Total amount:*** $18,499,000 (8% Federal, 2% state, 85% institutional, 5% external sources). ***Receiving aid:*** *Freshmen:* 56% (550); *all full-time undergraduates:* 59% (2,203). ***Average award:*** Freshmen: $6500; Undergraduates: $6750. ***Scholarships, grants, and awards:*** Federal Pell, FSEOG, state, private, college/university gift aid from institutional funds.

GIFT AID (NON-NEED-BASED) ***Total amount:*** $2,522,000 (93% institutional, 7% external sources). ***Receiving aid:*** *Freshmen:* 6% (56); *Undergraduates:* 6% (224). ***Scholarships, grants, and awards by category:*** *Academic Interests/Achievement:* business, general academic interests/achievements, military science, premedicine. *Creative Arts/Performance:* theater/drama. *Special Achievements/Activities:* community service. ***Tuition waivers:*** Full or partial for employees or children of employees. ***ROTC:*** Army.

LOANS ***Student loans:*** $10,459,000 (75% need-based, 25% non-need-based). 65% of past graduating class borrowed through all loan programs. Average indebtedness per student: $19,125. ***Average need-based loan:*** Freshmen: $3875; Undergraduates: $6000. ***Parent loans:*** $4,984,000 (100% non-need-based). ***Programs:*** Federal Direct (Subsidized and Unsubsidized Stafford, PLUS), Perkins.

WORK-STUDY ***Federal work-study:*** *Total amount:* $950,000; 594 jobs averaging $1600. ***State or other work-study/employment:*** *Total amount:* $920,000 (100% non-need-based). 511 part-time jobs averaging $1800.

Providence College (continued)

ATHLETIC AWARDS *Total amount:* 2,596,000 (30% need-based, 70% non-need-based).

APPLYING for FINANCIAL AID ***Required financial aid forms:*** FAFSA, CSS Financial Aid PROFILE, state aid form. ***Financial aid deadline:*** 2/1. ***Notification date:*** 4/15. Students must reply by 5/1.

CONTACT Mr. Herbert J. D'Arcy, Executive Director of Financial Aid, Providence College, River Avenue and Eaton Street, Providence, RI 02918, 401-865-2286 or toll-free 800-721-6444. *Fax:* 401-865-2826. *E-mail:* hdarcy@providence.edu

PUGET SOUND CHRISTIAN COLLEGE

Edmonds, WA

Tuition & fees: $6420 **Average undergraduate aid package: N/A**

ABOUT THE INSTITUTION Independent Christian, coed. Awards: associate and bachelor's degrees. 9 undergraduate majors. Total enrollment: 207. Undergraduates: 207. Freshmen: 42. Federal methodology is used as a basis for awarding need-based institutional aid.

UNDERGRADUATE EXPENSES for 1999–2000 ***Application fee:*** $25. ***Comprehensive fee:*** $10,570 includes full-time tuition ($6250), mandatory fees ($170), and room and board ($4150). ***College room only:*** $2550. Full-time tuition and fees vary according to class time. Room and board charges vary according to board plan. ***Part-time tuition:*** $290 per semester hour. ***Part-time fees:*** $40 per term part-time. Part-time tuition and fees vary according to class time and course load. ***Payment plans:*** tuition prepayment, installment.

GIFT AID (NEED-BASED) ***Scholarships, grants, and awards:*** Federal Pell, FSEOG, college/university gift aid from institutional funds.

GIFT AID (NON-NEED-BASED) ***Scholarships, grants, and awards by category:*** *Academic Interests/Achievement:* general academic interests/achievements, religion/biblical studies. *Special Characteristics:* children of faculty/staff, relatives of clergy, spouses of current students. ***Tuition waivers:*** Full or partial for employees or children of employees, senior citizens.

LOANS ***Programs:*** FFEL (Subsidized and Unsubsidized Stafford, PLUS), college/university.

WORK-STUDY Federal work-study jobs available.

APPLYING for FINANCIAL AID ***Required financial aid form:*** FAFSA.

CONTACT Carlene Krause, Financial Aid Officer, Puget Sound Christian College, 410 4th Avenue North, Edmonds, WA 98020-3171, 425-775-8686 Ext. 201. *Fax:* 425-775-8688. *E-mail:* psccfina@gte.net

PURCHASE COLLEGE, STATE UNIVERSITY OF NEW YORK

Purchase, NY

Tuition & fees (NY res): $3949 **Average undergraduate aid package: $8510**

ABOUT THE INSTITUTION State-supported, coed. Awards: bachelor's and master's degrees. 24 undergraduate majors. Total enrollment: 3,956. Undergraduates: 3,837. Freshmen: 646. Federal methodology is used as a basis for awarding need-based institutional aid.

UNDERGRADUATE EXPENSES for 1999–2000 ***Application fee:*** $30. ***Tuition, state resident:*** full-time $3400; part-time $137 per credit. ***Tuition, nonresident:*** full-time $8300; part-time $346 per credit. ***Required fees:*** full-time $549; $18 per credit. ***College room and board:*** $5942; ***room only:*** $3572. Room and board charges vary according to board plan and housing facility. ***Payment plan:*** installment.

FRESHMAN FINANCIAL AID (Fall 1999) 513 applied for aid; of those 76% were deemed to have need. 100% of freshmen with need received aid; of those 98% had need fully met. *Average percent of need met:* 64% (excluding resources awarded to replace EFC). *Average financial aid package:* $7505 (excluding resources awarded to replace EFC). 33% of all full-time freshmen had no need and received non-need-based aid.

UNDERGRADUATE FINANCIAL AID (Fall 1999) 2,004 applied for aid; of those 83% were deemed to have need. 100% of undergraduates with need received aid; of those 54% had need fully met. *Average percent of need met:* 76% (excluding resources awarded to replace EFC). *Average financial aid package:* $8510 (excluding resources awarded to replace EFC). 26% of all full-time undergraduates had no need and received non-need-based aid.

GIFT AID (NEED-BASED) ***Total amount:*** $5,373,160 (47% Federal, 42% state, 9% institutional, 2% external sources). ***Receiving aid:*** *Freshmen:* 47% (300); *all full-time undergraduates:* 50% (1,381). ***Average award:*** Freshmen: $2765; Undergraduates: $3230. ***Scholarships, grants, and awards:*** Federal Pell, FSEOG, state, private, college/university gift aid from institutional funds.

GIFT AID (NON-NEED-BASED) ***Total amount:*** $583,221 (4% state, 75% institutional, 21% external sources). ***Receiving aid:*** *Freshmen:* 14% (90); *Undergraduates:* 19% (528). ***Scholarships, grants, and awards by category:*** *Academic Interests/Achievement:* 114 awards ($232,214 total): area/ethnic studies, biological sciences, computer science, English, general academic interests/achievements, humanities, mathematics, social sciences. *Creative Arts/Performance:* 291 awards ($537,381 total): art/fine arts, cinema/film/broadcasting, creative writing, dance, general creative arts/performance, music, performing arts, theater/drama. *Special Characteristics:* 36 awards ($39,900 total): ethnic background, members of minority groups. ***Tuition waivers:*** Full or partial for employees or children of employees, senior citizens.

LOANS ***Student loans:*** $9,203,000 (74% need-based, 26% non-need-based). 59% of past graduating class borrowed through all loan programs. ***Average need-based loan:*** Freshmen: $3180; Undergraduates: $4270. ***Parent loans:*** $1,188,010 (35% need-based, 65% non-need-based). ***Programs:*** FFEL (Subsidized and Unsubsidized Stafford, PLUS), Perkins, college/university, alternative loans.

WORK-STUDY ***Federal work-study:*** *Total amount:* $225,000; 197 jobs averaging $1142. ***State or other work-study/employment:*** *Total amount:* $470,000 (100% non-need-based). 200 part-time jobs averaging $2350.

APPLYING for FINANCIAL AID ***Required financial aid forms:*** FAFSA, state aid form. ***Financial aid deadline (priority):*** 3/15. ***Notification date:*** Continuous. Students must reply within 2 weeks of notification.

CONTACT Ms. Emilie B. Devine, Director of Financial Aid and Scholarships, Purchase College, State University of New York, 735 Anderson Hill Road, Purchase, NY 10577-1400, 914-251-6355. *Fax:* 914-251-6356. *E-mail:* emilie.devine@purchase.edu

PURDUE UNIVERSITY

West Lafayette, IN

Tuition & fees (IN res): $3724 **Average undergraduate aid package: $6448**

ABOUT THE INSTITUTION State-supported, coed. Awards: associate, bachelor's, master's, doctoral, and first professional degrees. 81 undergraduate majors. Total enrollment: 37,762. Undergraduates: 30,835. Freshmen: 6,860. Federal methodology is used as a basis for awarding need-based institutional aid.

UNDERGRADUATE EXPENSES for 1999–2000 ***Application fee:*** $30. ***Tuition, state resident:*** full-time $3724; part-time $134 per semester hour. ***Tuition, nonresident:*** full-time $12,348; part-time $408 per semester hour. Full-time tuition and fees vary according to course load. Part-time tuition and fees vary according to course load. ***College room and board:*** $5500. Room and board charges vary according to board plan and housing facility. ***Payment plan:*** installment.

FRESHMAN FINANCIAL AID (Fall 1999, est.) 4711 applied for aid; of those 61% were deemed to have need. 95% of freshmen with need received aid; of those 34% had need fully met. *Average percent of need met:* 89% (excluding resources awarded to replace EFC). *Average financial aid package:* $6616 (excluding resources awarded to replace EFC). 4% of all full-time freshmen had no need and received non-need-based aid.

UNDERGRADUATE FINANCIAL AID (Fall 1999, est.) 16,355 applied for aid; of those 69% were deemed to have need. 96% of undergraduates with need received aid; of those 41% had need fully met. *Average percent*

of need met: 89% (excluding resources awarded to replace EFC). *Average financial aid package:* $6448 (excluding resources awarded to replace EFC). 4% of all full-time undergraduates had no need and received non-need-based aid.

GIFT AID (NEED-BASED) ***Total amount:*** $33,998,333 (28% Federal, 25% state, 47% institutional). ***Receiving aid:*** *Freshmen:* 24% (1,674); *all full-time undergraduates:* 23% (6,585). ***Scholarships, grants, and awards:*** Federal Pell, FSEOG, state, private, college/university gift aid from institutional funds.

GIFT AID (NON-NEED-BASED) ***Total amount:*** $5,976,749 (100% external sources). ***Receiving aid:*** *Freshmen:* 7% (485); *Undergraduates:* 4% (1,218). ***Scholarships, grants, and awards by category:*** *Academic Interests/Achievement:* agriculture, biological sciences, business, education, engineering/technologies, general academic interests/achievements, physical sciences. *Special Characteristics:* children of faculty/staff. ***Tuition waivers:*** Full or partial for employees or children of employees, senior citizens. ***ROTC:*** Army, Naval, Air Force.

LOANS ***Student loans:*** $65,965,478 (55% need-based, 45% non-need-based). 49% of past graduating class borrowed through all loan programs. Average indebtedness per student: $15,633. ***Average need-based loan:*** Freshmen: $2857; Undergraduates: $3506. ***Parent loans:*** $75,716,462 (13% need-based, 87% non-need-based). ***Programs:*** FFEL (Subsidized and Unsubsidized Stafford, PLUS), Perkins, college/university.

WORK-STUDY ***Federal work-study:*** *Total amount:* $2,024,365; 1,384 jobs averaging $1549.

ATHLETIC AWARDS *Total amount:* 3,983,842 (100% non-need-based).

APPLYING for FINANCIAL AID ***Required financial aid form:*** FAFSA. ***Financial aid deadline (priority):*** 3/1. ***Notification date:*** 4/15.

CONTACT Division of Financial Aid, Purdue University, Schleman Hall, Room 305, West Lafayette, IN 47907-1102, 765-494-5050.

PURDUE UNIVERSITY CALUMET

Hammond, IN

Tuition & fees (IN res): $2577 **Average undergraduate aid package: $4653**

ABOUT THE INSTITUTION State-supported, coed. Awards: associate, bachelor's, and master's degrees and post-bachelor's certificates. 76 undergraduate majors. Total enrollment: 9,974. Undergraduates: 7,885. Federal methodology is used as a basis for awarding need-based institutional aid.

UNDERGRADUATE EXPENSES for 1999–2000 ***Tuition, state resident:*** full-time $2341; part-time $98 per credit hour. ***Tuition, nonresident:*** full-time $5887; part-time $245 per credit hour. ***Required fees:*** full-time $236; $10 per credit hour. Full-time tuition and fees vary according to course load and program. Part-time tuition and fees vary according to program. ***Payment plan:*** deferred payment.

FRESHMAN FINANCIAL AID (Fall 1999, est.) 726 applied for aid; of those 74% were deemed to have need. 97% of freshmen with need received aid; of those 13% had need fully met. *Average percent of need met:* 71% (excluding resources awarded to replace EFC). *Average financial aid package:* $3666 (excluding resources awarded to replace EFC). 2% of all full-time freshmen had no need and received non-need-based aid.

UNDERGRADUATE FINANCIAL AID (Fall 1999, est.) 2,851 applied for aid; of those 80% were deemed to have need. 97% of undergraduates with need received aid; of those 15% had need fully met. *Average percent of need met:* 70% (excluding resources awarded to replace EFC). *Average financial aid package:* $4653 (excluding resources awarded to replace EFC). 1% of all full-time undergraduates had no need and received non-need-based aid.

GIFT AID (NEED-BASED) ***Total amount:*** $6,596,041 (63% Federal, 36% state, 1% institutional). ***Receiving aid:*** *Freshmen:* 31% (317); *all full-time undergraduates:* 42% (1,492). ***Average award:*** Freshmen: $3278; Undergraduates: $3498. ***Scholarships, grants, and awards:*** Federal Pell, FSEOG, state, private, college/university gift aid from institutional funds.

GIFT AID (NON-NEED-BASED) ***Total amount:*** $285,876 (68% institutional, 32% external sources). ***Receiving aid:*** *Freshmen:* 3% (33); *Undergraduates:* 5% (165). ***Scholarships, grants, and awards by category:*** *Academic Interests/Achievement:* general academic interests/achievements. ***Tuition waivers:*** Full or partial for employees or children of employees, senior citizens. ***ROTC:*** Army cooperative.

LOANS ***Student loans:*** $10,357,729 (66% need-based, 34% non-need-based). Average indebtedness per student: $10,309. ***Average need-based loan:*** Freshmen: $2228; Undergraduates: $2840. ***Parent loans:*** $119,624 (100% non-need-based). ***Programs:*** Federal Direct (Subsidized and Unsubsidized Stafford, PLUS), Perkins.

WORK-STUDY ***Federal work-study:*** *Total amount:* $312,888; jobs available. ***State or other work-study/employment:*** *Total amount:* $9600 (100% need-based). Part-time jobs available.

ATHLETIC AWARDS *Total amount:* 19,138 (100% non-need-based).

APPLYING for FINANCIAL AID ***Required financial aid form:*** FAFSA. ***Financial aid deadline (priority):*** 3/1. ***Notification date:*** Continuous beginning 6/1. Students must reply within 2 weeks of notification.

CONTACT Ms. Mary Ann Bishel, Director of Financial Aid, Purdue University Calumet, 2200 169th Street, Hammond, IN 46323-2094, 219-989-2660 or toll-free 800-447-8738 (in-state). *Fax:* 219-989-2775. *E-mail:* finaid@calumet.purdue.edu

PURDUE UNIVERSITY NORTH CENTRAL

Westville, IN

Tuition & fees (IN res): $3211 **Average undergraduate aid package: $5000**

ABOUT THE INSTITUTION State-supported, coed. Awards: associate, bachelor's, and master's degrees. 23 undergraduate majors. Total enrollment: 3,355. Undergraduates: 3,308. Freshmen: 710. Federal methodology is used as a basis for awarding need-based institutional aid.

UNDERGRADUATE EXPENSES for 1999–2000 ***Tuition, state resident:*** full-time $2927; part-time $98 per credit hour. ***Tuition, nonresident:*** full-time $7425; part-time $248 per credit hour. ***Required fees:*** full-time $284; $9 per credit hour. Full-time tuition and fees vary according to course load. Part-time tuition and fees vary according to course load. ***Payment plan:*** deferred payment.

FRESHMAN FINANCIAL AID (Fall 1999) 246 applied for aid; of those 91% were deemed to have need. 98% of freshmen with need received aid; of those 16% had need fully met. *Average percent of need met:* 88% (excluding resources awarded to replace EFC). *Average financial aid package:* $5000 (excluding resources awarded to replace EFC). 5% of all full-time freshmen had no need and received non-need-based aid.

UNDERGRADUATE FINANCIAL AID (Fall 1999) 893 applied for aid; of those 96% were deemed to have need. 99% of undergraduates with need received aid; of those 5% had need fully met. *Average percent of need met:* 88% (excluding resources awarded to replace EFC). *Average financial aid package:* $5000 (excluding resources awarded to replace EFC). 3% of all full-time undergraduates had no need and received non-need-based aid.

GIFT AID (NEED-BASED) ***Total amount:*** $2,710,907 (62% Federal, 38% state). ***Receiving aid:*** *Freshmen:* 28% (156); *all full-time undergraduates:* 23% (402). ***Average award:*** Freshmen: $3000; Undergraduates: $3000. ***Scholarships, grants, and awards:*** Federal Pell, FSEOG, state, private, college/university gift aid from institutional funds.

GIFT AID (NON-NEED-BASED) ***Total amount:*** $330,956 (21% institutional, 79% external sources). ***Receiving aid:*** *Freshmen:* 2% (11); *Undergraduates:* 4% (76). ***Scholarships, grants, and awards by category:*** *Academic Interests/Achievement:* general academic interests/achievements. *Special Achievements/Activities:* general special achievements/activities, leadership. *Special Characteristics:* adult students, children of faculty/staff, veterans' children. ***Tuition waivers:*** Full or partial for senior citizens.

LOANS ***Student loans:*** $6,599,963 (60% need-based, 40% non-need-based). 61% of past graduating class borrowed through all loan programs. ***Average need-based loan:*** Freshmen: $2000; Undergraduates: $2000. ***Parent loans:*** $29,824 (100% non-need-based). ***Programs:*** FFEL (Subsidized and Unsubsidized Stafford, PLUS), Perkins, college/university.

WORK-STUDY ***Federal work-study:*** *Total amount:* $326,831; jobs available. ***State or other work-study/employment:*** *Total amount:* $12,365 (100% need-based). Part-time jobs available.

Purdue University North Central (continued)

APPLYING for FINANCIAL AID ***Required financial aid forms:*** FAFSA, state aid form. ***Financial aid deadline (priority):*** 3/1. ***Notification date:*** Continuous beginning 5/20. Students must reply within 2 weeks of notification.

CONTACT Bryant Dabney, Financial Aid Systems Manager, Purdue University North Central, 1401 South US Highway 421, Westville, IN 46391-9528, 219-785-5279 Ext. 5502 or toll-free 800-872-1231 (in-state). *Fax:* 219-785-5538. *E-mail:* bdabney@purduenc.edu

QUEENS COLLEGE

Charlotte, NC

Tuition & fees: $10,680 **Average undergraduate aid package: $11,440**

ABOUT THE INSTITUTION Independent Presbyterian, coed. Awards: bachelor's and master's degrees and post-bachelor's certificates. 41 undergraduate majors. Total enrollment: 1,563. Undergraduates: 1,115. Freshmen: 123. Federal methodology is used as a basis for awarding need-based institutional aid.

UNDERGRADUATE EXPENSES for 2000–2001 ***Application fee:*** $25. ***Comprehensive fee:*** $16,570 includes full-time tuition ($10,680) and room and board ($5890). ***Part-time tuition:*** $225 per credit hour. ***Part-time fees:*** $15 per term part-time. ***Payment plan:*** installment.

FRESHMAN FINANCIAL AID (Fall 1999, est.) 91 applied for aid; of those 74% were deemed to have need. 100% of freshmen with need received aid; of those 28% had need fully met. *Average percent of need met:* 82% (excluding resources awarded to replace EFC). *Average financial aid package:* $9938 (excluding resources awarded to replace EFC). 23% of all full-time freshmen had no need and received non-need-based aid.

UNDERGRADUATE FINANCIAL AID (Fall 1999, est.) 386 applied for aid; of those 83% were deemed to have need. 100% of undergraduates with need received aid; of those 38% had need fully met. *Average percent of need met:* 85% (excluding resources awarded to replace EFC). *Average financial aid package:* $11,440 (excluding resources awarded to replace EFC). 28% of all full-time undergraduates had no need and received non-need-based aid.

GIFT AID (NEED-BASED) ***Total amount:*** $2,711,999 (12% Federal, 29% state, 58% institutional, 1% external sources). ***Receiving aid:*** *Freshmen:* 53% (67); *all full-time undergraduates:* 56% (317). ***Average award:*** Freshmen: $6533; Undergraduates: $6821. ***Scholarships, grants, and awards:*** Federal Pell, FSEOG, state, private, college/university gift aid from institutional funds.

GIFT AID (NON-NEED-BASED) ***Total amount:*** $1,433,350 (14% state, 84% institutional, 2% external sources). ***Receiving aid:*** *Freshmen:* 11% (14); *Undergraduates:* 19% (106). ***Scholarships, grants, and awards by category:*** *Academic Interests/Achievement:* 449 awards ($1,740,311 total): general academic interests/achievements. *Creative Arts/Performance:* 39 awards ($49,795 total): art/fine arts, music, theater/drama. *Special Achievements/Activities:* 105 awards ($120,663 total): community service, general special achievements/activities, leadership, religious involvement. *Special Characteristics:* 71 awards ($196,381 total): adult students, children of current students, children of faculty/staff, international students, members of minority groups, relatives of clergy, religious affiliation, siblings of current students. ***Tuition waivers:*** Full or partial for employees or children of employees. ***ROTC:*** Army cooperative, Air Force cooperative.

LOANS ***Student loans:*** $1,936,598 (70% need-based, 30% non-need-based). Average indebtedness per student: $15,300. ***Average need-based loan:*** Freshmen: $2600; Undergraduates: $4089. ***Parent loans:*** $400,989 (25% need-based, 75% non-need-based). ***Programs:*** FFEL (Subsidized and Unsubsidized Stafford, PLUS), Perkins.

WORK-STUDY ***Federal work-study:*** *Total amount:* $90,079; 60 jobs averaging $1500. ***State or other work-study/employment:*** *Total amount:* $90,371 (100% need-based). 60 part-time jobs averaging $1500.

ATHLETIC AWARDS *Total amount:* 515,010 (54% need-based, 46% non-need-based).

APPLYING for FINANCIAL AID ***Required financial aid form:*** FAFSA. ***Financial aid deadline (priority):*** 3/1. ***Notification date:*** Continuous. Students must reply by 5/1 or within 3 weeks of notification.

CONTACT Mr. Tony D. Carter, Director of Financial Aid, Queens College, 1900 Selwyn Avenue, Charlotte, NC 28274-0002, 704-337-2225 or toll-free 800-849-0202. *Fax:* 704-337-2416. *E-mail:* cartert@queens.edu

QUEENS COLLEGE OF THE CITY UNIVERSITY OF NEW YORK

Flushing, NY

Tuition & fees (NY res): $3403 **Average undergraduate aid package: $4500**

ABOUT THE INSTITUTION State and locally supported, coed. Awards: bachelor's and master's degrees. 92 undergraduate majors. Total enrollment: 15,686. Undergraduates: 11,566. Freshmen: 1,037. Federal methodology is used as a basis for awarding need-based institutional aid.

UNDERGRADUATE EXPENSES for 2000–2001 ***Application fee:*** $40. ***Tuition, state resident:*** full-time $3200; part-time $135 per credit. ***Tuition, nonresident:*** full-time $6800; part-time $285 per credit. ***Required fees:*** full-time $203; $71 per term part-time. Full-time tuition and fees vary according to program. Part-time tuition and fees vary according to program. ***Payment plan:*** installment.

FRESHMAN FINANCIAL AID (Fall 1999, est.) 989 applied for aid; of those 75% were deemed to have need. 93% of freshmen with need received aid; of those 57% had need fully met. *Average percent of need met:* 85% (excluding resources awarded to replace EFC). *Average financial aid package:* $3500 (excluding resources awarded to replace EFC). 5% of all full-time freshmen had no need and received non-need-based aid.

UNDERGRADUATE FINANCIAL AID (Fall 1999, est.) 4,275 applied for aid; of those 73% were deemed to have need. 93% of undergraduates with need received aid; of those 80% had need fully met. *Average percent of need met:* 85% (excluding resources awarded to replace EFC). *Average financial aid package:* $4500 (excluding resources awarded to replace EFC). 4% of all full-time undergraduates had no need and received non-need-based aid.

GIFT AID (NEED-BASED) ***Total amount:*** $14,421,299 (48% Federal, 52% state). ***Receiving aid:*** *Freshmen:* 46% (640); *all full-time undergraduates:* 18% (1,359). ***Average award:*** Freshmen: $1200; Undergraduates: $2800. ***Scholarships, grants, and awards:*** Federal Pell, FSEOG, state.

GIFT AID (NON-NEED-BASED) ***Total amount:*** $1,099,725 (45% institutional, 55% external sources). ***Receiving aid:*** *Freshmen:* 7% (98); *Undergraduates:* 10% (750). ***Scholarships, grants, and awards by category:*** *Academic Interests/Achievement:* general academic interests/achievements. ***Tuition waivers:*** Full or partial for employees or children of employees, senior citizens. ***ROTC:*** Army cooperative.

LOANS ***Student loans:*** $5,232,798 (100% need-based). Average indebtedness per student: $12,000. ***Parent loans:*** $54,500 (56% need-based, 44% non-need-based). ***Programs:*** Federal Direct (Subsidized and Unsubsidized Stafford, PLUS), Perkins.

WORK-STUDY ***Federal work-study:*** *Total amount:* $585,500; 650 jobs averaging $900.

ATHLETIC AWARDS *Total amount:* 270,725 (100% non-need-based).

APPLYING for FINANCIAL AID ***Required financial aid forms:*** FAFSA, institution's own form, state aid form. ***Financial aid deadline (priority):*** 5/1. ***Notification date:*** Continuous beginning 6/1.

CONTACT Office of Financial Aid, Queens College of the City University of New York, 65-30 Kissena Boulevard, Flushing, NY 11367-1597, 718-997-5100.

QUINCY UNIVERSITY

Quincy, IL

Tuition & fees: $14,700 **Average undergraduate aid package: $13,455**

ABOUT THE INSTITUTION Independent Roman Catholic, coed. Awards: associate, bachelor's, and master's degrees. 42 undergraduate majors. Total enrollment: 1,186. Undergraduates: 1,051. Freshmen: 274. Federal methodology is used as a basis for awarding need-based institutional aid.

UNDERGRADUATE EXPENSES for 2000–2001 ***Application fee:*** $25. ***Comprehensive fee:*** $19,480 includes full-time tuition ($14,300), mandatory fees ($400), and room and board ($4780). Room and board charges vary according to housing facility. ***Part-time tuition:*** $410 per credit hour. ***Payment plans:*** guaranteed tuition, installment.

FRESHMAN FINANCIAL AID (Fall 1999, est.) 270 applied for aid; of those 87% were deemed to have need. 100% of freshmen with need received aid; of those 78% had need fully met. *Average percent of need met:* 97% (excluding resources awarded to replace EFC). *Average financial aid package:* $14,015 (excluding resources awarded to replace EFC). 14% of all full-time freshmen had no need and received non-need-based aid.

UNDERGRADUATE FINANCIAL AID (Fall 1999, est.) 969 applied for aid; of those 87% were deemed to have need. 100% of undergraduates with need received aid. *Average financial aid package:* $13,455 (excluding resources awarded to replace EFC).

GIFT AID (NEED-BASED) ***Total amount:*** $5,067,880 (16% Federal, 37% state, 45% institutional, 2% external sources). ***Receiving aid:*** *Freshmen:* 70% (191); *all full-time undergraduates:* 72% (712). ***Scholarships, grants, and awards:*** Federal Pell, FSEOG, state, private, college/university gift aid from institutional funds.

GIFT AID (NON-NEED-BASED) ***Total amount:*** $2,731,367 (1% state, 99% institutional). ***Receiving aid:*** *Freshmen:* 84% (230). ***Scholarships, grants, and awards by category:*** *Academic Interests/Achievement:* 642 awards ($2,392,445 total): biological sciences, business, communication, computer science, education, English, general academic interests/achievements, health fields, international studies, mathematics, religion/biblical studies, social sciences. *Creative Arts/Performance:* 77 awards ($194,190 total): art/fine arts, cinema/film/broadcasting, music. *Special Achievements/Activities:* 5 awards ($3700 total): community service, leadership. *Special Characteristics:* 42 awards ($235,779 total): children of faculty/staff, relatives of clergy. ***Tuition waivers:*** Full or partial for employees or children of employees, senior citizens.

LOANS ***Student loans:*** $3,565,883 (67% need-based, 33% non-need-based). 87% of past graduating class borrowed through all loan programs. Average indebtedness per student: $13,475. ***Parent loans:*** $581,823 (100% non-need-based). ***Programs:*** FFEL (Subsidized and Unsubsidized Stafford, PLUS), Perkins.

WORK-STUDY ***Federal work-study:*** *Total amount:* $514,061; 350 jobs averaging $1500. ***State or other work-study/employment:*** *Total amount:* $64,047 (100% non-need-based). 45 part-time jobs averaging $1450.

ATHLETIC AWARDS *Total amount:* 1,318,383 (100% non-need-based).

APPLYING for FINANCIAL AID ***Required financial aid form:*** FAFSA. ***Financial aid deadline (priority):*** 4/15. ***Notification date:*** Continuous. Students must reply by 5/1 or within 2 weeks of notification.

CONTACT James D. Reed, Director of Financial Aid, Quincy University, 1800 College Avenue, Quincy, IL 62301-2699, 217-228-5260 or toll-free 800-688-4295. *Fax:* 217-228-5635. *E-mail:* jimr@quincy.edu

QUINNIPIAC UNIVERSITY

Hamden, CT

Tuition & fees: $17,780 **Average undergraduate aid package: $10,947**

ABOUT THE INSTITUTION Independent, coed. Awards: bachelor's, master's, and first professional degrees. 61 undergraduate majors. Total enrollment: 6,047. Undergraduates: 4,513. Freshmen: 1,164. Federal methodology is used as a basis for awarding need-based institutional aid.

UNDERGRADUATE EXPENSES for 2000–2001 ***Application fee:*** $45. ***Comprehensive fee:*** $25,955 includes full-time tuition ($17,000), mandatory fees ($780), and room and board ($8175). Room and board charges vary according to board plan and housing facility. ***Part-time tuition:*** $420 per semester hour. ***Part-time fees:*** $75 per course. Part-time tuition and fees vary according to course load. ***Payment plan:*** installment.

FRESHMAN FINANCIAL AID (Fall 1999) 937 applied for aid; of those 82% were deemed to have need. 100% of freshmen with need received aid; of those 9% had need fully met. *Average percent of need met:* 65% (excluding resources awarded to replace EFC). *Average financial aid package:* $10,908 (excluding resources awarded to replace EFC). 5% of all full-time freshmen had no need and received non-need-based aid.

UNDERGRADUATE FINANCIAL AID (Fall 1999) 2,975 applied for aid; of those 86% were deemed to have need. 99% of undergraduates with need received aid; of those 13% had need fully met. *Average percent of need met:* 67% (excluding resources awarded to replace EFC). *Average financial aid package:* $10,947 (excluding resources awarded to replace EFC). 4% of all full-time undergraduates had no need and received non-need-based aid.

GIFT AID (NEED-BASED) ***Total amount:*** $15,351,870 (6% Federal, 15% state, 74% institutional, 5% external sources). ***Receiving aid:*** *Freshmen:* 63% (728); *all full-time undergraduates:* 60% (2,405). ***Average award:*** Freshmen: $7012; Undergraduates: $6182. ***Scholarships, grants, and awards:*** Federal Pell, FSEOG, state, private, college/university gift aid from institutional funds.

GIFT AID (NON-NEED-BASED) ***Total amount:*** $2,089,098 (97% institutional, 3% external sources). ***Receiving aid:*** *Freshmen:* 18% (214); *Undergraduates:* 14% (580). ***Scholarships, grants, and awards by category:*** *Academic Interests/Achievement:* 664 awards ($1,888,358 total): general academic interests/achievements. *Special Achievements/Activities:* 8 awards ($74,000 total): leadership. *Special Characteristics:* 42 awards ($414,105 total): children of faculty/staff, local/state students, veterans. ***Tuition waivers:*** Full or partial for employees or children of employees, senior citizens. ***ROTC:*** Army cooperative, Air Force cooperative.

LOANS ***Student loans:*** $11,388,256 (75% need-based, 25% non-need-based). 68% of past graduating class borrowed through all loan programs. Average indebtedness per student: $13,177. ***Average need-based loan:*** Freshmen: $2766; Undergraduates: $3793. ***Parent loans:*** $5,987,085 (100% non-need-based). ***Programs:*** FFEL (Subsidized and Unsubsidized Stafford, PLUS), Perkins, Federal Nursing.

WORK-STUDY ***Federal work-study:*** *Total amount:* $1,793,384; 1,119 jobs averaging $1602. ***State or other work-study/employment:*** *Total amount:* $61,202 (100% need-based). 23 part-time jobs averaging $2661.

ATHLETIC AWARDS *Total amount:* 1,913,789 (100% non-need-based).

APPLYING for FINANCIAL AID ***Required financial aid forms:*** FAFSA, institution's own form. ***Financial aid deadline (priority):*** 3/1. ***Notification date:*** Continuous. Students must reply by 5/1 or within 2 weeks of notification.

CONTACT Mr. Dominic Yoia, Director of Financial Aid, Quinnipiac University, 275 Mount Carmel Avenue, Hamden, CT 06518-1904, 203-281-8750 or toll-free 800-462-1944 (out-of-state). *Fax:* 203-287-5238.

RABBINICAL ACADEMY MESIVTA RABBI CHAIM BERLIN

Brooklyn, NY

CONTACT Office of Financial Aid, Rabbinical Academy Mesivta Rabbi Chaim Berlin, 1605 Coney Island Avenue, Brooklyn, NY 11230-4715, 718-377-0777.

RABBINICAL COLLEGE BETH SHRAGA

Monsey, NY

CONTACT Financial Aid Office, Rabbinical College Beth Shraga, 28 Saddle River Road, Monsey, NY 10952-3035, 914-356-1980.

RABBINICAL COLLEGE BOBOVER YESHIVA B'NEI ZION

Brooklyn, NY

CONTACT Financial Aid Office, Rabbinical College Bobover Yeshiva B'nei Zion, 1577 48th Street, Brooklyn, NY 11219, 718-438-2018.

RABBINICAL COLLEGE CH'SAN SOFER

Brooklyn, NY

CONTACT Financial Aid Office, Rabbinical College Ch'san Sofer, 1876 50th Street, Brooklyn, NY 11204, 718-236-1171.

RABBINICAL COLLEGE OF AMERICA

Morristown, NJ

CONTACT Financial Aid Office, Rabbinical College of America, 226 Sussex Avenue, Morristown, NJ 07960, 973-267-9404. *Fax:* 973-267-5208.

RABBINICAL COLLEGE OF LONG ISLAND

Long Beach, NY

CONTACT Rabbi Cone, Financial Aid Administrator, Rabbinical College of Long Island, 201 Magnolia Boulevard, Long Beach, NY 11561-3305, 516-431-7414.

RABBINICAL SEMINARY ADAS YEREIM

Brooklyn, NY

CONTACT Mr. Israel Weingarten, Financial Aid Administrator, Rabbinical Seminary Adas Yereim, 185 Wilson Street, Brooklyn, NY 11211-7206, 718-388-1751.

RABBINICAL SEMINARY M'KOR CHAIM

Brooklyn, NY

CONTACT Financial Aid Office, Rabbinical Seminary M'kor Chaim, 1571 55th Street, Brooklyn, NY 11219, 718-851-0183.

RABBINICAL SEMINARY OF AMERICA

Forest Hills, NY

CONTACT Ms. Leah Eisenstein, Director of Financial Aid, Rabbinical Seminary of America, 92-15 69th Avenue, Forest Hills, NY 11375, 718-268-4700. *Fax:* 718-268-4684.

RADFORD UNIVERSITY

Radford, VA

Tuition & fees (VA res): $2887 **Average undergraduate aid package: $6738**

ABOUT THE INSTITUTION State-supported, coed. Awards: bachelor's and master's degrees and post-master's certificates. 45 undergraduate majors. Total enrollment: 8,579. Undergraduates: 7,406. Freshmen: 1,664. Federal methodology is used as a basis for awarding need-based institutional aid.

UNDERGRADUATE EXPENSES for 1999–2000 ***Application fee:*** $20. ***Tuition, state resident:*** full-time $1629; part-time $120 per semester hour. ***Tuition, nonresident:*** full-time $7384; part-time $360 per semester hour. ***Required fees:*** full-time $1258. ***College room and board:*** $4770; ***room only:*** $2614. Room and board charges vary according to board plan and housing facility. ***Payment plan:*** installment.

FRESHMAN FINANCIAL AID (Fall 1999, est.) 1184 applied for aid; of those 64% were deemed to have need. 96% of freshmen with need received aid. *Average percent of need met:* 73% (excluding resources awarded to replace EFC). *Average financial aid package:* $5797 (excluding resources awarded to replace EFC). 25% of all full-time freshmen had no need and received non-need-based aid.

UNDERGRADUATE FINANCIAL AID (Fall 1999, est.) 4,393 applied for aid; of those 70% were deemed to have need. 96% of undergraduates with need received aid. *Average percent of need met:* 76% (excluding resources awarded to replace EFC). *Average financial aid package:* $6738 (excluding resources awarded to replace EFC). 24% of all full-time undergraduates had no need and received non-need-based aid.

GIFT AID (NEED-BASED) ***Total amount:*** $7,596,803 (43% Federal, 40% state, 8% institutional, 9% external sources). ***Receiving aid:*** *Freshmen:* 28% (458); *all full-time undergraduates:* 29% (1,978). ***Average award:*** Freshmen: $3206; Undergraduates: $2976. ***Scholarships, grants, and awards:*** Federal Pell, FSEOG, state, private, college/university gift aid from institutional funds.

GIFT AID (NON-NEED-BASED) ***Total amount:*** $1,293,772 (4% state, 58% institutional, 38% external sources). ***Receiving aid:*** *Freshmen:* 17% (274); *Undergraduates:* 10% (718). ***Scholarships, grants, and awards by category:*** *Academic Interests/Achievement:* area/ethnic studies, biological sciences, business, communication, computer science, education, English, general academic interests/achievements, health fields, humanities, library science, mathematics, military science, physical sciences, premedicine, social sciences. *Creative Arts/Performance:* applied art and design, art/fine arts, cinema/film/broadcasting, dance, music, theater/drama. *Special Achievements/Activities:* leadership. *Special Characteristics:* children of faculty/staff, children of union members/company employees, general special characteristics, members of minority groups. ***Tuition waivers:*** Full or partial for employees or children of employees. ***ROTC:*** Army, Naval cooperative.

LOANS ***Student loans:*** $16,214,385 (74% need-based, 26% non-need-based). 61% of past graduating class borrowed through all loan programs. Average indebtedness per student: $13,727. ***Average need-based loan:*** Freshmen: $2496; Undergraduates: $3131. ***Parent loans:*** $2,936,781 (51% need-based, 49% non-need-based). ***Programs:*** FFEL (Subsidized and Unsubsidized Stafford, PLUS), Perkins, Federal Nursing, state, college/university.

WORK-STUDY ***Federal work-study:*** *Total amount:* $578,145; 377 jobs averaging $1496. ***State or other work-study/employment:*** *Total amount:* $1,568,359 (49% need-based, 51% non-need-based). 892 part-time jobs averaging $1303.

ATHLETIC AWARDS *Total amount:* 1,016,818 (38% need-based, 62% non-need-based).

APPLYING for FINANCIAL AID ***Required financial aid form:*** FAFSA. ***Financial aid deadline (priority):*** 3/1. ***Notification date:*** 4/15. Students must reply within 2 weeks of notification.

CONTACT Ms. Barbara Porter, Associate Director of Financial Aid, Radford University, PO Box 6905, Radford, VA 24142, 540-831-5408 or toll-free 800-890-4265. *Fax:* 540-831-5138. *E-mail:* bporter@runet.edu

RAMAPO COLLEGE OF NEW JERSEY

Mahwah, NJ

Tuition & fees (NJ res): $5110 **Average undergraduate aid package: $5594**

ABOUT THE INSTITUTION State-supported, coed. Awards: bachelor's and master's degrees. 28 undergraduate majors. Total enrollment: 4,869. Undergraduates: 4,656. Freshmen: 536. Federal methodology is used as a basis for awarding need-based institutional aid.

UNDERGRADUATE EXPENSES for 1999–2000 ***Application fee:*** $45. ***Tuition, state resident:*** full-time $3822; part-time $119 per credit. ***Tuition, nonresident:*** full-time $6688; part-time $209 per credit. ***Required fees:*** full-time $1288; $36 per credit; $65 per term part-time. Full-time tuition and fees vary according to reciprocity agreements. Part-time tuition and fees vary according to course load and reciprocity agreements. ***College room and board:*** $6790; ***room only:*** $4550. Room and board charges vary according to board plan and housing facility. ***Payment plan:*** installment.

FRESHMAN FINANCIAL AID (Fall 1998) 300 applied for aid; of those 77% were deemed to have need. 97% of freshmen with need received aid; of those 44% had need fully met. *Average percent of need met:* 88% (excluding resources awarded to replace EFC). *Average financial aid package:* $5967 (excluding resources awarded to replace EFC).

UNDERGRADUATE FINANCIAL AID (Fall 1998) 1,695 applied for aid; of those 77% were deemed to have need. 97% of undergraduates with need received aid; of those 45% had need fully met. *Average percent of need met:* 73% (excluding resources awarded to replace EFC). *Average financial aid package:* $5594 (excluding resources awarded to replace EFC).

GIFT AID (NEED-BASED) ***Total amount:*** $4,310,836 (43% Federal, 46% state, 11% institutional). ***Receiving aid:*** *Freshmen:* 40% (188); *all full-time undergraduates:* 36% (1,036). ***Average award:*** Freshmen: $6295; Undergraduates: $4501. ***Scholarships, grants, and awards:*** Federal Pell, FSEOG, state, private, college/university gift aid from institutional funds.

GIFT AID (NON-NEED-BASED) ***Total amount:*** $1,484,204 (6% state, 79% institutional, 15% external sources). ***Receiving aid:*** *Freshmen:* 10% (48); *Undergraduates:* 5% (140). ***Scholarships, grants, and awards by category:*** *Academic Interests/Achievement:* general academic interests/achievements. *Special Characteristics:* international students, out-of-state students, veterans. ***Tuition waivers:*** Full or partial for employees or children of employees, senior citizens.

LOANS ***Student loans:*** $7,168,437 (59% need-based, 41% non-need-based). Average indebtedness per student: $11,498. ***Average need-based loan:*** Freshmen: $2203; Undergraduates: $3515. ***Parent loans:*** $449,795 (100% non-need-based). ***Programs:*** Federal Direct (Subsidized and Unsubsidized Stafford, PLUS), Perkins, state.

WORK-STUDY ***Federal work-study:*** *Total amount:* $196,310; 173 jobs averaging $1135. ***State or other work-study/employment:*** *Total amount:* $467,908 (100% non-need-based). 347 part-time jobs averaging $1348.

APPLYING for FINANCIAL AID ***Required financial aid form:*** FAFSA. ***Financial aid deadline (priority):*** 3/1. ***Notification date:*** Continuous beginning 4/1. Students must reply by 5/1 or within 2 weeks of notification.

CONTACT Bernice Mulch, Assistant Director of Financial Aid, Ramapo College of New Jersey, 505 Ramapo Valley Road, Mahwah, NJ 07430-1680, 201-684-7252 or toll-free 800-9RAMAPO (in-state). *Fax:* 201-684-7085. *E-mail:* finaid@ramapo.edu

RANDOLPH-MACON COLLEGE

Ashland, VA

Tuition & fees: $17,660 **Average undergraduate aid package: $13,627**

ABOUT THE INSTITUTION Independent United Methodist, coed. Awards: bachelor's degrees. 30 undergraduate majors. Total enrollment: 1,145. Undergraduates: 1,145. Freshmen: 360. Federal methodology is used as a basis for awarding need-based institutional aid.

UNDERGRADUATE EXPENSES for 1999–2000 ***Application fee:*** $30. ***Comprehensive fee:*** $22,180 includes full-time tuition ($17,160), mandatory fees ($500), and room and board ($4520). ***College room only:*** $2305. Room and board charges vary according to board plan and housing facility. ***Part-time tuition:*** $175 per credit hour. Part-time tuition and fees vary according to course load. ***Payment plan:*** installment.

FRESHMAN FINANCIAL AID (Fall 1999) 299 applied for aid; of those 66% were deemed to have need. 100% of freshmen with need received aid; of those 23% had need fully met. *Average percent of need met:* 85% (excluding resources awarded to replace EFC). *Average financial aid package:* $12,525 (excluding resources awarded to replace EFC). 39% of all full-time freshmen had no need and received non-need-based aid.

UNDERGRADUATE FINANCIAL AID (Fall 1999) 752 applied for aid; of those 74% were deemed to have need. 100% of undergraduates with need received aid; of those 23% had need fully met. *Average percent of need met:* 88% (excluding resources awarded to replace EFC). *Average financial aid package:* $13,627 (excluding resources awarded to replace EFC). 37% of all full-time undergraduates had no need and received non-need-based aid.

GIFT AID (NEED-BASED) ***Total amount:*** $5,122,584 (6% Federal, 18% state, 71% institutional, 5% external sources). ***Receiving aid:*** *Freshmen:* 54% (196); *all full-time undergraduates:* 51% (559). ***Average award:*** Freshmen: $8997; Undergraduates: $9204. ***Scholarships, grants, and awards:*** Federal Pell, FSEOG, state, private, college/university gift aid from institutional funds.

GIFT AID (NON-NEED-BASED) ***Total amount:*** $2,273,208 (34% state, 63% institutional, 3% external sources). ***Receiving aid:*** *Freshmen:* 2% (6); *Undergraduates:* 1% (7). ***Scholarships, grants, and awards by category:*** *Academic Interests/Achievement:* 172 awards ($1,173,870 total): general academic interests/achievements. *Special Achievements/Activities:* 285 awards ($1,052,500 total): general special achievements/activities. *Special Characteristics:* 50 awards ($284,217 total): children and siblings of alumni, relatives of clergy, siblings of current students. ***Tuition waivers:*** Full or partial for employees or children of employees. ***ROTC:*** Army cooperative.

LOANS ***Student loans:*** $2,888,899 (85% need-based, 15% non-need-based). 54% of past graduating class borrowed through all loan programs. Average indebtedness per student: $16,832. ***Average need-based loan:*** Freshmen: $2994; Undergraduates: $3897. ***Parent loans:*** $2,105,278 (76% need-based, 24% non-need-based). ***Programs:*** FFEL (Subsidized and Unsubsidized Stafford, PLUS), Perkins, college/university.

WORK-STUDY ***Federal work-study:*** *Total amount:* $302,864; 226 jobs averaging $1340.

APPLYING for FINANCIAL AID ***Required financial aid form:*** FAFSA. ***Financial aid deadline (priority):*** 2/1. ***Notification date:*** 4/1. Students must reply by 5/1 or within 2 weeks of notification.

CONTACT Ms. Mary Neal, Director of Financial Aid, Randolph-Macon College, PO Box 5005, Ashland, VA 23005-5505, 804-752-7259 or toll-free 800-888-1762. *Fax:* 804-752-3719. *E-mail:* mneal@rmc.edu

RANDOLPH-MACON WOMAN'S COLLEGE

Lynchburg, VA

Tuition & fees: $17,080 **Average undergraduate aid package: $15,515**

ABOUT THE INSTITUTION Independent Methodist, women only. Awards: bachelor's degrees. 31 undergraduate majors. Total enrollment: 710. Undergraduates: 710. Freshmen: 201. Federal methodology is used as a basis for awarding need-based institutional aid.

UNDERGRADUATE EXPENSES for 1999–2000 ***Application fee:*** $25. ***Comprehensive fee:*** $24,090 includes full-time tuition ($16,730), mandatory fees ($350), and room and board ($7010). ***Part-time tuition:*** $700 per semester hour. Part-time tuition and fees vary according to course load. ***Payment plan:*** installment.

FRESHMAN FINANCIAL AID (Fall 1999, est.) 153 applied for aid; of those 81% were deemed to have need. 100% of freshmen with need received aid; of those 51% had need fully met. *Average percent of need met:* 93% (excluding resources awarded to replace EFC). *Average financial aid package:* $15,080 (excluding resources awarded to replace EFC). 38% of all full-time freshmen had no need and received non-need-based aid.

UNDERGRADUATE FINANCIAL AID (Fall 1999, est.) 441 applied for aid; of those 86% were deemed to have need. 100% of undergraduates with need received aid; of those 46% had need fully met. *Average percent of need met:* 92% (excluding resources awarded to replace EFC). *Average financial aid package:* $15,515 (excluding resources awarded to replace EFC). 40% of all full-time undergraduates had no need and received non-need-based aid.

GIFT AID (NEED-BASED) ***Total amount:*** $4,153,620 (9% Federal, 8% state, 80% institutional, 3% external sources). ***Receiving aid:*** *Freshmen:* 62% (124); *all full-time undergraduates:* 59% (378). ***Average award:*** Freshmen: $11,630; Undergraduates: $11,077. ***Scholarships, grants, and awards:*** Federal Pell, FSEOG, state, private, college/university gift aid from institutional funds.

GIFT AID (NON-NEED-BASED) ***Total amount:*** $2,792,102 (7% state, 91% institutional, 2% external sources). ***Receiving aid:*** *Freshmen:* 17% (34); *Undergraduates:* 11% (73). ***Scholarships, grants, and awards by category:*** *Academic Interests/Achievement:* 491 awards ($2,760,464 total): biological sciences, English, general academic interests/achievements, mathematics, social sciences. *Creative Arts/Performance:* 7 awards ($3700 total): art/fine arts, creative writing, music, theater/drama. *Special Achievements/Activities:* 161 awards ($443,500 total): community service, general special achievements/activities, leadership, religious involvement. *Special Characteristics:* 162 awards ($1,973,806 total): adult students, children of faculty/staff, international students, local/state students, relatives of clergy, religious affiliation, twins. ***Tuition waivers:*** Full or partial for employees or children of employees, adult students.

LOANS ***Student loans:*** $2,183,352 (66% need-based, 34% non-need-based). 74% of past graduating class borrowed through all loan programs. Average indebtedness per student: $15,495. ***Average need-based loan:***

Randolph-Macon Woman's College (continued)

Freshmen: $2392; Undergraduates: $3915. ***Parent loans:*** $775,755 (19% need-based, 81% non-need-based). ***Programs:*** FFEL (Subsidized and Unsubsidized Stafford, PLUS), Perkins, college/university.

WORK-STUDY ***Federal work-study:*** *Total amount:* $157,300; 86 jobs averaging $1860. ***State or other work-study/employment:*** *Total amount:* $453,037 (76% need-based, 24% non-need-based). 245 part-time jobs averaging $1860.

APPLYING for FINANCIAL AID ***Required financial aid forms:*** FAFSA, state aid form. ***Financial aid deadline:*** 3/1 (priority: 2/1). ***Notification date:*** Continuous. Students must reply by 5/1 or within 2 weeks of notification.

CONTACT Sharon M. Wilkes, Director of Financial Planning and Assistance, Randolph-Macon Woman's College, 2500 Rivermont Avenue, Lynchburg, VA 24503-1526, 804-947-8128 or toll-free 800-745-7692. *Fax:* 804-947-8996. *E-mail:* swilkes@rmwc.edu

REED COLLEGE

Portland, OR

Tuition & fees: $24,050 **Average undergraduate aid package: $21,116**

ABOUT THE INSTITUTION Independent, coed. Awards: bachelor's and master's degrees. 29 undergraduate majors. Total enrollment: 1,373. Undergraduates: 1,353. Freshmen: 334. Both federal and institutional methodology are used as a basis for awarding need-based institutional aid.

UNDERGRADUATE EXPENSES for 1999–2000 ***Application fee:*** $40. ***Comprehensive fee:*** $30,700 includes full-time tuition ($23,880), mandatory fees ($170), and room and board ($6650). ***College room only:*** $3450. Room and board charges vary according to board plan. ***Part-time tuition:*** $4110 per course. Part-time tuition and fees vary according to course load. ***Payment plan:*** installment.

FRESHMAN FINANCIAL AID (Fall 1999, est.) 233 applied for aid; of those 69% were deemed to have need. 76% of freshmen with need received aid; of those 100% had need fully met. *Average percent of need met:* 100% (excluding resources awarded to replace EFC). *Average financial aid package:* $22,208 (excluding resources awarded to replace EFC).

UNDERGRADUATE FINANCIAL AID (Fall 1999, est.) 807 applied for aid; of those 74% were deemed to have need. 92% of undergraduates with need received aid; of those 100% had need fully met. *Average percent of need met:* 100% (excluding resources awarded to replace EFC). *Average financial aid package:* $21,116 (excluding resources awarded to replace EFC).

GIFT AID (NEED-BASED) ***Total amount:*** $9,240,682 (8% Federal, 2% state, 86% institutional, 4% external sources). ***Receiving aid:*** *Freshmen:* 36% (123); *all full-time undergraduates:* 42% (549). ***Average award:*** Freshmen: $19,907; Undergraduates: $16,832. ***Scholarships, grants, and awards:*** Federal Pell, FSEOG, state, private, college/university gift aid from institutional funds.

GIFT AID (NON-NEED-BASED) ***Tuition waivers:*** Full or partial for employees or children of employees. ***ROTC:*** Army cooperative.

LOANS ***Student loans:*** $2,786,827 (91% need-based, 9% non-need-based). 45% of past graduating class borrowed through all loan programs. Average indebtedness per student: $14,010. ***Average need-based loan:*** Freshmen: $1748; Undergraduates: $3662. ***Parent loans:*** $1,798,109 (100% non-need-based). ***Programs:*** FFEL (Subsidized and Unsubsidized Stafford, PLUS), Perkins, college/university loans from institutional funds (for international students only).

WORK-STUDY ***Federal work-study:*** *Total amount:* $252,150; 380 jobs averaging $664. ***State or other work-study/employment:*** *Total amount:* $33,650 (100% need-based). 57 part-time jobs averaging $590.

APPLYING for FINANCIAL AID ***Required financial aid forms:*** FAFSA, institution's own form, CSS Financial Aid PROFILE, student's and parents' federal income tax forms (including all schedules and W-2 forms). ***Financial aid deadline:*** 1/15. ***Notification date:*** 4/1. Students must reply by 5/1 or within 2 weeks of notification.

CONTACT Ms. Sarah Duncan, Financial Aid Counselor, Reed College, 3203 Southeast Woodstock Boulevard, Portland, OR 97202-8199, 503-777-7223 or toll-free 800-547-4750 (out-of-state). *Fax:* 503-788-6682. *E-mail:* financial.aid@reed.edu

REFORMED BIBLE COLLEGE

Grand Rapids, MI

Tuition & fees: $7371 **Average undergraduate aid package: $4277**

ABOUT THE INSTITUTION Independent religious, coed. Awards: associate and bachelor's degrees. 22 undergraduate majors. Total enrollment: 301. Undergraduates: 301. Federal methodology is used as a basis for awarding need-based institutional aid.

UNDERGRADUATE EXPENSES for 1999–2000 ***Application fee:*** $25. ***Comprehensive fee:*** $11,471 includes full-time tuition ($7150), mandatory fees ($221), and room and board ($4100). ***Part-time tuition:*** $298 per credit. ***Part-time fees:*** $34 per term part-time. Part-time tuition and fees vary according to course load. ***Payment plan:*** deferred payment.

FRESHMAN FINANCIAL AID (Fall 1999, est.) 54 applied for aid; of those 87% were deemed to have need. 100% of freshmen with need received aid; of those 6% had need fully met. *Average percent of need met:* 34% (excluding resources awarded to replace EFC). *Average financial aid package:* $4277 (excluding resources awarded to replace EFC). 12% of all full-time freshmen had no need and received non-need-based aid.

UNDERGRADUATE FINANCIAL AID (Fall 1999, est.) 191 applied for aid; of those 85% were deemed to have need. 98% of undergraduates with need received aid; of those 6% had need fully met. *Average percent of need met:* 38% (excluding resources awarded to replace EFC). *Average financial aid package:* $4277 (excluding resources awarded to replace EFC). 7% of all full-time undergraduates had no need and received non-need-based aid.

GIFT AID (NEED-BASED) ***Total amount:*** $662,536 (30% Federal, 41% state, 21% institutional, 8% external sources). ***Receiving aid:*** *Freshmen:* 81% (46); *all full-time undergraduates:* 38% (111). ***Average award:*** Freshmen: $2150; Undergraduates: $2150. ***Scholarships, grants, and awards:*** Federal Pell, FSEOG, state, college/university gift aid from institutional funds.

GIFT AID (NON-NEED-BASED) ***Total amount:*** $12,115 (100% institutional). ***Receiving aid:*** *Freshmen:* 12% (7); *Undergraduates:* 8% (24). ***Scholarships, grants, and awards by category:*** *Academic Interests/Achievement:* 61 awards ($38,306 total): general academic interests/achievements. *Special Achievements/Activities:* 7 awards ($10,500 total): leadership, religious involvement. *Special Characteristics:* 20 awards ($177,231 total): children of faculty/staff, international students, spouses of current students. ***Tuition waivers:*** Full or partial for employees or children of employees.

LOANS ***Student loans:*** $437,819 (79% need-based, 21% non-need-based). 47% of past graduating class borrowed through all loan programs. Average indebtedness per student: $12,320. ***Average need-based loan:*** Freshmen: $3034; Undergraduates: $3034. ***Parent loans:*** $40,847 (100% need-based). ***Programs:*** FFEL (Subsidized and Unsubsidized Stafford, PLUS), college/university.

WORK-STUDY ***Federal work-study:*** *Total amount:* $44,652; 37 jobs averaging $1200. ***State or other work-study/employment:*** *Total amount:* $8200 (100% need-based). 7 part-time jobs averaging $1170.

APPLYING for FINANCIAL AID ***Required financial aid forms:*** FAFSA, institution's own form. ***Financial aid deadline (priority):*** 2/15. ***Notification date:*** 5/15. Students must reply within 2 weeks of notification.

CONTACT Ms. Agnes Russell, Financial Aid Administrator, Reformed Bible College, 3333 East Beltline NE, Grand Rapids, MI 49525-9749, 616-988-3656 Ext. 156. *Fax:* 616-222-3045. *E-mail:* amr@reformed.edu

REGENTS COLLEGE

Albany, NY

Tuition & fees: N/R **Average undergraduate aid package: N/A**

ABOUT THE INSTITUTION Independent, coed. Awards: associate, bachelor's, and master's degrees and post-bachelor's certificates (offers only external degree programs). 38 undergraduate majors. Total enrollment: 17,461. Undergraduates: 17,418. Both federal and institutional methodology are used as a basis for awarding need-based institutional aid.

UNDERGRADUATE EXPENSES for 1999–2000 ***Tuition:*** part-time $800 per year. ***Required fees:*** $350 per year part-time. Full-time tuition and fees vary according to degree level. Part-time tuition and fees vary according to degree level. ***Payment plans:*** tuition prepayment, installment, deferred payment.

GIFT AID (NEED-BASED) ***Total amount:*** $155,857 (21% state, 72% institutional, 7% external sources). ***Scholarships, grants, and awards:*** state, private, college/university gift aid from institutional funds.

GIFT AID (NON-NEED-BASED) ***Total amount:*** $46,501 (1% institutional, 99% external sources). ***Scholarships, grants, and awards by category:*** *Academic Interests/Achievement:* general academic interests/achievements. *Special Characteristics:* veterans, veterans' children. ***Tuition waivers:*** Full or partial for employees or children of employees.

LOANS ***Student loans:*** $513,895 (100% non-need-based). 1% of past graduating class borrowed through all loan programs. Average indebtedness per student: $4989. ***Programs:*** alternative loans, TERI Loans, PLATO loans.

APPLYING for FINANCIAL AID ***Required financial aid form:*** institution's own form. ***Financial aid deadline (priority):*** 7/1. ***Notification date:*** Continuous.

CONTACT Donna L. Eames, Associate Director of Financial Aid, Regents College, 7 Columbia Circle, Albany, NY 12203-5159, 518-464-8500 or toll-free 888-647-2388. *Fax:* 518-464-8777.

REGIS COLLEGE

Weston, MA

Tuition & fees: $16,860 **Average undergraduate aid package: $12,479**

ABOUT THE INSTITUTION Independent Roman Catholic, women only. Awards: associate, bachelor's, and master's degrees. 21 undergraduate majors. Total enrollment: 1,131. Undergraduates: 889. Freshmen: 175. Both federal and institutional methodology are used as a basis for awarding need-based institutional aid.

UNDERGRADUATE EXPENSES for 1999–2000 ***Application fee:*** $30. ***Comprehensive fee:*** $24,730 includes full-time tuition ($16,860) and room and board ($7870). ***Part-time tuition:*** $1950 per course. Part-time tuition and fees vary according to class time and course load. ***Payment plans:*** tuition prepayment, installment, deferred payment.

FRESHMAN FINANCIAL AID (Fall 1999) 173 applied for aid; of those 98% were deemed to have need. 100% of freshmen with need received aid; of those 81% had need fully met. *Average percent of need met:* 85% (excluding resources awarded to replace EFC). *Average financial aid package:* $15,156 (excluding resources awarded to replace EFC). 8% of all full-time freshmen had no need and received non-need-based aid.

UNDERGRADUATE FINANCIAL AID (Fall 1999) 669 applied for aid; of those 88% were deemed to have need. 100% of undergraduates with need received aid; of those 74% had need fully met. *Average percent of need met:* 83% (excluding resources awarded to replace EFC). *Average financial aid package:* $12,479 (excluding resources awarded to replace EFC). 8% of all full-time undergraduates had no need and received non-need-based aid.

GIFT AID (NEED-BASED) ***Total amount:*** $3,654,747 (16% Federal, 13% state, 66% institutional, 5% external sources). ***Receiving aid:*** *Freshmen:* 67% (123); *all full-time undergraduates:* 65% (443). ***Average award:*** Freshmen: $8457; Undergraduates: $7386. ***Scholarships, grants, and awards:*** Federal Pell, FSEOG, state, private, college/university gift aid from institutional funds.

GIFT AID (NON-NEED-BASED) ***Total amount:*** $2,113,675 (100% institutional). ***Receiving aid:*** *Freshmen:* 67% (124); *Undergraduates:* 58% (398). ***Scholarships, grants, and awards by category:*** *Academic Interests/Achievement:* general academic interests/achievements. ***Tuition waivers:*** Full or partial for employees or children of employees.

LOANS ***Student loans:*** $3,157,574 (76% need-based, 24% non-need-based). 81% of past graduating class borrowed through all loan programs. Average indebtedness per student: $18,443. ***Average need-based loan:*** Freshmen: $3826; Undergraduates: $4912. ***Parent loans:*** $557,003 (100% non-need-based). ***Programs:*** FFEL (Subsidized and Unsubsidized Stafford, PLUS), Perkins, state, college/university.

WORK-STUDY ***Federal work-study:*** *Total amount:* $283,886; 276 jobs averaging $1029. ***State or other work-study/employment:*** *Total amount:* $75,000 (100% non-need-based). 75 part-time jobs averaging $1000.

APPLYING for FINANCIAL AID ***Required financial aid forms:*** FAFSA, institution's own form, CSS Financial Aid PROFILE. ***Financial aid deadline (priority):*** 3/1. ***Notification date:*** Continuous. Students must reply within 2 weeks of notification.

CONTACT Jennifer Porter, Director of Financial Aid, Regis College, Box 81, 235 Wellesley Street, Weston, MA 02493, 781-768-7180 or toll-free 800-456-1820. *Fax:* 781-768-8339. *E-mail:* finaid@regiscollege.edu

REGIS UNIVERSITY

Denver, CO

Tuition & fees: $16,670 **Average undergraduate aid package: $14,594**

ABOUT THE INSTITUTION Independent Roman Catholic (Jesuit), coed. Awards: bachelor's and master's degrees. 33 undergraduate majors. Total enrollment: 1,022. Undergraduates: 1,022. Federal methodology is used as a basis for awarding need-based institutional aid.

UNDERGRADUATE EXPENSES for 1999–2000 ***Application fee:*** $40. ***Comprehensive fee:*** $23,370 includes full-time tuition ($16,500), mandatory fees ($170), and room and board ($6700). ***College room only:*** $3900. Room and board charges vary according to board plan and housing facility. ***Part-time tuition:*** $515 per semester hour. ***Part-time fees:*** $60 per term part-time. ***Payment plan:*** deferred payment.

FRESHMAN FINANCIAL AID (Fall 1999) 204 applied for aid; of those 57% were deemed to have need. 100% of freshmen with need received aid; of those 28% had need fully met. *Average percent of need met:* 65% (excluding resources awarded to replace EFC). *Average financial aid package:* $12,010 (excluding resources awarded to replace EFC). 24% of all full-time freshmen had no need and received non-need-based aid.

UNDERGRADUATE FINANCIAL AID (Fall 1999) 987 applied for aid; of those 64% were deemed to have need. 100% of undergraduates with need received aid; of those 39% had need fully met. *Average percent of need met:* 83% (excluding resources awarded to replace EFC). *Average financial aid package:* $14,594 (excluding resources awarded to replace EFC). 25% of all full-time undergraduates had no need and received non-need-based aid.

GIFT AID (NEED-BASED) ***Total amount:*** $4,513,589 (16% Federal, 27% state, 53% institutional, 4% external sources). ***Receiving aid:*** *Freshmen:* 38% (109); *all full-time undergraduates:* 50% (542). ***Average award:*** Freshmen: $6417; Undergraduates: $8210. ***Scholarships, grants, and awards:*** Federal Pell, FSEOG, state, college/university gift aid from institutional funds.

GIFT AID (NON-NEED-BASED) ***Total amount:*** $1,492,369 (3% state, 94% institutional, 3% external sources). ***Receiving aid:*** *Freshmen:* 4% (12); *Undergraduates:* 6% (65). ***Scholarships, grants, and awards by category:*** *Academic Interests/Achievement:* general academic interests/achievements, physical sciences. *Creative Arts/Performance:* debating. *Special Achievements/Activities:* leadership. *Special Characteristics:* children of faculty/staff, ethnic background, local/state students, members of minority groups. ***Tuition waivers:*** Full or partial for employees or children of employees, adult students, senior citizens. ***ROTC:*** Army cooperative, Naval cooperative, Air Force cooperative.

LOANS ***Student loans:*** $3,785,167 (68% need-based, 32% non-need-based). 65% of past graduating class borrowed through all loan programs. Average indebtedness per student: $20,000. ***Average need-based loan:*** Freshmen: $3911; Undergraduates: $4510. ***Programs:*** FFEL (Subsidized and Unsubsidized Stafford, PLUS), Perkins, Federal Nursing.

Regis University (continued)

WORK-STUDY ***Federal work-study:*** *Total amount:* $315,205; 146 jobs averaging $2200. ***State or other work-study/employment:*** *Total amount:* $1,005,642 (40% need-based, 60% non-need-based). 505 part-time jobs averaging $2000.

ATHLETIC AWARDS *Total amount:* 1,240,669 (53% need-based, 47% non-need-based).

APPLYING for FINANCIAL AID ***Required financial aid form:*** FAFSA. ***Financial aid deadline (priority):*** 3/5. ***Notification date:*** Continuous beginning 3/31.

CONTACT Ms. Lydia MacMillan, Director of Financial Aid, Regis University, 3333 Regis Boulevard, A-8, Denver, CO 80221-1099, 303-458-4066 or toll-free 800-388-2366 Ext. 4900. *Fax:* 303-964-5449. *E-mail:* regisfa@regis.edu

REINHARDT COLLEGE

Waleska, GA

Tuition & fees: $8800 **Average undergraduate aid package: N/A**

ABOUT THE INSTITUTION Independent religious, coed. Awards: associate and bachelor's degrees. 23 undergraduate majors. Total enrollment: 1,190. Undergraduates: 1,190. Freshmen: 300. Both federal and institutional methodology are used as a basis for awarding need-based institutional aid.

UNDERGRADUATE EXPENSES for 2000–2001 ***Application fee:*** $15. ***Comprehensive fee:*** $13,550 includes full-time tuition ($8800) and room and board ($4750). ***College room only:*** $2730. Full-time tuition and fees vary according to course load. Room and board charges vary according to board plan and housing facility. ***Part-time tuition:*** $275 per credit hour. Part-time tuition and fees vary according to course load and location. ***Payment plan:*** installment.

GIFT AID (NEED-BASED) ***Scholarships, grants, and awards:*** Federal Pell, FSEOG, state, private, college/university gift aid from institutional funds.

GIFT AID (NON-NEED-BASED) ***Scholarships, grants, and awards by category:*** *Academic Interests/Achievement:* biological sciences, business, communication, education, English, general academic interests/achievements, health fields, humanities, mathematics, religion/biblical studies, social sciences. *Creative Arts/Performance:* art/fine arts, music, performing arts. *Special Achievements/Activities:* leadership, religious involvement. *Special Characteristics:* adult students, children and siblings of alumni, children of educators, children of faculty/staff, local/state students, relatives of clergy, religious affiliation. ***Tuition waivers:*** Full or partial for children of alumni, employees or children of employees, senior citizens.

LOANS ***Programs:*** FFEL (Subsidized and Unsubsidized Stafford, PLUS), Perkins, state.

WORK-STUDY Federal work-study jobs available.

APPLYING for FINANCIAL AID ***Required financial aid forms:*** FAFSA, institution's own form, state aid form. ***Financial aid deadline (priority):*** 6/1. ***Notification date:*** Continuous. Students must reply within 2 weeks of notification.

CONTACT Ron Day, Director of Financial Aid, Reinhardt College, 7300 Reinhardt College Circle, Waleska, GA 30183-2981, 770-720-5603. *E-mail:* rhd@mail.reinhardt.edu

RENSSELAER POLYTECHNIC INSTITUTE

Troy, NY

Tuition & fees: $22,955 **Average undergraduate aid package: $17,537**

ABOUT THE INSTITUTION Independent, coed. Awards: bachelor's, master's, and doctoral degrees. 52 undergraduate majors. Total enrollment: 7,650. Undergraduates: 4,926. Freshmen: 1,323. Federal methodology is used as a basis for awarding need-based institutional aid.

UNDERGRADUATE EXPENSES for 1999–2000 ***Application fee:*** $50. ***Comprehensive fee:*** $30,647 includes full-time tuition ($22,300), mandatory fees ($655), and room and board ($7692). ***College room only:*** $4250. Room and board charges vary according to board plan, housing facility, and student level. ***Part-time tuition:*** $665 per credit hour. ***Part-time fees:*** $328 per term part-time. Part-time tuition and fees vary according to location. ***Payment plan:*** installment.

FRESHMAN FINANCIAL AID (Fall 1999, est.) 982 applied for aid; of those 100% were deemed to have need. 100% of freshmen with need received aid; of those 62% had need fully met. *Average percent of need met:* 89% (excluding resources awarded to replace EFC). *Average financial aid package:* $19,375 (excluding resources awarded to replace EFC). 12% of all full-time freshmen had no need and received non-need-based aid.

UNDERGRADUATE FINANCIAL AID (Fall 1999, est.) 3,480 applied for aid; of those 100% were deemed to have need. 100% of undergraduates with need received aid; of those 63% had need fully met. *Average percent of need met:* 84% (excluding resources awarded to replace EFC). *Average financial aid package:* $17,537 (excluding resources awarded to replace EFC). 15% of all full-time undergraduates had no need and received non-need-based aid.

GIFT AID (NEED-BASED) ***Total amount:*** $43,168,091 (6% Federal, 6% state, 85% institutional, 3% external sources). ***Receiving aid:*** *Freshmen:* 74% (982); *all full-time undergraduates:* 72% (3,480). ***Average award:*** Freshmen: $15,406; Undergraduates: $13,037. ***Scholarships, grants, and awards:*** Federal Pell, FSEOG, state, private, college/university gift aid from institutional funds.

GIFT AID (NON-NEED-BASED) ***Total amount:*** $10,044,157 (1% state, 56% institutional, 43% external sources). ***Receiving aid:*** *Freshmen:* 26% (346); *Undergraduates:* 24% (1,166). ***Scholarships, grants, and awards by category:*** *Academic Interests/Achievement:* general academic interests/achievements, military science. ***Tuition waivers:*** Full or partial for employees or children of employees. ***ROTC:*** Army, Naval, Air Force.

LOANS ***Student loans:*** $21,823,277 (73% need-based, 27% non-need-based). Average indebtedness per student: $22,300. ***Average need-based loan:*** Freshmen: $4973; Undergraduates: $5452. ***Parent loans:*** $5,011,220 (86% need-based, 14% non-need-based). ***Programs:*** Federal Direct (Subsidized and Unsubsidized Stafford, PLUS), Perkins, college/university, alternative loans.

WORK-STUDY ***Federal work-study:*** *Total amount:* $3,069,897; 1,863 jobs averaging $1648.

ATHLETIC AWARDS *Total amount:* 540,132 (100% non-need-based).

APPLYING for FINANCIAL AID ***Required financial aid forms:*** FAFSA, state aid form. ***Financial aid deadline (priority):*** 2/15. ***Notification date:*** 3/20.

CONTACT Mr. James Stevenson, Director of Financial Aid, Rensselaer Polytechnic Institute, Admissions and Financial Aid Building, 110 8th Street, Troy, NY 12180-3590, 518-276-6813 or toll-free 800-448-6562. *Fax:* 518-276-4797. *E-mail:* stevej@rpi.edu

RESEARCH COLLEGE OF NURSING

Kansas City, MO

Tuition & fees: $12,840 **Average undergraduate aid package: $8326**

ABOUT THE INSTITUTION Independent, coed. Awards: bachelor's and master's degrees (jointly with Rockhurst College). 1 undergraduate major. Total enrollment: 216. Undergraduates: 212. Freshmen: 19. Federal methodology is used as a basis for awarding need-based institutional aid.

UNDERGRADUATE EXPENSES for 1999–2000 ***Application fee:*** $20. ***One-time required fee:*** $40. ***Comprehensive fee:*** $18,070 includes full-time tuition ($12,500), mandatory fees ($340), and room and board ($5230). Full-time tuition and fees vary according to program. Room and board charges vary according to board plan. ***Part-time tuition:*** $420 per credit hour. ***Part-time fees:*** $170 per term part-time. Part-time tuition and fees vary according to class time and program. ***Payment plans:*** guaranteed tuition, installment, deferred payment.

UNDERGRADUATE FINANCIAL AID (Fall 1999, est.) 93 applied for aid; of those 94% were deemed to have need. 100% of undergraduates with need received aid; of those 34% had need fully met. *Average percent of need met:* 50% (excluding resources awarded to replace EFC). *Average*

financial aid package: $8326 (excluding resources awarded to replace EFC). 11% of all full-time undergraduates had no need and received non-need-based aid.

GIFT AID (NEED-BASED) ***Total amount:*** $303,056 (22% Federal, 9% state, 66% institutional, 3% external sources). ***Receiving aid:*** *All full-time undergraduates:* 32% (51). ***Average award:*** Undergraduates: $6700. ***Scholarships, grants, and awards:*** Federal Pell, FSEOG, state, private, college/university gift aid from institutional funds.

GIFT AID (NON-NEED-BASED) ***Total amount:*** $132,600 (2% state, 67% institutional, 31% external sources). ***Receiving aid:*** *Undergraduates:* 39% (62). ***Scholarships, grants, and awards by category:*** *Academic Interests/Achievement:* general academic interests/achievements, health fields. *Special Characteristics:* children and siblings of alumni, children of educators, siblings of current students. ***Tuition waivers:*** Full or partial for employees or children of employees, senior citizens. ***ROTC:*** Army cooperative.

LOANS ***Student loans:*** $369,754 (60% need-based, 40% non-need-based). ***Average need-based loan:*** Undergraduates: $3229. ***Parent loans:*** $2425 (100% need-based). ***Programs:*** FFEL (Subsidized and Unsubsidized Stafford, PLUS), Perkins, Federal Nursing, college/university.

WORK-STUDY Federal work-study jobs available.

APPLYING for FINANCIAL AID ***Required financial aid forms:*** FAFSA, institution's own form. ***Financial aid deadline (priority):*** 3/15. ***Notification date:*** Continuous. Students must reply within 2 weeks of notification.

CONTACT Ms. Stacie Withers, Financial Aid Director, Research College of Nursing, 2316 East Meyer Boulevard, Kansas City, MO 64132, 816-276-4732 or toll-free 800-842-6776. *Fax:* 816-276-3526. *E-mail:* sawithers@healthmidwest.org

RHODE ISLAND COLLEGE

Providence, RI

Tuition & fees: N/R **Average undergraduate aid package: N/A**

ABOUT THE INSTITUTION State-supported, coed. Awards: bachelor's, master's, and doctoral degrees and post-master's certificates. 66 undergraduate majors. Total enrollment: 8,683. Undergraduates: 6,873. Freshmen: 952. Institutional methodology is used as a basis for awarding need-based institutional aid.

GIFT AID (NEED-BASED) ***Scholarships, grants, and awards:*** Federal Pell, FSEOG, state, private, college/university gift aid from institutional funds.

GIFT AID (NON-NEED-BASED) ***Scholarships, grants, and awards by category:*** *Academic Interests/Achievement:* general academic interests/achievements. *Creative Arts/Performance:* art/fine arts, dance, debating, journalism/publications, music, theater/drama. *Special Achievements/Activities:* hobbies/interests. ***Tuition waivers:*** Full or partial for employees or children of employees, senior citizens. ***ROTC:*** Army cooperative.

LOANS ***Programs:*** FFEL (Subsidized and Unsubsidized Stafford, PLUS), Perkins, state.

WORK-STUDY Federal work-study jobs available.

APPLYING for FINANCIAL AID ***Required financial aid forms:*** FAFSA, institution's own form. ***Financial aid deadline (priority):*** 3/1. ***Notification date:*** Continuous beginning 3/15. Students must reply within 3 weeks of notification.

CONTACT Office of Financial Aid, Rhode Island College, 600 Mount Pleasant Avenue, Providence, RI 02908, 401-456-8033 or toll-free 800-669-5760 (in-state).

RHODE ISLAND SCHOOL OF DESIGN

Providence, RI

Tuition & fees: $21,405 **Average undergraduate aid package: N/A**

ABOUT THE INSTITUTION Independent, coed. Awards: bachelor's, master's, and first professional degrees. 16 undergraduate majors. Total enrollment: 2,112. Undergraduates: 1,861. Freshmen: 387. Institutional methodology is used as a basis for awarding need-based institutional aid.

UNDERGRADUATE EXPENSES for 1999–2000 ***Application fee:*** $45. ***Comprehensive fee:*** $27,895 includes full-time tuition ($21,020), mandatory fees ($385), and room and board ($6490). ***College room only:*** $3490. Room and board charges vary according to board plan. ***Payment plan:*** installment.

GIFT AID (NEED-BASED) ***Scholarships, grants, and awards:*** Federal Pell, FSEOG, state, private, college/university gift aid from institutional funds.

GIFT AID (NON-NEED-BASED) ***Scholarships, grants, and awards by category:*** *Academic Interests/Achievement:* general academic interests/achievements. *Creative Arts/Performance:* applied art and design, art/fine arts. ***Tuition waivers:*** Full or partial for employees or children of employees.

LOANS ***Programs:*** FFEL (Subsidized and Unsubsidized Stafford, PLUS), Perkins, college/university.

WORK-STUDY Federal work-study jobs available.

APPLYING for FINANCIAL AID ***Required financial aid forms:*** FAFSA, CSS Financial Aid PROFILE. ***Financial aid deadline (priority):*** 2/15. ***Notification date:*** 4/1. Students must reply by 5/1 or within 4 weeks of notification.

CONTACT Mr. Peter R. Riefler, Director of Financial Aid, Rhode Island School of Design, 2 College Street, Providence, RI 02903-2784, 401-454-6636 or toll-free 800-364-RISD. *Fax:* 401-454-6412.

RHODES COLLEGE

Memphis, TN

Tuition & fees: $19,303 **Average undergraduate aid package: $18,024**

ABOUT THE INSTITUTION Independent Presbyterian, coed. Awards: bachelor's and master's degrees (master's degree in accounting only). 33 undergraduate majors. Total enrollment: 1,510. Undergraduates: 1,499. Freshmen: 439. Both federal and institutional methodology are used as a basis for awarding need-based institutional aid.

UNDERGRADUATE EXPENSES for 2000–2001 ***Application fee:*** $40. ***Comprehensive fee:*** $24,656 includes full-time tuition ($19,303) and room and board ($5353). Room and board charges vary according to board plan. ***Part-time tuition:*** $780 per credit hour. ***Part-time fees:*** $155 per year part-time. ***Payment plan:*** installment.

FRESHMAN FINANCIAL AID (Fall 1999, est.) 251 applied for aid; of those 76% were deemed to have need. 100% of freshmen with need received aid; of those 55% had need fully met. *Average percent of need met:* 94% (excluding resources awarded to replace EFC). *Average financial aid package:* $18,393 (excluding resources awarded to replace EFC). 34% of all full-time freshmen had no need and received non-need-based aid.

UNDERGRADUATE FINANCIAL AID (Fall 1999, est.) 759 applied for aid; of those 83% were deemed to have need. 99% of undergraduates with need received aid; of those 57% had need fully met. *Average percent of need met:* 93% (excluding resources awarded to replace EFC). *Average financial aid package:* $18,024 (excluding resources awarded to replace EFC). 34% of all full-time undergraduates had no need and received non-need-based aid.

GIFT AID (NEED-BASED) ***Total amount:*** $6,068,477 (6% Federal, 2% state, 90% institutional, 2% external sources). ***Receiving aid:*** *Freshmen:* 42% (190); *all full-time undergraduates:* 42% (625). ***Average award:*** Freshmen: $11,759; Undergraduates: $9221. ***Scholarships, grants, and awards:*** Federal Pell, FSEOG, state, private, college/university gift aid from institutional funds.

GIFT AID (NON-NEED-BASED) ***Total amount:*** $5,213,833 (1% Federal, 1% state, 87% institutional, 11% external sources). ***Receiving aid:*** *Freshmen:* 11% (51); *Undergraduates:* 10% (153). ***Scholarships, grants, and awards by category:*** *Academic Interests/Achievement:* 656 awards ($5,244,043 total): general academic interests/achievements, humanities. *Creative Arts/Performance:* 23 awards ($238,300 total): art/fine arts, music, theater/drama. *Special Achievements/Activities:* 31 awards ($21,500 total): general special achievements/activities, hobbies/interests, memberships. *Special Characteristics:* 53 awards ($622,606 total): children of faculty/staff, ethnic background, relatives of clergy, religious affiliation. ***Tuition waivers:*** Full or partial for employees or children of employees. ***ROTC:*** Army cooperative, Air Force cooperative.

Rhodes College (continued)

LOANS ***Student loans:*** $2,655,138 (63% need-based, 37% non-need-based). 46% of past graduating class borrowed through all loan programs. Average indebtedness per student: $15,598. ***Average need-based loan:*** Freshmen: $3555; Undergraduates: $4114. ***Parent loans:*** $1,301,643 (100% non-need-based). ***Programs:*** FFEL (Subsidized and Unsubsidized Stafford, PLUS), Perkins.

WORK-STUDY ***Federal work-study:*** *Total amount:* $344,845; 220 jobs averaging $1567. ***State or other work-study/employment:*** *Total amount:* $368,300 (100% non-need-based). 257 part-time jobs averaging $1433.

APPLYING for FINANCIAL AID ***Required financial aid forms:*** FAFSA, CSS Financial Aid PROFILE. ***Financial aid deadline (priority):*** 3/1. ***Notification date:*** 4/1. Students must reply by 5/1 or within 2 weeks of notification.

CONTACT Art Weeden, Director of Financial Aid, Rhodes College, 2000 North Parkway, Memphis, TN 38112-1690, 901-843-3810 or toll-free 800-844-5969 (out-of-state). *Fax:* 901-843-3435. *E-mail:* weeden@rhodes.edu

RICE UNIVERSITY

Houston, TX

Tuition & fees: $15,796 **Average undergraduate aid package: N/A**

ABOUT THE INSTITUTION Independent, coed. Awards: bachelor's, master's, and doctoral degrees. 45 undergraduate majors. Total enrollment: 4,310. Undergraduates: 2,769. Both federal and institutional methodology are used as a basis for awarding need-based institutional aid.

UNDERGRADUATE EXPENSES for 1999–2000 ***Application fee:*** $35. ***Comprehensive fee:*** $22,396 includes full-time tuition ($15,350), mandatory fees ($446), and room and board ($6600). ***College room only:*** $3700. Full-time tuition and fees vary according to student level. Room and board charges vary according to board plan. ***Part-time tuition:*** $607 per semester hour. ***Part-time fees:*** $110 per term part-time. Part-time tuition and fees vary according to student level. ***Payment plan:*** installment.

FRESHMAN FINANCIAL AID (Fall 1999, est.) 442 applied for aid; of those 58% were deemed to have need. 100% of freshmen with need received aid; of those 100% had need fully met. *Average percent of need met:* 100% (excluding resources awarded to replace EFC).

UNDERGRADUATE FINANCIAL AID (Fall 1999, est.) 1,455 applied for aid; of those 87% were deemed to have need. 100% of undergraduates with need received aid; of those 100% had need fully met. *Average percent of need met:* 100% (excluding resources awarded to replace EFC).

GIFT AID (NEED-BASED) ***Total amount:*** $10,049,800 (9% Federal, 15% state, 76% institutional). ***Receiving aid:*** *Freshmen:* 35% (235); *all full-time undergraduates:* 39% (1,067). ***Average award:*** Freshmen: $12,000; Undergraduates: $9425. ***Scholarships, grants, and awards:*** Federal Pell, FSEOG, state, private, college/university gift aid from institutional funds.

GIFT AID (NON-NEED-BASED) ***Total amount:*** $4,513,948 (48% institutional, 52% external sources). ***Receiving aid:*** *Freshmen:* 31% (211); *Undergraduates:* 26% (708). ***Scholarships, grants, and awards by category:*** *Academic Interests/Achievement:* engineering/technologies, general academic interests/achievements. *Creative Arts/Performance:* music. ***Tuition waivers:*** Full or partial for employees or children of employees. ***ROTC:*** Army cooperative, Naval.

LOANS ***Student loans:*** $3,901,414 (58% need-based, 42% non-need-based). ***Parent loans:*** $2,219,928 (100% non-need-based). ***Programs:*** Federal Direct (Subsidized and Unsubsidized Stafford, PLUS), Perkins, state, college/university.

WORK-STUDY ***Federal work-study:*** *Total amount:* $400,000; 375 jobs averaging $1067. ***State or other work-study/employment:*** *Total amount:* $1,350,000 (100% non-need-based). Part-time jobs available.

ATHLETIC AWARDS *Total amount:* 3,436,197 (100% non-need-based).

APPLYING for FINANCIAL AID ***Required financial aid forms:*** FAFSA, institution's own form. ***Financial aid deadline (priority):*** 3/1. ***Notification date:*** Continuous. Students must reply by 5/1 or within 2 weeks of notification.

CONTACT Mr. Carl Buck, Director of Financial Aid, Rice University, 6100 South Main, MS 12, Houston, TX 77005-1892, 713-348-4958 or toll-free 800-527-OWLS. *Fax:* 713-348-5921. *E-mail:* chb@rice.edu

THE RICHARD STOCKTON COLLEGE OF NEW JERSEY

Pomona, NJ

Tuition & fees (NJ res): $4400 **Average undergraduate aid package: $7980**

ABOUT THE INSTITUTION State-supported, coed. Awards: bachelor's and master's degrees. 31 undergraduate majors. Total enrollment: 6,298. Undergraduates: 5,975. Freshmen: 732. Federal methodology is used as a basis for awarding need-based institutional aid.

UNDERGRADUATE EXPENSES for 1999–2000 ***Application fee:*** $35. ***Tuition, state resident:*** full-time $3280; part-time $102 per credit hour. ***Tuition, nonresident:*** full-time $5312; part-time $166 per credit hour. ***Required fees:*** full-time $1120; $35 per credit hour. Full-time tuition and fees vary according to course load. ***College room and board:*** $5381; ***room only:*** $3485. Room and board charges vary according to board plan and housing facility. ***Payment plan:*** installment.

FRESHMAN FINANCIAL AID (Fall 1999) 572 applied for aid; of those 92% were deemed to have need. 96% of freshmen with need received aid; of those 75% had need fully met. *Average percent of need met:* 89% (excluding resources awarded to replace EFC). *Average financial aid package:* $8565 (excluding resources awarded to replace EFC). 15% of all full-time freshmen had no need and received non-need-based aid.

UNDERGRADUATE FINANCIAL AID (Fall 1999) 3,588 applied for aid; of those 98% were deemed to have need. 87% of undergraduates with need received aid; of those 57% had need fully met. *Average percent of need met:* 90% (excluding resources awarded to replace EFC). *Average financial aid package:* $7980 (excluding resources awarded to replace EFC). 7% of all full-time undergraduates had no need and received non-need-based aid.

GIFT AID (NEED-BASED) ***Total amount:*** $7,328,994 (42% Federal, 52% state, 4% institutional, 2% external sources). ***Receiving aid:*** *Freshmen:* 71% (501); *all full-time undergraduates:* 37% (1,760). ***Average award:*** Freshmen: $4554; Undergraduates: $4040. ***Scholarships, grants, and awards:*** Federal Pell, FSEOG, state, college/university gift aid from institutional funds.

GIFT AID (NON-NEED-BASED) ***Total amount:*** $856,479 (25% state, 56% institutional, 19% external sources). ***Receiving aid:*** *Freshmen:* 31% (221); *Undergraduates:* 10% (481). ***Scholarships, grants, and awards by category:*** *Academic Interests/Achievement:* 195 awards ($299,900 total): area/ethnic studies, biological sciences, business, computer science, education, general academic interests/achievements, health fields, humanities, mathematics, physical sciences, social sciences. *Creative Arts/Performance:* 13 awards ($34,300 total): applied art and design, art/fine arts, creative writing, dance, journalism/publications, music, performing arts, theater/drama. *Special Achievements/Activities:* community service, general special achievements/activities, leadership. *Special Characteristics:* 37 awards ($212,885 total): adult students, children of faculty/staff, ethnic background, general special characteristics, local/state students, members of minority groups, previous college experience. ***Tuition waivers:*** Full or partial for senior citizens. ***ROTC:*** Army cooperative.

LOANS ***Student loans:*** $13,651,275 (78% need-based, 22% non-need-based). 62% of past graduating class borrowed through all loan programs. Average indebtedness per student: $13,135. ***Average need-based loan:*** Freshmen: $2579; Undergraduates: $3502. ***Parent loans:*** $1,343,405 (20% need-based, 80% non-need-based). ***Programs:*** Federal Direct (Subsidized and Unsubsidized Stafford, PLUS), Perkins, state.

WORK-STUDY ***Federal work-study:*** *Total amount:* $389,119; 286 jobs averaging $1361. ***State or other work-study/employment:*** *Total amount:* $659,108 (100% non-need-based). 860 part-time jobs averaging $767.

APPLYING for FINANCIAL AID ***Required financial aid form:*** FAFSA. ***Financial aid deadline (priority):*** 3/1. ***Notification date:*** Continuous beginning 4/1. Students must reply within 2 weeks of notification.

CONTACT Ms. Jeanne L. Lewis, Director of Financial Aid, The Richard Stockton College of New Jersey, Jimmie Leeds Road, Pomona, NJ 08240-9988, 609-652-4203. *Fax:* 609-748-5517. *E-mail:* iaprod91@pollux.stockton.edu

RIDER UNIVERSITY

Lawrenceville, NJ

Tuition & fees: $16,820 **Average undergraduate aid package: $14,637**

ABOUT THE INSTITUTION Independent, coed. Awards: associate, bachelor's, and master's degrees and post-bachelor's and post-master's certificates. 52 undergraduate majors. Total enrollment: 5,348. Undergraduates: 4,223. Freshmen: 829. Federal methodology is used as a basis for awarding need-based institutional aid.

UNDERGRADUATE EXPENSES for 1999–2000 ***Application fee:*** $35. ***Comprehensive fee:*** $23,590 includes full-time tuition ($16,520), mandatory fees ($300), and room and board ($6770). ***College room only:*** $4260. Full-time tuition and fees vary according to course load. Room and board charges vary according to housing facility. ***Part-time tuition:*** $550 per semester hour. ***Part-time fees:*** $10 per course. Part-time tuition and fees vary according to course load. ***Payment plan:*** installment.

FRESHMAN FINANCIAL AID (Fall 1999) 660 applied for aid; of those 87% were deemed to have need. 100% of freshmen with need received aid; of those 40% had need fully met. *Average percent of need met:* 92% (excluding resources awarded to replace EFC). *Average financial aid package:* $15,351 (excluding resources awarded to replace EFC). 18% of all full-time freshmen had no need and received non-need-based aid.

UNDERGRADUATE FINANCIAL AID (Fall 1999) 2,487 applied for aid; of those 88% were deemed to have need. 100% of undergraduates with need received aid; of those 27% had need fully met. *Average percent of need met:* 89% (excluding resources awarded to replace EFC). *Average financial aid package:* $14,637 (excluding resources awarded to replace EFC). 16% of all full-time undergraduates had no need and received non-need-based aid.

GIFT AID (NEED-BASED) ***Total amount:*** $19,841,295 (11% Federal, 25% state, 63% institutional, 1% external sources). ***Receiving aid:*** *Freshmen:* 61% (506); *all full-time undergraduates:* 58% (1,862). ***Average award:*** Freshmen: $7964; Undergraduates: $7283. ***Scholarships, grants, and awards:*** Federal Pell, FSEOG, state, private, college/university gift aid from institutional funds.

GIFT AID (NON-NEED-BASED) ***Total amount:*** $2,247,430 (1% state, 97% institutional, 2% external sources). ***Receiving aid:*** *Freshmen:* 38% (317); *Undergraduates:* 29% (953). ***Scholarships, grants, and awards by category:*** *Academic Interests/Achievement:* 642 awards ($4,411,717 total): general academic interests/achievements. *Creative Arts/Performance:* 5 awards ($77,654 total): art/fine arts, theater/drama. *Special Characteristics:* 23 awards ($132,718 total): members of minority groups. ***Tuition waivers:*** Full or partial for employees or children of employees. ***ROTC:*** Army cooperative, Air Force cooperative.

LOANS ***Student loans:*** $19,232,534 (73% need-based, 27% non-need-based). 66% of past graduating class borrowed through all loan programs. Average indebtedness per student: $12,500. ***Average need-based loan:*** Freshmen: $3854; Undergraduates: $4472. ***Parent loans:*** $2,226,588 (31% need-based, 69% non-need-based). ***Programs:*** FFEL (Subsidized and Unsubsidized Stafford, PLUS), Perkins, state, college/university, alternative loans.

WORK-STUDY ***Federal work-study:*** *Total amount:* $2,330,666; jobs available.

ATHLETIC AWARDS *Total amount:* 1,774,531 (55% need-based, 45% non-need-based).

APPLYING for FINANCIAL AID ***Required financial aid form:*** FAFSA. ***Financial aid deadline (priority):*** 3/1. ***Notification date:*** Continuous beginning 4/15.

CONTACT Mr. John J. Williams, Director of Student Financial Services, Rider University, 2083 Lawrenceville Road, Lawrenceville, NJ 08648-3001, 609-896-5360 or toll-free 800-257-9026. *Fax:* 609-219-4487. *E-mail:* williams@rider.edu

RINGLING SCHOOL OF ART AND DESIGN

Sarasota, FL

Tuition & fees: $15,600 **Average undergraduate aid package: $10,048**

ABOUT THE INSTITUTION Independent, coed. Awards: bachelor's degrees. 5 undergraduate majors. Total enrollment: 892. Undergraduates: 892. Freshmen: 159. Both federal and institutional methodology are used as a basis for awarding need-based institutional aid.

UNDERGRADUATE EXPENSES for 1999–2000 ***Application fee:*** $35. ***One-time required fee:*** $250. ***Comprehensive fee:*** $22,888 includes full-time tuition ($14,500), mandatory fees ($1100), and room and board ($7288). Full-time tuition and fees vary according to course level, course load, program, and student level. Room and board charges vary according to board plan and housing facility. ***Part-time tuition:*** $700 per credit hour. Part-time tuition and fees vary according to course level, course load, and program. ***Payment plan:*** installment.

FRESHMAN FINANCIAL AID (Fall 1999) 119 applied for aid; of those 86% were deemed to have need. 100% of freshmen with need received aid; of those 8% had need fully met. *Average percent of need met:* 47% (excluding resources awarded to replace EFC). *Average financial aid package:* $8805 (excluding resources awarded to replace EFC). 4% of all full-time freshmen had no need and received non-need-based aid.

UNDERGRADUATE FINANCIAL AID (Fall 1999) 698 applied for aid; of those 89% were deemed to have need. 100% of undergraduates with need received aid; of those 11% had need fully met. *Average percent of need met:* 45% (excluding resources awarded to replace EFC). *Average financial aid package:* $10,048 (excluding resources awarded to replace EFC). 4% of all full-time undergraduates had no need and received non-need-based aid.

GIFT AID (NEED-BASED) ***Total amount:*** $2,181,064 (26% Federal, 45% state, 20% institutional, 9% external sources). ***Receiving aid:*** *Freshmen:* 16% (25); *all full-time undergraduates:* 26% (225). ***Average award:*** Freshmen: $3427; Undergraduates: $2747. ***Scholarships, grants, and awards:*** Federal Pell, FSEOG, state, private, college/university gift aid from institutional funds.

GIFT AID (NON-NEED-BASED) ***Total amount:*** $187,847 (29% state, 16% institutional, 55% external sources). ***Receiving aid:*** *Freshmen:* 11% (17); *Undergraduates:* 10% (83). ***Scholarships, grants, and awards by category:*** *Creative Arts/Performance:* applied art and design, art/fine arts. ***Tuition waivers:*** Full or partial for employees or children of employees.

LOANS ***Student loans:*** $3,710,758 (86% need-based, 14% non-need-based). 67% of past graduating class borrowed through all loan programs. Average indebtedness per student: $21,966. ***Average need-based loan:*** Freshmen: $2374; Undergraduates: $4030. ***Parent loans:*** $1,921,835 (80% need-based, 20% non-need-based). ***Programs:*** FFEL (Subsidized and Unsubsidized Stafford, PLUS), alternative loans.

WORK-STUDY ***Federal work-study:*** *Total amount:* $149,000; 60 jobs averaging $2483. ***State or other work-study/employment:*** *Total amount:* $2326 (100% need-based). 1 part-time job averaging $2326.

APPLYING for FINANCIAL AID ***Required financial aid forms:*** FAFSA, institution's own form. ***Financial aid deadline (priority):*** 3/1. ***Notification date:*** Continuous beginning 3/15.

CONTACT Juanice Mullet, Financial Aid Counselor, Ringling School of Art and Design, 2700 North Tamiami Trail, Office of Financial Aid, Sarasota, FL 34234, 941-351-5100 or toll-free 800-255-7695. *Fax:* 941-359-7517.

RIPON COLLEGE

Ripon, WI

Tuition & fees: $18,240 **Average undergraduate aid package: $16,798**

ABOUT THE INSTITUTION Independent, coed. Awards: bachelor's degrees. 37 undergraduate majors. Total enrollment: 746. Undergraduates: 746. Freshmen: 283. Federal methodology is used as a basis for awarding need-based institutional aid.

Ripon College (continued)

UNDERGRADUATE EXPENSES for 1999–2000 ***Application fee:*** $25. ***Comprehensive fee:*** $22,640 includes full-time tuition ($18,000), mandatory fees ($240), and room and board ($4400). ***College room only:*** $2000. ***Part-time tuition:*** $775 per credit. ***Payment plans:*** guaranteed tuition, installment.

FRESHMAN FINANCIAL AID (Fall 1999) 264 applied for aid; of those 88% were deemed to have need. 100% of freshmen with need received aid; of those 100% had need fully met. *Average percent of need met:* 100% (excluding resources awarded to replace EFC). *Average financial aid package:* $16,973 (excluding resources awarded to replace EFC). 17% of all full-time freshmen had no need and received non-need-based aid.

UNDERGRADUATE FINANCIAL AID (Fall 1999) 605 applied for aid; of those 93% were deemed to have need. 100% of undergraduates with need received aid; of those 84% had need fully met. *Average percent of need met:* 99% (excluding resources awarded to replace EFC). *Average financial aid package:* $16,798 (excluding resources awarded to replace EFC). 16% of all full-time undergraduates had no need and received non-need-based aid.

GIFT AID (NEED-BASED) ***Total amount:*** $7,232,224 (7% Federal, 9% state, 79% institutional, 5% external sources). ***Receiving aid:*** *Freshmen:* 82% (232); *all full-time undergraduates:* 80% (560). ***Average award:*** Freshmen: $14,277; Undergraduates: $13,191. ***Scholarships, grants, and awards:*** Federal Pell, FSEOG, state, private, college/university gift aid from institutional funds.

GIFT AID (NON-NEED-BASED) ***Total amount:*** $1,230,139 (2% state, 85% institutional, 13% external sources). ***Receiving aid:*** *Freshmen:* 25% (70); *Undergraduates:* 18% (126). ***Scholarships, grants, and awards by category:*** *Academic Interests/Achievement:* 411 awards ($2,544,195 total): computer science, general academic interests/achievements, mathematics, military science, physical sciences. *Creative Arts/Performance:* 67 awards ($164,625 total): art/fine arts, debating, music, theater/drama. *Special Achievements/Activities:* 134 awards ($413,700 total): general special achievements/activities, leadership, memberships. *Special Characteristics:* 108 awards ($830,165 total): children and siblings of alumni, children of faculty/staff, international students, members of minority groups, out-of-state students, previous college experience, siblings of current students. ***Tuition waivers:*** Full or partial for children of alumni, employees or children of employees. ***ROTC:*** Army.

LOANS ***Student loans:*** $2,212,280 (76% need-based, 24% non-need-based). 83% of past graduating class borrowed through all loan programs. Average indebtedness per student: $15,507. ***Average need-based loan:*** Freshmen: $2658; Undergraduates: $3327. ***Parent loans:*** $241,450 (2% need-based, 98% non-need-based). ***Programs:*** FFEL (Subsidized and Unsubsidized Stafford, PLUS), Perkins, alternative loans.

WORK-STUDY ***Federal work-study:*** *Total amount:* $328,426; 249 jobs averaging $1320. ***State or other work-study/employment:*** *Total amount:* $317,735 (5% need-based, 95% non-need-based). 264 part-time jobs averaging $1200.

APPLYING for FINANCIAL AID ***Required financial aid form:*** FAFSA. ***Financial aid deadline:*** Continuous. ***Notification date:*** Continuous beginning 3/1. Students must reply within 2 weeks of notification.

CONTACT Michelle Krajnik, Director of Financial Aid, Ripon College, 300 Seward Street, Ripon, WI 54971, 920-748-8101 or toll-free 800-947-4766. *Fax:* 920-748-8335. *E-mail:* finaid@ripon.edu

RIVIER COLLEGE

Nashua, NH

Tuition & fees: $14,260 **Average undergraduate aid package: $11,730**

ABOUT THE INSTITUTION Independent Roman Catholic, coed. Awards: associate, bachelor's, and master's degrees and post-bachelor's and post-master's certificates. 44 undergraduate majors. Total enrollment: 2,592. Undergraduates: 1,546. Freshmen: 194. Federal methodology is used as a basis for awarding need-based institutional aid.

UNDERGRADUATE EXPENSES for 1999–2000 ***Application fee:*** $25. ***Comprehensive fee:*** $19,950 includes full-time tuition ($13,950), mandatory fees ($310), and room and board ($5690). ***Part-time tuition:*** $465 per credit hour. ***Part-time fees:*** $2 per credit hour; $25 per term part-time. Part-time tuition and fees vary according to class time. ***Payment plans:*** installment, deferred payment.

FRESHMAN FINANCIAL AID (Fall 1999, est.) 167 applied for aid; of those 96% were deemed to have need. 100% of freshmen with need received aid; of those 32% had need fully met. *Average percent of need met:* 80% (excluding resources awarded to replace EFC). *Average financial aid package:* $12,377 (excluding resources awarded to replace EFC). 12% of all full-time freshmen had no need and received non-need-based aid.

UNDERGRADUATE FINANCIAL AID (Fall 1999, est.) 576 applied for aid; of those 93% were deemed to have need. 100% of undergraduates with need received aid; of those 27% had need fully met. *Average percent of need met:* 77% (excluding resources awarded to replace EFC). *Average financial aid package:* $11,730 (excluding resources awarded to replace EFC). 24% of all full-time undergraduates had no need and received non-need-based aid.

GIFT AID (NEED-BASED) ***Total amount:*** $3,448,901 (16% Federal, 4% state, 78% institutional, 2% external sources). ***Receiving aid:*** *Freshmen:* 82% (150); *all full-time undergraduates:* 69% (487). ***Average award:*** Freshmen: $7841; Undergraduates: $6193. ***Scholarships, grants, and awards:*** Federal Pell, FSEOG, state, private, college/university gift aid from institutional funds.

GIFT AID (NON-NEED-BASED) ***Total amount:*** $194,992 (95% institutional, 5% external sources). ***Receiving aid:*** *Freshmen:* 4% (7); *Undergraduates:* 3% (21). ***Scholarships, grants, and awards by category:*** *Academic Interests/Achievement:* 155 awards ($622,500 total): general academic interests/achievements. *Special Characteristics:* 88 awards ($272,130 total): children and siblings of alumni, members of minority groups, religious affiliation, siblings of current students. ***Tuition waivers:*** Full or partial for employees or children of employees, senior citizens. ***ROTC:*** Air Force cooperative.

LOANS ***Student loans:*** $4,820,136 (71% need-based, 29% non-need-based). Average indebtedness per student: $16,555. ***Average need-based loan:*** Freshmen: $3666; Undergraduates: $4859. ***Parent loans:*** $527,161 (47% need-based, 53% non-need-based). ***Programs:*** FFEL (Subsidized and Unsubsidized Stafford, PLUS), Perkins.

WORK-STUDY ***Federal work-study:*** *Total amount:* $353,871; 184 jobs averaging $1923. ***State or other work-study/employment:*** *Total amount:* $97,200 (13% need-based, 87% non-need-based). Part-time jobs available.

APPLYING for FINANCIAL AID ***Required financial aid form:*** FAFSA. ***Financial aid deadline (priority):*** 2/1. ***Notification date:*** Continuous beginning 3/1. Students must reply within 4 weeks of notification.

CONTACT Leslie Bembridge, Director of Financial Aid, Rivier College, 420 Main Street, Nashua, NH 03060-5086, 603-897-8533 or toll-free 800-44RIVIER. *Fax:* 603-897-8810. *E-mail:* lbembridge@rivier.edu

ROANOKE BIBLE COLLEGE

Elizabeth City, NC

Tuition & fees: $5610 **Average undergraduate aid package: $6908**

ABOUT THE INSTITUTION Independent Christian, coed. Awards: associate and bachelor's degrees. 4 undergraduate majors. Total enrollment: 155. Undergraduates: 155. Freshmen: 30. Federal methodology is used as a basis for awarding need-based institutional aid.

UNDERGRADUATE EXPENSES for 1999–2000 ***Application fee:*** $25. ***Comprehensive fee:*** $9070 includes full-time tuition ($4960), mandatory fees ($650), and room and board ($3460). Room and board charges vary according to housing facility. ***Part-time tuition:*** $155 per semester hour. ***Part-time fees:*** $35 per semester hour. Part-time tuition and fees vary according to course load. ***Payment plans:*** installment, deferred payment.

FRESHMAN FINANCIAL AID (Fall 1998) 30 applied for aid; of those 90% were deemed to have need. 100% of freshmen with need received aid. *Average percent of need met:* 35% (excluding resources awarded to replace EFC). *Average financial aid package:* $4943 (excluding resources awarded to replace EFC). 9% of all full-time freshmen had no need and received non-need-based aid.

UNDERGRADUATE FINANCIAL AID (Fall 1998) 107 applied for aid; of those 93% were deemed to have need. 100% of undergraduates with need received aid. *Average percent of need met:* 40% (excluding resources awarded to replace EFC). *Average financial aid package:* $6908 (excluding resources awarded to replace EFC). 7% of all full-time undergraduates had no need and received non-need-based aid.

GIFT AID (NEED-BASED) ***Total amount:*** $360,157 (46% Federal, 50% institutional, 4% external sources). ***Receiving aid:*** *Freshmen:* 82% (27); *all full-time undergraduates:* 88% (99). ***Average award:*** Freshmen: $2454; Undergraduates: $3638. ***Scholarships, grants, and awards:*** Federal Pell, FSEOG, private, college/university gift aid from institutional funds.

GIFT AID (NON-NEED-BASED) ***Total amount:*** $35,059 (85% institutional, 15% external sources). ***Receiving aid:*** *Freshmen:* 24% (8); *Undergraduates:* 15% (17). ***Scholarships, grants, and awards by category:*** *Academic Interests/Achievement:* 16 awards ($27,859 total): general academic interests/achievements, religion/biblical studies. *Special Achievements/Activities:* 70 awards ($76,133 total): community service, general special achievements/activities, leadership, religious involvement. *Special Characteristics:* 27 awards ($47,321 total): children of faculty/staff, general special characteristics, handicapped students, international students, married students, spouses of current students. ***Tuition waivers:*** Full or partial for employees or children of employees, senior citizens.

LOANS ***Student loans:*** $322,107 (91% need-based, 9% non-need-based). 75% of past graduating class borrowed through all loan programs. Average indebtedness per student: $11,742. ***Average need-based loan:*** Freshmen: $2345; Undergraduates: $3126. ***Parent loans:*** $51,100 (64% need-based, 36% non-need-based). ***Programs:*** FFEL (Subsidized and Unsubsidized Stafford, PLUS).

APPLYING for FINANCIAL AID ***Required financial aid forms:*** FAFSA, institution's own form. ***Financial aid deadline (priority):*** 3/15. ***Notification date:*** Continuous beginning 4/1. Students must reply within 2 weeks of notification.

CONTACT Mrs. Julie Ann Fields, Financial Aid Administrator, Roanoke Bible College, 715 North Poindexter Street, Elizabeth City, NC 27909, 252-334-2020 or toll-free 800-RBC-8980. *Fax:* 252-334-2071. *E-mail:* jaf@roanokebible.edu

ROANOKE COLLEGE

Salem, VA

Tuition & fees: $17,095 **Average undergraduate aid package: $14,784**

ABOUT THE INSTITUTION Independent religious, coed. Awards: bachelor's degrees. 27 undergraduate majors. Total enrollment: 1,731. Undergraduates: 1,731. Freshmen: 450. Federal methodology is used as a basis for awarding need-based institutional aid.

UNDERGRADUATE EXPENSES for 1999–2000 ***Application fee:*** $30. ***Comprehensive fee:*** $22,545 includes full-time tuition ($16,655), mandatory fees ($440), and room and board ($5450). ***College room only:*** $2645. ***Part-time tuition:*** $830 per course. ***Part-time fees:*** $25 per term part-time. ***Payment plan:*** installment.

FRESHMAN FINANCIAL AID (Fall 1999) 353 applied for aid; of those 85% were deemed to have need. 100% of freshmen with need received aid; of those 30% had need fully met. *Average percent of need met:* 94% (excluding resources awarded to replace EFC). *Average financial aid package:* $14,725 (excluding resources awarded to replace EFC). 28% of all full-time freshmen had no need and received non-need-based aid.

UNDERGRADUATE FINANCIAL AID (Fall 1999) 1,122 applied for aid; of those 88% were deemed to have need. 100% of undergraduates with need received aid; of those 35% had need fully met. *Average percent of need met:* 92% (excluding resources awarded to replace EFC). *Average financial aid package:* $14,784 (excluding resources awarded to replace EFC). 32% of all full-time undergraduates had no need and received non-need-based aid.

GIFT AID (NEED-BASED) ***Total amount:*** $11,281,502 (6% Federal, 14% state, 76% institutional, 4% external sources). ***Receiving aid:*** *Freshmen:* 66% (297); *all full-time undergraduates:* 61% (983). ***Average award:*** Freshmen: $11,242; Undergraduates: $11,045. ***Scholarships, grants, and awards:*** Federal Pell, FSEOG, state, private, college/university gift aid from institutional funds.

GIFT AID (NON-NEED-BASED) ***Total amount:*** $4,093,572 (16% state, 81% institutional, 3% external sources). ***Receiving aid:*** *Freshmen:* 60% (272); *Undergraduates:* 57% (917). ***Scholarships, grants, and awards by category:*** *Academic Interests/Achievement:* 1,304 awards ($7,126,475 total): general academic interests/achievements. *Creative Arts/Performance:* 27 awards ($17,700 total): art/fine arts, music. *Special Characteristics:* 682 awards ($1,892,953 total): local/state students, members of minority groups, religious affiliation. ***Tuition waivers:*** Full or partial for employees or children of employees, senior citizens.

LOANS ***Student loans:*** $4,982,787 (90% need-based, 10% non-need-based). 66% of past graduating class borrowed through all loan programs. Average indebtedness per student: $14,784. ***Average need-based loan:*** Freshmen: $3290; Undergraduates: $3763. ***Parent loans:*** $1,403,052 (78% need-based, 22% non-need-based). ***Programs:*** FFEL (Subsidized and Unsubsidized Stafford, PLUS), Perkins, college/university.

WORK-STUDY ***Federal work-study:*** *Total amount:* $700,957; 489 jobs averaging $1433.

APPLYING for FINANCIAL AID ***Required financial aid forms:*** FAFSA, state aid form. ***Financial aid deadline (priority):*** 3/1. ***Notification date:*** Continuous. Students must reply within 2 weeks of notification.

CONTACT Mr. Thomas S. Blair Jr., Director of Financial Aid, Roanoke College, 221 College Lane, Salem, VA 24153-3794, 540-375-2235 or toll-free 800-388-2276. *E-mail:* finaid@roanoke.edu

ROBERT MORRIS COLLEGE

Chicago, IL

Tuition & fees: $10,950 **Average undergraduate aid package: $9371**

ABOUT THE INSTITUTION Independent, coed. Awards: bachelor's degrees. 14 undergraduate majors. Total enrollment: 4,311. Undergraduates: 4,311. Freshmen: 1,521. Federal methodology is used as a basis for awarding need-based institutional aid.

UNDERGRADUATE EXPENSES for 1999–2000 ***Application fee:*** $20. ***Tuition:*** full-time $10,950; part-time $920 per course. ***Payment plan:*** installment.

FRESHMAN FINANCIAL AID (Fall 1999, est.) 1321 applied for aid; of those 97% were deemed to have need. 100% of freshmen with need received aid; of those 7% had need fully met. *Average percent of need met:* 65% (excluding resources awarded to replace EFC). *Average financial aid package:* $9246 (excluding resources awarded to replace EFC). 11% of all full-time freshmen had no need and received non-need-based aid.

UNDERGRADUATE FINANCIAL AID (Fall 1999, est.) 3,556 applied for aid; of those 97% were deemed to have need. 100% of undergraduates with need received aid; of those 9% had need fully met. *Average percent of need met:* 63% (excluding resources awarded to replace EFC). *Average financial aid package:* $9371 (excluding resources awarded to replace EFC). 9% of all full-time undergraduates had no need and received non-need-based aid.

GIFT AID (NEED-BASED) ***Total amount:*** $22,487,000 (25% Federal, 52% state, 22% institutional, 1% external sources). ***Receiving aid:*** *Freshmen:* 83% (1,253); *all full-time undergraduates:* 89% (3,373). ***Average award:*** Freshmen: $6636; Undergraduates: $6446. ***Scholarships, grants, and awards:*** Federal Pell, FSEOG, state, private, college/university gift aid from institutional funds.

GIFT AID (NON-NEED-BASED) ***Total amount:*** $405,443 (2% state, 81% institutional, 17% external sources). ***Receiving aid:*** *Freshmen:* 2% (35); *Undergraduates:* 2% (94). ***Scholarships, grants, and awards by category:*** *Academic Interests/Achievement:* general academic interests/achievements. *Special Achievements/Activities:* community service, general special achievements/activities. *Special Characteristics:* children of faculty/staff, general special characteristics, out-of-state students, veterans. ***Tuition waivers:*** Full or partial for employees or children of employees.

LOANS ***Student loans:*** $11,529,677 (92% need-based, 8% non-need-based). 96% of past graduating class borrowed through all loan programs. Average indebtedness per student: $8511. ***Average need-based loan:***

Robert Morris College (continued)

Freshmen: $2610; Undergraduates: $2925. ***Parent loans:*** $849,384 (43% need-based, 57% non-need-based). ***Programs:*** FFEL (Subsidized and Unsubsidized Stafford, PLUS), Perkins.

WORK-STUDY ***Federal work-study:*** *Total amount:* $167,628; jobs available.

ATHLETIC AWARDS *Total amount:* 740,618 (71% need-based, 29% non-need-based).

APPLYING for FINANCIAL AID ***Required financial aid form:*** FAFSA. ***Financial aid deadline:*** Continuous. ***Notification date:*** Continuous.

CONTACT Ms. Alexandria Gonzalez, Associate Director of Financial Services, Robert Morris College, 401 South State Street, Chicago, IL 60605, 312-935-4070 or toll-free 800-225-1520.

ROBERT MORRIS COLLEGE

Moon Township, PA

Tuition & fees: $9919 **Average undergraduate aid package: $5600**

ABOUT THE INSTITUTION Independent, coed. Awards: associate, bachelor's, and master's degrees. 23 undergraduate majors. Total enrollment: 4,750. Undergraduates: 3,833. Freshmen: 567. Federal methodology is used as a basis for awarding need-based institutional aid.

UNDERGRADUATE EXPENSES for 1999–2000 ***Application fee:*** $20. ***Comprehensive fee:*** $15,981 includes full-time tuition ($8940), mandatory fees ($979), and room and board ($6062). ***Part-time tuition:*** $298 per credit. ***Part-time fees:*** $16 per credit. ***Payment plans:*** installment, deferred payment.

FRESHMAN FINANCIAL AID (Fall 1999, est.) 488 applied for aid; of those 86% were deemed to have need. 100% of freshmen with need received aid; of those .2% had need fully met. *Average financial aid package:* $6300 (excluding resources awarded to replace EFC). 10% of all full-time freshmen had no need and received non-need-based aid.

UNDERGRADUATE FINANCIAL AID (Fall 1999, est.) 2,324 applied for aid; of those 87% were deemed to have need. 100% of undergraduates with need received aid; of those 1% had need fully met. *Average financial aid package:* $5600 (excluding resources awarded to replace EFC). 14% of all full-time undergraduates had no need and received non-need-based aid.

GIFT AID (NEED-BASED) ***Total amount:*** $6,021,127 (38% Federal, 51% state, 4% institutional, 7% external sources). ***Receiving aid:*** *Freshmen:* 85% (421); *all full-time undergraduates:* 77% (2,017). ***Average award:*** Freshmen: $3000; Undergraduates: $2750. ***Scholarships, grants, and awards:*** Federal Pell, FSEOG, state, private, college/university gift aid from institutional funds, United Negro College Fund.

GIFT AID (NON-NEED-BASED) ***Total amount:*** $3,299,385 (100% institutional). ***Receiving aid:*** *Freshmen:* 85% (421); *Undergraduates:* 77% (2,017). ***Scholarships, grants, and awards by category:*** *Academic Interests/Achievement:* 1,114 awards ($1,649,275 total): business, communication, general academic interests/achievements, international studies. *Special Achievements/Activities:* 28 awards ($67,045 total): hobbies/interests, leadership. *Special Characteristics:* 90 awards ($249,759 total): children of faculty/staff, ethnic background, members of minority groups, out-of-state students. ***Tuition waivers:*** Full or partial for employees or children of employees, senior citizens. ***ROTC:*** Army cooperative, Air Force cooperative.

LOANS ***Student loans:*** $12,746,850 (45% need-based, 55% non-need-based). ***Average need-based loan:*** Freshmen: $3000; Undergraduates: $4250. ***Parent loans:*** $1,936,348 (100% non-need-based). ***Programs:*** Federal Direct (Subsidized and Unsubsidized Stafford, PLUS), Perkins, state.

WORK-STUDY ***Federal work-study:*** *Total amount:* $1,129,170; jobs available. ***State or other work-study/employment:*** *Total amount:* $606,452 (100% non-need-based). Part-time jobs available.

ATHLETIC AWARDS *Total amount:* 1,098,056 (100% non-need-based).

APPLYING for FINANCIAL AID ***Required financial aid form:*** FAFSA. ***Financial aid deadline (priority):*** 5/1. ***Notification date:*** Continuous.

CONTACT Mr. Andy Rahimi, Manager of Financial Aid, Daily Operations, Robert Morris College, 881 Narrows Run Road, Moon Township, PA 15108-1189, 412-262-8545 or toll-free 800-762-0097. *Fax:* 412-262-8601. *E-mail:* rahimi@robert-morris.edu

ROBERTS WESLEYAN COLLEGE

Rochester, NY

Tuition & fees: $13,614 **Average undergraduate aid package: $12,503**

ABOUT THE INSTITUTION Independent religious, coed. Awards: associate, bachelor's, and master's degrees. 44 undergraduate majors. Total enrollment: 1,405. Undergraduates: 1,149. Freshmen: 272. Federal methodology is used as a basis for awarding need-based institutional aid.

UNDERGRADUATE EXPENSES for 1999–2000 ***Application fee:*** $35. ***One-time required fee:*** $100. ***Comprehensive fee:*** $18,228 includes full-time tuition ($13,100), mandatory fees ($514), and room and board ($4614). ***College room only:*** $3174. Room and board charges vary according to board plan. ***Part-time tuition:*** $270 per hour. Part-time tuition and fees vary according to course load. ***Payment plan:*** installment.

FRESHMAN FINANCIAL AID (Fall 1998) 176 applied for aid; of those 94% were deemed to have need. 100% of freshmen with need received aid; of those 13% had need fully met. *Average percent of need met:* 84% (excluding resources awarded to replace EFC). *Average financial aid package:* $12,764 (excluding resources awarded to replace EFC). 35% of all full-time freshmen had no need and received non-need-based aid.

UNDERGRADUATE FINANCIAL AID (Fall 1998) 820 applied for aid; of those 95% were deemed to have need. 100% of undergraduates with need received aid; of those 25% had need fully met. *Average percent of need met:* 87% (excluding resources awarded to replace EFC). *Average financial aid package:* $12,503 (excluding resources awarded to replace EFC). 13% of all full-time undergraduates had no need and received non-need-based aid.

GIFT AID (NEED-BASED) ***Total amount:*** $5,055,970 (18% Federal, 22% state, 52% institutional, 8% external sources). ***Receiving aid:*** *Freshmen:* 65% (165); *all full-time undergraduates:* 81% (729). ***Average award:*** Freshmen: $7652; Undergraduates: $6403. ***Scholarships, grants, and awards:*** Federal Pell, FSEOG, state, private, college/university gift aid from institutional funds.

GIFT AID (NON-NEED-BASED) ***Total amount:*** $602,590 (2% state, 65% institutional, 33% external sources). ***Receiving aid:*** *Freshmen:* 2% (6); *Undergraduates:* 3% (23). ***Scholarships, grants, and awards by category:*** *Academic Interests/Achievement:* 422 awards ($1,129,009 total): business, computer science, education, general academic interests/achievements, health fields, mathematics, religion/biblical studies. *Creative Arts/Performance:* 159 awards ($219,536 total): art/fine arts, music. *Special Achievements/Activities:* 212 awards ($176,675 total): community service, junior miss, leadership, religious involvement. *Special Characteristics:* 449 awards ($502,101 total): children and siblings of alumni, children of faculty/staff, international students, out-of-state students, relatives of clergy, religious affiliation, siblings of current students. ***Tuition waivers:*** Full or partial for employees or children of employees. ***ROTC:*** Army cooperative, Air Force cooperative.

LOANS ***Student loans:*** $5,413,420 (85% need-based, 15% non-need-based). 90% of past graduating class borrowed through all loan programs. Average indebtedness per student: $17,436. ***Average need-based loan:*** Freshmen: $4156; Undergraduates: $5457. ***Parent loans:*** $740,510 (57% need-based, 43% non-need-based). ***Programs:*** Federal Direct (Subsidized and Unsubsidized Stafford, PLUS), Perkins.

WORK-STUDY ***Federal work-study:*** *Total amount:* $516,034; 481 jobs averaging $1073. ***State or other work-study/employment:*** *Total amount:* $73,225 (10% need-based, 90% non-need-based). 46 part-time jobs averaging $1592.

ATHLETIC AWARDS *Total amount:* 394,598 (67% need-based, 33% non-need-based).

APPLYING for FINANCIAL AID ***Required financial aid forms:*** FAFSA, institution's own form. ***Financial aid deadline (priority):*** 3/15. ***Notification date:*** Continuous. Students must reply by 5/1 or within 2 weeks of notification.

CONTACT Mr. Stephen Field, Director of Student Financial Services, Roberts Wesleyan College, 2301 Westside Drive, Rochester, NY 14624-1997, 716-594-6150 or toll-free 800-777-4RWC. *Fax:* 716-594-6036. *E-mail:* fields@roberts.edu

ROCHESTER COLLEGE

Rochester Hills, MI

Tuition & fees: $8304 **Average undergraduate aid package: N/A**

ABOUT THE INSTITUTION Independent religious, coed. Awards: associate and bachelor's degrees. 23 undergraduate majors. Total enrollment: 557. Undergraduates: 557. Freshmen: 108. Both federal and institutional methodology are used as a basis for awarding need-based institutional aid.

UNDERGRADUATE EXPENSES for 1999–2000 ***Application fee:*** $25. ***Comprehensive fee:*** $12,720 includes full-time tuition ($7808), mandatory fees ($496), and room and board ($4416). ***Part-time tuition:*** $244 per credit hour. ***Part-time fees:*** $108 per term part-time. Part-time tuition and fees vary according to course load. ***Payment plan:*** installment.

GIFT AID (NEED-BASED) ***Total amount:*** $740,891 (27% Federal, 73% state). ***Scholarships, grants, and awards:*** Federal Pell, FSEOG, state, private, college/university gift aid from institutional funds.

GIFT AID (NON-NEED-BASED) ***Scholarships, grants, and awards by category:*** *Academic Interests/Achievement:* computer science, general academic interests/achievements, mathematics, religion/biblical studies. *Creative Arts/Performance:* journalism/publications, music, theater/drama. *Special Achievements/Activities:* leadership. *Special Characteristics:* adult students, children and siblings of alumni, children of faculty/staff, first-generation college students, general special characteristics, out-of-state students, previous college experience, relatives of clergy, siblings of current students. ***Tuition waivers:*** Full or partial for children of alumni, employees or children of employees, senior citizens.

LOANS ***Student loans:*** $1,193,491 (59% need-based, 41% non-need-based). ***Parent loans:*** $481,070 (100% non-need-based). ***Programs:*** Federal Direct (Subsidized and Unsubsidized Stafford, PLUS), Perkins.

WORK-STUDY ***Federal work-study:*** *Total amount:* $54,380; jobs available. ***State or other work-study/employment:*** *Total amount:* $163,324 (8% need-based, 92% non-need-based).

ATHLETIC AWARDS *Total amount:* 222,678 (100% non-need-based).

APPLYING for FINANCIAL AID ***Required financial aid forms:*** FAFSA, scholarship application form. ***Financial aid deadline (priority):*** 3/1. ***Notification date:*** Continuous beginning 4/1. Students must reply within 4 weeks of notification.

CONTACT Ms. Lora McClelland, Director of Financial Aid, Rochester College, 800 West Avon Road, Rochester Hills, MI 48307, 248-218-2028 or toll-free 800-521-6010.

ROCHESTER INSTITUTE OF TECHNOLOGY

Rochester, NY

Tuition & fees: $17,637 **Average undergraduate aid package: $14,700**

ABOUT THE INSTITUTION Independent, coed. Awards: associate, bachelor's, master's, and doctoral degrees and post-bachelor's certificates. 90 undergraduate majors. Total enrollment: 12,775. Undergraduates: 10,746. Freshmen: 2,186. Both federal and institutional methodology are used as a basis for awarding need-based institutional aid.

UNDERGRADUATE EXPENSES for 1999–2000 ***Application fee:*** $40. ***Comprehensive fee:*** $24,489 includes full-time tuition ($17,328), mandatory fees ($309), and room and board ($6852). ***College room only:*** $3774. Full-time tuition and fees vary according to course load and program. Room and board charges vary according to board plan and housing facility. ***Part-time tuition:*** $414 per credit hour. ***Part-time fees:*** $22 per term part-time. Part-time tuition and fees vary according to class time, course level, course load, and program. ***Payment plans:*** tuition prepayment, installment, deferred payment.

FRESHMAN FINANCIAL AID (Fall 1998) 1713 applied for aid; of those 87% were deemed to have need. 100% of freshmen with need received aid; of those 90% had need fully met. *Average percent of need met:* 90% (excluding resources awarded to replace EFC). *Average financial aid package:* $14,900 (excluding resources awarded to replace EFC). 7% of all full-time freshmen had no need and received non-need-based aid.

UNDERGRADUATE FINANCIAL AID (Fall 1998) 6,668 applied for aid; of those 92% were deemed to have need. 100% of undergraduates with need received aid; of those 90% had need fully met. *Average percent of need met:* 90% (excluding resources awarded to replace EFC). *Average financial aid package:* $14,700 (excluding resources awarded to replace EFC). 5% of all full-time undergraduates had no need and received non-need-based aid.

GIFT AID (NEED-BASED) ***Total amount:*** $49,220,827 (13% Federal, 13% state, 74% institutional). ***Receiving aid:*** *Freshmen:* 64% (1,389); *all full-time undergraduates:* 67% (5,705). ***Average award:*** Freshmen: $8000; Undergraduates: $7650. ***Scholarships, grants, and awards:*** Federal Pell, FSEOG, state, private, college/university gift aid from institutional funds.

GIFT AID (NON-NEED-BASED) ***Total amount:*** $9,444,211 (13% Federal, 45% state, 28% institutional, 14% external sources). ***Receiving aid:*** *Freshmen:* 16% (350); *Undergraduates:* 17% (1,425). ***Scholarships, grants, and awards by category:*** *Academic Interests/Achievement:* biological sciences, business, communication, computer science, engineering/technologies, general academic interests/achievements, health fields, mathematics, military science, physical sciences, premedicine, social sciences. *Creative Arts/Performance:* applied art and design, art/fine arts, cinema/film/broadcasting. *Special Characteristics:* children of faculty/staff, international students, members of minority groups, veterans. ***Tuition waivers:*** Full or partial for employees or children of employees. ***ROTC:*** Army, Naval cooperative, Air Force.

LOANS ***Student loans:*** $35,567,436 (68% need-based, 32% non-need-based). ***Average need-based loan:*** Freshmen: $3750; Undergraduates: $4200. ***Parent loans:*** $5,857,669 (33% need-based, 67% non-need-based). ***Programs:*** Federal Direct (Subsidized and Unsubsidized Stafford, PLUS), Perkins, alternative loans.

WORK-STUDY ***Federal work-study:*** *Total amount:* $2,546,296; 2,090 jobs averaging $1218. ***State or other work-study/employment:*** *Total amount:* $4,453,704 (100% non-need-based). 2,500 part-time jobs averaging $1781.

APPLYING for FINANCIAL AID ***Required financial aid form:*** FAFSA. ***Financial aid deadline (priority):*** 3/15. ***Notification date:*** Continuous. Students must reply by 5/1 or within 2 weeks of notification.

CONTACT Mrs. Verna Hazen, Director of Financial Aid, Rochester Institute of Technology, 56 Lomb Memorial Drive, Rochester, NY 14623-5604, 716-475-2186. *Fax:* 716-475-7270. *E-mail:* finaid@rit.edu

ROCKFORD COLLEGE

Rockford, IL

Tuition & fees: $16,800 **Average undergraduate aid package: N/A**

ABOUT THE INSTITUTION Independent, coed. Awards: bachelor's and master's degrees. 50 undergraduate majors. Total enrollment: 1,328. Undergraduates: 1,019. Federal methodology is used as a basis for awarding need-based institutional aid.

UNDERGRADUATE EXPENSES for 2000–2001 ***Application fee:*** $35. ***Comprehensive fee:*** $22,230 includes full-time tuition ($16,800) and room and board ($5430). ***College room only:*** $3300. Room and board charges vary according to board plan and housing facility. ***Payment plans:*** installment, deferred payment.

GIFT AID (NEED-BASED) ***Scholarships, grants, and awards:*** Federal Pell, FSEOG, state, private, college/university gift aid from institutional funds.

GIFT AID (NON-NEED-BASED) ***Scholarships, grants, and awards by category:*** *Academic Interests/Achievement:* biological sciences, business, education, English, general academic interests/achievements, mathematics, physical sciences, premedicine. *Creative Arts/Performance:* dance,

Rockford College (continued)

music, theater/drama. *Special Characteristics:* children and siblings of alumni, children of current students, children of educators, children of faculty/staff, children of workers in trades, general special characteristics, handicapped students, international students, out-of-state students, parents of current students, relatives of clergy, siblings of current students. ***Tuition waivers:*** Full or partial for employees or children of employees. ***ROTC:*** Army cooperative.

LOANS ***Programs:*** FFEL (Subsidized and Unsubsidized Stafford, PLUS), Perkins, college/university, alternative loans.

WORK-STUDY Federal work-study jobs available.

APPLYING for FINANCIAL AID ***Required financial aid forms:*** FAFSA, institution's own form, financial aid transcript (for transfers). ***Financial aid deadline (priority):*** 4/15. ***Notification date:*** Continuous.

CONTACT Ms. Roberta Fitt, Director of Financial Aid, Rockford College, 5050 East State Street, Rockford, IL 61108, 815-226-3383 or toll-free 800-892-2984. *Fax:* 815-226-4119.

ROCKHURST UNIVERSITY

Kansas City, MO

Tuition & fees: $13,845 **Average undergraduate aid package: $12,785**

ABOUT THE INSTITUTION Independent Roman Catholic (Jesuit), coed. Awards: bachelor's and master's degrees and post-bachelor's certificates. 37 undergraduate majors. Total enrollment: 2,955. Undergraduates: 2,097. Freshmen: 309. Both federal and institutional methodology are used as a basis for awarding need-based institutional aid.

UNDERGRADUATE EXPENSES for 2000–2001 (est.) ***Application fee:*** $20. ***One-time required fee:*** $40. ***Comprehensive fee:*** $18,865 includes full-time tuition ($13,500), mandatory fees ($345), and room and board ($5020). ***College room only:*** $2375. Full-time tuition and fees vary according to course load. Room and board charges vary according to board plan, gender, and housing facility. ***Part-time tuition:*** $453 per semester hour. ***Part-time fees:*** $15 per term part-time. Part-time tuition and fees vary according to class time, course load, and program. ***Payment plans:*** installment, deferred payment.

FRESHMAN FINANCIAL AID (Fall 1999, est.) 238 applied for aid; of those 89% were deemed to have need. 100% of freshmen with need received aid. *Average financial aid package:* $13,175 (excluding resources awarded to replace EFC). 16% of all full-time freshmen had no need and received non-need-based aid.

UNDERGRADUATE FINANCIAL AID (Fall 1999, est.) 850 applied for aid; of those 89% were deemed to have need. 100% of undergraduates with need received aid. *Average financial aid package:* $12,785 (excluding resources awarded to replace EFC). 24% of all full-time undergraduates had no need and received non-need-based aid.

GIFT AID (NEED-BASED) ***Total amount:*** $3,445,495 (22% Federal, 13% state, 38% institutional, 27% external sources). ***Receiving aid:*** *Freshmen:* 55% (166); *all full-time undergraduates:* 46% (585). ***Average award:*** Freshmen: $3555; Undergraduates: $3203. ***Scholarships, grants, and awards:*** Federal Pell, FSEOG, state, private, college/university gift aid from institutional funds.

GIFT AID (NON-NEED-BASED) ***Total amount:*** $5,405,623 (3% state, 97% institutional). ***Receiving aid:*** *Freshmen:* 65% (198); *Undergraduates:* 51% (661). ***Scholarships, grants, and awards by category:*** *Academic Interests/Achievement:* 557 awards ($2,492,501 total): biological sciences, business, communication, computer science, education, English, foreign languages, general academic interests/achievements, health fields, humanities, international studies, mathematics, physical sciences, premedicine, religion/biblical studies, social sciences. *Creative Arts/Performance:* 42 awards ($72,066 total): creative writing, music, performing arts, theater/drama. *Special Achievements/Activities:* 172 awards ($325,000 total): community service, leadership, memberships, religious involvement. *Special Characteristics:* 292 awards ($622,381 total): children and siblings of alumni, children of faculty/staff, international students, local/state students, relatives of clergy, religious affiliation, siblings of current students. ***Tuition waivers:*** Full or partial for children of alumni, employees or children of employees, senior citizens. ***ROTC:*** Army cooperative.

LOANS ***Student loans:*** $4,267,008 (72% need-based, 28% non-need-based). 66% of past graduating class borrowed through all loan programs. Average indebtedness per student: $15,106. ***Average need-based loan:*** Freshmen: $4250; Undergraduates: $5184. ***Parent loans:*** $675,052 (100% need-based). ***Programs:*** FFEL (Subsidized and Unsubsidized Stafford, PLUS), Perkins, state.

WORK-STUDY ***Federal work-study:*** *Total amount:* $387,178; 237 jobs averaging $1634. ***State or other work-study/employment:*** *Total amount:* $77,228 (100% need-based). 44 part-time jobs averaging $1755.

ATHLETIC AWARDS *Total amount:* 1,070,891 (100% non-need-based).

APPLYING for FINANCIAL AID ***Required financial aid forms:*** FAFSA, institution's own form. ***Financial aid deadline (priority):*** 2/15. ***Notification date:*** Continuous beginning 3/1. Students must reply within 3 weeks of notification.

CONTACT Mr. Paul Gordon, Director of Financial Aid, Rockhurst University, 1100 Rockhurst Road, Kansas City, MO 64110-2561, 816-501-4100 or toll-free 800-842-6776. *Fax:* 816-501-4241. *E-mail:* paul.gordon@rockhurst.edu

ROCKY MOUNTAIN COLLEGE

Billings, MT

Tuition & fees: $12,243 **Average undergraduate aid package: $10,387**

ABOUT THE INSTITUTION Independent interdenominational, coed. Awards: associate and bachelor's degrees. 57 undergraduate majors. Total enrollment: 801. Undergraduates: 801. Freshmen: 147. Federal methodology is used as a basis for awarding need-based institutional aid.

UNDERGRADUATE EXPENSES for 2000–2001 (est.) ***Application fee:*** $25. ***Comprehensive fee:*** $16,390 includes full-time tuition ($12,088), mandatory fees ($155), and room and board ($4147). ***College room only:*** $1625. Full-time tuition and fees vary according to course load, program, and reciprocity agreements. Room and board charges vary according to board plan and housing facility. ***Part-time tuition:*** $504 per semester hour. ***Part-time fees:*** $35 per term part-time. Part-time tuition and fees vary according to course load and program. ***Payment plan:*** installment.

FRESHMAN FINANCIAL AID (Fall 1999, est.) 139 applied for aid; of those 78% were deemed to have need. 100% of freshmen with need received aid; of those 20% had need fully met. *Average percent of need met:* 69% (excluding resources awarded to replace EFC). *Average financial aid package:* $9311 (excluding resources awarded to replace EFC). 16% of all full-time freshmen had no need and received non-need-based aid.

UNDERGRADUATE FINANCIAL AID (Fall 1999, est.) 684 applied for aid; of those 82% were deemed to have need. 100% of undergraduates with need received aid; of those 13% had need fully met. *Average percent of need met:* 74% (excluding resources awarded to replace EFC). *Average financial aid package:* $10,387 (excluding resources awarded to replace EFC). 13% of all full-time undergraduates had no need and received non-need-based aid.

GIFT AID (NEED-BASED) ***Total amount:*** $2,601,012 (28% Federal, 52% institutional, 20% external sources). ***Receiving aid:*** *Freshmen:* 73% (108); *all full-time undergraduates:* 80% (564). ***Average award:*** Freshmen: $6063; Undergraduates: $5072. ***Scholarships, grants, and awards:*** Federal Pell, FSEOG, state, private, college/university gift aid from institutional funds.

GIFT AID (NON-NEED-BASED) ***Total amount:*** $341,019 (90% institutional, 10% external sources). ***Receiving aid:*** *Freshmen:* 7% (10); *Undergraduates:* 6% (42). ***Scholarships, grants, and awards by category:*** *Academic Interests/Achievement:* 285 awards ($602,678 total): biological sciences, business, education, English, general academic interests/achievements, health fields, humanities, mathematics, physical sciences, premedicine, religion/biblical studies, social sciences. *Creative Arts/Performance:* 79 awards ($116,950 total): art/fine arts, debating, music, theater/drama. *Special Characteristics:* 60 awards ($232,103 total): children and siblings of alumni, children of faculty/staff, international students, members of minority groups, religious affiliation. ***Tuition waivers:*** Full or partial for employees or children of employees.

LOANS ***Student loans:*** $3,733,948 (96% need-based, 4% non-need-based). 73% of past graduating class borrowed through all loan programs. Average indebtedness per student: $16,606. ***Average need-based loan:*** Freshmen: $2803; Undergraduates: $3995. ***Parent loans:*** $621,376 (100% need-based). ***Programs:*** FFEL (Subsidized and Unsubsidized Stafford, PLUS), Perkins.

WORK-STUDY ***Federal work-study:*** *Total amount:* $137,387; 296 jobs averaging $464. ***State or other work-study/employment:*** *Total amount:* $125,920 (70% need-based, 30% non-need-based). 135 part-time jobs averaging $655.

ATHLETIC AWARDS *Total amount:* 935,397 (81% need-based, 19% non-need-based).

APPLYING for FINANCIAL AID ***Required financial aid forms:*** FAFSA, institution's own form. ***Financial aid deadline (priority):*** 4/1. ***Notification date:*** Continuous. Students must reply within 4 weeks of notification.

CONTACT Ms. Judy Chapman, Director of Student Financial Assistance, Rocky Mountain College, 1511 Poly Drive, Billings, MT 59102-1796, 406-657-1031 or toll-free 800-877-6259. *Fax:* 406-259-9751. *E-mail:* chapmanj@rocky.edu

ROCKY MOUNTAIN COLLEGE OF ART & DESIGN

Denver, CO

Tuition & fees: $15,510 **Average undergraduate aid package: $3725**

ABOUT THE INSTITUTION Proprietary, coed. Awards: bachelor's degrees. 5 undergraduate majors. Total enrollment: 410. Undergraduates: 410. Freshmen: 80. Federal methodology is used as a basis for awarding need-based institutional aid.

UNDERGRADUATE EXPENSES for 1999–2000 ***Application fee:*** $50. ***Tuition:*** full-time $15,480; part-time $430 per credit. ***Required fees:*** full-time $30; $15 per term part-time. ***Payment plan:*** installment.

FRESHMAN FINANCIAL AID (Fall 1998) 92 applied for aid; of those 91% were deemed to have need. 76% of freshmen with need received aid; of those 5% had need fully met. *Average percent of need met:* 38% (excluding resources awarded to replace EFC). *Average financial aid package:* $3501 (excluding resources awarded to replace EFC). 2% of all full-time freshmen had no need and received non-need-based aid.

UNDERGRADUATE FINANCIAL AID (Fall 1998) 418 applied for aid; of those 93% were deemed to have need. 83% of undergraduates with need received aid; of those 5% had need fully met. *Average percent of need met:* 24% (excluding resources awarded to replace EFC). *Average financial aid package:* $3725 (excluding resources awarded to replace EFC). 2% of all full-time undergraduates had no need and received non-need-based aid.

GIFT AID (NEED-BASED) ***Total amount:*** $401,515 (80% Federal, 20% state). ***Receiving aid:*** *Freshmen:* 33% (36); *all full-time undergraduates:* 30% (147). ***Average award:*** Freshmen: $2505; Undergraduates: $2262. ***Scholarships, grants, and awards:*** Federal Pell, FSEOG, state, college/university gift aid from institutional funds.

GIFT AID (NON-NEED-BASED) ***Total amount:*** $215,462 (5% state, 95% institutional). ***Receiving aid:*** *Freshmen:* 13% (14); *Undergraduates:* 19% (95). ***Scholarships, grants, and awards by category:*** *Academic Interests/Achievement:* general academic interests/achievements. *Creative Arts/Performance:* applied art and design, art/fine arts. *Special Characteristics:* children of faculty/staff. ***Tuition waivers:*** Full or partial for employees or children of employees.

LOANS ***Student loans:*** $1,178,224 (100% need-based). 81% of past graduating class borrowed through all loan programs. ***Average need-based loan:*** Freshmen: $2625; Undergraduates: $3708. ***Parent loans:*** $455,372 (100% need-based). ***Programs:*** Federal Direct (Subsidized and Unsubsidized Stafford, PLUS), FFEL (Subsidized and Unsubsidized Stafford, PLUS), Perkins, alternative loans.

WORK-STUDY ***Federal work-study:*** *Total amount:* $36,795; 19 jobs averaging $1774. ***State or other work-study/employment:*** *Total amount:* $5000 (100% need-based). 3 part-time jobs averaging $1667.

APPLYING for FINANCIAL AID ***Required financial aid forms:*** FAFSA, institution's own form, state aid form. ***Financial aid deadline (priority):*** 3/1. ***Notification date:*** Continuous beginning 4/1. Students must reply within 3 weeks of notification.

CONTACT Sherri Thompson, Director of Financial Aid, Rocky Mountain College of Art & Design, 6875 East Evans Avenue, Denver, CO 80224-2329, 303-753-6046 or toll-free 800-888-ARTS. *Fax:* 303-759-4970. *E-mail:* sthompson@rmcad.edu

ROGER WILLIAMS UNIVERSITY

Bristol, RI

Tuition & fees: $17,980 **Average undergraduate aid package: $14,462**

ABOUT THE INSTITUTION Independent, coed. Awards: associate, bachelor's, master's, and first professional degrees. 42 undergraduate majors. Total enrollment: 3,833. Undergraduates: 3,375. Freshmen: 772. Both federal and institutional methodology are used as a basis for awarding need-based institutional aid.

UNDERGRADUATE EXPENSES for 2000–2001 (est.) ***Application fee:*** $35. ***One-time required fee:*** $100. ***Comprehensive fee:*** $26,180 includes full-time tuition ($17,300), mandatory fees ($680), and room and board ($8200). ***College room only:*** $4300. Full-time tuition and fees vary according to class time, course load, and program. Room and board charges vary according to board plan and housing facility. ***Part-time tuition:*** $725 per credit. ***Part-time fees:*** $350 per term part-time. Part-time tuition and fees vary according to class time. ***Payment plans:*** installment, deferred payment.

FRESHMAN FINANCIAL AID (Fall 1999, est.) 617 applied for aid; of those 87% were deemed to have need. 99% of freshmen with need received aid; of those 44% had need fully met. *Average percent of need met:* 93% (excluding resources awarded to replace EFC). *Average financial aid package:* $14,978 (excluding resources awarded to replace EFC). 9% of all full-time freshmen had no need and received non-need-based aid.

UNDERGRADUATE FINANCIAL AID (Fall 1999, est.) 1,704 applied for aid; of those 89% were deemed to have need. 97% of undergraduates with need received aid; of those 46% had need fully met. *Average percent of need met:* 93% (excluding resources awarded to replace EFC). *Average financial aid package:* $14,462 (excluding resources awarded to replace EFC). 8% of all full-time undergraduates had no need and received non-need-based aid.

GIFT AID (NEED-BASED) ***Total amount:*** $8,884,829 (14% Federal, 2% state, 84% institutional). ***Receiving aid:*** *Freshmen:* 54% (414); *all full-time undergraduates:* 53% (1,154). ***Average award:*** Freshmen: $7900; Undergraduates: $7664. ***Scholarships, grants, and awards:*** Federal Pell, FSEOG, state, private, college/university gift aid from institutional funds.

GIFT AID (NON-NEED-BASED) ***Total amount:*** $5,501,075 (95% institutional, 5% external sources). ***Receiving aid:*** *Freshmen:* 33% (253); *Undergraduates:* 25% (547). ***Scholarships, grants, and awards by category:*** *Academic Interests/Achievement:* general academic interests/achievements. ***Tuition waivers:*** Full or partial for employees or children of employees. ***ROTC:*** Army cooperative.

LOANS ***Student loans:*** $8,006,864 (69% need-based, 31% non-need-based). 75% of past graduating class borrowed through all loan programs. Average indebtedness per student: $17,125. ***Average need-based loan:*** Freshmen: $3265; Undergraduates: $4176. ***Parent loans:*** $5,187,718 (100% non-need-based). ***Programs:*** FFEL (Subsidized and Unsubsidized Stafford, PLUS), Perkins, state.

WORK-STUDY ***Federal work-study:*** *Total amount:* $536,250; 429 jobs averaging $1250. ***State or other work-study/employment:*** *Total amount:* $599,550 (100% need-based). 571 part-time jobs averaging $1050.

APPLYING for FINANCIAL AID ***Required financial aid forms:*** FAFSA, CSS Financial Aid PROFILE. ***Financial aid deadline (priority):*** 3/1. ***Notification date:*** Continuous beginning 4/1. Students must reply within 2 weeks of notification.

Roger Williams University (continued)

CONTACT Barry Paine, Director of Financial Aid, Roger Williams University, 1 Old Ferry Road, Bristol, RI 02809, 401-254-3100 or toll-free 800-458-7144 (out-of-state). *Fax:* 401-254-3356.

ROLLINS COLLEGE

Winter Park, FL

Tuition & fees: $21,852 **Average undergraduate aid package: $23,356**

ABOUT THE INSTITUTION Independent, coed. Awards: bachelor's and master's degrees. 35 undergraduate majors. Total enrollment: 2,256. Undergraduates: 1,519. Freshmen: 448. Federal methodology is used as a basis for awarding need-based institutional aid.

UNDERGRADUATE EXPENSES for 1999–2000 ***Application fee:*** $40. ***Comprehensive fee:*** $28,552 includes full-time tuition ($21,250), mandatory fees ($602), and room and board ($6700). ***College room only:*** $3850. ***Payment plans:*** tuition prepayment, installment.

FRESHMAN FINANCIAL AID (Fall 1999, est.) 247 applied for aid; of those 81% were deemed to have need. 97% of freshmen with need received aid; of those 31% had need fully met. *Average percent of need met:* 91% (excluding resources awarded to replace EFC). *Average financial aid package:* $22,703 (excluding resources awarded to replace EFC). 24% of all full-time freshmen had no need and received non-need-based aid.

UNDERGRADUATE FINANCIAL AID (Fall 1999, est.) 845 applied for aid; of those 86% were deemed to have need. 94% of undergraduates with need received aid; of those 36% had need fully met. *Average percent of need met:* 90% (excluding resources awarded to replace EFC). *Average financial aid package:* $23,356 (excluding resources awarded to replace EFC). 24% of all full-time undergraduates had no need and received non-need-based aid.

GIFT AID (NEED-BASED) ***Total amount:*** $10,342,621 (7% Federal, 14% state, 78% institutional, 1% external sources). ***Receiving aid:*** *Freshmen:* 40% (179); *all full-time undergraduates:* 44% (665). ***Average award:*** Freshmen: $17,869; Undergraduates: $17,648. ***Scholarships, grants, and awards:*** Federal Pell, FSEOG, state, private, college/university gift aid from institutional funds.

GIFT AID (NON-NEED-BASED) ***Total amount:*** $3,469,587 (1% Federal, 24% state, 73% institutional, 2% external sources). ***Receiving aid:*** *Freshmen:* 14% (62); *Undergraduates:* 9% (141). ***Scholarships, grants, and awards by category:*** *Academic Interests/Achievement:* computer science, engineering/technologies, general academic interests/achievements, mathematics, physical sciences. *Creative Arts/Performance:* art/fine arts, music, theater/drama. ***Tuition waivers:*** Full or partial for employees or children of employees.

LOANS ***Student loans:*** $3,087,406 (80% need-based, 20% non-need-based). Average indebtedness per student: $14,600. ***Average need-based loan:*** Freshmen: $3545; Undergraduates: $3973. ***Parent loans:*** $1,256,085 (6% need-based, 94% non-need-based). ***Programs:*** Federal Direct (Subsidized and Unsubsidized Stafford, PLUS), Perkins.

WORK-STUDY ***Federal work-study:*** *Total amount:* $321,724; jobs available. ***State or other work-study/employment:*** *Total amount:* $62,900 (15% need-based, 85% non-need-based). Part-time jobs available.

ATHLETIC AWARDS *Total amount:* 1,350,676 (21% need-based, 79% non-need-based).

APPLYING for FINANCIAL AID ***Required financial aid form:*** FAFSA. ***Financial aid deadline:*** 3/1.

CONTACT Mr. Phil Asbury, Director of Student Financial Planning, Rollins College, 1000 Holt Avenue-2721, Winter Park, FL 32789-4499, 407-646-2395. *Fax:* 407-646-2600. *E-mail:* pasbury@rollins.edu

ROOSEVELT UNIVERSITY

Chicago, IL

ABOUT THE INSTITUTION Independent, coed. Awards: bachelor's, master's, and doctoral degrees. 67 undergraduate majors. Total enrollment: 6,837. Undergraduates: 4,368. Freshmen: 266.

GIFT AID (NEED-BASED) ***Scholarships, grants, and awards:*** Federal Pell, FSEOG, state, private, college/university gift aid from institutional funds.

GIFT AID (NON-NEED-BASED) ***Scholarships, grants, and awards by category:*** *Academic Interests/Achievement:* general academic interests/achievements. *Creative Arts/Performance:* music, theater/drama.

LOANS ***Programs:*** FFEL (Subsidized and Unsubsidized Stafford, PLUS), Perkins, college/university.

WORK-STUDY ***Federal work-study:*** *Total amount:* $261,908; 119 jobs averaging $2413.

APPLYING for FINANCIAL AID ***Required financial aid form:*** FAFSA.

CONTACT Mr. Walter J. H. O'Neill, Director of Financial Aid, Roosevelt University, 430 South Michigan Avenue, Chicago, IL 60605-1394, 312-341-3565 or toll-free 877-APPLYRU. *Fax:* 312-341-3545. *E-mail:* woneill@roosevelt.edu

ROSE-HULMAN INSTITUTE OF TECHNOLOGY

Terre Haute, IN

Tuition & fees: $19,545 **Average undergraduate aid package: $12,274**

ABOUT THE INSTITUTION Independent, coed, primarily men. Awards: bachelor's and master's degrees. 11 undergraduate majors. Total enrollment: 1,678. Undergraduates: 1,545. Freshmen: 395. Federal methodology is used as a basis for awarding need-based institutional aid.

UNDERGRADUATE EXPENSES for 1999–2000 ***Application fee:*** $40. ***Comprehensive fee:*** $25,020 includes full-time tuition ($19,440), mandatory fees ($105), and room and board ($5475). ***College room only:*** $3000. Full-time tuition and fees vary according to course load and student level. Room and board charges vary according to board plan. ***Part-time tuition:*** $505 per credit. Part-time tuition and fees vary according to course load. ***Payment plans:*** tuition prepayment, installment.

FRESHMAN FINANCIAL AID (Fall 1999, est.) 346 applied for aid; of those 84% were deemed to have need. 100% of freshmen with need received aid; of those 29% had need fully met. *Average percent of need met:* 83% (excluding resources awarded to replace EFC). *Average financial aid package:* $14,017 (excluding resources awarded to replace EFC). 21% of all full-time freshmen had no need and received non-need-based aid.

UNDERGRADUATE FINANCIAL AID (Fall 1999, est.) 1,259 applied for aid; of those 92% were deemed to have need. 100% of undergraduates with need received aid; of those 20% had need fully met. *Average percent of need met:* 78% (excluding resources awarded to replace EFC). *Average financial aid package:* $12,274 (excluding resources awarded to replace EFC). 20% of all full-time undergraduates had no need and received non-need-based aid.

GIFT AID (NEED-BASED) ***Total amount:*** $5,190,725 (12% Federal, 30% state, 58% institutional). ***Receiving aid:*** *Freshmen:* 63% (250); *all full-time undergraduates:* 72% (1,074). ***Average award:*** Freshmen: $4575; Undergraduates: $4803. ***Scholarships, grants, and awards:*** Federal Pell, FSEOG, state, private, college/university gift aid from institutional funds.

GIFT AID (NON-NEED-BASED) ***Total amount:*** $6,285,216 (68% institutional, 32% external sources). ***Receiving aid:*** *Freshmen:* 61% (242); *Undergraduates:* 64% (949). ***Scholarships, grants, and awards by category:*** *Academic Interests/Achievement:* 1,421 awards ($3,493,261 total): computer science, engineering/technologies, general academic interests/achievements, mathematics, physical sciences. *Special Characteristics:* 95 awards ($389,816 total): local/state students, members of minority groups. ***Tuition waivers:*** Full or partial for employees or children of employees. ***ROTC:*** Army, Air Force.

LOANS ***Student loans:*** $7,122,723 (69% need-based, 31% non-need-based). 90% of past graduating class borrowed through all loan programs. Average indebtedness per student: $22,000. ***Average need-based loan:*** Freshmen: $5585; Undergraduates: $4078. ***Parent loans:*** $4,525,108 (100% non-need-based). ***Programs:*** Federal Direct (Subsidized and Unsubsidized Stafford, PLUS), Perkins, college/university.

WORK-STUDY ***Federal work-study:*** *Total amount:* $353,295; 231 jobs averaging $1529. ***State or other work-study/employment:*** *Total amount:* $1,166,493 (100% need-based). 809 part-time jobs averaging $1442.

APPLYING for FINANCIAL AID ***Required financial aid form:*** FAFSA. ***Financial aid deadline (priority):*** 3/1. ***Notification date:*** Continuous.

CONTACT Darin J. Greggs, Director of Financial Aid, Rose-Hulman Institute of Technology, 5500 Wabash Avenue, Box #5, Terre Haute, IN 47803, 812-877-8259 or toll-free 800-552-0725 (in-state), 800-248-7448 (out-of-state). *Fax:* 812-877-8746. *E-mail:* darin.greggs@rose-hulman.edu

ROSEMONT COLLEGE

Rosemont, PA

Tuition & fees: $15,270 **Average undergraduate aid package: N/A**

ABOUT THE INSTITUTION Independent Roman Catholic, women only. Awards: bachelor's and master's degrees. 24 undergraduate majors. Total enrollment: 1,174. Undergraduates: 953. Freshmen: 116.

UNDERGRADUATE EXPENSES for 2000–2001 ***Application fee:*** $35. ***Comprehensive fee:*** $22,300 includes full-time tuition ($14,580), mandatory fees ($690), and room and board ($7030). ***Part-time tuition:*** $1680 per course. ***Part-time fees:*** $64 per course. ***Payment plan:*** installment.

GIFT AID (NEED-BASED) ***Scholarships, grants, and awards:*** Federal Pell, FSEOG, state, college/university gift aid from institutional funds.

GIFT AID (NON-NEED-BASED) ***Scholarships, grants, and awards by category:*** *Academic Interests/Achievement:* general academic interests/achievements. *Creative Arts/Performance:* art/fine arts. *Special Characteristics:* children of educators, siblings of current students. ***Tuition waivers:*** Full or partial for employees or children of employees, senior citizens. ***ROTC:*** Army cooperative, Air Force cooperative.

LOANS ***Programs:*** FFEL (Subsidized and Unsubsidized Stafford, PLUS), Perkins.

WORK-STUDY Federal work-study jobs available.

APPLYING for FINANCIAL AID ***Required financial aid form:*** FAFSA. ***Financial aid deadline (priority):*** 3/1. ***Notification date:*** Continuous.

CONTACT Financial Aid Counselor, Rosemont College, 1400 Montgomery Avenue, Rosemont, PA 19010, 610-527-0200 Ext. 2221 or toll-free 800-331-0708.

ROWAN UNIVERSITY

Glassboro, NJ

Tuition & fees (NJ res): $4921 **Average undergraduate aid package: $5235**

ABOUT THE INSTITUTION State-supported, coed. Awards: bachelor's, master's, and doctoral degrees. 53 undergraduate majors. Total enrollment: 9,632. Undergraduates: 8,387. Freshmen: 1,129. Federal methodology is used as a basis for awarding need-based institutional aid.

UNDERGRADUATE EXPENSES for 1999–2000 ***Application fee:*** $50. ***Tuition, state resident:*** full-time $3750; part-time $114 per credit. ***Tuition, nonresident:*** full-time $7500; part-time $228 per credit. ***Required fees:*** full-time $1171; $37 per credit. ***College room and board:*** $5766; ***room only:*** $3660. Room and board charges vary according to board plan and housing facility. ***Payment plan:*** deferred payment.

FRESHMAN FINANCIAL AID (Fall 1998) 999 applied for aid; of those 76% were deemed to have need. 100% of freshmen with need received aid; of those 34% had need fully met. *Average percent of need met:* 82% (excluding resources awarded to replace EFC). *Average financial aid package:* $4610 (excluding resources awarded to replace EFC). 27% of all full-time freshmen had no need and received non-need-based aid.

UNDERGRADUATE FINANCIAL AID (Fall 1998) 4,866 applied for aid; of those 91% were deemed to have need. 100% of undergraduates with need received aid; of those 24% had need fully met. *Average percent of need met:* 84% (excluding resources awarded to replace EFC). *Average financial aid package:* $5235 (excluding resources awarded to replace EFC). 16% of all full-time undergraduates had no need and received non-need-based aid.

GIFT AID (NEED-BASED) ***Total amount:*** $7,956,851 (48% Federal, 46% state, 6% institutional). ***Receiving aid:*** *Freshmen:* 32% (358); *all full-time undergraduates:* 36% (2,409). ***Average award:*** Freshmen: $3839; Undergraduates: $3449. ***Scholarships, grants, and awards:*** Federal Pell, FSEOG, state, private, college/university gift aid from institutional funds.

GIFT AID (NON-NEED-BASED) ***Total amount:*** $1,689,701 (2% Federal, 17% state, 67% institutional, 14% external sources). ***Receiving aid:*** *Freshmen:* 35% (395); *Undergraduates:* 19% (1,266). ***Scholarships, grants, and awards by category:*** *Academic Interests/Achievement:* biological sciences, business, communication, computer science, education, engineering/technologies, general academic interests/achievements, humanities, physical sciences, social sciences. *Creative Arts/Performance:* art/fine arts, general creative arts/performance, music, performing arts. *Special Characteristics:* handicapped students, international students, members of minority groups. ***Tuition waivers:*** Full or partial for employees or children of employees. ***ROTC:*** Army cooperative.

LOANS ***Student loans:*** $15,552,710 (63% need-based, 37% non-need-based). ***Average need-based loan:*** Freshmen: $2542; Undergraduates: $3503. ***Parent loans:*** $1,538,983 (100% non-need-based). ***Programs:*** Federal Direct (Subsidized and Unsubsidized Stafford, PLUS).

WORK-STUDY ***Federal work-study:*** *Total amount:* $420,218; jobs available. ***State or other work-study/employment:*** *Total amount:* $300,000 (100% non-need-based). 298 part-time jobs averaging $1000.

APPLYING for FINANCIAL AID ***Required financial aid form:*** FAFSA. ***Financial aid deadline:*** 3/15. ***Notification date:*** Continuous beginning 5/1.

CONTACT Luis Tavarez, Acting Director of Financial Aid, Rowan University, 201 Mullica Hill Road, Glassboro, NJ 08028-1701, 856-256-4250 or toll-free 800-447-1165 (in-state). *Fax:* 856-256-4413. *E-mail:* tavarez@rowan.edu

RUSH UNIVERSITY

Chicago, IL

Tuition & fees: $12,270 **Average undergraduate aid package: N/A**

ABOUT THE INSTITUTION Independent, coed. Awards: bachelor's, master's, doctoral, and first professional degrees. 3 undergraduate majors. Total enrollment: 1,299. Undergraduates: 197. Both federal and institutional methodology are used as a basis for awarding need-based institutional aid.

UNDERGRADUATE EXPENSES for 1999–2000 ***Application fee:*** $40. ***Tuition:*** full-time $12,270; part-time $360 per quarter hour. Full-time tuition and fees vary according to program. Part-time tuition and fees vary according to program. Room and board charges vary according to housing facility. ***Payment plans:*** installment, deferred payment.

UNDERGRADUATE FINANCIAL AID (Fall 1999) 179 applied for aid; of those 89% were deemed to have need. 100% of undergraduates with need received aid; of those 100% had need fully met. *Average percent of need met:* 100% (excluding resources awarded to replace EFC). 3% of all full-time undergraduates had no need and received non-need-based aid.

GIFT AID (NEED-BASED) ***Total amount:*** $709,219 (31% Federal, 36% state, 28% institutional, 5% external sources). ***Receiving aid:*** *All full-time undergraduates:* 56% (136). ***Average award:*** Undergraduates: $6000. ***Scholarships, grants, and awards:*** Federal Pell, FSEOG, state, private, college/university gift aid from institutional funds.

GIFT AID (NON-NEED-BASED) ***Total amount:*** $282,210 (100% institutional). ***Receiving aid:*** *Undergraduates:* 6% (15). ***Scholarships, grants, and awards by category:*** *Academic Interests/Achievement:* 23 awards ($282,210 total): general academic interests/achievements. *Special Characteristics:* 6 awards ($58,030 total): children of faculty/staff, members of minority groups. ***Tuition waivers:*** Full or partial for employees or children of employees.

LOANS ***Student loans:*** $1,634,312 (100% need-based). 75% of past graduating class borrowed through all loan programs. Average indebtedness per student: $19,230. ***Average need-based loan:*** Undergraduates:

Rush University (continued)

$5500. ***Parent loans:*** $190,370 (100% need-based). ***Programs:*** FFEL (Subsidized and Unsubsidized Stafford, PLUS), Perkins, Federal Nursing, state, college/university.

WORK-STUDY ***Federal work-study:*** *Total amount:* $25,000; 12 jobs averaging $2083. ***State or other work-study/employment:*** *Total amount:* $190,000 (100% need-based). Part-time jobs available.

APPLYING for FINANCIAL AID ***Required financial aid forms:*** FAFSA, institution's own form. ***Financial aid deadline:*** 4/1 (priority: 3/1). ***Notification date:*** Continuous beginning 6/1. Students must reply within 3 weeks of notification.

CONTACT Mr. Robert A. Dame, Director, Student Financial Aid, Rush University, 600 South Paulina Street, Suite 440, Chicago, IL 60612-3832, 312-942-6256. *Fax:* 312-942-2219.

RUSSELL SAGE COLLEGE

Troy, NY

Tuition & fees: $15,300 **Average undergraduate aid package: $12,583**

ABOUT THE INSTITUTION Independent, women only. Awards: bachelor's degrees. 29 undergraduate majors. Total enrollment: 842. Undergraduates: 842. Freshmen: 109. Federal methodology is used as a basis for awarding need-based institutional aid.

UNDERGRADUATE EXPENSES for 1999–2000 ***Application fee:*** $30. ***Comprehensive fee:*** $21,650 includes full-time tuition ($14,920), mandatory fees ($380), and room and board ($6350). ***College room only:*** $3250. Room and board charges vary according to board plan and housing facility. ***Part-time tuition:*** $500 per credit hour. Part-time tuition and fees vary according to program.

FRESHMAN FINANCIAL AID (Fall 1999, est.) 155 applied for aid; of those 100% were deemed to have need. 100% of freshmen with need received aid. *Average percent of need met:* 60% (excluding resources awarded to replace EFC). *Average financial aid package:* $13,856 (excluding resources awarded to replace EFC).

UNDERGRADUATE FINANCIAL AID (Fall 1999, est.) 788 applied for aid; of those 100% were deemed to have need. 100% of undergraduates with need received aid. *Average percent of need met:* 55% (excluding resources awarded to replace EFC). *Average financial aid package:* $12,583 (excluding resources awarded to replace EFC).

GIFT AID (NEED-BASED) ***Total amount:*** $6,236,910 (13% Federal, 19% state, 65% institutional, 3% external sources). ***Receiving aid:*** *Freshmen:* 95% (154); *all full-time undergraduates:* 80% (731). ***Average award:*** Freshmen: $2919; Undergraduates: $3410. ***Scholarships, grants, and awards:*** Federal Pell, FSEOG, state, private, college/university gift aid from institutional funds.

GIFT AID (NON-NEED-BASED) ***Receiving aid:*** *Freshmen:* 28% (45); *Undergraduates:* 35% (325). ***Scholarships, grants, and awards by category:*** *Academic Interests/Achievement:* 423 awards ($1,462,755 total): general academic interests/achievements, health fields. *Special Characteristics:* 25 awards ($16,392 total): children and siblings of alumni. ***Tuition waivers:*** Full or partial for employees or children of employees, senior citizens. ***ROTC:*** Army cooperative, Air Force cooperative.

LOANS ***Student loans:*** $4,657,186 (66% need-based, 34% non-need-based). 66% of past graduating class borrowed through all loan programs. Average indebtedness per student: $11,350. ***Average need-based loan:*** Freshmen: $1916; Undergraduates: $4373. ***Parent loans:*** $947,300 (100% non-need-based). ***Programs:*** FFEL (Subsidized and Unsubsidized Stafford, PLUS), Perkins, college/university.

WORK-STUDY ***Federal work-study:*** *Total amount:* $352,106; 390 jobs averaging $1200. ***State or other work-study/employment:*** *Total amount:* $127,875 (100% non-need-based). 95 part-time jobs averaging $1200.

APPLYING for FINANCIAL AID ***Required financial aid forms:*** FAFSA, state aid form. ***Financial aid deadline (priority):*** 3/1. ***Notification date:*** Continuous beginning 4/1. Students must reply within 2 weeks of notification.

CONTACT Ms. Cathy Berrahou, Associate Director, Student Financial Services, Russell Sage College, 140 New Scotland Avenue, Albany, NY 12208-4115, 518-292-1758 or toll-free 888-VERY-SAGE (in-state), 888-VERY SAGE (out-of-state). *Fax:* 518-292-7701. *E-mail:* berrac@sage.edu

RUST COLLEGE

Holly Springs, MS

Tuition & fees: $5200 **Average undergraduate aid package: N/A**

ABOUT THE INSTITUTION Independent United Methodist, coed. Awards: associate and bachelor's degrees. 25 undergraduate majors. Total enrollment: 843. Undergraduates: 843. Freshmen: 208. Both federal and institutional methodology are used as a basis for awarding need-based institutional aid.

UNDERGRADUATE EXPENSES for 1999–2000 ***Application fee:*** $10. ***Comprehensive fee:*** $7600 includes full-time tuition ($5200) and room and board ($2400). ***Part-time tuition:*** $225 per credit hour. ***Payment plan:*** installment.

GIFT AID (NEED-BASED) ***Scholarships, grants, and awards:*** Federal Pell, FSEOG, state, private, college/university gift aid from institutional funds, United Negro College Fund.

GIFT AID (NON-NEED-BASED) ***Scholarships, grants, and awards by category:*** *Academic Interests/Achievement:* general academic interests/achievements. *Creative Arts/Performance:* music, theater/drama. *Special Characteristics:* children of faculty/staff, ethnic background, international students, local/state students, members of minority groups, relatives of clergy, religious affiliation, siblings of current students, veterans. ***Tuition waivers:*** Full or partial for employees or children of employees.

LOANS ***Programs:*** FFEL (Subsidized and Unsubsidized Stafford, PLUS), Perkins, United Methodist Student Loans.

WORK-STUDY Federal work-study jobs available.

APPLYING for FINANCIAL AID ***Required financial aid forms:*** FAFSA, institution's own form. ***Financial aid deadline (priority):*** 4/1. ***Notification date:*** 6/1. Students must reply within 2 weeks of notification.

CONTACT Mrs. Helen L. Street, Director of Financial Aid, Rust College, 150 Rust Avenue, Holly Springs, MS 38635, 662-252-8000 or toll-free 888-886-8492 Ext. 4065. *Fax:* 662-252-8895.

RUTGERS, THE STATE UNIVERSITY OF NEW JERSEY, CAMDEN COLLEGE OF ARTS AND SCIENCES

Camden, NJ

Tuition & fees (NJ res): $5874 **Average undergraduate aid package: $7720**

ABOUT THE INSTITUTION State-supported, coed. Awards: bachelor's degrees. 46 undergraduate majors. Total enrollment: 2,813. Undergraduates: 2,813. Freshmen: 299. Federal methodology is used as a basis for awarding need-based institutional aid.

UNDERGRADUATE EXPENSES for 1999–2000 ***Application fee:*** $50. ***Tuition, state resident:*** full-time $4762. ***Tuition, nonresident:*** full-time $9692. ***Required fees:*** full-time $1112. Full-time tuition and fees vary according to location. Part-time tuition and fees vary according to course load. ***College room and board:*** $5548; ***room only:*** $3348. Room and board charges vary according to board plan and housing facility. ***Payment plan:*** deferred payment.

FRESHMAN FINANCIAL AID (Fall 1999) 245 applied for aid; of those 79% were deemed to have need. 99% of freshmen with need received aid; of those 37% had need fully met. *Average percent of need met:* 87% (excluding resources awarded to replace EFC). *Average financial aid package:* $7811 (excluding resources awarded to replace EFC). 15% of all full-time freshmen had no need and received non-need-based aid.

UNDERGRADUATE FINANCIAL AID (Fall 1999) 1,674 applied for aid; of those 81% were deemed to have need. 98% of undergraduates with need received aid; of those 50% had need fully met. *Average percent of need met:* 88% (excluding resources awarded to replace EFC). *Average financial*

aid package: $7720 (excluding resources awarded to replace EFC). 10% of all full-time undergraduates had no need and received non-need-based aid.

GIFT AID (NEED-BASED) ***Total amount:*** $6,134,961 (31% Federal, 57% state, 11% institutional, 1% external sources). ***Receiving aid:*** *Freshmen:* 59% (173); *all full-time undergraduates:* 48% (1,089). ***Average award:*** Freshmen: $5609; Undergraduates: $5353. ***Scholarships, grants, and awards:*** Federal Pell, FSEOG, state, college/university gift aid from institutional funds.

GIFT AID (NON-NEED-BASED) ***Total amount:*** $279,512 (12% state, 80% institutional, 8% external sources). ***Receiving aid:*** *Freshmen:* 11% (33); *Undergraduates:* 8% (173). ***Scholarships, grants, and awards by category:*** *Academic Interests/Achievement:* 234 awards ($839,606 total): general academic interests/achievements. *Special Characteristics:* 7 awards ($27,657 total): children of faculty/staff. ***Tuition waivers:*** Full or partial for employees or children of employees. ***ROTC:*** Army cooperative, Air Force cooperative.

LOANS ***Student loans:*** $6,490,045 (84% need-based, 16% non-need-based). 74% of past graduating class borrowed through all loan programs. Average indebtedness per student: $15,709. ***Average need-based loan:*** Freshmen: $2880; Undergraduates: $3302. ***Parent loans:*** $34,910 (37% need-based, 63% non-need-based). ***Programs:*** Federal Direct (Subsidized and Unsubsidized Stafford, PLUS), Perkins, state, college/university.

WORK-STUDY ***Federal work-study:*** *Total amount:* $372,973; 251 jobs averaging $1480.

APPLYING for FINANCIAL AID ***Required financial aid form:*** FAFSA. ***Financial aid deadline (priority):*** 3/15. ***Notification date:*** Continuous. Students must reply within 2 weeks of notification.

CONTACT Ms. Marlene Martin, Assistant Funds Manager, Rutgers, The State University of New Jersey, Camden College of Arts and Sciences, 620 George Street, Room 140, New Brunswick, NJ 08901-1175, 732-932-7057. *Fax:* 732-932-7385. *E-mail:* mgmartin@rci.rutgers.edu

RUTGERS, THE STATE UNIVERSITY OF NEW JERSEY, COLLEGE OF NURSING

Newark, NJ

Tuition & fees (NJ res): $5792 **Average undergraduate aid package: $8444**

ABOUT THE INSTITUTION State-supported, coed. Awards: bachelor's, master's, and doctoral degrees (master's and doctoral degrees offered jointly with Rutgers Graduate School–Newark). 1 undergraduate major. Total enrollment: 466. Undergraduates: 466. Freshmen: 46. Federal methodology is used as a basis for awarding need-based institutional aid.

UNDERGRADUATE EXPENSES for 1999–2000 ***Application fee:*** $50. ***Tuition, state resident:*** full-time $4762. ***Tuition, nonresident:*** full-time $9692. ***Required fees:*** full-time $1030. Part-time tuition and fees vary according to course load and location. ***College room and board:*** $6110; ***room only:*** $3348. Room and board charges vary according to board plan and housing facility. ***Payment plan:*** deferred payment.

FRESHMAN FINANCIAL AID (Fall 1999) 40 applied for aid; of those 75% were deemed to have need. 97% of freshmen with need received aid; of those 28% had need fully met. *Average percent of need met:* 84% (excluding resources awarded to replace EFC). *Average financial aid package:* $8943 (excluding resources awarded to replace EFC). 20% of all full-time freshmen had no need and received non-need-based aid.

UNDERGRADUATE FINANCIAL AID (Fall 1999) 242 applied for aid; of those 82% were deemed to have need. 98% of undergraduates with need received aid; of those 43% had need fully met. *Average percent of need met:* 88% (excluding resources awarded to replace EFC). *Average financial aid package:* $8444 (excluding resources awarded to replace EFC). 8% of all full-time undergraduates had no need and received non-need-based aid.

GIFT AID (NEED-BASED) ***Total amount:*** $924,561 (34% Federal, 55% state, 10% institutional, 1% external sources). ***Receiving aid:*** *Freshmen:* 52% (24); *all full-time undergraduates:* 43% (142). ***Average award:*** Freshmen: $6083; Undergraduates: $6148. ***Scholarships, grants, and awards:*** Federal Pell, FSEOG, state, college/university gift aid from institutional funds.

GIFT AID (NON-NEED-BASED) ***Total amount:*** $88,606 (9% state, 73% institutional, 18% external sources). ***Receiving aid:*** *Freshmen:* 15% (7); *Undergraduates:* 11% (37). ***Scholarships, grants, and awards by category:*** *Academic Interests/Achievement:* 58 awards ($179,438 total): general academic interests/achievements. *Special Characteristics:* 4 awards ($19,030 total): children of faculty/staff. ***Tuition waivers:*** Full or partial for employees or children of employees. ***ROTC:*** Army cooperative, Air Force cooperative.

LOANS ***Student loans:*** $1,059,284 (86% need-based, 14% non-need-based). 68% of past graduating class borrowed through all loan programs. Average indebtedness per student: $17,701. ***Average need-based loan:*** Freshmen: $3283; Undergraduates: $3649. ***Parent loans:*** $23,850 (66% need-based, 34% non-need-based). ***Programs:*** Federal Direct (Subsidized and Unsubsidized Stafford, PLUS), Perkins, state, college/university.

WORK-STUDY ***Federal work-study:*** *Total amount:* $49,014; 33 jobs averaging $1485.

APPLYING for FINANCIAL AID ***Required financial aid form:*** FAFSA. ***Financial aid deadline (priority):*** 3/15. ***Notification date:*** Continuous. Students must reply within 2 weeks of notification.

CONTACT Ms. Marlene Martin, Assistant Funds Manager, Rutgers, The State University of New Jersey, College of Nursing, 620 George Street, Room 140, New Brunswick, NJ 08901-1175, 732-932-7057. *Fax:* 732-932-7385. *E-mail:* mgmartin@rci.rutgers.edu

RUTGERS, THE STATE UNIVERSITY OF NEW JERSEY, COLLEGE OF PHARMACY

Piscataway, NJ

Tuition & fees (NJ res): $6576 **Average undergraduate aid package: $8611**

ABOUT THE INSTITUTION State-supported, coed. Awards: doctoral and first professional degrees (6-year doctor of pharmacy [PharmD] degree program is offered to students applying directly from high school). 1 undergraduate major. Total enrollment: 1,016. Undergraduates: 825. Freshmen: 164. Federal methodology is used as a basis for awarding need-based institutional aid.

UNDERGRADUATE EXPENSES for 1999–2000 ***Application fee:*** $50. ***Tuition, state resident:*** full-time $5286; part-time $174 per credit hour. ***Tuition, nonresident:*** full-time $10,754; part-time $358 per credit hour. ***Required fees:*** full-time $1290. Full-time tuition and fees vary according to location. ***College room and board:*** $6098; ***room only:*** $3348. Room and board charges vary according to board plan, housing facility, and location. ***Payment plan:*** deferred payment.

FRESHMAN FINANCIAL AID (Fall 1999) 110 applied for aid; of those 67% were deemed to have need. 96% of freshmen with need received aid; of those 27% had need fully met. *Average percent of need met:* 80% (excluding resources awarded to replace EFC). *Average financial aid package:* $8916 (excluding resources awarded to replace EFC). 19% of all full-time freshmen had no need and received non-need-based aid.

UNDERGRADUATE FINANCIAL AID (Fall 1999) 507 applied for aid; of those 78% were deemed to have need. 98% of undergraduates with need received aid; of those 32% had need fully met. *Average percent of need met:* 82% (excluding resources awarded to replace EFC). *Average financial aid package:* $8611 (excluding resources awarded to replace EFC). 11% of all full-time undergraduates had no need and received non-need-based aid.

GIFT AID (NEED-BASED) ***Total amount:*** $1,636,383 (30% Federal, 59% state, 8% institutional, 3% external sources). ***Receiving aid:*** *Freshmen:* 29% (47); *all full-time undergraduates:* 31% (255). ***Average award:*** Freshmen: $6307; Undergraduates: $5746. ***Scholarships, grants, and awards:*** Federal Pell, FSEOG, state, college/university gift aid from institutional funds.

GIFT AID (NON-NEED-BASED) ***Total amount:*** $805,880 (17% state, 76% institutional, 7% external sources). ***Receiving aid:*** *Freshmen:* 22% (36); *Undergraduates:* 20% (161). ***Scholarships, grants, and awards by category:*** *Academic Interests/Achievement:* 352 awards ($1,092,654 total): general academic interests/achievements. *Special Characteristics:* 4 awards ($21,084 total): children of faculty/staff. ***Tuition waivers:*** Full or partial for employees or children of employees. ***ROTC:*** Army, Air Force.

Rutgers, The State University of New Jersey, College of Pharmacy (continued)

LOANS ***Student loans:*** $1,828,844 (85% need-based, 15% non-need-based). 67% of past graduating class borrowed through all loan programs. Average indebtedness per student: $16,760. ***Average need-based loan:*** Freshmen: $3572; Undergraduates: $4082. ***Parent loans:*** $80,326 (86% need-based, 14% non-need-based). ***Programs:*** Federal Direct (Subsidized and Unsubsidized Stafford, PLUS), Perkins, state, college/university.

WORK-STUDY ***Federal work-study:*** *Total amount:* $109,780; 72 jobs averaging $1503.

ATHLETIC AWARDS *Total amount:* 26,600 (44% need-based, 56% non-need-based).

APPLYING for FINANCIAL AID ***Required financial aid form:*** FAFSA. ***Financial aid deadline (priority):*** 3/15. ***Notification date:*** Continuous. Students must reply within 2 weeks of notification.

CONTACT Ms. Marlene Martin, Assistant Funds Manager, Rutgers, The State University of New Jersey, College of Pharmacy, 620 George Street, Room 140, New Brunswick, NJ 08901-1175, 732-932-7057. *Fax:* 732-932-7385. *E-mail:* mgmartin@rci.rutgers.edu

RUTGERS, THE STATE UNIVERSITY OF NEW JERSEY, COOK COLLEGE

New Brunswick, NJ

Tuition & fees (NJ res): $6544 **Average undergraduate aid package: $8198**

ABOUT THE INSTITUTION State-supported, coed. Awards: bachelor's degrees. 45 undergraduate majors. Total enrollment: 3,231. Undergraduates: 3,231. Freshmen: 464. Federal methodology is used as a basis for awarding need-based institutional aid.

UNDERGRADUATE EXPENSES for 1999–2000 ***Application fee:*** $50. ***Tuition, state resident:*** full-time $5286. ***Tuition, nonresident:*** full-time $10,754. ***Required fees:*** full-time $1258. Full-time tuition and fees vary according to location. ***College room and board:*** $6098; ***room only:*** $3348. Room and board charges vary according to board plan and housing facility. ***Payment plan:*** deferred payment.

FRESHMAN FINANCIAL AID (Fall 1999) 354 applied for aid; of those 73% were deemed to have need. 98% of freshmen with need received aid; of those 30% had need fully met. *Average percent of need met:* 81% (excluding resources awarded to replace EFC). *Average financial aid package:* $8231 (excluding resources awarded to replace EFC). 19% of all full-time freshmen had no need and received non-need-based aid.

UNDERGRADUATE FINANCIAL AID (Fall 1999) 1,860 applied for aid; of those 78% were deemed to have need. 97% of undergraduates with need received aid; of those 32% had need fully met. *Average percent of need met:* 82% (excluding resources awarded to replace EFC). *Average financial aid package:* $8198 (excluding resources awarded to replace EFC). 9% of all full-time undergraduates had no need and received non-need-based aid.

GIFT AID (NEED-BASED) ***Total amount:*** $5,611,348 (28% Federal, 61% state, 9% institutional, 2% external sources). ***Receiving aid:*** *Freshmen:* 35% (164); *all full-time undergraduates:* 32% (936). ***Average award:*** Freshmen: $5873; Undergraduates: $5541. ***Scholarships, grants, and awards:*** Federal Pell, FSEOG, state, college/university gift aid from institutional funds.

GIFT AID (NON-NEED-BASED) ***Total amount:*** $977,726 (13% state, 74% institutional, 13% external sources). ***Receiving aid:*** *Freshmen:* 15% (68); *Undergraduates:* 12% (345). ***Scholarships, grants, and awards by category:*** *Academic Interests/Achievement:* 609 awards ($1,979,759 total): biological sciences, general academic interests/achievements. *Special Characteristics:* 45 awards ($245,605 total): children of faculty/staff. ***Tuition waivers:*** Full or partial for employees or children of employees. ***ROTC:*** Army, Air Force.

LOANS ***Student loans:*** $7,075,628 (84% need-based, 16% non-need-based). 66% of past graduating class borrowed through all loan programs. Average indebtedness per student: $16,078. ***Average need-based loan:*** Freshmen: $3475; Undergraduates: $3638. ***Parent loans:*** $578,741 (72% need-based, 28% non-need-based). ***Programs:*** Federal Direct (Subsidized and Unsubsidized Stafford, PLUS), Perkins, state, college/university.

WORK-STUDY ***Federal work-study:*** *Total amount:* $527,284; 353 jobs averaging $1487.

ATHLETIC AWARDS *Total amount:* 253,554 (25% need-based, 75% non-need-based).

APPLYING for FINANCIAL AID ***Required financial aid form:*** FAFSA. ***Financial aid deadline (priority):*** 3/15. ***Notification date:*** Continuous. Students must reply within 2 weeks of notification.

CONTACT Ms. Marlene Martin, Assistant Funds Manager, Rutgers, The State University of New Jersey, Cook College, 620 George Street, Room 140, New Brunswick, NJ 08901-1175, 732-932-7057. *Fax:* 732-932-7385. *E-mail:* mgmartin@rci.rutgers.edu

RUTGERS, THE STATE UNIVERSITY OF NEW JERSEY, DOUGLASS COLLEGE

New Brunswick, NJ

Tuition & fees (NJ res): $6017 **Average undergraduate aid package: $8541**

ABOUT THE INSTITUTION State-supported, women only. Awards: bachelor's degrees. 79 undergraduate majors. Total enrollment: 3,099. Undergraduates: 3,099. Freshmen: 519. Federal methodology is used as a basis for awarding need-based institutional aid.

UNDERGRADUATE EXPENSES for 1999–2000 ***Application fee:*** $50. ***Tuition, state resident:*** full-time $4762. ***Tuition, nonresident:*** full-time $9692. ***Required fees:*** full-time $1255. Full-time tuition and fees vary according to location. Part-time tuition and fees vary according to course load and location. ***College room and board:*** $6098; ***room only:*** $3348. Room and board charges vary according to board plan and housing facility. ***Payment plan:*** deferred payment.

FRESHMAN FINANCIAL AID (Fall 1999) 382 applied for aid; of those 72% were deemed to have need. 99% of freshmen with need received aid; of those 30% had need fully met. *Average percent of need met:* 84% (excluding resources awarded to replace EFC). *Average financial aid package:* $8176 (excluding resources awarded to replace EFC). 16% of all full-time freshmen had no need and received non-need-based aid.

UNDERGRADUATE FINANCIAL AID (Fall 1999) 1,875 applied for aid; of those 78% were deemed to have need. 98% of undergraduates with need received aid; of those 36% had need fully met. *Average percent of need met:* 86% (excluding resources awarded to replace EFC). *Average financial aid package:* $8541 (excluding resources awarded to replace EFC). 9% of all full-time undergraduates had no need and received non-need-based aid.

GIFT AID (NEED-BASED) ***Total amount:*** $6,201,339 (32% Federal, 58% state, 8% institutional, 2% external sources). ***Receiving aid:*** *Freshmen:* 36% (185); *all full-time undergraduates:* 35% (1,031). ***Average award:*** Freshmen: $5999; Undergraduates: $5712. ***Scholarships, grants, and awards:*** Federal Pell, FSEOG, state, college/university gift aid from institutional funds.

GIFT AID (NON-NEED-BASED) ***Total amount:*** $634,283 (9% state, 80% institutional, 11% external sources). ***Receiving aid:*** *Freshmen:* 12% (60); *Undergraduates:* 11% (316). ***Scholarships, grants, and awards by category:*** *Academic Interests/Achievement:* 502 awards ($1,585,553 total): general academic interests/achievements. *Special Characteristics:* 55 awards ($273,648 total): children of faculty/staff. ***Tuition waivers:*** Full or partial for employees or children of employees. ***ROTC:*** Army, Air Force.

LOANS ***Student loans:*** $6,997,945 (84% need-based, 16% non-need-based). 61% of past graduating class borrowed through all loan programs. Average indebtedness per student: $16,496. ***Average need-based loan:*** Freshmen: $3457; Undergraduates: $3595. ***Parent loans:*** $515,763 (69% need-based, 31% non-need-based). ***Programs:*** Federal Direct (Subsidized and Unsubsidized Stafford, PLUS), Perkins, state, college/university.

WORK-STUDY ***Federal work-study:*** *Total amount:* $642,800; 431 jobs averaging $1484.

ATHLETIC AWARDS *Total amount:* 87,500 (53% need-based, 47% non-need-based).

APPLYING for FINANCIAL AID ***Required financial aid form:*** FAFSA. ***Financial aid deadline (priority):*** 3/15. ***Notification date:*** Continuous. Students must reply within 2 weeks of notification.

CONTACT Ms. Marlene Martin, Assistant Funds Manager, Rutgers, The State University of New Jersey, Douglass College, 620 George Street, Room 140, New Brunswick, NJ 08901-1175, 732-932-7057. *Fax:* 732-932-7385. *E-mail:* mgmartin@rci.rutgers.edu

RUTGERS, THE STATE UNIVERSITY OF NEW JERSEY, LIVINGSTON COLLEGE

Piscataway, NJ

Tuition & fees (NJ res): $6038 **Average undergraduate aid package: $8392**

ABOUT THE INSTITUTION State-supported, coed. Awards: bachelor's degrees. 75 undergraduate majors. Total enrollment: 3,536. Undergraduates: 3,536. Freshmen: 712. Federal methodology is used as a basis for awarding need-based institutional aid.

UNDERGRADUATE EXPENSES for 1999–2000 ***Application fee:*** $50. ***Tuition, state resident:*** full-time $4762. ***Tuition, nonresident:*** full-time $9692. ***Required fees:*** full-time $1276. Full-time tuition and fees vary according to location. Part-time tuition and fees vary according to course load. ***College room and board:*** $6098; ***room only:*** $3348. Room and board charges vary according to board plan and housing facility. ***Payment plan:*** deferred payment.

FRESHMAN FINANCIAL AID (Fall 1999) 504 applied for aid; of those 73% were deemed to have need. 98% of freshmen with need received aid; of those 25% had need fully met. *Average percent of need met:* 82% (excluding resources awarded to replace EFC). *Average financial aid package:* $8051 (excluding resources awarded to replace EFC). 15% of all full-time freshmen had no need and received non-need-based aid.

UNDERGRADUATE FINANCIAL AID (Fall 1999) 2,141 applied for aid; of those 78% were deemed to have need. 97% of undergraduates with need received aid; of those 33% had need fully met. *Average percent of need met:* 84% (excluding resources awarded to replace EFC). *Average financial aid package:* $8392 (excluding resources awarded to replace EFC). 9% of all full-time undergraduates had no need and received non-need-based aid.

GIFT AID (NEED-BASED) ***Total amount:*** $7,037,990 (33% Federal, 58% state, 8% institutional, 1% external sources). ***Receiving aid:*** *Freshmen:* 36% (259); *all full-time undergraduates:* 35% (1,165). ***Average award:*** Freshmen: $5740; Undergraduates: $5756. ***Scholarships, grants, and awards:*** Federal Pell, FSEOG, state, college/university gift aid from institutional funds.

GIFT AID (NON-NEED-BASED) ***Total amount:*** $172,571 (9% state, 66% institutional, 25% external sources). ***Receiving aid:*** *Freshmen:* 7% (50); *Undergraduates:* 7% (229). ***Scholarships, grants, and awards by category:*** *Academic Interests/Achievement:* 265 awards ($988,717 total): general academic interests/achievements. *Special Characteristics:* 35 awards ($166,310 total): children of faculty/staff. ***Tuition waivers:*** Full or partial for employees or children of employees. ***ROTC:*** Army, Air Force.

LOANS ***Student loans:*** $8,051,891 (83% need-based, 17% non-need-based). 66% of past graduating class borrowed through all loan programs. Average indebtedness per student: $15,942. ***Average need-based loan:*** Freshmen: $3541; Undergraduates: $3603. ***Parent loans:*** $819,279 (63% need-based, 37% non-need-based). ***Programs:*** Federal Direct (Subsidized and Unsubsidized Stafford, PLUS), Perkins, state, college/university.

WORK-STUDY ***Federal work-study:*** *Total amount:* $737,732; 493 jobs averaging $1490.

ATHLETIC AWARDS *Total amount:* 370,693 (42% need-based, 58% non-need-based).

APPLYING for FINANCIAL AID ***Required financial aid form:*** FAFSA. ***Financial aid deadline (priority):*** 3/15. ***Notification date:*** Continuous. Students must reply within 2 weeks of notification.

CONTACT Ms. Marlene Martin, Assistant Funds Manager, Rutgers, The State University of New Jersey, Livingston College, 620 George Street, Room 140, New Brunswick, NJ 08901-1175, 732-932-7057. *Fax:* 732-932-7385. *E-mail:* mgmartin@rci.rutgers.edu

RUTGERS, THE STATE UNIVERSITY OF NEW JERSEY, MASON GROSS SCHOOL OF THE ARTS

New Brunswick, NJ

Tuition & fees (NJ res): $6052 **Average undergraduate aid package: $7817**

ABOUT THE INSTITUTION State-supported, coed. Awards: bachelor's, master's, and doctoral degrees (also offers artist diploma). 14 undergraduate majors. Total enrollment: 851. Undergraduates: 617. Freshmen: 112. Federal methodology is used as a basis for awarding need-based institutional aid.

UNDERGRADUATE EXPENSES for 1999–2000 ***Application fee:*** $50. ***Tuition, state resident:*** full-time $4762; part-time $154 per credit hour. ***Tuition, nonresident:*** full-time $9692; part-time $314 per credit hour. ***Required fees:*** full-time $1290. Full-time tuition and fees vary according to location. ***College room and board:*** $6098; ***room only:*** $3348. Room and board charges vary according to board plan, housing facility, and location. ***Payment plan:*** deferred payment.

FRESHMAN FINANCIAL AID (Fall 1999) 69 applied for aid; of those 61% were deemed to have need. 95% of freshmen with need received aid; of those 22% had need fully met. *Average percent of need met:* 84% (excluding resources awarded to replace EFC). *Average financial aid package:* $8264 (excluding resources awarded to replace EFC). 21% of all full-time freshmen had no need and received non-need-based aid.

UNDERGRADUATE FINANCIAL AID (Fall 1999) 367 applied for aid; of those 69% were deemed to have need. 98% of undergraduates with need received aid; of those 33% had need fully met. *Average percent of need met:* 84% (excluding resources awarded to replace EFC). *Average financial aid package:* $7817 (excluding resources awarded to replace EFC). 13% of all full-time undergraduates had no need and received non-need-based aid.

GIFT AID (NEED-BASED) ***Total amount:*** $845,769 (31% Federal, 52% state, 13% institutional, 4% external sources). ***Receiving aid:*** *Freshmen:* 21% (23); *all full-time undergraduates:* 25% (149). ***Average award:*** Freshmen: $5787; Undergraduates: $5304. ***Scholarships, grants, and awards:*** Federal Pell, FSEOG, state, college/university gift aid from institutional funds.

GIFT AID (NON-NEED-BASED) ***Total amount:*** $138,650 (11% state, 80% institutional, 9% external sources). ***Receiving aid:*** *Freshmen:* 11% (12); *Undergraduates:* 8% (48). ***Scholarships, grants, and awards by category:*** *Academic Interests/Achievement:* 91 awards ($336,799 total): general academic interests/achievements. *Creative Arts/Performance:* 41 awards ($45,293 total): dance, music. *Special Characteristics:* 12 awards ($57,018 total): children of faculty/staff. ***Tuition waivers:*** Full or partial for employees or children of employees. ***ROTC:*** Army, Air Force.

LOANS ***Student loans:*** $1,456,775 (77% need-based, 23% non-need-based). 64% of past graduating class borrowed through all loan programs. Average indebtedness per student: $18,141. ***Average need-based loan:*** Freshmen: $3665; Undergraduates: $3819. ***Parent loans:*** $155,489 (86% need-based, 14% non-need-based). ***Programs:*** Federal Direct (Subsidized and Unsubsidized Stafford, PLUS), Perkins, state, college/university.

WORK-STUDY ***Federal work-study:*** *Total amount:* $80,700; 54 jobs averaging $1466.

ATHLETIC AWARDS *Total amount:* 6600 (62% need-based, 38% non-need-based).

APPLYING for FINANCIAL AID ***Required financial aid form:*** FAFSA. ***Financial aid deadline (priority):*** 3/15. ***Notification date:*** Continuous. Students must reply within 2 weeks of notification.

CONTACT Ms. Marlene Martin, Assistant Funds Manager, Rutgers, The State University of New Jersey, Mason Gross School of the Arts, 620

Rutgers, The State University of New Jersey, Mason Gross School of the Arts (continued)

George Street, Room 140, New Brunswick, NJ 08901-1175, 732-932-7057. *Fax:* 732-932-7385. *E-mail:* mgmartin@rci.rutgers.edu

RUTGERS, THE STATE UNIVERSITY OF NEW JERSEY, NEWARK COLLEGE OF ARTS AND SCIENCES

Newark, NJ

Tuition & fees (NJ res): $5814 **Average undergraduate aid package: $7876**

ABOUT THE INSTITUTION State-supported, coed. Awards: bachelor's degrees. 48 undergraduate majors. Total enrollment: 3,665. Undergraduates: 3,665. Freshmen: 598. Federal methodology is used as a basis for awarding need-based institutional aid.

UNDERGRADUATE EXPENSES for 1999–2000 ***Application fee:*** $50. ***Tuition, state resident:*** full-time $4762. ***Tuition, nonresident:*** full-time $9692. ***Required fees:*** full-time $1052. Full-time tuition and fees vary according to location. Part-time tuition and fees vary according to course load. ***College room and board:*** $6110; ***room only:*** $3348. Room and board charges vary according to board plan and housing facility. ***Payment plan:*** deferred payment.

FRESHMAN FINANCIAL AID (Fall 1999) 480 applied for aid; of those 80% were deemed to have need. 97% of freshmen with need received aid; of those 31% had need fully met. *Average percent of need met:* 84% (excluding resources awarded to replace EFC). *Average financial aid package:* $8185 (excluding resources awarded to replace EFC). 11% of all full-time freshmen had no need and received non-need-based aid.

UNDERGRADUATE FINANCIAL AID (Fall 1999) 2,211 applied for aid; of those 85% were deemed to have need. 98% of undergraduates with need received aid; of those 38% had need fully met. *Average percent of need met:* 84% (excluding resources awarded to replace EFC). *Average financial aid package:* $7876 (excluding resources awarded to replace EFC). 6% of all full-time undergraduates had no need and received non-need-based aid.

GIFT AID (NEED-BASED) ***Total amount:*** $9,288,687 (34% Federal, 54% state, 12% institutional). ***Receiving aid:*** *Freshmen:* 57% (331); *all full-time undergraduates:* 52% (1,595). ***Average award:*** Freshmen: $6154; Undergraduates: $5554. ***Scholarships, grants, and awards:*** Federal Pell, FSEOG, state, college/university gift aid from institutional funds.

GIFT AID (NON-NEED-BASED) ***Total amount:*** $392,879 (12% state, 82% institutional, 6% external sources). ***Receiving aid:*** *Freshmen:* 13% (78); *Undergraduates:* 9% (275). ***Scholarships, grants, and awards by category:*** *Academic Interests/Achievement:* 370 awards ($1,032,672 total): general academic interests/achievements. *Special Characteristics:* 5 awards ($23,810 total): children of faculty/staff. ***Tuition waivers:*** Full or partial for employees or children of employees. ***ROTC:*** Army cooperative, Air Force cooperative.

LOANS ***Student loans:*** $7,102,223 (89% need-based, 11% non-need-based). 67% of past graduating class borrowed through all loan programs. Average indebtedness per student: $14,313. ***Average need-based loan:*** Freshmen: $3024; Undergraduates: $3175. ***Parent loans:*** $88,069 (56% need-based, 44% non-need-based). ***Programs:*** Federal Direct (Subsidized and Unsubsidized Stafford, PLUS), Perkins, state, college/university.

WORK-STUDY ***Federal work-study:*** *Total amount:* $571,575; 385 jobs averaging $1495.

APPLYING for FINANCIAL AID ***Required financial aid form:*** FAFSA. ***Financial aid deadline (priority):*** 3/15. ***Notification date:*** Continuous. Students must reply within 2 weeks of notification.

CONTACT Ms. Marlene Martin, Assistant Funds Manager, Rutgers, The State University of New Jersey, Newark College of Arts and Sciences, 620 George Street, Room 140, New Brunswick, NJ 08901-1175, 732-932-7057. *Fax:* 732-932-7385. *E-mail:* mgmartin@rci.rutgers.edu

RUTGERS, THE STATE UNIVERSITY OF NEW JERSEY, RUTGERS COLLEGE

New Brunswick, NJ

Tuition & fees (NJ res): $6052 **Average undergraduate aid package: $8586**

ABOUT THE INSTITUTION State-supported, coed. Awards: bachelor's degrees. 73 undergraduate majors. Total enrollment: 10,993. Undergraduates: 10,993. Freshmen: 1,765. Federal methodology is used as a basis for awarding need-based institutional aid.

UNDERGRADUATE EXPENSES for 1999–2000 ***Application fee:*** $50. ***Tuition, state resident:*** full-time $4762. ***Tuition, nonresident:*** full-time $9692. ***Required fees:*** full-time $1290. Full-time tuition and fees vary according to location. ***College room and board:*** $6098; ***room only:*** $3348. Room and board charges vary according to board plan and housing facility. ***Payment plan:*** installment.

FRESHMAN FINANCIAL AID (Fall 1999) 1255 applied for aid; of those 69% were deemed to have need. 98% of freshmen with need received aid; of those 31% had need fully met. *Average percent of need met:* 85% (excluding resources awarded to replace EFC). *Average financial aid package:* $8469 (excluding resources awarded to replace EFC). 23% of all full-time freshmen had no need and received non-need-based aid.

UNDERGRADUATE FINANCIAL AID (Fall 1999) 6,165 applied for aid; of those 77% were deemed to have need. 97% of undergraduates with need received aid; of those 35% had need fully met. *Average percent of need met:* 84% (excluding resources awarded to replace EFC). *Average financial aid package:* $8586 (excluding resources awarded to replace EFC). 10% of all full-time undergraduates had no need and received non-need-based aid.

GIFT AID (NEED-BASED) ***Total amount:*** $19,786,313 (32% Federal, 57% state, 9% institutional, 2% external sources). ***Receiving aid:*** *Freshmen:* 33% (580); *all full-time undergraduates:* 30% (3,179). ***Average award:*** Freshmen: $5905; Undergraduates: $5751. ***Scholarships, grants, and awards:*** Federal Pell, FSEOG, state, college/university gift aid from institutional funds.

GIFT AID (NON-NEED-BASED) ***Total amount:*** $5,872,491 (14% state, 77% institutional, 9% external sources). ***Receiving aid:*** *Freshmen:* 17% (302); *Undergraduates:* 12% (1,223). ***Scholarships, grants, and awards by category:*** *Academic Interests/Achievement:* 2,366 awards ($8,959,362 total): general academic interests/achievements. *Special Characteristics:* 133 awards ($681,269 total): children of faculty/staff. ***Tuition waivers:*** Full or partial for employees or children of employees. ***ROTC:*** Army, Air Force.

LOANS ***Student loans:*** $21,877,566 (82% need-based, 18% non-need-based). 61% of past graduating class borrowed through all loan programs. Average indebtedness per student: $15,560. ***Average need-based loan:*** Freshmen: $3414; Undergraduates: $3645. ***Parent loans:*** $1,783,392 (69% need-based, 31% non-need-based). ***Programs:*** Federal Direct (Subsidized and Unsubsidized Stafford, PLUS), Perkins, state, college/university.

WORK-STUDY ***Federal work-study:*** *Total amount:* $1,827,094; 1,221 jobs averaging $1494.

ATHLETIC AWARDS *Total amount:* 2,834,932 (28% need-based, 72% non-need-based).

APPLYING for FINANCIAL AID ***Required financial aid form:*** FAFSA. ***Financial aid deadline (priority):*** 3/15. ***Notification date:*** Continuous. Students must reply within 2 weeks of notification.

CONTACT Ms. Marlene Martin, Assistant Funds Manager, Rutgers, The State University of New Jersey, Rutgers College, 620 George Street, Room 140, New Brunswick, NJ 08901-1175, 732-932-7057. *Fax:* 732-932-7385. *E-mail:* mgmartin@rci.rutgers.edu

RUTGERS, THE STATE UNIVERSITY OF NEW JERSEY, SCHOOL OF ENGINEERING

Piscataway, NJ

Tuition & fees (NJ res): $6576 **Average undergraduate aid package: $8988**

ABOUT THE INSTITUTION State-supported, coed. Awards: bachelor's degrees (master of science, master of philosophy, and doctor of philosophy degrees are offered through the Graduate School, New Brunswick). 12 undergraduate majors. Total university enrollment: 48,660. Total unit enrollment: 2,190. Undergraduates: 2,190. Freshmen: 394. Federal methodology is used as a basis for awarding need-based institutional aid.

UNDERGRADUATE EXPENSES for 1999–2000 ***Application fee:*** $50. ***Tuition, state resident:*** full-time $5286; part-time $174 per credit hour. ***Tuition, nonresident:*** full-time $10,754; part-time $358 per credit hour. ***Required fees:*** full-time $1290. Full-time tuition and fees vary according to location. ***College room and board:*** $6098; ***room only:*** $3348. Room and board charges vary according to board plan and housing facility. ***Payment plan:*** deferred payment.

FRESHMAN FINANCIAL AID (Fall 1999) 291 applied for aid; of those 68% were deemed to have need. 98% of freshmen with need received aid; of those 21% had need fully met. *Average percent of need met:* 79% (excluding resources awarded to replace EFC). *Average financial aid package:* $8848 (excluding resources awarded to replace EFC). 23% of all full-time freshmen had no need and received non-need-based aid.

UNDERGRADUATE FINANCIAL AID (Fall 1999) 1,272 applied for aid; of those 75% were deemed to have need. 98% of undergraduates with need received aid; of those 31% had need fully met. *Average percent of need met:* 83% (excluding resources awarded to replace EFC). *Average financial aid package:* $8988 (excluding resources awarded to replace EFC). 10% of all full-time undergraduates had no need and received non-need-based aid.

GIFT AID (NEED-BASED) ***Total amount:*** $4,400,888 (29% Federal, 59% state, 9% institutional, 3% external sources). ***Receiving aid:*** *Freshmen:* 36% (140); *all full-time undergraduates:* 32% (665). ***Average award:*** Freshmen: $6212; Undergraduates: $6043. ***Scholarships, grants, and awards:*** Federal Pell, FSEOG, state, college/university gift aid from institutional funds.

GIFT AID (NON-NEED-BASED) ***Total amount:*** $1,330,770 (12% state, 76% institutional, 12% external sources). ***Receiving aid:*** *Freshmen:* 16% (63); *Undergraduates:* 13% (270). ***Scholarships, grants, and awards by category:*** *Academic Interests/Achievement:* 531 awards ($2,005,843 total): engineering/technologies, general academic interests/achievements. *Special Characteristics:* 21 awards ($126,090 total): children of faculty/staff. ***Tuition waivers:*** Full or partial for employees or children of employees. ***ROTC:*** Army, Air Force.

LOANS ***Student loans:*** $4,418,990 (84% need-based, 16% non-need-based). 63% of past graduating class borrowed through all loan programs. Average indebtedness per student: $16,386. ***Average need-based loan:*** Freshmen: $3615; Undergraduates: $3640. ***Parent loans:*** $259,146 (71% need-based, 29% non-need-based). ***Programs:*** Federal Direct (Subsidized and Unsubsidized Stafford, PLUS), Perkins, state, college/university.

WORK-STUDY ***Federal work-study:*** *Total amount:* $404,150; 267 jobs averaging $1496.

ATHLETIC AWARDS *Total amount:* 61,098 (43% need-based, 57% non-need-based).

APPLYING for FINANCIAL AID ***Required financial aid form:*** FAFSA. ***Financial aid deadline (priority):*** 3/15. ***Notification date:*** Continuous. Students must reply within 2 weeks of notification.

CONTACT Ms. Marlene Martin, Assistant Funds Manager, Rutgers, The State University of New Jersey, School of Engineering, 620 George Street, Room 140, New Brunswick, NJ 08901-1175, 732-932-7057. *Fax:* 732-932-7385. *E-mail:* mgmartin@rci.rutgers.edu

RUTGERS, THE STATE UNIVERSITY OF NEW JERSEY, UNIVERSITY COLLEGE–CAMDEN

Camden, NJ

Tuition & fees: N/R **Average undergraduate aid package: $6692**

ABOUT THE INSTITUTION State-supported, coed. Awards: bachelor's degrees (offers primarily part-time evening degree programs). 47 undergraduate majors. Total enrollment: 724. Undergraduates: 724. Freshmen: 4. Federal methodology is used as a basis for awarding need-based institutional aid.

UNDERGRADUATE EXPENSES for 1999–2000 ***Application fee:*** $50. ***Tuition, state resident:*** part-time $154 per credit hour. ***Tuition, nonresident:*** part-time $314 per credit hour. ***Required fees:*** $170 per term part-time. Part-time tuition and fees vary according to course load. ***Payment plan:*** installment.

FRESHMAN FINANCIAL AID (Fall 1999) 3 applied for aid; of those 100% were deemed to have need. 100% of freshmen with need received aid; of those 33% had need fully met. *Average percent of need met:* 94% (excluding resources awarded to replace EFC). *Average financial aid package:* $7159 (excluding resources awarded to replace EFC).

UNDERGRADUATE FINANCIAL AID (Fall 1999) 226 applied for aid; of those 76% were deemed to have need. 99% of undergraduates with need received aid; of those 64% had need fully met. *Average percent of need met:* 92% (excluding resources awarded to replace EFC). *Average financial aid package:* $6692 (excluding resources awarded to replace EFC). 12% of all full-time undergraduates had no need and received non-need-based aid.

GIFT AID (NEED-BASED) ***Total amount:*** $714,882 (36% Federal, 60% state, 4% institutional). ***Receiving aid:*** *Freshmen:* 100% (3); *all full-time undergraduates:* 44% (133). ***Average award:*** Freshmen: $5860; Undergraduates: $5051. ***Scholarships, grants, and awards:*** Federal Pell, FSEOG, state, college/university gift aid from institutional funds.

GIFT AID (NON-NEED-BASED) ***Receiving aid:*** *Undergraduates:* 3% (9). ***Scholarships, grants, and awards by category:*** *Academic Interests/Achievement:* 8 awards ($28,380 total): general academic interests/achievements. *Special Characteristics:* 2 awards ($9524 total): children of faculty/staff. ***Tuition waivers:*** Full or partial for employees or children of employees. ***ROTC:*** Army cooperative, Air Force cooperative.

LOANS ***Student loans:*** $1,206,536 (82% need-based, 18% non-need-based). 76% of past graduating class borrowed through all loan programs. Average indebtedness per student: $15,780. ***Average need-based loan:*** Freshmen: $1299; Undergraduates: $3075. ***Parent loans:*** $2000 (100% non-need-based). ***Programs:*** Federal Direct (Subsidized and Unsubsidized Stafford, PLUS), Perkins, state, college/university.

WORK-STUDY ***Federal work-study:*** *Total amount:* $17,320; 13 jobs averaging $1332.

APPLYING for FINANCIAL AID ***Required financial aid form:*** FAFSA. ***Financial aid deadline (priority):*** 3/15. ***Notification date:*** Continuous. Students must reply within 2 weeks of notification.

CONTACT Ms. Marlene Martin, Assistant Funds Manager, Rutgers, The State University of New Jersey, University College–Camden, 620 George Street, Room 140, New Brunswick, NJ 08901-1175, 732-932-7057. *Fax:* 732-932-7385. *E-mail:* mgmartin@rci.rutgers.edu

RUTGERS, THE STATE UNIVERSITY OF NEW JERSEY, UNIVERSITY COLLEGE–NEWARK

Newark, NJ

Tuition & fees: N/R **Average undergraduate aid package: $7470**

ABOUT THE INSTITUTION State-supported, coed. Awards: bachelor's degrees (offers primarily part-time evening degree programs). 17 undergraduate majors. Total enrollment: 1,645. Undergraduates: 1,645. Freshmen: 70. Federal methodology is used as a basis for awarding need-based institutional aid.

UNDERGRADUATE EXPENSES for 1999–2000 ***Application fee:*** $50. ***Tuition, state resident:*** part-time $154 per credit hour. ***Tuition, nonresident:*** part-time $314 per credit hour. ***Required fees:*** $128 per term part-time. Part-time tuition and fees vary according to course load. ***Payment plan:*** deferred payment.

FRESHMAN FINANCIAL AID (Fall 1999) 49 applied for aid; of those 90% were deemed to have need. 100% of freshmen with need received aid; of those 55% had need fully met. *Average percent of need met:* 89% (exclud-

Rutgers, The State University of New Jersey, University College–Newark (continued)

ing resources awarded to replace EFC). *Average financial aid package:* $7209 (excluding resources awarded to replace EFC). 7% of all full-time freshmen had no need and received non-need-based aid.

UNDERGRADUATE FINANCIAL AID (Fall 1999) 448 applied for aid; of those 85% were deemed to have need. 97% of undergraduates with need received aid; of those 53% had need fully met. *Average percent of need met:* 88% (excluding resources awarded to replace EFC). *Average financial aid package:* $7470 (excluding resources awarded to replace EFC). 2% of all full-time undergraduates had no need and received non-need-based aid.

GIFT AID (NEED-BASED) ***Total amount:*** $2,024,087 (42% Federal, 49% state, 9% institutional). ***Receiving aid:*** *Freshmen:* 67% (41); *all full-time undergraduates:* 26% (319). ***Average award:*** Freshmen: $6263; Undergraduates: $5445. ***Scholarships, grants, and awards:*** Federal Pell, FSEOG, state, college/university gift aid from institutional funds.

GIFT AID (NON-NEED-BASED) ***Total amount:*** $30,100 (10% state, 77% institutional, 13% external sources). ***Receiving aid:*** *Freshmen:* 5% (3); *Undergraduates:* 2% (20). ***Scholarships, grants, and awards by category:*** *Academic Interests/Achievement:* 30 awards ($68,106 total): general academic interests/achievements. *Special Characteristics:* 2 awards ($9524 total): children of faculty/staff. ***Tuition waivers:*** Full or partial for employees or children of employees. ***ROTC:*** Army cooperative, Air Force cooperative.

LOANS ***Student loans:*** $2,698,330 (88% need-based, 12% non-need-based). 68% of past graduating class borrowed through all loan programs. Average indebtedness per student: $17,030. ***Average need-based loan:*** Freshmen: $1852; Undergraduates: $3256. ***Parent loans:*** $7760 (100% non-need-based). ***Programs:*** Federal Direct (Subsidized and Unsubsidized Stafford, PLUS), Perkins, state, college/university.

WORK-STUDY ***Federal work-study:*** *Total amount:* $42,333; 31 jobs averaging $1383.

ATHLETIC AWARDS *Total amount:* 6000 (100% non-need-based).

APPLYING for FINANCIAL AID ***Required financial aid form:*** FAFSA. ***Financial aid deadline (priority):*** 3/15. ***Notification date:*** Continuous. Students must reply within 2 weeks of notification.

CONTACT Ms. Marlene Martin, Assistant Funds Manager, Rutgers, The State University of New Jersey, University College–Newark, 620 George Street, Room 140, New Brunswick, NJ 08901-1175, 732-932-7057. *Fax:* 732-932-7385. *E-mail:* mgmartin@rci.rutgers.edu

RUTGERS, THE STATE UNIVERSITY OF NEW JERSEY, UNIVERSITY COLLEGE–NEW BRUNSWICK

New Brunswick, NJ

Tuition & fees: N/R **Average undergraduate aid package: $7559**

ABOUT THE INSTITUTION State-supported, coed. Awards: bachelor's degrees (offers primarily part-time degree programs). 73 undergraduate majors. Total enrollment: 3,306. Undergraduates: 3,306. Freshmen: 54. Federal methodology is used as a basis for awarding need-based institutional aid.

UNDERGRADUATE EXPENSES for 1999–2000 ***Application fee:*** $50. ***Tuition, state resident:*** part-time $154 per credit hour. ***Tuition, nonresident:*** part-time $314 per credit hour. Part-time tuition and fees vary according to course load. ***Payment plan:*** installment.

FRESHMAN FINANCIAL AID (Fall 1999) 17 applied for aid; of those 65% were deemed to have need. 100% of freshmen with need received aid; of those 27% had need fully met. *Average percent of need met:* 83% (excluding resources awarded to replace EFC). *Average financial aid package:* $6970 (excluding resources awarded to replace EFC). 12% of all full-time freshmen had no need and received non-need-based aid.

UNDERGRADUATE FINANCIAL AID (Fall 1999) 735 applied for aid; of those 76% were deemed to have need. 98% of undergraduates with need received aid; of those 48% had need fully met. *Average percent of need met:* 87% (excluding resources awarded to replace EFC). *Average financial aid package:* $7559 (excluding resources awarded to replace EFC). 5% of all full-time undergraduates had no need and received non-need-based aid.

GIFT AID (NEED-BASED) ***Total amount:*** $2,682,209 (37% Federal, 53% state, 9% institutional, 1% external sources). ***Receiving aid:*** *Freshmen:* 19% (8); *all full-time undergraduates:* 32% (419). ***Average award:*** Freshmen: $4844; Undergraduates: $5192. ***Scholarships, grants, and awards:*** Federal Pell, FSEOG, state, college/university gift aid from institutional funds.

GIFT AID (NON-NEED-BASED) ***Total amount:*** $22,090 (7% state, 77% institutional, 16% external sources). ***Receiving aid:*** *Freshmen:* 2% (1); *Undergraduates:* 3% (34). ***Scholarships, grants, and awards by category:*** *Academic Interests/Achievement:* 73 awards ($186,387 total): general academic interests/achievements. *Special Characteristics:* 11 awards ($49,397 total): children of faculty/staff. ***Tuition waivers:*** Full or partial for employees or children of employees. ***ROTC:*** Army, Air Force.

LOANS ***Student loans:*** $4,183,483 (88% need-based, 12% non-need-based). Average indebtedness per student: $16,737. ***Average need-based loan:*** Freshmen: $3549; Undergraduates: $3830. ***Parent loans:*** $71,382 (78% need-based, 22% non-need-based). ***Programs:*** Federal Direct (Subsidized and Unsubsidized Stafford, PLUS), Perkins, state, college/university.

WORK-STUDY ***Federal work-study:*** *Total amount:* $67,590; 44 jobs averaging $1467.

ATHLETIC AWARDS *Total amount:* 11,715 (100% non-need-based).

APPLYING for FINANCIAL AID ***Required financial aid form:*** FAFSA. ***Financial aid deadline (priority):*** 3/15. ***Notification date:*** Continuous. Students must reply within 2 weeks of notification.

CONTACT Ms. Marlene Martin, Assistant Funds Manager, Rutgers, The State University of New Jersey, University College–New Brunswick, 620 George Street, Room 140, New Brunswick, NJ 08901-1175, 732-932-7057. *Fax:* 732-932-7385. *E-mail:* mgmartin@rci.rutgers.edu

SACRED HEART MAJOR SEMINARY

Detroit, MI

Tuition & fees: $6114 **Average undergraduate aid package: N/A**

ABOUT THE INSTITUTION Independent Roman Catholic, coed. Awards: associate, bachelor's, master's, and first professional degrees. 2 undergraduate majors. Total enrollment: 349. Undergraduates: 249. Freshmen: 8. Federal methodology is used as a basis for awarding need-based institutional aid.

UNDERGRADUATE EXPENSES for 1999–2000 ***Application fee:*** $30. ***Comprehensive fee:*** $10,504 includes full-time tuition ($6074), mandatory fees ($40), and room and board ($4390). Full-time tuition and fees vary according to course load. ***Part-time tuition:*** $192 per credit. ***Part-time fees:*** $20 per term part-time. Part-time tuition and fees vary according to course load. ***Payment plans:*** installment, deferred payment.

GIFT AID (NEED-BASED) ***Scholarships, grants, and awards:*** Federal Pell, FSEOG, state, private, college/university gift aid from institutional funds.

GIFT AID (NON-NEED-BASED) ***Scholarships, grants, and awards by category:*** *Special Characteristics:* local/state students, religious affiliation. ***Tuition waivers:*** Full or partial for employees or children of employees.

LOANS ***Programs:*** FFEL (Subsidized and Unsubsidized Stafford, PLUS), college/university.

WORK-STUDY Federal work-study jobs available.

APPLYING for FINANCIAL AID ***Required financial aid forms:*** FAFSA, institution's own form. ***Financial aid deadline (priority):*** 4/1.

CONTACT Sr. Mary Ward, OP, Registrar, Sacred Heart Major Seminary, 2701 West Chicago Boulevard, Detroit, MI 48206, 313-883-8587.

SACRED HEART UNIVERSITY

Fairfield, CT

Tuition & fees: $14,720 **Average undergraduate aid package: $10,887**

ABOUT THE INSTITUTION Independent Roman Catholic, coed. Awards: associate, bachelor's, and master's degrees and post-master's certificates (also offers part-time program with significant enrollment not reflected in profile). 57 undergraduate majors. Total enrollment: 5,528. Undergraduates: 3,920. Freshmen: 755. Both federal and institutionai methodology are used as a basis for awarding need-based institutional aid.

UNDERGRADUATE EXPENSES for 1999–2000 ***Application fee:*** $45. ***Comprehensive fee:*** $21,920 includes full-time tuition ($14,670), mandatory fees ($50), and room and board ($7200). ***College room only:*** $5130. Room and board charges vary according to board plan. ***Part-time tuition:*** $305 per credit. ***Part-time fees:*** $58 per term part-time. ***Payment plans:*** installment, deferred payment.

FRESHMAN FINANCIAL AID (Fall 1999, est.) 599 applied for aid; of those 83% were deemed to have need. 100% of freshmen with need received aid; of those 32% had need fully met. *Average percent of need met:* 70% (excluding resources awarded to replace EFC). *Average financial aid package:* $10,595 (excluding resources awarded to replace EFC). 30% of all full-time freshmen had no need and received non-need-based aid.

UNDERGRADUATE FINANCIAL AID (Fall 1999, est.) 1,922 applied for aid; of those 85% were deemed to have need. 100% of undergraduates with need received aid; of those 31% had need fully met. *Average percent of need met:* 72% (excluding resources awarded to replace EFC). *Average financial aid package:* $10,887 (excluding resources awarded to replace EFC). 32% of all full-time undergraduates had no need and received non-need-based aid.

GIFT AID (NEED-BASED) ***Total amount:*** $11,496,439 (9% Federal, 21% state, 65% institutional, 5% external sources). ***Receiving aid:*** *Freshmen:* 66% (473); *all full-time undergraduates:* 64% (1,555). ***Average award:*** Freshmen: $6466; Undergraduates: $6366. ***Scholarships, grants, and awards:*** Federal Pell, FSEOG, state, private, college/university gift aid from institutional funds.

GIFT AID (NON-NEED-BASED) ***Total amount:*** $1,013,846 (2% state, 75% institutional, 23% external sources). ***Receiving aid:*** *Freshmen:* 5% (39); *Undergraduates:* 4% (99). ***Scholarships, grants, and awards by category:*** *Academic Interests/Achievement:* 814 awards ($2,882,000 total): biological sciences, business, computer science, education, English, general academic interests/achievements, health fields, mathematics, premedicine. *Creative Arts/Performance:* 42 awards ($42,200 total): art/fine arts, cinema/film/broadcasting, music. *Special Achievements/Activities:* 113 awards ($226,125 total): community service, general special achievements/activities, hobbies/interests, leadership, religious involvement. *Special Characteristics:* adult students, children and siblings of alumni, children of faculty/staff, children of union members/company employees, ethnic background, general special characteristics, members of minority groups, siblings of current students. ***Tuition waivers:*** Full or partial for employees or children of employees, senior citizens.

LOANS ***Student loans:*** $8,845,196 (66% need-based, 34% non-need-based). 87% of past graduating class borrowed through all loan programs. Average indebtedness per student: $16,880. ***Average need-based loan:*** Freshmen: $3638; Undergraduates: $4229. ***Parent loans:*** $6,212,995 (44% need-based, 56% non-need-based). ***Programs:*** FFEL (Subsidized and Unsubsidized Stafford, PLUS), Perkins, state, alternative loans.

WORK-STUDY ***Federal work-study:*** *Total amount:* $247,382; 306 jobs averaging $808. ***State or other work-study/employment:*** *Total amount:* $353,006 (64% need-based, 36% non-need-based). Part-time jobs available.

ATHLETIC AWARDS *Total amount:* 964,659 (61% need-based, 39% non-need-based).

APPLYING for FINANCIAL AID ***Required financial aid forms:*** FAFSA, CSS Financial Aid PROFILE. ***Financial aid deadline (priority):*** 2/15. ***Notification date:*** 3/1. Students must reply within 2 weeks of notification.

CONTACT Ms. Julie B. Savino, Dean of University Financial Assistance, Sacred Heart University, 5151 Park Avenue, Fairfield, CT 06432-1000, 203-371-7980. *Fax:* 203-365-7608. *E-mail:* savinoj@sacredheart.edu

SAGINAW VALLEY STATE UNIVERSITY

University Center, MI

Tuition & fees (MI res): $3512 **Average undergraduate aid package: N/A**

ABOUT THE INSTITUTION State-supported, coed. Awards: bachelor's and master's degrees and post-master's certificates. 47 undergraduate majors. Total enrollment: 8,334. Undergraduates: 6,822. Freshmen: 1,083. Federal methodology is used as a basis for awarding need-based institutional aid.

UNDERGRADUATE EXPENSES for 1999–2000 ***Application fee:*** $25. ***Tuition, state resident:*** full-time $3243; part-time $108 per credit hour. ***Tuition, nonresident:*** full-time $6782; part-time $226 per credit hour. ***Required fees:*** full-time $269; $9 per credit hour. Full-time tuition and fees vary according to course load, location, and program. Part-time tuition and fees vary according to course load, location, and program. ***College room and board:*** $4800. Room and board charges vary according to board plan and housing facility. ***Payment plan:*** installment.

GIFT AID (NEED-BASED) ***Scholarships, grants, and awards:*** Federal Pell, FSEOG, state, private, college/university gift aid from institutional funds.

GIFT AID (NON-NEED-BASED) ***Scholarships, grants, and awards by category:*** *Academic Interests/Achievement:* biological sciences, business, communication, computer science, education, engineering/technologies, general academic interests/achievements, health fields, international studies, mathematics, physical sciences, premedicine, social sciences. *Creative Arts/Performance:* music. *Special Characteristics:* children of faculty/staff, international students, out-of-state students. ***Tuition waivers:*** Full or partial for employees or children of employees.

LOANS ***Programs:*** Federal Direct (Subsidized and Unsubsidized Stafford, PLUS).

WORK-STUDY Federal work-study jobs available.

APPLYING for FINANCIAL AID ***Required financial aid forms:*** FAFSA, state aid form. ***Financial aid deadline (priority):*** 2/14. ***Notification date:*** Continuous beginning 3/20. Students must reply within 10 weeks of notification.

CONTACT Cindy Munger, Director of Scholarships and Student Financial Aid, Saginaw Valley State University, 7400 Bay Road, University Center, MI 48710, 517-790-5628 or toll-free 800-968-9500. *Fax:* 517-790-0180.

ST. AMBROSE UNIVERSITY

Davenport, IA

Tuition & fees: $13,580 **Average undergraduate aid package: $11,200**

ABOUT THE INSTITUTION Independent Roman Catholic, coed. Awards: bachelor's, master's, and doctoral degrees and post-bachelor's and post-master's certificates. 63 undergraduate majors. Total enrollment: 2,819. Undergraduates: 1,960. Freshmen: 300. Both federal and institutional methodology are used as a basis for awarding need-based institutional aid.

UNDERGRADUATE EXPENSES for 2000–2001 ***Application fee:*** $25. ***Comprehensive fee:*** $18,730 includes full-time tuition ($13,580) and room and board ($5150). ***College room only:*** $2270. Full-time tuition and fees vary according to course load and degree level. Room and board charges vary according to board plan and housing facility. ***Part-time tuition:*** $415 per credit. Part-time tuition and fees vary according to degree level. ***Payment plan:*** installment.

FRESHMAN FINANCIAL AID (Fall 1998) 280 applied for aid; of those 92% were deemed to have need. 98% of freshmen with need received aid; of those 25% had need fully met. *Average percent of need met:* 80% (excluding resources awarded to replace EFC). *Average financial aid package:* $12,000 (excluding resources awarded to replace EFC). 9% of all full-time freshmen had no need and received non-need-based aid.

UNDERGRADUATE FINANCIAL AID (Fall 1998) 1,427 applied for aid; of those 85% were deemed to have need. 96% of undergraduates with need received aid; of those 26% had need fully met. *Average percent of need met:* 74% (excluding resources awarded to replace EFC). *Average financial*

St. Ambrose University (continued)

aid package: $11,200 (excluding resources awarded to replace EFC). 6% of all full-time undergraduates had no need and received non-need-based aid.

GIFT AID (NEED-BASED) ***Total amount:*** $6,707,944 (14% Federal, 26% state, 60% institutional). ***Receiving aid:*** *Freshmen:* 47% (139); *all full-time undergraduates:* 40% (581). ***Average award:*** Freshmen: $7200; Undergraduates: $7285. ***Scholarships, grants, and awards:*** Federal Pell, FSEOG, state, private, college/university gift aid from institutional funds.

GIFT AID (NON-NEED-BASED) ***Total amount:*** $270,691 (2% state, 40% institutional, 58% external sources). ***Receiving aid:*** *Freshmen:* 68% (200); *Undergraduates:* 16% (238). ***Scholarships, grants, and awards by category:*** *Academic Interests/Achievement:* biological sciences, business, communication, computer science, education, engineering/technologies, English, foreign languages, general academic interests/achievements, health fields, mathematics, physical sciences, premedicine, religion/biblical studies, social sciences. *Creative Arts/Performance:* art/fine arts, music, theater/drama. *Special Characteristics:* adult students, children and siblings of alumni, children of educators, children of faculty/staff, general special characteristics, international students, relatives of clergy, religious affiliation, siblings of current students. ***Tuition waivers:*** Full or partial for minority students, children of alumni, employees or children of employees, adult students, senior citizens.

LOANS ***Student loans:*** $8,737,078 (64% need-based, 36% non-need-based). 80% of past graduating class borrowed through all loan programs. Average indebtedness per student: $13,000. ***Average need-based loan:*** Freshmen: $3000; Undergraduates: $4000. ***Parent loans:*** $671,004 (100% non-need-based). ***Programs:*** Federal Direct (Subsidized and Unsubsidized Stafford, PLUS), Perkins.

WORK-STUDY ***Federal work-study:*** *Total amount:* $235,495; jobs available. ***State or other work-study/employment:*** *Total amount:* $210,687 (26% need-based, 74% non-need-based). 118 part-time jobs averaging $1850.

ATHLETIC AWARDS *Total amount:* 1,011,349 (100% non-need-based).

APPLYING for FINANCIAL AID ***Required financial aid forms:*** FAFSA, institution's own form. ***Financial aid deadline (priority):*** 3/15. ***Notification date:*** Continuous. Students must reply within 2 weeks of notification.

CONTACT Mr. Jeff Griebel, Director of Financial Aid, St. Ambrose University, 518 West Locust Street, Davenport, IA 52803, 319-333-6314 or toll-free 800-383-2627. *Fax:* 319-333-6243.

ST. ANDREWS PRESBYTERIAN COLLEGE

Laurinburg, NC

Tuition & fees: $13,735 **Average undergraduate aid package: $12,388**

ABOUT THE INSTITUTION Independent Presbyterian, coed. Awards: bachelor's degrees. 33 undergraduate majors. Total enrollment: 638. Undergraduates: 638. Freshmen: 152. Federal methodology is used as a basis for awarding need-based institutional aid.

UNDERGRADUATE EXPENSES for 1999–2000 ***Application fee:*** $25. ***Comprehensive fee:*** $19,035 includes full-time tuition ($13,515), mandatory fees ($220), and room and board ($5300). ***College room only:*** $2115. ***Part-time tuition:*** $410 per credit. ***Payment plan:*** installment.

FRESHMAN FINANCIAL AID (Fall 1998) 246 applied for aid; of those 67% were deemed to have need. 100% of freshmen with need received aid; of those 29% had need fully met. *Average percent of need met:* 81% (excluding resources awarded to replace EFC). *Average financial aid package:* $11,334 (excluding resources awarded to replace EFC). 31% of all full-time freshmen had no need and received non-need-based aid.

UNDERGRADUATE FINANCIAL AID (Fall 1998) 543 applied for aid; of those 67% were deemed to have need. 100% of undergraduates with need received aid; of those 29% had need fully met. *Average percent of need met:* 87% (excluding resources awarded to replace EFC). *Average financial aid package:* $12,388 (excluding resources awarded to replace EFC). 31% of all full-time undergraduates had no need and received non-need-based aid.

GIFT AID (NEED-BASED) ***Total amount:*** $2,475,927 (19% Federal, 8% state, 73% institutional). ***Receiving aid:*** *Freshmen:* 39% (101); *all full-time undergraduates:* 39% (221). ***Scholarships, grants, and awards:*** Federal Pell, FSEOG, state, private, college/university gift aid from institutional funds.

GIFT AID (NON-NEED-BASED) ***Total amount:*** $1,280,942 (22% state, 70% institutional, 8% external sources). ***Receiving aid:*** *Freshmen:* 60% (155); *Undergraduates:* 39% (224). ***Scholarships, grants, and awards by category:*** *Academic Interests/Achievement:* general academic interests/achievements. ***Tuition waivers:*** Full or partial for employees or children of employees, adult students.

LOANS ***Student loans:*** $1,448,673 (94% need-based, 6% non-need-based). ***Parent loans:*** $646,311 (100% non-need-based). ***Programs:*** FFEL (Subsidized and Unsubsidized Stafford, PLUS), Perkins.

WORK-STUDY ***Federal work-study:*** *Total amount:* $191,078; jobs available. ***State or other work-study/employment:*** *Total amount:* $48,631 (100% non-need-based). Part-time jobs available.

ATHLETIC AWARDS *Total amount:* 471,395 (62% need-based, 38% non-need-based).

APPLYING for FINANCIAL AID ***Required financial aid form:*** FAFSA. ***Financial aid deadline:*** Continuous. ***Notification date:*** Continuous beginning 2/1. Students must reply within 2 weeks of notification.

CONTACT Susan Hartwell, Director of Student Financial Planning, St. Andrews Presbyterian College, 1700 Dogwood Mile, Laurinburg, NC 28352, 910-277-5560 or toll-free 800-763-0198. *Fax:* 910-277-5206.

SAINT ANSELM COLLEGE

Manchester, NH

Tuition & fees: $17,640 **Average undergraduate aid package: N/A**

ABOUT THE INSTITUTION Independent Roman Catholic, coed. Awards: bachelor's degrees. 36 undergraduate majors. Total enrollment: 2,003. Undergraduates: 2,003. Freshmen: 536. Federal methodology is used as a basis for awarding need-based institutional aid.

UNDERGRADUATE EXPENSES for 1999–2000 ***Application fee:*** $35. ***Comprehensive fee:*** $24,160 includes full-time tuition ($17,300), mandatory fees ($340), and room and board ($6520). Room and board charges vary according to housing facility. ***Part-time tuition:*** $1730 per course. ***Payment plans:*** installment, deferred payment.

FRESHMAN FINANCIAL AID (Fall 1999, est.) 513 applied for aid; of those 92% were deemed to have need. 99% of freshmen with need received aid; of those 27% had need fully met. *Average percent of need met:* 85% (excluding resources awarded to replace EFC). *Average financial aid package:* $16,515 (excluding resources awarded to replace EFC). 13% of all full-time freshmen had no need and received non-need-based aid.

UNDERGRADUATE FINANCIAL AID (Fall 1999, est.) 1,679 applied for aid; of those 97% were deemed to have need. 100% of undergraduates with need received aid; of those 19% had need fully met. *Average percent of need met:* 81% (excluding resources awarded to replace EFC). 12% of all full-time undergraduates had no need and received non-need-based aid.

GIFT AID (NEED-BASED) ***Total amount:*** $12,710,982 (8% Federal, 1% state, 88% institutional, 3% external sources). ***Receiving aid:*** *Freshmen:* 74% (401); *all full-time undergraduates:* 72% (1,375). ***Average award:*** Freshmen: $9027. ***Scholarships, grants, and awards:*** Federal Pell, FSEOG, state, private, college/university gift aid from institutional funds.

GIFT AID (NON-NEED-BASED) ***Total amount:*** $3,391,575 (100% institutional). ***Receiving aid:*** *Freshmen:* 5% (29). ***Scholarships, grants, and awards by category:*** *Academic Interests/Achievement:* 245 awards ($1,833,841 total): general academic interests/achievements. *Creative Arts/Performance:* 5 awards ($7000 total): debating. *Special Characteristics:* 145 awards ($1,301,147 total): children of faculty/staff, members of minority groups, siblings of current students. ***Tuition waivers:*** Full or partial for employees or children of employees, senior citizens. ***ROTC:*** Army cooperative, Air Force cooperative.

LOANS ***Student loans:*** $4,504,922 (100% need-based). 77% of past graduating class borrowed through all loan programs. Average indebtedness per student: $16,448. ***Average need-based loan:*** Freshmen: $2571;

Undergraduates: $3575. ***Parent loans:*** $2,616,911 (100% non-need-based). ***Programs:*** FFEL (Subsidized and Unsubsidized Stafford, PLUS), Perkins, Federal Nursing, GATE Loans, GATE Family Loans.

WORK-STUDY ***Federal work-study:*** *Total amount:* $836,800; jobs available. ***State or other work-study/employment:*** *Total amount:* $218,342 (100% non-need-based). Part-time jobs available.

ATHLETIC AWARDS *Total amount:* 476,400 (100% non-need-based).

APPLYING for FINANCIAL AID ***Required financial aid forms:*** FAFSA, CSS Financial Aid PROFILE. ***Financial aid deadline:*** 4/15 (priority: 3/1). ***Notification date:*** Continuous. Students must reply by 5/1 or within 2 weeks of notification.

CONTACT Francis X. Fraitzl, Director of Financial Aid, Saint Anselm College, 100 Saint Anselm Drive—1735, Manchester, NH 03102-1310, 603-641-7110 or toll-free 888-4ANSELM. *Fax:* 603-641-7222.

SAINT ANTHONY COLLEGE OF NURSING

Rockford, IL

Tuition & fees: $11,460 **Average undergraduate aid package: $6666**

ABOUT THE INSTITUTION Independent Roman Catholic, coed, primarily women. Awards: bachelor's degrees. 1 undergraduate major. Total enrollment: 74. Undergraduates: 74. Federal methodology is used as a basis for awarding need-based institutional aid.

UNDERGRADUATE EXPENSES for 2000–2001 ***Application fee:*** $50. ***One-time required fee:*** $65. ***Tuition:*** full-time $11,360; part-time $355 per credit. ***Required fees:*** full-time $100. Full-time tuition and fees vary according to program. Part-time tuition and fees vary according to program. ***Payment plan:*** installment.

UNDERGRADUATE FINANCIAL AID (Fall 1998) 81 applied for aid; of those 100% were deemed to have need. 100% of undergraduates with need received aid. *Average percent of need met:* 50% (excluding resources awarded to replace EFC). *Average financial aid package:* $6666 (excluding resources awarded to replace EFC).

GIFT AID (NEED-BASED) ***Total amount:*** $214,575 (22% Federal, 60% state, 5% institutional, 13% external sources). ***Receiving aid:*** *All full-time undergraduates:* 57% (48). ***Average award:*** Undergraduates: $3659. ***Scholarships, grants, and awards:*** Federal Pell, state, private, college/university gift aid from institutional funds.

GIFT AID (NON-NEED-BASED) ***Receiving aid:*** *Undergraduates:* 45% (38).

LOANS ***Student loans:*** $488,989 (67% need-based, 33% non-need-based). 90% of past graduating class borrowed through all loan programs. Average indebtedness per student: $13,000. ***Average need-based loan:*** Undergraduates: $4785. ***Parent loans:*** $22,200 (100% need-based). ***Programs:*** FFEL (Subsidized and Unsubsidized Stafford, PLUS).

APPLYING for FINANCIAL AID ***Required financial aid forms:*** FAFSA, institution's own form. ***Financial aid deadline (priority):*** 5/1. ***Notification date:*** 7/1.

CONTACT Mr. Steve Crick, Financial Aid Officer, Saint Anthony College of Nursing, 5658 East State Street, Rockford, IL 61108-2468, 815-395-5089. *Fax:* 815-395-2275.

ST. AUGUSTINE COLLEGE

Chicago, IL

CONTACT Ms. Maria Zambonino, Director of Financial Aid, St. Augustine College, 1333 West Argyle, Chicago, IL 60640-3501, 773-878-8756.

SAINT AUGUSTINE'S COLLEGE

Raleigh, NC

Tuition & fees: $7182 **Average undergraduate aid package: $8762**

ABOUT THE INSTITUTION Independent Episcopal, coed. Awards: bachelor's degrees. 41 undergraduate majors. Total enrollment: 1,492. Undergraduates: 1,492. Freshmen: 338. Both federal and institutional methodology are used as a basis for awarding need-based institutional aid.

UNDERGRADUATE EXPENSES for 1999–2000 ***Application fee:*** $25. ***One-time required fee:*** $275. ***Comprehensive fee:*** $11,690 includes full-time tuition ($5132), mandatory fees ($2050), and room and board ($4508). Full-time tuition and fees vary according to program. Room and board charges vary according to housing facility and location. ***Part-time tuition:*** $210 per semester hour. ***Part-time fees:*** $210 per term part-time. Part-time tuition and fees vary according to program. ***Payment plan:*** installment.

FRESHMAN FINANCIAL AID (Fall 1998) 299 applied for aid; of those 87% were deemed to have need. 100% of freshmen with need received aid; of those 70% had need fully met. *Average percent of need met:* 73% (excluding resources awarded to replace EFC). *Average financial aid package:* $9453 (excluding resources awarded to replace EFC). 5% of all full-time freshmen had no need and received non-need-based aid.

UNDERGRADUATE FINANCIAL AID (Fall 1998) 1,483 applied for aid; of those 90% were deemed to have need. 100% of undergraduates with need received aid; of those 70% had need fully met. *Average percent of need met:* 73% (excluding resources awarded to replace EFC). *Average financial aid package:* $8762 (excluding resources awarded to replace EFC). 6% of all full-time undergraduates had no need and received non-need-based aid.

GIFT AID (NEED-BASED) ***Total amount:*** $4,190,553 (79% Federal, 17% state, 4% external sources). ***Receiving aid:*** *Freshmen:* 70% (210); *all full-time undergraduates:* 68% (1,028). ***Average award:*** Freshmen: $4321; Undergraduates: $3965. ***Scholarships, grants, and awards:*** Federal Pell, FSEOG, state, private, college/university gift aid from institutional funds, United Negro College Fund.

GIFT AID (NON-NEED-BASED) ***Total amount:*** $2,251,155 (1% Federal, 49% state, 30% institutional, 20% external sources). ***Receiving aid:*** *Freshmen:* 63% (187); *Undergraduates:* 68% (1,028). ***Scholarships, grants, and awards by category:*** *Academic Interests/Achievement:* 310 awards ($542,247 total): general academic interests/achievements. *Creative Arts/Performance:* 48 awards ($128,474 total): art/fine arts, music, performing arts. *Special Characteristics:* 8 awards ($29,580 total): children of faculty/staff. ***Tuition waivers:*** Full or partial for employees or children of employees. ***ROTC:*** Army, Air Force cooperative.

LOANS ***Student loans:*** $6,410,672 (64% need-based, 36% non-need-based). 79% of past graduating class borrowed through all loan programs. Average indebtedness per student: $18,000. ***Average need-based loan:*** Freshmen: $3384; Undergraduates: $3834. ***Parent loans:*** $3000 (100% non-need-based). ***Programs:*** FFEL (Subsidized and Unsubsidized Stafford, PLUS), Perkins.

WORK-STUDY ***Federal work-study:*** *Total amount:* $717,681; 422 jobs averaging $1700. ***State or other work-study/employment:*** *Total amount:* $122,800 (100% need-based). 114 part-time jobs averaging $1077.

ATHLETIC AWARDS *Total amount:* 721,062 (100% non-need-based).

APPLYING for FINANCIAL AID ***Required financial aid forms:*** FAFSA, institution's own form. ***Financial aid deadline (priority):*** 4/15. ***Notification date:*** Continuous beginning 5/1. Students must reply within 2 weeks of notification.

CONTACT Ms. Wanda White, Director of Financial Aid, Saint Augustine's College, 1315 Oakwood Avenue, Raleigh, NC 27610-2298, 919-516-4133 or toll-free 800-948-1126. *Fax:* 919-516-4338. *E-mail:* wwhite@es.st-aug.edu

ST. BONAVENTURE UNIVERSITY

St. Bonaventure, NY

Tuition & fees: $14,430 **Average undergraduate aid package: $12,811**

ABOUT THE INSTITUTION Independent religious, coed. Awards: bachelor's and master's degrees and post-bachelor's and post-master's certificates. 43 undergraduate majors. Total enrollment: 2,822. Undergraduates: 2,200. Freshmen: 520. Federal methodology is used as a basis for awarding need-based institutional aid.

UNDERGRADUATE EXPENSES for 1999–2000 ***Application fee:*** $30. ***Comprehensive fee:*** $20,230 includes full-time tuition ($13,880), mandatory fees ($550), and room and board ($5800). ***Part-time tuition:*** $440 per credit hour. ***Payment plans:*** installment, deferred payment.

St. Bonaventure University (continued)

FRESHMAN FINANCIAL AID (Fall 1999) 457 applied for aid; of those 86% were deemed to have need. 100% of freshmen with need received aid; of those 27% had need fully met. *Average percent of need met:* 90% (excluding resources awarded to replace EFC). *Average financial aid package:* $12,416 (excluding resources awarded to replace EFC). 17% of all full-time freshmen had no need and received non-need-based aid.

UNDERGRADUATE FINANCIAL AID (Fall 1999) 1,727 applied for aid; of those 87% were deemed to have need. 100% of undergraduates with need received aid; of those 41% had need fully met. *Average percent of need met:* 86% (excluding resources awarded to replace EFC). *Average financial aid package:* $12,811 (excluding resources awarded to replace EFC). 19% of all full-time undergraduates had no need and received non-need-based aid.

GIFT AID (NEED-BASED) ***Total amount:*** $9,675,263 (15% Federal, 18% state, 65% institutional, 2% external sources). ***Receiving aid:*** *Freshmen:* 76% (394); *all full-time undergraduates:* 71% (1,477). ***Average award:*** Freshmen: $7278; Undergraduates: $6869. ***Scholarships, grants, and awards:*** Federal Pell, FSEOG, state, private, college/university gift aid from institutional funds.

GIFT AID (NON-NEED-BASED) ***Total amount:*** $4,330,288 (10% Federal, 87% institutional, 3% external sources). ***Scholarships, grants, and awards by category:*** *Academic Interests/Achievement:* general academic interests/achievements. *Creative Arts/Performance:* music. *Special Characteristics:* children of faculty/staff, local/state students, members of minority groups, relatives of clergy, religious affiliation, siblings of current students. ***Tuition waivers:*** Full or partial for employees or children of employees, senior citizens. ***ROTC:*** Army.

LOANS ***Student loans:*** $9,492,927 (68% need-based, 32% non-need-based). 82% of past graduating class borrowed through all loan programs. Average indebtedness per student: $16,402. ***Average need-based loan:*** Freshmen: $3040; Undergraduates: $4167. ***Parent loans:*** $2,162,715 (64% need-based, 36% non-need-based). ***Programs:*** FFEL (Subsidized and Unsubsidized Stafford, PLUS), Perkins.

WORK-STUDY ***Federal work-study:*** *Total amount:* $538,734; jobs available. ***State or other work-study/employment:*** *Total amount:* $321,938 (54% need-based, 46% non-need-based). Part-time jobs available.

ATHLETIC AWARDS *Total amount:* 1,391,965 (34% need-based, 66% non-need-based).

APPLYING for FINANCIAL AID ***Required financial aid forms:*** FAFSA, institution's own form, state aid form. ***Financial aid deadline:*** Continuous. ***Notification date:*** Continuous beginning 4/1. Students must reply by 5/1 or within 2 weeks of notification.

CONTACT Ms. Mary K. Piccioli, Director of Financial Aid, St. Bonaventure University, Route 417, St. Bonaventure, NY 14778-2284, 716-375-2435 or toll-free 800-462-5050. *Fax:* 716-375-2005.

ST. CHARLES BORROMEO SEMINARY, OVERBROOK

Wynnewood, PA

Tuition & fees: $7950 **Average undergraduate aid package: N/A**

ABOUT THE INSTITUTION Independent Roman Catholic, coed, primarily men. Awards: bachelor's, master's, and first professional degrees. 1 undergraduate major. Total enrollment: 468. Undergraduates: 256. Freshmen: 6. Federal methodology is used as a basis for awarding need-based institutional aid.

UNDERGRADUATE EXPENSES for 1999–2000 ***Comprehensive fee:*** $13,500 includes full-time tuition ($7950) and room and board ($5550). ***Part-time tuition:*** $75 per credit. ***Payment plan:*** installment.

GIFT AID (NEED-BASED) ***Scholarships, grants, and awards:*** Federal Pell, FSEOG, state, college/university gift aid from institutional funds.

GIFT AID (NON-NEED-BASED) ***Scholarships, grants, and awards by category:*** *Academic Interests/Achievement:* general academic interests/achievements. ***Tuition waivers:*** Full or partial for employees or children of employees.

LOANS ***Programs:*** Federal Direct (Subsidized and Unsubsidized Stafford, PLUS).

WORK-STUDY Federal work-study jobs available.

APPLYING for FINANCIAL AID ***Required financial aid form:*** FAFSA. ***Financial aid deadline (priority):*** 4/15.

CONTACT Ms. Bonnie L. Behm, Coordinator of Financial Aid, St. Charles Borromeo Seminary, Overbrook, 100 East Wynnewood Road, Wynnewood, PA 19096-3099, 610-667-3394 Ext. 201. *Fax:* 610-667-3971.

ST. CLOUD STATE UNIVERSITY

St. Cloud, MN

ABOUT THE INSTITUTION State-supported, coed. Awards: associate, bachelor's, master's, and doctoral degrees. 118 undergraduate majors. Total enrollment: 14,551. Undergraduates: 13,372. Freshmen: 2,404.

GIFT AID (NEED-BASED) ***Scholarships, grants, and awards:*** Federal Pell, FSEOG, state, private, college/university gift aid from institutional funds.

GIFT AID (NON-NEED-BASED) ***Scholarships, grants, and awards by category:*** *Academic Interests/Achievement:* biological sciences, business, communication, computer science, education, engineering/technologies, English, general academic interests/achievements, international studies, mathematics, physical sciences, social sciences. *Creative Arts/Performance:* applied art and design, art/fine arts, cinema/film/broadcasting, journalism/publications, music, performing arts, theater/drama. *Special Characteristics:* children of faculty/staff, children of union members/company employees, local/state students, members of minority groups, out-of-state students.

LOANS ***Programs:*** FFEL (Subsidized and Unsubsidized Stafford, PLUS), Perkins, state, college/university.

WORK-STUDY Federal work-study jobs available.

APPLYING for FINANCIAL AID ***Required financial aid forms:*** FAFSA, institution's own form.

CONTACT Mr. Michael Uran, Assistant Director of Financial Aid, St. Cloud State University, Administrative Services-106, 720 4th Avenue South, St. Cloud, MN 56301-4498, 320-255-2047 or toll-free 877-654-7278. *Fax:* 320-654-5424. *E-mail:* mturan@stcloudstate.edu

ST. EDWARD'S UNIVERSITY

Austin, TX

Tuition & fees: $11,438 **Average undergraduate aid package: $9587**

ABOUT THE INSTITUTION Independent Roman Catholic, coed. Awards: bachelor's and master's degrees and post-bachelor's certificates. 33 undergraduate majors. Total enrollment: 3,669. Undergraduates: 2,957. Freshmen: 381. Federal methodology is used as a basis for awarding need-based institutional aid.

UNDERGRADUATE EXPENSES for 1999–2000 ***Application fee:*** $30. ***Comprehensive fee:*** $16,438 includes full-time tuition ($11,438) and room and board ($5000). Room and board charges vary according to housing facility. ***Part-time tuition:*** $381 per credit hour. ***Payment plan:*** installment.

FRESHMAN FINANCIAL AID (Fall 1999, est.) 268 applied for aid; of those 86% were deemed to have need. 100% of freshmen with need received aid; of those 20% had need fully met. *Average percent of need met:* 81% (excluding resources awarded to replace EFC). *Average financial aid package:* $9607 (excluding resources awarded to replace EFC). 7% of all full-time freshmen had no need and received non-need-based aid.

UNDERGRADUATE FINANCIAL AID (Fall 1999, est.) 1,255 applied for aid; of those 87% were deemed to have need. 99% of undergraduates with need received aid; of those 16% had need fully met. *Average percent of need met:* 79% (excluding resources awarded to replace EFC). *Average financial aid package:* $9587 (excluding resources awarded to replace EFC). 6% of all full-time undergraduates had no need and received non-need-based aid.

GIFT AID (NEED-BASED) ***Total amount:*** $6,857,451 (27% Federal, 27% state, 46% institutional). ***Receiving aid:*** *Freshmen:* 61% (221); *all full-time undergraduates:* 53% (1,007). ***Average award:*** Freshmen: $10,920;

Undergraduates: $8972. ***Scholarships, grants, and awards:*** Federal Pell, FSEOG, state, private, college/university gift aid from institutional funds, endowed scholarships.

GIFT AID (NON-NEED-BASED) ***Total amount:*** $1,393,035 (89% institutional, 11% external sources). ***Receiving aid:*** *Freshmen:* 31% (114); *Undergraduates:* 23% (435). ***Scholarships, grants, and awards by category:*** *Academic Interests/Achievement:* 432 awards ($981,352 total): biological sciences, business, communication, computer science, education, English, general academic interests/achievements, humanities, mathematics, physical sciences, religion/biblical studies, social sciences. *Creative Arts/Performance:* 27 awards ($73,300 total): theater/drama. *Special Achievements/Activities:* 10 awards ($6380 total): general special achievements/activities, leadership. *Special Characteristics:* 102 awards ($235,430 total): adult students, children of faculty/staff, religious affiliation, spouses of current students. ***Tuition waivers:*** Full or partial for employees or children of employees. ***ROTC:*** Army cooperative, Air Force cooperative.

LOANS ***Student loans:*** $10,041,029 (49% need-based, 51% non-need-based). 62% of past graduating class borrowed through all loan programs. ***Average need-based loan:*** Freshmen: $2489; Undergraduates: $3896. ***Parent loans:*** $1,752,596 (100% non-need-based). ***Programs:*** FFEL (Subsidized and Unsubsidized Stafford, PLUS), Perkins, state, alternative loans.

WORK-STUDY ***Federal work-study:*** *Total amount:* $325,519; 175 jobs averaging $1860. ***State or other work-study/employment:*** *Total amount:* $123,041 (100% need-based). 68 part-time jobs averaging $1809.

ATHLETIC AWARDS *Total amount:* 913,088 (100% non-need-based).

APPLYING for FINANCIAL AID ***Required financial aid form:*** FAFSA. ***Financial aid deadline (priority):*** 4/15. ***Notification date:*** Continuous.

CONTACT Christopher Roche, Scholarship Coordinator, St. Edward's University, 3001 South Congress Avenue, Austin, TX 78704-6489, 512-448-8784 or toll-free 800-555-0164. *Fax:* 512-416-5837. *E-mail:* chrisnr@admin.stedwards.edu

SAINT FRANCIS COLLEGE

Fort Wayne, IN

See University of Saint Francis

ST. FRANCIS COLLEGE

Brooklyn Heights, NY

Tuition & fees: $8410 **Average undergraduate aid package: $7990**

ABOUT THE INSTITUTION Independent Roman Catholic, coed. Awards: associate and bachelor's degrees. 35 undergraduate majors. Total enrollment: 2,305. Undergraduates: 2,305. Federal methodology is used as a basis for awarding need-based institutional aid.

UNDERGRADUATE EXPENSES for 1999–2000 ***Application fee:*** $20. ***One-time required fee:*** $25. ***Tuition:*** full-time $8250; part-time $285 per credit. ***Required fees:*** full-time $160; $20 per term part-time. Full-time tuition and fees vary according to course load. Part-time tuition and fees vary according to course load. ***Payment plan:*** installment.

FRESHMAN FINANCIAL AID (Fall 1998) 419 applied for aid; of those 72% were deemed to have need. 99% of freshmen with need received aid; of those .3% had need fully met. *Average percent of need met:* 60% (excluding resources awarded to replace EFC). *Average financial aid package:* $8226 (excluding resources awarded to replace EFC). 20% of all full-time freshmen had no need and received non-need-based aid.

UNDERGRADUATE FINANCIAL AID (Fall 1998) 1,403 applied for aid; of those 78% were deemed to have need. 98% of undergraduates with need received aid; of those 3% had need fully met. *Average percent of need met:* 60% (excluding resources awarded to replace EFC). *Average financial aid package:* $7990 (excluding resources awarded to replace EFC). 14% of all full-time undergraduates had no need and received non-need-based aid.

GIFT AID (NEED-BASED) ***Total amount:*** $5,471,829 (33% Federal, 49% state, 18% institutional). ***Receiving aid:*** *Freshmen:* 60% (284); *all full-time undergraduates:* 60% (1,047). ***Average award:*** Freshmen: $2136; Undergraduates: $2090. ***Scholarships, grants, and awards:*** Federal Pell, FSEOG, state, private, college/university gift aid from institutional funds.

GIFT AID (NON-NEED-BASED) ***Total amount:*** $741,198 (89% institutional, 11% external sources). ***Receiving aid:*** *Freshmen:* 31% (146); *Undergraduates:* 21% (371). ***Scholarships, grants, and awards by category:*** *Academic Interests/Achievement:* general academic interests/achievements. ***Tuition waivers:*** Full or partial for employees or children of employees. ***ROTC:*** Army cooperative, Air Force cooperative.

LOANS ***Student loans:*** $3,663,763 (100% need-based). ***Average need-based loan:*** Freshmen: $2625; Undergraduates: $4000. ***Parent loans:*** $239,900 (36% need-based, 64% non-need-based). ***Programs:*** FFEL (Subsidized and Unsubsidized Stafford, PLUS), Perkins.

WORK-STUDY ***Federal work-study:*** *Total amount:* $179,365; jobs available.

ATHLETIC AWARDS *Total amount:* 578,899 (58% need-based, 42% non-need-based).

APPLYING for FINANCIAL AID ***Required financial aid forms:*** FAFSA, institution's own form, state aid form. ***Financial aid deadline (priority):*** 2/15. ***Notification date:*** Continuous beginning 4/15. Students must reply within 2 weeks of notification.

CONTACT Br. Thomas O'Neill, OSF, Director of Financial Aid, St. Francis College, 180 Remsen Street, Brooklyn Heights, NY 11201-4398, 718-489-5346. *Fax:* 718-522-1274.

SAINT FRANCIS COLLEGE

Loretto, PA

Tuition & fees: $15,040 **Average undergraduate aid package: $15,555**

ABOUT THE INSTITUTION Independent Roman Catholic, coed. Awards: associate, bachelor's, and master's degrees. 55 undergraduate majors. Total enrollment: 1,993. Undergraduates: 1,484. Freshmen: 313. Both federal and institutional methodology are used as a basis for awarding need-based institutional aid.

UNDERGRADUATE EXPENSES for 1999–2000 ***Application fee:*** $30. ***Comprehensive fee:*** $21,520 includes full-time tuition ($15,040) and room and board ($6480). ***College room only:*** $3080. Room and board charges vary according to board plan, housing facility, and location. ***Part-time tuition:*** $470 per credit. Part-time tuition and fees vary according to course load. ***Payment plans:*** installment, deferred payment.

FRESHMAN FINANCIAL AID (Fall 1998) 310 applied for aid; of those 92% were deemed to have need. 99% of freshmen with need received aid; of those 11% had need fully met. *Average percent of need met:* 85% (excluding resources awarded to replace EFC). *Average financial aid package:* $15,032 (excluding resources awarded to replace EFC). 5% of all full-time freshmen had no need and received non-need-based aid.

UNDERGRADUATE FINANCIAL AID (Fall 1998) 1,174 applied for aid; of those 94% were deemed to have need. 98% of undergraduates with need received aid; of those 25% had need fully met. *Average percent of need met:* 89% (excluding resources awarded to replace EFC). *Average financial aid package:* $15,555 (excluding resources awarded to replace EFC). 4% of all full-time undergraduates had no need and received non-need-based aid.

GIFT AID (NEED-BASED) ***Total amount:*** $6,870,666 (15% Federal, 25% state, 59% institutional, 1% external sources). ***Receiving aid:*** *Freshmen:* 79% (261); *all full-time undergraduates:* 78% (968). ***Scholarships, grants, and awards:*** Federal Pell, FSEOG, state, private, college/university gift aid from institutional funds.

GIFT AID (NON-NEED-BASED) ***Total amount:*** $1,605,773 (95% institutional, 5% external sources). ***Receiving aid:*** *Freshmen:* 52% (171); *Undergraduates:* 45% (553). ***Scholarships, grants, and awards by category:*** *Academic Interests/Achievement:* 424 awards ($1,102,348 total): general academic interests/achievements. *Creative Arts/Performance:* art/fine arts, music, theater/drama. *Special Achievements/Activities:* cheerleading/drum major, community service, junior miss, religious involvement. *Special Characteristics:* adult students, children of faculty/staff, siblings of current students. ***Tuition waivers:*** Full or partial for children of alumni, employees or children of employees. ***ROTC:*** Army cooperative.

Saint Francis College (continued)

LOANS ***Student loans:*** $5,059,080 (72% need-based, 28% non-need-based). 90% of past graduating class borrowed through all loan programs. Average indebtedness per student: $14,075. ***Average need-based loan:*** Freshmen: $1671; Undergraduates: $2162. ***Parent loans:*** $1,005,977 (100% non-need-based). ***Programs:*** FFEL (Subsidized and Unsubsidized Stafford, PLUS), Perkins.

WORK-STUDY ***Federal work-study:*** *Total amount:* $549,991; 731 jobs averaging $800. ***State or other work-study/employment:*** *Total amount:* $63,653 (100% non-need-based). Part-time jobs available.

ATHLETIC AWARDS *Total amount:* 1,360,577 (100% non-need-based).

APPLYING for FINANCIAL AID ***Required financial aid forms:*** FAFSA, institution's own form. ***Financial aid deadline:*** Continuous. ***Notification date:*** Continuous beginning 3/1. Students must reply within 4 weeks of notification.

CONTACT Valerie A. Mockus, Director of Financial Aid, Saint Francis College, PO Box 600, Loretto, PA 15940-0600, 814-472-3010 or toll-free 800-342-5732. *Fax:* 814-472-3335. *E-mail:* vmockus@sfcpa.edu

SAINT FRANCIS MEDICAL CENTER COLLEGE OF NURSING

Peoria, IL

Tuition & fees: $9200 **Average undergraduate aid package: $8024**

ABOUT THE INSTITUTION Independent Roman Catholic, coed, primarily women. Awards: bachelor's degrees. 1 undergraduate major. Total enrollment: 144. Undergraduates: 144. Federal methodology is used as a basis for awarding need-based institutional aid.

UNDERGRADUATE EXPENSES for 1999–2000 ***Application fee:*** $25. ***Tuition:*** full-time $8880; part-time $370 per semester hour. ***Required fees:*** full-time $320; $160 per term part-time. Full-time tuition and fees vary according to course load. Part-time tuition and fees vary according to course load. ***Payment plans:*** installment, deferred payment.

UNDERGRADUATE FINANCIAL AID (Fall 1998) 135 applied for aid; of those 81% were deemed to have need. 99% of undergraduates with need received aid; of those 17% had need fully met. *Average percent of need met:* 73% (excluding resources awarded to replace EFC). *Average financial aid package:* $8024 (excluding resources awarded to replace EFC). 5% of all full-time undergraduates had no need and received non-need-based aid.

GIFT AID (NEED-BASED) ***Total amount:*** $413,256 (19% Federal, 62% state, 14% institutional, 5% external sources). ***Receiving aid:*** *All full-time undergraduates:* 68% (103). ***Average award:*** Undergraduates: $4062. ***Scholarships, grants, and awards:*** Federal Pell, state, private, college/university gift aid from institutional funds.

GIFT AID (NON-NEED-BASED) ***Total amount:*** $128,443 (8% state, 91% institutional, 1% external sources). ***Receiving aid:*** *Undergraduates:* 55% (83). ***Scholarships, grants, and awards by category:*** *Academic Interests/Achievement:* 68 awards ($20,600 total): general academic interests/achievements, health fields. ***Tuition waivers:*** Full or partial for employees or children of employees.

LOANS ***Student loans:*** $478,114 (81% need-based, 19% non-need-based). 63% of past graduating class borrowed through all loan programs. ***Average need-based loan:*** Undergraduates: $3313. ***Parent loans:*** $19,948 (18% need-based, 82% non-need-based). ***Programs:*** FFEL (Subsidized and Unsubsidized Stafford, PLUS), college/university.

ATHLETIC AWARDS *Total amount:* 84,406 (33% need-based, 67% non-need-based).

APPLYING for FINANCIAL AID ***Required financial aid forms:*** FAFSA, institution's own form. ***Financial aid deadline (priority):*** 3/1. ***Notification date:*** Continuous beginning 5/1.

CONTACT Ms. Kathy Casey, Director of Financial Aid, Saint Francis Medical Center College of Nursing, 511 Northeast Greenleaf Street, Peoria, IL 61603-3783, 309-655-2291. *E-mail:* kathy.casey@osfhealthcare.org

ST. GREGORY'S UNIVERSITY

Shawnee, OK

Tuition & fees: $7866 **Average undergraduate aid package: $8467**

ABOUT THE INSTITUTION Independent Roman Catholic, coed. Awards: associate and bachelor's degrees. 8 undergraduate majors. Total enrollment: 742. Undergraduates: 742. Freshmen: 173. Federal methodology is used as a basis for awarding need-based institutional aid.

UNDERGRADUATE EXPENSES for 1999–2000 ***Application fee:*** $25. ***Comprehensive fee:*** $11,936 includes full-time tuition ($7126), mandatory fees ($740), and room and board ($4070). ***College room only:*** $2290. Full-time tuition and fees vary according to course load. Room and board charges vary according to board plan and housing facility. ***Part-time tuition:*** $225 per credit hour. ***Part-time fees:*** $30 per credit hour. Part-time tuition and fees vary according to course load. Additional technology fee: $150 full-time, $75 per term part-time for students who own laptop computers; $400 full-time, $32 per credit hour part-time for students who do not own laptop computers. ***Payment plans:*** installment, deferred payment.

FRESHMAN FINANCIAL AID (Fall 1998) 116 applied for aid; of those 59% were deemed to have need. 99% of freshmen with need received aid; of those 13% had need fully met.

UNDERGRADUATE FINANCIAL AID (Fall 1998) 451 applied for aid; of those 69% were deemed to have need. 99% of undergraduates with need received aid; of those 26% had need fully met. *Average percent of need met:* 76% (excluding resources awarded to replace EFC). *Average financial aid package:* $8467 (excluding resources awarded to replace EFC). 14% of all full-time undergraduates had no need and received non-need-based aid.

GIFT AID (NEED-BASED) ***Total amount:*** $1,121,310 (36% Federal, 9% state, 44% institutional, 11% external sources). ***Receiving aid:*** *Freshmen:* 40% (62); *all full-time undergraduates:* 61% (305). ***Average award:*** Undergraduates: $4875. ***Scholarships, grants, and awards:*** Federal Pell, FSEOG, state, private, college/university gift aid from institutional funds.

GIFT AID (NON-NEED-BASED) ***Total amount:*** $287,072 (78% institutional, 22% external sources). ***Receiving aid:*** *Freshmen:* 15% (23); *Undergraduates:* 14% (69). ***Scholarships, grants, and awards by category:*** *Academic Interests/Achievement:* 67 awards ($136,056 total): general academic interests/achievements. *Creative Arts/Performance:* 50 awards ($75,236 total): dance, journalism/publications, music, theater/drama. *Special Achievements/Activities:* 79 awards ($72,880 total): cheerleading/drum major, leadership, religious involvement. *Special Characteristics:* 121 awards ($242,615 total): children of faculty/staff, handicapped students, international students, religious affiliation. ***Tuition waivers:*** Full or partial for employees or children of employees, senior citizens. ***ROTC:*** Air Force cooperative.

LOANS ***Student loans:*** $998,997 (68% need-based, 32% non-need-based). 57% of past graduating class borrowed through all loan programs. ***Average need-based loan:*** Undergraduates: $2882. ***Parent loans:*** $225,912 (100% non-need-based). ***Programs:*** Federal Direct (Subsidized and Unsubsidized Stafford, PLUS), Perkins.

WORK-STUDY ***Federal work-study:*** *Total amount:* $54,169; 59 jobs averaging $918. ***State or other work-study/employment:*** *Total amount:* $73,250 (100% non-need-based). Part-time jobs available.

ATHLETIC AWARDS *Total amount:* 828,345 (53% need-based, 47% non-need-based).

APPLYING for FINANCIAL AID ***Required financial aid forms:*** FAFSA, institution's own form. ***Financial aid deadline:*** Continuous. ***Notification date:*** Continuous beginning 4/1. Students must reply within 2 weeks of notification.

CONTACT Financial Aid Office, St. Gregory's University, 1900 West MacArthur Drive, Shawnee, OK 74804, 888-STGREGS. *Fax:* 405-878-5198. *E-mail:* admissions@sgc.edu

ST. JOHN FISHER COLLEGE

Rochester, NY

Tuition & fees: $14,140 **Average undergraduate aid package: $10,794**

ABOUT THE INSTITUTION Independent religious, coed. Awards: bachelor's and master's degrees. 34 undergraduate majors. Total enrollment: 2,588. Undergraduates: 2,123. Federal methodology is used as a basis for awarding need-based institutional aid.

UNDERGRADUATE EXPENSES for 1999–2000 ***Application fee:*** $25. ***One-time required fee:*** $200. ***Comprehensive fee:*** $20,190 includes full-time tuition ($13,990), mandatory fees ($150), and room and board ($6050). Full-time tuition and fees vary according to course load. Room and board charges vary according to board plan. ***Part-time tuition:*** $395 per credit hour. Part-time tuition and fees vary according to course load. ***Payment plans:*** installment, deferred payment.

FRESHMAN FINANCIAL AID (Fall 1999, est.) 389 applied for aid; of those 100% were deemed to have need. 100% of freshmen with need received aid; of those 18% had need fully met. *Average percent of need met:* 81% (excluding resources awarded to replace EFC). *Average financial aid package:* $11,879 (excluding resources awarded to replace EFC). 6% of all full-time freshmen had no need and received non-need-based aid.

UNDERGRADUATE FINANCIAL AID (Fall 1999, est.) 1,452 applied for aid; of those 90% were deemed to have need. 100% of undergraduates with need received aid; of those 48% had need fully met. *Average percent of need met:* 84% (excluding resources awarded to replace EFC). *Average financial aid package:* $10,794 (excluding resources awarded to replace EFC). 6% of all full-time undergraduates had no need and received non-need-based aid.

GIFT AID (NEED-BASED) ***Total amount:*** $6,390,199 (21% Federal, 33% state, 44% institutional, 2% external sources). ***Receiving aid:*** *Freshmen:* 74% (303); *all full-time undergraduates:* 65% (1,050). ***Average award:*** Freshmen: $5418. ***Scholarships, grants, and awards:*** Federal Pell, FSEOG, state, private, college/university gift aid from institutional funds.

GIFT AID (NON-NEED-BASED) ***Total amount:*** $3,259,130 (100% institutional). ***Receiving aid:*** *Freshmen:* 13% (55); *Undergraduates:* 38% (615). ***Scholarships, grants, and awards by category:*** *Academic Interests/Achievement:* business, English, foreign languages, general academic interests/achievements, humanities, mathematics, physical sciences. *Special Achievements/Activities:* community service, junior miss. *Special Characteristics:* children and siblings of alumni, ethnic background, local/state students, members of minority groups. ***Tuition waivers:*** Full or partial for employees or children of employees, senior citizens. ***ROTC:*** Army cooperative, Air Force cooperative.

LOANS ***Student loans:*** $9,141,145 (60% need-based, 40% non-need-based). 76% of past graduating class borrowed through all loan programs. Average indebtedness per student: $18,400. ***Average need-based loan:*** Freshmen: $2264. ***Programs:*** FFEL (Subsidized and Unsubsidized Stafford, PLUS), Perkins.

WORK-STUDY ***Federal work-study:*** *Total amount:* $278,526; 260 jobs averaging $1600.

APPLYING for FINANCIAL AID ***Required financial aid forms:*** FAFSA, state aid form. ***Financial aid deadline (priority):*** 2/15. ***Notification date:*** Continuous beginning 3/21. Students must reply by 5/1 or within 3 weeks of notification.

CONTACT Mrs. Angela Monnat, Director of Financial Aid, St. John Fisher College, 3690 East Avenue, Rochester, NY 14618-3597, 716-385-8042 or toll-free 800-444-4640. *Fax:* 716-385-8129. *E-mail:* monnat@sjfc.edu

ST. JOHN'S COLLEGE

Springfield, IL

Tuition & fees: $7654 **Average undergraduate aid package: N/A**

ABOUT THE INSTITUTION Independent Roman Catholic, coed. Awards: bachelor's degrees. 1 undergraduate major. Total enrollment: 84. Undergraduates: 84. Federal methodology is used as a basis for awarding need-based institutional aid.

UNDERGRADUATE EXPENSES for 1999–2000 ***Application fee:*** $25. ***One-time required fee:*** $67. ***Tuition:*** full-time $7442. ***Required fees:*** full-time $212. Full-time tuition and fees vary according to course load and student level. Part-time tuition and fees vary according to course load and student level. ***Payment plans:*** installment, deferred payment.

UNDERGRADUATE FINANCIAL AID (Fall 1998) 81 applied for aid; of those 84% were deemed to have need. 100% of undergraduates with need received aid; of those 16% had need fully met. *Average percent of need met:* 52% (excluding resources awarded to replace EFC). 13% of all full-time undergraduates had no need and received non-need-based aid.

GIFT AID (NEED-BASED) ***Total amount:*** $291,584 (20% Federal, 54% state, 17% institutional, 9% external sources). ***Receiving aid:*** *All full-time undergraduates:* 73% (68). ***Scholarships, grants, and awards:*** Federal Pell, FSEOG, state, private, college/university gift aid from institutional funds, Federal Nursing.

LOANS ***Student loans:*** $468,392 (69% need-based, 31% non-need-based). ***Parent loans:*** $19,498 (100% need-based). ***Programs:*** FFEL (Subsidized and Unsubsidized Stafford, PLUS), Federal Nursing.

WORK-STUDY ***Federal work-study:*** *Total amount:* $17,500; 11 jobs averaging $851.

APPLYING for FINANCIAL AID ***Required financial aid forms:*** FAFSA, institution's own form. ***Financial aid deadline (priority):*** 5/1. ***Notification date:*** 5/15. Students must reply within 2 weeks of notification.

CONTACT Joann Williams, Financial Aid Administrator, St. John's College, 421 North Ninth Street, Springfield, IL 62702, 217-544-6464 Ext. 44705. *Fax:* 217-757-6870.

ST. JOHN'S COLLEGE

Annapolis, MD

Tuition & fees: $23,490 **Average undergraduate aid package: $20,763**

ABOUT THE INSTITUTION Independent, coed. Awards: bachelor's and master's degrees. 3 undergraduate majors. Total enrollment: 516. Undergraduates: 452. Freshmen: 133. Both federal and institutional methodology are used as a basis for awarding need-based institutional aid.

UNDERGRADUATE EXPENSES for 1999–2000 ***Comprehensive fee:*** $29,850 includes full-time tuition ($23,290), mandatory fees ($200), and room and board ($6360). ***College room only:*** $3150. Room and board charges vary according to board plan. ***Payment plans:*** tuition prepayment, installment.

FRESHMAN FINANCIAL AID (Fall 1999) 90 applied for aid; of those 84% were deemed to have need. 100% of freshmen with need received aid; of those 95% had need fully met. *Average percent of need met:* 95% (excluding resources awarded to replace EFC). *Average financial aid package:* $19,826 (excluding resources awarded to replace EFC).

UNDERGRADUATE FINANCIAL AID (Fall 1999) 300 applied for aid; of those 95% were deemed to have need. 100% of undergraduates with need received aid; of those 99% had need fully met. *Average percent of need met:* 95% (excluding resources awarded to replace EFC). *Average financial aid package:* $20,763 (excluding resources awarded to replace EFC).

GIFT AID (NEED-BASED) ***Total amount:*** $4,191,167 (9% Federal, 3% state, 84% institutional, 4% external sources). ***Receiving aid:*** *Freshmen:* 45% (60); *all full-time undergraduates:* 58% (264). ***Average award:*** Freshmen: $14,207; Undergraduates: $14,132. ***Scholarships, grants, and awards:*** Federal Pell, FSEOG, state, college/university gift aid from institutional funds.

GIFT AID (NON-NEED-BASED) ***Tuition waivers:*** Full or partial for employees or children of employees.

LOANS ***Student loans:*** $1,371,983 (100% need-based). 65% of past graduating class borrowed through all loan programs. Average indebtedness per student: $17,125. ***Average need-based loan:*** Freshmen: $3125; Undergraduates: $4280. ***Parent loans:*** $1,172,552 (100% need-based). ***Programs:*** FFEL (Subsidized and Unsubsidized Stafford, PLUS), Perkins, college/university.

St. John's College (continued)

WORK-STUDY ***Federal work-study:*** *Total amount:* $280,000; 200 jobs averaging $2350. ***State or other work-study/employment:*** *Total amount:* $35,000 (100% non-need-based). Part-time jobs available.

APPLYING for FINANCIAL AID ***Required financial aid forms:*** FAFSA, CSS Financial Aid PROFILE. ***Financial aid deadline (priority):*** 2/15. ***Notification date:*** Continuous. Students must reply by 5/5.

CONTACT Ms. Caroline Christensen, Director of Financial Aid, St. John's College, PO Box 2800, Annapolis, MD 21404, 410-626-2502 or toll-free 800-727-9238. *Fax:* 410-626-2885. *E-mail:* c-christensen@sjca.edu

ST. JOHN'S COLLEGE

Santa Fe, NM

Tuition & fees: $22,200 **Average undergraduate aid package: $20,220**

ABOUT THE INSTITUTION Independent, coed. Awards: bachelor's and master's degrees. 5 undergraduate majors. Total enrollment: 556. Undergraduates: 431. Freshmen: 109. Both federal and institutional methodology are used as a basis for awarding need-based institutional aid.

UNDERGRADUATE EXPENSES for 1999–2000 ***Comprehensive fee:*** $28,586 includes full-time tuition ($22,000), mandatory fees ($200), and room and board ($6386). Room and board charges vary according to board plan. ***Payment plans:*** tuition prepayment, installment.

FRESHMAN FINANCIAL AID (Fall 1999) 96 applied for aid; of those 81% were deemed to have need. 100% of freshmen with need received aid; of those 95% had need fully met. *Average percent of need met:* 99% (excluding resources awarded to replace EFC). *Average financial aid package:* $17,512 (excluding resources awarded to replace EFC). 15% of all full-time freshmen had no need and received non-need-based aid.

UNDERGRADUATE FINANCIAL AID (Fall 1999) 220 applied for aid; of those 89% were deemed to have need. 100% of undergraduates with need received aid; of those 96% had need fully met. *Average percent of need met:* 99% (excluding resources awarded to replace EFC). *Average financial aid package:* $20,220 (excluding resources awarded to replace EFC). 9% of all full-time undergraduates had no need and received non-need-based aid.

GIFT AID (NEED-BASED) ***Total amount:*** $3,513,921 (10% Federal, 3% state, 86% institutional, 1% external sources). ***Receiving aid:*** *Freshmen:* 58% (71); *all full-time undergraduates:* 44% (187). ***Average award:*** Freshmen: $14,046; Undergraduates: $13,172. ***Scholarships, grants, and awards:*** Federal Pell, FSEOG, state, private, college/university gift aid from institutional funds.

GIFT AID (NON-NEED-BASED) ***Total amount:*** $319,138 (1% Federal, 16% state, 63% institutional, 20% external sources). ***Receiving aid:*** *Freshmen:* 5% (6); *Undergraduates:* 3% (15). ***Scholarships, grants, and awards by category:*** *Special Characteristics:* children of faculty/staff. ***Tuition waivers:*** Full or partial for employees or children of employees.

LOANS ***Student loans:*** $1,587,439 (75% need-based, 25% non-need-based). 74% of past graduating class borrowed through all loan programs. Average indebtedness per student: $17,125. ***Average need-based loan:*** Freshmen: $3125; Undergraduates: $4850. ***Parent loans:*** $344,332 (100% non-need-based). ***Programs:*** Federal Direct (Subsidized and Unsubsidized Stafford, PLUS), FFEL (Subsidized and Unsubsidized Stafford, PLUS), Perkins, state, college/university.

WORK-STUDY ***Federal work-study:*** *Total amount:* $396,354; jobs available. ***State or other work-study/employment:*** *Total amount:* $39,940 (56% need-based, 44% non-need-based). Part-time jobs available.

APPLYING for FINANCIAL AID ***Required financial aid forms:*** FAFSA, CSS Financial Aid PROFILE, noncustodial (divorced/separated) parent's statement, business/farm supplement. ***Financial aid deadline:*** 2/15 (priority: 12/1). ***Notification date:*** Continuous. Students must reply by 5/1.

CONTACT Michael Rodriquez, Director of Financial Aid, St. John's College, 1160 Camino Cruz Blanca, Santa Fe, NM 87501-4599, 505-984-6058 or toll-free 800-331-5232. *Fax:* 505-984-6003.

ST. JOHN'S SEMINARY COLLEGE

Camarillo, CA

Tuition & fees: $7555 **Average undergraduate aid package: N/A**

ABOUT THE INSTITUTION Independent Roman Catholic, men only. Awards: bachelor's degrees. 4 undergraduate majors. Total enrollment: 90. Undergraduates: 90. Freshmen: 2. Federal methodology is used as a basis for awarding need-based institutional aid.

UNDERGRADUATE EXPENSES for 1999–2000 ***Application fee:*** $40. ***Comprehensive fee:*** $11,555 includes full-time tuition ($7270), mandatory fees ($285), and room and board ($4000). ***Payment plans:*** installment, deferred payment.

GIFT AID (NEED-BASED) ***Scholarships, grants, and awards:*** Federal Pell, FSEOG, state, private, college/university gift aid from institutional funds.

GIFT AID (NON-NEED-BASED) ***Scholarships, grants, and awards by category:*** *Academic Interests/Achievement:* general academic interests/achievements. *Special Characteristics:* religious affiliation, veterans.

LOANS ***Programs:*** FFEL (Subsidized Stafford), college/university.

WORK-STUDY Federal work-study jobs available.

APPLYING for FINANCIAL AID ***Required financial aid form:*** FAFSA. ***Financial aid deadline:*** Continuous. ***Notification date:*** Continuous beginning 6/15. Students must reply within 4 weeks of notification.

CONTACT Rain Delaney, Financial Aid Officer, St. John's Seminary College, 5118 Seminary Road, Camarillo, CA 93012, 805-482-2755 Ext. 1004. *Fax:* 805-484-4074. *E-mail:* rdelaney@sjs-sc.org

SAINT JOHN'S SEMINARY COLLEGE OF LIBERAL ARTS

Brighton, MA

Tuition & fees: $5800 **Average undergraduate aid package: N/A**

ABOUT THE INSTITUTION Independent Roman Catholic, men only. Awards: associate and bachelor's degrees. 1 undergraduate major. Total enrollment: 31. Undergraduates: 31. Freshmen: 7. Federal methodology is used as a basis for awarding need-based institutional aid.

UNDERGRADUATE EXPENSES for 1999–2000 ***Comprehensive fee:*** $8800 includes full-time tuition ($5800) and room and board ($3000). ***Part-time tuition:*** $200 per credit hour. ***Payment plan:*** installment.

GIFT AID (NEED-BASED) ***Scholarships, grants, and awards:*** Federal Pell, FSEOG, state.

GIFT AID (NON-NEED-BASED) ***Scholarships, grants, and awards by category:*** *Academic Interests/Achievement:* religion/biblical studies.

LOANS ***Programs:*** Federal Direct (Subsidized and Unsubsidized Stafford, PLUS), FFEL (Subsidized and Unsubsidized Stafford, PLUS), college/university.

WORK-STUDY Federal work-study jobs available.

APPLYING for FINANCIAL AID ***Required financial aid form:*** FAFSA. ***Financial aid deadline (priority):*** 5/1. ***Notification date:*** Continuous beginning 9/1. Students must reply within 3 weeks of notification.

CONTACT Mr. John B. Lynch Jr., Business Manager, Saint John's Seminary College of Liberal Arts, 197 Foster Street, Brighton, MA 02135-4644, 617-746-5450. *Fax:* 617-787-2336.

SAINT JOHN'S UNIVERSITY

Collegeville, MN

Tuition & fees: $16,441 **Average undergraduate aid package: $13,677**

ABOUT THE INSTITUTION Independent Roman Catholic, men only. Awards: bachelor's, master's, and first professional degrees. 49 undergraduate majors. Total enrollment: 1,932. Undergraduates: 1,803. Freshmen: 475. Federal methodology is used as a basis for awarding need-based institutional aid.

UNDERGRADUATE EXPENSES for 1999–2000 ***Application fee:*** $25. ***Comprehensive fee:*** $21,371 includes full-time tuition ($16,195), mandatory fees ($246), and room and board ($4930). ***College room only:*** $2364. Room and board charges vary according to board plan and housing facility. ***Part-time tuition:*** $675 per credit. ***Payment plans:*** tuition prepayment, installment, deferred payment.

FRESHMAN FINANCIAL AID (Fall 1999, est.) 423 applied for aid; of those 73% were deemed to have need. 100% of freshmen with need received aid; of those 88% had need fully met. *Average percent of need met:* 96% (excluding resources awarded to replace EFC). *Average financial aid package:* $13,719 (excluding resources awarded to replace EFC). 29% of all full-time freshmen had no need and received non-need-based aid.

UNDERGRADUATE FINANCIAL AID (Fall 1999, est.) 1,568 applied for aid; of those 66% were deemed to have need. 100% of undergraduates with need received aid; of those 88% had need fully met. *Average percent of need met:* 96% (excluding resources awarded to replace EFC). *Average financial aid package:* $13,677 (excluding resources awarded to replace EFC). 30% of all full-time undergraduates had no need and received non-need-based aid.

GIFT AID (NEED-BASED) ***Total amount:*** $9,013,210 (8% Federal, 21% state, 67% institutional, 4% external sources). ***Receiving aid:*** *Freshmen:* 64% (306); *all full-time undergraduates:* 57% (1,001). ***Average award:*** Freshmen: $9140; Undergraduates: $8680. ***Scholarships, grants, and awards:*** Federal Pell, FSEOG, state, private, college/university gift aid from institutional funds.

GIFT AID (NON-NEED-BASED) ***Total amount:*** $2,969,958 (10% Federal, 87% institutional, 3% external sources). ***Receiving aid:*** *Freshmen:* 31% (145); *Undergraduates:* 31% (550). ***Scholarships, grants, and awards by category:*** *Academic Interests/Achievement:* 406 awards ($2,026,847 total): general academic interests/achievements. *Creative Arts/Performance:* 38 awards ($53,725 total): art/fine arts, music, theater/drama. *Special Achievements/Activities:* 193 awards ($341,000 total): leadership. *Special Characteristics:* 21 awards ($177,030 total): international students. ***ROTC:*** Army.

LOANS ***Student loans:*** $5,475,485 (86% need-based, 14% non-need-based). 73% of past graduating class borrowed through all loan programs. Average indebtedness per student: $16,487. ***Average need-based loan:*** Freshmen: $3525; Undergraduates: $4815. ***Parent loans:*** $849,250 (100% non-need-based). ***Programs:*** FFEL (Subsidized and Unsubsidized Stafford, PLUS), Perkins, state, Student Educational Loan Fund (SELF), Norwest Collegiate Loans, GOAL Loans, Voyager Loan Program.

WORK-STUDY ***Federal work-study:*** *Total amount:* $360,000; 233 jobs averaging $1600. ***State or other work-study/employment:*** *Total amount:* $1,719,947 (80% need-based, 20% non-need-based). 717 part-time jobs averaging $2400.

APPLYING for FINANCIAL AID ***Required financial aid forms:*** FAFSA, institution's own form, parent and student federal income tax returns. ***Financial aid deadline (priority):*** 3/1. ***Notification date:*** Continuous. Students must reply within 3 weeks of notification.

CONTACT Ms. Mary Dehler, Associate Director of Financial Aid, Saint John's University, PO Box 5000, Collegeville, MN 56321-5000, 320-363-3664 or toll-free 800-24JOHNS. *Fax:* 320-363-3102. *E-mail:* mdehler@csbsju.edu

ST. JOHN'S UNIVERSITY

Jamaica, NY

Tuition & fees: $14,420 **Average undergraduate aid package: $10,517**

ABOUT THE INSTITUTION Independent religious, coed. Awards: associate, bachelor's, master's, doctoral, and first professional degrees and post-master's certificates. 69 undergraduate majors. Total enrollment: 18,478. Undergraduates: 14,035. Freshmen: 2,696. Federal methodology is used as a basis for awarding need-based institutional aid.

UNDERGRADUATE EXPENSES for 1999–2000 ***Application fee:*** $30. ***Comprehensive fee:*** $22,970 includes full-time tuition ($13,990), mandatory fees ($430), and room and board ($8550). Full-time tuition and fees vary according to class time, course level, course load, program, and student level. Room and board charges vary according to housing facility. ***Part-time tuition:*** $466 per credit. ***Part-time fees:*** $70 per term part-time. Part-time tuition and fees vary according to class time, course level, course load, program, and student level. ***Payment plans:*** guaranteed tuition, installment, deferred payment.

FRESHMAN FINANCIAL AID (Fall 1998) 2284 applied for aid; of those 86% were deemed to have need. 100% of freshmen with need received aid; of those 11% had need fully met. *Average percent of need met:* 85% (excluding resources awarded to replace EFC). *Average financial aid package:* $11,192 (excluding resources awarded to replace EFC). 11% of all full-time freshmen had no need and received non-need-based aid.

UNDERGRADUATE FINANCIAL AID (Fall 1998) 9,662 applied for aid; of those 85% were deemed to have need. 100% of undergraduates with need received aid; of those 8% had need fully met. *Average percent of need met:* 70% (excluding resources awarded to replace EFC). *Average financial aid package:* $10,517 (excluding resources awarded to replace EFC). 9% of all full-time undergraduates had no need and received non-need-based aid.

GIFT AID (NEED-BASED) ***Total amount:*** $37,689,532 (31% Federal, 43% state, 26% institutional). ***Receiving aid:*** *Freshmen:* 74% (1,848); *all full-time undergraduates:* 63% (6,750). ***Average award:*** Freshmen: $4461; Undergraduates: $3445. ***Scholarships, grants, and awards:*** Federal Pell, FSEOG, state, private, college/university gift aid from institutional funds.

GIFT AID (NON-NEED-BASED) ***Total amount:*** $18,757,888 (6% Federal, 1% state, 84% institutional, 9% external sources). ***Receiving aid:*** *Freshmen:* 30% (758); *Undergraduates:* 24% (2,511). ***Scholarships, grants, and awards by category:*** *Academic Interests/Achievement:* 2,964 awards ($12,735,142 total): biological sciences, computer science, general academic interests/achievements, health fields, mathematics, military science. *Creative Arts/Performance:* 154 awards ($332,842 total): art/fine arts, cinema/film/broadcasting, debating, journalism/publications, music, performing arts, theater/drama. *Special Achievements/Activities:* 138 awards ($154,376 total): community service, general special achievements/activities, hobbies/interests, leadership, religious involvement. *Special Characteristics:* 420 awards ($3,913,916 total): children and siblings of alumni, children of faculty/staff, general special characteristics, relatives of clergy, religious affiliation, siblings of current students, veterans, veterans' children. ***Tuition waivers:*** Full or partial for employees or children of employees, senior citizens. ***ROTC:*** Army.

LOANS ***Student loans:*** $34,957,673 (97% need-based, 3% non-need-based). 64% of past graduating class borrowed through all loan programs. Average indebtedness per student: $14,393. ***Average need-based loan:*** Freshmen: $3897; Undergraduates: $5476. ***Parent loans:*** $5,989,674 (100% non-need-based). ***Programs:*** FFEL (Subsidized and Unsubsidized Stafford, PLUS), Perkins, college/university, Health Professions Loans.

WORK-STUDY ***Federal work-study:*** *Total amount:* $2,035,669; 702 jobs available.

ATHLETIC AWARDS *Total amount:* 3,372,690 (100% non-need-based).

APPLYING for FINANCIAL AID ***Required financial aid form:*** FAFSA. ***Financial aid deadline (priority):*** 2/1. ***Notification date:*** 5/1. Students must reply within 2 weeks of notification.

CONTACT Mr. Jorge Rodriguez, Executive Director of Financial Aid, St. John's University, 8000 Utopia Parkway, Jamaica, NY 11439, 718-990-6403 or toll-free 800-232-4SJU (in-state). *Fax:* 718-990-5945.

ST. JOHN VIANNEY COLLEGE SEMINARY

Miami, FL

Tuition & fees: $7000 **Average undergraduate aid package: N/A**

ABOUT THE INSTITUTION Independent Roman Catholic, coed, primarily men. Awards: bachelor's degrees. 2 undergraduate majors. Total enrollment: 47. Undergraduates: 47. Freshmen: 11. Federal methodology is used as a basis for awarding need-based institutional aid.

UNDERGRADUATE EXPENSES for 1999–2000 ***Comprehensive fee:*** $11,000 includes full-time tuition ($6900), mandatory fees ($100), and room and board ($4000). ***Part-time tuition:*** $150 per credit. ***Part-time fees:*** $100 per year part-time. ***Payment plan:*** installment.

St. John Vianney College Seminary (continued)

GIFT AID (NEED-BASED) ***Scholarships, grants, and awards:*** Federal Pell, state.

LOANS ***Programs:*** FFEL (Subsidized and Unsubsidized Stafford).

APPLYING for FINANCIAL AID ***Required financial aid form:*** FAFSA. ***Financial aid deadline:*** Continuous.

CONTACT Ms. Bonnie DeAngulo, Director of Financial Aid, St. John Vianney College Seminary, 2900 Southwest 87th Avenue, Miami, FL 33165-3244, 305-223-4561 Ext. 10.

SAINT JOSEPH COLLEGE

West Hartford, CT

Tuition & fees: $16,150 **Average undergraduate aid package: $14,452**

ABOUT THE INSTITUTION Independent Roman Catholic, women only. Awards: bachelor's and master's degrees. 43 undergraduate majors. Total enrollment: 1,740. Undergraduates: 1,114. Freshmen: 147. Both federal and institutional methodology are used as a basis for awarding need-based institutional aid.

UNDERGRADUATE EXPENSES for 1999–2000 ***Application fee:*** $35. ***Comprehensive fee:*** $22,760 includes full-time tuition ($15,900), mandatory fees ($250), and room and board ($6610). ***College room only:*** $3110. Room and board charges vary according to board plan. ***Part-time tuition:*** $405 per credit. ***Part-time fees:*** $25 per credit. ***Payment plan:*** installment.

FRESHMAN FINANCIAL AID (Fall 1999, est.) 151 applied for aid; of those 91% were deemed to have need. 100% of freshmen with need received aid; of those 35% had need fully met. *Average financial aid package:* $14,082 (excluding resources awarded to replace EFC). 3% of all full-time freshmen had no need and received non-need-based aid.

UNDERGRADUATE FINANCIAL AID (Fall 1999, est.) 587 applied for aid; of those 98% were deemed to have need. 100% of undergraduates with need received aid; of those 33% had need fully met. *Average financial aid package:* $14,452 (excluding resources awarded to replace EFC). 3% of all full-time undergraduates had no need and received non-need-based aid.

GIFT AID (NEED-BASED) ***Total amount:*** $4,226,660 (14% Federal, 28% state, 55% institutional, 3% external sources). ***Receiving aid:*** *Freshmen:* 84% (137); *all full-time undergraduates:* 80% (531). ***Average award:*** Freshmen: $10,140; Undergraduates: $9014. ***Scholarships, grants, and awards:*** Federal Pell, FSEOG, state, private, college/university gift aid from institutional funds.

GIFT AID (NON-NEED-BASED) ***Total amount:*** $709,225 (4% state, 96% institutional). ***Receiving aid:*** *Freshmen:* 26% (42); *Undergraduates:* 24% (159). ***Scholarships, grants, and awards by category:*** *Academic Interests/Achievement:* 159 awards ($707,600 total): general academic interests/achievements. *Special Characteristics:* 16 awards ($16,000 total): siblings of current students. ***Tuition waivers:*** Full or partial for employees or children of employees, senior citizens.

LOANS ***Student loans:*** $2,966,086 (77% need-based, 23% non-need-based). Average indebtedness per student: $7541. ***Average need-based loan:*** Freshmen: $2692; Undergraduates: $5950. ***Parent loans:*** $421,731 (100% need-based). ***Programs:*** FFEL (Subsidized and Unsubsidized Stafford, PLUS), Perkins, state, Connecticut Family Education Loan Program.

WORK-STUDY ***Federal work-study:*** *Total amount:* $64,000; 40 jobs averaging $1500. ***State or other work-study/employment:*** *Total amount:* $175,000 (100% need-based). 125 part-time jobs averaging $1500.

APPLYING for FINANCIAL AID ***Required financial aid forms:*** FAFSA, institution's own form. ***Financial aid deadline (priority):*** 2/15. ***Notification date:*** 3/15. Students must reply within 3 weeks of notification.

CONTACT Mr. Philip T. Malinoski, Director of Financial Aid, Saint Joseph College, 1678 Asylum Avenue, West Hartford, CT 06117-2700, 860-231-5223 or toll-free 800-285-6565. *Fax:* 860-233-5695. *E-mail:* pmalinoski@mercy.sjc.edu

SAINT JOSEPH COLLEGE OF NURSING

Joliet, IL

See University of St. Francis

SAINT JOSEPH'S COLLEGE

Rensselaer, IN

Tuition & fees: $14,190 **Average undergraduate aid package: $12,350**

ABOUT THE INSTITUTION Independent Roman Catholic, coed. Awards: associate, bachelor's, and master's degrees. 43 undergraduate majors. Total enrollment: 934. Undergraduates: 934. Freshmen: 301. Both federal and institutional methodology are used as a basis for awarding need-based institutional aid.

UNDERGRADUATE EXPENSES for 1999–2000 ***Application fee:*** $25. ***Comprehensive fee:*** $19,270 includes full-time tuition ($14,070), mandatory fees ($120), and room and board ($5080). Full-time tuition and fees vary according to reciprocity agreements. ***Part-time tuition:*** $470 per credit. ***Part-time fees:*** $2 per credit hour; $60 per term part-time. Part-time tuition and fees vary according to course load and program. ***Payment plan:*** installment.

FRESHMAN FINANCIAL AID (Fall 1999, est.) 261 applied for aid; of those 92% were deemed to have need. 100% of freshmen with need received aid; of those 35% had need fully met. *Average percent of need met:* 81% (excluding resources awarded to replace EFC). *Average financial aid package:* $12,500 (excluding resources awarded to replace EFC). 7% of all full-time freshmen had no need and received non-need-based aid.

UNDERGRADUATE FINANCIAL AID (Fall 1999, est.) 795 applied for aid; of those 82% were deemed to have need. 100% of undergraduates with need received aid; of those 45% had need fully met. *Average percent of need met:* 84% (excluding resources awarded to replace EFC). *Average financial aid package:* $12,350 (excluding resources awarded to replace EFC). 7% of all full-time undergraduates had no need and received non-need-based aid.

GIFT AID (NEED-BASED) ***Total amount:*** $4,637,828 (13% Federal, 30% state, 55% institutional, 2% external sources). ***Receiving aid:*** *Freshmen:* 64% (175); *all full-time undergraduates:* 48% (399). ***Average award:*** Freshmen: $9000; Undergraduates: $8700. ***Scholarships, grants, and awards:*** Federal Pell, FSEOG, state, college/university gift aid from institutional funds.

GIFT AID (NON-NEED-BASED) ***Total amount:*** $442,879 (83% institutional, 17% external sources). ***Receiving aid:*** *Freshmen:* 58% (157); *Undergraduates:* 48% (401). ***Scholarships, grants, and awards by category:*** *Academic Interests/Achievement:* 309 awards ($1,606,912 total): general academic interests/achievements. *Creative Arts/Performance:* 149 awards ($229,250 total): cinema/film/broadcasting, debating, journalism/publications, music, theater/drama. *Special Achievements/Activities:* 12 awards ($18,000 total): cheerleading/drum major. *Special Characteristics:* 113 awards ($372,705 total): children and siblings of alumni, children of faculty/staff, members of minority groups, siblings of current students. ***Tuition waivers:*** Full or partial for minority students, children of alumni, employees or children of employees.

LOANS ***Student loans:*** $3,284,072 (60% need-based, 40% non-need-based). 70% of past graduating class borrowed through all loan programs. Average indebtedness per student: $16,730. ***Average need-based loan:*** Freshmen: $1532; Undergraduates: $2553. ***Parent loans:*** $1,419,681 (87% need-based, 13% non-need-based). ***Programs:*** FFEL (Subsidized and Unsubsidized Stafford, PLUS), Perkins.

WORK-STUDY ***Federal work-study:*** *Total amount:* $150,000; 100 jobs averaging $1500.

ATHLETIC AWARDS *Total amount:* 1,436,842 (70% need-based, 30% non-need-based).

APPLYING for FINANCIAL AID ***Required financial aid form:*** FAFSA. ***Financial aid deadline (priority):*** 3/1. ***Notification date:*** Continuous beginning 3/15. Students must reply by 5/1 or within 2 weeks of notification.

CONTACT Ms. Dianne Mickey, Director of Financial Aid, Saint Joseph's College, Box 971, Rensselaer, IN 47978-0850, 219-866-6149 or toll-free 800-447-8781 (out-of-state). *Fax:* 219-866-6122. *E-mail:* diannem@saintjoe.edu

SAINT JOSEPH'S COLLEGE

Standish, ME

Tuition & fees: $13,735 **Average undergraduate aid package: $12,276**

ABOUT THE INSTITUTION Independent religious, coed. Awards: associate, bachelor's, and master's degrees (profile does not include enrollment in distance learning master's program). 33 undergraduate majors. Total enrollment: 821. Undergraduates: 821. Freshmen: 281. Both federal and institutional methodology are used as a basis for awarding need-based institutional aid.

UNDERGRADUATE EXPENSES for 1999–2000 ***Comprehensive fee:*** $19,685 includes full-time tuition ($13,240), mandatory fees ($495), and room and board ($5950). ***Part-time tuition:*** $235 per credit hour. ***Part-time fees:*** $100 per term part-time. Part-time tuition and fees vary according to course load. ***Payment plan:*** installment.

FRESHMAN FINANCIAL AID (Fall 1999, est.) 289 applied for aid; of those 90% were deemed to have need. 100% of freshmen with need received aid; of those 18% had need fully met. *Average percent of need met:* 80% (excluding resources awarded to replace EFC). *Average financial aid package:* $12,287 (excluding resources awarded to replace EFC). 12% of all full-time freshmen had no need and received non-need-based aid.

UNDERGRADUATE FINANCIAL AID (Fall 1999, est.) 723 applied for aid; of those 93% were deemed to have need. 100% of undergraduates with need received aid; of those 22% had need fully met. *Average percent of need met:* 80% (excluding resources awarded to replace EFC). *Average financial aid package:* $12,276 (excluding resources awarded to replace EFC). 9% of all full-time undergraduates had no need and received non-need-based aid.

GIFT AID (NEED-BASED) ***Total amount:*** $4,867,005 (14% Federal, 6% state, 71% institutional, 9% external sources). ***Receiving aid:*** *Freshmen:* 77% (258); *all full-time undergraduates:* 84% (656). ***Average award:*** Freshmen: $8144; Undergraduates: $7293. ***Scholarships, grants, and awards:*** Federal Pell, FSEOG, state, private, college/university gift aid from institutional funds.

GIFT AID (NON-NEED-BASED) ***Total amount:*** $338,563 (73% institutional, 27% external sources). ***Receiving aid:*** *Freshmen:* 5% (18); *Undergraduates:* 4% (28). ***Scholarships, grants, and awards by category:*** *Academic Interests/Achievement:* 361 awards ($1,123,024 total): general academic interests/achievements. *Special Achievements/Activities:* 16 awards ($73,912 total): community service, general special achievements/activities, leadership, memberships. *Special Characteristics:* 26 awards ($182,616 total): children of faculty/staff, international students, local/state students, siblings of current students, spouses of current students. ***Tuition waivers:*** Full or partial for employees or children of employees, senior citizens. ***ROTC:*** Army cooperative.

LOANS ***Student loans:*** $3,230,331 (88% need-based, 12% non-need-based). 90% of past graduating class borrowed through all loan programs. Average indebtedness per student: $16,122. ***Average need-based loan:*** Freshmen: $3615; Undergraduates: $4554. ***Parent loans:*** $1,538,255 (39% need-based, 61% non-need-based). ***Programs:*** FFEL (Subsidized and Unsubsidized Stafford, PLUS), Perkins, Federal Nursing, state.

WORK-STUDY ***Federal work-study:*** *Total amount:* $288,530; 295 jobs averaging $1000.

APPLYING for FINANCIAL AID ***Required financial aid forms:*** FAFSA, institution's own form, noncustodial (divorced/separated) parent's statement. ***Financial aid deadline (priority):*** 3/1. ***Notification date:*** Continuous. Students must reply within 2 weeks of notification.

CONTACT Office of Financial Aid, Saint Joseph's College, 278 Whites Bridge Road, Standish, ME 04084-5263, 800-752-1266 or toll-free 800-338-7057. *Fax:* 207-893-7862. *E-mail:* finaid@sjcme.edu

ST. JOSEPH'S COLLEGE, NEW YORK

Brooklyn, NY

Tuition & fees: $8922 **Average undergraduate aid package: $7000**

ABOUT THE INSTITUTION Independent, coed. Awards: bachelor's degrees. 35 undergraduate majors. Total enrollment: 1,283. Undergraduates: 1,256. Freshmen: 91. Federal methodology is used as a basis for awarding need-based institutional aid.

UNDERGRADUATE EXPENSES for 1999–2000 ***Application fee:*** $25. ***Tuition:*** full-time $8600; part-time $276 per credit. ***Required fees:*** full-time $322; $11 per credit; $5 per term part-time. Part-time tuition and fees vary according to course load. ***Payment plans:*** installment, deferred payment.

FRESHMAN FINANCIAL AID (Fall 1999, est.) 73 applied for aid; of those 74% were deemed to have need. 100% of freshmen with need received aid; of those 24% had need fully met. *Average percent of need met:* 80% (excluding resources awarded to replace EFC). *Average financial aid package:* $8152 (excluding resources awarded to replace EFC). 18% of all full-time freshmen had no need and received non-need-based aid.

UNDERGRADUATE FINANCIAL AID (Fall 1999, est.) 500 applied for aid; of those 76% were deemed to have need. 100% of undergraduates with need received aid; of those 59% had need fully met. *Average percent of need met:* 70% (excluding resources awarded to replace EFC). *Average financial aid package:* $7000 (excluding resources awarded to replace EFC). 12% of all full-time undergraduates had no need and received non-need-based aid.

GIFT AID (NEED-BASED) ***Total amount:*** $1,670,000 (37% Federal, 47% state, 16% institutional). ***Receiving aid:*** *Freshmen:* 71% (54); *all full-time undergraduates:* 59% (350). ***Average award:*** Freshmen: $3412; Undergraduates: $3000. ***Scholarships, grants, and awards:*** Federal Pell, FSEOG, state, private, college/university gift aid from institutional funds.

GIFT AID (NON-NEED-BASED) ***Total amount:*** $1,066,000 (3% state, 93% institutional, 4% external sources). ***Receiving aid:*** *Freshmen:* 41% (31); *Undergraduates:* 42% (250). ***Scholarships, grants, and awards by category:*** *Academic Interests/Achievement:* general academic interests/achievements. *Special Characteristics:* children and siblings of alumni, children of faculty/staff. ***Tuition waivers:*** Full or partial for employees or children of employees.

LOANS ***Student loans:*** $2,205,000 (50% need-based, 50% non-need-based). Average indebtedness per student: $14,000. ***Average need-based loan:*** Freshmen: $2200; Undergraduates: $4200. ***Parent loans:*** $210,000 (100% non-need-based). ***Programs:*** FFEL (Subsidized and Unsubsidized Stafford, PLUS), Perkins.

WORK-STUDY ***Federal work-study:*** *Total amount:* $134,000; 64 jobs averaging $2000. ***State or other work-study/employment:*** *Total amount:* $50,000 (100% non-need-based). 27 part-time jobs averaging $1850.

APPLYING for FINANCIAL AID ***Required financial aid forms:*** FAFSA, institution's own form, state aid form. ***Financial aid deadline (priority):*** 2/25. ***Notification date:*** 4/15. Students must reply by 5/1 or within 2 weeks of notification.

CONTACT Ms. Carol Sullivan, Director of Financial Aid, St. Joseph's College, New York, 245 Clinton Avenue, Brooklyn, NY 11205-3688, 718-636-6808. *Fax:* 718-636-6827.

ST. JOSEPH'S COLLEGE, SUFFOLK CAMPUS

Patchogue, NY

Tuition & fees: $9182 **Average undergraduate aid package: $5000**

ABOUT THE INSTITUTION Independent, coed. Awards: bachelor's and master's degrees (master's degree in education only). 29 undergraduate majors. Total enrollment: 3,011. Undergraduates: 2,931. Freshmen: 246. Federal methodology is used as a basis for awarding need-based institutional aid.

St. Joseph's College, Suffolk Campus (continued)

UNDERGRADUATE EXPENSES for 1999–2000 ***Application fee:*** $25. ***Tuition:*** full-time $8850; part-time $286 per credit. ***Required fees:*** full-time $332; $96 per term part-time. Part-time tuition and fees vary according to course load. ***Payment plan:*** installment.

FRESHMAN FINANCIAL AID (Fall 1999, est.) 233 applied for aid; of those 89% were deemed to have need. 100% of freshmen with need received aid; of those 42% had need fully met. *Average percent of need met:* 55% (excluding resources awarded to replace EFC). *Average financial aid package:* $4600 (excluding resources awarded to replace EFC). 7% of all full-time freshmen had no need and received non-need-based aid.

UNDERGRADUATE FINANCIAL AID (Fall 1999, est.) 1,335 applied for aid; of those 90% were deemed to have need. 100% of undergraduates with need received aid; of those 10% had need fully met. *Average percent of need met:* 55% (excluding resources awarded to replace EFC). *Average financial aid package:* $5000 (excluding resources awarded to replace EFC). 5% of all full-time undergraduates had no need and received non-need-based aid.

GIFT AID (NEED-BASED) ***Total amount:*** $4,378,425 (25% Federal, 39% state, 36% institutional). ***Receiving aid:*** *Freshmen:* 73% (173); *all full-time undergraduates:* 27% (789). ***Average award:*** Freshmen: $1000; Undergraduates: $800. ***Scholarships, grants, and awards:*** Federal Pell, FSEOG, state, private, college/university gift aid from institutional funds.

GIFT AID (NON-NEED-BASED) ***Total amount:*** $44,250 (73% institutional, 27% external sources). ***Receiving aid:*** *Freshmen:* 11% (25); *Undergraduates:* 10% (306). ***Scholarships, grants, and awards by category:*** *Academic Interests/Achievement:* 450 awards ($1,512,749 total): general academic interests/achievements. ***Tuition waivers:*** Full or partial for employees or children of employees, senior citizens. ***ROTC:*** Army cooperative, Air Force cooperative.

LOANS ***Student loans:*** $5,604,904 (100% need-based). 88% of past graduating class borrowed through all loan programs. Average indebtedness per student: $13,000. ***Average need-based loan:*** Freshmen: $2625; Undergraduates: $3800. ***Parent loans:*** $2,751,725 (100% need-based). ***Programs:*** FFEL (Subsidized and Unsubsidized Stafford, PLUS), Perkins.

WORK-STUDY ***Federal work-study:*** *Total amount:* $183,850; 84 jobs averaging $2150. ***State or other work-study/employment:*** *Total amount:* $174,777 (100% need-based). 88 part-time jobs averaging $2080.

APPLYING for FINANCIAL AID ***Required financial aid forms:*** FAFSA, institution's own form, state aid form. ***Financial aid deadline (priority):*** 2/25. ***Notification date:*** 4/15. Students must reply within 2 weeks of notification.

CONTACT Joan Farley, Associate Director of Financial Aid, St. Joseph's College, Suffolk Campus, 155 West Roe Boulevard, Patchogue, NY 11772-2399, 631-447-3214. *Fax:* 631-447-1734.

SAINT JOSEPH SEMINARY COLLEGE

Saint Benedict, LA

Tuition & fees: N/R **Average undergraduate aid package: $12,386**

ABOUT THE INSTITUTION Independent Roman Catholic, coed, primarily men. Awards: bachelor's degrees. 1 undergraduate major. Federal methodology is used as a basis for awarding need-based institutional aid.

FRESHMAN FINANCIAL AID (Fall 1999, est.) 9 applied for aid; of those 11% were deemed to have need. 100% of freshmen with need received aid; of those 100% had need fully met. *Average percent of need met:* 100% (excluding resources awarded to replace EFC). *Average financial aid package:* $11,622 (excluding resources awarded to replace EFC). 38% of all full-time freshmen had no need and received non-need-based aid.

UNDERGRADUATE FINANCIAL AID (Fall 1999, est.) 33 applied for aid; of those 58% were deemed to have need. 100% of undergraduates with need received aid; of those 100% had need fully met. *Average percent of need met:* 100% (excluding resources awarded to replace EFC). *Average financial aid package:* $12,386 (excluding resources awarded to replace EFC). 18% of all full-time undergraduates had no need and received non-need-based aid.

GIFT AID (NEED-BASED) ***Total amount:*** $474,845 (10% Federal, 90% external sources). ***Receiving aid:*** *Freshmen:* 8% (1); *all full-time undergraduates:* 26% (19). ***Average award:*** Freshmen: $7225; Undergraduates: $9530. ***Scholarships, grants, and awards:*** Federal Pell, FSEOG, state, private, college/university gift aid from institutional funds.

GIFT AID (NON-NEED-BASED) ***Total amount:*** $34,712 (73% state, 14% institutional, 13% external sources). ***Receiving aid:*** *Freshmen:* 8% (1); *Undergraduates:* 5% (4). ***Scholarships, grants, and awards by category:*** *Academic Interests/Achievement:* 2 awards ($2000 total): general academic interests/achievements. *Special Achievements/Activities:* 6 awards ($3000 total): leadership. ***Tuition waivers:*** Full or partial for senior citizens.

LOANS ***Student loans:*** $261,600 (100% need-based). Average indebtedness per student: $12,400. ***Average need-based loan:*** Undergraduates: $1614. ***Programs:*** FFEL (Subsidized and Unsubsidized Stafford, PLUS), Perkins.

WORK-STUDY ***Federal work-study:*** *Total amount:* $16,950; 15 jobs averaging $1000. ***State or other work-study/employment:*** *Total amount:* $5000 (100% non-need-based). 8 part-time jobs averaging $1000.

APPLYING for FINANCIAL AID ***Required financial aid form:*** FAFSA. ***Financial aid deadline (priority):*** 3/15. ***Notification date:*** Continuous beginning 7/1. Students must reply within 4 weeks of notification.

CONTACT Mr. Les Lavergne, Financial Aid Officer, Saint Joseph Seminary College, Saint Benedict, LA 70457, 504-867-2229. *Fax:* 504-867-2270.

SAINT JOSEPH'S UNIVERSITY

Philadelphia, PA

Tuition & fees: $18,430 **Average undergraduate aid package: $11,150**

ABOUT THE INSTITUTION Independent Roman Catholic (Jesuit), coed. Awards: associate, bachelor's, master's, and doctoral degrees and post-master's certificates. 39 undergraduate majors. Total enrollment: 6,978. Undergraduates: 4,407. Freshmen: 971. Federal methodology is used as a basis for awarding need-based institutional aid.

UNDERGRADUATE EXPENSES for 1999–2000 ***Application fee:*** $40. ***Comprehensive fee:*** $25,944 includes full-time tuition ($18,140), mandatory fees ($290), and room and board ($7514). ***College room only:*** $4704. Full-time tuition and fees vary according to program. Room and board charges vary according to board plan and housing facility. ***Part-time tuition:*** $313 per credit. Part-time tuition and fees vary according to class time. ***Payment plans:*** installment, deferred payment.

FRESHMAN FINANCIAL AID (Fall 1999, est.) 713 applied for aid; of those 82% were deemed to have need. 99% of freshmen with need received aid. *Average financial aid package:* $10,825 (excluding resources awarded to replace EFC). 22% of all full-time freshmen had no need and received non-need-based aid.

UNDERGRADUATE FINANCIAL AID (Fall 1999, est.) 2,719 applied for aid; of those 79% were deemed to have need. 99% of undergraduates with need received aid. *Average financial aid package:* $11,150 (excluding resources awarded to replace EFC). 20% of all full-time undergraduates had no need and received non-need-based aid.

GIFT AID (NEED-BASED) ***Total amount:*** $18,078,621 (6% Federal, 9% state, 83% institutional, 2% external sources). ***Receiving aid:*** *Freshmen:* 52% (510); *all full-time undergraduates:* 55% (1,877). ***Average award:*** Freshmen: $7205; Undergraduates: $6915. ***Scholarships, grants, and awards:*** Federal Pell, FSEOG, state, private, college/university gift aid from institutional funds.

GIFT AID (NON-NEED-BASED) ***Total amount:*** $5,039,942 (98% institutional, 2% external sources). ***Receiving aid:*** *Freshmen:* 50% (493); *Undergraduates:* 24% (831). ***Scholarships, grants, and awards by category:*** *Academic Interests/Achievement:* general academic interests/achievements. *Creative Arts/Performance:* debating, theater/drama. ***Tuition waivers:*** Full or partial for employees or children of employees. ***ROTC:*** Army cooperative, Naval cooperative, Air Force.

LOANS ***Student loans:*** $9,443,767 (81% need-based, 19% non-need-based). ***Average need-based loan:*** Freshmen: $2665; Undergraduates: $4250. ***Parent loans:*** $5,804,055 (100% need-based). ***Programs:*** FFEL (Subsidized and Unsubsidized Stafford, PLUS), Perkins.

WORK-STUDY ***Federal work-study:*** *Total amount:* $342,808; jobs available.

ATHLETIC AWARDS *Total amount:* 2,119,589 (100% non-need-based).

APPLYING for FINANCIAL AID ***Required financial aid form:*** FAFSA. ***Financial aid deadline (priority):*** 2/15. ***Notification date:*** Continuous beginning 3/15. Students must reply by 5/1.

CONTACT Felicia R. Korenstein, Director of Financial Aid, Saint Joseph's University, 5600 City Avenue, Philadelphia, PA 19131-1395, 610-660-1556 or toll-free 888-BEAHAWK (in-state). *Fax:* 610-660-1342. *E-mail:* fkorenst@sju.edu

ST. LAWRENCE UNIVERSITY

Canton, NY

Tuition & fees: $23,165 **Average undergraduate aid package: $22,736**

ABOUT THE INSTITUTION Independent, coed. Awards: bachelor's and master's degrees and post-master's certificates. 31 undergraduate majors. Total enrollment: 1,978. Undergraduates: 1,875. Freshmen: 575. Federal methodology is used as a basis for awarding need-based institutional aid.

UNDERGRADUATE EXPENSES for 1999–2000 ***Application fee:*** $50. ***Comprehensive fee:*** $30,370 includes full-time tuition ($22,905), mandatory fees ($260), and room and board ($7205). ***College room only:*** $3875. Full-time tuition and fees vary according to student level. Room and board charges vary according to board plan. ***Payment plans:*** installment, deferred payment.

FRESHMAN FINANCIAL AID (Fall 1999) 393 applied for aid; of those 89% were deemed to have need. 100% of freshmen with need received aid; of those 42% had need fully met. *Average percent of need met:* 93% (excluding resources awarded to replace EFC). *Average financial aid package:* $23,664 (excluding resources awarded to replace EFC). 13% of all full-time freshmen had no need and received non-need-based aid.

UNDERGRADUATE FINANCIAL AID (Fall 1999) 1,293 applied for aid; of those 92% were deemed to have need. 100% of undergraduates with need received aid; of those 39% had need fully met. *Average percent of need met:* 91% (excluding resources awarded to replace EFC). *Average financial aid package:* $22,736 (excluding resources awarded to replace EFC). 11% of all full-time undergraduates had no need and received non-need-based aid.

GIFT AID (NEED-BASED) ***Total amount:*** $16,413,003 (5% Federal, 9% state, 83% institutional, 3% external sources). ***Receiving aid:*** *Freshmen:* 59% (339); *all full-time undergraduates:* 62% (1,143). ***Average award:*** Freshmen: $13,636; Undergraduates: $13,330. ***Scholarships, grants, and awards:*** Federal Pell, FSEOG, state, private, college/university gift aid from institutional funds.

GIFT AID (NON-NEED-BASED) ***Total amount:*** $5,564,850 (100% institutional). ***Receiving aid:*** *Freshmen:* 26% (149); *Undergraduates:* 23% (420). ***Scholarships, grants, and awards by category:*** *Academic Interests/Achievement:* general academic interests/achievements. *Special Achievements/Activities:* community service. *Special Characteristics:* children and siblings of alumni. ***Tuition waivers:*** Full or partial for employees or children of employees. ***ROTC:*** Army cooperative, Air Force cooperative.

LOANS ***Student loans:*** $6,762,401 (86% need-based, 14% non-need-based). 73% of past graduating class borrowed through all loan programs. ***Average need-based loan:*** Freshmen: $4552; Undergraduates: $5245. ***Programs:*** Federal Direct (Subsidized and Unsubsidized Stafford, PLUS), FFEL (Subsidized and Unsubsidized Stafford, PLUS), Perkins, college/university.

WORK-STUDY ***Federal work-study:*** *Total amount:* $1,153,026; 763 jobs available. ***State or other work-study/employment:*** *Total amount:* $676,350 (100% non-need-based). Part-time jobs available.

ATHLETIC AWARDS *Total amount:* 739,651 (100% need-based).

APPLYING for FINANCIAL AID ***Required financial aid forms:*** FAFSA, state aid form, noncustodial (divorced/separated) parent's statement. ***Financial aid deadline (priority):*** 2/15. ***Notification date:*** 3/15. Students must reply by 5/1.

CONTACT Mrs. Patricia J. B. Farmer, Director of Financial Aid, St. Lawrence University, Payson Hall, Park Street, Canton, NY 13617-1455, 315-229-5265 or toll-free 800-285-1856. *Fax:* 315-229-5502. *E-mail:* pfarmer@stlawu.edu

SAINT LEO UNIVERSITY

Saint Leo, FL

Tuition & fees: $11,650 **Average undergraduate aid package: $12,000**

ABOUT THE INSTITUTION Independent Roman Catholic, coed. Awards: associate, bachelor's, and master's degrees. 35 undergraduate majors. Total enrollment: 1,683. Undergraduates: 1,469. Freshmen: 202. Federal methodology is used as a basis for awarding need-based institutional aid.

UNDERGRADUATE EXPENSES for 1999–2000 ***Application fee:*** $35. ***Comprehensive fee:*** $17,700 includes full-time tuition ($11,450), mandatory fees ($200), and room and board ($6050). ***College room only:*** $3200. Full-time tuition and fees vary according to class time. Room and board charges vary according to board plan and housing facility. ***Part-time tuition:*** $300 per credit hour. Part-time tuition and fees vary according to class time. ***Payment plan:*** installment.

FRESHMAN FINANCIAL AID (Fall 1999, est.) 170 applied for aid; of those 97% were deemed to have need. 100% of freshmen with need received aid; of those 59% had need fully met. *Average percent of need met:* 88% (excluding resources awarded to replace EFC). *Average financial aid package:* $11,938 (excluding resources awarded to replace EFC). 17% of all full-time freshmen had no need and received non-need-based aid.

UNDERGRADUATE FINANCIAL AID (Fall 1999, est.) 865 applied for aid; of those 83% were deemed to have need. 100% of undergraduates with need received aid; of those 49% had need fully met. *Average percent of need met:* 85% (excluding resources awarded to replace EFC). *Average financial aid package:* $12,000 (excluding resources awarded to replace EFC). 6% of all full-time undergraduates had no need and received non-need-based aid.

GIFT AID (NEED-BASED) ***Total amount:*** $7,788,576 (15% Federal, 46% state, 37% institutional, 2% external sources). ***Receiving aid:*** *Freshmen:* 77% (155); *all full-time undergraduates:* 66% (685). ***Average award:*** Freshmen: $10,000; Undergraduates: $9700. ***Scholarships, grants, and awards:*** Federal Pell, FSEOG, state, private, college/university gift aid from institutional funds.

GIFT AID (NON-NEED-BASED) ***Total amount:*** $1,024,000 (46% state, 51% institutional, 3% external sources). ***Receiving aid:*** *Freshmen:* 6% (12); *Undergraduates:* 4% (37). ***Scholarships, grants, and awards by category:*** *Academic Interests/Achievement:* general academic interests/achievements. ***Tuition waivers:*** Full or partial for employees or children of employees. ***ROTC:*** Army cooperative, Air Force cooperative.

LOANS ***Student loans:*** $2,665,837 (89% need-based, 11% non-need-based). 72% of past graduating class borrowed through all loan programs. Average indebtedness per student: $12,000. ***Average need-based loan:*** Freshmen: $1897; Undergraduates: $3800. ***Parent loans:*** $340,000 (40% need-based, 60% non-need-based). ***Programs:*** FFEL (Subsidized and Unsubsidized Stafford, PLUS), Perkins.

WORK-STUDY ***Federal work-study:*** *Total amount:* $98,900; jobs available.

ATHLETIC AWARDS *Total amount:* 620,571 (71% need-based, 29% non-need-based).

APPLYING for FINANCIAL AID ***Required financial aid form:*** FAFSA. ***Financial aid deadline (priority):*** 3/1. ***Notification date:*** Continuous.

CONTACT Dr. Pat Watkins, Director of Financial Aid, Saint Leo University, PO Box 6665, MC 2228, Saint Leo, FL 33574-6665, 352-588-8270 or toll-free 800-334-5532.

ST. LOUIS CHRISTIAN COLLEGE

Florissant, MO

Tuition & fees: $4950 **Average undergraduate aid package: $5797**

St. Louis Christian College (continued)

ABOUT THE INSTITUTION Independent Christian, coed. Awards: associate and bachelor's degrees. 6 undergraduate majors. Total enrollment: 203. Undergraduates: 203. Freshmen: 38. Federal methodology is used as a basis for awarding need-based institutional aid.

UNDERGRADUATE EXPENSES for 1999–2000 ***Application fee:*** $20. ***Comprehensive fee:*** $8070 includes full-time tuition ($4950) and room and board ($3120). ***College room only:*** $1560. Room and board charges vary according to board plan and housing facility. ***Part-time tuition:*** $165 per credit hour. ***Payment plan:*** installment.

FRESHMAN FINANCIAL AID (Fall 1999, est.) 35 applied for aid; of those 86% were deemed to have need. 93% of freshmen with need received aid; of those 14% had need fully met. *Average percent of need met:* 73% (excluding resources awarded to replace EFC). *Average financial aid package:* $5627 (excluding resources awarded to replace EFC). 11% of all full-time freshmen had no need and received non-need-based aid.

UNDERGRADUATE FINANCIAL AID (Fall 1999, est.) 91 applied for aid; of those 89% were deemed to have need. 98% of undergraduates with need received aid; of those 13% had need fully met. *Average percent of need met:* 69% (excluding resources awarded to replace EFC). *Average financial aid package:* $5797 (excluding resources awarded to replace EFC). 19% of all full-time undergraduates had no need and received non-need-based aid.

GIFT AID (NEED-BASED) ***Total amount:*** $304,300 (50% Federal, 31% institutional, 19% external sources). ***Receiving aid:*** *Freshmen:* 69% (25); *all full-time undergraduates:* 53% (70). ***Average award:*** Freshmen: $4516; Undergraduates: $4579. ***Scholarships, grants, and awards:*** Federal Pell, FSEOG, private, college/university gift aid from institutional funds.

GIFT AID (NON-NEED-BASED) ***Total amount:*** $58,800 (79% institutional, 21% external sources). ***Receiving aid:*** *Freshmen:* 58% (21); *Undergraduates:* 42% (55). ***Scholarships, grants, and awards by category:*** *Academic Interests/Achievement:* general academic interests/achievements. *Creative Arts/Performance:* music. *Special Achievements/Activities:* leadership, religious involvement. *Special Characteristics:* local/state students, religious affiliation. ***Tuition waivers:*** Full or partial for employees or children of employees.

LOANS ***Student loans:*** $290,000 (66% need-based, 34% non-need-based). ***Average need-based loan:*** Freshmen: $2400; Undergraduates: $3468. ***Parent loans:*** $26,000 (100% non-need-based). ***Programs:*** FFEL (Subsidized and Unsubsidized Stafford, PLUS).

WORK-STUDY ***Federal work-study:*** *Total amount:* $11,678; 10 jobs averaging $1167. ***State or other work-study/employment:*** *Total amount:* $50,000 (100% non-need-based). Part-time jobs available.

APPLYING for FINANCIAL AID ***Required financial aid forms:*** FAFSA, institution's own form. ***Financial aid deadline (priority):*** 5/1. ***Notification date:*** Continuous. Students must reply within 2 weeks of notification.

CONTACT Mrs. Catherine Wilhoit, Director of Financial Aid, St. Louis Christian College, 1360 Grandview Drive, Florissant, MO 63033-6499, 314-837-6777 Ext. 1101. *Fax:* 314-837-8291. *E-mail:* 74721.424@compuserve.com

ST. LOUIS COLLEGE OF PHARMACY

St. Louis, MO

Tuition & fees: $13,370 **Average undergraduate aid package: $8469**

ABOUT THE INSTITUTION Independent, coed. Awards: bachelor's, master's, and first professional degrees. 1 undergraduate major. Total enrollment: 875. Undergraduates: 815. Freshmen: 132. Federal methodology is used as a basis for awarding need-based institutional aid.

UNDERGRADUATE EXPENSES for 2000–2001 (est.) ***Application fee:*** $35. ***Comprehensive fee:*** $18,745 includes full-time tuition ($13,250), mandatory fees ($120), and room and board ($5375). ***Payment plan:*** deferred payment.

FRESHMAN FINANCIAL AID (Fall 1999) 133 applied for aid; of those 100% were deemed to have need. *Average percent of need met:* 51% (excluding resources awarded to replace EFC). *Average financial aid package:* $10,654 (excluding resources awarded to replace EFC).

UNDERGRADUATE FINANCIAL AID (Fall 1999) 706 applied for aid; of those 80% were deemed to have need. *Average percent of need met:* 36% (excluding resources awarded to replace EFC). *Average financial aid package:* $8469 (excluding resources awarded to replace EFC).

GIFT AID (NEED-BASED) ***Total amount:*** $988,945 (54% Federal, 38% state, 8% institutional). ***Scholarships, grants, and awards:*** Federal Pell, FSEOG, state, private, college/university gift aid from institutional funds.

GIFT AID (NON-NEED-BASED) ***Total amount:*** $1,172,144 (3% state, 83% institutional, 14% external sources). ***Scholarships, grants, and awards by category:*** *Academic Interests/Achievement:* 277 awards ($856,197 total): general academic interests/achievements. *Special Achievements/Activities:* 122 awards ($106,439 total): community service, leadership. *Special Characteristics:* 55 awards ($47,895 total): children of faculty/staff, local/state students. ***Tuition waivers:*** Full or partial for employees or children of employees.

LOANS ***Student loans:*** $6,736,646 (45% need-based, 55% non-need-based). 80% of past graduating class borrowed through all loan programs. Average indebtedness per student: $45,108. ***Parent loans:*** $674,369 (100% non-need-based). ***Programs:*** FFEL (Subsidized and Unsubsidized Stafford, PLUS), Perkins, college/university.

WORK-STUDY ***Federal work-study:*** *Total amount:* $133,000; 111 jobs averaging $1200.

APPLYING for FINANCIAL AID ***Required financial aid forms:*** FAFSA, institution's own form. ***Financial aid deadline:*** 11/15 (priority: 4/1). ***Notification date:*** Continuous.

CONTACT Mr. David Rice, Director of Financial Aid, St. Louis College of Pharmacy, 4588 Parkview Place, St. Louis, MO 63110-1088, 314-367-8700 Ext. 1073 or toll-free 800-278-5267 (in-state). *Fax:* 314-367-2784.

SAINT LOUIS UNIVERSITY

St. Louis, MO

Tuition & fees: $17,268 **Average undergraduate aid package: N/A**

ABOUT THE INSTITUTION Independent Roman Catholic (Jesuit), coed. Awards: associate, bachelor's, master's, doctoral, and first professional degrees and post-bachelor's and post-master's certificates. 85 undergraduate majors. Total enrollment: 14,062. Undergraduates: 9,882. Freshmen: 1,274. Federal methodology is used as a basis for awarding need-based institutional aid.

UNDERGRADUATE EXPENSES for 1999–2000 ***Application fee:*** $25. ***Comprehensive fee:*** $23,168 includes full-time tuition ($17,230), mandatory fees ($38), and room and board ($5900). ***College room only:*** $3000. Room and board charges vary according to board plan and housing facility. ***Part-time tuition:*** $605 per credit hour. Part-time tuition and fees vary according to class time and program. ***Payment plan:*** installment.

FRESHMAN FINANCIAL AID (Fall 1999, est.) 1224 applied for aid; of those 85% were deemed to have need. 100% of freshmen with need received aid; of those 30% had need fully met. *Average percent of need met:* 78% (excluding resources awarded to replace EFC). 13% of all full-time freshmen had no need and received non-need-based aid.

UNDERGRADUATE FINANCIAL AID (Fall 1999, est.) 5,349 applied for aid; of those 84% were deemed to have need. 100% of undergraduates with need received aid; of those 33% had need fully met. *Average percent of need met:* 78% (excluding resources awarded to replace EFC). 12% of all full-time undergraduates had no need and received non-need-based aid.

GIFT AID (NEED-BASED) ***Total amount:*** $40,169,734 (18% Federal, 9% state, 70% institutional, 3% external sources). ***Receiving aid:*** *Freshmen:* 81% (1,022); *all full-time undergraduates:* 68% (4,351). ***Average award:*** Freshmen: $11,545; Undergraduates: $10,497. ***Scholarships, grants, and awards:*** Federal Pell, FSEOG, state, private, college/university gift aid from institutional funds.

GIFT AID (NON-NEED-BASED) ***Total amount:*** $4,782,068 (4% Federal, 2% state, 71% institutional, 23% external sources). ***Receiving aid:*** *Freshmen:* 68% (868); *Undergraduates:* 51% (3,291). ***Scholarships, grants, and awards by category:*** *Academic Interests/Achievement:* 3,110 awards

($15,878,703 total): business, communication, engineering/technologies, general academic interests/achievements, health fields, mathematics, physical sciences, social sciences. *Creative Arts/Performance:* 103 awards ($97,250 total): art/fine arts, music, performing arts, theater/drama. *Special Achievements/Activities:* 230 awards ($970,395 total): community service, leadership, memberships. *Special Characteristics:* 620 awards ($6,701,517 total): children of faculty/staff, general special characteristics, members of minority groups, siblings of current students. ***Tuition waivers:*** Full or partial for employees or children of employees. ***ROTC:*** Army cooperative, Air Force.

LOANS ***Student loans:*** $23,589,542 (98% need-based, 2% non-need-based). 74% of past graduating class borrowed through all loan programs. Average indebtedness per student: $19,058. ***Average need-based loan:*** Freshmen: $3242; Undergraduates: $4832. ***Parent loans:*** $4,490,278 (100% non-need-based). ***Programs:*** FFEL (Subsidized and Unsubsidized Stafford, PLUS), Perkins, Federal Nursing, state, college/university, alternative loans.

WORK-STUDY ***Federal work-study:*** *Total amount:* $3,469,588; 1,292 jobs averaging $2685.

ATHLETIC AWARDS *Total amount:* 2,269,212 (50% need-based, 50% non-need-based).

APPLYING for FINANCIAL AID ***Required financial aid form:*** FAFSA. ***Financial aid deadline (priority):*** 3/1. ***Notification date:*** Continuous. Students must reply by 5/1.

CONTACT Mr. Harold A. Deuser, Director of Scholarship and Financial Aid, Saint Louis University, 221 North Grand Boulevard, Room 121, St. Louis, MO 63103-2097, 314-977-2353 or toll-free 800-758-3678 (out-of-state). *Fax:* 314-977-3437. *E-mail:* deuserha@slu.edu

SAINT LUKE'S COLLEGE

Kansas City, MO

Tuition & fees: $8600 **Average undergraduate aid package: N/A**

ABOUT THE INSTITUTION Independent Episcopal, coed. Awards: bachelor's degrees. 1 undergraduate major. Total enrollment: 112. Undergraduates: 112. Both federal and institutional methodology are used as a basis for awarding need-based institutional aid.

UNDERGRADUATE EXPENSES for 1999–2000 ***Application fee:*** $20. ***Comprehensive fee:*** $11,600 includes full-time tuition ($8250), mandatory fees ($350), and room and board ($3000). Full-time tuition and fees vary according to course load. ***Part-time tuition:*** $275 per credit hour. Part-time tuition and fees vary according to course load.

GIFT AID (NEED-BASED) ***Total amount:*** $113,000 (48% Federal, 8% state, 40% institutional, 4% external sources). ***Scholarships, grants, and awards:*** Federal Pell, FSEOG, state, private, college/university gift aid from institutional funds.

GIFT AID (NON-NEED-BASED) ***Scholarships, grants, and awards by category:*** *Special Characteristics:* 3 awards ($6000 total): ethnic background.

LOANS ***Student loans:*** $714,179 (51% need-based, 49% non-need-based). 97% of past graduating class borrowed through all loan programs. Average indebtedness per student: $21,000. ***Programs:*** FFEL (Subsidized and Unsubsidized Stafford, PLUS), Perkins, Federal Nursing, college/university.

WORK-STUDY ***Federal work-study:*** *Total amount:* $4000; 3 jobs available.

APPLYING for FINANCIAL AID ***Required financial aid forms:*** FAFSA, institution's own form.

CONTACT Angie Comstock, Director of Financial Aid, Saint Luke's College, 4426 Wornall Road, Kansas City, MO 64111, 816-932-2194. *Fax:* 816-932-3831.

SAINT MARTIN'S COLLEGE

Lacey, WA

Tuition & fees: $14,180 **Average undergraduate aid package: $14,336**

ABOUT THE INSTITUTION Independent Roman Catholic, coed. Awards: associate, bachelor's, and master's degrees. 32 undergraduate majors. Total enrollment: 1,567. Undergraduates: 1,215. Federal methodology is used as a basis for awarding need-based institutional aid.

UNDERGRADUATE EXPENSES for 1999–2000 ***Comprehensive fee:*** $18,948 includes full-time tuition ($14,050), mandatory fees ($130), and room and board ($4768). ***Part-time tuition:*** $468 per credit. ***Payment plan:*** installment.

FRESHMAN FINANCIAL AID (Fall 1999) 68 applied for aid; of those 91% were deemed to have need. 100% of freshmen with need received aid; of those 48% had need fully met. *Average percent of need met:* 91% (excluding resources awarded to replace EFC). *Average financial aid package:* $13,907 (excluding resources awarded to replace EFC). 33% of all full-time freshmen had no need and received non-need-based aid.

UNDERGRADUATE FINANCIAL AID (Fall 1999) 483 applied for aid; of those 93% were deemed to have need. 100% of undergraduates with need received aid; of those 49% had need fully met. *Average percent of need met:* 89% (excluding resources awarded to replace EFC). *Average financial aid package:* $14,336 (excluding resources awarded to replace EFC). 12% of all full-time undergraduates had no need and received non-need-based aid.

GIFT AID (NEED-BASED) ***Total amount:*** $3,543,617 (21% Federal, 18% state, 47% institutional, 14% external sources). ***Receiving aid:*** *Freshmen:* 67% (62); *all full-time undergraduates:* 87% (441). ***Average award:*** Freshmen: $9516; Undergraduates: $7566. ***Scholarships, grants, and awards:*** Federal Pell, FSEOG, state, college/university gift aid from institutional funds.

GIFT AID (NON-NEED-BASED) ***Total amount:*** $243,896 (1% state, 65% institutional, 34% external sources). ***Receiving aid:*** *Freshmen:* 11% (10); *Undergraduates:* 6% (30). ***Scholarships, grants, and awards by category:*** *Academic Interests/Achievement:* business, education, engineering/technologies, general academic interests/achievements, humanities. *Creative Arts/Performance:* music, performing arts, theater/drama. *Special Achievements/Activities:* community service, leadership, memberships. *Special Characteristics:* children and siblings of alumni, children of current students, children of faculty/staff, ethnic background, general special characteristics, international students, local/state students, members of minority groups, religious affiliation, siblings of current students, spouses of current students. ***Tuition waivers:*** Full or partial for employees or children of employees. ***ROTC:*** Army cooperative.

LOANS ***Student loans:*** $3,887,843 (79% need-based, 21% non-need-based). 97% of past graduating class borrowed through all loan programs. Average indebtedness per student: $12,813. ***Average need-based loan:*** Freshmen: $2982; Undergraduates: $5463. ***Parent loans:*** $321,469 (49% need-based, 51% non-need-based). ***Programs:*** Federal Direct (Subsidized and Unsubsidized Stafford), FFEL (PLUS), Perkins, college/university.

WORK-STUDY ***Federal work-study:*** *Total amount:* $293,932; jobs available. ***State or other work-study/employment:*** *Total amount:* $591,666 (70% need-based, 30% non-need-based). Part-time jobs available.

ATHLETIC AWARDS *Total amount:* 375,395 (69% need-based, 31% non-need-based).

APPLYING for FINANCIAL AID ***Required financial aid form:*** FAFSA. ***Financial aid deadline (priority):*** 3/1. ***Notification date:*** 3/15. Students must reply within 3 weeks of notification.

CONTACT Director of Financial Aid, Saint Martin's College, 5300 Pacific Avenue, SE, Lacey, WA 98503-1297, 360-438-4397 or toll-free 800-368-8803. *Fax:* 360-459-4124.

SAINT MARY COLLEGE

Leavenworth, KS

Tuition & fees: $11,390 **Average undergraduate aid package: N/A**

ABOUT THE INSTITUTION Independent Roman Catholic, coed. Awards: associate, bachelor's, and master's degrees. 22 undergraduate majors. Total enrollment: 725. Undergraduates: 541. Freshmen: 121. Federal methodology is used as a basis for awarding need-based institutional aid.

UNDERGRADUATE EXPENSES for 2000–2001 ***Application fee:*** $25. ***Comprehensive fee:*** $15,990 includes full-time tuition ($11,390) and room and board ($4600). ***College room only:*** $2140. Full-time tuition and

Saint Mary College (continued)

fees vary according to class time. Room and board charges vary according to housing facility. ***Part-time tuition:*** $375 per credit hour. Part-time tuition and fees vary according to class time. ***Payment plan:*** installment.

GIFT AID (NEED-BASED) ***Total amount:*** $1,283,950 (23% Federal, 17% state, 57% institutional, 3% external sources). ***Scholarships, grants, and awards:*** Federal Pell, FSEOG, state, college/university gift aid from institutional funds.

GIFT AID (NON-NEED-BASED) ***Scholarships, grants, and awards by category:*** *Academic Interests/Achievement:* general academic interests/achievements. *Creative Arts/Performance:* art/fine arts, creative writing, journalism/publications, music, theater/drama. *Special Achievements/Activities:* community service. *Special Characteristics:* children of educators, siblings of current students. ***Tuition waivers:*** Full or partial for minority students, employees or children of employees, adult students. ***ROTC:*** Army cooperative.

LOANS ***Student loans:*** $1,747,029 (64% need-based, 36% non-need-based). ***Parent loans:*** $129,155 (100% need-based). ***Programs:*** FFEL (Subsidized and Unsubsidized Stafford, PLUS), Perkins.

WORK-STUDY ***Federal work-study:*** *Total amount:* $69,219; jobs available. ***State or other work-study/employment:*** *Total amount:* $16,170 (100% non-need-based). Part-time jobs available.

ATHLETIC AWARDS *Total amount:* 93,980 (100% need-based).

APPLYING for FINANCIAL AID ***Required financial aid form:*** FAFSA. ***Financial aid deadline (priority):*** 4/1. ***Notification date:*** Continuous. Students must reply within 2 weeks of notification.

CONTACT Mrs. Judy Wiedower, Financial Aid Director, Saint Mary College, 4100 South Fourth Street Trafficway, Leavenworth, KS 66048, 913-758-6314 or toll-free 800-758-6140 (out-of-state). *Fax:* 913-758-6140. *E-mail:* wiedower@hub.smcks.edu

SAINT MARY-OF-THE-WOODS COLLEGE

Saint Mary-of-the-Woods, IN

Tuition & fees: $14,660 **Average undergraduate aid package: $12,000**

ABOUT THE INSTITUTION Independent Roman Catholic, women only. Awards: associate, bachelor's, and master's degrees (also offers external degree program with significant enrollment reflected in profile). 50 undergraduate majors. Total enrollment: 1,356. Undergraduates: 1,270. Freshmen: 135. Federal methodology is used as a basis for awarding need-based institutional aid.

UNDERGRADUATE EXPENSES for 2000–2001 ***Application fee:*** $30. ***Comprehensive fee:*** $20,070 includes full-time tuition ($14,200), mandatory fees ($460), and room and board ($5410). ***College room only:*** $2000. ***Part-time tuition:*** $570 per credit hour. ***Part-time fees:*** $230 per term part-time. Part-time tuition and fees vary according to course load and program. ***Payment plan:*** installment.

FRESHMAN FINANCIAL AID (Fall 1999, est.) 91 applied for aid; of those 80% were deemed to have need. 100% of freshmen with need received aid; of those 38% had need fully met. *Average percent of need met:* 63% (excluding resources awarded to replace EFC). *Average financial aid package:* $12,000 (excluding resources awarded to replace EFC).

UNDERGRADUATE FINANCIAL AID (Fall 1999, est.) 352 applied for aid; of those 80% were deemed to have need. 100% of undergraduates with need received aid; of those 38% had need fully met. *Average percent of need met:* 63% (excluding resources awarded to replace EFC). *Average financial aid package:* $12,000 (excluding resources awarded to replace EFC).

GIFT AID (NEED-BASED) ***Total amount:*** $1,248,800 (75% state, 25% institutional). ***Receiving aid:*** *Freshmen:* 54% (55); *all full-time undergraduates:* 53% (210). ***Average award:*** Freshmen: $6000; Undergraduates: $7000. ***Scholarships, grants, and awards:*** Federal Pell, FSEOG, state, college/university gift aid from institutional funds.

GIFT AID (NON-NEED-BASED) ***Total amount:*** $1,174,366 (93% institutional, 7% external sources). ***Receiving aid:*** *Freshmen:* 72% (73); *Undergraduates:* 71% (281). ***Scholarships, grants, and awards by category:*** *Academic Interests/Achievement:* 159 awards ($518,000 total): general academic interests/achievements. *Creative Arts/Performance:* 41 awards ($77,000 total): applied art and design, art/fine arts, creative writing, dance, journalism/publications, music, performing arts, theater/drama. *Special Achievements/Activities:* 101 awards ($137,000 total): community service, general special achievements/activities, leadership, memberships, religious involvement. *Special Characteristics:* 582 awards ($639,000 total): adult students, children and siblings of alumni, children of current students, children of faculty/staff, ethnic background, first-generation college students, general special characteristics, international students, local/state students, members of minority groups, out-of-state students, parents of current students, religious affiliation, siblings of current students, spouses of current students. ***Tuition waivers:*** Full or partial for minority students, children of alumni, employees or children of employees. ***ROTC:*** Army cooperative, Air Force cooperative.

LOANS ***Student loans:*** $358,000 (30% need-based, 70% non-need-based). 85% of past graduating class borrowed through all loan programs. Average indebtedness per student: $15,000. ***Average need-based loan:*** Freshmen: $2500; Undergraduates: $2600. ***Programs:*** FFEL (Subsidized and Unsubsidized Stafford, PLUS), Perkins.

WORK-STUDY ***Federal work-study:*** *Total amount:* $120,000; 143 jobs averaging $800.

ATHLETIC AWARDS *Total amount:* 76,500 (100% non-need-based).

APPLYING for FINANCIAL AID ***Required financial aid forms:*** FAFSA, institution's own form. ***Financial aid deadline:*** 3/1. ***Notification date:*** Continuous. Students must reply by 5/1 or within 6 weeks of notification.

CONTACT Ms. Jan Benton, Director of Financial Aid, Saint Mary-of-the-Woods College, 106 Guerin Hall, Saint Mary-of-the-Woods, IN 47876, 812-535-5109 or toll-free 800-926-SMWC. *Fax:* 812-535-4900. *E-mail:* jbenton@smwc.edu

SAINT MARY'S COLLEGE

Notre Dame, IN

Tuition & fees: $16,994 **Average undergraduate aid package: $14,440**

ABOUT THE INSTITUTION Independent Roman Catholic, women only. Awards: bachelor's degrees. 43 undergraduate majors. Total enrollment: 1,417. Undergraduates: 1,409. Freshmen: 424. Both federal and institutional methodology are used as a basis for awarding need-based institutional aid.

UNDERGRADUATE EXPENSES for 1999–2000 ***Application fee:*** $30. ***Comprehensive fee:*** $22,956 includes full-time tuition ($16,994) and room and board ($5962). Full-time tuition and fees vary according to location. Room and board charges vary according to housing facility. ***Part-time tuition:*** $678 per semester hour. ***Payment plans:*** installment, deferred payment.

FRESHMAN FINANCIAL AID (Fall 1999, est.) 323 applied for aid; of those 82% were deemed to have need. 100% of freshmen with need received aid; of those 22% had need fully met. *Average percent of need met:* 85% (excluding resources awarded to replace EFC). *Average financial aid package:* $14,149 (excluding resources awarded to replace EFC). 19% of all full-time freshmen had no need and received non-need-based aid.

UNDERGRADUATE FINANCIAL AID (Fall 1999, est.) 998 applied for aid; of those 86% were deemed to have need. 98% of undergraduates with need received aid; of those 24% had need fully met. *Average percent of need met:* 86% (excluding resources awarded to replace EFC). *Average financial aid package:* $14,440 (excluding resources awarded to replace EFC). 14% of all full-time undergraduates had no need and received non-need-based aid.

GIFT AID (NEED-BASED) ***Total amount:*** $7,544,636 (6% Federal, 9% state, 81% institutional, 4% external sources). ***Receiving aid:*** *Freshmen:* 65% (260); *all full-time undergraduates:* 56% (765). ***Average award:*** Freshmen: $8364; Undergraduates: $8333. ***Scholarships, grants, and awards:*** Federal Pell, FSEOG, state, private, college/university gift aid from institutional funds.

GIFT AID (NON-NEED-BASED) ***Total amount:*** $898,030 (1% Federal, 92% institutional, 7% external sources). ***Receiving aid:*** *Freshmen:* 36% (145);

Undergraduates: 25% (340). ***Scholarships, grants, and awards by category:*** *Academic Interests/Achievement:* 434 awards ($2,362,862 total): general academic interests/achievements. *Creative Arts/Performance:* art/ fine arts, music. *Special Characteristics:* 70 awards ($571,312 total): children of faculty/staff, siblings of current students. ***Tuition waivers:*** Full or partial for employees or children of employees, adult students, senior citizens. ***ROTC:*** Army cooperative, Naval cooperative, Air Force cooperative.

LOANS ***Student loans:*** $4,610,178 (72% need-based, 28% non-need-based). 62% of past graduating class borrowed through all loan programs. Average indebtedness per student: $15,894. ***Average need-based loan:*** Freshmen: $3556; Undergraduates: $4400. ***Parent loans:*** $762,014 (32% need-based, 68% non-need-based). ***Programs:*** FFEL (Subsidized and Unsubsidized Stafford, PLUS), Perkins, college/university.

WORK-STUDY ***Federal work-study:*** *Total amount:* $220,772; 150 jobs averaging $1471. ***State or other work-study/employment:*** *Total amount:* $776,970 (80% need-based, 20% non-need-based). Part-time jobs available.

APPLYING for FINANCIAL AID ***Required financial aid forms:*** FAFSA, CSS Financial Aid PROFILE. ***Financial aid deadline (priority):*** 3/1. ***Notification date:*** Continuous. Students must reply by 5/1.

CONTACT Mrs. Mary Nucciarone, Director of Financial Aid, Saint Mary's College, 141 Le Mans Hall, Notre Dame, IN 46556, 219-284-4557 or toll-free 800-551-7621 (in-state), 219-284-4716 (out-of-state). *Fax:* 219-284-4707. *E-mail:* mnucciar@saintmarys.edu

SAINT MARY'S COLLEGE

Orchard Lake, MI

Tuition & fees: $7524 | **Average undergraduate aid package: $7657**

ABOUT THE INSTITUTION Independent Roman Catholic, coed. Awards: bachelor's degrees. 17 undergraduate majors. Total enrollment: 381. Undergraduates: 381. Freshmen: 176. Federal methodology is used as a basis for awarding need-based institutional aid.

UNDERGRADUATE EXPENSES for 1999–2000 ***Application fee:*** $25. ***Comprehensive fee:*** $12,024 includes full-time tuition ($7380), mandatory fees ($144), and room and board ($4500). ***College room only:*** $1900. Full-time tuition and fees vary according to course load. Room and board charges vary according to board plan and housing facility. ***Part-time tuition:*** $246 per credit hour. Part-time tuition and fees vary according to course load. ***Payment plan:*** installment.

FRESHMAN FINANCIAL AID (Fall 1999) 39 applied for aid; of those 100% were deemed to have need. 100% of freshmen with need received aid; of those 3% had need fully met. *Average percent of need met:* 55% (excluding resources awarded to replace EFC). *Average financial aid package:* $5580 (excluding resources awarded to replace EFC). 12% of all full-time freshmen had no need and received non-need-based aid.

UNDERGRADUATE FINANCIAL AID (Fall 1999) 131 applied for aid; of those 100% were deemed to have need. 100% of undergraduates with need received aid; of those 4% had need fully met. *Average percent of need met:* 52% (excluding resources awarded to replace EFC). *Average financial aid package:* $7657 (excluding resources awarded to replace EFC). 10% of all full-time undergraduates had no need and received non-need-based aid.

GIFT AID (NEED-BASED) ***Total amount:*** $574,689 (30% Federal, 47% state, 23% institutional). ***Receiving aid:*** *Freshmen:* 61% (39); *all full-time undergraduates:* 68% (131). ***Average award:*** Freshmen: $4637; Undergraduates: $5889. ***Scholarships, grants, and awards:*** Federal Pell, FSEOG, state, private, college/university gift aid from institutional funds.

GIFT AID (NON-NEED-BASED) ***Total amount:*** $51,697 (100% institutional). ***Receiving aid:*** *Freshmen:* 2% (1); *Undergraduates:* 3% (5). ***Scholarships, grants, and awards by category:*** *Academic Interests/Achievement:* 20 awards ($20,000 total): general academic interests/achievements. *Special Achievements/Activities:* 20 awards ($20,000 total): general special achievements/activities. ***Tuition waivers:*** Full or partial for employees or children of employees.

LOANS ***Student loans:*** $374,550 (74% need-based, 26% non-need-based). Average indebtedness per student: $12,344. ***Average need-based loan:*** Freshmen: $2616; Undergraduates: $4333. ***Parent loans:*** $13,700 (100% non-need-based). ***Programs:*** FFEL (Subsidized and Unsubsidized Stafford, PLUS), state.

WORK-STUDY ***Federal work-study:*** *Total amount:* $16,750; 20 jobs averaging $838.

APPLYING for FINANCIAL AID ***Required financial aid forms:*** FAFSA, institution's own form. ***Financial aid deadline:*** 4/30 (priority: 2/21). ***Notification date:*** 5/30. Students must reply within 2 weeks of notification.

CONTACT Ms. Carol Sturgis, Assistant Director of Financial Aid, Saint Mary's College, 3535 Indian Trail, Orchard Lake, MI 48324-1623, 248-683-0508 or toll-free 877-252 Ext. 3131 (in-state). *Fax:* 248-683-1756. *E-mail:* fastmcoll@aol.com

SAINT MARY'S COLLEGE OF CALIFORNIA

Moraga, CA

Tuition & fees: $17,475 | **Average undergraduate aid package: $18,886**

ABOUT THE INSTITUTION Independent Roman Catholic, coed. Awards: bachelor's, master's, and doctoral degrees. 45 undergraduate majors. Total enrollment: 4,063. Undergraduates: 2,863. Freshmen: 706. Federal methodology is used as a basis for awarding need-based institutional aid.

UNDERGRADUATE EXPENSES for 1999–2000 ***Application fee:*** $35. ***Comprehensive fee:*** $24,845 includes full-time tuition ($17,340), mandatory fees ($135), and room and board ($7370). ***College room only:*** $4020. Room and board charges vary according to board plan and housing facility. ***Part-time tuition:*** $2167 per course. ***Payment plans:*** tuition prepayment, installment.

FRESHMAN FINANCIAL AID (Fall 1999, est.) 508 applied for aid; of those 79% were deemed to have need. 100% of freshmen with need received aid; of those 51% had need fully met. *Average percent of need met:* 83% (excluding resources awarded to replace EFC). *Average financial aid package:* $16,133 (excluding resources awarded to replace EFC). 2% of all full-time freshmen had no need and received non-need-based aid.

UNDERGRADUATE FINANCIAL AID (Fall 1999, est.) 1,542 applied for aid; of those 89% were deemed to have need. 99% of undergraduates with need received aid; of those 55% had need fully met. *Average percent of need met:* 76% (excluding resources awarded to replace EFC). *Average financial aid package:* $18,886 (excluding resources awarded to replace EFC). 4% of all full-time undergraduates had no need and received non-need-based aid.

GIFT AID (NEED-BASED) ***Total amount:*** $14,761,132 (9% Federal, 32% state, 57% institutional, 2% external sources). ***Receiving aid:*** *Freshmen:* 60% (369); *all full-time undergraduates:* 53% (1,237). ***Average award:*** Freshmen: $13,229; Undergraduates: $14,027. ***Scholarships, grants, and awards:*** Federal Pell, FSEOG, state, private, college/university gift aid from institutional funds.

GIFT AID (NON-NEED-BASED) ***Total amount:*** $188,625 (100% institutional). ***Receiving aid:*** *Freshmen:* 13% (82); *Undergraduates:* 13% (305). ***Scholarships, grants, and awards by category:*** *Academic Interests/Achievement:* 268 awards ($510,517 total): general academic interests/achievements. *Special Achievements/Activities:* 25 awards ($161,990 total): memberships. *Special Characteristics:* 44 awards ($553,553 total): children and siblings of alumni, children of faculty/staff, relatives of clergy. ***Tuition waivers:*** Full or partial for employees or children of employees. ***ROTC:*** Army cooperative, Naval cooperative, Air Force cooperative.

LOANS ***Student loans:*** $5,459,574 (91% need-based, 9% non-need-based). 48% of past graduating class borrowed through all loan programs. Average indebtedness per student: $16,500. ***Average need-based loan:*** Freshmen: $2844; Undergraduates: $3905. ***Parent loans:*** $3,539,043 (71% need-based, 29% non-need-based). ***Programs:*** FFEL (Subsidized and Unsubsidized Stafford, PLUS), Perkins.

WORK-STUDY ***Federal work-study:*** *Total amount:* $509,242; 339 jobs averaging $1502.

ATHLETIC AWARDS *Total amount:* 2,158,548 (53% need-based, 47% non-need-based).

Saint Mary's College of California (continued)

APPLYING for FINANCIAL AID ***Required financial aid forms:*** FAFSA, state aid form. ***Financial aid deadline (priority):*** 3/2. ***Notification date:*** 4/15. Students must reply by 5/1 or within 2 weeks of notification.

CONTACT Ms. Billie C. Jones, Director of Financial Aid, Saint Mary's College of California, PO Box 4530, Moraga, CA 94575, 925-631-4370 or toll-free 800-800-4SMC. *Fax:* 925-376-2965. *E-mail:* bjones@stmarys-ca.edu

ST. MARY'S COLLEGE OF MARYLAND

St. Mary's City, MD

Tuition & fees (MD res): $7360 **Average undergraduate aid package: $5455**

ABOUT THE INSTITUTION State-supported, coed. Awards: bachelor's degrees. 23 undergraduate majors. Total enrollment: 1,613. Undergraduates: 1,613. Freshmen: 276. Federal methodology is used as a basis for awarding need-based institutional aid.

UNDERGRADUATE EXPENSES for 2000–2001 ***Application fee:*** $25. ***Tuition, state resident:*** full-time $6285; part-time $110 per credit. ***Tuition, nonresident:*** full-time $11,125; part-time $110 per credit. ***Required fees:*** full-time $1075; $250 per term part-time. Part-time tuition and fees vary according to course load. ***College room and board:*** $6325; ***room only:*** $3425. Room and board charges vary according to board plan and housing facility.

FRESHMAN FINANCIAL AID (Fall 1999) 232 applied for aid; of those 60% were deemed to have need. 98% of freshmen with need received aid; of those 20% had need fully met. *Average percent of need met:* 67% (excluding resources awarded to replace EFC). *Average financial aid package:* $5709 (excluding resources awarded to replace EFC). 22% of all full-time freshmen had no need and received non-need-based aid.

UNDERGRADUATE FINANCIAL AID (Fall 1999) 1,028 applied for aid; of those 60% were deemed to have need. 98% of undergraduates with need received aid; of those 20% had need fully met. *Average percent of need met:* 67% (excluding resources awarded to replace EFC). *Average financial aid package:* $5455 (excluding resources awarded to replace EFC). 22% of all full-time undergraduates had no need and received non-need-based aid.

GIFT AID (NEED-BASED) ***Total amount:*** $2,289,720 (18% Federal, 28% state, 47% institutional, 7% external sources). ***Receiving aid:*** *Freshmen:* 43% (118); *all full-time undergraduates:* 36% (503). ***Average award:*** Freshmen: $5568; Undergraduates: $4620. ***Scholarships, grants, and awards:*** Federal Pell, FSEOG, state, private, college/university gift aid from institutional funds.

GIFT AID (NON-NEED-BASED) ***Total amount:*** $971,848 (32% state, 57% institutional, 11% external sources). ***Receiving aid:*** *Freshmen:* 4% (10); *Undergraduates:* 3% (45). ***Scholarships, grants, and awards by category:*** *Academic Interests/Achievement:* 125 awards ($552,569 total): general academic interests/achievements. *Special Characteristics:* children and siblings of alumni. ***Tuition waivers:*** Full or partial for employees or children of employees, senior citizens.

LOANS ***Student loans:*** $3,126,358 (65% need-based, 35% non-need-based). 53% of past graduating class borrowed through all loan programs. Average indebtedness per student: $14,399. ***Average need-based loan:*** Freshmen: $2492; Undergraduates: $3881. ***Parent loans:*** $2,784,530 (35% need-based, 65% non-need-based). ***Programs:*** FFEL (Subsidized and Unsubsidized Stafford, PLUS), Perkins.

WORK-STUDY ***Federal work-study:*** *Total amount:* $58,275; 63 jobs averaging $925. ***State or other work-study/employment:*** *Total amount:* $112,523 (100% need-based). 111 part-time jobs averaging $1014.

APPLYING for FINANCIAL AID ***Required financial aid form:*** FAFSA. ***Financial aid deadline:*** 3/1. ***Notification date:*** 4/1. Students must reply by 5/1.

CONTACT Mr. George Bachman, Director of Financial Aid, St. Mary's College of Maryland, 18952 East Fisher Road, St. Mary's City, MD 20686-3001, 301-862-0300 or toll-free 800-492-7181. *Fax:* 301-862-0959. *E-mail:* gtbachman@osprey.smcm.edu

SAINT MARY'S UNIVERSITY OF MINNESOTA

Winona, MN

ABOUT THE INSTITUTION Independent Roman Catholic, coed. Awards: bachelor's, master's, and doctoral degrees and post-master's certificates. 54 undergraduate majors. Total enrollment: 6,356. Undergraduates: 1,799. Freshmen: 418.

GIFT AID (NEED-BASED) ***Scholarships, grants, and awards:*** Federal Pell, FSEOG, state, college/university gift aid from institutional funds.

GIFT AID (NON-NEED-BASED) ***Scholarships, grants, and awards by category:*** *Academic Interests/Achievement:* general academic interests/achievements. *Creative Arts/Performance:* debating, music, theater/drama. *Special Achievements/Activities:* leadership, memberships.

LOANS ***Programs:*** FFEL (Subsidized and Unsubsidized Stafford, PLUS), Perkins, state.

WORK-STUDY ***Federal work-study:*** *Total amount:* $271,346; 319 jobs averaging $1094. ***State or other work-study/employment:*** *Total amount:* $445,307 (71% need-based, 29% non-need-based).

APPLYING for FINANCIAL AID ***Required financial aid forms:*** FAFSA, institution's own form.

CONTACT Ms. Jayne P. Wobig, Director of Financial Aid, Saint Mary's University of Minnesota, 700 Terrace Heights, Winona, MN 55987-1399, 507-457-1437 or toll-free 800-635-5987. *Fax:* 507-457-1633. *E-mail:* jwobig@smumn.edu

ST. MARY'S UNIVERSITY OF SAN ANTONIO

San Antonio, TX

Tuition & fees: $11,880 **Average undergraduate aid package: $12,100**

ABOUT THE INSTITUTION Independent Roman Catholic, coed. Awards: bachelor's, master's, doctoral, and first professional degrees. 47 undergraduate majors. Total enrollment: 4,065. Undergraduates: 2,543. Freshmen: 489. Federal methodology is used as a basis for awarding need-based institutional aid.

UNDERGRADUATE EXPENSES for 1999–2000 ***Application fee:*** $30. ***Comprehensive fee:*** $17,131 includes full-time tuition ($11,500), mandatory fees ($380), and room and board ($5251). ***College room only:*** $3096. Room and board charges vary according to board plan and housing facility. ***Part-time tuition:*** $377 per semester hour. ***Part-time fees:*** $61 per term part-time. ***Payment plans:*** tuition prepayment, installment, deferred payment.

FRESHMAN FINANCIAL AID (Fall 1999) 394 applied for aid; of those 92% were deemed to have need. 100% of freshmen with need received aid; of those 25% had need fully met. *Average percent of need met:* 61% (excluding resources awarded to replace EFC). *Average financial aid package:* $11,864 (excluding resources awarded to replace EFC). 6% of all full-time freshmen had no need and received non-need-based aid.

UNDERGRADUATE FINANCIAL AID (Fall 1999) 1,660 applied for aid; of those 92% were deemed to have need. 100% of undergraduates with need received aid; of those 26% had need fully met. *Average percent of need met:* 64% (excluding resources awarded to replace EFC). *Average financial aid package:* $12,100 (excluding resources awarded to replace EFC). 6% of all full-time undergraduates had no need and received non-need-based aid.

GIFT AID (NEED-BASED) ***Total amount:*** $8,308,430 (26% Federal, 52% state, 22% institutional). ***Receiving aid:*** *Freshmen:* 72% (351); *all full-time undergraduates:* 66% (1,462). ***Average award:*** Freshmen: $5259; Undergraduates: $5498. ***Scholarships, grants, and awards:*** Federal Pell, FSEOG, state, college/university gift aid from institutional funds.

GIFT AID (NON-NEED-BASED) ***Total amount:*** $4,972,823 (8% Federal, 82% institutional, 10% external sources). ***Receiving aid:*** *Freshmen:* 39% (189); *Undergraduates:* 26% (568). ***Scholarships, grants, and awards by category:*** *Academic Interests/Achievement:* 1,146 awards ($5,407,173

total): general academic interests/achievements, military science. *Creative Arts/Performance:* 52 awards ($128,850 total): music. *Special Achievements/Activities:* 30 awards ($35,354 total): cheerleading/drum major. ***Tuition waivers:*** Full or partial for employees or children of employees. ***ROTC:*** Army.

LOANS ***Student loans:*** $10,133,198 (61% need-based, 39% non-need-based). 76% of past graduating class borrowed through all loan programs. Average indebtedness per student: $16,415. ***Average need-based loan:*** Freshmen: $3328; Undergraduates: $4322. ***Parent loans:*** $661,475 (100% non-need-based). ***Programs:*** FFEL (Subsidized and Unsubsidized Stafford, PLUS), Perkins, state, alternative loans.

WORK-STUDY ***Federal work-study:*** *Total amount:* $1,044,154; 570 jobs averaging $1831. ***State or other work-study/employment:*** *Total amount:* $169,797 (100% non-need-based). 108 part-time jobs averaging $1572.

ATHLETIC AWARDS *Total amount:* 943,327 (100% non-need-based).

APPLYING for FINANCIAL AID ***Required financial aid form:*** FAFSA. ***Financial aid deadline (priority):*** 4/1. ***Notification date:*** Continuous beginning 5/1. Students must reply within 2 weeks of notification.

CONTACT Mr. David R. Krause, Director of Financial Assistance, St. Mary's University of San Antonio, One Camino Santa Maria, San Antonio, TX 78228-8541, 210-436-3141 or toll-free 800-FOR-STMU (out-of-state). *Fax:* 210-431-2221. *E-mail:* dkrause@alvin.stmarytx.edu

SAINT MICHAEL'S COLLEGE

Colchester, VT

Tuition & fees: $17,662 **Average undergraduate aid package: $12,032**

ABOUT THE INSTITUTION Independent Roman Catholic, coed. Awards: bachelor's and master's degrees. 36 undergraduate majors. Total enrollment: 2,628. Undergraduates: 2,004. Freshmen: 506. Both federal and institutional methodology are used as a basis for awarding need-based institutional aid.

UNDERGRADUATE EXPENSES for 1999–2000 ***Application fee:*** $45. ***Comprehensive fee:*** $24,915 includes full-time tuition ($17,500), mandatory fees ($162), and room and board ($7253). ***College room only:*** $4508. Room and board charges vary according to board plan and housing facility. ***Part-time tuition:*** $585 per semester hour. ***Payment plan:*** installment.

FRESHMAN FINANCIAL AID (Fall 1998) 470 applied for aid; of those 94% were deemed to have need. 100% of freshmen with need received aid. *Average percent of need met:* 80% (excluding resources awarded to replace EFC). *Average financial aid package:* $12,634 (excluding resources awarded to replace EFC).

UNDERGRADUATE FINANCIAL AID (Fall 1998) 1,570 applied for aid; of those 89% were deemed to have need. 100% of undergraduates with need received aid. *Average percent of need met:* 80% (excluding resources awarded to replace EFC). *Average financial aid package:* $12,032 (excluding resources awarded to replace EFC).

GIFT AID (NEED-BASED) ***Total amount:*** $11,645,391 (7% Federal, 4% state, 86% institutional, 3% external sources). ***Receiving aid:*** *Freshmen:* 72% (364); *all full-time undergraduates:* 63% (1,172). ***Average award:*** Freshmen: $8560; Undergraduates: $7499. ***Scholarships, grants, and awards:*** Federal Pell, FSEOG, state, private, college/university gift aid from institutional funds.

GIFT AID (NON-NEED-BASED) ***Total amount:*** $1,337,471 (87% institutional, 13% external sources). ***Receiving aid:*** *Freshmen:* 25% (126); *Undergraduates:* 18% (339). ***Scholarships, grants, and awards by category:*** *Academic Interests/Achievement:* general academic interests/achievements. *Creative Arts/Performance:* art/fine arts. *Special Characteristics:* local/state students, members of minority groups, religious affiliation, siblings of current students. ***Tuition waivers:*** Full or partial for employees or children of employees. ***ROTC:*** Army cooperative, Air Force cooperative.

LOANS ***Student loans:*** $5,830,283 (73% need-based, 27% non-need-based). ***Average need-based loan:*** Freshmen: $3853; Undergraduates: $4185. ***Programs:*** FFEL (Subsidized and Unsubsidized Stafford, PLUS), Perkins.

WORK-STUDY ***Federal work-study:*** *Total amount:* $251,875; 216 jobs averaging $1050. ***State or other work-study/employment:*** *Total amount:* $542,875 (100% need-based). Part-time jobs available.

ATHLETIC AWARDS *Total amount:* 476,796 (100% non-need-based).

APPLYING for FINANCIAL AID ***Required financial aid forms:*** FAFSA, institution's own form. ***Financial aid deadline (priority):*** 3/15. ***Notification date:*** 4/1. Students must reply by 5/1 or within 2 weeks of notification.

CONTACT Mrs. Nelberta B. Lunde, Director of Financial Aid, Saint Michael's College, Winooski Park, Colchester, VT 05439, 802-654-3243 or toll-free 800-762-8000. *Fax:* 802-654-2591. *E-mail:* finaid@smcvt.edu

ST. NORBERT COLLEGE

De Pere, WI

Tuition & fees: $16,770 **Average undergraduate aid package: $13,045**

ABOUT THE INSTITUTION Independent Roman Catholic, coed. Awards: bachelor's and master's degrees. 38 undergraduate majors. Total enrollment: 1,959. Undergraduates: 1,950. Freshmen: 519. Both federal and institutional methodology are used as a basis for awarding need-based institutional aid.

UNDERGRADUATE EXPENSES for 2000–2001 ***Application fee:*** $25. ***Comprehensive fee:*** $21,932 includes full-time tuition ($16,570), mandatory fees ($200), and room and board ($5162). ***College room only:*** $2742. Full-time tuition and fees vary according to course load. Room and board charges vary according to board plan and housing facility. ***Part-time tuition:*** $518 per credit hour. ***Part-time fees:*** $12 per course; $20 per term part-time. Part-time tuition and fees vary according to course load. ***Payment plans:*** guaranteed tuition, installment, deferred payment.

FRESHMAN FINANCIAL AID (Fall 1999, est.) 428 applied for aid; of those 84% were deemed to have need. 100% of freshmen with need received aid; of those 46% had need fully met. *Average percent of need met:* 91% (excluding resources awarded to replace EFC). *Average financial aid package:* $13,481 (excluding resources awarded to replace EFC). 25% of all full-time freshmen had no need and received non-need-based aid.

UNDERGRADUATE FINANCIAL AID (Fall 1999, est.) 1,437 applied for aid; of those 87% were deemed to have need. 100% of undergraduates with need received aid; of those 51% had need fully met. *Average percent of need met:* 91% (excluding resources awarded to replace EFC). *Average financial aid package:* $13,045 (excluding resources awarded to replace EFC). 27% of all full-time undergraduates had no need and received non-need-based aid.

GIFT AID (NEED-BASED) ***Total amount:*** $10,334,182 (8% Federal, 12% state, 77% institutional, 3% external sources). ***Receiving aid:*** *Freshmen:* 69% (358); *all full-time undergraduates:* 65% (1,225). ***Average award:*** Freshmen: $10,024; Undergraduates: $8764. ***Scholarships, grants, and awards:*** Federal Pell, FSEOG, state, private, college/university gift aid from institutional funds.

GIFT AID (NON-NEED-BASED) ***Total amount:*** $2,873,324 (1% Federal, 1% state, 89% institutional, 9% external sources). ***Receiving aid:*** *Freshmen:* 10% (53); *Undergraduates:* 8% (158). ***Scholarships, grants, and awards by category:*** *Academic Interests/Achievement:* general academic interests/achievements. *Creative Arts/Performance:* art/fine arts, music, theater/drama. *Special Characteristics:* children of faculty/staff, children with a deceased or disabled parent, ethnic background, international students. ***Tuition waivers:*** Full or partial for employees or children of employees. ***ROTC:*** Army.

LOANS ***Student loans:*** $6,874,757 (65% need-based, 35% non-need-based). 85% of past graduating class borrowed through all loan programs. Average indebtedness per student: $14,088. ***Average need-based loan:*** Freshmen: $2504; Undergraduates: $3588. ***Parent loans:*** $919,188 (24% need-based, 76% non-need-based). ***Programs:*** Federal Direct (Subsidized and Unsubsidized Stafford, PLUS), Perkins.

WORK-STUDY ***Federal work-study:*** *Total amount:* $659,390; 348 jobs averaging $1895. ***State or other work-study/employment:*** *Total amount:* $1,595,471 (13% need-based, 87% non-need-based). 669 part-time jobs averaging $2385.

St. Norbert College (continued)

APPLYING for FINANCIAL AID ***Required financial aid forms:*** FAFSA, institution's own form, parent and student income tax returns. ***Financial aid deadline (priority):*** 3/1. ***Notification date:*** Continuous beginning 3/15. Students must reply within 2 weeks of notification.

CONTACT Mr. Jeffrey A. Zahn, Director of Financial Aid, St. Norbert College, 100 Grant Street, De Pere, WI 54115-2099, 920-403-3071 or toll-free 800-236-4878. *Fax:* 920-403-3062. *E-mail:* zahnja@mail.snc.edu

ST. OLAF COLLEGE

Northfield, MN

Tuition & fees: $19,400 **Average undergraduate aid package: $14,654**

ABOUT THE INSTITUTION Independent Lutheran, coed. Awards: bachelor's degrees. 63 undergraduate majors. Total enrollment: 2,998. Undergraduates: 2,998. Freshmen: 766. Both federal and institutional methodology are used as a basis for awarding need-based institutional aid.

UNDERGRADUATE EXPENSES for 2000–2001 ***Application fee:*** $35. ***Comprehensive fee:*** $23,900 includes full-time tuition ($19,400) and room and board ($4500). ***College room only:*** $2100. Room and board charges vary according to board plan. ***Part-time tuition:*** $2280 per course. ***Payment plans:*** tuition prepayment, installment.

FRESHMAN FINANCIAL AID (Fall 1999, est.) 670 applied for aid; of those 71% were deemed to have need. 100% of freshmen with need received aid; of those 100% had need fully met. *Average percent of need met:* 100% (excluding resources awarded to replace EFC). *Average financial aid package:* $13,970 (excluding resources awarded to replace EFC). 26% of all full-time freshmen had no need and received non-need-based aid.

UNDERGRADUATE FINANCIAL AID (Fall 1999, est.) 2,726 applied for aid; of those 65% were deemed to have need. 98% of undergraduates with need received aid; of those 100% had need fully met. *Average percent of need met:* 100% (excluding resources awarded to replace EFC). *Average financial aid package:* $14,654 (excluding resources awarded to replace EFC). 20% of all full-time undergraduates had no need and received non-need-based aid.

GIFT AID (NEED-BASED) ***Total amount:*** $17,319,361 (7% Federal, 11% state, 76% institutional, 6% external sources). ***Receiving aid:*** *Freshmen:* 61% (471); *all full-time undergraduates:* 60% (1,751). ***Average award:*** Freshmen: $9920; Undergraduates: $9895. ***Scholarships, grants, and awards:*** Federal Pell, FSEOG, state, private, college/university gift aid from institutional funds.

GIFT AID (NON-NEED-BASED) ***Total amount:*** $2,527,301 (1% Federal, 85% institutional, 14% external sources). ***Receiving aid:*** *Freshmen:* 31% (236); *Undergraduates:* 22% (651). ***Scholarships, grants, and awards by category:*** *Academic Interests/Achievement:* 1,020 awards ($3,784,575 total): general academic interests/achievements. *Creative Arts/Performance:* 141 awards ($226,050 total): music. *Special Achievements/Activities:* 193 awards ($357,375 total): community service, religious involvement. ***Tuition waivers:*** Full or partial for employees or children of employees.

LOANS ***Student loans:*** $9,272,160 (76% need-based, 24% non-need-based). 71% of past graduating class borrowed through all loan programs. Average indebtedness per student: $15,991. ***Average need-based loan:*** Freshmen: $3534; Undergraduates: $4489. ***Parent loans:*** $1,349,979 (100% non-need-based). ***Programs:*** FFEL (Subsidized and Unsubsidized Stafford, PLUS), Perkins, Federal Nursing, state, college/university.

WORK-STUDY ***Federal work-study:*** *Total amount:* $1,995,499; 1,208 jobs averaging $1652. ***State or other work-study/employment:*** *Total amount:* $942,506 (22% need-based, 78% non-need-based). 821 part-time jobs averaging $1148.

APPLYING for FINANCIAL AID ***Required financial aid forms:*** FAFSA, institution's own form. ***Financial aid deadline (priority):*** 3/1. ***Notification date:*** Continuous beginning 3/10. Students must reply by 5/1 or within 2 weeks of notification.

CONTACT Ms. Katharine Ruby, Director of Student Financial Services, St. Olaf College, 1520 Saint Olaf Avenue, Northfield, MN 55057-1098, 507-646-3019 or toll-free 800-800-3025 (in-state). *Fax:* 507-646-3832. *E-mail:* ruby@stolaf.edu

SAINT PAUL'S COLLEGE

Lawrenceville, VA

Tuition & fees: $8200 **Average undergraduate aid package: $9915**

ABOUT THE INSTITUTION Independent Episcopal, coed. Awards: bachelor's degrees. 13 undergraduate majors. Both federal and institutional methodology are used as a basis for awarding need-based institutional aid.

UNDERGRADUATE EXPENSES for 1999–2000 ***Application fee:*** $20. ***Comprehensive fee:*** $12,460 includes full-time tuition ($7760), mandatory fees ($440), and room and board ($4260). ***Part-time tuition:*** $323 per credit. ***Part-time fees:*** $220 per term part-time.

FRESHMAN FINANCIAL AID (Fall 1999, est.) 190 applied for aid; of those 95% were deemed to have need. 99% of freshmen with need received aid; of those 1% had need fully met. *Average percent of need met:* 90% (excluding resources awarded to replace EFC). *Average financial aid package:* $10,340 (excluding resources awarded to replace EFC).

UNDERGRADUATE FINANCIAL AID (Fall 1999, est.) 559 applied for aid; of those 91% were deemed to have need. 99% of undergraduates with need received aid; of those 6% had need fully met. *Average percent of need met:* 90% (excluding resources awarded to replace EFC). *Average financial aid package:* $9915 (excluding resources awarded to replace EFC).

GIFT AID (NEED-BASED) ***Total amount:*** $1,107,739 (88% Federal, 5% state, 7% external sources). ***Receiving aid:*** *Freshmen:* 84% (165); *all full-time undergraduates:* 74% (451). ***Average award:*** Freshmen: $4396; Undergraduates: $5091. ***Scholarships, grants, and awards:*** Federal Pell, FSEOG, state, private, college/university gift aid from institutional funds, United Negro College Fund.

GIFT AID (NON-NEED-BASED) ***Total amount:*** $1,688,005 (49% state, 32% institutional, 19% external sources). ***Receiving aid:*** *Freshmen:* 74% (145); *Undergraduates:* 58% (350). ***Scholarships, grants, and awards by category:*** *Academic Interests/Achievement:* biological sciences, general academic interests/achievements. *Special Achievements/Activities:* general special achievements/activities. *Special Characteristics:* children of faculty/staff, children of union members/company employees, general special characteristics, religious affiliation, twins. ***ROTC:*** Army.

LOANS ***Student loans:*** $1,788,114 (62% need-based, 38% non-need-based). 90% of past graduating class borrowed through all loan programs. Average indebtedness per student: $22,000. ***Average need-based loan:*** Freshmen: $2625. ***Parent loans:*** $293,449 (100% non-need-based). ***Programs:*** Federal Direct (Subsidized and Unsubsidized Stafford, PLUS), Perkins.

WORK-STUDY ***Federal work-study:*** *Total amount:* $279,959; jobs available.

ATHLETIC AWARDS *Total amount:* 167,653 (100% non-need-based).

APPLYING for FINANCIAL AID ***Required financial aid forms:*** FAFSA, state aid form. ***Financial aid deadline:*** Continuous. ***Notification date:*** Continuous beginning 4/20. Students must reply by 8/25.

CONTACT Financial Aid Department, Saint Paul's College, 115 College Drive, Lawrenceville, VA 23868-1202, 804-848-3111 or toll-free 800-678-7071.

SAINT PETER'S COLLEGE

Jersey City, NJ

Tuition & fees: $15,606 **Average undergraduate aid package: N/A**

ABOUT THE INSTITUTION Independent Roman Catholic (Jesuit), coed. Awards: associate, bachelor's, and master's degrees. 41 undergraduate majors. Total enrollment: 3,280. Undergraduates: 2,762. Freshmen: 601. Federal methodology is used as a basis for awarding need-based institutional aid.

UNDERGRADUATE EXPENSES for 2000–2001 ***Application fee:*** $30. ***Comprehensive fee:*** $22,052 includes full-time tuition ($15,240), mandatory fees ($366), and room and board ($6446). ***College room only:*** $3990. Full-time tuition and fees vary according to course load and location. Room and board charges vary according to board plan and housing facility. ***Part-time tuition:*** $508 per credit. Part-time tuition and fees vary according to class time and course load. ***Payment plans:*** installment, deferred payment.

GIFT AID (NEED-BASED) ***Scholarships, grants, and awards:*** Federal Pell, FSEOG, state, private, college/university gift aid from institutional funds.

GIFT AID (NON-NEED-BASED) ***Scholarships, grants, and awards by category:*** *Academic Interests/Achievement:* general academic interests/achievements. *Special Achievements/Activities:* leadership. *Special Characteristics:* children of faculty/staff, general special characteristics, relatives of clergy, religious affiliation. ***Tuition waivers:*** Full or partial for employees or children of employees. ***ROTC:*** Army, Air Force cooperative.

LOANS ***Programs:*** Federal Direct (Subsidized and Unsubsidized Stafford, PLUS), Perkins, state.

WORK-STUDY Federal work-study jobs available. ***State or other work-study/employment:*** Part-time jobs available.

APPLYING for FINANCIAL AID ***Required financial aid form:*** FAFSA. ***Financial aid deadline (priority):*** 4/15.

CONTACT Associate Vice President for Enrollment, Saint Peter's College, 2641 Kennedy Boulevard, Jersey City, NJ 07306, 201-915-9309 or toll-free 888-SPC-9933. *Fax:* 201-434-6878.

ST. THOMAS AQUINAS COLLEGE

Sparkill, NY

Tuition & fees: $12,120 **Average undergraduate aid package: N/A**

ABOUT THE INSTITUTION Independent, coed. Awards: bachelor's and master's degrees and post-master's certificates. 38 undergraduate majors. Total enrollment: 2,190. Undergraduates: 2,010. Freshmen: 312. Federal methodology is used as a basis for awarding need-based institutional aid.

UNDERGRADUATE EXPENSES for 1999–2000 ***Application fee:*** $30. ***Comprehensive fee:*** $19,270 includes full-time tuition ($11,800), mandatory fees ($320), and room and board ($7150). ***College room only:*** $4040. Room and board charges vary according to board plan and housing facility. ***Part-time tuition:*** $415 per credit. ***Part-time fees:*** $75 per term part-time. ***Payment plans:*** installment, deferred payment.

GIFT AID (NEED-BASED) ***Scholarships, grants, and awards:*** Federal Pell, FSEOG, state, private, college/university gift aid from institutional funds.

GIFT AID (NON-NEED-BASED) ***Scholarships, grants, and awards by category:*** *Academic Interests/Achievement:* business, communication, education, general academic interests/achievements, humanities, mathematics, social sciences. *Special Achievements/Activities:* community service, leadership. *Special Characteristics:* siblings of current students, spouses of current students, twins. ***Tuition waivers:*** Full or partial for employees or children of employees, senior citizens. ***ROTC:*** Air Force cooperative.

LOANS ***Programs:*** FFEL (Subsidized and Unsubsidized Stafford, PLUS), Perkins.

WORK-STUDY Federal work-study jobs available.

APPLYING for FINANCIAL AID ***Required financial aid forms:*** FAFSA, state aid form. ***Financial aid deadline (priority):*** 2/15. ***Notification date:*** Continuous beginning 3/1. Students must reply by 5/1 or within 2 weeks of notification.

CONTACT Margaret McGrail, Director of Financial Aid, St. Thomas Aquinas College, 125 Route 340, Sparkill, NY 10976, 914-398-4097 or toll-free 800-999-STAC.

ST. THOMAS UNIVERSITY

Miami, FL

Tuition & fees: $13,320 **Average undergraduate aid package: $12,674**

ABOUT THE INSTITUTION Independent Roman Catholic, coed. Awards: bachelor's, master's, and first professional degrees. 28 undergraduate majors. Total enrollment: 2,185. Undergraduates: 1,019. Freshmen: 128. Both federal and institutional methodology are used as a basis for awarding need-based institutional aid.

UNDERGRADUATE EXPENSES for 2000–2001 ***Application fee:*** $45. ***Comprehensive fee:*** $17,720 includes full-time tuition ($12,720), mandatory fees ($600), and room and board ($4400). Room and board charges vary according to housing facility. ***Part-time tuition:*** $454 per credit. ***Part-time fees:*** $45 per term part-time. ***Payment plan:*** installment.

FRESHMAN FINANCIAL AID (Fall 1999) 160 applied for aid; of those 69% were deemed to have need. 100% of freshmen with need received aid; of those 34% had need fully met. *Average percent of need met:* 88% (excluding resources awarded to replace EFC). *Average financial aid package:* $16,027 (excluding resources awarded to replace EFC). 4% of all full-time freshmen had no need and received non-need-based aid.

UNDERGRADUATE FINANCIAL AID (Fall 1999) 937 applied for aid; of those 95% were deemed to have need. 91% of undergraduates with need received aid; of those 39% had need fully met. *Average percent of need met:* 84% (excluding resources awarded to replace EFC). *Average financial aid package:* $12,674 (excluding resources awarded to replace EFC). 13% of all full-time undergraduates had no need and received non-need-based aid.

GIFT AID (NEED-BASED) ***Total amount:*** $1,557,360 (75% Federal, 13% state, 10% institutional, 2% external sources). ***Receiving aid:*** *Freshmen:* 40% (67); *all full-time undergraduates:* 66% (699). ***Scholarships, grants, and awards:*** Federal Pell, FSEOG, state, private, college/university gift aid from institutional funds.

GIFT AID (NON-NEED-BASED) ***Total amount:*** $3,896,339 (28% state, 69% institutional, 3% external sources). ***Receiving aid:*** *Freshmen:* 66% (110); *Undergraduates:* 77% (810). ***Scholarships, grants, and awards by category:*** *Academic Interests/Achievement:* 918 awards ($2,841,374 total): general academic interests/achievements. ***Tuition waivers:*** Full or partial for minority students, children of alumni, employees or children of employees. ***ROTC:*** Army cooperative, Air Force cooperative.

LOANS ***Student loans:*** $3,406,586 (100% need-based). 64% of past graduating class borrowed through all loan programs. ***Parent loans:*** $402,737 (100% need-based). ***Programs:*** Federal Direct (Subsidized and Unsubsidized Stafford, PLUS), FFEL (Subsidized and Unsubsidized Stafford, PLUS), Perkins, alternative loans.

WORK-STUDY ***Federal work-study:*** *Total amount:* $353,567; 164 jobs averaging $2410.

ATHLETIC AWARDS *Total amount:* 763,239 (100% non-need-based).

APPLYING for FINANCIAL AID ***Required financial aid forms:*** FAFSA, institution's own form. ***Financial aid deadline (priority):*** 4/15. ***Notification date:*** Continuous beginning 5/1. Students must reply within 2 weeks of notification.

CONTACT Lidiette Esquivel, Director of Financial Aid, St. Thomas University, 16400 Northwest 32nd Avenue, Miami, FL 33054-6459, 305-628-6547 or toll-free 800-367-9006 (in-state), 800-367-9010 (out-of-state). *Fax:* 305-628-6754. *E-mail:* lesquive@stu.edu

SAINT VINCENT COLLEGE

Latrobe, PA

Tuition & fees: $14,955 **Average undergraduate aid package: $11,420**

ABOUT THE INSTITUTION Independent Roman Catholic, coed. Awards: bachelor's degrees. 32 undergraduate majors. Total enrollment: 1,186. Undergraduates: 1,186. Freshmen: 272. Federal methodology is used as a basis for awarding need-based institutional aid.

UNDERGRADUATE EXPENSES for 1999–2000 ***Application fee:*** $25. ***Comprehensive fee:*** $20,069 includes full-time tuition ($14,725), mandatory fees ($230), and room and board ($5114). Full-time tuition and fees vary according to course load. Room and board charges vary according to board plan and housing facility. ***Part-time tuition:*** $475 per credit. ***Part-time fees:*** $115 per term part-time. Part-time tuition and fees vary according to course load. ***Payment plans:*** installment, deferred payment.

FRESHMAN FINANCIAL AID (Fall 1999, est.) 254 applied for aid; of those 87% were deemed to have need. 100% of freshmen with need received aid; of those 12% had need fully met. *Average percent of need met:* 83% (excluding resources awarded to replace EFC). *Average financial aid pack-*

Saint Vincent College (continued)

age: $12,337 (excluding resources awarded to replace EFC). 12% of all full-time freshmen had no need and received non-need-based aid.

UNDERGRADUATE FINANCIAL AID (Fall 1999, est.) 974 applied for aid; of those 86% were deemed to have need. 100% of undergraduates with need received aid; of those 17% had need fully met. *Average percent of need met:* 76% (excluding resources awarded to replace EFC). *Average financial aid package:* $11,420 (excluding resources awarded to replace EFC). 12% of all full-time undergraduates had no need and received non-need-based aid.

GIFT AID (NEED-BASED) ***Total amount:*** $6,968,698 (11% Federal, 22% state, 65% institutional, 2% external sources). ***Receiving aid:*** *Freshmen:* 81% (220); *all full-time undergraduates:* 79% (827). ***Average award:*** Freshmen: $8639; Undergraduates: $8429. ***Scholarships, grants, and awards:*** Federal Pell, FSEOG, state, private, college/university gift aid from institutional funds.

GIFT AID (NON-NEED-BASED) ***Total amount:*** $587,507 (86% institutional, 14% external sources). ***Receiving aid:*** *Freshmen:* 19% (51); *Undergraduates:* 17% (177). ***Scholarships, grants, and awards by category:*** *Academic Interests/Achievement:* 367 awards ($1,350,339 total): biological sciences, business, computer science, general academic interests/achievements, mathematics, physical sciences, social sciences. *Creative Arts/Performance:* 2 awards ($4500 total): music. *Special Achievements/Activities:* 325 awards ($397,350 total): leadership. *Special Characteristics:* 52 awards ($120,022 total): international students, members of minority groups. ***Tuition waivers:*** Full or partial for employees or children of employees, senior citizens. ***ROTC:*** Air Force cooperative.

LOANS ***Student loans:*** $3,684,444 (70% need-based, 30% non-need-based). 70% of past graduating class borrowed through all loan programs. Average indebtedness per student: $19,842. ***Average need-based loan:*** Freshmen: $3068; Undergraduates: $4081. ***Parent loans:*** $854,527 (30% need-based, 70% non-need-based). ***Programs:*** FFEL (Subsidized and Unsubsidized Stafford, PLUS), Perkins.

WORK-STUDY ***Federal work-study:*** *Total amount:* $198,251; 136 jobs averaging $1458. ***State or other work-study/employment:*** *Total amount:* $607,537 (13% need-based, 87% non-need-based). 367 part-time jobs averaging $1656.

ATHLETIC AWARDS *Total amount:* 553,146 (67% need-based, 33% non-need-based).

APPLYING for FINANCIAL AID ***Required financial aid form:*** FAFSA. ***Financial aid deadline (priority):*** 2/15. ***Notification date:*** Continuous beginning 3/1. Students must reply within 4 weeks of notification.

CONTACT Ms. Karen G. Squib, Assistant Director of Financial Aid, Saint Vincent College, 300 Fraser Purchase Road, Latrobe, PA 15650, 724-537-4540 or toll-free 800-SVC-5549. *Fax:* 724-532-5069. *E-mail:* ksquib@stvincent.edu

SAINT XAVIER UNIVERSITY

Chicago, IL

Tuition & fees: $13,760 **Average undergraduate aid package: $10,865**

ABOUT THE INSTITUTION Independent Roman Catholic, coed. Awards: bachelor's and master's degrees. 45 undergraduate majors. Total enrollment: 4,051. Undergraduates: 2,401. Freshmen: 323. Federal methodology is used as a basis for awarding need-based institutional aid.

UNDERGRADUATE EXPENSES for 1999–2000 ***Application fee:*** $25. ***Comprehensive fee:*** $19,313 includes full-time tuition ($13,650), mandatory fees ($110), and room and board ($5553). ***College room only:*** $3180. Full-time tuition and fees vary according to course load. Room and board charges vary according to board plan. ***Part-time tuition:*** $455 per semester hour. ***Part-time fees:*** $40 per term part-time. Part-time tuition and fees vary according to course load. ***Payment plan:*** installment.

FRESHMAN FINANCIAL AID (Fall 1998) 239 applied for aid; of those 93% were deemed to have need. 100% of freshmen with need received aid; of those 25% had need fully met. *Average percent of need met:* 82% (excluding resources awarded to replace EFC). *Average financial aid package:* $10,716 (excluding resources awarded to replace EFC). 19% of all full-time freshmen had no need and received non-need-based aid.

UNDERGRADUATE FINANCIAL AID (Fall 1998) 1,136 applied for aid; of those 91% were deemed to have need. 100% of undergraduates with need received aid; of those 42% had need fully met. *Average percent of need met:* 86% (excluding resources awarded to replace EFC). *Average financial aid package:* $10,865 (excluding resources awarded to replace EFC). 31% of all full-time undergraduates had no need and received non-need-based aid.

GIFT AID (NEED-BASED) ***Total amount:*** $8,798,443 (20% Federal, 49% state, 27% institutional, 4% external sources). ***Receiving aid:*** *Freshmen:* 80% (220); *all full-time undergraduates:* 67% (995). ***Average award:*** Freshmen: $8446; Undergraduates: $7201. ***Scholarships, grants, and awards:*** Federal Pell, FSEOG, state, private, college/university gift aid from institutional funds.

GIFT AID (NON-NEED-BASED) ***Total amount:*** $1,185,794 (7% state, 87% institutional, 6% external sources). ***Receiving aid:*** *Freshmen:* 10% (27); *Undergraduates:* 6% (87). ***Scholarships, grants, and awards by category:*** *Academic Interests/Achievement:* general academic interests/achievements. *Creative Arts/Performance:* music. *Special Achievements/Activities:* leadership. *Special Characteristics:* children of faculty/staff, international students. ***Tuition waivers:*** Full or partial for employees or children of employees, senior citizens. ***ROTC:*** Army cooperative.

LOANS ***Student loans:*** $8,291,160 (77% need-based, 23% non-need-based). 80% of past graduating class borrowed through all loan programs. Average indebtedness per student: $15,787. ***Average need-based loan:*** Freshmen: $2191; Undergraduates: $3566. ***Parent loans:*** $420,565 (100% non-need-based). ***Programs:*** FFEL (Subsidized and Unsubsidized Stafford, PLUS), Perkins.

WORK-STUDY ***Federal work-study:*** *Total amount:* $136,595; 169 jobs averaging $873.

ATHLETIC AWARDS *Total amount:* 883,494 (100% non-need-based).

APPLYING for FINANCIAL AID ***Required financial aid form:*** FAFSA. ***Financial aid deadline (priority):*** 3/1. ***Notification date:*** Continuous. Students must reply by 5/1 or within 2 weeks of notification.

CONTACT Ms. Susan Swisher, Director of Financial Aid, Saint Xavier University, 3700 West 103rd Street, Chicago, IL 60655-3105, 773-298-3070 or toll-free 800-462-9288. *Fax:* 773-779-3084. *E-mail:* swisher@sxu.edu

SALEM COLLEGE

Winston-Salem, NC

Tuition & fees: $13,415 **Average undergraduate aid package: $12,300**

ABOUT THE INSTITUTION Independent Moravian, women only. Awards: bachelor's and master's degrees (only students 23 or over are eligible to enroll part-time; men may attend evening program only). 29 undergraduate majors. Total enrollment: 1,025. Undergraduates: 918. Federal methodology is used as a basis for awarding need-based institutional aid.

UNDERGRADUATE EXPENSES for 1999–2000 ***Application fee:*** $25. ***Comprehensive fee:*** $21,335 includes full-time tuition ($13,200), mandatory fees ($215), and room and board ($7920). ***Part-time tuition:*** $720 per course. ***Payment plan:*** installment.

UNDERGRADUATE FINANCIAL AID (Fall 1998) *Average financial aid package:* $12,300 (excluding resources awarded to replace EFC).

GIFT AID (NEED-BASED) ***Scholarships, grants, and awards:*** Federal Pell, FSEOG, state, private, college/university gift aid from institutional funds.

GIFT AID (NON-NEED-BASED) ***Scholarships, grants, and awards by category:*** *Academic Interests/Achievement:* general academic interests/achievements. *Creative Arts/Performance:* music. *Special Achievements/Activities:* leadership. *Special Characteristics:* children of educators, children of faculty/staff, relatives of clergy. ***Tuition waivers:*** Full or partial for employees or children of employees. ***ROTC:*** Army cooperative.

LOANS ***Programs:*** FFEL (Subsidized and Unsubsidized Stafford, PLUS), Perkins.

WORK-STUDY Federal work-study jobs available.

APPLYING for FINANCIAL AID ***Required financial aid forms:*** FAFSA, institution's own form. ***Financial aid deadline (priority):*** 3/1.

CONTACT Julie Setzer, Director of Financial Aid, Salem College, PO Box 10548, Winston-Salem, NC 27108, 336-721-2808 or toll-free 800-327-2536. *Fax:* 336-917-5584.

SALEM STATE COLLEGE

Salem, MA

Tuition & fees (MA res): $2958 **Average undergraduate aid package: $5942**

ABOUT THE INSTITUTION State-supported, coed. Awards: bachelor's and master's degrees. 61 undergraduate majors. Total enrollment: 8,081. Undergraduates: 6,838. Freshmen: 671. Federal methodology is used as a basis for awarding need-based institutional aid.

UNDERGRADUATE EXPENSES for 1999–2000 ***Application fee:*** $10. ***Tuition, state resident:*** full-time $1030; part-time $43 per hour. ***Tuition, nonresident:*** full-time $7050; part-time $294 per hour. ***Required fees:*** full-time $1928; $80 per hour. Full-time tuition and fees vary according to class time. Part-time tuition and fees vary according to class time. ***College room and board:*** $4044; ***room only:*** $2500. Room and board charges vary according to board plan and housing facility. ***Payment plans:*** installment, deferred payment.

FRESHMAN FINANCIAL AID (Fall 1998) 755 applied for aid; of those 76% were deemed to have need. 93% of freshmen with need received aid; of those 81% had need fully met. *Average percent of need met:* 79% (excluding resources awarded to replace EFC). *Average financial aid package:* $5144 (excluding resources awarded to replace EFC). 14% of all full-time freshmen had no need and received non-need-based aid.

UNDERGRADUATE FINANCIAL AID (Fall 1998) 3,331 applied for aid; of those 82% were deemed to have need. 94% of undergraduates with need received aid; of those 35% had need fully met. *Average percent of need met:* 84% (excluding resources awarded to replace EFC). *Average financial aid package:* $5942 (excluding resources awarded to replace EFC). 11% of all full-time undergraduates had no need and received non-need-based aid.

GIFT AID (NEED-BASED) ***Total amount:*** $6,544,053 (52% Federal, 13% state, 32% institutional, 3% external sources). ***Receiving aid:*** *Freshmen:* 48% (472); *all full-time undergraduates:* 45% (2,097). ***Average award:*** Freshmen: $2587; Undergraduates: $2783. ***Scholarships, grants, and awards:*** Federal Pell, FSEOG, state, private, college/university gift aid from institutional funds.

GIFT AID (NON-NEED-BASED) ***Total amount:*** $531,000 (5% state, 49% institutional, 46% external sources). ***Receiving aid:*** *Freshmen:* 4% (35); *Undergraduates:* 4% (170). ***Scholarships, grants, and awards by category:*** *Academic Interests/Achievement:* 114 awards ($136,811 total): general academic interests/achievements. *Creative Arts/Performance:* 22 awards ($23,575 total): applied art and design, art/fine arts, creative writing, dance, music, performing arts, theater/drama. *Special Achievements/Activities:* 53 awards ($36,327 total): general special achievements/activities, memberships. *Special Characteristics:* 707 awards ($722,262 total): adult students, children and siblings of alumni, children of faculty/staff, children of public servants, children of union members/company employees, first-generation college students, general special characteristics, members of minority groups, public servants, veterans, veterans' children. ***Tuition waivers:*** Full or partial for minority students, employees or children of employees, senior citizens.

LOANS ***Student loans:*** $13,800,000 (77% need-based, 23% non-need-based). ***Average need-based loan:*** Freshmen: $2898; Undergraduates: $2926. ***Parent loans:*** $535,305 (100% non-need-based). ***Programs:*** Federal Direct (Subsidized and Unsubsidized Stafford), FFEL (PLUS), Perkins, Federal Nursing, state, MassPlan Loans, TERI Loans, PLATO Loans.

WORK-STUDY ***Federal work-study:*** *Total amount:* $559,040; 495 jobs averaging $1130. ***State or other work-study/employment:*** *Total amount:* $920,715 (72% need-based, 28% non-need-based). 581 part-time jobs averaging $1585.

APPLYING for FINANCIAL AID ***Required financial aid form:*** FAFSA. ***Financial aid deadline (priority):*** 4/1. ***Notification date:*** Continuous. Students must reply within 2 weeks of notification.

CONTACT Ms. Janet Lundstrom, Director of Financial Aid, Salem State College, 352 Lafayette Street, Salem, MA 01970-5353, 978-542-6060. *Fax:* 978-542-6876.

SALEM-TEIKYO UNIVERSITY

Salem, WV

Tuition & fees: $12,840 **Average undergraduate aid package: $14,200**

ABOUT THE INSTITUTION Independent, coed. Awards: associate, bachelor's, and master's degrees. 25 undergraduate majors. Total enrollment: 797. Undergraduates: 763. Freshmen: 171. Federal methodology is used as a basis for awarding need-based institutional aid.

UNDERGRADUATE EXPENSES for 1999–2000 ***Application fee:*** $25. ***Comprehensive fee:*** $17,168 includes full-time tuition ($12,800), mandatory fees ($40), and room and board ($4328). Full-time tuition and fees vary according to course load and program. ***Part-time tuition:*** $264 per credit. ***Part-time fees:*** $5 per term part-time. Part-time tuition and fees vary according to course load and program. ***Payment plan:*** installment.

FRESHMAN FINANCIAL AID (Fall 1999) 121 applied for aid; of those 98% were deemed to have need. 100% of freshmen with need received aid; of those 97% had need fully met. *Average percent of need met:* 97% (excluding resources awarded to replace EFC). *Average financial aid package:* $14,600 (excluding resources awarded to replace EFC). 19% of all full-time freshmen had no need and received non-need-based aid.

UNDERGRADUATE FINANCIAL AID (Fall 1999) 488 applied for aid; of those 92% were deemed to have need. 100% of undergraduates with need received aid; of those 97% had need fully met. *Average percent of need met:* 97% (excluding resources awarded to replace EFC). *Average financial aid package:* $14,200 (excluding resources awarded to replace EFC). 14% of all full-time undergraduates had no need and received non-need-based aid.

GIFT AID (NEED-BASED) ***Total amount:*** $1,103,915 (70% Federal, 13% state, 15% institutional, 2% external sources). ***Receiving aid:*** *Freshmen:* 47% (78); *all full-time undergraduates:* 54% (360). ***Average award:*** Freshmen: $3800; Undergraduates: $3800. ***Scholarships, grants, and awards:*** Federal Pell, FSEOG, state, private, college/university gift aid from institutional funds.

GIFT AID (NON-NEED-BASED) ***Total amount:*** $2,652,336 (2% Federal, 91% institutional, 7% external sources). ***Receiving aid:*** *Freshmen:* 67% (111); *Undergraduates:* 66% (444). ***Scholarships, grants, and awards by category:*** *Academic Interests/Achievement:* business, education, general academic interests/achievements, humanities. *Special Achievements/Activities:* memberships, religious involvement. *Special Characteristics:* religious affiliation. ***Tuition waivers:*** Full or partial for employees or children of employees, senior citizens.

LOANS ***Student loans:*** $1,786,652 (79% need-based, 21% non-need-based). 54% of past graduating class borrowed through all loan programs. Average indebtedness per student: $17,000. ***Average need-based loan:*** Freshmen: $4300; Undergraduates: $4600. ***Parent loans:*** $127,183 (100% non-need-based). ***Programs:*** Federal Direct (Subsidized and Unsubsidized Stafford, PLUS), Perkins, college/university.

WORK-STUDY ***Federal work-study:*** *Total amount:* $560,192; jobs available. ***State or other work-study/employment:*** *Total amount:* $53,400 (100% non-need-based). Part-time jobs available.

ATHLETIC AWARDS *Total amount:* 563,215 (100% non-need-based).

APPLYING for FINANCIAL AID ***Required financial aid form:*** FAFSA. ***Financial aid deadline:*** Continuous. ***Notification date:*** Continuous beginning 2/1. Students must reply within 4 weeks of notification.

CONTACT Mrs. Charlotte Lake, Director of Financial Aid, Salem-Teikyo University, 223 West Main Street, Salem, WV 26426-0500, 304-782-5303 or toll-free 800-283-4562. *E-mail:* lakec@salem.wvnet.edu

SALISBURY STATE UNIVERSITY

Salisbury, MD

Tuition & fees (MD res): $4156 **Average undergraduate aid package: $5120**

ABOUT THE INSTITUTION State-supported, coed. Awards: bachelor's and master's degrees. 32 undergraduate majors. Total enrollment: 6,060. Undergraduates: 5,536. Freshmen: 871. Federal methodology is used as a basis for awarding need-based institutional aid.

UNDERGRADUATE EXPENSES for 1999–2000 ***Application fee:*** $30. ***Tuition, state resident:*** full-time $2972; part-time $125 per semester hour. ***Tuition, nonresident:*** full-time $7366; part-time $308 per semester hour. ***Required fees:*** full-time $1184; $4 per semester hour. ***College room and board:*** $5590; ***room only:*** $2900. Room and board charges vary according to board plan and housing facility. ***Payment plan:*** installment.

FRESHMAN FINANCIAL AID (Fall 1999, est.) 644 applied for aid; of those 55% were deemed to have need. 93% of freshmen with need received aid; of those 24% had need fully met. *Average percent of need met:* 60% (excluding resources awarded to replace EFC). *Average financial aid package:* $4259 (excluding resources awarded to replace EFC). 23% of all full-time freshmen had no need and received non-need-based aid.

UNDERGRADUATE FINANCIAL AID (Fall 1999, est.) 3,467 applied for aid; of those 71% were deemed to have need. 77% of undergraduates with need received aid; of those 26% had need fully met. *Average percent of need met:* 65% (excluding resources awarded to replace EFC). *Average financial aid package:* $5120 (excluding resources awarded to replace EFC). 16% of all full-time undergraduates had no need and received non-need-based aid.

GIFT AID (NEED-BASED) ***Total amount:*** $2,785,344 (57% Federal, 36% state, 6% institutional, 1% external sources). ***Receiving aid:*** *Freshmen:* 17% (149); *all full-time undergraduates:* 21% (988). ***Average award:*** Freshmen: $3084; Undergraduates: $2668. ***Scholarships, grants, and awards:*** Federal Pell, FSEOG, state, college/university gift aid from institutional funds.

GIFT AID (NON-NEED-BASED) ***Total amount:*** $1,958,545 (36% state, 36% institutional, 28% external sources). ***Receiving aid:*** *Freshmen:* 14% (124); *Undergraduates:* 10% (458). ***Scholarships, grants, and awards by category:*** *Academic Interests/Achievement:* 302 awards ($704,956 total): biological sciences, business, communication, education, English, foreign languages, general academic interests/achievements, humanities, mathematics, physical sciences, premedicine, social sciences. ***Tuition waivers:*** Full or partial for employees or children of employees, senior citizens. ***ROTC:*** Air Force cooperative.

LOANS ***Student loans:*** $11,559,984 (56% need-based, 44% non-need-based). 50% of past graduating class borrowed through all loan programs. Average indebtedness per student: $14,000. ***Average need-based loan:*** Freshmen: $2412; Undergraduates: $3592. ***Parent loans:*** $6,151,823 (100% non-need-based). ***Programs:*** Federal Direct (Subsidized and Unsubsidized Stafford, PLUS), Perkins.

WORK-STUDY ***Federal work-study:*** *Total amount:* $130,985; 77 jobs averaging $1701.

APPLYING for FINANCIAL AID ***Required financial aid form:*** FAFSA. ***Financial aid deadline (priority):*** 2/15. ***Notification date:*** Continuous beginning 4/1. Students must reply within 2 weeks of notification.

CONTACT Ms. Beverly N. Horner, Director of Financial Aid, Salisbury State University, 1101 Camden Avenue, Salisbury, MD 21801-6837, 410-543-6165 or toll-free 888-543-0148. *E-mail:* bnhorner@ssu.edu

SALVE REGINA UNIVERSITY

Newport, RI

Tuition & fees: $16,850 **Average undergraduate aid package: $13,241**

ABOUT THE INSTITUTION Independent Roman Catholic, coed. Awards: associate, bachelor's, master's, and doctoral degrees and post-master's certificates. 47 undergraduate majors. Total enrollment: 2,257. Undergraduates: 1,800. Freshmen: 571. Institutional methodology is used as a basis for awarding need-based institutional aid.

UNDERGRADUATE EXPENSES for 1999–2000 ***Application fee:*** $25. ***Comprehensive fee:*** $24,350 includes full-time tuition ($16,500), mandatory fees ($350), and room and board ($7500). ***Part-time tuition:*** $550 per credit. ***Part-time fees:*** $35 per term part-time. Part-time tuition and fees vary according to course load.

FRESHMAN FINANCIAL AID (Fall 1999, est.) 397 applied for aid; of those 90% were deemed to have need. 100% of freshmen with need received aid; of those 16% had need fully met. *Average percent of need met:* 72% (excluding resources awarded to replace EFC). *Average financial aid package:* $13,262 (excluding resources awarded to replace EFC). 33% of all full-time freshmen had no need and received non-need-based aid.

UNDERGRADUATE FINANCIAL AID (Fall 1999, est.) 1,138 applied for aid; of those 91% were deemed to have need. 100% of undergraduates with need received aid; of those 19% had need fully met. *Average percent of need met:* 63% (excluding resources awarded to replace EFC). *Average financial aid package:* $13,241 (excluding resources awarded to replace EFC). 32% of all full-time undergraduates had no need and received non-need-based aid.

GIFT AID (NEED-BASED) ***Total amount:*** $7,148,479 (11% Federal, 2% state, 83% institutional, 4% external sources). ***Receiving aid:*** *Freshmen:* 63% (339); *all full-time undergraduates:* 59% (950). ***Average award:*** Freshmen: $8094; Undergraduates: $7130. ***Scholarships, grants, and awards:*** Federal Pell, FSEOG, state, private, college/university gift aid from institutional funds.

GIFT AID (NON-NEED-BASED) ***Total amount:*** $344,786 (1% state, 86% institutional, 13% external sources). ***Receiving aid:*** *Freshmen:* 1% (7); *Undergraduates:* 2% (31). ***Scholarships, grants, and awards by category:*** *Academic Interests/Achievement:* 207 awards ($1,202,650 total): general academic interests/achievements. ***Tuition waivers:*** Full or partial for employees or children of employees. ***ROTC:*** Army cooperative.

LOANS ***Student loans:*** $6,489,979 (83% need-based, 17% non-need-based). 77% of past graduating class borrowed through all loan programs. Average indebtedness per student: $19,125. ***Average need-based loan:*** Freshmen: $4077; Undergraduates: $5028. ***Parent loans:*** $2,771,322 (42% need-based, 58% non-need-based). ***Programs:*** FFEL (Subsidized and Unsubsidized Stafford, PLUS), Perkins, Federal Nursing.

WORK-STUDY ***Federal work-study:*** *Total amount:* $258,388; 319 jobs averaging $810. ***State or other work-study/employment:*** *Total amount:* $257,200 (5% need-based, 95% non-need-based). 355 part-time jobs averaging $718.

APPLYING for FINANCIAL AID ***Required financial aid forms:*** FAFSA, institution's own form, CSS Financial Aid PROFILE, noncustodial (divorced/separated) parent's statement, business/farm supplement. ***Financial aid deadline (priority):*** 3/1. ***Notification date:*** 4/1. Students must reply by 5/1.

CONTACT Aida Mirante, Director of Financial Aid, Salve Regina University, 100 Ochre Point Avenue, Newport, RI 02840-4192, 401-847-6650 Ext. 2901 or toll-free 888-GO SALVE. *Fax:* 401-341-2928. *E-mail:* srufa@salve.edu

SAMFORD UNIVERSITY

Birmingham, AL

Tuition & fees: $10,300 **Average undergraduate aid package: $8748**

ABOUT THE INSTITUTION Independent Baptist, coed. Awards: associate, bachelor's, master's, doctoral, and first professional degrees and post-bachelor's and post-master's certificates. 64 undergraduate majors. Total enrollment: 4,494. Undergraduates: 2,855. Freshmen: 675. Federal methodology is used as a basis for awarding need-based institutional aid.

UNDERGRADUATE EXPENSES for 1999–2000 ***Application fee:*** $25. ***Comprehensive fee:*** $14,860 includes full-time tuition ($10,300) and room and board ($4560). ***College room only:*** $2236. Room and board charges vary according to board plan and housing facility. ***Part-time tuition:*** $341 per semester hour. Part-time tuition and fees vary according to course load.

FRESHMAN FINANCIAL AID (Fall 1999) 481 applied for aid; of those 62% were deemed to have need. 100% of freshmen with need received aid; of

those 32% had need fully met. *Average percent of need met:* 77% (excluding resources awarded to replace EFC). *Average financial aid package:* $8403 (excluding resources awarded to replace EFC). 37% of all full-time freshmen had no need and received non-need-based aid.

UNDERGRADUATE FINANCIAL AID (Fall 1999) 1,449 applied for aid; of those 73% were deemed to have need. 99% of undergraduates with need received aid; of those 37% had need fully met. *Average percent of need met:* 80% (excluding resources awarded to replace EFC). *Average financial aid package:* $8748 (excluding resources awarded to replace EFC). 38% of all full-time undergraduates had no need and received non-need-based aid.

GIFT AID (NEED-BASED) ***Total amount:*** $4,995,438 (18% Federal, 7% state, 64% institutional, 11% external sources). ***Receiving aid:*** *Freshmen:* 43% (290); *all full-time undergraduates:* 37% (991). ***Average award:*** Freshmen: $5528; Undergraduates: $4711. ***Scholarships, grants, and awards:*** Federal Pell, FSEOG, state, private, college/university gift aid from institutional funds.

GIFT AID (NON-NEED-BASED) ***Total amount:*** $3,016,721 (10% state, 75% institutional, 15% external sources). ***Scholarships, grants, and awards by category:*** *Academic Interests/Achievement:* 287 awards ($962,924 total): general academic interests/achievements. *Creative Arts/Performance:* 21 awards ($22,550 total): music. *Special Achievements/Activities:* 41 awards ($90,500 total): leadership. *Special Characteristics:* 167 awards ($747,687 total): children of faculty/staff, relatives of clergy. ***Tuition waivers:*** Full or partial for employees or children of employees. ***ROTC:*** Army cooperative, Air Force.

LOANS ***Student loans:*** $5,169,497 (60% need-based, 40% non-need-based). 46% of past graduating class borrowed through all loan programs. Average indebtedness per student: $14,228. ***Average need-based loan:*** Freshmen: $2003; Undergraduates: $2826. ***Parent loans:*** $3,097,960 (100% non-need-based). ***Programs:*** Federal Direct (Subsidized and Unsubsidized Stafford), FFEL (Subsidized and Unsubsidized Stafford, PLUS), Perkins, college/university.

WORK-STUDY ***Federal work-study:*** *Total amount:* $347,082; 259 jobs averaging $1340. ***State or other work-study/employment:*** *Total amount:* $213,974 (43% need-based, 57% non-need-based). Part-time jobs available.

ATHLETIC AWARDS *Total amount:* 2,362,833 (36% need-based, 64% non-need-based).

APPLYING for FINANCIAL AID ***Required financial aid forms:*** FAFSA, state aid form. ***Financial aid deadline (priority):*** 3/1. ***Notification date:*** 4/1. Students must reply by 5/1 or within 2 weeks of notification.

CONTACT Ms. Ann P. Peeples, Director of Financial Aid, Samford University, 800 Lakeshore Drive, Birmingham, AL 35229-0002, 205-726-2905 or toll-free 800-888-7218. *Fax:* 205-726-2738. *E-mail:* appeeple@samford.edu

SAM HOUSTON STATE UNIVERSITY

Huntsville, TX

Tuition & fees (TX res): $1988 **Average undergraduate aid package: $5718**

ABOUT THE INSTITUTION State-supported, coed. Awards: bachelor's, master's, and doctoral degrees. 63 undergraduate majors. Total enrollment: 12,215. Undergraduates: 10,825. Freshmen: 1,608. Federal methodology is used as a basis for awarding need-based institutional aid.

UNDERGRADUATE EXPENSES for 1999–2000 ***Application fee:*** $20. ***Tuition, state resident:*** full-time $912; part-time $38 per semester hour. ***Tuition, nonresident:*** full-time $6096; part-time $254 per semester hour. ***Required fees:*** full-time $1076; $54 per semester hour; $97 per term part-time. Full-time tuition and fees vary according to course load. Part-time tuition and fees vary according to course load. ***College room and board:*** $3390; ***room only:*** $1750. Room and board charges vary according to board plan and housing facility. ***Payment plan:*** installment.

FRESHMAN FINANCIAL AID (Fall 1999, est.) 941 applied for aid; of those 72% were deemed to have need. 100% of freshmen with need received aid. *Average financial aid package:* $4666 (excluding resources awarded to replace EFC). 8% of all full-time freshmen had no need and received non-need-based aid.

UNDERGRADUATE FINANCIAL AID (Fall 1999, est.) 4,665 applied for aid; of those 74% were deemed to have need. 100% of undergraduates with need received aid. *Average financial aid package:* $5718 (excluding resources awarded to replace EFC). 8% of all full-time undergraduates had no need and received non-need-based aid.

GIFT AID (NEED-BASED) ***Total amount:*** $6,734,352 (76% Federal, 24% state). ***Receiving aid:*** *Freshmen:* 19% (545); *all full-time undergraduates:* 31% (2,634). ***Average award:*** Freshmen: $2697; Undergraduates: $2436. ***Scholarships, grants, and awards:*** Federal Pell, FSEOG, state, college/university gift aid from institutional funds.

GIFT AID (NON-NEED-BASED) ***Total amount:*** $3,436,351 (2% Federal, 46% institutional, 52% external sources). ***Receiving aid:*** *Freshmen:* 8% (223); *Undergraduates:* 7% (645). ***Scholarships, grants, and awards by category:*** *Academic Interests/Achievement:* 299 awards ($123,048 total): agriculture, biological sciences, business, communication, computer science, education, engineering/technologies, English, foreign languages, general academic interests/achievements, home economics, humanities, library science, mathematics, military science, physical sciences, social sciences. *Creative Arts/Performance:* 62 awards ($23,475 total): art/fine arts, cinema/film/broadcasting, dance, journalism/publications, music, performing arts, theater/drama. *Special Achievements/Activities:* 119 awards ($51,722 total): cheerleading/drum major, general special achievements/activities, leadership, rodeo. *Special Characteristics:* 1 award ($400 total): general special characteristics, handicapped students. ***ROTC:*** Army.

LOANS ***Student loans:*** $14,663,564 (63% need-based, 37% non-need-based). 53% of past graduating class borrowed through all loan programs. Average indebtedness per student: $8530. ***Average need-based loan:*** Freshmen: $2509; Undergraduates: $3694. ***Parent loans:*** $1,312,822 (100% non-need-based). ***Programs:*** FFEL (Subsidized and Unsubsidized Stafford, PLUS), Perkins, state, college/university.

WORK-STUDY ***Federal work-study:*** *Total amount:* $270,728; 154 jobs averaging $1997. ***State or other work-study/employment:*** *Total amount:* $29,703 (100% need-based). 17 part-time jobs averaging $1985.

ATHLETIC AWARDS *Total amount:* 1,015,375 (100% non-need-based).

APPLYING for FINANCIAL AID ***Required financial aid form:*** FAFSA. ***Financial aid deadline (priority):*** 3/31. ***Notification date:*** Continuous beginning 6/1. Students must reply within 4 weeks of notification.

CONTACT Mr. Jess Davis, Director of Student Financial Aid, Sam Houston State University, PO Box 2328, Huntsville, TX 77341, 409-294-1724.

SAMUEL MERRITT COLLEGE

Oakland, CA

Tuition & fees: $16,425 **Average undergraduate aid package: N/A**

ABOUT THE INSTITUTION Independent, coed, primarily women. Awards: bachelor's and master's degrees and post-master's certificates (bachelor's degree offered jointly with Saint Mary's College of California). 2 undergraduate majors. Total enrollment: 714. Undergraduates: 278. Freshmen: 12. Federal methodology is used as a basis for awarding need-based institutional aid.

UNDERGRADUATE EXPENSES for 1999–2000 ***Application fee:*** $35. ***Tuition:*** full-time $16,360; part-time $686 per unit. ***Required fees:*** full-time $65; $32 per term part-time. Full-time tuition and fees vary according to program. Part-time tuition and fees vary according to program. ***Payment plans:*** installment, deferred payment.

GIFT AID (NEED-BASED) ***Scholarships, grants, and awards:*** Federal Pell, FSEOG, state, private, college/university gift aid from institutional funds, Federal Nursing.

GIFT AID (NON-NEED-BASED) ***ROTC:*** Army cooperative, Naval cooperative, Air Force cooperative.

LOANS ***Programs:*** FFEL (Subsidized and Unsubsidized Stafford, PLUS), Federal Nursing, college/university.

WORK-STUDY Federal work-study jobs available.

APPLYING for FINANCIAL AID ***Required financial aid form:*** FAFSA. ***Financial aid deadline (priority):*** 3/2. ***Notification date:*** Continuous beginning 4/15. Students must reply within 2 weeks of notification.

Samuel Merritt College (continued)

CONTACT Financial Aid Office, Samuel Merritt College, 450 30th Street, Room 2710, Oakland, CA 94609, 510-869-6131 or toll-free 800-607-MERRITT.

SAN DIEGO STATE UNIVERSITY

San Diego, CA

Tuition & fees: N/R **Average undergraduate aid package: $7300**

ABOUT THE INSTITUTION State-supported, coed. Awards: bachelor's, master's, and doctoral degrees. 106 undergraduate majors. Total enrollment: 31,413. Undergraduates: 25,631. Freshmen: 3,813. Federal methodology is used as a basis for awarding need-based institutional aid.

UNDERGRADUATE EXPENSES for 2000–2001 ***Application fee:*** $55. ***Tuition, nonresident:*** full-time $7380; part-time $246 per unit. ***Required fees:*** full-time $1776; $612 per term part-time. ***College room and board:*** $7110; ***room only:*** $3413. Room and board charges vary according to board plan and housing facility. ***Payment plan:*** installment.

FRESHMAN FINANCIAL AID (Fall 1999, est.) 2500 applied for aid; of those 68% were deemed to have need. 88% of freshmen with need received aid; of those 27% had need fully met. *Average percent of need met:* 60% (excluding resources awarded to replace EFC). *Average financial aid package:* $4800 (excluding resources awarded to replace EFC). 11% of all full-time freshmen had no need and received non-need-based aid.

UNDERGRADUATE FINANCIAL AID (Fall 1999, est.) 12,500 applied for aid; of those 78% were deemed to have need. 94% of undergraduates with need received aid; of those 33% had need fully met. *Average percent of need met:* 85% (excluding resources awarded to replace EFC). *Average financial aid package:* $7300 (excluding resources awarded to replace EFC). 16% of all full-time undergraduates had no need and received non-need-based aid.

GIFT AID (NEED-BASED) ***Total amount:*** $35,980,000 (58% Federal, 14% state, 28% institutional). ***Receiving aid:*** *Freshmen:* 34% (1,200); *all full-time undergraduates:* 38% (7,500). ***Average award:*** Freshmen: $3700; Undergraduates: $3500. ***Scholarships, grants, and awards:*** Federal Pell, FSEOG, state, private, college/university gift aid from institutional funds.

GIFT AID (NON-NEED-BASED) ***Total amount:*** $1,200,000 (40% institutional, 60% external sources). ***Scholarships, grants, and awards by category:*** *Academic Interests/Achievement:* general academic interests/achievements. *Special Achievements/Activities:* community service, leadership. *Special Characteristics:* handicapped students, members of minority groups. ***Tuition waivers:*** Full or partial for employees or children of employees, senior citizens. ***ROTC:*** Army, Naval, Air Force.

LOANS ***Student loans:*** $48,400,000 (62% need-based, 38% non-need-based). Average indebtedness per student: $13,600. ***Average need-based loan:*** Freshmen: $2300; Undergraduates: $3700. ***Parent loans:*** $8,960,000 (100% non-need-based). ***Programs:*** Federal Direct (Subsidized and Unsubsidized Stafford, PLUS), Perkins, college/university.

WORK-STUDY ***Federal work-study:*** *Total amount:* $1,480,000; 500 jobs averaging $2960.

ATHLETIC AWARDS *Total amount:* 990,000 (100% non-need-based).

APPLYING for FINANCIAL AID ***Required financial aid forms:*** FAFSA, state aid form. ***Financial aid deadline:*** Continuous. ***Notification date:*** Continuous beginning 2/15.

CONTACT Mr. William D. Boyd, Director of Financial Aid, San Diego State University, 5500 Campanile Drive, SSW 3605, San Diego, CA 92182-7436, 619-594-6323.

SAN FRANCISCO ART INSTITUTE

San Francisco, CA

Tuition & fees: $19,300 **Average undergraduate aid package: $21,084**

ABOUT THE INSTITUTION Independent, coed. Awards: bachelor's and master's degrees and post-bachelor's certificates. 8 undergraduate majors. Total enrollment: 624. Undergraduates: 500. Freshmen: 40. Federal methodology is used as a basis for awarding need-based institutional aid.

UNDERGRADUATE EXPENSES for 1999–2000 ***Application fee:*** $50. ***Tuition:*** full-time $19,300; part-time $804 per semester hour. ***Payment plan:*** installment.

FRESHMAN FINANCIAL AID (Fall 1999, est.) 25 applied for aid; of those 92% were deemed to have need. 100% of freshmen with need received aid. *Average percent of need met:* 73% (excluding resources awarded to replace EFC). *Average financial aid package:* $18,578 (excluding resources awarded to replace EFC). 18% of all full-time freshmen had no need and received non-need-based aid.

UNDERGRADUATE FINANCIAL AID (Fall 1999, est.) 263 applied for aid; of those 94% were deemed to have need. 100% of undergraduates with need received aid; of those 18% had need fully met. *Average percent of need met:* 83% (excluding resources awarded to replace EFC). *Average financial aid package:* $21,084 (excluding resources awarded to replace EFC). 11% of all full-time undergraduates had no need and received non-need-based aid.

GIFT AID (NEED-BASED) ***Total amount:*** $3,633,216 (16% Federal, 19% state, 63% institutional, 2% external sources). ***Receiving aid:*** *Freshmen:* 59% (23); *all full-time undergraduates:* 58% (244). ***Average award:*** Freshmen: $12,438; Undergraduates: $11,676. ***Scholarships, grants, and awards:*** Federal Pell, FSEOG, state, college/university gift aid from institutional funds.

GIFT AID (NON-NEED-BASED) ***Total amount:*** $224,435 (98% institutional, 2% external sources). ***Receiving aid:*** *Undergraduates:* 1% (5). ***Scholarships, grants, and awards by category:*** *Creative Arts/Performance:* 191 awards ($809,251 total): art/fine arts. ***Tuition waivers:*** Full or partial for employees or children of employees.

LOANS ***Student loans:*** $2,657,271 (94% need-based, 6% non-need-based). 70% of past graduating class borrowed through all loan programs. ***Average need-based loan:*** Freshmen: $3671; Undergraduates: $7033. ***Parent loans:*** $686,121 (63% need-based, 37% non-need-based). ***Programs:*** Federal Direct (Subsidized and Unsubsidized Stafford, PLUS), alternative loans.

WORK-STUDY ***Federal work-study:*** *Total amount:* $767,405; 295 jobs averaging $2601.

APPLYING for FINANCIAL AID ***Required financial aid form:*** FAFSA. ***Financial aid deadline (priority):*** 3/1. ***Notification date:*** Continuous beginning 3/31. Students must reply within 3 weeks of notification.

CONTACT Ms. Leslie Wills, Director of Financial Aid, San Francisco Art Institute, 800 Chestnut Street, San Francisco, CA 94133-2299, 415-749-4520 or toll-free 800-345-SFAI. *Fax:* 415-749-4592. *E-mail:* admissions@sfair.edu

SAN FRANCISCO CONSERVATORY OF MUSIC

San Francisco, CA

Tuition & fees: $18,670 **Average undergraduate aid package: $12,281**

ABOUT THE INSTITUTION Independent, coed. Awards: bachelor's and master's degrees and post-master's certificates. 6 undergraduate majors. Total enrollment: 243. Undergraduates: 136. Freshmen: 21. Federal methodology is used as a basis for awarding need-based institutional aid.

UNDERGRADUATE EXPENSES for 1999–2000 ***Application fee:*** $60. ***Tuition:*** full-time $18,400; part-time $820 per semester hour. ***Required fees:*** full-time $270; $135 per term part-time. Part-time tuition and fees vary according to course load. ***Payment plan:*** installment.

FRESHMAN FINANCIAL AID (Fall 1998) 20 applied for aid; of those 85% were deemed to have need. 100% of freshmen with need received aid; of those 47% had need fully met. *Average percent of need met:* 83% (excluding resources awarded to replace EFC). *Average financial aid package:* $12,922 (excluding resources awarded to replace EFC). 4% of all full-time freshmen had no need and received non-need-based aid.

UNDERGRADUATE FINANCIAL AID (Fall 1998) 128 applied for aid; of those 92% were deemed to have need. 98% of undergraduates with need received aid; of those 34% had need fully met. *Average percent of need met:* 81% (excluding resources awarded to replace EFC). *Average financial aid package:* $12,281 (excluding resources awarded to replace EFC). 1% of all full-time undergraduates had no need and received non-need-based aid.

GIFT AID (NEED-BASED) ***Total amount:*** $991,179 (12% Federal, 14% state, 74% institutional). ***Receiving aid:*** *Freshmen:* 71% (17); *all full-time undergraduates:* 68% (104). ***Average award:*** Freshmen: $10,309; Undergraduates: $9597. ***Scholarships, grants, and awards:*** Federal Pell, FSEOG, state, private, college/university gift aid from institutional funds.

GIFT AID (NON-NEED-BASED) ***Total amount:*** $7000 (100% institutional). ***Tuition waivers:*** Full or partial for employees or children of employees.

LOANS ***Student loans:*** $527,859 (79% need-based, 21% non-need-based). 59% of past graduating class borrowed through all loan programs. Average indebtedness per student: $17,582. ***Average need-based loan:*** Freshmen: $3656; Undergraduates: $4771. ***Parent loans:*** $233,040 (60% need-based, 40% non-need-based). ***Programs:*** FFEL (Subsidized and Unsubsidized Stafford, PLUS), Perkins.

WORK-STUDY ***Federal work-study:*** *Total amount:* $11,383; jobs available.

APPLYING for FINANCIAL AID ***Required financial aid forms:*** FAFSA, institution's own form. ***Financial aid deadline (priority):*** 3/1. ***Notification date:*** Continuous. Students must reply by 5/1 or within 2 weeks of notification.

CONTACT Ms. Colleen Katzowitz, Director of Student Services, San Francisco Conservatory of Music, 1201 Ortega Street, San Francisco, CA 94122-4411, 415-759-3422. *Fax:* 415-759-3499. *E-mail:* cmk@sfcm.edu

SAN FRANCISCO STATE UNIVERSITY

San Francisco, CA

Tuition & fees (CA res): $1826 **Average undergraduate aid package: $6759**

ABOUT THE INSTITUTION State-supported, coed. Awards: bachelor's and master's degrees. 91 undergraduate majors. Total enrollment: 27,701. Undergraduates: 21,138. Freshmen: 2,101. Federal methodology is used as a basis for awarding need-based institutional aid.

UNDERGRADUATE EXPENSES for 1999–2000 ***Application fee:*** $55. ***Tuition, state resident:*** full-time $0. ***Tuition, nonresident:*** full-time $5904; part-time $246 per unit. ***Required fees:*** full-time $1826; $613 per term part-time. ***College room and board:*** $7380. Room and board charges vary according to board plan and housing facility. ***Payment plans:*** installment, deferred payment.

FRESHMAN FINANCIAL AID (Fall 1999, est.) 1315 applied for aid; of those 99% were deemed to have need. 95% of freshmen with need received aid; of those 16% had need fully met. *Average percent of need met:* 67% (excluding resources awarded to replace EFC). *Average financial aid package:* $5601 (excluding resources awarded to replace EFC). 8% of all full-time freshmen had no need and received non-need-based aid.

UNDERGRADUATE FINANCIAL AID (Fall 1999, est.) 8,726 applied for aid; of those 93% were deemed to have need. 93% of undergraduates with need received aid; of those 14% had need fully met. *Average percent of need met:* 80% (excluding resources awarded to replace EFC). *Average financial aid package:* $6759 (excluding resources awarded to replace EFC). 3% of all full-time undergraduates had no need and received non-need-based aid.

GIFT AID (NEED-BASED) ***Total amount:*** $27,564,741 (60% Federal, 40% state). ***Receiving aid:*** *Freshmen:* 35% (741); *all full-time undergraduates:* 40% (5,997). ***Average award:*** Freshmen: $4641; Undergraduates: $4089. ***Scholarships, grants, and awards:*** Federal Pell, FSEOG, state, private, college/university gift aid from institutional funds.

GIFT AID (NON-NEED-BASED) ***Total amount:*** $420,595 (96% institutional, 4% external sources). ***Scholarships, grants, and awards by category:*** *Academic Interests/Achievement:* general academic interests/achievements. ***Tuition waivers:*** Full or partial for employees or children of employees. ***ROTC:*** Army cooperative, Naval cooperative, Air Force cooperative.

LOANS ***Student loans:*** $43,710,230 (100% need-based). Average indebtedness per student: $12,000. ***Average need-based loan:*** Freshmen: $2162; Undergraduates: $4162. ***Parent loans:*** $5,150,896 (100% need-based). ***Programs:*** Federal Direct (Subsidized and Unsubsidized Stafford, PLUS), Perkins, college/university.

WORK-STUDY ***Federal work-study:*** *Total amount:* $1,600,000; 800 jobs averaging $2000.

ATHLETIC AWARDS *Total amount:* 50,000 (100% need-based).

APPLYING for FINANCIAL AID ***Required financial aid form:*** FAFSA. ***Financial aid deadline (priority):*** 3/2. ***Notification date:*** Continuous. Students must reply within 2 weeks of notification.

CONTACT Mr. Marlew Haskins, Assistant Director of Financial Aid, San Francisco State University, 1600 Holloway Avenue, San Francisco, CA 94132-1722, 415-338-2592. *Fax:* 415-338-7196. *E-mail:* poiu@sfsu.edu

SAN JOSE CHRISTIAN COLLEGE

San Jose, CA

ABOUT THE INSTITUTION Independent nondenominational, coed. Awards: associate and bachelor's degrees. 7 undergraduate majors. Total enrollment: 372. Undergraduates: 372. Freshmen: 31.

GIFT AID (NEED-BASED) ***Scholarships, grants, and awards:*** Federal Pell, FSEOG, state, private, college/university gift aid from institutional funds.

GIFT AID (NON-NEED-BASED) ***Scholarships, grants, and awards by category:*** *Academic Interests/Achievement:* education, general academic interests/achievements, international studies, religion/biblical studies. *Creative Arts/Performance:* music. *Special Achievements/Activities:* leadership, religious involvement. *Special Characteristics:* children of faculty/staff, international students, previous college experience, relatives of clergy, veterans, veterans' children.

LOANS ***Programs:*** FFEL (Subsidized and Unsubsidized Stafford, PLUS).

WORK-STUDY Federal work-study jobs available.

APPLYING for FINANCIAL AID ***Required financial aid forms:*** FAFSA, institution's own form.

CONTACT Danielle M. Brown, Financial Aid Administrator, San Jose Christian College, 790 South Twelfth Street, San Jose, CA 95112-2381, 408-278-4328 or toll-free 800-355-7522. *E-mail:* dbrown@sjchristian.edu

SAN JOSE STATE UNIVERSITY

San Jose, CA

Tuition & fees (CA res): $1939 **Average undergraduate aid package: $6999**

ABOUT THE INSTITUTION State-supported, coed. Awards: bachelor's and master's degrees. 118 undergraduate majors. Total enrollment: 26,937. Undergraduates: 20,732. Freshmen: 2,388. Federal methodology is used as a basis for awarding need-based institutional aid.

UNDERGRADUATE EXPENSES for 1999–2000 ***Application fee:*** $55. ***Tuition, state resident:*** full-time $0. ***Tuition, nonresident:*** full-time $5904; part-time $246 per unit. ***Required fees:*** full-time $1939; $654 per term part-time. Part-time tuition and fees vary according to course load. ***College room and board:*** $6248; ***room only:*** $3552. Room and board charges vary according to board plan.

FRESHMAN FINANCIAL AID (Fall 1999, est.) 2194 applied for aid; of those 75% were deemed to have need. 98% of freshmen with need received aid; of those 26% had need fully met. *Average percent of need met:* 73% (excluding resources awarded to replace EFC). *Average financial aid package:* $6714 (excluding resources awarded to replace EFC). 1% of all full-time freshmen had no need and received non-need-based aid.

UNDERGRADUATE FINANCIAL AID (Fall 1999, est.) 7,720 applied for aid; of those 83% were deemed to have need. 98% of undergraduates with need received aid; of those 28% had need fully met. *Average percent of need met:* 74% (excluding resources awarded to replace EFC). *Average financial aid package:* $6999 (excluding resources awarded to replace EFC). .5% of all full-time undergraduates had no need and received non-need-based aid.

GIFT AID (NEED-BASED) ***Total amount:*** $25,636,972 (58% Federal, 41% state, 1% institutional). ***Receiving aid:*** *Freshmen:* 37% (1,351); *all full-time undergraduates:* 37% (5,354). ***Average award:*** Freshmen: $4369;

San Jose State University (continued)

Undergraduates: $3983. ***Scholarships, grants, and awards:*** Federal Pell, FSEOG, state, private, college/university gift aid from institutional funds.

GIFT AID (NON-NEED-BASED) ***Total amount:*** $1,491,527 (100% external sources). ***Receiving aid:*** *Freshmen:* 5% (191); *Undergraduates:* 3% (476). ***Scholarships, grants, and awards by category:*** *Academic Interests/Achievement:* general academic interests/achievements. ***Tuition waivers:*** Full or partial for employees or children of employees, senior citizens. ***ROTC:*** Army, Naval cooperative, Air Force.

LOANS ***Student loans:*** $15,828,241 (88% need-based, 12% non-need-based). 37% of past graduating class borrowed through all loan programs. Average indebtedness per student: $9981. ***Average need-based loan:*** Freshmen: $2623; Undergraduates: $3791. ***Parent loans:*** $774,520 (100% non-need-based). ***Programs:*** FFEL (Subsidized and Unsubsidized Stafford, PLUS), Perkins, college/university.

WORK-STUDY ***Federal work-study:*** *Total amount:* $1,418,082; 696 jobs averaging $2037.

ATHLETIC AWARDS *Total amount:* 350,000 (100% non-need-based).

APPLYING for FINANCIAL AID ***Required financial aid form:*** FAFSA. ***Financial aid deadline (priority):*** 3/2. ***Notification date:*** Continuous beginning 5/1.

CONTACT Colleen S. Brown, Director of Financial Aid, San Jose State University, One Washington Square, San Jose, CA 95192-0036, 408-924-6060. *E-mail:* brownc@sjsu.edu

SANTA CLARA UNIVERSITY

Santa Clara, CA

Tuition & fees: $19,311 **Average undergraduate aid package: N/A**

ABOUT THE INSTITUTION Independent Roman Catholic (Jesuit), coed. Awards: bachelor's, master's, doctoral, and first professional degrees and post-bachelor's and post-master's certificates. 40 undergraduate majors. Total enrollment: 7,670. Undergraduates: 4,477. Freshmen: 1,103. Both federal and institutional methodology are used as a basis for awarding need-based institutional aid.

UNDERGRADUATE EXPENSES for 1999–2000 ***Application fee:*** $50. ***Comprehensive fee:*** $26,955 includes full-time tuition ($19,311) and room and board ($7644). ***College room only:*** $4828. Full-time tuition and fees vary according to program and student level. Room and board charges vary according to board plan and housing facility. ***Part-time tuition:*** $2088 per course. Part-time tuition and fees vary according to course load and student level. ***Payment plans:*** tuition prepayment, installment, deferred payment.

GIFT AID (NEED-BASED) ***Scholarships, grants, and awards:*** Federal Pell, FSEOG, state, private, college/university gift aid from institutional funds.

GIFT AID (NON-NEED-BASED) ***Scholarships, grants, and awards by category:*** *Academic Interests/Achievement:* business, engineering/technologies, general academic interests/achievements, military science. *Creative Arts/Performance:* debating, music, theater/drama. ***Tuition waivers:*** Full or partial for employees or children of employees. ***ROTC:*** Army, Air Force cooperative.

LOANS ***Programs:*** Federal Direct (Subsidized and Unsubsidized Stafford, PLUS), Perkins, CitiAssist Loans, GATE Loans.

WORK-STUDY Federal work-study jobs available.

APPLYING for FINANCIAL AID ***Required financial aid forms:*** FAFSA, CSS Financial Aid PROFILE. ***Financial aid deadline (priority):*** 2/1. ***Notification date:*** Continuous beginning 4/1. Students must reply by 5/1 or within 2 weeks of notification.

CONTACT Ms. Sandra L. Hayes, Director of Financial Aid, Santa Clara University, 500 El Camino Real, Santa Clara, CA 95053-0609, 408-554-4505. *Fax:* 408-554-2154.

SARAH LAWRENCE COLLEGE

Bronxville, NY

Tuition & fees: $25,406 **Average undergraduate aid package: $17,957**

ABOUT THE INSTITUTION Independent, coed. Awards: bachelor's and master's degrees. 71 undergraduate majors. Total enrollment: 1,495. Undergraduates: 1,178. Freshmen: 277. Both federal and institutional methodology are used as a basis for awarding need-based institutional aid.

UNDERGRADUATE EXPENSES for 1999–2000 ***Application fee:*** $50. ***Comprehensive fee:*** $34,054 includes full-time tuition ($24,810), mandatory fees ($596), and room and board ($8648). ***College room only:*** $5638. Full-time tuition and fees vary according to course load. Room and board charges vary according to board plan. ***Part-time tuition:*** $827 per credit. ***Part-time fees:*** $149 per term part-time. Part-time tuition and fees vary according to course load. ***Payment plan:*** installment.

FRESHMAN FINANCIAL AID (Fall 1998) 170 applied for aid; of those 90% were deemed to have need. 100% of freshmen with need received aid; of those 73% had need fully met. *Average percent of need met:* 96% (excluding resources awarded to replace EFC). *Average financial aid package:* $18,134 (excluding resources awarded to replace EFC). 6% of all full-time freshmen had no need and received non-need-based aid.

UNDERGRADUATE FINANCIAL AID (Fall 1998) 630 applied for aid; of those 91% were deemed to have need. 100% of undergraduates with need received aid; of those 70% had need fully met. *Average percent of need met:* 92% (excluding resources awarded to replace EFC). *Average financial aid package:* $17,957 (excluding resources awarded to replace EFC). 6% of all full-time undergraduates had no need and received non-need-based aid.

GIFT AID (NEED-BASED) ***Total amount:*** $7,582,108 (6% Federal, 2% state, 87% institutional, 5% external sources). ***Receiving aid:*** *Freshmen:* 45% (137); *all full-time undergraduates:* 48% (491). ***Average award:*** Freshmen: $14,747; Undergraduates: $12,905. ***Scholarships, grants, and awards:*** Federal Pell, FSEOG, state, private, college/university gift aid from institutional funds.

GIFT AID (NON-NEED-BASED) ***Total amount:*** $1500 (100% external sources). ***Receiving aid:*** *Freshmen:* 6% (17); *Undergraduates:* 6% (57). ***Tuition waivers:*** Full or partial for employees or children of employees.

LOANS ***Student loans:*** $2,658,609 (82% need-based, 18% non-need-based). Average indebtedness per student: $16,362. ***Average need-based loan:*** Freshmen: $2374; Undergraduates: $3814. ***Parent loans:*** $2,937,642 (100% non-need-based). ***Programs:*** FFEL (Subsidized and Unsubsidized Stafford, PLUS), Perkins, college/university, Achiever Loans, Signature Loans, CitiAssist Loans.

WORK-STUDY ***Federal work-study:*** *Total amount:* $706,134; jobs available.

APPLYING for FINANCIAL AID ***Required financial aid forms:*** FAFSA, CSS Financial Aid PROFILE. ***Financial aid deadline:*** 2/1. ***Notification date:*** 4/1. Students must reply by 5/1.

CONTACT Ms. Heather McDonnell, Director of Financial Aid, Sarah Lawrence College, One Meadway, Bronxville, NY 10708, 914-395-2570 or toll-free 800-888-2858. *Fax:* 914-395-2668. *E-mail:* hmcdonn@mail.slc.edu

SAVANNAH COLLEGE OF ART AND DESIGN

Savannah, GA

Tuition & fees: $16,200 **Average undergraduate aid package: $7600**

ABOUT THE INSTITUTION Independent, coed. Awards: bachelor's and master's degrees. 16 undergraduate majors. Total enrollment: 4,431. Undergraduates: 3,775. Freshmen: 881. Federal methodology is used as a basis for awarding need-based institutional aid.

UNDERGRADUATE EXPENSES for 2000–2001 ***Application fee:*** $50. ***One-time required fee:*** $500. ***Comprehensive fee:*** $22,950 includes full-time tuition ($16,200) and room and board ($6750). ***College room only:*** $4200. ***Part-time tuition:*** $1800 per course. ***Payment plan:*** installment.

FRESHMAN FINANCIAL AID (Fall 1999, est.) 590 applied for aid; of those 81% were deemed to have need. 83% of freshmen with need received aid; of those 22% had need fully met. *Average percent of need met:* 35% (excluding resources awarded to replace EFC). *Average financial aid package:* $5600 (excluding resources awarded to replace EFC). 23% of all full-time freshmen had no need and received non-need-based aid.

UNDERGRADUATE FINANCIAL AID (Fall 1999, est.) 2,420 applied for aid; of those 87% were deemed to have need. 87% of undergraduates with need received aid; of those 14% had need fully met. *Average percent of need met:* 35% (excluding resources awarded to replace EFC). *Average financial aid package:* $7600 (excluding resources awarded to replace EFC). 24% of all full-time undergraduates had no need and received non-need-based aid.

GIFT AID (NEED-BASED) ***Total amount:*** $8,350,000 (21% Federal, 8% state, 69% institutional, 2% external sources). ***Receiving aid:*** *Freshmen:* 33% (290); *all full-time undergraduates:* 42% (1,430). ***Average award:*** Freshmen: $3500; Undergraduates: $4000. ***Scholarships, grants, and awards:*** Federal Pell, FSEOG, state, private, college/university gift aid from institutional funds.

GIFT AID (NON-NEED-BASED) ***Total amount:*** $1,940,000 (18% state, 77% institutional, 5% external sources). ***Receiving aid:*** *Freshmen:* 6% (50); *Undergraduates:* 9% (300). ***Scholarships, grants, and awards by category:*** *Academic Interests/Achievement:* 550 awards ($2,500,000 total): architecture, general academic interests/achievements. *Creative Arts/Performance:* 450 awards ($2,500,000 total): art/fine arts, general creative arts/performance. *Special Achievements/Activities:* 350 awards ($1,500,000 total): general special achievements/activities. *Special Characteristics:* 150 awards ($800,000 total): general special characteristics. ***Tuition waivers:*** Full or partial for employees or children of employees.

LOANS ***Student loans:*** $8,450,000 (99% need-based, 1% non-need-based). 60% of past graduating class borrowed through all loan programs. Average indebtedness per student: $17,000. ***Average need-based loan:*** Freshmen: $2600; Undergraduates: $3500. ***Parent loans:*** $10,800,000 (100% need-based). ***Programs:*** Federal Direct (Subsidized and Unsubsidized Stafford, PLUS), Perkins.

WORK-STUDY ***Federal work-study:*** *Total amount:* $380,000; jobs available. ***State or other work-study/employment:*** *Total amount:* $200,000 (50% need-based, 50% non-need-based). Part-time jobs available.

APPLYING for FINANCIAL AID ***Required financial aid forms:*** FAFSA, institution's own form, state aid form. ***Financial aid deadline:*** Continuous. ***Notification date:*** Continuous.

CONTACT Ms. Cindy Bradley, Director of Financial Aid, Savannah College of Art and Design, PO Box 3146, 342 Bull Street, Savannah, GA 31402-3146, 912-525-6119 or toll-free 800-869-7223. *Fax:* 912-525-6263. *E-mail:* cbradley@scad.edu

SAVANNAH STATE UNIVERSITY

Savannah, GA

Tuition & fees (GA res): $2356 **Average undergraduate aid package: N/A**

ABOUT THE INSTITUTION State-supported, coed. Awards: bachelor's and master's degrees. 27 undergraduate majors. Total enrollment: 2,153. Undergraduates: 2,042. Freshmen: 332. Federal methodology is used as a basis for awarding need-based institutional aid.

UNDERGRADUATE EXPENSES for 1999–2000 ***Application fee:*** $20. ***Tuition, state resident:*** full-time $1808; part-time $76 per credit. ***Tuition, nonresident:*** full-time $7232; part-time $302 per credit. ***Required fees:*** full-time $548; $274 per term part-time. Part-time tuition and fees vary according to course load. ***College room and board:*** $4084; ***room only:*** $2120. Room and board charges vary according to board plan.

GIFT AID (NEED-BASED) ***Scholarships, grants, and awards:*** Federal Pell, FSEOG, state, private, college/university gift aid from institutional funds.

GIFT AID (NON-NEED-BASED) ***Scholarships, grants, and awards by category:*** *Academic Interests/Achievement:* biological sciences, business, computer science, engineering/technologies, English, general academic interests/achievements, humanities, mathematics, military science, physical sciences, social sciences. *Creative Arts/Performance:* music. ***Tuition waivers:*** Full or partial for employees or children of employees, senior citizens. ***ROTC:*** Army, Naval.

LOANS ***Programs:*** Federal Direct (Subsidized and Unsubsidized Stafford, PLUS), Perkins.

WORK-STUDY Federal work-study jobs available.

APPLYING for FINANCIAL AID ***Required financial aid form:*** FAFSA. ***Financial aid deadline (priority):*** 5/1. ***Notification date:*** Continuous. Students must reply within 2 weeks of notification.

CONTACT Mrs. Jerrie K. Huewitt, Assistant Director of Financial Aid, Savannah State University, PO Box 20523, Savannah, GA 31404, 912-356-2253 or toll-free 800-788-0478. *E-mail:* jerrie_huewitt@savstate.edu

SCHOOL OF THE ART INSTITUTE OF CHICAGO

Chicago, IL

Tuition & fees: $20,220 **Average undergraduate aid package: N/A**

ABOUT THE INSTITUTION Independent, coed. Awards: bachelor's and master's degrees. 14 undergraduate majors. Total enrollment: 2,370. Undergraduates: 1,819. Federal methodology is used as a basis for awarding need-based institutional aid.

UNDERGRADUATE EXPENSES for 2000–2001 (est.) ***Application fee:*** $45. ***Tuition:*** full-time $20,220; part-time $674 per semester hour. Room and board charges vary according to housing facility. ***Payment plan:*** installment.

GIFT AID (NEED-BASED) ***Scholarships, grants, and awards:*** Federal Pell, FSEOG, state, private, college/university gift aid from institutional funds.

GIFT AID (NON-NEED-BASED) ***Scholarships, grants, and awards by category:*** *Academic Interests/Achievement:* general academic interests/achievements. *Creative Arts/Performance:* art/fine arts. ***Tuition waivers:*** Full or partial for employees or children of employees.

LOANS ***Programs:*** FFEL (Subsidized and Unsubsidized Stafford, PLUS), Perkins.

WORK-STUDY Federal work-study jobs available. ***State or other work-study/employment:*** Part-time jobs available.

APPLYING for FINANCIAL AID ***Required financial aid forms:*** FAFSA, federal income tax form(s). ***Financial aid deadline (priority):*** 3/15. ***Notification date:*** Continuous. Students must reply within 4 weeks of notification.

CONTACT Financial Aid Office, School of the Art Institute of Chicago, 37 South Wabash, Suite 708, Chicago, IL 60603-3103, 312-899-5106 or toll-free 800-232-SAIC.

SCHOOL OF THE MUSEUM OF FINE ARTS

Boston, MA

Tuition & fees: $18,580 **Average undergraduate aid package: $8778**

ABOUT THE INSTITUTION Independent, coed. Awards: bachelor's and master's degrees and post-bachelor's certificates. 14 undergraduate majors. Total enrollment: 1,177. Undergraduates: 1,095. Both federal and institutional methodology are used as a basis for awarding need-based institutional aid.

UNDERGRADUATE EXPENSES for 2000–2001 ***Application fee:*** $35. ***Tuition:*** full-time $17,880. ***Required fees:*** full-time $700. Full-time tuition and fees vary according to program. Part-time tuition and fees vary according to program. ***Payment plan:*** installment.

FRESHMAN FINANCIAL AID (Fall 1998) 58 applied for aid; of those 100% were deemed to have need. 100% of freshmen with need received aid; of those 3% had need fully met. *Average percent of need met:* 53% (excluding resources awarded to replace EFC). *Average financial aid package:* $8324 (excluding resources awarded to replace EFC).

UNDERGRADUATE FINANCIAL AID (Fall 1998) 345 applied for aid; of those 100% were deemed to have need. 100% of undergraduates with need received aid; of those 12% had need fully met. *Average percent of*

School of the Museum of Fine Arts (continued)

need met: 55% (excluding resources awarded to replace EFC). *Average financial aid package:* $8778 (excluding resources awarded to replace EFC).

GIFT AID (NEED-BASED) ***Total amount:*** $2,136,905 (15% Federal, 6% state, 75% institutional, 4% external sources). ***Receiving aid:*** *Freshmen:* 64% (54); *all full-time undergraduates:* 51% (292). ***Average award:*** Freshmen: $5695; Undergraduates: $7318. ***Scholarships, grants, and awards:*** Federal Pell, FSEOG, state, private, college/university gift aid from institutional funds.

GIFT AID (NON-NEED-BASED) ***Receiving aid:*** *Freshmen:* 13% (11); *Undergraduates:* 4% (22). ***Scholarships, grants, and awards by category:*** *Creative Arts/Performance:* general creative arts/performance. ***Tuition waivers:*** Full or partial for employees or children of employees. ***ROTC:*** Army cooperative, Naval cooperative, Air Force cooperative.

LOANS ***Student loans:*** $1,391,626 (100% need-based). ***Average need-based loan:*** Freshmen: $2550; Undergraduates: $3536. ***Parent loans:*** $501,836 (100% need-based). ***Programs:*** FFEL (Subsidized and Unsubsidized Stafford, PLUS), state.

WORK-STUDY ***Federal work-study:*** *Total amount:* $74,548; jobs available.

APPLYING for FINANCIAL AID ***Required financial aid forms:*** FAFSA, institution's own form. ***Financial aid deadline (priority):*** 3/15. ***Notification date:*** 5/1. Students must reply within 2 weeks of notification.

CONTACT Ms. Elizabeth Goreham, Director of Financial Aid, School of the Museum of Fine Arts, 230 The Fenway, Boston, MA 02115, 617-369-3684 or toll-free 800-643-6078 (in-state). *Fax:* 617-369-3041. *E-mail:* elizabeth_goreham@smfa.edu

SCHOOL OF VISUAL ARTS

New York, NY

Tuition & fees: $15,320 **Average undergraduate aid package: N/A**

ABOUT THE INSTITUTION Proprietary, coed. Awards: bachelor's and master's degrees. 15 undergraduate majors. Total enrollment: 5,528. Undergraduates: 5,215. Freshmen: 513. Federal methodology is used as a basis for awarding need-based institutional aid.

UNDERGRADUATE EXPENSES for 1999–2000 ***Application fee:*** $45. ***Tuition:*** full-time $15,000; part-time $630 per credit. ***Required fees:*** full-time $320. Full-time tuition and fees vary according to program. Room and board charges vary according to gender and housing facility. ***Payment plan:*** installment.

GIFT AID (NEED-BASED) ***Scholarships, grants, and awards:*** Federal Pell, FSEOG, state, private, college/university gift aid from institutional funds.

GIFT AID (NON-NEED-BASED) ***Scholarships, grants, and awards by category:*** *Creative Arts/Performance:* applied art and design, art/fine arts. ***Tuition waivers:*** Full or partial for employees or children of employees.

LOANS ***Programs:*** FFEL (Subsidized and Unsubsidized Stafford, PLUS), Perkins, alternative loans.

WORK-STUDY Federal work-study jobs available.

APPLYING for FINANCIAL AID ***Required financial aid forms:*** FAFSA, state aid form. ***Financial aid deadline (priority):*** 2/1. ***Notification date:*** Continuous.

CONTACT Mr. Javier Vega, Director of Financial Aid, School of Visual Arts, 209 East 23rd Street, New York, NY 10010, 212-592-2030 or toll-free 800-436-4204. *Fax:* 212-592-2029. *E-mail:* jvega@adm.schoolofvisualarts.edu

SCHREINER COLLEGE

Kerrville, TX

Tuition & fees: $11,740 **Average undergraduate aid package: $10,720**

ABOUT THE INSTITUTION Independent Presbyterian, coed. Awards: associate, bachelor's, and master's degrees. 27 undergraduate majors. Total enrollment: 803. Undergraduates: 762. Freshmen: 230. Federal methodology is used as a basis for awarding need-based institutional aid.

UNDERGRADUATE EXPENSES for 2000–2001 ***Application fee:*** $20. ***Comprehensive fee:*** $18,260 includes full-time tuition ($11,540), mandatory fees ($200), and room and board ($6520). ***College room only:*** $3340. Room and board charges vary according to board plan and housing facility. ***Part-time tuition:*** $492 per credit hour. ***Payment plan:*** installment.

FRESHMAN FINANCIAL AID (Fall 1998) 137 applied for aid; of those 91% were deemed to have need. 98% of freshmen with need received aid; of those 6% had need fully met. *Average percent of need met:* 64% (excluding resources awarded to replace EFC). *Average financial aid package:* $9333 (excluding resources awarded to replace EFC). 6% of all full-time freshmen had no need and received non-need-based aid.

UNDERGRADUATE FINANCIAL AID (Fall 1998) 516 applied for aid; of those 94% were deemed to have need. 99% of undergraduates with need received aid; of those 11% had need fully met. *Average percent of need met:* 74% (excluding resources awarded to replace EFC). *Average financial aid package:* $10,720 (excluding resources awarded to replace EFC). 5% of all full-time undergraduates had no need and received non-need-based aid.

GIFT AID (NEED-BASED) ***Total amount:*** $3,391,617 (17% Federal, 11% state, 69% institutional, 3% external sources). ***Receiving aid:*** *Freshmen:* 84% (119); *all full-time undergraduates:* 86% (473). ***Average award:*** Freshmen: $6833; Undergraduates: $7729. ***Scholarships, grants, and awards:*** Federal Pell, FSEOG, state, private, college/university gift aid from institutional funds.

GIFT AID (NON-NEED-BASED) ***Total amount:*** $369,844 (96% institutional, 4% external sources). ***Receiving aid:*** *Freshmen:* 1% (1); *Undergraduates:* 10% (56). ***Scholarships, grants, and awards by category:*** *Academic Interests/Achievement:* 291 awards ($1,256,531 total): general academic interests/achievements. *Creative Arts/Performance:* 66 awards ($74,228 total): art/fine arts, journalism/publications, music, theater/drama. *Special Achievements/Activities:* 49 awards ($49,690 total): general special achievements/activities, leadership, religious involvement. *Special Characteristics:* 44 awards ($179,087 total): children of educators, children of faculty/staff, general special characteristics, religious affiliation. ***Tuition waivers:*** Full or partial for employees or children of employees.

LOANS ***Student loans:*** $1,883,805 (84% need-based, 16% non-need-based). 25% of past graduating class borrowed through all loan programs. Average indebtedness per student: $9476. ***Average need-based loan:*** Freshmen: $1890; Undergraduates: $2645. ***Parent loans:*** $597,433 (65% need-based, 35% non-need-based). ***Programs:*** Federal Direct (Subsidized and Unsubsidized Stafford, PLUS), FFEL (Subsidized and Unsubsidized Stafford, PLUS), state.

WORK-STUDY ***Federal work-study:*** *Total amount:* $37,994; 46 jobs averaging $856. ***State or other work-study/employment:*** *Total amount:* $259,005 (88% need-based, 12% non-need-based). 203 part-time jobs averaging $1336.

APPLYING for FINANCIAL AID ***Required financial aid forms:*** FAFSA, institution's own form. ***Financial aid deadline (priority):*** 4/15. ***Notification date:*** Continuous. Students must reply within 2 weeks of notification.

CONTACT Cathleen Wright, Financial Aid Director, Schreiner College, 2100 Memorial Boulevard, Kerrville, TX 78028, 830-792-7230 or toll-free 800-343-4919. *Fax:* 830-792-7226. *E-mail:* cfwright@schreiner.edu

SCRIPPS COLLEGE

Claremont, CA

Tuition & fees: $21,130 **Average undergraduate aid package: $19,799**

ABOUT THE INSTITUTION Independent, women only. Awards: bachelor's degrees and post-bachelor's certificates. 52 undergraduate majors. Total enrollment: 790. Undergraduates: 773. Freshmen: 212. Institutional methodology is used as a basis for awarding need-based institutional aid.

UNDERGRADUATE EXPENSES for 1999–2000 ***Application fee:*** $50. ***Comprehensive fee:*** $29,000 includes full-time tuition ($21,000), mandatory fees ($130), and room and board ($7870). ***College room only:*** $4170. Full-time tuition and fees vary according to program. Room and board charges vary according to board plan. ***Part-time tuition:*** $2625 per course. ***Part-time fees:*** $130 per year part-time. Part-time tuition and fees vary according to program. ***Payment plan:*** installment.

FRESHMAN FINANCIAL AID (Fall 1999) 147 applied for aid; of those 73% were deemed to have need. 100% of freshmen with need received aid; of those 100% had need fully met. *Average percent of need met:* 100% (excluding resources awarded to replace EFC). *Average financial aid package:* $20,177 (excluding resources awarded to replace EFC). 10% of all full-time freshmen had no need and received non-need-based aid.

UNDERGRADUATE FINANCIAL AID (Fall 1999) 421 applied for aid; of those 91% were deemed to have need. 100% of undergraduates with need received aid; of those 95% had need fully met. *Average percent of need met:* 97% (excluding resources awarded to replace EFC). *Average financial aid package:* $19,799 (excluding resources awarded to replace EFC). 7% of all full-time undergraduates had no need and received non-need-based aid.

GIFT AID (NEED-BASED) ***Total amount:*** $5,705,241 (7% Federal, 12% state, 78% institutional, 3% external sources). ***Receiving aid:*** *Freshmen:* 49% (105); *all full-time undergraduates:* 48% (368). ***Average award:*** Freshmen: $16,033; Undergraduates: $15,674. ***Scholarships, grants, and awards:*** Federal Pell, FSEOG, state, private, college/university gift aid from institutional funds.

GIFT AID (NON-NEED-BASED) ***Total amount:*** $537,228 (1% state, 93% institutional, 6% external sources). ***Receiving aid:*** *Freshmen:* 3% (6); *Undergraduates:* 1% (8). ***Scholarships, grants, and awards by category:*** *Academic Interests/Achievement:* 105 awards ($745,600 total): general academic interests/achievements. ***Tuition waivers:*** Full or partial for employees or children of employees. ***ROTC:*** Army cooperative, Air Force cooperative.

LOANS ***Student loans:*** $3,360,133 (59% need-based, 41% non-need-based). 62% of past graduating class borrowed through all loan programs. Average indebtedness per student: $18,278. ***Average need-based loan:*** Freshmen: $3037; Undergraduates: $4192. ***Parent loans:*** $852,219 (100% non-need-based). ***Programs:*** FFEL (Subsidized and Unsubsidized Stafford, PLUS), Perkins, college/university.

WORK-STUDY ***Federal work-study:*** *Total amount:* $538,644; 336 jobs averaging $1603.

APPLYING for FINANCIAL AID ***Required financial aid forms:*** FAFSA, CSS Financial Aid PROFILE, noncustodial (divorced/separated) parent's statement, business/farm supplement, federal verification worksheet, federal income tax return, W-2 forms (parent and student). ***Financial aid deadline (priority):*** 11/15. ***Notification date:*** 4/1. Students must reply by 5/1 or within 2 weeks of notification.

CONTACT Sean Smith, Director of Financial Aid, Scripps College, 1030 Columbia Avenue, Claremont, CA 91711-3948, 909-621-8275 or toll-free 800-770-1333. *Fax:* 909-607-7742. *E-mail:* ssmith@scrippscollege.edu

SEATTLE PACIFIC UNIVERSITY

Seattle, WA

Tuition & fees: $14,934 **Average undergraduate aid package: $12,576**

ABOUT THE INSTITUTION Independent Free Methodist, coed. Awards: bachelor's, master's, and doctoral degrees and post-master's certificates. 52 undergraduate majors. Total enrollment: 3,427. Undergraduates: 2,636. Freshmen: 571. Federal methodology is used as a basis for awarding need-based institutional aid.

UNDERGRADUATE EXPENSES for 1999–2000 ***Application fee:*** $35. ***Comprehensive fee:*** $20,658 includes full-time tuition ($14,934) and room and board ($5724). ***College room only:*** $2982. Room and board charges vary according to board plan and housing facility. ***Part-time tuition:*** $238 per credit. Part-time tuition and fees vary according to course load. ***Payment plan:*** installment.

FRESHMAN FINANCIAL AID (Fall 1999, est.) 474 applied for aid; of those 82% were deemed to have need. 100% of freshmen with need received aid; of those 25% had need fully met. *Average percent of need met:* 84% (excluding resources awarded to replace EFC). *Average financial aid package:* $12,721 (excluding resources awarded to replace EFC). 22% of all full-time freshmen had no need and received non-need-based aid.

UNDERGRADUATE FINANCIAL AID (Fall 1999, est.) 1,924 applied for aid; of those 87% were deemed to have need. 94% of undergraduates with need received aid; of those 27% had need fully met. *Average percent of need met:* 81% (excluding resources awarded to replace EFC). *Average financial aid package:* $12,576 (excluding resources awarded to replace EFC). 30% of all full-time undergraduates had no need and received non-need-based aid.

GIFT AID (NEED-BASED) ***Total amount:*** $10,751,539 (9% Federal, 6% state, 81% institutional, 4% external sources). ***Receiving aid:*** *Freshmen:* 54% (365); *all full-time undergraduates:* 41% (1,048). ***Average award:*** Freshmen: $7328; Undergraduates: $7186. ***Scholarships, grants, and awards:*** Federal Pell, FSEOG, state, private, college/university gift aid from institutional funds.

GIFT AID (NON-NEED-BASED) ***Total amount:*** $2,958,428 (1% state, 92% institutional, 7% external sources). ***Scholarships, grants, and awards by category:*** *Academic Interests/Achievement:* general academic interests/achievements. *Creative Arts/Performance:* art/fine arts, performing arts. *Special Achievements/Activities:* leadership. *Special Characteristics:* children and siblings of alumni, general special characteristics, relatives of clergy, religious affiliation. ***Tuition waivers:*** Full or partial for employees or children of employees, senior citizens. ***ROTC:*** Army cooperative, Naval cooperative, Air Force cooperative.

LOANS ***Student loans:*** $8,448,214 (92% need-based, 8% non-need-based). 65% of past graduating class borrowed through all loan programs. Average indebtedness per student: $16,550. ***Average need-based loan:*** Freshmen: $4863; Undergraduates: $5221. ***Parent loans:*** $1,668,218 (79% need-based, 21% non-need-based). ***Programs:*** FFEL (Subsidized and Unsubsidized Stafford, PLUS), Perkins, Federal Nursing, college/university.

WORK-STUDY ***Federal work-study:*** *Total amount:* $482,200; jobs available. ***State or other work-study/employment:*** *Total amount:* $759,841 (100% need-based). Part-time jobs available.

ATHLETIC AWARDS *Total amount:* 889,988 (56% need-based, 44% non-need-based).

APPLYING for FINANCIAL AID ***Required financial aid form:*** FAFSA. ***Financial aid deadline (priority):*** 1/31. ***Notification date:*** Continuous beginning 4/15. Students must reply by 5/1 or within 4 weeks of notification.

CONTACT Ms. Vickie Rekow, Director of Student Financial Services, Seattle Pacific University, 3307 Third Avenue West, Seattle, WA 98119-1997, 206-281-2469 or toll-free 800-366-3344. *E-mail:* vrekow@spu.edu

SEATTLE UNIVERSITY

Seattle, WA

Tuition & fees: $16,110 **Average undergraduate aid package: $17,567**

ABOUT THE INSTITUTION Independent Roman Catholic, coed. Awards: bachelor's, master's, doctoral, and first professional degrees and post-bachelor's and post-master's certificates. 54 undergraduate majors. Total enrollment: 5,829. Undergraduates: 3,245. Freshmen: 579. Federal methodology is used as a basis for awarding need-based institutional aid.

UNDERGRADUATE EXPENSES for 1999–2000 ***Application fee:*** $50. ***One-time required fee:*** $75. ***Comprehensive fee:*** $21,980 includes full-time tuition ($16,110) and room and board ($5870). ***College room only:*** $3825. Full-time tuition and fees vary according to course load. Room and board charges vary according to board plan and housing facility. ***Part-time tuition:*** $358 per credit hour. Part-time tuition and fees vary according to course load. ***Payment plan:*** installment.

FRESHMAN FINANCIAL AID (Fall 1999) 497 applied for aid; of those 77% were deemed to have need. 100% of freshmen with need received aid; of those 32% had need fully met. *Average percent of need met:* 83% (excluding resources awarded to replace EFC). *Average financial aid package:* $15,860 (excluding resources awarded to replace EFC). 15% of all full-time freshmen had no need and received non-need-based aid.

UNDERGRADUATE FINANCIAL AID (Fall 1999) 2,330 applied for aid; of those 79% were deemed to have need. 99% of undergraduates with need received aid; of those 34% had need fully met. *Average percent of need met:* 86% (excluding resources awarded to replace EFC). *Average financial*

Seattle University (continued)

aid package: $17,567 (excluding resources awarded to replace EFC). 11% of all full-time undergraduates had no need and received non-need-based aid.

GIFT AID (NEED-BASED) ***Total amount:*** $15,034,000 (17% Federal, 8% state, 72% institutional, 3% external sources). ***Receiving aid:*** *Freshmen:* 63% (369); *all full-time undergraduates:* 56% (1,602). ***Average award:*** Freshmen: $8532; Undergraduates: $3517. ***Scholarships, grants, and awards:*** Federal Pell, FSEOG, state, private, college/university gift aid from institutional funds.

GIFT AID (NON-NEED-BASED) ***Total amount:*** $3,684,831 (21% Federal, 67% institutional, 12% external sources). ***Receiving aid:*** *Freshmen:* 21% (120); *Undergraduates:* 22% (619). ***Scholarships, grants, and awards by category:*** *Academic Interests/Achievement:* general academic interests/achievements. *Creative Arts/Performance:* music. *Special Achievements/Activities:* leadership. *Special Characteristics:* children and siblings of alumni, children of educators, children of faculty/staff, members of minority groups. ***Tuition waivers:*** Full or partial for employees or children of employees. ***ROTC:*** Army, Naval cooperative, Air Force cooperative.

LOANS ***Student loans:*** $20,721,916 (57% need-based, 43% non-need-based). 61% of past graduating class borrowed through all loan programs. ***Average need-based loan:*** Freshmen: $3520; Undergraduates: $4920. ***Parent loans:*** $835,163 (10% need-based, 90% non-need-based). ***Programs:*** Federal Direct (Subsidized and Unsubsidized Stafford, PLUS), Perkins, Federal Nursing, alternative loans.

WORK-STUDY ***Federal work-study:*** *Total amount:* $2,420,345; jobs available. ***State or other work-study/employment:*** *Total amount:* $2,994,064 (100% need-based). Part-time jobs available.

ATHLETIC AWARDS *Total amount:* 303,345 (73% need-based, 27% non-need-based).

APPLYING for FINANCIAL AID ***Required financial aid form:*** FAFSA. ***Financial aid deadline (priority):*** 2/1. ***Notification date:*** Continuous beginning 4/1. Students must reply by 5/1 or within 4 weeks of notification.

CONTACT Mr. James White, Director of Financial Aid, Seattle University, Broadway & Madison, Seattle, WA 98122-4460, 206-296-5840 or toll-free 800-542-0833 (in-state), 800-426-7123 (out-of-state). *Fax:* 206-296-5755. *E-mail:* financial-aid@seattleu.edu

SETON HALL UNIVERSITY

South Orange, NJ

Tuition & fees: $17,360 **Average undergraduate aid package: $11,608**

ABOUT THE INSTITUTION Independent Roman Catholic, coed. Awards: bachelor's, master's, doctoral, and first professional degrees and post-master's certificates. 48 undergraduate majors. Total enrollment: 10,096. Undergraduates: 5,465. Freshmen: 1,083. Federal methodology is used as a basis for awarding need-based institutional aid.

UNDERGRADUATE EXPENSES for 1999–2000 ***Application fee:*** $45. ***Comprehensive fee:*** $24,856 includes full-time tuition ($15,480), mandatory fees ($1880), and room and board ($7496). ***College room only:*** $5290. Full-time tuition and fees vary according to course load and student level. Room and board charges vary according to board plan and housing facility. ***Part-time tuition:*** $516 per credit. ***Part-time fees:*** $185 per term part-time. Part-time tuition and fees vary according to course load and student level. ***Payment plans:*** installment, deferred payment.

FRESHMAN FINANCIAL AID (Fall 1998) 1016 applied for aid; of those 87% were deemed to have need. 100% of freshmen with need received aid; of those 10% had need fully met. *Average percent of need met:* 58% (excluding resources awarded to replace EFC). *Average financial aid package:* $10,841 (excluding resources awarded to replace EFC). 16% of all full-time freshmen had no need and received non-need-based aid.

UNDERGRADUATE FINANCIAL AID (Fall 1998) 3,430 applied for aid; of those 87% were deemed to have need. 100% of undergraduates with need received aid; of those 12% had need fully met. *Average percent of need met:* 63% (excluding resources awarded to replace EFC). *Average financial aid package:* $11,608 (excluding resources awarded to replace EFC). 14% of all full-time undergraduates had no need and received non-need-based aid.

GIFT AID (NEED-BASED) ***Total amount:*** $19,759,828 (18% Federal, 41% state, 41% institutional). ***Receiving aid:*** *Freshmen:* 64% (790); *all full-time undergraduates:* 56% (2,461). ***Average award:*** Freshmen: $8468; Undergraduates: $7742. ***Scholarships, grants, and awards:*** Federal Pell, FSEOG, state, private, college/university gift aid from institutional funds, Federal Nursing.

GIFT AID (NON-NEED-BASED) ***Total amount:*** $3,081,903 (8% Federal, 4% state, 87% institutional, 1% external sources). ***Receiving aid:*** *Freshmen:* 5% (63); *Undergraduates:* 3% (151). ***Scholarships, grants, and awards by category:*** *Academic Interests/Achievement:* 2,343 awards ($8,783,143 total): biological sciences, business, education, general academic interests/achievements, health fields, military science, physical sciences, premedicine. *Creative Arts/Performance:* 8 awards ($46,500 total): art/fine arts, cinema/film/broadcasting, debating, journalism/publications, music. *Special Achievements/Activities:* 12 awards ($45,000 total): community service, leadership. *Special Characteristics:* 487 awards ($2,372,862 total): children of faculty/staff, children of union members/company employees, ethnic background, members of minority groups, relatives of clergy, siblings of current students. ***Tuition waivers:*** Full or partial for employees or children of employees, senior citizens. ***ROTC:*** Army, Air Force cooperative.

LOANS ***Student loans:*** $13,668,304 (92% need-based, 8% non-need-based). 70% of past graduating class borrowed through all loan programs. Average indebtedness per student: $15,824. ***Average need-based loan:*** Freshmen: $4142; Undergraduates: $2803. ***Parent loans:*** $5,881,158 (59% need-based, 41% non-need-based). ***Programs:*** Federal Direct (Subsidized and Unsubsidized Stafford, PLUS), Perkins, Federal Nursing, state, college/university.

WORK-STUDY ***Federal work-study:*** *Total amount:* $893,651; 714 jobs averaging $1252. ***State or other work-study/employment:*** *Total amount:* $1,433,151 (39% need-based, 61% non-need-based). 841 part-time jobs averaging $1704.

ATHLETIC AWARDS *Total amount:* 3,159,485 (48% need-based, 52% non-need-based).

APPLYING for FINANCIAL AID ***Required financial aid form:*** FAFSA. ***Financial aid deadline:*** Continuous. ***Notification date:*** Continuous beginning 3/15. Students must reply by 5/1 or within 4 weeks of notification.

CONTACT Office of Enrollment Services, Seton Hall University, 400 South Orange Avenue, South Orange, NJ 07079, 973-761-9350 or toll-free 800-THE HALL (out-of-state).

SETON HILL COLLEGE

Greensburg, PA

Tuition & fees: $14,500 **Average undergraduate aid package: $14,350**

ABOUT THE INSTITUTION Independent Roman Catholic, coed, primarily women. Awards: bachelor's and master's degrees and post-master's certificates. 107 undergraduate majors. Total enrollment: 1,272. Undergraduates: 1,085. Freshmen: 165. Federal methodology is used as a basis for awarding need-based institutional aid.

UNDERGRADUATE EXPENSES for 1999–2000 ***Application fee:*** $30. ***Comprehensive fee:*** $19,350 includes full-time tuition ($14,500) and room and board ($4850). Room and board charges vary according to board plan. ***Part-time tuition:*** $360 per credit. ***Payment plan:*** installment.

FRESHMAN FINANCIAL AID (Fall 1998) 127 applied for aid; of those 98% were deemed to have need. 100% of freshmen with need received aid; of those 78% had need fully met. *Average percent of need met:* 78% (excluding resources awarded to replace EFC). *Average financial aid package:* $13,550 (excluding resources awarded to replace EFC). 5% of all full-time freshmen had no need and received non-need-based aid.

UNDERGRADUATE FINANCIAL AID (Fall 1998) 495 applied for aid; of those 91% were deemed to have need. 100% of undergraduates with need received aid; of those 68% had need fully met. *Average percent of need met:* 73% (excluding resources awarded to replace EFC). *Average*

financial aid package: $14,350 (excluding resources awarded to replace EFC). 7% of all full-time undergraduates had no need and received non-need-based aid.

GIFT AID (NEED-BASED) ***Total amount:*** $4,661,249 (23% Federal, 22% state, 55% institutional). ***Receiving aid:*** *Freshmen:* 93% (125); *all full-time undergraduates:* 85% (450). ***Average award:*** Freshmen: $9950; Undergraduates: $8675. ***Scholarships, grants, and awards:*** Federal Pell, FSEOG, state, private, college/university gift aid from institutional funds.

GIFT AID (NON-NEED-BASED) ***Total amount:*** $1,562,796 (97% institutional, 3% external sources). ***Receiving aid:*** *Freshmen:* 4% (5); *Undergraduates:* 23% (125). ***Scholarships, grants, and awards by category:*** *Academic Interests/Achievement:* biological sciences, computer science, education, English, general academic interests/achievements, home economics, humanities, mathematics, physical sciences, premedicine, religion/biblical studies. *Creative Arts/Performance:* art/fine arts, music, theater/drama. *Special Characteristics:* children and siblings of alumni, children of faculty/staff, children with a deceased or disabled parent, international students, parents of current students, siblings of current students. ***Tuition waivers:*** Full or partial for employees or children of employees. ***ROTC:*** Army cooperative.

LOANS ***Student loans:*** $3,688,355 (100% need-based). ***Average need-based loan:*** Freshmen: $4250; Undergraduates: $4790. ***Parent loans:*** $127,981 (100% non-need-based). ***Programs:*** FFEL (Subsidized and Unsubsidized Stafford, PLUS), Perkins, college/university.

WORK-STUDY ***Federal work-study:*** *Total amount:* $370,720; 357 jobs averaging $1250. ***State or other work-study/employment:*** *Total amount:* $75,556 (100% non-need-based). 63 part-time jobs averaging $1125.

ATHLETIC AWARDS *Total amount:* 51,900 (100% non-need-based).

APPLYING for FINANCIAL AID ***Required financial aid forms:*** FAFSA, institution's own form. ***Financial aid deadline:*** Continuous. ***Notification date:*** Continuous beginning 10/15. Students must reply within 2 weeks of notification.

CONTACT Sr. Mary Philip Aaron, Director of Financial Aid, Seton Hill College, Seton Hill Drive, Greensburg, PA 15601, 724-834-2200 or toll-free 800-826-6234. *Fax:* 724-830-4611. *E-mail:* aaron@setonhill.edu

SHASTA BIBLE COLLEGE

Redding, CA

Tuition & fees: $4830 **Average undergraduate aid package: N/A**

ABOUT THE INSTITUTION Independent nondenominational, coed. Awards: associate and bachelor's degrees. 3 undergraduate majors. Total enrollment: 212. Undergraduates: 212. Freshmen: 12. Institutional methodology is used as a basis for awarding need-based institutional aid.

UNDERGRADUATE EXPENSES for 1999–2000 ***Application fee:*** $30. ***Tuition:*** full-time $4650; part-time $155 per credit. ***Required fees:*** full-time $180; $70 per term part-time. Full-time tuition and fees vary according to course load. Room and board charges vary according to housing facility. ***Payment plan:*** deferred payment.

GIFT AID (NEED-BASED) ***Total amount:*** $61,676 (95% institutional, 5% external sources). ***Scholarships, grants, and awards:*** private, college/university gift aid from institutional funds.

GIFT AID (NON-NEED-BASED) ***Scholarships, grants, and awards by category:*** *Academic Interests/Achievement:* education, religion/biblical studies. *Special Characteristics:* relatives of clergy, religious affiliation, siblings of current students, spouses of current students, veterans. ***Tuition waivers:*** Full or partial for minority students, children of alumni, employees or children of employees.

APPLYING for FINANCIAL AID ***Required financial aid form:*** FAFSA. ***Financial aid deadline:*** Continuous. ***Notification date:*** Continuous.

CONTACT Dr. Sam Rodriguez, Dean of Professional Education, Shasta Bible College, 2980 Hartnell Avenue, Redding, CA 96002, 530-221-4275 or toll-free 800-800-45BC (in-state), 800-800-6929 (out-of-state). *Fax:* 530-221-6929. *E-mail:* samrod@shasta.edu

SHAWNEE STATE UNIVERSITY

Portsmouth, OH

Tuition & fees (area res): $3294 **Average undergraduate aid package: $3972**

ABOUT THE INSTITUTION State-supported, coed. Awards: associate and bachelor's degrees. 49 undergraduate majors. Total enrollment: 3,613. Undergraduates: 3,613. Freshmen: 564. Federal methodology is used as a basis for awarding need-based institutional aid.

UNDERGRADUATE EXPENSES for 1999–2000 ***Application fee:*** $30. ***Tuition, area resident:*** full-time $2745; part-time $76 per quarter hour. ***Tuition, state resident:*** full-time $3654; part-time $102 per quarter hour. ***Tuition, nonresident:*** full-time $5148; part-time $143 per quarter hour. ***Required fees:*** full-time $549; $16 per quarter hour. Full-time tuition and fees vary according to reciprocity agreements. Part-time tuition and fees vary according to reciprocity agreements. ***College room and board:*** $4431; ***room only:*** $3015. Room and board charges vary according to board plan and housing facility. ***Payment plan:*** installment.

FRESHMAN FINANCIAL AID (Fall 1999, est.) 526 applied for aid; of those 68% were deemed to have need. 94% of freshmen with need received aid; of those 100% had need fully met. *Average percent of need met:* 80% (excluding resources awarded to replace EFC). *Average financial aid package:* $3881 (excluding resources awarded to replace EFC).

UNDERGRADUATE FINANCIAL AID (Fall 1999, est.) 2,591 applied for aid; of those 70% were deemed to have need. 97% of undergraduates with need received aid; of those 100% had need fully met. *Average percent of need met:* 70% (excluding resources awarded to replace EFC). *Average financial aid package:* $3972 (excluding resources awarded to replace EFC).

GIFT AID (NEED-BASED) ***Total amount:*** $5,889,701 (67% Federal, 22% state, 3% institutional, 8% external sources). ***Receiving aid:*** *Freshmen:* 58% (307); *all full-time undergraduates:* 65% (1,702). ***Average award:*** Freshmen: $2788; Undergraduates: $2620. ***Scholarships, grants, and awards:*** Federal Pell, FSEOG, state, private, college/university gift aid from institutional funds.

GIFT AID (NON-NEED-BASED) ***Total amount:*** $1,321,790 (9% state, 62% institutional, 29% external sources). ***Receiving aid:*** *Freshmen:* 30% (160); *Undergraduates:* 28% (724). ***Scholarships, grants, and awards by category:*** *Academic Interests/Achievement:* general academic interests/achievements. *Creative Arts/Performance:* art/fine arts, performing arts. *Special Achievements/Activities:* memberships. *Special Characteristics:* ethnic background, first-generation college students, handicapped students, local/state students, members of minority groups, veterans. ***Tuition waivers:*** Full or partial for employees or children of employees, senior citizens.

LOANS ***Student loans:*** $5,211,243 (100% need-based). 56% of past graduating class borrowed through all loan programs. Average indebtedness per student: $10,944. ***Parent loans:*** $296,598 (100% need-based). ***Programs:*** FFEL (Subsidized and Unsubsidized Stafford, PLUS), college/university.

WORK-STUDY ***Federal work-study:*** *Total amount:* $209,898; 104 jobs averaging $2018.

ATHLETIC AWARDS *Total amount:* 113,813 (100% non-need-based).

APPLYING for FINANCIAL AID ***Required financial aid forms:*** FAFSA, institution's own form. ***Financial aid deadline (priority):*** 4/1. ***Notification date:*** 6/1.

CONTACT Director of Financial Aid, Shawnee State University, 940 Second Street, Portsmouth, OH 45662-4344, 740-355-2287 or toll-free 800-959-2SSU.

SHAW UNIVERSITY

Raleigh, NC

Tuition & fees: $6854 **Average undergraduate aid package: $5775**

ABOUT THE INSTITUTION Independent Baptist, coed. Awards: associate, bachelor's, and first professional degrees. 34 undergraduate majors. Total

Shaw University (continued)

enrollment: 2,670. Undergraduates: 2,529. Freshmen: 464. Federal methodology is used as a basis for awarding need-based institutional aid.

UNDERGRADUATE EXPENSES for 1999–2000 ***Application fee:*** $25. ***Comprehensive fee:*** $11,196 includes full-time tuition ($6272), mandatory fees ($582), and room and board ($4342). Full-time tuition and fees vary according to degree level. ***Part-time tuition:*** $261 per credit hour. ***Part-time fees:*** $134 per term part-time. Part-time tuition and fees vary according to degree level. ***Payment plans:*** installment, deferred payment.

FRESHMAN FINANCIAL AID (Fall 1998) 362 applied for aid; of those 89% were deemed to have need. 100% of freshmen with need received aid; of those 17% had need fully met. *Average percent of need met:* 85% (excluding resources awarded to replace EFC). *Average financial aid package:* $5775 (excluding resources awarded to replace EFC). 2% of all full-time freshmen had no need and received non-need-based aid.

UNDERGRADUATE FINANCIAL AID (Fall 1998) 2,054 applied for aid; of those 74% were deemed to have need. 100% of undergraduates with need received aid; of those 15% had need fully met. *Average percent of need met:* 85% (excluding resources awarded to replace EFC). *Average financial aid package:* $5775 (excluding resources awarded to replace EFC). 1% of all full-time undergraduates had no need and received non-need-based aid.

GIFT AID (NEED-BASED) ***Total amount:*** $6,672,115 (66% Federal, 22% state, 12% institutional). ***Receiving aid:*** *Freshmen:* 67% (255); *all full-time undergraduates:* 63% (1,371). ***Average award:*** Freshmen: $4250; Undergraduates: $4250. ***Scholarships, grants, and awards:*** Federal Pell, FSEOG, state, private, college/university gift aid from institutional funds, United Negro College Fund.

GIFT AID (NON-NEED-BASED) ***Total amount:*** $2,727,762 (81% state, 19% external sources). ***Receiving aid:*** *Freshmen:* 78% (297); *Undergraduates:* 60% (1,292). ***Scholarships, grants, and awards by category:*** *Academic Interests/Achievement:* biological sciences, education, engineering/technologies, general academic interests/achievements, mathematics, physical sciences. *Creative Arts/Performance:* music. *Special Characteristics:* children of faculty/staff. ***Tuition waivers:*** Full or partial for employees or children of employees. ***ROTC:*** Army cooperative, Air Force cooperative.

LOANS ***Student loans:*** $8,915,260 (75% need-based, 25% non-need-based). 93% of past graduating class borrowed through all loan programs. Average indebtedness per student: $17,125. ***Average need-based loan:*** Freshmen: $1313; Undergraduates: $1750. ***Parent loans:*** $1,161,011 (100% non-need-based). ***Programs:*** Federal Direct (Subsidized and Unsubsidized Stafford, PLUS), Perkins, state loans (for Education majors).

WORK-STUDY ***Federal work-study:*** *Total amount:* $481,632; 450 jobs averaging $1070.

ATHLETIC AWARDS *Total amount:* 490,532 (100% non-need-based).

APPLYING for FINANCIAL AID ***Required financial aid forms:*** FAFSA, institution's own form. ***Financial aid deadline (priority):*** 4/1. ***Notification date:*** Continuous beginning 5/1. Students must reply within 2 weeks of notification.

CONTACT Brenda Moore, Director of Financial Aid, Shaw University, 118 East South Street, Raleigh, NC 27601-2399, 919-546-8241 or toll-free 800-214-6683. *Fax:* 919-546-8356.

SHELDON JACKSON COLLEGE

Sitka, AK

Tuition & fees: $7250 | **Average undergraduate aid package: N/A**

ABOUT THE INSTITUTION Independent religious, coed. Awards: bachelor's degrees. 16 undergraduate majors. Total enrollment: 277. Undergraduates: 277. Freshmen: 52. Federal methodology is used as a basis for awarding need-based institutional aid.

UNDERGRADUATE EXPENSES for 2000–2001 (est.) ***Application fee:*** $25. ***Tuition:*** full-time $7250. Room and board charges vary according to housing facility. ***Payment plan:*** installment.

FRESHMAN FINANCIAL AID (Fall 1998) 88 applied for aid. *Average percent of need met:* 75% (excluding resources awarded to replace EFC).

GIFT AID (NEED-BASED) ***Total amount:*** $851,575 (32% Federal, 28% state, 28% institutional, 12% external sources). ***Scholarships, grants, and awards:*** Federal Pell, FSEOG, state, college/university gift aid from institutional funds.

GIFT AID (NON-NEED-BASED) ***Total amount:*** $202,779 (100% Federal). ***Scholarships, grants, and awards by category:*** *Academic Interests/Achievement:* general academic interests/achievements. *Creative Arts/Performance:* music, theater/drama. *Special Characteristics:* adult students, children and siblings of alumni, ethnic background, handicapped students, international students, religious affiliation. ***Tuition waivers:*** Full or partial for children of alumni, employees or children of employees.

LOANS ***Student loans:*** $970,027 (100% need-based). ***Parent loans:*** $43,742 (100% need-based). ***Programs:*** FFEL (Subsidized and Unsubsidized Stafford, PLUS), Perkins, state.

WORK-STUDY ***Federal work-study:*** *Total amount:* $148,267; 115 jobs averaging $1500. ***State or other work-study/employment:*** *Total amount:* $30,000 (100% need-based). 1 part-time job averaging $10,000.

APPLYING for FINANCIAL AID ***Required financial aid form:*** FAFSA. ***Financial aid deadline (priority):*** 3/1. ***Notification date:*** 5/1. Students must reply within 4 weeks of notification.

CONTACT Ms. September Horton, Financial Aid Director, Sheldon Jackson College, 801 Lincoln Street, Sitka, AK 99835-7699, 907-747-5221 or toll-free 800-478-5220 (in-state), 800-949-5220 (out-of-state). *Fax:* 907-747-6366. *E-mail:* shorton@sj-alaska.edu

SHENANDOAH UNIVERSITY

Winchester, VA

Tuition & fees: $15,700 | **Average undergraduate aid package: $10,544**

ABOUT THE INSTITUTION Independent United Methodist, coed. Awards: associate, bachelor's, master's, doctoral, and first professional degrees and post-bachelor's certificates. 30 undergraduate majors. Total enrollment: 2,269. Undergraduates: 1,285. Freshmen: 296. Federal methodology is used as a basis for awarding need-based institutional aid.

UNDERGRADUATE EXPENSES for 1999–2000 ***Application fee:*** $30. ***Comprehensive fee:*** $21,000 includes full-time tuition ($15,700) and room and board ($5300). Full-time tuition and fees vary according to course load. Room and board charges vary according to board plan. ***Part-time tuition:*** $490 per semester hour. Part-time tuition and fees vary according to course load. ***Payment plan:*** deferred payment.

FRESHMAN FINANCIAL AID (Fall 1999) 258 applied for aid; of those 81% were deemed to have need. 100% of freshmen with need received aid; of those 43% had need fully met. *Average percent of need met:* 81% (excluding resources awarded to replace EFC). *Average financial aid package:* $10,080 (excluding resources awarded to replace EFC).

UNDERGRADUATE FINANCIAL AID (Fall 1999) 1,018 applied for aid; of those 83% were deemed to have need. 100% of undergraduates with need received aid; of those 36% had need fully met. *Average percent of need met:* 83% (excluding resources awarded to replace EFC). *Average financial aid package:* $10,544 (excluding resources awarded to replace EFC).

GIFT AID (NEED-BASED) ***Total amount:*** $3,653,494 (25% Federal, 34% state, 35% institutional, 6% external sources). ***Receiving aid:*** *Freshmen:* 51% (148); *all full-time undergraduates:* 46% (502). ***Average award:*** Freshmen: $6508; Undergraduates: $6562. ***Scholarships, grants, and awards:*** Federal Pell, FSEOG, state, private, college/university gift aid from institutional funds.

GIFT AID (NON-NEED-BASED) ***Total amount:*** $257,671 (52% state, 40% institutional, 8% external sources). ***Receiving aid:*** *Freshmen:* 63% (184); *Undergraduates:* 69% (752). ***Scholarships, grants, and awards by category:*** *Academic Interests/Achievement:* 723 awards: business, general academic interests/achievements. *Creative Arts/Performance:* 193 awards: dance, music, performing arts, theater/drama. *Special Characteristics:* 569 awards: children of faculty/staff, local/state students, relatives of clergy, religious affiliation. ***Tuition waivers:*** Full or partial for employees or children of employees.

LOANS ***Student loans:*** $13,385,410 (98% need-based, 2% non-need-based). Average indebtedness per student: $13,618. ***Average need-based loan:*** Freshmen: $2186; Undergraduates: $2017. ***Parent loans:*** $2,020,727 (60% need-based, 40% non-need-based). ***Programs:*** Federal Direct (Subsidized and Unsubsidized Stafford, PLUS), Perkins, Federal Nursing, college/university.

WORK-STUDY ***Federal work-study:*** *Total amount:* $573,839; 389 jobs averaging $1475. ***State or other work-study/employment:*** *Total amount:* $236,500 (100% non-need-based). 168 part-time jobs averaging $1407.

APPLYING for FINANCIAL AID ***Required financial aid forms:*** FAFSA, state aid form. ***Financial aid deadline (priority):*** 3/1. ***Notification date:*** Continuous beginning 3/15. Students must reply within 2 weeks of notification.

CONTACT Nancy Bragg, Director of Financial Aid, Shenandoah University, 1460 University Drive, Winchester, VA 22601-5195, 540-665-4538 or toll-free 800-432-2266. *Fax:* 540-665-5433. *E-mail:* nbragg@su.edu

SHEPHERD COLLEGE

Shepherdstown, WV

Tuition & fees (WV res): $2430 **Average undergraduate aid package: $6609**

ABOUT THE INSTITUTION State-supported, coed. Awards: associate and bachelor's degrees. 34 undergraduate majors. Total enrollment: 4,597. Undergraduates: 4,597. Freshmen: 714. Federal methodology is used as a basis for awarding need-based institutional aid.

UNDERGRADUATE EXPENSES for 1999–2000 ***Application fee:*** $25. ***Tuition, state resident:*** full-time $2430; part-time $101 per semester hour. ***Tuition, nonresident:*** full-time $5754; part-time $240 per semester hour. Full-time tuition and fees vary according to location and reciprocity agreements. Part-time tuition and fees vary according to location. ***College room and board:*** $4432; ***room only:*** $2316. Room and board charges vary according to board plan and housing facility. ***Payment plan:*** installment.

FRESHMAN FINANCIAL AID (Fall 1999, est.) 526 applied for aid; of those 69% were deemed to have need. 93% of freshmen with need received aid; of those 16% had need fully met. *Average percent of need met:* 72% (excluding resources awarded to replace EFC). *Average financial aid package:* $4918 (excluding resources awarded to replace EFC). 11% of all full-time freshmen had no need and received non-need-based aid.

UNDERGRADUATE FINANCIAL AID (Fall 1999, est.) 1,959 applied for aid; of those 69% were deemed to have need. 95% of undergraduates with need received aid; of those 23% had need fully met. *Average percent of need met:* 78% (excluding resources awarded to replace EFC). *Average financial aid package:* $6609 (excluding resources awarded to replace EFC). 10% of all full-time undergraduates had no need and received non-need-based aid.

GIFT AID (NEED-BASED) ***Total amount:*** $2,342,143 (79% Federal, 19% state, 2% external sources). ***Receiving aid:*** *Freshmen:* 31% (211); *all full-time undergraduates:* 30% (826). ***Average award:*** Freshmen: $2467; Undergraduates: $2604. ***Scholarships, grants, and awards:*** Federal Pell, FSEOG, state, private, college/university gift aid from institutional funds, Federal Nursing.

GIFT AID (NON-NEED-BASED) ***Total amount:*** $574,084 (54% institutional, 46% external sources). ***Receiving aid:*** *Freshmen:* 6% (40); *Undergraduates:* 5% (152). ***Scholarships, grants, and awards by category:*** *Academic Interests/Achievement:* biological sciences, business, communication, computer science, education, engineering/technologies, English, foreign languages, general academic interests/achievements, health fields, home economics, humanities, mathematics, physical sciences, premedicine, social sciences. *Creative Arts/Performance:* applied art and design, art/fine arts, music, performing arts. *Special Achievements/Activities:* leadership. *Special Characteristics:* ethnic background, members of minority groups, veterans' children. ***Tuition waivers:*** Full or partial for minority students, employees or children of employees. ***ROTC:*** Army cooperative, Air Force cooperative.

LOANS ***Student loans:*** $6,770,863 (60% need-based, 40% non-need-based). Average indebtedness per student: $12,381. ***Average need-based loan:*** Freshmen: $2350; Undergraduates: $3599. ***Parent loans:*** $888,164 (100% non-need-based). ***Programs:*** Federal Direct (Subsidized and Unsubsidized Stafford, PLUS), Perkins, Federal Nursing, college/university.

WORK-STUDY ***Federal work-study:*** *Total amount:* $149,014; 160 jobs averaging $900. ***State or other work-study/employment:*** *Total amount:* $222,000 (100% non-need-based). 290 part-time jobs averaging $765.

ATHLETIC AWARDS *Total amount:* 193,326 (100% non-need-based).

APPLYING for FINANCIAL AID ***Required financial aid form:*** FAFSA. ***Financial aid deadline (priority):*** 3/1. ***Notification date:*** Continuous beginning 3/15. Students must reply within 2 weeks of notification.

CONTACT Financial Aid Office, Shepherd College, Gardiner Hall, Shepherdstown, WV 25443-3210, 304-876-5470 or toll-free 800-344-5231. *Fax:* 304-876-5238. *E-mail:* faoweb@shepherd.edu

SHIMER COLLEGE

Waukegan, IL

Tuition & fees: $14,180 **Average undergraduate aid package: $11,437**

ABOUT THE INSTITUTION Independent, coed. Awards: bachelor's degrees. 5 undergraduate majors. Total enrollment: 110. Undergraduates: 110. Freshmen: 15. Federal methodology is used as a basis for awarding need-based institutional aid.

UNDERGRADUATE EXPENSES for 1999–2000 ***Application fee:*** $10. ***Tuition:*** full-time $14,020; part-time $490 per credit hour. ***Required fees:*** full-time $160; $80 per term part-time. Room and board charges vary according to housing facility. ***Payment plan:*** installment.

FRESHMAN FINANCIAL AID (Fall 1998) 30 applied for aid; of those 97% were deemed to have need. 100% of freshmen with need received aid; of those 14% had need fully met. *Average percent of need met:* 68% (excluding resources awarded to replace EFC). *Average financial aid package:* $11,146 (excluding resources awarded to replace EFC). 3% of all full-time freshmen had no need and received non-need-based aid.

UNDERGRADUATE FINANCIAL AID (Fall 1998) 91 applied for aid; of those 95% were deemed to have need. 100% of undergraduates with need received aid; of those 20% had need fully met. *Average percent of need met:* 70% (excluding resources awarded to replace EFC). *Average financial aid package:* $11,437 (excluding resources awarded to replace EFC). 4% of all full-time undergraduates had no need and received non-need-based aid.

GIFT AID (NEED-BASED) ***Total amount:*** $725,800 (20% Federal, 17% state, 63% institutional). ***Receiving aid:*** *Freshmen:* 85% (29); *all full-time undergraduates:* 76% (86). ***Average award:*** Freshmen: $4239; Undergraduates: $3693. ***Scholarships, grants, and awards:*** Federal Pell, FSEOG, state, private, college/university gift aid from institutional funds.

GIFT AID (NON-NEED-BASED) ***Total amount:*** $12,450 (100% external sources). ***Scholarships, grants, and awards by category:*** *Academic Interests/Achievement:* 118 awards ($368,458 total): general academic interests/achievements. *Creative Arts/Performance:* art/fine arts, creative writing, theater/drama. *Special Achievements/Activities:* hobbies/interests. *Special Characteristics:* 59 awards ($93,542 total): children and siblings of alumni, out-of-state students. ***Tuition waivers:*** Full or partial for minority students, children of alumni, employees or children of employees, senior citizens.

LOANS ***Student loans:*** $589,330 (71% need-based, 29% non-need-based). 76% of past graduating class borrowed through all loan programs. Average indebtedness per student: $16,631. ***Average need-based loan:*** Freshmen: $3301; Undergraduates: $4049. ***Parent loans:*** $38,125 (64% need-based, 36% non-need-based). ***Programs:*** FFEL (Subsidized and Unsubsidized Stafford, PLUS), Perkins, college/university.

WORK-STUDY ***Federal work-study:*** *Total amount:* $79,142; 56 jobs averaging $1413. ***State or other work-study/employment:*** *Total amount:* $6509 (40% need-based, 60% non-need-based). 11 part-time jobs averaging $370.

APPLYING for FINANCIAL AID ***Required financial aid forms:*** FAFSA, institution's own form. ***Financial aid deadline (priority):*** 6/1. ***Notification date:*** 7/31. Students must reply by 9/1.

CONTACT Vincent D. Centeno, Director of Financial Aid, Shimer College, PO Box 500, Waukegan, IL 60079-0500, 847-249-7180 or toll-free 800-215-7173. *Fax:* 847-249-7171.

SHIPPENSBURG UNIVERSITY OF PENNSYLVANIA

Shippensburg, PA

Tuition & fees (PA res): $4550 **Average undergraduate aid package: $4962**

ABOUT THE INSTITUTION State-supported, coed. Awards: bachelor's and master's degrees. 35 undergraduate majors. Total enrollment: 6,676. Undergraduates: 5,735. Freshmen: 1,383. Federal methodology is used as a basis for awarding need-based institutional aid.

UNDERGRADUATE EXPENSES for 1999–2000 ***Application fee:*** $30. ***Tuition, state resident:*** full-time $3618; part-time $150 per credit hour. ***Tuition, nonresident:*** full-time $9046; part-time $377 per credit hour. ***Required fees:*** full-time $932; $15 per credit hour; $102 per term part-time. Part-time tuition and fees vary according to course load. ***College room and board:*** $4120; ***room only:*** $2468. Room and board charges vary according to board plan.

FRESHMAN FINANCIAL AID (Fall 1999, est.) 1108 applied for aid; of those 84% were deemed to have need. *Average financial aid package:* $3729 (excluding resources awarded to replace EFC).

UNDERGRADUATE FINANCIAL AID (Fall 1999, est.) 4,491 applied for aid; of those 74% were deemed to have need. *Average financial aid package:* $4962 (excluding resources awarded to replace EFC).

GIFT AID (NEED-BASED) ***Total amount:*** $5,976,495 (39% Federal, 60% state, 1% external sources). ***Scholarships, grants, and awards:*** Federal Pell, FSEOG, state, private, college/university gift aid from institutional funds.

GIFT AID (NON-NEED-BASED) ***Total amount:*** $950,640 (8% Federal, 1% state, 27% institutional, 64% external sources). ***Scholarships, grants, and awards by category:*** *Academic Interests/Achievement:* 135 awards ($297,425 total): area/ethnic studies, biological sciences, business, communication, computer science, education, English, general academic interests/achievements, military science, physical sciences, premedicine. *Special Characteristics:* 214 awards ($341,512 total): ethnic background, local/state students. ***Tuition waivers:*** Full or partial for employees or children of employees, senior citizens. ***ROTC:*** Army.

LOANS ***Student loans:*** $13,118,695 (52% need-based, 48% non-need-based). 62% of past graduating class borrowed through all loan programs. ***Parent loans:*** $2,013,857 (100% non-need-based). ***Programs:*** FFEL (Subsidized and Unsubsidized Stafford, PLUS), Perkins, state, college/university.

WORK-STUDY ***Federal work-study:*** *Total amount:* $478,979; 380 jobs averaging $1500. ***State or other work-study/employment:*** *Total amount:* $793,781 (100% non-need-based). 480 part-time jobs available.

ATHLETIC AWARDS *Total amount:* 283,811 (100% non-need-based).

APPLYING for FINANCIAL AID ***Required financial aid form:*** FAFSA. ***Financial aid deadline:*** 5/1 (priority: 3/15). ***Notification date:*** Continuous. Students must reply within 2 weeks of notification.

CONTACT Financial Aid Office, Shippensburg University of Pennsylvania, 1871 Old Main Drive, Shippensburg, PA 17257-2299, 717-477-1131 or toll-free 800-822-8028 (in-state). *E-mail:* finaid1@ark.ship.edu

SHORTER COLLEGE

Rome, GA

Tuition & fees: $9170 **Average undergraduate aid package: $6993**

ABOUT THE INSTITUTION Independent Baptist, coed. Awards: bachelor's and master's degrees. 36 undergraduate majors. Total enrollment: 1,772. Undergraduates: 1,739. Freshmen: 260. Federal methodology is used as a basis for awarding need-based institutional aid.

UNDERGRADUATE EXPENSES for 1999–2000 ***Application fee:*** $25. ***Comprehensive fee:*** $13,820 includes full-time tuition ($9050), mandatory fees ($120), and room and board ($4650). ***College room only:*** $2675. Full-time tuition and fees vary according to location and program. Room and board charges vary according to board plan and housing facility. ***Part-time tuition:*** $210 per credit hour. ***Payment plan:*** installment.

FRESHMAN FINANCIAL AID (Fall 1999) 255 applied for aid; of those 87% were deemed to have need. 100% of freshmen with need received aid; of those 35% had need fully met. *Average percent of need met:* 76% (excluding resources awarded to replace EFC). *Average financial aid package:* $9087 (excluding resources awarded to replace EFC). 13% of all full-time freshmen had no need and received non-need-based aid.

UNDERGRADUATE FINANCIAL AID (Fall 1999) 1,379 applied for aid; of those 86% were deemed to have need. 99% of undergraduates with need received aid; of those 20% had need fully met. *Average percent of need met:* 58% (excluding resources awarded to replace EFC). *Average financial aid package:* $6993 (excluding resources awarded to replace EFC). 10% of all full-time undergraduates had no need and received non-need-based aid.

GIFT AID (NEED-BASED) ***Total amount:*** $4,578,539 (11% Federal, 50% state, 36% institutional, 3% external sources). ***Receiving aid:*** *Freshmen:* 84% (218); *all full-time undergraduates:* 69% (1,163). ***Average award:*** Freshmen: $6565; Undergraduates: $4409. ***Scholarships, grants, and awards:*** Federal Pell, FSEOG, state, private, college/university gift aid from institutional funds.

GIFT AID (NON-NEED-BASED) ***Total amount:*** $1,203,863 (60% state, 32% institutional, 8% external sources). ***Receiving aid:*** *Freshmen:* 21% (55); *Undergraduates:* 8% (137). ***Scholarships, grants, and awards by category:*** *Academic Interests/Achievement:* 510 awards ($1,261,666 total): general academic interests/achievements, religion/biblical studies. *Creative Arts/Performance:* 105 awards ($135,410 total): art/fine arts, music, theater/drama. *Special Achievements/Activities:* 855 awards ($558,019 total): religious involvement. *Special Characteristics:* 420 awards ($332,105 total): children of faculty/staff, local/state students, out-of-state students, religious affiliation, siblings of current students. ***Tuition waivers:*** Full or partial for employees or children of employees, senior citizens.

LOANS ***Student loans:*** $5,003,084 (65% need-based, 35% non-need-based). 54% of past graduating class borrowed through all loan programs. Average indebtedness per student: $16,700. ***Average need-based loan:*** Freshmen: $2413; Undergraduates: $2092. ***Parent loans:*** $654,425 (32% need-based, 68% non-need-based). ***Programs:*** FFEL (Subsidized and Unsubsidized Stafford, PLUS), Perkins, state, college/university.

WORK-STUDY ***Federal work-study:*** *Total amount:* $148,550; 108 jobs averaging $1375. ***State or other work-study/employment:*** *Total amount:* $113,540 (46% need-based, 54% non-need-based). Part-time jobs available.

ATHLETIC AWARDS *Total amount:* 387,055 (87% need-based, 13% non-need-based).

APPLYING for FINANCIAL AID ***Required financial aid forms:*** FAFSA, institution's own form. ***Financial aid deadline:*** 8/1 (priority: 4/1). ***Notification date:*** Continuous. Students must reply within 2 weeks of notification.

CONTACT Mrs. Susan Tate, Associate Director for Financial Aid, Shorter College, 315 Shorter Avenue, Rome, GA 30165-4298, 706-233-7227 or toll-free 800-868-6980. *Fax:* 706-236-1515. *E-mail:* state@shorter.peachnet.edu

SH'OR YOSHUV RABBINICAL COLLEGE

Far Rockaway, NY

CONTACT Office of Financial Aid, Sh'or Yoshuv Rabbinical College, 1526 Central Avenue, Far Rockaway, NY 11691-4002, 718-327-2048.

SIENA COLLEGE

Loudonville, NY

Tuition & fees: $14,130 **Average undergraduate aid package: $10,440**

ABOUT THE INSTITUTION Independent Roman Catholic, coed. Awards: bachelor's and master's degrees. 27 undergraduate majors. Total enrollment: 3,024. Undergraduates: 3,002. Freshmen: 680. Federal methodology is used as a basis for awarding need-based institutional aid.

UNDERGRADUATE EXPENSES for 1999–2000 ***Application fee:*** $40. ***Comprehensive fee:*** $20,345 includes full-time tuition ($13,660), mandatory fees ($470), and room and board ($6215). ***College room only:***

$3795. Room and board charges vary according to board plan and housing facility. ***Part-time tuition:*** $250 per credit hour. ***Part-time fees:*** $25 per term part-time. ***Payment plan:*** installment.

FRESHMAN FINANCIAL AID (Fall 1999) 604 applied for aid; of those 82% were deemed to have need. 100% of freshmen with need received aid; of those 13% had need fully met. *Average percent of need met:* 74% (excluding resources awarded to replace EFC). *Average financial aid package:* $10,716 (excluding resources awarded to replace EFC). 15% of all full-time freshmen had no need and received non-need-based aid.

UNDERGRADUATE FINANCIAL AID (Fall 1999) 2,124 applied for aid; of those 87% were deemed to have need. 100% of undergraduates with need received aid; of those 18% had need fully met. *Average percent of need met:* 76% (excluding resources awarded to replace EFC). *Average financial aid package:* $10,440 (excluding resources awarded to replace EFC). 10% of all full-time undergraduates had no need and received non-need-based aid.

GIFT AID (NEED-BASED) ***Total amount:*** $12,074,932 (13% Federal, 17% state, 70% institutional). ***Receiving aid:*** *Freshmen:* 72% (485); *all full-time undergraduates:* 70% (1,797). ***Average award:*** Freshmen: $7880; Undergraduates: $6882. ***Scholarships, grants, and awards:*** Federal Pell, FSEOG, state, private, college/university gift aid from institutional funds, Siena Grants, Franciscan Community Grants.

GIFT AID (NON-NEED-BASED) ***Total amount:*** $1,430,507 (4% state, 78% institutional, 18% external sources). ***Receiving aid:*** *Freshmen:* 51% (346); *Undergraduates:* 29% (744). ***Scholarships, grants, and awards by category:*** *Academic Interests/Achievement:* biological sciences, business, communication, computer science, education, English, foreign languages, general academic interests/achievements, health fields, home economics, humanities, international studies, mathematics, military science, physical sciences, premedicine, religion/biblical studies, social sciences. *Creative Arts/Performance:* creative writing, journalism/publications, music. *Special Achievements/Activities:* community service, general special achievements/activities, hobbies/interests, leadership, memberships, religious involvement. *Special Characteristics:* adult students, children and siblings of alumni, children of faculty/staff, children of public servants, children of union members/company employees, children of workers in trades, children with a deceased or disabled parent, ethnic background, general special characteristics, local/state students, out-of-state students, previous college experience, relatives of clergy, religious affiliation, veterans' children. ***Tuition waivers:*** Full or partial for employees or children of employees, senior citizens. ***ROTC:*** Army, Air Force cooperative.

LOANS ***Student loans:*** $9,077,079 (71% need-based, 29% non-need-based). 58% of past graduating class borrowed through all loan programs. Average indebtedness per student: $14,000. ***Average need-based loan:*** Freshmen: $2872; Undergraduates: $3966. ***Parent loans:*** $3,245,704 (38% need-based, 62% non-need-based). ***Programs:*** FFEL (Subsidized and Unsubsidized Stafford, PLUS), Perkins.

WORK-STUDY ***Federal work-study:*** *Total amount:* $279,327; 340 jobs averaging $824.

ATHLETIC AWARDS *Total amount:* 1,202,944 (51% need-based, 49% non-need-based).

APPLYING for FINANCIAL AID ***Required financial aid forms:*** FAFSA, state aid form. ***Financial aid deadline (priority):*** 2/1. ***Notification date:*** 4/1. Students must reply by 5/1.

CONTACT Director of Financial Aid, Siena College, 515 Loudon Road, Loudonville, NY 12211-1462, 518-783-2427 or toll-free 800-45SIENA. *E-mail:* aid@siena.edu

SIENA HEIGHTS UNIVERSITY

Adrian, MI

Tuition & fees: $12,400 **Average undergraduate aid package: $12,500**

ABOUT THE INSTITUTION Independent Roman Catholic, coed. Awards: associate, bachelor's, and master's degrees. 36 undergraduate majors. Total enrollment: 1,951. Undergraduates: 1,716. Freshmen: 218. Both federal and institutional methodology are used as a basis for awarding need-based institutional aid.

UNDERGRADUATE EXPENSES for 2000–2001 ***Application fee:*** $25. ***Comprehensive fee:*** $16,902 includes full-time tuition ($12,100), mandatory fees ($300), and room and board ($4502). Room and board charges vary according to board plan and housing facility. ***Part-time tuition:*** $307 per credit. ***Part-time fees:*** $75 per term part-time. Part-time tuition and fees vary according to course load. ***Payment plans:*** installment, deferred payment.

FRESHMAN FINANCIAL AID (Fall 1999, est.) *Average percent of need met:* 90% (excluding resources awarded to replace EFC). *Average financial aid package:* $11,000 (excluding resources awarded to replace EFC).

UNDERGRADUATE FINANCIAL AID (Fall 1999, est.) *Average percent of need met:* 90% (excluding resources awarded to replace EFC). *Average financial aid package:* $12,500 (excluding resources awarded to replace EFC).

GIFT AID (NEED-BASED) ***Total amount:*** $1,875,000 ***Scholarships, grants, and awards:*** Federal Pell, FSEOG, state, private, college/university gift aid from institutional funds.

GIFT AID (NON-NEED-BASED) ***Total amount:*** $625,000 ***Scholarships, grants, and awards by category:*** *Academic Interests/Achievement:* business, computer science, foreign languages, general academic interests/achievements, mathematics, physical sciences, social sciences. *Creative Arts/Performance:* art/fine arts, music, theater/drama. *Special Achievements/Activities:* community service. *Special Characteristics:* children and siblings of alumni, general special characteristics, members of minority groups, relatives of clergy, religious affiliation. ***Tuition waivers:*** Full or partial for children of alumni, employees or children of employees, senior citizens.

LOANS ***Programs:*** FFEL (Subsidized and Unsubsidized Stafford, PLUS).

WORK-STUDY Federal work-study jobs available. ***State or other work-study/employment:*** Part-time jobs available.

APPLYING for FINANCIAL AID ***Required financial aid forms:*** FAFSA, institution's own form. ***Financial aid deadline (priority):*** 3/15. ***Notification date:*** Continuous. Students must reply within 2 weeks of notification.

CONTACT Office of Financial Aid, Siena Heights University, 1247 East Siena Heights Drive, Adrian, MI 49221, 517-263-0731 or toll-free 800-521-0009.

SIERRA NEVADA COLLEGE

Incline Village, NV

Tuition & fees: $11,600 **Average undergraduate aid package: N/A**

ABOUT THE INSTITUTION Independent, coed. Awards: bachelor's degrees and post-bachelor's certificates. 10 undergraduate majors. Total enrollment: 585. Undergraduates: 354. Freshmen: 125. Federal methodology is used as a basis for awarding need-based institutional aid.

UNDERGRADUATE EXPENSES for 1999–2000 ***Application fee:*** $35. ***One-time required fee:*** $630. ***Comprehensive fee:*** $17,200 includes full-time tuition ($11,400), mandatory fees ($200), and room and board ($5600). ***College room only:*** $2600. Full-time tuition and fees vary according to course load, location, and program. Room and board charges vary according to housing facility. ***Part-time tuition:*** $380 per semester hour. ***Part-time fees:*** $100 per term part-time. Part-time tuition and fees vary according to course load, location, and program. ***Payment plan:*** deferred payment.

UNDERGRADUATE FINANCIAL AID (Fall 1998) 344 applied for aid; of those 100% were deemed to have need. 100% of undergraduates with need received aid.

GIFT AID (NEED-BASED) ***Total amount:*** $893,381 (21% Federal, 74% institutional, 5% external sources). ***Receiving aid:*** *All full-time undergraduates:* 58% (344). ***Average award:*** Undergraduates: $2500. ***Scholarships, grants, and awards:*** Federal Pell, FSEOG, state, private, college/university gift aid from institutional funds.

GIFT AID (NON-NEED-BASED) ***Scholarships, grants, and awards by category:*** *Academic Interests/Achievement:* business, education, general academic interests/achievements, humanities. *Creative Arts/Performance:* art/fine arts, music. *Special Achievements/Activities:* community service. *Special Characteristics:* children of faculty/staff, ethnic background, local/

Sierra Nevada College (continued)

state students, members of minority groups. ***Tuition waivers:*** Full or partial for employees or children of employees. ***ROTC:*** Army cooperative.

LOANS ***Student loans:*** $2,390,623 (100% need-based). 60% of past graduating class borrowed through all loan programs. Average indebtedness per student: $12,250. ***Parent loans:*** $294,744 (100% need-based). ***Programs:*** FFEL (Subsidized and Unsubsidized Stafford, PLUS), alternative loans.

WORK-STUDY ***Federal work-study:*** *Total amount:* $29,018; 46 jobs available.

ATHLETIC AWARDS *Total amount:* 141,897 (100% need-based).

APPLYING for FINANCIAL AID ***Required financial aid forms:*** FAFSA, institution's own form, financial aid transcript (for transfers). ***Financial aid deadline:*** Continuous. ***Notification date:*** Continuous beginning 2/1. Students must reply within 4 weeks of notification.

CONTACT Ms. Laura Whitelaw, Director of Financial Aid, Sierra Nevada College, PO Box 4269, 999 Tahoe Boulevard, Incline Village, NV 89450-4269, 775-831-1314 Ext. 1651 or toll-free 800-332-8666 Ext. 1632 (out-of-state). *Fax:* 775-831-1347. *E-mail:* lwhitelaw@sierranevada.edu

SILVER LAKE COLLEGE

Manitowoc, WI

Tuition & fees: $11,150 **Average undergraduate aid package: $10,398**

ABOUT THE INSTITUTION Independent Roman Catholic, coed. Awards: associate, bachelor's, and master's degrees. 22 undergraduate majors. Total enrollment: 1,030. Undergraduates: 789. Freshmen: 27. Federal methodology is used as a basis for awarding need-based institutional aid.

UNDERGRADUATE EXPENSES for 1999–2000 ***Application fee:*** $25. ***Comprehensive fee:*** $15,515 includes full-time tuition ($11,150) and room and board ($4365). ***College room only:*** $2400. Full-time tuition and fees vary according to location and program. Room and board charges vary according to board plan and housing facility. ***Part-time tuition:*** $275 per credit. Part-time tuition and fees vary according to course load, location, and program. ***Payment plan:*** installment.

FRESHMAN FINANCIAL AID (Fall 1999) 25 applied for aid; of those 84% were deemed to have need. 100% of freshmen with need received aid; of those 24% had need fully met. *Average percent of need met:* 75% (excluding resources awarded to replace EFC). *Average financial aid package:* $10,272 (excluding resources awarded to replace EFC). 12% of all full-time freshmen had no need and received non-need-based aid.

UNDERGRADUATE FINANCIAL AID (Fall 1999) 222 applied for aid; of those 90% were deemed to have need. 96% of undergraduates with need received aid; of those 19% had need fully met. *Average percent of need met:* 71% (excluding resources awarded to replace EFC). *Average financial aid package:* $10,398 (excluding resources awarded to replace EFC). 9% of all full-time undergraduates had no need and received non-need-based aid.

GIFT AID (NEED-BASED) ***Total amount:*** $1,277,224 (31% Federal, 23% state, 42% institutional, 4% external sources). ***Receiving aid:*** *Freshmen:* 60% (15); *all full-time undergraduates:* 60% (133). ***Average award:*** Freshmen: $4187; Undergraduates: $4193. ***Scholarships, grants, and awards:*** Federal Pell, FSEOG, state, private, college/university gift aid from institutional funds.

GIFT AID (NON-NEED-BASED) ***Total amount:*** $101,577 (89% Federal, 3% state, 8% external sources). ***Receiving aid:*** *Freshmen:* 80% (20); *Undergraduates:* 68% (151). ***Scholarships, grants, and awards by category:*** *Academic Interests/Achievement:* general academic interests/achievements. *Creative Arts/Performance:* music. *Special Achievements/Activities:* religious involvement. *Special Characteristics:* children of faculty/staff, first-generation college students. ***Tuition waivers:*** Full or partial for employees or children of employees, senior citizens.

LOANS ***Student loans:*** $1,262,080 (69% need-based, 31% non-need-based). 52% of past graduating class borrowed through all loan programs. Average indebtedness per student: $15,344. ***Average need-based loan:*** Freshmen: $1821; Undergraduates: $3668. ***Parent loans:*** $32,495 (100% non-need-based). ***Programs:*** FFEL (Subsidized and Unsubsidized Stafford, PLUS), college/university.

WORK-STUDY ***Federal work-study:*** *Total amount:* $94,000; 70 jobs averaging $1342.

ATHLETIC AWARDS *Total amount:* 16,000 (100% need-based).

APPLYING for FINANCIAL AID ***Required financial aid forms:*** FAFSA, institution's own form. ***Financial aid deadline (priority):*** 4/15. ***Notification date:*** Continuous beginning 5/1. Students must reply within 2 weeks of notification.

CONTACT Sr. Mary Beth Kornely, Director of Financial Aid, Silver Lake College, 2406 South Alverno Road, Manitowoc, WI 54220-9319, 920-686-6127 or toll-free 800-236-4752 Ext. 175 (in-state). *Fax:* 920-684-7082. *E-mail:* smbkor@sl.edu

SIMMONS COLLEGE

Boston, MA

Tuition & fees: $20,134 **Average undergraduate aid package: $19,059**

ABOUT THE INSTITUTION Independent, women only. Awards: bachelor's, master's, and doctoral degrees and post-bachelor's and post-master's certificates. 50 undergraduate majors. Total enrollment: 3,295. Undergraduates: 1,235. Freshmen: 271. Institutional methodology is used as a basis for awarding need-based institutional aid.

UNDERGRADUATE EXPENSES for 1999–2000 ***Application fee:*** $35. ***Comprehensive fee:*** $28,180 includes full-time tuition ($19,520), mandatory fees ($614), and room and board ($8046). Full-time tuition and fees vary according to course load. ***Part-time tuition:*** $610 per semester hour. Part-time tuition and fees vary according to course load. ***Payment plan:*** installment.

FRESHMAN FINANCIAL AID (Fall 1998) 225 applied for aid; of those 88% were deemed to have need. 100% of freshmen with need received aid; of those 44% had need fully met. *Average percent of need met:* 97% (excluding resources awarded to replace EFC). *Average financial aid package:* $19,618 (excluding resources awarded to replace EFC). 5% of all full-time freshmen had no need and received non-need-based aid.

UNDERGRADUATE FINANCIAL AID (Fall 1998) 830 applied for aid; of those 92% were deemed to have need. 100% of undergraduates with need received aid; of those 49% had need fully met. *Average percent of need met:* 95% (excluding resources awarded to replace EFC). *Average financial aid package:* $19,059 (excluding resources awarded to replace EFC). 3% of all full-time undergraduates had no need and received non-need-based aid.

GIFT AID (NEED-BASED) ***Total amount:*** $10,029,093 (13% Federal, 8% state, 79% institutional). ***Receiving aid:*** *Freshmen:* 74% (191); *all full-time undergraduates:* 70% (727). ***Average award:*** Freshmen: $13,051; Undergraduates: $12,309. ***Scholarships, grants, and awards:*** Federal Pell, FSEOG, state, private, college/university gift aid from institutional funds.

GIFT AID (NON-NEED-BASED) ***Total amount:*** $557,543 (75% institutional, 25% external sources). ***Receiving aid:*** *Freshmen:* 18% (47); *Undergraduates:* 16% (163). ***Scholarships, grants, and awards by category:*** *Academic Interests/Achievement:* 92 awards ($895,000 total): general academic interests/achievements. *Special Achievements/Activities:* 29 awards ($203,000 total): community service, general special achievements/activities. *Special Characteristics:* 4 awards ($78,000 total): general special characteristics. ***Tuition waivers:*** Full or partial for employees or children of employees, adult students, senior citizens. ***ROTC:*** Army cooperative.

LOANS ***Student loans:*** $1,751,628 (100% non-need-based). 84% of past graduating class borrowed through all loan programs. Average indebtedness per student: $19,650. ***Average need-based loan:*** Freshmen: $3600; Undergraduates: $4623. ***Parent loans:*** $777,463 (100% non-need-based). ***Programs:*** FFEL (Subsidized and Unsubsidized Stafford, PLUS), Perkins, state, college/university.

WORK-STUDY Federal work-study jobs available.

APPLYING for FINANCIAL AID ***Required financial aid forms:*** FAFSA, CSS Financial Aid PROFILE, noncustodial (divorced/separated) parent's statement, business/farm supplement, federal income tax return. ***Financial aid deadline (priority):*** 2/1. ***Notification date:*** 4/1.

CONTACT Katherine M. Nolan, Director of Financial Aid, Simmons College, 300 The Fenway, Boston, MA 02115, 617-521-2036 or toll-free 800-345-8468 (out-of-state). *Fax:* 617-521-3195. *E-mail:* katherine.nolan@simmons.edu

SIMON'S ROCK COLLEGE OF BARD

Great Barrington, MA

Tuition & fees: $23,300 **Average undergraduate aid package: $15,908**

ABOUT THE INSTITUTION Independent, coed. Awards: associate and bachelor's degrees. 54 undergraduate majors. Total enrollment: 372. Undergraduates: 372. Freshmen: 143. Both federal and institutional methodology are used as a basis for awarding need-based institutional aid.

UNDERGRADUATE EXPENSES for 1999–2000 ***Application fee:*** $40. ***Comprehensive fee:*** $29,710 includes full-time tuition ($20,800), mandatory fees ($2500), and room and board ($6410). ***College room only:*** $3130. Full-time tuition and fees vary according to course load. Room and board charges vary according to board plan and housing facility. ***Part-time tuition:*** $795 per credit hour. ***Part-time fees:*** $150 per term part-time. Part-time tuition and fees vary according to course load. ***Payment plan:*** installment.

FRESHMAN FINANCIAL AID (Fall 1998) 113 applied for aid; of those 80% were deemed to have need. 100% of freshmen with need received aid; of those 21% had need fully met. *Average percent of need met:* 74% (excluding resources awarded to replace EFC). *Average financial aid package:* $15,654 (excluding resources awarded to replace EFC). 35% of all full-time freshmen had no need and received non-need-based aid.

UNDERGRADUATE FINANCIAL AID (Fall 1998) 275 applied for aid; of those 81% were deemed to have need. 100% of undergraduates with need received aid; of those 23% had need fully met. *Average percent of need met:* 76% (excluding resources awarded to replace EFC). *Average financial aid package:* $15,908 (excluding resources awarded to replace EFC). 35% of all full-time undergraduates had no need and received non-need-based aid.

GIFT AID (NEED-BASED) ***Total amount:*** $2,422,588 (8% Federal, 1% state, 89% institutional, 2% external sources). ***Receiving aid:*** *Freshmen:* 60% (86); *all full-time undergraduates:* 59% (215). ***Average award:*** Freshmen: $11,626; Undergraduates: $11,166. ***Scholarships, grants, and awards:*** Federal Pell, FSEOG, state, private, college/university gift aid from institutional funds.

GIFT AID (NON-NEED-BASED) ***Total amount:*** $1,034,501 (100% institutional). ***Receiving aid:*** *Freshmen:* 9% (13); *Undergraduates:* 8% (29). ***Scholarships, grants, and awards by category:*** *Academic Interests/Achievement:* general academic interests/achievements. *Creative Arts/Performance:* general creative arts/performance. *Special Achievements/Activities:* general special achievements/activities. *Special Characteristics:* children of faculty/staff, general special characteristics, local/state students, members of minority groups. ***Tuition waivers:*** Full or partial for employees or children of employees.

LOANS ***Student loans:*** $956,263 (88% need-based, 12% non-need-based). 67% of past graduating class borrowed through all loan programs. ***Average need-based loan:*** Freshmen: $2939; Undergraduates: $3752. ***Parent loans:*** $631,744 (100% need-based). ***Programs:*** Federal Direct (Subsidized and Unsubsidized Stafford, PLUS), FFEL (Subsidized and Unsubsidized Stafford, PLUS), Perkins, state.

WORK-STUDY ***Federal work-study:*** *Total amount:* $100,000; 161 jobs averaging $621.

APPLYING for FINANCIAL AID ***Required financial aid forms:*** FAFSA, CSS Financial Aid PROFILE, noncustodial (divorced/separated) parent's statement. ***Financial aid deadline (priority):*** 6/30. ***Notification date:*** Continuous. Students must reply within 2 weeks of notification.

CONTACT Ms. Eve Caimano, Director of Financial Aid, Simon's Rock College of Bard, 84 Alford Road, Great Barrington, MA 01230-9702, 413-528-0771 or toll-free 800-235-7186. *Fax:* 413-528-7339.

SIMPSON COLLEGE

Indianola, IA

Tuition & fees: $14,430 **Average undergraduate aid package: $15,174**

ABOUT THE INSTITUTION Independent United Methodist, coed. Awards: bachelor's degrees. 49 undergraduate majors. Total enrollment: 1,897. Undergraduates: 1,897. Freshmen: 352. Federal methodology is used as a basis for awarding need-based institutional aid.

UNDERGRADUATE EXPENSES for 1999–2000 ***Comprehensive fee:*** $19,230 includes full-time tuition ($14,300), mandatory fees ($130), and room and board ($4800). ***College room only:*** $2280. Room and board charges vary according to board plan and housing facility. ***Part-time tuition:*** $195 per credit. Part-time tuition and fees vary according to class time and course load. ***Payment plan:*** installment.

FRESHMAN FINANCIAL AID (Fall 1999) 345 applied for aid; of those 85% were deemed to have need. 100% of freshmen with need received aid; of those 30% had need fully met. *Average percent of need met:* 92% (excluding resources awarded to replace EFC). *Average financial aid package:* $15,084 (excluding resources awarded to replace EFC). 12% of all full-time freshmen had no need and received non-need-based aid.

UNDERGRADUATE FINANCIAL AID (Fall 1999) 1,291 applied for aid; of those 89% were deemed to have need. 100% of undergraduates with need received aid; of those 30% had need fully met. *Average percent of need met:* 91% (excluding resources awarded to replace EFC). *Average financial aid package:* $15,174 (excluding resources awarded to replace EFC). 10% of all full-time undergraduates had no need and received non-need-based aid.

GIFT AID (NEED-BASED) ***Total amount:*** $11,658,792 (8% Federal, 27% state, 62% institutional, 3% external sources). ***Receiving aid:*** *Freshmen:* 85% (294); *all full-time undergraduates:* 87% (1,142). ***Average award:*** Freshmen: $10,763; Undergraduates: $9877. ***Scholarships, grants, and awards:*** Federal Pell, FSEOG, state, private, college/university gift aid from institutional funds.

GIFT AID (NON-NEED-BASED) ***Total amount:*** $1,047,761 (92% institutional, 8% external sources). ***Receiving aid:*** *Freshmen:* 8% (28); *Undergraduates:* 7% (91). ***Scholarships, grants, and awards by category:*** *Academic Interests/Achievement:* general academic interests/achievements. *Creative Arts/Performance:* art/fine arts, music, theater/drama. *Special Characteristics:* children and siblings of alumni, children of faculty/staff, international students, members of minority groups, relatives of clergy, siblings of current students. ***Tuition waivers:*** Full or partial for employees or children of employees.

LOANS ***Student loans:*** $6,430,296 (75% need-based, 25% non-need-based). 91% of past graduating class borrowed through all loan programs. Average indebtedness per student: $16,851. ***Average need-based loan:*** Freshmen: $2925; Undergraduates: $3722. ***Parent loans:*** $832,829 (17% need-based, 83% non-need-based). ***Programs:*** FFEL (Subsidized and Unsubsidized Stafford, PLUS), Perkins, college/university.

WORK-STUDY ***Federal work-study:*** *Total amount:* $282,570; 382 jobs averaging $742. ***State or other work-study/employment:*** *Total amount:* $381,857 (8% need-based, 92% non-need-based). 399 part-time jobs averaging $881.

APPLYING for FINANCIAL AID ***Required financial aid form:*** FAFSA. ***Financial aid deadline (priority):*** 4/1. ***Notification date:*** Continuous. Students must reply by 5/1 or within 3 weeks of notification.

CONTACT Tracie Pavon, Director of Financial Assistance, Simpson College, 701 North C Street, Indianola, IA 50125-1297, 515-961-1630 or toll-free 800-362-2454. *Fax:* 515-961-1300. *E-mail:* pavon@storm.simpson.edu

SIMPSON COLLEGE AND GRADUATE SCHOOL

Redding, CA

Tuition & fees: $10,540 **Average undergraduate aid package: $10,815**

ABOUT THE INSTITUTION Independent religious, coed. Awards: associate, bachelor's, and master's degrees. 24 undergraduate majors. Total enrollment: 1,186. Undergraduates: 971. Freshmen: 191. Both federal and institutional methodology are used as a basis for awarding need-based institutional aid.

UNDERGRADUATE EXPENSES for 1999–2000 ***Application fee:*** $20. ***One-time required fee:*** $60. ***Comprehensive fee:*** $15,220 includes full-time tuition ($9400), mandatory fees ($1140), and room and board ($4680). Room and board charges vary according to board plan. ***Part-time tuition:*** $400 per credit. ***Part-time fees:*** $25 per credit. ***Payment plan:*** installment.

FRESHMAN FINANCIAL AID (Fall 1999, est.) 152 applied for aid; of those 95% were deemed to have need. 100% of freshmen with need received aid; of those 11% had need fully met. *Average percent of need met:* 81% (excluding resources awarded to replace EFC). *Average financial aid package:* $10,239 (excluding resources awarded to replace EFC). 7% of all full-time freshmen had no need and received non-need-based aid.

UNDERGRADUATE FINANCIAL AID (Fall 1999, est.) 667 applied for aid; of those 92% were deemed to have need. 100% of undergraduates with need received aid; of those 19% had need fully met. *Average percent of need met:* 82% (excluding resources awarded to replace EFC). *Average financial aid package:* $10,815 (excluding resources awarded to replace EFC). 7% of all full-time undergraduates had no need and received non-need-based aid.

GIFT AID (NEED-BASED) ***Total amount:*** $3,029,782 (33% Federal, 67% state). ***Receiving aid:*** *Freshmen:* 70% (133); *all full-time undergraduates:* 80% (587). ***Average award:*** Freshmen: $6139; Undergraduates: $6377. ***Scholarships, grants, and awards:*** Federal Pell, FSEOG, state, private, college/university gift aid from institutional funds.

GIFT AID (NON-NEED-BASED) ***Total amount:*** $1,413,248 (88% institutional, 12% external sources). ***Receiving aid:*** *Freshmen:* 58% (110); *Undergraduates:* 65% (482). ***Scholarships, grants, and awards by category:*** *Academic Interests/Achievement:* general academic interests/achievements. *Creative Arts/Performance:* music. *Special Achievements/Activities:* leadership, religious involvement. *Special Characteristics:* general special characteristics, international students, relatives of clergy, religious affiliation, siblings of current students, spouses of current students. ***Tuition waivers:*** Full or partial for employees or children of employees.

LOANS ***Student loans:*** $5,360,000 (76% need-based, 24% non-need-based). 85% of past graduating class borrowed through all loan programs. ***Average need-based loan:*** Freshmen: $2340; Undergraduates: $3181. ***Parent loans:*** $800,000 (100% non-need-based). ***Programs:*** FFEL (Subsidized and Unsubsidized Stafford, PLUS), Perkins, college/university, alternative loans.

WORK-STUDY ***Federal work-study:*** *Total amount:* $115,000; 210 jobs averaging $550.

APPLYING for FINANCIAL AID ***Required financial aid forms:*** FAFSA, institution's own form. ***Financial aid deadline (priority):*** 3/2. ***Notification date:*** Continuous. Students must reply within 3 weeks of notification.

CONTACT Christina Linton, Financial Aid Quality Control Coordinator, Simpson College and Graduate School, 2211 College View Drive, Redding, CA 96003-8606, 530-224-5606 Ext. 2604 or toll-free 800-598-2493. *Fax:* 530-224-5627. *E-mail:* chrisl@simpsonca.edu

SINTE GLESKA UNIVERSITY

Rosebud, SD

CONTACT Office of Financial Aid, Sinte Gleska University, PO Box 490, Rosebud, SD 57570-0490, 605-747-2263.

SKIDMORE COLLEGE

Saratoga Springs, NY

Comprehensive fee: $31,200 **Average undergraduate aid package: $18,355**

ABOUT THE INSTITUTION Independent, coed. Awards: bachelor's and master's degrees. 40 undergraduate majors. Total enrollment: 2,592. Undergraduates: 2,540. Freshmen: 648. Both federal and institutional methodology are used as a basis for awarding need-based institutional aid.

UNDERGRADUATE EXPENSES for 1999–2000 ***Application fee:*** $50. ***Comprehensive fee:*** $31,200 includes full-time tuition ($24,000), mandatory fees ($259), and room and board ($6950). ***College room only:*** $3900. Room and board charges vary according to board plan and housing facility. ***Part-time tuition:*** $800 per semester hour. ***Part-time fees:*** $25 per year part-time. ***Payment plans:*** tuition prepayment, installment.

FRESHMAN FINANCIAL AID (Fall 1999, est.) 336 applied for aid; of those 85% were deemed to have need. 100% of freshmen with need received aid; of those 61% had need fully met. *Average percent of need met:* 92% (excluding resources awarded to replace EFC). *Average financial aid package:* $18,786 (excluding resources awarded to replace EFC). 1% of all full-time freshmen had no need and received non-need-based aid.

UNDERGRADUATE FINANCIAL AID (Fall 1999, est.) 975 applied for aid; of those 94% were deemed to have need. 100% of undergraduates with need received aid; of those 67% had need fully met. *Average percent of need met:* 96% (excluding resources awarded to replace EFC). *Average financial aid package:* $18,355 (excluding resources awarded to replace EFC). 1% of all full-time undergraduates had no need and received non-need-based aid.

GIFT AID (NEED-BASED) ***Total amount:*** $12,952,000 (8% Federal, 7% state, 85% institutional). ***Receiving aid:*** *Freshmen:* 40% (262); *all full-time undergraduates:* 39% (873). ***Average award:*** Freshmen: $14,847; Undergraduates: $13,159. ***Scholarships, grants, and awards:*** Federal Pell, FSEOG, state, college/university gift aid from institutional funds.

GIFT AID (NON-NEED-BASED) ***Total amount:*** $608,000 (36% institutional, 64% external sources). ***Receiving aid:*** *Freshmen:* 20% (131); *Undergraduates:* 8% (176). ***Scholarships, grants, and awards by category:*** *Academic Interests/Achievement:* 9 awards ($90,000 total): biological sciences, computer science, mathematics, physical sciences. *Creative Arts/Performance:* 16 awards ($128,000 total): music. ***Tuition waivers:*** Full or partial for employees or children of employees. ***ROTC:*** Army cooperative, Air Force cooperative.

LOANS ***Student loans:*** $3,480,000 (89% need-based, 11% non-need-based). 43% of past graduating class borrowed through all loan programs. Average indebtedness per student: $14,400. ***Average need-based loan:*** Freshmen: $2412; Undergraduates: $3351. ***Parent loans:*** $3,500,000 (100% non-need-based). ***Programs:*** FFEL (Subsidized and Unsubsidized Stafford, PLUS), Perkins.

WORK-STUDY ***Federal work-study:*** *Total amount:* $600,000; 600 jobs averaging $1000. ***State or other work-study/employment:*** *Total amount:* $390,000 (100% non-need-based). 540 part-time jobs averaging $722.

APPLYING for FINANCIAL AID ***Required financial aid forms:*** FAFSA, CSS Financial Aid PROFILE, state aid form. ***Financial aid deadline:*** 2/1. ***Notification date:*** 4/1. Students must reply by 5/1.

CONTACT Mr. Robert D. Shorb, Director of Student Aid and Family Finance, Skidmore College, 815 North Broadway, Saratoga Springs, NY 12866-1632, 518-580-5750 or toll-free 800-867-6007. *Fax:* 518-580-5752. *E-mail:* rshorb@skidmore.edu

SLIPPERY ROCK UNIVERSITY OF PENNSYLVANIA

Slippery Rock, PA

Tuition & fees (PA res): $4484 **Average undergraduate aid package: $5619**

ABOUT THE INSTITUTION State-supported, coed. Awards: bachelor's, master's, and doctoral degrees. 64 undergraduate majors. Total enrollment: 6,803. Undergraduates: 6,130. Freshmen: 1,320. Federal methodology is used as a basis for awarding need-based institutional aid.

UNDERGRADUATE EXPENSES for 1999–2000 ***Application fee:*** $25. ***Tuition, state resident:*** full-time $3618; part-time $150 per credit. ***Tuition, nonresident:*** full-time $9046; part-time $377 per credit. ***Required fees:*** full-time $866; $38 per credit; $396 per term part-time. Part-time tuition and fees vary according to course load. ***College room and board:*** $3810; ***room only:*** $2038. Room and board charges vary according to board plan, housing facility, and location. ***Payment plan:*** installment.

FRESHMAN FINANCIAL AID (Fall 1998) 1250 applied for aid; of those 75% were deemed to have need. 96% of freshmen with need received aid; of those 46% had need fully met. *Average percent of need met:* 74% (excluding resources awarded to replace EFC). *Average financial aid package:* $4891 (excluding resources awarded to replace EFC). 18% of all full-time freshmen had no need and received non-need-based aid.

UNDERGRADUATE FINANCIAL AID (Fall 1998) 5,043 applied for aid; of those 75% were deemed to have need. 97% of undergraduates with need received aid; of those 65% had need fully met. *Average percent of need met:* 85% (excluding resources awarded to replace EFC). *Average financial aid package:* $5619 (excluding resources awarded to replace EFC). 19% of all full-time undergraduates had no need and received non-need-based aid.

GIFT AID (NEED-BASED) ***Total amount:*** $8,352,507 (48% Federal, 48% state, 4% external sources). ***Receiving aid:*** *Freshmen:* 53% (737); *all full-time undergraduates:* 49% (2,802). ***Average award:*** Freshmen: $2317; Undergraduates: $2171. ***Scholarships, grants, and awards:*** Federal Pell, FSEOG, state, private, college/university gift aid from institutional funds.

GIFT AID (NON-NEED-BASED) ***Total amount:*** $1,219,084 (21% institutional, 79% external sources). ***Receiving aid:*** *Freshmen:* 15% (204); *Undergraduates:* 11% (609). ***Scholarships, grants, and awards by category:*** *Academic Interests/Achievement:* biological sciences, business, computer science, education, English, general academic interests/achievements, social sciences. *Creative Arts/Performance:* art/fine arts, music. *Special Achievements/Activities:* general special achievements/activities, leadership. *Special Characteristics:* children of faculty/staff, children of union members/company employees, ethnic background, general special characteristics, members of minority groups. ***Tuition waivers:*** Full or partial for minority students, employees or children of employees, senior citizens. ***ROTC:*** Army.

LOANS ***Student loans:*** $16,697,081 (66% need-based, 34% non-need-based). 73% of past graduating class borrowed through all loan programs. Average indebtedness per student: $13,745. ***Average need-based loan:*** Freshmen: $2017; Undergraduates: $2799. ***Parent loans:*** $2,019,236 (100% non-need-based). ***Programs:*** FFEL (Subsidized and Unsubsidized Stafford, PLUS), Perkins.

WORK-STUDY ***Federal work-study:*** *Total amount:* $343,231; 285 jobs averaging $1204. ***State or other work-study/employment:*** *Total amount:* $1,251,855 (100% non-need-based). 1,043 part-time jobs averaging $1200.

ATHLETIC AWARDS *Total amount:* 447,446 (100% non-need-based).

APPLYING for FINANCIAL AID ***Required financial aid form:*** FAFSA. ***Financial aid deadline (priority):*** 5/1. ***Notification date:*** Continuous.

CONTACT Ms. Patty A. Hladio, Director of Financial Aid, Slippery Rock University of Pennsylvania, 107 Maltby Center, Slippery Rock, PA 16057, 724-738-2044 or toll-free 800-SRU-9111 (in-state), 724-738-2913 (out-of-state). *Fax:* 724-738-2922. *E-mail:* financial.aid@sru.edu

SMITH COLLEGE

Northampton, MA

Tuition & fees: $22,622 | **Average undergraduate aid package: $21,548**

ABOUT THE INSTITUTION Independent, women only. Awards: bachelor's, master's, and doctoral degrees and post-bachelor's and post-master's certificates. 45 undergraduate majors. Total enrollment: 3,168. Undergraduates: 2,665. Freshmen: 667. Both federal and institutional methodology are used as a basis for awarding need-based institutional aid.

UNDERGRADUATE EXPENSES for 1999–2000 ***Application fee:*** $50. ***Comprehensive fee:*** $30,442 includes full-time tuition ($22,440), mandatory fees ($182), and room and board ($7820). ***College room only:*** $3520. Room and board charges vary according to housing facility. ***Part-time tuition:*** $705 per credit. ***Payment plans:*** tuition prepayment, installment.

FRESHMAN FINANCIAL AID (Fall 1999) 491 applied for aid; of those 77% were deemed to have need. 100% of freshmen with need received aid; of those 100% had need fully met. *Average percent of need met:* 100% (excluding resources awarded to replace EFC). *Average financial aid package:* $21,320 (excluding resources awarded to replace EFC). 3% of all full-time freshmen had no need and received non-need-based aid.

UNDERGRADUATE FINANCIAL AID (Fall 1999) 1,882 applied for aid; of those 80% were deemed to have need. 100% of undergraduates with need received aid; of those 100% had need fully met. *Average percent of need met:* 100% (excluding resources awarded to replace EFC). *Average financial aid package:* $21,548 (excluding resources awarded to replace EFC). 2% of all full-time undergraduates had no need and received non-need-based aid.

GIFT AID (NEED-BASED) ***Total amount:*** $24,210,724 (5% Federal, 1% state, 90% institutional, 4% external sources). ***Receiving aid:*** *Freshmen:* 56% (376); *all full-time undergraduates:* 59% (1,509). ***Average award:*** Freshmen: $17,384; Undergraduates: $15,835. ***Scholarships, grants, and awards:*** Federal Pell, FSEOG, state, college/university gift aid from institutional funds.

GIFT AID (NON-NEED-BASED) ***Total amount:*** $304,460 (100% institutional). ***Scholarships, grants, and awards by category:*** *Academic Interests/Achievement:* general academic interests/achievements. *Special Characteristics:* local/state students. ***Tuition waivers:*** Full or partial for employees or children of employees. ***ROTC:*** Army cooperative, Air Force cooperative.

LOANS ***Student loans:*** $7,162,081 (88% need-based, 12% non-need-based). 67% of past graduating class borrowed through all loan programs. Average indebtedness per student: $15,142. ***Average need-based loan:*** Freshmen: $2451; Undergraduates: $4025. ***Programs:*** Federal Direct (Subsidized and Unsubsidized Stafford), FFEL (PLUS), Perkins, college/university.

WORK-STUDY ***Federal work-study:*** *Total amount:* $2,304,849; 1,327 jobs averaging $1777. ***State or other work-study/employment:*** *Total amount:* $349,585 (89% need-based, 11% non-need-based). 198 part-time jobs averaging $1765.

APPLYING for FINANCIAL AID ***Required financial aid forms:*** FAFSA, institution's own form, CSS Financial Aid PROFILE. ***Financial aid deadline:*** 2/1. ***Notification date:*** 4/1.

CONTACT Ms. Myra Baas Smith, Director of Financial Aid, Smith College, College Hall, Northampton, MA 01063, 413-585-2530. *Fax:* 413-585-2527. *E-mail:* pcounselor@ais.smith.edu

SOJOURNER-DOUGLASS COLLEGE

Baltimore, MD

Tuition & fees: $4470 | **Average undergraduate aid package: N/A**

ABOUT THE INSTITUTION Independent, coed. Awards: bachelor's degrees (offers only evening and weekend programs). 18 undergraduate majors. Federal methodology is used as a basis for awarding need-based institutional aid.

UNDERGRADUATE EXPENSES for 1999–2000 ***Tuition:*** full-time $4280; part-time $1838 per term. ***Required fees:*** full-time $190; $95 per term part-time. ***Payment plans:*** installment, deferred payment.

GIFT AID (NEED-BASED) ***Scholarships, grants, and awards:*** Federal Pell, FSEOG, state.

GIFT AID (NON-NEED-BASED) ***Tuition waivers:*** Full or partial for employees or children of employees.

LOANS ***Programs:*** FFEL (Subsidized and Unsubsidized Stafford, PLUS), college/university.

WORK-STUDY Federal work-study jobs available.

Sojourner-Douglass College (continued)

APPLYING for FINANCIAL AID ***Required financial aid forms:*** FAFSA, institution's own form. ***Financial aid deadline:*** Continuous.

CONTACT Ms. Rebecca Chalk, Financial Aid Director, Sojourner-Douglass College, 500 North Caroline Street, Baltimore, MD 21205, 410-276-0306.

SONOMA STATE UNIVERSITY

Rohnert Park, CA

Tuition & fees: N/R **Average undergraduate aid package: $8520**

ABOUT THE INSTITUTION State-supported, coed. Awards: bachelor's and master's degrees. 60 undergraduate majors. Total enrollment: 7,080. Undergraduates: 5,845. Freshmen: 860. Federal methodology is used as a basis for awarding need-based institutional aid.

UNDERGRADUATE EXPENSES for 1999–2000 ***Application fee:*** $55. ***Tuition, nonresident:*** full-time $5904; part-time $246 per unit. ***Required fees:*** full-time $1974; $687 per term part-time. Part-time tuition and fees vary according to course load. ***College room and board:*** $6217; ***room only:*** $4092. Room and board charges vary according to board plan and housing facility. ***Payment plan:*** deferred payment.

FRESHMAN FINANCIAL AID (Fall 1999, est.) 487 applied for aid; of those 67% were deemed to have need. 99% of freshmen with need received aid; of those 89% had need fully met. *Average percent of need met:* 65% (excluding resources awarded to replace EFC). *Average financial aid package:* $6589 (excluding resources awarded to replace EFC). 17% of all full-time freshmen had no need and received non-need-based aid.

UNDERGRADUATE FINANCIAL AID (Fall 1999, est.) 2,849 applied for aid; of those 80% were deemed to have need. 100% of undergraduates with need received aid; of those 59% had need fully met. *Average percent of need met:* 68% (excluding resources awarded to replace EFC). *Average financial aid package:* $8520 (excluding resources awarded to replace EFC). 10% of all full-time undergraduates had no need and received non-need-based aid.

GIFT AID (NEED-BASED) ***Total amount:*** $6,941,270 (58% Federal, 41% state, 1% external sources). ***Receiving aid:*** *Freshmen:* 26% (219); *all full-time undergraduates:* 33% (1,637). ***Average award:*** Freshmen: $3624; Undergraduates: $3022. ***Scholarships, grants, and awards:*** Federal Pell, FSEOG, state, private, college/university gift aid from institutional funds.

GIFT AID (NON-NEED-BASED) ***Total amount:*** $817,572 (18% state, 50% institutional, 32% external sources). ***Receiving aid:*** *Freshmen:* 17% (143); *Undergraduates:* 10% (465). ***Scholarships, grants, and awards by category:*** *Academic Interests/Achievement:* 544 awards ($340,000 total): area/ethnic studies, biological sciences, business, communication, computer science, education, English, foreign languages, general academic interests/achievements, health fields, humanities, international studies, mathematics, physical sciences, premedicine, social sciences. *Creative Arts/Performance:* 69 awards ($46,200 total): applied art and design, art/fine arts, cinema/film/broadcasting, creative writing, dance, journalism/publications, music, performing arts, theater/drama. *Special Achievements/Activities:* 7 awards ($6800 total): community service, leadership, memberships. *Special Characteristics:* 550 awards ($345,000 total): adult students, children and siblings of alumni, children of educators, children of faculty/staff, children of public servants, children of union members/company employees, children of workers in trades, ethnic background, first-generation college students, general special characteristics, handicapped students, international students, members of minority groups, previous college experience, veterans. ***Tuition waivers:*** Full or partial for employees or children of employees. ***ROTC:*** Army cooperative, Naval cooperative, Air Force cooperative.

LOANS ***Student loans:*** $15,740,000 (65% need-based, 35% non-need-based). ***Average need-based loan:*** Freshmen: $3218; Undergraduates: $4450. ***Parent loans:*** $2,000,000 (100% non-need-based). ***Programs:*** Federal Direct (Subsidized and Unsubsidized Stafford, PLUS), Perkins.

WORK-STUDY ***Federal work-study:*** *Total amount:* $320,000; jobs available. ***State or other work-study/employment:*** *Total amount:* $1,600,000 (100% non-need-based). Part-time jobs available.

ATHLETIC AWARDS *Total amount:* 40,000 (100% non-need-based).

APPLYING for FINANCIAL AID ***Required financial aid form:*** FAFSA. ***Financial aid deadline (priority):*** 1/31. ***Notification date:*** Continuous beginning 4/15. Students must reply within 4 weeks of notification.

CONTACT George Urdzik, Financial Aid Representative, Sonoma State University, 1801 East Cotati Avenue, Rohnert Park, CA 94928-3609, 707-664-2407. *Fax:* 707-664-4242.

SOUTHAMPTON COLLEGE OF LONG ISLAND UNIVERSITY

Southampton, NY

See Long Island University, Southampton College

SOUTH CAROLINA STATE UNIVERSITY

Orangeburg, SC

CONTACT Director, Financial Aid to Students, South Carolina State University, 300 College Street Northeast, Orangeburg, SC 29117-0001, 803-536-7067 or toll-free 800-260-5956.

SOUTH COLLEGE

Savannah, GA

Tuition & fees: N/R **Average undergraduate aid package: N/A**

ABOUT THE INSTITUTION Proprietary, coed, primarily women. Awards: associate and bachelor's degrees. 7 undergraduate majors. Total enrollment: 446. Undergraduates: 446. Freshmen: 46. Federal methodology is used as a basis for awarding need-based institutional aid.

FRESHMAN FINANCIAL AID (Fall 1998) *Average percent of need met:* 80% (excluding resources awarded to replace EFC).

UNDERGRADUATE FINANCIAL AID (Fall 1998) *Average percent of need met:* 85% (excluding resources awarded to replace EFC).

GIFT AID (NEED-BASED) ***Total amount:*** $1,708,750 (100% Federal). ***Scholarships, grants, and awards:*** Federal Pell, FSEOG, state, private, college/university gift aid from institutional funds.

GIFT AID (NON-NEED-BASED) ***Total amount:*** $466,283 (100% state). ***Scholarships, grants, and awards by category:*** *Academic Interests/Achievement:* general academic interests/achievements. ***Tuition waivers:*** Full or partial for employees or children of employees.

LOANS ***Student loans:*** $2,376,094 (50% need-based, 50% non-need-based). 75% of past graduating class borrowed through all loan programs. ***Parent loans:*** $127,736 (100% non-need-based). ***Programs:*** FFEL (Subsidized and Unsubsidized Stafford, PLUS), Perkins, state, college/university.

WORK-STUDY ***Federal work-study:*** *Total amount:* $83,677; jobs available.

APPLYING for FINANCIAL AID ***Required financial aid forms:*** FAFSA, state aid form. ***Financial aid deadline:*** Continuous. ***Notification date:*** Continuous. Students must reply within 4 weeks of notification.

CONTACT Tréssa A. Brush, Director of Financial Aid, South College, 709 Mall Boulevard, Savannah, GA 31406-4881, 912-691-6000. *Fax:* 912-691-6070. *E-mail:* tbrush@southcollege.edu

SOUTH DAKOTA SCHOOL OF MINES AND TECHNOLOGY

Rapid City, SD

Tuition & fees (SD res): $3850 **Average undergraduate aid package: $4058**

ABOUT THE INSTITUTION State-supported, coed. Awards: bachelor's, master's, and doctoral degrees. 17 undergraduate majors. Total enrollment: 2,272. Undergraduates: 2,020. Freshmen: 423. Federal methodology is used as a basis for awarding need-based institutional aid.

UNDERGRADUATE EXPENSES for 1999–2000 ***Application fee:*** $15. ***Tuition, state resident:*** full-time $1867; part-time $58 per semester hour. ***Tuition,***

nonresident: full-time $5941; part-time $186 per semester hour. ***Required fees:*** full-time $1983; $62 per semester hour. Full-time tuition and fees vary according to reciprocity agreements. Part-time tuition and fees vary according to reciprocity agreements. ***College room and board:*** $3122; ***room only:*** $1396. Room and board charges vary according to housing facility. ***Payment plan:*** installment.

FRESHMAN FINANCIAL AID (Fall 1998) 298 applied for aid; of those 68% were deemed to have need. 100% of freshmen with need received aid; of those 59% had need fully met. *Average percent of need met:* 97% (excluding resources awarded to replace EFC). *Average financial aid package:* $4126 (excluding resources awarded to replace EFC). 8% of all full-time freshmen had no need and received non-need-based aid.

UNDERGRADUATE FINANCIAL AID (Fall 1998) 1,659 applied for aid; of those 85% were deemed to have need. 100% of undergraduates with need received aid; of those 79% had need fully met. *Average percent of need met:* 97% (excluding resources awarded to replace EFC). *Average financial aid package:* $4058 (excluding resources awarded to replace EFC). 4% of all full-time undergraduates had no need and received non-need-based aid.

GIFT AID (NEED-BASED) ***Total amount:*** $1,025,333 (100% Federal). ***Receiving aid:*** *Freshmen:* 49% (179); *all full-time undergraduates:* 49% (898). ***Average award:*** Freshmen: $1207; Undergraduates: $1207. ***Scholarships, grants, and awards:*** Federal Pell, FSEOG, state, private, college/university gift aid from institutional funds.

GIFT AID (NON-NEED-BASED) ***Total amount:*** $915,940 (1% state, 40% institutional, 59% external sources). ***Scholarships, grants, and awards by category:*** *Academic Interests/Achievement:* 660 awards ($368,256 total): engineering/technologies. ***Tuition waivers:*** Full or partial for senior citizens. ***ROTC:*** Army.

LOANS ***Student loans:*** $4,680,198 (96% need-based, 4% non-need-based). 39% of past graduating class borrowed through all loan programs. Average indebtedness per student: $12,709. ***Average need-based loan:*** Freshmen: $2980; Undergraduates: $2980. ***Parent loans:*** $259,405 (100% non-need-based). ***Programs:*** FFEL (Subsidized and Unsubsidized Stafford, PLUS), Perkins.

WORK-STUDY ***Federal work-study:*** *Total amount:* $156,651; 104 jobs available.

ATHLETIC AWARDS *Total amount:* 105,750 (100% non-need-based).

APPLYING for FINANCIAL AID ***Required financial aid forms:*** FAFSA, freshmen scholarship application form. ***Financial aid deadline (priority):*** 4/15. ***Notification date:*** Continuous. Students must reply within 4 weeks of notification.

CONTACT Sharon Colombe, Director of Financial Aid, South Dakota School of Mines and Technology, 501 East Saint Joseph Street, Rapid City, SD 57701, 605-394-2400 or toll-free 800-544-8162 Ext. 2414. *Fax:* 605-394-1268. *E-mail:* scolombe@silver.sdsmt.edu

SOUTH DAKOTA STATE UNIVERSITY

Brookings, SD

Tuition & fees (SD res): $3357 **Average undergraduate aid package: $6115**

ABOUT THE INSTITUTION State-supported, coed. Awards: associate, bachelor's, master's, doctoral, and first professional degrees. 75 undergraduate majors. Total enrollment: 8,540. Undergraduates: 7,382. Freshmen: 1,452. Federal methodology is used as a basis for awarding need-based institutional aid.

UNDERGRADUATE EXPENSES for 1999–2000 ***Application fee:*** $15. ***Tuition, state resident:*** full-time $1867; part-time $58 per credit. ***Tuition, nonresident:*** full-time $5941; part-time $186 per credit. ***Required fees:*** full-time $1490; $47 per credit. Full-time tuition and fees vary according to location and reciprocity agreements. Part-time tuition and fees vary according to location and reciprocity agreements. ***College room and board:*** $2868; ***room only:*** $1364. Room and board charges vary according to board plan and housing facility. ***Payment plans:*** installment, deferred payment.

FRESHMAN FINANCIAL AID (Fall 1998) 1248 applied for aid; of those 89% were deemed to have need. 95% of freshmen with need received aid; of those 73% had need fully met. *Average percent of need met:* 84% (excluding resources awarded to replace EFC). *Average financial aid package:* $5230 (excluding resources awarded to replace EFC). 12% of all full-time freshmen had no need and received non-need-based aid.

UNDERGRADUATE FINANCIAL AID (Fall 1998) 5,342 applied for aid; of those 89% were deemed to have need. 94% of undergraduates with need received aid; of those 80% had need fully met. *Average percent of need met:* 82% (excluding resources awarded to replace EFC). *Average financial aid package:* $6115 (excluding resources awarded to replace EFC). 7% of all full-time undergraduates had no need and received non-need-based aid.

GIFT AID (NEED-BASED) ***Total amount:*** $4,967,163 (94% Federal, 4% institutional, 2% external sources). ***Receiving aid:*** *Freshmen:* 31% (474); *all full-time undergraduates:* 39% (2,510). ***Average award:*** Freshmen: $2760; Undergraduates: $2750. ***Scholarships, grants, and awards:*** Federal Pell, FSEOG, private, college/university gift aid from institutional funds, United Negro College Fund, Federal Nursing.

GIFT AID (NON-NEED-BASED) ***Total amount:*** $2,665,435 (13% Federal, 3% state, 53% institutional, 31% external sources). ***Receiving aid:*** *Freshmen:* 20% (310); *Undergraduates:* 32% (2,069). ***Scholarships, grants, and awards by category:*** *Academic Interests/Achievement:* 1,840 awards ($678,798 total): agriculture, area/ethnic studies, biological sciences, business, communication, computer science, education, engineering/technologies, English, foreign languages, general academic interests/achievements, health fields, home economics, humanities, international studies, mathematics, military science, physical sciences, premedicine, social sciences. *Creative Arts/Performance:* 121 awards ($117,612 total): art/fine arts, debating, general creative arts/performance, journalism/publications, music, performing arts, theater/drama. *Special Achievements/Activities:* 39 awards ($38,700 total): general special achievements/activities, hobbies/interests, junior miss, leadership, memberships, rodeo. *Special Characteristics:* 78 awards ($94,240 total): children of workers in trades, general special characteristics, handicapped students, members of minority groups, veterans, veterans' children. ***Tuition waivers:*** Full or partial for employees or children of employees, senior citizens. ***ROTC:*** Army, Air Force.

LOANS ***Student loans:*** $20,379,214 (70% need-based, 30% non-need-based). 83% of past graduating class borrowed through all loan programs. Average indebtedness per student: $14,084. ***Average need-based loan:*** Freshmen: $2450; Undergraduates: $3880. ***Parent loans:*** $757,999 (100% non-need-based). ***Programs:*** FFEL (Subsidized and Unsubsidized Stafford, PLUS), Perkins, Federal Nursing, college/university, alternative loans.

WORK-STUDY ***Federal work-study:*** *Total amount:* $624,763; 583 jobs averaging $1103. ***State or other work-study/employment:*** *Total amount:* $2,547,283 (100% non-need-based). 1,862 part-time jobs averaging $1243.

ATHLETIC AWARDS *Total amount:* 580,206 (100% non-need-based).

APPLYING for FINANCIAL AID ***Required financial aid forms:*** FAFSA, financial aid transcript (for transfers). ***Financial aid deadline (priority):*** 3/1. ***Notification date:*** Continuous beginning 4/5. Students must reply within 3 weeks of notification.

CONTACT Mr. Jay Larsen, Director of Financial Aid, South Dakota State University, Box 2201, Brookings, SD 57007, 605-688-4703 or toll-free 800-952-3541. *Fax:* 605-688-6384. *E-mail:* larsenj@adm.sdstate.edu

SOUTHEAST COLLEGE OF TECHNOLOGY

Mobile, AL

See Education America, Southeast College of Technology, Mobile Campus

SOUTHEASTERN BAPTIST COLLEGE

Laurel, MS

CONTACT Financial Aid Officer, Southeastern Baptist College, 4229 Highway 15 North, Laurel, MS 39440-1096, 601-426-6346. *Fax:* 601-426-6347.

SOUTHEASTERN BIBLE COLLEGE

Birmingham, AL

Tuition & fees: $5740 **Average undergraduate aid package: $6457**

ABOUT THE INSTITUTION Independent nondenominational, coed. Awards: associate and bachelor's degrees. 14 undergraduate majors. Total enrollment: 177. Undergraduates: 177. Freshmen: 29. Federal methodology is used as a basis for awarding need-based institutional aid.

UNDERGRADUATE EXPENSES for 1999–2000 ***Application fee:*** $20. ***Comprehensive fee:*** $8980 includes full-time tuition ($5740) and room and board ($3240). ***Part-time tuition:*** $205 per semester hour. ***Payment plan:*** installment.

FRESHMAN FINANCIAL AID (Fall 1999, est.) 44 applied for aid; of those 91% were deemed to have need. 100% of freshmen with need received aid; of those 12% had need fully met. *Average percent of need met:* 60% (excluding resources awarded to replace EFC). *Average financial aid package:* $5125 (excluding resources awarded to replace EFC).

UNDERGRADUATE FINANCIAL AID (Fall 1999, est.) 146 applied for aid; of those 97% were deemed to have need. 100% of undergraduates with need received aid; of those 6% had need fully met. *Average percent of need met:* 60% (excluding resources awarded to replace EFC). *Average financial aid package:* $6457 (excluding resources awarded to replace EFC).

GIFT AID (NEED-BASED) ***Total amount:*** $161,934 (100% Federal). ***Receiving aid:*** *Freshmen:* 87% (39); *all full-time undergraduates:* 40% (70). ***Average award:*** Freshmen: $1500; Undergraduates: $2870. ***Scholarships, grants, and awards:*** Federal Pell, FSEOG, college/university gift aid from institutional funds.

GIFT AID (NON-NEED-BASED) ***Total amount:*** $146,271 (2% state, 81% institutional, 17% external sources). ***Receiving aid:*** *Freshmen:* 47% (21); *Undergraduates:* 34% (59). ***Scholarships, grants, and awards by category:*** *Academic Interests/Achievement:* 41 awards ($20,000 total): general academic interests/achievements, religion/biblical studies. *Creative Arts/Performance:* 1 award ($2000 total): music. *Special Achievements/Activities:* cheerleading/drum major. *Special Characteristics:* 16 awards ($30,010 total): children of faculty/staff, local/state students, relatives of clergy, spouses of current students, veterans. ***Tuition waivers:*** Full or partial for children of alumni, employees or children of employees.

LOANS ***Student loans:*** $415,288 (100% need-based). 50% of past graduating class borrowed through all loan programs. Average indebtedness per student: $20,000. ***Average need-based loan:*** Freshmen: $2625; Undergraduates: $1720. ***Parent loans:*** $5000 (100% non-need-based). ***Programs:*** FFEL (Subsidized and Unsubsidized Stafford, PLUS).

WORK-STUDY ***Federal work-study:*** *Total amount:* $12,024; 10 jobs averaging $1200. ***State or other work-study/employment:*** *Total amount:* $20,000 (100% non-need-based). 10 part-time jobs averaging $2000.

APPLYING for FINANCIAL AID ***Required financial aid forms:*** FAFSA, institution's own form, state aid form. ***Financial aid deadline (priority):*** 5/1. ***Notification date:*** Continuous. Students must reply within 2 weeks of notification.

CONTACT Ms. Joanne Belin, Financial Aid Administrator, Southeastern Bible College, 3001 Highway 280 East, Birmingham, AL 35243-4181, 205-970-9215. *E-mail:* 102064.406@compuserve.com

SOUTHEASTERN COLLEGE OF THE ASSEMBLIES OF GOD

Lakeland, FL

Tuition & fees: $6023 **Average undergraduate aid package: $7456**

ABOUT THE INSTITUTION Independent religious, coed. Awards: bachelor's degrees. 23 undergraduate majors. Total enrollment: 1,118. Undergraduates: 1,118. Freshmen: 194. Federal methodology is used as a basis for awarding need-based institutional aid.

UNDERGRADUATE EXPENSES for 1999–2000 ***Application fee:*** $40. ***Comprehensive fee:*** $9531 includes full-time tuition ($5320), mandatory fees ($703), and room and board ($3508). Room and board charges vary according to board plan. ***Part-time tuition:*** $190 per credit. ***Part-time fees:*** $352 per term part-time. Part-time tuition and fees vary according to course load and program. ***Payment plan:*** installment.

FRESHMAN FINANCIAL AID (Fall 1999) 164 applied for aid; of those 85% were deemed to have need. 100% of freshmen with need received aid; of those 29% had need fully met. *Average percent of need met:* 77% (excluding resources awarded to replace EFC). *Average financial aid package:* $6410 (excluding resources awarded to replace EFC). 50% of all full-time freshmen had no need and received non-need-based aid.

UNDERGRADUATE FINANCIAL AID (Fall 1999) 825 applied for aid; of those 87% were deemed to have need. 100% of undergraduates with need received aid; of those 26% had need fully met. *Average percent of need met:* 78% (excluding resources awarded to replace EFC). *Average financial aid package:* $7456 (excluding resources awarded to replace EFC). 25% of all full-time undergraduates had no need and received non-need-based aid.

GIFT AID (NEED-BASED) ***Total amount:*** $2,462,158 (38% Federal, 36% state, 14% institutional, 12% external sources). ***Receiving aid:*** *Freshmen:* 43% (118); *all full-time undergraduates:* 66% (622). ***Average award:*** Freshmen: $3342; Undergraduates: $3370. ***Scholarships, grants, and awards:*** Federal Pell, FSEOG, state, private, college/university gift aid from institutional funds.

GIFT AID (NON-NEED-BASED) ***Total amount:*** $648,539 (45% state, 27% institutional, 28% external sources). ***Receiving aid:*** *Freshmen:* 6% (17); *Undergraduates:* 5% (46). ***Scholarships, grants, and awards by category:*** *Academic Interests/Achievement:* communication, general academic interests/achievements, religion/biblical studies. *Creative Arts/Performance:* music, theater/drama. *Special Achievements/Activities:* religious involvement. *Special Characteristics:* children of faculty/staff, general special characteristics, relatives of clergy, siblings of current students. ***Tuition waivers:*** Full or partial for employees or children of employees. ***ROTC:*** Army cooperative.

LOANS ***Student loans:*** $3,894,150 (74% need-based, 26% non-need-based). 91% of past graduating class borrowed through all loan programs. Average indebtedness per student: $9775. ***Average need-based loan:*** Freshmen: $2766; Undergraduates: $3911. ***Parent loans:*** $969,610 (31% need-based, 69% non-need-based). ***Programs:*** FFEL (Subsidized and Unsubsidized Stafford, PLUS), Perkins.

WORK-STUDY ***Federal work-study:*** *Total amount:* $127,258; 109 jobs averaging $1168.

APPLYING for FINANCIAL AID ***Required financial aid forms:*** FAFSA, institution's own form, state aid form (for Florida residents only). ***Financial aid deadline (priority):*** 4/1. ***Notification date:*** 5/15. Students must reply within 2 weeks of notification.

CONTACT Ms. Carol B. Bradley, Financial Aid Director, Southeastern College of the Assemblies of God, 1000 Longfellow Boulevard, Lakeland, FL 33801-6099, 941-667-5000 or toll-free 800-500-8760 (out-of-state). *Fax:* 941-667-5200. *E-mail:* cbbradle@secollege.edu

SOUTHEASTERN LOUISIANA UNIVERSITY

Hammond, LA

Tuition & fees (LA res): $2217 **Average undergraduate aid package: $5249**

ABOUT THE INSTITUTION State-supported, coed. Awards: associate, bachelor's, and master's degrees. 44 undergraduate majors. Total enrollment: 15,175. Undergraduates: 13,476. Freshmen: 2,448. Federal methodology is used as a basis for awarding need-based institutional aid.

UNDERGRADUATE EXPENSES for 1999–2000 ***Application fee:*** $10. ***Tuition, state resident:*** full-time $2030. ***Tuition, nonresident:*** full-time $7358. ***Required fees:*** full-time $187. Part-time tuition and fees vary according to course load. ***College room and board:*** $2770. Room and board charges vary according to board plan and housing facility. ***Payment plans:*** installment, deferred payment.

FRESHMAN FINANCIAL AID (Fall 1998) 2937 applied for aid; of those 84% were deemed to have need. 100% of freshmen with need received aid; of those 20% had need fully met. *Average percent of need met:* 55% (excluding resources awarded to replace EFC). *Average financial aid pack-*

age: $3584 (excluding resources awarded to replace EFC). 14% of all full-time freshmen had no need and received non-need-based aid.

UNDERGRADUATE FINANCIAL AID (Fall 1998) 9,946 applied for aid; of those 87% were deemed to have need. 100% of undergraduates with need received aid; of those 27% had need fully met. *Average percent of need met:* 67% (excluding resources awarded to replace EFC). *Average financial aid package:* $5249 (excluding resources awarded to replace EFC). 21% of all full-time undergraduates had no need and received non-need-based aid.

GIFT AID (NEED-BASED) ***Total amount:*** $19,510,794 (79% Federal, 15% state, 5% institutional, 1% external sources). ***Receiving aid:*** *Freshmen:* 34% (2,213); *all full-time undergraduates:* 49% (7,201). ***Average award:*** Freshmen: $2100; Undergraduates: $2006. ***Scholarships, grants, and awards:*** Federal Pell, FSEOG, state, private, college/university gift aid from institutional funds, Federal Nursing.

GIFT AID (NON-NEED-BASED) ***Total amount:*** $1,800,669 (1% Federal, 79% state, 15% institutional, 5% external sources). ***Receiving aid:*** *Freshmen:* 2% (139); *Undergraduates:* 2% (296). ***Scholarships, grants, and awards by category:*** *Academic Interests/Achievement:* agriculture, biological sciences, business, communication, education, engineering/technologies, English, general academic interests/achievements, home economics, humanities, mathematics, military science, physical sciences, premedicine, religion/biblical studies, social sciences. *Creative Arts/Performance:* debating, general creative arts/performance, journalism/publications, music. *Special Achievements/Activities:* cheerleading/drum major, community service, leadership, religious involvement. *Special Characteristics:* adult students, children and siblings of alumni, children of faculty/staff, handicapped students, local/state students, members of minority groups, out-of-state students, public servants, relatives of clergy, religious affiliation. ***Tuition waivers:*** Full or partial for employees or children of employees, senior citizens. ***ROTC:*** Army cooperative.

LOANS ***Student loans:*** $43,805,057 (81% need-based, 19% non-need-based). 62% of past graduating class borrowed through all loan programs. ***Average need-based loan:*** Freshmen: $1430; Undergraduates: $3176. ***Parent loans:*** $2,849,125 (30% need-based, 70% non-need-based). ***Programs:*** FFEL (Subsidized and Unsubsidized Stafford, PLUS), Perkins, college/university.

WORK-STUDY ***Federal work-study:*** *Total amount:* $634,999; 288 jobs averaging $2200. ***State or other work-study/employment:*** *Total amount:* $637,676 (100% non-need-based). 1,002 part-time jobs averaging $636.

ATHLETIC AWARDS *Total amount:* 242,896 (85% need-based, 15% non-need-based).

APPLYING for FINANCIAL AID ***Required financial aid forms:*** FAFSA, institution's own form. ***Financial aid deadline (priority):*** 5/1. ***Notification date:*** Continuous. Students must reply within 2 weeks of notification.

CONTACT Financial Aid Office, Southeastern Louisiana University, SLU 10768, 500 Western Avenue, Hammond, LA 70402, 504-549-2245 or toll-free 800-222-7358. *Fax:* 504-549-5077.

SOUTHEASTERN OKLAHOMA STATE UNIVERSITY

Durant, OK

CONTACT Director, Student Financial Aid, Southeastern Oklahoma State University, Fifth and University Avenues, Durant, OK 74701-0609, 405-924-0121 Ext. 2406 or toll-free 800-435-1327 Ext. 2307.

SOUTHEASTERN UNIVERSITY

Washington, DC

Tuition & fees: $7500 **Average undergraduate aid package: $5775**

ABOUT THE INSTITUTION Independent, coed. Awards: associate, bachelor's, and master's degrees. 12 undergraduate majors. Total enrollment: 1,011. Undergraduates: 508. Freshmen: 95. Federal methodology is used as a basis for awarding need-based institutional aid.

UNDERGRADUATE EXPENSES for 2000–2001 ***Application fee:*** $45. ***Tuition:*** full-time $7200; part-time $200 per credit hour. ***Required fees:*** full-time $300. ***Payment plan:*** installment.

FRESHMAN FINANCIAL AID (Fall 1998) 50 applied for aid; of those 94% were deemed to have need. 100% of freshmen with need received aid; of those 81% had need fully met. *Average percent of need met:* 95% (excluding resources awarded to replace EFC). *Average financial aid package:* $5025 (excluding resources awarded to replace EFC).

UNDERGRADUATE FINANCIAL AID (Fall 1998) 112 applied for aid; of those 96% were deemed to have need. 100% of undergraduates with need received aid; of those 81% had need fully met. *Average percent of need met:* 95% (excluding resources awarded to replace EFC). *Average financial aid package:* $5775 (excluding resources awarded to replace EFC).

GIFT AID (NEED-BASED) ***Total amount:*** $351,066 (96% Federal, 3% state, 1% external sources). ***Receiving aid:*** *Freshmen:* 55% (32); *all full-time undergraduates:* 32% (85). ***Average award:*** Freshmen: $2100; Undergraduates: $2100. ***Scholarships, grants, and awards:*** Federal Pell, FSEOG, state, private, college/university gift aid from institutional funds.

GIFT AID (NON-NEED-BASED) ***Total amount:*** $18,500 (19% institutional, 81% external sources). ***Scholarships, grants, and awards by category:*** *Academic Interests/Achievement:* general academic interests/achievements. *Special Characteristics:* general special characteristics, local/state students. ***Tuition waivers:*** Full or partial for employees or children of employees.

LOANS ***Student loans:*** $2,956,101 (57% need-based, 43% non-need-based). 57% of past graduating class borrowed through all loan programs. ***Average need-based loan:*** Freshmen: $2625; Undergraduates: $3500. ***Parent loans:*** $76,253 (100% non-need-based). ***Programs:*** FFEL (Subsidized and Unsubsidized Stafford, PLUS), college/university.

WORK-STUDY ***Federal work-study:*** *Total amount:* $17,753; 14 jobs averaging $3690.

APPLYING for FINANCIAL AID ***Required financial aid forms:*** FAFSA, institution's own form. ***Financial aid deadline:*** Continuous.

CONTACT Hope Gibbs, Assistant Director of Financial Aid, Southeastern University, 501 I Street, SW, Washington, DC 20024-2788, 202-488-8162 Ext. 234. *E-mail:* hgibbs@admin.seu.edu

SOUTHEAST MISSOURI STATE UNIVERSITY

Cape Girardeau, MO

Tuition & fees (MO res): $3225 **Average undergraduate aid package: $3940**

ABOUT THE INSTITUTION State-supported, coed. Awards: associate, bachelor's, and master's degrees. 90 undergraduate majors. Total enrollment: 8,863. Undergraduates: 7,474. Federal methodology is used as a basis for awarding need-based institutional aid.

UNDERGRADUATE EXPENSES for 1999–2000 ***Application fee:*** $20. ***Tuition, state resident:*** full-time $2979; part-time $99 per credit hour. ***Tuition, nonresident:*** full-time $5559; part-time $185 per credit hour. ***Required fees:*** full-time $246; $8 per credit hour. ***College room and board:*** $4401. Room and board charges vary according to board plan, housing facility, and location. ***Payment plans:*** installment, deferred payment.

FRESHMAN FINANCIAL AID (Fall 1999, est.) 1115 applied for aid; of those 56% were deemed to have need. 100% of freshmen with need received aid; of those 38% had need fully met. *Average financial aid package:* $3410 (excluding resources awarded to replace EFC). 24% of all full-time freshmen had no need and received non-need-based aid.

UNDERGRADUATE FINANCIAL AID (Fall 1999, est.) 2,620 applied for aid; of those 81% were deemed to have need. 100% of undergraduates with need received aid; of those 43% had need fully met. *Average financial aid package:* $3940 (excluding resources awarded to replace EFC). 21% of all full-time undergraduates had no need and received non-need-based aid.

GIFT AID (NEED-BASED) ***Total amount:*** $4,439,261 (59% Federal, 6% state, 28% institutional, 7% external sources). ***Receiving aid:*** *Freshmen:* 24% (341); *all full-time undergraduates:* 23% (1,323). ***Average award:*** Freshmen: $3195; Undergraduates: $2881. ***Scholarships, grants, and awards:*** Federal Pell, FSEOG, state, private, college/university gift aid from institutional funds.

Southeast Missouri State University (continued)

GIFT AID (NON-NEED-BASED) ***Total amount:*** $2,199,918 (10% state, 77% institutional, 13% external sources). ***Receiving aid:*** *Freshmen:* 18% (251); *Undergraduates:* 12% (711). ***Scholarships, grants, and awards by category:*** *Academic Interests/Achievement:* agriculture, biological sciences, business, communication, computer science, education, English, foreign languages, general academic interests/achievements, health fields, home economics, humanities, mathematics, military science, physical sciences, social sciences. *Creative Arts/Performance:* music, theater/drama. *Special Achievements/Activities:* cheerleading/drum major, leadership. *Special Characteristics:* children of faculty/staff, international students, members of minority groups, previous college experience. ***Tuition waivers:*** Full or partial for employees or children of employees, senior citizens. ***ROTC:*** Air Force.

LOANS ***Student loans:*** $9,061,114 (81% need-based, 19% non-need-based). 55% of past graduating class borrowed through all loan programs. Average indebtedness per student: $14,090. ***Average need-based loan:*** Freshmen: $2641; Undergraduates: $3489. ***Parent loans:*** $1,087,547 (56% need-based, 44% non-need-based). ***Programs:*** FFEL (Subsidized and Unsubsidized Stafford, PLUS), Perkins, Federal Nursing, state, college/university.

WORK-STUDY ***Federal work-study:*** *Total amount:* $343,930; 243 jobs averaging $1415. ***State or other work-study/employment:*** *Total amount:* $2,929,549 (100% non-need-based). 777 part-time jobs averaging $3770.

ATHLETIC AWARDS *Total amount:* 1,018,511 (39% need-based, 61% non-need-based).

APPLYING for FINANCIAL AID ***Required financial aid form:*** FAFSA. ***Financial aid deadline (priority):*** 3/1. ***Notification date:*** Continuous beginning 4/1.

CONTACT Karen Walker, Director of Financial Aid Services, Southeast Missouri State University, One University Plaza, Cape Girardeau, MO 63701-4799, 573-651-2840. *Fax:* 573-651-5155.

SOUTHERN ADVENTIST UNIVERSITY

Collegedale, TN

Tuition & fees: $10,620 **Average undergraduate aid package: $9894**

ABOUT THE INSTITUTION Independent Seventh-day Adventist, coed. Awards: associate, bachelor's, and master's degrees. 58 undergraduate majors. Total enrollment: 1,781. Undergraduates: 1,707. Freshmen: 421. Federal methodology is used as a basis for awarding need-based institutional aid.

UNDERGRADUATE EXPENSES for 1999–2000 ***Application fee:*** $25. ***Comprehensive fee:*** $14,350 includes full-time tuition ($10,300), mandatory fees ($320), and room and board ($3730). ***College room only:*** $1780. Full-time tuition and fees vary according to program. Room and board charges vary according to housing facility. ***Part-time tuition:*** $445 per semester hour. ***Part-time fees:*** $160 per term part-time. Part-time tuition and fees vary according to course load and program. ***Payment plans:*** tuition prepayment, installment, deferred payment.

FRESHMAN FINANCIAL AID (Fall 1999, est.) 397 applied for aid; of those 66% were deemed to have need. 100% of freshmen with need received aid; of those 31% had need fully met. *Average percent of need met:* 75% (excluding resources awarded to replace EFC). *Average financial aid package:* $9098 (excluding resources awarded to replace EFC). 34% of all full-time freshmen had no need and received non-need-based aid.

UNDERGRADUATE FINANCIAL AID (Fall 1999, est.) 1,166 applied for aid; of those 66% were deemed to have need. 100% of undergraduates with need received aid; of those 27% had need fully met. *Average percent of need met:* 76% (excluding resources awarded to replace EFC). *Average financial aid package:* $9894 (excluding resources awarded to replace EFC). 34% of all full-time undergraduates had no need and received non-need-based aid.

GIFT AID (NEED-BASED) ***Total amount:*** $3,879,595 (28% Federal, 2% state, 70% institutional). ***Receiving aid:*** *Freshmen:* 62% (247); *all full-time undergraduates:* 60% (697). ***Average award:*** Freshmen: $3977; Undergraduates: $4418. ***Scholarships, grants, and awards:*** Federal Pell, FSEOG, state, private, college/university gift aid from institutional funds.

GIFT AID (NON-NEED-BASED) ***Total amount:*** $1,008,292 (100% institutional). ***Receiving aid:*** *Freshmen:* 2% (7); *Undergraduates:* 1% (13). ***Scholarships, grants, and awards by category:*** *Academic Interests/Achievement:* 1,006 awards ($1,426,168 total): business, communication, education, English, general academic interests/achievements, health fields, mathematics, religion/biblical studies. *Creative Arts/Performance:* 156 awards ($159,556 total): art/fine arts, journalism/publications, music, theater/drama. *Special Achievements/Activities:* 320 awards ($175,719 total): community service, general special achievements/activities, leadership, religious involvement. *Special Characteristics:* children and siblings of alumni, general special characteristics, international students, local/state students, members of minority groups, out-of-state students, siblings of current students, spouses of current students. ***Tuition waivers:*** Full or partial for employees or children of employees, adult students, senior citizens.

LOANS ***Student loans:*** $3,724,048 (92% need-based, 8% non-need-based). 63% of past graduating class borrowed through all loan programs. Average indebtedness per student: $15,600. ***Average need-based loan:*** Freshmen: $3463; Undergraduates: $3912. ***Parent loans:*** $529,257 (36% need-based, 64% non-need-based). ***Programs:*** FFEL (Subsidized and Unsubsidized Stafford, PLUS), Perkins, Federal Nursing, college/university.

WORK-STUDY ***Federal work-study:*** *Total amount:* $1,178,515; 929 jobs available. ***State or other work-study/employment:*** *Total amount:* $79,881 (100% non-need-based). Part-time jobs available.

APPLYING for FINANCIAL AID ***Required financial aid form:*** FAFSA. ***Financial aid deadline (priority):*** 3/1. ***Notification date:*** Continuous. Students must reply within 2 weeks of notification.

CONTACT Mr. Marc Grundy, Director, Student Finance Office, Southern Adventist University, PO Box 370, Collegedale, TN 37315-0370, 423-238-2834 or toll-free 800-768-8437. *Fax:* 423-238-3007.

SOUTHERN ARKANSAS UNIVERSITY–MAGNOLIA

Magnolia, AR

Tuition & fees (AR res): $2232 **Average undergraduate aid package: $5047**

ABOUT THE INSTITUTION State-supported, coed. Awards: associate, bachelor's, and master's degrees. 43 undergraduate majors. Total enrollment: 2,871. Undergraduates: 2,602. Freshmen: 566. Federal methodology is used as a basis for awarding need-based institutional aid.

UNDERGRADUATE EXPENSES for 1999–2000 ***Tuition, state resident:*** full-time $2112; part-time $88 per credit hour. ***Tuition, nonresident:*** full-time $3240; part-time $135 per credit hour. ***Required fees:*** full-time $120; $4 per credit hour. Full-time tuition and fees vary according to course load. Part-time tuition and fees vary according to course load. ***College room and board:*** $2800. ***Payment plans:*** installment, deferred payment.

FRESHMAN FINANCIAL AID (Fall 1999) 396 applied for aid; of those 66% were deemed to have need. 96% of freshmen with need received aid; of those 96% had need fully met. *Average percent of need met:* 100% (excluding resources awarded to replace EFC). *Average financial aid package:* $4917 (excluding resources awarded to replace EFC). 16% of all full-time freshmen had no need and received non-need-based aid.

UNDERGRADUATE FINANCIAL AID (Fall 1999) 1,764 applied for aid; of those 65% were deemed to have need. 86% of undergraduates with need received aid; of those 96% had need fully met. *Average percent of need met:* 100% (excluding resources awarded to replace EFC). *Average financial aid package:* $5047 (excluding resources awarded to replace EFC). 24% of all full-time undergraduates had no need and received non-need-based aid.

GIFT AID (NEED-BASED) ***Total amount:*** $3,109,108 (80% Federal, 20% state). ***Receiving aid:*** *Freshmen:* 42% (235); *all full-time undergraduates:* 41% (909). ***Average award:*** Freshmen: $2896; Undergraduates: $2876. ***Scholarships, grants, and awards:*** Federal Pell, FSEOG, state, private, college/university gift aid from institutional funds.

GIFT AID (NON-NEED-BASED) ***Total amount:*** $1,654,215 (91% institutional, 9% external sources). ***Scholarships, grants, and awards by category:*** *Academic Interests/Achievement:* 19 awards ($43,796 total): agriculture, general academic interests/achievements. *Creative Arts/Performance:* 12 awards ($27,456 total): art/fine arts, music, theater/drama. *Special Achievements/Activities:* 18 awards ($32,432 total): cheerleading/drum major, leadership, rodeo. *Special Characteristics:* 340 awards ($157,174 total): adult students, children of faculty/staff, out-of-state students. ***Tuition waivers:*** Full or partial for children of alumni, employees or children of employees, senior citizens.

LOANS ***Student loans:*** $3,157,070 (61% need-based, 39% non-need-based). 45% of past graduating class borrowed through all loan programs. Average indebtedness per student: $9259. ***Average need-based loan:*** Freshmen: $1735; Undergraduates: $2429. ***Parent loans:*** $78,723 (100% non-need-based). ***Programs:*** FFEL (Subsidized and Unsubsidized Stafford, PLUS), Perkins.

WORK-STUDY ***Federal work-study:*** *Total amount:* $1,884,620; 703 jobs averaging $2681. ***State or other work-study/employment:*** *Total amount:* $551,448 (100% non-need-based). 234 part-time jobs averaging $2357.

ATHLETIC AWARDS *Total amount:* 341,955 (100% non-need-based).

APPLYING for FINANCIAL AID ***Required financial aid form:*** FAFSA. ***Financial aid deadline (priority):*** 7/1. ***Notification date:*** Continuous.

CONTACT Ms. Bronwyn C. Sneed, Director of Student Aid, Southern Arkansas University–Magnolia, PO Box 9344, Magnolia, AR 71754-9344, 870-235-4023. *Fax:* 870-235-5005. *E-mail:* fabronwyn@saumag.edu

SOUTHERN BAPTIST THEOLOGICAL SEMINARY

Louisville, KY

CONTACT Financial Aid Office, Southern Baptist Theological Seminary, 2825 Lexington Road, Louisville, KY 40280-0004, 502-897-4011.

SOUTHERN CALIFORNIA BIBLE COLLEGE & SEMINARY

El Cajon, CA

CONTACT Financial Aid Office, Southern California Bible College & Seminary, 2075 East Madison Avenue, El Cajon, CA 92019, 619-442-9841.

SOUTHERN CALIFORNIA COLLEGE

Costa Mesa, CA

See Vanguard University of Southern California

SOUTHERN CALIFORNIA INSTITUTE OF ARCHITECTURE

Los Angeles, CA

Tuition & fees: N/R **Average undergraduate aid package: N/A**

ABOUT THE INSTITUTION Independent, coed. Awards: bachelor's and master's degrees. 1 undergraduate major. Total enrollment: 430. Undergraduates: 218. Federal methodology is used as a basis for awarding need-based institutional aid.

GIFT AID (NEED-BASED) ***Scholarships, grants, and awards:*** Federal Pell, FSEOG, state, private, college/university gift aid from institutional funds.

GIFT AID (NON-NEED-BASED) ***Tuition waivers:*** Full or partial for employees or children of employees.

LOANS ***Programs:*** FFEL (Subsidized and Unsubsidized Stafford, PLUS), alternative loans.

WORK-STUDY Federal work-study jobs available.

APPLYING for FINANCIAL AID ***Required financial aid forms:*** FAFSA, institution's own form. ***Financial aid deadline (priority):*** 2/26.

CONTACT Financial Aid Office, Southern California Institute of Architecture, 5454 Beethoven Street, Los Angeles, CA 90066-7017, 310-574-1123.

SOUTHERN CHRISTIAN UNIVERSITY

Montgomery, AL

Tuition & fees: $8830 **Average undergraduate aid package: $4200**

ABOUT THE INSTITUTION Independent religious, coed. Awards: bachelor's, master's, doctoral, and first professional degrees. 4 undergraduate majors. Total enrollment: 307. Undergraduates: 97. Federal methodology is used as a basis for awarding need-based institutional aid.

UNDERGRADUATE EXPENSES for 1999–2000 ***Application fee:*** $35. ***Tuition:*** full-time $8280; part-time $230 per semester hour. ***Required fees:*** full-time $550; $275 per term part-time.

FRESHMAN FINANCIAL AID (Fall 1999) 6 applied for aid; of those 100% were deemed to have need. 100% of freshmen with need received aid. *Average percent of need met:* 26% (excluding resources awarded to replace EFC). *Average financial aid package:* $2700 (excluding resources awarded to replace EFC).

UNDERGRADUATE FINANCIAL AID (Fall 1999) 48 applied for aid; of those 96% were deemed to have need. 100% of undergraduates with need received aid. *Average percent of need met:* 38% (excluding resources awarded to replace EFC). *Average financial aid package:* $4200 (excluding resources awarded to replace EFC). 6% of all full-time undergraduates had no need and received non-need-based aid.

GIFT AID (NEED-BASED) ***Total amount:*** $121,700 (45% Federal, 40% institutional, 15% external sources). ***Receiving aid:*** *Freshmen:* 67% (6); *all full-time undergraduates:* 65% (42). ***Average award:*** Freshmen: $7000; Undergraduates: $1800. ***Scholarships, grants, and awards:*** Federal Pell, FSEOG, private, college/university gift aid from institutional funds.

GIFT AID (NON-NEED-BASED) ***Total amount:*** $1500 (100% institutional). ***Receiving aid:*** *Undergraduates:* 6% (4). ***Scholarships, grants, and awards by category:*** *Academic Interests/Achievement:* education, health fields, humanities, religion/biblical studies. *Special Achievements/Activities:* religious involvement. *Special Characteristics:* children of faculty/staff, religious affiliation, veterans.

LOANS ***Student loans:*** $211,700 (94% need-based, 6% non-need-based). 80% of past graduating class borrowed through all loan programs. Average indebtedness per student: $16,500. ***Average need-based loan:*** Freshmen: $1700; Undergraduates: $2400. ***Programs:*** FFEL (Subsidized and Unsubsidized Stafford, PLUS).

WORK-STUDY ***Federal work-study:*** *Total amount:* $5500; 4 jobs averaging $1500.

APPLYING for FINANCIAL AID ***Required financial aid forms:*** FAFSA, institution's own form. ***Financial aid deadline:*** Continuous. ***Notification date:*** 8/31. Students must reply within 2 weeks of notification.

CONTACT Mr. Steve Garrett, Director of Financial Aid, Southern Christian University, 1200 Taylor Road, Montgomery, AL 36117, 334-387-3877 Ext. 227 or toll-free 800-351-4040. *Fax:* 334-387-3878. *E-mail:* stevegarrett@southernchristian.edu

SOUTHERN CONNECTICUT STATE UNIVERSITY

New Haven, CT

Tuition & fees (CT res): $3773 **Average undergraduate aid package: $6130**

ABOUT THE INSTITUTION State-supported, coed. Awards: associate, bachelor's, and master's degrees and post-master's certificates. 56 undergraduate majors. Total enrollment: 11,264. Undergraduates: 7,445. Freshmen: 1,117. Federal methodology is used as a basis for awarding need-based institutional aid.

UNDERGRADUATE EXPENSES for 1999–2000 ***Application fee:*** $40. ***Tuition, state resident:*** full-time $2124; part-time $166 per credit. ***Tuition, nonresident:*** full-time $7802; part-time $166 per credit. ***Required fees:*** full-time $1649; $45 per term part-time. Full-time tuition and fees vary

Southern Connecticut State University (continued)

according to reciprocity agreements. ***College room and board:*** $5825; ***room only:*** $3115. Room and board charges vary according to housing facility. ***Payment plan:*** installment.

FRESHMAN FINANCIAL AID (Fall 1998) 816 applied for aid; of those 55% were deemed to have need. 100% of freshmen with need received aid; of those 100% had need fully met. *Average percent of need met:* 64% (excluding resources awarded to replace EFC). *Average financial aid package:* $4525 (excluding resources awarded to replace EFC). 3% of all full-time freshmen had no need and received non-need-based aid.

UNDERGRADUATE FINANCIAL AID (Fall 1998) 4,672 applied for aid; of those 79% were deemed to have need. 100% of undergraduates with need received aid; of those 63% had need fully met. *Average percent of need met:* 64% (excluding resources awarded to replace EFC). *Average financial aid package:* $6130 (excluding resources awarded to replace EFC). 2% of all full-time undergraduates had no need and received non-need-based aid.

GIFT AID (NEED-BASED) ***Total amount:*** $7,256,089 (36% Federal, 21% state, 32% institutional, 11% external sources). ***Receiving aid:*** *Freshmen:* 39% (424); *all full-time undergraduates:* 39% (2,169). ***Scholarships, grants, and awards:*** Federal Pell, FSEOG, state, college/university gift aid from institutional funds.

GIFT AID (NON-NEED-BASED) ***Total amount:*** $436,146 (100% institutional). ***Receiving aid:*** *Freshmen:* 4% (40); *Undergraduates:* 3% (146). ***Scholarships, grants, and awards by category:*** *Academic Interests/Achievement:* general academic interests/achievements. *Special Characteristics:* children of faculty/staff, veterans. ***Tuition waivers:*** Full or partial for employees or children of employees, senior citizens. ***ROTC:*** Army cooperative, Air Force cooperative.

LOANS ***Student loans:*** $15,275,335 (100% need-based). ***Parent loans:*** $298,350 (100% non-need-based). ***Programs:*** FFEL (Subsidized and Unsubsidized Stafford, PLUS), Perkins.

WORK-STUDY ***Federal work-study:*** *Total amount:* $278,000; jobs available. ***State or other work-study/employment:*** *Total amount:* $1,173,695 (2% need-based, 98% non-need-based). Part-time jobs available.

ATHLETIC AWARDS *Total amount:* 387,954 (100% non-need-based).

APPLYING for FINANCIAL AID ***Required financial aid forms:*** FAFSA, institution's own form, business/farm supplement, parent and student federal income tax forms. ***Financial aid deadline:*** 4/15. ***Notification date:*** Continuous beginning 4/21. Students must reply within 2 weeks of notification.

CONTACT Financial Aid Office, Southern Connecticut State University, 501 Crescent Street, New Haven, CT 06515-1355, 203-392-5222. *Fax:* 203-392-5229.

SOUTHERN ILLINOIS UNIVERSITY CARBONDALE

Carbondale, IL

Tuition & fees (IL res): $3936 **Average undergraduate aid package: $6217**

ABOUT THE INSTITUTION State-supported, coed. Awards: associate, bachelor's, master's, doctoral, and first professional degrees and post-bachelor's, post-master's, and first-professional certificates. 85 undergraduate majors. Total enrollment: 22,323. Undergraduates: 17,829. Freshmen: 2,595. Federal methodology is used as a basis for awarding need-based institutional aid.

UNDERGRADUATE EXPENSES for 1999–2000 ***Tuition, state resident:*** full-time $2865; part-time $96 per semester hour. ***Tuition, nonresident:*** full-time $5730; part-time $191 per semester hour. ***Required fees:*** full-time $1071; $36 per semester hour. Full-time tuition and fees vary according to course load. Part-time tuition and fees vary according to course load. ***College room and board:*** $3889. Room and board charges vary according to board plan and housing facility. ***Payment plan:*** installment.

FRESHMAN FINANCIAL AID (Fall 1998) 1809 applied for aid; of those 80% were deemed to have need. 96% of freshmen with need received aid; of those 26% had need fully met. *Average percent of need met:* 77% (excluding resources awarded to replace EFC). *Average financial aid package:* $5598 (excluding resources awarded to replace EFC). 18% of all full-time freshmen had no need and received non-need-based aid.

UNDERGRADUATE FINANCIAL AID (Fall 1998) 10,773 applied for aid; of those 85% were deemed to have need. 97% of undergraduates with need received aid; of those 42% had need fully met. *Average percent of need met:* 84% (excluding resources awarded to replace EFC). *Average financial aid package:* $6217 (excluding resources awarded to replace EFC). 21% of all full-time undergraduates had no need and received non-need-based aid.

GIFT AID (NEED-BASED) ***Total amount:*** $33,033,938 (42% Federal, 55% state, 2% institutional, 1% external sources). ***Receiving aid:*** *Freshmen:* 38% (912); *all full-time undergraduates:* 42% (6,513). ***Average award:*** Freshmen: $4716; Undergraduates: $4332. ***Scholarships, grants, and awards:*** Federal Pell, FSEOG, state, private, college/university gift aid from institutional funds.

GIFT AID (NON-NEED-BASED) ***Total amount:*** $5,241,255 (26% Federal, 37% state, 13% institutional, 24% external sources). ***Receiving aid:*** *Freshmen:* 12% (303); *Undergraduates:* 13% (1,986). ***Scholarships, grants, and awards by category:*** *Academic Interests/Achievement:* 764 awards ($653,230 total): agriculture, architecture, area/ethnic studies, biological sciences, business, communication, computer science, education, engineering/technologies, English, foreign languages, general academic interests/achievements, health fields, home economics, humanities, international studies, mathematics, military science, physical sciences, premedicine, religion/biblical studies, social sciences. *Creative Arts/Performance:* 27 awards ($17,281 total): applied art and design, art/fine arts, cinema/film/broadcasting, creative writing, dance, debating, general creative arts/performance, journalism/publications, music, performing arts, theater/drama. *Special Achievements/Activities:* 41 awards ($13,800 total): cheerleading/drum major, community service, general special achievements/activities, leadership. *Special Characteristics:* 243 awards ($259,056 total): children and siblings of alumni, children of educators, children of faculty/staff, children of public servants, children with a deceased or disabled parent, general special characteristics, handicapped students, international students, public servants, spouses of deceased or disabled public servants, veterans. ***Tuition waivers:*** Full or partial for employees or children of employees, senior citizens. ***ROTC:*** Army, Air Force.

LOANS ***Student loans:*** $29,389,669 (75% need-based, 25% non-need-based). Average indebtedness per student: $11,475. ***Average need-based loan:*** Freshmen: $2253; Undergraduates: $2892. ***Parent loans:*** $2,247,064 (18% need-based, 82% non-need-based). ***Programs:*** Federal Direct (Subsidized and Unsubsidized Stafford, PLUS), Perkins, college/university.

WORK-STUDY ***Federal work-study:*** *Total amount:* $2,489,928; 2,296 jobs averaging $1084. ***State or other work-study/employment:*** *Total amount:* $5,249,173 (15% need-based, 85% non-need-based). 4,401 part-time jobs averaging $1193.

ATHLETIC AWARDS *Total amount:* 1,547,671 (31% need-based, 69% non-need-based).

APPLYING for FINANCIAL AID ***Required financial aid form:*** FAFSA. ***Financial aid deadline (priority):*** 4/1. ***Notification date:*** Continuous. Students must reply within 3 weeks of notification.

CONTACT Mr. Dan Mann, Interim Director of Financial Aid, Southern Illinois University Carbondale, Woody Hall, Third Floor, B-Wing, Carbondale, IL 62901-4702, 618-453-4334 Ext. 21. *Fax:* 618-453-4606. *E-mail:* dmann@siu.edu

SOUTHERN ILLINOIS UNIVERSITY EDWARDSVILLE

Edwardsville, IL

Tuition & fees (IL res): $2827 **Average undergraduate aid package: $9553**

ABOUT THE INSTITUTION State-supported, coed. Awards: bachelor's, master's, and first professional degrees and first-professional certificates. 45 undergraduate majors. Total enrollment: 11,877. Undergraduates: 9,313. Federal methodology is used as a basis for awarding need-based institutional aid.

UNDERGRADUATE EXPENSES for 2000–2001 ***Tuition, state resident:*** full-time $2208. ***Tuition, nonresident:*** full-time $4416. ***Required fees:*** full-time $619. Full-time tuition and fees vary according to course load. Part-time tuition and fees vary according to course load. ***College room and board:*** $4290; ***room only:*** $2666. Room and board charges vary according to board plan and housing facility. ***Payment plan:*** installment.

FRESHMAN FINANCIAL AID (Fall 1998) 600 applied for aid; of those 97% were deemed to have need. 100% of freshmen with need received aid; of those 44% had need fully met. *Average percent of need met:* 98% (excluding resources awarded to replace EFC). *Average financial aid package:* $7829 (excluding resources awarded to replace EFC). 7% of all full-time freshmen had no need and received non-need-based aid.

UNDERGRADUATE FINANCIAL AID (Fall 1998) 3,004 applied for aid; of those 95% were deemed to have need. 100% of undergraduates with need received aid; of those 52% had need fully met. *Average percent of need met:* 98% (excluding resources awarded to replace EFC). *Average financial aid package:* $9553 (excluding resources awarded to replace EFC). 6% of all full-time undergraduates had no need and received non-need-based aid.

GIFT AID (NEED-BASED) ***Total amount:*** $11,502,507 (50% Federal, 44% state, 1% institutional, 5% external sources). ***Receiving aid:*** *Freshmen:* 35% (498); *all full-time undergraduates:* 35% (2,558). ***Average award:*** Freshmen: $5284; Undergraduates: $6053. ***Scholarships, grants, and awards:*** Federal Pell, FSEOG, state, private, college/university gift aid from institutional funds.

GIFT AID (NON-NEED-BASED) ***Total amount:*** $2,886,468 (10% Federal, 58% state, 32% institutional). ***Scholarships, grants, and awards by category:*** *Academic Interests/Achievement:* general academic interests/achievements. *Creative Arts/Performance:* art/fine arts, music, theater/drama. ***Tuition waivers:*** Full or partial for employees or children of employees. ***ROTC:*** Army, Air Force.

LOANS ***Student loans:*** $21,780,263 (59% need-based, 41% non-need-based). 60% of past graduating class borrowed through all loan programs. ***Average need-based loan:*** Freshmen: $2335; Undergraduates: $3300. ***Parent loans:*** $707,582 (100% non-need-based). ***Programs:*** Federal Direct (Subsidized and Unsubsidized Stafford, PLUS), Perkins.

WORK-STUDY ***Federal work-study:*** *Total amount:* $770,004; 596 jobs averaging $1292. ***State or other work-study/employment:*** *Total amount:* $2,506,629 (100% non-need-based). 1,617 part-time jobs averaging $1550.

ATHLETIC AWARDS *Total amount:* 274,634 (100% non-need-based).

APPLYING for FINANCIAL AID ***Required financial aid form:*** FAFSA. ***Financial aid deadline (priority):*** 3/1. ***Notification date:*** Continuous beginning 4/15. Students must reply within 2 weeks of notification.

CONTACT Ms. Marian Smithson, Director of Financial Aid, Southern Illinois University Edwardsville, Box 1060, Rendleman Hall, Room 2308, Edwardsville, IL 62026-1060, 618-650-3880 or toll-free 800-447-SIUE. *Fax:* 618-650-3885.

SOUTHERN METHODIST COLLEGE

Orangeburg, SC

CONTACT Financial Aid Office, Southern Methodist College, 541 Broughton Stret, PO Box 1027, Orangeburg, SC 29116-1027, 803-534-7826.

SOUTHERN METHODIST UNIVERSITY

Dallas, TX

Tuition & fees: $18,510 **Average undergraduate aid package: $19,298**

ABOUT THE INSTITUTION Independent religious, coed. Awards: bachelor's, master's, doctoral, and first professional degrees and post-bachelor's certificates. 65 undergraduate majors. Total enrollment: 10,361. Undergraduates: 5,552. Freshmen: 1,331. Both federal and institutional methodology are used as a basis for awarding need-based institutional aid.

UNDERGRADUATE EXPENSES for 1999–2000 ***Application fee:*** $40. ***Comprehensive fee:*** $25,411 includes full-time tuition ($16,422), mandatory fees ($2088), and room and board ($6901). Room and board charges vary according to board plan and housing facility. ***Part-time tuition:*** $686 per credit hour. ***Part-time fees:*** $88 per credit hour. Part-time tuition and fees vary according to class time and course load. ***Payment plans:*** tuition prepayment, installment.

FRESHMAN FINANCIAL AID (Fall 1999) 760 applied for aid; of those 82% were deemed to have need. 100% of freshmen with need received aid; of those 31% had need fully met. *Average percent of need met:* 92% (excluding resources awarded to replace EFC). *Average financial aid package:* $19,479 (excluding resources awarded to replace EFC). 33% of all full-time freshmen had no need and received non-need-based aid.

UNDERGRADUATE FINANCIAL AID (Fall 1999) 2,749 applied for aid; of those 89% were deemed to have need. 100% of undergraduates with need received aid; of those 34% had need fully met. *Average percent of need met:* 91% (excluding resources awarded to replace EFC). *Average financial aid package:* $19,298 (excluding resources awarded to replace EFC). 28% of all full-time undergraduates had no need and received non-need-based aid.

GIFT AID (NEED-BASED) ***Total amount:*** $18,576,445 (14% Federal, 20% state, 66% institutional). ***Receiving aid:*** *Freshmen:* 35% (470); *all full-time undergraduates:* 35% (1,820). ***Average award:*** Freshmen: $12,883; Undergraduates: $11,190. ***Scholarships, grants, and awards:*** Federal Pell, FSEOG, state, private, college/university gift aid from institutional funds.

GIFT AID (NON-NEED-BASED) ***Total amount:*** $17,297,427 (95% institutional, 5% external sources). ***Receiving aid:*** *Freshmen:* 37% (486); *Undergraduates:* 30% (1,581). ***Scholarships, grants, and awards by category:*** *Academic Interests/Achievement:* area/ethnic studies, biological sciences, business, communication, computer science, engineering/technologies, English, foreign languages, general academic interests/achievements, humanities, international studies, mathematics, physical sciences, religion/biblical studies, social sciences. *Creative Arts/Performance:* art/fine arts, cinema/film/broadcasting, creative writing, dance, journalism/publications, music, theater/drama. *Special Characteristics:* children of faculty/staff, relatives of clergy. ***Tuition waivers:*** Full or partial for employees or children of employees. ***ROTC:*** Army, Air Force cooperative.

LOANS ***Student loans:*** $14,520,328 (48% need-based, 52% non-need-based). ***Average need-based loan:*** Freshmen: $3253; Undergraduates: $5045. ***Parent loans:*** $3,728,041 (100% non-need-based). ***Programs:*** Federal Direct (Subsidized and Unsubsidized Stafford, PLUS), Perkins, state, college/university.

WORK-STUDY ***Federal work-study:*** *Total amount:* $2,756,341; jobs available. ***State or other work-study/employment:*** *Total amount:* $131,693 (77% need-based, 23% non-need-based). Part-time jobs available.

ATHLETIC AWARDS *Total amount:* 5,133,371 (100% non-need-based).

APPLYING for FINANCIAL AID ***Required financial aid form:*** FAFSA. ***Financial aid deadline (priority):*** 2/1. ***Notification date:*** Continuous beginning 3/15. Students must reply within 4 weeks of notification.

CONTACT Mr. Michael A. Novak, Executive Director of Financial Aid, Southern Methodist University, Box 750196, Dallas, TX 75275, 214-768-2414 or toll-free 800-323-0672. *Fax:* 214-768-0202.

SOUTHERN NAZARENE UNIVERSITY

Bethany, OK

Tuition & fees: $9380 **Average undergraduate aid package: N/A**

ABOUT THE INSTITUTION Independent Nazarene, coed. Awards: associate, bachelor's, and master's degrees. 71 undergraduate majors. Total enrollment: 1,950. Undergraduates: 1,652. Freshmen: 332. Federal methodology is used as a basis for awarding need-based institutional aid.

UNDERGRADUATE EXPENSES for 1999–2000 ***Application fee:*** $25. ***Comprehensive fee:*** $13,696 includes full-time tuition ($8850), mandatory fees ($530), and room and board ($4316). ***College room only:*** $2096. Room and board charges vary according to board plan and housing facility. ***Part-time tuition:*** $295 per credit hour. ***Part-time fees:*** $23 per credit. Part-time tuition and fees vary according to course load. ***Payment plans:*** tuition prepayment, installment.

FRESHMAN FINANCIAL AID (Fall 1999, est.) 389 applied for aid; of those 95% were deemed to have need. 96% of freshmen with need received aid.

Southern Nazarene University (continued)

UNDERGRADUATE FINANCIAL AID (Fall 1999, est.) 1,461 applied for aid; of those 94% were deemed to have need. 96% of undergraduates with need received aid.

GIFT AID (NEED-BASED) ***Total amount:*** $5,158,941 (23% Federal, 4% state, 66% institutional, 7% external sources). ***Scholarships, grants, and awards:*** Federal Pell, FSEOG, state, private, college/university gift aid from institutional funds.

GIFT AID (NON-NEED-BASED) ***Scholarships, grants, and awards by category:*** *Academic Interests/Achievement:* biological sciences, business, communication, education, English, general academic interests/ achievements, mathematics, religion/biblical studies. *Creative Arts/ Performance:* music, performing arts. *Special Characteristics:* children and siblings of alumni, children of faculty/staff, local/state students, religious affiliation. ***Tuition waivers:*** Full or partial for employees or children of employees, senior citizens. ***ROTC:*** Army cooperative, Air Force cooperative.

LOANS ***Student loans:*** $6,467,227 (100% need-based). ***Parent loans:*** $1,522,252 (100% need-based). ***Programs:*** FFEL (Subsidized and Unsubsidized Stafford, PLUS), Perkins.

WORK-STUDY ***Federal work-study:*** *Total amount:* $185,000; jobs available. ***State or other work-study/employment:*** *Total amount:* $20,000 (100% need-based). Part-time jobs available.

ATHLETIC AWARDS *Total amount:* 1,161,550 (100% need-based).

APPLYING for FINANCIAL AID ***Required financial aid forms:*** FAFSA, institution's own form. ***Financial aid deadline (priority):*** 3/1. ***Notification date:*** Continuous beginning 4/15. Students must reply within 2 weeks of notification.

CONTACT Ms. Diana Lee, Director of Financial Assistance, Southern Nazarene University, 6729 Northwest 39 Expressway, Bethany, OK 73008-2694, 405-491-6310 or toll-free 800-648-9899. *Fax:* 405-491-6320. *E-mail:* dlee@snu.edu

SOUTHERN OREGON UNIVERSITY

Ashland, OR

Tuition & fees (OR res): $3234 **Average undergraduate aid package: $6892**

ABOUT THE INSTITUTION State-supported, coed. Awards: bachelor's and master's degrees. 38 undergraduate majors. Total enrollment: 5,742. Undergraduates: 5,077. Freshmen: 746. Federal methodology is used as a basis for awarding need-based institutional aid.

UNDERGRADUATE EXPENSES for 1999–2000 ***Application fee:*** $50. ***Tuition, state resident:*** full-time $3234; part-time $518 per term. ***Tuition, nonresident:*** full-time $9897; part-time $518 per term. Full-time tuition and fees vary according to course load, location, and reciprocity agreements. Part-time tuition and fees vary according to course load, location, and reciprocity agreements. ***College room and board:*** $4658. Room and board charges vary according to board plan and housing facility. ***Payment plan:*** deferred payment.

FRESHMAN FINANCIAL AID (Fall 1999) 641 applied for aid; of those 85% were deemed to have need. 100% of freshmen with need received aid; of those 20% had need fully met. *Average percent of need met:* 59% (excluding resources awarded to replace EFC). *Average financial aid package:* $5819 (excluding resources awarded to replace EFC). 15% of all full-time freshmen had no need and received non-need-based aid.

UNDERGRADUATE FINANCIAL AID (Fall 1999) 2,814 applied for aid; of those 89% were deemed to have need. 100% of undergraduates with need received aid; of those 26% had need fully met. *Average percent of need met:* 66% (excluding resources awarded to replace EFC). *Average financial aid package:* $6892 (excluding resources awarded to replace EFC). 13% of all full-time undergraduates had no need and received non-need-based aid.

GIFT AID (NEED-BASED) ***Total amount:*** $7,155,981 (68% Federal, 14% state, 12% institutional, 6% external sources). ***Receiving aid:*** *Freshmen:* 52% (457); *all full-time undergraduates:* 58% (2,097). ***Average award:*** Freshmen: $3178; Undergraduates: $2935. ***Scholarships, grants, and awards:*** Federal Pell, FSEOG, state, private, college/university gift aid from institutional funds.

GIFT AID (NON-NEED-BASED) ***Total amount:*** $481,957 (1% Federal, 52% institutional, 47% external sources). ***Receiving aid:*** *Freshmen:* 3% (26); *Undergraduates:* 2% (69). ***Scholarships, grants, and awards by category:*** *Academic Interests/Achievement:* 4,009 awards ($1,242,191 total): biological sciences, business, education, English, general academic interests/ achievements, mathematics, physical sciences, social sciences. *Creative Arts/Performance:* 35 awards ($20,515 total): art/fine arts, music, theater/ drama. *Special Achievements/Activities:* 3 awards ($2400 total): general special achievements/activities, leadership, memberships. *Special Characteristics:* 460 awards ($2,285,000 total): members of minority groups, out-of-state students. ***Tuition waivers:*** Full or partial for employees or children of employees, senior citizens.

LOANS ***Student loans:*** $13,378,891 (84% need-based, 16% non-need-based). 57% of past graduating class borrowed through all loan programs. Average indebtedness per student: $13,404. ***Average need-based loan:*** Freshmen: $2495; Undergraduates: $3761. ***Parent loans:*** $3,298,694 (38% need-based, 62% non-need-based). ***Programs:*** Federal Direct (Subsidized and Unsubsidized Stafford, PLUS), Perkins, college/university.

WORK-STUDY ***Federal work-study:*** *Total amount:* $546,221; 553 jobs available.

ATHLETIC AWARDS *Total amount:* 63,200 (61% need-based, 39% non-need-based).

APPLYING for FINANCIAL AID ***Required financial aid form:*** FAFSA. ***Financial aid deadline (priority):*** 3/1. ***Notification date:*** Continuous beginning 4/1. Students must reply within 3 weeks of notification.

CONTACT Ms. Constance Alexander, Director of Financial Aid, Southern Oregon University, 1250 Siskiyou Boulevard, Ashland, OR 97520-5006, 541-552-6161 or toll-free 800-482-SOSC Ext. 6411 (in-state). *Fax:* 541-552-6035. *E-mail:* alexand@sou.edu

SOUTHERN POLYTECHNIC STATE UNIVERSITY

Marietta, GA

Tuition & fees (GA res): $2134 **Average undergraduate aid package: $4082**

ABOUT THE INSTITUTION State-supported, coed. Awards: associate, bachelor's, and master's degrees and post-bachelor's certificates. 16 undergraduate majors. Total enrollment: 3,628. Undergraduates: 3,008. Freshmen: 384. Federal methodology is used as a basis for awarding need-based institutional aid.

UNDERGRADUATE EXPENSES for 1999–2000 ***Application fee:*** $20. ***Tuition, state resident:*** full-time $1808; part-time $76 per hour. ***Tuition, nonresident:*** full-time $7232; part-time $302 per hour. ***Required fees:*** full-time $326; $163 per term part-time. Part-time tuition and fees vary according to course load. ***College room and board:*** $4452; ***room only:*** $2142.

FRESHMAN FINANCIAL AID (Fall 1999, est.) 238 applied for aid; of those 52% were deemed to have need. 56% of freshmen with need received aid; of those 31% had need fully met. *Average percent of need met:* 65% (excluding resources awarded to replace EFC). *Average financial aid package:* $3460 (excluding resources awarded to replace EFC). 9% of all full-time freshmen had no need and received non-need-based aid.

UNDERGRADUATE FINANCIAL AID (Fall 1999, est.) 1,369 applied for aid; of those 78% were deemed to have need. 72% of undergraduates with need received aid; of those 35% had need fully met. *Average percent of need met:* 78% (excluding resources awarded to replace EFC). *Average financial aid package:* $4082 (excluding resources awarded to replace EFC). 15% of all full-time undergraduates had no need and received non-need-based aid.

GIFT AID (NEED-BASED) ***Total amount:*** $1,417,752 (99% Federal, 1% institutional). ***Receiving aid:*** *Freshmen:* 8% (29); *all full-time undergraduates:* 17% (308). ***Average award:*** Freshmen: $1540; Undergraduates: $2270. ***Scholarships, grants, and awards:*** Federal Pell, FSEOG, state, private, college/university gift aid from institutional funds.

GIFT AID (NON-NEED-BASED) ***Total amount:*** $1,839,608 (86% state, 9% institutional, 5% external sources). ***Receiving aid:*** *Freshmen:* 15% (57); *Undergraduates:* 13% (231). ***Scholarships, grants, and awards by category:*** *Academic Interests/Achievement:* 16 awards ($20,000 total): general academic interests/achievements. ***Tuition waivers:*** Full or partial for senior citizens. ***ROTC:*** Army cooperative, Naval cooperative, Air Force cooperative.

LOANS ***Student loans:*** $6,518,143 (56% need-based, 44% non-need-based). Average indebtedness per student: $16,585. ***Average need-based loan:*** Freshmen: $2292; Undergraduates: $3572. ***Parent loans:*** $60,307 (100% non-need-based). ***Programs:*** Federal Direct (Subsidized and Unsubsidized Stafford, PLUS), Perkins, college/university.

WORK-STUDY ***Federal work-study:*** *Total amount:* $53,220; 30 jobs averaging $1774.

ATHLETIC AWARDS *Total amount:* 55,970 (100% non-need-based).

APPLYING for FINANCIAL AID ***Required financial aid form:*** FAFSA. ***Financial aid deadline (priority):*** 3/15. ***Notification date:*** Continuous beginning 5/15. Students must reply within 2 weeks of notification.

CONTACT Dr. Emerelle McNair, Director of Financial Aid, Southern Polytechnic State University, 1100 South Marietta Parkway, Marietta, GA 30060-2896, 770-528-7290 or toll-free 800-635-3204. *Fax:* 770-528-7301. *E-mail:* emcnair@spsu.edu

SOUTHERN UNIVERSITY AND AGRICULTURAL AND MECHANICAL COLLEGE

Baton Rouge, LA

Tuition & fees (LA res): $2286 **Average undergraduate aid package: N/A**

ABOUT THE INSTITUTION State-supported, coed. Awards: associate, bachelor's, master's, doctoral, and first professional degrees. 40 undergraduate majors. Total enrollment: 9,345. Undergraduates: 7,797. Federal methodology is used as a basis for awarding need-based institutional aid.

UNDERGRADUATE EXPENSES for 1999–2000 ***Application fee:*** $5. ***One-time required fee:*** $20. ***Tuition, state resident:*** full-time $2286; part-time $646 per term. ***Tuition, nonresident:*** full-time $5690. Part-time tuition and fees vary according to course load and location. ***College room and board:*** $3082. Room and board charges vary according to board plan and housing facility.

GIFT AID (NEED-BASED) ***Scholarships, grants, and awards:*** Federal Pell, FSEOG, state, private, college/university gift aid from institutional funds.

GIFT AID (NON-NEED-BASED) ***Scholarships, grants, and awards by category:*** *Academic Interests/Achievement:* general academic interests/achievements. ***Tuition waivers:*** Full or partial for children of alumni, employees or children of employees. ***ROTC:*** Army, Naval, Air Force cooperative.

LOANS ***Programs:*** Federal Direct (Subsidized and Unsubsidized Stafford, PLUS), FFEL (Subsidized and Unsubsidized Stafford, PLUS), college/university.

WORK-STUDY Federal work-study jobs available.

APPLYING for FINANCIAL AID ***Required financial aid form:*** FAFSA. ***Financial aid deadline (priority):*** 4/15.

CONTACT Mrs. Debra Ephrom, Director of Financial Aid, Southern University and Agricultural and Mechanical College, Baton Rouge, LA 70813, 225-771-2790 or toll-free 800-256-1531 (in-state). *Fax:* 225-771-5898.

SOUTHERN UNIVERSITY AT NEW ORLEANS

New Orleans, LA

Tuition & fees: N/R **Average undergraduate aid package: N/A**

ABOUT THE INSTITUTION State-supported, coed. Awards: associate, bachelor's, and master's degrees. 20 undergraduate majors.

GIFT AID (NEED-BASED) ***Scholarships, grants, and awards:*** Federal Pell, FSEOG, state.

GIFT AID (NON-NEED-BASED) ***Scholarships, grants, and awards by category:*** *Academic Interests/Achievement:* biological sciences, physical sciences. *Creative Arts/Performance:* music. ***ROTC:*** Army cooperative, Air Force cooperative.

LOANS ***Programs:*** Federal Direct (Subsidized and Unsubsidized Stafford), FFEL (Subsidized and Unsubsidized Stafford).

WORK-STUDY Federal work-study jobs available.

APPLYING for FINANCIAL AID ***Required financial aid form:*** FAFSA. ***Financial aid deadline (priority):*** 4/15.

CONTACT Director of Financial Aid, Southern University at New Orleans, 6400 Press Drive, New Orleans, LA 70126, 504-286-5000.

SOUTHERN UTAH UNIVERSITY

Cedar City, UT

Tuition & fees (UT res): $1965 **Average undergraduate aid package: $5148**

ABOUT THE INSTITUTION State-supported, coed. Awards: associate, bachelor's, and master's degrees. 49 undergraduate majors. Total enrollment: 6,025. Undergraduates: 5,867. Freshmen: 841. Federal methodology is used as a basis for awarding need-based institutional aid.

UNDERGRADUATE EXPENSES for 1999–2000 ***Application fee:*** $25. ***Tuition, state resident:*** full-time $1524; part-time $78 per credit hour. ***Tuition, nonresident:*** full-time $5754; part-time $1729 per term. ***Required fees:*** full-time $441; $148 per term part-time. Part-time tuition and fees vary according to course load. ***College room and board:*** $2520. Room and board charges vary according to board plan and housing facility.

FRESHMAN FINANCIAL AID (Fall 1998) 839 applied for aid; of those 56% were deemed to have need. 90% of freshmen with need received aid; of those 6% had need fully met. *Average percent of need met:* 60% (excluding resources awarded to replace EFC). *Average financial aid package:* $3447 (excluding resources awarded to replace EFC). 10% of all full-time freshmen had no need and received non-need-based aid.

UNDERGRADUATE FINANCIAL AID (Fall 1998) 3,011 applied for aid; of those 74% were deemed to have need. 97% of undergraduates with need received aid; of those 9% had need fully met. *Average percent of need met:* 74% (excluding resources awarded to replace EFC). *Average financial aid package:* $5148 (excluding resources awarded to replace EFC). 10% of all full-time undergraduates had no need and received non-need-based aid.

GIFT AID (NEED-BASED) ***Total amount:*** $4,855,161 (98% Federal, 2% state). ***Receiving aid:*** *Freshmen:* 26% (281); *all full-time undergraduates:* 47% (1,603). ***Average award:*** Freshmen: $1852; Undergraduates: $2324. ***Scholarships, grants, and awards:*** Federal Pell, FSEOG, state, private, college/university gift aid from institutional funds.

GIFT AID (NON-NEED-BASED) ***Total amount:*** $1,672,237 (2% Federal, 38% state, 36% institutional, 24% external sources). ***Receiving aid:*** *Freshmen:* 11% (122); *Undergraduates:* 20% (667). ***Scholarships, grants, and awards by category:*** *Academic Interests/Achievement:* business, communication, education, general academic interests/achievements. *Creative Arts/Performance:* dance, general creative arts/performance, journalism/publications, music, performing arts, theater/drama. *Special Achievements/Activities:* cheerleading/drum major, general special achievements/activities, leadership. *Special Characteristics:* ethnic background. ***Tuition waivers:*** Full or partial for employees or children of employees, senior citizens.

LOANS ***Student loans:*** $7,718,115 (93% need-based, 7% non-need-based). 58% of past graduating class borrowed through all loan programs. Average indebtedness per student: $10,712. ***Average need-based loan:*** Freshmen: $2167; Undergraduates: $3966. ***Parent loans:*** $292,438 (100% need-based). ***Programs:*** FFEL (Subsidized and Unsubsidized Stafford, PLUS), Perkins, college/university.

WORK-STUDY ***Federal work-study:*** *Total amount:* $290,022; jobs available. ***State or other work-study/employment:*** *Total amount:* $88,902 (100% need-based). Part-time jobs available.

ATHLETIC AWARDS *Total amount:* 704,411 (100% non-need-based).

Southern Utah University (continued)

APPLYING for FINANCIAL AID ***Required financial aid forms:*** FAFSA, institution's own form, institutional verification form. ***Financial aid deadline:*** Continuous. ***Notification date:*** Continuous.

CONTACT Mr. Rex Michie, Director of Financial Aid, Southern Utah University, 351 West Center Street, Cedar City, UT 84720-2498, 435-586-7735.

SOUTHERN VERMONT COLLEGE

Bennington, VT

Tuition & fees: $10,990 **Average undergraduate aid package: $11,505**

ABOUT THE INSTITUTION Independent, coed. Awards: associate and bachelor's degrees. 18 undergraduate majors. Total enrollment: 515. Undergraduates: 515. Freshmen: 83. Both federal and institutional methodology are used as a basis for awarding need-based institutional aid.

UNDERGRADUATE EXPENSES for 1999–2000 ***Application fee:*** $25. ***Comprehensive fee:*** $16,340 includes full-time tuition ($10,990) and room and board ($5350). ***College room only:*** $2560. Room and board charges vary according to board plan. ***Part-time tuition:*** $265 per credit. Part-time tuition and fees vary according to course load. ***Payment plans:*** installment, deferred payment.

FRESHMAN FINANCIAL AID (Fall 1999) 74 applied for aid; of those 96% were deemed to have need. 100% of freshmen with need received aid; of those 100% had need fully met. *Average percent of need met:* 98% (excluding resources awarded to replace EFC). *Average financial aid package:* $14,056 (excluding resources awarded to replace EFC). 12% of all full-time freshmen had no need and received non-need-based aid.

UNDERGRADUATE FINANCIAL AID (Fall 1999) 262 applied for aid; of those 98% were deemed to have need. 100% of undergraduates with need received aid; of those 100% had need fully met. *Average percent of need met:* 97% (excluding resources awarded to replace EFC). *Average financial aid package:* $11,505 (excluding resources awarded to replace EFC). 7% of all full-time undergraduates had no need and received non-need-based aid.

GIFT AID (NEED-BASED) ***Total amount:*** $2,092,647 (22% Federal, 9% state, 66% institutional, 3% external sources). ***Receiving aid:*** *Freshmen:* 80% (65); *all full-time undergraduates:* 71% (236). ***Average award:*** Freshmen: $8636; Undergraduates: $7399. ***Scholarships, grants, and awards:*** Federal Pell, FSEOG, state, private, college/university gift aid from institutional funds.

GIFT AID (NON-NEED-BASED) ***Receiving aid:*** *Freshmen:* 28% (23); *Undergraduates:* 7% (24). ***Scholarships, grants, and awards by category:*** *Special Characteristics:* children of union members/company employees. ***Tuition waivers:*** Full or partial for employees or children of employees, senior citizens.

LOANS ***Student loans:*** $2,702,554 (76% need-based, 24% non-need-based). 87% of past graduating class borrowed through all loan programs. Average indebtedness per student: $13,507. ***Average need-based loan:*** Freshmen: $2580; Undergraduates: $3927. ***Parent loans:*** $460,218 (100% non-need-based). ***Programs:*** FFEL (Subsidized and Unsubsidized Stafford, PLUS).

WORK-STUDY ***Federal work-study:*** *Total amount:* $234,877; jobs available.

APPLYING for FINANCIAL AID ***Required financial aid forms:*** FAFSA, institution's own form. ***Financial aid deadline (priority):*** 5/1. ***Notification date:*** Continuous. Students must reply within 2 weeks of notification.

CONTACT Ms. Cathleen Seaton, Director of Financial Aid, Southern Vermont College, 982 Mansion Drive, Bennington, VT 05201-2128, 802-447-6332 or toll-free 800-378-2782 (in-state).

SOUTHERN WESLEYAN UNIVERSITY

Central, SC

Tuition & fees: $11,498 **Average undergraduate aid package: $9500**

ABOUT THE INSTITUTION Independent religious, coed. Awards: associate, bachelor's, and master's degrees. 22 undergraduate majors. Total enrollment: 1,527. Undergraduates: 1,472. Freshmen: 102. Federal methodology is used as a basis for awarding need-based institutional aid.

UNDERGRADUATE EXPENSES for 1999–2000 ***Application fee:*** $15. ***Comprehensive fee:*** $15,350 includes full-time tuition ($11,148), mandatory fees ($350), and room and board ($3852). ***College room only:*** $1320. Full-time tuition and fees vary according to class time, course load, and degree level. Room and board charges vary according to housing facility. ***Part-time tuition:*** $400 per hour. ***Part-time fees:*** $50 per term part-time. Part-time tuition and fees vary according to course load and degree level. ***Payment plan:*** installment.

FRESHMAN FINANCIAL AID (Fall 1999, est.) 115 applied for aid; of those 72% were deemed to have need. 100% of freshmen with need received aid; of those 36% had need fully met. *Average percent of need met:* 75% (excluding resources awarded to replace EFC). *Average financial aid package:* $9575 (excluding resources awarded to replace EFC).

UNDERGRADUATE FINANCIAL AID (Fall 1999, est.) 405 applied for aid; of those 79% were deemed to have need. 100% of undergraduates with need received aid; of those 31% had need fully met. *Average percent of need met:* 85% (excluding resources awarded to replace EFC). *Average financial aid package:* $9500 (excluding resources awarded to replace EFC).

GIFT AID (NEED-BASED) ***Total amount:*** $1,960,000 (22% Federal, 17% state, 59% institutional, 2% external sources). ***Receiving aid:*** *Freshmen:* 61% (83); *all full-time undergraduates:* 73% (320). ***Average award:*** Freshmen: $3900; Undergraduates: $3800. ***Scholarships, grants, and awards:*** Federal Pell, FSEOG, state, private, college/university gift aid from institutional funds.

GIFT AID (NON-NEED-BASED) ***Total amount:*** $320,000 (16% state, 78% institutional, 6% external sources). ***Receiving aid:*** *Freshmen:* 10% (13); *Undergraduates:* 11% (50). ***Scholarships, grants, and awards by category:*** *Academic Interests/Achievement:* business, education, English, general academic interests/achievements, mathematics, religion/biblical studies, social sciences. *Creative Arts/Performance:* music, theater/drama. *Special Achievements/Activities:* community service, leadership, religious involvement. *Special Characteristics:* children of faculty/staff, relatives of clergy, religious affiliation, siblings of current students. ***Tuition waivers:*** Full or partial for employees or children of employees, senior citizens. ***ROTC:*** Army cooperative, Air Force cooperative.

LOANS ***Student loans:*** $1,330,000 (71% need-based, 29% non-need-based). 85% of past graduating class borrowed through all loan programs. Average indebtedness per student: $10,000. ***Average need-based loan:*** Freshmen: $1935; Undergraduates: $1950. ***Parent loans:*** $200,000 (50% need-based, 50% non-need-based). ***Programs:*** FFEL (Subsidized and Unsubsidized Stafford, PLUS), Perkins.

WORK-STUDY ***Federal work-study:*** *Total amount:* $110,000; jobs available. ***State or other work-study/employment:*** *Total amount:* $30,000 (100% non-need-based). Part-time jobs available.

ATHLETIC AWARDS *Total amount:* 500,000 (70% need-based, 30% non-need-based).

APPLYING for FINANCIAL AID ***Required financial aid forms:*** FAFSA, institution's own form. ***Financial aid deadline (priority):*** 6/30. ***Notification date:*** Continuous. Students must reply within 2 weeks of notification.

CONTACT Mrs. Rita Martin, Financial Aid Associate, Southern Wesleyan University, 907 Wesleyan Drive, Central, SC 29630-1020, 800-289-1292 Ext. 5501 or toll-free 800-CUATSWU. *Fax:* 864-644-5970.

SOUTHWEST BAPTIST UNIVERSITY

Bolivar, MO

Tuition & fees: $9290 **Average undergraduate aid package: $7885**

ABOUT THE INSTITUTION Independent Southern Baptist, coed. Awards: associate, bachelor's, and master's degrees. 40 undergraduate majors. Total enrollment: 3,634. Undergraduates: 2,801. Freshmen: 528. Federal methodology is used as a basis for awarding need-based institutional aid.

UNDERGRADUATE EXPENSES for 1999–2000 ***Application fee:*** $25. ***Comprehensive fee:*** $12,120 includes full-time tuition ($8940), mandatory fees ($350), and room and board ($2830). ***College room only:*** $1400. Full-time tuition and fees vary according to location. Room and board charges vary according to board plan and housing facility. ***Part-time tuition:*** $372 per credit hour. ***Part-time fees:*** $9 per credit hour. Part-time tuition and fees vary according to location. ***Payment plan:*** installment.

FRESHMAN FINANCIAL AID (Fall 1999, est.) 465 applied for aid; of those 92% were deemed to have need. 99% of freshmen with need received aid; of those 9% had need fully met. *Average percent of need met:* 57% (excluding resources awarded to replace EFC). *Average financial aid package:* $7618 (excluding resources awarded to replace EFC). 8% of all full-time freshmen had no need and received non-need-based aid.

UNDERGRADUATE FINANCIAL AID (Fall 1999, est.) 1,835 applied for aid; of those 96% were deemed to have need. 98% of undergraduates with need received aid; of those 6% had need fully met. *Average percent of need met:* 55% (excluding resources awarded to replace EFC). *Average financial aid package:* $7885 (excluding resources awarded to replace EFC). 5% of all full-time undergraduates had no need and received non-need-based aid.

GIFT AID (NEED-BASED) ***Total amount:*** $3,019,302 (75% Federal, 25% state). ***Receiving aid:*** *Freshmen:* 41% (194); *all full-time undergraduates:* 47% (910). ***Average award:*** Freshmen: $3100; Undergraduates: $2929. ***Scholarships, grants, and awards:*** Federal Pell, FSEOG, state, private.

GIFT AID (NON-NEED-BASED) ***Total amount:*** $4,934,353 (7% state, 80% institutional, 13% external sources). ***Receiving aid:*** *Freshmen:* 83% (394); *Undergraduates:* 78% (1,505). ***Scholarships, grants, and awards by category:*** *Academic Interests/Achievement:* 906 awards ($2,036,075 total): education, general academic interests/achievements. *Creative Arts/Performance:* 150 awards ($121,225 total): debating, general creative arts/performance, music, theater/drama. *Special Characteristics:* 1,032 awards ($738,638 total): local/state students, relatives of clergy. ***Tuition waivers:*** Full or partial for employees or children of employees. ***ROTC:*** Army cooperative.

LOANS ***Student loans:*** $7,979,608 (72% need-based, 28% non-need-based). 93% of past graduating class borrowed through all loan programs. Average indebtedness per student: $12,756. ***Average need-based loan:*** Freshmen: $2925; Undergraduates: $3968. ***Parent loans:*** $493,256 (100% non-need-based). ***Programs:*** FFEL (Subsidized and Unsubsidized Stafford, PLUS), Perkins, Federal Nursing.

WORK-STUDY ***Federal work-study:*** *Total amount:* $766,085; 733 jobs averaging $1045. ***State or other work-study/employment:*** *Total amount:* $49,140 (100% non-need-based). 48 part-time jobs averaging $1024.

ATHLETIC AWARDS *Total amount:* 1,024,719 (100% non-need-based).

APPLYING for FINANCIAL AID ***Required financial aid forms:*** FAFSA, institution's own form. ***Financial aid deadline (priority):*** 3/15. ***Notification date:*** Continuous beginning 4/1. Students must reply within 2 weeks of notification.

CONTACT Mr. Brad Gamble, Associate Director of Financial Assistance, Southwest Baptist University, 1600 University Avenue, Bolivar, MO 65613-2597, 417-328-1823 or toll-free 800-526-5859. *Fax:* 417-328-1514. *E-mail:* bgamble@sbuniv.edu

SOUTHWESTERN ADVENTIST UNIVERSITY

Keene, TX

Tuition & fees: $9062 **Average undergraduate aid package: $8694**

ABOUT THE INSTITUTION Independent Seventh-day Adventist, coed. Awards: associate, bachelor's, and master's degrees. 29 undergraduate majors. Total enrollment: 1,149. Undergraduates: 1,119. Freshmen: 197. Federal methodology is used as a basis for awarding need-based institutional aid.

UNDERGRADUATE EXPENSES for 1999–2000 ***Comprehensive fee:*** $13,396 includes full-time tuition ($8962), mandatory fees ($100), and room and board ($4334). Room and board charges vary according to board plan. ***Part-time tuition:*** $374 per semester hour. Part-time tuition and fees vary according to course load. ***Payment plan:*** installment.

FRESHMAN FINANCIAL AID (Fall 1998) 174 applied for aid; of those 68% were deemed to have need. 100% of freshmen with need received aid; of those 18% had need fully met. *Average percent of need met:* 76% (excluding resources awarded to replace EFC). *Average financial aid package:* $7779 (excluding resources awarded to replace EFC). 24% of all full-time freshmen had no need and received non-need-based aid.

UNDERGRADUATE FINANCIAL AID (Fall 1998) 667 applied for aid; of those 68% were deemed to have need. 100% of undergraduates with need received aid; of those 19% had need fully met. *Average percent of need met:* 79% (excluding resources awarded to replace EFC). *Average financial aid package:* $8694 (excluding resources awarded to replace EFC). 23% of all full-time undergraduates had no need and received non-need-based aid.

GIFT AID (NEED-BASED) ***Total amount:*** $1,473,625 (61% Federal, 23% state, 10% institutional, 6% external sources). ***Receiving aid:*** *Freshmen:* 44% (79); *all full-time undergraduates:* 49% (357). ***Average award:*** Freshmen: $3087; Undergraduates: $2861. ***Scholarships, grants, and awards:*** Federal Pell, FSEOG, state, private, college/university gift aid from institutional funds.

GIFT AID (NON-NEED-BASED) ***Total amount:*** $1,833,891 (58% institutional, 42% external sources). ***Receiving aid:*** *Freshmen:* 61% (110); *Undergraduates:* 45% (328). ***Scholarships, grants, and awards by category:*** *Academic Interests/Achievement:* business, communication, computer science, education, English, general academic interests/achievements, humanities, physical sciences, premedicine, religion/biblical studies, social sciences. *Creative Arts/Performance:* music, theater/drama. *Special Achievements/Activities:* community service, general special achievements/activities, leadership, religious involvement. *Special Characteristics:* children of faculty/staff, married students, siblings of current students. ***Tuition waivers:*** Full or partial for employees or children of employees.

LOANS ***Student loans:*** $3,044,933 (99% need-based, 1% non-need-based). 70% of past graduating class borrowed through all loan programs. Average indebtedness per student: $17,375. ***Average need-based loan:*** Freshmen: $2624; Undergraduates: $4437. ***Parent loans:*** $326,551 (100% need-based). ***Programs:*** FFEL (Subsidized and Unsubsidized Stafford, PLUS), Perkins, state.

WORK-STUDY ***Federal work-study:*** *Total amount:* $124,344; 100 jobs averaging $1243. ***State or other work-study/employment:*** *Total amount:* $4222 (100% need-based). 4 part-time jobs averaging $1056.

APPLYING for FINANCIAL AID ***Required financial aid forms:*** FAFSA, institution's own form. ***Financial aid deadline (priority):*** 3/15. ***Notification date:*** Continuous beginning 4/15.

CONTACT Patricia Norwood, Assistant Financial Vice President, Student Finance, Southwestern Adventist University, PO Box 567, Keene, TX 76059, 817-645-3921 Ext. 223 or toll-free 800-433-2240. *Fax:* 817-556-4744. *E-mail:* norwoodp@swau.edu

SOUTHWESTERN ASSEMBLIES OF GOD UNIVERSITY

Waxahachie, TX

Tuition & fees: $5858 **Average undergraduate aid package: $5156**

ABOUT THE INSTITUTION Independent religious, coed. Awards: associate, bachelor's, and master's degrees. 19 undergraduate majors. Federal methodology is used as a basis for awarding need-based institutional aid.

UNDERGRADUATE EXPENSES for 1999–2000 ***Application fee:*** $35. ***Comprehensive fee:*** $9804 includes full-time tuition ($5320), mandatory fees ($538), and room and board ($3946). ***Part-time tuition:*** $190 per hour. ***Part-time fees:*** $30 per hour; $19 per term part-time. Part-time tuition and fees vary according to course load. ***Payment plans:*** guaranteed tuition, installment.

FRESHMAN FINANCIAL AID (Fall 1998) 334 applied for aid; of those 78% were deemed to have need. 100% of freshmen with need received aid; of those 16% had need fully met. *Average percent of need met:* 49% (exclud-

Southwestern Assemblies of God University (continued)

ing resources awarded to replace EFC). *Average financial aid package:* $4485 (excluding resources awarded to replace EFC). 22% of all full-time freshmen had no need and received non-need-based aid.

UNDERGRADUATE FINANCIAL AID (Fall 1998) 1,336 applied for aid; of those 78% were deemed to have need. 100% of undergraduates with need received aid; of those 20% had need fully met. *Average percent of need met:* 53% (excluding resources awarded to replace EFC). *Average financial aid package:* $5156 (excluding resources awarded to replace EFC). 18% of all full-time undergraduates had no need and received non-need-based aid.

GIFT AID (NEED-BASED) ***Total amount:*** $1,801,294 (80% Federal, 19% state, 1% external sources). ***Receiving aid:*** *Freshmen:* 53% (177); *all full-time undergraduates:* 53% (707). ***Average award:*** Freshmen: $2226; Undergraduates: $2369. ***Scholarships, grants, and awards:*** Federal Pell, FSEOG, state, private, college/university gift aid from institutional funds.

GIFT AID (NON-NEED-BASED) ***Total amount:*** $741,068 (1% state, 56% institutional, 43% external sources). ***Receiving aid:*** *Freshmen:* 48% (161); *Undergraduates:* 40% (538). ***Scholarships, grants, and awards by category:*** *Academic Interests/Achievement:* 138 awards ($151,734 total): business, communication, education, foreign languages, general academic interests/achievements, religion/biblical studies, social sciences. *Creative Arts/Performance:* 192 awards ($124,750 total): art/fine arts, creative writing, general creative arts/performance, journalism/publications, music, performing arts, theater/drama. *Special Achievements/Activities:* 29 awards ($13,250 total): general special achievements/activities, leadership, religious involvement. *Special Characteristics:* 253 awards ($254,376 total): children of faculty/staff, relatives of clergy, spouses of current students. ***Tuition waivers:*** Full or partial for employees or children of employees.

LOANS ***Student loans:*** $4,092,863 (75% need-based, 25% non-need-based). 67% of past graduating class borrowed through all loan programs. Average indebtedness per student: $13,321. ***Average need-based loan:*** Freshmen: $2076; Undergraduates: $2884. ***Parent loans:*** $443,791 (100% non-need-based). ***Programs:*** FFEL (Subsidized and Unsubsidized Stafford, PLUS), Perkins, state.

WORK-STUDY ***Federal work-study:*** *Total amount:* $161,661; 151 jobs averaging $1070. ***State or other work-study/employment:*** *Total amount:* $7210 (100% need-based). 5 part-time jobs averaging $1442.

ATHLETIC AWARDS *Total amount:* 18,423 (100% non-need-based).

APPLYING for FINANCIAL AID ***Required financial aid forms:*** FAFSA, institution's own form, financial aid transcript (for transfers). ***Financial aid deadline:*** 7/1 (priority: 3/1). ***Notification date:*** Continuous. Students must reply within 3 weeks of notification.

CONTACT Ms. Myrna Wyckoff, Senior Director of Financial Aid, Southwestern Assemblies of God University, 1200 Sycamore Street, Waxahachie, TX 75165-2397, 972-937-4010 or toll-free 800-262-SAGU. *Fax:* 972-937-4001.

SOUTHWESTERN CHRISTIAN COLLEGE

Terrell, TX

Tuition & fees: N/R **Average undergraduate aid package: N/A**

ABOUT THE INSTITUTION Independent religious, coed. Awards: associate and bachelor's degrees. 12 undergraduate majors.

GIFT AID (NEED-BASED) ***Scholarships, grants, and awards:*** Federal Pell, FSEOG, state, private, college/university gift aid from institutional funds.

GIFT AID (NON-NEED-BASED) ***Scholarships, grants, and awards by category:*** *Academic Interests/Achievement:* general academic interests/achievements. *Creative Arts/Performance:* music. *Special Characteristics:* children of faculty/staff, local/state students.

LOANS ***Programs:*** FFEL (Subsidized and Unsubsidized Stafford, PLUS).

WORK-STUDY Federal work-study jobs available.

APPLYING for FINANCIAL AID ***Required financial aid forms:*** FAFSA, CSS Financial Aid PROFILE. ***Financial aid deadline (priority):*** 5/1.

CONTACT Ms. Felicia Robinson, Financial Aid Director, Southwestern Christian College, PO Box 10, Terrell, TX 75160, 972-524-3341. *Fax:* 972-563-7133.

SOUTHWESTERN COLLEGE

Phoenix, AZ

Tuition & fees: $7640 **Average undergraduate aid package: $4500**

ABOUT THE INSTITUTION Independent Conservative Baptist, coed. Awards: associate and bachelor's degrees. 9 undergraduate majors. Total enrollment: 259. Undergraduates: 259. Freshmen: 45. Federal methodology is used as a basis for awarding need-based institutional aid.

UNDERGRADUATE EXPENSES for 1999–2000 ***Application fee:*** $25. ***Comprehensive fee:*** $10,580 includes full-time tuition ($7400), mandatory fees ($240), and room and board ($2940). ***College room only:*** $2100. Full-time tuition and fees vary according to program. ***Part-time tuition:*** $315 per credit. ***Part-time fees:*** $120 per term part-time. Part-time tuition and fees vary according to program.

UNDERGRADUATE FINANCIAL AID (Fall 1998) 195 applied for aid; of those 95% were deemed to have need. 100% of undergraduates with need received aid; of those 3% had need fully met. *Average percent of need met:* 85% (excluding resources awarded to replace EFC). *Average financial aid package:* $4500 (excluding resources awarded to replace EFC). 11% of all full-time undergraduates had no need and received non-need-based aid.

GIFT AID (NEED-BASED) ***Total amount:*** $210,024 (96% Federal, 1% state, 3% external sources). ***Receiving aid:*** *All full-time undergraduates:* 4% (10). ***Average award:*** Undergraduates: $1000. ***Scholarships, grants, and awards:*** Federal Pell, FSEOG, state, private, college/university gift aid from institutional funds.

GIFT AID (NON-NEED-BASED) ***Total amount:*** $338,781 (100% institutional). ***Receiving aid:*** *Undergraduates:* 59% (165). ***Scholarships, grants, and awards by category:*** *Academic Interests/Achievement:* general academic interests/achievements. *Creative Arts/Performance:* music. *Special Achievements/Activities:* community service, hobbies/interests, leadership, religious involvement. *Special Characteristics:* children and siblings of alumni, children of faculty/staff, relatives of clergy, religious affiliation, siblings of current students, spouses of current students.

LOANS ***Student loans:*** $756,996 (100% need-based). 75% of past graduating class borrowed through all loan programs. Average indebtedness per student: $10,000. ***Average need-based loan:*** Undergraduates: $1000. ***Parent loans:*** $90,766 (100% need-based). ***Programs:*** FFEL (Subsidized and Unsubsidized Stafford, PLUS), Perkins.

WORK-STUDY ***Federal work-study:*** *Total amount:* $31,304; 32 jobs averaging $978.

APPLYING for FINANCIAL AID ***Required financial aid form:*** FAFSA. ***Financial aid deadline (priority):*** 3/30. ***Notification date:*** 5/20.

CONTACT Ms. Sheri Doerksen, Director of Financial Aid, Southwestern College, 2625 East Cactus Road, Phoenix, AZ 85032-7097, 602-992-6101 or toll-free 800-247-2697 (out-of-state). *Fax:* 602-404-2159.

SOUTHWESTERN COLLEGE

Winfield, KS

Tuition & fees: $10,560 **Average undergraduate aid package: $11,123**

ABOUT THE INSTITUTION Independent United Methodist, coed. Awards: bachelor's and master's degrees. 36 undergraduate majors. Total enrollment: 974. Undergraduates: 948. Freshmen: 136. Federal methodology is used as a basis for awarding need-based institutional aid.

UNDERGRADUATE EXPENSES for 1999–2000 ***Application fee:*** $20. ***Comprehensive fee:*** $14,830 includes full-time tuition ($10,560) and room and board ($4270). ***College room only:*** $1750. Full-time tuition and fees vary according to degree level and location. Room and board charges vary according to board plan, housing facility, and location. ***Part-time tuition:*** $440 per semester hour. Part-time tuition and fees vary according to degree level and location. ***Payment plan:*** installment.

FRESHMAN FINANCIAL AID (Fall 1999) 140 applied for aid; of those 79% were deemed to have need. 98% of freshmen with need received aid; of those 70% had need fully met. *Average percent of need met:* 100% (excluding resources awarded to replace EFC). *Average financial aid package:* $12,724 (excluding resources awarded to replace EFC). 10% of all full-time freshmen had no need and received non-need-based aid.

UNDERGRADUATE FINANCIAL AID (Fall 1999) 593 applied for aid; of those 77% were deemed to have need. 100% of undergraduates with need received aid; of those 62% had need fully met. *Average percent of need met:* 91% (excluding resources awarded to replace EFC). *Average financial aid package:* $11,123 (excluding resources awarded to replace EFC). 10% of all full-time undergraduates had no need and received non-need-based aid.

GIFT AID (NEED-BASED) ***Total amount:*** $1,302,028 (47% Federal, 30% state, 23% institutional). ***Receiving aid:*** *Freshmen:* 55% (78); *all full-time undergraduates:* 45% (306). ***Average award:*** Freshmen: $5376; Undergraduates: $4137. ***Scholarships, grants, and awards:*** Federal Pell, FSEOG, state, college/university gift aid from institutional funds.

GIFT AID (NON-NEED-BASED) ***Total amount:*** $1,911,305 (88% institutional, 12% external sources). ***Receiving aid:*** *Freshmen:* 75% (107); *Undergraduates:* 57% (385). ***Scholarships, grants, and awards by category:*** *Academic Interests/Achievement:* 322 awards ($992,969 total): biological sciences, business, general academic interests/achievements, humanities. *Creative Arts/Performance:* 148 awards ($186,375 total): cinema/film/broadcasting, debating, journalism/publications, music, theater/drama. *Special Achievements/Activities:* 110 awards ($122,250 total): cheerleading/drum major, community service, leadership, religious involvement. *Special Characteristics:* 150 awards ($338,640 total): children and siblings of alumni, children of current students, children of faculty/staff, ethnic background, international students, local/state students, members of minority groups, relatives of clergy, religious affiliation, siblings of current students. ***Tuition waivers:*** Full or partial for employees or children of employees, senior citizens.

LOANS ***Student loans:*** $2,874,524 (69% need-based, 31% non-need-based). 82% of past graduating class borrowed through all loan programs. Average indebtedness per student: $13,803. ***Average need-based loan:*** Freshmen: $2507; Undergraduates: $3766. ***Parent loans:*** $306,817 (100% non-need-based). ***Programs:*** Federal Direct (Subsidized and Unsubsidized Stafford, PLUS), FFEL (Subsidized and Unsubsidized Stafford, PLUS), Perkins.

WORK-STUDY ***Federal work-study:*** *Total amount:* $265,246; 201 jobs averaging $1320. ***State or other work-study/employment:*** *Total amount:* $46,900 (100% non-need-based). 145 part-time jobs averaging $323.

ATHLETIC AWARDS *Total amount:* 407,400 (100% non-need-based).

APPLYING for FINANCIAL AID ***Required financial aid form:*** institution's own form. ***Financial aid deadline:*** 8/1 (priority: 7/1). ***Notification date:*** Continuous. Students must reply within 2 weeks of notification.

CONTACT Mrs. Margaret Robinson, Director of Financial Aid, Southwestern College, 100 College Street, Winfield, KS 67156-2499, 316-221-8215 or toll-free 800-846-1543 Ext. 236. *Fax:* 316-221-8384.

SOUTHWESTERN COLLEGE OF CHRISTIAN MINISTRIES

Bethany, OK

Tuition & fees: $5916 **Average undergraduate aid package: $6025**

ABOUT THE INSTITUTION Independent religious, coed. Awards: associate, bachelor's, and master's degrees. 10 undergraduate majors. Total enrollment: 208. Undergraduates: 163. Freshmen: 54. Federal methodology is used as a basis for awarding need-based institutional aid.

UNDERGRADUATE EXPENSES for 1999–2000 ***Application fee:*** $25. ***Comprehensive fee:*** $8916 includes full-time tuition ($5600), mandatory fees ($316), and room and board ($3000). Full-time tuition and fees vary according to course load. ***Part-time tuition:*** $195 per credit. ***Part-time fees:*** $3 per credit; $70 per term part-time. Part-time tuition and fees vary according to course load. ***Payment plan:*** installment.

FRESHMAN FINANCIAL AID (Fall 1999, est.) 28 applied for aid; of those 93% were deemed to have need. 100% of freshmen with need received aid; of those 12% had need fully met. *Average percent of need met:* 72% (excluding resources awarded to replace EFC). *Average financial aid package:* $7450 (excluding resources awarded to replace EFC). 15% of all full-time freshmen had no need and received non-need-based aid.

UNDERGRADUATE FINANCIAL AID (Fall 1999, est.) 101 applied for aid; of those 93% were deemed to have need. 100% of undergraduates with need received aid; of those 5% had need fully met. *Average percent of need met:* 70% (excluding resources awarded to replace EFC). *Average financial aid package:* $6025 (excluding resources awarded to replace EFC). 10% of all full-time undergraduates had no need and received non-need-based aid.

GIFT AID (NEED-BASED) ***Total amount:*** $235,000 (77% Federal, 6% state, 17% institutional). ***Receiving aid:*** *Freshmen:* 79% (26); *all full-time undergraduates:* 67% (94). ***Average award:*** Freshmen: $2000; Undergraduates: $2000. ***Scholarships, grants, and awards:*** Federal Pell, FSEOG, state, private, college/university gift aid from institutional funds.

GIFT AID (NON-NEED-BASED) ***Total amount:*** $32,000 (6% state, 94% institutional). ***Receiving aid:*** *Freshmen:* 12% (4); *Undergraduates:* 4% (6). ***Scholarships, grants, and awards by category:*** *Academic Interests/Achievement:* 45 awards ($43,000 total): general academic interests/achievements, religion/biblical studies. *Creative Arts/Performance:* 12 awards ($15,000 total): music. *Special Characteristics:* 24 awards ($5800 total): children and siblings of alumni, relatives of clergy, religious affiliation. ***Tuition waivers:*** Full or partial for employees or children of employees.

LOANS ***Student loans:*** $400,000 (100% need-based). 73% of past graduating class borrowed through all loan programs. Average indebtedness per student: $12,250. ***Average need-based loan:*** Freshmen: $2500; Undergraduates: $4300. ***Parent loans:*** $25,000 (100% need-based). ***Programs:*** FFEL (Subsidized and Unsubsidized Stafford, PLUS), college/university.

WORK-STUDY ***Federal work-study:*** *Total amount:* $70,000; 50 jobs averaging $1600. ***State or other work-study/employment:*** *Total amount:* $20,000 (100% non-need-based). 15 part-time jobs averaging $1600.

APPLYING for FINANCIAL AID ***Required financial aid forms:*** FAFSA, institution's own form. ***Financial aid deadline (priority):*** 7/15. ***Notification date:*** Continuous.

CONTACT Mr. Mark Arthur, Financial Aid Director, Southwestern College of Christian Ministries, PO Box 340, Bethany, OK 73008, 405-789-7661 Ext. 3436. *Fax:* 405-495-0078. *E-mail:* mark@sccm.edu

SOUTHWESTERN OKLAHOMA STATE UNIVERSITY

Weatherford, OK

Tuition & fees (OK res): $1873 **Average undergraduate aid package: $948**

ABOUT THE INSTITUTION State-supported, coed. Awards: bachelor's, master's, and first professional degrees. 52 undergraduate majors. Total enrollment: 4,374. Undergraduates: 3,853. Freshmen: 790. Federal methodology is used as a basis for awarding need-based institutional aid.

UNDERGRADUATE EXPENSES for 1999–2000 ***Application fee:*** $15. ***Tuition, state resident:*** full-time $1470; part-time $49 per credit hour. ***Tuition, nonresident:*** full-time $3990; part-time $132 per credit hour. ***Required fees:*** full-time $403; $13 per credit hour; $10 per term part-time. Full-time tuition and fees vary according to course level and program. Part-time tuition and fees vary according to course level and program. ***College room and board:*** $2440; ***room only:*** $910. Room and board charges vary according to board plan and housing facility. ***Payment plan:*** installment.

FRESHMAN FINANCIAL AID (Fall 1999, est.) 542 applied for aid; of those 83% were deemed to have need. 97% of freshmen with need received aid; of those 7% had need fully met. *Average percent of need met:* 94% (excluding resources awarded to replace EFC). *Average financial aid package:* $727 (excluding resources awarded to replace EFC). 24% of all full-time freshmen had no need and received non-need-based aid.

UNDERGRADUATE FINANCIAL AID (Fall 1999, est.) 2,515 applied for aid; of those 86% were deemed to have need. 99% of undergraduates with need received aid; of those 17% had need fully met. *Average percent of need met:* 94% (excluding resources awarded to replace EFC). *Average*

Southwestern Oklahoma State University (continued)

financial aid package: $948 (excluding resources awarded to replace EFC). 11% of all full-time undergraduates had no need and received non-need-based aid.

GIFT AID (NEED-BASED) ***Total amount:*** $2,575,244 (70% Federal, 26% state, 4% external sources). ***Receiving aid:*** *Freshmen:* 53% (406); *all full-time undergraduates:* 54% (1,952). ***Average award:*** Freshmen: $795; Undergraduates: $831. ***Scholarships, grants, and awards:*** Federal Pell, FSEOG, state, private, college/university gift aid from institutional funds.

GIFT AID (NON-NEED-BASED) ***Total amount:*** $1,182,614 (50% institutional, 50% external sources). ***Receiving aid:*** *Freshmen:* 52% (395); *Undergraduates:* 51% (1,836). ***Scholarships, grants, and awards by category:*** *Academic Interests/Achievement:* biological sciences, business, communication, computer science, education, engineering/technologies, English, foreign languages, general academic interests/achievements, health fields, mathematics, physical sciences, social sciences. *Creative Arts/Performance:* applied art and design, art/fine arts, music, theater/drama. *Special Achievements/Activities:* cheerleading/drum major, rodeo. *Special Characteristics:* children and siblings of alumni, local/state students, out-of-state students. ***Tuition waivers:*** Full or partial for children of alumni, employees or children of employees, senior citizens.

LOANS ***Student loans:*** $3,373,193 (68% need-based, 32% non-need-based). 65% of past graduating class borrowed through all loan programs. Average indebtedness per student: $7500. ***Average need-based loan:*** Freshmen: $1031; Undergraduates: $1540. ***Parent loans:*** $72,004 (100% non-need-based). ***Programs:*** FFEL (Subsidized and Unsubsidized Stafford, PLUS), alternative loans.

WORK-STUDY ***Federal work-study:*** *Total amount:* $506,121; jobs available.

ATHLETIC AWARDS *Total amount:* 404,277 (100% non-need-based).

APPLYING for FINANCIAL AID ***Required financial aid forms:*** FAFSA, institution's own form. ***Financial aid deadline:*** 3/1. ***Notification date:*** 3/20. Students must reply by 4/30.

CONTACT Mr. Thomas M. Ratliff, Director of Student Financial Services, Southwestern Oklahoma State University, 100 Campus Drive, Weatherford, OK 73096-3098, 580-774-3786. *Fax:* 580-774-7066. *E-mail:* ratlift@swosu.edu

SOUTHWESTERN UNIVERSITY

Georgetown, TX

Tuition & fees: $15,750 **Average undergraduate aid package: $14,024**

ABOUT THE INSTITUTION Independent Methodist, coed. Awards: bachelor's degrees. 38 undergraduate majors. Total enrollment: 1,256. Undergraduates: 1,256. Freshmen: 354. Both federal and institutional methodology are used as a basis for awarding need-based institutional aid.

UNDERGRADUATE EXPENSES for 2000–2001 ***Application fee:*** $40. ***Comprehensive fee:*** $22,070 includes full-time tuition ($15,750) and room and board ($6320). ***College room only:*** $3090. Room and board charges vary according to board plan, housing facility, and student level. ***Part-time tuition:*** $650 per semester hour. ***Payment plans:*** tuition prepayment, installment, deferred payment.

FRESHMAN FINANCIAL AID (Fall 1999, est.) 304 applied for aid; of those 61% were deemed to have need. 100% of freshmen with need received aid; of those 100% had need fully met. *Average percent of need met:* 100% (excluding resources awarded to replace EFC). *Average financial aid package:* $13,264 (excluding resources awarded to replace EFC). 30% of all full-time freshmen had no need and received non-need-based aid.

UNDERGRADUATE FINANCIAL AID (Fall 1999, est.) 1,079 applied for aid; of those 57% were deemed to have need. 100% of undergraduates with need received aid; of those 100% had need fully met. *Average percent of need met:* 98% (excluding resources awarded to replace EFC). *Average financial aid package:* $14,024 (excluding resources awarded to replace EFC). 29% of all full-time undergraduates had no need and received non-need-based aid.

GIFT AID (NEED-BASED) ***Total amount:*** $5,485,540 (8% Federal, 19% state, 68% institutional, 5% external sources). ***Receiving aid:*** *Freshmen:* 51% (182); *all full-time undergraduates:* 47% (593). ***Average award:*** Freshmen: $10,087; Undergraduates: $9349. ***Scholarships, grants, and awards:*** Federal Pell, FSEOG, state, private, college/university gift aid from institutional funds.

GIFT AID (NON-NEED-BASED) ***Total amount:*** $2,436,521 (2% Federal, 2% state, 88% institutional, 8% external sources). ***Receiving aid:*** *Freshmen:* 35% (125); *Undergraduates:* 24% (303). ***Scholarships, grants, and awards by category:*** *Academic Interests/Achievement:* 633 awards ($3,344,960 total): general academic interests/achievements. *Creative Arts/Performance:* 82 awards ($142,925 total): art/fine arts, music, performing arts, theater/drama. *Special Characteristics:* 54 awards ($478,125 total): children of faculty/staff, relatives of clergy. ***Tuition waivers:*** Full or partial for employees or children of employees.

LOANS ***Student loans:*** $2,751,871 (85% need-based, 15% non-need-based). 59% of past graduating class borrowed through all loan programs. Average indebtedness per student: $18,879. ***Average need-based loan:*** Freshmen: $1694; Undergraduates: $3201. ***Parent loans:*** $537,119 (57% need-based, 43% non-need-based). ***Programs:*** FFEL (Subsidized and Unsubsidized Stafford, PLUS), Perkins, state, college/university, Gold and Silver STAR Private Educational Loan Program.

WORK-STUDY ***Federal work-study:*** *Total amount:* $326,496; 192 jobs averaging $1705. ***State or other work-study/employment:*** *Total amount:* $817,794 (67% need-based, 33% non-need-based). 464 part-time jobs averaging $1763.

APPLYING for FINANCIAL AID ***Required financial aid forms:*** FAFSA, institution's own form. ***Financial aid deadline (priority):*** 3/1. ***Notification date:*** Continuous. Students must reply by 5/1 or within 2 weeks of notification.

CONTACT Mr. James P. Gaeta, Director of Financial Aid, Southwestern University, 1001 East University Avenue, Georgetown, TX 78626, 512-863-1200 or toll-free 800-252-3166. *Fax:* 512-863-9601. *E-mail:* gaeta@southwestern.edu

SOUTHWEST MISSOURI STATE UNIVERSITY

Springfield, MO

Tuition & fees (MO res): $3564 **Average undergraduate aid package: $7000**

ABOUT THE INSTITUTION State-supported, coed. Awards: bachelor's and master's degrees and post-bachelor's certificates. 93 undergraduate majors. Total enrollment: 17,388. Undergraduates: 14,515. Freshmen: 2,673. Federal methodology is used as a basis for awarding need-based institutional aid.

UNDERGRADUATE EXPENSES for 2000–2001 ***Application fee:*** $25. ***Tuition, state resident:*** full-time $3180; part-time $106 per credit hour. ***Tuition, nonresident:*** full-time $6360; part-time $212 per credit hour. ***Required fees:*** full-time $384. Full-time tuition and fees vary according to course load. Part-time tuition and fees vary according to course load. ***College room and board:*** $3846. Room and board charges vary according to board plan and housing facility. ***Payment plan:*** deferred payment.

FRESHMAN FINANCIAL AID (Fall 1998) 2004 applied for aid; of those 68% were deemed to have need. 99% of freshmen with need received aid; of those 13% had need fully met. *Average percent of need met:* 38% (excluding resources awarded to replace EFC). *Average financial aid package:* $4425 (excluding resources awarded to replace EFC).

UNDERGRADUATE FINANCIAL AID (Fall 1998) 8,296 applied for aid; of those 70% were deemed to have need. 99% of undergraduates with need received aid; of those 24% had need fully met. *Average percent of need met:* 38% (excluding resources awarded to replace EFC). *Average financial aid package:* $7000 (excluding resources awarded to replace EFC).

GIFT AID (NEED-BASED) ***Total amount:*** $9,114,122 (82% Federal, 17% state, 1% institutional). ***Receiving aid:*** *Freshmen:* 26% (725); *all full-time undergraduates:* 29% (3,344). ***Average award:*** Freshmen: $1800; Undergraduates: $2426. ***Scholarships, grants, and awards:*** Federal Pell, FSEOG, state, private, college/university gift aid from institutional funds.

GIFT AID (NON-NEED-BASED) ***Total amount:*** $11,552,852 (1% Federal, 12% state, 70% institutional, 17% external sources). ***Receiving aid:*** *Freshmen:* 21% (588); *Undergraduates:* 14% (1,595). ***Scholarships, grants,***

and awards by category: *Academic Interests/Achievement:* agriculture, biological sciences, business, communication, computer science, education, foreign languages, general academic interests/achievements, health fields, home economics, mathematics, military science, physical sciences, premedicine, religion/biblical studies, social sciences. *Creative Arts/Performance:* applied art and design, art/fine arts, dance, debating, general creative arts/performance, journalism/publications, music, performing arts, theater/drama. *Special Achievements/Activities:* cheerleading/drum major, general special achievements/activities, hobbies/interests, memberships, rodeo. *Special Characteristics:* adult students, children and siblings of alumni, children of faculty/staff, ethnic background, first-generation college students, general special characteristics, handicapped students, international students, members of minority groups, out-of-state students, spouses of deceased or disabled public servants, veterans. ***Tuition waivers:*** Full or partial for employees or children of employees, senior citizens. ***ROTC:*** Army.

LOANS ***Student loans:*** $30,037,770 (71% need-based, 29% non-need-based). 60% of past graduating class borrowed through all loan programs. Average indebtedness per student: $13,455. ***Average need-based loan:*** Freshmen: $2105; Undergraduates: $3065. ***Parent loans:*** $1,720,988 (100% non-need-based). ***Programs:*** Federal Direct (Subsidized and Unsubsidized Stafford, PLUS), FFEL (Subsidized and Unsubsidized Stafford, PLUS), Perkins, state, college/university.

WORK-STUDY ***Federal work-study:*** *Total amount:* $581,057; jobs available. ***State or other work-study/employment:*** *Total amount:* $4,775,513 (100% non-need-based). Part-time jobs available.

ATHLETIC AWARDS *Total amount:* 1,467,018 (100% non-need-based).

APPLYING for FINANCIAL AID ***Required financial aid form:*** FAFSA. ***Financial aid deadline (priority):*** 3/31. ***Notification date:*** Continuous beginning 4/30. Students must reply within 4 weeks of notification.

CONTACT Assistant Director of Financial Aid, Southwest Missouri State University, 901 South National Avenue, Springfield, MO 65804, 417-836-5262 or toll-free 800-492-7900.

SOUTHWEST STATE UNIVERSITY

Marshall, MN

Tuition & fees (MN res): $3428 **Average undergraduate aid package: $6255**

ABOUT THE INSTITUTION State-supported, coed. Awards: associate, bachelor's, and master's degrees. 49 undergraduate majors. Total enrollment: 4,521. Undergraduates: 3,999. Freshmen: 528. Federal methodology is used as a basis for awarding need-based institutional aid.

UNDERGRADUATE EXPENSES for 2000–2001 (est.) ***Application fee:*** $20. ***Tuition, state resident:*** full-time $2790; part-time $93 per credit hour. ***Tuition, nonresident:*** full-time $6286; part-time $206 per credit hour. ***Required fees:*** full-time $638; $21 per credit hour. Full-time tuition and fees vary according to course load, location, and reciprocity agreements. Part-time tuition and fees vary according to course load, location, and reciprocity agreements. ***College room and board:*** $3588; ***room only:*** $2580. Room and board charges vary according to board plan and housing facility. ***Payment plans:*** installment, deferred payment.

FRESHMAN FINANCIAL AID (Fall 1998) 506 applied for aid; of those 82% were deemed to have need. 100% of freshmen with need received aid; of those 62% had need fully met. *Average percent of need met:* 90% (excluding resources awarded to replace EFC). *Average financial aid package:* $6521 (excluding resources awarded to replace EFC). 17% of all full-time freshmen had no need and received non-need-based aid.

UNDERGRADUATE FINANCIAL AID (Fall 1998) 1,538 applied for aid; of those 91% were deemed to have need. 100% of undergraduates with need received aid; of those 62% had need fully met. *Average percent of need met:* 91% (excluding resources awarded to replace EFC). *Average financial aid package:* $6255 (excluding resources awarded to replace EFC). 13% of all full-time undergraduates had no need and received non-need-based aid.

GIFT AID (NEED-BASED) ***Total amount:*** $2,949,766 (53% Federal, 42% state, 1% institutional, 4% external sources). ***Receiving aid:*** *Freshmen:* 62% (353); *all full-time undergraduates:* 54% (1,066). ***Scholarships, grants, and awards:*** Federal Pell, FSEOG, state, private, college/university gift aid from institutional funds.

GIFT AID (NON-NEED-BASED) ***Total amount:*** $667,537 (71% institutional, 29% external sources). ***Receiving aid:*** *Freshmen:* 5% (29); *Undergraduates:* 4% (77). ***Scholarships, grants, and awards by category:*** *Academic Interests/Achievement:* biological sciences, business, communication, education, general academic interests/achievements, mathematics, physical sciences, social sciences. *Creative Arts/Performance:* art/fine arts, creative writing, music, theater/drama. *Special Achievements/Activities:* leadership. *Special Characteristics:* children of union members/company employees, ethnic background, first-generation college students, handicapped students, international students, local/state students, members of minority groups, previous college experience, veterans, veterans' children. ***Tuition waivers:*** Full or partial for employees or children of employees, senior citizens.

LOANS ***Student loans:*** $5,745,839 (62% need-based, 38% non-need-based). ***Parent loans:*** $168,254 (100% non-need-based). ***Programs:*** FFEL (Subsidized and Unsubsidized Stafford, PLUS), Perkins, state.

WORK-STUDY ***Federal work-study:*** *Total amount:* $253,366; jobs available. ***State or other work-study/employment:*** *Total amount:* $714,472 (25% need-based, 75% non-need-based). Part-time jobs available.

ATHLETIC AWARDS *Total amount:* 202,423 (100% non-need-based).

APPLYING for FINANCIAL AID ***Required financial aid forms:*** FAFSA, institution's own form. ***Financial aid deadline (priority):*** 4/1. ***Notification date:*** Continuous beginning 5/15.

CONTACT Mr. Scott Crowell, Assistant Vice President for Student Affairs, Southwest State University, 1501 State Street, Marshall, MN 56258, 507-537-6136 or toll-free 800-642-0684. *E-mail:* crowells@southwest.msus.edu

SOUTHWEST TEXAS STATE UNIVERSITY

San Marcos, TX

Tuition & fees (TX res): $2756 **Average undergraduate aid package: $6217**

ABOUT THE INSTITUTION State-supported, coed. Awards: bachelor's, master's, and doctoral degrees. 84 undergraduate majors. Total enrollment: 21,769. Undergraduates: 18,856. Freshmen: 2,568. Federal methodology is used as a basis for awarding need-based institutional aid.

UNDERGRADUATE EXPENSES for 2000–2001 (est.) ***Application fee:*** $25. ***Tuition, state resident:*** full-time $960; part-time $40 per semester hour. ***Tuition, nonresident:*** full-time $6144; part-time $256 per semester hour. ***Required fees:*** full-time $1796; $62 per semester hour; $159 per term part-time. Full-time tuition and fees vary according to course load. Part-time tuition and fees vary according to course load. ***College room and board:*** $4583; ***room only:*** $2818. Room and board charges vary according to board plan and housing facility. ***Payment plan:*** installment.

FRESHMAN FINANCIAL AID (Fall 1998) 1540 applied for aid; of those 76% were deemed to have need. 91% of freshmen with need received aid; of those 9% had need fully met. *Average percent of need met:* 61% (excluding resources awarded to replace EFC). *Average financial aid package:* $5580 (excluding resources awarded to replace EFC). 11% of all full-time freshmen had no need and received non-need-based aid.

UNDERGRADUATE FINANCIAL AID (Fall 1998) 9,156 applied for aid; of those 80% were deemed to have need. 92% of undergraduates with need received aid; of those 20% had need fully met. *Average percent of need met:* 67% (excluding resources awarded to replace EFC). *Average financial aid package:* $6217 (excluding resources awarded to replace EFC). 9% of all full-time undergraduates had no need and received non-need-based aid.

GIFT AID (NEED-BASED) ***Total amount:*** $10,675,156 (74% Federal, 26% state). ***Receiving aid:*** *Freshmen:* 26% (628); *all full-time undergraduates:* 25% (4,169). ***Average award:*** Freshmen: $2624; Undergraduates: $2401. ***Scholarships, grants, and awards:*** Federal Pell, FSEOG, state, college/university gift aid from institutional funds.

GIFT AID (NON-NEED-BASED) ***Total amount:*** $4,029,301 (36% institutional, 64% external sources). ***Receiving aid:*** *Freshmen:* 13% (312); *Undergradu-*

Southwest Texas State University (continued)

ates: 6% (1,035). ***Scholarships, grants, and awards by category:*** *Academic Interests/Achievement:* agriculture, business, education, English, general academic interests/achievements, home economics, international studies, military science. *Creative Arts/Performance:* applied art and design, journalism/publications, music, theater/drama. *Special Characteristics:* children and siblings of alumni, first-generation college students, handicapped students. ***Tuition waivers:*** Full or partial for employees or children of employees. ***ROTC:*** Army, Air Force.

LOANS ***Student loans:*** $35,905,863 (63% need-based, 37% non-need-based). 50% of past graduating class borrowed through all loan programs. Average indebtedness per student: $13,511. ***Average need-based loan:*** Freshmen: $2444; Undergraduates: $3684. ***Parent loans:*** $4,412,112 (100% non-need-based). ***Programs:*** Federal Direct (Subsidized and Unsubsidized Stafford, PLUS), FFEL (Subsidized and Unsubsidized Stafford, PLUS), Perkins, state, college/university.

WORK-STUDY ***Federal work-study:*** *Total amount:* $1,117,251; jobs available. ***State or other work-study/employment:*** *Total amount:* $57,393 (100% need-based). 72 part-time jobs averaging $797.

ATHLETIC AWARDS *Total amount:* 1,305,478 (100% non-need-based).

APPLYING for FINANCIAL AID ***Required financial aid form:*** FAFSA. ***Financial aid deadline (priority):*** 4/1. ***Notification date:*** Continuous. Students must reply within 3 weeks of notification.

CONTACT Ms. Mariko Gomez, Director of Financial Aid, Southwest Texas State University, 601 University Drive, San Marcos, TX 78666-4602, 512-245-2315. *Fax:* 512-245-7920. *E-mail:* mg01@swt.edu

SPALDING UNIVERSITY

Louisville, KY

Tuition & fees: $10,996 **Average undergraduate aid package: $10,500**

ABOUT THE INSTITUTION Independent religious, coed. Awards: associate, bachelor's, master's, and doctoral degrees. 32 undergraduate majors. Total enrollment: 1,575. Undergraduates: 1,084. Freshmen: 116. Federal methodology is used as a basis for awarding need-based institutional aid.

UNDERGRADUATE EXPENSES for 1999–2000 ***Application fee:*** $20. ***Comprehensive fee:*** $13,806 includes full-time tuition ($10,900), mandatory fees ($96), and room and board ($2810). ***College room only:*** $1500. Room and board charges vary according to board plan. ***Part-time tuition:*** $335 per semester hour. ***Part-time fees:*** $4 per semester hour. Part-time tuition and fees vary according to program. ***Payment plan:*** installment.

FRESHMAN FINANCIAL AID (Fall 1999, est.) 227 applied for aid; of those 44% were deemed to have need. 100% of freshmen with need received aid; of those 34% had need fully met. *Average percent of need met:* 45% (excluding resources awarded to replace EFC). *Average financial aid package:* $9737 (excluding resources awarded to replace EFC). 43% of all full-time freshmen had no need and received non-need-based aid.

UNDERGRADUATE FINANCIAL AID (Fall 1999, est.) 596 applied for aid; of those 74% were deemed to have need. 100% of undergraduates with need received aid; of those 35% had need fully met. *Average percent of need met:* 65% (excluding resources awarded to replace EFC). *Average financial aid package:* $10,500 (excluding resources awarded to replace EFC). 30% of all full-time undergraduates had no need and received non-need-based aid.

GIFT AID (NEED-BASED) ***Total amount:*** $4,038,277 (22% Federal, 23% state, 44% institutional, 11% external sources). ***Receiving aid:*** *Freshmen:* 40% (101); *all full-time undergraduates:* 55% (435). ***Average award:*** Freshmen: $7779; Undergraduates: $6858. ***Scholarships, grants, and awards:*** Federal Pell, FSEOG, state, private, college/university gift aid from institutional funds.

GIFT AID (NON-NEED-BASED) ***Total amount:*** $1,606,702 (1% Federal, 1% state, 96% institutional, 2% external sources). ***Receiving aid:*** *Freshmen:* 6% (16); *Undergraduates:* 6% (47). ***Scholarships, grants, and awards by category:*** *Academic Interests/Achievement:* 255 awards ($883,377 total): general academic interests/achievements. *Creative Arts/Performance:* 13 awards ($30,000 total): applied art and design, art/fine arts, creative writing. *Special Achievements/Activities:* 57 awards ($301,800 total): community service, general special achievements/activities, leadership. *Special Characteristics:* 116 awards ($624,998 total): children and siblings of alumni, children of faculty/staff, general special characteristics, international students, siblings of current students, spouses of current students. ***Tuition waivers:*** Full or partial for children of alumni, employees or children of employees, senior citizens. ***ROTC:*** Army cooperative, Air Force cooperative.

LOANS ***Student loans:*** $3,901,210 (80% need-based, 20% non-need-based). 95% of past graduating class borrowed through all loan programs. Average indebtedness per student: $11,620. ***Average need-based loan:*** Freshmen: $1587; Undergraduates: $3410. ***Parent loans:*** $105,649 (26% need-based, 74% non-need-based). ***Programs:*** FFEL (Subsidized and Unsubsidized Stafford, PLUS), Perkins, Federal Nursing, college/university.

WORK-STUDY ***Federal work-study:*** *Total amount:* $127,641; 82 jobs averaging $1556. ***State or other work-study/employment:*** *Total amount:* $106,061 (8% need-based, 92% non-need-based). 64 part-time jobs averaging $1657.

ATHLETIC AWARDS *Total amount:* 689,797 (62% need-based, 38% non-need-based).

APPLYING for FINANCIAL AID ***Required financial aid forms:*** FAFSA, institution's own form. ***Financial aid deadline (priority):*** 3/1. ***Notification date:*** Continuous beginning 3/15. Students must reply within 2 weeks of notification.

CONTACT Pat King, Associate Director, Student Financial Aid, Spalding University, 851 South Fourth Street, Louisville, KY 40203, 502-588-7185 or toll-free 800-896-8941 Ext. 111. *Fax:* 502-585-7158. *E-mail:* paking@spalding.edu

SPELMAN COLLEGE

Atlanta, GA

CONTACT Ms. Vera Brooks, Director, Student Financial Services, Spelman College, 350 Spelman Lane, Southwest, Atlanta, GA 30314-4399, 404-681-3643 Ext. 1470 or toll-free 800-982-2411 (out-of-state).

SPRING ARBOR COLLEGE

Spring Arbor, MI

Tuition & fees: $11,706 **Average undergraduate aid package: N/A**

ABOUT THE INSTITUTION Independent Free Methodist, coed. Awards: associate, bachelor's, and master's degrees. 29 undergraduate majors. Total enrollment: 2,434. Undergraduates: 2,139. Freshmen: 185. Federal methodology is used as a basis for awarding need-based institutional aid.

UNDERGRADUATE EXPENSES for 1999–2000 ***Application fee:*** $15. ***Comprehensive fee:*** $16,166 includes full-time tuition ($11,600), mandatory fees ($106), and room and board ($4460). ***Part-time tuition:*** $215 per credit. ***Part-time fees:*** $25 per term part-time. Part-time tuition and fees vary according to course load. ***Payment plans:*** installment, deferred payment.

FRESHMAN FINANCIAL AID (Fall 1998) 194 applied for aid.

UNDERGRADUATE FINANCIAL AID (Fall 1998) 1,544 applied for aid; of those 90% were deemed to have need. 100% of undergraduates with need received aid.

GIFT AID (NEED-BASED) ***Total amount:*** $8,261,098 (19% Federal, 34% state, 41% institutional, 6% external sources). ***Receiving aid:*** *All full-time undergraduates:* 77% (1,319). ***Scholarships, grants, and awards:*** Federal Pell, FSEOG, state, private, college/university gift aid from institutional funds.

GIFT AID (NON-NEED-BASED) ***Scholarships, grants, and awards by category:*** *Academic Interests/Achievement:* 403 awards ($1,272,976 total): biological sciences, business, education, general academic interests/achievements, religion/biblical studies. *Creative Arts/Performance:* 86 awards ($50,537 total): art/fine arts, music. *Special Achievements/Activities:* junior miss. *Special Characteristics:* 419 awards ($823,828 total): children of faculty/staff, international students, members of minority groups, out-of-state students, relatives of clergy, religious affiliation. ***Tuition waivers:*** Full or partial for employees or children of employees, senior citizens.

LOANS ***Student loans:*** $4,867,057 (100% need-based). ***Parent loans:*** $246,137 (100% need-based). ***Programs:*** FFEL (Subsidized and Unsubsidized Stafford, PLUS), Perkins, MI-Loan Program, alternative loans.

WORK-STUDY ***Federal work-study:*** *Total amount:* $197,763; 218 jobs averaging $907. ***State or other work-study/employment:*** *Total amount:* $48,611 (100% need-based). 49 part-time jobs averaging $992.

ATHLETIC AWARDS *Total amount:* 314,554 (100% need-based).

APPLYING for FINANCIAL AID ***Required financial aid form:*** FAFSA. ***Financial aid deadline (priority):*** 2/15. ***Notification date:*** Continuous beginning 3/1.

CONTACT Lois M. Hardy, Director of Financial Aid, Spring Arbor College, 106 Main Street, Spring Arbor, MI 49283-9799, 517-750-6468 or toll-free 800-968-0011. *Fax:* 517-750-6620.

SPRINGFIELD COLLEGE

Springfield, MA

Tuition & fees: $16,898 **Average undergraduate aid package: $12,100**

ABOUT THE INSTITUTION Independent, coed. Awards: bachelor's, master's, and doctoral degrees. 52 undergraduate majors. Total enrollment: 2,490. Undergraduates: 1,890. Institutional methodology is used as a basis for awarding need-based institutional aid.

UNDERGRADUATE EXPENSES for 1999–2000 ***Application fee:*** $30. ***Comprehensive fee:*** $22,754 includes full-time tuition ($16,698), mandatory fees ($200), and room and board ($5856). ***College room only:*** $3106. Room and board charges vary according to board plan and housing facility. ***Part-time tuition:*** $506 per credit hour. ***Part-time fees:*** $100 per term part-time.

FRESHMAN FINANCIAL AID (Fall 1999, est.) 460 applied for aid; of those 90% were deemed to have need. 100% of freshmen with need received aid; of those 25% had need fully met. *Average percent of need met:* 79% (excluding resources awarded to replace EFC). *Average financial aid package:* $12,600 (excluding resources awarded to replace EFC). 5% of all full-time freshmen had no need and received non-need-based aid.

UNDERGRADUATE FINANCIAL AID (Fall 1999, est.) 1,616 applied for aid; of those 90% were deemed to have need. 100% of undergraduates with need received aid; of those 20% had need fully met. *Average percent of need met:* 76% (excluding resources awarded to replace EFC). *Average financial aid package:* $12,100 (excluding resources awarded to replace EFC). 2% of all full-time undergraduates had no need and received non-need-based aid.

GIFT AID (NEED-BASED) ***Total amount:*** $11,223,028 (10% Federal, 5% state, 84% institutional, 1% external sources). ***Receiving aid:*** *Freshmen:* 76% (391); *all full-time undergraduates:* 70% (1,361). ***Average award:*** Freshmen: $9700; Undergraduates: $7750. ***Scholarships, grants, and awards:*** Federal Pell, FSEOG, state, private, college/university gift aid from institutional funds, Project Spirit.

GIFT AID (NON-NEED-BASED) ***Total amount:*** $179,000 (72% institutional, 28% external sources). ***Receiving aid:*** *Freshmen:* 4% (19); *Undergraduates:* 1% (24). ***Scholarships, grants, and awards by category:*** *Special Characteristics:* 87 awards ($435,000 total): general special characteristics. ***ROTC:*** Army cooperative, Air Force cooperative.

LOANS ***Student loans:*** $6,100,000 (100% need-based). 79% of past graduating class borrowed through all loan programs. Average indebtedness per student: $16,500. ***Average need-based loan:*** Freshmen: $2705; Undergraduates: $4215. ***Parent loans:*** $3,125,160 (100% non-need-based). ***Programs:*** FFEL (Subsidized and Unsubsidized Stafford, PLUS), Perkins, state, alternative loans.

WORK-STUDY ***Federal work-study:*** *Total amount:* $475,000; jobs available. ***State or other work-study/employment:*** *Total amount:* $1,041,800 (34% need-based, 66% non-need-based). Part-time jobs available.

APPLYING for FINANCIAL AID ***Required financial aid forms:*** FAFSA, CSS Financial Aid PROFILE, federal income tax form(s). ***Financial aid deadline (priority):*** 3/15. ***Notification date:*** Continuous. Students must reply within 2 weeks of notification.

CONTACT Dr. Linda M. Dagradi, Director of Financial Aid, Springfield College, 263 Alden Street, Springfield, MA 01109-3797, 413-748-3108 or toll-free 800-343-1257 (out-of-state). *Fax:* 413-748-3462. *E-mail:* linda_dagradi@spfldcol.edu

SPRING HILL COLLEGE

Mobile, AL

Tuition & fees: $16,254 **Average undergraduate aid package: $14,654**

ABOUT THE INSTITUTION Independent Roman Catholic (Jesuit), coed. Awards: associate, bachelor's, and master's degrees and post-bachelor's certificates. 44 undergraduate majors. Total enrollment: 1,484. Undergraduates: 1,212. Freshmen: 310. Federal methodology is used as a basis for awarding need-based institutional aid.

UNDERGRADUATE EXPENSES for 2000–2001 ***Application fee:*** $25. ***Comprehensive fee:*** $22,022 includes full-time tuition ($15,254), mandatory fees ($1000), and room and board ($5768). ***College room only:*** $2992. Room and board charges vary according to board plan and housing facility. ***Part-time tuition:*** $565 per semester hour. ***Part-time fees:*** $32 per semester hour; $10 per term part-time. ***Payment plan:*** deferred payment.

FRESHMAN FINANCIAL AID (Fall 1999) 220 applied for aid; of those 84% were deemed to have need. 100% of freshmen with need received aid; of those 22% had need fully met. *Average percent of need met:* 86% (excluding resources awarded to replace EFC). *Average financial aid package:* $14,738 (excluding resources awarded to replace EFC). 31% of all full-time freshmen had no need and received non-need-based aid.

UNDERGRADUATE FINANCIAL AID (Fall 1999) 686 applied for aid; of those 88% were deemed to have need. 100% of undergraduates with need received aid; of those 28% had need fully met. *Average percent of need met:* 84% (excluding resources awarded to replace EFC). *Average financial aid package:* $14,654 (excluding resources awarded to replace EFC). 29% of all full-time undergraduates had no need and received non-need-based aid.

GIFT AID (NEED-BASED) ***Total amount:*** $5,691,544 (11% Federal, 4% state, 81% institutional, 4% external sources). ***Receiving aid:*** *Freshmen:* 61% (184); *all full-time undergraduates:* 62% (601). ***Average award:*** Freshmen: $11,193; Undergraduates: $10,199. ***Scholarships, grants, and awards:*** Federal Pell, FSEOG, state, private, college/university gift aid from institutional funds, Whitehead Scholarships, Bedsole Grants.

GIFT AID (NON-NEED-BASED) ***Total amount:*** $1,732,010 (8% state, 85% institutional, 7% external sources). ***Receiving aid:*** *Freshmen:* 8% (23); *Undergraduates:* 7% (71). ***Scholarships, grants, and awards by category:*** *Academic Interests/Achievement:* 224 awards ($1,332,325 total): general academic interests/achievements. *Special Achievements/Activities:* 72 awards ($139,260 total): community service, leadership. *Special Characteristics:* 7 awards ($51,551 total): children of faculty/staff, siblings of current students. ***Tuition waivers:*** Full or partial for employees or children of employees. ***ROTC:*** Army cooperative, Air Force cooperative.

LOANS ***Student loans:*** $3,106,560 (79% need-based, 21% non-need-based). ***Average need-based loan:*** Freshmen: $2916; Undergraduates: $3985. ***Parent loans:*** $1,082,195 (30% need-based, 70% non-need-based). ***Programs:*** FFEL (Subsidized and Unsubsidized Stafford, PLUS), Perkins, Key Corp Loans, Signature Loans.

WORK-STUDY ***Federal work-study:*** *Total amount:* $202,628; 163 jobs averaging $1243. ***State or other work-study/employment:*** *Total amount:* $159,223 (51% need-based, 49% non-need-based). 97 part-time jobs averaging $1641.

ATHLETIC AWARDS *Total amount:* 764,297 (47% need-based, 53% non-need-based).

APPLYING for FINANCIAL AID ***Required financial aid forms:*** FAFSA, institution's own form. ***Financial aid deadline (priority):*** 3/1. ***Notification date:*** Continuous. Students must reply by 5/1 or within 2 weeks of notification.

CONTACT Betty H. Harlan, Director of Financial Aid, Spring Hill College, 4000 Dauphin Street, Mobile, AL 36608-1791, 334-380-3460 or toll-free 800-SHC-6704. *Fax:* 334-460-2176. *E-mail:* bharlan@shc.edu

STANFORD UNIVERSITY
Stanford, CA

Tuition & fees: $23,058 **Average undergraduate aid package: $20,926**

ABOUT THE INSTITUTION Independent, coed. Awards: bachelor's, master's, doctoral, and first professional degrees. 59 undergraduate majors. Total enrollment: 18,083. Undergraduates: 7,784. Freshmen: 1,749. Institutional methodology is used as a basis for awarding need-based institutional aid.

UNDERGRADUATE EXPENSES for 1999–2000 ***Application fee:*** $60. ***One-time required fee:*** $275. ***Comprehensive fee:*** $30,939 includes full-time tuition ($23,058) and room and board ($7881). Room and board charges vary according to board plan and housing facility. ***Payment plans:*** installment, deferred payment.

FRESHMAN FINANCIAL AID (Fall 1998) 951 applied for aid; of those 70% were deemed to have need. 99% of freshmen with need received aid; of those 99% had need fully met. *Average percent of need met:* 99% (excluding resources awarded to replace EFC). *Average financial aid package:* $20,920 (excluding resources awarded to replace EFC). 22% of all full-time freshmen had no need and received non-need-based aid.

UNDERGRADUATE FINANCIAL AID (Fall 1998) 3,477 applied for aid; of those 84% were deemed to have need. 99% of undergraduates with need received aid; of those 97% had need fully met. *Average percent of need met:* 99% (excluding resources awarded to replace EFC). *Average financial aid package:* $20,926 (excluding resources awarded to replace EFC). 20% of all full-time undergraduates had no need and received non-need-based aid.

GIFT AID (NEED-BASED) ***Total amount:*** $46,320,214 (7% Federal, 7% state, 80% institutional, 6% external sources). ***Receiving aid:*** *Freshmen:* 38% (615); *all full-time undergraduates:* 42% (2,660). ***Average award:*** Freshmen: $18,138; Undergraduates: $17,524. ***Scholarships, grants, and awards:*** Federal Pell, FSEOG, state, private, college/university gift aid from institutional funds.

GIFT AID (NON-NEED-BASED) ***Total amount:*** $6,521,986 (12% Federal, 2% state, 28% institutional, 58% external sources). ***Receiving aid:*** *Freshmen:* 2% (33); *Undergraduates:* 2% (107). ***ROTC:*** Army cooperative, Naval cooperative, Air Force cooperative.

LOANS ***Student loans:*** $12,953,106 (88% need-based, 12% non-need-based). 48% of past graduating class borrowed through all loan programs. Average indebtedness per student: $15,892. ***Average need-based loan:*** Freshmen: $2923; Undergraduates: $3456. ***Parent loans:*** $6,331,519 (100% non-need-based). ***Programs:*** FFEL (Subsidized and Unsubsidized Stafford, PLUS), Perkins, college/university.

WORK-STUDY ***Federal work-study:*** *Total amount:* $859,013; 450 jobs averaging $1909. ***State or other work-study/employment:*** *Total amount:* $2,386,644 (99% need-based, 1% non-need-based). 1,422 part-time jobs averaging $1678.

ATHLETIC AWARDS *Total amount:* 8,614,138 (3% need-based, 97% non-need-based).

APPLYING for FINANCIAL AID ***Required financial aid forms:*** FAFSA, CSS Financial Aid PROFILE, noncustodial (divorced/separated) parent's statement. ***Financial aid deadline (priority):*** 2/1. ***Notification date:*** 4/1.

CONTACT Financial Aid Office, Stanford University, 520 Lasuen Mall, Old Union Building, Room 322, Stanford, CA 94305-3021, 650-723-3058.

STATE UNIVERSITY OF NEW YORK AT ALBANY
Albany, NY

Tuition & fees (NY res): $4338 **Average undergraduate aid package: $6962**

ABOUT THE INSTITUTION State-supported, coed. Awards: bachelor's, master's, and doctoral degrees and post-master's certificates. 60 undergraduate majors. Total enrollment: 16,901. Undergraduates: 11,737. Freshmen: 2,282. Federal methodology is used as a basis for awarding need-based institutional aid.

UNDERGRADUATE EXPENSES for 1999–2000 ***Application fee:*** $30. ***Tuition, state resident:*** full-time $3400; part-time $138 per credit hour. ***Tuition, nonresident:*** full-time $8300; part-time $347 per credit hour. ***Required fees:*** full-time $938; $27 per credit hour. Part-time tuition and fees vary according to course load. ***College room and board:*** $5828; ***room only:*** $3740. Room and board charges vary according to board plan and housing facility. ***Payment plan:*** installment.

FRESHMAN FINANCIAL AID (Fall 1999) 1843 applied for aid; of those 71% were deemed to have need. 99% of freshmen with need received aid; of those 12% had need fully met. *Average percent of need met:* 73% (excluding resources awarded to replace EFC). *Average financial aid package:* $6750 (excluding resources awarded to replace EFC). 5% of all full-time freshmen had no need and received non-need-based aid.

UNDERGRADUATE FINANCIAL AID (Fall 1999) 7,303 applied for aid; of those 78% were deemed to have need. 99% of undergraduates with need received aid; of those 18% had need fully met. *Average percent of need met:* 74% (excluding resources awarded to replace EFC). *Average financial aid package:* $6962 (excluding resources awarded to replace EFC). 3% of all full-time undergraduates had no need and received non-need-based aid.

GIFT AID (NEED-BASED) ***Total amount:*** $17,016,650 (45% Federal, 55% state). ***Receiving aid:*** *Freshmen:* 46% (1,052); *all full-time undergraduates:* 44% (4,544). ***Average award:*** Freshmen: $3904; Undergraduates: $3711. ***Scholarships, grants, and awards:*** Federal Pell, FSEOG, state, private, college/university gift aid from institutional funds.

GIFT AID (NON-NEED-BASED) ***Total amount:*** $2,458,289 (4% state, 64% institutional, 32% external sources). ***Receiving aid:*** *Freshmen:* 5% (112); *Undergraduates:* 3% (324). ***Scholarships, grants, and awards by category:*** *Academic Interests/Achievement:* general academic interests/achievements. ***Tuition waivers:*** Full or partial for senior citizens. ***ROTC:*** Army cooperative, Air Force cooperative.

LOANS ***Student loans:*** $28,493,997 (67% need-based, 33% non-need-based). ***Average need-based loan:*** Freshmen: $3102; Undergraduates: $3887. ***Parent loans:*** $3,517,343 (100% non-need-based). ***Programs:*** FFEL (Subsidized and Unsubsidized Stafford, PLUS), Perkins, college/university.

WORK-STUDY ***Federal work-study:*** *Total amount:* $1,676,158; 1,526 jobs averaging $1098.

ATHLETIC AWARDS *Total amount:* 820,938 (100% non-need-based).

APPLYING for FINANCIAL AID ***Required financial aid form:*** FAFSA. ***Financial aid deadline (priority):*** 3/15. ***Notification date:*** Continuous beginning 4/1. Students must reply within 2 weeks of notification.

CONTACT Mr. Dennis Tillman, Director of Financial Aid, State University of New York at Albany, 1400 Washington Avenue, Campus Center B52, Albany, NY 12222-0001, 518-442-5757. *Fax:* 518-442-5295.

STATE UNIVERSITY OF NEW YORK AT BINGHAMTON
Binghamton, NY

Tuition & fees (NY res): $4416 **Average undergraduate aid package: $9573**

ABOUT THE INSTITUTION State-supported, coed. Awards: bachelor's, master's, and doctoral degrees and post-master's certificates. 52 undergraduate majors. Total enrollment: 12,564. Undergraduates: 9,872. Freshmen: 2,050. Federal methodology is used as a basis for awarding need-based institutional aid.

UNDERGRADUATE EXPENSES for 1999–2000 ***Application fee:*** $30. ***Tuition, state resident:*** full-time $3400; part-time $137 per credit. ***Tuition, nonresident:*** full-time $8300; part-time $346 per credit. ***Required fees:*** full-time $1016; $38 per credit; $37 per term part-time. ***College room and board:*** $5516; ***room only:*** $3430. Room and board charges vary according to board plan and housing facility. ***Payment plan:*** installment.

FRESHMAN FINANCIAL AID (Fall 1999) 1668 applied for aid; of those 65% were deemed to have need. 97% of freshmen with need received aid; of those 55% had need fully met. *Average percent of need met:* 100% (excluding resources awarded to replace EFC). *Average financial aid pack-*

age: $9628 (excluding resources awarded to replace EFC). 5% of all full-time freshmen had no need and received non-need-based aid.

UNDERGRADUATE FINANCIAL AID (Fall 1999) 6,579 applied for aid; of those 74% were deemed to have need. 98% of undergraduates with need received aid; of those 37% had need fully met. *Average percent of need met:* 100% (excluding resources awarded to replace EFC). *Average financial aid package:* $9573 (excluding resources awarded to replace EFC). 2% of all full-time undergraduates had no need and received non-need-based aid.

GIFT AID (NEED-BASED) ***Total amount:*** $16,183,533 (45% Federal, 47% state, 2% institutional, 6% external sources). ***Receiving aid:*** *Freshmen:* 42% (854); *all full-time undergraduates:* 40% (3,833). ***Average award:*** Freshmen: $4187; Undergraduates: $4020. ***Scholarships, grants, and awards:*** Federal Pell, FSEOG, state, private, college/university gift aid from institutional funds, Federal Nursing.

GIFT AID (NON-NEED-BASED) ***Total amount:*** $1,527,782 (26% state, 74% institutional). ***Receiving aid:*** *Freshmen:* 8% (172); *Undergraduates:* 6% (538). ***Scholarships, grants, and awards by category:*** *Academic Interests/Achievement:* 163 awards ($304,400 total): business, computer science, engineering/technologies, general academic interests/achievements, health fields, humanities, physical sciences, premedicine. *Creative Arts/ Performance:* 3 awards ($2100 total): creative writing, music, theater/ drama. *Special Achievements/Activities:* 29 awards ($45,725 total): community service. *Special Characteristics:* 54 awards ($83,750 total): members of minority groups, out-of-state students. ***Tuition waivers:*** Full or partial for employees or children of employees. ***ROTC:*** Air Force cooperative.

LOANS ***Student loans:*** $30,683,639 (100% need-based). 58% of past graduating class borrowed through all loan programs. Average indebtedness per student: $11,856. ***Average need-based loan:*** Freshmen: $2820; Undergraduates: $3879. ***Parent loans:*** $27,232,162 (100% need-based). ***Programs:*** Federal Direct (Subsidized and Unsubsidized Stafford, PLUS), Perkins, Federal Nursing.

WORK-STUDY ***Federal work-study:*** *Total amount:* $2,440,001; jobs available.

ATHLETIC AWARDS *Total amount:* 678,862 (100% non-need-based).

APPLYING for FINANCIAL AID ***Required financial aid forms:*** FAFSA, CSS Financial Aid PROFILE, state aid form. ***Financial aid deadline (priority):*** 3/1. ***Notification date:*** Continuous beginning 3/15.

CONTACT Ms. Christina M. Knickerbocker, Director of Student Financial Aid and Employment, State University of New York at Binghamton, PO Box 6011, Binghamton, NY 13902-6011, 607-777-2428.

STATE UNIVERSITY OF NEW YORK AT BUFFALO

Buffalo, NY

Tuition & fees (NY res): $4655 **Average undergraduate aid package: $5940**

ABOUT THE INSTITUTION State-supported, coed. Awards: bachelor's, master's, doctoral, and first professional degrees and post-master's certificates. 61 undergraduate majors. Total enrollment: 24,257. Undergraduates: 16,259. Freshmen: 3,223. Federal methodology is used as a basis for awarding need-based institutional aid.

UNDERGRADUATE EXPENSES for 1999–2000 ***Application fee:*** $30. ***Tuition, state resident:*** full-time $3400; part-time $137 per credit hour. ***Tuition, nonresident:*** full-time $8300; part-time $346 per credit hour. ***Required fees:*** full-time $1255; $52 per credit hour. ***College room and board:*** $5904; ***room only:*** $3424. Room and board charges vary according to board plan and housing facility. ***Payment plan:*** installment.

FRESHMAN FINANCIAL AID (Fall 1999, est.) 3795 applied for aid; of those 76% were deemed to have need. *Average percent of need met:* 60% (excluding resources awarded to replace EFC). *Average financial aid package:* $5501 (excluding resources awarded to replace EFC). 4% of all full-time freshmen had no need and received non-need-based aid.

UNDERGRADUATE FINANCIAL AID (Fall 1999, est.) 9,895 applied for aid; of those 78% were deemed to have need. *Average percent of need met:* 70% (excluding resources awarded to replace EFC). *Average financial aid package:* $5940 (excluding resources awarded to replace EFC). 4% of all full-time undergraduates had no need and received non-need-based aid.

GIFT AID (NEED-BASED) ***Total amount:*** $29,039,129 (48% Federal, 44% state, 7% institutional, 1% external sources). ***Scholarships, grants, and awards:*** Federal Pell, FSEOG, state, private, college/university gift aid from institutional funds.

GIFT AID (NON-NEED-BASED) ***Total amount:*** $844,792 (100% institutional). ***Scholarships, grants, and awards by category:*** *Academic Interests/ Achievement:* general academic interests/achievements. *Creative Arts/ Performance:* music. *Special Achievements/Activities:* general special achievements/activities. *Special Characteristics:* local/state students. ***ROTC:*** Army cooperative.

LOANS ***Student loans:*** $77,993,790 (100% need-based). 60% of past graduating class borrowed through all loan programs. Average indebtedness per student: $15,250. ***Parent loans:*** $11,719,823 (100% non-need-based). ***Programs:*** Federal Direct (Subsidized and Unsubsidized Stafford, PLUS), Perkins, Federal Nursing, college/university.

WORK-STUDY ***Federal work-study:*** *Total amount:* $1,394,319; 1,206 jobs averaging $1156. ***State or other work-study/employment:*** *Total amount:* $4,740,649 (100% non-need-based). 894 part-time jobs averaging $5302.

ATHLETIC AWARDS *Total amount:* 2,542,711 (100% non-need-based).

APPLYING for FINANCIAL AID ***Required financial aid form:*** FAFSA. ***Financial aid deadline (priority):*** 3/1. ***Notification date:*** Continuous. Students must reply by 5/1.

CONTACT Customer Service Department, State University of New York at Buffalo, Hayes Annex C, 3435 Main Street, Buffalo, NY 14214, 716-829-3724. *Fax:* 716-829-2022. *E-mail:* st-finances-records@acsu.buffalo.edu

STATE UNIVERSITY OF NEW YORK AT FARMINGDALE

Farmingdale, NY

Tuition & fees (NY res): $4075 **Average undergraduate aid package: N/A**

ABOUT THE INSTITUTION State-supported, coed. Awards: associate and bachelor's degrees (one bachelor's degree program is upper level). 31 undergraduate majors. Total enrollment: 5,492. Undergraduates: 5,492. Freshmen: 1,058. Federal methodology is used as a basis for awarding need-based institutional aid.

UNDERGRADUATE EXPENSES for 1999–2000 ***Application fee:*** $30. ***Tuition, state resident:*** full-time $3400; part-time $137 per credit. ***Tuition, nonresident:*** full-time $8300; part-time $346 per credit. ***Required fees:*** full-time $675; $19 per credit. Full-time tuition and fees vary according to degree level. Part-time tuition and fees vary according to course load and degree level. ***College room and board:*** $6114; ***room only:*** $3390. Room and board charges vary according to board plan and housing facility. ***Payment plans:*** installment, deferred payment.

GIFT AID (NEED-BASED) ***Total amount:*** $3,392,565 (94% Federal, 6% state). ***Scholarships, grants, and awards:*** Federal Pell, FSEOG, state, college/university gift aid from institutional funds, Federal Nursing.

GIFT AID (NON-NEED-BASED) ***Total amount:*** $2,701,722 (1% Federal, 97% state, 1% institutional, 1% external sources). ***Scholarships, grants, and awards by category:*** *Academic Interests/Achievement:* general academic interests/achievements. *Special Achievements/Activities:* general special achievements/activities. *Special Characteristics:* general special characteristics. ***Tuition waivers:*** Full or partial for senior citizens. ***ROTC:*** Army cooperative, Air Force cooperative.

LOANS ***Student loans:*** $3,749,535 (62% need-based, 38% non-need-based). ***Parent loans:*** $209,784 (100% non-need-based). ***Programs:*** FFEL (Subsidized and Unsubsidized Stafford, PLUS), Perkins, alternative loans.

WORK-STUDY ***Federal work-study:*** *Total amount:* $187,258; 235 jobs available. ***State or other work-study/employment:*** *Total amount:* $220,000 (100% non-need-based). 130 part-time jobs available.

APPLYING for FINANCIAL AID ***Required financial aid forms:*** FAFSA, institution's own form, state aid form. ***Financial aid deadline (priority):*** 4/1. ***Notification date:*** Continuous.

State University of New York at Farmingdale (continued)

CONTACT Dionne Walker-Belgrave, Assistant Director of Financial Aid, State University of New York at Farmingdale, Route 110, Farmingdale, NY 11735, 631-420-2328 or toll-free 877-4-FARMINGDALE. *Fax:* 631-420-3662.

STATE UNIVERSITY OF NEW YORK AT NEW PALTZ

New Paltz, NY

Tuition & fees (NY res): $3985 **Average undergraduate aid package: $7500**

ABOUT THE INSTITUTION State-supported, coed. Awards: bachelor's, master's, and doctoral degrees and post-master's certificates. 75 undergraduate majors. Total enrollment: 7,745. Undergraduates: 6,082. Freshmen: 977. Federal methodology is used as a basis for awarding need-based institutional aid.

UNDERGRADUATE EXPENSES for 2000–2001 (est.) ***Application fee:*** $30. ***Tuition, state resident:*** full-time $3400; part-time $137 per credit. ***Tuition, nonresident:*** full-time $8300; part-time $346 per credit. ***Required fees:*** full-time $585; $19 per credit; $60 per term part-time. ***College room and board:*** $5368; ***room only:*** $3200. Room and board charges vary according to board plan. ***Payment plan:*** installment.

FRESHMAN FINANCIAL AID (Fall 1998) 597 applied for aid; of those 83% were deemed to have need. 98% of freshmen with need received aid; of those 30% had need fully met. *Average percent of need met:* 75% (excluding resources awarded to replace EFC). *Average financial aid package:* $7771 (excluding resources awarded to replace EFC). 20% of all full-time freshmen had no need and received non-need-based aid.

UNDERGRADUATE FINANCIAL AID (Fall 1998) 4,199 applied for aid; of those 80% were deemed to have need. 98% of undergraduates with need received aid; of those 19% had need fully met. *Average percent of need met:* 65% (excluding resources awarded to replace EFC). *Average financial aid package:* $7500 (excluding resources awarded to replace EFC). 20% of all full-time undergraduates had no need and received non-need-based aid.

GIFT AID (NEED-BASED) ***Total amount:*** $10,009,915 (43% Federal, 54% state, 1% institutional, 2% external sources). ***Receiving aid:*** *Freshmen:* 51% (388); *all full-time undergraduates:* 53% (2,624). ***Scholarships, grants, and awards:*** Federal Pell, FSEOG, state, college/university gift aid from institutional funds.

GIFT AID (NON-NEED-BASED) ***Total amount:*** $655,606 (38% state, 39% institutional, 23% external sources). ***Receiving aid:*** *Freshmen:* 7% (50); *Undergraduates:* 7% (347). ***Scholarships, grants, and awards by category:*** *Academic Interests/Achievement:* computer science, education, engineering/technologies, English, general academic interests/achievements, health fields, humanities, mathematics, physical sciences, premedicine. *Creative Arts/Performance:* art/fine arts, creative writing. *Special Achievements/Activities:* community service. *Special Characteristics:* members of minority groups.

LOANS ***Student loans:*** $15,381,982 (68% need-based, 32% non-need-based). ***Parent loans:*** $2,432,465 (20% need-based, 80% non-need-based). ***Programs:*** FFEL (Subsidized and Unsubsidized Stafford, PLUS), Perkins.

WORK-STUDY ***Federal work-study:*** *Total amount:* $673,475; jobs available. ***State or other work-study/employment:*** *Total amount:* $365,375 (35% need-based, 65% non-need-based). Part-time jobs available.

APPLYING for FINANCIAL AID ***Required financial aid forms:*** FAFSA, state aid form. ***Financial aid deadline (priority):*** 3/1. ***Notification date:*** 4/1. Students must reply within 2 weeks of notification.

CONTACT Mr. Daniel Sistarenik, Director of Financial Aid, State University of New York at New Paltz, 75 South Manheim Boulevard, Suite 2, New Paltz, NY 12561-2437, 914-257-3250 or toll-free 888-639-7589 (in-state). *Fax:* 914-257-3568. *E-mail:* fao@npvm.newpaltz.edu

STATE UNIVERSITY OF NEW YORK AT OSWEGO

Oswego, NY

Tuition & fees (NY res): $3975 **Average undergraduate aid package: $7049**

ABOUT THE INSTITUTION State-supported, coed. Awards: bachelor's and master's degrees and post-master's certificates. 52 undergraduate majors. Total enrollment: 7,944. Undergraduates: 6,849. Freshmen: 1,258. Federal methodology is used as a basis for awarding need-based institutional aid.

UNDERGRADUATE EXPENSES for 1999–2000 ***Application fee:*** $30. ***Tuition, state resident:*** full-time $3400; part-time $137 per credit hour. ***Tuition, nonresident:*** full-time $8300; part-time $346 per credit hour. ***Required fees:*** full-time $575; $18 per credit hour. Part-time tuition and fees vary according to class time and location. ***College room and board:*** $6160; ***room only:*** $3540. Room and board charges vary according to board plan and housing facility. ***Payment plans:*** installment, deferred payment.

FRESHMAN FINANCIAL AID (Fall 1998) 1081 applied for aid; of those 81% were deemed to have need. 98% of freshmen with need received aid; of those 21% had need fully met. *Average percent of need met:* 71% (excluding resources awarded to replace EFC). *Average financial aid package:* $5794 (excluding resources awarded to replace EFC). 16% of all full-time freshmen had no need and received non-need-based aid.

UNDERGRADUATE FINANCIAL AID (Fall 1998) 4,853 applied for aid; of those 84% were deemed to have need. 98% of undergraduates with need received aid; of those 34% had need fully met. *Average percent of need met:* 86% (excluding resources awarded to replace EFC). *Average financial aid package:* $7049 (excluding resources awarded to replace EFC). 12% of all full-time undergraduates had no need and received non-need-based aid.

GIFT AID (NEED-BASED) ***Total amount:*** $11,300,541 (43% Federal, 52% state, 2% institutional, 3% external sources). ***Receiving aid:*** *Freshmen:* 57% (719); *all full-time undergraduates:* 54% (3,272). ***Average award:*** Freshmen: $2945; Undergraduates: $2777. ***Scholarships, grants, and awards:*** Federal Pell, FSEOG, state, private, college/university gift aid from institutional funds.

GIFT AID (NON-NEED-BASED) ***Total amount:*** $375,412 (12% Federal, 13% state, 39% institutional, 36% external sources). ***Receiving aid:*** *Freshmen:* 18% (227); *Undergraduates:* 8% (496). ***Scholarships, grants, and awards by category:*** *Academic Interests/Achievement:* 211 awards ($149,994 total): area/ethnic studies, biological sciences, communication, education, English, general academic interests/achievements, humanities, international studies, mathematics, physical sciences, premedicine, social sciences. *Creative Arts/Performance:* 32 awards ($9160 total): art/fine arts, cinema/film/broadcasting, creative writing, journalism/publications, music, theater/drama. *Special Achievements/Activities:* 11 awards ($5500 total): leadership. *Special Characteristics:* 19 awards ($17,250 total): adult students, children and siblings of alumni, children of current students, children of union members/company employees, children of workers in trades, ethnic background, general special characteristics, international students, local/state students, members of minority groups, parents of current students.

LOANS ***Student loans:*** $21,886,526 (85% need-based, 15% non-need-based). 74% of past graduating class borrowed through all loan programs. Average indebtedness per student: $14,649. ***Average need-based loan:*** Freshmen: $2895; Undergraduates: $4231. ***Parent loans:*** $1,792,037 (68% need-based, 32% non-need-based). ***Programs:*** FFEL (Subsidized and Unsubsidized Stafford, PLUS), Perkins, college/university.

WORK-STUDY ***Federal work-study:*** *Total amount:* $312,633; 398 jobs averaging $786. ***State or other work-study/employment:*** *Total amount:* $512,727 (59% need-based, 41% non-need-based). 558 part-time jobs averaging $1781.

APPLYING for FINANCIAL AID ***Required financial aid forms:*** FAFSA, state aid form. ***Financial aid deadline (priority):*** 4/1. ***Notification date:*** Continuous. Students must reply by 5/1 or within 3 weeks of notification.

CONTACT Margaret Sternberg, Director of Financial Aid, State University of New York at Oswego, 206 Culkin Hall, Oswego, NY 13126, 315-341-2248. *Fax:* 315-341-3696.

STATE UNIVERSITY OF NEW YORK AT STONY BROOK

Stony Brook, NY

Tuition & fees (NY res): $4141 **Average undergraduate aid package: $7157**

ABOUT THE INSTITUTION State-supported, coed. Awards: bachelor's, master's, doctoral, and first professional degrees and post-master's certificates. 55 undergraduate majors. Total enrollment: 19,139. Undergraduates: 12,691. Freshmen: 2,269. Federal methodology is used as a basis for awarding need-based institutional aid.

UNDERGRADUATE EXPENSES for 1999–2000 ***Application fee:*** $30. ***Tuition, state resident:*** full-time $3400; part-time $137 per credit. ***Tuition, nonresident:*** full-time $8300; part-time $346 per credit. ***Required fees:*** full-time $741; $35 per credit. ***College room and board:*** $6421; ***room only:*** $4021. Room and board charges vary according to board plan and housing facility. ***Payment plans:*** installment, deferred payment.

FRESHMAN FINANCIAL AID (Fall 1998) 1513 applied for aid; of those 83% were deemed to have need. 97% of freshmen with need received aid; of those 15% had need fully met. *Average percent of need met:* 17% (excluding resources awarded to replace EFC). *Average financial aid package:* $6707 (excluding resources awarded to replace EFC). 13% of all full-time freshmen had no need and received non-need-based aid.

UNDERGRADUATE FINANCIAL AID (Fall 1998) 8,347 applied for aid; of those 87% were deemed to have need. 93% of undergraduates with need received aid; of those 17% had need fully met. *Average percent of need met:* 19% (excluding resources awarded to replace EFC). *Average financial aid package:* $7157 (excluding resources awarded to replace EFC). 10% of all full-time undergraduates had no need and received non-need-based aid.

GIFT AID (NEED-BASED) ***Total amount:*** $23,671,378 (51% Federal, 49% state). ***Receiving aid:*** *Freshmen:* 55% (1,158); *all full-time undergraduates:* 60% (6,608). ***Average award:*** Freshmen: $3819; Undergraduates: $3364. ***Scholarships, grants, and awards:*** Federal Pell, FSEOG, state, private, college/university gift aid from institutional funds.

GIFT AID (NON-NEED-BASED) ***Total amount:*** $1,898,468 (9% Federal, 15% state, 40% institutional, 36% external sources). ***Receiving aid:*** *Freshmen:* 5% (109); *Undergraduates:* 4% (427). ***Scholarships, grants, and awards by category:*** *Academic Interests/Achievement:* 317 awards ($793,031 total): biological sciences, computer science, engineering/technologies, general academic interests/achievements, health fields, physical sciences. *Creative Arts/Performance:* 2 awards ($8100 total): music. *Special Achievements/Activities:* 123 awards ($595,725 total): general special achievements/activities. ***Tuition waivers:*** Full or partial for minority students.

LOANS ***Student loans:*** $32,852,736 (71% need-based, 29% non-need-based). ***Average need-based loan:*** Freshmen: $2712; Undergraduates: $3851. ***Parent loans:*** $2,925,838 (100% non-need-based). ***Programs:*** FFEL (Subsidized and Unsubsidized Stafford, PLUS), Perkins, college/university.

WORK-STUDY ***Federal work-study:*** *Total amount:* $745,076; 637 jobs averaging $1170. ***State or other work-study/employment:*** *Total amount:* $710,205 (23% need-based, 77% non-need-based). 154 part-time jobs averaging $4612.

ATHLETIC AWARDS *Total amount:* 595,725 (100% non-need-based).

APPLYING for FINANCIAL AID ***Required financial aid form:*** FAFSA. ***Financial aid deadline (priority):*** 3/1. ***Notification date:*** Continuous. Students must reply within 2 weeks of notification.

CONTACT Ms. Ana Maria Torres, Director of Financial Aid and Student Employment, State University of New York at Stony Brook, Administration 230, Stony Brook, NY 11794-0851, 516-632-6840 or toll-free 800-USB-SUNY (out-of-state).

STATE UNIVERSITY OF NEW YORK COLLEGE AT BROCKPORT

Brockport, NY

Comprehensive fee: $9424 **Average undergraduate aid package: $7017**

ABOUT THE INSTITUTION State-supported, coed. Awards: bachelor's and master's degrees and post-bachelor's certificates. 81 undergraduate majors. Total enrollment: 8,525. Undergraduates: 6,719. Freshmen: 987. Federal methodology is used as a basis for awarding need-based institutional aid.

UNDERGRADUATE EXPENSES for 1999–2000 ***Application fee:*** $30. ***Comprehensive fee:*** $9424 includes mandatory fees ($614) and room and board ($5410). ***College room only:*** $3340. Full-time tuition and fees vary according to course load. Room and board charges vary according to board plan and housing facility. ***Part-time fees:*** $26 per credit hour. Part-time tuition and fees vary according to course load. ***Payment plans:*** installment, deferred payment.

FRESHMAN FINANCIAL AID (Fall 1999) 821 applied for aid; of those 79% were deemed to have need. 97% of freshmen with need received aid; of those 48% had need fully met. *Average percent of need met:* 84% (excluding resources awarded to replace EFC). *Average financial aid package:* $6358 (excluding resources awarded to replace EFC). 29% of all full-time freshmen had no need and received non-need-based aid.

UNDERGRADUATE FINANCIAL AID (Fall 1999) 4,462 applied for aid; of those 83% were deemed to have need. 96% of undergraduates with need received aid; of those 53% had need fully met. *Average percent of need met:* 86% (excluding resources awarded to replace EFC). *Average financial aid package:* $7017 (excluding resources awarded to replace EFC). 32% of all full-time undergraduates had no need and received non-need-based aid.

GIFT AID (NEED-BASED) ***Total amount:*** $8,660,304 (51% Federal, 49% state). ***Receiving aid:*** *Freshmen:* 52% (474); *all full-time undergraduates:* 51% (2,805). ***Average award:*** Freshmen: $2216; Undergraduates: $2277. ***Scholarships, grants, and awards:*** Federal Pell, FSEOG, state, private, college/university gift aid from institutional funds.

GIFT AID (NON-NEED-BASED) ***Total amount:*** $1,159,312 (2% Federal, 10% state, 57% institutional, 31% external sources). ***Receiving aid:*** *Freshmen:* 15% (133); *Undergraduates:* 6% (353). ***Scholarships, grants, and awards by category:*** *Academic Interests/Achievement:* biological sciences, education, English, foreign languages, general academic interests/achievements, mathematics, military science, physical sciences. *Creative Arts/Performance:* art/fine arts. *Special Achievements/Activities:* community service, leadership. *Special Characteristics:* children and siblings of alumni, local/state students, married students, members of minority groups. ***Tuition waivers:*** Full or partial for employees or children of employees, senior citizens. ***ROTC:*** Army, Naval cooperative, Air Force cooperative.

LOANS ***Student loans:*** $22,461,601 (68% need-based, 32% non-need-based). 74% of past graduating class borrowed through all loan programs. Average indebtedness per student: $15,514. ***Average need-based loan:*** Freshmen: $2822; Undergraduates: $3507. ***Parent loans:*** $1,210,243 (13% need-based, 87% non-need-based). ***Programs:*** Federal Direct (Subsidized and Unsubsidized Stafford, PLUS), Perkins, Federal Nursing, alternative loans.

WORK-STUDY ***Federal work-study:*** *Total amount:* $2,277,300; 800 jobs averaging $1500. ***State or other work-study/employment:*** *Total amount:* $1,220,180 (100% non-need-based). 1,235 part-time jobs averaging $988.

APPLYING for FINANCIAL AID ***Required financial aid forms:*** FAFSA, state aid form. ***Financial aid deadline (priority):*** 3/15.

CONTACT Mr. J. Scott Atkinson, Director of Financial Aid, State University of New York College at Brockport, 350 New Campus Drive, Brockport, NY 14420-2997, 716-395-2501 or toll-free 800-382-8447 (in-state). *Fax:* 716-395-5445. *E-mail:* satkinso@brockport.edu

STATE UNIVERSITY OF NEW YORK COLLEGE AT BUFFALO

Buffalo, NY

Tuition & fees (NY res): $3909 **Average undergraduate aid package: N/A**

ABOUT THE INSTITUTION State-supported, coed. Awards: bachelor's and master's degrees. 66 undergraduate majors. Total enrollment: 11,162. Undergraduates: 9,252. Federal methodology is used as a basis for awarding need-based institutional aid.

UNDERGRADUATE EXPENSES for 1999–2000 ***Application fee:*** $30. ***Tuition, state resident:*** full-time $3400; part-time $137 per semester hour. ***Tuition, nonresident:*** full-time $8300; part-time $346 per semester hour. ***Required fees:*** full-time $509; $21 per semester hour. ***College room and board:*** $5170; ***room only:*** $3190. Room and board charges vary according to board plan, housing facility, and student level. ***Payment plan:*** installment.

GIFT AID (NEED-BASED) ***Scholarships, grants, and awards:*** Federal Pell, FSEOG, state, private, college/university gift aid from institutional funds.

GIFT AID (NON-NEED-BASED) ***Scholarships, grants, and awards by category:*** *Academic Interests/Achievement:* general academic interests/achievements. *Special Characteristics:* members of minority groups. ***Tuition waivers:*** Full or partial for employees or children of employees. ***ROTC:*** Army cooperative.

LOANS ***Programs:*** FFEL (Subsidized and Unsubsidized Stafford, PLUS), Perkins.

WORK-STUDY Federal work-study jobs available. ***State or other work-study/employment:*** Part-time jobs available.

APPLYING for FINANCIAL AID ***Required financial aid form:*** FAFSA. ***Financial aid deadline:*** Continuous. ***Notification date:*** Continuous beginning 5/1. Students must reply within 4 weeks of notification.

CONTACT Mr. Kent McGowan, Director of Financial Aid, State University of New York College at Buffalo, 1300 Elmwood Avenue, Buffalo, NY 14222-1095, 716-878-4901. *Fax:* 716-878-4903.

STATE UNIVERSITY OF NEW YORK COLLEGE AT CORTLAND

Cortland, NY

Tuition & fees (NY res): $4104 **Average undergraduate aid package: $8400**

ABOUT THE INSTITUTION State-supported, coed. Awards: bachelor's and master's degrees and post-bachelor's and post-master's certificates. 47 undergraduate majors. Total enrollment: 6,947. Undergraduates: 5,660. Freshmen: 1,022. Federal methodology is used as a basis for awarding need-based institutional aid.

UNDERGRADUATE EXPENSES for 1999–2000 ***Application fee:*** $30. ***Tuition, state resident:*** full-time $3400; part-time $137 per credit. ***Tuition, nonresident:*** full-time $8300; part-time $346 per credit. ***Required fees:*** full-time $704; $28 per credit. Part-time tuition and fees vary according to course load. ***College room and board:*** $5530; ***room only:*** $3250. Room and board charges vary according to board plan. ***Payment plan:*** installment.

FRESHMAN FINANCIAL AID (Fall 1999, est.) 1047 applied for aid; of those 94% were deemed to have need. 100% of freshmen with need received aid; of those 44% had need fully met. *Average percent of need met:* 92% (excluding resources awarded to replace EFC). *Average financial aid package:* $5425 (excluding resources awarded to replace EFC).

UNDERGRADUATE FINANCIAL AID (Fall 1999, est.) 4,215 applied for aid; of those 91% were deemed to have need. 100% of undergraduates with need received aid; of those 42% had need fully met. *Average percent of need met:* 95% (excluding resources awarded to replace EFC). *Average financial aid package:* $8400 (excluding resources awarded to replace EFC).

GIFT AID (NEED-BASED) ***Total amount:*** $8,028,883 (48% Federal, 49% state, 3% institutional). ***Receiving aid:*** *Freshmen:* 76% (917); *all full-time undergraduates:* 76% (3,775). ***Average award:*** Freshmen: $2035; Undergraduates: $2100. ***Scholarships, grants, and awards:*** Federal Pell, FSEOG, state, private, college/university gift aid from institutional funds.

GIFT AID (NON-NEED-BASED) ***Total amount:*** $994,981 (1% Federal, 99% institutional). ***Receiving aid:*** *Freshmen:* 14% (170); *Undergraduates:* 8% (399). ***Scholarships, grants, and awards by category:*** *Academic Interests/Achievement:* general academic interests/achievements. *Creative Arts/Performance:* general creative arts/performance. ***Tuition waivers:*** Full or partial for employees or children of employees. ***ROTC:*** Army cooperative, Naval cooperative, Air Force cooperative.

LOANS ***Student loans:*** $21,183,945 (64% need-based, 36% non-need-based). Average indebtedness per student: $18,279. ***Average need-based loan:*** Freshmen: $3590; Undergraduates: $3500. ***Parent loans:*** $3,209,598 (100% need-based). ***Programs:*** FFEL (Subsidized and Unsubsidized Stafford, PLUS), Perkins.

WORK-STUDY ***Federal work-study:*** *Total amount:* $390,488; 266 jobs averaging $1468.

APPLYING for FINANCIAL AID ***Required financial aid form:*** FAFSA. ***Financial aid deadline:*** 4/1. ***Notification date:*** Continuous. Students must reply by 5/1 or within 2 weeks of notification.

CONTACT Financial Aid Office, State University of New York College at Cortland, PO Box 2000, Cortland, NY 13045, 607-753-4717. *Fax:* 607-753-5990.

STATE UNIVERSITY OF NEW YORK COLLEGE AT FREDONIA

Fredonia, NY

Tuition & fees (NY res): $4125 **Average undergraduate aid package: $6046**

ABOUT THE INSTITUTION State-supported, coed. Awards: bachelor's and master's degrees. 75 undergraduate majors. Total enrollment: 5,020. Undergraduates: 4,727. Freshmen: 1,073. Federal methodology is used as a basis for awarding need-based institutional aid.

UNDERGRADUATE EXPENSES for 1999–2000 ***Application fee:*** $30. ***Tuition, state resident:*** full-time 3400; part-time 137 per credit hour. ***Tuition, nonresident:*** full-time 8300; part-time 346 per credit hour. ***Required fees:*** full-time 725; 310 per credit hour. ***College room and board:*** 5200; ***room only:*** 3150. Room and board charges vary according to board plan and housing facility. ***Payment plan:*** installment.

FRESHMAN FINANCIAL AID (Fall 1999) 976 applied for aid; of those 72% were deemed to have need. 93% of freshmen with need received aid; of those 68% had need fully met. *Average percent of need met:* 56% (excluding resources awarded to replace EFC). *Average financial aid package:* $5329 (excluding resources awarded to replace EFC). 18% of all full-time freshmen had no need and received non-need-based aid.

UNDERGRADUATE FINANCIAL AID (Fall 1999) 3,518 applied for aid; of those 77% were deemed to have need. 94% of undergraduates with need received aid; of those 71% had need fully met. *Average percent of need met:* 65% (excluding resources awarded to replace EFC). *Average financial aid package:* $6046 (excluding resources awarded to replace EFC). 14% of all full-time undergraduates had no need and received non-need-based aid.

GIFT AID (NEED-BASED) ***Total amount:*** $6,294,458 (42% Federal, 48% state, 5% institutional, 5% external sources). ***Receiving aid:*** *Freshmen:* 50% (498); *all full-time undergraduates:* 45% (1,984). ***Average award:*** Freshmen: $856; Undergraduates: $416. ***Scholarships, grants, and awards:*** Federal Pell, FSEOG, state, private, college/university gift aid from institutional funds.

GIFT AID (NON-NEED-BASED) ***Receiving aid:*** *Freshmen:* 19% (191); *Undergraduates:* 12% (530). ***Scholarships, grants, and awards by category:*** *Academic Interests/Achievement:* 102 awards ($143,000 total): biological sciences, business, communication, education, English, foreign languages, general academic interests/achievements, humanities, international studies, mathematics, physical sciences, social sciences. *Creative Arts/Performance:* 55 awards ($60,000 total): applied art and design, dance, music, performing arts, theater/drama. *Special Achievements/Activities:* 60 awards ($60,000 total): general special achievements/activities, leadership. *Special Characteristics:* 50 awards ($42,000 total):

children and siblings of alumni, ethnic background, general special characteristics, international students, members of minority groups, out-of-state students, previous college experience, veterans, veterans' children. ***ROTC:*** Army cooperative.

LOANS ***Student loans:*** $14,432,542 (61% need-based, 39% non-need-based). 85% of past graduating class borrowed through all loan programs. Average indebtedness per student: $12,691. ***Average need-based loan:*** Freshmen: $1139; Undergraduates: $536. ***Parent loans:*** $1,389,599 (100% non-need-based). ***Programs:*** FFEL (Subsidized and Unsubsidized Stafford, PLUS), Perkins.

WORK-STUDY ***Federal work-study:*** *Total amount:* $369,250; 308 jobs averaging $1100.

APPLYING for FINANCIAL AID ***Required financial aid forms:*** FAFSA, state aid form. ***Financial aid deadline (priority):*** 2/15. ***Notification date:*** Continuous beginning 3/15.

CONTACT Mr. Daniel M. Tramuta, Interim Director of Financial Aid, State University of New York College at Fredonia, Maytum Hall, 212, Fredonia, NY 14063, 716-673-3253 or toll-free 800-252-1212. *Fax:* 716-673-3785. *E-mail:* tramuta@fredonia.edu

STATE UNIVERSITY OF NEW YORK COLLEGE AT GENESEO

Geneseo, NY

Tuition & fees (NY res): $4221 **Average undergraduate aid package: $6730**

ABOUT THE INSTITUTION State-supported, coed. Awards: bachelor's and master's degrees. 44 undergraduate majors. Total enrollment: 5,604. Undergraduates: 5,322. Freshmen: 1,169. Federal methodology is used as a basis for awarding need-based institutional aid.

UNDERGRADUATE EXPENSES for 1999–2000 ***Application fee:*** $30. ***Tuition, state resident:*** full-time $3400; part-time $137 per credit. ***Tuition, nonresident:*** full-time $8300; part-time $346 per credit. ***Required fees:*** full-time $821; $34 per credit. ***College room and board:*** $4940. Room and board charges vary according to board plan and housing facility. ***Payment plans:*** installment, deferred payment.

FRESHMAN FINANCIAL AID (Fall 1999, est.) 982 applied for aid; of those 55% were deemed to have need. 100% of freshmen with need received aid; of those 80% had need fully met. *Average percent of need met:* 80% (excluding resources awarded to replace EFC). *Average financial aid package:* $6080 (excluding resources awarded to replace EFC).

UNDERGRADUATE FINANCIAL AID (Fall 1999, est.) 3,723 applied for aid; of those 65% were deemed to have need. 100% of undergraduates with need received aid; of those 85% had need fully met. *Average percent of need met:* 85% (excluding resources awarded to replace EFC). *Average financial aid package:* $6730 (excluding resources awarded to replace EFC).

GIFT AID (NEED-BASED) ***Total amount:*** $4,853,175 (44% Federal, 56% state). ***Receiving aid:*** *Freshmen:* 36% (420); *all full-time undergraduates:* 40% (2,105). ***Average award:*** Freshmen: $2170; Undergraduates: $2305. ***Scholarships, grants, and awards:*** Federal Pell, FSEOG, state, private, college/university gift aid from institutional funds.

GIFT AID (NON-NEED-BASED) ***Total amount:*** $689,510 (2% Federal, 36% state, 62% institutional). ***Receiving aid:*** *Freshmen:* 10% (120); *Undergraduates:* 10% (530). ***Scholarships, grants, and awards by category:*** *Academic Interests/Achievement:* 294 awards ($289,675 total): area/ethnic studies, biological sciences, business, communication, computer science, education, English, foreign languages, general academic interests/achievements, humanities, mathematics, physical sciences, premedicine, social sciences. *Creative Arts/Performance:* 63 awards ($23,825 total): applied art and design, art/fine arts, creative writing, dance, general creative arts/performance, journalism/publications, music, performing arts, theater/drama. *Special Achievements/Activities:* 37 awards ($22,700 total): community service, general special achievements/activities, leadership. *Special Characteristics:* 30 awards ($25,009 total): local/state students, members of minority groups. ***ROTC:*** Army cooperative, Air Force cooperative.

LOANS ***Student loans:*** $13,858,160 (59% need-based, 41% non-need-based). 75% of past graduating class borrowed through all loan programs. Average indebtedness per student: $12,500. ***Average need-based loan:*** Freshmen: $3535; Undergraduates: $3450. ***Programs:*** FFEL (Subsidized and Unsubsidized Stafford, PLUS), Perkins, state.

WORK-STUDY ***Federal work-study:*** *Total amount:* $645,000; 500 jobs averaging $1350.

APPLYING for FINANCIAL AID ***Required financial aid forms:*** FAFSA, state aid form. ***Financial aid deadline (priority):*** 2/15. ***Notification date:*** Continuous beginning 3/15. Students must reply within 3 weeks of notification.

CONTACT Archie Cureton, Director of Financial Aid, State University of New York College at Geneseo, 1 College Circle, Erwin 104, Geneseo, NY 14454, 716-245-5731. *Fax:* 716-245-5717. *E-mail:* cureton@geneseo.edu

STATE UNIVERSITY OF NEW YORK COLLEGE AT OLD WESTBURY

Old Westbury, NY

ABOUT THE INSTITUTION State-supported, coed. Awards: bachelor's degrees. 27 undergraduate majors. Total enrollment: 3,245. Undergraduates: 3,245.

GIFT AID (NEED-BASED) ***Scholarships, grants, and awards:*** Federal Pell, FSEOG, state, private, college/university gift aid from institutional funds.

GIFT AID (NON-NEED-BASED) ***Scholarships, grants, and awards by category:*** *Academic Interests/Achievement:* biological sciences, health fields, physical sciences.

LOANS ***Programs:*** FFEL (Subsidized and Unsubsidized Stafford, PLUS), Perkins.

WORK-STUDY Federal work-study jobs available.

APPLYING for FINANCIAL AID ***Required financial aid forms:*** FAFSA, institution's own form, state aid form.

CONTACT Financial Aid Office, State University of New York College at Old Westbury, PO Box 210, Old Westbury, NY 11568-0210, 516-876-3222.

STATE UNIVERSITY OF NEW YORK COLLEGE AT ONEONTA

Oneonta, NY

Tuition & fees (NY res): $4123 **Average undergraduate aid package: $7997**

ABOUT THE INSTITUTION State-supported, coed. Awards: bachelor's and master's degrees and post-bachelor's certificates. 59 undergraduate majors. Total enrollment: 5,407. Undergraduates: 5,147. Freshmen: 1,152. Federal methodology is used as a basis for awarding need-based institutional aid.

UNDERGRADUATE EXPENSES for 2000–2001 (est.) ***Application fee:*** $30. ***Tuition, state resident:*** full-time $3400; part-time $137 per semester hour. ***Tuition, nonresident:*** full-time $8300; part-time $346 per semester hour. ***Required fees:*** full-time $723; $27 per semester hour. Part-time tuition and fees vary according to course load. ***College room and board:*** $5456; ***room only:*** $3006. Room and board charges vary according to board plan and housing facility. ***Payment plan:*** installment.

FRESHMAN FINANCIAL AID (Fall 1998) 865 applied for aid; of those 80% were deemed to have need. 95% of freshmen with need received aid; of those 28% had need fully met. *Average percent of need met:* 62% (excluding resources awarded to replace EFC). *Average financial aid package:* $7210 (excluding resources awarded to replace EFC). 25% of all full-time freshmen had no need and received non-need-based aid.

UNDERGRADUATE FINANCIAL AID (Fall 1998) 3,668 applied for aid; of those 84% were deemed to have need. 98% of undergraduates with need received aid; of those 33% had need fully met. *Average percent of need met:* 69% (excluding resources awarded to replace EFC). *Average financial aid package:* $7997 (excluding resources awarded to replace EFC). 28% of all full-time undergraduates had no need and received non-need-based aid.

GIFT AID (NEED-BASED) ***Total amount:*** $8,632,961 (43% Federal, 50% state, 3% institutional, 4% external sources). ***Receiving aid:*** *Freshmen:* 52% (553); *all full-time undergraduates:* 52% (2,403). ***Average award:***

State University of New York College at Oneonta (continued)

Freshmen: $3368; Undergraduates: $3297. ***Scholarships, grants, and awards:*** Federal Pell, FSEOG, state, private, college/university gift aid from institutional funds.

GIFT AID (NON-NEED-BASED) ***Total amount:*** $68,542 (10% institutional, 90% external sources). ***Scholarships, grants, and awards by category:*** *Academic Interests/Achievement:* 118 awards ($103,137 total): biological sciences, education, general academic interests/achievements, home economics, physical sciences. *Creative Arts/Performance:* 15 awards ($5950 total): music. *Special Achievements/Activities:* 15 awards ($13,022 total): community service, general special achievements/activities, leadership. *Special Characteristics:* 137 awards ($108,747 total): adult students, children and siblings of alumni, ethnic background, general special characteristics, handicapped students, international students, local/state students, members of minority groups. ***Tuition waivers:*** Full or partial for employees or children of employees.

LOANS ***Student loans:*** $15,265,037 (70% need-based, 30% non-need-based). 75% of past graduating class borrowed through all loan programs. Average indebtedness per student: $15,100. ***Average need-based loan:*** Freshmen: $1416; Undergraduates: $2242. ***Parent loans:*** $3,687,829 (100% non-need-based). ***Programs:*** FFEL (Subsidized and Unsubsidized Stafford, PLUS), Perkins, college/university.

WORK-STUDY ***Federal work-study:*** *Total amount:* $286,763; 439 jobs averaging $653. ***State or other work-study/employment:*** *Total amount:* $493,094 (100% non-need-based). 337 part-time jobs averaging $1463.

ATHLETIC AWARDS *Total amount:* 62,100 (10% need-based, 90% non-need-based).

APPLYING for FINANCIAL AID ***Required financial aid forms:*** FAFSA, state aid form. ***Financial aid deadline (priority):*** 3/15. ***Notification date:*** Continuous.

CONTACT Mr. Bill Goodhue, Director of Financial Aid, State University of New York College at Oneonta, Ravine Parkway, Oneonta, NY 13820, 607-436-2992 or toll-free 800-SUNY-123. *Fax:* 607-436-2659. *E-mail:* goodhucw@oneonta.edu

STATE UNIVERSITY OF NEW YORK COLLEGE AT PLATTSBURGH

Plattsburgh, NY

See Plattsburgh State University of New York

STATE UNIVERSITY OF NEW YORK COLLEGE AT POTSDAM

Potsdam, NY

Tuition & fees (NY res): $3935 **Average undergraduate aid package: $9133**

ABOUT THE INSTITUTION State-supported, coed. Awards: bachelor's and master's degrees. 57 undergraduate majors. Total enrollment: 4,127. Undergraduates: 3,587. Freshmen: 750. Federal methodology is used as a basis for awarding need-based institutional aid.

UNDERGRADUATE EXPENSES for 1999–2000 ***Application fee:*** $30. ***Tuition, state resident:*** full-time $3400; part-time $137 per credit hour. ***Tuition, nonresident:*** full-time $8300; part-time $346 per credit hour. ***Required fees:*** full-time $535; $28 per credit hour. ***College room and board:*** $5750; ***room only:*** $3300. Room and board charges vary according to board plan and housing facility. ***Payment plan:*** installment.

FRESHMAN FINANCIAL AID (Fall 1999) 691 applied for aid; of those 80% were deemed to have need. 98% of freshmen with need received aid; of those 82% had need fully met. *Average percent of need met:* 86% (excluding resources awarded to replace EFC). *Average financial aid package:* $8607 (excluding resources awarded to replace EFC). 15% of all full-time freshmen had no need and received non-need-based aid.

UNDERGRADUATE FINANCIAL AID (Fall 1999) 2,747 applied for aid; of those 84% were deemed to have need. 99% of undergraduates with need received aid; of those 82% had need fully met. *Average percent of need met:* 83% (excluding resources awarded to replace EFC). *Average financial aid package:* $9133 (excluding resources awarded to replace EFC). 15% of all full-time undergraduates had no need and received non-need-based aid.

GIFT AID (NEED-BASED) ***Total amount:*** $6,232,473 (52% Federal, 48% state). ***Receiving aid:*** *Freshmen:* 70% (526); *all full-time undergraduates:* 62% (2,104). ***Average award:*** Freshmen: $3548; Undergraduates: $3518. ***Scholarships, grants, and awards:*** Federal Pell, FSEOG, state, private, college/university gift aid from institutional funds.

GIFT AID (NON-NEED-BASED) ***Total amount:*** $1,736,317 (15% Federal, 6% state, 60% institutional, 19% external sources). ***Receiving aid:*** *Freshmen:* 34% (254); *Undergraduates:* 21% (722). ***Scholarships, grants, and awards by category:*** *Academic Interests/Achievement:* 409 awards ($431,400 total): biological sciences, business, communication, education, engineering/technologies, English, foreign languages, general academic interests/achievements, humanities, mathematics, physical sciences, social sciences. *Creative Arts/Performance:* 123 awards ($130,700 total): art/fine arts, dance, music, performing arts, theater/drama. *Special Achievements/Activities:* 11 awards ($11,000 total): community service, leadership. *Special Characteristics:* 48 awards ($46,000 total): children and siblings of alumni, ethnic background, handicapped students, members of minority groups. ***ROTC:*** Army cooperative, Air Force cooperative.

LOANS ***Student loans:*** $15,776,283 (62% need-based, 38% non-need-based). 56% of past graduating class borrowed through all loan programs. Average indebtedness per student: $15,303. ***Average need-based loan:*** Freshmen: $2994; Undergraduates: $3839. ***Parent loans:*** $3,023,630 (100% non-need-based). ***Programs:*** Federal Direct (Subsidized and Unsubsidized Stafford, PLUS), Perkins.

WORK-STUDY ***Federal work-study:*** *Total amount:* $297,824; 352 jobs averaging $800.

APPLYING for FINANCIAL AID ***Required financial aid forms:*** FAFSA, state aid form. ***Financial aid deadline:*** Continuous. ***Notification date:*** Continuous beginning 2/15.

CONTACT Mark J. Dougherty, Interim Director of Financial Aid, State University of New York College at Potsdam, 44 Pierrepont Avenue, Potsdam, NY 13676, 315-267-2162. *Fax:* 315-267-3067. *E-mail:* doughemj@potsdam.edu

STATE UNIVERSITY OF NEW YORK COLLEGE AT PURCHASE

Purchase, NY

See Purchase College, State University of New York

STATE UNIVERSITY OF NEW YORK COLLEGE OF ENVIRONMENTAL SCIENCE AND FORESTRY

Syracuse, NY

Tuition & fees (NY res): $3762 **Average undergraduate aid package: $8456**

ABOUT THE INSTITUTION State-supported, coed. Awards: bachelor's, master's, and doctoral degrees. 44 undergraduate majors. Total enrollment: 1,729. Undergraduates: 1,171. Freshmen: 142. Federal methodology is used as a basis for awarding need-based institutional aid.

UNDERGRADUATE EXPENSES for 1999–2000 ***Application fee:*** $30. ***Tuition, state resident:*** full-time $3400; part-time $137 per credit hour. ***Tuition, nonresident:*** full-time $8300; part-time $346 per credit hour. ***Required fees:*** full-time $362; $12 per credit hour. Full-time tuition and fees vary according to location. Part-time tuition and fees vary according to course load and location. ***College room and board:*** $8310; ***room only:*** $4170. Room and board charges vary according to board plan, housing facility, and location. College room and board are provided by Syracuse University. ***Payment plans:*** installment, deferred payment.

FRESHMAN FINANCIAL AID (Fall 1998) 132 applied for aid; of those 70% were deemed to have need. 100% of freshmen with need received aid; of

those 97% had need fully met. *Average percent of need met:* 97% (excluding resources awarded to replace EFC). *Average financial aid package:* $7550 (excluding resources awarded to replace EFC). 15% of all full-time freshmen had no need and received non-need-based aid.

UNDERGRADUATE FINANCIAL AID (Fall 1998) 965 applied for aid; of those 85% were deemed to have need. 100% of undergraduates with need received aid; of those 70% had need fully met. *Average percent of need met:* 85% (excluding resources awarded to replace EFC). *Average financial aid package:* $8456 (excluding resources awarded to replace EFC). 30% of all full-time undergraduates had no need and received non-need-based aid.

GIFT AID (NEED-BASED) ***Total amount:*** $2,232,314 (40% Federal, 41% state, 17% institutional, 2% external sources). ***Receiving aid:*** *Freshmen:* 61% (86); *all full-time undergraduates:* 60% (697). ***Average award:*** Freshmen: $4458; Undergraduates: $3203. ***Scholarships, grants, and awards:*** Federal Pell, FSEOG, state, private, college/university gift aid from institutional funds.

GIFT AID (NON-NEED-BASED) ***Total amount:*** $158,629 (21% Federal, 8% state, 39% institutional, 32% external sources). ***Receiving aid:*** *Freshmen:* 4% (5); *Undergraduates:* 3% (35). ***Scholarships, grants, and awards by category:*** *Academic Interests/Achievement:* 34 awards ($78,000 total): agriculture, biological sciences, engineering/technologies, physical sciences. *Special Achievements/Activities:* 6 awards ($10,000 total): leadership. *Special Characteristics:* members of minority groups. ***ROTC:*** Army cooperative, Air Force cooperative.

LOANS ***Student loans:*** $5,720,157 (75% need-based, 25% non-need-based). 80% of past graduating class borrowed through all loan programs. Average indebtedness per student: $15,000. ***Average need-based loan:*** Freshmen: $2904; Undergraduates: $5007. ***Parent loans:*** $563,643 (10% need-based, 90% non-need-based). ***Programs:*** FFEL (Subsidized and Unsubsidized Stafford, PLUS), Perkins, college/university.

WORK-STUDY ***Federal work-study:*** *Total amount:* $383,221; 290 jobs averaging $1100. ***State or other work-study/employment:*** *Total amount:* $295,000 (100% non-need-based). 118 part-time jobs averaging $1100.

APPLYING for FINANCIAL AID ***Required financial aid forms:*** FAFSA, state aid form. ***Financial aid deadline (priority):*** 3/1. ***Notification date:*** 4/1. Students must reply within 2 weeks of notification.

CONTACT Mr. John E. View, Director of Financial Aid, State University of New York College of Environmental Science and Forestry, 1 Forestry Drive, 115 Bray Hall, Syracuse, NY 13210-2779, 315-470-6670 or toll-free 800-777-7373. *E-mail:* jeview@esf.edu

STATE UNIVERSITY OF NEW YORK HEALTH SCIENCE CENTER AT BROOKLYN

Brooklyn, NY

CONTACT Office of Financial Aid, State University of New York Health Science Center at Brooklyn, 450 Clarkson Avenue, Brooklyn, NY 11203-2098, 718-270-2488.

STATE UNIVERSITY OF NEW YORK INSTITUTE OF TECHNOLOGY AT UTICA/ROME

Utica, NY

Tuition & fees (NY res): $3975 **Average undergraduate aid package: N/A**

ABOUT THE INSTITUTION State-supported, coed. Awards: bachelor's and master's degrees. 22 undergraduate majors. Total enrollment: 2,602. Undergraduates: 2,215. Federal methodology is used as a basis for awarding need-based institutional aid.

UNDERGRADUATE EXPENSES for 1999–2000 ***Application fee:*** $30. ***Tuition, state resident:*** full-time $3400; part-time $137 per semester hour. ***Tuition, nonresident:*** full-time $8300; part-time $346 per semester hour. ***Required fees:*** full-time $575; $22 per semester hour. Part-time tuition and fees vary according to course load. ***College room and board:*** $6100; ***room only:*** $3900. Room and board charges vary according to board plan and housing facility. ***Payment plan:*** installment.

GIFT AID (NEED-BASED) ***Total amount:*** $2,790,948 (60% Federal, 40% state). ***Scholarships, grants, and awards:*** Federal Pell, FSEOG, state.

GIFT AID (NON-NEED-BASED) ***Total amount:*** $462,771 (9% Federal, 46% state, 26% institutional, 19% external sources). ***Scholarships, grants, and awards by category:*** *Academic Interests/Achievement:* general academic interests/achievements. *Special Characteristics:* local/state students, members of minority groups, previous college experience. ***ROTC:*** Army cooperative, Naval cooperative, Air Force cooperative.

LOANS ***Student loans:*** $6,933,726 (59% need-based, 41% non-need-based). ***Parent loans:*** $411,405 (100% non-need-based). ***Programs:*** Federal Direct (Subsidized and Unsubsidized Stafford, PLUS), Perkins, Federal Nursing, college/university.

WORK-STUDY ***Federal work-study:*** *Total amount:* $324,483; 219 jobs averaging $1481.

APPLYING for FINANCIAL AID ***Required financial aid forms:*** FAFSA, institution's own form, state aid form. ***Financial aid deadline:*** Continuous. ***Notification date:*** Continuous. Students must reply within 2 weeks of notification.

CONTACT Mr. Edward Hutchinson, Director of Financial Aid, State University of New York Institute of Technology at Utica/Rome, PO Box 3050, Utica, NY 13504-3050, 315-792-7210 or toll-free 800-SUNYTEC. *Fax:* 315-792-7220. *E-mail:* finaid@sunyit.edu

STATE UNIVERSITY OF NEW YORK MARITIME COLLEGE

Throggs Neck, NY

Tuition & fees (NY res): $4195 **Average undergraduate aid package: $10,000**

ABOUT THE INSTITUTION State-supported, coed. Awards: associate, bachelor's, and master's degrees. 11 undergraduate majors. Total enrollment: 829. Undergraduates: 666. Freshmen: 156. Federal methodology is used as a basis for awarding need-based institutional aid.

UNDERGRADUATE EXPENSES for 1999–2000 ***Application fee:*** $30. ***One-time required fee:*** $1900. ***Tuition, state resident:*** full-time $3400; part-time $157 per credit. ***Tuition, nonresident:*** full-time $8300; part-time $546 per credit. ***Required fees:*** full-time $795; $11 per credit. Full-time tuition and fees vary according to reciprocity agreements. Part-time tuition and fees vary according to reciprocity agreements. ***College room and board:*** $5600; ***room only:*** $3400. Room and board charges vary according to board plan. Tuition and fees for mandatory summer sea term: $1600. ***Payment plan:*** installment.

FRESHMAN FINANCIAL AID (Fall 1998) 125 applied for aid; of those 80% were deemed to have need. 100% of freshmen with need received aid; of those 60% had need fully met. *Average percent of need met:* 85% (excluding resources awarded to replace EFC). *Average financial aid package:* $12,000 (excluding resources awarded to replace EFC). 20% of all full-time freshmen had no need and received non-need-based aid.

UNDERGRADUATE FINANCIAL AID (Fall 1998) 487 applied for aid; of those 82% were deemed to have need. 100% of undergraduates with need received aid; of those 90% had need fully met. *Average percent of need met:* 85% (excluding resources awarded to replace EFC). *Average financial aid package:* $10,000 (excluding resources awarded to replace EFC). 13% of all full-time undergraduates had no need and received non-need-based aid.

GIFT AID (NEED-BASED) ***Total amount:*** $999,956 (49% Federal, 34% state, 10% institutional, 7% external sources). ***Receiving aid:*** *Freshmen:* 46% (72); *all full-time undergraduates:* 45% (287). ***Average award:*** Freshmen: $2500; Undergraduates: $3346. ***Scholarships, grants, and awards:*** Federal Pell, FSEOG, state, private, college/university gift aid from institutional funds, Educational Opportunity Program (EOP).

GIFT AID (NON-NEED-BASED) ***Total amount:*** $623,535 (2% state, 19% institutional, 79% external sources). ***Receiving aid:*** *Freshmen:* 22% (35);

State University of New York Maritime College (continued)

Undergraduates: 28% (179). ***Scholarships, grants, and awards by category:*** *Academic Interests/Achievement:* general academic interests/achievements. ***ROTC:*** Naval, Air Force cooperative.

LOANS ***Student loans:*** $2,179,920 (100% need-based). 70% of past graduating class borrowed through all loan programs. Average indebtedness per student: $12,000. ***Average need-based loan:*** Freshmen: $2812; Undergraduates: $4184. ***Parent loans:*** $650,998 (100% need-based). ***Programs:*** FFEL (Subsidized and Unsubsidized Stafford, PLUS), Perkins, college/university, alternative loans.

WORK-STUDY ***Federal work-study:*** *Total amount:* $16,845; 55 jobs averaging $500. ***State or other work-study/employment:*** *Total amount:* $16,300 (100% non-need-based). 53 part-time jobs averaging $600.

APPLYING for FINANCIAL AID ***Required financial aid forms:*** FAFSA, institution's own form. ***Financial aid deadline (priority):*** 2/15. ***Notification date:*** Continuous beginning 3/1. Students must reply within 4 weeks of notification.

CONTACT Sandra J. Hebert, Director of Financial Aid, State University of New York Maritime College, 6 Pennyfield Avenue, Throgs Neck, NY 10465-4198, 718-409-7267 or toll-free 800-654-1874 (in-state), 800-642-1874 (out-of-state). *Fax:* 718-409-7275.

STATE UNIVERSITY OF NEW YORK UPSTATE MEDICAL UNIVERSITY

Syracuse, NY

Tuition & fees (NY res): $3810 **Average undergraduate aid package: N/A**

ABOUT THE INSTITUTION State-supported, coed. Awards: bachelor's, master's, doctoral, and first professional degrees. 10 undergraduate majors. Total enrollment: 1,173. Undergraduates: 320. Entering class: 6. Both federal and institutional methodology are used as a basis for awarding need-based institutional aid.

UNDERGRADUATE EXPENSES for 1999–2000 ***Application fee:*** $30. ***Tuition, state resident:*** full-time $3400; part-time $137 per credit. ***Tuition, nonresident:*** full-time $8300; part-time $346 per credit. ***Required fees:*** full-time $410; $9 per credit; $32 per term part-time. Full-time tuition and fees vary according to degree level. Part-time tuition and fees vary according to course load and degree level. ***College room and board:*** $6515; ***room only:*** $4175. Room and board charges vary according to housing facility. ***Payment plan:*** installment.

GIFT AID (NEED-BASED) ***Scholarships, grants, and awards:*** Federal Pell, FSEOG, state, private, college/university gift aid from institutional funds.

LOANS ***Programs:*** FFEL (Subsidized and Unsubsidized Stafford, PLUS), Perkins, college/university, Primary Care Loans.

WORK-STUDY Federal work-study jobs available.

APPLYING for FINANCIAL AID ***Required financial aid form:*** FAFSA. ***Financial aid deadline:*** 4/1 (priority: 3/1). ***Notification date:*** Continuous beginning 5/1.

CONTACT Office of Financial Aid, State University of New York Upstate Medical University, 750 East Adams Street, Syracuse, NY 13210-2375, 315-464-4329. *E-mail:* finaid@hscsyr.edu

STATE UNIVERSITY OF WEST GEORGIA

Carrollton, GA

Tuition & fees (GA res): $2212 **Average undergraduate aid package: $5406**

ABOUT THE INSTITUTION State-supported, coed. Awards: associate, bachelor's, and master's degrees. 51 undergraduate majors. Total enrollment: 8,665. Undergraduates: 6,772. Freshmen: 1,638. Federal methodology is used as a basis for awarding need-based institutional aid.

UNDERGRADUATE EXPENSES for 1999–2000 ***Application fee:*** $20. ***Tuition, state resident:*** full-time $1808; part-time $75 per semester hour. ***Tuition, nonresident:*** full-time $7232; part-time $301 per semester hour. ***Required fees:*** full-time $404; $14 per semester hour; $65 per term part-time. Part-time tuition and fees vary according to course load. ***College room and board:*** $3806; ***room only:*** $2026. Room and board charges vary according to board plan and housing facility.

FRESHMAN FINANCIAL AID (Fall 1999) 1461 applied for aid. *Average percent of need met:* 62% (excluding resources awarded to replace EFC). *Average financial aid package:* $6751 (excluding resources awarded to replace EFC). 35% of all full-time freshmen had no need and received non-need-based aid.

UNDERGRADUATE FINANCIAL AID (Fall 1999) 4,110 applied for aid. *Average percent of need met:* 75% (excluding resources awarded to replace EFC). *Average financial aid package:* $5406 (excluding resources awarded to replace EFC). 15% of all full-time undergraduates had no need and received non-need-based aid.

GIFT AID (NEED-BASED) ***Total amount:*** $9,288,007 (69% Federal, 31% state). ***Scholarships, grants, and awards:*** Federal Pell, FSEOG, state, private, college/university gift aid from institutional funds.

GIFT AID (NON-NEED-BASED) ***Total amount:*** $5,971,366 ***Scholarships, grants, and awards by category:*** *Academic Interests/Achievement:* biological sciences, business, communication, computer science, education, English, foreign languages, general academic interests/achievements, health fields, humanities, mathematics, physical sciences, social sciences. *Creative Arts/Performance:* art/fine arts, debating, journalism/publications, music, theater/drama. *Special Achievements/Activities:* memberships. *Special Characteristics:* adult students, children and siblings of alumni, children of union members/company employees, handicapped students, international students, local/state students, members of minority groups, previous college experience. ***Tuition waivers:*** Full or partial for minority students, adult students, senior citizens. ***ROTC:*** Army.

LOANS ***Student loans:*** $18,914,696 (70% need-based, 30% non-need-based). 76% of past graduating class borrowed through all loan programs. ***Parent loans:*** $488,262 (100% non-need-based). ***Programs:*** Federal Direct (Subsidized and Unsubsidized Stafford, PLUS), Perkins, college/university.

WORK-STUDY ***Federal work-study:*** *Total amount:* $1,227,902; jobs available.

ATHLETIC AWARDS *Total amount:* 2,418,547 (100% non-need-based).

APPLYING for FINANCIAL AID ***Required financial aid form:*** FAFSA. ***Financial aid deadline (priority):*** 4/15. ***Notification date:*** Continuous beginning 5/1. Students must reply within 4 weeks of notification.

CONTACT Kimberly Jordan, Director of Financial Aid, State University of West Georgia, 215 Mandeville Hall, Carrollton, GA 30118, 770-836-6421. *Fax:* 770-830-2339. *E-mail:* kjordan@westga.edu

STEPHEN F. AUSTIN STATE UNIVERSITY

Nacogdoches, TX

Tuition & fees (TX res): $2578 **Average undergraduate aid package: $2923**

ABOUT THE INSTITUTION State-supported, coed. Awards: bachelor's, master's, and doctoral degrees. 72 undergraduate majors. Total enrollment: 11,919. Undergraduates: 10,508. Freshmen: 2,257. Federal methodology is used as a basis for awarding need-based institutional aid.

UNDERGRADUATE EXPENSES for 1999–2000 ***Tuition, state resident:*** full-time $1860; part-time $62 per semester hour. ***Tuition, nonresident:*** full-time $8340; part-time $278 per semester hour. ***Required fees:*** full-time $718; $21 per semester hour; $10 per term part-time. Full-time tuition and fees vary according to course load and reciprocity agreements. Part-time tuition and fees vary according to course load and reciprocity agreements. ***College room and board:*** $4168. Room and board charges vary according to board plan and housing facility. ***Payment plan:*** installment.

FRESHMAN FINANCIAL AID (Fall 1999, est.) 1341 applied for aid; of those 66% were deemed to have need. 97% of freshmen with need received aid; of those 26% had need fully met. *Average percent of need met:* 60% (excluding resources awarded to replace EFC). *Average financial aid package:* $2817 (excluding resources awarded to replace EFC). 15% of all full-time freshmen had no need and received non-need-based aid.

UNDERGRADUATE FINANCIAL AID (Fall 1999, est.) 5,256 applied for aid; of those 72% were deemed to have need. 96% of undergraduates with need received aid; of those 26% had need fully met. *Average percent of*

need met: 63% (excluding resources awarded to replace EFC). *Average financial aid package:* $2923 (excluding resources awarded to replace EFC). 13% of all full-time undergraduates had no need and received non-need-based aid.

GIFT AID (NEED-BASED) ***Total amount:*** $8,730,896 (77% Federal, 9% state, 14% institutional). ***Receiving aid:*** *Freshmen:* 33% (660); *all full-time undergraduates:* 33% (2,792). ***Average award:*** Freshmen: $1465; Undergraduates: $1261. ***Scholarships, grants, and awards:*** Federal Pell, FSEOG, state, private, college/university gift aid from institutional funds.

GIFT AID (NON-NEED-BASED) ***Total amount:*** $2,882,051 (55% institutional, 45% external sources). ***Receiving aid:*** *Freshmen:* 17% (343); *Undergraduates:* 8% (702). ***Scholarships, grants, and awards by category:*** *Academic Interests/Achievement:* agriculture, biological sciences, business, communication, computer science, education, general academic interests/achievements, health fields, home economics, mathematics, military science, physical sciences, premedicine. *Creative Arts/Performance:* applied art and design, art/fine arts, journalism/publications, music, theater/drama. *Special Achievements/Activities:* cheerleading/drum major, general special achievements/activities, hobbies/interests, leadership, rodeo. *Special Characteristics:* adult students, children of union members/company employees, first-generation college students, general special characteristics, local/state students, previous college experience, religious affiliation. ***ROTC:*** Army.

LOANS ***Student loans:*** $24,094,869 (57% need-based, 43% non-need-based). 50% of past graduating class borrowed through all loan programs. Average indebtedness per student: $9000. ***Average need-based loan:*** Freshmen: $1187; Undergraduates: $1770. ***Parent loans:*** $2,316,693 (100% non-need-based). ***Programs:*** FFEL (Subsidized and Unsubsidized Stafford), Perkins, state, college/university.

WORK-STUDY ***Federal work-study:*** *Total amount:* $864,679; 395 jobs averaging $2189. ***State or other work-study/employment:*** *Total amount:* $57,609 (100% need-based). 35 part-time jobs averaging $1646.

ATHLETIC AWARDS *Total amount:* 1,116,639 (100% non-need-based).

APPLYING for FINANCIAL AID ***Required financial aid forms:*** FAFSA, institution's own form. ***Financial aid deadline (priority):*** 4/15. ***Notification date:*** Continuous beginning 5/1. Students must reply within 2 weeks of notification.

CONTACT Office of Financial Aid, Stephen F. Austin State University, PO Box 13052, SFA Station, Nacogdoches, TX 75962, 409-468-2403 or toll-free 800-731-2902. *Fax:* 409-468-1048. *E-mail:* finaid@sfasu.edu

STEPHENS COLLEGE

Columbia, MO

Tuition & fees: $15,770 **Average undergraduate aid package: N/A**

ABOUT THE INSTITUTION Independent, women only. Awards: associate, bachelor's, and master's degrees. 36 undergraduate majors. Total enrollment: 788. Undergraduates: 734. Freshmen: 134. Federal methodology is used as a basis for awarding need-based institutional aid.

UNDERGRADUATE EXPENSES for 2000–2001 ***Application fee:*** $25. ***Comprehensive fee:*** $21,640 includes full-time tuition ($15,770) and room and board ($5870). Room and board charges vary according to board plan. ***Payment plan:*** installment.

FRESHMAN FINANCIAL AID (Fall 1998) 105 applied for aid; of those 87% were deemed to have need. 100% of freshmen with need received aid.

GIFT AID (NEED-BASED) ***Receiving aid:*** *Freshmen:* 54% (69). ***Scholarships, grants, and awards:*** Federal Pell, FSEOG, state, private, college/university gift aid from institutional funds.

GIFT AID (NON-NEED-BASED) ***Receiving aid:*** *Freshmen:* 65% (82). ***Scholarships, grants, and awards by category:*** *Academic Interests/Achievement:* general academic interests/achievements. *Creative Arts/Performance:* dance, performing arts, theater/drama. *Special Achievements/Activities:* leadership. *Special Characteristics:* children of faculty/staff, local/state students, siblings of current students. ***Tuition waivers:*** Full or partial for employees or children of employees. ***ROTC:*** Army cooperative, Naval cooperative, Air Force cooperative.

LOANS ***Student loans:*** $1,931,006 (74% need-based, 26% non-need-based). ***Programs:*** FFEL (Subsidized and Unsubsidized Stafford, PLUS), Perkins, state, alternative loans.

WORK-STUDY ***Federal work-study:*** *Total amount:* $72,919; 83 jobs available. ***State or other work-study/employment:*** *Total amount:* $308,533 (100% non-need-based). 516 part-time jobs available.

APPLYING for FINANCIAL AID ***Required financial aid form:*** FAFSA. ***Financial aid deadline (priority):*** 3/15. ***Notification date:*** Continuous. Students must reply within 2 weeks of notification.

CONTACT Ms. Courtney Seibert, Director of Financial Aid, Stephens College, 1200 East Broadway, Campus Box 2124, Columbia, MO 65215-0002, 800-876-7207. *Fax:* 573-876-7237. *E-mail:* finaid@wc.stephens.edu

STERLING COLLEGE

Sterling, KS

Tuition & fees: $11,030 **Average undergraduate aid package: $9000**

ABOUT THE INSTITUTION Independent Presbyterian, coed. Awards: bachelor's degrees. 17 undergraduate majors. Total enrollment: 424. Undergraduates: 424. Freshmen: 115. Federal methodology is used as a basis for awarding need-based institutional aid.

UNDERGRADUATE EXPENSES for 1999–2000 ***Application fee:*** $10. ***One-time required fee:*** $100. ***Comprehensive fee:*** $15,616 includes full-time tuition ($11,030) and room and board ($4586). Full-time tuition and fees vary according to course load. Room and board charges vary according to board plan and housing facility. ***Part-time tuition:*** $236 per credit. Part-time tuition and fees vary according to course load. ***Payment plan:*** installment.

FRESHMAN FINANCIAL AID (Fall 1998) 170 applied for aid; of those 82% were deemed to have need. 100% of freshmen with need received aid; of those 71% had need fully met. *Average percent of need met:* 80% (excluding resources awarded to replace EFC). *Average financial aid package:* $9000 (excluding resources awarded to replace EFC). 6% of all full-time freshmen had no need and received non-need-based aid.

UNDERGRADUATE FINANCIAL AID (Fall 1998) 475 applied for aid; of those 92% were deemed to have need. 100% of undergraduates with need received aid; of those 48% had need fully met. *Average percent of need met:* 80% (excluding resources awarded to replace EFC). *Average financial aid package:* $9000 (excluding resources awarded to replace EFC). 6% of all full-time undergraduates had no need and received non-need-based aid.

GIFT AID (NEED-BASED) ***Total amount:*** $938,041 (45% Federal, 43% state, 12% institutional). ***Receiving aid:*** *Freshmen:* 82% (140); *all full-time undergraduates:* 92% (437). ***Scholarships, grants, and awards:*** Federal Pell, FSEOG, state, private, college/university gift aid from institutional funds.

GIFT AID (NON-NEED-BASED) ***Total amount:*** $1,174,133 (85% institutional, 15% external sources). ***Receiving aid:*** *Freshmen:* 26% (45); *Undergraduates:* 13% (60). ***Scholarships, grants, and awards by category:*** *Academic Interests/Achievement:* $719,936 total: general academic interests/achievements. *Creative Arts/Performance:* $141,752 total: debating, music, theater/drama. *Special Achievements/Activities:* $31,178 total: cheerleading/drum major, leadership. *Special Characteristics:* $126,789 total: general special characteristics, twins. ***Tuition waivers:*** Full or partial for employees or children of employees, senior citizens.

LOANS ***Student loans:*** $1,477,629 (72% need-based, 28% non-need-based). 74% of past graduating class borrowed through all loan programs. Average indebtedness per student: $12,287. ***Parent loans:*** $434,139 (100% need-based). ***Programs:*** FFEL (Subsidized and Unsubsidized Stafford, PLUS), Perkins, college/university.

WORK-STUDY ***Federal work-study:*** *Total amount:* $97,259; 151 jobs available. ***State or other work-study/employment:*** *Total amount:* $106,150 (100% non-need-based). Part-time jobs available.

ATHLETIC AWARDS *Total amount:* 631,172 (100% need-based).

APPLYING for FINANCIAL AID ***Required financial aid form:*** FAFSA. ***Financial aid deadline (priority):*** 3/15. ***Notification date:*** Continuous. Students must reply within 2 weeks of notification.

Sterling College (continued)

CONTACT Mrs. Kay Barnes, Director of Financial Aid, Sterling College, PO Box 98, Sterling, KS 67579-0098, 316-278-4226 or toll-free 800-346-1017. *Fax:* 316-278-2716.

STERLING COLLEGE

Craftsbury Common, VT

Tuition & fees: $13,355 **Average undergraduate aid package: $8000**

ABOUT THE INSTITUTION Independent, coed. Awards: associate and bachelor's degrees. 10 undergraduate majors. Total enrollment: 90. Undergraduates: 90. Freshmen: 28. Both federal and institutional methodology are used as a basis for awarding need-based institutional aid.

UNDERGRADUATE EXPENSES for 2000–2001 (est.) ***Application fee:*** $35. ***Comprehensive fee:*** $19,025 includes full-time tuition ($13,230), mandatory fees ($125), and room and board ($5670). Full-time tuition and fees vary according to course load, program, and reciprocity agreements. Room and board charges vary according to board plan, housing facility, and student level. ***Payment plan:*** installment.

FRESHMAN FINANCIAL AID (Fall 1999, est.) 36 applied for aid; of those 86% were deemed to have need. 100% of freshmen with need received aid; of those 23% had need fully met. *Average percent of need met:* 62% (excluding resources awarded to replace EFC). *Average financial aid package:* $7600 (excluding resources awarded to replace EFC). 5% of all full-time freshmen had no need and received non-need-based aid.

UNDERGRADUATE FINANCIAL AID (Fall 1999, est.) 72 applied for aid; of those 93% were deemed to have need. 100% of undergraduates with need received aid; of those 22% had need fully met. *Average percent of need met:* 62% (excluding resources awarded to replace EFC). *Average financial aid package:* $8000 (excluding resources awarded to replace EFC). 5% of all full-time undergraduates had no need and received non-need-based aid.

GIFT AID (NEED-BASED) ***Total amount:*** $443,729 (19% Federal, 8% state, 68% institutional, 5% external sources). ***Receiving aid:*** *Freshmen:* 59% (26); *all full-time undergraduates:* 66% (60). ***Average award:*** Freshmen: $4300; Undergraduates: $4300. ***Scholarships, grants, and awards:*** Federal Pell, FSEOG, state, private, college/university gift aid from institutional funds.

GIFT AID (NON-NEED-BASED) ***Total amount:*** $9200 (98% institutional, 2% external sources). ***Receiving aid:*** *Freshmen:* 5% (2); *Undergraduates:* 5% (5). ***Tuition waivers:*** Full or partial for employees or children of employees.

LOANS ***Student loans:*** $204,860 (93% need-based, 7% non-need-based). 52% of past graduating class borrowed through all loan programs. ***Average need-based loan:*** Freshmen: $2625; Undergraduates: $3000. ***Parent loans:*** $157,956 (71% need-based, 29% non-need-based). ***Programs:*** Federal Direct (Subsidized and Unsubsidized Stafford, PLUS), FFEL (Subsidized and Unsubsidized Stafford, PLUS).

WORK-STUDY ***Federal work-study:*** *Total amount:* $4000; 25 jobs averaging $450.

APPLYING for FINANCIAL AID ***Required financial aid forms:*** FAFSA, institution's own form, noncustodial (divorced/separated) parent's statement, business/farm supplement, federal income tax form(s). ***Financial aid deadline:*** Continuous. ***Notification date:*** Continuous beginning 5/1. Students must reply within 2 weeks of notification.

CONTACT Barbara Stuart, Financial Aid Coordinator, Sterling College, PO Box 72, 16 Sterling Drive, Kane Hall, Craftsbury Common, VT 05827, 800-648-3591 or toll-free 800-802-2596 (out-of-state). *Fax:* 802-586-2596. *E-mail:* bstuart@sterlingcollege.edu

STERN COLLEGE FOR WOMEN

New York, NY

See Yeshiva University

STETSON UNIVERSITY

DeLand, FL

Tuition & fees: $18,385 **Average undergraduate aid package: $17,540**

ABOUT THE INSTITUTION Independent, coed. Awards: bachelor's, master's, and first professional degrees and post-master's certificates. 56 undergraduate majors. Total enrollment: 3,053. Undergraduates: 2,062. Freshmen: 550. Federal methodology is used as a basis for awarding need-based institutional aid.

UNDERGRADUATE EXPENSES for 2000–2001 (est.) ***Application fee:*** $35. ***Comprehensive fee:*** $24,455 includes full-time tuition ($17,475), mandatory fees ($910), and room and board ($6070). ***College room only:*** $3380. Room and board charges vary according to board plan and housing facility. ***Part-time tuition:*** $580 per credit hour. Part-time tuition and fees vary according to course load. ***Payment plan:*** installment.

FRESHMAN FINANCIAL AID (Fall 1999) 529 applied for aid; of those 67% were deemed to have need. 100% of freshmen with need received aid; of those 38% had need fully met. *Average percent of need met:* 87% (excluding resources awarded to replace EFC). *Average financial aid package:* $17,163 (excluding resources awarded to replace EFC). 29% of all full-time freshmen had no need and received non-need-based aid.

UNDERGRADUATE FINANCIAL AID (Fall 1999) 1,832 applied for aid; of those 64% were deemed to have need. 99% of undergraduates with need received aid; of those 39% had need fully met. *Average percent of need met:* 86% (excluding resources awarded to replace EFC). *Average financial aid package:* $17,540 (excluding resources awarded to replace EFC). 29% of all full-time undergraduates had no need and received non-need-based aid.

GIFT AID (NEED-BASED) ***Total amount:*** $8,151,436 (18% Federal, 6% state, 76% institutional). ***Receiving aid:*** *Freshmen:* 64% (352); *all full-time undergraduates:* 59% (1,154). ***Average award:*** Freshmen: $12,355; Undergraduates: $11,395. ***Scholarships, grants, and awards:*** Federal Pell, FSEOG, state, private, college/university gift aid from institutional funds.

GIFT AID (NON-NEED-BASED) ***Total amount:*** $9,725,655 (49% state, 42% institutional, 9% external sources). ***Receiving aid:*** *Freshmen:* 61% (333); *Undergraduates:* 49% (961). ***Scholarships, grants, and awards by category:*** *Academic Interests/Achievement:* 550 awards ($2,860,376 total): area/ethnic studies, biological sciences, business, communication, computer science, education, English, foreign languages, general academic interests/achievements, humanities, mathematics, military science, physical sciences, premedicine, religion/biblical studies, social sciences. *Creative Arts/Performance:* 68 awards ($323,210 total): applied art and design, art/fine arts, music, theater/drama. *Special Achievements/Activities:* cheerleading/drum major, community service, general special achievements/activities, leadership, religious involvement. *Special Characteristics:* children and siblings of alumni, children of faculty/staff, ethnic background, general special characteristics, international students, local/state students, members of minority groups. ***Tuition waivers:*** Full or partial for employees or children of employees. ***ROTC:*** Army cooperative.

LOANS ***Student loans:*** $6,663,387 (78% need-based, 22% non-need-based). 59% of past graduating class borrowed through all loan programs. Average indebtedness per student: $17,500. ***Average need-based loan:*** Freshmen: $3597; Undergraduates: $5330. ***Parent loans:*** $980,408 (73% need-based, 27% non-need-based). ***Programs:*** FFEL (Subsidized and Unsubsidized Stafford, PLUS), Perkins, state, college/university.

WORK-STUDY ***Federal work-study:*** *Total amount:* $858,000; 598 jobs averaging $2195. ***State or other work-study/employment:*** *Total amount:* $574,049 (79% need-based, 21% non-need-based). 80 part-time jobs averaging $1487.

ATHLETIC AWARDS *Total amount:* 1,900,592 (44% need-based, 56% non-need-based).

APPLYING for FINANCIAL AID ***Required financial aid forms:*** FAFSA, institution's own form. ***Financial aid deadline (priority):*** 4/15. ***Notification date:*** Continuous.

CONTACT Robert E. Lynn, Director of Student Financial Planning, Stetson University, 421 North Woodland Boulevard, DeLand, FL 32720-3781, 904-822-7120 or toll-free 800-688-0101. *Fax:* 904-822-7126. *E-mail:* finaid@stetson.edu

STEVENS INSTITUTE OF TECHNOLOGY

Hoboken, NJ

Tuition & fees: $21,140 **Average undergraduate aid package: $19,815**

ABOUT THE INSTITUTION Independent, coed. Awards: bachelor's, master's, and doctoral degrees and post-bachelor's certificates. 20 undergraduate majors. Total enrollment: 3,467. Undergraduates: 1,564. Freshmen: 372. Both federal and institutional methodology are used as a basis for awarding need-based institutional aid.

UNDERGRADUATE EXPENSES for 1999–2000 ***Application fee:*** $45. ***Comprehensive fee:*** $28,420 includes full-time tuition ($20,890), mandatory fees ($250), and room and board ($7280). Room and board charges vary according to board plan and housing facility. ***Payment plan:*** installment.

FRESHMAN FINANCIAL AID (Fall 1999, est.) 316 applied for aid; of those 84% were deemed to have need. 100% of freshmen with need received aid; of those 27% had need fully met. *Average percent of need met:* 96% (excluding resources awarded to replace EFC). *Average financial aid package:* $19,137 (excluding resources awarded to replace EFC). 19% of all full-time freshmen had no need and received non-need-based aid.

UNDERGRADUATE FINANCIAL AID (Fall 1999, est.) 1,351 applied for aid; of those 85% were deemed to have need. 100% of undergraduates with need received aid; of those 15% had need fully met. *Average percent of need met:* 97% (excluding resources awarded to replace EFC). *Average financial aid package:* $19,815 (excluding resources awarded to replace EFC). 18% of all full-time undergraduates had no need and received non-need-based aid.

GIFT AID (NEED-BASED) ***Total amount:*** $7,670,000 (15% Federal, 27% state, 58% institutional). ***Receiving aid:*** *Freshmen:* 67% (249); *all full-time undergraduates:* 67% (1,050). ***Average award:*** Freshmen: $11,318; Undergraduates: $9022. ***Scholarships, grants, and awards:*** Federal Pell, FSEOG, state, private, college/university gift aid from institutional funds.

GIFT AID (NON-NEED-BASED) ***Total amount:*** $6,992,700 (3% state, 90% institutional, 7% external sources). ***Receiving aid:*** *Freshmen:* 53% (195); *Undergraduates:* 51% (804). ***Scholarships, grants, and awards by category:*** *Academic Interests/Achievement:* 1,000 awards ($6,292,000 total): computer science, engineering/technologies, general academic interests/achievements, humanities, mathematics, physical sciences, premedicine. *Special Characteristics:* 85 awards ($758,000 total): children and siblings of alumni, children of faculty/staff, international students, local/state students, members of minority groups. ***Tuition waivers:*** Full or partial for employees or children of employees. ***ROTC:*** Army cooperative, Air Force cooperative.

LOANS ***Student loans:*** $5,996,000 (72% need-based, 28% non-need-based). 68% of past graduating class borrowed through all loan programs. Average indebtedness per student: $12,900. ***Average need-based loan:*** Freshmen: $3909; Undergraduates: $4603. ***Parent loans:*** $2,122,000 (100% non-need-based). ***Programs:*** Federal Direct (Subsidized and Unsubsidized Stafford, PLUS), Perkins, state, Sallie Mae Signature Loans, TERI Loans, NJ Class Loans.

WORK-STUDY ***Federal work-study:*** *Total amount:* $828,000; jobs available.

APPLYING for FINANCIAL AID ***Required financial aid form:*** FAFSA. ***Financial aid deadline (priority):*** 2/15. ***Notification date:*** Continuous beginning 3/30. Students must reply by 5/1.

CONTACT Mr. David Sheridan, Dean of Enrollment Services, Stevens Institute of Technology, Castle Point on Hudson, Hoboken, NJ 07030, 201-216-5555 or toll-free 800-458-5323. *Fax:* 201-216-8050. *E-mail:* dsherida@stevens-tech.edu

STILLMAN COLLEGE

Tuscaloosa, AL

Tuition & fees: $5880 **Average undergraduate aid package: N/A**

ABOUT THE INSTITUTION Independent religious, coed. Awards: bachelor's degrees. 18 undergraduate majors. Total enrollment: 1,458. Undergraduates: 1,458. Both federal and institutional methodology are used as a basis for awarding need-based institutional aid.

UNDERGRADUATE EXPENSES for 1999–2000 ***Application fee:*** $15. ***Comprehensive fee:*** $9644 includes full-time tuition ($5570), mandatory fees ($310), and room and board ($3764). Room and board charges vary according to board plan and housing facility. ***Part-time tuition:*** $245 per semester hour. ***Part-time fees:*** $51 per term part-time. ***Payment plan:*** installment.

GIFT AID (NEED-BASED) ***Scholarships, grants, and awards:*** Federal Pell, FSEOG, state, private, college/university gift aid from institutional funds, United Negro College Fund.

GIFT AID (NON-NEED-BASED) ***Scholarships, grants, and awards by category:*** *Academic Interests/Achievement:* education, general academic interests/achievements. *Creative Arts/Performance:* music. *Special Characteristics:* children of faculty/staff. ***Tuition waivers:*** Full or partial for employees or children of employees. ***ROTC:*** Army cooperative.

LOANS ***Programs:*** Federal Direct (Subsidized and Unsubsidized Stafford, PLUS), Perkins.

WORK-STUDY Federal work-study jobs available.

APPLYING for FINANCIAL AID ***Required financial aid forms:*** FAFSA, state aid form. ***Financial aid deadline (priority):*** 4/1. ***Notification date:*** 6/1. Students must reply within 4 weeks of notification.

CONTACT Mr. Booker T. Crawford, Director of Financial Aid, Stillman College, PO Box 1430, Tuscaloosa, AL 35403, 205-349-4240 Ext. 8844 or toll-free 800-841-5722. *Fax:* 205-366-8996.

STONEHILL COLLEGE

Easton, MA

Tuition & fees: $16,336 **Average undergraduate aid package: $12,129**

ABOUT THE INSTITUTION Independent Roman Catholic, coed. Awards: bachelor's and master's degrees. 36 undergraduate majors. Total enrollment: 2,565. Undergraduates: 2,549. Freshmen: 589. Institutional methodology is used as a basis for awarding need-based institutional aid.

UNDERGRADUATE EXPENSES for 1999–2000 ***Application fee:*** $50. ***Comprehensive fee:*** $24,188 includes full-time tuition ($15,736), mandatory fees ($600), and room and board ($7852). Full-time tuition and fees vary according to class time and course load. Room and board charges vary according to board plan. ***Part-time tuition:*** $1574 per course. ***Part-time fees:*** $60 per course. Part-time tuition and fees vary according to class time. ***Payment plans:*** tuition prepayment, installment.

FRESHMAN FINANCIAL AID (Fall 1999) 523 applied for aid; of those 82% were deemed to have need. 100% of freshmen with need received aid; of those 32% had need fully met. *Average percent of need met:* 81% (excluding resources awarded to replace EFC). *Average financial aid package:* $11,866 (excluding resources awarded to replace EFC). 23% of all full-time freshmen had no need and received non-need-based aid.

UNDERGRADUATE FINANCIAL AID (Fall 1999) 1,749 applied for aid; of those 77% were deemed to have need. 100% of undergraduates with need received aid; of those 36% had need fully met. *Average percent of need met:* 84% (excluding resources awarded to replace EFC). *Average financial aid package:* $12,129 (excluding resources awarded to replace EFC). 18% of all full-time undergraduates had no need and received non-need-based aid.

GIFT AID (NEED-BASED) ***Total amount:*** $10,835,840 (5% Federal, 6% state, 84% institutional, 5% external sources). ***Receiving aid:*** *Freshmen:* 66% (401); *all full-time undergraduates:* 62% (1,280). ***Average award:***

Stonehill College (continued)

Freshmen: $8346; Undergraduates: $8084. ***Scholarships, grants, and awards:*** Federal Pell, FSEOG, state, private, college/university gift aid from institutional funds.

GIFT AID (NON-NEED-BASED) ***Total amount:*** $1,994,395 (89% institutional, 11% external sources). ***Receiving aid:*** *Freshmen:* 9% (56); *Undergraduates:* 9% (175). ***Scholarships, grants, and awards by category:*** *Academic Interests/Achievement:* general academic interests/achievements. ***Tuition waivers:*** Full or partial for minority students, employees or children of employees, senior citizens. ***ROTC:*** Army.

LOANS ***Student loans:*** $7,488,269 (64% need-based, 36% non-need-based). 95% of past graduating class borrowed through all loan programs. Average indebtedness per student: $10,115. ***Average need-based loan:*** Freshmen: $3182; Undergraduates: $3721. ***Parent loans:*** $4,165,757 (27% need-based, 73% non-need-based). ***Programs:*** Federal Direct (Subsidized and Unsubsidized Stafford, PLUS), Perkins, state.

WORK-STUDY ***Federal work-study:*** *Total amount:* $810,000; jobs available. ***State or other work-study/employment:*** *Total amount:* $125,765 (1% need-based, 99% non-need-based). 165 part-time jobs averaging $750.

ATHLETIC AWARDS *Total amount:* 521,062 (17% need-based, 83% non-need-based).

APPLYING for FINANCIAL AID ***Required financial aid forms:*** FAFSA, CSS Financial Aid PROFILE, noncustodial (divorced/separated) parent's statement, business/farm supplement. ***Financial aid deadline (priority):*** 2/1. ***Notification date:*** 4/1. Students must reply by 5/1.

CONTACT Judith Kellie, Assistant to the Director, Stonehill College, 320 Washington Street, Easton, MA 02357, 508-565-1347. *Fax:* 508-565-1426. *E-mail:* jkellie@stonehill.edu

STRAYER UNIVERSITY

Washington, DC

Tuition & fees: $7695 **Average undergraduate aid package: N/A**

ABOUT THE INSTITUTION Proprietary, coed. Awards: associate, bachelor's, and master's degrees. 6 undergraduate majors. Total enrollment: 10,449. Undergraduates: 9,111. Freshmen: 1,405. Federal methodology is used as a basis for awarding need-based institutional aid.

UNDERGRADUATE EXPENSES for 1999–2000 ***Application fee:*** $25. ***Tuition:*** full-time $7695; part-time $200 per quarter hour. Full-time tuition and fees vary according to course load. Part-time tuition and fees vary according to course load. ***Payment plan:*** installment.

GIFT AID (NEED-BASED) ***Scholarships, grants, and awards:*** Federal Pell, FSEOG, state.

GIFT AID (NON-NEED-BASED) ***Scholarships, grants, and awards by category:*** *Academic Interests/Achievement:* business, computer science, general academic interests/achievements. *Special Achievements/Activities:* general special achievements/activities. ***Tuition waivers:*** Full or partial for employees or children of employees.

LOANS ***Programs:*** FFEL (Subsidized and Unsubsidized Stafford, PLUS), Perkins, credit-based loans (for tuition and fees).

WORK-STUDY Federal work-study jobs available.

APPLYING for FINANCIAL AID ***Required financial aid form:*** FAFSA. ***Financial aid deadline:*** Continuous. ***Notification date:*** Continuous beginning 9/1. Students must reply within 2 weeks of notification.

CONTACT Mr. Michael Williams, Campus Coordinator, Strayer University, 1025 15th Street, NW, Washington, DC 20005-2603, 202-408-2400. *Fax:* 202-289-1831.

SUFFOLK UNIVERSITY

Boston, MA

Tuition & fees: $14,660 **Average undergraduate aid package: $11,402**

ABOUT THE INSTITUTION Independent, coed. Awards: associate, bachelor's, master's, doctoral, and first professional degrees and post-bachelor's and post-master's certificates (doctoral degree in law). 69 undergraduate majors. Total enrollment: 6,457. Undergraduates: 3,305. Freshmen: 678. Both federal and institutional methodology are used as a basis for awarding need-based institutional aid.

UNDERGRADUATE EXPENSES for 1999–2000 ***Application fee:*** $40. ***Comprehensive fee:*** $23,870 includes full-time tuition ($14,580), mandatory fees ($80), and room and board ($9210). Room and board charges vary according to housing facility. ***Part-time tuition:*** $386 per semester hour. ***Part-time fees:*** $10 per term part-time. ***Payment plans:*** installment, deferred payment.

FRESHMAN FINANCIAL AID (Fall 1999) 505 applied for aid; of those 82% were deemed to have need. 100% of freshmen with need received aid; of those 12% had need fully met. *Average percent of need met:* 71% (excluding resources awarded to replace EFC). *Average financial aid package:* $11,254 (excluding resources awarded to replace EFC). 11% of all full-time freshmen had no need and received non-need-based aid.

UNDERGRADUATE FINANCIAL AID (Fall 1999) 1,778 applied for aid; of those 86% were deemed to have need. 100% of undergraduates with need received aid; of those 16% had need fully met. *Average percent of need met:* 71% (excluding resources awarded to replace EFC). *Average financial aid package:* $11,402 (excluding resources awarded to replace EFC). 12% of all full-time undergraduates had no need and received non-need-based aid.

GIFT AID (NEED-BASED) ***Total amount:*** $8,008,755 (21% Federal, 13% state, 62% institutional, 4% external sources). ***Receiving aid:*** *Freshmen:* 59% (393); *all full-time undergraduates:* 53% (1,397). ***Average award:*** Freshmen: $6011; Undergraduates: $5792. ***Scholarships, grants, and awards:*** Federal Pell, FSEOG, state, private, college/university gift aid from institutional funds.

GIFT AID (NON-NEED-BASED) ***Total amount:*** $1,725,400 (1% state, 98% institutional, 1% external sources). ***Receiving aid:*** *Freshmen:* 15% (100); *Undergraduates:* 15% (405). ***Scholarships, grants, and awards by category:*** *Academic Interests/Achievement:* general academic interests/achievements. *Creative Arts/Performance:* debating. *Special Characteristics:* adult students, children of current students, parents of current students, siblings of current students. ***Tuition waivers:*** Full or partial for employees or children of employees, senior citizens. ***ROTC:*** Army cooperative.

LOANS ***Student loans:*** $9,796,197 (79% need-based, 21% non-need-based). 65% of past graduating class borrowed through all loan programs. Average indebtedness per student: $20,384. ***Average need-based loan:*** Freshmen: $3890; Undergraduates: $4442. ***Parent loans:*** $3,784,863 (100% non-need-based). ***Programs:*** Federal Direct (Subsidized and Unsubsidized Stafford), FFEL (PLUS), Perkins, state, college/university.

WORK-STUDY ***Federal work-study:*** *Total amount:* $2,050,584; jobs available. ***State or other work-study/employment:*** *Total amount:* $359,363 (100% non-need-based). Part-time jobs available.

APPLYING for FINANCIAL AID ***Required financial aid forms:*** FAFSA, institution's own form, parent and student federal income tax forms. ***Financial aid deadline (priority):*** 3/1. ***Notification date:*** Continuous. Students must reply within 2 weeks of notification.

CONTACT Ms. Christine A. Perry, Director of Financial Aid, Suffolk University, 8 Ashburton Place, Boston, MA 02108, 617-573-8470 or toll-free 800-6-SUFFOLK. *Fax:* 617-742-4291.

SULLIVAN COLLEGE

Louisville, KY

Tuition & fees: $9600 **Average undergraduate aid package: N/A**

ABOUT THE INSTITUTION Proprietary, coed. Awards: associate, bachelor's, and master's degrees (master's degree in business administration only). 12 undergraduate majors. Total enrollment: 2,975. Undergraduates: 2,915. Both federal and institutional methodology are used as a basis for awarding need-based institutional aid.

UNDERGRADUATE EXPENSES for 1999–2000 ***Application fee:*** $80. ***One-time required fee:*** $325. ***Tuition:*** full-time $9600; part-time $160 per credit. ***Required fees:*** $12 per course. Full-time tuition and fees vary according to program. Part-time tuition and fees vary according to program. ***Payment plans:*** installment, deferred payment.

GIFT AID (NEED-BASED) ***Scholarships, grants, and awards:*** Federal Pell, FSEOG, state, college/university gift aid from institutional funds, Job Training Partnership Act grants.

GIFT AID (NON-NEED-BASED) ***Scholarships, grants, and awards by category:*** *Academic Interests/Achievement:* general academic interests/achievements. *Creative Arts/Performance:* general creative arts/performance. ***Tuition waivers:*** Full or partial for employees or children of employees.

LOANS ***Programs:*** Federal Direct (Subsidized and Unsubsidized Stafford, PLUS), Perkins, college/university.

WORK-STUDY Federal work-study jobs available.

APPLYING for FINANCIAL AID ***Required financial aid forms:*** FAFSA, institution's own form. ***Financial aid deadline:*** Continuous.

CONTACT Charlene Geiser, Director of Financial Planning, Sullivan College, 3101 Bardstown Road, Louisville, KY 40205, 502-456-6504 Ext. 311 or toll-free 800-844-1354 (in-state).

SUL ROSS STATE UNIVERSITY

Alpine, TX

Tuition & fees (TX res): $2150 **Average undergraduate aid package: N/A**

ABOUT THE INSTITUTION State-supported, coed. Awards: associate, bachelor's, and master's degrees. 35 undergraduate majors. Total enrollment: 2,119. Undergraduates: 1,459. Freshmen: 268. Federal methodology is used as a basis for awarding need-based institutional aid.

UNDERGRADUATE EXPENSES for 1999–2000 ***Tuition, state resident:*** full-time $1140; part-time $38 per semester hour. ***Tuition, nonresident:*** full-time $7620; part-time $254 per semester hour. ***Required fees:*** full-time $1010; $41 per semester hour. Full-time tuition and fees vary according to course load. Part-time tuition and fees vary according to course load. ***College room and board:*** $3530; ***room only:*** $1690. Room and board charges vary according to board plan and housing facility. ***Payment plan:*** installment.

GIFT AID (NEED-BASED) ***Scholarships, grants, and awards:*** Federal Pell, FSEOG, state, private, college/university gift aid from institutional funds.

GIFT AID (NON-NEED-BASED) ***Scholarships, grants, and awards by category:*** *Academic Interests/Achievement:* agriculture, biological sciences, business, education, English, foreign languages, general academic interests/achievements, health fields. *Creative Arts/Performance:* art/fine arts, cinema/film/broadcasting, journalism/publications, music, theater/drama. *Special Achievements/Activities:* leadership.

LOANS ***Programs:*** Perkins, state, college/university.

APPLYING for FINANCIAL AID ***Required financial aid forms:*** FAFSA, institution's own form. ***Financial aid deadline:*** Continuous.

CONTACT Ms. Rena Gallego, Director of Financial Assistance and Recruiting, Sul Ross State University, PO Box C-113, Alpine, TX 79832, 915-837-8059.

SUOMI COLLEGE

Hancock, MI

See Finlandia University

SUSQUEHANNA UNIVERSITY

Selinsgrove, PA

Tuition & fees: $19,670 **Average undergraduate aid package: $16,518**

ABOUT THE INSTITUTION Independent religious, coed. Awards: bachelor's degrees (also offers associate degree through evening program to local students). 54 undergraduate majors. Total enrollment: 1,772. Undergraduates: 1,772. Freshmen: 464. Both federal and institutional methodology are used as a basis for awarding need-based institutional aid.

UNDERGRADUATE EXPENSES for 1999–2000 ***Application fee:*** $30. ***Comprehensive fee:*** $25,220 includes full-time tuition ($19,380), mandatory fees ($290), and room and board ($5550). ***College room only:*** $2950. Room and board charges vary according to board plan. ***Part-time tuition:*** $625 per semester hour. ***Payment plans:*** tuition prepayment, installment, deferred payment.

FRESHMAN FINANCIAL AID (Fall 1999) 358 applied for aid; of those 80% were deemed to have need. 100% of freshmen with need received aid; of those 52% had need fully met. *Average percent of need met:* 92% (excluding resources awarded to replace EFC). *Average financial aid package:* $16,176 (excluding resources awarded to replace EFC). 14% of all full-time freshmen had no need and received non-need-based aid.

UNDERGRADUATE FINANCIAL AID (Fall 1999) 1,288 applied for aid; of those 88% were deemed to have need. 100% of undergraduates with need received aid; of those 52% had need fully met. *Average percent of need met:* 91% (excluding resources awarded to replace EFC). *Average financial aid package:* $16,518 (excluding resources awarded to replace EFC). 8% of all full-time undergraduates had no need and received non-need-based aid.

GIFT AID (NEED-BASED) ***Total amount:*** $14,573,314 (6% Federal, 10% state, 81% institutional, 3% external sources). ***Receiving aid:*** *Freshmen:* 61% (284); *all full-time undergraduates:* 68% (1,116). ***Average award:*** Freshmen: $11,353; Undergraduates: $11,063. ***Scholarships, grants, and awards:*** Federal Pell, FSEOG, state, private, college/university gift aid from institutional funds.

GIFT AID (NON-NEED-BASED) ***Total amount:*** $1,270,926 (92% institutional, 8% external sources). ***Receiving aid:*** *Freshmen:* 9% (44); *Undergraduates:* 7% (121). ***Scholarships, grants, and awards by category:*** *Academic Interests/Achievement:* 473 awards ($3,425,000 total): general academic interests/achievements. *Creative Arts/Performance:* 73 awards ($125,000 total): music. *Special Achievements/Activities:* 500 awards ($2,500,000 total): general special achievements/activities. *Special Characteristics:* 100 awards ($1,100,000 total): members of minority groups, relatives of clergy. ***Tuition waivers:*** Full or partial for employees or children of employees. ***ROTC:*** Army cooperative.

LOANS ***Student loans:*** $4,840,126 (80% need-based, 20% non-need-based). 79% of past graduating class borrowed through all loan programs. Average indebtedness per student: $17,005. ***Average need-based loan:*** Freshmen: $2633; Undergraduates: $3386. ***Parent loans:*** $2,068,763 (33% need-based, 67% non-need-based). ***Programs:*** FFEL (Subsidized and Unsubsidized Stafford, PLUS), Perkins, college/university.

WORK-STUDY ***Federal work-study:*** *Total amount:* $1,337,569; 856 jobs averaging $1568.

APPLYING for FINANCIAL AID ***Required financial aid forms:*** FAFSA, CSS Financial Aid PROFILE, business/farm supplement, tax documents. ***Financial aid deadline (priority):*** 3/1. ***Notification date:*** Continuous. Students must reply by 5/1.

CONTACT Helen S. Nunn, Director of Financial Aid, Susquehanna University, 514 University Avenue, Selinsgrove, PA 17870, 570-372-4450 or toll-free 800-326-9672. *Fax:* 570-372-2722. *E-mail:* sufinaid@susqu.edu

SWARTHMORE COLLEGE

Swarthmore, PA

Tuition & fees: $24,190 **Average undergraduate aid package: $23,515**

ABOUT THE INSTITUTION Independent, coed. Awards: bachelor's degrees. 37 undergraduate majors. Total enrollment: 1,467. Undergraduates: 1,467. Freshmen: 368. Institutional methodology is used as a basis for awarding need-based institutional aid.

UNDERGRADUATE EXPENSES for 1999–2000 ***Application fee:*** $60. ***Comprehensive fee:*** $31,690 includes full-time tuition ($23,964), mandatory fees ($226), and room and board ($7500). ***College room only:*** $3850. ***Payment plan:*** installment.

FRESHMAN FINANCIAL AID (Fall 1999, est.) 263 applied for aid; of those 71% were deemed to have need. 100% of freshmen with need received aid; of those 100% had need fully met. *Average percent of need met:*

Swarthmore College (continued)

100% (excluding resources awarded to replace EFC). *Average financial aid package:* $23,314 (excluding resources awarded to replace EFC).

UNDERGRADUATE FINANCIAL AID (Fall 1999, est.) 800 applied for aid; of those 86% were deemed to have need. 100% of undergraduates with need received aid; of those 100% had need fully met. *Average percent of need met:* 100% (excluding resources awarded to replace EFC). *Average financial aid package:* $23,515 (excluding resources awarded to replace EFC). 1% of all full-time undergraduates had no need and received non-need-based aid.

GIFT AID (NEED-BASED) ***Total amount:*** $13,354,500 (6% Federal, 1% state, 90% institutional, 3% external sources). ***Receiving aid:*** *Freshmen:* 51% (188); *all full-time undergraduates:* 48% (692). ***Average award:*** Freshmen: $20,649; Undergraduates: $19,376. ***Scholarships, grants, and awards:*** Federal Pell, FSEOG, state, private, college/university gift aid from institutional funds.

GIFT AID (NON-NEED-BASED) ***Total amount:*** $1,023,756 (33% institutional, 67% external sources). ***Scholarships, grants, and awards by category:*** *Academic Interests/Achievement:* 4 awards ($95,856 total): general academic interests/achievements. ***Tuition waivers:*** Full or partial for employees or children of employees. ***ROTC:*** Army cooperative, Naval cooperative, Air Force cooperative.

LOANS ***Student loans:*** $2,116,146 (87% need-based, 13% non-need-based). 50% of past graduating class borrowed through all loan programs. Average indebtedness per student: $13,390. ***Average need-based loan:*** Freshmen: $2293; Undergraduates: $3508. ***Parent loans:*** $1,297,206 (100% non-need-based). ***Programs:*** FFEL (Subsidized and Unsubsidized Stafford, PLUS), Perkins, state, college/university.

WORK-STUDY ***Federal work-study:*** *Total amount:* $763,025; jobs available. ***State or other work-study/employment:*** *Total amount:* $428,160 (51% need-based, 49% non-need-based). Part-time jobs available.

APPLYING for FINANCIAL AID ***Required financial aid forms:*** FAFSA, institution's own form, CSS Financial Aid PROFILE, noncustodial (divorced/separated) parent's statement, business/farm supplement, copy of student and parent tax returns, W-2 forms. ***Financial aid deadline (priority):*** 2/15. ***Notification date:*** 4/1. Students must reply by 5/1.

CONTACT Ms. Patricia Serianni, Associate Director of Financial Aid, Swarthmore College, 500 College Avenue, Swarthmore, PA 19081-1397, 610-328-8357 or toll-free 800-667-3110. *Fax:* 610-328-8673. *E-mail:* pserian1@cc.swarthmore.edu

SWEET BRIAR COLLEGE

Sweet Briar, VA

Tuition & fees: $17,150 **Average undergraduate aid package: $14,621**

ABOUT THE INSTITUTION Independent, women only. Awards: bachelor's degrees. 32 undergraduate majors. Total enrollment: 710. Undergraduates: 710. Freshmen: 188. Federal methodology is used as a basis for awarding need-based institutional aid.

UNDERGRADUATE EXPENSES for 2000–2001 (est.) ***Application fee:*** $25. ***Comprehensive fee:*** $24,150 includes full-time tuition ($17,000), mandatory fees ($150), and room and board ($7000). ***College room only:*** $2850. Full-time tuition and fees vary according to program. ***Part-time tuition:*** $575 per semester hour. Part-time tuition and fees vary according to program. ***Payment plan:*** installment.

FRESHMAN FINANCIAL AID (Fall 1999) 131 applied for aid; of those 80% were deemed to have need. 100% of freshmen with need received aid; of those 31% had need fully met. *Average percent of need met:* 87% (excluding resources awarded to replace EFC). *Average financial aid package:* $14,776 (excluding resources awarded to replace EFC). 38% of all full-time freshmen had no need and received non-need-based aid.

UNDERGRADUATE FINANCIAL AID (Fall 1999) 391 applied for aid; of those 80% were deemed to have need. 100% of undergraduates with need received aid; of those 35% had need fully met. *Average percent of need met:* 86% (excluding resources awarded to replace EFC). *Average financial aid package:* $14,621 (excluding resources awarded to replace EFC). 31% of all full-time undergraduates had no need and received non-need-based aid.

GIFT AID (NEED-BASED) ***Total amount:*** $3,634,927 (7% Federal, 9% state, 83% institutional, 1% external sources). ***Receiving aid:*** *Freshmen:* 56% (105); *all full-time undergraduates:* 54% (309). ***Average award:*** Freshmen: $11,866; Undergraduates: $11,299. ***Scholarships, grants, and awards:*** Federal Pell, FSEOG, state, private, college/university gift aid from institutional funds.

GIFT AID (NON-NEED-BASED) ***Total amount:*** $2,009,299 (10% state, 89% institutional, 1% external sources). ***Receiving aid:*** *Freshmen:* 10% (19); *Undergraduates:* 9% (52). ***Scholarships, grants, and awards by category:*** *Academic Interests/Achievement:* 357 awards ($2,441,600 total): general academic interests/achievements, premedicine. *Creative Arts/Performance:* 2 awards ($4700 total): art/fine arts, general creative arts/performance, music. *Special Achievements/Activities:* 128 awards ($603,000 total): leadership. *Special Characteristics:* 40 awards ($273,152 total): adult students, general special characteristics, international students, local/state students. ***Tuition waivers:*** Full or partial for employees or children of employees, adult students, senior citizens.

LOANS ***Student loans:*** $1,063,826 (87% need-based, 13% non-need-based). 71% of past graduating class borrowed through all loan programs. Average indebtedness per student: $17,689. ***Average need-based loan:*** Freshmen: $2521; Undergraduates: $3007. ***Parent loans:*** $1,092,093 (79% need-based, 21% non-need-based). ***Programs:*** Federal Direct (Subsidized and Unsubsidized Stafford, PLUS), FFEL (Subsidized and Unsubsidized Stafford, PLUS), Perkins, college/university.

WORK-STUDY ***Federal work-study:*** *Total amount:* $58,628; 124 jobs averaging $840. ***State or other work-study/employment:*** *Total amount:* $100,822 (100% need-based). Part-time jobs available.

APPLYING for FINANCIAL AID ***Required financial aid forms:*** FAFSA, institution's own form, noncustodial (divorced/separated) parent's statement, business/farm supplement, state aid form (for Virginia residents only). ***Financial aid deadline (priority):*** 3/1. ***Notification date:*** Continuous. Students must reply by 5/1 or within 2 weeks of notification.

CONTACT Mr. Robert Steckel, Director, Financial Aid, Sweet Briar College, Box AS, Sweet Briar, VA 24595, 800-381-6156 or toll-free 800-381-6142. *Fax:* 804-381-6450. *E-mail:* financialaid@sbc.edu

SYRACUSE UNIVERSITY

Syracuse, NY

Tuition & fees: $19,784 **Average undergraduate aid package: $15,700**

ABOUT THE INSTITUTION Independent, coed. Awards: bachelor's, master's, doctoral, and first professional degrees and post-master's certificates. 133 undergraduate majors. Total enrollment: 14,668. Undergraduates: 10,685. Freshmen: 2,752. Both federal and institutional methodology are used as a basis for awarding need-based institutional aid.

UNDERGRADUATE EXPENSES for 1999–2000 ***Application fee:*** $40. ***One-time required fee:*** $50. ***Comprehensive fee:*** $28,184 includes full-time tuition ($19,360), mandatory fees ($424), and room and board ($8400). ***College room only:*** $4430. Room and board charges vary according to board plan and housing facility. ***Part-time tuition:*** $844 per credit hour. ***Part-time fees:*** $62 per year part-time. Part-time tuition and fees vary according to course load, location, and program. ***Payment plans:*** tuition prepayment, installment.

FRESHMAN FINANCIAL AID (Fall 1999) 2000 applied for aid; of those 77% were deemed to have need. 100% of freshmen with need received aid. *Average financial aid package:* $15,100 (excluding resources awarded to replace EFC). 16% of all full-time freshmen had no need and received non-need-based aid.

UNDERGRADUATE FINANCIAL AID (Fall 1999) 7,300 applied for aid; of those 87% were deemed to have need. 100% of undergraduates with need received aid. *Average financial aid package:* $15,700 (excluding resources awarded to replace EFC). 17% of all full-time undergraduates had no need and received non-need-based aid.

GIFT AID (NEED-BASED) ***Total amount:*** $76,160,000 (10% Federal, 9% state, 79% institutional, 2% external sources). ***Receiving aid:*** *Freshmen:* 50% (1,374); *all full-time undergraduates:* 57% (5,926). ***Average award:*** Freshmen: $9700; Undergraduates: $9300. ***Scholarships, grants, and awards:*** Federal Pell, FSEOG, state, college/university gift aid from institutional funds.

GIFT AID (NON-NEED-BASED) ***Total amount:*** $9,740,000 (97% institutional, 3% external sources). ***Receiving aid:*** *Freshmen:* 16% (427); *Undergraduates:* 16% (1,702). ***Scholarships, grants, and awards by category:*** *Academic Interests/Achievement:* architecture, general academic interests/achievements. *Creative Arts/Performance:* art/fine arts, music. *Special Characteristics:* children of faculty/staff. ***Tuition waivers:*** Full or partial for employees or children of employees. ***ROTC:*** Army, Air Force.

LOANS ***Student loans:*** $33,610,000 (90% need-based, 10% non-need-based). 67% of past graduating class borrowed through all loan programs. Average indebtedness per student: $18,600. ***Average need-based loan:*** Freshmen: $3500; Undergraduates: $4800. ***Parent loans:*** $13,800,000 (75% need-based, 25% non-need-based). ***Programs:*** FFEL (Subsidized and Unsubsidized Stafford, PLUS), Perkins, Federal Nursing.

WORK-STUDY ***Federal work-study:*** *Total amount:* $2,850,000; jobs available.

ATHLETIC AWARDS *Total amount:* 7,000,000 (17% need-based, 83% non-need-based).

APPLYING for FINANCIAL AID ***Required financial aid forms:*** FAFSA, state aid form. ***Financial aid deadline (priority):*** 2/15. ***Notification date:*** 4/1. Students must reply by 5/1.

CONTACT Mr. Christopher Walsh, Executive Director of Financial Aid, Syracuse University, 200 Archbold Gymnasium, Syracuse, NY 13244-1140, 315-443-1513. *E-mail:* finmail@syr.edu

SYRACUSE UNIVERSITY, UTICA COLLEGE

Utica, NY

See Utica College of Syracuse University

TABOR COLLEGE

Hillsboro, KS

Tuition & fees: $12,410 **Average undergraduate aid package: $11,260**

ABOUT THE INSTITUTION Independent Mennonite Brethren, coed. Awards: associate and bachelor's degrees. 57 undergraduate majors. Total enrollment: 538. Undergraduates: 538. Freshmen: 138. Federal methodology is used as a basis for awarding need-based institutional aid.

UNDERGRADUATE EXPENSES for 2000–2001 ***Application fee:*** $10. ***Comprehensive fee:*** $16,890 includes full-time tuition ($12,090), mandatory fees ($320), and room and board ($4480). ***College room only:*** $1700. Room and board charges vary according to board plan, housing facility, and location. Part-time tuition and fees vary according to course load. ***Payment plan:*** installment.

FRESHMAN FINANCIAL AID (Fall 1999) 120 applied for aid; of those 87% were deemed to have need. 100% of freshmen with need received aid; of those 23% had need fully met. *Average percent of need met:* 83% (excluding resources awarded to replace EFC). *Average financial aid package:* $11,220 (excluding resources awarded to replace EFC). 22% of all full-time freshmen had no need and received non-need-based aid.

UNDERGRADUATE FINANCIAL AID (Fall 1999) 340 applied for aid; of those 94% were deemed to have need. 100% of undergraduates with need received aid; of those 26% had need fully met. *Average percent of need met:* 87% (excluding resources awarded to replace EFC). *Average financial aid package:* $11,260 (excluding resources awarded to replace EFC). 19% of all full-time undergraduates had no need and received non-need-based aid.

GIFT AID (NEED-BASED) ***Total amount:*** $755,303 (51% Federal, 49% state). ***Receiving aid:*** *Freshmen:* 68% (93); *all full-time undergraduates:* 61% (270). ***Average award:*** Freshmen: $3294; Undergraduates: $3226. ***Scholarships, grants, and awards:*** Federal Pell, FSEOG, state, private, college/university gift aid from institutional funds.

GIFT AID (NON-NEED-BASED) ***Total amount:*** $1,648,597 (89% institutional, 11% external sources). ***Receiving aid:*** *Freshmen:* 76% (104); *Undergraduates:* 69% (307). ***Scholarships, grants, and awards by category:*** *Academic Interests/Achievement:* general academic interests/achievements. *Creative Arts/Performance:* journalism/publications, music, performing arts, theater/drama. *Special Achievements/Activities:* cheerleading/drum major, religious involvement. *Special Characteristics:* children and siblings of alumni, children of faculty/staff, general special characteristics, international students, relatives of clergy, religious affiliation, siblings of current students, spouses of current students. ***Tuition waivers:*** Full or partial for children of alumni, employees or children of employees, adult students, senior citizens.

LOANS ***Student loans:*** $1,371,858 (100% need-based). 80% of past graduating class borrowed through all loan programs. Average indebtedness per student: $16,452. ***Average need-based loan:*** Freshmen: $3466; Undergraduates: $4444. ***Parent loans:*** $178,025 (100% need-based). ***Programs:*** FFEL (Subsidized and Unsubsidized Stafford, PLUS), Perkins.

WORK-STUDY ***Federal work-study:*** *Total amount:* $85,789; 157 jobs averaging $798. ***State or other work-study/employment:*** *Total amount:* $80,000 (100% need-based). Part-time jobs available.

ATHLETIC AWARDS *Total amount:* 401,255 (100% non-need-based).

APPLYING for FINANCIAL AID ***Required financial aid form:*** FAFSA. ***Financial aid deadline:*** 8/15 (priority: 3/1). ***Notification date:*** Continuous. Students must reply within 5 weeks of notification.

CONTACT Mr. Mark Bandré, Director of Student Financial Assistance, Tabor College, 400 South Jefferson, Hillsboro, KS 67063, 316-947-3121 Ext. 1726 or toll-free 800-822-6799. *Fax:* 316-947-6276. *E-mail:* markb@tcnet.tabor.edu

TALLADEGA COLLEGE

Talladega, AL

Tuition & fees: $5873 **Average undergraduate aid package: N/A**

ABOUT THE INSTITUTION Independent, coed. Awards: bachelor's degrees. 25 undergraduate majors. Total enrollment: 455. Undergraduates: 455. Freshmen: 79. Federal methodology is used as a basis for awarding need-based institutional aid.

UNDERGRADUATE EXPENSES for 1999–2000 ***Application fee:*** $25. ***Comprehensive fee:*** $8837 includes full-time tuition ($5666), mandatory fees ($207), and room and board ($2964). ***College room only:*** $1424. Full-time tuition and fees vary according to student level. ***Part-time tuition:*** $236 per credit hour. ***Part-time fees:*** $104 per term part-time. Part-time tuition and fees vary according to course load and student level. ***Payment plan:*** installment.

FRESHMAN FINANCIAL AID (Fall 1999, est.) 74 applied for aid; of those 100% were deemed to have need. 100% of freshmen with need received aid; of those 7% had need fully met. 5% of all full-time freshmen had no need and received non-need-based aid.

UNDERGRADUATE FINANCIAL AID (Fall 1999, est.) 362 applied for aid; of those 100% were deemed to have need. 100% of undergraduates with need received aid; of those 4% had need fully met. 7% of all full-time undergraduates had no need and received non-need-based aid.

GIFT AID (NEED-BASED) ***Total amount:*** $3,026,788 (86% Federal, 7% institutional, 7% external sources). ***Receiving aid:*** *Freshmen:* 85% (66); *all full-time undergraduates:* 74% (327). ***Scholarships, grants, and awards:*** Federal Pell, FSEOG, state, private, college/university gift aid from institutional funds, United Negro College Fund.

GIFT AID (NON-NEED-BASED) ***Receiving aid:*** *Freshmen:* 10% (8); *Undergraduates:* 11% (50). ***Scholarships, grants, and awards by category:*** *Academic Interests/Achievement:* general academic interests/achievements. ***Tuition waivers:*** Full or partial for employees or children of employees. ***ROTC:*** Army cooperative.

LOANS ***Student loans:*** $1,383,304 (85% need-based, 15% non-need-based). ***Average need-based loan:*** Freshmen: $2546; Undergraduates: $3420. ***Parent loans:*** $225,594 (100% non-need-based). ***Programs:*** Federal

Talladega College (continued)

Direct (Subsidized and Unsubsidized Stafford, PLUS), FFEL (Subsidized and Unsubsidized Stafford, PLUS), Perkins, college/university.

WORK-STUDY ***Federal work-study:*** *Total amount:* $161,481; 150 jobs averaging $1077.

ATHLETIC AWARDS *Total amount:* 271,332 (100% non-need-based).

APPLYING for FINANCIAL AID ***Required financial aid form:*** FAFSA. ***Financial aid deadline:*** 6/30 (priority: 5/1). ***Notification date:*** Continuous. Students must reply within 2 weeks of notification.

CONTACT Mr. Johnny Byrd, Director of Financial Aid, Talladega College, 627 West Battle Street, Talladega, AL 35160, 256-761-6341 or toll-free 800-762-2168 (in-state), 800-633-2440 (out-of-state). *Fax:* 256-761-6440.

TALMUDICAL ACADEMY OF NEW JERSEY

Adelphia, NJ

CONTACT Office of Financial Aid, Talmudical Academy of New Jersey, Route 524, Adelphia, NJ 07710, 732-431-1600.

TALMUDICAL INSTITUTE OF UPSTATE NEW YORK

Rochester, NY

Tuition & fees: N/R **Average undergraduate aid package: N/A**

ABOUT THE INSTITUTION Independent Jewish, men only. Awards: also offers some graduate courses. 2 undergraduate majors. Total enrollment: 28. Undergraduates: 21. Freshmen: 8.

GIFT AID (NEED-BASED) ***Scholarships, grants, and awards:*** Federal Pell, FSEOG.

GIFT AID (NON-NEED-BASED) ***Scholarships, grants, and awards by category:*** *Academic Interests/Achievement:* religion/biblical studies.

WORK-STUDY Federal work-study jobs available.

APPLYING for FINANCIAL AID ***Required financial aid form:*** FAFSA.

CONTACT Mrs. Ilene Rocklin, Financial Aid Administrator, Talmudical Institute of Upstate New York, 769 Park Avenue, Rochester, NY 14607-3046, 716-473-2810.

TALMUDICAL SEMINARY OHOLEI TORAH

Brooklyn, NY

CONTACT Financial Aid Administrator, Talmudical Seminary Oholei Torah, 667 Eastern Parkway, Brooklyn, NY 11213-3310, 718-774-5050.

TALMUDICAL YESHIVA OF PHILADELPHIA

Philadelphia, PA

Tuition & fees: $5100 **Average undergraduate aid package: $4870**

ABOUT THE INSTITUTION Independent Jewish, men only. Awards: bachelor's degrees (also offers some graduate courses). 2 undergraduate majors. Total enrollment: 114. Undergraduates: 114. Freshmen: 30. Federal methodology is used as a basis for awarding need-based institutional aid.

UNDERGRADUATE EXPENSES for 1999–2000 ***Comprehensive fee:*** $9600 includes full-time tuition ($5000), mandatory fees ($100), and room and board ($4500). ***Payment plan:*** installment.

FRESHMAN FINANCIAL AID (Fall 1998) 20 applied for aid; of those 100% were deemed to have need. 100% of freshmen with need received aid; of those 100% had need fully met. *Average percent of need met:* 100% (excluding resources awarded to replace EFC). *Average financial aid package:* $5950 (excluding resources awarded to replace EFC).

UNDERGRADUATE FINANCIAL AID (Fall 1998) 71 applied for aid; of those 100% were deemed to have need. 100% of undergraduates with need received aid; of those 100% had need fully met. *Average percent of need met:* 100% (excluding resources awarded to replace EFC). *Average financial aid package:* $4870 (excluding resources awarded to replace EFC).

GIFT AID (NEED-BASED) ***Total amount:*** $362,369 (36% Federal, 64% institutional). ***Receiving aid:*** *Freshmen:* 53% (20); *all full-time undergraduates:* 63% (71). ***Scholarships, grants, and awards:*** Federal Pell, FSEOG, college/university gift aid from institutional funds.

GIFT AID (NON-NEED-BASED) ***Tuition waivers:*** Full or partial for employees or children of employees.

WORK-STUDY ***Federal work-study:*** *Total amount:* $28,372; 28 jobs averaging $1000.

APPLYING for FINANCIAL AID ***Required financial aid form:*** FAFSA.

CONTACT Rabbi Uri Mandelbaum, Director of Student Financial Aid/Registrar, Talmudical Yeshiva of Philadelphia, 6063 Drexel Road, Philadelphia, PA 19131-1296, 215-473-1212. *E-mail:* typp@juno.com

TALMUDIC COLLEGE OF FLORIDA

Miami Beach, FL

CONTACT Director of Financial Aid, Talmudic College of Florida, 1910 Alton Road, Miami Beach, FL 33139, 305-534-7050.

TARLETON STATE UNIVERSITY

Stephenville, TX

Tuition & fees (TX res): $2066 **Average undergraduate aid package: N/A**

ABOUT THE INSTITUTION State-supported, coed. Awards: bachelor's and master's degrees. 60 undergraduate majors. Total enrollment: 7,433. Undergraduates: 6,102. Freshmen: 937. Federal methodology is used as a basis for awarding need-based institutional aid.

UNDERGRADUATE EXPENSES for 2000–2001 ***Application fee:*** $25. ***Tuition, state resident:*** full-time $1608; part-time $67 per semester hour. ***Tuition, nonresident:*** full-time $6768; part-time $282 per semester hour. ***Required fees:*** full-time $458. Full-time tuition and fees vary according to course load. Part-time tuition and fees vary according to course load. ***College room and board:*** $3636; ***room only:*** $1956. Room and board charges vary according to board plan and housing facility. ***Payment plan:*** installment.

GIFT AID (NEED-BASED) ***Total amount:*** $4,350,400 (78% Federal, 21% state, 1% institutional). ***Scholarships, grants, and awards:*** Federal Pell, FSEOG, state, private, college/university gift aid from institutional funds.

GIFT AID (NON-NEED-BASED) ***Total amount:*** $1,517,145 (73% institutional, 27% external sources). ***Scholarships, grants, and awards by category:*** *Academic Interests/Achievement:* general academic interests/achievements. *Creative Arts/Performance:* music, theater/drama. *Special Achievements/Activities:* rodeo. *Special Characteristics:* 50 awards ($9000 total): children of faculty/staff. ***Tuition waivers:*** Full or partial for employees or children of employees, senior citizens. ***ROTC:*** Army.

LOANS ***Student loans:*** $20,064,148 (71% need-based, 29% non-need-based). Average indebtedness per student: $10,000. ***Parent loans:*** $1,510,670 (100% non-need-based). ***Programs:*** FFEL (Subsidized and Unsubsidized Stafford, PLUS), college/university.

WORK-STUDY ***Federal work-study:*** *Total amount:* $273,996; 82 jobs averaging $3300. ***State or other work-study/employment:*** *Total amount:* $22,287 (100% need-based). 10 part-time jobs averaging $3300.

ATHLETIC AWARDS *Total amount:* 209,693 (100% non-need-based).

APPLYING for FINANCIAL AID ***Required financial aid form:*** FAFSA. ***Financial aid deadline (priority):*** 6/1.

CONTACT Ms. Betty Murray, Director of Financial Aid, Tarleton State University, Box T-0310, Stephenville, TX 76402, 254-968-9070 or toll-free 800-687-4878. *Fax:* 254-968-9600. *E-mail:* finaid@tarleton.edu

TAYLOR UNIVERSITY

Upland, IN

Tuition & fees: $15,118 **Average undergraduate aid package: $11,273**

ABOUT THE INSTITUTION Independent interdenominational, coed. Awards: associate and bachelor's degrees. 62 undergraduate majors. Total enrollment: 1,897. Undergraduates: 1,897. Freshmen: 475. Both federal and institutional methodology are used as a basis for awarding need-based institutional aid.

UNDERGRADUATE EXPENSES for 1999–2000 ***Application fee:*** $20. ***Comprehensive fee:*** $19,748 includes full-time tuition ($14,900), mandatory fees ($218), and room and board ($4630). ***College room only:*** $2200. Room and board charges vary according to board plan and housing facility. Part-time tuition and fees vary according to course load. ***Payment plan:*** installment.

FRESHMAN FINANCIAL AID (Fall 1999, est.) 345 applied for aid; of those 76% were deemed to have need. 100% of freshmen with need received aid; of those 26% had need fully met. *Average percent of need met:* 81% (excluding resources awarded to replace EFC). *Average financial aid package:* $11,077 (excluding resources awarded to replace EFC). 27% of all full-time freshmen had no need and received non-need-based aid.

UNDERGRADUATE FINANCIAL AID (Fall 1999, est.) 1,231 applied for aid; of those 83% were deemed to have need. 100% of undergraduates with need received aid; of those 28% had need fully met. *Average percent of need met:* 82% (excluding resources awarded to replace EFC). *Average financial aid package:* $11,273 (excluding resources awarded to replace EFC). 27% of all full-time undergraduates had no need and received non-need-based aid.

GIFT AID (NEED-BASED) ***Total amount:*** $6,268,642 (11% Federal, 13% state, 69% institutional, 7% external sources). ***Receiving aid:*** *Freshmen:* 52% (246); *all full-time undergraduates:* 51% (940). ***Average award:*** Freshmen: $7225; Undergraduates: $6888. ***Scholarships, grants, and awards:*** Federal Pell, FSEOG, state, private, college/university gift aid from institutional funds.

GIFT AID (NON-NEED-BASED) ***Total amount:*** $1,299,885 (1% Federal, 3% state, 76% institutional, 20% external sources). ***Receiving aid:*** *Freshmen:* 5% (24); *Undergraduates:* 4% (70). ***Scholarships, grants, and awards by category:*** *Academic Interests/Achievement:* 701 awards ($1,237,980 total): general academic interests/achievements. *Creative Arts/Performance:* 34 awards ($43,700 total): music, theater/drama. *Special Achievements/Activities:* 58 awards ($300,235 total): leadership, religious involvement. *Special Characteristics:* 583 awards ($1,473,697 total): children and siblings of alumni, children of faculty/staff, ethnic background, international students, religious affiliation. ***Tuition waivers:*** Full or partial for employees or children of employees.

LOANS ***Student loans:*** $3,527,162 (82% need-based, 18% non-need-based). 54% of past graduating class borrowed through all loan programs. Average indebtedness per student: $14,655. ***Average need-based loan:*** Freshmen: $3135; Undergraduates: $3615. ***Parent loans:*** $2,274,804 (79% need-based, 21% non-need-based). ***Programs:*** FFEL (Subsidized and Unsubsidized Stafford, PLUS), Perkins, college/university.

WORK-STUDY ***Federal work-study:*** *Total amount:* $793,317; 813 jobs averaging $975.

ATHLETIC AWARDS *Total amount:* 577,576 (56% need-based, 44% non-need-based).

APPLYING for FINANCIAL AID ***Required financial aid forms:*** FAFSA, institution's own form. ***Financial aid deadline:*** 3/1. ***Notification date:*** Continuous. Students must reply by 5/1.

CONTACT Mr. Timothy A. Nace, Director of Financial Aid, Taylor University, 236 West Reade Avenue, Upland, IN 46989-1001, 765-998-5358 or toll-free 800-882-3456. *Fax:* 765-998-4910. *E-mail:* tmnace@tayloru.edu

TAYLOR UNIVERSITY, FORT WAYNE CAMPUS

Fort Wayne, IN

Tuition & fees: $12,600 **Average undergraduate aid package: $12,727**

ABOUT THE INSTITUTION Independent interdenominational, coed. Awards: associate and bachelor's degrees. 21 undergraduate majors. Total enrollment: 428. Undergraduates: 428. Freshmen: 122. Both federal and institutional methodology are used as a basis for awarding need-based institutional aid.

UNDERGRADUATE EXPENSES for 1999–2000 ***Application fee:*** $20. ***One-time required fee:*** $140. ***Comprehensive fee:*** $16,830 includes full-time tuition ($12,550), mandatory fees ($50), and room and board ($4230). ***College room only:*** $1800. Room and board charges vary according to board plan. ***Part-time tuition:*** $170 per hour. ***Part-time fees:*** $25 per term part-time. Part-time tuition and fees vary according to course load. ***Payment plan:*** installment.

FRESHMAN FINANCIAL AID (Fall 1999, est.) 87 applied for aid; of those 89% were deemed to have need. 100% of freshmen with need received aid; of those 14% had need fully met. *Average percent of need met:* 85% (excluding resources awarded to replace EFC). *Average financial aid package:* $12,450 (excluding resources awarded to replace EFC). 17% of all full-time freshmen had no need and received non-need-based aid.

UNDERGRADUATE FINANCIAL AID (Fall 1999, est.) 271 applied for aid; of those 94% were deemed to have need. 100% of undergraduates with need received aid; of those 24% had need fully met. *Average percent of need met:* 88% (excluding resources awarded to replace EFC). *Average financial aid package:* $12,727 (excluding resources awarded to replace EFC). 10% of all full-time undergraduates had no need and received non-need-based aid.

GIFT AID (NEED-BASED) ***Total amount:*** $2,226,251 (17% Federal, 31% state, 50% institutional, 2% external sources). ***Receiving aid:*** *Freshmen:* 67% (72); *all full-time undergraduates:* 77% (246). ***Average award:*** Freshmen: $8835; Undergraduates: $8680. ***Scholarships, grants, and awards:*** Federal Pell, FSEOG, state, private, college/university gift aid from institutional funds, endowed-donor scholarships.

GIFT AID (NON-NEED-BASED) ***Total amount:*** $104,921 (2% Federal, 3% state, 82% institutional, 13% external sources). ***Receiving aid:*** *Undergraduates:* 2% (6). ***Scholarships, grants, and awards by category:*** *Academic Interests/Achievement:* 127 awards ($161,700 total): general academic interests/achievements. *Special Achievements/Activities:* 9 awards ($9700 total): leadership. *Special Characteristics:* 46 awards ($152,544 total): children and siblings of alumni, children of faculty/staff, ethnic background, international students, members of minority groups. ***Tuition waivers:*** Full or partial for employees or children of employees, senior citizens.

LOANS ***Student loans:*** $954,550 (85% need-based, 15% non-need-based). ***Average need-based loan:*** Freshmen: $3198; Undergraduates: $3625. ***Parent loans:*** $307,453 (89% need-based, 11% non-need-based). ***Programs:*** FFEL (Subsidized and Unsubsidized Stafford, PLUS), Perkins, college/university.

WORK-STUDY ***Federal work-study:*** *Total amount:* $109,102; 229 jobs averaging $476.

ATHLETIC AWARDS *Total amount:* 2000 (100% need-based).

APPLYING for FINANCIAL AID ***Required financial aid forms:*** FAFSA, institution's own form. ***Financial aid deadline (priority):*** 3/1. ***Notification date:*** Continuous. Students must reply by 5/1 or within 2 weeks of notification.

CONTACT Mr. Charles Belknap, Director of Financial Aid, Taylor University, Fort Wayne Campus, 1025 West Rudisill Boulevard, Fort Wayne, IN 46807-2197, 219-456-2111 Ext. 32276 or toll-free 800-233-3922. *Fax:* 219-456-2119. *E-mail:* chbelknap@tayloru.edu

TEIKYO LORETTO HEIGHTS UNIVERSITY

Denver, CO

CONTACT Financial Aid Office, Teikyo Loretto Heights University, 3001 South Federal Boulevard, Denver, CO 80236-2711, 303-937-4200.

TEIKYO POST UNIVERSITY

Waterbury, CT

Tuition & fees: $13,400 **Average undergraduate aid package: $10,639**

Teikyo Post University (continued)

ABOUT THE INSTITUTION Independent, coed. Awards: associate and bachelor's degrees. 16 undergraduate majors. Total enrollment: 1,422. Undergraduates: 1,422. Freshmen: 188. Federal methodology is used as a basis for awarding need-based institutional aid.

UNDERGRADUATE EXPENSES for 1999–2000 ***Application fee:*** $40. ***Comprehensive fee:*** $19,300 includes full-time tuition ($13,125), mandatory fees ($275), and room and board ($5900). ***Part-time tuition:*** $440 per credit. Part-time tuition and fees vary according to class time and course load. ***Payment plans:*** installment, deferred payment.

FRESHMAN FINANCIAL AID (Fall 1998) 161 applied for aid; of those 96% were deemed to have need. 100% of freshmen with need received aid; of those 38% had need fully met. *Average percent of need met:* 80% (excluding resources awarded to replace EFC). *Average financial aid package:* $10,572 (excluding resources awarded to replace EFC). 3% of all full-time freshmen had no need and received non-need-based aid.

UNDERGRADUATE FINANCIAL AID (Fall 1998) 400 applied for aid; of those 96% were deemed to have need. 100% of undergraduates with need received aid; of those 32% had need fully met. *Average percent of need met:* 75% (excluding resources awarded to replace EFC). *Average financial aid package:* $10,639 (excluding resources awarded to replace EFC). 3% of all full-time undergraduates had no need and received non-need-based aid.

GIFT AID (NEED-BASED) ***Total amount:*** $1,718,595 (46% Federal, 54% state). ***Receiving aid:*** *Freshmen:* 46% (92); *all full-time undergraduates:* 47% (234). ***Average award:*** Freshmen: $9000; Undergraduates: $9000. ***Scholarships, grants, and awards:*** Federal Pell, FSEOG, state, private, college/university gift aid from institutional funds.

GIFT AID (NON-NEED-BASED) ***Total amount:*** $1,802,038 (2% state, 95% institutional, 3% external sources). ***Receiving aid:*** *Freshmen:* 75% (152); *Undergraduates:* 62% (308). ***Scholarships, grants, and awards by category:*** *Academic Interests/Achievement:* business, English, general academic interests/achievements, international studies, mathematics, social sciences. *Special Achievements/Activities:* community service, general special achievements/activities, leadership, rodeo. *Special Characteristics:* 25 awards ($30,000 total): children and siblings of alumni, general special characteristics, local/state students, members of minority groups, siblings of current students. ***Tuition waivers:*** Full or partial for minority students, employees or children of employees, senior citizens. ***ROTC:*** Army cooperative.

LOANS ***Student loans:*** $2,145,678 (68% need-based, 32% non-need-based). 92% of past graduating class borrowed through all loan programs. ***Average need-based loan:*** Freshmen: $4200; Undergraduates: $4200. ***Parent loans:*** $198,339 (100% non-need-based). ***Programs:*** FFEL (Subsidized and Unsubsidized Stafford, PLUS), Perkins, state.

WORK-STUDY ***Federal work-study:*** *Total amount:* $229,689; jobs available. ***State or other work-study/employment:*** *Total amount:* $60,675 (3% need-based, 97% non-need-based). Part-time jobs available.

ATHLETIC AWARDS *Total amount:* 436,250 (100% need-based).

APPLYING for FINANCIAL AID ***Required financial aid form:*** FAFSA. ***Financial aid deadline (priority):*** 3/1. ***Notification date:*** Continuous. Students must reply within 3 weeks of notification.

CONTACT Kathleen Crowley, Assistant Vice President, Student Services, Teikyo Post University, 800 Country Club Road, Waterbury, CT 06723-2540, 203-596-4526 or toll-free 800-345-2562. *Fax:* 203-756-5810. *E-mail:* kcrowley@teikyopost.edu

TELSHE YESHIVA–CHICAGO

Chicago, IL

CONTACT Office of Financial Aid, Telshe Yeshiva–Chicago, 3535 West Foster Avenue, Chicago, IL 60625-5598, 773-463-7738.

TEMPLE UNIVERSITY

Philadelphia, PA

Tuition & fees (PA res): $6622 **Average undergraduate aid package: $8947**

ABOUT THE INSTITUTION State-related, coed. Awards: associate, bachelor's, master's, doctoral, and first professional degrees and post-master's and first-professional certificates. 104 undergraduate majors. Total enrollment: 28,126. Undergraduates: 18,175. Freshmen: 2,777. Federal methodology is used as a basis for awarding need-based institutional aid.

UNDERGRADUATE EXPENSES for 1999–2000 ***Application fee:*** $35. ***Tuition, state resident:*** full-time $6332; part-time $224 per semester hour. ***Tuition, nonresident:*** full-time $11,450; part-time $342 per semester hour. ***Required fees:*** full-time $290. Full-time tuition and fees vary according to course load and program. Part-time tuition and fees vary according to course load, location, and program. ***College room and board:*** $6302. Room and board charges vary according to board plan and housing facility. ***Payment plan:*** installment.

FRESHMAN FINANCIAL AID (Fall 1998) 1988 applied for aid; of those 83% were deemed to have need. 96% of freshmen with need received aid; of those 14% had need fully met. *Average percent of need met:* 67% (excluding resources awarded to replace EFC). *Average financial aid package:* $8626 (excluding resources awarded to replace EFC). 12% of all full-time freshmen had no need and received non-need-based aid.

UNDERGRADUATE FINANCIAL AID (Fall 1998) 11,664 applied for aid; of those 84% were deemed to have need. 92% of undergraduates with need received aid; of those 20% had need fully met. *Average percent of need met:* 71% (excluding resources awarded to replace EFC). *Average financial aid package:* $8947 (excluding resources awarded to replace EFC). 13% of all full-time undergraduates had no need and received non-need-based aid.

GIFT AID (NEED-BASED) ***Total amount:*** $32,854,221 (43% Federal, 34% state, 23% institutional). ***Receiving aid:*** *Freshmen:* 57% (1,576); *all full-time undergraduates:* 64% (9,038). ***Average award:*** Freshmen: $3882; Undergraduates: $3514. ***Scholarships, grants, and awards:*** Federal Pell, FSEOG, state, private, college/university gift aid from institutional funds, Federal Nursing.

GIFT AID (NON-NEED-BASED) ***Total amount:*** $8,881,726 (33% institutional, 67% external sources). ***Receiving aid:*** *Freshmen:* 24% (663); *Undergraduates:* 18% (2,498). ***Scholarships, grants, and awards by category:*** *Academic Interests/Achievement:* general academic interests/achievements. *Creative Arts/Performance:* general creative arts/performance, music, performing arts. *Special Achievements/Activities:* cheerleading/drum major. *Special Characteristics:* general special characteristics. ***Tuition waivers:*** Full or partial for employees or children of employees. ***ROTC:*** Army, Naval cooperative, Air Force cooperative.

LOANS ***Student loans:*** $52,562,260 (69% need-based, 31% non-need-based). 85% of past graduating class borrowed through all loan programs. Average indebtedness per student: $14,500. ***Average need-based loan:*** Freshmen: $2262; Undergraduates: $3099. ***Parent loans:*** $985,884 (100% non-need-based). ***Programs:*** FFEL (Subsidized and Unsubsidized Stafford, PLUS), Perkins, Federal Nursing, college/university.

WORK-STUDY ***Federal work-study:*** *Total amount:* $1,754,755; 1,416 jobs averaging $1239.

ATHLETIC AWARDS *Total amount:* 4,535,294 (100% non-need-based).

APPLYING for FINANCIAL AID ***Required financial aid form:*** FAFSA. ***Financial aid deadline (priority):*** 3/1. ***Notification date:*** Continuous. Students must reply by 5/1 or within 3 weeks of notification.

CONTACT Dr. John F. Morris, Director, Student Services, Temple University, Conwell Hall, Ground Floor, 1801 North Broad Street, Philadelphia, PA 19122-6096, 215-204-8760 or toll-free 888-340-2222. *Fax:* 215-204-2016. *E-mail:* morrisj@mail.temple.edu

TENNESSEE STATE UNIVERSITY

Nashville, TN

Tuition & fees (TN res): $2730 **Average undergraduate aid package: $7689**

ABOUT THE INSTITUTION State-supported, coed. Awards: associate, bachelor's, master's, and doctoral degrees. 59 undergraduate majors. Total enrollment: 8,836. Undergraduates: 7,277. Freshmen: 1,368. Federal methodology is used as a basis for awarding need-based institutional aid.

UNDERGRADUATE EXPENSES for 1999–2000 ***Application fee:*** $15. ***Tuition, state resident:*** full-time $2308; part-time $138 per semester hour. ***Tuition, nonresident:*** full-time $7134; part-time $349 per semester hour. ***Required fees:*** full-time $422. Full-time tuition and fees vary according to course load. Part-time tuition and fees vary according to course load. ***College room and board:*** $3600; ***room only:*** $2090. Room and board charges vary according to board plan and housing facility. ***Payment plan:*** deferred payment.

FRESHMAN FINANCIAL AID (Fall 1999, est.) 1253 applied for aid. *Average percent of need met:* 58% (excluding resources awarded to replace EFC). *Average financial aid package:* $7405 (excluding resources awarded to replace EFC).

UNDERGRADUATE FINANCIAL AID (Fall 1999, est.) 5,828 applied for aid. *Average percent of need met:* 61% (excluding resources awarded to replace EFC). *Average financial aid package:* $7689 (excluding resources awarded to replace EFC).

GIFT AID (NEED-BASED) ***Total amount:*** $8,556,633 (54% Federal, 28% state, 14% institutional, 4% external sources). ***Scholarships, grants, and awards:*** Federal Pell, FSEOG, state, private, college/university gift aid from institutional funds.

GIFT AID (NON-NEED-BASED) ***Total amount:*** $657,865 (70% institutional, 30% external sources). ***Scholarships, grants, and awards by category:*** *Academic Interests/Achievement:* general academic interests/achievements. *Creative Arts/Performance:* music. *Special Achievements/Activities:* general special achievements/activities. *Special Characteristics:* local/state students, members of minority groups. ***Tuition waivers:*** Full or partial for minority students, employees or children of employees. ***ROTC:*** Army cooperative, Naval cooperative, Air Force.

LOANS ***Student loans:*** $25,267,068 (64% need-based, 36% non-need-based). ***Parent loans:*** $1,191,160 (100% non-need-based). ***Programs:*** Federal Direct (Subsidized and Unsubsidized Stafford), FFEL (Subsidized and Unsubsidized Stafford, PLUS), Perkins, college/university.

WORK-STUDY ***Federal work-study:*** *Total amount:* $1,154,310; jobs available. ***State or other work-study/employment:*** *Total amount:* $514,199 (31% need-based, 69% non-need-based). Part-time jobs available.

ATHLETIC AWARDS *Total amount:* 1,077,134 (100% non-need-based).

APPLYING for FINANCIAL AID ***Required financial aid form:*** FAFSA. ***Financial aid deadline (priority):*** 4/1. ***Notification date:*** 6/1. Students must reply within 2 weeks of notification.

CONTACT Michael Jones, Assistant Director of Financial Aid, Tennessee State University, 3500 John Merritt Boulevard, Nashville, TN 37209-1561, 615-963-5701. *Fax:* 615-963-5108.

TENNESSEE TECHNOLOGICAL UNIVERSITY

Cookeville, TN

Tuition & fees (TN res): $2390 **Average undergraduate aid package: $2992**

ABOUT THE INSTITUTION State-supported, coed. Awards: bachelor's, master's, and doctoral degrees. 66 undergraduate majors. Total enrollment: 8,584. Undergraduates: 7,043. Freshmen: 1,183. Federal methodology is used as a basis for awarding need-based institutional aid.

UNDERGRADUATE EXPENSES for 1999–2000 ***Application fee:*** $15. ***Tuition, state resident:*** full-time $2390; part-time $111 per semester hour. ***Tuition, nonresident:*** full-time $8028; part-time $335 per semester hour. Part-time tuition and fees vary according to course load. ***College room and board:*** $4170; ***room only:*** $1784. Room and board charges vary according to board plan and housing facility.

FRESHMAN FINANCIAL AID (Fall 1999) 1054 applied for aid; of those 56% were deemed to have need. 97% of freshmen with need received aid; of those 21% had need fully met. *Average percent of need met:* 77% (excluding resources awarded to replace EFC). *Average financial aid package:* $4506 (excluding resources awarded to replace EFC). 23% of all full-time freshmen had no need and received non-need-based aid.

UNDERGRADUATE FINANCIAL AID (Fall 1999) 4,311 applied for aid; of those 53% were deemed to have need. 97% of undergraduates with need received aid; of those 24% had need fully met. *Average percent of need met:* 73% (excluding resources awarded to replace EFC). *Average financial aid package:* $2992 (excluding resources awarded to replace EFC). 18% of all full-time undergraduates had no need and received non-need-based aid.

GIFT AID (NEED-BASED) ***Total amount:*** $4,739,718 (84% Federal, 16% state). ***Receiving aid:*** *Freshmen:* 30% (346); *all full-time undergraduates:* 23% (1,407). ***Average award:*** Freshmen: $2401; Undergraduates: $2092. ***Scholarships, grants, and awards:*** Federal Pell, FSEOG, state, private, college/university gift aid from institutional funds, United Negro College Fund.

GIFT AID (NON-NEED-BASED) ***Total amount:*** $2,907,752 (1% Federal, 22% state, 49% institutional, 28% external sources). ***Receiving aid:*** *Freshmen:* 17% (200); *Undergraduates:* 10% (620). ***Scholarships, grants, and awards by category:*** *Academic Interests/Achievement:* agriculture, biological sciences, business, communication, computer science, education, engineering/technologies, English, foreign languages, general academic interests/achievements, health fields, home economics, humanities, mathematics, military science, physical sciences, premedicine, social sciences. *Creative Arts/Performance:* art/fine arts, debating, journalism/publications, music. *Special Achievements/Activities:* cheerleading/drum major, memberships. *Special Characteristics:* children of educators, children of faculty/staff, children of public servants, ethnic background, first-generation college students, members of minority groups, out-of-state students, public servants. ***Tuition waivers:*** Full or partial for employees or children of employees. ***ROTC:*** Army, Air Force cooperative.

LOANS ***Student loans:*** $9,355,024 (66% need-based, 34% non-need-based). ***Average need-based loan:*** Freshmen: $920; Undergraduates: $1491. ***Parent loans:*** $450,552 (100% non-need-based). ***Programs:*** Federal Direct (Subsidized and Unsubsidized Stafford), FFEL (PLUS), Perkins, college/university.

WORK-STUDY ***Federal work-study:*** *Total amount:* $652,029; 408 jobs averaging $1598. ***State or other work-study/employment:*** *Total amount:* $806,929 (100% non-need-based).

ATHLETIC AWARDS *Total amount:* 1,618,631 (100% non-need-based).

APPLYING for FINANCIAL AID ***Required financial aid forms:*** FAFSA, parent and student income tax returns. ***Financial aid deadline (priority):*** 3/15. ***Notification date:*** Continuous beginning 4/15. Students must reply within 2 weeks of notification.

CONTACT Dr. Raymond L. Holbrook, Director of Student Financial Aid, Tennessee Technological University, Box 5076, University Center, Cookeville, TN 38505, 931-372-3073 or toll-free 800-255-8881. *Fax:* 931-372-6309. *E-mail:* rholbrook@tntech.edu

TENNESSEE TEMPLE UNIVERSITY

Chattanooga, TN

Tuition & fees: $5250 **Average undergraduate aid package: $8100**

ABOUT THE INSTITUTION Independent Baptist, coed. Awards: associate, bachelor's, and master's degrees. 25 undergraduate majors. Total enrollment: 743. Undergraduates: 723. Freshmen: 171. Federal methodology is used as a basis for awarding need-based institutional aid.

UNDERGRADUATE EXPENSES for 1999–2000 ***Application fee:*** $30. ***Comprehensive fee:*** $10,000 includes full-time tuition ($4650), mandatory fees ($600), and room and board ($4750). ***Part-time tuition:*** $210 per credit hour. ***Payment plan:*** installment.

FRESHMAN FINANCIAL AID (Fall 1999) 259 applied for aid; of those 53% were deemed to have need. 100% of freshmen with need received aid; of those 85% had need fully met. *Average percent of need met:* 70% (excluding resources awarded to replace EFC). *Average financial aid package:* $7500 (excluding resources awarded to replace EFC). 39% of all full-time freshmen had no need and received non-need-based aid.

UNDERGRADUATE FINANCIAL AID (Fall 1999) 681 applied for aid; of those 72% were deemed to have need. 100% of undergraduates with need received aid; of those 92% had need fully met. *Average percent of*

Tennessee Temple University (continued)

need met: 70% (excluding resources awarded to replace EFC). *Average financial aid package:* $8100 (excluding resources awarded to replace EFC). 28% of all full-time undergraduates had no need and received non-need-based aid.

GIFT AID (NEED-BASED) ***Total amount:*** $876,652 (96% Federal, 4% state). ***Receiving aid:*** *Freshmen:* 47% (121); *all full-time undergraduates:* 62% (424). ***Average award:*** Freshmen: $1500; Undergraduates: $2000. ***Scholarships, grants, and awards:*** Federal Pell, FSEOG, state, private, college/university gift aid from institutional funds.

GIFT AID (NON-NEED-BASED) ***Total amount:*** $1,736,402 (96% institutional, 4% external sources). ***Receiving aid:*** *Freshmen:* 53% (136); *Undergraduates:* 72% (488). ***Scholarships, grants, and awards by category:*** *Academic Interests/Achievement:* 359 awards ($641,532 total): general academic interests/achievements, religion/biblical studies. *Creative Arts/Performance:* 18 awards ($49,837 total): music. *Special Achievements/Activities:* 12 awards ($42,656 total): leadership. *Special Characteristics:* 106 awards ($251,883 total): children of faculty/staff, local/state students, siblings of current students, spouses of current students. ***Tuition waivers:*** Full or partial for employees or children of employees.

LOANS ***Student loans:*** $1,260,311 (27% need-based, 73% non-need-based). 45% of past graduating class borrowed through all loan programs. Average indebtedness per student: $9000. ***Average need-based loan:*** Freshmen: $3500; Undergraduates: $4500. ***Parent loans:*** $56,062 (100% non-need-based). ***Programs:*** FFEL (Subsidized and Unsubsidized Stafford, PLUS), Perkins.

WORK-STUDY ***Federal work-study:*** *Total amount:* $119,892; 72 jobs averaging $1600. ***State or other work-study/employment:*** *Total amount:* $150,071 (100% need-based). 95 part-time jobs averaging $1500.

ATHLETIC AWARDS *Total amount:* 212,140 (100% non-need-based).

APPLYING for FINANCIAL AID ***Required financial aid forms:*** FAFSA, institution's own form. ***Financial aid deadline:*** Continuous. ***Notification date:*** Continuous. Students must reply within 4 weeks of notification.

CONTACT Mr. Dell Hamilton, Director of Financial Aid, Tennessee Temple University, 1815 Union Avenue, Chattanooga, TN 37404-3587, 423-493-4207 or toll-free 800-553-4050. *Fax:* 423-493-4497. *E-mail:* dell@tntemple.edu

TENNESSEE WESLEYAN COLLEGE

Athens, TN

Tuition & fees: $7550 **Average undergraduate aid package: $7668**

ABOUT THE INSTITUTION Independent United Methodist, coed. Awards: bachelor's degrees (all information given is for both main and branch campuses). 37 undergraduate majors. Total enrollment: 835. Undergraduates: 835. Freshmen: 145. Federal methodology is used as a basis for awarding need-based institutional aid.

UNDERGRADUATE EXPENSES for 1999–2000 ***Application fee:*** $25. ***Comprehensive fee:*** $11,630 includes full-time tuition ($7400), mandatory fees ($150), and room and board ($4080). ***College room only:*** $1580. ***Part-time tuition:*** $205 per semester hour. Part-time tuition and fees vary according to class time and location. ***Payment plan:*** deferred payment.

FRESHMAN FINANCIAL AID (Fall 1999, est.) 128 applied for aid; of those 90% were deemed to have need. 100% of freshmen with need received aid; of those 25% had need fully met. *Average percent of need met:* 96% (excluding resources awarded to replace EFC). *Average financial aid package:* $6940 (excluding resources awarded to replace EFC).

UNDERGRADUATE FINANCIAL AID (Fall 1999, est.) 425 applied for aid; of those 87% were deemed to have need. 100% of undergraduates with need received aid; of those 23% had need fully met. *Average percent of need met:* 95% (excluding resources awarded to replace EFC). *Average financial aid package:* $7668 (excluding resources awarded to replace EFC).

GIFT AID (NEED-BASED) ***Total amount:*** $1,839,558 (30% Federal, 21% state, 43% institutional, 6% external sources). ***Receiving aid:*** *Freshmen:* 50% (114); *all full-time undergraduates:* 66% (357). ***Average award:*** Freshmen: $5119; Undergraduates: $5234. ***Scholarships, grants, and awards:*** Federal Pell, FSEOG, state, private, college/university gift aid from institutional funds, Federal Nursing.

GIFT AID (NON-NEED-BASED) ***Total amount:*** $391,122 (92% institutional, 8% external sources). ***Receiving aid:*** *Freshmen:* 7% (16); *Undergraduates:* 7% (37). ***Scholarships, grants, and awards by category:*** *Academic Interests/Achievement:* 301 awards ($917,786 total): biological sciences, business, communication, computer science, education, English, foreign languages, general academic interests/achievements, health fields, humanities, international studies, mathematics, physical sciences, premedicine, religion/biblical studies, social sciences. *Creative Arts/Performance:* 16 awards ($32,200 total): music. *Special Achievements/Activities:* 96 awards ($120,982 total): cheerleading/drum major, general special achievements/activities, junior miss, leadership, memberships, religious involvement. *Special Characteristics:* 96 awards ($228,139 total): children of faculty/staff, general special characteristics, international students, members of minority groups, relatives of clergy, religious affiliation. ***Tuition waivers:*** Full or partial for minority students, employees or children of employees.

LOANS ***Student loans:*** $1,353,583 (79% need-based, 21% non-need-based). 64% of past graduating class borrowed through all loan programs. Average indebtedness per student: $11,746. ***Average need-based loan:*** Freshmen: $1648; Undergraduates: $2206. ***Parent loans:*** $152,247 (40% need-based, 60% non-need-based). ***Programs:*** FFEL (Subsidized and Unsubsidized Stafford, PLUS), Perkins, state, United Methodist Student Loans.

WORK-STUDY ***Federal work-study:*** *Total amount:* $91,212; 115 jobs averaging $793. ***State or other work-study/employment:*** *Total amount:* $31,101 (22% need-based, 78% non-need-based). 24 part-time jobs averaging $1296.

ATHLETIC AWARDS *Total amount:* 673,954 (50% need-based, 50% non-need-based).

APPLYING for FINANCIAL AID ***Required financial aid forms:*** FAFSA, institution's own form. ***Financial aid deadline:*** 5/1 (priority: 2/28). ***Notification date:*** Continuous beginning 5/2. Students must reply within 2 weeks of notification.

CONTACT Ms. Bobbie Pennington, Financial Aid Officer, Tennessee Wesleyan College, PO Box 40, Athens, TN 37371-0040, 423-746-5215 or toll-free 800-PICK-TWC. *Fax:* 423-744-9968. *E-mail:* weisberg@twcnet.edu

TEXAS A&M INTERNATIONAL UNIVERSITY

Laredo, TX

Tuition & fees (TX res): $2579 **Average undergraduate aid package: $3932**

ABOUT THE INSTITUTION State-supported, coed. Awards: bachelor's and master's degrees. 34 undergraduate majors. Total enrollment: 3,209. Undergraduates: 2,241. Freshmen: 268. Federal methodology is used as a basis for awarding need-based institutional aid.

UNDERGRADUATE EXPENSES for 2000–2001 ***One-time required fee:*** $10. ***Tuition, state resident:*** full-time $1984; part-time $62 per semester hour. ***Tuition, nonresident:*** full-time $8310; part-time $277 per semester hour. ***Required fees:*** full-time $595; $20 per semester hour; $34 per term part-time. Full-time tuition and fees vary according to course load. Part-time tuition and fees vary according to course load. ***Payment plan:*** installment.

FRESHMAN FINANCIAL AID (Fall 1998) 200 applied for aid; of those 80% were deemed to have need. 94% of freshmen with need received aid; of those 80% had need fully met. *Average percent of need met:* 55% (excluding resources awarded to replace EFC). *Average financial aid package:* $6432 (excluding resources awarded to replace EFC).

UNDERGRADUATE FINANCIAL AID (Fall 1998) 1,387 applied for aid; of those 83% were deemed to have need. 96% of undergraduates with need received aid; of those 53% had need fully met. *Average percent of need met:* 52% (excluding resources awarded to replace EFC). *Average financial*

aid package: $3932 (excluding resources awarded to replace EFC). 6% of all full-time undergraduates had no need and received non-need-based aid.

GIFT AID (NEED-BASED) ***Total amount:*** $3,244,894 (67% Federal, 8% state, 25% institutional). ***Receiving aid:*** *Freshmen:* 65% (143); *all full-time undergraduates:* 75% (1,051). ***Average award:*** Freshmen: $1000; Undergraduates: $1000. ***Scholarships, grants, and awards:*** Federal Pell, FSEOG, state, college/university gift aid from institutional funds.

GIFT AID (NON-NEED-BASED) ***Receiving aid:*** *Freshmen:* 16% (35); *Undergraduates:* 42% (584). ***Scholarships, grants, and awards by category:*** *Academic Interests/Achievement:* 2,103 awards ($801,897 total): general academic interests/achievements. *Creative Arts/Performance:* 30 awards ($5000 total): dance, music, performing arts. ***Tuition waivers:*** Full or partial for employees or children of employees, senior citizens.

LOANS ***Student loans:*** $3,193,147 (70% need-based, 30% non-need-based). 39% of past graduating class borrowed through all loan programs. Average indebtedness per student: $10,000. ***Average need-based loan:*** Freshmen: $1300; Undergraduates: $1500. ***Programs:*** FFEL (Subsidized and Unsubsidized Stafford, PLUS), college/university, Hinson-Hazelwood Loan Program.

WORK-STUDY ***Federal work-study:*** *Total amount:* $154,808; 38 jobs available. ***State or other work-study/employment:*** *Total amount:* $5927 (100% need-based). 2 part-time jobs available.

APPLYING for FINANCIAL AID ***Required financial aid form:*** FAFSA. ***Financial aid deadline (priority):*** 3/15. ***Notification date:*** Continuous beginning 4/15.

CONTACT Araceli S. Rangel, Director of Financial Aid, Texas A&M International University, 5201 University Boulevard, Laredo, TX 78041, 956-326-2225. *Fax:* 956-326-2224. *E-mail:* arangel@tamiu.edu

TEXAS A&M UNIVERSITY

College Station, TX

Tuition & fees (TX res): $2639 **Average undergraduate aid package: $6959**

ABOUT THE INSTITUTION State-supported, coed. Awards: bachelor's, master's, doctoral, and first professional degrees and post-bachelor's certificates. 93 undergraduate majors. Total enrollment: 43,442. Undergraduates: 36,082. Freshmen: 6,695. Federal methodology is used as a basis for awarding need-based institutional aid.

UNDERGRADUATE EXPENSES for 1999–2000 ***Application fee:*** $50. ***Tuition, state resident:*** full-time $1824; part-time $76 per credit hour. ***Tuition, nonresident:*** full-time $7008; part-time $292 per credit hour. ***Required fees:*** full-time $815; $23 per credit hour; $132 per term part-time. Full-time tuition and fees vary according to course load, location, and program. ***College room and board:*** $4898; ***room only:*** $2970. Room and board charges vary according to board plan and housing facility. ***Payment plan:*** installment.

FRESHMAN FINANCIAL AID (Fall 1998) 3530 applied for aid; of those 62% were deemed to have need. 96% of freshmen with need received aid; of those 97% had need fully met. *Average percent of need met:* 75% (excluding resources awarded to replace EFC). *Average financial aid package:* $6561 (excluding resources awarded to replace EFC). 35% of all full-time freshmen had no need and received non-need-based aid.

UNDERGRADUATE FINANCIAL AID (Fall 1998) 15,075 applied for aid; of those 73% were deemed to have need. 96% of undergraduates with need received aid; of those 68% had need fully met. *Average percent of need met:* 77% (excluding resources awarded to replace EFC). *Average financial aid package:* $6959 (excluding resources awarded to replace EFC). 25% of all full-time undergraduates had no need and received non-need-based aid.

GIFT AID (NEED-BASED) ***Total amount:*** $19,128,276 (62% Federal, 16% state, 12% institutional, 10% external sources). ***Receiving aid:*** *Freshmen:* 26% (1,875); *all full-time undergraduates:* 25% (8,259). ***Average award:*** Freshmen: $5168; Undergraduates: $3727. ***Scholarships, grants, and awards:*** Federal Pell, FSEOG, state, private, college/university gift aid from institutional funds.

GIFT AID (NON-NEED-BASED) ***Total amount:*** $24,419,144 (5% Federal, 12% state, 50% institutional, 33% external sources). ***Receiving aid:*** *Freshmen:* 24% (1,771); *Undergraduates:* 14% (4,577). ***Scholarships, grants, and awards by category:*** *Academic Interests/Achievement:* agriculture, architecture, biological sciences, business, computer science, education, engineering/technologies, general academic interests/achievements, health fields, physical sciences. *Creative Arts/Performance:* journalism/publications, performing arts, theater/drama. *Special Achievements/Activities:* general special achievements/activities, leadership, memberships, rodeo. *Special Characteristics:* children of faculty/staff, veterans, veterans' children. ***ROTC:*** Army, Naval, Air Force.

LOANS ***Student loans:*** $53,002,704 (37% need-based, 63% non-need-based). Average indebtedness per student: $12,401. ***Average need-based loan:*** Freshmen: $2270; Undergraduates: $3073. ***Parent loans:*** $5,845,409 (4% need-based, 96% non-need-based). ***Programs:*** FFEL (Subsidized and Unsubsidized Stafford, PLUS), Perkins, state, college/university.

WORK-STUDY ***Federal work-study:*** *Total amount:* $1,262,322; 902 jobs averaging $1400. ***State or other work-study/employment:*** *Total amount:* $15,065,866 (22% need-based, 78% non-need-based). 7,522 part-time jobs averaging $2003.

ATHLETIC AWARDS *Total amount:* 2,780,893 (28% need-based, 72% non-need-based).

APPLYING for FINANCIAL AID ***Required financial aid forms:*** FAFSA, institution's own form, financial aid transcript (for transfers). ***Financial aid deadline (priority):*** 4/1. ***Notification date:*** Continuous beginning 4/5.

CONTACT Mrs. Debra J. Riding-LaGrone, Assistant Director of Student Financial Aid, Texas A&M University, Department of Student Financial Aid, PO Box 30016, College Station, TX 77842-3016, 409-845-3917. *Fax:* 409-847-9061. *E-mail:* financialaid@tamu.edu

TEXAS A&M UNIVERSITY AT GALVESTON

Galveston, TX

Tuition & fees (TX res): $2855 **Average undergraduate aid package: N/A**

ABOUT THE INSTITUTION State-supported, coed. Awards: bachelor's degrees. 8 undergraduate majors. Total enrollment: 1,288. Undergraduates: 1,288. Federal methodology is used as a basis for awarding need-based institutional aid.

UNDERGRADUATE EXPENSES for 1999–2000 ***Application fee:*** $35. ***Tuition, state resident:*** full-time $1140; part-time $38 per credit hour. ***Tuition, nonresident:*** full-time $7620; part-time $254 per credit hour. ***Required fees:*** full-time $1715; $56 per credit hour; $42 per term part-time. Part-time tuition and fees vary according to program. ***College room and board:*** $3977; ***room only:*** $1780. Room and board charges vary according to board plan. ***Payment plan:*** installment.

GIFT AID (NEED-BASED) ***Scholarships, grants, and awards:*** Federal Pell, FSEOG, state.

GIFT AID (NON-NEED-BASED) ***Scholarships, grants, and awards by category:*** *Academic Interests/Achievement:* general academic interests/achievements. ***ROTC:*** Naval.

LOANS ***Programs:*** FFEL (Subsidized and Unsubsidized Stafford, PLUS), Perkins.

WORK-STUDY Federal work-study jobs available. ***State or other work-study/employment:*** Part-time jobs available.

APPLYING for FINANCIAL AID ***Required financial aid forms:*** FAFSA, institution's own form, financial aid transcript (for transfers). ***Financial aid deadline (priority):*** 4/1. ***Notification date:*** Continuous.

CONTACT Office of Financial Aid, Texas A&M University at Galveston, PO Box 1675, Galveston, TX 77553-1675, 409-740-4500 or toll-free 800-850-6376. *Fax:* 409-741-4396. *E-mail:* 4finaid@tamug.tamu.edu

TEXAS A&M UNIVERSITY–COMMERCE

Commerce, TX

Tuition & fees (TX res): $2526 **Average undergraduate aid package: N/A**

Texas A&M University–Commerce (continued)

ABOUT THE INSTITUTION State-supported, coed. Awards: bachelor's, master's, and doctoral degrees. 68 undergraduate majors. Total enrollment: 7,908. Undergraduates: 4,574. Freshmen: 481. Federal methodology is used as a basis for awarding need-based institutional aid.

UNDERGRADUATE EXPENSES for 1999–2000 ***Tuition, state resident:*** full-time $1980. ***Tuition, nonresident:*** full-time $8460. ***Required fees:*** full-time $546. Full-time tuition and fees vary according to course load. Part-time tuition and fees vary according to course load. ***College room and board:*** $4055; ***room only:*** $2125. Room and board charges vary according to board plan and housing facility. ***Payment plan:*** installment.

GIFT AID (NON-NEED-BASED) ***Scholarships, grants, and awards by category:*** *Academic Interests/Achievement:* agriculture, general academic interests/achievements. *Creative Arts/Performance:* art/fine arts, music, theater/drama. *Special Achievements/Activities:* general special achievements/activities, leadership. *Special Characteristics:* ethnic background, members of minority groups. ***Tuition waivers:*** Full or partial for senior citizens.

LOANS ***Programs:*** Federal Direct (Subsidized Stafford), state.

WORK-STUDY Federal work-study jobs available.

APPLYING for FINANCIAL AID ***Required financial aid forms:*** FAFSA, institution's own form. ***Financial aid deadline (priority):*** 5/1. ***Notification date:*** Continuous beginning 6/1. Students must reply within 2 weeks of notification.

CONTACT Mr. John E. Patton, Director of Financial Aid, Texas A&M University–Commerce, PO Box 3011, Commerce, TX 75429, 903-886-5096 or toll-free 800-331-3878.

TEXAS A&M UNIVERSITY–CORPUS CHRISTI

Corpus Christi, TX

Tuition & fees (TX res): $2306 **Average undergraduate aid package: $5082**

ABOUT THE INSTITUTION State-supported, coed. Awards: bachelor's, master's, and doctoral degrees. 30 undergraduate majors. Total enrollment: 6,621. Undergraduates: 5,049. Freshmen: 735. Federal methodology is used as a basis for awarding need-based institutional aid.

UNDERGRADUATE EXPENSES for 2000–2001 ***Application fee:*** $10. ***Tuition, state resident:*** full-time $1680; part-time $70 per semester hour. ***Tuition, nonresident:*** full-time $6840; part-time $285 per semester hour. ***Required fees:*** full-time $626. Full-time tuition and fees vary according to course load. Part-time tuition and fees vary according to course load. ***College room and board:*** $5661. Room and board charges vary according to housing facility. ***Payment plans:*** guaranteed tuition, installment, deferred payment.

FRESHMAN FINANCIAL AID (Fall 1999, est.) 569 applied for aid; of those 75% were deemed to have need. 94% of freshmen with need received aid; of those 22% had need fully met. *Average percent of need met:* 81% (excluding resources awarded to replace EFC). *Average financial aid package:* $5378 (excluding resources awarded to replace EFC). 7% of all full-time freshmen had no need and received non-need-based aid.

UNDERGRADUATE FINANCIAL AID (Fall 1999, est.) 1,819 applied for aid; of those 81% were deemed to have need. 95% of undergraduates with need received aid; of those 10% had need fully met. *Average percent of need met:* 74% (excluding resources awarded to replace EFC). *Average financial aid package:* $5082 (excluding resources awarded to replace EFC). 9% of all full-time undergraduates had no need and received non-need-based aid.

GIFT AID (NEED-BASED) ***Total amount:*** $4,076,972 (78% Federal, 18% state, 4% institutional). ***Receiving aid:*** *Freshmen:* 31% (278); *all full-time undergraduates:* 36% (1,038). ***Average award:*** Freshmen: $3197; Undergraduates: $2701. ***Scholarships, grants, and awards:*** Federal Pell, FSEOG, state, private, college/university gift aid from institutional funds.

GIFT AID (NON-NEED-BASED) ***Total amount:*** $1,043,739 (63% institutional, 37% external sources). ***Receiving aid:*** *Freshmen:* 8% (73); *Undergraduates:* 7% (205). ***Scholarships, grants, and awards by category:*** *Academic Interests/Achievement:* 303 awards ($563,871 total): general academic interests/achievements. *Creative Arts/Performance:* 67 awards ($37,050 total): art/fine arts. ***Tuition waivers:*** Full or partial for employees or children of employees. ***ROTC:*** Army.

LOANS ***Student loans:*** $9,143,747 (60% need-based, 40% non-need-based). Average indebtedness per student: $11,000. ***Average need-based loan:*** Freshmen: $2417; Undergraduates: $3519. ***Parent loans:*** $994,236 (100% non-need-based). ***Programs:*** FFEL (Subsidized and Unsubsidized Stafford, PLUS), Perkins, college/university.

WORK-STUDY ***Federal work-study:*** *Total amount:* $245,543; 136 jobs averaging $1800. ***State or other work-study/employment:*** *Total amount:* $15,377 (100% need-based). 6 part-time jobs averaging $2400.

ATHLETIC AWARDS *Total amount:* 303,823 (100% non-need-based).

APPLYING for FINANCIAL AID ***Required financial aid forms:*** FAFSA, institution's own form. ***Financial aid deadline (priority):*** 4/1. ***Notification date:*** 5/1. Students must reply within 2 weeks of notification.

CONTACT Financial Aid Counselor, Texas A&M University–Corpus Christi, 6300 Ocean Drive, Corpus Christi, TX 78412-5503, 800-482-6822. *Fax:* 361-825-6095. *E-mail:* faoweb@falcon.tamucc.edu

TEXAS A&M UNIVERSITY–KINGSVILLE

Kingsville, TX

Tuition & fees (TX res): $2542 **Average undergraduate aid package: $6492**

ABOUT THE INSTITUTION State-supported, coed. Awards: bachelor's, master's, and doctoral degrees. 72 undergraduate majors. Total enrollment: 5,843. Undergraduates: 4,644. Freshmen: 720. Federal methodology is used as a basis for awarding need-based institutional aid.

UNDERGRADUATE EXPENSES for 1999–2000 ***Application fee:*** $15. ***Tuition, state resident:*** full-time $1200; part-time $38 per credit. ***Tuition, nonresident:*** full-time $7620; part-time $254 per credit. ***Required fees:*** full-time $1342; $48 per credit; $41 per term part-time. Full-time tuition and fees vary according to course load. Part-time tuition and fees vary according to course load. ***College room and board:*** $3484. Room and board charges vary according to board plan. ***Payment plan:*** installment.

FRESHMAN FINANCIAL AID (Fall 1998) 912 applied for aid; of those 100% were deemed to have need. 100% of freshmen with need received aid; of those 78% had need fully met. *Average percent of need met:* 72% (excluding resources awarded to replace EFC). *Average financial aid package:* $5875 (excluding resources awarded to replace EFC).

UNDERGRADUATE FINANCIAL AID (Fall 1998) 5,087 applied for aid; of those 100% were deemed to have need. 100% of undergraduates with need received aid; of those 76% had need fully met. *Average percent of need met:* 87% (excluding resources awarded to replace EFC). *Average financial aid package:* $6492 (excluding resources awarded to replace EFC).

GIFT AID (NEED-BASED) ***Total amount:*** $8,051,919 (87% Federal, 13% state). ***Receiving aid:*** *Freshmen:* 83% (879); *all full-time undergraduates:* 80% (4,224). ***Average award:*** Freshmen: $5875; Undergraduates: $6492. ***Scholarships, grants, and awards:*** Federal Pell, FSEOG, state, private, college/university gift aid from institutional funds.

GIFT AID (NON-NEED-BASED) ***Receiving aid:*** *Freshmen:* 8% (88); *Undergraduates:* 25% (1,299). ***Scholarships, grants, and awards by category:*** *Academic Interests/Achievement:* agriculture, biological sciences, business, communication, computer science, education, English, general academic interests/achievements, health fields, home economics, mathematics, military science, physical sciences, social sciences. *Creative Arts/Performance:* music. *Special Achievements/Activities:* rodeo. *Special Characteristics:* general special characteristics. ***Tuition waivers:*** Full or partial for employees or children of employees, senior citizens. ***ROTC:*** Army.

LOANS ***Student loans:*** $18,499,374 (100% need-based). 50% of past graduating class borrowed through all loan programs. Average indebtedness per student: $8500. ***Average need-based loan:*** Freshmen: $4225; Undergraduates: $5500. ***Parent loans:*** $817,672 (100% need-based). ***Programs:*** FFEL (Subsidized and Unsubsidized Stafford, PLUS), Perkins, state, college/university.

WORK-STUDY ***Federal work-study:*** *Total amount:* $539,872; jobs available. ***State or other work-study/employment:*** *Total amount:* $101,903 (100% need-based). Part-time jobs available.

ATHLETIC AWARDS *Total amount:* 351,417 (100% need-based).

APPLYING for FINANCIAL AID ***Required financial aid form:*** FAFSA. ***Financial aid deadline (priority):*** 4/15.

CONTACT Director, Student Financial Aid, Texas A&M University–Kingsville, 700 University Boulevard, Kingsville, TX 78363, 361-593-3911 or toll-free 800-687-6000.

TEXAS A&M UNIVERSITY–TEXARKANA

Texarkana, TX

Tuition & fees (TX res): $1692 **Average undergraduate aid package: N/A**

ABOUT THE INSTITUTION State-supported, coed. Awards: bachelor's and master's degrees. 15 undergraduate majors. Total enrollment: 1,152. Undergraduates: 781. Entering class: . Federal methodology is used as a basis for awarding need-based institutional aid.

UNDERGRADUATE EXPENSES for 1999–2000 ***Tuition, state resident:*** full-time $1392; part-time $58 per semester hour. ***Tuition, nonresident:*** full-time $6576; part-time $274 per semester hour. ***Required fees:*** full-time $300; $12 per semester hour; $6 per term part-time. Part-time tuition and fees vary according to course load. ***Payment plan:*** installment.

GIFT AID (NEED-BASED) ***Total amount:*** $696,136 (63% Federal, 18% state, 7% institutional, 12% external sources). ***Scholarships, grants, and awards:*** Federal Pell, FSEOG, state, private, college/university gift aid from institutional funds.

GIFT AID (NON-NEED-BASED) ***Scholarships, grants, and awards by category:*** *Academic Interests/Achievement:* business, education, English, general academic interests/achievements, mathematics, social sciences. *Special Achievements/Activities:* community service, general special achievements/activities, leadership, memberships. ***Tuition waivers:*** Full or partial for senior citizens.

LOANS ***Student loans:*** $448,979 (100% need-based). ***Programs:*** FFEL (Subsidized and Unsubsidized Stafford, PLUS), college/university.

WORK-STUDY ***Federal work-study:*** *Total amount:* $17,533; 13 jobs averaging $1349.

APPLYING for FINANCIAL AID ***Required financial aid forms:*** FAFSA, institution's own form. ***Financial aid deadline (priority):*** 5/1. ***Notification date:*** Continuous beginning 6/1. Students must reply within 6 weeks of notification.

CONTACT Marilyn Raney, Director of Financial Aid and Veterans' Services, Texas A&M University–Texarkana, 2600 North Robison Road, Texarkana, TX 75505, 903-223-3060. *Fax:* 903-223-3118. *E-mail:* marilyn.raney@tamut.edu

TEXAS CHIROPRACTIC COLLEGE

Pasadena, TX

Tuition & fees: $13,935 **Average undergraduate aid package: N/A**

ABOUT THE INSTITUTION Independent, coed. Awards: first professional degrees. 1 undergraduate major. Total enrollment: 470. Federal methodology is used as a basis for awarding need-based institutional aid.

UNDERGRADUATE EXPENSES for 1999–2000 ***Application fee:*** $50. ***Tuition:*** full-time $13,800. ***Required fees:*** full-time $135. ***Payment plans:*** installment, deferred payment.

GIFT AID (NEED-BASED) ***Scholarships, grants, and awards:*** Federal Pell, FSEOG, state, private, college/university gift aid from institutional funds.

GIFT AID (NON-NEED-BASED) ***Scholarships, grants, and awards by category:*** *Academic Interests/Achievement:* general academic interests/achievements.

LOANS ***Programs:*** FFEL (Subsidized and Unsubsidized Stafford, PLUS), state, college/university, Chiroloans, alternative loans.

WORK-STUDY Federal work-study jobs available.

APPLYING for FINANCIAL AID ***Required financial aid forms:*** FAFSA, institution's own form, verification worksheet, copy of tax return, financial aid transcript (for transfers). ***Financial aid deadline (priority):*** 4/15. ***Notification date:*** Continuous beginning 6/1. Students must reply within 2 weeks of notification.

CONTACT Ms. Billie Ford, Financial Aid Director, Texas Chiropractic College, 5912 Spencer Highway, Pasadena, TX 77417, 281-998-6020 or toll-free 800-468-6839. *Fax:* 281-991-5237. *E-mail:* bford@txchiro.edu

TEXAS CHRISTIAN UNIVERSITY

Fort Worth, TX

Tuition & fees: $12,290 **Average undergraduate aid package: $12,006**

ABOUT THE INSTITUTION Independent religious, coed. Awards: bachelor's, master's, doctoral, and first professional degrees. 64 undergraduate majors. Total enrollment: 7,551. Undergraduates: 6,456. Freshmen: 1,424. Both federal and institutional methodology are used as a basis for awarding need-based institutional aid.

UNDERGRADUATE EXPENSES for 1999–2000 ***Application fee:*** $30. ***One-time required fee:*** $200. ***Comprehensive fee:*** $16,260 includes full-time tuition ($10,950), mandatory fees ($1340), and room and board ($3970). ***College room only:*** $2770. Room and board charges vary according to board plan and housing facility. ***Part-time tuition:*** $365 per semester hour. ***Part-time fees:*** $55 per semester hour. ***Payment plan:*** installment.

FRESHMAN FINANCIAL AID (Fall 1999) 901 applied for aid; of those 62% were deemed to have need. 97% of freshmen with need received aid; of those 36% had need fully met. *Average percent of need met:* 94% (excluding resources awarded to replace EFC). *Average financial aid package:* $12,111 (excluding resources awarded to replace EFC).

UNDERGRADUATE FINANCIAL AID (Fall 1999) 3,005 applied for aid; of those 72% were deemed to have need. 94% of undergraduates with need received aid; of those 43% had need fully met. *Average percent of need met:* 94% (excluding resources awarded to replace EFC). *Average financial aid package:* $12,006 (excluding resources awarded to replace EFC).

GIFT AID (NEED-BASED) ***Total amount:*** $9,635,503 (16% Federal, 37% state, 45% institutional, 2% external sources). ***Receiving aid:*** *Freshmen:* 33% (470); *all full-time undergraduates:* 28% (1,671). ***Average award:*** Freshmen: $4794; Undergraduates: $4508. ***Scholarships, grants, and awards:*** Federal Pell, FSEOG, state, private, college/university gift aid from institutional funds.

GIFT AID (NON-NEED-BASED) ***Total amount:*** $9,553,590 (86% institutional, 14% external sources). ***Receiving aid:*** *Freshmen:* 22% (312); *Undergraduates:* 17% (1,006). ***Scholarships, grants, and awards by category:*** *Academic Interests/Achievement:* education, engineering/technologies, general academic interests/achievements, international studies, military science, premedicine, religion/biblical studies. *Creative Arts/Performance:* art/fine arts, cinema/film/broadcasting, dance, journalism/publications, music, performing arts, theater/drama. *Special Achievements/Activities:* general special achievements/activities, leadership, religious involvement. *Special Characteristics:* adult students, children of faculty/staff, children of union members/company employees, international students, local/state students, relatives of clergy, religious affiliation. ***Tuition waivers:*** Full or partial for employees or children of employees. ***ROTC:*** Army, Air Force.

LOANS ***Student loans:*** $12,928,790 (58% need-based, 42% non-need-based). ***Average need-based loan:*** Freshmen: $4705; Undergraduates: $4678. ***Parent loans:*** $2,282,457 (100% non-need-based). ***Programs:*** FFEL (Subsidized and Unsubsidized Stafford, PLUS), Perkins, Federal Nursing, state, college/university.

WORK-STUDY ***Federal work-study:*** *Total amount:* $1,682,238; jobs available. ***State or other work-study/employment:*** *Total amount:* $2500 (100% need-based). Part-time jobs available.

ATHLETIC AWARDS *Total amount:* 3,517,274 (15% need-based, 85% non-need-based).

APPLYING for FINANCIAL AID ***Required financial aid forms:*** FAFSA, institution's own form. ***Financial aid deadline:*** 5/1. ***Notification date:*** Continuous. Students must reply within 2 weeks of notification.

Texas Christian University (continued)

CONTACT Michael Scott, Director, Scholarships and Student Financial Aid, Texas Christian University, PO Box 297012, Fort Worth, TX 76129-0002, 817-257-7858 or toll-free 800-828-3764. *Fax:* 817-257-7462. *E-mail:* m.scott@tcu.edu

TEXAS COLLEGE

Tyler, TX

CONTACT Ms. Cynthia Thornton, Director of Financial Aid, Texas College, 2404 North Grand Avenue, PO Box 4500, Tyler, TX 75712-4500, 903-593-8311.

TEXAS LUTHERAN UNIVERSITY

Seguin, TX

Tuition & fees: $11,444 **Average undergraduate aid package: $11,319**

ABOUT THE INSTITUTION Independent religious, coed. Awards: bachelor's degrees. 31 undergraduate majors. Total enrollment: 1,547. Undergraduates: 1,547. Freshmen: 386. Federal methodology is used as a basis for awarding need-based institutional aid.

UNDERGRADUATE EXPENSES for 1999–2000 ***Application fee:*** $25. ***Comprehensive fee:*** $15,810 includes full-time tuition ($11,374), mandatory fees ($70), and room and board ($4366). ***College room only:*** $1786. Room and board charges vary according to board plan and housing facility. ***Part-time tuition:*** $380 per credit hour. ***Part-time fees:*** $35 per term part-time. ***Payment plan:*** installment.

FRESHMAN FINANCIAL AID (Fall 1999) 360 applied for aid; of those 71% were deemed to have need. 100% of freshmen with need received aid; of those 22% had need fully met. *Average percent of need met:* 90% (excluding resources awarded to replace EFC). *Average financial aid package:* $11,527 (excluding resources awarded to replace EFC). 28% of all full-time freshmen had no need and received non-need-based aid.

UNDERGRADUATE FINANCIAL AID (Fall 1999) 1,153 applied for aid; of those 68% were deemed to have need. 100% of undergraduates with need received aid; of those 22% had need fully met. *Average percent of need met:* 89% (excluding resources awarded to replace EFC). *Average financial aid package:* $11,319 (excluding resources awarded to replace EFC). 32% of all full-time undergraduates had no need and received non-need-based aid.

GIFT AID (NEED-BASED) ***Total amount:*** $4,812,714 (16% Federal, 25% state, 56% institutional, 3% external sources). ***Receiving aid:*** *Freshmen:* 64% (230); *all full-time undergraduates:* 61% (706). ***Average award:*** Freshmen: $7045; Undergraduates: $6394. ***Scholarships, grants, and awards:*** Federal Pell, FSEOG, state, private, college/university gift aid from institutional funds.

GIFT AID (NON-NEED-BASED) ***Total amount:*** $1,285,535 (92% institutional, 8% external sources). ***Receiving aid:*** *Freshmen:* 53% (192); *Undergraduates:* 51% (586). ***Scholarships, grants, and awards by category:*** *Academic Interests/Achievement:* 486 awards ($1,564,305 total): general academic interests/achievements. *Creative Arts/Performance:* 155 awards ($358,075 total): journalism/publications, music, theater/drama. *Special Achievements/Activities:* 396 awards ($721,892 total): general special achievements/activities, leadership, religious involvement. *Special Characteristics:* 598 awards ($1,109,439 total): children and siblings of alumni, first-generation college students, general special characteristics, international students, religious affiliation. ***Tuition waivers:*** Full or partial for employees or children of employees. ***ROTC:*** Army cooperative, Air Force cooperative.

LOANS ***Student loans:*** $4,346,883 (89% need-based, 11% non-need-based). 55% of past graduating class borrowed through all loan programs. Average indebtedness per student: $18,519. ***Average need-based loan:*** Freshmen: $4158; Undergraduates: $4576. ***Parent loans:*** $1,182,043 (56% need-based, 44% non-need-based). ***Programs:*** FFEL (Subsidized and Unsubsidized Stafford, PLUS), Perkins, state, alternative loans.

WORK-STUDY ***Federal work-study:*** *Total amount:* $138,625; 161 jobs averaging $994. ***State or other work-study/employment:*** *Total amount:* $366,721 (60% need-based, 40% non-need-based). Part-time jobs available.

ATHLETIC AWARDS *Total amount:* 521,750 (51% need-based, 49% non-need-based).

APPLYING for FINANCIAL AID ***Required financial aid form:*** FAFSA. ***Financial aid deadline (priority):*** 4/1. ***Notification date:*** Continuous. Students must reply within 2 weeks of notification.

CONTACT Ms. Carol Hamilton, Director, Financial Aid, Texas Lutheran University, 1000 West Court Street, Seguin, TX 78155-5999, 830-372-8075 or toll-free 800-771-8521. *Fax:* 830-372-8096. *E-mail:* chamilton@txlutheran.edu

TEXAS SOUTHERN UNIVERSITY

Houston, TX

CONTACT Financial Aid Office, Texas Southern University, 3100 Cleburne, Houston, TX 77004-4584, 713-313-7011.

TEXAS TECH UNIVERSITY

Lubbock, TX

Tuition & fees (TX res): $3107 **Average undergraduate aid package: $5322**

ABOUT THE INSTITUTION State-supported, coed. Awards: bachelor's, master's, doctoral, and first professional degrees. 102 undergraduate majors. Total enrollment: 24,249. Undergraduates: 20,227. Freshmen: 3,536. Federal methodology is used as a basis for awarding need-based institutional aid.

UNDERGRADUATE EXPENSES for 1999–2000 ***Application fee:*** $25. ***Tuition, state resident:*** full-time $1140; part-time $38 per credit hour. ***Tuition, nonresident:*** full-time $7620; part-time $254 per credit hour. ***Required fees:*** full-time $1967; $38 per credit hour. Full-time tuition and fees vary according to course load. Part-time tuition and fees vary according to course load. ***College room and board:*** $4787; ***room only:*** $2633. Room and board charges vary according to board plan and housing facility. ***Payment plan:*** installment.

FRESHMAN FINANCIAL AID (Fall 1998) 1912 applied for aid; of those 61% were deemed to have need. 89% of freshmen with need received aid. *Average financial aid package:* $4306 (excluding resources awarded to replace EFC). 2% of all full-time freshmen had no need and received non-need-based aid.

UNDERGRADUATE FINANCIAL AID (Fall 1998) 10,539 applied for aid; of those 87% were deemed to have need. 78% of undergraduates with need received aid. *Average financial aid package:* $5322 (excluding resources awarded to replace EFC). 1% of all full-time undergraduates had no need and received non-need-based aid.

GIFT AID (NEED-BASED) ***Total amount:*** $16,455,004 (56% Federal, 1% state, 43% institutional). ***Receiving aid:*** *Freshmen:* 22% (713); *all full-time undergraduates:* 30% (5,335). ***Average award:*** Freshmen: $2382; Undergraduates: $2514. ***Scholarships, grants, and awards:*** Federal Pell, FSEOG, state, college/university gift aid from institutional funds.

GIFT AID (NON-NEED-BASED) ***Total amount:*** $4,133,838 (2% Federal, 52% institutional, 46% external sources). ***Receiving aid:*** *Freshmen:* 4% (127); *Undergraduates:* 9% (1,560). ***Scholarships, grants, and awards by category:*** *Academic Interests/Achievement:* agriculture, architecture, biological sciences, business, communication, computer science, education, engineering/technologies, English, foreign languages, general academic interests/achievements, home economics, international studies, mathematics, military science, physical sciences, premedicine, social sciences. *Creative Arts/Performance:* applied art and design, art/fine arts, dance, journalism/publications, music, performing arts, theater/drama. *Special Achievements/Activities:* community service, memberships, rodeo. *Special Characteristics:* children of faculty/staff, handicapped students, out-of-state students, veterans, veterans' children. ***ROTC:*** Army, Air Force.

LOANS ***Student loans:*** $37,801,638 (60% need-based, 40% non-need-based). ***Average need-based loan:*** Freshmen: $2337; Undergraduates: $3539. ***Parent loans:*** $6,156,547 (100% need-based). ***Programs:*** FFEL (Subsidized and Unsubsidized Stafford, PLUS), Perkins, state, college/university.

WORK-STUDY ***Federal work-study:*** *Total amount:* $656,345; 450 jobs averaging $1457.

ATHLETIC AWARDS *Total amount:* 2,140,881 (100% non-need-based).

APPLYING for FINANCIAL AID ***Required financial aid forms:*** FAFSA, institution's own form. ***Financial aid deadline (priority):*** 5/1. ***Notification date:*** Continuous. Students must reply within 2 weeks of notification.

CONTACT Mr. Edwin Earl Hudgins, Director of Financial Aid, Texas Tech University, PO Box 45011, Lubbock, TX 79409-5011, 806-742-3681. *Fax:* 806-742-0980.

TEXAS WESLEYAN UNIVERSITY

Fort Worth, TX

Tuition & fees: $9250 **Average undergraduate aid package: N/A**

ABOUT THE INSTITUTION Independent United Methodist, coed. Awards: bachelor's, master's, and first professional degrees. 70 undergraduate majors. Total enrollment: 3,049. Undergraduates: 2,034. Freshmen: 281. Federal methodology is used as a basis for awarding need-based institutional aid.

UNDERGRADUATE EXPENSES for 1999–2000 ***Application fee:*** $25. ***Comprehensive fee:*** $13,136 includes full-time tuition ($8500), mandatory fees ($750), and room and board ($3886). ***College room only:*** $1500. Full-time tuition and fees vary according to program. Room and board charges vary according to board plan and student level. ***Part-time tuition:*** $280 per credit hour. ***Part-time fees:*** $30 per credit hour. Part-time tuition and fees vary according to program. ***Payment plans:*** installment, deferred payment.

FRESHMAN FINANCIAL AID (Fall 1998) 264 applied for aid; of those 100% were deemed to have need. 100% of freshmen with need received aid.

GIFT AID (NEED-BASED) ***Total amount:*** $4,962,634 (28% Federal, 34% state, 34% institutional, 4% external sources). ***Scholarships, grants, and awards:*** Federal Pell, FSEOG, state, private, college/university gift aid from institutional funds.

GIFT AID (NON-NEED-BASED) ***Scholarships, grants, and awards by category:*** *Academic Interests/Achievement:* general academic interests/achievements. *Creative Arts/Performance:* art/fine arts, general creative arts/performance. *Special Achievements/Activities:* cheerleading/drum major, general special achievements/activities, leadership, religious involvement. *Special Characteristics:* relatives of clergy, religious affiliation. ***Tuition waivers:*** Full or partial for employees or children of employees. ***ROTC:*** Army cooperative, Air Force cooperative.

LOANS ***Student loans:*** $14,685,346 (100% need-based). ***Parent loans:*** $163,674 (100% need-based). ***Programs:*** FFEL (Subsidized and Unsubsidized Stafford, PLUS), state, college/university.

WORK-STUDY ***Federal work-study:*** *Total amount:* $142,515; 132 jobs averaging $1075.

ATHLETIC AWARDS *Total amount:* 849,904 (100% need-based).

APPLYING for FINANCIAL AID ***Required financial aid forms:*** FAFSA, institution's own form. ***Financial aid deadline:*** Continuous. ***Notification date:*** Continuous. Students must reply within 4 weeks of notification.

CONTACT Mrs. Karen Krause, Director of Financial Aid, Texas Wesleyan University, 1201 Wesleyan Street, Fort Worth, TX 76105-1536, 817-531-4420 or toll-free 800-580-8980 (in-state). *Fax:* 817-531-4231. *E-mail:* finaid@txwes.edu

TEXAS WOMAN'S UNIVERSITY

Denton, TX

Tuition & fees (TX res): $2072 **Average undergraduate aid package: $7571**

ABOUT THE INSTITUTION State-supported, coed, primarily women. Awards: bachelor's, master's, and doctoral degrees. 55 undergraduate majors. Total enrollment: 8,624. Undergraduates: 4,730. Freshmen: 340. Federal methodology is used as a basis for awarding need-based institutional aid.

UNDERGRADUATE EXPENSES for 1999–2000 ***Application fee:*** $30. ***Tuition, state resident:*** full-time $912; part-time $38 per semester hour. ***Tuition, nonresident:*** full-time $6096; part-time $254 per semester hour. ***Required fees:*** full-time $1160; $43 per semester hour; $120 per term part-time. Full-time tuition and fees vary according to course load and location. Part-time tuition and fees vary according to course load. ***College room and board:*** $3872. Room and board charges vary according to board plan and housing facility. ***Payment plan:*** installment.

FRESHMAN FINANCIAL AID (Fall 1999) 340 applied for aid; of those 79% were deemed to have need. 95% of freshmen with need received aid; of those 45% had need fully met. *Average percent of need met:* 98% (excluding resources awarded to replace EFC). *Average financial aid package:* $6821 (excluding resources awarded to replace EFC). 17% of all full-time freshmen had no need and received non-need-based aid.

UNDERGRADUATE FINANCIAL AID (Fall 1999) 2,934 applied for aid; of those 79% were deemed to have need. 95% of undergraduates with need received aid; of those 50% had need fully met. *Average percent of need met:* 90% (excluding resources awarded to replace EFC). *Average financial aid package:* $7571 (excluding resources awarded to replace EFC). 12% of all full-time undergraduates had no need and received non-need-based aid.

GIFT AID (NEED-BASED) ***Total amount:*** $4,420,408 (74% Federal, 6% state, 20% institutional). ***Receiving aid:*** *Freshmen:* 66% (242); *all full-time undergraduates:* 63% (2,114). ***Average award:*** Freshmen: $2908; Undergraduates: $2676. ***Scholarships, grants, and awards:*** Federal Pell, FSEOG, state, private, college/university gift aid from institutional funds.

GIFT AID (NON-NEED-BASED) ***Total amount:*** $1,649,298 (75% institutional, 25% external sources). ***Receiving aid:*** *Freshmen:* 22% (81); *Undergraduates:* 17% (587). ***Scholarships, grants, and awards by category:*** *Academic Interests/Achievement:* biological sciences, business, communication, computer science, education, English, foreign languages, general academic interests/achievements, health fields, home economics, humanities, mathematics, physical sciences, premedicine, social sciences. *Creative Arts/Performance:* applied art and design, art/fine arts, cinema/film/broadcasting, dance, journalism/publications, music, theater/drama. ***Tuition waivers:*** Full or partial for senior citizens.

LOANS ***Student loans:*** $13,062,274 (56% need-based, 44% non-need-based). Average indebtedness per student: $18,912. ***Average need-based loan:*** Freshmen: $2167; Undergraduates: $3653. ***Parent loans:*** $502,015 (13% need-based, 87% non-need-based). ***Programs:*** FFEL (Subsidized and Unsubsidized Stafford, PLUS), Perkins, Federal Nursing, state, college/university.

WORK-STUDY ***Federal work-study:*** *Total amount:* $204,408; 176 jobs averaging $1161. ***State or other work-study/employment:*** *Total amount:* $891,608 (3% need-based, 97% non-need-based). Part-time jobs available.

ATHLETIC AWARDS *Total amount:* 162,366 (100% non-need-based).

APPLYING for FINANCIAL AID ***Required financial aid forms:*** FAFSA, institution's own form. ***Financial aid deadline (priority):*** 4/1. ***Notification date:*** 5/1. Students must reply within 2 weeks of notification.

CONTACT Mr. Governor Jackson, Director of Financial Aid, Texas Woman's University, PO Box 425408, Denton, TX 76204-5408, 940-898-3051 or toll-free 888-948-9984. *Fax:* 940-898-3068. *E-mail:* gjackson@twu.edu

THIEL COLLEGE

Greenville, PA

Tuition & fees: $10,785 **Average undergraduate aid package: $13,740**

ABOUT THE INSTITUTION Independent religious, coed. Awards: associate and bachelor's degrees. 38 undergraduate majors. Total enrollment: 980. Undergraduates: 980. Freshmen: 287. Federal methodology is used as a basis for awarding need-based institutional aid.

UNDERGRADUATE EXPENSES for 1999–2000 ***Application fee:*** $25. ***Comprehensive fee:*** $16,275 includes full-time tuition ($9990), mandatory fees ($795), and room and board ($5490). ***College room only:*** $2798. Full-time tuition and fees vary according to student level. ***Part-time tuition:*** $270 per credit. ***Part-time fees:*** $20 per credit. Part-time tuition and fees vary according to course load. ***Payment plan:*** installment.

Thiel College (continued)

FRESHMAN FINANCIAL AID (Fall 1999) 257 applied for aid; of those 100% were deemed to have need. 100% of freshmen with need received aid; of those 26% had need fully met. *Average percent of need met:* 84% (excluding resources awarded to replace EFC). *Average financial aid package:* $10,880 (excluding resources awarded to replace EFC). 9% of all full-time freshmen had no need and received non-need-based aid.

UNDERGRADUATE FINANCIAL AID (Fall 1999) 780 applied for aid; of those 100% were deemed to have need. 100% of undergraduates with need received aid; of those 26% had need fully met. *Average percent of need met:* 84% (excluding resources awarded to replace EFC). *Average financial aid package:* $13,740 (excluding resources awarded to replace EFC). 7% of all full-time undergraduates had no need and received non-need-based aid.

GIFT AID (NEED-BASED) ***Total amount:*** $5,186,516 (20% Federal, 26% state, 53% institutional, 1% external sources). ***Receiving aid:*** *Freshmen:* 90% (257); *all full-time undergraduates:* 91% (780). ***Average award:*** Freshmen: $6460; Undergraduates: $8244. ***Scholarships, grants, and awards:*** Federal Pell, FSEOG, state, private, college/university gift aid from institutional funds.

GIFT AID (NON-NEED-BASED) ***Total amount:*** $2,004,650 (89% institutional, 11% external sources). ***Receiving aid:*** *Freshmen:* 40% (114); *Undergraduates:* 40% (343). ***Scholarships, grants, and awards by category:*** *Academic Interests/Achievement:* general academic interests/achievements. *Creative Arts/Performance:* music. *Special Achievements/Activities:* junior miss, leadership. *Special Characteristics:* children of faculty/staff, religious affiliation, siblings of current students. ***Tuition waivers:*** Full or partial for employees or children of employees, senior citizens.

LOANS ***Student loans:*** $3,733,288 (76% need-based, 24% non-need-based). 91% of past graduating class borrowed through all loan programs. Average indebtedness per student: $20,069. ***Average need-based loan:*** Freshmen: $3540; Undergraduates: $4500. ***Parent loans:*** $439,221 (100% non-need-based). ***Programs:*** FFEL (Subsidized and Unsubsidized Stafford, PLUS), Perkins, college/university.

WORK-STUDY ***Federal work-study:*** *Total amount:* $145,892; 95 jobs averaging $1224. ***State or other work-study/employment:*** *Total amount:* $283,078 (70% need-based, 30% non-need-based). Part-time jobs available.

APPLYING for FINANCIAL AID ***Required financial aid forms:*** FAFSA, state aid form. ***Financial aid deadline:*** Continuous. ***Notification date:*** Continuous. Students must reply within 2 weeks of notification.

CONTACT Ms. Cynthia H. Farrell, Director of Financial Aid, Thiel College, 75 College Avenue, Greenville, PA 16125-2181, 724-589-2178 or toll-free 800-24THIEL. *Fax:* 724-589-2850. *E-mail:* cfarrell@thiel.edu

THOMAS AQUINAS COLLEGE

Santa Paula, CA

Tuition & fees: $14,900 **Average undergraduate aid package: $13,015**

ABOUT THE INSTITUTION Independent Roman Catholic, coed. Awards: bachelor's degrees. 3 undergraduate majors. Total enrollment: 267. Undergraduates: 267. Freshmen: 86. Both federal and institutional methodology are used as a basis for awarding need-based institutional aid.

UNDERGRADUATE EXPENSES for 1999–2000 ***Comprehensive fee:*** $19,200 includes full-time tuition ($14,900) and room and board ($4300). ***Payment plan:*** installment.

FRESHMAN FINANCIAL AID (Fall 1999) 71 applied for aid; of those 85% were deemed to have need. 100% of freshmen with need received aid; of those 100% had need fully met. *Average percent of need met:* 100% (excluding resources awarded to replace EFC). *Average financial aid package:* $12,485 (excluding resources awarded to replace EFC). 8% of all full-time freshmen had no need and received non-need-based aid.

UNDERGRADUATE FINANCIAL AID (Fall 1999) 225 applied for aid; of those 92% were deemed to have need. 100% of undergraduates with need received aid; of those 100% had need fully met. *Average percent of need met:* 100% (excluding resources awarded to replace EFC). *Average financial aid package:* $13,015 (excluding resources awarded to replace EFC). 3% of all full-time undergraduates had no need and received non-need-based aid.

GIFT AID (NEED-BASED) ***Total amount:*** $1,560,840 (18% state, 78% institutional, 4% external sources). ***Receiving aid:*** *Freshmen:* 63% (54); *all full-time undergraduates:* 72% (193). ***Average award:*** Freshmen: $8085; Undergraduates: $8062. ***Scholarships, grants, and awards:*** state, private, college/university gift aid from institutional funds.

GIFT AID (NON-NEED-BASED) ***Total amount:*** $6000 (100% external sources).

LOANS ***Student loans:*** $690,444 (92% need-based, 8% non-need-based). 80% of past graduating class borrowed through all loan programs. Average indebtedness per student: $12,675. ***Average need-based loan:*** Freshmen: $2685; Undergraduates: $3308. ***Parent loans:*** $80,370 (100% non-need-based). ***Programs:*** FFEL (Subsidized and Unsubsidized Stafford, PLUS), college/university, Canadian Student Loans.

WORK-STUDY ***State or other work-study/employment:*** *Total amount:* $518,870 (98% need-based, 2% non-need-based). 177 part-time jobs averaging $2931.

APPLYING for FINANCIAL AID ***Required financial aid forms:*** FAFSA, institution's own form, state aid form, noncustodial (divorced/separated) parent's statement, income tax returns. ***Financial aid deadline:*** Continuous. ***Notification date:*** Continuous beginning 11/1. Students must reply within 4 weeks of notification.

CONTACT Mr. Gregory Becher, Director of Financial Aid, Thomas Aquinas College, 10000 North Ojai Road, Santa Paula, CA 93060-9980, 805-525-4419 Ext. 308 or toll-free 800-634-9797. *Fax:* 805-525-9342. *E-mail:* gbecher@thomasaquinas.edu

THOMAS COLLEGE

Waterville, ME

Tuition & fees: $12,290 **Average undergraduate aid package: $15,018**

ABOUT THE INSTITUTION Independent, coed. Awards: associate, bachelor's, and master's degrees. 19 undergraduate majors. Total enrollment: 944. Undergraduates: 759. Freshmen: 164. Federal methodology is used as a basis for awarding need-based institutional aid.

UNDERGRADUATE EXPENSES for 1999–2000 ***Application fee:*** $25. ***One-time required fee:*** $75. ***Comprehensive fee:*** $17,840 includes full-time tuition ($12,000), mandatory fees ($290), and room and board ($5550). Room and board charges vary according to housing facility. ***Part-time tuition:*** $1500 per course. ***Part-time fees:*** $145 per term part-time. Part-time tuition and fees vary according to class time and course load. ***Payment plan:*** installment.

FRESHMAN FINANCIAL AID (Fall 1999, est.) 149 applied for aid; of those 98% were deemed to have need. *Average percent of need met:* 86% (excluding resources awarded to replace EFC). *Average financial aid package:* $15,027 (excluding resources awarded to replace EFC). 5% of all full-time freshmen had no need and received non-need-based aid.

UNDERGRADUATE FINANCIAL AID (Fall 1999, est.) 436 applied for aid; of those 98% were deemed to have need. *Average percent of need met:* 85% (excluding resources awarded to replace EFC). *Average financial aid package:* $15,018 (excluding resources awarded to replace EFC). 2% of all full-time undergraduates had no need and received non-need-based aid.

GIFT AID (NEED-BASED) ***Total amount:*** $2,283,890 (40% Federal, 11% state, 49% institutional). ***Scholarships, grants, and awards:*** Federal Pell, FSEOG, state, private, college/university gift aid from institutional funds.

GIFT AID (NON-NEED-BASED) ***Total amount:*** $678,559 (72% institutional, 28% external sources). ***Scholarships, grants, and awards by category:*** *Academic Interests/Achievement:* education, general academic interests/achievements. *Special Achievements/Activities:* 12 awards: leadership. *Special Characteristics:* children of union members/company employees, local/state students. ***Tuition waivers:*** Full or partial for employees or children of employees.

LOANS ***Student loans:*** $2,277,973 (66% need-based, 34% non-need-based). 78% of past graduating class borrowed through all loan programs.

Average indebtedness per student: $19,125. ***Parent loans:*** $296,402 (100% non-need-based). ***Programs:*** Federal Direct (Subsidized and Unsubsidized Stafford, PLUS), Perkins.

WORK-STUDY ***Federal work-study:*** *Total amount:* $142,800; 102 jobs averaging $1400.

APPLYING for FINANCIAL AID ***Required financial aid form:*** FAFSA. ***Financial aid deadline (priority):*** 2/15. ***Notification date:*** Continuous beginning 3/15. Students must reply within 2 weeks of notification.

CONTACT Angela Dostie, Student Financial Services Counselor, Thomas College, 180 West River Road, Waterville, ME 04901-5097, 800-339-7001. *Fax:* 207-859-1114. *E-mail:* dostiea@thomas.edu

THOMAS JEFFERSON UNIVERSITY

Philadelphia, PA

Tuition & fees: $16,785 **Average undergraduate aid package: N/A**

ABOUT THE INSTITUTION Independent, coed. Awards: bachelor's and master's degrees and post-bachelor's certificates. 8 undergraduate majors. Total enrollment: 2,273. Undergraduates: 838. Both federal and institutional methodology are used as a basis for awarding need-based institutional aid.

UNDERGRADUATE EXPENSES for 1999–2000 ***Application fee:*** $45. ***Tuition:*** full-time $16,785; part-time $582 per credit. Full-time tuition and fees vary according to course level. Part-time tuition and fees vary according to course level. Room and board charges vary according to housing facility. ***Payment plan:*** installment.

UNDERGRADUATE FINANCIAL AID (Fall 1998) 381 applied for aid; of those 99% were deemed to have need. 100% of undergraduates with need received aid.

GIFT AID (NEED-BASED) ***Total amount:*** $842,492 (31% Federal, 29% state, 31% institutional, 9% external sources). ***Receiving aid:*** *All full-time undergraduates:* 52% (214). ***Scholarships, grants, and awards:*** Federal Pell, FSEOG, state, private, college/university gift aid from institutional funds.

GIFT AID (NON-NEED-BASED) ***Total amount:*** $280,351 (100% institutional). ***Receiving aid:*** *Undergraduates:* 66% (270). ***Scholarships, grants, and awards by category:*** *Academic Interests/Achievement:* health fields. ***Tuition waivers:*** Full or partial for employees or children of employees. ***ROTC:*** Air Force cooperative.

LOANS ***Student loans:*** $5,145,559 (73% need-based, 27% non-need-based). 73% of past graduating class borrowed through all loan programs. ***Average need-based loan:*** Undergraduates: $9993. ***Parent loans:*** $98,626 (100% non-need-based). ***Programs:*** FFEL (Subsidized and Unsubsidized Stafford, PLUS), Perkins, Federal Nursing, college/university.

WORK-STUDY ***Federal work-study:*** *Total amount:* $112,120; 100 jobs averaging $1121.

APPLYING for FINANCIAL AID ***Required financial aid forms:*** FAFSA, institution's own form, state aid form, parent and student income tax returns. ***Financial aid deadline (priority):*** 5/1. ***Notification date:*** Continuous. Students must reply within 2 weeks of notification.

CONTACT Dr. Raelynn Cooter, University Director of Financial Aid, Thomas Jefferson University, 1025 Walnut Street, Room G-1, College Building, Philadelphia, PA 19107, 215-955-2867 or toll-free 877-533-3247. *E-mail:* financial.aid@jefferson.edu

THOMAS MORE COLLEGE

Crestview Hills, KY

Tuition & fees: $12,580 **Average undergraduate aid package: $10,865**

ABOUT THE INSTITUTION Independent Roman Catholic, coed. Awards: associate, bachelor's, and master's degrees. 41 undergraduate majors. Total enrollment: 1,481. Undergraduates: 1,325. Freshmen: 287. Federal methodology is used as a basis for awarding need-based institutional aid.

UNDERGRADUATE EXPENSES for 1999–2000 ***Application fee:*** $25. ***Comprehensive fee:*** $16,336 includes full-time tuition ($12,300), mandatory fees ($280), and room and board ($3756). ***College room only:*** $2156. Room and board charges vary according to board plan and housing facility. ***Part-time tuition:*** $314 per credit hour. ***Part-time fees:*** $10 per credit hour; $10 per term part-time. Part-time tuition and fees vary according to course load and program. ***Payment plans:*** installment, deferred payment.

FRESHMAN FINANCIAL AID (Fall 1999) 181 applied for aid; of those 75% were deemed to have need. 100% of freshmen with need received aid; of those 95% had need fully met. *Average percent of need met:* 94% (excluding resources awarded to replace EFC). *Average financial aid package:* $11,343 (excluding resources awarded to replace EFC). 22% of all full-time freshmen had no need and received non-need-based aid.

UNDERGRADUATE FINANCIAL AID (Fall 1999) 754 applied for aid; of those 79% were deemed to have need. 100% of undergraduates with need received aid; of those 89% had need fully met. *Average percent of need met:* 91% (excluding resources awarded to replace EFC). *Average financial aid package:* $10,865 (excluding resources awarded to replace EFC). 10% of all full-time undergraduates had no need and received non-need-based aid.

GIFT AID (NEED-BASED) ***Total amount:*** $2,636,594 (19% Federal, 19% state, 36% institutional, 26% external sources). ***Receiving aid:*** *Freshmen:* 70% (130); *all full-time undergraduates:* 37% (477). ***Average award:*** Freshmen: $5167; Undergraduates: $5167. ***Scholarships, grants, and awards:*** Federal Pell, FSEOG, state, private, college/university gift aid from institutional funds.

GIFT AID (NON-NEED-BASED) ***Total amount:*** $2,227,680 (5% state, 86% institutional, 9% external sources). ***Receiving aid:*** *Freshmen:* 11% (21); *Undergraduates:* 7% (86). ***Scholarships, grants, and awards by category:*** *Academic Interests/Achievement:* general academic interests/achievements. *Creative Arts/Performance:* art/fine arts, theater/drama. *Special Achievements/Activities:* leadership, religious involvement. *Special Characteristics:* adult students, children and siblings of alumni, children of faculty/staff, international students, out-of-state students, religious affiliation. ***Tuition waivers:*** Full or partial for children of alumni, employees or children of employees. ***ROTC:*** Army cooperative, Air Force cooperative.

LOANS ***Student loans:*** $3,085,611 (97% need-based, 3% non-need-based). 42% of past graduating class borrowed through all loan programs. Average indebtedness per student: $18,931. ***Average need-based loan:*** Freshmen: $4001; Undergraduates: $4001. ***Parent loans:*** $460,417 (100% non-need-based). ***Programs:*** FFEL (Subsidized and Unsubsidized Stafford, PLUS), Perkins, Federal Nursing, college/university.

WORK-STUDY ***Federal work-study:*** *Total amount:* $133,512; 84 jobs averaging $1589. ***State or other work-study/employment:*** *Total amount:* $272,989 (73% need-based, 27% non-need-based). 171 part-time jobs averaging $1589.

APPLYING for FINANCIAL AID ***Required financial aid form:*** FAFSA. ***Financial aid deadline (priority):*** 3/1. ***Notification date:*** 3/15. Students must reply within 3 weeks of notification.

CONTACT Ms. Dolores Fink, Assistant Director of Financial Aid, Thomas More College, 333 Thomas More Parkway, Crestview Hills, KY 41017-3428, 606-344-3334 or toll-free 800-825-4557. *Fax:* 606-344-3638. *E-mail:* finkd@thomasmore.edu

THOMAS MORE COLLEGE OF LIBERAL ARTS

Merrimack, NH

Tuition & fees: $9600 **Average undergraduate aid package: $10,318**

ABOUT THE INSTITUTION Independent religious, coed. Awards: bachelor's degrees. 4 undergraduate majors. Total enrollment: 72. Undergraduates: 72. Freshmen: 17. Federal methodology is used as a basis for awarding need-based institutional aid.

UNDERGRADUATE EXPENSES for 1999–2000 ***Application fee:*** $25. ***Comprehensive fee:*** $17,000 includes full-time tuition ($9600) and room and board ($7400). ***Payment plans:*** installment, deferred payment.

FRESHMAN FINANCIAL AID (Fall 1998) 16 applied for aid; of those 100% were deemed to have need. 100% of freshmen with need received aid; of

Thomas More College of Liberal Arts (continued)

those 25% had need fully met. *Average percent of need met:* 80% (excluding resources awarded to replace EFC). *Average financial aid package:* $8768 (excluding resources awarded to replace EFC).

UNDERGRADUATE FINANCIAL AID (Fall 1998) 54 applied for aid; of those 100% were deemed to have need. 100% of undergraduates with need received aid; of those 20% had need fully met. *Average percent of need met:* 80% (excluding resources awarded to replace EFC). *Average financial aid package:* $10,318 (excluding resources awarded to replace EFC).

GIFT AID (NEED-BASED) ***Total amount:*** $300,978 (18% Federal, 1% state, 81% institutional). ***Receiving aid:*** *Freshmen:* 65% (13); *all full-time undergraduates:* 77% (46). ***Average award:*** Freshmen: $6117; Undergraduates: $5328. ***Scholarships, grants, and awards:*** Federal Pell, FSEOG, state, college/university gift aid from institutional funds.

GIFT AID (NON-NEED-BASED) ***Scholarships, grants, and awards by category:*** *Academic Interests/Achievement:* general academic interests/achievements. ***Tuition waivers:*** Full or partial for employees or children of employees.

LOANS ***Student loans:*** $172,375 (100% need-based). 90% of past graduating class borrowed through all loan programs. Average indebtedness per student: $13,056. ***Average need-based loan:*** Freshmen: $2625; Undergraduates: $2653. ***Parent loans:*** $55,088 (100% need-based). ***Programs:*** FFEL (Subsidized and Unsubsidized Stafford, PLUS).

WORK-STUDY ***State or other work-study/employment:*** *Total amount:* $41,940 (100% need-based). 36 part-time jobs averaging $1493.

APPLYING for FINANCIAL AID ***Required financial aid form:*** FAFSA. ***Financial aid deadline (priority):*** 5/1. ***Notification date:*** Continuous beginning 5/15. Students must reply within 2 weeks of notification.

CONTACT Mrs. Pam Bernstein, Business Manager, Thomas More College of Liberal Arts, 6 Manchester Street, Merrimack, NH 03054-4818, 603-324-1494. *Fax:* 603-880-9280.

THOMAS UNIVERSITY

Thomasville, GA

Tuition & fees: $7870 **Average undergraduate aid package: $4349**

ABOUT THE INSTITUTION Independent, coed. Awards: associate, bachelor's, and master's degrees. 25 undergraduate majors. Total enrollment: 604. Undergraduates: 589. Freshmen: 73. Federal methodology is used as a basis for awarding need-based institutional aid.

UNDERGRADUATE EXPENSES for 1999–2000 ***Application fee:*** $25. ***Tuition:*** full-time $7500; part-time $250 per semester hour. ***Required fees:*** full-time $370; $92 per term part-time. Full-time tuition and fees vary according to course load. Room and board charges vary according to board plan. ***Payment plans:*** guaranteed tuition, installment, deferred payment.

UNDERGRADUATE FINANCIAL AID (Fall 1999, est.) 550 applied for aid; of those 89% were deemed to have need. 100% of undergraduates with need received aid; of those 20% had need fully met. *Average percent of need met:* 20% (excluding resources awarded to replace EFC). *Average financial aid package:* $4349 (excluding resources awarded to replace EFC). 5% of all full-time undergraduates had no need and received non-need-based aid.

GIFT AID (NEED-BASED) ***Total amount:*** $1,178,690 (52% Federal, 48% state). ***Receiving aid:*** *All full-time undergraduates:* 65% (390). ***Average award:*** Undergraduates: $3023. ***Scholarships, grants, and awards:*** Federal Pell, FSEOG, state, private, college/university gift aid from institutional funds.

GIFT AID (NON-NEED-BASED) ***Total amount:*** $29,364 (93% institutional, 7% external sources). ***Receiving aid:*** *Undergraduates:* 17% (100). ***Scholarships, grants, and awards by category:*** *Academic Interests/Achievement:* 2 awards ($4214 total): business, education, general academic interests/achievements, library science, social sciences. *Creative Arts/Performance:* music. *Special Achievements/Activities:* 1 award ($300 total): cheerleading/drum major, junior miss. *Special Characteristics:* 17 awards ($14,900 total): children of faculty/staff, out-of-state students, veterans. ***Tuition waivers:*** Full or partial for employees or children of employees, senior citizens. ***ROTC:*** Army.

LOANS ***Student loans:*** $1,405,550 (53% need-based, 47% non-need-based). 60% of past graduating class borrowed through all loan programs. ***Average need-based loan:*** Undergraduates: $5060. ***Parent loans:*** $6000 (100% non-need-based). ***Programs:*** FFEL (Subsidized and Unsubsidized Stafford, PLUS), college/university.

WORK-STUDY ***Federal work-study:*** *Total amount:* $27,216; 9 jobs averaging $3024.

ATHLETIC AWARDS *Total amount:* 186,902 (100% need-based).

APPLYING for FINANCIAL AID ***Required financial aid forms:*** FAFSA, institution's own form, state aid form. ***Financial aid deadline:*** Continuous. ***Notification date:*** Continuous.

CONTACT Mrs. Debbie Wiggins, Director of Financial Aid, Thomas University, 1501 Millpond Road, Thomasville, GA 31792-7499, 912-226-1621 Ext. 158 or toll-free 800-538-9784. *Fax:* 912-226-1653. *E-mail:* dwiggins@thomascollege.edu

TIFFIN UNIVERSITY

Tiffin, OH

Tuition & fees: $10,500 **Average undergraduate aid package: $3790**

ABOUT THE INSTITUTION Independent, coed. Awards: associate, bachelor's, and master's degrees. 23 undergraduate majors. Total enrollment: 1,445. Undergraduates: 1,265. Freshmen: 347. Federal methodology is used as a basis for awarding need-based institutional aid.

UNDERGRADUATE EXPENSES for 1999–2000 ***Application fee:*** $20. ***Comprehensive fee:*** $15,350 includes full-time tuition ($10,500) and room and board ($4850). ***College room only:*** $2450. Room and board charges vary according to board plan and housing facility. ***Part-time tuition:*** $1050 per course. ***Payment plan:*** installment.

FRESHMAN FINANCIAL AID (Fall 1998) 247 applied for aid; of those 90% were deemed to have need. 100% of freshmen with need received aid; of those 15% had need fully met. *Average percent of need met:* 57% (excluding resources awarded to replace EFC). *Average financial aid package:* $3561 (excluding resources awarded to replace EFC). 5% of all full-time freshmen had no need and received non-need-based aid.

UNDERGRADUATE FINANCIAL AID (Fall 1998) 625 applied for aid; of those 89% were deemed to have need. 100% of undergraduates with need received aid; of those 10% had need fully met. *Average percent of need met:* 61% (excluding resources awarded to replace EFC). *Average financial aid package:* $3790 (excluding resources awarded to replace EFC). 3% of all full-time undergraduates had no need and received non-need-based aid.

GIFT AID (NEED-BASED) ***Total amount:*** $2,883,938 (37% Federal, 40% state, 21% institutional, 2% external sources). ***Receiving aid:*** *Freshmen:* 45% (120); *all full-time undergraduates:* 41% (285). ***Average award:*** Freshmen: $1903; Undergraduates: $1791. ***Scholarships, grants, and awards:*** Federal Pell, FSEOG, state, college/university gift aid from institutional funds.

GIFT AID (NON-NEED-BASED) ***Receiving aid:*** *Freshmen:* 71% (188); *Undergraduates:* 69% (485). ***Scholarships, grants, and awards by category:*** *Academic Interests/Achievement:* 199 awards ($469,519 total): business, general academic interests/achievements. *Creative Arts/Performance:* 39 awards ($30,850 total): music. *Special Achievements/Activities:* 11 awards ($9500 total): cheerleading/drum major. *Special Characteristics:* 109 awards ($77,868 total): local/state students, out-of-state students. ***Tuition waivers:*** Full or partial for employees or children of employees. ***ROTC:*** Army cooperative.

LOANS ***Student loans:*** $4,444,220 (67% need-based, 33% non-need-based). 85% of past graduating class borrowed through all loan programs. Average indebtedness per student: $16,670. ***Average need-based loan:*** Freshmen: $1450; Undergraduates: $1835. ***Parent loans:*** $825,234 (85% need-based, 15% non-need-based). ***Programs:*** Federal Direct (Subsidized and Unsubsidized Stafford, PLUS), Perkins, state, college/university.

WORK-STUDY ***Federal work-study:*** *Total amount:* $115,540; 127 jobs averaging $910. ***State or other work-study/employment:*** *Total amount:* $168,394 (100% non-need-based). Part-time jobs available.

ATHLETIC AWARDS *Total amount:* 657,629 (91% need-based, 9% non-need-based).

APPLYING for FINANCIAL AID ***Required financial aid form:*** FAFSA. ***Financial aid deadline (priority):*** 3/31. ***Notification date:*** Continuous beginning 4/1. Students must reply within 2 weeks of notification.

CONTACT Deb Brickner, Assistant Director of Financial Aid, Tiffin University, 155 Miami Street, Tiffin, OH 44883-2161, 419-448-3357 or toll-free 800-968-6446. *Fax:* 419-443-5006. *E-mail:* dbrickne@tiffin.edu

TOCCOA FALLS COLLEGE

Toccoa Falls, GA

Tuition & fees: $8424 **Average undergraduate aid package: N/A**

ABOUT THE INSTITUTION Independent interdenominational, coed. Awards: associate, bachelor's, and master's degrees. 33 undergraduate majors. Total enrollment: 961. Undergraduates: 924. Freshmen: 314. Federal methodology is used as a basis for awarding need-based institutional aid.

UNDERGRADUATE EXPENSES for 1999–2000 ***Application fee:*** $20. ***One-time required fee:*** $20. ***Comprehensive fee:*** $12,320 includes full-time tuition ($8384), mandatory fees ($40), and room and board ($3896). ***Part-time tuition:*** $350 per credit hour. ***Part-time fees:*** $20 per term part-time. ***Payment plan:*** installment.

GIFT AID (NEED-BASED) ***Scholarships, grants, and awards:*** Federal Pell, FSEOG, state, private, college/university gift aid from institutional funds.

GIFT AID (NON-NEED-BASED) ***Scholarships, grants, and awards by category:*** *Academic Interests/Achievement:* general academic interests/achievements. *Creative Arts/Performance:* music. *Special Achievements/Activities:* general special achievements/activities, leadership. *Special Characteristics:* international students, relatives of clergy. ***Tuition waivers:*** Full or partial for children of alumni, employees or children of employees, senior citizens.

LOANS ***Programs:*** Federal Direct (Subsidized and Unsubsidized Stafford, PLUS), Perkins.

WORK-STUDY Federal work-study jobs available.

APPLYING for FINANCIAL AID ***Required financial aid form:*** FAFSA. ***Financial aid deadline (priority):*** 3/1. ***Notification date:*** Continuous.

CONTACT John Gailer, Financial Aid Director, Toccoa Falls College, PO Box 777, Toccoa Falls, GA 30598-1000, 706-886-6831 or toll-free 800-868-3257. *Fax:* 706-886-0210.

TORAH TEMIMAH TALMUDICAL SEMINARY

Brooklyn, NY

CONTACT Financial Aid Office, Torah Temimah Talmudical Seminary, 507 Ocean Parkway, Brooklyn, NY 11218-5913, 718-853-8500.

TOUGALOO COLLEGE

Tougaloo, MS

Tuition & fees: $7110 **Average undergraduate aid package: N/A**

ABOUT THE INSTITUTION Independent religious, coed. Awards: associate and bachelor's degrees. 23 undergraduate majors. Total enrollment: 967. Undergraduates: 967. Freshmen: 251. Federal methodology is used as a basis for awarding need-based institutional aid.

UNDERGRADUATE EXPENSES for 1999–2000 ***Application fee:*** $5. ***Comprehensive fee:*** $10,170 includes full-time tuition ($6400), mandatory fees ($710), and room and board ($3060). ***College room only:*** $1760. ***Part-time tuition:*** $240 per hour. ***Part-time fees:*** $710 per year part-time. ***Payment plans:*** installment, deferred payment.

GIFT AID (NEED-BASED) ***Scholarships, grants, and awards:*** Federal Pell, FSEOG, state, private, college/university gift aid from institutional funds, United Negro College Fund.

GIFT AID (NON-NEED-BASED) ***Scholarships, grants, and awards by category:*** *Academic Interests/Achievement:* general academic interests/achievements. *Creative Arts/Performance:* music. *Special Characteristics:* general special characteristics. ***Tuition waivers:*** Full or partial for employees or children of employees, adult students, senior citizens. ***ROTC:*** Army.

LOANS ***Programs:*** Federal Direct (Subsidized and Unsubsidized Stafford, PLUS), FFEL (Subsidized and Unsubsidized Stafford, PLUS), Perkins.

WORK-STUDY Federal work-study jobs available.

APPLYING for FINANCIAL AID ***Required financial aid forms:*** FAFSA, institution's own form, state aid form. ***Financial aid deadline (priority):*** 4/15. ***Notification date:*** Continuous. Students must reply within 2 weeks of notification.

CONTACT Mrs. Janis Evans, Director of Financial Aid, Tougaloo College, 500 West County Line Road, Tougaloo, MS 39174, 601-977-7766 or toll-free 888-42GALOO.

TOURO COLLEGE

New York, NY

Tuition & fees: $9250 **Average undergraduate aid package: N/A**

ABOUT THE INSTITUTION Independent, coed. Awards: associate, bachelor's, master's, doctoral, and first professional degrees. 37 undergraduate majors. Total enrollment: 8,202. Undergraduates: 6,661. Federal methodology is used as a basis for awarding need-based institutional aid.

UNDERGRADUATE EXPENSES for 1999–2000 ***Application fee:*** $35. ***Tuition:*** full-time $9250; part-time $390 per credit. Full-time tuition and fees vary according to program. Part-time tuition and fees vary according to program. Room and board charges vary according to gender.

GIFT AID (NEED-BASED) ***Scholarships, grants, and awards:*** Federal Pell, FSEOG, state, private, college/university gift aid from institutional funds.

GIFT AID (NON-NEED-BASED) ***Scholarships, grants, and awards by category:*** *Academic Interests/Achievement:* general academic interests/achievements. *Special Characteristics:* children of faculty/staff. ***Tuition waivers:*** Full or partial for employees or children of employees.

LOANS ***Programs:*** FFEL (Subsidized and Unsubsidized Stafford, PLUS), Perkins, alternative loans.

WORK-STUDY Federal work-study jobs available.

APPLYING for FINANCIAL AID ***Required financial aid form:*** FAFSA. ***Financial aid deadline (priority):*** 5/15.

CONTACT Office of Financial Aid, Touro College, 27 West 23rd Street, New York, NY 10010, 212-463-0400.

TOWSON UNIVERSITY

Towson, MD

Tuition & fees (MD res): $4710 **Average undergraduate aid package: $7851**

ABOUT THE INSTITUTION State-supported, coed. Awards: bachelor's and master's degrees and post-bachelor's and post-master's certificates. 49 undergraduate majors. Total enrollment: 16,597. Undergraduates: 13,931. Freshmen: 2,079. Federal methodology is used as a basis for awarding need-based institutional aid.

UNDERGRADUATE EXPENSES for 1999–2000 ***Application fee:*** $30. ***Tuition, state resident:*** full-time $3466; part-time $150 per credit hour. ***Tuition, nonresident:*** full-time $9896; part-time $362 per credit hour. ***Required fees:*** full-time $1244; $43 per credit hour. ***College room and board:*** $5800; ***room only:*** $3350. Room and board charges vary according to board plan and housing facility. ***Payment plan:*** installment.

FRESHMAN FINANCIAL AID (Fall 1998) 1355 applied for aid; of those 72% were deemed to have need. 97% of freshmen with need received aid; of those 30% had need fully met. *Average percent of need met:* 39% (excluding resources awarded to replace EFC). *Average financial aid package:* $7878 (excluding resources awarded to replace EFC). 49% of all full-time freshmen had no need and received non-need-based aid.

UNDERGRADUATE FINANCIAL AID (Fall 1998) 6,262 applied for aid; of those 80% were deemed to have need. 97% of undergraduates with need

Towson University (continued)

received aid; of those 30% had need fully met. *Average percent of need met:* 43% (excluding resources awarded to replace EFC). *Average financial aid package:* $7851 (excluding resources awarded to replace EFC). 47% of all full-time undergraduates had no need and received non-need-based aid.

GIFT AID (NEED-BASED) ***Total amount:*** $8,924,252 (50% Federal, 37% state, 13% institutional). ***Receiving aid:*** *Freshmen:* 31% (597); *all full-time undergraduates:* 28% (3,001). ***Average award:*** Freshmen: $4514; Undergraduates: $4318. ***Scholarships, grants, and awards:*** Federal Pell, FSEOG, state, private, college/university gift aid from institutional funds.

GIFT AID (NON-NEED-BASED) ***Total amount:*** $7,632,514 (9% state, 81% institutional, 10% external sources). ***Receiving aid:*** *Freshmen:* 27% (512); *Undergraduates:* 17% (1,866). ***Scholarships, grants, and awards by category:*** *Academic Interests/Achievement:* general academic interests/achievements. *Creative Arts/Performance:* art/fine arts, dance, music, theater/drama. ***Tuition waivers:*** Full or partial for employees or children of employees, senior citizens. ***ROTC:*** Army cooperative.

LOANS ***Student loans:*** $28,771,186 (60% need-based, 40% non-need-based). ***Average need-based loan:*** Freshmen: $2577; Undergraduates: $3723. ***Parent loans:*** $8,650,749 (100% non-need-based). ***Programs:*** Federal Direct (Subsidized and Unsubsidized Stafford, PLUS), Perkins.

WORK-STUDY ***Federal work-study:*** *Total amount:* $359,776; 275 jobs averaging $1308. ***State or other work-study/employment:*** *Total amount:* $2,132,000 (100% non-need-based). 1,452 part-time jobs averaging $1446.

ATHLETIC AWARDS *Total amount:* 168,120 (100% non-need-based).

APPLYING for FINANCIAL AID ***Required financial aid form:*** FAFSA. ***Financial aid deadline (priority):*** 2/15. ***Notification date:*** Continuous beginning 4/1. Students must reply within 2 weeks of notification.

CONTACT Vince Pecora, Director, Financial Aid, Towson University, 8000 York Road, Towson, MD 21252-0001, 410-830-4236 or toll-free 888-4TOWSON. *E-mail:* finaid@towson.edu

TRANSYLVANIA UNIVERSITY

Lexington, KY

Tuition & fees: $14,600 **Average undergraduate aid package: $13,021**

ABOUT THE INSTITUTION Independent religious, coed. Awards: bachelor's degrees. 29 undergraduate majors. Total enrollment: 1,070. Undergraduates: 1,070. Freshmen: 308. Federal methodology is used as a basis for awarding need-based institutional aid.

UNDERGRADUATE EXPENSES for 1999–2000 ***Application fee:*** $30. ***Comprehensive fee:*** $19,950 includes full-time tuition ($14,050), mandatory fees ($550), and room and board ($5350). ***College room only:*** $2996. Room and board charges vary according to board plan and housing facility. ***Part-time tuition:*** $1561 per course. ***Part-time fees:*** $61 per course. ***Payment plans:*** tuition prepayment, installment, deferred payment.

FRESHMAN FINANCIAL AID (Fall 1999, est.) 309 applied for aid; of those 63% were deemed to have need. 100% of freshmen with need received aid; of those 44% had need fully met. *Average percent of need met:* 92% (excluding resources awarded to replace EFC). *Average financial aid package:* $12,939 (excluding resources awarded to replace EFC). 35% of all full-time freshmen had no need and received non-need-based aid.

UNDERGRADUATE FINANCIAL AID (Fall 1999, est.) 1,068 applied for aid; of those 59% were deemed to have need. 100% of undergraduates with need received aid; of those 45% had need fully met. *Average percent of need met:* 90% (excluding resources awarded to replace EFC). *Average financial aid package:* $13,021 (excluding resources awarded to replace EFC). 40% of all full-time undergraduates had no need and received non-need-based aid.

GIFT AID (NEED-BASED) ***Total amount:*** $5,603,731 (9% Federal, 15% state, 72% institutional, 4% external sources). ***Receiving aid:*** *Freshmen:* 63% (194); *all full-time undergraduates:* 59% (625). ***Average award:*** Freshmen: $9811; Undergraduates: $9352. ***Scholarships, grants, and awards:*** Federal Pell, FSEOG, state, private, college/university gift aid from institutional funds.

GIFT AID (NON-NEED-BASED) ***Total amount:*** $3,355,621 (3% state, 93% institutional, 4% external sources). ***Receiving aid:*** *Freshmen:* 13% (40); *Undergraduates:* 9% (94). ***Scholarships, grants, and awards by category:*** *Academic Interests/Achievement:* 1,148 awards ($5,791,905 total): computer science, education, general academic interests/achievements. *Creative Arts/Performance:* 72 awards ($159,000 total): art/fine arts, music. *Special Achievements/Activities:* 95 awards ($101,067 total): cheerleading/drum major, general special achievements/activities, religious involvement. *Special Characteristics:* 154 awards ($303,165 total): children of faculty/staff, members of minority groups, out-of-state students, relatives of clergy, religious affiliation. ***Tuition waivers:*** Full or partial for employees or children of employees. ***ROTC:*** Army cooperative, Air Force cooperative.

LOANS ***Student loans:*** $2,377,381 (74% need-based, 26% non-need-based). Average indebtedness per student: $14,650. ***Average need-based loan:*** Freshmen: $3178; Undergraduates: $3847. ***Parent loans:*** $615,380 (23% need-based, 77% non-need-based). ***Programs:*** FFEL (Subsidized and Unsubsidized Stafford, PLUS), Perkins, college/university.

WORK-STUDY ***Federal work-study:*** *Total amount:* $512,840; 296 jobs averaging $1733. ***State or other work-study/employment:*** *Total amount:* $102,106 (47% need-based, 53% non-need-based). 27 part-time jobs averaging $3781.

ATHLETIC AWARDS *Total amount:* 587,925 (37% need-based, 63% non-need-based).

APPLYING for FINANCIAL AID ***Required financial aid form:*** FAFSA. ***Financial aid deadline (priority):*** 3/1. ***Notification date:*** Continuous beginning 3/15. Students must reply within 2 weeks of notification.

CONTACT Mr. Dave Cecil, Director of Financial Aid, Transylvania University, 300 North Broadway, Lexington, KY 40508-1797, 606-233-8239 or toll-free 800-872-6798. *E-mail:* financialaid@mail.transy.edu

TREVECCA NAZARENE UNIVERSITY

Nashville, TN

Tuition & fees: $10,656 **Average undergraduate aid package: $9584**

ABOUT THE INSTITUTION Independent Nazarene, coed. Awards: associate, bachelor's, master's, and doctoral degrees and post-master's certificates. 40 undergraduate majors. Total enrollment: 1,615. Undergraduates: 1,004. Freshmen: 200. Federal methodology is used as a basis for awarding need-based institutional aid.

UNDERGRADUATE EXPENSES for 1999–2000 ***Application fee:*** $25. ***Comprehensive fee:*** $15,104 includes full-time tuition ($10,016), mandatory fees ($640), and room and board ($4448). ***College room only:*** $1926. Full-time tuition and fees vary according to course load. Room and board charges vary according to board plan. ***Part-time tuition:*** $313 per semester hour. Part-time tuition and fees vary according to course load. ***Payment plan:*** installment.

FRESHMAN FINANCIAL AID (Fall 1999) 164 applied for aid; of those 88% were deemed to have need. 100% of freshmen with need received aid; of those 21% had need fully met. *Average percent of need met:* 79% (excluding resources awarded to replace EFC). *Average financial aid package:* $9775 (excluding resources awarded to replace EFC). 8% of all full-time freshmen had no need and received non-need-based aid.

UNDERGRADUATE FINANCIAL AID (Fall 1999) 526 applied for aid; of those 89% were deemed to have need. 100% of undergraduates with need received aid; of those 16% had need fully met. *Average percent of need met:* 83% (excluding resources awarded to replace EFC). *Average financial aid package:* $9584 (excluding resources awarded to replace EFC). 3% of all full-time undergraduates had no need and received non-need-based aid.

GIFT AID (NEED-BASED) ***Total amount:*** $476,038 (37% Federal, 30% state, 33% institutional). ***Receiving aid:*** *Freshmen:* 34% (68); *all full-time undergraduates:* 29% (233). ***Average award:*** Freshmen: $3004; Undergraduates: $3210. ***Scholarships, grants, and awards:*** Federal Pell, FSEOG, state, private, college/university gift aid from institutional funds.

GIFT AID (NON-NEED-BASED) ***Total amount:*** $1,239,517 (90% institutional, 10% external sources). ***Receiving aid:*** *Freshmen:* 66% (131); *Undergraduates:* 56% (455). ***Scholarships, grants, and awards by category:*** *Academic Interests/Achievement:* business, communication, education, general academic interests/achievements, physical sciences, religion/biblical studies, social sciences. *Creative Arts/Performance:* music. *Special Achievements/Activities:* general special achievements/activities, memberships. *Special Characteristics:* children and siblings of alumni, general special characteristics, handicapped students, relatives of clergy, religious affiliation. ***Tuition waivers:*** Full or partial for employees or children of employees, senior citizens. ***ROTC:*** Army cooperative.

LOANS ***Student loans:*** $2,712,242 (72% need-based, 28% non-need-based). 86% of past graduating class borrowed through all loan programs. Average indebtedness per student: $19,532. ***Average need-based loan:*** Freshmen: $4224; Undergraduates: $4883. ***Parent loans:*** $989,562 (100% non-need-based). ***Programs:*** FFEL (Subsidized and Unsubsidized Stafford, PLUS), Perkins.

WORK-STUDY ***Federal work-study:*** *Total amount:* $396,927; 90 jobs available.

ATHLETIC AWARDS *Total amount:* 481,948 (100% non-need-based).

APPLYING for FINANCIAL AID ***Required financial aid form:*** FAFSA. ***Financial aid deadline (priority):*** 3/1. ***Notification date:*** Continuous beginning 3/20.

CONTACT Ms. Joanie Hall, Senior Counselor, Undergraduate Studies, Trevecca Nazarene University, 333 Murfreesboro Road, Nashville, TN 37210-2834, 615-248-1242 or toll-free 888-210-4TNU. *Fax:* 615-248-7728. *E-mail:* jhall@trevecca.edu

TRINITY BAPTIST COLLEGE

Jacksonville, FL

Tuition & fees: $3980 **Average undergraduate aid package: $5485**

ABOUT THE INSTITUTION Independent Baptist, coed. Awards: associate and bachelor's degrees. 7 undergraduate majors. Total enrollment: 336. Undergraduates: 336. Freshmen: 68. Federal methodology is used as a basis for awarding need-based institutional aid.

UNDERGRADUATE EXPENSES for 1999–2000 ***Application fee:*** $25. ***Comprehensive fee:*** $6980 includes full-time tuition ($3580), mandatory fees ($400), and room and board ($3000). ***College room only:*** $1700. Full-time tuition and fees vary according to location. Room and board charges vary according to board plan. ***Part-time tuition:*** $150 per semester hour. ***Part-time fees:*** $200 per term part-time. Part-time tuition and fees vary according to course load and location. ***Payment plan:*** installment.

FRESHMAN FINANCIAL AID (Fall 1998) 65 applied for aid; of those 89% were deemed to have need. 98% of freshmen with need received aid; of those 37% had need fully met. *Average percent of need met:* 54% (excluding resources awarded to replace EFC). *Average financial aid package:* $4130 (excluding resources awarded to replace EFC). 3% of all full-time freshmen had no need and received non-need-based aid.

UNDERGRADUATE FINANCIAL AID (Fall 1998) 202 applied for aid; of those 87% were deemed to have need. 90% of undergraduates with need received aid; of those 48% had need fully met. *Average percent of need met:* 69% (excluding resources awarded to replace EFC). *Average financial aid package:* $5485 (excluding resources awarded to replace EFC). 3% of all full-time undergraduates had no need and received non-need-based aid.

GIFT AID (NEED-BASED) ***Total amount:*** $433,143 (67% Federal, 9% state, 23% institutional, 1% external sources). ***Receiving aid:*** *Freshmen:* 56% (50); *all full-time undergraduates:* 46% (151). ***Average award:*** Freshmen: $2380; Undergraduates: $2691. ***Scholarships, grants, and awards:*** Federal Pell, FSEOG, state, private, college/university gift aid from institutional funds.

GIFT AID (NON-NEED-BASED) ***Total amount:*** $70,743 (100% institutional). ***Receiving aid:*** *Freshmen:* 3% (3); *Undergraduates:* 1% (3). ***Scholarships, grants, and awards by category:*** *Academic Interests/Achievement:* 15 awards ($11,000 total): education, general academic interests/achievements, religion/biblical studies. *Special Achievements/Activities:* 7 awards ($4500 total): leadership, religious involvement. *Special Characteristics:* 92 awards ($106,558 total): relatives of clergy, religious affiliation, spouses of current students. ***Tuition waivers:*** Full or partial for employees or children of employees.

LOANS ***Student loans:*** $314,911 (86% need-based, 14% non-need-based). 36% of past graduating class borrowed through all loan programs. Average indebtedness per student: $6096. ***Average need-based loan:*** Freshmen: $2131; Undergraduates: $2444. ***Parent loans:*** $29,100 (16% need-based, 84% non-need-based). ***Programs:*** FFEL (Subsidized and Unsubsidized Stafford, PLUS).

APPLYING for FINANCIAL AID ***Required financial aid forms:*** FAFSA, institution's own form, state aid form. ***Financial aid deadline:*** 6/15 (priority: 5/15). ***Notification date:*** 7/15. Students must reply within 2 weeks of notification.

CONTACT Donald Schaffer, Financial Aid Administrator, Trinity Baptist College, 800 Hammond Boulevard, Jacksonville, FL 32221, 904-596-2445 or toll-free 800-786-2206 (out-of-state). *Fax:* 904-596-2531. *E-mail:* financialaid@tbc.edu

TRINITY BIBLE COLLEGE

Ellendale, ND

Tuition & fees: $6294 **Average undergraduate aid package: $7236**

ABOUT THE INSTITUTION Independent religious, coed. Awards: associate and bachelor's degrees. 11 undergraduate majors. Total enrollment: 344. Undergraduates: 344. Freshmen: 91. Federal methodology is used as a basis for awarding need-based institutional aid.

UNDERGRADUATE EXPENSES for 1999–2000 ***Application fee:*** $25. ***Comprehensive fee:*** $9974 includes full-time tuition ($5490), mandatory fees ($804), and room and board ($3680). Full-time tuition and fees vary according to course load. Room and board charges vary according to gender and housing facility. ***Part-time tuition:*** $183 per credit. ***Part-time fees:*** $175 per term part-time. Part-time tuition and fees vary according to course load. ***Payment plans:*** installment, deferred payment.

FRESHMAN FINANCIAL AID (Fall 1999) 82 applied for aid; of those 94% were deemed to have need. 99% of freshmen with need received aid; of those 7% had need fully met. *Average percent of need met:* 68% (excluding resources awarded to replace EFC). *Average financial aid package:* $6962 (excluding resources awarded to replace EFC). 5% of all full-time freshmen had no need and received non-need-based aid.

UNDERGRADUATE FINANCIAL AID (Fall 1999) 291 applied for aid; of those 92% were deemed to have need. 100% of undergraduates with need received aid; of those 11% had need fully met. *Average percent of need met:* 69% (excluding resources awarded to replace EFC). *Average financial aid package:* $7236 (excluding resources awarded to replace EFC). 5% of all full-time undergraduates had no need and received non-need-based aid.

GIFT AID (NEED-BASED) ***Total amount:*** $526,145 (96% Federal, 4% state). ***Receiving aid:*** *Freshmen:* 56% (51); *all full-time undergraduates:* 63% (188). ***Average award:*** Freshmen: $2836; Undergraduates: $2799. ***Scholarships, grants, and awards:*** Federal Pell, FSEOG, state, private, college/university gift aid from institutional funds.

GIFT AID (NON-NEED-BASED) ***Total amount:*** $545,509 (1% state, 79% institutional, 20% external sources). ***Scholarships, grants, and awards by category:*** *Academic Interests/Achievement:* business, education, general academic interests/achievements, religion/biblical studies. *Creative Arts/Performance:* art/fine arts, creative writing, music, theater/drama. *Special Achievements/Activities:* general special achievements/activities, leadership, religious involvement. *Special Characteristics:* children of current students, children of faculty/staff, general special characteristics, international students, relatives of clergy, siblings of current students, spouses of current students. ***Tuition waivers:*** Full or partial for employees or children of employees.

LOANS ***Student loans:*** $1,460,363 (59% need-based, 41% non-need-based). 87% of past graduating class borrowed through all loan programs. ***Average need-based loan:*** Freshmen: $2397; Undergraduates: $3631.

Trinity Bible College (continued)

Parent loans: $82,750 (100% non-need-based). ***Programs:*** FFEL (Subsidized and Unsubsidized Stafford, PLUS), Perkins, alternative loans, Norwest Collegiate Loans.

WORK-STUDY ***Federal work-study:*** *Total amount:* $177,071; 148 jobs averaging $1196.

ATHLETIC AWARDS *Total amount:* 19,995 (100% non-need-based).

APPLYING for FINANCIAL AID ***Required financial aid form:*** FAFSA. ***Financial aid deadline:*** 9/1 (priority: 3/1). ***Notification date:*** Continuous. Students must reply within 3 weeks of notification.

CONTACT Financial Aid Secretary, Trinity Bible College, 50 South 6th Avenue, Ellendale, ND 58436-7150, 701-349-3621 Ext. 2025 or toll-free 800-TBC-2DAY. *Fax:* 701-349-5443. *E-mail:* tbcfnaid@drtel.net

TRINITY CHRISTIAN COLLEGE

Palos Heights, IL

Tuition & fees: $12,730 **Average undergraduate aid package: $10,251**

ABOUT THE INSTITUTION Independent interdenominational, coed. Awards: bachelor's degrees. 59 undergraduate majors. Total enrollment: 723. Undergraduates: 723. Freshmen: 182. Federal methodology is used as a basis for awarding need-based institutional aid.

UNDERGRADUATE EXPENSES for 1999–2000 ***Application fee:*** $20. ***Comprehensive fee:*** $17,740 includes full-time tuition ($12,730) and room and board ($5010). ***College room only:*** $2580. Room and board charges vary according to board plan. ***Part-time tuition:*** $425 per credit hour. Part-time tuition and fees vary according to course load. ***Payment plan:*** installment.

FRESHMAN FINANCIAL AID (Fall 1999, est.) 156 applied for aid; of those 93% were deemed to have need. 100% of freshmen with need received aid; of those 66% had need fully met. *Average percent of need met:* 79% (excluding resources awarded to replace EFC). *Average financial aid package:* $11,173 (excluding resources awarded to replace EFC). 16% of all full-time freshmen had no need and received non-need-based aid.

UNDERGRADUATE FINANCIAL AID (Fall 1999, est.) 520 applied for aid; of those 92% were deemed to have need. 100% of undergraduates with need received aid; of those 30% had need fully met. *Average percent of need met:* 75% (excluding resources awarded to replace EFC). *Average financial aid package:* $10,251 (excluding resources awarded to replace EFC). 17% of all full-time undergraduates had no need and received non-need-based aid.

GIFT AID (NEED-BASED) ***Total amount:*** $1,693,484 (21% Federal, 46% state, 32% institutional, 1% external sources). ***Receiving aid:*** *Freshmen:* 60% (109); *all full-time undergraduates:* 45% (324). ***Average award:*** Freshmen: $5185; Undergraduates: $4889. ***Scholarships, grants, and awards:*** Federal Pell, FSEOG, state, private, college/university gift aid from institutional funds.

GIFT AID (NON-NEED-BASED) ***Total amount:*** $1,317,909 (1% state, 91% institutional, 8% external sources). ***Receiving aid:*** *Freshmen:* 67% (122); *Undergraduates:* 52% (373). ***Scholarships, grants, and awards by category:*** *Academic Interests/Achievement:* 255 awards ($653,015 total): business, English, general academic interests/achievements, health fields, mathematics. *Creative Arts/Performance:* 81 awards ($120,000 total): journalism/publications, music, theater/drama. *Special Achievements/Activities:* 14 awards ($13,500 total): general special achievements/activities, leadership. *Special Characteristics:* 26 awards ($106,775 total): children and siblings of alumni, children of faculty/staff, local/state students, members of minority groups, out-of-state students. ***Tuition waivers:*** Full or partial for employees or children of employees, senior citizens.

LOANS ***Student loans:*** $1,769,422 (100% need-based). 56% of past graduating class borrowed through all loan programs. ***Average need-based loan:*** Freshmen: $3415; Undergraduates: $4022. ***Programs:*** FFEL (Subsidized and Unsubsidized Stafford, PLUS), Perkins, Federal Nursing.

WORK-STUDY ***Federal work-study:*** *Total amount:* $58,729; jobs available. ***State or other work-study/employment:*** *Total amount:* $92,471 (100% need-based). Part-time jobs available.

ATHLETIC AWARDS *Total amount:* 209,000 (100% non-need-based).

APPLYING for FINANCIAL AID ***Required financial aid forms:*** FAFSA, institution's own form. ***Financial aid deadline (priority):*** 2/15. ***Notification date:*** Continuous beginning 4/1.

CONTACT Kristine Medema, Associate Director of Financial Aid, Trinity Christian College, 6601 West College Drive, Palos Heights, IL 60463-0929, 708-597-3000 Ext. 4706 or toll-free 800-748-0085. *Fax:* 708-385-5665. *E-mail:* financial.aid@trnty.edu

TRINITY COLLEGE

Hartford, CT

Tuition & fees: $24,490 **Average undergraduate aid package: $22,495**

ABOUT THE INSTITUTION Independent, coed. Awards: bachelor's and master's degrees. 41 undergraduate majors. Total enrollment: 2,371. Undergraduates: 2,169. Freshmen: 566. Both federal and institutional methodology are used as a basis for awarding need-based institutional aid.

UNDERGRADUATE EXPENSES for 1999–2000 ***Application fee:*** $50. ***One-time required fee:*** $25. ***Comprehensive fee:*** $31,380 includes full-time tuition ($23,730), mandatory fees ($760), and room and board ($6890). ***College room only:*** $4150. Room and board charges vary according to board plan. ***Part-time tuition:*** $7910 per term. Part-time tuition and fees vary according to program. ***Payment plan:*** installment.

FRESHMAN FINANCIAL AID (Fall 1999) 314 applied for aid; of those 85% were deemed to have need. 100% of freshmen with need received aid; of those 100% had need fully met. *Average percent of need met:* 100% (excluding resources awarded to replace EFC). *Average financial aid package:* $21,199 (excluding resources awarded to replace EFC). 1% of all full-time freshmen had no need and received non-need-based aid.

UNDERGRADUATE FINANCIAL AID (Fall 1999) 963 applied for aid; of those 94% were deemed to have need. 100% of undergraduates with need received aid; of those 100% had need fully met. *Average percent of need met:* 100% (excluding resources awarded to replace EFC). *Average financial aid package:* $22,495 (excluding resources awarded to replace EFC). .4% of all full-time undergraduates had no need and received non-need-based aid.

GIFT AID (NEED-BASED) ***Total amount:*** $14,402,969 (5% Federal, 4% state, 88% institutional, 3% external sources). ***Receiving aid:*** *Freshmen:* 45% (253); *all full-time undergraduates:* 41% (786). ***Average award:*** Freshmen: $18,348; Undergraduates: $15,404. ***Scholarships, grants, and awards:*** Federal Pell, FSEOG, state, private, college/university gift aid from institutional funds.

GIFT AID (NON-NEED-BASED) ***Total amount:*** $50,000 (100% institutional). ***Scholarships, grants, and awards by category:*** *Academic Interests/Achievement:* general academic interests/achievements. ***Tuition waivers:*** Full or partial for employees or children of employees, adult students. ***ROTC:*** Army cooperative.

LOANS ***Student loans:*** $3,832,334 (91% need-based, 9% non-need-based). Average indebtedness per student: $13,761. ***Parent loans:*** $2,578,398 (100% non-need-based). ***Programs:*** Federal Direct (Subsidized and Unsubsidized Stafford, PLUS), Perkins, college/university.

WORK-STUDY ***Federal work-study:*** *Total amount:* $870,652; 653 jobs averaging $1333. ***State or other work-study/employment:*** *Total amount:* $3900 (100% need-based). Part-time jobs available.

APPLYING for FINANCIAL AID ***Required financial aid forms:*** FAFSA, CSS Financial Aid PROFILE, noncustodial (divorced/separated) parent's statement, business/farm supplement, federal income tax return. ***Financial aid deadline:*** 3/1 (priority: 2/1). ***Notification date:*** 4/1. Students must reply by 5/1 or within 2 weeks of notification.

CONTACT Ms. Kelly O'Brien, Director of Financial Aid, Trinity College, 300 Summit Street, Hartford, CT 06106-3100, 860-297-2046. *Fax:* 860-297-5203.

TRINITY COLLEGE
Washington, DC

Tuition & fees: $14,025 **Average undergraduate aid package: $15,093**

ABOUT THE INSTITUTION Independent Roman Catholic, women only. Awards: bachelor's and master's degrees and post-bachelor's certificates. 27 undergraduate majors. Total enrollment: 1,576. Undergraduates: 1,096. Federal methodology is used as a basis for awarding need-based institutional aid.

UNDERGRADUATE EXPENSES for 1999–2000 ***Application fee:*** $35. ***Comprehensive fee:*** $20,525 includes full-time tuition ($13,875), mandatory fees ($150), and room and board ($6500). ***College room only:*** $2860. Room and board charges vary according to board plan and housing facility. ***Part-time tuition:*** $465 per credit hour. ***Part-time fees:*** $30 per term part-time. Part-time tuition and fees vary according to class time. ***Payment plans:*** installment, deferred payment.

FRESHMAN FINANCIAL AID (Fall 1999, est.) 100 applied for aid; of those 95% were deemed to have need. 100% of freshmen with need received aid; of those 7% had need fully met. *Average percent of need met:* 79% (excluding resources awarded to replace EFC). *Average financial aid package:* $14,654 (excluding resources awarded to replace EFC). 4% of all full-time freshmen had no need and received non-need-based aid.

UNDERGRADUATE FINANCIAL AID (Fall 1999, est.) 417 applied for aid; of those 91% were deemed to have need. 100% of undergraduates with need received aid; of those 20% had need fully met. *Average percent of need met:* 86% (excluding resources awarded to replace EFC). *Average financial aid package:* $15,093 (excluding resources awarded to replace EFC). 6% of all full-time undergraduates had no need and received non-need-based aid.

GIFT AID (NEED-BASED) ***Total amount:*** $3,298,550 (26% Federal, 1% state, 72% institutional, 1% external sources). ***Receiving aid:*** *Freshmen:* 74% (90); *all full-time undergraduates:* 63% (360). ***Average award:*** Freshmen: $9351; Undergraduates: $8207. ***Scholarships, grants, and awards:*** Federal Pell, FSEOG, state, private, college/university gift aid from institutional funds.

GIFT AID (NON-NEED-BASED) ***Total amount:*** $217,795 (97% institutional, 3% external sources). ***Receiving aid:*** *Freshmen:* 4% (5); *Undergraduates:* 6% (35). ***Scholarships, grants, and awards by category:*** *Academic Interests/Achievement:* general academic interests/achievements. *Special Characteristics:* siblings of current students. ***Tuition waivers:*** Full or partial for employees or children of employees. ***ROTC:*** Army cooperative, Naval cooperative, Air Force cooperative.

LOANS ***Student loans:*** $4,861,215 (90% need-based, 10% non-need-based). 67% of past graduating class borrowed through all loan programs. ***Average need-based loan:*** Freshmen: $3306; Undergraduates: $3966. ***Parent loans:*** $385,687 (58% need-based, 42% non-need-based). ***Programs:*** FFEL (Subsidized and Unsubsidized Stafford, PLUS), Perkins.

WORK-STUDY ***Federal work-study:*** *Total amount:* $160,000; 106 jobs averaging $1500.

APPLYING for FINANCIAL AID ***Required financial aid form:*** FAFSA. ***Financial aid deadline (priority):*** 4/1. ***Notification date:*** Continuous. Students must reply within 2 weeks of notification.

CONTACT Catherine H. Geier, Director of Student Financial Services, Trinity College, 125 Michigan Avenue, NE, Washington, DC 20017-1094, 202-884-9530. *Fax:* 202-884-9524. *E-mail:* financialaid@trinitydc.edu

TRINITY COLLEGE OF FLORIDA
New Port Richey, FL

Tuition & fees: $4730 **Average undergraduate aid package: N/A**

ABOUT THE INSTITUTION Independent nondenominational, coed. Awards: associate and bachelor's degrees. 4 undergraduate majors. Total enrollment: 128. Undergraduates: 128. Freshmen: 23. Federal methodology is used as a basis for awarding need-based institutional aid.

UNDERGRADUATE EXPENSES for 1999–2000 ***Application fee:*** $25. ***Comprehensive fee:*** $7750 includes full-time tuition ($4420), mandatory fees ($310), and room and board ($3020). ***Part-time tuition:*** $170 per credit hour. ***Part-time fees:*** $155 per term part-time. Part-time tuition and fees vary according to course load. ***Payment plan:*** deferred payment.

GIFT AID (NEED-BASED) ***Total amount:*** $76,599 (94% Federal, 6% state). ***Scholarships, grants, and awards:*** Federal Pell, state, private, college/university gift aid from institutional funds.

GIFT AID (NON-NEED-BASED) ***Scholarships, grants, and awards by category:*** *Academic Interests/Achievement:* general academic interests/achievements. ***Tuition waivers:*** Full or partial for employees or children of employees, senior citizens.

LOANS ***Student loans:*** $96,804 (100% need-based). ***Parent loans:*** $4224 (100% need-based). ***Programs:*** Federal Direct (Subsidized and Unsubsidized Stafford, PLUS).

WORK-STUDY ***State or other work-study/employment:*** Part-time jobs available.

APPLYING for FINANCIAL AID ***Required financial aid forms:*** FAFSA, institution's own form.

CONTACT Sue Wayne, Director of Financial Aid, Trinity College of Florida, 2430 Welbilt Boulevard, New Port Richey, FL 34655, 727-376-6911 or toll-free 888-776-4999 Ext. 1120. *Fax:* 727-376-0781.

TRINITY COLLEGE OF NURSING
Moline, IL

CONTACT Ms. JoAnne Cunningham, Director of Student Services, Trinity College of Nursing, 555 6th Street, Suite 300, Moline, IL 61265-1216, 309-757-2903.

TRINITY COLLEGE OF VERMONT
Burlington, VT

Tuition & fees: $14,120 **Average undergraduate aid package: $13,993**

ABOUT THE INSTITUTION Independent Roman Catholic, coed, primarily women. Awards: associate, bachelor's, and master's degrees and post-bachelor's and post-master's certificates. 12 undergraduate majors. Total enrollment: 660. Undergraduates: 600. Freshmen: 77. Federal methodology is used as a basis for awarding need-based institutional aid.

UNDERGRADUATE EXPENSES for 1999–2000 ***Application fee:*** $40. ***Comprehensive fee:*** $20,820 includes full-time tuition ($13,620), mandatory fees ($500), and room and board ($6700). ***College room only:*** $3800. Room and board charges vary according to board plan. ***Part-time tuition:*** $454 per credit. ***Part-time fees:*** $20 per credit. Part-time tuition and fees vary according to class time and program. ***Payment plans:*** installment, deferred payment.

FRESHMAN FINANCIAL AID (Fall 1999) 67 applied for aid; of those 94% were deemed to have need. 100% of freshmen with need received aid; of those 13% had need fully met. *Average percent of need met:* 80% (excluding resources awarded to replace EFC). *Average financial aid package:* $14,821 (excluding resources awarded to replace EFC). 6% of all full-time freshmen had no need and received non-need-based aid.

UNDERGRADUATE FINANCIAL AID (Fall 1999) 272 applied for aid; of those 95% were deemed to have need. 100% of undergraduates with need received aid; of those 19% had need fully met. *Average percent of need met:* 81% (excluding resources awarded to replace EFC). *Average financial aid package:* $13,993 (excluding resources awarded to replace EFC). 4% of all full-time undergraduates had no need and received non-need-based aid.

GIFT AID (NEED-BASED) ***Total amount:*** $2,358,627 (22% Federal, 20% state, 53% institutional, 5% external sources). ***Receiving aid:*** *Freshmen:* 88% (63); *all full-time undergraduates:* 77% (254). ***Average award:*** Freshmen: $9946; Undergraduates: $8233. ***Scholarships, grants, and awards:*** Federal Pell, FSEOG, state, private, college/university gift aid from institutional funds.

GIFT AID (NON-NEED-BASED) ***Total amount:*** $119,940 (100% institutional). ***Receiving aid:*** *Freshmen:* 1% (1); *Undergraduates:* 2% (8). ***Scholar-***

Trinity College of Vermont (continued)

ships, grants, and awards by category: *Academic Interests/Achievement:* 18 awards ($45,000 total): general academic interests/achievements. ***Tuition waivers:*** Full or partial for employees or children of employees, senior citizens.

LOANS ***Student loans:*** $2,413,203 (87% need-based, 13% non-need-based). 82% of past graduating class borrowed through all loan programs. Average indebtedness per student: $16,462. ***Average need-based loan:*** Freshmen: $3437; Undergraduates: $4646. ***Parent loans:*** $653,990 (42% need-based, 58% non-need-based). ***Programs:*** FFEL (Subsidized and Unsubsidized Stafford, PLUS), Perkins, college/university, alternative loans.

WORK-STUDY ***Federal work-study:*** *Total amount:* $272,598; 147 jobs averaging $1850. ***State or other work-study/employment:*** *Total amount:* $24,901 (33% need-based, 67% non-need-based). 8 part-time jobs averaging $1500.

APPLYING for FINANCIAL AID ***Required financial aid forms:*** FAFSA, state aid form. ***Financial aid deadline:*** Continuous. ***Notification date:*** Continuous beginning 2/15.

CONTACT Yvonne Whitaker, Assistant Director, VSAC Financial Aid Services, Trinity College of Vermont, PO Box 2000, Winooski, VT 05404, 802-654-3793 or toll-free 888-277-5975 (out-of-state). *Fax:* 802-654-3765.

TRINITY INTERNATIONAL UNIVERSITY

Deerfield, IL

ABOUT THE INSTITUTION Independent religious, coed. Awards: bachelor's, master's, doctoral, and first professional degrees. 30 undergraduate majors. Total enrollment: 2,571. Undergraduates: 964.

GIFT AID (NEED-BASED) ***Scholarships, grants, and awards:*** Federal Pell, FSEOG, state, private, college/university gift aid from institutional funds.

GIFT AID (NON-NEED-BASED) ***Scholarships, grants, and awards by category:*** *Academic Interests/Achievement:* communication, English, general academic interests/achievements. *Creative Arts/Performance:* debating, journalism/publications, music. *Special Achievements/Activities:* leadership, religious involvement. *Special Characteristics:* religious affiliation.

LOANS ***Programs:*** FFEL (Subsidized and Unsubsidized Stafford, PLUS), Perkins, alternative loans.

WORK-STUDY Federal work-study jobs available.

APPLYING for FINANCIAL AID ***Required financial aid form:*** FAFSA.

CONTACT Mr. Brian K. Pomeroy, Director of Financial Aid, Trinity International University, 2065 Half Day Road, Deerfield, IL 60015-1284, 847-317-8060 or toll-free 800-822-3225 (out-of-state). *Fax:* 847-317-7081.

TRINITY INTERNATIONAL UNIVERSITY, SOUTH FLORIDA CAMPUS

Miami, FL

Tuition & fees: $8850 **Average undergraduate aid package: $9175**

ABOUT THE INSTITUTION Independent nondenominational, coed. Awards: bachelor's and master's degrees. 9 undergraduate majors. Total enrollment: 525. Undergraduates: 525. Federal methodology is used as a basis for awarding need-based institutional aid.

UNDERGRADUATE EXPENSES for 1999–2000 ***Application fee:*** $15. ***Tuition:*** full-time $8650; part-time $365 per semester hour. ***Required fees:*** full-time $200; $50 per term part-time. ***Payment plan:*** installment.

FRESHMAN FINANCIAL AID (Fall 1998) 38 applied for aid; of those 84% were deemed to have need. 100% of freshmen with need received aid; of those 3% had need fully met. *Average percent of need met:* 65% (excluding resources awarded to replace EFC). *Average financial aid package:* $6500 (excluding resources awarded to replace EFC). 17% of all full-time freshmen had no need and received non-need-based aid.

UNDERGRADUATE FINANCIAL AID (Fall 1998) 325 applied for aid; of those 90% were deemed to have need. 100% of undergraduates with need received aid; of those 2% had need fully met. *Average percent of need met:* 71% (excluding resources awarded to replace EFC). *Average financial aid package:* $9175 (excluding resources awarded to replace EFC). 10% of all full-time undergraduates had no need and received non-need-based aid.

GIFT AID (NEED-BASED) ***Total amount:*** $664,264 (67% Federal, 24% institutional, 9% external sources). ***Receiving aid:*** *Freshmen:* 66% (27); *all full-time undergraduates:* 59% (208). ***Average award:*** Freshmen: $3315; Undergraduates: $3890. ***Scholarships, grants, and awards:*** Federal Pell, FSEOG, state, private, college/university gift aid from institutional funds.

GIFT AID (NON-NEED-BASED) ***Total amount:*** $118,835 (6% state, 74% institutional, 20% external sources). ***Receiving aid:*** *Freshmen:* 63% (26); *Undergraduates:* 33% (116). ***Scholarships, grants, and awards by category:*** *Academic Interests/Achievement:* 53 awards ($46,375 total): general academic interests/achievements. *Special Achievements/Activities:* 33 awards ($30,375 total): leadership. *Special Characteristics:* 10 awards ($11,496 total): general special characteristics. ***Tuition waivers:*** Full or partial for employees or children of employees.

LOANS ***Student loans:*** $1,805,938 (61% need-based, 39% non-need-based). Average indebtedness per student: $15,000. ***Average need-based loan:*** Freshmen: $2330; Undergraduates: $3568. ***Parent loans:*** $29,800 (100% non-need-based). ***Programs:*** FFEL (Subsidized and Unsubsidized Stafford, PLUS).

WORK-STUDY ***Federal work-study:*** *Total amount:* $87,785; 41 jobs averaging $2117.

ATHLETIC AWARDS *Total amount:* 102,225 (100% non-need-based).

APPLYING for FINANCIAL AID ***Required financial aid forms:*** FAFSA, institution's own form. ***Financial aid deadline (priority):*** 4/1. ***Notification date:*** Continuous beginning 5/1. Students must reply within 4 weeks of notification.

CONTACT Anh Do, Director of Financial Aid, Trinity International University, South Florida Campus, 500 Northeast 1st Avenue, Miami, FL 33132, 305-577-4600 Ext. 145 or toll-free 800-288-1138 (out-of-state). *Fax:* 305-577-4614.

TRINITY LUTHERAN COLLEGE

Issaquah, WA

Tuition & fees: $7746 **Average undergraduate aid package: N/A**

ABOUT THE INSTITUTION Independent Lutheran, coed. Awards: associate and bachelor's degrees and post-bachelor's certificates. 3 undergraduate majors. Total enrollment: 142. Undergraduates: 142. Freshmen: 14. Federal methodology is used as a basis for awarding need-based institutional aid.

UNDERGRADUATE EXPENSES for 1999–2000 ***Application fee:*** $30. ***Comprehensive fee:*** $12,271 includes full-time tuition ($6900), mandatory fees ($846), and room and board ($4525). ***Part-time tuition:*** $198 per credit. ***Part-time fees:*** $27 per credit. ***Payment plan:*** installment.

GIFT AID (NEED-BASED) ***Total amount:*** $198,353 (41% Federal, 53% institutional, 6% external sources). ***Scholarships, grants, and awards:*** Federal Pell, FSEOG, private, college/university gift aid from institutional funds.

GIFT AID (NON-NEED-BASED) ***Total amount:*** $27,150 (100% institutional). ***Scholarships, grants, and awards by category:*** *Academic Interests/Achievement:* religion/biblical studies. *Creative Arts/Performance:* music. *Special Achievements/Activities:* leadership, religious involvement. *Special Characteristics:* international students, relatives of clergy, religious affiliation. ***Tuition waivers:*** Full or partial for employees or children of employees, senior citizens.

LOANS ***Student loans:*** $286,824 (100% need-based). ***Parent loans:*** $45,821 (100% need-based). ***Programs:*** FFEL (Subsidized and Unsubsidized Stafford, PLUS), college/university.

WORK-STUDY ***Federal work-study:*** *Total amount:* $20,632; jobs available.

APPLYING for FINANCIAL AID ***Required financial aid forms:*** FAFSA, institution's own form. ***Financial aid deadline (priority):*** 3/1. ***Notification date:*** Continuous. Students must reply within 4 weeks of notification.

CONTACT Ms. Susan Dalgleish, Director of Financial Aid, Trinity Lutheran College, 4221 228th Avenue Southeast, Issaquah, WA 98029-9299, 425-961-5514 or toll-free 800-843-5659. *Fax:* 425-392-0404. *E-mail:* finaid@tlc.edu

TRINITY UNIVERSITY

San Antonio, TX

Tuition & fees: $15,804 **Average undergraduate aid package: $15,745**

ABOUT THE INSTITUTION Independent religious, coed. Awards: bachelor's and master's degrees. 49 undergraduate majors. Total enrollment: 2,515. Undergraduates: 2,278. Freshmen: 637. Both federal and institutional methodology are used as a basis for awarding need-based institutional aid.

UNDERGRADUATE EXPENSES for 2000–2001 (est.) ***Application fee:*** $30. ***Comprehensive fee:*** $22,134 includes full-time tuition ($15,660), mandatory fees ($144), and room and board ($6330). ***College room only:*** $4070. Room and board charges vary according to board plan. ***Part-time tuition:*** $653 per semester hour. ***Part-time fees:*** $6 per semester hour. ***Payment plans:*** tuition prepayment, installment.

FRESHMAN FINANCIAL AID (Fall 1999, est.) 533 applied for aid; of those 53% were deemed to have need. 100% of freshmen with need received aid; of those 100% had need fully met. *Average percent of need met:* 100% (excluding resources awarded to replace EFC). *Average financial aid package:* $15,258 (excluding resources awarded to replace EFC). 29% of all full-time freshmen had no need and received non-need-based aid.

UNDERGRADUATE FINANCIAL AID (Fall 1999, est.) 1,850 applied for aid; of those 54% were deemed to have need. 100% of undergraduates with need received aid; of those 100% had need fully met. *Average percent of need met:* 100% (excluding resources awarded to replace EFC). *Average financial aid package:* $15,745 (excluding resources awarded to replace EFC). 26% of all full-time undergraduates had no need and received non-need-based aid.

GIFT AID (NEED-BASED) ***Total amount:*** $10,941,882 (10% Federal, 13% state, 72% institutional, 5% external sources). ***Receiving aid:*** *Freshmen:* 45% (285); *all full-time undergraduates:* 45% (1,002). ***Average award:*** Freshmen: $11,240; Undergraduates: $10,805. ***Scholarships, grants, and awards:*** Federal Pell, FSEOG, state, private, college/university gift aid from institutional funds.

GIFT AID (NON-NEED-BASED) ***Total amount:*** $3,628,198 (93% institutional, 7% external sources). ***Receiving aid:*** *Freshmen:* 22% (138); *Undergraduates:* 16% (350). ***Scholarships, grants, and awards by category:*** *Academic Interests/Achievement:* 926 awards ($4,209,334 total): general academic interests/achievements. *Creative Arts/Performance:* 115 awards ($103,900 total): music. ***Tuition waivers:*** Full or partial for employees or children of employees. ***ROTC:*** Air Force cooperative.

LOANS ***Student loans:*** $9,264,090 (38% need-based, 62% non-need-based). Average indebtedness per student: $14,272. ***Average need-based loan:*** Freshmen: $2800; Undergraduates: $3530. ***Parent loans:*** $1,434,853 (100% non-need-based). ***Programs:*** FFEL (Subsidized and Unsubsidized Stafford, PLUS), Perkins, state, college/university.

WORK-STUDY ***Federal work-study:*** *Total amount:* $1,389,760; 813 jobs averaging $1700. ***State or other work-study/employment:*** *Total amount:* $14,350 (100% need-based). 10 part-time jobs averaging $1435.

APPLYING for FINANCIAL AID ***Required financial aid forms:*** FAFSA, CSS Financial Aid PROFILE, noncustodial (divorced/separated) parent's statement. ***Financial aid deadline (priority):*** 2/1. ***Notification date:*** 4/1. Students must reply by 5/1 or within 4 weeks of notification.

CONTACT Ms. Estelle Frerichs, Director of Financial Aid, Trinity University, 715 Stadium Drive, San Antonio, TX 78212-7200, 210-999-8315 or toll-free 800-TRINITY. *Fax:* 210-999-8316. *E-mail:* efrerich@trinity.edu

TRI-STATE UNIVERSITY

Angola, IN

Tuition & fees: $13,700 **Average undergraduate aid package: $11,453**

ABOUT THE INSTITUTION Independent, coed. Awards: associate and bachelor's degrees. 38 undergraduate majors. Total enrollment: 1,231. Undergraduates: 1,231. Freshmen: 368. Federal methodology is used as a basis for awarding need-based institutional aid.

UNDERGRADUATE EXPENSES for 2000–2001 (est.) ***Application fee:*** $20. ***Comprehensive fee:*** $18,650 includes full-time tuition ($13,450), mandatory fees ($250), and room and board ($4950). Full-time tuition and fees vary according to class time and program. ***Part-time tuition:*** $420 per semester hour. ***Part-time fees:*** $50 per term part-time. Part-time tuition and fees vary according to class time and program. ***Payment plan:*** installment.

FRESHMAN FINANCIAL AID (Fall 1999) 365 applied for aid; of those 73% were deemed to have need. 100% of freshmen with need received aid; of those 56% had need fully met. *Average percent of need met:* 86% (excluding resources awarded to replace EFC). *Average financial aid package:* $10,096 (excluding resources awarded to replace EFC). 9% of all full-time freshmen had no need and received non-need-based aid.

UNDERGRADUATE FINANCIAL AID (Fall 1999) 1,109 applied for aid; of those 77% were deemed to have need. 100% of undergraduates with need received aid; of those 35% had need fully met. *Average percent of need met:* 84% (excluding resources awarded to replace EFC). *Average financial aid package:* $11,453 (excluding resources awarded to replace EFC). 11% of all full-time undergraduates had no need and received non-need-based aid.

GIFT AID (NEED-BASED) ***Total amount:*** $2,637,184 (26% Federal, 53% state, 21% institutional). ***Receiving aid:*** *Freshmen:* 73% (267); *all full-time undergraduates:* 66% (729). ***Average award:*** Freshmen: $1392; Undergraduates: $1293. ***Scholarships, grants, and awards:*** Federal Pell, FSEOG, state, private, college/university gift aid from institutional funds.

GIFT AID (NON-NEED-BASED) ***Total amount:*** $5,395,027 (94% institutional, 6% external sources). ***Receiving aid:*** *Freshmen:* 73% (267); *Undergraduates:* 77% (857). ***Scholarships, grants, and awards by category:*** *Academic Interests/Achievement:* general academic interests/achievements. *Special Achievements/Activities:* cheerleading/drum major, hobbies/interests. *Special Characteristics:* children and siblings of alumni, siblings of current students. ***Tuition waivers:*** Full or partial for employees or children of employees, senior citizens.

LOANS ***Student loans:*** $2,881,680 (94% need-based, 6% non-need-based). 61% of past graduating class borrowed through all loan programs. Average indebtedness per student: $14,000. ***Average need-based loan:*** Freshmen: $2204; Undergraduates: $3065. ***Parent loans:*** $1,311,981 (100% non-need-based). ***Programs:*** FFEL (Subsidized and Unsubsidized Stafford, PLUS), alternative loans.

WORK-STUDY ***Federal work-study:*** *Total amount:* $195,000; 309 jobs averaging $874. ***State or other work-study/employment:*** *Total amount:* $2136 (100% need-based). Part-time jobs available.

ATHLETIC AWARDS *Total amount:* 1,302,212 (100% non-need-based).

APPLYING for FINANCIAL AID ***Required financial aid form:*** FAFSA. ***Financial aid deadline (priority):*** 3/1. ***Notification date:*** Continuous. Students must reply by 4/15.

CONTACT Ms. Angela Metzger-Raub, Director of Admission and Financial Aid, Tri-State University, 1 University Avenue, Angola, IN 46703-1764, 219-665-4175 or toll-free 800-347-4TSU. *Fax:* 219-665-4292. *E-mail:* rauba@alpha.tristate.edu

TROY STATE UNIVERSITY

Troy, AL

Tuition & fees (AL res): $2900 **Average undergraduate aid package: $3609**

ABOUT THE INSTITUTION State-supported, coed. Awards: associate, bachelor's, and master's degrees. 41 undergraduate majors. Total enrollment: 6,266. Undergraduates: 4,695. Freshmen: 733. Federal methodology is used as a basis for awarding need-based institutional aid.

UNDERGRADUATE EXPENSES for 1999–2000 ***Application fee:*** $20. ***Tuition, state resident:*** full-time $2660; part-time $110 per credit hour. ***Tuition, nonresident:*** full-time $5320; part-time $220 per credit hour. ***Required fees:*** full-time $240; $10 per credit hour. ***College room and board:***

Troy State University (continued)

$3854; ***room only:*** $1970. Room and board charges vary according to board plan and housing facility. ***Payment plan:*** installment.

FRESHMAN FINANCIAL AID (Fall 1999) 524 applied for aid; of those 89% were deemed to have need. 99% of freshmen with need received aid. *Average percent of need met:* 59% (excluding resources awarded to replace EFC). *Average financial aid package:* $2056 (excluding resources awarded to replace EFC).

UNDERGRADUATE FINANCIAL AID (Fall 1999) 3,565 applied for aid; of those 92% were deemed to have need. 97% of undergraduates with need received aid; of those 8% had need fully met. *Average percent of need met:* 83% (excluding resources awarded to replace EFC). *Average financial aid package:* $3609 (excluding resources awarded to replace EFC).

GIFT AID (NEED-BASED) ***Total amount:*** $5,055,180 (99% Federal, 1% state). ***Receiving aid:*** *Freshmen:* 366; *all full-time undergraduates:* 2,295. ***Average award:*** Undergraduates: $1732. ***Scholarships, grants, and awards:*** Federal Pell, FSEOG, state, private, college/university gift aid from institutional funds.

GIFT AID (NON-NEED-BASED) ***Total amount:*** $3,056,308 (90% institutional, 10% external sources). ***Receiving aid:*** *Freshmen:* 380; *Undergraduates:* 1,542. ***Scholarships, grants, and awards by category:*** *Academic Interests/Achievement:* general academic interests/achievements. *Creative Arts/Performance:* journalism/publications, music, performing arts, theater/drama. *Special Characteristics:* general special characteristics. ***Tuition waivers:*** Full or partial for employees or children of employees. ***ROTC:*** Army, Air Force.

LOANS ***Student loans:*** $8,989,645 (67% need-based, 33% non-need-based). Average indebtedness per student: $17,125. ***Average need-based loan:*** Freshmen: $2625; Undergraduates: $4281. ***Parent loans:*** $424,513 (100% non-need-based). ***Programs:*** FFEL (Subsidized and Unsubsidized Stafford, PLUS), Perkins.

WORK-STUDY ***Federal work-study:*** *Total amount:* $481,850; 306 jobs averaging $1574.

ATHLETIC AWARDS *Total amount:* 1,634,868 (100% non-need-based).

APPLYING for FINANCIAL AID ***Required financial aid forms:*** FAFSA, institution's own form. ***Financial aid deadline (priority):*** 5/1. ***Notification date:*** Continuous. Students must reply within 2 weeks of notification.

CONTACT Ms. Carol Supri, Director of Financial Aid, Troy State University, Adams Administration 141, Troy, AL 36082, 334-670-3186 or toll-free 800-551-9716 (in-state). *Fax:* 334-670-3702.

TROY STATE UNIVERSITY DOTHAN

Dothan, AL

Tuition & fees (AL res): $2832 **Average undergraduate aid package: N/A**

ABOUT THE INSTITUTION State-supported, coed. Awards: associate, bachelor's, and master's degrees and post-master's certificates. 22 undergraduate majors. Total enrollment: 1,998. Undergraduates: 1,552. Freshmen: 47. Federal methodology is used as a basis for awarding need-based institutional aid.

UNDERGRADUATE EXPENSES for 1999–2000 ***Application fee:*** $20. ***Tuition, state resident:*** full-time $2760; part-time $115 per semester hour. ***Tuition, nonresident:*** full-time $5640; part-time $230 per semester hour. ***Required fees:*** full-time $72; $3 per semester hour. ***Payment plan:*** installment.

FRESHMAN FINANCIAL AID (Fall 1999) 23 applied for aid; of those 43% were deemed to have need. 100% of freshmen with need received aid. *Average percent of need met:* 11% (excluding resources awarded to replace EFC). 67% of all full-time freshmen had no need and received non-need-based aid.

UNDERGRADUATE FINANCIAL AID (Fall 1999) 1,274 applied for aid; of those 89% were deemed to have need. 67% of undergraduates with need received aid; of those 56% had need fully met. *Average percent of need met:* 37% (excluding resources awarded to replace EFC). 27% of all full-time undergraduates had no need and received non-need-based aid.

GIFT AID (NEED-BASED) ***Total amount:*** $1,204,104 (95% Federal, 1% state, 4% institutional). ***Receiving aid:*** *Freshmen:* 33% (10); *all full-time undergraduates:* 39% (609). ***Average award:*** Freshmen: $1622; Undergraduates: $1925. ***Scholarships, grants, and awards:*** Federal Pell, FSEOG, state.

GIFT AID (NON-NEED-BASED) ***Total amount:*** $348,591 (100% Federal). ***Scholarships, grants, and awards by category:*** *Academic Interests/Achievement:* general academic interests/achievements. ***Tuition waivers:*** Full or partial for employees or children of employees, senior citizens.

LOANS ***Student loans:*** $2,176,245 (86% need-based, 14% non-need-based). ***Average need-based loan:*** Freshmen: $4665; Undergraduates: $4791. ***Programs:*** FFEL (Subsidized and Unsubsidized Stafford).

WORK-STUDY ***Federal work-study:*** *Total amount:* $32,100; 18 jobs averaging $1783.

APPLYING for FINANCIAL AID ***Required financial aid forms:*** FAFSA, institution's own form. ***Financial aid deadline (priority):*** 5/1. ***Notification date:*** Continuous.

CONTACT Jonua Byrd, Director, Financial Aid and Veterans' Affairs, Troy State University Dothan, PO Box 8368, Dothan, AL 36304-8368, 334-983-6556 Ext. 255. *Fax:* 334-983-6322.

TROY STATE UNIVERSITY MONTGOMERY

Montgomery, AL

Tuition & fees (AL res): $2460 **Average undergraduate aid package: N/A**

ABOUT THE INSTITUTION State-supported, coed. Awards: associate, bachelor's, and master's degrees. 16 undergraduate majors. Total enrollment: 3,363. Undergraduates: 2,799. Freshmen: 169. Federal methodology is used as a basis for awarding need-based institutional aid.

UNDERGRADUATE EXPENSES for 1999–2000 ***Application fee:*** $15. ***Tuition, state resident:*** full-time $2430; part-time $58 per quarter hour. ***Tuition, nonresident:*** full-time $4860; part-time $116 per quarter hour. ***Required fees:*** full-time $30; $10 per term part-time. ***Payment plan:*** deferred payment.

FRESHMAN FINANCIAL AID (Fall 1999) 104 applied for aid; of those 100% were deemed to have need. 100% of freshmen with need received aid; of those 61% had need fully met. *Average percent of need met:* 61% (excluding resources awarded to replace EFC). 4% of all full-time freshmen had no need and received non-need-based aid.

UNDERGRADUATE FINANCIAL AID (Fall 1999) 746 applied for aid; of those 100% were deemed to have need. 100% of undergraduates with need received aid; of those 29% had need fully met. *Average percent of need met:* 39% (excluding resources awarded to replace EFC). 5% of all full-time undergraduates had no need and received non-need-based aid.

GIFT AID (NEED-BASED) ***Total amount:*** $1,849,059 (100% Federal). ***Receiving aid:*** *Freshmen:* 62% (104); *all full-time undergraduates:* 27% (746). ***Average award:*** Freshmen: $3125; Undergraduates: $3125. ***Scholarships, grants, and awards:*** Federal Pell, FSEOG, state.

GIFT AID (NON-NEED-BASED) ***Scholarships, grants, and awards by category:*** *Academic Interests/Achievement:* general academic interests/achievements. ***Tuition waivers:*** Full or partial for employees or children of employees. ***ROTC:*** Army cooperative, Air Force cooperative.

LOANS ***Student loans:*** $1,225,605 (71% need-based, 29% non-need-based). ***Average need-based loan:*** Freshmen: $2625; Undergraduates: $4282. ***Programs:*** FFEL (Subsidized and Unsubsidized Stafford, PLUS), Perkins.

WORK-STUDY ***Federal work-study:*** *Total amount:* $36,400; 23 jobs averaging $1583.

APPLYING for FINANCIAL AID ***Required financial aid forms:*** FAFSA, institution's own form. ***Financial aid deadline (priority):*** 5/1.

CONTACT Ms. Carol Supri, Director of Financial Aid, Troy State University Montgomery, Adams Administration Building, Troy, AL 36082, 334-670-3182 or toll-free 800-355-TSUM.

TRUMAN STATE UNIVERSITY

Kirksville, MO

Tuition & fees (MO res): $3562 **Average undergraduate aid package: $5200**

ABOUT THE INSTITUTION State-supported, coed. Awards: bachelor's and master's degrees. 49 undergraduate majors. Total enrollment: 6,236. Undergraduates: 5,963. Freshmen: 1,457. Federal methodology is used as a basis for awarding need-based institutional aid.

UNDERGRADUATE EXPENSES for 1999–2000 ***Tuition, state resident:*** full-time $3544. ***Tuition, nonresident:*** full-time $6344. ***Required fees:*** full-time $18. Part-time tuition and fees vary according to course load. ***College room and board:*** $4400. Room and board charges vary according to board plan and housing facility. ***Payment plan:*** installment.

FRESHMAN FINANCIAL AID (Fall 1999) 948 applied for aid; of those 59% were deemed to have need. *Average percent of need met:* 83% (excluding resources awarded to replace EFC). *Average financial aid package:* $5319 (excluding resources awarded to replace EFC).

UNDERGRADUATE FINANCIAL AID (Fall 1999) 3,338 applied for aid; of those 60% were deemed to have need. *Average percent of need met:* 82% (excluding resources awarded to replace EFC). *Average financial aid package:* $5200 (excluding resources awarded to replace EFC).

GIFT AID (NEED-BASED) ***Total amount:*** $1,752,373 (89% Federal, 11% state). ***Scholarships, grants, and awards:*** Federal Pell, FSEOG, state, private.

GIFT AID (NON-NEED-BASED) ***Total amount:*** $12,424,229 (18% state, 71% institutional, 11% external sources). ***Scholarships, grants, and awards by category:*** *Academic Interests/Achievement:* 3,107 awards ($8,124,758 total): biological sciences, business, communication, education, English, foreign languages, general academic interests/achievements, mathematics, military science, physical sciences, premedicine, social sciences. *Creative Arts/Performance:* 173 awards ($86,529 total): art/fine arts, debating, music, theater/drama. *Special Achievements/Activities:* 317 awards ($637,448 total): leadership. *Special Characteristics:* 300 awards ($803,109 total): children and siblings of alumni, children of faculty/staff, ethnic background, international students. ***Tuition waivers:*** Full or partial for employees or children of employees, senior citizens. ***ROTC:*** Army.

LOANS ***Student loans:*** $10,439,255 (65% need-based, 35% non-need-based). 51% of past graduating class borrowed through all loan programs. Average indebtedness per student: $15,357. ***Parent loans:*** $829,195 (100% non-need-based). ***Programs:*** FFEL (Subsidized and Unsubsidized Stafford, PLUS), Perkins, Federal Nursing, state, college/university.

WORK-STUDY ***Federal work-study:*** *Total amount:* $360,153; 358 jobs averaging $1006. ***State or other work-study/employment:*** *Total amount:* $1,158,412 (100% non-need-based). 1,392 part-time jobs averaging $832.

ATHLETIC AWARDS *Total amount:* 787,371 (100% non-need-based).

APPLYING for FINANCIAL AID ***Required financial aid forms:*** FAFSA, institution's own form. ***Financial aid deadline (priority):*** 4/1. ***Notification date:*** Continuous. Students must reply within 4 weeks of notification.

CONTACT Ms. Melinda Wood, Director of Financial Aid, Truman State University, 103 McClain Hall, Kirksville, MO 63501-4221, 660-785-4130 or toll-free 800-892-7792 (in-state). *Fax:* 660-785-7389. *E-mail:* mwood@truman.edu

TUFTS UNIVERSITY

Medford, MA

Tuition & fees: $24,751 **Average undergraduate aid package: $19,785**

ABOUT THE INSTITUTION Independent, coed. Awards: bachelor's, master's, doctoral, and first professional degrees and post-master's certificates. 63 undergraduate majors. Total enrollment: 9,269. Undergraduates: 4,977. Freshmen: 1,351. Institutional methodology is used as a basis for awarding need-based institutional aid.

UNDERGRADUATE EXPENSES for 1999–2000 ***Application fee:*** $55. ***Comprehensive fee:*** $32,126 includes full-time tuition ($24,126), mandatory fees ($625), and room and board ($7375). ***College room only:*** $3775. Room and board charges vary according to board plan. ***Payment plans:*** tuition prepayment, installment.

FRESHMAN FINANCIAL AID (Fall 1999, est.) 729 applied for aid; of those 79% were deemed to have need. 100% of freshmen with need received aid; of those 100% had need fully met. *Average percent of need met:* 100% (excluding resources awarded to replace EFC). *Average financial aid package:* $19,765 (excluding resources awarded to replace EFC). 3% of all full-time freshmen had no need and received non-need-based aid.

UNDERGRADUATE FINANCIAL AID (Fall 1999, est.) 2,018 applied for aid; of those 90% were deemed to have need. 100% of undergraduates with need received aid; of those 100% had need fully met. *Average percent of need met:* 100% (excluding resources awarded to replace EFC). *Average financial aid package:* $19,785 (excluding resources awarded to replace EFC). 4% of all full-time undergraduates had no need and received non-need-based aid.

GIFT AID (NEED-BASED) ***Total amount:*** $26,235,464 (7% Federal, 3% state, 87% institutional, 3% external sources). ***Receiving aid:*** *Freshmen:* 37% (504); *all full-time undergraduates:* 34% (1,668). ***Average award:*** Freshmen: $17,320; Undergraduates: $15,729. ***Scholarships, grants, and awards:*** Federal Pell, FSEOG, state, private, college/university gift aid from institutional funds.

GIFT AID (NON-NEED-BASED) ***Total amount:*** $402,198 (84% Federal, 9% institutional, 7% external sources). ***Scholarships, grants, and awards by category:*** *Academic Interests/Achievement:* 87 awards ($120,625 total): general academic interests/achievements. *Special Characteristics:* 70 awards ($1,688,820 total): children of faculty/staff. ***Tuition waivers:*** Full or partial for employees or children of employees. ***ROTC:*** Army cooperative, Naval cooperative, Air Force cooperative.

LOANS ***Student loans:*** $7,596,749 (95% need-based, 5% non-need-based). 47% of past graduating class borrowed through all loan programs. Average indebtedness per student: $14,834. ***Average need-based loan:*** Freshmen: $3419; Undergraduates: $4276. ***Parent loans:*** $6,437,050 (100% non-need-based). ***Programs:*** FFEL (Subsidized and Unsubsidized Stafford, PLUS), Perkins, state, college/university.

WORK-STUDY ***Federal work-study:*** *Total amount:* $2,571,630; 1,470 jobs averaging $1749. ***State or other work-study/employment:*** *Total amount:* $40,000 (100% need-based). 22 part-time jobs averaging $1818.

APPLYING for FINANCIAL AID ***Required financial aid forms:*** FAFSA, CSS Financial Aid PROFILE, noncustodial (divorced/separated) parent's statement, business/farm supplement, parent and student federal income tax forms. ***Financial aid deadline:*** 2/15 (priority: 2/1). ***Notification date:*** 4/10. Students must reply by 5/1.

CONTACT Mr. William F. Eastwood, Financial Aid Director, Tufts University, 128 Professors Row, Medford, MA 02155, 617-627-3528. *Fax:* 617-627-3848. *E-mail:* william.eastwood@tufts.edu

TULANE UNIVERSITY

New Orleans, LA

Tuition & fees: $24,214 **Average undergraduate aid package: $22,948**

ABOUT THE INSTITUTION Independent, coed. Awards: associate, bachelor's, master's, doctoral, and first professional degrees. 70 undergraduate majors. Total enrollment: 11,438. Undergraduates: 7,163. Freshmen: 2,445. Both federal and institutional methodology are used as a basis for awarding need-based institutional aid.

UNDERGRADUATE EXPENSES for 1999–2000 ***Application fee:*** $45. ***Comprehensive fee:*** $31,256 includes full-time tuition ($22,590), mandatory fees ($1624), and room and board ($7042). ***College room only:*** $3892. Room and board charges vary according to board plan and housing facility. ***Part-time tuition:*** $941 per credit hour. ***Part-time fees:*** $195 per credit hour; $60 per term part-time. ***Payment plan:*** installment.

FRESHMAN FINANCIAL AID (Fall 1999) 1127 applied for aid; of those 69% were deemed to have need. 100% of freshmen with need received aid; of those 68% had need fully met. *Average percent of need met:* 95% (excluding resources awarded to replace EFC). *Average financial aid pack-*

Tulane University (continued)

age: $21,980 (excluding resources awarded to replace EFC). 32% of all full-time freshmen had no need and received non-need-based aid.

UNDERGRADUATE FINANCIAL AID (Fall 1999) 3,137 applied for aid; of those 81% were deemed to have need. 99% of undergraduates with need received aid; of those 69% had need fully met. *Average percent of need met:* 94% (excluding resources awarded to replace EFC). *Average financial aid package:* $22,948 (excluding resources awarded to replace EFC). 24% of all full-time undergraduates had no need and received non-need-based aid.

GIFT AID (NEED-BASED) ***Total amount:*** $37,829,294 (8% Federal, 2% state, 86% institutional, 4% external sources). ***Receiving aid:*** *Freshmen:* 51% (742); *all full-time undergraduates:* 45% (2,429). ***Average award:*** Freshmen: $15,918; Undergraduates: $16,286. ***Scholarships, grants, and awards:*** Federal Pell, FSEOG, state, private, college/university gift aid from institutional funds.

GIFT AID (NON-NEED-BASED) ***Total amount:*** $19,812,337 (3% state, 78% institutional, 19% external sources). ***Receiving aid:*** *Freshmen:* 15% (219); *Undergraduates:* 8% (453). ***Scholarships, grants, and awards by category:*** *Academic Interests/Achievement:* general academic interests/achievements. *Special Characteristics:* children of faculty/staff, local/state students. ***Tuition waivers:*** Full or partial for employees or children of employees. ***ROTC:*** Army, Naval, Air Force.

LOANS ***Student loans:*** $15,034,466 (80% need-based, 20% non-need-based). Average indebtedness per student: $20,040. ***Average need-based loan:*** Freshmen: $4159; Undergraduates: $5217. ***Parent loans:*** $5,548,779 (9% need-based, 91% non-need-based). ***Programs:*** FFEL (Subsidized and Unsubsidized Stafford, PLUS), Perkins.

WORK-STUDY ***Federal work-study:*** *Total amount:* $2,495,584; jobs available. ***State or other work-study/employment:*** *Total amount:* $474,538 (29% need-based, 71% non-need-based). Part-time jobs available.

ATHLETIC AWARDS *Total amount:* 6,046,585 (94% need-based, 6% non-need-based).

APPLYING for FINANCIAL AID ***Required financial aid forms:*** FAFSA, CSS Financial Aid PROFILE, noncustodial (divorced/separated) parent's statement. ***Financial aid deadline:*** 2/1 (priority: 1/15). ***Notification date:*** Continuous beginning 3/1. Students must reply by 5/1 or within 2 weeks of notification.

CONTACT Ms. Elaine Rivera, Director of Financial Aid, Tulane University, 6823 St. Charles Avenue, New Orleans, LA 70118-5669, 504-865-5723 or toll-free 800-873-9283.

TUSCULUM COLLEGE

Greeneville, TN

Tuition & fees: $12,500 **Average undergraduate aid package: $7150**

ABOUT THE INSTITUTION Independent Presbyterian, coed. Awards: bachelor's and master's degrees. 27 undergraduate majors. Total enrollment: 1,562. Undergraduates: 1,285. Freshmen: 183. Federal methodology is used as a basis for awarding need-based institutional aid.

UNDERGRADUATE EXPENSES for 1999–2000 ***Comprehensive fee:*** $16,600 includes full-time tuition ($12,500) and room and board ($4100). Full-time tuition and fees vary according to course load and reciprocity agreements. ***Part-time tuition:*** $500 per credit hour. Part-time tuition and fees vary according to course load and reciprocity agreements. ***Payment plan:*** installment.

FRESHMAN FINANCIAL AID (Fall 1999, est.) 172 applied for aid; of those 76% were deemed to have need. 100% of freshmen with need received aid; of those 18% had need fully met. *Average percent of need met:* 60% (excluding resources awarded to replace EFC). *Average financial aid package:* $7547 (excluding resources awarded to replace EFC). 21% of all full-time freshmen had no need and received non-need-based aid.

UNDERGRADUATE FINANCIAL AID (Fall 1999, est.) 1,015 applied for aid; of those 66% were deemed to have need. 100% of undergraduates with need received aid; of those 23% had need fully met. *Average percent of need met:* 70% (excluding resources awarded to replace EFC). *Average financial aid package:* $7150 (excluding resources awarded to replace EFC). 22% of all full-time undergraduates had no need and received non-need-based aid.

GIFT AID (NEED-BASED) ***Total amount:*** $1,095,686 (63% Federal, 21% state, 16% institutional). ***Receiving aid:*** *Freshmen:* 45% (80); *all full-time undergraduates:* 17% (216). ***Average award:*** Freshmen: $1169; Undergraduates: $1152. ***Scholarships, grants, and awards:*** Federal Pell, FSEOG, state, private, college/university gift aid from institutional funds.

GIFT AID (NON-NEED-BASED) ***Total amount:*** $1,484,049 (4% state, 92% institutional, 4% external sources). ***Receiving aid:*** *Freshmen:* 66% (117); *Undergraduates:* 33% (411). ***Scholarships, grants, and awards by category:*** *Academic Interests/Achievement:* 451 awards ($1,087,412 total): general academic interests/achievements. *Special Characteristics:* 75 awards ($116,500 total): children of faculty/staff, local/state students. ***Tuition waivers:*** Full or partial for employees or children of employees.

LOANS ***Student loans:*** $5,304,020 (42% need-based, 58% non-need-based). 64% of past graduating class borrowed through all loan programs. Average indebtedness per student: $12,675. ***Average need-based loan:*** Freshmen: $2250; Undergraduates: $3161. ***Parent loans:*** $558,675 (100% non-need-based). ***Programs:*** FFEL (Subsidized and Unsubsidized Stafford, PLUS), Perkins.

WORK-STUDY ***Federal work-study:*** *Total amount:* $214,060; 127 jobs averaging $1734. ***State or other work-study/employment:*** *Total amount:* $60,300 (100% non-need-based). 75 part-time jobs averaging $1372.

ATHLETIC AWARDS *Total amount:* 1,047,695 (100% non-need-based).

APPLYING for FINANCIAL AID ***Required financial aid form:*** FAFSA. ***Financial aid deadline (priority):*** 3/1. ***Notification date:*** Continuous. Students must reply within 2 weeks of notification.

CONTACT Mr. J. Pat Shannon, Director of Financial Aid, Tusculum College, 5049 Tusculum Station, Greeneville, TN 37743-9997, 423-636-7300 Ext. 373 or toll-free 800-729-0256. *Fax:* 423-638-5181. *E-mail:* pshannon@tusculum.edu

TUSKEGEE UNIVERSITY

Tuskegee, AL

Tuition & fees: $9690 **Average undergraduate aid package: $10,100**

ABOUT THE INSTITUTION Independent, coed. Awards: bachelor's, master's, and first professional degrees. 40 undergraduate majors. Total enrollment: 3,009. Undergraduates: 2,616. Freshmen: 694. Federal methodology is used as a basis for awarding need-based institutional aid.

UNDERGRADUATE EXPENSES for 1999–2000 ***Application fee:*** $25. ***Comprehensive fee:*** $14,790 includes full-time tuition ($9500), mandatory fees ($190), and room and board ($5100). ***Part-time tuition:*** $384 per credit. ***Part-time fees:*** $95 per term part-time. Part-time tuition and fees vary according to course load. ***Payment plan:*** installment.

FRESHMAN FINANCIAL AID (Fall 1998) 573 applied for aid; of those 85% were deemed to have need. 100% of freshmen with need received aid; of those 40% had need fully met. *Average percent of need met:* 85% (excluding resources awarded to replace EFC). *Average financial aid package:* $11,832 (excluding resources awarded to replace EFC). 12% of all full-time freshmen had no need and received non-need-based aid.

UNDERGRADUATE FINANCIAL AID (Fall 1998) 2,377 applied for aid; of those 85% were deemed to have need. 100% of undergraduates with need received aid; of those 40% had need fully met. *Average percent of need met:* 85% (excluding resources awarded to replace EFC). *Average financial aid package:* $10,100 (excluding resources awarded to replace EFC). 9% of all full-time undergraduates had no need and received non-need-based aid.

GIFT AID (NEED-BASED) ***Total amount:*** $4,483,742 (91% Federal, 1% state, 8% external sources). ***Receiving aid:*** *Freshmen:* 60% (385); *all full-time undergraduates:* 57% (1,597). ***Average award:*** Freshmen: $4700; Undergraduates: $3850. ***Scholarships, grants, and awards:*** Federal Pell, FSEOG, state, private, college/university gift aid from institutional funds, United Negro College Fund.

GIFT AID (NON-NEED-BASED) ***Total amount:*** $4,442,041 (61% institutional, 39% external sources). ***Receiving aid:*** *Freshmen:* 16% (102); *Undergradu-*

ates: 15% (424). ***Scholarships, grants, and awards by category:*** *Academic Interests/Achievement:* 1,729 awards ($3,483,770 total): general academic interests/achievements. *Creative Arts/Performance:* 126 awards ($69,400 total): music. *Special Characteristics:* 43 awards ($145,855 total): children of faculty/staff, local/state students. ***Tuition waivers:*** Full or partial for employees or children of employees. ***ROTC:*** Army, Air Force.

LOANS ***Student loans:*** $10,104,697 (66% need-based, 34% non-need-based). 70% of past graduating class borrowed through all loan programs. Average indebtedness per student: $17,125. ***Average need-based loan:*** Freshmen: $3625; Undergraduates: $4282. ***Parent loans:*** $2,419,132 (100% non-need-based). ***Programs:*** Federal Direct (Subsidized and Unsubsidized Stafford, PLUS), Perkins, Federal Nursing, college/university.

WORK-STUDY ***Federal work-study:*** *Total amount:* $970,258; 495 jobs averaging $1777. ***State or other work-study/employment:*** *Total amount:* $235,750 (100% non-need-based). Part-time jobs available.

ATHLETIC AWARDS *Total amount:* 662,678 (100% non-need-based).

APPLYING for FINANCIAL AID ***Required financial aid forms:*** FAFSA, institution's own form, CSS Financial Aid PROFILE. ***Financial aid deadline (priority):*** 3/31. ***Notification date:*** Continuous beginning 4/15. Students must reply within 2 weeks of notification.

CONTACT Mrs. Dorothy Body, Director of Financial Aid, Tuskegee University, Office of Financial Aid Services, Tuskegee, AL 36088, 334-727-8201 or toll-free 800-622-6531. *Fax:* 334-724-4227. *E-mail:* dbody@acd.tusk.edu

UNION COLLEGE

Barbourville, KY

Tuition & fees: $11,320 **Average undergraduate aid package: $9579**

ABOUT THE INSTITUTION Independent United Methodist, coed. Awards: bachelor's and master's degrees. 41 undergraduate majors. Total enrollment: 835. Undergraduates: 541. Freshmen: 93. Federal methodology is used as a basis for awarding need-based institutional aid.

UNDERGRADUATE EXPENSES for 2000–2001 ***Application fee:*** $20. ***Tuition:*** full-time $11,070; part-time $225 per hour. ***Required fees:*** full-time $250. Room and board charges vary according to board plan and housing facility. ***Payment plan:*** installment.

FRESHMAN FINANCIAL AID (Fall 1999, est.) 92 applied for aid; of those 90% were deemed to have need. 100% of freshmen with need received aid; of those 61% had need fully met. *Average percent of need met:* 71% (excluding resources awarded to replace EFC). *Average financial aid package:* $8764 (excluding resources awarded to replace EFC). 4% of all full-time freshmen had no need and received non-need-based aid.

UNDERGRADUATE FINANCIAL AID (Fall 1999, est.) 479 applied for aid; of those 93% were deemed to have need. 100% of undergraduates with need received aid; of those 58% had need fully met. *Average percent of need met:* 77% (excluding resources awarded to replace EFC). *Average financial aid package:* $9579 (excluding resources awarded to replace EFC). 6% of all full-time undergraduates had no need and received non-need-based aid.

GIFT AID (NEED-BASED) ***Total amount:*** $4,237,379 (19% Federal, 17% state, 64% institutional). ***Receiving aid:*** *Freshmen:* 84% (81); *all full-time undergraduates:* 87% (445). ***Average award:*** Freshmen: $5605; Undergraduates: $6088. ***Scholarships, grants, and awards:*** Federal Pell, FSEOG, state, college/university gift aid from institutional funds.

GIFT AID (NON-NEED-BASED) ***Total amount:*** $186,511 (8% state, 90% institutional, 2% external sources). ***Receiving aid:*** *Freshmen:* 4% (4); *Undergraduates:* 6% (33). ***Scholarships, grants, and awards by category:*** *Academic Interests/Achievement:* 376 awards ($600,534 total): general academic interests/achievements. *Creative Arts/Performance:* 15 awards ($20,350 total): music. *Special Achievements/Activities:* 12 awards ($11,600 total): cheerleading/drum major. *Special Characteristics:* 60 awards ($58,973 total): children and siblings of alumni, religious affiliation. ***Tuition waivers:*** Full or partial for minority students, children of alumni, employees or children of employees, senior citizens.

LOANS ***Student loans:*** $1,512,311 (85% need-based, 15% non-need-based). 76% of past graduating class borrowed through all loan programs. Average indebtedness per student: $11,283. ***Average need-based loan:*** Freshmen: $2403; Undergraduates: $2919. ***Programs:*** FFEL (Subsidized and Unsubsidized Stafford, PLUS), Perkins, college/university.

WORK-STUDY ***Federal work-study:*** *Total amount:* $189,499; 233 jobs averaging $813. ***State or other work-study/employment:*** *Total amount:* $29,250 (100% need-based). 15 part-time jobs averaging $1950.

APPLYING for FINANCIAL AID ***Required financial aid form:*** FAFSA. ***Financial aid deadline (priority):*** 3/15. ***Notification date:*** 4/1. Students must reply within 2 weeks of notification.

CONTACT Mrs. Debra L. Smith, Director of Financial Aid, Union College, 310 College Street, Barbourville, KY 40906-1499, 606-546-4151 Ext. 1223 or toll-free 800-489-8646. *Fax:* 606-546-1667.

UNION COLLEGE

Lincoln, NE

Tuition & fees: $10,696 **Average undergraduate aid package: $8245**

ABOUT THE INSTITUTION Independent Seventh-day Adventist, coed. Awards: associate and bachelor's degrees. 51 undergraduate majors. Total enrollment: 856. Undergraduates: 856. Freshmen: 184. Federal methodology is used as a basis for awarding need-based institutional aid.

UNDERGRADUATE EXPENSES for 1999–2000 ***Comprehensive fee:*** $13,726 includes full-time tuition ($10,590), mandatory fees ($106), and room and board ($3030). ***College room only:*** $2080. Full-time tuition and fees vary according to course load. ***Part-time tuition:*** $442 per semester hour. ***Payment plans:*** tuition prepayment, installment.

FRESHMAN FINANCIAL AID (Fall 1999, est.) 119 applied for aid; of those 100% were deemed to have need. 100% of freshmen with need received aid; of those 12% had need fully met. *Average percent of need met:* 74% (excluding resources awarded to replace EFC). *Average financial aid package:* $7548 (excluding resources awarded to replace EFC). 38% of all full-time freshmen had no need and received non-need-based aid.

UNDERGRADUATE FINANCIAL AID (Fall 1999, est.) 486 applied for aid; of those 100% were deemed to have need. 100% of undergraduates with need received aid; of those 17% had need fully met. *Average percent of need met:* 72% (excluding resources awarded to replace EFC). *Average financial aid package:* $8245 (excluding resources awarded to replace EFC). 35% of all full-time undergraduates had no need and received non-need-based aid.

GIFT AID (NEED-BASED) ***Total amount:*** $1,823,220 (36% Federal, 2% state, 62% institutional). ***Receiving aid:*** *Freshmen:* 60% (119); *all full-time undergraduates:* 54% (462). ***Average award:*** Freshmen: $4799; Undergraduates: $4163. ***Scholarships, grants, and awards:*** Federal Pell, FSEOG, state, private, college/university gift aid from institutional funds.

GIFT AID (NON-NEED-BASED) ***Total amount:*** $790,647 (100% institutional). ***Scholarships, grants, and awards by category:*** *Academic Interests/Achievement:* general academic interests/achievements. *Creative Arts/Performance:* music. *Special Achievements/Activities:* community service, leadership, religious involvement. ***Tuition waivers:*** Full or partial for employees or children of employees, senior citizens.

LOANS ***Student loans:*** $2,606,585 (80% need-based, 20% non-need-based). 76% of past graduating class borrowed through all loan programs. Average indebtedness per student: $10,736. ***Average need-based loan:*** Freshmen: $3239; Undergraduates: $5070. ***Parent loans:*** $390,787 (100% non-need-based). ***Programs:*** FFEL (Subsidized and Unsubsidized Stafford, PLUS), Perkins, Federal Nursing, college/university.

WORK-STUDY ***Federal work-study:*** *Total amount:* $210,000; 125 jobs averaging $1650.

APPLYING for FINANCIAL AID ***Required financial aid form:*** FAFSA. ***Financial aid deadline (priority):*** 5/1. ***Notification date:*** Continuous. Students must reply within 3 weeks of notification.

CONTACT Mr. Dan Duff, Director of Financial Aid, Union College, 3800 South 48th Street, Lincoln, NE 68506-4300, 402-486-2505 or toll-free 800-228-4600 (out-of-state). *Fax:* 402-486-2895. *E-mail:* daduff@ucollege.edu

UNION COLLEGE

Schenectady, NY

Tuition & fees: $24,099 **Average undergraduate aid package: $21,084**

ABOUT THE INSTITUTION Independent, coed. Awards: bachelor's and master's degrees. 27 undergraduate majors. Total enrollment: 2,432. Undergraduates: 2,150. Freshmen: 535. Institutional methodology is used as a basis for awarding need-based institutional aid.

UNDERGRADUATE EXPENSES for 1999–2000 ***Application fee:*** $50. ***Comprehensive fee:*** $30,573 includes full-time tuition ($23,892), mandatory fees ($207), and room and board ($6474). ***College room only:*** $3492. Room and board charges vary according to board plan. ***Part-time tuition:*** $2655 per course. ***Payment plan:*** installment.

FRESHMAN FINANCIAL AID (Fall 1998) 336 applied for aid; of those 92% were deemed to have need. 100% of freshmen with need received aid; of those 100% had need fully met. *Average percent of need met:* 100% (excluding resources awarded to replace EFC). *Average financial aid package:* $22,348 (excluding resources awarded to replace EFC). 1% of all full-time freshmen had no need and received non-need-based aid.

UNDERGRADUATE FINANCIAL AID (Fall 1998) 1,221 applied for aid; of those 95% were deemed to have need. 100% of undergraduates with need received aid; of those 86% had need fully met. *Average percent of need met:* 97% (excluding resources awarded to replace EFC). *Average financial aid package:* $21,084 (excluding resources awarded to replace EFC). .4% of all full-time undergraduates had no need and received non-need-based aid.

GIFT AID (NEED-BASED) ***Total amount:*** $17,972,551 (6% Federal, 7% state, 85% institutional, 2% external sources). ***Receiving aid:*** *Freshmen:* 57% (309); *all full-time undergraduates:* 56% (1,149). ***Average award:*** Freshmen: $18,458; Undergraduates: $15,917. ***Scholarships, grants, and awards:*** Federal Pell, FSEOG, state, private, college/university gift aid from institutional funds.

GIFT AID (NON-NEED-BASED) ***Total amount:*** $55,031 (48% Federal, 52% state). ***Tuition waivers:*** Full or partial for employees or children of employees, senior citizens. ***ROTC:*** Army cooperative, Naval cooperative, Air Force cooperative.

LOANS ***Student loans:*** $5,798,560 (87% need-based, 13% non-need-based). 54% of past graduating class borrowed through all loan programs. Average indebtedness per student: $17,650. ***Average need-based loan:*** Freshmen: $3138; Undergraduates: $4508. ***Parent loans:*** $2,718,745 (100% non-need-based). ***Programs:*** FFEL (Subsidized and Unsubsidized Stafford, PLUS), Perkins, college/university.

WORK-STUDY ***Federal work-study:*** *Total amount:* $739,326; 657 jobs averaging $1127. ***State or other work-study/employment:*** *Total amount:* $59,200 (100% need-based). 44 part-time jobs averaging $1345.

APPLYING for FINANCIAL AID ***Required financial aid forms:*** FAFSA, CSS Financial Aid PROFILE, state aid form, noncustodial (divorced/separated) parent's statement, business/farm supplement. ***Financial aid deadline (priority):*** 2/1. ***Notification date:*** 4/1. Students must reply by 5/1.

CONTACT Mr. Michael Brown, Director of Financial Aid, Union College, Becker Hall, Schenectady, NY 12308-2311, 518-388-6123 or toll-free 888-843-6688 (in-state). *Fax:* 518-388-6986. *E-mail:* brownm@alice.union.edu

THE UNION INSTITUTE

Cincinnati, OH

Tuition & fees: $6288 **Average undergraduate aid package: N/A**

ABOUT THE INSTITUTION Independent, coed. Awards: bachelor's and doctoral degrees. 12 undergraduate majors. Total enrollment: 1,859. Undergraduates: 681. Freshmen: 14. Federal methodology is used as a basis for awarding need-based institutional aid.

UNDERGRADUATE EXPENSES for 1999–2000 ***Application fee:*** $50. ***Tuition:*** full-time $6288; part-time $262 per credit. ***Payment plan:*** installment.

FRESHMAN FINANCIAL AID (Fall 1998) 13 applied for aid; of those 100% were deemed to have need. *Average percent of need met:* 25% (excluding resources awarded to replace EFC).

UNDERGRADUATE FINANCIAL AID (Fall 1998) 616 applied for aid; of those 90% were deemed to have need. *Average percent of need met:* 75% (excluding resources awarded to replace EFC).

GIFT AID (NEED-BASED) ***Total amount:*** $832,140 (90% Federal, 9% state, 1% institutional). ***Scholarships, grants, and awards:*** Federal Pell, FSEOG, state, private, college/university gift aid from institutional funds.

GIFT AID (NON-NEED-BASED) ***Total amount:*** $71,004 (60% state, 40% institutional). ***Scholarships, grants, and awards by category:*** *Academic Interests/Achievement:* general academic interests/achievements. ***Tuition waivers:*** Full or partial for employees or children of employees.

LOANS ***Student loans:*** $6,316,813 (45% need-based, 55% non-need-based). 80% of past graduating class borrowed through all loan programs. ***Parent loans:*** $16,000 (62% need-based, 38% non-need-based). ***Programs:*** FFEL (Subsidized and Unsubsidized Stafford, PLUS), Perkins.

WORK-STUDY ***Federal work-study:*** *Total amount:* $23,836; 11 jobs available.

APPLYING for FINANCIAL AID ***Required financial aid forms:*** FAFSA, institution's own form, federal income tax form(s). ***Financial aid deadline (priority):*** 4/15. ***Notification date:*** Continuous beginning 5/1. Students must reply within 4 weeks of notification.

CONTACT Ms. Rebecca Zackerman, Director of Financial Aid, The Union Institute, 440 East McMillan Street, Cincinnati, OH 45206-1925, 513-861-6400 or toll-free 800-486-3116. *Fax:* 513-861-0779. *E-mail:* rzackerman@tui.edu

UNION UNIVERSITY

Jackson, TN

Tuition & fees: $11,900 **Average undergraduate aid package: $7800**

ABOUT THE INSTITUTION Independent Southern Baptist, coed. Awards: associate, bachelor's, and master's degrees. 62 undergraduate majors. Total enrollment: 2,297. Undergraduates: 1,931. Freshmen: 424. Federal methodology is used as a basis for awarding need-based institutional aid.

UNDERGRADUATE EXPENSES for 2000–2001 ***Application fee:*** $25. ***Comprehensive fee:*** $15,750 includes full-time tuition ($11,550), mandatory fees ($350), and room and board ($3850). Full-time tuition and fees vary according to class time, course load, location, and program. Room and board charges vary according to board plan and location. ***Part-time tuition:*** $385 per credit hour. ***Part-time fees:*** $150 per term part-time. ***Payment plans:*** installment, deferred payment.

FRESHMAN FINANCIAL AID (Fall 1999, est.) 360 applied for aid; of those 74% were deemed to have need. 97% of freshmen with need received aid; of those 16% had need fully met. *Average percent of need met:* 80% (excluding resources awarded to replace EFC). *Average financial aid package:* $6500 (excluding resources awarded to replace EFC). 30% of all full-time freshmen had no need and received non-need-based aid.

UNDERGRADUATE FINANCIAL AID (Fall 1999, est.) 1,240 applied for aid; of those 82% were deemed to have need. 92% of undergraduates with need received aid; of those 20% had need fully met. *Average percent of need met:* 80% (excluding resources awarded to replace EFC). *Average financial aid package:* $7800 (excluding resources awarded to replace EFC). 8% of all full-time undergraduates had no need and received non-need-based aid.

GIFT AID (NEED-BASED) ***Total amount:*** $1,543,011 (51% Federal, 28% state, 21% institutional). ***Receiving aid:*** *Freshmen:* 60% (230); *all full-time undergraduates:* 48% (728). ***Average award:*** Freshmen: $1800; Undergraduates: $2325. ***Scholarships, grants, and awards:*** Federal Pell, FSEOG, state, private, college/university gift aid from institutional funds.

GIFT AID (NON-NEED-BASED) ***Total amount:*** $3,922,734 (97% institutional, 3% external sources). ***Receiving aid:*** *Freshmen:* 35% (135); *Undergraduates:* 46% (690). ***Scholarships, grants, and awards by category:*** *Academic Interests/Achievement:* business, communication, general academic interests/achievements, religion/biblical studies. *Creative Arts/Performance:* art/fine arts, cinema/film/broadcasting, journalism/publications, music, theater/drama. *Special Achievements/Activities:* leadership. *Special Characteristics:* children and siblings of alumni, relatives of clergy. ***Tuition waivers:*** Full or partial for employees or children of employees.

LOANS ***Student loans:*** $4,497,502 (65% need-based, 35% non-need-based). 48% of past graduating class borrowed through all loan programs. Average indebtedness per student: $7800. ***Average need-based loan:*** Freshmen: $1800; Undergraduates: $2100. ***Parent loans:*** $737,057 (100% non-need-based). ***Programs:*** FFEL (Subsidized and Unsubsidized Stafford, PLUS), Perkins, college/university.

WORK-STUDY ***Federal work-study:*** *Total amount:* $125,000; 156 jobs averaging $800. ***State or other work-study/employment:*** *Total amount:* $215,000 (53% need-based, 47% non-need-based). 200 part-time jobs averaging $1075.

ATHLETIC AWARDS *Total amount:* 944,000 (100% non-need-based).

APPLYING for FINANCIAL AID ***Required financial aid forms:*** FAFSA, institution's own form. ***Financial aid deadline (priority):*** 2/15. ***Notification date:*** Continuous beginning 3/15. Students must reply within 2 weeks of notification.

CONTACT Mr. Don Morris, Assistant Vice President/Director of Financial Aid, Union University, 1050 Union University Drive, Jackson, TN 38305-3697, 901-661-5015 or toll-free 800-33-UNION. *Fax:* 901-661-5017. *E-mail:* dmorris@uu.edu

UNITED STATES INTERNATIONAL UNIVERSITY

San Diego, CA

Tuition & fees: $13,611 **Average undergraduate aid package: $11,659**

ABOUT THE INSTITUTION Independent, coed. Awards: bachelor's, master's, and doctoral degrees. 19 undergraduate majors. Total enrollment: 1,363. Undergraduates: 510. Freshmen: 110. Federal methodology is used as a basis for awarding need-based institutional aid.

UNDERGRADUATE EXPENSES for 2000–2001 (est.) ***Application fee:*** $40. ***Comprehensive fee:*** $19,386 includes full-time tuition ($13,200), mandatory fees ($411), and room and board ($5775). Full-time tuition and fees vary according to course load and location. Room and board charges vary according to board plan. ***Part-time tuition:*** $320 per unit. ***Part-time fees:*** $117 per term part-time. Part-time tuition and fees vary according to course load and location. ***Payment plans:*** installment, deferred payment.

FRESHMAN FINANCIAL AID (Fall 1999, est.) 103 applied for aid; of those 63% were deemed to have need. 100% of freshmen with need received aid; of those 82% had need fully met. *Average percent of need met:* 80% (excluding resources awarded to replace EFC). *Average financial aid package:* $12,482 (excluding resources awarded to replace EFC). 15% of all full-time freshmen had no need and received non-need-based aid.

UNDERGRADUATE FINANCIAL AID (Fall 1999, est.) 410 applied for aid; of those 60% were deemed to have need. 100% of undergraduates with need received aid; of those 85% had need fully met. *Average percent of need met:* 78% (excluding resources awarded to replace EFC). *Average financial aid package:* $11,659 (excluding resources awarded to replace EFC). 20% of all full-time undergraduates had no need and received non-need-based aid.

GIFT AID (NEED-BASED) ***Total amount:*** $1,589,991 (53% Federal, 36% state, 11% institutional). ***Receiving aid:*** *Freshmen:* 55% (61); *all full-time undergraduates:* 47% (225). ***Average award:*** Freshmen: $7457; Undergraduates: $6945. ***Scholarships, grants, and awards:*** Federal Pell, FSEOG, state, private, college/university gift aid from institutional funds.

GIFT AID (NON-NEED-BASED) ***Total amount:*** $1,316,982 (96% institutional, 4% external sources). ***Receiving aid:*** *Freshmen:* 55% (61); *Undergraduates:* 51% (243). ***Scholarships, grants, and awards by category:*** *Academic Interests/Achievement:* business, communication, computer science, education, foreign languages, general academic interests/achievements, humanities, international studies, social sciences. *Special Achievements/Activities:* community service, general special achievements/activities, leadership. *Special Characteristics:* children of faculty/staff, ethnic background, international students, local/state students, members of minority groups. ***Tuition waivers:*** Full or partial for employees or children of employees. ***ROTC:*** Army cooperative.

LOANS ***Student loans:*** $1,367,769 (70% need-based, 30% non-need-based). Average indebtedness per student: $16,210. ***Average need-based loan:*** Freshmen: $3742; Undergraduates: $4470. ***Parent loans:*** $299,277 (100% non-need-based). ***Programs:*** FFEL (Subsidized and Unsubsidized Stafford, PLUS), Perkins, alternative loans.

WORK-STUDY ***Federal work-study:*** *Total amount:* $616,923; 210 jobs averaging $3000. ***State or other work-study/employment:*** *Total amount:* $1215 (100% non-need-based). Part-time jobs available.

ATHLETIC AWARDS *Total amount:* 164,361 (100% non-need-based).

APPLYING for FINANCIAL AID ***Required financial aid forms:*** FAFSA, institution's own form. ***Financial aid deadline (priority):*** 3/2. ***Notification date:*** Continuous. Students must reply within 3 weeks of notification.

CONTACT Tina Moncada, Assistant Dean, United States International University, 10455 Pomerado Road, San Diego, CA 92131-1799, 858-635-4559. *Fax:* 858-635-4848. *E-mail:* tmoncada@usiu.edu

UNITED STATES OPEN UNIVERSITY

Wilmington, DE

CONTACT Financial Aid Office, United States Open University, 901 Market Street, Wilmington, DE 19801, 302-778-0300 or toll-free 800-232-7705.

UNITED TALMUDICAL SEMINARY

Brooklyn, NY

CONTACT Financial Aid Office, United Talmudical Seminary, 82 Lee Avenue, Brooklyn, NY 11211-7900, 718-963-9770 Ext. 309.

UNITY COLLEGE

Unity, ME

Tuition & fees: $12,780 **Average undergraduate aid package: $9022**

ABOUT THE INSTITUTION Independent, coed. Awards: associate and bachelor's degrees. 14 undergraduate majors. Total enrollment: 512. Undergraduates: 512. Freshmen: 146. Federal methodology is used as a basis for awarding need-based institutional aid.

UNDERGRADUATE EXPENSES for 2000–2001 ***Application fee:*** $25. ***One-time required fee:*** $150. ***Comprehensive fee:*** $18,080 includes full-time tuition ($12,330), mandatory fees ($450), and room and board ($5300). ***Part-time tuition:*** $415 per credit hour. Part-time tuition and fees vary according to course load. ***Payment plan:*** installment.

FRESHMAN FINANCIAL AID (Fall 1998) 117 applied for aid; of those 89% were deemed to have need. 100% of freshmen with need received aid; of those 69% had need fully met. *Average percent of need met:* 91% (excluding resources awarded to replace EFC). *Average financial aid package:* $9406 (excluding resources awarded to replace EFC). 4% of all full-time freshmen had no need and received non-need-based aid.

UNDERGRADUATE FINANCIAL AID (Fall 1998) 462 applied for aid; of those 88% were deemed to have need. 100% of undergraduates with need received aid; of those 70% had need fully met. *Average percent of need met:* 93% (excluding resources awarded to replace EFC). *Average financial aid package:* $9022 (excluding resources awarded to replace EFC). 4% of all full-time undergraduates had no need and received non-need-based aid.

GIFT AID (NEED-BASED) ***Total amount:*** $1,808,953 (30% Federal, 9% state, 53% institutional, 8% external sources). ***Receiving aid:*** *Freshmen:* 78% (99); *all full-time undergraduates:* 65% (336). ***Scholarships, grants, and awards:*** Federal Pell, FSEOG, state, private, college/university gift aid from institutional funds.

GIFT AID (NON-NEED-BASED) ***Total amount:*** $29,605 (75% institutional, 25% external sources). ***Receiving aid:*** *Freshmen:* 22% (28); *Undergraduates:* 18% (92). ***Scholarships, grants, and awards by category:*** *Academic Interests/Achievement:* general academic interests/achievements. *Special*

Unity College (continued)

Achievements/Activities: community service, leadership. *Special Characteristics:* children of educators, general special characteristics, local/state students, members of minority groups. ***Tuition waivers:*** Full or partial for employees or children of employees. ***ROTC:*** Army cooperative.

LOANS ***Student loans:*** $2,272,061 (85% need-based, 15% non-need-based). ***Parent loans:*** $675,788 (55% need-based, 45% non-need-based). ***Programs:*** FFEL (Subsidized and Unsubsidized Stafford, PLUS), Perkins.

WORK-STUDY ***Federal work-study:*** *Total amount:* $482,725; 294 jobs averaging $1632. ***State or other work-study/employment:*** *Total amount:* $4000 (100% non-need-based). Part-time jobs available.

APPLYING for FINANCIAL AID ***Required financial aid forms:*** FAFSA, institution's own form, state aid form. ***Financial aid deadline (priority):*** 3/1. ***Notification date:*** Continuous. Students must reply within 4 weeks of notification.

CONTACT Mr. Rand E. Newell, Director of Financial Aid, Unity College, HC 78, Box 1, Unity, ME 04988, 207-948-3131 Ext. 201. *Fax:* 207-948-6277. *E-mail:* rnewell@unity.unity.edu

UNIVERSIDAD ADVENTISTA DE LAS ANTILLAS

Mayagüez, PR

Tuition & fees: $3690 **Average undergraduate aid package: $1769**

ABOUT THE INSTITUTION Independent Seventh-day Adventist, coed. Awards: associate and bachelor's degrees. 19 undergraduate majors. Total enrollment: 762. Undergraduates: 731. Freshmen: 327. Federal methodology is used as a basis for awarding need-based institutional aid.

UNDERGRADUATE EXPENSES for 1999–2000 ***Application fee:*** $20. ***One-time required fee:*** $75. ***Comprehensive fee:*** $5840 includes full-time tuition ($3150), mandatory fees ($540), and room and board ($2150). Full-time tuition and fees vary according to course load. Room and board charges vary according to board plan. ***Part-time tuition:*** $110 per credit. Part-time tuition and fees vary according to course load. ***Payment plans:*** tuition prepayment, installment, deferred payment.

FRESHMAN FINANCIAL AID (Fall 1999, est.) 100 applied for aid; of those 100% were deemed to have need. 100% of freshmen with need received aid; of those 5% had need fully met. *Average percent of need met:* 44% (excluding resources awarded to replace EFC). *Average financial aid package:* $3356 (excluding resources awarded to replace EFC).

UNDERGRADUATE FINANCIAL AID (Fall 1999, est.) 621 applied for aid; of those 100% were deemed to have need. 87% of undergraduates with need received aid; of those 3% had need fully met. *Average percent of need met:* 36% (excluding resources awarded to replace EFC). *Average financial aid package:* $1769 (excluding resources awarded to replace EFC).

GIFT AID (NEED-BASED) ***Total amount:*** $1,852,862 (92% Federal, 8% state). ***Receiving aid:*** *Freshmen:* 100% (100); *all full-time undergraduates:* 87% (538). ***Average award:*** Freshmen: $305. ***Scholarships, grants, and awards:*** Federal Pell, FSEOG, state, college/university gift aid from institutional funds.

GIFT AID (NON-NEED-BASED) ***Tuition waivers:*** Full or partial for employees or children of employees.

LOANS ***Student loans:*** $800,000 (100% need-based). 12% of past graduating class borrowed through all loan programs. ***Average need-based loan:*** Freshmen: $670; Undergraduates: $3500. ***Programs:*** FFEL (Subsidized Stafford, PLUS), college/university.

WORK-STUDY ***Federal work-study:*** *Total amount:* $136,232; 145 jobs averaging $940. ***State or other work-study/employment:*** *Total amount:* $216,200 (46% need-based, 54% non-need-based). Part-time jobs available.

APPLYING for FINANCIAL AID ***Required financial aid form:*** FAFSA. ***Financial aid deadline:*** Continuous.

CONTACT Mr. Heriberto Juarbe, Director of Financial Aid, Universidad Adventista de las Antillas, Box 118, Mayagüez, PR 00681-0118, 787-834-9595 Ext. 2200. *Fax:* 787-834-9597. *E-mail:* hjuarbe@uaa.edu

UNIVERSIDAD DEL TURABO

Turabo, PR

CONTACT Ms. Ivette Vázquez Ríos, Directora Oficina de Asistencia Económica, Universidad del Turabo, Apartado 3030, Gurabo, PR 00778-3030, 787-743-7979 Ext. 4352. *Fax:* 787-743-7979.

UNIVERSIDAD METROPOLITANA

Río Piedras, PR

CONTACT Economic Assistant Director, Universidad Metropolitana, Call Box 21150, Rio Piedras, PR 00928-1150, 787-766-1717 Ext. 6586.

UNIVERSIDAD POLITÉCNICA DE PUERTO RICO

Hato Rey, PR

See Polytechnic University of Puerto Rico

UNIVERSITY AT ALBANY, STATE UNIVERSITY OF NEW YORK

Albany, NY

See State University of New York at Albany

UNIVERSITY OF ADVANCING COMPUTER TECHNOLOGY

Tempe, AZ

Tuition & fees: N/R **Average undergraduate aid package: N/A**

ABOUT THE INSTITUTION Proprietary, coed. Awards: associate, bachelor's, and master's degrees. 8 undergraduate majors. Total enrollment: 1,055. Undergraduates: 1,055. Federal methodology is used as a basis for awarding need-based institutional aid.

GIFT AID (NEED-BASED) ***Scholarships, grants, and awards:*** Federal Pell, FSEOG, college/university gift aid from institutional funds.

GIFT AID (NON-NEED-BASED) ***Scholarships, grants, and awards by category:*** *Academic Interests/Achievement:* computer science, general academic interests/achievements. *Special Characteristics:* local/state students, out-of-state students.

LOANS ***Programs:*** Federal Direct (Subsidized and Unsubsidized Stafford, PLUS).

WORK-STUDY Federal work-study jobs available.

APPLYING for FINANCIAL AID ***Required financial aid forms:*** FAFSA, institution's own form. ***Financial aid deadline:*** Continuous.

CONTACT Director of Financial Aid, University of Advancing Computer Technology, 2625 West Baseline Road, Tempe, AZ 85283-1042, 602-383-8228 or toll-free 800-658-5744 (out-of-state).

THE UNIVERSITY OF AKRON

Akron, OH

Tuition & fees (OH res): $4152 **Average undergraduate aid package: $4495**

ABOUT THE INSTITUTION State-supported, coed. Awards: associate, bachelor's, master's, doctoral, and first professional degrees. 150 undergraduate majors. Total enrollment: 23,264. Undergraduates: 19,248. Freshmen: 3,423. Federal methodology is used as a basis for awarding need-based institutional aid.

UNDERGRADUATE EXPENSES for 1999–2000 ***Application fee:*** $25. ***One-time required fee:*** $100. ***Tuition, state resident:*** full-time $3755; part-time $156 per credit. ***Tuition, nonresident:*** full-time $8716; part-time $363 per credit. ***Required fees:*** full-time $397; $17 per credit. Full-time tuition and fees vary according to course level and location. Part-time tuition and fees vary according to course level and location. ***College room and board:*** $5010; ***room only:*** $3150. Room and board charges vary according to board plan and housing facility. ***Payment plan:*** installment.

FRESHMAN FINANCIAL AID (Fall 1999, est.) 2045 applied for aid; of those 84% were deemed to have need. 100% of freshmen with need received aid; of those 20% had need fully met. *Average financial aid package:* $3790 (excluding resources awarded to replace EFC).

UNDERGRADUATE FINANCIAL AID (Fall 1999, est.) 7,669 applied for aid; of those 88% were deemed to have need. 100% of undergraduates with need received aid; of those 20% had need fully met. *Average financial aid package:* $4495 (excluding resources awarded to replace EFC).

GIFT AID (NEED-BASED) ***Total amount:*** $14,850,670 (75% Federal, 25% state). ***Receiving aid:*** *Freshmen:* 33% (907); *all full-time undergraduates:* 33% (3,928). ***Average award:*** Freshmen: $3144; Undergraduates: $3075. ***Scholarships, grants, and awards:*** Federal Pell, FSEOG, state.

GIFT AID (NON-NEED-BASED) ***Total amount:*** $7,627,058 (17% state, 63% institutional, 20% external sources). ***Receiving aid:*** *Freshmen:* 43% (1,201); *Undergraduates:* 28% (3,259). ***Scholarships, grants, and awards by category:*** *Academic Interests/Achievement:* 2,312 awards ($3,912,992 total): biological sciences, business, communication, computer science, education, engineering/technologies, English, foreign languages, general academic interests/achievements, health fields, home economics, humanities, international studies, mathematics, military science, physical sciences, premedicine, social sciences. *Creative Arts/Performance:* 220 awards ($226,614 total): applied art and design, art/fine arts, creative writing, dance, debating, general creative arts/performance, journalism/publications, music, performing arts, theater/drama. *Special Achievements/Activities:* 208 awards ($372,502 total): memberships. *Special Characteristics:* 124 awards ($259,350 total): adult students, general special characteristics, handicapped students, local/state students, members of minority groups, out-of-state students. ***Tuition waivers:*** Full or partial for employees or children of employees, senior citizens. ***ROTC:*** Army, Air Force.

LOANS ***Student loans:*** $31,809,407 (100% need-based). Average indebtedness per student: $15,421. ***Average need-based loan:*** Freshmen: $2686; Undergraduates: $3286. ***Parent loans:*** $1,287,010 (100% non-need-based). ***Programs:*** FFEL (Subsidized and Unsubsidized Stafford, PLUS), Perkins, Federal Nursing, college/university.

WORK-STUDY ***Federal work-study:*** *Total amount:* $1,098,730; jobs available. ***State or other work-study/employment:*** *Total amount:* $4,100,000 (100% non-need-based). Part-time jobs available.

ATHLETIC AWARDS *Total amount:* 2,434,695 (100% non-need-based).

APPLYING for FINANCIAL AID ***Required financial aid forms:*** FAFSA, institution's own form. ***Financial aid deadline (priority):*** 3/1. ***Notification date:*** Continuous beginning 4/15. Students must reply within 2 weeks of notification.

CONTACT Mr. Doug McNutt, Director of Financial Aid, The University of Akron, Office of Student Financial Aid, Akron, OH 44325-6211, 330-972-6343 or toll-free 800-655-4884. *Fax:* 330-972-7139. *E-mail:* dmcnutt@uakron.edu

THE UNIVERSITY OF ALABAMA

Tuscaloosa, AL

Tuition & fees (AL res): $2872 **Average undergraduate aid package: $3866**

ABOUT THE INSTITUTION State-supported, coed. Awards: bachelor's, master's, doctoral, and first professional degrees and post-master's certificates. 80 undergraduate majors. Total enrollment: 18,744. Undergraduates: 14,645. Freshmen: 2,720. Federal methodology is used as a basis for awarding need-based institutional aid.

UNDERGRADUATE EXPENSES for 1999–2000 ***Application fee:*** $25. ***Tuition, state resident:*** full-time $2872; part-time $614 per course. ***Tuition, nonresident:*** full-time $7722; part-time $1241 per course. Full-time tuition and fees vary according to course load. Part-time tuition and fees vary according to course load. ***College room and board:*** $4154; ***room only:*** $2454. Room and board charges vary according to board plan and housing facility. ***Payment plans:*** installment, deferred payment.

FRESHMAN FINANCIAL AID (Fall 1999, est.) 2002 applied for aid; of those 89% were deemed to have need. 61% of freshmen with need received aid; of those 39% had need fully met. *Average percent of need met:* 58% (excluding resources awarded to replace EFC). *Average financial aid package:* $3590 (excluding resources awarded to replace EFC). 7% of all full-time freshmen had no need and received non-need-based aid.

UNDERGRADUATE FINANCIAL AID (Fall 1999, est.) 8,643 applied for aid; of those 91% were deemed to have need. 66% of undergraduates with need received aid; of those 40% had need fully met. *Average percent of need met:* 64% (excluding resources awarded to replace EFC). *Average financial aid package:* $3866 (excluding resources awarded to replace EFC). 4% of all full-time undergraduates had no need and received non-need-based aid.

GIFT AID (NEED-BASED) ***Total amount:*** $8,708,535 (76% Federal, 2% state, 22% institutional). ***Receiving aid:*** *Freshmen:* 20% (581); *all full-time undergraduates:* 22% (2,830). ***Average award:*** Freshmen: $727; Undergraduates: $779. ***Scholarships, grants, and awards:*** Federal Pell, FSEOG, state, private, college/university gift aid from institutional funds.

GIFT AID (NON-NEED-BASED) ***Receiving aid:*** *Freshmen:* 16% (458); *Undergraduates:* 12% (1,540). ***Scholarships, grants, and awards by category:*** *Academic Interests/Achievement:* 582 awards ($569,929 total): computer science, general academic interests/achievements. *Creative Arts/Performance:* 108 awards ($157,274 total): art/fine arts, dance, music, theater/drama. *Special Achievements/Activities:* 289 awards ($949,124 total): general special achievements/activities. *Special Characteristics:* 4 awards ($2100 total): general special characteristics. ***Tuition waivers:*** Full or partial for employees or children of employees. ***ROTC:*** Army, Air Force.

LOANS ***Student loans:*** $30,987,854 (60% need-based, 40% non-need-based). 44% of past graduating class borrowed through all loan programs. Average indebtedness per student: $18,994. ***Average need-based loan:*** Freshmen: $1101; Undergraduates: $722. ***Parent loans:*** $8,432,912 (100% non-need-based). ***Programs:*** Federal Direct (Subsidized and Unsubsidized Stafford, PLUS), Perkins, college/university.

WORK-STUDY ***Federal work-study:*** *Total amount:* $1,356,407; 600 jobs averaging $2260. ***State or other work-study/employment:*** *Total amount:* $5,438,481 (100% non-need-based). Part-time jobs available.

ATHLETIC AWARDS *Total amount:* 1,941,118 (100% non-need-based).

APPLYING for FINANCIAL AID ***Required financial aid form:*** FAFSA. ***Financial aid deadline (priority):*** 3/1. ***Notification date:*** 4/1. Students must reply within 3 weeks of notification.

CONTACT Helen Leathers, Assistant Director of Financial Aid, The University of Alabama, Box 870162, Tuscaloosa, AL 35487-0162, 205-348-6756 or toll-free 800-933-BAMA. *Fax:* 205-348-2989. *E-mail:* hleather@enroll.ua.edu

THE UNIVERSITY OF ALABAMA AT BIRMINGHAM

Birmingham, AL

Tuition & fees (AL res): $3240 **Average undergraduate aid package: N/A**

ABOUT THE INSTITUTION State-supported, coed. Awards: bachelor's, master's, doctoral, and first professional degrees and post-bachelor's and post-master's certificates. 50 undergraduate majors. Total enrollment: 15,098. Undergraduates: 10,420. Freshmen: 1,233. Both federal and institutional methodology are used as a basis for awarding need-based institutional aid.

UNDERGRADUATE EXPENSES for 1999–2000 ***Application fee:*** $25. ***Tuition, state resident:*** full-time $2730; part-time $91 per hour. ***Tuition, nonresident:*** full-time $5460; part-time $182 per hour. ***Required fees:*** full-time $510; $13 per hour; $40 per term part-time. Full-time tuition and fees vary according to course load and program. Part-time tuition and fees vary according to course load and program. ***College room and board: room only:*** $2438. Room and board charges vary according to housing facility.

FRESHMAN FINANCIAL AID (Fall 1998) 750 applied for aid; of those 64% were deemed to have need. 98% of freshmen with need received aid; of

The University of Alabama at Birmingham (continued)

those 13% had need fully met. *Average percent of need met:* 39% (excluding resources awarded to replace EFC). 19% of all full-time freshmen had no need and received non-need-based aid.

UNDERGRADUATE FINANCIAL AID (Fall 1998) 4,276 applied for aid; of those 72% were deemed to have need. 99% of undergraduates with need received aid; of those 15% had need fully met. *Average percent of need met:* 45% (excluding resources awarded to replace EFC). 13% of all full-time undergraduates had no need and received non-need-based aid.

GIFT AID (NEED-BASED) ***Total amount:*** $6,571,458 (95% Federal, 2% state, 3% institutional). ***Receiving aid:*** *Freshmen:* 28% (305); *all full-time undergraduates:* 28% (1,855). ***Average award:*** Freshmen: $2629; Undergraduates: $2698. ***Scholarships, grants, and awards:*** Federal Pell, FSEOG, state, college/university gift aid from institutional funds.

GIFT AID (NON-NEED-BASED) ***Total amount:*** $2,642,820 (70% institutional, 30% external sources). ***Receiving aid:*** *Freshmen:* 21% (228); *Undergraduates:* 18% (1,219). ***Scholarships, grants, and awards by category:*** *Academic Interests/Achievement:* business, engineering/technologies, general academic interests/achievements. *Creative Arts/Performance:* art/fine arts, music, performing arts, theater/drama. *Special Achievements/Activities:* cheerleading/drum major, leadership, memberships. *Special Characteristics:* adult students, children and siblings of alumni, children of current students, children of educators, children of faculty/staff, children of public servants, children of union members/company employees, children of workers in trades, children with a deceased or disabled parent, ethnic background, first-generation college students, general special characteristics, handicapped students, local/state students, married students, out-of-state students, parents of current students, previous college experience, public servants, relatives of clergy, religious affiliation, siblings of current students, spouses of current students, spouses of deceased or disabled public servants, twins, veterans, veterans' children. ***Tuition waivers:*** Full or partial for employees or children of employees. ***ROTC:*** Army, Air Force cooperative.

LOANS ***Student loans:*** $30,873,596 (68% need-based, 32% non-need-based). Average indebtedness per student: $15,459. ***Average need-based loan:*** Freshmen: $3012; Undergraduates: $4277. ***Parent loans:*** $1,150,560 (100% non-need-based). ***Programs:*** Federal Direct (Subsidized and Unsubsidized Stafford, PLUS), Perkins, state, college/university.

WORK-STUDY ***Federal work-study:*** *Total amount:* $1,463,966; jobs available.

ATHLETIC AWARDS *Total amount:* 2,413,439 (100% non-need-based).

APPLYING for FINANCIAL AID ***Required financial aid forms:*** FAFSA, institution's own form. ***Financial aid deadline (priority):*** 5/1. ***Notification date:*** Continuous. Students must reply within 2 weeks of notification.

CONTACT Ms. Janet B. May, Financial Aid Director, The University of Alabama at Birmingham, HUC 317, 1530 3rd Avenue South, Birmingham, AL 35294-1150, 205-934-8223 or toll-free 800-421-8743 (in-state).

THE UNIVERSITY OF ALABAMA IN HUNTSVILLE

Huntsville, AL

Tuition & fees (AL res): $3112 **Average undergraduate aid package: $6145**

ABOUT THE INSTITUTION State-supported, coed. Awards: bachelor's, master's, and doctoral degrees and post-bachelor's and post-master's certificates. 33 undergraduate majors. Total enrollment: 6,874. Undergraduates: 5,513. Freshmen: 574. Both federal and institutional methodology are used as a basis for awarding need-based institutional aid.

UNDERGRADUATE EXPENSES for 1999–2000 ***Application fee:*** $20. ***Tuition, state resident:*** full-time $3112; part-time $698 per term. ***Tuition, nonresident:*** full-time $6516; part-time $1458 per term. Full-time tuition and fees vary according to course load. Part-time tuition and fees vary according to course load. ***College room and board:*** $3780; ***room only:*** $2780. Room and board charges vary according to board plan and housing facility. ***Payment plan:*** deferred payment.

FRESHMAN FINANCIAL AID (Fall 1999) 505 applied for aid; of those 37% were deemed to have need. 98% of freshmen with need received aid; of those 17% had need fully met. *Average percent of need met:* 57% (excluding resources awarded to replace EFC). *Average financial aid package:* $4599 (excluding resources awarded to replace EFC). 51% of all full-time freshmen had no need and received non-need-based aid.

UNDERGRADUATE FINANCIAL AID (Fall 1999) 2,209 applied for aid; of those 58% were deemed to have need. 93% of undergraduates with need received aid; of those 34% had need fully met. *Average percent of need met:* 67% (excluding resources awarded to replace EFC). *Average financial aid package:* $6145 (excluding resources awarded to replace EFC). 19% of all full-time undergraduates had no need and received non-need-based aid.

GIFT AID (NEED-BASED) ***Total amount:*** $2,855,145 (82% Federal, 1% state, 9% institutional, 8% external sources). ***Receiving aid:*** *Freshmen:* 17% (92); *all full-time undergraduates:* 25% (731). ***Average award:*** Freshmen: $2486; Undergraduates: $2494. ***Scholarships, grants, and awards:*** Federal Pell, FSEOG, state, private, college/university gift aid from institutional funds.

GIFT AID (NON-NEED-BASED) ***Total amount:*** $1,123,816 (64% institutional, 36% external sources). ***Receiving aid:*** *Freshmen:* 27% (146); *Undergraduates:* 13% (378). ***Scholarships, grants, and awards by category:*** *Academic Interests/Achievement:* business, computer science, education, engineering/technologies, English, general academic interests/achievements, health fields, physical sciences. *Creative Arts/Performance:* art/fine arts, music. *Special Achievements/Activities:* community service, general special achievements/activities, leadership. *Special Characteristics:* general special characteristics, local/state students, members of minority groups. ***Tuition waivers:*** Full or partial for employees or children of employees. ***ROTC:*** Army cooperative, Air Force.

LOANS ***Student loans:*** $7,357,736 (100% need-based). Average indebtedness per student: $15,146. ***Average need-based loan:*** Freshmen: $2907; Undergraduates: $4898. ***Parent loans:*** $281,239 (100% need-based). ***Programs:*** Federal Direct (Subsidized and Unsubsidized Stafford, PLUS), college/university.

WORK-STUDY ***Federal work-study:*** *Total amount:* $142,649; 47 jobs averaging $3035.

ATHLETIC AWARDS *Total amount:* 825,710 (18% need-based, 82% non-need-based).

APPLYING for FINANCIAL AID ***Required financial aid forms:*** FAFSA, institution's own form. ***Financial aid deadline (priority):*** 4/1. ***Notification date:*** Continuous beginning 7/1. Students must reply within 2 weeks of notification.

CONTACT Mr. Andrew Weaver, Director of Financial Aid, The University of Alabama in Huntsville, Office of Financial Aid, 301 Sparkman Drive, Huntsville, AL 35899, 256-890-6241 or toll-free 800-UAH-CALL. *Fax:* 256-890-6073. *E-mail:* weavera@email.uah.edu

UNIVERSITY OF ALASKA ANCHORAGE

Anchorage, AK

Tuition & fees: N/R **Average undergraduate aid package: N/A**

ABOUT THE INSTITUTION State-supported, coed. Awards: associate, bachelor's, and master's degrees. 67 undergraduate majors. Total enrollment: 14,765. Undergraduates: 14,235.

GIFT AID (NEED-BASED) ***Scholarships, grants, and awards:*** Federal Pell, FSEOG, state, private, college/university gift aid from institutional funds.

GIFT AID (NON-NEED-BASED) ***Scholarships, grants, and awards by category:*** *Academic Interests/Achievement:* biological sciences, business, communication, computer science, education, engineering/technologies, English, general academic interests/achievements, health fields, humanities, mathematics, social sciences. *Creative Arts/Performance:* art/fine arts, music. *Special Achievements/Activities:* general special achievements/activities. *Special Characteristics:* children of faculty/staff, ethnic background, general special characteristics, international students, members of minority groups, spouses of deceased or disabled public servants. ***Tuition***

waivers: Full or partial for minority students, children of alumni, employees or children of employees, adult students, senior citizens.

LOANS ***Programs:*** FFEL (Subsidized and Unsubsidized Stafford, PLUS), Perkins, state, college/university.

WORK-STUDY Federal work-study jobs available.

APPLYING for FINANCIAL AID ***Required financial aid form:*** FAFSA. ***Financial aid deadline (priority):*** 6/1. ***Notification date:*** 8/1.

CONTACT Linda S. Williams, Coordinator, Student Financial Aid, University of Alaska Anchorage, 3211 Providence Drive, Anchorage, AK 99508, 907-786-1586. *Fax:* 907-786-6122.

UNIVERSITY OF ALASKA FAIRBANKS

Fairbanks, AK

Tuition & fees (AK res): $3412 **Average undergraduate aid package: N/A**

ABOUT THE INSTITUTION State-supported, coed. Awards: associate, bachelor's, master's, and doctoral degrees. 91 undergraduate majors. Total enrollment: 6,768. Undergraduates: 6,028. Freshmen: 790. Federal methodology is used as a basis for awarding need-based institutional aid.

UNDERGRADUATE EXPENSES for 2000–2001 ***Application fee:*** $35. ***Tuition, state resident:*** full-time $2460; part-time $77 per credit. ***Tuition, nonresident:*** full-time $7380; part-time $241 per credit. ***Required fees:*** full-time $952. Full-time tuition and fees vary according to course level, course load, program, reciprocity agreements, and student level. Part-time tuition and fees vary according to course level, course load, program, and reciprocity agreements. ***College room and board:*** $4150; ***room only:*** $2150. Room and board charges vary according to board plan, housing facility, and location. ***Payment plan:*** deferred payment.

FRESHMAN FINANCIAL AID (Fall 1999) 470 applied for aid; of those 53% were deemed to have need. 78% of freshmen with need received aid; of those 14% had need fully met. 28% of all full-time freshmen had no need and received non-need-based aid.

UNDERGRADUATE FINANCIAL AID (Fall 1999) 2,154 applied for aid; of those 55% were deemed to have need. 88% of undergraduates with need received aid; of those 11% had need fully met. 28% of all full-time undergraduates had no need and received non-need-based aid.

GIFT AID (NEED-BASED) ***Total amount:*** $2,409,173 (100% Federal). ***Receiving aid:*** *Freshmen:* 24% (156); *all full-time undergraduates:* 27% (814). ***Average award:*** Freshmen: $1168; Undergraduates: $1123. ***Scholarships, grants, and awards:*** Federal Pell, FSEOG, private, college/university gift aid from institutional funds.

GIFT AID (NON-NEED-BASED) ***Total amount:*** $2,327,388 (53% institutional, 47% external sources). ***Scholarships, grants, and awards by category:*** *Academic Interests/Achievement:* general academic interests/achievements. *Creative Arts/Performance:* creative writing, music, theater/drama. *Special Achievements/Activities:* general special achievements/activities. *Special Characteristics:* general special characteristics. ***Tuition waivers:*** Full or partial for children of alumni, employees or children of employees, senior citizens. ***ROTC:*** Army.

LOANS ***Student loans:*** $11,761,380 (23% need-based, 77% non-need-based). ***Average need-based loan:*** Freshmen: $1311; Undergraduates: $2073. ***Parent loans:*** $196,488 (100% non-need-based). ***Programs:*** FFEL (Subsidized and Unsubsidized Stafford, PLUS), state, college/university.

WORK-STUDY ***Federal work-study:*** *Total amount:* $252,207; jobs available.

ATHLETIC AWARDS *Total amount:* 429,375 (100% non-need-based).

APPLYING for FINANCIAL AID ***Required financial aid form:*** FAFSA. ***Financial aid deadline (priority):*** 6/1.

CONTACT Financial Aid Office, University of Alaska Fairbanks, 101 Eielson Building, Fairbanks, AK 99775-6360, 907-474-7256 or toll-free 800-478-1823 (out-of-state).

UNIVERSITY OF ALASKA SOUTHEAST

Juneau, AK

Tuition & fees: N/R **Average undergraduate aid package: N/A**

ABOUT THE INSTITUTION State-supported, coed. Awards: associate, bachelor's, and master's degrees. 17 undergraduate majors. Total enrollment: 1,803. Undergraduates: 1,803. Federal methodology is used as a basis for awarding need-based institutional aid.

FRESHMAN FINANCIAL AID (Fall 1999) 83 applied for aid; of those 27% were deemed to have need. 95% of freshmen with need received aid; of those 38% had need fully met. 47% of all full-time freshmen had no need and received non-need-based aid.

UNDERGRADUATE FINANCIAL AID (Fall 1999) 390 applied for aid; of those 48% were deemed to have need. 96% of undergraduates with need received aid; of those 29% had need fully met. 31% of all full-time undergraduates had no need and received non-need-based aid.

GIFT AID (NEED-BASED) ***Total amount:*** $465,678 (72% Federal, 3% institutional, 25% external sources). ***Receiving aid:*** *Freshmen:* 22% (21); *all full-time undergraduates:* 32% (161). ***Average award:*** Freshmen: $1078; Undergraduates: $1000. ***Scholarships, grants, and awards:*** Federal Pell, FSEOG, state, private, college/university gift aid from institutional funds.

GIFT AID (NON-NEED-BASED) ***Total amount:*** $433,290 (67% institutional, 33% external sources). ***Scholarships, grants, and awards by category:*** *Academic Interests/Achievement:* 58 awards ($69,203 total): biological sciences, business, communication, education, general academic interests/achievements, social sciences. *Special Achievements/Activities:* 29 awards ($18,200 total): general special achievements/activities, leadership. *Special Characteristics:* 8 awards ($15,184 total): international students. ***Tuition waivers:*** Full or partial for employees or children of employees, senior citizens.

LOANS ***Student loans:*** $1,674,772 (31% need-based, 69% non-need-based). ***Average need-based loan:*** Freshmen: $1145; Undergraduates: $1781. ***Parent loans:*** $14,721 (100% non-need-based). ***Programs:*** FFEL (Subsidized and Unsubsidized Stafford, PLUS), state.

WORK-STUDY ***Federal work-study:*** 10 jobs averaging $3840. ***State or other work-study/employment:*** *Total amount:* $27,124 (100% non-need-based).

APPLYING for FINANCIAL AID ***Required financial aid form:*** FAFSA. ***Financial aid deadline:*** Continuous. ***Notification date:*** Continuous beginning 3/1. Students must reply within 3 weeks of notification.

CONTACT Ms. Barbara Carlson Burnett, Financial Aid Director, University of Alaska Southeast, 11120 Glacier Highway, Juneau, AK 99801-8680, 907-465-6255. *Fax:* 907-465-1394.

THE UNIVERSITY OF ARIZONA

Tucson, AZ

Tuition & fees (AZ res): $2264 **Average undergraduate aid package: $8808**

ABOUT THE INSTITUTION State-supported, coed. Awards: bachelor's, master's, doctoral, and first professional degrees. 125 undergraduate majors. Total enrollment: 34,326. Undergraduates: 26,258. Freshmen: 5,365. Federal methodology is used as a basis for awarding need-based institutional aid.

UNDERGRADUATE EXPENSES for 1999–2000 ***Application fee:*** $40 for nonresidents. ***Tuition, state resident:*** full-time $2264; part-time $115 per unit. ***Tuition, nonresident:*** full-time $9416; part-time $389 per unit. ***Required fees:*** $7 per unit. Part-time tuition and fees vary according to course load. ***College room and board:*** $5548. Room and board charges vary according to board plan and housing facility.

FRESHMAN FINANCIAL AID (Fall 1998) 3681 applied for aid; of those 57% were deemed to have need. 100% of freshmen with need received aid. *Average financial aid package:* $7580 (excluding resources awarded to replace EFC). 30% of all full-time freshmen had no need and received non-need-based aid.

UNDERGRADUATE FINANCIAL AID (Fall 1998) 18,476 applied for aid; of those 61% were deemed to have need. 100% of undergraduates with need received aid. *Average financial aid package:* $8808 (excluding resources awarded to replace EFC). 27% of all full-time undergraduates had no need and received non-need-based aid.

The University of Arizona (continued)

GIFT AID (NEED-BASED) ***Total amount:*** $15,428,818 (98% Federal, 2% state). ***Scholarships, grants, and awards:*** Federal Pell, FSEOG, state, college/university gift aid from institutional funds.

GIFT AID (NON-NEED-BASED) ***Scholarships, grants, and awards by category:*** *Academic Interests/Achievement:* agriculture, architecture, biological sciences, business, education, engineering/technologies, general academic interests/achievements, humanities, military science, physical sciences, religion/biblical studies. *Creative Arts/Performance:* art/fine arts, dance, music, performing arts, theater/drama. *Special Characteristics:* children of faculty/staff, ethnic background, international students. ***Tuition waivers:*** Full or partial for minority students, employees or children of employees. ***ROTC:*** Army, Naval, Air Force.

LOANS ***Student loans:*** $70,641,596 (84% need-based, 16% non-need-based). Average indebtedness per student: $17,143. ***Parent loans:*** $13,063,991 (100% non-need-based). ***Programs:*** FFEL (Subsidized and Unsubsidized Stafford, PLUS), Perkins, Federal Nursing, state, college/university.

WORK-STUDY ***Federal work-study:*** *Total amount:* $1,470,241; 896 jobs averaging $1640. ***State or other work-study/employment:*** *Total amount:* $13,530,338 (78% need-based, 22% non-need-based). 6,293 part-time jobs averaging $2150.

ATHLETIC AWARDS *Total amount:* 3,596,657 (100% non-need-based).

APPLYING for FINANCIAL AID ***Required financial aid form:*** FAFSA. ***Financial aid deadline (priority):*** 3/1. ***Notification date:*** Continuous beginning 4/1.

CONTACT Phyllis Bolt Bannister, Executive Director, Office of Student Financial Aid, The University of Arizona, PO Box 210066, Tucson, AZ 85721-0066, 520-621-1643. *Fax:* 520-621-9473. *E-mail:* askaid@u.arizona.edu

UNIVERSITY OF ARKANSAS

Fayetteville, AR

Tuition & fees (AR res): $3660 **Average undergraduate aid package: $7191**

ABOUT THE INSTITUTION State-supported, coed. Awards: bachelor's, master's, doctoral, and first professional degrees. 79 undergraduate majors. Total enrollment: 15,167. Undergraduates: 12,240. Freshmen: 2,268. Federal methodology is used as a basis for awarding need-based institutional aid.

UNDERGRADUATE EXPENSES for 2000–2001 ***Application fee:*** $30. ***Tuition, area resident:*** part-time $106 per credit hour. ***Tuition, state resident:*** full-time $2968; part-time $295 per credit hour. ***Tuition, nonresident:*** full-time $8260. ***Required fees:*** full-time $692. Full-time tuition and fees vary according to course load, degree level, program, and student level. Part-time tuition and fees vary according to course load, degree level, program, and student level. ***College room and board:*** $4358. Room and board charges vary according to board plan and housing facility. ***Payment plan:*** installment.

FRESHMAN FINANCIAL AID (Fall 1999, est.) 1622 applied for aid; of those 68% were deemed to have need. 98% of freshmen with need received aid; of those 49% had need fully met. *Average percent of need met:* 92% (excluding resources awarded to replace EFC). *Average financial aid package:* $7861 (excluding resources awarded to replace EFC). 28% of all full-time freshmen had no need and received non-need-based aid.

UNDERGRADUATE FINANCIAL AID (Fall 1999, est.) 5,925 applied for aid; of those 79% were deemed to have need. 92% of undergraduates with need received aid; of those 38% had need fully met. *Average percent of need met:* 77% (excluding resources awarded to replace EFC). *Average financial aid package:* $7191 (excluding resources awarded to replace EFC). 24% of all full-time undergraduates had no need and received non-need-based aid.

GIFT AID (NEED-BASED) ***Total amount:*** $10,619,805 (60% Federal, 40% state). ***Receiving aid:*** *Freshmen:* 39% (865); *all full-time undergraduates:* 28% (2,907). ***Average award:*** Freshmen: $3358; Undergraduates: $3202. ***Scholarships, grants, and awards:*** Federal Pell, FSEOG, state, private, college/university gift aid from institutional funds.

GIFT AID (NON-NEED-BASED) ***Total amount:*** $15,526,598 (9% state, 84% institutional, 7% external sources). ***Receiving aid:*** *Freshmen:* 32% (702); *Undergraduates:* 16% (1,707). ***Scholarships, grants, and awards by category:*** *Academic Interests/Achievement:* general academic interests/achievements. *Creative Arts/Performance:* music. *Special Achievements/Activities:* community service, general special achievements/activities, leadership. *Special Characteristics:* children and siblings of alumni, children of faculty/staff, ethnic background, international students, out-of-state students, previous college experience. ***Tuition waivers:*** Full or partial for employees or children of employees, senior citizens. ***ROTC:*** Army, Air Force.

LOANS ***Student loans:*** $18,717,486 (61% need-based, 39% non-need-based). 47% of past graduating class borrowed through all loan programs. Average indebtedness per student: $14,910. ***Average need-based loan:*** Freshmen: $2356; Undergraduates: $3804. ***Parent loans:*** $1,748,985 (100% non-need-based). ***Programs:*** FFEL (Subsidized and Unsubsidized Stafford, PLUS), Perkins, state, college/university.

WORK-STUDY ***Federal work-study:*** *Total amount:* $1,000,000; 633 jobs averaging $1580.

ATHLETIC AWARDS *Total amount:* 1,155,804 (100% non-need-based).

APPLYING for FINANCIAL AID ***Required financial aid form:*** FAFSA. ***Financial aid deadline (priority):*** 3/15. ***Notification date:*** Continuous. Students must reply by 5/1 or within 2 weeks of notification.

CONTACT Arlene Cash, Dean of Enrollment Services, University of Arkansas, 114 Silas H. Hunt Hall, Fayetteville, AR 72701-1201, 501-575-3806 or toll-free 800-377-8632.

UNIVERSITY OF ARKANSAS AT LITTLE ROCK

Little Rock, AR

Tuition & fees (AR res): $2820 **Average undergraduate aid package: N/A**

ABOUT THE INSTITUTION State-supported, coed. Awards: associate, bachelor's, master's, doctoral, and first professional degrees and post-bachelor's certificates. 55 undergraduate majors. Total enrollment: 10,541. Undergraduates: 8,383. Both federal and institutional methodology are used as a basis for awarding need-based institutional aid.

UNDERGRADUATE EXPENSES for 1999–2000 ***Tuition, state resident:*** full-time $2424; part-time $101 per credit hour. ***Tuition, nonresident:*** full-time $6240; part-time $260 per credit hour. ***Required fees:*** full-time $396; $16 per credit hour. ***College room and board: room only:*** $2500. Room and board charges vary according to housing facility. ***Payment plan:*** deferred payment.

GIFT AID (NEED-BASED) ***Scholarships, grants, and awards:*** Federal Pell, FSEOG, state, private, college/university gift aid from institutional funds.

GIFT AID (NON-NEED-BASED) ***Scholarships, grants, and awards by category:*** *Academic Interests/Achievement:* biological sciences, business, communication, computer science, education, engineering/technologies, English, foreign languages, general academic interests/achievements, health fields, humanities, international studies, mathematics, physical sciences, social sciences. *Creative Arts/Performance:* art/fine arts, music, theater/drama. *Special Achievements/Activities:* community service, leadership, memberships. *Special Characteristics:* local/state students, members of minority groups, previous college experience. ***Tuition waivers:*** Full or partial for employees or children of employees, senior citizens. ***ROTC:*** Army.

LOANS ***Programs:*** FFEL (Subsidized and Unsubsidized Stafford, PLUS).

WORK-STUDY Federal work-study jobs available.

APPLYING for FINANCIAL AID ***Required financial aid form:*** FAFSA. ***Financial aid deadline (priority):*** 3/1. ***Notification date:*** 4/15.

CONTACT Financial Aid Office, University of Arkansas at Little Rock, 2801 South University Avenue, Little Rock, AR 72204-1099, 501-569-3130 or toll-free 800-482-8892 (in-state).

UNIVERSITY OF ARKANSAS AT MONTICELLO

Monticello, AR

Tuition & fees (AR res): $2530 **Average undergraduate aid package: N/A**

ABOUT THE INSTITUTION State-supported, coed. Awards: associate, bachelor's, and master's degrees. 33 undergraduate majors. Total enrollment: 2,094. Undergraduates: 2,094. Federal methodology is used as a basis for awarding need-based institutional aid.

UNDERGRADUATE EXPENSES for 1999–2000 ***Tuition, state resident:*** full-time $2100; part-time $70 per hour. ***Tuition, nonresident:*** full-time $4860; part-time $162 per hour. ***Required fees:*** full-time $430; $14 per hour; $5 per term part-time. Full-time tuition and fees vary according to reciprocity agreements. Part-time tuition and fees vary according to reciprocity agreements. ***College room and board:*** $2580. Room and board charges vary according to board plan and housing facility.

UNDERGRADUATE FINANCIAL AID (Fall 1998) 1,460 applied for aid; of those 88% were deemed to have need. 97% of undergraduates with need received aid.

GIFT AID (NEED-BASED) ***Total amount:*** $3,506,709 (66% Federal, 19% state, 12% institutional, 3% external sources). ***Scholarships, grants, and awards:*** Federal Pell, FSEOG, state, private, college/university gift aid from institutional funds.

GIFT AID (NON-NEED-BASED) ***Total amount:*** $633,571 (17% state, 74% institutional, 9% external sources). ***Scholarships, grants, and awards by category:*** *Academic Interests/Achievement:* 144 awards ($286,390 total): general academic interests/achievements. *Creative Arts/Performance:* 200 awards ($192,001 total): debating, music. *Special Achievements/Activities:* 62 awards ($93,035 total): cheerleading/drum major, leadership. *Special Characteristics:* 255 awards ($425,559 total): children of faculty/staff, out-of-state students. ***Tuition waivers:*** Full or partial for employees or children of employees, senior citizens.

LOANS ***Student loans:*** $3,255,330 (77% need-based, 23% non-need-based). Average indebtedness per student: $13,599. ***Parent loans:*** $55,054 (100% non-need-based). ***Programs:*** FFEL (Subsidized and Unsubsidized Stafford, PLUS), Perkins.

WORK-STUDY ***Federal work-study:*** *Total amount:* $163,913; 189 jobs averaging $846. ***State or other work-study/employment:*** *Total amount:* $297,682 (100% non-need-based). 269 part-time jobs averaging $1100.

ATHLETIC AWARDS *Total amount:* 213,593 (68% need-based, 32% non-need-based).

APPLYING for FINANCIAL AID ***Required financial aid forms:*** FAFSA, institution's own form. ***Financial aid deadline:*** Continuous. ***Notification date:*** Continuous beginning 4/1. Students must reply within 2 weeks of notification.

CONTACT Susan Brewer, Director of Financial Aid, University of Arkansas at Monticello, PO Box 3470, Monticello, AR 71656, 870-460-1050 or toll-free 800-844-1826 (in-state).

UNIVERSITY OF ARKANSAS AT PINE BLUFF

Pine Bluff, AR

Tuition & fees (AR res): $2620 **Average undergraduate aid package: N/A**

ABOUT THE INSTITUTION State-supported, coed. Awards: associate, bachelor's, and master's degrees. 52 undergraduate majors. Total enrollment: 3,040. Undergraduates: 2,974. Freshmen: 705. Federal methodology is used as a basis for awarding need-based institutional aid.

UNDERGRADUATE EXPENSES for 1999–2000 ***One-time required fee:*** $25. ***Tuition, state resident:*** full-time $2058; part-time $74 per semester hour. ***Tuition, nonresident:*** full-time $4760; part-time $170 per semester hour. ***Required fees:*** full-time $562; $14 per semester hour; $48 per term part-time. Full-time tuition and fees vary according to course load. Part-time tuition and fees vary according to course load. ***College room and board:*** $3940. Room and board charges vary according to board plan and housing facility. ***Payment plan:*** installment.

GIFT AID (NEED-BASED) ***Scholarships, grants, and awards:*** Federal Pell, FSEOG, state.

GIFT AID (NON-NEED-BASED) ***Scholarships, grants, and awards by category:*** *Academic Interests/Achievement:* agriculture, biological sciences, business, education, English, general academic interests/achievements, mathematics. *Creative Arts/Performance:* art/fine arts, music. *Special Achievements/Activities:* leadership. ***Tuition waivers:*** Full or partial for employees or children of employees, senior citizens. ***ROTC:*** Army.

LOANS ***Programs:*** FFEL (Subsidized and Unsubsidized Stafford, PLUS), Perkins, state.

WORK-STUDY Federal work-study jobs available.

APPLYING for FINANCIAL AID ***Required financial aid form:*** FAFSA. ***Financial aid deadline (priority):*** 4/15.

CONTACT Marilyn Cobbs, Financial Aid Officer, University of Arkansas at Pine Bluff, 1200 North University, PO Box 4985, Pine Bluff, AR 71611, 870-543-8302 or toll-free 800-264-6585 (in-state). *Fax:* 870-543-8019. *E-mail:* fnaid@vx4500.uapb.edu

UNIVERSITY OF ARKANSAS FOR MEDICAL SCIENCES

Little Rock, AR

CONTACT Financial Aid Office, University of Arkansas for Medical Sciences, 4301 West Markham, Little Rock, AR 72205-7199, 501-686-5000.

UNIVERSITY OF BALTIMORE

Baltimore, MD

Tuition & fees (MD res): $4122 **Average undergraduate aid package: N/A**

ABOUT THE INSTITUTION State-supported, coed. Awards: bachelor's, master's, doctoral, and first professional degrees. 23 undergraduate majors. Total enrollment: 4,611. Undergraduates: 1,934. Federal methodology is used as a basis for awarding need-based institutional aid.

UNDERGRADUATE EXPENSES for 1999–2000 ***Application fee:*** $20. ***Tuition, state resident:*** full-time $3542; part-time $163 per credit. ***Tuition, nonresident:*** full-time $10,884; part-time $454 per credit. ***Required fees:*** full-time $580; $20 per credit; $60 per term part-time. Full-time tuition and fees vary according to course level. ***Payment plan:*** deferred payment.

GIFT AID (NEED-BASED) ***Total amount:*** $1,292,593 (77% Federal, 23% state). ***Scholarships, grants, and awards:*** Federal Pell, FSEOG, state, college/university gift aid from institutional funds.

GIFT AID (NON-NEED-BASED) ***Total amount:*** $515,454 (100% institutional). ***Tuition waivers:*** Full or partial for employees or children of employees, senior citizens. ***ROTC:*** Army cooperative.

LOANS ***Student loans:*** $2,942,967 (100% need-based). ***Parent loans:*** $6596 (100% non-need-based). ***Programs:*** FFEL (Subsidized and Unsubsidized Stafford, PLUS), Perkins, college/university.

WORK-STUDY ***Federal work-study:*** *Total amount:* $135,162; jobs available.

ATHLETIC AWARDS *Total amount:* 29,496 (100% non-need-based).

APPLYING for FINANCIAL AID ***Required financial aid forms:*** FAFSA, institution's own form. ***Financial aid deadline (priority):*** 4/1.

CONTACT Financial Aid Office, University of Baltimore, 1420 North Charles Street, CH 123, Baltimore, MD 21201-5779, 410-837-4763 or toll-free 877-APPLYUB (in-state). *Fax:* 410-837-5493.

UNIVERSITY OF BIBLICAL STUDIES AND SEMINARY

Oklahoma City, OK

See American Bible College and Seminary

UNIVERSITY OF BRIDGEPORT

Bridgeport, CT

Tuition & fees: $14,641 **Average undergraduate aid package: $14,270**

ABOUT THE INSTITUTION Independent, coed. Awards: associate, bachelor's, master's, doctoral, and first professional degrees and post-master's certificates. 35 undergraduate majors. Total enrollment: 2,686. Undergraduates: 1,212. Freshmen: 195. Federal methodology is used as a basis for awarding need-based institutional aid.

UNDERGRADUATE EXPENSES for 1999–2000 ***Application fee:*** $40. ***Comprehensive fee:*** $21,611 includes full-time tuition ($13,800), mandatory fees ($841), and room and board ($6970). ***College room only:*** $3780. Full-time tuition and fees vary according to program. Room and board charges vary according to board plan. ***Part-time tuition:*** $330 per credit. ***Part-time fees:*** $50 per term part-time. Part-time tuition and fees vary according to program. ***Payment plans:*** installment, deferred payment.

FRESHMAN FINANCIAL AID (Fall 1998) 243 applied for aid. *Average percent of need met:* 95% (excluding resources awarded to replace EFC). *Average financial aid package:* $17,527 (excluding resources awarded to replace EFC). 1% of all full-time freshmen had no need and received non-need-based aid.

UNDERGRADUATE FINANCIAL AID (Fall 1998) 893 applied for aid. *Average percent of need met:* 88% (excluding resources awarded to replace EFC). *Average financial aid package:* $14,270 (excluding resources awarded to replace EFC). 1% of all full-time undergraduates had no need and received non-need-based aid.

GIFT AID (NEED-BASED) ***Total amount:*** $2,957,255 (36% Federal, 10% state, 54% institutional). ***Scholarships, grants, and awards:*** Federal Pell, FSEOG, state, college/university gift aid from institutional funds.

GIFT AID (NON-NEED-BASED) ***Total amount:*** $5,986,123 (88% institutional, 12% external sources). ***Scholarships, grants, and awards by category:*** *Academic Interests/Achievement:* general academic interests/achievements. *Special Characteristics:* children of faculty/staff, local/state students, parents of current students, siblings of current students, spouses of current students. ***Tuition waivers:*** Full or partial for employees or children of employees, senior citizens. ***ROTC:*** Army.

LOANS ***Student loans:*** $2,351,050 (80% need-based, 20% non-need-based). ***Parent loans:*** $129,794 (100% non-need-based). ***Programs:*** FFEL (Subsidized and Unsubsidized Stafford, PLUS), Perkins.

WORK-STUDY ***Federal work-study:*** *Total amount:* $215,432; jobs available. ***State or other work-study/employment:*** *Total amount:* $154,000 (100% non-need-based). Part-time jobs available.

ATHLETIC AWARDS *Total amount:* 839,710 (100% non-need-based).

APPLYING for FINANCIAL AID ***Required financial aid forms:*** FAFSA, institution's own form. ***Financial aid deadline (priority):*** 4/15. ***Notification date:*** Continuous. Students must reply within 4 weeks of notification.

CONTACT Jacklyn C. Stoltz, Director of Financial Aid, University of Bridgeport, 126 Park Avenue, Bridgeport, CT 06601, 203-576-4568 or toll-free 800-EXCEL-UB (in-state), 800-243-9496 (out-of-state). *Fax:* 203-576-4941. *E-mail:* jstoltz@bridgeport.edu

UNIVERSITY OF CALIFORNIA, BERKELEY

Berkeley, CA

Tuition & fees (CA res): $4046 **Average undergraduate aid package: $11,330**

ABOUT THE INSTITUTION State-supported, coed. Awards: bachelor's, master's, doctoral, and first professional degrees. 79 undergraduate majors. Total enrollment: 31,011. Undergraduates: 22,261. Freshmen: 3,727. Both federal and institutional methodology are used as a basis for awarding need-based institutional aid.

UNDERGRADUATE EXPENSES for 1999–2000 ***Application fee:*** $40. ***Tuition, state resident:*** full-time $0. ***Tuition, nonresident:*** full-time $9804. ***Required fees:*** full-time $4046. ***College room and board:*** $8266. Room and board charges vary according to housing facility. ***Payment plan:*** installment.

FRESHMAN FINANCIAL AID (Fall 1999) 2912 applied for aid; of those 62% were deemed to have need. 98% of freshmen with need received aid; of those 82% had need fully met. *Average percent of need met:* 99% (excluding resources awarded to replace EFC). *Average financial aid package:* $11,546 (excluding resources awarded to replace EFC). 29% of all full-time freshmen had no need and received non-need-based aid.

UNDERGRADUATE FINANCIAL AID (Fall 1999) 14,194 applied for aid; of those 73% were deemed to have need. 98% of undergraduates with need received aid; of those 82% had need fully met. *Average percent of need met:* 99% (excluding resources awarded to replace EFC). *Average financial aid package:* $11,330 (excluding resources awarded to replace EFC). 16% of all full-time undergraduates had no need and received non-need-based aid.

GIFT AID (NEED-BASED) ***Total amount:*** $68,453,260 (24% Federal, 27% state, 45% institutional, 4% external sources). ***Receiving aid:*** *Freshmen:* 39% (1,377); *all full-time undergraduates:* 42% (8,788). ***Average award:*** Freshmen: $7145; Undergraduates: $6701. ***Scholarships, grants, and awards:*** Federal Pell, FSEOG, state, private, college/university gift aid from institutional funds.

GIFT AID (NON-NEED-BASED) ***Total amount:*** $3,505,023 (44% institutional, 56% external sources). ***Receiving aid:*** *Freshmen:* 25% (873); *Undergraduates:* 14% (2,831). ***Scholarships, grants, and awards by category:*** *Academic Interests/Achievement:* engineering/technologies, general academic interests/achievements. *Creative Arts/Performance:* general creative arts/performance. *Special Achievements/Activities:* general special achievements/activities. *Special Characteristics:* general special characteristics. ***ROTC:*** Army, Naval, Air Force.

LOANS ***Student loans:*** $54,578,065 (81% need-based, 19% non-need-based). ***Average need-based loan:*** Freshmen: $3947; Undergraduates: $3537. ***Parent loans:*** $55,509,462 (52% need-based, 48% non-need-based). ***Programs:*** Federal Direct (Subsidized and Unsubsidized Stafford, PLUS), Perkins, college/university, alternative loans, TERI Loans, PLATO Loans.

WORK-STUDY ***Federal work-study:*** *Total amount:* $9,608,992; jobs available. ***State or other work-study/employment:*** *Total amount:* $837,488 (100% need-based). Part-time jobs available.

ATHLETIC AWARDS *Total amount:* 3,817,032 (35% need-based, 65% non-need-based).

APPLYING for FINANCIAL AID ***Required financial aid forms:*** FAFSA, state aid form. ***Financial aid deadline (priority):*** 3/2. ***Notification date:*** 4/14.

CONTACT Sandy Jensen, Executive Assistant to the Director of Financial Aid, University of California, Berkeley, 225 Sproul Hall, Berkeley, CA 94720-1960, 510-642-0649. *Fax:* 510-643-5526.

UNIVERSITY OF CALIFORNIA, DAVIS

Davis, CA

Tuition & fees (CA res): $4214 **Average undergraduate aid package: $9651**

ABOUT THE INSTITUTION State-supported, coed. Awards: bachelor's, master's, doctoral, and first professional degrees and post-bachelor's certificates. 77 undergraduate majors. Total enrollment: 25,092. Undergraduates: 19,517. Freshmen: 3,819. Both federal and institutional methodology are used as a basis for awarding need-based institutional aid.

UNDERGRADUATE EXPENSES for 1999–2000 ***Application fee:*** $40. ***Tuition, state resident:*** full-time $0. ***Tuition, nonresident:*** full-time $10,322; part-time $1596 per term. ***Required fees:*** full-time $4214; $903 per term part-time. ***College room and board:*** $7012. Room and board charges vary according to board plan and housing facility.

FRESHMAN FINANCIAL AID (Fall 1999, est.) 2604 applied for aid; of those 52% were deemed to have need. 96% of freshmen with need received aid; of those 35% had need fully met. *Average percent of need met:* 86% (excluding resources awarded to replace EFC). *Average financial aid package:* $10,412 (excluding resources awarded to replace EFC). 14% of all full-time freshmen had no need and received non-need-based aid.

UNDERGRADUATE FINANCIAL AID (Fall 1999, est.) 12,191 applied for aid; of those 72% were deemed to have need. 97% of undergraduates with need received aid; of those 29% had need fully met. *Average percent*

of need met: 86% (excluding resources awarded to replace EFC). *Average financial aid package:* $9651 (excluding resources awarded to replace EFC). 8% of all full-time undergraduates had no need and received non-need-based aid.

GIFT AID (NEED-BASED) ***Total amount:*** $44,461,340 (32% Federal, 34% state, 32% institutional, 2% external sources). ***Receiving aid:*** *Freshmen:* 37% (1,010); *all full-time undergraduates:* 41% (7,145). ***Average award:*** Freshmen: $5427; Undergraduates: $5255. ***Scholarships, grants, and awards:*** Federal Pell, FSEOG, state, private, college/university gift aid from institutional funds, Bureau of Indian Affairs Grants.

GIFT AID (NON-NEED-BASED) ***Total amount:*** $1,830,910 (58% institutional, 42% external sources). ***Scholarships, grants, and awards by category:*** *Academic Interests/Achievement:* agriculture, general academic interests/ achievements. ***Tuition waivers:*** Full or partial for employees or children of employees. ***ROTC:*** Army, Air Force cooperative.

LOANS ***Student loans:*** $46,123,474 (94% need-based, 6% non-need-based). ***Average need-based loan:*** Freshmen: $4053; Undergraduates: $4158. ***Parent loans:*** $10,476,052 (74% need-based, 26% non-need-based). ***Programs:*** Federal Direct (Subsidized and Unsubsidized Stafford, PLUS), Perkins, college/university.

WORK-STUDY ***Federal work-study:*** *Total amount:* $1,674,678; jobs available.

ATHLETIC AWARDS *Total amount:* 395,705 (42% need-based, 58% non-need-based).

APPLYING for FINANCIAL AID ***Required financial aid forms:*** FAFSA, state aid form. ***Financial aid deadline (priority):*** 3/2. ***Notification date:*** Continuous beginning 3/15. Students must reply within 3 weeks of notification.

CONTACT Ms. Patricia A. Kearney, Director of Financial Aid, University of California, Davis, 1 Shields Avenue, Davis, CA 95616, 530-752-2396. *Fax:* 530-752-7339.

UNIVERSITY OF CALIFORNIA, IRVINE

Irvine, CA

Tuition & fees (CA res): $3870 **Average undergraduate aid package: $11,254**

ABOUT THE INSTITUTION State-supported, coed. Awards: bachelor's, master's, doctoral, and first professional degrees. 47 undergraduate majors. Total enrollment: 19,149. Undergraduates: 15,235. Freshmen: 3,629. Federal methodology is used as a basis for awarding need-based institutional aid.

UNDERGRADUATE EXPENSES for 1999–2000 ***Application fee:*** $40. ***Tuition, state resident:*** full-time $0. ***Tuition, nonresident:*** full-time $9804; part-time $2475 per term. ***Required fees:*** full-time $3,870; $779 per term part-time. ***College room and board:*** $6407. Room and board charges vary according to board plan and housing facility. ***Payment plan:*** installment.

FRESHMAN FINANCIAL AID (Fall 1999) 2684 applied for aid; of those 71% were deemed to have need. 95% of freshmen with need received aid; of those 98% had need fully met. *Average percent of need met:* 89% (excluding resources awarded to replace EFC). *Average financial aid package:* $9244 (excluding resources awarded to replace EFC). 4% of all full-time freshmen had no need and received non-need-based aid.

UNDERGRADUATE FINANCIAL AID (Fall 1999) 10,434 applied for aid; of those 81% were deemed to have need. 95% of undergraduates with need received aid; of those 99% had need fully met. *Average percent of need met:* 90% (excluding resources awarded to replace EFC). *Average financial aid package:* $11,254 (excluding resources awarded to replace EFC). 3% of all full-time undergraduates had no need and received non-need-based aid.

GIFT AID (NEED-BASED) ***Total amount:*** $39,164,509 (34% Federal, 37% state, 29% institutional). ***Receiving aid:*** *Freshmen:* 37% (1,360); *all full-time undergraduates:* 40% (6,251). ***Average award:*** Freshmen: $3910; Undergraduates: $3835. ***Scholarships, grants, and awards:*** Federal Pell, FSEOG, state, private, college/university gift aid from institutional funds.

GIFT AID (NON-NEED-BASED) ***Total amount:*** $2,835,733 (4% state, 58% institutional, 38% external sources). ***Receiving aid:*** *Freshmen:* 9% (333); *Undergraduates:* 5% (770). ***Scholarships, grants, and awards by category:*** *Academic Interests/Achievement:* general academic interests/achievements. ***ROTC:*** Army cooperative, Air Force cooperative.

LOANS ***Student loans:*** $38,084,406 (71% need-based, 29% non-need-based). Average indebtedness per student: $13,199. ***Average need-based loan:*** Freshmen: $4362; Undergraduates: $4756. ***Parent loans:*** $40,233,429 (12% need-based, 88% non-need-based). ***Programs:*** Federal Direct (Subsidized and Unsubsidized Stafford, PLUS), Perkins, college/university.

WORK-STUDY ***Federal work-study:*** *Total amount:* $3,208,494; 1,973 jobs averaging $1626. ***State or other work-study/employment:*** *Total amount:* $130,205 (100% need-based). 70 part-time jobs averaging $1860.

ATHLETIC AWARDS *Total amount:* 939,773 (100% non-need-based).

APPLYING for FINANCIAL AID ***Required financial aid form:*** FAFSA. ***Financial aid deadline (priority):*** 3/2. ***Notification date:*** Continuous beginning 4/1. Students must reply by 5/1 or within 3 weeks of notification.

CONTACT Pat Wilhoit, Associate Director of Financial Aid, University of California, Irvine, 102 Administration Building, Irvine, CA 92697-2825, 949-824-7435. *E-mail:* pcwilhoi@uci.edu

UNIVERSITY OF CALIFORNIA, LOS ANGELES

Los Angeles, CA

Tuition & fees (CA res): $3683 **Average undergraduate aid package: $8764**

ABOUT THE INSTITUTION State-supported, coed. Awards: bachelor's, master's, doctoral, and first professional degrees. 86 undergraduate majors. Total enrollment: 36,350. Undergraduates: 24,668. Freshmen: 3,751. Federal methodology is used as a basis for awarding need-based institutional aid.

UNDERGRADUATE EXPENSES for 1999–2000 ***Application fee:*** $40. ***Tuition, state resident:*** full-time $3683. ***Tuition, nonresident:*** full-time $10,174. ***College room and board:*** $8565; ***room only:*** $2925. Room and board charges vary according to board plan and housing facility.

FRESHMAN FINANCIAL AID (Fall 1999) 2283 applied for aid; of those 94% were deemed to have need. 99% of freshmen with need received aid; of those 79% had need fully met. *Average percent of need met:* 71% (excluding resources awarded to replace EFC). *Average financial aid package:* $8409 (excluding resources awarded to replace EFC). 2% of all full-time freshmen had no need and received non-need-based aid.

UNDERGRADUATE FINANCIAL AID (Fall 1999) 14,397 applied for aid; of those 94% were deemed to have need. 98% of undergraduates with need received aid; of those 83% had need fully met. *Average percent of need met:* 79% (excluding resources awarded to replace EFC). *Average financial aid package:* $8764 (excluding resources awarded to replace EFC). 3% of all full-time undergraduates had no need and received non-need-based aid.

GIFT AID (NEED-BASED) ***Total amount:*** $72,592,002 (28% Federal, 32% state, 36% institutional, 4% external sources). ***Receiving aid:*** *Freshmen:* 39% (1,438); *all full-time undergraduates:* 46% (10,729). ***Average award:*** Freshmen: $7251; Undergraduates: $6570. ***Scholarships, grants, and awards:*** Federal Pell, FSEOG, state, private, college/university gift aid from institutional funds, United Negro College Fund, Federal Nursing, National Merit Scholarships.

GIFT AID (NON-NEED-BASED) ***Total amount:*** $1,595,794 (49% institutional, 51% external sources). ***Receiving aid:*** *Freshmen:* 23% (828); *Undergraduates:* 13% (3,126). ***Scholarships, grants, and awards by category:*** *Academic Interests/Achievement:* general academic interests/achievements. ***ROTC:*** Army, Naval, Air Force.

LOANS ***Student loans:*** $47,433,769 (100% need-based). 54% of past graduating class borrowed through all loan programs. Average indebtedness per student: $16,187. ***Average need-based loan:*** Freshmen: $2832; Undergraduates: $3594. ***Parent loans:*** $8,783,141 (10% need-based, 90% non-need-based). ***Programs:*** FFEL (Subsidized and Unsubsidized Stafford, PLUS), Perkins, Federal Nursing, state, college/university.

WORK-STUDY ***Federal work-study:*** *Total amount:* $5,437,000; jobs available. ***State or other work-study/employment:*** *Total amount:* $140,000 (100% need-based). Part-time jobs available.

ATHLETIC AWARDS *Total amount:* 3,642,672 (42% need-based, 58% non-need-based).

University of California, Los Angeles (continued)

APPLYING for FINANCIAL AID ***Required financial aid form:*** FAFSA. ***Financial aid deadline (priority):*** 3/2. ***Notification date:*** Continuous beginning 4/1.

CONTACT Ms. Yolanda Tan, Administrative Assistant, University of California, Los Angeles, Financial Aid Office, A-129 Murphy Hall, Los Angeles, CA 90095-1435, 310-206-0404. *E-mail:* finaid@saonet.ucla.edu

UNIVERSITY OF CALIFORNIA, RIVERSIDE

Riverside, CA

Tuition & fees (CA res): $4126 **Average undergraduate aid package: $8655**

ABOUT THE INSTITUTION State-supported, coed. Awards: bachelor's, master's, and doctoral degrees. 60 undergraduate majors. Total enrollment: 11,600. Undergraduates: 10,120. Freshmen: 2,721. Federal methodology is used as a basis for awarding need-based institutional aid.

UNDERGRADUATE EXPENSES for 1999–2000 ***Application fee:*** $40. ***Tuition, state resident:*** full-time $0. ***Tuition, nonresident:*** full-time $9804. ***Required fees:*** full-time $4126. ***College room and board:*** $6579. Room and board charges vary according to board plan and housing facility. ***Payment plans:*** installment, deferred payment.

FRESHMAN FINANCIAL AID (Fall 1999) 1808 applied for aid; of those 75% were deemed to have need. 97% of freshmen with need received aid; of those 45% had need fully met. *Average percent of need met:* 87% (excluding resources awarded to replace EFC). *Average financial aid package:* $8927 (excluding resources awarded to replace EFC). 19% of all full-time freshmen had no need and received non-need-based aid.

UNDERGRADUATE FINANCIAL AID (Fall 1999) 7,471 applied for aid; of those 81% were deemed to have need. 97% of undergraduates with need received aid; of those 43% had need fully met. *Average percent of need met:* 88% (excluding resources awarded to replace EFC). *Average financial aid package:* $8655 (excluding resources awarded to replace EFC). 15% of all full-time undergraduates had no need and received non-need-based aid.

GIFT AID (NEED-BASED) ***Total amount:*** $31,171,833 (35% Federal, 31% state, 32% institutional, 2% external sources). ***Receiving aid:*** *Freshmen:* 54% (1,183); *all full-time undergraduates:* 53% (5,182). ***Average award:*** Freshmen: $6877; Undergraduates: $5927. ***Scholarships, grants, and awards:*** Federal Pell, FSEOG, state, private, college/university gift aid from institutional funds.

GIFT AID (NON-NEED-BASED) ***Total amount:*** $1,566,083 (32% Federal, 3% state, 53% institutional, 12% external sources). ***Receiving aid:*** *Freshmen:* 13% (291); *Undergraduates:* 8% (755). ***Scholarships, grants, and awards by category:*** *Academic Interests/Achievement:* agriculture, area/ethnic studies, biological sciences, business, education, engineering/technologies, English, general academic interests/achievements, humanities, mathematics, physical sciences, premedicine, social sciences. *Creative Arts/Performance:* art/fine arts, creative writing, dance, music, theater/drama. ***ROTC:*** Army cooperative, Air Force cooperative.

LOANS ***Student loans:*** $23,939,820 (82% need-based, 18% non-need-based). ***Average need-based loan:*** Freshmen: $2362; Undergraduates: $3394. ***Parent loans:*** $8,586,166 (40% need-based, 60% non-need-based). ***Programs:*** Federal Direct (Subsidized and Unsubsidized Stafford, PLUS), Perkins, college/university.

WORK-STUDY ***Federal work-study:*** *Total amount:* $3,593,598; 2,085 jobs averaging $1875. ***State or other work-study/employment:*** *Total amount:* $89,083 (100% need-based). Part-time jobs available.

ATHLETIC AWARDS *Total amount:* 182,910 (29% need-based, 71% non-need-based).

APPLYING for FINANCIAL AID ***Required financial aid form:*** FAFSA. ***Financial aid deadline (priority):*** 3/2. ***Notification date:*** Continuous. Students must reply by 5/1 or within 3 weeks of notification.

CONTACT Ms. Sheryl Hayes, Director of Financial Aid, University of California, Riverside, 900 University Avenue, 1156 Hinderaker Hall, Riverside, CA 92521-0209, 909-787-3878. *E-mail:* finaid@pop.ucr.edu

UNIVERSITY OF CALIFORNIA, SAN DIEGO

La Jolla, CA

Tuition & fees (CA res): $3849 **Average undergraduate aid package: $9205**

ABOUT THE INSTITUTION State-supported, coed. Awards: bachelor's, master's, doctoral, and first professional degrees. 72 undergraduate majors. Total enrollment: 19,918. Undergraduates: 16,230. Federal methodology is used as a basis for awarding need-based institutional aid.

UNDERGRADUATE EXPENSES for 1999–2000 ***Application fee:*** $40. ***Tuition, state resident:*** full-time $0. ***Tuition, nonresident:*** full-time $10,174. ***Required fees:*** full-time $3849. ***College room and board:*** $7134. Room and board charges vary according to board plan. ***Payment plan:*** deferred payment.

FRESHMAN FINANCIAL AID (Fall 1999, est.) 2435 applied for aid; of those 66% were deemed to have need. 95% of freshmen with need received aid; of those 99% had need fully met. *Average financial aid package:* $9094 (excluding resources awarded to replace EFC). 6% of all full-time freshmen had no need and received non-need-based aid.

UNDERGRADUATE FINANCIAL AID (Fall 1999, est.) 10,768 applied for aid; of those 73% were deemed to have need. 96% of undergraduates with need received aid; of those 99% had need fully met. *Average financial aid package:* $9205 (excluding resources awarded to replace EFC). 8% of all full-time undergraduates had no need and received non-need-based aid.

GIFT AID (NEED-BASED) ***Total amount:*** $42,657,952 (30% Federal, 34% state, 33% institutional, 3% external sources). ***Receiving aid:*** *Freshmen:* 52% (1,372); *all full-time undergraduates:* 54% (6,722). ***Average award:*** Freshmen: $6034; Undergraduates: $6056. ***Scholarships, grants, and awards:*** Federal Pell, FSEOG, state, private, college/university gift aid from institutional funds.

GIFT AID (NON-NEED-BASED) ***Total amount:*** $2,980,126 (11% Federal, 50% state, 15% institutional, 24% external sources). ***Receiving aid:*** *Freshmen:* 15% (385); *Undergraduates:* 9% (1,112). ***Scholarships, grants, and awards by category:*** *Academic Interests/Achievement:* 861 awards ($1,480,452 total): biological sciences, business, communication, computer science, engineering/technologies, general academic interests/achievements, mathematics, physical sciences, premedicine, social sciences. *Creative Arts/Performance:* 3 awards ($11,000 total): journalism/publications, music, performing arts. *Special Achievements/Activities:* 48 awards ($64,500 total): community service, leadership. *Special Characteristics:* 126 awards ($180,111 total): ethnic background, first-generation college students, handicapped students, veterans' children.

LOANS ***Student loans:*** $35,384,491 (88% need-based, 12% non-need-based). Average indebtedness per student: $11,000. ***Average need-based loan:*** Freshmen: $3039; Undergraduates: $3742. ***Parent loans:*** $12,366,612 (59% need-based, 41% non-need-based). ***Programs:*** FFEL (Subsidized and Unsubsidized Stafford, PLUS), Perkins, college/university, alternative loans.

WORK-STUDY ***Federal work-study:*** *Total amount:* $7,764,514; 3,820 jobs averaging $2033. ***State or other work-study/employment:*** *Total amount:* $248,348 (100% need-based). 160 part-time jobs averaging $1552.

APPLYING for FINANCIAL AID ***Required financial aid forms:*** FAFSA, state aid form. ***Financial aid deadline (priority):*** 3/2. ***Notification date:*** Continuous beginning 3/15. Students must reply within 3 weeks of notification.

CONTACT Mr. Vincent DeAnda, Director of Student Financial Services, University of California, San Diego, 9500 Gilman Drive, La Jolla, CA 92093-0013, 858-534-3800. *E-mail:* vdeanda@ucsd.edu

UNIVERSITY OF CALIFORNIA, SANTA BARBARA

Santa Barbara, CA

Tuition & fees (CA res): $3844 **Average undergraduate aid package: $8851**

ABOUT THE INSTITUTION State-supported, coed. Awards: bachelor's, master's, and doctoral degrees. 63 undergraduate majors. Total enrollment: 20,056. Undergraduates: 17,699. Freshmen: 3,781. Federal methodology is used as a basis for awarding need-based institutional aid.

UNDERGRADUATE EXPENSES for 1999–2000 ***Application fee:*** $40. ***Tuition, state resident:*** full-time $0. ***Tuition, nonresident:*** full-time $10,174. ***Required fees:*** full-time $3844. ***College room and board:*** $7156. Room and board charges vary according to housing facility.

FRESHMAN FINANCIAL AID (Fall 1999) 2190 applied for aid; of those 77% were deemed to have need. 100% of freshmen with need received aid; of those 52% had need fully met. *Average percent of need met:* 89% (excluding resources awarded to replace EFC). *Average financial aid package:* $9446 (excluding resources awarded to replace EFC). 12% of all full-time freshmen had no need and received non-need-based aid.

UNDERGRADUATE FINANCIAL AID (Fall 1999) 9,276 applied for aid; of those 79% were deemed to have need. 100% of undergraduates with need received aid; of those 40% had need fully met. *Average percent of need met:* 87% (excluding resources awarded to replace EFC). *Average financial aid package:* $8851 (excluding resources awarded to replace EFC). 10% of all full-time undergraduates had no need and received non-need-based aid.

GIFT AID (NEED-BASED) ***Total amount:*** $36,539,264 (28% Federal, 30% state, 39% institutional, 3% external sources). ***Receiving aid:*** *Freshmen:* 36% (1,326); *all full-time undergraduates:* 34% (5,728). ***Average award:*** Freshmen: $7557; Undergraduates: $5923. ***Scholarships, grants, and awards:*** Federal Pell, FSEOG, state, college/university gift aid from institutional funds, endowed scholarships.

GIFT AID (NON-NEED-BASED) ***Total amount:*** $889,536 (58% institutional, 42% external sources). ***Receiving aid:*** *Freshmen:* 11% (427); *Undergraduates:* 5% (834). ***Scholarships, grants, and awards by category:*** *Academic Interests/Achievement:* general academic interests/achievements. ***Tuition waivers:*** Full or partial for employees or children of employees. ***ROTC:*** Army.

LOANS ***Student loans:*** $36,343,457 (81% need-based, 19% non-need-based). ***Average need-based loan:*** Freshmen: $3125; Undergraduates: $3767. ***Parent loans:*** $18,863,208 (56% need-based, 44% non-need-based). ***Programs:*** Federal Direct (Subsidized and Unsubsidized Stafford, PLUS), Perkins.

WORK-STUDY ***Federal work-study:*** *Total amount:* $1,530,637; jobs available.

ATHLETIC AWARDS *Total amount:* 1,257,441 (31% need-based, 69% non-need-based).

APPLYING for FINANCIAL AID ***Required financial aid form:*** FAFSA. ***Financial aid deadline:*** 5/31 (priority: 3/2). ***Notification date:*** Continuous. Students must reply by 8/15.

CONTACT Office of Financial Aid, University of California, Santa Barbara, Santa Barbara, CA 93106, 805-893-2432. *Fax:* 805-893-8793.

UNIVERSITY OF CALIFORNIA, SANTA CRUZ

Santa Cruz, CA

Tuition & fees (CA res): $4377 **Average undergraduate aid package: $10,036**

ABOUT THE INSTITUTION State-supported, coed. Awards: bachelor's, master's, and doctoral degrees. 58 undergraduate majors. Total enrollment: 11,302. Undergraduates: 10,269. Freshmen: 2,365. Both federal and institutional methodology are used as a basis for awarding need-based institutional aid.

UNDERGRADUATE EXPENSES for 1999–2000 ***Application fee:*** $40. ***Tuition, state resident:*** full-time $0. ***Tuition, nonresident:*** full-time $10,322. ***Required fees:*** full-time $4377. ***College room and board:*** $7337. Room and board charges vary according to board plan and housing facility. ***Payment plans:*** installment, deferred payment.

FRESHMAN FINANCIAL AID (Fall 1999) 1666 applied for aid; of those 62% were deemed to have need. 97% of freshmen with need received aid; of those 75% had need fully met. *Average percent of need met:* 96% (excluding resources awarded to replace EFC). *Average financial aid package:* $9539 (excluding resources awarded to replace EFC). 11% of all full-time freshmen had no need and received non-need-based aid.

UNDERGRADUATE FINANCIAL AID (Fall 1999) 6,190 applied for aid; of those 77% were deemed to have need. 97% of undergraduates with need received aid; of those 72% had need fully met. *Average percent of need met:* 96% (excluding resources awarded to replace EFC). *Average financial aid package:* $10,036 (excluding resources awarded to replace EFC). 8% of all full-time undergraduates had no need and received non-need-based aid.

GIFT AID (NEED-BASED) ***Total amount:*** $23,605,129 (29% Federal, 27% state, 41% institutional, 3% external sources). ***Receiving aid:*** *Freshmen:* 32% (727); *all full-time undergraduates:* 39% (3,797). ***Average award:*** Freshmen: $6145; Undergraduates: $5682. ***Scholarships, grants, and awards:*** Federal Pell, FSEOG, state, private, college/university gift aid from institutional funds.

GIFT AID (NON-NEED-BASED) ***Total amount:*** $939,171 (57% institutional, 43% external sources). ***Receiving aid:*** *Freshmen:* 10% (227); *Undergraduates:* 6% (536). ***Tuition waivers:*** Full or partial for senior citizens. ***ROTC:*** Army cooperative, Naval cooperative, Air Force cooperative.

LOANS ***Student loans:*** $21,745,638 (90% need-based, 10% non-need-based). 36% of past graduating class borrowed through all loan programs. Average indebtedness per student: $13,569. ***Average need-based loan:*** Freshmen: $3379; Undergraduates: $4034. ***Parent loans:*** $5,350,701 (49% need-based, 51% non-need-based). ***Programs:*** Federal Direct (Subsidized and Unsubsidized Stafford, PLUS), Perkins, college/university.

WORK-STUDY ***Federal work-study:*** *Total amount:* $5,897,020; jobs available. ***State or other work-study/employment:*** *Total amount:* $6170 (100% need-based). Part-time jobs available.

APPLYING for FINANCIAL AID ***Required financial aid form:*** FAFSA. ***Financial aid deadline (priority):*** 3/2. ***Notification date:*** Continuous beginning 5/1. Students must reply within 3 weeks of notification.

CONTACT Ms. Ann Draper, Associate Director of Financial Aid, University of California, Santa Cruz, 201 Hahn Student Services Building, Santa Cruz, CA 95064, 831-459-4358. *Fax:* 831-459-4631. *E-mail:* ann@cats.ucsc.edu

UNIVERSITY OF CENTRAL ARKANSAS

Conway, AR

Tuition & fees (AR res): $3402 **Average undergraduate aid package: N/A**

ABOUT THE INSTITUTION State-supported, coed. Awards: associate, bachelor's, master's, and doctoral degrees and post-master's certificates. 68 undergraduate majors. Total enrollment: 8,848. Undergraduates: 7,833. Freshmen: 1,837. Federal methodology is used as a basis for awarding need-based institutional aid.

UNDERGRADUATE EXPENSES for 2000–2001 ***Tuition, state resident:*** full-time $2856; part-time $119 per credit hour. ***Tuition, nonresident:*** full-time $5598; part-time $234 per credit hour. ***Required fees:*** full-time $546; $20 per credit hour; $29 per term part-time. Part-time tuition and fees vary according to course load. ***College room and board:*** $3290; ***room only:*** $1860. Room and board charges vary according to board plan and housing facility. ***Payment plan:*** installment.

GIFT AID (NEED-BASED) ***Scholarships, grants, and awards:*** Federal Pell, FSEOG, state, private.

GIFT AID (NON-NEED-BASED) ***Scholarships, grants, and awards by category:*** *Academic Interests/Achievement:* biological sciences, business, communication, computer science, education, English, general academic interests/achievements, home economics, humanities, library science, mathematics, physical sciences, social sciences. *Creative Arts/Performance:* applied art and design, art/fine arts, cinema/film/broadcasting, journalism/publications, music, performing arts, theater/drama. *Special Achievements/Activities:* cheerleading/drum major, junior miss, leadership. *Special Characteristics:* children of educators, children of faculty/staff, handicapped students. ***Tuition waivers:*** Full or partial for employees or children of employees, senior citizens. ***ROTC:*** Army.

LOANS ***Programs:*** Federal Direct (Subsidized and Unsubsidized Stafford, PLUS), Perkins.

WORK-STUDY Federal work-study jobs available.

APPLYING for FINANCIAL AID ***Required financial aid forms:*** FAFSA, institution's own form. ***Financial aid deadline (priority):*** 4/15.

University of Central Arkansas (continued)

CONTACT Ms. Terri Powers, Coordinator of Financial and Administrative Services, University of Central Arkansas, 201 Donaghey Avenue, Bernard Hall, Room 202, Conway, AR 72035, 501-450-5151 or toll-free 800-243-8245 (in-state). *Fax:* 501-450-5168. *E-mail:* terrip@ecom.uca.edu

UNIVERSITY OF CENTRAL FLORIDA

Orlando, FL

Tuition & fees (FL res): $2297 **Average undergraduate aid package: $2907**

ABOUT THE INSTITUTION State-supported, coed. Awards: associate, bachelor's, master's, and doctoral degrees. 74 undergraduate majors. Total enrollment: 31,673. Undergraduates: 26,485. Freshmen: 4,297. Federal methodology is used as a basis for awarding need-based institutional aid.

UNDERGRADUATE EXPENSES for 1999–2000 ***Application fee:*** $20. ***One-time required fee:*** $10. ***Tuition, state resident:*** full-time $2202; part-time $73 per semester hour. ***Tuition, nonresident:*** full-time $9191; part-time $306 per semester hour. ***Required fees:*** full-time $95; $47 per term part-time. Full-time tuition and fees vary according to course load. Part-time tuition and fees vary according to course load. ***College room and board:*** $5215; ***room only:*** $3000. Room and board charges vary according to board plan and housing facility. ***Payment plans:*** tuition prepayment, deferred payment.

FRESHMAN FINANCIAL AID (Fall 1999, est.) 2866 applied for aid; of those 49% were deemed to have need. 96% of freshmen with need received aid. *Average financial aid package:* $2650 (excluding resources awarded to replace EFC). 46% of all full-time freshmen had no need and received non-need-based aid.

UNDERGRADUATE FINANCIAL AID (Fall 1999, est.) 13,203 applied for aid; of those 62% were deemed to have need. 92% of undergraduates with need received aid. *Average financial aid package:* $2907 (excluding resources awarded to replace EFC). 29% of all full-time undergraduates had no need and received non-need-based aid.

GIFT AID (NEED-BASED) ***Total amount:*** $14,316,371 (76% Federal, 14% state, 10% institutional). ***Receiving aid:*** *Freshmen:* 17% (585); *all full-time undergraduates:* 22% (3,917). ***Average award:*** Freshmen: $1248; Undergraduates: $1388. ***Scholarships, grants, and awards:*** Federal Pell, FSEOG, state, private, college/university gift aid from institutional funds.

GIFT AID (NON-NEED-BASED) ***Total amount:*** $13,839,263 (52% state, 32% institutional, 16% external sources). ***Receiving aid:*** *Freshmen:* 33% (1,127); *Undergraduates:* 19% (3,432). ***Scholarships, grants, and awards by category:*** *Academic Interests/Achievement:* general academic interests/achievements. *Creative Arts/Performance:* music, theater/drama. *Special Achievements/Activities:* general special achievements/activities. *Special Characteristics:* members of minority groups. ***Tuition waivers:*** Full or partial for employees or children of employees, senior citizens. ***ROTC:*** Army, Air Force.

LOANS ***Student loans:*** $50,245,021 (62% need-based, 38% non-need-based). ***Average need-based loan:*** Freshmen: $1162; Undergraduates: $1975. ***Parent loans:*** $2,795,886 (100% non-need-based). ***Programs:*** FFEL (Subsidized and Unsubsidized Stafford, PLUS), Perkins, college/university.

WORK-STUDY ***Federal work-study:*** *Total amount:* $1,275,797; jobs available. ***State or other work-study/employment:*** *Total amount:* $27,486 (100% non-need-based). Part-time jobs available.

ATHLETIC AWARDS *Total amount:* 1,814,029 (100% non-need-based).

APPLYING for FINANCIAL AID ***Required financial aid forms:*** FAFSA, institution's own form. ***Financial aid deadline (priority):*** 3/1. ***Notification date:*** 4/1. Students must reply within 3 weeks of notification.

CONTACT Mr. Thomas S. Silarek, Financial Aid Coordinator, University of Central Florida, 4000 Central Florida Boulevard, Orlando, FL 32816, 407-823-3361. *Fax:* 407-823-5241.

UNIVERSITY OF CENTRAL OKLAHOMA

Edmond, OK

Tuition & fees (OK res): $1936 **Average undergraduate aid package: $4750**

ABOUT THE INSTITUTION State-supported, coed. Awards: bachelor's and master's degrees. 85 undergraduate majors. Total enrollment: 14,183. Undergraduates: 11,476. Freshmen: 1,626. Federal methodology is used as a basis for awarding need-based institutional aid.

UNDERGRADUATE EXPENSES for 1999–2000 ***Application fee:*** $15. ***Tuition, state resident:*** full-time $1470; part-time $49 per credit hour. ***Tuition, nonresident:*** full-time $3990; part-time $133 per credit hour. ***Required fees:*** full-time $466; $14 per credit hour; $20 per term part-time. Full-time tuition and fees vary according to course level, course load, program, and student level. Part-time tuition and fees vary according to course level, course load, program, and student level. ***College room and board:*** $2743. Room and board charges vary according to board plan and housing facility.

FRESHMAN FINANCIAL AID (Fall 1998) 743 applied for aid; of those 70% were deemed to have need. 83% of freshmen with need received aid; of those 86% had need fully met. *Average percent of need met:* 75% (excluding resources awarded to replace EFC). *Average financial aid package:* $3200 (excluding resources awarded to replace EFC). 33% of all full-time freshmen had no need and received non-need-based aid.

UNDERGRADUATE FINANCIAL AID (Fall 1998) 4,821 applied for aid; of those 84% were deemed to have need. 88% of undergraduates with need received aid; of those 56% had need fully met. *Average percent of need met:* 75% (excluding resources awarded to replace EFC). *Average financial aid package:* $4750 (excluding resources awarded to replace EFC). 23% of all full-time undergraduates had no need and received non-need-based aid.

GIFT AID (NEED-BASED) ***Total amount:*** $7,955,114 (70% Federal, 16% state, 3% institutional, 11% external sources). ***Receiving aid:*** *Freshmen:* 32% (374); *all full-time undergraduates:* 30% (2,209). ***Average award:*** Freshmen: $1200; Undergraduates: $1250. ***Scholarships, grants, and awards:*** Federal Pell, FSEOG, state, private, college/university gift aid from institutional funds.

GIFT AID (NON-NEED-BASED) ***Total amount:*** $1,067,118 (100% external sources). ***Receiving aid:*** *Freshmen:* 30% (349); *Undergraduates:* 20% (1,483). ***Scholarships, grants, and awards by category:*** *Academic Interests/Achievement:* biological sciences, business, computer science, education, foreign languages, general academic interests/achievements, health fields, home economics, mathematics, military science, physical sciences, social sciences. *Creative Arts/Performance:* applied art and design, art/fine arts, journalism/publications, music, theater/drama. *Special Achievements/Activities:* general special achievements/activities, leadership. *Special Characteristics:* ethnic background, members of minority groups. ***Tuition waivers:*** Full or partial for employees or children of employees. ***ROTC:*** Army.

LOANS ***Student loans:*** $17,082,649 (70% need-based, 30% non-need-based). Average indebtedness per student: $10,000. ***Average need-based loan:*** Freshmen: $1031; Undergraduates: $2020. ***Parent loans:*** $276,843 (100% non-need-based). ***Programs:*** FFEL (Subsidized and Unsubsidized Stafford, PLUS), Perkins.

WORK-STUDY ***Federal work-study:*** *Total amount:* $331,602; 210 jobs averaging $1684. ***State or other work-study/employment:*** *Total amount:* $1,451,711 (100% non-need-based). 581 part-time jobs available.

ATHLETIC AWARDS *Total amount:* 549,997 (35% need-based, 65% non-need-based).

APPLYING for FINANCIAL AID ***Required financial aid forms:*** FAFSA, institution's own form. ***Financial aid deadline (priority):*** 3/31. ***Notification date:*** Continuous beginning 5/1. Students must reply within 3 weeks of notification.

CONTACT Ms. Becky Garrett, Assistant Director, Technical Services, University of Central Oklahoma, 100 North University Drive, Edmond, OK 73034-5209, 405-974-2303 or toll-free 800-254-4215 (in-state). *Fax:* 405-340-7658. *E-mail:* bgarrett@ucok.edu

UNIVERSITY OF CHARLESTON

Charleston, WV

Tuition & fees: $13,200 **Average undergraduate aid package: $10,350**

ABOUT THE INSTITUTION Independent, coed. Awards: associate, bachelor's, and master's degrees. 38 undergraduate majors. Total enrollment: 1,214. Undergraduates: 1,162. Freshmen: 184. Federal methodology is used as a basis for awarding need-based institutional aid.

UNDERGRADUATE EXPENSES for 2000–2001 ***Application fee:*** $25. ***Comprehensive fee:*** $18,730 includes full-time tuition ($13,200) and room and board ($5530). Room and board charges vary according to board plan and housing facility. ***Part-time tuition:*** $275 per credit. Part-time tuition and fees vary according to course load and program. ***Payment plan:*** installment.

FRESHMAN FINANCIAL AID (Fall 1999, est.) 212 applied for aid; of those 71% were deemed to have need. 100% of freshmen with need received aid; of those 44% had need fully met. *Average percent of need met:* 87% (excluding resources awarded to replace EFC). *Average financial aid package:* $9875 (excluding resources awarded to replace EFC). 11% of all full-time freshmen had no need and received non-need-based aid.

UNDERGRADUATE FINANCIAL AID (Fall 1999, est.) 743 applied for aid; of those 88% were deemed to have need. 98% of undergraduates with need received aid; of those 49% had need fully met. *Average percent of need met:* 84% (excluding resources awarded to replace EFC). *Average financial aid package:* $10,350 (excluding resources awarded to replace EFC). 8% of all full-time undergraduates had no need and received non-need-based aid.

GIFT AID (NEED-BASED) ***Total amount:*** $2,408,500 (41% Federal, 19% state, 40% institutional). ***Receiving aid:*** *Freshmen:* 47% (109); *all full-time undergraduates:* 38% (310). ***Average award:*** Freshmen: $2550; Undergraduates: $2850. ***Scholarships, grants, and awards:*** Federal Pell, FSEOG, state, private, college/university gift aid from institutional funds, Council of Independent Colleges Tuition Exchange grants, Tuition Exchange Inc. grants.

GIFT AID (NON-NEED-BASED) ***Total amount:*** $1,498,312 (7% state, 74% institutional, 19% external sources). ***Receiving aid:*** *Freshmen:* 62% (143); *Undergraduates:* 62% (511). ***Scholarships, grants, and awards by category:*** *Academic Interests/Achievement:* general academic interests/achievements. *Creative Arts/Performance:* music. *Special Achievements/Activities:* community service, general special achievements/activities, leadership. *Special Characteristics:* children of educators, children of faculty/staff, international students, local/state students. ***Tuition waivers:*** Full or partial for employees or children of employees, senior citizens. ***ROTC:*** Army.

LOANS ***Student loans:*** $3,857,443 (62% need-based, 38% non-need-based). 86% of past graduating class borrowed through all loan programs. Average indebtedness per student: $18,950. ***Average need-based loan:*** Freshmen: $2650; Undergraduates: $4250. ***Parent loans:*** $371,110 (100% need-based). ***Programs:*** FFEL (Subsidized and Unsubsidized Stafford, PLUS), Perkins, Federal Nursing.

WORK-STUDY ***Federal work-study:*** *Total amount:* $136,518; jobs available. ***State or other work-study/employment:*** *Total amount:* $13,250 (100% need-based). 12 part-time jobs averaging $1104.

ATHLETIC AWARDS *Total amount:* 884,168 (100% non-need-based).

APPLYING for FINANCIAL AID ***Required financial aid forms:*** FAFSA, institution's own form. ***Financial aid deadline (priority):*** 3/1. ***Notification date:*** Continuous. Students must reply by 5/1 or within 4 weeks of notification.

CONTACT Ms. Janet M. Ruge, Director of Financial Aid, University of Charleston, 2300 MacCorkle Avenue SE, Charleston, WV 25304-1099, 304-357-4760 or toll-free 800-995-GOUC. *Fax:* 304-357-4769. *E-mail:* finaid@uchaswv.edu

UNIVERSITY OF CHICAGO

Chicago, IL

Tuition & fees: $24,234 **Average undergraduate aid package: N/A**

ABOUT THE INSTITUTION Independent, coed. Awards: bachelor's, master's, doctoral, and first professional degrees. 63 undergraduate majors. Total enrollment: 12,003. Undergraduates: 3,844. Freshmen: 1,005. Both federal and institutional methodology are used as a basis for awarding need-based institutional aid.

UNDERGRADUATE EXPENSES for 1999–2000 ***Application fee:*** $60. ***Comprehensive fee:*** $32,068 includes full-time tuition ($23,820), mandatory fees ($414), and room and board ($7834). ***College room only:*** $4378. ***Part-time tuition:*** $3337 per course. ***Part-time fees:*** $138 per term part-time. Part-time tuition and fees vary according to course load. ***Payment plans:*** tuition prepayment, installment.

GIFT AID (NEED-BASED) ***Scholarships, grants, and awards:*** Federal Pell, FSEOG, state, college/university gift aid from institutional funds.

GIFT AID (NON-NEED-BASED) ***Scholarships, grants, and awards by category:*** *Academic Interests/Achievement:* general academic interests/achievements. ***Tuition waivers:*** Full or partial for employees or children of employees. ***ROTC:*** Army cooperative, Air Force cooperative.

LOANS ***Student loans:*** 58% of past graduating class borrowed through all loan programs. Average indebtedness per student: $13,770. ***Programs:*** Federal Direct (Subsidized and Unsubsidized Stafford, PLUS), FFEL (Subsidized and Unsubsidized Stafford, PLUS), Perkins, college/university, alternative loans.

WORK-STUDY Federal work-study jobs available.

APPLYING for FINANCIAL AID ***Required financial aid forms:*** FAFSA, institution's own form, CSS Financial Aid PROFILE, noncustodial (divorced/separated) parent's statement, business/farm supplement. ***Financial aid deadline (priority):*** 2/1. ***Notification date:*** 4/5. Students must reply by 5/1.

CONTACT Ms. Alicia Reyes, Director of College Aid, University of Chicago, 1116 East 59th Street, Chicago, IL 60637, 773-702-8666. *Fax:* 773-702-5846. *E-mail:* areyes1@midway.uchicago.edu

UNIVERSITY OF CINCINNATI

Cincinnati, OH

Tuition & fees (OH res): $4998 **Average undergraduate aid package: $5087**

ABOUT THE INSTITUTION State-supported, coed. Awards: associate, bachelor's, master's, doctoral, and first professional degrees. 143 undergraduate majors. Total enrollment: 28,162. Undergraduates: 20,656. Freshmen: 3,846. Federal methodology is used as a basis for awarding need-based institutional aid.

UNDERGRADUATE EXPENSES for 1999–2000 ***Application fee:*** $30. ***Tuition, state resident:*** full-time $4257; part-time $139 per credit hour. ***Tuition, nonresident:*** full-time $12,138; part-time $358 per credit hour. ***Required fees:*** full-time $741. Full-time tuition and fees vary according to location. Part-time tuition and fees vary according to location. ***College room and board:*** $6399. ***Payment plan:*** installment.

FRESHMAN FINANCIAL AID (Fall 1998) 2151 applied for aid; of those 82% were deemed to have need. 97% of freshmen with need received aid; of those 43% had need fully met. *Average financial aid package:* $4546 (excluding resources awarded to replace EFC). 12% of all full-time freshmen had no need and received non-need-based aid.

UNDERGRADUATE FINANCIAL AID (Fall 1998) 6,679 applied for aid; of those 85% were deemed to have need. 99% of undergraduates with need received aid; of those 35% had need fully met. *Average financial aid package:* $5087 (excluding resources awarded to replace EFC). 8% of all full-time undergraduates had no need and received non-need-based aid.

GIFT AID (NEED-BASED) ***Total amount:*** $27,312,322 (52% Federal, 16% state, 27% institutional, 5% external sources). ***Receiving aid:*** *Freshmen:*

University of Cincinnati (continued)

36% (1,060); *all full-time undergraduates:* 20% (2,755). ***Scholarships, grants, and awards:*** Federal Pell, FSEOG, state, private, college/university gift aid from institutional funds, Federal Nursing.

GIFT AID (NON-NEED-BASED) ***Scholarships, grants, and awards by category:*** *Academic Interests/Achievement:* architecture, area/ethnic studies, biological sciences, business, communication, computer science, education, engineering/technologies, English, foreign languages, general academic interests/achievements, health fields, humanities, mathematics, military science, physical sciences, premedicine, social sciences. *Creative Arts/ Performance:* applied art and design, art/fine arts, music. *Special Achievements/Activities:* general special achievements/activities. *Special Characteristics:* children of faculty/staff, members of minority groups, out-of-state students. ***Tuition waivers:*** Full or partial for employees or children of employees. ***ROTC:*** Army, Air Force.

LOANS ***Student loans:*** $62,034,415 (61% need-based, 39% non-need-based). ***Parent loans:*** $25,345,167 (100% non-need-based). ***Programs:*** FFEL (Subsidized and Unsubsidized Stafford, PLUS), Perkins, Federal Nursing, state, college/university.

WORK-STUDY ***Federal work-study:*** *Total amount:* $2,940,270; 1,130 jobs averaging $2602.

ATHLETIC AWARDS *Total amount:* 3,130,769 (100% non-need-based).

APPLYING for FINANCIAL AID ***Required financial aid form:*** FAFSA. ***Financial aid deadline:*** Continuous. ***Notification date:*** Continuous beginning 4/1. Students must reply within 2 weeks of notification.

CONTACT Ms. Ann Sexton, Associate Director of Student Financial Aid, University of Cincinnati, 52 Beecher Hall, Cincinnati, OH 45221-0125, 513-556-6994 or toll-free 800-827-8728 (in-state). *Fax:* 513-556-9171. *E-mail:* ann.sexton@uc.edu

UNIVERSITY OF COLORADO AT BOULDER

Boulder, CO

Tuition & fees (CO res): $3118 **Average undergraduate aid package: $8470**

ABOUT THE INSTITUTION State-supported, coed. Awards: bachelor's, master's, doctoral, and first professional degrees. 68 undergraduate majors. Total enrollment: 28,373. Undergraduates: 22,660. Freshmen: 4,596. Federal methodology is used as a basis for awarding need-based institutional aid.

UNDERGRADUATE EXPENSES for 1999–2000 ***Application fee:*** $40. ***One-time required fee:*** $35. ***Tuition, state resident:*** full-time $2444; part-time $148 per credit. ***Tuition, nonresident:*** full-time $15,224. ***Required fees:*** full-time $674; $215 per term part-time. Full-time tuition and fees vary according to program. Part-time tuition and fees vary according to course load and program. ***College room and board:*** $5202; ***room only:*** $2728. Room and board charges vary according to board plan, housing facility, and location. ***Payment plan:*** deferred payment.

FRESHMAN FINANCIAL AID (Fall 1998) 2509 applied for aid; of those 50% were deemed to have need. 100% of freshmen with need received aid; of those 19% had need fully met. *Average percent of need met:* 63% (excluding resources awarded to replace EFC). *Average financial aid package:* $6826 (excluding resources awarded to replace EFC). 23% of all full-time freshmen had no need and received non-need-based aid.

UNDERGRADUATE FINANCIAL AID (Fall 1998) 11,134 applied for aid; of those 59% were deemed to have need. 99% of undergraduates with need received aid; of those 22% had need fully met. *Average percent of need met:* 69% (excluding resources awarded to replace EFC). *Average financial aid package:* $8470 (excluding resources awarded to replace EFC). 16% of all full-time undergraduates had no need and received non-need-based aid.

GIFT AID (NEED-BASED) ***Total amount:*** $15,445,630 (47% Federal, 26% state, 24% institutional, 3% external sources). ***Receiving aid:*** *Freshmen:* 20% (856); *all full-time undergraduates:* 24% (4,814). ***Average award:*** Freshmen: $2847; Undergraduates: $2929. ***Scholarships, grants, and awards:*** Federal Pell, FSEOG, state, private, college/university gift aid from institutional funds.

GIFT AID (NON-NEED-BASED) ***Total amount:*** $8,651,674 (27% Federal, 8% state, 29% institutional, 36% external sources). ***Receiving aid:*** *Freshmen:* 13% (569); *Undergraduates:* 8% (1,620). ***Scholarships, grants, and awards by category:*** *Academic Interests/Achievement:* architecture, area/ethnic studies, biological sciences, business, communication, computer science, education, engineering/technologies, English, foreign languages, general academic interests/achievements, health fields, humanities, international studies, mathematics, military science, physical sciences, premedicine, religion/biblical studies, social sciences. *Creative Arts/ Performance:* art/fine arts, cinema/film/broadcasting, creative writing, dance, journalism/publications, music, performing arts, theater/drama. *Special Achievements/Activities:* community service, general special achievements/ activities, leadership. *Special Characteristics:* first-generation college students, general special characteristics, local/state students. ***Tuition waivers:*** Full or partial for senior citizens. ***ROTC:*** Army, Naval, Air Force.

LOANS ***Student loans:*** $44,024,511 (58% need-based, 42% non-need-based). 48% of past graduating class borrowed through all loan programs. Average indebtedness per student: $16,422. ***Average need-based loan:*** Freshmen: $2654; Undergraduates: $4023. ***Parent loans:*** $49,287,415 (100% non-need-based). ***Programs:*** Federal Direct (Subsidized and Unsubsidized Stafford, PLUS), Perkins, college/university, alternative loans.

WORK-STUDY ***Federal work-study:*** *Total amount:* $734,832; jobs available. ***State or other work-study/employment:*** *Total amount:* $1,902,951 (98% need-based, 2% non-need-based). 986 part-time jobs averaging $2104.

ATHLETIC AWARDS *Total amount:* 3,449,199 (100% non-need-based).

APPLYING for FINANCIAL AID ***Required financial aid forms:*** FAFSA, tax return. ***Financial aid deadline (priority):*** 4/1. ***Notification date:*** Continuous. Students must reply within 3 weeks of notification.

CONTACT Financial Aid Office, University of Colorado at Boulder, Room 2, Environmental Design Building, Campus Box 106, Boulder, CO 80309, 303-492-5091. *Fax:* 303-492-0838. *E-mail:* finaid@colorado.edu

UNIVERSITY OF COLORADO AT COLORADO SPRINGS

Colorado Springs, CO

Tuition & fees (CO res): $3191 **Average undergraduate aid package: $5787**

ABOUT THE INSTITUTION State-supported, coed. Awards: bachelor's, master's, and doctoral degrees. 34 undergraduate majors. Total enrollment: 6,615. Undergraduates: 4,957. Freshmen: 619. Federal methodology is used as a basis for awarding need-based institutional aid.

UNDERGRADUATE EXPENSES for 1999–2000 ***Application fee:*** $45. ***One-time required fee:*** $25. ***Tuition, state resident:*** full-time $2820; part-time $94 per credit. ***Tuition, nonresident:*** full-time $11,190; part-time $373 per credit. ***Required fees:*** full-time $371; $12 per credit; $371 per term part-time. Full-time tuition and fees vary according to program and student level. Part-time tuition and fees vary according to program and student level. ***College room and board:*** $5683. Room and board charges vary according to board plan and housing facility. ***Payment plan:*** deferred payment.

FRESHMAN FINANCIAL AID (Fall 1999, est.) 414 applied for aid; of those 60% were deemed to have need. 89% of freshmen with need received aid; of those 19% had need fully met. *Average percent of need met:* 62% (excluding resources awarded to replace EFC). *Average financial aid package:* $5086 (excluding resources awarded to replace EFC). 33% of all full-time freshmen had no need and received non-need-based aid.

UNDERGRADUATE FINANCIAL AID (Fall 1999, est.) 2,578 applied for aid; of those 70% were deemed to have need. 94% of undergraduates with need received aid; of those 13% had need fully met. *Average percent of need met:* 60% (excluding resources awarded to replace EFC). *Average financial aid package:* $5787 (excluding resources awarded to replace EFC). 10% of all full-time undergraduates had no need and received non-need-based aid.

GIFT AID (NEED-BASED) ***Total amount:*** $5,132,963 (49% Federal, 27% state, 17% institutional, 7% external sources). ***Receiving aid:*** *Freshmen:* 30% (171); *all full-time undergraduates:* 34% (1,170). ***Average award:***

Freshmen: $3323; Undergraduates: $3187. ***Scholarships, grants, and awards:*** Federal Pell, FSEOG, state, private, college/university gift aid from institutional funds.

GIFT AID (NON-NEED-BASED) ***Total amount:*** $43,050 (100% institutional). ***Receiving aid:*** *Freshmen:* 17% (98); *Undergraduates:* 12% (426). ***Scholarships, grants, and awards by category:*** *Academic Interests/Achievement:* biological sciences, business, computer science, education, engineering/technologies, English, general academic interests/achievements, health fields, mathematics, military science, physical sciences, premedicine. *Special Achievements/Activities:* community service, leadership. *Special Characteristics:* children and siblings of alumni, ethnic background, first-generation college students, general special characteristics, handicapped students, out-of-state students. ***Tuition waivers:*** Full or partial for employees or children of employees. ***ROTC:*** Army.

LOANS ***Student loans:*** $8,546,699 (100% need-based). Average indebtedness per student: $15,067. ***Average need-based loan:*** Freshmen: $2664; Undergraduates: $3581. ***Parent loans:*** $768,406 (100% need-based). ***Programs:*** FFEL (Subsidized and Unsubsidized Stafford, PLUS), Perkins, college/university.

WORK-STUDY ***Federal work-study:*** *Total amount:* $526,230; 147 jobs averaging $3580. ***State or other work-study/employment:*** *Total amount:* $538,971 (100% need-based). Part-time jobs available.

ATHLETIC AWARDS *Total amount:* 205,513 (100% non-need-based).

APPLYING for FINANCIAL AID ***Required financial aid form:*** FAFSA. ***Financial aid deadline (priority):*** 4/1. ***Notification date:*** Continuous beginning 4/15. Students must reply within 3 weeks of notification.

CONTACT Ms. Lee Ingalls-Noble, Director of Financial Aid, University of Colorado at Colorado Springs, 1420 Austin Bluffs Parkway, Colorado Springs, CO 80933-7150, 719-262-3466 or toll-free 800-990-8227 Ext. 3383.

UNIVERSITY OF COLORADO AT DENVER

Denver, CO

Tuition & fees (CO res): $2418 **Average undergraduate aid package: $5268**

ABOUT THE INSTITUTION State-supported, coed. Awards: bachelor's, master's, and doctoral degrees. 28 undergraduate majors. Total enrollment: 14,075. Undergraduates: 8,354. Freshmen: 454. Federal methodology is used as a basis for awarding need-based institutional aid.

UNDERGRADUATE EXPENSES for 1999–2000 ***Application fee:*** $40. ***One-time required fee:*** $25. ***Tuition, state resident:*** full-time $2068; part-time $126 per semester hour. ***Tuition, nonresident:*** full-time $11,194; part-time $672 per semester hour. ***Required fees:*** full-time $350; $3 per semester hour; $130 per term part-time. Full-time tuition and fees vary according to program. Part-time tuition and fees vary according to course load and program. ***Payment plans:*** installment, deferred payment.

FRESHMAN FINANCIAL AID (Fall 1998) 205 applied for aid; of those 85% were deemed to have need. 94% of freshmen with need received aid; of those 18% had need fully met. *Average percent of need met:* 54% (excluding resources awarded to replace EFC). *Average financial aid package:* $3514 (excluding resources awarded to replace EFC). 5% of all full-time freshmen had no need and received non-need-based aid.

UNDERGRADUATE FINANCIAL AID (Fall 1998) 1,966 applied for aid; of those 90% were deemed to have need. 89% of undergraduates with need received aid; of those 21% had need fully met. *Average percent of need met:* 58% (excluding resources awarded to replace EFC). *Average financial aid package:* $5268 (excluding resources awarded to replace EFC). 4% of all full-time undergraduates had no need and received non-need-based aid.

GIFT AID (NEED-BASED) ***Total amount:*** $3,767,588 (81% Federal, 14% state, 4% institutional, 1% external sources). ***Receiving aid:*** *Freshmen:* 23% (106); *all full-time undergraduates:* 26% (952). ***Average award:*** Freshmen: $2557; Undergraduates: $3143. ***Scholarships, grants, and awards:*** Federal Pell, FSEOG, state, private, college/university gift aid from institutional funds.

GIFT AID (NON-NEED-BASED) ***Total amount:*** $1,523,630 (2% Federal, 49% state, 34% institutional, 15% external sources). ***Receiving aid:*** *Freshmen:* 22% (99); *Undergraduates:* 14% (499). ***Scholarships, grants, and awards by category:*** *Academic Interests/Achievement:* 728 awards ($649,972 total): business, engineering/technologies, general academic interests/achievements. *Creative Arts/Performance:* 6 awards ($4938 total): general creative arts/performance. *Special Achievements/Activities:* 33 awards ($48,818 total): leadership. *Special Characteristics:* 371 awards ($654,190 total): children and siblings of alumni, children of educators, children of faculty/staff, children of public servants, first-generation college students, general special characteristics, handicapped students. ***Tuition waivers:*** Full or partial for employees or children of employees. ***ROTC:*** Army, Air Force cooperative.

LOANS ***Student loans:*** $11,234,919 (51% need-based, 49% non-need-based). Average indebtedness per student: $15,275. ***Average need-based loan:*** Freshmen: $1879; Undergraduates: $3499. ***Parent loans:*** $189,815 (100% non-need-based). ***Programs:*** FFEL (Subsidized and Unsubsidized Stafford, PLUS), Perkins, college/university.

WORK-STUDY ***Federal work-study:*** *Total amount:* $527,773; 158 jobs averaging $3340. ***State or other work-study/employment:*** *Total amount:* $701,172 (80% need-based, 20% non-need-based). 174 part-time jobs averaging $4029.

APPLYING for FINANCIAL AID ***Required financial aid forms:*** FAFSA, institution's own form. ***Financial aid deadline (priority):*** 3/1. ***Notification date:*** 5/1. Students must reply within 2 weeks of notification.

CONTACT Mr. Rodney C. Anderson, Executive Director, Student Financial Services, University of Colorado at Denver, PO Box 173364, Denver, CO 80217-3364, 303-556-3590. *Fax:* 303-556-2299.

UNIVERSITY OF COLORADO HEALTH SCIENCES CENTER

Denver, CO

ABOUT THE INSTITUTION State-supported, coed. Awards: bachelor's, master's, doctoral, and first professional degrees and post-master's and first-professional certificates. 3 undergraduate majors. Total enrollment: 2,224. Undergraduates: 513.

GIFT AID (NEED-BASED) ***Scholarships, grants, and awards:*** Federal Pell, FSEOG, state, private, college/university gift aid from institutional funds, Title VII scholarships.

GIFT AID (NON-NEED-BASED) ***Scholarships, grants, and awards by category:*** *Academic Interests/Achievement:* general academic interests/achievements, health fields. *Special Characteristics:* children of public servants, first-generation college students, general special characteristics, members of minority groups, parents of current students, previous college experience.

LOANS ***Programs:*** Federal Direct (Subsidized and Unsubsidized Stafford, PLUS), Perkins, Federal Nursing, college/university, Loans for Disadvantaged Students program (LDS).

WORK-STUDY Federal work-study jobs available.

APPLYING for FINANCIAL AID ***Required financial aid forms:*** FAFSA, institution's own form.

CONTACT Veronica Van Gulick, Manager, Client Services and Consumer Information, University of Colorado Health Sciences Center, 4200 East 9th Avenue, Box A088, Denver, CO 80262, 303-315-8364. *Fax:* 303-315-8539.

UNIVERSITY OF CONNECTICUT

Storrs, CT

Tuition & fees (CT res): $5404 **Average undergraduate aid package: $6904**

ABOUT THE INSTITUTION State-supported, coed. Awards: associate, bachelor's, master's, doctoral, and first professional degrees and post-master's certificates. 88 undergraduate majors. Total enrollment: 18,853. Undergraduates: 12,353. Freshmen: 2,956. Federal methodology is used as a basis for awarding need-based institutional aid.

UNDERGRADUATE EXPENSES for 1999–2000 ***Application fee:*** $50. ***Tuition, state resident:*** full-time $4158; part-time $173 per credit. ***Tuition, nonresident:*** full-time $12,676; part-time $528 per credit. ***Required fees:***

University of Connecticut (continued)

full-time $1246; $117 per credit. Part-time tuition and fees vary according to course load. ***College room and board:*** $5694; ***room only:*** $2894. Room and board charges vary according to board plan and housing facility. ***Payment plans:*** installment, deferred payment.

FRESHMAN FINANCIAL AID (Fall 1999) 75% of freshmen with need received aid; of those 28% had need fully met. *Average percent of need met:* 74% (excluding resources awarded to replace EFC). *Average financial aid package:* $6714 (excluding resources awarded to replace EFC).

UNDERGRADUATE FINANCIAL AID (Fall 1999) 83% of undergraduates with need received aid; of those 45% had need fully met. *Average percent of need met:* 83% (excluding resources awarded to replace EFC). *Average financial aid package:* $6904 (excluding resources awarded to replace EFC).

GIFT AID (NEED-BASED) ***Total amount:*** $15,347,627 (29% Federal, 31% state, 31% institutional, 9% external sources). ***Receiving aid:*** *Freshmen:* 1,316; *all full-time undergraduates:* 2,514. ***Average award:*** Freshmen: $2621; Undergraduates: $2326. ***Scholarships, grants, and awards:*** Federal Pell, FSEOG, state, private, college/university gift aid from institutional funds.

GIFT AID (NON-NEED-BASED) ***Total amount:*** $6,397,080 (84% institutional, 16% external sources). ***Receiving aid:*** *Freshmen:* 1,108; *Undergraduates:* 1,720. ***Scholarships, grants, and awards by category:*** *Academic Interests/Achievement:* general academic interests/achievements. *Creative Arts/Performance:* art/fine arts, music, theater/drama. ***Tuition waivers:*** Full or partial for employees or children of employees. ***ROTC:*** Army, Air Force.

LOANS ***Student loans:*** $28,991,566 (62% need-based, 38% non-need-based). 74% of past graduating class borrowed through all loan programs. Average indebtedness per student: $16,598. ***Average need-based loan:*** Freshmen: $3094; Undergraduates: $4533. ***Parent loans:*** $5,502,405 (50% need-based, 50% non-need-based). ***Programs:*** FFEL (Subsidized and Unsubsidized Stafford, PLUS), Perkins, state.

WORK-STUDY ***Federal work-study:*** *Total amount:* $2,800,014; 1,700 jobs averaging $1647.

ATHLETIC AWARDS *Total amount:* 3,651,381 (31% need-based, 69% non-need-based).

APPLYING for FINANCIAL AID ***Required financial aid form:*** FAFSA. ***Financial aid deadline (priority):*** 3/1. ***Notification date:*** Continuous. Students must reply within 3 weeks of notification.

CONTACT Client Service Staff, University of Connecticut, 233 Glenbrook Road, U-116, Storrs, CT 06269-4116, 860-486-2819.

UNIVERSITY OF DALLAS

Irving, TX

Tuition & fees: $14,420 **Average undergraduate aid package: $13,365**

ABOUT THE INSTITUTION Independent Roman Catholic, coed. Awards: bachelor's, master's, and doctoral degrees. 33 undergraduate majors. Total enrollment: 3,211. Undergraduates: 1,184. Freshmen: 310. Federal methodology is used as a basis for awarding need-based institutional aid.

UNDERGRADUATE EXPENSES for 1999–2000 ***Application fee:*** $40. ***Comprehensive fee:*** $19,866 includes full-time tuition ($14,354), mandatory fees ($66), and room and board ($5446). ***College room only:*** $2764. Room and board charges vary according to board plan and housing facility. ***Part-time tuition:*** $600 per credit. ***Part-time fees:*** $33 per term part-time. ***Payment plans:*** installment, deferred payment.

FRESHMAN FINANCIAL AID (Fall 1999) 300 applied for aid; of those 72% were deemed to have need. 100% of freshmen with need received aid; of those 20% had need fully met. *Average percent of need met:* 81% (excluding resources awarded to replace EFC). *Average financial aid package:* $13,665 (excluding resources awarded to replace EFC). 26% of all full-time freshmen had no need and received non-need-based aid.

UNDERGRADUATE FINANCIAL AID (Fall 1999) 1,051 applied for aid; of those 69% were deemed to have need. 100% of undergraduates with need received aid; of those 17% had need fully met. *Average percent of need met:* 80% (excluding resources awarded to replace EFC). *Average financial aid package:* $13,365 (excluding resources awarded to replace EFC). 26% of all full-time undergraduates had no need and received non-need-based aid.

GIFT AID (NEED-BASED) ***Total amount:*** $6,409,565 (10% Federal, 14% state, 73% institutional, 3% external sources). ***Receiving aid:*** *Freshmen:* 70% (216); *all full-time undergraduates:* 61% (720). ***Average award:*** Freshmen: $9838; Undergraduates: $9056. ***Scholarships, grants, and awards:*** Federal Pell, FSEOG, state, private, college/university gift aid from institutional funds.

GIFT AID (NON-NEED-BASED) ***Total amount:*** $2,485,296 (1% Federal, 96% institutional, 3% external sources). ***Receiving aid:*** *Freshmen:* 69% (213); *Undergraduates:* 58% (690). ***Scholarships, grants, and awards by category:*** *Academic Interests/Achievement:* foreign languages, general academic interests/achievements. *Creative Arts/Performance:* art/fine arts, performing arts. *Special Achievements/Activities:* leadership. *Special Characteristics:* children of faculty/staff, members of minority groups, siblings of current students. ***Tuition waivers:*** Full or partial for employees or children of employees. ***ROTC:*** Army cooperative, Air Force cooperative.

LOANS ***Student loans:*** $4,337,002 (75% need-based, 25% non-need-based). 85% of past graduating class borrowed through all loan programs. Average indebtedness per student: $15,300. ***Average need-based loan:*** Freshmen: $3378; Undergraduates: $4201. ***Parent loans:*** $828,360 (34% need-based, 66% non-need-based). ***Programs:*** Federal Direct (Subsidized and Unsubsidized Stafford, PLUS), Perkins, state, alternative loans.

WORK-STUDY ***Federal work-study:*** *Total amount:* $819,585; 399 jobs averaging $2054. ***State or other work-study/employment:*** *Total amount:* $143,061 (10% need-based, 90% non-need-based). 110 part-time jobs averaging $1290.

APPLYING for FINANCIAL AID ***Required financial aid forms:*** FAFSA, institution's own form, financial aid transcript (for transfers). ***Financial aid deadline (priority):*** 3/1. ***Notification date:*** Continuous. Students must reply within 2 weeks of notification.

CONTACT Larry Webb, Director of Enrollment, University of Dallas, 1845 East Northgate Drive, Irving, TX 75062, 972-721-5266 or toll-free 800-628-6999. *Fax:* 972-721-5017. *E-mail:* undadmis@acad.udallas.edu

UNIVERSITY OF DAYTON

Dayton, OH

Tuition & fees: $15,530 **Average undergraduate aid package: $11,032**

ABOUT THE INSTITUTION Independent Roman Catholic, coed. Awards: bachelor's, master's, doctoral, and first professional degrees. 75 undergraduate majors. Total enrollment: 10,185. Undergraduates: 6,906. Freshmen: 1,800. Both federal and institutional methodology are used as a basis for awarding need-based institutional aid.

UNDERGRADUATE EXPENSES for 1999–2000 ***Application fee:*** $30. ***Comprehensive fee:*** $20,400 includes full-time tuition ($15,020), mandatory fees ($510), and room and board ($4870). ***College room only:*** $2620. Full-time tuition and fees vary according to program. Room and board charges vary according to board plan, housing facility, and student level. ***Part-time tuition:*** $501 per semester hour. ***Part-time fees:*** $25 per term part-time. Part-time tuition and fees vary according to course load and program. ***Payment plans:*** installment, deferred payment.

FRESHMAN FINANCIAL AID (Fall 1999, est.) 1425 applied for aid; of those 77% were deemed to have need. 100% of freshmen with need received aid; of those 64% had need fully met. *Average percent of need met:* 81% (excluding resources awarded to replace EFC). *Average financial aid package:* $9904 (excluding resources awarded to replace EFC). 35% of all full-time freshmen had no need and received non-need-based aid.

UNDERGRADUATE FINANCIAL AID (Fall 1999, est.) 4,399 applied for aid; of those 80% were deemed to have need. 100% of undergraduates with need received aid; of those 70% had need fully met. *Average percent of need met:* 77% (excluding resources awarded to replace EFC). *Average financial aid package:* $11,032 (excluding resources awarded to replace EFC). 42% of all full-time undergraduates had no need and received non-need-based aid.

GIFT AID (NEED-BASED) ***Total amount:*** $25,528,572 (9% Federal, 13% state, 78% institutional). ***Receiving aid:*** *Freshmen:* 61% (1,092); *all full-time undergraduates:* 55% (3,534). ***Average award:*** Freshmen: $6731; Undergraduates: $7122. ***Scholarships, grants, and awards:*** Federal Pell, FSEOG, state, private, college/university gift aid from institutional funds.

GIFT AID (NON-NEED-BASED) ***Total amount:*** $10,792,910 (3% Federal, 14% state, 70% institutional, 13% external sources). ***Scholarships, grants, and awards by category:*** *Academic Interests/Achievement:* 3,231 awards ($14,319,388 total): business, education, engineering/technologies, general academic interests/achievements, humanities. *Creative Arts/Performance:* 78 awards ($162,600 total): art/fine arts, music. *Special Achievements/ Activities:* 420 awards ($652,000 total): general special achievements/ activities. *Special Characteristics:* 16 awards ($105,922 total): religious affiliation. ***Tuition waivers:*** Full or partial for employees or children of employees, senior citizens. ***ROTC:*** Army, Air Force cooperative.

LOANS ***Student loans:*** $15,387,806 (76% need-based, 24% non-need-based). 65% of past graduating class borrowed through all loan programs. Average indebtedness per student: $16,357. ***Average need-based loan:*** Freshmen: $2091; Undergraduates: $3328. ***Parent loans:*** $4,525,963 (77% need-based, 23% non-need-based). ***Programs:*** FFEL (Subsidized and Unsubsidized Stafford, PLUS), Perkins, state, college/university.

WORK-STUDY ***Federal work-study:*** *Total amount:* $648,309; 1,061 jobs averaging $1280. ***State or other work-study/employment:*** *Total amount:* $4,214,818 (100% non-need-based). Part-time jobs available.

ATHLETIC AWARDS *Total amount:* 1,601,634 (37% need-based, 63% non-need-based).

APPLYING for FINANCIAL AID ***Required financial aid form:*** FAFSA. ***Financial aid deadline (priority):*** 3/31. ***Notification date:*** Continuous.

CONTACT Joyce Wilkins, Director of Financial Aid, University of Dayton, 300 College Park Drive, Dayton, OH 45469-1621, 800-427-5029 or toll-free 800-837-7433. *Fax:* 937-229-4338. *E-mail:* jwilkins@udayton.edu

UNIVERSITY OF DELAWARE

Newark, DE

Tuition & fees (DE res): $4858 **Average undergraduate aid package: $8200**

ABOUT THE INSTITUTION State-related, coed. Awards: associate, bachelor's, master's, and doctoral degrees. 133 undergraduate majors. Total enrollment: 20,507. Undergraduates: 17,399. Freshmen: 3,503. Federal methodology is used as a basis for awarding need-based institutional aid.

UNDERGRADUATE EXPENSES for 1999–2000 ***Application fee:*** $45. ***Tuition, state resident:*** full-time $4380; part-time $183 per credit hour. ***Tuition, nonresident:*** full-time $12,750; part-time $531 per credit hour. ***Required fees:*** full-time $478; $15 per term part-time. ***College room and board:*** $5132; ***room only:*** $2810. Room and board charges vary according to housing facility. ***Payment plans:*** tuition prepayment, installment.

FRESHMAN FINANCIAL AID (Fall 1999, est.) 2400 applied for aid; of those 57% were deemed to have need. 100% of freshmen with need received aid; of those 54% had need fully met. *Average percent of need met:* 81% (excluding resources awarded to replace EFC). *Average financial aid package:* $7500 (excluding resources awarded to replace EFC). 21% of all full-time freshmen had no need and received non-need-based aid.

UNDERGRADUATE FINANCIAL AID (Fall 1999, est.) 7,778 applied for aid; of those 64% were deemed to have need. 100% of undergraduates with need received aid; of those 55% had need fully met. *Average percent of need met:* 82% (excluding resources awarded to replace EFC). *Average financial aid package:* $8200 (excluding resources awarded to replace EFC). 18% of all full-time undergraduates had no need and received non-need-based aid.

GIFT AID (NEED-BASED) ***Total amount:*** $17,900,000 (20% Federal, 22% state, 42% institutional, 16% external sources). ***Receiving aid:*** *Freshmen:* 31% (1,092); *all full-time undergraduates:* 28% (4,005). ***Average award:*** Freshmen: $5100; Undergraduates: $4700. ***Scholarships, grants, and awards:*** Federal Pell, FSEOG, state, private, college/university gift aid from institutional funds.

GIFT AID (NON-NEED-BASED) ***Total amount:*** $10,100,000 (12% state, 70% institutional, 18% external sources). ***Receiving aid:*** *Freshmen:* 12% (428); *Undergraduates:* 9% (1,248). ***Scholarships, grants, and awards by category:*** *Academic Interests/Achievement:* agriculture, biological sciences, business, education, engineering/technologies, general academic interests/achievements, home economics, humanities, physical sciences. *Creative Arts/Performance:* art/fine arts, music. *Special Achievements/ Activities:* cheerleading/drum major, leadership. *Special Characteristics:* children and siblings of alumni, children of public servants, general special characteristics, local/state students. ***Tuition waivers:*** Full or partial for employees or children of employees, senior citizens. ***ROTC:*** Army, Air Force.

LOANS ***Student loans:*** $31,100,000 (69% need-based, 31% non-need-based). Average indebtedness per student: $14,000. ***Average need-based loan:*** Freshmen: $3200; Undergraduates: $4000. ***Parent loans:*** $13,100,000 (63% need-based, 37% non-need-based). ***Programs:*** Federal Direct (Subsidized and Unsubsidized Stafford, PLUS), Perkins, Federal Nursing.

WORK-STUDY ***Federal work-study:*** *Total amount:* $1,520,000; jobs available. ***State or other work-study/employment:*** *Total amount:* $240,000 (100% need-based). Part-time jobs available.

ATHLETIC AWARDS *Total amount:* 3,400,000 (29% need-based, 71% non-need-based).

APPLYING for FINANCIAL AID ***Required financial aid form:*** FAFSA. ***Financial aid deadline:*** 3/15 (priority: 2/1). ***Notification date:*** Continuous. Students must reply by 5/1 or within 2 weeks of notification.

CONTACT Mr. Johnie A. Burton, Director of Scholarships and Financial Aid, University of Delaware, 224 Hullihen Hall, Newark, DE 19716, 302-831-8081.

UNIVERSITY OF DENVER

Denver, CO

CONTACT Mrs. Colleen Hillmeyer, Director of Financial Aid, University of Denver, Office of Financial Aid, MRB 222, Denver, CO 80208, 303-871-2331 or toll-free 800-525-9495 (out-of-state). *E-mail:* fao1@denver.du.edu

UNIVERSITY OF DETROIT MERCY

Detroit, MI

Tuition & fees: $14,332 **Average undergraduate aid package: $13,602**

ABOUT THE INSTITUTION Independent Roman Catholic (Jesuit), coed. Awards: associate, bachelor's, master's, doctoral, and first professional degrees and post-bachelor's and post-master's certificates. 59 undergraduate majors. Total enrollment: 6,212. Undergraduates: 3,932. Freshmen: 448. Federal methodology is used as a basis for awarding need-based institutional aid.

UNDERGRADUATE EXPENSES for 1999–2000 ***Application fee:*** $25. ***One-time required fee:*** $694. ***Comprehensive fee:*** $19,802 includes full-time tuition ($14,100), mandatory fees ($232), and room and board ($5470). ***College room only:*** $3300. Full-time tuition and fees vary according to program. Room and board charges vary according to board plan and housing facility. ***Part-time tuition:*** $350 per credit hour. ***Part-time fees:*** $83 per term part-time. Part-time tuition and fees vary according to program. ***Payment plans:*** installment, deferred payment.

FRESHMAN FINANCIAL AID (Fall 1999, est.) 423 applied for aid; of those 88% were deemed to have need. 100% of freshmen with need received aid; of those 25% had need fully met. *Average percent of need met:* 77% (excluding resources awarded to replace EFC). *Average financial aid package:* $14,827 (excluding resources awarded to replace EFC). 13% of all full-time freshmen had no need and received non-need-based aid.

UNDERGRADUATE FINANCIAL AID (Fall 1999, est.) 1,793 applied for aid; of those 93% were deemed to have need. 100% of undergraduates with need received aid; of those 18% had need fully met. *Average percent of need met:* 69% (excluding resources awarded to replace EFC). *Average financial aid package:* $13,602 (excluding resources awarded to replace EFC). 10% of all full-time undergraduates had no need and received non-need-based aid.

University of Detroit Mercy (continued)

GIFT AID (NEED-BASED) ***Total amount:*** $17,128,570 (23% Federal, 24% state, 53% institutional). ***Receiving aid:*** *Freshmen:* 84% (374); *all full-time undergraduates:* 79% (1,653). ***Average award:*** Freshmen: $10,281; Undergraduates: $8920. ***Scholarships, grants, and awards:*** Federal Pell, FSEOG, state, private, college/university gift aid from institutional funds, Federal Nursing.

GIFT AID (NON-NEED-BASED) ***Total amount:*** $2,544,774 (91% institutional, 9% external sources). ***Scholarships, grants, and awards by category:*** *Academic Interests/Achievement:* general academic interests/achievements. *Creative Arts/Performance:* theater/drama. *Special Achievements/Activities:* religious involvement. *Special Characteristics:* children and siblings of alumni, children of faculty/staff, members of minority groups. ***Tuition waivers:*** Full or partial for children of alumni, employees or children of employees, senior citizens. ***ROTC:*** Army cooperative.

LOANS ***Student loans:*** $15,850,620 (61% need-based, 39% non-need-based). 69% of past graduating class borrowed through all loan programs. Average indebtedness per student: $14,881. ***Average need-based loan:*** Freshmen: $2533; Undergraduates: $3015. ***Parent loans:*** $300,000 (100% non-need-based). ***Programs:*** FFEL (Subsidized and Unsubsidized Stafford, PLUS), Perkins, Federal Nursing, college/university.

WORK-STUDY ***Federal work-study:*** *Total amount:* $956,199; jobs available. ***State or other work-study/employment:*** *Total amount:* $137,110 (100% need-based).

ATHLETIC AWARDS *Total amount:* 1,735,740 (79% need-based, 21% non-need-based).

APPLYING for FINANCIAL AID ***Required financial aid form:*** FAFSA. ***Financial aid deadline (priority):*** 4/1. ***Notification date:*** Continuous. Students must reply within 2 weeks of notification.

CONTACT Sandy Ross, Financial Aid Officer, University of Detroit Mercy, PO Box 19900, Detroit, MI 48219-0900, 313-993-3350 or toll-free 800-635-5020 (out-of-state). *Fax:* 313-993-3347.

UNIVERSITY OF DUBUQUE

Dubuque, IA

Tuition & fees: $13,530 — **Average undergraduate aid package: $14,582**

ABOUT THE INSTITUTION Independent Presbyterian, coed. Awards: associate, bachelor's, master's, and first professional degrees. 20 undergraduate majors. Total enrollment: 956. Undergraduates: 680. Freshmen: 126. Federal methodology is used as a basis for awarding need-based institutional aid.

UNDERGRADUATE EXPENSES for 1999–2000 ***Application fee:*** $25. ***Comprehensive fee:*** $17,810 includes full-time tuition ($13,390), mandatory fees ($140), and room and board ($4280). ***College room only:*** $2220. Room and board charges vary according to board plan. ***Part-time tuition:*** $290 per semester hour. ***Payment plans:*** installment, deferred payment.

FRESHMAN FINANCIAL AID (Fall 1999, est.) 110 applied for aid; of those 95% were deemed to have need. 100% of freshmen with need received aid; of those 48% had need fully met. *Average percent of need met:* 91% (excluding resources awarded to replace EFC). *Average financial aid package:* $16,286 (excluding resources awarded to replace EFC).

UNDERGRADUATE FINANCIAL AID (Fall 1999, est.) 510 applied for aid; of those 96% were deemed to have need. 100% of undergraduates with need received aid; of those 37% had need fully met. *Average percent of need met:* 87% (excluding resources awarded to replace EFC). *Average financial aid package:* $14,582 (excluding resources awarded to replace EFC).

GIFT AID (NEED-BASED) ***Total amount:*** $4,102,556 (14% Federal, 19% state, 66% institutional, 1% external sources). ***Receiving aid:*** *Freshmen:* 88% (104); *all full-time undergraduates:* 93% (482). ***Average award:*** Freshmen: $8539; Undergraduates: $8268. ***Scholarships, grants, and awards:*** Federal Pell, FSEOG, state, private, college/university gift aid from institutional funds.

GIFT AID (NON-NEED-BASED) ***Total amount:*** $219,039 (90% institutional, 10% external sources). ***Receiving aid:*** *Freshmen:* 1% (1); *Undergraduates:* 3% (18). ***Scholarships, grants, and awards by category:*** *Academic Interests/Achievement:* general academic interests/achievements. *Creative Arts/Performance:* music. *Special Characteristics:* children and siblings of alumni, children of educators, children of faculty/staff, ethnic background, members of minority groups, out-of-state students, relatives of clergy, religious affiliation, siblings of current students. ***Tuition waivers:*** Full or partial for children of alumni, employees or children of employees, senior citizens.

LOANS ***Student loans:*** $3,807,212 (76% need-based, 24% non-need-based). 96% of past graduating class borrowed through all loan programs. Average indebtedness per student: $14,157. ***Average need-based loan:*** Freshmen: $6799; Undergraduates: $5719. ***Parent loans:*** $224,976 (33% need-based, 67% non-need-based). ***Programs:*** FFEL (Subsidized and Unsubsidized Stafford, PLUS), Perkins, state, college/university.

WORK-STUDY ***Federal work-study:*** *Total amount:* $292,484; jobs available.

APPLYING for FINANCIAL AID ***Required financial aid form:*** FAFSA. ***Financial aid deadline (priority):*** 4/1. ***Notification date:*** Continuous. Students must reply within 4 weeks of notification.

CONTACT Mr. Timothy Kremer, Director of Financial Aid, University of Dubuque, 2000 University Avenue, Dubuque, IA 52001-5050, 319-589-3170 or toll-free 800-722-5583 (in-state). *Fax:* 319-589-3690.

UNIVERSITY OF EVANSVILLE

Evansville, IN

Tuition & fees: N/R — **Average undergraduate aid package: $12,606**

ABOUT THE INSTITUTION Independent religious, coed. Awards: associate, bachelor's, and master's degrees. 71 undergraduate majors. Total enrollment: 2,821. Undergraduates: 2,796. Freshmen: 596. Both federal and institutional methodology are used as a basis for awarding need-based institutional aid.

FRESHMAN FINANCIAL AID (Fall 1999, est.) 521 applied for aid; of those 79% were deemed to have need. 100% of freshmen with need received aid; of those 32% had need fully met. *Average percent of need met:* 87% (excluding resources awarded to replace EFC). *Average financial aid package:* $13,261 (excluding resources awarded to replace EFC). 24% of all full-time freshmen had no need and received non-need-based aid.

UNDERGRADUATE FINANCIAL AID (Fall 1999, est.) 2,123 applied for aid; of those 75% were deemed to have need. 100% of undergraduates with need received aid; of those 32% had need fully met. *Average percent of need met:* 82% (excluding resources awarded to replace EFC). *Average financial aid package:* $12,606 (excluding resources awarded to replace EFC). 24% of all full-time undergraduates had no need and received non-need-based aid.

GIFT AID (NEED-BASED) ***Total amount:*** $12,949,362 (10% Federal, 24% state, 60% institutional, 6% external sources). ***Receiving aid:*** *Freshmen:* 68% (409); *all full-time undergraduates:* 59% (1,511). ***Average award:*** Freshmen: $6165; Undergraduates: $5804. ***Scholarships, grants, and awards:*** Federal Pell, FSEOG, state, private, college/university gift aid from institutional funds.

GIFT AID (NON-NEED-BASED) ***Total amount:*** $3,404,619 (92% institutional, 8% external sources). ***Receiving aid:*** *Freshmen:* 49% (295); *Undergraduates:* 50% (1,291). ***Scholarships, grants, and awards by category:*** *Academic Interests/Achievement:* 1,151 awards ($5,261,349 total): biological sciences, business, communication, computer science, education, engineering/technologies, English, foreign languages, general academic interests/achievements, health fields, humanities, international studies, mathematics, physical sciences, premedicine, religion/biblical studies, social sciences. *Creative Arts/Performance:* 212 awards ($998,895 total): art/fine arts, music, theater/drama. *Special Achievements/Activities:* 322 awards ($803,749 total): leadership. *Special Characteristics:* 254 awards ($1,060,245 total): children and siblings of alumni, international students, members of minority groups, religious affiliation, siblings of current students. ***Tuition waivers:*** Full or partial for employees or children of employees.

LOANS ***Student loans:*** $6,262,297 (91% need-based, 9% non-need-based). 60% of past graduating class borrowed through all loan programs. Average indebtedness per student: $15,688. ***Average need-based loan:***

Freshmen: $3936; Undergraduates: $4120. ***Parent loans:*** $3,048,989 (85% need-based, 15% non-need-based). ***Programs:*** FFEL (Subsidized and Unsubsidized Stafford, PLUS), Perkins, Federal Nursing, college/university.

WORK-STUDY ***Federal work-study:*** *Total amount:* $509,465; 399 jobs averaging $1277. ***State or other work-study/employment:*** *Total amount:* $75,750 (100% non-need-based). 77 part-time jobs averaging $1127.

ATHLETIC AWARDS *Total amount:* 2,433,363 (41% need-based, 59% non-need-based).

APPLYING for FINANCIAL AID ***Required financial aid forms:*** FAFSA, institution's own form. ***Financial aid deadline (priority):*** 3/1. ***Notification date:*** 3/21. Students must reply by 5/1.

CONTACT Ms. JoAnn E. Laugel, Director of Financial Aid, University of Evansville, 1800 Lincoln Avenue, Evansville, IN 47722-0002, 812-479-2364 or toll-free 800-992-5877 (in-state), 800-423-8633 (out-of-state). *Fax:* 812-479-2320. *E-mail:* jl25@evansville.edu

THE UNIVERSITY OF FINDLAY

Findlay, OH

Tuition & fees: $15,260 **Average undergraduate aid package: $14,200**

ABOUT THE INSTITUTION Independent religious, coed. Awards: associate, bachelor's, and master's degrees. 59 undergraduate majors. Total enrollment: 4,191. Undergraduates: 3,327. Freshmen: 653. Both federal and institutional methodology are used as a basis for awarding need-based institutional aid.

UNDERGRADUATE EXPENSES for 1999–2000 ***Comprehensive fee:*** $21,000 includes full-time tuition ($15,080), mandatory fees ($180), and room and board ($5740). ***College room only:*** $2800. Full-time tuition and fees vary according to location and program. ***Part-time tuition:*** $328 per semester hour. ***Part-time fees:*** $30 per term part-time. Part-time tuition and fees vary according to location and program. ***Payment plan:*** installment.

FRESHMAN FINANCIAL AID (Fall 1999, est.) 550 applied for aid; of those 91% were deemed to have need. 100% of freshmen with need received aid; of those 8% had need fully met. *Average percent of need met:* 87% (excluding resources awarded to replace EFC). *Average financial aid package:* $11,200 (excluding resources awarded to replace EFC). 6% of all full-time freshmen had no need and received non-need-based aid.

UNDERGRADUATE FINANCIAL AID (Fall 1999, est.) 2,225 applied for aid; of those 85% were deemed to have need. 100% of undergraduates with need received aid; of those 21% had need fully met. *Average percent of need met:* 94% (excluding resources awarded to replace EFC). *Average financial aid package:* $14,200 (excluding resources awarded to replace EFC). 8% of all full-time undergraduates had no need and received non-need-based aid.

GIFT AID (NEED-BASED) ***Total amount:*** $10,701,000 (15% Federal, 8% state, 77% institutional). ***Receiving aid:*** *Freshmen:* 84% (485); *all full-time undergraduates:* 59% (1,600). ***Average award:*** Freshmen: $7400; Undergraduates: $8700. ***Scholarships, grants, and awards:*** Federal Pell, FSEOG, state, college/university gift aid from institutional funds.

GIFT AID (NON-NEED-BASED) ***Total amount:*** $12,556,600 (14% state, 83% institutional, 3% external sources). ***Receiving aid:*** *Freshmen:* 19% (110); *Undergraduates:* 15% (400). ***Scholarships, grants, and awards by category:*** *Academic Interests/Achievement:* 960 awards ($3,900,000 total): foreign languages, general academic interests/achievements, physical sciences. *Creative Arts/Performance:* 110 awards ($94,000 total): music, theater/drama. *Special Characteristics:* 300 awards ($1,300,000 total): children and siblings of alumni, children of faculty/staff, parents of current students, religious affiliation, siblings of current students. ***Tuition waivers:*** Full or partial for employees or children of employees, senior citizens. ***ROTC:*** Air Force cooperative.

LOANS ***Student loans:*** $9,159,000 (66% need-based, 34% non-need-based). 80% of past graduating class borrowed through all loan programs. Average indebtedness per student: $17,500. ***Average need-based loan:*** Freshmen: $2400; Undergraduates: $4300. ***Parent loans:*** $2,000,000 (100% non-need-based). ***Programs:*** Federal Direct (Subsidized and Unsubsidized Stafford, PLUS), Perkins, college/university.

WORK-STUDY ***Federal work-study:*** *Total amount:* $370,000; 425 jobs averaging $800.

ATHLETIC AWARDS *Total amount:* 1,600,000 (100% non-need-based).

APPLYING for FINANCIAL AID ***Required financial aid form:*** FAFSA. ***Financial aid deadline:*** Continuous. ***Notification date:*** Continuous beginning 3/1.

CONTACT Mr. Charles Ernst, Assistant Director of Financial Aid, The University of Findlay, 1000 North Main Street, Findlay, OH 45840-3653, 419-424-4792 or toll-free 800-548-0932. *Fax:* 419-424-4898.

UNIVERSITY OF FLORIDA

Gainesville, FL

Tuition & fees (FL res): $2141 **Average undergraduate aid package: $7908**

ABOUT THE INSTITUTION State-supported, coed. Awards: associate, bachelor's, master's, doctoral, and first professional degrees. 100 undergraduate majors. Total enrollment: 43,382. Undergraduates: 31,633. Freshmen: 5,462. Federal methodology is used as a basis for awarding need-based institutional aid.

UNDERGRADUATE EXPENSES for 1999–2000 ***Application fee:*** $20. ***Tuition, state resident:*** full-time $2141; part-time $71 per semester hour. ***Tuition, nonresident:*** full-time $9130; part-time $304 per semester hour. ***College room and board:*** $5040; ***room only:*** $2670. Room and board charges vary according to board plan and housing facility. ***Payment plan:*** tuition prepayment.

FRESHMAN FINANCIAL AID (Fall 1998) 2848 applied for aid; of those 69% were deemed to have need. 99% of freshmen with need received aid. *Average percent of need met:* 78% (excluding resources awarded to replace EFC). *Average financial aid package:* $7028 (excluding resources awarded to replace EFC). 54% of all full-time freshmen had no need and received non-need-based aid.

UNDERGRADUATE FINANCIAL AID (Fall 1998) 15,644 applied for aid; of those 85% were deemed to have need. 99% of undergraduates with need received aid. *Average percent of need met:* 81% (excluding resources awarded to replace EFC). *Average financial aid package:* $7908 (excluding resources awarded to replace EFC). 34% of all full-time undergraduates had no need and received non-need-based aid.

GIFT AID (NEED-BASED) ***Total amount:*** $26,991,979 (65% Federal, 12% state, 23% institutional). ***Receiving aid:*** *Freshmen:* 18% (1,053); *all full-time undergraduates:* 24% (7,796). ***Average award:*** Freshmen: $3233; Undergraduates: $3318. ***Scholarships, grants, and awards:*** Federal Pell, FSEOG, state, private, college/university gift aid from institutional funds.

GIFT AID (NON-NEED-BASED) ***Total amount:*** $56,861,280 (1% Federal, 57% state, 14% institutional, 28% external sources). ***Receiving aid:*** *Freshmen:* 31% (1,787); *Undergraduates:* 20% (6,716). ***Scholarships, grants, and awards by category:*** *Academic Interests/Achievement:* agriculture, architecture, business, education, engineering/technologies, general academic interests/achievements. *Creative Arts/Performance:* art/fine arts, dance, general creative arts/performance, journalism/publications, music, performing arts, theater/drama. *Special Achievements/Activities:* community service, general special achievements/activities, leadership. *Special Characteristics:* members of minority groups, out-of-state students. ***Tuition waivers:*** Full or partial for employees or children of employees, senior citizens. ***ROTC:*** Army, Naval, Air Force.

LOANS ***Student loans:*** $54,973,036 (58% need-based, 42% non-need-based). ***Average need-based loan:*** Freshmen: $2491; Undergraduates: $3702. ***Parent loans:*** $8,090,976 (100% non-need-based). ***Programs:*** Federal Direct (Subsidized and Unsubsidized Stafford, PLUS), Perkins, state, college/university.

WORK-STUDY ***Federal work-study:*** *Total amount:* $1,787,715; 1,525 jobs averaging $1172. ***State or other work-study/employment:*** *Total amount:* $6,707,341 (100% non-need-based). 4,736 part-time jobs averaging $1416.

ATHLETIC AWARDS *Total amount:* 2,322,373 (100% non-need-based).

APPLYING for FINANCIAL AID ***Required financial aid form:*** FAFSA. ***Financial aid deadline (priority):*** 3/15. ***Notification date:*** Continuous beginning 4/1.

University of Florida (continued)

CONTACT Ms. Karen L. Fooks, Director of Student Financial Affairs, University of Florida, S-107 Criser Hall, PO Box 114025, Gainesville, FL 32611-4025, 352-392-1275. *Fax:* 352-392-2861. *E-mail:* kfooks@ufl.edu

UNIVERSITY OF GEORGIA

Athens, GA

Tuition & fees (GA res): $3024 **Average undergraduate aid package: $5371**

ABOUT THE INSTITUTION State-supported, coed. Awards: associate, bachelor's, master's, doctoral, and first professional degrees. 118 undergraduate majors. Total enrollment: 30,912. Undergraduates: 24,040. Freshmen: 4,398. Federal methodology is used as a basis for awarding need-based institutional aid.

UNDERGRADUATE EXPENSES for 1999–2000 ***Application fee:*** $25. ***Tuition, state resident:*** full-time $2414; part-time $101 per hour. ***Tuition, nonresident:*** full-time $9656; part-time $403 per hour. ***Required fees:*** full-time $610; $310 per term part-time. Full-time tuition and fees vary according to program. Part-time tuition and fees vary according to program. ***College room and board:*** $4902; ***room only:*** $2626. Room and board charges vary according to board plan and housing facility.

FRESHMAN FINANCIAL AID (Fall 1999, est.) 4048 applied for aid; of those 37% were deemed to have need. 99% of freshmen with need received aid; of those 40% had need fully met. *Average percent of need met:* 71% (excluding resources awarded to replace EFC). *Average financial aid package:* $4974 (excluding resources awarded to replace EFC). 59% of all full-time freshmen had no need and received non-need-based aid.

UNDERGRADUATE FINANCIAL AID (Fall 1999, est.) 17,489 applied for aid; of those 42% were deemed to have need. 98% of undergraduates with need received aid; of those 32% had need fully met. *Average percent of need met:* 66% (excluding resources awarded to replace EFC). *Average financial aid package:* $5371 (excluding resources awarded to replace EFC). 43% of all full-time undergraduates had no need and received non-need-based aid.

GIFT AID (NEED-BASED) ***Total amount:*** $20,872,891 (34% Federal, 60% state, 2% institutional, 4% external sources). ***Receiving aid:*** *Freshmen:* 33% (1,423); *all full-time undergraduates:* 28% (5,962). ***Average award:*** Freshmen: $3850; Undergraduates: $3542. ***Scholarships, grants, and awards:*** Federal Pell, FSEOG, state, private, college/university gift aid from institutional funds.

GIFT AID (NON-NEED-BASED) ***Total amount:*** $34,180,936 (92% state, 4% institutional, 4% external sources). ***Receiving aid:*** *Freshmen:* 9% (414); *Undergraduates:* 6% (1,210). ***Scholarships, grants, and awards by category:*** *Academic Interests/Achievement:* 21,261 awards ($47,870,618 total): agriculture, business, education, general academic interests/achievements. *Creative Arts/Performance:* 2 awards ($2150 total): debating, journalism/publications. *Special Characteristics:* 34 awards ($34,479 total): local/state students. ***Tuition waivers:*** Full or partial for employees or children of employees, senior citizens. ***ROTC:*** Army, Air Force.

LOANS ***Student loans:*** $35,571,094 (61% need-based, 39% non-need-based). 47% of past graduating class borrowed through all loan programs. Average indebtedness per student: $13,597. ***Average need-based loan:*** Freshmen: $2356; Undergraduates: $3680. ***Parent loans:*** $10,270,689 (22% need-based, 78% non-need-based). ***Programs:*** Federal Direct (Subsidized and Unsubsidized Stafford, PLUS), Perkins, state, college/university.

WORK-STUDY ***Federal work-study:*** *Total amount:* $832,067; 328 jobs averaging $2537.

ATHLETIC AWARDS *Total amount:* 3,150,977 (26% need-based, 74% non-need-based).

APPLYING for FINANCIAL AID ***Required financial aid form:*** FAFSA. ***Financial aid deadline (priority):*** 3/1. ***Notification date:*** 5/1. Students must reply within 2 weeks of notification.

CONTACT Mr. D. Ray Tripp, Director of Financial Aid, University of Georgia, 220 Academic Building, Athens, GA 30602-6114, 706-542-8208. *Fax:* 706-542-8217. *E-mail:* rtripp@arches.uga.edu

UNIVERSITY OF GREAT FALLS

Great Falls, MT

Tuition & fees: $8420 **Average undergraduate aid package: $9165**

ABOUT THE INSTITUTION Independent Roman Catholic, coed. Awards: associate, bachelor's, and master's degrees. 34 undergraduate majors. Total enrollment: 936. Undergraduates: 825. Freshmen: 119. Federal methodology is used as a basis for awarding need-based institutional aid.

UNDERGRADUATE EXPENSES for 1999–2000 ***Application fee:*** $25. ***One-time required fee:*** $8. ***Tuition:*** full-time $8160; part-time $255 per credit. ***Required fees:*** full-time $260; $5 per credit; $70 per term part-time. Full-time tuition and fees vary according to course load. Part-time tuition and fees vary according to course load. Room and board charges vary according to board plan. ***Payment plan:*** deferred payment.

FRESHMAN FINANCIAL AID (Fall 1999) 73 applied for aid; of those 100% were deemed to have need. 100% of freshmen with need received aid; of those 36% had need fully met. *Average percent of need met:* 80% (excluding resources awarded to replace EFC). *Average financial aid package:* $9771 (excluding resources awarded to replace EFC). 1% of all full-time freshmen had no need and received non-need-based aid.

UNDERGRADUATE FINANCIAL AID (Fall 1999) 467 applied for aid; of those 100% were deemed to have need. 100% of undergraduates with need received aid; of those 35% had need fully met. *Average percent of need met:* 90% (excluding resources awarded to replace EFC). *Average financial aid package:* $9165 (excluding resources awarded to replace EFC). 4% of all full-time undergraduates had no need and received non-need-based aid.

GIFT AID (NEED-BASED) ***Total amount:*** $1,825,263 (79% Federal, 10% state, 11% institutional). ***Receiving aid:*** *Freshmen:* 80% (66); *all full-time undergraduates:* 43% (237). ***Average award:*** Freshmen: $3115; Undergraduates: $3908. ***Scholarships, grants, and awards:*** Federal Pell, FSEOG, state, private, college/university gift aid from institutional funds, Junior Training Partnership Act and AFL-CIO Scholarships.

GIFT AID (NON-NEED-BASED) ***Total amount:*** $359,599 (86% institutional, 14% external sources). ***Receiving aid:*** *Freshmen:* 76% (62); *Undergraduates:* 56% (308). ***Scholarships, grants, and awards by category:*** *Academic Interests/Achievement:* 103 awards ($359,595 total): biological sciences, business, communication, computer science, education, general academic interests/achievements, health fields, humanities, mathematics, physical sciences, premedicine, religion/biblical studies, social sciences. *Special Characteristics:* 271 awards ($117,964 total): adult students, children of current students, children of faculty/staff, ethnic background, first-generation college students, general special characteristics, international students, religious affiliation. ***Tuition waivers:*** Full or partial for employees or children of employees, senior citizens.

LOANS ***Student loans:*** $5,265,371 (100% need-based). 90% of past graduating class borrowed through all loan programs. Average indebtedness per student: $20,750. ***Average need-based loan:*** Freshmen: $2526; Undergraduates: $5006. ***Parent loans:*** $390,347 (100% need-based). ***Programs:*** FFEL (Subsidized and Unsubsidized Stafford, PLUS), Perkins, college/university.

WORK-STUDY ***Federal work-study:*** *Total amount:* $434,129; 145 jobs averaging $2994. ***State or other work-study/employment:*** *Total amount:* $86,362 (100% need-based). Part-time jobs available.

APPLYING for FINANCIAL AID ***Required financial aid forms:*** FAFSA, institution's own form. ***Financial aid deadline (priority):*** 4/1. ***Notification date:*** 5/1. Students must reply within 2 weeks of notification.

CONTACT Ms. Sally Schuman, Director of Financial Aid, University of Great Falls, 1301 20th Street South, Great Falls, MT 59405, 406-791-5235 or toll-free 800-856-9544. *E-mail:* sschuman@ugf.edu

UNIVERSITY OF GUAM

Mangilao, GU

Tuition & fees: N/R **Average undergraduate aid package: N/A**

ABOUT THE INSTITUTION Territory-supported, coed. Awards: bachelor's and master's degrees. 36 undergraduate majors. Federal methodology is used as a basis for awarding need-based institutional aid.

GIFT AID (NEED-BASED) ***Scholarships, grants, and awards:*** Federal Pell, FSEOG, state, private.

GIFT AID (NON-NEED-BASED) ***Scholarships, grants, and awards by category:*** *Academic Interests/Achievement:* agriculture, business, communication, computer science, education, general academic interests/achievements, health fields. *Creative Arts/Performance:* art/fine arts, general creative arts/performance, journalism/publications, music, performing arts. *Special Characteristics:* children and siblings of alumni, children of faculty/staff, children of union members/company employees, international students. ***Tuition waivers:*** Full or partial for senior citizens. ***ROTC:*** Army.

LOANS ***Programs:*** Federal Direct (Subsidized and Unsubsidized Stafford), FFEL (Subsidized and Unsubsidized Stafford), territory.

WORK-STUDY Federal work-study jobs available.

APPLYING for FINANCIAL AID ***Required financial aid form:*** FAFSA. ***Financial aid deadline (priority):*** 6/30.

CONTACT Office of Financial Aid, University of Guam, UOG Station, Mangilao, GU 96923, 671-735-2280.

UNIVERSITY OF HARTFORD

West Hartford, CT

Tuition & fees: $19,696 **Average undergraduate aid package: $14,715**

ABOUT THE INSTITUTION Independent, coed. Awards: associate, bachelor's, master's, and doctoral degrees. 80 undergraduate majors. Total enrollment: 6,882. Undergraduates: 5,340. Freshmen: 1,410. Federal methodology is used as a basis for awarding need-based institutional aid.

UNDERGRADUATE EXPENSES for 2000–2001 ***Application fee:*** $35. ***Comprehensive fee:*** $27,536 includes full-time tuition ($18,626), mandatory fees ($1070), and room and board ($7840). ***College room only:*** $4836. Room and board charges vary according to board plan and housing facility. ***Part-time tuition:*** $285 per credit. ***Part-time fees:*** $110 per term part-time. Part-time tuition and fees vary according to course load. ***Payment plans:*** tuition prepayment, installment.

FRESHMAN FINANCIAL AID (Fall 1998) 736 applied for aid; of those 94% were deemed to have need. 99% of freshmen with need received aid. *Average percent of need met:* 70% (excluding resources awarded to replace EFC). *Average financial aid package:* $13,814 (excluding resources awarded to replace EFC). 21% of all full-time freshmen had no need and received non-need-based aid.

UNDERGRADUATE FINANCIAL AID (Fall 1998) 2,638 applied for aid; of those 93% were deemed to have need. 98% of undergraduates with need received aid. *Average percent of need met:* 70% (excluding resources awarded to replace EFC). *Average financial aid package:* $14,715 (excluding resources awarded to replace EFC). 13% of all full-time undergraduates had no need and received non-need-based aid.

GIFT AID (NEED-BASED) ***Total amount:*** $25,090,241 (9% Federal, 1% state, 89% institutional, 1% external sources). ***Receiving aid:*** *Freshmen:* 65% (657); *all full-time undergraduates:* 61% (2,267). ***Scholarships, grants, and awards:*** Federal Pell, FSEOG, state, private, college/university gift aid from institutional funds.

GIFT AID (NON-NEED-BASED) ***Total amount:*** $4,609,898 (96% institutional, 4% external sources). ***Receiving aid:*** *Freshmen:* 17% (173); *Undergraduates:* 16% (604). ***Scholarships, grants, and awards by category:*** *Academic Interests/Achievement:* general academic interests/achievements. *Creative Arts/Performance:* art/fine arts, dance, music, performing arts, theater/drama. *Special Characteristics:* children of current students, children of faculty/staff, international students, local/state students, parents of current students, siblings of current students, twins. ***Tuition waivers:*** Full or partial for employees or children of employees, senior citizens. ***ROTC:*** Army cooperative, Air Force cooperative.

LOANS ***Student loans:*** $17,586,541 (61% need-based, 39% non-need-based). ***Parent loans:*** $6,073,181 (100% need-based). ***Programs:*** FFEL (Subsidized and Unsubsidized Stafford, PLUS), Perkins.

WORK-STUDY ***Federal work-study:*** *Total amount:* $450,709; jobs available.

ATHLETIC AWARDS *Total amount:* 2,142,275 (25% need-based, 75% non-need-based).

APPLYING for FINANCIAL AID ***Required financial aid form:*** FAFSA. ***Financial aid deadline (priority):*** 2/1. ***Notification date:*** Continuous beginning 3/1. Students must reply by 5/1.

CONTACT Office of Admission and Student Financial Assistance, University of Hartford, 200 Bloomfield Avenue, West Hartford, CT 06117-1599, 860-768-4296 or toll-free 800-947-4303. *Fax:* 860-768-4961.

UNIVERSITY OF HAWAII AT HILO

Hilo, HI

Tuition & fees (HI res): $1466 **Average undergraduate aid package: $4248**

ABOUT THE INSTITUTION State-supported, coed. Awards: bachelor's degrees. 29 undergraduate majors. Total enrollment: 2,462. Undergraduates: 2,462. Freshmen: 345. Federal methodology is used as a basis for awarding need-based institutional aid.

UNDERGRADUATE EXPENSES for 1999–2000 ***Application fee:*** $25. ***Tuition, state resident:*** full-time $1416; part-time $59 per credit. ***Tuition, nonresident:*** full-time $7032; part-time $293 per credit. ***Required fees:*** full-time $50; $2 per credit; $5 per term part-time. Full-time tuition and fees vary according to course level and student level. Part-time tuition and fees vary according to course level and student level. ***College room and board:*** $4992. Room and board charges vary according to board plan and housing facility.

FRESHMAN FINANCIAL AID (Fall 1998) 240 applied for aid; of those 82% were deemed to have need. 85% of freshmen with need received aid; of those 33% had need fully met. *Average percent of need met:* 49% (excluding resources awarded to replace EFC). *Average financial aid package:* $5492 (excluding resources awarded to replace EFC). 1% of all full-time freshmen had no need and received non-need-based aid.

UNDERGRADUATE FINANCIAL AID (Fall 1998) 1,398 applied for aid; of those 93% were deemed to have need. 98% of undergraduates with need received aid; of those 51% had need fully met. *Average percent of need met:* 71% (excluding resources awarded to replace EFC). *Average financial aid package:* $4248 (excluding resources awarded to replace EFC). 1% of all full-time undergraduates had no need and received non-need-based aid.

GIFT AID (NEED-BASED) ***Total amount:*** $2,080,114 (98% Federal, 2% institutional). ***Receiving aid:*** *Freshmen:* 39% (137); *all full-time undergraduates:* 46% (936). ***Average award:*** Freshmen: $2232; Undergraduates: $3261. ***Scholarships, grants, and awards:*** Federal Pell, FSEOG, state, private, college/university gift aid from institutional funds.

GIFT AID (NON-NEED-BASED) ***Total amount:*** $1,773,324 (1% institutional, 99% external sources). ***Receiving aid:*** *Freshmen:* 7% (24); *Undergraduates:* 10% (198). ***Scholarships, grants, and awards by category:*** *Academic Interests/Achievement:* 21 awards ($12,810 total): agriculture, business, computer science, English, general academic interests/achievements, health fields, social sciences. *Creative Arts/Performance:* 5 awards ($1950 total): art/fine arts, music, performing arts, theater/drama. *Special Achievements/Activities:* 1 award ($500 total): community service, leadership. ***ROTC:*** Army cooperative.

LOANS ***Student loans:*** $2,039,614 (70% need-based, 30% non-need-based). 35% of past graduating class borrowed through all loan programs. Average indebtedness per student: $7600. ***Average need-based loan:*** Freshmen: $1362; Undergraduates: $4806. ***Parent loans:*** $180,315 (100% non-need-based). ***Programs:*** FFEL (Subsidized and Unsubsidized Stafford, PLUS), Perkins, state.

WORK-STUDY ***Federal work-study:*** *Total amount:* $379,293; 128 jobs averaging $2964. ***State or other work-study/employment:*** *Total amount:* $801,201 (100% non-need-based). 306 part-time jobs averaging $2618.

ATHLETIC AWARDS *Total amount:* 220,335 (100% non-need-based).

APPLYING for FINANCIAL AID ***Required financial aid forms:*** FAFSA, institution's own form. ***Financial aid deadline (priority):*** 3/1. ***Notification date:*** Continuous beginning 4/15. Students must reply within 2 weeks of notification.

University of Hawaii at Hilo (continued)

CONTACT Ms. Jean Coffman, Financial Aid Coordinator, University of Hawaii at Hilo, 200 West Kawili Street, Hilo, HI 96720-4091, 808-974-7324 or toll-free 800-897-4456. *Fax:* 808-974-7691. *E-mail:* jcoffman@uhhadc.uhh.hawaii.edu

UNIVERSITY OF HAWAII AT MANOA

Honolulu, HI

Tuition & fees (HI res): $3141   Average undergraduate aid package: $5686

ABOUT THE INSTITUTION State-supported, coed. Awards: bachelor's, master's, doctoral, and first professional degrees and post-bachelor's certificates. 72 undergraduate majors. Total enrollment: 17,612. Undergraduates: 11,939. Freshmen: 1,529. Federal methodology is used as a basis for awarding need-based institutional aid.

UNDERGRADUATE EXPENSES for 1999–2000 ***Application fee:*** $25. ***Tuition, state resident:*** full-time $3024; part-time $126 per credit. ***Tuition, nonresident:*** full-time $9504; part-time $396 per credit. ***Required fees:*** full-time $117; $48 per term part-time. Full-time tuition and fees vary according to class time, course load, and program. Part-time tuition and fees vary according to class time, course load, and program. ***College room and board:*** $5297; ***room only:*** $3125. Room and board charges vary according to board plan and housing facility.

FRESHMAN FINANCIAL AID (Fall 1998) 776 applied for aid; of those 52% were deemed to have need. 96% of freshmen with need received aid; of those 22% had need fully met. *Average percent of need met:* 70% (excluding resources awarded to replace EFC). *Average financial aid package:* $4026 (excluding resources awarded to replace EFC). 9% of all full-time freshmen had no need and received non-need-based aid.

UNDERGRADUATE FINANCIAL AID (Fall 1998) 4,278 applied for aid; of those 71% were deemed to have need. 97% of undergraduates with need received aid; of those 37% had need fully met. *Average percent of need met:* 77% (excluding resources awarded to replace EFC). *Average financial aid package:* $5686 (excluding resources awarded to replace EFC). 6% of all full-time undergraduates had no need and received non-need-based aid.

GIFT AID (NEED-BASED) ***Total amount:*** $7,473,140 (67% Federal, 3% state, 3% institutional, 27% external sources). ***Receiving aid:*** *Freshmen:* 23% (328); *all full-time undergraduates:* 25% (2,487). ***Average award:*** Freshmen: $2651; Undergraduates: $2811. ***Scholarships, grants, and awards:*** Federal Pell, FSEOG, state, private, college/university gift aid from institutional funds, Federal Nursing.

GIFT AID (NON-NEED-BASED) ***Total amount:*** $1,758,531 (36% institutional, 64% external sources). ***Receiving aid:*** *Freshmen:* 7% (97); *Undergraduates:* 6% (559). ***Scholarships, grants, and awards by category:*** *Academic Interests/Achievement:* general academic interests/achievements. *Creative Arts/Performance:* art/fine arts, dance, journalism/publications, music, performing arts, theater/drama. ***Tuition waivers:*** Full or partial for minority students, employees or children of employees, adult students. ***ROTC:*** Army, Air Force.

LOANS ***Student loans:*** $12,065,619 (72% need-based, 28% non-need-based). 29% of past graduating class borrowed through all loan programs. Average indebtedness per student: $12,161. ***Average need-based loan:*** Freshmen: $1353; Undergraduates: $2580. ***Parent loans:*** $1,266,511 (100% non-need-based). ***Programs:*** FFEL (Subsidized and Unsubsidized Stafford, PLUS), Perkins, Federal Nursing, state, college/university.

WORK-STUDY ***Federal work-study:*** *Total amount:* $551,163; jobs available.

ATHLETIC AWARDS *Total amount:* 3,912,905 (100% non-need-based).

APPLYING for FINANCIAL AID ***Required financial aid forms:*** FAFSA, institution's own form. ***Financial aid deadline (priority):*** 3/1. ***Notification date:*** Continuous beginning 4/1. Students must reply within 2 weeks of notification.

CONTACT Ms. Gail C. Koki, Director of Financial Aid Services, University of Hawaii at Manoa, 2600 Campus Road, Suite 112, Honolulu, HI 96822, 808-956-7251 or toll-free 800-823-9771. *Fax:* 808-956-3985. *E-mail:* finaid@kala.ssc.hawaii.edu

UNIVERSITY OF HAWAII–WEST OAHU

Pearl City, HI

Tuition & fees (HI res): $1906   Average undergraduate aid package: $4193

ABOUT THE INSTITUTION State-supported, coed. Awards: bachelor's degrees. 18 undergraduate majors. Total enrollment: 685. Undergraduates: 685. Federal methodology is used as a basis for awarding need-based institutional aid.

UNDERGRADUATE EXPENSES for 1999–2000 ***Application fee:*** $25. ***Tuition, state resident:*** full-time $1896; part-time $79 per credit. ***Tuition, nonresident:*** full-time $7032; part-time $293 per credit. ***Required fees:*** full-time $10; $5 per term part-time.

UNDERGRADUATE FINANCIAL AID (Fall 1999, est.) 135 applied for aid; of those 96% were deemed to have need. 84% of undergraduates with need received aid; of those 24% had need fully met. *Average percent of need met:* 62% (excluding resources awarded to replace EFC). *Average financial aid package:* $4193 (excluding resources awarded to replace EFC).

GIFT AID (NEED-BASED) ***Total amount:*** $475,000 (58% Federal, 42% external sources). ***Receiving aid:*** *All full-time undergraduates:* 28% (93). ***Average award:*** Undergraduates: $2999. ***Scholarships, grants, and awards:*** Federal Pell, FSEOG, state, college/university gift aid from institutional funds.

GIFT AID (NON-NEED-BASED) ***Total amount:*** $12,000 (42% institutional, 58% external sources). ***Receiving aid:*** *Undergraduates:* 1% (2). ***Scholarships, grants, and awards by category:*** *Academic Interests/Achievement:* 5 awards ($5000 total): general academic interests/achievements. ***Tuition waivers:*** Full or partial for senior citizens. ***ROTC:*** Army cooperative.

LOANS ***Student loans:*** $465,000 (97% need-based, 3% non-need-based). 18% of past graduating class borrowed through all loan programs. Average indebtedness per student: $7700. ***Average need-based loan:*** Undergraduates: $5400. ***Programs:*** FFEL (Subsidized and Unsubsidized Stafford), college/university.

WORK-STUDY ***Federal work-study:*** *Total amount:* $5500; 3 jobs averaging $1833. ***State or other work-study/employment:*** *Total amount:* $97,000 (100% non-need-based). Part-time jobs available.

APPLYING for FINANCIAL AID ***Required financial aid forms:*** FAFSA, institution's own form. ***Financial aid deadline (priority):*** 5/1. ***Notification date:*** 7/1. Students must reply within 2 weeks of notification.

CONTACT Lillian Yasuhara, Financial Aid Clerk, University of Hawaii–West Oahu, 96-129 Ala Ike, Pearl City, HI 96782-3366, 808-454-4700.

UNIVERSITY OF HOUSTON

Houston, TX

Tuition & fees (TX res): $2444   Average undergraduate aid package: N/A

ABOUT THE INSTITUTION State-supported, coed. Awards: bachelor's, master's, doctoral, and first professional degrees. 85 undergraduate majors. Total enrollment: 32,651. Undergraduates: 24,672. Freshmen: 3,303. Federal methodology is used as a basis for awarding need-based institutional aid.

UNDERGRADUATE EXPENSES for 2000–2001 (est.) ***Application fee:*** $40. ***Tuition, state resident:*** full-time $960; part-time $40 per credit hour. ***Tuition, nonresident:*** full-time $6120; part-time $255 per credit hour. ***Required fees:*** full-time $1484; $696 per term part-time. Full-time tuition and fees vary according to program. Part-time tuition and fees vary according to course load and program. ***College room and board:*** $4513; ***room only:*** $2553. Room and board charges vary according to board plan and housing facility. ***Payment plan:*** installment.

GIFT AID (NEED-BASED) ***Scholarships, grants, and awards:*** Federal Pell, FSEOG, state, private, college/university gift aid from institutional funds.

GIFT AID (NON-NEED-BASED) ***Scholarships, grants, and awards by category:*** *Academic Interests/Achievement:* biological sciences, business, computer science, education, engineering/technologies, English, general academic interests/achievements, health fields, humanities, military science, physical sciences, social sciences. *Creative Arts/Performance:* art/fine arts, creative writing, music, theater/drama. *Special Achievements/Activities:* leadership. ***ROTC:*** Army, Naval cooperative.

LOANS *Programs:* FFEL (Subsidized and Unsubsidized Stafford, PLUS), Perkins, college/university, alternative loans.

WORK-STUDY Federal work-study jobs available.

APPLYING for FINANCIAL AID *Required financial aid form:* FAFSA. ***Financial aid deadline (priority):*** 4/1. ***Notification date:*** 5/1.

CONTACT Financial Aid Office, University of Houston, 4800 Calhoun Road, Houston, TX 77204-2160, 713-743-1010. *Fax:* 713-743-9098. *E-mail:* sfa@bayou.uh.edu

UNIVERSITY OF HOUSTON–CLEAR LAKE

Houston, TX

Tuition & fees (TX res): $2138 **Average undergraduate aid package: $5597**

ABOUT THE INSTITUTION State-supported, coed. Awards: bachelor's and master's degrees. 31 undergraduate majors. Total enrollment: 6,806. Undergraduates: 3,484. Federal methodology is used as a basis for awarding need-based institutional aid.

UNDERGRADUATE EXPENSES for 1999–2000 *Application fee:* $30. ***Tuition, state resident:*** full-time $912; part-time $38 per semester hour. ***Tuition, nonresident:*** full-time $6096; part-time $254 per semester hour. ***Required fees:*** full-time $1226; $428 per term part-time. Part-time tuition and fees vary according to course load. ***Payment plan:*** installment.

UNDERGRADUATE FINANCIAL AID (Fall 1999, est.) 1,722 applied for aid; of those 90% were deemed to have need. 74% of undergraduates with need received aid; of those 27% had need fully met. *Average percent of need met:* 80% (excluding resources awarded to replace EFC). *Average financial aid package:* $5597 (excluding resources awarded to replace EFC).

GIFT AID (NEED-BASED) *Total amount:* $1,766,847 (90% Federal, 2% state, 8% institutional). ***Receiving aid:*** *All full-time undergraduates:* 53% (936). ***Average award:*** Undergraduates: $1266. ***Scholarships, grants, and awards:*** Federal Pell, FSEOG, state, college/university gift aid from institutional funds.

GIFT AID (NON-NEED-BASED) *Total amount:* $48,028 (82% institutional, 18% external sources). ***Receiving aid:*** *Undergraduates:* 22% (386). ***Scholarships, grants, and awards by category:*** *Academic Interests/Achievement:* biological sciences, business, computer science, education, humanities, mathematics, social sciences. *Special Achievements/Activities:* community service, general special achievements/activities, leadership. *Special Characteristics:* veterans, veterans' children. ***Tuition waivers:*** Full or partial for senior citizens. ***ROTC:*** Army cooperative.

LOANS *Student loans:* $4,938,915 (99% need-based, 1% non-need-based). ***Average need-based loan:*** Undergraduates: $2452. ***Programs:*** FFEL (Subsidized and Unsubsidized Stafford, PLUS), Perkins, state.

WORK-STUDY *Federal work-study:* *Total amount:* $69,305; 52 jobs available. ***State or other work-study/employment:*** *Total amount:* $9817 (100% need-based). 5 part-time jobs averaging $3000.

APPLYING for FINANCIAL AID *Required financial aid forms:* FAFSA, institution's own form. ***Financial aid deadline (priority):*** 6/1.

CONTACT Ms. JoAnne M. Greene, Director, Financial Aid and Veterans' Affairs, University of Houston–Clear Lake, 2700 Bay Area Boulevard, Houston, TX 77058-1098, 281-283-2485. *Fax:* 281-283-2502. *E-mail:* greene@cl.uh.edu

UNIVERSITY OF HOUSTON–DOWNTOWN

Houston, TX

Tuition & fees (TX res): $2316 **Average undergraduate aid package: $5201**

ABOUT THE INSTITUTION State-supported, coed. Awards: bachelor's degrees. 28 undergraduate majors. Total enrollment: 8,712. Undergraduates: 8,712. Freshmen: 970. Federal methodology is used as a basis for awarding need-based institutional aid.

UNDERGRADUATE EXPENSES for 1999–2000 *Application fee:* $10. ***Tuition, state resident:*** full-time $1140; part-time $38 per credit hour. ***Tuition, nonresident:*** full-time $7620; part-time $254 per credit hour. ***Required fees:*** full-time $1176; $275 per term part-time. Full-time tuition and fees vary according to course load. Part-time tuition and fees vary according to course load. ***Payment plan:*** installment.

FRESHMAN FINANCIAL AID (Fall 1999, est.) 418 applied for aid; of those 85% were deemed to have need. 100% of freshmen with need received aid; of those 14% had need fully met. *Average percent of need met:* 65% (excluding resources awarded to replace EFC). *Average financial aid package:* $4756 (excluding resources awarded to replace EFC). 7% of all full-time freshmen had no need and received non-need-based aid.

UNDERGRADUATE FINANCIAL AID (Fall 1999, est.) 1,718 applied for aid; of those 96% were deemed to have need. 100% of undergraduates with need received aid; of those 29% had need fully met. *Average percent of need met:* 71% (excluding resources awarded to replace EFC). *Average financial aid package:* $5201 (excluding resources awarded to replace EFC). 12% of all full-time undergraduates had no need and received non-need-based aid.

GIFT AID (NEED-BASED) *Total amount:* $6,065,759 (77% Federal, 4% state, 16% institutional, 3% external sources). ***Receiving aid:*** *Freshmen:* 48% (339); *all full-time undergraduates:* 42% (1,488). ***Average award:*** Freshmen: $2979; Undergraduates: $2674. ***Scholarships, grants, and awards:*** Federal Pell, FSEOG, state, college/university gift aid from institutional funds.

GIFT AID (NON-NEED-BASED) *Total amount:* $435,482 (1% state, 62% institutional, 37% external sources). ***Receiving aid:*** *Freshmen:* 2; *Undergraduates:* 6. ***Scholarships, grants, and awards by category:*** *Academic Interests/Achievement:* biological sciences, business, computer science, education, engineering/technologies, general academic interests/achievements, physical sciences. *Creative Arts/Performance:* art/fine arts, theater/drama. *Special Achievements/Activities:* community service, general special achievements/activities, leadership. ***Tuition waivers:*** Full or partial for senior citizens. ***ROTC:*** Army cooperative, Naval cooperative.

LOANS *Student loans:* $4,904,737 (75% need-based, 25% non-need-based). ***Average need-based loan:*** Freshmen: $357; Undergraduates: $1443. ***Parent loans:*** $13,829 (16% need-based, 84% non-need-based). ***Programs:*** FFEL (Subsidized and Unsubsidized Stafford, PLUS), state, college/university.

WORK-STUDY *Federal work-study:* *Total amount:* $309,335; 120 jobs averaging $2578. ***State or other work-study/employment:*** *Total amount:* $17,570 (100% need-based). 5 part-time jobs averaging $3514.

APPLYING for FINANCIAL AID *Required financial aid forms:* FAFSA, institution's own form. ***Financial aid deadline (priority):*** 4/1. ***Notification date:*** Continuous beginning 6/1.

CONTACT Lisa Beaudo, Director of Financial Aid, University of Houston–Downtown, One Main Street, Houston, TX 77002-1001, 713-221-8162. *Fax:* 713-221-8468. *E-mail:* beaudo@dt.uh.edu

UNIVERSITY OF HOUSTON–VICTORIA

Victoria, TX

Tuition & fees (TX res): $2004 **Average undergraduate aid package: $6709**

ABOUT THE INSTITUTION State-supported, coed. Awards: bachelor's and master's degrees. 6 undergraduate majors. Total enrollment: 1,526. Undergraduates: 832. Federal methodology is used as a basis for awarding need-based institutional aid.

UNDERGRADUATE EXPENSES for 1999–2000 *Tuition, state resident:* full-time $912; part-time $38 per credit hour. ***Tuition, nonresident:*** full-time $6096; part-time $254 per credit hour. ***Required fees:*** full-time $1092; $46 per credit hour. Full-time tuition and fees vary according to course load. Part-time tuition and fees vary according to course load. ***Payment plans:*** tuition prepayment, installment.

UNDERGRADUATE FINANCIAL AID (Fall 1998) 114 applied for aid; of those 94% were deemed to have need. 100% of undergraduates with need received aid; of those 17% had need fully met. *Average percent of need met:* 71% (excluding resources awarded to replace EFC). *Average*

University of Houston–Victoria (continued)

financial aid package: $6709 (excluding resources awarded to replace EFC). 21% of all full-time undergraduates had no need and received non-need-based aid.

GIFT AID (NEED-BASED) ***Total amount:*** $723,768 (62% Federal, 17% state, 19% institutional, 2% external sources). ***Receiving aid:*** *All full-time undergraduates:* 70% (94). ***Average award:*** Undergraduates: $2364. ***Scholarships, grants, and awards:*** Federal Pell, FSEOG, state, private, college/university gift aid from institutional funds.

GIFT AID (NON-NEED-BASED) ***Total amount:*** $152,520 (95% institutional, 5% external sources). ***Receiving aid:*** *Undergraduates:* 1% (2). ***Scholarships, grants, and awards by category:*** *Academic Interests/Achievement:* $281,112 total: business, communication, computer science, education, general academic interests/achievements, humanities, mathematics, social sciences. *Special Achievements/Activities:* $2475 total: leadership, memberships. ***Tuition waivers:*** Full or partial for senior citizens.

LOANS ***Student loans:*** $1,513,779 (84% need-based, 16% non-need-based). 97% of past graduating class borrowed through all loan programs. Average indebtedness per student: $12,530. ***Average need-based loan:*** Undergraduates: $4256. ***Parent loans:*** $6838 (100% non-need-based). ***Programs:*** FFEL (Subsidized and Unsubsidized Stafford, PLUS), state, college/university.

WORK-STUDY ***Federal work-study:*** *Total amount:* $39,344; 32 jobs averaging $1230. ***State or other work-study/employment:*** *Total amount:* $3340 (100% need-based). 2 part-time jobs averaging $1670.

APPLYING for FINANCIAL AID ***Required financial aid forms:*** FAFSA, institution's own form. ***Financial aid deadline (priority):*** 4/15. ***Notification date:*** Continuous beginning 7/1. Students must reply within 3 weeks of notification.

CONTACT Carolyn Mallory, Coordinator, Financial Aid, University of Houston–Victoria, 2506 East Red River, Victoria, TX 77901-4450, 361-788-6267 or toll-free 800-687-8648 (in-state). *Fax:* 361-582-1188. *E-mail:* malloryc@vic.uh.edu

UNIVERSITY OF IDAHO

Moscow, ID

Tuition & fees (ID res): $2348 **Average undergraduate aid package: $4800**

ABOUT THE INSTITUTION State-supported, coed. Awards: bachelor's, master's, doctoral, and first professional degrees and post-master's certificates. 109 undergraduate majors. Total enrollment: 11,305. Undergraduates: 8,591. Freshmen: 1,453. Federal methodology is used as a basis for awarding need-based institutional aid.

UNDERGRADUATE EXPENSES for 1999–2000 ***Application fee:*** $30. ***Tuition, state resident:*** full-time $0. ***Tuition, nonresident:*** full-time $6000; part-time $95 per credit. ***Required fees:*** full-time $2348; $117 per credit. Full-time tuition and fees vary according to program and reciprocity agreements. Part-time tuition and fees vary according to course load. ***College room and board:*** $3952. Room and board charges vary according to board plan and housing facility. ***Payment plan:*** deferred payment.

FRESHMAN FINANCIAL AID (Fall 1999) 1100 applied for aid; of those 80% were deemed to have need. 100% of freshmen with need received aid; of those 84% had need fully met. *Average percent of need met:* 80% (excluding resources awarded to replace EFC). *Average financial aid package:* $4200 (excluding resources awarded to replace EFC).

UNDERGRADUATE FINANCIAL AID (Fall 1999) 5,600 applied for aid; of those 92% were deemed to have need. 100% of undergraduates with need received aid; of those 83% had need fully met. *Average percent of need met:* 80% (excluding resources awarded to replace EFC). *Average financial aid package:* $4800 (excluding resources awarded to replace EFC).

GIFT AID (NEED-BASED) ***Total amount:*** $6,975,237 (89% Federal, 2% state, 9% institutional). ***Receiving aid:*** *Freshmen:* 40% (540); *all full-time undergraduates:* 43% (3,200). ***Scholarships, grants, and awards:*** Federal Pell, FSEOG, state, private, college/university gift aid from institutional funds.

GIFT AID (NON-NEED-BASED) ***Total amount:*** $6,156,029 (2% state, 79% institutional, 19% external sources). ***Receiving aid:*** *Freshmen:* 34% (460); *Undergraduates:* 34% (2,500). ***Scholarships, grants, and awards by category:*** *Academic Interests/Achievement:* agriculture, architecture, biological sciences, business, communication, computer science, education, engineering/technologies, English, foreign languages, general academic interests/achievements, home economics, humanities, mathematics, military science, physical sciences, premedicine, social sciences. *Creative Arts/Performance:* applied art and design, art/fine arts, creative writing, dance, general creative arts/performance, journalism/publications, music, performing arts, theater/drama. *Special Achievements/Activities:* cheerleading/drum major, general special achievements/activities, junior miss, leadership, rodeo. *Special Characteristics:* children and siblings of alumni, children of faculty/staff, ethnic background, first-generation college students, general special characteristics, handicapped students, international students, local/state students, members of minority groups, out-of-state students. ***Tuition waivers:*** Full or partial for employees or children of employees. ***ROTC:*** Army, Naval, Air Force cooperative.

LOANS ***Student loans:*** $28,752,736 (61% need-based, 39% non-need-based). 70% of past graduating class borrowed through all loan programs. Average indebtedness per student: $18,465. ***Parent loans:*** $632,635 (100% non-need-based). ***Programs:*** Federal Direct (Subsidized and Unsubsidized Stafford, PLUS), Perkins, college/university.

WORK-STUDY ***Federal work-study:*** *Total amount:* $745,675; jobs available. ***State or other work-study/employment:*** *Total amount:* $328,461 (100% need-based). Part-time jobs available.

ATHLETIC AWARDS *Total amount:* 2,163,388 (100% non-need-based).

APPLYING for FINANCIAL AID ***Required financial aid form:*** FAFSA. ***Financial aid deadline (priority):*** 2/15. ***Notification date:*** 4/1. Students must reply within 3 weeks of notification.

CONTACT Mr. Dan Davenport, Director of Admissions and Financial Aid, University of Idaho, Financial Aid Office, Moscow, ID 83844-4291, 208-885-6312 or toll-free 888-884-3246 (out-of-state). *Fax:* 208-885-5592. *E-mail:* dand@uidaho.edu

UNIVERSITY OF ILLINOIS AT CHICAGO

Chicago, IL

Tuition & fees (IL res): $4780 **Average undergraduate aid package: $11,200**

ABOUT THE INSTITUTION State-supported, coed. Awards: bachelor's, master's, doctoral, and first professional degrees and first-professional certificates. 76 undergraduate majors. Total enrollment: 24,429. Undergraduates: 16,160. Freshmen: 2,616. Federal methodology is used as a basis for awarding need-based institutional aid.

UNDERGRADUATE EXPENSES for 2000–2001 ***Application fee:*** $40. ***Tuition, state resident:*** full-time $3232; part-time $1077 per term. ***Tuition, nonresident:*** full-time $9696; part-time $3232 per term. ***Required fees:*** full-time $1548; $774 per term part-time. Full-time tuition and fees vary according to program. Part-time tuition and fees vary according to course load and program. ***College room and board:*** $5856. Room and board charges vary according to board plan and housing facility.

FRESHMAN FINANCIAL AID (Fall 1998) 2300 applied for aid; of those 78% were deemed to have need. 78% of freshmen with need received aid; of those 36% had need fully met. *Average percent of need met:* 85% (excluding resources awarded to replace EFC). *Average financial aid package:* $11,000 (excluding resources awarded to replace EFC). 27% of all full-time freshmen had no need and received non-need-based aid.

UNDERGRADUATE FINANCIAL AID (Fall 1998) 11,500 applied for aid; of those 84% were deemed to have need. 90% of undergraduates with need received aid; of those 31% had need fully met. *Average percent of need met:* 86% (excluding resources awarded to replace EFC). *Average financial aid package:* $11,200 (excluding resources awarded to replace EFC). 22% of all full-time undergraduates had no need and received non-need-based aid.

GIFT AID (NEED-BASED) ***Total amount:*** $40,784,000 (35% Federal, 61% state, 4% institutional). ***Receiving aid:*** *Freshmen:* 46% (1,200); *all full-time undergraduates:* 50% (8,100). ***Average award:*** Freshmen: $5200;

Undergraduates: $4700. ***Scholarships, grants, and awards:*** Federal Pell, FSEOG, state, private, college/university gift aid from institutional funds.

GIFT AID (NON-NEED-BASED) ***Total amount:*** $1,712,000 (8% state, 51% institutional, 41% external sources). ***Receiving aid:*** *Freshmen:* 12% (300); *Undergraduates:* 8% (1,300). ***Scholarships, grants, and awards by category:*** *Academic Interests/Achievement:* general academic interests/achievements. *Creative Arts/Performance:* applied art and design, art/fine arts, music, performing arts, theater/drama. *Special Achievements/Activities:* general special achievements/activities. *Special Characteristics:* children of faculty/staff, general special characteristics, members of minority groups, veterans, veterans' children. ***Tuition waivers:*** Full or partial for employees or children of employees, senior citizens. ***ROTC:*** Army, Naval cooperative, Air Force cooperative.

LOANS ***Student loans:*** $31,167,000 (65% need-based, 35% non-need-based). ***Average need-based loan:*** Freshmen: $2400; Undergraduates: $3100. ***Parent loans:*** $817,000 (40% need-based, 60% non-need-based). ***Programs:*** Federal Direct (Subsidized and Unsubsidized Stafford, PLUS), Perkins, Federal Nursing, college/university.

WORK-STUDY ***Federal work-study:*** *Total amount:* $829,000; jobs available. ***State or other work-study/employment:*** *Total amount:* $6,674,000 (100% non-need-based). Part-time jobs available.

ATHLETIC AWARDS *Total amount:* 1,427,000 (100% non-need-based).

APPLYING for FINANCIAL AID ***Required financial aid form:*** FAFSA. ***Financial aid deadline (priority):*** 3/1. ***Notification date:*** Continuous beginning 4/1. Students must reply within 2 weeks of notification.

CONTACT Ms. Paula C. Luff, Associate Director of Financial Aid, University of Illinois at Chicago, 1200 West Harrison, M/C 334, Chicago, IL 60607-7128, 312-996-5563. *Fax:* 312-996-3385. *E-mail:* pluff@uic.edu

UNIVERSITY OF ILLINOIS AT SPRINGFIELD

Springfield, IL

Tuition & fees (IL res): $3042 **Average undergraduate aid package: $7526**

ABOUT THE INSTITUTION State-supported, coed. Awards: bachelor's and master's degrees. 27 undergraduate majors. Total enrollment: 4,079. Undergraduates: 2,183. Federal methodology is used as a basis for awarding need-based institutional aid.

UNDERGRADUATE EXPENSES for 1999–2000 ***Tuition, state resident:*** full-time $2790; part-time $93 per semester hour. ***Tuition, nonresident:*** full-time $8370; part-time $279 per semester hour. ***Required fees:*** full-time $252; $4 per semester hour; $42 per term part-time. ***College room and board: room only:*** $2376. Room and board charges vary according to housing facility. ***Payment plan:*** installment.

UNDERGRADUATE FINANCIAL AID (Fall 1999) 763 applied for aid; of those 87% were deemed to have need. 100% of undergraduates with need received aid; of those 22% had need fully met. *Average percent of need met:* 74% (excluding resources awarded to replace EFC). *Average financial aid package:* $7526 (excluding resources awarded to replace EFC). 4% of all full-time undergraduates had no need and received non-need-based aid.

GIFT AID (NEED-BASED) ***Total amount:*** $2,530,928 (49% Federal, 47% state, 4% institutional). ***Receiving aid:*** *All full-time undergraduates:* 51% (599). ***Average award:*** Undergraduates: $3342. ***Scholarships, grants, and awards:*** Federal Pell, FSEOG, state, private, college/university gift aid from institutional funds.

GIFT AID (NON-NEED-BASED) ***Total amount:*** $635,129 (62% state, 11% institutional, 27% external sources). ***Receiving aid:*** *Undergraduates:* 15% (177). ***Scholarships, grants, and awards by category:*** *Academic Interests/Achievement:* biological sciences, business, communication, computer science, education, English, general academic interests/achievements, health fields, humanities, mathematics. *Creative Arts/Performance:* art/fine arts, journalism/publications. *Special Achievements/Activities:* community service, leadership. *Special Characteristics:* adult students, children of faculty/staff, children of union members/company employees, children of workers in trades, ethnic background, first-generation college students, general special characteristics, international students, local/state students, members of minority groups, out-of-state students, public servants, veterans, veterans' children. ***Tuition waivers:*** Full or partial for employees or children of employees.

LOANS ***Student loans:*** $3,172,884 (80% need-based, 20% non-need-based). ***Average need-based loan:*** Undergraduates: $4458. ***Parent loans:*** $24,323 (100% non-need-based). ***Programs:*** FFEL (Subsidized and Unsubsidized Stafford, PLUS), Perkins, college/university.

WORK-STUDY ***Federal work-study:*** *Total amount:* $58,255; 38 jobs averaging $1533. ***State or other work-study/employment:*** *Total amount:* $188,328 (100% non-need-based). Part-time jobs available.

ATHLETIC AWARDS *Total amount:* 50,000 (100% non-need-based).

APPLYING for FINANCIAL AID ***Required financial aid forms:*** FAFSA, institution's own form. ***Financial aid deadline:*** 11/15 (priority: 4/1). ***Notification date:*** Continuous. Students must reply within 2 weeks of notification.

CONTACT Ms. Mary Beth Maloney, Financial Aid Advisor IV, University of Illinois at Springfield, PO Box 19243, Springfield, IL 62794-9243, 217-206-6724 or toll-free 800-252-8533 (in-state). *Fax:* 217-206-6620. *E-mail:* maloney.mary@uis.edu

UNIVERSITY OF ILLINOIS AT URBANA–CHAMPAIGN

Urbana, IL

Tuition & fees (IL res): $4752 **Average undergraduate aid package: $7800**

ABOUT THE INSTITUTION State-supported, coed. Awards: bachelor's, master's, doctoral, and first professional degrees. 132 undergraduate majors. Total enrollment: 38,851. Undergraduates: 28,916. Freshmen: 6,479. Federal methodology is used as a basis for awarding need-based institutional aid.

UNDERGRADUATE EXPENSES for 2000–2001 ***Application fee:*** $40. ***Tuition, state resident:*** full-time $3724. ***Tuition, nonresident:*** full-time $11,172. ***Required fees:*** full-time $1028. Full-time tuition and fees vary according to program and student level. Part-time tuition and fees vary according to course load and student level. ***College room and board:*** $5424. Room and board charges vary according to board plan and housing facility. ***Payment plan:*** installment.

FRESHMAN FINANCIAL AID (Fall 1998) 4887 applied for aid; of those 61% were deemed to have need. *Average percent of need met:* 79% (excluding resources awarded to replace EFC). *Average financial aid package:* $7500 (excluding resources awarded to replace EFC). 19% of all full-time freshmen had no need and received non-need-based aid.

UNDERGRADUATE FINANCIAL AID (Fall 1998) 14,930 applied for aid; of those 84% were deemed to have need. *Average percent of need met:* 83% (excluding resources awarded to replace EFC). *Average financial aid package:* $7800 (excluding resources awarded to replace EFC). 13% of all full-time undergraduates had no need and received non-need-based aid.

GIFT AID (NEED-BASED) ***Total amount:*** $42,749,341 (26% Federal, 52% state, 16% institutional, 6% external sources). ***Scholarships, grants, and awards:*** Federal Pell, FSEOG, state, private, college/university gift aid from institutional funds.

GIFT AID (NON-NEED-BASED) ***Total amount:*** $7,510,676 (4% Federal, 38% state, 34% institutional, 24% external sources). ***Tuition waivers:*** Full or partial for employees or children of employees, senior citizens. ***ROTC:*** Army, Naval, Air Force.

LOANS ***Student loans:*** $43,323,178 (82% need-based, 18% non-need-based). 46% of past graduating class borrowed through all loan programs. Average indebtedness per student: $10,394. ***Programs:*** Federal Direct (Subsidized and Unsubsidized Stafford, PLUS), Perkins, college/university.

WORK-STUDY ***Federal work-study:*** *Total amount:* $1,716,760; jobs available.

APPLYING for FINANCIAL AID ***Required financial aid form:*** FAFSA. ***Financial aid deadline (priority):*** 3/15. ***Notification date:*** 4/1.

CONTACT Orlo Austin, Director of Student Financial Aid, University of Illinois at Urbana–Champaign, 610 East John Street, Champaign, IL 61820-5711, 217-333-0100.

UNIVERSITY OF INDIANAPOLIS
Indianapolis, IN

Tuition & fees: $14,630 **Average undergraduate aid package: $12,118**

ABOUT THE INSTITUTION Independent religious, coed. Awards: associate, bachelor's, master's, and doctoral degrees. 69 undergraduate majors. Total enrollment: 3,632. Undergraduates: 2,781. Freshmen: 606. Federal methodology is used as a basis for awarding need-based institutional aid.

UNDERGRADUATE EXPENSES for 2000–2001 ***Application fee:*** $20. ***Comprehensive fee:*** $19,855 includes full-time tuition ($14,630) and room and board ($5225). Full-time tuition and fees vary according to course load and program. Room and board charges vary according to board plan. ***Part-time tuition:*** $610 per credit hour. Part-time tuition and fees vary according to class time and course load. ***Payment plans:*** installment, deferred payment.

FRESHMAN FINANCIAL AID (Fall 1999) 525 applied for aid; of those 86% were deemed to have need. 100% of freshmen with need received aid; of those 24% had need fully met. *Average percent of need met:* 78% (excluding resources awarded to replace EFC). *Average financial aid package:* $11,576 (excluding resources awarded to replace EFC). 11% of all full-time freshmen had no need and received non-need-based aid.

UNDERGRADUATE FINANCIAL AID (Fall 1999) 985 applied for aid; of those 89% were deemed to have need. 100% of undergraduates with need received aid; of those 29% had need fully met. *Average percent of need met:* 82% (excluding resources awarded to replace EFC). *Average financial aid package:* $12,118 (excluding resources awarded to replace EFC). 12% of all full-time undergraduates had no need and received non-need-based aid.

GIFT AID (NEED-BASED) ***Total amount:*** $5,022,315 (25% Federal, 67% state, 8% institutional). ***Receiving aid:*** *Freshmen:* 71% (398); *all full-time undergraduates:* 63% (789). ***Average award:*** Freshmen: $6780; Undergraduates: $7189. ***Scholarships, grants, and awards:*** Federal Pell, FSEOG, state, private, college/university gift aid from institutional funds.

GIFT AID (NON-NEED-BASED) ***Total amount:*** $5,521,178 (98% institutional, 2% external sources). ***Receiving aid:*** *Freshmen:* 70% (392); *Undergraduates:* 58% (731). ***Scholarships, grants, and awards by category:*** *Academic Interests/Achievement:* general academic interests/achievements. *Creative Arts/Performance:* art/fine arts, music, theater/drama. *Special Achievements/Activities:* community service, religious involvement. *Special Characteristics:* adult students, children of faculty/staff, international students, relatives of clergy. ***Tuition waivers:*** Full or partial for employees or children of employees, senior citizens. ***ROTC:*** Army cooperative.

LOANS ***Student loans:*** $11,725,135 (64% need-based, 36% non-need-based). 66% of past graduating class borrowed through all loan programs. Average indebtedness per student: $16,418. ***Average need-based loan:*** Freshmen: $1258; Undergraduates: $3678. ***Parent loans:*** $1,184,712 (100% non-need-based). ***Programs:*** FFEL (Subsidized and Unsubsidized Stafford, PLUS), Perkins.

WORK-STUDY ***Federal work-study:*** *Total amount:* $194,918; jobs available.

ATHLETIC AWARDS *Total amount:* 2,026,525 (100% non-need-based).

APPLYING for FINANCIAL AID ***Required financial aid forms:*** FAFSA, institution's own form. ***Financial aid deadline (priority):*** 3/1. ***Notification date:*** 4/1. Students must reply within 3 weeks of notification.

CONTACT Ms. Linda B. Handy, Director of Financial Aid, University of Indianapolis, 1400 East Hanna Avenue, Indianapolis, IN 46227-3697, 317-788-3217 or toll-free 800-232-8634 Ext. 3216.

THE UNIVERSITY OF IOWA
Iowa City, IA

Tuition & fees (IA res): $2998 **Average undergraduate aid package: $5981**

ABOUT THE INSTITUTION State-supported, coed. Awards: bachelor's, master's, doctoral, and first professional degrees. 141 undergraduate majors. Total enrollment: 28,846. Undergraduates: 19,537. Freshmen: 3,859. Federal methodology is used as a basis for awarding need-based institutional aid.

UNDERGRADUATE EXPENSES for 1999–2000 ***Application fee:*** $30. ***Tuition, state resident:*** full-time $2786; part-time $117 per semester hour. ***Tuition, nonresident:*** full-time $10,228; part-time $427 per semester hour. ***Required fees:*** full-time $212; $106 per term part-time. Full-time tuition and fees vary according to course load and program. Part-time tuition and fees vary according to course load. ***College room and board:*** $4370; ***room only:*** $2415. Room and board charges vary according to board plan and housing facility. ***Payment plan:*** installment.

FRESHMAN FINANCIAL AID (Fall 1999, est.) 2669 applied for aid; of those 63% were deemed to have need. 94% of freshmen with need received aid; of those 56% had need fully met. *Average percent of need met:* 68% (excluding resources awarded to replace EFC). *Average financial aid package:* $4105 (excluding resources awarded to replace EFC). 49% of all full-time freshmen had no need and received non-need-based aid.

UNDERGRADUATE FINANCIAL AID (Fall 1999, est.) 10,241 applied for aid; of those 73% were deemed to have need. 94% of undergraduates with need received aid; of those 74% had need fully met. *Average percent of need met:* 75% (excluding resources awarded to replace EFC). *Average financial aid package:* $5981 (excluding resources awarded to replace EFC). 32% of all full-time undergraduates had no need and received non-need-based aid.

GIFT AID (NEED-BASED) ***Total amount:*** $14,781,130 (45% Federal, 6% state, 49% institutional). ***Receiving aid:*** *Freshmen:* 24% (922); *all full-time undergraduates:* 24% (4,081). ***Average award:*** Freshmen: $1600; Undergraduates: $1762. ***Scholarships, grants, and awards:*** Federal Pell, FSEOG, state, private, college/university gift aid from institutional funds.

GIFT AID (NON-NEED-BASED) ***Total amount:*** $13,999,071 (9% Federal, 2% state, 37% institutional, 52% external sources). ***Receiving aid:*** *Freshmen:* 28% (1,088); *Undergraduates:* 29% (4,891). ***Scholarships, grants, and awards by category:*** *Academic Interests/Achievement:* business, engineering/technologies, general academic interests/achievements. *Creative Arts/Performance:* music, performing arts, theater/drama. *Special Achievements/Activities:* general special achievements/activities. *Special Characteristics:* general special characteristics. ***ROTC:*** Army, Air Force.

LOANS ***Student loans:*** $37,883,725 (56% need-based, 44% non-need-based). 57% of past graduating class borrowed through all loan programs. Average indebtedness per student: $11,018. ***Average need-based loan:*** Freshmen: $1882; Undergraduates: $2916. ***Parent loans:*** $15,496,588 (100% non-need-based). ***Programs:*** Federal Direct (Subsidized and Unsubsidized Stafford, PLUS), Perkins, Federal Nursing, college/university.

WORK-STUDY ***Federal work-study:*** *Total amount:* $4,898,259; 1,100 jobs available. ***State or other work-study/employment:*** *Total amount:* $2,579,560 (100% need-based). Part-time jobs available.

ATHLETIC AWARDS *Total amount:* 3,617,160 (100% non-need-based).

APPLYING for FINANCIAL AID ***Required financial aid forms:*** FAFSA, institution's own form. ***Financial aid deadline (priority):*** 1/1. ***Notification date:*** 3/1.

CONTACT Director, Student Financial Aid, The University of Iowa, 208 Calvin Hall, Iowa City, IA 52242, 319-335-1449 or toll-free 800-553-4692.

UNIVERSITY OF JUDAISM
Bel Air, CA

Tuition & fees: N/R **Average undergraduate aid package: $18,250**

ABOUT THE INSTITUTION Independent Jewish, coed. Awards: bachelor's and master's degrees. 8 undergraduate majors. Total enrollment: 209. Undergraduates: 102. Federal methodology is used as a basis for awarding need-based institutional aid.

FRESHMAN FINANCIAL AID (Fall 1999) 20 applied for aid; of those 85% were deemed to have need. 100% of freshmen with need received aid; of those 41% had need fully met. *Average percent of need met:* 99% (excluding resources awarded to replace EFC). *Average financial aid package:* $18,674 (excluding resources awarded to replace EFC). 26% of all full-time freshmen had no need and received non-need-based aid.

UNDERGRADUATE FINANCIAL AID (Fall 1999) 79 applied for aid; of those 87% were deemed to have need. 100% of undergraduates with need received aid; of those 86% had need fully met. *Average percent of need met:* 99% (excluding resources awarded to replace EFC). *Average financial aid package:* $18,250 (excluding resources awarded to replace EFC). 11% of all full-time undergraduates had no need and received non-need-based aid.

GIFT AID (NEED-BASED) ***Total amount:*** $594,196 (13% Federal, 16% state, 68% institutional, 3% external sources). ***Receiving aid:*** *Freshmen:* 74% (17); *all full-time undergraduates:* 63% (59). ***Average award:*** Freshmen: $12,541; Undergraduates: $10,750. ***Scholarships, grants, and awards:*** Federal Pell, FSEOG, state, private, college/university gift aid from institutional funds.

GIFT AID (NON-NEED-BASED) ***Total amount:*** $271,553 (100% institutional). ***Receiving aid:*** *Freshmen:* 43% (10); *Undergraduates:* 53% (50). ***Scholarships, grants, and awards by category:*** *Academic Interests/Achievement:* 40 awards ($325,000 total): general academic interests/achievements. ***Tuition waivers:*** Full or partial for employees or children of employees.

LOANS ***Student loans:*** $262,167 (82% need-based, 18% non-need-based). 65% of past graduating class borrowed through all loan programs. Average indebtedness per student: $12,448. ***Average need-based loan:*** Freshmen: $3292; Undergraduates: $5648. ***Parent loans:*** $131,464 (44% need-based, 56% non-need-based). ***Programs:*** FFEL (Subsidized and Unsubsidized Stafford, PLUS), alternative loans.

WORK-STUDY ***Federal work-study:*** *Total amount:* $82,013; 46 jobs averaging $1783.

APPLYING for FINANCIAL AID ***Required financial aid forms:*** FAFSA, institution's own form, state aid form. ***Financial aid deadline (priority):*** 3/2. ***Notification date:*** Continuous beginning 3/15. Students must reply within 3 weeks of notification.

CONTACT Ms. Jodi Valpey, Director of Financial Aid, University of Judaism, 15600 Mulholland Drive, Bel Air, CA 90077-1599, 310-476-9777 Ext. 252 or toll-free 888-853-6763. *Fax:* 310-471-3657. *E-mail:* jvalpey@uj.edu

UNIVERSITY OF KANSAS

Lawrence, KS

Tuition & fees (KS res): $2518 **Average undergraduate aid package: $5686**

ABOUT THE INSTITUTION State-supported, coed. Awards: bachelor's, master's, doctoral, and first professional degrees and post-master's and first-professional certificates (University of Kansas is a single institution with academic programs and facilities at two primary locations: Lawrence and Kansas City. Undergraduate, graduate, and professional education are the principal missions of the Lawrence campus, with medicine and related professional education the focus of the Kansas City campus). 99 undergraduate majors. Total enrollment: 27,838. Undergraduates: 19,477. Freshmen: 3,878. Federal methodology is used as a basis for awarding need-based institutional aid.

UNDERGRADUATE EXPENSES for 1999–2000 ***Application fee:*** $20. ***Tuition, state resident:*** full-time $2090; part-time $70 per credit hour. ***Tuition, nonresident:*** full-time $8693; part-time $290 per credit hour. ***Required fees:*** full-time $428; $31 per credit hour. Full-time tuition and fees vary according to course load and program. Part-time tuition and fees vary according to course load and program. ***College room and board:*** $3941. Room and board charges vary according to board plan and housing facility. ***Payment plan:*** installment.

FRESHMAN FINANCIAL AID (Fall 1998) 2083 applied for aid; of those 73% were deemed to have need. 99% of freshmen with need received aid; of those 24% had need fully met. *Average percent of need met:* 66% (excluding resources awarded to replace EFC). *Average financial aid package:* $5054 (excluding resources awarded to replace EFC). 13% of all full-time freshmen had no need and received non-need-based aid.

UNDERGRADUATE FINANCIAL AID (Fall 1998) 8,011 applied for aid; of those 78% were deemed to have need. 99% of undergraduates with need received aid; of those 28% had need fully met. *Average percent of need met:* 71% (excluding resources awarded to replace EFC). *Average financial aid package:* $5686 (excluding resources awarded to replace EFC). 10% of all full-time undergraduates had no need and received non-need-based aid.

GIFT AID (NEED-BASED) ***Total amount:*** $13,595,066 (48% Federal, 9% state, 29% institutional, 14% external sources). ***Receiving aid:*** *Freshmen:* 29% (1,082); *all full-time undergraduates:* 24% (4,023). ***Average award:*** Freshmen: $3310; Undergraduates: $2850. ***Scholarships, grants, and awards:*** Federal Pell, FSEOG, state, private, college/university gift aid from institutional funds.

GIFT AID (NON-NEED-BASED) ***Total amount:*** $3,465,119 (84% institutional, 16% external sources). ***Receiving aid:*** *Freshmen:* 5; *Undergraduates:* 17. ***Scholarships, grants, and awards by category:*** *Academic Interests/Achievement:* architecture, area/ethnic studies, biological sciences, business, communication, computer science, education, engineering/technologies, English, foreign languages, general academic interests/achievements, health fields, humanities, international studies, library science, mathematics, military science, physical sciences, premedicine, religion/biblical studies, social sciences. *Creative Arts/Performance:* applied art and design, art/fine arts, cinema/film/broadcasting, creative writing, dance, debating, general creative arts/performance, journalism/publications, music, performing arts, theater/drama. *Special Achievements/Activities:* community service, leadership. *Special Characteristics:* adult students, ethnic background, first-generation college students, general special characteristics, international students, local/state students, married students, members of minority groups, out-of-state students. ***Tuition waivers:*** Full or partial for employees or children of employees, senior citizens. ***ROTC:*** Army, Naval, Air Force.

LOANS ***Student loans:*** $29,868,557 (66% need-based, 34% non-need-based). ***Average need-based loan:*** Freshmen: $2530; Undergraduates: $3508. ***Parent loans:*** $8,242,878 (100% non-need-based). ***Programs:*** Federal Direct (Subsidized and Unsubsidized Stafford, PLUS), Perkins, college/university.

WORK-STUDY ***Federal work-study:*** *Total amount:* $872,323; 560 jobs averaging $1557. ***State or other work-study/employment:*** *Total amount:* $390,285 (100% non-need-based). 87 part-time jobs averaging $4486.

ATHLETIC AWARDS *Total amount:* 3,541,634 (33% need-based, 67% non-need-based).

APPLYING for FINANCIAL AID ***Required financial aid form:*** FAFSA. ***Financial aid deadline (priority):*** 3/1. ***Notification date:*** Continuous beginning 4/1. Students must reply within 2 weeks of notification.

CONTACT Ms. Diane Del Buono, Director of Student Financial Aid, University of Kansas, Office of Student Financial Aid, 50 Strong Hall, Lawrence, KS 66045-1920, 785-864-4700 or toll-free 888-686-7323 (in-state). *Fax:* 785-864-5469. *E-mail:* osfa@ukans.edu

UNIVERSITY OF KENTUCKY

Lexington, KY

ABOUT THE INSTITUTION State-supported, coed. Awards: bachelor's, master's, doctoral, and first professional degrees. 80 undergraduate majors. Total enrollment: 23,060. Undergraduates: 16,841. Freshmen: 2,681.

GIFT AID (NEED-BASED) ***Scholarships, grants, and awards:*** Federal Pell, FSEOG, state, private, college/university gift aid from institutional funds.

GIFT AID (NON-NEED-BASED) ***Scholarships, grants, and awards by category:*** *Academic Interests/Achievement:* agriculture, biological sciences, communication, education, engineering/technologies, foreign languages, general academic interests/achievements, health fields, home economics, military science. *Creative Arts/Performance:* debating, general creative arts/performance, music. *Special Achievements/Activities:* general special achievements/activities. *Special Characteristics:* adult students, children of union members/company employees, children of workers in trades, children with a deceased or disabled parent, international students, members of minority groups, spouses of deceased or disabled public servants, veterans, veterans' children.

LOANS ***Programs:*** Federal Direct (Subsidized and Unsubsidized Stafford, PLUS), Perkins, Federal Nursing, college/university.

WORK-STUDY Federal work-study jobs available.

APPLYING for FINANCIAL AID ***Required financial aid form:*** FAFSA.

University of Kentucky (continued)

CONTACT Ms. Lynda S. George, Director of Financial Aid, University of Kentucky, 128 Funkhouser Building, Lexington, KY 40506-0054, 606-257-3172 Ext. 241 or toll-free 800-432-0967 (in-state). *Fax:* 606-257-4398. *E-mail:* lgeorge@pop.uky.edu

UNIVERSITY OF LA VERNE

La Verne, CA

Tuition & fees: $16,860 **Average undergraduate aid package: $14,792**

ABOUT THE INSTITUTION Independent, coed. Awards: associate, bachelor's, master's, doctoral, and first professional degrees and post-master's certificates (also offers continuing education program with significant enrollment not reflected in profile). 54 undergraduate majors. Total enrollment: 2,955. Undergraduates: 1,300. Freshmen: 321. Federal methodology is used as a basis for awarding need-based institutional aid.

UNDERGRADUATE EXPENSES for 2000–2001 ***Application fee:*** $35. ***One-time required fee:*** $110. ***Tuition:*** full-time $16,800; part-time $525 per unit. ***Required fees:*** full-time $60; $30 per term part-time. Full-time tuition and fees vary according to course load, degree level, location, and program. Part-time tuition and fees vary according to course load, degree level, location, and program. Room and board charges vary according to board plan, housing facility, and location. ***Payment plans:*** installment, deferred payment.

FRESHMAN FINANCIAL AID (Fall 1999) 311 applied for aid; of those 90% were deemed to have need. 100% of freshmen with need received aid; of those 16% had need fully met. *Average percent of need met:* 85% (excluding resources awarded to replace EFC). *Average financial aid package:* $14,912 (excluding resources awarded to replace EFC). 8% of all full-time freshmen had no need and received non-need-based aid.

UNDERGRADUATE FINANCIAL AID (Fall 1999) 1,132 applied for aid; of those 93% were deemed to have need. 100% of undergraduates with need received aid; of those 24% had need fully met. *Average percent of need met:* 84% (excluding resources awarded to replace EFC). *Average financial aid package:* $14,792 (excluding resources awarded to replace EFC). 5% of all full-time undergraduates had no need and received non-need-based aid.

GIFT AID (NEED-BASED) ***Total amount:*** $15,142,814 (10% Federal, 19% state, 21% institutional, 50% external sources). ***Receiving aid:*** *Freshmen:* 76% (245); *all full-time undergraduates:* 78% (971). ***Average award:*** Freshmen: $7340; Undergraduates: $7731. ***Scholarships, grants, and awards:*** Federal Pell, FSEOG, state, private, college/university gift aid from institutional funds.

GIFT AID (NON-NEED-BASED) ***Total amount:*** $3,637,673 (96% institutional, 4% external sources). ***Receiving aid:*** *Freshmen:* 81% (261); *Undergraduates:* 58% (728). ***Scholarships, grants, and awards by category:*** *Academic Interests/Achievement:* 763 awards ($3,356,041 total): general academic interests/achievements. *Creative Arts/Performance:* 27 awards ($116,983 total): debating, journalism/publications, music, theater/drama. *Special Achievements/Activities:* 72 awards ($38,000 total): community service, leadership. *Special Characteristics:* 201 awards ($593,313 total): children and siblings of alumni, children of faculty/staff, first-generation college students, general special characteristics, international students, religious affiliation. ***Tuition waivers:*** Full or partial for employees or children of employees, adult students.

LOANS ***Student loans:*** $5,448,261 (61% need-based, 39% non-need-based). ***Average need-based loan:*** Freshmen: $3264; Undergraduates: $3935. ***Parent loans:*** $2,578,265 (100% non-need-based). ***Programs:*** FFEL (Subsidized and Unsubsidized Stafford, PLUS), Perkins, college/university.

WORK-STUDY ***Federal work-study:*** *Total amount:* $1,013,166; 529 jobs averaging $1907.

APPLYING for FINANCIAL AID ***Required financial aid form:*** FAFSA. ***Financial aid deadline:*** Continuous. ***Notification date:*** Continuous beginning 4/15. Students must reply by 5/1 or within 2 weeks of notification.

CONTACT Mr. Edward J. Mervine, Director of Financial Aid, University of La Verne, 1950 3rd Street, La Verne, CA 91750-4443, 909-593-3511 Ext. 4135 or toll-free 800-876-4858. *Fax:* 909-392-2751. *E-mail:* mervinee@ulv.edu

UNIVERSITY OF LOUISIANA AT LAFAYETTE

Lafayette, LA

Tuition & fees (LA res): $2013 **Average undergraduate aid package: $5400**

ABOUT THE INSTITUTION State-supported, coed. Awards: associate, bachelor's, master's, and doctoral degrees and post-master's certificates. 56 undergraduate majors. Total enrollment: 16,351. Undergraduates: 14,900. Freshmen: 2,529. Federal methodology is used as a basis for awarding need-based institutional aid.

UNDERGRADUATE EXPENSES for 1999–2000 ***Application fee:*** $20. ***One-time required fee:*** $7.50. ***Tuition, state resident:*** full-time $2013; part-time $525 per term. ***Tuition, nonresident:*** full-time $7245; part-time $1833 per term. Part-time tuition and fees vary according to course load. ***College room and board:*** $2656. Room and board charges vary according to board plan. ***Payment plan:*** deferred payment.

FRESHMAN FINANCIAL AID (Fall 1998) 2652 applied for aid; of those 97% were deemed to have need. 98% of freshmen with need received aid. *Average percent of need met:* 92% (excluding resources awarded to replace EFC). *Average financial aid package:* $3200 (excluding resources awarded to replace EFC).

UNDERGRADUATE FINANCIAL AID (Fall 1998) 10,665 applied for aid; of those 73% were deemed to have need. 93% of undergraduates with need received aid. *Average percent of need met:* 92% (excluding resources awarded to replace EFC). *Average financial aid package:* $5400 (excluding resources awarded to replace EFC).

GIFT AID (NEED-BASED) ***Total amount:*** $11,030,362 (99% Federal, 1% state). ***Receiving aid:*** *Freshmen:* 49% (1,440); *all full-time undergraduates:* 38% (4,748). ***Scholarships, grants, and awards:*** Federal Pell, FSEOG, state, college/university gift aid from institutional funds.

GIFT AID (NON-NEED-BASED) ***Scholarships, grants, and awards by category:*** *Academic Interests/Achievement:* general academic interests/achievements. *Creative Arts/Performance:* general creative arts/performance. *Special Achievements/Activities:* general special achievements/activities. ***Tuition waivers:*** Full or partial for employees or children of employees, senior citizens. ***ROTC:*** Army.

LOANS ***Student loans:*** $19,435,526 (100% need-based). ***Parent loans:*** $1,259,294 (100% need-based). ***Programs:*** FFEL (Subsidized and Unsubsidized Stafford, PLUS), Perkins.

WORK-STUDY ***Federal work-study:*** *Total amount:* $1,189,429; jobs available.

ATHLETIC AWARDS *Total amount:* 960,608 (100% need-based).

APPLYING for FINANCIAL AID ***Required financial aid form:*** FAFSA. ***Financial aid deadline (priority):*** 3/1. ***Notification date:*** Continuous. Students must reply within 2 weeks of notification.

CONTACT Director of Financial Aid, University of Louisiana at Lafayette, 104 University Circle, PO Box 41206, Lafayette, LA 70504, 337-482-6497 or toll-free 800-752-6553 (in-state).

UNIVERSITY OF LOUISIANA AT MONROE

Monroe, LA

Tuition & fees (LA res): $2052 **Average undergraduate aid package: N/A**

ABOUT THE INSTITUTION State-supported, coed. Awards: associate, bachelor's, master's, and doctoral degrees. 61 undergraduate majors. Total enrollment: 9,947. Undergraduates: 8,669. Freshmen: 1,529. Federal methodology is used as a basis for awarding need-based institutional aid.

UNDERGRADUATE EXPENSES for 1999–2000 ***Application fee:*** $15. ***Tuition, state resident:*** full-time $1644; part-time $414 per term. ***Tuition, nonresident:*** full-time $8024; part-time $1488 per term. ***Required fees:*** full-time $408; $153 per term part-time. Part-time tuition and fees vary according to course load. ***College room and board:*** $3660; ***room only:*** $2560. Room and board charges vary according to board plan and housing facility.

GIFT AID (NEED-BASED) ***Scholarships, grants, and awards:*** Federal Pell, FSEOG, state, private, college/university gift aid from institutional funds, Leveraging Educational Assistance Partnership Program (LEAPP).

GIFT AID (NON-NEED-BASED) ***Scholarships, grants, and awards by category:*** *Academic Interests/Achievement:* agriculture, biological sciences, business, communication, computer science, education, English, foreign languages, general academic interests/achievements, health fields, home economics, library science, mathematics, military science, physical sciences, social sciences. *Creative Arts/Performance:* art/fine arts, creative writing, debating, journalism/publications, music, performing arts, theater/drama. *Special Achievements/Activities:* cheerleading/drum major, community service, leadership. *Special Characteristics:* children of faculty/staff, children with a deceased or disabled parent, international students, out-of-state students. ***Tuition waivers:*** Full or partial for children of alumni, employees or children of employees, senior citizens. ***ROTC:*** Army.

LOANS ***Programs:*** FFEL (Subsidized and Unsubsidized Stafford, PLUS), Perkins, college/university, Federal Health Professions Student Loans.

WORK-STUDY Federal work-study jobs available. ***State or other work-study/employment:*** Part-time jobs available.

APPLYING for FINANCIAL AID ***Required financial aid forms:*** FAFSA, institution's own form. ***Financial aid deadline (priority):*** 4/1. ***Notification date:*** 6/15.

CONTACT Roslynn Pogue, Assistant Director, Financial Aid, University of Louisiana at Monroe, 700 University Avenue, Monroe, LA 71209-1120, 318-342-5320 or toll-free 800-372-5127. *Fax:* 318-342-3539. *E-mail:* sspogue@ulm.edu

UNIVERSITY OF LOUISVILLE

Louisville, KY

Tuition & fees (KY res): $3246 **Average undergraduate aid package: $6488**

ABOUT THE INSTITUTION State-supported, coed. Awards: associate, bachelor's, master's, doctoral, and first professional degrees and post-bachelor's and post-master's certificates. 59 undergraduate majors. Total enrollment: 19,892. Undergraduates: 14,694. Freshmen: 2,447. Federal methodology is used as a basis for awarding need-based institutional aid.

UNDERGRADUATE EXPENSES for 1999–2000 ***Application fee:*** $25. ***Tuition, state resident:*** full-time $2960; part-time $123 per hour. ***Tuition, nonresident:*** full-time $8880; part-time $370 per hour. ***Required fees:*** full-time $286; $10 per hour; $15 per term part-time. Part-time tuition and fees vary according to course load. ***College room and board:*** $3400. Room and board charges vary according to board plan and housing facility. ***Payment plan:*** installment.

FRESHMAN FINANCIAL AID (Fall 1998) 1474 applied for aid; of those 66% were deemed to have need. 96% of freshmen with need received aid; of those 29% had need fully met. *Average percent of need met:* 70% (excluding resources awarded to replace EFC). *Average financial aid package:* $5538 (excluding resources awarded to replace EFC). 17% of all full-time freshmen had no need and received non-need-based aid.

UNDERGRADUATE FINANCIAL AID (Fall 1998) 6,232 applied for aid; of those 69% were deemed to have need. 94% of undergraduates with need received aid; of those 30% had need fully met. *Average percent of need met:* 72% (excluding resources awarded to replace EFC). *Average financial aid package:* $6488 (excluding resources awarded to replace EFC). 14% of all full-time undergraduates had no need and received non-need-based aid.

GIFT AID (NEED-BASED) ***Total amount:*** $9,288,007 (69% Federal, 31% state). ***Receiving aid:*** *Freshmen:* 28% (554); *all full-time undergraduates:* 17% (1,607). ***Scholarships, grants, and awards:*** Federal Pell, FSEOG, state, private, college/university gift aid from institutional funds.

GIFT AID (NON-NEED-BASED) ***Total amount:*** $5,971,366 (81% institutional, 19% external sources). ***Receiving aid:*** *Freshmen:* 10% (203); *Undergraduates:* 5% (517). ***Scholarships, grants, and awards by category:*** *Academic Interests/Achievement:* general academic interests/achievements. *Special Achievements/Activities:* general special achievements/activities, memberships. *Special Characteristics:* general special characteristics. ***Tuition waivers:*** Full or partial for employees or children of employees, senior citizens. ***ROTC:*** Army, Air Force.

LOANS ***Student loans:*** $13,355,485 (100% need-based). ***Parent loans:*** $488,262 (100% non-need-based). ***Programs:*** FFEL (Subsidized and Unsubsidized Stafford, PLUS), Perkins, college/university.

WORK-STUDY ***Federal work-study:*** *Total amount:* $1,227,902; jobs available.

ATHLETIC AWARDS *Total amount:* 2,418,547 (100% non-need-based).

APPLYING for FINANCIAL AID ***Required financial aid form:*** FAFSA. ***Financial aid deadline (priority):*** 3/15. ***Notification date:*** 6/1.

CONTACT Ms. Patricia O. Arauz, Director of Financial Aid, University of Louisville, 2301 South Third Street, Louisville, KY 40292-0001, 502-852-6145 or toll-free 502-852-6531 (in-state), 800-334-8635 (out-of-state). *Fax:* 502-852-0182. *E-mail:* p.arauz@louisville.edu

UNIVERSITY OF MAINE

Orono, ME

Tuition & fees (ME res): $4656 **Average undergraduate aid package: $7888**

ABOUT THE INSTITUTION State-supported, coed. Awards: bachelor's, master's, and doctoral degrees and post-bachelor's and post-master's certificates. 76 undergraduate majors. Total enrollment: 9,945. Undergraduates: 7,882. Freshmen: 1,573. Federal methodology is used as a basis for awarding need-based institutional aid.

UNDERGRADUATE EXPENSES for 1999–2000 ***Application fee:*** $25. ***One-time required fee:*** $15. ***Tuition, state resident:*** full-time $3960; part-time $132 per credit hour. ***Tuition, nonresident:*** full-time $11,250; part-time $375 per credit hour. ***Required fees:*** full-time $696; $135 per term part-time. Full-time tuition and fees vary according to course load and reciprocity agreements. Part-time tuition and fees vary according to course load and reciprocity agreements. ***College room and board:*** $5256. Room and board charges vary according to board plan and housing facility. ***Payment plan:*** installment.

FRESHMAN FINANCIAL AID (Fall 1999) 1335 applied for aid; of those 84% were deemed to have need. 99% of freshmen with need received aid; of those 26% had need fully met. *Average percent of need met:* 87% (excluding resources awarded to replace EFC). *Average financial aid package:* $7825 (excluding resources awarded to replace EFC). 11% of all full-time freshmen had no need and received non-need-based aid.

UNDERGRADUATE FINANCIAL AID (Fall 1999) 5,263 applied for aid; of those 88% were deemed to have need. 95% of undergraduates with need received aid; of those 26% had need fully met. *Average percent of need met:* 86% (excluding resources awarded to replace EFC). *Average financial aid package:* $7888 (excluding resources awarded to replace EFC). 9% of all full-time undergraduates had no need and received non-need-based aid.

GIFT AID (NEED-BASED) ***Total amount:*** $16,786,269 (42% Federal, 13% state, 36% institutional, 9% external sources). ***Receiving aid:*** *Freshmen:* 62% (991); *all full-time undergraduates:* 59% (3,704). ***Average award:*** Freshmen: $5017; Undergraduates: $4454. ***Scholarships, grants, and awards:*** Federal Pell, FSEOG, state, private, college/university gift aid from institutional funds.

GIFT AID (NON-NEED-BASED) ***Total amount:*** $4,182,726 (25% institutional, 75% external sources). ***Receiving aid:*** *Freshmen:* 6% (96); *Undergraduates:* 4% (257). ***Scholarships, grants, and awards by category:*** *Academic Interests/Achievement:* engineering/technologies, general academic interests/achievements, military science, physical sciences. *Creative Arts/Performance:* art/fine arts, performing arts. *Special Achievements/Activities:* community service, leadership. *Special Characteristics:* children and siblings of alumni, children of faculty/staff, children of union members/company employees, children with a deceased or disabled parent, ethnic background, first-generation college students, handicapped students, international students, local/state students, members of minority groups, out-of-state students, veterans, veterans' children. ***Tuition waivers:*** Full or partial for employees or children of employees. ***ROTC:*** Army, Naval.

University of Maine (continued)

LOANS ***Student loans:*** $20,349,289 (79% need-based, 21% non-need-based). 80% of past graduating class borrowed through all loan programs. Average indebtedness per student: $15,000. ***Average need-based loan:*** Freshmen: $2602; Undergraduates: $3735. ***Parent loans:*** $1,704,737 (100% non-need-based). ***Programs:*** FFEL (Subsidized and Unsubsidized Stafford, PLUS), Perkins, state, college/university.

WORK-STUDY ***Federal work-study:*** *Total amount:* $3,060,805; jobs available.

ATHLETIC AWARDS *Total amount:* 1,850,856 (100% need-based).

APPLYING for FINANCIAL AID ***Required financial aid form:*** FAFSA. ***Financial aid deadline (priority):*** 3/1. ***Notification date:*** Continuous beginning 3/15. Students must reply by 5/1 or within 2 weeks of notification.

CONTACT Ms. Peggy L. Crawford, Director of Student Aid, University of Maine, 5781 Wingate Hall, Orono, ME 04469, 207-581-1324 or toll-free 877-486-2364. *Fax:* 207-581-3261.

THE UNIVERSITY OF MAINE AT AUGUSTA

Augusta, ME

Tuition & fees (ME res): $3366 **Average undergraduate aid package: N/A**

ABOUT THE INSTITUTION State-supported, coed. Awards: associate and bachelor's degrees (also offers some graduate courses and continuing education program with significant enrollment not reflected in profile). 19 undergraduate majors. Total enrollment: 5,611. Undergraduates: 5,611. Freshmen: 654. Federal methodology is used as a basis for awarding need-based institutional aid.

UNDERGRADUATE EXPENSES for 1999–2000 ***Tuition, state resident:*** full-time $3090; part-time $103 per credit. ***Tuition, nonresident:*** full-time $7590; part-time $252 per credit. ***Required fees:*** full-time $276; $12 per credit. Full-time tuition and fees vary according to reciprocity agreements. Part-time tuition and fees vary according to reciprocity agreements. ***Payment plan:*** installment.

FRESHMAN FINANCIAL AID (Fall 1999) 398 applied for aid; of those 93% were deemed to have need. 96% of freshmen with need received aid; of those 11% had need fully met. *Average percent of need met:* 63% (excluding resources awarded to replace EFC).

UNDERGRADUATE FINANCIAL AID (Fall 1999) 1,535 applied for aid; of those 95% were deemed to have need. 96% of undergraduates with need received aid; of those 16% had need fully met. *Average percent of need met:* 70% (excluding resources awarded to replace EFC).

GIFT AID (NEED-BASED) ***Total amount:*** $7,457,528 (64% Federal, 15% state, 7% institutional, 14% external sources). ***Receiving aid:*** *Freshmen:* 300; *all full-time undergraduates:* 1,223. ***Average award:*** Freshmen: $3571; Undergraduates: $4085. ***Scholarships, grants, and awards:*** Federal Pell, FSEOG, state, private, college/university gift aid from institutional funds.

GIFT AID (NON-NEED-BASED) ***Total amount:*** $188,079 (62% institutional, 38% external sources). ***Receiving aid:*** *Freshmen:* 9; *Undergraduates:* 21. ***Scholarships, grants, and awards by category:*** *Academic Interests/Achievement:* 85 awards ($263,768 total): architecture, biological sciences, business, health fields. *Creative Arts/Performance:* 16 awards ($12,367 total): music. *Special Achievements/Activities:* 8 awards ($9888 total): leadership, memberships. ***Tuition waivers:*** Full or partial for employees or children of employees, senior citizens.

LOANS ***Student loans:*** $8,379,683 (79% need-based, 21% non-need-based). 63% of past graduating class borrowed through all loan programs. ***Average need-based loan:*** Freshmen: $2649; Undergraduates: $3360. ***Parent loans:*** $79,101 (100% non-need-based). ***Programs:*** Federal Direct (Subsidized and Unsubsidized Stafford), FFEL (Subsidized and Unsubsidized Stafford, PLUS), Perkins, Federal Nursing, college/university.

WORK-STUDY ***Federal work-study:*** *Total amount:* $360,738; 230 jobs averaging $1524.

APPLYING for FINANCIAL AID ***Required financial aid form:*** FAFSA.

CONTACT Office of Financial Aid, The University of Maine at Augusta, 46 University Drive, Augusta, ME 04330-9410, 207-621-3455 or toll-free 800-696-6000 Ext. 3185 (in-state).

UNIVERSITY OF MAINE AT FARMINGTON

Farmington, ME

Tuition & fees (ME res): $3776 **Average undergraduate aid package: $7839**

ABOUT THE INSTITUTION State-supported, coed. Awards: bachelor's degrees. 40 undergraduate majors. Total enrollment: 2,411. Undergraduates: 2,411. Freshmen: 480. Federal methodology is used as a basis for awarding need-based institutional aid.

UNDERGRADUATE EXPENSES for 1999–2000 ***Application fee:*** $25. ***One-time required fee:*** $15. ***Tuition, state resident:*** full-time $3390; part-time $113 per credit hour. ***Tuition, nonresident:*** full-time $8280; part-time $276 per credit hour. ***Required fees:*** full-time $386; $5 per credit hour; $59 per term part-time. Full-time tuition and fees vary according to course load and reciprocity agreements. Part-time tuition and fees vary according to course load and reciprocity agreements. ***College room and board:*** $4614; ***room only:*** $2384. Room and board charges vary according to board plan and housing facility. ***Payment plan:*** installment.

FRESHMAN FINANCIAL AID (Fall 1998) 379 applied for aid; of those 85% were deemed to have need. 99% of freshmen with need received aid; of those 43% had need fully met. *Average percent of need met:* 88% (excluding resources awarded to replace EFC). *Average financial aid package:* $7517 (excluding resources awarded to replace EFC). 10% of all full-time freshmen had no need and received non-need-based aid.

UNDERGRADUATE FINANCIAL AID (Fall 1998) 1,514 applied for aid; of those 88% were deemed to have need. 99% of undergraduates with need received aid; of those 49% had need fully met. *Average percent of need met:* 86% (excluding resources awarded to replace EFC). *Average financial aid package:* $7839 (excluding resources awarded to replace EFC). 8% of all full-time undergraduates had no need and received non-need-based aid.

GIFT AID (NEED-BASED) ***Total amount:*** $3,880,951 (45% Federal, 18% state, 20% institutional, 17% external sources). ***Receiving aid:*** *Freshmen:* 59% (295); *all full-time undergraduates:* 54% (1,080). ***Average award:*** Freshmen: $3791; Undergraduates: $3118. ***Scholarships, grants, and awards:*** Federal Pell, FSEOG, state, private, college/university gift aid from institutional funds, Maine Student Incentive Scholarship Program.

GIFT AID (NON-NEED-BASED) ***Total amount:*** $303,706 (100% institutional). ***Receiving aid:*** *Freshmen:* 14% (71); *Undergraduates:* 12% (229). ***Scholarships, grants, and awards by category:*** *Academic Interests/Achievement:* general academic interests/achievements. *Special Characteristics:* members of minority groups. ***Tuition waivers:*** Full or partial for minority students, employees or children of employees, senior citizens.

LOANS ***Student loans:*** $6,581,091 (70% need-based, 30% non-need-based). 80% of past graduating class borrowed through all loan programs. Average indebtedness per student: $15,474. ***Average need-based loan:*** Freshmen: $2699; Undergraduates: $3552. ***Parent loans:*** $485,541 (100% non-need-based). ***Programs:*** FFEL (Subsidized and Unsubsidized Stafford, PLUS), Perkins, state, college/university.

WORK-STUDY ***Federal work-study:*** *Total amount:* $623,460; 420 jobs averaging $1484. ***State or other work-study/employment:*** *Total amount:* $654,998 (27% need-based, 73% non-need-based). 580 part-time jobs averaging $1434.

APPLYING for FINANCIAL AID ***Required financial aid form:*** FAFSA. ***Financial aid deadline (priority):*** 3/1. ***Notification date:*** Continuous.

CONTACT Mr. Ronald P. Milliken, Director of Financial Aid, University of Maine at Farmington, 86 Main Street, Farmington, ME 04938-1990, 207-778-7100. *Fax:* 207-788-8178.

UNIVERSITY OF MAINE AT FORT KENT

Fort Kent, ME

Tuition & fees (ME res): $3375 **Average undergraduate aid package: $5150**

ABOUT THE INSTITUTION State-supported, coed. Awards: associate and bachelor's degrees. 16 undergraduate majors. Total enrollment: 926. Undergraduates: 926. Freshmen: 130. Federal methodology is used as a basis for awarding need-based institutional aid.

UNDERGRADUATE EXPENSES for 1999–2000 ***Application fee:*** $25. ***One-time required fee:*** $15. ***Tuition, state resident:*** full-time $3120; part-time $104 per credit hour. ***Tuition, nonresident:*** full-time $7590; part-time $253 per credit hour. ***Required fees:*** full-time $255; $8 per credit hour. Full-time tuition and fees vary according to course load and reciprocity agreements. Part-time tuition and fees vary according to course load and reciprocity agreements. ***College room and board:*** $4000; ***room only:*** $2020. Room and board charges vary according to board plan. ***Payment plan:*** installment.

FRESHMAN FINANCIAL AID (Fall 1999, est.) 125 applied for aid; of those 88% were deemed to have need. 81% of freshmen with need received aid; of those 15% had need fully met. *Average percent of need met:* 79% (excluding resources awarded to replace EFC). *Average financial aid package:* $3780 (excluding resources awarded to replace EFC). 9% of all full-time freshmen had no need and received non-need-based aid.

UNDERGRADUATE FINANCIAL AID (Fall 1999, est.) 454 applied for aid; of those 87% were deemed to have need. 80% of undergraduates with need received aid; of those 28% had need fully met. *Average percent of need met:* 85% (excluding resources awarded to replace EFC). *Average financial aid package:* $5150 (excluding resources awarded to replace EFC). 5% of all full-time undergraduates had no need and received non-need-based aid.

GIFT AID (NEED-BASED) ***Total amount:*** $1,016,858 (68% Federal, 15% state, 10% institutional, 7% external sources). ***Receiving aid:*** *Freshmen:* 61% (79); *all full-time undergraduates:* 47% (283). ***Average award:*** Freshmen: $3475; Undergraduates: $3182. ***Scholarships, grants, and awards:*** Federal Pell, FSEOG, state, private, college/university gift aid from institutional funds.

GIFT AID (NON-NEED-BASED) ***Total amount:*** $87,471 (40% institutional, 60% external sources). ***Receiving aid:*** *Freshmen:* 4% (5); *Undergraduates:* 2% (12). ***Scholarships, grants, and awards by category:*** *Academic Interests/Achievement:* business, education, foreign languages, general academic interests/achievements. *Creative Arts/Performance:* general creative arts/performance, performing arts. *Special Achievements/Activities:* general special achievements/activities. *Special Characteristics:* adult students, children of faculty/staff, general special characteristics, international students, members of minority groups. ***Tuition waivers:*** Full or partial for employees or children of employees, senior citizens.

LOANS ***Student loans:*** $1,089,679 (72% need-based, 28% non-need-based). 81% of past graduating class borrowed through all loan programs. Average indebtedness per student: $10,483. ***Average need-based loan:*** Freshmen: $2923; Undergraduates: $3194. ***Parent loans:*** $313,366 (100% non-need-based). ***Programs:*** FFEL (Subsidized and Unsubsidized Stafford, PLUS), Perkins, state, college/university.

WORK-STUDY ***Federal work-study:*** *Total amount:* $211,578; 209 jobs averaging $1012. ***State or other work-study/employment:*** *Total amount:* $38,644 (39% need-based, 61% non-need-based). 41 part-time jobs averaging $943.

APPLYING for FINANCIAL AID ***Required financial aid form:*** FAFSA. ***Financial aid deadline (priority):*** 3/15. ***Notification date:*** Continuous.

CONTACT Mr. John Murphy, Vice President for Administration, University of Maine at Fort Kent, 25 Pleasant Street, Fort Kent, ME 04743-1292, 207-834-7500 or toll-free 888-TRY-UMFK.

UNIVERSITY OF MAINE AT MACHIAS

Machias, ME

Tuition & fees (ME res): $3445 **Average undergraduate aid package: N/A**

ABOUT THE INSTITUTION State-supported, coed. Awards: associate and bachelor's degrees. 26 undergraduate majors. Total enrollment: 908. Undergraduates: 908. Freshmen: 144. Federal methodology is used as a basis for awarding need-based institutional aid.

UNDERGRADUATE EXPENSES for 1999–2000 ***Application fee:*** $25. ***One-time required fee:*** $15. ***Tuition, state resident:*** full-time $3090; part-time $103 per credit. ***Tuition, nonresident:*** full-time $7620; part-time $254 per credit. ***Required fees:*** full-time $355; $11 per credit; $20 per term part-time. Full-time tuition and fees vary according to course load and reciprocity agreements. Part-time tuition and fees vary according to course load and reciprocity agreements. ***College room and board:*** $4330; ***room only:*** $2140. ***Payment plans:*** installment, deferred payment.

GIFT AID (NEED-BASED) ***Scholarships, grants, and awards:*** Federal Pell, FSEOG, state, private, college/university gift aid from institutional funds.

GIFT AID (NON-NEED-BASED) ***Scholarships, grants, and awards by category:*** *Academic Interests/Achievement:* education, general academic interests/achievements, social sciences. *Special Achievements/Activities:* leadership. *Special Characteristics:* children of workers in trades, local/state students. ***Tuition waivers:*** Full or partial for employees or children of employees, senior citizens.

LOANS ***Programs:*** FFEL (Subsidized and Unsubsidized Stafford, PLUS), Perkins.

WORK-STUDY Federal work-study jobs available.

APPLYING for FINANCIAL AID ***Required financial aid form:*** FAFSA. ***Financial aid deadline (priority):*** 3/1. ***Notification date:*** Continuous beginning 3/15. Students must reply within 2 weeks of notification.

CONTACT Ms. Stephanie Larrabee, Director of Financial Aid, University of Maine at Machias, 9 O'Brien Avenue, Machias, ME 04654, 207-255-1203 or toll-free 888-GOTOUMM. *Fax:* 207-255-4864.

UNIVERSITY OF MAINE AT PRESQUE ISLE

Presque Isle, ME

Tuition & fees (ME res): $3390 **Average undergraduate aid package: $5765**

ABOUT THE INSTITUTION State-supported, coed. Awards: associate and bachelor's degrees. 33 undergraduate majors. Total enrollment: 1,378. Undergraduates: 1,378. Freshmen: 223. Federal methodology is used as a basis for awarding need-based institutional aid.

UNDERGRADUATE EXPENSES for 1999–2000 ***Application fee:*** $25. ***One-time required fee:*** $15. ***Tuition, state resident:*** full-time $3090; part-time $103 per credit hour. ***Tuition, nonresident:*** full-time $7560; part-time $252 per credit hour. ***Required fees:*** full-time $300; $8 per credit hour; $20 per term part-time. Full-time tuition and fees vary according to course load and reciprocity agreements. Part-time tuition and fees vary according to course load and reciprocity agreements. ***College room and board:*** $4048; ***room only:*** $2060. Room and board charges vary according to board plan. ***Payment plans:*** installment, deferred payment.

FRESHMAN FINANCIAL AID (Fall 1999) 225 applied for aid; of those 87% were deemed to have need. 90% of freshmen with need received aid; of those 44% had need fully met. *Average percent of need met:* 90% (excluding resources awarded to replace EFC). *Average financial aid package:* $5710 (excluding resources awarded to replace EFC). 8% of all full-time freshmen had no need and received non-need-based aid.

UNDERGRADUATE FINANCIAL AID (Fall 1999) 857 applied for aid; of those 88% were deemed to have need. 86% of undergraduates with need received aid; of those 46% had need fully met. *Average percent of need met:* 90% (excluding resources awarded to replace EFC). *Average financial aid package:* $5765 (excluding resources awarded to replace EFC). 8% of all full-time undergraduates had no need and received non-need-based aid.

GIFT AID (NEED-BASED) ***Total amount:*** $2,489,987 (64% Federal, 16% state, 11% institutional, 9% external sources). ***Receiving aid:*** *Freshmen:* 74% (167); *all full-time undergraduates:* 62% (602). ***Average award:*** Freshmen: $4298; Undergraduates: $3875. ***Scholarships, grants, and awards:*** Federal Pell, FSEOG, state, private, college/university gift aid from institutional funds.

GIFT AID (NON-NEED-BASED) ***Total amount:*** $135,940 (54% institutional, 46% external sources). ***Receiving aid:*** *Freshmen:* 4% (10); *Undergraduates:* 2% (18). ***Scholarships, grants, and awards by category:*** *Academic Interests/Achievement:* 90 awards ($143,057 total): general academic interests/achievements. *Creative Arts/Performance:* 2 awards ($6004 total): art/fine arts. *Special Achievements/Activities:* 3 awards ($1500 total): community service. *Special Characteristics:* 88 awards ($264,068 total): children of faculty/staff, ethnic background, international students, veterans' children. ***Tuition waivers:*** Full or partial for minority students, children of alumni, employees or children of employees, adult students, senior citizens.

University of Maine at Presque Isle (continued)

LOANS ***Student loans:*** $2,031,983 (67% need-based, 33% non-need-based). 52% of past graduating class borrowed through all loan programs. Average indebtedness per student: $10,186. ***Average need-based loan:*** Freshmen: $2132; Undergraduates: $2881. ***Parent loans:*** $69,999 (100% non-need-based). ***Programs:*** Federal Direct (Subsidized and Unsubsidized Stafford, PLUS), FFEL (Subsidized and Unsubsidized Stafford, PLUS), Perkins, state, college/university.

WORK-STUDY ***Federal work-study:*** *Total amount:* $416,139; 259 jobs averaging $1533.

APPLYING for FINANCIAL AID ***Required financial aid form:*** FAFSA. ***Financial aid deadline (priority):*** 4/1. ***Notification date:*** Continuous. Students must reply within 2 weeks of notification.

CONTACT Ms. Barbara J. Bridges, Director of Financial Aid, University of Maine at Presque Isle, 181 Main Street, Presque Isle, ME 04769-2888, 207-768-9513. *Fax:* 207-768-9608. *E-mail:* bridges@maine.maine.edu

UNIVERSITY OF MARY

Bismarck, ND

Tuition & fees: $8300 **Average undergraduate aid package: $7470**

ABOUT THE INSTITUTION Independent Roman Catholic, coed. Awards: associate, bachelor's, and master's degrees. 32 undergraduate majors. Total enrollment: 2,148. Undergraduates: 1,934. Freshmen: 383. Federal methodology is used as a basis for awarding need-based institutional aid.

UNDERGRADUATE EXPENSES for 1999–2000 ***Application fee:*** $15. ***Comprehensive fee:*** $11,838 includes full-time tuition ($8200), mandatory fees ($100), and room and board ($3538). ***College room only:*** $1698. Full-time tuition and fees vary according to course load. Room and board charges vary according to board plan, housing facility, and location. ***Part-time tuition:*** $260 per credit hour. ***Payment plan:*** installment.

FRESHMAN FINANCIAL AID (Fall 1998) 403 applied for aid; of those 71% were deemed to have need. 100% of freshmen with need received aid; of those 52% had need fully met. *Average percent of need met:* 90% (excluding resources awarded to replace EFC). *Average financial aid package:* $7700 (excluding resources awarded to replace EFC). 5% of all full-time freshmen had no need and received non-need-based aid.

UNDERGRADUATE FINANCIAL AID (Fall 1998) 1,740 applied for aid; of those 61% were deemed to have need. 100% of undergraduates with need received aid; of those 81% had need fully met. *Average percent of need met:* 85% (excluding resources awarded to replace EFC). *Average financial aid package:* $7470 (excluding resources awarded to replace EFC).

GIFT AID (NEED-BASED) ***Total amount:*** $1,976,647 (89% Federal, 11% state). ***Receiving aid:*** *Freshmen:* 51% (207); *all full-time undergraduates:* 54% (984). ***Average award:*** Freshmen: $2100; Undergraduates: $2000. ***Scholarships, grants, and awards:*** Federal Pell, FSEOG, state, private, college/university gift aid from institutional funds.

GIFT AID (NON-NEED-BASED) ***Total amount:*** $3,646,154 (88% institutional, 12% external sources). ***Receiving aid:*** *Freshmen:* 71% (286); *Undergraduates:* 56% (1,025). ***Scholarships, grants, and awards by category:*** *Academic Interests/Achievement:* 1,426 awards ($1,775,696 total): communication, general academic interests/achievements. *Creative Arts/Performance:* 293 awards ($215,262 total): debating, music, theater/drama. *Special Characteristics:* children of faculty/staff, spouses of current students. ***Tuition waivers:*** Full or partial for employees or children of employees, senior citizens.

LOANS ***Student loans:*** $9,683,648 (64% need-based, 36% non-need-based). 79% of past graduating class borrowed through all loan programs. Average indebtedness per student: $15,691. ***Average need-based loan:*** Freshmen: $3400; Undergraduates: $3800. ***Parent loans:*** $312,659 (100% non-need-based). ***Programs:*** FFEL (Subsidized and Unsubsidized Stafford, PLUS), Perkins, Federal Nursing, college/university.

WORK-STUDY ***Federal work-study:*** *Total amount:* $257,769; 260 jobs averaging $1000.

ATHLETIC AWARDS *Total amount:* 1,167,676 (100% non-need-based).

APPLYING for FINANCIAL AID ***Required financial aid form:*** FAFSA. ***Financial aid deadline (priority):*** 5/1. ***Notification date:*** Continuous. Students must reply within 2 weeks of notification.

CONTACT Jeff Jacobs, Director of Financial Aid, University of Mary, 7500 University Drive, Bismarck, ND 58504-9652, 701-225-7500 Ext. 383 or toll-free 800-288-6279. *E-mail:* jjacobs@umary.edu

UNIVERSITY OF MARY HARDIN-BAYLOR

Belton, TX

Tuition & fees: $8430 **Average undergraduate aid package: $7477**

ABOUT THE INSTITUTION Independent Southern Baptist, coed. Awards: bachelor's and master's degrees. 44 undergraduate majors. Total enrollment: 2,566. Undergraduates: 2,342. Freshmen: 473. Federal methodology is used as a basis for awarding need-based institutional aid.

UNDERGRADUATE EXPENSES for 1999–2000 ***Application fee:*** $35. ***Comprehensive fee:*** $11,972 includes full-time tuition ($7950), mandatory fees ($480), and room and board ($3542). ***College room only:*** $1550. Full-time tuition and fees vary according to degree level. Room and board charges vary according to housing facility. ***Part-time tuition:*** $265 per semester hour. ***Part-time fees:*** $16 per semester hour. Part-time tuition and fees vary according to degree level. ***Payment plan:*** installment.

FRESHMAN FINANCIAL AID (Fall 1998) 446 applied for aid; of those 87% were deemed to have need. 97% of freshmen with need received aid; of those 46% had need fully met. *Average percent of need met:* 49% (excluding resources awarded to replace EFC). *Average financial aid package:* $6546 (excluding resources awarded to replace EFC). 7% of all full-time freshmen had no need and received non-need-based aid.

UNDERGRADUATE FINANCIAL AID (Fall 1998) 1,559 applied for aid; of those 87% were deemed to have need. 97% of undergraduates with need received aid; of those 46% had need fully met. *Average percent of need met:* 49% (excluding resources awarded to replace EFC). *Average financial aid package:* $7477 (excluding resources awarded to replace EFC). 3% of all full-time undergraduates had no need and received non-need-based aid.

GIFT AID (NEED-BASED) ***Total amount:*** $5,220,735 (35% Federal, 48% state, 17% institutional). ***Receiving aid:*** *Freshmen:* 67% (356); *all full-time undergraduates:* 65% (1,250). ***Scholarships, grants, and awards:*** Federal Pell, FSEOG, state, private, college/university gift aid from institutional funds.

GIFT AID (NON-NEED-BASED) ***Total amount:*** $1,806,719 (80% institutional, 20% external sources). ***Receiving aid:*** *Freshmen:* 30% (161); *Undergraduates:* 29% (566). ***Scholarships, grants, and awards by category:*** *Academic Interests/Achievement:* 382 awards ($586,184 total): biological sciences, business, communication, education, English, foreign languages, general academic interests/achievements, health fields, humanities, international studies, mathematics, physical sciences, premedicine, religion/biblical studies, social sciences. *Creative Arts/Performance:* 91 awards ($119,050 total): art/fine arts, journalism/publications, music. *Special Achievements/Activities:* 90 awards ($163,600 total): cheerleading/drum major, leadership, religious involvement. *Special Characteristics:* 278 awards ($362,832 total): children and siblings of alumni, children of current students, children of faculty/staff, handicapped students, international students, local/state students, parents of current students, relatives of clergy, religious affiliation, siblings of current students. ***Tuition waivers:*** Full or partial for employees or children of employees. ***ROTC:*** Air Force cooperative.

LOANS ***Student loans:*** $8,545,167 (71% need-based, 29% non-need-based). 63% of past graduating class borrowed through all loan programs. Average indebtedness per student: $15,300. ***Parent loans:*** $608,493 (100% non-need-based). ***Programs:*** FFEL (Subsidized and Unsubsidized Stafford, PLUS), Perkins, state, college/university.

WORK-STUDY ***Federal work-study:*** *Total amount:* $433,490; 219 jobs averaging $2100. ***State or other work-study/employment:*** *Total amount:* $330,000 (22% need-based, 78% non-need-based). 107 part-time jobs averaging $2100.

APPLYING for FINANCIAL AID ***Required financial aid form:*** FAFSA. ***Financial aid deadline (priority):*** 3/1. ***Notification date:*** Continuous. Students must reply within 2 weeks of notification.

CONTACT Mr. Victor Howard, Assistant Director of Financial Aid, University of Mary Hardin-Baylor, Box 8004, UMHB Station, Belton, TX 76513, 254-295-4517 or toll-free 800-727-8642. *Fax:* 254-295-5049. *E-mail:* vhoward@umhb.edu

UNIVERSITY OF MARYLAND, BALTIMORE COUNTY

Baltimore, MD

Tuition & fees (MD res): $5160 **Average undergraduate aid package: $6000**

ABOUT THE INSTITUTION State-supported, coed. Awards: bachelor's, master's, and doctoral degrees. 47 undergraduate majors. Total enrollment: 10,265. Undergraduates: 8,854. Freshmen: 1,398. Federal methodology is used as a basis for awarding need-based institutional aid.

UNDERGRADUATE EXPENSES for 1999–2000 ***Application fee:*** $45. ***Tuition, state resident:*** full-time $4046; part-time $170 per credit hour. ***Tuition, nonresident:*** full-time $8518; part-time $353 per credit hour. ***Required fees:*** full-time $1114; $57 per credit hour. Part-time tuition and fees vary according to course load. ***College room and board:*** $5694; ***room only:*** $3414. Room and board charges vary according to board plan and housing facility. ***Payment plan:*** installment.

FRESHMAN FINANCIAL AID (Fall 1999) 996 applied for aid. *Average percent of need met:* 65% (excluding resources awarded to replace EFC). *Average financial aid package:* $6000 (excluding resources awarded to replace EFC).

UNDERGRADUATE FINANCIAL AID (Fall 1999) 5,328 applied for aid. *Average percent of need met:* 65% (excluding resources awarded to replace EFC). *Average financial aid package:* $6000 (excluding resources awarded to replace EFC).

GIFT AID (NEED-BASED) ***Total amount:*** $7,777,410 (53% Federal, 38% state, 9% institutional). ***Scholarships, grants, and awards:*** Federal Pell, FSEOG, state, private, college/university gift aid from institutional funds.

GIFT AID (NON-NEED-BASED) ***Total amount:*** $7,738,823 (1% Federal, 8% state, 56% institutional, 35% external sources). ***Scholarships, grants, and awards by category:*** *Academic Interests/Achievement:* 878 awards ($4,687,479 total): biological sciences, computer science, engineering/technologies, English, foreign languages, general academic interests/achievements, humanities, mathematics, physical sciences. *Creative Arts/Performance:* 87 awards ($485,297 total): art/fine arts, cinema/film/broadcasting, creative writing, dance, music, performing arts, theater/drama. ***Tuition waivers:*** Full or partial for employees or children of employees, senior citizens. ***ROTC:*** Army cooperative, Air Force cooperative.

LOANS ***Student loans:*** $16,288,983 (60% need-based, 40% non-need-based). Average indebtedness per student: $12,000. ***Parent loans:*** $2,475,037 (100% non-need-based). ***Programs:*** FFEL (Subsidized and Unsubsidized Stafford, PLUS), Perkins.

WORK-STUDY ***Federal work-study:*** *Total amount:* $131,270; jobs available.

ATHLETIC AWARDS *Total amount:* 1,565,583 (100% non-need-based).

APPLYING for FINANCIAL AID ***Required financial aid form:*** FAFSA. ***Financial aid deadline (priority):*** 3/1. ***Notification date:*** Continuous beginning 3/15. Students must reply by 5/1 or within 3 weeks of notification.

CONTACT Ms. Janice B. Doyle, Director of Financial Aid and Scholarships, University of Maryland, Baltimore County, 1000 Hilltop Circle, Baltimore, MD 21250, 410-455-2387 or toll-free 800-UMBC-4U2 (in-state), 800-862-2402 (out-of-state). *Fax:* 410-455-1094. *E-mail:* doyle@umbc.edu

UNIVERSITY OF MARYLAND, COLLEGE PARK

College Park, MD

Tuition & fees (MD res): $4939 **Average undergraduate aid package: $7019**

ABOUT THE INSTITUTION State-supported, coed. Awards: bachelor's, master's, and doctoral degrees and post-master's certificates. 125 undergraduate majors. Total enrollment: 32,864. Undergraduates: 24,717. Freshmen: 3,916. Federal methodology is used as a basis for awarding need-based institutional aid.

UNDERGRADUATE EXPENSES for 1999–2000 ***Application fee:*** $45. ***Tuition, state resident:*** full-time $4050; part-time $170 per semester hour. ***Tuition, nonresident:*** full-time $10,938; part-time $456 per semester hour. ***Required fees:*** full-time $889; $198 per term part-time. ***College room and board:*** $6306; ***room only:*** $3686. Room and board charges vary according to board plan. ***Payment plans:*** installment, deferred payment.

FRESHMAN FINANCIAL AID (Fall 1998) 3245 applied for aid; of those 60% were deemed to have need. 94% of freshmen with need received aid; of those 30% had need fully met. *Average percent of need met:* 69% (excluding resources awarded to replace EFC). *Average financial aid package:* $7258 (excluding resources awarded to replace EFC). 19% of all full-time freshmen had no need and received non-need-based aid.

UNDERGRADUATE FINANCIAL AID (Fall 1998) 15,961 applied for aid; of those 68% were deemed to have need. 95% of undergraduates with need received aid; of those 26% had need fully met. *Average percent of need met:* 67% (excluding resources awarded to replace EFC). *Average financial aid package:* $7019 (excluding resources awarded to replace EFC). 13% of all full-time undergraduates had no need and received non-need-based aid.

GIFT AID (NEED-BASED) ***Total amount:*** $21,965,054 (49% Federal, 31% state, 20% institutional). ***Receiving aid:*** *Freshmen:* 30% (1,230); *all full-time undergraduates:* 32% (6,894). ***Average award:*** Freshmen: $4635; Undergraduates: $3105. ***Scholarships, grants, and awards:*** Federal Pell, FSEOG, state, private, college/university gift aid from institutional funds.

GIFT AID (NON-NEED-BASED) ***Total amount:*** $18,265,962 (15% state, 67% institutional, 18% external sources). ***Receiving aid:*** *Freshmen:* 19% (763); *Undergraduates:* 12% (2,579). ***Scholarships, grants, and awards by category:*** *Academic Interests/Achievement:* 4,314 awards ($14,914,993 total): general academic interests/achievements, military science. *Creative Arts/Performance:* 178 awards ($537,411 total): art/fine arts, music, theater/drama. ***Tuition waivers:*** Full or partial for employees or children of employees, senior citizens. ***ROTC:*** Army cooperative, Naval cooperative, Air Force.

LOANS ***Student loans:*** $52,418,937 (77% need-based, 23% non-need-based). Average indebtedness per student: $14,076. ***Average need-based loan:*** Freshmen: $2692; Undergraduates: $3714. ***Parent loans:*** $12,010,745 (41% need-based, 59% non-need-based). ***Programs:*** FFEL (Subsidized and Unsubsidized Stafford, PLUS), Perkins.

WORK-STUDY ***Federal work-study:*** *Total amount:* $1,102,443; 721 jobs averaging $1529.

ATHLETIC AWARDS *Total amount:* 4,708,635 (100% non-need-based).

APPLYING for FINANCIAL AID ***Required financial aid form:*** FAFSA. ***Financial aid deadline (priority):*** 2/15. ***Notification date:*** 4/1.

CONTACT Mr. William D. Leith Jr., Director of Financial Aid, University of Maryland, College Park, Lee Building, College Park, MD 20742, 301-314-9000 or toll-free 800-422-5867. *Fax:* 301-314-9587. *E-mail:* umfinaid@umdacc.umd.edu

UNIVERSITY OF MARYLAND EASTERN SHORE

Princess Anne, MD

ABOUT THE INSTITUTION State-supported, coed. Awards: bachelor's, master's, and doctoral degrees. 53 undergraduate majors. Total enrollment: 3,204. Undergraduates: 2,908.

GIFT AID (NEED-BASED) ***Scholarships, grants, and awards:*** Federal Pell, FSEOG, state, college/university gift aid from institutional funds.

GIFT AID (NON-NEED-BASED) ***Scholarships, grants, and awards by category:*** *Academic Interests/Achievement:* agriculture, business, education, engineering/technologies, English, general academic interests/achievements, home economics. *Creative Arts/Performance:* art/fine arts,

University of Maryland Eastern Shore (continued)

music, performing arts, theater/drama. *Special Achievements/Activities:* community service, leadership. *Special Characteristics:* children of faculty/staff, first-generation college students.

LOANS ***Programs:*** Federal Direct (Subsidized and Unsubsidized Stafford, PLUS), Perkins.

WORK-STUDY Federal work-study jobs available.

APPLYING for FINANCIAL AID ***Required financial aid forms:*** FAFSA, institution's own form.

CONTACT Ms. Dorothy J. Body, Director of Financial Aid, University of Maryland Eastern Shore, Backbone Road, Princess Anne, MD 21853-1299, 410-651-6172. *Fax:* 410-651-7670.

UNIVERSITY OF MARYLAND UNIVERSITY COLLEGE

College Park, MD

Tuition & fees (MD res): $4416 Average undergraduate aid package: $1480

ABOUT THE INSTITUTION State-supported, coed. Awards: associate, bachelor's, master's, and doctoral degrees and post-bachelor's and post-master's certificates (offers primarily part-time evening and weekend degree programs at more than 30 off-campus locations in Maryland and the Washington, DC area, and more than 180 military communities in Europe and Asia with military enrollment not reflected in this profile; associate of arts program available to military students only). 29 undergraduate majors. Total enrollment: 15,673. Undergraduates: 11,603. Freshmen: 516. Federal methodology is used as a basis for awarding need-based institutional aid.

UNDERGRADUATE EXPENSES for 1999–2000 ***Application fee:*** $30. ***Tuition, state resident:*** full-time $4416; part-time $184 per semester hour. ***Tuition, nonresident:*** full-time $5664; part-time $236 per semester hour.

FRESHMAN FINANCIAL AID (Fall 1998) 20 applied for aid; of those 95% were deemed to have need. 84% of freshmen with need received aid. *Average percent of need met:* 18% (excluding resources awarded to replace EFC). *Average financial aid package:* $1201 (excluding resources awarded to replace EFC).

UNDERGRADUATE FINANCIAL AID (Fall 1998) 835 applied for aid; of those 89% were deemed to have need. 91% of undergraduates with need received aid; of those .1% had need fully met. *Average percent of need met:* 22% (excluding resources awarded to replace EFC). *Average financial aid package:* $1480 (excluding resources awarded to replace EFC). 1% of all full-time undergraduates had no need and received non-need-based aid.

GIFT AID (NEED-BASED) ***Total amount:*** $3,283,203 (58% Federal, 13% state, 29% institutional). ***Receiving aid:*** *Freshmen:* 32% (12); *all full-time undergraduates:* 36% (505). ***Average award:*** Freshmen: $895; Undergraduates: $827. ***Scholarships, grants, and awards:*** Federal Pell, FSEOG, state, private, college/university gift aid from institutional funds.

GIFT AID (NON-NEED-BASED) ***Total amount:*** $150,109 (42% state, 37% institutional, 21% external sources). ***Receiving aid:*** *Freshmen:* 3% (1); *Undergraduates:* 2% (28). ***Scholarships, grants, and awards by category:*** *Academic Interests/Achievement:* general academic interests/achievements. ***Tuition waivers:*** Full or partial for employees or children of employees, senior citizens.

LOANS ***Student loans:*** $21,888,905 (54% need-based, 46% non-need-based). 8% of past graduating class borrowed through all loan programs. Average indebtedness per student: $1799. ***Average need-based loan:*** Freshmen: $1289; Undergraduates: $1958. ***Parent loans:*** $9378 (100% non-need-based). ***Programs:*** Federal Direct (Subsidized and Unsubsidized Stafford, PLUS), Perkins.

WORK-STUDY ***Federal work-study:*** *Total amount:* $24,838; jobs available. ***State or other work-study/employment:*** *Total amount:* $194,213 (100% non-need-based). Part-time jobs available.

APPLYING for FINANCIAL AID ***Required financial aid forms:*** FAFSA, institution's own form, financial aid transcript (for mid-year transfers). ***Financial aid deadline (priority):*** 6/1. ***Notification date:*** Continuous. Students must reply within 3 weeks of notification.

CONTACT Financial Aid Counselor, University of Maryland University College, University Boulevard at Adelphi Road, College Park, MD 20742-1600, 301-985-7000 or toll-free 800-888-UMUC (in-state). *Fax:* 301-985-7226. *E-mail:* umucinfo@nova.umuc.edu

UNIVERSITY OF MASSACHUSETTS AMHERST

Amherst, MA

Tuition & fees (MA res): $5323 Average undergraduate aid package: $8069

ABOUT THE INSTITUTION State-supported, coed. Awards: associate, bachelor's, master's, and doctoral degrees and post-master's certificates. 89 undergraduate majors. Total enrollment: 25,031. Undergraduates: 19,372. Freshmen: 4,196. Federal methodology is used as a basis for awarding need-based institutional aid.

UNDERGRADUATE EXPENSES for 1999–2000 ***Application fee:*** $25; $40 for nonresidents. ***One-time required fee:*** $153. ***Tuition, state resident:*** full-time $1714; part-time $72 per credit. ***Tuition, nonresident:*** full-time $9756; part-time $406 per credit. ***Required fees:*** full-time $3609; $494 per term part-time. Full-time tuition and fees vary according to reciprocity agreements. Part-time tuition and fees vary according to course load and reciprocity agreements. ***College room and board:*** $4790; ***room only:*** $2638. Room and board charges vary according to board plan. ***Payment plan:*** installment.

FRESHMAN FINANCIAL AID (Fall 1999, est.) 3529 applied for aid; of those 64% were deemed to have need. 95% of freshmen with need received aid; of those 21% had need fully met. *Average percent of need met:* 80% (excluding resources awarded to replace EFC). *Average financial aid package:* $6965 (excluding resources awarded to replace EFC).

UNDERGRADUATE FINANCIAL AID (Fall 1999, est.) 13,133 applied for aid; of those 70% were deemed to have need. 97% of undergraduates with need received aid; of those 40% had need fully met. *Average percent of need met:* 86% (excluding resources awarded to replace EFC). *Average financial aid package:* $8069 (excluding resources awarded to replace EFC).

GIFT AID (NEED-BASED) ***Total amount:*** $28,900,322 (38% Federal, 16% state, 39% institutional, 7% external sources). ***Receiving aid:*** *Freshmen:* 1,732; *all full-time undergraduates:* 7,084. ***Average award:*** Freshmen: $5164; Undergraduates: $5305. ***Scholarships, grants, and awards:*** Federal Pell, FSEOG, state, private, college/university gift aid from institutional funds.

GIFT AID (NON-NEED-BASED) ***Total amount:*** $3,473,284 (79% institutional, 21% external sources). ***Receiving aid:*** *Freshmen:* 31; *Undergraduates:* 60. ***Scholarships, grants, and awards by category:*** *Academic Interests/Achievement:* agriculture, architecture, biological sciences, business, communication, computer science, education, engineering/technologies, general academic interests/achievements, health fields, humanities, mathematics, military science, physical sciences, premedicine, social sciences. *Creative Arts/Performance:* art/fine arts, dance, music, theater/drama. *Special Achievements/Activities:* cheerleading/drum major, general special achievements/activities, leadership. *Special Characteristics:* children and siblings of alumni, children of faculty/staff, handicapped students, veterans. ***Tuition waivers:*** Full or partial for employees or children of employees, senior citizens. ***ROTC:*** Army, Air Force.

LOANS ***Student loans:*** $45,581,100 (69% need-based, 31% non-need-based). 42% of past graduating class borrowed through all loan programs. Average indebtedness per student: $16,255. ***Average need-based loan:*** Freshmen: $2784; Undergraduates: $3594. ***Parent loans:*** $10,803,254 (36% need-based, 64% non-need-based). ***Programs:*** Federal Direct (Subsidized and Unsubsidized Stafford, PLUS), Perkins, state.

WORK-STUDY ***Federal work-study:*** *Total amount:* $8,354,075; jobs available.

ATHLETIC AWARDS *Total amount:* 3,889,062 (32% need-based, 68% non-need-based).

APPLYING for FINANCIAL AID ***Required financial aid form:*** FAFSA. ***Financial aid deadline (priority):*** 3/1. ***Notification date:*** Continuous beginning 4/1. Students must reply within 6 weeks of notification.

CONTACT Office of Financial Aid Services, University of Massachusetts Amherst, 255 Whitmore Administration Building, Amherst, MA 01003, 413-545-0801.

UNIVERSITY OF MASSACHUSETTS BOSTON

Boston, MA

Tuition & fees (MA res): $4307 **Average undergraduate aid package: $7447**

ABOUT THE INSTITUTION State-supported, coed. Awards: bachelor's, master's, and doctoral degrees and post-master's certificates. 44 undergraduate majors. Total enrollment: 13,778. Undergraduates: 10,579. Freshmen: 789. Federal methodology is used as a basis for awarding need-based institutional aid.

UNDERGRADUATE EXPENSES for 1999–2000 ***Application fee:*** $25. ***One-time required fee:*** $150. ***Tuition, state resident:*** full-time $1714; part-time $72 per credit. ***Tuition, nonresident:*** full-time $9758; part-time $406 per credit. ***Required fees:*** full-time $2593; $482 per term part-time. Part-time tuition and fees vary according to course load. Additional part-time mandatory fees per term: $15 for nonresidents. ***Payment plan:*** installment.

FRESHMAN FINANCIAL AID (Fall 1999) 539 applied for aid; of those 91% were deemed to have need. 85% of freshmen with need received aid; of those 36% had need fully met. *Average percent of need met:* 100% (excluding resources awarded to replace EFC). *Average financial aid package:* $6676 (excluding resources awarded to replace EFC). 3% of all full-time freshmen had no need and received non-need-based aid.

UNDERGRADUATE FINANCIAL AID (Fall 1999) 3,860 applied for aid; of those 92% were deemed to have need. 85% of undergraduates with need received aid; of those 40% had need fully met. *Average percent of need met:* 79% (excluding resources awarded to replace EFC). *Average financial aid package:* $7447 (excluding resources awarded to replace EFC). 5% of all full-time undergraduates had no need and received non-need-based aid.

GIFT AID (NEED-BASED) ***Receiving aid:*** *Freshmen:* 61% (412); *all full-time undergraduates:* 48% (2,892). ***Average award:*** Freshmen: $3514; Undergraduates: $3682. ***Scholarships, grants, and awards:*** Federal Pell, FSEOG, state, private, college/university gift aid from institutional funds.

GIFT AID (NON-NEED-BASED) ***Receiving aid:*** *Freshmen:* 13% (85); *Undergraduates:* 5% (326). ***Scholarships, grants, and awards by category:*** *Academic Interests/Achievement:* general academic interests/achievements. ***Tuition waivers:*** Full or partial for employees or children of employees, senior citizens.

LOANS ***Student loans:*** Average indebtedness per student: $17,340. ***Average need-based loan:*** Freshmen: $2469; Undergraduates: $3561. ***Programs:*** FFEL (Subsidized and Unsubsidized Stafford, PLUS), Perkins, state, TERI Loans, CitiAssist Loans.

WORK-STUDY Federal work-study jobs available.

APPLYING for FINANCIAL AID ***Required financial aid form:*** FAFSA. ***Financial aid deadline (priority):*** 3/1. ***Notification date:*** Continuous beginning 4/1.

CONTACT Ms. Ernestine Whiting-Settles, Director of Financial Aid Services, University of Massachusetts Boston, 100 Morrissey Boulevard, Boston, MA 02125-3393, 617-287-6300. *E-mail:* ernestine.whiting@umb.edu

UNIVERSITY OF MASSACHUSETTS DARTMOUTH

North Dartmouth, MA

Tuition & fees (MA res): $4129 **Average undergraduate aid package: $6912**

ABOUT THE INSTITUTION State-supported, coed. Awards: bachelor's, master's, and doctoral degrees and post-bachelor's and post-master's certificates. 45 undergraduate majors. Total enrollment: 6,963. Undergraduates: 6,162. Freshmen: 1,142. Federal methodology is used as a basis for awarding need-based institutional aid.

UNDERGRADUATE EXPENSES for 1999–2000 ***Application fee:*** $20; $40 for nonresidents. ***Tuition, state resident:*** full-time $1417; part-time $59 per credit hour. ***Tuition, nonresident:*** full-time $9071; part-time $327 per credit hour. ***Required fees:*** full-time $2712; $113 per credit hour. Part-time tuition and fees vary according to course load and program. ***College room and board:*** $4992; ***room only:*** $2827. Room and board charges vary according to board plan and housing facility. ***Payment plan:*** installment.

UNDERGRADUATE FINANCIAL AID (Fall 1998) 2,118 applied for aid; of those 80% were deemed to have need. 100% of undergraduates with need received aid; of those 70% had need fully met. *Average percent of need met:* 90% (excluding resources awarded to replace EFC). *Average financial aid package:* $6912 (excluding resources awarded to replace EFC). 6% of all full-time undergraduates had no need and received non-need-based aid.

GIFT AID (NEED-BASED) ***Receiving aid:*** *All full-time undergraduates:* 36% (1,576). ***Average award:*** Undergraduates: $2669. ***Scholarships, grants, and awards:*** Federal Pell, FSEOG, state, private, college/university gift aid from institutional funds.

GIFT AID (NON-NEED-BASED) ***Scholarships, grants, and awards by category:*** *Academic Interests/Achievement:* general academic interests/achievements. ***Tuition waivers:*** Full or partial for employees or children of employees, senior citizens. ***ROTC:*** Army cooperative.

LOANS ***Student loans:*** 65% of past graduating class borrowed through all loan programs. Average indebtedness per student: $13,446. ***Average need-based loan:*** Undergraduates: $3498. ***Programs:*** Federal Direct (Subsidized and Unsubsidized Stafford, PLUS), Perkins, Federal Nursing, state.

WORK-STUDY Federal work-study jobs available.

APPLYING for FINANCIAL AID ***Required financial aid form:*** FAFSA. ***Financial aid deadline (priority):*** 3/1. ***Notification date:*** Continuous.

CONTACT Gerald Coutinho, Director of Financial Aid, University of Massachusetts Dartmouth, 285 Old Westport Road, North Dartmouth, MA 02747-2300, 508-999-8631. *Fax:* 508-999-8935. *E-mail:* gcoutinho@umassd.edu

UNIVERSITY OF MASSACHUSETTS LOWELL

Lowell, MA

Tuition & fees (MA res): $4255 **Average undergraduate aid package: $6702**

ABOUT THE INSTITUTION State-supported, coed. Awards: associate, bachelor's, master's, and doctoral degrees. 34 undergraduate majors. Total enrollment: 12,038. Undergraduates: 9,354. Freshmen: 950. Federal methodology is used as a basis for awarding need-based institutional aid.

UNDERGRADUATE EXPENSES for 1999–2000 ***Application fee:*** $20; $35 for nonresidents. ***Tuition, state resident:*** full-time $1454; part-time $61 per credit. ***Tuition, nonresident:*** full-time $8091; part-time $328 per credit. ***Required fees:*** full-time $2801; $129 per credit. ***College room and board:*** $4726; ***room only:*** $2800. Room and board charges vary according to board plan and housing facility. ***Payment plan:*** installment.

FRESHMAN FINANCIAL AID (Fall 1999, est.) 768 applied for aid; of those 72% were deemed to have need. 96% of freshmen with need received aid; of those 86% had need fully met. *Average percent of need met:* 98% (excluding resources awarded to replace EFC). *Average financial aid package:* $6565 (excluding resources awarded to replace EFC). 3% of all full-time freshmen had no need and received non-need-based aid.

UNDERGRADUATE FINANCIAL AID (Fall 1999, est.) 3,286 applied for aid; of those 74% were deemed to have need. 98% of undergraduates with need received aid; of those 90% had need fully met. *Average percent of need met:* 97% (excluding resources awarded to replace EFC). *Average financial aid package:* $6702 (excluding resources awarded to replace EFC). 3% of all full-time undergraduates had no need and received non-need-based aid.

GIFT AID (NEED-BASED) ***Total amount:*** $5,389,777 (57% Federal, 42% state, 1% institutional). ***Receiving aid:*** *Freshmen:* 50% (464); *all full-time undergraduates:* 40% (2,067). ***Average award:*** Freshmen: $1175; Undergradu-

University of Massachusetts Lowell (continued)

ates: $1171. ***Scholarships, grants, and awards:*** Federal Pell, FSEOG, state, private, college/university gift aid from institutional funds.

GIFT AID (NON-NEED-BASED) ***Total amount:*** $1,098,930 (1% state, 62% institutional, 37% external sources). ***Receiving aid:*** *Freshmen:* 6% (60); *Undergraduates:* 7% (365). ***Scholarships, grants, and awards by category:*** *Academic Interests/Achievement:* computer science, engineering/technologies, general academic interests/achievements, health fields, humanities. *Creative Arts/Performance:* music. *Special Achievements/Activities:* community service, general special achievements/activities. *Special Characteristics:* general special characteristics. ***Tuition waivers:*** Full or partial for employees or children of employees, senior citizens. ***ROTC:*** Air Force.

LOANS ***Student loans:*** $12,834,222 (47% need-based, 53% non-need-based). 68% of past graduating class borrowed through all loan programs. Average indebtedness per student: $15,735. ***Average need-based loan:*** Freshmen: $2158; Undergraduates: $2821. ***Parent loans:*** $682,765 (100% non-need-based). ***Programs:*** Federal Direct (Subsidized and Unsubsidized Stafford, PLUS), Perkins, state.

WORK-STUDY ***Federal work-study:*** *Total amount:* $542,000; jobs available. ***State or other work-study/employment:*** *Total amount:* $2,000,000 (100% need-based). Part-time jobs available.

ATHLETIC AWARDS *Total amount:* 502,780 (100% non-need-based).

APPLYING for FINANCIAL AID ***Required financial aid form:*** FAFSA. ***Financial aid deadline (priority):*** 3/1. ***Notification date:*** 4/1.

CONTACT Ms. Judy Keyes, Director of Student Financial Assistance, University of Massachusetts Lowell, 71 Wilder Street, Lowell, MA 01854-2881, 978-934-4232 or toll-free 800-410-4607.

UNIVERSITY OF MEDICINE AND DENTISTRY OF NEW JERSEY

Newark, NJ

CONTACT Financial Aid Office, University of Medicine and Dentistry of New Jersey, 65 Bergen Street, Newark, NJ 07107-3001, 973-972-4300.

THE UNIVERSITY OF MEMPHIS

Memphis, TN

Tuition & fees (TN res): $2818 **Average undergraduate aid package: $4118**

ABOUT THE INSTITUTION State-supported, coed. Awards: bachelor's, master's, doctoral, and first professional degrees and post-bachelor's, post-master's, and first-professional certificates. 49 undergraduate majors. Total enrollment: 20,301. Undergraduates: 15,428. Freshmen: 1,939. Federal methodology is used as a basis for awarding need-based institutional aid.

UNDERGRADUATE EXPENSES for 1999–2000 ***Application fee:*** $15. ***Tuition, state resident:*** full-time $2730; part-time $130 per credit hour. ***Tuition, nonresident:*** full-time $7990; part-time $360 per credit hour. ***Required fees:*** full-time $88; $6 per credit hour. Part-time tuition and fees vary according to course load. ***College room and board:*** $3320; ***room only:*** $1820. Room and board charges vary according to housing facility. ***Payment plan:*** installment.

FRESHMAN FINANCIAL AID (Fall 1998) 739 applied for aid; of those 65% were deemed to have need. 96% of freshmen with need received aid; of those 11% had need fully met. *Average percent of need met:* 82% (excluding resources awarded to replace EFC). *Average financial aid package:* $3796 (excluding resources awarded to replace EFC). 7% of all full-time freshmen had no need and received non-need-based aid.

UNDERGRADUATE FINANCIAL AID (Fall 1998) 6,866 applied for aid; of those 64% were deemed to have need. 96% of undergraduates with need received aid; of those 18% had need fully met. *Average percent of need met:* 76% (excluding resources awarded to replace EFC). *Average financial aid package:* $4118 (excluding resources awarded to replace EFC). 10% of all full-time undergraduates had no need and received non-need-based aid.

GIFT AID (NEED-BASED) ***Total amount:*** $14,804,617 (64% Federal, 11% state, 21% institutional, 4% external sources). ***Receiving aid:*** *Freshmen:* 18% (301); *all full-time undergraduates:* 25% (2,741). ***Average award:*** Freshmen: $2339; Undergraduates: $2347. ***Scholarships, grants, and awards:*** Federal Pell, FSEOG, state, college/university gift aid from institutional funds, Federal Nursing.

GIFT AID (NON-NEED-BASED) ***Total amount:*** $2,658,121 (90% institutional, 10% external sources). ***Receiving aid:*** *Freshmen:* 5% (88); *Undergraduates:* 6% (709). ***Scholarships, grants, and awards by category:*** *Academic Interests/Achievement:* biological sciences, business, communication, education, engineering/technologies, English, general academic interests/achievements, health fields, humanities, international studies, mathematics, military science, physical sciences, premedicine, social sciences. *Creative Arts/Performance:* art/fine arts, cinema/film/broadcasting, dance, journalism/publications, music. *Special Achievements/Activities:* cheerleading/drum major, general special achievements/activities, leadership. *Special Characteristics:* adult students, children of educators, children of faculty/staff, children of public servants, handicapped students, members of minority groups, public servants. ***Tuition waivers:*** Full or partial for employees or children of employees, senior citizens. ***ROTC:*** Army, Naval, Air Force.

LOANS ***Student loans:*** $31,042,193 (63% need-based, 37% non-need-based). Average indebtedness per student: $17,257. ***Average need-based loan:*** Freshmen: $900; Undergraduates: $1779. ***Parent loans:*** $771,666 (100% non-need-based). ***Programs:*** Federal Direct (Subsidized and Unsubsidized Stafford, PLUS), Perkins, college/university.

WORK-STUDY ***Federal work-study:*** *Total amount:* $486,491; 398 jobs averaging $1222.

ATHLETIC AWARDS *Total amount:* 3,062,600 (66% need-based, 34% non-need-based).

APPLYING for FINANCIAL AID ***Required financial aid form:*** FAFSA. ***Financial aid deadline (priority):*** 3/1. ***Notification date:*** Continuous.

CONTACT Dr. Charles Boudreau, Director of Student Aid, The University of Memphis, Scates Hall 312, Memphis, TN 38152, 901-678-2832. *Fax:* 901-678-3590. *E-mail:* cboudrea@memphis.edu

UNIVERSITY OF MIAMI

Coral Gables, FL

Tuition & fees: $21,344 **Average undergraduate aid package: $19,537**

ABOUT THE INSTITUTION Independent, coed. Awards: bachelor's, master's, doctoral, and first professional degrees and post-bachelor's and post-master's certificates. 96 undergraduate majors. Total enrollment: 13,715. Undergraduates: 8,628. Freshmen: 1,859. Federal methodology is used as a basis for awarding need-based institutional aid.

UNDERGRADUATE EXPENSES for 1999–2000 ***Application fee:*** $45. ***Comprehensive fee:*** $29,126 includes full-time tuition ($20,950), mandatory fees ($394), and room and board ($7782). ***College room only:*** $4424. Room and board charges vary according to board plan and housing facility. ***Payment plans:*** tuition prepayment, installment.

FRESHMAN FINANCIAL AID (Fall 1999) 1308 applied for aid; of those 83% were deemed to have need. 100% of freshmen with need received aid; of those 20% had need fully met. *Average percent of need met:* 85% (excluding resources awarded to replace EFC). *Average financial aid package:* $18,948 (excluding resources awarded to replace EFC). 24% of all full-time freshmen had no need and received non-need-based aid.

UNDERGRADUATE FINANCIAL AID (Fall 1999) 4,907 applied for aid; of those 89% were deemed to have need. 100% of undergraduates with need received aid; of those 25% had need fully met. *Average percent of need met:* 85% (excluding resources awarded to replace EFC). *Average financial aid package:* $19,537 (excluding resources awarded to replace EFC). 21% of all full-time undergraduates had no need and received non-need-based aid.

GIFT AID (NEED-BASED) ***Total amount:*** $55,298,520 (10% Federal, 18% state, 70% institutional, 2% external sources). ***Receiving aid:*** *Freshmen:* 57% (1,051); *all full-time undergraduates:* 56% (4,309). ***Average award:***

Freshmen: $14,133; Undergraduates: $13,616. ***Scholarships, grants, and awards:*** Federal Pell, FSEOG, state, private, college/university gift aid from institutional funds, Federal Nursing.

GIFT AID (NON-NEED-BASED) ***Total amount:*** $19,418,642 (1% Federal, 27% state, 70% institutional, 2% external sources). ***Receiving aid:*** *Freshmen:* 8% (155); *Undergraduates:* 6% (485). ***Scholarships, grants, and awards by category:*** *Academic Interests/Achievement:* 3,116 awards ($29,801,425 total): general academic interests/achievements. *Creative Arts/Performance:* art/fine arts, debating, music, theater/drama. *Special Achievements/Activities:* general special achievements/activities. *Special Characteristics:* 534 awards ($1,809,190 total): ethnic background. ***Tuition waivers:*** Full or partial for employees or children of employees. ***ROTC:*** Army cooperative, Air Force.

LOANS ***Student loans:*** $30,656,759 (79% need-based, 21% non-need-based). 59% of past graduating class borrowed through all loan programs. Average indebtedness per student: $19,108. ***Average need-based loan:*** Freshmen: $3330; Undergraduates: $4587. ***Parent loans:*** $7,790,848 (42% need-based, 58% non-need-based). ***Programs:*** FFEL (Subsidized and Unsubsidized Stafford, PLUS), Perkins, Federal Nursing, Signature Loans.

WORK-STUDY ***Federal work-study:*** *Total amount:* $5,770,252; 2,424 jobs averaging $2196. ***State or other work-study/employment:*** *Total amount:* $847,813 (23% need-based, 77% non-need-based). 246 part-time jobs averaging $3446.

ATHLETIC AWARDS *Total amount:* 5,334,919 (34% need-based, 66% non-need-based).

APPLYING for FINANCIAL AID ***Required financial aid forms:*** FAFSA, state aid form. ***Financial aid deadline (priority):*** 2/15. ***Notification date:*** Continuous beginning 3/1. Students must reply by 5/1.

CONTACT Mr. Martin J. Carney, Director, Financial Assistance Services, University of Miami, 1204 Dickinson Drive, PO Box 248187, Coral Gables, FL 33124-5240, 305-284-5212. *Fax:* 305-284-4491. *E-mail:* mcarney@miami.edu

UNIVERSITY OF MICHIGAN

Ann Arbor, MI

Tuition & fees (MI res): $6333 **Average undergraduate aid package: $10,405**

ABOUT THE INSTITUTION State-supported, coed. Awards: bachelor's, master's, doctoral, and first professional degrees and post-master's certificates. 144 undergraduate majors. Total enrollment: 37,846. Undergraduates: 24,493. Freshmen: 5,559. Federal methodology is used as a basis for awarding need-based institutional aid.

UNDERGRADUATE EXPENSES for 1999–2000 ***Application fee:*** $40. ***Tuition, state resident:*** full-time $6148; part-time $232 per credit hour. ***Tuition, nonresident:*** full-time $19,576; part-time $792 per credit hour. ***Required fees:*** full-time $185. Full-time tuition and fees vary according to program and student level. Part-time tuition and fees vary according to course load, program, and student level. ***College room and board:*** $5614. Room and board charges vary according to board plan and housing facility. ***Payment plan:*** installment.

FRESHMAN FINANCIAL AID (Fall 1998) 2298 applied for aid; of those 70% were deemed to have need. 100% of freshmen with need received aid; of those 90% had need fully met. *Average percent of need met:* 90% (excluding resources awarded to replace EFC). *Average financial aid package:* $9401 (excluding resources awarded to replace EFC). 15% of all full-time freshmen had no need and received non-need-based aid.

UNDERGRADUATE FINANCIAL AID (Fall 1998) 11,466 applied for aid; of those 80% were deemed to have need. 100% of undergraduates with need received aid; of those 90% had need fully met. *Average percent of need met:* 90% (excluding resources awarded to replace EFC). *Average financial aid package:* $10,405 (excluding resources awarded to replace EFC). 18% of all full-time undergraduates had no need and received non-need-based aid.

GIFT AID (NEED-BASED) ***Total amount:*** $38,842,698 (20% Federal, 80% institutional). ***Receiving aid:*** *Freshmen:* 21% (1,127); *all full-time undergraduates:* 27% (6,481). ***Average award:*** Freshmen: $5607; Undergraduates: $5993. ***Scholarships, grants, and awards:*** Federal Pell, FSEOG, state, private, college/university gift aid from institutional funds.

GIFT AID (NON-NEED-BASED) ***Total amount:*** $28,660,122 (9% Federal, 15% state, 53% institutional, 23% external sources). ***Receiving aid:*** *Freshmen:* 18% (961); *Undergraduates:* 23% (5,459). ***Scholarships, grants, and awards by category:*** *Academic Interests/Achievement:* architecture, area/ethnic studies, biological sciences, business, communication, computer science, education, engineering/technologies, English, foreign languages, general academic interests/achievements, health fields, humanities, international studies, library science, mathematics, military science, physical sciences, premedicine, social sciences. *Creative Arts/Performance:* journalism/publications, music, theater/drama. *Special Achievements/Activities:* community service, general special achievements/activities, leadership. *Special Characteristics:* children of faculty/staff, children of workers in trades, handicapped students, international students, local/state students, members of minority groups, out-of-state students. ***Tuition waivers:*** Full or partial for employees or children of employees, senior citizens. ***ROTC:*** Army, Naval, Air Force.

LOANS ***Student loans:*** $59,638,818 (75% need-based, 25% non-need-based). Average indebtedness per student: $14,534. ***Average need-based loan:*** Freshmen: $1470; Undergraduates: $3837. ***Parent loans:*** $9,028,098 (100% non-need-based). ***Programs:*** Federal Direct (Subsidized and Unsubsidized Stafford, PLUS), Perkins, Federal Nursing, state, college/university, MI-Loan Program, Health Professions Student Loans (HPSL).

WORK-STUDY ***Federal work-study:*** *Total amount:* $9,171,299; 5,198 jobs averaging $1764. ***State or other work-study/employment:*** *Total amount:* $2,749,158 (100% need-based). 1,124 part-time jobs averaging $2446.

ATHLETIC AWARDS *Total amount:* 8,170,374 (100% non-need-based).

APPLYING for FINANCIAL AID ***Required financial aid forms:*** FAFSA, parent and student federal income tax forms. ***Financial aid deadline:*** 9/30 (priority: 2/15). ***Notification date:*** Continuous. Students must reply within 2 weeks of notification.

CONTACT Financial Aid Counseling and Advising Office, University of Michigan, 2011 Student Activities Building, Ann Arbor, MI 48109-1316, 734-763-6600. *Fax:* 734-647-3081. *E-mail:* financial.aid@umich.edu

UNIVERSITY OF MICHIGAN–DEARBORN

Dearborn, MI

Tuition & fees (MI res): $4361 **Average undergraduate aid package: $6535**

ABOUT THE INSTITUTION State-supported, coed. Awards: bachelor's and master's degrees. 60 undergraduate majors. Total enrollment: 8,076. Undergraduates: 6,523. Freshmen: 767. Federal methodology is used as a basis for awarding need-based institutional aid.

UNDERGRADUATE EXPENSES for 1999–2000 ***Application fee:*** $30. ***Tuition, state resident:*** full-time $4077; part-time $161 per credit. ***Tuition, nonresident:*** full-time $11,565; part-time $460 per credit. ***Required fees:*** full-time $284; $10 per credit; $62 per term part-time. Full-time tuition and fees vary according to course level, course load, program, and student level. Part-time tuition and fees vary according to course level, course load, program, and student level. ***Payment plan:*** installment.

FRESHMAN FINANCIAL AID (Fall 1998) 513 applied for aid; of those 59% were deemed to have need. 97% of freshmen with need received aid; of those 23% had need fully met. *Average percent of need met:* 53% (excluding resources awarded to replace EFC). *Average financial aid package:* $3450 (excluding resources awarded to replace EFC). 1% of all full-time freshmen had no need and received non-need-based aid.

UNDERGRADUATE FINANCIAL AID (Fall 1998) 2,197 applied for aid; of those 65% were deemed to have need. 98% of undergraduates with need received aid; of those 21% had need fully met. *Average percent of need met:* 84% (excluding resources awarded to replace EFC). *Average financial aid package:* $6535 (excluding resources awarded to replace EFC). 1% of all full-time undergraduates had no need and received non-need-based aid.

GIFT AID (NEED-BASED) ***Total amount:*** $3,449,877 (60% Federal, 15% state, 25% institutional). ***Receiving aid:*** *Freshmen:* 28% (210); *all full-time undergraduates:* 27% (978). ***Average award:*** Freshmen: $2516;

University of Michigan–Dearborn (continued)

Undergraduates: $2517. ***Scholarships, grants, and awards:*** Federal Pell, FSEOG, state, private, college/university gift aid from institutional funds.

GIFT AID (NON-NEED-BASED) ***Total amount:*** $2,160,462 (1% state, 48% institutional, 51% external sources). ***Receiving aid:*** *Freshmen:* 22% (164); *Undergraduates:* 16% (604). ***Scholarships, grants, and awards by category:*** *Academic Interests/Achievement:* 235 awards ($499,100 total): biological sciences, business, computer science, engineering/technologies, general academic interests/achievements, international studies, physical sciences, social sciences. *Creative Arts/Performance:* 9 awards ($1825 total): art/fine arts, creative writing, journalism/publications. *Special Achievements/Activities:* 8 awards ($3076 total): community service. *Special Characteristics:* 193 awards ($463,644 total): children and siblings of alumni, children of current students, ethnic background, general special characteristics, members of minority groups, previous college experience, religious affiliation. ***Tuition waivers:*** Full or partial for employees or children of employees, senior citizens. ***ROTC:*** Army, Naval cooperative, Air Force cooperative.

LOANS ***Student loans:*** $9,924,270 (99% need-based, 1% non-need-based). Average indebtedness per student: $14,314. ***Average need-based loan:*** Freshmen: $1044; Undergraduates: $3148. ***Parent loans:*** $59,455 (100% non-need-based). ***Programs:*** Federal Direct (Subsidized and Unsubsidized Stafford, PLUS), Perkins, state, college/university.

WORK-STUDY ***Federal work-study:*** *Total amount:* $29,200; 27 jobs averaging $1081. ***State or other work-study/employment:*** *Total amount:* $55,250 (100% need-based). 40 part-time jobs averaging $1381.

ATHLETIC AWARDS *Total amount:* 73,805 (100% non-need-based).

APPLYING for FINANCIAL AID ***Required financial aid form:*** FAFSA. ***Financial aid deadline (priority):*** 4/1. ***Notification date:*** Continuous. Students must reply within 3 weeks of notification.

CONTACT Mr. John A. Mason, Director of Financial Aid, University of Michigan–Dearborn, 4901 Evergreen Road, 205 SSC, Dearborn, MI 48128-1491, 313-593-5300. *Fax:* 313-593-5313. *E-mail:* jamason@umd.umich.edu

UNIVERSITY OF MICHIGAN–FLINT

Flint, MI

Tuition & fees (MI res): $3800 **Average undergraduate aid package: $8300**

ABOUT THE INSTITUTION State-supported, coed. Awards: bachelor's and master's degrees and post-bachelor's certificates. 52 undergraduate majors. Total enrollment: 6,524. Undergraduates: 5,994. Federal methodology is used as a basis for awarding need-based institutional aid.

UNDERGRADUATE EXPENSES for 1999–2000 ***Application fee:*** $30. ***Tuition, state resident:*** full-time $3546; part-time $152 per credit. ***Tuition, nonresident:*** full-time $10,736; part-time $450 per credit. ***Required fees:*** full-time $254; $116 per term part-time. Full-time tuition and fees vary according to program and student level. Part-time tuition and fees vary according to program and student level. ***Payment plan:*** deferred payment.

FRESHMAN FINANCIAL AID (Fall 1999, est.) 290 applied for aid; of those 93% were deemed to have need. 100% of freshmen with need received aid; of those 94% had need fully met. *Average percent of need met:* 90% (excluding resources awarded to replace EFC). *Average financial aid package:* $7700 (excluding resources awarded to replace EFC). 31% of all full-time freshmen had no need and received non-need-based aid.

UNDERGRADUATE FINANCIAL AID (Fall 1999, est.) 3,100 applied for aid; of those 90% were deemed to have need. 100% of undergraduates with need received aid; of those 89% had need fully met. *Average percent of need met:* 90% (excluding resources awarded to replace EFC). *Average financial aid package:* $8300 (excluding resources awarded to replace EFC). 16% of all full-time undergraduates had no need and received non-need-based aid.

GIFT AID (NEED-BASED) ***Total amount:*** $6,400,000 (55% Federal, 8% state, 36% institutional, 1% external sources). ***Receiving aid:*** *Freshmen:* 55% (270); *all full-time undergraduates:* 84% (2,800). ***Average award:*** Freshmen: $2100; Undergraduates: $2200. ***Scholarships, grants, and awards:*** Federal Pell, FSEOG, state, private, college/university gift aid from institutional funds.

GIFT AID (NON-NEED-BASED) ***Total amount:*** $480,000 (83% institutional, 17% external sources). ***Receiving aid:*** *Freshmen:* 29% (140); *Undergraduates:* 15% (500). ***Scholarships, grants, and awards by category:*** *Academic Interests/Achievement:* 60 awards ($60,000 total): business, education, general academic interests/achievements. *Creative Arts/Performance:* 20 awards ($25,000 total): art/fine arts, music, theater/drama. *Special Achievements/Activities:* 20 awards ($20,000 total): community service, leadership. ***Tuition waivers:*** Full or partial for minority students, senior citizens.

LOANS ***Student loans:*** $20,200,000 (50% need-based, 50% non-need-based). 62% of past graduating class borrowed through all loan programs. Average indebtedness per student: $10,600. ***Average need-based loan:*** Freshmen: $3000; Undergraduates: $4100. ***Parent loans:*** $60,000 (100% non-need-based). ***Programs:*** Federal Direct (Subsidized and Unsubsidized Stafford, PLUS), Perkins.

WORK-STUDY ***Federal work-study:*** *Total amount:* $1,600,000; jobs available. ***State or other work-study/employment:*** *Total amount:* $120,000 (100% need-based). Part-time jobs available.

APPLYING for FINANCIAL AID ***Required financial aid form:*** FAFSA. ***Financial aid deadline (priority):*** 2/21. ***Notification date:*** Continuous beginning 3/15. Students must reply within 3 weeks of notification.

CONTACT Financial Aid Office, University of Michigan–Flint, Room 277 UPAV, Flint, MI 48502-1950, 810-762-3444 or toll-free 800-942-5636 (in-state).

UNIVERSITY OF MINNESOTA, CROOKSTON

Crookston, MN

Tuition & fees (MN res): $5020 **Average undergraduate aid package: N/A**

ABOUT THE INSTITUTION State-supported, coed. Awards: associate and bachelor's degrees. 25 undergraduate majors. Total enrollment: 2,464. Undergraduates: 2,464. Freshmen: 303. Federal methodology is used as a basis for awarding need-based institutional aid.

UNDERGRADUATE EXPENSES for 2000–2001 ***Tuition, state resident:*** full-time $3780; part-time $126 per credit. ***Tuition, nonresident:*** full-time $3780; part-time $126 per credit. ***Required fees:*** full-time $1240; $480 per term part-time. Full-time tuition and fees vary according to reciprocity agreements. Part-time tuition and fees vary according to course load. ***College room and board:*** $4046; ***room only:*** $1861. Room and board charges vary according to board plan and housing facility. ***Payment plans:*** guaranteed tuition, installment.

FRESHMAN FINANCIAL AID (Fall 1998) 272 applied for aid; of those 89% were deemed to have need. 89% of freshmen with need received aid; of those 60% had need fully met. *Average percent of need met:* 90% (excluding resources awarded to replace EFC).

GIFT AID (NEED-BASED) ***Total amount:*** $1,799,452 (50% Federal, 50% state). ***Receiving aid:*** *Freshmen:* 55% (169). ***Scholarships, grants, and awards:*** Federal Pell, FSEOG, state, college/university gift aid from institutional funds.

GIFT AID (NON-NEED-BASED) ***Total amount:*** $329,000 (100% institutional). ***Receiving aid:*** *Freshmen:* 5% (16). ***Scholarships, grants, and awards by category:*** *Academic Interests/Achievement:* agriculture, business, communication, computer science, engineering/technologies, general academic interests/achievements, health fields. *Special Achievements/Activities:* general special achievements/activities, leadership. *Special Characteristics:* children and siblings of alumni, children of faculty/staff, ethnic background, general special characteristics, members of minority groups, out-of-state students, previous college experience. ***Tuition waivers:*** Full or partial for senior citizens. ***ROTC:*** Air Force cooperative.

LOANS ***Student loans:*** $2,007,739 (100% need-based). ***Parent loans:*** $383,170 (100% non-need-based). ***Programs:*** Federal Direct (Subsidized and Unsubsidized Stafford, PLUS), Perkins, state, college/university.

WORK-STUDY ***Federal work-study:*** *Total amount:* $181,367; jobs available. ***State or other work-study/employment:*** *Total amount:* $23,944 (100% need-based). Part-time jobs available.

ATHLETIC AWARDS *Total amount:* 131,000 (100% non-need-based).

APPLYING for FINANCIAL AID ***Required financial aid form:*** FAFSA. ***Financial aid deadline (priority):*** 3/31. ***Notification date:*** 4/1.

CONTACT Heidi Patterson, Associate Director of Financial Aid, University of Minnesota, Crookston, 170 Owen Hall, Crookston, MN 56716-5001, 218-281-8561 or toll-free 800-232-6466. *Fax:* 218-281-8575.

UNIVERSITY OF MINNESOTA, DULUTH

Duluth, MN

Tuition & fees (MN res): $4903 Average undergraduate aid package: $6494

ABOUT THE INSTITUTION State-supported, coed. Awards: bachelor's, master's, and first professional degrees. 68 undergraduate majors. Total enrollment: 8,504. Undergraduates: 7,959. Freshmen: 1,922. Federal methodology is used as a basis for awarding need-based institutional aid.

UNDERGRADUATE EXPENSES for 1999–2000 ***Application fee:*** $25. ***Tuition, state resident:*** full-time $4230; part-time $141 per credit. ***Tuition, nonresident:*** full-time $12,000; part-time $400 per credit. ***Required fees:*** full-time $673; $302 per term part-time. Full-time tuition and fees vary according to course level, course load, reciprocity agreements, and student level. Part-time tuition and fees vary according to course level, course load, reciprocity agreements, and student level. ***College room and board:*** $4132. Room and board charges vary according to board plan and housing facility. Additional part-time mandatory fees per term: $124 for nonresidents. ***Payment plan:*** installment.

FRESHMAN FINANCIAL AID (Fall 1999, est.) 1998 applied for aid; of those 83% were deemed to have need. *Average percent of need met:* 64% (excluding resources awarded to replace EFC). *Average financial aid package:* $5818 (excluding resources awarded to replace EFC). 18% of all full-time freshmen had no need and received non-need-based aid.

UNDERGRADUATE FINANCIAL AID (Fall 1999, est.) 4,928 applied for aid; of those 82% were deemed to have need. *Average percent of need met:* 64% (excluding resources awarded to replace EFC). *Average financial aid package:* $6494 (excluding resources awarded to replace EFC). 37% of all full-time undergraduates had no need and received non-need-based aid.

GIFT AID (NEED-BASED) ***Total amount:*** $7,824,750 (35% Federal, 56% state, 9% institutional). ***Scholarships, grants, and awards:*** Federal Pell, FSEOG, state, private, college/university gift aid from institutional funds.

GIFT AID (NON-NEED-BASED) ***Total amount:*** $3,702,452 (51% institutional, 49% external sources). ***Scholarships, grants, and awards by category:*** *Academic Interests/Achievement:* general academic interests/achievements. *Creative Arts/Performance:* art/fine arts, music, theater/drama. *Special Characteristics:* general special characteristics. ***Tuition waivers:*** Full or partial for employees or children of employees, senior citizens. ***ROTC:*** Air Force.

LOANS ***Student loans:*** $16,276,199 (59% need-based, 41% non-need-based). 71% of past graduating class borrowed through all loan programs. Average indebtedness per student: $11,500. ***Parent loans:*** $654,921 (100% non-need-based). ***Programs:*** Federal Direct (Subsidized and Unsubsidized Stafford, PLUS), Perkins, state, college/university, Primary Care Loans.

WORK-STUDY ***Federal work-study:*** *Total amount:* $490,678; 324 jobs averaging $1514. ***State or other work-study/employment:*** *Total amount:* $378,509 (100% need-based). 231 part-time jobs averaging $1639.

ATHLETIC AWARDS *Total amount:* 437,718 (100% need-based).

APPLYING for FINANCIAL AID ***Required financial aid form:*** FAFSA. ***Financial aid deadline (priority):*** 3/1. ***Notification date:*** Continuous.

CONTACT Ms. Brenda Herzig, Director of Financial Aid, University of Minnesota, Duluth, 10 University Drive, 184 Darland Administration Building, Duluth, MN 55812-2496, 218-726-8794 or toll-free 800-232-1339. *Fax:* 218-726-8219.

UNIVERSITY OF MINNESOTA, MORRIS

Morris, MN

Tuition & fees (MN res): $5312 Average undergraduate aid package: $6496

ABOUT THE INSTITUTION State-supported, coed. Awards: bachelor's degrees. 38 undergraduate majors. Total enrollment: 1,867. Undergraduates: 1,867. Freshmen: 457. Federal methodology is used as a basis for awarding need-based institutional aid.

UNDERGRADUATE EXPENSES for 1999–2000 ***Application fee:*** $25. ***Tuition, state resident:*** full-time $4778; part-time $159 per credit. ***Tuition, nonresident:*** full-time $9480; part-time $318 per credit. ***Required fees:*** full-time $534; $267 per term part-time. Part-time tuition and fees vary according to course load. ***College room and board:*** $3910; ***room only:*** $2080. Room and board charges vary according to board plan and housing facility. ***Payment plans:*** installment, deferred payment.

FRESHMAN FINANCIAL AID (Fall 1998) 476 applied for aid; of those 85% were deemed to have need. 100% of freshmen with need received aid; of those 93% had need fully met. *Average percent of need met:* 93% (excluding resources awarded to replace EFC). *Average financial aid package:* $6173 (excluding resources awarded to replace EFC). 19% of all full-time freshmen had no need and received non-need-based aid.

UNDERGRADUATE FINANCIAL AID (Fall 1998) 1,411 applied for aid; of those 89% were deemed to have need. 100% of undergraduates with need received aid; of those 91% had need fully met. *Average percent of need met:* 92% (excluding resources awarded to replace EFC). *Average financial aid package:* $6496 (excluding resources awarded to replace EFC). 18% of all full-time undergraduates had no need and received non-need-based aid.

GIFT AID (NEED-BASED) ***Total amount:*** $3,761,883 (50% Federal, 45% state, 5% institutional). ***Receiving aid:*** *Freshmen:* 59% (357); *all full-time undergraduates:* 60% (1,093). ***Average award:*** Freshmen: $4392; Undergraduates: $5389. ***Scholarships, grants, and awards:*** Federal Pell, FSEOG, state, private, college/university gift aid from institutional funds.

GIFT AID (NON-NEED-BASED) ***Total amount:*** $2,558,170 (6% Federal, 1% state, 60% institutional, 33% external sources). ***Receiving aid:*** *Freshmen:* 52% (314); *Undergraduates:* 23% (427). ***Scholarships, grants, and awards by category:*** *Academic Interests/Achievement:* general academic interests/achievements. *Creative Arts/Performance:* music. *Special Achievements/Activities:* general special achievements/activities. *Special Characteristics:* ethnic background, general special characteristics, international students, members of minority groups, out-of-state students, veterans, veterans' children. ***Tuition waivers:*** Full or partial for minority students.

LOANS ***Student loans:*** $5,709,512 (76% need-based, 24% non-need-based). 70% of past graduating class borrowed through all loan programs. Average indebtedness per student: $11,600. ***Average need-based loan:*** Freshmen: $1423; Undergraduates: $2328. ***Parent loans:*** $12,200 (100% non-need-based). ***Programs:*** Federal Direct (Subsidized and Unsubsidized Stafford, PLUS), Perkins, state, college/university, SELF Loans.

WORK-STUDY ***Federal work-study:*** *Total amount:* $414,458; jobs available. ***State or other work-study/employment:*** *Total amount:* $363,101 (53% need-based, 47% non-need-based). Part-time jobs available.

APPLYING for FINANCIAL AID ***Required financial aid form:*** FAFSA. ***Financial aid deadline (priority):*** 4/1. ***Notification date:*** Continuous. Students must reply within 3 weeks of notification.

CONTACT Ms. Pam Engebretson, Assistant Director of Financial Aid, University of Minnesota, Morris, 600 East 4th Street, Morris, MN 56267, 320-589-6035 or toll-free 800-992-8863. *Fax:* 320-589-1673. *E-mail:* engebrpj@mrs.umn.edu

UNIVERSITY OF MINNESOTA, TWIN CITIES CAMPUS

Minneapolis, MN

Tuition & fees (MN res): $4649 Average undergraduate aid package: $7854

University of Minnesota, Twin Cities Campus (continued)

ABOUT THE INSTITUTION State-supported, coed. Awards: bachelor's, master's, doctoral, and first professional degrees and post-bachelor's and post-master's certificates. 132 undergraduate majors. Total enrollment: 45,361. Undergraduates: 32,342. Freshmen: 5,141. Federal methodology is used as a basis for awarding need-based institutional aid.

UNDERGRADUATE EXPENSES for 1999–2000 ***Application fee:*** $25. ***Tuition, state resident:*** full-time $4172; part-time $154 per credit. ***Tuition, nonresident:*** full-time $12,312; part-time $456 per credit. ***Required fees:*** full-time $477; $238 per term part-time. Full-time tuition and fees vary according to program, reciprocity agreements, and student level. Part-time tuition and fees vary according to course load, program, reciprocity agreements, and student level. ***College room and board:*** $4494. Room and board charges vary according to board plan, housing facility, and location. ***Payment plans:*** guaranteed tuition, installment.

FRESHMAN FINANCIAL AID (Fall 1998) 3064 applied for aid; of those 80% were deemed to have need. 94% of freshmen with need received aid; of those 42% had need fully met. *Average percent of need met:* 84% (excluding resources awarded to replace EFC). *Average financial aid package:* $6934 (excluding resources awarded to replace EFC). 30% of all full-time freshmen had no need and received non-need-based aid.

UNDERGRADUATE FINANCIAL AID (Fall 1998) 13,738 applied for aid; of those 84% were deemed to have need. 97% of undergraduates with need received aid; of those 46% had need fully met. *Average percent of need met:* 85% (excluding resources awarded to replace EFC). *Average financial aid package:* $7854 (excluding resources awarded to replace EFC). 33% of all full-time undergraduates had no need and received non-need-based aid.

GIFT AID (NEED-BASED) ***Total amount:*** $36,217,756 (41% Federal, 32% state, 23% institutional, 4% external sources). ***Receiving aid:*** *Freshmen:* 35% (1,585); *all full-time undergraduates:* 34% (7,461). ***Average award:*** Freshmen: $4284; Undergraduates: $4292. ***Scholarships, grants, and awards:*** Federal Pell, FSEOG, state, private, college/university gift aid from institutional funds, Federal Nursing.

GIFT AID (NON-NEED-BASED) ***Total amount:*** $11,455,863 (4% Federal, 3% state, 78% institutional, 15% external sources). ***Receiving aid:*** *Freshmen:* 7% (327); *Undergraduates:* 5% (986). ***Scholarships, grants, and awards by category:*** *Academic Interests/Achievement:* agriculture, architecture, area/ethnic studies, biological sciences, business, communication, computer science, education, engineering/technologies, English, foreign languages, general academic interests/achievements, health fields, home economics, humanities, international studies, library science, mathematics, military science, physical sciences, premedicine, religion/biblical studies, social sciences. *Creative Arts/Performance:* general creative arts/performance. *Special Achievements/Activities:* hobbies/interests. ***Tuition waivers:*** Full or partial for employees or children of employees, senior citizens. ***ROTC:*** Army, Naval, Air Force.

LOANS ***Student loans:*** $57,868,639 (59% need-based, 41% non-need-based). ***Average need-based loan:*** Freshmen: $2603; Undergraduates: $3587. ***Parent loans:*** $22,285,067 (100% non-need-based). ***Programs:*** Federal Direct (Subsidized and Unsubsidized Stafford, PLUS), Perkins, Federal Nursing, state, college/university, Health Professions Loans, alternative loans.

WORK-STUDY ***Federal work-study:*** *Total amount:* $2,813,896; jobs available. ***State or other work-study/employment:*** *Total amount:* $4,411,953 (100% need-based). Part-time jobs available.

APPLYING for FINANCIAL AID ***Required financial aid form:*** FAFSA. ***Financial aid deadline (priority):*** 2/15. ***Notification date:*** Continuous.

CONTACT Mr. John Kellogg, Analyst, University of Minnesota, Twin Cities Campus, 100 Church Street, SE, 160 Morrill Hall, Minneapolis, MN 55455-0213, 612-625-3387 or toll-free 800-752-1000. *Fax:* 612-624-6057. *E-mail:* j-kell@maroon.tc.umn.edu

UNIVERSITY OF MISSISSIPPI

Oxford, MS

Tuition & fees (MS res): $3053 **Average undergraduate aid package: $6523**

ABOUT THE INSTITUTION State-supported, coed. Awards: bachelor's, master's, doctoral, and first professional degrees. 63 undergraduate majors. Total enrollment: 11,637. Undergraduates: 9,222. Freshmen: 1,826. Federal methodology is used as a basis for awarding need-based institutional aid.

UNDERGRADUATE EXPENSES for 1999–2000 ***Application fee:*** $25 for nonresidents. ***Tuition, state resident:*** full-time $3053; part-time $127 per semester hour. ***Tuition, nonresident:*** full-time $6155; part-time $256 per semester hour. Part-time tuition and fees vary according to course load. ***College room and board:*** $3414. Room and board charges vary according to board plan and housing facility. ***Payment plans:*** tuition prepayment, deferred payment.

FRESHMAN FINANCIAL AID (Fall 1998) 882 applied for aid; of those 69% were deemed to have need. 99% of freshmen with need received aid; of those 36% had need fully met. *Average percent of need met:* 73% (excluding resources awarded to replace EFC). *Average financial aid package:* $5573 (excluding resources awarded to replace EFC). 16% of all full-time freshmen had no need and received non-need-based aid.

UNDERGRADUATE FINANCIAL AID (Fall 1998) 4,387 applied for aid; of those 74% were deemed to have need. 99% of undergraduates with need received aid; of those 43% had need fully met. *Average percent of need met:* 76% (excluding resources awarded to replace EFC). *Average financial aid package:* $6523 (excluding resources awarded to replace EFC). 14% of all full-time undergraduates had no need and received non-need-based aid.

GIFT AID (NEED-BASED) ***Total amount:*** $4,524,239 (96% Federal, 4% state). ***Receiving aid:*** *Freshmen:* 34% (549); *all full-time undergraduates:* 35% (2,824). ***Average award:*** Freshmen: $3960; Undergraduates: $3837. ***Scholarships, grants, and awards:*** Federal Pell, FSEOG, state, private, college/university gift aid from institutional funds.

GIFT AID (NON-NEED-BASED) ***Total amount:*** $13,401,278 (1% Federal, 23% state, 70% institutional, 6% external sources). ***Receiving aid:*** *Freshmen:* 28% (456); *Undergraduates:* 26% (2,064). ***Scholarships, grants, and awards by category:*** *Academic Interests/Achievement:* general academic interests/achievements. *Creative Arts/Performance:* art/fine arts, music, theater/drama. *Special Achievements/Activities:* leadership. *Special Characteristics:* children and siblings of alumni, local/state students, out-of-state students. ***Tuition waivers:*** Full or partial for children of alumni, employees or children of employees, senior citizens. ***ROTC:*** Army, Naval, Air Force.

LOANS ***Student loans:*** $17,691,941 (60% need-based, 40% non-need-based). 69% of past graduating class borrowed through all loan programs. Average indebtedness per student: $14,795. ***Average need-based loan:*** Freshmen: $2421; Undergraduates: $3939. ***Parent loans:*** $2,049,772 (100% non-need-based). ***Programs:*** FFEL (Subsidized and Unsubsidized Stafford, PLUS), Perkins, college/university.

WORK-STUDY ***Federal work-study:*** *Total amount:* $465,696; 455 jobs averaging $924.

ATHLETIC AWARDS *Total amount:* 2,175,335 (100% non-need-based).

APPLYING for FINANCIAL AID ***Required financial aid form:*** FAFSA. ***Financial aid deadline (priority):*** 3/15. ***Notification date:*** Continuous beginning 4/15. Students must reply within 3 weeks of notification.

CONTACT Mr. Larry D. Ridgeway, Director of Financial Aid, University of Mississippi, 257 Martindale Center, Suite E, University, MS 38677-9702, 915-662-7175 or toll-free 662-915-7226 (in-state), 662-915-5869 (out-of-state). *Fax:* 915-662-1164. *E-mail:* lridgewa@olemiss.edu

UNIVERSITY OF MISSISSIPPI MEDICAL CENTER

Jackson, MS

Tuition & fees (MS res): $3168 **Average undergraduate aid package: N/A**

ABOUT THE INSTITUTION State-supported, coed. Awards: bachelor's, master's, doctoral, and first professional degrees. 6 undergraduate majors. Total enrollment: 1,780. Undergraduates: 552. Entering class: . Federal methodology is used as a basis for awarding need-based institutional aid.

UNDERGRADUATE EXPENSES for 1999–2000 ***Application fee:*** $10. ***Tuition, state resident:*** full-time $3168. ***Tuition, nonresident:*** full-time $8819. ***College room and board: room only:*** $1530. Room and board charges vary according to housing facility. ***Payment plans:*** installment, deferred payment.

UNDERGRADUATE FINANCIAL AID (Fall 1998) 587 applied for aid; of those 51% were deemed to have need. 100% of undergraduates with need received aid; of those 50% had need fully met. *Average percent of need met:* 75% (excluding resources awarded to replace EFC). 43% of all full-time undergraduates had no need and received non-need-based aid.

GIFT AID (NEED-BASED) ***Total amount:*** $386,301 (92% Federal, 1% state, 7% external sources). ***Receiving aid:*** *All full-time undergraduates:* 26% (178). ***Average award:*** Undergraduates: $2176. ***Scholarships, grants, and awards:*** Federal Pell, FSEOG, state, Federal Nursing, Lettie Pate Whitehead Foundation Scholarships.

GIFT AID (NON-NEED-BASED) ***Total amount:*** $989,669 (2% Federal, 50% state, 12% institutional, 36% external sources). ***Receiving aid:*** *Undergraduates:* 29% (198). ***Scholarships, grants, and awards by category:*** *Special Characteristics:* 336 awards ($317,565 total): children of faculty/staff, local/state students. ***Tuition waivers:*** Full or partial for employees or children of employees.

LOANS ***Student loans:*** $1,583,597 (58% need-based, 42% non-need-based). 75% of past graduating class borrowed through all loan programs. Average indebtedness per student: $9500. ***Average need-based loan:*** Undergraduates: $3888. ***Parent loans:*** $6760 (100% non-need-based). ***Programs:*** FFEL (Subsidized and Unsubsidized Stafford, PLUS), Perkins, Federal Nursing, state, college/university.

WORK-STUDY ***Federal work-study:*** *Total amount:* $25,277; 11 jobs averaging $2298.

APPLYING for FINANCIAL AID ***Required financial aid forms:*** FAFSA, institution's own form, state aid form. ***Financial aid deadline (priority):*** 4/1. ***Notification date:*** 7/15. Students must reply within 2 weeks of notification.

CONTACT Steve Greenough, Director of Student Financial Aid, University of Mississippi Medical Center, 2500 North State Street, Jackson, MS 39216-4505, 601-984-1117. *Fax:* 601-984-6984. *E-mail:* sgreenough@registrar.umsmed.edu

UNIVERSITY OF MISSOURI–COLUMBIA

Columbia, MO

Tuition & fees (MO res): $4581 **Average undergraduate aid package: $6159**

ABOUT THE INSTITUTION State-supported, coed. Awards: bachelor's, master's, doctoral, and first professional degrees. 88 undergraduate majors. Total enrollment: 22,930. Undergraduates: 17,811. Freshmen: 3,932. Both federal and institutional methodology are used as a basis for awarding need-based institutional aid.

UNDERGRADUATE EXPENSES for 1999–2000 ***Application fee:*** $25. ***Tuition, state resident:*** full-time $3978; part-time $133 per credit hour. ***Tuition, nonresident:*** full-time $11,892; part-time $396 per credit hour. ***Required fees:*** full-time $603; $18 per credit hour. ***College room and board:*** $4545. Room and board charges vary according to board plan and housing facility. ***Payment plan:*** installment.

FRESHMAN FINANCIAL AID (Fall 1999) 2631 applied for aid; of those 65% were deemed to have need. 98% of freshmen with need received aid; of those 43% had need fully met. *Average percent of need met:* 84% (excluding resources awarded to replace EFC). *Average financial aid package:* $6224 (excluding resources awarded to replace EFC). 50% of all full-time freshmen had no need and received non-need-based aid.

UNDERGRADUATE FINANCIAL AID (Fall 1999) 9,994 applied for aid; of those 73% were deemed to have need. 98% of undergraduates with need received aid; of those 41% had need fully met. *Average percent of need met:* 84% (excluding resources awarded to replace EFC). *Average financial aid package:* $6159 (excluding resources awarded to replace EFC). 44% of all full-time undergraduates had no need and received non-need-based aid.

GIFT AID (NEED-BASED) ***Total amount:*** $24,369,254 (28% Federal, 8% state, 47% institutional, 17% external sources). ***Receiving aid:*** *Freshmen:* 37% (1,449); *all full-time undergraduates:* 33% (5,877). ***Average award:*** Freshmen: $4518; Undergraduates: $4236. ***Scholarships, grants, and awards:*** Federal Pell, FSEOG, state, private, college/university gift aid from institutional funds, Federal Nursing.

GIFT AID (NON-NEED-BASED) ***Total amount:*** $20,278,781 (3% Federal, 15% state, 64% institutional, 18% external sources). ***Receiving aid:*** *Freshmen:* 32% (1,234); *Undergraduates:* 26% (4,664). ***Scholarships, grants, and awards by category:*** *Academic Interests/Achievement:* general academic interests/achievements. *Creative Arts/Performance:* journalism/publications, music, theater/drama. *Special Achievements/Activities:* general special achievements/activities. *Special Characteristics:* members of minority groups, out-of-state students. ***Tuition waivers:*** Full or partial for employees or children of employees. ***ROTC:*** Army, Naval, Air Force.

LOANS ***Student loans:*** $33,359,936 (75% need-based, 25% non-need-based). Average indebtedness per student: $16,161. ***Average need-based loan:*** Freshmen: $3065; Undergraduates: $4196. ***Parent loans:*** $10,480,926 (46% need-based, 54% non-need-based). ***Programs:*** Federal Direct (Subsidized and Unsubsidized Stafford, PLUS), Perkins, Federal Nursing, state, college/university.

WORK-STUDY ***Federal work-study:*** *Total amount:* $2,024,955; 1,231 jobs averaging $1646.

ATHLETIC AWARDS *Total amount:* 3,383,171 (24% need-based, 76% non-need-based).

APPLYING for FINANCIAL AID ***Required financial aid form:*** FAFSA. ***Financial aid deadline (priority):*** 3/1. ***Notification date:*** Continuous beginning 4/1. Students must reply within 4 weeks of notification.

CONTACT Billie Jo Hamilton, Associate Director, Student Financial Aid, University of Missouri–Columbia, 11 Jesse Hall, Columbia, MO 65211, 573-882-3569 or toll-free 800-225-6075 (in-state). *Fax:* 573-884-5335. *E-mail:* hamiltonbj@missouri.edu

UNIVERSITY OF MISSOURI–KANSAS CITY

Kansas City, MO

Tuition & fees (MO res): $3852 **Average undergraduate aid package: $11,920**

ABOUT THE INSTITUTION State-supported, coed. Awards: bachelor's, master's, doctoral, and first professional degrees and first-professional certificates. 54 undergraduate majors. Total enrollment: 11,518. Undergraduates: 6,790. Freshmen: 688. Federal methodology is used as a basis for awarding need-based institutional aid.

UNDERGRADUATE EXPENSES for 2000–2001 ***Application fee:*** $25. ***Tuition, state resident:*** full-time $3822; part-time $137 per credit hour. ***Tuition, nonresident:*** full-time $10,357; part-time $409 per credit hour. ***Required fees:*** full-time $30; $22 per credit hour; $30 per term part-time. Full-time tuition and fees vary according to student level. Part-time tuition and fees vary according to student level. Room and board charges vary according to board plan and housing facility.

FRESHMAN FINANCIAL AID (Fall 1999) 615 applied for aid; of those 58% were deemed to have need. 100% of freshmen with need received aid; of those 95% had need fully met. *Average percent of need met:* 69% (excluding resources awarded to replace EFC). *Average financial aid package:* $12,227 (excluding resources awarded to replace EFC). 30% of all full-time freshmen had no need and received non-need-based aid.

UNDERGRADUATE FINANCIAL AID (Fall 1999) 3,102 applied for aid; of those 67% were deemed to have need. 100% of undergraduates with need received aid; of those 74% had need fully met. *Average percent of need met:* 75% (excluding resources awarded to replace EFC). *Average financial aid package:* $11,920 (excluding resources awarded to replace EFC). 20% of all full-time undergraduates had no need and received non-need-based aid.

GIFT AID (NEED-BASED) ***Total amount:*** $5,801,451 (50% Federal, 10% state, 32% institutional, 8% external sources). ***Receiving aid:*** *Freshmen:* 34% (237); *all full-time undergraduates:* 34% (1,305). ***Average award:*** Freshmen: $4992; Undergraduates: $4007. ***Scholarships, grants, and***

University of Missouri–Kansas City (continued)

awards: Federal Pell, FSEOG, state, private, college/university gift aid from institutional funds, United Negro College Fund, Federal Nursing.

GIFT AID (NON-NEED-BASED) ***Total amount:*** $3,628,851 (11% state, 79% institutional, 10% external sources). ***Receiving aid:*** *Freshmen:* 46% (315); *Undergraduates:* 27% (1,051). ***Scholarships, grants, and awards by category:*** *Academic Interests/Achievement:* general academic interests/achievements. *Creative Arts/Performance:* debating, general creative arts/performance, music, performing arts. *Special Characteristics:* members of minority groups, out-of-state students. ***Tuition waivers:*** Full or partial for employees or children of employees. ***ROTC:*** Army.

LOANS ***Student loans:*** $17,023,989 (73% need-based, 27% non-need-based). 81% of past graduating class borrowed through all loan programs. Average indebtedness per student: $22,127. ***Average need-based loan:*** Freshmen: $3492; Undergraduates: $5502. ***Parent loans:*** $1,185,887 (34% need-based, 66% non-need-based). ***Programs:*** Federal Direct (Subsidized and Unsubsidized Stafford, PLUS), Perkins, Federal Nursing, state, college/university, alternative loans.

WORK-STUDY ***Federal work-study:*** *Total amount:* $1,795,974; 584 jobs averaging $3075.

ATHLETIC AWARDS *Total amount:* 1,284,651 (17% need-based, 83% non-need-based).

APPLYING for FINANCIAL AID ***Required financial aid form:*** FAFSA. ***Financial aid deadline (priority):*** 3/15. ***Notification date:*** Continuous beginning 4/15. Students must reply within 2 weeks of notification.

CONTACT Office of Financial Services, University of Missouri–Kansas City, Administrative Center, 5100 Rockhill Road, Kansas City, MO 64110-2499, 816-235-5446. *Fax:* 816-235-5511.

UNIVERSITY OF MISSOURI–ROLLA

Rolla, MO

Tuition & fees (MO res): $4665 **Average undergraduate aid package: $8067**

ABOUT THE INSTITUTION State-supported, coed. Awards: bachelor's, master's, and doctoral degrees. 30 undergraduate majors. Total enrollment: 4,715. Undergraduates: 3,882. Freshmen: 688. Federal methodology is used as a basis for awarding need-based institutional aid.

UNDERGRADUATE EXPENSES for 1999–2000 ***Application fee:*** $25. ***Tuition, state resident:*** full-time $3978; part-time $133 per credit hour. ***Tuition, nonresident:*** full-time $11,892; part-time $396 per credit hour. ***Required fees:*** full-time $687; $24 per credit hour; $60 per term part-time. Full-time tuition and fees vary according to course load and program. Part-time tuition and fees vary according to course load and program. ***College room and board:*** $4557; ***room only:*** $2670. Room and board charges vary according to board plan and housing facility. ***Payment plan:*** installment.

FRESHMAN FINANCIAL AID (Fall 1998) 506 applied for aid; of those 77% were deemed to have need. 100% of freshmen with need received aid; of those 52% had need fully met. *Average percent of need met:* 88% (excluding resources awarded to replace EFC). *Average financial aid package:* $9011 (excluding resources awarded to replace EFC). 40% of all full-time freshmen had no need and received non-need-based aid.

UNDERGRADUATE FINANCIAL AID (Fall 1998) 2,261 applied for aid; of those 85% were deemed to have need. 100% of undergraduates with need received aid; of those 40% had need fully met. *Average percent of need met:* 81% (excluding resources awarded to replace EFC). *Average financial aid package:* $8067 (excluding resources awarded to replace EFC). 33% of all full-time undergraduates had no need and received non-need-based aid.

GIFT AID (NEED-BASED) ***Total amount:*** $7,767,090 (26% Federal, 3% state, 71% institutional). ***Receiving aid:*** *Freshmen:* 53% (382); *all full-time undergraduates:* 47% (1,690). ***Average award:*** Freshmen: $5713; Undergraduates: $4563. ***Scholarships, grants, and awards:*** Federal Pell, FSEOG, state, private, college/university gift aid from institutional funds.

GIFT AID (NON-NEED-BASED) ***Total amount:*** $7,325,214 (25% state, 41% institutional, 34% external sources). ***Receiving aid:*** *Freshmen:* 14% (104); *Undergraduates:* 8% (294). ***Scholarships, grants, and awards by category:*** *Academic Interests/Achievement:* computer science, education, engineering/technologies, English, general academic interests/achievements, humanities, mathematics, military science, physical sciences, premedicine, social sciences. *Creative Arts/Performance:* music, theater/drama. *Special Characteristics:* children and siblings of alumni, international students, members of minority groups, out-of-state students. ***Tuition waivers:*** Full or partial for minority students, children of alumni, employees or children of employees. ***ROTC:*** Army, Air Force.

LOANS ***Student loans:*** $10,423,151 (64% need-based, 36% non-need-based). Average indebtedness per student: $15,000. ***Average need-based loan:*** Freshmen: $2989; Undergraduates: $4290. ***Parent loans:*** $592,620 (100% non-need-based). ***Programs:*** Federal Direct (Subsidized and Unsubsidized Stafford, PLUS), Perkins, state, college/university.

WORK-STUDY ***Federal work-study:*** *Total amount:* $344,258; 291 jobs averaging $1183. ***State or other work-study/employment:*** *Total amount:* $1,284,686 (100% non-need-based). 1,295 part-time jobs averaging $992.

ATHLETIC AWARDS *Total amount:* 703,790 (100% non-need-based).

APPLYING for FINANCIAL AID ***Required financial aid forms:*** FAFSA, institution's own form. ***Financial aid deadline (priority):*** 3/1. ***Notification date:*** Continuous beginning 4/1. Students must reply within 3 weeks of notification.

CONTACT Mr. Robert W. Whites, Associate Director, Admission and Student Financial Assistance, University of Missouri–Rolla, G1 Parker Hall, Rolla, MO 65409, 573-341-4282 or toll-free 800-522-0938. *Fax:* 573-341-4274.

UNIVERSITY OF MISSOURI–ST. LOUIS

St. Louis, MO

Tuition & fees (MO res): $4798 **Average undergraduate aid package: $6898**

ABOUT THE INSTITUTION State-supported, coed. Awards: bachelor's, master's, doctoral, and first professional degrees. 78 undergraduate majors. Total enrollment: 15,594. Undergraduates: 12,986. Freshmen: 655. Federal methodology is used as a basis for awarding need-based institutional aid.

UNDERGRADUATE EXPENSES for 1999–2000 ***Application fee:*** $25. ***Tuition, state resident:*** full-time $3978; part-time $133 per credit hour. ***Tuition, nonresident:*** full-time $11,892; part-time $396 per credit hour. ***Required fees:*** full-time $820; $32 per credit hour. Part-time tuition and fees vary according to course load. ***College room and board:*** $4500; ***room only:*** $2900. Room and board charges vary according to board plan and housing facility. ***Payment plan:*** installment.

UNDERGRADUATE FINANCIAL AID (Fall 1998) of those 98% had need fully met. *Average percent of need met:* 98% (excluding resources awarded to replace EFC). *Average financial aid package:* $6898 (excluding resources awarded to replace EFC).

GIFT AID (NEED-BASED) ***Total amount:*** $5,542,436 (69% Federal, 10% state, 3% institutional, 18% external sources). ***Receiving aid:*** *All full-time undergraduates:* 3,502. ***Average award:*** Undergraduates: $1583. ***Scholarships, grants, and awards:*** Federal Pell, FSEOG, state, private, college/university gift aid from institutional funds.

GIFT AID (NON-NEED-BASED) ***Total amount:*** $5,281,844 (15% state, 85% institutional). ***Receiving aid:*** *Undergraduates:* 1,787. ***Scholarships, grants, and awards by category:*** *Academic Interests/Achievement:* biological sciences, business, communication, computer science, education, engineering/technologies, English, foreign languages, general academic interests/achievements, health fields, humanities, international studies, mathematics. *Creative Arts/Performance:* art/fine arts, music. *Special Achievements/Activities:* memberships. *Special Characteristics:* ethnic background, general special characteristics, local/state students, members of minority groups. ***Tuition waivers:*** Full or partial for employees or children of employees. ***ROTC:*** Army cooperative, Air Force cooperative.

LOANS ***Student loans:*** $23,685,285 (100% need-based). ***Average need-based loan:*** Undergraduates: $3428. ***Parent loans:*** $292,468 (100% need-based). ***Programs:*** Federal Direct (Subsidized and Unsubsidized Stafford, PLUS), Perkins, Federal Nursing, college/university.

WORK-STUDY ***Federal work-study:*** *Total amount:* $335,014; jobs available.

ATHLETIC AWARDS *Total amount:* 337,508 (100% need-based).

APPLYING for FINANCIAL AID ***Required financial aid form:*** FAFSA. ***Financial aid deadline (priority):*** 4/1. ***Notification date:*** Continuous beginning 4/15. Students must reply within 4 weeks of notification.

CONTACT Thuy Bigham, Assistant Director, Student Financial Aid, University of Missouri–St. Louis, 8001 Natural Bridge Road, 209 Woods Hall, St. Louis, MO 63121-4499, 314-516-6302. *Fax:* 314-516-5408.

UNIVERSITY OF MOBILE

Mobile, AL

Tuition & fees: $7830 **Average undergraduate aid package: $8250**

ABOUT THE INSTITUTION Independent Southern Baptist, coed. Awards: associate, bachelor's, and master's degrees. 33 undergraduate majors. Total enrollment: 1,978. Undergraduates: 1,772. Freshmen: 251. Federal methodology is used as a basis for awarding need-based institutional aid.

UNDERGRADUATE EXPENSES for 1999–2000 ***Application fee:*** $30. ***Comprehensive fee:*** $12,110 includes full-time tuition ($7710), mandatory fees ($120), and room and board ($4280). Full-time tuition and fees vary according to course load. Room and board charges vary according to board plan. ***Part-time tuition:*** $257 per semester hour. ***Part-time fees:*** $15 per term part-time. Part-time tuition and fees vary according to course load. ***Payment plan:*** installment.

FRESHMAN FINANCIAL AID (Fall 1999, est.) 242 applied for aid; of those 92% were deemed to have need. 100% of freshmen with need received aid. *Average percent of need met:* 55% (excluding resources awarded to replace EFC). *Average financial aid package:* $7550 (excluding resources awarded to replace EFC). 8% of all full-time freshmen had no need and received non-need-based aid.

UNDERGRADUATE FINANCIAL AID (Fall 1999, est.) 1,312 applied for aid; of those 66% were deemed to have need. 100% of undergraduates with need received aid. *Average percent of need met:* 55% (excluding resources awarded to replace EFC). *Average financial aid package:* $8250 (excluding resources awarded to replace EFC). 12% of all full-time undergraduates had no need and received non-need-based aid.

GIFT AID (NEED-BASED) ***Total amount:*** $2,517,326 (99% Federal, 1% state). ***Receiving aid:*** *Freshmen:* 83% (202); *all full-time undergraduates:* 55% (785). ***Average award:*** Freshmen: $2300; Undergraduates: $3200. ***Scholarships, grants, and awards:*** Federal Pell, FSEOG, state, private, college/university gift aid from institutional funds.

GIFT AID (NON-NEED-BASED) ***Total amount:*** $3,413,819 (4% Federal, 26% state, 61% institutional, 9% external sources). ***Scholarships, grants, and awards by category:*** *Academic Interests/Achievement:* general academic interests/achievements, religion/biblical studies. *Creative Arts/Performance:* art/fine arts, dance, general creative arts/performance, music. *Special Achievements/Activities:* cheerleading/drum major, community service, junior miss, leadership, religious involvement. ***Tuition waivers:*** Full or partial for employees or children of employees. ***ROTC:*** Army cooperative, Air Force cooperative.

LOANS ***Student loans:*** $8,229,421 (51% need-based, 49% non-need-based). 86% of past graduating class borrowed through all loan programs. Average indebtedness per student: $14,000. ***Average need-based loan:*** Freshmen: $2625; Undergraduates: $4625. ***Parent loans:*** $352,313 (100% non-need-based). ***Programs:*** FFEL (Subsidized and Unsubsidized Stafford, PLUS), Perkins.

WORK-STUDY ***Federal work-study:*** *Total amount:* $143,711; 93 jobs averaging $1545. ***State or other work-study/employment:*** *Total amount:* $50,603 (100% non-need-based). Part-time jobs available.

ATHLETIC AWARDS *Total amount:* 898,199 (100% non-need-based).

APPLYING for FINANCIAL AID ***Required financial aid forms:*** FAFSA, institution's own form, state aid form. ***Financial aid deadline (priority):*** 3/21. ***Notification date:*** Continuous beginning 4/1. Students must reply within 2 weeks of notification.

CONTACT Ms. Lydia Husley, Director of Financial Aid, University of Mobile, PO Box 13220, Mobile, AL 36663-0220, 334-442-2252 or toll-free 800-946-7267. *Fax:* 334-442-2498.

THE UNIVERSITY OF MONTANA–MISSOULA

Missoula, MT

Tuition & fees (MT res): $2967 **Average undergraduate aid package: N/A**

ABOUT THE INSTITUTION State-supported, coed. Awards: associate, bachelor's, master's, doctoral, and first professional degrees. 115 undergraduate majors. Total enrollment: 12,208. Undergraduates: 10,457. Freshmen: 2,060. Federal methodology is used as a basis for awarding need-based institutional aid.

UNDERGRADUATE EXPENSES for 1999–2000 ***Application fee:*** $30. ***Tuition, state resident:*** full-time $2048. ***Tuition, nonresident:*** full-time $7158. ***Required fees:*** full-time $919. Full-time tuition and fees vary according to program and student level. Part-time tuition and fees vary according to course load and program. ***College room and board:*** $4496; ***room only:*** $2054. Room and board charges vary according to board plan and housing facility. ***Payment plan:*** installment.

FRESHMAN FINANCIAL AID (Fall 1998) 1357 applied for aid; of those 76% were deemed to have need. 89% of freshmen with need received aid; of those 26% had need fully met. 18% of all full-time freshmen had no need and received non-need-based aid.

UNDERGRADUATE FINANCIAL AID (Fall 1998) 5,827 applied for aid; of those 79% were deemed to have need. 91% of undergraduates with need received aid; of those 38% had need fully met. 14% of all full-time undergraduates had no need and received non-need-based aid.

GIFT AID (NEED-BASED) ***Total amount:*** $8,675,211 (75% Federal, 2% state, 23% institutional). ***Receiving aid:*** *Freshmen:* 34% (648); *all full-time undergraduates:* 35% (2,997). ***Scholarships, grants, and awards:*** Federal Pell, FSEOG, state, private, college/university gift aid from institutional funds.

GIFT AID (NON-NEED-BASED) ***Total amount:*** $1,132,226 (46% institutional, 54% external sources). ***Receiving aid:*** *Freshmen:* 5% (100); *Undergraduates:* 3% (220). ***Scholarships, grants, and awards by category:*** *Academic Interests/Achievement:* biological sciences, business, computer science, education, English, foreign languages, general academic interests/achievements, health fields, humanities, international studies, mathematics, military science, physical sciences, premedicine, social sciences. *Creative Arts/Performance:* art/fine arts, creative writing, dance, journalism/publications, music, performing arts, theater/drama. *Special Achievements/Activities:* leadership, rodeo. *Special Characteristics:* children and siblings of alumni, members of minority groups. ***Tuition waivers:*** Full or partial for minority students, senior citizens. ***ROTC:*** Army.

LOANS ***Student loans:*** $26,191,789 (100% need-based). ***Parent loans:*** $2,607,288 (100% non-need-based). ***Programs:*** FFEL (Subsidized and Unsubsidized Stafford, PLUS), Perkins, college/university.

WORK-STUDY ***Federal work-study:*** *Total amount:* $1,235,456; jobs available. ***State or other work-study/employment:*** *Total amount:* $144,645 (100% need-based). Part-time jobs available.

ATHLETIC AWARDS *Total amount:* 1,368,121 (100% non-need-based).

APPLYING for FINANCIAL AID ***Required financial aid forms:*** FAFSA, institution's own form. ***Financial aid deadline (priority):*** 3/1. ***Notification date:*** Continuous beginning 3/17.

CONTACT Financial Aid Office, The University of Montana–Missoula, Arthur and University Avenues, Missoula, MT 59812-0002, 406-243-5373 or toll-free 800-462-8636. *Fax:* 406-243-4930. *E-mail:* faid@selway.umt.edu

UNIVERSITY OF MONTEVALLO

Montevallo, AL

Tuition & fees (AL res): $3290 **Average undergraduate aid package: $2984**

ABOUT THE INSTITUTION State-supported, coed. Awards: bachelor's and master's degrees and post-master's certificates. 49 undergraduate majors. Total enrollment: 3,147. Undergraduates: 2,691. Freshmen: 538. Federal methodology is used as a basis for awarding need-based institutional aid.

UNDERGRADUATE EXPENSES for 1999–2000 ***Application fee:*** $25. ***Tuition, state resident:*** full-time $3150; part-time $105 per semester hour. ***Tuition,***

University of Montevallo (continued)

nonresident: full-time $6300; part-time $210 per semester hour. ***Required fees:*** full-time $140; $35 per term part-time. Full-time tuition and fees vary according to course load. Part-time tuition and fees vary according to course load. ***College room and board:*** $3354; ***room only:*** $2144. Room and board charges vary according to board plan and housing facility. ***Payment plan:*** deferred payment.

FRESHMAN FINANCIAL AID (Fall 1998) 408 applied for aid; of those 50% were deemed to have need. 96% of freshmen with need received aid; of those 29% had need fully met. *Average percent of need met:* 75% (excluding resources awarded to replace EFC). *Average financial aid package:* $4608 (excluding resources awarded to replace EFC). 25% of all full-time freshmen had no need and received non-need-based aid.

UNDERGRADUATE FINANCIAL AID (Fall 1998) 1,747 applied for aid; of those 56% were deemed to have need. 96% of undergraduates with need received aid; of those 37% had need fully met. *Average percent of need met:* 67% (excluding resources awarded to replace EFC). *Average financial aid package:* $2984 (excluding resources awarded to replace EFC). 17% of all full-time undergraduates had no need and received non-need-based aid.

GIFT AID (NEED-BASED) ***Total amount:*** $1,434,890 (100% Federal). ***Receiving aid:*** *Freshmen:* 19% (100); *all full-time undergraduates:* 22% (527). ***Average award:*** Freshmen: $1927; Undergraduates: $1802. ***Scholarships, grants, and awards:*** Federal Pell, FSEOG, state, college/university gift aid from institutional funds.

GIFT AID (NON-NEED-BASED) ***Total amount:*** $2,865,075 (26% state, 64% institutional, 10% external sources). ***Receiving aid:*** *Freshmen:* 19% (99); *Undergraduates:* 13% (318). ***Scholarships, grants, and awards by category:*** *Academic Interests/Achievement:* biological sciences, education, general academic interests/achievements, physical sciences. *Creative Arts/Performance:* art/fine arts, music. *Special Achievements/Activities:* junior miss. *Special Characteristics:* international students, out-of-state students, veterans, veterans' children. ***Tuition waivers:*** Full or partial for employees or children of employees, senior citizens. ***ROTC:*** Army cooperative, Air Force cooperative.

LOANS ***Student loans:*** $5,665,872 (53% need-based, 47% non-need-based). Average indebtedness per student: $14,131. ***Average need-based loan:*** Freshmen: $796; Undergraduates: $1513. ***Parent loans:*** $386,543 (100% non-need-based). ***Programs:*** Perkins, college/university.

WORK-STUDY ***Federal work-study:*** *Total amount:* $145,880; 137 jobs averaging $1288. ***State or other work-study/employment:*** *Total amount:* $568,220 (100% need-based). Part-time jobs available.

ATHLETIC AWARDS *Total amount:* 521,258 (100% non-need-based).

APPLYING for FINANCIAL AID ***Required financial aid form:*** FAFSA. ***Financial aid deadline (priority):*** 4/15.

CONTACT Mr. Clark Aldridge, Director of Student Financial Services, University of Montevallo, Station 6050, Montevallo, AL 35115, 205-665-6050 or toll-free 800-292-4349. *Fax:* 205-665-6047. *E-mail:* aldridge@montevallo.edu

UNIVERSITY OF NEBRASKA AT KEARNEY

Kearney, NE

Tuition & fees (NE res): $2728 **Average undergraduate aid package: N/A**

ABOUT THE INSTITUTION State-supported, coed. Awards: bachelor's and master's degrees and post-master's certificates. 41 undergraduate majors. Total enrollment: 6,780. Undergraduates: 5,805. Freshmen: 1,224. Federal methodology is used as a basis for awarding need-based institutional aid.

UNDERGRADUATE EXPENSES for 1999–2000 ***Application fee:*** $25. ***One-time required fee:*** $30. ***Tuition, state resident:*** full-time $2122; part-time $71 per semester hour. ***Tuition, nonresident:*** full-time $3975; part-time $132 per semester hour. ***Required fees:*** full-time $606; $11 per semester hour; $5 per term part-time. Full-time tuition and fees vary according to course load. Part-time tuition and fees vary according to course load. ***College room and board:*** $3430; ***room only:*** $1720. Room and board charges vary according to board plan and housing facility. ***Payment plan:*** installment.

FRESHMAN FINANCIAL AID (Fall 1998) 1158 applied for aid.

GIFT AID (NEED-BASED) ***Total amount:*** $4,025,439 (86% Federal, 2% state, 12% institutional). ***Scholarships, grants, and awards:*** Federal Pell, FSEOG, state, college/university gift aid from institutional funds.

GIFT AID (NON-NEED-BASED) ***Total amount:*** $1,213,430 (27% state, 17% institutional, 56% external sources). ***Scholarships, grants, and awards by category:*** *Academic Interests/Achievement:* business, English, foreign languages, general academic interests/achievements. *Creative Arts/Performance:* applied art and design, art/fine arts, cinema/film/broadcasting, creative writing, dance, debating, journalism/publications, music, theater/drama. *Special Achievements/Activities:* cheerleading/drum major, general special achievements/activities, leadership, memberships. *Special Characteristics:* children of faculty/staff, international students, out-of-state students, veterans, veterans' children. ***Tuition waivers:*** Full or partial for employees or children of employees.

LOANS ***Student loans:*** $13,965,789 (100% need-based). ***Parent loans:*** $537,494 (100% need-based). ***Programs:*** FFEL (Subsidized and Unsubsidized Stafford, PLUS), Perkins.

WORK-STUDY ***Federal work-study:*** *Total amount:* $367,701; jobs available.

ATHLETIC AWARDS *Total amount:* 521,675 (100% non-need-based).

APPLYING for FINANCIAL AID ***Required financial aid forms:*** FAFSA, institution's own form, federal income tax return. ***Financial aid deadline:*** Continuous. ***Notification date:*** Continuous beginning 4/15. Students must reply within 2 weeks of notification.

CONTACT Financial Aid Office, University of Nebraska at Kearney, 905 West 25th Street, Kearney, NE 68849-0001, 308-865-8520 or toll-free 800-445-3434. *Fax:* 308-865-8096.

UNIVERSITY OF NEBRASKA AT OMAHA

Omaha, NE

Tuition & fees (NE res): $2823 **Average undergraduate aid package: N/A**

ABOUT THE INSTITUTION State-supported, coed. Awards: associate, bachelor's, master's, and doctoral degrees. 94 undergraduate majors. Total enrollment: 13,264. Undergraduates: 10,659. Freshmen: 1,620. Federal methodology is used as a basis for awarding need-based institutional aid.

UNDERGRADUATE EXPENSES for 1999–2000 ***Application fee:*** $25. ***Tuition, state resident:*** full-time $2393; part-time $80 per semester hour. ***Tuition, nonresident:*** full-time $6458; part-time $215 per semester hour. ***Required fees:*** full-time $430; $12 per semester hour; $60 per term part-time. Full-time tuition and fees vary according to course load and program. Part-time tuition and fees vary according to program. ***College room and board:*** $5290; ***room only:*** $2151. ***Payment plan:*** deferred payment.

FRESHMAN FINANCIAL AID (Fall 1998) 812 applied for aid; of those 74% were deemed to have need. 99% of freshmen with need received aid.

UNDERGRADUATE FINANCIAL AID (Fall 1998) 4,184 applied for aid; of those 82% were deemed to have need. 99% of undergraduates with need received aid.

GIFT AID (NEED-BASED) ***Total amount:*** $6,352,686 (73% Federal, 17% state, 10% institutional). ***Receiving aid:*** *Freshmen:* 22% (311); *all full-time undergraduates:* 28% (2,049). ***Scholarships, grants, and awards:*** Federal Pell, FSEOG, state, private, college/university gift aid from institutional funds.

GIFT AID (NON-NEED-BASED) ***Total amount:*** $4,131,681 (2% Federal, 36% state, 38% institutional, 24% external sources). ***Receiving aid:*** *Freshmen:* 34% (481); *Undergraduates:* 25% (1,849). ***Scholarships, grants, and awards by category:*** *Academic Interests/Achievement:* biological sciences, business, communication, computer science, education, engineering/technologies, English, foreign languages, general academic interests/achievements, home economics, mathematics, physical sciences, premedicine, social sciences. *Creative Arts/Performance:* art/fine arts, debating, journalism/publications, music, theater/drama. *Special Achievements/Activities:* general special achievements/activities, leadership, memberships. *Special Characteristics:* adult students, children of faculty/staff, ethnic background, first-generation college students, handicapped students, international students, members of minority groups, out-of-state students, veterans' children. ***ROTC:*** Army cooperative, Air Force.

LOANS ***Student loans:*** $23,442,570 (59% need-based, 41% non-need-based). 58% of past graduating class borrowed through all loan programs. Average indebtedness per student: $14,200. ***Parent loans:*** $279,967 (100% non-need-based). ***Programs:*** FFEL (Subsidized and Unsubsidized Stafford, PLUS), Perkins, college/university.

WORK-STUDY ***Federal work-study:*** *Total amount:* $485,113; 305 jobs averaging $1591.

ATHLETIC AWARDS *Total amount:* 907,531 (100% non-need-based).

APPLYING for FINANCIAL AID ***Required financial aid form:*** FAFSA. ***Financial aid deadline (priority):*** 3/1. ***Notification date:*** Continuous beginning 4/15. Students must reply within 2 weeks of notification.

CONTACT Office of Financial Aid, University of Nebraska at Omaha, 103 Eppley Administration Building, 6001 Dodge Street, Omaha, NE 68182-0187, 402-554-2327 or toll-free 800-858-8648 (in-state). *Fax:* 402-554-3472.

UNIVERSITY OF NEBRASKA–LINCOLN

Lincoln, NE

Tuition & fees (NE res): $3338 **Average undergraduate aid package: $5394**

ABOUT THE INSTITUTION State-supported, coed. Awards: associate, bachelor's, master's, doctoral, and first professional degrees and post-master's certificates. 120 undergraduate majors. Total enrollment: 22,142. Undergraduates: 17,804. Both federal and institutional methodology are used as a basis for awarding need-based institutional aid.

UNDERGRADUATE EXPENSES for 1999–2000 ***Application fee:*** $25. ***Tuition, state resident:*** full-time $2618; part-time $87 per credit hour. ***Tuition, nonresident:*** full-time $7125; part-time $238 per credit hour. ***Required fees:*** full-time $720; $5 per credit hour; $119 per term part-time. Full-time tuition and fees vary according to course load. Part-time tuition and fees vary according to course load. ***College room and board:*** $4070; ***room only:*** $1880. Room and board charges vary according to board plan and housing facility.

FRESHMAN FINANCIAL AID (Fall 1998) 2169 applied for aid; of those 71% were deemed to have need. 96% of freshmen with need received aid; of those 23% had need fully met. *Average percent of need met:* 67% (excluding resources awarded to replace EFC). *Average financial aid package:* $4955 (excluding resources awarded to replace EFC). 14% of all full-time freshmen had no need and received non-need-based aid.

UNDERGRADUATE FINANCIAL AID (Fall 1998) 9,530 applied for aid; of those 77% were deemed to have need. 96% of undergraduates with need received aid; of those 33% had need fully met. *Average percent of need met:* 74% (excluding resources awarded to replace EFC). *Average financial aid package:* $5394 (excluding resources awarded to replace EFC). 11% of all full-time undergraduates had no need and received non-need-based aid.

GIFT AID (NEED-BASED) ***Total amount:*** $13,697,775 (56% Federal, 1% state, 29% institutional, 14% external sources). ***Receiving aid:*** *Freshmen:* 31% (1,141); *all full-time undergraduates:* 26% (4,666). ***Average award:*** Freshmen: $2920; Undergraduates: $2699. ***Scholarships, grants, and awards:*** Federal Pell, FSEOG, state, private, college/university gift aid from institutional funds.

GIFT AID (NON-NEED-BASED) ***Total amount:*** $8,003,819 (6% Federal, 69% institutional, 25% external sources). ***Receiving aid:*** *Freshmen:* 3% (128); *Undergraduates:* 2% (357). ***Scholarships, grants, and awards by category:*** *Academic Interests/Achievement:* agriculture, architecture, biological sciences, business, computer science, education, engineering/technologies, English, foreign languages, general academic interests/achievements, health fields, home economics, humanities, international studies, mathematics, physical sciences, premedicine, social sciences. *Creative Arts/Performance:* art/fine arts, cinema/film/broadcasting, dance, journalism/publications, music, performing arts, theater/drama. *Special Achievements/Activities:* cheerleading/drum major, community service, leadership. *Special Characteristics:* children and siblings of alumni, ethnic background, handicapped students, international students, members of minority groups, out-of-state students, veterans' children. ***Tuition waivers:*** Full or partial for employees or children of employees. ***ROTC:*** Army, Naval, Air Force.

LOANS ***Student loans:*** $37,054,841 (69% need-based, 31% non-need-based). 61% of past graduating class borrowed through all loan programs. Average indebtedness per student: $15,540. ***Average need-based loan:*** Freshmen: $2433; Undergraduates: $3410. ***Parent loans:*** $4,399,276 (68% need-based, 32% non-need-based). ***Programs:*** Federal Direct (Subsidized and Unsubsidized Stafford, PLUS), Perkins, college/university.

WORK-STUDY ***Federal work-study:*** *Total amount:* $1,217,875; 648 jobs averaging $1879.

ATHLETIC AWARDS *Total amount:* 3,327,838 (29% need-based, 71% non-need-based).

APPLYING for FINANCIAL AID ***Required financial aid form:*** FAFSA. ***Financial aid deadline:*** Continuous. ***Notification date:*** Continuous beginning 4/15.

CONTACT Ms. Jo Tederman, Assistant Director of Scholarships and Financial Aid, University of Nebraska–Lincoln, PO Box 880411, Lincoln, NE 68588-0411, 402-472-0561 or toll-free 800-742-8800. *Fax:* 402-472-9826.

UNIVERSITY OF NEBRASKA MEDICAL CENTER

Omaha, NE

Tuition & fees (NE res): $2838 **Average undergraduate aid package: N/A**

ABOUT THE INSTITUTION State-supported, coed. Awards: bachelor's, master's, doctoral, and first professional degrees and post-bachelor's, post-master's, and first-professional certificates. 6 undergraduate majors. Total enrollment: 2,590. Undergraduates: 764. Federal methodology is used as a basis for awarding need-based institutional aid.

UNDERGRADUATE EXPENSES for 1999–2000 ***Application fee:*** $25. ***Tuition, state resident:*** full-time $2618; part-time $87 per hour. ***Tuition, nonresident:*** full-time $7125; part-time $238 per hour. ***Required fees:*** full-time $220; $110 per term part-time. Full-time tuition and fees vary according to location and program. Part-time tuition and fees vary according to course load, location, and program.

UNDERGRADUATE FINANCIAL AID (Fall 1999, est.) 705 applied for aid; of those 100% were deemed to have need. 100% of undergraduates with need received aid. *Average percent of need met:* 62% (excluding resources awarded to replace EFC).

GIFT AID (NEED-BASED) ***Total amount:*** $1,703,346 (28% Federal, 16% state, 55% institutional, 1% external sources). ***Receiving aid:*** *All full-time undergraduates:* 80% (684). ***Average award:*** Undergraduates: $2453. ***Scholarships, grants, and awards:*** Federal Pell, FSEOG, state, private, college/university gift aid from institutional funds.

GIFT AID (NON-NEED-BASED) ***Scholarships, grants, and awards by category:*** *Academic Interests/Achievement:* general academic interests/achievements. *Special Achievements/Activities:* community service, leadership. ***ROTC:*** Army cooperative, Naval cooperative, Air Force cooperative.

LOANS ***Student loans:*** $4,041,865 (100% need-based). 85% of past graduating class borrowed through all loan programs. Average indebtedness per student: $24,100. ***Average need-based loan:*** Undergraduates: $6474. ***Parent loans:*** $515,616 (100% need-based). ***Programs:*** FFEL (Subsidized and Unsubsidized Stafford, PLUS), Perkins, Federal Nursing, state, college/university.

WORK-STUDY ***Federal work-study:*** *Total amount:* $68,692; 29 jobs averaging $2367.

ATHLETIC AWARDS *Total amount:* 5000 (100% need-based).

APPLYING for FINANCIAL AID ***Required financial aid forms:*** FAFSA, institution's own form. ***Financial aid deadline (priority):*** 2/1. ***Notification date:*** Continuous. Students must reply within 2 weeks of notification.

CONTACT Ms. Tammy Reese, Assistant Director, Financial Aid, University of Nebraska Medical Center, 984265 Nebraska Medical Center, Omaha, NE 68198-4265, 402-559-7265 or toll-free 800-626-8431. *Fax:* 402-559-6796. *E-mail:* tbatterm@unmc.edu

UNIVERSITY OF NEVADA, LAS VEGAS

Las Vegas, NV

Tuition & fees (NV res): $2386 **Average undergraduate aid package: $6765**

ABOUT THE INSTITUTION State-supported, coed. Awards: bachelor's, master's, doctoral, and first professional degrees and post-bachelor's and post-master's certificates. 81 undergraduate majors. Total enrollment: 20,475. Undergraduates: 16,195. Freshmen: 1,794. Federal methodology is used as a basis for awarding need-based institutional aid.

UNDERGRADUATE EXPENSES for 1999–2000 ***Application fee:*** $40. ***Tuition, state resident:*** full-time $2340; part-time $72 per credit hour. ***Tuition, nonresident:*** full-time $9320; part-time $150 per credit hour. ***Required fees:*** full-time $46; $23 per term part-time. Full-time tuition and fees vary according to course load and reciprocity agreements. Part-time tuition and fees vary according to course load and reciprocity agreements. ***College room and board:*** $5694; ***room only:*** $3522. Room and board charges vary according to board plan. ***Payment plan:*** deferred payment.

FRESHMAN FINANCIAL AID (Fall 1998) 1052 applied for aid; of those 55% were deemed to have need. 82% of freshmen with need received aid; of those 58% had need fully met. *Average percent of need met:* 59% (excluding resources awarded to replace EFC). *Average financial aid package:* $5322 (excluding resources awarded to replace EFC). 12% of all full-time freshmen had no need and received non-need-based aid.

UNDERGRADUATE FINANCIAL AID (Fall 1998) 6,470 applied for aid; of those 67% were deemed to have need. 89% of undergraduates with need received aid; of those 60% had need fully met. *Average percent of need met:* 76% (excluding resources awarded to replace EFC). *Average financial aid package:* $6765 (excluding resources awarded to replace EFC). 39% of all full-time undergraduates had no need and received non-need-based aid.

GIFT AID (NEED-BASED) ***Total amount:*** $8,031,536 (71% Federal, 26% state, 3% institutional). ***Receiving aid:*** *Freshmen:* 23% (360); *all full-time undergraduates:* 28% (2,745). ***Average award:*** Freshmen: $2277; Undergraduates: $2389. ***Scholarships, grants, and awards:*** Federal Pell, FSEOG, state, private, college/university gift aid from institutional funds.

GIFT AID (NON-NEED-BASED) ***Total amount:*** $3,897,773 (3% Federal, 10% state, 57% institutional, 30% external sources). ***Receiving aid:*** *Freshmen:* 25% (379); *Undergraduates:* 17% (1,627). ***Scholarships, grants, and awards by category:*** *Academic Interests/Achievement:* architecture, biological sciences, business, communication, computer science, education, engineering/technologies, English, general academic interests/achievements, health fields, humanities, international studies, mathematics, physical sciences, premedicine, social sciences. *Creative Arts/Performance:* applied art and design, art/fine arts, cinema/film/broadcasting, dance, journalism/publications, music, performing arts, theater/drama. *Special Achievements/Activities:* cheerleading/drum major, community service, general special achievements/activities, hobbies/interests, leadership, memberships, rodeo. *Special Characteristics:* children and siblings of alumni, children of faculty/staff, children of public servants, children of workers in trades, ethnic background, first-generation college students, general special characteristics, handicapped students, international students, local/state students, members of minority groups, out-of-state students. ***Tuition waivers:*** Full or partial for children of alumni, employees or children of employees, senior citizens.

LOANS ***Student loans:*** $24,551,906 (55% need-based, 45% non-need-based). Average indebtedness per student: $11,500. ***Average need-based loan:*** Freshmen: $2369; Undergraduates: $3700. ***Parent loans:*** $3,619,449 (100% non-need-based). ***Programs:*** Federal Direct (Subsidized and Unsubsidized Stafford, PLUS), Perkins, college/university.

WORK-STUDY ***Federal work-study:*** *Total amount:* $566,167; jobs available. ***State or other work-study/employment:*** *Total amount:* $2,134,877 (26% need-based, 74% non-need-based). Part-time jobs available.

ATHLETIC AWARDS *Total amount:* 3,249,628 (100% non-need-based).

APPLYING for FINANCIAL AID ***Required financial aid forms:*** FAFSA, institution's own form. ***Financial aid deadline (priority):*** 2/1. ***Notification date:*** Continuous beginning 3/25. Students must reply within 2 weeks of notification.

CONTACT Ms. Cheryl Dedrickson, Assistant Director, Student Financial Services, University of Nevada, Las Vegas, 4505 Maryland Parkway, Box 452016, Las Vegas, NV 89154-2016, 702-895-4113 or toll-free 800-334-UNLV. *Fax:* 702-895-1353.

UNIVERSITY OF NEVADA, RENO

Reno, NV

Tuition & fees (NV res): $2259 **Average undergraduate aid package: $9500**

ABOUT THE INSTITUTION State-supported, coed. Awards: bachelor's, master's, doctoral, and first professional degrees and post-bachelor's and post-master's certificates. 97 undergraduate majors. Total enrollment: 12,532. Undergraduates: 9,402. Freshmen: 1,548. Federal methodology is used as a basis for awarding need-based institutional aid.

UNDERGRADUATE EXPENSES for 1999–2000 ***Application fee:*** $40. ***Tuition, state resident:*** full-time $2145; part-time $72 per credit. ***Tuition, nonresident:*** full-time $8492; part-time $150 per credit. ***Required fees:*** full-time $114; $57 per term part-time. Full-time tuition and fees vary according to course load. Part-time tuition and fees vary according to course load. ***College room and board:*** $5295; ***room only:*** $2860. Room and board charges vary according to board plan and housing facility. ***Payment plan:*** deferred payment.

FRESHMAN FINANCIAL AID (Fall 1999, est.) 585 applied for aid; of those 67% were deemed to have need. 72% of freshmen with need received aid; of those 21% had need fully met. *Average percent of need met:* 85% (excluding resources awarded to replace EFC). *Average financial aid package:* $8300 (excluding resources awarded to replace EFC). 4% of all full-time freshmen had no need and received non-need-based aid.

UNDERGRADUATE FINANCIAL AID (Fall 1999, est.) 2,335 applied for aid; of those 82% were deemed to have need. 84% of undergraduates with need received aid; of those 29% had need fully met. *Average percent of need met:* 80% (excluding resources awarded to replace EFC). *Average financial aid package:* $9500 (excluding resources awarded to replace EFC). 3% of all full-time undergraduates had no need and received non-need-based aid.

GIFT AID (NEED-BASED) ***Total amount:*** $4,084,620 (68% Federal, 26% state, 6% institutional). ***Receiving aid:*** *Freshmen:* 12% (175); *all full-time undergraduates:* 16% (1,030). ***Average award:*** Freshmen: $850; Undergraduates: $900. ***Scholarships, grants, and awards:*** Federal Pell, FSEOG, state, private.

GIFT AID (NON-NEED-BASED) ***Total amount:*** $7,586,270 (85% institutional, 15% external sources). ***Receiving aid:*** *Freshmen:* 17% (245); *Undergraduates:* 12% (820). ***Scholarships, grants, and awards by category:*** *Academic Interests/Achievement:* agriculture, area/ethnic studies, biological sciences, business, computer science, education, engineering/technologies, English, foreign languages, general academic interests/achievements, health fields, humanities, international studies, mathematics, military science, physical sciences, premedicine, social sciences. *Creative Arts/Performance:* applied art and design, art/fine arts, dance, debating, journalism/publications, music, theater/drama. *Special Achievements/Activities:* cheerleading/drum major, leadership. *Special Characteristics:* children and siblings of alumni, children of faculty/staff, ethnic background, first-generation college students, members of minority groups. ***Tuition waivers:*** Full or partial for children of alumni, employees or children of employees, senior citizens. ***ROTC:*** Army.

LOANS ***Student loans:*** $13,825,035 (60% need-based, 40% non-need-based). ***Average need-based loan:*** Freshmen: $1000; Undergraduates: $2000. ***Parent loans:*** $1,997,595 (100% non-need-based). ***Programs:*** FFEL (Subsidized and Unsubsidized Stafford, PLUS), Perkins, Federal Nursing, college/university.

WORK-STUDY ***Federal work-study:*** *Total amount:* $664,100; jobs available. ***State or other work-study/employment:*** *Total amount:* $31,850 (100% non-need-based). Part-time jobs available.

ATHLETIC AWARDS *Total amount:* 2,200,000 (100% non-need-based).

APPLYING for FINANCIAL AID ***Required financial aid form:*** FAFSA. ***Financial aid deadline (priority):*** 2/1. ***Notification date:*** Continuous beginning 4/1. Students must reply within 2 weeks of notification.

CONTACT Dr. Nancee Langley, Director of Student Financial Services, University of Nevada, Reno, 200 Thompson, Mail Stop 076, Reno, NV 89557, 702-784-1288 or toll-free 800-622-4867 (in-state). *Fax:* 702-784-1025. *E-mail:* langley@admin.unr.edu

UNIVERSITY OF NEW ENGLAND
Biddeford, ME

Tuition & fees: $15,500 **Average undergraduate aid package: N/A**

ABOUT THE INSTITUTION Independent, coed. Awards: associate, bachelor's, master's, and first professional degrees. 39 undergraduate majors. Total enrollment: 2,945. Undergraduates: 1,695. Freshmen: 310. Federal methodology is used as a basis for awarding need-based institutional aid.

UNDERGRADUATE EXPENSES for 1999–2000 ***Application fee:*** $40. ***Comprehensive fee:*** $21,700 includes full-time tuition ($14,990), mandatory fees ($510), and room and board ($6200). Room and board charges vary according to housing facility. ***Part-time tuition:*** $500 per credit. ***Part-time fees:*** $230 per year part-time. Part-time tuition and fees vary according to course load. ***Payment plans:*** installment, deferred payment.

GIFT AID (NEED-BASED) ***Scholarships, grants, and awards:*** Federal Pell, FSEOG, state, private, college/university gift aid from institutional funds.

GIFT AID (NON-NEED-BASED) ***Scholarships, grants, and awards by category:*** *Academic Interests/Achievement:* biological sciences, general academic interests/achievements. *Special Achievements/Activities:* community service, hobbies/interests, leadership. ***Tuition waivers:*** Full or partial for employees or children of employees. ***ROTC:*** Army cooperative.

LOANS ***Programs:*** FFEL (Subsidized and Unsubsidized Stafford, PLUS), Perkins, Federal Nursing, college/university.

WORK-STUDY Federal work-study jobs available.

APPLYING for FINANCIAL AID ***Required financial aid forms:*** FAFSA, institution's own form. ***Financial aid deadline:*** 5/1 (priority: 3/1). ***Notification date:*** Continuous. Students must reply within 2 weeks of notification.

CONTACT Lisa M. Connor, Director of Financial Aid, University of New England, 11 Hills Beach Road, Biddeford, ME 04005, 207-283-0171 Ext. 2342 or toll-free 800-477-4UNE. *Fax:* 207-282-6379. *E-mail:* finaid@mailbox.une.edu

UNIVERSITY OF NEW HAMPSHIRE
Durham, NH

Tuition & fees (NH res): $6939 **Average undergraduate aid package: $10,405**

ABOUT THE INSTITUTION State-supported, coed. Awards: associate, bachelor's, master's, and doctoral degrees and post-master's certificates. 131 undergraduate majors. Total enrollment: 13,591. Undergraduates: 10,877. Freshmen: 2,556. Federal methodology is used as a basis for awarding need-based institutional aid.

UNDERGRADUATE EXPENSES for 1999–2000 ***Application fee:*** $35; $50 for nonresidents. ***Tuition, state resident:*** full-time $5450; part-time $227 per credit. ***Tuition, nonresident:*** full-time $14,340; part-time $598 per credit. ***Required fees:*** full-time $1489; $15 per term part-time. Full-time tuition and fees vary according to program. Part-time tuition and fees vary according to course load. ***College room and board:*** $4798; ***room only:*** $2820. Room and board charges vary according to board plan and housing facility.

FRESHMAN FINANCIAL AID (Fall 1999) 1902 applied for aid; of those 75% were deemed to have need. 98% of freshmen with need received aid; of those 27% had need fully met. *Average percent of need met:* 81% (excluding resources awarded to replace EFC). *Average financial aid package:* $12,322 (excluding resources awarded to replace EFC). 17% of all full-time freshmen had no need and received non-need-based aid.

UNDERGRADUATE FINANCIAL AID (Fall 1999) 6,600 applied for aid; of those 80% were deemed to have need. 99% of undergraduates with need received aid; of those 23% had need fully met. *Average percent of need met:* 85% (excluding resources awarded to replace EFC). *Average financial aid package:* $10,405 (excluding resources awarded to replace EFC). 16% of all full-time undergraduates had no need and received non-need-based aid.

GIFT AID (NEED-BASED) ***Total amount:*** $15,592,660 (36% Federal, 3% state, 43% institutional, 18% external sources). ***Receiving aid:*** *Freshmen:* 39% (1,003); *all full-time undergraduates:* 32% (3,086). ***Average award:*** Freshmen: $2024; Undergraduates: $2086. ***Scholarships, grants, and awards:*** Federal Pell, FSEOG, state, private, college/university gift aid from institutional funds.

GIFT AID (NON-NEED-BASED) ***Total amount:*** $8,051,885 (100% institutional). ***Receiving aid:*** *Freshmen:* 4% (109); *Undergraduates:* 3% (248). ***Scholarships, grants, and awards by category:*** *Academic Interests/Achievement:* agriculture, business, education, engineering/technologies, English, general academic interests/achievements, health fields, humanities, mathematics, military science. *Creative Arts/Performance:* art/fine arts, dance, music, theater/drama. *Special Achievements/Activities:* community service. *Special Characteristics:* children and siblings of alumni, children of faculty/staff, handicapped students, international students, local/state students. ***Tuition waivers:*** Full or partial for minority students, employees or children of employees, senior citizens. ***ROTC:*** Army, Air Force.

LOANS ***Student loans:*** $36,239,833 (70% need-based, 30% non-need-based). 69% of past graduating class borrowed through all loan programs. Average indebtedness per student: $19,712. ***Average need-based loan:*** Freshmen: $2282; Undergraduates: $3376. ***Parent loans:*** $9,048,606 (100% non-need-based). ***Programs:*** FFEL (Subsidized and Unsubsidized Stafford, PLUS), Perkins, state, college/university.

WORK-STUDY ***Federal work-study:*** *Total amount:* $5,526,280; 2,943 jobs averaging $1878. ***State or other work-study/employment:*** *Total amount:* $3,271,040 (100% non-need-based).

ATHLETIC AWARDS *Total amount:* 3,651,248 (100% non-need-based).

APPLYING for FINANCIAL AID ***Required financial aid form:*** FAFSA. ***Financial aid deadline:*** 3/1. ***Notification date:*** Continuous beginning 3/15.

CONTACT Susan K. Allen, Associate Director of Financial Aid, University of New Hampshire, 11 Garrison Avenue, Stoke Hall, Durham, NH 03824, 603-862-3600. *Fax:* 603-862-1947. *E-mail:* financial.aid@unh.edu

UNIVERSITY OF NEW HAMPSHIRE AT MANCHESTER
Manchester, NH

Tuition & fees (NH res): $4684 **Average undergraduate aid package: N/A**

ABOUT THE INSTITUTION State-supported, coed. Awards: associate and bachelor's degrees. 13 undergraduate majors. Total enrollment: 1,086. Undergraduates: 1,016. Freshmen: 107. Federal methodology is used as a basis for awarding need-based institutional aid.

UNDERGRADUATE EXPENSES for 1999–2000 ***Application fee:*** $35; $50 for nonresidents. ***Tuition, state resident:*** full-time $4630; part-time $172 per credit. ***Tuition, nonresident:*** full-time $12,190; part-time $190 per credit. ***Required fees:*** full-time $54; $17 per term part-time. Part-time tuition and fees vary according to program. ***Payment plan:*** installment.

GIFT AID (NEED-BASED) ***Scholarships, grants, and awards:*** Federal Pell, FSEOG, state, private, college/university gift aid from institutional funds.

GIFT AID (NON-NEED-BASED) ***Scholarships, grants, and awards by category:*** *Academic Interests/Achievement:* general academic interests/achievements. *Special Characteristics:* children of faculty/staff, ethnic background, members of minority groups. ***Tuition waivers:*** Full or partial for employees or children of employees, senior citizens. ***ROTC:*** Army cooperative, Air Force cooperative.

LOANS ***Programs:*** FFEL (Subsidized and Unsubsidized Stafford, PLUS), Perkins.

WORK-STUDY Federal work-study jobs available. ***State or other work-study/employment:*** Part-time jobs available.

APPLYING for FINANCIAL AID ***Required financial aid form:*** FAFSA. ***Financial aid deadline (priority):*** 5/1.

University of New Hampshire at Manchester (continued)

CONTACT Kim Tracey, Assistant Director of Financial Aid, University of New Hampshire at Manchester, French Hall, 400 Commercial Street, Manchester, NH 03101-1113, 603-629-4114. *Fax:* 603-623-2745.

UNIVERSITY OF NEW HAVEN

West Haven, CT

Tuition & fees: $14,550 **Average undergraduate aid package: $12,800**

ABOUT THE INSTITUTION Independent, coed. Awards: associate, bachelor's, master's, and doctoral degrees and post-bachelor's and post-master's certificates. 58 undergraduate majors. Total enrollment: 4,463. Undergraduates: 2,585. Freshmen: 417. Both federal and institutional methodology are used as a basis for awarding need-based institutional aid.

UNDERGRADUATE EXPENSES for 1999–2000 ***Application fee:*** $25. ***Comprehensive fee:*** $21,110 includes full-time tuition ($14,250), mandatory fees ($300), and room and board ($6560). Full-time tuition and fees vary according to program. Room and board charges vary according to board plan and housing facility. ***Part-time tuition:*** $270 per credit hour. ***Part-time fees:*** $10 per term part-time. Part-time tuition and fees vary according to class time, location, and program. ***Payment plans:*** installment, deferred payment.

FRESHMAN FINANCIAL AID (Fall 1999, est.) 241 applied for aid; of those 92% were deemed to have need. 100% of freshmen with need received aid; of those 25% had need fully met. *Average percent of need met:* 81% (excluding resources awarded to replace EFC). *Average financial aid package:* $12,314 (excluding resources awarded to replace EFC). 14% of all full-time freshmen had no need and received non-need-based aid.

UNDERGRADUATE FINANCIAL AID (Fall 1999, est.) 1,081 applied for aid; of those 92% were deemed to have need. 100% of undergraduates with need received aid; of those 31% had need fully met. *Average percent of need met:* 75% (excluding resources awarded to replace EFC). *Average financial aid package:* $12,800 (excluding resources awarded to replace EFC). 13% of all full-time undergraduates had no need and received non-need-based aid.

GIFT AID (NEED-BASED) ***Total amount:*** $6,376,113 (16% Federal, 27% state, 51% institutional, 6% external sources). ***Receiving aid:*** *Freshmen:* 77% (198); *all full-time undergraduates:* 80% (916). ***Average award:*** Freshmen: $7178; Undergraduates: $7237. ***Scholarships, grants, and awards:*** Federal Pell, FSEOG, state, private, college/university gift aid from institutional funds.

GIFT AID (NON-NEED-BASED) ***Total amount:*** $414,025 (2% state, 91% institutional, 7% external sources). ***Receiving aid:*** *Freshmen:* 4% (10); *Undergraduates:* 5% (63). ***Scholarships, grants, and awards by category:*** *Academic Interests/Achievement:* 203 awards ($961,626 total): general academic interests/achievements. *Special Achievements/Activities:* general special achievements/activities. *Special Characteristics:* children of faculty/staff. ***Tuition waivers:*** Full or partial for employees or children of employees, senior citizens. ***ROTC:*** Air Force cooperative.

LOANS ***Student loans:*** $7,601,187 (76% need-based, 24% non-need-based). 65% of past graduating class borrowed through all loan programs. Average indebtedness per student: $15,500. ***Average need-based loan:*** Freshmen: $4890; Undergraduates: $5416. ***Parent loans:*** $1,546,904 (100% non-need-based). ***Programs:*** FFEL (Subsidized and Unsubsidized Stafford, PLUS), Perkins.

WORK-STUDY ***Federal work-study:*** *Total amount:* $122,764; 87 jobs averaging $1400. ***State or other work-study/employment:*** *Total amount:* $59,295 (100% non-need-based). Part-time jobs available.

ATHLETIC AWARDS *Total amount:* 1,247,987 (69% need-based, 31% non-need-based).

APPLYING for FINANCIAL AID ***Required financial aid forms:*** FAFSA, institution's own form, CSS Financial Aid PROFILE. ***Financial aid deadline (priority):*** 3/1. ***Notification date:*** Continuous beginning 3/15. Students must reply by 5/1 or within 2 weeks of notification.

CONTACT Ms. Jane Sangeloty, Director of Financial Aid, University of New Haven, 300 Orange Avenue, West Haven, CT 06516-1916, 203-932-7315 or toll-free 800-DIAL-UNH (out-of-state). *Fax:* 203-931-6050. *E-mail:* finaid@charger.newhaven.edu

UNIVERSITY OF NEW MEXICO

Albuquerque, NM

Tuition & fees (NM res): $2430 **Average undergraduate aid package: $8074**

ABOUT THE INSTITUTION State-supported, coed. Awards: associate, bachelor's, master's, doctoral, and first professional degrees and post-master's certificates. 91 undergraduate majors. Total enrollment: 23,852. Undergraduates: 16,295. Freshmen: 2,649. Federal methodology is used as a basis for awarding need-based institutional aid.

UNDERGRADUATE EXPENSES for 1999–2000 ***Application fee:*** $15. ***Tuition, state resident:*** full-time $2430; part-time $101 per credit hour. ***Tuition, nonresident:*** full-time $9170; part-time $101 per credit hour. Part-time tuition and fees vary according to course load. ***College room and board:*** $4800. Room and board charges vary according to board plan and housing facility. ***Payment plan:*** installment.

FRESHMAN FINANCIAL AID (Fall 1999, est.) 1375 applied for aid; of those 80% were deemed to have need. 99% of freshmen with need received aid; of those 28% had need fully met. *Average percent of need met:* 76% (excluding resources awarded to replace EFC). *Average financial aid package:* $6402 (excluding resources awarded to replace EFC). 51% of all full-time freshmen had no need and received non-need-based aid.

UNDERGRADUATE FINANCIAL AID (Fall 1999, est.) 6,986 applied for aid; of those 88% were deemed to have need. 97% of undergraduates with need received aid; of those 29% had need fully met. *Average percent of need met:* 75% (excluding resources awarded to replace EFC). *Average financial aid package:* $8074 (excluding resources awarded to replace EFC). 30% of all full-time undergraduates had no need and received non-need-based aid.

GIFT AID (NEED-BASED) ***Total amount:*** $19,291,563 (53% Federal, 26% state, 11% institutional, 10% external sources). ***Receiving aid:*** *Freshmen:* 37% (1,015); *all full-time undergraduates:* 38% (4,910). ***Average award:*** Freshmen: $3432; Undergraduates: $2951. ***Scholarships, grants, and awards:*** Federal Pell, FSEOG, state, private, college/university gift aid from institutional funds, Federal Nursing.

GIFT AID (NON-NEED-BASED) ***Total amount:*** $8,733,698 (1% Federal, 58% state, 31% institutional, 10% external sources). ***Receiving aid:*** *Freshmen:* 4% (116); *Undergraduates:* 2% (255). ***Scholarships, grants, and awards by category:*** *Academic Interests/Achievement:* engineering/technologies, general academic interests/achievements. *Creative Arts/Performance:* art/fine arts, music, theater/drama. *Special Achievements/Activities:* general special achievements/activities. *Special Characteristics:* children of faculty/staff, children of union members/company employees, members of minority groups, out-of-state students, veterans. ***Tuition waivers:*** Full or partial for employees or children of employees, senior citizens. ***ROTC:*** Army, Air Force.

LOANS ***Student loans:*** $29,142,714 (85% need-based, 15% non-need-based). 52% of past graduating class borrowed through all loan programs. Average indebtedness per student: $15,896. ***Average need-based loan:*** Freshmen: $2818; Undergraduates: $4925. ***Programs:*** Federal Direct (Subsidized and Unsubsidized Stafford), Perkins, Federal Nursing, state, college/university.

WORK-STUDY ***Federal work-study:*** *Total amount:* $2,917,413; 1,521 jobs available. ***State or other work-study/employment:*** *Total amount:* $1,688,447 (96% need-based, 4% non-need-based). 865 part-time jobs available.

ATHLETIC AWARDS *Total amount:* 1,499,438 (34% need-based, 66% non-need-based).

APPLYING for FINANCIAL AID ***Required financial aid form:*** FAFSA. ***Financial aid deadline (priority):*** 3/1. ***Notification date:*** Continuous beginning 4/15.

CONTACT Office of Financial Aid, University of New Mexico, Mesa Vista North, Albuquerque, NM 87131-2081, 505-277-5017 or toll-free 800-CALLUNM (in-state). *Fax:* 505-277-6326. *E-mail:* finaid@unm.edu

UNIVERSITY OF NEW ORLEANS

New Orleans, LA

Tuition & fees (LA res): $2532 **Average undergraduate aid package: N/A**

ABOUT THE INSTITUTION State-supported, coed. Awards: bachelor's, master's, and doctoral degrees. 49 undergraduate majors. Total enrollment: 15,868. Undergraduates: 11,872. Freshmen: 1,872. Federal methodology is used as a basis for awarding need-based institutional aid.

UNDERGRADUATE EXPENSES for 1999–2000 ***Application fee:*** $20. ***Tuition, state resident:*** full-time $2362; part-time $735 per term. ***Tuition, nonresident:*** full-time $7888; part-time $2119 per term. ***Required fees:*** full-time $170; $5 per semester hour; $10 per term part-time. Part-time tuition and fees vary according to course load. ***College room and board:*** $3175; ***room only:*** $1575. Room and board charges vary according to board plan and housing facility. ***Payment plan:*** deferred payment.

GIFT AID (NEED-BASED) ***Scholarships, grants, and awards:*** Federal Pell, FSEOG, state, private.

GIFT AID (NON-NEED-BASED) ***Scholarships, grants, and awards by category:*** *Academic Interests/Achievement:* general academic interests/achievements. *Creative Arts/Performance:* music. *Special Characteristics:* children and siblings of alumni. ***Tuition waivers:*** Full or partial for employees or children of employees, senior citizens. ***ROTC:*** Army cooperative, Air Force cooperative.

LOANS ***Programs:*** FFEL (Subsidized and Unsubsidized Stafford, PLUS), Perkins.

WORK-STUDY Federal work-study jobs available.

APPLYING for FINANCIAL AID ***Required financial aid forms:*** FAFSA, financial aid transcript (for transfers). ***Financial aid deadline:*** Continuous. ***Notification date:*** Continuous.

CONTACT Director of Student Financial Aid, University of New Orleans, Administration Building, Room 1005, Lakefront, New Orleans, LA 70148, 504-286-6687 or toll-free 888-514-4275.

UNIVERSITY OF NORTH ALABAMA

Florence, AL

Tuition & fees (AL res): $2512 **Average undergraduate aid package: N/A**

ABOUT THE INSTITUTION State-supported, coed. Awards: bachelor's and master's degrees. 35 undergraduate majors. Total enrollment: 5,805. Undergraduates: 5,099. Freshmen: 809. Federal methodology is used as a basis for awarding need-based institutional aid.

UNDERGRADUATE EXPENSES for 1999–2000 ***Application fee:*** $25. ***Tuition, state resident:*** full-time $2232; part-time $93 per semester hour. ***Tuition, nonresident:*** full-time $4464; part-time $186 per semester hour. ***Required fees:*** full-time $280; $13 per semester hour; $26 per term part-time. Part-time tuition and fees vary according to course load. ***College room and board:*** $3672.

FRESHMAN FINANCIAL AID (Fall 1998) 522 applied for aid; of those 84% were deemed to have need. 97% of freshmen with need received aid; of those 28% had need fully met. *Average percent of need met:* 75% (excluding resources awarded to replace EFC). 23% of all full-time freshmen had no need and received non-need-based aid.

UNDERGRADUATE FINANCIAL AID (Fall 1998) 3,166 applied for aid; of those 84% were deemed to have need. 94% of undergraduates with need received aid; of those 44% had need fully met. *Average percent of need met:* 67% (excluding resources awarded to replace EFC). 17% of all full-time undergraduates had no need and received non-need-based aid.

GIFT AID (NEED-BASED) ***Total amount:*** $3,429,164 (100% Federal). ***Receiving aid:*** *Freshmen:* 36% (287); *all full-time undergraduates:* 39% (1,715). ***Average award:*** Freshmen: $3099; Undergraduates: $2023. ***Scholarships, grants, and awards:*** Federal Pell, FSEOG, state, private.

GIFT AID (NON-NEED-BASED) ***Total amount:*** $1,499,765 (81% institutional, 19% external sources). ***Scholarships, grants, and awards by category:*** *Academic Interests/Achievement:* general academic interests/achievements. *Creative Arts/Performance:* art/fine arts, journalism/publications, music. *Special Achievements/Activities:* cheerleading/drum major, general special achievements/activities, leadership. *Special Characteristics:* children of faculty/staff, first-generation college students, general special characteristics, out-of-state students. ***Tuition waivers:*** Full or partial for employees or children of employees. ***ROTC:*** Army.

LOANS ***Student loans:*** $10,457,326 (61% need-based, 39% non-need-based). 46% of past graduating class borrowed through all loan programs. Average indebtedness per student: $16,466. ***Parent loans:*** $202,751 (100% non-need-based). ***Programs:*** FFEL (Subsidized and Unsubsidized Stafford, PLUS), Perkins.

WORK-STUDY ***Federal work-study:*** *Total amount:* $307,629; jobs available. ***State or other work-study/employment:*** *Total amount:* $466,813 (100% non-need-based). Part-time jobs available.

ATHLETIC AWARDS *Total amount:* 608,514 (100% non-need-based).

APPLYING for FINANCIAL AID ***Required financial aid form:*** FAFSA. ***Financial aid deadline (priority):*** 4/1. ***Notification date:*** 5/1. Students must reply within 2 weeks of notification.

CONTACT Dr. Jo Bennett, Director of Student Financial Services, University of North Alabama, PO Box 5014, Florence, AL 35632-0001, 256-765-4278 or toll-free 800-TALKUNA. *Fax:* 256-765-4920. *E-mail:* jbennett@unanov.una.edu

THE UNIVERSITY OF NORTH CAROLINA AT ASHEVILLE

Asheville, NC

Tuition & fees (NC res): $1960 **Average undergraduate aid package: $6014**

ABOUT THE INSTITUTION State-supported, coed. Awards: bachelor's and master's degrees. 28 undergraduate majors. Total enrollment: 3,164. Undergraduates: 3,125. Freshmen: 460. Federal methodology is used as a basis for awarding need-based institutional aid.

UNDERGRADUATE EXPENSES for 1999–2000 ***Application fee:*** $45. ***Tuition, state resident:*** full-time $806; part-time $302 per term. ***Tuition, nonresident:*** full-time $7426; part-time $2785 per term. ***Required fees:*** full-time $1154; $432 per term part-time. Part-time tuition and fees vary according to course load. ***College room and board:*** $4179; ***room only:*** $2039. Room and board charges vary according to board plan and housing facility. ***Payment plan:*** installment.

FRESHMAN FINANCIAL AID (Fall 1998) 333 applied for aid; of those 57% were deemed to have need. 100% of freshmen with need received aid; of those 22% had need fully met. *Average percent of need met:* 72% (excluding resources awarded to replace EFC). *Average financial aid package:* $4804 (excluding resources awarded to replace EFC). 35% of all full-time freshmen had no need and received non-need-based aid.

UNDERGRADUATE FINANCIAL AID (Fall 1998) 1,583 applied for aid; of those 59% were deemed to have need. 100% of undergraduates with need received aid; of those 39% had need fully met. *Average percent of need met:* 78% (excluding resources awarded to replace EFC). *Average financial aid package:* $6014 (excluding resources awarded to replace EFC). 37% of all full-time undergraduates had no need and received non-need-based aid.

GIFT AID (NEED-BASED) ***Total amount:*** $1,642,332 (74% Federal, 22% state, 1% institutional, 3% external sources). ***Receiving aid:*** *Freshmen:* 31% (145); *all full-time undergraduates:* 32% (729). ***Average award:*** Freshmen: $1810; Undergraduates: $1963. ***Scholarships, grants, and awards:*** Federal Pell, FSEOG, state, private, college/university gift aid from institutional funds.

GIFT AID (NON-NEED-BASED) ***Total amount:*** $1,225,146 (2% Federal, 54% state, 28% institutional, 16% external sources). ***Receiving aid:*** *Freshmen:* 19% (89); *Undergraduates:* 11% (250). ***Scholarships, grants, and awards by category:*** *Academic Interests/Achievement:* 298 awards ($723,226 total): biological sciences, computer science, education, engineering/technologies, English, general academic interests/achievements, mathematics, physical sciences, premedicine, social sciences. *Creative Arts/Performance:* 20 awards ($16,910 total): art/fine arts, music, theater/drama. *Special Achievements/Activities:* 139 awards ($178,027 total): community service, general special achievements/activities, junior miss,

The University of North Carolina at Asheville (continued)

leadership. *Special Characteristics:* 55 awards ($63,937 total): adult students, children and siblings of alumni, children of faculty/staff, ethnic background, first-generation college students, general special characteristics, handicapped students, international students, local/state students, members of minority groups, veterans, veterans' children. ***Tuition waivers:*** Full or partial for employees or children of employees, senior citizens.

LOANS ***Student loans:*** $4,867,839 (63% need-based, 37% non-need-based). Average indebtedness per student: $13,118. ***Average need-based loan:*** Freshmen: $2344; Undergraduates: $3468. ***Parent loans:*** $390,447 (100% non-need-based). ***Programs:*** Federal Direct (Subsidized and Unsubsidized Stafford, PLUS), Perkins, state, college/university.

WORK-STUDY ***Federal work-study:*** *Total amount:* $136,340; 132 jobs averaging $1033. ***State or other work-study/employment:*** *Total amount:* $734,468 (100% non-need-based). 626 part-time jobs averaging $1173.

ATHLETIC AWARDS *Total amount:* 701,945 (100% non-need-based).

APPLYING for FINANCIAL AID ***Required financial aid form:*** FAFSA. ***Financial aid deadline (priority):*** 3/1. ***Notification date:*** Continuous beginning 4/15. Students must reply within 2 weeks of notification.

CONTACT Mrs. V. Carolyn McElrath, Director of Financial Aid, The University of North Carolina at Asheville, 1 University Heights, Asheville, NC 28804-8510, 828-251-6535 or toll-free 800-531-9842. *Fax:* 828-251-6841. *E-mail:* cmcelrath@unca.edu

THE UNIVERSITY OF NORTH CAROLINA AT CHAPEL HILL

Chapel Hill, NC

Tuition & fees (NC res): $2365 **Average undergraduate aid package: $6772**

ABOUT THE INSTITUTION State-supported, coed. Awards: bachelor's, master's, doctoral, and first professional degrees and post-master's certificates. 65 undergraduate majors. Total enrollment: 24,353. Undergraduates: 15,434. Freshmen: 3,396. Both federal and institutional methodology are used as a basis for awarding need-based institutional aid.

UNDERGRADUATE EXPENSES for 1999–2000 ***Application fee:*** $55. ***Tuition, state resident:*** full-time $1528. ***Tuition, nonresident:*** full-time $10,694. ***Required fees:*** full-time $837. Full-time tuition and fees vary according to program and student level. Part-time tuition and fees vary according to course load and program. ***College room and board:*** $5280; ***room only:*** $2460. Room and board charges vary according to board plan, housing facility, and location. ***Payment plan:*** deferred payment.

FRESHMAN FINANCIAL AID (Fall 1998) 2316 applied for aid; of those 45% were deemed to have need. 99% of freshmen with need received aid; of those 93% had need fully met. *Average percent of need met:* 95% (excluding resources awarded to replace EFC). *Average financial aid package:* $6114 (excluding resources awarded to replace EFC). 27% of all full-time freshmen had no need and received non-need-based aid.

UNDERGRADUATE FINANCIAL AID (Fall 1998) 7,810 applied for aid; of those 53% were deemed to have need. 99% of undergraduates with need received aid; of those 93% had need fully met. *Average percent of need met:* 92% (excluding resources awarded to replace EFC). *Average financial aid package:* $6772 (excluding resources awarded to replace EFC). 18% of all full-time undergraduates had no need and received non-need-based aid.

GIFT AID (NEED-BASED) ***Total amount:*** $16,086,138 (31% Federal, 10% state, 49% institutional, 10% external sources). ***Receiving aid:*** *Freshmen:* 28% (970); *all full-time undergraduates:* 28% (4,026). ***Average award:*** Freshmen: $3880; Undergraduates: $3668. ***Scholarships, grants, and awards:*** Federal Pell, FSEOG, state, private, college/university gift aid from institutional funds.

GIFT AID (NON-NEED-BASED) ***Total amount:*** $8,608,683 (12% Federal, 18% state, 44% institutional, 26% external sources). ***Receiving aid:*** *Freshmen:* 29% (1,008); *Undergraduates:* 28% (4,035). ***Scholarships, grants, and awards by category:*** *Academic Interests/Achievement:* business, communication, education, English, general academic interests/achievements, health fields, mathematics. *Creative Arts/Performance:* applied art and design, art/fine arts, journalism/publications, music, theater/drama. *Special Achievements/Activities:* community service, general special achievements/activities, leadership. *Special Characteristics:* children of faculty/staff, international students, out-of-state students. ***Tuition waivers:*** Full or partial for employees or children of employees, senior citizens. ***ROTC:*** Army, Naval, Air Force.

LOANS ***Student loans:*** $17,175,613 (79% need-based, 21% non-need-based). 61% of past graduating class borrowed through all loan programs. Average indebtedness per student: $12,800. ***Average need-based loan:*** Freshmen: $3175; Undergraduates: $3574. ***Parent loans:*** $4,518,282 (36% need-based, 64% non-need-based). ***Programs:*** FFEL (Subsidized and Unsubsidized Stafford, PLUS), Perkins, state, college/university, alternative loans.

WORK-STUDY ***Federal work-study:*** *Total amount:* $646,490; 690 jobs averaging $937.

ATHLETIC AWARDS *Total amount:* 4,176,449 (23% need-based, 77% non-need-based).

APPLYING for FINANCIAL AID ***Required financial aid forms:*** FAFSA, CSS Financial Aid PROFILE. ***Financial aid deadline (priority):*** 3/1. ***Notification date:*** Continuous.

CONTACT Ms. Shirley A. Ort, Director, Office of Scholarships and Student Aid, The University of North Carolina at Chapel Hill, PO Box 1080, Chapel Hill, NC 27514, 919-962-9246. *E-mail:* sao@unc.edu

THE UNIVERSITY OF NORTH CAROLINA AT CHARLOTTE

Charlotte, NC

Tuition & fees (NC res): $1920 **Average undergraduate aid package: $6629**

ABOUT THE INSTITUTION State-supported, coed. Awards: bachelor's, master's, and doctoral degrees and post-master's certificates. 64 undergraduate majors. Total enrollment: 16,950. Undergraduates: 14,195. Freshmen: 2,122. Federal methodology is used as a basis for awarding need-based institutional aid.

UNDERGRADUATE EXPENSES for 1999–2000 ***Application fee:*** $35. ***Tuition, state resident:*** full-time $962; part-time $240 per term. ***Tuition, nonresident:*** full-time $8232; part-time $2058 per term. ***Required fees:*** full-time $958; $252 per term part-time. Full-time tuition and fees vary according to course load. Part-time tuition and fees vary according to course load. ***College room and board:*** $3816; ***room only:*** $1996. Room and board charges vary according to board plan and housing facility.

FRESHMAN FINANCIAL AID (Fall 1999, est.) 1227 applied for aid; of those 69% were deemed to have need. 96% of freshmen with need received aid; of those 20% had need fully met. *Average percent of need met:* 65% (excluding resources awarded to replace EFC). *Average financial aid package:* $4873 (excluding resources awarded to replace EFC). 16% of all full-time freshmen had no need and received non-need-based aid.

UNDERGRADUATE FINANCIAL AID (Fall 1999, est.) 5,673 applied for aid; of those 78% were deemed to have need. 99% of undergraduates with need received aid; of those 33% had need fully met. *Average percent of need met:* 79% (excluding resources awarded to replace EFC). *Average financial aid package:* $6629 (excluding resources awarded to replace EFC). 17% of all full-time undergraduates had no need and received non-need-based aid.

GIFT AID (NEED-BASED) ***Total amount:*** $8,067,292 (79% Federal, 11% state, 4% institutional, 6% external sources). ***Receiving aid:*** *Freshmen:* 26% (558); *all full-time undergraduates:* 27% (2,889). ***Average award:*** Freshmen: $2663; Undergraduates: $2640. ***Scholarships, grants, and awards:*** Federal Pell, FSEOG, state, private, college/university gift aid from institutional funds.

GIFT AID (NON-NEED-BASED) ***Total amount:*** $256,304 (29% state, 31% institutional, 40% external sources). ***Receiving aid:*** *Freshmen:* 10% (215); *Undergraduates:* 5% (525). ***Scholarships, grants, and awards by category:*** *Academic Interests/Achievement:* 190 awards ($480,000 total): architecture, business, computer science, education, engineering/technologies, general academic interests/achievements, health fields, mathematics. *Creative Arts/Performance:* 24 awards ($36,650 total): music, performing arts. *Special*

Characteristics: 58 awards ($58,000 total): adult students. ***Tuition waivers:*** Full or partial for senior citizens. ***ROTC:*** Army, Air Force.

LOANS ***Student loans:*** $29,100,000 (56% need-based, 44% non-need-based). 38% of past graduating class borrowed through all loan programs. Average indebtedness per student: $7848. ***Average need-based loan:*** Freshmen: $2676; Undergraduates: $3680. ***Parent loans:*** $2,411,600 (100% non-need-based). ***Programs:*** Federal Direct (Subsidized and Unsubsidized Stafford, PLUS), Perkins, state, college/university.

WORK-STUDY ***Federal work-study:*** *Total amount:* $585,000; 488 jobs averaging $1200. ***State or other work-study/employment:*** *Total amount:* $2,520,000 (100% non-need-based). 1,200 part-time jobs averaging $2000.

ATHLETIC AWARDS *Total amount:* 1,199,246 (34% need-based, 66% non-need-based).

APPLYING for FINANCIAL AID ***Required financial aid form:*** FAFSA. ***Financial aid deadline (priority):*** 4/1. ***Notification date:*** 4/2. Students must reply within 3 weeks of notification.

CONTACT Curtis Whalen, Director of Financial Aid, The University of North Carolina at Charlotte, 9201 University City Boulevard, Charlotte, NC 28223-0001, 704-547-2461. *Fax:* 704-547-3132. *E-mail:* finaid@email.uncc.edu

THE UNIVERSITY OF NORTH CAROLINA AT GREENSBORO

Greensboro, NC

Tuition & fees (NC res): $2136 **Average undergraduate aid package: $5000**

ABOUT THE INSTITUTION State-supported, coed. Awards: bachelor's, master's, and doctoral degrees. 78 undergraduate majors. Total enrollment: 12,998. Undergraduates: 10,286. Freshmen: 1,939. Federal methodology is used as a basis for awarding need-based institutional aid.

UNDERGRADUATE EXPENSES for 1999–2000 ***Application fee:*** $35. ***Tuition, state resident:*** full-time $1086; part-time $136 per credit. ***Tuition, nonresident:*** full-time $9540; part-time $1193 per credit. ***Required fees:*** full-time $1050; $43 per credit. Part-time tuition and fees vary according to course load. ***College room and board:*** $4064; ***room only:*** $2164. Room and board charges vary according to board plan and housing facility.

FRESHMAN FINANCIAL AID (Fall 1999, est.) 1355 applied for aid; of those 52% were deemed to have need. 97% of freshmen with need received aid; of those 53% had need fully met. *Average percent of need met:* 80% (excluding resources awarded to replace EFC). *Average financial aid package:* $4600 (excluding resources awarded to replace EFC). 31% of all full-time freshmen had no need and received non-need-based aid.

UNDERGRADUATE FINANCIAL AID (Fall 1999, est.) 6,073 applied for aid; of those 52% were deemed to have need. 90% of undergraduates with need received aid; of those 42% had need fully met. *Average percent of need met:* 70% (excluding resources awarded to replace EFC). *Average financial aid package:* $5000 (excluding resources awarded to replace EFC). 24% of all full-time undergraduates had no need and received non-need-based aid.

GIFT AID (NEED-BASED) ***Total amount:*** $7,024,032 (81% Federal, 15% state, 4% institutional). ***Receiving aid:*** *Freshmen:* 26% (512); *all full-time undergraduates:* 25% (2,131). ***Average award:*** Freshmen: $1000; Undergraduates: $1000. ***Scholarships, grants, and awards:*** Federal Pell, FSEOG, state, private, college/university gift aid from institutional funds.

GIFT AID (NON-NEED-BASED) ***Total amount:*** $5,832,514 (1% Federal, 35% state, 41% institutional, 23% external sources). ***Receiving aid:*** *Freshmen:* 5% (103); *Undergraduates:* 5% (425). ***Scholarships, grants, and awards by category:*** *Academic Interests/Achievement:* 320 awards ($350,000 total): biological sciences, business, communication, education, English, foreign languages, general academic interests/achievements, health fields, home economics, humanities, library science, mathematics, physical sciences, premedicine, religion/biblical studies, social sciences. *Creative Arts/Performance:* 100 awards ($150,000 total): art/fine arts, cinema/film/broadcasting, dance, music, performing arts, theater/drama. *Special Achievements/Activities:* 5 awards ($5000 total): community service, general special achievements/activities, junior miss, leadership, religious involvement. *Special Characteristics:* 500 awards ($500,000 total): adult students, ethnic background, general special characteristics, handicapped students, members of minority groups, out-of-state students, religious affiliation, veterans, veterans' children. ***Tuition waivers:*** Full or partial for employees or children of employees, senior citizens. ***ROTC:*** Army cooperative, Air Force cooperative.

LOANS ***Student loans:*** $23,730,834 (49% need-based, 51% non-need-based). 58% of past graduating class borrowed through all loan programs. Average indebtedness per student: $10,026. ***Average need-based loan:*** Freshmen: $2625; Undergraduates: $3000. ***Parent loans:*** $6,096,380 (100% non-need-based). ***Programs:*** FFEL (Subsidized and Unsubsidized Stafford, PLUS), Perkins, college/university.

WORK-STUDY ***Federal work-study:*** *Total amount:* $482,583; 305 jobs averaging $1500.

ATHLETIC AWARDS *Total amount:* 1,026,959 (100% non-need-based).

APPLYING for FINANCIAL AID ***Required financial aid form:*** FAFSA. ***Financial aid deadline (priority):*** 3/1. ***Notification date:*** Continuous beginning 4/1. Students must reply within 3 weeks of notification.

CONTACT Mr. Bruce Cabiness, Associate Director of Financial Aid, The University of North Carolina at Greensboro, PO Box 26177, Greensboro, NC 27402-6177, 336-334-5702. *Fax:* 336-334-3010. *E-mail:* bruce_cabiness@uncg.edu

THE UNIVERSITY OF NORTH CAROLINA AT PEMBROKE

Pembroke, NC

Tuition & fees (NC res): $1706 **Average undergraduate aid package: $4630**

ABOUT THE INSTITUTION State-supported, coed. Awards: bachelor's and master's degrees. 43 undergraduate majors. Total enrollment: 3,062. Undergraduates: 2,789. Freshmen: 481. Federal methodology is used as a basis for awarding need-based institutional aid.

UNDERGRADUATE EXPENSES for 1999–2000 ***Application fee:*** $25. ***Tuition, state resident:*** full-time $962; part-time $241 per term. ***Tuition, nonresident:*** full-time $8232; part-time $2058 per term. ***Required fees:*** full-time $744; $158 per term part-time. Part-time tuition and fees vary according to course load. ***College room and board:*** $3358; ***room only:*** $1758. Room and board charges vary according to board plan and housing facility. ***Payment plan:*** installment.

FRESHMAN FINANCIAL AID (Fall 1999) 356 applied for aid; of those 70% were deemed to have need. 95% of freshmen with need received aid; of those 36% had need fully met. *Average percent of need met:* 81% (excluding resources awarded to replace EFC). *Average financial aid package:* $4277 (excluding resources awarded to replace EFC). 24% of all full-time freshmen had no need and received non-need-based aid.

UNDERGRADUATE FINANCIAL AID (Fall 1999) 1,407 applied for aid; of those 78% were deemed to have need. 95% of undergraduates with need received aid; of those 46% had need fully met. *Average percent of need met:* 83% (excluding resources awarded to replace EFC). *Average financial aid package:* $4630 (excluding resources awarded to replace EFC). 23% of all full-time undergraduates had no need and received non-need-based aid.

GIFT AID (NEED-BASED) ***Total amount:*** $3,790,721 (56% Federal, 31% state, 3% institutional, 10% external sources). ***Receiving aid:*** *Freshmen:* 43% (205); *all full-time undergraduates:* 47% (928). ***Average award:*** Freshmen: $2733; Undergraduates: $2852. ***Scholarships, grants, and awards:*** Federal Pell, FSEOG, state, private, college/university gift aid from institutional funds.

GIFT AID (NON-NEED-BASED) ***Total amount:*** $84,803 (58% state, 42% institutional). ***Receiving aid:*** *Freshmen:* 11% (51); *Undergraduates:* 10% (190). ***Scholarships, grants, and awards by category:*** *Academic Interests/Achievement:* 48 awards ($22,103 total): business, communication, education, English, general academic interests/achievements, health fields, physical sciences. *Creative Arts/Performance:* 16 awards ($6700 total): journalism/publications, music. *Special Characteristics:* 53 awards ($56,000 total): children and siblings of alumni, general special characteristics. ***Tuition waivers:*** Full or partial for senior citizens. ***ROTC:*** Army, Air Force.

The University of North Carolina at Pembroke (continued)

LOANS ***Student loans:*** $2,837,752 (66% need-based, 34% non-need-based). ***Average need-based loan:*** Freshmen: $2412; Undergraduates: $2704. ***Parent loans:*** $192,133 (100% non-need-based). ***Programs:*** FFEL (Subsidized and Unsubsidized Stafford, PLUS), Perkins, college/university.

WORK-STUDY ***Federal work-study:*** *Total amount:* $206,312; 147 jobs averaging $1403. ***State or other work-study/employment:*** *Total amount:* $69,921 (75% need-based, 25% non-need-based). 54 part-time jobs averaging $1295.

ATHLETIC AWARDS *Total amount:* 362,549 (99% need-based, 1% non-need-based).

APPLYING for FINANCIAL AID ***Required financial aid forms:*** FAFSA, institution's own form. ***Financial aid deadline (priority):*** 3/15. ***Notification date:*** 4/15. Students must reply within 2 weeks of notification.

CONTACT Mildred Weber, Systems Coordinator, The University of North Carolina at Pembroke, PO Box 1510, Pembroke, NC 28372-1510, 910-521-6612 or toll-free 800-822-2185 (in-state). *E-mail:* weber@papa.uncp.edu

THE UNIVERSITY OF NORTH CAROLINA AT WILMINGTON

Wilmington, NC

Tuition & fees (NC res): $2068 **Average undergraduate aid package: $7282**

ABOUT THE INSTITUTION State-supported, coed. Awards: bachelor's and master's degrees. 35 undergraduate majors. Total enrollment: 9,757. Undergraduates: 9,067. Freshmen: 1,670. Federal methodology is used as a basis for awarding need-based institutional aid.

UNDERGRADUATE EXPENSES for 1999–2000 ***Application fee:*** $45. ***Tuition, state resident:*** full-time $962. ***Tuition, nonresident:*** full-time $8232. ***Required fees:*** full-time $1106. Part-time tuition and fees vary according to course load and program. ***College room and board:*** $4656. Room and board charges vary according to board plan and housing facility. ***Payment plan:*** installment.

FRESHMAN FINANCIAL AID (Fall 1999, est.) 923 applied for aid; of those 59% were deemed to have need. 100% of freshmen with need received aid; of those 29% had need fully met. *Average percent of need met:* 69% (excluding resources awarded to replace EFC). *Average financial aid package:* $6694 (excluding resources awarded to replace EFC). 19% of all full-time freshmen had no need and received non-need-based aid.

UNDERGRADUATE FINANCIAL AID (Fall 1999, est.) 3,604 applied for aid; of those 76% were deemed to have need. 100% of undergraduates with need received aid; of those 29% had need fully met. *Average percent of need met:* 75% (excluding resources awarded to replace EFC). *Average financial aid package:* $7282 (excluding resources awarded to replace EFC). 19% of all full-time undergraduates had no need and received non-need-based aid.

GIFT AID (NEED-BASED) ***Total amount:*** $5,379,812 (64% Federal, 19% state, 8% institutional, 9% external sources). ***Receiving aid:*** *Freshmen:* 20% (335); *all full-time undergraduates:* 22% (1,707). ***Average award:*** Freshmen: $2869; Undergraduates: $2870. ***Scholarships, grants, and awards:*** Federal Pell, FSEOG, state, private, college/university gift aid from institutional funds.

GIFT AID (NON-NEED-BASED) ***Total amount:*** $1,636,978 (46% state, 25% institutional, 29% external sources). ***Receiving aid:*** *Freshmen:* 3% (43); *Undergraduates:* 2% (148). ***Scholarships, grants, and awards by category:*** *Academic Interests/Achievement:* biological sciences, business, communication, computer science, education, English, foreign languages, general academic interests/achievements, health fields, humanities, international studies, mathematics, physical sciences, religion/biblical studies, social sciences. *Creative Arts/Performance:* art/fine arts, music. *Special Achievements/Activities:* cheerleading/drum major, community service, general special achievements/activities, leadership. *Special Characteristics:* local/state students. ***Tuition waivers:*** Full or partial for employees or children of employees, senior citizens.

LOANS ***Student loans:*** $16,607,694 (57% need-based, 43% non-need-based). 80% of past graduating class borrowed through all loan programs. Average indebtedness per student: $12,559. ***Average need-based loan:*** Freshmen: $2613; Undergraduates: $3712. ***Parent loans:*** $7,494,647 (100% non-need-based). ***Programs:*** Federal Direct (Subsidized and Unsubsidized Stafford, PLUS), Perkins, state, college/university.

WORK-STUDY ***Federal work-study:*** *Total amount:* $630,145; 291 jobs averaging $2165. ***State or other work-study/employment:*** *Total amount:* $1,557,804 (100% non-need-based). Part-time jobs available.

ATHLETIC AWARDS *Total amount:* 1,000,924 (27% need-based, 73% non-need-based).

APPLYING for FINANCIAL AID ***Required financial aid form:*** FAFSA. ***Financial aid deadline:*** Continuous. ***Notification date:*** Continuous beginning 1/15. Students must reply within 3 weeks of notification.

CONTACT Mark S. Williams, Director of Financial Aid and Veterans Services Office, The University of North Carolina at Wilmington, 601 South College Road, Wilmington, NC 28403, 910-962-3177 or toll-free 800-228-5571 (out-of-state). *Fax:* 910-962-3851. *E-mail:* finaid@uncwil.edu

UNIVERSITY OF NORTH DAKOTA

Grand Forks, ND

Tuition & fees (ND res): $2956 **Average undergraduate aid package: $4609**

ABOUT THE INSTITUTION State-supported, coed. Awards: bachelor's, master's, doctoral, and first professional degrees. 72 undergraduate majors. Total enrollment: 10,590. Undergraduates: 8,680. Freshmen: 1,754. Federal methodology is used as a basis for awarding need-based institutional aid.

UNDERGRADUATE EXPENSES for 1999–2000 ***Application fee:*** $25. ***Tuition, state resident:*** full-time $2480; part-time $103 per credit hour. ***Tuition, nonresident:*** full-time $6622; part-time $276 per credit hour. ***Required fees:*** full-time $476; $15 per credit hour; $32 per term part-time. Full-time tuition and fees vary according to program and reciprocity agreements. Part-time tuition and fees vary according to course load, program, and reciprocity agreements. ***College room and board:*** $3406; ***room only:*** $1346. Room and board charges vary according to board plan and housing facility.

FRESHMAN FINANCIAL AID (Fall 1998) 1349 applied for aid; of those 73% were deemed to have need. 100% of freshmen with need received aid; of those 14% had need fully met. *Average percent of need met:* 73% (excluding resources awarded to replace EFC). *Average financial aid package:* $4287 (excluding resources awarded to replace EFC). 16% of all full-time freshmen had no need and received non-need-based aid.

UNDERGRADUATE FINANCIAL AID (Fall 1998) 5,828 applied for aid; of those 77% were deemed to have need. 100% of undergraduates with need received aid; of those 21% had need fully met. *Average percent of need met:* 85% (excluding resources awarded to replace EFC). *Average financial aid package:* $4609 (excluding resources awarded to replace EFC). 16% of all full-time undergraduates had no need and received non-need-based aid.

GIFT AID (NEED-BASED) ***Total amount:*** $5,689,098 (92% Federal, 8% state). ***Receiving aid:*** *Freshmen:* 15% (332); *all full-time undergraduates:* 22% (1,897). ***Average award:*** Freshmen: $3270; Undergraduates: $2553. ***Scholarships, grants, and awards:*** Federal Pell, FSEOG, state, private, college/university gift aid from institutional funds.

GIFT AID (NON-NEED-BASED) ***Total amount:*** $9,323,221 (24% Federal, 6% state, 34% institutional, 36% external sources). ***Receiving aid:*** *Freshmen:* 11% (248); *Undergraduates:* 11% (966). ***Scholarships, grants, and awards by category:*** *Academic Interests/Achievement:* 2,181 awards ($2,679,569 total): business, communication, computer science, education, engineering/technologies, English, foreign languages, general academic interests/achievements, mathematics, premedicine. *Creative Arts/Performance:* 97 awards ($60,800 total): art/fine arts, music, theater/drama. *Special Characteristics:* 85 awards ($202,994 total): members of minority groups. ***Tuition waivers:*** Full or partial for employees or children of employees, senior citizens. ***ROTC:*** Army, Air Force.

LOANS ***Student loans:*** $22,793,721 (69% need-based, 31% non-need-based). 68% of past graduating class borrowed through all loan programs.

Average indebtedness per student: $19,143. ***Average need-based loan:*** Freshmen: $2859; Undergraduates: $3280. ***Parent loans:*** $1,398,215 (100% non-need-based). ***Programs:*** FFEL (Subsidized and Unsubsidized Stafford, PLUS), Perkins, Federal Nursing, college/university.

WORK-STUDY ***Federal work-study:*** *Total amount:* $1,304,613; 1,383 jobs averaging $943. ***State or other work-study/employment:*** *Total amount:* $5,601,161 (100% non-need-based). 1,947 part-time jobs averaging $2876.

ATHLETIC AWARDS *Total amount:* 789,168 (100% non-need-based).

APPLYING for FINANCIAL AID ***Required financial aid form:*** FAFSA. ***Financial aid deadline (priority):*** 4/15. ***Notification date:*** 6/8. Students must reply within 4 weeks of notification.

CONTACT Ms. Alice Hoffert, Director, Student Financial Aid, University of North Dakota, Box 8371, Grand Forks, ND 58202, 701-777-3121 or toll-free 800-CALL UND. *Fax:* 701-777-2040. *E-mail:* alice_hoffert@mail.und.nodak.edu

UNIVERSITY OF NORTHERN COLORADO

Greeley, CO

Tuition & fees (CO res): $2754 **Average undergraduate aid package: $6170**

ABOUT THE INSTITUTION State-supported, coed. Awards: bachelor's, master's, and doctoral degrees. 36 undergraduate majors. Total enrollment: 12,045. Undergraduates: 9,953. Freshmen: 2,177. Federal methodology is used as a basis for awarding need-based institutional aid.

UNDERGRADUATE EXPENSES for 1999–2000 ***Application fee:*** $30. ***Tuition, state resident:*** full-time $2014; part-time $112 per hour. ***Tuition, nonresident:*** full-time $8997; part-time $500 per hour. ***Required fees:*** full-time $740; $38 per hour. Full-time tuition and fees vary according to course load. ***College room and board:*** $4796; ***room only:*** $2286. Room and board charges vary according to board plan and housing facility. ***Payment plan:*** deferred payment.

FRESHMAN FINANCIAL AID (Fall 1998) 1852 applied for aid; of those 60% were deemed to have need. 95% of freshmen with need received aid; of those 13% had need fully met. *Average percent of need met:* 62% (excluding resources awarded to replace EFC). *Average financial aid package:* $4883 (excluding resources awarded to replace EFC). 33% of all full-time freshmen had no need and received non-need-based aid.

UNDERGRADUATE FINANCIAL AID (Fall 1998) 6,868 applied for aid; of those 65% were deemed to have need. 96% of undergraduates with need received aid; of those 22% had need fully met. *Average percent of need met:* 74% (excluding resources awarded to replace EFC). *Average financial aid package:* $6170 (excluding resources awarded to replace EFC). 26% of all full-time undergraduates had no need and received non-need-based aid.

GIFT AID (NEED-BASED) ***Total amount:*** $6,141,988 (66% Federal, 34% state). ***Receiving aid:*** *Freshmen:* 32% (701); *all full-time undergraduates:* 32% (2,808). ***Average award:*** Freshmen: $2060; Undergraduates: $2135. ***Scholarships, grants, and awards:*** Federal Pell, FSEOG, state, private, college/university gift aid from institutional funds, Robert C. Byrd Scholarships.

GIFT AID (NON-NEED-BASED) ***Total amount:*** $4,209,049 (17% state, 32% institutional, 51% external sources). ***Receiving aid:*** *Freshmen:* 24% (534); *Undergraduates:* 16% (1,420). ***Scholarships, grants, and awards by category:*** *Academic Interests/Achievement:* 1,053 awards ($853,291 total): biological sciences, business, communication, education, English, general academic interests/achievements, health fields, home economics, mathematics, military science, physical sciences, social sciences. *Creative Arts/Performance:* 247 awards ($188,054 total): dance, music, performing arts, theater/drama. *Special Characteristics:* 1,945 awards ($2,778,150 total): adult students, children and siblings of alumni, children of faculty/staff, children of union members/company employees, ethnic background, general special characteristics, handicapped students, international students, local/state students, members of minority groups, out-of-state students, veterans. ***Tuition waivers:*** Full or partial for employees or children of employees. ***ROTC:*** Army, Air Force.

LOANS ***Student loans:*** $18,610,714 (64% need-based, 36% non-need-based). ***Average need-based loan:*** Freshmen: $2612; Undergraduates: $3404. ***Parent loans:*** $5,366,852 (100% non-need-based). ***Programs:*** FFEL (Subsidized and Unsubsidized Stafford, PLUS), Perkins, college/university.

WORK-STUDY ***Federal work-study:*** *Total amount:* $463,207; 307 jobs averaging $1509. ***State or other work-study/employment:*** *Total amount:* $3,475,053 (26% need-based, 74% non-need-based). Part-time jobs available.

ATHLETIC AWARDS *Total amount:* 504,890 (100% non-need-based).

APPLYING for FINANCIAL AID ***Required financial aid form:*** FAFSA. ***Financial aid deadline (priority):*** 3/1. ***Notification date:*** 4/15. Students must reply within 4 weeks of notification.

CONTACT Donni Clark, Director of Student Financial Resources, University of Northern Colorado, Carter Hall 1005, Greeley, CO 80639, 970-351-2502. *Fax:* 970-351-3737. *E-mail:* sfrinfo@unco.edu

UNIVERSITY OF NORTHERN IOWA

Cedar Falls, IA

Tuition & fees (IA res): $3130 **Average undergraduate aid package: $4771**

ABOUT THE INSTITUTION State-supported, coed. Awards: bachelor's, master's, and doctoral degrees. 93 undergraduate majors. Total enrollment: 13,811. Undergraduates: 12,100. Freshmen: 2,176. Federal methodology is used as a basis for awarding need-based institutional aid.

UNDERGRADUATE EXPENSES for 2000–2001 ***Application fee:*** $20. ***Tuition, state resident:*** full-time $2906; part-time $122 per semester hour. ***Tuition, nonresident:*** full-time $7870; part-time $328 per semester hour. ***Required fees:*** full-time $224; $15 per term part-time. Part-time tuition and fees vary according to course load. ***College room and board:*** $4200; ***room only:*** $1927. Room and board charges vary according to board plan and housing facility. ***Payment plan:*** installment.

FRESHMAN FINANCIAL AID (Fall 1999, est.) 1653 applied for aid; of those 70% were deemed to have need. 99% of freshmen with need received aid; of those 26% had need fully met. *Average percent of need met:* 76% (excluding resources awarded to replace EFC). *Average financial aid package:* $4270 (excluding resources awarded to replace EFC). 28% of all full-time freshmen had no need and received non-need-based aid.

UNDERGRADUATE FINANCIAL AID (Fall 1999, est.) 7,426 applied for aid; of those 77% were deemed to have need. 99% of undergraduates with need received aid; of those 32% had need fully met. *Average percent of need met:* 77% (excluding resources awarded to replace EFC). *Average financial aid package:* $4771 (excluding resources awarded to replace EFC). 22% of all full-time undergraduates had no need and received non-need-based aid.

GIFT AID (NEED-BASED) ***Total amount:*** $7,121,209 (76% Federal, 6% state, 18% institutional). ***Receiving aid:*** *Freshmen:* 26% (560); *all full-time undergraduates:* 26% (2,759). ***Average award:*** Freshmen: $2393; Undergraduates: $2277. ***Scholarships, grants, and awards:*** Federal Pell, FSEOG, state, private, college/university gift aid from institutional funds.

GIFT AID (NON-NEED-BASED) ***Total amount:*** $5,885,213 (6% state, 69% institutional, 25% external sources). ***Receiving aid:*** *Freshmen:* 27% (584); *Undergraduates:* 15% (1,576). ***Scholarships, grants, and awards by category:*** *Academic Interests/Achievement:* biological sciences, business, education, general academic interests/achievements, mathematics, physical sciences, social sciences. *Creative Arts/Performance:* applied art and design, art/fine arts, music, theater/drama. *Special Achievements/Activities:* leadership. *Special Characteristics:* general special characteristics, members of minority groups. ***ROTC:*** Army.

LOANS ***Student loans:*** $39,180,431 (58% need-based, 42% non-need-based). 72% of past graduating class borrowed through all loan programs. Average indebtedness per student: $16,983. ***Average need-based loan:*** Freshmen: $2540; Undergraduates: $3849. ***Parent loans:*** $6,447,840 (100% non-need-based). ***Programs:*** Federal Direct (Subsidized and Unsubsidized Stafford, PLUS), Perkins, alternative loans.

WORK-STUDY ***Federal work-study:*** *Total amount:* $934,144; jobs available. ***State or other work-study/employment:*** *Total amount:* $596,282 (92% need-based, 8% non-need-based). Part-time jobs available.

ATHLETIC AWARDS *Total amount:* 1,366,775 (100% non-need-based).

University of Northern Iowa (continued)

APPLYING for FINANCIAL AID ***Required financial aid form:*** FAFSA. ***Financial aid deadline:*** Continuous. ***Notification date:*** Continuous beginning 3/20. Students must reply within 2 weeks of notification.

CONTACT Joyce Morrow, Assistant Director of Scholarships, University of Northern Iowa, 116 Gilchrist Hall, Cedar Falls, IA 50614-0024, 319-273-2700 or toll-free 800-772-2037. *Fax:* 319-273-6950. *E-mail:* joyce.morrow@uni.edu

UNIVERSITY OF NORTH FLORIDA

Jacksonville, FL

Tuition & fees (FL res): $1820 **Average undergraduate aid package: $2184**

ABOUT THE INSTITUTION State-supported, coed. Awards: associate, bachelor's, master's, and doctoral degrees and post-bachelor's certificates (doctoral degree in education only). 47 undergraduate majors. Total enrollment: 12,077. Undergraduates: 10,267. Freshmen: 1,505. Federal methodology is used as a basis for awarding need-based institutional aid.

UNDERGRADUATE EXPENSES for 1999–2000 ***Application fee:*** $20. ***Tuition, state resident:*** full-time $1820; part-time $76 per semester hour. ***Tuition, nonresident:*** full-time $7411; part-time $309 per semester hour. ***College room and board:*** $5100; ***room only:*** $2790. Room and board charges vary according to board plan and housing facility. ***Payment plan:*** deferred payment.

FRESHMAN FINANCIAL AID (Fall 1999, est.) 1198 applied for aid; of those 42% were deemed to have need. 97% of freshmen with need received aid; of those 37% had need fully met. *Average percent of need met:* 77% (excluding resources awarded to replace EFC). *Average financial aid package:* $1693 (excluding resources awarded to replace EFC). 44% of all full-time freshmen had no need and received non-need-based aid.

UNDERGRADUATE FINANCIAL AID (Fall 1999, est.) 4,400 applied for aid; of those 55% were deemed to have need. 95% of undergraduates with need received aid; of those 37% had need fully met. *Average percent of need met:* 71% (excluding resources awarded to replace EFC). *Average financial aid package:* $2184 (excluding resources awarded to replace EFC). 28% of all full-time undergraduates had no need and received non-need-based aid.

GIFT AID (NEED-BASED) ***Total amount:*** $6,889,328 (45% Federal, 28% state, 23% institutional, 4% external sources). ***Receiving aid:*** *Freshmen:* 22% (320); *all full-time undergraduates:* 24% (1,485). ***Average award:*** Freshmen: $1411; Undergraduates: $1457. ***Scholarships, grants, and awards:*** Federal Pell, FSEOG, state, college/university gift aid from institutional funds, 2+2 Scholarships (jointly sponsored with Florida public community colleges).

GIFT AID (NON-NEED-BASED) ***Total amount:*** $3,907,490 (74% state, 20% institutional, 6% external sources). ***Receiving aid:*** *Freshmen:* 26% (370); *Undergraduates:* 15% (945). ***Scholarships, grants, and awards by category:*** *Academic Interests/Achievement:* 433 awards ($761,664 total): business, education, general academic interests/achievements. *Creative Arts/Performance:* 83 awards ($87,800 total): music. *Special Achievements/Activities:* 89 awards ($86,323 total): community service, general special achievements/activities, leadership. *Special Characteristics:* 26 awards ($23,039 total): first-generation college students, general special characteristics, members of minority groups. ***Tuition waivers:*** Full or partial for employees or children of employees, senior citizens. ***ROTC:*** Naval cooperative.

LOANS ***Student loans:*** $11,527,713 (86% need-based, 14% non-need-based). Average indebtedness per student: $11,141. ***Average need-based loan:*** Freshmen: $2284; Undergraduates: $3707. ***Parent loans:*** $624,396 (51% need-based, 49% non-need-based). ***Programs:*** FFEL (Subsidized and Unsubsidized Stafford, PLUS), Perkins.

WORK-STUDY ***Federal work-study:*** *Total amount:* $191,799; 160 jobs averaging $1199.

ATHLETIC AWARDS *Total amount:* 467,189 (25% need-based, 75% non-need-based).

APPLYING for FINANCIAL AID ***Required financial aid forms:*** FAFSA, financial aid transcript (for transfers). ***Financial aid deadline (priority):*** 4/1. ***Notification date:*** Continuous beginning 5/1. Students must reply within 2 weeks of notification.

CONTACT Mrs. Janice Nowak, Director of Financial Aid, University of North Florida, 4567 St. Johns Bluff Road, South, Jacksonville, FL 32224-2645, 904-620-2604. *E-mail:* jnowak@unf.edu

UNIVERSITY OF NORTH TEXAS

Denton, TX

Tuition & fees (TX res): $2769 **Average undergraduate aid package: $5145**

ABOUT THE INSTITUTION State-supported, coed. Awards: bachelor's, master's, and doctoral degrees. 113 undergraduate majors. Total enrollment: 26,501. Undergraduates: 20,452. Federal methodology is used as a basis for awarding need-based institutional aid.

UNDERGRADUATE EXPENSES for 1999–2000 ***Application fee:*** $25. ***Tuition, state resident:*** full-time $2070; part-time $69 per credit. ***Tuition, nonresident:*** full-time $8550; part-time $285 per credit. ***Required fees:*** full-time $699; $18 per credit; $80 per term part-time. Full-time tuition and fees vary according to course load. Part-time tuition and fees vary according to course load. ***College room and board:*** $4096; ***room only:*** $2100. Room and board charges vary according to board plan. ***Payment plan:*** installment.

FRESHMAN FINANCIAL AID (Fall 1999) 1641 applied for aid; of those 63% were deemed to have need. 97% of freshmen with need received aid; of those 26% had need fully met. *Average percent of need met:* 72% (excluding resources awarded to replace EFC). *Average financial aid package:* $4901 (excluding resources awarded to replace EFC). 28% of all full-time freshmen had no need and received non-need-based aid.

UNDERGRADUATE FINANCIAL AID (Fall 1999) 8,031 applied for aid; of those 73% were deemed to have need. 94% of undergraduates with need received aid; of those 24% had need fully met. *Average percent of need met:* 67% (excluding resources awarded to replace EFC). *Average financial aid package:* $5145 (excluding resources awarded to replace EFC). 18% of all full-time undergraduates had no need and received non-need-based aid.

GIFT AID (NEED-BASED) ***Total amount:*** $12,906,049 (65% Federal, 22% state, 8% institutional, 5% external sources). ***Receiving aid:*** *Freshmen:* 28% (795); *all full-time undergraduates:* 26% (4,059). ***Average award:*** Freshmen: $2842; Undergraduates: $2449. ***Scholarships, grants, and awards:*** Federal Pell, FSEOG, state, college/university gift aid from institutional funds.

GIFT AID (NON-NEED-BASED) ***Total amount:*** $2,751,340 (71% institutional, 29% external sources). ***Receiving aid:*** *Freshmen:* 13% (366); *Undergraduates:* 7% (1,059). ***Scholarships, grants, and awards by category:*** *Academic Interests/Achievement:* general academic interests/achievements. *Creative Arts/Performance:* dance, music, theater/drama. ***Tuition waivers:*** Full or partial for employees or children of employees, senior citizens. ***ROTC:*** Army cooperative, Air Force.

LOANS ***Student loans:*** $38,048,044 (79% need-based, 21% non-need-based). Average indebtedness per student: $14,955. ***Average need-based loan:*** Freshmen: $1822; Undergraduates: $3391. ***Parent loans:*** $7,789,084 (41% need-based, 59% non-need-based). ***Programs:*** FFEL (Subsidized and Unsubsidized Stafford, PLUS), Perkins, state, college/university.

WORK-STUDY ***Federal work-study:*** *Total amount:* $2,338,779; jobs available. ***State or other work-study/employment:*** *Total amount:* $156,330 (100% need-based). Part-time jobs available.

ATHLETIC AWARDS *Total amount:* 642,536 (35% need-based, 65% non-need-based).

APPLYING for FINANCIAL AID ***Required financial aid form:*** FAFSA. ***Financial aid deadline (priority):*** 6/1.

CONTACT Mrs. Carolyn Cunningham, Director of Financial Aid, University of North Texas, PO Box 311370, Denton, TX 76203-1370, 940-565-2302 or toll-free 800-868-8211 (in-state). *Fax:* 940-565-2738.

UNIVERSITY OF NOTRE DAME

Notre Dame, IN

Tuition & fees: $22,187 **Average undergraduate aid package: $17,992**

ABOUT THE INSTITUTION Independent Roman Catholic, coed. Awards: bachelor's, master's, doctoral, and first professional degrees. 50 undergraduate majors. Total enrollment: 10,654. Undergraduates: 8,014. Freshmen: 1,967. Both federal and institutional methodology are used as a basis for awarding need-based institutional aid.

UNDERGRADUATE EXPENSES for 1999–2000 ***Application fee:*** $40. ***Comprehensive fee:*** $27,937 includes full-time tuition ($22,030), mandatory fees ($157), and room and board ($5750). Full-time tuition and fees vary according to program. Room and board charges vary according to housing facility. ***Part-time tuition:*** $918 per credit. ***Part-time fees:*** $40 per term part-time. Part-time tuition and fees vary according to course load and program. ***Payment plan:*** installment.

FRESHMAN FINANCIAL AID (Fall 1999) 1312 applied for aid; of those 67% were deemed to have need. 100% of freshmen with need received aid; of those 100% had need fully met. *Average percent of need met:* 100% (excluding resources awarded to replace EFC). *Average financial aid package:* $18,242 (excluding resources awarded to replace EFC). 8% of all full-time freshmen had no need and received non-need-based aid.

UNDERGRADUATE FINANCIAL AID (Fall 1999) 4,371 applied for aid; of those 78% were deemed to have need. 100% of undergraduates with need received aid; of those 86% had need fully met. *Average percent of need met:* 96% (excluding resources awarded to replace EFC). *Average financial aid package:* $17,992 (excluding resources awarded to replace EFC). 4% of all full-time undergraduates had no need and received non-need-based aid.

GIFT AID (NEED-BASED) ***Total amount:*** $35,140,380 (16% Federal, 2% state, 76% institutional, 6% external sources). ***Receiving aid:*** *Freshmen:* 42% (835); *all full-time undergraduates:* 38% (3,053). ***Average award:*** Freshmen: $13,101; Undergraduates: $12,309. ***Scholarships, grants, and awards:*** Federal Pell, FSEOG, state, private, college/university gift aid from institutional funds.

GIFT AID (NON-NEED-BASED) ***Total amount:*** $8,604,641 (49% Federal, 1% state, 20% institutional, 30% external sources). ***Receiving aid:*** *Freshmen:* 13% (249); *Undergraduates:* 10% (829). ***Scholarships, grants, and awards by category:*** *Special Characteristics:* children of faculty/staff. ***Tuition waivers:*** Full or partial for employees or children of employees. ***ROTC:*** Army, Naval, Air Force.

LOANS ***Student loans:*** $27,354,934 (63% need-based, 37% non-need-based). 53% of past graduating class borrowed through all loan programs. Average indebtedness per student: $19,635. ***Average need-based loan:*** Freshmen: $3985; Undergraduates: $5291. ***Parent loans:*** $7,174,364 (5% need-based, 95% non-need-based). ***Programs:*** FFEL (Subsidized and Unsubsidized Stafford, PLUS), Perkins, Notre Dame Undergraduate Loans.

WORK-STUDY ***Federal work-study:*** *Total amount:* $3,443,942; 1,875 jobs averaging $1837. ***State or other work-study/employment:*** *Total amount:* $4,334,175 (12% need-based, 88% non-need-based). 1,795 part-time jobs averaging $2415.

ATHLETIC AWARDS *Total amount:* 6,976,117 (22% need-based, 78% non-need-based).

APPLYING for FINANCIAL AID ***Required financial aid forms:*** FAFSA, CSS Financial Aid PROFILE, noncustodial (divorced/separated) parent's statement, business/farm supplement. ***Financial aid deadline (priority):*** 2/15. ***Notification date:*** 3/31. Students must reply by 5/1.

CONTACT Mr. Joseph A. Russo, Director of Financial Aid, University of Notre Dame, 115 Main Building, Notre Dame, IN 46556, 219-631-6436. *Fax:* 219-631-6899. *E-mail:* finaid.1@nd.edu

UNIVERSITY OF OKLAHOMA

Norman, OK

Tuition & fees (OK res): $2456 **Average undergraduate aid package: $5991**

ABOUT THE INSTITUTION State-supported, coed. Awards: bachelor's, master's, doctoral, and first professional degrees. 97 undergraduate majors. Total enrollment: 21,320. Undergraduates: 17,245. Freshmen: 3,298. Federal methodology is used as a basis for awarding need-based institutional aid.

UNDERGRADUATE EXPENSES for 1999–2000 ***Application fee:*** $25. ***Tuition, state resident:*** full-time $1890; part-time $63 per credit. ***Tuition, nonresident:*** full-time $6225; part-time $208 per credit. ***Required fees:*** full-time $566; $13 per credit; $93 per term part-time. Full-time tuition and fees vary according to course level, course load, location, program, and reciprocity agreements. Part-time tuition and fees vary according to course level, course load, location, program, and reciprocity agreements. ***College room and board:*** $4384. Room and board charges vary according to board plan and housing facility. ***Payment plan:*** installment.

FRESHMAN FINANCIAL AID (Fall 1998) 1760 applied for aid; of those 91% were deemed to have need. 100% of freshmen with need received aid; of those 89% had need fully met. *Average percent of need met:* 89% (excluding resources awarded to replace EFC). *Average financial aid package:* $5089 (excluding resources awarded to replace EFC). 15% of all full-time freshmen had no need and received non-need-based aid.

UNDERGRADUATE FINANCIAL AID (Fall 1998) 7,663 applied for aid; of those 96% were deemed to have need. 100% of undergraduates with need received aid; of those 89% had need fully met. *Average percent of need met:* 89% (excluding resources awarded to replace EFC). *Average financial aid package:* $5991 (excluding resources awarded to replace EFC). 13% of all full-time undergraduates had no need and received non-need-based aid.

GIFT AID (NEED-BASED) ***Total amount:*** $15,062,807 (62% Federal, 22% state, 10% institutional, 6% external sources). ***Receiving aid:*** *Freshmen:* 16% (508); *all full-time undergraduates:* 23% (3,353). ***Average award:*** Freshmen: $2663; Undergraduates: $2607. ***Scholarships, grants, and awards:*** Federal Pell, FSEOG, state, private, college/university gift aid from institutional funds.

GIFT AID (NON-NEED-BASED) ***Total amount:*** $7,116,880 (3% Federal, 65% state, 17% institutional, 15% external sources). ***Receiving aid:*** *Freshmen:* 27% (852); *Undergraduates:* 16% (2,429). ***Scholarships, grants, and awards by category:*** *Academic Interests/Achievement:* 5,402 awards ($10,087,063 total): architecture, area/ethnic studies, biological sciences, business, communication, computer science, education, engineering/technologies, general academic interests/achievements, humanities, international studies, library science, mathematics, military science, physical sciences, social sciences. *Creative Arts/Performance:* 124 awards ($116,032 total): art/fine arts, dance, debating, journalism/publications, music, performing arts, theater/drama. *Special Achievements/Activities:* 64 awards ($72,323 total): leadership. *Special Characteristics:* 771 awards ($1,732,107 total): children and siblings of alumni, members of minority groups, previous college experience. ***Tuition waivers:*** Full or partial for children of alumni, employees or children of employees, senior citizens. ***ROTC:*** Army, Naval, Air Force.

LOANS ***Student loans:*** $37,366,712 (100% need-based). Average indebtedness per student: $18,976. ***Average need-based loan:*** Freshmen: $2688; Undergraduates: $3877. ***Parent loans:*** $5,285,664 (83% need-based, 17% non-need-based). ***Programs:*** FFEL (Subsidized and Unsubsidized Stafford, PLUS), Perkins, college/university.

WORK-STUDY ***Federal work-study:*** *Total amount:* $953,146; 524 jobs averaging $1819.

ATHLETIC AWARDS *Total amount:* 2,511,863 (35% need-based, 65% non-need-based).

APPLYING for FINANCIAL AID ***Required financial aid form:*** FAFSA. ***Financial aid deadline:*** 6/1 (priority: 3/1). ***Notification date:*** Continuous. Students must reply within 6 weeks of notification.

CONTACT Financial Aid Assistant, University of Oklahoma, Office of Financial Aid Services, 731 Elm, Robertson Hall, Norman, OK 73019-0230, 405-325-4521 or toll-free 800-234-6868. *Fax:* 405-325-7608. *E-mail:* financialaid@ou.edu

UNIVERSITY OF OREGON

Eugene, OR

Tuition & fees (OR res): $3810 **Average undergraduate aid package: $8204**

ABOUT THE INSTITUTION State-supported, coed. Awards: bachelor's, master's, doctoral, and first professional degrees. 83 undergraduate majors. Total enrollment: 17,236. Undergraduates: 13,610. Freshmen: 2,503. Federal methodology is used as a basis for awarding need-based institutional aid.

UNDERGRADUATE EXPENSES for 1999–2000 ***Application fee:*** $50. ***Tuition, state resident:*** full-time $2694; part-time $75 per credit hour. ***Tuition, nonresident:*** full-time $12,081; part-time $336 per credit hour. ***Required fees:*** full-time $1116; $255 per term part-time. Part-time tuition and fees vary according to course load. ***College room and board:*** $5350. Room and board charges vary according to housing facility. ***Payment plan:*** deferred payment.

UNDERGRADUATE FINANCIAL AID (Fall 1999, est.) of those 33% had need fully met. *Average percent of need met:* 60% (excluding resources awarded to replace EFC). *Average financial aid package:* $8204 (excluding resources awarded to replace EFC).

GIFT AID (NEED-BASED) ***Total amount:*** $9,497,000 (73% Federal, 19% state, 8% institutional). ***Receiving aid:*** *All full-time undergraduates:* 5,600. ***Average award:*** Undergraduates: $1865. ***Scholarships, grants, and awards:*** Federal Pell, FSEOG, state, private, college/university gift aid from institutional funds.

GIFT AID (NON-NEED-BASED) ***Total amount:*** $9,356,300 (90% Federal, 2% institutional, 8% external sources). ***Receiving aid:*** *Undergraduates:* 2,200. ***Scholarships, grants, and awards by category:*** *Academic Interests/Achievement:* general academic interests/achievements. *Creative Arts/Performance:* art/fine arts, journalism/publications, performing arts. *Special Characteristics:* general special characteristics. ***Tuition waivers:*** Full or partial for minority students. ***ROTC:*** Army, Air Force cooperative.

LOANS ***Student loans:*** $43,433,000 (66% need-based, 34% non-need-based). ***Average need-based loan:*** Undergraduates: $2709. ***Parent loans:*** $8,480,000 (100% need-based). ***Programs:*** Federal Direct (Subsidized and Unsubsidized Stafford, PLUS), FFEL (Subsidized and Unsubsidized Stafford, PLUS), Perkins, state, college/university.

WORK-STUDY ***Federal work-study:*** *Total amount:* $1,800,000; jobs available. ***State or other work-study/employment:*** *Total amount:* $300,000 (100% need-based). Part-time jobs available.

APPLYING for FINANCIAL AID ***Required financial aid form:*** FAFSA. ***Financial aid deadline (priority):*** 2/1. ***Notification date:*** 4/15. Students must reply within 4 weeks of notification.

CONTACT Mr. James Gilmour, Associate Director of Financial Aid, University of Oregon, 260 Oregon Hall, Eugene, OR 97403, 541-346-1178 or toll-free 800-232-3825 (in-state). *Fax:* 541-346-1175. *E-mail:* jgilmour@oregon.uoregon.edu

UNIVERSITY OF PENNSYLVANIA

Philadelphia, PA

Tuition & fees: $24,230 **Average undergraduate aid package: $21,788**

ABOUT THE INSTITUTION Independent, coed. Awards: associate, bachelor's, master's, doctoral, and first professional degrees (also offers evening program with significant enrollment not reflected in profile). 86 undergraduate majors. Total enrollment: 18,042. Undergraduates: 9,827. Freshmen: 2,507. Institutional methodology is used as a basis for awarding need-based institutional aid.

UNDERGRADUATE EXPENSES for 1999–2000 ***Application fee:*** $55. ***Comprehensive fee:*** $31,592 includes full-time tuition ($21,746), mandatory fees ($2484), and room and board ($7362). ***College room only:*** $4592. Room and board charges vary according to board plan and housing facility. ***Part-time tuition:*** $2777 per course. ***Part-time fees:*** $253 per course. Part-time tuition and fees vary according to course load. ***Payment plans:*** tuition prepayment, installment.

FRESHMAN FINANCIAL AID (Fall 1998) 1264 applied for aid; of those 78% were deemed to have need. 100% of freshmen with need received aid; of those 100% had need fully met. *Average percent of need met:* 100% (excluding resources awarded to replace EFC). *Average financial aid package:* $21,460 (excluding resources awarded to replace EFC).

UNDERGRADUATE FINANCIAL AID (Fall 1998) 4,919 applied for aid; of those 88% were deemed to have need. 100% of undergraduates with need received aid; of those 100% had need fully met. *Average percent of need met:* 100% (excluding resources awarded to replace EFC). *Average financial aid package:* $21,788 (excluding resources awarded to replace EFC).

GIFT AID (NEED-BASED) ***Total amount:*** $60,571,000 (8% Federal, 3% state, 84% institutional, 5% external sources). ***Receiving aid:*** *Freshmen:* 38% (910); *all full-time undergraduates:* 39% (3,857). ***Average award:*** Freshmen: $16,606; Undergraduates: $15,888. ***Scholarships, grants, and awards:*** Federal Pell, FSEOG, state, private, college/university gift aid from institutional funds.

GIFT AID (NON-NEED-BASED) ***Total amount:*** $3,429,000 (100% external sources). ***Tuition waivers:*** Full or partial for employees or children of employees. ***ROTC:*** Army, Naval, Air Force cooperative.

LOANS ***Student loans:*** $25,434,000 (89% need-based, 11% non-need-based). 51% of past graduating class borrowed through all loan programs. Average indebtedness per student: $20,200. ***Average need-based loan:*** Freshmen: $4069; Undergraduates: $5260. ***Parent loans:*** $11,191,000 (58% need-based, 42% non-need-based). ***Programs:*** FFEL (Subsidized and Unsubsidized Stafford, PLUS), Perkins, Federal Nursing, college/university, supplemental third-party loans (guaranteed by institution).

WORK-STUDY ***Federal work-study:*** *Total amount:* $8,337,000; 3,838 jobs averaging $2172.

APPLYING for FINANCIAL AID ***Required financial aid forms:*** FAFSA, institution's own form, CSS Financial Aid PROFILE, state aid form, parent and student federal income tax returns (for verification). ***Financial aid deadline (priority):*** 2/15. ***Notification date:*** 4/1. Students must reply by 5/1.

CONTACT Mr. William Schilling, Director of Financial Aid, University of Pennsylvania, 212 Franklin Building, 3451 Walnut Street, Philadelphia, PA 19104-6270, 215-898-6784. *Fax:* 215-573-2208. *E-mail:* schilling@sfs.upenn.edu

UNIVERSITY OF PITTSBURGH

Pittsburgh, PA

Tuition & fees (PA res): $6698 **Average undergraduate aid package: $8185**

ABOUT THE INSTITUTION State-related, coed. Awards: bachelor's, master's, doctoral, and first professional degrees and post-master's certificates. 84 undergraduate majors. Total enrollment: 26,162. Undergraduates: 17,168. Freshmen: 3,190. Federal methodology is used as a basis for awarding need-based institutional aid.

UNDERGRADUATE EXPENSES for 1999–2000 ***Application fee:*** $35. ***Tuition, state resident:*** full-time $6118; part-time $212 per credit. ***Tuition, nonresident:*** full-time $13,434; part-time $459 per credit. ***Required fees:*** full-time $580; $103 per term part-time. Full-time tuition and fees vary according to degree level and program. Part-time tuition and fees vary according to degree level and program. ***College room and board:*** $5766; ***room only:*** $3356. Room and board charges vary according to board plan and housing facility. ***Payment plans:*** installment, deferred payment.

FRESHMAN FINANCIAL AID (Fall 1999) 2527 applied for aid; of those 80% were deemed to have need. 100% of freshmen with need received aid; of those 14% had need fully met. *Average percent of need met:* 85% (excluding resources awarded to replace EFC). *Average financial aid package:* $8185 (excluding resources awarded to replace EFC). 11% of all full-time freshmen had no need and received non-need-based aid.

UNDERGRADUATE FINANCIAL AID (Fall 1999) 11,390 applied for aid; of those 80% were deemed to have need. 100% of undergraduates with need received aid; of those 13% had need fully met. *Average percent of need met:* 85% (excluding resources awarded to replace EFC). *Average*

financial aid package: $8185 (excluding resources awarded to replace EFC). 9% of all full-time undergraduates had no need and received non-need-based aid.

GIFT AID (NEED-BASED) ***Total amount:*** $24,453,631 (40% Federal, 45% state, 15% institutional). ***Receiving aid:*** *Freshmen:* 50% (1,541); *all full-time undergraduates:* 49% (6,876). ***Average award:*** Freshmen: $4193; Undergraduates: $4082. ***Scholarships, grants, and awards:*** Federal Pell, FSEOG, state, college/university gift aid from institutional funds.

GIFT AID (NON-NEED-BASED) ***Total amount:*** $9,958,718 (85% institutional, 15% external sources). ***Receiving aid:*** *Freshmen:* 26% (796); *Undergraduates:* 22% (3,038). ***Scholarships, grants, and awards by category:*** *Academic Interests/Achievement:* 2,204 awards ($1,459,855 total): general academic interests/achievements. *Special Characteristics:* $1,891,408 total: children of faculty/staff. ***Tuition waivers:*** Full or partial for employees or children of employees, senior citizens. ***ROTC:*** Army, Naval cooperative, Air Force.

LOANS ***Student loans:*** $52,906,697 (72% need-based, 28% non-need-based). 60% of past graduating class borrowed through all loan programs. Average indebtedness per student: $16,000. ***Average need-based loan:*** Freshmen: $3341; Undergraduates: $4000. ***Parent loans:*** $7,770,000 (100% non-need-based). ***Programs:*** FFEL (Subsidized and Unsubsidized Stafford, PLUS), Perkins, Federal Nursing, college/university.

WORK-STUDY ***Federal work-study:*** *Total amount:* $1,900,000; 1,282 jobs averaging $1482. ***State or other work-study/employment:*** Part-time jobs available.

ATHLETIC AWARDS *Total amount:* 3,663,359 (100% non-need-based).

APPLYING for FINANCIAL AID ***Required financial aid forms:*** FAFSA, institution's own form. ***Financial aid deadline (priority):*** 3/1. ***Notification date:*** Continuous beginning 3/15.

CONTACT Dr. Betsy A. Porter, Director, Office of Admissions and Financial Aid, University of Pittsburgh, 4227 Fifth Avenue, First Floor, Pittsburgh, PA 15213, 412-624-7488. *Fax:* 412-648-8815. *E-mail:* oafa@pitt.edu

UNIVERSITY OF PITTSBURGH AT BRADFORD

Bradford, PA

Tuition & fees (PA res): $6598 **Average undergraduate aid package: N/A**

ABOUT THE INSTITUTION State-related, coed. Awards: associate and bachelor's degrees. 64 undergraduate majors. Total enrollment: 1,175. Undergraduates: 1,175. Freshmen: 228. Federal methodology is used as a basis for awarding need-based institutional aid.

UNDERGRADUATE EXPENSES for 1999–2000 ***Application fee:*** $35. ***Tuition, state resident:*** full-time $6118; part-time $212 per credit. ***Tuition, nonresident:*** full-time $13,434; part-time $459 per credit. ***Required fees:*** full-time $480; $48 per term part-time. Full-time tuition and fees vary according to course load and program. Part-time tuition and fees vary according to course load and program. ***College room and board:*** $5070; ***room only:*** $2540. Room and board charges vary according to board plan and housing facility. ***Payment plans:*** installment, deferred payment.

FRESHMAN FINANCIAL AID (Fall 1999, est.) 203 applied for aid.

UNDERGRADUATE FINANCIAL AID (Fall 1999, est.) 780 applied for aid.

GIFT AID (NEED-BASED) ***Total amount:*** $2,646,920 (40% Federal, 37% state, 11% institutional, 12% external sources). ***Scholarships, grants, and awards:*** Federal Pell, FSEOG, state, private, college/university gift aid from institutional funds.

GIFT AID (NON-NEED-BASED) ***Total amount:*** $1,530,179 (100% institutional). ***Scholarships, grants, and awards by category:*** *Academic Interests/Achievement:* biological sciences, general academic interests/achievements, humanities, social sciences. *Creative Arts/Performance:* general creative arts/performance. *Special Characteristics:* out-of-state students. ***Tuition waivers:*** Full or partial for employees or children of employees. ***ROTC:*** Army, Air Force cooperative.

LOANS ***Student loans:*** $3,436,718 (100% need-based). 85% of past graduating class borrowed through all loan programs. Average indebtedness per student: $16,000. ***Parent loans:*** $431,136 (100% need-based). ***Programs:*** FFEL (Subsidized and Unsubsidized Stafford, PLUS), Perkins.

WORK-STUDY ***Federal work-study:*** *Total amount:* $159,445; 164 jobs averaging $972.

APPLYING for FINANCIAL AID ***Required financial aid form:*** FAFSA. ***Financial aid deadline (priority):*** 3/1. ***Notification date:*** Continuous beginning 4/1. Students must reply within 4 weeks of notification.

CONTACT Melissa Ibañez, Director of Financial Aid, University of Pittsburgh at Bradford, 300 Campus Drive, Bradford, PA 16701-2812, 814-362-7550 or toll-free 800-872-1787. *Fax:* 814-362-7578.

UNIVERSITY OF PITTSBURGH AT GREENSBURG

Greensburg, PA

ABOUT THE INSTITUTION State-related, coed. Awards: bachelor's degrees. 22 undergraduate majors. Total enrollment: 1,548. Undergraduates: 1,548. Freshmen: 463.

GIFT AID (NEED-BASED) ***Scholarships, grants, and awards:*** Federal Pell, FSEOG, state, private, college/university gift aid from institutional funds.

GIFT AID (NON-NEED-BASED) ***Scholarships, grants, and awards by category:*** *Academic Interests/Achievement:* general academic interests/achievements. *Special Characteristics:* general special characteristics.

LOANS ***Programs:*** FFEL (Subsidized and Unsubsidized Stafford, PLUS), Perkins, college/university.

WORK-STUDY Federal work-study jobs available.

APPLYING for FINANCIAL AID ***Required financial aid forms:*** FAFSA, institution's own form, state aid form.

CONTACT Mr. John R. Sparks, Director of Admissions and Financial Aid, University of Pittsburgh at Greensburg, 1150 Mt. Pleasant Road, Greensburg, PA 15601-5860, 724-836-9880. *Fax:* 724-836-7160. *E-mail:* upgadmits@pitt.edu

UNIVERSITY OF PITTSBURGH AT JOHNSTOWN

Johnstown, PA

Tuition & fees (PA res): $6630 **Average undergraduate aid package: $8472**

ABOUT THE INSTITUTION State-related, coed. Awards: associate and bachelor's degrees. 46 undergraduate majors. Total enrollment: 3,147. Undergraduates: 3,147. Freshmen: 740. Federal methodology is used as a basis for awarding need-based institutional aid.

UNDERGRADUATE EXPENSES for 1999–2000 ***Application fee:*** $35. ***Tuition, state resident:*** full-time $6118; part-time $212 per credit. ***Tuition, nonresident:*** full-time $13,434; part-time $459 per credit. ***Required fees:*** full-time $512; $42 per term part-time. Full-time tuition and fees vary according to program. Part-time tuition and fees vary according to program. ***College room and board:*** $5460; ***room only:*** $2930. Room and board charges vary according to board plan and housing facility. ***Payment plans:*** installment, deferred payment.

FRESHMAN FINANCIAL AID (Fall 1999, est.) 702 applied for aid; of those 80% were deemed to have need. 96% of freshmen with need received aid; of those 12% had need fully met. *Average percent of need met:* 79% (excluding resources awarded to replace EFC). *Average financial aid package:* $8661 (excluding resources awarded to replace EFC). 3% of all full-time freshmen had no need and received non-need-based aid.

UNDERGRADUATE FINANCIAL AID (Fall 1999, est.) 2,289 applied for aid; of those 85% were deemed to have need. 95% of undergraduates with need received aid; of those 16% had need fully met. *Average percent of need met:* 75% (excluding resources awarded to replace EFC). *Average financial aid package:* $8472 (excluding resources awarded to replace EFC). 2% of all full-time undergraduates had no need and received non-need-based aid.

GIFT AID (NEED-BASED) ***Total amount:*** $5,307,880 (36% Federal, 59% state, 2% institutional, 3% external sources). ***Receiving aid:*** *Freshmen:*

University of Pittsburgh at Johnstown (continued)

59% (431); *all full-time undergraduates:* 54% (1,506). ***Average award:*** Freshmen: $7994; Undergraduates: $7557. ***Scholarships, grants, and awards:*** Federal Pell, FSEOG, state, private, college/university gift aid from institutional funds.

GIFT AID (NON-NEED-BASED) ***Total amount:*** $1,096,953 (71% institutional, 29% external sources). ***Receiving aid:*** *Freshmen:* 20% (144); *Undergraduates:* 14% (384). ***Scholarships, grants, and awards by category:*** *Academic Interests/Achievement:* 160 awards ($387,750 total): general academic interests/achievements. *Special Achievements/Activities:* 76 awards ($71,350 total): leadership. *Special Characteristics:* 83 awards ($426,030 total): children of faculty/staff. ***Tuition waivers:*** Full or partial for employees or children of employees.

LOANS ***Student loans:*** $8,405,412 (73% need-based, 27% non-need-based). 86% of past graduating class borrowed through all loan programs. Average indebtedness per student: $15,800. ***Average need-based loan:*** Freshmen: $2809; Undergraduates: $2947. ***Parent loans:*** $1,678,086 (100% non-need-based). ***Programs:*** FFEL (Subsidized and Unsubsidized Stafford, PLUS), Perkins.

WORK-STUDY ***Federal work-study:*** *Total amount:* $385,040; 256 jobs averaging $1500. ***State or other work-study/employment:*** *Total amount:* $421,398 (100% non-need-based). 312 part-time jobs averaging $1350.

ATHLETIC AWARDS *Total amount:* 257,902 (100% non-need-based).

APPLYING for FINANCIAL AID ***Required financial aid forms:*** FAFSA, state aid form. ***Financial aid deadline (priority):*** 4/1. ***Notification date:*** Continuous. Students must reply within 2 weeks of notification.

CONTACT Ms. Julie A. Salem, Director, Student Financial Aid, University of Pittsburgh at Johnstown, 125 Biddle Hall, Johnstown, PA 15904-2990, 814-269-7045 or toll-free 800-765-4875. *Fax:* 814-269-7061. *E-mail:* jasalem+@pitt.edu

UNIVERSITY OF PORTLAND

Portland, OR

Tuition & fees: $17,299 **Average undergraduate aid package: $15,143**

ABOUT THE INSTITUTION Independent Roman Catholic, coed. Awards: bachelor's and master's degrees and post-master's certificates. 42 undergraduate majors. Total enrollment: 2,847. Undergraduates: 2,392. Freshmen: 626. Federal methodology is used as a basis for awarding need-based institutional aid.

UNDERGRADUATE EXPENSES for 1999–2000 ***Application fee:*** $40. ***Comprehensive fee:*** $22,489 includes full-time tuition ($16,930), mandatory fees ($369), and room and board ($5190). Full-time tuition and fees vary according to program. Room and board charges vary according to board plan and housing facility. ***Part-time tuition:*** $538 per credit hour. Part-time tuition and fees vary according to program. ***Payment plans:*** installment, deferred payment.

FRESHMAN FINANCIAL AID (Fall 1999) 502 applied for aid; of those 75% were deemed to have need. 99% of freshmen with need received aid; of those 42% had need fully met. *Average percent of need met:* 83% (excluding resources awarded to replace EFC). *Average financial aid package:* $14,205 (excluding resources awarded to replace EFC). 29% of all full-time freshmen had no need and received non-need-based aid.

UNDERGRADUATE FINANCIAL AID (Fall 1999) 1,642 applied for aid; of those 81% were deemed to have need. 99% of undergraduates with need received aid; of those 42% had need fully met. *Average percent of need met:* 84% (excluding resources awarded to replace EFC). *Average financial aid package:* $15,143 (excluding resources awarded to replace EFC). 30% of all full-time undergraduates had no need and received non-need-based aid.

GIFT AID (NEED-BASED) ***Total amount:*** $10,419,203 ***Receiving aid:*** *Freshmen:* 56% (352); *all full-time undergraduates:* 56% (1,272). ***Average award:*** Freshmen: $10,646; Undergraduates: $9843. ***Scholarships, grants, and awards:*** Federal Pell, FSEOG, state, private, college/university gift aid from institutional funds.

GIFT AID (NON-NEED-BASED) ***Total amount:*** $8,843,263 (69% institutional, 31% external sources). ***Receiving aid:*** *Freshmen:* 31% (192); *Undergraduates:* 24% (555). ***Scholarships, grants, and awards by category:*** *Academic Interests/Achievement:* biological sciences, business, communication, computer science, education, engineering/technologies, English, foreign languages, general academic interests/achievements, health fields, humanities, mathematics, military science, physical sciences, premedicine, religion/biblical studies, social sciences. *Creative Arts/Performance:* journalism/publications, music, performing arts, theater/drama. *Special Characteristics:* children of faculty/staff, relatives of clergy. ***Tuition waivers:*** Full or partial for employees or children of employees. ***ROTC:*** Army, Air Force.

LOANS ***Student loans:*** $6,174,198 (89% need-based, 11% non-need-based). 67% of past graduating class borrowed through all loan programs. Average indebtedness per student: $19,319. ***Average need-based loan:*** Freshmen: $3362; Undergraduates: $6159. ***Parent loans:*** $2,195,679 (29% need-based, 71% non-need-based). ***Programs:*** FFEL (Subsidized and Unsubsidized Stafford, PLUS), Perkins, Federal Nursing, college/university.

WORK-STUDY ***Federal work-study:*** *Total amount:* $959,211; 540 jobs averaging $1801. ***State or other work-study/employment:*** *Total amount:* $1,118,119 (2% need-based, 98% non-need-based). 491 part-time jobs available.

ATHLETIC AWARDS *Total amount:* 2,028,897 (23% need-based, 77% non-need-based).

APPLYING for FINANCIAL AID ***Required financial aid forms:*** FAFSA, institution's own form. ***Financial aid deadline (priority):*** 3/1. ***Notification date:*** 4/1. Students must reply within 3 weeks of notification.

CONTACT Ms. Rita Lambert, Director of Financial Aid, University of Portland, 5000 North Willamette Boulevard, Portland, OR 97203-5798, 503-943-7311 or toll-free 888-627-5601 (out-of-state). *Fax:* 503-943-7508. *E-mail:* lambert@up.edu

UNIVERSITY OF PUERTO RICO, AGUADILLA UNIVERSITY COLLEGE

Aguadilla, PR

CONTACT Director of Financial Aid, University of Puerto Rico, Aguadilla University College, PO Box 250-160, Aguadilla, PR 00604-0160, 787-890-2681 Ext. 273.

UNIVERSITY OF PUERTO RICO AT ARECIBO

Arecibo, PR

Tuition & fees: N/R **Average undergraduate aid package: N/A**

ABOUT THE INSTITUTION Commonwealth-supported, coed. Awards: associate and bachelor's degrees. 12 undergraduate majors. Total enrollment: 4,580. Undergraduates: 4,580. Freshmen: 1,124. Federal methodology is used as a basis for awarding need-based institutional aid.

FRESHMAN FINANCIAL AID (Fall 1999) 940 applied for aid; of those 100% were deemed to have need. 100% of freshmen with need received aid. *Average percent of need met:* 72% (excluding resources awarded to replace EFC).

GIFT AID (NEED-BASED) ***Total amount:*** $10,711,751 (88% Federal, 12% state). ***Scholarships, grants, and awards:*** Federal Pell, FSEOG, state.

GIFT AID (NON-NEED-BASED) ***Scholarships, grants, and awards by category:*** *Academic Interests/Achievement:* general academic interests/achievements. *Creative Arts/Performance:* general creative arts/performance. *Special Characteristics:* children of union members/company employees, general special characteristics, local/state students. ***Tuition waivers:*** Full or partial for employees or children of employees. ***ROTC:*** Army.

LOANS ***Student loans:*** $1,443,739 (100% need-based). ***Programs:*** Federal Direct (Subsidized and Unsubsidized Stafford, PLUS), Perkins.

WORK-STUDY ***Federal work-study:*** *Total amount:* $294,504; 274 jobs averaging $1100.

APPLYING for FINANCIAL AID ***Required financial aid forms:*** FAFSA, institution's own form. ***Financial aid deadline:*** 6/2 (priority: 5/16). ***Notification date:*** Continuous beginning 7/1. Students must reply within 4 weeks of notification.

CONTACT Mr. Luis Rodriguez, Director of Financial Aid, University of Puerto Rico at Arecibo, PO Box 4010, Arecibo, PR 00613, 787-878-2830 Ext. 2008.

UNIVERSITY OF PUERTO RICO AT PONCE

Ponce, PR

ABOUT THE INSTITUTION Commonwealth-supported, coed. Awards: associate and bachelor's degrees. 13 undergraduate majors. Total enrollment: 4,265. Undergraduates: 4,265. Freshmen: 1,054.

GIFT AID (NEED-BASED) ***Scholarships, grants, and awards:*** Federal Pell, FSEOG, state, private.

LOANS ***Programs:*** FFEL (Subsidized Stafford).

WORK-STUDY ***Federal work-study:*** *Total amount:* $352,078; jobs available.

APPLYING for FINANCIAL AID ***Required financial aid forms:*** FAFSA, institution's own form, noncustodial (divorced/separated) parent's statement.

CONTACT Carmelo Vega Montes, Director of Financial Aid, University of Puerto Rico at Ponce, Box 7186, Ponce, PR 00732-7186, 787-844-8181. *Fax:* 787-840-8108.

UNIVERSITY OF PUERTO RICO, CAYEY UNIVERSITY COLLEGE

Cayey, PR

Tuition & fees: N/R **Average undergraduate aid package: $4025**

ABOUT THE INSTITUTION Commonwealth-supported, coed. Awards: associate and bachelor's degrees. 30 undergraduate majors. Total enrollment: 3,944. Undergraduates: 3,944. Federal methodology is used as a basis for awarding need-based institutional aid.

FRESHMAN FINANCIAL AID (Fall 1999, est.) 738 applied for aid; of those 99% were deemed to have need. 100% of freshmen with need received aid; of those 38% had need fully met. *Average financial aid package:* $4025 (excluding resources awarded to replace EFC). 3% of all full-time freshmen had no need and received non-need-based aid.

UNDERGRADUATE FINANCIAL AID (Fall 1999, est.) 2,681 applied for aid; of those 98% were deemed to have need. 100% of undergraduates with need received aid; of those 32% had need fully met. *Average financial aid package:* $4025 (excluding resources awarded to replace EFC). 3% of all full-time undergraduates had no need and received non-need-based aid.

GIFT AID (NEED-BASED) ***Total amount:*** $4,872,757 (78% Federal, 15% state, 7% institutional). ***Receiving aid:*** *Freshmen:* 79% (728); *all full-time undergraduates:* 73% (2,636). ***Average award:*** Freshmen: $3125; Undergraduates: $3125. ***Scholarships, grants, and awards:*** Federal Pell, FSEOG, state, private, college/university gift aid from institutional funds, America Reads Challenge.

GIFT AID (NON-NEED-BASED) ***Total amount:*** $22,470 (100% external sources). ***Receiving aid:*** *Freshmen:* 1% (6); *Undergraduates:* 18. ***Scholarships, grants, and awards by category:*** *Creative Arts/Performance:* music, theater/drama. *Special Achievements/Activities:* cheerleading/drum major, general special achievements/activities. *Special Characteristics:* children of faculty/staff, children of public servants, veterans. ***Tuition waivers:*** Full or partial for employees or children of employees. ***ROTC:*** Army.

LOANS ***Student loans:*** $818,933 (100% need-based). 27% of past graduating class borrowed through all loan programs. Average indebtedness per student: $3500. ***Average need-based loan:*** Freshmen: $3000; Undergraduates: $3000. ***Parent loans:*** $3500 (100% need-based). ***Programs:*** FFEL (Subsidized and Unsubsidized Stafford, PLUS), Perkins, college/university.

WORK-STUDY ***Federal work-study:*** *Total amount:* $354,860; 300 jobs averaging $1182.

ATHLETIC AWARDS *Total amount:* 54,010 (100% non-need-based).

APPLYING for FINANCIAL AID ***Required financial aid forms:*** FAFSA, institution's own form. ***Financial aid deadline (priority):*** 3/31. ***Notification date:*** 5/30. Students must reply by 9/30.

CONTACT Mr. Hector Maldonado Otero, Director of Financial Aid, University of Puerto Rico, Cayey University College, Antonio Barcelo, Cayey, PR 00737, 787-738-2161. *Fax:* 787-263-0676.

UNIVERSITY OF PUERTO RICO, HUMACAO UNIVERSITY COLLEGE

Humacao, PR

Tuition & fees (PR res): $1095 **Average undergraduate aid package: N/A**

ABOUT THE INSTITUTION Commonwealth-supported, coed. Awards: associate and bachelor's degrees. 20 undergraduate majors. Total enrollment: 4,469. Undergraduates: 4,469. Freshmen: 889. Both federal and institutional methodology are used as a basis for awarding need-based institutional aid.

UNDERGRADUATE EXPENSES for 1999–2000 ***Application fee:*** $15. ***Tuition, state resident:*** full-time $1020; part-time $30 per credit. ***Required fees:*** full-time $75; $38 per term part-time. Full-time tuition and fees vary according to course load, program, and reciprocity agreements. Part-time tuition and fees vary according to program. Nonresidents who are U.S. citizens pay an amount equal to the rate for nonresidents at a state university in their home state. ***Payment plan:*** deferred payment.

FRESHMAN FINANCIAL AID (Fall 1998) 858 applied for aid; of those 93% were deemed to have need. 100% of freshmen with need received aid. *Average percent of need met:* 55% (excluding resources awarded to replace EFC).

UNDERGRADUATE FINANCIAL AID (Fall 1998) 2,898 applied for aid; of those 98% were deemed to have need. 100% of undergraduates with need received aid. *Average percent of need met:* 55% (excluding resources awarded to replace EFC). 1% of all full-time undergraduates had no need and received non-need-based aid.

GIFT AID (NEED-BASED) ***Total amount:*** $5,371,473 (94% Federal, 4% state, 2% institutional). ***Receiving aid:*** *Freshmen:* 83% (799); *all full-time undergraduates:* 79% (2,839). ***Scholarships, grants, and awards:*** Federal Pell, FSEOG, state, college/university gift aid from institutional funds.

GIFT AID (NON-NEED-BASED) ***Total amount:*** $81,869 (38% institutional, 62% external sources). ***Receiving aid:*** *Freshmen:* 4; *Undergraduates:* 1% (26). ***Scholarships, grants, and awards by category:*** *Academic Interests/Achievement:* biological sciences, business, computer science, education, English, general academic interests/achievements, humanities, library science, mathematics, social sciences. *Creative Arts/Performance:* music, theater/drama. *Special Characteristics:* children of faculty/staff. ***Tuition waivers:*** Full or partial for employees or children of employees.

LOANS ***Student loans:*** $761,900 (100% need-based). ***Programs:*** Federal Direct (Subsidized and Unsubsidized Stafford), FFEL (Subsidized and Unsubsidized Stafford), Perkins, college/university.

WORK-STUDY ***Federal work-study:*** *Total amount:* $390,766; 278 jobs averaging $1318.

ATHLETIC AWARDS *Total amount:* 81,450 (100% non-need-based).

APPLYING for FINANCIAL AID ***Required financial aid forms:*** FAFSA, institution's own form. ***Financial aid deadline:*** 6/30. ***Notification date:*** 9/10. Students must reply by 9/17 or within 1 week of notification.

CONTACT Larry Cruz, Director of Financial Aid, University of Puerto Rico, Humacao University College, HUC Station, Humacao, PR 00791-4300, 787-850-9342.

UNIVERSITY OF PUERTO RICO, MAYAGÜEZ CAMPUS

Mayagüez, PR

Tuition & fees: N/R **Average undergraduate aid package: $4025**

ABOUT THE INSTITUTION Commonwealth-supported, coed. Awards: bachelor's, master's, and doctoral degrees. 50 undergraduate majors.

University of Puerto Rico, Mayagüez Campus (continued)

Total enrollment: 12,883. Undergraduates: 12,019. Federal methodology is used as a basis for awarding need-based institutional aid.

FRESHMAN FINANCIAL AID (Fall 1999) 1875 applied for aid; of those 83% were deemed to have need. 100% of freshmen with need received aid. *Average percent of need met:* 54% (excluding resources awarded to replace EFC). *Average financial aid package:* $4025 (excluding resources awarded to replace EFC). .1% of all full-time freshmen had no need and received non-need-based aid.

UNDERGRADUATE FINANCIAL AID (Fall 1999) 8,307 applied for aid; of those 86% were deemed to have need. 100% of undergraduates with need received aid. *Average percent of need met:* 54% (excluding resources awarded to replace EFC). *Average financial aid package:* $4025 (excluding resources awarded to replace EFC). .1% of all full-time undergraduates had no need and received non-need-based aid.

GIFT AID (NEED-BASED) ***Total amount:*** $23,163,468 (86% Federal, 13% state, 1% external sources). ***Receiving aid:*** *Freshmen:* 67% (1,526); *all full-time undergraduates:* 59% (6,971). ***Average award:*** Freshmen: $900; Undergraduates: $900. ***Scholarships, grants, and awards:*** Federal Pell, FSEOG, state, private, college/university gift aid from institutional funds.

GIFT AID (NON-NEED-BASED) ***Total amount:*** $6000 (100% external sources). ***Receiving aid:*** *Undergraduates:* 2. ***Tuition waivers:*** Full or partial for employees or children of employees. ***ROTC:*** Army, Air Force.

LOANS ***Student loans:*** $6,967,175 (98% need-based, 2% non-need-based). 44% of past graduating class borrowed through all loan programs. Average indebtedness per student: $5000. ***Programs:*** FFEL (Subsidized and Unsubsidized Stafford), college/university.

WORK-STUDY ***Federal work-study:*** *Total amount:* $432,000; 384 jobs averaging $1133. ***State or other work-study/employment:*** *Total amount:* $31,462 (100% need-based). Part-time jobs available.

ATHLETIC AWARDS *Total amount:* 287,290 (100% non-need-based).

APPLYING for FINANCIAL AID ***Required financial aid forms:*** FAFSA, institution's own form, noncustodial (divorced/separated) parent's statement, business/farm supplement.

CONTACT Ms. Ana I. Rodríguez, Assistant Director of Financial Aid, University of Puerto Rico, Mayagüez Campus, Box 9035, Mayagüez, PR 00681, 787-265-3863. *Fax:* 787-265-1920.

UNIVERSITY OF PUERTO RICO, MEDICAL SCIENCES CAMPUS

San Juan, PR

Tuition & fees (PR res): $1700 **Average undergraduate aid package: $3000**

ABOUT THE INSTITUTION Commonwealth-supported, coed, primarily women. Awards: associate, bachelor's, master's, doctoral, and first professional degrees and post-bachelor's and first-professional certificates (bachelor's degree is upper-level). 14 undergraduate majors. Total enrollment: 2,822. Undergraduates: 1,153. Entering class: . Both federal and institutional methodology are used as a basis for awarding need-based institutional aid.

UNDERGRADUATE FINANCIAL AID (Fall 1998) 898 applied for aid; of those 95% were deemed to have need. 100% of undergraduates with need received aid; of those 70% had need fully met. *Average percent of need met:* 70% (excluding resources awarded to replace EFC). *Average financial aid package:* $3000 (excluding resources awarded to replace EFC).

GIFT AID (NEED-BASED) ***Total amount:*** $2,634,770 (96% Federal, 2% state, 2% institutional). ***Receiving aid:*** *Entering class:* 83% (290); *all full-time undergraduates:* 76% (856). ***Average award:*** Freshmen: $3000; Undergraduates: $3000. ***Scholarships, grants, and awards:*** Federal Pell, FSEOG, state, college/university gift aid from institutional funds, Department of Health and Human Services Scholarships.

GIFT AID (NON-NEED-BASED) ***Tuition waivers:*** Full or partial for employees or children of employees.

LOANS ***Student loans:*** $1,154,872 (100% need-based). 33% of past graduating class borrowed through all loan programs. Average indebtedness per student: $4500. ***Average need-based loan:*** Freshmen: $4500; Undergraduates: $4500.

WORK-STUDY ***Federal work-study:*** *Total amount:* $56,749; 97 jobs averaging $618.

APPLYING for FINANCIAL AID ***Required financial aid forms:*** FAFSA, institution's own form. ***Financial aid deadline:*** 6/15. ***Notification date:*** Continuous beginning 8/1. Students must reply within 2 weeks of notification.

CONTACT Lourdes Pont, Financial Aid Director, University of Puerto Rico, Medical Sciences Campus, Terreno Centro Médico-Edificio Decanato Farmacia y Estudiantes, Rio Piedras, PR 00936-5067, 787-763-2525. *Fax:* 787-282-7117.

UNIVERSITY OF PUERTO RICO, RÍO PIEDRAS

San Juan, PR

CONTACT Mr. Efraim Williams, EDP Manager, University of Puerto Rico, Río Piedras, PO Box 23353, San Juan, PR 00931, 787-764-0000 Ext. 5573.

UNIVERSITY OF PUGET SOUND

Tacoma, WA

Tuition & fees: $20,605 **Average undergraduate aid package: $16,939**

ABOUT THE INSTITUTION Independent, coed. Awards: bachelor's and master's degrees. 40 undergraduate majors. Total enrollment: 2,973. Undergraduates: 2,695. Freshmen: 684. Federal methodology is used as a basis for awarding need-based institutional aid.

UNDERGRADUATE EXPENSES for 1999–2000 ***Application fee:*** $40. ***Comprehensive fee:*** $25,875 includes full-time tuition ($20,450), mandatory fees ($155), and room and board ($5270). ***College room only:*** $2880. Room and board charges vary according to board plan. ***Part-time tuition:*** $2580 per unit. ***Payment plans:*** installment, deferred payment.

FRESHMAN FINANCIAL AID (Fall 1999, est.) 488 applied for aid; of those 82% were deemed to have need. 100% of freshmen with need received aid; of those 42% had need fully met. *Average percent of need met:* 89% (excluding resources awarded to replace EFC). *Average financial aid package:* $16,392 (excluding resources awarded to replace EFC). 21% of all full-time freshmen had no need and received non-need-based aid.

UNDERGRADUATE FINANCIAL AID (Fall 1999, est.) 1,798 applied for aid; of those 85% were deemed to have need. 100% of undergraduates with need received aid; of those 39% had need fully met. *Average percent of need met:* 88% (excluding resources awarded to replace EFC). *Average financial aid package:* $16,939 (excluding resources awarded to replace EFC). 21% of all full-time undergraduates had no need and received non-need-based aid.

GIFT AID (NEED-BASED) ***Total amount:*** $15,504,000 (11% Federal, 2% state, 82% institutional, 5% external sources). ***Receiving aid:*** *Freshmen:* 56% (383); *all full-time undergraduates:* 56% (1,459). ***Average award:*** Freshmen: $10,056; Undergraduates: $9226. ***Scholarships, grants, and awards:*** Federal Pell, FSEOG, state, private, college/university gift aid from institutional funds.

GIFT AID (NON-NEED-BASED) ***Total amount:*** $3,520,000 (1% Federal, 3% state, 84% institutional, 12% external sources). ***Receiving aid:*** *Freshmen:* 42% (285); *Undergraduates:* 38% (983). ***Scholarships, grants, and awards by category:*** *Academic Interests/Achievement:* 450 awards ($2,600,000 total): biological sciences, business, communication, computer science, English, foreign languages, general academic interests/achievements, humanities, mathematics, physical sciences, premedicine, social sciences. *Creative Arts/Performance:* 45 awards ($205,000 total): art/fine arts, debating, music, theater/drama. *Special Achievements/Activities:* 10 awards ($85,000 total): leadership, religious involvement.

Special Characteristics: children of faculty/staff, international students. ***Tuition waivers:*** Full or partial for employees or children of employees. ***ROTC:*** Army cooperative.

LOANS ***Student loans:*** $10,146,000 (92% need-based, 8% non-need-based). 62% of past graduating class borrowed through all loan programs. Average indebtedness per student: $20,259. ***Average need-based loan:*** Freshmen: $5576; Undergraduates: $6873. ***Parent loans:*** $1,933,000 (100% non-need-based). ***Programs:*** FFEL (Subsidized and Unsubsidized Stafford, PLUS), Perkins, college/university, Alaska Loans.

WORK-STUDY ***Federal work-study:*** *Total amount:* $1,168,000; 672 jobs averaging $1738. ***State or other work-study/employment:*** *Total amount:* $1,444,000 (40% need-based, 60% non-need-based). 706 part-time jobs averaging $2045.

APPLYING for FINANCIAL AID ***Required financial aid form:*** FAFSA. ***Financial aid deadline (priority):*** 2/1. ***Notification date:*** 3/15. Students must reply by 5/1.

CONTACT Mr. Steven Thorndill, Director of Financial Aid, University of Puget Sound, 1500 North Warner Street, Tacoma, WA 98416-0005, 253-879-3214 or toll-free 800-396-7191. *Fax:* 253-879-8508. *E-mail:* finaid@ups.edu

UNIVERSITY OF REDLANDS

Redlands, CA

Tuition & fees: $19,811 **Average undergraduate aid package: $18,959**

ABOUT THE INSTITUTION Independent, coed. Awards: bachelor's and master's degrees and post-bachelor's and post-master's certificates. 42 undergraduate majors. Total enrollment: 1,736. Undergraduates: 1,669. Freshmen: 474. Federal methodology is used as a basis for awarding need-based institutional aid.

UNDERGRADUATE EXPENSES for 1999–2000 ***Application fee:*** $40. ***One-time required fee:*** $140. ***Comprehensive fee:*** $27,179 includes full-time tuition ($19,490), mandatory fees ($321), and room and board ($7368). Room and board charges vary according to board plan and housing facility. ***Part-time tuition:*** $609 per credit. ***Part-time fees:*** $40 per term part-time. Part-time tuition and fees vary according to course load. ***Payment plan:*** installment.

FRESHMAN FINANCIAL AID (Fall 1999, est.) 430 applied for aid; of those 76% were deemed to have need. 100% of freshmen with need received aid; of those 46% had need fully met. *Average percent of need met:* 92% (excluding resources awarded to replace EFC). *Average financial aid package:* $19,271 (excluding resources awarded to replace EFC). 14% of all full-time freshmen had no need and received non-need-based aid.

UNDERGRADUATE FINANCIAL AID (Fall 1999, est.) 1,491 applied for aid; of those 81% were deemed to have need. 100% of undergraduates with need received aid; of those 43% had need fully met. *Average percent of need met:* 91% (excluding resources awarded to replace EFC). *Average financial aid package:* $18,959 (excluding resources awarded to replace EFC). 11% of all full-time undergraduates had no need and received non-need-based aid.

GIFT AID (NEED-BASED) ***Total amount:*** $12,607,264 (11% Federal, 21% state, 65% institutional, 3% external sources). ***Receiving aid:*** *Freshmen:* 69% (325); *all full-time undergraduates:* 71% (1,176). ***Average award:*** Freshmen: $10,146; Undergraduates: $10,317. ***Scholarships, grants, and awards:*** Federal Pell, FSEOG, state, private, college/university gift aid from institutional funds.

GIFT AID (NON-NEED-BASED) ***Total amount:*** $5,083,644 (99% institutional, 1% external sources). ***Receiving aid:*** *Freshmen:* 41% (193); *Undergraduates:* 36% (587). ***Scholarships, grants, and awards by category:*** *Academic Interests/Achievement:* general academic interests/achievements. *Creative Arts/Performance:* art/fine arts, creative writing, debating, music. *Special Achievements/Activities:* general special achievements/activities. *Special Characteristics:* general special characteristics, international students. ***Tuition waivers:*** Full or partial for employees or children of employees. ***ROTC:*** Army cooperative, Air Force cooperative.

LOANS ***Student loans:*** $7,373,342 (63% need-based, 37% non-need-based). 79% of past graduating class borrowed through all loan programs. Average indebtedness per student: $22,072. ***Average need-based loan:*** Freshmen: $3802; Undergraduates: $4687. ***Parent loans:*** $1,416,841 (100% non-need-based). ***Programs:*** FFEL (Subsidized and Unsubsidized Stafford, PLUS), Perkins, college/university, alternative loans.

WORK-STUDY ***Federal work-study:*** *Total amount:* $970,095; 542 jobs averaging $1790. ***State or other work-study/employment:*** *Total amount:* $1,131,621 (100% need-based). 625 part-time jobs averaging $1811.

APPLYING for FINANCIAL AID ***Required financial aid forms:*** FAFSA, GPA Verification form (for CA residents). ***Financial aid deadline (priority):*** 2/15. ***Notification date:*** Continuous beginning 3/1.

CONTACT Ms. Bethann Corey, Director of Financial Aid, University of Redlands, PO Box 3080, Redlands, CA 92373-0999, 909-335-4047 or toll-free 800-455-5064. *Fax:* 909-335-4089. *E-mail:* fabcorey@uor.edu

UNIVERSITY OF RHODE ISLAND

Kingston, RI

Tuition & fees (RI res): $4928 **Average undergraduate aid package: N/A**

ABOUT THE INSTITUTION State-supported, coed. Awards: bachelor's, master's, doctoral, and first professional degrees and post-bachelor's certificates. 76 undergraduate majors. Total enrollment: 14,577. Undergraduates: 10,639. Freshmen: 2,150. Federal methodology is used as a basis for awarding need-based institutional aid.

UNDERGRADUATE EXPENSES for 1999–2000 ***Application fee:*** $35; $45 for nonresidents. ***Tuition, state resident:*** full-time $3372; part-time $226 per credit. ***Tuition, nonresident:*** full-time $11,592; part-time $568 per credit. ***Required fees:*** full-time $1556; $42 per credit; $43 per term part-time. Part-time tuition and fees vary according to reciprocity agreements. ***College room and board:*** $6378; ***room only:*** $3592. Room and board charges vary according to board plan and housing facility. ***Payment plan:*** installment.

GIFT AID (NEED-BASED) ***Scholarships, grants, and awards:*** Federal Pell, FSEOG, state, college/university gift aid from institutional funds.

GIFT AID (NON-NEED-BASED) ***Scholarships, grants, and awards by category:*** *Academic Interests/Achievement:* general academic interests/achievements. *Creative Arts/Performance:* music. ***Tuition waivers:*** Full or partial for minority students, employees or children of employees, senior citizens. ***ROTC:*** Army.

LOANS ***Programs:*** Federal Direct (Subsidized and Unsubsidized Stafford, PLUS), Perkins, Federal Nursing, state, college/university, Health Professions Loans.

WORK-STUDY Federal work-study jobs available. ***State or other work-study/employment:*** Part-time jobs available.

APPLYING for FINANCIAL AID ***Required financial aid form:*** FAFSA. ***Financial aid deadline:*** Continuous. ***Notification date:*** Continuous beginning 3/15. Students must reply within 2 weeks of notification.

CONTACT Mr. Horace J. Amaral, Assistant Dean of Financial Aid, University of Rhode Island, 90 Lower College Road, Roosevelt Hall, Suite 11, Kingston, RI 02881-0891, 401-874-2314.

UNIVERSITY OF RICHMOND

Richmond, VA

Tuition & fees: $19,610 **Average undergraduate aid package: $15,111**

ABOUT THE INSTITUTION Independent, coed. Awards: associate, bachelor's, master's, and first professional degrees. 53 undergraduate majors. Total enrollment: 3,777. Undergraduates: 3,034. Freshmen: 854. Federal methodology is used as a basis for awarding need-based institutional aid.

UNDERGRADUATE EXPENSES for 1999–2000 ***Application fee:*** $40. ***Comprehensive fee:*** $23,660 includes full-time tuition ($19,340), mandatory fees ($270), and room and board ($4050). ***College room only:*** $1716. Room and board charges vary according to board plan and housing facility. ***Part-time tuition:*** $965 per semester hour. Part-time tuition and fees vary according to class time. ***Payment plan:*** installment.

University of Richmond (continued)

FRESHMAN FINANCIAL AID (Fall 1999) 480 applied for aid; of those 61% were deemed to have need. 100% of freshmen with need received aid; of those 41% had need fully met. *Average percent of need met:* 93% (excluding resources awarded to replace EFC). *Average financial aid package:* $14,667 (excluding resources awarded to replace EFC). 24% of all full-time freshmen had no need and received non-need-based aid.

UNDERGRADUATE FINANCIAL AID (Fall 1999) 1,374 applied for aid; of those 70% were deemed to have need. 100% of undergraduates with need received aid; of those 52% had need fully met. *Average percent of need met:* 93% (excluding resources awarded to replace EFC). *Average financial aid package:* $15,111 (excluding resources awarded to replace EFC). 25% of all full-time undergraduates had no need and received non-need-based aid.

GIFT AID (NEED-BASED) ***Total amount:*** $8,842,644 (7% Federal, 6% state, 82% institutional, 5% external sources). ***Receiving aid:*** *Freshmen:* 31% (273); *all full-time undergraduates:* 29% (876). ***Average award:*** Freshmen: $10,407; Undergraduates: $10,071. ***Scholarships, grants, and awards:*** Federal Pell, FSEOG, state, private, college/university gift aid from institutional funds.

GIFT AID (NON-NEED-BASED) ***Total amount:*** $4,887,416 (13% Federal, 16% state, 63% institutional, 8% external sources). ***Receiving aid:*** *Freshmen:* 22% (190); *Undergraduates:* 23% (688). ***Scholarships, grants, and awards by category:*** *Academic Interests/Achievement:* 188 awards ($2,198,630 total): biological sciences, computer science, general academic interests/achievements, mathematics, physical sciences. *Creative Arts/Performance:* 17 awards ($47,500 total): music. *Special Achievements/Activities:* 14 awards ($27,300 total): community service. *Special Characteristics:* 53 awards ($459,600 total): members of minority groups. ***Tuition waivers:*** Full or partial for employees or children of employees. ***ROTC:*** Army.

LOANS ***Student loans:*** $4,888,291 (56% need-based, 44% non-need-based). 41% of past graduating class borrowed through all loan programs. Average indebtedness per student: $14,300. ***Average need-based loan:*** Freshmen: $3165; Undergraduates: $3853. ***Parent loans:*** $2,788,821 (8% need-based, 92% non-need-based). ***Programs:*** Federal Direct (Subsidized and Unsubsidized Stafford, PLUS), Perkins, Charles B. Keesee Educational Loans (VA and NC residents).

WORK-STUDY ***Federal work-study:*** *Total amount:* $371,986; 300 jobs averaging $1240.

ATHLETIC AWARDS *Total amount:* 4,157,535 (23% need-based, 77% non-need-based).

APPLYING for FINANCIAL AID ***Required financial aid forms:*** FAFSA, institution's own form. ***Financial aid deadline:*** 2/25. ***Notification date:*** 4/1. Students must reply within 4 weeks of notification.

CONTACT Financial Aid Office, University of Richmond, Sarah Brunet Hall, University of Richmond, VA 23173, 804-289-8438 or toll-free 800-700-1662. *Fax:* 804-287-6003.

UNIVERSITY OF RIO GRANDE

Rio Grande, OH

Tuition & fees (area res): $2961 **Average undergraduate aid package: N/A**

ABOUT THE INSTITUTION Independent, coed. Awards: associate, bachelor's, and master's degrees. 67 undergraduate majors. Total enrollment: 1,952. Undergraduates: 1,851. Federal methodology is used as a basis for awarding need-based institutional aid.

UNDERGRADUATE EXPENSES for 1999–2000 ***Application fee:*** $15. ***Tuition, area resident:*** full-time $2520; part-time $52 per quarter hour. ***Tuition, state resident:*** full-time $3000; part-time $62 per quarter hour. ***Tuition, nonresident:*** full-time $8784; part-time $244 per quarter hour. ***Required fees:*** full-time $441; $7 per credit hour; $15 per term part-time. Full-time tuition and fees vary according to reciprocity agreements and student level. Part-time tuition and fees vary according to reciprocity agreements and student level. ***College room and board:*** $4995. Area and state resident tuition rates apply only for the first 2 years. ***Payment plans:*** installment, deferred payment.

FRESHMAN FINANCIAL AID (Fall 1998) 342 applied for aid; of those 85% were deemed to have need. 100% of freshmen with need received aid; of those 25% had need fully met.

UNDERGRADUATE FINANCIAL AID (Fall 1998) 1,305 applied for aid; of those 90% were deemed to have need. 100% of undergraduates with need received aid; of those 25% had need fully met.

GIFT AID (NEED-BASED) ***Total amount:*** $2,641,235 (61% Federal, 24% state, 14% institutional, 1% external sources). ***Receiving aid:*** *Freshmen:* 45% (175); *all full-time undergraduates:* 43% (646). ***Scholarships, grants, and awards:*** Federal Pell, FSEOG, state, private, college/university gift aid from institutional funds.

GIFT AID (NON-NEED-BASED) ***Total amount:*** $1,868,335 (23% state, 74% institutional, 3% external sources). ***Receiving aid:*** *Freshmen:* 15% (58); *Undergraduates:* 51% (776). ***Scholarships, grants, and awards by category:*** *Academic Interests/Achievement:* biological sciences, business, communication, computer science, education, general academic interests/achievements, health fields, physical sciences, social sciences. *Creative Arts/Performance:* music. *Special Characteristics:* children and siblings of alumni, children of faculty/staff, local/state students, out-of-state students. ***Tuition waivers:*** Full or partial for employees or children of employees. ***ROTC:*** Army cooperative.

LOANS ***Student loans:*** $4,190,122 (73% need-based, 27% non-need-based). 84% of past graduating class borrowed through all loan programs. Average indebtedness per student: $13,750. ***Parent loans:*** $148,046 (100% non-need-based). ***Programs:*** Federal Direct (Subsidized and Unsubsidized Stafford, PLUS), Perkins.

WORK-STUDY ***Federal work-study:*** *Total amount:* $114,958; jobs available. ***State or other work-study/employment:*** *Total amount:* $86,000 (100% non-need-based). Part-time jobs available.

ATHLETIC AWARDS *Total amount:* 347,083 (100% non-need-based).

APPLYING for FINANCIAL AID ***Required financial aid forms:*** FAFSA, institution's own form. ***Financial aid deadline:*** Continuous. ***Notification date:*** Continuous beginning 2/1. Students must reply within 3 weeks of notification.

CONTACT Dr. John Hill, Director of Financial Aid, University of Rio Grande, 218 North College Avenue, Rio Grande, OH 45674, 740-245-7218 or toll-free 800-282-7201 (in-state). *Fax:* 740-245-7102.

UNIVERSITY OF ROCHESTER

Rochester, NY

Tuition & fees: $22,864 **Average undergraduate aid package: $21,103**

ABOUT THE INSTITUTION Independent, coed. Awards: bachelor's, master's, doctoral, and first professional degrees. 57 undergraduate majors. Total enrollment: 7,697. Undergraduates: 4,529. Freshmen: 1,212. Both federal and institutional methodology are used as a basis for awarding need-based institutional aid.

UNDERGRADUATE EXPENSES for 1999–2000 ***Application fee:*** $50. ***Comprehensive fee:*** $30,376 includes full-time tuition ($22,300), mandatory fees ($564), and room and board ($7512). ***College room only:*** $4560. Room and board charges vary according to board plan. ***Part-time tuition:*** $697 per credit hour. ***Payment plans:*** tuition prepayment, installment.

FRESHMAN FINANCIAL AID (Fall 1999) 769 applied for aid; of those 84% were deemed to have need. 100% of freshmen with need received aid; of those 100% had need fully met. *Average percent of need met:* 100% (excluding resources awarded to replace EFC). *Average financial aid package:* $19,725 (excluding resources awarded to replace EFC). 30% of all full-time freshmen had no need and received non-need-based aid.

UNDERGRADUATE FINANCIAL AID (Fall 1999) 2,654 applied for aid; of those 89% were deemed to have need. 100% of undergraduates with need received aid; of those 100% had need fully met. *Average percent of need met:* 100% (excluding resources awarded to replace EFC). *Average financial aid package:* $21,103 (excluding resources awarded to replace EFC). 28% of all full-time undergraduates had no need and received non-need-based aid.

GIFT AID (NEED-BASED) ***Total amount:*** $38,652,257 (7% Federal, 7% state, 80% institutional, 6% external sources). ***Receiving aid:*** *Freshmen:* 65% (636); *all full-time undergraduates:* 64% (2,326). ***Average award:*** Freshmen: $15,841; Undergraduates: $16,315. ***Scholarships, grants, and awards:*** Federal Pell, FSEOG, state, private, college/university gift aid from institutional funds.

GIFT AID (NON-NEED-BASED) ***Total amount:*** $9,686,751 (93% institutional, 7% external sources). ***Receiving aid:*** *Freshmen:* 53% (520); *Undergraduates:* 48% (1,726). ***Scholarships, grants, and awards by category:*** *Academic Interests/Achievement:* biological sciences, general academic interests/achievements, humanities, mathematics, physical sciences, social sciences. *Special Achievements/Activities:* leadership. *Special Characteristics:* children and siblings of alumni, ethnic background, local/state students, members of minority groups, out-of-state students. ***Tuition waivers:*** Full or partial for children of alumni, employees or children of employees. ***ROTC:*** Army cooperative, Naval, Air Force cooperative.

LOANS ***Student loans:*** $9,654,202 (94% need-based, 6% non-need-based). ***Average need-based loan:*** Freshmen: $3724; Undergraduates: $4549. ***Parent loans:*** $2,988,034 (88% need-based, 12% non-need-based). ***Programs:*** Federal Direct (Subsidized and Unsubsidized Stafford, PLUS), Perkins, Federal Nursing, college/university, alternative loans.

WORK-STUDY ***Federal work-study:*** *Total amount:* $2,918,841; 1,512 jobs averaging $1904.

APPLYING for FINANCIAL AID ***Required financial aid forms:*** FAFSA, CSS Financial Aid PROFILE, state aid form, noncustodial (divorced/separated) parent's statement. ***Financial aid deadline (priority):*** 2/1. ***Notification date:*** 4/1. Students must reply by 5/1 or within 2 weeks of notification.

CONTACT Ginny Abamonte, Senior Programmer/Analyst, University of Rochester, River Campus, PO Box 270261, Rochester, NY 14627-0001, 716-275-8642 or toll-free 888-822-2256. *Fax:* 716-756-7664. *E-mail:* gabamonte@finaid.rochester.edu

UNIVERSITY OF ST. FRANCIS

Joliet, IL

Tuition & fees: $13,082 **Average undergraduate aid package: $11,127**

ABOUT THE INSTITUTION Independent Roman Catholic, coed. Awards: bachelor's and master's degrees. 37 undergraduate majors. Total enrollment: 2,604. Undergraduates: 1,403. Freshmen: 170. Federal methodology is used as a basis for awarding need-based institutional aid.

UNDERGRADUATE EXPENSES for 1999–2000 ***Application fee:*** $20. ***Comprehensive fee:*** $18,202 includes full-time tuition ($12,800), mandatory fees ($282), and room and board ($5120). ***Part-time tuition:*** $370 per credit. ***Part-time fees:*** $15 per term part-time. Part-time tuition and fees vary according to course load. ***Payment plan:*** installment.

FRESHMAN FINANCIAL AID (Fall 1999) 170 applied for aid; of those 73% were deemed to have need. 100% of freshmen with need received aid; of those 63% had need fully met. *Average percent of need met:* 88% (excluding resources awarded to replace EFC). *Average financial aid package:* $12,388 (excluding resources awarded to replace EFC). 24% of all full-time freshmen had no need and received non-need-based aid.

UNDERGRADUATE FINANCIAL AID (Fall 1999) 942 applied for aid; of those 69% were deemed to have need. 100% of undergraduates with need received aid; of those 78% had need fully met. *Average percent of need met:* 89% (excluding resources awarded to replace EFC). *Average financial aid package:* $11,127 (excluding resources awarded to replace EFC). 23% of all full-time undergraduates had no need and received non-need-based aid.

GIFT AID (NEED-BASED) ***Total amount:*** $3,116,638 (19% Federal, 58% state, 23% institutional). ***Receiving aid:*** *Freshmen:* 47% (80); *all full-time undergraduates:* 51% (487). ***Average award:*** Freshmen: $6046; Undergraduates: $6400. ***Scholarships, grants, and awards:*** Federal Pell, FSEOG, state, private, college/university gift aid from institutional funds.

GIFT AID (NON-NEED-BASED) ***Total amount:*** $2,040,795 (2% state, 95% institutional, 3% external sources). ***Receiving aid:*** *Freshmen:* 69% (118); *Undergraduates:* 47% (450). ***Scholarships, grants, and awards by category:*** *Academic Interests/Achievement:* biological sciences, general academic interests/achievements. *Creative Arts/Performance:* music. *Special Achievements/Activities:* cheerleading/drum major. *Special Characteristics:* children of educators, ethnic background, siblings of current students. ***Tuition waivers:*** Full or partial for children of alumni, employees or children of employees.

LOANS ***Student loans:*** $3,209,641 (54% need-based, 46% non-need-based). 66% of past graduating class borrowed through all loan programs. Average indebtedness per student: $11,506. ***Average need-based loan:*** Freshmen: $2796; Undergraduates: $3567. ***Parent loans:*** $903,661 (100% non-need-based). ***Programs:*** Federal Direct (Subsidized and Unsubsidized Stafford, PLUS), Perkins.

WORK-STUDY ***Federal work-study:*** *Total amount:* $249,168; 155 jobs averaging $1638. ***State or other work-study/employment:*** *Total amount:* $200,000 (100% non-need-based). Part-time jobs available.

ATHLETIC AWARDS *Total amount:* 1,327,928 (35% need-based, 65% non-need-based).

APPLYING for FINANCIAL AID ***Required financial aid forms:*** FAFSA, institution's own form. ***Financial aid deadline:*** Continuous. ***Notification date:*** Continuous beginning 2/15. Students must reply within 2 weeks of notification.

CONTACT Mr. Bruce A. Foote, Director of Financial Aid, University of St. Francis, 500 North Wilcox Street, Joliet, IL 60435-6188, 815-740-3403 or toll-free 800-735-7500. *Fax:* 815-740-3822. *E-mail:* bfoote@stfrancis.edu

UNIVERSITY OF SAINT FRANCIS

Fort Wayne, IN

Tuition & fees: $12,495 **Average undergraduate aid package: N/A**

ABOUT THE INSTITUTION Independent Roman Catholic, coed. Awards: associate, bachelor's, and master's degrees and post-bachelor's certificates. 38 undergraduate majors. Total enrollment: 1,518. Undergraduates: 1,428. Freshmen: 241. Federal methodology is used as a basis for awarding need-based institutional aid.

UNDERGRADUATE EXPENSES for 2000–2001 ***Application fee:*** $20. ***Comprehensive fee:*** $17,295 includes full-time tuition ($12,080), mandatory fees ($415), and room and board ($4800). Full-time tuition and fees vary according to class time. ***Part-time tuition:*** $380 per semester hour. ***Part-time fees:*** $8 per semester hour; $70 per term part-time. Part-time tuition and fees vary according to class time and course load. ***Payment plan:*** installment.

GIFT AID (NEED-BASED) ***Scholarships, grants, and awards:*** Federal Pell, state, private, college/university gift aid from institutional funds.

GIFT AID (NON-NEED-BASED) ***Scholarships, grants, and awards by category:*** *Academic Interests/Achievement:* biological sciences, general academic interests/achievements, health fields, physical sciences. *Creative Arts/Performance:* art/fine arts. *Special Characteristics:* adult students, children and siblings of alumni, first-generation college students, out-of-state students, siblings of current students. ***Tuition waivers:*** Full or partial for children of alumni, employees or children of employees, senior citizens.

LOANS ***Programs:*** Federal Direct (Subsidized and Unsubsidized Stafford, PLUS), Perkins, college/university.

APPLYING for FINANCIAL AID ***Required financial aid form:*** FAFSA. ***Financial aid deadline (priority):*** 3/1. ***Notification date:*** Continuous beginning 3/15. Students must reply within 2 weeks of notification.

CONTACT Sherri Shockey, Director of Financial Aid, University of Saint Francis, 2701 Spring Street, Fort Wayne, IN 46808, 219-434-3244 or toll-free 800-729-4732.

UNIVERSITY OF ST. THOMAS

St. Paul, MN

Tuition & fees: $16,340 **Average undergraduate aid package: $13,310**

ABOUT THE INSTITUTION Independent Roman Catholic, coed. Awards: bachelor's, master's, doctoral, and first professional degrees and post-bachelor's and post-master's certificates. 64 undergraduate majors. Total

University of St. Thomas (continued)

enrollment: 10,929. Undergraduates: 5,399. Freshmen: 1,055. Both federal and institutional methodology are used as a basis for awarding need-based institutional aid.

UNDERGRADUATE EXPENSES for 1999–2000 ***Application fee:*** $30. ***Comprehensive fee:*** $21,520 includes full-time tuition ($16,128), mandatory fees ($212), and room and board ($5180). ***College room only:*** $3058. Full-time tuition and fees vary according to course load. Room and board charges vary according to board plan and housing facility. ***Part-time tuition:*** $504 per credit. ***Part-time fees:*** $78 per term part-time. Part-time tuition and fees vary according to course load. ***Payment plans:*** installment, deferred payment.

FRESHMAN FINANCIAL AID (Fall 1999) 811 applied for aid; of those 77% were deemed to have need. 100% of freshmen with need received aid; of those 27% had need fully met. *Average percent of need met:* 89% (excluding resources awarded to replace EFC). *Average financial aid package:* $13,482 (excluding resources awarded to replace EFC). 16% of all full-time freshmen had no need and received non-need-based aid.

UNDERGRADUATE FINANCIAL AID (Fall 1999) 3,336 applied for aid; of those 82% were deemed to have need. 100% of undergraduates with need received aid; of those 28% had need fully met. *Average percent of need met:* 88% (excluding resources awarded to replace EFC). *Average financial aid package:* $13,310 (excluding resources awarded to replace EFC). 11% of all full-time undergraduates had no need and received non-need-based aid.

GIFT AID (NEED-BASED) ***Total amount:*** $21,473,222 (9% Federal, 21% state, 66% institutional, 4% external sources). ***Receiving aid:*** *Freshmen:* 59% (617); *all full-time undergraduates:* 58% (2,648). ***Average award:*** Freshmen: $8338; Undergraduates: $7332. ***Scholarships, grants, and awards:*** Federal Pell, FSEOG, state, private, college/university gift aid from institutional funds.

GIFT AID (NON-NEED-BASED) ***Total amount:*** $4,743,280 (1% state, 87% institutional, 12% external sources). ***Receiving aid:*** *Freshmen:* 6% (59); *Undergraduates:* 4% (169). ***Scholarships, grants, and awards by category:*** *Academic Interests/Achievement:* 2,105 awards ($7,893,606 total): biological sciences, business, education, English, general academic interests/achievements, humanities, international studies, mathematics, physical sciences, social sciences. *Creative Arts/Performance:* 34 awards ($81,750 total): journalism/publications, music. *Special Characteristics:* 207 awards ($1,553,194 total): children of educators, children of faculty/staff, parents of current students. ***Tuition waivers:*** Full or partial for employees or children of employees, senior citizens. ***ROTC:*** Army cooperative, Naval cooperative, Air Force.

LOANS ***Student loans:*** $16,583,850 (69% need-based, 31% non-need-based). 76% of past graduating class borrowed through all loan programs. Average indebtedness per student: $16,245. ***Average need-based loan:*** Freshmen: $2764; Undergraduates: $3649. ***Parent loans:*** $2,013,900 (16% need-based, 84% non-need-based). ***Programs:*** FFEL (Subsidized and Unsubsidized Stafford, PLUS), Perkins, state, alternative loans.

WORK-STUDY ***Federal work-study:*** *Total amount:* $1,406,201; 666 jobs averaging $2111. ***State or other work-study/employment:*** *Total amount:* $4,010,368 (46% need-based, 54% non-need-based). 1,797 part-time jobs averaging $2232.

APPLYING for FINANCIAL AID ***Required financial aid form:*** FAFSA. ***Financial aid deadline (priority):*** 4/1. ***Notification date:*** Continuous. Students must reply within 3 weeks of notification.

CONTACT Ms. Ginny Reese, Associate Director, Student Financial Services, University of St. Thomas, 2115 Summit Avenue, CHC156, St. Paul, MN 55105-1096, 651-962-6557 or toll-free 800-328-6819 Ext. 26150. *Fax:* 651-962-6599. *E-mail:* vmreese@stthomas.edu

UNIVERSITY OF ST. THOMAS
Houston, TX

Tuition & fees: $12,416 **Average undergraduate aid package: $9883**

ABOUT THE INSTITUTION Independent Roman Catholic, coed. Awards: bachelor's, master's, doctoral, and first professional degrees. 35 undergraduate majors. Total enrollment: 3,345. Undergraduates: 1,666. Freshmen: 225. Both federal and institutional methodology are used as a basis for awarding need-based institutional aid.

UNDERGRADUATE EXPENSES for 2000–2001 ***Application fee:*** $35. ***Comprehensive fee:*** $17,466 includes full-time tuition ($12,300), mandatory fees ($116), and room and board ($5050). ***College room only:*** $2900. Full-time tuition and fees vary according to degree level. Room and board charges vary according to board plan and housing facility. ***Part-time tuition:*** $418 per credit hour. Part-time tuition and fees vary according to degree level. ***Payment plans:*** installment, deferred payment.

FRESHMAN FINANCIAL AID (Fall 1999, est.) 169 applied for aid; of those 61% were deemed to have need. 100% of freshmen with need received aid. *Average financial aid package:* $10,965 (excluding resources awarded to replace EFC). 32% of all full-time freshmen had no need and received non-need-based aid.

UNDERGRADUATE FINANCIAL AID (Fall 1999, est.) 874 applied for aid; of those 65% were deemed to have need. 98% of undergraduates with need received aid. *Average financial aid package:* $9883 (excluding resources awarded to replace EFC). 24% of all full-time undergraduates had no need and received non-need-based aid.

GIFT AID (NEED-BASED) ***Total amount:*** $2,108,964 (38% Federal, 50% state, 12% institutional). ***Receiving aid:*** *Freshmen:* 44% (85); *all full-time undergraduates:* 42% (456). ***Average award:*** Freshmen: $3846; Undergraduates: $4206. ***Scholarships, grants, and awards:*** Federal Pell, FSEOG, state, college/university gift aid from institutional funds.

GIFT AID (NON-NEED-BASED) ***Total amount:*** $3,969,747 (94% institutional, 6% external sources). ***Receiving aid:*** *Freshmen:* 53% (103); *Undergraduates:* 38% (410). ***Scholarships, grants, and awards by category:*** *Academic Interests/Achievement:* 717 awards ($3,718,374 total): general academic interests/achievements. *Creative Arts/Performance:* 16 awards ($48,380 total): debating, music, theater/drama. *Special Achievements/Activities:* community service. *Special Characteristics:* children of educators, children of faculty/staff, general special characteristics, members of minority groups, relatives of clergy, religious affiliation. ***Tuition waivers:*** Full or partial for employees or children of employees, senior citizens. ***ROTC:*** Army cooperative.

LOANS ***Student loans:*** $3,366,033 (55% need-based, 45% non-need-based). ***Average need-based loan:*** Freshmen: $2248; Undergraduates: $4020. ***Parent loans:*** $509,149 (100% non-need-based). ***Programs:*** Federal Direct (Subsidized and Unsubsidized Stafford, PLUS), Perkins, state.

WORK-STUDY ***Federal work-study:*** *Total amount:* $84,779; 42 jobs averaging $2019. ***State or other work-study/employment:*** *Total amount:* $7200 (100% need-based). 22 part-time jobs averaging $328.

APPLYING for FINANCIAL AID ***Required financial aid forms:*** FAFSA, institution's own form, CSS Financial Aid PROFILE. ***Financial aid deadline (priority):*** 2/1. ***Notification date:*** Continuous.

CONTACT Ms. Linda Ballard, Director of Student Financial Aid, University of St. Thomas, 3800 Montrose Boulevard, Houston, TX 77006-4694, 713-525-2175 or toll-free 800-856-8565. *Fax:* 713-525-2142. *E-mail:* ballard@stthom.edu

UNIVERSITY OF SAN DIEGO
San Diego, CA

Tuition & fees: $19,128 **Average undergraduate aid package: $14,958**

ABOUT THE INSTITUTION Independent Roman Catholic, coed. Awards: bachelor's, master's, doctoral, and first professional degrees. 39 undergraduate majors. Total enrollment: 6,858. Undergraduates: 4,623. Freshmen: 992. Both federal and institutional methodology are used as a basis for awarding need-based institutional aid.

UNDERGRADUATE EXPENSES for 2000–2001 ***Application fee:*** $55. ***Comprehensive fee:*** $27,568 includes full-time tuition ($19,020), mandatory fees ($108), and room and board ($8440). ***College room only:*** $4400. Room and board charges vary according to board plan and housing facility. ***Part-time tuition:*** $660 per unit. ***Part-time fees:*** $19 per term part-time. Part-time tuition and fees vary according to course load. ***Payment plan:*** installment.

FRESHMAN FINANCIAL AID (Fall 1998) 785 applied for aid; of those 70% were deemed to have need. 100% of freshmen with need received aid; of those 49% had need fully met. *Average percent of need met:* 94% (excluding resources awarded to replace EFC). *Average financial aid package:* $15,346 (excluding resources awarded to replace EFC). 16% of all full-time freshmen had no need and received non-need-based aid.

UNDERGRADUATE FINANCIAL AID (Fall 1998) 3,004 applied for aid; of those 72% were deemed to have need. 100% of undergraduates with need received aid; of those 47% had need fully met. *Average percent of need met:* 90% (excluding resources awarded to replace EFC). *Average financial aid package:* $14,958 (excluding resources awarded to replace EFC). 20% of all full-time undergraduates had no need and received non-need-based aid.

GIFT AID (NEED-BASED) ***Total amount:*** $21,654,387 (16% Federal, 20% state, 62% institutional, 2% external sources). ***Receiving aid:*** *Freshmen:* 35% (512); *all full-time undergraduates:* 45% (1,903). ***Average award:*** Freshmen: $12,955; Undergraduates: $11,790. ***Scholarships, grants, and awards:*** Federal Pell, FSEOG, state, private, college/university gift aid from institutional funds.

GIFT AID (NON-NEED-BASED) ***Total amount:*** $4,535,965 (25% Federal, 71% institutional, 4% external sources). ***Receiving aid:*** *Freshmen:* 22% (320); *Undergraduates:* 14% (578). ***Scholarships, grants, and awards by category:*** *Academic Interests/Achievement:* 847 awards ($6,074,319 total): general academic interests/achievements. *Creative Arts/Performance:* 11 awards ($78,750 total): music. *Special Characteristics:* 94 awards ($844,800 total): children of faculty/staff. ***Tuition waivers:*** Full or partial for employees or children of employees. ***ROTC:*** Army cooperative, Naval, Air Force cooperative.

LOANS ***Student loans:*** $11,641,422 (94% need-based, 6% non-need-based). 48% of past graduating class borrowed through all loan programs. Average indebtedness per student: $23,100. ***Average need-based loan:*** Freshmen: $3601; Undergraduates: $4800. ***Parent loans:*** $8,374,729 (75% need-based, 25% non-need-based). ***Programs:*** FFEL (Subsidized and Unsubsidized Stafford, PLUS), Perkins, Federal Nursing, college/university.

WORK-STUDY ***Federal work-study:*** *Total amount:* $1,162,147; 552 jobs averaging $2105. ***State or other work-study/employment:*** *Total amount:* $434,995 (60% need-based, 40% non-need-based). 116 part-time jobs averaging $3750.

ATHLETIC AWARDS *Total amount:* 1,993,779 (20% need-based, 80% non-need-based).

APPLYING for FINANCIAL AID ***Required financial aid forms:*** FAFSA, institution's own form. ***Financial aid deadline (priority):*** 2/20. ***Notification date:*** Continuous beginning 3/1. Students must reply within 3 weeks of notification.

CONTACT Ms. Judith Lewis Logue, Director of Financial Aid, University of San Diego, 5998 Alcala Park, San Diego, CA 92110-2492, 619-260-4514 or toll-free 800-248-4873 Ext. 4506.

UNIVERSITY OF SAN FRANCISCO

San Francisco, CA

Tuition & fees: $19,060 **Average undergraduate aid package: $15,159**

ABOUT THE INSTITUTION Independent Roman Catholic (Jesuit), coed. Awards: bachelor's, master's, doctoral, and first professional degrees and post-master's certificates. 68 undergraduate majors. Total enrollment: 7,797. Undergraduates: 4,572. Freshmen: 762. Federal methodology is used as a basis for awarding need-based institutional aid.

UNDERGRADUATE EXPENSES for 2000–2001 ***Application fee:*** $45. ***Comprehensive fee:*** $27,302 includes full-time tuition ($18,860), mandatory fees ($200), and room and board ($8242). ***College room only:*** $5112. Room and board charges vary according to board plan and housing facility. ***Part-time tuition:*** $689 per unit. ***Part-time fees:*** $200 per year part-time. ***Payment plan:*** installment.

FRESHMAN FINANCIAL AID (Fall 1999, est.) 574 applied for aid; of those 85% were deemed to have need. 97% of freshmen with need received aid; of those 19% had need fully met. *Average percent of need met:* 73% (excluding resources awarded to replace EFC). *Average financial aid package:* $15,693 (excluding resources awarded to replace EFC). 6% of all full-time freshmen had no need and received non-need-based aid.

UNDERGRADUATE FINANCIAL AID (Fall 1999, est.) 2,651 applied for aid; of those 88% were deemed to have need. 97% of undergraduates with need received aid; of those 20% had need fully met. *Average percent of need met:* 73% (excluding resources awarded to replace EFC). *Average financial aid package:* $15,159 (excluding resources awarded to replace EFC). 6% of all full-time undergraduates had no need and received non-need-based aid.

GIFT AID (NEED-BASED) ***Total amount:*** $11,155,631 (22% Federal, 38% state, 34% institutional, 6% external sources). ***Receiving aid:*** *Freshmen:* 51% (390); *all full-time undergraduates:* 40% (1,725). ***Average award:*** Freshmen: $12,445; Undergraduates: $10,282. ***Scholarships, grants, and awards:*** Federal Pell, FSEOG, state, private, college/university gift aid from institutional funds.

GIFT AID (NON-NEED-BASED) ***Total amount:*** $2,143,390 (100% institutional). ***Receiving aid:*** *Freshmen:* 6% (48); *Undergraduates:* 5% (212). ***Scholarships, grants, and awards by category:*** *Academic Interests/Achievement:* 189 awards ($2,045,692 total): general academic interests/achievements. *Creative Arts/Performance:* 3 awards ($40,000 total): performing arts. *Special Achievements/Activities:* 39 awards ($315,213 total): general special achievements/activities. *Special Characteristics:* 89 awards ($1,089,827 total): children of faculty/staff, general special characteristics. ***Tuition waivers:*** Full or partial for employees or children of employees. ***ROTC:*** Army, Air Force cooperative.

LOANS ***Student loans:*** $15,067,939 (65% need-based, 35% non-need-based). 58% of past graduating class borrowed through all loan programs. Average indebtedness per student: $22,238. ***Average need-based loan:*** Freshmen: $3599; Undergraduates: $4692. ***Parent loans:*** $5,286,514 (100% non-need-based). ***Programs:*** Federal Direct (Subsidized and Unsubsidized Stafford, PLUS), Perkins, Federal Nursing, college/university.

WORK-STUDY ***Federal work-study:*** *Total amount:* $1,619,093; 705 jobs averaging $2297. ***State or other work-study/employment:*** *Total amount:* $628,480 (100% non-need-based). 273 part-time jobs averaging $2302.

ATHLETIC AWARDS *Total amount:* 2,222,773 (100% non-need-based).

APPLYING for FINANCIAL AID ***Required financial aid form:*** FAFSA. ***Financial aid deadline (priority):*** 2/15. ***Notification date:*** Continuous beginning 4/1. Students must reply within 4 weeks of notification.

CONTACT Ms. Susan Murphy, Director of Financial Aid, University of San Francisco, 2130 Fulton Street, San Francisco, CA 94117-1080, 415-422-2620 or toll-free 800-CALL USF (out-of-state). *Fax:* 415-422-2217. *E-mail:* murphy@usfca.edu

UNIVERSITY OF SARASOTA

Sarasota, FL

CONTACT Financial Aid Office, University of Sarasota, 5250 17th Street, Sarasota, FL 34235-8246, 941-379-0404.

UNIVERSITY OF SCIENCE AND ARTS OF OKLAHOMA

Chickasha, OK

Tuition & fees (OK res): $1878 **Average undergraduate aid package: $6946**

ABOUT THE INSTITUTION State-supported, coed. Awards: bachelor's degrees. 27 undergraduate majors. Total enrollment: 1,393. Undergraduates: 1,393. Freshmen: 286. Federal methodology is used as a basis for awarding need-based institutional aid.

UNDERGRADUATE EXPENSES for 1999–2000 ***Tuition, state resident:*** full-time $1470; part-time $49 per hour. ***Tuition, nonresident:*** full-time $3990; part-time $133 per hour. ***Required fees:*** full-time $408; $14 per hour. Full-time tuition and fees vary according to course level and student level. Part-time tuition and fees vary according to course level and student level. ***College room and board:*** $2320; ***room only:*** $690. Room and board charges vary according to board plan and housing facility. ***Payment plan:*** installment.

University of Science and Arts of Oklahoma (continued)

FRESHMAN FINANCIAL AID (Fall 1999, est.) 232 applied for aid; of those 83% were deemed to have need. 94% of freshmen with need received aid; of those 46% had need fully met. *Average percent of need met:* 93% (excluding resources awarded to replace EFC). *Average financial aid package:* $6534 (excluding resources awarded to replace EFC). 6% of all full-time freshmen had no need and received non-need-based aid.

UNDERGRADUATE FINANCIAL AID (Fall 1999, est.) 838 applied for aid; of those 81% were deemed to have need. 92% of undergraduates with need received aid; of those 59% had need fully met. *Average percent of need met:* 90% (excluding resources awarded to replace EFC). *Average financial aid package:* $6946 (excluding resources awarded to replace EFC). 3% of all full-time undergraduates had no need and received non-need-based aid.

GIFT AID (NEED-BASED) ***Total amount:*** $2,158,979 (79% Federal, 14% state, 4% institutional, 3% external sources). ***Receiving aid:*** *Freshmen:* 63% (166); *all full-time undergraduates:* 59% (574). ***Average award:*** Freshmen: $5097; Undergraduates: $3959. ***Scholarships, grants, and awards:*** Federal Pell, FSEOG, state, private, college/university gift aid from institutional funds, USAO Foundation Grants.

GIFT AID (NON-NEED-BASED) ***Total amount:*** $159,473 (14% Federal, 45% state, 21% institutional, 20% external sources). ***Receiving aid:*** *Freshmen:* 59% (154); *Undergraduates:* 32% (315). ***Scholarships, grants, and awards by category:*** *Academic Interests/Achievement:* 162 awards ($127,393 total): general academic interests/achievements. *Creative Arts/Performance:* 38 awards ($38,382 total): art/fine arts, music, theater/drama. *Special Achievements/Activities:* 39 awards ($20,830 total): cheerleading/drum major, leadership. *Special Characteristics:* 24 awards ($42,376 total): international students, out-of-state students, previous college experience. ***Tuition waivers:*** Full or partial for senior citizens.

LOANS ***Student loans:*** $1,622,672 (85% need-based, 15% non-need-based). 51% of past graduating class borrowed through all loan programs. Average indebtedness per student: $11,120. ***Average need-based loan:*** Freshmen: $1400; Undergraduates: $2100. ***Parent loans:*** $21,865 (10% need-based, 90% non-need-based). ***Programs:*** FFEL (Subsidized and Unsubsidized Stafford, PLUS), Perkins, college/university.

WORK-STUDY ***Federal work-study:*** *Total amount:* $386,324; 183 jobs averaging $1849.

ATHLETIC AWARDS *Total amount:* 240,034 (35% need-based, 65% non-need-based).

APPLYING for FINANCIAL AID ***Required financial aid forms:*** FAFSA, institution's own form. ***Financial aid deadline (priority):*** 3/15. ***Notification date:*** Continuous beginning 4/1. Students must reply within 4 weeks of notification.

CONTACT Laura Coponiti, Assistant Director, Financial Aid, University of Science and Arts of Oklahoma, PO Box 82345, Chickasha, OK 73018-0001, 405-574-1350 or toll-free 800-933-8726 Ext. 1204. *Fax:* 405-522-3176.

THE UNIVERSITY OF SCRANTON

Scranton, PA

Tuition & fees: $17,740 **Average undergraduate aid package: $12,759**

ABOUT THE INSTITUTION Independent Roman Catholic (Jesuit), coed. Awards: associate, bachelor's, and master's degrees and post-master's certificates. 49 undergraduate majors. Total enrollment: 4,773. Undergraduates: 4,099. Freshmen: 969. Institutional methodology is used as a basis for awarding need-based institutional aid.

UNDERGRADUATE EXPENSES for 1999–2000 ***Application fee:*** $40. ***One-time required fee:*** $20. ***Comprehensive fee:*** $25,450 includes full-time tuition ($17,540), mandatory fees ($200), and room and board ($7710). ***College room only:*** $4490. Full-time tuition and fees vary according to degree level, program, and student level. Room and board charges vary according to board plan and housing facility. ***Part-time tuition:*** $410 per credit hour. ***Part-time fees:*** $35 per term part-time. Part-time tuition and fees vary according to degree level and student level. ***Payment plan:*** installment.

FRESHMAN FINANCIAL AID (Fall 1999, est.) 764 applied for aid; of those 79% were deemed to have need. 98% of freshmen with need received aid; of those 19% had need fully met. *Average percent of need met:* 78% (excluding resources awarded to replace EFC). *Average financial aid package:* $14,445 (excluding resources awarded to replace EFC). 10% of all full-time freshmen had no need and received non-need-based aid.

UNDERGRADUATE FINANCIAL AID (Fall 1999, est.) 2,591 applied for aid; of those 84% were deemed to have need. 96% of undergraduates with need received aid; of those 24% had need fully met. *Average percent of need met:* 76% (excluding resources awarded to replace EFC). *Average financial aid package:* $12,759 (excluding resources awarded to replace EFC). 7% of all full-time undergraduates had no need and received non-need-based aid.

GIFT AID (NEED-BASED) ***Total amount:*** $20,914,334 (8% Federal, 11% state, 81% institutional). ***Receiving aid:*** *Freshmen:* 61% (585); *all full-time undergraduates:* 57% (2,043). ***Average award:*** Freshmen: $9446; Undergraduates: $8724. ***Scholarships, grants, and awards:*** Federal Pell, FSEOG, state, private, college/university gift aid from institutional funds.

GIFT AID (NON-NEED-BASED) ***Total amount:*** $2,675,447 (97% institutional, 3% external sources). ***Receiving aid:*** *Freshmen:* 7% (67); *Undergraduates:* 5% (185). ***Scholarships, grants, and awards by category:*** *Academic Interests/Achievement:* general academic interests/achievements. *Special Characteristics:* children of educators, children of faculty/staff, members of minority groups, siblings of current students. ***Tuition waivers:*** Full or partial for employees or children of employees, senior citizens. ***ROTC:*** Army, Air Force cooperative.

LOANS ***Student loans:*** $11,732,000 (100% need-based). 60% of past graduating class borrowed through all loan programs. Average indebtedness per student: $14,800. ***Average need-based loan:*** Freshmen: $4522; Undergraduates: $3675. ***Parent loans:*** $3,331,934 (86% need-based, 14% non-need-based). ***Programs:*** FFEL (Subsidized and Unsubsidized Stafford, PLUS), Perkins.

WORK-STUDY ***Federal work-study:*** *Total amount:* $1,036,494; 525 jobs averaging $2000. ***State or other work-study/employment:*** *Total amount:* $63,250 (100% need-based). Part-time jobs available.

APPLYING for FINANCIAL AID ***Required financial aid forms:*** FAFSA, institution's own form, CSS Financial Aid PROFILE. ***Financial aid deadline (priority):*** 2/15. ***Notification date:*** Continuous beginning 3/10. Students must reply by 5/1 or within 2 weeks of notification.

CONTACT Mr. William R. Burke, Director of Financial Aid, The University of Scranton, St. Thomas Hall 401, Scranton, PA 18510, 570-941-7887 or toll-free 888-SCRANTON. *Fax:* 570-941-4370. *E-mail:* finaid@uofs.edu

UNIVERSITY OF SIOUX FALLS

Sioux Falls, SD

ABOUT THE INSTITUTION Independent American Baptist, coed. Awards: associate, bachelor's, and master's degrees. 57 undergraduate majors. Total enrollment: 1,107. Undergraduates: 946. Freshmen: 181.

GIFT AID (NEED-BASED) ***Scholarships, grants, and awards:*** Federal Pell, FSEOG, private, college/university gift aid from institutional funds.

GIFT AID (NON-NEED-BASED) ***Scholarships, grants, and awards by category:*** *Academic Interests/Achievement:* biological sciences, business, communication, computer science, education, engineering/technologies, English, general academic interests/achievements, humanities, mathematics, physical sciences, premedicine, religion/biblical studies, social sciences. *Creative Arts/Performance:* music, theater/drama. *Special Achievements/Activities:* leadership, memberships. *Special Characteristics:* international students, out-of-state students, religious affiliation.

LOANS ***Programs:*** Federal Direct (Subsidized and Unsubsidized Stafford, PLUS), FFEL (Subsidized and Unsubsidized Stafford, PLUS), Perkins, state.

WORK-STUDY ***Federal work-study:*** *Total amount:* $207,545; 180 jobs averaging $1200.

APPLYING for FINANCIAL AID ***Required financial aid forms:*** FAFSA, institution's own form.

CONTACT Director of Financial Aid, University of Sioux Falls, 1101 West 22nd Street, Sioux Falls, SD 57105-1699, 605-331-6623 or toll-free 800-888-1047 (out-of-state).

UNIVERSITY OF SOUTH ALABAMA

Mobile, AL

Tuition & fees (AL res): $2670 **Average undergraduate aid package: $5702**

ABOUT THE INSTITUTION State-supported, coed. Awards: bachelor's, master's, doctoral, and first professional degrees. 75 undergraduate majors. Total enrollment: 11,185. Undergraduates: 9,029. Freshmen: 1,210. Federal methodology is used as a basis for awarding need-based institutional aid.

UNDERGRADUATE EXPENSES for 2000–2001 ***Application fee:*** $25. ***Tuition, state resident:*** full-time $2670; part-time $89 per semester hour. ***Tuition, nonresident:*** full-time $5340; part-time $178 per semester hour. ***Required fees:*** $90 per term part-time. Full-time tuition and fees vary according to course level, course load, and program. Part-time tuition and fees vary according to course level, course load, and program. ***College room and board:*** $3114; ***room only:*** $1604. Room and board charges vary according to board plan and student level.

FRESHMAN FINANCIAL AID (Fall 1998) 1290 applied for aid; of those 99% were deemed to have need. 94% of freshmen with need received aid; of those 2% had need fully met. *Average percent of need met:* 45% (excluding resources awarded to replace EFC). *Average financial aid package:* $4046 (excluding resources awarded to replace EFC).

UNDERGRADUATE FINANCIAL AID (Fall 1998) 4,077 applied for aid; of those 99% were deemed to have need. 96% of undergraduates with need received aid; of those 3% had need fully met. *Average percent of need met:* 45% (excluding resources awarded to replace EFC). *Average financial aid package:* $5702 (excluding resources awarded to replace EFC).

GIFT AID (NEED-BASED) ***Total amount:*** $6,198,087 (91% Federal, 2% state, 7% external sources). ***Receiving aid:*** *Freshmen:* 33% (668); *all full-time undergraduates:* 37% (2,370). ***Scholarships, grants, and awards:*** Federal Pell, FSEOG, state, college/university gift aid from institutional funds.

GIFT AID (NON-NEED-BASED) ***Total amount:*** $1,513,103 (100% institutional). ***Receiving aid:*** *Freshmen:* 16% (322); *Undergraduates:* 12% (756). ***Scholarships, grants, and awards by category:*** *Academic Interests/Achievement:* 500 awards ($1,367,527 total): business, general academic interests/achievements. *Creative Arts/Performance:* 87 awards ($63,776 total): art/fine arts, journalism/publications, music, theater/drama. *Special Achievements/Activities:* 120 awards ($72,000 total): general special achievements/activities, hobbies/interests, junior miss, leadership. *Special Characteristics:* 11 awards ($9800 total): children and siblings of alumni, children of faculty/staff, members of minority groups. ***Tuition waivers:*** Full or partial for employees or children of employees. ***ROTC:*** Army, Air Force.

LOANS ***Student loans:*** $31,636,799 (55% need-based, 45% non-need-based). 55% of past graduating class borrowed through all loan programs. ***Parent loans:*** $804,803 (100% non-need-based). ***Programs:*** FFEL (Subsidized and Unsubsidized Stafford, PLUS), Perkins.

WORK-STUDY ***Federal work-study:*** *Total amount:* $386,594; 120 jobs available. ***State or other work-study/employment:*** *Total amount:* $1,000,000 (100% non-need-based). 400 part-time jobs available.

ATHLETIC AWARDS *Total amount:* 1,077,822 (100% non-need-based).

APPLYING for FINANCIAL AID ***Required financial aid forms:*** FAFSA, institution's own form. ***Financial aid deadline:*** Continuous. ***Notification date:*** Continuous beginning 5/1.

CONTACT Financial Aid Office, University of South Alabama, 260 Administration Building, Mobile, AL 36688-0002, 334-460-6231 or toll-free 800-872-5247. *Fax:* 334-460-7023. *E-mail:* finaid@usamail.usouthal.edu

UNIVERSITY OF SOUTH CAROLINA

Columbia, SC

Tuition & fees (SC res): $3740 **Average undergraduate aid package: $3211**

ABOUT THE INSTITUTION State-supported, coed. Awards: associate, bachelor's, master's, doctoral, and first professional degrees and post-master's certificates. 62 undergraduate majors. Total enrollment: 23,430. Undergraduates: 15,551. Freshmen: 2,668. Federal methodology is used as a basis for awarding need-based institutional aid.

UNDERGRADUATE EXPENSES for 1999–2000 ***Application fee:*** $35. ***One-time required fee:*** $25. ***Tuition, state resident:*** full-time $3640; part-time $172 per credit hour. ***Tuition, nonresident:*** full-time $9714; part-time $442 per credit hour. ***Required fees:*** full-time $100; $4 per credit hour. Full-time tuition and fees vary according to program and reciprocity agreements. Part-time tuition and fees vary according to course load. ***College room and board:*** $4167; ***room only:*** $2352. Room and board charges vary according to board plan, housing facility, and location. ***Payment plans:*** installment, deferred payment.

FRESHMAN FINANCIAL AID (Fall 1998) 1417 applied for aid; of those 79% were deemed to have need. 97% of freshmen with need received aid; of those 25% had need fully met. *Average percent of need met:* 63% (excluding resources awarded to replace EFC). *Average financial aid package:* $2720 (excluding resources awarded to replace EFC). 11% of all full-time freshmen had no need and received non-need-based aid.

UNDERGRADUATE FINANCIAL AID (Fall 1998) 7,877 applied for aid; of those 90% were deemed to have need. 98% of undergraduates with need received aid; of those 28% had need fully met. *Average percent of need met:* 65% (excluding resources awarded to replace EFC). *Average financial aid package:* $3211 (excluding resources awarded to replace EFC). 12% of all full-time undergraduates had no need and received non-need-based aid.

GIFT AID (NEED-BASED) ***Total amount:*** $10,242,168 (80% Federal, 20% state). ***Receiving aid:*** *Freshmen:* 15% (412); *all full-time undergraduates:* 27% (3,397). ***Average award:*** Freshmen: $900; Undergraduates: $1100. ***Scholarships, grants, and awards:*** Federal Pell, FSEOG, state, private, college/university gift aid from institutional funds, United Negro College Fund, Federal Nursing.

GIFT AID (NON-NEED-BASED) ***Total amount:*** $18,222,513 (47% state, 33% institutional, 20% external sources). ***Receiving aid:*** *Freshmen:* 8% (227); *Undergraduates:* 17% (2,113). ***Scholarships, grants, and awards by category:*** *Academic Interests/Achievement:* 3,402 awards ($4,769,911 total): biological sciences, business, communication, computer science, education, engineering/technologies, English, general academic interests/achievements, health fields, humanities, international studies, library science, mathematics, military science, physical sciences, premedicine, religion/biblical studies, social sciences. *Creative Arts/Performance:* 649 awards ($874,461 total): art/fine arts, creative writing, debating, general creative arts/performance, journalism/publications, music, performing arts, theater/drama. *Special Achievements/Activities:* 530 awards ($750,901 total): cheerleading/drum major, community service, general special achievements/activities, hobbies/interests, leadership, religious involvement. *Special Characteristics:* 1,089 awards ($1,554,246 total): adult students, children and siblings of alumni, children of faculty/staff, children of public servants, children of union members/company employees, children of workers in trades, children with a deceased or disabled parent, ethnic background, first-generation college students, general special characteristics, handicapped students, international students, members of minority groups, public servants, relatives of clergy, religious affiliation, spouses of deceased or disabled public servants. ***Tuition waivers:*** Full or partial for employees or children of employees, senior citizens. ***ROTC:*** Army, Naval, Air Force.

LOANS ***Student loans:*** $32,921,722 (88% need-based, 12% non-need-based). 60% of past graduating class borrowed through all loan programs. Average indebtedness per student: $16,200. ***Average need-based loan:*** Freshmen: $1900; Undergraduates: $2300. ***Parent loans:*** $5,916,552 (100% non-need-based). ***Programs:*** FFEL (Subsidized and Unsubsidized Stafford, PLUS), Perkins, Federal Nursing.

WORK-STUDY ***Federal work-study:*** *Total amount:* $1,161,315; 934 jobs averaging $1243. ***State or other work-study/employment:*** *Total amount:* $8,953,200 (100% non-need-based). 2,700 part-time jobs averaging $3316.

ATHLETIC AWARDS *Total amount:* 2,685,516 (100% non-need-based).

APPLYING for FINANCIAL AID ***Required financial aid form:*** FAFSA. ***Financial aid deadline (priority):*** 4/15. ***Notification date:*** Continuous beginning 5/1.

University of South Carolina (continued)

CONTACT Dr. Ed Miller, Financial Aid Director, University of South Carolina, 1714 College Street, Columbia, SC 29208, 803-777-8134 or toll-free 800-868-5872 (in-state). *Fax:* 803-777-0941.

UNIVERSITY OF SOUTH CAROLINA AIKEN

Aiken, SC

Tuition & fees (SC res): $3358 **Average undergraduate aid package: N/A**

ABOUT THE INSTITUTION State-supported, coed. Awards: associate, bachelor's, and master's degrees. 18 undergraduate majors. Total enrollment: 3,179. Undergraduates: 3,107. Freshmen: 536. Federal methodology is used as a basis for awarding need-based institutional aid.

UNDERGRADUATE EXPENSES for 1999–2000 ***Application fee:*** $25. ***One-time required fee:*** $50. ***Tuition, state resident:*** full-time $3218; part-time $141 per semester hour. ***Tuition, nonresident:*** full-time $7744; part-time $340 per semester hour. ***Required fees:*** full-time $140; $5 per semester hour; $10 per term part-time. ***College room and board:*** $3940; ***room only:*** $2390. Room and board charges vary according to board plan. ***Payment plan:*** deferred payment.

GIFT AID (NEED-BASED) ***Scholarships, grants, and awards:*** Federal Pell, FSEOG, state, private, college/university gift aid from institutional funds.

GIFT AID (NON-NEED-BASED) ***Scholarships, grants, and awards by category:*** *Academic Interests/Achievement:* biological sciences, business, communication, computer science, education, engineering/technologies, English, general academic interests/achievements, humanities, mathematics, physical sciences, social sciences. *Creative Arts/Performance:* art/fine arts, creative writing, journalism/publications, music. *Special Achievements/Activities:* cheerleading/drum major. ***Tuition waivers:*** Full or partial for employees or children of employees, senior citizens.

LOANS ***Programs:*** FFEL (Subsidized and Unsubsidized Stafford, PLUS), Perkins, college/university.

WORK-STUDY Federal work-study jobs available.

APPLYING for FINANCIAL AID ***Required financial aid form:*** FAFSA. ***Financial aid deadline (priority):*** 3/15. ***Notification date:*** Continuous beginning 5/1. Students must reply within 4 weeks of notification.

CONTACT Mr. A. Glenn Shumpert, Director of Financial Aid, University of South Carolina Aiken, 471 University Parkway, Aiken, SC 29801, 803-641-3476 or toll-free 888-WOW-USCA.

UNIVERSITY OF SOUTH CAROLINA SPARTANBURG

Spartanburg, SC

Tuition & fees (SC res): $3428 **Average undergraduate aid package: $3507**

ABOUT THE INSTITUTION State-supported, coed. Awards: associate, bachelor's, and master's degrees. 20 undergraduate majors. Total enrollment: 3,778. Undergraduates: 3,492. Freshmen: 601. Federal methodology is used as a basis for awarding need-based institutional aid.

UNDERGRADUATE EXPENSES for 1999–2000 ***Application fee:*** $25. ***One-time required fee:*** $50. ***Tuition, state resident:*** full-time $3250; part-time $143 per semester hour. ***Tuition, nonresident:*** full-time $7776; part-time $342 per semester hour. ***Required fees:*** full-time $178; $5 per semester hour; $20 per term part-time. Part-time tuition and fees vary according to course load. ***College room and board:*** $3950; ***room only:*** $2370. Room and board charges vary according to board plan. ***Payment plan:*** deferred payment.

FRESHMAN FINANCIAL AID (Fall 1999, est.) 404 applied for aid; of those 69% were deemed to have need. 96% of freshmen with need received aid. *Average percent of need met:* 30% (excluding resources awarded to replace EFC). *Average financial aid package:* $2762 (excluding resources awarded to replace EFC). 16% of all full-time freshmen had no need and received non-need-based aid.

UNDERGRADUATE FINANCIAL AID (Fall 1999, est.) 1,779 applied for aid; of those 75% were deemed to have need. 95% of undergraduates with need received aid. *Average percent of need met:* 37% (excluding resources awarded to replace EFC). *Average financial aid package:* $3507 (excluding resources awarded to replace EFC). 13% of all full-time undergraduates had no need and received non-need-based aid.

GIFT AID (NEED-BASED) ***Total amount:*** $2,633,571 (87% Federal, 13% state). ***Receiving aid:*** *Freshmen:* 33% (183); *all full-time undergraduates:* 33% (861). ***Average award:*** Freshmen: $1526; Undergraduates: $1446. ***Scholarships, grants, and awards:*** Federal Pell, FSEOG, state, private, college/university gift aid from institutional funds.

GIFT AID (NON-NEED-BASED) ***Total amount:*** $1,205,039 (68% state, 32% institutional). ***Receiving aid:*** *Freshmen:* 16% (92); *Undergraduates:* 10% (268). ***Scholarships, grants, and awards by category:*** *Academic Interests/Achievement:* 362 awards ($395,579 total): general academic interests/achievements. ***Tuition waivers:*** Full or partial for senior citizens. ***ROTC:*** Army cooperative.

LOANS ***Student loans:*** $4,818,228 (96% need-based, 4% non-need-based). 56% of past graduating class borrowed through all loan programs. Average indebtedness per student: $13,597. ***Average need-based loan:*** Freshmen: $1269; Undergraduates: $1772. ***Parent loans:*** $280,787 (100% non-need-based). ***Programs:*** FFEL (Subsidized and Unsubsidized Stafford, PLUS), Perkins.

WORK-STUDY ***Federal work-study:*** *Total amount:* $190,389; 121 jobs averaging $1573.

ATHLETIC AWARDS *Total amount:* 357,148 (100% non-need-based).

APPLYING for FINANCIAL AID ***Required financial aid form:*** FAFSA. ***Financial aid deadline (priority):*** 3/1. ***Notification date:*** Continuous beginning 4/1. Students must reply within 2 weeks of notification.

CONTACT Kay Cash Walton, Director of Financial Aid, University of South Carolina Spartanburg, 800 University Way, Spartanburg, SC 29303-4932, 864-503-5340 or toll-free 800-277-8727. *Fax:* 864-503-5974.

UNIVERSITY OF SOUTH DAKOTA

Vermillion, SD

Tuition & fees (SD res): $3459 **Average undergraduate aid package: $5820**

ABOUT THE INSTITUTION State-supported, coed. Awards: associate, bachelor's, master's, doctoral, and first professional degrees. 79 undergraduate majors. Total enrollment: 6,904. Undergraduates: 5,138. Freshmen: 966. Federal methodology is used as a basis for awarding need-based institutional aid.

UNDERGRADUATE EXPENSES for 1999–2000 ***Application fee:*** $15. ***Tuition, state resident:*** full-time $1867; part-time $58 per credit hour. ***Tuition, nonresident:*** full-time $5941; part-time $186 per credit hour. ***Required fees:*** full-time $1592; $50 per credit hour. Full-time tuition and fees vary according to course load and reciprocity agreements. Part-time tuition and fees vary according to course load and reciprocity agreements. ***College room and board:*** $3094; ***room only:*** $1408. Room and board charges vary according to board plan and housing facility. ***Payment plans:*** installment, deferred payment.

UNDERGRADUATE FINANCIAL AID (Fall 1998) 3,980 applied for aid; of those 94% were deemed to have need. 100% of undergraduates with need received aid; of those 80% had need fully met. *Average percent of need met:* 77% (excluding resources awarded to replace EFC). *Average financial aid package:* $5820 (excluding resources awarded to replace EFC). 14% of all full-time undergraduates had no need and received non-need-based aid.

GIFT AID (NEED-BASED) ***Total amount:*** $4,057,403 (85% Federal, 11% institutional, 4% external sources). ***Receiving aid:*** *All full-time undergraduates:* 33% (1,472). ***Average award:*** Undergraduates: $1164. ***Scholarships, grants, and awards:*** Federal Pell, FSEOG, private, college/university gift aid from institutional funds, Federal Nursing.

GIFT AID (NON-NEED-BASED) ***Total amount:*** $1,397,529 (2% Federal, 13% state, 63% institutional, 22% external sources). ***Receiving aid:*** *Undergraduates:* 3% (123). ***Scholarships, grants, and awards by category:*** *Academic Interests/Achievement:* biological sciences, business, communication, computer science, education, English, foreign languages, general academic interests/achievements, humanities, mathematics, military science, premedicine, social sciences. *Creative Arts/Performance:* art/fine arts, creative writing, debating, music, theater/drama. *Special Achievements/Activities:* leadership. *Special Characteristics:* members of minority groups. ***Tuition waivers:*** Full or partial for children of alumni, senior citizens. ***ROTC:*** Army.

LOANS ***Student loans:*** $15,747,636 (71% need-based, 29% non-need-based). ***Average need-based loan:*** Undergraduates: $4281. ***Parent loans:*** $1,495,486 (100% non-need-based). ***Programs:*** FFEL (Subsidized and Unsubsidized Stafford, PLUS), Perkins, Federal Nursing, alternative loans.

WORK-STUDY ***Federal work-study:*** *Total amount:* $801,677; jobs available. ***State or other work-study/employment:*** *Total amount:* $88,986 (100% non-need-based). Part-time jobs available.

ATHLETIC AWARDS *Total amount:* 430,823 (100% non-need-based).

APPLYING for FINANCIAL AID ***Required financial aid form:*** FAFSA. ***Financial aid deadline (priority):*** 3/1. ***Notification date:*** 5/1. Students must reply within 2 weeks of notification.

CONTACT Julie Pier, Director of Student Financial Aid, University of South Dakota, Slagle Hall, Room 14, 414 East Clark Street, Vermillion, SD 57069-2390, 605-677-5446 or toll-free 877-269-6837. *Fax:* 605-677-5238.

UNIVERSITY OF SOUTHERN CALIFORNIA

Los Angeles, CA

Tuition & fees: $22,636 **Average undergraduate aid package: $23,393**

ABOUT THE INSTITUTION Independent, coed. Awards: bachelor's, master's, doctoral, and first professional degrees and post-master's certificates. 126 undergraduate majors. Total enrollment: 28,739. Undergraduates: 15,553. Freshmen: 2,980. Institutional methodology is used as a basis for awarding need-based institutional aid.

UNDERGRADUATE EXPENSES for 1999–2000 ***Application fee:*** $55. ***Comprehensive fee:*** $29,918 includes full-time tuition ($22,198), mandatory fees ($438), and room and board ($7282). Room and board charges vary according to board plan and housing facility. ***Part-time tuition:*** $748 per unit. ***Part-time fees:*** $219 per term part-time. Part-time tuition and fees vary according to course load. ***Payment plans:*** tuition prepayment, installment.

FRESHMAN FINANCIAL AID (Fall 1999) 1652 applied for aid; of those 86% were deemed to have need. 100% of freshmen with need received aid; of those 100% had need fully met. *Average percent of need met:* 100% (excluding resources awarded to replace EFC). *Average financial aid package:* $22,354 (excluding resources awarded to replace EFC). 15% of all full-time freshmen had no need and received non-need-based aid.

UNDERGRADUATE FINANCIAL AID (Fall 1999) 8,850 applied for aid; of those 91% were deemed to have need. 100% of undergraduates with need received aid; of those 88% had need fully met. *Average percent of need met:* 97% (excluding resources awarded to replace EFC). *Average financial aid package:* $23,393 (excluding resources awarded to replace EFC). 11% of all full-time undergraduates had no need and received non-need-based aid.

GIFT AID (NEED-BASED) ***Total amount:*** $102,643,427 (12% Federal, 23% state, 65% institutional). ***Receiving aid:*** *Freshmen:* 47% (1,340); *all full-time undergraduates:* 49% (7,159). ***Average award:*** Freshmen: $16,854; Undergraduates: $14,338. ***Scholarships, grants, and awards:*** Federal Pell, FSEOG, state, college/university gift aid from institutional funds.

GIFT AID (NON-NEED-BASED) ***Total amount:*** $30,352,782 (78% institutional, 22% external sources). ***Receiving aid:*** *Freshmen:* 8% (226); *Undergraduates:* 6% (826). ***Scholarships, grants, and awards by category:*** *Academic Interests/Achievement:* general academic interests/achievements. *Creative Arts/Performance:* debating. *Special Characteristics:* children and siblings of alumni, local/state students, members of minority groups. ***Tuition waivers:*** Full or partial for employees or children of employees. ***ROTC:*** Army, Naval, Air Force.

LOANS ***Student loans:*** $59,948,555 (52% need-based, 48% non-need-based). 71% of past graduating class borrowed through all loan programs. Average indebtedness per student: $14,722. ***Average need-based loan:*** Freshmen: $2492; Undergraduates: $4025. ***Parent loans:*** $19,093,684 (100% non-need-based). ***Programs:*** FFEL (Subsidized and Unsubsidized Stafford, PLUS), Perkins, college/university.

WORK-STUDY ***Federal work-study:*** *Total amount:* $10,648,172; 5,679 jobs averaging $1875.

ATHLETIC AWARDS *Total amount:* 7,223,386 (21% need-based, 79% non-need-based).

APPLYING for FINANCIAL AID ***Required financial aid forms:*** FAFSA, CSS Financial Aid PROFILE, state aid form, parent and student federal income tax forms (with all schedules and W-2 forms). ***Financial aid deadline (priority):*** 1/31. ***Notification date:*** Continuous beginning 3/1. Students must reply by 5/1.

CONTACT Catherine C. Thomas, Associate Dean of Admissions and Financial Aid, University of Southern California, University Park Campus, Los Angeles, CA 90089-0914, 213-740-1111. *Fax:* 213-740-0680.

UNIVERSITY OF SOUTHERN COLORADO

Pueblo, CO

Tuition & fees (CO res): $2307 **Average undergraduate aid package: $6891**

ABOUT THE INSTITUTION State-supported, coed. Awards: bachelor's and master's degrees. 68 undergraduate majors. Total enrollment: 5,791. Undergraduates: 5,122. Freshmen: 646. Federal methodology is used as a basis for awarding need-based institutional aid.

UNDERGRADUATE EXPENSES for 1999–2000 ***Application fee:*** $25. ***Tuition, state resident:*** full-time $1808; part-time $90 per semester hour. ***Tuition, nonresident:*** full-time $8448; part-time $422 per semester hour. ***Required fees:*** full-time $499; $23 per semester hour. Full-time tuition and fees vary according to reciprocity agreements. Part-time tuition and fees vary according to reciprocity agreements. ***College room and board:*** $4768; ***room only:*** $2088. Room and board charges vary according to board plan and housing facility. ***Payment plans:*** installment, deferred payment.

FRESHMAN FINANCIAL AID (Fall 1999, est.) *Average percent of need met:* 58% (excluding resources awarded to replace EFC). *Average financial aid package:* $5268 (excluding resources awarded to replace EFC).

UNDERGRADUATE FINANCIAL AID (Fall 1999, est.) *Average percent of need met:* 64% (excluding resources awarded to replace EFC). *Average financial aid package:* $6891 (excluding resources awarded to replace EFC).

GIFT AID (NEED-BASED) ***Total amount:*** $6,636,407 (62% Federal, 22% state, 11% institutional, 5% external sources). ***Scholarships, grants, and awards:*** Federal Pell, FSEOG, state, private, college/university gift aid from institutional funds.

GIFT AID (NON-NEED-BASED) ***Total amount:*** $820,731 (18% state, 57% institutional, 25% external sources). ***Scholarships, grants, and awards by category:*** *Academic Interests/Achievement:* biological sciences, business, computer science, engineering/technologies, general academic interests/achievements, international studies, mathematics, premedicine. *Creative Arts/Performance:* applied art and design, art/fine arts, cinema/film/broadcasting, journalism/publications, music, performing arts, theater/drama. *Special Achievements/Activities:* community service, general special achievements/activities, leadership. *Special Characteristics:* first-generation college students, general special characteristics. ***Tuition waivers:*** Full or partial for employees or children of employees, senior citizens. ***ROTC:*** Army cooperative.

LOANS ***Student loans:*** $12,983,898 (90% need-based, 10% non-need-based). 57% of past graduating class borrowed through all loan programs. ***Parent loans:*** $2,216,344 (39% need-based, 61% non-need-based). ***Programs:*** FFEL (Subsidized and Unsubsidized Stafford, PLUS), Perkins.

WORK-STUDY ***Federal work-study:*** *Total amount:* $607,437; 325 jobs averaging $1800. ***State or other work-study/employment:*** *Total amount:* $673,697 (81% need-based, 19% non-need-based). Part-time jobs available.

ATHLETIC AWARDS *Total amount:* 136,795 (47% need-based, 53% non-need-based).

University of Southern Colorado (continued)

APPLYING for FINANCIAL AID ***Required financial aid form:*** FAFSA. ***Financial aid deadline (priority):*** 3/1. ***Notification date:*** Continuous. Students must reply within 3 weeks of notification.

CONTACT Mr. Donald Ortega, Director of Student Financial Services, University of Southern Colorado, 2200 Bonforte Boulevard, Pueblo, CO 81001-4901, 719-549-2232 or toll-free 877-872-9653. *Fax:* 719-549-2088. *E-mail:* ortega@uscolo.edu

UNIVERSITY OF SOUTHERN INDIANA

Evansville, IN

Tuition & fees (IN res): $2920 **Average undergraduate aid package: $4394**

ABOUT THE INSTITUTION State-supported, coed. Awards: associate, bachelor's, and master's degrees and post-bachelor's certificates. 48 undergraduate majors. Total enrollment: 8,695. Undergraduates: 8,217. Freshmen: 1,809. Federal methodology is used as a basis for awarding need-based institutional aid.

UNDERGRADUATE EXPENSES for 1999–2000 ***Application fee:*** $25. ***One-time required fee:*** $62. ***Tuition, state resident:*** full-time $2860; part-time $92 per semester hour. ***Tuition, nonresident:*** full-time $7006; part-time $226 per semester hour. ***Required fees:*** full-time $60; $23 per term part-time. Part-time tuition and fees vary according to course load. ***College room and board: room only:*** $2286. Room and board charges vary according to housing facility. ***Payment plan:*** installment.

FRESHMAN FINANCIAL AID (Fall 1999) 1432 applied for aid; of those 70% were deemed to have need. 89% of freshmen with need received aid; of those 23% had need fully met. *Average percent of need met:* 41% (excluding resources awarded to replace EFC). *Average financial aid package:* $3925 (excluding resources awarded to replace EFC). 21% of all full-time freshmen had no need and received non-need-based aid.

UNDERGRADUATE FINANCIAL AID (Fall 1999) 4,826 applied for aid; of those 76% were deemed to have need. 91% of undergraduates with need received aid; of those 30% had need fully met. *Average percent of need met:* 44% (excluding resources awarded to replace EFC). *Average financial aid package:* $4394 (excluding resources awarded to replace EFC). 20% of all full-time undergraduates had no need and received non-need-based aid.

GIFT AID (NEED-BASED) ***Total amount:*** $7,219,643 (47% Federal, 34% state, 10% institutional, 9% external sources). ***Receiving aid:*** *Freshmen:* 36% (609); *all full-time undergraduates:* 35% (2,215). ***Average award:*** Freshmen: $3092; Undergraduates: $3040. ***Scholarships, grants, and awards:*** Federal Pell, FSEOG, state, private, college/university gift aid from institutional funds.

GIFT AID (NON-NEED-BASED) ***Total amount:*** $1,094,890 (63% institutional, 37% external sources). ***Receiving aid:*** *Freshmen:* 2% (37); *Undergraduates:* 5% (298). ***Scholarships, grants, and awards by category:*** *Academic Interests/Achievement:* business, communication, education, engineering/technologies, foreign languages, general academic interests/achievements, health fields, humanities, mathematics, physical sciences, premedicine, social sciences. *Creative Arts/Performance:* art/fine arts, creative writing, music, theater/drama. *Special Achievements/Activities:* leadership. *Special Characteristics:* children of faculty/staff, out-of-state students, spouses of current students. ***Tuition waivers:*** Full or partial for employees or children of employees, senior citizens.

LOANS ***Student loans:*** $11,062,549 (74% need-based, 26% non-need-based). 39% of past graduating class borrowed through all loan programs. Average indebtedness per student: $13,695. ***Average need-based loan:*** Freshmen: $2599; Undergraduates: $3421. ***Parent loans:*** $249,233 (100% need-based). ***Programs:*** FFEL (Subsidized and Unsubsidized Stafford, PLUS), Perkins.

WORK-STUDY ***Federal work-study:*** *Total amount:* $253,640; jobs available.

ATHLETIC AWARDS *Total amount:* 447,988 (46% need-based, 54% non-need-based).

APPLYING for FINANCIAL AID ***Required financial aid forms:*** FAFSA, institution's own form. ***Financial aid deadline (priority):*** 3/1. ***Notification date:*** Continuous beginning 4/15.

CONTACT Ms. Rebecca Horton, Financial Assistance Counselor, University of Southern Indiana, 8600 University Boulevard, Evansville, IN 47712-3590, 812-464-1767 or toll-free 800-467-1965. *Fax:* 812-465-7154. *E-mail:* finaid@usi.edu

UNIVERSITY OF SOUTHERN MAINE

Portland, ME

Tuition & fees (ME res): $4192 **Average undergraduate aid package: $7446**

ABOUT THE INSTITUTION State-supported, coed. Awards: associate, bachelor's, master's, doctoral, and first professional degrees and post-master's certificates. 46 undergraduate majors. Total enrollment: 10,645. Undergraduates: 8,703. Freshmen: 953. Federal methodology is used as a basis for awarding need-based institutional aid.

UNDERGRADUATE EXPENSES for 1999–2000 ***Application fee:*** $25. ***One-time required fee:*** $15. ***Tuition, state resident:*** full-time $3630; part-time $121 per credit hour. ***Tuition, nonresident:*** full-time $10,110; part-time $337 per credit hour. ***Required fees:*** full-time $562; $13 per credit hour; $70 per term part-time. Full-time tuition and fees vary according to course load, degree level, location, and reciprocity agreements. Part-time tuition and fees vary according to course load, degree level, location, and reciprocity agreements. ***College room and board:*** $4926; ***room only:*** $2548. Room and board charges vary according to housing facility. ***Payment plan:*** installment.

FRESHMAN FINANCIAL AID (Fall 1999) 693 applied for aid; of those 85% were deemed to have need. 96% of freshmen with need received aid; of those 15% had need fully met. *Average percent of need met:* 73% (excluding resources awarded to replace EFC). *Average financial aid package:* $6079 (excluding resources awarded to replace EFC). 9% of all full-time freshmen had no need and received non-need-based aid.

UNDERGRADUATE FINANCIAL AID (Fall 1999) 3,260 applied for aid; of those 88% were deemed to have need. 97% of undergraduates with need received aid; of those 27% had need fully met. *Average percent of need met:* 82% (excluding resources awarded to replace EFC). *Average financial aid package:* $7446 (excluding resources awarded to replace EFC). 8% of all full-time undergraduates had no need and received non-need-based aid.

GIFT AID (NEED-BASED) ***Total amount:*** $8,655,497 (65% Federal, 15% state, 7% institutional, 13% external sources). ***Receiving aid:*** *Freshmen:* 56% (462); *all full-time undergraduates:* 56% (2,186). ***Average award:*** Freshmen: $3394; Undergraduates: $3352. ***Scholarships, grants, and awards:*** Federal Pell, FSEOG, state, college/university gift aid from institutional funds.

GIFT AID (NON-NEED-BASED) ***Total amount:*** $599,660 (76% institutional, 24% external sources). ***Receiving aid:*** *Freshmen:* 2% (15); *Undergraduates:* 1% (49). ***Scholarships, grants, and awards by category:*** *Academic Interests/Achievement:* general academic interests/achievements. *Creative Arts/Performance:* music, theater/drama. *Special Achievements/Activities:* community service. *Special Characteristics:* general special characteristics, local/state students. ***Tuition waivers:*** Full or partial for minority students, employees or children of employees, senior citizens. ***ROTC:*** Air Force cooperative.

LOANS ***Student loans:*** $15,844,967 (69% need-based, 31% non-need-based). ***Average need-based loan:*** Freshmen: $2704; Undergraduates: $3709. ***Programs:*** FFEL (Subsidized and Unsubsidized Stafford, PLUS), Perkins, Federal Nursing, college/university.

WORK-STUDY ***Federal work-study:*** *Total amount:* $3,069,799; jobs available.

APPLYING for FINANCIAL AID ***Required financial aid form:*** FAFSA. ***Financial aid deadline (priority):*** 2/15. ***Notification date:*** Continuous beginning 3/15. Students must reply within 2 weeks of notification.

CONTACT Mr. Keith P. Dubois, Director of Student Financial Aid, University of Southern Maine, 96 Falmouth Street, PO Box 9300, Portland, ME 04104-9300, 207-780-5250 or toll-free 800-800-4USM Ext. 5670. *E-mail:* dubois@maine.maine.edu

UNIVERSITY OF SOUTHERN MISSISSIPPI

Hattiesburg, MS

Tuition & fees (MS res): $2870 **Average undergraduate aid package: $6297**

ABOUT THE INSTITUTION State-supported, coed. Awards: bachelor's, master's, and doctoral degrees. 61 undergraduate majors. Total enrollment: 14,362. Undergraduates: 11,987. Freshmen: 1,307. Federal methodology is used as a basis for awarding need-based institutional aid.

UNDERGRADUATE EXPENSES for 1999–2000 ***Tuition, state resident:*** full-time $2870; part-time $105 per credit. ***Tuition, nonresident:*** full-time $5972; part-time $234 per credit. Part-time tuition and fees vary according to course load. ***College room and board:*** $3345; ***room only:*** $1785. Room and board charges vary according to board plan and housing facility. ***Payment plans:*** tuition prepayment, installment.

FRESHMAN FINANCIAL AID (Fall 1999, est.) 659 applied for aid; of those 56% were deemed to have need. 100% of freshmen with need received aid; of those 9% had need fully met. *Average percent of need met:* 94% (excluding resources awarded to replace EFC). *Average financial aid package:* $6652 (excluding resources awarded to replace EFC).

UNDERGRADUATE FINANCIAL AID (Fall 1999, est.) 8,730 applied for aid; of those 64% were deemed to have need. 100% of undergraduates with need received aid; of those 10% had need fully met. *Average percent of need met:* 85% (excluding resources awarded to replace EFC). *Average financial aid package:* $6297 (excluding resources awarded to replace EFC).

GIFT AID (NEED-BASED) ***Total amount:*** $13,946,300 (65% Federal, 11% state, 16% institutional, 8% external sources). ***Receiving aid:*** *Freshmen:* 32% (230); *all full-time undergraduates:* 38% (3,701). ***Average award:*** Freshmen: $2409; Undergraduates: $2425. ***Scholarships, grants, and awards:*** Federal Pell, FSEOG, state, private, college/university gift aid from institutional funds.

GIFT AID (NON-NEED-BASED) ***Total amount:*** $5,812,723 (23% state, 58% institutional, 19% external sources). ***Receiving aid:*** *Freshmen:* 32% (231); *Undergraduates:* 31% (3,054). ***Scholarships, grants, and awards by category:*** *Academic Interests/Achievement:* 1,963 awards ($2,930,339 total): general academic interests/achievements. *Creative Arts/Performance:* 386 awards ($921,573 total): art/fine arts, dance, music, theater/drama. *Special Achievements/Activities:* 275 awards ($389,610 total): cheerleading/drum major, leadership. *Special Characteristics:* 825 awards ($1,465,111 total): children and siblings of alumni, children of faculty/staff, ethnic background, out-of-state students, veterans. ***Tuition waivers:*** Full or partial for children of alumni, employees or children of employees, senior citizens. ***ROTC:*** Army, Air Force.

LOANS ***Student loans:*** $28,193,421 (74% need-based, 26% non-need-based). 62% of past graduating class borrowed through all loan programs. Average indebtedness per student: $16,558. ***Average need-based loan:*** Freshmen: $2849; Undergraduates: $3013. ***Parent loans:*** $821,951 (29% need-based, 71% non-need-based). ***Programs:*** FFEL (Subsidized and Unsubsidized Stafford, PLUS), Perkins, Federal Nursing, college/university.

WORK-STUDY ***Federal work-study:*** *Total amount:* $1,047,524; 461 jobs averaging $2275.

ATHLETIC AWARDS *Total amount:* 2,186,565 (100% non-need-based).

APPLYING for FINANCIAL AID ***Required financial aid forms:*** FAFSA, institution's own form, state aid form. ***Financial aid deadline (priority):*** 3/15. ***Notification date:*** Continuous. Students must reply within 2 weeks of notification.

CONTACT James B. Gibson Sr., Director of Financial Aid, University of Southern Mississippi, Box 5101, Hattiesburg, MS 39406-5101, 601-266-4774. *E-mail:* james.b.gibson@usm.edu

UNIVERSITY OF SOUTH FLORIDA

Tampa, FL

Tuition & fees (FL res): $2256 **Average undergraduate aid package: $8336**

ABOUT THE INSTITUTION State-supported, coed. Awards: associate, bachelor's, master's, doctoral, and first professional degrees and post-bachelor's certificates. 78 undergraduate majors. Total enrollment: 35,118. Undergraduates: 28,916. Freshmen: 3,588. Federal methodology is used as a basis for awarding need-based institutional aid.

UNDERGRADUATE EXPENSES for 1999–2000 ***Application fee:*** $20. ***Tuition, state resident:*** full-time $2256; part-time $75 per semester hour. ***Tuition, nonresident:*** full-time $9245; part-time $308 per semester hour. Full-time tuition and fees vary according to course level, course load, and location. Part-time tuition and fees vary according to course level, course load, and location. ***College room and board:*** $4606; ***room only:*** $2406. Room and board charges vary according to board plan, housing facility, and location. ***Payment plans:*** tuition prepayment, installment.

FRESHMAN FINANCIAL AID (Fall 1999) 1801 applied for aid; of those 76% were deemed to have need. 99% of freshmen with need received aid; of those 26% had need fully met. *Average percent of need met:* 83% (excluding resources awarded to replace EFC). *Average financial aid package:* $6774 (excluding resources awarded to replace EFC). 12% of all full-time freshmen had no need and received non-need-based aid.

UNDERGRADUATE FINANCIAL AID (Fall 1999) 9,499 applied for aid; of those 84% were deemed to have need. 99% of undergraduates with need received aid; of those 25% had need fully met. *Average percent of need met:* 69% (excluding resources awarded to replace EFC). *Average financial aid package:* $8336 (excluding resources awarded to replace EFC). 5% of all full-time undergraduates had no need and received non-need-based aid.

GIFT AID (NEED-BASED) ***Total amount:*** $34,373,850 (56% Federal, 44% institutional). ***Receiving aid:*** *Freshmen:* 24% (703); *all full-time undergraduates:* 38% (6,188). ***Average award:*** Freshmen: $920; Undergraduates: $840. ***Scholarships, grants, and awards:*** Federal Pell, FSEOG, state, private, college/university gift aid from institutional funds.

GIFT AID (NON-NEED-BASED) ***Total amount:*** $37,660,424 (67% state, 27% institutional, 6% external sources). ***Receiving aid:*** *Freshmen:* 36% (1,069); *Undergraduates:* 21% (3,445). ***Scholarships, grants, and awards by category:*** *Academic Interests/Achievement:* architecture, biological sciences, business, communication, computer science, education, engineering/technologies, English, foreign languages, general academic interests/achievements, health fields, humanities, international studies, library science, mathematics, military science, physical sciences, premedicine, religion/biblical studies, social sciences. *Creative Arts/Performance:* applied art and design, art/fine arts, cinema/film/broadcasting, creative writing, dance, debating, journalism/publications, music, performing arts, theater/drama. *Special Achievements/Activities:* general special achievements/activities. *Special Characteristics:* general special characteristics. ***Tuition waivers:*** Full or partial for senior citizens. ***ROTC:*** Army, Air Force.

LOANS ***Student loans:*** $80,921,046 (59% need-based, 41% non-need-based). Average indebtedness per student: $16,900. ***Average need-based loan:*** Freshmen: $2530; Undergraduates: $3870. ***Parent loans:*** $1,849,214 (100% non-need-based). ***Programs:*** FFEL (Subsidized and Unsubsidized Stafford, PLUS), Perkins, Federal Nursing, college/university.

WORK-STUDY ***Federal work-study:*** *Total amount:* $3,893,379; jobs available.

ATHLETIC AWARDS *Total amount:* 1,504,889 (100% non-need-based).

APPLYING for FINANCIAL AID ***Required financial aid form:*** FAFSA. ***Financial aid deadline (priority):*** 3/1. ***Notification date:*** 4/10. Students must reply within 3 weeks of notification.

CONTACT Mr. Leonard Gude, Director of Financial Aid, University of South Florida, 4202 East Fowler Avenue, SVC 1102, Tampa, FL 33620-9951, 813-974-3039. *Fax:* 813-974-9689. *E-mail:* lgude@admin.usf.edu

UNIVERSITY OF SOUTH FLORIDA, NEW COLLEGE

Sarasota, FL

See New College of the University of South Florida

UNIVERSITY OF SOUTHWESTERN LOUISIANA

Lafayette, LA

See University of Louisiana at Lafayette

THE UNIVERSITY OF TAMPA

Tampa, FL

Tuition & fees: $15,542 **Average undergraduate aid package: $13,624**

ABOUT THE INSTITUTION Independent, coed. Awards: associate, bachelor's, and master's degrees. 43 undergraduate majors. Total enrollment: 3,316. Undergraduates: 2,761. Freshmen: 614. Federal methodology is used as a basis for awarding need-based institutional aid.

UNDERGRADUATE EXPENSES for 1999–2000 ***Application fee:*** $30. ***Comprehensive fee:*** $20,717 includes full-time tuition ($14,740), mandatory fees ($802), and room and board ($5175). Room and board charges vary according to housing facility. ***Part-time tuition:*** $315 per hour. ***Part-time fees:*** $35 per term part-time. Part-time tuition and fees vary according to class time. ***Payment plan:*** installment.

FRESHMAN FINANCIAL AID (Fall 1999, est.) 553 applied for aid; of those 76% were deemed to have need. 100% of freshmen with need received aid; of those 16% had need fully met. *Average percent of need met:* 76% (excluding resources awarded to replace EFC). *Average financial aid package:* $12,623 (excluding resources awarded to replace EFC). 9% of all full-time freshmen had no need and received non-need-based aid.

UNDERGRADUATE FINANCIAL AID (Fall 1999, est.) 1,972 applied for aid; of those 81% were deemed to have need. 99% of undergraduates with need received aid; of those 21% had need fully met. *Average percent of need met:* 86% (excluding resources awarded to replace EFC). *Average financial aid package:* $13,624 (excluding resources awarded to replace EFC). 11% of all full-time undergraduates had no need and received non-need-based aid.

GIFT AID (NEED-BASED) ***Total amount:*** $12,008,606 (14% Federal, 15% state, 63% institutional, 8% external sources). ***Receiving aid:*** *Freshmen:* 63% (390); *all full-time undergraduates:* 62% (1,390). ***Average award:*** Freshmen: $7268; Undergraduates: $7850. ***Scholarships, grants, and awards:*** Federal Pell, FSEOG, state, private, college/university gift aid from institutional funds, Federal Nursing.

GIFT AID (NON-NEED-BASED) ***Total amount:*** $3,094,140 (19% state, 66% institutional, 15% external sources). ***Receiving aid:*** *Freshmen:* 19% (117); *Undergraduates:* 12% (281). ***Scholarships, grants, and awards by category:*** *Academic Interests/Achievement:* biological sciences, business, communication, education, general academic interests/achievements, health fields, military science, social sciences. *Creative Arts/Performance:* art/fine arts, creative writing, journalism/publications, music, performing arts. *Special Achievements/Activities:* general special achievements/activities, leadership. *Special Characteristics:* children and siblings of alumni, children of faculty/staff, international students. ***Tuition waivers:*** Full or partial for employees or children of employees. ***ROTC:*** Army, Air Force cooperative.

LOANS ***Student loans:*** $9,287,000 (76% need-based, 24% non-need-based). 66% of past graduating class borrowed through all loan programs. Average indebtedness per student: $17,130. ***Average need-based loan:*** Freshmen: $2477; Undergraduates: $3843. ***Parent loans:*** $2,167,903 (60% need-based, 40% non-need-based). ***Programs:*** Federal Direct (Subsidized and Unsubsidized Stafford, PLUS), Perkins, college/university.

WORK-STUDY ***Federal work-study:*** *Total amount:* $778,200; 376 jobs available.

ATHLETIC AWARDS *Total amount:* 681,359 (62% need-based, 38% non-need-based).

APPLYING for FINANCIAL AID ***Required financial aid form:*** FAFSA. ***Financial aid deadline (priority):*** 5/1. ***Notification date:*** Continuous. Students must reply within 3 weeks of notification.

CONTACT Financial Aid Office, The University of Tampa, 401 West Kennedy Boulevard, Tampa, FL 33606-1490, 813-253-6219 or toll-free 800-733-4773. *Fax:* 813-254-4955. *E-mail:* finaid@alpha.utampa.edu

THE UNIVERSITY OF TENNESSEE AT CHATTANOOGA

Chattanooga, TN

Tuition & fees (TN res): $2660 **Average undergraduate aid package: $7853**

ABOUT THE INSTITUTION State-supported, coed. Awards: bachelor's and master's degrees and post-master's certificates. 68 undergraduate majors. Total enrollment: 8,604. Undergraduates: 7,216. Freshmen: 1,106. Federal methodology is used as a basis for awarding need-based institutional aid.

UNDERGRADUATE EXPENSES for 1999–2000 ***Application fee:*** $25. ***Tuition, state resident:*** full-time $2660; part-time $115 per semester hour. ***Tuition, nonresident:*** full-time $7920; part-time $319 per semester hour. ***College room and board: room only:*** $2000. Room and board charges vary according to housing facility. ***Payment plan:*** deferred payment.

FRESHMAN FINANCIAL AID (Fall 1998) 776 applied for aid; of those 64% were deemed to have need. 83% of freshmen with need received aid; of those 48% had need fully met. *Average percent of need met:* 83% (excluding resources awarded to replace EFC). *Average financial aid package:* $7853 (excluding resources awarded to replace EFC). 24% of all full-time freshmen had no need and received non-need-based aid.

UNDERGRADUATE FINANCIAL AID (Fall 1998) 3,677 applied for aid; of those 86% were deemed to have need. 79% of undergraduates with need received aid; of those 17% had need fully met. *Average percent of need met:* 83% (excluding resources awarded to replace EFC). *Average financial aid package:* $7853 (excluding resources awarded to replace EFC). 13% of all full-time undergraduates had no need and received non-need-based aid.

GIFT AID (NEED-BASED) ***Total amount:*** $4,071,048 (83% Federal, 17% state). ***Receiving aid:*** *Freshmen:* 27% (331); *all full-time undergraduates:* 32% (1,862). ***Average award:*** Freshmen: $3300; Undergraduates: $2900. ***Scholarships, grants, and awards:*** Federal Pell, FSEOG, state, private, college/university gift aid from institutional funds, Federal Nursing.

GIFT AID (NON-NEED-BASED) ***Total amount:*** $1,523,093 (45% state, 21% institutional, 34% external sources). ***Receiving aid:*** *Freshmen:* 26% (324); *Undergraduates:* 21% (1,208). ***Scholarships, grants, and awards by category:*** *Academic Interests/Achievement:* general academic interests/achievements. *Creative Arts/Performance:* art/fine arts, music, theater/drama. *Special Achievements/Activities:* cheerleading/drum major, leadership. *Special Characteristics:* members of minority groups. ***Tuition waivers:*** Full or partial for employees or children of employees, senior citizens. ***ROTC:*** Army.

LOANS ***Student loans:*** $14,419,189 (67% need-based, 33% non-need-based). Average indebtedness per student: $12,445. ***Average need-based loan:*** Freshmen: $2500; Undergraduates: $4250. ***Parent loans:*** $640,201 (100% non-need-based). ***Programs:*** FFEL (Subsidized and Unsubsidized Stafford, PLUS), Perkins.

WORK-STUDY ***Federal work-study:*** *Total amount:* $333,230; jobs available. ***State or other work-study/employment:*** *Total amount:* $859,149 (100% non-need-based). Part-time jobs available.

ATHLETIC AWARDS *Total amount:* 1,895,909 (100% non-need-based).

APPLYING for FINANCIAL AID ***Required financial aid forms:*** FAFSA, institution's own form. ***Financial aid deadline (priority):*** 4/1. ***Notification date:*** Continuous. Students must reply within 2 weeks of notification.

CONTACT Jonathan Looney, Financial Aid Director, The University of Tennessee at Chattanooga, 615 McCallie Avenue, Chattanooga, TN 37403-2598, 423-755-4677 or toll-free 800-UTC-6627 (in-state). *Fax:* 423-785-2216. *E-mail:* jonathan-looney@utc.edu

THE UNIVERSITY OF TENNESSEE AT MARTIN

Martin, TN

Tuition & fees (TN res): $2656 **Average undergraduate aid package: $5867**

ABOUT THE INSTITUTION State-supported, coed. Awards: bachelor's and master's degrees. 77 undergraduate majors. Total enrollment: 5,741.

Undergraduates: 5,385. Freshmen: 948. Federal methodology is used as a basis for awarding need-based institutional aid.

UNDERGRADUATE EXPENSES for 1999–2000 ***Application fee:*** $25. ***Tuition, state resident:*** full-time $2656; part-time $112 per semester hour. ***Tuition, nonresident:*** full-time $7916; part-time $332 per semester hour. ***College room and board:*** $3606; ***room only:*** $1760. Room and board charges vary according to board plan and housing facility. ***Payment plan:*** deferred payment.

FRESHMAN FINANCIAL AID (Fall 1999) 1112 applied for aid; of those 57% were deemed to have need. 97% of freshmen with need received aid; of those 17% had need fully met. *Average percent of need met:* 70% (excluding resources awarded to replace EFC). *Average financial aid package:* $5253 (excluding resources awarded to replace EFC). 23% of all full-time freshmen had no need and received non-need-based aid.

UNDERGRADUATE FINANCIAL AID (Fall 1999) 3,841 applied for aid; of those 59% were deemed to have need. 97% of undergraduates with need received aid; of those 22% had need fully met. *Average percent of need met:* 74% (excluding resources awarded to replace EFC). *Average financial aid package:* $5867 (excluding resources awarded to replace EFC). 18% of all full-time undergraduates had no need and received non-need-based aid.

GIFT AID (NEED-BASED) ***Total amount:*** $4,826,996 (72% Federal, 28% state). ***Receiving aid:*** *Freshmen:* 29% (361); *all full-time undergraduates:* 30% (1,370). ***Average award:*** Freshmen: $3087; Undergraduates: $2911. ***Scholarships, grants, and awards:*** Federal Pell, FSEOG, state, private, TN Minority Teaching Fellowships, TN Teachers Scholars Programs.

GIFT AID (NON-NEED-BASED) ***Total amount:*** $2,643,133 (11% state, 72% institutional, 17% external sources). ***Receiving aid:*** *Freshmen:* 21% (261); *Undergraduates:* 16% (747). ***Scholarships, grants, and awards by category:*** *Academic Interests/Achievement:* 1,039 awards ($1,367,040 total): agriculture, biological sciences, business, communication, computer science, education, engineering/technologies, English, general academic interests/achievements, health fields, home economics, humanities, mathematics, military science, physical sciences, premedicine, social sciences. *Creative Arts/Performance:* 128 awards ($72,174 total): journalism/publications, music, theater/drama. *Special Achievements/Activities:* 200 awards ($122,793 total): cheerleading/drum major, leadership, rodeo. *Special Characteristics:* 1,897 awards ($1,893,504 total): children of educators, ethnic background, handicapped students, members of minority groups, out-of-state students. ***Tuition waivers:*** Full or partial for employees or children of employees, senior citizens. ***ROTC:*** Army.

LOANS ***Student loans:*** $8,854,215 (69% need-based, 31% non-need-based). Average indebtedness per student: $10,500. ***Average need-based loan:*** Freshmen: $2989; Undergraduates: $3972. ***Parent loans:*** $343,767 (100% non-need-based). ***Programs:*** FFEL (Subsidized and Unsubsidized Stafford, PLUS), Perkins.

WORK-STUDY ***Federal work-study:*** *Total amount:* $511,379; 260 jobs averaging $2000.

ATHLETIC AWARDS *Total amount:* 1,473,571 (100% non-need-based).

APPLYING for FINANCIAL AID ***Required financial aid form:*** FAFSA. ***Financial aid deadline (priority):*** 3/1. ***Notification date:*** 5/1.

CONTACT Bobbie McClain, Director of Student Financial Assistance, The University of Tennessee at Martin, 205 Administration Building, Martin, TN 38238-1000, 901-587-7040 or toll-free 800-829-8861. *Fax:* 901-587-7036. *E-mail:* bmcclain@utm.edu

THE UNIVERSITY OF TENNESSEE KNOXVILLE

Knoxville, TN

Tuition & fees (TN res): $3104   **Average undergraduate aid package: $5892**

ABOUT THE INSTITUTION State-supported, coed. Awards: bachelor's, master's, doctoral, and first professional degrees. 96 undergraduate majors. Total enrollment: 26,437. Undergraduates: 20,259. Freshmen: 4,155. Federal methodology is used as a basis for awarding need-based institutional aid.

UNDERGRADUATE EXPENSES for 1999–2000 ***Application fee:*** $25. ***Tuition, state resident:*** full-time $2604; part-time $109 per semester hour. ***Tuition, nonresident:*** full-time $8672; part-time $362 per semester hour. ***Required fees:*** full-time $500; $22 per semester hour. ***College room and board:*** $4030; ***room only:*** $2030. Room and board charges vary according to board plan and housing facility. ***Payment plans:*** installment, deferred payment.

FRESHMAN FINANCIAL AID (Fall 1999) 2275 applied for aid; of those 65% were deemed to have need. 93% of freshmen with need received aid; of those 17% had need fully met. *Average percent of need met:* 67% (excluding resources awarded to replace EFC). *Average financial aid package:* $5548 (excluding resources awarded to replace EFC). .4% of all full-time freshmen had no need and received non-need-based aid.

UNDERGRADUATE FINANCIAL AID (Fall 1999) 8,497 applied for aid; of those 74% were deemed to have need. 95% of undergraduates with need received aid; of those 21% had need fully met. *Average percent of need met:* 67% (excluding resources awarded to replace EFC). *Average financial aid package:* $5892 (excluding resources awarded to replace EFC). .2% of all full-time undergraduates had no need and received non-need-based aid.

GIFT AID (NEED-BASED) ***Total amount:*** $15,052,124 (50% Federal, 12% state, 27% institutional, 11% external sources). ***Receiving aid:*** *Freshmen:* 22% (906); *all full-time undergraduates:* 21% (3,756). ***Average award:*** Freshmen: $4379; Undergraduates: $3603. ***Scholarships, grants, and awards:*** Federal Pell, FSEOG, state, private, college/university gift aid from institutional funds.

GIFT AID (NON-NEED-BASED) ***Scholarships, grants, and awards by category:*** *Academic Interests/Achievement:* agriculture, architecture, business, communication, education, engineering/technologies, general academic interests/achievements, military science, premedicine. *Creative Arts/Performance:* music, theater/drama. *Special Achievements/Activities:* cheerleading/drum major, hobbies/interests, leadership. *Special Characteristics:* adult students, children of union members/company employees, ethnic background, first-generation college students, handicapped students, local/state students, members of minority groups, previous college experience, veterans' children. ***Tuition waivers:*** Full or partial for employees or children of employees, senior citizens. ***ROTC:*** Army, Air Force.

LOANS ***Student loans:*** $32,966,948 (98% need-based, 2% non-need-based). 43% of past graduating class borrowed through all loan programs. Average indebtedness per student: $19,624. ***Average need-based loan:*** Freshmen: $2502; Undergraduates: $3467. ***Parent loans:*** $5,778,883 (100% need-based). ***Programs:*** FFEL (Subsidized and Unsubsidized Stafford, PLUS), Perkins, Federal Nursing, state, college/university.

WORK-STUDY ***Federal work-study:*** *Total amount:* $685,667; jobs available.

ATHLETIC AWARDS *Total amount:* 2,196,006 (100% need-based).

APPLYING for FINANCIAL AID ***Required financial aid forms:*** FAFSA, institution's own form, scholarship application form. ***Financial aid deadline (priority):*** 3/1. ***Notification date:*** Continuous beginning 4/1. Students must reply within 3 weeks of notification.

CONTACT Mr. Jeff Gerkin, Acting Director of Financial Aid, The University of Tennessee Knoxville, 115 Student Services Building, Knoxville, TN 37996-0210, 865-974-3131 or toll-free 800-221-8657 (in-state). *Fax:* 865-974-2175. *E-mail:* finaid@utk.edu

THE UNIVERSITY OF TENNESSEE MEMPHIS

Memphis, TN

Tuition & fees (TN res): $2634   **Average undergraduate aid package: $9200**

ABOUT THE INSTITUTION State-supported, coed. Awards: bachelor's, master's, doctoral, and first professional degrees. 6 undergraduate majors. Federal methodology is used as a basis for awarding need-based institutional aid.

UNDERGRADUATE EXPENSES for 1999–2000 ***Application fee:*** $25. ***Tuition, state resident:*** full-time $2634. ***Tuition, nonresident:*** full-time $8590. Full-time tuition and fees vary according to program. ***College room and board: room only:*** $3600. ***Payment plan:*** installment.

The University of Tennessee Memphis (continued)

UNDERGRADUATE FINANCIAL AID (Fall 1998) 413 applied for aid; of those 90% were deemed to have need. 100% of undergraduates with need received aid; of those 31% had need fully met. *Average percent of need met:* 75% (excluding resources awarded to replace EFC). *Average financial aid package:* $9200 (excluding resources awarded to replace EFC).

GIFT AID (NEED-BASED) ***Total amount:*** $750,533 (52% Federal, 12% state, 32% institutional, 4% external sources). ***Receiving aid:*** *All full-time undergraduates:* 47% (206). ***Average award:*** Undergraduates: $2100. ***Scholarships, grants, and awards:*** Federal Pell, FSEOG, state, private, college/university gift aid from institutional funds, Department of Health and Human Services Scholarships.

GIFT AID (NON-NEED-BASED) ***Total amount:*** $65,772 (3% state, 83% institutional, 14% external sources). ***Receiving aid:*** *Undergraduates:* 2% (7). ***Scholarships, grants, and awards by category:*** *Special Characteristics:* 40 awards ($247,392 total): members of minority groups. ***Tuition waivers:*** Full or partial for employees or children of employees.

LOANS ***Student loans:*** $2,930,686 (82% need-based, 18% non-need-based). 98% of past graduating class borrowed through all loan programs. Average indebtedness per student: $15,545. ***Average need-based loan:*** Undergraduates: $6700. ***Parent loans:*** $62,913 (20% need-based, 80% non-need-based). ***Programs:*** FFEL (Subsidized and Unsubsidized Stafford, PLUS), Perkins, Federal Nursing, college/university, Federal Health Professions Student Loans, alternative loans.

WORK-STUDY ***Federal work-study:*** *Total amount:* $164,137; 140 jobs averaging $897.

APPLYING for FINANCIAL AID ***Required financial aid forms:*** FAFSA, institution's own form. ***Financial aid deadline (priority):*** 4/1. ***Notification date:*** Continuous beginning 5/1. Students must reply within 2 weeks of notification.

CONTACT Ms. Lori A. Hartman, Director, Student Financial Aid, The University of Tennessee Memphis, 800 Madison Avenue, SAC 311, Memphis, TN 38163-0002, 901-448-5568. *Fax:* 901-448-1570. *E-mail:* lhartman@utmem.edu

THE UNIVERSITY OF TEXAS AT ARLINGTON

Arlington, TX

Tuition & fees (TX res): $2670 **Average undergraduate aid package: $7149**

ABOUT THE INSTITUTION State-supported, coed. Awards: bachelor's, master's, and doctoral degrees and post-bachelor's and post-master's certificates. 67 undergraduate majors. Total enrollment: 19,149. Undergraduates: 15,266. Freshmen: 1,481. Federal methodology is used as a basis for awarding need-based institutional aid.

UNDERGRADUATE EXPENSES for 1999–2000 ***Application fee:*** $25. ***Tuition, state resident:*** full-time $1824. ***Tuition, nonresident:*** full-time $7008. ***Required fees:*** full-time $846. Full-time tuition and fees vary according to course load. Part-time tuition and fees vary according to course load. ***College room and board: room only:*** $1686. Room and board charges vary according to housing facility. ***Payment plan:*** installment.

FRESHMAN FINANCIAL AID (Fall 1999) 789 applied for aid; of those 71% were deemed to have need. 100% of freshmen with need received aid; of those 14% had need fully met. *Average percent of need met:* 79% (excluding resources awarded to replace EFC). *Average financial aid package:* $5969 (excluding resources awarded to replace EFC). 20% of all full-time freshmen had no need and received non-need-based aid.

UNDERGRADUATE FINANCIAL AID (Fall 1999) 5,213 applied for aid; of those 79% were deemed to have need. 100% of undergraduates with need received aid; of those 19% had need fully met. *Average percent of need met:* 80% (excluding resources awarded to replace EFC). *Average financial aid package:* $7149 (excluding resources awarded to replace EFC). 12% of all full-time undergraduates had no need and received non-need-based aid.

GIFT AID (NEED-BASED) ***Total amount:*** $12,074,110 (58% Federal, 25% state, 9% institutional, 8% external sources). ***Receiving aid:*** *Freshmen:* 27% (373); *all full-time undergraduates:* 29% (2,809). ***Average award:*** Freshmen: $3711; Undergraduates: $3270. ***Scholarships, grants, and awards:*** Federal Pell, FSEOG, state, private, college/university gift aid from institutional funds.

GIFT AID (NON-NEED-BASED) ***Total amount:*** $2,161,276 (71% institutional, 29% external sources). ***Receiving aid:*** *Freshmen:* 18% (256); *Undergraduates:* 11% (1,130). ***Scholarships, grants, and awards by category:*** *Academic Interests/Achievement:* biological sciences, business, communication, computer science, engineering/technologies, general academic interests/achievements, humanities, international studies, mathematics, military science, physical sciences. *Creative Arts/Performance:* art/fine arts, debating, journalism/publications, music, theater/drama. *Special Achievements/Activities:* cheerleading/drum major, general special achievements/activities, junior miss, leadership. *Special Characteristics:* first-generation college students, general special characteristics, handicapped students. ***ROTC:*** Army, Air Force cooperative.

LOANS ***Student loans:*** $21,523,140 (84% need-based, 16% non-need-based). Average indebtedness per student: $13,055. ***Average need-based loan:*** Freshmen: $2700; Undergraduates: $4753. ***Parent loans:*** $801,211 (55% need-based, 45% non-need-based). ***Programs:*** FFEL (Subsidized and Unsubsidized Stafford, PLUS), Perkins, state, college/university.

WORK-STUDY ***Federal work-study:*** *Total amount:* $3,781,074; 1,443 jobs averaging $2620.

ATHLETIC AWARDS *Total amount:* 916,048 (30% need-based, 70% non-need-based).

APPLYING for FINANCIAL AID ***Required financial aid form:*** FAFSA. ***Financial aid deadline (priority):*** 6/1. ***Notification date:*** Continuous. Students must reply within 3 weeks of notification.

CONTACT Ms. Judy Schneider, Assistant Vice President, Student Enrollment, The University of Texas at Arlington, PO Box 19199, Arlington, TX 76019, 817-272-3568. *Fax:* 817-272-3555. *E-mail:* judy.schneider@uta.edu

THE UNIVERSITY OF TEXAS AT AUSTIN

Austin, TX

Tuition & fees (TX res): $3128 **Average undergraduate aid package: $7452**

ABOUT THE INSTITUTION State-supported, coed. Awards: bachelor's, master's, doctoral, and first professional degrees. 89 undergraduate majors. Total enrollment: 49,009. Undergraduates: 37,159. Freshmen: 7,040. Federal methodology is used as a basis for awarding need-based institutional aid.

UNDERGRADUATE EXPENSES for 1999–2000 ***Application fee:*** $50. ***Tuition, state resident:*** full-time $2280; part-time $76 per semester hour. ***Tuition, nonresident:*** full-time $8760; part-time $292 per semester hour. ***Required fees:*** full-time $848; $21 per semester hour; $142 per term part-time. Full-time tuition and fees vary according to course load and program. Part-time tuition and fees vary according to course load and program. ***College room and board:*** $4854; ***room only:*** $2521. Room and board charges vary according to board plan and housing facility. ***Payment plan:*** installment.

FRESHMAN FINANCIAL AID (Fall 1998) 3980 applied for aid; of those 71% were deemed to have need. 99% of freshmen with need received aid; of those 85% had need fully met. *Average percent of need met:* 92% (excluding resources awarded to replace EFC). *Average financial aid package:* $7260 (excluding resources awarded to replace EFC). 10% of all full-time freshmen had no need and received non-need-based aid.

UNDERGRADUATE FINANCIAL AID (Fall 1998) 20,200 applied for aid; of those 72% were deemed to have need. 94% of undergraduates with need received aid; of those 91% had need fully met. *Average percent of need met:* 96% (excluding resources awarded to replace EFC). *Average financial aid package:* $7452 (excluding resources awarded to replace EFC). 16% of all full-time undergraduates had no need and received non-need-based aid.

GIFT AID (NEED-BASED) ***Total amount:*** $30,910,000 (39% Federal, 5% state, 50% institutional, 6% external sources). ***Receiving aid:*** *Freshmen:* 32% (2,225); *all full-time undergraduates:* 26% (8,400). ***Average award:***

Freshmen: $4440; Undergraduates: $3678. ***Scholarships, grants, and awards:*** Federal Pell, FSEOG, state, private, college/university gift aid from institutional funds, Federal Nursing.

GIFT AID (NON-NEED-BASED) ***Total amount:*** $16,250,000 (3% state, 83% institutional, 14% external sources). ***Scholarships, grants, and awards by category:*** *Academic Interests/Achievement:* general academic interests/achievements. *Creative Arts/Performance:* general creative arts/performance. *Special Achievements/Activities:* general special achievements/activities. *Special Characteristics:* general special characteristics. ***ROTC:*** Army, Naval, Air Force.

LOANS ***Student loans:*** $79,500,000 (80% need-based, 20% non-need-based). Average indebtedness per student: $17,000. ***Average need-based loan:*** Freshmen: $2950; Undergraduates: $3970. ***Parent loans:*** $10,400,000 (39% need-based, 61% non-need-based). ***Programs:*** FFEL (Subsidized and Unsubsidized Stafford, PLUS), Perkins, state, college/university.

WORK-STUDY ***Federal work-study:*** *Total amount:* $2,500,000; 2,100 jobs averaging $1190. ***State or other work-study/employment:*** *Total amount:* $22,720,000 (1% need-based, 99% non-need-based). Part-time jobs available.

APPLYING for FINANCIAL AID ***Required financial aid form:*** FAFSA. ***Financial aid deadline (priority):*** 4/1. ***Notification date:*** Continuous. Students must reply within 4 weeks of notification.

CONTACT Don C. Davis, Associate Director of Student Financial Services, The University of Texas at Austin, PO Box 7758, UT Station, Austin, TX 78713-7758, 512-475-6203. *Fax:* 512-475-6349. *E-mail:* fadcd@utxdp.dp.utexas.edu

THE UNIVERSITY OF TEXAS AT BROWNSVILLE

Brownsville, TX

Tuition & fees (area res): $1722 **Average undergraduate aid package: N/A**

ABOUT THE INSTITUTION State-supported, coed. Awards: bachelor's and master's degrees. 21 undergraduate majors. Federal methodology is used as a basis for awarding need-based institutional aid.

UNDERGRADUATE EXPENSES for 1999–2000 ***Tuition, area resident:*** full-time $660; part-time $22 per credit. ***Tuition, state resident:*** full-time $1260; part-time $42 per credit. ***Tuition, nonresident:*** full-time $7620; part-time $254 per credit. ***Required fees:*** full-time $1062; $32 per credit; $49 per term part-time. Full-time tuition and fees vary according to student level. Part-time tuition and fees vary according to course load and student level. ***Payment plan:*** installment.

UNDERGRADUATE FINANCIAL AID (Fall 1999) 2,361 applied for aid; of those 99% were deemed to have need. 100% of undergraduates with need received aid.

GIFT AID (NEED-BASED) ***Total amount:*** $6,973,393 (82% Federal, 2% state, 7% institutional, 9% external sources). ***Receiving aid:*** *All full-time undergraduates:* 96% (2,267). ***Scholarships, grants, and awards:*** Federal Pell, FSEOG, state, private, college/university gift aid from institutional funds, institutional nursing scholarships.

GIFT AID (NON-NEED-BASED) ***Receiving aid:*** *Undergraduates:* 7% (161). ***Scholarships, grants, and awards by category:*** *Academic Interests/Achievement:* biological sciences, education, general academic interests/achievements, mathematics. *Creative Arts/Performance:* art/fine arts, music.

LOANS ***Student loans:*** $4,121,772 (100% need-based). ***Parent loans:*** $7359 (100% non-need-based). ***Programs:*** FFEL (Subsidized and Unsubsidized Stafford, PLUS), college/university.

WORK-STUDY ***Federal work-study:*** *Total amount:* $259,300; jobs available. ***State or other work-study/employment:*** *Total amount:* $58,302 (100% need-based). Part-time jobs available.

ATHLETIC AWARDS *Total amount:* 49,845 (100% need-based).

APPLYING for FINANCIAL AID ***Required financial aid forms:*** FAFSA, institution's own form. ***Financial aid deadline (priority):*** 4/1. ***Notification date:*** Continuous beginning 6/15. Students must reply within 6 weeks of notification.

CONTACT Mr. Albert Barreda, Financial Aid Director, The University of Texas at Brownsville, 80 Fort Brown, Brownsville, TX 78520-4991, 956-544-8265. *Fax:* 956-544-8229. *E-mail:* abarreda@utb1.utb.edu

THE UNIVERSITY OF TEXAS AT DALLAS

Richardson, TX

Tuition & fees (TX res): $2912 **Average undergraduate aid package: $4072**

ABOUT THE INSTITUTION State-supported, coed. Awards: bachelor's, master's, and doctoral degrees. 30 undergraduate majors. Total enrollment: 10,097. Undergraduates: 5,974. Both federal and institutional methodology are used as a basis for awarding need-based institutional aid.

UNDERGRADUATE EXPENSES for 1999–2000 ***Application fee:*** $25. ***One-time required fee:*** $10. ***Tuition, state resident:*** full-time $912; part-time $38 per semester hour. ***Tuition, nonresident:*** full-time $6096; part-time $254 per semester hour. ***Required fees:*** full-time $2000; $67 per semester hour; $118 per term part-time. Full-time tuition and fees vary according to course level, course load, degree level, and program. Part-time tuition and fees vary according to course level, course load, degree level, and program. ***College room and board: room only:*** $1700. Room and board charges vary according to board plan and housing facility. ***Payment plan:*** installment.

FRESHMAN FINANCIAL AID (Fall 1999) 396 applied for aid; of those 99% were deemed to have need. 100% of freshmen with need received aid; of those 94% had need fully met. *Average percent of need met:* 98% (excluding resources awarded to replace EFC). *Average financial aid package:* $4595 (excluding resources awarded to replace EFC).

UNDERGRADUATE FINANCIAL AID (Fall 1999) 1,996 applied for aid; of those 100% were deemed to have need. 100% of undergraduates with need received aid; of those 88% had need fully met. *Average percent of need met:* 98% (excluding resources awarded to replace EFC). *Average financial aid package:* $4072 (excluding resources awarded to replace EFC).

GIFT AID (NEED-BASED) ***Total amount:*** $2,518,141 (81% Federal, 19% state). ***Receiving aid:*** *Freshmen:* 20% (114); *all full-time undergraduates:* 23% (816). ***Average award:*** Freshmen: $2064; Undergraduates: $2312. ***Scholarships, grants, and awards:*** Federal Pell, FSEOG, state, private, college/university gift aid from institutional funds.

GIFT AID (NON-NEED-BASED) ***Total amount:*** $3,483,648 (1% state, 91% institutional, 8% external sources). ***Receiving aid:*** *Freshmen:* 46% (268); *Undergraduates:* 24% (870). ***Scholarships, grants, and awards by category:*** *Academic Interests/Achievement:* biological sciences, business, computer science, engineering/technologies, general academic interests/achievements, mathematics, physical sciences. *Special Achievements/Activities:* general special achievements/activities, leadership. *Special Characteristics:* adult students, children of public servants, general special characteristics, handicapped students, international students, local/state students, members of minority groups, out-of-state students, public servants, veterans, veterans' children. ***Tuition waivers:*** Full or partial for senior citizens. ***ROTC:*** Army cooperative, Air Force cooperative.

LOANS ***Student loans:*** $2,158,170 (55% need-based, 45% non-need-based). ***Average need-based loan:*** Freshmen: $2340; Undergraduates: $4069. ***Parent loans:*** $583,910 (100% non-need-based). ***Programs:*** FFEL (Subsidized and Unsubsidized Stafford, PLUS), Perkins, state, college/university.

WORK-STUDY ***Federal work-study:*** *Total amount:* $180,197; jobs available. ***State or other work-study/employment:*** *Total amount:* $2924 (100% need-based). 1 part-time job averaging $1500.

APPLYING for FINANCIAL AID ***Required financial aid form:*** FAFSA. ***Financial aid deadline:*** 4/30 (priority: 3/4). ***Notification date:*** Continuous. Students must reply within 4 weeks of notification.

CONTACT Maria Ramos, Director of Financial Aid, The University of Texas at Dallas, 2601 North Floyd Road, PO Box 830688, Richardson, TX 75083, 972-883-2941 or toll-free 800-889-2443. *Fax:* 972-883-2947. *E-mail:* ramos@utdallas.edu

THE UNIVERSITY OF TEXAS AT EL PASO

El Paso, TX

Tuition & fees (TX res): $2244 **Average undergraduate aid package: $6741**

ABOUT THE INSTITUTION State-supported, coed. Awards: bachelor's, master's, and doctoral degrees. 62 undergraduate majors. Total enrollment: 14,677. Undergraduates: 12,545. Freshmen: 1,811. Federal methodology is used as a basis for awarding need-based institutional aid.

UNDERGRADUATE EXPENSES for 1999–2000 ***Tuition, state resident:*** full-time $912; part-time $38 per semester hour. ***Tuition, nonresident:*** full-time $6096; part-time $254 per semester hour. ***Required fees:*** full-time $1332; $50 per semester hour; $60 per term part-time. Full-time tuition and fees vary according to course load and reciprocity agreements. Part-time tuition and fees vary according to reciprocity agreements. ***College room and board: room only:*** $2058. Room and board charges vary according to housing facility. ***Payment plan:*** installment.

FRESHMAN FINANCIAL AID (Fall 1998) 1257 applied for aid; of those 80% were deemed to have need. 98% of freshmen with need received aid; of those 23% had need fully met. *Average percent of need met:* 78% (excluding resources awarded to replace EFC). *Average financial aid package:* $6255 (excluding resources awarded to replace EFC). 7% of all full-time freshmen had no need and received non-need-based aid.

UNDERGRADUATE FINANCIAL AID (Fall 1998) 5,733 applied for aid; of those 77% were deemed to have need. 96% of undergraduates with need received aid; of those 38% had need fully met. *Average percent of need met:* 79% (excluding resources awarded to replace EFC). *Average financial aid package:* $6741 (excluding resources awarded to replace EFC). 5% of all full-time undergraduates had no need and received non-need-based aid.

GIFT AID (NEED-BASED) ***Total amount:*** $14,760,605 (81% Federal, 19% state). ***Receiving aid:*** *Freshmen:* 55% (883); *all full-time undergraduates:* 49% (3,773). ***Average award:*** Freshmen: $3624; Undergraduates: $2942. ***Scholarships, grants, and awards:*** Federal Pell, FSEOG, state, college/university gift aid from institutional funds.

GIFT AID (NON-NEED-BASED) ***Total amount:*** $1,318,384 (6% state, 69% institutional, 25% external sources). ***Receiving aid:*** *Freshmen:* 15% (242); *Undergraduates:* 9% (669). ***Scholarships, grants, and awards by category:*** *Academic Interests/Achievement:* biological sciences, business, communication, computer science, education, engineering/technologies, English, general academic interests/achievements, health fields, humanities, international studies, mathematics, military science, physical sciences. *Creative Arts/Performance:* applied art and design, art/fine arts, journalism/publications, music, performing arts, theater/drama. *Special Achievements/Activities:* cheerleading/drum major, leadership. *Special Characteristics:* 9,747 awards: ethnic background, international students, local/state students, members of minority groups, out-of-state students. ***ROTC:*** Army, Air Force.

LOANS ***Student loans:*** $24,591,315 (100% need-based). 26% of past graduating class borrowed through all loan programs. Average indebtedness per student: $5647. ***Average need-based loan:*** Freshmen: $2508; Undergraduates: $4164. ***Parent loans:*** $92,344 (100% non-need-based). ***Programs:*** FFEL (Subsidized and Unsubsidized Stafford, PLUS), Perkins, college/university.

WORK-STUDY ***Federal work-study:*** *Total amount:* $2,932,423; jobs available.

ATHLETIC AWARDS *Total amount:* 575,260 (100% non-need-based).

APPLYING for FINANCIAL AID ***Required financial aid forms:*** FAFSA, institution's own form. ***Financial aid deadline (priority):*** 3/15. ***Notification date:*** 6/30. Students must reply within 2 weeks of notification.

CONTACT Ms. Linda Gonzales-Hensgen, Director of Financial Aid, The University of Texas at El Paso, 500 West University Avenue, El Paso, TX 79968-0001, 915-747-5204. *Fax:* 915-747-5122.

THE UNIVERSITY OF TEXAS AT SAN ANTONIO

San Antonio, TX

Tuition & fees (TX res): $2974 **Average undergraduate aid package: N/A**

ABOUT THE INSTITUTION State-supported, coed. Awards: bachelor's, master's, and doctoral degrees. 56 undergraduate majors. Total enrollment: 18,608. Undergraduates: 15,796. Freshmen: 2,098. Federal methodology is used as a basis for awarding need-based institutional aid.

UNDERGRADUATE EXPENSES for 1999–2000 ***Application fee:*** $25. ***Tuition, state resident:*** full-time $2160; part-time $72 per semester hour. ***Tuition, nonresident:*** full-time $8640; part-time $288 per semester hour. ***Required fees:*** full-time $814; $34 per semester hour; $24 per term part-time. Full-time tuition and fees vary according to course load. Part-time tuition and fees vary according to course load. ***College room and board: room only:*** $2832. Room and board charges vary according to housing facility. ***Payment plan:*** installment.

FRESHMAN FINANCIAL AID (Fall 1998) 1965 applied for aid. *Average percent of need met:* 63% (excluding resources awarded to replace EFC).

UNDERGRADUATE FINANCIAL AID (Fall 1998) 6,456 applied for aid. *Average percent of need met:* 65% (excluding resources awarded to replace EFC).

GIFT AID (NEED-BASED) ***Total amount:*** $14,976,872 (80% Federal, 20% state). ***Scholarships, grants, and awards:*** Federal Pell, FSEOG, state, private, college/university gift aid from institutional funds.

GIFT AID (NON-NEED-BASED) ***Scholarships, grants, and awards by category:*** *Academic Interests/Achievement:* 1,058 awards ($822,292 total): agriculture, architecture, area/ethnic studies, biological sciences, business, communication, computer science, education, engineering/technologies, English, foreign languages, general academic interests/achievements, humanities, mathematics, physical sciences, social sciences. *Creative Arts/Performance:* 72 awards ($38,450 total): art/fine arts, debating, music. *Special Achievements/Activities:* 56 awards ($41,300 total): general special achievements/activities. *Special Characteristics:* 141 awards ($210,892 total): ethnic background, general special characteristics, handicapped students, local/state students, out-of-state students. ***ROTC:*** Army, Air Force.

LOANS ***Student loans:*** $44,439,841 (99% need-based, 1% non-need-based). ***Parent loans:*** $164,679 (100% need-based). ***Programs:*** FFEL (Subsidized and Unsubsidized Stafford, PLUS), Perkins, state, college/university.

WORK-STUDY ***Federal work-study:*** *Total amount:* $1,071,852; 525 jobs averaging $2042. ***State or other work-study/employment:*** *Total amount:* $85,844 (100% need-based). 41 part-time jobs averaging $2094.

ATHLETIC AWARDS *Total amount:* 320,580 (100% non-need-based).

APPLYING for FINANCIAL AID ***Required financial aid form:*** FAFSA. ***Financial aid deadline (priority):*** 3/31. ***Notification date:*** Continuous beginning 4/1.

CONTACT Ms. Judy Curry, Assistant Director of Student Financial Aid, The University of Texas at San Antonio, 6900 North Loop 1604 West, San Antonio, TX 78249-0687, 210-458-4635 or toll-free 800-669-0919 (out-of-state).

THE UNIVERSITY OF TEXAS AT TYLER

Tyler, TX

Tuition & fees (TX res): $2240 **Average undergraduate aid package: $6900**

ABOUT THE INSTITUTION State-supported, coed. Awards: bachelor's and master's degrees. 29 undergraduate majors. Total enrollment: 3,393. Undergraduates: 2,455. Freshmen: 103. Federal methodology is used as a basis for awarding need-based institutional aid.

UNDERGRADUATE EXPENSES for 1999–2000 ***Tuition, state resident:*** full-time $912; part-time $38 per semester hour. ***Tuition, nonresident:*** full-time $6096; part-time $254 per semester hour. ***Required fees:*** full-time $1328; $49 per semester hour; $76 per term part-time. Full-time tuition and fees vary according to course load. ***College room and board: room only:*** $3199. Room and board charges vary according to board plan and housing facility. ***Payment plan:*** installment.

FRESHMAN FINANCIAL AID (Fall 1999, est.) 76 applied for aid; of those 70% were deemed to have need. 77% of freshmen with need received aid; of those 100% had need fully met. *Average percent of need met:* 90% (excluding resources awarded to replace EFC). *Average financial aid package:* $5300 (excluding resources awarded to replace EFC). 37% of all full-time freshmen had no need and received non-need-based aid.

UNDERGRADUATE FINANCIAL AID (Fall 1999, est.) 940 applied for aid; of those 90% were deemed to have need. 95% of undergraduates with need received aid; of those 39% had need fully met. *Average percent of need met:* 70% (excluding resources awarded to replace EFC). *Average financial aid package:* $6900 (excluding resources awarded to replace EFC). 16% of all full-time undergraduates had no need and received non-need-based aid.

GIFT AID (NEED-BASED) ***Total amount:*** $2,655,996 (76% Federal, 24% state). ***Receiving aid:*** *Freshmen:* 40% (34); *all full-time undergraduates:* 62% (785). ***Average award:*** Freshmen: $2600; Undergraduates: $2100. ***Scholarships, grants, and awards:*** Federal Pell, FSEOG, state, private, college/university gift aid from institutional funds.

GIFT AID (NON-NEED-BASED) ***Total amount:*** $325,857 (58% institutional, 42% external sources). ***Receiving aid:*** *Freshmen:* 20% (17); *Undergraduates:* 37% (468). ***Scholarships, grants, and awards by category:*** *Academic Interests/Achievement:* biological sciences, business, communication, engineering/technologies, general academic interests/achievements, health fields, social sciences. *Creative Arts/Performance:* art/fine arts, debating, journalism/publications.

LOANS ***Student loans:*** $8,859,646 (59% need-based, 41% non-need-based). 41% of past graduating class borrowed through all loan programs. Average indebtedness per student: $6900. ***Average need-based loan:*** Freshmen: $2100; Undergraduates: $4500. ***Parent loans:*** $52,384 (100% non-need-based). ***Programs:*** FFEL (Subsidized and Unsubsidized Stafford, PLUS), Perkins.

WORK-STUDY ***Federal work-study:*** *Total amount:* $129,098; 68 jobs averaging $2400. ***State or other work-study/employment:*** *Total amount:* $12,204 (100% need-based). 12 part-time jobs averaging $2400.

APPLYING for FINANCIAL AID ***Required financial aid forms:*** FAFSA, financial aid transcript (for transfers). ***Financial aid deadline (priority):*** 4/1. ***Notification date:*** Continuous. Students must reply within 3 weeks of notification.

CONTACT Ms. Candice A. Garner, Associate Dean of Enrollment Management, The University of Texas at Tyler, 3900 University Boulevard, Tyler, TX 75799-0001, 903-566-7180 or toll-free 800-UTTYLER (in-state). *Fax:* 903-566-7183.

THE UNIVERSITY OF TEXAS HEALTH SCIENCE CENTER AT SAN ANTONIO

San Antonio, TX

Tuition & fees (TX res): $1520 **Average undergraduate aid package: N/A**

ABOUT THE INSTITUTION State-supported, coed. Awards: bachelor's, master's, doctoral, and first professional degrees. 6 undergraduate majors. Federal methodology is used as a basis for awarding need-based institutional aid.

UNDERGRADUATE EXPENSES for 1999–2000 ***Application fee:*** $50. ***One-time required fee:*** $10. ***Tuition, state resident:*** full-time $1140; part-time $38 per semester hour. ***Tuition, nonresident:*** full-time $7620; part-time $254 per semester hour. ***Required fees:*** full-time $380; $8 per semester hour; $80 per term part-time. ***Payment plan:*** installment.

GIFT AID (NEED-BASED) ***Scholarships, grants, and awards:*** Federal Pell, FSEOG, college/university gift aid from institutional funds.

GIFT AID (NON-NEED-BASED) ***Scholarships, grants, and awards by category:*** *Academic Interests/Achievement:* general academic interests/achievements. ***ROTC:*** Army cooperative, Air Force cooperative.

LOANS ***Programs:*** college/university.

APPLYING for FINANCIAL AID ***Required financial aid forms:*** FAFSA, institution's own form, CSS Financial Aid PROFILE. ***Financial aid deadline:*** Continuous.

CONTACT Financial Aid Administrator, The University of Texas Health Science Center at San Antonio, 7703 Floyd Curl Drive, San Antonio, TX 78284, 210-567-2635.

THE UNIVERSITY OF TEXAS–HOUSTON HEALTH SCIENCE CENTER

Houston, TX

Tuition & fees (TX res): $3477 **Average undergraduate aid package: $9371**

ABOUT THE INSTITUTION State-supported, coed. Awards: bachelor's, master's, doctoral, and first professional degrees and post-master's certificates. 1 undergraduate major. Total enrollment: 3,170. Undergraduates: 262. Entering class: . Federal methodology is used as a basis for awarding need-based institutional aid.

UNDERGRADUATE EXPENSES for 2000–2001 ***Application fee:*** $10. ***Tuition, state resident:*** full-time $2880; part-time $58 per semester hour. ***Tuition, nonresident:*** full-time $12,510; part-time $274 per semester hour. ***Required fees:*** full-time $597; $13 per semester hour; $20 per term part-time. Part-time tuition and fees vary according to course load. ***Payment plan:*** installment.

UNDERGRADUATE FINANCIAL AID (Fall 1998) 123 applied for aid; of those 100% were deemed to have need. 100% of undergraduates with need received aid; of those 8% had need fully met. *Average percent of need met:* 83% (excluding resources awarded to replace EFC). *Average financial aid package:* $9371 (excluding resources awarded to replace EFC).

GIFT AID (NEED-BASED) ***Total amount:*** $305,034 (46% Federal, 7% state, 41% institutional, 6% external sources). ***Receiving aid:*** *All full-time undergraduates:* 70% (86). ***Average award:*** Undergraduates: $3309. ***Scholarships, grants, and awards:*** Federal Pell, FSEOG, state, private, college/university gift aid from institutional funds.

GIFT AID (NON-NEED-BASED) ***ROTC:*** Army cooperative.

LOANS ***Student loans:*** $962,028 (100% need-based). 90% of past graduating class borrowed through all loan programs. Average indebtedness per student: $15,504. ***Average need-based loan:*** Undergraduates: $4636. ***Parent loans:*** $14,506 (100% need-based). ***Programs:*** FFEL (Subsidized and Unsubsidized Stafford, PLUS), Perkins, Federal Nursing, college/university.

APPLYING for FINANCIAL AID ***Required financial aid forms:*** FAFSA, institution's own form. ***Financial aid deadline:*** Continuous. ***Notification date:*** Continuous.

CONTACT Mr. Carl W. Gordon, Assistant Director of Student Financial Aid, The University of Texas–Houston Health Science Center, PO Box 20036, Houston, TX 77225-0036, 713-500-3860. *Fax:* 713-500-3863. *E-mail:* cgordon@admin4.hsc.uth.tmc.edu

THE UNIVERSITY OF TEXAS MEDICAL BRANCH AT GALVESTON

Galveston, TX

Tuition & fees (TX res): $1832 **Average undergraduate aid package: N/A**

ABOUT THE INSTITUTION State-supported, coed. Awards: bachelor's, master's, doctoral, and first professional degrees. 4 undergraduate majors. Total enrollment: 1,953. Undergraduates: 654. Federal methodology is used as a basis for awarding need-based institutional aid.

UNDERGRADUATE EXPENSES for 1999–2000 ***Application fee:*** $30. ***One-time required fee:*** $10. ***Tuition, state resident:*** full-time $1368; part-time $38 per semester hour. ***Tuition, nonresident:*** full-time $9144; part-time $254 per semester hour. ***Required fees:*** full-time $464; $12 per semester hour; $45 per term part-time. Full-time tuition and fees vary according to course load and program. Part-time tuition and fees vary according to

The University of Texas Medical Branch at Galveston (continued)

course load and program. ***College room and board: room only:*** $1755. Room and board charges vary according to housing facility. ***Payment plan:*** installment.

UNDERGRADUATE FINANCIAL AID (Fall 1998) 424 applied for aid; of those 94% were deemed to have need. 99% of undergraduates with need received aid; of those 49% had need fully met. *Average percent of need met:* 83% (excluding resources awarded to replace EFC). 3% of all full-time undergraduates had no need and received non-need-based aid.

GIFT AID (NEED-BASED) ***Total amount:*** $786,866 (53% Federal, 35% state, 5% institutional, 7% external sources). ***Receiving aid:*** *All full-time undergraduates:* 49% (332). ***Average award:*** Undergraduates: $2760. ***Scholarships, grants, and awards:*** Federal Pell, FSEOG, state, private, college/university gift aid from institutional funds.

GIFT AID (NON-NEED-BASED) ***Total amount:*** $2750 (100% institutional). ***Receiving aid:*** *Undergraduates:* 3. ***Scholarships, grants, and awards by category:*** *Academic Interests/Achievement:* health fields.

LOANS ***Student loans:*** $4,792,168 (94% need-based, 6% non-need-based). 74% of past graduating class borrowed through all loan programs. Average indebtedness per student: $19,674. ***Average need-based loan:*** Undergraduates: $8709. ***Parent loans:*** $55,399 (97% need-based, 3% non-need-based). ***Programs:*** Federal Direct (Subsidized and Unsubsidized Stafford, PLUS), Perkins, Federal Nursing, state, college/university.

WORK-STUDY ***Federal work-study:*** *Total amount:* $108,933; 34 jobs averaging $3204.

APPLYING for FINANCIAL AID ***Required financial aid forms:*** FAFSA, institution's own form, credit report. ***Financial aid deadline (priority):*** 3/1. ***Notification date:*** Continuous. Students must reply within 4 weeks of notification.

CONTACT Ms. Betty J. Hazelbaker, Director, Student Fiscal Planning and Management, The University of Texas Medical Branch at Galveston, 301 University Boulevard, Galveston, TX 77555-1312, 409-772-4952. *Fax:* 409-772-4466. *E-mail:* bhazelba@utmb.edu

THE UNIVERSITY OF TEXAS OF THE PERMIAN BASIN

Odessa, TX

Tuition & fees (TX res): $2320 **Average undergraduate aid package: $6844**

ABOUT THE INSTITUTION State-supported, coed. Awards: bachelor's and master's degrees. 25 undergraduate majors. Total enrollment: 2,224. Undergraduates: 1,970. Federal methodology is used as a basis for awarding need-based institutional aid.

UNDERGRADUATE EXPENSES for 1999–2000 ***Tuition, state resident:*** full-time $1890. ***Tuition, nonresident:*** full-time $8370; part-time $279 per credit hour. ***Required fees:*** full-time $430. ***Payment plan:*** installment.

FRESHMAN FINANCIAL AID (Fall 1998) 133 applied for aid; of those 74% were deemed to have need. 99% of freshmen with need received aid; of those 27% had need fully met. *Average percent of need met:* 65% (excluding resources awarded to replace EFC). *Average financial aid package:* $5373 (excluding resources awarded to replace EFC). 34% of all full-time freshmen had no need and received non-need-based aid.

UNDERGRADUATE FINANCIAL AID (Fall 1998) 1,016 applied for aid; of those 82% were deemed to have need. 100% of undergraduates with need received aid; of those 31% had need fully met. *Average percent of need met:* 74% (excluding resources awarded to replace EFC). *Average financial aid package:* $6844 (excluding resources awarded to replace EFC). 32% of all full-time undergraduates had no need and received non-need-based aid.

GIFT AID (NEED-BASED) ***Total amount:*** $2,190,583 (74% Federal, 13% state, 10% institutional, 3% external sources). ***Receiving aid:*** *Freshmen:* 64% (97); *all full-time undergraduates:* 60% (774). ***Average award:*** Freshmen: $4930; Undergraduates: $6234. ***Scholarships, grants, and awards:*** Federal Pell, FSEOG, state, private, college/university gift aid from institutional funds.

GIFT AID (NON-NEED-BASED) ***Total amount:*** $308,518 (11% Federal, 65% institutional, 24% external sources). ***Receiving aid:*** *Freshmen:* 3% (4); *Undergraduates:* 3% (44). ***Scholarships, grants, and awards by category:*** *Academic Interests/Achievement:* 215 awards ($236,905 total): general academic interests/achievements. *Creative Arts/Performance:* 5 awards ($2100 total): art/fine arts, general creative arts/performance.

LOANS ***Student loans:*** $4,813,038 (79% need-based, 21% non-need-based). 65% of past graduating class borrowed through all loan programs. Average indebtedness per student: $10,414. ***Average need-based loan:*** Freshmen: $2339; Undergraduates: $3824. ***Parent loans:*** $13,396 (22% need-based, 78% non-need-based). ***Programs:*** FFEL (Subsidized and Unsubsidized Stafford, PLUS), state, college/university.

WORK-STUDY ***Federal work-study:*** *Total amount:* $91,533; 42 jobs averaging $2179. ***State or other work-study/employment:*** *Total amount:* $4653 (100% need-based). 3 part-time jobs averaging $1000.

APPLYING for FINANCIAL AID ***Required financial aid forms:*** FAFSA, institution's own form. ***Financial aid deadline (priority):*** 5/1. ***Notification date:*** Continuous beginning 6/1.

CONTACT Mr. Robert L. Vasquez, Director of Financial Aid, The University of Texas of the Permian Basin, 4901 East University, Odessa, TX 79762-0001, 915-552-2620. *Fax:* 915-552-2621. *E-mail:* vasquez_r@utpb.edu

THE UNIVERSITY OF TEXAS–PAN AMERICAN

Edinburg, TX

Tuition & fees (TX res): $2017 **Average undergraduate aid package: $2650**

ABOUT THE INSTITUTION State-supported, coed. Awards: bachelor's, master's, and doctoral degrees. 68 undergraduate majors. Total enrollment: 12,569. Undergraduates: 10,922. Freshmen: 1,464. Federal methodology is used as a basis for awarding need-based institutional aid.

UNDERGRADUATE EXPENSES for 1999–2000 ***Tuition, state resident:*** full-time $1800; part-time $60 per semester hour. ***Tuition, nonresident:*** full-time $8700; part-time $290 per semester hour. ***Required fees:*** full-time $217; $16 per semester hour; $19 per term part-time. Part-time tuition and fees vary according to course load. ***College room and board:*** $2663; ***room only:*** $1540. Room and board charges vary according to board plan and housing facility.

FRESHMAN FINANCIAL AID (Fall 1998) 2241 applied for aid; of those 96% were deemed to have need. 93% of freshmen with need received aid; of those .1% had need fully met. *Average percent of need met:* 23% (excluding resources awarded to replace EFC). *Average financial aid package:* $1987 (excluding resources awarded to replace EFC).

UNDERGRADUATE FINANCIAL AID (Fall 1998) 5,597 applied for aid; of those 97% were deemed to have need. 92% of undergraduates with need received aid; of those .1% had need fully met. *Average percent of need met:* 27% (excluding resources awarded to replace EFC). *Average financial aid package:* $2650 (excluding resources awarded to replace EFC).

GIFT AID (NEED-BASED) ***Total amount:*** $16,813,532 (86% Federal, 13% state, 1% institutional). ***Receiving aid:*** *Freshmen:* 63% (1,727); *all full-time undergraduates:* 51% (3,653). ***Average award:*** Freshmen: $1959; Undergraduates: $2302. ***Scholarships, grants, and awards:*** Federal Pell, FSEOG, state, private, college/university gift aid from institutional funds.

GIFT AID (NON-NEED-BASED) ***Total amount:*** $2,171,704 (15% state, 48% institutional, 37% external sources). ***Receiving aid:*** *Freshmen:* 2% (58); *Undergraduates:* 3% (182). ***Scholarships, grants, and awards by category:*** *Academic Interests/Achievement:* 547 awards ($719,776 total): biological sciences, business, communication, computer science, education, engineering/technologies, English, general academic interests/achievements, health fields, mathematics, military science, premedicine. *Creative Arts/Performance:* 18 awards ($12,190 total): art/fine arts, music, theater/drama. *Special Achievements/Activities:* 136 awards ($100,650 total): general special achievements/activities. *Special Characteristics:* 21 awards ($21,100 total): general special characteristics, international students, veterans. ***ROTC:*** Army.

LOANS ***Student loans:*** $15,890,495 (83% need-based, 17% non-need-based). ***Average need-based loan:*** Freshmen: $1188; Undergraduates:

$1828. ***Parent loans:*** $45,407 (100% non-need-based). ***Programs:*** FFEL (Subsidized and Unsubsidized Stafford, PLUS), Perkins, state, college/university.

WORK-STUDY ***Federal work-study:*** *Total amount:* $1,512,650; 935 jobs averaging $1600. ***State or other work-study/employment:*** *Total amount:* $84,314 (100% need-based). 123 part-time jobs averaging $686.

ATHLETIC AWARDS *Total amount:* 503,891 (100% non-need-based).

APPLYING for FINANCIAL AID ***Required financial aid form:*** FAFSA. ***Financial aid deadline:*** 4/15 (priority: 2/28). ***Notification date:*** Continuous beginning 6/1. Students must reply within 2 weeks of notification.

CONTACT Ms. Lucile Shabowich, Associate Director of Financial Aid, The University of Texas–Pan American, 1201 West University Drive, Edinburg, TX 78539-2999, 956-381-2507. *E-mail:* els28ad@panam.edu

THE UNIVERSITY OF TEXAS SOUTHWESTERN MEDICAL CENTER AT DALLAS

Dallas, TX

Tuition & fees (TX res): $1940 **Average undergraduate aid package: N/A**

ABOUT THE INSTITUTION State-supported, coed. Awards: bachelor's, master's, doctoral, and first professional degrees. 6 undergraduate majors. Total enrollment: 1,552. Undergraduates: 246. Federal methodology is used as a basis for awarding need-based institutional aid.

UNDERGRADUATE EXPENSES for 2000–2001 ***Application fee:*** $10. ***Tuition, state resident:*** full-time $1500; part-time $50 per semester hour. ***Tuition, nonresident:*** full-time $7950; part-time $265 per semester hour. ***Required fees:*** full-time $440. ***Payment plan:*** installment.

UNDERGRADUATE FINANCIAL AID (Fall 1998) 196 applied for aid; of those 100% were deemed to have need. 100% of undergraduates with need received aid.

GIFT AID (NEED-BASED) ***Total amount:*** $416,789 (69% Federal, 2% state, 27% institutional, 2% external sources). ***Scholarships, grants, and awards:*** Federal Pell, FSEOG, state, private, college/university gift aid from institutional funds.

GIFT AID (NON-NEED-BASED) ***Total amount:*** $47,698 (100% external sources). ***Scholarships, grants, and awards by category:*** *Academic Interests/Achievement:* health fields. *Special Achievements/Activities:* community service.

LOANS ***Student loans:*** $1,743,213 (72% need-based, 28% non-need-based). 54% of past graduating class borrowed through all loan programs. ***Parent loans:*** $17,000 (100% need-based). ***Programs:*** FFEL (Subsidized and Unsubsidized Stafford, PLUS), Perkins, state, college/university.

WORK-STUDY ***Federal work-study:*** *Total amount:* $2836; 3 jobs averaging $945.

APPLYING for FINANCIAL AID ***Required financial aid form:*** FAFSA. ***Financial aid deadline (priority):*** 3/15. ***Notification date:*** 4/15. Students must reply within 2 weeks of notification.

CONTACT Ms. Karen T. Mangum, Associate Director of Student Financial Aid, The University of Texas Southwestern Medical Center at Dallas, 5323 Harry Hines Boulevard, Dallas, TX 75235-9064, 214-648-3611. *Fax:* 214-648-3289. *E-mail:* karen.mangum@email.swmed.edu

THE UNIVERSITY OF THE ARTS

Philadelphia, PA

Tuition & fees: $16,800 **Average undergraduate aid package: N/A**

ABOUT THE INSTITUTION Independent, coed. Awards: bachelor's and master's degrees and post-bachelor's certificates. 31 undergraduate majors. Total enrollment: 1,938. Undergraduates: 1,806. Freshmen: 431. Federal methodology is used as a basis for awarding need-based institutional aid.

UNDERGRADUATE EXPENSES for 1999–2000 ***Application fee:*** $40. ***Tuition:*** full-time $16,200; part-time $700 per credit. ***Required fees:*** full-time $600. Room and board charges vary according to housing facility. ***Payment plans:*** installment, deferred payment.

GIFT AID (NEED-BASED) ***Scholarships, grants, and awards:*** Federal Pell, FSEOG, state, private, college/university gift aid from institutional funds.

GIFT AID (NON-NEED-BASED) ***Scholarships, grants, and awards by category:*** *Academic Interests/Achievement:* general academic interests/achievements. *Creative Arts/Performance:* applied art and design, dance, music, performing arts, theater/drama. ***Tuition waivers:*** Full or partial for children of alumni, employees or children of employees.

LOANS ***Programs:*** FFEL (Subsidized and Unsubsidized Stafford, PLUS).

WORK-STUDY Federal work-study jobs available. ***State or other work-study/employment:*** Part-time jobs available.

APPLYING for FINANCIAL AID ***Required financial aid form:*** FAFSA. ***Financial aid deadline (priority):*** 2/15. ***Notification date:*** Continuous. Students must reply within 2 weeks of notification.

CONTACT Office of Financial Aid, The University of the Arts, 320 South Broad Street, Philadelphia, PA 19102-4944, 800-616-ARTS.

UNIVERSITY OF THE DISTRICT OF COLUMBIA

Washington, DC

Tuition & fees (DC res): $2070 **Average undergraduate aid package: N/A**

ABOUT THE INSTITUTION District-supported, coed. Awards: associate, bachelor's, and master's degrees. 91 undergraduate majors. Total enrollment: 5,181. Undergraduates: 4,944. Freshmen: 1,171. Federal methodology is used as a basis for awarding need-based institutional aid.

UNDERGRADUATE EXPENSES for 1999–2000 ***Application fee:*** $20. ***Tuition, state resident:*** full-time $1800; part-time $75 per semester hour. ***Tuition, nonresident:*** full-time $4440; part-time $185 per semester hour. ***Required fees:*** full-time $270; $135 per term part-time. Full-time tuition and fees vary according to course load. Part-time tuition and fees vary according to course load. ***Payment plans:*** installment, deferred payment.

FRESHMAN FINANCIAL AID (Fall 1999, est.) 200 applied for aid; of those 88% were deemed to have need. 86% of freshmen with need received aid. *Average percent of need met:* 25% (excluding resources awarded to replace EFC). 1% of all full-time freshmen had no need and received non-need-based aid.

UNDERGRADUATE FINANCIAL AID (Fall 1999, est.) 850 applied for aid; of those 50% were deemed to have need. 88% of undergraduates with need received aid. *Average percent of need met:* 33% (excluding resources awarded to replace EFC). 1% of all full-time undergraduates had no need and received non-need-based aid.

GIFT AID (NEED-BASED) ***Total amount:*** $2,124,803 (84% Federal, 11% state, 5% external sources). ***Receiving aid:*** *Freshmen:* 32% (125); *all full-time undergraduates:* 20% (321). ***Average award:*** Freshmen: $3125; Undergraduates: $5925. ***Scholarships, grants, and awards:*** college/university gift aid from institutional funds.

GIFT AID (NON-NEED-BASED) ***Total amount:*** $14,484 (100% state). ***Receiving aid:*** *Freshmen:* 4% (15); *Undergraduates:* 2% (25). ***Scholarships, grants, and awards by category:*** *Academic Interests/Achievement:* general academic interests/achievements. *Creative Arts/Performance:* music. *Special Characteristics:* children of faculty/staff. ***Tuition waivers:*** Full or partial for employees or children of employees, senior citizens. ***ROTC:*** Army cooperative, Air Force cooperative.

LOANS ***Student loans:*** $1,665,731 (68% need-based, 32% non-need-based). Average indebtedness per student: $19,000. ***Average need-based loan:*** Freshmen: $2625; Undergraduates: $3500. ***Parent loans:*** $5040 (100% non-need-based). ***Programs:*** Federal Direct (Subsidized and Unsubsidized Stafford, PLUS), college/university.

WORK-STUDY ***Federal work-study:*** *Total amount:* $129,639; 53 jobs averaging $2000. ***State or other work-study/employment:*** *Total amount:* $311,251 (100% non-need-based). Part-time jobs available.

University of the District of Columbia (continued)

APPLYING for FINANCIAL AID ***Required financial aid form:*** FAFSA. ***Financial aid deadline (priority):*** 3/15. ***Notification date:*** Continuous beginning 7/1. Students must reply within 2 weeks of notification.

CONTACT Director of Financial Aid, University of the District of Columbia, 4200 Connecticut Avenue, NW, Washington, DC 20008-1175, 202-274-5060.

UNIVERSITY OF THE INCARNATE WORD

San Antonio, TX

Tuition & fees: $12,140 **Average undergraduate aid package: $13,715**

ABOUT THE INSTITUTION Independent Roman Catholic, coed. Awards: bachelor's, master's, and doctoral degrees. 58 undergraduate majors. Total enrollment: 3,637. Undergraduates: 2,905. Freshmen: 385. Federal methodology is used as a basis for awarding need-based institutional aid.

UNDERGRADUATE EXPENSES for 1999–2000 ***Application fee:*** $20. ***Comprehensive fee:*** $17,010 includes full-time tuition ($11,850), mandatory fees ($290), and room and board ($4870). ***College room only:*** $2820. Room and board charges vary according to board plan. ***Part-time tuition:*** $370 per semester hour. ***Part-time fees:*** $92 per term part-time. Part-time tuition and fees vary according to course load. ***Payment plan:*** installment.

FRESHMAN FINANCIAL AID (Fall 1998) 377 applied for aid; of those 84% were deemed to have need. 98% of freshmen with need received aid; of those 37% had need fully met. *Average percent of need met:* 82% (excluding resources awarded to replace EFC). *Average financial aid package:* $12,578 (excluding resources awarded to replace EFC). 11% of all full-time freshmen had no need and received non-need-based aid.

UNDERGRADUATE FINANCIAL AID (Fall 1998) 1,860 applied for aid; of those 82% were deemed to have need. 98% of undergraduates with need received aid; of those 40% had need fully met. *Average percent of need met:* 85% (excluding resources awarded to replace EFC). *Average financial aid package:* $13,715 (excluding resources awarded to replace EFC). 8% of all full-time undergraduates had no need and received non-need-based aid.

GIFT AID (NEED-BASED) ***Total amount:*** $8,151,685 (32% Federal, 22% state, 39% institutional, 7% external sources). ***Receiving aid:*** *Freshmen:* 77% (303); *all full-time undergraduates:* 74% (1,431). ***Scholarships, grants, and awards:*** Federal Pell, FSEOG, state, private, college/university gift aid from institutional funds, Federal Nursing.

GIFT AID (NON-NEED-BASED) ***Total amount:*** $807,933 (1% Federal, 95% institutional, 4% external sources). ***Scholarships, grants, and awards by category:*** *Academic Interests/Achievement:* general academic interests/achievements. *Creative Arts/Performance:* art/fine arts, dance, music, theater/drama. *Special Achievements/Activities:* religious involvement. *Special Characteristics:* children of union members/company employees. ***Tuition waivers:*** Full or partial for employees or children of employees. ***ROTC:*** Army cooperative, Air Force cooperative.

LOANS ***Student loans:*** $14,282,585 (96% need-based, 4% non-need-based). ***Parent loans:*** $367,675 (77% need-based, 23% non-need-based). ***Programs:*** FFEL (Subsidized and Unsubsidized Stafford, PLUS), Perkins, Federal Nursing, state, alternative loans.

WORK-STUDY ***Federal work-study:*** *Total amount:* $840,487; jobs available. ***State or other work-study/employment:*** *Total amount:* $63,244 (70% need-based, 30% non-need-based). Part-time jobs available.

ATHLETIC AWARDS *Total amount:* 695,305 (64% need-based, 36% non-need-based).

APPLYING for FINANCIAL AID ***Required financial aid forms:*** FAFSA, institution's own form. ***Financial aid deadline:*** 4/1. ***Notification date:*** Continuous. Students must reply within 2 weeks of notification.

CONTACT Ms. Lisa Blazer, Director of Financial Assistance, University of the Incarnate Word, 4301 Broadway, Box 308, San Antonio, TX 78209, 210-829-6008 or toll-free 800-749-WORD. *Fax:* 210-283-5053. *E-mail:* blazer@universe.uiwtx.edu

UNIVERSITY OF THE OZARKS

Clarksville, AR

Tuition & fees: $8530 **Average undergraduate aid package: $9295**

ABOUT THE INSTITUTION Independent Presbyterian, coed. Awards: associate and bachelor's degrees. 30 undergraduate majors. Total enrollment: 596. Undergraduates: 596. Both federal and institutional methodology are used as a basis for awarding need-based institutional aid.

UNDERGRADUATE EXPENSES for 1999–2000 ***Application fee:*** $10. ***Comprehensive fee:*** $12,454 includes full-time tuition ($8290), mandatory fees ($240), and room and board ($3924). ***Part-time tuition:*** $350 per semester hour. Part-time tuition and fees vary according to course load. ***Payment plan:*** installment.

FRESHMAN FINANCIAL AID (Fall 1999, est.) 146 applied for aid; of those 64% were deemed to have need. 100% of freshmen with need received aid; of those 34% had need fully met. *Average percent of need met:* 76% (excluding resources awarded to replace EFC). *Average financial aid package:* $9252 (excluding resources awarded to replace EFC). 31% of all full-time freshmen had no need and received non-need-based aid.

UNDERGRADUATE FINANCIAL AID (Fall 1999, est.) 526 applied for aid; of those 62% were deemed to have need. 100% of undergraduates with need received aid; of those 23% had need fully met. *Average percent of need met:* 70% (excluding resources awarded to replace EFC). *Average financial aid package:* $9295 (excluding resources awarded to replace EFC). 36% of all full-time undergraduates had no need and received non-need-based aid.

GIFT AID (NEED-BASED) ***Total amount:*** $1,196,317 (41% Federal, 31% state, 28% institutional). ***Receiving aid:*** *Freshmen:* 54% (93); *all full-time undergraduates:* 58% (325). ***Average award:*** Freshmen: $5741; Undergraduates: $4634. ***Scholarships, grants, and awards:*** Federal Pell, FSEOG, state, private, college/university gift aid from institutional funds.

GIFT AID (NON-NEED-BASED) ***Total amount:*** $2,060,351 (4% state, 94% institutional, 2% external sources). ***Receiving aid:*** *Freshmen:* 50% (85); *Undergraduates:* 57% (317). ***Scholarships, grants, and awards by category:*** *Academic Interests/Achievement:* 239 awards ($572,307 total): biological sciences, business, communication, education, English, general academic interests/achievements, humanities, mathematics, premedicine, religion/biblical studies, social sciences. *Creative Arts/Performance:* 18 awards ($15,596 total): art/fine arts. *Special Achievements/Activities:* 112 awards ($301,675 total): leadership. *Special Characteristics:* 87 awards ($247,195 total): children of faculty/staff, general special characteristics, members of minority groups, relatives of clergy. ***Tuition waivers:*** Full or partial for employees or children of employees.

LOANS ***Student loans:*** $1,005,533 (57% need-based, 43% non-need-based). 42% of past graduating class borrowed through all loan programs. Average indebtedness per student: $15,000. ***Average need-based loan:*** Freshmen: $1801; Undergraduates: $2515. ***Parent loans:*** $85,204 (65% need-based, 35% non-need-based). ***Programs:*** FFEL (Subsidized and Unsubsidized Stafford, PLUS), Perkins.

WORK-STUDY ***Federal work-study:*** *Total amount:* $222,488; 114 jobs averaging $1950. ***State or other work-study/employment:*** *Total amount:* $323,337 (100% non-need-based). Part-time jobs available.

APPLYING for FINANCIAL AID ***Required financial aid form:*** FAFSA. ***Financial aid deadline (priority):*** 2/15. ***Notification date:*** Continuous beginning 3/15. Students must reply within 2 weeks of notification.

CONTACT Ms. Jana D. Hart, Director of Financial Aid, University of the Ozarks, 415 North College Avenue, Clarksville, AR 72830-2880, 501-979-1221 or toll-free 800-264-8636. *Fax:* 501-979-1355. *E-mail:* jhart@ozarks.edu

UNIVERSITY OF THE PACIFIC

Stockton, CA

Tuition & fees: $20,725 **Average undergraduate aid package: $20,468**

ABOUT THE INSTITUTION Independent, coed. Awards: bachelor's, master's, doctoral, and first professional degrees. 92 undergraduate majors. Total enrollment: 5,640. Undergraduates: 2,944. Freshmen: 746. Federal methodology is used as a basis for awarding need-based institutional aid.

UNDERGRADUATE EXPENSES for 2000–2001 ***Application fee:*** $50. ***One-time required fee:*** $100. ***Comprehensive fee:*** $27,103 includes full-time tuition ($20,350), mandatory fees ($375), and room and board ($6378). Room and board charges vary according to board plan and housing facility. ***Payment plan:*** deferred payment.

FRESHMAN FINANCIAL AID (Fall 1999) 627 applied for aid; of those 87% were deemed to have need. 99% of freshmen with need received aid; of those 42% had need fully met. *Average percent of need met:* 88% (excluding resources awarded to replace EFC). *Average financial aid package:* $20,141 (excluding resources awarded to replace EFC). 10% of all full-time freshmen had no need and received non-need-based aid.

UNDERGRADUATE FINANCIAL AID (Fall 1999) 2,304 applied for aid; of those 91% were deemed to have need. 100% of undergraduates with need received aid; of those 30% had need fully met. *Average percent of need met:* 86% (excluding resources awarded to replace EFC). *Average financial aid package:* $20,468 (excluding resources awarded to replace EFC). 5% of all full-time undergraduates had no need and received non-need-based aid.

GIFT AID (NEED-BASED) ***Total amount:*** $28,813,698 (8% Federal, 29% state, 63% institutional). ***Receiving aid:*** *Freshmen:* 70% (525); *all full-time undergraduates:* 69% (2,023). ***Average award:*** Freshmen: $15,796; Undergraduates: $14,679. ***Scholarships, grants, and awards:*** Federal Pell, FSEOG, state, private, college/university gift aid from institutional funds.

GIFT AID (NON-NEED-BASED) ***Total amount:*** $1,440,768 (100% institutional). ***Scholarships, grants, and awards by category:*** *Academic Interests/Achievement:* general academic interests/achievements. *Creative Arts/Performance:* music. *Special Achievements/Activities:* religious involvement. ***Tuition waivers:*** Full or partial for employees or children of employees. ***ROTC:*** Air Force cooperative.

LOANS ***Student loans:*** $10,947,731 (93% need-based, 7% non-need-based). ***Average need-based loan:*** Freshmen: $3102; Undergraduates: $4248. ***Parent loans:*** $2,913,857 (86% need-based, 14% non-need-based). ***Programs:*** Federal Direct (Subsidized and Unsubsidized Stafford, PLUS), FFEL (Subsidized and Unsubsidized Stafford, PLUS), Perkins, state.

WORK-STUDY ***Federal work-study:*** *Total amount:* $2,820,502; jobs available. ***State or other work-study/employment:*** *Total amount:* $85,112 (100% need-based). Part-time jobs available.

ATHLETIC AWARDS *Total amount:* 2,771,630 (37% need-based, 63% non-need-based).

APPLYING for FINANCIAL AID ***Required financial aid form:*** FAFSA. ***Financial aid deadline (priority):*** 2/15. ***Notification date:*** Continuous beginning 3/15.

CONTACT Director of Financial Aid, University of the Pacific, 3601 Pacific Avenue, Stockton, CA 95211-0197, 209-946-2421 or toll-free 800-959-2867.

UNIVERSITY OF THE SACRED HEART

San Juan, PR

Tuition & fees: $4660 **Average undergraduate aid package: N/A**

ABOUT THE INSTITUTION Independent Roman Catholic, coed. Awards: associate, bachelor's, and master's degrees. 36 undergraduate majors. Total enrollment: 5,184. Undergraduates: 4,772. Freshmen: 841. Federal methodology is used as a basis for awarding need-based institutional aid.

UNDERGRADUATE EXPENSES for 1999–2000 ***Application fee:*** $15. ***One-time required fee:*** $10. ***Tuition:*** full-time $4280; part-time $130 per credit. ***Required fees:*** full-time $380. Full-time tuition and fees vary according to student level. Part-time tuition and fees vary according to student level. Room and board charges vary according to student level. ***Payment plan:*** deferred payment.

GIFT AID (NEED-BASED) ***Scholarships, grants, and awards:*** Federal Pell, FSEOG, state, private, college/university gift aid from institutional funds.

GIFT AID (NON-NEED-BASED) ***Scholarships, grants, and awards by category:*** *Academic Interests/Achievement:* general academic interests/achievements. *Creative Arts/Performance:* music, theater/drama. *Special Achievements/Activities:* memberships. *Special Characteristics:* children of faculty/staff. ***Tuition waivers:*** Full or partial for employees or children of employees.

LOANS ***Programs:*** Federal Direct (Subsidized and Unsubsidized Stafford, PLUS), Perkins.

WORK-STUDY Federal work-study jobs available.

APPLYING for FINANCIAL AID ***Required financial aid forms:*** FAFSA, institution's own form, Territory of Puerto Rico income tax form(s). ***Financial aid deadline (priority):*** 5/30. ***Notification date:*** 7/30.

CONTACT Ms. Maria Torres, Director of Financial Aid, University of the Sacred Heart, PO Box 12383, San Juan, PR 00914-0383, 787-728-1515 Ext. 3605.

UNIVERSITY OF THE SCIENCES IN PHILADELPHIA

Philadelphia, PA

Tuition & fees: $15,204 **Average undergraduate aid package: $10,481**

ABOUT THE INSTITUTION Independent, coed. Awards: bachelor's, master's, doctoral, and first professional degrees. 18 undergraduate majors. Total enrollment: 2,250. Undergraduates: 966. Federal methodology is used as a basis for awarding need-based institutional aid.

UNDERGRADUATE EXPENSES for 2000–2001 (est.) ***Application fee:*** $45. ***Comprehensive fee:*** $22,804 includes full-time tuition ($14,700), mandatory fees ($504), and room and board ($7600). ***College room only:*** $4958. Full-time tuition and fees vary according to program and student level. Room and board charges vary according to board plan and housing facility. ***Part-time tuition:*** $591 per credit hour. ***Part-time fees:*** $21 per credit hour. ***Payment plans:*** installment, deferred payment.

FRESHMAN FINANCIAL AID (Fall 1999, est.) 286 applied for aid; of those 88% were deemed to have need. 99% of freshmen with need received aid; of those 10% had need fully met. *Average percent of need met:* 36% (excluding resources awarded to replace EFC). *Average financial aid package:* $8362 (excluding resources awarded to replace EFC). 12% of all full-time freshmen had no need and received non-need-based aid.

UNDERGRADUATE FINANCIAL AID (Fall 1999, est.) 1,471 applied for aid; of those 92% were deemed to have need. 97% of undergraduates with need received aid; of those 7% had need fully met. *Average percent of need met:* 36% (excluding resources awarded to replace EFC). *Average financial aid package:* $10,481 (excluding resources awarded to replace EFC). 9% of all full-time undergraduates had no need and received non-need-based aid.

GIFT AID (NEED-BASED) ***Total amount:*** $3,129,140 (41% Federal, 38% state, 21% institutional). ***Receiving aid:*** *Freshmen:* 54% (168); *all full-time undergraduates:* 51% (932). ***Average award:*** Freshmen: $3745; Undergraduates: $3354. ***Scholarships, grants, and awards:*** Federal Pell, FSEOG, state, college/university gift aid from institutional funds, Scholarships for Disadvantaged Students (SDS).

GIFT AID (NON-NEED-BASED) ***Total amount:*** $2,729,927 (99% institutional, 1% external sources). ***Receiving aid:*** *Freshmen:* 31% (98); *Undergraduates:* 20% (363). ***Scholarships, grants, and awards by category:*** *Academic Interests/Achievement:* general academic interests/achievements. *Special Characteristics:* children of union members/company employees, local/state students, members of minority groups. ***Tuition waivers:*** Full or partial for employees or children of employees. ***ROTC:*** Army cooperative.

LOANS ***Student loans:*** $8,549,322 (71% need-based, 29% non-need-based). 64% of past graduating class borrowed through all loan programs. ***Average need-based loan:*** Freshmen: $3727; Undergraduates: $4888. ***Parent loans:*** $1,257,125 (100% non-need-based). ***Programs:*** FFEL (Subsidized and Unsubsidized Stafford, PLUS), Perkins, college/university.

WORK-STUDY ***Federal work-study:*** *Total amount:* $109,625; 172 jobs averaging $700.

ATHLETIC AWARDS *Total amount:* 175,012 (100% non-need-based).

University of the Sciences in Philadelphia (continued)

APPLYING for FINANCIAL AID ***Required financial aid form:*** FAFSA. ***Financial aid deadline (priority):*** 3/15. ***Notification date:*** Continuous. Students must reply within 2 weeks of notification.

CONTACT Mr. Mike Colahan, Director of Financial Aid, University of the Sciences in Philadelphia, 600 South 43rd Street, Philadelphia, PA 19104-4495, 215-596-8894 or toll-free 888-996-8747 (in-state). *Fax:* 215-895-1100. *E-mail:* m.colaha@usip.edu

UNIVERSITY OF THE SOUTH

Sewanee, TN

Tuition & fees: $19,080 **Average undergraduate aid package: $16,600**

ABOUT THE INSTITUTION Independent Episcopal, coed. Awards: bachelor's, master's, doctoral, and first professional degrees. 41 undergraduate majors. Total enrollment: 1,438. Undergraduates: 1,332. Freshmen: 392. Both federal and institutional methodology are used as a basis for awarding need-based institutional aid.

UNDERGRADUATE EXPENSES for 1999–2000 ***Application fee:*** $45. ***Comprehensive fee:*** $24,310 includes full-time tuition ($18,900), mandatory fees ($180), and room and board ($5230). ***College room only:*** $2680. ***Part-time tuition:*** $705 per semester hour. ***Payment plans:*** installment, deferred payment.

FRESHMAN FINANCIAL AID (Fall 1998) 209 applied for aid; of those 78% were deemed to have need. 100% of freshmen with need received aid; of those 100% had need fully met. *Average percent of need met:* 100% (excluding resources awarded to replace EFC). *Average financial aid package:* $16,333 (excluding resources awarded to replace EFC). 19% of all full-time freshmen had no need and received non-need-based aid.

UNDERGRADUATE FINANCIAL AID (Fall 1998) 611 applied for aid; of those 82% were deemed to have need. 100% of undergraduates with need received aid; of those 100% had need fully met. *Average percent of need met:* 100% (excluding resources awarded to replace EFC). *Average financial aid package:* $16,600 (excluding resources awarded to replace EFC). 17% of all full-time undergraduates had no need and received non-need-based aid.

GIFT AID (NEED-BASED) ***Total amount:*** $6,367,920 (8% Federal, 2% state, 87% institutional, 3% external sources). ***Receiving aid:*** *Freshmen:* 42% (162); *all full-time undergraduates:* 39% (503). ***Average award:*** Freshmen: $11,779; Undergraduates: $12,660. ***Scholarships, grants, and awards:*** Federal Pell, FSEOG, state, private, college/university gift aid from institutional funds.

GIFT AID (NON-NEED-BASED) ***Total amount:*** $1,206,193 (1% Federal, 1% state, 84% institutional, 14% external sources). ***Scholarships, grants, and awards by category:*** *Academic Interests/Achievement:* 88 awards ($890,340 total): general academic interests/achievements. *Special Characteristics:* 87 awards ($436,890 total): children of faculty/staff, ethnic background, members of minority groups, relatives of clergy, religious affiliation. ***Tuition waivers:*** Full or partial for employees or children of employees.

LOANS ***Student loans:*** $1,678,760 (82% need-based, 18% non-need-based). 36% of past graduating class borrowed through all loan programs. Average indebtedness per student: $13,103. ***Average need-based loan:*** Freshmen: $3306; Undergraduates: $3440. ***Parent loans:*** $2,189,380 (34% need-based, 66% non-need-based). ***Programs:*** FFEL (Subsidized and Unsubsidized Stafford, PLUS), Perkins, state, college/university.

WORK-STUDY ***Federal work-study:*** *Total amount:* $500,520; 430 jobs averaging $1167. ***State or other work-study/employment:*** *Total amount:* $169,670 (42% need-based, 58% non-need-based). 156 part-time jobs averaging $1088.

APPLYING for FINANCIAL AID ***Required financial aid forms:*** FAFSA, institution's own form. ***Financial aid deadline (priority):*** 3/1. ***Notification date:*** 4/1. Students must reply within 4 weeks of notification.

CONTACT Mr. David R. Gelinas, Director of Financial Aid, University of the South, 735 University Avenue, Sewanee, TN 37383-1000, 931-598-1312 or toll-free 800-522-2234. *Fax:* 931-598-3273. *E-mail:* finaid@sewanee.edu

UNIVERSITY OF THE STATE OF NEW YORK, REGENTS COLLEGE

Albany, NY

See Regents College

UNIVERSITY OF THE VIRGIN ISLANDS

Charlotte Amalie, VI

Tuition & fees (VI res): $4946 **Average undergraduate aid package: N/A**

ABOUT THE INSTITUTION Territory-supported, coed. Awards: associate, bachelor's, and master's degrees. 23 undergraduate majors. Total enrollment: 2,742. Undergraduates: 2,539. Freshmen: 316. Federal methodology is used as a basis for awarding need-based institutional aid.

UNDERGRADUATE EXPENSES for 1999–2000 ***Application fee:*** $20. ***Tuition, state resident:*** full-time $2730; part-time $91 per credit. ***Tuition, nonresident:*** full-time $8190; part-time $273 per credit. ***Required fees:*** full-time $2216; $55 per term part-time. ***College room and board:*** $5830.

GIFT AID (NEED-BASED) ***Total amount:*** $2,961,984 (73% Federal, 13% institutional, 14% external sources). ***Scholarships, grants, and awards:*** Federal Pell, FSEOG, state, college/university gift aid from institutional funds.

GIFT AID (NON-NEED-BASED) ***Scholarships, grants, and awards by category:*** *Creative Arts/Performance:* music. *Special Characteristics:* children of faculty/staff, veterans. ***Tuition waivers:*** Full or partial for employees or children of employees, senior citizens.

LOANS ***Student loans:*** $871,666 (100% need-based). ***Parent loans:*** $3000 (100% need-based). ***Programs:*** Federal Direct (Subsidized and Unsubsidized Stafford, PLUS), Perkins, college/university.

WORK-STUDY ***Federal work-study:*** *Total amount:* $113,854; jobs available. ***State or other work-study/employment:*** *Total amount:* $110,000 (100% need-based). Part-time jobs available.

ATHLETIC AWARDS *Total amount:* 12,315 (100% need-based).

APPLYING for FINANCIAL AID ***Required financial aid form:*** FAFSA. ***Financial aid deadline:*** 3/1. ***Notification date:*** Continuous beginning 5/15. Students must reply within 2 weeks of notification.

CONTACT Ardrina Scott-Elliott, Financial Aid Supervisor, University of the Virgin Islands, No. 2 John Brewers Bay, St. Thomas, VI 00802-9990, 340-693-1096. *E-mail:* ascott@uvi.edu

UNIVERSITY OF TOLEDO

Toledo, OH

Tuition & fees (OH res): $4416 **Average undergraduate aid package: N/A**

ABOUT THE INSTITUTION State-supported, coed. Awards: associate, bachelor's, master's, doctoral, and first professional degrees and post-bachelor's and post-master's certificates. 118 undergraduate majors. Total enrollment: 20,411. Undergraduates: 16,729. Freshmen: 3,068. Federal methodology is used as a basis for awarding need-based institutional aid.

UNDERGRADUATE EXPENSES for 1999–2000 ***Application fee:*** $30. ***Tuition, state resident:*** full-time $3611; part-time $150 per semester hour. ***Tuition, nonresident:*** full-time $9980; part-time $416 per semester hour. ***Required fees:*** full-time $805; $34 per semester hour. ***College room and board:*** $4538. Room and board charges vary according to board plan and housing facility. ***Payment plan:*** installment.

GIFT AID (NEED-BASED) ***Scholarships, grants, and awards:*** Federal Pell, FSEOG, state, private, college/university gift aid from institutional funds.

GIFT AID (NON-NEED-BASED) ***Scholarships, grants, and awards by category:*** *Academic Interests/Achievement:* area/ethnic studies, business, communication, computer science, education, engineering/technologies, English, general academic interests/achievements, health fields, humanities, mathematics, military science, physical sciences, premedicine, social sciences. *Creative Arts/Performance:* art/fine arts, dance, journalism/publications, music, theater/drama. *Special Achievements/Activities:* general special achievements/activities, leadership, memberships. *Special Characteristics:* adult students, children and siblings of alumni, children of educators, children of faculty/staff, ethnic background, general special characteristics, handicapped students, local/state students, members of minority groups, previous college experience, siblings of current students, spouses of current students, veterans' children. ***Tuition waivers:*** Full or partial for minority students, employees or children of employees, senior citizens. ***ROTC:*** Army, Air Force cooperative.

LOANS ***Programs:*** Federal Direct (Subsidized and Unsubsidized Stafford, PLUS), Perkins, state.

WORK-STUDY Federal work-study jobs available.

APPLYING for FINANCIAL AID ***Required financial aid form:*** FAFSA. ***Financial aid deadline (priority):*** 4/1. ***Notification date:*** Continuous. Students must reply within 4 weeks of notification.

CONTACT Laura Smith, Senior Technical Analyst, University of Toledo, Office of Student Financial Aid, 1200 Rocket Hall, Toledo, OH 43606-3390, 419-530-5800 or toll-free 800-5TOLEDO (in-state). *Fax:* 419-530-5835.

UNIVERSITY OF TULSA

Tulsa, OK

Tuition & fees: $13,480 **Average undergraduate aid package: $14,439**

ABOUT THE INSTITUTION Independent religious, coed. Awards: bachelor's, master's, doctoral, and first professional degrees. 58 undergraduate majors. Total enrollment: 4,192. Undergraduates: 2,924. Freshmen: 615. Federal methodology is used as a basis for awarding need-based institutional aid.

UNDERGRADUATE EXPENSES for 1999–2000 ***Application fee:*** $25. ***One-time required fee:*** $200. ***Comprehensive fee:*** $18,140 includes full-time tuition ($13,400), mandatory fees ($80), and room and board ($4660). ***College room only:*** $2480. Room and board charges vary according to board plan and housing facility. ***Part-time tuition:*** $480 per credit hour. ***Part-time fees:*** $3 per credit hour. ***Payment plans:*** tuition prepayment, installment.

FRESHMAN FINANCIAL AID (Fall 1999, est.) 437 applied for aid; of those 85% were deemed to have need. 100% of freshmen with need received aid; of those 28% had need fully met. *Average percent of need met:* 83% (excluding resources awarded to replace EFC). *Average financial aid package:* $13,705 (excluding resources awarded to replace EFC). 9% of all full-time freshmen had no need and received non-need-based aid.

UNDERGRADUATE FINANCIAL AID (Fall 1999, est.) 1,657 applied for aid; of those 89% were deemed to have need. 100% of undergraduates with need received aid; of those 36% had need fully met. *Average percent of need met:* 86% (excluding resources awarded to replace EFC). *Average financial aid package:* $14,439 (excluding resources awarded to replace EFC). 5% of all full-time undergraduates had no need and received non-need-based aid.

GIFT AID (NEED-BASED) ***Total amount:*** $5,451,546 (33% Federal, 5% state, 62% institutional). ***Receiving aid:*** *Freshmen:* 43% (260); *all full-time undergraduates:* 42% (1,097). ***Average award:*** Freshmen: $4365; Undergraduates: $4810. ***Scholarships, grants, and awards:*** Federal Pell, FSEOG, state, private, college/university gift aid from institutional funds.

GIFT AID (NON-NEED-BASED) ***Total amount:*** $8,157,364 (6% state, 87% institutional, 7% external sources). ***Receiving aid:*** *Freshmen:* 48% (291); *Undergraduates:* 32% (853). ***Scholarships, grants, and awards by category:*** *Academic Interests/Achievement:* 840 awards ($3,737,360 total): biological sciences, business, communication, computer science, engineering/technologies, English, foreign languages, general academic interests/achievements, international studies, mathematics, premedicine, religion/biblical studies, social sciences. *Creative Arts/Performance:* 183 awards ($962,746 total): art/fine arts, music, performing arts, theater/drama. *Special Achievements/Activities:* 103 awards ($182,600 total): cheerleading/drum major, community service, leadership. *Special Characteristics:* 193 awards ($188,500 total): children and siblings of alumni. ***Tuition waivers:*** Full or partial for employees or children of employees.

LOANS ***Student loans:*** $7,759,539 (69% need-based, 31% non-need-based). 68% of past graduating class borrowed through all loan programs. Average indebtedness per student: $21,376. ***Average need-based loan:*** Freshmen: $2438; Undergraduates: $3535. ***Parent loans:*** $1,873,034 (100% non-need-based). ***Programs:*** FFEL (Subsidized and Unsubsidized Stafford, PLUS), Perkins, college/university.

WORK-STUDY ***Federal work-study:*** *Total amount:* $1,303,700; 786 jobs averaging $1710. ***State or other work-study/employment:*** *Total amount:* $24,800 (100% non-need-based). Part-time jobs available.

ATHLETIC AWARDS *Total amount:* 4,115,813 (100% non-need-based).

APPLYING for FINANCIAL AID ***Required financial aid forms:*** FAFSA, institution's own form. ***Financial aid deadline (priority):*** 3/1. ***Notification date:*** Continuous beginning 3/15. Students must reply by 5/1 or within 2 weeks of notification.

CONTACT Ms. Vicki Hendrickson, Director of Student Financial Services, University of Tulsa, 600 South College, Tulsa, OK 74104-3189, 918-631-2526 or toll-free 800-331-3050. *Fax:* 918-631-5105. *E-mail:* vicki-hendrickson@utulsa.edu

UNIVERSITY OF UTAH

Salt Lake City, UT

Tuition & fees (UT res): $2790 **Average undergraduate aid package: $7627**

ABOUT THE INSTITUTION State-supported, coed. Awards: bachelor's, master's, doctoral, and first professional degrees. 84 undergraduate majors. Total enrollment: 26,988. Undergraduates: 21,956. Federal methodology is used as a basis for awarding need-based institutional aid.

UNDERGRADUATE EXPENSES for 1999–2000 ***Application fee:*** $30. ***Tuition, state resident:*** full-time $2278; part-time $563 per term. ***Tuition, nonresident:*** full-time $7983; part-time $2009 per term. ***Required fees:*** full-time $512; $173 per term part-time. Full-time tuition and fees vary according to course load. Part-time tuition and fees vary according to course load. ***College room and board:*** $5179; ***room only:*** $1840. Room and board charges vary according to board plan and housing facility. ***Payment plans:*** installment, deferred payment.

FRESHMAN FINANCIAL AID (Fall 1998) 984 applied for aid; of those 48% were deemed to have need. 100% of freshmen with need received aid; of those 16% had need fully met. *Average percent of need met:* 54% (excluding resources awarded to replace EFC). *Average financial aid package:* $6193 (excluding resources awarded to replace EFC).

UNDERGRADUATE FINANCIAL AID (Fall 1998) 6,588 applied for aid; of those 71% were deemed to have need. 100% of undergraduates with need received aid; of those 17% had need fully met. *Average percent of need met:* 63% (excluding resources awarded to replace EFC). *Average financial aid package:* $7627 (excluding resources awarded to replace EFC).

GIFT AID (NEED-BASED) ***Total amount:*** $13,745,416 (61% Federal, 4% state, 6% institutional, 29% external sources). ***Receiving aid:*** *Freshmen:* 14% (261); *all full-time undergraduates:* 24% (3,038). ***Average award:*** Freshmen: $2125; Undergraduates: $2218. ***Scholarships, grants, and awards:*** Federal Pell, FSEOG, state, private, college/university gift aid from institutional funds.

GIFT AID (NON-NEED-BASED) ***Receiving aid:*** *Freshmen:* 8% (156); *Undergraduates:* 7% (830). ***Scholarships, grants, and awards by category:*** *Academic Interests/Achievement:* architecture, area/ethnic studies, biological sciences, business, communication, computer science, education, engineering/technologies, English, foreign languages, general academic interests/achievements, health fields, humanities, mathematics, physical sciences, social sciences. *Creative Arts/Performance:* art/fine arts, cinema/film/broadcasting, dance, music, theater/drama. *Special Achievements/Activities:* general special achievements/activities, leadership. *Special Characteristics:* children of faculty/staff. ***Tuition waivers:*** Full or partial for employees or children of employees, senior citizens. ***ROTC:*** Army, Naval, Air Force.

LOANS ***Student loans:*** $34,236,567 (90% need-based, 10% non-need-based). ***Average need-based loan:*** Freshmen: $2899; Undergraduates: $4988. ***Parent loans:*** $462,598 (100% need-based). ***Programs:*** FFEL (Subsidized and Unsubsidized Stafford, PLUS), Perkins, Federal Nursing, state, college/university.

University of Utah (continued)

WORK-STUDY ***Federal work-study:*** *Total amount:* $1,233,783; 422 jobs averaging $2924. ***State or other work-study/employment:*** *Total amount:* $94,024 (100% need-based). 37 part-time jobs averaging $2541.

ATHLETIC AWARDS *Total amount:* 4,287,028 (100% need-based).

APPLYING for FINANCIAL AID ***Required financial aid form:*** FAFSA. ***Financial aid deadline (priority):*** 3/15. ***Notification date:*** 4/1. Students must reply within 8 weeks of notification.

CONTACT Wendy Clark, Financial Aid Supervisor, University of Utah, 201 South 1460 East, Room 105, Salt Lake City, UT 84112-9055, 801-581-6211 or toll-free 800-444-8638. *Fax:* 801-585-6350. *E-mail:* fawin1@saff.utah.edu

UNIVERSITY OF VERMONT

Burlington, VT

Tuition & fees (VT res): $8044 **Average undergraduate aid package: $16,500**

ABOUT THE INSTITUTION State-supported, coed. Awards: associate, bachelor's, master's, doctoral, and first professional degrees and post-bachelor's and post-master's certificates. 108 undergraduate majors. Total enrollment: 10,206. Undergraduates: 8,739. Freshmen: 1,818. Both federal and institutional methodology are used as a basis for awarding need-based institutional aid.

UNDERGRADUATE EXPENSES for 1999–2000 ***Application fee:*** $45. ***Tuition, state resident:*** full-time $7464; part-time $311 per credit. ***Tuition, nonresident:*** full-time $18,672; part-time $778 per credit. ***Required fees:*** full-time $580; $130 per term part-time. Part-time tuition and fees vary according to course load and program. ***College room and board:*** $5620; ***room only:*** $3700. Room and board charges vary according to board plan. ***Payment plans:*** installment, deferred payment.

FRESHMAN FINANCIAL AID (Fall 1998) 1142 applied for aid; of those 85% were deemed to have need. 100% of freshmen with need received aid; of those 92% had need fully met. *Average percent of need met:* 94% (excluding resources awarded to replace EFC). *Average financial aid package:* $15,000 (excluding resources awarded to replace EFC). 6% of all full-time freshmen had no need and received non-need-based aid.

UNDERGRADUATE FINANCIAL AID (Fall 1998) 4,950 applied for aid; of those 88% were deemed to have need. 100% of undergraduates with need received aid; of those 93% had need fully met. *Average percent of need met:* 92% (excluding resources awarded to replace EFC). *Average financial aid package:* $16,500 (excluding resources awarded to replace EFC). 6% of all full-time undergraduates had no need and received non-need-based aid.

GIFT AID (NEED-BASED) ***Total amount:*** $20,165,517 (23% Federal, 9% state, 61% institutional, 7% external sources). ***Receiving aid:*** *Freshmen:* 35% (644); *all full-time undergraduates:* 33% (2,461). ***Average award:*** Freshmen: $6799; Undergraduates: $5857. ***Scholarships, grants, and awards:*** Federal Pell, FSEOG, state, private, college/university gift aid from institutional funds.

GIFT AID (NON-NEED-BASED) ***Scholarships, grants, and awards by category:*** *Academic Interests/Achievement:* $600,000 total: general academic interests/achievements. ***Tuition waivers:*** Full or partial for employees or children of employees, senior citizens. ***ROTC:*** Army.

LOANS ***Student loans:*** $20,727,770 (89% need-based, 11% non-need-based). 50% of past graduating class borrowed through all loan programs. Average indebtedness per student: $21,500. ***Average need-based loan:*** Freshmen: $4420; Undergraduates: $5267. ***Parent loans:*** $12,902,724 (100% need-based). ***Programs:*** FFEL (Subsidized and Unsubsidized Stafford, PLUS), Perkins, Federal Nursing, college/university.

WORK-STUDY ***Federal work-study:*** *Total amount:* $3,647,170; 1,791 jobs averaging $2030.

ATHLETIC AWARDS *Total amount:* 1,995,713 (100% non-need-based).

APPLYING for FINANCIAL AID ***Required financial aid forms:*** FAFSA, institution's own form. ***Financial aid deadline (priority):*** 2/10. ***Notification date:*** Continuous beginning 3/15. Students must reply within 4 weeks of notification.

CONTACT Financial Aid Office, University of Vermont, 330 Waterman, South Prospect Street, Burlington, VT 05405-0160, 802-656-3156. *Fax:* 802-656-4076. *E-mail:* finaid@zoo.uvm.edu

UNIVERSITY OF VIRGINIA

Charlottesville, VA

Tuition & fees (VA res): $4160 **Average undergraduate aid package: $10,042**

ABOUT THE INSTITUTION State-supported, coed. Awards: bachelor's, master's, doctoral, and first professional degrees and post-master's certificates. 44 undergraduate majors. Total enrollment: 22,433. Undergraduates: 13,570. Freshmen: 2,924. Federal methodology is used as a basis for awarding need-based institutional aid.

UNDERGRADUATE EXPENSES for 2000–2001 ***Tuition, state resident:*** full-time $3046. ***Tuition, nonresident:*** full-time $16,295. ***Required fees:*** full-time $1114. Full-time tuition and fees vary according to program. ***College room and board:*** $4767; ***room only:*** $2137. Room and board charges vary according to board plan and housing facility. ***Payment plan:*** installment.

FRESHMAN FINANCIAL AID (Fall 1999) 1610 applied for aid; of those 43% were deemed to have need. 93% of freshmen with need received aid; of those 52% had need fully met. *Average percent of need met:* 91% (excluding resources awarded to replace EFC). *Average financial aid package:* $9197 (excluding resources awarded to replace EFC). 24% of all full-time freshmen had no need and received non-need-based aid.

UNDERGRADUATE FINANCIAL AID (Fall 1999) 5,004 applied for aid; of those 61% were deemed to have need. 96% of undergraduates with need received aid; of those 51% had need fully met. *Average percent of need met:* 92% (excluding resources awarded to replace EFC). *Average financial aid package:* $10,042 (excluding resources awarded to replace EFC). 16% of all full-time undergraduates had no need and received non-need-based aid.

GIFT AID (NEED-BASED) ***Total amount:*** $17,600,706 (19% Federal, 19% state, 55% institutional, 7% external sources). ***Receiving aid:*** *Freshmen:* 18% (540); *all full-time undergraduates:* 19% (2,352). ***Average award:*** Freshmen: $7289; Undergraduates: $7764. ***Scholarships, grants, and awards:*** Federal Pell, FSEOG, state, private, college/university gift aid from institutional funds.

GIFT AID (NON-NEED-BASED) ***Total amount:*** $3,010,979 (10% state, 29% institutional, 61% external sources). ***Receiving aid:*** *Freshmen:* 5% (158); *Undergraduates:* 3% (349). ***Scholarships, grants, and awards by category:*** *Academic Interests/Achievement:* general academic interests/achievements. ***Tuition waivers:*** Full or partial for employees or children of employees, senior citizens. ***ROTC:*** Army, Naval, Air Force.

LOANS ***Student loans:*** $13,877,911 (61% need-based, 39% non-need-based). 34% of past graduating class borrowed through all loan programs. Average indebtedness per student: $13,913. ***Average need-based loan:*** Freshmen: $3126; Undergraduates: $3776. ***Parent loans:*** $6,575,545 (5% need-based, 95% non-need-based). ***Programs:*** Federal Direct (Subsidized and Unsubsidized Stafford, PLUS), Perkins, Federal Nursing, college/university.

WORK-STUDY ***Federal work-study:*** *Total amount:* $556,520; 413 jobs averaging $1348.

ATHLETIC AWARDS *Total amount:* 4,548,233 (18% need-based, 82% non-need-based).

APPLYING for FINANCIAL AID ***Required financial aid forms:*** FAFSA, institution's own form. ***Financial aid deadline (priority):*** 3/1. ***Notification date:*** 4/5. Students must reply by 5/1.

CONTACT Ms. Yvonne B. Hubbard, Director of Financial Aid, University of Virginia, PO Box 9021, Charlottesville, VA 22906, 804-982-6000. *E-mail:* faid@virginia.edu

UNIVERSITY OF VIRGINIA'S COLLEGE AT WISE

Wise, VA

Tuition & fees (VA res): $3192 **Average undergraduate aid package: N/A**

ABOUT THE INSTITUTION State-supported, coed. Awards: bachelor's degrees and post-bachelor's certificates. 22 undergraduate majors. Total enrollment: 1,551. Undergraduates: 1,551. Freshmen: 299. Federal methodology is used as a basis for awarding need-based institutional aid.

UNDERGRADUATE EXPENSES for 1999–2000 ***Application fee:*** $15. ***Tuition, state resident:*** full-time $3192; part-time $77 per semester hour. ***Tuition, nonresident:*** full-time $9286; part-time $330 per semester hour. ***Required fees:*** $5 per semester hour. Part-time tuition and fees vary according to course load. ***College room and board:*** $4938; ***room only:*** $2774. Room and board charges vary according to board plan and housing facility. ***Payment plan:*** installment.

GIFT AID (NEED-BASED) ***Scholarships, grants, and awards:*** Federal Pell, FSEOG, state, private, college/university gift aid from institutional funds.

GIFT AID (NON-NEED-BASED) ***Scholarships, grants, and awards by category:*** *Academic Interests/Achievement:* agriculture, biological sciences, business, computer science, education, English, general academic interests/achievements, health fields, humanities, mathematics, physical sciences, premedicine, social sciences. *Creative Arts/Performance:* creative writing, general creative arts/performance, journalism/publications, music, performing arts, theater/drama. *Special Achievements/Activities:* community service, religious involvement. *Special Characteristics:* children with a deceased or disabled parent, ethnic background, local/state students, veterans, veterans' children. ***Tuition waivers:*** Full or partial for senior citizens.

LOANS ***Programs:*** FFEL (Subsidized and Unsubsidized Stafford, PLUS), Perkins, state, college/university.

WORK-STUDY Federal work-study jobs available.

APPLYING for FINANCIAL AID ***Required financial aid form:*** FAFSA. ***Financial aid deadline (priority):*** 4/1. ***Notification date:*** Continuous beginning 4/2. Students must reply within 4 weeks of notification.

CONTACT Debra Wharton, Coordinator of Financial Aid Services, University of Virginia's College at Wise, 1 College Avenue, Wise, VA 24293, 540-328-0103 or toll-free 888-282-9324. *Fax:* 540-328-0251. *E-mail:* d_wharton@clinch.edu

UNIVERSITY OF WASHINGTON

Seattle, WA

Tuition & fees (WA res): $3638 **Average undergraduate aid package: $8167**

ABOUT THE INSTITUTION State-supported, coed. Awards: bachelor's, master's, doctoral, and first professional degrees. 156 undergraduate majors. Total enrollment: 35,559. Undergraduates: 25,638. Freshmen: 4,353. Federal methodology is used as a basis for awarding need-based institutional aid.

UNDERGRADUATE EXPENSES for 1999–2000 ***Application fee:*** $35. ***Tuition, state resident:*** full-time $3638. ***Tuition, nonresident:*** full-time $12,029. Part-time tuition and fees vary according to course load. ***College room and board:*** $4905. Room and board charges vary according to board plan. Part-time tuition per term ranges from $242 to $1092 for state residents, $802 to $3609 for nonresidents. ***Payment plan:*** installment.

FRESHMAN FINANCIAL AID (Fall 1999) 3255 applied for aid; of those 50% were deemed to have need. 91% of freshmen with need received aid; of those 79% had need fully met. *Average percent of need met:* 86% (excluding resources awarded to replace EFC). *Average financial aid package:* $6937 (excluding resources awarded to replace EFC). 5% of all full-time freshmen had no need and received non-need-based aid.

UNDERGRADUATE FINANCIAL AID (Fall 1999) 13,345 applied for aid; of those 77% were deemed to have need. 92% of undergraduates with need received aid; of those 60% had need fully met. *Average percent of need met:* 86% (excluding resources awarded to replace EFC). *Average financial aid package:* $8167 (excluding resources awarded to replace EFC). 5% of all full-time undergraduates had no need and received non-need-based aid.

GIFT AID (NEED-BASED) ***Total amount:*** $30,677,084 (51% Federal, 33% state, 13% institutional, 3% external sources). ***Receiving aid:*** *Freshmen:* 19% (810); *all full-time undergraduates:* 24% (6,095). ***Average award:*** Freshmen: $4687; Undergraduates: $4368. ***Scholarships, grants, and awards:*** Federal Pell, FSEOG, state, private, college/university gift aid from institutional funds.

GIFT AID (NON-NEED-BASED) ***Total amount:*** $2,210,837 (72% institutional, 28% external sources). ***Receiving aid:*** *Freshmen:* 10% (428); *Undergraduates:* 3% (838). ***Scholarships, grants, and awards by category:*** *Academic Interests/Achievement:* architecture, biological sciences, business, communication, engineering/technologies, English, foreign languages, general academic interests/achievements, health fields, humanities, mathematics, physical sciences, social sciences. *Creative Arts/Performance:* art/fine arts, creative writing, dance, general creative arts/performance, journalism/publications, music, performing arts, theater/drama. *Special Achievements/Activities:* community service, general special achievements/activities, leadership. *Special Characteristics:* international students. ***Tuition waivers:*** Full or partial for employees or children of employees. ***ROTC:*** Army, Naval, Air Force.

LOANS ***Student loans:*** $53,316,891 (75% need-based, 25% non-need-based). ***Average need-based loan:*** Freshmen: $2789; Undergraduates: $4039. ***Parent loans:*** $18,014,467 (30% need-based, 70% non-need-based). ***Programs:*** Federal Direct (Subsidized and Unsubsidized Stafford, PLUS), Perkins, Federal Nursing, alternative loans.

WORK-STUDY ***Federal work-study:*** *Total amount:* $4,067,554; 1,440 jobs averaging $2825. ***State or other work-study/employment:*** *Total amount:* $716,290 (100% need-based). 198 part-time jobs averaging $3618.

ATHLETIC AWARDS *Total amount:* 3,736,535 (100% non-need-based).

APPLYING for FINANCIAL AID ***Required financial aid form:*** FAFSA. ***Financial aid deadline (priority):*** 2/28. ***Notification date:*** 4/1. Students must reply within 3 weeks of notification.

CONTACT Financial Aid Office, University of Washington, Box 355880, Seattle, WA 98195, 206-543-6101. *E-mail:* osfa@u.washington.edu

THE UNIVERSITY OF WEST ALABAMA

Livingston, AL

Tuition & fees (AL res): $2688 **Average undergraduate aid package: N/A**

ABOUT THE INSTITUTION State-supported, coed. Awards: associate, bachelor's, and master's degrees. 19 undergraduate majors. Total enrollment: 1,980. Undergraduates: 1,681. Freshmen: 327. Federal methodology is used as a basis for awarding need-based institutional aid.

UNDERGRADUATE EXPENSES for 1999–2000 ***Application fee:*** $20. ***Tuition, state resident:*** full-time $2280; part-time $95 per semester hour. ***Tuition, nonresident:*** full-time $4560; part-time $190 per semester hour. ***Required fees:*** full-time $408; $55 per term part-time. Part-time tuition and fees vary according to course load. ***College room and board:*** $2740; ***room only:*** $1110. Room and board charges vary according to board plan and housing facility. ***Payment plan:*** deferred payment.

GIFT AID (NEED-BASED) ***Scholarships, grants, and awards:*** Federal Pell, FSEOG, state, private, college/university gift aid from institutional funds.

GIFT AID (NON-NEED-BASED) ***Scholarships, grants, and awards by category:*** *Academic Interests/Achievement:* computer science, English, general academic interests/achievements. *Creative Arts/Performance:* creative writing, dance, journalism/publications, music. *Special Achievements/Activities:* cheerleading/drum major, rodeo. *Special Characteristics:* children of educators, children of faculty/staff. ***Tuition waivers:*** Full or partial for employees or children of employees. ***ROTC:*** Army cooperative, Air Force cooperative.

LOANS ***Programs:*** FFEL (Subsidized and Unsubsidized Stafford, PLUS), Perkins.

WORK-STUDY Federal work-study jobs available.

The University of West Alabama (continued)

APPLYING for FINANCIAL AID ***Required financial aid form:*** FAFSA. ***Financial aid deadline (priority):*** 4/1. ***Notification date:*** Continuous beginning 5/1.

CONTACT Mrs. Pat Reedy, Director of Financial Aid, The University of West Alabama, Station 3, Livingston, AL 35470, 205-652-3576 or toll-free 800-621-7742 (in-state), 800-621-8044 (out-of-state).

UNIVERSITY OF WEST FLORIDA

Pensacola, FL

Tuition & fees (FL res): $2294 **Average undergraduate aid package: N/A**

ABOUT THE INSTITUTION State-supported, coed. Awards: bachelor's, master's, and doctoral degrees. 52 undergraduate majors. Total enrollment: 8,091. Undergraduates: 6,414. Freshmen: 730. Federal methodology is used as a basis for awarding need-based institutional aid.

UNDERGRADUATE EXPENSES for 1999–2000 ***Application fee:*** $20. ***Tuition, state resident:*** full-time $2294; part-time $76 per semester hour. ***Tuition, nonresident:*** full-time $9282; part-time $309 per semester hour. ***College room and board: room only:*** $2310. Room and board charges vary according to housing facility.

GIFT AID (NEED-BASED) ***Total amount:*** $1,919,783 (34% Federal, 27% state, 39% institutional). ***Scholarships, grants, and awards:*** Federal Pell, FSEOG, state, college/university gift aid from institutional funds.

GIFT AID (NON-NEED-BASED) ***Total amount:*** $2,658,949 (1% Federal, 63% state, 26% institutional, 10% external sources). ***Scholarships, grants, and awards by category:*** *Academic Interests/Achievement:* 500 awards ($580,000 total): general academic interests/achievements. *Creative Arts/Performance:* 80 awards ($54,000 total): applied art and design, art/fine arts, music, theater/drama. *Special Characteristics:* 70 awards ($70,000 total): members of minority groups. ***Tuition waivers:*** Full or partial for employees or children of employees, senior citizens. ***ROTC:*** Army, Air Force.

LOANS ***Student loans:*** $16,355,954 (64% need-based, 36% non-need-based). ***Parent loans:*** $462,807 (100% non-need-based). ***Programs:*** Federal Direct (Subsidized and Unsubsidized Stafford, PLUS), Perkins, college/university.

WORK-STUDY ***Federal work-study:*** *Total amount:* $219,640; 100 jobs averaging $2400. ***State or other work-study/employment:*** *Total amount:* $2,869,060 (100% non-need-based). 1,397 part-time jobs averaging $2054.

ATHLETIC AWARDS *Total amount:* 414,590 (100% non-need-based).

APPLYING for FINANCIAL AID ***Required financial aid forms:*** FAFSA, institution's own form. ***Financial aid deadline:*** Continuous. ***Notification date:*** Continuous beginning 3/1.

CONTACT Ms. Georganne E. Major, Senior Financial Aid Officer, University of West Florida, 11000 University Parkway, Pensacola, FL 32514-5750, 850-474-2397. *E-mail:* gmajor@uwf.edu

UNIVERSITY OF WEST LOS ANGELES

Inglewood, CA

Tuition & fees: $6030 **Average undergraduate aid package: N/A**

ABOUT THE INSTITUTION Independent, coed. Awards: bachelor's and first professional degrees. 1 undergraduate major. Total enrollment: 397. Undergraduates: 102. Federal methodology is used as a basis for awarding need-based institutional aid.

UNDERGRADUATE EXPENSES for 1999–2000 ***Application fee:*** $45. ***Tuition:*** full-time $5670; part-time $210 per unit. ***Required fees:*** full-time $360; $120 per term part-time. ***Payment plan:*** installment.

GIFT AID (NEED-BASED) ***Scholarships, grants, and awards:*** Federal Pell, FSEOG, state, private, college/university gift aid from institutional funds.

GIFT AID (NON-NEED-BASED) ***Scholarships, grants, and awards by category:*** *Academic Interests/Achievement:* general academic interests/achievements. *Special Characteristics:* siblings of current students, spouses of current students. ***Tuition waivers:*** Full or partial for employees or children of employees.

LOANS ***Programs:*** Federal Direct (Subsidized and Unsubsidized Stafford), FFEL (Subsidized and Unsubsidized Stafford), alternative loans.

WORK-STUDY Federal work-study jobs available.

APPLYING for FINANCIAL AID ***Required financial aid form:*** FAFSA. ***Financial aid deadline:*** Continuous.

CONTACT Edward Reed, Director of Financial Aid, University of West Los Angeles, 1155 West Arbor Vitae Street, Inglewood, CA 90301-2902, 310-342-5257. *Fax:* 310-342-5295.

UNIVERSITY OF WISCONSIN–EAU CLAIRE

Eau Claire, WI

Tuition & fees (WI res): $3210 **Average undergraduate aid package: $5225**

ABOUT THE INSTITUTION State-supported, coed. Awards: associate, bachelor's, and master's degrees and post-bachelor's and post-master's certificates. 45 undergraduate majors. Total enrollment: 10,395. Undergraduates: 9,919. Freshmen: 2,016. Federal methodology is used as a basis for awarding need-based institutional aid.

UNDERGRADUATE EXPENSES for 1999–2000 ***Application fee:*** $35. ***Tuition, state resident:*** full-time $3210; part-time $136 per credit. ***Tuition, nonresident:*** full-time $10,074; part-time $422 per credit. Full-time tuition and fees vary according to reciprocity agreements. Part-time tuition and fees vary according to reciprocity agreements. ***College room and board:*** $3301; ***room only:*** $1985. Room and board charges vary according to board plan. ***Payment plan:*** installment.

FRESHMAN FINANCIAL AID (Fall 1998) 1387 applied for aid; of those 68% were deemed to have need. 97% of freshmen with need received aid; of those 70% had need fully met. *Average percent of need met:* 70% (excluding resources awarded to replace EFC). *Average financial aid package:* $5089 (excluding resources awarded to replace EFC). 19% of all full-time freshmen had no need and received non-need-based aid.

UNDERGRADUATE FINANCIAL AID (Fall 1998) 5,571 applied for aid; of those 74% were deemed to have need. 98% of undergraduates with need received aid; of those 69% had need fully met. *Average percent of need met:* 69% (excluding resources awarded to replace EFC). *Average financial aid package:* $5225 (excluding resources awarded to replace EFC). 17% of all full-time undergraduates had no need and received non-need-based aid.

GIFT AID (NEED-BASED) ***Total amount:*** $7,161,958 (63% Federal, 25% state, 3% institutional, 9% external sources). ***Receiving aid:*** *Freshmen:* 27% (582); *all full-time undergraduates:* 26% (2,375). ***Average award:*** Freshmen: $2818; Undergraduates: $2843. ***Scholarships, grants, and awards:*** Federal Pell, FSEOG, state, private, college/university gift aid from institutional funds.

GIFT AID (NON-NEED-BASED) ***Total amount:*** $1,097,030 (3% Federal, 21% state, 25% institutional, 51% external sources). ***Receiving aid:*** *Freshmen:* 6% (124); *Undergraduates:* 2% (231). ***Scholarships, grants, and awards by category:*** *Academic Interests/Achievement:* biological sciences, business, communication, computer science, education, English, foreign languages, general academic interests/achievements, health fields, international studies, mathematics, physical sciences, premedicine, social sciences. *Creative Arts/Performance:* debating, music, theater/drama. *Special Achievements/Activities:* community service, general special achievements/activities, hobbies/interests, leadership, memberships. *Special Characteristics:* adult students, ethnic background, first-generation college students, general special characteristics, international students, local/state students, members of minority groups, previous college experience. ***Tuition waivers:*** Full or partial for minority students, senior citizens.

LOANS ***Student loans:*** $16,693,333 (68% need-based, 32% non-need-based). 61% of past graduating class borrowed through all loan programs. Average indebtedness per student: $13,252. ***Average need-based loan:*** Freshmen: $2354; Undergraduates: $2890. ***Programs:*** Federal Direct (Subsidized and Unsubsidized Stafford, PLUS), Perkins, college/university.

WORK-STUDY ***Federal work-study:*** *Total amount:* $4,207,536; 2,220 jobs averaging $1895. ***State or other work-study/employment:*** *Total amount:* $1,961,346 (37% need-based, 63% non-need-based). 2,034 part-time jobs averaging $964.

APPLYING for FINANCIAL AID ***Required financial aid form:*** FAFSA. ***Financial aid deadline (priority):*** 4/15. ***Notification date:*** Continuous. Students must reply within 3 weeks of notification.

CONTACT Ms. Kathleen Sahlhoff, Director, Financial Aid, University of Wisconsin–Eau Claire, 115 Schofield Hall, Eau Claire, WI 54701, 715-836-3373. *Fax:* 715-836-3846.

UNIVERSITY OF WISCONSIN–GREEN BAY

Green Bay, WI

Tuition & fees (WI res): $3184 **Average undergraduate aid package: $5477**

ABOUT THE INSTITUTION State-supported, coed. Awards: associate, bachelor's, and master's degrees and post-bachelor's certificates. 33 undergraduate majors. Total enrollment: 5,428. Undergraduates: 5,274. Freshmen: 918. Federal methodology is used as a basis for awarding need-based institutional aid.

UNDERGRADUATE EXPENSES for 1999–2000 ***Application fee:*** $35. ***Tuition, state resident:*** full-time $2594; part-time $109 per credit. ***Tuition, nonresident:*** full-time $9458; part-time $395 per credit. ***Required fees:*** full-time $590; $20 per credit. Full-time tuition and fees vary according to reciprocity agreements. Part-time tuition and fees vary according to reciprocity agreements. ***College room and board: room only:*** $2035. Room and board charges vary according to housing facility. ***Payment plan:*** installment.

FRESHMAN FINANCIAL AID (Fall 1998) 682 applied for aid; of those 74% were deemed to have need. 92% of freshmen with need received aid; of those 44% had need fully met. *Average percent of need met:* 85% (excluding resources awarded to replace EFC). *Average financial aid package:* $4973 (excluding resources awarded to replace EFC).

UNDERGRADUATE FINANCIAL AID (Fall 1998) 2,806 applied for aid; of those 77% were deemed to have need. 94% of undergraduates with need received aid; of those 56% had need fully met. *Average percent of need met:* 92% (excluding resources awarded to replace EFC). *Average financial aid package:* $5477 (excluding resources awarded to replace EFC).

GIFT AID (NEED-BASED) ***Total amount:*** $3,789,043 (64% Federal, 36% state). ***Receiving aid:*** *Freshmen:* 33% (229); *all full-time undergraduates:* 39% (1,115). ***Average award:*** Freshmen: $1576; Undergraduates: $1770. ***Scholarships, grants, and awards:*** Federal Pell, FSEOG, state, private, college/university gift aid from institutional funds.

GIFT AID (NON-NEED-BASED) ***Total amount:*** $794,918 (6% Federal, 29% institutional, 65% external sources). ***Receiving aid:*** *Freshmen:* 21% (143); *Undergraduates:* 11% (330). ***Scholarships, grants, and awards by category:*** *Academic Interests/Achievement:* business, engineering/technologies, general academic interests/achievements. *Creative Arts/Performance:* art/fine arts, dance, music, theater/drama. ***Tuition waivers:*** Full or partial for senior citizens. ***ROTC:*** Army.

LOANS ***Student loans:*** $8,994,785 (65% need-based, 35% non-need-based). 59% of past graduating class borrowed through all loan programs. ***Average need-based loan:*** Freshmen: $2494; Undergraduates: $3068. ***Parent loans:*** $412,377 (100% non-need-based). ***Programs:*** FFEL (Subsidized and Unsubsidized Stafford, PLUS), Perkins.

WORK-STUDY ***Federal work-study:*** *Total amount:* $333,796; jobs available. ***State or other work-study/employment:*** *Total amount:* $1,589,895 (100% non-need-based). Part-time jobs available.

ATHLETIC AWARDS *Total amount:* 1,011,971 (100% non-need-based).

APPLYING for FINANCIAL AID ***Required financial aid form:*** FAFSA. ***Financial aid deadline (priority):*** 4/15. ***Notification date:*** Continuous. Students must reply within 3 weeks of notification.

CONTACT Mr. Ron Ronnenberg, Director of Financial Aid, University of Wisconsin–Green Bay, 2420 Nicolet Drive, Green Bay, WI 54311-7001, 920-465-2075 or toll-free 888-367-8942 (out-of-state). *E-mail:* ronnenbr@uwgb.edu

UNIVERSITY OF WISCONSIN–LA CROSSE

La Crosse, WI

Tuition & fees (WI res): $3242 **Average undergraduate aid package: $5370**

ABOUT THE INSTITUTION State-supported, coed. Awards: associate, bachelor's, and master's degrees. 57 undergraduate majors. Total enrollment: 9,309. Undergraduates: 8,650. Freshmen: 1,639. Federal methodology is used as a basis for awarding need-based institutional aid.

UNDERGRADUATE EXPENSES for 1999–2000 ***Application fee:*** $35. ***Tuition, state resident:*** full-time $3242; part-time $153 per credit. ***Tuition, nonresident:*** full-time $10,106; part-time $439 per credit. Full-time tuition and fees vary according to program and reciprocity agreements. Part-time tuition and fees vary according to course load and reciprocity agreements. ***College room and board:*** $3300; ***room only:*** $1740. ***Payment plan:*** installment.

FRESHMAN FINANCIAL AID (Fall 1999, est.) 1185 applied for aid; of those 73% were deemed to have need. 100% of freshmen with need received aid; of those 89% had need fully met. *Average percent of need met:* 90% (excluding resources awarded to replace EFC). *Average financial aid package:* $4120 (excluding resources awarded to replace EFC). 2% of all full-time freshmen had no need and received non-need-based aid.

UNDERGRADUATE FINANCIAL AID (Fall 1999, est.) 5,680 applied for aid; of those 76% were deemed to have need. 100% of undergraduates with need received aid; of those 94% had need fully met. *Average percent of need met:* 91% (excluding resources awarded to replace EFC). *Average financial aid package:* $5370 (excluding resources awarded to replace EFC). 5% of all full-time undergraduates had no need and received non-need-based aid.

GIFT AID (NEED-BASED) ***Total amount:*** $5,228,200 (52% Federal, 33% state, 15% institutional). ***Receiving aid:*** *Freshmen:* 28% (460); *all full-time undergraduates:* 36% (2,810). ***Average award:*** Freshmen: $1320; Undergraduates: $1710. ***Scholarships, grants, and awards:*** Federal Pell, FSEOG, state, college/university gift aid from institutional funds.

GIFT AID (NON-NEED-BASED) ***Total amount:*** $949,900 (31% state, 28% institutional, 41% external sources). ***Receiving aid:*** *Freshmen:* 3% (52); *Undergraduates:* 6% (450). ***Scholarships, grants, and awards by category:*** *Academic Interests/Achievement:* 275 awards ($250,000 total): business, education, English, general academic interests/achievements, health fields, mathematics, physical sciences. *Creative Arts/Performance:* 40 awards ($23,500 total): art/fine arts, music, theater/drama. *Special Characteristics:* 32 awards ($48,700 total): adult students, ethnic background, members of minority groups, out-of-state students. ***Tuition waivers:*** Full or partial for minority students, senior citizens. ***ROTC:*** Army.

LOANS ***Student loans:*** $20,280,600 (73% need-based, 27% non-need-based). 56% of past graduating class borrowed through all loan programs. Average indebtedness per student: $13,800. ***Average need-based loan:*** Freshmen: $1830; Undergraduates: $3150. ***Parent loans:*** $430,500 (5% need-based, 95% non-need-based). ***Programs:*** FFEL (Subsidized and Unsubsidized Stafford, PLUS), Perkins, college/university.

WORK-STUDY ***Federal work-study:*** *Total amount:* $475,700; 465 jobs averaging $1100. ***State or other work-study/employment:*** *Total amount:* $1,410,400 (100% non-need-based). Part-time jobs available.

APPLYING for FINANCIAL AID ***Required financial aid forms:*** FAFSA, institution's own form, federal income tax form(s). ***Financial aid deadline (priority):*** 3/15. ***Notification date:*** Continuous beginning 4/15. Students must reply by 5/10 or within 3 weeks of notification.

CONTACT Mr. A. C. Stadthaus, Director of Financial Aid, University of Wisconsin–La Crosse, 1725 State Street, La Crosse, WI 54601-3742, 608-785-8604. *Fax:* 608-785-8843.

UNIVERSITY OF WISCONSIN–MADISON

Madison, WI

Tuition & fees (WI res): $3738 **Average undergraduate aid package: N/A**

ABOUT THE INSTITUTION State-supported, coed. Awards: bachelor's, master's, doctoral, and first professional degrees. 139 undergraduate

University of Wisconsin–Madison (continued)

majors. Total enrollment: 28,996. Undergraduates: 28,996. Freshmen: 5,880. Both federal and institutional methodology are used as a basis for awarding need-based institutional aid.

UNDERGRADUATE EXPENSES for 1999–2000 ***Application fee:*** $35. ***Tuition, state resident:*** full-time $3290; part-time $828 per term. ***Tuition, nonresident:*** full-time $12,604; part-time $3156 per term. ***Required fees:*** full-time $448; $113 per term part-time. Full-time tuition and fees vary according to reciprocity agreements. Part-time tuition and fees vary according to course load and reciprocity agreements. ***College room and board:*** $4206.

FRESHMAN FINANCIAL AID (Fall 1998) 3297 applied for aid; of those 61% were deemed to have need. 86% of freshmen with need received aid.

UNDERGRADUATE FINANCIAL AID (Fall 1998) 13,744 applied for aid; of those 65% were deemed to have need. 89% of undergraduates with need received aid.

GIFT AID (NEED-BASED) ***Total amount:*** $13,829,323 (68% Federal, 18% state, 14% institutional). ***Receiving aid:*** *Freshmen:* 13% (771); *all full-time undergraduates:* 13% (3,352). ***Average award:*** Freshmen: $2914; Undergraduates: $2753. ***Scholarships, grants, and awards:*** Federal Pell, FSEOG, state, private, college/university gift aid from institutional funds.

GIFT AID (NON-NEED-BASED) ***Total amount:*** $11,910,225 (5% Federal, 31% state, 29% institutional, 35% external sources). ***Receiving aid:*** *Freshmen:* 29% (1,661); *Undergraduates:* 11% (2,922). ***Scholarships, grants, and awards by category:*** *Academic Interests/Achievement:* general academic interests/achievements. *Creative Arts/Performance:* general creative arts/performance. *Special Achievements/Activities:* general special achievements/activities. *Special Characteristics:* general special characteristics. ***ROTC:*** Army, Naval, Air Force.

LOANS ***Student loans:*** $43,976,209 (66% need-based, 34% non-need-based). 44% of past graduating class borrowed through all loan programs. Average indebtedness per student: $15,813. ***Average need-based loan:*** Freshmen: $3589; Undergraduates: $3935. ***Parent loans:*** $5,216,610 (100% non-need-based). ***Programs:*** FFEL (Subsidized and Unsubsidized Stafford, PLUS), Perkins, Federal Nursing, state, college/university.

WORK-STUDY ***Federal work-study:*** *Total amount:* $4,937,249; jobs available. ***State or other work-study/employment:*** Part-time jobs available.

ATHLETIC AWARDS *Total amount:* 3,694,681 (100% non-need-based).

APPLYING for FINANCIAL AID ***Required financial aid forms:*** FAFSA, institution's own form. ***Financial aid deadline:*** Continuous. ***Notification date:*** Continuous beginning 4/1. Students must reply within 3 weeks of notification.

CONTACT Office of Student Financial Services, University of Wisconsin–Madison, 432 North Murray Street, Madison, WI 53706-1380, 608-262-3060. *Fax:* 608-262-9068. *E-mail:* financial-aid.uw-madison@mail.admin.wisc.edu

UNIVERSITY OF WISCONSIN–MILWAUKEE

Milwaukee, WI

Tuition & fees (WI res): $3741 **Average undergraduate aid package: N/A**

ABOUT THE INSTITUTION State-supported, coed. Awards: bachelor's, master's, and doctoral degrees. 106 undergraduate majors. Total enrollment: 21,525. Undergraduates: 17,032. Freshmen: 2,248. Federal methodology is used as a basis for awarding need-based institutional aid.

UNDERGRADUATE EXPENSES for 1999–2000 ***Application fee:*** $35. ***Tuition, state resident:*** full-time $3741; part-time $134 per credit. ***Tuition, nonresident:*** full-time $12,361; part-time $493 per credit. Full-time tuition and fees vary according to location and reciprocity agreements. Part-time tuition and fees vary according to course load, location, and reciprocity agreements. ***College room and board: room only:*** $2542. Room and board charges vary according to board plan. ***Payment plan:*** installment.

FRESHMAN FINANCIAL AID (Fall 1998) 1535 applied for aid; of those 84% were deemed to have need. 100% of freshmen with need received aid; of those 48% had need fully met. *Average percent of need met:* 73% (excluding resources awarded to replace EFC). 2% of all full-time freshmen had no need and received non-need-based aid.

UNDERGRADUATE FINANCIAL AID (Fall 1998) 7,239 applied for aid; of those 84% were deemed to have need. 100% of undergraduates with need received aid; of those 45% had need fully met. *Average percent of need met:* 83% (excluding resources awarded to replace EFC). 1% of all full-time undergraduates had no need and received non-need-based aid.

GIFT AID (NEED-BASED) ***Total amount:*** $13,856,344 (62% Federal, 33% state, 5% institutional). ***Receiving aid:*** *Freshmen:* 45% (922); *all full-time undergraduates:* 33% (3,804). ***Average award:*** Undergraduates: $3240. ***Scholarships, grants, and awards:*** Federal Pell, FSEOG, state, private, college/university gift aid from institutional funds.

GIFT AID (NON-NEED-BASED) ***Total amount:*** $2,472,056 (37% Federal, 17% state, 25% institutional, 21% external sources). ***Receiving aid:*** *Freshmen:* 2% (35); *Undergraduates:* 1% (154). ***Scholarships, grants, and awards by category:*** *Academic Interests/Achievement:* general academic interests/achievements. *Special Achievements/Activities:* general special achievements/activities.

LOANS ***Student loans:*** $34,863,341 (100% need-based). ***Parent loans:*** $1,223,330 (100% need-based). ***Programs:*** Federal Direct (Subsidized and Unsubsidized Stafford, PLUS), Perkins, Federal Nursing.

WORK-STUDY ***Federal work-study:*** *Total amount:* $689,903; jobs available.

ATHLETIC AWARDS *Total amount:* 143,136 (100% non-need-based).

APPLYING for FINANCIAL AID ***Required financial aid form:*** FAFSA. ***Financial aid deadline (priority):*** 3/1. ***Notification date:*** 4/15.

CONTACT Ms. Mary E. Roggeman, Director of Financial Aid, University of Wisconsin–Milwaukee, Mellencamp Hall 162, Milwaukee, WI 53201, 414-229-6300. *E-mail:* roggeman@uwm.edu

UNIVERSITY OF WISCONSIN–OSHKOSH

Oshkosh, WI

Tuition & fees (WI res): $3001 **Average undergraduate aid package: N/A**

ABOUT THE INSTITUTION State-supported, coed. Awards: associate, bachelor's, and master's degrees. 55 undergraduate majors. Total enrollment: 10,960. Undergraduates: 9,295. Federal methodology is used as a basis for awarding need-based institutional aid.

UNDERGRADUATE EXPENSES for 1999–2000 ***Application fee:*** $35. ***Tuition, state resident:*** full-time $3001; part-time $126 per credit. ***Tuition, nonresident:*** full-time $9865; part-time $412 per credit. Full-time tuition and fees vary according to reciprocity agreements. Part-time tuition and fees vary according to reciprocity agreements. ***College room and board:*** $3130; ***room only:*** $1850. Room and board charges vary according to housing facility. ***Payment plan:*** installment.

GIFT AID (NEED-BASED) ***Scholarships, grants, and awards:*** Federal Pell, FSEOG, state, private, college/university gift aid from institutional funds.

GIFT AID (NON-NEED-BASED) ***Scholarships, grants, and awards by category:*** *Academic Interests/Achievement:* business, computer science, general academic interests/achievements, mathematics, physical sciences. *Creative Arts/Performance:* art/fine arts, debating, music, theater/drama. *Special Achievements/Activities:* general special achievements/activities. *Special Characteristics:* children and siblings of alumni, local/state students, members of minority groups. ***ROTC:*** Army.

LOANS ***Programs:*** FFEL (Subsidized and Unsubsidized Stafford, PLUS), Perkins, Federal Nursing, college/university.

WORK-STUDY Federal work-study jobs available.

APPLYING for FINANCIAL AID ***Required financial aid form:*** FAFSA. ***Financial aid deadline (priority):*** 3/15. ***Notification date:*** 5/1.

CONTACT Ms. Sheila Denney, Financial Aid Counselor, University of Wisconsin–Oshkosh, 800 Algoma Boulevard, Oshkosh, WI 54901, 920-424-3377. *E-mail:* denney@uwosh.edu

UNIVERSITY OF WISCONSIN–PARKSIDE

Kenosha, WI

Tuition & fees (WI res): $3200 **Average undergraduate aid package: $5651**

ABOUT THE INSTITUTION State-supported, coed. Awards: bachelor's and master's degrees. 51 undergraduate majors. Total enrollment: 4,884. Undergraduates: 4,744. Freshmen: 888. Federal methodology is used as a basis for awarding need-based institutional aid.

UNDERGRADUATE EXPENSES for 1999–2000 ***Application fee:*** $35. ***Tuition, state resident:*** full-time $3200; part-time $777 per term. ***Tuition, nonresident:*** full-time $10,400; part-time $2,493 per term. Full-time tuition and fees vary according to course load and reciprocity agreements. Part-time tuition and fees vary according to course load. ***College room and board:*** $4230; ***room only:*** $2860. Room and board charges vary according to board plan and housing facility. ***Payment plan:*** installment.

FRESHMAN FINANCIAL AID (Fall 1998) 609 applied for aid; of those 79% were deemed to have need. 93% of freshmen with need received aid; of those 36% had need fully met. *Average percent of need met:* 79% (excluding resources awarded to replace EFC). *Average financial aid package:* $4691 (excluding resources awarded to replace EFC). 11% of all full-time freshmen had no need and received non-need-based aid.

UNDERGRADUATE FINANCIAL AID (Fall 1998) 1,613 applied for aid; of those 77% were deemed to have need. 96% of undergraduates with need received aid; of those 46% had need fully met. *Average percent of need met:* 83% (excluding resources awarded to replace EFC). *Average financial aid package:* $5651 (excluding resources awarded to replace EFC). 9% of all full-time undergraduates had no need and received non-need-based aid.

GIFT AID (NEED-BASED) ***Total amount:*** $3,908,630 (66% Federal, 30% state, 4% institutional). ***Receiving aid:*** *Freshmen:* 28% (230); *all full-time undergraduates:* 22% (700). ***Average award:*** Freshmen: $3392; Undergraduates: $3421. ***Scholarships, grants, and awards:*** Federal Pell, FSEOG, state, private, college/university gift aid from institutional funds.

GIFT AID (NON-NEED-BASED) ***Total amount:*** $2,888,889 (10% Federal, 71% state, 9% institutional, 10% external sources). ***Receiving aid:*** *Freshmen:* 16% (137); *Undergraduates:* 11% (360). ***Scholarships, grants, and awards by category:*** *Academic Interests/Achievement:* 136 awards ($152,405 total): biological sciences, business, communication, education, engineering/technologies, English, general academic interests/achievements, health fields, mathematics, premedicine. *Creative Arts/Performance:* 20 awards ($7800 total): applied art and design, music. *Special Characteristics:* 144 awards ($291,212 total): adult students, children of union members/company employees, children of workers in trades, ethnic background, local/state students, married students, members of minority groups, out-of-state students. ***Tuition waivers:*** Full or partial for minority students, employees or children of employees. ***ROTC:*** Army cooperative.

LOANS ***Student loans:*** $5,982,349 (56% need-based, 44% non-need-based). 43% of past graduating class borrowed through all loan programs. Average indebtedness per student: $7725. ***Average need-based loan:*** Freshmen: $2519; Undergraduates: $3354. ***Parent loans:*** $339,261 (100% non-need-based). ***Programs:*** FFEL (Subsidized and Unsubsidized Stafford, PLUS), Perkins, Federal Nursing, college/university.

WORK-STUDY ***Federal work-study:*** *Total amount:* $174,877; 108 jobs averaging $1619.

ATHLETIC AWARDS *Total amount:* 618,370 (82% need-based, 18% non-need-based).

APPLYING for FINANCIAL AID ***Required financial aid forms:*** FAFSA, institution's own form. ***Financial aid deadline (priority):*** 4/1. ***Notification date:*** Continuous beginning 5/1. Students must reply within 2 weeks of notification.

CONTACT Ms. Ingrid Austin, Acting Director of Financial Aid and Scholarships, University of Wisconsin–Parkside, 900 Wood Road, Kenosha, WI 53141-2000, 414-595-2574 or toll-free 877-633-3897 (in-state). *E-mail:* ingrid.austin@uwp.edu

UNIVERSITY OF WISCONSIN–PLATTEVILLE

Platteville, WI

Tuition & fees (WI res): $3132 **Average undergraduate aid package: N/A**

ABOUT THE INSTITUTION State-supported, coed. Awards: associate, bachelor's, and master's degrees. 48 undergraduate majors. Total enrollment: 5,558. Undergraduates: 5,304. Freshmen: 1,157. Federal methodology is used as a basis for awarding need-based institutional aid.

UNDERGRADUATE EXPENSES for 1999–2000 ***Application fee:*** $35. ***Tuition, state resident:*** full-time $2594; part-time $109 per credit. ***Tuition, nonresident:*** full-time $9458. ***Required fees:*** full-time $538; $27 per credit. Full-time tuition and fees vary according to reciprocity agreements. Part-time tuition and fees vary according to course load and reciprocity agreements. ***College room and board:*** $3338; ***room only:*** $1608. Room and board charges vary according to board plan. ***Payment plan:*** installment.

GIFT AID (NEED-BASED) ***Total amount:*** $3,147,791 (75% Federal, 25% state). ***Scholarships, grants, and awards:*** Federal Pell, FSEOG, state.

GIFT AID (NON-NEED-BASED) ***Total amount:*** $790,548 (45% institutional, 55% external sources). ***Scholarships, grants, and awards by category:*** *Academic Interests/Achievement:* agriculture, biological sciences, business, communication, education, engineering/technologies, general academic interests/achievements, health fields, mathematics. *Creative Arts/Performance:* art/fine arts, music, theater/drama. *Special Achievements/Activities:* leadership.

LOANS ***Student loans:*** $10,319,389 (100% need-based). 60% of past graduating class borrowed through all loan programs. Average indebtedness per student: $8500. ***Parent loans:*** $554,306 (100% non-need-based). ***Programs:*** FFEL (Subsidized and Unsubsidized Stafford, PLUS), Perkins.

WORK-STUDY ***Federal work-study:*** *Total amount:* $560,000; jobs available. ***State or other work-study/employment:*** *Total amount:* $1,120,000 (100% non-need-based). Part-time jobs available.

APPLYING for FINANCIAL AID ***Required financial aid form:*** FAFSA. ***Financial aid deadline (priority):*** 3/15. ***Notification date:*** Continuous.

CONTACT Elizabeth Tucker, Director of Financial Aid, University of Wisconsin–Platteville, 1 University Plaza, Platteville, WI 53818-3099, 608-342-1836 or toll-free 800-362-5515 (in-state).

UNIVERSITY OF WISCONSIN–RIVER FALLS

River Falls, WI

Tuition & fees (WI res): $3102 **Average undergraduate aid package: $4429**

ABOUT THE INSTITUTION State-supported, coed. Awards: bachelor's and master's degrees. 80 undergraduate majors. Total enrollment: 5,728. Undergraduates: 5,399. Federal methodology is used as a basis for awarding need-based institutional aid.

UNDERGRADUATE EXPENSES for 1999–2000 ***Application fee:*** $35. ***Tuition, state resident:*** full-time $3102; part-time $840 per term. ***Tuition, nonresident:*** full-time $9936; part-time $2,556 per term. Full-time tuition and fees vary according to reciprocity agreements. Part-time tuition and fees vary according to course load and reciprocity agreements. ***College room and board:*** $3350; ***room only:*** $1800. Room and board charges vary according to board plan. ***Payment plan:*** installment.

FRESHMAN FINANCIAL AID (Fall 1999) 1091 applied for aid; of those 72% were deemed to have need. 100% of freshmen with need received aid; of those 32% had need fully met. *Average percent of need met:* 64% (excluding resources awarded to replace EFC). *Average financial aid package:* $3764 (excluding resources awarded to replace EFC).

UNDERGRADUATE FINANCIAL AID (Fall 1999) 3,631 applied for aid; of those 75% were deemed to have need. 100% of undergraduates with need received aid; of those 45% had need fully met. *Average percent of need met:* 77% (excluding resources awarded to replace EFC). *Average financial aid package:* $4429 (excluding resources awarded to replace EFC).

University of Wisconsin–River Falls (continued)

GIFT AID (NEED-BASED) ***Total amount:*** $4,582,996 (70% Federal, 13% state, 8% institutional, 9% external sources). ***Receiving aid:*** *Freshmen:* 51% (563); *all full-time undergraduates:* 36% (1,701). ***Average award:*** Freshmen: $1777; Undergraduates: $1652. ***Scholarships, grants, and awards:*** Federal Pell, FSEOG, state, private, college/university gift aid from institutional funds.

GIFT AID (NON-NEED-BASED) ***Total amount:*** $351,788 (18% state, 30% institutional, 52% external sources). ***Receiving aid:*** *Freshmen:* 2% (22); *Undergraduates:* 1% (48). ***Scholarships, grants, and awards by category:*** *Academic Interests/Achievement:* agriculture, area/ethnic studies, biological sciences, business, communication, computer science, education, English, foreign languages, general academic interests/achievements, health fields, humanities, international studies, mathematics, physical sciences, premedicine, social sciences. *Creative Arts/Performance:* art/fine arts, music, theater/drama.

LOANS ***Student loans:*** $11,428,160 (63% need-based, 37% non-need-based). 65% of past graduating class borrowed through all loan programs. Average indebtedness per student: $12,500. ***Average need-based loan:*** Freshmen: $1508; Undergraduates: $2353. ***Parent loans:*** $356,572 (100% non-need-based). ***Programs:*** FFEL (Subsidized and Unsubsidized Stafford, PLUS), Perkins, state.

WORK-STUDY ***Federal work-study:*** *Total amount:* $1,219,498; jobs available. ***State or other work-study/employment:*** *Total amount:* $800,000 (100% non-need-based). Part-time jobs available.

APPLYING for FINANCIAL AID ***Required financial aid forms:*** FAFSA, institution's own form. ***Financial aid deadline (priority):*** 3/15. ***Notification date:*** 4/1. Students must reply within 3 weeks of notification.

CONTACT Mr. David Woodward, Director of Financial Aid, University of Wisconsin–River Falls, 410 South Third Street, River Falls, WI 54022-5001, 715-425-3272. *Fax:* 715-425-0708.

UNIVERSITY OF WISCONSIN–STEVENS POINT

Stevens Point, WI

Tuition & fees (WI res): $3140 **Average undergraduate aid package: $5152**

ABOUT THE INSTITUTION State-supported, coed. Awards: associate, bachelor's, and master's degrees. 55 undergraduate majors. Total enrollment: 8,968. Undergraduates: 8,400. Freshmen: 1,492. Federal methodology is used as a basis for awarding need-based institutional aid.

UNDERGRADUATE EXPENSES for 1999–2000 ***Application fee:*** $35. ***Tuition, state resident:*** full-time $3140; part-time $158 per credit. ***Tuition, nonresident:*** full-time $10,004; part-time $444 per credit. Full-time tuition and fees vary according to reciprocity agreements. Part-time tuition and fees vary according to course load and reciprocity agreements. ***College room and board:*** $3524; ***room only:*** $2076. Room and board charges vary according to board plan. ***Payment plan:*** deferred payment.

FRESHMAN FINANCIAL AID (Fall 1998) 1154 applied for aid; of those 67% were deemed to have need. 91% of freshmen with need received aid; of those 20% had need fully met. *Average percent of need met:* 89% (excluding resources awarded to replace EFC). *Average financial aid package:* $4200 (excluding resources awarded to replace EFC). 16% of all full-time freshmen had no need and received non-need-based aid.

UNDERGRADUATE FINANCIAL AID (Fall 1998) 6,326 applied for aid; of those 63% were deemed to have need. 95% of undergraduates with need received aid; of those 20% had need fully met. *Average percent of need met:* 87% (excluding resources awarded to replace EFC). *Average financial aid package:* $5152 (excluding resources awarded to replace EFC). 13% of all full-time undergraduates had no need and received non-need-based aid.

GIFT AID (NEED-BASED) ***Total amount:*** $6,197,713 (69% Federal, 26% state, 3% institutional, 2% external sources). ***Receiving aid:*** *Freshmen:* 23% (353); *all full-time undergraduates:* 26% (2,054). ***Average award:*** Freshmen: $2607; Undergraduates: $2814. ***Scholarships, grants, and awards:*** Federal Pell, FSEOG, state, college/university gift aid from institutional funds.

GIFT AID (NON-NEED-BASED) ***Total amount:*** $1,215,772 (8% state, 36% institutional, 56% external sources). ***Receiving aid:*** *Freshmen:* 10% (154); *Undergraduates:* 5% (421). ***Scholarships, grants, and awards by category:*** *Academic Interests/Achievement:* 329 awards ($179,300 total): architecture, biological sciences, business, communication, computer science, education, English, foreign languages, general academic interests/achievements, health fields, home economics, humanities, international studies, mathematics, military science, physical sciences, premedicine, social sciences. *Creative Arts/Performance:* applied art and design, creative writing, dance, music, performing arts, theater/drama. *Special Achievements/Activities:* 56 awards ($15,050 total): general special achievements/activities, leadership. *Special Characteristics:* 20 awards ($18,500 total): general special characteristics, out-of-state students. ***ROTC:*** Army.

LOANS ***Student loans:*** $15,592,997 (80% need-based, 20% non-need-based). 77% of past graduating class borrowed through all loan programs. Average indebtedness per student: $12,921. ***Average need-based loan:*** Freshmen: $2587; Undergraduates: $3465. ***Parent loans:*** $722,033 (4% need-based, 96% non-need-based). ***Programs:*** Perkins, college/university.

WORK-STUDY ***Federal work-study:*** *Total amount:* $1,871,051; jobs available.

APPLYING for FINANCIAL AID ***Required financial aid form:*** FAFSA. ***Financial aid deadline (priority):*** 6/15. ***Notification date:*** Continuous. Students must reply within 4 weeks of notification.

CONTACT Mr. Philip George, Director, Financial Aid, University of Wisconsin–Stevens Point, 105 Student Services Center, Stevens Point, WI 54481-3897, 715-346-4771. *Fax:* 715-346-3526. *E-mail:* pgeorge@uwsp.edu

UNIVERSITY OF WISCONSIN–STOUT

Menomonie, WI

Tuition & fees (WI res): $3256 **Average undergraduate aid package: $5865**

ABOUT THE INSTITUTION State-supported, coed. Awards: bachelor's and master's degrees. 21 undergraduate majors. Total enrollment: 7,518. Undergraduates: 6,932. Federal methodology is used as a basis for awarding need-based institutional aid.

UNDERGRADUATE EXPENSES for 1999–2000 ***Application fee:*** $35. ***Tuition, state resident:*** full-time $2594; part-time $114 per credit. ***Tuition, nonresident:*** full-time $9458; part-time $400 per credit. ***Required fees:*** full-time $662; $24 per credit. Full-time tuition and fees vary according to reciprocity agreements. Part-time tuition and fees vary according to reciprocity agreements. ***College room and board:*** $3284; ***room only:*** $1816. Room and board charges vary according to board plan. ***Payment plan:*** installment.

FRESHMAN FINANCIAL AID (Fall 1998) 958 applied for aid; of those 80% were deemed to have need. 98% of freshmen with need received aid; of those 23% had need fully met. *Average percent of need met:* 65% (excluding resources awarded to replace EFC). *Average financial aid package:* $4630 (excluding resources awarded to replace EFC). 13% of all full-time freshmen had no need and received non-need-based aid.

UNDERGRADUATE FINANCIAL AID (Fall 1998) 4,051 applied for aid; of those 81% were deemed to have need. 99% of undergraduates with need received aid; of those 40% had need fully met. *Average percent of need met:* 74% (excluding resources awarded to replace EFC). *Average financial aid package:* $5865 (excluding resources awarded to replace EFC). 15% of all full-time undergraduates had no need and received non-need-based aid.

GIFT AID (NEED-BASED) ***Total amount:*** $5,513,814 (74% Federal, 26% state). ***Receiving aid:*** *Freshmen:* 28% (382); *all full-time undergraduates:* 29% (1,781). ***Scholarships, grants, and awards:*** Federal Pell, FSEOG, state, private, college/university gift aid from institutional funds.

GIFT AID (NON-NEED-BASED) ***Total amount:*** $1,424,949 (5% state, 8% institutional, 87% external sources). ***Receiving aid:*** *Freshmen:* 17% (227); *Undergraduates:* 9% (564). ***Scholarships, grants, and awards by category:*** *Academic Interests/Achievement:* business, education, engineering/

technologies, general academic interests/achievements, home economics, mathematics. *Creative Arts/Performance:* applied art and design, art/fine arts, music. *Special Achievements/Activities:* general special achievements/activities, memberships. *Special Characteristics:* adult students, international students, local/state students, members of minority groups, out-of-state students, previous college experience, veterans, veterans' children.

LOANS ***Student loans:*** $16,148,883 (63% need-based, 37% non-need-based). ***Parent loans:*** $591,639 (100% non-need-based). ***Programs:*** FFEL (Subsidized and Unsubsidized Stafford, PLUS), Perkins.

WORK-STUDY ***Federal work-study:*** *Total amount:* $624,182; 556 jobs averaging $1193.

APPLYING for FINANCIAL AID ***Required financial aid form:*** FAFSA. ***Financial aid deadline (priority):*** 4/1. ***Notification date:*** Continuous beginning 5/1. Students must reply within 2 weeks of notification.

CONTACT Office of Financial Aid, University of Wisconsin–Stout, 210 Bowman Hall, Menomonie, WI 54751, 715-232-1363 or toll-free 800-HI-STOUT (in-state). *Fax:* 715-232-5246.

UNIVERSITY OF WISCONSIN–SUPERIOR

Superior, WI

Tuition & fees (WI res): $2974 **Average undergraduate aid package: $5026**

ABOUT THE INSTITUTION State-supported, coed. Awards: associate, bachelor's, and master's degrees. 61 undergraduate majors. Total enrollment: 2,660. Undergraduates: 2,264. Federal methodology is used as a basis for awarding need-based institutional aid.

UNDERGRADUATE EXPENSES for 1999–2000 ***Application fee:*** $35. ***Tuition, state resident:*** full-time $2594; part-time $109 per credit hour. ***Tuition, nonresident:*** full-time $9458; part-time $395 per credit hour. ***Required fees:*** full-time $380. Full-time tuition and fees vary according to course load and reciprocity agreements. Part-time tuition and fees vary according to course load and reciprocity agreements. ***College room and board:*** $3426; ***room only:*** $1740. ***Payment plan:*** installment.

FRESHMAN FINANCIAL AID (Fall 1999) 315 applied for aid; of those 76% were deemed to have need. 100% of freshmen with need received aid; of those 40% had need fully met. *Average percent of need met:* 75% (excluding resources awarded to replace EFC). *Average financial aid package:* $4318 (excluding resources awarded to replace EFC).

UNDERGRADUATE FINANCIAL AID (Fall 1999) 1,499 applied for aid; of those 82% were deemed to have need. 100% of undergraduates with need received aid; of those 54% had need fully met. *Average percent of need met:* 82% (excluding resources awarded to replace EFC). *Average financial aid package:* $5026 (excluding resources awarded to replace EFC).

GIFT AID (NEED-BASED) ***Total amount:*** $2,953,332 (55% Federal, 30% state, 8% institutional, 7% external sources). ***Receiving aid:*** *Freshmen:* 34% (179); *all full-time undergraduates:* 51% (902). ***Average award:*** Freshmen: $2104; Undergraduates: $2200. ***Scholarships, grants, and awards:*** Federal Pell, FSEOG, state, private, college/university gift aid from institutional funds.

GIFT AID (NON-NEED-BASED) ***Total amount:*** $1,013,118 (66% state, 20% institutional, 14% external sources). ***Receiving aid:*** *Freshmen:* 2% (11); *Undergraduates:* 2% (36). ***Scholarships, grants, and awards by category:*** *Academic Interests/Achievement:* biological sciences, business, communication, computer science, education, English, general academic interests/achievements, health fields, humanities, mathematics, physical sciences, social sciences. *Creative Arts/Performance:* art/fine arts, cinema/film/broadcasting, general creative arts/performance, journalism/publications, music, performing arts, theater/drama. ***Tuition waivers:*** Full or partial for minority students, children of alumni, employees or children of employees, adult students. ***ROTC:*** Air Force cooperative.

LOANS ***Student loans:*** $5,586,298 (64% need-based, 36% non-need-based). 65% of past graduating class borrowed through all loan programs. Average indebtedness per student: $12,500. ***Average need-based loan:*** Freshmen: $1890; Undergraduates: $2578. ***Parent loans:*** $130,389 (29% need-based, 71% non-need-based). ***Programs:*** Federal Direct (Subsidized and Unsubsidized Stafford, PLUS), Perkins, state, college/university.

WORK-STUDY ***Federal work-study:*** *Total amount:* $302,152; 260 jobs averaging $1320. ***State or other work-study/employment:*** *Total amount:* $78,360 (25% need-based, 75% non-need-based). Part-time jobs available.

APPLYING for FINANCIAL AID ***Required financial aid form:*** FAFSA. ***Financial aid deadline (priority):*** 1/3. ***Notification date:*** 4/15. Students must reply within 2 weeks of notification.

CONTACT Financial Aid Office, University of Wisconsin–Superior, 1800 Grand Avenue, Superior, WI 54880-2873, 715-394-8200. *Fax:* 715-394-8027.

UNIVERSITY OF WISCONSIN–WHITEWATER

Whitewater, WI

Tuition & fees (WI res): $3105 **Average undergraduate aid package: $5729**

ABOUT THE INSTITUTION State-supported, coed. Awards: associate, bachelor's, and master's degrees. 51 undergraduate majors. Total enrollment: 10,654. Undergraduates: 9,583. Federal methodology is used as a basis for awarding need-based institutional aid.

UNDERGRADUATE EXPENSES for 1999–2000 ***Application fee:*** $35. ***Tuition, state resident:*** full-time $3105; part-time $130 per credit. ***Tuition, nonresident:*** full-time $9969; part-time $416 per credit. Full-time tuition and fees vary according to reciprocity agreements. Part-time tuition and fees vary according to reciprocity agreements. ***College room and board:*** $3204; ***room only:*** $1810. Room and board charges vary according to board plan. ***Payment plan:*** installment.

UNDERGRADUATE FINANCIAL AID (Fall 1998) 5,411 applied for aid; of those 80% were deemed to have need. 100% of undergraduates with need received aid. *Average percent of need met:* 86% (excluding resources awarded to replace EFC). *Average financial aid package:* $5729 (excluding resources awarded to replace EFC). 25% of all full-time undergraduates had no need and received non-need-based aid.

GIFT AID (NEED-BASED) ***Total amount:*** $5,394,380 (70% Federal, 30% state). ***Receiving aid:*** *All full-time undergraduates:* 26% (2,135). ***Average award:*** Undergraduates: $2999. ***Scholarships, grants, and awards:*** Federal Pell, FSEOG, state, private, college/university gift aid from institutional funds.

GIFT AID (NON-NEED-BASED) ***Total amount:*** $1,798,782 (2% Federal, 20% state, 29% institutional, 49% external sources). ***Receiving aid:*** *Undergraduates:* 9% (782). ***Scholarships, grants, and awards by category:*** *Academic Interests/Achievement:* biological sciences, business, communication, computer science, education, English, foreign languages, general academic interests/achievements, humanities, mathematics, physical sciences, premedicine, social sciences. *Creative Arts/Performance:* art/fine arts, cinema/film/broadcasting, creative writing, journalism/publications, music, theater/drama. *Special Achievements/Activities:* leadership. *Special Characteristics:* adult students, ethnic background, handicapped students, international students, local/state students, members of minority groups, out-of-state students. ***ROTC:*** Army, Air Force.

LOANS ***Student loans:*** $21,266,497 (63% need-based, 37% non-need-based). 86% of past graduating class borrowed through all loan programs. Average indebtedness per student: $10,451. ***Average need-based loan:*** Undergraduates: $3089. ***Parent loans:*** $918,910 (100% non-need-based). ***Programs:*** Federal Direct (Subsidized and Unsubsidized Stafford, PLUS), Perkins.

WORK-STUDY ***Federal work-study:*** *Total amount:* $679,695; 585 jobs averaging $1161. ***State or other work-study/employment:*** *Total amount:* $2,578,469 (100% non-need-based). Part-time jobs available.

APPLYING for FINANCIAL AID ***Required financial aid form:*** FAFSA. ***Financial aid deadline (priority):*** 3/15. ***Notification date:*** Continuous beginning 4/15. Students must reply within 2 weeks of notification.

CONTACT Ms. Carol Miller, Director of Financial Aid, University of Wisconsin–Whitewater, 800 West Main Street, Whitewater, WI 53190-1790, 262-472-1130. *Fax:* 262-472-5655.

UNIVERSITY OF WYOMING

Laramie, WY

Tuition & fees (WY res): $2416 **Average undergraduate aid package: $5814**

ABOUT THE INSTITUTION State-supported, coed. Awards: bachelor's, master's, doctoral, and first professional degrees and post-master's certificates. 84 undergraduate majors. Total enrollment: 10,940. Undergraduates: 8,438. Freshmen: 1,225. Federal methodology is used as a basis for awarding need-based institutional aid.

UNDERGRADUATE EXPENSES for 1999–2000 ***Application fee:*** $30. ***Tuition, state resident:*** full-time $2016; part-time $84 per semester hour. ***Tuition, nonresident:*** full-time $7284; part-time $304 per semester hour. ***Required fees:*** full-time $400; $7 per semester hour. ***College room and board:*** $4618; ***room only:*** $1846. Room and board charges vary according to board plan. ***Payment plans:*** installment, deferred payment.

FRESHMAN FINANCIAL AID (Fall 1998) 1166 applied for aid; of those 70% were deemed to have need. 92% of freshmen with need received aid; of those 66% had need fully met. *Average percent of need met:* 75% (excluding resources awarded to replace EFC). *Average financial aid package:* $4959 (excluding resources awarded to replace EFC). 30% of all full-time freshmen had no need and received non-need-based aid.

UNDERGRADUATE FINANCIAL AID (Fall 1998) 6,810 applied for aid; of those 60% were deemed to have need. 85% of undergraduates with need received aid; of those 69% had need fully met. *Average percent of need met:* 74% (excluding resources awarded to replace EFC). *Average financial aid package:* $5814 (excluding resources awarded to replace EFC). 36% of all full-time undergraduates had no need and received non-need-based aid.

GIFT AID (NEED-BASED) ***Total amount:*** $6,420,838 (82% Federal, 9% institutional, 9% external sources). ***Receiving aid:*** *Freshmen:* 24% (298); *all full-time undergraduates:* 17% (1,348). ***Average award:*** Freshmen: $1915; Undergraduates: $1915. ***Scholarships, grants, and awards:*** Federal Pell, FSEOG, state, private, college/university gift aid from institutional funds.

GIFT AID (NON-NEED-BASED) ***Total amount:*** $7,918,937 (13% Federal, 2% state, 69% institutional, 16% external sources). ***Receiving aid:*** *Freshmen:* 27% (331); *Undergraduates:* 14% (1,085). ***Scholarships, grants, and awards by category:*** *Academic Interests/Achievement:* agriculture, business, communication, computer science, education, engineering/technologies, English, foreign languages, general academic interests/achievements, health fields, home economics, mathematics, military science, physical sciences, social sciences. *Creative Arts/Performance:* dance, debating, music, theater/drama. *Special Achievements/Activities:* leadership, rodeo. *Special Characteristics:* adult students, children and siblings of alumni, ethnic background, first-generation college students, handicapped students, international students, local/state students, out-of-state students, veterans. ***Tuition waivers:*** Full or partial for children of alumni, employees or children of employees, senior citizens. ***ROTC:*** Army, Air Force.

LOANS ***Student loans:*** $16,192,654 (62% need-based, 38% non-need-based). 76% of past graduating class borrowed through all loan programs. Average indebtedness per student: $16,168. ***Average need-based loan:*** Freshmen: $2096; Undergraduates: $3192. ***Parent loans:*** $974,346 (100% non-need-based). ***Programs:*** FFEL (Subsidized and Unsubsidized Stafford, PLUS), alternative loans.

WORK-STUDY ***Federal work-study:*** *Total amount:* $372,806; 342 jobs averaging $1090.

ATHLETIC AWARDS *Total amount:* 2,224,194 (100% non-need-based).

APPLYING for FINANCIAL AID ***Required financial aid forms:*** FAFSA, institution's own form. ***Financial aid deadline (priority):*** 3/1. ***Notification date:*** Continuous beginning 5/1. Students must reply within 2 weeks of notification.

CONTACT Mr. John Nutter, Director, Student Financial Aid, University of Wyoming, PO Box 3335, Laramie, WY 82071-3335, 307-766-2116 or toll-free 800-342-5996. *Fax:* 307-766-3800. *E-mail:* finaid@uwyo.edu

UPPER IOWA UNIVERSITY

Fayette, IA

Tuition & fees: $10,752 **Average undergraduate aid package: $6000**

ABOUT THE INSTITUTION Independent, coed. Awards: associate, bachelor's, and master's degrees (also offers continuing education program with significant enrollment not reflected in profile). 41 undergraduate majors. Total enrollment: 671. Undergraduates: 671. Freshmen: 140. Federal methodology is used as a basis for awarding need-based institutional aid.

UNDERGRADUATE EXPENSES for 1999–2000 ***Application fee:*** $15. ***Comprehensive fee:*** $14,908 includes full-time tuition ($10,752) and room and board ($4156). Full-time tuition and fees vary according to location. ***Part-time tuition:*** $360 per semester hour. Part-time tuition and fees vary according to location. ***Payment plan:*** installment.

FRESHMAN FINANCIAL AID (Fall 1999, est.) 875 applied for aid; of those 100% were deemed to have need. 100% of freshmen with need received aid. *Average percent of need met:* 50% (excluding resources awarded to replace EFC). *Average financial aid package:* $10,500 (excluding resources awarded to replace EFC).

UNDERGRADUATE FINANCIAL AID (Fall 1999, est.) 3,700 applied for aid; of those 100% were deemed to have need. 100% of undergraduates with need received aid. *Average percent of need met:* 50% (excluding resources awarded to replace EFC). *Average financial aid package:* $6000 (excluding resources awarded to replace EFC).

GIFT AID (NEED-BASED) ***Total amount:*** $4,743,329 (46% Federal, 33% state, 21% institutional). ***Receiving aid:*** *Freshmen:* 75% (800); *all full-time undergraduates:* 75% (3,300). ***Average award:*** Freshmen: $6875; Undergraduates: $4000. ***Scholarships, grants, and awards:*** Federal Pell, FSEOG, state, private, college/university gift aid from institutional funds.

GIFT AID (NON-NEED-BASED) ***Total amount:*** $841,475 (92% institutional, 8% external sources). ***Scholarships, grants, and awards by category:*** *Academic Interests/Achievement:* general academic interests/achievements. *Creative Arts/Performance:* art/fine arts, music, theater/drama. *Special Characteristics:* children and siblings of alumni, children of current students, parents of current students, religious affiliation, spouses of current students. ***Tuition waivers:*** Full or partial for employees or children of employees.

LOANS ***Student loans:*** $9,394,969 (59% need-based, 41% non-need-based). 96% of past graduating class borrowed through all loan programs. Average indebtedness per student: $17,125. ***Average need-based loan:*** Freshmen: $2000; Undergraduates: $3500. ***Parent loans:*** $554,373 (100% non-need-based). ***Programs:*** FFEL (Subsidized and Unsubsidized Stafford, PLUS), Perkins, college/university, TERI Loans, Norwest Collegiate Loans, partnership loan.

WORK-STUDY ***Federal work-study:*** *Total amount:* $361,811; 219 jobs averaging $1650. ***State or other work-study/employment:*** *Total amount:* $48,000 (100% need-based). 29 part-time jobs averaging $1650.

APPLYING for FINANCIAL AID ***Required financial aid form:*** FAFSA. ***Financial aid deadline (priority):*** 6/1. ***Notification date:*** Continuous. Students must reply within 3 weeks of notification.

CONTACT Jobyna Johnston, Director of Financial Aid, Upper Iowa University, Parker Fox Hall, Box 1859, Fayette, IA 52142-1859, 319-425-5393 or toll-free 800-553-4150. *Fax:* 319-425-5277. *E-mail:* jobyna@uiu.edu

URBANA UNIVERSITY

Urbana, OH

Tuition & fees: $11,488 **Average undergraduate aid package: N/A**

ABOUT THE INSTITUTION Independent religious, coed. Awards: associate, bachelor's, and master's degrees. 28 undergraduate majors. Total enrollment: 1,144. Undergraduates: 1,111. Freshmen: 167. Federal methodology is used as a basis for awarding need-based institutional aid.

UNDERGRADUATE EXPENSES for 1999–2000 ***Application fee:*** $25. ***Comprehensive fee:*** $16,488 includes full-time tuition ($11,388), mandatory fees ($100), and room and board ($5000). ***College room only:*** $2100. Full-time tuition and fees vary according to location. Room and board charges vary according to student level. ***Part-time tuition:*** $232 per credit hour. ***Part-time fees:*** $25 per term part-time. Part-time tuition and fees vary according to location. ***Payment plans:*** installment, deferred payment.

GIFT AID (NEED-BASED) ***Total amount:*** $968,187 (71% Federal, 29% state). ***Scholarships, grants, and awards:*** Federal Pell, FSEOG, state, private, college/university gift aid from institutional funds.

GIFT AID (NON-NEED-BASED) ***Total amount:*** $1,710,655 (22% state, 74% institutional, 4% external sources). ***Scholarships, grants, and awards by category:*** *Academic Interests/Achievement:* general academic interests/achievements. *Creative Arts/Performance:* music, performing arts, theater/drama. *Special Achievements/Activities:* community service, leadership, religious involvement. *Special Characteristics:* children and siblings of alumni, children of faculty/staff. ***Tuition waivers:*** Full or partial for children of alumni, employees or children of employees, senior citizens.

LOANS ***Student loans:*** $2,479,952 (58% need-based, 42% non-need-based). ***Parent loans:*** $326,268 (100% need-based). ***Programs:*** FFEL (Subsidized and Unsubsidized Stafford, PLUS), Perkins.

WORK-STUDY ***Federal work-study:*** *Total amount:* $112,900; jobs available.

ATHLETIC AWARDS *Total amount:* 400,491 (100% non-need-based).

APPLYING for FINANCIAL AID ***Required financial aid forms:*** FAFSA, institution's own form. ***Financial aid deadline (priority):*** 5/1. ***Notification date:*** Continuous. Students must reply within 2 weeks of notification.

CONTACT Mrs. Jean Rabe, Director of Financial Aid, Urbana University, 579 College Way, Urbana, OH 43078-2091, 937-484-1355 or toll-free 800-787-2262 (in-state). *Fax:* 937-484-1389. *E-mail:* jrabe@urbana.edu

URSINUS COLLEGE

Collegeville, PA

Tuition & fees: $20,230 **Average undergraduate aid package: $15,223**

ABOUT THE INSTITUTION Independent religious, coed. Awards: bachelor's degrees. 48 undergraduate majors. Total enrollment: 1,240. Undergraduates: 1,240. Freshmen: 353. Both federal and institutional methodology are used as a basis for awarding need-based institutional aid.

UNDERGRADUATE EXPENSES for 1999–2000 ***Application fee:*** $30. ***Comprehensive fee:*** $26,200 includes full-time tuition ($19,950), mandatory fees ($280), and room and board ($5970). ***Part-time tuition:*** $685 per semester hour. Part-time tuition and fees vary according to class time and program. ***Payment plan:*** installment.

FRESHMAN FINANCIAL AID (Fall 1999) 309 applied for aid; of those 76% were deemed to have need. 100% of freshmen with need received aid; of those 68% had need fully met. *Average percent of need met:* 90% (excluding resources awarded to replace EFC). *Average financial aid package:* $16,217 (excluding resources awarded to replace EFC). 24% of all full-time freshmen had no need and received non-need-based aid.

UNDERGRADUATE FINANCIAL AID (Fall 1999) 1,136 applied for aid; of those 88% were deemed to have need. 100% of undergraduates with need received aid; of those 75% had need fully met. *Average percent of need met:* 90% (excluding resources awarded to replace EFC). *Average financial aid package:* $15,223 (excluding resources awarded to replace EFC). 13% of all full-time undergraduates had no need and received non-need-based aid.

GIFT AID (NEED-BASED) ***Total amount:*** $11,166,413 (5% Federal, 9% state, 83% institutional, 3% external sources). ***Receiving aid:*** *Freshmen:* 67% (225); *all full-time undergraduates:* 70% (857). ***Average award:*** Freshmen: $12,915; Undergraduates: $11,061. ***Scholarships, grants, and awards:*** Federal Pell, FSEOG, state, private, college/university gift aid from institutional funds, Office of Vocational Rehabilitation Awards.

GIFT AID (NON-NEED-BASED) ***Total amount:*** $1,531,983 (100% institutional). ***Receiving aid:*** *Freshmen:* 6% (20); *Undergraduates:* 7% (80). ***Scholarships, grants, and awards by category:*** *Academic Interests/Achievement:* general academic interests/achievements. *Creative Arts/Performance:* art/fine arts, creative writing, music. *Special Achievements/Activities:* leadership. *Special Characteristics:* general special characteristics, siblings of current students. ***Tuition waivers:*** Full or partial for employees or children of employees, senior citizens.

LOANS ***Student loans:*** $5,230,371 (100% need-based). 79% of past graduating class borrowed through all loan programs. Average indebtedness per student: $16,000. ***Average need-based loan:*** Freshmen: $2562; Undergraduates: $3483. ***Parent loans:*** $1,320,902 (100% need-based). ***Programs:*** FFEL (Subsidized and Unsubsidized Stafford, PLUS), Perkins, college/university.

WORK-STUDY ***Federal work-study:*** *Total amount:* $777,650; 538 jobs averaging $1445.

APPLYING for FINANCIAL AID ***Required financial aid forms:*** FAFSA, institution's own form, CSS Financial Aid PROFILE. ***Financial aid deadline (priority):*** 2/15. ***Notification date:*** 4/1. Students must reply by 5/1.

CONTACT Ms. Suzanne B. Sparrow, Financial Aid Officer, Ursinus College, PO Box 1000, Collegeville, PA 19426-1000, 610-409-3600 Ext. 2242. *Fax:* 610-489-0627. *E-mail:* ssparrow@acad.ursinus.edu

URSULINE COLLEGE

Pepper Pike, OH

Tuition & fees: $13,760 **Average undergraduate aid package: N/A**

ABOUT THE INSTITUTION Independent Roman Catholic, coed, primarily women. Awards: bachelor's and master's degrees. 32 undergraduate majors. Total enrollment: 1,259. Undergraduates: 1,040. Federal methodology is used as a basis for awarding need-based institutional aid.

UNDERGRADUATE EXPENSES for 1999–2000 ***Application fee:*** $25. ***Comprehensive fee:*** $18,320 includes full-time tuition ($13,760) and room and board ($4560). ***Part-time tuition:*** $430 per credit hour. ***Payment plan:*** installment.

GIFT AID (NEED-BASED) ***Total amount:*** $3,006,549 (26% Federal, 31% state, 39% institutional, 4% external sources). ***Scholarships, grants, and awards:*** Federal Pell, FSEOG, state, college/university gift aid from institutional funds.

GIFT AID (NON-NEED-BASED) ***Total amount:*** $2000 (100% state). ***Scholarships, grants, and awards by category:*** *Academic Interests/Achievement:* general academic interests/achievements. *Creative Arts/Performance:* general creative arts/performance. *Special Achievements/Activities:* community service, leadership. *Special Characteristics:* children and siblings of alumni, children of faculty/staff, relatives of clergy, religious affiliation, siblings of current students. ***Tuition waivers:*** Full or partial for employees or children of employees. ***ROTC:*** Army cooperative.

LOANS ***Student loans:*** $4,206,790 (62% need-based, 38% non-need-based). 66% of past graduating class borrowed through all loan programs. ***Parent loans:*** $101,987 (100% non-need-based). ***Programs:*** FFEL (Subsidized and Unsubsidized Stafford, PLUS), Perkins, college/university.

WORK-STUDY ***Federal work-study:*** *Total amount:* $83,669; jobs available.

APPLYING for FINANCIAL AID ***Required financial aid form:*** FAFSA. ***Financial aid deadline (priority):*** 4/1. ***Notification date:*** Continuous.

CONTACT Ms. Mary Lynn Perri, Director of Financial Aid, Ursuline College, 2550 Lander Road, Pepper Pike, OH 44124-4398, 440-646-8331.

UTAH STATE UNIVERSITY

Logan, UT

Tuition & fees (UT res): $2314 **Average undergraduate aid package: $5400**

ABOUT THE INSTITUTION State-supported, coed. Awards: associate, bachelor's, master's, and doctoral degrees. 107 undergraduate majors. Total enrollment: 20,865. Undergraduates: 17,228. Freshmen: 2,564. Federal methodology is used as a basis for awarding need-based institutional aid.

UNDERGRADUATE EXPENSES for 1999–2000 ***Application fee:*** $35. ***Tuition, state resident:*** full-time $1871. ***Tuition, nonresident:*** full-time $6560. ***Required fees:*** full-time $443. Full-time tuition and fees vary according to course load. Part-time tuition and fees vary according to course load. ***College room and board:*** $3938; ***room only:*** $1558. Room and board charges vary according to board plan and housing facility. ***Payment plan:*** deferred payment.

Utah State University (continued)

FRESHMAN FINANCIAL AID (Fall 1998) 917 applied for aid; of those 84% were deemed to have need. 93% of freshmen with need received aid; of those 8% had need fully met. *Average percent of need met:* 54% (excluding resources awarded to replace EFC). *Average financial aid package:* $5137 (excluding resources awarded to replace EFC). 13% of all full-time freshmen had no need and received non-need-based aid.

UNDERGRADUATE FINANCIAL AID (Fall 1998) 5,992 applied for aid; of those 92% were deemed to have need. 97% of undergraduates with need received aid; of those 38% had need fully met. *Average percent of need met:* 60% (excluding resources awarded to replace EFC). *Average financial aid package:* $5400 (excluding resources awarded to replace EFC). 10% of all full-time undergraduates had no need and received non-need-based aid.

GIFT AID (NEED-BASED) ***Total amount:*** $10,818,726 (98% Federal, 2% state). ***Receiving aid:*** *Freshmen:* 19% (488); *all full-time undergraduates:* 37% (4,122). ***Average award:*** Freshmen: $2200; Undergraduates: $2300. ***Scholarships, grants, and awards:*** Federal Pell, FSEOG, state, private, college/university gift aid from institutional funds.

GIFT AID (NON-NEED-BASED) ***Total amount:*** $3,292,000 (82% institutional, 18% external sources). ***Receiving aid:*** *Freshmen:* 7% (195); *Undergraduates:* 11% (1,165). ***Scholarships, grants, and awards by category:*** *Academic Interests/Achievement:* 4,282 awards: agriculture, architecture, biological sciences, business, communication, computer science, education, engineering/technologies, English, foreign languages, general academic interests/achievements, health fields, home economics, humanities, international studies, library science, mathematics, physical sciences, premedicine, social sciences. *Creative Arts/Performance:* 123 awards ($111,561 total): applied art and design, art/fine arts, general creative arts/performance, journalism/publications, music, performing arts, theater/drama. *Special Achievements/Activities:* 424 awards ($384,496 total): cheerleading/drum major, general special achievements/activities, junior miss, leadership, memberships, religious involvement, rodeo. *Special Characteristics:* 2,271 awards ($3,605,704 total): adult students, children and siblings of alumni, children of faculty/staff, ethnic background, handicapped students, international students, local/state students, members of minority groups, out-of-state students, religious affiliation. ***Tuition waivers:*** Full or partial for minority students, children of alumni, employees or children of employees, adult students, senior citizens. ***ROTC:*** Air Force.

LOANS ***Student loans:*** $18,929,571 (78% need-based, 22% non-need-based). 50% of past graduating class borrowed through all loan programs. Average indebtedness per student: $13,400. ***Average need-based loan:*** Freshmen: $2480; Undergraduates: $3760. ***Parent loans:*** $427,000 (100% non-need-based). ***Programs:*** FFEL (Subsidized and Unsubsidized Stafford, PLUS), Perkins, college/university.

WORK-STUDY ***Federal work-study:*** *Total amount:* $1,066,252; 410 jobs averaging $2600. ***State or other work-study/employment:*** *Total amount:* $110,000 (100% need-based). 55 part-time jobs averaging $2000.

ATHLETIC AWARDS *Total amount:* 1,780,000 (100% non-need-based).

APPLYING for FINANCIAL AID ***Required financial aid forms:*** FAFSA, institution's own form, federal income tax form(s). ***Financial aid deadline:*** Continuous. ***Notification date:*** Continuous beginning 4/1. Students must reply within 4 weeks of notification.

CONTACT Karen Marshall, Business Manager, Utah State University, 1800 Old Main Hill, Logan, UT 84322-1800, 435-797-0174. *Fax:* 435-797-0654. *E-mail:* karenm@admissions.usu.edu

UTICA COLLEGE OF SYRACUSE UNIVERSITY

Utica, NY

Tuition & fees: $16,410 **Average undergraduate aid package: N/A**

ABOUT THE INSTITUTION Independent, coed. Awards: bachelor's and master's degrees. 41 undergraduate majors. Total enrollment: 2,059. Undergraduates: 2,017. Freshmen: 366. Federal methodology is used as a basis for awarding need-based institutional aid.

UNDERGRADUATE EXPENSES for 1999–2000 ***Application fee:*** $35. ***Comprehensive fee:*** $22,760 includes full-time tuition ($16,150), mandatory fees ($260), and room and board ($6350). ***College room only:*** $3200. Room and board charges vary according to board plan and housing facility. ***Part-time tuition:*** $545 per credit hour. ***Payment plan:*** deferred payment.

FRESHMAN FINANCIAL AID (Fall 1999, est.) 361 applied for aid; of those 94% were deemed to have need. 100% of freshmen with need received aid; of those 15% had need fully met.

UNDERGRADUATE FINANCIAL AID (Fall 1999, est.) 1,557 applied for aid; of those 93% were deemed to have need. 100% of undergraduates with need received aid; of those 16% had need fully met.

GIFT AID (NEED-BASED) ***Total amount:*** $13,739,632 (12% Federal, 19% state, 67% institutional, 2% external sources). ***Receiving aid:*** *Freshmen:* 339; *all full-time undergraduates:* 1,414. ***Average award:*** Freshmen: $11,830; Undergraduates: $9271. ***Scholarships, grants, and awards:*** Federal Pell, FSEOG, state, private, college/university gift aid from institutional funds.

GIFT AID (NON-NEED-BASED) ***Total amount:*** $363,243 (6% state, 85% institutional, 9% external sources). ***Receiving aid:*** *Freshmen:* 122; *Undergraduates:* 418. ***Scholarships, grants, and awards by category:*** *Academic Interests/Achievement:* 326 awards ($1,372,010 total): general academic interests/achievements. ***Tuition waivers:*** Full or partial for employees or children of employees, senior citizens. ***ROTC:*** Army cooperative, Air Force.

LOANS ***Student loans:*** $7,360,824 (96% need-based, 4% non-need-based). 94% of past graduating class borrowed through all loan programs. ***Average need-based loan:*** Freshmen: $2524; Undergraduates: $3885. ***Parent loans:*** $1,763,026 (94% need-based, 6% non-need-based). ***Programs:*** Federal Direct (Subsidized and Unsubsidized Stafford, PLUS), Perkins, GATE Loans.

WORK-STUDY ***Federal work-study:*** *Total amount:* $952,176; 696 jobs averaging $1368. ***State or other work-study/employment:*** *Total amount:* $308,223 (84% need-based, 16% non-need-based). 230 part-time jobs averaging $1122.

APPLYING for FINANCIAL AID ***Required financial aid forms:*** FAFSA, state aid form. ***Financial aid deadline (priority):*** 2/15. ***Notification date:*** Continuous beginning 3/1. Students must reply by 5/1 or within 4 weeks of notification.

CONTACT Mrs. Elizabeth C. Wilson, Director of Financial Aid, Utica College of Syracuse University, Burrstone Road, Utica, NY 13502-4892, 888-458-8422 or toll-free 800-782-8884. *Fax:* 315-792-3368.

VALDOSTA STATE UNIVERSITY

Valdosta, GA

Tuition & fees (GA res): $2290 **Average undergraduate aid package: $7557**

ABOUT THE INSTITUTION State-supported, coed. Awards: associate, bachelor's, master's, and doctoral degrees. 66 undergraduate majors. Total enrollment: 8,752. Undergraduates: 7,635. Freshmen: 1,259. Federal methodology is used as a basis for awarding need-based institutional aid.

UNDERGRADUATE EXPENSES for 1999–2000 ***Application fee:*** $20. ***Tuition, state resident:*** full-time $2290; part-time $76 per semester hour. ***Tuition, nonresident:*** full-time $7714; part-time $302 per semester hour. Part-time tuition and fees vary according to course load. ***College room and board:*** $3954; ***room only:*** $1844. Room and board charges vary according to board plan.

FRESHMAN FINANCIAL AID (Fall 1999, est.) 1019 applied for aid; of those 56% were deemed to have need. 100% of freshmen with need received aid; of those 51% had need fully met. *Average percent of need met:* 80% (excluding resources awarded to replace EFC). *Average financial aid package:* $5683 (excluding resources awarded to replace EFC). 40% of all full-time freshmen had no need and received non-need-based aid.

UNDERGRADUATE FINANCIAL AID (Fall 1999, est.) 4,566 applied for aid; of those 68% were deemed to have need. 97% of undergraduates with need received aid; of those 36% had need fully met. *Average percent of need met:* 88% (excluding resources awarded to replace EFC). *Average*

financial aid package: $7557 (excluding resources awarded to replace EFC). 39% of all full-time undergraduates had no need and received non-need-based aid.

GIFT AID (NEED-BASED) ***Total amount:*** $9,339,546 (53% Federal, 44% state, 2% institutional, 1% external sources). ***Receiving aid:*** *Freshmen:* 25% (281); *all full-time undergraduates:* 32% (1,624). ***Average award:*** Freshmen: $1995; Undergraduates: $2150. ***Scholarships, grants, and awards:*** Federal Pell, FSEOG, state, private, college/university gift aid from institutional funds.

GIFT AID (NON-NEED-BASED) ***Total amount:*** $2,610,969 (84% state, 9% institutional, 7% external sources). ***Receiving aid:*** *Freshmen:* 46% (509); *Undergraduates:* 28% (1,449). ***Scholarships, grants, and awards by category:*** *Academic Interests/Achievement:* 405 awards ($430,500 total): business, education, general academic interests/achievements, health fields, military science, social sciences. *Creative Arts/Performance:* 35 awards ($42,550 total): art/fine arts, journalism/publications, music, theater/drama. *Special Achievements/Activities:* 22 awards ($25,000 total): community service, general special achievements/activities, hobbies/interests. *Special Characteristics:* 38 awards ($34,800 total): children of public servants, general special characteristics, international students. ***Tuition waivers:*** Full or partial for employees or children of employees, senior citizens. ***ROTC:*** Air Force.

LOANS ***Student loans:*** $27,226,771 (61% need-based, 39% non-need-based). 61% of past graduating class borrowed through all loan programs. Average indebtedness per student: $12,725. ***Average need-based loan:*** Freshmen: $2016; Undergraduates: $3020. ***Parent loans:*** $11,000,174 (32% need-based, 68% non-need-based). ***Programs:*** Federal Direct (Subsidized and Unsubsidized Stafford, PLUS), college/university.

WORK-STUDY ***Federal work-study:*** *Total amount:* $491,906; 193 jobs averaging $2549.

ATHLETIC AWARDS *Total amount:* 361,582 (50% need-based, 50% non-need-based).

APPLYING for FINANCIAL AID ***Required financial aid forms:*** FAFSA, institution's own form, state aid form. ***Financial aid deadline (priority):*** 4/1. ***Notification date:*** Continuous beginning 5/1.

CONTACT Mr. Douglas R. Tanner, Manager of Operations, Valdosta State University, 1500 North Patterson Street, Valdosta, GA 31698, 912-333-5935 or toll-free 800-618-1878 Ext. 1. *Fax:* 912-333-5430.

VALLEY CITY STATE UNIVERSITY

Valley City, ND

Tuition & fees (ND res): $3097 **Average undergraduate aid package: $5662**

ABOUT THE INSTITUTION State-supported, coed. Awards: bachelor's degrees. 29 undergraduate majors. Total enrollment: 1,077. Undergraduates: 1,077. Freshmen: 173. Federal methodology is used as a basis for awarding need-based institutional aid.

UNDERGRADUATE EXPENSES for 1999–2000 ***Application fee:*** $25. ***Tuition, state resident:*** full-time $1906; part-time $129 per semester hour. ***Tuition, nonresident:*** full-time $5089; part-time $262 per semester hour. ***Required fees:*** full-time $1191. Full-time tuition and fees vary according to reciprocity agreements. Part-time tuition and fees vary according to course load and reciprocity agreements. ***College room and board:*** $2800; ***room only:*** $1050. Room and board charges vary according to board plan and housing facility.

FRESHMAN FINANCIAL AID (Fall 1998) 179 applied for aid; of those 77% were deemed to have need. 99% of freshmen with need received aid; of those 65% had need fully met. *Average percent of need met:* 73% (excluding resources awarded to replace EFC). *Average financial aid package:* $4877 (excluding resources awarded to replace EFC). 21% of all full-time freshmen had no need and received non-need-based aid.

UNDERGRADUATE FINANCIAL AID (Fall 1998) 584 applied for aid; of those 77% were deemed to have need. 99% of undergraduates with need received aid; of those 69% had need fully met. *Average percent of need met:* 86% (excluding resources awarded to replace EFC). *Average financial aid package:* $5662 (excluding resources awarded to replace EFC). 20% of all full-time undergraduates had no need and received non-need-based aid.

GIFT AID (NEED-BASED) ***Total amount:*** $1,157,764 (75% Federal, 6% state, 15% institutional, 4% external sources). ***Receiving aid:*** *Freshmen:* 65% (131); *all full-time undergraduates:* 44% (363). ***Average award:*** Freshmen: $2628; Undergraduates: $1567. ***Scholarships, grants, and awards:*** Federal Pell, FSEOG, state, private, college/university gift aid from institutional funds.

GIFT AID (NON-NEED-BASED) ***Total amount:*** $107,138 (4% Federal, 2% state, 75% institutional, 19% external sources). ***Receiving aid:*** *Freshmen:* 4% (8); *Undergraduates:* 2% (19). ***Scholarships, grants, and awards by category:*** *Academic Interests/Achievement:* biological sciences, business, communication, education, engineering/technologies, English, general academic interests/achievements, library science, mathematics, physical sciences, social sciences. *Creative Arts/Performance:* art/fine arts, journalism/publications, music, theater/drama. *Special Characteristics:* children and siblings of alumni, ethnic background, international students, local/state students. ***Tuition waivers:*** Full or partial for children of alumni, employees or children of employees.

LOANS ***Student loans:*** $2,469,850 (79% need-based, 21% non-need-based). ***Average need-based loan:*** Freshmen: $2464; Undergraduates: $3465. ***Parent loans:*** $48,274 (8% need-based, 92% non-need-based). ***Programs:*** FFEL (Subsidized and Unsubsidized Stafford, PLUS), Perkins, college/university.

WORK-STUDY ***Federal work-study:*** *Total amount:* $107,175; jobs available. ***State or other work-study/employment:*** *Total amount:* $244,353 (100% non-need-based). Part-time jobs available.

ATHLETIC AWARDS *Total amount:* 59,150 (79% need-based, 21% non-need-based).

APPLYING for FINANCIAL AID ***Required financial aid form:*** FAFSA. ***Financial aid deadline (priority):*** 4/15. ***Notification date:*** Continuous beginning 6/1. Students must reply within 2 weeks of notification.

CONTACT Mr. Ryan Graalum, Assistant Director, Financial Aid, Valley City State University, 101 College Street SW, Valley City, ND 58072, 701-845-7541 or toll-free 800-532-8641 Ext. 37101. *E-mail:* ryan_graalum@mail.vcsu.nodak.edu

VALLEY FORGE CHRISTIAN COLLEGE

Phoenixville, PA

Tuition & fees: $6936 **Average undergraduate aid package: N/A**

ABOUT THE INSTITUTION Independent religious, coed. Awards: associate and bachelor's degrees. 6 undergraduate majors. Total enrollment: 532. Undergraduates: 532. Freshmen: 155. Federal methodology is used as a basis for awarding need-based institutional aid.

UNDERGRADUATE EXPENSES for 1999–2000 ***Application fee:*** $25. ***Comprehensive fee:*** $10,726 includes full-time tuition ($6196), mandatory fees ($740), and room and board ($3790). ***College room only:*** $1700. Full-time tuition and fees vary according to course load. Room and board charges vary according to board plan and housing facility. ***Part-time tuition:*** $243 per credit. ***Part-time fees:*** $210 per term part-time. Part-time tuition and fees vary according to course load. ***Payment plan:*** installment.

GIFT AID (NEED-BASED) ***Total amount:*** $1,679,657 (37% Federal, 22% state, 28% institutional, 13% external sources). ***Scholarships, grants, and awards:*** Federal Pell, FSEOG, state, private, college/university gift aid from institutional funds.

GIFT AID (NON-NEED-BASED) ***Scholarships, grants, and awards by category:*** *Academic Interests/Achievement:* general academic interests/achievements. *Creative Arts/Performance:* art/fine arts, music. *Special Achievements/Activities:* community service, general special achievements/activities, leadership, religious involvement. *Special Characteristics:* children of current students, children of faculty/staff, general special characteristics, married students, relatives of clergy, siblings of current students, spouses of current students. ***Tuition waivers:*** Full or partial for employees or children of employees, adult students.

Valley Forge Christian College (continued)

LOANS ***Student loans:*** $2,100,070 (63% need-based, 37% non-need-based). ***Parent loans:*** $336,126 (100% non-need-based). ***Programs:*** FFEL (Subsidized and Unsubsidized Stafford, PLUS), Perkins, state.

WORK-STUDY ***Federal work-study:*** *Total amount:* $71,421; 87 jobs averaging $821.

APPLYING for FINANCIAL AID ***Required financial aid form:*** FAFSA. ***Financial aid deadline (priority):*** 5/1. ***Notification date:*** Continuous. Students must reply within 2 weeks of notification.

CONTACT Mrs. Evie Meyer, Director of Financial Aid, Valley Forge Christian College, 1401 Charlestown Road, Phoenixville, PA 19460-2399, 610-917-1417 or toll-free 800-432-8322. *Fax:* 610-935-9353. *E-mail:* eemeyer@vfcc.edu

VALPARAISO UNIVERSITY

Valparaiso, IN

Tuition & fees: $17,636 **Average undergraduate aid package: $16,640**

ABOUT THE INSTITUTION Independent religious, coed. Awards: associate, bachelor's, master's, and first professional degrees. 65 undergraduate majors. Total enrollment: 3,650. Undergraduates: 2,986. Freshmen: 734. Both federal and institutional methodology are used as a basis for awarding need-based institutional aid.

UNDERGRADUATE EXPENSES for 2000–2001 ***Application fee:*** $30. ***Comprehensive fee:*** $22,296 includes full-time tuition ($17,100), mandatory fees ($536), and room and board ($4660). ***College room only:*** $2970. Full-time tuition and fees vary according to program. Room and board charges vary according to board plan and housing facility. ***Part-time tuition:*** $380 per credit. ***Part-time fees:*** $35 per term part-time. Part-time tuition and fees vary according to course load. ***Payment plan:*** installment.

FRESHMAN FINANCIAL AID (Fall 1999, est.) 610 applied for aid; of those 78% were deemed to have need. 100% of freshmen with need received aid; of those 63% had need fully met. *Average percent of need met:* 95% (excluding resources awarded to replace EFC). *Average financial aid package:* $15,189 (excluding resources awarded to replace EFC). 28% of all full-time freshmen had no need and received non-need-based aid.

UNDERGRADUATE FINANCIAL AID (Fall 1999, est.) 2,081 applied for aid; of those 85% were deemed to have need. 100% of undergraduates with need received aid; of those 68% had need fully met. *Average percent of need met:* 90% (excluding resources awarded to replace EFC). *Average financial aid package:* $16,640 (excluding resources awarded to replace EFC). 24% of all full-time undergraduates had no need and received non-need-based aid.

GIFT AID (NEED-BASED) ***Total amount:*** $16,117,500 (11% Federal, 11% state, 74% institutional, 4% external sources). ***Receiving aid:*** *Freshmen:* 61% (473); *all full-time undergraduates:* 62% (1,713). ***Average award:*** Freshmen: $9730; Undergraduates: $8777. ***Scholarships, grants, and awards:*** Federal Pell, FSEOG, state, private, college/university gift aid from institutional funds.

GIFT AID (NON-NEED-BASED) ***Total amount:*** $6,950,000 (95% institutional, 5% external sources). ***Receiving aid:*** *Freshmen:* 14% (110); *Undergraduates:* 30% (837). ***Scholarships, grants, and awards by category:*** *Academic Interests/Achievement:* engineering/technologies, foreign languages, general academic interests/achievements, health fields, physical sciences. *Creative Arts/Performance:* art/fine arts, music, performing arts, theater/drama. *Special Achievements/Activities:* religious involvement. *Special Characteristics:* children and siblings of alumni, children of faculty/staff, ethnic background, first-generation college students, international students, members of minority groups, relatives of clergy, religious affiliation. ***Tuition waivers:*** Full or partial for employees or children of employees.

LOANS ***Student loans:*** $10,200,000 (70% need-based, 30% non-need-based). 71% of past graduating class borrowed through all loan programs. Average indebtedness per student: $17,435. ***Average need-based loan:*** Freshmen: $3643; Undergraduates: $4500. ***Parent loans:*** $1,450,000 (10% need-based, 90% non-need-based). ***Programs:*** Federal Direct (Subsidized and Unsubsidized Stafford, PLUS), Perkins, college/university.

WORK-STUDY ***Federal work-study:*** *Total amount:* $385,000; 380 jobs averaging $1013. ***State or other work-study/employment:*** *Total amount:* $800,000 (34% need-based, 66% non-need-based). 770 part-time jobs averaging $1039.

ATHLETIC AWARDS *Total amount:* 1,840,000 (41% need-based, 59% non-need-based).

APPLYING for FINANCIAL AID ***Required financial aid form:*** FAFSA. ***Financial aid deadline (priority):*** 3/1. ***Notification date:*** Continuous. Students must reply by 5/1.

CONTACT Mr. David Fevig, Director of Financial Aid, Valparaiso University, O. P. Kretzmann Hall, Valparaiso, IN 46383-6493, 219-464-5015 or toll-free 888-GO-VALPO (out-of-state). *Fax:* 219-464-5381. *E-mail:* dave.fevig@valpo.edu

VANDERBILT UNIVERSITY

Nashville, TN

Tuition & fees: $23,598 **Average undergraduate aid package: $23,905**

ABOUT THE INSTITUTION Independent, coed. Awards: bachelor's, master's, doctoral, and first professional degrees. 56 undergraduate majors. Total enrollment: 10,022. Undergraduates: 5,780. Freshmen: 1,633. Both federal and institutional methodology are used as a basis for awarding need-based institutional aid.

UNDERGRADUATE EXPENSES for 1999–2000 ***Application fee:*** $50. ***Comprehensive fee:*** $31,630 includes full-time tuition ($22,990), mandatory fees ($608), and room and board ($8032). ***College room only:*** $5172. Room and board charges vary according to board plan and housing facility. ***Part-time tuition:*** $958 per credit hour. ***Part-time fees:*** $300 per term part-time. Part-time tuition and fees vary according to course load. ***Payment plans:*** tuition prepayment, installment, deferred payment.

FRESHMAN FINANCIAL AID (Fall 1999, est.) 871 applied for aid; of those 79% were deemed to have need. 100% of freshmen with need received aid; of those 98% had need fully met. *Average percent of need met:* 98% (excluding resources awarded to replace EFC). *Average financial aid package:* $24,073 (excluding resources awarded to replace EFC). 13% of all full-time freshmen had no need and received non-need-based aid.

UNDERGRADUATE FINANCIAL AID (Fall 1999, est.) 2,465 applied for aid; of those 86% were deemed to have need. 100% of undergraduates with need received aid; of those 98% had need fully met. *Average percent of need met:* 98% (excluding resources awarded to replace EFC). *Average financial aid package:* $23,905 (excluding resources awarded to replace EFC). 13% of all full-time undergraduates had no need and received non-need-based aid.

GIFT AID (NEED-BASED) ***Total amount:*** $32,571,525 (6% Federal, 1% state, 89% institutional, 4% external sources). ***Receiving aid:*** *Freshmen:* 37% (603); *all full-time undergraduates:* 32% (1,881). ***Average award:*** Freshmen: $14,934; Undergraduates: $14,225. ***Scholarships, grants, and awards:*** Federal Pell, FSEOG, state, private, college/university gift aid from institutional funds.

GIFT AID (NON-NEED-BASED) ***Total amount:*** $9,607,009 (29% Federal, 3% state, 55% institutional, 13% external sources). ***Receiving aid:*** *Freshmen:* 22% (357); *Undergraduates:* 14% (821). ***Scholarships, grants, and awards by category:*** *Academic Interests/Achievement:* education, engineering/technologies, general academic interests/achievements, humanities. *Creative Arts/Performance:* journalism/publications, music. *Special Achievements/Activities:* community service, leadership. *Special Characteristics:* local/state students, members of minority groups. ***Tuition waivers:*** Full or partial for employees or children of employees. ***ROTC:*** Army, Naval, Air Force cooperative.

LOANS ***Student loans:*** $12,923,902 (89% need-based, 11% non-need-based). 40% of past graduating class borrowed through all loan programs. Average indebtedness per student: $19,900. ***Average need-based loan:*** Freshmen: $5214; Undergraduates: $5904. ***Parent loans:*** $6,281,356 (100% non-need-based). ***Programs:*** FFEL (Subsidized and Unsubsidized Stafford, PLUS), Perkins, Federal Nursing, college/university.

WORK-STUDY ***Federal work-study:*** *Total amount:* $2,351,711; jobs available.

ATHLETIC AWARDS *Total amount:* 5,618,911 (24% need-based, 76% non-need-based).

APPLYING for FINANCIAL AID ***Required financial aid forms:*** FAFSA, CSS Financial Aid PROFILE. ***Financial aid deadline (priority):*** 2/1. ***Notification date:*** Continuous beginning 4/7.

CONTACT Office of Student Financial Aid, Vanderbilt University, 2309 West End Avenue, Nashville, TN 37203-1725, 615-322-3591 or toll-free 800-288-0432. *E-mail:* askfinad@uansv2.vanderbilt.edu

VANDERCOOK COLLEGE OF MUSIC

Chicago, IL

ABOUT THE INSTITUTION Independent, coed. Awards: bachelor's and master's degrees. 1 undergraduate major. Total enrollment: 160. Undergraduates: 79.

GIFT AID (NEED-BASED) ***Scholarships, grants, and awards:*** Federal Pell, state, private, college/university gift aid from institutional funds.

GIFT AID (NON-NEED-BASED) ***Scholarships, grants, and awards by category:*** *Academic Interests/Achievement:* general academic interests/achievements. *Creative Arts/Performance:* music. *Special Characteristics:* ethnic background.

LOANS ***Programs:*** FFEL (Subsidized and Unsubsidized Stafford, PLUS).

APPLYING for FINANCIAL AID ***Required financial aid form:*** FAFSA.

CONTACT George Pierard, Admissions Counselor, VanderCook College of Music, 3140 South Federal Street, Chicago, IL 60616, 312-225-6288 or toll-free 800-448-2655. *Fax:* 312-225-5211. *E-mail:* vcmusic@mcs.com

VANGUARD UNIVERSITY OF SOUTHERN CALIFORNIA

Costa Mesa, CA

Tuition & fees: $13,778 **Average undergraduate aid package: N/A**

ABOUT THE INSTITUTION Independent religious, coed. Awards: bachelor's and master's degrees. 34 undergraduate majors. Total enrollment: 1,440. Undergraduates: 1,289. Freshmen: 330. Federal methodology is used as a basis for awarding need-based institutional aid.

UNDERGRADUATE EXPENSES for 2000–2001 (est.) ***Application fee:*** $30. ***Comprehensive fee:*** $18,838 includes full-time tuition ($13,230), mandatory fees ($548), and room and board ($5060). ***College room only:*** $2820. Room and board charges vary according to board plan and housing facility. ***Part-time tuition:*** $514 per unit. ***Payment plan:*** installment.

GIFT AID (NEED-BASED) ***Total amount:*** $4,151,207 (19% Federal, 49% state, 32% institutional). ***Scholarships, grants, and awards:*** Federal Pell, FSEOG, state, college/university gift aid from institutional funds.

GIFT AID (NON-NEED-BASED) ***Total amount:*** $2,250,084 (95% institutional, 5% external sources). ***Scholarships, grants, and awards by category:*** *Academic Interests/Achievement:* general academic interests/achievements. *Creative Arts/Performance:* debating, music, theater/drama. *Special Characteristics:* children of faculty/staff, relatives of clergy, religious affiliation. ***Tuition waivers:*** Full or partial for employees or children of employees. ***ROTC:*** Army cooperative, Naval cooperative, Air Force cooperative.

LOANS ***Student loans:*** $4,950,004 (59% need-based, 41% non-need-based). ***Parent loans:*** $906,539 (100% non-need-based). ***Programs:*** FFEL (Subsidized and Unsubsidized Stafford, PLUS), Perkins, college/university.

WORK-STUDY ***Federal work-study:*** *Total amount:* $61,097; jobs available.

ATHLETIC AWARDS *Total amount:* 790,971 (100% non-need-based).

APPLYING for FINANCIAL AID ***Required financial aid form:*** FAFSA. ***Financial aid deadline (priority):*** 3/2. ***Notification date:*** 4/1. Students must reply within 3 weeks of notification.

CONTACT Admissions Office, Vanguard University of Southern California, 55 Fair Drive, Costa Mesa, CA 92626-6597, 800-SCC-6279 or toll-free 800-722-6279. *Fax:* 714-966-5471.

VASSAR COLLEGE

Poughkeepsie, NY

Tuition & fees: $24,030 **Average undergraduate aid package: $20,820**

ABOUT THE INSTITUTION Independent, coed. Awards: bachelor's and master's degrees. 44 undergraduate majors. Total enrollment: 2,322. Undergraduates: 2,322. Freshmen: 635. Institutional methodology is used as a basis for awarding need-based institutional aid.

UNDERGRADUATE EXPENSES for 1999–2000 ***Application fee:*** $60. ***Comprehensive fee:*** $30,800 includes full-time tuition ($23,700), mandatory fees ($330), and room and board ($6770). ***College room only:*** $3600. Room and board charges vary according to board plan. ***Part-time tuition:*** $2790 per unit. Part-time tuition and fees vary according to program. ***Payment plan:*** installment.

FRESHMAN FINANCIAL AID (Fall 1999, est.) 412 applied for aid; of those 81% were deemed to have need. 100% of freshmen with need received aid; of those 100% had need fully met. *Average percent of need met:* 100% (excluding resources awarded to replace EFC). *Average financial aid package:* $20,027 (excluding resources awarded to replace EFC). 10% of all full-time freshmen had no need and received non-need-based aid.

UNDERGRADUATE FINANCIAL AID (Fall 1999, est.) 1,509 applied for aid; of those 85% were deemed to have need. 100% of undergraduates with need received aid; of those 100% had need fully met. *Average percent of need met:* 100% (excluding resources awarded to replace EFC). *Average financial aid package:* $20,820 (excluding resources awarded to replace EFC). 7% of all full-time undergraduates had no need and received non-need-based aid.

GIFT AID (NEED-BASED) ***Total amount:*** $19,451,400 (6% Federal, 3% state, 88% institutional, 3% external sources). ***Receiving aid:*** *Freshmen:* 52% (331); *all full-time undergraduates:* 55% (1,246). ***Average award:*** Freshmen: $16,651; Undergraduates: $15,556. ***Scholarships, grants, and awards:*** Federal Pell, FSEOG, state, private, college/university gift aid from institutional funds.

GIFT AID (NON-NEED-BASED) ***Total amount:*** $82,312 (22% state, 78% external sources). ***Tuition waivers:*** Full or partial for employees or children of employees.

LOANS ***Student loans:*** $6,468,633 (76% need-based, 24% non-need-based). 59% of past graduating class borrowed through all loan programs. Average indebtedness per student: $15,772. ***Average need-based loan:*** Freshmen: $2295; Undergraduates: $4161. ***Parent loans:*** $2,136,851 (100% non-need-based). ***Programs:*** FFEL (Subsidized and Unsubsidized Stafford, PLUS), Perkins, college/university.

WORK-STUDY ***Federal work-study:*** *Total amount:* $1,353,260; 944 jobs averaging $1434. ***State or other work-study/employment:*** *Total amount:* $434,196 (99% need-based, 1% non-need-based). 299 part-time jobs averaging $1452.

APPLYING for FINANCIAL AID ***Required financial aid forms:*** FAFSA, institution's own form, CSS Financial Aid PROFILE, state aid form, noncustodial (divorced/separated) parent's statement, business/farm supplement. ***Financial aid deadline:*** 1/10. ***Notification date:*** 4/3. Students must reply by 5/1.

CONTACT Mr. Michael P. Fraher, Director of Financial Aid, Vassar College, 124 Raymond Avenue, Poughkeepsie, NY 12604-0008, 914-437-5320 or toll-free 800-827-7270. *Fax:* 914-437-5325. *E-mail:* mifraher@vassar.edu

VILLA JULIE COLLEGE

Stevenson, MD

Tuition & fees: $10,980 **Average undergraduate aid package: $10,554**

ABOUT THE INSTITUTION Independent, coed. Awards: associate, bachelor's, and master's degrees. 48 undergraduate majors. Total enrollment: 2,158. Undergraduates: 2,091. Freshmen: 430. Both federal and institutional methodology are used as a basis for awarding need-based institutional aid.

Villa Julie College (continued)

UNDERGRADUATE EXPENSES for 1999–2000 ***Application fee:*** $25. ***Tuition:*** full-time $10,250; part-time $305 per credit. ***Required fees:*** full-time $730; $30 per term part-time.

FRESHMAN FINANCIAL AID (Fall 1999, est.) 399 applied for aid; of those 77% were deemed to have need. 95% of freshmen with need received aid; of those 45% had need fully met. *Average percent of need met:* 58% (excluding resources awarded to replace EFC). *Average financial aid package:* $10,265 (excluding resources awarded to replace EFC). 24% of all full-time freshmen had no need and received non-need-based aid.

UNDERGRADUATE FINANCIAL AID (Fall 1999, est.) 1,220 applied for aid; of those 75% were deemed to have need. 94% of undergraduates with need received aid; of those 53% had need fully met. *Average percent of need met:* 48% (excluding resources awarded to replace EFC). *Average financial aid package:* $10,554 (excluding resources awarded to replace EFC). 17% of all full-time undergraduates had no need and received non-need-based aid.

GIFT AID (NEED-BASED) ***Total amount:*** $2,896,869 (24% Federal, 61% state, 15% institutional). ***Receiving aid:*** *Freshmen:* 30% (128); *all full-time undergraduates:* 25% (375). ***Average award:*** Freshmen: $1654; Undergraduates: $1622. ***Scholarships, grants, and awards:*** Federal Pell, FSEOG, state, private, college/university gift aid from institutional funds.

GIFT AID (NON-NEED-BASED) ***Total amount:*** $3,830,228 (4% state, 89% institutional, 7% external sources). ***Receiving aid:*** *Freshmen:* 43% (183); *Undergraduates:* 31% (462). ***Scholarships, grants, and awards by category:*** *Academic Interests/Achievement:* 321 awards ($565,880 total): general academic interests/achievements. *Creative Arts/Performance:* 4 awards ($13,500 total): art/fine arts, cinema/film/broadcasting, creative writing. *Special Achievements/Activities:* 610 awards ($2,833,425 total): community service, general special achievements/activities, leadership. ***Tuition waivers:*** Full or partial for employees or children of employees. ***ROTC:*** Army cooperative.

LOANS ***Student loans:*** $4,412,296 (55% need-based, 45% non-need-based). Average indebtedness per student: $13,344. ***Average need-based loan:*** Freshmen: $2806; Undergraduates: $3505. ***Parent loans:*** $960,300 (100% non-need-based). ***Programs:*** FFEL (Subsidized and Unsubsidized Stafford, PLUS), Perkins.

WORK-STUDY ***Federal work-study:*** *Total amount:* $91,123; 76 jobs averaging $1200.

APPLYING for FINANCIAL AID ***Required financial aid forms:*** FAFSA, institution's own form. ***Financial aid deadline (priority):*** 3/1. ***Notification date:*** Continuous beginning 3/15. Students must reply within 2 weeks of notification.

CONTACT Ms. Debra Bottomms, Director of Financial Aid, Villa Julie College, 1525 Greenspring Valley Road, Stevenson, MD 21153, 410-602-7559 or toll-free 877-468-6852 (in-state), 877-468-3852 (out-of-state). *Fax:* 410-602-6600. *E-mail:* fa-deb1@mail.vjc.edu

VILLANOVA UNIVERSITY

Villanova, PA

Tuition & fees: $20,850 **Average undergraduate aid package: $13,966**

ABOUT THE INSTITUTION Independent Roman Catholic, coed. Awards: associate, bachelor's, master's, doctoral, and first professional degrees. 47 undergraduate majors. Total enrollment: 9,968. Undergraduates: 7,144. Freshmen: 1,680. Both federal and institutional methodology are used as a basis for awarding need-based institutional aid.

UNDERGRADUATE EXPENSES for 1999–2000 ***Application fee:*** $50. ***Comprehensive fee:*** $28,850 includes full-time tuition ($20,550), mandatory fees ($300), and room and board ($8000). ***College room only:*** $4400. Full-time tuition and fees vary according to program and student level. Room and board charges vary according to board plan and housing facility. ***Part-time tuition:*** $475 per credit hour. ***Part-time fees:*** $150 per term part-time. Part-time tuition and fees vary according to class time and program. ***Payment plan:*** installment.

FRESHMAN FINANCIAL AID (Fall 1999) 1141 applied for aid; of those 76% were deemed to have need. 98% of freshmen with need received aid; of those 15% had need fully met. *Average percent of need met:* 86% (excluding resources awarded to replace EFC). *Average financial aid package:* $15,033 (excluding resources awarded to replace EFC). 9% of all full-time freshmen had no need and received non-need-based aid.

UNDERGRADUATE FINANCIAL AID (Fall 1999) 3,814 applied for aid; of those 81% were deemed to have need. 98% of undergraduates with need received aid; of those 15% had need fully met. *Average percent of need met:* 80% (excluding resources awarded to replace EFC). *Average financial aid package:* $13,966 (excluding resources awarded to replace EFC). 8% of all full-time undergraduates had no need and received non-need-based aid.

GIFT AID (NEED-BASED) ***Total amount:*** $25,054,549 (7% Federal, 6% state, 87% institutional). ***Receiving aid:*** *Freshmen:* 43% (716); *all full-time undergraduates:* 39% (2,474). ***Average award:*** Freshmen: $10,315; Undergraduates: $8876. ***Scholarships, grants, and awards:*** Federal Pell, FSEOG, state, private, college/university gift aid from institutional funds, endowed and restricted grants.

GIFT AID (NON-NEED-BASED) ***Total amount:*** $7,608,055 (41% Federal, 1% state, 39% institutional, 19% external sources). ***Receiving aid:*** *Freshmen:* 9% (155); *Undergraduates:* 7% (428). ***Scholarships, grants, and awards by category:*** *Academic Interests/Achievement:* 368 awards ($3,651,798 total): general academic interests/achievements, international studies, military science. *Special Achievements/Activities:* 19 awards ($15,500 total): general special achievements/activities. *Special Characteristics:* 111 awards ($1,645,451 total): children of educators, general special characteristics, members of minority groups, religious affiliation. ***Tuition waivers:*** Full or partial for employees or children of employees. ***ROTC:*** Army, Naval, Air Force cooperative.

LOANS ***Student loans:*** $21,786,492 (79% need-based, 21% non-need-based). 52% of past graduating class borrowed through all loan programs. Average indebtedness per student: $16,652. ***Average need-based loan:*** Freshmen: $2835; Undergraduates: $4242. ***Parent loans:*** $7,634,497 (100% non-need-based). ***Programs:*** FFEL (Subsidized and Unsubsidized Stafford, PLUS), Perkins, Federal Nursing, Villanova Loan.

WORK-STUDY ***Federal work-study:*** *Total amount:* $1,346,639; 778 jobs averaging $1732.

ATHLETIC AWARDS *Total amount:* 5,061,495 (26% need-based, 74% non-need-based).

APPLYING for FINANCIAL AID ***Required financial aid forms:*** FAFSA, institution's own form, W-2 forms, federal income tax forms (student and parent). ***Financial aid deadline (priority):*** 2/15. ***Notification date:*** 4/1. Students must reply by 5/1.

CONTACT Mr. George Walter, Director of Financial Assistance, Villanova University, 800 Lancaster Avenue, Villanova, PA 19085-1699, 610-519-4010 or toll-free 800-338-7927. *Fax:* 610-519-7599. *E-mail:* finaid@email.villanova.edu

VIRGINIA COLLEGE AT BIRMINGHAM

Birmingham, AL

Tuition & fees: $7000 **Average undergraduate aid package: N/A**

ABOUT THE INSTITUTION Proprietary, coed. Awards: associate and bachelor's degrees. 8 undergraduate majors. Total enrollment: 837. Undergraduates: 837. Freshmen: 129. Federal methodology is used as a basis for awarding need-based institutional aid.

UNDERGRADUATE EXPENSES for 1999–2000 ***Tuition:*** full-time $7000; part-time $175 per quarter hour. Full-time tuition and fees vary according to program. Part-time tuition and fees vary according to program. ***Payment plans:*** guaranteed tuition, installment.

FRESHMAN FINANCIAL AID (Fall 1999, est.) 243 applied for aid; of those 100% were deemed to have need. 100% of freshmen with need received aid. *Average percent of need met:* 25% (excluding resources awarded to replace EFC).

UNDERGRADUATE FINANCIAL AID (Fall 1999, est.) 709 applied for aid; of those 100% were deemed to have need. 100% of undergraduates with need received aid. *Average percent of need met:* 36% (excluding resources awarded to replace EFC).

GIFT AID (NEED-BASED) ***Total amount:*** $191,979 (86% Federal, 8% state, 5% institutional, 1% external sources). ***Scholarships, grants, and awards:*** Federal Pell, FSEOG, state, private, college/university gift aid from institutional funds.

GIFT AID (NON-NEED-BASED) ***Tuition waivers:*** Full or partial for employees or children of employees.

LOANS ***Student loans:*** $8,000,000 (100% need-based). ***Parent loans:*** $400,000 (100% non-need-based). ***Programs:*** Federal Direct (Subsidized and Unsubsidized Stafford, PLUS), FFEL (Subsidized and Unsubsidized Stafford, PLUS), alternative loans.

WORK-STUDY ***Federal work-study:*** *Total amount:* $3000; jobs available.

APPLYING for FINANCIAL AID ***Required financial aid forms:*** FAFSA, institution's own form, noncustodial (divorced/separated) parent's statement. ***Financial aid deadline:*** Continuous. ***Notification date:*** Continuous.

CONTACT Wanda Upton, Financial Aid Director, Virginia College at Birmingham, 65 Bagby Drive, Suite 100, Birmingham, AL 35209, 205-802-1200 Ext. 206. *Fax:* 205-802-7045.

VIRGINIA COMMONWEALTH UNIVERSITY

Richmond, VA

Tuition & fees (VA res): $3587 **Average undergraduate aid package: $5377**

ABOUT THE INSTITUTION State-supported, coed. Awards: bachelor's, master's, doctoral, and first professional degrees and post-bachelor's and post-master's certificates. 95 undergraduate majors. Total enrollment: 23,481. Undergraduates: 15,824. Freshmen: 2,460. Federal methodology is used as a basis for awarding need-based institutional aid.

UNDERGRADUATE EXPENSES for 1999–2000 ***Application fee:*** $25. ***Tuition, state resident:*** full-time $2492; part-time $104 per credit. ***Tuition, nonresident:*** full-time $11,946; part-time $498 per credit. ***Required fees:*** full-time $1095; $40 per credit. Full-time tuition and fees vary according to location and program. Part-time tuition and fees vary according to course load and location. ***College room and board:*** $4839; ***room only:*** $2824. Room and board charges vary according to board plan and housing facility. ***Payment plan:*** installment.

FRESHMAN FINANCIAL AID (Fall 1998) 2424 applied for aid; of those 79% were deemed to have need. 96% of freshmen with need received aid; of those 17% had need fully met. *Average percent of need met:* 53% (excluding resources awarded to replace EFC). *Average financial aid package:* $4839 (excluding resources awarded to replace EFC). 5% of all full-time freshmen had no need and received non-need-based aid.

UNDERGRADUATE FINANCIAL AID (Fall 1998) 8,211 applied for aid; of those 81% were deemed to have need. 98% of undergraduates with need received aid; of those 16% had need fully met. *Average percent of need met:* 47% (excluding resources awarded to replace EFC). *Average financial aid package:* $5377 (excluding resources awarded to replace EFC). 5% of all full-time undergraduates had no need and received non-need-based aid.

GIFT AID (NEED-BASED) ***Total amount:*** $17,024,304 (53% Federal, 44% state, 1% institutional, 2% external sources). ***Receiving aid:*** *Freshmen:* 66% (1,616); *all full-time undergraduates:* 49% (5,314). ***Average award:*** Freshmen: $3032; Undergraduates: $3209. ***Scholarships, grants, and awards:*** Federal Pell, FSEOG, state, private, college/university gift aid from institutional funds, Federal Nursing.

GIFT AID (NON-NEED-BASED) ***Total amount:*** $5,125,853 (2% Federal, 13% state, 66% institutional, 19% external sources). ***Receiving aid:*** *Freshmen:* 12% (285); *Undergraduates:* 12% (1,311). ***Scholarships, grants, and awards by category:*** *Academic Interests/Achievement:* engineering/technologies, general academic interests/achievements, health fields. *Creative Arts/Performance:* applied art and design, art/fine arts, dance, music, performing arts, theater/drama. *Special Characteristics:* children of union members/company employees, general special characteristics, veterans' children. ***Tuition waivers:*** Full or partial for senior citizens. ***ROTC:*** Army.

LOANS ***Student loans:*** $43,501,212 (62% need-based, 38% non-need-based). 71% of past graduating class borrowed through all loan programs. Average indebtedness per student: $22,379. ***Average need-based loan:*** Freshmen: $1608; Undergraduates: $2106. ***Parent loans:*** $3,234,446 (43% need-based, 57% non-need-based). ***Programs:*** Federal Direct (Subsidized and Unsubsidized Stafford, PLUS), Perkins, Federal Nursing, state, college/university.

WORK-STUDY ***Federal work-study:*** *Total amount:* $1,325,205; jobs available.

ATHLETIC AWARDS *Total amount:* 1,490,402 (25% need-based, 75% non-need-based).

APPLYING for FINANCIAL AID ***Required financial aid form:*** FAFSA. ***Financial aid deadline (priority):*** 4/1. ***Notification date:*** Continuous. Students must reply by 5/1 or within 4 weeks of notification.

CONTACT Janel Schaefer, Director, Financial Aid, Virginia Commonwealth University, PO Box 843026, Richmond, VA 23284-3026, 804-828-6669 or toll-free 800-841-3638. *Fax:* 804-828-6187. *E-mail:* faidmail@vcu.edu

VIRGINIA INTERMONT COLLEGE

Bristol, VA

Tuition & fees: $11,750 **Average undergraduate aid package: $5054**

ABOUT THE INSTITUTION Independent religious, coed. Awards: associate and bachelor's degrees. 32 undergraduate majors. Total enrollment: 795. Undergraduates: 795. Freshmen: 116. Federal methodology is used as a basis for awarding need-based institutional aid.

UNDERGRADUATE EXPENSES for 2000–2001 ***Application fee:*** $15. ***Comprehensive fee:*** $16,950 includes full-time tuition ($11,430), mandatory fees ($320), and room and board ($5200). ***College room only:*** $2600. ***Part-time tuition:*** $150 per credit. ***Part-time fees:*** $60 per term part-time. Part-time tuition and fees vary according to course load. ***Payment plan:*** installment.

FRESHMAN FINANCIAL AID (Fall 1999) 54 applied for aid; of those 96% were deemed to have need. 100% of freshmen with need received aid; of those 94% had need fully met. *Average percent of need met:* 71% (excluding resources awarded to replace EFC). *Average financial aid package:* $3744 (excluding resources awarded to replace EFC). 14% of all full-time freshmen had no need and received non-need-based aid.

UNDERGRADUATE FINANCIAL AID (Fall 1999) 511 applied for aid; of those 96% were deemed to have need. 100% of undergraduates with need received aid; of those 96% had need fully met. *Average percent of need met:* 57% (excluding resources awarded to replace EFC). *Average financial aid package:* $5054 (excluding resources awarded to replace EFC). 24% of all full-time undergraduates had no need and received non-need-based aid.

GIFT AID (NEED-BASED) ***Total amount:*** $1,118,109 (60% Federal, 3% state, 37% institutional). ***Receiving aid:*** *Freshmen:* 39% (37); *all full-time undergraduates:* 42% (277). ***Average award:*** Freshmen: $2288; Undergraduates: $2425. ***Scholarships, grants, and awards:*** Federal Pell, FSEOG, state, private, college/university gift aid from institutional funds.

GIFT AID (NON-NEED-BASED) ***Total amount:*** $1,071,999 (8% state, 91% institutional, 1% external sources). ***Receiving aid:*** *Freshmen:* 36% (34); *Undergraduates:* 65% (429). ***Scholarships, grants, and awards by category:*** *Academic Interests/Achievement:* general academic interests/achievements. *Creative Arts/Performance:* applied art and design, art/fine arts, dance, general creative arts/performance, performing arts, theater/drama. *Special Characteristics:* religious affiliation. ***Tuition waivers:*** Full or partial for employees or children of employees.

LOANS ***Student loans:*** $1,896,257 (73% need-based, 27% non-need-based). 82% of past graduating class borrowed through all loan programs. Average indebtedness per student: $17,125. ***Average need-based loan:*** Freshmen: $3239; Undergraduates: $3629. ***Parent loans:*** $491,259 (100% non-need-based). ***Programs:*** FFEL (Subsidized and Unsubsidized Stafford, PLUS).

WORK-STUDY ***Federal work-study:*** *Total amount:* $204,297; 250 jobs available.

ATHLETIC AWARDS *Total amount:* 510,323 (100% non-need-based).

Virginia Intermont College (continued)

APPLYING for FINANCIAL AID ***Required financial aid forms:*** FAFSA, state aid form. ***Financial aid deadline:*** Continuous. ***Notification date:*** Continuous beginning 3/1. Students must reply within 4 weeks of notification.

CONTACT Mrs. Nancy Roberts, Director of Financial Aid, Virginia Intermont College, 1013 Moore Street, Bristol, VA 24201-4298, 540-466-7873 or toll-free 800-451-1842. *Fax:* 540-669-5763.

VIRGINIA MILITARY INSTITUTE

Lexington, VA

Tuition & fees (VA res): $5014 **Average undergraduate aid package: $8873**

ABOUT THE INSTITUTION State-supported, coed, primarily men. Awards: bachelor's degrees. 14 undergraduate majors. Total enrollment: 1,335. Undergraduates: 1,335. Freshmen: 374. Federal methodology is used as a basis for awarding need-based institutional aid.

UNDERGRADUATE EXPENSES for 1999–2000 ***Application fee:*** $25. ***Tuition, state resident:*** full-time $2924. ***Tuition, nonresident:*** full-time $12,364. ***Required fees:*** full-time $2090. ***College room and board:*** $4376. Additional mandatory fees per year: $1000 quartermaster charge. ***Payment plan:*** installment.

FRESHMAN FINANCIAL AID (Fall 1999) 223 applied for aid; of those 78% were deemed to have need. 100% of freshmen with need received aid; of those 70% had need fully met. *Average percent of need met:* 92% (excluding resources awarded to replace EFC). *Average financial aid package:* $8607 (excluding resources awarded to replace EFC). 27% of all full-time freshmen had no need and received non-need-based aid.

UNDERGRADUATE FINANCIAL AID (Fall 1999) 654 applied for aid; of those 81% were deemed to have need. 100% of undergraduates with need received aid; of those 76% had need fully met. *Average percent of need met:* 92% (excluding resources awarded to replace EFC). *Average financial aid package:* $8873 (excluding resources awarded to replace EFC). 27% of all full-time undergraduates had no need and received non-need-based aid.

GIFT AID (NEED-BASED) ***Total amount:*** $2,404,442 (19% Federal, 23% state, 54% institutional, 4% external sources). ***Receiving aid:*** *Freshmen:* 29% (125); *all full-time undergraduates:* 32% (434). ***Average award:*** Freshmen: $7089; Undergraduates: $6564. ***Scholarships, grants, and awards:*** Federal Pell, FSEOG, state, private, college/university gift aid from institutional funds.

GIFT AID (NON-NEED-BASED) ***Total amount:*** $3,975,613 (51% Federal, 46% institutional, 3% external sources). ***Receiving aid:*** *Freshmen:* 2% (9); *Undergraduates:* 3% (35). ***Scholarships, grants, and awards by category:*** *Academic Interests/Achievement:* 60 awards ($550,000 total): biological sciences, business, computer science, engineering/technologies, English, general academic interests/achievements, international studies, mathematics, military science, premedicine. *Creative Arts/Performance:* 12 awards ($6000 total): music. *Special Achievements/Activities:* 15 awards ($75,000 total): general special achievements/activities, leadership. *Special Characteristics:* 275 awards ($1,169,000 total): children and siblings of alumni, children of faculty/staff, local/state students, members of minority groups, out-of-state students. ***ROTC:*** Army, Naval, Air Force.

LOANS ***Student loans:*** $1,471,395 (68% need-based, 32% non-need-based). Average indebtedness per student: $14,000. ***Average need-based loan:*** Freshmen: $3558; Undergraduates: $3571. ***Parent loans:*** $613,696 (100% non-need-based). ***Programs:*** Federal Direct (Subsidized and Unsubsidized Stafford, PLUS), Perkins, college/university.

WORK-STUDY ***Federal work-study:*** *Total amount:* $75,000; 71 jobs averaging $1050.

ATHLETIC AWARDS *Total amount:* 1,458,352 (22% need-based, 78% non-need-based).

APPLYING for FINANCIAL AID ***Required financial aid forms:*** FAFSA, institution's own form. ***Financial aid deadline:*** 4/1 (priority: 3/1). ***Notification date:*** Continuous. Students must reply by 5/1.

CONTACT Col. Timothy P. Golden, Director of Financial Aid, Virginia Military Institute, 306 Carroll Hall, Lexington, VA 24450, 540-464-7208 or toll-free 800-767-4207. *Fax:* 540-464-7629. *E-mail:* goldentp@mail.vmi.edu

VIRGINIA POLYTECHNIC INSTITUTE AND STATE UNIVERSITY

Blacksburg, VA

Tuition & fees (VA res): $3620 **Average undergraduate aid package: $6015**

ABOUT THE INSTITUTION State-supported, coed. Awards: associate, bachelor's, master's, doctoral, and first professional degrees. 73 undergraduate majors. Total enrollment: 25,452. Undergraduates: 21,479. Freshmen: 4,613. Federal methodology is used as a basis for awarding need-based institutional aid.

UNDERGRADUATE EXPENSES for 1999–2000 ***Application fee:*** $25. ***Tuition, state resident:*** full-time $2792; part-time $116 per credit hour. ***Tuition, nonresident:*** full-time $11,016; part-time $459 per credit hour. ***Required fees:*** full-time $828; $107 per term part-time. Full-time tuition and fees vary according to location. Part-time tuition and fees vary according to course load. ***College room and board:*** $3722; ***room only:*** $1838. Room and board charges vary according to board plan and housing facility. ***Payment plan:*** installment.

FRESHMAN FINANCIAL AID (Fall 1998) 3604 applied for aid; of those 75% were deemed to have need. 94% of freshmen with need received aid; of those 19% had need fully met. *Average percent of need met:* 60% (excluding resources awarded to replace EFC). *Average financial aid package:* $6353 (excluding resources awarded to replace EFC). 18% of all full-time freshmen had no need and received non-need-based aid.

UNDERGRADUATE FINANCIAL AID (Fall 1998) 13,550 applied for aid; of those 77% were deemed to have need. 92% of undergraduates with need received aid; of those 26% had need fully met. *Average percent of need met:* 63% (excluding resources awarded to replace EFC). *Average financial aid package:* $6015 (excluding resources awarded to replace EFC). 27% of all full-time undergraduates had no need and received non-need-based aid.

GIFT AID (NEED-BASED) ***Total amount:*** $18,781,261 (35% Federal, 54% state, 7% institutional, 4% external sources). ***Receiving aid:*** *Freshmen:* 36% (2,121); *all full-time undergraduates:* 33% (7,077). ***Average award:*** Freshmen: $3816; Undergraduates: $3665. ***Scholarships, grants, and awards:*** Federal Pell, FSEOG, state, private, college/university gift aid from institutional funds, General Scholarship Program.

GIFT AID (NON-NEED-BASED) ***Total amount:*** $12,996,242 (36% institutional, 64% external sources). ***Receiving aid:*** *Freshmen:* 18% (1,084); *Undergraduates:* 10% (2,114). ***Scholarships, grants, and awards by category:*** *Academic Interests/Achievement:* agriculture, business, education, engineering/technologies, general academic interests/achievements, home economics, international studies, mathematics, military science. *Creative Arts/Performance:* art/fine arts, journalism/publications, music, performing arts, theater/drama. *Special Achievements/Activities:* community service, general special achievements/activities, leadership, memberships. *Special Characteristics:* children of faculty/staff, local/state students, members of minority groups, out-of-state students, twins. ***Tuition waivers:*** Full or partial for employees or children of employees. ***ROTC:*** Army, Naval, Air Force.

LOANS ***Student loans:*** $47,308,924 (60% need-based, 40% non-need-based). 59% of past graduating class borrowed through all loan programs. Average indebtedness per student: $14,530. ***Average need-based loan:*** Freshmen: $3197; Undergraduates: $4263. ***Parent loans:*** $14,594,325 (100% non-need-based). ***Programs:*** Federal Direct (Subsidized and Unsubsidized Stafford, PLUS), Perkins, college/university, Health Professions Loans.

WORK-STUDY ***Federal work-study:*** *Total amount:* $1,055,181; 1,094 jobs averaging $793. ***State or other work-study/employment:*** *Total amount:* $4,683,645 (100% non-need-based). 4,402 part-time jobs averaging $823.

ATHLETIC AWARDS *Total amount:* 3,236,010 (100% non-need-based).

APPLYING for FINANCIAL AID ***Required financial aid form:*** FAFSA. ***Financial aid deadline (priority):*** 3/1. ***Notification date:*** Continuous beginning 4/1. Students must reply within 4 weeks of notification.

CONTACT Tony A. Sutphin, Special Projects Coordinator, Virginia Polytechnic Institute and State University, 222 Burruss Hall, Blacksburg, VA 24061, 540-231-9555. *Fax:* 540-231-9139. *E-mail:* sutphint@vt.edu

VIRGINIA STATE UNIVERSITY

Petersburg, VA

Tuition & fees (VA res): $3086 **Average undergraduate aid package: $6413**

ABOUT THE INSTITUTION State-supported, coed. Awards: bachelor's and master's degrees and post-master's certificates. 26 undergraduate majors. Total enrollment: 4,341. Undergraduates: 3,369. Freshmen: 881. Federal methodology is used as a basis for awarding need-based institutional aid.

UNDERGRADUATE EXPENSES for 1999–2000 ***Application fee:*** $25. ***Tuition, state resident:*** full-time $1588; part-time $69 per credit hour. ***Tuition, nonresident:*** full-time $7132; part-time $311 per credit hour. ***Required fees:*** full-time $1498; $29 per credit hour. Full-time tuition and fees vary according to course level, course load, and program. Part-time tuition and fees vary according to course level, course load, and program. ***College room and board:*** $5096. Room and board charges vary according to board plan and housing facility. ***Payment plan:*** deferred payment.

FRESHMAN FINANCIAL AID (Fall 1999, est.) 890 applied for aid; of those 90% were deemed to have need. 100% of freshmen with need received aid. *Average percent of need met:* 70% (excluding resources awarded to replace EFC). *Average financial aid package:* $5315 (excluding resources awarded to replace EFC). 15% of all full-time freshmen had no need and received non-need-based aid.

UNDERGRADUATE FINANCIAL AID (Fall 1999, est.) 2,989 applied for aid; of those 90% were deemed to have need. 100% of undergraduates with need received aid. *Average percent of need met:* 78% (excluding resources awarded to replace EFC). *Average financial aid package:* $6413 (excluding resources awarded to replace EFC). 5% of all full-time undergraduates had no need and received non-need-based aid.

GIFT AID (NEED-BASED) ***Total amount:*** $7,258,251 (66% Federal, 34% state). ***Receiving aid:*** *Freshmen:* 55% (520); *all full-time undergraduates:* 56% (1,748). ***Average award:*** Freshmen: $2122; Undergraduates: $2122. ***Scholarships, grants, and awards:*** Federal Pell, FSEOG, state, private, college/university gift aid from institutional funds.

GIFT AID (NON-NEED-BASED) ***Total amount:*** $1,336,674 (11% Federal, 62% institutional, 27% external sources). ***Receiving aid:*** *Freshmen:* 6% (56); *Undergraduates:* 9% (269). ***Scholarships, grants, and awards by category:*** *Academic Interests/Achievement:* agriculture, biological sciences, business, education, engineering/technologies, general academic interests/achievements, health fields, home economics, mathematics, military science, premedicine, social sciences. *Creative Arts/Performance:* art/fine arts, music, performing arts. *Special Achievements/Activities:* community service, hobbies/interests, religious involvement. *Special Characteristics:* veterans. ***Tuition waivers:*** Full or partial for senior citizens. ***ROTC:*** Army.

LOANS ***Student loans:*** $11,487,355 (67% need-based, 33% non-need-based). 86% of past graduating class borrowed through all loan programs. Average indebtedness per student: $18,500. ***Average need-based loan:*** Freshmen: $2232; Undergraduates: $2815. ***Parent loans:*** $2,380,640 (100% non-need-based). ***Programs:*** Federal Direct (Subsidized and Unsubsidized Stafford, PLUS), Perkins, college/university.

WORK-STUDY ***Federal work-study:*** *Total amount:* $417,843; 290 jobs averaging $1200. ***State or other work-study/employment:*** *Total amount:* $329,843 (100% non-need-based). 75 part-time jobs averaging $4398.

ATHLETIC AWARDS *Total amount:* 378,461 (100% non-need-based).

APPLYING for FINANCIAL AID ***Required financial aid forms:*** FAFSA, institution's own form. ***Financial aid deadline:*** 5/1 (priority: 3/31). ***Notification date:*** Continuous. Students must reply within 2 weeks of notification.

CONTACT Assistant Director, Student Services, Virginia State University, 101 Gandy Hall, PO Box 9031, Petersburg, VA 23806-2096, 804-524-6854 or toll-free 800-871-7611. *Fax:* 804-524-5055.

VIRGINIA UNION UNIVERSITY

Richmond, VA

Tuition & fees: $9580 **Average undergraduate aid package: $9386**

ABOUT THE INSTITUTION Independent Baptist, coed. Awards: bachelor's, doctoral, and first professional degrees. 22 undergraduate majors. Total enrollment: 1,700. Undergraduates: 1,500. Federal methodology is used as a basis for awarding need-based institutional aid.

UNDERGRADUATE EXPENSES for 1999–2000 ***Application fee:*** $15. ***Comprehensive fee:*** $13,830 includes full-time tuition ($8780), mandatory fees ($800), and room and board ($4250). ***Part-time tuition:*** $366 per semester hour. ***Part-time fees:*** $400 per term part-time. ***Payment plans:*** installment, deferred payment.

FRESHMAN FINANCIAL AID (Fall 1999, est.) 404 applied for aid; of those 95% were deemed to have need. 100% of freshmen with need received aid; of those 9% had need fully met. *Average percent of need met:* 77% (excluding resources awarded to replace EFC). *Average financial aid package:* $8368 (excluding resources awarded to replace EFC). 2% of all full-time freshmen had no need and received non-need-based aid.

UNDERGRADUATE FINANCIAL AID (Fall 1999, est.) 933 applied for aid; of those 93% were deemed to have need. 100% of undergraduates with need received aid; of those 21% had need fully met. *Average percent of need met:* 82% (excluding resources awarded to replace EFC). *Average financial aid package:* $9386 (excluding resources awarded to replace EFC). 3% of all full-time undergraduates had no need and received non-need-based aid.

GIFT AID (NEED-BASED) ***Total amount:*** $1,879,048 (91% Federal, 4% state, 5% external sources). ***Receiving aid:*** *Freshmen:* 53% (251); *all full-time undergraduates:* 43% (550). ***Scholarships, grants, and awards:*** Federal Pell, FSEOG, state, private, college/university gift aid from institutional funds, United Negro College Fund.

GIFT AID (NON-NEED-BASED) ***Total amount:*** $2,976,293 (2% Federal, 44% state, 45% institutional, 9% external sources). ***Receiving aid:*** *Freshmen:* 59% (278); *Undergraduates:* 54% (693). ***Scholarships, grants, and awards by category:*** *Academic Interests/Achievement:* general academic interests/achievements. *Creative Arts/Performance:* music. *Special Characteristics:* children of faculty/staff. ***Tuition waivers:*** Full or partial for employees or children of employees. ***ROTC:*** Army cooperative.

LOANS ***Student loans:*** $3,818,317 (73% need-based, 27% non-need-based). ***Parent loans:*** $1,287,995 (100% non-need-based). ***Programs:*** Federal Direct (Subsidized and Unsubsidized Stafford), FFEL (PLUS), Perkins.

WORK-STUDY ***Federal work-study:*** *Total amount:* $636,745; 347 jobs averaging $1835.

ATHLETIC AWARDS *Total amount:* 671,406 (100% non-need-based).

APPLYING for FINANCIAL AID ***Required financial aid form:*** FAFSA. ***Financial aid deadline (priority):*** 5/1. ***Notification date:*** Continuous. Students must reply within 2 weeks of notification.

CONTACT Michele E. Cherry, Reports Coordinator, Virginia Union University, 1500 North Lombardy Street, Richmond, VA 23220-1170, 804-257-5763 or toll-free 800-368-3227 (out-of-state). *Fax:* 804-257-5797.

VIRGINIA WESLEYAN COLLEGE

Norfolk, VA

Tuition & fees: $14,050 **Average undergraduate aid package: $10,874**

ABOUT THE INSTITUTION Independent United Methodist, coed. Awards: bachelor's degrees. 44 undergraduate majors. Total enrollment: 1,409. Undergraduates: 1,409. Freshmen: 292. Federal methodology is used as a basis for awarding need-based institutional aid.

UNDERGRADUATE EXPENSES for 1999–2000 ***Application fee:*** $35. ***Comprehensive fee:*** $19,700 includes full-time tuition ($14,050) and room and board ($5650). Full-time tuition and fees vary according to class time. Room and board charges vary according to board plan and

Virginia Wesleyan College (continued)

housing facility. ***Part-time tuition:*** $586 per semester hour. Part-time tuition and fees vary according to class time and course load. ***Payment plans:*** installment, deferred payment.

FRESHMAN FINANCIAL AID (Fall 1999, est.) 265 applied for aid; of those 77% were deemed to have need. 100% of freshmen with need received aid; of those 15% had need fully met. *Average percent of need met:* 73% (excluding resources awarded to replace EFC). *Average financial aid package:* $10,852 (excluding resources awarded to replace EFC). 11% of all full-time freshmen had no need and received non-need-based aid.

UNDERGRADUATE FINANCIAL AID (Fall 1999, est.) 1,062 applied for aid; of those 77% were deemed to have need. 100% of undergraduates with need received aid; of those 14% had need fully met. *Average percent of need met:* 72% (excluding resources awarded to replace EFC). *Average financial aid package:* $10,874 (excluding resources awarded to replace EFC). 8% of all full-time undergraduates had no need and received non-need-based aid.

GIFT AID (NEED-BASED) ***Total amount:*** $975,063 (88% Federal, 5% state, 7% institutional). ***Receiving aid:*** *Freshmen:* 30% (81); *all full-time undergraduates:* 30% (329). ***Average award:*** Freshmen: $2903; Undergraduates: $2747. ***Scholarships, grants, and awards:*** Federal Pell, FSEOG, state, college/university gift aid from institutional funds.

GIFT AID (NON-NEED-BASED) ***Total amount:*** $6,046,883 (27% state, 69% institutional, 4% external sources). ***Receiving aid:*** *Freshmen:* 75% (204); *Undergraduates:* 74% (809). ***Scholarships, grants, and awards by category:*** *Academic Interests/Achievement:* general academic interests/achievements. *Creative Arts/Performance:* art/fine arts, music, theater/drama. *Special Achievements/Activities:* leadership, religious involvement. *Special Characteristics:* children of educators, children of faculty/staff, local/state students, relatives of clergy. ***Tuition waivers:*** Full or partial for employees or children of employees, senior citizens. ***ROTC:*** Army cooperative.

LOANS ***Student loans:*** $4,996,302 (58% need-based, 42% non-need-based). 71% of past graduating class borrowed through all loan programs. Average indebtedness per student: $16,292. ***Average need-based loan:*** Freshmen: $2989; Undergraduates: $3948. ***Parent loans:*** $1,421,836 (100% non-need-based). ***Programs:*** FFEL (Subsidized and Unsubsidized Stafford, PLUS), Perkins.

WORK-STUDY ***Federal work-study:*** *Total amount:* $315,227; 226 jobs averaging $1500.

APPLYING for FINANCIAL AID ***Required financial aid forms:*** FAFSA, state aid form. ***Financial aid deadline:*** Continuous. ***Notification date:*** Continuous beginning 2/15. Students must reply by 5/1 or within 2 weeks of notification.

CONTACT Ms. Eugenia F. Hickman, Director of Financial Aid, Virginia Wesleyan College, 1584 Wesleyan Drive, Norfolk, VA 23502-5599, 757-455-3207 or toll-free 800-737-8684. *Fax:* 757-455-6779. *E-mail:* dhickman@vwc.edu

VITERBO UNIVERSITY

La Crosse, WI

Tuition & fees: $12,490 **Average undergraduate aid package: $11,647**

ABOUT THE INSTITUTION Independent Roman Catholic, coed. Awards: bachelor's and master's degrees. 45 undergraduate majors. Total enrollment: 2,574. Undergraduates: 1,790. Both federal and institutional methodology are used as a basis for awarding need-based institutional aid.

UNDERGRADUATE EXPENSES for 1999–2000 ***Application fee:*** $15. ***Comprehensive fee:*** $16,890 includes full-time tuition ($12,220), mandatory fees ($270), and room and board ($4400). ***College room only:*** $1930. ***Part-time tuition:*** $355 per credit. ***Part-time fees:*** $14 per credit. Part-time tuition and fees vary according to course load. ***Payment plan:*** installment.

FRESHMAN FINANCIAL AID (Fall 1999) 294 applied for aid; of those 91% were deemed to have need. 100% of freshmen with need received aid; of those 17% had need fully met. *Average percent of need met:* 81% (excluding resources awarded to replace EFC). *Average financial aid package:* $11,856 (excluding resources awarded to replace EFC). 13% of all full-time freshmen had no need and received non-need-based aid.

UNDERGRADUATE FINANCIAL AID (Fall 1999) 1,186 applied for aid; of those 93% were deemed to have need. 100% of undergraduates with need received aid; of those 26% had need fully met. *Average percent of need met:* 84% (excluding resources awarded to replace EFC). *Average financial aid package:* $11,647 (excluding resources awarded to replace EFC).

GIFT AID (NEED-BASED) ***Total amount:*** $8,185,761 (18% Federal, 15% state, 65% institutional, 2% external sources). ***Receiving aid:*** *Freshmen:* 86% (269); *all full-time undergraduates:* 1,080. ***Average award:*** Freshmen: $8717; Undergraduates: $7625. ***Scholarships, grants, and awards:*** Federal Pell, FSEOG, state, private, college/university gift aid from institutional funds.

GIFT AID (NON-NEED-BASED) ***Total amount:*** $1,305,294 (16% Federal, 79% institutional, 5% external sources). ***Receiving aid:*** *Freshmen:* 8% (26); *Undergraduates:* 85. ***Scholarships, grants, and awards by category:*** *Academic Interests/Achievement:* general academic interests/achievements, health fields. *Creative Arts/Performance:* art/fine arts, music, performing arts, theater/drama. *Special Achievements/Activities:* community service, general special achievements/activities, leadership. *Special Characteristics:* children and siblings of alumni, children of faculty/staff. ***Tuition waivers:*** Full or partial for minority students, employees or children of employees, senior citizens. ***ROTC:*** Army cooperative.

LOANS ***Student loans:*** $6,088,585 (82% need-based, 18% non-need-based). 82% of past graduating class borrowed through all loan programs. Average indebtedness per student: $15,338. ***Average need-based loan:*** Freshmen: $2809; Undergraduates: $3990. ***Parent loans:*** $1,057,127 (32% need-based, 68% non-need-based). ***Programs:*** FFEL (Subsidized and Unsubsidized Stafford, PLUS), Perkins, Federal Nursing.

WORK-STUDY ***Federal work-study:*** *Total amount:* $410,697; 268 jobs averaging $1532. ***State or other work-study/employment:*** *Total amount:* $68,252 (74% need-based, 26% non-need-based). 47 part-time jobs averaging $1452.

ATHLETIC AWARDS *Total amount:* 46,122 (81% need-based, 19% non-need-based).

APPLYING for FINANCIAL AID ***Required financial aid form:*** FAFSA. ***Financial aid deadline (priority):*** 3/15. ***Notification date:*** Continuous. Students must reply within 2 weeks of notification.

CONTACT Ms. Terry Norman, Director of Financial Aid, Viterbo University, 815 South Ninth Street, La Crosse, WI 54601-4797, 608-796-3900 or toll-free 800-VIT-ERBO. *Fax:* 608-796-3050. *E-mail:* twnorman@mail.viterbo.edu

VOORHEES COLLEGE

Denmark, SC

Tuition & fees: $5860 **Average undergraduate aid package: $8566**

ABOUT THE INSTITUTION Independent Episcopal, coed. Awards: bachelor's degrees. 16 undergraduate majors. Total enrollment: 943. Undergraduates: 943. Federal methodology is used as a basis for awarding need-based institutional aid.

UNDERGRADUATE EXPENSES for 1999–2000 ***Application fee:*** $25. ***Comprehensive fee:*** $9050 includes full-time tuition ($5860) and room and board ($3190). ***Part-time tuition:*** $200 per credit hour. ***Payment plans:*** installment, deferred payment.

FRESHMAN FINANCIAL AID (Fall 1999, est.) 119 applied for aid; of those 100% were deemed to have need. 100% of freshmen with need received aid; of those 6% had need fully met. *Average percent of need met:* 58% (excluding resources awarded to replace EFC). *Average financial aid package:* $8468 (excluding resources awarded to replace EFC).

UNDERGRADUATE FINANCIAL AID (Fall 1999, est.) 769 applied for aid; of those 98% were deemed to have need. 100% of undergraduates with need received aid; of those 5% had need fully met. *Average percent of need met:* 58% (excluding resources awarded to replace EFC). *Average financial aid package:* $8566 (excluding resources awarded to replace EFC).

GIFT AID (NEED-BASED) ***Total amount:*** $2,925,645 (71% Federal, 19% state, 7% institutional, 3% external sources). ***Receiving aid:*** *Freshmen:* 91% (115); *all full-time undergraduates:* 77% (684). ***Average award:*** Freshmen: $4734; Undergraduates: $4363. ***Scholarships, grants, and awards:*** Federal Pell, FSEOG, state, private, college/university gift aid from institutional funds, United Negro College Fund.

GIFT AID (NON-NEED-BASED) ***Scholarships, grants, and awards by category:*** *Academic Interests/Achievement:* biological sciences, business, computer science, education, general academic interests/achievements, premedicine. *Creative Arts/Performance:* general creative arts/performance. *Special Achievements/Activities:* community service. *Special Characteristics:* 16 awards ($18,337 total): children of faculty/staff, general special characteristics, international students. ***Tuition waivers:*** Full or partial for employees or children of employees. ***ROTC:*** Army cooperative.

LOANS ***Student loans:*** $2,898,186 (100% need-based). 80% of past graduating class borrowed through all loan programs. ***Average need-based loan:*** Freshmen: $2417; Undergraduates: $3536. ***Parent loans:*** $168,985 (100% need-based). ***Programs:*** FFEL (Subsidized and Unsubsidized Stafford, PLUS), Perkins, state.

WORK-STUDY ***Federal work-study:*** *Total amount:* $473,667; 297 jobs averaging $1589. ***State or other work-study/employment:*** *Total amount:* $3326 (100% need-based). 2 part-time jobs averaging $1663.

ATHLETIC AWARDS *Total amount:* 71,367 (100% need-based).

APPLYING for FINANCIAL AID ***Required financial aid forms:*** FAFSA, institution's own form. ***Financial aid deadline (priority):*** 4/15. ***Notification date:*** Continuous beginning 5/1. Students must reply within 2 weeks of notification.

CONTACT Ms. Carolyn B. White, Director of Financial Aid, Voorhees College, Voorhees Road, Denmark, SC 29042, 803-703-7109 or toll-free 800-446-6250. *Fax:* 803-793-0831. *E-mail:* white@voorhees.edu

WABASH COLLEGE

Crawfordsville, IN

Tuition & fees: $17,275 **Average undergraduate aid package: $16,872**

ABOUT THE INSTITUTION Independent, men only. Awards: bachelor's degrees. 24 undergraduate majors. Total enrollment: 861. Undergraduates: 861. Freshmen: 292. Both federal and institutional methodology are used as a basis for awarding need-based institutional aid.

UNDERGRADUATE EXPENSES for 1999–2000 ***Application fee:*** $30. ***Comprehensive fee:*** $22,710 includes full-time tuition ($16,975), mandatory fees ($300), and room and board ($5435). ***College room only:*** $2025. Room and board charges vary according to housing facility. ***Part-time tuition:*** $2830 per course. Part-time tuition and fees vary according to course load. ***Payment plans:*** tuition prepayment, installment.

FRESHMAN FINANCIAL AID (Fall 1999) 263 applied for aid; of those 85% were deemed to have need. 100% of freshmen with need received aid; of those 100% had need fully met. *Average percent of need met:* 100% (excluding resources awarded to replace EFC). *Average financial aid package:* $17,569 (excluding resources awarded to replace EFC). 20% of all full-time freshmen had no need and received non-need-based aid.

UNDERGRADUATE FINANCIAL AID (Fall 1999) 676 applied for aid; of those 89% were deemed to have need. 100% of undergraduates with need received aid; of those 100% had need fully met. *Average percent of need met:* 100% (excluding resources awarded to replace EFC). *Average financial aid package:* $16,872 (excluding resources awarded to replace EFC).

GIFT AID (NEED-BASED) ***Total amount:*** $7,300,576 (5% Federal, 16% state, 76% institutional, 3% external sources). ***Receiving aid:*** *Freshmen:* 76% (223); *all full-time undergraduates:* 70% (599). ***Average award:*** Freshmen: $13,983; Undergraduates: $12,961. ***Scholarships, grants, and awards:*** Federal Pell, state, private, college/university gift aid from institutional funds.

GIFT AID (NON-NEED-BASED) ***Total amount:*** $2,650,908 (91% institutional, 9% external sources). ***Receiving aid:*** *Freshmen:* 19% (55); *Undergraduates:* 11% (98). ***Scholarships, grants, and awards by category:*** *Academic Interests/Achievement:* 207 awards ($939,421 total): computer science, education, general academic interests/achievements. *Creative Arts/Performance:* 46 awards ($178,000 total): art/fine arts, creative writing, journalism/publications, music, theater/drama. *Special Achievements/Activities:* 298 awards ($1,728,302 total): community service, leadership. *Special Characteristics:* 99 awards ($989,626 total): children of faculty/staff, ethnic background, international students. ***Tuition waivers:*** Full or partial for employees or children of employees.

LOANS ***Student loans:*** $2,344,761 (74% need-based, 26% non-need-based). 68% of past graduating class borrowed through all loan programs. Average indebtedness per student: $13,925. ***Average need-based loan:*** Freshmen: $2670; Undergraduates: $3463. ***Parent loans:*** $47,910 (32% need-based, 68% non-need-based). ***Programs:*** FFEL (Subsidized and Unsubsidized Stafford, PLUS), college/university.

WORK-STUDY ***State or other work-study/employment:*** *Total amount:* $496,409 (90% need-based, 10% non-need-based). 432 part-time jobs averaging $1149.

APPLYING for FINANCIAL AID ***Required financial aid forms:*** FAFSA, CSS Financial Aid PROFILE. ***Financial aid deadline:*** 3/1 (priority: 2/15). ***Notification date:*** Continuous beginning 3/15. Students must reply by 5/1 or within 2 weeks of notification.

CONTACT Mr. Clint Gasaway, Financial Aid Director, Wabash College, PO Box 352, Crawfordsville, IN 47933-0352, 800-718-9746 or toll-free 800-345-5385. *Fax:* 765-361-6166.

WADHAMS HALL SEMINARY-COLLEGE

Ogdensburg, NY

Tuition & fees: $5525 **Average undergraduate aid package: $10,500**

ABOUT THE INSTITUTION Independent Roman Catholic, coed, primarily men. Awards: bachelor's degrees and post-bachelor's certificates. 2 undergraduate majors. Total enrollment: 22. Undergraduates: 22. Freshmen: 4. Both federal and institutional methodology are used as a basis for awarding need-based institutional aid.

UNDERGRADUATE EXPENSES for 1999–2000 ***Application fee:*** $15. ***Comprehensive fee:*** $10,300 includes full-time tuition ($5100), mandatory fees ($425), and room and board ($4775). ***College room only:*** $2275. ***Part-time tuition:*** $170 per credit hour. ***Payment plans:*** installment, deferred payment.

FRESHMAN FINANCIAL AID (Fall 1998) 7 applied for aid; of those 86% were deemed to have need. 100% of freshmen with need received aid; of those 17% had need fully met. *Average percent of need met:* 80% (excluding resources awarded to replace EFC). *Average financial aid package:* $10,500 (excluding resources awarded to replace EFC).

UNDERGRADUATE FINANCIAL AID (Fall 1998) 27 applied for aid; of those 59% were deemed to have need. 100% of undergraduates with need received aid; of those 44% had need fully met. *Average percent of need met:* 82% (excluding resources awarded to replace EFC). *Average financial aid package:* $10,500 (excluding resources awarded to replace EFC).

GIFT AID (NEED-BASED) ***Total amount:*** $128,682 (20% Federal, 17% state, 14% institutional, 49% external sources). ***Receiving aid:*** *Freshmen:* 57% (4); *all full-time undergraduates:* 32% (9). ***Average award:*** Freshmen: $500; Undergraduates: $750. ***Scholarships, grants, and awards:*** Federal Pell, FSEOG, state, private, college/university gift aid from institutional funds.

GIFT AID (NON-NEED-BASED) ***Total amount:*** $12,100 (92% institutional, 8% external sources). ***Receiving aid:*** *Freshmen:* 14% (1); *Undergraduates:* 11% (3). ***Scholarships, grants, and awards by category:*** *Academic Interests/Achievement:* $3000 total: general academic interests/achievements. *Special Achievements/Activities:* 2 awards ($2000 total): general special achievements/activities. *Special Characteristics:* 3 awards ($7100 total): international students, out-of-state students.

LOANS ***Student loans:*** $31,731 (100% need-based). 20% of past graduating class borrowed through all loan programs. Average indebtedness per student: $6800. ***Average need-based loan:*** Freshmen: $2625; Undergraduates: $3500. ***Parent loans:*** $10,550 (100% need-based). ***Programs:*** FFEL (Subsidized and Unsubsidized Stafford, PLUS).

Wadhams Hall Seminary-College (continued)

WORK-STUDY ***Federal work-study:*** *Total amount:* $2341; 4 jobs averaging $585. ***State or other work-study/employment:*** *Total amount:* $2000 (100% need-based). 4 part-time jobs averaging $500.

APPLYING for FINANCIAL AID ***Required financial aid forms:*** FAFSA, institution's own form, state aid form. ***Financial aid deadline (priority):*** 7/1. ***Notification date:*** 7/30. Students must reply within 2 weeks of notification.

CONTACT Mrs. Beth Turner, Financial Aid Administrator, Wadhams Hall Seminary-College, 6866 State Highway 37, Ogdensburg, NY 13669, 315-393-4231. *Fax:* 315-393-4249. *E-mail:* whsc@gisco.net

WAGNER COLLEGE

Staten Island, NY

Tuition & fees: $18,000 **Average undergraduate aid package: $12,103**

ABOUT THE INSTITUTION Independent, coed. Awards: bachelor's and master's degrees. 35 undergraduate majors. Total enrollment: 2,000. Undergraduates: 1,616. Freshmen: 478. Federal methodology is used as a basis for awarding need-based institutional aid.

UNDERGRADUATE EXPENSES for 1999–2000 ***Application fee:*** $45. ***Comprehensive fee:*** $24,500 includes full-time tuition ($18,000) and room and board ($6500). ***Part-time tuition:*** $600 per credit. Part-time tuition and fees vary according to course load. ***Payment plan:*** installment.

FRESHMAN FINANCIAL AID (Fall 1998) 418 applied for aid; of those 86% were deemed to have need. 100% of freshmen with need received aid; of those 16% had need fully met. *Average percent of need met:* 79% (excluding resources awarded to replace EFC). *Average financial aid package:* $12,472 (excluding resources awarded to replace EFC). 25% of all full-time freshmen had no need and received non-need-based aid.

UNDERGRADUATE FINANCIAL AID (Fall 1998) 1,165 applied for aid; of those 90% were deemed to have need. 100% of undergraduates with need received aid; of those 21% had need fully met. *Average percent of need met:* 77% (excluding resources awarded to replace EFC). *Average financial aid package:* $12,103 (excluding resources awarded to replace EFC). 30% of all full-time undergraduates had no need and received non-need-based aid.

GIFT AID (NEED-BASED) ***Total amount:*** $7,613,687 (12% Federal, 14% state, 72% institutional, 2% external sources). ***Receiving aid:*** *Freshmen:* 74% (356); *all full-time undergraduates:* 66% (1,021). ***Average award:*** Freshmen: $7512; Undergraduates: $7100. ***Scholarships, grants, and awards:*** Federal Pell, FSEOG, state, private, college/university gift aid from institutional funds.

GIFT AID (NON-NEED-BASED) ***Total amount:*** $2,524,370 (98% institutional, 2% external sources). ***Receiving aid:*** *Freshmen:* 74% (356); *Undergraduates:* 31% (474). ***Scholarships, grants, and awards by category:*** *Academic Interests/Achievement:* general academic interests/achievements. *Creative Arts/Performance:* music, theater/drama. *Special Achievements/Activities:* general special achievements/activities. ***Tuition waivers:*** Full or partial for employees or children of employees, senior citizens. ***ROTC:*** Army cooperative, Air Force cooperative.

LOANS ***Student loans:*** $5,889,029 (92% need-based, 8% non-need-based). ***Average need-based loan:*** Freshmen: $2946; Undergraduates: $4060. ***Parent loans:*** $2,671,044 (83% need-based, 17% non-need-based). ***Programs:*** FFEL (Subsidized and Unsubsidized Stafford, PLUS), Perkins, Federal Nursing.

WORK-STUDY ***Federal work-study:*** *Total amount:* $295,000; jobs available. ***State or other work-study/employment:*** *Total amount:* $125,000 (20% need-based, 80% non-need-based). Part-time jobs available.

ATHLETIC AWARDS *Total amount:* 2,804,440 (65% need-based, 35% non-need-based).

APPLYING for FINANCIAL AID ***Required financial aid forms:*** FAFSA, institution's own form. ***Financial aid deadline (priority):*** 2/15. ***Notification date:*** 3/15. Students must reply by 5/1.

CONTACT Mr. Edward Keough, Director of Financial Aid, Wagner College, One Campus Road, Staten Island, NY 10301, 718-390-3183 or toll-free 800-221-1010 (out-of-state). *Fax:* 718-390-3105.

WAKE FOREST UNIVERSITY

Winston-Salem, NC

Tuition & fees: $21,452 **Average undergraduate aid package: $17,451**

ABOUT THE INSTITUTION Independent religious, coed. Awards: bachelor's, master's, doctoral, and first professional degrees. 35 undergraduate majors. Total enrollment: 6,082. Undergraduates: 3,990. Freshmen: 971. Both federal and institutional methodology are used as a basis for awarding need-based institutional aid.

UNDERGRADUATE EXPENSES for 1999–2000 ***Application fee:*** $40. ***Comprehensive fee:*** $27,352 includes full-time tuition ($21,420), mandatory fees ($32), and room and board ($5900). ***College room only:*** $3250. Room and board charges vary according to board plan and housing facility. ***Part-time tuition:*** $575 per credit. ***Payment plan:*** installment.

FRESHMAN FINANCIAL AID (Fall 1999) 530 applied for aid; of those 70% were deemed to have need. 100% of freshmen with need received aid; of those 54% had need fully met. *Average percent of need met:* 91% (excluding resources awarded to replace EFC). *Average financial aid package:* $17,400 (excluding resources awarded to replace EFC). 31% of all full-time freshmen had no need and received non-need-based aid.

UNDERGRADUATE FINANCIAL AID (Fall 1999) 1,546 applied for aid; of those 80% were deemed to have need. 100% of undergraduates with need received aid; of those 52% had need fully met. *Average percent of need met:* 90% (excluding resources awarded to replace EFC). *Average financial aid package:* $17,451 (excluding resources awarded to replace EFC). 32% of all full-time undergraduates had no need and received non-need-based aid.

GIFT AID (NEED-BASED) ***Total amount:*** $13,794,664 (7% Federal, 13% state, 73% institutional, 7% external sources). ***Receiving aid:*** *Freshmen:* 35% (340); *all full-time undergraduates:* 30% (1,141). ***Average award:*** Freshmen: $13,061; Undergraduates: $12,233. ***Scholarships, grants, and awards:*** Federal Pell, FSEOG, state, college/university gift aid from institutional funds.

GIFT AID (NON-NEED-BASED) ***Total amount:*** $6,745,772 (1% Federal, 17% state, 59% institutional, 23% external sources). ***Receiving aid:*** *Freshmen:* 7% (69); *Undergraduates:* 5% (198). ***Scholarships, grants, and awards by category:*** *Academic Interests/Achievement:* biological sciences, business, education, English, foreign languages, general academic interests/achievements, international studies, mathematics, military science, physical sciences, religion/biblical studies. *Creative Arts/Performance:* art/fine arts, cinema/film/broadcasting, creative writing, dance, debating, journalism/publications, music, performing arts, theater/drama. *Special Achievements/Activities:* community service, leadership, religious involvement. *Special Characteristics:* children of faculty/staff, members of minority groups, relatives of clergy. ***Tuition waivers:*** Full or partial for employees or children of employees. ***ROTC:*** Army.

LOANS ***Student loans:*** $8,603,007 (60% need-based, 40% non-need-based). Average indebtedness per student: $17,661. ***Average need-based loan:*** Freshmen: $2989; Undergraduates: $4120. ***Parent loans:*** $3,018,848 (13% need-based, 87% non-need-based). ***Programs:*** FFEL (Subsidized and Unsubsidized Stafford, PLUS), Perkins, college/university, alternative loans.

WORK-STUDY ***Federal work-study:*** *Total amount:* $1,364,399; 745 jobs averaging $1831.

ATHLETIC AWARDS *Total amount:* 5,062,093 (23% need-based, 77% non-need-based).

APPLYING for FINANCIAL AID ***Required financial aid forms:*** FAFSA, CSS Financial Aid PROFILE, noncustodial (divorced/separated) parent's statement, federal income tax forms and all schedules (student and parent), W-2 forms. ***Financial aid deadline (priority):*** 2/1. ***Notification date:*** Continuous beginning 4/15. Students must reply by 5/1 or within 2 weeks of notification.

CONTACT Office of Financial Aid, Wake Forest University, PO Box 7246, Winston-Salem, NC 27109, 336-758-5154. *Fax:* 336-758-4924.

WALLA WALLA COLLEGE

College Place, WA

Tuition & fees: $13,941 **Average undergraduate aid package: $14,166**

ABOUT THE INSTITUTION Independent Seventh-day Adventist, coed. Awards: associate, bachelor's, and master's degrees. 62 undergraduate majors. Total enrollment: 1,782. Undergraduates: 1,535. Freshmen: 321. Federal methodology is used as a basis for awarding need-based institutional aid.

UNDERGRADUATE EXPENSES for 1999–2000 ***Application fee:*** $30. ***Comprehensive fee:*** $16,962 includes full-time tuition ($13,806), mandatory fees ($135), and room and board ($3021). ***College room only:*** $2034. Full-time tuition and fees vary according to course load, degree level, and location. Room and board charges vary according to gender, housing facility, and location. ***Part-time tuition:*** $365 per quarter hour. ***Part-time fees:*** $45 per term part-time. ***Payment plan:*** installment.

FRESHMAN FINANCIAL AID (Fall 1998) 310 applied for aid; of those 78% were deemed to have need. 100% of freshmen with need received aid; of those 25% had need fully met. *Average percent of need met:* 81% (excluding resources awarded to replace EFC). *Average financial aid package:* $13,125 (excluding resources awarded to replace EFC). 10% of all full-time freshmen had no need and received non-need-based aid.

UNDERGRADUATE FINANCIAL AID (Fall 1998) 1,295 applied for aid; of those 75% were deemed to have need. 100% of undergraduates with need received aid; of those 22% had need fully met. *Average percent of need met:* 85% (excluding resources awarded to replace EFC). *Average financial aid package:* $14,166 (excluding resources awarded to replace EFC). 10% of all full-time undergraduates had no need and received non-need-based aid.

GIFT AID (NEED-BASED) ***Total amount:*** $4,222,895 (33% Federal, 9% state, 58% institutional). ***Receiving aid:*** *Freshmen:* 67% (211); *all full-time undergraduates:* 60% (824). ***Average award:*** Freshmen: $6509; Undergraduates: $6479. ***Scholarships, grants, and awards:*** Federal Pell, FSEOG, state, private, college/university gift aid from institutional funds.

GIFT AID (NON-NEED-BASED) ***Total amount:*** $4,404,986 (38% institutional, 62% external sources). ***Receiving aid:*** *Freshmen:* 69% (218); *Undergraduates:* 58% (802). ***Scholarships, grants, and awards by category:*** *Academic Interests/Achievement:* general academic interests/achievements. *Creative Arts/Performance:* general creative arts/performance, music. *Special Achievements/Activities:* community service, leadership. *Special Characteristics:* children of faculty/staff. ***Tuition waivers:*** Full or partial for employees or children of employees, senior citizens.

LOANS ***Student loans:*** $5,692,285 (100% need-based). 73% of past graduating class borrowed through all loan programs. Average indebtedness per student: $18,876. ***Average need-based loan:*** Freshmen: $6275; Undergraduates: $6392. ***Parent loans:*** $760,253 (100% need-based). ***Programs:*** FFEL (Subsidized and Unsubsidized Stafford, PLUS), Perkins, Federal Nursing, college/university.

WORK-STUDY ***Federal work-study:*** *Total amount:* $1,256,404; jobs available. ***State or other work-study/employment:*** *Total amount:* $232,929 (100% need-based). Part-time jobs available.

APPLYING for FINANCIAL AID ***Required financial aid forms:*** FAFSA, institution's own form. ***Financial aid deadline:*** Continuous. ***Notification date:*** Continuous beginning 3/15.

CONTACT Ms. Nancy Caldera, Associate Director of Financial Aid, Walla Walla College, 204 South College Avenue, College Place, WA 99324-1198, 509-527-2315 or toll-free 800-541-8900. *Fax:* 509-527-2253. *E-mail:* caldna@wwc.edu

WALSH COLLEGE OF ACCOUNTANCY AND BUSINESS ADMINISTRATION

Troy, MI

Tuition & fees: $5275 **Average undergraduate aid package: N/A**

ABOUT THE INSTITUTION Independent, coed. Awards: bachelor's and master's degrees. 5 undergraduate majors. Total enrollment: 2,929. Undergraduates: 1,179. Federal methodology is used as a basis for awarding need-based institutional aid.

UNDERGRADUATE EXPENSES for 1999–2000 ***Application fee:*** $25. ***Tuition:*** full-time $5125; part-time $205 per credit hour. ***Required fees:*** full-time $150; $75 per term part-time. Full-time tuition and fees vary according to course load. Part-time tuition and fees vary according to course load. ***Payment plan:*** deferred payment.

UNDERGRADUATE FINANCIAL AID (Fall 1998) 93 applied for aid; of those 78% were deemed to have need. 100% of undergraduates with need received aid.

GIFT AID (NEED-BASED) ***Total amount:*** $897,228 (28% Federal, 46% state, 26% institutional). ***Receiving aid:*** *All full-time undergraduates:* 28% (50). ***Scholarships, grants, and awards:*** Federal Pell, FSEOG, state, private, college/university gift aid from institutional funds.

GIFT AID (NON-NEED-BASED) ***Total amount:*** $25,958 (100% institutional). ***Scholarships, grants, and awards by category:*** *Academic Interests/Achievement:* business. *Special Characteristics:* previous college experience. ***Tuition waivers:*** Full or partial for employees or children of employees.

LOANS ***Student loans:*** $1,422,085 (86% need-based, 14% non-need-based). Average indebtedness per student: $12,700. ***Parent loans:*** $7584 (100% need-based). ***Programs:*** FFEL (Subsidized and Unsubsidized Stafford, PLUS), alternative loans.

WORK-STUDY ***Federal work-study:*** *Total amount:* $9222; 8 jobs averaging $1153. ***State or other work-study/employment:*** *Total amount:* $4600 (100% need-based). 1 part-time job averaging $4000.

APPLYING for FINANCIAL AID ***Required financial aid forms:*** FAFSA, institution's own form. ***Financial aid deadline:*** Continuous. ***Notification date:*** Continuous beginning 6/1.

CONTACT Howard Thomas, Director of Student Financial Resources, Walsh College of Accountancy and Business Administration, 3838 Livernois Road, PO Box 7006, Troy, MI 48007-7006, 248-689-8282 Ext. 285. *Fax:* 248-524-2520. *E-mail:* hthomas@walshcol.edu

WALSH UNIVERSITY

North Canton, OH

Tuition & fees: $11,728 **Average undergraduate aid package: $9972**

ABOUT THE INSTITUTION Independent Roman Catholic, coed. Awards: associate, bachelor's, and master's degrees. 45 undergraduate majors. Total enrollment: 1,580. Undergraduates: 1,406. Freshmen: 319. Federal methodology is used as a basis for awarding need-based institutional aid.

UNDERGRADUATE EXPENSES for 1999–2000 ***Application fee:*** $25. ***Comprehensive fee:*** $17,128 includes full-time tuition ($11,350), mandatory fees ($378), and room and board ($5400). Full-time tuition and fees vary according to course load. ***Part-time tuition:*** $378 per credit hour. ***Part-time fees:*** $11 per credit hour. ***Payment plans:*** installment, deferred payment.

FRESHMAN FINANCIAL AID (Fall 1999) 251 applied for aid; of those 86% were deemed to have need. 100% of freshmen with need received aid; of those 23% had need fully met. *Average percent of need met:* 78% (excluding resources awarded to replace EFC). *Average financial aid package:* $10,088 (excluding resources awarded to replace EFC).

UNDERGRADUATE FINANCIAL AID (Fall 1999) 871 applied for aid; of those 87% were deemed to have need. 100% of undergraduates with need received aid; of those 30% had need fully met. *Average percent of need met:* 79% (excluding resources awarded to replace EFC). *Average financial aid package:* $9972 (excluding resources awarded to replace EFC).

Walsh University (continued)

GIFT AID (NEED-BASED) ***Total amount:*** $3,934,637 (19% Federal, 29% state, 48% institutional, 4% external sources). ***Receiving aid:*** *Freshmen:* 79% (216); *all full-time undergraduates:* 76% (742). ***Average award:*** Freshmen: $7046; Undergraduates: $5999. ***Scholarships, grants, and awards:*** Federal Pell, FSEOG, state, private, college/university gift aid from institutional funds.

GIFT AID (NON-NEED-BASED) ***Total amount:*** $545,332 (45% state, 46% institutional, 9% external sources). ***Receiving aid:*** *Freshmen:* 8% (23); *Undergraduates:* 7% (72). ***Scholarships, grants, and awards by category:*** *Academic Interests/Achievement:* 486 awards ($1,091,625 total): biological sciences, business, communication, computer science, education, English, general academic interests/achievements, health fields, humanities, mathematics, physical sciences, premedicine, social sciences. *Creative Arts/Performance:* 9 awards ($3500 total): music. *Special Achievements/Activities:* 140 awards ($118,901 total): community service, leadership, religious involvement. *Special Characteristics:* 164 awards ($183,963 total): children and siblings of alumni, international students, local/state students, members of minority groups, out-of-state students, siblings of current students. ***Tuition waivers:*** Full or partial for children of alumni, employees or children of employees, senior citizens.

LOANS ***Student loans:*** $5,375,325 (79% need-based, 21% non-need-based). 85% of past graduating class borrowed through all loan programs. Average indebtedness per student: $17,000. ***Average need-based loan:*** Freshmen: $2439; Undergraduates: $3614. ***Parent loans:*** $506,756 (50% need-based, 50% non-need-based). ***Programs:*** Federal Direct (Subsidized and Unsubsidized Stafford), FFEL (Subsidized and Unsubsidized Stafford), Perkins, state, college/university.

WORK-STUDY ***Federal work-study:*** *Total amount:* $271,294; jobs available. ***State or other work-study/employment:*** *Total amount:* $38,000 (6% need-based, 94% non-need-based). 32 part-time jobs averaging $1269.

ATHLETIC AWARDS *Total amount:* 597,855 (69% need-based, 31% non-need-based).

APPLYING for FINANCIAL AID ***Required financial aid form:*** FAFSA. ***Financial aid deadline:*** Continuous.

CONTACT Mrs. Amy Baker, Director of Financial Aid, Walsh University, 2020 Easton Street, NW, North Canton, OH 44720-3396, 330-490-7146 or toll-free 800-362-9846 (in-state), 800-362-8846 (out-of-state). *Fax:* 330-490-7372. *E-mail:* abaker@alex.walsh.edu

WARNER PACIFIC COLLEGE

Portland, OR

Tuition & fees: $135,000 **Average undergraduate aid package: $9944**

ABOUT THE INSTITUTION Independent religious, coed. Awards: associate, bachelor's, and master's degrees and first-professional certificates. 35 undergraduate majors. Total enrollment: 650. Undergraduates: 645. Freshmen: 72. Federal methodology is used as a basis for awarding need-based institutional aid.

UNDERGRADUATE EXPENSES for 2000–2001 (est.) ***Application fee:*** $25. ***Comprehensive fee:*** $139,567 includes full-time tuition ($135,000) and room and board ($4567). Room and board charges vary according to board plan and housing facility. ***Part-time tuition:*** $562 per semester hour. Part-time tuition and fees vary according to course load. ***Payment plan:*** installment.

FRESHMAN FINANCIAL AID (Fall 1998) 71 applied for aid; of those 93% were deemed to have need. 100% of freshmen with need received aid; of those 21% had need fully met. *Average percent of need met:* 83% (excluding resources awarded to replace EFC). *Average financial aid package:* $10,390 (excluding resources awarded to replace EFC).

UNDERGRADUATE FINANCIAL AID (Fall 1998) 351 applied for aid; of those 91% were deemed to have need. 99% of undergraduates with need received aid; of those 11% had need fully met. *Average percent of need met:* 74% (excluding resources awarded to replace EFC). *Average financial aid package:* $9944 (excluding resources awarded to replace EFC). 1% of all full-time undergraduates had no need and received non-need-based aid.

GIFT AID (NEED-BASED) ***Total amount:*** $1,127,898 (44% Federal, 11% state, 45% institutional). ***Receiving aid:*** *Freshmen:* 49% (35); *all full-time undergraduates:* 46% (188). ***Average award:*** Freshmen: $2470; Undergraduates: $2535. ***Scholarships, grants, and awards:*** Federal Pell, FSEOG, state, private, college/university gift aid from institutional funds.

GIFT AID (NON-NEED-BASED) ***Total amount:*** $1,166,029 (85% institutional, 15% external sources). ***Receiving aid:*** *Freshmen:* 85% (61); *Undergraduates:* 53% (217). ***Scholarships, grants, and awards by category:*** *Academic Interests/Achievement:* 186 awards ($377,617 total): general academic interests/achievements, premedicine. *Creative Arts/Performance:* 43 awards ($39,300 total): music. *Special Achievements/Activities:* 74 awards ($74,365 total): leadership, religious involvement. *Special Characteristics:* 156 awards ($347,200 total): children and siblings of alumni, members of minority groups, religious affiliation. ***Tuition waivers:*** Full or partial for children of alumni, employees or children of employees. ***ROTC:*** Army cooperative, Air Force cooperative.

LOANS ***Student loans:*** $2,654,141 (66% need-based, 34% non-need-based). 71% of past graduating class borrowed through all loan programs. Average indebtedness per student: $12,908. ***Average need-based loan:*** Freshmen: $3003; Undergraduates: $4211. ***Parent loans:*** $75,346 (100% non-need-based). ***Programs:*** FFEL (Subsidized and Unsubsidized Stafford, PLUS), Perkins, college/university.

WORK-STUDY ***Federal work-study:*** *Total amount:* $223,088; 133 jobs averaging $1678.

ATHLETIC AWARDS *Total amount:* 29,750 (100% non-need-based).

APPLYING for FINANCIAL AID ***Required financial aid form:*** FAFSA. ***Financial aid deadline (priority):*** 5/1. ***Notification date:*** Continuous. Students must reply within 2 weeks of notification.

CONTACT Jackie Gresham, Director of Financial Aid, Warner Pacific College, 2219 Southeast 68th Avenue, Portland, OR 97215-4099, 503-517-1018 or toll-free 800-582-7885. *E-mail:* jgresham@warnerpacific.edu

WARNER SOUTHERN COLLEGE

Lake Wales, FL

Tuition & fees: $8980 **Average undergraduate aid package: N/A**

ABOUT THE INSTITUTION Independent religious, coed. Awards: associate and bachelor's degrees. 27 undergraduate majors. Total enrollment: 844. Undergraduates: 844. Freshmen: 78. Both federal and institutional methodology are used as a basis for awarding need-based institutional aid.

UNDERGRADUATE EXPENSES for 1999–2000 ***Application fee:*** $20. ***Comprehensive fee:*** $13,338 includes full-time tuition ($8340), mandatory fees ($640), and room and board ($4358). ***College room only:*** $2090. Room and board charges vary according to board plan. ***Part-time tuition:*** $205 per semester hour. ***Part-time fees:*** $45 per term part-time. Part-time tuition and fees vary according to course load. ***Payment plan:*** installment.

GIFT AID (NEED-BASED) ***Scholarships, grants, and awards:*** Federal Pell, FSEOG, state, private, college/university gift aid from institutional funds.

GIFT AID (NON-NEED-BASED) ***Scholarships, grants, and awards by category:*** *Academic Interests/Achievement:* business, communication, education, English, general academic interests/achievements, humanities. *Special Achievements/Activities:* leadership. *Special Characteristics:* children and siblings of alumni, children of educators, children of faculty/staff, international students, out-of-state students, relatives of clergy, siblings of current students, veterans, veterans' children. ***Tuition waivers:*** Full or partial for employees or children of employees, senior citizens.

LOANS ***Programs:*** FFEL (Subsidized and Unsubsidized Stafford, PLUS), Perkins.

WORK-STUDY Federal work-study jobs available.

APPLYING for FINANCIAL AID ***Required financial aid form:*** FAFSA. ***Financial aid deadline (priority):*** 4/1. ***Notification date:*** Continuous. Students must reply within 2 weeks of notification.

CONTACT Financial Aid Office, Warner Southern College, 5301 US Highway 27 South, Lake Wales, FL 33853, 800-949-7248. *E-mail:* financialaid@warner.edu

WARREN WILSON COLLEGE

Asheville, NC

Tuition & fees: $13,600 **Average undergraduate aid package: $11,809**

ABOUT THE INSTITUTION Independent religious, coed. Awards: bachelor's and master's degrees. 36 undergraduate majors. Total enrollment: 831. Undergraduates: 763. Freshmen: 193. Both federal and institutional methodology are used as a basis for awarding need-based institutional aid.

UNDERGRADUATE EXPENSES for 1999–2000 ***Comprehensive fee:*** $18,044 includes full-time tuition ($13,350), mandatory fees ($250), and room and board ($4444). Full-time tuition and fees vary according to course load. Room and board charges vary according to board plan. Part-time tuition and fees vary according to course load. Full-time students work 15 hours per week to lower the cost of tuition. ***Payment plan:*** installment.

FRESHMAN FINANCIAL AID (Fall 1999) 133 applied for aid; of those 81% were deemed to have need. 100% of freshmen with need received aid; of those 18% had need fully met. *Average percent of need met:* 76% (excluding resources awarded to replace EFC). *Average financial aid package:* $11,397 (excluding resources awarded to replace EFC). 24% of all full-time freshmen had no need and received non-need-based aid.

UNDERGRADUATE FINANCIAL AID (Fall 1999) 446 applied for aid; of those 85% were deemed to have need. 100% of undergraduates with need received aid; of those 18% had need fully met. *Average percent of need met:* 78% (excluding resources awarded to replace EFC). *Average financial aid package:* $11,809 (excluding resources awarded to replace EFC). 27% of all full-time undergraduates had no need and received non-need-based aid.

GIFT AID (NEED-BASED) ***Total amount:*** $2,475,890 (17% Federal, 12% state, 66% institutional, 5% external sources). ***Receiving aid:*** *Freshmen:* 49% (95); *all full-time undergraduates:* 44% (335). ***Average award:*** Freshmen: $7968; Undergraduates: $7391. ***Scholarships, grants, and awards:*** Federal Pell, FSEOG, state, college/university gift aid from institutional funds.

GIFT AID (NON-NEED-BASED) ***Total amount:*** $511,408 (23% state, 61% institutional, 16% external sources). ***Receiving aid:*** *Freshmen:* 31% (59); *Undergraduates:* 21% (156). ***Scholarships, grants, and awards by category:*** *Academic Interests/Achievement:* 68 awards ($95,000 total): general academic interests/achievements. *Creative Arts/Performance:* 2 awards ($2000 total): creative writing. *Special Achievements/Activities:* 46 awards ($55,000 total): general special achievements/activities, leadership. *Special Characteristics:* 4 awards ($3500 total): religious affiliation. ***Tuition waivers:*** Full or partial for employees or children of employees.

LOANS ***Student loans:*** $1,377,122 (87% need-based, 13% non-need-based). 61% of past graduating class borrowed through all loan programs. Average indebtedness per student: $13,880. ***Average need-based loan:*** Freshmen: $2446; Undergraduates: $3446. ***Parent loans:*** $523,905 (77% need-based, 23% non-need-based). ***Programs:*** FFEL (Subsidized and Unsubsidized Stafford, PLUS), Perkins, college/university.

WORK-STUDY ***Federal work-study:*** *Total amount:* $500,000; 379 jobs available. ***State or other work-study/employment:*** *Total amount:* $1,057,000 (35% need-based, 65% non-need-based). Part-time jobs available.

APPLYING for FINANCIAL AID ***Required financial aid forms:*** FAFSA, institution's own form, state aid form. ***Financial aid deadline (priority):*** 4/1. ***Notification date:*** Continuous. Students must reply within 3 weeks of notification.

CONTACT Admissions Office, Warren Wilson College, PO Box 9000, Asheville, NC 28815-9000, 800-934-3536. *Fax:* 828-298-1440.

WARTBURG COLLEGE

Waverly, IA

Tuition & fees: $15,765 **Average undergraduate aid package: $14,306**

ABOUT THE INSTITUTION Independent Lutheran, coed. Awards: bachelor's degrees. 51 undergraduate majors. Total enrollment: 1,546. Undergraduates: 1,546. Freshmen: 411. Federal methodology is used as a basis for awarding need-based institutional aid.

UNDERGRADUATE EXPENSES for 2000–2001 ***Application fee:*** $20. ***Comprehensive fee:*** $20,165 includes full-time tuition ($15,510), mandatory fees ($255), and room and board ($4400). ***College room only:*** $2100. Room and board charges vary according to board plan and housing facility. Part-time tuition and fees vary according to class time and course load. ***Payment plan:*** installment.

FRESHMAN FINANCIAL AID (Fall 1999, est.) 358 applied for aid; of those 67% were deemed to have need. 100% of freshmen with need received aid; of those 15% had need fully met. *Average percent of need met:* 87% (excluding resources awarded to replace EFC). *Average financial aid package:* $13,630 (excluding resources awarded to replace EFC).

UNDERGRADUATE FINANCIAL AID (Fall 1999, est.) 1,392 applied for aid; of those 66% were deemed to have need. 99% of undergraduates with need received aid; of those 20% had need fully met. *Average percent of need met:* 88% (excluding resources awarded to replace EFC). *Average financial aid package:* $14,306 (excluding resources awarded to replace EFC).

GIFT AID (NEED-BASED) ***Total amount:*** $9,192,717 (11% Federal, 28% state, 57% institutional, 4% external sources). ***Receiving aid:*** *Freshmen:* 59% (241); *all full-time undergraduates:* 62% (920). ***Average award:*** Freshmen: $10,145; Undergraduates: $9713. ***Scholarships, grants, and awards:*** Federal Pell, FSEOG, state, private, college/university gift aid from institutional funds.

GIFT AID (NON-NEED-BASED) ***Total amount:*** $3,288,147 (92% institutional, 8% external sources). ***Scholarships, grants, and awards by category:*** *Academic Interests/Achievement:* biological sciences, English, general academic interests/achievements, mathematics, physical sciences. *Creative Arts/Performance:* 30 awards ($11,980 total): music. *Special Characteristics:* children and siblings of alumni, children of faculty/staff, ethnic background, members of minority groups, out-of-state students, religious affiliation, siblings of current students. ***Tuition waivers:*** Full or partial for employees or children of employees, senior citizens.

LOANS ***Student loans:*** $6,293,919 (84% need-based, 16% non-need-based). 76% of past graduating class borrowed through all loan programs. Average indebtedness per student: $14,826. ***Average need-based loan:*** Freshmen: $3038; Undergraduates: $3650. ***Parent loans:*** $600,837 (64% need-based, 36% non-need-based). ***Programs:*** FFEL (Subsidized and Unsubsidized Stafford, PLUS), Perkins, alternative loans.

WORK-STUDY ***Federal work-study:*** *Total amount:* $775,222; 548 jobs averaging $1405. ***State or other work-study/employment:*** *Total amount:* $561,696 (30% need-based, 70% non-need-based). 446 part-time jobs averaging $1256.

APPLYING for FINANCIAL AID ***Required financial aid form:*** FAFSA. ***Financial aid deadline (priority):*** 3/1. ***Notification date:*** Continuous beginning 3/22. Students must reply within 2 weeks of notification.

CONTACT Mr. David Best, Director of Financial Aid, Wartburg College, 222 9th Street, NW, Waverly, IA 50677-1003, 319-352-8262 or toll-free 800-772-2085. *Fax:* 319-352-8247. *E-mail:* best@wartburg.edu

WASHBURN UNIVERSITY OF TOPEKA

Topeka, KS

Tuition & fees (KS res): $2934 **Average undergraduate aid package: $5814**

ABOUT THE INSTITUTION City-supported, coed. Awards: associate, bachelor's, master's, and first professional degrees. 68 undergraduate majors. Total enrollment: 6,065. Undergraduates: 4,829. Freshmen: 627. Federal methodology is used as a basis for awarding need-based institutional aid.

UNDERGRADUATE EXPENSES for 1999–2000 ***Tuition, state resident:*** full-time $2884; part-time $103 per credit hour. ***Tuition, nonresident:*** full-time $6496; part-time $232 per credit hour. ***Required fees:*** full-time $50; $25 per term part-time. Part-time tuition and fees vary according to

Washburn University of Topeka (continued)

course load. ***College room and board:*** $3320. Room and board charges vary according to board plan and housing facility. ***Payment plan:*** installment.

FRESHMAN FINANCIAL AID (Fall 1998) 341 applied for aid; of those 78% were deemed to have need. 100% of freshmen with need received aid. *Average financial aid package:* $4175 (excluding resources awarded to replace EFC).

UNDERGRADUATE FINANCIAL AID (Fall 1998) 1,542 applied for aid; of those 94% were deemed to have need. 100% of undergraduates with need received aid. *Average financial aid package:* $5814 (excluding resources awarded to replace EFC).

GIFT AID (NEED-BASED) ***Total amount:*** $4,484,947 (54% Federal, 2% state, 39% institutional, 5% external sources). ***Receiving aid:*** *Freshmen:* 30% (155); *all full-time undergraduates:* 31% (844). ***Scholarships, grants, and awards:*** Federal Pell, FSEOG, state, private, college/university gift aid from institutional funds.

GIFT AID (NON-NEED-BASED) ***Scholarships, grants, and awards by category:*** *Academic Interests/Achievement:* general academic interests/achievements. *Creative Arts/Performance:* debating, music. *Special Characteristics:* children of faculty/staff. ***ROTC:*** Army, Air Force cooperative.

LOANS ***Parent loans:*** $187,912 (100% need-based). ***Programs:*** FFEL (Subsidized and Unsubsidized Stafford, PLUS), Perkins.

WORK-STUDY ***Federal work-study:*** 159 jobs averaging $2310. ***State or other work-study/employment:*** Part-time jobs available.

ATHLETIC AWARDS *Total amount:* 642,183 (100% need-based).

APPLYING for FINANCIAL AID ***Required financial aid form:*** FAFSA. ***Financial aid deadline (priority):*** 3/1. ***Notification date:*** Continuous beginning 4/1. Students must reply within 2 weeks of notification.

CONTACT Annita Huff, Director, Financial Aid, Washburn University of Topeka, 1700 SW College Avenue, Topeka, KS 66621, 785-231-1151 or toll-free 800-332-0291 (in-state).

WASHINGTON & JEFFERSON COLLEGE

Washington, PA

Tuition & fees: $19,000 | **Average undergraduate aid package: $14,489**

ABOUT THE INSTITUTION Independent, coed. Awards: associate and bachelor's degrees. 18 undergraduate majors. Total enrollment: 1,217. Undergraduates: 1,217. Freshmen: 327. Both federal and institutional methodology are used as a basis for awarding need-based institutional aid.

UNDERGRADUATE EXPENSES for 1999–2000 ***Application fee:*** $25. ***One-time required fee:*** $30. ***Comprehensive fee:*** $23,750 includes full-time tuition ($18,675), mandatory fees ($325), and room and board ($4750). ***College room only:*** $2410. Room and board charges vary according to board plan. ***Part-time tuition:*** $1850 per course. ***Payment plans:*** installment, deferred payment.

FRESHMAN FINANCIAL AID (Fall 1999, est.) 294 applied for aid; of those 92% were deemed to have need. 99% of freshmen with need received aid; of those 11% had need fully met. *Average percent of need met:* 77% (excluding resources awarded to replace EFC). *Average financial aid package:* $14,596 (excluding resources awarded to replace EFC). 10% of all full-time freshmen had no need and received non-need-based aid.

UNDERGRADUATE FINANCIAL AID (Fall 1999, est.) 975 applied for aid; of those 93% were deemed to have need. 97% of undergraduates with need received aid; of those 14% had need fully met. *Average percent of need met:* 76% (excluding resources awarded to replace EFC). *Average financial aid package:* $14,489 (excluding resources awarded to replace EFC). 9% of all full-time undergraduates had no need and received non-need-based aid.

GIFT AID (NEED-BASED) ***Total amount:*** $11,251,521 (8% Federal, 13% state, 79% institutional). ***Receiving aid:*** *Freshmen:* 82% (266); *all full-time undergraduates:* 78% (871). ***Average award:*** Freshmen: $13,119; Undergraduates: $13,401. ***Scholarships, grants, and awards:*** Federal Pell, FSEOG, state, private, college/university gift aid from institutional funds.

GIFT AID (NON-NEED-BASED) ***Total amount:*** $1,430,197 (84% institutional, 16% external sources). ***Receiving aid:*** *Freshmen:* 4% (13); *Undergraduates:* 1% (13). ***Scholarships, grants, and awards by category:*** *Academic Interests/Achievement:* business, general academic interests/achievements. *Special Achievements/Activities:* general special achievements/activities. *Special Characteristics:* children and siblings of alumni, children of faculty/staff. ***Tuition waivers:*** Full or partial for employees or children of employees. ***ROTC:*** Army cooperative.

LOANS ***Student loans:*** $3,102,500 (84% need-based, 16% non-need-based). 69% of past graduating class borrowed through all loan programs. ***Average need-based loan:*** Freshmen: $2400; Undergraduates: $2530. ***Parent loans:*** $760,000 (100% non-need-based). ***Programs:*** FFEL (Subsidized and Unsubsidized Stafford, PLUS), Perkins, college/university.

WORK-STUDY ***Federal work-study:*** *Total amount:* $275,000; 190 jobs averaging $1447. ***State or other work-study/employment:*** *Total amount:* $102,000 (100% non-need-based). 100 part-time jobs averaging $1020.

APPLYING for FINANCIAL AID ***Required financial aid forms:*** FAFSA, state aid form. ***Financial aid deadline (priority):*** 2/15. ***Notification date:*** Continuous beginning 3/10. Students must reply by 5/1.

CONTACT Ms. Nancy R. Sninsky, Director of Financial Aid, Washington & Jefferson College, 60 South Lincoln Street, Washington, PA 15301-4801, 724-223-6019 or toll-free 888-WANDJAY. *Fax:* 724-223-5271. *E-mail:* nsninsky@washjeff.edu

WASHINGTON AND LEE UNIVERSITY

Lexington, VA

Tuition & fees: $17,105 | **Average undergraduate aid package: $13,560**

ABOUT THE INSTITUTION Independent, coed. Awards: bachelor's and first professional degrees. 38 undergraduate majors. Total enrollment: 2,096. Undergraduates: 1,729. Freshmen: 467. Both federal and institutional methodology are used as a basis for awarding need-based institutional aid.

UNDERGRADUATE EXPENSES for 1999–2000 ***Application fee:*** $40. ***Comprehensive fee:*** $22,652 includes full-time tuition ($16,950), mandatory fees ($155), and room and board ($5547). ***College room only:*** $3000. Room and board charges vary according to board plan and housing facility. ***Part-time tuition:*** $565 per credit hour.

FRESHMAN FINANCIAL AID (Fall 1998) 218 applied for aid; of those 64% were deemed to have need. 100% of freshmen with need received aid; of those 95% had need fully met. *Average percent of need met:* 98% (excluding resources awarded to replace EFC). *Average financial aid package:* $14,465 (excluding resources awarded to replace EFC). 24% of all full-time freshmen had no need and received non-need-based aid.

UNDERGRADUATE FINANCIAL AID (Fall 1998) 618 applied for aid; of those 73% were deemed to have need. 99% of undergraduates with need received aid; of those 88% had need fully met. *Average percent of need met:* 98% (excluding resources awarded to replace EFC). *Average financial aid package:* $13,560 (excluding resources awarded to replace EFC). 25% of all full-time undergraduates had no need and received non-need-based aid.

GIFT AID (NEED-BASED) ***Total amount:*** $4,421,719 (5% Federal, 3% state, 85% institutional, 7% external sources). ***Receiving aid:*** *Freshmen:* 27% (124); *all full-time undergraduates:* 21% (351). ***Scholarships, grants, and awards:*** Federal Pell, FSEOG, state, private, college/university gift aid from institutional funds.

GIFT AID (NON-NEED-BASED) ***Total amount:*** $2,393,422 (3% Federal, 13% state, 75% institutional, 9% external sources). ***Receiving aid:*** *Freshmen:* 9% (43); *Undergraduates:* 6% (101). ***Scholarships, grants, and awards by category:*** *Academic Interests/Achievement:* general academic interests/achievements. *Special Characteristics:* local/state students. ***Tuition waivers:*** Full or partial for employees or children of employees. ***ROTC:*** Army cooperative.

LOANS ***Student loans:*** $1,910,020 (80% need-based, 20% non-need-based). ***Parent loans:*** $2,637,453 (50% need-based, 50% non-need-based). ***Programs:*** FFEL (Subsidized and Unsubsidized Stafford, PLUS), Perkins, college/university.

WORK-STUDY ***Federal work-study:*** *Total amount:* $307,520; jobs available. ***State or other work-study/employment:*** *Total amount:* $412,831 (43% need-based, 57% non-need-based). Part-time jobs available.

APPLYING for FINANCIAL AID ***Required financial aid forms:*** FAFSA, CSS Financial Aid PROFILE, noncustodial (divorced/separated) parent's statement, business/farm supplement. ***Financial aid deadline (priority):*** 2/1. ***Notification date:*** 4/3. Students must reply by 5/1.

CONTACT Ms. E. McClain Stradtner, Associate Director, Financial Aid, Washington and Lee University, Gilliam House, Letcher Avenue, Lexington, VA 24450, 540-463-8729.

WASHINGTON BIBLE COLLEGE

Lanham, MD

Tuition & fees: $6460 **Average undergraduate aid package: N/A**

ABOUT THE INSTITUTION Independent nondenominational, coed. Awards: associate and bachelor's degrees. 8 undergraduate majors. Total enrollment: 335. Undergraduates: 335. Freshmen: 34. Both federal and institutional methodology are used as a basis for awarding need-based institutional aid.

UNDERGRADUATE EXPENSES for 1999–2000 ***Application fee:*** $15. ***Comprehensive fee:*** $10,710 includes full-time tuition ($6240), mandatory fees ($220), and room and board ($4250). ***College room only:*** $1770. Room and board charges vary according to board plan. ***Part-time tuition:*** $260 per credit hour. Part-time tuition and fees vary according to course load and location. ***Payment plans:*** installment, deferred payment.

GIFT AID (NEED-BASED) ***Scholarships, grants, and awards:*** Federal Pell, FSEOG, state, private, college/university gift aid from institutional funds.

GIFT AID (NON-NEED-BASED) ***Scholarships, grants, and awards by category:*** *Academic Interests/Achievement:* general academic interests/ achievements. *Special Achievements/Activities:* leadership, religious involvement. *Special Characteristics:* children of faculty/staff, relatives of clergy, religious affiliation, spouses of current students. ***Tuition waivers:*** Full or partial for employees or children of employees.

LOANS ***Programs:*** FFEL (Subsidized and Unsubsidized Stafford, PLUS).

WORK-STUDY Federal work-study jobs available.

APPLYING for FINANCIAL AID ***Required financial aid forms:*** FAFSA, institution's own form, CSS Financial Aid PROFILE, verification form. ***Financial aid deadline (priority):*** 6/1. ***Notification date:*** Continuous beginning 7/1. Students must reply within 2 weeks of notification.

CONTACT Wanda Rounds, Financial Aid Administrator, Washington Bible College, 6511 Princess Garden Parkway, Lanham, MD 20706-3599, 301-552-1400 Ext. 222 or toll-free 800-787-0256 Ext. 212. *E-mail:* wrounds@ bible.edu

WASHINGTON COLLEGE

Chestertown, MD

Tuition & fees: $20,200 **Average undergraduate aid package: $17,977**

ABOUT THE INSTITUTION Independent, coed. Awards: bachelor's and master's degrees. 30 undergraduate majors. Total enrollment: 1,194. Undergraduates: 1,117. Freshmen: 282. Both federal and institutional methodology are used as a basis for awarding need-based institutional aid.

UNDERGRADUATE EXPENSES for 1999–2000 ***Application fee:*** $40. ***Comprehensive fee:*** $25,940 includes full-time tuition ($19,750), mandatory fees ($450), and room and board ($5740). ***College room only:*** $2600. Full-time tuition and fees vary according to program. Room and board charges vary according to board plan and housing facility. ***Part-time tuition:*** $3291 per course. ***Part-time fees:*** $75 per course. Part-time tuition and fees vary according to course load and program. ***Payment plan:*** installment.

FRESHMAN FINANCIAL AID (Fall 1999) 209 applied for aid; of those 84% were deemed to have need. 100% of freshmen with need received aid; of those 70% had need fully met. *Average percent of need met:* 87% (excluding resources awarded to replace EFC). *Average financial aid package:* $16,113 (excluding resources awarded to replace EFC). 16% of all full-time freshmen had no need and received non-need-based aid.

UNDERGRADUATE FINANCIAL AID (Fall 1999) 636 applied for aid; of those 83% were deemed to have need. 100% of undergraduates with need received aid; of those 90% had need fully met. *Average percent of need met:* 89% (excluding resources awarded to replace EFC). *Average financial aid package:* $17,977 (excluding resources awarded to replace EFC). 23% of all full-time undergraduates had no need and received non-need-based aid.

GIFT AID (NEED-BASED) ***Total amount:*** $7,030,436 (5% Federal, 9% state, 86% institutional). ***Receiving aid:*** *Freshmen:* 56% (174); *all full-time undergraduates:* 50% (524). ***Average award:*** Freshmen: $13,625; Undergraduates: $14,372. ***Scholarships, grants, and awards:*** Federal Pell, FSEOG, state, private, college/university gift aid from institutional funds.

GIFT AID (NON-NEED-BASED) ***Total amount:*** $2,654,225 (3% state, 88% institutional, 9% external sources). ***Receiving aid:*** *Freshmen:* 34% (105); *Undergraduates:* 22% (236). ***Scholarships, grants, and awards by category:*** *Creative Arts/Performance:* 16 awards ($24,000 total): creative writing. *Special Achievements/Activities:* 591 awards ($5,910,000 total): memberships. *Special Characteristics:* 72 awards ($1,186,332 total): children of faculty/staff, children of union members/company employees, international students. ***Tuition waivers:*** Full or partial for employees or children of employees, adult students.

LOANS ***Student loans:*** $2,742,335 (55% need-based, 45% non-need-based). 61% of past graduating class borrowed through all loan programs. Average indebtedness per student: $17,278. ***Average need-based loan:*** Freshmen: $2625; Undergraduates: $5602. ***Parent loans:*** $1,756,469 (100% non-need-based). ***Programs:*** FFEL (Subsidized and Unsubsidized Stafford, PLUS), Perkins, college/university.

WORK-STUDY ***Federal work-study:*** *Total amount:* $212,470; 213 jobs averaging $1200.

APPLYING for FINANCIAL AID ***Required financial aid forms:*** FAFSA, institution's own form, federal income tax form(s). ***Financial aid deadline (priority):*** 2/15. ***Notification date:*** Continuous beginning 3/1. Students must reply by 5/1.

CONTACT Ms. Jean M. Narcum, Director of Financial Aid, Washington College, 300 Washington Avenue, Chestertown, MD 21620-1197, 410-778-7214 or toll-free 800-422-1782. *Fax:* 410-778-7287. *E-mail:* jean-narcum@ washcoll.edu

WASHINGTON STATE UNIVERSITY

Pullman, WA

Tuition & fees (WA res): $3662 **Average undergraduate aid package: $10,500**

ABOUT THE INSTITUTION State-supported, coed. Awards: bachelor's, master's, doctoral, and first professional degrees. 108 undergraduate majors. Total enrollment: 20,799. Undergraduates: 17,087. Freshmen: 2,487. Federal methodology is used as a basis for awarding need-based institutional aid.

UNDERGRADUATE EXPENSES for 1999–2000 ***Application fee:*** $35. ***Tuition, state resident:*** full-time $3233; part-time $177 per credit. ***Tuition, nonresident:*** full-time $10,267; part-time $528 per credit. ***Required fees:*** full-time $429. Full-time tuition and fees vary according to reciprocity agreements. Part-time tuition and fees vary according to course load and reciprocity agreements. ***College room and board:*** $4618. Room and board charges vary according to board plan and housing facility. ***Payment plans:*** tuition prepayment, installment.

FRESHMAN FINANCIAL AID (Fall 1999, est.) 1578 applied for aid; of those 66% were deemed to have need. 100% of freshmen with need received aid; of those 46% had need fully met. *Average percent of need met:* 98% (excluding resources awarded to replace EFC). *Average financial aid package:* $7972 (excluding resources awarded to replace EFC). 10% of all full-time freshmen had no need and received non-need-based aid.

UNDERGRADUATE FINANCIAL AID (Fall 1999, est.) 8,991 applied for aid; of those 79% were deemed to have need. 100% of undergraduates with

Washington State University (continued)

need received aid; of those 62% had need fully met. *Average percent of need met:* 98% (excluding resources awarded to replace EFC). *Average financial aid package:* $10,500 (excluding resources awarded to replace EFC). 3% of all full-time undergraduates had no need and received non-need-based aid.

GIFT AID (NEED-BASED) ***Total amount:*** $18,790,000 (52% Federal, 35% state, 13% institutional). ***Receiving aid:*** *Freshmen:* 26% (659); *all full-time undergraduates:* 26% (4,510). ***Average award:*** Freshmen: $3038; Undergraduates: $3591. ***Scholarships, grants, and awards:*** Federal Pell, FSEOG, state, private, college/university gift aid from institutional funds.

GIFT AID (NON-NEED-BASED) ***Total amount:*** $5,705,000 (12% state, 53% institutional, 35% external sources). ***Receiving aid:*** *Freshmen:* 27% (666); *Undergraduates:* 14% (2,419). ***Scholarships, grants, and awards by category:*** *Academic Interests/Achievement:* agriculture, architecture, area/ethnic studies, biological sciences, business, communication, computer science, education, engineering/technologies, English, foreign languages, general academic interests/achievements, health fields, home economics, humanities, international studies, mathematics, physical sciences, premedicine, social sciences. *Creative Arts/Performance:* applied art and design, art/fine arts, cinema/film/broadcasting, creative writing, general creative arts/performance, journalism/publications, music, performing arts, theater/drama. *Special Achievements/Activities:* general special achievements/activities, junior miss, leadership, rodeo. *Special Characteristics:* international students, members of minority groups. ***Tuition waivers:*** Full or partial for children of alumni, employees or children of employees, senior citizens. ***ROTC:*** Army, Naval, Air Force.

LOANS ***Student loans:*** $60,000,000 (58% need-based, 42% non-need-based). 80% of past graduating class borrowed through all loan programs. Average indebtedness per student: $15,000. ***Average need-based loan:*** Freshmen: $3180; Undergraduates: $6031. ***Parent loans:*** $13,000,000 (100% non-need-based). ***Programs:*** FFEL (Subsidized and Unsubsidized Stafford, PLUS), Perkins, Federal Nursing, college/university, alternative loans.

WORK-STUDY ***Federal work-study:*** *Total amount:* $1,000,000; 625 jobs averaging $1600. ***State or other work-study/employment:*** *Total amount:* $1,500,000 (100% need-based). 833 part-time jobs averaging $1800.

ATHLETIC AWARDS *Total amount:* 3,300,000 (100% non-need-based).

APPLYING for FINANCIAL AID ***Required financial aid form:*** FAFSA. ***Financial aid deadline (priority):*** 3/1. ***Notification date:*** 4/15.

CONTACT Office of Student Financial Aid, Washington State University, PO Box 641068, Pullman, WA 99164-1068, 509-335-9711. *E-mail:* finaid@wsunix.wsu.edu

WASHINGTON UNIVERSITY IN ST. LOUIS

St. Louis, MO

Tuition & fees: $24,745 **Average undergraduate aid package: $20,682**

ABOUT THE INSTITUTION Independent, coed. Awards: bachelor's, master's, doctoral, and first professional degrees and post-bachelor's certificates. 135 undergraduate majors. Total enrollment: 12,088. Undergraduates: 6,509. Freshmen: 1,384. Both federal and institutional methodology are used as a basis for awarding need-based institutional aid.

UNDERGRADUATE EXPENSES for 2000–2001 ***Application fee:*** $55. ***Comprehensive fee:*** $32,469 includes full-time tuition ($24,500), mandatory fees ($245), and room and board ($7724). ***College room only:*** $4602. Room and board charges vary according to board plan and housing facility. Part-time tuition and fees vary according to class time. ***Payment plans:*** tuition prepayment, installment.

FRESHMAN FINANCIAL AID (Fall 1999, est.) 990 applied for aid; of those 65% were deemed to have need. 99% of freshmen with need received aid; of those 100% had need fully met. *Average percent of need met:* 100% (excluding resources awarded to replace EFC). *Average financial aid package:* $19,879 (excluding resources awarded to replace EFC).

UNDERGRADUATE FINANCIAL AID (Fall 1999, est.) 4,030 applied for aid; of those 70% were deemed to have need. 99% of undergraduates with need received aid; of those 100% had need fully met. *Average percent of need met:* 100% (excluding resources awarded to replace EFC). *Average financial aid package:* $20,682 (excluding resources awarded to replace EFC).

GIFT AID (NEED-BASED) ***Total amount:*** $42,423,099 (5% Federal, 2% state, 88% institutional, 5% external sources). ***Receiving aid:*** *Freshmen:* 46% (633); *all full-time undergraduates:* 49% (2,754). ***Scholarships, grants, and awards:*** Federal Pell, FSEOG, state, private, college/university gift aid from institutional funds, United Negro College Fund.

GIFT AID (NON-NEED-BASED) ***Total amount:*** $6,267,695 (3% state, 87% institutional, 10% external sources). ***Receiving aid:*** *Freshmen:* 17% (233); *Undergraduates:* 12% (677). ***Scholarships, grants, and awards by category:*** *Academic Interests/Achievement:* architecture, biological sciences, business, computer science, engineering/technologies, English, general academic interests/achievements, humanities, mathematics, physical sciences, social sciences. *Creative Arts/Performance:* applied art and design, art/fine arts, creative writing, dance, music. ***Tuition waivers:*** Full or partial for employees or children of employees. ***ROTC:*** Army, Air Force cooperative.

LOANS ***Student loans:*** $14,688,700 (94% need-based, 6% non-need-based). ***Parent loans:*** $2,407,523 (60% need-based, 40% non-need-based). ***Programs:*** FFEL (Subsidized and Unsubsidized Stafford, PLUS), Perkins, college/university.

WORK-STUDY ***Federal work-study:*** *Total amount:* $2,954,029; 1,527 jobs averaging $1935.

APPLYING for FINANCIAL AID ***Required financial aid forms:*** FAFSA, CSS Financial Aid PROFILE, parent and student federal income tax returns. ***Financial aid deadline:*** 2/15. ***Notification date:*** 4/1. Students must reply by 5/1.

CONTACT Mr. William Witbrodt, Director of Financial Aid, Washington University in St. Louis, Campus Box 1041, 1 Brookings Drive, St. Louis, MO 63130-4899, 314-935-5900 or toll-free 800-638-0700. *Fax:* 314-935-4037. *E-mail:* financial@wustl.edu

WAYLAND BAPTIST UNIVERSITY

Plainview, TX

Tuition & fees: $7400 **Average undergraduate aid package: $8485**

ABOUT THE INSTITUTION Independent Baptist, coed. Awards: associate, bachelor's, and master's degrees (branch locations: Anchorage, AK; Amarillo, TX; Luke Airforce Base, AZ; Glorieta, NM; Aiea, HI; Lubbock, TX; San Antonio, TX; Wichita Falls, TX). 28 undergraduate majors. Total enrollment: 4,586. Undergraduates: 4,130. Freshmen: 221. Federal methodology is used as a basis for awarding need-based institutional aid.

UNDERGRADUATE EXPENSES for 1999–2000 ***Application fee:*** $35. ***Comprehensive fee:*** $10,521 includes full-time tuition ($7050), mandatory fees ($350), and room and board ($3121). ***College room only:*** $1216. Room and board charges vary according to board plan and housing facility. ***Part-time tuition:*** $235 per semester hour. ***Part-time fees:*** $40 per term part-time. Part-time tuition and fees vary according to course load. ***Payment plan:*** installment.

FRESHMAN FINANCIAL AID (Fall 1999, est.) 208 applied for aid; of those 84% were deemed to have need. 99% of freshmen with need received aid; of those 26% had need fully met. *Average percent of need met:* 79% (excluding resources awarded to replace EFC). *Average financial aid package:* $7878 (excluding resources awarded to replace EFC). 14% of all full-time freshmen had no need and received non-need-based aid.

UNDERGRADUATE FINANCIAL AID (Fall 1999, est.) 809 applied for aid; of those 89% were deemed to have need. 99% of undergraduates with need received aid; of those 26% had need fully met. *Average percent of need met:* 80% (excluding resources awarded to replace EFC). *Average financial aid package:* $8485 (excluding resources awarded to replace EFC). 7% of all full-time undergraduates had no need and received non-need-based aid.

GIFT AID (NEED-BASED) ***Total amount:*** $4,948,581 (34% Federal, 17% state, 44% institutional, 5% external sources). ***Receiving aid:*** *Freshmen:* 81% (171); *all full-time undergraduates:* 80% (697). ***Average award:***

Freshmen: $5226; Undergraduates: $5011. ***Scholarships, grants, and awards:*** Federal Pell, FSEOG, state, private, college/university gift aid from institutional funds.

GIFT AID (NON-NEED-BASED) ***Receiving aid:*** *Freshmen:* 14% (30); *Undergraduates:* 8% (72). ***Scholarships, grants, and awards by category:*** *Academic Interests/Achievement:* biological sciences, business, communication, education, English, general academic interests/achievements, mathematics, physical sciences, religion/biblical studies. *Creative Arts/Performance:* music, theater/drama. *Special Achievements/Activities:* cheerleading/drum major, leadership, memberships, religious involvement. *Special Characteristics:* children of faculty/staff, ethnic background, general special characteristics, local/state students, members of minority groups, relatives of clergy. ***Tuition waivers:*** Full or partial for employees or children of employees.

LOANS ***Student loans:*** $5,626,077 (52% need-based, 48% non-need-based). ***Average need-based loan:*** Freshmen: $2330; Undergraduates: $2979. ***Parent loans:*** $998,475 (100% non-need-based). ***Programs:*** FFEL (Subsidized and Unsubsidized Stafford, PLUS), Perkins, state, college/university.

WORK-STUDY ***Federal work-study:*** *Total amount:* $544,920; 183 jobs averaging $2978. ***State or other work-study/employment:*** *Total amount:* $318,616 (2% need-based, 98% non-need-based). Part-time jobs available.

ATHLETIC AWARDS *Total amount:* 424,047 (100% need-based).

APPLYING for FINANCIAL AID ***Required financial aid forms:*** FAFSA, institution's own form. ***Financial aid deadline (priority):*** 5/1. ***Notification date:*** Continuous. Students must reply within 4 weeks of notification.

CONTACT Ms. Julie Hacker, Director of Financial Aid, Wayland Baptist University, 1900 West 7th Street, 597 WBU, Plainview, TX 79072-6998, 806-296-4713 or toll-free 800-588-1-WBU. *Fax:* 806-296-4531.

WAYNESBURG COLLEGE

Waynesburg, PA

Tuition & fees: $11,430 **Average undergraduate aid package: $11,425**

ABOUT THE INSTITUTION Independent religious, coed. Awards: associate, bachelor's, and master's degrees. 37 undergraduate majors. Total enrollment: 1,498. Undergraduates: 1,323. Freshmen: 287. Federal methodology is used as a basis for awarding need-based institutional aid.

UNDERGRADUATE EXPENSES for 1999–2000 ***Application fee:*** $15. ***Comprehensive fee:*** $16,020 includes full-time tuition ($11,160), mandatory fees ($270), and room and board ($4590). ***College room only:*** $2340. Full-time tuition and fees vary according to class time. Room and board charges vary according to board plan. ***Part-time tuition:*** $465 per credit hour. Part-time tuition and fees vary according to class time, course load, and location. ***Payment plan:*** installment.

FRESHMAN FINANCIAL AID (Fall 1999, est.) 277 applied for aid; of those 93% were deemed to have need. 100% of freshmen with need received aid; of those 21% had need fully met. *Average percent of need met:* 92% (excluding resources awarded to replace EFC). *Average financial aid package:* $12,094 (excluding resources awarded to replace EFC). 3% of all full-time freshmen had no need and received non-need-based aid.

UNDERGRADUATE FINANCIAL AID (Fall 1999, est.) 1,201 applied for aid; of those 94% were deemed to have need. 98% of undergraduates with need received aid; of those 28% had need fully met. *Average percent of need met:* 94% (excluding resources awarded to replace EFC). *Average financial aid package:* $11,425 (excluding resources awarded to replace EFC). 2% of all full-time undergraduates had no need and received non-need-based aid.

GIFT AID (NEED-BASED) ***Total amount:*** $6,558,527 (18% Federal, 25% state, 52% institutional, 5% external sources). ***Receiving aid:*** *Freshmen:* 90% (255); *all full-time undergraduates:* 87% (1,054). ***Average award:*** Freshmen: $8245; Undergraduates: $7147. ***Scholarships, grants, and awards:*** Federal Pell, FSEOG, state, private, college/university gift aid from institutional funds.

GIFT AID (NON-NEED-BASED) ***Total amount:*** $825,738 (6% Federal, 94% institutional). ***Receiving aid:*** *Freshmen:* 40% (114); *Undergraduates:* 26% (312). ***Scholarships, grants, and awards by category:*** *Academic Interests/Achievement:* general academic interests/achievements. *Creative Arts/Performance:* journalism/publications. *Special Achievements/Activities:* community service, leadership. *Special Characteristics:* children of faculty/staff, children of union members/company employees. ***Tuition waivers:*** Full or partial for employees or children of employees.

LOANS ***Student loans:*** $4,902,798 (77% need-based, 23% non-need-based). 81% of past graduating class borrowed through all loan programs. Average indebtedness per student: $15,000. ***Average need-based loan:*** Freshmen: $2946; Undergraduates: $4088. ***Parent loans:*** $647,732 (83% need-based, 17% non-need-based). ***Programs:*** FFEL (Subsidized and Unsubsidized Stafford, PLUS), Perkins, Federal Nursing, college/university, alternative loans.

WORK-STUDY ***Federal work-study:*** *Total amount:* $125,307; 200 jobs averaging $626. ***State or other work-study/employment:*** *Total amount:* $235,396 (100% non-need-based). Part-time jobs available.

APPLYING for FINANCIAL AID ***Required financial aid forms:*** FAFSA, institution's own form, state aid form. ***Financial aid deadline (priority):*** 3/15. ***Notification date:*** Continuous. Students must reply within 2 weeks of notification.

CONTACT Ms. Sheree K. Fetcho, Director of Financial Aid, Waynesburg College, 51 West College Street, Waynesburg, PA 15370-1222, 724-852-3227 or toll-free 800-225-7393. *Fax:* 724-627-6416. *E-mail:* sfetcho@waynesburg.edu

WAYNE STATE COLLEGE

Wayne, NE

Tuition & fees (NE res): $2271 **Average undergraduate aid package: $3066**

ABOUT THE INSTITUTION State-supported, coed. Awards: bachelor's and master's degrees and post-master's certificates. 61 undergraduate majors. Total enrollment: 3,601. Undergraduates: 3,036. Freshmen: 668. Federal methodology is used as a basis for awarding need-based institutional aid.

UNDERGRADUATE EXPENSES for 1999–2000 ***Application fee:*** $10. ***Tuition, state resident:*** full-time $1875; part-time $62 per semester hour. ***Tuition, nonresident:*** full-time $3750; part-time $125 per semester hour. ***Required fees:*** full-time $396; $16 per semester hour. ***College room and board:*** $3300; ***room only:*** $1520. Room and board charges vary according to board plan and housing facility. ***Payment plan:*** installment.

FRESHMAN FINANCIAL AID (Fall 1999, est.) 542 applied for aid; of those 76% were deemed to have need. 98% of freshmen with need received aid; of those 34% had need fully met. *Average percent of need met:* 41% (excluding resources awarded to replace EFC). *Average financial aid package:* $2842 (excluding resources awarded to replace EFC).

UNDERGRADUATE FINANCIAL AID (Fall 1999, est.) 2,074 applied for aid; of those 77% were deemed to have need. 98% of undergraduates with need received aid; of those 58% had need fully met. *Average percent of need met:* 44% (excluding resources awarded to replace EFC). *Average financial aid package:* $3066 (excluding resources awarded to replace EFC).

GIFT AID (NEED-BASED) ***Total amount:*** $2,211,344 (89% Federal, 11% state). ***Receiving aid:*** *Freshmen:* 43% (282); *all full-time undergraduates:* 41% (1,129). ***Average award:*** Freshmen: $1016; Undergraduates: $1033. ***Scholarships, grants, and awards:*** Federal Pell, FSEOG, state, college/university gift aid from institutional funds.

GIFT AID (NON-NEED-BASED) ***Total amount:*** $821,368 (57% institutional, 43% external sources). ***Receiving aid:*** *Freshmen:* 6% (40); *Undergraduates:* 7% (201). ***Scholarships, grants, and awards by category:*** *Academic Interests/Achievement:* general academic interests/achievements. *Creative Arts/Performance:* art/fine arts, cinema/film/broadcasting, creative writing, general creative arts/performance, journalism/publications, music, theater/drama. *Special Achievements/Activities:* leadership. *Special Characteristics:* children of faculty/staff, general special characteristics, international students, members of minority groups, out-of-state students, veterans' children. ***Tuition waivers:*** Full or partial for employees or children of employees. ***ROTC:*** Army cooperative.

LOANS ***Student loans:*** $7,444,712 (51% need-based, 49% non-need-based). ***Average need-based loan:*** Freshmen: $1250; Undergraduates:

Wayne State College (continued)

$1428. ***Parent loans:*** $187,532 (100% non-need-based). ***Programs:*** FFEL (Subsidized and Unsubsidized Stafford, PLUS), Perkins.

WORK-STUDY ***Federal work-study:*** *Total amount:* $178,350; jobs available.

ATHLETIC AWARDS *Total amount:* 305,969 (100% non-need-based).

APPLYING for FINANCIAL AID ***Required financial aid forms:*** FAFSA, institution's own form. ***Financial aid deadline:*** Continuous. ***Notification date:*** Continuous beginning 4/1. Students must reply within 3 weeks of notification.

CONTACT Mrs. Kyle M. Rose, Director of Financial Aid, Wayne State College, 1111 Main Street, Wayne, NE 68787, 402-375-7230 or toll-free 800-228-9972 (in-state). *Fax:* 402-375-7204. *E-mail:* krose@wscgate.wsc.edu

WAYNE STATE UNIVERSITY

Detroit, MI

Tuition & fees (MI res): $3809 **Average undergraduate aid package: $4804**

ABOUT THE INSTITUTION State-supported, coed. Awards: bachelor's, master's, doctoral, and first professional degrees and post-bachelor's and post-master's certificates. 88 undergraduate majors. Total enrollment: 31,025. Undergraduates: 18,393. Freshmen: 2,014. Federal methodology is used as a basis for awarding need-based institutional aid.

UNDERGRADUATE EXPENSES for 1999–2000 ***Application fee:*** $20. ***Tuition, state resident:*** full-time $3420; part-time $114 per semester hour. ***Tuition, nonresident:*** full-time $7860; part-time $262 per semester hour. ***Required fees:*** full-time $389; $10 per semester hour; $71 per term part-time. Full-time tuition and fees vary according to course level and student level. Part-time tuition and fees vary according to course level and student level. ***College room and board: room only:*** $4152. Room and board charges vary according to housing facility. ***Payment plan:*** installment.

FRESHMAN FINANCIAL AID (Fall 1998) 1532 applied for aid; of those 87% were deemed to have need. 93% of freshmen with need received aid; of those 4% had need fully met. *Average percent of need met:* 33% (excluding resources awarded to replace EFC). *Average financial aid package:* $3724 (excluding resources awarded to replace EFC). 6% of all full-time freshmen had no need and received non-need-based aid.

UNDERGRADUATE FINANCIAL AID (Fall 1998) 6,363 applied for aid; of those 92% were deemed to have need. 94% of undergraduates with need received aid; of those 5% had need fully met. *Average percent of need met:* 50% (excluding resources awarded to replace EFC). *Average financial aid package:* $4804 (excluding resources awarded to replace EFC). 4% of all full-time undergraduates had no need and received non-need-based aid.

GIFT AID (NEED-BASED) ***Total amount:*** $13,314,665 (86% Federal, 7% state, 7% institutional). ***Receiving aid:*** *Freshmen:* 35% (606); *all full-time undergraduates:* 29% (2,697). ***Average award:*** Freshmen: $2483; Undergraduates: $2645. ***Scholarships, grants, and awards:*** Federal Pell, FSEOG, state, private, college/university gift aid from institutional funds.

GIFT AID (NON-NEED-BASED) ***Total amount:*** $8,494,583 (2% state, 73% institutional, 25% external sources). ***Receiving aid:*** *Freshmen:* 39% (681); *Undergraduates:* 30% (2,800). ***Scholarships, grants, and awards by category:*** *Academic Interests/Achievement:* general academic interests/achievements. *Creative Arts/Performance:* dance, debating, music. *Special Achievements/Activities:* memberships. ***Tuition waivers:*** Full or partial for employees or children of employees, senior citizens. ***ROTC:*** Army cooperative, Air Force cooperative.

LOANS ***Student loans:*** $23,668,554 (74% need-based, 26% non-need-based). Average indebtedness per student: $14,834. ***Average need-based loan:*** Freshmen: $2300; Undergraduates: $3784. ***Parent loans:*** $159,007 (100% non-need-based). ***Programs:*** Federal Direct (Subsidized and Unsubsidized Stafford), FFEL (Subsidized and Unsubsidized Stafford, PLUS), Perkins, state, college/university.

WORK-STUDY ***Federal work-study:*** *Total amount:* $2,236,117; 619 jobs averaging $3613. ***State or other work-study/employment:*** *Total amount:* $933,987 (100% need-based). 259 part-time jobs averaging $3606.

ATHLETIC AWARDS *Total amount:* 551,276 (100% non-need-based).

APPLYING for FINANCIAL AID ***Required financial aid forms:*** FAFSA, income tax forms, W-2 forms. ***Financial aid deadline (priority):*** 3/1. ***Notification date:*** Continuous beginning 4/1. Students must reply within 2 weeks of notification.

CONTACT Adalberto Andino, Director, Scholarships and Financial Aid, Wayne State University, 3W HNJ Student Services Building, Detroit, MI 48202, 313-577-3378. *Fax:* 313-577-6648. *E-mail:* adalberto.andino@wayne.edu

WEBBER COLLEGE

Babson Park, FL

Tuition & fees: $8160 **Average undergraduate aid package: $8224**

ABOUT THE INSTITUTION Independent, coed. Awards: associate, bachelor's, and master's degrees. 11 undergraduate majors. Total enrollment: 458. Undergraduates: 421. Freshmen: 75. Federal methodology is used as a basis for awarding need-based institutional aid.

UNDERGRADUATE EXPENSES for 1999–2000 ***Application fee:*** $35. ***Comprehensive fee:*** $11,730 includes full-time tuition ($8160) and room and board ($3570). Room and board charges vary according to board plan. ***Part-time tuition:*** $155 per credit. Part-time tuition and fees vary according to course load. ***Payment plan:*** installment.

FRESHMAN FINANCIAL AID (Fall 1999) 74 applied for aid; of those 51% were deemed to have need. 100% of freshmen with need received aid; of those 47% had need fully met. *Average percent of need met:* 82% (excluding resources awarded to replace EFC). *Average financial aid package:* $9056 (excluding resources awarded to replace EFC). 24% of all full-time freshmen had no need and received non-need-based aid.

UNDERGRADUATE FINANCIAL AID (Fall 1999) 335 applied for aid; of those 50% were deemed to have need. 100% of undergraduates with need received aid; of those 51% had need fully met. *Average percent of need met:* 74% (excluding resources awarded to replace EFC). *Average financial aid package:* $8224 (excluding resources awarded to replace EFC). 16% of all full-time undergraduates had no need and received non-need-based aid.

GIFT AID (NEED-BASED) ***Total amount:*** $770,603 (27% Federal, 49% state, 18% institutional, 6% external sources). ***Receiving aid:*** *Freshmen:* 51% (38); *all full-time undergraduates:* 47% (166). ***Average award:*** Freshmen: $7545; Undergraduates: $6226. ***Scholarships, grants, and awards:*** Federal Pell, FSEOG, state, private, college/university gift aid from institutional funds.

GIFT AID (NON-NEED-BASED) ***Total amount:*** $300,024 (36% state, 60% institutional, 4% external sources). ***Receiving aid:*** *Freshmen:* 51% (38); *Undergraduates:* 47% (166). ***Scholarships, grants, and awards by category:*** *Academic Interests/Achievement:* 101 awards ($106,100 total): general academic interests/achievements. *Creative Arts/Performance:* 29 awards ($28,500 total): journalism/publications. *Special Achievements/Activities:* 105 awards ($96,405 total): community service, general special achievements/activities, leadership, memberships. *Special Characteristics:* 123 awards ($120,660 total): children and siblings of alumni, children of faculty/staff, general special characteristics, local/state students. ***Tuition waivers:*** Full or partial for children of alumni, employees or children of employees, adult students, senior citizens.

LOANS ***Student loans:*** $667,854 (81% need-based, 19% non-need-based). Average indebtedness per student: $11,923. ***Average need-based loan:*** Freshmen: $2498; Undergraduates: $3805. ***Parent loans:*** $53,053 (67% need-based, 33% non-need-based). ***Programs:*** FFEL (Subsidized and Unsubsidized Stafford, PLUS), Perkins.

WORK-STUDY ***Federal work-study:*** *Total amount:* $29,148; 30 jobs averaging $971. ***State or other work-study/employment:*** *Total amount:* $39,028 (23% need-based, 77% non-need-based). 41 part-time jobs averaging $951.

ATHLETIC AWARDS *Total amount:* 330,300 (50% need-based, 50% non-need-based).

APPLYING for FINANCIAL AID ***Required financial aid forms:*** FAFSA, state aid form. ***Financial aid deadline (priority):*** 5/1. ***Notification date:*** Continuous. Students must reply within 4 weeks of notification.

CONTACT Ms. Kathleen Wilson, Director of Financial Aid, Webber College, PO Box 96, Babson Park, FL 33827-0096, 863-638-2930. *Fax:* 863-638-1317.

WEBB INSTITUTE

Glen Cove, NY

Tuition & fees: **Average undergraduate aid package: $5250**

ABOUT THE INSTITUTION Independent, coed. Awards: bachelor's degrees. 1 undergraduate major. Total enrollment: 81. Undergraduates: 81. Freshmen: 22. Federal methodology is used as a basis for awarding need-based institutional aid.

UNDERGRADUATE EXPENSES for 2000–2001 ***Application fee:*** $25. includes room and board ($6250). ***College room only:*** $2800.

FRESHMAN FINANCIAL AID (Fall 1999) 8 applied for aid; of those 38% were deemed to have need. 100% of freshmen with need received aid; of those 100% had need fully met. *Average percent of need met:* 100% (excluding resources awarded to replace EFC). *Average financial aid package:* $4700 (excluding resources awarded to replace EFC).

UNDERGRADUATE FINANCIAL AID (Fall 1999) 18 applied for aid; of those 50% were deemed to have need. 100% of undergraduates with need received aid; of those 100% had need fully met. *Average percent of need met:* 100% (excluding resources awarded to replace EFC). *Average financial aid package:* $5250 (excluding resources awarded to replace EFC).

GIFT AID (NEED-BASED) ***Total amount:*** $6125 (100% Federal). ***Scholarships, grants, and awards:*** Federal Pell, private.

GIFT AID (NON-NEED-BASED) ***Total amount:*** $13,500 (30% state, 70% external sources). ***Scholarships, grants, and awards by category:*** *Academic Interests/Achievement:* engineering/technologies.

LOANS ***Student loans:*** $35,050 (100% need-based). 14% of past graduating class borrowed through all loan programs. Average indebtedness per student: $16,600. ***Programs:*** FFEL (Subsidized and Unsubsidized Stafford, PLUS).

APPLYING for FINANCIAL AID ***Required financial aid form:*** FAFSA. ***Financial aid deadline (priority):*** 7/1. ***Notification date:*** Continuous beginning 8/15.

CONTACT William G. Murray, Director of Financial Aid, Webb Institute, Crescent Beach Road, Glen Cove, NY 11542-1398, 516-671-2213. *Fax:* 516-674-9838. *E-mail:* bmurray@webb-institute.edu

WEBER STATE UNIVERSITY

Ogden, UT

Tuition & fees (UT res): $2042 **Average undergraduate aid package: N/A**

ABOUT THE INSTITUTION State-supported, coed. Awards: associate, bachelor's, and master's degrees. 106 undergraduate majors. Total enrollment: 14,984. Undergraduates: 14,813. Freshmen: 2,712. Both federal and institutional methodology are used as a basis for awarding need-based institutional aid.

UNDERGRADUATE EXPENSES for 1999–2000 ***Application fee:*** $30. ***Tuition, state resident:*** full-time $1606; part-time $485 per term. ***Tuition, nonresident:*** full-time $5622; part-time $1698 per term. ***Required fees:*** full-time $436; $143 per term part-time. Part-time tuition and fees vary according to course load. ***College room and board:*** $3878; ***room only:*** $1680. Room and board charges vary according to board plan and housing facility. ***Payment plans:*** installment, deferred payment.

GIFT AID (NEED-BASED) ***Scholarships, grants, and awards:*** Federal Pell, FSEOG, state.

GIFT AID (NON-NEED-BASED) ***Scholarships, grants, and awards by category:*** *Academic Interests/Achievement:* general academic interests/achievements. *Creative Arts/Performance:* art/fine arts, debating, performing arts, theater/drama. *Special Achievements/Activities:* leadership, rodeo. *Special Characteristics:* adult students, members of minority groups. ***Tuition waivers:*** Full or partial for employees or children of employees, senior citizens. ***ROTC:*** Army, Naval, Air Force.

LOANS ***Programs:*** FFEL (Subsidized and Unsubsidized Stafford, PLUS), Perkins, college/university.

WORK-STUDY Federal work-study jobs available.

APPLYING for FINANCIAL AID ***Required financial aid form:*** FAFSA. ***Financial aid deadline (priority):*** 3/1. ***Notification date:*** Continuous beginning 3/30. Students must reply within 2 weeks of notification.

CONTACT Mr. Richard O. Effiong, Financial Aid Director, Weber State University, 120 Student Service Center, 1136 University Circle, Ogden, UT 84408-1136, 801-626-7569 or toll-free 800-634-6568 (in-state). *E-mail:* finaid@weber.edu

WEBSTER UNIVERSITY

St. Louis, MO

Tuition & fees: $12,450 **Average undergraduate aid package: $12,709**

ABOUT THE INSTITUTION Independent, coed. Awards: bachelor's, master's, and doctoral degrees. 71 undergraduate majors. Total enrollment: 12,826. Undergraduates: 3,489. Freshmen: 404. Federal methodology is used as a basis for awarding need-based institutional aid.

UNDERGRADUATE EXPENSES for 1999–2000 ***Application fee:*** $25. ***Comprehensive fee:*** $17,890 includes full-time tuition ($12,150), mandatory fees ($300), and room and board ($5440). Full-time tuition and fees vary according to program. Room and board charges vary according to board plan and housing facility. ***Part-time tuition:*** $368 per credit hour. Part-time tuition and fees vary according to location. ***Payment plan:*** installment.

FRESHMAN FINANCIAL AID (Fall 1999) 453 applied for aid; of those 56% were deemed to have need. 100% of freshmen with need received aid. *Average financial aid package:* $12,910 (excluding resources awarded to replace EFC).

UNDERGRADUATE FINANCIAL AID (Fall 1999) 2,018 applied for aid; of those 67% were deemed to have need. 100% of undergraduates with need received aid. *Average financial aid package:* $12,709 (excluding resources awarded to replace EFC).

GIFT AID (NEED-BASED) ***Total amount:*** $9,153,620 (17% Federal, 12% state, 55% institutional, 16% external sources). ***Receiving aid:*** *Freshmen:* 230; *all full-time undergraduates:* 1,093. ***Average award:*** Freshmen: $3239; Undergraduates: $3064. ***Scholarships, grants, and awards:*** Federal Pell, FSEOG, state, private, college/university gift aid from institutional funds.

GIFT AID (NON-NEED-BASED) ***Total amount:*** $1,925,480 (4% state, 80% institutional, 16% external sources). ***Receiving aid:*** *Freshmen:* 196; *Undergraduates:* 796. ***Scholarships, grants, and awards by category:*** *Academic Interests/Achievement:* biological sciences, business, communication, computer science, education, English, foreign languages, general academic interests/achievements, humanities, international studies, mathematics, premedicine, social sciences. *Creative Arts/Performance:* art/fine arts, cinema/film/broadcasting, creative writing, dance, debating, journalism/publications, music, performing arts, theater/drama. *Special Achievements/Activities:* leadership. ***Tuition waivers:*** Full or partial for employees or children of employees.

LOANS ***Student loans:*** $9,851,539 (92% need-based, 8% non-need-based). 47% of past graduating class borrowed through all loan programs. ***Average need-based loan:*** Freshmen: $2658; Undergraduates: $4403. ***Parent loans:*** $1,039,744 (78% need-based, 22% non-need-based). ***Programs:*** FFEL (Subsidized and Unsubsidized Stafford, PLUS), Perkins.

WORK-STUDY ***Federal work-study:*** *Total amount:* $753,806; 322 jobs averaging $2299. ***State or other work-study/employment:*** *Total amount:* $493,208 (100% need-based). 209 part-time jobs averaging $2345.

APPLYING for FINANCIAL AID ***Required financial aid forms:*** FAFSA, institution's own form. ***Financial aid deadline (priority):*** 4/1. ***Notification date:*** Continuous. Students must reply within 2 weeks of notification.

Webster University (continued)

CONTACT Amy Cagle, Office Supervisor, Webster University, Financial Aid Office, 470 East Lockwood Avenue, St. Louis, MO 63119, 314-968-6992 or toll-free 800-75-ENROL. *Fax:* 314-968-7125. *E-mail:* acagle@webster.edu

WELLESLEY COLLEGE

Wellesley, MA

Tuition & fees: $23,320 **Average undergraduate aid package: $18,704**

ABOUT THE INSTITUTION Independent, women only. Awards: bachelor's degrees (double bachelor's degree with Massachusetts Institute of Technology). 46 undergraduate majors. Total enrollment: 2,333. Undergraduates: 2,333. Freshmen: 596. Both federal and institutional methodology are used as a basis for awarding need-based institutional aid.

UNDERGRADUATE EXPENSES for 1999–2000 ***Application fee:*** $50. ***Comprehensive fee:*** $30,554 includes full-time tuition ($22,894), mandatory fees ($426), and room and board ($7234). ***College room only:*** $3664. Room and board charges vary according to board plan. ***Part-time tuition:*** $2916 per course. ***Payment plans:*** tuition prepayment, installment.

FRESHMAN FINANCIAL AID (Fall 1999) 389 applied for aid; of those 78% were deemed to have need. 100% of freshmen with need received aid; of those 100% had need fully met. *Average percent of need met:* 100% (excluding resources awarded to replace EFC). *Average financial aid package:* $18,657 (excluding resources awarded to replace EFC).

UNDERGRADUATE FINANCIAL AID (Fall 1999) 1,405 applied for aid; of those 83% were deemed to have need. 100% of undergraduates with need received aid; of those 100% had need fully met. *Average percent of need met:* 100% (excluding resources awarded to replace EFC). *Average financial aid package:* $18,704 (excluding resources awarded to replace EFC).

GIFT AID (NEED-BASED) ***Total amount:*** $18,455,002 (7% Federal, 1% state, 87% institutional, 5% external sources). ***Receiving aid:*** *Freshmen:* 47% (277); *all full-time undergraduates:* 49% (1,091). ***Average award:*** Freshmen: $16,918; Undergraduates: $15,921. ***Scholarships, grants, and awards:*** Federal Pell, FSEOG, state, private, college/university gift aid from institutional funds.

GIFT AID (NON-NEED-BASED) ***Tuition waivers:*** Full or partial for employees or children of employees. ***ROTC:*** Army cooperative, Air Force cooperative.

LOANS ***Student loans:*** $4,088,477 (85% need-based, 15% non-need-based). 44% of past graduating class borrowed through all loan programs. Average indebtedness per student: $17,664. ***Average need-based loan:*** Freshmen: $2654; Undergraduates: $3233. ***Parent loans:*** $3,775,443 (100% non-need-based). ***Programs:*** FFEL (Subsidized and Unsubsidized Stafford, PLUS), Perkins, state, college/university.

WORK-STUDY ***Federal work-study:*** *Total amount:* $1,063,297; 900 jobs averaging $1088. ***State or other work-study/employment:*** *Total amount:* $83,670 (100% need-based). 62 part-time jobs averaging $1350.

APPLYING for FINANCIAL AID ***Required financial aid forms:*** FAFSA, institution's own form, CSS Financial Aid PROFILE, noncustodial (divorced/separated) parent's statement, business/farm supplement, federal income tax form(s). ***Financial aid deadline (priority):*** 1/15. ***Notification date:*** 4/1. Students must reply by 5/1.

CONTACT Ms. Kathryn Osmond, Director of Financial Aid, Wellesley College, 106 Central Street, Wellesley, MA 02481-8291, 781-283-2360. *Fax:* 781-283-3946. *E-mail:* finaid@wellesley.edu

WELLS COLLEGE

Aurora, NY

Tuition & fees: $12,300 **Average undergraduate aid package: $13,807**

ABOUT THE INSTITUTION Independent, women only. Awards: bachelor's degrees. 40 undergraduate majors. Total enrollment: 404. Undergraduates: 404. Freshmen: 135. Federal methodology is used as a basis for awarding need-based institutional aid.

UNDERGRADUATE EXPENSES for 1999–2000 ***Application fee:*** $40. ***Comprehensive fee:*** $18,400 includes full-time tuition ($11,850), mandatory fees ($450), and room and board ($6100). ***Part-time tuition:*** $250 per semester hour. ***Payment plan:*** installment.

FRESHMAN FINANCIAL AID (Fall 1998) 128 applied for aid; of those 86% were deemed to have need. 100% of freshmen with need received aid; of those 31% had need fully met. *Average percent of need met:* 90% (excluding resources awarded to replace EFC). *Average financial aid package:* $13,682 (excluding resources awarded to replace EFC). 5% of all full-time freshmen had no need and received non-need-based aid.

UNDERGRADUATE FINANCIAL AID (Fall 1998) 327 applied for aid; of those 94% were deemed to have need. 100% of undergraduates with need received aid; of those 35% had need fully met. *Average percent of need met:* 90% (excluding resources awarded to replace EFC). *Average financial aid package:* $13,807 (excluding resources awarded to replace EFC). 10% of all full-time undergraduates had no need and received non-need-based aid.

GIFT AID (NEED-BASED) ***Total amount:*** $3,625,398 (10% Federal, 11% state, 76% institutional, 3% external sources). ***Receiving aid:*** *Freshmen:* 81% (110); *all full-time undergraduates:* 81% (304). ***Average award:*** Freshmen: $9307; Undergraduates: $8839. ***Scholarships, grants, and awards:*** Federal Pell, FSEOG, state, private, college/university gift aid from institutional funds.

GIFT AID (NON-NEED-BASED) ***Total amount:*** $260,606 (3% state, 95% institutional, 2% external sources). ***Receiving aid:*** *Freshmen:* 21% (28); *Undergraduates:* 38% (143). ***Scholarships, grants, and awards by category:*** *Special Achievements/Activities:* leadership. *Special Characteristics:* children and siblings of alumni. ***Tuition waivers:*** Full or partial for employees or children of employees, senior citizens. ***ROTC:*** Air Force cooperative.

LOANS ***Student loans:*** $1,375,271 (82% need-based, 18% non-need-based). 85% of past graduating class borrowed through all loan programs. Average indebtedness per student: $17,125. ***Average need-based loan:*** Freshmen: $2621; Undergraduates: $3740. ***Parent loans:*** $303,415 (100% non-need-based). ***Programs:*** FFEL (Subsidized and Unsubsidized Stafford, PLUS), Perkins.

WORK-STUDY ***Federal work-study:*** *Total amount:* $108,879; 103 jobs averaging $1057. ***State or other work-study/employment:*** *Total amount:* $175,383 (83% need-based, 17% non-need-based). 192 part-time jobs averaging $913.

APPLYING for FINANCIAL AID ***Required financial aid form:*** FAFSA. ***Financial aid deadline (priority):*** 2/15. ***Notification date:*** 3/1. Students must reply by 5/1.

CONTACT Ms. Cathleen A. Bellomo, Director of Financial Aid, Wells College, Route 90, Aurora, NY 13026, 315-364-3289 or toll-free 800-952-9355. *Fax:* 315-364-3227. *E-mail:* cbellomo@henry.wells.edu

WENTWORTH INSTITUTE OF TECHNOLOGY

Boston, MA

Tuition & fees: $12,450 **Average undergraduate aid package: $7681**

ABOUT THE INSTITUTION Independent, coed, primarily men. Awards: associate and bachelor's degrees. 21 undergraduate majors. Total enrollment: 3,225. Undergraduates: 3,225. Freshmen: 972. Federal methodology is used as a basis for awarding need-based institutional aid.

UNDERGRADUATE EXPENSES for 1999–2000 ***Application fee:*** $30. ***Comprehensive fee:*** $18,950 includes full-time tuition ($12,450) and room and board ($6500). Room and board charges vary according to board plan and housing facility. ***Part-time tuition:*** $330 per credit. Part-time tuition and fees vary according to class time. ***Payment plan:*** installment.

FRESHMAN FINANCIAL AID (Fall 1998) 591 applied for aid; of those 91% were deemed to have need. 100% of freshmen with need received aid. *Average financial aid package:* $6307 (excluding resources awarded to replace EFC).

UNDERGRADUATE FINANCIAL AID (Fall 1998) 1,938 applied for aid; of those 91% were deemed to have need. 100% of undergraduates with need received aid. *Average financial aid package:* $7681 (excluding resources awarded to replace EFC).

GIFT AID (NEED-BASED) ***Total amount:*** $4,886,691 (39% Federal, 15% state, 46% institutional). ***Receiving aid:*** *Freshmen:* 18% (163); *all full-time undergraduates:* 37% (898). ***Average award:*** Freshmen: $2877; Undergraduates: $2321. ***Scholarships, grants, and awards:*** Federal Pell, FSEOG, state, private, college/university gift aid from institutional funds.

GIFT AID (NON-NEED-BASED) ***Total amount:*** $942,206 (100% institutional). ***Receiving aid:*** *Freshmen:* 43% (379); *Undergraduates:* 39% (948). ***Scholarships, grants, and awards by category:*** *Academic Interests/Achievement:* architecture, computer science, engineering/technologies, general academic interests/achievements. ***Tuition waivers:*** Full or partial for employees or children of employees. ***ROTC:*** Army cooperative, Air Force cooperative.

LOANS ***Student loans:*** $7,465,360 (77% need-based, 23% non-need-based). 66% of past graduating class borrowed through all loan programs. Average indebtedness per student: $19,500. ***Parent loans:*** $3,259,655 (62% need-based, 38% non-need-based). ***Programs:*** Federal Direct (Subsidized and Unsubsidized Stafford, PLUS), Perkins, state.

WORK-STUDY ***Federal work-study:*** *Total amount:* $598,215; 536 jobs averaging $1200.

APPLYING for FINANCIAL AID ***Required financial aid forms:*** FAFSA, state aid form. ***Financial aid deadline (priority):*** 3/1. ***Notification date:*** Continuous beginning 3/15. Students must reply within 2 weeks of notification.

CONTACT Ms. Carrie Glass, Director of Financial Aid, Wentworth Institute of Technology, 550 Huntington Avenue, Boston, MA 02115-5998, 617-989-4038 or toll-free 800-556-0610. *Fax:* 617-989-4015.

WESLEYAN COLLEGE

Macon, GA

Tuition & fees: $16,300 **Average undergraduate aid package: $12,420**

ABOUT THE INSTITUTION Independent United Methodist, women only. Awards: bachelor's and master's degrees. 25 undergraduate majors. Total enrollment: 607. Undergraduates: 585. Freshmen: 160. Federal methodology is used as a basis for awarding need-based institutional aid.

UNDERGRADUATE EXPENSES for 1999–2000 ***Application fee:*** $30. ***Comprehensive fee:*** $22,900 includes full-time tuition ($15,450), mandatory fees ($850), and room and board ($6600). Full-time tuition and fees vary according to class time and course load. Room and board charges vary according to housing facility. ***Part-time tuition:*** $390 per semester hour. Part-time tuition and fees vary according to class time, course load, and program. ***Payment plan:*** installment.

FRESHMAN FINANCIAL AID (Fall 1999, est.) 131 applied for aid; of those 80% were deemed to have need. 100% of freshmen with need received aid; of those 96% had need fully met. *Average percent of need met:* 83% (excluding resources awarded to replace EFC). *Average financial aid package:* $13,623 (excluding resources awarded to replace EFC). 8% of all full-time freshmen had no need and received non-need-based aid.

UNDERGRADUATE FINANCIAL AID (Fall 1999, est.) 424 applied for aid; of those 94% were deemed to have need. 100% of undergraduates with need received aid; of those 85% had need fully met. *Average percent of need met:* 83% (excluding resources awarded to replace EFC). *Average financial aid package:* $12,420 (excluding resources awarded to replace EFC). 10% of all full-time undergraduates had no need and received non-need-based aid.

GIFT AID (NEED-BASED) ***Total amount:*** $5,050,493 (10% Federal, 17% state, 69% institutional, 4% external sources). ***Receiving aid:*** *Freshmen:* 76% (100); *all full-time undergraduates:* 61% (382). ***Average award:*** Freshmen: $11,950; Undergraduates: $10,855. ***Scholarships, grants, and awards:*** Federal Pell, FSEOG, state, private, college/university gift aid from institutional funds.

GIFT AID (NON-NEED-BASED) ***Total amount:*** $1,250,615 (17% state, 79% institutional, 4% external sources). ***Receiving aid:*** *Freshmen:* 79% (104); *Undergraduates:* 59% (370). ***Scholarships, grants, and awards by category:*** *Academic Interests/Achievement:* general academic interests/achievements. *Creative Arts/Performance:* art/fine arts, music, theater/drama. *Special Achievements/Activities:* community service, leadership. *Special Characteristics:* children and siblings of alumni, children of current students, children of faculty/staff, general special characteristics, relatives of clergy. ***Tuition waivers:*** Full or partial for children of alumni, employees or children of employees, senior citizens.

LOANS ***Student loans:*** $2,226,024 (80% need-based, 20% non-need-based). 82% of past graduating class borrowed through all loan programs. Average indebtedness per student: $16,250. ***Average need-based loan:*** Freshmen: $2871; Undergraduates: $2871. ***Parent loans:*** $267,889 (29% need-based, 71% non-need-based). ***Programs:*** Federal Direct (Subsidized and Unsubsidized Stafford, PLUS), Perkins, state, college/university, GATE Loans, CitiAssist Loans.

WORK-STUDY ***Federal work-study:*** *Total amount:* $159,416; 127 jobs averaging $1255. ***State or other work-study/employment:*** *Total amount:* $118,820 (100% non-need-based). 98 part-time jobs averaging $1212.

APPLYING for FINANCIAL AID ***Required financial aid forms:*** FAFSA, institution's own form, state aid form, noncustodial (divorced/separated) parent's statement. ***Financial aid deadline (priority):*** 3/1. ***Notification date:*** Continuous beginning 3/18. Students must reply within 2 weeks of notification.

CONTACT Parker Leake, Director of Financial Aid, Wesleyan College, 4760 Forsyth Road, Macon, GA 31210-4462, 912-757-5205 or toll-free 800-447-6610. *Fax:* 912-757-4030. *E-mail:* pleake@wesleyancollege.edu

WESLEYAN UNIVERSITY

Middletown, CT

Tuition & fees: $25,120 **Average undergraduate aid package: $21,135**

ABOUT THE INSTITUTION Independent, coed. Awards: bachelor's, master's, and doctoral degrees and post-master's certificates. 45 undergraduate majors. Total enrollment: 3,201. Undergraduates: 2,759. Freshmen: 732. Both federal and institutional methodology are used as a basis for awarding need-based institutional aid.

UNDERGRADUATE EXPENSES for 2000–2001 ***Application fee:*** $55. ***Comprehensive fee:*** $31,630 includes full-time tuition ($24,330), mandatory fees ($790), and room and board ($6510). ***College room only:*** $3860. Full-time tuition and fees vary according to program. Room and board charges vary according to board plan and housing facility. Part-time tuition and fees vary according to program. ***Payment plan:*** installment.

FRESHMAN FINANCIAL AID (Fall 1998) 409 applied for aid; of those 86% were deemed to have need. 100% of freshmen with need received aid; of those 100% had need fully met. *Average percent of need met:* 100% (excluding resources awarded to replace EFC). *Average financial aid package:* $20,775 (excluding resources awarded to replace EFC).

UNDERGRADUATE FINANCIAL AID (Fall 1998) 1,498 applied for aid; of those 91% were deemed to have need. 100% of undergraduates with need received aid; of those 100% had need fully met. *Average percent of need met:* 100% (excluding resources awarded to replace EFC). *Average financial aid package:* $21,135 (excluding resources awarded to replace EFC).

GIFT AID (NEED-BASED) ***Total amount:*** $18,190,450 (9% Federal, 3% state, 85% institutional, 3% external sources). ***Receiving aid:*** *Freshmen:* 44% (308); *all full-time undergraduates:* 41% (1,184). ***Average award:*** Freshmen: $15,974; Undergraduates: $15,248. ***Scholarships, grants, and awards:*** Federal Pell, FSEOG, state, private, college/university gift aid from institutional funds.

GIFT AID (NON-NEED-BASED) ***Total amount:*** $3,251,428 (100% external sources). ***Tuition waivers:*** Full or partial for employees or children of employees. ***ROTC:*** Army cooperative, Naval cooperative, Air Force cooperative.

LOANS ***Student loans:*** $8,885,216 (100% need-based). 49% of past graduating class borrowed through all loan programs. Average indebtedness per student: $24,430. ***Average need-based loan:*** Freshmen: $5270; Undergraduates: $6502. ***Parent loans:*** $3,515,307 (100% non-need-based). ***Programs:*** FFEL (Subsidized and Unsubsidized Stafford, PLUS), Perkins, college/university.

Wesleyan University (continued)

WORK-STUDY ***Federal work-study:*** *Total amount:* $1,777,619; 1,347 jobs averaging $1322. ***State or other work-study/employment:*** *Total amount:* $28,300 (100% need-based). 19 part-time jobs averaging $1322.

APPLYING for FINANCIAL AID ***Required financial aid forms:*** FAFSA, CSS Financial Aid PROFILE, noncustodial (divorced/separated) parent's statement, business/farm supplement. ***Financial aid deadline:*** 2/1. ***Notification date:*** 4/1. Students must reply by 5/1 or within 2 weeks of notification.

CONTACT Ms. Karen Hook, Assistant Director of Financial Aid, Wesleyan University, 237 High Street, Middletown, CT 06459-0260, 860-685-2800. *Fax:* 860-685-2801. *E-mail:* finaid@wesleyan.edu

WESLEY COLLEGE

Dover, DE

Tuition & fees: $11,919 **Average undergraduate aid package: N/A**

ABOUT THE INSTITUTION Independent United Methodist, coed. Awards: associate, bachelor's, and master's degrees and post-bachelor's certificates. 21 undergraduate majors. Total enrollment: 1,706. Undergraduates: 1,613. Freshmen: 689. Federal methodology is used as a basis for awarding need-based institutional aid.

UNDERGRADUATE EXPENSES for 2000–2001 ***Application fee:*** $20. ***Comprehensive fee:*** $16,937 includes full-time tuition ($11,314), mandatory fees ($605), and room and board ($5018). ***College room only:*** $2572. Full-time tuition and fees vary according to class time and program. Room and board charges vary according to board plan. ***Part-time tuition:*** $471 per credit hour. ***Part-time fees:*** $10 per term part-time. ***Payment plan:*** installment.

GIFT AID (NEED-BASED) ***Scholarships, grants, and awards:*** Federal Pell, FSEOG, state, private, college/university gift aid from institutional funds.

GIFT AID (NON-NEED-BASED) ***Scholarships, grants, and awards by category:*** *Academic Interests/Achievement:* general academic interests/achievements. *Special Achievements/Activities:* religious involvement. *Special Characteristics:* international students. ***Tuition waivers:*** Full or partial for employees or children of employees, senior citizens. ***ROTC:*** Army cooperative.

LOANS ***Programs:*** FFEL (Subsidized and Unsubsidized Stafford, PLUS), Perkins, state, college/university.

WORK-STUDY Federal work-study jobs available.

APPLYING for FINANCIAL AID ***Required financial aid form:*** FAFSA. ***Financial aid deadline (priority):*** 4/15. ***Notification date:*** Continuous. Students must reply within 2 weeks of notification.

CONTACT Director of Student Financial Planning, Wesley College, 120 North State Street, Dover, DE 19901-3875, 302-736-2338 or toll-free 800-937-5398 (out-of-state).

WESLEY COLLEGE

Florence, MS

Tuition & fees: $2800 **Average undergraduate aid package: N/A**

ABOUT THE INSTITUTION Independent Congregational Methodist, coed. Awards: bachelor's degrees. 2 undergraduate majors. Total enrollment: 101. Undergraduates: 101. Freshmen: 29. Federal methodology is used as a basis for awarding need-based institutional aid.

UNDERGRADUATE EXPENSES for 1999–2000 ***Application fee:*** $20. ***Comprehensive fee:*** $5250 includes full-time tuition ($2500), mandatory fees ($300), and room and board ($2450). Full-time tuition and fees vary according to course load. Room and board charges vary according to housing facility. ***Part-time tuition:*** $105 per semester hour. ***Part-time fees:*** $75 per term part-time. Part-time tuition and fees vary according to course load. ***Payment plan:*** installment.

GIFT AID (NEED-BASED) ***Scholarships, grants, and awards:*** Federal Pell, FSEOG, state.

GIFT AID (NON-NEED-BASED) ***Scholarships, grants, and awards by category:*** *Academic Interests/Achievement:* general academic interests/achievements. *Special Achievements/Activities:* religious involvement. ***Tuition waivers:*** Full or partial for employees or children of employees, senior citizens.

LOANS ***Programs:*** Federal Direct (Subsidized and Unsubsidized Stafford, PLUS).

WORK-STUDY Federal work-study jobs available.

APPLYING for FINANCIAL AID ***Required financial aid form:*** FAFSA. ***Financial aid deadline (priority):*** 8/20. ***Notification date:*** Continuous.

CONTACT Mr. William Devore Jr., Director of Financial Aid, Wesley College, PO Box 1070, Florence, MS 39073-1070, 601-845-2265 or toll-free 800-748-9972. *Fax:* 601-845-2266.

WESTBROOK COLLEGE

Biddeford, ME

See University of New England

WEST CHESTER UNIVERSITY OF PENNSYLVANIA

West Chester, PA

Tuition & fees (PA res): $4422 **Average undergraduate aid package: $5931**

ABOUT THE INSTITUTION State-supported, coed. Awards: associate, bachelor's, and master's degrees. 82 undergraduate majors. Total enrollment: 11,892. Undergraduates: 10,078. Freshmen: 1,720. Federal methodology is used as a basis for awarding need-based institutional aid.

UNDERGRADUATE EXPENSES for 1999–2000 ***Application fee:*** $30. ***Tuition, state resident:*** full-time $3618; part-time $150 per credit. ***Tuition, nonresident:*** full-time $9046; part-time $377 per credit. ***Required fees:*** full-time $804; $34 per credit. ***College room and board:*** $4518; ***room only:*** $3888. Room and board charges vary according to board plan, housing facility, and location. ***Payment plans:*** tuition prepayment, installment, deferred payment.

FRESHMAN FINANCIAL AID (Fall 1998) 1567 applied for aid; of those 93% were deemed to have need. 92% of freshmen with need received aid; of those 45% had need fully met. *Average percent of need met:* 72% (excluding resources awarded to replace EFC). *Average financial aid package:* $5359 (excluding resources awarded to replace EFC). 9% of all full-time freshmen had no need and received non-need-based aid.

UNDERGRADUATE FINANCIAL AID (Fall 1998) 5,136 applied for aid; of those 81% were deemed to have need. 97% of undergraduates with need received aid; of those 44% had need fully met. *Average percent of need met:* 74% (excluding resources awarded to replace EFC). *Average financial aid package:* $5931 (excluding resources awarded to replace EFC). 6% of all full-time undergraduates had no need and received non-need-based aid.

GIFT AID (NEED-BASED) ***Total amount:*** $8,115,155 (46% Federal, 54% state). ***Receiving aid:*** *Freshmen:* 32% (783); *all full-time undergraduates:* 27% (2,199). ***Average award:*** Freshmen: $3645; Undergraduates: $3526. ***Scholarships, grants, and awards:*** Federal Pell, FSEOG, state, private, college/university gift aid from institutional funds.

GIFT AID (NON-NEED-BASED) ***Total amount:*** $2,256,129 (16% institutional, 84% external sources). ***Receiving aid:*** *Freshmen:* 12% (293); *Undergraduates:* 7% (535). ***Scholarships, grants, and awards by category:*** *Academic Interests/Achievement:* 183 awards ($547,518 total): business, general academic interests/achievements, social sciences. *Creative Arts/Performance:* 35 awards ($17,021 total): music. ***Tuition waivers:*** Full or partial for employees or children of employees, senior citizens. ***ROTC:*** Army cooperative, Air Force cooperative.

LOANS ***Student loans:*** $19,282,892 (57% need-based, 43% non-need-based). 52% of past graduating class borrowed through all loan programs. Average indebtedness per student: $17,000. ***Average need-based loan:*** Freshmen: $1675; Undergraduates: $2214. ***Parent loans:*** $3,051,449 (100% non-need-based). ***Programs:*** FFEL (Subsidized and Unsubsidized Stafford, PLUS), Perkins, Federal Nursing.

WORK-STUDY ***Federal work-study:*** *Total amount:* $360,156; 373 jobs averaging $966. ***State or other work-study/employment:*** *Total amount:* $1,769,185 (100% non-need-based). 913 part-time jobs averaging $1938.

ATHLETIC AWARDS *Total amount:* 311,832 (100% non-need-based).

APPLYING for FINANCIAL AID ***Required financial aid form:*** FAFSA. ***Financial aid deadline (priority):*** 3/1. ***Notification date:*** 4/15. Students must reply within 3 weeks of notification.

CONTACT Financial Aid Office, West Chester University of Pennsylvania, 138 E.O. Bull Center, West Chester, PA 19383, 610-436-2627. *Fax:* 610-436-2574. *E-mail:* finaid@wcupa.edu

WESTERN BAPTIST COLLEGE

Salem, OR

Tuition & fees: $13,690 **Average undergraduate aid package: $10,354**

ABOUT THE INSTITUTION Independent religious, coed. Awards: associate and bachelor's degrees. 26 undergraduate majors. Total enrollment: 683. Undergraduates: 683. Freshmen: 126. Federal methodology is used as a basis for awarding need-based institutional aid.

UNDERGRADUATE EXPENSES for 2000–2001 ***Application fee:*** $35. ***Comprehensive fee:*** $18,630 includes full-time tuition ($13,224), mandatory fees ($466), and room and board ($4940). Room and board charges vary according to board plan. ***Part-time tuition:*** $551 per credit hour. ***Part-time fees:*** $30 per term part-time. Part-time tuition and fees vary according to course load. ***Payment plan:*** installment.

FRESHMAN FINANCIAL AID (Fall 1999, est.) 126 applied for aid; of those 92% were deemed to have need. 100% of freshmen with need received aid; of those 39% had need fully met. *Average percent of need met:* 80% (excluding resources awarded to replace EFC). *Average financial aid package:* $11,453 (excluding resources awarded to replace EFC). 8% of all full-time freshmen had no need and received non-need-based aid.

UNDERGRADUATE FINANCIAL AID (Fall 1999, est.) 600 applied for aid; of those 89% were deemed to have need. 100% of undergraduates with need received aid; of those 42% had need fully met. *Average percent of need met:* 80% (excluding resources awarded to replace EFC). *Average financial aid package:* $10,354 (excluding resources awarded to replace EFC). 12% of all full-time undergraduates had no need and received non-need-based aid.

GIFT AID (NEED-BASED) ***Total amount:*** $1,675,103 (23% Federal, 9% state, 68% institutional). ***Receiving aid:*** *Freshmen:* 71% (90); *all full-time undergraduates:* 60% (411). ***Average award:*** Freshmen: $7558; Undergraduates: $6326. ***Scholarships, grants, and awards:*** Federal Pell, FSEOG, state, private, college/university gift aid from institutional funds.

GIFT AID (NON-NEED-BASED) ***Total amount:*** $1,870,726 (88% institutional, 12% external sources). ***Receiving aid:*** *Freshmen:* 32% (40); *Undergraduates:* 31% (210). ***Scholarships, grants, and awards by category:*** *Academic Interests/Achievement:* general academic interests/achievements. *Creative Arts/Performance:* journalism/publications, music, performing arts. *Special Achievements/Activities:* general special achievements/activities, hobbies/interests, leadership, memberships, religious involvement. *Special Characteristics:* children and siblings of alumni, children of faculty/staff, general special characteristics, international students, relatives of clergy, siblings of current students. ***Tuition waivers:*** Full or partial for employees or children of employees. ***ROTC:*** Army cooperative, Air Force cooperative.

LOANS ***Student loans:*** $2,661,352 (60% need-based, 40% non-need-based). 79% of past graduating class borrowed through all loan programs. Average indebtedness per student: $13,498. ***Average need-based loan:*** Freshmen: $2999; Undergraduates: $3891. ***Parent loans:*** $330,558 (100% non-need-based). ***Programs:*** Federal Direct (Subsidized and Unsubsidized Stafford, PLUS), Perkins, state, alternative loans.

WORK-STUDY ***Federal work-study:*** *Total amount:* $133,356; 133 jobs averaging $1000.

ATHLETIC AWARDS *Total amount:* 558,503 (100% non-need-based).

APPLYING for FINANCIAL AID ***Required financial aid form:*** FAFSA. ***Financial aid deadline (priority):*** 2/15. ***Notification date:*** Continuous beginning 3/1. Students must reply within 4 weeks of notification.

CONTACT Nathan Warthan, Director of Financial Aid, Western Baptist College, 5000 Deer Park Drive, SE, Salem, OR 97301-9392, 503-375-7005 or toll-free 800-845-3005 (out-of-state). *Fax:* 503-585-4316. *E-mail:* nwarthan@wbc.edu

WESTERN CAROLINA UNIVERSITY

Cullowhee, NC

Tuition & fees (NC res): $2082 **Average undergraduate aid package: $5107**

ABOUT THE INSTITUTION State-supported, coed. Awards: bachelor's, master's, and doctoral degrees and post-master's certificates. 65 undergraduate majors. Total enrollment: 6,353. Undergraduates: 5,352. Freshmen: 1,156. Federal methodology is used as a basis for awarding need-based institutional aid.

UNDERGRADUATE EXPENSES for 1999–2000 ***Application fee:*** $35. ***Tuition, state resident:*** full-time $962; part-time $241 per term. ***Tuition, nonresident:*** full-time $8232; part-time $2058 per term. ***Required fees:*** full-time $1120; $263. Part-time tuition and fees vary according to course load. ***College room and board:*** $3260; ***room only:*** $1540. Room and board charges vary according to board plan and housing facility. ***Payment plan:*** installment.

FRESHMAN FINANCIAL AID (Fall 1999) 683 applied for aid; of those 71% were deemed to have need. 97% of freshmen with need received aid; of those 93% had need fully met. *Average percent of need met:* 90% (excluding resources awarded to replace EFC). *Average financial aid package:* $5400 (excluding resources awarded to replace EFC). 14% of all full-time freshmen had no need and received non-need-based aid.

UNDERGRADUATE FINANCIAL AID (Fall 1999) 2,742 applied for aid; of those 73% were deemed to have need. 98% of undergraduates with need received aid; of those 97% had need fully met. *Average percent of need met:* 96% (excluding resources awarded to replace EFC). *Average financial aid package:* $5107 (excluding resources awarded to replace EFC). 14% of all full-time undergraduates had no need and received non-need-based aid.

GIFT AID (NEED-BASED) ***Total amount:*** $3,773,907 (69% Federal, 15% state, 7% institutional, 9% external sources). ***Receiving aid:*** *Freshmen:* 31% (363); *all full-time undergraduates:* 30% (1,442). ***Average award:*** Freshmen: $2008; Undergraduates: $1784. ***Scholarships, grants, and awards:*** Federal Pell, FSEOG, state, private, college/university gift aid from institutional funds.

GIFT AID (NON-NEED-BASED) ***Total amount:*** $1,176,411 (1% Federal, 38% state, 33% institutional, 28% external sources). ***Receiving aid:*** *Freshmen:* 2% (25); *Undergraduates:* 1% (55). ***Scholarships, grants, and awards by category:*** *Academic Interests/Achievement:* English, general academic interests/achievements, mathematics. *Creative Arts/Performance:* art/fine arts, music. *Special Characteristics:* ethnic background, local/state students, members of minority groups. ***Tuition waivers:*** Full or partial for senior citizens. ***ROTC:*** Army.

LOANS ***Student loans:*** $8,482,885 (49% need-based, 51% non-need-based). 41% of past graduating class borrowed through all loan programs. Average indebtedness per student: $15,500. ***Average need-based loan:*** Freshmen: $2779; Undergraduates: $2955. ***Parent loans:*** $1,837,273 (23% need-based, 77% non-need-based). ***Programs:*** Federal Direct (Subsidized and Unsubsidized Stafford, PLUS), Perkins.

WORK-STUDY ***Federal work-study:*** *Total amount:* $1,163,428; 689 jobs averaging $1688.

ATHLETIC AWARDS *Total amount:* 836,887 (44% need-based, 56% non-need-based).

APPLYING for FINANCIAL AID ***Required financial aid forms:*** FAFSA, institution's own form. ***Financial aid deadline (priority):*** 3/31. ***Notification date:*** Continuous beginning 4/1.

CONTACT Ms. Nancy B. Dillard, Associate Director, Financial Aid, Western Carolina University, 230 H. F. Robinson Administration Building, Cullowhee, NC 28723, 828-227-7290. *Fax:* 828-227-7042. *E-mail:* dillard@wcuvax1.wcu.edu

WESTERN CONNECTICUT STATE UNIVERSITY

Danbury, CT

Tuition & fees (CT res): $3758 **Average undergraduate aid package: $4732**

ABOUT THE INSTITUTION State-supported, coed. Awards: associate, bachelor's, and master's degrees. 40 undergraduate majors. Total enrollment: 5,589. Undergraduates: 4,658. Freshmen: 811. Federal methodology is used as a basis for awarding need-based institutional aid.

UNDERGRADUATE EXPENSES for 1999–2000 ***Application fee:*** $40. ***Tuition, state resident:*** full-time $2062; part-time $154 per semester hour. ***Tuition, nonresident:*** full-time $7602; part-time $154 per semester hour. ***Required fees:*** full-time $1696; $30 per term part-time. Full-time tuition and fees vary according to reciprocity agreements. ***College room and board:*** $5434; ***room only:*** $3750. Room and board charges vary according to housing facility.

FRESHMAN FINANCIAL AID (Fall 1998) 478 applied for aid; of those 68% were deemed to have need. 96% of freshmen with need received aid; of those 2% had need fully met. *Average percent of need met:* 61% (excluding resources awarded to replace EFC). *Average financial aid package:* $4493 (excluding resources awarded to replace EFC). 8% of all full-time freshmen had no need and received non-need-based aid.

UNDERGRADUATE FINANCIAL AID (Fall 1998) 1,879 applied for aid; of those 67% were deemed to have need. 96% of undergraduates with need received aid; of those 2% had need fully met. *Average percent of need met:* 62% (excluding resources awarded to replace EFC). *Average financial aid package:* $4732 (excluding resources awarded to replace EFC). 8% of all full-time undergraduates had no need and received non-need-based aid.

GIFT AID (NEED-BASED) ***Total amount:*** $2,728,948 (46% Federal, 50% state, 2% institutional, 2% external sources). ***Receiving aid:*** *Freshmen:* 39% (252); *all full-time undergraduates:* 34% (1,008). ***Average award:*** Freshmen: $3351; Undergraduates: $2590. ***Scholarships, grants, and awards:*** Federal Pell, FSEOG, state, private, college/university gift aid from institutional funds.

GIFT AID (NON-NEED-BASED) ***Total amount:*** $140,949 (22% state, 74% institutional, 4% external sources). ***Receiving aid:*** *Freshmen:* 1% (4); *Undergraduates:* 9. ***Scholarships, grants, and awards by category:*** *Academic Interests/Achievement:* 67 awards ($140,949 total): general academic interests/achievements. ***Tuition waivers:*** Full or partial for employees or children of employees, senior citizens. ***ROTC:*** Army cooperative, Air Force cooperative.

LOANS ***Student loans:*** $4,667,251 (75% need-based, 25% non-need-based). ***Average need-based loan:*** Freshmen: $2170; Undergraduates: $3067. ***Parent loans:*** $546,869 (41% need-based, 59% non-need-based). ***Programs:*** Federal Direct (Subsidized and Unsubsidized Stafford, PLUS), FFEL (Subsidized and Unsubsidized Stafford, PLUS), Perkins.

WORK-STUDY ***Federal work-study:*** *Total amount:* $132,939; 116 jobs averaging $1146.

APPLYING for FINANCIAL AID ***Required financial aid forms:*** FAFSA, institution's own form. ***Financial aid deadline:*** 4/15 (priority: 3/15). ***Notification date:*** Continuous. Students must reply by 5/1 or within 2 weeks of notification.

CONTACT Nancy Barton, Associate Director of Financial Aid, Western Connecticut State University, 181 White Street, Danbury, CT 06810-6860, 203-837-8580 or toll-free 877-837-9278. *Fax:* 203-837-8528. *E-mail:* bartonn@wcsu.ctstateu.edu

WESTERN ILLINOIS UNIVERSITY

Macomb, IL

Tuition & fees (IL res): $3610 **Average undergraduate aid package: $6526**

ABOUT THE INSTITUTION State-supported, coed. Awards: bachelor's and master's degrees. 45 undergraduate majors. Total enrollment: 12,934. Undergraduates: 10,434. Freshmen: 1,707. Federal methodology is used as a basis for awarding need-based institutional aid.

UNDERGRADUATE EXPENSES for 1999–2000 ***Tuition, state resident:*** full-time $2730; part-time $91 per credit hour. ***Tuition, nonresident:*** full-time $5460; part-time $182 per credit hour. ***Required fees:*** full-time $880; $29 per credit hour. ***College room and board:*** $4392; ***room only:*** $2570. Room and board charges vary according to board plan. ***Payment plans:*** guaranteed tuition, installment.

FRESHMAN FINANCIAL AID (Fall 1999) 1470 applied for aid; of those 62% were deemed to have need. 95% of freshmen with need received aid; of those 30% had need fully met. *Average percent of need met:* 71% (excluding resources awarded to replace EFC). *Average financial aid package:* $5492 (excluding resources awarded to replace EFC). 28% of all full-time freshmen had no need and received non-need-based aid.

UNDERGRADUATE FINANCIAL AID (Fall 1999) 7,912 applied for aid; of those 62% were deemed to have need. 98% of undergraduates with need received aid; of those 42% had need fully met. *Average percent of need met:* 74% (excluding resources awarded to replace EFC). *Average financial aid package:* $6526 (excluding resources awarded to replace EFC). 32% of all full-time undergraduates had no need and received non-need-based aid.

GIFT AID (NEED-BASED) ***Total amount:*** $16,051,675 (40% Federal, 52% state, 6% institutional, 2% external sources). ***Receiving aid:*** *Freshmen:* 41% (692); *all full-time undergraduates:* 47% (4,180). ***Average award:*** Freshmen: $4136; Undergraduates: $3901. ***Scholarships, grants, and awards:*** Federal Pell, FSEOG, state, private, college/university gift aid from institutional funds.

GIFT AID (NON-NEED-BASED) ***Total amount:*** $2,329,360 (32% Federal, 27% state, 34% institutional, 7% external sources). ***Scholarships, grants, and awards by category:*** *Academic Interests/Achievement:* 1,901 awards ($934,596 total): agriculture, biological sciences, business, education, foreign languages, general academic interests/achievements, home economics, mathematics, physical sciences, social sciences. *Creative Arts/Performance:* 481 awards ($331,455 total): applied art and design, cinema/film/broadcasting, dance, debating, journalism/publications, music, performing arts, theater/drama. *Special Achievements/Activities:* 243 awards ($102,102 total): community service, leadership. *Special Characteristics:* 1,033 awards ($1,277,429 total): children of faculty/staff, general special characteristics, international students, members of minority groups, veterans' children. ***Tuition waivers:*** Full or partial for employees or children of employees, senior citizens. ***ROTC:*** Army.

LOANS ***Student loans:*** $21,954,633 (66% need-based, 34% non-need-based). 61% of past graduating class borrowed through all loan programs. Average indebtedness per student: $13,463. ***Average need-based loan:*** Freshmen: $2394; Undergraduates: $3273. ***Parent loans:*** $2,767,562 (71% need-based, 29% non-need-based). ***Programs:*** FFEL (Subsidized and Unsubsidized Stafford, PLUS), Perkins.

WORK-STUDY ***Federal work-study:*** *Total amount:* $649,942; 432 jobs available. ***State or other work-study/employment:*** *Total amount:* $1,007,562 (64% need-based, 36% non-need-based). Part-time jobs available.

ATHLETIC AWARDS *Total amount:* 1,126,018 (41% need-based, 59% non-need-based).

APPLYING for FINANCIAL AID ***Required financial aid form:*** FAFSA. ***Financial aid deadline:*** Continuous. ***Notification date:*** Continuous beginning 2/15.

CONTACT Financial Aid Office, Western Illinois University, 1 University Circle, 127 Sherman Hall, Macomb, IL 61455-1390, 309-298-2446. *Fax:* 309-298-2353. *E-mail:* mifina@wiu.edu

WESTERN KENTUCKY UNIVERSITY

Bowling Green, KY

Tuition & fees (KY res): $2390 **Average undergraduate aid package: $5795**

ABOUT THE INSTITUTION State-supported, coed. Awards: associate, bachelor's, and master's degrees. 86 undergraduate majors. Total enrollment: 15,114. Undergraduates: 12,912. Freshmen: 2,552. Federal methodology is used as a basis for awarding need-based institutional aid.

UNDERGRADUATE EXPENSES for 1999–2000 ***Application fee:*** $25. ***Tuition, state resident:*** full-time $2020; part-time $97 per semester hour. ***Tuition, nonresident:*** full-time $6060; part-time $265 per semester hour. ***Required fees:*** full-time $370; $18 per semester hour. Full-time tuition and fees vary according to reciprocity agreements. Part-time tuition and fees vary according to reciprocity agreements. ***College room and board:*** $3460; ***room only:*** $1660. Room and board charges vary according to board plan and housing facility. ***Payment plans:*** installment, deferred payment.

FRESHMAN FINANCIAL AID (Fall 1999, est.) 1636 applied for aid; of those 73% were deemed to have need. 99% of freshmen with need received aid; of those 55% had need fully met. *Average percent of need met:* 55% (excluding resources awarded to replace EFC). *Average financial aid package:* $5544 (excluding resources awarded to replace EFC). 38% of all full-time freshmen had no need and received non-need-based aid.

UNDERGRADUATE FINANCIAL AID (Fall 1999, est.) 6,396 applied for aid; of those 75% were deemed to have need. 96% of undergraduates with need received aid; of those 59% had need fully met. *Average percent of need met:* 57% (excluding resources awarded to replace EFC). *Average financial aid package:* $5795 (excluding resources awarded to replace EFC). 24% of all full-time undergraduates had no need and received non-need-based aid.

GIFT AID (NEED-BASED) ***Total amount:*** $11,590,692 (71% Federal, 29% state). ***Receiving aid:*** *Freshmen:* 31% (706); *all full-time undergraduates:* 31% (2,981). ***Average award:*** Freshmen: $3004; Undergraduates: $3133. ***Scholarships, grants, and awards:*** Federal Pell, FSEOG, state.

GIFT AID (NON-NEED-BASED) ***Total amount:*** $6,415,115 (23% Federal, 18% state, 41% institutional, 18% external sources). ***Receiving aid:*** *Freshmen:* 37% (854); *Undergraduates:* 16% (1,563). ***Scholarships, grants, and awards by category:*** *Academic Interests/Achievement:* 1,977 awards ($4,591,021 total): agriculture, biological sciences, general academic interests/achievements, physical sciences. *Creative Arts/Performance:* 55 awards ($35,400 total): music. *Special Achievements/Activities:* 229 awards ($237,961 total): general special achievements/activities, leadership. *Special Characteristics:* 184 awards ($296,995 total): children of public servants, general special characteristics, members of minority groups, veterans' children. ***Tuition waivers:*** Full or partial for children of alumni, employees or children of employees, senior citizens. ***ROTC:*** Army, Air Force cooperative.

LOANS ***Student loans:*** $18,761,449 (60% need-based, 40% non-need-based). ***Average need-based loan:*** Freshmen: $2328; Undergraduates: $2968. ***Parent loans:*** $790,263 (100% non-need-based). ***Programs:*** Federal Direct (Subsidized and Unsubsidized Stafford, PLUS), Perkins, state, college/university.

WORK-STUDY ***Federal work-study:*** *Total amount:* $1,272,791; 792 jobs averaging $1607. ***State or other work-study/employment:*** *Total amount:* $3,178,878 (100% non-need-based). 1,511 part-time jobs averaging $2104.

ATHLETIC AWARDS *Total amount:* 1,603,542 (100% non-need-based).

APPLYING for FINANCIAL AID ***Required financial aid form:*** FAFSA. ***Financial aid deadline (priority):*** 3/1. ***Notification date:*** Continuous beginning 4/1. Students must reply within 3 weeks of notification.

CONTACT Marilyn Clark, Director, Student Financial Assistance, Western Kentucky University, Potter Hall, Room 317, 1 Big Red Way, Bowling Green, KY 42101-3576, 270-745-2758 or toll-free 800-495-8463 (in-state). *Fax:* 270-745-6586. *E-mail:* marilyn.clark@wku.edu

WESTERN MARYLAND COLLEGE

Westminster, MD

Tuition & fees: $19,600 **Average undergraduate aid package: $17,067**

ABOUT THE INSTITUTION Independent, coed. Awards: bachelor's and master's degrees. 33 undergraduate majors. Total enrollment: 3,328. Undergraduates: 1,636. Freshmen: 412. Both federal and institutional methodology are used as a basis for awarding need-based institutional aid.

UNDERGRADUATE EXPENSES for 2000–2001 ***Application fee:*** $40. ***One-time required fee:*** $300. ***Comprehensive fee:*** $24,950 includes full-time tuition ($19,600) and room and board ($5350). ***College room only:*** $2540. Room and board charges vary according to board plan and housing facility. ***Part-time tuition:*** $613 per semester hour. ***Payment plans:*** tuition prepayment, installment.

FRESHMAN FINANCIAL AID (Fall 1999, est.) 326 applied for aid; of those 85% were deemed to have need. 100% of freshmen with need received aid; of those 33% had need fully met. *Average percent of need met:* 93% (excluding resources awarded to replace EFC). *Average financial aid package:* $18,028 (excluding resources awarded to replace EFC). 25% of all full-time freshmen had no need and received non-need-based aid.

UNDERGRADUATE FINANCIAL AID (Fall 1999, est.) 1,145 applied for aid; of those 88% were deemed to have need. 100% of undergraduates with need received aid; of those 33% had need fully met. *Average percent of need met:* 98% (excluding resources awarded to replace EFC). *Average financial aid package:* $17,067 (excluding resources awarded to replace EFC). 7% of all full-time undergraduates had no need and received non-need-based aid.

GIFT AID (NEED-BASED) ***Total amount:*** $6,436,541 (12% Federal, 19% state, 69% institutional). ***Receiving aid:*** *Freshmen:* 51% (206); *all full-time undergraduates:* 57% (837). ***Average award:*** Freshmen: $5885; Undergraduates: $6412. ***Scholarships, grants, and awards:*** Federal Pell, FSEOG, state, private, college/university gift aid from institutional funds.

GIFT AID (NON-NEED-BASED) ***Total amount:*** $9,936,870 (3% state, 92% institutional, 5% external sources). ***Receiving aid:*** *Freshmen:* 52% (209); *Undergraduates:* 48% (707). ***Scholarships, grants, and awards by category:*** *Academic Interests/Achievement:* 948 awards ($7,426,837 total): general academic interests/achievements. *Special Achievements/Activities:* 8 awards ($20,000 total): junior miss, leadership, memberships. *Special Characteristics:* 287 awards ($420,268 total): local/state students, previous college experience, siblings of current students. ***Tuition waivers:*** Full or partial for employees or children of employees. ***ROTC:*** Army, Air Force cooperative.

LOANS ***Student loans:*** $4,567,028 (69% need-based, 31% non-need-based). 54% of past graduating class borrowed through all loan programs. Average indebtedness per student: $15,799. ***Average need-based loan:*** Freshmen: $3987; Undergraduates: $4991. ***Parent loans:*** $1,281,785 (100% non-need-based). ***Programs:*** FFEL (Subsidized and Unsubsidized Stafford, PLUS), Perkins, college/university.

WORK-STUDY ***Federal work-study:*** *Total amount:* $195,616; jobs available. ***State or other work-study/employment:*** *Total amount:* $106,078 (100% non-need-based). 121 part-time jobs averaging $847.

APPLYING for FINANCIAL AID ***Required financial aid forms:*** FAFSA, institution's own form. ***Financial aid deadline (priority):*** 3/1. ***Notification date:*** Continuous beginning 3/15. Students must reply by 5/1 or within 2 weeks of notification.

CONTACT Financial Aid Office, Western Maryland College, 2 College Hill, Westminster, MD 21157-4390, 410-857-2233 or toll-free 800-638-5005. *Fax:* 410-857-2729.

WESTERN MICHIGAN UNIVERSITY

Kalamazoo, MI

Tuition & fees (MI res): $3944 **Average undergraduate aid package: $4078**

ABOUT THE INSTITUTION State-supported, coed. Awards: bachelor's, master's, and doctoral degrees and post-master's certificates. 118 undergraduate majors. Total enrollment: 27,744. Undergraduates: 21,829. Freshmen: 4,344. Federal methodology is used as a basis for awarding need-based institutional aid.

UNDERGRADUATE EXPENSES for 1999–2000 ***Application fee:*** $25. ***Tuition, state resident:*** full-time $3342; part-time $111 per credit hour. ***Tuition, nonresident:*** full-time $8388; part-time $280 per credit hour. ***Required fees:*** full-time $602; $132 per term part-time. Full-time tuition and fees vary according to course load and student level. Part-time tuition and fees vary according to course load and student level. ***College room and board:*** $4831. Room and board charges vary according to board plan. ***Payment plan:*** installment.

Western Michigan University (continued)

FRESHMAN FINANCIAL AID (Fall 1998) 4947 applied for aid; of those 100% were deemed to have need. 96% of freshmen with need received aid. *Average financial aid package:* $4078 (excluding resources awarded to replace EFC).

UNDERGRADUATE FINANCIAL AID (Fall 1998) 16,579 applied for aid; of those 100% were deemed to have need. 95% of undergraduates with need received aid. *Average financial aid package:* $4078 (excluding resources awarded to replace EFC).

GIFT AID (NEED-BASED) ***Total amount:*** $11,130,835 (75% Federal, 25% state). ***Receiving aid:*** *Freshmen:* 24% (1,177); *all full-time undergraduates:* 24% (3,923). ***Average award:*** Freshmen: $3186; Undergraduates: $3186. ***Scholarships, grants, and awards:*** Federal Pell, FSEOG, state, private, college/university gift aid from institutional funds.

GIFT AID (NON-NEED-BASED) ***Total amount:*** $15,677,040 (9% Federal, 64% institutional, 27% external sources). ***Receiving aid:*** *Freshmen:* 26% (1,285); *Undergraduates:* 26% (4,283). ***Scholarships, grants, and awards by category:*** *Academic Interests/Achievement:* biological sciences, business, education, engineering/technologies, English, foreign languages, general academic interests/achievements, health fields, humanities, international studies, mathematics, military science, physical sciences, social sciences. *Creative Arts/Performance:* applied art and design, art/fine arts, dance, music, performing arts, theater/drama. *Special Achievements/Activities:* community service, general special achievements/activities, memberships. *Special Characteristics:* adult students, children and siblings of alumni, children of faculty/staff, children of union members/company employees, ethnic background, general special characteristics, international students, members of minority groups, out-of-state students. ***Tuition waivers:*** Full or partial for employees or children of employees, senior citizens. ***ROTC:*** Army.

LOANS ***Student loans:*** $46,102,205 (65% need-based, 35% non-need-based). 52% of past graduating class borrowed through all loan programs. Average indebtedness per student: $16,000. ***Average need-based loan:*** Freshmen: $4007; Undergraduates: $4007. ***Parent loans:*** $11,049,807 (100% non-need-based). ***Programs:*** Federal Direct (Subsidized and Unsubsidized Stafford, PLUS), Perkins.

WORK-STUDY ***Federal work-study:*** *Total amount:* $616,893; jobs available. ***State or other work-study/employment:*** *Total amount:* $529,465 (100% need-based). Part-time jobs available.

ATHLETIC AWARDS *Total amount:* 1,593,031 (100% non-need-based).

APPLYING for FINANCIAL AID ***Required financial aid form:*** FAFSA. ***Financial aid deadline (priority):*** 1/31. ***Notification date:*** Continuous beginning 4/1.

CONTACT Mr. David Ladd, Business Manager, Western Michigan University, Office of Student Financial Aid, 3306 Faunce Building, Kalamazoo, MI 49008, 616-387-6000 or toll-free 800-400-4968 (in-state). *E-mail:* david.ladd@wmich.edu

WESTERN MONTANA COLLEGE OF THE UNIVERSITY OF MONTANA

Dillon, MT

Tuition & fees (MT res): $2545 **Average undergraduate aid package: $5728**

ABOUT THE INSTITUTION State-supported, coed. Awards: associate and bachelor's degrees. 44 undergraduate majors. Total enrollment: 1,081. Undergraduates: 1,081. Freshmen: 226. Federal methodology is used as a basis for awarding need-based institutional aid.

UNDERGRADUATE EXPENSES for 1999–2000 ***Application fee:*** $30. ***Tuition, state resident:*** full-time $1880; part-time $78 per credit. ***Tuition, nonresident:*** full-time $6762; part-time $282 per credit. ***Required fees:*** full-time $665; $7 per credit; $84 per term part-time. Full-time tuition and fees vary according to course level, course load, and reciprocity agreements. Part-time tuition and fees vary according to course level, course load, and reciprocity agreements. ***College room and board:*** $3810. Room and board charges vary according to board plan and housing facility. ***Payment plan:*** deferred payment.

FRESHMAN FINANCIAL AID (Fall 1999, est.) 186 applied for aid; of those 100% were deemed to have need. 81% of freshmen with need received aid. *Average percent of need met:* 44% (excluding resources awarded to replace EFC). *Average financial aid package:* $4532 (excluding resources awarded to replace EFC). 9% of all full-time freshmen had no need and received non-need-based aid.

UNDERGRADUATE FINANCIAL AID (Fall 1999, est.) 811 applied for aid; of those 86% were deemed to have need. 95% of undergraduates with need received aid. *Average percent of need met:* 64% (excluding resources awarded to replace EFC). *Average financial aid package:* $5728 (excluding resources awarded to replace EFC). 20% of all full-time undergraduates had no need and received non-need-based aid.

GIFT AID (NEED-BASED) ***Total amount:*** $1,475,540 (79% Federal, 4% state, 12% institutional, 5% external sources). ***Receiving aid:*** *Freshmen:* 72% (146); *all full-time undergraduates:* 51% (549). ***Average award:*** Freshmen: $2611; Undergraduates: $2097. ***Scholarships, grants, and awards:*** Federal Pell, FSEOG, state, private, college/university gift aid from institutional funds.

GIFT AID (NON-NEED-BASED) ***Total amount:*** $905,516 (90% Federal, 3% state, 3% institutional, 4% external sources). ***Receiving aid:*** *Freshmen:* 25% (52); *Undergraduates:* 36% (390). ***Scholarships, grants, and awards by category:*** *Academic Interests/Achievement:* business, education, English, general academic interests/achievements, social sciences. *Creative Arts/Performance:* art/fine arts. *Special Achievements/Activities:* rodeo. *Special Characteristics:* 304 awards ($173,823 total): members of minority groups. ***Tuition waivers:*** Full or partial for minority students, employees or children of employees, senior citizens.

LOANS ***Student loans:*** $3,158,801 (80% need-based, 20% non-need-based). 63% of past graduating class borrowed through all loan programs. Average indebtedness per student: $13,867. ***Average need-based loan:*** Freshmen: $2521; Undergraduates: $3631. ***Parent loans:*** $294,937 (59% need-based, 41% non-need-based). ***Programs:*** FFEL (Subsidized and Unsubsidized Stafford, PLUS), Perkins, college/university.

WORK-STUDY ***Federal work-study:*** *Total amount:* $236,845; 158 jobs averaging $1499. ***State or other work-study/employment:*** *Total amount:* $169,667 (15% need-based, 85% non-need-based). Part-time jobs available.

ATHLETIC AWARDS *Total amount:* 89,046 (73% need-based, 27% non-need-based).

APPLYING for FINANCIAL AID ***Required financial aid form:*** FAFSA. ***Financial aid deadline (priority):*** 3/1. ***Notification date:*** Continuous. Students must reply within 2 weeks of notification.

CONTACT Arlene Williams, Financial Aid Director, Western Montana College of The University of Montana, 710 South Atlantic, Dillon, MT 59725, 406-683-7511 or toll-free 800-WMC-MONT. *Fax:* 406-683-7493. *E-mail:* a_williams@wmc.edu

WESTERN NEW ENGLAND COLLEGE

Springfield, MA

Tuition & fees: $15,504 **Average undergraduate aid package: $9909**

ABOUT THE INSTITUTION Independent, coed. Awards: associate, bachelor's, master's, and first professional degrees. 29 undergraduate majors. Total enrollment: 5,094. Undergraduates: 3,344. Freshmen: 612. Federal methodology is used as a basis for awarding need-based institutional aid.

UNDERGRADUATE EXPENSES for 2000–2001 ***Application fee:*** $30. ***Comprehensive fee:*** $22,554 includes full-time tuition ($14,354), mandatory fees ($1150), and room and board ($7050). Room and board charges vary according to board plan and housing facility. ***Part-time tuition:*** $356 per semester hour. ***Part-time fees:*** $9 per semester hour; $20 per term part-time. ***Payment plans:*** tuition prepayment, installment, deferred payment.

FRESHMAN FINANCIAL AID (Fall 1999, est.) 574 applied for aid; of those 90% were deemed to have need. 100% of freshmen with need received aid; of those 20% had need fully met. *Average percent of need met:* 83% (excluding resources awarded to replace EFC). *Average financial aid package:* $10,130 (excluding resources awarded to replace EFC). 3% of all full-time freshmen had no need and received non-need-based aid.

UNDERGRADUATE FINANCIAL AID (Fall 1999, est.) 1,595 applied for aid; of those 93% were deemed to have need. 100% of undergraduates with need received aid; of those 11% had need fully met. *Average percent of need met:* 77% (excluding resources awarded to replace EFC). *Average financial aid package:* $9909 (excluding resources awarded to replace EFC). 1% of all full-time undergraduates had no need and received non-need-based aid.

GIFT AID (NEED-BASED) ***Total amount:*** $7,291,881 (15% Federal, 7% state, 70% institutional, 8% external sources). ***Receiving aid:*** *Freshmen:* 78% (510); *all full-time undergraduates:* 75% (1,457). ***Average award:*** Freshmen: $5482; Undergraduates: $4681. ***Scholarships, grants, and awards:*** Federal Pell, FSEOG, state, private, college/university gift aid from institutional funds.

GIFT AID (NON-NEED-BASED) ***Total amount:*** $764,020 (100% institutional). ***Receiving aid:*** *Freshmen:* 16% (104); *Undergraduates:* 7% (145). ***Scholarships, grants, and awards by category:*** *Academic Interests/Achievement:* general academic interests/achievements. *Special Characteristics:* children of faculty/staff, siblings of current students. ***Tuition waivers:*** Full or partial for employees or children of employees, senior citizens. ***ROTC:*** Army, Air Force.

LOANS ***Student loans:*** $8,983,165 (64% need-based, 36% non-need-based). Average indebtedness per student: $23,000. ***Parent loans:*** $2,950,047 (100% non-need-based). ***Programs:*** Federal Direct (Subsidized and Unsubsidized Stafford, PLUS), Perkins, state.

WORK-STUDY ***Federal work-study:*** *Total amount:* $1,245,380; 789 jobs averaging $1578.

APPLYING for FINANCIAL AID ***Required financial aid forms:*** FAFSA, institution's own form, federal income tax form(s), W-2 forms. ***Financial aid deadline:*** Continuous. ***Notification date:*** 3/15. Students must reply by 5/1 or within 2 weeks of notification.

CONTACT Mrs. Kathy M. Chambers, Associate Director of Student Administrative Services, Western New England College, 1215 Wilbraham Road, Springfield, MA 01119-2654, 413-796-2080 or toll-free 800-325-1122 Ext. 1321.

WESTERN NEW MEXICO UNIVERSITY

Silver City, NM

Tuition & fees (NM res): $1768 **Average undergraduate aid package: $5792**

ABOUT THE INSTITUTION State-supported, coed. Awards: associate, bachelor's, and master's degrees. 53 undergraduate majors. Total enrollment: 2,580. Undergraduates: 2,104. Freshmen: 321. Both federal and institutional methodology are used as a basis for awarding need-based institutional aid.

UNDERGRADUATE EXPENSES for 1999–2000 ***Application fee:*** $10. ***Tuition, state resident:*** full-time $1768; part-time $57 per hour. ***Tuition, nonresident:*** full-time $6456; part-time $57 per hour. Full-time tuition and fees vary according to program. Part-time tuition and fees vary according to course load and program. ***College room and board:*** $2938; ***room only:*** $1122. ***Payment plan:*** deferred payment.

FRESHMAN FINANCIAL AID (Fall 1998) 261 applied for aid; of those 68% were deemed to have need. 98% of freshmen with need received aid; of those 10% had need fully met. *Average percent of need met:* 65% (excluding resources awarded to replace EFC). *Average financial aid package:* $4356 (excluding resources awarded to replace EFC). 7% of all full-time freshmen had no need and received non-need-based aid.

UNDERGRADUATE FINANCIAL AID (Fall 1998) 1,237 applied for aid; of those 73% were deemed to have need. 98% of undergraduates with need received aid; of those 20% had need fully met. *Average percent of need met:* 77% (excluding resources awarded to replace EFC). *Average financial aid package:* $5792 (excluding resources awarded to replace EFC). 6% of all full-time undergraduates had no need and received non-need-based aid.

GIFT AID (NEED-BASED) ***Total amount:*** $2,876,357 (79% Federal, 10% state, 11% institutional). ***Receiving aid:*** *Freshmen:* 57% (160); *all full-time undergraduates:* 58% (808). ***Scholarships, grants, and awards:*** Federal Pell, FSEOG, state, private, college/university gift aid from institutional funds.

GIFT AID (NON-NEED-BASED) ***Total amount:*** $132,546 (100% external sources). ***Receiving aid:*** *Freshmen:* 21% (59); *Undergraduates:* 19% (270). ***Scholarships, grants, and awards by category:*** *Academic Interests/Achievement:* general academic interests/achievements. *Creative Arts/Performance:* performing arts. *Special Achievements/Activities:* general special achievements/activities. *Special Characteristics:* veterans. ***Tuition waivers:*** Full or partial for employees or children of employees, senior citizens.

LOANS ***Student loans:*** $1,566,003 (100% need-based). ***Parent loans:*** $6200 (100% need-based). ***Programs:*** FFEL (Subsidized and Unsubsidized Stafford, PLUS), Perkins, state, college/university.

WORK-STUDY ***Federal work-study:*** *Total amount:* $244,576; 98 jobs averaging $2040. ***State or other work-study/employment:*** *Total amount:* $512,109 (32% need-based, 68% non-need-based). Part-time jobs available.

ATHLETIC AWARDS *Total amount:* 332,574 (100% non-need-based).

APPLYING for FINANCIAL AID ***Required financial aid forms:*** FAFSA, institution's own form. ***Financial aid deadline (priority):*** 4/1.

CONTACT Debra Reyes, Grant Counselor, Western New Mexico University, PO Box 680, Silver City, NM 88062, 505-538-6173 or toll-free 800-872-WNMU (in-state). *Fax:* 505-538-6155.

WESTERN OREGON UNIVERSITY

Monmouth, OR

Tuition & fees (OR res): $3276 **Average undergraduate aid package: $6649**

ABOUT THE INSTITUTION State-supported, coed. Awards: associate, bachelor's, and master's degrees. 33 undergraduate majors. Total enrollment: 4,515. Undergraduates: 4,045. Freshmen: 786. Federal methodology is used as a basis for awarding need-based institutional aid.

UNDERGRADUATE EXPENSES for 1999–2000 ***Application fee:*** $50. ***Tuition, state resident:*** full-time $3276; part-time $516 per term. ***Tuition, nonresident:*** full-time $10,293; part-time $516 per term. Part-time tuition and fees vary according to course load. ***College room and board:*** $5004. Room and board charges vary according to board plan and housing facility. ***Payment plans:*** installment, deferred payment.

FRESHMAN FINANCIAL AID (Fall 1999, est.) 556 applied for aid; of those 78% were deemed to have need. 100% of freshmen with need received aid; of those 39% had need fully met. *Average percent of need met:* 80% (excluding resources awarded to replace EFC). *Average financial aid package:* $5904 (excluding resources awarded to replace EFC). 30% of all full-time freshmen had no need and received non-need-based aid.

UNDERGRADUATE FINANCIAL AID (Fall 1999, est.) 2,500 applied for aid; of those 83% were deemed to have need. 100% of undergraduates with need received aid; of those 45% had need fully met. *Average percent of need met:* 83% (excluding resources awarded to replace EFC). *Average financial aid package:* $6649 (excluding resources awarded to replace EFC). 24% of all full-time undergraduates had no need and received non-need-based aid.

GIFT AID (NEED-BASED) ***Total amount:*** $4,936,656 (54% Federal, 17% state, 8% institutional, 21% external sources). ***Receiving aid:*** *Freshmen:* 57% (356); *all full-time undergraduates:* 56% (1,517). ***Average award:*** Freshmen: $2937; Undergraduates: $2560. ***Scholarships, grants, and awards:*** Federal Pell, FSEOG, state, private, college/university gift aid from institutional funds.

GIFT AID (NON-NEED-BASED) ***Total amount:*** $369,776 (5% state, 43% institutional, 52% external sources). ***Receiving aid:*** *Freshmen:* 4% (27); *Undergraduates:* 3% (73). ***Scholarships, grants, and awards by category:*** *Academic Interests/Achievement:* 465 awards ($513,922 total): general academic interests/achievements. *Creative Arts/Performance:* 24 awards ($8051 total): art/fine arts, music, theater/drama. *Special Achievements/Activities:* 87 awards ($145,287 total): general special achievements/activities. *Special Characteristics:* 94 awards ($311,394 total): general special characteristics, international students. ***Tuition waivers:*** Full or partial for minority students. ***ROTC:*** Army, Air Force cooperative.

Western Oregon University (continued)

LOANS ***Student loans:*** $12,012,022 (73% need-based, 27% non-need-based). 73% of past graduating class borrowed through all loan programs. Average indebtedness per student: $14,301. ***Average need-based loan:*** Freshmen: $2558; Undergraduates: $3826. ***Parent loans:*** $1,317,847 (23% need-based, 77% non-need-based). ***Programs:*** Federal Direct (Subsidized and Unsubsidized Stafford, PLUS), Perkins, college/university.

WORK-STUDY ***Federal work-study:*** *Total amount:* $578,543; 670 jobs averaging $830.

ATHLETIC AWARDS *Total amount:* 97,392 (59% need-based, 41% non-need-based).

APPLYING for FINANCIAL AID ***Required financial aid form:*** FAFSA. ***Financial aid deadline (priority):*** 3/1. ***Notification date:*** Continuous beginning 4/15. Students must reply within 2 weeks of notification.

CONTACT Ms. Sandra Mountain, Director of Financial Aid, Western Oregon University, 345 North Monmouth Avenue, Monmouth, OR 97361, 503-838-8684 or toll-free 877-877-1593. *E-mail:* mountas@wou.edu

WESTERN STATE COLLEGE OF COLORADO

Gunnison, CO

Tuition & fees (CO res): $2208 **Average undergraduate aid package: $9880**

ABOUT THE INSTITUTION State-supported, coed. Awards: bachelor's degrees. 52 undergraduate majors. Total enrollment: 2,440. Undergraduates: 2,440. Freshmen: 576. Federal methodology is used as a basis for awarding need-based institutional aid.

UNDERGRADUATE EXPENSES for 1999–2000 ***Application fee:*** $25. ***Tuition, state resident:*** full-time $1516; part-time $76 per credit. ***Tuition, nonresident:*** full-time $7028; part-time $351 per credit. ***Required fees:*** full-time $692; $23 per credit; $64 per term part-time. Full-time tuition and fees vary according to course load. Part-time tuition and fees vary according to course load. ***College room and board:*** $4890; ***room only:*** $2650. Room and board charges vary according to board plan and housing facility. ***Payment plans:*** installment, deferred payment.

FRESHMAN FINANCIAL AID (Fall 1999, est.) 418 applied for aid; of those 60% were deemed to have need. 85% of freshmen with need received aid; of those 30% had need fully met. *Average percent of need met:* 59% (excluding resources awarded to replace EFC). *Average financial aid package:* $6625 (excluding resources awarded to replace EFC). 40% of all full-time freshmen had no need and received non-need-based aid.

UNDERGRADUATE FINANCIAL AID (Fall 1999, est.) 1,659 applied for aid; of those 60% were deemed to have need. 85% of undergraduates with need received aid; of those 25% had need fully met. *Average percent of need met:* 65% (excluding resources awarded to replace EFC). *Average financial aid package:* $9880 (excluding resources awarded to replace EFC). 20% of all full-time undergraduates had no need and received non-need-based aid.

GIFT AID (NEED-BASED) ***Total amount:*** $1,548,000 (74% Federal, 23% state, 2% institutional, 1% external sources). ***Receiving aid:*** *Freshmen:* 33% (182); *all full-time undergraduates:* 32% (718). ***Average award:*** Freshmen: $2500; Undergraduates: $2500. ***Scholarships, grants, and awards:*** Federal Pell, FSEOG, state, private, college/university gift aid from institutional funds.

GIFT AID (NON-NEED-BASED) ***Total amount:*** $1,210,000 (7% state, 56% institutional, 37% external sources). ***Receiving aid:*** *Freshmen:* 15% (85); *Undergraduates:* 15% (338). ***Scholarships, grants, and awards by category:*** *Academic Interests/Achievement:* 290 awards ($150,000 total): biological sciences, business, communication, computer science, education, English, general academic interests/achievements, mathematics, social sciences. *Creative Arts/Performance:* 75 awards ($35,000 total): art/fine arts, music. *Special Achievements/Activities:* 65 awards ($30,000 total): leadership. ***Tuition waivers:*** Full or partial for employees or children of employees, senior citizens.

LOANS ***Student loans:*** $5,750,000 (65% need-based, 35% non-need-based). 63% of past graduating class borrowed through all loan programs. Average indebtedness per student: $12,500. ***Average need-based loan:*** Freshmen: $2625; Undergraduates: $4880. ***Parent loans:*** $1,200,000 (100% non-need-based). ***Programs:*** FFEL (Subsidized and Unsubsidized Stafford, PLUS), Perkins, college/university.

WORK-STUDY ***Federal work-study:*** *Total amount:* $225,000; jobs available. ***State or other work-study/employment:*** *Total amount:* $708,910 (29% need-based, 71% non-need-based). 190 part-time jobs available.

ATHLETIC AWARDS *Total amount:* 450,000 (100% non-need-based).

APPLYING for FINANCIAL AID ***Required financial aid form:*** FAFSA. ***Financial aid deadline (priority):*** 4/1. ***Notification date:*** Continuous. Students must reply within 3 weeks of notification.

CONTACT Mr. Marty Somero, Director of Financial Aid, Western State College of Colorado, 600 North Adams Street, Gunnison, CO 81231, 970-943-3026 or toll-free 800-876-5309. *Fax:* 970-943-7069.

WESTERN WASHINGTON UNIVERSITY

Bellingham, WA

Tuition & fees (WA res): $2992 **Average undergraduate aid package: $6370**

ABOUT THE INSTITUTION State-supported, coed. Awards: bachelor's and master's degrees and post-bachelor's certificates. 104 undergraduate majors. Total enrollment: 11,708. Undergraduates: 11,050. Freshmen: 2,086. Federal methodology is used as a basis for awarding need-based institutional aid.

UNDERGRADUATE EXPENSES for 1999–2000 ***Application fee:*** $35. ***Tuition, state resident:*** full-time $2738; part-time $91 per quarter hour. ***Tuition, nonresident:*** full-time $9740; part-time $325 per quarter hour. ***Required fees:*** full-time $254; $84 per term part-time. Part-time tuition and fees vary according to course load. ***College room and board:*** $5076. Room and board charges vary according to board plan and housing facility. ***Payment plan:*** installment.

FRESHMAN FINANCIAL AID (Fall 1998) 2104 applied for aid; of those 40% were deemed to have need. 94% of freshmen with need received aid; of those 69% had need fully met. *Average percent of need met:* 87% (excluding resources awarded to replace EFC). *Average financial aid package:* $5134 (excluding resources awarded to replace EFC). 6% of all full-time freshmen had no need and received non-need-based aid.

UNDERGRADUATE FINANCIAL AID (Fall 1998) 7,054 applied for aid; of those 61% were deemed to have need. 96% of undergraduates with need received aid; of those 77% had need fully met. *Average percent of need met:* 91% (excluding resources awarded to replace EFC). *Average financial aid package:* $6370 (excluding resources awarded to replace EFC). 4% of all full-time undergraduates had no need and received non-need-based aid.

GIFT AID (NEED-BASED) ***Total amount:*** $9,576,799 (52% Federal, 30% state, 11% institutional, 7% external sources). ***Receiving aid:*** *Freshmen:* 28% (586); *all full-time undergraduates:* 30% (3,082). ***Average award:*** Freshmen: $2585; Undergraduates: $3024. ***Scholarships, grants, and awards:*** Federal Pell, FSEOG, state, private, college/university gift aid from institutional funds.

GIFT AID (NON-NEED-BASED) ***Total amount:*** $841,878 (2% Federal, 8% state, 21% institutional, 69% external sources). ***Receiving aid:*** *Freshmen:* 1; *Undergraduates:* 3. ***Scholarships, grants, and awards by category:*** *Academic Interests/Achievement:* biological sciences, business, communication, computer science, education, engineering/technologies, English, foreign languages, general academic interests/achievements, health fields, humanities, library science, mathematics, physical sciences, premedicine, social sciences. *Creative Arts/Performance:* applied art and design, art/fine arts, cinema/film/broadcasting, creative writing, dance, general creative arts/performance, journalism/publications, music, performing arts, theater/drama. *Special Achievements/Activities:* community service, leadership, memberships. *Special Characteristics:* children of public servants, children of union members/company employees, ethnic background, general special characteristics, international students, local/state students, members of minority groups, previous college experience, veterans. ***Tuition waivers:*** Full or partial for employees or children of employees, senior citizens.

LOANS ***Student loans:*** $21,537,151 (71% need-based, 29% non-need-based). ***Average need-based loan:*** Freshmen: $1295; Undergraduates:

$3716. ***Parent loans:*** $2,331,823 (16% need-based, 84% non-need-based). ***Programs:*** Federal Direct (Subsidized and Unsubsidized Stafford), FFEL (PLUS), Perkins, college/university.

WORK-STUDY ***Federal work-study:*** *Total amount:* $683,947; jobs available. ***State or other work-study/employment:*** *Total amount:* $930,662 (100% need-based). 498 part-time jobs averaging $1843.

ATHLETIC AWARDS *Total amount:* 378,275 (40% need-based, 60% non-need-based).

APPLYING for FINANCIAL AID ***Required financial aid forms:*** FAFSA, business/farm supplement. ***Financial aid deadline (priority):*** 2/15. ***Notification date:*** 5/1. Students must reply within 3 weeks of notification.

CONTACT Ms. Jean Meyer, Systems Coordinator, Student Financial Resources, Western Washington University, OM 240 MS 9006, Bellingham, WA 98225-9006, 360-650-3470.

WESTFIELD STATE COLLEGE

Westfield, MA

Tuition & fees (MA res): $2974 **Average undergraduate aid package: $5081**

ABOUT THE INSTITUTION State-supported, coed. Awards: bachelor's and master's degrees and post-bachelor's and post-master's certificates. 49 undergraduate majors. Total enrollment: 4,985. Undergraduates: 4,282. Freshmen: 899. Federal methodology is used as a basis for awarding need-based institutional aid.

UNDERGRADUATE EXPENSES for 1999–2000 ***Application fee:*** $10. ***Tuition, state resident:*** full-time $1090; part-time $135 per credit hour. ***Tuition, nonresident:*** full-time $7050. ***Required fees:*** full-time $1884. Full-time tuition and fees vary according to reciprocity agreements and student level. ***College room and board:*** $4174; ***room only:*** $2440. Room and board charges vary according to board plan and housing facility. ***Payment plan:*** installment.

FRESHMAN FINANCIAL AID (Fall 1998) 630 applied for aid; of those 72% were deemed to have need. 100% of freshmen with need received aid; of those 29% had need fully met. *Average percent of need met:* 82% (excluding resources awarded to replace EFC). *Average financial aid package:* $4502 (excluding resources awarded to replace EFC). 17% of all full-time freshmen had no need and received non-need-based aid.

UNDERGRADUATE FINANCIAL AID (Fall 1998) 2,198 applied for aid; of those 75% were deemed to have need. 100% of undergraduates with need received aid; of those 47% had need fully met. *Average percent of need met:* 88% (excluding resources awarded to replace EFC). *Average financial aid package:* $5081 (excluding resources awarded to replace EFC). 15% of all full-time undergraduates had no need and received non-need-based aid.

GIFT AID (NEED-BASED) ***Total amount:*** $2,993,194 (54% Federal, 33% state, 4% institutional, 9% external sources). ***Receiving aid:*** *Freshmen:* 34% (295); *all full-time undergraduates:* 32% (1,029). ***Scholarships, grants, and awards:*** Federal Pell, FSEOG, state, private, college/university gift aid from institutional funds.

GIFT AID (NON-NEED-BASED) ***Total amount:*** $41,532 (2% state, 70% institutional, 28% external sources). ***Receiving aid:*** *Freshmen:* 3; *Undergraduates:* 7. ***Scholarships, grants, and awards by category:*** *Academic Interests/Achievement:* general academic interests/achievements. *Special Achievements/Activities:* community service. ***Tuition waivers:*** Full or partial for employees or children of employees, senior citizens. ***ROTC:*** Army cooperative.

LOANS ***Student loans:*** $8,474,292 (64% need-based, 36% non-need-based). ***Parent loans:*** $284,583 (15% need-based, 85% non-need-based). ***Programs:*** FFEL (Subsidized and Unsubsidized Stafford, PLUS), Perkins, state.

WORK-STUDY ***Federal work-study:*** *Total amount:* $486,675; jobs available.

APPLYING for FINANCIAL AID ***Required financial aid form:*** FAFSA. ***Financial aid deadline (priority):*** 3/1. ***Notification date:*** 4/15.

CONTACT Ms. Michelle Mattie, Director of Admission and Financial Aid, Westfield State College, 577 Western Avenue, Westfield, MA 01086, 413-572-5407 or toll-free 800-322-8401 (in-state).

WEST LIBERTY STATE COLLEGE

West Liberty, WV

Tuition & fees (WV res): $2320 **Average undergraduate aid package: $4235**

ABOUT THE INSTITUTION State-supported, coed. Awards: associate and bachelor's degrees. 34 undergraduate majors. Total enrollment: 2,579. Undergraduates: 2,579. Freshmen: 503. Federal methodology is used as a basis for awarding need-based institutional aid.

UNDERGRADUATE EXPENSES for 1999–2000 ***Tuition, state resident:*** full-time $2320; part-time $97 per semester hour. ***Tuition, nonresident:*** full-time $5760; part-time $240 per semester hour. ***College room and board:*** $3200. Room and board charges vary according to board plan and housing facility. ***Payment plans:*** installment, deferred payment.

FRESHMAN FINANCIAL AID (Fall 1999, est.) 387 applied for aid; of those 69% were deemed to have need. 100% of freshmen with need received aid; of those 39% had need fully met. *Average percent of need met:* 79% (excluding resources awarded to replace EFC). *Average financial aid package:* $4998 (excluding resources awarded to replace EFC). 13% of all full-time freshmen had no need and received non-need-based aid.

UNDERGRADUATE FINANCIAL AID (Fall 1999, est.) 1,758 applied for aid; of those 69% were deemed to have need. 100% of undergraduates with need received aid; of those 39% had need fully met. *Average percent of need met:* 84% (excluding resources awarded to replace EFC). *Average financial aid package:* $4235 (excluding resources awarded to replace EFC). 16% of all full-time undergraduates had no need and received non-need-based aid.

GIFT AID (NEED-BASED) ***Total amount:*** $2,414,408 (79% Federal, 21% state). ***Receiving aid:*** *Freshmen:* 43% (211); *all full-time undergraduates:* 39% (899). ***Average award:*** Freshmen: $2879; Undergraduates: $2686. ***Scholarships, grants, and awards:*** Federal Pell, FSEOG, state, private.

GIFT AID (NON-NEED-BASED) ***Total amount:*** $392,184 (75% institutional, 25% external sources). ***Receiving aid:*** *Freshmen:* 4% (21); *Undergraduates:* 4% (94). ***Scholarships, grants, and awards by category:*** *Academic Interests/Achievement:* 140 awards ($270,000 total): business, communication, education, English, general academic interests/achievements, mathematics, physical sciences. *Creative Arts/Performance:* 48 awards ($76,500 total): art/fine arts, music, theater/drama. *Special Characteristics:* 1 award ($500 total): children of faculty/staff.

LOANS ***Student loans:*** $5,006,871 (52% need-based, 48% non-need-based). 53% of past graduating class borrowed through all loan programs. Average indebtedness per student: $10,890. ***Average need-based loan:*** Freshmen: $2456; Undergraduates: $2721. ***Parent loans:*** $589,019 (100% non-need-based). ***Programs:*** Federal Direct (Subsidized and Unsubsidized Stafford, PLUS), Perkins, Federal Nursing.

WORK-STUDY ***Federal work-study:*** *Total amount:* $133,593; 146 jobs available. ***State or other work-study/employment:*** *Total amount:* $152,399 (100% non-need-based). 49 part-time jobs available.

ATHLETIC AWARDS *Total amount:* 215,181 (100% non-need-based).

APPLYING for FINANCIAL AID ***Required financial aid form:*** FAFSA. ***Financial aid deadline (priority):*** 3/1. ***Notification date:*** Continuous. Students must reply within 2 weeks of notification.

CONTACT Mr. Scott A. Cook, Director of Financial Aid, West Liberty State College, PO Box 295, West Liberty, WV 26074-0295, 304-336-8016 or toll-free 800-732-6204 Ext. 8076. *Fax:* 304-336-8088. *E-mail:* cookscot@wlsc.wvnet.edu

WESTMINSTER CHOIR COLLEGE OF RIDER UNIVERSITY

Princeton, NJ

Tuition & fees: $16,760 **Average undergraduate aid package: $14,534**

ABOUT THE INSTITUTION Independent, coed. Awards: bachelor's and master's degrees. 7 undergraduate majors. Total enrollment: 417. Undergraduates: 275. Federal methodology is used as a basis for awarding need-based institutional aid.

Westminster Choir College of Rider University (continued)

UNDERGRADUATE EXPENSES for 1999–2000 ***Application fee:*** $40. ***Comprehensive fee:*** $23,840 includes full-time tuition ($16,520), mandatory fees ($240), and room and board ($7080). ***College room only:*** $3220. ***Part-time tuition:*** $550 per credit. ***Part-time fees:*** $120 per term part-time. ***Payment plan:*** installment.

FRESHMAN FINANCIAL AID (Fall 1999, est.) 83 applied for aid; of those 86% were deemed to have need. 100% of freshmen with need received aid; of those 30% had need fully met. *Average percent of need met:* 92% (excluding resources awarded to replace EFC). *Average financial aid package:* $14,724 (excluding resources awarded to replace EFC).

UNDERGRADUATE FINANCIAL AID (Fall 1999, est.) 271 applied for aid; of those 87% were deemed to have need. 100% of undergraduates with need received aid; of those 24% had need fully met. *Average percent of need met:* 89% (excluding resources awarded to replace EFC). *Average financial aid package:* $14,534 (excluding resources awarded to replace EFC).

GIFT AID (NEED-BASED) ***Total amount:*** $2,073,028 (10% Federal, 14% state, 74% institutional, 2% external sources). ***Receiving aid:*** *Freshmen:* 69; *all full-time undergraduates:* 215. ***Average award:*** Freshmen: $6913; Undergraduates: $6751. ***Scholarships, grants, and awards:*** Federal Pell, FSEOG, state, private, college/university gift aid from institutional funds.

GIFT AID (NON-NEED-BASED) ***Total amount:*** $270,930 (1% state, 92% institutional, 7% external sources). ***Receiving aid:*** *Freshmen:* 32; *Undergraduates:* 99. ***Scholarships, grants, and awards by category:*** *Creative Arts/Performance:* 99 awards ($536,356 total): music. ***Tuition waivers:*** Full or partial for employees or children of employees.

LOANS ***Student loans:*** $1,863,378 (80% need-based, 20% non-need-based). 86% of past graduating class borrowed through all loan programs. Average indebtedness per student: $12,500. ***Average need-based loan:*** Freshmen: $3909; Undergraduates: $4355. ***Parent loans:*** $314,143 (35% need-based, 65% non-need-based). ***Programs:*** FFEL (Subsidized and Unsubsidized Stafford, PLUS), Perkins, state, college/university, alternative loans.

WORK-STUDY ***Federal work-study:*** *Total amount:* $247,844; 186 jobs averaging $1332.

APPLYING for FINANCIAL AID ***Required financial aid form:*** FAFSA. ***Financial aid deadline (priority):*** 3/1. ***Notification date:*** Continuous beginning 4/1. Students must reply by 5/1.

CONTACT Mr. John J. Williams, Director of Student Financial Services, Westminster Choir College of Rider University, 2083 Lawrenceville Road, Lawrenceville, NJ 08648, 609-896-5360 or toll-free 800-96-CHOIR. *Fax:* 609-219-4487. *E-mail:* williams@rider.edu

WESTMINSTER COLLEGE

Fulton, MO

Tuition & fees: $14,070 **Average undergraduate aid package: $12,400**

ABOUT THE INSTITUTION Independent religious, coed. Awards: bachelor's degrees. 41 undergraduate majors. Total enrollment: 686. Undergraduates: 686. Freshmen: 201. Federal methodology is used as a basis for awarding need-based institutional aid.

UNDERGRADUATE EXPENSES for 1999–2000 ***Application fee:*** $25. ***Comprehensive fee:*** $18,950 includes full-time tuition ($13,490), mandatory fees ($580), and room and board ($4880). ***College room only:*** $2460. Full-time tuition and fees vary according to course load. Room and board charges vary according to housing facility and student level. ***Part-time tuition:*** $562 per credit hour. ***Part-time fees:*** $120 per term part-time. Part-time tuition and fees vary according to course load. ***Payment plan:*** installment.

FRESHMAN FINANCIAL AID (Fall 1999, est.) 236 applied for aid; of those 61% were deemed to have need. 100% of freshmen with need received aid; of those 45% had need fully met. *Average percent of need met:* 88% (excluding resources awarded to replace EFC). *Average financial aid package:* $12,300 (excluding resources awarded to replace EFC). 41% of all full-time freshmen had no need and received non-need-based aid.

UNDERGRADUATE FINANCIAL AID (Fall 1999, est.) 667 applied for aid; of those 56% were deemed to have need. 100% of undergraduates with need received aid; of those 42% had need fully met. *Average percent of need met:* 85% (excluding resources awarded to replace EFC). *Average financial aid package:* $12,400 (excluding resources awarded to replace EFC). 42% of all full-time undergraduates had no need and received non-need-based aid.

GIFT AID (NEED-BASED) ***Total amount:*** $3,190,379 (10% Federal, 10% state, 77% institutional, 3% external sources). ***Receiving aid:*** *Freshmen:* 59% (143); *all full-time undergraduates:* 55% (374). ***Average award:*** Freshmen: $9000; Undergraduates: $8500. ***Scholarships, grants, and awards:*** Federal Pell, FSEOG, state, private, college/university gift aid from institutional funds.

GIFT AID (NON-NEED-BASED) ***Total amount:*** $1,923,563 (2% state, 94% institutional, 4% external sources). ***Receiving aid:*** *Freshmen:* 12% (29); *Undergraduates:* 9% (62). ***Scholarships, grants, and awards by category:*** *Academic Interests/Achievement:* 508 awards ($2,693,678 total): general academic interests/achievements. *Special Achievements/Activities:* 433 awards ($576,688 total): general special achievements/activities, leadership. *Special Characteristics:* 75 awards ($72,600 total): children and siblings of alumni, religious affiliation. ***Tuition waivers:*** Full or partial for employees or children of employees. ***ROTC:*** Army cooperative, Air Force cooperative.

LOANS ***Student loans:*** $1,972,557 (60% need-based, 40% non-need-based). 55% of past graduating class borrowed through all loan programs. Average indebtedness per student: $12,600. ***Average need-based loan:*** Freshmen: $2500; Undergraduates: $3100. ***Parent loans:*** $593,307 (26% need-based, 74% non-need-based). ***Programs:*** FFEL (Subsidized and Unsubsidized Stafford, PLUS), Perkins, state.

WORK-STUDY ***Federal work-study:*** *Total amount:* $283,059; 270 jobs averaging $1048. ***State or other work-study/employment:*** *Total amount:* $420,005 (7% need-based, 93% non-need-based). 326 part-time jobs averaging $1288.

APPLYING for FINANCIAL AID ***Required financial aid form:*** FAFSA. ***Financial aid deadline (priority):*** 2/28. ***Notification date:*** Continuous. Students must reply within 3 weeks of notification.

CONTACT Ms. Karla Albert, Associate Dean of Enrollment/Director of Financial Aid, Westminster College, 501 Westminster Avenue, Fulton, MO 65251-1299, 800-475-3361. *Fax:* 573-592-5255. *E-mail:* albertkj@jaynet.wcmo.edu

WESTMINSTER COLLEGE

New Wilmington, PA

Tuition & fees: $16,270 **Average undergraduate aid package: $14,503**

ABOUT THE INSTITUTION Independent religious, coed. Awards: bachelor's and master's degrees. 52 undergraduate majors. Total enrollment: 1,599. Undergraduates: 1,450. Freshmen: 356. Federal methodology is used as a basis for awarding need-based institutional aid.

UNDERGRADUATE EXPENSES for 1999–2000 ***Application fee:*** $20. ***Comprehensive fee:*** $20,800 includes full-time tuition ($15,485), mandatory fees ($785), and room and board ($4530). ***College room only:*** $2370. Room and board charges vary according to board plan. ***Part-time tuition:*** $480 per semester hour. ***Part-time fees:*** $10 per semester hour; $232 per term part-time. ***Payment plan:*** installment.

FRESHMAN FINANCIAL AID (Fall 1999) 324 applied for aid; of those 89% were deemed to have need. 100% of freshmen with need received aid; of those 42% had need fully met. *Average percent of need met:* 98% (excluding resources awarded to replace EFC). *Average financial aid package:* $14,954 (excluding resources awarded to replace EFC). 14% of all full-time freshmen had no need and received non-need-based aid.

UNDERGRADUATE FINANCIAL AID (Fall 1999) 1,169 applied for aid; of those 91% were deemed to have need. 100% of undergraduates with need received aid; of those 50% had need fully met. *Average percent of need met:* 97% (excluding resources awarded to replace EFC). *Average financial aid package:* $14,503 (excluding resources awarded to replace EFC). 16% of all full-time undergraduates had no need and received non-need-based aid.

GIFT AID (NEED-BASED) ***Total amount:*** $10,438,512 (8% Federal, 15% state, 73% institutional, 4% external sources). ***Receiving aid:*** *Freshmen:* 77% (271); *all full-time undergraduates:* 70% (966). ***Average award:*** Freshmen: $7695; Undergraduates: $7793. ***Scholarships, grants, and awards:*** Federal Pell, FSEOG, state, private, college/university gift aid from institutional funds.

GIFT AID (NON-NEED-BASED) ***Total amount:*** $1,526,762 (2% Federal, 96% institutional, 2% external sources). ***Receiving aid:*** *Freshmen:* 60% (210); *Undergraduates:* 48% (658). ***Scholarships, grants, and awards by category:*** *Academic Interests/Achievement:* 435 awards ($2,679,300 total): biological sciences, computer science, general academic interests/achievements, mathematics. *Creative Arts/Performance:* 131 awards ($186,721 total): cinema/film/broadcasting, music, theater/drama. *Special Achievements/Activities:* 4 awards ($19,458 total): leadership. *Special Characteristics:* 339 awards ($1,060,724 total): children and siblings of alumni, general special characteristics, international students. ***Tuition waivers:*** Full or partial for children of alumni, employees or children of employees, adult students. ***ROTC:*** Army cooperative.

LOANS ***Student loans:*** $3,352,173 (100% need-based). 80% of past graduating class borrowed through all loan programs. Average indebtedness per student: $14,896. ***Average need-based loan:*** Freshmen: $3416; Undergraduates: $3831. ***Parent loans:*** $1,299,265 (89% need-based, 11% non-need-based). ***Programs:*** FFEL (Subsidized and Unsubsidized Stafford, PLUS), Perkins.

WORK-STUDY ***Federal work-study:*** *Total amount:* $315,578; 244 jobs averaging $1299. ***State or other work-study/employment:*** *Total amount:* $316,122 (70% need-based, 30% non-need-based). Part-time jobs available.

ATHLETIC AWARDS *Total amount:* 605,940 (83% need-based, 17% non-need-based).

APPLYING for FINANCIAL AID ***Required financial aid forms:*** FAFSA, institution's own form, federal income tax form(s). ***Financial aid deadline (priority):*** 5/1. ***Notification date:*** Continuous. Students must reply within 3 weeks of notification.

CONTACT Mr. Robert A. Latta, Director of Financial Aid, Westminster College, South Market Street, New Wilmington, PA 16172-0001, 724-946-7102 or toll-free 800-942-8033 (in-state). *E-mail:* lattara@westminster.edu

WESTMINSTER COLLEGE

Salt Lake City, UT

Tuition & fees: $12,726 **Average undergraduate aid package: $10,686**

ABOUT THE INSTITUTION Independent, coed. Awards: bachelor's and master's degrees and post-bachelor's certificates. 31 undergraduate majors. Total enrollment: 2,274. Undergraduates: 1,737. Freshmen: 320. Federal methodology is used as a basis for awarding need-based institutional aid.

UNDERGRADUATE EXPENSES for 1999–2000 ***Application fee:*** $25. ***Comprehensive fee:*** $17,476 includes full-time tuition ($12,456), mandatory fees ($270), and room and board ($4750). Full-time tuition and fees vary according to course load. Room and board charges vary according to board plan and housing facility. ***Part-time tuition:*** $492 per credit hour. ***Part-time fees:*** $100 per term. Part-time tuition and fees vary according to course load. ***Payment plans:*** installment, deferred payment.

FRESHMAN FINANCIAL AID (Fall 1998) 365 applied for aid; of those 72% were deemed to have need. 100% of freshmen with need received aid; of those 25% had need fully met. *Average percent of need met:* 81% (excluding resources awarded to replace EFC). *Average financial aid package:* $11,569 (excluding resources awarded to replace EFC). 29% of all full-time freshmen had no need and received non-need-based aid.

UNDERGRADUATE FINANCIAL AID (Fall 1998) 1,293 applied for aid; of those 72% were deemed to have need. 100% of undergraduates with need received aid; of those 30% had need fully met. *Average percent of need met:* 82% (excluding resources awarded to replace EFC). *Average financial aid package:* $10,686 (excluding resources awarded to replace EFC). 27% of all full-time undergraduates had no need and received non-need-based aid.

GIFT AID (NEED-BASED) ***Total amount:*** $7,097,139 (16% Federal, 1% state, 75% institutional, 8% external sources). ***Receiving aid:*** *Freshmen:* 71% (263); *all full-time undergraduates:* 70% (927). ***Scholarships, grants, and awards:*** Federal Pell, FSEOG, state, private, college/university gift aid from institutional funds.

GIFT AID (NON-NEED-BASED) ***Total amount:*** $1,935,788 (74% institutional, 26% external sources). ***Receiving aid:*** *Freshmen:* 5% (17); *Undergraduates:* 4% (49). ***Scholarships, grants, and awards by category:*** *Academic Interests/Achievement:* biological sciences, business, communication, computer science, education, English, general academic interests/achievements, health fields, international studies, mathematics, physical sciences, premedicine. *Creative Arts/Performance:* art/fine arts, journalism/publications, music, theater/drama. *Special Characteristics:* adult students, children and siblings of alumni, children of public servants, ethnic background, international students, local/state students, members of minority groups, public servants, relatives of clergy, religious affiliation, siblings of current students. ***Tuition waivers:*** Full or partial for employees or children of employees. ***ROTC:*** Army cooperative, Naval cooperative, Air Force cooperative.

LOANS ***Student loans:*** $6,050,485 (85% need-based, 15% non-need-based). ***Parent loans:*** $600,000 (25% need-based, 75% non-need-based). ***Programs:*** FFEL (Subsidized and Unsubsidized Stafford, PLUS), Perkins, college/university.

WORK-STUDY ***Federal work-study:*** *Total amount:* $385,000; jobs available. ***State or other work-study/employment:*** *Total amount:* $200,000 (100% non-need-based). Part-time jobs available.

APPLYING for FINANCIAL AID ***Required financial aid form:*** FAFSA. ***Financial aid deadline:*** Continuous. ***Notification date:*** Continuous beginning 3/1. Students must reply within 3 weeks of notification.

CONTACT Ms. Ruth Henneman, Director of Financial Aid, Westminster College, 1840 South 1300 East, Salt Lake City, UT 84105-3697, 801-484-7651 or toll-free 800-748-4753. *Fax:* 801-466-6916. *E-mail:* r-hennem@wcslc.edu

WESTMONT COLLEGE

Santa Barbara, CA

Tuition & fees: $20,965 **Average undergraduate aid package: $15,299**

ABOUT THE INSTITUTION Independent nondenominational, coed. Awards: bachelor's degrees. 43 undergraduate majors. Total enrollment: 1,335. Undergraduates: 1,323. Freshmen: 318. Federal methodology is used as a basis for awarding need-based institutional aid.

UNDERGRADUATE EXPENSES for 2000–2001 ***Application fee:*** $40. ***Comprehensive fee:*** $28,033 includes full-time tuition ($20,379), mandatory fees ($586), and room and board ($7068). ***College room only:*** $4104. Room and board charges vary according to board plan. ***Payment plans:*** installment, deferred payment.

FRESHMAN FINANCIAL AID (Fall 1999) 236 applied for aid; of those 84% were deemed to have need. 100% of freshmen with need received aid; of those 23% had need fully met. *Average percent of need met:* 75% (excluding resources awarded to replace EFC). *Average financial aid package:* $13,798 (excluding resources awarded to replace EFC).

UNDERGRADUATE FINANCIAL AID (Fall 1999) 1,256 applied for aid; of those 69% were deemed to have need. 100% of undergraduates with need received aid; of those 19% had need fully met. *Average percent of need met:* 78% (excluding resources awarded to replace EFC). *Average financial aid package:* $15,299 (excluding resources awarded to replace EFC).

GIFT AID (NEED-BASED) ***Total amount:*** $8,107,154 (8% Federal, 24% state, 63% institutional, 5% external sources). ***Receiving aid:*** *Freshmen:* 193; *all full-time undergraduates:* 852. ***Average award:*** Freshmen: $9924; Undergraduates: $10,115. ***Scholarships, grants, and awards:*** Federal Pell, FSEOG, state, private, college/university gift aid from institutional funds.

GIFT AID (NON-NEED-BASED) ***Total amount:*** $1,744,810 (95% institutional, 5% external sources). ***Receiving aid:*** *Freshmen:* 30; *Undergraduates:* 72. ***Scholarships, grants, and awards by category:*** *Academic Interests/*

Westmont College (continued)

Achievement: 1,087 awards ($4,455,887 total): general academic interests/achievements. *Creative Arts/Performance:* 82 awards ($59,250 total): art/fine arts, music, theater/drama. *Special Achievements/Activities:* 10 awards ($5750 total): leadership. *Special Characteristics:* 108 awards ($713,342 total): ethnic background, international students. ***Tuition waivers:*** Full or partial for employees or children of employees. ***ROTC:*** Army cooperative, Air Force cooperative.

LOANS ***Student loans:*** $797,526 (100% non-need-based). 77% of past graduating class borrowed through all loan programs. Average indebtedness per student: $18,319. ***Average need-based loan:*** Freshmen: $3074; Undergraduates: $4525. ***Parent loans:*** $2,021,446 (38% need-based, 62% non-need-based). ***Programs:*** FFEL (Subsidized and Unsubsidized Stafford, PLUS), Perkins, college/university, alternative loans.

WORK-STUDY ***Federal work-study:*** 173 jobs averaging $1188.

ATHLETIC AWARDS *Total amount:* 508,400 (67% need-based, 33% non-need-based).

APPLYING for FINANCIAL AID ***Required financial aid form:*** FAFSA. ***Financial aid deadline:*** 3/2 (priority: 3/1). ***Notification date:*** Continuous beginning 4/1. Students must reply by 5/1 or within 2 weeks of notification.

CONTACT Mrs. Diane L. Horvath, Director of Financial Aid, Westmont College, 955 La Paz Road, Santa Barbara, CA 93108-1089, 888-963-4624 or toll-free 800-777-9011. *Fax:* 805-565-6234. *E-mail:* dhorvath@westmont.edu

WEST TEXAS A&M UNIVERSITY

Canyon, TX

Tuition & fees (TX res): $1974 **Average undergraduate aid package: $7425**

ABOUT THE INSTITUTION State-supported, coed. Awards: bachelor's and master's degrees. 52 undergraduate majors. Total enrollment: 6,651. Undergraduates: 5,521. Freshmen: 980. Federal methodology is used as a basis for awarding need-based institutional aid.

UNDERGRADUATE EXPENSES for 1999–2000 ***Tuition, state resident:*** full-time $1404; part-time $58 per semester hour. ***Tuition, nonresident:*** full-time $6588; part-time $274 per semester hour. ***Required fees:*** full-time $570; $55 per term part-time. Full-time tuition and fees vary according to course load and reciprocity agreements. Part-time tuition and fees vary according to course load and reciprocity agreements. ***College room and board:*** $3310; ***room only:*** $1484. Room and board charges vary according to board plan and housing facility. ***Payment plan:*** installment.

FRESHMAN FINANCIAL AID (Fall 1999, est.) 251 applied for aid; of those 84% were deemed to have need. 88% of freshmen with need received aid; of those 40% had need fully met. *Average percent of need met:* 61% (excluding resources awarded to replace EFC). *Average financial aid package:* $4750 (excluding resources awarded to replace EFC). 12% of all full-time freshmen had no need and received non-need-based aid.

UNDERGRADUATE FINANCIAL AID (Fall 1999, est.) 2,226 applied for aid; of those 76% were deemed to have need. 97% of undergraduates with need received aid; of those 69% had need fully met. *Average percent of need met:* 66% (excluding resources awarded to replace EFC). *Average financial aid package:* $7425 (excluding resources awarded to replace EFC). 14% of all full-time undergraduates had no need and received non-need-based aid.

GIFT AID (NEED-BASED) ***Total amount:*** $4,226,105 (69% Federal, 31% state). ***Receiving aid:*** *Freshmen:* 20% (177); *all full-time undergraduates:* 33% (1,401). ***Average award:*** Freshmen: $2125; Undergraduates: $2425. ***Scholarships, grants, and awards:*** Federal Pell, FSEOG, state, college/university gift aid from institutional funds.

GIFT AID (NON-NEED-BASED) ***Total amount:*** $1,504,807 (3% state, 69% institutional, 28% external sources). ***Receiving aid:*** *Freshmen:* 6% (52); *Undergraduates:* 13% (549). ***Scholarships, grants, and awards by category:*** *Academic Interests/Achievement:* 670 awards ($669,577 total): agriculture, business, communication, computer science, education, English, general academic interests/achievements, health fields, humanities, mathematics, social sciences. *Creative Arts/Performance:* 130 awards ($129,756 total): dance, journalism/publications, music, theater/drama. *Special Achievements/Activities:* 62 awards ($61,780 total): cheerleading/drum major, leadership, memberships, rodeo. *Special Characteristics:* 90 awards ($89,948 total): children of faculty/staff, first-generation college students, handicapped students. ***Tuition waivers:*** Full or partial for senior citizens.

LOANS ***Student loans:*** $6,581,299 (65% need-based, 35% non-need-based). Average indebtedness per student: $17,125. ***Average need-based loan:*** Freshmen: $2625; Undergraduates: $5000. ***Parent loans:*** $246,854 (100% non-need-based). ***Programs:*** FFEL (Subsidized and Unsubsidized Stafford, PLUS), Perkins, state, college/university.

WORK-STUDY ***Federal work-study:*** *Total amount:* $250,398; 209 jobs averaging $1200. ***State or other work-study/employment:*** *Total amount:* $221,000 (7% need-based, 93% non-need-based). Part-time jobs available.

ATHLETIC AWARDS *Total amount:* 595,729 (100% non-need-based).

APPLYING for FINANCIAL AID ***Required financial aid form:*** FAFSA. ***Financial aid deadline (priority):*** 5/1. ***Notification date:*** Continuous. Students must reply within 2 weeks of notification.

CONTACT Mrs. Lynda R. Tinsley, Director of Financial Aid, West Texas A&M University, WTAMU Box 60939, Canyon, TX 79016-0001, 806-651-2055 or toll-free 800-99-WTAMU (in-state), 800-99-WTMAU (out-of-state). *E-mail:* lynda.tinsley@mail.wtamu.edu

WEST VIRGINIA STATE COLLEGE

Institute, WV

Tuition & fees (WV res): $2836 **Average undergraduate aid package: N/A**

ABOUT THE INSTITUTION State-supported, coed. Awards: associate and bachelor's degrees and post-bachelor's certificates. 48 undergraduate majors. Total enrollment: 4,794. Undergraduates: 4,794. Freshmen: 715.

UNDERGRADUATE EXPENSES for 1999–2000 ***One-time required fee:*** $5. ***Tuition, state resident:*** full-time $2836; part-time $99 per semester hour. ***Tuition, nonresident:*** full-time $5588; part-time $233 per semester hour. Full-time tuition and fees vary according to program. Part-time tuition and fees vary according to course load and program. ***College room and board:*** $3600; ***room only:*** $1700. ***Payment plans:*** tuition prepayment, installment.

GIFT AID (NEED-BASED) ***Scholarships, grants, and awards:*** Federal Pell, FSEOG, state, private, college/university gift aid from institutional funds.

GIFT AID (NON-NEED-BASED) ***Scholarships, grants, and awards by category:*** *Academic Interests/Achievement:* biological sciences, business, communication, English, foreign languages, general academic interests/achievements, mathematics, military science. *Creative Arts/Performance:* art/fine arts, music. *Special Achievements/Activities:* general special achievements/activities, leadership. *Special Characteristics:* ethnic background, general special characteristics. ***ROTC:*** Army.

LOANS ***Programs:*** Federal Direct (Subsidized and Unsubsidized Stafford, PLUS), Perkins, college/university.

WORK-STUDY Federal work-study jobs available.

APPLYING for FINANCIAL AID ***Required financial aid form:*** FAFSA. ***Financial aid deadline:*** 6/30. ***Notification date:*** Continuous.

CONTACT Mrs. Mary Blizzard, Director, Office of Student Financial Assistance, West Virginia State College, PO Box 1000, Ferrell Hall 324, Institute, WV 25112-1000, 304-766-3131 or toll-free 800-987-2112.

WEST VIRGINIA UNIVERSITY

Morgantown, WV

Tuition & fees (WV res): $2748 **Average undergraduate aid package: $4590**

ABOUT THE INSTITUTION State-supported, coed. Awards: bachelor's, master's, doctoral, and first professional degrees. 68 undergraduate majors. Total enrollment: 22,315. Undergraduates: 15,417. Freshmen: 3,567. Federal methodology is used as a basis for awarding need-based institutional aid.

UNDERGRADUATE EXPENSES for 1999–2000 ***Application fee:*** $15; $35 for nonresidents. ***Tuition, state resident:*** full-time $2748; part-time $109 per credit hour. ***Tuition, nonresident:*** full-time $8100; part-time $332 per credit hour. Full-time tuition and fees vary according to location, program, and reciprocity agreements. Part-time tuition and fees vary according to course load, location, program, and reciprocity agreements. ***College room and board:*** $4990. Room and board charges vary according to board plan, housing facility, and location. ***Payment plans:*** installment, deferred payment.

FRESHMAN FINANCIAL AID (Fall 1999, est.) 2301 applied for aid; of those 80% were deemed to have need. 96% of freshmen with need received aid; of those 53% had need fully met. *Average percent of need met:* 79% (excluding resources awarded to replace EFC). *Average financial aid package:* $4594 (excluding resources awarded to replace EFC). 12% of all full-time freshmen had no need and received non-need-based aid.

UNDERGRADUATE FINANCIAL AID (Fall 1999, est.) 10,200 applied for aid; of those 91% were deemed to have need. 98% of undergraduates with need received aid; of those 37% had need fully met. *Average percent of need met:* 81% (excluding resources awarded to replace EFC). *Average financial aid package:* $4590 (excluding resources awarded to replace EFC). 7% of all full-time undergraduates had no need and received non-need-based aid.

GIFT AID (NEED-BASED) ***Total amount:*** $14,154,377 (65% Federal, 26% state, 9% institutional). ***Receiving aid:*** *Freshmen:* 32% (1,125); *all full-time undergraduates:* 32% (4,692). ***Average award:*** Freshmen: $2592; Undergraduates: $2566. ***Scholarships, grants, and awards:*** Federal Pell, FSEOG, state, private, college/university gift aid from institutional funds, Federal Nursing.

GIFT AID (NON-NEED-BASED) ***Total amount:*** $3,203,493 (2% Federal, 62% institutional, 36% external sources). ***Receiving aid:*** *Freshmen:* 23% (810); *Undergraduates:* 19% (2,706). ***Scholarships, grants, and awards by category:*** *Academic Interests/Achievement:* agriculture, architecture, area/ethnic studies, biological sciences, business, communication, computer science, education, engineering/technologies, English, foreign languages, general academic interests/achievements, health fields, home economics, humanities, international studies, library science, mathematics, military science, physical sciences, premedicine, religion/biblical studies, social sciences. *Creative Arts/Performance:* art/fine arts, debating, music, theater/drama. *Special Achievements/Activities:* general special achievements/activities, leadership. *Special Characteristics:* children of faculty/staff, children of union members/company employees, children of workers in trades, ethnic background, general special characteristics, international students, local/state students, members of minority groups. ***Tuition waivers:*** Full or partial for employees or children of employees. ***ROTC:*** Army, Air Force.

LOANS ***Student loans:*** $40,032,498 (71% need-based, 29% non-need-based). 56% of past graduating class borrowed through all loan programs. Average indebtedness per student: $15,864. ***Average need-based loan:*** Freshmen: $3212; Undergraduates: $4031. ***Parent loans:*** $11,715,293 (100% non-need-based). ***Programs:*** Federal Direct (Subsidized and Unsubsidized Stafford, PLUS), Perkins, Federal Nursing, state, college/university, alternative loans.

WORK-STUDY ***Federal work-study:*** *Total amount:* $1,507,567; 1,730 jobs averaging $886. ***State or other work-study/employment:*** *Total amount:* $1,339,025 (100% non-need-based). Part-time jobs available.

ATHLETIC AWARDS *Total amount:* 2,894,197 (100% non-need-based).

APPLYING for FINANCIAL AID ***Required financial aid form:*** FAFSA. ***Financial aid deadline:*** 3/1 (priority: 2/15). ***Notification date:*** Continuous beginning 3/15. Students must reply within 3 weeks of notification.

CONTACT Ms. Brenda Thompson, Director of Financial Aid, West Virginia University, PO Box 6004, Morgantown, WV 26506-6004, 304-293-5242 or toll-free 800-344-9881. *Fax:* 304-293-4890. *E-mail:* bthompso@wvu.edu

WEST VIRGINIA UNIVERSITY INSTITUTE OF TECHNOLOGY

Montgomery, WV

Tuition & fees (WV res): $2646 **Average undergraduate aid package: $5567**

ABOUT THE INSTITUTION State-supported, coed. Awards: associate, bachelor's, and master's degrees. 38 undergraduate majors. Total enrollment: 2,593. Undergraduates: 2,587. Freshmen: 440. Federal methodology is used as a basis for awarding need-based institutional aid.

UNDERGRADUATE EXPENSES for 1999–2000 ***Tuition, state resident:*** full-time $2646; part-time $110 per semester hour. ***Tuition, nonresident:*** full-time $6458; part-time $269 per semester hour. Full-time tuition and fees vary according to location and program. Part-time tuition and fees vary according to location. ***College room and board:*** $4048; ***room only:*** $2090. Room and board charges vary according to board plan. ***Payment plan:*** installment.

FRESHMAN FINANCIAL AID (Fall 1998) 332 applied for aid; of those 78% were deemed to have need. 92% of freshmen with need received aid; of those 18% had need fully met. *Average percent of need met:* 96% (excluding resources awarded to replace EFC). *Average financial aid package:* $4900 (excluding resources awarded to replace EFC). 26% of all full-time freshmen had no need and received non-need-based aid.

UNDERGRADUATE FINANCIAL AID (Fall 1998) 1,194 applied for aid; of those 83% were deemed to have need. 96% of undergraduates with need received aid; of those 20% had need fully met. *Average percent of need met:* 91% (excluding resources awarded to replace EFC). *Average financial aid package:* $5567 (excluding resources awarded to replace EFC). 19% of all full-time undergraduates had no need and received non-need-based aid.

GIFT AID (NEED-BASED) ***Total amount:*** $2,246,587 (72% Federal, 20% state, 3% institutional, 5% external sources). ***Receiving aid:*** *Freshmen:* 50% (201); *all full-time undergraduates:* 44% (756). ***Average award:*** Freshmen: $2235; Undergraduates: $2557. ***Scholarships, grants, and awards:*** Federal Pell, FSEOG, state, private, college/university gift aid from institutional funds.

GIFT AID (NON-NEED-BASED) ***Total amount:*** $185,996 (6% Federal, 33% institutional, 61% external sources). ***Receiving aid:*** *Undergraduates:* 8% (142). ***Scholarships, grants, and awards by category:*** *Academic Interests/Achievement:* 84 awards ($71,178 total): engineering/technologies, general academic interests/achievements. *Creative Arts/Performance:* 21 awards ($13,289 total): music. *Special Achievements/Activities:* 10 awards ($2000 total): cheerleading/drum major. ***Tuition waivers:*** Full or partial for employees or children of employees. ***ROTC:*** Army.

LOANS ***Student loans:*** $3,143,236 (88% need-based, 12% non-need-based). 50% of past graduating class borrowed through all loan programs. Average indebtedness per student: $9337. ***Average need-based loan:*** Freshmen: $1376; Undergraduates: $1652. ***Parent loans:*** $250,357 (65% need-based, 35% non-need-based). ***Programs:*** FFEL (Subsidized and Unsubsidized Stafford, PLUS), Perkins, college/university.

WORK-STUDY ***Federal work-study:*** *Total amount:* $218,284; 350 jobs averaging $624. ***State or other work-study/employment:*** *Total amount:* $152,992 (100% non-need-based). 250 part-time jobs averaging $612.

ATHLETIC AWARDS *Total amount:* 272,967 (68% need-based, 32% non-need-based).

APPLYING for FINANCIAL AID ***Required financial aid forms:*** FAFSA, institution's own form. ***Financial aid deadline (priority):*** 3/1. ***Notification date:*** Continuous beginning 3/15. Students must reply within 3 weeks of notification.

CONTACT Nina M. Morton, Director of Financial Aid, West Virginia University Institute of Technology, Box 51, 405 Fayette Pike, Montgomery, WV 25136, 304-442-3228 or toll-free 888-554-8324. *Fax:* 304-442-3464. *E-mail:* nmorton@wvutech.edu

WEST VIRGINIA WESLEYAN COLLEGE

Buckhannon, WV

Tuition & fees: $18,050 **Average undergraduate aid package: $16,796**

ABOUT THE INSTITUTION Independent religious, coed. Awards: bachelor's and master's degrees. 49 undergraduate majors. Total enrollment: 1,648. Undergraduates: 1,601. Freshmen: 472. Federal methodology is used as a basis for awarding need-based institutional aid.

UNDERGRADUATE EXPENSES for 1999–2000 ***Application fee:*** $25. ***One-time required fee:*** $250. ***Comprehensive fee:*** $22,400 includes full-time tuition ($16,800), mandatory fees ($1250), and room and board ($4350).

West Virginia Wesleyan College (continued)

Full-time tuition and fees vary according to student level. Room and board charges vary according to board plan and housing facility. Part-time tuition and fees vary according to course load. ***Payment plan:*** installment.

FRESHMAN FINANCIAL AID (Fall 1999) 468 applied for aid; of those 84% were deemed to have need. 100% of freshmen with need received aid; of those 62% had need fully met. *Average percent of need met:* 95% (excluding resources awarded to replace EFC). *Average financial aid package:* $16,844 (excluding resources awarded to replace EFC). 12% of all full-time freshmen had no need and received non-need-based aid.

UNDERGRADUATE FINANCIAL AID (Fall 1999) 1,496 applied for aid; of those 78% were deemed to have need. 100% of undergraduates with need received aid; of those 67% had need fully met. *Average percent of need met:* 96% (excluding resources awarded to replace EFC). *Average financial aid package:* $16,796 (excluding resources awarded to replace EFC). 16% of all full-time undergraduates had no need and received non-need-based aid.

GIFT AID (NEED-BASED) ***Total amount:*** $13,048,034 (9% Federal, 4% state, 86% institutional, 1% external sources). ***Receiving aid:*** *Freshmen:* 83% (390); *all full-time undergraduates:* 77% (1,165). ***Average award:*** Freshmen: $12,819; Undergraduates: $11,988. ***Scholarships, grants, and awards:*** Federal Pell, FSEOG, state, private, college/university gift aid from institutional funds, Federal Nursing.

GIFT AID (NON-NEED-BASED) ***Total amount:*** $2,187,270 (2% Federal, 4% state, 94% institutional). ***Receiving aid:*** *Freshmen:* 51% (241); *Undergraduates:* 52% (783). ***Scholarships, grants, and awards by category:*** *Academic Interests/Achievement:* general academic interests/achievements. *Creative Arts/Performance:* art/fine arts, music, theater/drama. *Special Achievements/Activities:* community service, leadership, religious involvement. *Special Characteristics:* children of faculty/staff, general special characteristics, international students, members of minority groups, relatives of clergy. ***Tuition waivers:*** Full or partial for employees or children of employees.

LOANS ***Student loans:*** $5,020,462 (72% need-based, 28% non-need-based). 68% of past graduating class borrowed through all loan programs. Average indebtedness per student: $15,787. ***Average need-based loan:*** Freshmen: $3169; Undergraduates: $3850. ***Parent loans:*** $1,971,275 (100% non-need-based). ***Programs:*** Federal Direct (Subsidized and Unsubsidized Stafford, PLUS), Perkins, Federal Nursing, college/university.

WORK-STUDY ***Federal work-study:*** *Total amount:* $1,035,550; 740 jobs averaging $1400. ***State or other work-study/employment:*** *Total amount:* $941,823 (100% non-need-based). 675 part-time jobs averaging $1395.

ATHLETIC AWARDS *Total amount:* 1,467,390 (60% need-based, 40% non-need-based).

APPLYING for FINANCIAL AID ***Required financial aid form:*** FAFSA. ***Financial aid deadline (priority):*** 2/15. ***Notification date:*** Continuous beginning 4/15.

CONTACT Ms. Lana Golden, Director of Financial Aid, West Virginia Wesleyan College, 59 College Avenue, Buckhannon, WV 26201, 304-473-8080 or toll-free 800-722-9933 (out-of-state). *Fax:* 304-472-2571.

WESTWOOD COLLEGE OF TECHNOLOGY

Denver, CO

Tuition & fees: $8919 | **Average undergraduate aid package: N/A**

ABOUT THE INSTITUTION Proprietary, coed. Awards: associate and bachelor's degrees. 14 undergraduate majors. Total enrollment: 1,925. Undergraduates: 1,925. Freshmen: 719. Both federal and institutional methodology are used as a basis for awarding need-based institutional aid.

UNDERGRADUATE EXPENSES for 1999–2000 ***Application fee:*** $100. ***One-time required fee:*** $50. ***Tuition:*** full-time $8919; part-time $388 per credit hour. Full-time tuition and fees vary according to course load, degree level, and program. Part-time tuition and fees vary according to course load, degree level, and program. ***Payment plans:*** installment, deferred payment.

GIFT AID (NEED-BASED) ***Scholarships, grants, and awards:*** Federal Pell, FSEOG, state, private, college/university gift aid from institutional funds, Bureau of Indian Affairs Grants.

GIFT AID (NON-NEED-BASED) ***Scholarships, grants, and awards by category:*** *Academic Interests/Achievement:* general academic interests/achievements. ***Tuition waivers:*** Full or partial for employees or children of employees.

LOANS ***Programs:*** Federal Direct (Subsidized and Unsubsidized Stafford, PLUS), FFEL (Subsidized and Unsubsidized Stafford, PLUS), Perkins, TERI Loans.

WORK-STUDY Federal work-study jobs available.

APPLYING for FINANCIAL AID ***Required financial aid forms:*** FAFSA, institution's own form. ***Financial aid deadline:*** Continuous. ***Notification date:*** Continuous beginning 1/1. Students must reply within 2 weeks of notification.

CONTACT Admissions Office, Westwood College of Technology, 7350 North Broadway, Denver, CO 80221, 800-875-6050 or toll-free 800-992-5050.

WHEATON COLLEGE

Wheaton, IL

Tuition & fees: $14,930 | **Average undergraduate aid package: $13,109**

ABOUT THE INSTITUTION Independent nondenominational, coed. Awards: bachelor's, master's, and doctoral degrees and post-bachelor's certificates. 46 undergraduate majors. Total enrollment: 2,732. Undergraduates: 2,338. Freshmen: 583. Both federal and institutional methodology are used as a basis for awarding need-based institutional aid.

UNDERGRADUATE EXPENSES for 1999–2000 ***Application fee:*** $35. ***Comprehensive fee:*** $20,010 includes full-time tuition ($14,930) and room and board ($5080). ***College room only:*** $2930. Room and board charges vary according to board plan and housing facility. ***Part-time tuition:*** $625 per hour. ***Payment plan:*** installment.

FRESHMAN FINANCIAL AID (Fall 1999) 467 applied for aid; of those 64% were deemed to have need. 95% of freshmen with need received aid; of those 6% had need fully met. *Average percent of need met:* 85% (excluding resources awarded to replace EFC). *Average financial aid package:* $13,280 (excluding resources awarded to replace EFC). 26% of all full-time freshmen had no need and received non-need-based aid.

UNDERGRADUATE FINANCIAL AID (Fall 1999) 1,623 applied for aid; of those 74% were deemed to have need. 96% of undergraduates with need received aid; of those 5% had need fully met. *Average percent of need met:* 80% (excluding resources awarded to replace EFC). *Average financial aid package:* $13,109 (excluding resources awarded to replace EFC). 21% of all full-time undergraduates had no need and received non-need-based aid.

GIFT AID (NEED-BASED) ***Total amount:*** $10,059,469 (12% Federal, 7% state, 72% institutional, 9% external sources). ***Receiving aid:*** *Freshmen:* 41% (238); *all full-time undergraduates:* 42% (968). ***Average award:*** Freshmen: $9285; Undergraduates: $8557. ***Scholarships, grants, and awards:*** Federal Pell, FSEOG, state, college/university gift aid from institutional funds.

GIFT AID (NON-NEED-BASED) ***Total amount:*** $925,271 (4% Federal, 1% state, 71% institutional, 24% external sources). ***Receiving aid:*** *Freshmen:* 19% (110); *Undergraduates:* 16% (357). ***Scholarships, grants, and awards by category:*** *Academic Interests/Achievement:* general academic interests/achievements. *Creative Arts/Performance:* music. ***Tuition waivers:*** Full or partial for employees or children of employees. ***ROTC:*** Army, Air Force cooperative.

LOANS ***Student loans:*** $6,249,164 (93% need-based, 7% non-need-based). 56% of past graduating class borrowed through all loan programs. Average indebtedness per student: $14,496. ***Average need-based loan:*** Freshmen: $3540; Undergraduates: $4568. ***Parent loans:*** $1,700,307 (65% need-based, 35% non-need-based). ***Programs:*** FFEL (Subsidized and Unsubsidized Stafford, PLUS), Perkins, college/university.

WORK-STUDY ***Federal work-study:*** *Total amount:* $362,185; jobs available.

APPLYING for FINANCIAL AID ***Required financial aid forms:*** FAFSA, institution's own form, CSS Financial Aid PROFILE. ***Financial aid deadline (priority):*** 2/15. ***Notification date:*** Continuous beginning 3/15. Students must reply by 7/1.

CONTACT Mrs. Donna Peltz, Director of Financial Aid, Wheaton College, 501 College Avenue, Wheaton, IL 60187-5593, 630-752-5021 or toll-free 800-222-2419 (out-of-state). *E-mail:* finaid@wheaton.edu

WHEATON COLLEGE

Norton, MA

Tuition & fees: $23,150 **Average undergraduate aid package: $18,068**

ABOUT THE INSTITUTION Independent, coed. Awards: bachelor's degrees. 36 undergraduate majors. Total enrollment: 1,500. Undergraduates: 1,500. Freshmen: 427. Institutional methodology is used as a basis for awarding need-based institutional aid.

UNDERGRADUATE EXPENSES for 1999–2000 ***Application fee:*** $50. ***Comprehensive fee:*** $29,880 includes full-time tuition ($22,950), mandatory fees ($200), and room and board ($6730). ***College room only:*** $3550. ***Part-time tuition:*** $2869 per course. ***Payment plans:*** tuition prepayment, installment, deferred payment.

FRESHMAN FINANCIAL AID (Fall 1999) 295 applied for aid; of those 86% were deemed to have need. 100% of freshmen with need received aid; of those 51% had need fully met. *Average percent of need met:* 93% (excluding resources awarded to replace EFC). *Average financial aid package:* $16,559 (excluding resources awarded to replace EFC). 10% of all full-time freshmen had no need and received non-need-based aid.

UNDERGRADUATE FINANCIAL AID (Fall 1999) 988 applied for aid; of those 92% were deemed to have need. 100% of undergraduates with need received aid; of those 52% had need fully met. *Average percent of need met:* 95% (excluding resources awarded to replace EFC). *Average financial aid package:* $18,068 (excluding resources awarded to replace EFC). 9% of all full-time undergraduates had no need and received non-need-based aid.

GIFT AID (NEED-BASED) ***Total amount:*** $11,957,436 (7% Federal, 4% state, 84% institutional, 5% external sources). ***Receiving aid:*** *Freshmen:* 54% (230); *all full-time undergraduates:* 55% (816). ***Average award:*** Freshmen: $12,101; Undergraduates: $12,464. ***Scholarships, grants, and awards:*** Federal Pell, FSEOG, state, private, college/university gift aid from institutional funds.

GIFT AID (NON-NEED-BASED) ***Total amount:*** $669,000 (100% institutional). ***Receiving aid:*** *Undergraduates:* 5. ***Scholarships, grants, and awards by category:*** *Academic Interests/Achievement:* general academic interests/achievements. ***Tuition waivers:*** Full or partial for employees or children of employees. ***ROTC:*** Army cooperative.

LOANS ***Student loans:*** $4,150,134 (92% need-based, 8% non-need-based). 65% of past graduating class borrowed through all loan programs. Average indebtedness per student: $16,193. ***Average need-based loan:*** Freshmen: $3134; Undergraduates: $4238. ***Parent loans:*** $4,270,049 (100% non-need-based). ***Programs:*** FFEL (Subsidized and Unsubsidized Stafford, PLUS), Perkins, state, college/university, alternative loans.

WORK-STUDY ***Federal work-study:*** *Total amount:* $1,173,161; 805 jobs averaging $1460. ***State or other work-study/employment:*** *Total amount:* $455,000 (16% need-based, 84% non-need-based). 242 part-time jobs averaging $1885.

APPLYING for FINANCIAL AID ***Required financial aid forms:*** FAFSA, CSS Financial Aid PROFILE, noncustodial (divorced/separated) parent's statement, business/farm supplement, parent and student federal income tax returns. ***Financial aid deadline:*** 2/1. ***Notification date:*** 4/1. Students must reply by 5/1.

CONTACT Ms. Susan Beard, Senior Associate Director of Student Aid, Wheaton College, East Main Street, Norton, MA 02766, 508-286-8232 or toll-free 800-394-6003. *Fax:* 508-286-3787. *E-mail:* sfs@wheatonma.edu

WHEELING JESUIT UNIVERSITY

Wheeling, WV

Tuition & fees: $15,220 **Average undergraduate aid package: $15,840**

ABOUT THE INSTITUTION Independent Roman Catholic (Jesuit), coed. Awards: bachelor's and master's degrees. 50 undergraduate majors. Total enrollment: 1,495. Undergraduates: 1,277. Freshmen: 323. Both federal and institutional methodology are used as a basis for awarding need-based institutional aid.

UNDERGRADUATE EXPENSES for 1999–2000 ***Application fee:*** $25. ***Comprehensive fee:*** $20,420 includes full-time tuition ($15,000), mandatory fees ($220), and room and board ($5200). Full-time tuition and fees vary according to program. Room and board charges vary according to board plan, gender, and housing facility. ***Part-time tuition:*** $405 per credit hour. ***Part-time fees:*** $55 per term part-time. Part-time tuition and fees vary according to class time and program. ***Payment plan:*** guaranteed tuition.

FRESHMAN FINANCIAL AID (Fall 1999) 284 applied for aid; of those 95% were deemed to have need. 98% of freshmen with need received aid; of those 50% had need fully met. *Average percent of need met:* 98% (excluding resources awarded to replace EFC). *Average financial aid package:* $16,294 (excluding resources awarded to replace EFC). 13% of all full-time freshmen had no need and received non-need-based aid.

UNDERGRADUATE FINANCIAL AID (Fall 1999) 856 applied for aid; of those 93% were deemed to have need. 99% of undergraduates with need received aid; of those 62% had need fully met. *Average percent of need met:* 96% (excluding resources awarded to replace EFC). *Average financial aid package:* $15,840 (excluding resources awarded to replace EFC). 13% of all full-time undergraduates had no need and received non-need-based aid.

GIFT AID (NEED-BASED) ***Total amount:*** $3,991,542 (22% Federal, 5% state, 73% institutional). ***Receiving aid:*** *Freshmen:* 77% (241); *all full-time undergraduates:* 66% (628). ***Scholarships, grants, and awards:*** Federal Pell, FSEOG, state, private, college/university gift aid from institutional funds.

GIFT AID (NON-NEED-BASED) ***Total amount:*** $2,854,124 (2% Federal, 93% institutional, 5% external sources). ***Receiving aid:*** *Freshmen:* 62% (195); *Undergraduates:* 59% (559). ***Scholarships, grants, and awards by category:*** *Academic Interests/Achievement:* 565 awards ($1,937,453 total): biological sciences, business, communication, computer science, education, engineering/technologies, English, foreign languages, general academic interests/achievements, health fields, humanities, international studies, mathematics, physical sciences, premedicine, religion/biblical studies, social sciences. *Creative Arts/Performance:* 35 awards ($76,000 total): creative writing, music. *Special Achievements/Activities:* 128 awards ($146,995 total): cheerleading/drum major, community service, religious involvement. *Special Characteristics:* 287 awards ($1,121,204 total): children and siblings of alumni, children of faculty/staff, children of union members/company employees, general special characteristics, international students, religious affiliation. ***Tuition waivers:*** Full or partial for employees or children of employees, senior citizens.

LOANS ***Student loans:*** $5,009,244 (63% need-based, 37% non-need-based). 90% of past graduating class borrowed through all loan programs. Average indebtedness per student: $15,000. ***Parent loans:*** $833,728 (100% non-need-based). ***Programs:*** Federal Direct (Subsidized and Unsubsidized Stafford, PLUS), Perkins, Federal Nursing.

WORK-STUDY ***Federal work-study:*** *Total amount:* $532,126; 372 jobs averaging $1430. ***State or other work-study/employment:*** *Total amount:* $509,713 (100% non-need-based). 430 part-time jobs averaging $1185.

ATHLETIC AWARDS *Total amount:* 870,601 (100% non-need-based).

APPLYING for FINANCIAL AID ***Required financial aid form:*** FAFSA. ***Financial aid deadline (priority):*** 3/1. ***Notification date:*** Continuous beginning 3/15. Students must reply within 2 weeks of notification.

CONTACT Karen Mackay, Director of Financial Aid, Wheeling Jesuit University, 316 Washington Avenue, Wheeling, WV 26003-6295, 304-243-2304 or toll-free 800-624-6992. *Fax:* 304-243-4397. *E-mail:* finaid@wju.edu

WHEELOCK COLLEGE

Boston, MA

Tuition & fees: $17,410 **Average undergraduate aid package: $13,557**

ABOUT THE INSTITUTION Independent, coed, primarily women. Awards: bachelor's and master's degrees. 7 undergraduate majors. Total enrollment: 1,360. Undergraduates: 632. Freshmen: 127. Both federal and institutional methodology are used as a basis for awarding need-based institutional aid.

UNDERGRADUATE EXPENSES for 2000–2001 ***Application fee:*** $30. ***Comprehensive fee:*** $24,355 includes full-time tuition ($17,410) and room and board ($6945). ***Part-time tuition:*** $544 per credit. ***Payment plan:*** installment.

FRESHMAN FINANCIAL AID (Fall 1999) 109 applied for aid; of those 90% were deemed to have need. 100% of freshmen with need received aid; of those 15% had need fully met. *Average percent of need met:* 80% (excluding resources awarded to replace EFC). *Average financial aid package:* $14,145 (excluding resources awarded to replace EFC). 17% of all full-time freshmen had no need and received non-need-based aid.

UNDERGRADUATE FINANCIAL AID (Fall 1999) 492 applied for aid; of those 93% were deemed to have need. 100% of undergraduates with need received aid; of those 17% had need fully met. *Average percent of need met:* 80% (excluding resources awarded to replace EFC). *Average financial aid package:* $13,557 (excluding resources awarded to replace EFC). 10% of all full-time undergraduates had no need and received non-need-based aid.

GIFT AID (NEED-BASED) ***Total amount:*** $3,879,843 (9% Federal, 9% state, 74% institutional, 8% external sources). ***Receiving aid:*** *Freshmen:* 81% (97); *all full-time undergraduates:* 84% (442). ***Average award:*** Freshmen: $9810; Undergraduates: $8665. ***Scholarships, grants, and awards:*** Federal Pell, FSEOG, state, college/university gift aid from institutional funds.

GIFT AID (NON-NEED-BASED) ***Total amount:*** $123,983 (95% institutional, 5% external sources). ***Receiving aid:*** *Freshmen:* 1% (1); *Undergraduates:* 1% (7). ***Scholarships, grants, and awards by category:*** *Academic Interests/Achievement:* 64 awards ($213,600 total): general academic interests/achievements. *Special Achievements/Activities:* general special achievements/activities. ***Tuition waivers:*** Full or partial for employees or children of employees.

LOANS ***Student loans:*** $3,225,436 (75% need-based, 25% non-need-based). 95% of past graduating class borrowed through all loan programs. Average indebtedness per student: $20,000. ***Average need-based loan:*** Freshmen: $3807; Undergraduates: $4707. ***Parent loans:*** $572,848 (46% need-based, 54% non-need-based). ***Programs:*** FFEL (Subsidized and Unsubsidized Stafford, PLUS), Perkins, state, college/university.

WORK-STUDY ***Federal work-study:*** *Total amount:* $259,483; jobs available. ***State or other work-study/employment:*** *Total amount:* $19,892 (84% need-based, 16% non-need-based). Part-time jobs available.

APPLYING for FINANCIAL AID ***Required financial aid forms:*** FAFSA, CSS Financial Aid PROFILE. ***Financial aid deadline (priority):*** 3/1. ***Notification date:*** Continuous. Students must reply by 5/1.

CONTACT Office of Financial Aid, Wheelock College, 200 The Riverway, Boston, MA 02215, 617-879-2206 or toll-free 800-734-5212 (out-of-state). *Fax:* 617-566-4453.

WHITE PINES COLLEGE

Chester, NH

Tuition & fees: $10,100 **Average undergraduate aid package: N/A**

ABOUT THE INSTITUTION Independent, coed. Awards: associate and bachelor's degrees. 5 undergraduate majors. Total enrollment: 102. Undergraduates: 102. Freshmen: 70.

UNDERGRADUATE EXPENSES for 2000–2001 ***Application fee:*** $25. ***Comprehensive fee:*** $15,600 includes full-time tuition ($10,100) and room and board ($5500). ***Part-time tuition:*** $340 per credit. ***Payment plan:*** installment.

GIFT AID (NEED-BASED) ***Scholarships, grants, and awards:*** Federal Pell, FSEOG, state, private, college/university gift aid from institutional funds.

GIFT AID (NON-NEED-BASED) ***Tuition waivers:*** Full or partial for employees or children of employees.

LOANS ***Programs:*** FFEL (Subsidized and Unsubsidized Stafford, PLUS), Perkins, alternative loans.

WORK-STUDY ***Federal work-study:*** 25 jobs averaging $1200. ***State or other work-study/employment:*** 25 part-time jobs averaging $1200.

APPLYING for FINANCIAL AID ***Required financial aid forms:*** FAFSA, institution's own form. ***Financial aid deadline (priority):*** 3/1. ***Notification date:*** Continuous. Students must reply within 2 weeks of notification.

CONTACT Financial Aid Director, White Pines College, 40 Chester Street, Chester, NH 03036-4331, 603-887-4401 or toll-free 800-974-6372. *Fax:* 603-887-1777.

WHITMAN COLLEGE

Walla Walla, WA

Tuition & fees: $21,742 **Average undergraduate aid package: $13,533**

ABOUT THE INSTITUTION Independent, coed. Awards: bachelor's degrees. 24 undergraduate majors. Total enrollment: 1,400. Undergraduates: 1,400. Freshmen: 368. Institutional methodology is used as a basis for awarding need-based institutional aid.

UNDERGRADUATE EXPENSES for 2000–2001 ***Application fee:*** $45. ***Comprehensive fee:*** $27,832 includes full-time tuition ($21,550), mandatory fees ($192), and room and board ($6090). ***College room only:*** $2790. Room and board charges vary according to board plan and housing facility. ***Part-time tuition:*** $900 per credit. ***Payment plan:*** deferred payment.

FRESHMAN FINANCIAL AID (Fall 1999) 220 applied for aid; of those 88% were deemed to have need. 100% of freshmen with need received aid; of those 61% had need fully met. *Average percent of need met:* 89% (excluding resources awarded to replace EFC). *Average financial aid package:* $13,761 (excluding resources awarded to replace EFC). 41% of all full-time freshmen had no need and received non-need-based aid.

UNDERGRADUATE FINANCIAL AID (Fall 1999) 900 applied for aid; of those 78% were deemed to have need. 100% of undergraduates with need received aid; of those 71% had need fully met. *Average percent of need met:* 90% (excluding resources awarded to replace EFC). *Average financial aid package:* $13,533 (excluding resources awarded to replace EFC). 43% of all full-time undergraduates had no need and received non-need-based aid.

GIFT AID (NEED-BASED) ***Total amount:*** $7,675,895 (7% Federal, 1% state, 92% institutional). ***Receiving aid:*** *Freshmen:* 50% (193); *all full-time undergraduates:* 55% (700). ***Average award:*** Freshmen: $11,318; Undergraduates: $11,124. ***Scholarships, grants, and awards:*** Federal Pell, FSEOG, state, private, college/university gift aid from institutional funds.

GIFT AID (NON-NEED-BASED) ***Total amount:*** $2,629,870 (82% institutional, 18% external sources). ***Receiving aid:*** *Freshmen:* 33% (129); *Undergraduates:* 39% (495). ***Scholarships, grants, and awards by category:*** *Academic Interests/Achievement:* 509 awards ($2,759,900 total): general academic interests/achievements. *Creative Arts/Performance:* 96 awards ($204,945 total): art/fine arts, debating, music, theater/drama. *Special Characteristics:* 14 awards ($240,100 total): ethnic background, first-generation college students, international students. ***Tuition waivers:*** Full or partial for employees or children of employees.

LOANS ***Student loans:*** $2,840,230 (76% need-based, 24% non-need-based). 50% of past graduating class borrowed through all loan programs. Average indebtedness per student: $12,431. ***Parent loans:*** $1,549,804 (100% non-need-based). ***Programs:*** FFEL (Subsidized and Unsubsidized Stafford, PLUS), Perkins, alternative loans.

WORK-STUDY ***Federal work-study:*** *Total amount:* $203,500; jobs available. ***State or other work-study/employment:*** *Total amount:* $419,200 (24% need-based, 76% non-need-based). 285 part-time jobs averaging $1470.

APPLYING for FINANCIAL AID ***Required financial aid forms:*** FAFSA, CSS Financial Aid PROFILE. ***Financial aid deadline (priority):*** 11/15. ***Notification date:*** Continuous beginning 12/20. Students must reply within 3 weeks of notification.

CONTACT Vanessa Prull, Financial Aid Assistant, Whitman College, 515 Boyer Avenue, Walla Walla, WA 99362-2046, 509-526-4782. *Fax:* 509-527-4967.

WHITTIER COLLEGE

Whittier, CA

Tuition & fees: $20,128 **Average undergraduate aid package: $17,150**

ABOUT THE INSTITUTION Independent, coed. Awards: bachelor's, master's, and first professional degrees. 25 undergraduate majors. Total enrollment: 2,203. Undergraduates: 1,296. Freshmen: 381. Both federal and institutional methodology are used as a basis for awarding need-based institutional aid.

UNDERGRADUATE EXPENSES for 1999–2000 ***Application fee:*** $35. ***Comprehensive fee:*** $26,864 includes full-time tuition ($19,828), mandatory fees ($300), and room and board ($6736). ***College room only:*** $3694. Room and board charges vary according to board plan and housing facility. ***Part-time tuition:*** $720 per credit. ***Payment plan:*** installment.

FRESHMAN FINANCIAL AID (Fall 1999) 303 applied for aid; of those 83% were deemed to have need. 98% of freshmen with need received aid; of those 72% had need fully met. *Average percent of need met:* 91% (excluding resources awarded to replace EFC). *Average financial aid package:* $17,240 (excluding resources awarded to replace EFC).

UNDERGRADUATE FINANCIAL AID (Fall 1999) 1,032 applied for aid; of those 95% were deemed to have need. 96% of undergraduates with need received aid; of those 70% had need fully met. *Average percent of need met:* 92% (excluding resources awarded to replace EFC). *Average financial aid package:* $17,150 (excluding resources awarded to replace EFC).

GIFT AID (NEED-BASED) ***Total amount:*** $9,243,522 (13% Federal, 20% state, 65% institutional, 2% external sources). ***Receiving aid:*** *Freshmen:* 61% (230); *all full-time undergraduates:* 54% (695). ***Average award:*** Freshmen: $14,200; Undergraduates: $13,300. ***Scholarships, grants, and awards:*** Federal Pell, FSEOG, state, private, college/university gift aid from institutional funds.

GIFT AID (NON-NEED-BASED) ***Total amount:*** $4,891,043 (100% institutional). ***Receiving aid:*** *Freshmen:* 62% (235); *Undergraduates:* 52% (675). ***Scholarships, grants, and awards by category:*** *Academic Interests/Achievement:* general academic interests/achievements. *Creative Arts/Performance:* art/fine arts, music, theater/drama. *Special Characteristics:* children and siblings of alumni, international students. ***Tuition waivers:*** Full or partial for children of alumni, employees or children of employees. ***ROTC:*** Army cooperative, Air Force cooperative.

LOANS ***Student loans:*** $5,977,573 (75% need-based, 25% non-need-based). ***Average need-based loan:*** Freshmen: $4740; Undergraduates: $4950. ***Parent loans:*** $1,300,507 (100% non-need-based). ***Programs:*** FFEL (Subsidized and Unsubsidized Stafford, PLUS), Perkins, college/university.

WORK-STUDY ***Federal work-study:*** *Total amount:* $1,686,923; 763 jobs averaging $2212. ***State or other work-study/employment:*** *Total amount:* $286,000 (73% need-based, 27% non-need-based). 112 part-time jobs averaging $2468.

APPLYING for FINANCIAL AID ***Required financial aid forms:*** FAFSA, CSS Financial Aid PROFILE. ***Financial aid deadline:*** 3/2 (priority: 2/1). ***Notification date:*** Continuous beginning 4/1. Students must reply by 5/1 or within 4 weeks of notification.

CONTACT Ms. Catherine Graham, Director of Student Finance, Whittier College, 13406 East Philadelphia Street, PO Box 634, Whittier, CA 90608-0634, 562-907-4285. *Fax:* 562-907-4870. *E-mail:* cgraham@whittier.edu

WHITWORTH COLLEGE

Spokane, WA

Tuition & fees: $16,924 **Average undergraduate aid package: $14,550**

ABOUT THE INSTITUTION Independent Presbyterian, coed. Awards: bachelor's and master's degrees. 44 undergraduate majors. Total enrollment: 2,034. Undergraduates: 1,780. Freshmen: 404. Federal methodology is used as a basis for awarding need-based institutional aid.

UNDERGRADUATE EXPENSES for 2000–2001 ***Application fee:*** $25. ***Comprehensive fee:*** $22,424 includes full-time tuition ($16,700), mandatory fees ($224), and room and board ($5500). Room and board charges vary according to board plan and housing facility. Part-time tuition and fees vary according to class time. ***Payment plans:*** tuition prepayment, installment.

FRESHMAN FINANCIAL AID (Fall 1999) 348 applied for aid; of those 86% were deemed to have need. 100% of freshmen with need received aid; of those 21% had need fully met. *Average percent of need met:* 86% (excluding resources awarded to replace EFC). *Average financial aid package:* $14,819 (excluding resources awarded to replace EFC). 22% of all full-time freshmen had no need and received non-need-based aid.

UNDERGRADUATE FINANCIAL AID (Fall 1999) 1,250 applied for aid; of those 89% were deemed to have need. 100% of undergraduates with need received aid; of those 24% had need fully met. *Average percent of need met:* 86% (excluding resources awarded to replace EFC). *Average financial aid package:* $14,550 (excluding resources awarded to replace EFC). 22% of all full-time undergraduates had no need and received non-need-based aid.

GIFT AID (NEED-BASED) ***Total amount:*** $9,403,466 (9% Federal, 6% state, 77% institutional, 8% external sources). ***Receiving aid:*** *Freshmen:* 73% (296); *all full-time undergraduates:* 66% (1,087). ***Average award:*** Freshmen: $9715; Undergraduates: $8566. ***Scholarships, grants, and awards:*** Federal Pell, FSEOG, state, private, college/university gift aid from institutional funds.

GIFT AID (NON-NEED-BASED) ***Total amount:*** $2,406,309 (2% Federal, 1% state, 87% institutional, 10% external sources). ***Receiving aid:*** *Freshmen:* 7% (29); *Undergraduates:* 5% (88). ***Scholarships, grants, and awards by category:*** *Academic Interests/Achievement:* general academic interests/achievements. *Creative Arts/Performance:* art/fine arts, music, theater/drama. *Special Characteristics:* children and siblings of alumni, international students, relatives of clergy, siblings of current students. ***Tuition waivers:*** Full or partial for children of alumni, employees or children of employees. ***ROTC:*** Army cooperative.

LOANS ***Student loans:*** $5,749,415 (82% need-based, 18% non-need-based). 75% of past graduating class borrowed through all loan programs. ***Average need-based loan:*** Freshmen: $3713; Undergraduates: $4444. ***Parent loans:*** $1,739,893 (34% need-based, 66% non-need-based). ***Programs:*** Federal Direct (Subsidized and Unsubsidized Stafford, PLUS), Perkins, college/university.

WORK-STUDY ***Federal work-study:*** *Total amount:* $837,326; jobs available. ***State or other work-study/employment:*** *Total amount:* $929,982 (100% need-based). Part-time jobs available.

APPLYING for FINANCIAL AID ***Required financial aid form:*** FAFSA. ***Financial aid deadline (priority):*** 3/1. ***Notification date:*** Continuous beginning 4/1. Students must reply by 5/1 or within 3 weeks of notification.

CONTACT Ms. Wendy Z. Olson, Director of Financial Aid, Whitworth College, 300 West Hawthorne Road, Spokane, WA 99251-0001, 509-777-4306 or toll-free 800-533-4668 (out-of-state). *Fax:* 509-777-3725. *E-mail:* wolson@whitworth.edu

WICHITA STATE UNIVERSITY

Wichita, KS

Tuition & fees (KS res): $2573 **Average undergraduate aid package: $4966**

ABOUT THE INSTITUTION State-supported, coed. Awards: associate, bachelor's, master's, and doctoral degrees and post-master's certificates.

Wichita State University (continued)

59 undergraduate majors. Total enrollment: 14,062. Undergraduates: 10,876. Freshmen: 1,316. Federal methodology is used as a basis for awarding need-based institutional aid.

UNDERGRADUATE EXPENSES for 1999–2000 ***Application fee:*** $20. ***Tuition, state resident:*** full-time $1976; part-time $66 per credit hour. ***Tuition, nonresident:*** full-time $8429; part-time $281 per credit hour. ***Required fees:*** full-time $597; $19 per credit hour; $17 per term part-time. Full-time tuition and fees vary according to course load. ***College room and board:*** $4070. Room and board charges vary according to board plan and housing facility. ***Payment plan:*** deferred payment.

FRESHMAN FINANCIAL AID (Fall 1999, est.) 1071 applied for aid; of those 83% were deemed to have need. 86% of freshmen with need received aid; of those 7% had need fully met. *Average percent of need met:* 35% (excluding resources awarded to replace EFC). *Average financial aid package:* $4094 (excluding resources awarded to replace EFC). 12% of all full-time freshmen had no need and received non-need-based aid.

UNDERGRADUATE FINANCIAL AID (Fall 1999, est.) 3,454 applied for aid; of those 86% were deemed to have need. 90% of undergraduates with need received aid; of those 8% had need fully met. *Average percent of need met:* 42% (excluding resources awarded to replace EFC). *Average financial aid package:* $4966 (excluding resources awarded to replace EFC). 6% of all full-time undergraduates had no need and received non-need-based aid.

GIFT AID (NEED-BASED) ***Total amount:*** $5,985,391 (86% Federal, 13% state, 1% external sources). ***Receiving aid:*** *Freshmen:* 41% (445); *all full-time undergraduates:* 25% (1,521). ***Average award:*** Freshmen: $1182; Undergraduates: $1166. ***Scholarships, grants, and awards:*** Federal Pell, FSEOG, state, private, college/university gift aid from institutional funds, Bureau of Indian Affairs Grants.

GIFT AID (NON-NEED-BASED) ***Total amount:*** $3,094,398 (83% institutional, 17% external sources). ***Receiving aid:*** *Freshmen:* 36% (382); *Undergraduates:* 19% (1,185). ***Scholarships, grants, and awards by category:*** *Academic Interests/Achievement:* area/ethnic studies, business, communication, computer science, education, engineering/technologies, English, foreign languages, general academic interests/achievements, health fields, humanities, international studies, mathematics, physical sciences, premedicine, social sciences. *Creative Arts/Performance:* applied art and design, art/fine arts, dance, debating, journalism/publications, music, performing arts, theater/drama. *Special Achievements/Activities:* general special achievements/activities, leadership. *Special Characteristics:* adult students, first-generation college students, international students, members of minority groups. ***Tuition waivers:*** Full or partial for senior citizens.

LOANS ***Student loans:*** $20,489,524 (71% need-based, 29% non-need-based). ***Parent loans:*** $254,158 (100% non-need-based). ***Programs:*** FFEL (Subsidized and Unsubsidized Stafford, PLUS), Perkins, college/university, alternative loans, CitiAssist Loans, Keybank Loans, TERI Loans.

WORK-STUDY ***Federal work-study:*** *Total amount:* $312,170; 160 jobs averaging $1951. ***State or other work-study/employment:*** *Total amount:* $99,148 (100% need-based). Part-time jobs available.

ATHLETIC AWARDS *Total amount:* 917,907 (100% non-need-based).

APPLYING for FINANCIAL AID ***Required financial aid forms:*** FAFSA, state aid form, scholarship application form. ***Financial aid deadline (priority):*** 3/15. ***Notification date:*** Continuous beginning 4/1. Students must reply within 2 weeks of notification.

CONTACT Deborah D. Byers, Director of Financial Aid, Wichita State University, 1845 Fairmount, Wichita, KS 67260-0024, 316-978-3430 or toll-free 800-362-2594. *Fax:* 316-978-3396.

WIDENER UNIVERSITY

Chester, PA

Tuition & fees: $16,750 **Average undergraduate aid package: $14,388**

ABOUT THE INSTITUTION Independent, coed. Awards: associate, bachelor's, master's, doctoral, and first professional degrees. 39 undergraduate majors. Total enrollment: 6,999. Undergraduates: 3,587. Freshmen: 606. Institutional methodology is used as a basis for awarding need-based institutional aid.

UNDERGRADUATE EXPENSES for 1999–2000 ***Application fee:*** $30. ***Comprehensive fee:*** $23,670 includes full-time tuition ($16,750) and room and board ($6920). Full-time tuition and fees vary according to course level, course load, program, and student level. Room and board charges vary according to housing facility. ***Part-time tuition:*** $560 per credit. ***Part-time fees:*** $15 per term part-time. Part-time tuition and fees vary according to class time, course level, program, and student level. ***Payment plan:*** installment.

FRESHMAN FINANCIAL AID (Fall 1999, est.) 489 applied for aid; of those 91% were deemed to have need. 100% of freshmen with need received aid; of those 16% had need fully met. *Average percent of need met:* 82% (excluding resources awarded to replace EFC). *Average financial aid package:* $14,559 (excluding resources awarded to replace EFC). 14% of all full-time freshmen had no need and received non-need-based aid.

UNDERGRADUATE FINANCIAL AID (Fall 1999, est.) 1,710 applied for aid; of those 91% were deemed to have need. 99% of undergraduates with need received aid; of those 17% had need fully met. *Average percent of need met:* 81% (excluding resources awarded to replace EFC). *Average financial aid package:* $14,388 (excluding resources awarded to replace EFC). 10% of all full-time undergraduates had no need and received non-need-based aid.

GIFT AID (NEED-BASED) ***Total amount:*** $13,486,290 (17% Federal, 16% state, 64% institutional, 3% external sources). ***Receiving aid:*** *Freshmen:* 79% (443); *all full-time undergraduates:* 72% (1,550). ***Average award:*** Freshmen: $9390; Undergraduates: $7889. ***Scholarships, grants, and awards:*** Federal Pell, FSEOG, state, private, college/university gift aid from institutional funds.

GIFT AID (NON-NEED-BASED) ***Total amount:*** $2,027,153 (8% Federal, 87% institutional, 5% external sources). ***Receiving aid:*** *Freshmen:* 13% (70); *Undergraduates:* 11% (232). ***Scholarships, grants, and awards by category:*** *Academic Interests/Achievement:* business, engineering/technologies, general academic interests/achievements, health fields, humanities, military science. *Creative Arts/Performance:* music. *Special Achievements/Activities:* leadership. *Special Characteristics:* adult students, children of faculty/staff, ethnic background, international students, siblings of current students. ***Tuition waivers:*** Full or partial for employees or children of employees, senior citizens. ***ROTC:*** Army, Air Force cooperative.

LOANS ***Student loans:*** $10,207,471 (87% need-based, 13% non-need-based). 58% of past graduating class borrowed through all loan programs. Average indebtedness per student: $17,690. ***Average need-based loan:*** Freshmen: $3434; Undergraduates: $4765. ***Parent loans:*** $3,669,951 (37% need-based, 63% non-need-based). ***Programs:*** Federal Direct (PLUS), FFEL (Subsidized and Unsubsidized Stafford, PLUS), Perkins.

WORK-STUDY ***Federal work-study:*** *Total amount:* $1,912,270; 1,329 jobs available.

APPLYING for FINANCIAL AID ***Required financial aid forms:*** FAFSA, institution's own form. ***Financial aid deadline (priority):*** 2/15. ***Notification date:*** Continuous beginning 3/1. Students must reply within 3 weeks of notification.

CONTACT Ms. Ethel M. Desmarais, Director of Financial Aid, Widener University, One University Place, Chester, PA 19013-5792, 610-499-4194 or toll-free 888-WIDENER (in-state). *Fax:* 610-499-4687. *E-mail:* ethel.m.desmarais@widener.edu

WILBERFORCE UNIVERSITY

Wilberforce, OH

Tuition & fees: $9130 **Average undergraduate aid package: N/A**

ABOUT THE INSTITUTION Independent religious, coed. Awards: bachelor's degrees. 21 undergraduate majors. Total enrollment: 825. Undergraduates: 825. Both federal and institutional methodology are used as a basis for awarding need-based institutional aid.

UNDERGRADUATE EXPENSES for 1999–2000 ***Application fee:*** $20. ***Comprehensive fee:*** $13,920 includes full-time tuition ($8200), mandatory fees ($930), and room and board ($4790). ***Part-time tuition:*** $355 per credit hour. ***Part-time fees:*** $465 per term part-time. ***Payment plans:*** installment, deferred payment.

GIFT AID (NEED-BASED) ***Scholarships, grants, and awards:*** Federal Pell, FSEOG, state, private, college/university gift aid from institutional funds.

GIFT AID (NON-NEED-BASED) ***Scholarships, grants, and awards by category:*** *Academic Interests/Achievement:* general academic interests/achievements. ***Tuition waivers:*** Full or partial for employees or children of employees. ***ROTC:*** Army cooperative, Air Force cooperative.

LOANS ***Programs:*** Federal Direct (Subsidized and Unsubsidized Stafford, PLUS), FFEL (Subsidized and Unsubsidized Stafford, PLUS), Perkins.

WORK-STUDY Federal work-study jobs available. ***State or other work-study/employment:*** Part-time jobs available.

APPLYING for FINANCIAL AID ***Required financial aid forms:*** FAFSA, institution's own form. ***Financial aid deadline:*** 6/1 (priority: 4/30). ***Notification date:*** Continuous.

CONTACT Director of Financial Aid, Wilberforce University, 1055 North Bickett Road, Wilberforce, OH 45384, 937-376-2911 Ext. 724 or toll-free 800-367-8568.

WILEY COLLEGE

Marshall, TX

CONTACT Financial Aid Office, Wiley College, 711 Wiley Avenue, Marshall, TX 75670-5199, 800-658-6889 Ext. 215 or toll-free 800-658-6889.

WILKES UNIVERSITY

Wilkes-Barre, PA

Tuition & fees: $16,362 **Average undergraduate aid package: N/A**

ABOUT THE INSTITUTION Independent, coed. Awards: bachelor's, master's, and first professional degrees. 39 undergraduate majors. Total enrollment: 3,320. Undergraduates: 1,752. Freshmen: 387. Federal methodology is used as a basis for awarding need-based institutional aid.

UNDERGRADUATE EXPENSES for 1999–2000 ***Application fee:*** $30. ***Comprehensive fee:*** $23,464 includes full-time tuition ($15,652), mandatory fees ($710), and room and board ($7102). Room and board charges vary according to board plan and housing facility. ***Part-time tuition:*** $434 per credit. ***Part-time fees:*** $12 per credit. ***Payment plan:*** installment.

GIFT AID (NEED-BASED) ***Scholarships, grants, and awards:*** Federal Pell, FSEOG, state, private, college/university gift aid from institutional funds.

GIFT AID (NON-NEED-BASED) ***Scholarships, grants, and awards by category:*** *Academic Interests/Achievement:* engineering/technologies, general academic interests/achievements, health fields, physical sciences. *Creative Arts/Performance:* music, performing arts. *Special Achievements/Activities:* general special achievements/activities, leadership. *Special Characteristics:* children of current students, children of faculty/staff, ethnic background, members of minority groups, siblings of current students, spouses of current students. ***Tuition waivers:*** Full or partial for children of alumni, employees or children of employees, senior citizens. ***ROTC:*** Army cooperative, Air Force.

LOANS ***Programs:*** Perkins, Federal Nursing, Gulf Oil Loan Fund, Rulison Evans Loan Fund.

WORK-STUDY Federal work-study jobs available. ***State or other work-study/employment:*** Part-time jobs available.

APPLYING for FINANCIAL AID ***Required financial aid forms:*** FAFSA, institution's own form. ***Financial aid deadline:*** Continuous.

CONTACT Mrs. Rachael L. Lohman, Director of Financial Aid, Wilkes University, 170 South Franklin Street, PO Box 111, Wilkes-Barre, PA 18766-0002, 570-408-4346 or toll-free 800-945-5378 Ext. 4400.

WILLAMETTE UNIVERSITY

Salem, OR

Tuition & fees: $21,822 **Average undergraduate aid package: $18,285**

ABOUT THE INSTITUTION Independent United Methodist, coed. Awards: bachelor's, master's, and first professional degrees. 38 undergraduate majors. Total enrollment: 2,364. Undergraduates: 1,724. Freshmen: 363. Federal methodology is used as a basis for awarding need-based institutional aid.

UNDERGRADUATE EXPENSES for 1999–2000 ***Application fee:*** $35. ***Comprehensive fee:*** $27,522 includes full-time tuition ($21,700), mandatory fees ($122), and room and board ($5700). Full-time tuition and fees vary according to course load. Room and board charges vary according to board plan and housing facility. ***Part-time tuition:*** $2713 per course. Part-time tuition and fees vary according to course load. ***Payment plans:*** tuition prepayment, installment.

FRESHMAN FINANCIAL AID (Fall 1999, est.) 300 applied for aid; of those 83% were deemed to have need. 100% of freshmen with need received aid; of those 59% had need fully met. *Average percent of need met:* 93% (excluding resources awarded to replace EFC). *Average financial aid package:* $18,850 (excluding resources awarded to replace EFC). 18% of all full-time freshmen had no need and received non-need-based aid.

UNDERGRADUATE FINANCIAL AID (Fall 1999, est.) 1,186 applied for aid; of those 87% were deemed to have need. 100% of undergraduates with need received aid; of those 55% had need fully met. *Average percent of need met:* 93% (excluding resources awarded to replace EFC). *Average financial aid package:* $18,285 (excluding resources awarded to replace EFC). 19% of all full-time undergraduates had no need and received non-need-based aid.

GIFT AID (NEED-BASED) ***Total amount:*** $14,104,258 (10% Federal, 3% state, 80% institutional, 7% external sources). ***Receiving aid:*** *Freshmen:* 67% (245); *all full-time undergraduates:* 62% (1,008). ***Average award:*** Freshmen: $14,100; Undergraduates: $11,945. ***Scholarships, grants, and awards:*** Federal Pell, FSEOG, state, private, college/university gift aid from institutional funds.

GIFT AID (NON-NEED-BASED) ***Total amount:*** $2,536,190 (95% institutional, 5% external sources). ***Receiving aid:*** *Freshmen:* 17% (60); *Undergraduates:* 14% (226). ***Scholarships, grants, and awards by category:*** *Academic Interests/Achievement:* general academic interests/achievements. *Creative Arts/Performance:* debating, music, theater/drama. *Special Achievements/Activities:* community service, leadership. *Special Characteristics:* international students, members of minority groups. ***Tuition waivers:*** Full or partial for employees or children of employees. ***ROTC:*** Air Force cooperative.

LOANS ***Student loans:*** $3,476,559 (73% need-based, 27% non-need-based). 70% of past graduating class borrowed through all loan programs. Average indebtedness per student: $16,800. ***Average need-based loan:*** Freshmen: $4500; Undergraduates: $5320. ***Parent loans:*** $1,451,890 (76% need-based, 24% non-need-based). ***Programs:*** FFEL (Subsidized and Unsubsidized Stafford, PLUS), Perkins.

WORK-STUDY ***Federal work-study:*** *Total amount:* $1,069,016; 643 jobs averaging $1880.

APPLYING for FINANCIAL AID ***Required financial aid form:*** FAFSA. ***Financial aid deadline (priority):*** 2/1. ***Notification date:*** 4/1. Students must reply by 5/1 or within 2 weeks of notification.

CONTACT Ms. Leslie Limper, Director of Financial Aid, Willamette University, 900 State Street, Salem, OR 97301-3931, 503-370-6273 or toll-free 877-542-2787. *Fax:* 503-370-6588. *E-mail:* llimper@willamette.edu

WILLIAM CAREY COLLEGE

Hattiesburg, MS

Tuition & fees: $5910 **Average undergraduate aid package: $8000**

ABOUT THE INSTITUTION Independent Southern Baptist, coed. Awards: bachelor's and master's degrees. 42 undergraduate majors. Federal methodology is used as a basis for awarding need-based institutional aid.

UNDERGRADUATE EXPENSES for 1999–2000 ***Application fee:*** $10. ***Comprehensive fee:*** $7800 includes full-time tuition ($5805), mandatory fees ($105), and room and board ($1890). Room and board charges vary according to student level. ***Part-time tuition:*** $215 per hour. ***Part-time fees:*** $35 per term part-time.

UNDERGRADUATE FINANCIAL AID (Fall 1998) 1,280 applied for aid; of those 92% were deemed to have need. 100% of undergraduates with need received aid; of those 90% had need fully met. *Average percent of*

William Carey College (continued)

need met: 74% (excluding resources awarded to replace EFC). *Average financial aid package:* $8000 (excluding resources awarded to replace EFC). 8% of all full-time undergraduates had no need and received non-need-based aid.

GIFT AID (NEED-BASED) ***Total amount:*** $4,804,999 (34% Federal, 11% state, 54% institutional, 1% external sources). ***Receiving aid:*** *All full-time undergraduates:* 92% (1,172). ***Average award:*** Undergraduates: $5200. ***Scholarships, grants, and awards:*** Federal Pell, FSEOG, state, private, college/university gift aid from institutional funds.

GIFT AID (NON-NEED-BASED) ***Receiving aid:*** *Undergraduates:* 67% (863). ***Scholarships, grants, and awards by category:*** *Academic Interests/Achievement:* general academic interests/achievements. *Creative Arts/Performance:* art/fine arts, debating, music, theater/drama. *Special Achievements/Activities:* cheerleading/drum major, junior miss, leadership, religious involvement. *Special Characteristics:* children and siblings of alumni, children of educators, children of faculty/staff, first-generation college students, international students, relatives of clergy, religious affiliation, veterans. ***ROTC:*** Army cooperative, Air Force cooperative.

LOANS ***Student loans:*** $8,311,424 (100% need-based). 80% of past graduating class borrowed through all loan programs. Average indebtedness per student: $15,000. ***Average need-based loan:*** Undergraduates: $4300. ***Parent loans:*** $103,692 (100% need-based). ***Programs:*** FFEL (Subsidized and Unsubsidized Stafford, PLUS), Perkins, college/university.

WORK-STUDY ***Federal work-study:*** *Total amount:* $316,907; 237 jobs averaging $1337.

ATHLETIC AWARDS *Total amount:* 625,000 (100% need-based).

APPLYING for FINANCIAL AID ***Required financial aid forms:*** FAFSA, institution's own form. ***Financial aid deadline (priority):*** 3/1. ***Notification date:*** Continuous beginning 5/1. Students must reply within 2 weeks of notification.

CONTACT Ms. Brenda Pittman, Assistant Director of Financial Aid, William Carey College, 498 Tuscan Avenue, Hattiesburg, MS 39401-5499, 601-582-6153 or toll-free 800-962-5991 (in-state).

WILLIAM JEWELL COLLEGE

Liberty, MO

Tuition & fees: $13,020 **Average undergraduate aid package: N/A**

ABOUT THE INSTITUTION Independent Baptist, coed. Awards: bachelor's degrees (also offers evening program with significant enrollment not reflected in profile). 42 undergraduate majors. Total enrollment: 1,145. Undergraduates: 1,145. Freshmen: 285. Federal methodology is used as a basis for awarding need-based institutional aid.

UNDERGRADUATE EXPENSES for 1999–2000 ***Application fee:*** $25. ***Comprehensive fee:*** $17,030 includes full-time tuition ($13,020) and room and board ($4010). Full-time tuition and fees vary according to class time and course load. Room and board charges vary according to board plan and housing facility. ***Part-time tuition:*** $525 per semester hour. Part-time tuition and fees vary according to class time. ***Payment plans:*** tuition prepayment, installment.

FRESHMAN FINANCIAL AID (Fall 1999) 224 applied for aid; of those 84% were deemed to have need. 99% of freshmen with need received aid.

UNDERGRADUATE FINANCIAL AID (Fall 1999) 1,006 applied for aid; of those 63% were deemed to have need. 100% of undergraduates with need received aid.

GIFT AID (NEED-BASED) ***Total amount:*** $4,628,251 (18% Federal, 8% state, 69% institutional, 5% external sources). ***Receiving aid:*** *Freshmen:* 56% (162); *all full-time undergraduates:* 50% (546). ***Average award:*** Freshmen: $4789; Undergraduates: $4191. ***Scholarships, grants, and awards:*** Federal Pell, FSEOG, state, private, college/university gift aid from institutional funds.

GIFT AID (NON-NEED-BASED) ***Total amount:*** $2,068,570 (11% state, 82% institutional, 7% external sources). ***Scholarships, grants, and awards by category:*** *Academic Interests/Achievement:* 583 awards ($2,299,991 total): education, general academic interests/achievements. *Creative Arts/Performance:* 206 awards ($423,865 total): art/fine arts, cinema/film/broadcasting, debating, journalism/publications, music, theater/drama. *Special Achievements/Activities:* 223 awards ($198,663 total): cheerleading/drum major, leadership, religious involvement. *Special Characteristics:* 63 awards ($392,045 total): children of faculty/staff, relatives of clergy. ***Tuition waivers:*** Full or partial for employees or children of employees, senior citizens.

LOANS ***Student loans:*** $3,099,022 (86% need-based, 14% non-need-based). 62% of past graduating class borrowed through all loan programs. Average indebtedness per student: $17,908. ***Average need-based loan:*** Freshmen: $3358; Undergraduates: $4267. ***Parent loans:*** $1,256,261 (61% need-based, 39% non-need-based). ***Programs:*** Federal Direct (Subsidized and Unsubsidized Stafford, PLUS), Perkins, Federal Nursing, alternative loans.

WORK-STUDY ***Federal work-study:*** *Total amount:* $754,515; 482 jobs averaging $1565. ***State or other work-study/employment:*** *Total amount:* $321,780 (42% need-based, 58% non-need-based). 157 part-time jobs averaging $2050.

ATHLETIC AWARDS *Total amount:* 856,275 (50% need-based, 50% non-need-based).

APPLYING for FINANCIAL AID ***Required financial aid forms:*** FAFSA, institution's own form, scholarship application form. ***Financial aid deadline (priority):*** 3/1. ***Notification date:*** Continuous beginning 3/15. Students must reply within 2 weeks of notification.

CONTACT Ms. Sue Armstrong, Director of Student Financial Planning, William Jewell College, 500 College Hill, Liberty, MO 64068-1896, 816-781-7700 Ext. 5146 or toll-free 800-753-7009. *Fax:* 816-415-5006. *E-mail:* armstrongs@william.jewell.edu

WILLIAM PATERSON UNIVERSITY OF NEW JERSEY

Wayne, NJ

Tuition & fees (NJ res): $4690 **Average undergraduate aid package: $6675**

ABOUT THE INSTITUTION State-supported, coed. Awards: bachelor's and master's degrees. 53 undergraduate majors. Total enrollment: 9,384. Undergraduates: 8,071. Freshmen: 1,261. Federal methodology is used as a basis for awarding need-based institutional aid.

UNDERGRADUATE EXPENSES for 1999–2000 ***Application fee:*** $35. ***Tuition, state resident:*** full-time $4690; part-time $106 per credit. ***Tuition, nonresident:*** full-time $7360; part-time $238 per credit. ***Required fees:*** $44 per credit. ***College room and board:*** $5650; ***room only:*** $3700. Room and board charges vary according to board plan and housing facility. ***Payment plan:*** installment.

FRESHMAN FINANCIAL AID (Fall 1999, est.) 858 applied for aid; of those 76% were deemed to have need. 92% of freshmen with need received aid; of those 30% had need fully met. *Average percent of need met:* 60% (excluding resources awarded to replace EFC). *Average financial aid package:* $6558 (excluding resources awarded to replace EFC). 18% of all full-time freshmen had no need and received non-need-based aid.

UNDERGRADUATE FINANCIAL AID (Fall 1999, est.) 3,936 applied for aid; of those 81% were deemed to have need. 94% of undergraduates with need received aid; of those 26% had need fully met. *Average percent of need met:* 63% (excluding resources awarded to replace EFC). *Average financial aid package:* $6675 (excluding resources awarded to replace EFC). 13% of all full-time undergraduates had no need and received non-need-based aid.

GIFT AID (NEED-BASED) ***Total amount:*** $9,265,000 (42% Federal, 51% state, 7% institutional). ***Receiving aid:*** *Freshmen:* 36% (411); *all full-time undergraduates:* 33% (2,047). ***Average award:*** Freshmen: $4675; Undergraduates: $4370. ***Scholarships, grants, and awards:*** Federal Pell, FSEOG, state, college/university gift aid from institutional funds.

GIFT AID (NON-NEED-BASED) ***Total amount:*** $2,926,760 (3% state, 88% institutional, 9% external sources). ***Receiving aid:*** *Freshmen:* 18% (203); *Undergraduates:* 10% (661). ***Scholarships, grants, and awards by category:*** *Academic Interests/Achievement:* 420 awards ($2,375,000 total): general academic interests/achievements. *Creative Arts/Performance:* 17

awards ($3150 total): music. *Special Characteristics:* 120 awards ($120,000 total): members of minority groups. ***ROTC:*** Air Force cooperative.

LOANS ***Student loans:*** $12,750,000 (60% need-based, 40% non-need-based). Average indebtedness per student: $11,728. ***Average need-based loan:*** Freshmen: $2512; Undergraduates: $3214. ***Parent loans:*** $1,700,000 (100% non-need-based). ***Programs:*** Federal Direct (Subsidized and Unsubsidized Stafford, PLUS), Perkins, state.

WORK-STUDY ***Federal work-study:*** *Total amount:* $280,000; 190 jobs averaging $1474. ***State or other work-study/employment:*** *Total amount:* $435,000 (100% non-need-based). 310 part-time jobs averaging $1403.

APPLYING for FINANCIAL AID ***Required financial aid form:*** FAFSA. ***Financial aid deadline (priority):*** 4/1. ***Notification date:*** Continuous.

CONTACT Robert Baumel, Director of Financial Aid, William Paterson University of New Jersey, 300 Pompton Road, Wayne, NJ 07470-8420, 973-720-2202. *Fax:* 973-720-3133. *E-mail:* baumelr@wpunj.edu

WILLIAM PENN UNIVERSITY

Oskaloosa, IA

Tuition & fees: $12,770 **Average undergraduate aid package: $9305**

ABOUT THE INSTITUTION Independent religious, coed. Awards: bachelor's degrees. 34 undergraduate majors. Total enrollment: 1,252. Undergraduates: 1,252. Freshmen: 440. Federal methodology is used as a basis for awarding need-based institutional aid.

UNDERGRADUATE EXPENSES for 2000–2001 ***Application fee:*** $20. ***Comprehensive fee:*** $16,910 includes full-time tuition ($12,400), mandatory fees ($370), and room and board ($4140). ***Part-time tuition:*** $200 per credit hour. ***Part-time fees:*** $12 per credit hour. Part-time tuition and fees vary according to course load. ***Payment plan:*** installment.

FRESHMAN FINANCIAL AID (Fall 1999, est.) 271 applied for aid; of those 99% were deemed to have need. 100% of freshmen with need received aid; of those 93% had need fully met. *Average percent of need met:* 93% (excluding resources awarded to replace EFC). *Average financial aid package:* $9271 (excluding resources awarded to replace EFC). 1% of all full-time freshmen had no need and received non-need-based aid.

UNDERGRADUATE FINANCIAL AID (Fall 1999, est.) 554 applied for aid; of those 99% were deemed to have need. 99% of undergraduates with need received aid; of those 92% had need fully met. *Average percent of need met:* 92% (excluding resources awarded to replace EFC). *Average financial aid package:* $9305 (excluding resources awarded to replace EFC). 1% of all full-time undergraduates had no need and received non-need-based aid.

GIFT AID (NEED-BASED) ***Total amount:*** $3,871,163 (30% Federal, 24% state, 43% institutional, 3% external sources). ***Receiving aid:*** *Freshmen:* 92% (268); *all full-time undergraduates:* 90% (545). ***Average award:*** Freshmen: $4285; Undergraduates: $4434. ***Scholarships, grants, and awards:*** Federal Pell, FSEOG, state, private, college/university gift aid from institutional funds.

GIFT AID (NON-NEED-BASED) ***Total amount:*** $52,200 (100% institutional). ***Scholarships, grants, and awards by category:*** *Academic Interests/Achievement:* 123 awards ($669,386 total): general academic interests/achievements. *Creative Arts/Performance:* 8 awards ($16,500 total): art/fine arts, creative writing, journalism/publications, music, theater/drama. *Special Achievements/Activities:* 16 awards ($39,000 total): junior miss, leadership, religious involvement. *Special Characteristics:* 237 awards ($713,052 total): children and siblings of alumni, out-of-state students, religious affiliation. ***Tuition waivers:*** Full or partial for employees or children of employees, senior citizens.

LOANS ***Student loans:*** $5,258,677 (100% need-based). ***Average need-based loan:*** Freshmen: $4281; Undergraduates: $4833. ***Parent loans:*** $148,200 (100% need-based). ***Programs:*** FFEL (Subsidized and Unsubsidized Stafford, PLUS), Perkins, state.

WORK-STUDY ***Federal work-study:*** *Total amount:* $213,926; 335 jobs averaging $692. ***State or other work-study/employment:*** *Total amount:* $41,340 (41% need-based, 59% non-need-based). 33 part-time jobs averaging $510.

APPLYING for FINANCIAL AID ***Required financial aid form:*** FAFSA. ***Financial aid deadline (priority):*** 4/15. ***Notification date:*** Continuous. Students must reply within 2 weeks of notification.

CONTACT Ms. Nancy Ferguson, Director of Financial Aid, William Penn University, 201 Trueblood Avenue, Oskaloosa, IA 52577-1799, 515-673-1060 or toll-free 800-779-7366. *E-mail:* fergusonn@wmpenn.edu

WILLIAMS BAPTIST COLLEGE

Walnut Ridge, AR

Tuition & fees: $6270 **Average undergraduate aid package: N/A**

ABOUT THE INSTITUTION Independent Southern Baptist, coed. Awards: associate and bachelor's degrees. 26 undergraduate majors. Total enrollment: 637. Undergraduates: 637. Freshmen: 160. Federal methodology is used as a basis for awarding need-based institutional aid.

UNDERGRADUATE EXPENSES for 1999–2000 ***Application fee:*** $20. ***Comprehensive fee:*** $9470 includes full-time tuition ($6000), mandatory fees ($270), and room and board ($3200). ***Part-time tuition:*** $250 per hour. ***Part-time fees:*** $135 per term part-time. Part-time tuition and fees vary according to course load. ***Payment plan:*** installment.

FRESHMAN FINANCIAL AID (Fall 1999) 146 applied for aid; of those 66% were deemed to have need. 100% of freshmen with need received aid. 20% of all full-time freshmen had no need and received non-need-based aid.

UNDERGRADUATE FINANCIAL AID (Fall 1999) 500 applied for aid; of those 74% were deemed to have need. 100% of undergraduates with need received aid. 17% of all full-time undergraduates had no need and received non-need-based aid.

GIFT AID (NEED-BASED) ***Total amount:*** $917,420 (77% Federal, 23% state). ***Receiving aid:*** *Freshmen:* 66% (96); *all full-time undergraduates:* 73% (369). ***Average award:*** Freshmen: $4169; Undergraduates: $4748. ***Scholarships, grants, and awards:*** Federal Pell, FSEOG, state, private, college/university gift aid from institutional funds.

GIFT AID (NON-NEED-BASED) ***Total amount:*** $839,502 (2% state, 87% institutional, 11% external sources). ***Receiving aid:*** *Freshmen:* 59% (86); *Undergraduates:* 61% (308). ***Scholarships, grants, and awards by category:*** *Academic Interests/Achievement:* 331 awards ($552,739 total): general academic interests/achievements. *Creative Arts/Performance:* 26 awards ($39,554 total): art/fine arts, music. *Special Achievements/Activities:* leadership. *Special Characteristics:* 50 awards ($54,907 total): children of faculty/staff, members of minority groups, relatives of clergy, religious affiliation. ***Tuition waivers:*** Full or partial for employees or children of employees, senior citizens. ***ROTC:*** Army cooperative.

LOANS ***Student loans:*** $1,278,239 (74% need-based, 26% non-need-based). 62% of past graduating class borrowed through all loan programs. Average indebtedness per student: $15,450. ***Average need-based loan:*** Freshmen: $2664; Undergraduates: $3208. ***Parent loans:*** $38,175 (100% non-need-based). ***Programs:*** Federal Direct (Subsidized and Unsubsidized Stafford, PLUS), college/university.

WORK-STUDY ***Federal work-study:*** *Total amount:* $241,105; 178 jobs averaging $1354. ***State or other work-study/employment:*** *Total amount:* $53,491 (100% non-need-based). Part-time jobs available.

ATHLETIC AWARDS *Total amount:* 276,888 (100% non-need-based).

APPLYING for FINANCIAL AID ***Required financial aid form:*** FAFSA. ***Financial aid deadline:*** Continuous. ***Notification date:*** Continuous beginning 4/1. Students must reply within 2 weeks of notification.

CONTACT Financial Aid Department, Williams Baptist College, 60 West Fulbright Avenue, Walnut Ridge, AR 72476, 870-886-6741 Ext. 121 or toll-free 800-722-4434. *Fax:* 870-886-3924.

WILLIAMS COLLEGE

Williamstown, MA

Tuition & fees: $24,790 **Average undergraduate aid package: $21,955**

Williams College (continued)

ABOUT THE INSTITUTION Independent, coed. Awards: bachelor's and master's degrees. 31 undergraduate majors. Total enrollment: 2,162. Undergraduates: 2,113. Freshmen: 544. Institutional methodology is used as a basis for awarding need-based institutional aid.

UNDERGRADUATE EXPENSES for 1999–2000 ***Application fee:*** $50. ***Comprehensive fee:*** $31,520 includes full-time tuition ($24,619), mandatory fees ($171), and room and board ($6730). ***College room only:*** $3340. Room and board charges vary according to board plan. ***Payment plan:*** installment.

FRESHMAN FINANCIAL AID (Fall 1999) 304 applied for aid; of those 79% were deemed to have need. 100% of freshmen with need received aid; of those 100% had need fully met. *Average percent of need met:* 100% (excluding resources awarded to replace EFC). *Average financial aid package:* $22,099 (excluding resources awarded to replace EFC). 6% of all full-time freshmen had no need and received non-need-based aid.

UNDERGRADUATE FINANCIAL AID (Fall 1999) 980 applied for aid; of those 92% were deemed to have need. 100% of undergraduates with need received aid; of those 100% had need fully met. *Average percent of need met:* 100% (excluding resources awarded to replace EFC). *Average financial aid package:* $21,955 (excluding resources awarded to replace EFC). 3% of all full-time undergraduates had no need and received non-need-based aid.

GIFT AID (NEED-BASED) ***Total amount:*** $15,219,952 (7% Federal, 1% state, 88% institutional, 4% external sources). ***Receiving aid:*** *Freshmen:* 43% (234); *all full-time undergraduates:* 40% (870). ***Average award:*** Freshmen: $19,807; Undergraduates: $17,494. ***Scholarships, grants, and awards:*** Federal Pell, FSEOG, state, private, college/university gift aid from institutional funds.

GIFT AID (NON-NEED-BASED) ***Tuition waivers:*** Full or partial for employees or children of employees.

LOANS ***Student loans:*** $3,682,024 (92% need-based, 8% non-need-based). Average indebtedness per student: $14,328. ***Average need-based loan:*** Freshmen: $2190; Undergraduates: $4113. ***Programs:*** Federal Direct (Subsidized and Unsubsidized Stafford, PLUS), Perkins, college/university.

WORK-STUDY ***Federal work-study:*** *Total amount:* $586,492; 378 jobs averaging $1552. ***State or other work-study/employment:*** *Total amount:* $707,701 (100% need-based). 433 part-time jobs averaging $1634.

APPLYING for FINANCIAL AID ***Required financial aid forms:*** FAFSA, CSS Financial Aid PROFILE. ***Financial aid deadline:*** 2/1. ***Notification date:*** 4/1. Students must reply by 5/1.

CONTACT Paul J. Boyer, Director of Financial Aid, Williams College, PO Box 37, Williamstown, MA 01267, 413-597-4181. *Fax:* 413-597-2999. *E-mail:* paul.j.boyer@williams.edu

WILLIAM SMITH COLLEGE

Geneva, NY

See Hobart and William Smith Colleges

WILLIAM TYNDALE COLLEGE

Farmington Hills, MI

Tuition & fees: $7050 **Average undergraduate aid package: $4782**

ABOUT THE INSTITUTION Independent religious, coed. Awards: associate and bachelor's degrees. 19 undergraduate majors. Total enrollment: 637. Undergraduates: 637. Freshmen: 90. Both federal and institutional methodology are used as a basis for awarding need-based institutional aid.

UNDERGRADUATE EXPENSES for 2000–2001 ***Application fee:*** $25. ***Comprehensive fee:*** $9850 includes full-time tuition ($7050) and room and board ($2800). Room and board charges vary according to housing facility. ***Part-time tuition:*** $235 per credit. ***Payment plan:*** deferred payment.

FRESHMAN FINANCIAL AID (Fall 1999) 67 applied for aid; of those 94% were deemed to have need. 100% of freshmen with need received aid; of those 11% had need fully met. *Average percent of need met:* 60% (excluding resources awarded to replace EFC). *Average financial aid package:* $4667 (excluding resources awarded to replace EFC). 9% of all full-time freshmen had no need and received non-need-based aid.

UNDERGRADUATE FINANCIAL AID (Fall 1999) 327 applied for aid; of those 99% were deemed to have need. 99% of undergraduates with need received aid; of those 10% had need fully met. *Average percent of need met:* 60% (excluding resources awarded to replace EFC). *Average financial aid package:* $4782 (excluding resources awarded to replace EFC). 9% of all full-time undergraduates had no need and received non-need-based aid.

GIFT AID (NEED-BASED) ***Total amount:*** $621,404 (38% Federal, 62% state). ***Receiving aid:*** *Freshmen:* 48% (33); *all full-time undergraduates:* 39% (160). ***Average award:*** Freshmen: $3884; Undergraduates: $3884. ***Scholarships, grants, and awards:*** Federal Pell, FSEOG, state, private, college/university gift aid from institutional funds.

GIFT AID (NON-NEED-BASED) ***Total amount:*** $894,517 (58% institutional, 42% external sources). ***Receiving aid:*** *Freshmen:* 38% (26); *Undergraduates:* 24% (100). ***Scholarships, grants, and awards by category:*** *Academic Interests/Achievement:* 116 awards ($497,389 total): general academic interests/achievements. *Creative Arts/Performance:* 3 awards ($9900 total): music. *Special Characteristics:* 6 awards ($10,368 total): children and siblings of alumni, children of faculty/staff, international students, previous college experience, relatives of clergy. ***Tuition waivers:*** Full or partial for employees or children of employees, senior citizens.

LOANS ***Student loans:*** $832,488 (55% need-based, 45% non-need-based). 80% of past graduating class borrowed through all loan programs. Average indebtedness per student: $9500. ***Average need-based loan:*** Freshmen: $1740; Undergraduates: $2147. ***Parent loans:*** $8000 (100% non-need-based). ***Programs:*** FFEL (Subsidized and Unsubsidized Stafford, PLUS).

WORK-STUDY ***Federal work-study:*** *Total amount:* $5000; 2 jobs averaging $2500. ***State or other work-study/employment:*** *Total amount:* $20,980 (100% need-based). 13 part-time jobs averaging $1614.

APPLYING for FINANCIAL AID ***Required financial aid forms:*** FAFSA, institution's own form. ***Financial aid deadline:*** 6/30 (priority: 2/21). ***Notification date:*** 8/15. Students must reply within 3 weeks of notification.

CONTACT Priscilla Oster, Director of Financial Aid, William Tyndale College, 35700 West Twelve Mile Road, Farmington Hills, MI 48331, 800-483-0707 Ext. 321 or toll-free 800-483-0707. *Fax:* 248-553-5963.

WILLIAM WOODS UNIVERSITY

Fulton, MO

Tuition & fees: $13,050 **Average undergraduate aid package: N/A**

ABOUT THE INSTITUTION Independent religious, coed. Awards: associate, bachelor's, and master's degrees. 39 undergraduate majors. Total enrollment: 1,317. Undergraduates: 905. Freshmen: 130. Federal methodology is used as a basis for awarding need-based institutional aid.

UNDERGRADUATE EXPENSES for 1999–2000 ***Application fee:*** $25. ***Comprehensive fee:*** $18,450 includes full-time tuition ($12,900), mandatory fees ($150), and room and board ($5400). ***College room only:*** $2640. Full-time tuition and fees vary according to program. ***Part-time tuition:*** $225 per credit hour. ***Part-time fees:*** $15 per term part-time. ***Payment plan:*** installment.

GIFT AID (NEED-BASED) ***Scholarships, grants, and awards:*** Federal Pell, FSEOG, state, private, college/university gift aid from institutional funds.

GIFT AID (NON-NEED-BASED) ***Scholarships, grants, and awards by category:*** *Academic Interests/Achievement:* communication, general academic interests/achievements, health fields. *Creative Arts/Performance:* applied art and design, art/fine arts, journalism/publications, performing arts, theater/drama. *Special Achievements/Activities:* community service, general special achievements/activities, leadership, memberships. *Special Characteristics:* children and siblings of alumni, children of current students, children of faculty/staff, local/state students, parents of current students, previous college experience, siblings of current students, spouses of current students. ***Tuition waivers:*** Full or partial for employees or children of employees.

LOANS ***Programs:*** FFEL (Subsidized and Unsubsidized Stafford, PLUS), Perkins, college/university.

WORK-STUDY Federal work-study jobs available.

APPLYING for FINANCIAL AID ***Required financial aid forms:*** FAFSA, institution's own form. ***Financial aid deadline:*** 9/1 (priority: 3/1). ***Notification date:*** Continuous. Students must reply within 2 weeks of notification.

CONTACT Mrs. Liz Bennett, Director for Student Financial Services, William Woods University, 200 West Twelfth Street, Fulton, MO 65251-1098, 573-592-4232 or toll-free 800-995-3159 Ext. 4221. *Fax:* 573-592-1180.

WILMINGTON COLLEGE

New Castle, DE

CONTACT Director of Admissions and Financial Aid, Wilmington College, 320 DuPont Highway, New Castle, DE 19720-6491, 302-328-9401 Ext. 102 or toll-free 877-967-5464.

WILMINGTON COLLEGE

Wilmington, OH

Tuition & fees: $14,666 **Average undergraduate aid package: $12,853**

ABOUT THE INSTITUTION Independent Friends, coed. Awards: bachelor's degrees. 42 undergraduate majors. Total enrollment: 1,153. Undergraduates: 1,153. Freshmen: 335. Federal methodology is used as a basis for awarding need-based institutional aid.

UNDERGRADUATE EXPENSES for 2000–2001 ***Application fee:*** $20. ***Comprehensive fee:*** $19,886 includes full-time tuition ($14,330), mandatory fees ($336), and room and board ($5220). Room and board charges vary according to housing facility. Part-time tuition and fees vary according to course load. ***Payment plan:*** installment.

FRESHMAN FINANCIAL AID (Fall 1999, est.) 291 applied for aid; of those 82% were deemed to have need. 100% of freshmen with need received aid; of those 44% had need fully met. *Average percent of need met:* 91% (excluding resources awarded to replace EFC). *Average financial aid package:* $13,104 (excluding resources awarded to replace EFC). 25% of all full-time freshmen had no need and received non-need-based aid.

UNDERGRADUATE FINANCIAL AID (Fall 1999, est.) 942 applied for aid; of those 86% were deemed to have need. 100% of undergraduates with need received aid; of those 50% had need fully met. *Average percent of need met:* 93% (excluding resources awarded to replace EFC). *Average financial aid package:* $12,853 (excluding resources awarded to replace EFC). 22% of all full-time undergraduates had no need and received non-need-based aid.

GIFT AID (NEED-BASED) ***Total amount:*** $3,526,208 (34% Federal, 16% state, 49% institutional, 1% external sources). ***Receiving aid:*** *Freshmen:* 70% (227); *all full-time undergraduates:* 70% (728). ***Average award:*** Freshmen: $5211; Undergraduates: $4833. ***Scholarships, grants, and awards:*** Federal Pell, FSEOG, state, private, college/university gift aid from institutional funds.

GIFT AID (NON-NEED-BASED) ***Total amount:*** $3,902,255 (1% Federal, 24% state, 68% institutional, 7% external sources). ***Receiving aid:*** *Freshmen:* 66% (213); *Undergraduates:* 74% (772). ***Scholarships, grants, and awards by category:*** *Academic Interests/Achievement:* 2 awards ($6000 total): agriculture, biological sciences, education, general academic interests/achievements, physical sciences. *Creative Arts/Performance:* 76 awards ($472,500 total): theater/drama. *Special Achievements/Activities:* 51 awards ($120,317 total): leadership. *Special Characteristics:* children and siblings of alumni, members of minority groups. ***Tuition waivers:*** Full or partial for employees or children of employees.

LOANS ***Student loans:*** $4,680,670 (72% need-based, 28% non-need-based). 90% of past graduating class borrowed through all loan programs. Average indebtedness per student: $19,800. ***Average need-based loan:*** Freshmen: $4049; Undergraduates: $4105. ***Parent loans:*** $1,306,964 (100% non-need-based). ***Programs:*** FFEL (Subsidized and Unsubsidized Stafford, PLUS), Perkins, college/university.

WORK-STUDY ***Federal work-study:*** *Total amount:* $697,031; jobs available. ***State or other work-study/employment:*** *Total amount:* $98,900 (100% non-need-based). Part-time jobs available.

APPLYING for FINANCIAL AID ***Required financial aid forms:*** FAFSA, institution's own form. ***Financial aid deadline:*** 6/30 (priority: 3/1). ***Notification date:*** Continuous. Students must reply within 2 weeks of notification.

CONTACT Office of Financial Aid, Wilmington College, Pyle Center Box 1184, Wilmington, OH 45177, 937-382-6661 Ext. 249 or toll-free 800-341-9318 Ext. 260. *Fax:* 937-383-8564.

WILSON COLLEGE

Chambersburg, PA

Tuition & fees: $13,588 **Average undergraduate aid package: $12,250**

ABOUT THE INSTITUTION Independent religious, women only. Awards: associate and bachelor's degrees. 21 undergraduate majors. Total enrollment: 819. Undergraduates: 819. Freshmen: 105. Both federal and institutional methodology are used as a basis for awarding need-based institutional aid.

UNDERGRADUATE EXPENSES for 1999–2000 ***Application fee:*** $20. ***Comprehensive fee:*** $19,740 includes full-time tuition ($13,238), mandatory fees ($350), and room and board ($6152). Room and board charges vary according to board plan. ***Part-time tuition:*** $536 per course. ***Payment plans:*** tuition prepayment, installment.

FRESHMAN FINANCIAL AID (Fall 1998) 122 applied for aid; of those 83% were deemed to have need. 100% of freshmen with need received aid; of those 98% had need fully met. *Average percent of need met:* 100% (excluding resources awarded to replace EFC). *Average financial aid package:* $13,425 (excluding resources awarded to replace EFC). 11% of all full-time freshmen had no need and received non-need-based aid.

UNDERGRADUATE FINANCIAL AID (Fall 1998) 445 applied for aid; of those 90% were deemed to have need. 100% of undergraduates with need received aid; of those 98% had need fully met. *Average percent of need met:* 100% (excluding resources awarded to replace EFC). *Average financial aid package:* $12,250 (excluding resources awarded to replace EFC). 5% of all full-time undergraduates had no need and received non-need-based aid.

GIFT AID (NEED-BASED) ***Total amount:*** $2,448,843 (28% Federal, 16% state, 56% institutional). ***Receiving aid:*** *Freshmen:* 60% (101); *all full-time undergraduates:* 48% (401). ***Average award:*** Freshmen: $2994; Undergraduates: $3226. ***Scholarships, grants, and awards:*** Federal Pell, FSEOG, state, private, college/university gift aid from institutional funds.

GIFT AID (NON-NEED-BASED) ***Total amount:*** $362,813 (24% Federal, 1% state, 75% institutional). ***Receiving aid:*** *Freshmen:* 26% (44); *Undergraduates:* 12% (101). ***Scholarships, grants, and awards by category:*** *Academic Interests/Achievement:* 203 awards ($732,860 total): general academic interests/achievements. *Creative Arts/Performance:* music. *Special Achievements/Activities:* 19 awards ($6900 total): community service, religious involvement. *Special Characteristics:* 71 awards ($173,809 total): children and siblings of alumni, local/state students, previous college experience, religious affiliation. ***Tuition waivers:*** Full or partial for children of alumni, employees or children of employees. ***ROTC:*** Army cooperative.

LOANS ***Student loans:*** $1,363,675 (73% need-based, 27% non-need-based). 98% of past graduating class borrowed through all loan programs. Average indebtedness per student: $14,667. ***Average need-based loan:*** Freshmen: $2625; Undergraduates: $3291. ***Parent loans:*** $247,182 (100% non-need-based). ***Programs:*** FFEL (Subsidized and Unsubsidized Stafford, PLUS), Perkins, college/university.

WORK-STUDY ***Federal work-study:*** *Total amount:* $74,272; 72 jobs averaging $1032. ***State or other work-study/employment:*** *Total amount:* $116,595 (100% non-need-based). 111 part-time jobs averaging $1050.

APPLYING for FINANCIAL AID ***Required financial aid forms:*** FAFSA, institution's own form, state aid form. ***Financial aid deadline:*** 4/30. ***Notification date:*** Continuous.

Wilson College (continued)

CONTACT Ms. Crystal A. Filer-Ogden, Director of Financial Aid, Wilson College, 1015 Philadelphia Avenue, Chambersburg, PA 17201-1285, 717-262-2016 or toll-free 800-421-8402. *Fax:* 717-264-1578. *E-mail:* finaid@wilson.edu

WINGATE UNIVERSITY

Wingate, NC

Tuition & fees: $13,050 **Average undergraduate aid package: $11,500**

ABOUT THE INSTITUTION Independent Baptist, coed. Awards: bachelor's and master's degrees. 54 undergraduate majors. Total enrollment: 1,214. Undergraduates: 1,115. Freshmen: 303. Both federal and institutional methodology are used as a basis for awarding need-based institutional aid.

UNDERGRADUATE EXPENSES for 2000–2001 ***Application fee:*** $25. ***Comprehensive fee:*** $18,250 includes full-time tuition ($12,300), mandatory fees ($750), and room and board ($5200). ***Part-time tuition:*** $410 per credit hour. ***Payment plan:*** installment.

FRESHMAN FINANCIAL AID (Fall 1999, est.) 264 applied for aid; of those 84% were deemed to have need. 100% of freshmen with need received aid; of those 19% had need fully met. *Average percent of need met:* 83% (excluding resources awarded to replace EFC). *Average financial aid package:* $10,750 (excluding resources awarded to replace EFC). 3% of all full-time freshmen had no need and received non-need-based aid.

UNDERGRADUATE FINANCIAL AID (Fall 1999, est.) 776 applied for aid; of those 88% were deemed to have need. 100% of undergraduates with need received aid; of those 20% had need fully met. *Average percent of need met:* 83% (excluding resources awarded to replace EFC). *Average financial aid package:* $11,500 (excluding resources awarded to replace EFC). 3% of all full-time undergraduates had no need and received non-need-based aid.

GIFT AID (NEED-BASED) ***Total amount:*** $2,479,864 (28% Federal, 27% state, 45% institutional). ***Receiving aid:*** *Freshmen:* 60% (183); *all full-time undergraduates:* 53% (587). ***Average award:*** Freshmen: $4000; Undergraduates: $5250. ***Scholarships, grants, and awards:*** Federal Pell, FSEOG, state, college/university gift aid from institutional funds.

GIFT AID (NON-NEED-BASED) ***Total amount:*** $3,925,063 (25% state, 71% institutional, 4% external sources). ***Scholarships, grants, and awards by category:*** *Academic Interests/Achievement:* 648 awards ($2,529,959 total): general academic interests/achievements. *Creative Arts/Performance:* 60 awards ($80,200 total): music. *Special Achievements/Activities:* religious involvement. *Special Characteristics:* 65 awards ($145,000 total): children and siblings of alumni, local/state students, relatives of clergy. ***Tuition waivers:*** Full or partial for employees or children of employees. ***ROTC:*** Army cooperative, Air Force cooperative.

LOANS ***Student loans:*** $4,642,134 (37% need-based, 63% non-need-based). 58% of past graduating class borrowed through all loan programs. Average indebtedness per student: $15,250. ***Average need-based loan:*** Freshmen: $2625; Undergraduates: $3500. ***Parent loans:*** $962,213 (100% non-need-based). ***Programs:*** FFEL (Subsidized and Unsubsidized Stafford, PLUS).

WORK-STUDY ***Federal work-study:*** *Total amount:* $140,124; jobs available. ***State or other work-study/employment:*** *Total amount:* $290,000 (100% non-need-based). Part-time jobs available.

ATHLETIC AWARDS *Total amount:* 1,124,908 (100% non-need-based).

APPLYING for FINANCIAL AID ***Required financial aid form:*** FAFSA. ***Financial aid deadline (priority):*** 3/1. ***Notification date:*** Continuous. Students must reply within 2 weeks of notification.

CONTACT Terry Jeffries, Director of Student Financial Planning, Wingate University, Box 3001, Wingate, NC 28174, 704-233-8209 or toll-free 800-755-5550. *E-mail:* jeffries@wingate.edu

WINONA STATE UNIVERSITY

Winona, MN

Tuition & fees (MN res): $3300 **Average undergraduate aid package: $4875**

ABOUT THE INSTITUTION State-supported, coed. Awards: associate, bachelor's, and master's degrees and post-master's certificates. 113 undergraduate majors. Total enrollment: 7,056. Undergraduates: 6,402. Freshmen: 1,479. Federal methodology is used as a basis for awarding need-based institutional aid.

UNDERGRADUATE EXPENSES for 2000–2001 ***Application fee:*** $20. ***Tuition, state resident:*** full-time $2800; part-time $93 per semester hour. ***Tuition, nonresident:*** full-time $6200; part-time $206 per semester hour. ***Required fees:*** full-time $500; $19 per semester hour. Full-time tuition and fees vary according to course load and reciprocity agreements. Part-time tuition and fees vary according to course load and reciprocity agreements. ***College room and board:*** $3500. Room and board charges vary according to board plan, housing facility, and location.

FRESHMAN FINANCIAL AID (Fall 1998) 1097 applied for aid; of those 68% were deemed to have need. 100% of freshmen with need received aid; of those 27% had need fully met. *Average percent of need met:* 60% (excluding resources awarded to replace EFC). *Average financial aid package:* $4275 (excluding resources awarded to replace EFC). 15% of all full-time freshmen had no need and received non-need-based aid.

UNDERGRADUATE FINANCIAL AID (Fall 1998) 3,752 applied for aid; of those 75% were deemed to have need. 100% of undergraduates with need received aid; of those 27% had need fully met. *Average percent of need met:* 65% (excluding resources awarded to replace EFC). *Average financial aid package:* $4875 (excluding resources awarded to replace EFC). 10% of all full-time undergraduates had no need and received non-need-based aid.

GIFT AID (NEED-BASED) ***Total amount:*** $4,569,936 (57% Federal, 39% state, 2% institutional, 2% external sources). ***Receiving aid:*** *Freshmen:* 30% (364); *all full-time undergraduates:* 29% (1,529). ***Average award:*** Freshmen: $1465; Undergraduates: $1476. ***Scholarships, grants, and awards:*** Federal Pell, FSEOG, state, private, college/university gift aid from institutional funds.

GIFT AID (NON-NEED-BASED) ***Total amount:*** $2,463,739 (67% institutional, 33% external sources). ***Receiving aid:*** *Freshmen:* 22% (270); *Undergraduates:* 14% (750). ***Scholarships, grants, and awards by category:*** *Academic Interests/Achievement:* 1,303 awards ($1,086,556 total): general academic interests/achievements. *Creative Arts/Performance:* 24 awards ($7950 total): art/fine arts, debating, music, theater/drama. *Special Characteristics:* 1,050 awards ($1,522,362 total): children and siblings of alumni, children of faculty/staff, local/state students, members of minority groups, out-of-state students. ***Tuition waivers:*** Full or partial for employees or children of employees, senior citizens. ***ROTC:*** Army cooperative.

LOANS ***Student loans:*** $14,015,531 (53% need-based, 47% non-need-based). 60% of past graduating class borrowed through all loan programs. ***Average need-based loan:*** Freshmen: $2310; Undergraduates: $3107. ***Parent loans:*** $479,634 (100% non-need-based). ***Programs:*** FFEL (Subsidized and Unsubsidized Stafford, PLUS), Perkins, state, college/university.

WORK-STUDY ***Federal work-study:*** *Total amount:* $295,825; 270 jobs averaging $1095. ***State or other work-study/employment:*** *Total amount:* $2,114,942 (18% need-based, 82% non-need-based). Part-time jobs available.

ATHLETIC AWARDS *Total amount:* 162,925 (100% non-need-based).

APPLYING for FINANCIAL AID ***Required financial aid form:*** FAFSA. ***Financial aid deadline:*** Continuous. ***Notification date:*** 5/1. Students must reply within 3 weeks of notification.

CONTACT Mr. Greg Peterson, Director of Financial Aid, Winona State University, PO Box 5838, Winona, MN 55987-5838, 507-457-5090 or toll-free 800-DIAL WSU.

WINSTON-SALEM STATE UNIVERSITY

Winston-Salem, NC

Tuition & fees (NC res): $1704 **Average undergraduate aid package: $4580**

ABOUT THE INSTITUTION State-supported, coed. Awards: bachelor's degrees. 32 undergraduate majors. Total enrollment: 2,679. Undergraduates: 2,679. Freshmen: 489. Federal methodology is used as a basis for awarding need-based institutional aid.

UNDERGRADUATE EXPENSES for 1999–2000 ***Application fee:*** $20. ***Tuition, state resident:*** full-time $806; part-time $202 per term. ***Tuition, nonresident:*** full-time $7224; part-time $1806 per term. ***Required fees:*** full-time $898; $235 per term part-time. Full-time tuition and fees vary according to course load. Part-time tuition and fees vary according to course load. ***College room and board:*** $3503; ***room only:*** $1893. Room and board charges vary according to board plan and housing facility. ***Payment plan:*** installment.

FRESHMAN FINANCIAL AID (Fall 1999) 418 applied for aid; of those 85% were deemed to have need. 99% of freshmen with need received aid; of those 10% had need fully met. *Average percent of need met:* 82% (excluding resources awarded to replace EFC). *Average financial aid package:* $3125 (excluding resources awarded to replace EFC). 9% of all full-time freshmen had no need and received non-need-based aid.

UNDERGRADUATE FINANCIAL AID (Fall 1999) 1,795 applied for aid; of those 87% were deemed to have need. 98% of undergraduates with need received aid; of those 14% had need fully met. *Average percent of need met:* 80% (excluding resources awarded to replace EFC). *Average financial aid package:* $4580 (excluding resources awarded to replace EFC). 7% of all full-time undergraduates had no need and received non-need-based aid.

GIFT AID (NEED-BASED) ***Total amount:*** $4,049,537 (88% Federal, 12% state). ***Receiving aid:*** *Freshmen:* 58% (267); *all full-time undergraduates:* 54% (1,183). ***Average award:*** Freshmen: $2799; Undergraduates: $3064. ***Scholarships, grants, and awards:*** Federal Pell, FSEOG, state, private, college/university gift aid from institutional funds, United Negro College Fund.

GIFT AID (NON-NEED-BASED) ***Total amount:*** $854,454 (39% state, 21% institutional, 40% external sources). ***Receiving aid:*** *Freshmen:* 7% (30); *Undergraduates:* 5% (100). ***Scholarships, grants, and awards by category:*** *Academic Interests/Achievement:* 117 awards ($298,050 total): business, computer science, education, general academic interests/achievements, health fields, mathematics. *Creative Arts/Performance:* 77 awards ($84,700 total): music. ***Tuition waivers:*** Full or partial for employees or children of employees, senior citizens. ***ROTC:*** Army.

LOANS ***Student loans:*** $5,675,812 (61% need-based, 39% non-need-based). Average indebtedness per student: $10,900. ***Average need-based loan:*** Freshmen: $500; Undergraduates: $900. ***Parent loans:*** $334,452 (100% non-need-based). ***Programs:*** FFEL (Subsidized and Unsubsidized Stafford, PLUS), Perkins, state, college/university.

WORK-STUDY ***Federal work-study:*** *Total amount:* $598,849; 466 jobs averaging $1285. ***State or other work-study/employment:*** *Total amount:* $14,630 (100% non-need-based). 12 part-time jobs averaging $2500.

ATHLETIC AWARDS *Total amount:* 255,028 (100% non-need-based).

APPLYING for FINANCIAL AID ***Required financial aid forms:*** FAFSA, institution's own form. ***Financial aid deadline:*** 4/1 (priority: 3/1). ***Notification date:*** 5/15. Students must reply within 2 weeks of notification.

CONTACT Mrs. Shirley P. Carter, Assistant Director of Financial Aid Office, Winston-Salem State University, 601 Martin Luther King, Jr. Drive, Winston-Salem, NC 27110-0003, 336-750-3280 or toll-free 800-257-4052. *Fax:* 336-750-2079.

WINTHROP UNIVERSITY

Rock Hill, SC

Tuition & fees (SC res): $4146 **Average undergraduate aid package: $5641**

ABOUT THE INSTITUTION State-supported, coed. Awards: bachelor's and master's degrees. 32 undergraduate majors. Total enrollment: 5,840. Undergraduates: 4,611. Freshmen: 971. Federal methodology is used as a basis for awarding need-based institutional aid.

UNDERGRADUATE EXPENSES for 1999–2000 ***Application fee:*** $35. ***Tuition, state resident:*** full-time $4126; part-time $172 per semester hour. ***Tuition, nonresident:*** full-time $7434; part-time $310 per semester hour. ***Required fees:*** full-time $20; $10 per term part-time. ***College room and board:*** $4022. Room and board charges vary according to board plan and housing facility. ***Payment plan:*** installment.

FRESHMAN FINANCIAL AID (Fall 1999, est.) 790 applied for aid; of those 73% were deemed to have need. 95% of freshmen with need received aid; of those 36% had need fully met. *Average percent of need met:* 66% (excluding resources awarded to replace EFC). *Average financial aid package:* $5177 (excluding resources awarded to replace EFC). 21% of all full-time freshmen had no need and received non-need-based aid.

UNDERGRADUATE FINANCIAL AID (Fall 1999, est.) 2,953 applied for aid; of those 75% were deemed to have need. 95% of undergraduates with need received aid; of those 33% had need fully met. *Average percent of need met:* 72% (excluding resources awarded to replace EFC). *Average financial aid package:* $5641 (excluding resources awarded to replace EFC). 16% of all full-time undergraduates had no need and received non-need-based aid.

GIFT AID (NEED-BASED) ***Total amount:*** $4,438,250 (56% Federal, 23% state, 16% institutional, 5% external sources). ***Receiving aid:*** *Freshmen:* 51% (488); *all full-time undergraduates:* 39% (1,518). ***Average award:*** Freshmen: $2863; Undergraduates: $2857. ***Scholarships, grants, and awards:*** Federal Pell, FSEOG, state, private, college/university gift aid from institutional funds.

GIFT AID (NON-NEED-BASED) ***Total amount:*** $4,496,815 (38% state, 48% institutional, 14% external sources). ***Receiving aid:*** *Freshmen:* 22% (210); *Undergraduates:* 14% (531). ***Scholarships, grants, and awards by category:*** *Academic Interests/Achievement:* 760 awards ($1,745,958 total): general academic interests/achievements. *Creative Arts/Performance:* 95 awards ($46,975 total): art/fine arts, dance, music, performing arts. *Special Characteristics:* 370 awards ($1,033,316 total): adult students, out-of-state students. ***Tuition waivers:*** Full or partial for employees or children of employees, senior citizens.

LOANS ***Student loans:*** $11,432,016 (61% need-based, 39% non-need-based). 58% of past graduating class borrowed through all loan programs. Average indebtedness per student: $14,751. ***Average need-based loan:*** Freshmen: $2500; Undergraduates: $3400. ***Parent loans:*** $1,059,611 (100% non-need-based). ***Programs:*** Federal Direct (Subsidized and Unsubsidized Stafford), FFEL (PLUS), Perkins, state.

WORK-STUDY ***Federal work-study:*** *Total amount:* $200,000; 200 jobs averaging $1000. ***State or other work-study/employment:*** *Total amount:* $1,358,657 (100% non-need-based). Part-time jobs available.

ATHLETIC AWARDS *Total amount:* 506,818 (40% need-based, 60% non-need-based).

APPLYING for FINANCIAL AID ***Required financial aid form:*** FAFSA. ***Financial aid deadline (priority):*** 3/1. ***Notification date:*** Continuous beginning 4/1. Students must reply within 2 weeks of notification.

CONTACT Ms. Geneva Drakeford, Assistant Director, Financial Resource Center, Winthrop University, 119 Tillman Hall, Rock Hill, SC 29733, 803-323-2189 or toll-free 800-763-0230. *Fax:* 803-323-2557. *E-mail:* wufrc@winthrop.edu

WISCONSIN LUTHERAN COLLEGE

Milwaukee, WI

Tuition & fees: $13,106 **Average undergraduate aid package: $12,046**

ABOUT THE INSTITUTION Independent religious, coed. Awards: bachelor's degrees. 15 undergraduate majors. Total enrollment: 551. Undergraduates: 551. Freshmen: 161. Federal methodology is used as a basis for awarding need-based institutional aid.

UNDERGRADUATE EXPENSES for 2000–2001 ***Application fee:*** $20. ***Comprehensive fee:*** $17,856 includes full-time tuition ($12,980), manda-

Wisconsin Lutheran College (continued)

tory fees ($126), and room and board ($4750). ***College room only:*** $2300. Room and board charges vary according to board plan and housing facility. ***Part-time tuition:*** $400 per credit. ***Part-time fees:*** $30 per term part-time. ***Payment plan:*** installment.

FRESHMAN FINANCIAL AID (Fall 1999) 161 applied for aid; of those 76% were deemed to have need. 100% of freshmen with need received aid; of those 28% had need fully met. *Average percent of need met:* 88% (excluding resources awarded to replace EFC). *Average financial aid package:* $11,899 (excluding resources awarded to replace EFC). 24% of all full-time freshmen had no need and received non-need-based aid.

UNDERGRADUATE FINANCIAL AID (Fall 1999) 515 applied for aid; of those 76% were deemed to have need. 100% of undergraduates with need received aid; of those 46% had need fully met. *Average percent of need met:* 92% (excluding resources awarded to replace EFC). *Average financial aid package:* $12,046 (excluding resources awarded to replace EFC). 23% of all full-time undergraduates had no need and received non-need-based aid.

GIFT AID (NEED-BASED) ***Total amount:*** $3,157,729 (7% Federal, 12% state, 78% institutional, 3% external sources). ***Receiving aid:*** *Freshmen:* 75% (121); *all full-time undergraduates:* 75% (390). ***Average award:*** Freshmen: $8753; Undergraduates: $8081. ***Scholarships, grants, and awards:*** Federal Pell, FSEOG, state, private, college/university gift aid from institutional funds.

GIFT AID (NON-NEED-BASED) ***Total amount:*** $637,474 (1% state, 96% institutional, 3% external sources). ***Scholarships, grants, and awards by category:*** *Academic Interests/Achievement:* 469 awards ($2,287,827 total): biological sciences, business, communication, education, general academic interests/achievements, international studies, mathematics. *Creative Arts/Performance:* 32 awards ($32,000 total): art/fine arts, music, theater/drama. *Special Achievements/Activities:* 9 awards ($23,000 total): general special achievements/activities, leadership. *Special Characteristics:* 21 awards ($191,450 total): children of faculty/staff, international students. ***Tuition waivers:*** Full or partial for employees or children of employees.

LOANS ***Student loans:*** $1,750,708 (91% need-based, 9% non-need-based). 81% of past graduating class borrowed through all loan programs. Average indebtedness per student: $13,830. ***Average need-based loan:*** Freshmen: $2463; Undergraduates: $3468. ***Parent loans:*** $212,615 (93% need-based, 7% non-need-based). ***Programs:*** FFEL (Subsidized and Unsubsidized Stafford, PLUS), state.

WORK-STUDY ***Federal work-study:*** *Total amount:* $340,690; 209 jobs averaging $1600. ***State or other work-study/employment:*** *Total amount:* $75,200 (78% need-based, 22% non-need-based). 18 part-time jobs averaging $4178.

APPLYING for FINANCIAL AID ***Required financial aid forms:*** FAFSA, institution's own form, business/farm supplement. ***Financial aid deadline (priority):*** 3/1. ***Notification date:*** Continuous beginning 3/15. Students must reply within 2 weeks of notification.

CONTACT Mrs. Linda Loeffel, Director of Financial Aid, Wisconsin Lutheran College, 8800 West Bluemound Road, Milwaukee, WI 53226-4699, 414-443-8842 or toll-free 888-WIS LUTH. *Fax:* 414-443-8514. *E-mail:* lloeffel@wlc.edu

WITTENBERG UNIVERSITY

Springfield, OH

Tuition & fees: $20,906 **Average undergraduate aid package: $19,361**

ABOUT THE INSTITUTION Independent religious, coed. Awards: bachelor's degrees. 78 undergraduate majors. Total enrollment: 1,940. Undergraduates: 1,940. Freshmen: 616. Federal methodology is used as a basis for awarding need-based institutional aid.

UNDERGRADUATE EXPENSES for 1999–2000 ***Application fee:*** $40. ***One-time required fee:*** $112. ***Comprehensive fee:*** $26,112 includes full-time tuition ($19,716), mandatory fees ($1190), and room and board ($5206). ***College room only:*** $2588. Room and board charges vary according to board plan and housing facility. ***Part-time tuition:*** $657 per credit. ***Payment plans:*** tuition prepayment, installment, deferred payment.

FRESHMAN FINANCIAL AID (Fall 1999) 520 applied for aid; of those 88% were deemed to have need. 100% of freshmen with need received aid; of those 37% had need fully met. *Average percent of need met:* 98% (excluding resources awarded to replace EFC). *Average financial aid package:* $19,863 (excluding resources awarded to replace EFC). 24% of all full-time freshmen had no need and received non-need-based aid.

UNDERGRADUATE FINANCIAL AID (Fall 1999) 1,539 applied for aid; of those 91% were deemed to have need. 100% of undergraduates with need received aid; of those 37% had need fully met. *Average percent of need met:* 96% (excluding resources awarded to replace EFC). *Average financial aid package:* $19,361 (excluding resources awarded to replace EFC). 27% of all full-time undergraduates had no need and received non-need-based aid.

GIFT AID (NEED-BASED) ***Total amount:*** $19,897,473 (6% Federal, 8% state, 83% institutional, 3% external sources). ***Receiving aid:*** *Freshmen:* 63% (392); *all full-time undergraduates:* 57% (1,139). ***Average award:*** Freshmen: $17,952; Undergraduates: $16,264. ***Scholarships, grants, and awards:*** Federal Pell, FSEOG, state, private, college/university gift aid from institutional funds.

GIFT AID (NON-NEED-BASED) ***Total amount:*** $4,184,436 (8% state, 90% institutional, 2% external sources). ***Receiving aid:*** *Freshmen:* 74% (458); *Undergraduates:* 69% (1,379). ***Scholarships, grants, and awards by category:*** *Academic Interests/Achievement:* general academic interests/achievements. *Creative Arts/Performance:* art/fine arts, dance, music, theater/drama. *Special Achievements/Activities:* community service, general special achievements/activities, leadership. *Special Characteristics:* adult students, children and siblings of alumni, children of faculty/staff, ethnic background, international students, local/state students, members of minority groups, relatives of clergy, religious affiliation. ***Tuition waivers:*** Full or partial for children of alumni, employees or children of employees, adult students, senior citizens. ***ROTC:*** Army cooperative, Air Force cooperative.

LOANS ***Student loans:*** $7,340,168 (93% need-based, 7% non-need-based). ***Average need-based loan:*** Freshmen: $4375; Undergraduates: $4336. ***Parent loans:*** $2,073,209 (84% need-based, 16% non-need-based). ***Programs:*** FFEL (Subsidized and Unsubsidized Stafford, PLUS), Perkins, college/university.

WORK-STUDY ***Federal work-study:*** *Total amount:* $473,418; jobs available. ***State or other work-study/employment:*** *Total amount:* $1,444,124 (75% need-based, 25% non-need-based). Part-time jobs available.

APPLYING for FINANCIAL AID ***Required financial aid form:*** FAFSA. ***Financial aid deadline:*** 3/15 (priority: 2/15). ***Notification date:*** Continuous. Students must reply by 5/1 or within 2 weeks of notification.

CONTACT Mr. J. Randy Green, Director of Financial Aid, Wittenberg University, PO Box 720, Springfield, OH 45501-0720, 937-327-6406 or toll-free 800-677-7558 Ext. 6314. *Fax:* 937-327-6379. *E-mail:* jgreen@wittenberg.edu

WOFFORD COLLEGE

Spartanburg, SC

Tuition & fees: $16,975 **Average undergraduate aid package: $14,278**

ABOUT THE INSTITUTION Independent religious, coed. Awards: bachelor's degrees. 27 undergraduate majors. Total enrollment: 1,100. Undergraduates: 1,100. Freshmen: 307. Both federal and institutional methodology are used as a basis for awarding need-based institutional aid.

UNDERGRADUATE EXPENSES for 1999–2000 ***Application fee:*** $35. ***Comprehensive fee:*** $21,990 includes full-time tuition ($16,410), mandatory fees ($565), and room and board ($5015). ***Part-time tuition:*** $600 per semester hour. ***Payment plan:*** installment.

FRESHMAN FINANCIAL AID (Fall 1998) *Average percent of need met:* 90% (excluding resources awarded to replace EFC). *Average financial aid package:* $13,898 (excluding resources awarded to replace EFC). 21% of all full-time freshmen had no need and received non-need-based aid.

UNDERGRADUATE FINANCIAL AID (Fall 1998) *Average percent of need met:* 89% (excluding resources awarded to replace EFC). *Average financial*

aid package: $14,278 (excluding resources awarded to replace EFC). 12% of all full-time undergraduates had no need and received non-need-based aid.

GIFT AID (NEED-BASED) ***Total amount:*** $5,718,623 (7% Federal, 34% state, 51% institutional, 8% external sources). ***Scholarships, grants, and awards:*** Federal Pell, FSEOG, state, private, college/university gift aid from institutional funds.

GIFT AID (NON-NEED-BASED) ***Total amount:*** $1,776,219 (20% state, 69% institutional, 11% external sources). ***Scholarships, grants, and awards by category:*** *Academic Interests/Achievement:* general academic interests/achievements. *Creative Arts/Performance:* music. *Special Achievements/Activities:* cheerleading/drum major, community service, general special achievements/activities, leadership, religious involvement. *Special Characteristics:* children of faculty/staff, general special characteristics, relatives of clergy. ***Tuition waivers:*** Full or partial for employees or children of employees. ***ROTC:*** Army.

LOANS ***Student loans:*** $2,003,232 (80% need-based, 20% non-need-based). ***Parent loans:*** $883,468 (51% need-based, 49% non-need-based). ***Programs:*** FFEL (Subsidized and Unsubsidized Stafford, PLUS).

WORK-STUDY ***Federal work-study:*** *Total amount:* $95,350; jobs available. ***State or other work-study/employment:*** *Total amount:* $16,500 (36% need-based, 64% non-need-based). Part-time jobs available.

ATHLETIC AWARDS *Total amount:* 1,946,922 (57% need-based, 43% non-need-based).

APPLYING for FINANCIAL AID ***Required financial aid forms:*** FAFSA, institution's own form, CSS Financial Aid PROFILE. ***Financial aid deadline (priority):*** 3/15. ***Notification date:*** Continuous beginning 3/25. Students must reply by 5/1.

CONTACT Donna D. Hawkins, Director of Financial Aid, Wofford College, Campus PO Box 171, 429 North Church Street, Spartanburg, SC 29303-3663, 864-597-4160. *Fax:* 864-597-4149. *E-mail:* hawkinsdd@wofford.edu

WOODBURY UNIVERSITY

Burbank, CA

Tuition & fees: $16,710 **Average undergraduate aid package: $14,150**

ABOUT THE INSTITUTION Independent, coed. Awards: bachelor's and master's degrees. 17 undergraduate majors. Total enrollment: 1,208. Undergraduates: 1,035. Freshmen: 136. Federal methodology is used as a basis for awarding need-based institutional aid.

UNDERGRADUATE EXPENSES for 1999–2000 ***Application fee:*** $30. ***One-time required fee:*** $950. ***Comprehensive fee:*** $22,700 includes full-time tuition ($16,590), mandatory fees ($120), and room and board ($5990). ***College room only:*** $3390. Full-time tuition and fees vary according to program. Room and board charges vary according to board plan and housing facility. ***Part-time tuition:*** $540 per unit. ***Part-time fees:*** $135 per term part-time. Part-time tuition and fees vary according to class time and program. ***Payment plans:*** installment, deferred payment.

FRESHMAN FINANCIAL AID (Fall 1998) 88 applied for aid; of those 100% were deemed to have need. 100% of freshmen with need received aid; of those 19% had need fully met. *Average percent of need met:* 65% (excluding resources awarded to replace EFC). *Average financial aid package:* $14,150 (excluding resources awarded to replace EFC). 5% of all full-time freshmen had no need and received non-need-based aid.

UNDERGRADUATE FINANCIAL AID (Fall 1998) 908 applied for aid; of those 83% were deemed to have need. 95% of undergraduates with need received aid; of those 8% had need fully met. *Average percent of need met:* 65% (excluding resources awarded to replace EFC). *Average financial aid package:* $14,150 (excluding resources awarded to replace EFC). 9% of all full-time undergraduates had no need and received non-need-based aid.

GIFT AID (NEED-BASED) ***Total amount:*** $4,597,587 (22% Federal, 28% state, 50% institutional). ***Receiving aid:*** *Freshmen:* 75% (75); *all full-time undergraduates:* 47% (507). ***Average award:*** Freshmen: $6000; Undergraduates: $6000. ***Scholarships, grants, and awards:*** Federal Pell, FSEOG, state, private, college/university gift aid from institutional funds.

GIFT AID (NON-NEED-BASED) ***Total amount:*** $32,984 (3% institutional, 97% external sources). ***Receiving aid:*** *Freshmen:* 25% (25); *Undergraduates:* 15% (160). ***Scholarships, grants, and awards by category:*** *Academic Interests/Achievement:* 6 awards ($39,000 total): general academic interests/achievements. ***Tuition waivers:*** Full or partial for employees or children of employees.

LOANS ***Student loans:*** $5,343,835 (95% need-based, 5% non-need-based). ***Average need-based loan:*** Freshmen: $1000; Undergraduates: $1500. ***Parent loans:*** $1,149,964 (100% non-need-based). ***Programs:*** FFEL (Subsidized and Unsubsidized Stafford, PLUS), Perkins, alternative loans.

WORK-STUDY ***Federal work-study:*** *Total amount:* $103,418; 90 jobs averaging $1200.

APPLYING for FINANCIAL AID ***Required financial aid forms:*** FAFSA, institution's own form. ***Financial aid deadline (priority):*** 3/2. ***Notification date:*** Continuous beginning 4/1. Students must reply within 2 weeks of notification.

CONTACT Celeastia Williams, Director, Financial Aid, Woodbury University, 7500 Glenoaks Boulevard, Burbank, CA 91510-7846, 818-767-0888 Ext. 273 or toll-free 800-784-WOOD. *Fax:* 818-767-4816. *E-mail:* cwilliams@vaxb.woodbury.edu

WORCESTER POLYTECHNIC INSTITUTE

Worcester, MA

Tuition & fees: $22,108 **Average undergraduate aid package: $17,122**

ABOUT THE INSTITUTION Independent, coed. Awards: bachelor's, master's, and doctoral degrees. 70 undergraduate majors. Total enrollment: 3,875. Undergraduates: 2,784. Freshmen: 664. Both federal and institutional methodology are used as a basis for awarding need-based institutional aid.

UNDERGRADUATE EXPENSES for 1999–2000 ***Application fee:*** $60. ***One-time required fee:*** $180. ***Comprehensive fee:*** $29,020 includes full-time tuition ($21,770), mandatory fees ($338), and room and board ($6912). ***College room only:*** $3600. Room and board charges vary according to board plan and housing facility. ***Part-time tuition:*** $1,814 per course.

FRESHMAN FINANCIAL AID (Fall 1999, est.) 601 applied for aid; of those 87% were deemed to have need. 99% of freshmen with need received aid; of those 50% had need fully met. *Average percent of need met:* 85% (excluding resources awarded to replace EFC). *Average financial aid package:* $15,944 (excluding resources awarded to replace EFC). 9% of all full-time freshmen had no need and received non-need-based aid.

UNDERGRADUATE FINANCIAL AID (Fall 1999, est.) 2,102 applied for aid; of those 92% were deemed to have need. 100% of undergraduates with need received aid; of those 60% had need fully met. *Average percent of need met:* 90% (excluding resources awarded to replace EFC). *Average financial aid package:* $17,122 (excluding resources awarded to replace EFC). 10% of all full-time undergraduates had no need and received non-need-based aid.

GIFT AID (NEED-BASED) ***Total amount:*** $22,664,418 (8% Federal, 4% state, 88% institutional). ***Receiving aid:*** *Freshmen:* 77% (510); *all full-time undergraduates:* 70% (1,872). ***Scholarships, grants, and awards:*** Federal Pell, FSEOG, state, private, college/university gift aid from institutional funds.

GIFT AID (NON-NEED-BASED) ***Total amount:*** $3,446,804 (32% institutional, 68% external sources). ***Receiving aid:*** *Freshmen:* 8% (50); *Undergraduates:* 5% (138). ***Scholarships, grants, and awards by category:*** *Academic Interests/Achievement:* general academic interests/achievements. *Special Characteristics:* 24 awards ($96,924 total): children of workers in trades. ***Tuition waivers:*** Full or partial for employees or children of employees. ***ROTC:*** Army, Naval cooperative, Air Force.

LOANS ***Student loans:*** $12,270,754 (100% need-based). 90% of past graduating class borrowed through all loan programs. Average indebtedness per student: $18,596. ***Parent loans:*** $4,600,000 (100% non-need-based). ***Programs:*** FFEL (Subsidized and Unsubsidized Stafford, PLUS), Perkins, state, college/university.

Worcester Polytechnic Institute (continued)

WORK-STUDY ***Federal work-study:*** *Total amount:* $450,000; 778 jobs averaging $1188. ***State or other work-study/employment:*** *Total amount:* $544,000 (100% need-based). Part-time jobs available.

APPLYING for FINANCIAL AID ***Required financial aid forms:*** FAFSA, CSS Financial Aid PROFILE, noncustodial (divorced/separated) parent's statement. ***Financial aid deadline (priority):*** 3/1. ***Notification date:*** 4/1. Students must reply by 5/1.

CONTACT Office of Financial Aid, Worcester Polytechnic Institute, 100 Institute Road, Worcester, MA 01609-2280, 508-831-5469.

WORCESTER STATE COLLEGE

Worcester, MA

Tuition & fees (MA res): $2458 **Average undergraduate aid package: N/A**

ABOUT THE INSTITUTION State-supported, coed. Awards: bachelor's and master's degrees. 31 undergraduate majors. Total enrollment: 5,212. Undergraduates: 4,465. Freshmen: 461. Federal methodology is used as a basis for awarding need-based institutional aid.

UNDERGRADUATE EXPENSES for 1999–2000 ***Application fee:*** $10; $40 for nonresidents. ***Tuition, state resident:*** full-time $1090; part-time $45 per credit. ***Tuition, nonresident:*** full-time $7050; part-time $294 per credit. ***Required fees:*** full-time $1368; $57 per credit. Full-time tuition and fees vary according to reciprocity agreements. Part-time tuition and fees vary according to reciprocity agreements. ***College room and board:*** $4369; ***room only:*** $2985. Room and board charges vary according to board plan and housing facility. ***Payment plan:*** deferred payment.

GIFT AID (NEED-BASED) ***Scholarships, grants, and awards:*** Federal Pell, FSEOG, state, private, college/university gift aid from institutional funds.

GIFT AID (NON-NEED-BASED) ***Scholarships, grants, and awards by category:*** *Academic Interests/Achievement:* biological sciences, business, education, English, foreign languages, health fields. *Creative Arts/Performance:* art/fine arts. *Special Achievements/Activities:* community service, general special achievements/activities. *Special Characteristics:* children and siblings of alumni, children of faculty/staff, children with a deceased or disabled parent, general special characteristics, handicapped students, local/state students, veterans. ***Tuition waivers:*** Full or partial for employees or children of employees, senior citizens. ***ROTC:*** Army cooperative, Naval cooperative, Air Force cooperative.

LOANS ***Programs:*** FFEL (Subsidized and Unsubsidized Stafford, PLUS), Perkins, Massachusetts No-Interest Loans (NIL).

WORK-STUDY Federal work-study jobs available. ***State or other work-study/employment:*** Part-time jobs available.

APPLYING for FINANCIAL AID ***Required financial aid forms:*** FAFSA, institution's own form. ***Financial aid deadline (priority):*** 3/1. ***Notification date:*** Continuous. Students must reply within 2 weeks of notification.

CONTACT Ms. Carole Lapierre-Denning, Director of Financial Aid, Worcester State College, 486 Chandler Street, Worcester, MA 01602, 508-929-8110. *Fax:* 508-929-8194. *E-mail:* clapierredenning@worcester.edu

WRIGHT STATE UNIVERSITY

Dayton, OH

CONTACT Mr. David R. Darr, Director of Financial Aid, Wright State University, Colonel Glenn Highway, Dayton, OH 45435, 937-873-5721 or toll-free 800-247-1770.

XAVIER UNIVERSITY

Cincinnati, OH

Tuition & fees: $15,880 **Average undergraduate aid package: $11,619**

ABOUT THE INSTITUTION Independent Roman Catholic, coed. Awards: associate, bachelor's, master's, and doctoral degrees and post-bachelor's and post-master's certificates. 49 undergraduate majors. Total enrollment: 6,466. Undergraduates: 3,958. Freshmen: 774. Federal methodology is used as a basis for awarding need-based institutional aid.

UNDERGRADUATE EXPENSES for 2000–2001 ***Application fee:*** $25. ***Comprehensive fee:*** $22,560 includes full-time tuition ($15,680), mandatory fees ($200), and room and board ($6680). ***College room only:*** $3540. Full-time tuition and fees vary according to program. Room and board charges vary according to board plan and housing facility. ***Part-time tuition:*** $365 per credit. Part-time tuition and fees vary according to class time and course load. ***Payment plans:*** installment, deferred payment.

FRESHMAN FINANCIAL AID (Fall 1999, est.) 566 applied for aid; of those 75% were deemed to have need. 100% of freshmen with need received aid; of those 30% had need fully met. *Average percent of need met:* 79% (excluding resources awarded to replace EFC). *Average financial aid package:* $11,447 (excluding resources awarded to replace EFC). 34% of all full-time freshmen had no need and received non-need-based aid.

UNDERGRADUATE FINANCIAL AID (Fall 1999, est.) 1,920 applied for aid; of those 81% were deemed to have need. 100% of undergraduates with need received aid; of those 35% had need fully met. *Average percent of need met:* 81% (excluding resources awarded to replace EFC). *Average financial aid package:* $11,619 (excluding resources awarded to replace EFC). 32% of all full-time undergraduates had no need and received non-need-based aid.

GIFT AID (NEED-BASED) ***Total amount:*** $12,605,650 (10% Federal, 12% state, 68% institutional, 10% external sources). ***Receiving aid:*** *Freshmen:* 55% (422); *all full-time undergraduates:* 45% (1,543). ***Average award:*** Freshmen: $7813; Undergraduates: $7656. ***Scholarships, grants, and awards:*** Federal Pell, FSEOG, state, private, college/university gift aid from institutional funds.

GIFT AID (NON-NEED-BASED) ***Total amount:*** $6,602,930 (13% state, 71% institutional, 16% external sources). ***Receiving aid:*** *Freshmen:* 10% (79); *Undergraduates:* 8% (277). ***Scholarships, grants, and awards by category:*** *Academic Interests/Achievement:* business, education, foreign languages, general academic interests/achievements, mathematics, military science, physical sciences, social sciences. *Creative Arts/Performance:* art/fine arts, music, performing arts, theater/drama. *Special Achievements/Activities:* community service, leadership. *Special Characteristics:* general special characteristics, international students, members of minority groups, siblings of current students. ***Tuition waivers:*** Full or partial for minority students, children of alumni, employees or children of employees, senior citizens. ***ROTC:*** Army, Air Force cooperative.

LOANS ***Student loans:*** $14,402,463 (81% need-based, 19% non-need-based). 63% of past graduating class borrowed through all loan programs. Average indebtedness per student: $10,988. ***Average need-based loan:*** Freshmen: $2815; Undergraduates: $3466. ***Parent loans:*** $2,195,490 (31% need-based, 69% non-need-based). ***Programs:*** FFEL (Subsidized and Unsubsidized Stafford, PLUS), Perkins, college/university.

WORK-STUDY ***Federal work-study:*** *Total amount:* $535,800; 310 jobs averaging $1730. ***State or other work-study/employment:*** *Total amount:* $250,984 (16% need-based, 84% non-need-based). 167 part-time jobs averaging $1500.

ATHLETIC AWARDS *Total amount:* 1,833,504 (28% need-based, 72% non-need-based).

APPLYING for FINANCIAL AID ***Required financial aid forms:*** FAFSA, financial aid transcript (for transfers). ***Financial aid deadline (priority):*** 2/15. ***Notification date:*** Continuous beginning 3/1. Students must reply by 5/1.

CONTACT Ms. Marie Toon, Associate Director of Financial Aid, Xavier University, 3800 Victory Parkway, Cincinnati, OH 45207-5411, 513-745-3142 or toll-free 800-344-4698. *Fax:* 513-745-2806. *E-mail:* toon@admin.xu.edu

XAVIER UNIVERSITY OF LOUISIANA

New Orleans, LA

Tuition & fees: $9700 **Average undergraduate aid package: N/A**

ABOUT THE INSTITUTION Independent Roman Catholic, coed. Awards: bachelor's, master's, and first professional degrees. 47 undergraduate majors. Total enrollment: 3,820. Undergraduates: 3,278. Freshmen: 898. Federal methodology is used as a basis for awarding need-based institutional aid.

UNDERGRADUATE EXPENSES for 1999–2000 ***Application fee:*** $25. ***Comprehensive fee:*** $14,800 includes full-time tuition ($8900), mandatory fees ($800), and room and board ($5100). Full-time tuition and fees vary according to program. Room and board charges vary according to housing facility. ***Part-time tuition:*** $375 per semester hour. ***Part-time fees:*** $75 per term part-time. Part-time tuition and fees vary according to course load and program. ***Payment plan:*** installment.

GIFT AID (NEED-BASED) ***Scholarships, grants, and awards:*** Federal Pell, FSEOG, state, private, college/university gift aid from institutional funds, United Negro College Fund.

GIFT AID (NON-NEED-BASED) ***Scholarships, grants, and awards by category:*** *Academic Interests/Achievement:* biological sciences, business, computer science, education, engineering/technologies, foreign languages, general academic interests/achievements, humanities, mathematics, physical sciences, premedicine, social sciences. *Creative Arts/Performance:* art/fine arts, music, performing arts. *Special Achievements/Activities:* religious involvement. *Special Characteristics:* children of faculty/staff. ***Tuition waivers:*** Full or partial for employees or children of employees, senior citizens. ***ROTC:*** Naval cooperative, Air Force cooperative.

LOANS ***Programs:*** Federal Direct (Subsidized and Unsubsidized Stafford, PLUS), FFEL (Subsidized and Unsubsidized Stafford, PLUS), Perkins.

WORK-STUDY Federal work-study jobs available.

APPLYING for FINANCIAL AID ***Required financial aid form:*** FAFSA. ***Financial aid deadline:*** Continuous. ***Notification date:*** Continuous beginning 4/1. Students must reply within 2 weeks of notification.

CONTACT Mrs. Mildred Higgins, Director of Financial Aid, Xavier University of Louisiana, 7325 Palmetto Street, Box 40A, New Orleans, LA 70125-1098, 504-486-7411.

YALE UNIVERSITY

New Haven, CT

Tuition & fees: $24,500 **Average undergraduate aid package: N/A**

ABOUT THE INSTITUTION Independent, coed. Awards: bachelor's, master's, doctoral, and first professional degrees. 56 undergraduate majors. Total enrollment: 11,032. Undergraduates: 5,440. Freshmen: 1,296. Both federal and institutional methodology are used as a basis for awarding need-based institutional aid.

UNDERGRADUATE EXPENSES for 1999–2000 ***Application fee:*** $65. ***Comprehensive fee:*** $31,940 includes full-time tuition ($24,500) and room and board ($7440). ***College room only:*** $4070. ***Payment plan:*** installment.

GIFT AID (NEED-BASED) ***Scholarships, grants, and awards:*** Federal Pell, FSEOG, state, private, college/university gift aid from institutional funds, Alumni Club awards.

GIFT AID (NON-NEED-BASED) ***Tuition waivers:*** Full or partial for employees or children of employees. ***ROTC:*** Army cooperative, Air Force cooperative.

LOANS ***Programs:*** FFEL (Subsidized and Unsubsidized Stafford, PLUS), Perkins, college/university, Connecticut Family Education Loan Program.

WORK-STUDY Federal work-study jobs available. ***State or other work-study/employment:*** Part-time jobs available.

APPLYING for FINANCIAL AID ***Required financial aid forms:*** FAFSA, CSS Financial Aid PROFILE, parent and student federal income tax returns and W-2 forms. ***Financial aid deadline (priority):*** 2/1. ***Notification date:*** 4/1. Students must reply by 5/1 or within 1 week of notification.

CONTACT Mr. Donald Routh, University Director of Financial Aid, Yale University, PO Box 208288, New Haven, CT 06520-8288, 203-432-0360. *Fax:* 203-432-0359. *E-mail:* donald.routh@yale.edu

YESHIVA BETH MOSHE

Scranton, PA

CONTACT Financial Aid Office, Yeshiva Beth Moshe, 930 Hickory Street, Scranton, PA 18505-2124, 717-346-1747.

YESHIVA COLLEGE

New York, NY

See Yeshiva University

YESHIVA DERECH CHAIM

Brooklyn, NY

CONTACT Financial Aid Office, Yeshiva Derech Chaim, 1573 39th Street, Brooklyn, NY 11218, 718-438-5426.

YESHIVA GEDDOLAH OF GREATER DETROIT RABBINICAL COLLEGE

Oak Park, MI

CONTACT Rabbi P. Rushnawitz, Executive Administrator, Yeshiva Geddolah of Greater Detroit Rabbinical College, 24600 Greenfield Road, Oak Park, MI 48237-1544, 810-968-3360. *Fax:* 810-968-8613.

YESHIVA KARLIN STOLIN RABBINICAL INSTITUTE

Brooklyn, NY

Tuition & fees: $5200 **Average undergraduate aid package: N/A**

ABOUT THE INSTITUTION Independent Jewish, men only. 3 undergraduate majors. Total enrollment: 53. Undergraduates: 38. Freshmen: 14.

UNDERGRADUATE EXPENSES for 1999–2000 ***Comprehensive fee:*** $8400 includes full-time tuition ($5200) and room and board ($3200). ***College room only:*** $1800. ***Payment plan:*** installment.

GIFT AID (NEED-BASED) ***Scholarships, grants, and awards:*** Federal Pell, FSEOG.

LOANS ***Programs:*** Perkins.

WORK-STUDY Federal work-study jobs available.

APPLYING for FINANCIAL AID ***Required financial aid forms:*** FAFSA, institution's own form. ***Financial aid deadline (priority):*** 11/1.

CONTACT Mr. Daniel Ross, Financial Aid Administrator, Yeshiva Karlin Stolin Rabbinical Institute, 1818 Fifty-fourth Street, Brooklyn, NY 11204, 718-232-7800 Ext. 16. *Fax:* 718-331-4833.

YESHIVA OF NITRA RABBINICAL COLLEGE

Mount Kisco, NY

CONTACT Mr. Yosef Rosen, Financial Aid Administrator, Yeshiva of Nitra Rabbinical College, 194 Division Avenue, Mount Kisco, NY 10549, 718-384-5460. *Fax:* 718-387-9400.

YESHIVA OHR ELCHONON CHABAD/WEST COAST TALMUDICAL SEMINARY

Los Angeles, CA

CONTACT Ms. Hendy Tauber, Director of Financial Aid, Yeshiva Ohr Elchonon Chabad/West Coast Talmudical Seminary, 7215 Waring Avenue, Los Angeles, CA 90046-7660, 213-937-3763. *Fax:* 213-937-9456.

YESHIVA SHAAR HATORAH TALMUDIC RESEARCH INSTITUTE

Kew Gardens, NY

CONTACT Mr. Yoel Yankelewitz, Executive Director, Financial Aid, Yeshiva Shaar Hatorah Talmudic Research Institute, 117-06 84th Avenue, Kew Gardens, NY 11418-1469, 718-846-1940.

YESHIVATH VIZNITZ

Monsey, NY

CONTACT Financial Aid Office, Yeshivath Viznitz, Phyllis Terrace, PO Box 446, Monsey, NY 10952, 914-356-1010.

YESHIVATH ZICHRON MOSHE

South Fallsburg, NY

CONTACT Ms. Miryom R. Miller, Director of Financial Aid, Yeshivath Zichron Moshe, Laurel Park Road, South Fallsburg, NY 12779, 914-434-5240. *Fax:* 914-434-1009. *E-mail:* lehus@aol.com

YESHIVAT MIKDASH MELECH

Brooklyn, NY

CONTACT Financial Aid Office, Yeshivat Mikdash Melech, 1326 Ocean Parkway, Brooklyn, NY 11230-5601, 718-339-1090.

YESHIVA TORAS CHAIM TALMUDICAL SEMINARY

Denver, CO

CONTACT Office of Financial Aid, Yeshiva Toras Chaim Talmudical Seminary, 1400 Quitman Street, Denver, CO 80204-1415, 303-629-8200.

YESHIVA UNIVERSITY

New York, NY

Tuition & fees: $15,960 **Average undergraduate aid package: N/A**

ABOUT THE INSTITUTION Independent, coed. Awards: bachelor's, master's, doctoral, and first professional degrees (Yeshiva College and Stern College for Women are coordinate undergraduate colleges of arts and sciences for men and women, respectively. Sy Syms School of Business offers programs at both campuses). 33 undergraduate majors. Total enrollment: 5,481. Undergraduates: 2,529. Freshmen: 671.

UNDERGRADUATE EXPENSES for 1999–2000 ***Application fee:*** $40. ***Comprehensive fee:*** $21,230 includes full-time tuition ($15,650), mandatory fees ($310), and room and board ($5270). ***College room only:*** $3770. ***Part-time tuition:*** $560 per credit. ***Part-time fees:*** $25 per term part-time. ***Payment plan:*** installment.

GIFT AID (NEED-BASED) ***Scholarships, grants, and awards:*** Federal Pell, FSEOG, state, private, college/university gift aid from institutional funds.

GIFT AID (NON-NEED-BASED) ***Scholarships, grants, and awards by category:*** *Academic Interests/Achievement:* general academic interests/achievements. ***Tuition waivers:*** Full or partial for employees or children of employees.

LOANS ***Programs:*** FFEL (Subsidized and Unsubsidized Stafford, PLUS), Perkins, college/university.

WORK-STUDY Federal work-study jobs available. ***State or other work-study/employment:*** Part-time jobs available.

APPLYING for FINANCIAL AID ***Required financial aid form:*** FAFSA. ***Financial aid deadline:*** Continuous.

CONTACT Mr. Neal Harris, Associate Director, Student Finances, Yeshiva University, 500 West 185th Street, New York, NY 10033-3201, 212-960-5400.

YORK COLLEGE

York, NE

Tuition & fees: $8000 **Average undergraduate aid package: $7681**

ABOUT THE INSTITUTION Independent religious, coed. Awards: associate and bachelor's degrees. 47 undergraduate majors. Total enrollment: 485. Undergraduates: 485. Institutional methodology is used as a basis for awarding need-based institutional aid.

UNDERGRADUATE EXPENSES for 1999–2000 ***Application fee:*** $20. ***Comprehensive fee:*** $11,300 includes full-time tuition ($7200), mandatory fees ($800), and room and board ($3300). ***College room only:*** $1400. Full-time tuition and fees vary according to course load. Room and board charges vary according to board plan and housing facility. ***Part-time tuition:*** $225 per credit hour. ***Part-time fees:*** $50 per term part-time. Part-time tuition and fees vary according to course load. ***Payment plan:*** installment.

FRESHMAN FINANCIAL AID (Fall 1998) 163 applied for aid; of those 89% were deemed to have need. 100% of freshmen with need received aid; of those 23% had need fully met. *Average percent of need met:* 84% (excluding resources awarded to replace EFC). *Average financial aid package:* $7311 (excluding resources awarded to replace EFC). 4% of all full-time freshmen had no need and received non-need-based aid.

UNDERGRADUATE FINANCIAL AID (Fall 1998) 402 applied for aid; of those 91% were deemed to have need. 100% of undergraduates with need received aid; of those 13% had need fully met. *Average percent of need met:* 79% (excluding resources awarded to replace EFC). *Average financial aid package:* $7681 (excluding resources awarded to replace EFC). 13% of all full-time undergraduates had no need and received non-need-based aid.

GIFT AID (NEED-BASED) ***Total amount:*** $585,768 (84% Federal, 16% state). ***Receiving aid:*** *Freshmen:* 42% (78); *all full-time undergraduates:* 43% (203). ***Average award:*** Freshmen: $4606; Undergraduates: $2783. ***Scholarships, grants, and awards:*** Federal Pell, FSEOG, state, private, college/university gift aid from institutional funds.

GIFT AID (NON-NEED-BASED) ***Total amount:*** $621,180 (89% institutional, 11% external sources). ***Receiving aid:*** *Freshmen:* 73% (137); *Undergraduates:* 70% (333). ***Scholarships, grants, and awards by category:*** *Academic Interests/Achievement:* biological sciences, business, communication, education, English, general academic interests/achievements, mathematics, premedicine, religion/biblical studies. *Creative Arts/Performance:* art/fine arts, debating, music, performing arts, theater/drama. *Special Achievements/Activities:* leadership. *Special Characteristics:* children and siblings of alumni, children of faculty/staff, previous college experience, siblings of current students. ***Tuition waivers:*** Full or partial for employees or children of employees. ***ROTC:*** Army cooperative, Naval cooperative, Air Force cooperative.

LOANS ***Student loans:*** $1,719,662 (70% need-based, 30% non-need-based). ***Average need-based loan:*** Freshmen: $2524; Undergraduates: $3060. ***Parent loans:*** $411,319 (100% non-need-based). ***Programs:*** FFEL (Subsidized and Unsubsidized Stafford, PLUS), Perkins, college/university.

WORK-STUDY ***Federal work-study:*** *Total amount:* $109,430; jobs available. ***State or other work-study/employment:*** *Total amount:* $6412 (100% non-need-based). 10 part-time jobs averaging $825.

ATHLETIC AWARDS *Total amount:* 346,200 (100% non-need-based).

APPLYING for FINANCIAL AID ***Required financial aid form:*** FAFSA. ***Financial aid deadline (priority):*** 4/1. ***Notification date:*** Continuous. Students must reply within 4 weeks of notification.

CONTACT Ms. Debra Lowry, Director of Financial Aid, York College, 1125 East 8th Street, York, NE 68467-2699, 402-363-5624 or toll-free 800-950-9675. *Fax:* 402-363-5623. *E-mail:* dlowry@york.edu

YORK COLLEGE OF PENNSYLVANIA

York, PA

Tuition & fees: $6630 **Average undergraduate aid package: $5655**

ABOUT THE INSTITUTION Independent, coed. Awards: associate, bachelor's, and master's degrees. 58 undergraduate majors. Total enrollment: 5,214. Undergraduates: 5,025. Freshmen: 741. Both federal and institutional methodology are used as a basis for awarding need-based institutional aid.

UNDERGRADUATE EXPENSES for 1999–2000 ***Application fee:*** $20. ***Comprehensive fee:*** $11,300 includes full-time tuition ($6280), mandatory fees ($350), and room and board ($4670). ***College room only:*** $2300. Room and board charges vary according to housing facility. ***Part-time tuition:*** $200 per credit hour. ***Part-time fees:*** $76 per term part-time. ***Payment plan:*** installment.

FRESHMAN FINANCIAL AID (Fall 1999) 738 applied for aid; of those 82% were deemed to have need. 93% of freshmen with need received aid; of those 23% had need fully met. *Average percent of need met:* 71% (excluding resources awarded to replace EFC). *Average financial aid package:* $5167 (excluding resources awarded to replace EFC). 21% of all full-time freshmen had no need and received non-need-based aid.

UNDERGRADUATE FINANCIAL AID (Fall 1999) 2,926 applied for aid; of those 69% were deemed to have need. 90% of undergraduates with need received aid; of those 31% had need fully met. *Average percent of need met:* 72% (excluding resources awarded to replace EFC). *Average financial aid package:* $5655 (excluding resources awarded to replace EFC). 18% of all full-time undergraduates had no need and received non-need-based aid.

GIFT AID (NEED-BASED) ***Total amount:*** $5,036,475 (25% Federal, 35% state, 33% institutional, 7% external sources). ***Receiving aid:*** *Freshmen:* 35% (324); *all full-time undergraduates:* 33% (1,277). ***Average award:*** Freshmen: $2957; Undergraduates: $3011. ***Scholarships, grants, and awards:*** Federal Pell, FSEOG, state, private, college/university gift aid from institutional funds.

GIFT AID (NON-NEED-BASED) ***Total amount:*** $727,866 (100% institutional). ***Receiving aid:*** *Freshmen:* 19% (175); *Undergraduates:* 7% (265). ***Scholarships, grants, and awards by category:*** *Academic Interests/Achievement:* 461 awards ($1,042,800 total): engineering/technologies, general academic interests/achievements, health fields. *Creative Arts/Performance:* 18 awards ($8371 total): music. *Special Achievements/Activities:* memberships. *Special Characteristics:* 32 awards ($42,900 total): children and siblings of alumni, children of union members/company employees, international students, members of minority groups. ***Tuition waivers:*** Full or partial for employees or children of employees.

LOANS ***Student loans:*** $10,581,383 (53% need-based, 47% non-need-based). 64% of past graduating class borrowed through all loan programs. Average indebtedness per student: $14,350. ***Average need-based loan:*** Freshmen: $2363; Undergraduates: $3250. ***Parent loans:*** $1,985,820 (14% need-based, 86% non-need-based). ***Programs:*** Federal Direct (Subsidized and Unsubsidized Stafford, PLUS), Perkins, Federal Nursing, college/university.

WORK-STUDY ***Federal work-study:*** *Total amount:* $378,592; 250 jobs averaging $1515. ***State or other work-study/employment:*** *Total amount:* $112,800 (100% non-need-based). Part-time jobs available.

APPLYING for FINANCIAL AID ***Required financial aid forms:*** FAFSA, institution's own form. ***Financial aid deadline (priority):*** 3/1. ***Notification date:*** Continuous. Students must reply within 4 weeks of notification.

CONTACT Calvin Williams, Director of Financial Aid, York College of Pennsylvania, Country Club Road, York, PA 17405-7199, 717-849-1682 or toll-free 800-455-8018. *Fax:* 717-849-1607. *E-mail:* admissions@ycp.edu

YORK COLLEGE OF THE CITY UNIVERSITY OF NEW YORK

Jamaica, NY

Tuition & fees (NY res): $3292 **Average undergraduate aid package: N/A**

ABOUT THE INSTITUTION State and locally supported, coed. Awards: bachelor's degrees. 36 undergraduate majors. Total enrollment: 5,362. Undergraduates: 5,362. Freshmen: 461. Both federal and institutional methodology are used as a basis for awarding need-based institutional aid.

UNDERGRADUATE EXPENSES for 1999–2000 ***Application fee:*** $40. ***Tuition, state resident:*** full-time $3200; part-time $135 per credit. ***Tuition, nonresident:*** full-time $6800; part-time $285 per credit. ***Required fees:*** full-time $92; $26 per term part-time.

GIFT AID (NEED-BASED) ***Total amount:*** $11,627,417 (52% Federal, 48% state). ***Scholarships, grants, and awards:*** Federal Pell, FSEOG, state, private.

GIFT AID (NON-NEED-BASED) ***ROTC:*** Army cooperative, Naval cooperative, Air Force cooperative.

LOANS ***Student loans:*** $3,298,228 (100% need-based). ***Parent loans:*** $3840 (100% need-based). ***Programs:*** Federal Direct (Subsidized and Unsubsidized Stafford, PLUS), FFEL (Subsidized Stafford, PLUS), Perkins.

WORK-STUDY ***Federal work-study:*** *Total amount:* $238,960; 280 jobs averaging $1200.

APPLYING for FINANCIAL AID ***Required financial aid forms:*** FAFSA, state aid form. ***Financial aid deadline:*** 5/1.

CONTACT Mr. Alan R. Rumberg, Director of Finance, York College of the City University of New York, 9420 Guy Brewer Boulevard, Jamaica, NY 11451-0001, 718-262-2230.

YOUNGSTOWN STATE UNIVERSITY

Youngstown, OH

Tuition & fees (OH res): $3762 **Average undergraduate aid package: N/A**

ABOUT THE INSTITUTION State-supported, coed. Awards: associate, bachelor's, master's, and doctoral degrees and post-bachelor's certificates. 147 undergraduate majors. Total enrollment: 12,222. Undergraduates: 11,025. Freshmen: 2,104. Federal methodology is used as a basis for awarding need-based institutional aid.

UNDERGRADUATE EXPENSES for 1999–2000 ***Application fee:*** $25. ***Tuition, state resident:*** full-time $2940; part-time $79 per credit. ***Tuition, nonresident:*** full-time $7101; part-time $195 per credit. ***Required fees:*** full-time $822; $20 per credit; $31 per term part-time. Full-time tuition and fees vary according to course load, reciprocity agreements, and student level. Part-time tuition and fees vary according to course load, reciprocity agreements, and student level. ***College room and board:*** $4695. Room and board charges vary according to board plan and housing facility. ***Payment plan:*** installment.

GIFT AID (NEED-BASED) ***Total amount:*** $9,222,290 (73% Federal, 24% state, 1% institutional, 2% external sources). ***Scholarships, grants, and awards:*** Federal Pell, FSEOG, state, private, college/university gift aid from institutional funds.

GIFT AID (NON-NEED-BASED) ***Total amount:*** $7,326,415 (2% Federal, 20% state, 78% external sources). ***Scholarships, grants, and awards by category:*** *Academic Interests/Achievement:* business, education, English, general academic interests/achievements, military science. *Creative Arts/Performance:* music. *Special Achievements/Activities:* cheerleading/drum major, leadership. *Special Characteristics:* adult students, children and siblings of alumni, children of faculty/staff, children of union members/company employees, children of workers in trades, children with a deceased or disabled parent, handicapped students, members of minority groups, spouses of deceased or disabled public servants, veterans, veterans' children. ***Tuition waivers:*** Full or partial for employees or children of employees, senior citizens. ***ROTC:*** Army.

LOANS ***Student loans:*** $20,081,887 (100% need-based). ***Parent loans:*** $823,879 (100% non-need-based). ***Programs:*** FFEL (Subsidized and Unsubsidized Stafford, PLUS), Perkins, state, college/university.

WORK-STUDY ***Federal work-study:*** *Total amount:* $434,695; 231 jobs averaging $1882. ***State or other work-study/employment:*** *Total amount:* $2,293,102 (100% non-need-based). Part-time jobs available.

ATHLETIC AWARDS *Total amount:* 1,488,769 (100% non-need-based).

APPLYING for FINANCIAL AID ***Required financial aid forms:*** FAFSA, institution's own form. ***Financial aid deadline (priority):*** 2/15. ***Notification date:*** 5/1. Students must reply within 4 weeks of notification.

Youngstown State University (continued)

CONTACT Ms. Beth Bartlett, Administrative Assistant, Youngstown State University, 1 University Plaza, Youngstown, OH 44555-0002, 330-742-3504 or toll-free 877-468-6978. *Fax:* 330-742-1659. *E-mail:* ysufinaid@ysu.edu

SECTION 8

College Financial Aid Indexes

NON-NEED SCHOLARSHIPS FOR UNDERGRADUATES

This index lists the colleges that report that they offer scholarships to freshmen based on academic interests, abilities, achievements, or personal characteristics other than financial need. For any college listed in this index, refer to the *Non-Need Awards* section of that college's profile for specific information on the number and total dollar value of the scholarships offered.

Specific categories appear in alphabetical order under the following broad groups:

Academic Interests/Achievements

General Academic, Agricultural, Architecture, Area/Ethnic Studies, Biological Sciences, Business, Communication, Computer Science, Education, Engineering/Technologies, English, Foreign Languages, Health Fields, Home Economics, Humanities, International Studies, Library Science, Mathematics, Military Science, Physical Sciences, Premedicine, Religion/Biblical Studies, Social Sciences

Creative Arts/Performance

Applied Art and Design, Art/Fine Arts, Cinema/Film/Broadcasting, Creative Writing, Dance, Debating, Journalism/Publications, Music, Performing Arts, Theater/Drama

Special Achievements/Activities

Cheerleading/Drum Major, Community Service, Hobbies/Interests, Junior Miss, Leadership, Memberships, Religious Involvement, Rodeo

Special Characteristics

Adult Students, Children/Siblings of Alumni, Children of Current Students, Children of Educators, Children of Faculty/Staff, Children of Public Servants, Children of Union Members/Company Employees, Children of Workers in Trades, Children with a Deceased or Disabled Parent, Ethnic Background, First-Generation College Students, Handicapped Students, International Students, Local/State Students, Married Students, Members of Minority Groups, Out-of-State Students, Parents of Current Students, Previous College Experience, Public Servants, Relatives of Clergy, Religious Affiliation, Siblings of Current Students, Spouses of Current Students, Spouses of Deceased or Disabled Public Servants, Twins, Veterans, Veterans' Children

---

ACADEMIC INTERESTS/ ACHIEVEMENTS

AGRICULTURE

Texas A&M University–Commerce, TX
Texas A&M University–Kingsville, TX
Texas Tech University, TX
The University of Arizona, AZ
University of Arkansas at Pine Bluff, AR
U of Calif, Davis, CA
U of Calif, Riverside, CA
University of Delaware, DE
University of Florida, FL
University of Georgia, GA
University of Guam, GU
University of Hawaii at Hilo, HI
University of Idaho, ID
University of Louisiana at Monroe, LA
University of Massachusetts Amherst, MA
University of Minnesota, Crookston, MN
University of Minnesota, Twin Cities Campus, MN
University of Nebraska–Lincoln, NE
University of Nevada, Reno, NV
University of New Hampshire, NH
The University of Tennessee at Martin, TN
The University of Tennessee Knoxville, TN
The University of Texas at San Antonio, TX
University of Virginia's College at Wise, VA
University of Wisconsin–Platteville, WI
University of Wisconsin–River Falls, WI
University of Wyoming, WY
Utah State University, UT
Virginia Polytechnic Institute and State U, VA
Virginia State University, VA
Washington State University, WA
Western Illinois University, IL
Western Kentucky University, KY
West Texas A&M University, TX
West Virginia University, WV
Wilmington College, OH

ARCHITECTURE

Arizona State University, AZ
Auburn University, AL
Ball State University, IN
Boston Architectural Center, MA
California Polytechnic State U, San Luis Obispo, CA
California State Polytechnic University, Pomona, CA
California State University, Fresno, CA
Clemson University, SC
Drury University, MO
Eastern Michigan University, MI
Florida International University, FL
Illinois Institute of Technology, IL
Iowa State University of Science and Technology, IA
James Madison University, VA
Judson College, IL
Kansas State University, KS
Kent State University, OH
Lawrence Technological University, MI
Louisiana State University and A&M College, LA
Louisiana Tech University, LA
Miami University, OH
Michigan State University, MI
Mississippi State University, MS
Montana State U–Bozeman, MT
New Jersey Institute of Technology, NJ
Newschool of Architecture, CA
North Dakota State University, ND
The Ohio State University, OH
Oklahoma State U, OK
Polytechnic University of Puerto Rico, PR
Prairie View A&M University, TX
Pratt Institute, NY
Savannah College of Art and Design, GA
Southern Illinois University Carbondale, IL
Syracuse University, NY
Texas A&M University, TX
Texas Tech University, TX
The University of Arizona, AZ
University of Cincinnati, OH
University of Colorado at Boulder, CO
University of Florida, FL
University of Idaho, ID
University of Kansas, KS
The University of Maine at Augusta, ME
University of Massachusetts Amherst, MA
University of Michigan, MI
University of Minnesota, Twin Cities Campus, MN
University of Nebraska–Lincoln, NE
University of Nevada, Las Vegas, NV
The University of North Carolina at Charlotte, NC
University of Oklahoma, OK
University of South Florida, FL
The University of Tennessee Knoxville, TN
The University of Texas at San Antonio, TX
University of Utah, UT
University of Washington, WA
University of Wisconsin–Stevens Point, WI
Utah State University, UT
Washington State University, WA
Washington University in St. Louis, MO
Wentworth Institute of Technology, MA
West Virginia University, WV

AREA/ETHNIC STUDIES

American University, DC
Arizona State University, AZ
Brigham Young University, UT
Brigham Young University–Hawaii Campus, HI
California State University, Chico, CA
California State University, Fresno, CA
The College of New Rochelle, NY
Eastern Connecticut State University, CT
Georgia State University, GA
Indiana University of Pennsylvania, PA
Iowa State University of Science and Technology, IA
Kent State University, OH
Loyola University Chicago, IL
Mississippi State University, MS
Montana State U–Bozeman, MT
The Ohio State University, OH
Ohio University, OH
Ohio University–Eastern, OH
Ohio University–Lancaster, OH
Oklahoma State U, OK
Ouachita Baptist University, AR
Plattsburgh State U of NY, NY
Purchase College, State U of NY, NY
Radford University, VA
The Richard Stockton College of New Jersey, NJ
Shippensburg University of Pennsylvania, PA
Sonoma State University, CA
South Dakota State University, SD
Southern Illinois University Carbondale, IL
Southern Methodist University, TX
State U of NY at Oswego, NY
State U of NY College at Geneseo, NY
Stetson University, FL
U of Calif, Riverside, CA
University of Cincinnati, OH
University of Colorado at Boulder, CO
University of Kansas, KS
University of Michigan, MI
University of Minnesota, Twin Cities Campus, MN
University of Nevada, Reno, NV
University of Oklahoma, OK
The University of Texas at San Antonio, TX
University of Toledo, OH
University of Utah, UT
University of Wisconsin–River Falls, WI
Washington State University, WA
West Virginia University, WV
Wichita State University, KS

BIOLOGICAL SCIENCES

Abilene Christian University, TX
Adams State College, CO
Agnes Scott College, GA
Alabama State University, AL
Albany State University, GA
Albertson College of Idaho, ID
Albertus Magnus College, CT
Alfred University, NY
Allentown College of St. Francis de Sales, PA
American University, DC
Anderson College, SC
Angelo State University, TX
Antioch College, OH
Arizona State University, AZ
Arkansas State University, AR
Armstrong Atlantic State University, GA
Ashland University, OH
Athens State University, AL
Auburn University, AL
Augsburg College, MN
Augustana College, IL
Augustana College, SD
Austin College, TX
Avila College, MO
Azusa Pacific University, CA
Baker University, KS
Ball State University, IN
Barat College, IL
Bard College, NY
Bartlesville Wesleyan College, OK
Barton College, NC
Bellarmine College, KY
Benedictine University, IL
Bethel College, IN
Black Hills State University, SD
Bloomsburg University of Pennsylvania, PA
Boise State University, ID
Bowie State University, MD
Bowling Green State University, OH
Brenau University, GA
Brescia University, KY
Briar Cliff College, IA
Brigham Young University, UT
Brigham Young University–Hawaii Campus, HI
Bryan College, TN
Buena Vista University, IA

Biological Sciences (continued)

Butler University, IN
California Lutheran University, CA
California Polytechnic State U, San Luis Obispo, CA
California State Polytechnic University, Pomona, CA
California State University, Bakersfield, CA
California State University, Chico, CA
California State University, Fresno, CA
California State University, Los Angeles, CA
California State University, Stanislaus, CA
Calvin College, MI
Cameron University, OK
Carlow College, PA
Carroll College, WI
Carson-Newman College, TN
Carthage College, WI
Centenary College of Louisiana, LA
Central College, IA
Central Methodist College, MO
Central Michigan University, MI
Central Missouri State University, MO
Chaminade University of Honolulu, HI
Cheyney University of Pennsylvania, PA
Citadel, The Military Coll of South Carolina, SC
Clarion University of Pennsylvania, PA
Clarkson University, NY
Clemson University, SC
Coastal Carolina University, SC
Coe College, IA
College of Charleston, SC
The College of New Rochelle, NY
The College of Wooster, OH
Columbia College, MO
Columbia College, SC
Concordia University, IL
Concordia University, NE
Dakota Wesleyan University, SD
Davidson College, NC
Davis & Elkins College, WV
Defiance College, OH
Delaware Valley College, PA
Delta State University, MS
Denison University, OH
DePaul University, IL
DePauw University, IN
Doane College, NE
Drury University, MO
D'Youville College, NY
East Carolina University, NC
Eastern Connecticut State University, CT
Eastern Mennonite University, VA
Eastern Michigan University, MI
Eastern New Mexico University, NM
Eastern Oregon University, OR
Eastern Washington University, WA
East Stroudsburg University of Pennsylvania, PA
East Tennessee State University, TN
East Texas Baptist University, TX
Edinboro University of Pennsylvania, PA
Elizabethtown College, PA
Elmhurst College, IL
Elon College, NC
Felician College, NJ
Fitchburg State College, MA
Florida Gulf Coast University, FL
Florida Institute of Technology, FL
Florida International University, FL
Florida Memorial College, FL
Florida Southern College, FL
Fort Hays State University, KS
Fort Lewis College, CO
Framingham State College, MA
Francis Marion University, SC
Friends University, KS
Frostburg State University, MD
Furman University, SC
Gannon University, PA
Gardner-Webb University, NC
George Fox University, OR
Georgian Court College, NJ
Georgia Southern University, GA
Georgia State University, GA
Goucher College, MD
Governors State University, IL
Grambling State University, LA
Grand Canyon University, AZ
Greenville College, IL
Grove City College, PA
Guilford College, NC
Gwynedd-Mercy College, PA
Hamline University, MN
Hardin-Simmons University, TX
Henderson State University, AR
Heritage College, WA
High Point University, NC
Hillsdale College, MI
Howard Payne University, TX
Idaho State University, ID
Illinois Institute of Technology, IL
Illinois State University, IL
Indiana University of Pennsylvania, PA
Indiana U–Purdue U Fort Wayne, IN
Iowa State University of Science and Technology, IA
Iowa Wesleyan College, IA
Jacksonville State University, AL
James Madison University, VA
John Carroll University, OH
Juniata College, PA
Kalamazoo College, MI
Kansas State University, KS
Kansas Wesleyan University, KS
Kennesaw State University, GA
Kent State University, OH
King's College, PA
Lake Erie College, OH
Lander University, SC
Lebanon Valley College, PA
Lee University, TN
Limestone College, SC
Lincoln University, MO
Lincoln University, PA
Lock Haven University of Pennsylvania, PA
Louisiana State University and A&M College, LA
Louisiana State University in Shreveport, LA
Loyola University Chicago, IL
Lycoming College, PA
MacMurray College, IL
Maine Maritime Academy, ME
Malone College, OH
Manhattan College, NY
Mansfield University of Pennsylvania, PA
Marquette University, WI
Marycrest International University, IA
Marymount University, VA
Massachusetts College of Liberal Arts, MA
The Master's College and Seminary, CA
Mayville State University, ND
McKendree College, IL
McNeese State University, LA
Mercer University, GA
Mesa State College, CO
Michigan State University, MI
Michigan Technological University, MI
Middle Tennessee State University, TN
Mills College, CA
Mississippi College, MS
Mississippi State University, MS
Missouri Western State College, MO
Montana State U–Billings, MT
Montana State U–Bozeman, MT
Morningside College, IA
Mount St. Clare College, IA
Murray State University, KY
Muskingum College, OH
Newberry College, SC
Norfolk State University, VA
North Carolina Central University, NC
North Carolina State University, NC
North Dakota State University, ND
Northeastern State University, OK
Northern Arizona University, AZ
Northwestern College, IA
Northwestern Oklahoma State University, OK
Northwest Missouri State University, MO
Northwest Nazarene University, ID
Oakland University, MI
Ohio Northern University, OH
The Ohio State University, OH
Ohio University, OH
Ohio University–Eastern, OH
Ohio University–Lancaster, OH
Oklahoma State U, OK
Old Dominion University, VA
Oral Roberts University, OK
Ottawa University, KS
Ouachita Baptist University, AR
Palmer College of Chiropractic, IA
Peace College, NC
Pepperdine University, CA
Piedmont College, GA
Pine Manor College, MA
Pittsburg State University, KS
Plattsburgh State U of NY, NY
Point Loma Nazarene University, CA
Prescott College, AZ
Purchase College, State U of NY, NY
Purdue University, IN
Quincy University, IL
Radford University, VA
Randolph-Macon Woman's College, VA
Reinhardt College, GA
The Richard Stockton College of New Jersey, NJ
Rochester Institute of Technology, NY
Rockford College, IL
Rockhurst University, MO
Rocky Mountain College, MT
Rowan University, NJ
Rutgers, State U of NJ, Cook College, NJ
Sacred Heart University, CT
Saginaw Valley State University, MI
St. Ambrose University, IA
St. Edward's University, TX

St. John's University, NY
Saint Paul's College, VA
Saint Vincent College, PA
Salisbury State University, MD
Sam Houston State University, TX
Savannah State University, GA
Seton Hall University, NJ
Seton Hill College, PA
Shaw University, NC
Shepherd College, WV
Shippensburg University of Pennsylvania, PA
Siena College, NY
Skidmore College, NY
Slippery Rock University of Pennsylvania, PA
Sonoma State University, CA
South Dakota State University, SD
Southeastern Louisiana University, LA
Southeast Missouri State University, MO
Southern Illinois University Carbondale, IL
Southern Methodist University, TX
Southern Nazarene University, OK
Southern Oregon University, OR
Southern University at New Orleans, LA
Southwestern College, KS
Southwestern Oklahoma State University, OK
Southwest Missouri State University, MO
Southwest State University, MN
Spring Arbor College, MI
State U of NY at Oswego, NY
State U of NY at Stony Brook, NY
State U of NY College at Brockport, NY
State U of NY College at Fredonia, NY
State U of NY College at Geneseo, NY
State U of NY College at Oneonta, NY
State U of NY College at Potsdam, NY
State U of NY Coll of Environ Sci and Forestry, NY
State University of West Georgia, GA
Stephen F. Austin State University, TX
Stetson University, FL
Sul Ross State University, TX
Tennessee Technological University, TN
Tennessee Wesleyan College, TN
Texas A&M University, TX
Texas A&M University–Kingsville, TX
Texas Tech University, TX
Texas Woman's University, TX
Truman State University, MO
The University of Akron, OH
U of Alaska Anchorage, AK
U of Alaska Southeast, AK
The University of Arizona, AZ
University of Arkansas at Little Rock, AR
University of Arkansas at Pine Bluff, AR
U of Calif, Riverside, CA
U of Calif, San Diego, CA
University of Central Arkansas, AR
University of Central Oklahoma, OK
University of Cincinnati, OH
University of Colorado at Boulder, CO
University of Colorado at Colorado Springs, CO
University of Delaware, DE
University of Evansville, IN
University of Great Falls, MT
University of Houston, TX
University of Houston–Clear Lake, TX
University of Houston–Downtown, TX
University of Idaho, ID
University of Illinois at Springfield, IL
University of Kansas, KS
University of Louisiana at Monroe, LA
The University of Maine at Augusta, ME
University of Mary Hardin-Baylor, TX
University of Maryland, Baltimore County, MD
University of Massachusetts Amherst, MA
The University of Memphis, TN
University of Michigan, MI
University of Michigan–Dearborn, MI
University of Minnesota, Twin Cities Campus, MN
University of Missouri–St. Louis, MO
The University of Montana–Missoula, MT
University of Montevallo, AL
University of Nebraska at Omaha, NE
University of Nebraska–Lincoln, NE
University of Nevada, Las Vegas, NV
University of Nevada, Reno, NV
University of New England, ME
The University of North Carolina at Asheville, NC
The University of North Carolina at Greensboro, NC
The University of North Carolina at Wilmington, NC
University of Northern Colorado, CO
University of Northern Iowa, IA
University of Oklahoma, OK
University of Pittsburgh at Bradford, PA
University of Portland, OR
U of Puerto Rico, Humacao University College, PR
University of Puget Sound, WA
University of Richmond, VA
University of Rio Grande, OH
University of Rochester, NY
University of St. Francis, IL
University of Saint Francis, IN
University of St. Thomas, MN
University of South Carolina, SC
University of South Carolina Aiken, SC
University of South Dakota, SD
University of Southern Colorado, CO
University of South Florida, FL
The University of Tampa, FL
The University of Tennessee at Martin, TN
The University of Texas at Arlington, TX
The University of Texas at Brownsville, TX
The University of Texas at Dallas, TX
The University of Texas at El Paso, TX
The University of Texas at San Antonio, TX
The University of Texas at Tyler, TX
The University of Texas–Pan American, TX
University of the Ozarks, AR
University of Tulsa, OK
University of Utah, UT
University of Virginia's College at Wise, VA
University of Washington, WA
University of Wisconsin–Eau Claire, WI
University of Wisconsin–Parkside, WI
University of Wisconsin–Platteville, WI
University of Wisconsin–River Falls, WI
University of Wisconsin–Stevens Point, WI
University of Wisconsin–Superior, WI
University of Wisconsin–Whitewater, WI
Utah State University, UT
Valley City State University, ND
Virginia Military Institute, VA
Virginia State University, VA
Voorhees College, SC
Wake Forest University, NC
Walsh University, OH
Wartburg College, IA
Washington State University, WA
Washington University in St. Louis, MO
Wayland Baptist University, TX
Webster University, MO
Western Illinois University, IL
Western Kentucky University, KY
Western Michigan University, MI
Western State College of Colorado, CO
Western Washington University, WA
Westminster College, PA
Westminster College, UT
West Virginia State College, WV
West Virginia University, WV
Wheeling Jesuit University, WV
Wilmington College, OH
Wisconsin Lutheran College, WI
Worcester State College, MA
Xavier University of Louisiana, LA
York College, NE

BUSINESS

Abilene Christian University, TX
Adams State College, CO
Adrian College, MI
Albertson College of Idaho, ID
Albertus Magnus College, CT
Albion College, MI
Alfred University, NY
Allentown College of St. Francis de Sales, PA
American University, DC
Anderson College, SC
Angelo State University, TX
Aquinas College, TN
Arizona State University, AZ
Arkansas State University, AR
Ashland University, OH
Athens State University, AL
Auburn University, AL
Augsburg College, MN
Augustana College, SD
Augusta State University, GA
Austin College, TX
Baker University, KS
Ball State University, IN
Barber-Scotia College, NC
Barton College, NC
Baylor University, TX
Bellarmine College, KY
Bellevue University, NE
Bethel College, IN
Birmingham-Southern College, AL
Black Hills State University, SD
Bloomsburg University of Pennsylvania, PA
Boise State University, ID
Bowie State University, MD
Bowling Green State University, OH
Brescia University, KY
Brevard College, NC
Briar Cliff College, IA
Brigham Young University, UT
Brigham Young University–Hawaii Campus, HI
Bryan College, TN
Butler University, IN
California Baptist University, CA
California Lutheran University, CA

Business (continued)

California Polytechnic State U, San Luis Obispo, CA
California State Polytechnic University, Pomona, CA
California State University, Bakersfield, CA
California State University, Chico, CA
California State University, Fresno, CA
California State University, Fullerton, CA
California State University, Los Angeles, CA
California State University, Northridge, CA
California State University, San Bernardino, CA
California State University, Stanislaus, CA
Calvin College, MI
Cameron University, OK
Carlow College, PA
Carson-Newman College, TN
Centenary College of Louisiana, LA
Central College, IA
Central Methodist College, MO
Central Missouri State University, MO
Central State University, OH
Chaminade University of Honolulu, HI
Circleville Bible College, OH
Clarion University of Pennsylvania, PA
Clarkson College, NE
Clarkson University, NY
Clearwater Christian College, FL
Clemson University, SC
Coastal Carolina University, SC
College of Charleston, SC
College of Insurance, NY
The College of New Rochelle, NY
College of St. Catherine, MN
The College of Saint Rose, NY
College of the Southwest, NM
The College of West Virginia, WV
Colorado Christian University, CO
Colorado School of Mines, CO
Columbia College, MO
Columbia College, SC
Concordia College, AL
Concordia University, IL
Concordia University, NE
Creighton University, NE
Crown College, MN
Dakota State University, SD
Dakota Wesleyan University, SD
Dalton State College, GA
Daniel Webster College, NH
David N. Myers College, OH
Defiance College, OH
Delaware Valley College, PA
DePaul University, IL
DePauw University, IN
Detroit College of Business, MI
Detroit College of Business–Flint, MI
Detroit College of Business, Warren Campus, MI
DeVry Institute of Technology, AZ
DeVry Institute of Technology, CA
DeVry Institute of Technology, CA
DeVry Institute of Technology, CA
DeVry Institute of Technology, GA
DeVry Institute of Technology, GA
DeVry Institute of Technology, IL
DeVry Institute of Technology, IL
DeVry Institute of Technology, MO
DeVry Institute of Technology, OH
DeVry Institute of Technology, TX
Doane College, NE
Dordt College, IA
Dowling College, NY
Drury University, MO
D'Youville College, NY
East Carolina University, NC
Eastern Connecticut State University, CT
Eastern Mennonite University, VA
Eastern Michigan University, MI
Eastern Nazarene College, MA
Eastern New Mexico University, NM
Eastern Oregon University, OR
Eastern Washington University, WA
East Stroudsburg University of Pennsylvania, PA
East Tennessee State University, TN
East Texas Baptist University, TX
Edinboro University of Pennsylvania, PA
Elizabethtown College, PA
Elmhurst College, IL
Elon College, NC
Emmanuel College, GA
Endicott College, MA
Fairmont State College, WV
Fitchburg State College, MA
Five Towns College, NY
Flagler College, FL
Florida Agricultural and Mechanical University, FL
Florida Atlantic University, FL
Florida Gulf Coast University, FL
Florida Institute of Technology, FL
Florida International University, FL
Florida Memorial College, FL
Florida Metropolitan U-Fort Lauderdale Coll, FL
Florida Metropolitan U-Tampa Coll, Lakeland, FL
Florida Southern College, FL
Fort Hays State University, KS
Fort Lewis College, CO
Fort Valley State University, GA
Francis Marion University, SC
Friends University, KS
Frostburg State University, MD
Furman University, SC
Gannon University, PA
Gardner-Webb University, NC
Georgia College and State University, GA
Georgia Southern University, GA
Georgia State University, GA
Goldey-Beacom College, DE
Gonzaga University, WA
Goshen College, IN
Goucher College, MD
Governors State University, IL
Grace University, NE
Grambling State University, LA
Grand Canyon University, AZ
Greenville College, IL
Grove City College, PA
Gwynedd-Mercy College, PA
Hardin-Simmons University, TX
Heritage College, WA
High Point University, NC
Hillsdale College, MI
Hillsdale Free Will Baptist College, OK
Howard Payne University, TX
Humphreys College, CA
Husson College, ME
Idaho State University, ID
Illinois State University, IL
Indiana Institute of Technology, IN
Indiana University of Pennsylvania, PA
Indiana U–Purdue U Fort Wayne, IN
Iowa State University of Science and Technology, IA
Jacksonville State University, AL
Jacksonville University, FL
James Madison University, VA
Johnson & Wales University, FL
Johnson & Wales University, RI
Johnson State College, VT
Juniata College, PA
Kansas State University, KS
Kansas Wesleyan University, KS
Kean University, NJ
Kennesaw State University, GA
Kent State University, OH
Kentucky Christian College, KY
Kettering University, MI
King's College, PA
Lakeland College, WI
Lander University, SC
Langston University, OK
Lawrence Technological University, MI
Lee University, TN
Limestone College, SC
Lincoln University, PA
Long Island U, Southampton College, NY
Longwood College, VA
Louisiana College, LA
Louisiana State University and A&M College, LA
Louisiana State University in Shreveport, LA
Louisiana Tech University, LA
Loyola University Chicago, IL
Loyola University New Orleans, LA
Lubbock Christian University, TX
Lycoming College, PA
Lyndon State College, VT
Lynn University, FL
Madonna University, MI
Malone College, OH
Manchester College, IN
Manhattan College, NY
Marquette University, WI
Marycrest International University, IA
Marymount University, VA
Mary Washington College, VA
Massachusetts College of Liberal Arts, MA
The Master's College and Seminary, CA
Mayville State University, ND
McKendree College, IL
McNeese State University, LA
Mesa State College, CO
Michigan State University, MI
Michigan Technological University, MI
Mid-America Bible College, OK
Middle Tennessee State University, TN
Millsaps College, MS
Milwaukee School of Engineering, WI
Minnesota State University, Mankato, MN
Minot State University, ND
Mississippi State University, MS
Missouri Western State College, MO
Montana State U–Billings, MT
Montana State U–Bozeman, MT

Montana Tech of The University of Montana, MT
Morehead State University, KY
Morningside College, IA
Morrison University, NV
Mount Mary College, WI
Mount St. Clare College, IA
Mount Vernon Nazarene College, OH
Murray State University, KY
Newberry College, SC
North Carolina State University, NC
North Dakota State University, ND
Northeastern State University, OK
Northern Arizona University, AZ
Northern Michigan University, MI
Northwestern College, IA
Northwestern Oklahoma State University, OK
Northwest Missouri State University, MO
Northwest Nazarene University, ID
Northwood University, MI
Northwood University, Florida Campus, FL
Northwood University, Texas Campus, TX
Oglala Lakota College, SD
Ohio Northern University, OH
The Ohio State University, OH
Ohio University, OH
Ohio University–Eastern, OH
Ohio University–Lancaster, OH
Ohio Valley College, WV
Oklahoma Christian U of Science and Arts, OK
Oklahoma City University, OK
Oklahoma State U, OK
Old Dominion University, VA
Oral Roberts University, OK
Ottawa University, KS
Ouachita Baptist University, AR
Paine College, GA
Peace College, NC
Pepperdine University, CA
Pittsburg State University, KS
Plattsburgh State U of NY, NY
Point Loma Nazarene University, CA
Portland State University, OR
Presentation College, SD
Providence College, RI
Purdue University, IN
Quincy University, IL
Radford University, VA
Reinhardt College, GA
The Richard Stockton College of New Jersey, NJ
Robert Morris College, PA
Roberts Wesleyan College, NY
Rochester Institute of Technology, NY
Rockford College, IL
Rockhurst University, MO
Rocky Mountain College, MT
Rowan University, NJ
Sacred Heart University, CT
Saginaw Valley State University, MI
St. Ambrose University, IA
St. Edward's University, TX
St. John Fisher College, NY
Saint Louis University, MO
Saint Martin's College, WA
St. Thomas Aquinas College, NY
Saint Vincent College, PA
Salem Teikyo University, WV
Salisbury State University, MD
Sam Houston State University, TX
Santa Clara University, CA
Savannah State University, GA
Seton Hall University, NJ
Shenandoah University, VA
Shepherd College, WV
Shippensburg University of Pennsylvania, PA
Siena College, NY
Siena Heights University, MI
Sierra Nevada College, NV
Slippery Rock University of Pennsylvania, PA
Sonoma State University, CA
South Dakota State University, SD
Southeastern Louisiana University, LA
Southeast Missouri State University, MO
Southern Adventist University, TN
Southern Illinois University Carbondale, IL
Southern Methodist University, TX
Southern Nazarene University, OK
Southern Oregon University, OR
Southern Utah University, UT
Southern Wesleyan University, SC
Southwestern Adventist University, TX
Southwestern Assemblies of God University, TX
Southwestern College, KS
Southwestern Oklahoma State University, OK
Southwest Missouri State University, MO
Southwest State University, MN
Southwest Texas State University, TX
Spring Arbor College, MI
State U of NY at Binghamton, NY
State U of NY College at Fredonia, NY
State U of NY College at Geneseo, NY
State U of NY College at Potsdam, NY
State University of West Georgia, GA
Stephen F. Austin State University, TX
Stetson University, FL
Strayer University, DC
Sul Ross State University, TX
Teikyo Post University, CT
Tennessee Technological University, TN
Tennessee Wesleyan College, TN
Texas A&M University, TX
Texas A&M University–Kingsville, TX
Texas A&M University–Texarkana, TX
Texas Tech University, TX
Texas Woman's University, TX
Thomas University, GA
Tiffin University, OH
Trevecca Nazarene University, TN
Trinity Bible College, ND
Trinity Christian College, IL
Truman State University, MO
Union University, TN
United States International University, CA
The University of Akron, OH
The University of Alabama at Birmingham, AL
The University of Alabama in Huntsville, AL
U of Alaska Anchorage, AK
U of Alaska Southeast, AK
The University of Arizona, AZ
University of Arkansas at Little Rock, AR
University of Arkansas at Pine Bluff, AR
U of Calif, Riverside, CA
U of Calif, San Diego, CA
University of Central Arkansas, AR
University of Central Oklahoma, OK
University of Cincinnati, OH
University of Colorado at Boulder, CO
University of Colorado at Colorado Springs, CO
University of Colorado at Denver, CO
University of Dayton, OH
University of Delaware, DE
University of Evansville, IN
University of Florida, FL
University of Georgia, GA
University of Great Falls, MT
University of Guam, GU
University of Hawaii at Hilo, HI
University of Houston, TX
University of Houston–Clear Lake, TX
University of Houston–Downtown, TX
University of Houston–Victoria, TX
University of Idaho, ID
University of Illinois at Springfield, IL
The University of Iowa, IA
University of Kansas, KS
University of Louisiana at Monroe, LA
The University of Maine at Augusta, ME
University of Maine at Fort Kent, ME
University of Mary Hardin-Baylor, TX
University of Massachusetts Amherst, MA
The University of Memphis, TN
University of Michigan, MI
University of Michigan–Dearborn, MI
University of Michigan–Flint, MI
University of Minnesota, Crookston, MN
University of Minnesota, Twin Cities Campus, MN
University of Missouri–St. Louis, MO
The University of Montana–Missoula, MT
University of Nebraska at Kearney, NE
University of Nebraska at Omaha, NE
University of Nebraska–Lincoln, NE
University of Nevada, Las Vegas, NV
University of Nevada, Reno, NV
University of New Hampshire, NH
The University of North Carolina at Chapel Hill, NC
The University of North Carolina at Charlotte, NC
The University of North Carolina at Greensboro, NC
The University of North Carolina at Pembroke, NC
The University of North Carolina at Wilmington, NC
University of North Dakota, ND
University of Northern Colorado, CO
University of Northern Iowa, IA
University of North Florida, FL
University of Oklahoma, OK
University of Portland, OR
U of Puerto Rico, Humacao University College, PR
University of Puget Sound, WA
University of Rio Grande, OH
University of St. Thomas, MN
University of South Alabama, AL
University of South Carolina, SC
University of South Carolina Aiken, SC
University of South Dakota, SD
University of Southern Colorado, CO
University of Southern Indiana, IN
University of South Florida, FL
The University of Tampa, FL
The University of Tennessee at Martin, TN

Business (continued)

The University of Tennessee Knoxville, TN
The University of Texas at Arlington, TX
The University of Texas at Dallas, TX
The University of Texas at El Paso, TX
The University of Texas at San Antonio, TX
The University of Texas at Tyler, TX
The University of Texas–Pan American, TX
University of the Ozarks, AR
University of Toledo, OH
University of Tulsa, OK
University of Utah, UT
University of Virginia's College at Wise, VA
University of Washington, WA
University of Wisconsin–Eau Claire, WI
University of Wisconsin–Green Bay, WI
University of Wisconsin–La Crosse, WI
University of Wisconsin–Oshkosh, WI
University of Wisconsin–Parkside, WI
University of Wisconsin–Platteville, WI
University of Wisconsin–River Falls, WI
University of Wisconsin–Stevens Point, WI
University of Wisconsin–Stout, WI
University of Wisconsin–Superior, WI
University of Wisconsin–Whitewater, WI
University of Wyoming, WY
Utah State University, UT
Valdosta State University, GA
Valley City State University, ND
Virginia Military Institute, VA
Virginia Polytechnic Institute and State U, VA
Virginia State University, VA
Voorhees College, SC
Wake Forest University, NC
Walsh College of Accountancy and Business Admin, MI
Walsh University, OH
Warner Southern College, FL
Washington & Jefferson College, PA
Washington State University, WA
Washington University in St. Louis, MO
Wayland Baptist University, TX
Webster University, MO
West Chester University of Pennsylvania, PA
Western Illinois University, IL
Western Michigan University, MI
Western Montana College of The U of Montana, MT
Western State College of Colorado, CO
Western Washington University, WA
West Liberty State College, WV
Westminster College, UT
West Texas A&M University, TX
West Virginia State College, WV
West Virginia University, WV
Wheeling Jesuit University, WV
Wichita State University, KS
Widener University, PA
Winston-Salem State University, NC
Wisconsin Lutheran College, WI
Worcester State College, MA
Xavier University, OH
Xavier University of Louisiana, LA
York College, NE
Youngstown State University, OH

COMMUNICATION

Abilene Christian University, TX
Adams State College, CO
Albertus Magnus College, CT
Alfred University, NY
Allentown College of St. Francis de Sales, PA
American University, DC
Anderson College, SC
Angelo State University, TX
Arizona State University, AZ
Arkansas State University, AR
Ashland University, OH
Auburn University, AL
Augsburg College, MN
Augustana College, SD
Austin College, TX
Avila College, MO
Baker University, KS
Ball State University, IN
Barber-Scotia College, NC
Barton College, NC
Baylor University, TX
Beaver College, PA
Berry College, GA
Bethel College, IN
Biola University, CA
Black Hills State University, SD
Bloomsburg University of Pennsylvania, PA
Boise State University, ID
Bowie State University, MD
Bowling Green State University, OH
Brenau University, GA
Briar Cliff College, IA
Brigham Young University, UT
Brigham Young University–Hawaii Campus, HI
Bryan College, TN
Butler University, IN
California Lutheran University, CA
California Polytechnic State U, San Luis Obispo, CA
California State University, Bakersfield, CA
California State University, Chico, CA
California State University, Fresno, CA
California State University, Fullerton, CA
California State University, Los Angeles, CA
California State University, Stanislaus, CA
Calvin College, MI
Cameron University, OK
Carlow College, PA
Centenary College of Louisiana, LA
Central College, IA
Central Methodist College, MO
Central Missouri State University, MO
Chaminade University of Honolulu, HI
Clarion University of Pennsylvania, PA
Clemson University, SC
College of Charleston, SC
The College of New Rochelle, NY
Columbia College, SC
Columbia International University, SC
Concordia University, IL
Concordia University, NE
Dakota State University, SD
Dana College, NE
Defiance College, OH
Denison University, OH
DePauw University, IN
Doane College, NE
Dordt College, IA
Drury University, MO
East Central University, OK
Eastern Connecticut State University, CT
Eastern Michigan University, MI
Eastern New Mexico University, NM
East Stroudsburg University of Pennsylvania, PA
East Texas Baptist University, TX
Edinboro University of Pennsylvania, PA
Elizabethtown College, PA
Elmhurst College, IL
Elon College, NC
Emmanuel College, GA
Fitchburg State College, MA
Flagler College, FL
Florida Institute of Technology, FL
Florida International University, FL
Florida Memorial College, FL
Florida Southern College, FL
Fordham University, NY
Fort Hays State University, KS
Fort Lewis College, CO
Franklin Pierce College, NH
Friends University, KS
Frostburg State University, MD
Gardner-Webb University, NC
Georgia State University, GA
Goshen College, IN
Governors State University, IL
Grambling State University, LA
Grand Canyon University, AZ
Grove City College, PA
Gwynedd-Mercy College, PA
Hardin-Simmons University, TX
Heritage College, WA
Hofstra University, NY
Howard Payne University, TX
Idaho State University, ID
Illinois State University, IL
Indiana University of Pennsylvania, PA
Indiana U–Purdue U Fort Wayne, IN
Iowa State University of Science and Technology, IA
Iowa Wesleyan College, IA
Jacksonville State University, AL
Juniata College, PA
Kansas State University, KS
Kansas Wesleyan University, KS
Kent State University, OH
King's College, PA
Lee University, TN
Lewis & Clark College, OR
Limestone College, SC
Lincoln University, PA
Lock Haven University of Pennsylvania, PA
Louisiana State University and A&M College, LA
Loyola University Chicago, IL
Lubbock Christian University, TX
Lycoming College, PA
Madonna University, MI
Malone College, OH
Mansfield University of Pennsylvania, PA
Marquette University, WI
Marycrest International University, IA
Marymount University, VA
Massachusetts College of Liberal Arts, MA
McNeese State University, LA
Mesa State College, CO
Michigan Technological University, MI
Middle Tennessee State University, TN
Milligan College, TN
Milwaukee School of Engineering, WI
Minot State University, ND

Mississippi College, MS
Mississippi State University, MS
Missouri Western State College, MO
Montana State U–Billings, MT
Montana State U–Bozeman, MT
Morningside College, IA
Mount Mary College, WI
Mount St. Clare College, IA
Multnomah Bible College and Biblical Seminary, OR
Murray State University, KY
Newberry College, SC
New Mexico Institute of Mining and Technology, NM
North Dakota State University, ND
Northeastern State University, OK
Northern Arizona University, AZ
Northwestern College, IA
Northwestern Oklahoma State University, OK
Northwest Missouri State University, MO
Ohio Northern University, OH
The Ohio State University, OH
Ohio University, OH
Ohio University–Eastern, OH
Ohio University–Lancaster, OH
Oklahoma Christian U of Science and Arts, OK
Oklahoma City University, OK
Oklahoma State U, OK
Oral Roberts University, OK
Ottawa University, KS
Ouachita Baptist University, AR
Paine College, GA
Peace College, NC
Pepperdine University, CA
Pittsburg State University, KS
Plattsburgh State U of NY, NY
Point Loma Nazarene University, CA
Presentation College, SD
Quincy University, IL
Radford University, VA
Reinhardt College, GA
Robert Morris College, PA
Rochester Institute of Technology, NY
Rockhurst University, MO
Rowan University, NJ
Saginaw Valley State University, MI
St. Ambrose University, IA
St. Edward's University, TX
Saint Louis University, MO
St. Thomas Aquinas College, NY
Salisbury State University, MD
Sam Houston State University, TX
Shepherd College, WV
Shippensburg University of Pennsylvania, PA
Siena College, NY
Sonoma State University, CA
South Dakota State University, SD
Southeastern College of the Assemblies of God, FL
Southeastern Louisiana University, LA
Southeast Missouri State University, MO
Southern Adventist University, TN
Southern Illinois University Carbondale, IL
Southern Methodist University, TX
Southern Nazarene University, OK
Southern Utah University, UT
Southwestern Adventist University, TX
Southwestern Assemblies of God University, TX
Southwestern Oklahoma State University, OK
Southwest Missouri State University, MO
Southwest State University, MN
State U of NY at Oswego, NY
State U of NY College at Fredonia, NY
State U of NY College at Geneseo, NY
State U of NY College at Potsdam, NY
State University of West Georgia, GA
Stephen F. Austin State University, TX
Stetson University, FL
Tennessee Technological University, TN
Tennessee Wesleyan College, TN
Texas A&M University–Kingsville, TX
Texas Tech University, TX
Texas Woman's University, TX
Trevecca Nazarene University, TN
Truman State University, MO
Union University, TN
United States International University, CA
The University of Akron, OH
U of Alaska Anchorage, AK
U of Alaska Southeast, AK
University of Arkansas at Little Rock, AR
U of Calif, San Diego, CA
University of Central Arkansas, AR
University of Cincinnati, OH
University of Colorado at Boulder, CO
University of Evansville, IN
University of Great Falls, MT
University of Guam, GU
University of Houston–Victoria, TX
University of Idaho, ID
University of Illinois at Springfield, IL
University of Kansas, KS
University of Louisiana at Monroe, LA
University of Mary, ND
University of Mary Hardin-Baylor, TX
University of Massachusetts Amherst, MA
The University of Memphis, TN
University of Michigan, MI
University of Minnesota, Crookston, MN
University of Minnesota, Twin Cities Campus, MN
University of Missouri–St. Louis, MO
University of Nebraska at Omaha, NE
University of Nevada, Las Vegas, NV
The University of North Carolina at Chapel Hill, NC
The University of North Carolina at Greensboro, NC
The University of North Carolina at Pembroke, NC
The University of North Carolina at Wilmington, NC
University of North Dakota, ND
University of Northern Colorado, CO
University of Oklahoma, OK
University of Portland, OR
University of Puget Sound, WA
University of Rio Grande, OH
University of South Carolina, SC
University of South Carolina Aiken, SC
University of South Dakota, SD
University of Southern Indiana, IN
University of South Florida, FL
The University of Tampa, FL
The University of Tennessee at Martin, TN
The University of Tennessee Knoxville, TN
The University of Texas at Arlington, TX
The University of Texas at El Paso, TX
The University of Texas at San Antonio, TX
The University of Texas at Tyler, TX
The University of Texas–Pan American, TX
University of the Ozarks, AR
University of Toledo, OH
University of Tulsa, OK
University of Utah, UT
University of Washington, WA
University of Wisconsin–Eau Claire, WI
University of Wisconsin–Parkside, WI
University of Wisconsin–Platteville, WI
University of Wisconsin–River Falls, WI
University of Wisconsin–Stevens Point, WI
University of Wisconsin–Superior, WI
University of Wisconsin–Whitewater, WI
University of Wyoming, WY
Utah State University, UT
Valley City State University, ND
Walsh University, OH
Warner Southern College, FL
Washington State University, WA
Wayland Baptist University, TX
Webster University, MO
Western State College of Colorado, CO
Western Washington University, WA
West Liberty State College, WV
Westminster College, UT
West Texas A&M University, TX
West Virginia State College, WV
West Virginia University, WV
Wheeling Jesuit University, WV
Wichita State University, KS
William Woods University, MO
Wisconsin Lutheran College, WI
York College, NE

COMPUTER SCIENCE

Adams State College, CO
Albany State University, GA
Albertson College of Idaho, ID
Albertus Magnus College, CT
Alfred University, NY
Allentown College of St. Francis de Sales, PA
American University, DC
Anderson College, SC
Angelo State University, TX
Arizona State University, AZ
Arkansas State University, AR
Armstrong Atlantic State University, GA
Ashland University, OH
Athens State University, AL
Auburn University, AL
Augsburg College, MN
Baker University, KS
Bartlesville Wesleyan College, OK
Barton College, NC
Baylor University, TX
Bethel College, IN
Birmingham-Southern College, AL
Black Hills State University, SD
Bloomsburg University of Pennsylvania, PA
Boise State University, ID
Bowie State University, MD
Bowling Green State University, OH
Briar Cliff College, IA
Brigham Young University, UT
Brigham Young University–Hawaii Campus, HI
Buena Vista University, IA
Butler University, IN

Computer Science (continued)

California Lutheran University, CA
California Polytechnic State U, San Luis Obispo, CA
California State Polytechnic University, Pomona, CA
California State University, Chico, CA
California State University, Fresno, CA
California State University, Los Angeles, CA
California State University, Northridge, CA
California State University, San Bernardino, CA
California State University, Stanislaus, CA
Cameron University, OK
Carlow College, PA
Carroll College, WI
Central College, IA
Central Methodist College, MO
Central Missouri State University, MO
Central State University, OH
Cheyney University of Pennsylvania, PA
Clarion University of Pennsylvania, PA
Clarke College, IA
Clarkson University, NY
Clemson University, SC
Cogswell Polytechnical College, CA
College of Charleston, SC
The College of West Virginia, WV
Colorado School of Mines, CO
Concordia College, AL
Concordia University, IL
Concordia University, NE
Dakota State University, SD
Daniel Webster College, NH
Defiance College, OH
Delaware Valley College, PA
DePaul University, IL
DePauw University, IN
Detroit College of Business, MI
Detroit College of Business, Warren Campus, MI
DeVry Institute of Technology, AZ
DeVry Institute of Technology, CA
DeVry Institute of Technology, CA
DeVry Institute of Technology, CA
DeVry Institute of Technology, GA
DeVry Institute of Technology, GA
DeVry Institute of Technology, IL
DeVry Institute of Technology, IL
DeVry Institute of Technology, MO
DeVry Institute of Technology, OH
DeVry Institute of Technology, TX
Dordt College, IA
Eastern Connecticut State University, CT
Eastern Michigan University, MI
Eastern New Mexico University, NM
East Stroudsburg University of Pennsylvania, PA
East Tennessee State University, TN
East Texas Baptist University, TX
Edinboro University of Pennsylvania, PA
Elizabethtown College, PA
Elon College, NC
Fitchburg State College, MA
Florida Institute of Technology, FL
Florida International University, FL
Florida Memorial College, FL
Florida Metropolitan U-Fort Lauderdale Coll, FL
Fontbonne College, MO
Fort Hays State University, KS
Fort Lewis College, CO
Friends University, KS
Furman University, SC
Gardner-Webb University, NC
Georgia State University, GA
Grambling State University, LA
Gwynedd-Mercy College, PA
Heritage College, WA
Humphreys College, CA
Husson College, ME
Idaho State University, ID
Illinois Institute of Technology, IL
Illinois State University, IL
Indiana Institute of Technology, IN
Indiana University of Pennsylvania, PA
Indiana U–Purdue U Fort Wayne, IN
Iowa State University of Science and Technology, IA
Jacksonville State University, AL
James Madison University, VA
Juniata College, PA
Kansas State University, KS
Kansas Wesleyan University, KS
Kettering University, MI
King's College, PA
Lander University, SC
La Roche College, PA
Lawrence Technological University, MI
Limestone College, SC
Lincoln University, PA
Longwood College, VA
Louisiana State University and A&M College, LA
Louisiana State University in Shreveport, LA
Louisiana Tech University, LA
Loyola University Chicago, IL
Lubbock Christian University, TX
Lycoming College, PA
Madonna University, MI
Malone College, OH
Manhattan College, NY
Marycrest International University, IA
Marymount University, VA
Mary Washington College, VA
Massachusetts College of Liberal Arts, MA
McNeese State University, LA
Mesa State College, CO
Michigan State University, MI
Michigan Technological University, MI
Middle Tennessee State University, TN
Mills College, CA
Milwaukee School of Engineering, WI
Minnesota State University, Mankato, MN
Minot State University, ND
Mississippi State University, MS
Missouri Western State College, MO
Montana State U–Bozeman, MT
Montana Tech of The University of Montana, MT
Mount St. Clare College, IA
Mount Vernon Nazarene College, OH
Murray State University, KY
Muskingum College, OH
Norfolk State University, VA
North Dakota State University, ND
Northeastern State University, OK
Northwestern College, IA
Northwestern Oklahoma State University, OK
Northwest Missouri State University, MO
Northwest Nazarene University, ID
Ohio Northern University, OH
The Ohio State University, OH
Ohio University, OH
Ohio University–Eastern, OH
Ohio University–Lancaster, OH
Oklahoma Christian U of Science and Arts, OK
Oklahoma State U, OK
Ouachita Baptist University, AR
Paine College, GA
Pittsburg State University, KS
Plattsburgh State U of NY, NY
Polytechnic U, Brooklyn Campus, NY
Presentation College, SD
Purchase College, State U of NY, NY
Quincy University, IL
Radford University, VA
The Richard Stockton College of New Jersey, NJ
Ripon College, WI
Roberts Wesleyan College, NY
Rochester College, MI
Rochester Institute of Technology, NY
Rockhurst University, MO
Rollins College, FL
Rose-Hulman Institute of Technology, IN
Rowan University, NJ
Sacred Heart University, CT
Saginaw Valley State University, MI
St. Ambrose University, IA
St. Edward's University, TX
St. John's University, NY
Saint Vincent College, PA
Sam Houston State University, TX
Savannah State University, GA
Seton Hill College, PA
Shepherd College, WV
Shippensburg University of Pennsylvania, PA
Siena College, NY
Siena Heights University, MI
Skidmore College, NY
Slippery Rock University of Pennsylvania, PA
Sonoma State University, CA
South Dakota State University, SD
Southeast Missouri State University, MO
Southern Illinois University Carbondale, IL
Southern Methodist University, TX
Southwestern Adventist University, TX
Southwestern Oklahoma State University, OK
Southwest Missouri State University, MO
State U of NY at Binghamton, NY
State U of NY at New Paltz, NY
State U of NY at Stony Brook, NY
State U of NY College at Geneseo, NY
State University of West Georgia, GA
Stephen F. Austin State University, TX
Stetson University, FL
Stevens Institute of Technology, NJ
Strayer University, DC
Tennessee Technological University, TN
Tennessee Wesleyan College, TN
Texas A&M University, TX
Texas A&M University–Kingsville, TX
Texas Tech University, TX
Texas Woman's University, TX
Transylvania University, KY
United States International University, CA

University of Advancing Computer Technology, AZ
The University of Akron, OH
The University of Alabama, AL
The University of Alabama in Huntsville, AL
U of Alaska Anchorage, AK
University of Arkansas at Little Rock, AR
U of Calif, San Diego, CA
University of Central Arkansas, AR
University of Central Oklahoma, OK
University of Cincinnati, OH
University of Colorado at Boulder, CO
University of Colorado at Colorado Springs, CO
University of Evansville, IN
University of Great Falls, MT
University of Guam, GU
University of Hawaii at Hilo, HI
University of Houston, TX
University of Houston–Clear Lake, TX
University of Houston–Downtown, TX
University of Houston–Victoria, TX
University of Idaho, ID
University of Illinois at Springfield, IL
University of Kansas, KS
University of Louisiana at Monroe, LA
University of Maryland, Baltimore County, MD
University of Massachusetts Amherst, MA
University of Massachusetts Lowell, MA
University of Michigan, MI
University of Michigan–Dearborn, MI
University of Minnesota, Crookston, MN
University of Minnesota, Twin Cities Campus, MN
University of Missouri–Rolla, MO
University of Missouri–St. Louis, MO
The University of Montana–Missoula, MT
University of Nebraska at Omaha, NE
University of Nebraska–Lincoln, NE
University of Nevada, Las Vegas, NV
University of Nevada, Reno, NV
The University of North Carolina at Asheville, NC
The University of North Carolina at Charlotte, NC
The University of North Carolina at Wilmington, NC
University of North Dakota, ND
University of Oklahoma, OK
University of Portland, OR
U of Puerto Rico, Humacao University College, PR
University of Puget Sound, WA
University of Richmond, VA
University of Rio Grande, OH
University of South Carolina, SC
University of South Carolina Aiken, SC
University of South Dakota, SD
University of Southern Colorado, CO
University of South Florida, FL
The University of Tennessee at Martin, TN
The University of Texas at Arlington, TX
The University of Texas at Dallas, TX
The University of Texas at El Paso, TX
The University of Texas at San Antonio, TX
The University of Texas–Pan American, TX
University of Toledo, OH
University of Tulsa, OK
University of Utah, UT
University of Virginia's College at Wise, VA
The University of West Alabama, AL
University of Wisconsin–Eau Claire, WI
University of Wisconsin–Oshkosh, WI
University of Wisconsin–River Falls, WI
University of Wisconsin–Stevens Point, WI
University of Wisconsin–Superior, WI
University of Wisconsin–Whitewater, WI
University of Wyoming, WY
Utah State University, UT
Virginia Military Institute, VA
Voorhees College, SC
Wabash College, IN
Walsh University, OH
Washington State University, WA
Washington University in St. Louis, MO
Webster University, MO
Wentworth Institute of Technology, MA
Western State College of Colorado, CO
Western Washington University, WA
Westminster College, PA
Westminster College, UT
West Texas A&M University, TX
West Virginia University, WV
Wheeling Jesuit University, WV
Wichita State University, KS
Winston-Salem State University, NC
Xavier University of Louisiana, LA

EDUCATION

Abilene Christian University, TX
Adams State College, CO
Alabama State University, AL
Albany State University, GA
Albertson College of Idaho, ID
Albertus Magnus College, CT
Alfred University, NY
Allentown College of St. Francis de Sales, PA
American University, DC
Anderson College, SC
Angelo State University, TX
Antioch College, OH
Aquinas College, TN
Arizona State University, AZ
Arkansas State University, AR
Armstrong Atlantic State University, GA
Ashland University, OH
Athens State University, AL
Auburn University, AL
Augsburg College, MN
Augustana College, SD
Augusta State University, GA
Austin College, TX
Baker University, KS
Ball State University, IN
Baptist Bible College of Pennsylvania, PA
Barber-Scotia College, NC
Bartlesville Wesleyan College, OK
Barton College, NC
Baylor University, TX
Bellarmine College, KY
Bethel College, IN
Bethune-Cookman College, FL
Birmingham-Southern College, AL
Black Hills State University, SD
Bloomsburg University of Pennsylvania, PA
Boise State University, ID
Boston University, MA
Bowie State University, MD
Bowling Green State University, OH
Brenau University, GA
Brescia University, KY
Briar Cliff College, IA
Brigham Young University, UT
Brigham Young University–Hawaii Campus, HI
Bryan College, TN
Buena Vista University, IA
Butler University, IN
California Lutheran University, CA
California Polytechnic State U, San Luis Obispo, CA
California State Polytechnic University, Pomona, CA
California State University, Bakersfield, CA
California State University, Chico, CA
California State University, Fresno, CA
California State University, Los Angeles, CA
California State University, Northridge, CA
California State University, San Bernardino, CA
California State University, Stanislaus, CA
Calvin College, MI
Cambridge College, MA
Cameron University, OK
Carlow College, PA
Carson-Newman College, TN
Centenary College of Louisiana, LA
Central College, IA
Central Methodist College, MO
Central Missouri State University, MO
Central State University, OH
Central Washington University, WA
Chaminade University of Honolulu, HI
Cheyney University of Pennsylvania, PA
Christopher Newport University, VA
Circleville Bible College, OH
Clarion University of Pennsylvania, PA
Clarke College, IA
Clearwater Christian College, FL
Clemson University, SC
Cleveland College of Jewish Studies, OH
Coastal Carolina University, SC
College of Charleston, SC
The College of New Rochelle, NY
College of St. Catherine, MN
The College of Saint Rose, NY
College of the Southwest, NM
The College of West Virginia, WV
Columbia College, MO
Columbia College, SC
Columbia International University, SC
Concordia College, AL
Concordia College, NY
Concordia University, CA
Concordia University, IL
Concordia University, NE
Crown College, MN
Daemen College, NY
Dakota State University, SD
Dakota Wesleyan University, SD
Dallas Baptist University, TX
Dallas Christian College, TX
Dana College, NE
Davidson College, NC
Defiance College, OH
Delaware Valley College, PA
DePaul University, IL
Doane College, NE
Dordt College, IA

Education (continued)

Dowling College, NY
Drury University, MO
D'Youville College, NY
East Carolina University, NC
Eastern Connecticut State University, CT
Eastern Illinois University, IL
Eastern Mennonite University, VA
Eastern Michigan University, MI
Eastern Nazarene College, MA
Eastern New Mexico University, NM
Eastern Oregon University, OR
Eastern Washington University, WA
East Stroudsburg University of Pennsylvania, PA
East Tennessee State University, TN
East Texas Baptist University, TX
Edinboro University of Pennsylvania, PA
Elizabethtown College, PA
Elmhurst College, IL
Elon College, NC
Emmanuel College, GA
Endicott College, MA
Fairmont State College, WV
Felician College, NJ
Fitchburg State College, MA
Five Towns College, NY
Flagler College, FL
Florida Gulf Coast University, FL
Florida Institute of Technology, FL
Florida International University, FL
Florida Memorial College, FL
Fort Hays State University, KS
Fort Lewis College, CO
Framingham State College, MA
Francis Marion University, SC
Friends University, KS
Frostburg State University, MD
Furman University, SC
Gannon University, PA
Gardner-Webb University, NC
George Fox University, OR
Georgia Southern University, GA
Georgia State University, GA
Goshen College, IN
Governors State University, IL
Grambling State University, LA
Grand Canyon University, AZ
Greenville College, IL
Guilford College, NC
Gwynedd-Mercy College, PA
Hardin-Simmons University, TX
Heritage College, WA
High Point University, NC
Hillsdale College, MI
Hillsdale Free Will Baptist College, OK
Howard Payne University, TX
Husson College, ME
Idaho State University, ID
Illinois State University, IL
Indiana University of Pennsylvania, PA
Indiana U–Purdue U Fort Wayne, IN
Iowa State University of Science and Technology, IA
Jacksonville State University, AL
James Madison University, VA
Jarvis Christian College, TX
Johnson State College, VT
John Wesley College, NC
Juniata College, PA
Kansas State University, KS
Kansas Wesleyan University, KS
Kean University, NJ
Kennesaw State University, GA
Kent State University, OH
Kentucky Christian College, KY
King's College, PA
Lander University, SC
Langston University, OK
Lawrence Technological University, MI
Lee University, TN
Lesley College, MA
Lewis-Clark State College, ID
Limestone College, SC
Lincoln University, MO
Lincoln University, PA
Lock Haven University of Pennsylvania, PA
Long Island U, Southampton College, NY
Longwood College, VA
Louisiana State University and A&M College, LA
Louisiana State University in Shreveport, LA
Louisiana Tech University, LA
Loyola University Chicago, IL
Lubbock Christian University, TX
Lycoming College, PA
Lyndon State College, VT
Madonna University, MI
Malone College, OH
Mansfield University of Pennsylvania, PA
Marycrest International University, IA
Maryville University of Saint Louis, MO
Mary Washington College, VA
Massachusetts College of Liberal Arts, MA
The Master's College and Seminary, CA
Mayville State University, ND
McNeese State University, LA
Mercer University, GA
Meredith College, NC
Mesa State College, CO
Messenger College, MO
Miami University, OH
Michigan State University, MI
Mid-America Bible College, OK
Mid-Continent College, KY
Middle Tennessee State University, TN
Minot State University, ND
Mississippi College, MS
Mississippi State University, MS
Missouri Western State College, MO
Montana State U–Billings, MT
Montana State U–Bozeman, MT
Morningside College, IA
Mount Mary College, WI
Mount St. Clare College, IA
Mount St. Mary's College, CA
Mount Vernon Nazarene College, OH
Murray State University, KY
Newberry College, SC
North Carolina State University, NC
North Central College, IL
North Dakota State University, ND
Northeastern Illinois University, IL
Northeastern State University, OK
North Greenville College, SC
Northwest College, WA
Northwestern College, IA
Northwestern Oklahoma State University, OK
Northwest Missouri State University, MO
Northwest Nazarene University, ID
Oglala Lakota College, SD
Ohio Northern University, OH
The Ohio State University, OH
Ohio University, OH
Ohio University–Eastern, OH
Ohio University–Lancaster, OH
Ohio Valley College, WV
Oklahoma Christian U of Science and Arts, OK
Oklahoma City University, OK
Oklahoma Panhandle State University, OK
Oklahoma State U, OK
Oral Roberts University, OK
Ottawa University, KS
Ouachita Baptist University, AR
Ozark Christian College, MO
Paine College, GA
Pepperdine University, CA
Piedmont College, GA
Pine Manor College, MA
Pittsburg State University, KS
Plattsburgh State U of NY, NY
Point Loma Nazarene University, CA
Prairie View A&M University, TX
Purdue University, IN
Quincy University, IL
Radford University, VA
Reinhardt College, GA
The Richard Stockton College of New Jersey, NJ
Roberts Wesleyan College, NY
Rockford College, IL
Rockhurst University, MO
Rocky Mountain College, MT
Rowan University, NJ
Sacred Heart University, CT
Saginaw Valley State University, MI
St. Ambrose University, IA
St. Edward's University, TX
Saint Martin's College, WA
St. Thomas Aquinas College, NY
Salem-Teikyo University, WV
Salisbury State University, MD
Sam Houston State University, TX
Seton Hall University, NJ
Seton Hill College, PA
Shasta Bible College, CA
Shaw University, NC
Shepherd College, WV
Shippensburg University of Pennsylvania, PA
Siena College, NY
Sierra Nevada College, NV
Slippery Rock University of Pennsylvania, PA
Sonoma State University, CA
South Dakota State University, SD
Southeastern Louisiana University, LA
Southeast Missouri State University, MO
Southern Adventist University, TN
Southern Christian University, AL
Southern Illinois University Carbondale, IL
Southern Nazarene University, OK
Southern Oregon University, OR
Southern Utah University, UT
Southern Wesleyan University, SC
Southwest Baptist University, MO
Southwestern Adventist University, TX
Southwestern Assemblies of God University, TX
Southwestern Oklahoma State University, OK

Southwest Missouri State University, MO
Southwest State University, MN
Southwest Texas State University, TX
Spring Arbor College, MI
State U of NY at New Paltz, NY
State U of NY at Oswego, NY
State U of NY College at Brockport, NY
State U of NY College at Fredonia, NY
State U of NY College at Geneseo, NY
State U of NY College at Oneonta, NY
State U of NY College at Potsdam, NY
State University of West Georgia, GA
Stephen F. Austin State University, TX
Stetson University, FL
Stillman College, AL
Sul Ross State University, TX
Tennessee Technological University, TN
Tennessee Wesleyan College, TN
Texas A&M University, TX
Texas A&M University–Kingsville, TX
Texas A&M University–Texarkana, TX
Texas Christian University, TX
Texas Tech University, TX
Texas Woman's University, TX
Thomas College, ME
Thomas University, GA
Transylvania University, KY
Trevecca Nazarene University, TN
Trinity Baptist College, FL
Trinity Bible College, ND
Truman State University, MO
United States International University, CA
The University of Akron, OH
The University of Alabama in Huntsville, AL
U of Alaska Anchorage, AK
U of Alaska Southeast, AK
The University of Arizona, AZ
University of Arkansas at Little Rock, AR
University of Arkansas at Pine Bluff, AR
U of Calif, Riverside, CA
University of Central Arkansas, AR
University of Central Oklahoma, OK
University of Cincinnati, OH
University of Colorado at Boulder, CO
University of Colorado at Colorado Springs, CO
University of Dayton, OH
University of Delaware, DE
University of Evansville, IN
University of Florida, FL
University of Georgia, GA
University of Great Falls, MT
University of Guam, GU
University of Houston, TX
University of Houston–Clear Lake, TX
University of Houston–Downtown, TX
University of Houston–Victoria, TX
University of Idaho, ID
University of Illinois at Springfield, IL
University of Kansas, KS
University of Louisiana at Monroe, LA
University of Maine at Fort Kent, ME
University of Maine at Machias, ME
University of Mary Hardin-Baylor, TX
University of Massachusetts Amherst, MA
The University of Memphis, TN
University of Michigan, MI
University of Michigan–Flint, MI
University of Minnesota, Twin Cities Campus, MN
University of Missouri–Rolla, MO
University of Missouri–St. Louis, MO
The University of Montana–Missoula, MT
University of Montevallo, AL
University of Nebraska at Omaha, NE
University of Nebraska–Lincoln, NE
University of Nevada, Las Vegas, NV
University of Nevada, Reno, NV
University of New Hampshire, NH
The University of North Carolina at Asheville, NC
The University of North Carolina at Chapel Hill, NC
The University of North Carolina at Charlotte, NC
The University of North Carolina at Greensboro, NC
The University of North Carolina at Pembroke, NC
The University of North Carolina at Wilmington, NC
University of North Dakota, ND
University of Northern Colorado, CO
University of Northern Iowa, IA
University of North Florida, FL
University of Oklahoma, OK
University of Portland, OR
U of Puerto Rico, Humacao University College, PR
University of Rio Grande, OH
University of St. Thomas, MN
University of South Carolina, SC
University of South Carolina Aiken, SC
University of South Dakota, SD
University of Southern Indiana, IN
University of South Florida, FL
The University of Tampa, FL
The University of Tennessee at Martin, TN
The University of Tennessee Knoxville, TN
The University of Texas at Brownsville, TX
The University of Texas at El Paso, TX
The University of Texas at San Antonio, TX
The University of Texas–Pan American, TX
University of the Ozarks, AR
University of Toledo, OH
University of Utah, UT
University of Virginia's College at Wise, VA
University of Wisconsin–Eau Claire, WI
University of Wisconsin–La Crosse, WI
University of Wisconsin–Parkside, WI
University of Wisconsin–Platteville, WI
University of Wisconsin–River Falls, WI
University of Wisconsin–Stevens Point, WI
University of Wisconsin–Stout, WI
University of Wisconsin–Superior, WI
University of Wisconsin–Whitewater, WI
University of Wyoming, WY
Utah State University, UT
Valdosta State University, GA
Valley City State University, ND
Vanderbilt University, TN
Virginia Polytechnic Institute and State U, VA
Virginia State University, VA
Voorhees College, SC
Wabash College, IN
Wake Forest University, NC
Walsh University, OH
Warner Southern College, FL
Washington State University, WA
Wayland Baptist University, TX
Webster University, MO
Western Illinois University, IL
Western Michigan University, MI
Western Montana College of The U of Montana, MT
Western State College of Colorado, CO
Western Washington University, WA
West Liberty State College, WV
Westminster College, UT
West Texas A&M University, TX
West Virginia University, WV
Wheeling Jesuit University, WV
Wichita State University, KS
William Jewell College, MO
Wilmington College, OH
Winston-Salem State University, NC
Wisconsin Lutheran College, WI
Worcester State College, MA
Xavier University, OH
Xavier University of Louisiana, LA
York College, NE
Youngstown State University, OH

ENGINEERING/TECHNOLOGIES

Alfred University, NY
Arizona State University, AZ
Arkansas State University, AR
Armstrong Atlantic State University, GA
Auburn University, AL
Austin College, TX
Baker University, KS
Baylor University, TX
Bluefield State College, WV
Boise State University, ID
Boston University, MA
Bowie State University, MD
Bowling Green State University, OH
Brigham Young University, UT
Butler University, IN
California Polytechnic State U, San Luis Obispo, CA
California State Polytechnic University, Pomona, CA
California State University, Bakersfield, CA
California State University, Chico, CA
California State University, Fresno, CA
California State University, Fullerton, CA
California State University, Los Angeles, CA
California State University, Northridge, CA
Calvin College, MI
Cameron University, OK
Carthage College, WI
Centenary College of Louisiana, LA
Central Missouri State University, MO
Central State University, OH
Citadel, The Military Coll of South Carolina, SC
Clarkson University, NY
Clemson University, SC
Cogswell Polytechnical College, CA
College of Charleston, SC
The College of New Jersey, NJ
The College of Saint Rose, NY
Colorado School of Mines, CO
Daniel Webster College, NH
Davis & Elkins College, WV
DeVry Institute of Technology, AZ
DeVry Institute of Technology, CA
DeVry Institute of Technology, CA
DeVry Institute of Technology, CA

Engineering/Technologies (continued)

DeVry Institute of Technology, GA
DeVry Institute of Technology, GA
DeVry Institute of Technology, IL
DeVry Institute of Technology, IL
DeVry Institute of Technology, MO
DeVry Institute of Technology, OH
DeVry Institute of Technology, TX
Dordt College, IA
Eastern Michigan University, MI
Eastern Nazarene College, MA
Eastern New Mexico University, NM
East Tennessee State University, TN
Edinboro University of Pennsylvania, PA
Elizabethtown College, PA
Elon College, NC
Fairmont State College, WV
Florida Agricultural and Mechanical University, FL
Florida Atlantic University, FL
Florida Institute of Technology, FL
Florida International University, FL
Fort Hays State University, KS
Fort Lewis College, CO
Furman University, SC
Gannon University, PA
Geneva College, PA
The George Washington University, DC
Georgia Southern University, GA
Gonzaga University, WA
Greenville College, IL
Grove City College, PA
Idaho State University, ID
Illinois Institute of Technology, IL
Illinois State University, IL
Indiana Institute of Technology, IN
Indiana University of Pennsylvania, PA
Indiana U–Purdue U Fort Wayne, IN
Iowa State University of Science and Technology, IA
James Madison University, VA
Kansas State University, KS
Kettering University, MI
Lakeland College, WI
Lander University, SC
Lawrence Technological University, MI
Loras College, IA
Louisiana State University and A&M College, LA
Louisiana Tech University, LA
Maharishi University of Management, IA
Maine Maritime Academy, ME
Marquette University, WI
McNeese State University, LA
Mesa State College, CO
Miami University, OH
Michigan State University, MI
Michigan Technological University, MI
Milwaukee School of Engineering, WI
Minnesota State University, Mankato, MN
Mississippi State University, MS
Missouri Western State College, MO
Montana State U–Bozeman, MT
Montana Tech of The University of Montana, MT
New Mexico Institute of Mining and Technology, NM
North Carolina State University, NC
North Dakota State University, ND
Northern Arizona University, AZ
Northern Michigan University, MI
Northwestern College, IA
Oakland University, MI
Ohio Northern University, OH
The Ohio State University, OH
Ohio University, OH
Ohio University–Eastern, OH
Ohio University–Lancaster, OH
Oklahoma Christian U of Science and Arts, OK
Oklahoma State U, OK
Old Dominion University, VA
Oral Roberts University, OK
Ouachita Baptist University, AR
Pittsburg State University, KS
Plattsburgh State U of NY, NY
Point Loma Nazarene University, CA
Polytechnic U, Brooklyn Campus, NY
Polytechnic University of Puerto Rico, PR
Portland State University, OR
Purdue University, IN
Rice University, TX
Rochester Institute of Technology, NY
Rollins College, FL
Rose-Hulman Institute of Technology, IN
Rowan University, NJ
Rutgers, State U of NJ, College of Engineering, NJ
Saginaw Valley State University, MI
St. Ambrose University, IA
Saint Louis University, MO
Saint Martin's College, WA
Sam Houston State University, TX
Santa Clara University, CA
Savannah State University, GA
Shaw University, NC
Shepherd College, WV
South Dakota School of Mines and Technology, SD
South Dakota State University, SD
Southeastern Louisiana University, LA
Southern Illinois University Carbondale, IL
Southern Methodist University, TX
Southwestern Oklahoma State University, OK
State U of NY at Binghamton, NY
State U of NY at New Paltz, NY
State U of NY at Stony Brook, NY
State U of NY College at Potsdam, NY
State U of NY Coll of Environ Sci and Forestry, NY
Stevens Institute of Technology, NJ
Tennessee Technological University, TN
Texas A&M University, TX
Texas Christian University, TX
Texas Tech University, TX
The University of Akron, OH
The University of Alabama at Birmingham, AL
The University of Alabama in Huntsville, AL
U of Alaska Anchorage, AK
The University of Arizona, AZ
University of Arkansas at Little Rock, AR
U of Calif, Berkeley, CA
U of Calif, Riverside, CA
U of Calif, San Diego, CA
University of Cincinnati, OH
University of Colorado at Boulder, CO
University of Colorado at Colorado Springs, CO
University of Colorado at Denver, CO
University of Dayton, OH
University of Delaware, DE
University of Evansville, IN
University of Florida, FL
University of Houston, TX
University of Houston–Downtown, TX
University of Idaho, ID
The University of Iowa, IA
University of Kansas, KS
University of Maine, ME
University of Maryland, Baltimore County, MD
University of Massachusetts Amherst, MA
University of Massachusetts Lowell, MA
The University of Memphis, TN
University of Michigan, MI
University of Michigan–Dearborn, MI
University of Minnesota, Crookston, MN
University of Minnesota, Twin Cities Campus, MN
University of Missouri–Rolla, MO
University of Missouri–St. Louis, MO
University of Nebraska at Omaha, NE
University of Nebraska–Lincoln, NE
University of Nevada, Las Vegas, NV
University of Nevada, Reno, NV
University of New Hampshire, NH
University of New Mexico, NM
The University of North Carolina at Asheville, NC
The University of North Carolina at Charlotte, NC
University of North Dakota, ND
University of Oklahoma, OK
University of Portland, OR
University of South Carolina, SC
University of South Carolina Aiken, SC
University of Southern Colorado, CO
University of Southern Indiana, IN
University of South Florida, FL
The University of Tennessee at Martin, TN
The University of Tennessee Knoxville, TN
The University of Texas at Arlington, TX
The University of Texas at Dallas, TX
The University of Texas at El Paso, TX
The University of Texas at San Antonio, TX
The University of Texas at Tyler, TX
The University of Texas–Pan American, TX
University of Toledo, OH
University of Tulsa, OK
University of Utah, UT
University of Washington, WA
University of Wisconsin–Green Bay, WI
University of Wisconsin–Parkside, WI
University of Wisconsin–Platteville, WI
University of Wisconsin–Stout, WI
University of Wyoming, WY
Utah State University, UT
Valley City State University, ND
Valparaiso University, IN
Vanderbilt University, TN
Virginia Commonwealth University, VA
Virginia Military Institute, VA
Virginia Polytechnic Institute and State U, VA
Virginia State University, VA
Washington State University, WA
Washington University in St. Louis, MO
Webb Institute, NY
Wentworth Institute of Technology, MA

Western Michigan University, MI
Western Washington University, WA
West Virginia University, WV
West Virginia University Institute of Technology, WV
Wheeling Jesuit University, WV
Wichita State University, KS
Widener University, PA
Wilkes University, PA
Xavier University of Louisiana, LA
York College of Pennsylvania, PA

ENGLISH

Abilene Christian University, TX
Adams State College, CO
Agnes Scott College, GA
Albertus Magnus College, CT
Alfred University, NY
Allentown College of St. Francis de Sales, PA
American University, DC
Anderson College, SC
Angelo State University, TX
Arizona State University, AZ
Arkansas State University, AR
Armstrong Atlantic State University, GA
Ashland University, OH
Athens State University, AL
Auburn University, AL
Augsburg College, MN
Augustana College, SD
Augusta State University, GA
Austin College, TX
Baker University, KS
Ball State University, IN
Barton College, NC
Baylor University, TX
Beaver College, PA
Berry College, GA
Bethel College, IN
Black Hills State University, SD
Bloomsburg University of Pennsylvania, PA
Boise State University, ID
Bowling Green State University, OH
Brescia University, KY
Brevard College, NC
Briar Cliff College, IA
Brigham Young University, UT
Brigham Young University–Hawaii Campus, HI
Bryan College, TN
Butler University, IN
California Lutheran University, CA
California Polytechnic State U, San Luis Obispo, CA
California State University, Chico, CA
California State University, Fresno, CA
California State University, Los Angeles, CA
California State University, Stanislaus, CA
Calvin College, MI
Cameron University, OK
Carlow College, PA
Centenary College of Louisiana, LA
Central Methodist College, MO
Central Missouri State University, MO
Central Washington University, WA
Chaminade University of Honolulu, HI
Clarion University of Pennsylvania, PA
Clemson University, SC
College of Charleston, SC
The College of New Rochelle, NY
College of St. Catherine, MN
The College of Saint Rose, NY
College of the Southwest, NM
Columbia College, SC
Columbia International University, SC
Concordia University, IL
Concordia University, NE
Crown College, MN
Dakota State University, SD
Dakota Wesleyan University, SD
Dana College, NE
Delaware Valley College, PA
Denison University, OH
Dordt College, IA
Drury University, MO
Duke University, NC
D'Youville College, NY
Eastern Connecticut State University, CT
Eastern Mennonite University, VA
Eastern Michigan University, MI
Eastern Nazarene College, MA
Eastern New Mexico University, NM
East Stroudsburg University of Pennsylvania, PA
East Tennessee State University, TN
East Texas Baptist University, TX
Edinboro University of Pennsylvania, PA
Elizabethtown College, PA
Emmanuel College, GA
Felician College, NJ
Fitchburg State College, MA
Florida International University, FL
Florida Memorial College, FL
Fontbonne College, MO
Fort Hays State University, KS
Fort Lewis College, CO
Francis Marion University, SC
Friends University, KS
Frostburg State University, MD
Furman University, SC
Gannon University, PA
Gardner-Webb University, NC
Governors State University, IL
Grambling State University, LA
Grand Canyon University, AZ
Green Mountain College, VT
Gwynedd-Mercy College, PA
Hardin-Simmons University, TX
High Point University, NC
Hillsdale College, MI
Hillsdale Free Will Baptist College, OK
Idaho State University, ID
Illinois State University, IL
Indiana University of Pennsylvania, PA
Indiana U–Purdue U Fort Wayne, IN
Iowa State University of Science and Technology, IA
Jacksonville State University, AL
James Madison University, VA
Juniata College, PA
Kalamazoo College, MI
Kansas State University, KS
Kansas Wesleyan University, KS
Kennesaw State University, GA
Kent State University, OH
King's College, PA
LaGrange College, GA
Lakeland College, WI
Lander University, SC
La Roche College, PA
Lee University, TN
Limestone College, SC
Lock Haven University of Pennsylvania, PA
Longwood College, VA
Louisiana State University and A&M College, LA
Louisiana State University in Shreveport, LA
Loyola University Chicago, IL
Lubbock Christian University, TX
Lycoming College, PA
MacMurray College, IL
Malone College, OH
Manchester College, IN
Marycrest International University, IA
Marymount University, VA
Mary Washington College, VA
Massachusetts College of Liberal Arts, MA
Mayville State University, ND
McNeese State University, LA
Mercer University, GA
Meredith College, NC
Mesa State College, CO
Mid-America Bible College, OK
Middle Tennessee State University, TN
Milligan College, TN
Minot State University, ND
Mississippi State University, MS
Missouri Western State College, MO
Montana State U–Billings, MT
Montana State U–Bozeman, MT
Morningside College, IA
Mount Mary College, WI
Mount St. Clare College, IA
Murray State University, KY
North Dakota State University, ND
Northeastern State University, OK
Northern Arizona University, AZ
Northwestern College, IA
Northwestern Oklahoma State University, OK
Northwest Missouri State University, MO
Northwest Nazarene University, ID
Ohio Northern University, OH
The Ohio State University, OH
Ohio University, OH
Ohio University–Eastern, OH
Ohio University–Lancaster, OH
Ohio Valley College, WV
Oklahoma Panhandle State University, OK
Oklahoma State U, OK
Old Dominion University, VA
Ottawa University, KS
Ouachita Baptist University, AR
Paine College, GA
Piedmont College, GA
Pittsburg State University, KS
Plattsburgh State U of NY, NY
Purchase College, State U of NY, NY
Quincy University, IL
Radford University, VA
Randolph-Macon Woman's College, VA
Reinhardt College, GA
Rockford College, IL
Rockhurst University, MO
Rocky Mountain College, MT
Sacred Heart University, CT
St. Ambrose University, IA
St. Edward's University, TX
St. John Fisher College, NY
Salisbury State University, MD
Sam Houston State University, TX

English (continued)

Savannah State University, GA
Seton Hill College, PA
Shepherd College, WV
Shippensburg University of Pennsylvania, PA
Siena College, NY
Slippery Rock University of Pennsylvania, PA
Sonoma State University, CA
South Dakota State University, SD
Southeastern Louisiana University, LA
Southeast Missouri State University, MO
Southern Adventist University, TN
Southern Illinois University Carbondale, IL
Southern Methodist University, TX
Southern Nazarene University, OK
Southern Oregon University, OR
Southern Wesleyan University, SC
Southwestern Adventist University, TX
Southwestern Oklahoma State University, OK
Southwest Texas State University, TX
State U of NY at New Paltz, NY
State U of NY at Oswego, NY
State U of NY College at Brockport, NY
State U of NY College at Fredonia, NY
State U of NY College at Geneseo, NY
State U of NY College at Potsdam, NY
State University of West Georgia, GA
Stetson University, FL
Sul Ross State University, TX
Teikyo Post University, CT
Tennessee Technological University, TN
Tennessee Wesleyan College, TN
Texas A&M University–Kingsville, TX
Texas A&M University–Texarkana, TX
Texas Tech University, TX
Texas Woman's University, TX
Trinity Christian College, IL
Truman State University, MO
The University of Akron, OH
The University of Alabama in Huntsville, AL
U of Alaska Anchorage, AK
University of Arkansas at Little Rock, AR
University of Arkansas at Pine Bluff, AR
U of Calif, Riverside, CA
University of Central Arkansas, AR
University of Cincinnati, OH
University of Colorado at Boulder, CO
University of Colorado at Colorado Springs, CO
University of Evansville, IN
University of Hawaii at Hilo, HI
University of Houston, TX
University of Idaho, ID
University of Illinois at Springfield, IL
University of Kansas, KS
University of Louisiana at Monroe, LA
University of Mary Hardin-Baylor, TX
University of Maryland, Baltimore County, MD
The University of Memphis, TN
University of Michigan, MI
University of Minnesota, Twin Cities Campus, MN
University of Missouri–Rolla, MO
University of Missouri–St. Louis, MO
The University of Montana–Missoula, MT
University of Nebraska at Kearney, NE
University of Nebraska at Omaha, NE
University of Nebraska–Lincoln, NE
University of Nevada, Las Vegas, NV
University of Nevada, Reno, NV
University of New Hampshire, NH
The University of North Carolina at Asheville, NC
The University of North Carolina at Chapel Hill, NC
The University of North Carolina at Greensboro, NC
The University of North Carolina at Pembroke, NC
The University of North Carolina at Wilmington, NC
University of North Dakota, ND
University of Northern Colorado, CO
University of Portland, OR
U of Puerto Rico, Humacao University College, PR
University of Puget Sound, WA
University of St. Thomas, MN
University of South Carolina, SC
University of South Carolina Aiken, SC
University of South Dakota, SD
University of South Florida, FL
The University of Tennessee at Martin, TN
The University of Texas at El Paso, TX
The University of Texas at San Antonio, TX
The University of Texas–Pan American, TX
University of the Ozarks, AR
University of Toledo, OH
University of Tulsa, OK
University of Utah, UT
University of Virginia's College at Wise, VA
University of Washington, WA
The University of West Alabama, AL
University of Wisconsin–Eau Claire, WI
University of Wisconsin–La Crosse, WI
University of Wisconsin–Parkside, WI
University of Wisconsin–River Falls, WI
University of Wisconsin–Stevens Point, WI
University of Wisconsin–Superior, WI
University of Wisconsin–Whitewater, WI
University of Wyoming, WY
Utah State University, UT
Valley City State University, ND
Virginia Military Institute, VA
Wake Forest University, NC
Walsh University, OH
Warner Southern College, FL
Wartburg College, IA
Washington State University, WA
Washington University in St. Louis, MO
Wayland Baptist University, TX
Webster University, MO
Western Carolina University, NC
Western Michigan University, MI
Western Montana College of The U of Montana, MT
Western State College of Colorado, CO
Western Washington University, WA
West Liberty State College, WV
Westminster College, UT
West Texas A&M University, TX
West Virginia State College, WV
West Virginia University, WV
Wheeling Jesuit University, WV
Wichita State University, KS
Worcester State College, MA
York College, NE
Youngstown State University, OH

FOREIGN LANGUAGES

Abilene Christian University, TX
Adams State College, CO
Adelphi University, NY
Albertson College of Idaho, ID
Albertus Magnus College, CT
Alfred University, NY
Allentown College of St. Francis de Sales, PA
American University, DC
Arizona State University, AZ
Ashland University, OH
Auburn University, AL
Augsburg College, MN
Austin College, TX
Baker University, KS
Ball State University, IN
Barton College, NC
Baylor University, TX
Black Hills State University, SD
Bloomsburg University of Pennsylvania, PA
Boise State University, ID
Boston University, MA
Briar Cliff College, IA
Brigham Young University, UT
Brigham Young University–Hawaii Campus, HI
Bryan College, TN
Butler University, IN
California Lutheran University, CA
California Polytechnic State U, San Luis Obispo, CA
California State University, Chico, CA
California State University, Los Angeles, CA
Carthage College, WI
Castleton State College, VT
Centenary College of Louisiana, LA
Central College, IA
Central Methodist College, MO
Central Michigan University, MI
Central Missouri State University, MO
Clarion University of Pennsylvania, PA
Clarke College, IA
Clemson University, SC
Coe College, IA
College of Charleston, SC
The College of New Rochelle, NY
College of St. Catherine, MN
The College of Saint Rose, NY
Columbia College, SC
Concordia University, IL
Davidson College, NC
Denison University, OH
Dordt College, IA
Eastern Connecticut State University, CT
Eastern Mennonite University, VA
Eastern Michigan University, MI
Eastern New Mexico University, NM
Eastern Washington University, WA
East Texas Baptist University, TX
Edinboro University of Pennsylvania, PA
Elizabethtown College, PA
Elmhurst College, IL
Fairmont State College, WV
Flagler College, FL
Florida International University, FL
Florida Memorial College, FL
Fordham University, NY
Fort Hays State University, KS
Fort Lewis College, CO
Friends University, KS

Frostburg State University, MD
Gannon University, PA
Gardner-Webb University, NC
Georgian Court College, NJ
Georgia Southern University, GA
Grove City College, PA
High Point University, NC
Hillsdale College, MI
Idaho State University, ID
Illinois State University, IL
Indiana University of Pennsylvania, PA
Indiana U–Purdue U Fort Wayne, IN
Iowa State University of Science and Technology, IA
John Carroll University, OH
Juniata College, PA
Kalamazoo College, MI
Kansas State University, KS
Kansas Wesleyan University, KS
King's College, PA
Lander University, SC
La Roche College, PA
Lock Haven University of Pennsylvania, PA
Louisiana State University and A&M College, LA
Loyola University Chicago, IL
Lubbock Christian University, TX
Lycoming College, PA
MacMurray College, IL
Malone College, OH
Manchester College, IN
Manhattan College, NY
Marquette University, WI
Mary Washington College, VA
McNeese State University, LA
Middle Tennessee State University, TN
Mississippi State University, MS
Montana State U–Bozeman, MT
Moravian College, PA
Mount St. Clare College, IA
Murray State University, KY
Newberry College, SC
North Dakota State University, ND
Northeastern State University, OK
Northwestern College, IA
Northwestern Oklahoma State University, OK
Northwest Missouri State University, MO
Ohio Northern University, OH
The Ohio State University, OH
Ohio University, OH
Ohio University–Eastern, OH
Ohio University–Lancaster, OH
Oklahoma State U, OK
Ottawa University, KS
Ouachita Baptist University, AR
Piedmont College, GA
Pittsburg State University, KS
Portland State University, OR
Rockhurst University, MO
St. Ambrose University, IA
St. John Fisher College, NY
Salisbury State University, MD
Sam Houston State University, TX
Shepherd College, WV
Siena College, NY
Siena Heights University, MI
Sonoma State University, CA
South Dakota State University, SD
Southeast Missouri State University, MO
Southern Illinois University Carbondale, IL
Southern Methodist University, TX
Southwestern Assemblies of God University, TX
Southwestern Oklahoma State University, OK
Southwest Missouri State University, MO
State U of NY College at Brockport, NY
State U of NY College at Fredonia, NY
State U of NY College at Geneseo, NY
State U of NY College at Potsdam, NY
State University of West Georgia, GA
Stetson University, FL
Sul Ross State University, TX
Tennessee Technological University, TN
Tennessee Wesleyan College, TN
Texas Tech University, TX
Texas Woman's University, TX
Truman State University, MO
United States International University, CA
The University of Akron, OH
University of Arkansas at Little Rock, AR
University of Central Oklahoma, OK
University of Cincinnati, OH
University of Colorado at Boulder, CO
University of Dallas, TX
University of Evansville, IN
The University of Findlay, OH
University of Idaho, ID
University of Kansas, KS
University of Louisiana at Monroe, LA
University of Maine at Fort Kent, ME
University of Mary Hardin-Baylor, TX
University of Maryland, Baltimore County, MD
University of Michigan, MI
University of Minnesota, Twin Cities Campus, MN
University of Missouri–St. Louis, MO
The University of Montana–Missoula, MT
University of Nebraska at Kearney, NE
University of Nebraska at Omaha, NE
University of Nebraska–Lincoln, NE
University of Nevada, Reno, NV
The University of North Carolina at Greensboro, NC
The University of North Carolina at Wilmington, NC
University of North Dakota, ND
University of Portland, OR
University of Puget Sound, WA
University of South Dakota, SD
University of Southern Indiana, IN
University of South Florida, FL
The University of Texas at San Antonio, TX
University of Tulsa, OK
University of Utah, UT
University of Washington, WA
University of Wisconsin–Eau Claire, WI
University of Wisconsin–River Falls, WI
University of Wisconsin–Stevens Point, WI
University of Wisconsin–Whitewater, WI
University of Wyoming, WY
Utah State University, UT
Valparaiso University, IN
Wake Forest University, NC
Washington State University, WA
Webster University, MO
Western Illinois University, IL
Western Michigan University, MI
Western Washington University, WA
West Virginia State College, WV
West Virginia University, WV
Wheeling Jesuit University, WV
Wichita State University, KS
Worcester State College, MA
Xavier University, OH
Xavier University of Louisiana, LA

HEALTH FIELDS

Adams State College, CO
Alabama State University, AL
Albany State University, GA
Allen College, IA
Allentown College of St. Francis de Sales, PA
American University, DC
Aquinas College, TN
Arizona State University, AZ
Arkansas State University, AR
Armstrong Atlantic State University, GA
Auburn University, AL
Augsburg College, MN
Augusta State University, GA
Austin College, TX
Azusa Pacific University, CA
Baker University, KS
Ball State University, IN
Barton College, NC
Bastyr University, WA
Baylor University, TX
Bellarmine College, KY
Bethel College, IN
Biola University, CA
Birmingham-Southern College, AL
Black Hills State University, SD
Bloomsburg University of Pennsylvania, PA
Boise State University, ID
Bowie State University, MD
Bowling Green State University, OH
Brenau University, GA
Brescia University, KY
Briar Cliff College, IA
Brigham Young University, UT
California Polytechnic State U, San Luis Obispo, CA
California State University, Bakersfield, CA
California State University, Chico, CA
California State University, Fresno, CA
California State University, Los Angeles, CA
California State University, San Bernardino, CA
Calvin College, MI
Carroll College, WI
Carthage College, WI
Central College, IA
Central Methodist College, MO
Central Missouri State University, MO
Chadron State College, NE
Clarkson College, NE
Clemson University, SC
College of Charleston, SC
The College of New Rochelle, NY
College of St. Catherine, MN
The College of West Virginia, WV
Comm Hospital Roanoke Valley–Coll of Health Scis, VA
Concordia University, NE
Daemen College, NY
Dalton State College, GA
Dana College, NE
Davis & Elkins College, WV
Deaconess College of Nursing, MO

Health Fields (continued)

Drury University, MO
D'Youville College, NY
East Carolina University, NC
Eastern Michigan University, MI
Eastern New Mexico University, NM
Eastern Washington University, WA
East Stroudsburg University of Pennsylvania, PA
East Tennessee State University, TN
East Texas Baptist University, TX
Edinboro University of Pennsylvania, PA
Elizabethtown College, PA
Elmhurst College, IL
Endicott College, MA
Fairmont State College, WV
Felician College, NJ
Fitchburg State College, MA
Florida Agricultural and Mechanical University, FL
Florida International University, FL
Florida Memorial College, FL
Fort Hays State University, KS
Francis Marion University, SC
Friends University, KS
Furman University, SC
Gardner-Webb University, NC
Georgia Baptist College of Nursing, GA
Georgia College and State University, GA
Georgia Southern University, GA
Georgia State University, GA
Governors State University, IL
Grace University, NE
Grambling State University, LA
Grand Canyon University, AZ
Gwynedd-Mercy College, PA
Hillsdale College, MI
Houston Baptist University, TX
Husson College, ME
Idaho State University, ID
Illinois State University, IL
Indiana University of Pennsylvania, PA
Indiana U–Purdue U Fort Wayne, IN
Iowa State University of Science and Technology, IA
Jacksonville State University, AL
James Madison University, VA
Juniata College, PA
Kansas State University, KS
Kean University, NJ
Kennesaw State University, GA
Kent State University, OH
King's College, PA
Lakeview College of Nursing, IL
Lander University, SC
Langston University, OK
Lee University, TN
Lewis-Clark State College, ID
Long Island U, Brooklyn Campus, NY
Louisiana College, LA
Louisiana Tech University, LA
Loyola University Chicago, IL
Lycoming College, PA
Lynn University, FL
MacMurray College, IL
Malone College, OH
Mansfield University of Pennsylvania, PA
Marquette University, WI
Marycrest International University, IA
Marymount University, VA
Massachusetts College of Liberal Arts, MA
McNeese State University, LA
Medcenter One College of Nursing, ND
Mesa State College, CO
MidAmerica Nazarene University, KS
Middle Tennessee State University, TN
Milligan College, TN
Milwaukee School of Engineering, WI
Minot State University, ND
Mississippi College, MS
Mississippi State University, MS
Missouri Western State College, MO
Montana State U–Bozeman, MT
Montana Tech of The University of Montana, MT
Mount St. Clare College, IA
Mount Vernon Nazarene College, OH
Murray State University, KY
North Dakota State University, ND
Northeastern State University, OK
Northern Arizona University, AZ
Northern Michigan University, MI
Northwestern College, IA
Northwest Missouri State University, MO
Northwest Nazarene University, ID
Oglala Lakota College, SD
Ohio Northern University, OH
The Ohio State University, OH
Ohio University, OH
Ohio University–Eastern, OH
Ohio University–Lancaster, OH
Old Dominion University, VA
Oral Roberts University, OK
Oregon Health Sciences University, OR
Ottawa University, KS
Ouachita Baptist University, AR
Palmer College of Chiropractic, IA
Piedmont College, GA
Pine Manor College, MA
Pittsburg State University, KS
Plattsburgh State U of NY, NY
Point Loma Nazarene University, CA
Presentation College, SD
Quincy University, IL
Radford University, VA
Reinhardt College, GA
Research College of Nursing, MO
The Richard Stockton College of New Jersey, NJ
Roberts Wesleyan College, NY
Rochester Institute of Technology, NY
Rockhurst University, MO
Rocky Mountain College, MT
Russell Sage College, NY
Sacred Heart University, CT
Saginaw Valley State University, MI
St. Ambrose University, IA
Saint Francis Medical Center College of Nursing, IL
St. John's University, NY
Saint Louis University, MO
Seton Hall University, NJ
Shepherd College, WV
Siena College, NY
Sonoma State University, CA
South Dakota State University, SD
Southeast Missouri State University, MO
Southern Adventist University, TN
Southern Christian University, AL
Southern Illinois University Carbondale, IL
Southwestern Oklahoma State University, OK
Southwest Missouri State University, MO
State U of NY at Binghamton, NY
State U of NY at New Paltz, NY
State U of NY at Stony Brook, NY
State University of West Georgia, GA
Stephen F. Austin State University, TX
Sul Ross State University, TX
Tennessee Technological University, TN
Tennessee Wesleyan College, TN
Texas A&M University, TX
Texas A&M University–Kingsville, TX
Texas Woman's University, TX
Thomas Jefferson University, PA
Trinity Christian College, IL
The University of Akron, OH
The University of Alabama in Huntsville, AL
U of Alaska Anchorage, AK
University of Arkansas at Little Rock, AR
University of Central Oklahoma, OK
University of Cincinnati, OH
University of Colorado at Boulder, CO
University of Colorado at Colorado Springs, CO
University of Evansville, IN
University of Great Falls, MT
University of Guam, GU
University of Hawaii at Hilo, HI
University of Houston, TX
University of Illinois at Springfield, IL
University of Kansas, KS
University of Louisiana at Monroe, LA
The University of Maine at Augusta, ME
University of Mary Hardin-Baylor, TX
University of Massachusetts Amherst, MA
University of Massachusetts Lowell, MA
The University of Memphis, TN
University of Michigan, MI
University of Minnesota, Crookston, MN
University of Minnesota, Twin Cities Campus, MN
University of Missouri–St. Louis, MO
The University of Montana–Missoula, MT
University of Nebraska–Lincoln, NE
University of Nevada, Las Vegas, NV
University of Nevada, Reno, NV
University of New Hampshire, NH
The University of North Carolina at Chapel Hill, NC
The University of North Carolina at Charlotte, NC
The University of North Carolina at Greensboro, NC
The University of North Carolina at Pembroke, NC
The University of North Carolina at Wilmington, NC
University of Northern Colorado, CO
University of Portland, OR
University of Rio Grande, OH
University of Saint Francis, IN
University of South Carolina, SC
University of Southern Indiana, IN
University of South Florida, FL
The University of Tampa, FL
The University of Tennessee at Martin, TN
The University of Texas at El Paso, TX
The University of Texas at Tyler, TX
U of Texas Medical Branch at Galveston, TX

The University of Texas–Pan American, TX
U of Texas Southwestern Medical Center at Dallas, TX
University of Toledo, OH
University of Utah, UT
University of Virginia's College at Wise, VA
University of Washington, WA
University of Wisconsin–Eau Claire, WI
University of Wisconsin–La Crosse, WI
University of Wisconsin–Parkside, WI
University of Wisconsin–Platteville, WI
University of Wisconsin–River Falls, WI
University of Wisconsin–Stevens Point, WI
University of Wisconsin–Superior, WI
University of Wyoming, WY
Utah State University, UT
Valdosta State University, GA
Valparaiso University, IN
Virginia Commonwealth University, VA
Virginia State University, VA
Viterbo University, WI
Walsh University, OH
Washington State University, WA
Western Michigan University, MI
Western Washington University, WA
Westminster College, UT
West Texas A&M University, TX
West Virginia University, WV
Wheeling Jesuit University, WV
Wichita State University, KS
Widener University, PA
Wilkes University, PA
William Woods University, MO
Winston-Salem State University, NC
Worcester State College, MA
York College of Pennsylvania, PA

HOME ECONOMICS

Abilene Christian University, TX
Arizona State University, AZ
Ashland University, OH
Baylor University, TX
Bowling Green State University, OH
Brigham Young University, UT
California Polytechnic State U, San Luis Obispo, CA
California State University, Fresno, CA
Carson-Newman College, TN
Central Missouri State University, MO
College of St. Catherine, MN
East Carolina University, NC
Eastern Michigan University, MI
Eastern New Mexico University, NM
Fort Valley State University, GA
Framingham State College, MA
Idaho State University, ID
Illinois State University, IL
Indiana University of Pennsylvania, PA
Iowa State University of Science and Technology, IA
Jacksonville State University, AL
Kansas State University, KS
Louisiana State University and A&M College, LA
Louisiana Tech University, LA
McNeese State University, LA
Middle Tennessee State University, TN
Mississippi State University, MS
Montana State U–Bozeman, MT
Mount Mary College, WI
Mount Vernon Nazarene College, OH
Murray State University, KY
North Dakota State University, ND
Northeastern State University, OK
Northwest Missouri State University, MO
The Ohio State University, OH
Ohio University, OH
Ohio University–Eastern, OH
Ohio University–Lancaster, OH
Oklahoma State U, OK
Ouachita Baptist University, AR
Pittsburg State University, KS
Plattsburgh State U of NY, NY
Point Loma Nazarene University, CA
Sam Houston State University, TX
Seton Hill College, PA
Shepherd College, WV
Siena College, NY
South Dakota State University, SD
Southeastern Louisiana University, LA
Southeast Missouri State University, MO
Southern Illinois University Carbondale, IL
Southwest Missouri State University, MO
Southwest Texas State University, TX
State U of NY College at Oneonta, NY
Stephen F. Austin State University, TX
Tennessee Technological University, TN
Texas A&M University–Kingsville, TX
Texas Tech University, TX
Texas Woman's University, TX
The University of Akron, OH
University of Central Arkansas, AR
University of Central Oklahoma, OK
University of Delaware, DE
University of Idaho, ID
University of Louisiana at Monroe, LA
University of Minnesota, Twin Cities Campus, MN
University of Nebraska at Omaha, NE
University of Nebraska–Lincoln, NE
The University of North Carolina at Greensboro, NC
University of Northern Colorado, CO
The University of Tennessee at Martin, TN
University of Wisconsin–Stevens Point, WI
University of Wisconsin–Stout, WI
University of Wyoming, WY
Utah State University, UT
Virginia Polytechnic Institute and State U, VA
Virginia State University, VA
Washington State University, WA
Western Illinois University, IL
West Virginia University, WV

HUMANITIES

Adams State College, CO
Agnes Scott College, GA
Albertson College of Idaho, ID
Albertus Magnus College, CT
Alfred University, NY
Allentown College of St. Francis de Sales, PA
Alma College, MI
American University, DC
Antioch College, OH
Arizona State University, AZ
Arkansas State University, AR
Armstrong Atlantic State University, GA
Ashland University, OH
Athens State University, AL
Auburn University, AL
Austin College, TX
Avila College, MO
Baker University, KS
Barton College, NC
Baylor University, TX
Bellevue University, NE
Benedictine University, IL
Berry College, GA
Black Hills State University, SD
Bloomsburg University of Pennsylvania, PA
Bowie State University, MD
Bowling Green State University, OH
Brenau University, GA
Briar Cliff College, IA
Brigham Young University, UT
Brigham Young University–Hawaii Campus, HI
Bryan College, TN
Buena Vista University, IA
Butler University, IN
California Institute of Integral Studies, CA
California Polytechnic State U, San Luis Obispo, CA
California State Polytechnic University, Pomona, CA
California State University, Chico, CA
California State University, Fresno, CA
California State University, Fullerton, CA
California State University, San Bernardino, CA
Calvin College, MI
Carlow College, PA
Carroll College, WI
Centenary College of Louisiana, LA
Central College, IA
Central Methodist College, MO
Central Missouri State University, MO
Chaminade University of Honolulu, HI
Clarion University of Pennsylvania, PA
Clarkson University, NY
Clemson University, SC
Coastal Carolina University, SC
College Misericordia, PA
College of Charleston, SC
The College of New Rochelle, NY
College of St. Catherine, MN
College of the Holy Cross, MA
The College of West Virginia, WV
Colorado Christian University, CO
Columbia College, SC
Columbia International University, SC
Concordia University, NE
Defiance College, OH
Denison University, OH
DePauw University, IN
Doane College, NE
Dordt College, IA
Drury University, MO
D'Youville College, NY
East Carolina University, NC
Eastern Connecticut State University, CT
Eastern Mennonite University, VA
Eastern Michigan University, MI
Eastern New Mexico University, NM
Edinboro University of Pennsylvania, PA
Elizabethtown College, PA
Elmhurst College, IL
Fairmont State College, WV
Florida Gulf Coast University, FL
Florida Institute of Technology, FL

Humanities (continued)

Florida International University, FL
Florida Memorial College, FL
Fort Hays State University, KS
Fort Lewis College, CO
Francis Marion University, SC
Friends University, KS
Furman University, SC
Gardner-Webb University, NC
Grand Canyon University, AZ
Gwynedd-Mercy College, PA
High Point University, NC
Hillsdale College, MI
Idaho State University, ID
Illinois State University, IL
Indiana University of Pennsylvania, PA
Indiana U–Purdue U Fort Wayne, IN
Iowa State University of Science and Technology, IA
Jacksonville State University, AL
James Madison University, VA
Juniata College, PA
Kansas State University, KS
Kean University, NJ
King's College, PA
Lander University, SC
Lawrence Technological University, MI
Lee University, TN
Limestone College, SC
Lincoln University, PA
Long Island U, Southampton College, NY
Longwood College, VA
Louisiana State University and A&M College, LA
Louisiana Tech University, LA
Loyola University Chicago, IL
Lubbock Christian University, TX
Lycoming College, PA
Lyndon State College, VT
Madonna University, MI
Malone College, OH
Marycrest International University, IA
Marymount University, VA
Massachusetts College of Liberal Arts, MA
McNeese State University, LA
Mesa State College, CO
Michigan Technological University, MI
Middle Tennessee State University, TN
Minot State University, ND
Mississippi College, MS
Mississippi State University, MS
Missouri Western State College, MO
Montana State U–Billings, MT
Montana State U–Bozeman, MT
Morningside College, IA
Mount Mary College, WI
Mount St. Clare College, IA
North Carolina State University, NC
North Dakota State University, ND
Northeastern State University, OK
Northern Arizona University, AZ
Northwestern College, IA
Northwestern Oklahoma State University, OK
Northwest Missouri State University, MO
Ohio Northern University, OH
The Ohio State University, OH
Ohio University, OH
Ohio University–Eastern, OH
Ohio University–Lancaster, OH
Ohio Wesleyan University, OH
Oklahoma State U, OK
Old Dominion University, VA
Ottawa University, KS
Ouachita Baptist University, AR
Paine College, GA
Pepperdine University, CA
Piedmont College, GA
Plattsburgh State U of NY, NY
Point Loma Nazarene University, CA
Portland State University, OR
Purchase College, State U of NY, NY
Radford University, VA
Reinhardt College, GA
Rhodes College, TN
The Richard Stockton College of New Jersey, NJ
Rockhurst University, MO
Rocky Mountain College, MT
Rowan University, NJ
St. Edward's University, TX
St. John Fisher College, NY
Saint Martin's College, WA
St. Thomas Aquinas College, NY
Salem-Teikyo University, WV
Salisbury State University, MD
Sam Houston State University, TX
Savannah State University, GA
Seton Hill College, PA
Shepherd College, WV
Siena College, NY
Sierra Nevada College, NV
Sonoma State University, CA
South Dakota State University, SD
Southeastern Louisiana University, LA
Southeast Missouri State University, MO
Southern Christian University, AL
Southern Illinois University Carbondale, IL
Southern Methodist University, TX
Southwestern Adventist University, TX
Southwestern College, KS
State U of NY at Binghamton, NY
State U of NY at New Paltz, NY
State U of NY at Oswego, NY
State U of NY College at Fredonia, NY
State U of NY College at Geneseo, NY
State U of NY College at Potsdam, NY
State University of West Georgia, GA
Stetson University, FL
Stevens Institute of Technology, NJ
Tennessee Technological University, TN
Tennessee Wesleyan College, TN
Texas Woman's University, TX
United States International University, CA
The University of Akron, OH
U of Alaska Anchorage, AK
The University of Arizona, AZ
University of Arkansas at Little Rock, AR
U of Calif, Riverside, CA
University of Central Arkansas, AR
University of Cincinnati, OH
University of Colorado at Boulder, CO
University of Dayton, OH
University of Delaware, DE
University of Evansville, IN
University of Great Falls, MT
University of Houston, TX
University of Houston–Clear Lake, TX
University of Houston–Victoria, TX
University of Idaho, ID
University of Illinois at Springfield, IL
University of Kansas, KS
University of Mary Hardin-Baylor, TX
University of Maryland, Baltimore County, MD
University of Massachusetts Amherst, MA
University of Massachusetts Lowell, MA
The University of Memphis, TN
University of Michigan, MI
University of Minnesota, Twin Cities Campus, MN
University of Missouri–Rolla, MO
University of Missouri–St. Louis, MO
The University of Montana–Missoula, MT
University of Nebraska–Lincoln, NE
University of Nevada, Las Vegas, NV
University of Nevada, Reno, NV
University of New Hampshire, NH
The University of North Carolina at Greensboro, NC
The University of North Carolina at Wilmington, NC
University of Oklahoma, OK
University of Pittsburgh at Bradford, PA
University of Portland, OR
U of Puerto Rico, Humacao University College, PR
University of Puget Sound, WA
University of Rochester, NY
University of St. Thomas, MN
University of South Carolina, SC
University of South Carolina Aiken, SC
University of South Dakota, SD
University of Southern Indiana, IN
University of South Florida, FL
The University of Tennessee at Martin, TN
The University of Texas at Arlington, TX
The University of Texas at El Paso, TX
The University of Texas at San Antonio, TX
University of the Ozarks, AR
University of Toledo, OH
University of Utah, UT
University of Virginia's College at Wise, VA
University of Washington, WA
University of Wisconsin–River Falls, WI
University of Wisconsin–Stevens Point, WI
University of Wisconsin–Superior, WI
University of Wisconsin–Whitewater, WI
Utah State University, UT
Vanderbilt University, TN
Walsh University, OH
Warner Southern College, FL
Washington State University, WA
Washington University in St. Louis, MO
Webster University, MO
Western Michigan University, MI
Western Washington University, WA
West Texas A&M University, TX
West Virginia University, WV
Wheeling Jesuit University, WV
Wichita State University, KS
Widener University, PA
Xavier University of Louisiana, LA

INTERNATIONAL STUDIES

Albertus Magnus College, CT
Alfred University, NY
American University, DC
Angelo State University, TX
Antioch College, OH

Ashland University, OH
Auburn University, AL
Augsburg College, MN
Austin College, TX
Baker University, KS
Barton College, NC
Baylor University, TX
Bloomsburg University of Pennsylvania, PA
Brigham Young University, UT
Brigham Young University–Hawaii Campus, HI
Butler University, IN
California Polytechnic State U, San Luis Obispo, CA
California State University, Bakersfield, CA
California State University, Chico, CA
Calvin College, MI
Central College, IA
Clarion University of Pennsylvania, PA
Clemson University, SC
Columbia International University, SC
Dana College, NE
D'Youville College, NY
Elizabethtown College, PA
Fort Hays State University, KS
Frostburg State University, MD
Gannon University, PA
Georgia College and State University, GA
Georgia State University, GA
Grace University, NE
Hampshire College, MA
High Point University, NC
Hillsdale College, MI
Idaho State University, ID
Illinois State University, IL
Indiana University of Pennsylvania, PA
Iowa State University of Science and Technology, IA
James Madison University, VA
Johnson & Wales University, RI
Juniata College, PA
Kennesaw State University, GA
Kent State University, OH
Lock Haven University of Pennsylvania, PA
Loyola University Chicago, IL
Lycoming College, PA
Malone College, OH
Marycrest International University, IA
Mercer University, GA
Middle Tennessee State University, TN
Mississippi State University, MS
Monterey Institute of International Studies, CA
North Central College, IL
North Dakota State University, ND
Ohio Northern University, OH
The Ohio State University, OH
Ohio University, OH
Ohio University–Eastern, OH
Ohio University–Lancaster, OH
Oklahoma State U, OK
Ottawa University, KS
Ouachita Baptist University, AR
Pepperdine University, CA
Pfeiffer University, NC
Plattsburgh State U of NY, NY
Quincy University, IL
Robert Morris College, PA
Rockhurst University, MO
Saginaw Valley State University, MI
Siena College, NY
Sonoma State University, CA
South Dakota State University, SD
Southern Illinois University Carbondale, IL
Southern Methodist University, TX
Southwest Texas State University, TX
State U of NY at Oswego, NY
State U of NY College at Fredonia, NY
Teikyo Post University, CT
Tennessee Wesleyan College, TN
Texas Christian University, TX
Texas Tech University, TX
United States International University, CA
The University of Akron, OH
University of Arkansas at Little Rock, AR
University of Colorado at Boulder, CO
University of Evansville, IN
University of Kansas, KS
University of Mary Hardin-Baylor, TX
The University of Memphis, TN
University of Michigan, MI
University of Michigan–Dearborn, MI
University of Minnesota, Twin Cities Campus, MN
University of Missouri–St. Louis, MO
The University of Montana–Missoula, MT
University of Nebraska–Lincoln, NE
University of Nevada, Las Vegas, NV
University of Nevada, Reno, NV
The University of North Carolina at Wilmington, NC
University of Oklahoma, OK
University of St. Thomas, MN
University of South Carolina, SC
University of Southern Colorado, CO
University of South Florida, FL
The University of Texas at Arlington, TX
The University of Texas at El Paso, TX
University of Tulsa, OK
University of Wisconsin–Eau Claire, WI
University of Wisconsin–River Falls, WI
University of Wisconsin–Stevens Point, WI
Utah State University, UT
Villanova University, PA
Virginia Military Institute, VA
Virginia Polytechnic Institute and State U, VA
Wake Forest University, NC
Washington State University, WA
Webster University, MO
Western Michigan University, MI
Westminster College, UT
West Virginia University, WV
Wheeling Jesuit University, WV
Wichita State University, KS
Wisconsin Lutheran College, WI

LIBRARY SCIENCE

Arkansas State University, AR
Brigham Young University–Hawaii Campus, HI
California Polytechnic State U, San Luis Obispo, CA
Clarion University of Pennsylvania, PA
Fort Hays State University, KS
Illinois State University, IL
Iowa State University of Science and Technology, IA
Kent State University, OH
Lock Haven University of Pennsylvania, PA
Mayville State University, ND
McNeese State University, LA
Mississippi State University, MS
Northeastern State University, OK
Northwestern Oklahoma State University, OK
Radford University, VA
Sam Houston State University, TX
Thomas University, GA
University of Central Arkansas, AR
University of Kansas, KS
University of Louisiana at Monroe, LA
University of Michigan, MI
University of Minnesota, Twin Cities Campus, MN
The University of North Carolina at Greensboro, NC
University of Oklahoma, OK
U of Puerto Rico, Humacao University College, PR
University of South Carolina, SC
University of South Florida, FL
Utah State University, UT
Valley City State University, ND
Western Washington University, WA
West Virginia University, WV

MATHEMATICS

Abilene Christian University, TX
Adams State College, CO
Agnes Scott College, GA
Alabama State University, AL
Albany State University, GA
Albertson College of Idaho, ID
Albertus Magnus College, CT
Albion College, MI
Alfred University, NY
Allentown College of St. Francis de Sales, PA
American University, DC
Antioch College, OH
Arizona State University, AZ
Arkansas State University, AR
Armstrong Atlantic State University, GA
Ashland University, OH
Athens State University, AL
Auburn University, AL
Augsburg College, MN
Augustana College, SD
Augusta State University, GA
Baker University, KS
Ball State University, IN
Barton College, NC
Baylor University, TX
Beaver College, PA
Bellevue University, NE
Benedictine University, IL
Bethel College, IN
Black Hills State University, SD
Bloomsburg University of Pennsylvania, PA
Boise State University, ID
Bowie State University, MD
Bowling Green State University, OH
Brevard College, NC
Briar Cliff College, IA
Brigham Young University, UT
Brigham Young University–Hawaii Campus, HI
Bryan College, TN
Buena Vista University, IA
Butler University, IN
California Lutheran University, CA

Mathematics (continued)

California Polytechnic State U, San Luis Obispo, CA
California State Polytechnic University, Pomona, CA
California State University, Chico, CA
California State University, Fresno, CA
California State University, Fullerton, CA
California State University, Los Angeles, CA
California State University, San Bernardino, CA
California State University, San Marcos, CA
California State University, Stanislaus, CA
Cameron University, OK
Carlow College, PA
Carroll College, WI
Carson-Newman College, TN
Carthage College, WI
Centenary College of Louisiana, LA
Central College, IA
Central Methodist College, MO
Central Missouri State University, MO
Central Washington University, WA
Cheyney University of Pennsylvania, PA
Clarion University of Pennsylvania, PA
Clarkson University, NY
Clearwater Christian College, FL
Clemson University, SC
Coastal Carolina University, SC
College of Insurance, NY
The College of New Rochelle, NY
College of St. Catherine, MN
The College of Saint Rose, NY
College of the Southwest, NM
The College of Wooster, OH
Colorado School of Mines, CO
Columbia College, SC
Concordia University, NE
Dakota State University, SD
Dallas Baptist University, TX
Davidson College, NC
Defiance College, OH
Delaware Valley College, PA
DePauw University, IN
Dordt College, IA
Drury University, MO
Duke University, NC
Eastern Connecticut State University, CT
Eastern Illinois University, IL
Eastern Mennonite University, VA
Eastern Michigan University, MI
Eastern Nazarene College, MA
Eastern New Mexico University, NM
Eastern Oregon University, OR
East Stroudsburg University of Pennsylvania, PA
East Tennessee State University, TN
East Texas Baptist University, TX
Edinboro University of Pennsylvania, PA
Elizabethtown College, PA
Elmhurst College, IL
Elon College, NC
Fairmont State College, WV
Fitchburg State College, MA
Florida Institute of Technology, FL
Florida International University, FL
Florida Memorial College, FL
Fort Hays State University, KS
Fort Lewis College, CO
Francis Marion University, SC
Franklin College of Indiana, IN
Friends University, KS
Frostburg State University, MD
Furman University, SC
Gannon University, PA
Gardner-Webb University, NC
George Fox University, OR
The George Washington University, DC
Georgian Court College, NJ
Georgia State University, GA
Governors State University, IL
Grambling State University, LA
Grand Canyon University, AZ
Greenville College, IL
Guilford College, NC
Gwynedd-Mercy College, PA
Hardin-Simmons University, TX
Heidelberg College, OH
High Point University, NC
Hillsdale College, MI
Hillsdale Free Will Baptist College, OK
Howard Payne University, TX
Idaho State University, ID
Illinois Institute of Technology, IL
Illinois State University, IL
Indiana University of Pennsylvania, PA
Indiana U–Purdue U Fort Wayne, IN
Iowa State University of Science and Technology, IA
Jacksonville State University, AL
James Madison University, VA
John Carroll University, OH
Johnson State College, VT
Juniata College, PA
Kalamazoo College, MI
Kansas State University, KS
Kansas Wesleyan University, KS
Kennesaw State University, GA
Kent State University, OH
Kettering University, MI
King's College, PA
Knox College, IL
LaGrange College, GA
Lander University, SC
Lawrence Technological University, MI
Lee University, TN
Lewis-Clark State College, ID
Limestone College, SC
Lincoln University, PA
Lock Haven University of Pennsylvania, PA
Longwood College, VA
Louisiana State University and A&M College, LA
Loyola University Chicago, IL
Lycoming College, PA
Malone College, OH
Manhattan College, NY
Mansfield University of Pennsylvania, PA
Marquette University, WI
Marymount University, VA
Mary Washington College, VA
Massachusetts College of Liberal Arts, MA
The Master's College and Seminary, CA
Mayville State University, ND
McKendree College, IL
McNeese State University, LA
Meredith College, NC
Mesa State College, CO
Michigan Technological University, MI
Middle Tennessee State University, TN
Mills College, CA
Minnesota State University, Mankato, MN
Minot State University, ND
Mississippi College, MS
Mississippi State University, MS
Missouri Western State College, MO
Montana State U–Billings, MT
Montana State U–Bozeman, MT
Montana Tech of The University of Montana, MT
Morningside College, IA
Mount Mary College, WI
Mount Olive College, NC
Mount St. Clare College, IA
Murray State University, KY
Muskingum College, OH
Norfolk State University, VA
North Carolina State University, NC
North Dakota State University, ND
Northeastern State University, OK
Northern Arizona University, AZ
Northwestern College, IA
Northwestern Oklahoma State University, OK
Northwest Missouri State University, MO
Northwest Nazarene University, ID
Ohio Northern University, OH
The Ohio State University, OH
Ohio University, OH
Ohio University–Eastern, OH
Ohio University–Lancaster, OH
Ohio Wesleyan University, OH
Oklahoma Christian U of Science and Arts, OK
Oklahoma Panhandle State University, OK
Oklahoma State U, OK
Ottawa University, KS
Ouachita Baptist University, AR
Paine College, GA
Piedmont College, GA
Pittsburg State University, KS
Plattsburgh State U of NY, NY
Point Loma Nazarene University, CA
Purchase College, State U of NY, NY
Quincy University, IL
Radford University, VA
Randolph-Macon Woman's College, VA
Reinhardt College, GA
The Richard Stockton College of New Jersey, NJ
Ripon College, WI
Roberts Wesleyan College, NY
Rochester College, MI
Rochester Institute of Technology, NY
Rockford College, IL
Rockhurst University, MO
Rocky Mountain College, MT
Rollins College, FL
Rose-Hulman Institute of Technology, IN
Sacred Heart University, CT
Saginaw Valley State University, MI
St. Ambrose University, IA
St. Edward's University, TX
St. John Fisher College, NY
St. John's University, NY
Saint Louis University, MO
St. Thomas Aquinas College, NY
Saint Vincent College, PA
Salisbury State University, MD
Sam Houston State University, TX

Savannah State University, GA
Seton Hill College, PA
Shaw University, NC
Shepherd College, WV
Siena College, NY
Siena Heights University, MI
Skidmore College, NY
Sonoma State University, CA
South Dakota State University, SD
Southeastern Louisiana University, LA
Southeast Missouri State University, MO
Southern Adventist University, TN
Southern Illinois University Carbondale, IL
Southern Methodist University, TX
Southern Nazarene University, OK
Southern Oregon University, OR
Southern Wesleyan University, SC
Southwestern Oklahoma State University, OK
Southwest Missouri State University, MO
Southwest State University, MN
State U of NY at New Paltz, NY
State U of NY at Oswego, NY
State U of NY College at Brockport, NY
State U of NY College at Fredonia, NY
State U of NY College at Geneseo, NY
State U of NY College at Potsdam, NY
State University of West Georgia, GA
Stephen F. Austin State University, TX
Stetson University, FL
Stevens Institute of Technology, NJ
Teikyo Post University, CT
Tennessee Technological University, TN
Tennessee Wesleyan College, TN
Texas A&M University–Kingsville, TX
Texas A&M University–Texarkana, TX
Texas Tech University, TX
Texas Woman's University, TX
Trinity Christian College, IL
Truman State University, MO
The University of Akron, OH
U of Alaska Anchorage, AK
University of Arkansas at Little Rock, AR
University of Arkansas at Pine Bluff, AR
U of Calif, Riverside, CA
U of Calif, San Diego, CA
University of Central Arkansas, AR
University of Central Oklahoma, OK
University of Cincinnati, OH
University of Colorado at Boulder, CO
University of Colorado at Colorado Springs, CO
University of Evansville, IN
University of Great Falls, MT
University of Houston–Clear Lake, TX
University of Houston–Victoria, TX
University of Idaho, ID
University of Illinois at Springfield, IL
University of Kansas, KS
University of Louisiana at Monroe, LA
University of Mary Hardin-Baylor, TX
University of Maryland, Baltimore County, MD
University of Massachusetts Amherst, MA
The University of Memphis, TN
University of Michigan, MI
University of Minnesota, Twin Cities Campus, MN
University of Missouri–Rolla, MO
University of Missouri–St. Louis, MO
The University of Montana–Missoula, MT
University of Nebraska at Omaha, NE
University of Nebraska–Lincoln, NE
University of Nevada, Las Vegas, NV
University of Nevada, Reno, NV
University of New Hampshire, NH
The University of North Carolina at Asheville, NC
The University of North Carolina at Chapel Hill, NC
The University of North Carolina at Charlotte, NC
The University of North Carolina at Greensboro, NC
The University of North Carolina at Wilmington, NC
University of North Dakota, ND
University of Northern Colorado, CO
University of Northern Iowa, IA
University of Oklahoma, OK
University of Portland, OR
U of Puerto Rico, Humacao University College, PR
University of Puget Sound, WA
University of Richmond, VA
University of Rochester, NY
University of St. Thomas, MN
University of South Carolina, SC
University of South Carolina Aiken, SC
University of South Dakota, SD
University of Southern Colorado, CO
University of Southern Indiana, IN
University of South Florida, FL
The University of Tennessee at Martin, TN
The University of Texas at Arlington, TX
The University of Texas at Brownsville, TX
The University of Texas at Dallas, TX
The University of Texas at El Paso, TX
The University of Texas at San Antonio, TX
The University of Texas–Pan American, TX
University of the Ozarks, AR
University of Toledo, OH
University of Tulsa, OK
University of Utah, UT
University of Virginia's College at Wise, VA
University of Washington, WA
University of Wisconsin–Eau Claire, WI
University of Wisconsin–La Crosse, WI
University of Wisconsin–Oshkosh, WI
University of Wisconsin–Parkside, WI
University of Wisconsin–Platteville, WI
University of Wisconsin–River Falls, WI
University of Wisconsin–Stevens Point, WI
University of Wisconsin–Stout, WI
University of Wisconsin–Superior, WI
University of Wisconsin–Whitewater, WI
University of Wyoming, WY
Utah State University, UT
Valley City State University, ND
Virginia Military Institute, VA
Virginia Polytechnic Institute and State U, VA
Virginia State University, VA
Wake Forest University, NC
Walsh University, OH
Wartburg College, IA
Washington State University, WA
Washington University in St. Louis, MO
Wayland Baptist University, TX
Webster University, MO
Western Carolina University, NC
Western Illinois University, IL
Western Michigan University, MI
Western State College of Colorado, CO
Western Washington University, WA
West Liberty State College, WV
Westminster College, PA
Westminster College, UT
West Texas A&M University, TX
West Virginia State College, WV
West Virginia University, WV
Wheeling Jesuit University, WV
Wichita State University, KS
Winston-Salem State University, NC
Wisconsin Lutheran College, WI
Xavier University, OH
Xavier University of Louisiana, LA
York College, NE

MILITARY SCIENCE

Alfred University, NY
Allentown College of St. Francis de Sales, PA
Angelo State University, TX
Arizona State University, AZ
Arkansas State University, AR
Armstrong Atlantic State University, GA
Augusta State University, GA
Black Hills State University, SD
Boise State University, ID
Bowie State University, MD
Bowling Green State University, OH
Brigham Young University, UT
California Polytechnic State U, San Luis Obispo, CA
California State University, Fullerton, CA
California State University, San Bernardino, CA
Cameron University, OK
Carson-Newman College, TN
Central Missouri State University, MO
Chaminade University of Honolulu, HI
Christopher Newport University, VA
Citadel, The Military Coll of South Carolina, SC
Clarkson University, NY
Clemson University, SC
College of the Holy Cross, MA
Colorado School of Mines, CO
Creighton University, NE
Dickinson College, PA
East Carolina University, NC
East Central University, OK
Eastern New Mexico University, NM
East Tennessee State University, TN
Edinboro University of Pennsylvania, PA
Florida Institute of Technology, FL
Fort Valley State University, GA
Furman University, SC
Georgia Southern University, GA
Grambling State University, LA
Grand Canyon University, AZ
Illinois State University, IL
Jacksonville State University, AL
James Madison University, VA
John Carroll University, OH
Kansas State University, KS
Kent State University, OH
Lincoln University, MO
Louisiana State University and A&M College, LA
Manhattan College, NY
Mercer University, GA

Military Science (continued)

Michigan State University, MI
Middle Tennessee State University, TN
Mississippi State University, MS
Missouri Western State College, MO
Montana State U–Bozeman, MT
North Carolina Agricultural and Technical State U, NC
North Dakota State University, ND
Northern Arizona University, AZ
Northern Michigan University, MI
North Georgia College & State University, GA
North Greenville College, SC
Northwest Nazarene University, ID
The Ohio State University, OH
Ohio University, OH
Ohio University–Eastern, OH
Ohio University–Lancaster, OH
Oklahoma State U, OK
Old Dominion University, VA
Paine College, GA
Pittsburg State University, KS
Providence College, RI
Radford University, VA
Rensselaer Polytechnic Institute, NY
Ripon College, WI
Rochester Institute of Technology, NY
St. John's University, NY
St. Mary's University of San Antonio, TX
Sam Houston State University, TX
Santa Clara University, CA
Savannah State University, GA
Seton Hall University, NJ
Shippensburg University of Pennsylvania, PA
Siena College, NY
South Dakota State University, SD
Southeastern Louisiana University, LA
Southeast Missouri State University, MO
Southern Illinois University Carbondale, IL
Southwest Missouri State University, MO
Southwest Texas State University, TX
State U of NY College at Brockport, NY
Stephen F. Austin State University, TX
Stetson University, FL
Tennessee Technological University, TN
Texas A&M University–Kingsville, TX
Texas Christian University, TX
Texas Tech University, TX
Truman State University, MO
The University of Akron, OH
The University of Arizona, AZ
University of Central Oklahoma, OK
University of Cincinnati, OH
University of Colorado at Boulder, CO
University of Colorado at Colorado Springs, CO
University of Houston, TX
University of Idaho, ID
University of Kansas, KS
University of Louisiana at Monroe, LA
University of Maine, ME
University of Maryland, College Park, MD
University of Massachusetts Amherst, MA
The University of Memphis, TN
University of Michigan, MI
University of Minnesota, Twin Cities Campus, MN
University of Missouri–Rolla, MO
The University of Montana–Missoula, MT
University of Nevada, Reno, NV
University of New Hampshire, NH
University of Northern Colorado, CO
University of Oklahoma, OK
University of Portland, OR
University of South Carolina, SC
University of South Dakota, SD
University of South Florida, FL
The University of Tampa, FL
The University of Tennessee at Martin, TN
The University of Tennessee Knoxville, TN
The University of Texas at Arlington, TX
The University of Texas at El Paso, TX
The University of Texas–Pan American, TX
University of Toledo, OH
University of Wisconsin–Stevens Point, WI
University of Wyoming, WY
Valdosta State University, GA
Villanova University, PA
Virginia Military Institute, VA
Virginia Polytechnic Institute and State U, VA
Virginia State University, VA
Wake Forest University, NC
Western Michigan University, MI
West Virginia State College, WV
West Virginia University, WV
Widener University, PA
Xavier University, OH
Youngstown State University, OH

PHYSICAL SCIENCES

Abilene Christian University, TX
Agnes Scott College, GA
Albertson College of Idaho, ID
Albertus Magnus College, CT
Alfred University, NY
Allentown College of St. Francis de Sales, PA
Anderson College, SC
Angelo State University, TX
Antioch College, OH
Arizona State University, AZ
Arkansas State University, AR
Armstrong Atlantic State University, GA
Ashland University, OH
Athens State University, AL
Auburn University, AL
Augsburg College, MN
Augustana College, SD
Augusta State University, GA
Austin College, TX
Baker University, KS
Barat College, IL
Bard College, NY
Barton College, NC
Baylor University, TX
Benedictine University, IL
Bethel College, IN
Black Hills State University, SD
Bloomsburg University of Pennsylvania, PA
Boise State University, ID
Bowie State University, MD
Bowling Green State University, OH
Brescia University, KY
Brevard College, NC
Briar Cliff College, IA
Brigham Young University, UT
Brigham Young University–Hawaii Campus, HI
Bryan College, TN
Butler University, IN
California Lutheran University, CA
California Polytechnic State U, San Luis Obispo, CA
California State Polytechnic University, Pomona, CA
California State University, Bakersfield, CA
California State University, Chico, CA
California State University, Fresno, CA
California State University, Los Angeles, CA
California State University, Stanislaus, CA
Calvin College, MI
Carroll College, WI
Carthage College, WI
Centenary College of Louisiana, LA
Central College, IA
Central Missouri State University, MO
Central State University, OH
Central Washington University, WA
Chicago State University, IL
Clarion University of Pennsylvania, PA
Clarkson University, NY
Clemson University, SC
Coe College, IA
College of Charleston, SC
The College of New Rochelle, NY
College of St. Catherine, MN
The College of Wooster, OH
The Colorado College, CO
Colorado School of Mines, CO
Columbia College, MO
Concordia University, NE
Davidson College, NC
Davis & Elkins College, WV
Defiance College, OH
Denison University, OH
DePauw University, IN
Doane College, NE
Dordt College, IA
Drury University, MO
Earlham College, IN
Eastern Connecticut State University, CT
Eastern Illinois University, IL
Eastern Mennonite University, VA
Eastern Michigan University, MI
Eastern Nazarene College, MA
Eastern New Mexico University, NM
Eastern Oregon University, OR
Eastern Washington University, WA
East Stroudsburg University of Pennsylvania, PA
East Texas Baptist University, TX
Edinboro University of Pennsylvania, PA
Elizabethtown College, PA
Elmhurst College, IL
Elon College, NC
Fairmont State College, WV
Florida Atlantic University, FL
Florida Institute of Technology, FL
Florida International University, FL
Florida Southern College, FL
Fort Hays State University, KS
Fort Lewis College, CO
Framingham State College, MA
Friends University, KS
Frostburg State University, MD
Furman University, SC
Gardner-Webb University, NC
George Fox University, OR
Georgian Court College, NJ

Georgia State University, GA
Goucher College, MD
Governors State University, IL
Grambling State University, LA
Grand Canyon University, AZ
Grove City College, PA
Heidelberg College, OH
Heritage College, WA
High Point University, NC
Hillsdale College, MI
Hiram College, OH
Idaho State University, ID
Illinois Institute of Technology, IL
Illinois State University, IL
Indiana University of Pennsylvania, PA
Indiana U–Purdue U Fort Wayne, IN
Iowa State University of Science and Technology, IA
Jacksonville State University, AL
Jacksonville University, FL
James Madison University, VA
John Carroll University, OH
Juniata College, PA
Kalamazoo College, MI
Kansas State University, KS
Kansas Wesleyan University, KS
Kennesaw State University, GA
Kent State University, OH
Kettering University, MI
King's College, PA
LaGrange College, GA
Lander University, SC
Lawrence Technological University, MI
Lee University, TN
Lincoln University, MO
Lincoln University, PA
Lock Haven University of Pennsylvania, PA
Long Island U, Southampton College, NY
Loras College, IA
Louisiana State University and A&M College, LA
Louisiana Tech University, LA
Loyola University Chicago, IL
Lubbock Christian University, TX
Lycoming College, PA
MacMurray College, IL
Malone College, OH
Mansfield University of Pennsylvania, PA
Mary Washington College, VA
Massachusetts College of Liberal Arts, MA
The Master's College and Seminary, CA
Mayville State University, ND
McKendree College, IL
McNeese State University, LA
Mesa State College, CO
Michigan Technological University, MI
Middle Tennessee State University, TN
Mills College, CA
Minnesota State University, Mankato, MN
Mississippi College, MS
Mississippi State University, MS
Missouri Western State College, MO
Montana State U–Bozeman, MT
Montana Tech of The University of Montana, MT
Moravian College, PA
Morehead State University, KY
Mount Mary College, WI
Mount St. Clare College, IA
Murray State University, KY
Muskingum College, OH
New Mexico Institute of Mining and Technology, NM
North Carolina Central University, NC
North Carolina State University, NC
North Dakota State University, ND
Northeastern State University, OK
Northern Arizona University, AZ
Northwestern College, IA
Northwest Missouri State University, MO
Northwest Nazarene University, ID
Ohio Northern University, OH
The Ohio State University, OH
Ohio University, OH
Ohio University–Eastern, OH
Ohio University–Lancaster, OH
Ohio Wesleyan University, OH
Oklahoma Christian U of Science and Arts, OK
Oklahoma State U, OK
Old Dominion University, VA
Ottawa University, KS
Ouachita Baptist University, AR
Paine College, GA
Pittsburg State University, KS
Plattsburgh State U of NY, NY
Portland State University, OR
Purdue University, IN
Radford University, VA
Regis University, CO
The Richard Stockton College of New Jersey, NJ
Ripon College, WI
Rochester Institute of Technology, NY
Rockford College, IL
Rockhurst University, MO
Rocky Mountain College, MT
Rollins College, FL
Rose-Hulman Institute of Technology, IN
Rowan University, NJ
Saginaw Valley State University, MI
St. Ambrose University, IA
St. Edward's University, TX
St. John Fisher College, NY
Saint Louis University, MO
Saint Vincent College, PA
Salisbury State University, MD
Sam Houston State University, TX
Savannah State University, GA
Seton Hall University, NJ
Seton Hill College, PA
Shaw University, NC
Shepherd College, WV
Shippensburg University of Pennsylvania, PA
Siena College, NY
Siena Heights University, MI
Skidmore College, NY
Sonoma State University, CA
South Dakota State University, SD
Southeastern Louisiana University, LA
Southeast Missouri State University, MO
Southern Illinois University Carbondale, IL
Southern Methodist University, TX
Southern Oregon University, OR
Southern University at New Orleans, LA
Southwestern Adventist University, TX
Southwestern Oklahoma State University, OK
Southwest Missouri State University, MO
Southwest State University, MN
State U of NY at Binghamton, NY
State U of NY at New Paltz, NY
State U of NY at Oswego, NY
State U of NY at Stony Brook, NY
State U of NY College at Brockport, NY
State U of NY College at Fredonia, NY
State U of NY College at Geneseo, NY
State U of NY College at Oneonta, NY
State U of NY College at Potsdam, NY
State U of NY Coll of Environ Sci and Forestry, NY
State University of West Georgia, GA
Stephen F. Austin State University, TX
Stetson University, FL
Stevens Institute of Technology, NJ
Tennessee Technological University, TN
Tennessee Wesleyan College, TN
Texas A&M University, TX
Texas A&M University–Kingsville, TX
Texas Tech University, TX
Texas Woman's University, TX
Trevecca Nazarene University, TN
Truman State University, MO
The University of Akron, OH
The University of Alabama in Huntsville, AL
The University of Arizona, AZ
University of Arkansas at Little Rock, AR
U of Calif, Riverside, CA
U of Calif, San Diego, CA
University of Central Arkansas, AR
University of Central Oklahoma, OK
University of Cincinnati, OH
University of Colorado at Boulder, CO
University of Colorado at Colorado Springs, CO
University of Delaware, DE
University of Evansville, IN
The University of Findlay, OH
University of Great Falls, MT
University of Houston, TX
University of Houston–Downtown, TX
University of Idaho, ID
University of Kansas, KS
University of Louisiana at Monroe, LA
University of Maine, ME
University of Mary Hardin-Baylor, TX
University of Maryland, Baltimore County, MD
University of Massachusetts Amherst, MA
The University of Memphis, TN
University of Michigan, MI
University of Michigan–Dearborn, MI
University of Minnesota, Twin Cities Campus, MN
University of Missouri–Rolla, MO
The University of Montana–Missoula, MT
University of Montevallo, AL
University of Nebraska at Omaha, NE
University of Nebraska–Lincoln, NE
University of Nevada, Las Vegas, NV
University of Nevada, Reno, NV
The University of North Carolina at Asheville, NC
The University of North Carolina at Greensboro, NC
The University of North Carolina at Pembroke, NC
The University of North Carolina at Wilmington, NC
University of Northern Colorado, CO
University of Northern Iowa, IA

Physical Sciences (continued)

University of Oklahoma, OK
University of Portland, OR
University of Puget Sound, WA
University of Richmond, VA
University of Rio Grande, OH
University of Rochester, NY
University of Saint Francis, IN
University of St. Thomas, MN
University of South Carolina, SC
University of South Carolina Aiken, SC
University of Southern Indiana, IN
University of South Florida, FL
The University of Tennessee at Martin, TN
The University of Texas at Arlington, TX
The University of Texas at Dallas, TX
The University of Texas at El Paso, TX
The University of Texas at San Antonio, TX
University of Toledo, OH
University of Utah, UT
University of Virginia's College at Wise, VA
University of Washington, WA
University of Wisconsin–Eau Claire, WI
University of Wisconsin–La Crosse, WI
University of Wisconsin–Oshkosh, WI
University of Wisconsin–River Falls, WI
University of Wisconsin–Stevens Point, WI
University of Wisconsin–Superior, WI
University of Wisconsin–Whitewater, WI
University of Wyoming, WY
Utah State University, UT
Valley City State University, ND
Valparaiso University, IN
Wake Forest University, NC
Walsh University, OH
Wartburg College, IA
Washington State University, WA
Washington University in St. Louis, MO
Wayland Baptist University, TX
Western Illinois University, IL
Western Kentucky University, KY
Western Michigan University, MI
Western Washington University, WA
West Liberty State College, WV
Westminster College, UT
West Virginia University, WV
Wheeling Jesuit University, WV
Wichita State University, KS
Wilkes University, PA
Wilmington College, OH
Xavier University, OH
Xavier University of Louisiana, LA

PREMEDICINE

Adams State College, CO
Albertson College of Idaho, ID
Albertus Magnus College, CT
Alfred University, NY
Allentown College of St. Francis de Sales, PA
Alma College, MI
Angelo State University, TX
Arizona State University, AZ
Arkansas State University, AR
Auburn University, AL
Augustana College, SD
Austin College, TX
Avila College, MO
Baker University, KS
Baylor University, TX
Birmingham-Southern College, AL
Boise State University, ID
Bowie State University, MD
Brescia University, KY
Brigham Young University, UT
California State University, Fresno, CA
Calvin College, MI
Carroll College, WI
Carthage College, WI
Centenary College of Louisiana, LA
Central Methodist College, MO
Central Missouri State University, MO
Central Washington University, WA
Cheyney University of Pennsylvania, PA
Clarion University of Pennsylvania, PA
Clearwater Christian College, FL
Clemson University, SC
Coe College, IA
College of Charleston, SC
The College of New Rochelle, NY
College of St. Catherine, MN
The College of Saint Rose, NY
Concordia University, NE
Dallas Baptist University, TX
Dana College, NE
Davidson College, NC
Defiance College, OH
Delaware Valley College, PA
Dordt College, IA
Drury University, MO
D'Youville College, NY
Eastern Mennonite University, VA
Eastern Nazarene College, MA
Eastern New Mexico University, NM
Edinboro University of Pennsylvania, PA
Elon College, NC
Florida Institute of Technology, FL
Florida Memorial College, FL
Fort Hays State University, KS
Fort Valley State University, GA
Francis Marion University, SC
Friends University, KS
Gannon University, PA
Gardner-Webb University, NC
Grambling State University, LA
Grand Canyon University, AZ
Gwynedd-Mercy College, PA
Hardin-Simmons University, TX
High Point University, NC
Hillsdale College, MI
Idaho State University, ID
Illinois Institute of Technology, IL
Illinois State University, IL
Indiana University of Pennsylvania, PA
Indiana U–Purdue U Fort Wayne, IN
Iowa State University of Science and Technology, IA
James Madison University, VA
Juniata College, PA
Kansas State University, KS
Kansas Wesleyan University, KS
Kennesaw State University, GA
King's College, PA
Lee University, TN
Louisiana State University and A&M College, LA
Louisiana State University in Shreveport, LA
Loyola University Chicago, IL
Lycoming College, PA
Lynn University, FL
Malone College, OH
McNeese State University, LA
Michigan Technological University, MI
Middle Tennessee State University, TN
Mills College, CA
Mississippi State University, MS
Morningside College, IA
Mount St. Clare College, IA
Murray State University, KY
Muskingum College, OH
North Dakota State University, ND
Northeastern State University, OK
Northern Michigan University, MI
Northwestern College, IA
Northwestern Oklahoma State University, OK
Northwest Nazarene University, ID
Ohio Northern University, OH
The Ohio State University, OH
Ohio University, OH
Ohio University–Eastern, OH
Ohio University–Lancaster, OH
Ohio Wesleyan University, OH
Oklahoma Christian U of Science and Arts, OK
Oklahoma State U, OK
Ottawa University, KS
Ouachita Baptist University, AR
Paine College, GA
Piedmont College, GA
Plattsburgh State U of NY, NY
Prairie View A&M University, TX
Providence College, RI
Radford University, VA
Rochester Institute of Technology, NY
Rockford College, IL
Rockhurst University, MO
Rocky Mountain College, MT
Sacred Heart University, CT
Saginaw Valley State University, MI
St. Ambrose University, IA
Salisbury State University, MD
Seton Hall University, NJ
Seton Hill College, PA
Shepherd College, WV
Shippensburg University of Pennsylvania, PA
Siena College, NY
Sonoma State University, CA
South Dakota State University, SD
Southeastern Louisiana University, LA
Southern Illinois University Carbondale, IL
Southwestern Adventist University, TX
Southwest Missouri State University, MO
State U of NY at Binghamton, NY
State U of NY at New Paltz, NY
State U of NY at Oswego, NY
State U of NY College at Geneseo, NY
Stephen F. Austin State University, TX
Stetson University, FL
Stevens Institute of Technology, NJ
Sweet Briar College, VA
Tennessee Technological University, TN
Tennessee Wesleyan College, TN
Texas Christian University, TX
Texas Tech University, TX
Texas Woman's University, TX
Truman State University, MO
The University of Akron, OH
U of Calif, Riverside, CA
U of Calif, San Diego, CA
University of Cincinnati, OH
University of Colorado at Boulder, CO

University of Colorado at Colorado Springs, CO
University of Evansville, IN
University of Great Falls, MT
University of Idaho, ID
University of Kansas, KS
University of Mary Hardin-Baylor, TX
University of Massachusetts Amherst, MA
The University of Memphis, TN
University of Michigan, MI
University of Minnesota, Twin Cities Campus, MN
University of Missouri–Rolla, MO
The University of Montana–Missoula, MT
University of Nebraska at Omaha, NE
University of Nebraska–Lincoln, NE
University of Nevada, Las Vegas, NV
University of Nevada, Reno, NV
The University of North Carolina at Asheville, NC
The University of North Carolina at Greensboro, NC
University of North Dakota, ND
University of Portland, OR
University of Puget Sound, WA
University of South Carolina, SC
University of South Dakota, SD
University of Southern Colorado, CO
University of Southern Indiana, IN
University of South Florida, FL
The University of Tennessee at Martin, TN
The University of Tennessee Knoxville, TN
The University of Texas–Pan American, TX
University of the Ozarks, AR
University of Toledo, OH
University of Tulsa, OK
University of Virginia's College at Wise, VA
University of Wisconsin–Eau Claire, WI
University of Wisconsin–Parkside, WI
University of Wisconsin–River Falls, WI
University of Wisconsin–Stevens Point, WI
University of Wisconsin–Whitewater, WI
Utah State University, UT
Virginia Military Institute, VA
Virginia State University, VA
Voorhees College, SC
Walsh University, OH
Warner Pacific College, OR
Washington State University, WA
Webster University, MO
Western Washington University, WA
Westminster College, UT
West Virginia University, WV
Wheeling Jesuit University, WV
Wichita State University, KS
Xavier University of Louisiana, LA
York College, NE

RELIGION/BIBLICAL STUDIES

Abilene Christian University, TX
Alaska Bible College, AK
Albertson College of Idaho, ID
Albertus Magnus College, CT
Allentown College of St. Francis de Sales, PA
Anderson College, SC
Ashland University, OH
Augsburg College, MN
Augustana College, SD
Austin College, TX
Azusa Pacific University, CA
Baker University, KS
Baptist Bible College of Pennsylvania, PA
Barber-Scotia College, NC
Bartlesville Wesleyan College, OK
Barton College, NC
Baylor University, TX
Belhaven College, MS
Belmont University, TN
Berry College, GA
Bethel College, IN
Bethel College, TN
Bloomsburg University of Pennsylvania, PA
Boise Bible College, ID
Briar Cliff College, IA
Brigham Young University, UT
Brigham Young University–Hawaii Campus, HI
Bryan College, TN
California Baptist University, CA
California Lutheran University, CA
Calvin College, MI
Carson-Newman College, TN
Centenary College of Louisiana, LA
Central College, IA
Central Missouri State University, MO
Cincinnati Bible College and Seminary, OH
Circleville Bible College, OH
Clearwater Christian College, FL
Cleveland College of Jewish Studies, OH
The College of New Rochelle, NY
Colorado Christian University, CO
Columbia College, SC
Columbia International University, SC
Conception Seminary College, MO
Concordia College, AL
Concordia College, MI
Concordia College, NY
Concordia University, CA
Concordia University, IL
Concordia University, NE
Cornerstone University, MI
Crown College, MN
Dallas Baptist University, TX
Dallas Christian College, TX
Dana College, NE
Davis & Elkins College, WV
Defiance College, OH
Dordt College, IA
Eastern Mennonite University, VA
Eastern Michigan University, MI
Eastern Nazarene College, MA
Eastern New Mexico University, NM
East Texas Baptist University, TX
Edinboro University of Pennsylvania, PA
Elizabethtown College, PA
Elmhurst College, IL
Emmanuel College, GA
Eugene Bible College, OR
Eureka College, IL
Faulkner University, AL
Felician College, NJ
Florida Baptist Theological College, FL
Florida Memorial College, FL
Florida Southern College, FL
Friends University, KS
Furman University, SC
Gannon University, PA
Gardner-Webb University, NC
George Fox University, OR
Grace University, NE
Grand Canyon University, AZ
Greenville College, IL
Hampden-Sydney College, VA
Hannibal-LaGrange College, MO
Hardin-Simmons University, TX
Hellenic College, MA
High Point University, NC
Hillsdale College, MI
Hillsdale Free Will Baptist College, OK
Hiram College, OH
Houston Baptist University, TX
Howard Payne University, TX
Idaho State University, ID
Institute for Christian Studies, TX
James Madison University, VA
John Wesley College, NC
Kansas Wesleyan University, KS
Kentucky Christian College, KY
King's College, PA
LaGrange College, GA
Lee University, TN
Limestone College, SC
Lincoln University, MO
Louisiana College, LA
Lubbock Christian University, TX
Lycoming College, PA
MacMurray College, IL
Malone College, OH
Manchester College, IN
Manhattan Christian College, KS
The Master's College and Seminary, CA
McKendree College, IL
McMurry University, TX
Mercer University, GA
Messenger College, MO
Mid-America Bible College, OK
Mid-Continent College, KY
Milligan College, TN
Minnesota Bible College, MN
Mississippi College, MS
Mississippi State University, MS
Missouri Baptist College, MO
Morningside College, IA
Mount Vernon Nazarene College, OH
Multnomah Bible College and Biblical Seminary, OR
Nazarene Indian Bible College, NM
North Greenville College, SC
Northwest College, WA
Northwestern College, IA
Northwest Nazarene University, ID
Ohio Northern University, OH
Ohio Valley College, WV
Oklahoma Baptist University, OK
Oklahoma Christian U of Science and Arts, OK
Oklahoma City University, OK
Oral Roberts University, OK
Ottawa University, KS
Ouachita Baptist University, AR
Ozark Christian College, MO
Pepperdine University, CA
Piedmont College, GA
Point Loma Nazarene University, CA
Practical Bible College, NY
Presentation College, SD
Puget Sound Christian College, WA
Quincy University, IL
Reinhardt College, GA
Roanoke Bible College, NC

Religion/Biblical Studies (continued)

Roberts Wesleyan College, NY
Rochester College, MI
Rockhurst University, MO
Rocky Mountain College, MT
St. Ambrose University, IA
St. Edward's University, TX
Saint John's Seminary College of Liberal Arts, MA
Seton Hill College, PA
Shasta Bible College, CA
Shorter College, GA
Siena College, NY
Southeastern Bible College, AL
Southeastern College of the Assemblies of God, FL
Southeastern Louisiana University, LA
Southern Adventist University, TN
Southern Christian University, AL
Southern Illinois University Carbondale, IL
Southern Methodist University, TX
Southern Nazarene University, OK
Southern Wesleyan University, SC
Southwestern Adventist University, TX
Southwestern Assemblies of God University, TX
Southwestern College of Christian Ministries, OK
Southwest Missouri State University, MO
Spring Arbor College, MI
Stetson University, FL
Talmudical Institute of Upstate New York, NY
Tennessee Temple University, TN
Tennessee Wesleyan College, TN
Texas Christian University, TX
Trevecca Nazarene University, TN
Trinity Baptist College, FL
Trinity Bible College, ND
Trinity Lutheran College, WA
Union University, TN
The University of Arizona, AZ
University of Colorado at Boulder, CO
University of Evansville, IN
University of Great Falls, MT
University of Kansas, KS
University of Mary Hardin-Baylor, TX
University of Minnesota, Twin Cities Campus, MN
University of Mobile, AL
The University of North Carolina at Greensboro, NC
The University of North Carolina at Wilmington, NC
University of Portland, OR
University of South Carolina, SC
University of South Florida, FL
University of the Ozarks, AR
University of Tulsa, OK
Wake Forest University, NC
Wayland Baptist University, TX
West Virginia University, WV
Wheeling Jesuit University, WV
York College, NE

SOCIAL SCIENCES

Abilene Christian University, TX
Adams State College, CO
Agnes Scott College, GA
Albany State University, GA
Albertson College of Idaho, ID
Albertus Magnus College, CT
Alfred University, NY
Allentown College of St. Francis de Sales, PA
American University, DC
Antioch College, OH
Arizona State University, AZ
Arkansas State University, AR
Ashland University, OH
Athens State University, AL
Auburn University, AL
Augsburg College, MN
Augustana College, SD
Austin College, TX
Baker University, KS
Ball State University, IN
Barber-Scotia College, NC
Barton College, NC
Baylor University, TX
Bellevue University, NE
Bethel College, IN
Black Hills State University, SD
Bloomsburg University of Pennsylvania, PA
Boise State University, ID
Bowie State University, MD
Bowling Green State University, OH
Brescia University, KY
Briar Cliff College, IA
Brigham Young University, UT
Brigham Young University–Hawaii Campus, HI
Bryan College, TN
Butler University, IN
California Institute of Integral Studies, CA
California Lutheran University, CA
California Polytechnic State U, San Luis Obispo, CA
California State Polytechnic University, Pomona, CA
California State University, Bakersfield, CA
California State University, Chico, CA
California State University, Fresno, CA
California State University, Fullerton, CA
California State University, Los Angeles, CA
California State University, Northridge, CA
California State University, Stanislaus, CA
Calvin College, MI
Cameron University, OK
Carlow College, PA
Centenary College of Louisiana, LA
Central Methodist College, MO
Central Missouri State University, MO
Chaminade University of Honolulu, HI
Chapman University, CA
Clarion University of Pennsylvania, PA
Clemson University, SC
College of Charleston, SC
The College of New Rochelle, NY
College of St. Catherine, MN
The College of Saint Rose, NY
College of the Southwest, NM
The College of West Virginia, WV
The College of Wooster, OH
Columbia College, MO
Concordia College, NY
Concordia University, NE
Dana College, NE
Defiance College, OH
Delaware Valley College, PA
Doane College, NE
Dordt College, IA
Drury University, MO
D'Youville College, NY
Eastern Connecticut State University, CT
Eastern Mennonite University, VA
Eastern Michigan University, MI
Eastern Nazarene College, MA
Eastern New Mexico University, NM
Eastern Washington University, WA
East Stroudsburg University of Pennsylvania, PA
East Tennessee State University, TN
Edinboro University of Pennsylvania, PA
Elizabethtown College, PA
Elmhurst College, IL
Fairmont State College, WV
Fitchburg State College, MA
Flagler College, FL
Florida Atlantic University, FL
Florida Gulf Coast University, FL
Florida International University, FL
Florida Memorial College, FL
Florida Southern College, FL
Fort Hays State University, KS
Fort Lewis College, CO
Fort Valley State University, GA
Francis Marion University, SC
Friends University, KS
Frostburg State University, MD
Furman University, SC
Gardner-Webb University, NC
Georgia State University, GA
Goucher College, MD
Governors State University, IL
Grambling State University, LA
Grand Canyon University, AZ
Gwynedd-Mercy College, PA
Hampshire College, MA
Hardin-Simmons University, TX
Heritage College, WA
Hiram College, OH
Howard Payne University, TX
Idaho State University, ID
Illinois Institute of Technology, IL
Illinois State University, IL
Indiana University of Pennsylvania, PA
Indiana U–Purdue U Fort Wayne, IN
Iowa State University of Science and Technology, IA
Jacksonville State University, AL
James Madison University, VA
Juniata College, PA
Kalamazoo College, MI
Kansas State University, KS
Kansas Wesleyan University, KS
Kennesaw State University, GA
Kent State University, OH
King's College, PA
LaGrange College, GA
Lee University, TN
Limestone College, SC
Lock Haven University of Pennsylvania, PA
Long Island U, Southampton College, NY
Loyola University Chicago, IL
Loyola University New Orleans, LA
Lubbock Christian University, TX
Lycoming College, PA
MacMurray College, IL
Malone College, OH
Marycrest International University, IA

Marymount University, VA
Mary Washington College, VA
Massachusetts College of Liberal Arts, MA
The Master's College and Seminary, CA
McNeese State University, LA
Mesa State College, CO
Michigan State University, MI
Michigan Technological University, MI
Middle Tennessee State University, TN
Minot State University, ND
Mississippi State University, MS
Missouri Western State College, MO
Montana State U–Billings, MT
Montana State U–Bozeman, MT
Morningside College, IA
Mount Mary College, WI
Mount St. Clare College, IA
Murray State University, KY
North Carolina Central University, NC
North Carolina State University, NC
North Dakota State University, ND
Northeastern State University, OK
Northern Arizona University, AZ
Northwestern College, IA
Northwestern Oklahoma State University, OK
Northwest Missouri State University, MO
Northwest Nazarene University, ID
Oglala Lakota College, SD
Ohio Northern University, OH
The Ohio State University, OH
Ohio University, OH
Ohio University–Eastern, OH
Ohio University–Lancaster, OH
Oklahoma State U, OK
Ottawa University, KS
Ouachita Baptist University, AR
Pepperdine University, CA
Pittsburg State University, KS
Plattsburgh State U of NY, NY
Point Loma Nazarene University, CA
Presentation College, SD
Purchase College, State U of NY, NY
Quincy University, IL
Radford University, VA
Randolph-Macon Woman's College, VA
Reinhardt College, GA
The Richard Stockton College of New Jersey, NJ
Rochester Institute of Technology, NY
Rockhurst University, MO
Rocky Mountain College, MT
Rowan University, NJ
Saginaw Valley State University, MI
St. Ambrose University, IA
St. Edward's University, TX
Saint Louis University, MO
St. Thomas Aquinas College, NY
Saint Vincent College, PA
Salisbury State University, MD
Sam Houston State University, TX
Savannah State University, GA
Shepherd College, WV
Siena College, NY
Siena Heights University, MI
Slippery Rock University of Pennsylvania, PA
Sonoma State University, CA
South Dakota State University, SD
Southeastern Louisiana University, LA
Southeast Missouri State University, MO
Southern Illinois University Carbondale, IL
Southern Methodist University, TX
Southern Oregon University, OR
Southern Wesleyan University, SC
Southwestern Adventist University, TX
Southwestern Assemblies of God University, TX
Southwestern Oklahoma State University, OK
Southwest Missouri State University, MO
Southwest State University, MN
State U of NY at Oswego, NY
State U of NY College at Fredonia, NY
State U of NY College at Geneseo, NY
State U of NY College at Potsdam, NY
State University of West Georgia, GA
Stetson University, FL
Teikyo Post University, CT
Tennessee Technological University, TN
Tennessee Wesleyan College, TN
Texas A&M University–Kingsville, TX
Texas A&M University–Texarkana, TX
Texas Tech University, TX
Texas Woman's University, TX
Thomas University, GA
Trevecca Nazarene University, TN
Truman State University, MO
United States International University, CA
The University of Akron, OH
U of Alaska Anchorage, AK
U of Alaska Southeast, AK
University of Arkansas at Little Rock, AR
U of Calif, Riverside, CA
U of Calif, San Diego, CA
University of Central Arkansas, AR
University of Central Oklahoma, OK
University of Cincinnati, OH
University of Colorado at Boulder, CO
University of Evansville, IN
University of Great Falls, MT
University of Hawaii at Hilo, HI
University of Houston, TX
University of Houston–Clear Lake, TX
University of Houston–Victoria, TX
University of Idaho, ID
University of Kansas, KS
University of Louisiana at Monroe, LA
University of Maine at Machias, ME
University of Mary Hardin-Baylor, TX
University of Massachusetts Amherst, MA
The University of Memphis, TN
University of Michigan, MI
University of Michigan–Dearborn, MI
University of Minnesota, Twin Cities Campus, MN
University of Missouri–Rolla, MO
The University of Montana–Missoula, MT
University of Nebraska at Omaha, NE
University of Nebraska–Lincoln, NE
University of Nevada, Las Vegas, NV
University of Nevada, Reno, NV
The University of North Carolina at Asheville, NC
The University of North Carolina at Greensboro, NC
The University of North Carolina at Wilmington, NC
University of Northern Colorado, CO
University of Northern Iowa, IA
University of Oklahoma, OK
University of Pittsburgh at Bradford, PA
University of Portland, OR
U of Puerto Rico, Humacao University College, PR
University of Puget Sound, WA
University of Rio Grande, OH
University of Rochester, NY
University of St. Thomas, MN
University of South Carolina, SC
University of South Carolina Aiken, SC
University of South Dakota, SD
University of Southern Indiana, IN
University of South Florida, FL
The University of Tampa, FL
The University of Tennessee at Martin, TN
The University of Texas at San Antonio, TX
The University of Texas at Tyler, TX
University of the Ozarks, AR
University of Toledo, OH
University of Tulsa, OK
University of Utah, UT
University of Virginia's College at Wise, VA
University of Washington, WA
University of Wisconsin–Eau Claire, WI
University of Wisconsin–River Falls, WI
University of Wisconsin–Stevens Point, WI
University of Wisconsin–Superior, WI
University of Wisconsin–Whitewater, WI
University of Wyoming, WY
Utah State University, UT
Valdosta State University, GA
Valley City State University, ND
Virginia State University, VA
Walsh University, OH
Washington State University, WA
Washington University in St. Louis, MO
Webster University, MO
West Chester University of Pennsylvania, PA
Western Illinois University, IL
Western Michigan University, MI
Western Montana College of The U of Montana, MT
Western State College of Colorado, CO
Western Washington University, WA
West Texas A&M University, TX
West Virginia University, WV
Wheeling Jesuit University, WV
Wichita State University, KS
Xavier University, OH
Xavier University of Louisiana, LA

CREATIVE ARTS/ PERFORMANCE

APPLIED ART AND DESIGN

Al Collins Graphic Design School, AZ
American InterContinental University, CA
Anderson College, SC
Arizona State University, AZ
Art Academy of Cincinnati, OH
The Art Institute of Colorado, CO
Art Institute of Southern California, CA
Barry University, FL
Belhaven College, MS
Bowie State University, MD
Brenau University, GA
Brigham Young University, UT
Brooks Institute of Photography, CA
California College of Arts and Crafts, CA
California Institute of the Arts, CA

Applied Art and Design (continued)

California Polytechnic State U, San Luis Obispo, CA
California State University, Chico, CA
California State University, Long Beach, CA
Castleton State College, VT
Ctr for Creative Studies—Coll of Art and Design, MI
Central Missouri State University, MO
Claflin University, SC
The College of New Rochelle, NY
Columbia College, MO
Columbia College, SC
Columbia College Chicago, IL
Converse College, SC
The Corcoran College of Art and Design, DC
Dana College, NE
East Carolina University, NC
Eastern Michigan University, MI
Eastern New Mexico University, NM
East Stroudsburg University of Pennsylvania, PA
The Evergreen State College, WA
Fort Hays State University, KS
Friends University, KS
Georgia State University, GA
Graceland College, IA
Grand Canyon University, AZ
Greenville College, IL
Huntingdon College, AL
Illinois State University, IL
Indiana University of Pennsylvania, PA
International Academy of Design, FL
Kendall College of Art and Design, MI
Kutztown University of Pennsylvania, PA
La Roche College, PA
Louisiana State University and A&M College, LA
Marian College, IN
Maryland Institute, College of Art, MD
Maryville University of Saint Louis, MO
Massachusetts College of Art, MA
Massachusetts College of Liberal Arts, MA
Memphis College of Art, TN
Meredith College, NC
Milwaukee Institute of Art and Design, WI
Minneapolis College of Art and Design, MN
Minnesota State University, Mankato, MN
Mississippi College, MS
Mississippi State University, MS
Montserrat College of Art, MA
Mount Mary College, WI
Murray State University, KY
North Carolina School of the Arts, NC
Northeastern Illinois University, IL
Northeastern State University, OK
Northern Michigan University, MI
North Georgia College & State University, GA
Northwest College of Art, WA
Ohio University, OH
Ohio University–Chillicothe, OH
Ohio University–Eastern, OH
Ohio University–Lancaster, OH
Oral Roberts University, OK
Otis College of Art and Design, CA
Peace College, NC
Pratt Institute, NY
Radford University, VA
Rhode Island School of Design, RI
The Richard Stockton College of New Jersey, NJ
Ringling School of Art and Design, FL
Rochester Institute of Technology, NY
Rocky Mountain College of Art & Design, CO
Saint Mary-of-the-Woods College, IN
Salem State College, MA
School of Visual Arts, NY
Shepherd College, WV
Sonoma State University, CA
Southern Illinois University Carbondale, IL
Southwestern Oklahoma State University, OK
Southwest Missouri State University, MO
Southwest Texas State University, TX
Spalding University, KY
State U of NY College at Fredonia, NY
State U of NY College at Geneseo, NY
Stephen F. Austin State University, TX
Stetson University, FL
Texas Tech University, TX
Texas Woman's University, TX
The University of Akron, OH
University of Central Arkansas, AR
University of Central Oklahoma, OK
University of Cincinnati, OH
University of Idaho, ID
University of Illinois at Chicago, IL
University of Kansas, KS
University of Nebraska at Kearney, NE
University of Nevada, Las Vegas, NV
University of Nevada, Reno, NV
The University of North Carolina at Chapel Hill, NC
University of Northern Iowa, IA
University of Southern Colorado, CO
University of South Florida, FL
The University of Texas at El Paso, TX
The University of the Arts, PA
University of West Florida, FL
University of Wisconsin–Parkside, WI
University of Wisconsin–Stevens Point, WI
University of Wisconsin–Stout, WI
Utah State University, UT
Virginia Commonwealth University, VA
Virginia Intermont College, VA
Washington State University, WA
Washington University in St. Louis, MO
Western Illinois University, IL
Western Michigan University, MI
Western Washington University, WA
Wichita State University, KS
William Woods University, MO

ART/FINE ARTS

Abilene Christian University, TX
Adams State College, CO
Adelphi University, NY
Adrian College, MI
Alabama State University, AL
Albertson College of Idaho, ID
Albertus Magnus College, CT
Albion College, MI
Albright College, PA
Alfred University, NY
Alma College, MI
Alverno College, WI
Anderson College, SC
Arizona State University, AZ
Arkansas State University, AR
Armstrong Atlantic State University, GA
Art Academy of Cincinnati, OH
The Art Institute of Colorado, CO
Art Institute of Southern California, CA
Ashland University, OH
Atlanta College of Art, GA
Augustana College, IL
Augustana College, SD
Augusta State University, GA
Austin College, TX
Austin Peay State University, TN
Avila College, MO
Baker University, KS
Ball State University, IN
Barat College, IL
Barclay College, KS
Barry University, FL
Barton College, NC
Baylor University, TX
Beaver College, PA
Belhaven College, MS
Bellarmine College, KY
Bellevue University, NE
Benedictine College, KS
Berry College, GA
Bethany College, KS
Bethel College, IN
Bethel College, KS
Bethel College, MN
Biola University, CA
Birmingham-Southern College, AL
Black Hills State University, SD
Bluefield College, VA
Bluffton College, OH
Boise State University, ID
Boston University, MA
Bowie State University, MD
Bowling Green State University, OH
Bradley University, IL
Brenau University, GA
Brescia University, KY
Brevard College, NC
Briar Cliff College, IA
Brigham Young University, UT
Brigham Young University–Hawaii Campus, HI
Bryan College, TN
Buena Vista University, IA
Butler University, IN
Caldwell College, NJ
California Baptist University, CA
California College of Arts and Crafts, CA
California Institute of the Arts, CA
California Lutheran University, CA
California Polytechnic State U, San Luis Obispo, CA
California State University, Bakersfield, CA
California State University, Chico, CA
California State University, Fullerton, CA
California State University, Los Angeles, CA
California State University, Stanislaus, CA
Calvin College, MI
Cameron University, OK
Campbellsville University, KY
Campbell University, NC
Canisius College, NY
Cardinal Stritch University, WI
Carlow College, PA
Carson-Newman College, TN

Carthage College, WI
Case Western Reserve University, OH
Castleton State College, VT
Cedar Crest College, PA
Centenary College of Louisiana, LA
Ctr for Creative Studies—Coll of Art and Design, MI
Central Bible College, MO
Central College, IA
Central Missouri State University, MO
Chadron State College, NE
Chapman University, CA
Charleston Southern University, SC
Chicago State University, IL
Christopher Newport University, VA
Claflin University, SC
Clarion University of Pennsylvania, PA
Clarke College, IA
Cleveland Institute of Art, OH
Coastal Carolina University, SC
Coe College, IA
Coker College, SC
Colby-Sawyer College, NH
College of Charleston, SC
College of Mount St. Joseph, OH
The College of New Rochelle, NY
College of Notre Dame of Maryland, MD
College of Saint Benedict, MN
College of St. Catherine, MN
College of Saint Elizabeth, NJ
The College of Saint Rose, NY
College of Visual Arts, MN
Colorado Christian University, CO
Colorado State University, CO
Columbia College, MO
Columbia College, SC
Columbia College Chicago, IL
Columbus College of Art and Design, OH
Columbus State University, GA
Concord College, WV
Concordia College, MI
Concordia University, IL
Concordia University, NE
Cornell College, IA
Cornish College of the Arts, WA
Creighton University, NE
Culver-Stockton College, MO
Cumberland College, KY
Cumberland University, TN
Daemen College, NY
Dakota Wesleyan University, SD
Dana College, NE
David Lipscomb University, TN
Davidson College, NC
Davis & Elkins College, WV
Delta State University, MS
Denison University, OH
DePaul University, IL
DePauw University, IN
Doane College, NE
Drake University, IA
Drury University, MO
East Carolina University, NC
Eastern Mennonite University, VA
Eastern Michigan University, MI
Eastern New Mexico University, NM
Eastern Oregon University, OR
Eastern Washington University, WA
East Tennessee State University, TN
Eckerd College, FL
Edgewood College, WI
Edinboro University of Pennsylvania, PA
Elon College, NC
Emporia State University, KS
Endicott College, MA
Eureka College, IL
Evangel University, MO
The Evergreen State College, WA
Fairmont State College, WV
Finlandia University, MI
Florida Agricultural and Mechanical University, FL
Florida Southern College, FL
Fontbonne College, MO
Fort Hays State University, KS
Fort Lewis College, CO
Francis Marion University, SC
Fresno Pacific University, CA
Friends University, KS
Frostburg State University, MD
Furman University, SC
Georgetown College, KY
Georgian Court College, NJ
Georgia Southern University, GA
Georgia Southwestern State University, GA
Georgia State University, GA
Glenville State College, WV
Goucher College, MD
Grace College, IN
Grand Canyon University, AZ
Grand Valley State University, MI
Grand View College, IA
Green Mountain College, VT
Greensboro College, NC
Greenville College, IL
Guilford College, NC
Hannibal-LaGrange College, MO
Hardin-Simmons University, TX
Hastings College, NE
Hendrix College, AR
Hillsdale College, MI
Hobart and William Smith Colleges, NY
Hofstra University, NY
Hollins University, VA
Hope College, MI
Houghton College, NY
Houston Baptist University, TX
Howard Payne University, TX
Huntington College, IN
Idaho State University, ID
Illinois College, IL
Illinois State University, IL
Illinois Wesleyan University, IL
Indiana State University, IN
Indiana University of Pennsylvania, PA
Indiana U–Purdue U Fort Wayne, IN
Indiana Wesleyan University, IN
Iowa Wesleyan College, IA
Jacksonville State University, AL
Jacksonville University, FL
James Madison University, VA
Johnson State College, VT
Judson College, AL
Judson College, IL
Kalamazoo College, MI
Kansas City Art Institute, MO
Kansas State University, KS
Keene State College, NH
Kendall College of Art and Design, MI
Kennesaw State University, GA
Kent State University, OH
Kentucky Wesleyan College, KY
Knox College, IL
LaGrange College, GA
Lake Erie College, OH
Lake Forest College, IL
Lander University, SC
Lewis-Clark State College, ID
Limestone College, SC
Lincoln University, MO
Lock Haven University of Pennsylvania, PA
Long Island U, Brooklyn Campus, NY
Long Island U, C.W. Post Campus, NY
Long Island U, Southampton College, NY
Longwood College, VA
Louisiana State University and A&M College, LA
Lourdes College, OH
Loyola University Chicago, IL
Loyola University New Orleans, LA
Lubbock Christian University, TX
Lycoming College, PA
Lyme Academy of Fine Arts, CT
Lyon College, AR
MacMurray College, IL
Maine College of Art, ME
Manchester College, IN
Mansfield University of Pennsylvania, PA
Marian College, IN
Marietta College, OH
Martin Methodist College, TN
Marycrest International University, IA
Maryland Institute, College of Art, MD
Marymount College, NY
Marymount Manhattan College, NY
Maryville College, TN
Maryville University of Saint Louis, MO
Mary Washington College, VA
Marywood University, PA
Massachusetts College of Art, MA
Massachusetts College of Liberal Arts, MA
McMurry University, TX
McNeese State University, LA
Memphis College of Art, TN
Mercer University, GA
Mercyhurst College, PA
Meredith College, NC
Merrimack College, MA
Mesa State College, CO
Messiah College, PA
Miami University, OH
Midland Lutheran College, NE
Midway College, KY
Milligan College, TN
Millikin University, IL
Millsaps College, MS
Mills College, CA
Milwaukee Institute of Art and Design, WI
Minneapolis College of Art and Design, MN
Minnesota Bible College, MN
Minnesota State University, Mankato, MN
Minnesota State University Moorhead, MN
Mississippi College, MS
Mississippi State University, MS
Mississippi University for Women, MS
Mississippi Valley State University, MS
Missouri Southern State College, MO
Missouri Western State College, MO
Monmouth College, IL
Montana State U–Billings, MT

Art/Fine Arts (continued)

Montana State U–Bozeman, MT
Montana State U–Northern, MT
Montreat College, NC
Montserrat College of Art, MA
Moore College of Art and Design, PA
Morehead State University, KY
Morningside College, IA
Mount Mary College, WI
Mount Mercy College, IA
Mount Olive College, NC
Mount St. Clare College, IA
Mount Senario College, WI
Mount Union College, OH
Murray State University, KY
Muskingum College, OH
Nazareth College of Rochester, NY
Nebraska Wesleyan University, NE
New England College, NH
New Mexico Highlands University, NM
North Central College, IL
North Dakota State University, ND
Northeastern Illinois University, IL
Northeastern State University, OK
Northern Arizona University, AZ
Northern Illinois University, IL
Northern Kentucky University, KY
North Greenville College, SC
Northwest College, WA
Northwest College of Art, WA
Northwestern College, IA
Northwest Missouri State University, MO
Northwest Nazarene University, ID
Oakland City University, IN
Ohio Northern University, OH
Ohio University, OH
Ohio University–Chillicothe, OH
Ohio University–Eastern, OH
Ohio University–Lancaster, OH
Ohio Wesleyan University, OH
Oklahoma Baptist University, OK
Oklahoma Christian U of Science and Arts, OK
Old Dominion University, VA
Olivet Nazarene University, IL
Oral Roberts University, OK
Oregon College of Art and Craft, OR
Otis College of Art and Design, CA
Ottawa University, KS
Otterbein College, OH
Ouachita Baptist University, AR
Our Lady of the Lake University of San Antonio, TX
Pacific Northwest College of Art, OR
Park University, MO
Peace College, NC
Pepperdine University, CA
Piedmont College, GA
Plattsburgh State U of NY, NY
Point Loma Nazarene University, CA
Portland State University, OR
Prairie View A&M University, TX
Purchase College, State U of NY, NY
Queens College, NC
Quincy University, IL
Radford University, VA
Randolph-Macon Woman's College, VA
Reinhardt College, GA
Rhode Island College, RI
Rhode Island School of Design, RI
Rhodes College, TN
The Richard Stockton College of New Jersey, NJ
Rider University, NJ
Ringling School of Art and Design, FL
Ripon College, WI
Roanoke College, VA
Roberts Wesleyan College, NY
Rochester Institute of Technology, NY
Rocky Mountain College, MT
Rocky Mountain College of Art & Design, CO
Rollins College, FL
Rosemont College, PA
Rowan University, NJ
Sacred Heart University, CT
St. Ambrose University, IA
Saint Augustine's College, NC
Saint Francis College, PA
Saint John's University, MN
St. John's University, NY
Saint Louis University, MO
Saint Mary College, KS
Saint Mary-of-the-Woods College, IN
Saint Mary's College, IN
Saint Michael's College, VT
St. Norbert College, WI
Salem State College, MA
Sam Houston State University, TX
San Francisco Art Institute, CA
Savannah College of Art and Design, GA
School of the Art Institute of Chicago, IL
School of Visual Arts, NY
Schreiner College, TX
Seattle Pacific University, WA
Seton Hall University, NJ
Seton Hill College, PA
Shawnee State University, OH
Shepherd College, WV
Shimer College, IL
Shorter College, GA
Siena Heights University, MI
Sierra Nevada College, NV
Simpson College, IA
Slippery Rock University of Pennsylvania, PA
Sonoma State University, CA
South Dakota State University, SD
Southern Adventist University, TN
Southern Arkansas University–Magnolia, AR
Southern Illinois University Carbondale, IL
Southern Illinois University Edwardsville, IL
Southern Methodist University, TX
Southern Oregon University, OR
Southwestern Assemblies of God University, TX
Southwestern Oklahoma State University, OK
Southwestern University, TX
Southwest Missouri State University, MO
Southwest State University, MN
Spalding University, KY
Spring Arbor College, MI
State U of NY at New Paltz, NY
State U of NY at Oswego, NY
State U of NY College at Brockport, NY
State U of NY College at Geneseo, NY
State U of NY College at Potsdam, NY
State University of West Georgia, GA
Stephen F. Austin State University, TX
Stetson University, FL
Sul Ross State University, TX
Sweet Briar College, VA
Syracuse University, NY
Tennessee Technological University, TN
Texas A&M University–Commerce, TX
Texas A&M University–Corpus Christi, TX
Texas Christian University, TX
Texas Tech University, TX
Texas Wesleyan University, TX
Texas Woman's University, TX
Thomas More College, KY
Towson University, MD
Transylvania University, KY
Trinity Bible College, ND
Truman State University, MO
Union University, TN
The University of Akron, OH
The University of Alabama, AL
The University of Alabama at Birmingham, AL
The University of Alabama in Huntsville, AL
U of Alaska Anchorage, AK
The University of Arizona, AZ
University of Arkansas at Little Rock, AR
University of Arkansas at Pine Bluff, AR
U of Calif, Riverside, CA
University of Central Arkansas, AR
University of Central Oklahoma, OK
University of Cincinnati, OH
University of Colorado at Boulder, CO
University of Connecticut, CT
University of Dallas, TX
University of Dayton, OH
University of Delaware, DE
University of Evansville, IN
University of Florida, FL
University of Guam, GU
University of Hartford, CT
University of Hawaii at Hilo, HI
University of Hawaii at Manoa, HI
University of Houston, TX
University of Houston–Downtown, TX
University of Idaho, ID
University of Illinois at Chicago, IL
University of Illinois at Springfield, IL
University of Indianapolis, IN
University of Kansas, KS
University of Louisiana at Monroe, LA
University of Maine, ME
University of Maine at Presque Isle, ME
University of Mary Hardin-Baylor, TX
University of Maryland, Baltimore County, MD
University of Maryland, College Park, MD
University of Massachusetts Amherst, MA
The University of Memphis, TN
University of Miami, FL
University of Michigan–Dearborn, MI
University of Michigan–Flint, MI
University of Minnesota, Duluth, MN
University of Mississippi, MS
University of Missouri–St. Louis, MO
University of Mobile, AL
The University of Montana–Missoula, MT
University of Montevallo, AL
University of Nebraska at Kearney, NE
University of Nebraska at Omaha, NE
University of Nebraska–Lincoln, NE
University of Nevada, Las Vegas, NV
University of Nevada, Reno, NV

University of New Hampshire, NH
University of New Mexico, NM
University of North Alabama, AL
The University of North Carolina at Asheville, NC
The University of North Carolina at Chapel Hill, NC
The University of North Carolina at Greensboro, NC
The University of North Carolina at Wilmington, NC
University of North Dakota, ND
University of Northern Iowa, IA
University of Oklahoma, OK
University of Oregon, OR
University of Puget Sound, WA
University of Redlands, CA
University of Saint Francis, IN
University of Science and Arts of Oklahoma, OK
University of South Alabama, AL
University of South Carolina, SC
University of South Carolina Aiken, SC
University of South Dakota, SD
University of Southern Colorado, CO
University of Southern Indiana, IN
University of Southern Mississippi, MS
University of South Florida, FL
The University of Tampa, FL
The University of Tennessee at Chattanooga, TN
The University of Texas at Arlington, TX
The University of Texas at Brownsville, TX
The University of Texas at El Paso, TX
The University of Texas at San Antonio, TX
The University of Texas at Tyler, TX
The University of Texas of the Permian Basin, TX
The University of Texas–Pan American, TX
University of the Incarnate Word, TX
University of the Ozarks, AR
University of Toledo, OH
University of Tulsa, OK
University of Utah, UT
University of Washington, WA
University of West Florida, FL
University of Wisconsin–Green Bay, WI
University of Wisconsin–La Crosse, WI
University of Wisconsin–Oshkosh, WI
University of Wisconsin–Platteville, WI
University of Wisconsin–River Falls, WI
University of Wisconsin–Stout, WI
University of Wisconsin–Superior, WI
University of Wisconsin–Whitewater, WI
Upper Iowa University, IA
Ursinus College, PA
Utah State University, UT
Valdosta State University, GA
Valley City State University, ND
Valley Forge Christian College, PA
Valparaiso University, IN
Villa Julie College, MD
Virginia Commonwealth University, VA
Virginia Intermont College, VA
Virginia Polytechnic Institute and State U, VA
Virginia State University, VA
Virginia Wesleyan College, VA
Viterbo University, WI
Wabash College, IN
Wake Forest University, NC
Washington State University, WA
Washington University in St. Louis, MO
Wayne State College, NE
Weber State University, UT
Webster University, MO
Wesleyan College, GA
Western Carolina University, NC
Western Michigan University, MI
Western Montana College of The U of Montana, MT
Western Oregon University, OR
Western State College of Colorado, CO
Western Washington University, WA
West Liberty State College, WV
Westminster College, UT
Westmont College, CA
West Virginia State College, WV
West Virginia University, WV
West Virginia Wesleyan College, WV
Whitman College, WA
Whittier College, CA
Whitworth College, WA
Wichita State University, KS
William Carey College, MS
William Jewell College, MO
William Penn University, IA
Williams Baptist College, AR
William Woods University, MO
Winona State University, MN
Winthrop University, SC
Wisconsin Lutheran College, WI
Wittenberg University, OH
Worcester State College, MA
Xavier University, OH
Xavier University of Louisiana, LA
York College, NE

CINEMA/FILM/BROADCASTING

Allentown College of St. Francis de Sales, PA
Arizona State University, AZ
Arkansas State University, AR
The Art Institute of Colorado, CO
Baker University, KS
Baylor University, TX
Bowling Green State University, OH
Brigham Young University, UT
Butler University, IN
California Institute of the Arts, CA
California Polytechnic State U, San Luis Obispo, CA
California State University, Chico, CA
California State University, Long Beach, CA
Central Michigan University, MI
Central Missouri State University, MO
Chapman University, CA
The College of New Rochelle, NY
Columbia College Chicago, IL
DePauw University, IN
Eastern Michigan University, MI
Eastern New Mexico University, NM
Edinboro University of Pennsylvania, PA
Five Towns College, NY
Fort Hays State University, KS
Grace University, NE
Henderson State University, AR
Howard Payne University, TX
Illinois State University, IL
Kalamazoo College, MI
Lee University, TN
Long Island U, Brooklyn Campus, NY
Long Island U, C.W. Post Campus, NY
Lynn University, FL
Manchester College, IN
Marywood University, PA
Massachusetts College of Liberal Arts, MA
MidAmerica Nazarene University, KS
Mississippi State University, MS
Montana State U–Bozeman, MT
Morehead State University, KY
Morningside College, IA
Mount Union College, OH
Muskingum College, OH
North Carolina School of the Arts, NC
North Central College, IL
Northern Arizona University, AZ
Ohio University, OH
Ohio University–Eastern, OH
Ohio University–Lancaster, OH
Oklahoma Panhandle State University, OK
Oral Roberts University, OK
Purchase College, State U of NY, NY
Quincy University, IL
Radford University, VA
Rochester Institute of Technology, NY
Sacred Heart University, CT
St. John's University, NY
Saint Joseph's College, IN
Sam Houston State University, TX
Seton Hall University, NJ
Sonoma State University, CA
Southern Illinois University Carbondale, IL
Southern Methodist University, TX
Southwestern College, KS
State U of NY at Oswego, NY
Sul Ross State University, TX
Texas Christian University, TX
Texas Woman's University, TX
Union University, TN
University of Central Arkansas, AR
University of Colorado at Boulder, CO
University of Kansas, KS
University of Maryland, Baltimore County, MD
The University of Memphis, TN
University of Nebraska at Kearney, NE
University of Nebraska–Lincoln, NE
University of Nevada, Las Vegas, NV
The University of North Carolina at Greensboro, NC
University of Southern Colorado, CO
University of South Florida, FL
University of Utah, UT
University of Wisconsin–Superior, WI
University of Wisconsin–Whitewater, WI
Villa Julie College, MD
Wake Forest University, NC
Washington State University, WA
Wayne State College, NE
Webster University, MO
Western Illinois University, IL
Western Washington University, WA
Westminster College, PA
William Jewell College, MO

CREATIVE WRITING

Allentown College of St. Francis de Sales, PA
Arizona State University, AZ
Arkansas Tech University, AR
Augustana College, IL
Austin Peay State University, TN

Creative Writing (continued)

Bowling Green State University, OH
Brescia University, KY
Brigham Young University, UT
Brigham Young University–Hawaii Campus, HI
California Institute of the Arts, CA
California Polytechnic State U, San Luis Obispo, CA
California State University, Chico, CA
Cameron University, OK
Campbell University, NC
Carlow College, PA
Case Western Reserve University, OH
Central Missouri State University, MO
Chapman University, CA
Coe College, IA
Colby-Sawyer College, NH
The College of New Rochelle, NY
Colorado State University, CO
Columbia College Chicago, IL
Converse College, SC
The Corcoran College of Art and Design, DC
Davidson College, NC
Dominican University, IL
Drury University, MO
Duke University, NC
Eastern Michigan University, MI
Eastern New Mexico University, NM
Eckerd College, FL
Edgewood College, WI
The Evergreen State College, WA
Fontbonne College, MO
Fort Hays State University, KS
Free Will Baptist Bible College, TN
Furman University, SC
Graceland College, IA
Green Mountain College, VT
Grove City College, PA
Hamline University, MN
Hobart and William Smith Colleges, NY
Hollins University, VA
Hood College, MD
Illinois State University, IL
Knox College, IL
Lewis-Clark State College, ID
Long Island U, Southampton College, NY
Lycoming College, PA
Maharishi University of Management, IA
Marycrest International University, IA
Mesa State College, CO
Michigan State University, MI
Midwestern State University, TX
Minnesota State University, Mankato, MN
Mississippi State University, MS
Mount Marty College, SD
Murray State University, KY
Northwest College, WA
The Ohio State University, OH
Plymouth State College, NH
Purchase College, State U of NY, NY
Randolph-Macon Woman's College, VA
The Richard Stockton College of New Jersey, NJ
Rockhurst University, MO
Saint Mary College, KS
Saint Mary-of-the-Woods College, IN
Salem State College, MA
Shimer College, IL
Siena College, NY
Sonoma State University, CA
Southern Illinois University Carbondale, IL
Southern Methodist University, TX
Southwestern Assemblies of God University, TX
Southwest State University, MN
Spalding University, KY
State U of NY at Binghamton, NY
State U of NY at New Paltz, NY
State U of NY at Oswego, NY
State U of NY College at Geneseo, NY
Trinity Bible College, ND
The University of Akron, OH
U of Alaska Fairbanks, AK
U of Calif, Riverside, CA
University of Colorado at Boulder, CO
University of Houston, TX
University of Idaho, ID
University of Kansas, KS
University of Louisiana at Monroe, LA
University of Maryland, Baltimore County, MD
University of Michigan–Dearborn, MI
The University of Montana–Missoula, MT
University of Nebraska at Kearney, NE
University of Redlands, CA
University of South Carolina, SC
University of South Carolina Aiken, SC
University of South Dakota, SD
University of Southern Indiana, IN
University of South Florida, FL
The University of Tampa, FL
University of Virginia's College at Wise, VA
University of Washington, WA
The University of West Alabama, AL
University of Wisconsin–Stevens Point, WI
University of Wisconsin–Whitewater, WI
Ursinus College, PA
Villa Julie College, MD
Wabash College, IN
Wake Forest University, NC
Warren Wilson College, NC
Washington College, MD
Washington State University, WA
Washington University in St. Louis, MO
Wayne State College, NE
Webster University, MO
Western Washington University, WA
Wheeling Jesuit University, WV
William Penn University, IA

DANCE

Adelphi University, NY
Allentown College of St. Francis de Sales, PA
Alma College, MI
Arizona State University, AZ
Ball State University, IN
Barat College, IL
Bay Path College, MA
Belhaven College, MS
Birmingham-Southern College, AL
Boise State University, ID
Boston Conservatory, MA
Bowling Green State University, OH
Brenau University, GA
Brigham Young University, UT
Butler University, IN
California Institute of the Arts, CA
California Polytechnic State U, San Luis Obispo, CA
California State University, Chico, CA
California State University, Long Beach, CA
Case Western Reserve University, OH
Cedar Crest College, PA
Centenary College of Louisiana, LA
Chapman University, CA
Coker College, SC
The College of New Rochelle, NY
The College of Wooster, OH
Colorado State University, CO
Columbia College, SC
Columbia College Chicago, IL
Cornish College of the Arts, WA
Denison University, OH
Drexel University, PA
Duquesne University, PA
Eastern Michigan University, MI
Eastern New Mexico University, NM
Florida International University, FL
Friends University, KS
Goucher College, MD
Grambling State University, LA
Hawaii Pacific University, HI
Hobart and William Smith Colleges, NY
Hofstra University, NY
Hollins University, VA
Hope College, MI
Huntingdon College, AL
Indiana University of Pennsylvania, PA
Jacksonville University, FL
James Madison University, VA
Johnson State College, VT
The Juilliard School, NY
Kansas Wesleyan University, KS
Lambuth University, TN
Lees-McRae College, NC
Lewis University, IL
Long Island U, Brooklyn Campus, NY
Long Island U, C.W. Post Campus, NY
Lyon College, AR
Mars Hill College, NC
Marymount Manhattan College, NY
Mary Washington College, VA
Mercyhurst College, PA
Methodist College, NC
Middle Tennessee State University, TN
Millikin University, IL
Mississippi State University, MS
Mississippi University for Women, MS
Missouri Western State College, MO
Montana State U–Bozeman, MT
Muhlenberg College, PA
Murray State University, KY
North Carolina School of the Arts, NC
Northeastern Illinois University, IL
Northeastern State University, OK
Northwestern State University of Louisiana, LA
Ohio Northern University, OH
The Ohio State University, OH
Ohio University, OH
Ohio University–Eastern, OH
Ohio University–Lancaster, OH
Oklahoma City University, OK
Old Dominion University, VA
Plymouth State College, NH
Point Park College, PA
Purchase College, State U of NY, NY

Radford University, VA
Rhode Island College, RI
The Richard Stockton College of New Jersey, NJ
Rockford College, IL
Rutgers, State U of NJ, Mason Gross School of Arts, NJ
St. Gregory's University, OK
Saint Mary-of-the-Woods College, IN
Salem State College, MA
Sam Houston State University, TX
Shenandoah University, VA
Sonoma State University, CA
Southern Illinois University Carbondale, IL
Southern Methodist University, TX
Southern Utah University, UT
Southwest Missouri State University, MO
State U of NY College at Fredonia, NY
State U of NY College at Geneseo, NY
State U of NY College at Potsdam, NY
Stephens College, MO
Texas A&M International University, TX
Texas Christian University, TX
Texas Tech University, TX
Texas Woman's University, TX
Towson University, MD
The University of Akron, OH
The University of Alabama, AL
The University of Arizona, AZ
U of Calif, Riverside, CA
University of Colorado at Boulder, CO
University of Florida, FL
University of Hartford, CT
University of Hawaii at Manoa, HI
University of Idaho, ID
University of Kansas, KS
University of Maryland, Baltimore County, MD
University of Massachusetts Amherst, MA
The University of Memphis, TN
University of Mobile, AL
The University of Montana–Missoula, MT
University of Nebraska at Kearney, NE
University of Nebraska–Lincoln, NE
University of Nevada, Las Vegas, NV
University of Nevada, Reno, NV
University of New Hampshire, NH
The University of North Carolina at Greensboro, NC
University of Northern Colorado, CO
University of North Texas, TX
University of Oklahoma, OK
University of Southern Mississippi, MS
University of South Florida, FL
The University of the Arts, PA
University of the Incarnate Word, TX
University of Toledo, OH
University of Utah, UT
University of Washington, WA
The University of West Alabama, AL
University of Wisconsin–Green Bay, WI
University of Wisconsin–Stevens Point, WI
University of Wyoming, WY
Virginia Commonwealth University, VA
Virginia Intermont College, VA
Wake Forest University, NC
Washington University in St. Louis, MO
Wayne State University, MI
Webster University, MO
Western Illinois University, IL
Western Michigan University, MI
Western Washington University, WA
West Texas A&M University, TX
Wichita State University, KS
Winthrop University, SC
Wittenberg University, OH

DEBATING

Abilene Christian University, TX
Albertson College of Idaho, ID
Allentown College of St. Francis de Sales, PA
Arizona State University, AZ
Arkansas State University, AR
Augustana College, IL
Augustana College, SD
Austin Peay State University, TN
Azusa Pacific University, CA
Bartlesville Wesleyan College, OK
Baylor University, TX
Berry College, GA
Bethel College, MN
Biola University, CA
Bluefield State College, WV
Boise State University, ID
Bowling Green State University, OH
Bradley University, IL
California Polytechnic State U, San Luis Obispo, CA
California State University, Chico, CA
Cameron University, OK
Carroll College, MT
Carson-Newman College, TN
Cedarville College, OH
Central Methodist College, MO
Central Missouri State University, MO
The College of New Rochelle, NY
Colorado State University, CO
Concordia College, MN
Creighton University, NE
Culver-Stockton College, MO
Dakota Wesleyan University, SD
Dana College, NE
DePaul University, IL
DePauw University, IN
Eastern Illinois University, IL
Eastern Michigan University, MI
Eastern New Mexico University, NM
Emory University, GA
Emporia State University, KS
Evangel University, MO
Fairmont State College, WV
Ferris State University, MI
Florida College, FL
Fort Hays State University, KS
George Fox University, OR
The George Washington University, DC
Georgia College and State University, GA
Gonzaga University, WA
Graceland College, IA
Hastings College, NE
Henderson State University, AR
Idaho State University, ID
Illinois College, IL
Illinois State University, IL
Kansas State University, KS
Kentucky Christian College, KY
King's College, PA
Lewis & Clark College, OR
Liberty University, VA
Linfield College, OR
Louisiana Tech University, LA
Loyola Marymount University, CA
Loyola University Chicago, IL
Malone College, OH
Marist College, NY
McNeese State University, LA
Mercer University, GA
Methodist College, NC
Michigan State University, MI
Midland Lutheran College, NE
Minnesota State University, Mankato, MN
Mississippi State University, MS
Missouri Southern State College, MO
Mount Union College, OH
Murray State University, KY
Muskingum College, OH
Newman University, KS
North Central College, IL
North Dakota State University, ND
Northeastern State University, OK
Northern Arizona University, AZ
Northwest College, WA
Northwestern State University of Louisiana, LA
Northwest Missouri State University, MO
Northwest Nazarene University, ID
Ohio University, OH
Ohio University–Eastern, OH
Ohio University–Lancaster, OH
Oklahoma Panhandle State University, OK
Pacific University, OR
Palm Beach Atlantic College, FL
Pepperdine University, CA
Point Loma Nazarene University, CA
Regis University, CO
Rhode Island College, RI
Ripon College, WI
Rocky Mountain College, MT
Saint Anselm College, NH
St. John's University, NY
Saint Joseph's College, IN
Saint Joseph's University, PA
Santa Clara University, CA
Seton Hall University, NJ
South Dakota State University, SD
Southeastern Louisiana University, LA
Southern Illinois University Carbondale, IL
Southwest Baptist University, MO
Southwestern College, KS
Southwest Missouri State University, MO
State University of West Georgia, GA
Sterling College, KS
Suffolk University, MA
Tennessee Technological University, TN
Truman State University, MO
The University of Akron, OH
University of Arkansas at Monticello, AR
University of Georgia, GA
University of Kansas, KS
University of La Verne, CA
University of Louisiana at Monroe, LA
University of Mary, ND
University of Miami, FL
University of Missouri–Kansas City, MO
University of Nebraska at Kearney, NE
University of Nebraska at Omaha, NE
University of Nevada, Reno, NV
University of Oklahoma, OK
University of Puget Sound, WA
University of Redlands, CA

Debating (continued)

University of St. Thomas, TX
University of South Carolina, SC
University of South Dakota, SD
University of Southern California, CA
University of South Florida, FL
The University of Texas at Arlington, TX
The University of Texas at San Antonio, TX
The University of Texas at Tyler, TX
University of Wisconsin–Eau Claire, WI
University of Wisconsin–Oshkosh, WI
University of Wyoming, WY
Vanguard University of Southern California, CA
Wake Forest University, NC
Washburn University of Topeka, KS
Wayne State University, MI
Weber State University, UT
Webster University, MO
Western Illinois University, IL
West Virginia University, WV
Whitman College, WA
Wichita State University, KS
Willamette University, OR
William Carey College, MS
William Jewell College, MO
Winona State University, MN
York College, NE

JOURNALISM/PUBLICATIONS

Abilene Christian University, TX
Anderson College, SC
Arizona State University, AZ
Arkansas State University, AR
Arkansas Tech University, AR
Athens State University, AL
Austin College, TX
Baker University, KS
Ball State University, IN
Baylor University, TX
Benedictine College, KS
Berry College, GA
Biola University, CA
Boise State University, ID
Bowling Green State University, OH
Brevard College, NC
Brigham Young University, UT
Brigham Young University–Hawaii Campus, HI
Bryan College, TN
California Polytechnic State U, San Luis Obispo, CA
California State University, Chico, CA
California State University, Fresno, CA
California State University, Los Angeles, CA
California State University, Northridge, CA
Cameron University, OK
Campbellsville University, KY
Campbell University, NC
Carroll College, WI
Carson-Newman College, TN
Central Missouri State University, MO
Chapman University, CA
Chicago State University, IL
Citadel, The Military Coll of South Carolina, SC
The College of New Rochelle, NY
Columbia College Chicago, IL
David Lipscomb University, TN
Delta State University, MS
DePauw University, IN
Dordt College, IA
Eastern New Mexico University, NM
Eastern Washington University, WA
East Tennessee State University, TN
Edinboro University of Pennsylvania, PA
Faulkner University, AL
Ferris State University, MI
Florida Agricultural and Mechanical University, FL
Florida College, FL
Fort Hays State University, KS
Fort Valley State University, GA
Franklin College of Indiana, IN
Georgia College and State University, GA
Georgia State University, GA
Hannibal-LaGrange College, MO
Henderson State University, AR
Huntington College, IN
Indiana University of Pennsylvania, PA
Jacksonville State University, AL
James Madison University, VA
John Brown University, AR
Judson College, IL
Kent State University, OH
Lakeland College, WI
Lees-McRae College, NC
Lee University, TN
LeTourneau University, TX
Liberty University, VA
Lincoln University, MO
Lock Haven University of Pennsylvania, PA
Louisiana State University and A&M College, LA
Louisiana Tech University, LA
Loyola University Chicago, IL
Lubbock Christian University, TX
Malone College, OH
Manchester College, IN
Mansfield University of Pennsylvania, PA
Marycrest International University, IA
Mary Washington College, VA
Massachusetts College of Liberal Arts, MA
Mesa State College, CO
Michigan State University, MI
Midland Lutheran College, NE
Midwestern State University, TX
Mississippi State University, MS
Mississippi University for Women, MS
Mississippi Valley State University, MS
Missouri Southern State College, MO
Morehead State University, KY
Morningside College, IA
Mount St. Clare College, IA
Mount Union College, OH
Murray State University, KY
Northeastern State University, OK
Northern Arizona University, AZ
North Greenville College, SC
Northwest College, WA
Northwestern College, IA
Northwest Missouri State University, MO
Northwest Nazarene University, ID
Nyack College, NY
Oglethorpe University, GA
The Ohio State University, OH
Ohio University, OH
Ohio University–Eastern, OH
Ohio University–Lancaster, OH
Oklahoma Christian U of Science and Arts, OK
Oral Roberts University, OK
Ouachita Baptist University, AR
Pepperdine University, CA
Point Park College, PA
Rhode Island College, RI
The Richard Stockton College of New Jersey, NJ
Rochester College, MI
St. Gregory's University, OK
St. John's University, NY
Saint Joseph's College, IN
Saint Mary College, KS
Saint Mary-of-the-Woods College, IN
Sam Houston State University, TX
Schreiner College, TX
Seton Hall University, NJ
Siena College, NY
Sonoma State University, CA
South Dakota State University, SD
Southeastern Louisiana University, LA
Southern Adventist University, TN
Southern Illinois University Carbondale, IL
Southern Methodist University, TX
Southern Utah University, UT
Southwestern Assemblies of God University, TX
Southwestern College, KS
Southwest Missouri State University, MO
Southwest Texas State University, TX
State U of NY at Oswego, NY
State U of NY College at Geneseo, NY
State University of West Georgia, GA
Stephen F. Austin State University, TX
Sul Ross State University, TX
Tabor College, KS
Tennessee Technological University, TN
Texas A&M University, TX
Texas Christian University, TX
Texas Lutheran University, TX
Texas Tech University, TX
Texas Woman's University, TX
Trinity Christian College, IL
Troy State University, AL
Union University, TN
The University of Akron, OH
U of Calif, San Diego, CA
University of Central Arkansas, AR
University of Central Oklahoma, OK
University of Colorado at Boulder, CO
University of Florida, FL
University of Georgia, GA
University of Guam, GU
University of Hawaii at Manoa, HI
University of Idaho, ID
University of Illinois at Springfield, IL
University of Kansas, KS
University of La Verne, CA
University of Louisiana at Monroe, LA
University of Mary Hardin-Baylor, TX
The University of Memphis, TN
University of Michigan, MI
University of Michigan–Dearborn, MI
University of Missouri–Columbia, MO
The University of Montana–Missoula, MT
University of Nebraska at Kearney, NE
University of Nebraska at Omaha, NE
University of Nebraska–Lincoln, NE
University of Nevada, Las Vegas, NV

University of Nevada, Reno, NV
University of North Alabama, AL
The University of North Carolina at Chapel Hill, NC
The University of North Carolina at Pembroke, NC
University of Oklahoma, OK
University of Oregon, OR
University of Portland, OR
University of St. Thomas, MN
University of South Alabama, AL
University of South Carolina, SC
University of South Carolina Aiken, SC
University of Southern Colorado, CO
University of South Florida, FL
The University of Tampa, FL
The University of Tennessee at Martin, TN
The University of Texas at Arlington, TX
The University of Texas at El Paso, TX
The University of Texas at Tyler, TX
University of Toledo, OH
University of Virginia's College at Wise, VA
University of Washington, WA
The University of West Alabama, AL
University of Wisconsin–Superior, WI
University of Wisconsin–Whitewater, WI
Utah State University, UT
Valdosta State University, GA
Valley City State University, ND
Vanderbilt University, TN
Virginia Polytechnic Institute and State U, VA
Wabash College, IN
Wake Forest University, NC
Washington State University, WA
Waynesburg College, PA
Wayne State College, NE
Webber College, FL
Webster University, MO
Western Baptist College, OR
Western Illinois University, IL
Western Washington University, WA
Westminster College, UT
West Texas A&M University, TX
Wichita State University, KS
William Jewell College, MO
William Penn University, IA
William Woods University, MO

MUSIC

Abilene Christian University, TX
Adams State College, CO
Adelphi University, NY
Adrian College, MI
Agnes Scott College, GA
Alabama Agricultural and Mechanical University, AL
Alabama State University, AL
Alaska Bible College, AK
Albany State University, GA
Albertson College of Idaho, ID
Albion College, MI
Albright College, PA
Alcorn State University, MS
Allentown College of St. Francis de Sales, PA
Allen University, SC
Alma College, MI
Alverno College, WI
American University, DC
Anderson College, SC
Anderson University, IN
Andrews University, MI
Angelo State University, TX
Anna Maria College, MA
Arizona State University, AZ
Arkansas State University, AR
Arkansas Tech University, AR
Armstrong Atlantic State University, GA
Asbury College, KY
Ashland University, OH
Athens State University, AL
Atlanta Christian College, GA
Atlantic Union College, MA
Auburn University, AL
Augsburg College, MN
Augustana College, IL
Augustana College, SD
Augusta State University, GA
Austin College, TX
Austin Peay State University, TN
Avila College, MO
Azusa Pacific University, CA
Baker University, KS
Baldwin-Wallace College, OH
Ball State University, IN
Baptist Bible College of Pennsylvania, PA
Barber-Scotia College, NC
Barclay College, KS
Bartlesville Wesleyan College, OK
Barton College, NC
Baylor University, TX
Belhaven College, MS
Bellarmine College, KY
Belmont University, TN
Beloit College, WI
Bemidji State University, MN
Benedictine College, KS
Benedictine University, IL
Berklee College of Music, MA
Berry College, GA
Bethany College, KS
Bethany College, WV
Bethany College of the Assemblies of God, CA
Bethel College, KS
Bethel College, MN
Bethel College, TN
Bethune-Cookman College, FL
Biola University, CA
Birmingham-Southern College, AL
Black Hills State University, SD
Bluefield College, VA
Blue Mountain College, MS
Bluffton College, OH
Boise Bible College, ID
Boise State University, ID
Boston Conservatory, MA
Boston University, MA
Bowie State University, MD
Bowling Green State University, OH
Bradley University, IL
Brenau University, GA
Brescia University, KY
Brevard College, NC
Briar Cliff College, IA
Bridgewater College, VA
Brigham Young University, UT
Brigham Young University–Hawaii Campus, HI
Bryan College, TN
Buena Vista University, IA
Butler University, IN
Caldwell College, NJ
California Baptist University, CA
California Institute of the Arts, CA
California Lutheran University, CA
California Polytechnic State U, San Luis Obispo, CA
California State University, Bakersfield, CA
California State University, Chico, CA
California State University, Fresno, CA
California State University, Fullerton, CA
California State University, Hayward, CA
California State University, Long Beach, CA
California State University, Los Angeles, CA
California State University, Northridge, CA
California State University, San Bernardino, CA
California State University, Stanislaus, CA
Calvin College, MI
Cameron University, OK
Campbellsville University, KY
Campbell University, NC
Canisius College, NY
Capital University, OH
Carleton College, MN
Carroll College, MT
Carroll College, WI
Carson-Newman College, TN
Carthage College, WI
Cascade College, OR
Case Western Reserve University, OH
Castleton State College, VT
The Catholic University of America, DC
Cedarville College, OH
Centenary College of Louisiana, LA
Central Bible College, MO
Central Christian College of the Bible, MO
Central College, IA
Central Methodist College, MO
Central Michigan University, MI
Central Missouri State University, MO
Central State University, OH
Central Washington University, WA
Chapman University, CA
Charleston Southern University, SC
Chatham College, PA
Chicago State University, IL
Chowan College, NC
Christian Heritage College, CA
Christopher Newport University, VA
Cincinnati Bible College and Seminary, OH
Circleville Bible College, OH
Citadel, The Military Coll of South Carolina, SC
Claflin University, SC
Clark Atlanta University, GA
Clarke College, IA
Clayton College & State University, GA
Clear Creek Baptist Bible College, KY
Clearwater Christian College, FL
Cleveland Institute of Music, OH
Coastal Carolina University, SC
Coe College, IA
Coker College, SC
Colby-Sawyer College, NH
College of Charleston, SC
College of Mount St. Joseph, OH
The College of New Jersey, NJ
The College of New Rochelle, NY
College of Saint Benedict, MN

Music (continued)

College of St. Catherine, MN
The College of Saint Rose, NY
The College of St. Scholastica, MN
College of the Holy Cross, MA
College of the Southwest, NM
The College of Wooster, OH
Colorado Christian University, CO
Colorado School of Mines, CO
Colorado State University, CO
Columbia College, MO
Columbia College, SC
Columbia International University, SC
Columbia Union College, MD
Columbus State University, GA
Concord College, WV
Concordia College, AL
Concordia College, MI
Concordia College, MN
Concordia College, NY
Concordia University, CA
Concordia University, IL
Concordia University, NE
Concordia University, OR
Concordia University at Austin, TX
Concordia University at St. Paul, MN
Concordia University Wisconsin, WI
Conservatory of Music of Puerto Rico, PR
Converse College, SC
Cornell College, IA
Cornerstone University, MI
Cornish College of the Arts, WA
Covenant College, GA
Crichton College, TN
Crown College, MN
Culver-Stockton College, MO
Cumberland College, KY
Cumberland University, TN
Dakota State University, SD
Dakota Wesleyan University, SD
Dallas Baptist University, TX
Dallas Christian College, TX
Dana College, NE
David Lipscomb University, TN
Davidson College, NC
Davis & Elkins College, WV
Defiance College, OH
Delaware State University, DE
Delta State University, MS
Denison University, OH
DePaul University, IL
DePauw University, IN
Dickinson College, PA
Dillard University, LA
Doane College, NE
Dominican University of California, CA
Dordt College, IA
Drake University, IA
Drexel University, PA
Drury University, MO
Duke University, NC
Duquesne University, PA
East Carolina University, NC
East Central University, OK
Eastern Connecticut State University, CT
Eastern Illinois University, IL
Eastern Kentucky University, KY
Eastern Mennonite University, VA
Eastern Michigan University, MI
Eastern Nazarene College, MA
Eastern New Mexico University, NM
Eastern Oregon University, OR
Eastern Washington University, WA
East Stroudsburg University of Pennsylvania, PA
East Tennessee State University, TN
East Texas Baptist University, TX
Eckerd College, FL
Edgewood College, WI
Edinboro University of Pennsylvania, PA
Elizabethtown College, PA
Elmhurst College, IL
Elon College, NC
Emmanuel College, GA
Emmaus Bible College, IA
Emory University, GA
Emporia State University, KS
Erskine College, SC
Eugene Bible College, OR
Evangel University, MO
Fairfield University, CT
Fairmont State College, WV
Faith Baptist Bible Coll and Theological Seminary, IA
Faulkner University, AL
Fayetteville State University, NC
Ferris State University, MI
Ferrum College, VA
Five Towns College, NY
Florida Agricultural and Mechanical University, FL
Florida Baptist Theological College, FL
Florida College, FL
Florida International University, FL
Florida Southern College, FL
Florida State University, FL
Fordham University, NY
Fort Hays State University, KS
Fort Lewis College, CO
Fort Valley State University, GA
Francis Marion University, SC
Franklin College of Indiana, IN
Free Will Baptist Bible College, TN
Fresno Pacific University, CA
Friends University, KS
Frostburg State University, MD
Furman University, SC
Gannon University, PA
Gardner-Webb University, NC
Geneva College, PA
George Fox University, OR
Georgetown College, KY
The George Washington University, DC
Georgia College and State University, GA
Georgia Southern University, GA
Georgia Southwestern State University, GA
Georgia State University, GA
Glenville State College, WV
Gonzaga University, WA
Gordon College, MA
Goshen College, IN
Goucher College, MD
Grace Bible College, MI
Grace College, IN
Graceland College, IA
Grace University, NE
Grambling State University, LA
Grand Canyon University, AZ
Grand Valley State University, MI
Grand View College, IA
Green Mountain College, VT
Greensboro College, NC
Greenville College, IL
Grove City College, PA
Guilford College, NC
Gustavus Adolphus College, MN
Hampton University, VA
Hannibal-LaGrange College, MO
Hanover College, IN
Harding University, AR
Hardin-Simmons University, TX
Harris-Stowe State College, MO
Hastings College, NE
Hawaii Pacific University, HI
Heidelberg College, OH
Henderson State University, AR
Hendrix College, AR
High Point University, NC
Hillsdale College, MI
Hillsdale Free Will Baptist College, OK
Hiram College, OH
Hobart and William Smith Colleges, NY
Hofstra University, NY
Hollins University, VA
Holy Names College, CA
Hope College, MI
Hope International University, CA
Houghton College, NY
Houston Baptist University, TX
Howard Payne University, TX
Huntingdon College, AL
Huntington College, IN
Huron University, SD
Huston-Tillotson College, TX
Idaho State University, ID
Illinois College, IL
Illinois State University, IL
Illinois Wesleyan University, IL
Immaculata College, PA
Indiana University of Pennsylvania, PA
Indiana U–Purdue U Fort Wayne, IN
Indiana Wesleyan University, IN
Iona College, NY
Iowa State University of Science and Technology, IA
Iowa Wesleyan College, IA
Ithaca College, NY
Jacksonville State University, AL
Jacksonville University, FL
James Madison University, VA
John Brown University, AR
Johnson C. Smith University, NC
Johnson State College, VT
Judson College, AL
Judson College, IL
The Juilliard School, NY
Juniata College, PA
Kalamazoo College, MI
Kansas State University, KS
Kansas Wesleyan University, KS
Keene State College, NH
Kennesaw State University, GA
Kent State University, OH
Kentucky Christian College, KY
Kentucky Mountain Bible College, KY
Kentucky Wesleyan College, KY
King College, TN
Knox College, IL
Kutztown University of Pennsylvania, PA

LaGrange College, GA
Lake Forest College, IL
Lakeland College, WI
Lambuth University, TN
Lancaster Bible College, PA
Lander University, SC
Langston University, OK
Lawrence University, WI
Lebanon Valley College, PA
Lee University, TN
Lehigh University, PA
LeMoyne-Owen College, TN
LeTourneau University, TX
Lewis & Clark College, OR
Lewis-Clark State College, ID
Liberty University, VA
Limestone College, SC
Lincoln Memorial University, TN
Lincoln University, MO
Lincoln University, PA
Linfield College, OR
Lock Haven University of Pennsylvania, PA
Long Island U, Brooklyn Campus, NY
Long Island U, C.W. Post Campus, NY
Longwood College, VA
Loras College, IA
Louisiana College, LA
Louisiana State University and A&M College, LA
Louisiana Tech University, LA
Lourdes College, OH
Loyola Marymount University, CA
Loyola University Chicago, IL
Loyola University New Orleans, LA
Lubbock Christian University, TX
Luther College, IA
Lycoming College, PA
Lynn University, FL
MacMurray College, IL
Magnolia Bible College, MS
Maharishi University of Management, IA
Malone College, OH
Manchester College, IN
Manhattan Christian College, KS
Manhattan College, NY
Manhattan School of Music, NY
Mansfield University of Pennsylvania, PA
Marian College, IN
Marian College of Fond du Lac, WI
Marist College, NY
Mars Hill College, NC
Martin Luther College, MN
Martin Methodist College, TN
Martin University, IN
Maryville College, TN
Mary Washington College, VA
Marywood University, PA
Massachusetts College of Liberal Arts, MA
The Master's College and Seminary, CA
McKendree College, IL
McMurry University, TX
McNeese State University, LA
Mercer University, GA
Mercyhurst College, PA
Meredith College, NC
Mesa State College, CO
Messiah College, PA
Methodist College, NC
Metropolitan State College of Denver, CO
Miami University, OH
Michigan State University, MI
Mid-America Bible College, OK
MidAmerica Nazarene University, KS
Middle Tennessee State University, TN
Midland Lutheran College, NE
Midway College, KY
Midwestern State University, TX
Milligan College, TN
Millikin University, IL
Millsaps College, MS
Mills College, CA
Minnesota Bible College, MN
Minnesota State University, Mankato, MN
Minnesota State University Moorhead, MN
Minot State University, ND
Mississippi College, MS
Mississippi State University, MS
Mississippi University for Women, MS
Mississippi Valley State University, MS
Missouri Baptist College, MO
Missouri Southern State College, MO
Missouri Western State College, MO
Monmouth College, IL
Montana State U–Billings, MT
Montana State U–Bozeman, MT
Montreat College, NC
Moravian College, PA
Morehead State University, KY
Morningside College, IA
Mount Aloysius College, PA
Mount Marty College, SD
Mount Mary College, WI
Mount Mercy College, IA
Mount Olive College, NC
Mount St. Clare College, IA
Mount Union College, OH
Mount Vernon Nazarene College, OH
Muhlenberg College, PA
Murray State University, KY
Muskingum College, OH
Nazareth College of Rochester, NY
Nebraska Christian College, NE
Nebraska Wesleyan University, NE
Newberry College, SC
New England Conservatory of Music, MA
Newman University, KS
New Mexico Highlands University, NM
Norfolk State University, VA
North Carolina Agricultural and Technical State U, NC
North Carolina School of the Arts, NC
North Central College, IL
North Dakota State University, ND
Northeastern Illinois University, IL
Northeastern State University, OK
Northern Arizona University, AZ
Northern Illinois University, IL
Northern Michigan University, MI
North Georgia College & State University, GA
North Greenville College, SC
Northland College, WI
Northwest Christian College, OR
Northwest College, WA
Northwestern College, IA
Northwestern College, MN
Northwestern Oklahoma State University, OK
Northwestern State University of Louisiana, LA
Northwest Missouri State University, MO
Northwest Nazarene University, ID
Nyack College, NY
Oakland City University, IN
Oakland University, MI
Oberlin College, OH
Occidental College, CA
Oglethorpe University, GA
Ohio Northern University, OH
The Ohio State University, OH
Ohio University, OH
Ohio University–Eastern, OH
Ohio University–Lancaster, OH
Ohio Valley College, WV
Ohio Wesleyan University, OH
Oklahoma Baptist University, OK
Oklahoma Christian U of Science and Arts, OK
Oklahoma City University, OK
Oklahoma Panhandle State University, OK
Oklahoma State U, OK
Old Dominion University, VA
Olivet College, MI
Olivet Nazarene University, IL
Oral Roberts University, OK
Oregon State University, OR
Ottawa University, KS
Otterbein College, OH
Ouachita Baptist University, AR
Our Lady of the Lake University of San Antonio, TX
Ozark Christian College, MO
Pacific University, OR
Paine College, GA
Palm Beach Atlantic College, FL
Paul Quinn College, TX
Peabody Conserv of Music of Johns Hopkins U, MD
Peace College, NC
Pepperdine University, CA
Pfeiffer University, NC
Philadelphia College of Bible, PA
Philander Smith College, AR
Piedmont College, GA
Pikeville College, KY
Pittsburg State University, KS
Plattsburgh State U of NY, NY
Plymouth State College, NH
Point Loma Nazarene University, CA
Pontifical Catholic University of Puerto Rico, PR
Portland State University, OR
Practical Bible College, NY
Prairie View A&M University, TX
Presbyterian College, SC
Purchase College, State U of NY, NY
Queens College, NC
Quincy University, IL
Radford University, VA
Randolph-Macon Woman's College, VA
Reinhardt College, GA
Rhode Island College, RI
Rhodes College, TN
Rice University, TX
The Richard Stockton College of New Jersey, NJ
Ripon College, WI
Roanoke College, VA
Roberts Wesleyan College, NY
Rochester College, MI
Rockford College, IL

Music (continued)

Rockhurst University, MO
Rocky Mountain College, MT
Rollins College, FL
Rowan University, NJ
Rust College, MS
Rutgers, State U of NJ, Mason Gross School of Arts, NJ
Sacred Heart University, CT
Saginaw Valley State University, MI
St. Ambrose University, IA
Saint Augustine's College, NC
St. Bonaventure University, NY
Saint Francis College, PA
St. Gregory's University, OK
Saint John's University, MN
St. John's University, NY
Saint Joseph's College, IN
St. Louis Christian College, MO
Saint Louis University, MO
Saint Martin's College, WA
Saint Mary College, KS
Saint Mary-of-the-Woods College, IN
Saint Mary's College, IN
St. Mary's University of San Antonio, TX
St. Norbert College, WI
St. Olaf College, MN
Saint Vincent College, PA
Saint Xavier University, IL
Salem College, NC
Salem State College, MA
Samford University, AL
Sam Houston State University, TX
Santa Clara University, CA
Savannah State University, GA
Schreiner College, TX
Seattle University, WA
Seton Hall University, NJ
Seton Hill College, PA
Shaw University, NC
Sheldon Jackson College, AK
Shenandoah University, VA
Shepherd College, WV
Shorter College, GA
Siena College, NY
Siena Heights University, MI
Sierra Nevada College, NV
Silver Lake College, WI
Simpson College, IA
Simpson College and Graduate School, CA
Skidmore College, NY
Slippery Rock University of Pennsylvania, PA
Sonoma State University, CA
South Dakota State University, SD
Southeastern Bible College, AL
Southeastern College of the Assemblies of God, FL
Southeastern Louisiana University, LA
Southeast Missouri State University, MO
Southern Adventist University, TN
Southern Arkansas University–Magnolia, AR
Southern Illinois University Carbondale, IL
Southern Illinois University Edwardsville, IL
Southern Methodist University, TX
Southern Nazarene University, OK
Southern Oregon University, OR
Southern University at New Orleans, LA
Southern Utah University, UT
Southern Wesleyan University, SC
Southwest Baptist University, MO
Southwestern Adventist University, TX
Southwestern Assemblies of God University, TX
Southwestern Christian College, TX
Southwestern College, AZ
Southwestern College, KS
Southwestern College of Christian Ministries, OK
Southwestern Oklahoma State University, OK
Southwestern University, TX
Southwest Missouri State University, MO
Southwest State University, MN
Southwest Texas State University, TX
Spring Arbor College, MI
State U of NY at Binghamton, NY
State U of NY at Buffalo, NY
State U of NY at Oswego, NY
State U of NY at Stony Brook, NY
State U of NY College at Fredonia, NY
State U of NY College at Geneseo, NY
State U of NY College at Oneonta, NY
State U of NY College at Potsdam, NY
State University of West Georgia, GA
Stephen F. Austin State University, TX
Sterling College, KS
Stetson University, FL
Stillman College, AL
Sul Ross State University, TX
Susquehanna University, PA
Sweet Briar College, VA
Syracuse University, NY
Tabor College, KS
Tarleton State University, TX
Taylor University, IN
Temple University, PA
Tennessee State University, TN
Tennessee Technological University, TN
Tennessee Temple University, TN
Tennessee Wesleyan College, TN
Texas A&M International University, TX
Texas A&M University–Commerce, TX
Texas A&M University–Kingsville, TX
Texas Christian University, TX
Texas Lutheran University, TX
Texas Tech University, TX
Texas Woman's University, TX
Thiel College, PA
Thomas University, GA
Tiffin University, OH
Toccoa Falls College, GA
Tougaloo College, MS
Towson University, MD
Transylvania University, KY
Trevecca Nazarene University, TN
Trinity Bible College, ND
Trinity Christian College, IL
Trinity Lutheran College, WA
Trinity University, TX
Troy State University, AL
Truman State University, MO
Tuskegee University, AL
Union College, KY
Union College, NE
Union University, TN
The University of Akron, OH
The University of Alabama, AL
The University of Alabama at Birmingham, AL
The University of Alabama in Huntsville, AL
U of Alaska Anchorage, AK
U of Alaska Fairbanks, AK
The University of Arizona, AZ
University of Arkansas, AR
University of Arkansas at Little Rock, AR
University of Arkansas at Monticello, AR
University of Arkansas at Pine Bluff, AR
U of Calif, Riverside, CA
U of Calif, San Diego, CA
University of Central Arkansas, AR
University of Central Florida, FL
University of Central Oklahoma, OK
University of Charleston, WV
University of Cincinnati, OH
University of Colorado at Boulder, CO
University of Connecticut, CT
University of Dayton, OH
University of Delaware, DE
University of Dubuque, IA
University of Evansville, IN
The University of Findlay, OH
University of Florida, FL
University of Guam, GU
University of Hartford, CT
University of Hawaii at Hilo, HI
University of Hawaii at Manoa, HI
University of Houston, TX
University of Idaho, ID
University of Illinois at Chicago, IL
University of Indianapolis, IN
The University of Iowa, IA
University of Kansas, KS
University of La Verne, CA
University of Louisiana at Monroe, LA
The University of Maine at Augusta, ME
University of Mary, ND
University of Mary Hardin-Baylor, TX
University of Maryland, Baltimore County, MD
University of Maryland, College Park, MD
University of Massachusetts Amherst, MA
University of Massachusetts Lowell, MA
The University of Memphis, TN
University of Miami, FL
University of Michigan, MI
University of Michigan–Flint, MI
University of Minnesota, Duluth, MN
University of Minnesota, Morris, MN
University of Mississippi, MS
University of Missouri–Columbia, MO
University of Missouri–Kansas City, MO
University of Missouri–Rolla, MO
University of Missouri–St. Louis, MO
University of Mobile, AL
The University of Montana–Missoula, MT
University of Montevallo, AL
University of Nebraska at Kearney, NE
University of Nebraska at Omaha, NE
University of Nebraska–Lincoln, NE
University of Nevada, Las Vegas, NV
University of Nevada, Reno, NV
University of New Hampshire, NH
University of New Mexico, NM
University of New Orleans, LA
University of North Alabama, AL
The University of North Carolina at Asheville, NC
The University of North Carolina at Chapel Hill, NC

The University of North Carolina at Charlotte, NC
The University of North Carolina at Greensboro, NC
The University of North Carolina at Pembroke, NC
The University of North Carolina at Wilmington, NC
University of North Dakota, ND
University of Northern Colorado, CO
University of Northern Iowa, IA
University of North Florida, FL
University of North Texas, TX
University of Oklahoma, OK
University of Portland, OR
U of Puerto Rico, Cayey University College, PR
U of Puerto Rico, Humacao University College, PR
University of Puget Sound, WA
University of Redlands, CA
University of Rhode Island, RI
University of Richmond, VA
University of Rio Grande, OH
University of St. Francis, IL
University of St. Thomas, MN
University of St. Thomas, TX
University of San Diego, CA
University of Science and Arts of Oklahoma, OK
University of South Alabama, AL
University of South Carolina, SC
University of South Carolina Aiken, SC
University of South Dakota, SD
University of Southern Colorado, CO
University of Southern Indiana, IN
University of Southern Maine, ME
University of Southern Mississippi, MS
University of South Florida, FL
The University of Tampa, FL
The University of Tennessee at Chattanooga, TN
The University of Tennessee at Martin, TN
The University of Tennessee Knoxville, TN
The University of Texas at Arlington, TX
The University of Texas at Brownsville, TX
The University of Texas at El Paso, TX
The University of Texas at San Antonio, TX
The University of Texas–Pan American, TX
The University of the Arts, PA
University of the District of Columbia, DC
University of the Incarnate Word, TX
University of the Pacific, CA
University of the Sacred Heart, PR
University of the Virgin Islands, VI
University of Toledo, OH
University of Tulsa, OK
University of Utah, UT
University of Virginia's College at Wise, VA
University of Washington, WA
The University of West Alabama, AL
University of West Florida, FL
University of Wisconsin–Eau Claire, WI
University of Wisconsin–Green Bay, WI
University of Wisconsin–La Crosse, WI
University of Wisconsin–Oshkosh, WI
University of Wisconsin–Parkside, WI
University of Wisconsin–Platteville, WI
University of Wisconsin–River Falls, WI
University of Wisconsin–Stevens Point, WI
University of Wisconsin–Stout, WI
University of Wisconsin–Superior, WI
University of Wisconsin–Whitewater, WI
University of Wyoming, WY
Upper Iowa University, IA
Urbana University, OH
Ursinus College, PA
Utah State University, UT
Valdosta State University, GA
Valley City State University, ND
Valley Forge Christian College, PA
Valparaiso University, IN
Vanderbilt University, TN
Vanguard University of Southern California, CA
Virginia Commonwealth University, VA
Virginia Military Institute, VA
Virginia Polytechnic Institute and State U, VA
Virginia State University, VA
Virginia Union University, VA
Virginia Wesleyan College, VA
Viterbo University, WI
Wabash College, IN
Wagner College, NY
Wake Forest University, NC
Walla Walla College, WA
Walsh University, OH
Warner Pacific College, OR
Wartburg College, IA
Washburn University of Topeka, KS
Washington State University, WA
Washington University in St. Louis, MO
Wayland Baptist University, TX
Wayne State College, NE
Wayne State University, MI
Webster University, MO
Wesleyan College, GA
West Chester University of Pennsylvania, PA
Western Baptist College, OR
Western Carolina University, NC
Western Illinois University, IL
Western Kentucky University, KY
Western Michigan University, MI
Western Oregon University, OR
Western State College of Colorado, CO
Western Washington University, WA
West Liberty State College, WV
Westminster Choir Coll of Rider U, NJ
Westminster College, PA
Westminster College, UT
Westmont College, CA
West Texas A&M University, TX
West Virginia State College, WV
West Virginia University, WV
West Virginia University Institute of Technology, WV
West Virginia Wesleyan College, WV
Wheaton College, IL
Wheeling Jesuit University, WV
Whitman College, WA
Whittier College, CA
Whitworth College, WA
Wichita State University, KS
Widener University, PA
Wilkes University, PA
Willamette University, OR
William Carey College, MS
William Jewell College, MO
William Paterson University of New Jersey, NJ
William Penn University, IA
Williams Baptist College, AR
William Tyndale College, MI
Wilson College, PA
Wingate University, NC
Winona State University, MN
Winston-Salem State University, NC
Winthrop University, SC
Wisconsin Lutheran College, WI
Wittenberg University, OH
Wofford College, SC
Xavier University, OH
Xavier University of Louisiana, LA
York College, NE
York College of Pennsylvania, PA
Youngstown State University, OH

PERFORMING ARTS

Adams State College, CO
Adelphi University, NY
Alabama State University, AL
Albertus Magnus College, CT
Alfred University, NY
Allentown College of St. Francis de Sales, PA
Alma College, MI
American University, DC
Arizona State University, AZ
Arkansas State University, AR
Augsburg College, MN
Avila College, MO
Bay Path College, MA
Belhaven College, MS
Bethune-Cookman College, FL
Biola University, CA
Birmingham-Southern College, AL
Bluefield College, VA
Boise State University, ID
Bowie State University, MD
Bowling Green State University, OH
Brigham Young University, UT
Bryan College, TN
California Institute of the Arts, CA
California Polytechnic State U, San Luis Obispo, CA
California State University, Chico, CA
California State University, Long Beach, CA
California State University, San Bernardino, CA
Calvin College, MI
Carroll College, WI
Cedar Crest College, PA
Central Missouri State University, MO
Charleston Southern University, SC
Christian Brothers University, TN
Clarion University of Pennsylvania, PA
Coe College, IA
College of Charleston, SC
The College of New Rochelle, NY
Columbia College Chicago, IL
Concordia College, MI
Concordia University Wisconsin, WI
Cumberland University, TN
Davis & Elkins College, WV
Delta State University, MS
DePaul University, IL
Dillard University, LA
Drexel University, PA
East Central University, OK
Eastern Illinois University, IL
Eastern Michigan University, MI

Performing Arts (continued)

Eastern New Mexico University, NM
Edgewood College, WI
Elon College, NC
Emerson College, MA
Emory University, GA
Eureka College, IL
Ferrum College, VA
Fitchburg State College, MA
Florida International University, FL
Fort Hays State University, KS
Fort Lewis College, CO
Franklin College of Indiana, IN
Franklin Pierce College, NH
Friends University, KS
Georgetown College, KY
The George Washington University, DC
Georgia State University, GA
Grand Canyon University, AZ
Greenville College, IL
Hannibal-LaGrange College, MO
Hastings College, NE
Hillsdale Free Will Baptist College, OK
Hobart and William Smith Colleges, NY
Hope College, MI
Idaho State University, ID
Illinois State University, IL
Indiana State University, IN
Indiana University of Pennsylvania, PA
Johnson State College, VT
Judson College, IL
The Juilliard School, NY
Juniata College, PA
Kennesaw State University, GA
Kentucky Christian College, KY
King College, TN
Lake Erie College, OH
Lakeland College, WI
Lees-McRae College, NC
Lee University, TN
Lehigh University, PA
Liberty University, VA
Limestone College, SC
Louisiana College, LA
Louisiana State University and A&M College, LA
Louisiana Tech University, LA
Lubbock Christian University, TX
Lyon College, AR
Manchester College, IN
Marian College, IN
Marywood University, PA
Massachusetts College of Liberal Arts, MA
Michigan State University, MI
Mississippi State University, MS
Mississippi University for Women, MS
Muhlenberg College, PA
Norfolk State University, VA
North Carolina School of the Arts, NC
Northeastern Illinois University, IL
Northeastern State University, OK
Northern Arizona University, AZ
Northern Illinois University, IL
Northwest Nazarene University, ID
Nyack College, NY
Oakland University, MI
Oglethorpe University, GA
Ohio Northern University, OH
The Ohio State University, OH
Ohio University, OH
Ohio University–Eastern, OH
Ohio University–Lancaster, OH
Ohio Valley College, WV
Oklahoma Baptist University, OK
Oklahoma Christian U of Science and Arts, OK
Oklahoma City University, OK
Old Dominion University, VA
Ouachita Baptist University, AR
Paul Quinn College, TX
Pepperdine University, CA
Point Park College, PA
Pontifical Catholic University of Puerto Rico, PR
Prairie View A&M University, TX
Purchase College, State U of NY, NY
Reinhardt College, GA
The Richard Stockton College of New Jersey, NJ
Rockhurst University, MO
Rowan University, NJ
Saint Augustine's College, NC
St. John's University, NY
Saint Louis University, MO
Saint Martin's College, WA
Saint Mary-of-the-Woods College, IN
Salem State College, MA
Sam Houston State University, TX
Seattle Pacific University, WA
Shawnee State University, OH
Shenandoah University, VA
Shepherd College, WV
Sonoma State University, CA
South Dakota State University, SD
Southern Illinois University Carbondale, IL
Southern Nazarene University, OK
Southern Utah University, UT
Southwestern Assemblies of God University, TX
Southwestern University, TX
Southwest Missouri State University, MO
State U of NY College at Fredonia, NY
State U of NY College at Geneseo, NY
State U of NY College at Potsdam, NY
Stephens College, MO
Tabor College, KS
Temple University, PA
Texas A&M International University, TX
Texas A&M University, TX
Texas Christian University, TX
Texas Tech University, TX
Troy State University, AL
The University of Akron, OH
The University of Alabama at Birmingham, AL
The University of Arizona, AZ
U of Calif, San Diego, CA
University of Central Arkansas, AR
University of Colorado at Boulder, CO
University of Dallas, TX
University of Florida, FL
University of Guam, GU
University of Hartford, CT
University of Hawaii at Hilo, HI
University of Hawaii at Manoa, HI
University of Idaho, ID
University of Illinois at Chicago, IL
The University of Iowa, IA
University of Kansas, KS
University of Louisiana at Monroe, LA
University of Maine, ME
University of Maine at Fort Kent, ME
University of Maryland, Baltimore County, MD
University of Missouri–Kansas City, MO
The University of Montana–Missoula, MT
University of Nebraska–Lincoln, NE
University of Nevada, Las Vegas, NV
The University of North Carolina at Charlotte, NC
The University of North Carolina at Greensboro, NC
University of Northern Colorado, CO
University of Oklahoma, OK
University of Oregon, OR
University of Portland, OR
University of San Francisco, CA
University of South Carolina, SC
University of Southern Colorado, CO
University of South Florida, FL
The University of Tampa, FL
The University of Texas at El Paso, TX
The University of the Arts, PA
University of Tulsa, OK
University of Virginia's College at Wise, VA
University of Washington, WA
University of Wisconsin–Stevens Point, WI
University of Wisconsin–Superior, WI
Urbana University, OH
Utah State University, UT
Valparaiso University, IN
Virginia Commonwealth University, VA
Virginia Intermont College, VA
Virginia Polytechnic Institute and State U, VA
Virginia State University, VA
Viterbo University, WI
Wake Forest University, NC
Washington State University, WA
Weber State University, UT
Webster University, MO
Western Baptist College, OR
Western Illinois University, IL
Western Michigan University, MI
Western New Mexico University, NM
Western Washington University, WA
Wichita State University, KS
Wilkes University, PA
William Woods University, MO
Winthrop University, SC
Xavier University, OH
Xavier University of Louisiana, LA
York College, NE

THEATER/DRAMA

Abilene Christian University, TX
Adams State College, CO
Adelphi University, NY
Adrian College, MI
Alabama Agricultural and Mechanical University, AL
Alabama State University, AL
Albertson College of Idaho, ID
Albertus Magnus College, CT
Albion College, MI
Albright College, PA
Allentown College of St. Francis de Sales, PA
Alma College, MI
American University, DC
Anderson College, SC

Angelo State University, TX
Arizona State University, AZ
Arkansas State University, AR
Ashland University, OH
Augsburg College, MN
Augustana College, IL
Augustana College, SD
Augusta State University, GA
Austin College, TX
Austin Peay State University, TN
Avila College, MO
Azusa Pacific University, CA
Baker University, KS
Ball State University, IN
Barat College, IL
Barry University, FL
Barton College, NC
Baylor University, TX
Bay Path College, MA
Belhaven College, MS
Bemidji State University, MN
Benedictine College, KS
Berry College, GA
Bethany College, KS
Bethany College of the Assemblies of God, CA
Bethel College, IN
Bethel College, KS
Bethel College, MN
Biola University, CA
Birmingham-Southern College, AL
Black Hills State University, SD
Boise State University, ID
Boston Conservatory, MA
Boston University, MA
Bowie State University, MD
Bowling Green State University, OH
Bradley University, IL
Brenau University, GA
Brevard College, NC
Briar Cliff College, IA
Brigham Young University, UT
Brigham Young University–Hawaii Campus, HI
Buena Vista University, IA
Butler University, IN
California Baptist University, CA
California Institute of the Arts, CA
California Lutheran University, CA
California Polytechnic State U, San Luis Obispo, CA
California State University, Bakersfield, CA
California State University, Chico, CA
California State University, Fresno, CA
California State University, Long Beach, CA
California State University, Los Angeles, CA
Calvin College, MI
Cameron University, OK
Campbellsville University, KY
Campbell University, NC
Carroll College, MT
Carroll College, WI
Carthage College, WI
Cascade College, OR
Case Western Reserve University, OH
Cedar Crest College, PA
Centenary College of Louisiana, LA
Central Bible College, MO
Central College, IA
Central Methodist College, MO
Central Michigan University, MI
Central Missouri State University, MO
Central Washington University, WA
Chapman University, CA
Chatham College, PA
Clarion University of Pennsylvania, PA
Clarke College, IA
Clear Creek Baptist Bible College, KY
Coastal Carolina University, SC
Coe College, IA
Coker College, SC
College of Charleston, SC
The College of New Rochelle, NY
College of Saint Benedict, MN
College of the Southwest, NM
The College of Wooster, OH
Colorado Christian University, CO
Colorado State University, CO
Columbia College Chicago, IL
Concord College, WV
Concordia College, MI
Concordia College, MN
Concordia University, CA
Concordia University, NE
Concordia University, OR
Converse College, SC
Cornell College, IA
Cornish College of the Arts, WA
Crichton College, TN
Culver-Stockton College, MO
Cumberland University, TN
Dakota Wesleyan University, SD
Dana College, NE
David Lipscomb University, TN
Davis & Elkins College, WV
Defiance College, OH
Denison University, OH
DePaul University, IL
DePauw University, IN
Dillard University, LA
Doane College, NE
Dordt College, IA
Drake University, IA
Drexel University, PA
Drury University, MO
Duke University, NC
Eastern Connecticut State University, CT
Eastern Illinois University, IL
Eastern Michigan University, MI
Eastern Nazarene College, MA
Eastern New Mexico University, NM
Eastern Oregon University, OR
Eastern Washington University, WA
East Stroudsburg University of Pennsylvania, PA
East Tennessee State University, TN
East Texas Baptist University, TX
Eckerd College, FL
Edgewood College, WI
Elmhurst College, IL
Elon College, NC
Emmanuel College, GA
Emporia State University, KS
Erskine College, SC
Fairfield University, CT
Fairmont State College, WV
Faulkner University, AL
Ferris State University, MI
Ferrum College, VA
Five Towns College, NY
Florida Agricultural and Mechanical University, FL
Florida College, FL
Florida International University, FL
Florida Southern College, FL
Fontbonne College, MO
Fort Hays State University, KS
Fort Lewis College, CO
Francis Marion University, SC
Franklin College of Indiana, IN
Fresno Pacific University, CA
Friends University, KS
Frostburg State University, MD
Furman University, SC
Gannon University, PA
Gardner-Webb University, NC
George Fox University, OR
Georgetown College, KY
The George Washington University, DC
Georgia College and State University, GA
Georgia State University, GA
Goucher College, MD
Grace College, IN
Graceland College, IA
Grambling State University, LA
Grand Canyon University, AZ
Grand Valley State University, MI
Grand View College, IA
Green Mountain College, VT
Greensboro College, NC
Gustavus Adolphus College, MN
Hannibal-LaGrange College, MO
Hardin-Simmons University, TX
Harris-Stowe State College, MO
Hastings College, NE
Henderson State University, AR
Hendrix College, AR
Hofstra University, NY
Hope College, MI
Howard Payne University, TX
Huntingdon College, AL
Huntington College, IN
Idaho State University, ID
Illinois State University, IL
Illinois Wesleyan University, IL
Indiana University of Pennsylvania, PA
Indiana U–Purdue U Fort Wayne, IN
Ithaca College, NY
Jacksonville State University, AL
Jacksonville University, FL
James Madison University, VA
Johnson State College, VT
Judson College, IL
The Juilliard School, NY
Kalamazoo College, MI
Kansas State University, KS
Kansas Wesleyan University, KS
Keene State College, NH
Kent State University, OH
Kentucky Christian College, KY
Kentucky Wesleyan College, KY
King College, TN
Knox College, IL
LaGrange College, GA
Lake Forest College, IL
Lambuth University, TN
Lander University, SC
Lees-McRae College, NC
Lee University, TN
Lehigh University, PA

Theater/Drama (continued)

Lewis University, IL
Limestone College, SC
Lincoln University, MO
Long Island U, C.W. Post Campus, NY
Longwood College, VA
Louisiana College, LA
Louisiana State University and A&M College, LA
Louisiana Tech University, LA
Loyola University Chicago, IL
Loyola University New Orleans, LA
Lubbock Christian University, TX
Lycoming College, PA
Lyon College, AR
Malone College, OH
Manchester College, IN
Marian College, IN
Marquette University, WI
Mars Hill College, NC
Martin Methodist College, TN
Marymount Manhattan College, NY
Maryville College, TN
Mary Washington College, VA
Marywood University, PA
Massachusetts College of Liberal Arts, MA
McMurry University, TX
McNeese State University, LA
Mercer University, GA
Merrimack College, MA
Mesa State College, CO
Methodist College, NC
Miami University, OH
Michigan State University, MI
Midland Lutheran College, NE
Midwestern State University, TX
Milligan College, TN
Millikin University, IL
Millsaps College, MS
Minnesota State University, Mankato, MN
Minnesota State University Moorhead, MN
Minot State University, ND
Mississippi State University, MS
Mississippi University for Women, MS
Missouri Southern State College, MO
Monmouth College, IL
Montana State U–Billings, MT
Montana State U–Bozeman, MT
Montreat College, NC
Morehead State University, KY
Morningside College, IA
Mount Marty College, SD
Mount Mercy College, IA
Mount Union College, OH
Muhlenberg College, PA
Murray State University, KY
Muskingum College, OH
National-Louis University, IL
Nazareth College of Rochester, NY
Nebraska Wesleyan University, NE
Newberry College, SC
New England Conservatory of Music, MA
Newman University, KS
New Mexico Highlands University, NM
Niagara University, NY
North Carolina Agricultural and Technical State U, NC
North Carolina Central University, NC
North Carolina School of the Arts, NC
North Central College, IL
North Dakota State University, ND
Northeastern Illinois University, IL
Northeastern State University, OK
Northern Arizona University, AZ
Northern Illinois University, IL
Northern Michigan University, MI
North Greenville College, SC
Northwest College, WA
Northwestern College, IA
Northwestern Oklahoma State University, OK
Northwestern State University of Louisiana, LA
Northwest Missouri State University, MO
Northwest Nazarene University, ID
Nyack College, NY
Oakland City University, IN
Oglethorpe University, GA
Ohio Northern University, OH
The Ohio State University, OH
Ohio University, OH
Ohio University–Eastern, OH
Ohio University–Lancaster, OH
Ohio Wesleyan University, OH
Oklahoma Christian U of Science and Arts, OK
Oklahoma Panhandle State University, OK
Old Dominion University, VA
Ottawa University, KS
Otterbein College, OH
Ouachita Baptist University, AR
Ozark Christian College, MO
Pacific University, OR
Palm Beach Atlantic College, FL
Park University, MO
Peace College, NC
Pepperdine University, CA
Piedmont College, GA
Plymouth State College, NH
Point Loma Nazarene University, CA
Point Park College, PA
Pontifical Catholic University of Puerto Rico, PR
Portland State University, OR
Providence College, RI
Purchase College, State U of NY, NY
Queens College, NC
Radford University, VA
Randolph-Macon Woman's College, VA
Rhode Island College, RI
Rhodes College, TN
The Richard Stockton College of New Jersey, NJ
Rider University, NJ
Ripon College, WI
Rochester College, MI
Rockford College, IL
Rockhurst University, MO
Rocky Mountain College, MT
Rollins College, FL
Rust College, MS
St. Ambrose University, IA
St. Edward's University, TX
Saint Francis College, PA
St. Gregory's University, OK
Saint John's University, MN
St. John's University, NY
Saint Joseph's College, IN
Saint Joseph's University, PA
Saint Louis University, MO
Saint Martin's College, WA
Saint Mary College, KS
Saint Mary-of-the-Woods College, IN
St. Norbert College, WI
Salem State College, MA
Sam Houston State University, TX
Santa Clara University, CA
Schreiner College, TX
Seton Hill College, PA
Sheldon Jackson College, AK
Shenandoah University, VA
Shimer College, IL
Shorter College, GA
Siena Heights University, MI
Simpson College, IA
Sonoma State University, CA
South Dakota State University, SD
Southeastern College of the Assemblies of God, FL
Southeast Missouri State University, MO
Southern Adventist University, TN
Southern Arkansas University–Magnolia, AR
Southern Illinois University Carbondale, IL
Southern Illinois University Edwardsville, IL
Southern Methodist University, TX
Southern Oregon University, OR
Southern Utah University, UT
Southern Wesleyan University, SC
Southwest Baptist University, MO
Southwestern Adventist University, TX
Southwestern Assemblies of God University, TX
Southwestern College, KS
Southwestern Oklahoma State University, OK
Southwestern University, TX
Southwest Missouri State University, MO
Southwest State University, MN
Southwest Texas State University, TX
State U of NY at Binghamton, NY
State U of NY at Oswego, NY
State U of NY College at Fredonia, NY
State U of NY College at Geneseo, NY
State U of NY College at Potsdam, NY
State University of West Georgia, GA
Stephen F. Austin State University, TX
Stephens College, MO
Sterling College, KS
Stetson University, FL
Sul Ross State University, TX
Tabor College, KS
Tarleton State University, TX
Taylor University, IN
Texas A&M University, TX
Texas A&M University–Commerce, TX
Texas Christian University, TX
Texas Lutheran University, TX
Texas Tech University, TX
Texas Woman's University, TX
Thomas More College, KY
Towson University, MD
Trinity Bible College, ND
Trinity Christian College, IL
Troy State University, AL
Truman State University, MO
Union University, TN
The University of Akron, OH
The University of Alabama, AL
The University of Alabama at Birmingham, AL
U of Alaska Fairbanks, AK

The University of Arizona, AZ
University of Arkansas at Little Rock, AR
U of Calif, Riverside, CA
University of Central Arkansas, AR
University of Central Florida, FL
University of Central Oklahoma, OK
University of Colorado at Boulder, CO
University of Connecticut, CT
University of Detroit Mercy, MI
University of Evansville, IN
The University of Findlay, OH
University of Florida, FL
University of Hartford, CT
University of Hawaii at Hilo, HI
University of Hawaii at Manoa, HI
University of Houston, TX
University of Houston–Downtown, TX
University of Idaho, ID
University of Illinois at Chicago, IL
University of Indianapolis, IN
The University of Iowa, IA
University of Kansas, KS
University of La Verne, CA
University of Louisiana at Monroe, LA
University of Mary, ND
University of Maryland, Baltimore County, MD
University of Maryland, College Park, MD
University of Massachusetts Amherst, MA
University of Miami, FL
University of Michigan, MI
University of Michigan–Flint, MI
University of Minnesota, Duluth, MN
University of Mississippi, MS
University of Missouri–Columbia, MO
University of Missouri–Rolla, MO
The University of Montana–Missoula, MT
University of Nebraska at Kearney, NE
University of Nebraska at Omaha, NE
University of Nebraska–Lincoln, NE
University of Nevada, Las Vegas, NV
University of Nevada, Reno, NV
University of New Hampshire, NH
University of New Mexico, NM
The University of North Carolina at Asheville, NC
The University of North Carolina at Chapel Hill, NC
The University of North Carolina at Greensboro, NC
University of North Dakota, ND
University of Northern Colorado, CO
University of Northern Iowa, IA
University of North Texas, TX
University of Oklahoma, OK
University of Portland, OR
U of Puerto Rico, Cayey University College, PR
U of Puerto Rico, Humacao University College, PR
University of Puget Sound, WA
University of St. Thomas, TX
University of Science and Arts of Oklahoma, OK
University of South Alabama, AL
University of South Carolina, SC
University of South Dakota, SD
University of Southern Colorado, CO
University of Southern Indiana, IN
University of Southern Maine, ME
University of Southern Mississippi, MS
University of South Florida, FL
The University of Tennessee at Chattanooga, TN
The University of Tennessee at Martin, TN
The University of Tennessee Knoxville, TN
The University of Texas at Arlington, TX
The University of Texas at El Paso, TX
The University of Texas–Pan American, TX
The University of the Arts, PA
University of the Incarnate Word, TX
University of the Sacred Heart, PR
University of Toledo, OH
University of Tulsa, OK
University of Utah, UT
University of Virginia's College at Wise, VA
University of Washington, WA
University of West Florida, FL
University of Wisconsin–Eau Claire, WI
University of Wisconsin–Green Bay, WI
University of Wisconsin–La Crosse, WI
University of Wisconsin–Oshkosh, WI
University of Wisconsin–Platteville, WI
University of Wisconsin–River Falls, WI
University of Wisconsin–Stevens Point, WI
University of Wisconsin–Superior, WI
University of Wisconsin–Whitewater, WI
University of Wyoming, WY
Upper Iowa University, IA
Urbana University, OH
Utah State University, UT
Valdosta State University, GA
Valley City State University, ND
Valparaiso University, IN
Vanguard University of Southern California, CA
Virginia Commonwealth University, VA
Virginia Intermont College, VA
Virginia Polytechnic Institute and State U, VA
Virginia Wesleyan College, VA
Viterbo University, WI
Wabash College, IN
Wagner College, NY
Wake Forest University, NC
Washington State University, WA
Wayland Baptist University, TX
Wayne State College, NE
Weber State University, UT
Webster University, MO
Wesleyan College, GA
Western Illinois University, IL
Western Michigan University, MI
Western Oregon University, OR
Western Washington University, WA
West Liberty State College, WV
Westminster College, PA
Westminster College, UT
Westmont College, CA
West Texas A&M University, TX
West Virginia University, WV
West Virginia Wesleyan College, WV
Whitman College, WA
Whittier College, CA
Whitworth College, WA
Wichita State University, KS
Willamette University, OR
William Carey College, MS
William Jewell College, MO
William Penn University, IA
William Woods University, MO
Wilmington College, OH
Winona State University, MN
Wisconsin Lutheran College, WI
Wittenberg University, OH
Xavier University, OH
York College, NE

SPECIAL ACHIEVEMENTS/ ACTIVITIES

CHEERLEADING/DRUM MAJOR

Abilene Christian University, TX
Alabama State University, AL
Anderson College, SC
Angelo State University, TX
Arizona State University, AZ
Arkansas State University, AR
Arkansas Tech University, AR
Athens State University, AL
Auburn University, AL
Austin Peay State University, TN
Azusa Pacific University, CA
Baker University, KS
Barber-Scotia College, NC
Belhaven College, MS
Bellarmine College, KY
Bethany College, KS
Bethany College of the Assemblies of God, CA
Bethel College, IN
Bluefield State College, WV
Boise State University, ID
Brigham Young University, UT
Brigham Young University–Hawaii Campus, HI
Bryan College, TN
Campbell University, NC
Carroll College, MT
Central Methodist College, MO
Central Missouri State University, MO
Claflin University, SC
Concordia College, AL
Cumberland College, KY
David Lipscomb University, TN
Delta State University, MS
Drexel University, PA
Drury University, MO
East Central University, OK
East Texas Baptist University, TX
Emporia State University, KS
Faulkner University, AL
Fort Hays State University, KS
Francis Marion University, SC
Gardner-Webb University, NC
Georgia College and State University, GA
Grambling State University, LA
Harding University, AR
Hastings College, NE
Hawaii Pacific University, HI
Huron University, SD
Iowa Wesleyan College, IA
Jacksonville State University, AL
James Madison University, VA
John Brown University, AR
Judson College, IL
Kansas Wesleyan University, KS
King College, TN
Lambuth University, TN
Lees-McRae College, NC

Cheerleading/Drum Major (continued)

Liberty University, VA
Limestone College, SC
Lincoln Memorial University, TN
Long Island U, Brooklyn Campus, NY
Louisiana Tech University, LA
Lubbock Christian University, TX
Mars Hill College, NC
Martin Methodist College, TN
McKendree College, IL
McNeese State University, LA
MidAmerica Nazarene University, KS
Middle Tennessee State University, TN
Midwestern State University, TX
Mississippi State University, MS
Missouri Baptist College, MO
Missouri Western State College, MO
Morehead State University, KY
Mount Senario College, WI
Northeastern State University, OK
North Georgia College & State University, GA
North Greenville College, SC
Northwestern Oklahoma State University, OK
Northwestern State University of Louisiana, LA
Northwest Missouri State University, MO
Northwest Nazarene University, ID
The Ohio State University, OH
Oklahoma City University, OK
Oklahoma Panhandle State University, OK
Oklahoma State U, OK
Old Dominion University, VA
Oral Roberts University, OK
Ottawa University, KS
Park University, MO
Saint Francis College, PA
St. Gregory's University, OK
Saint Joseph's College, IN
St. Mary's University of San Antonio, TX
Sam Houston State University, TX
Southeastern Bible College, AL
Southeastern Louisiana University, LA
Southeast Missouri State University, MO
Southern Arkansas University–Magnolia, AR
Southern Illinois University Carbondale, IL
Southern Utah University, UT
Southwestern College, KS
Southwestern Oklahoma State University, OK
Southwest Missouri State University, MO
Stephen F. Austin State University, TX
Sterling College, KS
Stetson University, FL
Tabor College, KS
Temple University, PA
Tennessee Technological University, TN
Tennessee Wesleyan College, TN
Texas Wesleyan University, TX
Thomas University, GA
Tiffin University, OH
Transylvania University, KY
Tri-State University, IN
Union College, KY
The University of Alabama at Birmingham, AL
University of Arkansas at Monticello, AR
University of Central Arkansas, AR
University of Delaware, DE
University of Idaho, ID
University of Louisiana at Monroe, LA
University of Mary Hardin-Baylor, TX
University of Massachusetts Amherst, MA
The University of Memphis, TN
University of Mobile, AL
University of Nebraska at Kearney, NE
University of Nebraska–Lincoln, NE
University of Nevada, Las Vegas, NV
University of Nevada, Reno, NV
University of North Alabama, AL
The University of North Carolina at Wilmington, NC
U of Puerto Rico, Cayey University College, PR
University of St. Francis, IL
University of Science and Arts of Oklahoma, OK
University of South Carolina, SC
University of South Carolina Aiken, SC
University of Southern Mississippi, MS
The University of Tennessee at Chattanooga, TN
The University of Tennessee at Martin, TN
The University of Tennessee Knoxville, TN
The University of Texas at Arlington, TX
The University of Texas at El Paso, TX
University of Tulsa, OK
The University of West Alabama, AL
Utah State University, UT
Wayland Baptist University, TX
West Texas A&M University, TX
West Virginia University Institute of Technology, WV
Wheeling Jesuit University, WV
William Carey College, MS
William Jewell College, MO
Wofford College, SC
Youngstown State University, OH

COMMUNITY SERVICE

Adams State College, CO
Agnes Scott College, GA
Albertus Magnus College, CT
Allen College, IA
Allentown College of St. Francis de Sales, PA
Alvernia College, PA
Alverno College, WI
Andrews University, MI
Antioch College, OH
Aquinas College, MI
Arizona State University, AZ
Arkansas State University, AR
Auburn University Montgomery, AL
Augsburg College, MN
Aurora University, IL
Barry University, FL
Baylor University, TX
Beaver College, PA
Bellarmine College, KY
Beloit College, WI
Bentley College, MA
Berry College, GA
Bethel College, MN
Biola University, CA
Bowie State University, MD
Bradley University, IL
Brevard College, NC
Brigham Young University, UT
Brigham Young University–Hawaii Campus, HI
Bryan College, TN
California Institute of Integral Studies, CA
California Maritime Academy, CA
California Polytechnic State U, San Luis Obispo, CA
California State University, Bakersfield, CA
California State University, Chico, CA
California State University, Fresno, CA
California State University, Los Angeles, CA
Calvin College, MI
Canisius College, NY
Cedar Crest College, PA
Centenary College of Louisiana, LA
Central Bible College, MO
Central College, IA
Chaminade University of Honolulu, HI
Cleary College, MI
Coe College, IA
Colby-Sawyer College, NH
The College of New Rochelle, NY
College of Notre Dame of Maryland, MD
College of St. Catherine, MN
College of St. Joseph, VT
The College of Saint Rose, NY
The College of Wooster, OH
Colorado Christian University, CO
Concord College, WV
Concordia College, NY
Cumberland College, KY
Davidson College, NC
Defiance College, OH
DePaul University, IL
DePauw University, IN
Dominican University of California, CA
Eastern Connecticut State University, CT
Eastern Nazarene College, MA
Eastern New Mexico University, NM
Eastern Oregon University, OR
Eckerd College, FL
Edgewood College, WI
Endicott College, MA
Eugene Bible College, OR
The Evergreen State College, WA
Ferrum College, VA
Finlandia University, MI
Florida Gulf Coast University, FL
Florida Memorial College, FL
Florida Southern College, FL
Fontbonne College, MO
Franklin and Marshall College, PA
Fresno Pacific University, CA
Frostburg State University, MD
Gannon University, PA
Georgia College and State University, GA
Georgia State University, GA
Goddard College, VT
Green Mountain College, VT
Greensboro College, NC
Guilford College, NC
Gustavus Adolphus College, MN
Gwynedd-Mercy College, PA
Hampshire College, MA
Hillsdale College, MI
Hillsdale Free Will Baptist College, OK
Hollins University, VA
Holy Names College, CA
Howard Payne University, TX
Humphreys College, CA
Illinois Institute of Technology, IL
Illinois State University, IL

Illinois Wesleyan University, IL
Immaculata College, PA
Indiana University of Pennsylvania, PA
Iowa State University of Science and Technology, IA
Jacksonville University, FL
John Carroll University, OH
Johnson Bible College, TN
Johnson C. Smith University, NC
Johnson State College, VT
Juniata College, PA
Kean University, NJ
Kennesaw State University, GA
Kent State University, OH
Kentucky Christian College, KY
King College, TN
King's College, PA
Knox College, IL
LaGrange College, GA
Lakeland College, WI
La Roche College, PA
La Salle University, PA
Lasell College, MA
Lesley College, MA
Lewis & Clark College, OR
Lewis University, IL
Loras College, IA
Loyola Marymount University, CA
Loyola University Chicago, IL
Lyndon State College, VT
Lynn University, FL
Malone College, OH
Manchester College, IN
Manhattan College, NY
Manhattanville College, NY
Marian College, IN
Marycrest International University, IA
Marymount College, NY
Maryville College, TN
Maryville University of Saint Louis, MO
Marywood University, PA
Massachusetts College of Art, MA
The Master's College and Seminary, CA
McKendree College, IL
McNeese State University, LA
Mercer University, GA
Mercyhurst College, PA
Michigan State University, MI
Mid-America Bible College, OK
Midland Lutheran College, NE
Millikin University, IL
Minnesota State University Moorhead, MN
Missouri Western State College, MO
Montana State U–Northern, MT
Mount Angel Seminary, OR
Mount St. Clare College, IA
Mount St. Mary's College, CA
National-Louis University, IL
New England College, NH
Newman University, KS
Niagara University, NY
Norwich University, VT
Oglethorpe University, GA
Ohio Wesleyan University, OH
Oklahoma State U, OK
Old Dominion University, VA
Olivet College, MI
Oral Roberts University, OK
Otterbein College, OH
Ouachita Baptist University, AR
Palmer College of Chiropractic, IA
Paul Quinn College, TX
Peirce College, PA
Pikeville College, KY
Pitzer College, CA
Plattsburgh State U of NY, NY
Point Park College, PA
Portland State University, OR
Providence College, RI
Queens College, NC
Quincy University, IL
Randolph-Macon Woman's College, VA
The Richard Stockton College of New Jersey, NJ
Roanoke Bible College, NC
Robert Morris College, IL
Roberts Wesleyan College, NY
Rockhurst University, MO
Sacred Heart University, CT
Saint Francis College, PA
St. John Fisher College, NY
St. John's University, NY
Saint Joseph's College, ME
St. Lawrence University, NY
St. Louis College of Pharmacy, MO
Saint Louis University, MO
Saint Martin's College, WA
Saint Mary College, KS
Saint Mary-of-the-Woods College, IN
St. Olaf College, MN
St. Thomas Aquinas College, NY
San Diego State University, CA
Seton Hall University, NJ
Siena College, NY
Siena Heights University, MI
Sierra Nevada College, NV
Simmons College, MA
Sonoma State University, CA
Southeastern Louisiana University, LA
Southern Adventist University, TN
Southern Illinois University Carbondale, IL
Southern Wesleyan University, SC
Southwestern Adventist University, TX
Southwestern College, AZ
Southwestern College, KS
Spalding University, KY
Spring Hill College, AL
State U of NY at Binghamton, NY
State U of NY at New Paltz, NY
State U of NY College at Brockport, NY
State U of NY College at Geneseo, NY
State U of NY College at Oneonta, NY
State U of NY College at Potsdam, NY
Stetson University, FL
Teikyo Post University, CT
Texas A&M University–Texarkana, TX
Texas Tech University, TX
Union College, NE
United States International University, CA
Unity College, ME
The University of Alabama in Huntsville, AL
University of Arkansas, AR
University of Arkansas at Little Rock, AR
U of Calif, San Diego, CA
University of Charleston, WV
University of Colorado at Boulder, CO
University of Colorado at Colorado Springs, CO
University of Florida, FL
University of Hawaii at Hilo, HI
University of Houston–Clear Lake, TX
University of Houston–Downtown, TX
University of Illinois at Springfield, IL
University of Indianapolis, IN
University of Kansas, KS
University of La Verne, CA
University of Louisiana at Monroe, LA
University of Maine, ME
University of Maine at Presque Isle, ME
University of Massachusetts Lowell, MA
University of Michigan, MI
University of Michigan–Dearborn, MI
University of Michigan–Flint, MI
University of Mobile, AL
University of Nebraska–Lincoln, NE
University of Nebraska Medical Center, NE
University of Nevada, Las Vegas, NV
University of New England, ME
University of New Hampshire, NH
The University of North Carolina at Asheville, NC
The University of North Carolina at Chapel Hill, NC
The University of North Carolina at Greensboro, NC
The University of North Carolina at Wilmington, NC
University of North Florida, FL
University of Richmond, VA
University of St. Thomas, TX
University of South Carolina, SC
University of Southern Colorado, CO
University of Southern Maine, ME
U of Texas Southwestern Medical Center at Dallas, TX
University of Tulsa, OK
University of Virginia's College at Wise, VA
University of Washington, WA
University of Wisconsin–Eau Claire, WI
Urbana University, OH
Ursuline College, OH
Valdosta State University, GA
Valley Forge Christian College, PA
Vanderbilt University, TN
Villa Julie College, MD
Virginia Polytechnic Institute and State U, VA
Virginia State University, VA
Viterbo University, WI
Voorhees College, SC
Wabash College, IN
Wake Forest University, NC
Walla Walla College, WA
Walsh University, OH
Waynesburg College, PA
Webber College, FL
Wesleyan College, GA
Western Illinois University, IL
Western Michigan University, MI
Western Washington University, WA
Westfield State College, MA
West Virginia Wesleyan College, WV
Wheeling Jesuit University, WV
Willamette University, OR
William Woods University, MO
Wilson College, PA
Wittenberg University, OH
Wofford College, SC
Worcester State College, MA
Xavier University, OH

HOBBIES/INTERESTS

Arizona State University, AZ
Augusta State University, GA
California State Polytechnic University, Pomona, CA
California State University, Chico, CA
Capital University, OH
Central Washington University, WA
The College of New Rochelle, NY
Eastern New Mexico University, NM
Edgewood College, WI
Emmaus Bible College, IA
Emporia State University, KS
Eugene Bible College, OR
Frostburg State University, MD
Hawaii Pacific University, HI
Illinois State University, IL
Illinois Wesleyan University, IL
Indiana University of Pennsylvania, PA
Lake Erie College, OH
Lawrence Technological University, MI
McNeese State University, LA
Mesa State College, CO
Michigan State University, MI
Montana State U–Northern, MT
Northeastern State University, OK
The Ohio State University, OH
Rhode Island College, RI
Rhodes College, TN
Robert Morris College, PA
Sacred Heart University, CT
St. John's University, NY
Shimer College, IL
Siena College, NY
South Dakota State University, SD
Southwestern College, AZ
Southwest Missouri State University, MO
Stephen F. Austin State University, TX
Tri-State University, IN
University of Minnesota, Twin Cities Campus, MN
University of Nevada, Las Vegas, NV
University of New England, ME
University of South Alabama, AL
University of South Carolina, SC
The University of Tennessee Knoxville, TN
University of Wisconsin–Eau Claire, WI
Valdosta State University, GA
Virginia State University, VA
Western Baptist College, OR

JUNIOR MISS

Albertson College of Idaho, ID
Albright College, PA
Alvernia College, PA
Arizona State University, AZ
The Art Institute of Colorado, CO
Augsburg College, MN
Belhaven College, MS
Bethel College, MN
Birmingham-Southern College, AL
Bluefield State College, WV
Brigham Young University–Hawaii Campus, HI
Caldwell College, NJ
Campbell University, NC
Carroll College, WI
Cedar Crest College, PA
The College of New Rochelle, NY
College of Saint Benedict, MN
College of Saint Elizabeth, NJ
Columbia College, MO
Elizabethtown College, PA
Georgian Court College, NJ
Hardin-Simmons University, TX
Hawaii Pacific University, HI
Huntingdon College, AL
Idaho State University, ID
Judson College, AL
Kentucky Wesleyan College, KY
Lewis-Clark State College, ID
Malone College, OH
McMurry University, TX
Mercer University, GA
Michigan State University, MI
Midway College, KY
Mississippi University for Women, MS
Mount Vernon Nazarene College, OH
Murray State University, KY
Northeastern State University, OK
North Greenville College, SC
Ohio Northern University, OH
Oklahoma City University, OK
Ottawa University, KS
Palmer College of Chiropractic, IA
Peace College, NC
Roberts Wesleyan College, NY
Saint Francis College, PA
St. John Fisher College, NY
South Dakota State University, SD
Spring Arbor College, MI
Tennessee Wesleyan College, TN
Thiel College, PA
Thomas University, GA
University of Central Arkansas, AR
University of Idaho, ID
University of Mobile, AL
University of Montevallo, AL
The University of North Carolina at Asheville, NC
The University of North Carolina at Greensboro, NC
University of South Alabama, AL
The University of Texas at Arlington, TX
Utah State University, UT
Washington State University, WA
Western Maryland College, MD
William Carey College, MS
William Penn University, IA

LEADERSHIP

Abilene Christian University, TX
Adams State College, CO
Alabama State University, AL
Albertus Magnus College, CT
Alfred University, NY
Allen College, IA
Allentown College of St. Francis de Sales, PA
Allen University, SC
American University, DC
Anderson College, SC
Anderson University, IN
Andrews University, MI
Anna Maria College, MA
Aquinas College, MI
Aquinas College, TN
Arizona State University, AZ
Ashland University, OH
Athens State University, AL
Atlantic Union College, MA
Auburn University Montgomery, AL
Augsburg College, MN
Augustana College, SD
Aurora University, IL
Austin College, TX
Austin Peay State University, TN
Baldwin-Wallace College, OH
Ball State University, IN
Baptist Bible College of Pennsylvania, PA
Barber-Scotia College, NC
Barclay College, KS
Bard College, NY
Barry University, FL
Barton College, NC
Baylor University, TX
Beaver College, PA
Becker College, MA
Belhaven College, MS
Bellarmine College, KY
Bellevue University, NE
Belmont Abbey College, NC
Bethany College, WV
Bethany College of the Assemblies of God, CA
Bethel College, IN
Bethel College, MN
Bluefield State College, WV
Bluffton College, OH
Boise Bible College, ID
Boise State University, ID
Boston University, MA
Bowie State University, MD
Bowling Green State University, OH
Bradley University, IL
Brevard College, NC
Briar Cliff College, IA
Brigham Young University, UT
Brigham Young University–Hawaii Campus, HI
Bryan College, TN
Bryant College, RI
Buena Vista University, IA
Cabrini College, PA
Caldwell College, NJ
California Lutheran University, CA
California Maritime Academy, CA
California Polytechnic State U, San Luis Obispo, CA
California State Polytechnic University, Pomona, CA
California State University, Bakersfield, CA
California State University, Chico, CA
California State University, Fresno, CA
California State University, Fullerton, CA
California State University, Stanislaus, CA
Calumet College of Saint Joseph, IN
Cameron University, OK
Canisius College, NY
Capital University, OH
Cardinal Stritch University, WI
Carlow College, PA
Carroll College, MT
Carson-Newman College, TN
Carthage College, WI
Case Western Reserve University, OH
Cedar Crest College, PA
Cedarville College, OH
Centenary College, NJ
Centenary College of Louisiana, LA
Central Christian College of the Bible, MO

Central College, IA
Central Methodist College, MO
Central Michigan University, MI
Central Missouri State University, MO
Chaminade University of Honolulu, HI
Chicago State University, IL
Chowan College, NC
Christian Heritage College, CA
Circleville Bible College, OH
Citadel, The Military Coll of South Carolina, SC
Clark Atlanta University, GA
Clarke College, IA
Clarkson University, NY
Coe College, IA
Colby-Sawyer College, NH
College of Mount St. Joseph, OH
College of Mount Saint Vincent, NY
The College of New Rochelle, NY
College of Notre Dame of Maryland, MD
College of St. Catherine, MN
College of St. Joseph, VT
College of Saint Mary, NE
Colorado Christian University, CO
Columbia College, MO
Columbia College, SC
Columbia College Chicago, IL
Columbia International University, SC
Columbia Union College, MD
Concordia University, OR
Concordia University at Austin, TX
Concordia University Wisconsin, WI
Converse College, SC
Cornerstone University, MI
Covenant College, GA
Crichton College, TN
Crown College, MN
The Culinary Institute of America, NY
Cumberland University, TN
Dakota Wesleyan University, SD
Dallas Baptist University, TX
Daniel Webster College, NH
David Lipscomb University, TN
Davidson College, NC
Davis & Elkins College, WV
Deaconess College of Nursing, MO
Defiance College, OH
Delta State University, MS
Denison University, OH
DePauw University, IN
Dickinson State University, ND
Doane College, NE
Dordt College, IA
Drury University, MO
Duke University, NC
East Carolina University, NC
Eastern Connecticut State University, CT
Eastern Michigan University, MI
Eastern Nazarene College, MA
Eastern New Mexico University, NM
Eastern Oregon University, OR
East Tennessee State University, TN
East Texas Baptist University, TX
Eckerd College, FL
Edgewood College, WI
Elmira College, NY
Elon College, NC
Embry-Riddle Aeronautical University, AZ
Embry-Riddle Aeronautical University, FL
Embry-Riddle Aeronautical U, Extended Campus, FL
Emmanuel College, GA
Emmaus Bible College, IA
Emporia State University, KS
Endicott College, MA
Erskine College, SC
Eugene Bible College, OR
Eureka College, IL
Evangel University, MO
Fairleigh Dickinson U, Florham-Madison Campus, NJ
Fairleigh Dickinson U, Teaneck-Hackensack Campus, NJ
Faith Baptist Bible Coll and Theological Seminary, IA
Faulkner University, AL
Finlandia University, MI
Fitchburg State College, MA
Florida Gulf Coast University, FL
Florida Memorial College, FL
Florida Southern College, FL
Fontbonne College, MO
Franklin University, OH
Fresno Pacific University, CA
Friends University, KS
Frostburg State University, MD
Gannon University, PA
George Fox University, OR
The George Washington University, DC
Georgia Institute of Technology, GA
Georgia Southwestern State University, GA
Georgia State University, GA
Golden Gate University, CA
Gordon College, MA
Graceland College, IA
Grace University, NE
Grambling State University, LA
Grand Canyon University, AZ
Green Mountain College, VT
Greensboro College, NC
Greenville College, IL
Grove City College, PA
Gwynedd-Mercy College, PA
Hampshire College, MA
Hardin-Simmons University, TX
Hellenic College, MA
Henderson State University, AR
Hendrix College, AR
Hilbert College, NY
Hillsdale College, MI
Hiram College, OH
Hobart and William Smith Colleges, NY
Hofstra University, NY
Hollins University, VA
Holy Names College, CA
Hood College, MD
Hope International University, CA
Howard Payne University, TX
Huntingdon College, AL
Husson College, ME
Idaho State University, ID
Illinois Institute of Technology, IL
Illinois State University, IL
Illinois Wesleyan University, IL
Immaculata College, PA
Indiana University of Pennsylvania, PA
Iowa State University of Science and Technology, IA
Ithaca College, NY
Jacksonville State University, AL
Jacksonville University, FL
James Madison University, VA
John Brown University, AR
John Carroll University, OH
Johnson & Wales University, FL
Johnson & Wales University, RI
Johnson & Wales University, SC
Johnson Bible College, TN
Johnson C. Smith University, NC
Johnson State College, VT
Judson College, IL
Juniata College, PA
Kansas State University, KS
Kean University, NJ
Kendall College, IL
Kent State University, OH
Kentucky Christian College, KY
Kentucky Wesleyan College, KY
King's College, PA
LaGrange College, GA
Lake Forest College, IL
Lakeland College, WI
Lancaster Bible College, PA
Lander University, SC
Langston University, OK
Lasell College, MA
Lees-McRae College, NC
Lee University, TN
Le Moyne College, NY
Lesley College, MA
Lewis-Clark State College, ID
Liberty University, VA
Limestone College, SC
Linfield College, OR
Lock Haven University of Pennsylvania, PA
Long Island U, Brooklyn Campus, NY
Louisiana College, LA
Louisiana State University and A&M College, LA
Loyola University Chicago, IL
Lubbock Christian University, TX
Lycoming College, PA
Lyndon State College, VT
Lyon College, AR
MacMurray College, IL
Maharishi University of Management, IA
Malone College, OH
Manhattan Christian College, KS
Manhattan College, NY
Mary Baldwin College, VA
Marycrest International University, IA
Marymount College, NY
Marymount Manhattan College, NY
Marymount University, VA
Maryville College, TN
Maryville University of Saint Louis, MO
Marywood University, PA
Massachusetts College of Liberal Arts, MA
The Master's College and Seminary, CA
McKendree College, IL
McNeese State University, LA
Menlo College, CA
Mercyhurst College, PA
Meredith College, NC
Merrimack College, MA
Messiah College, PA
Michigan State University, MI
Michigan Technological University, MI
Mid-America Bible College, OK

Leadership (continued)

MidAmerica Nazarene University, KS
Middle Tennessee State University, TN
Midland Lutheran College, NE
Midwestern State University, TX
Minnesota Bible College, MN
Minnesota State University, Mankato, MN
Mississippi State University, MS
Missouri Western State College, MO
Moody Bible Institute, IL
Morehead State University, KY
Mount Marty College, SD
Mount Mary College, WI
Mount Mercy College, IA
Mount Olive College, NC
Mount St. Clare College, IA
Mount St. Mary's College, CA
Muhlenberg College, PA
Murray State University, KY
National-Louis University, IL
National University, CA
New England College, NH
New Hampshire College, NH
Newman University, KS
Northeastern Illinois University, IL
Northern Michigan University, MI
North Georgia College & State University, GA
Northland College, WI
Northwest Christian College, OR
Northwest College, WA
Northwestern College, MN
Northwestern State University of Louisiana, LA
Northwest Missouri State University, MO
Northwest Nazarene University, ID
Norwich University, VT
Nyack College, NY
Oakland University, MI
Ohio Dominican College, OH
The Ohio State University, OH
Ohio Valley College, WV
Oklahoma Baptist University, OK
Oklahoma Christian U of Science and Arts, OK
Oklahoma City University, OK
Oklahoma State U, OK
Old Dominion University, VA
Olivet College, MI
Oral Roberts University, OK
Otterbein College, OH
Ouachita Baptist University, AR
Pacific Lutheran University, WA
Pacific Union College, CA
Palm Beach Atlantic College, FL
Palmer College of Chiropractic, IA
Peace College, NC
Peirce College, PA
Philadelphia College of Bible, PA
Piedmont College, GA
Pine Manor College, MA
Pitzer College, CA
Plattsburgh State U of NY, NY
Practical Bible College, NY
Presbyterian College, SC
Purdue University North Central, IN
Queens College, NC
Quincy University, IL
Quinnipiac University, CT
Radford University, VA
Randolph-Macon Woman's College, VA
Reformed Bible College, MI
Regis University, CO
Reinhardt College, GA
The Richard Stockton College of New Jersey, NJ
Ripon College, WI
Roanoke Bible College, NC
Robert Morris College, PA
Roberts Wesleyan College, NY
Rochester College, MI
Rockhurst University, MO
Sacred Heart University, CT
St. Edward's University, TX
St. Gregory's University, OK
Saint John's University, MN
St. John's University, NY
Saint Joseph's College, ME
Saint Joseph Seminary College, LA
St. Louis Christian College, MO
St. Louis College of Pharmacy, MO
Saint Louis University, MO
Saint Martin's College, WA
Saint Mary-of-the-Woods College, IN
Saint Peter's College, NJ
St. Thomas Aquinas College, NY
Saint Vincent College, PA
Saint Xavier University, IL
Salem College, NC
Samford University, AL
Sam Houston State University, TX
San Diego State University, CA
Schreiner College, TX
Seattle Pacific University, WA
Seattle University, WA
Seton Hall University, NJ
Shepherd College, WV
Siena College, NY
Simpson College and Graduate School, CA
Slippery Rock University of Pennsylvania, PA
Sonoma State University, CA
South Dakota State University, SD
Southeastern Louisiana University, LA
Southeast Missouri State University, MO
Southern Adventist University, TN
Southern Arkansas University–Magnolia, AR
Southern Illinois University Carbondale, IL
Southern Oregon University, OR
Southern Utah University, UT
Southern Wesleyan University, SC
Southwestern Adventist University, TX
Southwestern Assemblies of God University, TX
Southwestern College, AZ
Southwestern College, KS
Southwest State University, MN
Spalding University, KY
Spring Hill College, AL
State U of NY at Oswego, NY
State U of NY College at Brockport, NY
State U of NY College at Fredonia, NY
State U of NY College at Geneseo, NY
State U of NY College at Oneonta, NY
State U of NY College at Potsdam, NY
State U of NY Coll of Environ Sci and Forestry, NY
Stephen F. Austin State University, TX
Stephens College, MO
Sterling College, KS
Stetson University, FL
Sul Ross State University, TX
Sweet Briar College, VA
Taylor University, IN
Taylor University, Fort Wayne Campus, IN
Teikyo Post University, CT
Tennessee Temple University, TN
Tennessee Wesleyan College, TN
Texas A&M University, TX
Texas A&M University–Commerce, TX
Texas A&M University–Texarkana, TX
Texas Christian University, TX
Texas Lutheran University, TX
Texas Wesleyan University, TX
Thiel College, PA
Thomas College, ME
Thomas More College, KY
Toccoa Falls College, GA
Trinity Baptist College, FL
Trinity Bible College, ND
Trinity Christian College, IL
Trinity International U, South Florida Campus, FL
Trinity Lutheran College, WA
Truman State University, MO
Union College, NE
Union University, TN
United States International University, CA
Unity College, ME
The University of Alabama at Birmingham, AL
The University of Alabama in Huntsville, AL
U of Alaska Southeast, AK
University of Arkansas, AR
University of Arkansas at Little Rock, AR
University of Arkansas at Monticello, AR
University of Arkansas at Pine Bluff, AR
U of Calif, San Diego, CA
University of Central Arkansas, AR
University of Central Oklahoma, OK
University of Charleston, WV
University of Colorado at Boulder, CO
University of Colorado at Colorado Springs, CO
University of Colorado at Denver, CO
University of Dallas, TX
University of Delaware, DE
University of Evansville, IN
University of Florida, FL
University of Hawaii at Hilo, HI
University of Houston, TX
University of Houston–Clear Lake, TX
University of Houston–Downtown, TX
University of Houston–Victoria, TX
University of Idaho, ID
University of Illinois at Springfield, IL
University of Kansas, KS
University of La Verne, CA
University of Louisiana at Monroe, LA
University of Maine, ME
The University of Maine at Augusta, ME
University of Maine at Machias, ME
University of Mary Hardin-Baylor, TX
University of Massachusetts Amherst, MA
The University of Memphis, TN
University of Michigan, MI
University of Michigan–Flint, MI
University of Minnesota, Crookston, MN
University of Mississippi, MS
University of Mobile, AL

The University of Montana–Missoula, MT
University of Nebraska at Kearney, NE
University of Nebraska at Omaha, NE
University of Nebraska–Lincoln, NE
University of Nebraska Medical Center, NE
University of Nevada, Las Vegas, NV
University of Nevada, Reno, NV
University of New England, ME
University of North Alabama, AL
The University of North Carolina at Asheville, NC
The University of North Carolina at Chapel Hill, NC
The University of North Carolina at Greensboro, NC
The University of North Carolina at Wilmington, NC
University of Northern Iowa, IA
University of North Florida, FL
University of Oklahoma, OK
University of Pittsburgh at Johnstown, PA
University of Puget Sound, WA
University of Rochester, NY
University of Science and Arts of Oklahoma, OK
University of South Alabama, AL
University of South Carolina, SC
University of South Dakota, SD
University of Southern Colorado, CO
University of Southern Indiana, IN
University of Southern Mississippi, MS
The University of Tampa, FL
The University of Tennessee at Chattanooga, TN
The University of Tennessee at Martin, TN
The University of Tennessee Knoxville, TN
The University of Texas at Arlington, TX
The University of Texas at Dallas, TX
The University of Texas at El Paso, TX
University of the Ozarks, AR
University of Toledo, OH
University of Tulsa, OK
University of Utah, UT
University of Washington, WA
University of Wisconsin–Eau Claire, WI
University of Wisconsin–Platteville, WI
University of Wisconsin–Stevens Point, WI
University of Wisconsin–Whitewater, WI
University of Wyoming, WY
Urbana University, OH
Ursinus College, PA
Ursuline College, OH
Utah State University, UT
Valley Forge Christian College, PA
Vanderbilt University, TN
Villa Julie College, MD
Virginia Military Institute, VA
Virginia Polytechnic Institute and State U, VA
Virginia Wesleyan College, VA
Viterbo University, WI
Wabash College, IN
Wake Forest University, NC
Walla Walla College, WA
Walsh University, OH
Warner Pacific College, OR
Warner Southern College, FL
Warren Wilson College, NC
Washington Bible College, MD
Washington State University, WA
Wayland Baptist University, TX
Waynesburg College, PA
Wayne State College, NE
Webber College, FL
Weber State University, UT
Webster University, MO
Wells College, NY
Wesleyan College, GA
Western Baptist College, OR
Western Illinois University, IL
Western Kentucky University, KY
Western Maryland College, MD
Western State College of Colorado, CO
Western Washington University, WA
Westminster College, MO
Westminster College, PA
Westmont College, CA
West Texas A&M University, TX
West Virginia State College, WV
West Virginia University, WV
West Virginia Wesleyan College, WV
Wichita State University, KS
Widener University, PA
Wilkes University, PA
Willamette University, OR
William Carey College, MS
William Jewell College, MO
William Penn University, IA
Williams Baptist College, AR
William Woods University, MO
Wilmington College, OH
Wisconsin Lutheran College, WI
Wittenberg University, OH
Wofford College, SC
Xavier University, OH
York College, NE
Youngstown State University, OH

MEMBERSHIPS

Adams State College, CO
Adelphi University, NY
Albright College, PA
Allentown College of St. Francis de Sales, PA
Andrews University, MI
Aquinas College, MI
Arizona State University, AZ
Atlanta Christian College, GA
Auburn University, AL
Barry University, FL
Bay Path College, MA
Birmingham-Southern College, AL
Blue Mountain College, MS
Boston University, MA
Brigham Young University, UT
California State University, Chico, CA
Carroll College, WI
Carson-Newman College, TN
Cedar Crest College, PA
Central Washington University, WA
The College of New Rochelle, NY
College of Notre Dame of Maryland, MD
College of Saint Benedict, MN
College of St. Catherine, MN
Columbia College, MO
Columbia Union College, MD
Dallas Baptist University, TX
Delta State University, MS
Eastern Connecticut State University, CT
Eastern New Mexico University, NM
East Tennessee State University, TN
Erskine College, SC
Florida Gulf Coast University, FL
Georgia Southern University, GA
Georgia State University, GA
Grand Canyon University, AZ
Grove City College, PA
Hawaii Pacific University, HI
Hood College, MD
Idaho State University, ID
Illinois Institute of Technology, IL
Immaculata College, PA
Johnson & Wales University, FL
Johnson & Wales University, RI
Johnson & Wales University, SC
Johnson State College, VT
Kettering University, MI
Laboratory Institute of Merchandising, NY
Lincoln University, MO
Lock Haven University of Pennsylvania, PA
Longwood College, VA
Loras College, IA
Loyola University Chicago, IL
Manchester College, IN
Massachusetts College of Liberal Arts, MA
McNeese State University, LA
Mercer University, GA
Michigan State University, MI
Mid-America Bible College, OK
Midwestern State University, TX
Mississippi State University, MS
Montana State U–Northern, MT
Mount Marty College, SD
Mount St. Clare College, IA
Muhlenberg College, PA
New Hampshire College, NH
Newman University, KS
Northwestern Oklahoma State University, OK
Northwest Missouri State University, MO
Northwood University, Florida Campus, FL
Northwood University, Texas Campus, TX
The Ohio State University, OH
Old Dominion University, VA
Oral Roberts University, OK
Peirce College, PA
Portland State University, OR
Rhodes College, TN
Ripon College, WI
Rockhurst University, MO
Saint Joseph's College, ME
Saint Louis University, MO
Saint Martin's College, WA
Saint Mary-of-the-Woods College, IN
Saint Mary's College of California, CA
Salem State College, MA
Salem-Teikyo University, WV
Shawnee State University, OH
Siena College, NY
Sonoma State University, CA
South Dakota State University, SD
Southern Oregon University, OR
Southwest Missouri State University, MO
State University of West Georgia, GA
Tennessee Technological University, TN
Tennessee Wesleyan College, TN
Texas A&M University, TX
Texas A&M University–Texarkana, TX
Texas Tech University, TX
Trevecca Nazarene University, TN
The University of Akron, OH
The University of Alabama at Birmingham, AL

Memberships (continued)

University of Arkansas at Little Rock, AR
University of Houston–Victoria, TX
University of Louisville, KY
The University of Maine at Augusta, ME
University of Missouri–St. Louis, MO
University of Nebraska at Kearney, NE
University of Nebraska at Omaha, NE
University of Nevada, Las Vegas, NV
University of the Sacred Heart, PR
University of Toledo, OH
University of Wisconsin–Eau Claire, WI
University of Wisconsin–Stout, WI
Utah State University, UT
Virginia Polytechnic Institute and State U, VA
Washington College, MD
Wayland Baptist University, TX
Wayne State University, MI
Webber College, FL
Western Baptist College, OR
Western Maryland College, MD
Western Michigan University, MI
Western Washington University, WA
West Texas A&M University, TX
William Woods University, MO
York College of Pennsylvania, PA

RELIGIOUS INVOLVEMENT

Adrian College, MI
Alaska Bible College, AK
Allentown College of St. Francis de Sales, PA
Alvernia College, PA
Anderson College, SC
Andrews University, MI
Anna Maria College, MA
Ashland University, OH
Atlanta Christian College, GA
Augsburg College, MN
Austin College, TX
Baker University, KS
Baptist Bible College of Pennsylvania, PA
Barry University, FL
Bartlesville Wesleyan College, OK
Barton College, NC
Baylor University, TX
Bellarmine College, KY
Berry College, GA
Bethany College, WV
Birmingham-Southern College, AL
Bluefield College, VA
Blue Mountain College, MS
Boise Bible College, ID
Briar Cliff College, IA
Brigham Young University, UT
Brigham Young University–Hawaii Campus, HI
Bryan College, TN
Caldwell College, NJ
California Lutheran University, CA
Calvin College, MI
Campbellsville University, KY
Campbell University, NC
Canisius College, NY
Capital University, OH
Carlow College, PA
Carroll College, MT
Carthage College, WI
Cedar Crest College, PA
Centenary College of Louisiana, LA
Central Bible College, MO
Central Christian College of the Bible, MO
Central College, IA
Central Methodist College, MO
Chaminade University of Honolulu, HI
Chapman University, CA
Charleston Southern University, SC
Citadel, The Military Coll of South Carolina, SC
Clear Creek Baptist Bible College, KY
The College of New Rochelle, NY
College of Notre Dame of Maryland, MD
College of Saint Mary, NE
The College of Wooster, OH
Colorado Christian University, CO
Columbia College, MO
Columbia Union College, MD
Concordia University, CA
Concordia University, OR
Cornerstone University, MI
The Criswell College, TX
Cumberland College, KY
Dakota Wesleyan University, SD
Dana College, NE
David Lipscomb University, TN
Davidson College, NC
Defiance College, OH
Dominican University, IL
Drury University, MO
Eastern Mennonite University, VA
Eastern Michigan University, MI
East Texas Baptist University, TX
Emmanuel College, GA
Emmaus Bible College, IA
Eugene Bible College, OR
Faulkner University, AL
Finlandia University, MI
Flagler College, FL
Franciscan University of Steubenville, OH
Furman University, SC
Gardner-Webb University, NC
George Fox University, OR
Georgetown College, KY
Georgia Baptist College of Nursing, GA
Graceland College, IA
Grace University, NE
Green Mountain College, VT
Greensboro College, NC
Grove City College, PA
Guilford College, NC
Hamline University, MN
Harding University, AR
Hellenic College, MA
Hendrix College, AR
Hillsdale Free Will Baptist College, OK
Hope International University, CA
Houghton College, NY
Howard Payne University, TX
Immaculata College, PA
Johnson Bible College, TN
John Wesley College, NC
Kentucky Christian College, KY
LaGrange College, GA
Lakeland College, WI
Lancaster Bible College, PA
Liberty University, VA
Limestone College, SC
Loras College, IA
Loyola Marymount University, CA
MacMurray College, IL
Malone College, OH
Marian College, IN
Marycrest International University, IA
Mercyhurst College, PA
Messenger College, MO
Michigan State University, MI
Mid-America Bible College, OK
Midland Lutheran College, NE
Midway College, KY
Minnesota Bible College, MN
Missouri Baptist College, MO
Moravian College, PA
Mount Marty College, SD
Mount St. Clare College, IA
Mount Vernon Nazarene College, OH
Newman University, KS
North Central College, IL
North Greenville College, SC
Northwest Christian College, OR
Northwest College, WA
Northwest Nazarene University, ID
Nyack College, NY
Oakland City University, IN
Oglethorpe University, GA
Ohio Wesleyan University, OH
Oklahoma Baptist University, OK
Oklahoma Christian U of Science and Arts, OK
Oklahoma City University, OK
Olivet Nazarene University, IL
Oral Roberts University, OK
Ottawa University, KS
Ouachita Baptist University, AR
Ozark Christian College, MO
Pacific Union College, CA
Palm Beach Atlantic College, FL
Paul Quinn College, TX
Peace College, NC
Philadelphia College of Bible, PA
Presbyterian College, SC
Queens College, NC
Randolph-Macon Woman's College, VA
Reformed Bible College, MI
Reinhardt College, GA
Roanoke Bible College, NC
Roberts Wesleyan College, NY
Rockhurst University, MO
Sacred Heart University, CT
Saint Francis College, PA
St. Gregory's University, OK
St. John's University, NY
St. Louis Christian College, MO
Saint Mary-of-the-Woods College, IN
St. Olaf College, MN
Salem-Teikyo University, WV
Schreiner College, TX
Shorter College, GA
Siena College, NY
Silver Lake College, WI
Simpson College and Graduate School, CA
Southeastern College of the Assemblies of God, FL
Southeastern Louisiana University, LA
Southern Adventist University, TN
Southern Christian University, AL
Southern Wesleyan University, SC
Southwestern Adventist University, TX
Southwestern Assemblies of God University, TX
Southwestern College, AZ
Southwestern College, KS

Stetson University, FL
Tabor College, KS
Taylor University, IN
Tennessee Wesleyan College, TN
Texas Christian University, TX
Texas Lutheran University, TX
Texas Wesleyan University, TX
Thomas More College, KY
Transylvania University, KY
Trinity Baptist College, FL
Trinity Bible College, ND
Trinity Lutheran College, WA
Union College, NE
University of Detroit Mercy, MI
University of Indianapolis, IN
University of Mary Hardin-Baylor, TX
University of Mobile, AL
The University of North Carolina at Greensboro, NC
University of Puget Sound, WA
University of South Carolina, SC
University of the Incarnate Word, TX
University of the Pacific, CA
University of Virginia's College at Wise, VA
Urbana University, OH
Utah State University, UT
Valley Forge Christian College, PA
Valparaiso University, IN
Virginia State University, VA
Virginia Wesleyan College, VA
Wake Forest University, NC
Walsh University, OH
Warner Pacific College, OR
Washington Bible College, MD
Wayland Baptist University, TX
Wesley College, DE
Wesley College, MS
Western Baptist College, OR
West Virginia Wesleyan College, WV
Wheeling Jesuit University, WV
William Carey College, MS
William Jewell College, MO
William Penn University, IA
Wilson College, PA
Wingate University, NC
Wofford College, SC
Xavier University of Louisiana, LA

RODEO

Albertson College of Idaho, ID
Arizona State University, AZ
Boise State University, ID
California Polytechnic State U, San Luis Obispo, CA
Chadron State College, NE
Dakota Wesleyan University, SD
Dickinson State University, ND
Eastern New Mexico University, NM
Eastern Oregon University, OR
Fort Hays State University, KS
Idaho State University, ID
Lewis-Clark State College, ID
McNeese State University, LA
Montana State U–Northern, MT
Murray State University, KY
Northwestern Oklahoma State University, OK
Oklahoma Panhandle State University, OK
Sam Houston State University, TX
South Dakota State University, SD
Southern Arkansas University–Magnolia, AR
Southwestern Oklahoma State University, OK
Southwest Missouri State University, MO
Stephen F. Austin State University, TX
Tarleton State University, TX
Teikyo Post University, CT
Texas A&M University, TX
Texas A&M University–Kingsville, TX
Texas Tech University, TX
University of Idaho, ID
The University of Montana–Missoula, MT
University of Nevada, Las Vegas, NV
The University of Tennessee at Martin, TN
The University of West Alabama, AL
University of Wyoming, WY
Utah State University, UT
Washington State University, WA
Weber State University, UT
Western Montana College of The U of Montana, MT
West Texas A&M University, TX

SPECIAL CHARACTERISTICS

ADULT STUDENTS

Agnes Scott College, GA
Allentown College of St. Francis de Sales, PA
Anderson College, SC
Anderson University, IN
Arkansas State University, AR
Arkansas Tech University, AR
Baltimore Hebrew University, MD
Barry University, FL
Bay Path College, MA
Bellarmine College, KY
Berry College, GA
Bethel College, IN
Beulah Heights Bible College, GA
Biola University, CA
Brigham Young University, UT
California Lutheran University, CA
California State University, Bakersfield, CA
California State University, Chico, CA
California State University, Fresno, CA
Calumet College of Saint Joseph, IN
Cedar Crest College, PA
Central Missouri State University, MO
Central Washington University, WA
Charleston Southern University, SC
College of Mount St. Joseph, OH
College of St. Catherine, MN
The College of Saint Rose, NY
David Lipscomb University, TN
Detroit College of Business, MI
Detroit College of Business–Flint, MI
Detroit College of Business, Warren Campus, MI
East Carolina University, NC
Eastern Oregon University, OR
Eastern Washington University, WA
East Stroudsburg University of Pennsylvania, PA
Edinboro University of Pennsylvania, PA
Emmanuel College, GA
The Evergreen State College, WA
Faulkner University, AL
Fort Hays State University, KS
Francis Marion University, SC
Franklin Pierce College, NH
Frostburg State University, MD
Gannon University, PA
Grace University, NE
Greensboro College, NC
Guilford College, NC
Hastings College, NE
Hillsdale Free Will Baptist College, OK
Indiana University of Pennsylvania, PA
Inter Amer U of PR, Barranquitas Campus, PR
Iowa State University of Science and Technology, IA
Juniata College, PA
Kent State University, OH
Lambuth University, TN
Lancaster Bible College, PA
La Roche College, PA
Long Island U, C.W. Post Campus, NY
Loyola University Chicago, IL
Lyndon State College, VT
Marian College, IN
Mary Washington College, VA
Marywood University, PA
McNeese State University, LA
Medaille College, NY
Mercer University, GA
Messiah College, PA
Middle Tennessee State University, TN
Millsaps College, MS
Mississippi State University, MS
Mississippi University for Women, MS
Monmouth University, NJ
Montana State U–Northern, MT
Moravian College, PA
Morehead State University, KY
Morningside College, IA
Mount Angel Seminary, OR
Murray State University, KY
North Central College, IL
Northern Michigan University, MI
Northwestern College, IA
Northwestern State University of Louisiana, LA
The Ohio State University, OH
Oklahoma State U, OK
Paul Quinn College, TX
Piedmont College, GA
Purdue University North Central, IN
Queens College, NC
Randolph-Macon Woman's College, VA
Reinhardt College, GA
The Richard Stockton College of New Jersey, NJ
Rochester College, MI
Sacred Heart University, CT
St. Ambrose University, IA
St. Edward's University, TX
Saint Francis College, PA
Saint Mary-of-the-Woods College, IN
Salem State College, MA
Sheldon Jackson College, AK
Siena College, NY
Sonoma State University, CA
Southeastern Louisiana University, LA
Southern Arkansas University–Magnolia, AR
Southwest Missouri State University, MO
State U of NY at Oswego, NY
State U of NY College at Oneonta, NY
State University of West Georgia, GA
Stephen F. Austin State University, TX
Suffolk University, MA

Adult Students (continued)

Sweet Briar College, VA
Texas Christian University, TX
Thomas More College, KY
The University of Akron, OH
The University of Alabama at Birmingham, AL
University of Great Falls, MT
University of Illinois at Springfield, IL
University of Indianapolis, IN
University of Kansas, KS
University of Maine at Fort Kent, ME
The University of Memphis, TN
University of Nebraska at Omaha, NE
The University of North Carolina at Asheville, NC
The University of North Carolina at Charlotte, NC
The University of North Carolina at Greensboro, NC
University of Northern Colorado, CO
University of Saint Francis, IN
University of South Carolina, SC
The University of Tennessee Knoxville, TN
The University of Texas at Dallas, TX
University of Toledo, OH
University of Wisconsin–Eau Claire, WI
University of Wisconsin–La Crosse, WI
University of Wisconsin–Parkside, WI
University of Wisconsin–Stout, WI
University of Wisconsin–Whitewater, WI
University of Wyoming, WY
Utah State University, UT
Weber State University, UT
Western Michigan University, MI
Westminster College, UT
Wichita State University, KS
Widener University, PA
Winthrop University, SC
Wittenberg University, OH
Youngstown State University, OH

CHILDREN AND SIBLINGS OF ALUMNI

Adelphi University, NY
Adrian College, MI
Albany College of Pharmacy of Union University, NY
Albertson College of Idaho, ID
Albright College, PA
Alvernia College, PA
Alverno College, WI
American University, DC
Anderson College, SC
Andrews University, MI
Anna Maria College, MA
Appalachian Bible College, WV
Aquinas College, MI
Arkansas State University, AR
Asbury College, KY
Ashland University, OH
Athens State University, AL
Augsburg College, MN
Augustana College, IL
Augustana College, SD
Aurora University, IL
Avila College, MO
Baldwin-Wallace College, OH
Baptist Bible College of Pennsylvania, PA
Barclay College, KS
Barry University, FL
Bartlesville Wesleyan College, OK
Barton College, NC
Beaver College, PA
Benedictine University, IL
Bethany College, WV
Bethel College, KS
Bethel College, MN
Birmingham-Southern College, AL
Bloomfield College, NJ
Boston University, MA
Bowling Green State University, OH
Bradley University, IL
Brescia University, KY
Briar Cliff College, IA
Bryan College, TN
Bryant College, RI
Cabrini College, PA
Caldwell College, NJ
California Lutheran University, CA
California State Polytechnic University, Pomona, CA
California State University, Fresno, CA
Calvin College, MI
Canisius College, NY
Capital University, OH
Carroll College, MT
Carroll College, WI
Carson-Newman College, TN
Carthage College, WI
Cedar Crest College, PA
Centenary College, NJ
Central Christian College of the Bible, MO
Central College, IA
Central Missouri State University, MO
Centre College, KY
Chaminade University of Honolulu, HI
Chapman University, CA
Chatham College, PA
Citadel, The Military Coll of South Carolina, SC
Clarke College, IA
Clarkson College, NE
Coe College, IA
Coker College, SC
Coleman College, CA
College of Mount St. Joseph, OH
College of Mount Saint Vincent, NY
College of St. Catherine, MN
College of Saint Elizabeth, NJ
The College of Saint Rose, NY
The College of St. Scholastica, MN
The College of West Virginia, WV
Colorado School of Mines, CO
Columbia College, MO
Columbia International University, SC
Concordia College, MI
Concordia University, IL
Concordia University, NE
Crichton College, TN
Culver-Stockton College, MO
Cumberland College, KY
Daemen College, NY
Dallas Baptist University, TX
Dallas Christian College, TX
Dana College, NE
Delta State University, MS
DePauw University, IN
Detroit College of Business, MI
Detroit College of Business–Flint, MI
Detroit College of Business, Warren Campus, MI
Dominican University, IL
Dominican University of California, CA
Dordt College, IA
Dowling College, NY
Drake University, IA
Drexel University, PA
Drury University, MO
Duke University, NC
Eastern Mennonite University, VA
Eastern Michigan University, MI
Eastern Nazarene College, MA
Eastern New Mexico University, NM
Eastern Washington University, WA
East Texas Baptist University, TX
Edinboro University of Pennsylvania, PA
Embry-Riddle Aeronautical University, AZ
Embry-Riddle Aeronautical University, FL
Emmanuel College, MA
Emporia State University, KS
Endicott College, MA
Erskine College, SC
Fairleigh Dickinson U, Florham-Madison Campus, NJ
Fairleigh Dickinson U, Teaneck-Hackensack Campus, NJ
Fitchburg State College, MA
Florida Institute of Technology, FL
Florida Southern College, FL
Fordham University, NY
Francis Marion University, SC
Franklin College of Indiana, IN
Free Will Baptist Bible College, TN
Friends University, KS
Frostburg State University, MD
George Fox University, OR
Georgia Baptist College of Nursing, GA
Georgian Court College, NJ
Gonzaga University, WA
Gordon College, MA
Goshen College, IN
Grace University, NE
Grambling State University, LA
Grand Canyon University, AZ
Greensboro College, NC
Greenville College, IL
Gustavus Adolphus College, MN
Gwynedd-Mercy College, PA
Hartwick College, NY
Hellenic College, MA
Hillsdale Free Will Baptist College, OK
Hiram College, OH
Hollins University, VA
Hope International University, CA
Howard Payne University, TX
Huntington College, IN
Idaho State University, ID
Illinois Institute of Technology, IL
Indiana State University, IN
Indiana U–Purdue U Fort Wayne, IN
Indiana Wesleyan University, IN
Iona College, NY
James Madison University, VA
John Brown University, AR
Judson College, IL
Juniata College, PA
Kansas Wesleyan University, KS
Kennesaw State University, GA
Kent State University, OH

Kentucky Christian College, KY
Kentucky Wesleyan College, KY
Lake Forest College, IL
Lancaster Bible College, PA
Lasell College, MA
Lebanon Valley College, PA
Le Moyne College, NY
Lewis University, IL
LIFE Bible College, CA
Life University, GA
Limestone College, SC
Long Island U, Brooklyn Campus, NY
Long Island U, Southampton College, NY
Longwood College, VA
Loras College, IA
Louisiana State University and A&M College, LA
Lourdes College, OH
Lyon College, AR
MacMurray College, IL
Maharishi University of Management, IA
Malone College, OH
Manchester College, IN
Maranatha Baptist Bible College, WI
Marian College, IN
Marietta College, OH
Marlboro College, VT
Marycrest International University, IA
Marymount Manhattan College, NY
Marymount University, VA
Mary Washington College, VA
McNeese State University, LA
Merrimack College, MA
Messiah College, PA
Michigan State University, MI
Michigan Technological University, MI
Mid-Continent College, KY
Midway College, KY
Milwaukee School of Engineering, WI
Mississippi State University, MS
Mississippi University for Women, MS
Missouri Baptist College, MO
Monmouth University, NJ
Montana State U–Billings, MT
Montana State U–Northern, MT
Moravian College, PA
Morehead State University, KY
Morningside College, IA
Mount St. Clare College, IA
Mount St. Mary's College, CA
Mount Senario College, WI
Mount Union College, OH
Murray State University, KY
Muskingum College, OH
Nazareth College of Rochester, NY
Newman University, KS
Northern Arizona University, AZ
Northwestern College, IA
Northwestern State University of Louisiana, LA
Northwest Missouri State University, MO
Northwest Nazarene University, ID
Northwood University, MI
Northwood University, Florida Campus, FL
Northwood University, Texas Campus, TX
Notre Dame College, NH
Notre Dame College of Ohio, OH
Nyack College, NY
The Ohio State University, OH
Ohio Wesleyan University, OH
Oklahoma Baptist University, OK
Oklahoma Christian U of Science and Arts, OK
Oklahoma State U, OK
Oral Roberts University, OK
Ottawa University, KS
Otterbein College, OH
Pacific Lutheran University, WA
Pacific University, OR
Paine College, GA
Peace College, NC
Philadelphia College of Bible, PA
Pine Manor College, MA
Point Loma Nazarene University, CA
Point Park College, PA
Practical Bible College, NY
Presentation College, SD
Principia College, IL
Randolph-Macon College, VA
Reinhardt College, GA
Research College of Nursing, MO
Ripon College, WI
Rivier College, NH
Roberts Wesleyan College, NY
Rochester College, MI
Rockford College, IL
Rockhurst University, MO
Rocky Mountain College, MT
Russell Sage College, NY
Sacred Heart University, CT
St. Ambrose University, IA
St. John Fisher College, NY
St. John's University, NY
Saint Joseph's College, IN
St. Joseph's College, New York, NY
St. Lawrence University, NY
Saint Martin's College, WA
Saint Mary-of-the-Woods College, IN
Saint Mary's College of California, CA
St. Mary's College of Maryland, MD
Salem State College, MA
Seattle Pacific University, WA
Seattle University, WA
Seton Hill College, PA
Sheldon Jackson College, AK
Shimer College, IL
Siena College, NY
Siena Heights University, MI
Simpson College, IA
Sonoma State University, CA
Southeastern Louisiana University, LA
Southern Adventist University, TN
Southern Illinois University Carbondale, IL
Southern Nazarene University, OK
Southwestern College, AZ
Southwestern College, KS
Southwestern College of Christian Ministries, OK
Southwestern Oklahoma State University, OK
Southwest Missouri State University, MO
Southwest Texas State University, TX
Spalding University, KY
State U of NY at Oswego, NY
State U of NY College at Brockport, NY
State U of NY College at Fredonia, NY
State U of NY College at Oneonta, NY
State U of NY College at Potsdam, NY
State University of West Georgia, GA
Stetson University, FL
Stevens Institute of Technology, NJ
Tabor College, KS
Taylor University, IN
Taylor University, Fort Wayne Campus, IN
Teikyo Post University, CT
Texas Lutheran University, TX
Thomas More College, KY
Trevecca Nazarene University, TN
Trinity Christian College, IL
Tri-State University, IN
Truman State University, MO
Union College, KY
Union University, TN
The University of Alabama at Birmingham, AL
University of Arkansas, AR
University of Colorado at Colorado Springs, CO
University of Colorado at Denver, CO
University of Delaware, DE
University of Detroit Mercy, MI
University of Dubuque, IA
University of Evansville, IN
The University of Findlay, OH
University of Guam, GU
University of Idaho, ID
University of La Verne, CA
University of Maine, ME
University of Mary Hardin-Baylor, TX
University of Massachusetts Amherst, MA
University of Michigan–Dearborn, MI
University of Minnesota, Crookston, MN
University of Mississippi, MS
University of Missouri–Rolla, MO
The University of Montana–Missoula, MT
University of Nebraska–Lincoln, NE
University of Nevada, Las Vegas, NV
University of Nevada, Reno, NV
University of New Hampshire, NH
University of New Orleans, LA
The University of North Carolina at Asheville, NC
The University of North Carolina at Pembroke, NC
University of Northern Colorado, CO
University of Oklahoma, OK
University of Rio Grande, OH
University of Rochester, NY
University of Saint Francis, IN
University of South Alabama, AL
University of South Carolina, SC
University of Southern California, CA
University of Southern Mississippi, MS
The University of Tampa, FL
University of Toledo, OH
University of Tulsa, OK
University of Wisconsin–Oshkosh, WI
University of Wyoming, WY
Upper Iowa University, IA
Urbana University, OH
Ursuline College, OH
Utah State University, UT
Valley City State University, ND
Valparaiso University, IN
Virginia Military Institute, VA
Viterbo University, WI
Walsh University, OH
Warner Pacific College, OR
Warner Southern College, FL
Wartburg College, IA
Washington & Jefferson College, PA

Children and Siblings of Alumni (continued)

Webber College, FL
Wells College, NY
Wesleyan College, GA
Western Baptist College, OR
Western Michigan University, MI
Westminster College, MO
Westminster College, PA
Westminster College, UT
Wheeling Jesuit University, WV
Whittier College, CA
Whitworth College, WA
William Carey College, MS
William Penn University, IA
William Tyndale College, MI
William Woods University, MO
Wilmington College, OH
Wilson College, PA
Wingate University, NC
Winona State University, MN
Wittenberg University, OH
Worcester State College, MA
York College, NE
York College of Pennsylvania, PA
Youngstown State University, OH

CHILDREN OF CURRENT STUDENTS

Anderson College, SC
Arkansas State University, AR
Asbury College, KY
Augustana College, SD
Avila College, MO
Becker College, MA
Bloomfield College, NJ
Bryan College, TN
California State Polytechnic University, Pomona, CA
Carlow College, PA
Carroll College, WI
Chaminade University of Honolulu, HI
The College of New Rochelle, NY
Columbia College, MO
Huntington College, IN
Jacksonville University, FL
Johnson & Wales University, FL
Johnson & Wales University, RI
Johnson & Wales University, SC
Johnson Bible College, TN
Lasell College, MA
Lee University, TN
Maryville University of Saint Louis, MO
Marywood University, PA
Messiah College, PA
Minnesota Bible College, MN
Missouri Baptist College, MO
Mount Marty College, SD
Mount St. Clare College, IA
Multnomah Bible College and Biblical Seminary, OR
Northwest College, WA
Nyack College, NY
Oklahoma Christian U of Science and Arts, OK
Olivet Nazarene University, IL
Palm Beach Atlantic College, FL
Presentation College, SD
Queens College, NC
Rockford College, IL
Saint Martin's College, WA
Saint Mary-of-the-Woods College, IN
Southwestern College, KS
State U of NY at Oswego, NY
Suffolk University, MA
Trinity Bible College, ND
The University of Alabama at Birmingham, AL
University of Great Falls, MT
University of Hartford, CT
University of Mary Hardin-Baylor, TX
University of Michigan–Dearborn, MI
Upper Iowa University, IA
Valley Forge Christian College, PA
Wesleyan College, GA
Wilkes University, PA
William Woods University, MO

CHILDREN OF EDUCATORS

Agnes Scott College, GA
Alfred University, NY
Allentown College of St. Francis de Sales, PA
Aurora University, IL
Austin Peay State University, TN
Bartlesville Wesleyan College, OK
Benedictine College, KS
Bennington College, VT
Brigham Young University–Hawaii Campus, HI
California Institute of the Arts, CA
Canisius College, NY
Carlow College, PA
Carroll College, MT
Carthage College, WI
Centenary College of Louisiana, LA
Clearwater Christian College, FL
College of St. Catherine, MN
Colorado Christian University, CO
Columbia College, MO
Cornell College, IA
Crown College, MN
David Lipscomb University, TN
Delaware Valley College, PA
Dowling College, NY
Eastern Nazarene College, MA
East Texas Baptist University, TX
Emmanuel College, MA
Endicott College, MA
Ferrum College, VA
Florida College, FL
Gallaudet University, DC
Governors State University, IL
Hastings College, NE
Hilbert College, NY
Illinois College, IL
John Brown University, AR
Judson College, AL
Lees-McRae College, NC
LeMoyne-Owen College, TN
Lycoming College, PA
Maranatha Baptist Bible College, WI
Mary Baldwin College, VA
Marycrest International University, IA
Messiah College, PA
Minnesota Bible College, MN
Mississippi State University, MS
Moravian College, PA
Nebraska Christian College, NE
New England College, NH
New York Institute of Technology, NY
Northern Arizona University, AZ
Northwest Nazarene University, ID
Oklahoma Christian U of Science and Arts, OK
Pacific Lutheran University, WA
Paul Quinn College, TX
Practical Bible College, NY
Reinhardt College, GA
Research College of Nursing, MO
Rockford College, IL
Rosemont College, PA
St. Ambrose University, IA
Saint Mary College, KS
Salem College, NC
Schreiner College, TX
Seattle University, WA
Sonoma State University, CA
Southern Illinois University Carbondale, IL
Tennessee Technological University, TN
Unity College, ME
The University of Alabama at Birmingham, AL
University of Central Arkansas, AR
University of Charleston, WV
University of Colorado at Denver, CO
University of Dubuque, IA
The University of Memphis, TN
University of St. Francis, IL
University of St. Thomas, MN
University of St. Thomas, TX
The University of Scranton, PA
The University of Tennessee at Martin, TN
University of Toledo, OH
The University of West Alabama, AL
Villanova University, PA
Virginia Wesleyan College, VA
Warner Southern College, FL
William Carey College, MS

CHILDREN OF FACULTY/STAFF

Abilene Christian University, TX
Adelphi University, NY
Adrian College, MI
Agnes Scott College, GA
Alabama Agricultural and Mechanical University, AL
Alaska Bible College, AK
Albertson College of Idaho, ID
Albright College, PA
Alcorn State University, MS
Alfred University, NY
Allentown College of St. Francis de Sales, PA
Alma College, MI
Alvernia College, PA
Anderson College, SC
Anderson University, IN
Andrews University, MI
Anna Maria College, MA
Appalachian Bible College, WV
Aquinas College, MI
Arkansas Tech University, AR
Arlington Baptist College, TX
The Art Institute of Portland, OR
Asbury College, KY
Ashland University, OH
Athens State University, AL
Atlanta Christian College, GA
Augustana College, IL
Augustana College, SD
Aurora University, IL
Austin College, TX

Austin Peay State University, TN
Avila College, MO
Azusa Pacific University, CA
Baker University, KS
Ball State University, IN
Barclay College, KS
Barry University, FL
Bartlesville Wesleyan College, OK
Barton College, NC
Baylor University, TX
Bay Path College, MA
Becker College, MA
Belhaven College, MS
Bellarmine College, KY
Belmont Abbey College, NC
Belmont University, TN
Benedictine College, KS
Bennett College, NC
Bennington College, VT
Berry College, GA
Bethany College, WV
Bethel College, IN
Bethel College, KS
Bethel College, MN
Bethel College, TN
Biola University, CA
Birmingham-Southern College, AL
Bloomsburg University of Pennsylvania, PA
Bluffton College, OH
Boise Bible College, ID
Boston College, MA
Bowling Green State University, OH
Bradley University, IL
Brenau University, GA
Brescia University, KY
Brevard College, NC
Brigham Young University–Hawaii Campus, HI
Bryan College, TN
Cabrini College, PA
Caldwell College, NJ
California Baptist University, CA
California Institute of the Arts, CA
California Lutheran University, CA
California State University, Bakersfield, CA
California State University, Chico, CA
California State University, Fresno, CA
California State University, Stanislaus, CA
Calumet College of Saint Joseph, IN
Calvin College, MI
Campbell University, NC
Canisius College, NY
Capital University, OH
Carlow College, PA
Carroll College, MT
Carroll College, WI
Cascade College, OR
Case Western Reserve University, OH
Catawba College, NC
The Catholic University of America, DC
Cedarville College, OH
Centenary College of Louisiana, LA
Central Bible College, MO
Central Christian College of the Bible, MO
Central College, IA
Central Methodist College, MO
Central Michigan University, MI
Central Missouri State University, MO
Central State University, OH
Centre College, KY
Chadron State College, NE
Chaminade University of Honolulu, HI
Charleston Southern University, SC
Chatham College, PA
Cheyney University of Pennsylvania, PA
Chowan College, NC
Christian Heritage College, CA
Circleville Bible College, OH
Claflin University, SC
Clarke College, IA
Clarkson College, NE
Clarkson University, NY
Cleary College, MI
Clemson University, SC
Colby-Sawyer College, NH
College of Insurance, NY
College of Mount Saint Vincent, NY
The College of New Rochelle, NY
College of Our Lady of the Elms, MA
College of St. Catherine, MN
College of Saint Elizabeth, NJ
The College of St. Scholastica, MN
College of the Holy Cross, MA
The College of West Virginia, WV
The College of Wooster, OH
Colorado Christian University, CO
Columbia College, MO
Columbia College, SC
Columbia International University, SC
Concordia College, NY
Concordia University, CA
Concordia University, IL
Concordia University, NE
Concordia University, OR
Concordia University at St. Paul, MN
Concordia University Wisconsin, WI
Cornell College, IA
Cornerstone University, MI
Covenant College, GA
Creighton University, NE
Crown College, MN
Cumberland College, KY
Cumberland University, TN
Daemen College, NY
Dallas Baptist University, TX
Dallas Christian College, TX
Dana College, NE
David Lipscomb University, TN
David N. Myers College, OH
Davidson College, NC
Defiance College, OH
Delaware Valley College, PA
Delta State University, MS
DePaul University, IL
DePauw University, IN
Detroit College of Business, MI
Dickinson College, PA
Dillard University, LA
Dominican University, IL
Dordt College, IA
Dowling College, NY
Drury University, MO
Duke University, NC
Duquesne University, PA
East Carolina University, NC
Eastern Connecticut State University, CT
Eastern Mennonite University, VA
East Texas Baptist University, TX
Eckerd College, FL
Edinboro University of Pennsylvania, PA
Elizabethtown College, PA
Elmira College, NY
Elon College, NC
Embry-Riddle Aeronautical University, AZ
Embry-Riddle Aeronautical University, FL
Emmanuel College, GA
Emmanuel College, MA
Emmaus Bible College, IA
Emory & Henry College, VA
Emory University, GA
Emporia State University, KS
Erskine College, SC
Evangel University, MO
Faith Baptist Bible Coll and Theological Seminary, IA
Faulkner University, AL
Ferris State University, MI
Ferrum College, VA
Finlandia University, MI
Fisk University, TN
Flagler College, FL
Florida College, FL
Florida Institute of Technology, FL
Florida Metropolitan U-Orlando Coll, North, FL
Florida Southern College, FL
Fordham University, NY
Framingham State College, MA
Franciscan University of Steubenville, OH
Francis Marion University, SC
Franklin College of Indiana, IN
Franklin Pierce College, NH
Gallaudet University, DC
Gardner-Webb University, NC
Geneva College, PA
Georgetown College, KY
Georgetown University, DC
The George Washington University, DC
Georgia College and State University, GA
Georgia Institute of Technology, GA
Grace College, IN
Graceland College, IA
Grace University, NE
Grambling State University, LA
Grand Canyon University, AZ
Grand Valley State University, MI
Grand View College, IA
Green Mountain College, VT
Greensboro College, NC
Greenville College, IL
Grove City College, PA
Guilford College, NC
Hamline University, MN
Hampden-Sydney College, VA
Hampshire College, MA
Hannibal-LaGrange College, MO
Hanover College, IN
Hardin-Simmons University, TX
Hartwick College, NY
Hastings College, NE
Hawaii Pacific University, HI
Hellenic College, MA
Henderson State University, AR
Hendrix College, AR
Hillsdale College, MI
Hope International University, CA
Howard Payne University, TX
Huntington College, IN
Idaho State University, ID
Illinois College, IL

Children of Faculty/Staff (continued)

Illinois Institute of Technology, IL
Illinois State University, IL
Immaculata College, PA
Indiana Institute of Technology, IN
Indiana State University, IN
Indiana U–Purdue U Fort Wayne, IN
Iowa Wesleyan College, IA
Jacksonville University, FL
James Madison University, VA
Jamestown College, ND
John Brown University, AR
John Carroll University, OH
Johns Hopkins University, MD
Johnson & Wales University, FL
Johnson & Wales University, RI
Johnson & Wales University, SC
Johnson Bible College, TN
John Wesley College, NC
Judson College, AL
Judson College, IL
Juniata College, PA
Kalamazoo College, MI
Kansas Wesleyan University, KS
Kendall College, IL
Kent State University, OH
Kentucky Christian College, KY
Kentucky Mountain Bible College, KY
Kentucky Wesleyan College, KY
King College, TN
King's College, PA
Kutztown University of Pennsylvania, PA
Lake Erie College, OH
Lambuth University, TN
Lancaster Bible College, PA
La Salle University, PA
Lasell College, MA
Lawrence Technological University, MI
Lees-McRae College, NC
Lee University, TN
Lehigh University, PA
LeMoyne-Owen College, TN
LeTourneau University, TX
LIFE Bible College, CA
Limestone College, SC
Lincoln Memorial University, TN
Lincoln University, MO
Linfield College, OR
Logan University of Chiropractic, MO
Long Island U, Brooklyn Campus, NY
Long Island U, C.W. Post Campus, NY
Long Island U, Southampton College, NY
Louisiana College, LA
Louisiana Tech University, LA
Lourdes College, OH
Loyola Marymount University, CA
Loyola University New Orleans, LA
Lycoming College, PA
Lynchburg College, VA
Lyndon State College, VT
Lynn University, FL
MacMurray College, IL
Maharishi University of Management, IA
Maine Maritime Academy, ME
Malone College, OH
Manhattan Christian College, KS
Manhattan College, NY
Marian College, IN
Marian College of Fond du Lac, WI
Mary Baldwin College, VA
Maryland Institute, College of Art, MD
Marymount University, VA
Mary Washington College, VA
Massachusetts College of Art, MA
The Master's College and Seminary, CA
McKendree College, IL
McMurry University, TX
McNeese State University, LA
Mercer University, GA
Mercyhurst College, PA
Merrimack College, MA
Messiah College, PA
Methodist College, NC
Miami University, OH
Michigan State University, MI
Michigan Technological University, MI
Mid-America Bible College, OK
MidAmerica Nazarene University, KS
Midway College, KY
Milligan College, TN
Millsaps College, MS
Mills College, CA
Milwaukee Institute of Art and Design, WI
Milwaukee School of Engineering, WI
Minnesota Bible College, MN
Mississippi College, MS
Mississippi State University, MS
Mississippi University for Women, MS
Missouri Baptist College, MO
Missouri Southern State College, MO
Missouri Western State College, MO
Monmouth University, NJ
Montana State U–Billings, MT
Montreat College, NC
Moravian College, PA
Morningside College, IA
Mount Marty College, SD
Mount Mary College, WI
Mount Olive College, NC
Mount St. Clare College, IA
Mount Saint Mary College, NY
Mount Senario College, WI
Mount Union College, OH
Mount Vernon Nazarene College, OH
Murray State University, KY
Nazareth College of Rochester, NY
Nebraska Christian College, NE
Neumann College, PA
Newberry College, SC
New England College, NH
New Hampshire College, NH
New Mexico Institute of Mining and Technology, NM
New York Institute of Technology, NY
Niagara University, NY
Nichols College, MA
North Central College, IL
Northeastern Illinois University, IL
Northeastern University, MA
Northern Illinois University, IL
North Greenville College, SC
Northwest Christian College, OR
Northwest College, WA
Northwestern College, IA
Northwestern College, MN
Northwood University, MI
Northwood University, Florida Campus, FL
Northwood University, Texas Campus, TX
Notre Dame College of Ohio, OH
Nova Southeastern University, FL
Nyack College, NY
Oak Hills Christian College, MN
Oglethorpe University, GA
Ohio Northern University, OH
The Ohio State University, OH
Ohio University, OH
Ohio University–Eastern, OH
Ohio University–Lancaster, OH
Ohio Valley College, WV
Ohio Wesleyan University, OH
Oklahoma Baptist University, OK
Oklahoma Christian U of Science and Arts, OK
Oklahoma City University, OK
Oklahoma Panhandle State University, OK
Old Dominion University, VA
Olivet Nazarene University, IL
Oral Roberts University, OK
Ottawa University, KS
Otterbein College, OH
Ouachita Baptist University, AR
Our Lady of Holy Cross College, LA
Our Lady of the Lake University of San Antonio, TX
Ozark Christian College, MO
Pacific Lutheran University, WA
Pacific University, OR
Paine College, GA
Park University, MO
Paul Quinn College, TX
Peace College, NC
Philadelphia College of Bible, PA
Piedmont Baptist College, NC
Piedmont College, GA
Plymouth State College, NH
Point Loma Nazarene University, CA
Pontifical Catholic University of Puerto Rico, PR
Practical Bible College, NY
Presbyterian College, SC
Presentation College, SD
Puget Sound Christian College, WA
Purdue University, IN
Purdue University North Central, IN
Queens College, NC
Quincy University, IL
Quinnipiac University, CT
Radford University, VA
Randolph-Macon Woman's College, VA
Reformed Bible College, MI
Regis University, CO
Reinhardt College, GA
Rhodes College, TN
The Richard Stockton College of New Jersey, NJ
Ripon College, WI
Roanoke Bible College, NC
Robert Morris College, IL
Robert Morris College, PA
Roberts Wesleyan College, NY
Rochester College, MI
Rochester Institute of Technology, NY
Rockford College, IL
Rockhurst University, MO
Rocky Mountain College, MT
Rocky Mountain College of Art & Design, CO
Rush University, IL
Rust College, MS

Rutgers, State U of NJ, Camden Coll of Arts & Scis, NJ
Rutgers, State U of NJ, College of Nursing, NJ
Rutgers, State U of NJ, College of Pharmacy, NJ
Rutgers, State U of NJ, Cook College, NJ
Rutgers, State U of NJ, Douglass College, NJ
Rutgers, State U of NJ, Livingston College, NJ
Rutgers, State U of NJ, Mason Gross School of Arts, NJ
Rutgers, State U of NJ, Newark Coll of Arts & Scis, NJ
Rutgers, State U of NJ, Rutgers College, NJ
Rutgers, State U of NJ, College of Engineering, NJ
Rutgers, State U of NJ, U Coll–Camden, NJ
Rutgers, State U of NJ, U Coll–Newark, NJ
Rutgers, State U of NJ, U Coll–New Brunswick, NJ
Sacred Heart University, CT
Saginaw Valley State University, MI
St. Ambrose University, IA
Saint Anselm College, NH
Saint Augustine's College, NC
St. Bonaventure University, NY
St. Edward's University, TX
Saint Francis College, PA
St. Gregory's University, OK
St. John's College, NM
St. John's University, NY
Saint Joseph's College, IN
Saint Joseph's College, ME
St. Joseph's College, New York, NY
St. Louis College of Pharmacy, MO
Saint Louis University, MO
Saint Martin's College, WA
Saint Mary-of-the-Woods College, IN
Saint Mary's College, IN
Saint Mary's College of California, CA
St. Norbert College, WI
Saint Paul's College, VA
Saint Peter's College, NJ
Saint Xavier University, IL
Salem College, NC
Salem State College, MA
Samford University, AL
Schreiner College, TX
Seattle University, WA
Seton Hall University, NJ
Seton Hill College, PA
Shaw University, NC
Shenandoah University, VA
Shorter College, GA
Siena College, NY
Sierra Nevada College, NV
Silver Lake College, WI
Simon's Rock College of Bard, MA
Simpson College, IA
Slippery Rock University of Pennsylvania, PA
Sonoma State University, CA
Southeastern Bible College, AL
Southeastern College of the Assemblies of God, FL
Southeastern Louisiana University, LA
Southeast Missouri State University, MO
Southern Arkansas University–Magnolia, AR
Southern Christian University, AL
Southern Connecticut State University, CT
Southern Illinois University Carbondale, IL
Southern Methodist University, TX
Southern Nazarene University, OK
Southern Wesleyan University, SC
Southwestern Adventist University, TX
Southwestern Assemblies of God University, TX
Southwestern Christian College, TX
Southwestern College, AZ
Southwestern College, KS
Southwestern University, TX
Southwest Missouri State University, MO
Spalding University, KY
Spring Arbor College, MI
Spring Hill College, AL
Stephens College, MO
Stetson University, FL
Stevens Institute of Technology, NJ
Stillman College, AL
Syracuse University, NY
Tabor College, KS
Tarleton State University, TX
Taylor University, IN
Taylor University, Fort Wayne Campus, IN
Tennessee Technological University, TN
Tennessee Temple University, TN
Tennessee Wesleyan College, TN
Texas A&M University, TX
Texas Christian University, TX
Texas Tech University, TX
Thiel College, PA
Thomas More College, KY
Thomas University, GA
Touro College, NY
Transylvania University, KY
Trinity Bible College, ND
Trinity Christian College, IL
Truman State University, MO
Tufts University, MA
Tulane University, LA
Tusculum College, TN
Tuskegee University, AL
United States International University, CA
The University of Alabama at Birmingham, AL
U of Alaska Anchorage, AK
The University of Arizona, AZ
University of Arkansas, AR
University of Arkansas at Monticello, AR
University of Bridgeport, CT
University of Central Arkansas, AR
University of Charleston, WV
University of Cincinnati, OH
University of Colorado at Denver, CO
University of Dallas, TX
University of Detroit Mercy, MI
University of Dubuque, IA
The University of Findlay, OH
University of Great Falls, MT
University of Guam, GU
University of Hartford, CT
University of Idaho, ID
University of Illinois at Chicago, IL
University of Illinois at Springfield, IL
University of Indianapolis, IN
University of La Verne, CA
University of Louisiana at Monroe, LA
University of Maine, ME
University of Maine at Fort Kent, ME
University of Maine at Presque Isle, ME
University of Mary, ND
University of Mary Hardin-Baylor, TX
University of Massachusetts Amherst, MA
The University of Memphis, TN
University of Michigan, MI
University of Minnesota, Crookston, MN
University of Mississippi Medical Center, MS
University of Nebraska at Kearney, NE
University of Nebraska at Omaha, NE
University of Nevada, Las Vegas, NV
University of Nevada, Reno, NV
University of New Hampshire, NH
University of New Hampshire at Manchester, NH
University of New Haven, CT
University of New Mexico, NM
University of North Alabama, AL
The University of North Carolina at Asheville, NC
The University of North Carolina at Chapel Hill, NC
University of Northern Colorado, CO
University of Notre Dame, IN
University of Pittsburgh, PA
University of Pittsburgh at Johnstown, PA
University of Portland, OR
U of Puerto Rico, Cayey University College, PR
U of Puerto Rico, Humacao University College, PR
University of Puget Sound, WA
University of Rio Grande, OH
University of St. Thomas, MN
University of St. Thomas, TX
University of San Diego, CA
University of San Francisco, CA
The University of Scranton, PA
University of South Alabama, AL
University of South Carolina, SC
University of Southern Indiana, IN
University of Southern Mississippi, MS
The University of Tampa, FL
University of the District of Columbia, DC
University of the Ozarks, AR
University of the Sacred Heart, PR
University of the South, TN
University of the Virgin Islands, VI
University of Toledo, OH
University of Utah, UT
The University of West Alabama, AL
Urbana University, OH
Ursuline College, OH
Utah State University, UT
Valley Forge Christian College, PA
Valparaiso University, IN
Vanguard University of Southern California, CA
Virginia Military Institute, VA
Virginia Polytechnic Institute and State U, VA
Virginia Union University, VA
Virginia Wesleyan College, VA
Viterbo University, WI
Voorhees College, SC
Wabash College, IN
Wake Forest University, NC
Walla Walla College, WA
Warner Southern College, FL
Wartburg College, IA
Washburn University of Topeka, KS
Washington & Jefferson College, PA

Children of Faculty/Staff (continued)
Washington Bible College, MD
Washington College, MD
Wayland Baptist University, TX
Waynesburg College, PA
Wayne State College, NE
Webber College, FL
Wesleyan College, GA
Western Baptist College, OR
Western Illinois University, IL
Western Michigan University, MI
Western New England College, MA
West Liberty State College, WV
West Texas A&M University, TX
West Virginia University, WV
West Virginia Wesleyan College, WV
Wheeling Jesuit University, WV
Widener University, PA
Wilkes University, PA
William Carey College, MS
William Jewell College, MO
Williams Baptist College, AR
William Tyndale College, MI
William Woods University, MO
Winona State University, MN
Wisconsin Lutheran College, WI
Wittenberg University, OH
Wofford College, SC
Worcester State College, MA
Xavier University of Louisiana, LA
York College, NE
Youngstown State University, OH

CHILDREN OF PUBLIC SERVANTS

Bay Path College, MA
Carthage College, WI
Detroit College of Business, MI
Detroit College of Business–Flint, MI
Detroit College of Business, Warren Campus, MI
Dowling College, NY
Framingham State College, MA
Governors State University, IL
Graceland College, IA
Mercer University, GA
Mississippi State University, MS
New York Institute of Technology, NY
The Ohio State University, OH
Peirce College, PA
Salem State College, MA
Siena College, NY
Sonoma State University, CA
Southern Illinois University Carbondale, IL
Tennessee Technological University, TN
The University of Alabama at Birmingham, AL
University of Colorado at Denver, CO
University of Delaware, DE
The University of Memphis, TN
University of Nevada, Las Vegas, NV
U of Puerto Rico, Cayey University College, PR
University of South Carolina, SC
The University of Texas at Dallas, TX
Valdosta State University, GA
Western Kentucky University, KY
Western Washington University, WA
Westminster College, UT

CHILDREN OF UNION MEMBERS/ COMPANY EMPLOYEES

Alabama State University, AL
Arkansas State University, AR
Barton College, NC
Calvin College, MI
Carroll College, MT
Cincinnati Bible College and Seminary, OH
The College of Saint Rose, NY
The College of West Virginia, WV
Columbia College, MO
Cornerstone University, MI
Dowling College, NY
Eastern Connecticut State University, CT
East Tennessee State University, TN
Edinboro University of Pennsylvania, PA
Emporia State University, KS
Fordham University, NY
Framingham State College, MA
Frostburg State University, MD
Grand Valley State University, MI
Husson College, ME
Illinois State University, IL
Kent State University, OH
Kentucky Wesleyan College, KY
Massachusetts College of Art, MA
Mayville State University, ND
Mercer University, GA
Michigan State University, MI
Mid-Continent College, KY
Millersville University of Pennsylvania, PA
Millikin University, IL
Minnesota State University, Mankato, MN
Montana State U–Billings, MT
Nichols College, MA
Northern Michigan University, MI
Northwood University, Florida Campus, FL
Oakland University, MI
The Ohio State University, OH
Radford University, VA
Sacred Heart University, CT
Saint Paul's College, VA
Salem State College, MA
Seton Hall University, NJ
Siena College, NY
Slippery Rock University of Pennsylvania, PA
Sonoma State University, CA
Southern Vermont College, VT
Southwest State University, MN
State U of NY at Oswego, NY
State University of West Georgia, GA
Stephen F. Austin State University, TX
Texas Christian University, TX
Thomas College, ME
The University of Alabama at Birmingham, AL
University of Guam, GU
University of Illinois at Springfield, IL
University of Maine, ME
University of New Mexico, NM
University of Northern Colorado, CO
U of Puerto Rico at Arecibo, PR
University of South Carolina, SC
The University of Tennessee Knoxville, TN
University of the Incarnate Word, TX
University of the Sciences in Philadelphia, PA
University of Wisconsin–Parkside, WI
Virginia Commonwealth University, VA
Washington College, MD
Waynesburg College, PA
Western Michigan University, MI
Western Washington University, WA
West Virginia University, WV
Wheeling Jesuit University, WV
York College of Pennsylvania, PA
Youngstown State University, OH

CHILDREN OF WORKERS IN TRADES

Adrian College, MI
Arkansas State University, AR
Dowling College, NY
Kennesaw State University, GA
McNeese State University, LA
The Ohio State University, OH
Rockford College, IL
Siena College, NY
Sonoma State University, CA
South Dakota State University, SD
State U of NY at Oswego, NY
The University of Alabama at Birmingham, AL
University of Illinois at Springfield, IL
University of Maine at Machias, ME
University of Michigan, MI
University of Nevada, Las Vegas, NV
University of South Carolina, SC
University of Wisconsin–Parkside, WI
West Virginia University, WV
Worcester Polytechnic Institute, MA
Youngstown State University, OH

CHILDREN WITH A DECEASED OR DISABLED PARENT

Arkansas State University, AR
Bay Path College, MA
California State University, San Bernardino, CA
Citadel, The Military Coll of South Carolina, SC
College of Saint Elizabeth, NJ
Columbia College, MO
David Lipscomb University, TN
Defiance College, OH
Edinboro University of Pennsylvania, PA
Erskine College, SC
Florida Agricultural and Mechanical University, FL
Fordham University, NY
Harding University, AR
Illinois State University, IL
Indiana State University, IN
Indiana U–Purdue U Fort Wayne, IN
Kent State University, OH
Lees-McRae College, NC
Louisiana State University and A&M College, LA
Louisiana Tech University, LA
Marian College of Fond du Lac, WI
McNeese State University, LA
The Ohio State University, OH
St. Norbert College, WI
Seton Hill College, PA
Siena College, NY
Southern Illinois University Carbondale, IL
The University of Alabama at Birmingham, AL
University of Louisiana at Monroe, LA
University of Maine, ME
University of South Carolina, SC
University of Virginia's College at Wise, VA

Worcester State College, MA
Youngstown State University, OH

ETHNIC BACKGROUND

Abilene Christian University, TX
Alabama State University, AL
Albertson College of Idaho, ID
Albion College, MI
Allentown College of St. Francis de Sales, PA
American University, DC
Anna Maria College, MA
Arkansas State University, AR
Assumption College, MA
Auburn University, AL
Austin College, TX
Azusa Pacific University, CA
Baker University, KS
Barton College, NC
Bellarmine College, KY
Benedictine College, KS
Berry College, GA
Bethany College, WV
Bethel College, MN
Biola University, CA
Boise State University, ID
Brenau University, GA
Brescia University, KY
Bridgewater College, VA
Brigham Young University, UT
Brigham Young University–Hawaii Campus, HI
California College of Arts and Crafts, CA
California Institute of the Arts, CA
California State University, Chico, CA
California State University, Dominguez Hills, CA
California State University, San Bernardino, CA
California University of Pennsylvania, PA
Calvin College, MI
Capital University, OH
Cedar Crest College, PA
Centenary College, NJ
Central Bible College, MO
Central Missouri State University, MO
Chaminade University of Honolulu, HI
Cheyney University of Pennsylvania, PA
Claremont McKenna College, CA
Clarkson College, NE
Clemson University, SC
College of Saint Benedict, MN
College of St. Catherine, MN
The College of Saint Rose, NY
Colorado School of Mines, CO
Columbia College Chicago, IL
Columbia International University, SC
Concordia University, CA
Cornerstone University, MI
Dakota Wesleyan University, SD
Dana College, NE
Davidson College, NC
DePauw University, IN
Dickinson State University, ND
Drake University, IA
Duke University, NC
East Carolina University, NC
Eastern Mennonite University, VA
Eastern Michigan University, MI
Eastern Nazarene College, MA
Eastern New Mexico University, NM
Eastern Washington University, WA
Emporia State University, KS
Florida Agricultural and Mechanical University, FL
Fort Lewis College, CO
Gannon University, PA
George Fox University, OR
Georgia Institute of Technology, GA
Goshen College, IN
Grambling State University, LA
Grand Canyon University, AZ
Guilford College, NC
Hardin-Simmons University, TX
Hawaii Pacific University, HI
Humphreys College, CA
Illinois Institute of Technology, IL
Indiana University of Pennsylvania, PA
Iowa State University of Science and Technology, IA
John Brown University, AR
Johnson Bible College, TN
Juniata College, PA
Kent State University, OH
Kenyon College, OH
Lebanon Valley College, PA
Lesley College, MA
Lewis-Clark State College, ID
Life University, GA
Long Island U, Brooklyn Campus, NY
Long Island U, Southampton College, NY
Loyola University Chicago, IL
Lyon College, AR
Maharishi University of Management, IA
Manchester College, IN
Marycrest International University, IA
Marywood University, PA
McNeese State University, LA
Messiah College, PA
Michigan State University, MI
Michigan Technological University, MI
Millikin University, IL
Millsaps College, MS
Milwaukee Institute of Art and Design, WI
Minot State University, ND
Mississippi University for Women, MS
Montana State U–Billings, MT
Moravian College, PA
Nazarene Indian Bible College, NM
Newman University, KS
North Carolina Agricultural and Technical State U, NC
North Dakota State University, ND
Northland College, WI
Northwest Nazarene University, ID
The Ohio State University, OH
Oregon Health Sciences University, OR
Oregon Institute of Technology, OR
Pine Manor College, MA
Prairie View A&M University, TX
Purchase College, State U of NY, NY
Regis University, CO
Rhodes College, TN
The Richard Stockton College of New Jersey, NJ
Robert Morris College, PA
Rust College, MS
Sacred Heart University, CT
St. John Fisher College, NY
Saint Luke's College, MO
Saint Martin's College, WA
Saint Mary-of-the-Woods College, IN
St. Norbert College, WI
Seton Hall University, NJ
Shawnee State University, OH
Sheldon Jackson College, AK
Shepherd College, WV
Shippensburg University of Pennsylvania, PA
Siena College, NY
Sierra Nevada College, NV
Slippery Rock University of Pennsylvania, PA
Sonoma State University, CA
Southern Utah University, UT
Southwestern College, KS
Southwest Missouri State University, MO
Southwest State University, MN
State U of NY at Oswego, NY
State U of NY College at Fredonia, NY
State U of NY College at Oneonta, NY
State U of NY College at Potsdam, NY
Stetson University, FL
Taylor University, IN
Taylor University, Fort Wayne Campus, IN
Tennessee Technological University, TN
Texas A&M University–Commerce, TX
Truman State University, MO
United States International University, CA
The University of Alabama at Birmingham, AL
U of Alaska Anchorage, AK
The University of Arizona, AZ
University of Arkansas, AR
U of Calif, San Diego, CA
University of Central Oklahoma, OK
University of Colorado at Colorado Springs, CO
University of Dubuque, IA
University of Great Falls, MT
University of Idaho, ID
University of Illinois at Springfield, IL
University of Kansas, KS
University of Maine, ME
University of Maine at Presque Isle, ME
University of Miami, FL
University of Michigan–Dearborn, MI
University of Minnesota, Crookston, MN
University of Minnesota, Morris, MN
University of Missouri–St. Louis, MO
University of Nebraska at Omaha, NE
University of Nebraska–Lincoln, NE
University of Nevada, Las Vegas, NV
University of Nevada, Reno, NV
University of New Hampshire at Manchester, NH
The University of North Carolina at Asheville, NC
The University of North Carolina at Greensboro, NC
University of Northern Colorado, CO
University of Rochester, NY
University of St. Francis, IL
University of South Carolina, SC
University of Southern Mississippi, MS
The University of Tennessee at Martin, TN
The University of Tennessee Knoxville, TN
The University of Texas at El Paso, TX
The University of Texas at San Antonio, TX
University of the South, TN
University of Toledo, OH
University of Virginia's College at Wise, VA
University of Wisconsin–Eau Claire, WI

Ethnic Background (continued)

University of Wisconsin–La Crosse, WI
University of Wisconsin–Parkside, WI
University of Wisconsin–Whitewater, WI
University of Wyoming, WY
Utah State University, UT
Valley City State University, ND
Valparaiso University, IN
Wabash College, IN
Wartburg College, IA
Wayland Baptist University, TX
Western Carolina University, NC
Western Michigan University, MI
Western Washington University, WA
Westminster College, UT
Westmont College, CA
West Virginia State College, WV
West Virginia University, WV
Whitman College, WA
Widener University, PA
Wilkes University, PA
Wittenberg University, OH

FIRST-GENERATION COLLEGE STUDENTS

Abilene Christian University, TX
Arkansas State University, AR
Assumption College, MA
Austin College, TX
Boise State University, ID
Bowie State University, MD
California Maritime Academy, CA
California State University, Bakersfield, CA
California State University, Chico, CA
California State University, San Bernardino, CA
California State University, Stanislaus, CA
Central College, IA
Central Missouri State University, MO
Clearwater Christian College, FL
Coastal Carolina University, SC
The College of West Virginia, WV
Colorado State University, CO
Columbia College Chicago, IL
Concordia University, CA
David N. Myers College, OH
Defiance College, OH
Dowling College, NY
Eastern New Mexico University, NM
Edgewood College, WI
Edinboro University of Pennsylvania, PA
Finlandia University, MI
Fort Lewis College, CO
Glenville State College, WV
Goshen College, IN
Idaho State University, ID
Illinois State University, IL
Iowa State University of Science and Technology, IA
Lewis-Clark State College, ID
Long Island U, Brooklyn Campus, NY
Lyon College, AR
Massachusetts College of Liberal Arts, MA
McNeese State University, LA
Mesa State College, CO
Michigan State University, MI
Mississippi State University, MS
Morningside College, IA
Nyack College, NY
Paul Quinn College, TX
Pontifical Catholic University of Puerto Rico, PR
Rochester College, MI
Saint Mary-of-the-Woods College, IN
Salem State College, MA
Shawnee State University, OH
Silver Lake College, WI
Sonoma State University, CA
Southwest Missouri State University, MO
Southwest State University, MN
Southwest Texas State University, TX
Stephen F. Austin State University, TX
Tennessee Technological University, TN
Texas Lutheran University, TX
The University of Alabama at Birmingham, AL
U of Calif, San Diego, CA
University of Colorado at Boulder, CO
University of Colorado at Colorado Springs, CO
University of Colorado at Denver, CO
University of Great Falls, MT
University of Idaho, ID
University of Illinois at Springfield, IL
University of Kansas, KS
University of La Verne, CA
University of Maine, ME
University of Nebraska at Omaha, NE
University of Nevada, Las Vegas, NV
University of Nevada, Reno, NV
University of North Alabama, AL
The University of North Carolina at Asheville, NC
University of North Florida, FL
University of Saint Francis, IN
University of South Carolina, SC
University of Southern Colorado, CO
The University of Tennessee Knoxville, TN
The University of Texas at Arlington, TX
University of Wisconsin–Eau Claire, WI
University of Wyoming, WY
Valparaiso University, IN
West Texas A&M University, TX
Whitman College, WA
Wichita State University, KS
William Carey College, MS

HANDICAPPED STUDENTS

Agnes Scott College, GA
Alabama State University, AL
Arkansas State University, AR
Austin College, TX
Barry University, FL
Barton College, NC
Bloomfield College, NJ
Boise State University, ID
Bowie State University, MD
Brigham Young University, UT
Bryan College, TN
California State University, Chico, CA
California State University, Fresno, CA
Calvin College, MI
College of Saint Elizabeth, NJ
The College of Wooster, OH
Columbia College Chicago, IL
Dordt College, IA
East Carolina University, NC
Eastern Washington University, WA
East Stroudsburg University of Pennsylvania, PA
Edgewood College, WI
Edinboro University of Pennsylvania, PA
Emporia State University, KS
Fordham University, NY
Fort Valley State University, GA
Francis Marion University, SC
Frostburg State University, MD
Gallaudet University, DC
Gardner-Webb University, NC
Georgia Southern University, GA
Grand Valley State University, MI
Idaho State University, ID
Illinois State University, IL
Indiana U–Purdue U Fort Wayne, IN
Kent State University, OH
Lebanon Valley College, PA
LeMoyne-Owen College, TN
Lock Haven University of Pennsylvania, PA
Massachusetts College of Liberal Arts, MA
Midland Lutheran College, NE
Miles College, AL
Mississippi State University, MS
Murray State University, KY
North Carolina Agricultural and Technical State U, NC
Northern Arizona University, AZ
The Ohio State University, OH
Old Dominion University, VA
Roanoke Bible College, NC
Rockford College, IL
Rowan University, NJ
St. Gregory's University, OK
Sam Houston State University, TX
San Diego State University, CA
Shawnee State University, OH
Sheldon Jackson College, AK
Sonoma State University, CA
South Dakota State University, SD
Southeastern Louisiana University, LA
Southern Illinois University Carbondale, IL
Southwest Missouri State University, MO
Southwest State University, MN
Southwest Texas State University, TX
State U of NY College at Oneonta, NY
State U of NY College at Potsdam, NY
State University of West Georgia, GA
Texas Tech University, TX
Trevecca Nazarene University, TN
The University of Akron, OH
The University of Alabama at Birmingham, AL
U of Calif, San Diego, CA
University of Central Arkansas, AR
University of Colorado at Colorado Springs, CO
University of Colorado at Denver, CO
University of Idaho, ID
University of Maine, ME
University of Mary Hardin-Baylor, TX
University of Massachusetts Amherst, MA
The University of Memphis, TN
University of Michigan, MI
University of Nebraska at Omaha, NE
University of Nebraska–Lincoln, NE
University of Nevada, Las Vegas, NV
University of New Hampshire, NH
The University of North Carolina at Asheville, NC
The University of North Carolina at Greensboro, NC

University of Northern Colorado, CO
University of South Carolina, SC
The University of Tennessee at Martin, TN
The University of Tennessee Knoxville, TN
The University of Texas at Arlington, TX
The University of Texas at Dallas, TX
The University of Texas at San Antonio, TX
University of Toledo, OH
University of Wisconsin–Whitewater, WI
University of Wyoming, WY
Utah State University, UT
West Texas A&M University, TX
Worcester State College, MA
Youngstown State University, OH

INTERNATIONAL STUDENTS

Agnes Scott College, GA
Albright College, PA
Alfred University, NY
Allentown College of St. Francis de Sales, PA
Alvernia College, PA
Anderson University, IN
Appalachian Bible College, WV
Asbury College, KY
Augsburg College, MN
Augustana College, IL
Augustana College, SD
Austin College, TX
Azusa Pacific University, CA
Baker University, KS
Baltimore Hebrew University, MD
Barclay College, KS
Barry University, FL
Barton College, NC
Bay Path College, MA
Belhaven College, MS
Bellarmine College, KY
Bellevue University, NE
Belmont Abbey College, NC
Benedictine College, KS
Bethany College, KS
Bethel College, IN
Bethel College, KS
Bethel College, MN
Beulah Heights Bible College, GA
Biola University, CA
Bloomsburg University of Pennsylvania, PA
Bluffton College, OH
Boise Bible College, ID
Boise State University, ID
Bowling Green State University, OH
Brescia University, KY
Briar Cliff College, IA
Brigham Young University, UT
Brigham Young University–Hawaii Campus, HI
Bryan College, TN
Buena Vista University, IA
Caldwell College, NJ
California Lutheran University, CA
California State University, Chico, CA
California University of Pennsylvania, PA
Calvin College, MI
Canisius College, NY
Capital University, OH
Carlow College, PA
Carroll College, MT
Carroll College, WI
Cascade College, OR
Centenary College of Louisiana, LA
Central College, IA
Central Methodist College, MO
Central Michigan University, MI
Chadron State College, NE
Chaminade University of Honolulu, HI
Chatham College, PA
Chowan College, NC
Christian Heritage College, CA
Cincinnati Bible College and Seminary, OH
Circleville Bible College, OH
Clarke College, IA
Clarkson College, NE
Clarkson University, NY
Coastal Carolina University, SC
Coe College, IA
College of Notre Dame of Maryland, MD
College of Saint Benedict, MN
College of St. Catherine, MN
College of Saint Elizabeth, NJ
The College of St. Scholastica, MN
The College of Wooster, OH
The Colorado College, CO
Columbia International University, SC
Concordia College, MN
Concordia University, CA
Concordia University, IL
Concordia University, NE
Cornerstone University, MI
Covenant College, GA
Dana College, NE
David Lipscomb University, TN
DePauw University, IN
Dickinson College, PA
Dickinson State University, ND
Dominican University, IL
Dordt College, IA
Drake University, IA
Duquesne University, PA
Eastern Connecticut State University, CT
Eastern Kentucky University, KY
Eastern Mennonite University, VA
Eastern Michigan University, MI
Eastern Nazarene College, MA
Eastern New Mexico University, NM
Eastern Oregon University, OR
Eastern Washington University, WA
East Stroudsburg University of Pennsylvania, PA
East Texas Baptist University, TX
Eckerd College, FL
Edinboro University of Pennsylvania, PA
Elizabethtown College, PA
Elmira College, NY
Emmanuel College, MA
Emmaus Bible College, IA
Emporia State University, KS
Fairleigh Dickinson U, Florham-Madison Campus, NJ
Fairleigh Dickinson U, Teaneck-Hackensack Campus, NJ
Ferrum College, VA
Fort Valley State University, GA
Franciscan University of Steubenville, OH
Francis Marion University, SC
Franklin Pierce College, NH
Fresno Pacific University, CA
Friends University, KS
Gallaudet University, DC
Gannon University, PA
George Fox University, OR
The George Washington University, DC
Georgia College and State University, GA
Goshen College, IN
Graceland College, IA
Grambling State University, LA
Greensboro College, NC
Greenville College, IL
Hampton University, VA
Hanover College, IN
Harding University, AR
Hawaii Pacific University, HI
Henderson State University, AR
Hendrix College, AR
Hillsdale College, MI
Hope International University, CA
Huntingdon College, AL
Huntington College, IN
Illinois Institute of Technology, IL
Illinois Wesleyan University, IL
Iowa State University of Science and Technology, IA
Iowa Wesleyan College, IA
John Brown University, AR
Johnson Bible College, TN
Johnson State College, VT
Judson College, IL
Juniata College, PA
Kalamazoo College, MI
Kendall College, IL
Kent State University, OH
King's College, PA
Lancaster Bible College, PA
Lawrence University, WI
Lees-McRae College, NC
LeMoyne-Owen College, TN
LeTourneau University, TX
Liberty University, VA
Life University, GA
Long Island U, Brooklyn Campus, NY
Long Island U, C.W. Post Campus, NY
Lourdes College, OH
Lyon College, AR
MacMurray College, IL
Maharishi University of Management, IA
Maine College of Art, ME
Malone College, OH
Manchester College, IN
Marian College, IN
Marycrest International University, IA
Maryland Institute, College of Art, MD
Marymount Manhattan College, NY
Marywood University, PA
The Master's College and Seminary, CA
Mayville State University, ND
McMurry University, TX
McNeese State University, LA
Mercer University, GA
Messiah College, PA
Michigan Technological University, MI
Mid-America Bible College, OK
Midland Lutheran College, NE
Millikin University, IL
Minnesota Bible College, MN
Minot State University, ND
Mississippi University for Women, MS
Monmouth University, NJ
Montana State U–Northern, MT
Montreat College, NC
Moravian College, PA
Morningside College, IA

International Students (continued)

Mount Marty College, SD
Mount Mary College, WI
Mount St. Clare College, IA
Mount Senario College, WI
Mount Union College, OH
Mount Vernon Nazarene College, OH
Multnomah Bible College and Biblical Seminary, OR
Murray State University, KY
Nebraska Christian College, NE
Newman University, KS
North Dakota State University, ND
Northern Arizona University, AZ
Northern Illinois University, IL
Northwest College, WA
Northwestern College, IA
Northwest Nazarene University, ID
Nyack College, NY
Oak Hills Christian College, MN
Ohio Wesleyan University, OH
Oklahoma Christian U of Science and Arts, OK
Old Dominion University, VA
Olivet Nazarene University, IL
Oral Roberts University, OK
Otterbein College, OH
Ouachita Baptist University, AR
Ozark Christian College, MO
Pacific Lutheran University, WA
Pacific Union College, CA
Pacific University, OR
Palmer College of Chiropractic, IA
Philadelphia College of Bible, PA
Piedmont College, GA
Pine Manor College, MA
Plattsburgh State U of NY, NY
Plymouth State College, NH
Practical Bible College, NY
Queens College, NC
Ramapo College of New Jersey, NJ
Randolph-Macon Woman's College, VA
Reformed Bible College, MI
Ripon College, WI
Roanoke Bible College, NC
Roberts Wesleyan College, NY
Rochester Institute of Technology, NY
Rockford College, IL
Rockhurst University, MO
Rocky Mountain College, MT
Rowan University, NJ
Rust College, MS
Saginaw Valley State University, MI
St. Ambrose University, IA
St. Gregory's University, OK
Saint John's University, MN
Saint Joseph's College, ME
Saint Martin's College, WA
Saint Mary-of-the-Woods College, IN
St. Norbert College, WI
Saint Vincent College, PA
Saint Xavier University, IL
Seton Hill College, PA
Sheldon Jackson College, AK
Simpson College, IA
Simpson College and Graduate School, CA
Sonoma State University, CA
Southeast Missouri State University, MO
Southern Adventist University, TN
Southern Illinois University Carbondale, IL
Southwestern College, KS
Southwest Missouri State University, MO
Southwest State University, MN
Spalding University, KY
Spring Arbor College, MI
State U of NY at Oswego, NY
State U of NY College at Fredonia, NY
State U of NY College at Oneonta, NY
State University of West Georgia, GA
Stetson University, FL
Stevens Institute of Technology, NJ
Sweet Briar College, VA
Tabor College, KS
Taylor University, IN
Taylor University, Fort Wayne Campus, IN
Tennessee Wesleyan College, TN
Texas Christian University, TX
Texas Lutheran University, TX
Thomas More College, KY
Toccoa Falls College, GA
Trinity Bible College, ND
Trinity Lutheran College, WA
Truman State University, MO
United States International University, CA
U of Alaska Anchorage, AK
U of Alaska Southeast, AK
The University of Arizona, AZ
University of Arkansas, AR
University of Charleston, WV
University of Evansville, IN
University of Great Falls, MT
University of Guam, GU
University of Hartford, CT
University of Idaho, ID
University of Illinois at Springfield, IL
University of Indianapolis, IN
University of Kansas, KS
University of La Verne, CA
University of Louisiana at Monroe, LA
University of Maine, ME
University of Maine at Fort Kent, ME
University of Maine at Presque Isle, ME
University of Mary Hardin-Baylor, TX
University of Michigan, MI
University of Minnesota, Morris, MN
University of Missouri–Rolla, MO
University of Montevallo, AL
University of Nebraska at Kearney, NE
University of Nebraska at Omaha, NE
University of Nebraska–Lincoln, NE
University of Nevada, Las Vegas, NV
University of New Hampshire, NH
The University of North Carolina at Asheville, NC
The University of North Carolina at Chapel Hill, NC
University of Northern Colorado, CO
University of Puget Sound, WA
University of Redlands, CA
University of Science and Arts of Oklahoma, OK
University of South Carolina, SC
The University of Tampa, FL
The University of Texas at Dallas, TX
The University of Texas at El Paso, TX
The University of Texas–Pan American, TX
University of Washington, WA
University of Wisconsin–Eau Claire, WI
University of Wisconsin–Stout, WI
University of Wisconsin–Whitewater, WI
University of Wyoming, WY
Utah State University, UT
Valdosta State University, GA
Valley City State University, ND
Valparaiso University, IN
Voorhees College, SC
Wabash College, IN
Wadhams Hall Seminary-College, NY
Walsh University, OH
Warner Southern College, FL
Washington College, MD
Washington State University, WA
Wayne State College, NE
Wesley College, DE
Western Baptist College, OR
Western Illinois University, IL
Western Michigan University, MI
Western Oregon University, OR
Western Washington University, WA
Westminster College, PA
Westminster College, UT
Westmont College, CA
West Virginia University, WV
West Virginia Wesleyan College, WV
Wheeling Jesuit University, WV
Whitman College, WA
Whittier College, CA
Whitworth College, WA
Wichita State University, KS
Widener University, PA
Willamette University, OR
William Carey College, MS
William Tyndale College, MI
Wisconsin Lutheran College, WI
Wittenberg University, OH
Xavier University, OH
York College of Pennsylvania, PA

LOCAL/STATE STUDENTS

Abilene Christian University, TX
Agnes Scott College, GA
Alabama State University, AL
Alaska Bible College, AK
Albertson College of Idaho, ID
Albright College, PA
Alcorn State University, MS
Allen College, IA
Allentown College of St. Francis de Sales, PA
Antioch College, OH
Assumption College, MA
Augusta State University, GA
Austin College, TX
Barber-Scotia College, NC
Barclay College, KS
Barton College, NC
Bellarmine College, KY
Belmont Abbey College, NC
Benedictine College, KS
Berry College, GA
Bethany College, WV
Bluefield College, VA
Boise State University, ID
Boston University, MA
Brevard College, NC
Brigham Young University, UT
Bryan College, TN
California Maritime Academy, CA
California State University, Chico, CA
California State University, Fresno, CA

California State University, San Bernardino, CA
California State University, Stanislaus, CA
Calumet College of Saint Joseph, IN
Carroll College, MT
Carthage College, WI
Centenary College, NJ
Centenary College of Louisiana, LA
Central College, IA
Central Michigan University, MI
Centre College, KY
Chadron State College, NE
Chaminade University of Honolulu, HI
Chowan College, NC
Citadel, The Military Coll of South Carolina, SC
Clarion University of Pennsylvania, PA
Clarkson University, NY
Clearwater Christian College, FL
Clemson University, SC
Coastal Carolina University, SC
College of St. Catherine, MN
The College of Wooster, OH
Columbia College, MO
Columbia Union College, MD
Columbus College of Art and Design, OH
Comm Hospital Roanoke Valley–Coll of Health Scis, VA
Concordia University, NE
Creighton University, NE
Culver-Stockton College, MO
Dana College, NE
Davis & Elkins College, WV
Defiance College, OH
Detroit College of Business, MI
Detroit College of Business–Flint, MI
Detroit College of Business, Warren Campus, MI
Dordt College, IA
Dowling College, NY
Duke University, NC
East Carolina University, NC
Eastern Connecticut State University, CT
East Texas Baptist University, TX
Eckerd College, FL
Edgewood College, WI
Edinboro University of Pennsylvania, PA
Elizabethtown College, PA
Elmira College, NY
Emporia State University, KS
Endicott College, MA
Fayetteville State University, NC
Ferrum College, VA
Florida Institute of Technology, FL
Florida Southern College, FL
Florida State University, FL
Fort Lewis College, CO
Fort Valley State University, GA
Framingham State College, MA
Franciscan University of Steubenville, OH
Franklin and Marshall College, PA
Franklin College of Indiana, IN
Franklin Pierce College, NH
Frostburg State University, MD
Gardner-Webb University, NC
The George Washington University, DC
Georgia Southern University, GA
Georgia Southwestern State University, GA
Goddard College, VT
Graceland College, IA
Grambling State University, LA
Grand Valley State University, MI
Green Mountain College, VT
Greenville College, IL
Hamline University, MN
Heidelberg College, OH
Hollins University, VA
Hope International University, CA
Idaho State University, ID
Illinois College, IL
Illinois Institute of Technology, IL
Illinois State University, IL
Indiana Institute of Technology, IN
Indiana U–Purdue U Fort Wayne, IN
Johnson State College, VT
Judson College, IL
Juniata College, PA
Kennesaw State University, GA
Kettering University, MI
Laboratory Institute of Merchandising, NY
Lawrence University, WI
Lees-McRae College, NC
Lesley College, MA
LeTourneau University, TX
Limestone College, SC
Lincoln University, MO
Lock Haven University of Pennsylvania, PA
Long Island U, Southampton College, NY
Longwood College, VA
Lourdes College, OH
Loyola College in Maryland, MD
Lyon College, AR
Maharishi University of Management, IA
Maine Maritime Academy, ME
Mansfield University of Pennsylvania, PA
Martin Methodist College, TN
Maryland Institute, College of Art, MD
Maryville College, TN
Mary Washington College, VA
Marywood University, PA
Massachusetts College of Liberal Arts, MA
Mayville State University, ND
McMurry University, TX
McNeese State University, LA
Medcenter One College of Nursing, ND
Mercer University, GA
Mercyhurst College, PA
Meredith College, NC
Mesa State College, CO
Metropolitan College of Court Reporting, NM
Miami University, OH
Michigan Technological University, MI
Milwaukee Institute of Art and Design, WI
Minnesota State University, Mankato, MN
Minot State University, ND
Mississippi State University, MS
Montana State U–Billings, MT
Montreat College, NC
Morehead State University, KY
Morningside College, IA
Mount St. Clare College, IA
Mount Senario College, WI
Mount Vernon Nazarene College, OH
Murray State University, KY
Muskingum College, OH
Newberry College, SC
New England College, NH
New Hampshire College, NH
New York Institute of Technology, NY
North Dakota State University, ND
Northern Arizona University, AZ
Northwood University, Florida Campus, FL
Northwood University, Texas Campus, TX
Ohio University–Chillicothe, OH
Ohio Wesleyan University, OH
Oklahoma Baptist University, OK
Oklahoma Panhandle State University, OK
Old Dominion University, VA
Ottawa University, KS
Paine College, GA
Paul Quinn College, TX
Peirce College, PA
Pine Manor College, MA
Point Loma Nazarene University, CA
Pontifical College Josephinum, OH
Quinnipiac University, CT
Randolph-Macon Woman's College, VA
Regis University, CO
Reinhardt College, GA
The Richard Stockton College of New Jersey, NJ
Roanoke College, VA
Rockhurst University, MO
Rose-Hulman Institute of Technology, IN
Rust College, MS
Sacred Heart Major Seminary, MI
St. Bonaventure University, NY
St. John Fisher College, NY
Saint Joseph's College, ME
St. Louis Christian College, MO
St. Louis College of Pharmacy, MO
Saint Martin's College, WA
Saint Mary-of-the-Woods College, IN
Saint Michael's College, VT
Shawnee State University, OH
Shenandoah University, VA
Shippensburg University of Pennsylvania, PA
Shorter College, GA
Siena College, NY
Sierra Nevada College, NV
Simon's Rock College of Bard, MA
Smith College, MA
Southeastern Bible College, AL
Southeastern Louisiana University, LA
Southeastern University, DC
Southern Adventist University, TN
Southern Nazarene University, OK
Southwest Baptist University, MO
Southwestern Christian College, TX
Southwestern College, KS
Southwestern Oklahoma State University, OK
Southwest State University, MN
State U of NY at Buffalo, NY
State U of NY at Oswego, NY
State U of NY College at Brockport, NY
State U of NY College at Geneseo, NY
State U of NY College at Oneonta, NY
State U of NY Institute of Tech at Utica/Rome, NY
State University of West Georgia, GA
Stephen F. Austin State University, TX
Stephens College, MO
Stetson University, FL
Stevens Institute of Technology, NJ
Sweet Briar College, VA
Teikyo Post University, CT
Tennessee State University, TN
Tennessee Temple University, TN
Texas Christian University, TX
Thomas College, ME

Local/State Students (continued)

Tiffin University, OH
Trinity Christian College, IL
Tulane University, LA
Tusculum College, TN
Tuskegee University, AL
United States International University, CA
Unity College, ME
University of Advancing Computer Technology, AZ
The University of Akron, OH
The University of Alabama at Birmingham, AL
The University of Alabama in Huntsville, AL
University of Arkansas at Little Rock, AR
University of Bridgeport, CT
University of Charleston, WV
University of Colorado at Boulder, CO
University of Delaware, DE
University of Georgia, GA
University of Hartford, CT
University of Idaho, ID
University of Illinois at Springfield, IL
University of Kansas, KS
University of Maine, ME
University of Maine at Machias, ME
University of Mary Hardin-Baylor, TX
University of Michigan, MI
University of Mississippi, MS
University of Mississippi Medical Center, MS
University of Missouri–St. Louis, MO
University of Nevada, Las Vegas, NV
University of New Hampshire, NH
The University of North Carolina at Asheville, NC
The University of North Carolina at Wilmington, NC
University of Northern Colorado, CO
U of Puerto Rico at Arecibo, PR
University of Rio Grande, OH
University of Rochester, NY
University of Southern California, CA
University of Southern Maine, ME
The University of Tennessee Knoxville, TN
The University of Texas at Dallas, TX
The University of Texas at El Paso, TX
The University of Texas at San Antonio, TX
University of the Sciences in Philadelphia, PA
University of Toledo, OH
University of Virginia's College at Wise, VA
University of Wisconsin–Eau Claire, WI
University of Wisconsin–Oshkosh, WI
University of Wisconsin–Parkside, WI
University of Wisconsin–Stout, WI
University of Wisconsin–Whitewater, WI
University of Wyoming, WY
Utah State University, UT
Valley City State University, ND
Vanderbilt University, TN
Virginia Military Institute, VA
Virginia Polytechnic Institute and State U, VA
Virginia Wesleyan College, VA
Walsh University, OH
Washington and Lee University, VA
Wayland Baptist University, TX
Webber College, FL
Western Carolina University, NC
Western Maryland College, MD
Western Washington University, WA
Westminster College, UT
West Virginia University, WV
William Woods University, MO
Wilson College, PA
Wingate University, NC
Winona State University, MN
Wittenberg University, OH
Worcester State College, MA

MARRIED STUDENTS

Appalachian Bible College, WV
Baltimore Hebrew University, MD
Baptist Bible College of Pennsylvania, PA
Beulah Heights Bible College, GA
California State University, Chico, CA
Columbia International University, SC
Eugene Bible College, OR
Johnson Bible College, TN
John Wesley College, NC
Lancaster Bible College, PA
Messiah College, PA
Metropolitan College of Court Reporting, NM
Mid-Continent College, KY
Northwest College, WA
Paul Quinn College, TX
Practical Bible College, NY
Roanoke Bible College, NC
Southwestern Adventist University, TX
State U of NY College at Brockport, NY
The University of Alabama at Birmingham, AL
University of Kansas, KS
University of Wisconsin–Parkside, WI
Valley Forge Christian College, PA

MEMBERS OF MINORITY GROUPS

Abilene Christian University, TX
Alabama State University, AL
Albertson College of Idaho, ID
Albright College, PA
Alcorn State University, MS
Alice Lloyd College, KY
Allentown College of St. Francis de Sales, PA
American University, DC
Anna Maria College, MA
Assumption College, MA
Auburn University, AL
Augsburg College, MN
Augustana College, IL
Augustana College, SD
Aurora University, IL
Baker University, KS
Baldwin-Wallace College, OH
Barry University, FL
Barton College, NC
Beloit College, WI
Benedictine College, KS
Bentley College, MA
Berry College, GA
Bethel College, MN
Bluefield College, VA
Bluffton College, OH
Bowling Green State University, OH
Bradley University, IL
Brescia University, KY
Briar Cliff College, IA
Brigham Young University, UT
Bryant College, RI
California Institute of the Arts, CA
California State Polytechnic University, Pomona, CA
California State University, Chico, CA
California State University, Dominguez Hills, CA
California State University, Stanislaus, CA
California University of Pennsylvania, PA
Calvin College, MI
Cameron University, OK
Capital University, OH
Carson-Newman College, TN
Centenary College of Louisiana, LA
Central College, IA
Central Connecticut State University, CT
Central Michigan University, MI
Centre College, KY
Chadron State College, NE
Clarion University of Pennsylvania, PA
Clarkson University, NY
Clemson University, SC
The College of New Jersey, NJ
College of Saint Elizabeth, NJ
The College of Saint Rose, NY
The College of Wooster, OH
Colorado School of Mines, CO
Columbia College Chicago, IL
Columbia International University, SC
Concordia College, MN
Concordia University, CA
Concordia University, NE
Cornerstone University, MI
Covenant College, GA
Creighton University, NE
Crichton College, TN
Dana College, NE
David Lipscomb University, TN
Davidson College, NC
Defiance College, OH
Denison University, OH
DePauw University, IN
Dominican University of California, CA
Dordt College, IA
Drake University, IA
Duquesne University, PA
East Central University, OK
Eastern Connecticut State University, CT
Eastern Michigan University, MI
Eastern Nazarene College, MA
Eastern New Mexico University, NM
Eastern Oregon University, OR
East Stroudsburg University of Pennsylvania, PA
East Tennessee State University, TN
Edgewood College, WI
Edinboro University of Pennsylvania, PA
Elizabethtown College, PA
Elmhurst College, IL
Emporia State University, KS
The Evergreen State College, WA
Flagler College, FL
Florida International University, FL
Fort Hays State University, KS
Fort Lewis College, CO
Fort Valley State University, GA
Franklin University, OH
Gannon University, PA
Gardner-Webb University, NC
George Fox University, OR
Georgia College and State University, GA
Georgia Institute of Technology, GA

Golden Gate University, CA
Gonzaga University, WA
Governors State University, IL
Graceland College, IA
Grambling State University, LA
Grand Canyon University, AZ
Grand Valley State University, MI
Grove City College, PA
Guilford College, NC
Hampton University, VA
Hanover College, IN
Hendrix College, AR
Hilbert College, NY
Hiram College, OH
Humphreys College, CA
Idaho State University, ID
Illinois College, IL
Illinois Institute of Technology, IL
Illinois State University, IL
Indiana State University, IN
Iowa State University of Science and Technology, IA
Iowa Wesleyan College, IA
James Madison University, VA
John Brown University, AR
Johnson Bible College, TN
Johnson State College, VT
Kalamazoo College, MI
Kendall College, IL
Kennesaw State University, GA
Kent State University, OH
Kentucky Christian College, KY
King College, TN
Lander University, SC
La Roche College, PA
La Salle University, PA
Lawrence University, WI
Le Moyne College, NY
Lesley College, MA
Lewis-Clark State College, ID
Lock Haven University of Pennsylvania, PA
Lourdes College, OH
Loyola College in Maryland, MD
Manchester College, IN
Mansfield University of Pennsylvania, PA
Marian College, IN
Marycrest International University, IA
Maryville College, TN
Maryville University of Saint Louis, MO
Mary Washington College, VA
Mayville State University, ND
McNeese State University, LA
Mercer University, GA
Mercyhurst College, PA
Mesa State College, CO
Messiah College, PA
Miami University, OH
Michigan State University, MI
Michigan Technological University, MI
Mid-America Bible College, OK
Middle Tennessee State University, TN
Midland Lutheran College, NE
Midway College, KY
Millsaps College, MS
Milwaukee Institute of Art and Design, WI
Minnesota State University Moorhead, MN
Minot State University, ND
Mississippi College, MS
Mississippi University for Women, MS
Mississippi Valley State University, MS
Missouri Western State College, MO
Montana State U–Northern, MT
Moody Bible Institute, IL
Morehead State University, KY
Mount Angel Seminary, OR
Mount Saint Mary's College and Seminary, MD
Murray State University, KY
Muskingum College, OH
North Carolina Agricultural and Technical State U, NC
North Dakota State University, ND
Northeastern Illinois University, IL
Northern Illinois University, IL
Northern Kentucky University, KY
Northern Michigan University, MI
Northwest Missouri State University, MO
Northwest Nazarene University, ID
The Ohio State University, OH
Ohio University, OH
Ohio University–Chillicothe, OH
Ohio University–Eastern, OH
Ohio University–Lancaster, OH
Ohio Wesleyan University, OH
Oklahoma State U, OK
Old Dominion University, VA
Oregon Institute of Technology, OR
Otterbein College, OH
Pacific Union College, CA
Palmer College of Chiropractic, IA
Pikeville College, KY
Pine Manor College, MA
Plattsburgh State U of NY, NY
Purchase College, State U of NY, NY
Queens College, NC
Radford University, VA
Regis University, CO
The Richard Stockton College of New Jersey, NJ
Rider University, NJ
Ripon College, WI
Rivier College, NH
Roanoke College, VA
Robert Morris College, PA
Rochester Institute of Technology, NY
Rocky Mountain College, MT
Rose-Hulman Institute of Technology, IN
Rowan University, NJ
Rush University, IL
Rust College, MS
Sacred Heart University, CT
Saint Anselm College, NH
St. Bonaventure University, NY
St. John Fisher College, NY
Saint Joseph's College, IN
Saint Louis University, MO
Saint Martin's College, WA
Saint Mary-of-the-Woods College, IN
Saint Michael's College, VT
Saint Vincent College, PA
Salem State College, MA
San Diego State University, CA
Seattle University, WA
Seton Hall University, NJ
Shawnee State University, OH
Shepherd College, WV
Siena Heights University, MI
Sierra Nevada College, NV
Simon's Rock College of Bard, MA
Simpson College, IA
Slippery Rock University of Pennsylvania, PA
Sonoma State University, CA
South Dakota State University, SD
Southeastern Louisiana University, LA
Southeast Missouri State University, MO
Southern Adventist University, TN
Southern Oregon University, OR
Southwestern College, KS
Southwest Missouri State University, MO
Southwest State University, MN
Spring Arbor College, MI
State U of NY at Binghamton, NY
State U of NY at New Paltz, NY
State U of NY at Oswego, NY
State U of NY College at Brockport, NY
State U of NY College at Buffalo, NY
State U of NY College at Fredonia, NY
State U of NY College at Geneseo, NY
State U of NY College at Oneonta, NY
State U of NY College at Potsdam, NY
State U of NY Coll of Environ Sci and Forestry, NY
State U of NY Institute of Tech at Utica/Rome, NY
State University of West Georgia, GA
Stetson University, FL
Stevens Institute of Technology, NJ
Susquehanna University, PA
Taylor University, Fort Wayne Campus, IN
Teikyo Post University, CT
Tennessee State University, TN
Tennessee Technological University, TN
Tennessee Wesleyan College, TN
Texas A&M University–Commerce, TX
Transylvania University, KY
Trinity Christian College, IL
United States International University, CA
Unity College, ME
The University of Akron, OH
The University of Alabama in Huntsville, AL
U of Alaska Anchorage, AK
University of Arkansas at Little Rock, AR
University of Central Florida, FL
University of Central Oklahoma, OK
University of Cincinnati, OH
University of Dallas, TX
University of Detroit Mercy, MI
University of Dubuque, IA
University of Evansville, IN
University of Florida, FL
University of Idaho, ID
University of Illinois at Chicago, IL
University of Illinois at Springfield, IL
University of Kansas, KS
University of Maine, ME
University of Maine at Farmington, ME
University of Maine at Fort Kent, ME
The University of Memphis, TN
University of Michigan, MI
University of Michigan–Dearborn, MI
University of Minnesota, Crookston, MN
University of Minnesota, Morris, MN
University of Missouri–Columbia, MO
University of Missouri–Kansas City, MO
University of Missouri–Rolla, MO
University of Missouri–St. Louis, MO
The University of Montana–Missoula, MT
University of Nebraska at Omaha, NE
University of Nebraska–Lincoln, NE
University of Nevada, Las Vegas, NV

Members of Minority Groups (continued)

University of Nevada, Reno, NV
University of New Hampshire at Manchester, NH
University of New Mexico, NM
The University of North Carolina at Asheville, NC
The University of North Carolina at Greensboro, NC
University of North Dakota, ND
University of Northern Colorado, CO
University of Northern Iowa, IA
University of North Florida, FL
University of Oklahoma, OK
University of Richmond, VA
University of Rochester, NY
University of St. Thomas, TX
The University of Scranton, PA
University of South Alabama, AL
University of South Carolina, SC
University of South Dakota, SD
University of Southern California, CA
The University of Tennessee at Chattanooga, TN
The University of Tennessee at Martin, TN
The University of Tennessee Knoxville, TN
The University of Tennessee Memphis, TN
The University of Texas at Dallas, TX
The University of Texas at El Paso, TX
University of the Ozarks, AR
University of the Sciences in Philadelphia, PA
University of the South, TN
University of Toledo, OH
University of West Florida, FL
University of Wisconsin–Eau Claire, WI
University of Wisconsin–La Crosse, WI
University of Wisconsin–Oshkosh, WI
University of Wisconsin–Parkside, WI
University of Wisconsin–Stout, WI
University of Wisconsin–Whitewater, WI
Utah State University, UT
Valparaiso University, IN
Vanderbilt University, TN
Villanova University, PA
Virginia Military Institute, VA
Virginia Polytechnic Institute and State U, VA
Wake Forest University, NC
Walsh University, OH
Warner Pacific College, OR
Wartburg College, IA
Washington State University, WA
Wayland Baptist University, TX
Wayne State College, NE
Weber State University, UT
Western Carolina University, NC
Western Illinois University, IL
Western Kentucky University, KY
Western Michigan University, MI
Western Montana College of The U of Montana, MT
Western Washington University, WA
Westminster College, UT
West Virginia University, WV
West Virginia Wesleyan College, WV
Wichita State University, KS
Wilkes University, PA
Willamette University, OR
William Paterson University of New Jersey, NJ
Williams Baptist College, AR
Wilmington College, OH
Winona State University, MN
Wittenberg University, OH
Xavier University, OH
York College of Pennsylvania, PA
Youngstown State University, OH

OUT-OF-STATE STUDENTS

Abilene Christian University, TX
Adams State College, CO
Alabama State University, AL
Alvernia College, PA
Anderson College, SC
Arkansas State University, AR
Aurora University, IL
Baker University, KS
Bay Path College, MA
Bellarmine College, KY
Bemidji State University, MN
Benedictine University, IL
Bethel College, MN
Bluffton College, OH
Boise State University, ID
Bowie State University, MD
Brigham Young University, UT
Buena Vista University, IA
Caldwell College, NJ
California Maritime Academy, CA
California State University, Chico, CA
Centenary College, NJ
Central College, IA
Central Michigan University, MI
Central Missouri State University, MO
Chadron State College, NE
Chaminade University of Honolulu, HI
Charleston Southern University, SC
Christian Heritage College, CA
Circleville Bible College, OH
Coastal Carolina University, SC
The College of New Rochelle, NY
College of St. Catherine, MN
College of Saint Mary, NE
Concordia University, IL
Concordia University Wisconsin, WI
Cornerstone University, MI
Dana College, NE
Defiance College, OH
Delaware State University, DE
Delta State University, MS
Dordt College, IA
Eastern Kentucky University, KY
Eastern Michigan University, MI
Eastern New Mexico University, NM
Eastern Oregon University, OR
Eastern Washington University, WA
Edinboro University of Pennsylvania, PA
Emmaus Bible College, IA
Emporia State University, KS
Ferrum College, VA
Florida Southern College, FL
Fort Lewis College, CO
Fort Valley State University, GA
Francis Marion University, SC
Franklin Pierce College, NH
Frostburg State University, MD
Gardner-Webb University, NC
George Fox University, OR
Georgia College and State University, GA
Grambling State University, LA
Grand Canyon University, AZ
Grand Valley State University, MI
Greenville College, IL
Grove City College, PA
Hamline University, MN
Henderson State University, AR
Idaho State University, ID
Illinois Institute of Technology, IL
Indiana Institute of Technology, IN
Iowa State University of Science and Technology, IA
Judson College, IL
Kent State University, OH
Kentucky Christian College, KY
Kentucky Wesleyan College, KY
Lander University, SC
Lewis-Clark State College, ID
Limestone College, SC
Louisiana Tech University, LA
MacMurray College, IL
Maine Maritime Academy, ME
Marycrest International University, IA
Massachusetts College of Liberal Arts, MA
McKendree College, IL
McNeese State University, LA
Mesa State College, CO
Miami University, OH
Michigan State University, MI
Michigan Technological University, MI
Minnesota State University, Mankato, MN
Mississippi State University, MS
Mississippi University for Women, MS
Missouri Western State College, MO
Monmouth University, NJ
Montana State U–Billings, MT
Montana State U–Northern, MT
Morehead State University, KY
Mount Angel Seminary, OR
New Jersey Institute of Technology, NJ
Newman University, KS
Northern Arizona University, AZ
Northern Kentucky University, KY
Northern Michigan University, MI
Northwest Nazarene University, ID
Nyack College, NY
Oak Hills Christian College, MN
Oakland University, MI
The Ohio State University, OH
Ohio Wesleyan University, OH
Oklahoma Baptist University, OK
Oklahoma Panhandle State University, OK
Oklahoma State U, OK
Palmer College of Chiropractic, IA
Paul Quinn College, TX
Peace College, NC
Peirce College, PA
Piedmont College, GA
Plattsburgh State U of NY, NY
Ramapo College of New Jersey, NJ
Ripon College, WI
Robert Morris College, IL
Robert Morris College, PA
Roberts Wesleyan College, NY
Rochester College, MI
Rockford College, IL
Saginaw Valley State University, MI
Saint Mary-of-the-Woods College, IN
Shimer College, IL
Shorter College, GA
Siena College, NY

Southeastern Louisiana University, LA
Southern Adventist University, TN
Southern Arkansas University–Magnolia, AR
Southern Oregon University, OR
Southwestern Oklahoma State University, OK
Southwest Missouri State University, MO
Spring Arbor College, MI
State U of NY at Binghamton, NY
State U of NY College at Fredonia, NY
Tennessee Technological University, TN
Texas Tech University, TX
Thomas More College, KY
Thomas University, GA
Tiffin University, OH
Transylvania University, KY
Trinity Christian College, IL
University of Advancing Computer Technology, AZ
The University of Akron, OH
The University of Alabama at Birmingham, AL
University of Arkansas, AR
University of Arkansas at Monticello, AR
University of Cincinnati, OH
University of Colorado at Colorado Springs, CO
University of Dubuque, IA
University of Florida, FL
University of Idaho, ID
University of Illinois at Springfield, IL
University of Kansas, KS
University of Louisiana at Monroe, LA
University of Maine, ME
University of Michigan, MI
University of Minnesota, Crookston, MN
University of Minnesota, Morris, MN
University of Mississippi, MS
University of Missouri–Columbia, MO
University of Missouri–Kansas City, MO
University of Missouri–Rolla, MO
University of Montevallo, AL
University of Nebraska at Kearney, NE
University of Nebraska at Omaha, NE
University of Nebraska–Lincoln, NE
University of Nevada, Las Vegas, NV
University of New Mexico, NM
University of North Alabama, AL
The University of North Carolina at Chapel Hill, NC
The University of North Carolina at Greensboro, NC
University of Northern Colorado, CO
University of Pittsburgh at Bradford, PA
University of Rio Grande, OH
University of Rochester, NY
University of Saint Francis, IN
University of Science and Arts of Oklahoma, OK
University of Southern Indiana, IN
University of Southern Mississippi, MS
The University of Tennessee at Martin, TN
The University of Texas at Dallas, TX
The University of Texas at El Paso, TX
The University of Texas at San Antonio, TX
University of Wisconsin–La Crosse, WI
University of Wisconsin–Parkside, WI
University of Wisconsin–Stevens Point, WI
University of Wisconsin–Stout, WI
University of Wisconsin–Whitewater, WI
University of Wyoming, WY
Utah State University, UT
Virginia Military Institute, VA
Virginia Polytechnic Institute and State U, VA
Wadhams Hall Seminary-College, NY
Walsh University, OH
Warner Southern College, FL
Wartburg College, IA
Wayne State College, NE
Western Michigan University, MI
William Penn University, IA
Winona State University, MN
Winthrop University, SC

PARENTS OF CURRENT STUDENTS

Alabama Agricultural and Mechanical University, AL
Anderson College, SC
Aurora University, IL
Becker College, MA
Canisius College, NY
Chaminade University of Honolulu, HI
The College of New Rochelle, NY
Columbia College, MO
Fairleigh Dickinson U, Florham-Madison Campus, NJ
Fairleigh Dickinson U, Teaneck-Hackensack Campus, NJ
Houghton College, NY
Huntington College, IN
Johnson Bible College, TN
Lee University, TN
Malone College, OH
Maryville University of Saint Louis, MO
Messiah College, PA
Minnesota Bible College, MN
Missouri Baptist College, MO
Mount Marty College, SD
Mount Mary College, WI
Mount St. Clare College, IA
Northwest College, WA
Oklahoma Christian U of Science and Arts, OK
Olivet Nazarene University, IL
Presentation College, SD
Rockford College, IL
Saint Mary-of-the-Woods College, IN
Seton Hill College, PA
State U of NY at Oswego, NY
Suffolk University, MA
The University of Alabama at Birmingham, AL
University of Bridgeport, CT
The University of Findlay, OH
University of Hartford, CT
University of Mary Hardin-Baylor, TX
University of St. Thomas, MN
Upper Iowa University, IA
William Woods University, MO

PREVIOUS COLLEGE EXPERIENCE

Abilene Christian University, TX
Allentown College of St. Francis de Sales, PA
Alma College, MI
Alvernia College, PA
Bellarmine College, KY
Benedictine College, KS
Benedictine University, IL
Calumet College of Saint Joseph, IN
Carthage College, WI
Cedar Crest College, PA
Centenary College, NJ
Central Missouri State University, MO
Chaminade University of Honolulu, HI
The College of New Rochelle, NY
Defiance College, OH
Eastern Connecticut State University, CT
East Texas Baptist University, TX
Elmira College, NY
Hendrix College, AR
Illinois College, IL
Illinois Institute of Technology, IL
Illinois State University, IL
Johnson & Wales University, FL
Johnson & Wales University, RI
Johnson & Wales University, SC
Lake Forest College, IL
Lees-McRae College, NC
Lock Haven University of Pennsylvania, PA
MacMurray College, IL
Manchester College, IN
McMurry University, TX
Michigan Technological University, MI
Mississippi State University, MS
Mount Senario College, WI
Newman University, KS
New York Institute of Technology, NY
North Dakota State University, ND
The Ohio State University, OH
Old Dominion University, VA
Otterbein College, OH
Pacific Lutheran University, WA
Paul Quinn College, TX
Peirce College, PA
The Richard Stockton College of New Jersey, NJ
Ripon College, WI
Rochester College, MI
Siena College, NY
Sonoma State University, CA
Southeast Missouri State University, MO
Southwest State University, MN
State U of NY College at Fredonia, NY
State U of NY Institute of Tech at Utica/Rome, NY
State University of West Georgia, GA
Stephen F. Austin State University, TX
The University of Alabama at Birmingham, AL
University of Arkansas, AR
University of Arkansas at Little Rock, AR
University of Michigan–Dearborn, MI
University of Minnesota, Crookston, MN
University of Oklahoma, OK
University of Science and Arts of Oklahoma, OK
The University of Tennessee Knoxville, TN
University of Toledo, OH
University of Wisconsin–Eau Claire, WI
University of Wisconsin–Stout, WI
Walsh College of Accountancy and Business Admin, MI
Western Maryland College, MD
Western Washington University, WA
William Tyndale College, MI
William Woods University, MO
Wilson College, PA
York College, NE

PUBLIC SERVANTS

David N. Myers College, OH
Dowling College, NY
Hannibal-LaGrange College, MO
Hardin-Simmons University, TX
Louisiana Tech University, LA
Michigan State University, MI
Missouri Baptist College, MO
New York Institute of Technology, NY
Salem State College, MA
Southeastern Louisiana University, LA
Southern Illinois University Carbondale, IL
Tennessee Technological University, TN
The University of Alabama at Birmingham, AL
University of Illinois at Springfield, IL
The University of Memphis, TN
University of South Carolina, SC
The University of Texas at Dallas, TX
Westminster College, UT

RELATIVES OF CLERGY

Abilene Christian University, TX
Albion College, MI
Allentown College of St. Francis de Sales, PA
Anderson College, SC
Anderson University, IN
Appalachian Bible College, WV
Augsburg College, MN
Austin College, TX
Azusa Pacific University, CA
Baker University, KS
Baptist Bible College of Pennsylvania, PA
Barclay College, KS
Bartlesville Wesleyan College, OK
Barton College, NC
Beaver College, PA
Belhaven College, MS
Bennett College, NC
Bethany College, KS
Bethany College, WV
Bethany College of the Assemblies of God, CA
Bethel College, IN
Bethel College, KS
Bethel College, MN
Biola University, CA
Birmingham-Southern College, AL
Bloomfield College, NJ
Bluefield College, VA
Bluffton College, OH
Boise Bible College, ID
Boston University, MA
Brevard College, NC
Bryan College, TN
California Baptist University, CA
California Lutheran University, CA
Campbell University, NC
Capital University, OH
Carson-Newman College, TN
Carthage College, WI
Cedar Crest College, PA
Centenary College of Louisiana, LA
Central Bible College, MO
Central College, IA
Central Methodist College, MO
Chapman University, CA
Charleston Southern University, SC
Chowan College, NC
Christian Heritage College, CA
Circleville Bible College, OH
Claflin University, SC
Clarke College, IA
Columbia College, SC
Columbia International University, SC
Concordia College, MI
Concordia College, NY
Concordia University, CA
Concordia University, OR
Crichton College, TN
Crown College, MN
Cumberland College, KY
Dallas Baptist University, TX
Dana College, NE
David Lipscomb University, TN
Davidson College, NC
Defiance College, OH
DePauw University, IN
Dominican College of Blauvelt, NY
Drury University, MO
Duquesne University, PA
Eastern Nazarene College, MA
Elon College, NC
Emmanuel College, GA
Emory & Henry College, VA
Emory University, GA
Erskine College, SC
Eugene Bible College, OR
Faith Baptist Bible Coll and Theological Seminary, IA
Faulkner University, AL
Ferrum College, VA
Florida Southern College, FL
Fresno Pacific University, CA
Friends University, KS
Furman University, SC
Gardner-Webb University, NC
Geneva College, PA
George Fox University, OR
Georgetown College, KY
Georgia Baptist College of Nursing, GA
Gordon College, MA
Grace College, IN
Grace University, NE
Grand Canyon University, AZ
Greensboro College, NC
Greenville College, IL
Hamline University, MN
Hannibal-LaGrange College, MO
Hastings College, NE
Hawaii Pacific University, HI
Hendrix College, AR
High Point University, NC
Hillsdale Free Will Baptist College, OK
Hope International University, CA
Houghton College, NY
Howard Payne University, TX
Huntingdon College, AL
Huntington College, IN
Immaculata College, PA
Indiana Wesleyan University, IN
Iowa Wesleyan College, IA
John Brown University, AR
Johnson Bible College, TN
Judson College, AL
Kentucky Wesleyan College, KY
King College, TN
King's College, PA
LaGrange College, GA
Lambuth University, TN
Lancaster Bible College, PA
Lees-McRae College, NC
LeTourneau University, TX
Liberty University, VA
LIFE Bible College, CA
Lycoming College, PA
Malone College, OH
Maranatha Baptist Bible College, WI
Maryville College, TN
McMurry University, TX
Mercer University, GA
Merrimack College, MA
Messiah College, PA
MidAmerica Nazarene University, KS
Mid-Continent College, KY
Midway College, KY
Millikin University, IL
Millsaps College, MS
Mississippi College, MS
Missouri Baptist College, MO
Montreat College, NC
Moravian College, PA
Morningside College, IA
Mount St. Clare College, IA
Mount Union College, OH
Mount Vernon Nazarene College, OH
Muhlenberg College, PA
Nebraska Christian College, NE
Nebraska Wesleyan University, NE
Newberry College, SC
Niagara University, NY
North Central College, IL
Northwest Christian College, OR
Northwest College, WA
Northwestern College, MN
Northwest Nazarene University, ID
Notre Dame College of Ohio, OH
Nyack College, NY
Ohio Northern University, OH
Ohio Wesleyan University, OH
Oklahoma Baptist University, OK
Oklahoma City University, OK
Olivet Nazarene University, IL
Oral Roberts University, OK
Otterbein College, OH
Ouachita Baptist University, AR
Our Lady of Holy Cross College, LA
Pacific Lutheran University, WA
Pacific University, OR
Palm Beach Atlantic College, FL
Peace College, NC
Philadelphia College of Bible, PA
Piedmont Baptist College, NC
Point Loma Nazarene University, CA
Practical Bible College, NY
Presbyterian College, SC
Puget Sound Christian College, WA
Queens College, NC
Quincy University, IL
Randolph-Macon College, VA
Randolph-Macon Woman's College, VA
Reinhardt College, GA
Rhodes College, TN
Roberts Wesleyan College, NY
Rochester College, MI
Rockford College, IL
Rockhurst University, MO
Rust College, MS
St. Ambrose University, IA
St. Bonaventure University, NY

St. John's University, NY
Saint Mary's College of California, CA
Saint Peter's College, NJ
Salem College, NC
Samford University, AL
Seattle Pacific University, WA
Seton Hall University, NJ
Shasta Bible College, CA
Shenandoah University, VA
Siena College, NY
Siena Heights University, MI
Simpson College, IA
Simpson College and Graduate School, CA
Southeastern Bible College, AL
Southeastern College of the Assemblies of God, FL
Southeastern Louisiana University, LA
Southern Methodist University, TX
Southern Wesleyan University, SC
Southwest Baptist University, MO
Southwestern Assemblies of God University, TX
Southwestern College, AZ
Southwestern College, KS
Southwestern College of Christian Ministries, OK
Southwestern University, TX
Spring Arbor College, MI
Susquehanna University, PA
Tabor College, KS
Tennessee Wesleyan College, TN
Texas Christian University, TX
Texas Wesleyan University, TX
Toccoa Falls College, GA
Transylvania University, KY
Trevecca Nazarene University, TN
Trinity Baptist College, FL
Trinity Bible College, ND
Trinity Lutheran College, WA
Union University, TN
The University of Alabama at Birmingham, AL
University of Dubuque, IA
University of Indianapolis, IN
University of Mary Hardin-Baylor, TX
University of Portland, OR
University of St. Thomas, TX
University of South Carolina, SC
University of the Ozarks, AR
University of the South, TN
Ursuline College, OH
Valley Forge Christian College, PA
Valparaiso University, IN
Vanguard University of Southern California, CA
Virginia Wesleyan College, VA
Wake Forest University, NC
Warner Southern College, FL
Washington Bible College, MD
Wayland Baptist University, TX
Wesleyan College, GA
Western Baptist College, OR
Westminster College, UT
West Virginia Wesleyan College, WV
Whitworth College, WA
William Carey College, MS
William Jewell College, MO
Williams Baptist College, AR
William Tyndale College, MI
Wingate University, NC
Wittenberg University, OH
Wofford College, SC

RELIGIOUS AFFILIATION

Abilene Christian University, TX
Alabama State University, AL
Alaska Bible College, AK
Albertson College of Idaho, ID
Albertus Magnus College, CT
Albright College, PA
Allentown College of St. Francis de Sales, PA
Allen University, SC
Alvernia College, PA
American Baptist Coll of American Baptist Theol Sem, TN
Anderson College, SC
Ashland University, OH
Augustana College, IL
Augustana College, SD
Avila College, MO
Azusa Pacific University, CA
Baldwin-Wallace College, OH
Barber-Scotia College, NC
Barclay College, KS
Barry University, FL
Bartlesville Wesleyan College, OK
Barton College, NC
Beaver College, PA
Belmont Abbey College, NC
Belmont University, TN
Benedictine College, KS
Bennett College, NC
Bethany College, WV
Bethel College, IN
Bethel College, MN
Bethel College, TN
Bethune-Cookman College, FL
Birmingham-Southern College, AL
Bluffton College, OH
Boston University, MA
Brevard College, NC
Bridgewater College, VA
Brigham Young University, UT
Brigham Young University–Hawaii Campus, HI
Bryan College, TN
Buena Vista University, IA
Caldwell College, NJ
California Lutheran University, CA
Calumet College of Saint Joseph, IN
Calvin College, MI
Campbellsville University, KY
Canisius College, NY
Capital University, OH
Carlow College, PA
Carthage College, WI
Catawba College, NC
The Catholic University of America, DC
Cedar Crest College, PA
Cedarville College, OH
Centenary College, NJ
Centenary College of Louisiana, LA
Central Bible College, MO
Central College, IA
Central Methodist College, MO
Chaminade University of Honolulu, HI
Chapman University, CA
Charleston Southern University, SC
Chowan College, NC
Circleville Bible College, OH
Claflin University, SC
Coe College, IA
College of Our Lady of the Elms, MA
College of St. Catherine, MN
College of St. Joseph, VT
Colorado Christian University, CO
Columbia College, MO
Columbia International University, SC
Conception Seminary College, MO
Concordia College, MI
Concordia College, NY
Concordia University, CA
Concordia University, IL
Concordia University at Austin, TX
Concordia University Wisconsin, WI
Covenant College, GA
Creighton University, NE
Crichton College, TN
Culver-Stockton College, MO
Dakota Wesleyan University, SD
Dallas Baptist University, TX
Dallas Christian College, TX
Dana College, NE
Davis & Elkins College, WV
Defiance College, OH
DePauw University, IN
Dillard University, LA
Doane College, NE
Dordt College, IA
Drury University, MO
Duquesne University, PA
Earlham College, IN
Eastern Mennonite University, VA
Eastern Michigan University, MI
Eastern Nazarene College, MA
East Texas Baptist University, TX
Eckerd College, FL
Edgewood College, WI
Edinboro University of Pennsylvania, PA
Elizabethtown College, PA
Elmhurst College, IL
Emmanuel College, GA
Emmanuel College, MA
Emory University, GA
Emporia State University, KS
Erskine College, SC
Eureka College, IL
Ferrum College, VA
Finlandia University, MI
Florida Baptist Theological College, FL
Fontbonne College, MO
Franciscan University of Steubenville, OH
Franklin College of Indiana, IN
Fresno Pacific University, CA
Friends University, KS
Furman University, SC
Gannon University, PA
Geneva College, PA
George Fox University, OR
Georgetown College, KY
Georgia Baptist College of Nursing, GA
Georgian Court College, NJ
Graceland College, IA
Grace University, NE
Grand Canyon University, AZ
Greensboro College, NC
Greenville College, IL
Guilford College, NC
Hannibal-LaGrange College, MO
Hanover College, IN

Religious Affiliation (continued)

Hardin-Simmons University, TX
Hastings College, NE
Hawaii Pacific University, HI
Heidelberg College, OH
Hellenic College, MA
Hillsdale Free Will Baptist College, OK
Hiram College, OH
Holy Names College, CA
Houghton College, NY
Howard Payne University, TX
Huntingdon College, AL
Huntington College, IN
Indiana Wesleyan University, IN
Iowa Wesleyan College, IA
Jarvis Christian College, TX
Johnson Bible College, TN
Judson College, AL
Judson College, IL
Kentucky Christian College, KY
Kentucky Wesleyan College, KY
Lakeland College, WI
Lambuth University, TN
Lancaster Bible College, PA
Lees-McRae College, NC
Liberty University, VA
Loyola University Chicago, IL
Luther College, IA
Lyon College, AR
MacMurray College, IL
Malone College, OH
Manchester College, IN
Maranatha Baptist Bible College, WI
Marian College, IN
Martin Methodist College, TN
Maryland Institute, College of Art, MD
Maryville College, TN
Maryville University of Saint Louis, MO
Marywood University, PA
McKendree College, IL
McMurry University, TX
McNeese State University, LA
Mercer University, GA
Messenger College, MO
Messiah College, PA
Michigan State University, MI
Mid-America Bible College, OK
MidAmerica Nazarene University, KS
Midland Lutheran College, NE
Midway College, KY
Millikin University, IL
Millsaps College, MS
Minnesota Bible College, MN
Missouri Baptist College, MO
Moravian College, PA
Morningside College, IA
Mount Marty College, SD
Mount Olive College, NC
Mount Vernon Nazarene College, OH
Multnomah Bible College and Biblical Seminary, OR
Muskingum College, OH
Newberry College, SC
Newman University, KS
Northwest Christian College, OR
Northwest College, WA
Northwestern College, IA
Northwest Nazarene University, ID
Nyack College, NY
Oakland City University, IN
Ohio Northern University, OH
Ohio Valley College, WV
Ohio Wesleyan University, OH
Oklahoma Baptist University, OK
Olivet Nazarene University, IL
Ottawa University, KS
Ouachita Baptist University, AR
Our Lady of Holy Cross College, LA
Ozark Christian College, MO
Paine College, GA
Park University, MO
Peace College, NC
Point Loma Nazarene University, CA
Presbyterian College, SC
Queens College, NC
Randolph-Macon Woman's College, VA
Reinhardt College, GA
Rhodes College, TN
Rivier College, NH
Roanoke College, VA
Roberts Wesleyan College, NY
Rockhurst University, MO
Rocky Mountain College, MT
Rust College, MS
Sacred Heart Major Seminary, MI
St. Ambrose University, IA
St. Bonaventure University, NY
St. Edward's University, TX
St. Gregory's University, OK
St. John's Seminary College, CA
St. John's University, NY
St. Louis Christian College, MO
Saint Martin's College, WA
Saint Mary-of-the-Woods College, IN
Saint Michael's College, VT
Saint Paul's College, VA
Saint Peter's College, NJ
Salem-Teikyo University, WV
Schreiner College, TX
Seattle Pacific University, WA
Shasta Bible College, CA
Sheldon Jackson College, AK
Shenandoah University, VA
Shorter College, GA
Siena College, NY
Siena Heights University, MI
Simpson College and Graduate School, CA
Southeastern Louisiana University, LA
Southern Christian University, AL
Southern Nazarene University, OK
Southern Wesleyan University, SC
Southwestern College, AZ
Southwestern College, KS
Southwestern College of Christian Ministries, OK
Spring Arbor College, MI
Stephen F. Austin State University, TX
Tabor College, KS
Taylor University, IN
Tennessee Wesleyan College, TN
Texas Christian University, TX
Texas Lutheran University, TX
Texas Wesleyan University, TX
Thiel College, PA
Thomas More College, KY
Transylvania University, KY
Trevecca Nazarene University, TN
Trinity Baptist College, FL
Trinity Lutheran College, WA
Union College, KY
The University of Alabama at Birmingham, AL
University of Dayton, OH
University of Dubuque, IA
University of Evansville, IN
The University of Findlay, OH
University of Great Falls, MT
University of La Verne, CA
University of Mary Hardin-Baylor, TX
University of Michigan–Dearborn, MI
The University of North Carolina at Greensboro, NC
University of St. Thomas, TX
University of South Carolina, SC
University of the South, TN
Upper Iowa University, IA
Ursuline College, OH
Utah State University, UT
Valparaiso University, IN
Vanguard University of Southern California, CA
Villanova University, PA
Virginia Intermont College, VA
Warner Pacific College, OR
Warren Wilson College, NC
Wartburg College, IA
Washington Bible College, MD
Westminster College, MO
Westminster College, UT
Wheeling Jesuit University, WV
William Carey College, MS
William Penn University, IA
Williams Baptist College, AR
Wilson College, PA
Wittenberg University, OH

SIBLINGS OF CURRENT STUDENTS

Albright College, PA
Allentown College of St. Francis de Sales, PA
Alvernia College, PA
Alverno College, WI
Anderson College, SC
Anna Maria College, MA
Asbury College, KY
Ashland University, OH
Assumption College, MA
Augsburg College, MN
Augustana College, IL
Augustana College, SD
Aurora University, IL
Avila College, MO
Azusa Pacific University, CA
Baptist Bible College of Pennsylvania, PA
Barry University, FL
Barton College, NC
Bay Path College, MA
Becker College, MA
Belmont Abbey College, NC
Beloit College, WI
Benedictine University, IL
Bethel College, IN
Bloomfield College, NJ
Bridgewater College, VA
Bryant College, RI
Buena Vista University, IA
Cabrini College, PA
Caldwell College, NJ
California Baptist University, CA
Canisius College, NY

Capital University, OH
Carlow College, PA
Carroll College, MT
Carroll College, WI
Carson-Newman College, TN
Carthage College, WI
Cascade College, OR
The Catholic University of America, DC
Cedar Crest College, PA
Centenary College, NJ
Central Bible College, MO
Central College, IA
Central Methodist College, MO
Chaminade University of Honolulu, HI
Circleville Bible College, OH
Clarke College, IA
College of Mount Saint Vincent, NY
The College of New Rochelle, NY
College of St. Catherine, MN
The College of Saint Rose, NY
The College of St. Scholastica, MN
Columbia College, MO
Concordia University, CA
Creighton University, NE
Cumberland College, KY
Daemen College, NY
Dana College, NE
Doane College, NE
Dominican University, IL
Drexel University, PA
Eastern Nazarene College, MA
East Texas Baptist University, TX
Elizabethtown College, PA
Elmira College, NY
Emmanuel College, GA
Erskine College, SC
Fairleigh Dickinson U, Florham-Madison Campus, NJ
Fairleigh Dickinson U, Teaneck-Hackensack Campus, NJ
Faulkner University, AL
Ferrum College, VA
Florida Southern College, FL
Fontbonne College, MO
Franciscan University of Steubenville, OH
Franklin Pierce College, NH
The George Washington University, DC
Georgian Court College, NJ
Gonzaga University, WA
Goshen College, IN
Grace University, NE
Green Mountain College, VT
Greensboro College, NC
Greenville College, IL
Harding University, AR
Hartwick College, NY
Hastings College, NE
Hillsdale Free Will Baptist College, OK
Hope International University, CA
Houghton College, NY
Huntington College, IN
Illinois Institute of Technology, IL
Immaculata College, PA
Indiana Institute of Technology, IN
Indiana Wesleyan University, IN
Iona College, NY
Ithaca College, NY
Jacksonville University, FL
James Madison University, VA
John Brown University, AR
Johnson & Wales University, FL
Johnson & Wales University, RI
Johnson & Wales University, SC
Johnson Bible College, TN
Judson College, IL
Kansas Wesleyan University, KS
Kentucky Wesleyan College, KY
King's College, PA
Lakeland College, WI
Lancaster Bible College, PA
Lasell College, MA
Lee University, TN
Limestone College, SC
Long Island U, Southampton College, NY
Loras College, IA
Lyndon State College, VT
Lynn University, FL
MacMurray College, IL
Malone College, OH
Marian College, IN
Marian College of Fond du Lac, WI
Marietta College, OH
Marymount University, VA
Maryville University of Saint Louis, MO
Marywood University, PA
Mercer University, GA
Mercyhurst College, PA
Merrimack College, MA
Messiah College, PA
Midland Lutheran College, NE
Minnesota Bible College, MN
Missouri Baptist College, MO
Montserrat College of Art, MA
Mount Marty College, SD
Mount Mary College, WI
Mount St. Clare College, IA
Mount Saint Mary's College and Seminary, MD
Mount Senario College, WI
Mount Vernon Nazarene College, OH
Multnomah Bible College and Biblical Seminary, OR
Muskingum College, OH
Nazareth College of Rochester, NY
Nebraska Wesleyan University, NE
New England College, NH
New Hampshire College, NH
Newman University, KS
Nichols College, MA
North Greenville College, SC
Northwest College, WA
Northwestern College, IA
Northwestern College, MN
Northwood University, MI
Northwood University, Florida Campus, FL
Northwood University, Texas Campus, TX
Notre Dame College, NH
Notre Dame College of Ohio, OH
Oak Hills Christian College, MN
Oglethorpe University, GA
Ohio Northern University, OH
Oklahoma Christian U of Science and Arts, OK
Olivet Nazarene University, IL
Oral Roberts University, OK
Otterbein College, OH
Paine College, GA
Palm Beach Atlantic College, FL
Park University, MO
Philadelphia College of Bible, PA
Pine Manor College, MA
Point Loma Nazarene University, CA
Point Park College, PA
Practical Bible College, NY
Presentation College, SD
Queens College, NC
Randolph-Macon College, VA
Research College of Nursing, MO
Ripon College, WI
Rivier College, NH
Roberts Wesleyan College, NY
Rochester College, MI
Rockford College, IL
Rockhurst University, MO
Rosemont College, PA
Rust College, MS
Sacred Heart University, CT
St. Ambrose University, IA
Saint Anselm College, NH
St. Bonaventure University, NY
Saint Francis College, PA
St. John's University, NY
Saint Joseph College, CT
Saint Joseph's College, IN
Saint Joseph's College, ME
Saint Louis University, MO
Saint Martin's College, WA
Saint Mary College, KS
Saint Mary-of-the-Woods College, IN
Saint Mary's College, IN
Saint Michael's College, VT
St. Thomas Aquinas College, NY
Seton Hall University, NJ
Seton Hill College, PA
Shasta Bible College, CA
Shorter College, GA
Simpson College, IA
Simpson College and Graduate School, CA
Southeastern College of the Assemblies of God, FL
Southern Adventist University, TN
Southern Wesleyan University, SC
Southwestern Adventist University, TX
Southwestern College, AZ
Southwestern College, KS
Spalding University, KY
Spring Hill College, AL
Stephens College, MO
Suffolk University, MA
Tabor College, KS
Teikyo Post University, CT
Tennessee Temple University, TN
Thiel College, PA
Trinity Bible College, ND
Trinity College, DC
Tri-State University, IN
The University of Alabama at Birmingham, AL
University of Bridgeport, CT
University of Dallas, TX
University of Dubuque, IA
University of Evansville, IN
The University of Findlay, OH
University of Hartford, CT
University of Mary Hardin-Baylor, TX
University of St. Francis, IL
University of Saint Francis, IN
The University of Scranton, PA
University of Toledo, OH
University of West Los Angeles, CA

Siblings of Current Students (continued)

Ursinus College, PA
Ursuline College, OH
Valley Forge Christian College, PA
Walsh University, OH
Warner Southern College, FL
Wartburg College, IA
Western Baptist College, OR
Western Maryland College, MD
Western New England College, MA
Westminster College, UT
Whitworth College, WA
Widener University, PA
Wilkes University, PA
William Woods University, MO
Xavier University, OH
York College, NE

SPOUSES OF CURRENT STUDENTS

Alaska Bible College, AK
Anderson College, SC
Arlington Baptist College, TX
Atlanta Christian College, GA
Augustana College, SD
Aurora University, IL
Avila College, MO
Becker College, MA
Bethel College, IN
Bloomfield College, NJ
Boise Bible College, ID
Bryan College, TN
Canisius College, NY
Carlow College, PA
Carroll College, MT
Carroll College, WI
Central Methodist College, MO
Chaminade University of Honolulu, HI
Cincinnati Bible College and Seminary, OH
The College of New Rochelle, NY
Dana College, NE
Dominican University, IL
Emmaus Bible College, IA
Fairleigh Dickinson U, Florham-Madison Campus, NJ
Fairleigh Dickinson U, Teaneck-Hackensack Campus, NJ
Faith Baptist Bible Coll and Theological Seminary, IA
Georgian Court College, NJ
Grace University, NE
Hillsdale Free Will Baptist College, OK
Hope International University, CA
Huntington College, IN
Illinois Institute of Technology, IL
Jacksonville University, FL
Johnson & Wales University, FL
Johnson & Wales University, RI
Johnson & Wales University, SC
Johnson Bible College, TN
John Wesley College, NC
Lancaster Bible College, PA
Lee University, TN
LeMoyne-Owen College, TN
LeTourneau University, TX
LIFE Bible College, CA
Magnolia Bible College, MS
Malone College, OH
Marian College, IN
Maryville University of Saint Louis, MO
Marywood University, PA
Messiah College, PA
Mid-America Bible College, OK
Minnesota Bible College, MN
Mount Marty College, SD
Mount St. Clare College, IA
Mount Vernon Nazarene College, OH
Nebraska Christian College, NE
Northwest College, WA
Oak Hills Christian College, MN
Oklahoma Christian U of Science and Arts, OK
Olivet Nazarene University, IL
Ozark Christian College, MO
Palm Beach Atlantic College, FL
Paul Quinn College, TX
Piedmont Baptist College, NC
Pontifical Catholic University of Puerto Rico, PR
Practical Bible College, NY
Presentation College, SD
Puget Sound Christian College, WA
Reformed Bible College, MI
Roanoke Bible College, NC
St. Edward's University, TX
Saint Joseph's College, ME
Saint Martin's College, WA
Saint Mary-of-the-Woods College, IN
St. Thomas Aquinas College, NY
Shasta Bible College, CA
Simpson College and Graduate School, CA
Southeastern Bible College, AL
Southern Adventist University, TN
Southwestern Assemblies of God University, TX
Southwestern College, AZ
Spalding University, KY
Tabor College, KS
Tennessee Temple University, TN
Trinity Baptist College, FL
Trinity Bible College, ND
The University of Alabama at Birmingham, AL
University of Bridgeport, CT
University of Mary, ND
University of Southern Indiana, IN
University of Toledo, OH
University of West Los Angeles, CA
Upper Iowa University, IA
Valley Forge Christian College, PA
Washington Bible College, MD
Wilkes University, PA
William Woods University, MO

SPOUSES OF DECEASED OR DISABLED PUBLIC SERVANTS

California State University, Bakersfield, CA
Francis Marion University, SC
Indiana U–Purdue U Fort Wayne, IN
Louisiana Tech University, LA
Michigan State University, MI
Mississippi State University, MS
New York Institute of Technology, NY
Northern Kentucky University, KY
Southern Illinois University Carbondale, IL
Southwest Missouri State University, MO
The University of Alabama at Birmingham, AL
U of Alaska Anchorage, AK
University of South Carolina, SC
Youngstown State University, OH

TWINS

Allentown College of St. Francis de Sales, PA
Anderson College, SC
Bay Path College, MA
Becker College, MA
Bloomfield College, NJ
Cabrini College, PA
The College of Saint Rose, NY
Dominican University, IL
Drexel University, PA
East Texas Baptist University, TX
Kansas Wesleyan University, KS
Lasell College, MA
Maryville University of Saint Louis, MO
Mount St. Clare College, IA
Notre Dame College of Ohio, OH
Paul Quinn College, TX
Randolph-Macon Woman's College, VA
Saint Paul's College, VA
St. Thomas Aquinas College, NY
Sterling College, KS
The University of Alabama at Birmingham, AL
University of Hartford, CT
Virginia Polytechnic Institute and State U, VA

VETERANS

Alabama State University, AL
Appalachian Bible College, WV
Arkansas State University, AR
Augustana College, SD
Barton College, NC
Boise State University, ID
California Baptist University, CA
California State University, Fresno, CA
California University of Pennsylvania, PA
Carlos Albizu University, FL
Cedarville College, OH
Central Michigan University, MI
Central State University, OH
Chadron State College, NE
Chaminade University of Honolulu, HI
Circleville Bible College, OH
Clarkson College, NE
Columbia College, MO
Columbia International University, SC
David N. Myers College, OH
East Central University, OK
Eastern Connecticut State University, CT
Eastern New Mexico University, NM
Edinboro University of Pennsylvania, PA
Emporia State University, KS
Ferrum College, VA
Fordham University, NY
Framingham State College, MA
Francis Marion University, SC
Frostburg State University, MD
Georgian Court College, NJ
Governors State University, IL
Grambling State University, LA
Greensboro College, NC
Grove City College, PA
Hope International University, CA
Illinois State University, IL
Inter Amer U of PR, Barranquitas Campus, PR
Lees-McRae College, NC
Lincoln University, MO
Loyola University Chicago, IL
Maharishi University of Management, IA

McMurry University, TX
McNeese State University, LA
Metropolitan College of Court Reporting, NM
Michigan State University, MI
Minot State University, ND
Montana State U–Northern, MT
Mount Vernon Nazarene College, OH
Nazarene Indian Bible College, NM
New York Institute of Technology, NY
North Dakota State University, ND
Northern Illinois University, IL
Northwest Nazarene University, ID
Oklahoma Panhandle State University, OK
Paul Quinn College, TX
Piedmont Baptist College, NC
Pontifical Catholic University of Puerto Rico, PR
Quinnipiac University, CT
Ramapo College of New Jersey, NJ
Regents College, NY
Robert Morris College, IL
Rochester Institute of Technology, NY
Rust College, MS
St. John's Seminary College, CA
St. John's University, NY
Salem State College, MA
Shasta Bible College, CA
Shawnee State University, OH
Sonoma State University, CA
South Dakota State University, SD
Southeastern Bible College, AL
Southern Christian University, AL
Southern Connecticut State University, CT
Southern Illinois University Carbondale, IL
Southwest Missouri State University, MO
Southwest State University, MN
State U of NY College at Fredonia, NY
Texas A&M University, TX
Texas Tech University, TX
Thomas University, GA
The University of Alabama at Birmingham, AL
University of Houston–Clear Lake, TX
University of Illinois at Chicago, IL
University of Illinois at Springfield, IL
University of Maine, ME
University of Massachusetts Amherst, MA
University of Minnesota, Morris, MN
University of Montevallo, AL
University of Nebraska at Kearney, NE
University of New Mexico, NM
The University of North Carolina at Asheville, NC
The University of North Carolina at Greensboro, NC
University of Northern Colorado, CO
U of Puerto Rico, Cayey University College, PR
University of Southern Mississippi, MS
The University of Texas at Dallas, TX
The University of Texas–Pan American, TX
University of the Virgin Islands, VI
University of Virginia's College at Wise, VA
University of Wisconsin–Stout, WI
University of Wyoming, WY
Virginia State University, VA
Warner Southern College, FL
Western New Mexico University, NM
Western Washington University, WA
William Carey College, MS
Worcester State College, MA
Youngstown State University, OH

VETERANS' CHILDREN

Alabama State University, AL
Arkansas State University, AR
Boise State University, ID
California State University, Fresno, CA
Central Michigan University, MI
Central State University, OH
Chadron State College, NE
Circleville Bible College, OH
Coastal Carolina University, SC
David N. Myers College, OH
East Central University, OK
Edinboro University of Pennsylvania, PA
Emporia State University, KS
Florida Agricultural and Mechanical University, FL
Fordham University, NY
Francis Marion University, SC
Frostburg State University, MD
Glenville State College, WV
Grambling State University, LA
Hope International University, CA
Illinois State University, IL
Indiana State University, IN
Maharishi University of Management, IA
Marshall University, WV
McNeese State University, LA
Michigan State University, MI
Minot State University, ND
Mount Vernon Nazarene College, OH
North Dakota State University, ND
Northern Kentucky University, KY
Oklahoma Panhandle State University, OK
Old Dominion University, VA
Pontifical Catholic University of Puerto Rico, PR
Purdue University North Central, IN
Regents College, NY
St. John's University, NY
Salem State College, MA
Shepherd College, WV
Siena College, NY
South Dakota State University, SD
Southwest State University, MN
State U of NY College at Fredonia, NY
Texas A&M University, TX
Texas Tech University, TX
The University of Alabama at Birmingham, AL
U of Calif, San Diego, CA
University of Houston–Clear Lake, TX
University of Illinois at Chicago, IL
University of Illinois at Springfield, IL
University of Maine, ME
University of Maine at Presque Isle, ME
University of Minnesota, Morris, MN
University of Montevallo, AL
University of Nebraska at Kearney, NE
University of Nebraska at Omaha, NE
University of Nebraska–Lincoln, NE
The University of North Carolina at Asheville, NC
The University of North Carolina at Greensboro, NC
The University of Tennessee Knoxville, TN
The University of Texas at Dallas, TX
University of Toledo, OH
University of Virginia's College at Wise, VA
University of Wisconsin–Stout, WI
Virginia Commonwealth University, VA
Warner Southern College, FL
Wayne State College, NE
Western Illinois University, IL
Western Kentucky University, KY
Youngstown State University, OH

ATHLETIC GRANTS FOR UNDERGRADUATES

This index lists the colleges that report offering scholarships for undergraduates on the basis of athletic achievements or abilities. For each college listed in this index, refer to the *Non-Need Awards* section of the college's profile for specific information on the number and value of the scholarships offered. Under each sport, each college is marked with an *M* (Men) to indicate scholarship programs awarded to men in that sport, a *W* (Women) to indicate women's scholarships, or *M,W* to show grants in the specified sport to students of both sexes.

These are the categories and the order in which they appear: Archery, Baseball, Basketball, Bowling, Crew, Cross-Country Running, Equestrian Sports, Fencing, Field Hockey, Football, Golf, Gymnastics, Ice Hockey, Lacrosse, Riflery, Rugby, Sailing, Skiing—Cross Country, Skiing—Downhill, Soccer, Softball, Swimming, Table Tennis, Tennis, Track and Field, Volleyball, Water Polo, Weight Lifting, Wrestling.

Erskine College, SC	M
Evangel University, MO	M
Fairfield University, CT	M
Fairleigh Dickinson U, Teaneck-Hackensack Campus, NJ	M
Faulkner University, AL	M
Felician College, NJ	M
Flagler College, FL	M
Florida Atlantic University, FL	M
Florida College, FL	M
Florida Institute of Technology, FL	M
Florida International University, FL	M
Florida Southern College, FL	M
Florida State University, FL	M
Fordham University, NY	M
Fort Hays State University, KS	M
Francis Marion University, SC	M
Franklin Pierce College, NH	M
Friends University, KS	M
Furman University, SC	M
Gannon University, PA	M
Geneva College, PA	M
George Mason University, VA	M
Georgetown College, KY	M
Georgetown University, DC	M
The George Washington University, DC	M
Georgia College and State University, GA	M
Georgia Institute of Technology, GA	M
Georgia Southern University, GA	M
Georgia Southwestern State University, GA	M
Georgia State University, GA	M
Gonzaga University, WA	M
Goshen College, IN	M
Grace College, IN	M
Graceland College, IA	M
Grambling State University, LA	M
Grand Canyon University, AZ	M
Grand Valley State University, MI	M
Grand View College, IA	M
Hannibal-LaGrange College, MO	M
Harris-Stowe State College, MO	M
Hastings College, NE	M
Hawaii Pacific University, HI	M
Henderson State University, AR	M
High Point University, NC	M
Hillsdale College, MI	M
Hofstra University, NY	M
Houston Baptist University, TX	M
Huntingdon College, AL	M
Huntington College, IN	M
Huron University, SD	M
Illinois Institute of Technology, IL	M
Illinois State University, IL	M
Indiana Institute of Technology, IN	M
Indiana State University, IN	M
Indiana University Bloomington, IN	M
Indiana U–Purdue U Fort Wayne, IN	M
Indiana U–Purdue U Indianapolis, IN	M
Indiana Wesleyan University, IN	M
Inter American U of PR, San Germán Campus, PR	M
Iowa State University of Science and Technology, IA	M
Iowa Wesleyan College, IA	M
Jacksonville State University, AL	M
Jacksonville University, FL	M
James Madison University, VA	M
Jamestown College, ND	M
Judson College, IL	M
Kansas State University, KS	M
Kansas Wesleyan University, KS	M
Kennesaw State University, GA	M
Kent State University, OH	M
Kentucky Wesleyan College, KY	M
King College, TN	M
Kutztown University of Pennsylvania, PA	M
Lamar University, TX	M
Lambuth University, TN	M
La Salle University, PA	M
Lehigh University, PA	M
Le Moyne College, NY	M
LeMoyne-Owen College, TN	M
Lewis-Clark State College, ID	M
Lewis University, IL	M
Liberty University, VA	M
Limestone College, SC	M
Lincoln Memorial University, TN	M
Lincoln University, MO	M
Lock Haven University of Pennsylvania, PA	M
Long Island U, Brooklyn Campus, NY	M
Long Island U, C.W. Post Campus, NY	M
Longwood College, VA	M
Louisiana State University and A&M College, LA	M
Louisiana State University in Shreveport, LA	M
Louisiana Tech University, LA	M
Loyola Marymount University, CA	M
Lubbock Christian University, TX	M
Lynn University, FL	M
Lyon College, AR	M
Madonna University, MI	M
Malone College, OH	M
Manhattan College, NY	M
Mansfield University of Pennsylvania, PA	M
Marian College, IN	M
Marist College, NY	M
Marshall University, WV	M
Martin Methodist College, TN	M
The Master's College and Seminary, CA	M
Mayville State University, ND	M
McKendree College, IL	M
McNeese State University, LA	M
Mercer University, GA	M
Mercyhurst College, PA	M
Mesa State College, CO	M
Metropolitan State College of Denver, CO	M
Miami University, OH	M
MidAmerica Nazarene University, KS	M
Mid-Continent College, KY	M
Middle Tennessee State University, TN	M
Midland Lutheran College, NE	M
Millersville University of Pennsylvania, PA	M
Milligan College, TN	M
Minnesota State University, Mankato, MN	M
Mississippi State University, MS	M
Mississippi Valley State University, MS	M
Missouri Baptist College, MO	M
Missouri Southern State College, MO	M
Missouri Valley College, MO	M
Missouri Western State College, MO	M
Monmouth University, NJ	M
Montreat College, NC	M
Morehead State University, KY	M
Morningside College, IA	M
Mount Marty College, SD	M
Mount Olive College, NC	M
Mount St. Clare College, IA	M
Mount Saint Mary's College and Seminary, MD	M
Mount Vernon Nazarene College, OH	M
Murray State University, KY	M
Newberry College, SC	M
Newman University, KS	M
New Mexico Highlands University, NM	M
New York Institute of Technology, NY	M
Niagara University, NY	M
North Carolina Agricultural and Technical State U, NC	M
North Carolina State University, NC	M
North Dakota State University, ND	M
Northeastern State University, OK	M
Northeastern University, MA	M
Northern Illinois University, IL	M
Northern Kentucky University, KY	M
North Greenville College, SC	M
Northwestern College, IA	M
Northwestern Oklahoma State University, OK	M
Northwestern State University of Louisiana, LA	M
Northwestern University, IL	M
Northwest Missouri State University, MO	M
Northwest Nazarene University, ID	M
Northwood University, MI	M
Northwood University, Florida Campus, FL	M
Northwood University, Texas Campus, TX	M
Nova Southeastern University, FL	M
Oakland City University, IN	M
Oakland University, MI	M
Ohio Dominican College, OH	M
The Ohio State University, OH	M
Ohio University, OH	M
Ohio Valley College, WV	M
Oklahoma Baptist University, OK	M
Oklahoma Christian U of Science and Arts, OK	M
Oklahoma City University, OK	M
Oklahoma State U, OK	M
Old Dominion University, VA	M
Olivet Nazarene University, IL	M
Oral Roberts University, OK	M
Oregon State University, OR	M
Ottawa University, KS	M
Ouachita Baptist University, AR	M
Paine College, GA	M
Palm Beach Atlantic College, FL	M
Penn State U Univ Park Campus, PA	M
Pepperdine University, CA	M
Pfeiffer University, NC	M
Philadelphia University, PA	M
Piedmont College, GA	M
Pikeville College, KY	M
Pittsburg State University, KS	M
Point Loma Nazarene University, CA	M
Point Park College, PA	M
Portland State University, OR	M
Prairie View A&M University, TX	M
Presbyterian College, SC	M

Baseball (continued)

Purdue University, IN M
Queens Coll of the City U of NY, NY M
Quincy University, IL M
Quinnipiac University, CT M
Radford University, VA M
Regis University, CO M
Research College of Nursing, MO M
Rice University, TX M
Rider University, NJ M
Robert Morris College, IL M
Rochester College, MI M
Rockhurst University, MO M
Rollins College, FL M
Rutgers, State U of NJ, College of Pharmacy, NJ M
Rutgers, State U of NJ, Cook College, NJ M
Rutgers, State U of NJ, Livingston College, NJ M
Rutgers, State U of NJ, Mason Gross School of Arts, NJ M
Rutgers, State U of NJ, Rutgers College, NJ M
Rutgers, State U of NJ, College of Engineering, NJ M
Saginaw Valley State University, MI M
St. Ambrose University, IA M
St. Andrews Presbyterian College, NC M
Saint Augustine's College, NC M
St. Bonaventure University, NY M
St. Edward's University, TX M
St. Francis College, NY M
St. Gregory's University, OK M
St. John's University, NY M
Saint Joseph's College, IN M
Saint Joseph's University, PA M
Saint Leo University, FL M
Saint Louis University, MO M
Saint Martin's College, WA M
Saint Mary College, KS M
Saint Mary's College of California, CA M
St. Mary's University of San Antonio, TX M
Saint Paul's College, VA M
Saint Peter's College, NJ M
St. Thomas Aquinas College, NY M
St. Thomas University, FL M
Saint Vincent College, PA M
Saint Xavier University, IL M
Salem-Teikyo University, WV M
Samford University, AL M
Sam Houston State University, TX M
San Diego State University, CA M
San Francisco State University, CA M,W
San Jose State University, CA M
Santa Clara University, CA M
Savannah State University, GA M
Seton Hall University, NJ M
Shaw University, NC M
Shippensburg University of Pennsylvania, PA M
Shorter College, GA M
Siena College, NY M
Siena Heights University, MI M
Slippery Rock University of Pennsylvania, PA M
South Dakota State University, SD M
Southeastern Louisiana University, LA M
Southeast Missouri State University, MO M
Southern Arkansas University–Magnolia, AR M
Southern Illinois University Carbondale, IL M
Southern Illinois University Edwardsville, IL M
Southern Nazarene University, OK M
Southern Polytechnic State University, GA M
Southern Utah University, UT M
Southern Wesleyan University, SC M
Southwest Baptist University, MO M
Southwestern Oklahoma State University, OK M
Southwest Missouri State University, MO M
Southwest State University, MN M
Southwest Texas State University, TX M
Spalding University, KY M
Spring Arbor College, MI M
Spring Hill College, AL M
Stanford University, CA M
State U of NY at Albany, NY M
State U of NY at Binghamton, NY M
State U of NY at Buffalo, NY M
State U of NY at Stony Brook, NY M
State University of West Georgia, GA M
Sterling College, KS M
Stetson University, FL M
Stonehill College, MA M
Tabor College, KS M
Talladega College, AL M
Tarleton State University, TX M
Taylor University, IN M
Teikyo Post University, CT M
Temple University, PA M
Tennessee Technological University, TN M
Tennessee Temple University, TN M
Tennessee Wesleyan College, TN M
Texas A&M University, TX M
Texas A&M University–Kingsville, TX M
Texas Christian University, TX M
Texas Lutheran University, TX M
Texas Tech University, TX M
Texas Wesleyan University, TX M
Thomas University, GA M
Tiffin University, OH M
Towson University, MD M
Trevecca Nazarene University, TN M
Trinity Christian College, IL M
Tri-State University, IN M
Troy State University, AL M
Truman State University, MO M
Tulane University, LA M
Tusculum College, TN M
Tuskegee University, AL M
Union College, KY M
Union University, TN M
The University of Akron, OH M
The University of Alabama, AL M
The University of Alabama at Birmingham, AL M
The University of Alabama in Huntsville, AL M
The University of Arizona, AZ M
University of Arkansas, AR M
University of Arkansas at Little Rock, AR M
University of Arkansas at Monticello, AR M
University of Bridgeport, CT M
U of Calif, Berkeley, CA M
U of Calif, Los Angeles, CA M
U of Calif, Riverside, CA M
U of Calif, Santa Barbara, CA M
University of Central Florida, FL M
University of Central Oklahoma, OK M
University of Charleston, WV M
University of Connecticut, CT M
University of Dayton, OH M
University of Delaware, DE M
University of Detroit Mercy, MI M
University of Evansville, IN M
The University of Findlay, OH M
University of Florida, FL M
University of Georgia, GA M
University of Hartford, CT M
University of Hawaii at Hilo, HI M
University of Hawaii at Manoa, HI M
University of Houston, TX M
University of Illinois at Chicago, IL M
University of Illinois at Urbana–Champaign, IL M
University of Indianapolis, IN M
The University of Iowa, IA M
University of Kansas, KS M
University of Louisiana at Lafayette, LA M
University of Louisiana at Monroe, LA M
University of Louisville, KY M
University of Maine, ME M
University of Mary, ND M
University of Maryland, Baltimore County, MD M
University of Maryland, College Park, MD M
University of Massachusetts Amherst, MA M
The University of Memphis, TN M
University of Miami, FL M
University of Michigan, MI M
University of Minnesota, Crookston, MN M
University of Minnesota, Duluth, MN M
University of Minnesota, Twin Cities Campus, MN M
University of Mississippi, MS M
University of Missouri–Columbia, MO M
University of Missouri–Rolla, MO M
University of Missouri–St. Louis, MO M
University of Mobile, AL M
University of Montevallo, AL M
University of Nebraska at Kearney, NE M
University of Nebraska at Omaha, NE M
University of Nebraska–Lincoln, NE M
University of Nevada, Las Vegas, NV M
University of Nevada, Reno, NV M
University of New Haven, CT M
University of New Orleans, LA M
University of North Alabama, AL M
The University of North Carolina at Asheville, NC M
The University of North Carolina at Chapel Hill, NC M
The University of North Carolina at Charlotte, NC M
The University of North Carolina at Greensboro, NC M

The University of North Carolina at Pembroke, NC M
The University of North Carolina at Wilmington, NC M
University of North Dakota, ND M
University of Northern Colorado, CO M
University of Northern Iowa, IA M
University of North Florida, FL M
University of Notre Dame, IN M
University of Oklahoma, OK M
University of Pittsburgh, PA M
University of Portland, OR M
University of Rhode Island, RI M
University of Richmond, VA M
University of Rio Grande, OH M
University of St. Francis, IL M
University of Saint Francis, IN M
University of San Diego, CA M
University of San Francisco, CA M
University of Science and Arts of Oklahoma, OK M
University of South Alabama, AL M
University of South Carolina, SC M
University of South Carolina Aiken, SC M
U of South Carolina Spartanburg, SC M
University of South Dakota, SD M
University of Southern California, CA M
University of Southern Indiana, IN M
University of Southern Mississippi, MS M
University of South Florida, FL M
The University of Tampa, FL M
The University of Tennessee at Martin, TN M
The University of Tennessee Knoxville, TN M
The University of Texas at Arlington, TX M
The University of Texas at Austin, TX M
The University of Texas at San Antonio, TX M
The University of Texas–Pan American, TX M
University of the Incarnate Word, TX M
University of the Pacific, CA M
University of the Sciences in Philadelphia, PA M
University of Toledo, OH M
University of Utah, UT M
University of Vermont, VT M
University of Virginia, VA M
University of Virginia's College at Wise, VA M
University of Washington, WA M
The University of West Alabama, AL M
University of West Florida, FL M
Urbana University, OH M
Valdosta State University, GA M
Valley City State University, ND M
Valparaiso University, IN M
Vanderbilt University, TN M
Vanguard University of Southern California, CA M
Villanova University, PA M
Virginia Commonwealth University, VA M
Virginia Intermont College, VA M
Virginia Military Institute, VA M
Virginia Polytechnic Institute and State U, VA M
Wagner College, NY M
Wake Forest University, NC M
Walsh University, OH M
Warner Southern College, FL M
Washburn University of Topeka, KS M
Washington State University, WA M
Wayland Baptist University, TX M
Wayne State College, NE M
Wayne State University, MI M
Webber College, FL M
West Chester University of Pennsylvania, PA M
Western Baptist College, OR M
Western Carolina University, NC M
Western Illinois University, IL M
Western Kentucky University, KY M
Western Michigan University, MI M
West Liberty State College, WV M
Westmont College, CA M
West Texas A&M University, TX M
West Virginia University, WV M
West Virginia University Institute of Technology, WV M
Wichita State University, KS M
William Carey College, MS M
William Jewell College, MO M
Williams Baptist College, AR M
William Woods University, MO M
Wingate University, NC M
Winona State University, MN M
Winthrop University, SC M
Wofford College, SC M
Xavier University, OH M
York College, NE M
Youngstown State University, OH M

BASKETBALL

Abilene Christian University, TX M,W
Adams State College, CO M,W
Adelphi University, NY M,W
Alabama Agricultural and Mechanical University, AL M,W
Alabama State University, AL M,W
Albany State University, GA M,W
Albertson College of Idaho, ID M,W
Alcorn State University, MS M,W
Alice Lloyd College, KY M,W
Allen University, SC M,W
American International College, MA M,W
American University, DC M,W
Anderson College, SC M,W
Angelo State University, TX M,W
Appalachian State University, NC M,W
Aquinas College, MI M,W
Aquinas College, TN M
Arizona State University, AZ M,W
Arkansas State University, AR M,W
Arkansas Tech University, AR M,W
Armstrong Atlantic State University, GA M,W
Ashland University, OH M,W
Assumption College, MA M,W
Athens State University, AL M
Atlantic Union College, MA M,W
Auburn University, AL M,W
Auburn University Montgomery, AL M,W
Augustana College, SD M,W
Augusta State University, GA M,W
Austin Peay State University, TN M,W
Avila College, MO M,W
Azusa Pacific University, CA M,W
Baker University, KS M,W
Ball State University, IN M,W
Barat College, IL M
Barber-Scotia College, NC M,W
Barry University, FL M,W
Bartlesville Wesleyan College, OK M,W
Barton College, NC M,W
Bayamón Central University, PR M,W
Baylor University, TX M,W
Belhaven College, MS M,W
Bellarmine College, KY M,W
Bellevue University, NE M
Belmont Abbey College, NC M,W
Belmont University, TN M,W
Bemidji State University, MN M,W
Benedictine College, KS M,W
Bentley College, MA M,W
Berry College, GA M,W
Bethany College, KS M,W
Bethany College of the Assemblies of God, CA M,W
Bethel College, IN M,W
Bethel College, KS M,W
Bethel College, TN M,W
Bethune-Cookman College, FL M,W
Biola University, CA M,W
Birmingham-Southern College, AL M
Black Hills State University, SD M,W
Bloomfield College, NJ M,W
Bloomsburg University of Pennsylvania, PA M,W
Bluefield College, VA M,W
Bluefield State College, WV M,W
Blue Mountain College, MS W
Boise State University, ID M,W
Boston College, MA M,W
Boston University, MA M,W
Bowie State University, MD M,W
Bowling Green State University, OH M,W
Bradley University, IL M,W
Brescia University, KY M,W
Brevard College, NC M,W
Briar Cliff College, IA M,W
Brigham Young University, UT M,W
Brigham Young University–Hawaii Campus, HI M
Bryan College, TN M,W
Bryant College, RI M,W
Butler University, IN M,W
Caldwell College, NJ M,W
California Baptist University, CA M,W
California Polytechnic State U, San Luis Obispo, CA M,W
California State Polytechnic University, Pomona, CA M,W
California State University, Bakersfield, CA M
California State University, Dominguez Hills, CA M,W
California State University, Fresno, CA M,W
California State University, Fullerton, CA M,W
California State University, Long Beach, CA M,W
California State University, Los Angeles, CA M,W
California State University, Northridge, CA M,W
California State University, Sacramento, CA M,W
California State University, San Bernardino, CA M,W

Basketball (continued)

California University of Pennsylvania, PA M,W
Cameron University, OK M,W
Campbellsville University, KY M,W
Campbell University, NC M,W
Canisius College, NY M,W
Carlow College, PA W
Carroll College, MT M,W
Carson-Newman College, TN M,W
Catawba College, NC M,W
Cedarville College, OH M,W
Centenary College of Louisiana, LA M,W
Central Connecticut State University, CT M,W
Central Methodist College, MO M,W
Central Michigan University, MI M,W
Central Missouri State University, MO M,W
Central State University, OH M,W
Central Washington University, WA M,W
Chadron State College, NE M,W
Chaminade University of Honolulu, HI M
Champlain College, VT M
Charleston Southern University, SC M,W
Cheyney University of Pennsylvania, PA M,W
Chicago State University, IL M,W
Christian Brothers University, TN M,W
Christian Heritage College, CA M,W
Citadel, The Military Coll of South Carolina, SC M
Claflin University, SC M,W
Clarion University of Pennsylvania, PA M,W
Clark Atlanta University, GA M,W
Clayton College & State University, GA M,W
Clemson University, SC M,W
Coastal Carolina University, SC M,W
Coker College, SC M,W
College of Charleston, SC M,W
College of St. Joseph, VT M,W
College of Saint Mary, NE W
The College of Saint Rose, NY M,W
College of the Ozarks, MO M,W
The College of West Virginia, WV M
The College of William and Mary, VA M,W
Colorado Christian University, CO M,W
Colorado School of Mines, CO M,W
Colorado State University, CO M,W
Columbia College, MO M
Columbia Union College, MD M,W
Columbus State University, GA M,W
Concord College, WV M,W
Concordia College, AL M
Concordia College, MI M,W
Concordia College, NY M,W
Concordia University, CA M,W
Concordia University, NE M,W
Concordia University, OR M,W
Concordia University at St. Paul, MN M,W
Converse College, SC W
Coppin State College, MD M,W
Cornerstone University, MI M,W
Covenant College, GA M,W
Creighton University, NE M,W
Culver-Stockton College, MO M,W
Cumberland College, KY M,W
Cumberland University, TN M,W
Daemen College, NY M,W
Dakota State University, SD M,W
Dakota Wesleyan University, SD M,W
Dana College, NE M,W
David Lipscomb University, TN M,W
Davidson College, NC M,W
Davis & Elkins College, WV M,W
Delaware State University, DE M,W
Delta State University, MS M,W
DePaul University, IL M,W
Dickinson State University, ND M,W
Dillard University, LA M,W
Doane College, NE M,W
Dominican College of Blauvelt, NY M,W
Dominican University of California, CA M,W
Dordt College, IA M,W
Dowling College, NY M,W
Drake University, IA M,W
Drexel University, PA M
Drury University, MO M,W
Duke University, NC M,W
Duquesne University, PA M,W
D'Youville College, NY M,W
East Carolina University, NC M,W
East Central University, OK M,W
Eastern Illinois University, IL M,W
Eastern Kentucky University, KY M,W
Eastern Michigan University, MI M,W
Eastern New Mexico University, NM M,W
Eastern Washington University, WA M,W
East Stroudsburg University of Pennsylvania, PA M,W
East Tennessee State University, TN M,W
Eckerd College, FL M,W
Edinboro University of Pennsylvania, PA M,W
Edward Waters College, FL M,W
Elon College, NC M,W
Embry-Riddle Aeronautical University, FL M
Emmanuel College, GA M,W
Emporia State University, KS M,W
Erskine College, SC M,W
Evangel University, MO M,W
Fairfield University, CT M,W
Fairleigh Dickinson U, Teaneck-Hackensack Campus, NJ M,W
Fairmont State College, WV M,W
Faulkner University, AL M
Fayetteville State University, NC M
Felician College, NJ M,W
Ferris State University, MI M,W
Five Towns College, NY M
Flagler College, FL M,W
Florida Agricultural and Mechanical University, FL M,W
Florida Atlantic University, FL M,W
Florida College, FL M
Florida Institute of Technology, FL M,W
Florida International University, FL M,W
Florida Memorial College, FL M
Florida Southern College, FL M,W
Florida State University, FL M,W
Fordham University, NY M,W
Fort Hays State University, KS M,W
Fort Lewis College, CO M,W
Fort Valley State University, GA M,W
Francis Marion University, SC M,W
Franklin Pierce College, NH M,W
Fresno Pacific University, CA M,W
Friends University, KS M,W
Furman University, SC M,W
Gannon University, PA M,W
Gardner-Webb University, NC M,W
Geneva College, PA M,W
George Mason University, VA M,W
Georgetown College, KY M,W
Georgetown University, DC M,W
The George Washington University, DC M,W
Georgia College and State University, GA M,W
Georgia Institute of Technology, GA M,W
Georgian Court College, NJ W
Georgia Southern University, GA M,W
Georgia Southwestern State University, GA M,W
Georgia State University, GA M,W
Glenville State College, WV M,W
Goldey-Beacom College, DE M,W
Gonzaga University, WA M,W
Goshen College, IN M,W
Grace College, IN M,W
Graceland College, IA M,W
Grambling State University, LA M,W
Grand Canyon University, AZ M,W
Grand Valley State University, MI M,W
Grand View College, IA M,W
Green Mountain College, VT M,W
Hampton University, VA M,W
Hannibal-LaGrange College, MO M,W
Harding University, AR M,W
Harris-Stowe State College, MO M,W
Hastings College, NE M,W
Hawaii Pacific University, HI M
Henderson State University, AR M,W
High Point University, NC M,W
Hillsdale College, MI M,W
Hofstra University, NY M,W
Holy Family College, PA M,W
Holy Names College, CA M,W
Hope International University, CA M,W
Houghton College, NY M,W
Houston Baptist University, TX M,W
Humboldt State University, CA M,W
Huntington College, IN M,W
Huron University, SD M,W
Idaho State University, ID M,W
Illinois Institute of Technology, IL M,W
Illinois State University, IL M,W
Indiana Institute of Technology, IN M,W
Indiana State University, IN M,W
Indiana University Bloomington, IN M,W
Indiana University of Pennsylvania, PA M,W
Indiana U–Purdue U Fort Wayne, IN M,W
Indiana U–Purdue U Indianapolis, IN M,W
Indiana University South Bend, IN M,W
Indiana University Southeast, IN M,W
Indiana Wesleyan University, IN M,W
Inter American U of PR, Arecibo Campus, PR M,W
Inter American U of PR, San Germán Campus, PR M,W
Iona College, NY M,W
Iowa State University of Science and Technology, IA M,W
Iowa Wesleyan College, IA M,W
Jacksonville State University, AL M,W
Jacksonville University, FL M
James Madison University, VA M,W
Jamestown College, ND M,W
John Brown University, AR M,W
Johnson C. Smith University, NC M,W
Judson College, AL W

Judson College, IL M,W
Kansas State University, KS M,W
Kansas Wesleyan University, KS M,W
Kennesaw State University, GA M,W
Kent State University, OH M,W
Kentucky Wesleyan College, KY M,W
King College, TN M,W
Kutztown University of Pennsylvania, PA M,W
Lake Superior State University, MI M,W
Lamar University, TX M,W
Lambuth University, TN M,W
Lander University, SC M,W
Langston University, OK M,W
La Salle University, PA M,W
Lees-McRae College, NC M,W
Lee University, TN M,W
Lehigh University, PA M
Le Moyne College, NY M,W
LeMoyne-Owen College, TN M,W
Lewis-Clark State College, ID M,W
Lewis University, IL M,W
Liberty University, VA M,W
Limestone College, SC M,W
Lincoln Memorial University, TN M,W
Lincoln University, MO M,W
Lock Haven University of Pennsylvania, PA M,W
Long Island U, Brooklyn Campus, NY M,W
Long Island U, C.W. Post Campus, NY M,W
Long Island U, Southampton College, NY M,W
Longwood College, VA M,W
Louisiana State University and A&M College, LA M,W
Louisiana Tech University, LA M,W
Loyola Marymount University, CA M,W
Loyola University Chicago, IL M,W
Lubbock Christian University, TX M,W
Lynn University, FL M,W
Lyon College, AR M,W
Madonna University, MI M,W
Malone College, OH M,W
Manhattan College, NY M,W
Mansfield University of Pennsylvania, PA M,W
Marian College, IN M,W
Marist College, NY M,W
Marquette University, WI M,W
Marshall University, WV M,W
Mars Hill College, NC M,W
Martin Methodist College, TN M,W
Marycrest International University, IA M,W
The Master's College and Seminary, CA M,W
Mayville State University, ND M,W
McKendree College, IL M,W
McNeese State University, LA M,W
Mercer University, GA M,W
Mercy College, NY M,W
Mercyhurst College, PA M,W
Merrimack College, MA M,W
Mesa State College, CO M,W
Metropolitan State College of Denver, CO M,W
Miami University, OH M,W
Michigan State University, MI M,W
Michigan Technological University, MI M,W
MidAmerica Nazarene University, KS M,W
Middle Tennessee State University, TN M,W
Midland Lutheran College, NE M,W
Midway College, KY W
Midwestern State University, TX M,W
Millersville University of Pennsylvania, PA M,W
Milligan College, TN M,W
Minnesota State University, Mankato, MN M,W
Minnesota State University Moorhead, MN M,W
Minot State University, ND M,W
Mississippi State University, MS M,W
Mississippi University for Women, MS W
Mississippi Valley State University, MS M,W
Missouri Baptist College, MO M,W
Missouri Southern State College, MO M,W
Missouri Valley College, MO M,W
Missouri Western State College, MO M,W
Monmouth University, NJ M,W
Montana State U–Billings, MT M,W
Montana State U–Bozeman, MT M,W
Montana State U–Northern, MT M,W
Montana Tech of The University of Montana, MT M,W
Montreat College, NC M,W
Morehead State University, KY M,W
Morgan State University, MD M,W
Morningside College, IA M,W
Mount Aloysius College, PA M,W
Mount Marty College, SD M,W
Mount Olive College, NC M,W
Mount St. Clare College, IA M,W
Mount Saint Mary's College and Seminary, MD M,W
Mount Vernon Nazarene College, OH M,W
Murray State University, KY M,W
Newberry College, SC M,W
New Hampshire College, NH M,W
Newman University, KS M,W
New Mexico Highlands University, NM M,W
New York Institute of Technology, NY M
Niagara University, NY M,W
Norfolk State University, VA M,W
North Carolina Agricultural and Technical State U, NC M,W
North Carolina Central University, NC M,W
North Carolina State University, NC M,W
North Dakota State University, ND M,W
Northeastern State University, OK M,W
Northeastern University, MA M,W
Northern Arizona University, AZ M,W
Northern Illinois University, IL M,W
Northern Kentucky University, KY M,W
Northern Michigan University, MI M,W
North Georgia College & State University, GA M,W
North Greenville College, SC M,W
Northwest Christian College, OR M
Northwest College, WA M,W
Northwestern College, IA M,W
Northwestern Oklahoma State University, OK M,W
Northwestern State University of Louisiana, LA M,W
Northwestern University, IL M,W
Northwest Missouri State University, MO M,W
Northwest Nazarene University, ID M,W
Northwood University, MI M,W
Notre Dame College, NH M,W
Nova Southeastern University, FL M
Nyack College, NY M,W
Oakland City University, IN M,W
Oakland University, MI M,W
Ohio Dominican College, OH M,W
The Ohio State University, OH M,W
Ohio University, OH M,W
Ohio Valley College, WV M,W
Oklahoma Baptist University, OK M,W
Oklahoma Christian U of Science and Arts, OK M,W
Oklahoma City University, OK M,W
Oklahoma Panhandle State University, OK M,W
Oklahoma State U, OK M,W
Old Dominion University, VA M,W
Olivet Nazarene University, IL M,W
Oral Roberts University, OK M,W
Oregon Institute of Technology, OR M
Oregon State University, OR M,W
Ottawa University, KS M,W
Ouachita Baptist University, AR M,W
Paine College, GA M,W
Palm Beach Atlantic College, FL M,W
Park University, MO M,W
Penn State U Univ Park Campus, PA M,W
Pepperdine University, CA M,W
Pfeiffer University, NC M,W
Philadelphia University, PA M,W
Piedmont College, GA M,W
Pikeville College, KY M,W
Pittsburg State University, KS M,W
Point Loma Nazarene University, CA M,W
Point Park College, PA M,W
Portland State University, OR M,W
Prairie View A&M University, TX M,W
Presbyterian College, SC M,W
Providence College, RI M,W
Purdue University, IN M,W
Purdue University Calumet, IN M,W
Queens College, NC M,W
Queens Coll of the City U of NY, NY M,W
Quincy University, IL M,W
Quinnipiac University, CT M,W
Radford University, VA M,W
Regis University, CO M,W
Reinhardt College, GA M,W
Research College of Nursing, MO M,W
Rice University, TX M,W
Rider University, NJ M,W
Robert Morris College, IL M,W
Robert Morris College, PA M,W
Roberts Wesleyan College, NY M,W
Rochester College, MI M,W
Rockhurst University, MO M,W
Rocky Mountain College, MT M,W
Rollins College, FL M,W
Rutgers, State U of NJ, College of Pharmacy, NJ M,W
Rutgers, State U of NJ, Cook College, NJ M,W
Rutgers, State U of NJ, Douglass College, NJ W
Rutgers, State U of NJ, Livingston College, NJ M,W
Rutgers, State U of NJ, Mason Gross School of Arts, NJ M,W
Rutgers, State U of NJ, Rutgers College, NJ M,W
Rutgers, State U of NJ, College of Engineering, NJ M,W

Basketball (continued)

Sacred Heart University, CT M,W
Saginaw Valley State University, MI M,W
St. Ambrose University, IA M,W
St. Andrews Presbyterian College, NC M,W
Saint Anselm College, NH M,W
Saint Augustine's College, NC M,W
St. Bonaventure University, NY M,W
St. Edward's University, TX M,W
St. Francis College, NY M,W
Saint Francis College, PA M,W
St. Gregory's University, OK M,W
St. John's University, NY M,W
Saint Joseph's College, IN M,W
Saint Joseph's University, PA M,W
Saint Leo University, FL M,W
Saint Louis University, MO M,W
Saint Martin's College, WA M,W
Saint Mary College, KS M,W
Saint Mary-of-the-Woods College, IN W
Saint Mary's College of California, CA M,W
St. Mary's University of San Antonio, TX M,W
Saint Michael's College, VT M,W
Saint Paul's College, VA M,W
Saint Peter's College, NJ M,W
St. Thomas Aquinas College, NY M,W
Saint Vincent College, PA M,W
Saint Xavier University, IL M
Salem-Teikyo University, WV M,W
Samford University, AL M,W
Sam Houston State University, TX M,W
San Diego State University, CA M,W
San Francisco State University, CA M,W
San Jose State University, CA M,W
Santa Clara University, CA M,W
Savannah State University, GA M,W
Seattle Pacific University, WA M,W
Seton Hall University, NJ M,W
Seton Hill College, PA W
Shaw University, NC M,W
Shepherd College, WV M,W
Shippensburg University of Pennsylvania, PA M,W
Shorter College, GA M,W
Siena College, NY M,W
Siena Heights University, MI M,W
Slippery Rock University of Pennsylvania, PA M,W
South Dakota School of Mines and Technology, SD M,W
South Dakota State University, SD M,W
Southeastern Louisiana University, LA M,W
Southeast Missouri State University, MO M,W
Southern Arkansas University–Magnolia, AR M,W
Southern Illinois University Carbondale, IL M,W
Southern Illinois University Edwardsville, IL M,W
Southern Methodist University, TX M,W
Southern Nazarene University, OK M,W
Southern Oregon University, OR M,W
Southern Polytechnic State University, GA M
Southern University and A&M College, LA M,W
Southern University at New Orleans, LA M
Southern Utah University, UT M,W
Southern Wesleyan University, SC M,W
Southwest Baptist University, MO M,W
Southwestern Adventist University, TX M,W
Southwestern Christian College, TX M,W
Southwestern College, KS M,W
Southwestern Oklahoma State University, OK M,W
Southwest Missouri State University, MO M,W
Southwest State University, MN M,W
Southwest Texas State University, TX M,W
Spalding University, KY M,W
Spring Arbor College, MI M,W
Spring Hill College, AL M,W
Stanford University, CA M,W
State U of NY at Albany, NY M,W
State U of NY at Binghamton, NY M,W
State U of NY at Buffalo, NY M,W
State University of West Georgia, GA M,W
Stephen F. Austin State University, TX M,W
Sterling College, KS M,W
Stetson University, FL M,W
Stonehill College, MA M,W
Sullivan College, KY M,W
Syracuse University, NY M,W
Tabor College, KS M,W
Talladega College, AL M,W
Tarleton State University, TX M,W
Taylor University, IN M,W
Teikyo Post University, CT M,W
Temple University, PA M,W
Tennessee State University, TN M,W
Tennessee Technological University, TN M,W
Tennessee Temple University, TN M,W
Tennessee Wesleyan College, TN M,W
Texas A&M University, TX M,W
Texas A&M University–Commerce, TX M,W
Texas A&M University–Kingsville, TX M,W
Texas Christian University, TX M,W
Texas Lutheran University, TX M,W
Texas Tech University, TX M,W
Texas Wesleyan University, TX M,W
Texas Woman's University, TX W
Thomas University, GA M
Tiffin University, OH M,W
Tougaloo College, MS M,W
Towson University, MD M,W
Trevecca Nazarene University, TN M,W
Trinity Christian College, IL M,W
Tri-State University, IN M,W
Troy State University, AL M,W
Truman State University, MO M,W
Tulane University, LA M,W
Tusculum College, TN M,W
Tuskegee University, AL M,W
Union College, KY M,W
Union University, TN M,W
Unity College, ME M
The University of Akron, OH M,W
The University of Alabama, AL M,W
The University of Alabama at Birmingham, AL M,W
The University of Alabama in Huntsville, AL M,W
U of Alaska Anchorage, AK M,W
U of Alaska Fairbanks, AK M,W
The University of Arizona, AZ M,W
University of Arkansas, AR M,W
University of Arkansas at Little Rock, AR M
University of Arkansas at Monticello, AR M,W
University of Arkansas at Pine Bluff, AR M,W
University of Bridgeport, CT M,W
U of Calif, Berkeley, CA M,W
U of Calif, Irvine, CA M,W
U of Calif, Los Angeles, CA M,W
U of Calif, Riverside, CA M,W
U of Calif, Santa Barbara, CA M,W
University of Central Arkansas, AR M,W
University of Central Florida, FL M,W
University of Central Oklahoma, OK M,W
University of Charleston, WV M,W
University of Cincinnati, OH M,W
University of Colorado at Boulder, CO M,W
University of Colorado at Colorado Springs, CO M,W
University of Connecticut, CT M,W
University of Dayton, OH M,W
University of Delaware, DE M,W
University of Detroit Mercy, MI M,W
University of Evansville, IN M,W
The University of Findlay, OH M,W
University of Florida, FL M,W
University of Georgia, GA M,W
University of Great Falls, MT M,W
University of Guam, GU M,W
University of Hartford, CT M,W
University of Hawaii at Hilo, HI M
University of Hawaii at Manoa, HI M,W
University of Houston, TX M,W
University of Idaho, ID M,W
University of Illinois at Chicago, IL M,W
University of Illinois at Springfield, IL W
University of Illinois at Urbana–Champaign, IL M,W
University of Indianapolis, IN M,W
The University of Iowa, IA M,W
University of Kansas, KS M,W
University of Louisiana at Lafayette, LA M,W
University of Louisiana at Monroe, LA M,W
University of Louisville, KY M,W
University of Maine, ME M,W
University of Mary, ND M,W
University of Maryland, Baltimore County, MD M,W
University of Maryland, College Park, MD M,W
University of Massachusetts Amherst, MA M,W
University of Massachusetts Lowell, MA M,W
The University of Memphis, TN M,W
University of Miami, FL M,W
University of Michigan, MI M,W
University of Michigan–Dearborn, MI M,W
University of Minnesota, Crookston, MN M,W
University of Minnesota, Duluth, MN M,W
University of Minnesota, Twin Cities Campus, MN M,W
University of Mississippi, MS M,W
University of Missouri–Columbia, MO M,W
University of Missouri–Kansas City, MO M,W
University of Missouri–Rolla, MO M,W

University of Missouri–St. Louis, MO M,W
University of Mobile, AL M,W
The University of Montana–Missoula, MT M,W
University of Montevallo, AL M,W
University of Nebraska at Kearney, NE M,W
University of Nebraska at Omaha, NE M,W
University of Nebraska–Lincoln, NE M,W
University of Nevada, Las Vegas, NV M,W
University of Nevada, Reno, NV M,W
University of New Hampshire, NH M,W
University of New Haven, CT M,W
University of New Mexico, NM M,W
University of New Orleans, LA M,W
University of North Alabama, AL M,W
The University of North Carolina at Asheville, NC M,W
The University of North Carolina at Chapel Hill, NC M,W
The University of North Carolina at Charlotte, NC M,W
The University of North Carolina at Greensboro, NC M,W
The University of North Carolina at Pembroke, NC M,W
The University of North Carolina at Wilmington, NC M,W
University of North Dakota, ND M,W
University of Northern Colorado, CO M,W
University of Northern Iowa, IA M,W
University of North Florida, FL M,W
University of North Texas, TX M,W
University of Notre Dame, IN M,W
University of Oklahoma, OK M,W
University of Oregon, OR M,W
University of Pittsburgh, PA M,W
University of Pittsburgh at Johnstown, PA M,W
University of Portland, OR M,W
U of Puerto Rico, Cayey University College, PR M,W
U of Puerto Rico, Mayagüez Campus, PR M,W
University of Rhode Island, RI M,W
University of Richmond, VA M,W
University of Rio Grande, OH M,W
University of St. Francis, IL M,W
University of Saint Francis, IN M,W
University of San Diego, CA M,W
University of San Francisco, CA M,W
University of Science and Arts of Oklahoma, OK M,W
University of South Alabama, AL M,W
University of South Carolina, SC M,W
University of South Carolina Aiken, SC M,W
U of South Carolina Spartanburg, SC M,W
University of South Dakota, SD M,W
University of Southern California, CA M,W
University of Southern Colorado, CO M,W
University of Southern Indiana, IN M,W
University of Southern Mississippi, MS M,W
University of South Florida, FL M,W
The University of Tampa, FL M,W
The University of Tennessee at Chattanooga, TN M,W
The University of Tennessee at Martin, TN M,W
The University of Tennessee Knoxville, TN M,W
The University of Texas at Arlington, TX M,W
The University of Texas at Austin, TX M,W
The University of Texas at El Paso, TX M,W
The University of Texas at San Antonio, TX M,W
The University of Texas–Pan American, TX M,W
University of the District of Columbia, DC M,W
University of the Incarnate Word, TX M,W
University of the Pacific, CA M,W
University of the Sacred Heart, PR M
University of the Sciences in Philadelphia, PA M,W
University of Toledo, OH M,W
University of Tulsa, OK M,W
University of Utah, UT M,W
University of Vermont, VT M,W
University of Virginia, VA M,W
University of Virginia's College at Wise, VA M,W
University of Washington, WA M,W
The University of West Alabama, AL M,W
University of West Florida, FL M,W
University of Wisconsin–Green Bay, WI M,W
University of Wisconsin–Madison, WI M,W
University of Wisconsin–Milwaukee, WI M,W
University of Wisconsin–Parkside, WI M,W
University of Wyoming, WY M,W
Urbana University, OH M,W
Utah State University, UT M
Valdosta State University, GA M,W
Valley City State University, ND M,W
Valparaiso University, IN M,W
Vanderbilt University, TN M,W
Vanguard University of Southern California, CA M,W
Villanova University, PA M,W
Virginia Commonwealth University, VA M,W
Virginia Intermont College, VA M,W
Virginia Military Institute, VA M
Virginia Polytechnic Institute and State U, VA M,W
Virginia State University, VA M,W
Virginia Union University, VA M,W
Voorhees College, SC M,W
Wagner College, NY M,W
Wake Forest University, NC M,W
Walsh University, OH M,W
Warner Pacific College, OR M,W
Warner Southern College, FL M,W
Washburn University of Topeka, KS M,W
Washington State University, WA M,W
Wayland Baptist University, TX M,W
Wayne State College, NE M,W
Wayne State University, MI M,W
Webber College, FL M,W
Weber State University, UT M,W
West Chester University of Pennsylvania, PA M,W
Western Baptist College, OR M,W
Western Carolina University, NC M,W
Western Illinois University, IL M,W
Western Kentucky University, KY M,W
Western Michigan University, MI M,W
Western Montana College of The U of Montana, MT M,W
Western New Mexico University, NM M,W
Western State College of Colorado, CO M,W
Western Washington University, WA M,W
West Liberty State College, WV M
Westminster College, PA M,W
Westmont College, CA M,W
West Texas A&M University, TX M,W
West Virginia State College, WV M,W
West Virginia University, WV M,W
West Virginia University Institute of Technology, WV M,W
West Virginia Wesleyan College, WV M,W
Wheeling Jesuit University, WV M,W
Wichita State University, KS M,W
William Carey College, MS M,W
William Jewell College, MO M,W
Williams Baptist College, AR M,W
William Woods University, MO W
Wingate University, NC M,W
Winona State University, MN M,W
Winston-Salem State University, NC M,W
Winthrop University, SC M,W
Wofford College, SC M,W
Xavier University, OH M,W
Xavier University of Louisiana, LA M,W
York College, NE M,W
Youngstown State University, OH M,W

BOWLING

Briarcliffe College, NY M,W
Delaware State University, DE W
Prairie View A&M University, TX W
Saginaw Valley State University, MI M
Southern University and A&M College, LA W
West Texas A&M University, TX M,W

CREW

Barry University, FL W
Bloomfield College, NJ M
Boston University, MA M,W
Brenau University, GA W
California State University, Sacramento, CA M,W
Clemson University, SC W
Creighton University, NE W
Drexel University, PA M
Duke University, NC W
Duquesne University, PA W
Florida Institute of Technology, FL M,W
Florida State University, FL W
Fordham University, NY W
The George Washington University, DC M,W
Indiana University Bloomington, IN W
Jacksonville University, FL M,W
Kansas State University, KS W
La Salle University, PA M,W
Mercyhurst College, PA M,W
Michigan State University, MI W
Northeastern University, MA M,W
The Ohio State University, OH W
Robert Morris College, PA W
Rutgers, State U of NJ, College of Pharmacy, NJ M,W
Rutgers, State U of NJ, Cook College, NJ M,W
Rutgers, State U of NJ, Douglass College, NJ W
Rutgers, State U of NJ, Livingston College, NJ M,W
Rutgers, State U of NJ, Mason Gross School of Arts, NJ M,W

Crew (continued)

Rutgers, State U of NJ, Rutgers College, NJ M,W
Rutgers, State U of NJ, College of Engineering, NJ M,W
Southern Methodist University, TX W
Stanford University, CA W
State U of NY at Buffalo, NY W
Stetson University, FL M,W
Syracuse University, NY M,W
Temple University, PA M,W
U of Calif, Berkeley, CA M,W
University of Charleston, WV M,W
University of Delaware, DE W
The University of Iowa, IA W
University of Kansas, KS W
University of Massachusetts Amherst, MA W
University of Miami, FL W
University of New Hampshire, NH W
The University of North Carolina at Chapel Hill, NC W
University of Southern California, CA W
The University of Tampa, FL W
The University of Tennessee Knoxville, TN W
The University of Texas at Austin, TX W
University of Tulsa, OK W
University of Virginia, VA W
University of Washington, WA M,W
University of Wisconsin–Madison, WI M,W
Villanova University, PA W
Washington State University, WA W

CROSS-COUNTRY RUNNING

Abilene Christian University, TX M,W
Adams State College, CO M,W
Adelphi University, NY M,W
Alabama Agricultural and Mechanical University, AL M,W
Alabama State University, AL M,W
Albany State University, GA M,W
Alcorn State University, MS M,W
American University, DC M,W
Anderson College, SC M,W
Angelo State University, TX M,W
Appalachian State University, NC M,W
Aquinas College, MI M,W
Arizona State University, AZ M,W
Arkansas State University, AR M,W
Arkansas Tech University, AR W
Armstrong Atlantic State University, GA M
Ashland University, OH M,W
Auburn University, AL M,W
Augustana College, SD M,W
Augusta State University, GA M,W
Austin Peay State University, TN M,W
Azusa Pacific University, CA M,W
Baker University, KS M,W
Ball State University, IN M,W
Barber-Scotia College, NC M,W
Barton College, NC M,W
Bayamón Central University, PR M,W
Baylor University, TX M,W
Belhaven College, MS M,W
Bellarmine College, KY M,W
Belmont Abbey College, NC M,W
Belmont University, TN M,W
Benedictine College, KS M,W
Bentley College, MA M,W
Berry College, GA M,W
Bethany College, KS M,W
Bethel College, IN M,W
Bethune-Cookman College, FL M,W
Biola University, CA M,W
Black Hills State University, SD M,W
Bloomsburg University of Pennsylvania, PA W
Bluefield State College, WV M,W
Boise State University, ID M,W
Boston College, MA W
Boston University, MA M,W
Bowling Green State University, OH M,W
Bradley University, IL M,W
Brenau University, GA W
Brevard College, NC M,W
Briar Cliff College, IA M,W
Brigham Young University, UT M,W
Brigham Young University–Hawaii Campus, HI M,W
Butler University, IN M,W
California Baptist University, CA M,W
California Polytechnic State U, San Luis Obispo, CA M,W
California State Polytechnic University, Pomona, CA M,W
California State University, Fresno, CA M,W
California State University, Fullerton, CA M,W
California State University, Long Beach, CA M,W
California State University, Los Angeles, CA M,W
California State University, Northridge, CA M,W
California State University, Sacramento, CA M,W
California University of Pennsylvania, PA M,W
Campbellsville University, KY M,W
Campbell University, NC M,W
Canisius College, NY M,W
Carson-Newman College, TN M,W
Catawba College, NC M,W
Cedarville College, OH M,W
Centenary College of Louisiana, LA M,W
Central Connecticut State University, CT M,W
Central Methodist College, MO M,W
Central Michigan University, MI M,W
Central Missouri State University, MO M,W
Central Washington University, WA M,W
Chaminade University of Honolulu, HI M,W
Charleston Southern University, SC M,W
Cheyney University of Pennsylvania, PA M,W
Chicago State University, IL M,W
Citadel, The Military Coll of South Carolina, SC M,W
Clarion University of Pennsylvania, PA M,W
Clayton College & State University, GA M,W
Clemson University, SC M,W
Coastal Carolina University, SC M,W
Coker College, SC M,W
College of Charleston, SC M,W
College of St. Joseph, VT M,W
College of Saint Mary, NE W
The College of Saint Rose, NY M,W
The College of William and Mary, VA M,W
Colorado School of Mines, CO M,W
Colorado State University, CO M,W
Columbia Union College, MD M,W
Columbus State University, GA M,W
Concordia College, MI M,W
Concordia University, CA M,W
Concordia University, NE M,W
Concordia University at St. Paul, MN M,W
Converse College, SC W
Coppin State College, MD M,W
Cornerstone University, MI M,W
Covenant College, GA M,W
Creighton University, NE M,W
Cumberland College, KY M,W
Cumberland University, TN M,W
Daemen College, NY M,W
Dakota State University, SD M,W
Dakota Wesleyan University, SD M,W
Dallas Baptist University, TX W
Dana College, NE M,W
David Lipscomb University, TN M,W
Davidson College, NC M,W
Davis & Elkins College, WV M,W
Delaware State University, DE M,W
Delta State University, MS W
DePaul University, IL M,W
Dickinson State University, ND M,W
Doane College, NE M,W
Dominican College of Blauvelt, NY M,W
Dominican University of California, CA M,W
Dordt College, IA M,W
Drake University, IA M,W
Drexel University, PA M
Duquesne University, PA M,W
D'Youville College, NY M,W
East Carolina University, NC M,W
East Central University, OK M,W
Eastern Illinois University, IL M,W
Eastern Kentucky University, KY M,W
Eastern Michigan University, MI M,W
Eastern Washington University, WA M,W
East Stroudsburg University of Pennsylvania, PA M,W
East Tennessee State University, TN M,W
Eckerd College, FL W
Edinboro University of Pennsylvania, PA M,W
Elon College, NC M,W
Emporia State University, KS M,W
Erskine College, SC M,W
Evangel University, MO M,W
Fairleigh Dickinson U, Teaneck-Hackensack Campus, NJ M,W
Felician College, NJ M,W
Ferris State University, MI W
Flagler College, FL M,W
Florida Agricultural and Mechanical University, FL M,W
Florida Atlantic University, FL M,W
Florida Institute of Technology, FL M,W
Florida International University, FL M,W
Florida Southern College, FL M,W
Florida State University, FL M,W
Fordham University, NY M,W
Fort Hays State University, KS M,W
Fort Lewis College, CO M,W
Francis Marion University, SC M,W
Fresno Pacific University, CA M,W
Friends University, KS M,W
Furman University, SC M,W
Gannon University, PA M,W
Gardner-Webb University, NC M

Geneva College, PA M,W
George Mason University, VA M,W
Georgetown College, KY M,W
Georgetown University, DC M,W
The George Washington University, DC M,W
Georgia College and State University, GA M,W
Georgia Institute of Technology, GA M,W
Georgian Court College, NJ W
Georgia Southern University, GA W
Georgia State University, GA M,W
Glenville State College, WV M,W
Goshen College, IN M,W
Grace College, IN M,W
Graceland College, IA M,W
Grand Valley State University, MI M,W
Green Mountain College, VT M,W
Hampton University, VA M,W
Harding University, AR M,W
Hastings College, NE M,W
Hawaii Pacific University, HI M,W
Henderson State University, AR W
High Point University, NC M,W
Hillsdale College, MI M,W
Hofstra University, NY M,W
Holy Family College, PA W
Holy Names College, CA M,W
Houghton College, NY M,W
Humboldt State University, CA M,W
Huntington College, IN M,W
Idaho State University, ID M,W
Illinois Institute of Technology, IL M,W
Illinois State University, IL M,W
Indiana State University, IN M,W
Indiana University Bloomington, IN M,W
Indiana University of Pennsylvania, PA M,W
Indiana U–Purdue U Fort Wayne, IN M,W
Indiana U–Purdue U Indianapolis, IN M,W
Indiana Wesleyan University, IN M,W
Inter American U of PR, San Germán Campus, PR M,W
Iowa State University of Science and Technology, IA M,W
Iowa Wesleyan College, IA M,W
Jacksonville State University, AL M,W
Jacksonville University, FL M,W
James Madison University, VA M,W
Jamestown College, ND M,W
Judson College, IL M,W
Kansas State University, KS M,W
Kansas Wesleyan University, KS M,W
Kennesaw State University, GA M,W
Kent State University, OH M,W
Kutztown University of Pennsylvania, PA M,W
Lake Superior State University, MI M,W
Lamar University, TX M,W
Lambuth University, TN M,W
Lander University, SC M,W
La Salle University, PA M,W
Lees-McRae College, NC M,W
Lee University, TN M,W
Lehigh University, PA M,W
Le Moyne College, NY M,W
LeMoyne-Owen College, TN M
Lewis-Clark State College, ID M,W
Lewis University, IL M,W
Liberty University, VA M,W
Lincoln Memorial University, TN M,W
Lincoln University, MO M,W
Lock Haven University of Pennsylvania, PA M,W
Long Island U, Brooklyn Campus, NY W
Long Island U, C.W. Post Campus, NY M,W
Louisiana State University and A&M College, LA M,W
Louisiana Tech University, LA M,W
Loyola University Chicago, IL M,W
Lyon College, AR M,W
Malone College, OH M,W
Manhattan College, NY M,W
Marian College, IN M,W
Marist College, NY M,W
Marquette University, WI M,W
Marshall University, WV M,W
Mars Hill College, NC M,W
The Master's College and Seminary, CA M,W
McKendree College, IL M,W
McNeese State University, LA M,W
Mercer University, GA M,W
Mercy College, NY M,W
Mercyhurst College, PA M,W
Merrimack College, MA W
Mesa State College, CO W
Miami University, OH M,W
Michigan State University, MI M,W
MidAmerica Nazarene University, KS M,W
Middle Tennessee State University, TN M,W
Midland Lutheran College, NE M,W
Midway College, KY W
Millersville University of Pennsylvania, PA M,W
Milligan College, TN M,W
Minnesota State University, Mankato, MN M,W
Minot State University, ND M,W
Mississippi State University, MS W
Mississippi Valley State University, MS M,W
Missouri Southern State College, MO M,W
Missouri Valley College, MO M,W
Monmouth University, NJ M,W
Montana State U–Billings, MT M,W
Montana State U–Bozeman, MT M,W
Montreat College, NC M,W
Morehead State University, KY M,W
Morgan State University, MD M,W
Morningside College, IA M,W
Mount Marty College, SD M,W
Mount Olive College, NC M,W
Mount St. Clare College, IA M,W
Mount Saint Mary's College and Seminary, MD M,W
Murray State University, KY M,W
Newberry College, SC M,W
New Mexico Highlands University, NM M,W
New York Institute of Technology, NY M,W
Niagara University, NY M,W
Norfolk State University, VA M
North Carolina Agricultural and Technical State U, NC M,W
North Carolina State University, NC M,W
North Dakota State University, ND M,W
Northeastern University, MA M,W
Northern Arizona University, AZ M,W
Northern Kentucky University, KY M,W
Northern Michigan University, MI W
North Greenville College, SC M,W
Northwest College, WA M,W
Northwestern College, IA M,W
Northwestern State University of Louisiana, LA M,W
Northwestern University, IL W
Northwest Missouri State University, MO M,W
Northwest Nazarene University, ID M,W
Northwood University, MI M,W
Northwood University, Texas Campus, TX M,W
Nova Southeastern University, FL M,W
Oakland City University, IN M,W
Oakland University, MI M,W
The Ohio State University, OH M,W
Ohio University, OH M,W
Ohio Valley College, WV M,W
Oklahoma Baptist University, OK M,W
Oklahoma Christian U of Science and Arts, OK M,W
Oklahoma State U, OK M,W
Old Dominion University, VA W
Olivet Nazarene University, IL M,W
Oral Roberts University, OK M,W
Oregon Institute of Technology, OR M,W
Ottawa University, KS M,W
Paine College, GA M,W
Palm Beach Atlantic College, FL M,W
Park University, MO M,W
Penn State U Univ Park Campus, PA M,W
Pepperdine University, CA M,W
Pfeiffer University, NC M,W
Pikeville College, KY M,W
Pittsburg State University, KS M
Point Loma Nazarene University, CA M,W
Portland State University, OR M,W
Presbyterian College, SC M,W
Providence College, RI M,W
Purdue University, IN M,W
Queens College, NC M,W
Quinnipiac University, CT M,W
Radford University, VA M,W
Regis University, CO M,W
Rice University, TX M,W
Rider University, NJ M,W
Robert Morris College, IL M,W
Robert Morris College, PA M,W
Roberts Wesleyan College, NY M,W
Rochester College, MI M,W
Rockhurst University, MO M,W
Rutgers, State U of NJ, College of Pharmacy, NJ M,W
Rutgers, State U of NJ, Cook College, NJ M,W
Rutgers, State U of NJ, Douglass College, NJ W
Rutgers, State U of NJ, Livingston College, NJ M,W
Rutgers, State U of NJ, Mason Gross School of Arts, NJ M,W
Rutgers, State U of NJ, Rutgers College, NJ M,W
Rutgers, State U of NJ, College of Engineering, NJ M,W
Saginaw Valley State University, MI M,W
St. Ambrose University, IA M,W
St. Andrews Presbyterian College, NC M,W
Saint Augustine's College, NC M,W
St. Bonaventure University, NY M,W
St. Francis College, NY M,W
Saint Francis College, PA M,W
St. Gregory's University, OK M,W

Cross-country running (continued)

St. John's University, NY M,W
Saint Joseph's College, IN M,W
Saint Joseph's University, PA M,W
Saint Louis University, MO M,W
Saint Martin's College, WA M,W
Saint Mary's College of California, CA M,W
Saint Peter's College, NJ M,W
St. Thomas Aquinas College, NY M,W
St. Thomas University, FL M,W
Saint Vincent College, PA M,W
Saint Xavier University, IL W
Samford University, AL M,W
San Diego State University, CA W
San Francisco State University, CA M,W
San Jose State University, CA M,W
Santa Clara University, CA M,W
Savannah State University, GA W
Seattle Pacific University, WA M,W
Seton Hall University, NJ M,W
Seton Hill College, PA W
Shippensburg University of Pennsylvania, PA M,W
Shorter College, GA M,W
Siena Heights University, MI M,W
Slippery Rock University of Pennsylvania, PA M,W
South Dakota School of Mines and Technology, SD M,W
South Dakota State University, SD M,W
Southeastern Louisiana University, LA M,W
Southeast Missouri State University, MO M,W
Southern Arkansas University–Magnolia, AR W
Southern Illinois University Carbondale, IL M,W
Southern Illinois University Edwardsville, IL M,W
Southern Methodist University, TX M,W
Southern Nazarene University, OK M,W
Southern Oregon University, OR M,W
Southern University and A&M College, LA M
Southern University at New Orleans, LA M,W
Southern Wesleyan University, SC M,W
Southwest Baptist University, MO M,W
Southwestern College, KS M,W
Southwestern Oklahoma State University, OK W
Southwest Missouri State University, MO M,W
Southwest Texas State University, TX M,W
Spring Arbor College, MI M,W
Spring Hill College, AL M,W
Stanford University, CA M,W
State U of NY at Albany, NY M,W
State U of NY at Binghamton, NY M,W
State U of NY at Buffalo, NY M,W
State University of West Georgia, GA M,W
Stephen F. Austin State University, TX M,W
Sterling College, KS M,W
Stetson University, FL M,W
Stonehill College, MA M,W
Syracuse University, NY M,W
Tabor College, KS M,W
Taylor University, IN M,W
Teikyo Post University, CT M,W
Tennessee State University, TN M,W
Tennessee Technological University, TN M,W
Texas A&M University, TX M,W
Texas A&M University–Commerce, TX M,W
Texas A&M University–Kingsville, TX M,W
Texas Christian University, TX M,W
Texas Tech University, TX M,W
Tiffin University, OH M,W
Tougaloo College, MS M,W
Towson University, MD M,W
Tri-State University, IN M,W
Troy State University, AL M
Truman State University, MO M,W
Tulane University, LA M,W
Tusculum College, TN M,W
Union College, KY M,W
Union University, TN W
United States International University, CA M,W
Unity College, ME M,W
The University of Akron, OH M,W
The University of Alabama, AL M,W
The University of Alabama at Birmingham, AL W
The University of Alabama in Huntsville, AL M,W
U of Alaska Anchorage, AK M
U of Alaska Fairbanks, AK M,W
The University of Arizona, AZ M,W
University of Arkansas, AR M,W
University of Arkansas at Little Rock, AR M,W
U of Calif, Berkeley, CA M,W
U of Calif, Irvine, CA W
U of Calif, Los Angeles, CA M,W
U of Calif, Riverside, CA M,W
U of Calif, Santa Barbara, CA M,W
University of Central Florida, FL M,W
University of Central Oklahoma, OK M,W
University of Charleston, WV M,W
University of Cincinnati, OH M,W
University of Colorado at Boulder, CO M,W
University of Colorado at Colorado Springs, CO M,W
University of Connecticut, CT M,W
University of Dayton, OH M,W
University of Detroit Mercy, MI M,W
University of Evansville, IN M,W
The University of Findlay, OH M,W
University of Florida, FL M,W
University of Georgia, GA M,W
University of Hartford, CT M,W
University of Hawaii at Hilo, HI M,W
University of Hawaii at Manoa, HI W
University of Houston, TX M,W
University of Idaho, ID M,W
University of Illinois at Chicago, IL M,W
University of Illinois at Urbana–Champaign, IL M,W
University of Indianapolis, IN M,W
The University of Iowa, IA M,W
University of Kansas, KS M,W
University of Louisiana at Lafayette, LA M,W
University of Louisiana at Monroe, LA M,W
University of Louisville, KY M,W
University of Maine, ME M,W
University of Mary, ND M,W
University of Maryland, Baltimore County, MD M,W
University of Massachusetts Amherst, MA M,W
University of Massachusetts Lowell, MA M,W
The University of Memphis, TN M,W
University of Miami, FL M,W
University of Michigan, MI M,W
University of Minnesota, Duluth, MN M,W
University of Minnesota, Twin Cities Campus, MN M,W
University of Mississippi, MS M,W
University of Missouri–Columbia, MO M,W
University of Missouri–Kansas City, MO M,W
University of Missouri–Rolla, MO M,W
University of Mobile, AL M,W
The University of Montana–Missoula, MT M,W
University of Nebraska at Kearney, NE M,W
University of Nebraska at Omaha, NE W
University of Nebraska–Lincoln, NE M,W
University of Nevada, Las Vegas, NV W
University of Nevada, Reno, NV W
University of New Hampshire, NH W
University of New Haven, CT M,W
University of New Mexico, NM M,W
University of New Orleans, LA M,W
University of North Alabama, AL M,W
The University of North Carolina at Asheville, NC M,W
The University of North Carolina at Chapel Hill, NC M,W
The University of North Carolina at Charlotte, NC M,W
The University of North Carolina at Greensboro, NC M,W
The University of North Carolina at Pembroke, NC M,W
The University of North Carolina at Wilmington, NC M,W
University of Northern Colorado, CO W
University of Northern Iowa, IA M,W
University of North Florida, FL M,W
University of North Texas, TX M,W
University of Notre Dame, IN M,W
University of Oklahoma, OK M,W
University of Oregon, OR M,W
University of Pittsburgh, PA M,W
University of Portland, OR M,W
U of Puerto Rico, Cayey University College, PR M,W
U of Puerto Rico, Mayagüez Campus, PR M,W
University of Rhode Island, RI M,W
University of Richmond, VA W
University of Rio Grande, OH M,W
University of St. Francis, IL W
University of Saint Francis, IN M,W
University of San Diego, CA M,W
University of South Alabama, AL M,W
University of South Carolina, SC M,W
University of South Carolina Aiken, SC M,W
U of South Carolina Spartanburg, SC M,W
University of South Dakota, SD M,W
University of Southern California, CA W
University of Southern Colorado, CO M,W
University of Southern Indiana, IN M,W
University of Southern Mississippi, MS M,W
University of South Florida, FL M,W
The University of Tampa, FL M,W

The University of Tennessee at Chattanooga, TN M,W
The University of Tennessee at Martin, TN W
The University of Tennessee Knoxville, TN M,W
The University of Texas at Arlington, TX M,W
The University of Texas at Austin, TX M,W
The University of Texas at El Paso, TX M,W
The University of Texas at San Antonio, TX M,W
The University of Texas–Pan American, TX M,W
University of the Incarnate Word, TX M,W
University of the Sacred Heart, PR M,W
University of Toledo, OH M,W
University of Tulsa, OK M,W
University of Utah, UT M,W
University of Virginia, VA M,W
University of Washington, WA M,W
The University of West Alabama, AL M,W
University of West Florida, FL M,W
University of Wisconsin–Green Bay, WI M,W
University of Wisconsin–Madison, WI M,W
University of Wisconsin–Milwaukee, WI M,W
University of Wisconsin–Parkside, WI M,W
University of Wyoming, WY M,W
Utah State University, UT M,W
Valdosta State University, GA M,W
Valley City State University, ND M,W
Valparaiso University, IN M,W
Vanderbilt University, TN M,W
Vanguard University of Southern California, CA M,W
Villanova University, PA M,W
Virginia Commonwealth University, VA M,W
Virginia Military Institute, VA M,W
Virginia Polytechnic Institute and State U, VA M,W
Virginia State University, VA M,W
Virginia Union University, VA M,W
Wagner College, NY M,W
Wake Forest University, NC M,W
Walsh University, OH M,W
Warner Pacific College, OR M,W
Warner Southern College, FL M,W
Washington State University, WA M,W
Wayland Baptist University, TX M,W
Wayne State College, NE M,W
Wayne State University, MI M,W
Webber College, FL M,W
Weber State University, UT M,W
Western Carolina University, NC M,W
Western Illinois University, IL M,W
Western Kentucky University, KY M,W
Western Michigan University, MI M,W
Western State College of Colorado, CO M,W
Western Washington University, WA M,W
Westminster College, PA W
Westmont College, CA M,W
West Texas A&M University, TX M,W
West Virginia University, WV M,W
West Virginia Wesleyan College, WV M,W
Wheeling Jesuit University, WV M,W
Wichita State University, KS M,W
William Jewell College, MO M,W
Wingate University, NC M
Winona State University, MN W
Winston-Salem State University, NC M,W
Winthrop University, SC M,W
Wofford College, SC M,W
Xavier University, OH M,W
York College, NE M,W
Youngstown State University, OH M,W

EQUESTRIAN SPORTS

California State University, Fresno, CA W
Midway College, KY W
Oklahoma Panhandle State University, OK M,W
Oklahoma State U, OK W
Queens College, NC M
St. Andrews Presbyterian College, NC M,W
Southwestern Oklahoma State University, OK M,W
Teikyo Post University, CT M,W
University of South Carolina, SC W
Virginia Intermont College, VA M,W
West Texas A&M University, TX W

FENCING

California State University, Fullerton, CA M,W
Fairleigh Dickinson U, Teaneck-Hackensack Campus, NJ W
Northwestern University, IL W
The Ohio State University, OH W
Penn State U Univ Park Campus, PA M,W
Rutgers, State U of NJ, College of Pharmacy, NJ M,W
Rutgers, State U of NJ, Cook College, NJ M,W
Rutgers, State U of NJ, Douglass College, NJ W
Rutgers, State U of NJ, Livingston College, NJ M,W
Rutgers, State U of NJ, Mason Gross School of Arts, NJ M,W
Rutgers, State U of NJ, Rutgers College, NJ M,W
Rutgers, State U of NJ, College of Engineering, NJ M,W
St. John's University, NY M,W
Stanford University, CA M,W
Temple University, PA W
University of Detroit Mercy, MI M,W
University of Notre Dame, IN M,W
U of Puerto Rico, Cayey University College, PR M,W
Wayne State University, MI M,W

FIELD HOCKEY

American International College, MA W
American University, DC W
Appalachian State University, NC W
Ball State University, IN W
Bellarmine College, KY W
Bentley College, MA W
Bloomsburg University of Pennsylvania, PA W
Boston College, MA W
Boston University, MA W
Catawba College, NC W
Central Michigan University, MI W
The College of William and Mary, VA W
Davidson College, NC W
Davis & Elkins College, WV W
Drexel University, PA W
Duke University, NC W
East Stroudsburg University of Pennsylvania, PA W
Fairfield University, CT W
Hofstra University, NY W
Houghton College, NY W
James Madison University, VA W
Kent State University, OH W
Kutztown University of Pennsylvania, PA W
La Salle University, PA W
Lehigh University, PA W
Lock Haven University of Pennsylvania, PA W
Long Island U, C.W. Post Campus, NY W
Longwood College, VA W
Mansfield University of Pennsylvania, PA W
Mercyhurst College, PA W
Merrimack College, MA W
Miami University, OH W
Michigan State University, MI W
Millersville University of Pennsylvania, PA W
Monmouth University, NJ W
Northeastern University, MA W
Northwestern University, IL W
The Ohio State University, OH W
Ohio University, OH W
Old Dominion University, VA W
Penn State U Univ Park Campus, PA W
Philadelphia University, PA W
Providence College, RI W
Quinnipiac University, CT W
Radford University, VA W
Rider University, NJ W
Rutgers, State U of NJ, College of Pharmacy, NJ W
Rutgers, State U of NJ, Cook College, NJ W
Rutgers, State U of NJ, Douglass College, NJ W
Rutgers, State U of NJ, Livingston College, NJ W
Rutgers, State U of NJ, Mason Gross School of Arts, NJ W
Rutgers, State U of NJ, Rutgers College, NJ W
Rutgers, State U of NJ, College of Engineering, NJ W
Saint Louis University, MO W
Shippensburg University of Pennsylvania, PA W
Slippery Rock University of Pennsylvania, PA W
Southwest Missouri State University, MO W
Stanford University, CA W
State U of NY at Albany, NY W
Stonehill College, MA W
Syracuse University, NY W
Temple University, PA W
Towson University, MD W
U of Calif, Berkeley, CA W
University of Connecticut, CT W
University of Delaware, DE W
The University of Iowa, IA W
University of Louisville, KY W
University of Maine, ME W
University of Maryland, College Park, MD W

Field hockey (continued)

University of Massachusetts Amherst, MA W
University of Massachusetts Lowell, MA W
University of Michigan, MI W
University of New Hampshire, NH W
The University of North Carolina at Chapel Hill, NC W
University of Rhode Island, RI W
University of Richmond, VA W
University of the Pacific, CA W
University of Vermont, VT W
University of Virginia, VA W
Villanova University, PA W
Virginia Commonwealth University, VA W
Wake Forest University, NC W
West Chester University of Pennsylvania, PA W

FOOTBALL

Abilene Christian University, TX M
Adams State College, CO M
Alabama Agricultural and Mechanical University, AL M
Alabama State University, AL M
Albany State University, GA M
Alcorn State University, MS M
American International College, MA M
Angelo State University, TX M
Appalachian State University, NC M
Arizona State University, AZ M
Arkansas State University, AR M
Arkansas Tech University, AR M
Ashland University, OH M
Auburn University, AL M
Augustana College, SD M
Azusa Pacific University, CA M
Baker University, KS M
Ball State University, IN M
Baylor University, TX M
Belhaven College, MS M
Bemidji State University, MN M
Benedictine College, KS M
Bethany College, KS M
Bethel College, KS M
Bethune-Cookman College, FL M
Black Hills State University, SD M
Bloomsburg University of Pennsylvania, PA M
Boise State University, ID M
Boston College, MA M
Bowie State University, MD M
Bowling Green State University, OH M
Brigham Young University, UT M
California Polytechnic State U, San Luis Obispo, CA M
California State University, Fresno, CA M
California State University, Northridge, CA M
California State University, Sacramento, CA M
California University of Pennsylvania, PA M
Campbellsville University, KY M
Carroll College, MT M
Carson-Newman College, TN M
Catawba College, NC M
Central Methodist College, MO M
Central Michigan University, MI M
Central Missouri State University, MO M
Central Washington University, WA M
Chadron State College, NE M
Cheyney University of Pennsylvania, PA M
Citadel, The Military Coll of South Carolina, SC M
Clarion University of Pennsylvania, PA M
Clark Atlanta University, GA M
Clemson University, SC M
The College of William and Mary, VA M
Colorado School of Mines, CO M
Colorado State University, CO M
Concord College, WV M
Concordia University, NE M
Concordia University at St. Paul, MN M
Culver-Stockton College, MO M
Cumberland College, KY M
Cumberland University, TN M
Dakota State University, SD M
Dakota Wesleyan University, SD M
Dana College, NE M
Davidson College, NC M
Delaware State University, DE M
Delta State University, MS M
Dickinson State University, ND M
Doane College, NE M
Duke University, NC M
East Carolina University, NC M
East Central University, OK M
Eastern Illinois University, IL M
Eastern Kentucky University, KY M
Eastern Michigan University, MI M
Eastern New Mexico University, NM M
Eastern Washington University, WA M
East Stroudsburg University of Pennsylvania, PA M
East Tennessee State University, TN M
Edinboro University of Pennsylvania, PA M
Elon College, NC M
Emporia State University, KS M
Evangel University, MO M
Fairmont State College, WV M
Fayetteville State University, NC M
Ferris State University, MI M
Florida Agricultural and Mechanical University, FL M
Florida State University, FL M
Fort Hays State University, KS M
Fort Lewis College, CO M
Fort Valley State University, GA M
Friends University, KS M
Furman University, SC M
Gardner-Webb University, NC M
Geneva College, PA M
Georgetown College, KY M
Georgia Institute of Technology, GA M
Georgia Southern University, GA M
Glenville State College, WV M
Graceland College, IA M
Grambling State University, LA M
Grand Valley State University, MI M
Hampton University, VA M
Harding University, AR M
Hastings College, NE M
Henderson State University, AR M
Hillsdale College, MI M
Hofstra University, NY M
Humboldt State University, CA M
Huron University, SD M
Idaho State University, ID M
Illinois State University, IL M
Indiana State University, IN M
Indiana University Bloomington, IN M
Indiana University of Pennsylvania, PA M
Iowa State University of Science and Technology, IA M
Iowa Wesleyan College, IA M
Jacksonville State University, AL M
James Madison University, VA M
Jamestown College, ND M
Johnson C. Smith University, NC M
Kansas State University, KS M
Kansas Wesleyan University, KS M
Kent State University, OH M
Kentucky Wesleyan College, KY M
Kutztown University of Pennsylvania, PA M
Lamar University, TX M
Langston University, OK M
Lehigh University, PA M
Liberty University, VA M
Lincoln University, MO M
Lock Haven University of Pennsylvania, PA M
Louisiana State University and A&M College, LA M
Louisiana Tech University, LA M
Malone College, OH M
Mansfield University of Pennsylvania, PA M
Marshall University, WV M
Mars Hill College, NC M
Mayville State University, ND M
McKendree College, IL M
McNeese State University, LA M
Mesa State College, CO M
Miami University, OH M
Michigan State University, MI M
Michigan Technological University, MI M
MidAmerica Nazarene University, KS M
Middle Tennessee State University, TN M
Midland Lutheran College, NE M
Midwestern State University, TX M
Millersville University of Pennsylvania, PA M
Minnesota State University, Mankato, MN M
Minnesota State University Moorhead, MN M
Minot State University, ND M
Mississippi State University, MS M
Mississippi Valley State University, MS M
Missouri Southern State College, MO M
Missouri Valley College, MO M
Missouri Western State College, MO M
Montana State U–Bozeman, MT M
Montana Tech of The University of Montana, MT M
Morgan State University, MD M
Morningside College, IA M
Murray State University, KY M
Newberry College, SC M
New Mexico Highlands University, NM M
Norfolk State University, VA M
North Carolina Agricultural and Technical State U, NC M
North Carolina Central University, NC M
North Carolina State University, NC M
North Dakota State University, ND M

Northeastern State University, OK M
Northeastern University, MA M
Northern Arizona University, AZ M
Northern Illinois University, IL M
Northern Michigan University, MI M
North Greenville College, SC M
Northwestern College, IA M
Northwestern Oklahoma State University, OK M
Northwestern State University of Louisiana, LA M
Northwestern University, IL M
Northwest Missouri State University, MO M
Northwood University, MI M
The Ohio State University, OH M
Ohio University, OH M
Oklahoma Panhandle State University, OK M
Oklahoma State U, OK M
Olivet Nazarene University, IL M
Oregon State University, OR M
Ottawa University, KS M
Ouachita Baptist University, AR M
Penn State U Univ Park Campus, PA M
Pittsburg State University, KS M
Portland State University, OR M
Prairie View A&M University, TX M
Presbyterian College, SC M
Purdue University, IN M
Quincy University, IL M
Rice University, TX M
Rocky Mountain College, MT M
Rutgers, State U of NJ, College of Pharmacy, NJ M
Rutgers, State U of NJ, Cook College, NJ M
Rutgers, State U of NJ, Livingston College, NJ M
Rutgers, State U of NJ, Mason Gross School of Arts, NJ M
Rutgers, State U of NJ, Rutgers College, NJ M
Rutgers, State U of NJ, College of Engineering, NJ M
Sacred Heart University, CT M
Saginaw Valley State University, MI M
St. Ambrose University, IA M
Saint Joseph's College, IN M
Saint Mary College, KS M
Saint Mary's College of California, CA M
Saint Xavier University, IL M
Samford University, AL M
Sam Houston State University, TX M
San Diego State University, CA M
San Jose State University, CA M
Savannah State University, GA M
Shepherd College, WV M
Shippensburg University of Pennsylvania, PA M
Slippery Rock University of Pennsylvania, PA M
South Dakota School of Mines and Technology, SD M
South Dakota State University, SD M
Southeast Missouri State University, MO M
Southern Arkansas University–Magnolia, AR M
Southern Illinois University Carbondale, IL M
Southern Methodist University, TX M
Southern Oregon University, OR M
Southern University and A&M College, LA M
Southern Utah University, UT M
Southwest Baptist University, MO M
Southwestern College, KS M
Southwestern Oklahoma State University, OK M
Southwest Missouri State University, MO M
Southwest State University, MN M
Southwest Texas State University, TX M
Stanford University, CA M
State U of NY at Albany, NY M
State U of NY at Buffalo, NY M
State U of NY at Stony Brook, NY M
State University of West Georgia, GA M
Stephen F. Austin State University, TX M
Sterling College, KS M
Stonehill College, MA M
Syracuse University, NY M
Tabor College, KS M
Tarleton State University, TX M
Taylor University, IN M
Temple University, PA M
Tennessee State University, TN M
Tennessee Technological University, TN M
Texas A&M University, TX M
Texas A&M University–Commerce, TX M
Texas A&M University–Kingsville, TX M
Texas Christian University, TX M
Texas Tech University, TX M
Tiffin University, OH M
Tri-State University, IN M
Troy State University, AL M
Truman State University, MO M
Tulane University, LA M
Tusculum College, TN M
Tuskegee University, AL M
Union College, KY M
The University of Akron, OH M
The University of Alabama, AL M
The University of Alabama at Birmingham, AL M
The University of Arizona, AZ M
University of Arkansas, AR M
University of Arkansas at Monticello, AR M
University of Arkansas at Pine Bluff, AR M
U of Calif, Berkeley, CA M
U of Calif, Los Angeles, CA M
University of Central Arkansas, AR M
University of Central Florida, FL M
University of Central Oklahoma, OK M
University of Cincinnati, OH M
University of Colorado at Boulder, CO M
University of Delaware, DE M
The University of Findlay, OH M
University of Florida, FL M
University of Georgia, GA M
University of Hawaii at Manoa, HI M
University of Houston, TX M
University of Idaho, ID M
University of Illinois at Urbana–Champaign, IL M
University of Indianapolis, IN M
The University of Iowa, IA M
University of Kansas, KS M
University of Louisiana at Lafayette, LA M
University of Louisiana at Monroe, LA M
University of Louisville, KY M
University of Maine, ME M
University of Mary, ND M
University of Maryland, College Park, MD M
University of Massachusetts Amherst, MA M
The University of Memphis, TN M
University of Miami, FL M
University of Michigan, MI M
University of Minnesota, Crookston, MN M
University of Minnesota, Duluth, MN M
University of Minnesota, Twin Cities Campus, MN M
University of Mississippi, MS M
University of Missouri–Columbia, MO M
University of Missouri–Rolla, MO M
The University of Montana–Missoula, MT M
University of Nebraska at Kearney, NE M
University of Nebraska at Omaha, NE M
University of Nebraska–Lincoln, NE M
University of Nevada, Las Vegas, NV M
University of Nevada, Reno, NV M
University of New Hampshire, NH M
University of New Haven, CT M
University of New Mexico, NM M
University of North Alabama, AL M
The University of North Carolina at Chapel Hill, NC M
University of North Dakota, ND M
University of Northern Colorado, CO M
University of Northern Iowa, IA M
University of North Texas, TX M
University of Notre Dame, IN M
University of Oklahoma, OK M
University of Oregon, OR M
University of Pittsburgh, PA M
U of Puerto Rico, Cayey University College, PR M
University of Rhode Island, RI M
University of Richmond, VA M
University of St. Francis, IL M
University of Saint Francis, IN M
University of South Carolina, SC M
University of South Dakota, SD M
University of Southern California, CA M
University of Southern Mississippi, MS M
University of South Florida, FL M
The University of Tennessee at Chattanooga, TN M
The University of Tennessee at Martin, TN M
The University of Tennessee Knoxville, TN M
The University of Texas at Austin, TX M
The University of Texas at El Paso, TX M
University of Toledo, OH M
University of Tulsa, OK M
University of Utah, UT M
University of Virginia, VA M
University of Virginia's College at Wise, VA M
University of Washington, WA M
The University of West Alabama, AL M

Football (continued)

University of Wisconsin–Madison, WI M
University of Wyoming, WY M
Urbana University, OH M
Utah State University, UT M
Valdosta State University, GA M
Valley City State University, ND M
Vanderbilt University, TN M
Villanova University, PA M
Virginia Military Institute, VA M
Virginia Polytechnic Institute and State U, VA M
Virginia State University, VA M
Virginia Union University, VA M
Wake Forest University, NC M
Walsh University, OH M
Washburn University of Topeka, KS M
Washington State University, WA M
Wayne State College, NE M
Wayne State University, MI M
Weber State University, UT M
West Chester University of Pennsylvania, PA M
Western Carolina University, NC M
Western Illinois University, IL M
Western Kentucky University, KY M
Western Michigan University, MI M
Western Montana College of The U of Montana, MT M
Western New Mexico University, NM M
Western State College of Colorado, CO M
Western Washington University, WA M
West Liberty State College, WV M
Westminster College, PA M
West Texas A&M University, TX M
West Virginia State College, WV M
West Virginia University, WV M
West Virginia University Institute of Technology, WV M
West Virginia Wesleyan College, WV M
William Jewell College, MO M
Wingate University, NC M
Winona State University, MN M
Winston-Salem State University, NC M
Wofford College, SC M
Youngstown State University, OH M

GOLF

Abilene Christian University, TX M
Adams State College, CO M
Adelphi University, NY M
Alabama Agricultural and Mechanical University, AL M
Alabama State University, AL M,W
Albertson College of Idaho, ID M,W
Alcorn State University, MS M,W
American University, DC M
Anderson College, SC M,W
Appalachian State University, NC M,W
Aquinas College, MI M,W
Arizona State University, AZ M,W
Arkansas State University, AR M,W
Arkansas Tech University, AR M
Ashland University, OH M,W
Auburn University, AL M,W
Austin Peay State University, TN M
Azusa Pacific University, CA M
Baker University, KS M,W
Ball State University, IN M
Barry University, FL M,W
Bartlesville Wesleyan College, OK M
Barton College, NC M
Baylor University, TX M,W
Belhaven College, MS M,W
Bellarmine College, KY M,W
Belmont Abbey College, NC M
Belmont University, TN M,W
Benedictine College, KS M,W
Berry College, GA M
Bethany College, KS M
Bethel College, IN M
Bethel College, TN M
Bethune-Cookman College, FL M,W
Bluefield College, VA M
Bluefield State College, WV M
Boise State University, ID M,W
Bowling Green State University, OH M,W
Bradley University, IL M,W
Brescia University, KY M,W
Brevard College, NC M
Briar Cliff College, IA M,W
Brigham Young University, UT M,W
Butler University, IN M,W
Caldwell College, NJ M,W
California Baptist University, CA M
California Polytechnic State U, San Luis Obispo, CA M
California State University, Bakersfield, CA M
California State University, Fresno, CA M
California State University, Northridge, CA M
California State University, Sacramento, CA M
California State University, San Bernardino, CA M
California State University, San Marcos, CA M
California University of Pennsylvania, PA M
Cameron University, OK M
Campbellsville University, KY M,W
Campbell University, NC M,W
Canisius College, NY M
Carroll College, MT W
Carson-Newman College, TN M
Catawba College, NC M
Cedarville College, OH M
Centenary College of Louisiana, LA M,W
Central Connecticut State University, CT M,W
Central Methodist College, MO M,W
Central Missouri State University, MO M
Central State University, OH M,W
Chadron State College, NE W
Charleston Southern University, SC M,W
Citadel, The Military Coll of South Carolina, SC M
Clarion University of Pennsylvania, PA M
Clark Atlanta University, GA M
Clayton College & State University, GA M
Clemson University, SC M
Coastal Carolina University, SC M,W
Coker College, SC M
College of Charleston, SC M,W
College of Saint Mary, NE W
Colorado Christian University, CO M
Colorado School of Mines, CO M
Columbus State University, GA M
Concordia University, NE M,W
Cornerstone University, MI M
Creighton University, NE M,W
Culver-Stockton College, MO M,W
Cumberland College, KY M,W
Daemen College, NY M
Dakota Wesleyan University, SD M,W
David Lipscomb University, TN M,W
Davidson College, NC M
Davis & Elkins College, WV M
Delta State University, MS M
DePaul University, IL M,W
Doane College, NE M,W
Dominican College of Blauvelt, NY M,W
Dordt College, IA M
Drake University, IA M
Drury University, MO M
Duke University, NC M,W
Duquesne University, PA M
East Carolina University, NC M
East Central University, OK M
Eastern Illinois University, IL M,W
Eastern Kentucky University, KY M
Eastern Michigan University, MI M,W
Eastern Washington University, WA M,W
East Tennessee State University, TN M,W
Eckerd College, FL M
Elon College, NC M
Embry-Riddle Aeronautical University, FL M
Evangel University, MO M,W
Fairleigh Dickinson U, Teaneck-Hackensack Campus, NJ M
Fairmont State College, WV M
Ferris State University, MI M,W
Flagler College, FL M
Florida Agricultural and Mechanical University, FL M,W
Florida Atlantic University, FL M,W
Florida International University, FL W
Florida Southern College, FL M,W
Florida State University, FL M,W
Fort Hays State University, KS M
Fort Lewis College, CO M
Fort Valley State University, GA M
Francis Marion University, SC M
Franklin Pierce College, NH M
Friends University, KS M
Furman University, SC M,W
Gannon University, PA M,W
Gardner-Webb University, NC M
George Mason University, VA M
Georgetown College, KY M,W
Georgetown University, DC M
The George Washington University, DC M
Georgia College and State University, GA M
Georgia Institute of Technology, GA M
Georgia Southern University, GA M
Georgia State University, GA M,W
Glenville State College, WV M
Goshen College, IN M
Grace College, IN M
Graceland College, IA M,W
Grambling State University, LA M
Grand Canyon University, AZ M
Grand Valley State University, MI M,W
Green Mountain College, VT M,W
Hannibal-LaGrange College, MO M
Hastings College, NE M,W
High Point University, NC M

Hillsdale College, MI M
Hofstra University, NY M
Holy Family College, PA M
Holy Names College, CA M
Huntington College, IN M,W
Idaho State University, ID M,W
Illinois State University, IL M,W
Indiana University Bloomington, IN M,W
Indiana U–Purdue U Indianapolis, IN M
Indiana Wesleyan University, IN M
Iowa State University of Science and Technology, IA M,W
Iowa Wesleyan College, IA M,W
Jacksonville State University, AL M,W
Jacksonville University, FL M,W
James Madison University, VA M,W
Jamestown College, ND M,W
Johnson C. Smith University, NC M
Kansas State University, KS M,W
Kansas Wesleyan University, KS M,W
Kennesaw State University, GA M
Kent State University, OH M,W
Kentucky Wesleyan College, KY M,W
King College, TN M
Kutztown University of Pennsylvania, PA W
Lamar University, TX M,W
Lambuth University, TN M
La Salle University, PA M,W
Lees-McRae College, NC M
Lee University, TN M
Lehigh University, PA M
Le Moyne College, NY M
LeMoyne-Owen College, TN M,W
Lewis-Clark State College, ID M,W
Lewis University, IL M,W
Liberty University, VA M
Limestone College, SC M
Lincoln Memorial University, TN M
Lincoln University, MO M
Long Island U, Brooklyn Campus, NY M
Longwood College, VA M,W
Louisiana State University and A&M College, LA M,W
Louisiana Tech University, LA M
Loyola Marymount University, CA M
Loyola University Chicago, IL M,W
Lynn University, FL M,W
Lyon College, AR M,W
Malone College, OH M,W
Marian College, IN M,W
Marquette University, WI M
Marshall University, WV M
Mars Hill College, NC M
Martin Methodist College, TN M
McKendree College, IL M,W
McNeese State University, LA M
Mercer University, GA M,W
Mercyhurst College, PA M,W
Mesa State College, CO W
Miami University, OH M
Michigan State University, MI M,W
Middle Tennessee State University, TN M
Midland Lutheran College, NE M,W
Millersville University of Pennsylvania, PA M
Milligan College, TN M
Minnesota State University, Mankato, MN M,W
Mississippi State University, MS M,W
Mississippi Valley State University, MS M
Missouri Baptist College, MO M
Missouri Southern State College, MO M
Missouri Valley College, MO M
Missouri Western State College, MO M
Monmouth University, NJ M,W
Montana State U–Bozeman, MT W
Montana Tech of The University of Montana, MT M,W
Montreat College, NC M
Morehead State University, KY M
Morningside College, IA W
Mount Aloysius College, PA M
Mount Marty College, SD M,W
Mount Olive College, NC M
Mount St. Clare College, IA M
Mount Saint Mary's College and Seminary, MD M,W
Mount Vernon Nazarene College, OH M
Murray State University, KY M,W
Newberry College, SC M,W
Newman University, KS M,W
Niagara University, NY M
Norfolk State University, VA M
North Carolina State University, NC M
Northeastern State University, OK M,W
Northern Arizona University, AZ W
Northern Illinois University, IL M,W
Northern Kentucky University, KY M,W
Northern Michigan University, MI M
North Greenville College, SC M
Northwestern College, IA M,W
Northwestern State University of Louisiana, LA M
Northwestern University, IL M,W
Northwest Missouri State University, MO M
Northwest Nazarene University, ID M
Northwood University, MI M
Northwood University, Florida Campus, FL M
Northwood University, Texas Campus, TX M,W
Nova Southeastern University, FL M,W
Oakland University, MI M,W
The Ohio State University, OH M,W
Ohio University, OH M,W
Ohio Valley College, WV M
Oklahoma Baptist University, OK M,W
Oklahoma Christian U of Science and Arts, OK M
Oklahoma City University, OK M,W
Oklahoma State U, OK M,W
Old Dominion University, VA M
Olivet Nazarene University, IL M
Oral Roberts University, OK M,W
Oregon State University, OR M,W
Ottawa University, KS M
Ouachita Baptist University, AR M
Palm Beach Atlantic College, FL M
Penn State U Univ Park Campus, PA M,W
Pepperdine University, CA M,W
Pfeiffer University, NC M
Philadelphia University, PA M
Pikeville College, KY M
Pittsburg State University, KS M
Point Loma Nazarene University, CA M
Portland State University, OR M,W
Prairie View A&M University, TX M,W
Presbyterian College, SC M
Purdue University, IN M,W
Queens College, NC M
Quincy University, IL M,W
Quinnipiac University, CT M,W
Radford University, VA M,W
Regis University, CO M
Research College of Nursing, MO M,W
Rice University, TX M
Rider University, NJ M
Robert Morris College, PA M
Rockhurst University, MO M,W
Rocky Mountain College, MT M,W
Rollins College, FL M,W
Rutgers, State U of NJ, College of Pharmacy, NJ M,W
Rutgers, State U of NJ, Cook College, NJ M,W
Rutgers, State U of NJ, Douglass College, NJ W
Rutgers, State U of NJ, Livingston College, NJ M,W
Rutgers, State U of NJ, Mason Gross School of Arts, NJ M,W
Rutgers, State U of NJ, Rutgers College, NJ M,W
Rutgers, State U of NJ, College of Engineering, NJ M,W
Saginaw Valley State University, MI M
St. Ambrose University, IA M,W
St. Andrews Presbyterian College, NC M
Saint Augustine's College, NC M
St. Bonaventure University, NY M
St. Edward's University, TX M
Saint Francis College, PA M,W
St. Gregory's University, OK M,W
St. John's University, NY M
Saint Joseph's College, IN M,W
Saint Joseph's University, PA M
Saint Louis University, MO M
Saint Martin's College, WA M,W
Saint Mary's College of California, CA M
St. Mary's University of San Antonio, TX M
Saint Peter's College, NJ M
St. Thomas University, FL M,W
Saint Xavier University, IL M
Samford University, AL M,W
Sam Houston State University, TX M
San Diego State University, CA M,W
San Jose State University, CA M,W
Santa Clara University, CA M,W
Seton Hall University, NJ M
Seton Hill College, PA W
Siena Heights University, MI M
Slippery Rock University of Pennsylvania, PA M,W
South Dakota State University, SD M,W
Southeastern Louisiana University, LA M
Southeast Missouri State University, MO M
Southern Illinois University Carbondale, IL M,W
Southern Methodist University, TX M,W
Southern Nazarene University, OK M,W
Southern University and A&M College, LA M,W
Southern Utah University, UT M
Southern Wesleyan University, SC M
Southwest Baptist University, MO M
Southwestern College, KS M,W

Golf (continued)

Southwestern Oklahoma State University, OK M,W
Southwest Missouri State University, MO M,W
Southwest State University, MN W
Southwest Texas State University, TX M
Spring Arbor College, MI M
Spring Hill College, AL M,W
Stanford University, CA M,W
State U of NY at Albany, NY W
State U of NY at Binghamton, NY M
Stephen F. Austin State University, TX M
Stetson University, FL M,W
Tabor College, KS M,W
Taylor University, IN M
Temple University, PA M
Tennessee State University, TN M
Tennessee Technological University, TN M,W
Tennessee Wesleyan College, TN M
Texas A&M University, TX M,W
Texas A&M University–Commerce, TX M,W
Texas Christian University, TX M,W
Texas Lutheran University, TX M,W
Texas Tech University, TX M,W
Texas Wesleyan University, TX M
Thomas University, GA M
Tiffin University, OH M,W
Towson University, MD M
Tri-State University, IN M,W
Troy State University, AL M
Truman State University, MO M,W
Tulane University, LA M,W
Tuskegee University, AL M
Union College, KY M,W
Union University, TN M
The University of Akron, OH M
The University of Alabama, AL M,W
The University of Alabama at Birmingham, AL M,W
The University of Arizona, AZ M,W
University of Arkansas, AR M,W
University of Arkansas at Little Rock, AR M,W
University of Arkansas at Monticello, AR M
University of Arkansas at Pine Bluff, AR M
U of Calif, Berkeley, CA M,W
U of Calif, Irvine, CA M
U of Calif, Los Angeles, CA M,W
U of Calif, Santa Barbara, CA M
University of Central Florida, FL M,W
University of Central Oklahoma, OK M
University of Charleston, WV M
University of Cincinnati, OH M
University of Colorado at Boulder, CO M,W
University of Colorado at Colorado Springs, CO M
University of Dayton, OH M,W
University of Detroit Mercy, MI M
University of Evansville, IN M
The University of Findlay, OH M,W
University of Florida, FL M,W
University of Georgia, GA M,W
University of Hawaii at Hilo, HI M
University of Hawaii at Manoa, HI M,W
University of Houston, TX M
University of Idaho, ID M,W
University of Illinois at Urbana–Champaign, IL M,W
University of Indianapolis, IN M,W
The University of Iowa, IA M,W
University of Kansas, KS M,W
University of Louisiana at Lafayette, LA M
University of Louisiana at Monroe, LA M
University of Louisville, KY M
University of Mary, ND M
University of Maryland, Baltimore County, MD M,W
University of Maryland, College Park, MD M,W
The University of Memphis, TN M,W
University of Miami, FL W
University of Michigan, MI M,W
University of Minnesota, Crookston, MN M
University of Minnesota, Twin Cities Campus, MN M,W
University of Mississippi, MS M,W
University of Missouri–Columbia, MO M,W
University of Missouri–Kansas City, MO M,W
University of Missouri–Rolla, MO M
University of Missouri–St. Louis, MO M,W
University of Mobile, AL M,W
University of Montevallo, AL M,W
University of Nebraska at Kearney, NE M,W
University of Nebraska–Lincoln, NE M,W
University of Nevada, Las Vegas, NV M
University of Nevada, Reno, NV M,W
University of New Mexico, NM M,W
University of New Orleans, LA M,W
University of North Alabama, AL M
The University of North Carolina at Chapel Hill, NC M,W
The University of North Carolina at Charlotte, NC M
The University of North Carolina at Greensboro, NC M,W
The University of North Carolina at Pembroke, NC M
The University of North Carolina at Wilmington, NC M,W
University of Northern Colorado, CO M,W
University of Northern Iowa, IA M,W
University of North Florida, FL M
University of North Texas, TX M,W
University of Notre Dame, IN M,W
University of Oklahoma, OK M,W
University of Oregon, OR M,W
University of Portland, OR M,W
U of Puerto Rico, Cayey University College, PR M
University of Rhode Island, RI M
University of St. Francis, IL M,W
University of Saint Francis, IN M
University of San Diego, CA M
University of San Francisco, CA M,W
University of South Carolina, SC M,W
University of South Carolina Aiken, SC M
University of Southern California, CA M,W
University of Southern Colorado, CO M,W
University of Southern Indiana, IN M,W
University of Southern Mississippi, MS M,W
University of South Florida, FL M,W
The University of Tampa, FL M
The University of Tennessee at Chattanooga, TN M
The University of Tennessee at Martin, TN M
The University of Tennessee Knoxville, TN M,W
The University of Texas at Arlington, TX M
The University of Texas at Austin, TX M,W
The University of Texas at El Paso, TX M
The University of Texas at San Antonio, TX M
The University of Texas–Pan American, TX M,W
University of the District of Columbia, DC M
University of the Incarnate Word, TX M,W
University of the Pacific, CA M
University of Toledo, OH M,W
University of Tulsa, OK M,W
University of Utah, UT M
University of Virginia, VA M
University of Washington, WA M,W
University of West Florida, FL M
University of Wisconsin–Madison, WI M,W
University of Wisconsin–Parkside, WI M
University of Wyoming, WY M,W
Urbana University, OH M
Utah State University, UT M
Valdosta State University, GA M
Vanderbilt University, TN M,W
Virginia Commonwealth University, VA M
Virginia Military Institute, VA M
Virginia Polytechnic Institute and State U, VA M
Virginia Union University, VA M
Wagner College, NY M,W
Wake Forest University, NC M,W
Walsh University, OH M
Warner Southern College, FL M
Washburn University of Topeka, KS M
Washington State University, WA M,W
Wayne State University, MI M
Webber College, FL M,W
Weber State University, UT M,W
West Chester University of Pennsylvania, PA M
Western Carolina University, NC M,W
Western Illinois University, IL M
Western Kentucky University, KY M,W
Western Michigan University, MI W
Western Montana College of The U of Montana, MT M,W
Western New Mexico University, NM M,W
Western Washington University, WA M
West Texas A&M University, TX M,W
West Virginia State College, WV M
West Virginia University Institute of Technology, WV M
West Virginia Wesleyan College, WV M
Wheeling Jesuit University, WV M
Wichita State University, KS M,W
William Jewell College, MO M,W
Williams Baptist College, AR M
William Woods University, MO M,W
Wingate University, NC M,W
Winona State University, MN M,W
Winston-Salem State University, NC M
Winthrop University, SC M,W
Wofford College, SC M,W
Xavier University, OH M,W
Youngstown State University, OH M

GYMNASTICS

Arizona State University, AZ	W
Auburn University, AL	W
Ball State University, IN	W
Boise State University, ID	W
Bowling Green State University, OH	W
Brigham Young University, UT	M,W
California Polytechnic State U, San Luis Obispo, CA	W
California State University, Fullerton, CA	W
California State University, Sacramento, CA	W
Centenary College of Louisiana, LA	W
Central Michigan University, MI	W
The College of William and Mary, VA	M,W
Columbia Union College, MD	M,W
Eastern Michigan University, MI	W
The George Washington University, DC	W
Illinois State University, IL	W
Iowa State University of Science and Technology, IA	W
James Madison University, VA	M,W
Kent State University, OH	W
Louisiana State University and A&M College, LA	W
Michigan State University, MI	M,W
North Carolina State University, NC	W
Northern Illinois University, IL	W
The Ohio State University, OH	M,W
Oregon State University, OR	W
Penn State U Univ Park Campus, PA	M,W
Radford University, VA	W
Rutgers, State U of NJ, College of Pharmacy, NJ	W
Rutgers, State U of NJ, Cook College, NJ	W
Rutgers, State U of NJ, Douglass College, NJ	W
Rutgers, State U of NJ, Livingston College, NJ	W
Rutgers, State U of NJ, Mason Gross School of Arts, NJ	W
Rutgers, State U of NJ, Rutgers College, NJ	W
Rutgers, State U of NJ, College of Engineering, NJ	W
San Jose State University, CA	W
Seattle Pacific University, WA	W
Southeast Missouri State University, MO	W
Southern Utah University, UT	W
Stanford University, CA	M,W
Syracuse University, NY	M
Temple University, PA	M,W
Texas Woman's University, TX	W
Towson University, MD	W
The University of Alabama, AL	W
U of Alaska Anchorage, AK	W
The University of Arizona, AZ	W
University of Bridgeport, CT	W
U of Calif, Berkeley, CA	M,W
U of Calif, Los Angeles, CA	W
U of Calif, Santa Barbara, CA	W
University of Florida, FL	W
University of Georgia, GA	W
University of Illinois at Chicago, IL	M,W
University of Illinois at Urbana–Champaign, IL	M,W
The University of Iowa, IA	M,W
University of Maryland, College Park, MD	W
University of Massachusetts Amherst, MA	M,W
University of Michigan, MI	M,W
University of Minnesota, Twin Cities Campus, MN	M,W
University of Missouri–Columbia, MO	W
University of Nebraska–Lincoln, NE	M,W
University of New Hampshire, NH	W
The University of North Carolina at Chapel Hill, NC	W
University of Oklahoma, OK	M,W
University of Pittsburgh, PA	W
University of Rhode Island, RI	W
University of Utah, UT	W
University of Washington, WA	W
Utah State University, UT	W
West Chester University of Pennsylvania, PA	W
Western Michigan University, MI	W
West Virginia University, WV	W
Winona State University, MN	W

ICE HOCKEY

American International College, MA	M
Bemidji State University, MN	M,W
Bentley College, MA	M
Boston College, MA	M
Boston University, MA	M
Bowling Green State University, OH	M
Canisius College, NY	M
Clarkson University, NY	M
The Colorado College, CO	M
Fairfield University, CT	M
Ferris State University, MI	M
Lake Superior State University, MI	M
Mercyhurst College, PA	M,W
Merrimack College, MA	M
Miami University, OH	M
Michigan State University, MI	M
Michigan Technological University, MI	M
Minnesota State University, Mankato, MN	M,W
Niagara University, NY	M,W
Northeastern University, MA	M,W
Northern Michigan University, MI	M
The Ohio State University, OH	M,W
Providence College, RI	M,W
Quinnipiac University, CT	M,W
Sacred Heart University, CT	M
St. Lawrence University, NY	M,W
Stonehill College, MA	M
The University of Alabama in Huntsville, AL	M
U of Alaska Anchorage, AK	M
U of Alaska Fairbanks, AK	M
University of Connecticut, CT	M
The University of Findlay, OH	M,W
University of Maine, ME	M,W
University of Massachusetts Amherst, MA	M
University of Massachusetts Lowell, MA	M
University of Michigan, MI	M
University of Minnesota, Crookston, MN	M
University of Minnesota, Duluth, MN	M
University of Minnesota, Twin Cities Campus, MN	M,W
University of Nebraska at Omaha, NE	M
University of New Hampshire, NH	M,W
University of North Dakota, ND	M
University of Notre Dame, IN	M
University of Vermont, VT	M
University of Wisconsin–Madison, WI	M,W
Western Michigan University, MI	M

LACROSSE

Adelphi University, NY	M
American International College, MA	W
American University, DC	W
Bentley College, MA	M,W
Boston College, MA	W
Boston University, MA	W
Butler University, IN	M
Canisius College, NY	M
The College of William and Mary, VA	W
Davidson College, NC	W
Drexel University, PA	M
Duke University, NC	M,W
Duquesne University, PA	W
East Stroudsburg University of Pennsylvania, PA	W
Fairfield University, CT	M,W
Fairleigh Dickinson U, Teaneck-Hackensack Campus, NJ	W
Gannon University, PA	W
George Mason University, VA	W
Georgetown University, DC	M,W
Hofstra University, NY	M,W
James Madison University, VA	W
Johns Hopkins University, MD	M,W
La Salle University, PA	W
Lees-McRae College, NC	M
Lehigh University, PA	M,W
Limestone College, SC	M,W
Lock Haven University of Pennsylvania, PA	W
Long Island U, C.W. Post Campus, NY	M,W
Long Island U, Southampton College, NY	M
Manhattan College, NY	M,W
Mars Hill College, NC	M
Mercyhurst College, PA	M,W
Merrimack College, MA	W
Millersville University of Pennsylvania, PA	W
Monmouth University, NJ	W
Mount Saint Mary's College and Seminary, MD	M,W
New York Institute of Technology, NY	M
Niagara University, NY	W
Northwood University, MI	M
The Ohio State University, OH	M,W
Old Dominion University, VA	W
Penn State U Univ Park Campus, PA	M,W
Pfeiffer University, NC	M,W
Philadelphia University, PA	W
Quinnipiac University, CT	M,W
Radford University, VA	M
Regis University, CO	M,W
Rutgers, State U of NJ, College of Pharmacy, NJ	M,W
Rutgers, State U of NJ, Cook College, NJ	M,W
Rutgers, State U of NJ, Douglass College, NJ	W
Rutgers, State U of NJ, Livingston College, NJ	M,W

Lacrosse (continued)

Rutgers, State U of NJ, Mason Gross School of Arts, NJ M,W
Rutgers, State U of NJ, Rutgers College, NJ M,W
Rutgers, State U of NJ, College of Engineering, NJ M,W
St. Andrews Presbyterian College, NC M
Saint Joseph's University, PA M,W
Saint Vincent College, PA M,W
Shippensburg University of Pennsylvania, PA W
State U of NY at Albany, NY M,W
State U of NY at Stony Brook, NY M
Stonehill College, MA W
Syracuse University, NY M,W
Temple University, PA W
Towson University, MD M,W
U of Calif, Berkeley, CA W
University of Delaware, DE M,W
University of Hartford, CT M
University of Maryland, Baltimore County, MD M,W
University of Maryland, College Park, MD M,W
University of Massachusetts Amherst, MA M,W
University of New Hampshire, NH W
The University of North Carolina at Chapel Hill, NC M,W
University of Notre Dame, IN W
University of Richmond, VA W
University of Virginia, VA M,W
University of Wisconsin–Madison, WI W
Vanderbilt University, TN W
Virginia Military Institute, VA M
Virginia Polytechnic Institute and State U, VA W
Wagner College, NY M,W
West Chester University of Pennsylvania, PA M,W
Wingate University, NC M

RIFLERY

Austin Peay State University, TN W
Canisius College, NY M,W
Centenary College of Louisiana, LA M,W
DePaul University, IL M,W
Duquesne University, PA M,W
Jacksonville State University, AL M,W
Mercer University, GA M,W
Morehead State University, KY M,W
Murray State University, KY M,W
North Georgia College & State University, GA M,W
Saint Louis University, MO M,W
Tennessee Technological University, TN M,W
U of Alaska Fairbanks, AK M,W
The University of Memphis, TN M,W
University of Mississippi, MS W
University of Missouri–Kansas City, MO M,W
University of Nebraska–Lincoln, NE W
University of Nevada, Reno, NV M,W
The University of Tennessee at Martin, TN M,W
Virginia Military Institute, VA M,W
West Virginia University, WV M,W
Xavier University, OH M,W

RUGBY

Eastern Illinois University, IL W
U of Calif, Berkeley, CA M

SAILING

Old Dominion University, VA M,W

SKIING (CROSS-COUNTRY)

Montana State U–Bozeman, MT W
Northern Michigan University, MI M,W
U of Alaska Anchorage, AK M,W
U of Alaska Fairbanks, AK M,W
University of Colorado at Boulder, CO M,W
University of Nevada, Reno, NV M,W
University of New Hampshire, NH M,W
University of New Mexico, NM M,W
University of Utah, UT M,W
University of Vermont, VT M,W
University of Wisconsin–Green Bay, WI M,W
Western State College of Colorado, CO M,W

SKIING (DOWNHILL)

Albertson College of Idaho, ID M,W
Green Mountain College, VT M,W
Lees-McRae College, NC M,W
Montana State U–Bozeman, MT W
Northern Michigan University, MI W
Rocky Mountain College, MT M,W
Sierra Nevada College, NV M,W
U of Alaska Anchorage, AK M,W
University of Colorado at Boulder, CO M,W
University of Massachusetts Amherst, MA M,W
University of Nevada, Reno, NV M,W
University of New Hampshire, NH M,W
University of New Mexico, NM M,W
University of Utah, UT M,W
University of Vermont, VT M,W
Western State College of Colorado, CO M,W

SOCCER

Adelphi University, NY M,W
Alabama Agricultural and Mechanical University, AL M
Albertson College of Idaho, ID M,W
American International College, MA W
American University, DC M,W
Anderson College, SC M,W
Angelo State University, TX W
Appalachian State University, NC M,W
Aquinas College, MI M,W
Arizona State University, AZ W
Arkansas State University, AR W
Ashland University, OH M,W
Auburn University, AL W
Auburn University Montgomery, AL M,W
Augustana College, SD W
Augusta State University, GA M
Avila College, MO M,W
Azusa Pacific University, CA M,W
Baker University, KS M,W
Barry University, FL M,W
Bartlesville Wesleyan College, OK M,W
Barton College, NC M,W
Baylor University, TX W
Belhaven College, MS M,W
Bellarmine College, KY M,W
Bellevue University, NE M
Belmont Abbey College, NC M,W
Belmont University, TN M,W
Bemidji State University, MN W
Benedictine College, KS M,W
Bentley College, MA M,W
Berry College, GA M,W
Bethany College, KS M,W
Bethel College, IN M,W
Bethel College, KS M,W
Bethel College, TN M,W
Biola University, CA M,W
Birmingham-Southern College, AL M,W
Bloomfield College, NJ M,W
Bloomsburg University of Pennsylvania, PA W
Bluefield College, VA M
Boston College, MA M,W
Boston University, MA M,W
Bowling Green State University, OH M,W
Bradley University, IL M
Brenau University, GA W
Brescia University, KY M,W
Brevard College, NC M,W
Briar Cliff College, IA M,W
Briarcliffe College, NY W
Brigham Young University, UT W
Brigham Young University–Hawaii Campus, HI M
Bryan College, TN M,W
Butler University, IN M,W
Caldwell College, NJ M,W
California Baptist University, CA M,W
California State Polytechnic University, Pomona, CA M,W
California State University, Bakersfield, CA M
California State University, Dominguez Hills, CA M,W
California State University, Fresno, CA M,W
California State University, Fullerton, CA M,W
California State University, Los Angeles, CA M,W
California State University, Northridge, CA M
California State University, Sacramento, CA M,W
California State University, San Bernardino, CA M,W
California University of Pennsylvania, PA M
Campbellsville University, KY M,W
Campbell University, NC M,W
Canisius College, NY M,W
Carlow College, PA W
Carroll College, MT W
Carson-Newman College, TN M,W
Catawba College, NC M,W
Cedarville College, OH M,W
Centenary College of Louisiana, LA M,W
Central Connecticut State University, CT M,W
Central Methodist College, MO M,W
Central Michigan University, MI W
Central Missouri State University, MO W
Central Washington University, WA W
Champlain College, VT M,W
Charleston Southern University, SC M,W
Christian Brothers University, TN M,W
Christian Heritage College, CA M
Citadel, The Military Coll of South Carolina, SC M
Clayton College & State University, GA M,W

Clemson University, SC M,W
Coastal Carolina University, SC M,W
Coker College, SC M,W
College of Charleston, SC M,W
College of St. Joseph, VT M,W
College of Saint Mary, NE W
The College of Saint Rose, NY M,W
College of the Southwest, NM W
The College of William and Mary, VA M,W
Colorado Christian University, CO M,W
The Colorado College, CO W
Columbia College, MO M
Columbia College, SC W
Columbia Union College, MD M
Concordia College, MI M,W
Concordia College, NY M,W
Concordia University, CA M
Concordia University, NE M,W
Concordia University, OR M,W
Concordia University at St. Paul, MN W
Converse College, SC W
Cornerstone University, MI M,W
Covenant College, GA M,W
Creighton University, NE M,W
Culver-Stockton College, MO M,W
Cumberland College, KY M,W
Cumberland University, TN M,W
Daemen College, NY M,W
Dallas Baptist University, TX W
Dana College, NE W
David Lipscomb University, TN M,W
Davidson College, NC M,W
Davis & Elkins College, WV M
DePaul University, IL M,W
Doane College, NE M,W
Dominican College of Blauvelt, NY M,W
Dominican University of California, CA M,W
Dordt College, IA M,W
Dowling College, NY M
Drake University, IA M
Drexel University, PA M
Drury University, MO M,W
Duke University, NC M,W
Duquesne University, PA M,W
East Carolina University, NC M,W
East Central University, OK W
Eastern Illinois University, IL M,W
Eastern Michigan University, MI M,W
Eastern Washington University, WA W
East Stroudsburg University of Pennsylvania, PA M,W
Eckerd College, FL M,W
Edinboro University of Pennsylvania, PA W
Elon College, NC M,W
Embry-Riddle Aeronautical University, FL M,W
Emmanuel College, GA M
Erskine College, SC M,W
Fairfield University, CT M,W
Fairleigh Dickinson U, Teaneck-Hackensack Campus, NJ M,W
Felician College, NJ M,W
Flagler College, FL M,W
Florida Atlantic University, FL M,W
Florida Institute of Technology, FL M
Florida International University, FL M,W
Florida Southern College, FL M,W
Florida State University, FL W
Fordham University, NY M,W
Fort Lewis College, CO M,W
Francis Marion University, SC M,W
Franklin Pierce College, NH M,W
Fresno Pacific University, CA M
Friends University, KS M,W
Furman University, SC M,W
Gannon University, PA M,W
Gardner-Webb University, NC M
Geneva College, PA M,W
George Mason University, VA M,W
Georgetown College, KY M,W
Georgetown University, DC M,W
The George Washington University, DC M,W
Georgian Court College, NJ W
Georgia Southern University, GA M,W
Georgia State University, GA M
Goldey-Beacom College, DE M,W
Gonzaga University, WA M,W
Goshen College, IN M,W
Grace College, IN M,W
Graceland College, IA M,W
Grand Canyon University, AZ M,W
Grand Valley State University, MI W
Grand View College, IA M,W
Green Mountain College, VT M,W
Harris-Stowe State College, MO M,W
Hartwick College, NY M
Hastings College, NE M,W
Hawaii Pacific University, HI M,W
High Point University, NC M,W
Hillsdale College, MI M,W
Hofstra University, NY M,W
Holy Family College, PA M,W
Hope International University, CA M,W
Houghton College, NY M,W
Humboldt State University, CA M,W
Huntington College, IN M
Huron University, SD M,W
Illinois State University, IL W
Indiana Institute of Technology, IN M,W
Indiana University Bloomington, IN M,W
Indiana U–Purdue U Fort Wayne, IN M,W
Indiana U–Purdue U Indianapolis, IN M,W
Indiana Wesleyan University, IN M,W
Inter American U of PR, San Germán Campus, PR M
Iowa State University of Science and Technology, IA W
Iowa Wesleyan College, IA M,W
Jacksonville State University, AL W
Jacksonville University, FL M,W
James Madison University, VA M,W
Jamestown College, ND W
John Brown University, AR M
Judson College, IL M,W
Kansas Wesleyan University, KS M,W
Kent State University, OH W
Kentucky Wesleyan College, KY M,W
King College, TN M,W
Kutztown University of Pennsylvania, PA M,W
Lambuth University, TN M,W
Lander University, SC M,W
La Salle University, PA M,W
Lees-McRae College, NC M,W
Lee University, TN M,W
Lehigh University, PA M,W
Le Moyne College, NY M,W
Lewis University, IL M,W
Liberty University, VA M,W
Limestone College, SC M,W
Lincoln Memorial University, TN M,W
Lincoln University, MO M
Lock Haven University of Pennsylvania, PA M,W
Long Island U, Brooklyn Campus, NY M,W
Long Island U, C.W. Post Campus, NY M,W
Long Island U, Southampton College, NY M,W
Longwood College, VA M
Louisiana State University and A&M College, LA W
Loyola Marymount University, CA M,W
Loyola University Chicago, IL M,W
Lynn University, FL M,W
Madonna University, MI M
Malone College, OH M,W
Manhattan College, NY M,W
Marian College, IN M,W
Marist College, NY M,W
Marquette University, WI M,W
Marshall University, WV M,W
Mars Hill College, NC M,W
Martin Methodist College, TN M,W
Marycrest International University, IA M,W
The Master's College and Seminary, CA M,W
McKendree College, IL M,W
Mercer University, GA M,W
Mercy College, NY M,W
Mercyhurst College, PA M,W
Merrimack College, MA W
Mesa State College, CO W
Metropolitan State College of Denver, CO M,W
Miami University, OH W
Michigan State University, MI M
Midland Lutheran College, NE W
Midway College, KY W
Midwestern State University, TX M,W
Millersville University of Pennsylvania, PA M,W
Milligan College, TN M,W
Minnesota State University, Mankato, MN W
Minnesota State University Moorhead, MN W
Minot State University, ND W
Mississippi State University, MS W
Missouri Baptist College, MO M,W
Missouri Southern State College, MO M,W
Missouri Valley College, MO M,W
Monmouth University, NJ M,W
Montana State U–Billings, MT M,W
Montreat College, NC M,W
Mount Aloysius College, PA M,W
Mount Marty College, SD M
Mount Olive College, NC M,W
Mount St. Clare College, IA M,W
Mount Saint Mary's College and Seminary, MD M,W
Mount Vernon Nazarene College, OH M,W
Newberry College, SC M,W
New Hampshire College, NH M,W
Newman University, KS M,W
New Mexico Highlands University, NM W
New York Institute of Technology, NY M,W
Niagara University, NY M,W
North Carolina State University, NC M,W
North Dakota State University, ND W
Northeastern State University, OK M,W

Soccer (continued)

Institution	Grants
Northeastern University, MA	M,W
Northern Arizona University, AZ	W
Northern Illinois University, IL	M,W
Northern Kentucky University, KY	M,W
Northern Michigan University, MI	W
North Greenville College, SC	M,W
Northwest College, WA	M
Northwestern College, IA	M,W
Northwestern State University of Louisiana, LA	W
Northwestern University, IL	W
Northwest Missouri State University, MO	W
Northwest Nazarene University, ID	M,W
Northwood University, MI	W
Northwood University, Florida Campus, FL	M
Northwood University, Texas Campus, TX	M
Notre Dame College, NH	M,W
Nova Southeastern University, FL	M,W
Nyack College, NY	M,W
Oakland University, MI	M,W
Ohio Dominican College, OH	M
The Ohio State University, OH	M,W
Ohio University, OH	W
Ohio Valley College, WV	M
Oklahoma Christian U of Science and Arts, OK	M,W
Oklahoma City University, OK	M,W
Old Dominion University, VA	M,W
Olivet Nazarene University, IL	M,W
Oral Roberts University, OK	M,W
Oregon State University, OR	M,W
Ottawa University, KS	M,W
Palm Beach Atlantic College, FL	M,W
Park University, MO	M,W
Penn State U Univ Park Campus, PA	M,W
Pepperdine University, CA	W
Pfeiffer University, NC	M,W
Philadelphia University, PA	M,W
Piedmont College, GA	M,W
Point Loma Nazarene University, CA	M
Point Park College, PA	M
Portland State University, OR	W
Presbyterian College, SC	M,W
Providence College, RI	M,W
Purdue University, IN	W
Purdue University Calumet, IN	M
Queens College, NC	M,W
Queens Coll of the City U of NY, NY	M
Quincy University, IL	M,W
Quinnipiac University, CT	M,W
Radford University, VA	M,W
Regis University, CO	M,W
Reinhardt College, GA	M,W
Research College of Nursing, MO	M,W
Rider University, NJ	M,W
Robert Morris College, IL	M,W
Robert Morris College, PA	M,W
Roberts Wesleyan College, NY	M,W
Rochester College, MI	M
Rockhurst University, MO	M,W
Rocky Mountain College, MT	W
Rollins College, FL	M
Rutgers, State U of NJ, College of Pharmacy, NJ	M,W
Rutgers, State U of NJ, Cook College, NJ	M,W
Rutgers, State U of NJ, Douglass College, NJ	W
Rutgers, State U of NJ, Livingston College, NJ	M,W
Rutgers, State U of NJ, Mason Gross School of Arts, NJ	M,W
Rutgers, State U of NJ, Rutgers College, NJ	M,W
Rutgers, State U of NJ, College of Engineering, NJ	M,W
Saginaw Valley State University, MI	M,W
St. Ambrose University, IA	M,W
St. Andrews Presbyterian College, NC	M,W
St. Bonaventure University, NY	M,W
St. Edward's University, TX	M,W
St. Francis College, NY	M
Saint Francis College, PA	M,W
St. Gregory's University, OK	M,W
St. John's University, NY	M,W
Saint Joseph's College, IN	M,W
Saint Joseph's University, PA	M,W
Saint Leo University, FL	M,W
Saint Louis University, MO	M,W
Saint Mary College, KS	M,W
Saint Mary's College of California, CA	M,W
St. Mary's University of San Antonio, TX	M,W
Saint Peter's College, NJ	M,W
St. Thomas Aquinas College, NY	M,W
St. Thomas University, FL	M,W
Saint Vincent College, PA	M,W
Saint Xavier University, IL	M,W
Salem-Teikyo University, WV	M
Samford University, AL	W
San Diego State University, CA	M,W
San Francisco State University, CA	M,W
San Jose State University, CA	M,W
Santa Clara University, CA	M,W
Seattle Pacific University, WA	M
Seton Hall University, NJ	M,W
Seton Hill College, PA	W
Shippensburg University of Pennsylvania, PA	M,W
Siena College, NY	M,W
Siena Heights University, MI	M,W
Slippery Rock University of Pennsylvania, PA	M,W
Southeastern Louisiana University, LA	W
Southern Illinois University Edwardsville, IL	M,W
Southern Methodist University, TX	M,W
Southern Nazarene University, OK	M,W
Southern Oregon University, OR	W
Southern Wesleyan University, SC	M,W
Southwest Baptist University, MO	M,W
Southwestern College, KS	M,W
Southwestern Oklahoma State University, OK	M,W
Southwest Missouri State University, MO	M,W
Southwest State University, MN	W
Southwest Texas State University, TX	W
Spalding University, KY	M,W
Spring Arbor College, MI	M,W
Spring Hill College, AL	M,W
Stanford University, CA	M,W
State U of NY at Albany, NY	M,W
State U of NY at Binghamton, NY	M,W
State U of NY at Buffalo, NY	M,W
State U of NY at Stony Brook, NY	M,W
Stephen F. Austin State University, TX	W
Sterling College, KS	M,W
Stetson University, FL	M,W
Stonehill College, MA	M,W
Syracuse University, NY	M,W
Tabor College, KS	M,W
Taylor University, IN	M,W
Teikyo Post University, CT	M,W
Temple University, PA	M,W
Tennessee Technological University, TN	W
Tennessee Temple University, TN	M
Tennessee Wesleyan College, TN	M,W
Texas A&M University, TX	W
Texas A&M University–Commerce, TX	W
Texas Christian University, TX	W
Texas Lutheran University, TX	M,W
Texas Tech University, TX	W
Texas Wesleyan University, TX	M,W
Thomas University, GA	M
Tiffin University, OH	M,W
Towson University, MD	M,W
Trinity Christian College, IL	M,W
Tri-State University, IN	M,W
Truman State University, MO	M,W
Tulane University, LA	W
Tusculum College, TN	M,W
Union College, KY	M,W
Union University, TN	M
United States International University, CA	M,W
Unity College, ME	M
The University of Akron, OH	M
The University of Alabama, AL	W
The University of Alabama at Birmingham, AL	M,W
The University of Alabama in Huntsville, AL	M,W
The University of Arizona, AZ	W
University of Arkansas, AR	W
University of Arkansas at Little Rock, AR	W
University of Bridgeport, CT	M,W
U of Calif, Berkeley, CA	M,W
U of Calif, Los Angeles, CA	M,W
U of Calif, Santa Barbara, CA	M,W
University of Central Florida, FL	M,W
University of Charleston, WV	M,W
University of Cincinnati, OH	M,W
University of Colorado at Boulder, CO	W
University of Colorado at Colorado Springs, CO	M
University of Connecticut, CT	M,W
University of Dayton, OH	M,W
University of Delaware, DE	M,W
University of Detroit Mercy, MI	M,W
University of Evansville, IN	M
The University of Findlay, OH	M,W
University of Florida, FL	W
University of Georgia, GA	W
University of Guam, GU	M
University of Hartford, CT	M,W
University of Hawaii at Manoa, HI	W
University of Houston, TX	W
University of Idaho, ID	W
University of Illinois at Chicago, IL	M
University of Illinois at Springfield, IL	M
University of Illinois at Urbana–Champaign, IL	W

University of Indianapolis, IN M,W
The University of Iowa, IA W
University of Kansas, KS W
University of Louisiana at Monroe, LA W
University of Louisville, KY M,W
University of Maine, ME M,W
University of Mary, ND M,W
University of Maryland, Baltimore County, MD M,W
University of Maryland, College Park, MD M,W
University of Massachusetts Amherst, MA M,W
The University of Memphis, TN M,W
University of Miami, FL W
University of Minnesota, Crookston, MN W
University of Minnesota, Duluth, MN W
University of Mississippi, MS W
University of Missouri–Columbia, MO W
University of Missouri–Kansas City, MO M
University of Missouri–Rolla, MO M,W
University of Missouri–St. Louis, MO M,W
University of Mobile, AL M,W
University of Montevallo, AL M,W
University of Nebraska–Lincoln, NE W
University of Nevada, Las Vegas, NV M,W
University of Nevada, Reno, NV W
University of New Hampshire, NH M,W
University of New Haven, CT M,W
University of New Mexico, NM M,W
University of North Alabama, AL W
The University of North Carolina at Asheville, NC M,W
The University of North Carolina at Chapel Hill, NC M,W
The University of North Carolina at Charlotte, NC M,W
The University of North Carolina at Greensboro, NC M,W
The University of North Carolina at Pembroke, NC M
The University of North Carolina at Wilmington, NC M,W
University of Northern Colorado, CO W
University of North Florida, FL M,W
University of Notre Dame, IN M,W
University of Oklahoma, OK W
University of Oregon, OR W
University of Pittsburgh, PA M,W
University of Portland, OR M,W
U of Puerto Rico, Cayey University College, PR M
University of Rhode Island, RI M,W
University of Richmond, VA M,W
University of Rio Grande, OH M
University of St. Francis, IL M,W
University of Saint Francis, IN M,W
University of San Diego, CA M,W
University of San Francisco, CA M,W
University of Science and Arts of Oklahoma, OK M,W
University of South Alabama, AL W
University of South Carolina, SC M,W
University of South Carolina Aiken, SC M,W
U of South Carolina Spartanburg, SC M,W
University of Southern California, CA W
University of Southern Indiana, IN M,W
University of South Florida, FL M,W
The University of Tampa, FL M,W
The University of Tennessee at Chattanooga, TN M,W
The University of Tennessee at Martin, TN W
The University of Tennessee Knoxville, TN W
The University of Texas at Austin, TX W
University of the District of Columbia, DC M
University of the Incarnate Word, TX M,W
University of the Pacific, CA W
University of Toledo, OH W
University of Tulsa, OK M,W
University of Utah, UT W
University of Vermont, VT M,W
University of Virginia, VA M,W
University of Washington, WA M
University of West Florida, FL M,W
University of Wisconsin–Green Bay, WI M,W
University of Wisconsin–Madison, WI M,W
University of Wisconsin–Milwaukee, WI M,W
University of Wisconsin–Parkside, WI M,W
University of Wyoming, WY W
Urbana University, OH M,W
Utah State University, UT W
Valparaiso University, IN M,W
Vanderbilt University, TN M,W
Vanguard University of Southern California, CA M,W
Villanova University, PA M,W
Virginia Commonwealth University, VA M,W
Virginia Military Institute, VA M
Virginia Polytechnic Institute and State U, VA M,W
Wagner College, NY W
Wake Forest University, NC M,W
Walsh University, OH M,W
Warner Pacific College, OR M
Washington State University, WA W
Webber College, FL M,W
Weber State University, UT W
West Chester University of Pennsylvania, PA M,W
Western Baptist College, OR M,W
Western Carolina University, NC W
Western Illinois University, IL M
Western Kentucky University, KY M
Western Michigan University, MI M,W
Western Washington University, WA M,W
Westmont College, CA M,W
West Texas A&M University, TX M,W
West Virginia University, WV M,W
West Virginia Wesleyan College, WV M,W
Wheeling Jesuit University, WV M,W
William Carey College, MS M,W
William Jewell College, MO M,W
Williams Baptist College, AR M
William Woods University, MO M,W
Wingate University, NC M
Winona State University, MN W
Winthrop University, SC M
Wofford College, SC M,W
Xavier University, OH M,W
York College, NE M,W

SOFTBALL

Abilene Christian University, TX W
Adams State College, CO W
Adelphi University, NY W
Alabama State University, AL W
Alcorn State University, MS W
American International College, MA W
Anderson College, SC W
Angelo State University, TX W
Aquinas College, MI W
Arizona State University, AZ W
Ashland University, OH W
Athens State University, AL W
Auburn University, AL W
Augustana College, SD W
Austin Peay State University, TN W
Avila College, MO W
Azusa Pacific University, CA W
Baker University, KS W
Ball State University, IN W
Barber-Scotia College, NC W
Barry University, FL W
Bartlesville Wesleyan College, OK W
Barton College, NC W
Bayamón Central University, PR M,W
Baylor University, TX W
Belhaven College, MS W
Bellarmine College, KY W
Bellevue University, NE W
Belmont Abbey College, NC W
Belmont University, TN W
Bemidji State University, MN W
Benedictine College, KS W
Bentley College, MA W
Bethany College, KS W
Bethany College of the Assemblies of God, CA W
Bethel College, IN W
Bethel College, TN W
Bethune-Cookman College, FL W
Biola University, CA W
Bloomfield College, NJ W
Bloomsburg University of Pennsylvania, PA W
Bluefield College, VA W
Bluefield State College, WV W
Boston College, MA W
Boston University, MA W
Bowie State University, MD W
Bowling Green State University, OH W
Bradley University, IL W
Brescia University, KY W
Brevard College, NC W
Briar Cliff College, IA W
Briarcliffe College, NY W
Brigham Young University–Hawaii Campus, HI W
Butler University, IN W
Caldwell College, NJ W
California Baptist University, CA W
California Polytechnic State U, San Luis Obispo, CA W
California State University, Bakersfield, CA W
California State University, Fresno, CA W
California State University, Fullerton, CA W
California State University, Long Beach, CA W
California State University, Northridge, CA W
California State University, Sacramento, CA W

Softball (continued)

California State University, San Bernardino, CA W
Cameron University, OK W
Campbellsville University, KY W
Campbell University, NC W
Canisius College, NY W
Carlow College, PA W
Carson-Newman College, TN W
Catawba College, NC W
Cedarville College, OH W
Centenary College of Louisiana, LA W
Central Connecticut State University, CT W
Central Methodist College, MO W
Central Michigan University, MI W
Central Missouri State University, MO W
Central Washington University, WA W
Chaminade University of Honolulu, HI W
Charleston Southern University, SC W
Christian Brothers University, TN W
Clarion University of Pennsylvania, PA W
Coastal Carolina University, SC W
Coker College, SC W
College of Charleston, SC W
College of Saint Mary, NE W
The College of Saint Rose, NY W
The College of West Virginia, WV W
Colorado School of Mines, CO W
Columbia College, MO W
Columbia Union College, MD W
Columbus State University, GA W
Concordia College, MI W
Concordia College, NY W
Concordia University, CA W
Concordia University, NE W
Concordia University, OR W
Concordia University at St. Paul, MN W
Cornerstone University, MI W
Creighton University, NE W
Culver-Stockton College, MO W
Cumberland College, KY W
Cumberland University, TN W
Dakota Wesleyan University, SD W
Dana College, NE W
David Lipscomb University, TN W
Davis & Elkins College, WV W
Delaware State University, DE W
DePaul University, IL W
Doane College, NE W
Dominican College of Blauvelt, NY W
Dominican University of California, CA W
Dordt College, IA W
Dowling College, NY W
Drake University, IA W
Drexel University, PA W
East Carolina University, NC W
East Central University, OK W
Eastern Illinois University, IL W
Eastern Kentucky University, KY W
Eastern Michigan University, MI W
Eastern New Mexico University, NM W
East Stroudsburg University of Pennsylvania, PA W
East Tennessee State University, TN W
Eckerd College, FL W
Edinboro University of Pennsylvania, PA W
Elon College, NC W
Emmanuel College, GA W
Emporia State University, KS W
Erskine College, SC W
Evangel University, MO W
Fairfield University, CT W
Fairleigh Dickinson U, Teaneck-Hackensack Campus, NJ W
Faulkner University, AL W
Felician College, NJ W
Ferris State University, MI W
Florida Institute of Technology, FL W
Florida International University, FL W
Florida Southern College, FL W
Florida State University, FL W
Fordham University, NY W
Fort Lewis College, CO W
Francis Marion University, SC W
Franklin Pierce College, NH W
Friends University, KS W
Furman University, SC W
Gannon University, PA W
Gardner-Webb University, NC W
Geneva College, PA W
George Mason University, VA W
Georgetown College, KY W
Georgia College and State University, GA W
Georgia Institute of Technology, GA W
Georgian Court College, NJ W
Georgia Southern University, GA W
Georgia Southwestern State University, GA W
Georgia State University, GA W
Goldey-Beacom College, DE W
Goshen College, IN W
Grace College, IN W
Graceland College, IA W
Grand Valley State University, MI W
Grand View College, IA W
Green Mountain College, VT W
Hampton University, VA W
Hannibal-LaGrange College, MO W
Hastings College, NE W
Hawaii Pacific University, HI W
Henderson State University, AR W
Hillsdale College, MI W
Hofstra University, NY W
Hope International University, CA W
Houston Baptist University, TX W
Humboldt State University, CA W
Huntington College, IN W
Huron University, SD W
Illinois State University, IL W
Indiana Institute of Technology, IN W
Indiana State University, IN W
Indiana University Bloomington, IN W
Indiana U–Purdue U Fort Wayne, IN W
Indiana U–Purdue U Indianapolis, IN W
Indiana Wesleyan University, IN W
Iowa State University of Science and Technology, IA W
Iowa Wesleyan College, IA W
Jacksonville State University, AL W
Jamestown College, ND W
Judson College, AL W
Judson College, IL W
Kansas Wesleyan University, KS W
Kennesaw State University, GA W
Kent State University, OH W
Kentucky Wesleyan College, KY W
Kutztown University of Pennsylvania, PA W
Lambuth University, TN W
Lander University, SC W
La Salle University, PA W
Lees-McRae College, NC W
Lee University, TN W
Lehigh University, PA W
Le Moyne College, NY W
LeMoyne-Owen College, TN W
Lewis University, IL W
Liberty University, VA W
Limestone College, SC W
Lincoln Memorial University, TN W
Lincoln University, MO W
Lock Haven University of Pennsylvania, PA W
Long Island U, C.W. Post Campus, NY W
Long Island U, Southampton College, NY W
Louisiana State University and A&M College, LA W
Louisiana Tech University, LA W
Loyola University Chicago, IL W
Madonna University, MI W
Malone College, OH W
Manhattan College, NY W
Mansfield University of Pennsylvania, PA W
Marian College, IN W
Marist College, NY W
Marshall University, WV W
Mars Hill College, NC W
Martin Methodist College, TN W
Marycrest International University, IA W
Mayville State University, ND W
McKendree College, IL W
McNeese State University, LA W
Mercer University, GA W
Mercyhurst College, PA W
Merrimack College, MA W
Mesa State College, CO W
Miami University, OH W
MidAmerica Nazarene University, KS W
Mid-Continent College, KY W
Middle Tennessee State University, TN W
Midland Lutheran College, NE W
Midway College, KY W
Millersville University of Pennsylvania, PA W
Milligan College, TN W
Minnesota State University, Mankato, MN W
Minnesota State University Moorhead, MN W
Minot State University, ND W
Mississippi State University, MS W
Mississippi University for Women, MS W
Missouri Baptist College, MO W
Missouri Southern State College, MO W
Missouri Valley College, MO W
Missouri Western State College, MO W
Monmouth University, NJ W
Montreat College, NC W
Morehead State University, KY W
Morningside College, IA W
Mount Marty College, SD W
Mount Olive College, NC W
Mount St. Clare College, IA W

Mount Saint Mary's College and Seminary, MD W
Mount Vernon Nazarene College, OH W
Newberry College, SC W
Newman University, KS W
New Mexico Highlands University, NM W
New York Institute of Technology, NY W
Niagara University, NY W
North Dakota State University, ND W
Northeastern State University, OK W
Northern Illinois University, IL W
Northern Kentucky University, KY W
North Greenville College, SC W
Northwest Christian College, OR W
Northwestern College, IA W
Northwestern State University of Louisiana, LA W
Northwestern University, IL W
Northwest Missouri State University, MO W
Northwood University, MI W
Northwood University, Florida Campus, FL W
Northwood University, Texas Campus, TX W
Notre Dame College, NH W
Nova Southeastern University, FL W
Oakland City University, IN W
Ohio Dominican College, OH W
The Ohio State University, OH W
Ohio University, OH W
Ohio Valley College, WV W
Oklahoma Baptist University, OK W
Oklahoma Christian U of Science and Arts, OK W
Oklahoma City University, OK W
Oklahoma State U, OK W
Olivet Nazarene University, IL W
Oregon Institute of Technology, OR W
Oregon State University, OR W
Ottawa University, KS W
Park University, MO W
Penn State U Univ Park Campus, PA W
Pfeiffer University, NC W
Philadelphia University, PA W
Piedmont College, GA W
Pikeville College, KY W
Pittsburg State University, KS W
Point Loma Nazarene University, CA W
Point Park College, PA W
Portland State University, OR W
Prairie View A&M University, TX W
Presbyterian College, SC W
Providence College, RI W
Purdue University, IN W
Queens College, NC W
Queens Coll of the City U of NY, NY M
Quincy University, IL W
Quinnipiac University, CT W
Radford University, VA W
Regis University, CO W
Rider University, NJ W
Robert Morris College, IL W
Robert Morris College, PA W
Rochester College, MI W
Rutgers, State U of NJ, College of Pharmacy, NJ W
Rutgers, State U of NJ, Cook College, NJ W
Rutgers, State U of NJ, Douglass College, NJ W
Rutgers, State U of NJ, Livingston College, NJ W
Rutgers, State U of NJ, Mason Gross School of Arts, NJ W
Rutgers, State U of NJ, Rutgers College, NJ W
Rutgers, State U of NJ, College of Engineering, NJ W
Saginaw Valley State University, MI W
St. Ambrose University, IA W
St. Andrews Presbyterian College, NC W
Saint Augustine's College, NC W
St. Bonaventure University, NY W
St. Edward's University, TX W
St. Francis College, NY W
Saint Francis College, PA W
St. Gregory's University, OK W
St. John's University, NY W
Saint Joseph's College, IN W
Saint Joseph's University, PA W
Saint Leo University, FL W
Saint Louis University, MO W
Saint Martin's College, WA W
Saint Mary College, KS W
Saint Mary-of-the-Woods College, IN W
Saint Mary's College of California, CA W
Saint Peter's College, NJ W
St. Thomas Aquinas College, NY W
St. Thomas University, FL W
Saint Vincent College, PA W
Saint Xavier University, IL W
Salem-Teikyo University, WV W
Samford University, AL W
San Diego State University, CA W
San Francisco State University, CA W
Santa Clara University, CA W
Seton Hall University, NJ W
Seton Hill College, PA W
Shaw University, NC W
Shippensburg University of Pennsylvania, PA W
Siena College, NY W
Siena Heights University, MI W
Slippery Rock University of Pennsylvania, PA W
South Dakota State University, SD W
Southeastern Louisiana University, LA W
Southeast Missouri State University, MO W
Southern Arkansas University–Magnolia, AR W
Southern Illinois University Carbondale, IL W
Southern Illinois University Edwardsville, IL W
Southern Nazarene University, OK W
Southern Oregon University, OR W
Southern University and A&M College, LA W
Southern Utah University, UT W
Southern Wesleyan University, SC W
Southwest Baptist University, MO W
Southwestern Oklahoma State University, OK W
Southwest Missouri State University, MO W
Southwest State University, MN W
Southwest Texas State University, TX W
Spring Arbor College, MI W
Spring Hill College, AL W
Stanford University, CA W
State U of NY at Albany, NY W
State U of NY at Binghamton, NY W
State U of NY at Buffalo, NY W
State U of NY at Stony Brook, NY W
State University of West Georgia, GA W
Stephen F. Austin State University, TX W
Sterling College, KS W
Stetson University, FL W
Stonehill College, MA W
Syracuse University, NY W
Tabor College, KS W
Tarleton State University, TX W
Taylor University, IN W
Teikyo Post University, CT W
Temple University, PA M,W
Tennessee Technological University, TN W
Tennessee Wesleyan College, TN W
Texas A&M University, TX W
Texas A&M University–Kingsville, TX W
Texas Lutheran University, TX W
Texas Tech University, TX W
Texas Wesleyan University, TX W
Texas Woman's University, TX W
Thomas University, GA W
Tiffin University, OH W
Towson University, MD W
Trevecca Nazarene University, TN W
Trinity Christian College, IL W
Tri-State University, IN W
Truman State University, MO W
Tusculum College, TN W
Union College, KY W
Union University, TN W
The University of Akron, OH W
The University of Alabama, AL W
The University of Alabama at Birmingham, AL W
The University of Arizona, AZ W
University of Arkansas, AR W
University of Arkansas at Monticello, AR W
University of Bridgeport, CT W
U of Calif, Berkeley, CA W
U of Calif, Los Angeles, CA W
U of Calif, Riverside, CA W
U of Calif, Santa Barbara, CA W
University of Central Oklahoma, OK W
University of Charleston, WV W
University of Colorado at Colorado Springs, CO W
University of Connecticut, CT W
University of Dayton, OH W
University of Delaware, DE W
University of Detroit Mercy, MI W
The University of Findlay, OH W
University of Florida, FL W
University of Hartford, CT W
University of Hawaii at Hilo, HI W
University of Hawaii at Manoa, HI W
University of Houston, TX W
University of Illinois at Chicago, IL W
University of Illinois at Urbana–Champaign, IL W
University of Indianapolis, IN W
The University of Iowa, IA W
University of Kansas, KS W
University of Louisiana at Lafayette, LA W

Softball (continued)

University of Louisiana at Monroe, LA W
University of Louisville, KY W
University of Maine, ME W
University of Mary, ND W
University of Maryland, Baltimore County, MD W
University of Maryland, College Park, MD W
University of Massachusetts Amherst, MA W
University of Michigan, MI W
University of Minnesota, Crookston, MN W
University of Minnesota, Duluth, MN W
University of Mississippi, MS W
University of Missouri–Columbia, MO W
University of Missouri–Kansas City, MO W
University of Missouri–Rolla, MO W
University of Missouri–St. Louis, MO W
University of Mobile, AL W
University of Nebraska at Kearney, NE W
University of Nebraska at Omaha, NE W
University of Nebraska–Lincoln, NE W
University of Nevada, Las Vegas, NV W
University of New Haven, CT W
University of New Mexico, NM W
University of North Alabama, AL W
The University of North Carolina at Asheville, NC W
The University of North Carolina at Chapel Hill, NC W
The University of North Carolina at Charlotte, NC W
The University of North Carolina at Greensboro, NC W
The University of North Carolina at Pembroke, NC W
The University of North Carolina at Wilmington, NC W
University of North Dakota, ND W
University of Northern Colorado, CO W
University of Northern Iowa, IA W
University of North Florida, FL W
University of Notre Dame, IN W
University of Oklahoma, OK W
University of Oregon, OR W
University of Pittsburgh, PA W
University of Rhode Island, RI W
University of Rio Grande, OH W
University of St. Francis, IL W
University of Saint Francis, IN W
University of Science and Arts of Oklahoma, OK W
University of South Carolina, SC W
University of South Carolina Aiken, SC W
U of South Carolina Spartanburg, SC W
University of South Dakota, SD W
University of Southern Colorado, CO W
University of Southern Indiana, IN W
University of South Florida, FL W
The University of Tampa, FL W
The University of Tennessee at Chattanooga, TN W
The University of Tennessee at Martin, TN W
The University of Tennessee Knoxville, TN W
The University of Texas at Arlington, TX W
The University of Texas at Austin, TX W
The University of Texas at San Antonio, TX W
University of the Incarnate Word, TX W
University of the Pacific, CA W
University of the Sciences in Philadelphia, PA W
University of Toledo, OH W
University of Tulsa, OK W
University of Vermont, VT W
University of Virginia, VA W
University of Virginia's College at Wise, VA W
University of Washington, WA W
The University of West Alabama, AL W
University of West Florida, FL W
University of Wisconsin–Green Bay, WI W
University of Wisconsin–Madison, WI W
Urbana University, OH W
Utah State University, UT W
Valdosta State University, GA W
Valley City State University, ND W
Valparaiso University, IN W
Vanguard University of Southern California, CA W
Villanova University, PA W
Virginia Intermont College, VA W
Virginia State University, VA W
Virginia Union University, VA W
Wagner College, NY W
Walsh University, OH W
Warner Southern College, FL W
Washburn University of Topeka, KS W
Wayne State College, NE W
Wayne State University, MI W
Webber College, FL W
West Chester University of Pennsylvania, PA W
Western Illinois University, IL W
Western Kentucky University, KY W
Western Michigan University, MI W
Western New Mexico University, NM W
Western Washington University, WA W
West Liberty State College, WV W
Westminster College, PA W
West Virginia State College, WV W
West Virginia University Institute of Technology, WV W
West Virginia Wesleyan College, WV W
Wichita State University, KS W
William Jewell College, MO W
Williams Baptist College, AR W
William Woods University, MO W
Wingate University, NC W
Winona State University, MN W
Winston-Salem State University, NC W
Winthrop University, SC W
York College, NE W
Youngstown State University, OH W

SWIMMING

Adelphi University, NY M,W
American University, DC M,W
Arizona State University, AZ M,W
Ashland University, OH M,W
Auburn University, AL M,W
Ball State University, IN M,W
Bayamón Central University, PR M,W
Bentley College, MA M,W
Biola University, CA M,W
Bloomsburg University of Pennsylvania, PA M,W
Boston College, MA W
Boston University, MA M,W
Bowling Green State University, OH M,W
Bradley University, IL M,W
Brigham Young University, UT M,W
Butler University, IN M,W
California Baptist University, CA M,W
California State University, Bakersfield, CA M,W
California State University, Fresno, CA W
California State University, Long Beach, CA M,W
California State University, Northridge, CA M,W
California State University, San Bernardino, CA M,W
Campbellsville University, KY M,W
Canisius College, NY W
Catawba College, NC W
Central Connecticut State University, CT M,W
Central Washington University, WA M,W
Chicago State University, IL M,W
Clarion University of Pennsylvania, PA M,W
Clemson University, SC M,W
College of Charleston, SC M,W
The College of Saint Rose, NY M,W
The College of William and Mary, VA M
Colorado School of Mines, CO M,W
Colorado State University, CO W
Cumberland College, KY M,W
Davidson College, NC M,W
Delta State University, MS M,W
Drexel University, PA M,W
Drury University, MO M,W
Duquesne University, PA M,W
East Carolina University, NC M,W
Eastern Illinois University, IL M,W
Eastern Michigan University, MI M,W
East Stroudsburg University of Pennsylvania, PA W
Edinboro University of Pennsylvania, PA M,W
Fairfield University, CT M,W
Fairmont State College, WV M,W
Florida Agricultural and Mechanical University, FL M,W
Florida Atlantic University, FL M,W
Florida State University, FL M,W
Fordham University, NY M,W
Gannon University, PA M,W
George Mason University, VA M,W
The George Washington University, DC M,W
Georgia Institute of Technology, GA M
Georgia Southern University, GA W
Grand Valley State University, MI M,W
Henderson State University, AR M,W
Hillsdale College, MI M,W
Illinois Institute of Technology, IL M,W
Illinois State University, IL W
Indiana University Bloomington, IN M,W
Indiana U–Purdue U Indianapolis, IN M,W
Iowa State University of Science and Technology, IA M,W
James Madison University, VA M,W
John Brown University, AR M,W

Kutztown University of Pennsylvania, PA M,W
La Salle University, PA M,W
Lehigh University, PA M,W
Lewis University, IL M,W
Limestone College, SC W
Lock Haven University of Pennsylvania, PA W
Louisiana State University and A&M College, LA M,W
Marist College, NY M,W
Metropolitan State College of Denver, CO M,W
Miami University, OH M,W
Michigan State University, MI M,W
Millersville University of Pennsylvania, PA W
Minnesota State University, Mankato, MN M,W
Niagara University, NY M,W
North Carolina Agricultural and Technical State U, NC W
North Carolina State University, NC M,W
Northeastern University, MA W
Northern Arizona University, AZ W
Northern Illinois University, IL M,W
Northern Michigan University, MI W
Northwestern University, IL M,W
Oakland University, MI M,W
The Ohio State University, OH M,W
Ohio University, OH M,W
Old Dominion University, VA M,W
Oregon State University, OR W
Ouachita Baptist University, AR M,W
Penn State U Univ Park Campus, PA M,W
Pepperdine University, CA W
Pfeiffer University, NC W
Purdue University, IN M,W
Queens Coll of the City U of NY, NY M,W
Rice University, TX W
Rider University, NJ M,W
Rutgers, State U of NJ, College of Pharmacy, NJ M,W
Rutgers, State U of NJ, Cook College, NJ M,W
Rutgers, State U of NJ, Douglass College, NJ W
Rutgers, State U of NJ, Livingston College, NJ M,W
Rutgers, State U of NJ, Mason Gross School of Arts, NJ M,W
Rutgers, State U of NJ, Rutgers College, NJ M,W
Rutgers, State U of NJ, College of Engineering, NJ M,W
St. Ambrose University, IA W
St. Bonaventure University, NY M,W
St. Francis College, NY M,W
Saint Francis College, PA W
St. John's University, NY M,W
Saint Louis University, MO M,W
Saint Peter's College, NJ M,W
Salem-Teikyo University, WV M,W
San Diego State University, CA W
San Francisco State University, CA M,W
San Jose State University, CA W
Seton Hall University, NJ M,W
Shippensburg University of Pennsylvania, PA M,W
Slippery Rock University of Pennsylvania, PA M,W
South Dakota State University, SD M,W
Southern Arkansas University–Magnolia, AR M,W
Southern Illinois University Carbondale, IL M,W
Southern Methodist University, TX M,W
Southwest Missouri State University, MO M,W
Stanford University, CA M,W
State U of NY at Binghamton, NY M,W
State U of NY at Buffalo, NY M,W
State U of NY at Stony Brook, NY M,W
Syracuse University, NY M,W
Texas A&M University, TX M,W
Texas Christian University, TX M,W
Towson University, MD M,W
Tri-State University, IN M,W
Truman State University, MO M,W
Union College, KY M,W
The University of Alabama, AL M,W
The University of Alabama at Birmingham, AL W
U of Alaska Anchorage, AK M
The University of Arizona, AZ M,W
University of Arkansas, AR W
U of Calif, Berkeley, CA M,W
U of Calif, Irvine, CA M,W
U of Calif, Los Angeles, CA W
U of Calif, Santa Barbara, CA M,W
University of Charleston, WV M,W
University of Cincinnati, OH M,W
University of Connecticut, CT M,W
University of Delaware, DE W
University of Evansville, IN M,W
The University of Findlay, OH M,W
University of Florida, FL M,W
University of Georgia, GA M,W
University of Hawaii at Manoa, HI M,W
University of Houston, TX W
University of Illinois at Chicago, IL M,W
University of Illinois at Urbana–Champaign, IL W
University of Indianapolis, IN M,W
The University of Iowa, IA M,W
University of Kansas, KS M,W
University of Louisiana at Monroe, LA M,W
University of Louisville, KY M,W
University of Maine, ME M,W
University of Maryland, Baltimore County, MD M,W
University of Maryland, College Park, MD M,W
University of Massachusetts Amherst, MA M,W
University of Massachusetts Lowell, MA M
University of Miami, FL M,W
University of Michigan, MI M,W
University of Minnesota, Twin Cities Campus, MN M,W
University of Missouri–Columbia, MO M,W
University of Missouri–Rolla, MO M
University of Nebraska at Kearney, NE W
University of Nebraska–Lincoln, NE M,W
University of Nevada, Las Vegas, NV M,W
University of Nevada, Reno, NV W
University of New Hampshire, NH W
University of New Mexico, NM W
The University of North Carolina at Chapel Hill, NC M,W
The University of North Carolina at Wilmington, NC M,W
University of North Dakota, ND W
University of Northern Colorado, CO W
University of Northern Iowa, IA M,W
University of North Florida, FL W
University of Notre Dame, IN M,W
University of Pittsburgh, PA M,W
U of Puerto Rico, Cayey University College, PR M
U of Puerto Rico, Mayagüez Campus, PR M,W
University of Rhode Island, RI M,W
University of Richmond, VA W
University of San Diego, CA W
University of South Carolina, SC M,W
University of South Dakota, SD M
University of Southern California, CA M,W
The University of Tampa, FL M,W
The University of Tennessee Knoxville, TN M,W
The University of Texas at Austin, TX M,W
University of the Pacific, CA M,W
University of the Sacred Heart, PR M,W
University of Toledo, OH M,W
University of Utah, UT M,W
University of Virginia, VA M,W
University of Washington, WA M,W
University of Wisconsin–Green Bay, WI M,W
University of Wisconsin–Madison, WI M,W
University of Wisconsin–Milwaukee, WI M,W
University of Wyoming, WY M,W
Valparaiso University, IN M,W
Villanova University, PA W
Virginia Military Institute, VA M
Virginia Polytechnic Institute and State U, VA M,W
Wagner College, NY W
Walsh University, OH W
Washington State University, WA W
Wayne State University, MI M,W
West Chester University of Pennsylvania, PA M,W
Western Illinois University, IL M,W
Western Kentucky University, KY M,W
Westminster College, PA W
West Virginia University, WV M,W
West Virginia Wesleyan College, WV M,W
Wheeling Jesuit University, WV M
Wingate University, NC W
Xavier University, OH M,W

TABLE TENNIS

Inter American U of PR, San Germán Campus, PR M,W
U of Puerto Rico, Cayey University College, PR M
U of Puerto Rico, Mayagüez Campus, PR M,W

TENNIS

Abilene Christian University, TX M,W
Adelphi University, NY M,W
Alabama State University, AL M,W
Albany State University, GA M
Albertson College of Idaho, ID M,W
Alcorn State University, MS M,W
American University, DC M,W

Tennis (continued)

Anderson College, SC M,W
Appalachian State University, NC M,W
Aquinas College, MI M,W
Arizona State University, AZ M,W
Arkansas State University, AR W
Arkansas Tech University, AR W
Armstrong Atlantic State University, GA M,W
Auburn University, AL M,W
Auburn University Montgomery, AL M,W
Augustana College, SD M,W
Augusta State University, GA M,W
Austin Peay State University, TN M,W
Azusa Pacific University, CA M
Baker University, KS M,W
Ball State University, IN M,W
Barber-Scotia College, NC M
Barry University, FL M,W
Barton College, NC M,W
Baylor University, TX M,W
Belhaven College, MS M,W
Bellarmine College, KY M,W
Belmont Abbey College, NC M,W
Belmont University, TN M,W
Bemidji State University, MN W
Benedictine College, KS M,W
Berry College, GA M,W
Bethany College, KS M,W
Bethel College, IN M,W
Bethel College, KS M,W
Bethune-Cookman College, FL M,W
Biola University, CA W
Birmingham-Southern College, AL M,W
Bloomsburg University of Pennsylvania, PA M,W
Bluefield College, VA M,W
Bluefield State College, WV M,W
Blue Mountain College, MS W
Boise State University, ID M,W
Boston College, MA W
Boston University, MA W
Bowling Green State University, OH M,W
Bradley University, IL M,W
Brenau University, GA W
Brescia University, KY W
Brevard College, NC W
Brigham Young University, UT M,W
Brigham Young University–Hawaii Campus, HI M,W
Butler University, IN M,W
Caldwell College, NJ M,W
California Baptist University, CA M,W
California State Polytechnic University, Pomona, CA M,W
California State University, Bakersfield, CA W
California State University, Fresno, CA M,W
California State University, Fullerton, CA W
California State University, Long Beach, CA W
California State University, Los Angeles, CA M,W
California State University, Northridge, CA W
California State University, Sacramento, CA M,W
California University of Pennsylvania, PA W
Cameron University, OK M,W
Campbellsville University, KY M,W
Campbell University, NC M,W
Canisius College, NY M,W
Carlow College, PA W
Carson-Newman College, TN M,W
Catawba College, NC M,W
Cedarville College, OH M,W
Centenary College of Louisiana, LA M,W
Central Connecticut State University, CT M,W
Central Methodist College, MO M,W
Chaminade University of Honolulu, HI M,W
Charleston Southern University, SC M,W
Cheyney University of Pennsylvania, PA M,W
Citadel, The Military Coll of South Carolina, SC M
Clarion University of Pennsylvania, PA W
Clark Atlanta University, GA M,W
Clayton College & State University, GA W
Clemson University, SC M,W
Coastal Carolina University, SC M,W
Coker College, SC M,W
College of Charleston, SC M,W
College of Saint Mary, NE W
The College of William and Mary, VA M,W
Colorado Christian University, CO M,W
Colorado School of Mines, CO M,W
Columbia College, SC W
Columbus State University, GA M,W
Concordia College, NY M,W
Concordia University, NE M,W
Converse College, SC W
Coppin State College, MD M,W
Cornerstone University, MI M
Creighton University, NE M,W
Cumberland College, KY M,W
Cumberland University, TN M,W
David Lipscomb University, TN M,W
Davidson College, NC M,W
Davis & Elkins College, WV M,W
Delaware State University, DE M,W
Delta State University, MS M,W
DePaul University, IL M,W
Dominican University of California, CA M,W
Dordt College, IA M,W
Dowling College, NY M,W
Drake University, IA M,W
Drexel University, PA M
Drury University, MO M,W
Duke University, NC M,W
Duquesne University, PA M,W
East Carolina University, NC M,W
East Central University, OK M,W
Eastern Illinois University, IL M,W
Eastern Kentucky University, KY M,W
Eastern Michigan University, MI M,W
Eastern New Mexico University, NM W
Eastern Washington University, WA M,W
East Tennessee State University, TN M,W
Eckerd College, FL M,W
Edinboro University of Pennsylvania, PA M,W
Edward Waters College, FL M,W
Elon College, NC M,W
Embry-Riddle Aeronautical University, FL M
Emmanuel College, GA M,W
Emporia State University, KS M,W
Erskine College, SC M,W
Evangel University, MO M,W
Fairfield University, CT M,W
Fairleigh Dickinson U, Teaneck-Hackensack Campus, NJ M,W
Fairmont State College, WV M,W
Ferris State University, MI M,W
Flagler College, FL M,W
Florida Agricultural and Mechanical University, FL M,W
Florida Atlantic University, FL M,W
Florida International University, FL W
Florida Southern College, FL M,W
Florida State University, FL M,W
Fordham University, NY M,W
Fort Hays State University, KS W
Fort Valley State University, GA M,W
Francis Marion University, SC M,W
Franklin Pierce College, NH M,W
Friends University, KS M,W
Furman University, SC M,W
Gannon University, PA M,W
Gardner-Webb University, NC M,W
Geneva College, PA M,W
George Mason University, VA M,W
Georgetown College, KY M,W
Georgetown University, DC W
The George Washington University, DC M,W
Georgia College and State University, GA M,W
Georgia Institute of Technology, GA M,W
Georgia Southern University, GA M,W
Georgia Southwestern State University, GA M,W
Georgia State University, GA M,W
Gonzaga University, WA M,W
Goshen College, IN M,W
Grace College, IN M,W
Graceland College, IA M,W
Grambling State University, LA M
Grand Canyon University, AZ W
Grand Valley State University, MI M,W
Green Mountain College, VT M,W
Hampton University, VA M
Harding University, AR M,W
Hastings College, NE M,W
Hawaii Pacific University, HI M,W
Henderson State University, AR M,W
High Point University, NC M,W
Hillsdale College, MI M,W
Hofstra University, NY M,W
Hope International University, CA M,W
Huntington College, IN M,W
Idaho State University, ID M,W
Illinois State University, IL M,W
Indiana State University, IN M,W
Indiana University Bloomington, IN M,W
Indiana U–Purdue U Fort Wayne, IN M,W
Indiana U–Purdue U Indianapolis, IN M,W
Indiana Wesleyan University, IN M,W
Inter American U of PR, San Germán Campus, PR M,W
Iona College, NY M
Iowa State University of Science and Technology, IA W
Jacksonville State University, AL M,W
Jacksonville University, FL M,W
James Madison University, VA M,W
John Brown University, AR M,W
Johnson C. Smith University, NC M
Judson College, AL W

Judson College, IL M,W
Kansas State University, KS W
Kennesaw State University, GA W
King College, TN M,W
Kutztown University of Pennsylvania, PA M,W
Lake Superior State University, MI M,W
Lamar University, TX M,W
Lambuth University, TN M,W
Lander University, SC M
La Salle University, PA M,W
Lees-McRae College, NC M,W
Lee University, TN M,W
Lehigh University, PA M,W
Le Moyne College, NY M,W
LeMoyne-Owen College, TN M,W
Lewis-Clark State College, ID M,W
Lewis University, IL M,W
Liberty University, VA M
Limestone College, SC M,W
Lincoln Memorial University, TN M,W
Lincoln University, MO W
Long Island U, C.W. Post Campus, NY W
Longwood College, VA W
Louisiana State University and A&M College, LA M,W
Louisiana Tech University, LA W
Loyola Marymount University, CA W
Lynn University, FL M,W
Lyon College, AR M,W
Malone College, OH M,W
Manhattan College, NY M,W
Marian College, IN M,W
Marist College, NY M,W
Marquette University, WI M,W
Marshall University, WV W
Mars Hill College, NC M,W
Martin Methodist College, TN M,W
McKendree College, IL M,W
McNeese State University, LA W
Mercer University, GA M,W
Mercyhurst College, PA M,W
Merrimack College, MA W
Mesa State College, CO M,W
Metropolitan State College of Denver, CO M,W
Miami University, OH W
Michigan State University, MI M,W
Michigan Technological University, MI W
Middle Tennessee State University, TN M,W
Midland Lutheran College, NE M,W
Midway College, KY W
Midwestern State University, TX M,W
Millersville University of Pennsylvania, PA M,W
Milligan College, TN M,W
Minnesota State University, Mankato, MN M,W
Mississippi State University, MS M,W
Mississippi University for Women, MS W
Mississippi Valley State University, MS M
Missouri Southern State College, MO W
Missouri Western State College, MO W
Monmouth University, NJ M,W
Montana State U–Billings, MT M,W
Montana State U–Bozeman, MT M,W
Montreat College, NC M,W
Morehead State University, KY M,W
Morgan State University, MD M,W
Morningside College, IA W
Mount Olive College, NC M,W
Mount St. Clare College, IA M,W
Mount Saint Mary's College and Seminary, MD M,W
Murray State University, KY M,W
Newberry College, SC M,W
Niagara University, NY M,W
North Carolina Agricultural and Technical State U, NC M,W
North Carolina State University, NC M,W
Northeastern State University, OK M,W
Northern Arizona University, AZ M,W
Northern Illinois University, IL M,W
Northern Kentucky University, KY M,W
Northern Michigan University, MI W
North Georgia College & State University, GA M,W
North Greenville College, SC M,W
Northwestern College, IA M,W
Northwestern State University of Louisiana, LA W
Northwestern University, IL M,W
Northwest Missouri State University, MO M,W
Northwest Nazarene University, ID M,W
Northwood University, MI M,W
Oakland University, MI W
The Ohio State University, OH M,W
Oklahoma Baptist University, OK M,W
Oklahoma Christian U of Science and Arts, OK M,W
Oklahoma City University, OK M,W
Oklahoma State U, OK M,W
Old Dominion University, VA M,W
Olivet Nazarene University, IL M,W
Oral Roberts University, OK M,W
Ouachita Baptist University, AR M,W
Palm Beach Atlantic College, FL M,W
Penn State U Univ Park Campus, PA M,W
Pepperdine University, CA M,W
Pfeiffer University, NC M,W
Philadelphia University, PA M,W
Pikeville College, KY M,W
Point Loma Nazarene University, CA M,W
Portland State University, OR M,W
Prairie View A&M University, TX M,W
Presbyterian College, SC M,W
Providence College, RI W
Purdue University, IN M,W
Queens College, NC M,W
Queens Coll of the City U of NY, NY M,W
Quincy University, IL M,W
Quinnipiac University, CT M,W
Radford University, VA M,W
Rice University, TX M,W
Rider University, NJ M,W
Robert Morris College, PA M,W
Rockhurst University, MO M,W
Rollins College, FL M,W
Rust College, MS M,W
Rutgers, State U of NJ, College of Pharmacy, NJ M,W
Rutgers, State U of NJ, Cook College, NJ M,W
Rutgers, State U of NJ, Douglass College, NJ W
Rutgers, State U of NJ, Livingston College, NJ M,W
Rutgers, State U of NJ, Mason Gross School of Arts, NJ M,W
Rutgers, State U of NJ, Rutgers College, NJ M,W
Rutgers, State U of NJ, College of Engineering, NJ M,W
Saginaw Valley State University, MI W
St. Ambrose University, IA M,W
St. Bonaventure University, NY M,W
St. Edward's University, TX M,W
St. Francis College, NY M,W
Saint Francis College, PA M,W
St. Gregory's University, OK W
St. John's University, NY M,W
Saint Joseph's College, IN M,W
Saint Joseph's University, PA M,W
Saint Leo University, FL M,W
Saint Louis University, MO M,W
Saint Mary College, KS M,W
Saint Mary's College of California, CA M,W
St. Mary's University of San Antonio, TX M,W
Saint Peter's College, NJ M,W
St. Thomas University, FL M,W
Saint Vincent College, PA M
Samford University, AL M,W
Sam Houston State University, TX M,W
San Diego State University, CA M,W
San Jose State University, CA W
Santa Clara University, CA M,W
Savannah State University, GA W
Seton Hall University, NJ M,W
Seton Hill College, PA W
Shaw University, NC M,W
Shippensburg University of Pennsylvania, PA W
Shorter College, GA M,W
Slippery Rock University of Pennsylvania, PA M,W
Southeastern Louisiana University, LA M,W
Southeast Missouri State University, MO W
Southern Arkansas University–Magnolia, AR W
Southern Illinois University Carbondale, IL M,W
Southern Illinois University Edwardsville, IL M,W
Southern Methodist University, TX M,W
Southern Nazarene University, OK M,W
Southern Oregon University, OR W
Southern Polytechnic State University, GA M
Southern University and A&M College, LA M,W
Southern Utah University, UT W
Southwest Baptist University, MO M,W
Southwestern College, KS M,W
Southwest Missouri State University, MO M,W
Southwest State University, MN W
Southwest Texas State University, TX W
Spring Arbor College, MI M,W
Spring Hill College, AL M,W
Stanford University, CA M,W
State U of NY at Albany, NY W
State U of NY at Binghamton, NY M,W
State U of NY at Buffalo, NY M,W
State U of NY at Stony Brook, NY M,W
State University of West Georgia, GA M,W
Stephen F. Austin State University, TX W
Sterling College, KS M,W

Tennis (continued)

Stetson University, FL	M,W
Stonehill College, MA	M,W
Syracuse University, NY	W
Tabor College, KS	M,W
Taylor University, IN	M,W
Temple University, PA	M
Tennessee State University, TN	M,W
Tennessee Technological University, TN	M,W
Tennessee Wesleyan College, TN	W
Texas A&M University, TX	M,W
Texas A&M University–Kingsville, TX	M,W
Texas Christian University, TX	M,W
Texas Lutheran University, TX	M,W
Texas Tech University, TX	M,W
Texas Wesleyan University, TX	M,W
Texas Woman's University, TX	W
Thomas University, GA	W
Tiffin University, OH	M,W
Towson University, MD	M,W
Tri-State University, IN	M,W
Troy State University, AL	M,W
Truman State University, MO	M,W
Tulane University, LA	M,W
Tusculum College, TN	M,W
Tuskegee University, AL	M,W
Union University, TN	M,W
United States International University, CA	M,W
The University of Akron, OH	M,W
The University of Alabama, AL	M,W
The University of Alabama at Birmingham, AL	M,W
The University of Alabama in Huntsville, AL	M,W
The University of Arizona, AZ	M,W
University of Arkansas, AR	M,W
University of Arkansas at Little Rock, AR	M,W
U of Calif, Berkeley, CA	M,W
U of Calif, Irvine, CA	M,W
U of Calif, Los Angeles, CA	M,W
U of Calif, Riverside, CA	M,W
U of Calif, Santa Barbara, CA	M,W
University of Central Florida, FL	M,W
University of Central Oklahoma, OK	M,W
University of Charleston, WV	M,W
University of Cincinnati, OH	M,W
University of Colorado at Boulder, CO	M,W
University of Colorado at Colorado Springs, CO	M,W
University of Dayton, OH	M,W
University of Detroit Mercy, MI	W
University of Evansville, IN	M,W
The University of Findlay, OH	M,W
University of Florida, FL	M,W
University of Georgia, GA	M,W
University of Hartford, CT	M,W
University of Hawaii at Manoa, HI	M,W
University of Houston, TX	W
University of Idaho, ID	M,W
University of Illinois at Chicago, IL	M,W
University of Illinois at Springfield, IL	M,W
University of Illinois at Urbana–Champaign, IL	M,W
University of Indianapolis, IN	M,W
The University of Iowa, IA	M,W
University of Kansas, KS	M,W
University of Louisiana at Lafayette, LA	M,W
University of Louisiana at Monroe, LA	M,W
University of Louisville, KY	M,W
University of Mary, ND	M,W
University of Maryland, Baltimore County, MD	M,W
University of Maryland, College Park, MD	W
University of Massachusetts Amherst, MA	M,W
University of Massachusetts Lowell, MA	M,W
The University of Memphis, TN	M,W
University of Miami, FL	M,W
University of Michigan, MI	M,W
University of Minnesota, Crookston, MN	W
University of Minnesota, Duluth, MN	M,W
University of Minnesota, Twin Cities Campus, MN	M,W
University of Mississippi, MS	M,W
University of Missouri–Columbia, MO	W
University of Missouri–Kansas City, MO	M,W
University of Missouri–Rolla, MO	M
University of Missouri–St. Louis, MO	M,W
The University of Montana–Missoula, MT	M,W
University of Montevallo, AL	W
University of Nebraska at Kearney, NE	M,W
University of Nebraska–Lincoln, NE	M,W
University of Nevada, Las Vegas, NV	M,W
University of Nevada, Reno, NV	M,W
University of New Hampshire, NH	W
University of New Haven, CT	W
University of New Mexico, NM	M,W
University of New Orleans, LA	M,W
University of North Alabama, AL	M,W
The University of North Carolina at Asheville, NC	M,W
The University of North Carolina at Chapel Hill, NC	M,W
The University of North Carolina at Charlotte, NC	M,W
The University of North Carolina at Greensboro, NC	M,W
The University of North Carolina at Pembroke, NC	W
The University of North Carolina at Wilmington, NC	M,W
University of Northern Colorado, CO	M,W
University of Northern Iowa, IA	W
University of North Florida, FL	M,W
University of North Texas, TX	W
University of Notre Dame, IN	M,W
University of Oklahoma, OK	M,W
University of Oregon, OR	M,W
University of Pittsburgh, PA	W
University of Portland, OR	M,W
U of Puerto Rico, Cayey University College, PR	M,W
U of Puerto Rico, Mayagüez Campus, PR	M,W
University of Rhode Island, RI	W
University of Richmond, VA	W
University of St. Francis, IL	M,W
University of Saint Francis, IN	W
University of San Diego, CA	M,W
University of San Francisco, CA	M,W
University of Science and Arts of Oklahoma, OK	M,W
University of South Alabama, AL	M,W
University of South Carolina, SC	M,W
University of South Carolina Aiken, SC	M,W
U of South Carolina Spartanburg, SC	M,W
University of South Dakota, SD	M,W
University of Southern California, CA	M,W
University of Southern Colorado, CO	M,W
University of Southern Indiana, IN	M,W
University of Southern Mississippi, MS	M,W
University of South Florida, FL	M,W
The University of Tampa, FL	W
The University of Tennessee at Chattanooga, TN	M,W
The University of Tennessee at Martin, TN	M,W
The University of Tennessee Knoxville, TN	M,W
The University of Texas at Arlington, TX	M,W
The University of Texas at Austin, TX	M,W
The University of Texas at El Paso, TX	W
The University of Texas at San Antonio, TX	M,W
The University of Texas–Pan American, TX	M,W
University of the District of Columbia, DC	M,W
University of the Incarnate Word, TX	M,W
University of the Pacific, CA	M,W
University of the Sacred Heart, PR	M,W
University of Toledo, OH	M,W
University of Tulsa, OK	M,W
University of Utah, UT	M,W
University of Virginia, VA	M,W
University of Virginia's College at Wise, VA	M,W
University of Washington, WA	M,W
University of West Florida, FL	M,W
University of Wisconsin–Green Bay, WI	M,W
University of Wisconsin–Madison, WI	M,W
University of Wisconsin–Milwaukee, WI	M,W
University of Wyoming, WY	W
Utah State University, UT	M,W
Valdosta State University, GA	M,W
Valparaiso University, IN	M,W
Vanderbilt University, TN	M,W
Vanguard University of Southern California, CA	M,W
Virginia Commonwealth University, VA	M,W
Virginia Intermont College, VA	M,W
Virginia Military Institute, VA	M
Virginia Polytechnic Institute and State U, VA	M,W
Virginia State University, VA	M,W
Virginia Union University, VA	M
Wagner College, NY	M,W
Wake Forest University, NC	M,W
Walsh University, OH	M,W
Washburn University of Topeka, KS	M,W
Washington State University, WA	W
Wayne State University, MI	M,W
Webber College, FL	M,W
Weber State University, UT	M,W
West Chester University of Pennsylvania, PA	M,W
Western Carolina University, NC	W
Western Illinois University, IL	M,W
Western Kentucky University, KY	M,W
Western Michigan University, MI	M,W
Western New Mexico University, NM	M,W

West Liberty State College, WV M,W
Westminster College, PA W
Westmont College, CA M,W
West Texas A&M University, TX M,W
West Virginia University, WV M,W
West Virginia University Institute of Technology, WV M,W
West Virginia Wesleyan College, WV M,W
Wichita State University, KS M,W
William Carey College, MS M,W
William Jewell College, MO M,W
William Woods University, MO W
Wingate University, NC M,W
Winona State University, MN M,W
Winston-Salem State University, NC M,W
Winthrop University, SC M,W
Wofford College, SC M,W
Xavier University, OH M,W
Xavier University of Louisiana, LA M,W
York College, NE M,W
Youngstown State University, OH M,W

TRACK AND FIELD

Abilene Christian University, TX M,W
Adams State College, CO M,W
Alabama Agricultural and Mechanical University, AL M,W
Alabama State University, AL M,W
Albany State University, GA M,W
Alcorn State University, MS M,W
American University, DC M,W
Anderson College, SC M,W
Angelo State University, TX M,W
Appalachian State University, NC M,W
Aquinas College, MI M,W
Arizona State University, AZ M,W
Arkansas State University, AR M,W
Ashland University, OH M,W
Auburn University, AL M,W
Augustana College, SD M,W
Austin Peay State University, TN W
Azusa Pacific University, CA M,W
Baker University, KS M,W
Ball State University, IN M,W
Barber-Scotia College, NC M,W
Bayamón Central University, PR M,W
Baylor University, TX M,W
Bellarmine College, KY M,W
Belmont University, TN M,W
Bemidji State University, MN M,W
Benedictine College, KS M,W
Bentley College, MA M,W
Berry College, GA M,W
Bethany College, KS M,W
Bethel College, IN M,W
Bethel College, KS M,W
Bethune-Cookman College, FL M,W
Biola University, CA M,W
Black Hills State University, SD M,W
Bloomsburg University of Pennsylvania, PA M,W
Boise State University, ID M,W
Boston College, MA M,W
Boston University, MA M,W
Bowie State University, MD M,W
Bowling Green State University, OH M,W
Brevard College, NC M,W
Briar Cliff College, IA M,W
Brigham Young University, UT M,W
California Baptist University, CA M,W
California Polytechnic State U, San Luis Obispo, CA M,W
California State Polytechnic University, Pomona, CA M,W
California State University, Bakersfield, CA M,W
California State University, Fresno, CA M,W
California State University, Fullerton, CA M,W
California State University, Long Beach, CA M,W
California State University, Los Angeles, CA M,W
California State University, Northridge, CA M,W
California State University, Sacramento, CA M,W
California University of Pennsylvania, PA M,W
Campbell University, NC M,W
Canisius College, NY M,W
Carson-Newman College, TN M,W
Cedarville College, OH M,W
Central Connecticut State University, CT M,W
Central Methodist College, MO M,W
Central Michigan University, MI M,W
Central Missouri State University, MO M,W
Central State University, OH M,W
Central Washington University, WA M,W
Chadron State College, NE M,W
Charleston Southern University, SC M,W
Cheyney University of Pennsylvania, PA M,W
Chicago State University, IL M,W
Citadel, The Military Coll of South Carolina, SC M,W
Clarion University of Pennsylvania, PA M,W
Clark Atlanta University, GA M
Clemson University, SC M,W
Coastal Carolina University, SC M,W
The College of William and Mary, VA M,W
Colorado School of Mines, CO M,W
Colorado State University, CO M,W
Columbia Union College, MD M,W
Concordia College, MI M,W
Concordia University, NE M,W
Concordia University at St. Paul, MN M,W
Coppin State College, MD M,W
Cumberland College, KY M,W
Dakota State University, SD M,W
Dakota Wesleyan University, SD M,W
Dana College, NE M,W
Davidson College, NC M,W
Delaware State University, DE M,W
DePaul University, IL M,W
Dickinson State University, ND M,W
Doane College, NE M,W
Dordt College, IA M,W
Drake University, IA M,W
Drexel University, PA M
Duquesne University, PA W
East Carolina University, NC M,W
Eastern Illinois University, IL M,W
Eastern Kentucky University, KY M,W
Eastern Michigan University, MI M,W
Eastern Washington University, WA M,W
East Stroudsburg University of Pennsylvania, PA M,W
East Tennessee State University, TN M,W
Edinboro University of Pennsylvania, PA M,W
Edward Waters College, FL M,W
Emporia State University, KS M,W
Evangel University, MO M,W
Fairleigh Dickinson U, Teaneck-Hackensack Campus, NJ M,W
Felician College, NJ M,W
Ferris State University, MI M,W
Florida Agricultural and Mechanical University, FL M,W
Florida International University, FL M,W
Florida State University, FL M,W
Fordham University, NY M,W
Fort Hays State University, KS M,W
Fort Valley State University, GA M,W
Francis Marion University, SC M,W
Fresno Pacific University, CA M,W
Friends University, KS M,W
Furman University, SC M,W
Geneva College, PA M,W
George Mason University, VA M,W
Georgetown University, DC M,W
Georgia Institute of Technology, GA M,W
Georgia Southern University, GA W
Georgia State University, GA M
Glenville State College, WV M,W
Goshen College, IN M,W
Grace College, IN M,W
Graceland College, IA M,W
Grambling State University, LA M,W
Grand Valley State University, MI M,W
Hampton University, VA M,W
Harding University, AR M,W
Harris-Stowe State College, MO W
Hastings College, NE M,W
High Point University, NC W
Hillsdale College, MI M,W
Houghton College, NY M,W
Humboldt State University, CA M,W
Huntington College, IN M,W
Huron University, SD M,W
Idaho State University, ID M,W
Illinois State University, IL M,W
Indiana State University, IN M,W
Indiana University Bloomington, IN M,W
Indiana U–Purdue U Fort Wayne, IN M,W
Indiana Wesleyan University, IN M,W
Inter American U of PR, Arecibo Campus, PR M
Inter American U of PR, San Germán Campus, PR M,W
Iona College, NY M
Iowa State University of Science and Technology, IA M,W
Iowa Wesleyan College, IA M,W
Jacksonville University, FL W
James Madison University, VA M,W
Jamestown College, ND M,W
Johnson C. Smith University, NC M,W
Kansas State University, KS M,W
Kansas Wesleyan University, KS M,W
Kent State University, OH M,W
Kutztown University of Pennsylvania, PA M,W
Lake Superior State University, MI M,W
Lamar University, TX M,W
Langston University, OK M,W
La Salle University, PA M,W
Lehigh University, PA M,W

Track and field (continued)

Lewis University, IL M,W
Liberty University, VA M,W
Lincoln University, MO M,W
Lock Haven University of Pennsylvania, PA M,W
Long Island U, Brooklyn Campus, NY W
Long Island U, C.W. Post Campus, NY M,W
Louisiana State University and A&M College, LA M,W
Louisiana Tech University, LA M,W
Loyola University Chicago, IL M,W
Malone College, OH M,W
Manhattan College, NY M,W
Marian College, IN M,W
Marist College, NY M,W
Marquette University, WI M,W
Marshall University, WV M,W
McKendree College, IL M,W
McNeese State University, LA M,W
Miami University, OH M,W
Michigan State University, MI M,W
MidAmerica Nazarene University, KS M,W
Middle Tennessee State University, TN M,W
Midland Lutheran College, NE M,W
Midway College, KY W
Millersville University of Pennsylvania, PA M,W
Minnesota State University, Mankato, MN M,W
Minnesota State University Moorhead, MN M,W
Minot State University, ND M,W
Mississippi State University, MS M,W
Mississippi Valley State University, MS M,W
Missouri Southern State College, MO M,W
Missouri Valley College, MO M,W
Monmouth University, NJ M,W
Montana State U–Bozeman, MT M,W
Morehead State University, KY M,W
Morgan State University, MD M,W
Morningside College, IA M,W
Mount Marty College, SD M,W
Mount St. Clare College, IA M,W
Mount Saint Mary's College and Seminary, MD M,W
Murray State University, KY M,W
New York Institute of Technology, NY M,W
North Carolina Agricultural and Technical State U, NC M,W
North Carolina State University, NC M,W
North Dakota State University, ND M,W
Northeastern University, MA M,W
Northern Arizona University, AZ M,W
Northwest College, WA M,W
Northwestern College, IA M,W
Northwestern State University of Louisiana, LA M,W
Northwest Missouri State University, MO M,W
Northwest Nazarene University, ID M,W
Northwood University, MI M,W
Northwood University, Texas Campus, TX M,W
The Ohio State University, OH M,W
Ohio University, OH M,W
Oklahoma Baptist University, OK M,W
Oklahoma Christian U of Science and Arts, OK M,W
Oklahoma State U, OK M,W
Olivet Nazarene University, IL M,W
Oral Roberts University, OK M,W
Oregon Institute of Technology, OR M,W
Ottawa University, KS M,W
Paine College, GA M,W
Park University, MO M,W
Penn State U Univ Park Campus, PA M,W
Pittsburg State University, KS M,W
Point Loma Nazarene University, CA M,W
Pontifical Catholic University of Puerto Rico, PR M,W
Portland State University, OR M,W
Prairie View A&M University, TX M,W
Providence College, RI M,W
Purdue University, IN M,W
Queens Coll of the City U of NY, NY M,W
Quinnipiac University, CT M,W
Radford University, VA M,W
Rice University, TX M,W
Rider University, NJ M,W
Robert Morris College, PA M,W
Roberts Wesleyan College, NY M,W
Rochester College, MI M,W
Rust College, MS M,W
Rutgers, State U of NJ, College of Pharmacy, NJ M,W
Rutgers, State U of NJ, Cook College, NJ M,W
Rutgers, State U of NJ, Douglass College, NJ W
Rutgers, State U of NJ, Livingston College, NJ M,W
Rutgers, State U of NJ, Mason Gross School of Arts, NJ M,W
Rutgers, State U of NJ, Rutgers College, NJ M,W
Rutgers, State U of NJ, College of Engineering, NJ M,W
Saginaw Valley State University, MI M,W
St. Ambrose University, IA M,W
Saint Augustine's College, NC M,W
St. Francis College, NY M,W
Saint Francis College, PA M,W
St. John's University, NY M,W
Saint Joseph's College, IN M,W
Saint Joseph's University, PA M,W
Saint Martin's College, WA M,W
Saint Peter's College, NJ M,W
Samford University, AL M,W
San Diego State University, CA W
San Francisco State University, CA M,W
Savannah State University, GA M,W
Seattle Pacific University, WA M,W
Seton Hall University, NJ M,W
Shaw University, NC M,W
Shippensburg University of Pennsylvania, PA M,W
Shorter College, GA M,W
Siena Heights University, MI M,W
Slippery Rock University of Pennsylvania, PA M,W
South Dakota School of Mines and Technology, SD M,W
South Dakota State University, SD M,W
Southeastern Louisiana University, LA M,W
Southeast Missouri State University, MO M,W
Southern Illinois University Carbondale, IL M,W
Southern Illinois University Edwardsville, IL M,W
Southern Methodist University, TX M,W
Southern Nazarene University, OK M,W
Southern Oregon University, OR M,W
Southern University and A&M College, LA M,W
Southern University at New Orleans, LA M,W
Southern Utah University, UT M,W
Southwestern Christian College, TX M,W
Southwestern College, KS M,W
Southwest Missouri State University, MO M,W
Southwest Texas State University, TX M,W
Spring Arbor College, MI M,W
Stanford University, CA M,W
State U of NY at Albany, NY M,W
State U of NY at Binghamton, NY M,W
State U of NY at Buffalo, NY M,W
State U of NY at Stony Brook, NY M,W
Stephen F. Austin State University, TX M,W
Sterling College, KS M,W
Stonehill College, MA M,W
Syracuse University, NY M,W
Tabor College, KS M,W
Tarleton State University, TX M,W
Taylor University, IN M,W
Temple University, PA M,W
Tennessee State University, TN M,W
Tennessee Technological University, TN W
Texas A&M University, TX M,W
Texas A&M University–Commerce, TX M,W
Texas A&M University–Kingsville, TX M,W
Texas Christian University, TX M,W
Texas Tech University, TX M,W
Tiffin University, OH M,W
Towson University, MD M,W
Trinity Christian College, IL M,W
Tri-State University, IN M,W
Troy State University, AL M
Truman State University, MO M,W
Tulane University, LA M,W
Tuskegee University, AL M,W
The University of Akron, OH M,W
The University of Alabama, AL M,W
The University of Alabama at Birmingham, AL W
The University of Arizona, AZ M,W
University of Arkansas, AR M,W
University of Arkansas at Little Rock, AR W
U of Calif, Berkeley, CA M,W
U of Calif, Irvine, CA W
U of Calif, Los Angeles, CA M,W
U of Calif, Riverside, CA M,W
U of Calif, Santa Barbara, CA M,W
University of Central Oklahoma, OK M,W
University of Charleston, WV M,W
University of Cincinnati, OH M
University of Colorado at Boulder, CO M,W
University of Connecticut, CT M,W
University of Delaware, DE W
University of Detroit Mercy, MI M,W
The University of Findlay, OH M,W
University of Florida, FL M,W
University of Georgia, GA M,W
University of Houston, TX M,W
University of Idaho, ID M,W

University of Illinois at Urbana–Champaign, IL M,W
University of Indianapolis, IN M,W
The University of Iowa, IA M,W
University of Kansas, KS M,W
University of Louisiana at Lafayette, LA M,W
University of Louisiana at Monroe, LA M,W
University of Louisville, KY M,W
University of Maine, ME M,W
University of Mary, ND M,W
University of Maryland, Baltimore County, MD M,W
University of Maryland, College Park, MD M,W
University of Massachusetts Amherst, MA M,W
University of Massachusetts Lowell, MA M,W
University of Miami, FL M,W
University of Michigan, MI M,W
University of Minnesota, Duluth, MN M,W
University of Minnesota, Twin Cities Campus, MN M,W
University of Mississippi, MS M,W
University of Missouri–Columbia, MO M,W
University of Missouri–Kansas City, MO M,W
University of Missouri–Rolla, MO M,W
University of Mobile, AL M,W
The University of Montana–Missoula, MT M,W
University of Nebraska at Kearney, NE M,W
University of Nebraska–Lincoln, NE M,W
University of Nevada, Las Vegas, NV W
University of Nevada, Reno, NV W
University of New Hampshire, NH W
University of New Haven, CT M,W
University of New Mexico, NM M,W
University of New Orleans, LA M,W
The University of North Carolina at Asheville, NC M,W
The University of North Carolina at Chapel Hill, NC M,W
The University of North Carolina at Charlotte, NC M,W
The University of North Carolina at Pembroke, NC M
The University of North Carolina at Wilmington, NC M
University of North Dakota, ND M,W
University of Northern Colorado, CO M,W
University of Northern Iowa, IA M,W
University of North Florida, FL M,W
University of North Texas, TX M,W
University of Notre Dame, IN M,W
University of Oklahoma, OK M,W
University of Oregon, OR M,W
University of Pittsburgh, PA M,W
University of Portland, OR M,W
U of Puerto Rico, Cayey University College, PR M,W
U of Puerto Rico, Mayagüez Campus, PR M,W
University of Rhode Island, RI M,W
University of Rio Grande, OH M,W
University of Saint Francis, IN M,W
University of South Alabama, AL M,W
University of South Carolina, SC M,W
University of South Dakota, SD M,W
University of Southern California, CA M,W
University of Southern Mississippi, MS M,W
University of South Florida, FL M,W
The University of Tennessee at Martin, TN M,W
The University of Tennessee Knoxville, TN M,W
The University of Texas at Arlington, TX M,W
The University of Texas at Austin, TX M,W
The University of Texas at El Paso, TX M,W
The University of Texas at San Antonio, TX M,W
The University of Texas–Pan American, TX M,W
University of the District of Columbia, DC M,W
University of the Sacred Heart, PR M,W
University of Toledo, OH M,W
University of Tulsa, OK M,W
University of Utah, UT M,W
University of Vermont, VT W
University of Virginia, VA M,W
University of Washington, WA M,W
University of Wisconsin–Madison, WI M,W
University of Wisconsin–Milwaukee, WI M,W
University of Wisconsin–Parkside, WI M,W
University of Wyoming, WY M,W
Utah State University, UT M,W
Valley City State University, ND M,W
Vanderbilt University, TN W
Vanguard University of Southern California, CA M,W
Villanova University, PA M,W
Virginia Commonwealth University, VA M,W
Virginia Military Institute, VA M,W
Virginia Polytechnic Institute and State U, VA M,W
Virginia State University, VA M,W
Virginia Union University, VA M,W
Voorhees College, SC M
Wagner College, NY M,W
Wake Forest University, NC M,W
Walsh University, OH M,W
Washington State University, WA M,W
Wayland Baptist University, TX M,W
Wayne State College, NE M,W
Weber State University, UT M,W
West Chester University of Pennsylvania, PA M,W
Western Carolina University, NC M,W
Western Illinois University, IL M,W
Western Kentucky University, KY M,W
Western Michigan University, MI M,W
Western State College of Colorado, CO M,W
Western Washington University, WA M,W
Westmont College, CA M,W
West Virginia University, WV M,W
West Virginia Wesleyan College, WV M,W
Wheeling Jesuit University, WV M,W
Wichita State University, KS M,W
William Jewell College, MO M,W
Winona State University, MN W
Winston-Salem State University, NC M,W
Winthrop University, SC M,W
Wofford College, SC W
York College, NE M,W
Youngstown State University, OH M,W

VOLLEYBALL

Abilene Christian University, TX W
Adams State College, CO W
Adelphi University, NY W
Alabama Agricultural and Mechanical University, AL W
Alabama State University, AL W
Albany State University, GA W
Albertson College of Idaho, ID W
Alcorn State University, MS W
American International College, MA W
American University, DC W
Anderson College, SC W
Angelo State University, TX W
Appalachian State University, NC W
Aquinas College, MI W
Arizona State University, AZ W
Arkansas State University, AR W
Arkansas Tech University, AR W
Armstrong Atlantic State University, GA W
Ashland University, OH W
Atlantic Union College, MA W
Auburn University, AL W
Augustana College, SD W
Augusta State University, GA W
Austin Peay State University, TN W
Avila College, MO W
Azusa Pacific University, CA W
Baker University, KS W
Ball State University, IN M,W
Barat College, IL W
Barber-Scotia College, NC W
Barry University, FL W
Bartlesville Wesleyan College, OK W
Barton College, NC W
Bayamón Central University, PR M,W
Baylor University, TX W
Belhaven College, MS W
Bellarmine College, KY W
Bellevue University, NE W
Belmont University, TN W
Bemidji State University, MN W
Benedictine College, KS W
Bentley College, MA W
Bethany College, KS W
Bethany College of the Assemblies of God, CA M,W
Bethel College, IN W
Bethel College, KS W
Bethel College, TN W
Bethune-Cookman College, FL W
Biola University, CA W
Birmingham-Southern College, AL W
Black Hills State University, SD W
Bloomfield College, NJ W
Bluefield College, VA W
Boise State University, ID W
Boston College, MA W
Bowie State University, MD W
Bowling Green State University, OH W
Bradley University, IL W
Brenau University, GA W
Brescia University, KY W
Brevard College, NC W
Briar Cliff College, IA W
Brigham Young University, UT M,W
Brigham Young University–Hawaii Campus, HI W
Bryan College, TN W
Butler University, IN W
California Baptist University, CA M,W

Volleyball (continued)

California Polytechnic State U, San Luis Obispo, CA W
California State Polytechnic University, Pomona, CA W
California State University, Bakersfield, CA W
California State University, Dominguez Hills, CA W
California State University, Fresno, CA W
California State University, Fullerton, CA W
California State University, Long Beach, CA M,W
California State University, Los Angeles, CA W
California State University, Northridge, CA M,W
California State University, Sacramento, CA W
California State University, San Bernardino, CA W
California University of Pennsylvania, PA W
Cameron University, OK W
Campbellsville University, KY W
Campbell University, NC W
Canisius College, NY W
Carlow College, PA W
Carroll College, MT W
Carson-Newman College, TN W
Catawba College, NC W
Cedarville College, OH W
Centenary College of Louisiana, LA W
Central Connecticut State University, CT W
Central Methodist College, MO W
Central Michigan University, MI W
Central Missouri State University, MO W
Central State University, OH W
Central Washington University, WA W
Chadron State College, NE W
Chaminade University of Honolulu, HI W
Charleston Southern University, SC W
Cheyney University of Pennsylvania, PA W
Chicago State University, IL W
Christian Brothers University, TN W
Christian Heritage College, CA W
Citadel, The Military Coll of South Carolina, SC W
Clarion University of Pennsylvania, PA W
Clemson University, SC W
Coastal Carolina University, SC W
Coker College, SC W
College of Charleston, SC W
College of Saint Mary, NE W
The College of Saint Rose, NY W
College of the Ozarks, MO W
College of the Southwest, NM W
The College of William and Mary, VA W
Colorado Christian University, CO W
Colorado School of Mines, CO W
Colorado State University, CO W
Columbia College, MO M,W
Columbia College, SC W
Columbia Union College, MD M,W
Concord College, WV W
Concordia College, MI W
Concordia College, NY M,W
Concordia University, CA W
Concordia University, NE W
Concordia University, OR W
Concordia University at St. Paul, MN W
Converse College, SC W
Coppin State College, MD W
Cornerstone University, MI W
Covenant College, GA W
Creighton University, NE W
Culver-Stockton College, MO W
Cumberland College, KY W
Cumberland University, TN W
Daemen College, NY W
Dakota State University, SD W
Dakota Wesleyan University, SD W
Dallas Baptist University, TX W
Dana College, NE W
David Lipscomb University, TN W
Davidson College, NC W
Delaware State University, DE W
DePaul University, IL W
Dickinson State University, ND W
Doane College, NE W
Dominican College of Blauvelt, NY W
Dominican University of California, CA W
Dordt College, IA W
Dowling College, NY W
Drake University, IA W
Drury University, MO W
Duke University, NC W
Duquesne University, PA W
East Carolina University, NC W
Eastern Illinois University, IL W
Eastern Kentucky University, KY W
Eastern Michigan University, MI W
Eastern New Mexico University, NM W
Eastern Washington University, WA W
East Tennessee State University, TN W
Eckerd College, FL W
Edinboro University of Pennsylvania, PA W
Elon College, NC W
Embry-Riddle Aeronautical University, AZ W
Embry-Riddle Aeronautical University, FL W
Emporia State University, KS W
Evangel University, MO W
Fairfield University, CT W
Fairleigh Dickinson U, Teaneck-Hackensack Campus, NJ W
Faulkner University, AL W
Ferris State University, MI W
Flagler College, FL W
Florida Agricultural and Mechanical University, FL W
Florida Atlantic University, FL W
Florida College, FL W
Florida Institute of Technology, FL W
Florida International University, FL W
Florida Southern College, FL W
Florida State University, FL W
Fordham University, NY W
Fort Hays State University, KS W
Fort Lewis College, CO W
Fort Valley State University, GA W
Francis Marion University, SC W
Franklin Pierce College, NH W
Fresno Pacific University, CA W
Friends University, KS W
Furman University, SC W
Gannon University, PA W
Gardner-Webb University, NC W
Geneva College, PA W
George Mason University, VA M,W
Georgetown College, KY W
Georgetown University, DC W
The George Washington University, DC W
Georgia Institute of Technology, GA W
Georgia Southern University, GA W
Georgia Southwestern State University, GA W
Georgia State University, GA W
Glenville State College, WV W
Goldey-Beacom College, DE W
Gonzaga University, WA W
Goshen College, IN W
Grace College, IN W
Graceland College, IA M,W
Grand Canyon University, AZ W
Grand Valley State University, MI W
Grand View College, IA W
Green Mountain College, VT W
Hampton University, VA W
Hannibal-LaGrange College, MO W
Harding University, AR W
Harris-Stowe State College, MO W
Hastings College, NE W
Hawaii Pacific University, HI W
Henderson State University, AR W
High Point University, NC W
Hillsdale College, MI W
Hofstra University, NY W
Holy Names College, CA W
Hope International University, CA M,W
Houghton College, NY W
Houston Baptist University, TX W
Humboldt State University, CA W
Huntington College, IN W
Huron University, SD W
Idaho State University, ID W
Illinois Institute of Technology, IL W
Illinois State University, IL W
Indiana State University, IN W
Indiana University Bloomington, IN W
Indiana U–Purdue U Fort Wayne, IN M,W
Indiana U–Purdue U Indianapolis, IN W
Indiana University Southeast, IN W
Indiana Wesleyan University, IN W
Inter American U of PR, San Germán Campus, PR M,W
Iowa State University of Science and Technology, IA W
Iowa Wesleyan College, IA W
Jacksonville State University, AL W
Jacksonville University, FL W
James Madison University, VA W
Jamestown College, ND W
John Brown University, AR W
Judson College, AL W
Judson College, IL W
Kansas State University, KS W
Kansas Wesleyan University, KS W
Kent State University, OH W
Kentucky Wesleyan College, KY W
King College, TN W
Kutztown University of Pennsylvania, PA W
Lake Superior State University, MI W
Lamar University, TX W

Lambuth University, TN W
Lander University, SC W
La Salle University, PA W
Lees-McRae College, NC W
Lee University, TN W
Lehigh University, PA W
Le Moyne College, NY W
LeMoyne-Owen College, TN W
Lewis-Clark State College, ID M,W
Lewis University, IL M,W
Liberty University, VA W
Limestone College, SC W
Lincoln Memorial University, TN W
Lock Haven University of Pennsylvania, PA W
Long Island U, Brooklyn Campus, NY W
Long Island U, C.W. Post Campus, NY W
Long Island U, Southampton College, NY M,W
Louisiana State University and A&M College, LA W
Louisiana Tech University, LA W
Loyola Marymount University, CA M,W
Loyola University Chicago, IL M,W
Lubbock Christian University, TX W
Lyon College, AR W
Madonna University, MI W
Malone College, OH W
Manhattan College, NY W
Marian College, IN W
Marist College, NY W
Marquette University, WI W
Marshall University, WV W
Mars Hill College, NC W
Martin Methodist College, TN W
Marycrest International University, IA M
The Master's College and Seminary, CA W
Mayville State University, ND W
McKendree College, IL W
McNeese State University, LA W
Mercer University, GA W
Mercy College, NY W
Mercyhurst College, PA M,W
Merrimack College, MA W
Mesa State College, CO W
Metropolitan State College of Denver, CO W
Miami University, OH W
Michigan State University, MI W
Michigan Technological University, MI W
MidAmerica Nazarene University, KS W
Middle Tennessee State University, TN W
Midland Lutheran College, NE W
Midway College, KY W
Midwestern State University, TX W
Millersville University of Pennsylvania, PA W
Milligan College, TN W
Minnesota State University, Mankato, MN W
Minnesota State University Moorhead, MN W
Minot State University, ND W
Mississippi State University, MS W
Mississippi University for Women, MS W
Missouri Baptist College, MO M,W
Missouri Southern State College, MO W
Missouri Valley College, MO W
Missouri Western State College, MO W
Montana State U–Billings, MT W
Montana State U–Bozeman, MT W
Montana State U–Northern, MT W
Montana Tech of The University of Montana, MT W
Montreat College, NC W
Morehead State University, KY W
Morningside College, IA W
Mount Aloysius College, PA W
Mount Marty College, SD W
Mount Olive College, NC W
Mount St. Clare College, IA W
Mount Vernon Nazarene College, OH W
Murray State University, KY W
Newberry College, SC W
Newman University, KS W
New Mexico Highlands University, NM W
New York Institute of Technology, NY W
Niagara University, NY W
North Carolina Agricultural and Technical State U, NC W
North Carolina State University, NC W
North Dakota State University, ND W
Northeastern University, MA W
Northern Arizona University, AZ W
Northern Illinois University, IL W
Northern Kentucky University, KY W
Northern Michigan University, MI W
North Greenville College, SC W
Northwest College, WA W
Northwestern College, IA W
Northwestern State University of Louisiana, LA W
Northwestern University, IL W
Northwest Missouri State University, MO W
Northwest Nazarene University, ID W
Northwood University, MI W
Nova Southeastern University, FL W
Nyack College, NY W
Oakland City University, IN W
Oakland University, MI W
Ohio Dominican College, OH W
The Ohio State University, OH M,W
Ohio University, OH W
Ohio Valley College, WV W
Olivet Nazarene University, IL W
Oral Roberts University, OK W
Oregon Institute of Technology, OR W
Oregon State University, OR W
Ottawa University, KS W
Ouachita Baptist University, AR W
Paine College, GA W
Palm Beach Atlantic College, FL W
Park University, MO M,W
Penn State U Univ Park Campus, PA M,W
Pepperdine University, CA M,W
Pfeiffer University, NC W
Philadelphia University, PA W
Piedmont College, GA W
Pikeville College, KY W
Pittsburg State University, KS W
Point Loma Nazarene University, CA W
Point Park College, PA W
Portland State University, OR W
Prairie View A&M University, TX W
Presbyterian College, SC W
Providence College, RI W
Purdue University, IN W
Purdue University Calumet, IN W
Queens College, NC W
Queens Coll of the City U of NY, NY W
Quincy University, IL M,W
Quinnipiac University, CT W
Radford University, VA W
Regis University, CO W
Research College of Nursing, MO W
Rice University, TX W
Rider University, NJ W
Robert Morris College, IL W
Robert Morris College, PA W
Roberts Wesleyan College, NY W
Rochester College, MI W
Rockhurst University, MO W
Rocky Mountain College, MT W
Rollins College, FL W
Rutgers, State U of NJ, College of Nursing, NJ M
Rutgers, State U of NJ, Livingston College, NJ W
Rutgers, State U of NJ, Mason Gross School of Arts, NJ W
Rutgers, State U of NJ, Newark Coll of Arts & Scis, NJ M
Saginaw Valley State University, MI W
St. Ambrose University, IA M,W
St. Andrews Presbyterian College, NC W
Saint Augustine's College, NC W
St. Bonaventure University, NY W
St. Edward's University, TX W
St. Francis College, NY W
Saint Francis College, PA M,W
St. John's University, NY W
Saint Joseph's College, IN W
Saint Leo University, FL W
Saint Louis University, MO W
Saint Martin's College, WA W
Saint Mary College, KS W
Saint Mary's College of California, CA W
St. Mary's University of San Antonio, TX W
Saint Peter's College, NJ W
St. Thomas Aquinas College, NY W
St. Thomas University, FL W
Saint Vincent College, PA W
Saint Xavier University, IL W
Salem-Teikyo University, WV W
Samford University, AL W
Sam Houston State University, TX W
San Diego State University, CA M,W
San Francisco State University, CA W
San Jose State University, CA W
Santa Clara University, CA W
Savannah State University, GA W
Seattle Pacific University, WA W
Seton Hall University, NJ W
Seton Hill College, PA W
Shaw University, NC M,W
Shepherd College, WV W
Shippensburg University of Pennsylvania, PA W
Siena Heights University, MI W
Slippery Rock University of Pennsylvania, PA W
South Dakota School of Mines and Technology, SD W
South Dakota State University, SD W
Southeastern Louisiana University, LA W
Southeast Missouri State University, MO W

Volleyball (continued)

Institution	
Southern Arkansas University–Magnolia, AR	W
Southern Illinois University Carbondale, IL	W
Southern Methodist University, TX	W
Southern Nazarene University, OK	W
Southern Oregon University, OR	W
Southern University and A&M College, LA	W
Southern Wesleyan University, SC	W
Southwest Baptist University, MO	W
Southwestern Adventist University, TX	W
Southwestern College, KS	W
Southwest Missouri State University, MO	W
Southwest State University, MN	W
Southwest Texas State University, TX	W
Spalding University, KY	W
Spring Arbor College, MI	W
Stanford University, CA	M,W
State U of NY at Albany, NY	W
State U of NY at Binghamton, NY	W
State U of NY at Buffalo, NY	W
State U of NY at Stony Brook, NY	W
State University of West Georgia, GA	W
Stephen F. Austin State University, TX	W
Sterling College, KS	W
Stetson University, FL	W
Stonehill College, MA	W
Syracuse University, NY	W
Tabor College, KS	W
Tarleton State University, TX	W
Taylor University, IN	W
Teikyo Post University, CT	W
Temple University, PA	W
Tennessee Technological University, TN	W
Tennessee Temple University, TN	W
Tennessee Wesleyan College, TN	W
Texas A&M University, TX	W
Texas A&M University–Commerce, TX	W
Texas A&M University–Kingsville, TX	W
Texas Christian University, TX	W
Texas Lutheran University, TX	W
Texas Tech University, TX	W
Texas Wesleyan University, TX	W
Texas Woman's University, TX	W
Tiffin University, OH	W
Towson University, MD	W
Trevecca Nazarene University, TN	W
Trinity Christian College, IL	M,W
Tri-State University, IN	M,W
Troy State University, AL	W
Truman State University, MO	W
Tulane University, LA	W
Tusculum College, TN	W
Tuskegee University, AL	W
Union College, KY	W
Union University, TN	W
United States International University, CA	W
Unity College, ME	W
The University of Akron, OH	W
The University of Alabama, AL	W
The University of Alabama at Birmingham, AL	W
The University of Alabama in Huntsville, AL	W
U of Alaska Anchorage, AK	W
U of Alaska Fairbanks, AK	W
The University of Arizona, AZ	W
University of Arkansas, AR	W
University of Arkansas at Little Rock, AR	W
University of Arkansas at Pine Bluff, AR	W
University of Bridgeport, CT	W
U of Calif, Berkeley, CA	W
U of Calif, Irvine, CA	W
U of Calif, Los Angeles, CA	M,W
U of Calif, Riverside, CA	W
U of Calif, Santa Barbara, CA	M,W
University of Central Arkansas, AR	W
University of Central Florida, FL	W
University of Central Oklahoma, OK	W
University of Charleston, WV	W
University of Cincinnati, OH	W
University of Colorado at Boulder, CO	W
University of Colorado at Colorado Springs, CO	W
University of Connecticut, CT	W
University of Dayton, OH	W
University of Delaware, DE	W
University of Evansville, IN	W
The University of Findlay, OH	M,W
University of Florida, FL	W
University of Georgia, GA	W
University of Guam, GU	M,W
University of Hartford, CT	W
University of Hawaii at Hilo, HI	W
University of Hawaii at Manoa, HI	M,W
University of Houston, TX	W
University of Idaho, ID	W
University of Illinois at Chicago, IL	W
University of Illinois at Springfield, IL	W
University of Illinois at Urbana–Champaign, IL	W
University of Indianapolis, IN	W
The University of Iowa, IA	W
University of Kansas, KS	W
University of Louisiana at Lafayette, LA	W
University of Louisiana at Monroe, LA	W
University of Louisville, KY	W
University of Maine, ME	W
University of Mary, ND	W
University of Maryland, Baltimore County, MD	W
University of Maryland, College Park, MD	W
University of Massachusetts Amherst, MA	W
University of Massachusetts Lowell, MA	W
The University of Memphis, TN	W
University of Michigan, MI	W
University of Michigan–Dearborn, MI	W
University of Minnesota, Crookston, MN	W
University of Minnesota, Duluth, MN	W
University of Minnesota, Twin Cities Campus, MN	W
University of Mississippi, MS	W
University of Missouri–Columbia, MO	W
University of Missouri–Kansas City, MO	W
University of Missouri–St. Louis, MO	W
The University of Montana–Missoula, MT	W
University of Montevallo, AL	W
University of Nebraska at Kearney, NE	W
University of Nebraska at Omaha, NE	W
University of Nebraska–Lincoln, NE	W
University of Nevada, Las Vegas, NV	W
University of Nevada, Reno, NV	W
University of New Hampshire, NH	W
University of New Haven, CT	W
University of New Mexico, NM	W
University of New Orleans, LA	W
University of North Alabama, AL	W
The University of North Carolina at Asheville, NC	W
The University of North Carolina at Chapel Hill, NC	W
The University of North Carolina at Charlotte, NC	W
The University of North Carolina at Greensboro, NC	W
The University of North Carolina at Pembroke, NC	W
The University of North Carolina at Wilmington, NC	W
University of North Dakota, ND	W
University of Northern Colorado, CO	W
University of Northern Iowa, IA	W
University of North Florida, FL	W
University of North Texas, TX	W
University of Notre Dame, IN	W
University of Oklahoma, OK	W
University of Oregon, OR	W
University of Pittsburgh, PA	W
University of Portland, OR	W
U of Puerto Rico, Cayey University College, PR	M,W
U of Puerto Rico, Mayagüez Campus, PR	M,W
University of Rhode Island, RI	W
University of Rio Grande, OH	W
University of St. Francis, IL	W
University of Saint Francis, IN	W
University of San Diego, CA	W
University of San Francisco, CA	W
University of South Alabama, AL	W
University of South Carolina, SC	W
University of South Carolina Aiken, SC	W
U of South Carolina Spartanburg, SC	W
University of South Dakota, SD	W
University of Southern California, CA	M,W
University of Southern Colorado, CO	W
University of Southern Indiana, IN	W
University of Southern Mississippi, MS	W
University of South Florida, FL	W
The University of Tampa, FL	W
The University of Tennessee at Chattanooga, TN	W
The University of Tennessee at Martin, TN	W
The University of Tennessee Knoxville, TN	W
The University of Texas at Arlington, TX	W
The University of Texas at Austin, TX	W
The University of Texas at El Paso, TX	W
The University of Texas at San Antonio, TX	W
University of the District of Columbia, DC	W
University of the Incarnate Word, TX	W
University of the Pacific, CA	M,W
University of the Sacred Heart, PR	M,W

University of the Sciences in Philadelphia, PA W
University of Toledo, OH W
University of Tulsa, OK W
University of Utah, UT W
University of Virginia, VA W
University of Virginia's College at Wise, VA W
University of Washington, WA W
The University of West Alabama, AL W
University of Wisconsin–Green Bay, WI W
University of Wisconsin–Madison, WI M,W
University of Wisconsin–Milwaukee, WI W
University of Wisconsin–Parkside, WI W
University of Wyoming, WY W
Urbana University, OH W
Utah State University, UT W
Valdosta State University, GA W
Valley City State University, ND W
Valparaiso University, IN W
Vanguard University of Southern California, CA W
Villanova University, PA W
Virginia Commonwealth University, VA W
Virginia Polytechnic Institute and State U, VA W
Virginia State University, VA W
Virginia Union University, VA W
Wagner College, NY W
Wake Forest University, NC W
Walsh University, OH W
Warner Pacific College, OR W
Warner Southern College, FL W
Washburn University of Topeka, KS W
Washington State University, WA W
Wayland Baptist University, TX W
Wayne State College, NE W
Wayne State University, MI W
Webber College, FL W
Weber State University, UT W
West Chester University of Pennsylvania, PA W
Western Baptist College, OR W
Western Carolina University, NC W
Western Illinois University, IL W
Western Kentucky University, KY W
Western Michigan University, MI W
Western Montana College of The U of Montana, MT W
Western New Mexico University, NM W
Western State College of Colorado, CO W
Western Washington University, WA W
West Liberty State College, WV W
Westminster College, PA W
Westmont College, CA W
West Texas A&M University, TX W
West Virginia University, WV W
West Virginia University Institute of Technology, WV W
West Virginia Wesleyan College, WV W
Wheeling Jesuit University, WV W
Wichita State University, KS W
William Jewell College, MO W
Williams Baptist College, AR W
William Woods University, MO M,W
Wingate University, NC W
Winona State University, MN W
Winston-Salem State University, NC W
Winthrop University, SC W
Wofford College, SC W
Xavier University, OH W
York College, NE W
Youngstown State University, OH W

WATER POLO

Bayamón Central University, PR M,W
California Baptist University, CA M,W
California State University, Bakersfield, CA W
California State University, Long Beach, CA M
Chaminade University of Honolulu, HI M
Fordham University, NY M
The George Washington University, DC M
Hartwick College, NY W
Indiana University Bloomington, IN W
Pepperdine University, CA M
Queens Coll of the City U of NY, NY M
St. Francis College, NY M,W
Salem-Teikyo University, WV M,W
San Diego State University, CA W
San Jose State University, CA W
Santa Clara University, CA M
Stanford University, CA M,W
U of Calif, Berkeley, CA M,W
U of Calif, Irvine, CA M
U of Calif, Los Angeles, CA M,W
U of Calif, Santa Barbara, CA M
University of Hawaii at Manoa, HI W
University of Massachusetts Amherst, MA M,W
U of Puerto Rico, Mayagüez Campus, PR M
University of Southern California, CA M,W
University of the Pacific, CA M,W

WEIGHT LIFTING

Coppin State College, MD M,W
Inter American U of PR, San Germán Campus, PR M
U of Puerto Rico, Mayagüez Campus, PR M
University of the Sacred Heart, PR M

WRESTLING

Adams State College, CO M
American University, DC M
Anderson College, SC M
Appalachian State University, NC M
Arizona State University, AZ M
Ashland University, OH M
Augustana College, SD M
Bloomsburg University of Pennsylvania, PA M
Boise State University, ID M
Boston University, MA M
Briar Cliff College, IA M
Brigham Young University, UT M
California Polytechnic State U, San Luis Obispo, CA M
California State University, Bakersfield, CA M
California State University, Fresno, CA M
California State University, Fullerton, CA M
Campbell University, NC M
Carson-Newman College, TN M
Central Michigan University, MI M
Central Missouri State University, MO M
Central Washington University, WA M
Chadron State College, NE M
Cheyney University of Pennsylvania, PA M
Chicago State University, IL M
Citadel, The Military Coll of South Carolina, SC M
Clarion University of Pennsylvania, PA M
Colorado School of Mines, CO M
Coppin State College, MD M
Cumberland College, KY M,W
Dakota Wesleyan University, SD M
Dana College, NE M
Davidson College, NC M
Delaware State University, DE M
Dickinson State University, ND M
Drexel University, PA M
Duquesne University, PA M
Eastern Illinois University, IL M
Eastern Michigan University, MI M
East Stroudsburg University of Pennsylvania, PA M
Edinboro University of Pennsylvania, PA M
Embry-Riddle Aeronautical University, AZ M
Fort Hays State University, KS M
Gannon University, PA M
Gardner-Webb University, NC M
George Mason University, VA M
Hofstra University, NY M
Huron University, SD M
Indiana University Bloomington, IN M
Inter American U of PR, San Germán Campus, PR M
Iowa State University of Science and Technology, IA M
James Madison University, VA M
Jamestown College, ND M
Kent State University, OH M
Kutztown University of Pennsylvania, PA M
Lehigh University, PA M
Lock Haven University of Pennsylvania, PA M
Longwood College, VA M
Marquette University, WI M
Michigan State University, MI M
Millersville University of Pennsylvania, PA M
Minnesota State University, Mankato, MN M
Minnesota State University Moorhead, MN M
Missouri Valley College, MO M,W
Montana State U–Northern, MT M
Mount St. Clare College, IA M
North Carolina State University, NC M
North Dakota State University, ND M
Northern Illinois University, IL M
Northwestern College, IA M
Northwestern University, IL M
The Ohio State University, OH M
Ohio University, OH M
Oklahoma State U, OK M
Old Dominion University, VA M
Oregon State University, OR M
Penn State U Univ Park Campus, PA M
Portland State University, OR M
Purdue University, IN M
Rider University, NJ M
Rutgers, State U of NJ, College of Pharmacy, NJ M

Wrestling (continued)

Rutgers, State U of NJ, Cook College, NJ M
Rutgers, State U of NJ, Livingston College, NJ M
Rutgers, State U of NJ, Mason Gross School of Arts, NJ M
Rutgers, State U of NJ, Rutgers College, NJ M
Rutgers, State U of NJ, College of Engineering, NJ M
San Francisco State University, CA M
Seton Hall University, NJ M
Shippensburg University of Pennsylvania, PA M
Slippery Rock University of Pennsylvania, PA M
South Dakota State University, SD M
Southern Connecticut State University, CT M
Southern Illinois University Edwardsville, IL M
Southern Oregon University, OR M
Southwest State University, MN M
Stanford University, CA M
State U of NY at Binghamton, NY M
State U of NY at Buffalo, NY M
Truman State University, MO M
University of Central Oklahoma, OK M
The University of Findlay, OH M
University of Illinois at Urbana–Champaign, IL M
University of Indianapolis, IN M
The University of Iowa, IA M
University of Mary, ND M
University of Maryland, College Park, MD M
University of Massachusetts Lowell, MA M
University of Michigan, MI M
University of Minnesota, Twin Cities Campus, MN M
University of Missouri–Columbia, MO M
University of Nebraska at Kearney, NE M
University of Nebraska at Omaha, NE M
University of Nebraska–Lincoln, NE M
The University of North Carolina at Chapel Hill, NC M
The University of North Carolina at Greensboro, NC M
The University of North Carolina at Pembroke, NC M
University of Northern Colorado, CO M
University of Northern Iowa, IA M
University of Oklahoma, OK M
University of Oregon, OR M
University of Pittsburgh, PA M
University of Pittsburgh at Johnstown, PA M
U of Puerto Rico, Mayagüez Campus, PR M
University of Southern Colorado, CO M
The University of Tennessee at Chattanooga, TN M
University of the Sacred Heart, PR M
University of Virginia, VA M
University of Wisconsin–Madison, WI M
University of Wisconsin–Parkside, WI M
University of Wyoming, WY M
Virginia Military Institute, VA M
Virginia Polytechnic Institute and State U, VA M
Wagner College, NY M
Western State College of Colorado, CO M
West Virginia University, WV M

CO-OP PROGRAMS

This index lists the colleges that report offering cooperative education programs. These are formal arrangements with off-campus employers that are designed to allow students to combine study and work, often in a position related to the field of study. Salaries typically are set at a regular marketplace level, and sometimes academic credit is given for the work experience.

Abilene Christian University, TX
Adrian College, MI
Alabama Agricultural and Mechanical University, AL
Alabama State University, AL
Albany State University, GA
Alcorn State University, MS
Alfred University, NY
American Baptist Coll of American Baptist Theol Sem, TN
American InterContinental University, GA
American International College, MA
American University, DC
American University of Puerto Rico, PR
Anderson University, IN
Antioch College, OH
Aquinas College, MI
Arizona State University, AZ
Arkansas State University, AR
Armstrong Atlantic State University, GA
Athens State University, AL
Atlantic Union College, MA
Auburn University, AL
Auburn University Montgomery, AL
Audrey Cohen College, NY
Augsburg College, MN
Augustana College, IL
Augustana College, SD
Augusta State University, GA
Avila College, MO
Azusa Pacific University, CA
Ball State University, IN
Baltimore Hebrew University, MD
Barber-Scotia College, NC
Bartlesville Wesleyan College, OK
Barton College, NC
Bastyr University, WA
Beaver College, PA
Becker College, MA
Bellevue University, NE
Belmont Abbey College, NC
Belmont University, TN
Bemidji State University, MN
Benedictine College, KS
Bennett College, NC
Berry College, GA
Bethel College, KS
Bethune-Cookman College, FL
Beulah Heights Bible College, GA
Biola University, CA
Blackburn College, IL
Black Hills State University, SD
Bloomfield College, NJ
Bloomsburg University of Pennsylvania, PA
Boise Bible College, ID
Boston Architectural Center, MA
Boston University, MA
Bowie State University, MD
Bowling Green State University, OH
Bradley University, IL
Brenau University, GA
Brigham Young University, UT
Brigham Young University–Hawaii Campus, HI
Burlington College, VT
Butler University, IN
Cabrini College, PA
Caldwell College, NJ
California Baptist University, CA
California Lutheran University, CA
California Polytechnic State U, San Luis Obispo, CA
California State Polytechnic University, Pomona, CA
California State University, Bakersfield, CA
California State University, Chico, CA
California State University, Dominguez Hills, CA
California State University, Fresno, CA
California State University, Fullerton, CA
California State University, Hayward, CA
California State University, Los Angeles, CA
California State University, Sacramento, CA
California State University, San Bernardino, CA
California State University, Stanislaus, CA
California University of Pennsylvania, PA
Calumet College of Saint Joseph, IN
Calvin College, MI
Campbell University, NC
Capitol College, MD
Cardinal Stritch University, WI
Carnegie Mellon University, PA
Carroll College, MT
Carthage College, WI
Case Western Reserve University, OH
Castleton State College, VT
Cazenovia College, NY
Ctr for Creative Studies—Coll of Art and Design, MI
Central Connecticut State University, CT
Central State University, OH
Central Washington University, WA
Chadron State College, NE
Champlain College, VT
Chapman University, CA
Chatham College, PA
Cheyney University of Pennsylvania, PA
Chicago State University, IL
Christendom College, VA
Christopher Newport University, VA
City Coll of the City U of NY, NY
Claflin University, SC
Clarion University of Pennsylvania, PA
Clark Atlanta University, GA
Clarke College, IA
Clarkson College, NE
Clarkson University, NY
Clayton College & State University, GA
Cleary College, MI
Clemson University, SC
Cleveland College of Jewish Studies, OH
Coker College, SC
College Misericordia, PA
College of Aeronautics, NY
College of Charleston, SC
College of Insurance, NY
College of Mount St. Joseph, OH
The College of New Rochelle, NY
College of the Atlantic, ME
College of the Ozarks, MO
The College of West Virginia, WV
Colorado Christian University, CO
The Colorado College, CO
Colorado School of Mines, CO
Colorado State University, CO
Colorado Technical University, CO
Colorado Technical University Denver Campus, CO
Columbia College, MO
Columbia International University, SC
Columbia Union College, MD
Columbus State University, GA
Concordia College, MN
Concordia University, CA
Concordia University, NE
Concordia University at Austin, TX
Concordia University at St. Paul, MN
Coppin State College, MD
Cornell University, NY
Crichton College, TN
The Culinary Institute of America, NY
Cumberland University, TN
Daemen College, NY
Dakota State University, SD
Dakota Wesleyan University, SD
Davenport College of Business, Kalamazoo Campus, MI
Davenport College of Business, Lansing Campus, MI
David N. Myers College, OH
Davis & Elkins College, WV
Defiance College, OH
Delaware State University, DE
Delaware Valley College, PA
Denison University, OH
DePaul University, IL
Detroit College of Business, MI

Detroit College of Business–Flint, MI
Detroit College of Business, Warren Campus, MI
DeVry Institute of Technology, AZ
DeVry Institute of Technology, CA
DeVry Institute of Technology, CA
DeVry Institute of Technology, GA
DeVry Institute of Technology, GA
DeVry Institute of Technology, IL
DeVry Institute of Technology, IL
DeVry Institute of Technology, MO
DeVry Institute of Technology, NY
DeVry Institute of Technology, OH
DeVry Institute of Technology, TX
Dickinson State University, ND
Dillard University, LA
Doane College, NE
Dominican College of Blauvelt, NY
Dowling College, NY
Drake University, IA
Drexel University, PA
Duquesne University, PA
East Carolina University, NC
Eastern Connecticut State University, CT
Eastern Kentucky University, KY
Eastern Michigan University, MI
Eastern New Mexico University, NM
Eastern Oregon University, OR
Eastern Washington University, WA
East Tennessee State University, TN
Edward Waters College, FL
Elmhurst College, IL
Elon College, NC
Embry-Riddle Aeronautical University, AZ
Embry-Riddle Aeronautical University, FL
Embry-Riddle Aeronautical U, Extended Campus, FL
Emporia State University, KS
Escuela de Artes Plasticas de Puerto Rico, PR
The Evergreen State College, WA
Fairleigh Dickinson U, Florham-Madison Campus, NJ
Fairleigh Dickinson U, Teaneck-Hackensack Campus, NJ
Fashion Institute of Technology, NY
Fayetteville State University, NC
Ferris State University, MI
Ferrum College, VA
Fisk University, TN
Five Towns College, NY
Florida Agricultural and Mechanical University, FL
Florida Atlantic University, FL
Florida Gulf Coast University, FL
Florida Institute of Technology, FL
Florida International University, FL
Florida Memorial College, FL
Florida Metropolitan U-Orlando Coll, South, FL
Florida Metropolitan U-Tampa Coll, FL
Florida Metropolitan U-Tampa Coll, Brandon, FL
Florida State University, FL
Fontbonne College, MO
Fort Lewis College, CO
Fort Valley State University, GA
Francis Marion University, SC
Franklin University, OH
Fresno Pacific University, CA
Friends University, KS
Furman University, SC
Gannon University, PA
Geneva College, PA
George Fox University, OR
George Mason University, VA
Georgetown College, KY
The George Washington University, DC
Georgia College and State University, GA
Georgia Institute of Technology, GA
Georgia Southern University, GA
Georgia Southwestern State University, GA
Georgia State University, GA
Goddard College, VT
Golden Gate University, CA
Goldey-Beacom College, DE
Gordon College, MA
Goshen College, IN
Grace University, NE
Grambling State University, LA
Grand Valley State University, MI
Grand View College, IA
Greenville College, IL
Gustavus Adolphus College, MN
Gwynedd-Mercy College, PA
Hamline University, MN
Hampton University, VA
Hannibal-LaGrange College, MO
Harding University, AR
Harvey Mudd College, CA
Hawaii Pacific University, HI
Heritage College, WA
Hilbert College, NY
Holy Family College, PA
Hood College, MD
Humboldt State University, CA
Humphreys College, CA
Huntingdon College, AL
Huron University, SD
Husson College, ME
Huston-Tillotson College, TX
The Illinois Institute of Art, IL
Illinois Institute of Technology, IL
Illinois State University, IL
Illinois Wesleyan University, IL
Indiana State University, IN
Indiana University Bloomington, IN
Indiana University Northwest, IN
Indiana University of Pennsylvania, PA
Indiana U–Purdue U Fort Wayne, IN
Indiana U–Purdue U Indianapolis, IN
Inter American U of PR, Arecibo Campus, PR
Inter American U of PR, San Germán Campus, PR
International Academy of Design, FL
International College, FL
Iowa State University of Science and Technology, IA
Jacksonville State University, AL
Jacksonville University, FL
Jamestown College, ND
Jarvis Christian College, TX
John Carroll University, OH
John Jay Coll of Criminal Justice, the City U of NY, NY
Johns Hopkins University, MD
Johnson & Wales University, FL
Johnson & Wales University, RI
Johnson & Wales University, SC
Johnson Bible College, TN
Johnson C. Smith University, NC
Johnson State College, VT
Kalamazoo College, MI
Kansas City Art Institute, MO
Kansas State University, KS
Kean University, NJ
Keene State College, NH
Kendall College, IL
Kennesaw State University, GA
Kent State University, OH
Kentucky Christian College, KY
Kettering University, MI
Keuka College, NY
Laboratory Institute of Merchandising, NY
Lake Superior State University, MI
Lamar University, TX
Lander University, SC
Lane College, TN
Langston University, OK
La Roche College, PA
La Salle University, PA
Lawrence Technological University, MI
Lees-McRae College, NC
Lee University, TN
Lehigh University, PA
Lehman Coll of the City U of NY, NY
LeMoyne-Owen College, TN
LeTourneau University, TX
Lewis-Clark State College, ID
Lewis University, IL
Lincoln University, MO
Lincoln University, PA
Linfield College, OR
Lock Haven University of Pennsylvania, PA
Long Island U, Brooklyn Campus, NY
Long Island U, C.W. Post Campus, NY
Long Island U, Southampton College, NY
Louisiana State University and A&M College, LA
Louisiana State University in Shreveport, LA
Louisiana Tech University, LA
Lourdes College, OH
Loyola Marymount University, CA
Lyme Academy of Fine Arts, CT
Lyndon State College, VT
Macalester College, MN
Macon State College, GA
Madonna University, MI
Maharishi University of Management, IA
Maine College of Art, ME
Malone College, OH
Manhattan College, NY
Marian College, IN
Marian College of Fond du Lac, WI
Marist College, NY
Marquette University, WI
Marshall University, WV
Mars Hill College, NC
Marycrest International University, IA
Maryville University of Saint Louis, MO
Mary Washington College, VA
Massachusetts College of Art, MA
Massachusetts Institute of Technology, MA
Massachusetts Maritime Academy, MA
The Master's College and Seminary, CA
Mayo School of Health-Related Sciences, MN
Mayville State University, ND
The McGregor School of Antioch University, OH
McNeese State University, LA
McPherson College, KS

Medgar Evers College of the City U of NY, NY
Mercer University, GA
Mercy College, NY
Mercyhurst College, PA
Meredith College, NC
Merrimack College, MA
Mesa State College, CO
Metropolitan State College of Denver, CO
Miami University, OH
Michigan State University, MI
Michigan Technological University, MI
Middle Tennessee State University, TN
Midland Lutheran College, NE
Miles College, AL
Millersville University of Pennsylvania, PA
Milligan College, TN
Milwaukee Institute of Art and Design, WI
Minneapolis College of Art and Design, MN
Minot State University, ND
Mississippi College, MS
Mississippi State University, MS
Mississippi University for Women, MS
Mississippi Valley State University, MS
Missouri Baptist College, MO
Missouri Valley College, MO
Monmouth University, NJ
Montana State U–Billings, MT
Montana State U–Northern, MT
Montana Tech of The University of Montana, MT
Montclair State University, NJ
Monterey Institute of International Studies, CA
Montreat College, NC
Moravian College, PA
Morehead State University, KY
Morgan State University, MD
Mount Ida College, MA
Mount Marty College, SD
Mount Olive College, NC
Mount Saint Mary College, NY
Mount Saint Mary's College and Seminary, MD
Mount Senario College, WI
Mount Union College, OH
Murray State University, KY
NAES College, IL
Naropa University, CO
The National Hispanic University, CA
Nazareth College of Rochester, NY
Neumann College, PA
New England College, NH
New Hampshire College, NH
New Jersey Institute of Technology, NJ
Newman University, KS
New Mexico Highlands University, NM
New Mexico Institute of Mining and Technology, NM
Newschool of Architecture, CA
New York Institute of Technology, NY
Niagara University, NY
Norfolk State University, VA
North Carolina Agricultural and Technical State U, NC
North Carolina Central University, NC
North Carolina State University, NC
North Carolina Wesleyan College, NC
North Central College, IL
North Dakota State University, ND
Northeastern Illinois University, IL
Northeastern University, MA
Northern Arizona University, AZ
Northern Illinois University, IL
Northern Kentucky University, KY
North Georgia College & State University, GA
Northland College, WI
Northwest Christian College, OR
Northwestern College, IA
Northwestern State University of Louisiana, LA
Northwestern University, IL
Northwest Nazarene University, ID
Norwich University, VT
Notre Dame College of Ohio, OH
Nova Southeastern University, FL
Oakland University, MI
Oakwood College, AL
Oglala Lakota College, SD
Oglethorpe University, GA
Ohio Northern University, OH
The Ohio State University, OH
Ohio University, OH
Oklahoma Baptist University, OK
Oklahoma City University, OK
Oklahoma Panhandle State University, OK
Oklahoma State U, OK
Old Dominion University, VA
Olivet College, MI
O'More College of Design, TN
Oregon Institute of Technology, OR
Oregon State University, OR
Otis College of Art and Design, CA
Ouachita Baptist University, AR
Our Lady of Holy Cross College, LA
Pacific Lutheran University, WA
Pacific Union College, CA
Pacific University, OR
Paine College, GA
Paul Quinn College, TX
Peirce College, PA
Pennsylvania School of Art & Design, PA
Penn State U Univ Park Campus, PA
Pfeiffer University, NC
Philadelphia University, PA
Philander Smith College, AR
Pittsburg State University, KS
Pitzer College, CA
Plattsburgh State U of NY, NY
Polytechnic U, Brooklyn Campus, NY
Pontifical Catholic University of Puerto Rico, PR
Portland State University, OR
Practical Bible College, NY
Prairie View A&M University, TX
Pratt Institute, NY
Prescott College, AZ
Presentation College, SD
Princeton University, NJ
Providence College, RI
Purdue University, IN
Purdue University Calumet, IN
Purdue University North Central, IN
Queens Coll of the City U of NY, NY
Ramapo College of New Jersey, NJ
Reformed Bible College, MI
Regis University, CO
Reinhardt College, GA
Rensselaer Polytechnic Institute, NY
Rider University, NJ
Robert Morris College, IL
Robert Morris College, PA
Roberts Wesleyan College, NY
Rochester Institute of Technology, NY
Rockhurst University, MO
Rocky Mountain College, MT
Roger Williams University, RI
Rose-Hulman Institute of Technology, IN
Rowan University, NJ
Russell Sage College, NY
Rust College, MS
Rutgers, State U of NJ, Cook College, NJ
Rutgers, State U of NJ, College of Engineering, NJ
Sacred Heart University, CT
Saginaw Valley State University, MI
St. Ambrose University, IA
Saint Augustine's College, NC
St. Edward's University, TX
Saint Joseph's College, ME
Saint Joseph's University, PA
Saint Leo University, FL
Saint Louis University, MO
Saint Martin's College, WA
Saint Mary's College, MI
St. Mary's University of San Antonio, TX
Saint Paul's College, VA
Saint Peter's College, NJ
St. Thomas University, FL
Saint Vincent College, PA
Saint Xavier University, IL
Salisbury State University, MD
Samford University, AL
Sam Houston State University, TX
San Francisco Art Institute, CA
San Francisco State University, CA
San Jose State University, CA
Santa Clara University, CA
Savannah State University, GA
School of the Art Institute of Chicago, IL
Schreiner College, TX
Seattle Pacific University, WA
Seton Hall University, NJ
Seton Hill College, PA
Shepherd College, WV
Shimer College, IL
Shippensburg University of Pennsylvania, PA
Siena Heights University, MI
Sierra Nevada College, NV
Silver Lake College, WI
Simpson College, IA
Sonoma State University, CA
South Dakota School of Mines and Technology, SD
South Dakota State University, SD
Southeastern University, DC
Southeast Missouri State University, MO
Southern California Institute of Architecture, CA
Southern Connecticut State University, CT
Southern Illinois University Carbondale, IL
Southern Illinois University Edwardsville, IL
Southern Methodist University, TX
Southern Oregon University, OR
Southern Polytechnic State University, GA
Southern University and A&M College, LA
Southern Utah University, UT
Southwest Baptist University, MO
Southwestern Adventist University, TX

Southwestern Oklahoma State University, OK
Southwest Missouri State University, MO
Springfield College, MA
Spring Hill College, AL
State U of NY at Oswego, NY
State U of NY College at Brockport, NY
State U of NY College at Cortland, NY
State U of NY College at Potsdam, NY
State U of NY Institute of Tech at Utica/Rome, NY
State U of NY Maritime College, NY
State University of West Georgia, GA
Stephen F. Austin State University, TX
Stephens College, MO
Stevens Institute of Technology, NJ
Stillman College, AL
Strayer University, DC
Suffolk University, MA
Sullivan College, KY
Syracuse University, NY
Talladega College, AL
Tarleton State University, TX
Taylor University, Fort Wayne Campus, IN
Teikyo Post University, CT
Temple University, PA
Tennessee State University, TN
Tennessee Technological University, TN
Tennessee Temple University, TN
Texas A&M University, TX
Texas A&M University at Galveston, TX
Texas A&M University–Commerce, TX
Texas A&M University–Corpus Christi, TX
Texas A&M University–Kingsville, TX
Texas Tech University, TX
Texas Woman's University, TX
Thiel College, PA
Thomas College, ME
Thomas More College, KY
Thomas University, GA
Tougaloo College, MS
Towson University, MD
Trinity College, DC
Tri-State University, IN
Tulane University, LA
Tuskegee University, AL
Union College, KY
Union College, NE
Union College, NY
Unity College, ME
Universidad Adventista de las Antillas, PR
The University of Akron, OH
The University of Alabama, AL
The University of Alabama at Birmingham, AL
The University of Alabama in Huntsville, AL
U of Alaska Anchorage, AK
U of Alaska Fairbanks, AK
U of Alaska Southeast, AK
The University of Arizona, AZ
University of Arkansas, AR
University of Arkansas at Little Rock, AR
University of Arkansas at Pine Bluff, AR
University of Baltimore, MD
University of Bridgeport, CT
U of Calif, Berkeley, CA
U of Calif, Irvine, CA
U of Calif, Riverside, CA
U of Calif, San Diego, CA
U of Calif, Santa Cruz, CA
University of Central Arkansas, AR
University of Central Florida, FL
University of Cincinnati, OH
University of Colorado at Boulder, CO
University of Colorado at Colorado Springs, CO
University of Colorado at Denver, CO
University of Connecticut, CT
University of Dayton, OH
University of Delaware, DE
University of Detroit Mercy, MI
University of Evansville, IN
The University of Findlay, OH
University of Florida, FL
University of Georgia, GA
University of Great Falls, MT
University of Hartford, CT
University of Hawaii at Manoa, HI
University of Houston, TX
University of Houston–Clear Lake, TX
University of Houston–Downtown, TX
University of Idaho, ID
University of Illinois at Chicago, IL
University of Illinois at Springfield, IL
University of Illinois at Urbana–Champaign, IL
University of Indianapolis, IN
The University of Iowa, IA
University of Kansas, KS
University of Louisiana at Lafayette, LA
University of Louisiana at Monroe, LA
University of Louisville, KY
University of Maine, ME
The University of Maine at Augusta, ME
University of Maine at Machias, ME
University of Mary, ND
University of Maryland, Baltimore County, MD
University of Maryland, College Park, MD
University of Maryland University College, MD
University of Massachusetts Amherst, MA
University of Massachusetts Boston, MA
University of Massachusetts Dartmouth, MA
University of Massachusetts Lowell, MA
The University of Memphis, TN
University of Michigan, MI
University of Michigan–Dearborn, MI
University of Michigan–Flint, MI
University of Minnesota, Twin Cities Campus, MN
University of Missouri–Columbia, MO
University of Missouri–Kansas City, MO
University of Missouri–Rolla, MO
University of Missouri–St. Louis, MO
The University of Montana–Missoula, MT
University of Nebraska at Kearney, NE
University of Nebraska at Omaha, NE
University of Nebraska–Lincoln, NE
University of Nevada, Las Vegas, NV
University of New England, ME
University of New Haven, CT
University of New Mexico, NM
University of New Orleans, LA
University of North Alabama, AL
The University of North Carolina at Charlotte, NC
The University of North Carolina at Pembroke, NC
The University of North Carolina at Wilmington, NC
University of North Dakota, ND
University of Northern Colorado, CO
University of Northern Iowa, IA
University of North Florida, FL
University of North Texas, TX
University of Oklahoma, OK
University of Pittsburgh, PA
University of Pittsburgh at Johnstown, PA
University of Portland, OR
U of Puerto Rico, Mayagüez Campus, PR
University of Puget Sound, WA
University of Rhode Island, RI
University of Richmond, VA
University of Rio Grande, OH
University of St. Francis, IL
University of Saint Francis, IN
University of St. Thomas, TX
University of San Francisco, CA
University of Science and Arts of Oklahoma, OK
University of South Alabama, AL
University of South Carolina, SC
University of South Carolina Aiken, SC
U of South Carolina Spartanburg, SC
University of Southern California, CA
University of Southern Colorado, CO
University of Southern Indiana, IN
University of Southern Maine, ME
University of Southern Mississippi, MS
University of South Florida, FL
The University of Tampa, FL
The University of Tennessee at Chattanooga, TN
The University of Tennessee at Martin, TN
The University of Tennessee Knoxville, TN
The University of Texas at Arlington, TX
The University of Texas at Austin, TX
The University of Texas at Brownsville, TX
The University of Texas at Dallas, TX
The University of Texas at El Paso, TX
The University of Texas at San Antonio, TX
The University of Texas–Pan American, TX
University of the District of Columbia, DC
University of the Pacific, CA
University of the Sacred Heart, PR
University of the Sciences in Philadelphia, PA
University of Toledo, OH
University of Utah, UT
University of Vermont, VT
University of Virginia, VA
University of Virginia's College at Wise, VA
University of Washington, WA
University of West Florida, FL
University of Wisconsin–Eau Claire, WI
University of Wisconsin–Green Bay, WI
University of Wisconsin–Madison, WI
University of Wisconsin–Milwaukee, WI
University of Wisconsin–Platteville, WI
University of Wisconsin–River Falls, WI
University of Wisconsin–Stevens Point, WI
University of Wisconsin–Stout, WI
University of Wisconsin–Superior, WI
Urbana University, OH
Ursuline College, OH
Utah State University, UT
Utica College of Syracuse University, NY
Valdosta State University, GA
Valley City State University, ND
Valparaiso University, IN
Vanderbilt University, TN

Villa Julie College, MD
Virginia Commonwealth University, VA
Virginia Polytechnic Institute and State U, VA
Virginia State University, VA
Virginia Union University, VA
Virginia Wesleyan College, VA
Viterbo University, WI
Voorhees College, SC
Wabash College, IN
Walla Walla College, WA
Warner Pacific College, OR
Warren Wilson College, NC
Washburn University of Topeka, KS
Washington Bible College, MD
Washington College, MD
Washington State University, WA
Washington University in St. Louis, MO
Wayne State College, NE
Wayne State University, MI
Webber College, FL
Webb Institute, NY
Weber State University, UT
Webster University, MO
Wentworth Institute of Technology, MA
Western Carolina University, NC
Western Connecticut State University, CT
Western Kentucky University, KY
Western Michigan University, MI
Western Montana College of The U of Montana, MT
Western New Mexico University, NM
Western State College of Colorado, CO
Western Washington University, WA
Westfield State College, MA
Westmont College, CA
West Texas A&M University, TX
West Virginia State College, WV
West Virginia University, WV
West Virginia University Institute of Technology, WV
Wheeling Jesuit University, WV
Whitman College, WA
Whitworth College, WA
Wichita State University, KS
Widener University, PA
Wilberforce University, OH
Wilkes University, PA
Willamette University, OR
William Penn University, IA
Wilson College, PA
Winston-Salem State University, NC
Winthrop University, SC
Wofford College, SC
Worcester Polytechnic Institute, MA
Xavier University, OH
Xavier University of Louisiana, LA
Yeshiva Karlin Stolin Rabbinical Institute, NY
York College, NE
York College of the City University of New York, NY
Youngstown State University, OH

ROTC PROGRAMS

This index lists the colleges that offer ROTC programs. This is arranged in three categories by branch of the service that sponsors the program, in this order: Army, Navy, Air Force.

ARMY

Adelphi University, NY*
Alabama Agricultural and Mechanical University, AL
Alabama State University, AL*
Albany College of Pharmacy of Union University, NY*
Albany State University, GA
Alcorn State University, MS
Alfred University, NY*
Allegheny College, PA*
Allen College, IA*
Allentown College of St. Francis de Sales, PA*
Allen University, SC*
Alma College, MI*
Alvernia College, PA*
Alverno College, WI*
American International College, MA*
American University, DC*
American University of Puerto Rico, PR*
Anderson College, SC*
Anna Maria College, MA*
Appalachian State University, NC
Aquinas College, TN*
Arizona State University, AZ
Arizona State University East, AZ*
Arkansas State University, AR
Arkansas Tech University, AR
Armstrong Atlantic State University, GA
Art Academy of Cincinnati, OH*
Asbury College, KY*
Assumption College, MA*
Athens State University, AL*
Auburn University, AL
Auburn University Montgomery, AL
Augsburg College, MN*
Augusta State University, GA
Aurora University, IL*
Austin Peay State University, TN
Avila College, MO*
Azusa Pacific University, CA*
Babson College, MA*
Baker University, KS*
Baldwin-Wallace College, OH*
Ball State University, IN
Baptist Bible College, MO*
Baptist Bible College of Pennsylvania, PA*
Barber-Scotia College, NC*
Bayamón Central University, PR*
Bay Path College, MA*
Beaver College, PA*
Becker College, MA*
Bellarmine College, KY*
Bellevue University, NE*
Bellin College of Nursing, WI*
Belmont Abbey College, NC*
Belmont University, TN*
Benedictine College, KS
Benedictine University, IL*
Bennett College, NC*
Bentley College, MA*
Bethel College, IN*
Bethel College, MN*
Bethune-Cookman College, FL*
Biola University, CA*
Birmingham-Southern College, AL*
Black Hills State University, SD
Bloomfield College, NJ*
Bloomsburg University of Pennsylvania, PA
Boise State University, ID
Boston College, MA*
Boston University, MA
Bowie State University, MD
Bowling Green State University, OH
Bradley University, IL
Brandeis University, MA*
Bridgewater State College, MA*
Brigham Young University, UT
Brigham Young University–Hawaii Campus, HI*
Brown University, RI*
Bryant College, RI
Bucknell University, PA
Butler University, IN*
Cabrini College, PA*
Caldwell College, NJ*
California Baptist University, CA*
California Institute of Technology, CA*
California Lutheran University, CA*
California Polytechnic State U, San Luis Obispo, CA
California State Polytechnic University, Pomona, CA
California State University, Dominguez Hills, CA*
California State University, Fresno, CA
California State University, Fullerton, CA
California State University, Long Beach, CA
California State University, Los Angeles, CA*
California State University, Northridge, CA*
California State University, Sacramento, CA*
California State University, San Bernardino, CA
Calvin College, MI*
Cameron University, OK
Campbell University, NC
Canisius College, NY
Capital University, OH
Capitol College, MD*
Caribbean University, PR*
Carlow College, PA*
Carnegie Mellon University, PA
Carson-Newman College, TN
Cascade College, OR*
Case Western Reserve University, OH*
Catawba College, NC*
The Catholic University of America, DC*
Cazenovia College, NY*
Cedar Crest College, PA*
Cedarville College, OH*
Centenary College of Louisiana, LA*
Central Connecticut State University, CT*
Central Methodist College, MO*
Central Michigan University, MI
Central Missouri State University, MO
Central State University, OH
Central Washington University, WA
Centre College, KY*
Chaminade University of Honolulu, HI*
Champlain College, VT*
Chapman University, CA*
Chatham College, PA*
Cheyney University of Pennsylvania, PA
Chicago State University, IL
Christian Brothers University, TN*
Christian Heritage College, CA*
Christopher Newport University, VA
Citadel, The Military Coll of South Carolina, SC
City Coll of the City U of NY, NY*
Claflin University, SC*
Claremont McKenna College, CA
Clark Atlanta University, GA
Clarkson College, NE*
Clarkson University, NY
Clark University, MA*
Clayton College & State University, GA*
Clearwater Christian College, FL*
Clemson University, SC
Cleveland Institute of Music, OH*
Coe College, IA*
Colby College, ME*
Colby-Sawyer College, NH*
Colgate University, NY*
College Misericordia, PA*
College of Aeronautics, NY*
College of Mount St. Joseph, OH*
College of Mount Saint Vincent, NY*
The College of New Jersey, NJ*
The College of New Rochelle, NY*
College of Notre Dame of Maryland, MD*
College of Our Lady of the Elms, MA*
College of Saint Benedict, MN*
College of Saint Mary, NE*
The College of Saint Rose, NY*
The College of St. Scholastica, MN*
College of the Holy Cross, MA*
College of the Ozarks, MO
The College of William and Mary, VA
Colorado Christian University, CO*
The Colorado College, CO*
Colorado School of Mines, CO*
Colorado State University, CO

**program is offered at another college's campus*

Colorado Technical University, CO*
Columbia College, MO*
Columbia College, SC*
Columbus State University, GA
Concordia College, MI*
Concordia College, MN*
Concordia University at Austin, TX*
Concordia University at St. Paul, MN*
Conservatory of Music of Puerto Rico, PR*
Converse College, SC*
Coppin State College, MD
Cornell University, NY
Cornerstone University, MI*
Creighton University, NE
Curry College, MA*
Daemen College, NY*
Dallas Baptist University, TX*
Dana College, NE*
Daniel Webster College, NH*
Dartmouth College, NH
Davenport College of Business, Lansing Campus, MI*
David Lipscomb University, TN*
Davidson College, NC
Delaware State University, DE
DePaul University, IL
DePauw University, IN*
DeVry Institute of Technology, OH*
Dickinson College, PA
Dillard University, LA
Doane College, NE*
Dominican College of Blauvelt, NY*
Dominican University of California, CA*
Dowling College, NY*
Drake University, IA
Drexel University, PA
Drury University, MO*
Duke University, NC
Duquesne University, PA*
D'Youville College, NY*
East Carolina University, NC
Eastern Connecticut State University, CT*
Eastern Illinois University, IL
Eastern Kentucky University, KY
Eastern Michigan University, MI
Eastern Nazarene College, MA*
Eastern Washington University, WA
East Stroudsburg University of Pennsylvania, PA*
East Tennessee State University, TN
Eckerd College, FL*
Edinboro University of Pennsylvania, PA
Edward Waters College, FL*
Elmhurst College, IL*
Elmira College, NY*
Elon College, NC
Embry-Riddle Aeronautical University, AZ
Embry-Riddle Aeronautical University, FL
Emmanuel College, MA*
Evangel University, MO
Fairfield University, CT*
Fairleigh Dickinson U, Teaneck-Hackensack Campus, NJ*
Fairmont State College, WV
Ferris State University, MI*
Finlandia University, MI*
Fisk University, TN*
Florida Agricultural and Mechanical University, FL
Florida Atlantic University, FL*
Florida College, FL*
Florida Institute of Technology, FL
Florida International University, FL
Florida Memorial College, FL
Florida Southern College, FL
Florida State University, FL
Fontbonne College, MO*
Fordham University, NY
Fort Valley State University, GA
Framingham State College, MA*
Franklin College of Indiana, IN*
Franklin University, OH*
Free Will Baptist Bible College, TN*
Furman University, SC
Gannon University, PA
Geneva College, PA*
George Mason University, VA
Georgetown College, KY
Georgetown University, DC
The George Washington University, DC*
Georgia College and State University, GA
Georgia Institute of Technology, GA
Georgia Southern University, GA
Georgia State University, GA
Gonzaga University, WA
Gordon College, MA*
Governors State University, IL*
Grambling State University, LA
Grand Canyon University, AZ
Grand View College, IA*
Green Mountain College, VT*
Greensboro College, NC*
Guilford College, NC*
Gustavus Adolphus College, MN*
Hamilton College, NY*
Hampden-Sydney College, VA*
Hampton University, VA
Harding University, AR*
Harvard University, MA*
Harvey Mudd College, CA*
Hawaii Pacific University, HI*
Hendrix College, AR*
High Point University, NC*
Hillsdale College, MI*
Hofstra University, NY
Holy Names College, CA*
Hood College, MD*
Houghton College, NY*
Houston Baptist University, TX*
Howard Payne University, TX*
Huntingdon College, AL*
Husson College, ME*
Idaho State University, ID*
Illinois Institute of Technology, IL
Illinois State University, IL
Illinois Wesleyan University, IL*
Indiana State University, IN
Indiana University Bloomington, IN
Indiana University Kokomo, IN*
Indiana University Northwest, IN
Indiana University of Pennsylvania, PA
Indiana U–Purdue U Indianapolis, IN
Indiana University South Bend, IN*
Indiana University Southeast, IN*
Inter American U of PR, Arecibo Campus, PR*
Inter Amer U of PR, Barranquitas Campus, PR*
Inter American U of PR, Guayama Campus, PR*
Inter American U of PR, San Germán Campus, PR*
Iona College, NY*
Iowa State University of Science and Technology, IA
Ithaca College, NY*
Jacksonville State University, AL
James Madison University, VA
John Brown University, AR*
John Carroll University, OH
Johns Hopkins University, MD
Johnson & Wales University, RI*
Johnson C. Smith University, NC
Johnson State College, VT*
Judson College, AL*
Judson College, IL*
Kalamazoo College, MI*
Kansas State University, KS
Keene State College, NH*
Kennesaw State University, GA
Kent State University, OH
King College, TN*
King's College, PA
Kutztown University of Pennsylvania, PA*
Lafayette College, PA*
Lander University, SC
Langston University, OK*
La Roche College, PA*
La Salle University, PA*
Lawrence Technological University, MI*
Lebanon Valley College, PA*
Lees-McRae College, NC*
Lehigh University, PA
Lehman Coll of the City U of NY, NY*
Le Moyne College, NY*
LeMoyne-Owen College, TN*
Lewis-Clark State College, ID
Lewis University, IL
Limestone College, SC*
Lincoln University, MO
Lincoln University, PA*
Lock Haven University of Pennsylvania, PA
Long Island U, C.W. Post Campus, NY*
Longwood College, VA
Louisiana State University and A&M College, LA
Louisiana State University in Shreveport, LA
Louisiana Tech University, LA*
Lourdes College, OH*
Loyola College in Maryland, MD
Loyola Marymount University, CA*
Loyola University Chicago, IL*
Loyola University New Orleans, LA*
Lubbock Christian University, TX*
Lycoming College, PA*
Manhattan College, NY*
Marian College, IN*
Marian College of Fond du Lac, WI
Marquette University, WI
Marshall University, WV
Mary Baldwin College, VA
Maryland Institute, College of Art, MD*
Marymount University, VA*
Maryville University of Saint Louis, MO*
Marywood University, PA*
Mass Coll of Pharmacy and Allied Health Sciences, MA*
Massachusetts Institute of Technology, MA
Massachusetts Maritime Academy, MA*
Mayville State University, ND*

program is offered at another college's campus

Army (continued)

McKendree College, IL*
Medaille College, NY*
Menlo College, CA*
Mercer University, GA*
Mercyhurst College, PA*
Meredith College, NC*
Methodist College, NC
Miami University, OH*
Michigan State University, MI
Michigan Technological University, MI
MidAmerica Nazarene University, KS*
Middle Tennessee State University, TN
Midway College, KY*
Miles College, AL*
Milligan College, TN*
Millsaps College, MS*
Mills College, CA*
Milwaukee School of Engineering, WI*
Minnesota State University, Mankato, MN
Minnesota State University Moorhead, MN*
Mississippi College, MS*
Mississippi State University, MS
Mississippi University for Women, MS*
Mississippi Valley State University, MS
Missouri Baptist College, MO*
Missouri Western State College, MO
Monmouth College, IL*
Montana State U–Bozeman, MT
Moravian College, PA*
Morehead State University, KY
Morgan State University, MD
Mount Holyoke College, MA*
Mount Marty College, SD*
Mount Mary College, WI*
Mount Saint Mary College, NY*
Mount St. Mary's College, CA*
Mount Saint Mary's College and Seminary, MD*
Mount Union College, OH*
Muhlenberg College, PA*
Murray State University, KY*
National University, CA*
Nebraska Methodist Coll of Nursing & Allied Health, NE*
Nebraska Wesleyan University, NE*
Neumann College, PA*
Newberry College, SC
New College of the University of South Florida, FL*
New England College, NH*
New Hampshire College, NH*
New York University, NY*
Niagara University, NY
Nichols College, MA
Norfolk State University, VA
North Carolina Agricultural and Technical State U, NC
North Carolina Central University, NC*
North Carolina State University, NC
North Central College, IL*
North Dakota State University, ND
Northeastern Illinois University, IL*
Northeastern University, MA
Northern Arizona University, AZ
Northern Illinois University, IL
Northern Kentucky University, KY*
Northern Michigan University, MI
North Georgia College & State University, GA
North Greenville College, SC*
Northwest Christian College, OR*
Northwestern College, MN*
Northwestern State University of Louisiana, LA
Northwestern University, IL*
Northwest Nazarene University, ID
Norwich University, VT
Occidental College, CA*
Ohio Dominican College, OH*
Ohio Northern University, OH*
The Ohio State University, OH
Ohio University, OH
Ohio University–Chillicothe, OH
Ohio University–Lancaster, OH*
Ohio Wesleyan University, OH*
Oklahoma Christian U of Science and Arts, OK*
Oklahoma City University, OK*
Oklahoma State U, OK
Old Dominion University, VA
Olivet Nazarene University, IL*
Oregon Health Sciences University, OR*
Oregon Institute of Technology, OR
Oregon State University, OR
Otterbein College, OH*
Ouachita Baptist University, AR*
Our Lady of Holy Cross College, LA*
Our Lady of the Lake University of San Antonio, TX*
Pacific Lutheran University, WA
Pacific University, OR*
Paine College, GA*
Park University, MO
Peace College, NC*
Penn State U Abington College, PA
Penn State U Altoona College, PA
Penn State U Berks Cmps of Berks-Lehigh Valley Coll, PA
Penn State U Harrisburg Campus of the Capital Coll, PA*
Penn State U Schuylkill Campus of the Capital Coll, PA
Penn State U Univ Park Campus, PA
Pepperdine University, CA*
Pfeiffer University, NC*
Philander Smith College, AR*
Piedmont College, GA*
Pittsburg State University, KS
Plymouth State College, NH*
Point Loma Nazarene University, CA*
Point Park College, PA*
Polytechnic University of Puerto Rico, PR*
Pontifical Catholic University of Puerto Rico, PR*
Portland State University, OR
Prairie View A&M University, TX
Pratt Institute, NY*
Presbyterian College, SC
Princeton University, NJ
Providence College, RI
Purdue University, IN
Purdue University Calumet, IN*
Queens College, NC*
Queens Coll of the City U of NY, NY*
Quinnipiac University, CT*
Radford University, VA
Randolph-Macon College, VA*
Reed College, OR*
Regis University, CO*
Rensselaer Polytechnic Institute, NY
Research College of Nursing, MO*
Rhode Island College, RI*
Rhodes College, TN*
Rice University, TX*
The Richard Stockton College of New Jersey, NJ*
Rider University, NJ*
Ripon College, WI
Robert Morris College, PA*
Roberts Wesleyan College, NY*
Rochester Institute of Technology, NY
Rockford College, IL*
Rockhurst University, MO*
Roger Williams University, RI*
Rose-Hulman Institute of Technology, IN
Rosemont College, PA*
Rowan University, NJ*
Russell Sage College, NY*
Rutgers, State U of NJ, Camden Coll of Arts & Scis, NJ*
Rutgers, State U of NJ, College of Nursing, NJ*
Rutgers, State U of NJ, College of Pharmacy, NJ
Rutgers, State U of NJ, Cook College, NJ
Rutgers, State U of NJ, Douglass College, NJ
Rutgers, State U of NJ, Livingston College, NJ
Rutgers, State U of NJ, Mason Gross School of Arts, NJ
Rutgers, State U of NJ, Newark Coll of Arts & Scis, NJ*
Rutgers, State U of NJ, Rutgers College, NJ
Rutgers, State U of NJ, College of Engineering, NJ
Rutgers, State U of NJ, U Coll–Camden, NJ*
Rutgers, State U of NJ, U Coll–Newark, NJ*
Rutgers, State U of NJ, U Coll–New Brunswick, NJ
Saint Anselm College, NH*
Saint Augustine's College, NC
St. Bonaventure University, NY
St. Edward's University, TX*
St. Francis College, NY*
Saint Francis College, PA*
St. John Fisher College, NY*
Saint John's University, MN
St. John's University, NY
Saint Joseph's College, ME*
St. Joseph's College, Suffolk Campus, NY*
Saint Joseph's University, PA*
St. Lawrence University, NY*
Saint Leo University, FL*
Saint Louis University, MO*
Saint Martin's College, WA*
Saint Mary College, KS*
Saint Mary-of-the-Woods College, IN*
Saint Mary's College, IN*
Saint Mary's College of California, CA*
St. Mary's University of San Antonio, TX
Saint Michael's College, VT*
St. Norbert College, WI
Saint Paul's College, VA
Saint Peter's College, NJ
St. Thomas University, FL*
Saint Xavier University, IL*
Salem College, NC*

**program is offered at another college's campus*

Salve Regina University, RI*
Samford University, AL*
Sam Houston State University, TX
Samuel Merritt College, CA*
San Diego State University, CA
San Francisco State University, CA*
San Jose State University, CA
Santa Clara University, CA
Savannah State University, GA
School of the Museum of Fine Arts, MA*
Scripps College, CA*
Seattle Pacific University, WA*
Seattle University, WA
Seton Hall University, NJ
Seton Hill College, PA*
Shaw University, NC*
Shepherd College, WV*
Shippensburg University of Pennsylvania, PA
Siena College, NY
Sierra Nevada College, NV*
Simmons College, MA*
Skidmore College, NY*
Slippery Rock University of Pennsylvania, PA
Smith College, MA*
Sonoma State University, CA*
South Dakota School of Mines and Technology, SD
South Dakota State University, SD
Southeastern College of the Assemblies of God, FL*
Southeastern Louisiana University, LA*
Southern Connecticut State University, CT*
Southern Illinois University Carbondale, IL
Southern Illinois University Edwardsville, IL
Southern Methodist University, TX
Southern Nazarene University, OK*
Southern Polytechnic State University, GA*
Southern University and A&M College, LA
Southern University at New Orleans, LA*
Southern Wesleyan University, SC*
Southwest Baptist University, MO*
Southwest Missouri State University, MO
Southwest Texas State University, TX
Spalding University, KY*
Springfield College, MA*
Spring Hill College, AL*
Stanford University, CA*
State U of NY at Albany, NY*
State U of NY at Buffalo, NY*
State U of NY at Farmingdale, NY*
State U of NY College at Brockport, NY
State U of NY College at Buffalo, NY*
State U of NY College at Cortland, NY*
State U of NY College at Fredonia, NY*
State U of NY College at Geneseo, NY*
State U of NY College at Potsdam, NY*
State U of NY Coll of Environ Sci and Forestry, NY*
State U of NY Institute of Tech at Utica/Rome, NY*
State University of West Georgia, GA
Stephen F. Austin State University, TX
Stephens College, MO*
Stetson University, FL*
Stevens Institute of Technology, NJ*
Stillman College, AL*
Stonehill College, MA
Suffolk University, MA*
Susquehanna University, PA*
Swarthmore College, PA*
Syracuse University, NY
Talladega College, AL*
Tarleton State University, TX
Teikyo Post University, CT*
Temple University, PA
Tennessee State University, TN*
Tennessee Technological University, TN
Texas A&M University, TX
Texas A&M University–Corpus Christi, TX
Texas A&M University–Kingsville, TX
Texas Christian University, TX
Texas Lutheran University, TX*
Texas Tech University, TX
Texas Wesleyan University, TX*
Thomas More College, KY*
Thomas University, GA
Tiffin University, OH*
Tougaloo College, MS
Towson University, MD*
Transylvania University, KY*
Trevecca Nazarene University, TN*
Trinity College, CT*
Trinity College, DC*
Troy State University, AL
Troy State University Montgomery, AL*
Truman State University, MO
Tufts University, MA*
Tulane University, LA
Tuskegee University, AL
Union College, NY*
United States International University, CA*
Unity College, ME*
The University of Akron, OH
The University of Alabama, AL
The University of Alabama at Birmingham, AL
The University of Alabama in Huntsville, AL*
U of Alaska Fairbanks, AK
The University of Arizona, AZ
University of Arkansas, AR
University of Arkansas at Little Rock, AR
University of Arkansas at Pine Bluff, AR
University of Baltimore, MD*
University of Bridgeport, CT
U of Calif, Berkeley, CA
U of Calif, Davis, CA
U of Calif, Irvine, CA*
U of Calif, Los Angeles, CA
U of Calif, Riverside, CA*
U of Calif, Santa Barbara, CA
U of Calif, Santa Cruz, CA*
University of Central Arkansas, AR
University of Central Florida, FL
University of Central Oklahoma, OK
University of Charleston, WV
University of Chicago, IL*
University of Cincinnati, OH
University of Colorado at Boulder, CO
University of Colorado at Colorado Springs, CO
University of Colorado at Denver, CO
University of Connecticut, CT
University of Dallas, TX*
University of Dayton, OH
University of Delaware, DE
University of Detroit Mercy, MI*
University of Florida, FL
University of Georgia, GA
University of Guam, GU
University of Hartford, CT*
University of Hawaii at Hilo, HI*
University of Hawaii at Manoa, HI
University of Hawaii–West Oahu, HI*
University of Houston, TX
University of Houston–Clear Lake, TX*
University of Houston–Downtown, TX*
University of Idaho, ID
University of Illinois at Chicago, IL
University of Illinois at Urbana–Champaign, IL
University of Indianapolis, IN*
The University of Iowa, IA
University of Kansas, KS
University of Louisiana at Lafayette, LA
University of Louisiana at Monroe, LA
University of Louisville, KY
University of Maine, ME
University of Maryland, Baltimore County, MD*
University of Maryland, College Park, MD*
University of Massachusetts Amherst, MA
University of Massachusetts Dartmouth, MA*
The University of Memphis, TN
University of Miami, FL*
University of Michigan, MI
University of Michigan–Dearborn, MI
University of Minnesota, Twin Cities Campus, MN
University of Mississippi, MS
University of Missouri–Columbia, MO
University of Missouri–Kansas City, MO
University of Missouri–Rolla, MO
University of Missouri–St. Louis, MO*
University of Mobile, AL*
The University of Montana–Missoula, MT
University of Montevallo, AL*
University of Nebraska at Omaha, NE*
University of Nebraska–Lincoln, NE
University of Nebraska Medical Center, NE*
University of Nevada, Reno, NV
University of New England, ME*
University of New Hampshire, NH
University of New Hampshire at Manchester, NH*
University of New Mexico, NM
University of New Orleans, LA*
University of North Alabama, AL
The University of North Carolina at Chapel Hill, NC
The University of North Carolina at Charlotte, NC
The University of North Carolina at Greensboro, NC*
The University of North Carolina at Pembroke, NC
University of North Dakota, ND
University of Northern Colorado, CO
University of Northern Iowa, IA
University of North Texas, TX*
University of Notre Dame, IN
University of Oklahoma, OK
University of Oregon, OR
University of Pennsylvania, PA
University of Pittsburgh, PA
University of Pittsburgh at Bradford, PA
University of Portland, OR
U of Puerto Rico at Arecibo, PR
U of Puerto Rico, Cayey University College, PR

program is offered at another college's campus

Army (continued)

U of Puerto Rico, Mayagüez Campus, PR
University of Puget Sound, WA*
University of Redlands, CA*
University of Rhode Island, RI
University of Richmond, VA
University of Rio Grande, OH*
University of Rochester, NY*
University of St. Thomas, MN*
University of St. Thomas, TX*
University of San Diego, CA*
University of San Francisco, CA
The University of Scranton, PA
University of South Alabama, AL
University of South Carolina, SC
U of South Carolina Spartanburg, SC*
University of South Dakota, SD
University of Southern California, CA
University of Southern Colorado, CO*
University of Southern Mississippi, MS
University of South Florida, FL
The University of Tampa, FL
The University of Tennessee at Chattanooga, TN
The University of Tennessee at Martin, TN
The University of Tennessee Knoxville, TN
The University of Texas at Arlington, TX
The University of Texas at Austin, TX
The University of Texas at Dallas, TX*
The University of Texas at El Paso, TX
The University of Texas at San Antonio, TX
U of Texas Health Science Center at San Antonio, TX*
U of Texas-Houston Health Science Center, TX*
The University of Texas–Pan American, TX
University of the District of Columbia, DC*
University of the Incarnate Word, TX*
University of the Sciences in Philadelphia, PA*
University of Toledo, OH
University of Utah, UT
University of Vermont, VT
University of Virginia, VA
University of Washington, WA
The University of West Alabama, AL*
University of West Florida, FL
University of Wisconsin–Green Bay, WI
University of Wisconsin–La Crosse, WI
University of Wisconsin–Madison, WI
University of Wisconsin–Oshkosh, WI
University of Wisconsin–Parkside, WI*
University of Wisconsin–Stevens Point, WI
University of Wisconsin–Whitewater, WI
University of Wyoming, WY
Ursuline College, OH*
Utica College of Syracuse University, NY*
Vanderbilt University, TN
Vanguard University of Southern California, CA*
Villa Julie College, MD*
Villanova University, PA
Virginia Commonwealth University, VA
Virginia Military Institute, VA
Virginia Polytechnic Institute and State U, VA
Virginia State University, VA
Virginia Union University, VA*
Virginia Wesleyan College, VA*
Viterbo University, WI*
Voorhees College, SC*
Wagner College, NY*
Wake Forest University, NC
Warner Pacific College, OR*
Washburn University of Topeka, KS
Washington & Jefferson College, PA*
Washington and Lee University, VA*
Washington State University, WA
Washington University in St. Louis, MO
Wayne State College, NE*
Wayne State University, MI*
Weber State University, UT
Wellesley College, MA*
Wentworth Institute of Technology, MA*
Wesleyan University, CT*
Wesley College, DE*
West Chester University of Pennsylvania, PA*
Western Baptist College, OR*
Western Carolina University, NC
Western Connecticut State University, CT*
Western Illinois University, IL
Western Kentucky University, KY
Western Maryland College, MD
Western Michigan University, MI
Western New England College, MA
Western Oregon University, OR
Westfield State College, MA*
Westminster College, MO*
Westminster College, PA*
Westminster College, UT*
Westmont College, CA*
West Virginia State College, WV
West Virginia University, WV
West Virginia University Institute of Technology, WV
Wheaton College, IL
Wheaton College, MA*
Whittier College, CA*
Whitworth College, WA*
Widener University, PA
Wilberforce University, OH*
Wilkes University, PA*
William Carey College, MS*
Williams Baptist College, AR*
Wilson College, PA*
Wingate University, NC*
Winona State University, MN*
Winston-Salem State University, NC
Wittenberg University, OH*
Wofford College, SC
Worcester Polytechnic Institute, MA
Worcester State College, MA*
Xavier University, OH
Yale University, CT*
York College, NE*
York College of the City University of New York, NY*
Youngstown State University, OH

NAVAL

Agnes Scott College, GA*
Alabama State University, AL
Albany College of Pharmacy of Union University, NY*
Armstrong Atlantic State University, GA
Art Academy of Cincinnati, OH*
Assumption College, MA*
Auburn University, AL
Augsburg College, MN*
Babson College, MA*
Becker College, MA*
Bethel College, MN*
Biola University, CA*
Boston College, MA*
Boston University, MA
Brigham Young University–Hawaii Campus, HI*
California Maritime Academy, CA*
Capitol College, MD*
Carlow College, PA*
Carnegie Mellon University, PA
The Catholic University of America, DC*
Chatham College, PA*
Chicago State University, IL*
Christian Brothers University, TN*
Citadel, The Military Coll of South Carolina, SC
Claremont McKenna College, CA*
Clark Atlanta University, GA
The College of Saint Rose, NY*
College of the Holy Cross, MA
Columbia College, MO*
Concordia University at St. Paul, MN*
Cornell University, NY
Dillard University, LA*
Dowling College, NY*
Drexel University, PA*
Duke University, NC
Eastern Michigan University, MI*
Florida Agricultural and Mechanical University, FL
Florida State University, FL*
Fordham University, NY*
Georgetown University, DC*
The George Washington University, DC
Georgia Institute of Technology, GA
Georgia State University, GA*
Green Mountain College, VT*
Hampton University, VA
Harvard University, MA*
Hillsdale College, MI*
Houston Baptist University, TX*
Husson College, ME*
Illinois Institute of Technology, IL
Indiana University South Bend, IN*
Inter American U of PR, San Germán Campus, PR*
Iowa State University of Science and Technology, IA
Jacksonville University, FL
John Jay Coll of Criminal Justice, the City U of NY, NY*
Lewis-Clark State College, ID*
Louisiana State University and A&M College, LA*
Loyola Marymount University, CA*
Loyola University Chicago, IL*
Loyola University New Orleans, LA*
Lubbock Christian University, TX*
Macalester College, MN*
Maine Maritime Academy, ME
Marquette University, WI
Mary Baldwin College, VA
Mass Coll of Pharmacy and Allied Health Sciences, MA*
Massachusetts Institute of Technology, MA
Miami University, OH
Mount St. Mary's College, CA*
Norfolk State University, VA
North Carolina Central University, NC*

**program is offered at another college's campus*

North Carolina State University, NC
North Central College, IL*
Northeastern Illinois University, IL*
Northeastern University, MA*
Northwestern University, IL
Norwich University, VT
Occidental College, CA*
The Ohio State University, OH
Old Dominion University, VA
Oregon State University, OR
Our Lady of Holy Cross College, LA*
Peace College, NC*
Penn State U Univ Park Campus, PA
Pepperdine University, CA*
Point Loma Nazarene University, CA*
Prairie View A&M University, TX
Purdue University, IN
Radford University, VA*
Regis University, CO*
Rensselaer Polytechnic Institute, NY
Rice University, TX
Rochester Institute of Technology, NY*
Saint Joseph's University, PA*
Saint Mary's College, IN*
Saint Mary's College of California, CA*
Samuel Merritt College, CA*
San Diego State University, CA
San Francisco State University, CA*
San Jose State University, CA*
Savannah State University, GA
School of the Museum of Fine Arts, MA*
Seattle Pacific University, WA*
Seattle University, WA*
Sonoma State University, CA*
Southern Polytechnic State University, GA*
Southern University and A&M College, LA
Stanford University, CA*
State U of NY College at Brockport, NY*
State U of NY College at Cortland, NY*
State U of NY Institute of Tech at Utica/Rome, NY*
State U of NY Maritime College, NY
Stephens College, MO*
Swarthmore College, PA*
Temple University, PA*
Tennessee State University, TN*
Texas A&M University, TX
Texas A&M University at Galveston, TX
Trinity College, DC*
Tufts University, MA*
Tulane University, LA
Union College, NY*
The University of Arizona, AZ
U of Calif, Berkeley, CA
U of Calif, Los Angeles, CA
U of Calif, Santa Cruz, CA*
University of Colorado at Boulder, CO
University of Florida, FL
University of Houston, TX*
University of Houston–Downtown, TX*
University of Idaho, ID
University of Illinois at Chicago, IL*
University of Illinois at Urbana–Champaign, IL
University of Kansas, KS
University of Maine, ME
University of Maryland, College Park, MD*
The University of Memphis, TN
University of Michigan, MI
University of Michigan–Dearborn, MI*
University of Minnesota, Twin Cities Campus, MN
University of Mississippi, MS
University of Missouri–Columbia, MO
University of Nebraska–Lincoln, NE
University of Nebraska Medical Center, NE*
The University of North Carolina at Chapel Hill, NC
University of North Florida, FL*
University of Notre Dame, IN
University of Oklahoma, OK
University of Pennsylvania, PA
University of Pittsburgh, PA*
University of Rochester, NY
University of St. Thomas, MN*
University of San Diego, CA
University of South Carolina, SC
University of Southern California, CA
The University of Texas at Austin, TX
University of Utah, UT
University of Virginia, VA
University of Washington, WA
University of Wisconsin–Madison, WI
Vanderbilt University, TN
Vanguard University of Southern California, CA*
Villanova University, PA
Virginia Military Institute, VA
Virginia Polytechnic Institute and State U, VA
Washington State University, WA
Weber State University, UT
Wesleyan University, CT*
Westminster College, UT*
Worcester Polytechnic Institute, MA*
Worcester State College, MA*
Xavier University of Louisiana, LA*
York College, NE*
York College of the City University of New York, NY*

AIR FORCE

Adelphi University, NY*
Agnes Scott College, GA*
Albany College of Pharmacy of Union University, NY*
Allentown College of St. Francis de Sales, PA*
Alverno College, WI*
American International College, MA*
American University, DC*
Anderson College, SC*
Angelo State University, TX
Aquinas College, TN*
Arizona State University, AZ
Arizona State University East, AZ*
Art Academy of Cincinnati, OH*
Asbury College, KY*
Ashland University, OH*
Assumption College, MA*
Auburn University, AL
Auburn University Montgomery, AL*
Augsburg College, MN*
Babson College, MA*
Baldwin-Wallace College, OH*
Barber-Scotia College, NC
Barry University, FL*
Bayamón Central University, PR*
Baylor University, TX
Bay Path College, MA*
Becker College, MA*
Bellarmine College, KY*
Bellevue University, NE*
Belmont Abbey College, NC*
Bennett College, NC*
Bethel College, IN*
Bethel College, MN*
Bethune-Cookman College, FL*
Biola University, CA*
Birmingham-Southern College, AL*
Bloomsburg University of Pennsylvania, PA*
Boston College, MA*
Boston University, MA
Bowling Green State University, OH
Brandeis University, MA*
Bridgewater State College, MA
Brigham Young University, UT
Brigham Young University–Hawaii Campus, HI*
Bryn Mawr College, PA*
Butler University, IN*
California Baptist University, CA*
California Institute of Technology, CA*
California Lutheran University, CA*
California State Polytechnic University, Pomona, CA*
California State University, Dominguez Hills, CA*
California State University, Fresno, CA
California State University, Los Angeles, CA*
California State University, Northridge, CA*
California State University, Sacramento, CA
California State University, San Bernardino, CA
California State University, San Marcos, CA*
Capitol College, MD*
Carlow College, PA*
Carnegie Mellon University, PA
Carson-Newman College, TN*
Carthage College, WI*
Cascade College, OR*
Case Western Reserve University, OH*
The Catholic University of America, DC*
Cedarville College, OH*
Central Connecticut State University, CT*
Central Washington University, WA
Centre College, KY*
Chaminade University of Honolulu, HI*
Chapman University, CA*
Charleston Southern University, SC
Chatham College, PA*
Cheyney University of Pennsylvania, PA*
Chicago State University, IL*
Christian Brothers University, TN*
Christian Heritage College, CA*
Citadel, The Military Coll of South Carolina, SC
City Coll of the City U of NY, NY*
Claremont McKenna College, CA*
Clarkson College, NE*
Clarkson University, NY
Clark University, MA*
Clearwater Christian College, FL*
Cleary College, MI*
Clemson University, SC
Cleveland Institute of Music, OH*
Coe College, IA*
Colby-Sawyer College, NH*
College Misericordia, PA*
College of Aeronautics, NY*
College of Charleston, SC*

program is offered at another college's campus

Air Force (continued)

College of Mount St. Joseph, OH*
College of Mount Saint Vincent, NY*
The College of New Jersey, NJ*
College of Our Lady of the Elms, MA*
College of St. Catherine, MN*
College of Saint Mary, NE*
The College of Saint Rose, NY*
The College of St. Scholastica, MN*
College of the Holy Cross, MA*
Colorado Christian University, CO*
Colorado State University, CO
Columbia College, MO*
Concordia College, MI*
Concordia College, MN*
Concordia University, OR*
Concordia University at Austin, TX*
Concordia University at St. Paul, MN*
Cornell University, NY
Creighton University, NE*
Dakota State University, SD*
Dallas Baptist University, TX*
Dana College, NE*
Daniel Webster College, NH*
David Lipscomb University, TN*
Davidson College, NC*
Delaware State University, DE
Delta State University, MS
DePauw University, IN*
DeVry Institute of Technology, AZ
Dillard University, LA*
Doane College, NE*
Dominican University of California, CA*
Dowling College, NY*
Drake University, IA*
Drexel University, PA*
Duke University, NC
Duquesne University, PA*
East Carolina University, NC
Eastern Connecticut State University, CT*
Eastern Kentucky University, KY*
Eastern Michigan University, MI*
East Stroudsburg University of Pennsylvania, PA*
Eckerd College, FL*
Elmhurst College, IL*
Elmira College, NY*
Embry-Riddle Aeronautical University, AZ
Embry-Riddle Aeronautical University, FL
Emory University, GA*
Fairleigh Dickinson U, Teaneck-Hackensack Campus, NJ*
Fairmont State College, WV*
Fayetteville State University, NC
Finlandia University, MI*
Fisk University, TN*
Florida Agricultural and Mechanical University, FL*
Florida Atlantic University, FL*
Florida College, FL*
Florida International University, FL
Florida Memorial College, FL*
Florida State University, FL
Fordham University, NY*
Franklin Pierce College, NH*
Franklin University, OH*
Free Will Baptist Bible College, TN*
George Fox University, OR*
George Mason University, VA*
Georgetown College, KY*
Georgetown University, DC*
The George Washington University, DC*
Georgia Institute of Technology, GA
Gordon College, MA*
Governors State University, IL*
Grambling State University, LA
Grand Canyon University, AZ*
Grand View College, IA*
Green Mountain College, VT*
Greensboro College, NC*
Guilford College, NC*
Hamilton College, NY*
Hamline University, MN*
Harris-Stowe State College, MO*
Harvard University, MA*
Harvey Mudd College, CA
Hawaii Pacific University, HI*
High Point University, NC*
Hillsdale College, MI*
Holy Names College, CA*
Huntingdon College, AL*
Illinois Institute of Technology, IL
Indiana State University, IN
Indiana University Bloomington, IN
Indiana U–Purdue U Indianapolis, IN*
Indiana University South Bend, IN*
Indiana University Southeast, IN*
Inter American U of PR, San Germán Campus, PR*
Iowa State University of Science and Technology, IA
Ithaca College, NY*
John Jay Coll of Criminal Justice, the City U of NY, NY*
Johns Hopkins University, MD*
Johnson C. Smith University, NC
Kansas State University, KS
Kean University, NJ*
Keene State College, NH*
Kennesaw State University, GA*
Kent State University, OH
King's College, PA*
Kutztown University of Pennsylvania, PA*
La Roche College, PA*
La Salle University, PA*
Lawrence Technological University, MI*
Le Moyne College, NY*
LeMoyne-Owen College, TN*
Lewis-Clark State College, ID
Lewis University, IL*
Lincoln University, PA*
Linfield College, OR*
Long Island U, C.W. Post Campus, NY*
Louisiana State University and A&M College, LA
Louisiana Tech University, LA
Loyola College in Maryland, MD*
Loyola Marymount University, CA
Loyola University Chicago, IL*
Loyola University New Orleans, LA*
Lubbock Christian University, TX*
Lyndon State College, VT
Macalester College, MN*
Manhattan College, NY
Maranatha Baptist Bible College, WI*
Marian College, IN*
Marquette University, WI
Mary Baldwin College, VA
Marywood University, PA*
Mass Coll of Pharmacy and Allied Health Sciences, MA*
Massachusetts Institute of Technology, MA
McKendree College, IL*
McMurry University, TX*
Mercy College, NY*
Meredith College, NC*
Merrimack College, MA*
Methodist College, NC*
Metropolitan State College of Denver, CO*
Miami University, OH
Michigan State University, MI
Michigan Technological University, MI
MidAmerica Nazarene University, KS*
Middle Tennessee State University, TN*
Miles College, AL*
Milwaukee School of Engineering, WI*
Minnesota State University Moorhead, MN*
Mississippi State University, MS
Mississippi University for Women, MS*
Mississippi Valley State University, MS
Montana State U–Bozeman, MT
Mount Holyoke College, MA*
Mount St. Mary's College, CA*
Mount Union College, OH*
National University, CA*
Nazareth College of Rochester, NY*
Nebraska Wesleyan University, NE*
New College of the University of South Florida, FL*
New Hampshire College, NH*
New Jersey Institute of Technology, NJ
New York Institute of Technology, NY
New York University, NY*
North Carolina Agricultural and Technical State U, NC
North Carolina Central University, NC*
North Carolina State University, NC
North Central College, IL*
North Dakota State University, ND
Northeastern Illinois University, IL*
Northeastern University, MA*
Northern Arizona University, AZ
Northern Illinois University, IL*
Northern Kentucky University, KY*
Northwestern College, MN*
Northwestern University, IL*
Norwich University, VT
Notre Dame College, NH*
Occidental College, CA*
Ohio Dominican College, OH*
Ohio Northern University, OH*
The Ohio State University, OH
Ohio University, OH
Ohio University–Chillicothe, OH*
Ohio University–Lancaster, OH*
Ohio Valley College, WV*
Oklahoma Baptist University, OK*
Oklahoma Christian U of Science and Arts, OK*
Oklahoma City University, OK*
Oklahoma State U, OK
Oregon State University, OR
Otterbein College, OH*
Our Lady of Holy Cross College, LA*
Our Lady of the Lake University of San Antonio, TX*
Pacific University, OR*
Peace College, NC*
Penn State U Abington College, PA*

**program is offered at another college's campus*

Penn State U Univ Park Campus, PA
Pepperdine University, CA*
Piedmont College, GA*
Plymouth State College, NH*
Point Loma Nazarene University, CA*
Point Park College, PA*
Polytechnic U, Brooklyn Campus, NY*
Portland State University, OR*
Princeton University, NJ*
Purdue University, IN
Queens College, NC*
Quinnipiac University, CT*
Regis University, CO*
Rensselaer Polytechnic Institute, NY
Rhodes College, TN*
Rider University, NJ*
Rivier College, NH*
Robert Morris College, PA*
Roberts Wesleyan College, NY*
Rochester Institute of Technology, NY
Rose-Hulman Institute of Technology, IN
Rosemont College, PA*
Russell Sage College, NY*
Rutgers, State U of NJ, Camden Coll of Arts & Scis, NJ*
Rutgers, State U of NJ, College of Nursing, NJ*
Rutgers, State U of NJ, College of Pharmacy, NJ
Rutgers, State U of NJ, Cook College, NJ
Rutgers, State U of NJ, Douglass College, NJ
Rutgers, State U of NJ, Livingston College, NJ
Rutgers, State U of NJ, Mason Gross School of Arts, NJ
Rutgers, State U of NJ, Newark Coll of Arts & Scis, NJ*
Rutgers, State U of NJ, Rutgers College, NJ
Rutgers, State U of NJ, College of Engineering, NJ
Rutgers, State U of NJ, U Coll–Camden, NJ*
Rutgers, State U of NJ, U Coll–Newark, NJ*
Rutgers, State U of NJ, U Coll–New Brunswick, NJ
Saint Anselm College, NH*
Saint Augustine's College, NC*
St. Edward's University, TX*
St. Francis College, NY*
St. Gregory's University, OK*
St. John Fisher College, NY*
St. Joseph's College, Suffolk Campus, NY*
Saint Joseph's University, PA
St. Lawrence University, NY*
Saint Leo University, FL*
Saint Louis University, MO
Saint Mary-of-the-Woods College, IN*
Saint Mary's College, IN*
Saint Mary's College of California, CA*
Saint Michael's College, VT*
Saint Peter's College, NJ*
St. Thomas Aquinas College, NY*
St. Thomas University, FL*
Saint Vincent College, PA*
Salisbury State University, MD*
Samford University, AL
Samuel Merritt College, CA*
San Diego State University, CA
San Francisco State University, CA*
San Jose State University, CA
Santa Clara University, CA*
School of the Museum of Fine Arts, MA*
Scripps College, CA*
Seattle Pacific University, WA*
Seattle University, WA*
Seton Hall University, NJ*
Shaw University, NC*
Shepherd College, WV*
Siena College, NY*
Skidmore College, NY*
Smith College, MA*
Sonoma State University, CA*
South Dakota State University, SD
Southeast Missouri State University, MO
Southern Connecticut State University, CT*
Southern Illinois University Carbondale, IL
Southern Illinois University Edwardsville, IL
Southern Methodist University, TX*
Southern Nazarene University, OK*
Southern Polytechnic State University, GA*
Southern University and A&M College, LA*
Southern University at New Orleans, LA*
Southern Wesleyan University, SC*
Southwest Texas State University, TX
Spalding University, KY*
Springfield College, MA*
Spring Hill College, AL*
Stanford University, CA*
State U of NY at Albany, NY*
State U of NY at Binghamton, NY*
State U of NY at Farmingdale, NY*
State U of NY College at Brockport, NY*
State U of NY College at Cortland, NY*
State U of NY College at Geneseo, NY*
State U of NY College at Potsdam, NY*
State U of NY Coll of Environ Sci and Forestry, NY*
State U of NY Institute of Tech at Utica/ Rome, NY*
State U of NY Maritime College, NY*
Stephens College, MO*
Stevens Institute of Technology, NJ*
Swarthmore College, PA*
Syracuse University, NY
Temple University, PA*
Tennessee State University, TN
Tennessee Technological University, TN*
Texas A&M University, TX
Texas Christian University, TX
Texas Lutheran University, TX*
Texas Tech University, TX
Texas Wesleyan University, TX*
Thomas Jefferson University, PA*
Thomas More College, KY*
Transylvania University, KY*
Trinity College, DC*
Trinity University, TX*
Troy State University, AL
Troy State University Montgomery, AL*
Tufts University, MA*
Tulane University, LA
Tuskegee University, AL
Union College, NY*
The University of Akron, OH
The University of Alabama, AL
The University of Alabama at Birmingham, AL*
The University of Alabama in Huntsville, AL
The University of Arizona, AZ
University of Arkansas, AR
U of Calif, Berkeley, CA
U of Calif, Davis, CA*
U of Calif, Irvine, CA*
U of Calif, Los Angeles, CA
U of Calif, Riverside, CA*
U of Calif, Santa Cruz, CA*
University of Central Florida, FL
University of Chicago, IL*
University of Cincinnati, OH
University of Colorado at Boulder, CO
University of Colorado at Denver, CO*
University of Connecticut, CT
University of Dallas, TX*
University of Dayton, OH*
University of Delaware, DE
The University of Findlay, OH*
University of Florida, FL
University of Georgia, GA
University of Hartford, CT*
University of Hawaii at Manoa, HI
University of Idaho, ID*
University of Illinois at Chicago, IL*
University of Illinois at Urbana–Champaign, IL
The University of Iowa, IA
University of Kansas, KS
University of Louisville, KY
University of Mary Hardin-Baylor, TX*
University of Maryland, Baltimore County, MD*
University of Maryland, College Park, MD
University of Massachusetts Amherst, MA
University of Massachusetts Lowell, MA
The University of Memphis, TN
University of Miami, FL
University of Michigan, MI
University of Michigan–Dearborn, MI*
University of Minnesota, Crookston, MN*
University of Minnesota, Duluth, MN
University of Minnesota, Twin Cities Campus, MN
University of Mississippi, MS
University of Missouri–Columbia, MO
University of Missouri–Rolla, MO
University of Missouri–St. Louis, MO*
University of Mobile, AL*
University of Montevallo, AL*
University of Nebraska at Omaha, NE
University of Nebraska–Lincoln, NE
University of Nebraska Medical Center, NE*
University of New Hampshire, NH
University of New Hampshire at Manchester, NH*
University of New Haven, CT*
University of New Mexico, NM
University of New Orleans, LA*
The University of North Carolina at Chapel Hill, NC
The University of North Carolina at Charlotte, NC
The University of North Carolina at Greensboro, NC*
The University of North Carolina at Pembroke, NC
University of North Dakota, ND
University of Northern Colorado, CO
University of North Texas, TX
University of Notre Dame, IN
University of Oklahoma, OK
University of Oregon, OR*
University of Pennsylvania, PA*

**program is offered at another college's campus*

Air Force (continued)

University of Pittsburgh, PA
University of Pittsburgh at Bradford, PA*
University of Portland, OR
U of Puerto Rico, Mayagüez Campus, PR
University of Redlands, CA*
University of Rochester, NY*
University of St. Thomas, MN
University of San Diego, CA*
University of San Francisco, CA*
The University of Scranton, PA*
University of South Alabama, AL
University of South Carolina, SC
University of Southern California, CA
University of Southern Maine, ME*
University of Southern Mississippi, MS
University of South Florida, FL
The University of Tampa, FL*
The University of Tennessee Knoxville, TN
The University of Texas at Arlington, TX*
The University of Texas at Austin, TX
The University of Texas at Dallas, TX*
The University of Texas at El Paso, TX
The University of Texas at San Antonio, TX
U of Texas Health Science Center at San Antonio, TX*
University of the District of Columbia, DC*
University of the Incarnate Word, TX*
University of the Pacific, CA*
University of Toledo, OH*
University of Utah, UT
University of Virginia, VA
University of Washington, WA
The University of West Alabama, AL*
University of West Florida, FL
University of Wisconsin–Madison, WI
University of Wisconsin–Superior, WI*
University of Wisconsin–Whitewater, WI
University of Wyoming, WY
Utah State University, UT
Utica College of Syracuse University, NY
Valdosta State University, GA
Vanderbilt University, TN*
Vanguard University of Southern California, CA*
Villanova University, PA*
Virginia Military Institute, VA
Virginia Polytechnic Institute and State U, VA
Wagner College, NY*
Warner Pacific College, OR*
Washburn University of Topeka, KS*
Washington State University, WA
Washington University in St. Louis, MO*
Wayne State University, MI*
Weber State University, UT
Wellesley College, MA*
Wells College, NY*
Wentworth Institute of Technology, MA*
Wesleyan University, CT*
West Chester University of Pennsylvania, PA*
Western Baptist College, OR*
Western Connecticut State University, CT*
Western Kentucky University, KY*
Western Maryland College, MD*
Western New England College, MA
Western Oregon University, OR*
Westminster College, MO*
Westminster College, UT*
Westmont College, CA*
West Virginia University, WV
Wheaton College, IL*
Whittier College, CA*
Widener University, PA*
Wilberforce University, OH*
Wilkes University, PA
Willamette University, OR*
William Carey College, MS*
William Paterson University of New Jersey, NJ*
Wingate University, NC*
Wittenberg University, OH*
Worcester Polytechnic Institute, MA
Worcester State College, MA*
Xavier University, OH*
Xavier University of Louisiana, LA*
Yale University, CT*
York College, NE*
York College of the City University of New York, NY*

**program is offered at another college's campus*

TUITION WAIVERS

This index lists the colleges that report offering tuition waivers for certain categories of students. For each college listed in this index, refer to the *Other Money-Saving Options* section of the college's profile for specific information on whether a full or partial tuition waiver is offered. A majority of colleges offer tuition waivers to employees or children of employees. Because this benefit is so common and the affected employees usually are aware of it, no separate index of schools offering this option is provided. However, this information is included in the individual college profiles.

Within each category, the colleges are arranged alphabetically by school name. These are the categories and their order: Minority Students, Children of Alumni, Adult Students, Senior Citizens.

MINORITY STUDENTS

Alabama Agricultural and Mechanical University, AL
Assumption College, MA
Bloomsburg University of Pennsylvania, PA
Bridgewater College, VA
California State University, Fullerton, CA
Campbellsville University, KY
Carlos Albizu University, FL
Clarkson College, NE
Columbia U, School of Engineering & Applied Sci, NY
Crichton College, TN
The Culinary Institute of America, NY
David Lipscomb University, TN
Dickinson State University, ND
Dowling College, NY
D'Youville College, NY
Fort Lewis College, CO
George Fox University, OR
Hellenic College, MA
Huntington College, IN
Illinois State University, IL
Indiana University of Pennsylvania, PA
John Brown University, AR
Kentucky Christian College, KY
Lake Superior State University, MI
Lock Haven University of Pennsylvania, PA
Mary Washington College, VA
Mayville State University, ND
Messiah College, PA
Minot State University, ND
Mississippi University for Women, MS
Montana State U–Bozeman, MT
Montana State U–Northern, MT
Montana Tech of The University of Montana, MT
Newman University, KS
North Dakota State University, ND
Northern Illinois University, IL
Oakland City University, IN
Oklahoma State U, OK
Polytechnic U, Brooklyn Campus, NY
Portland State University, OR
St. Ambrose University, IA
Saint Joseph's College, IN
Saint Mary College, KS
Saint Mary-of-the-Woods College, IN
St. Thomas University, FL
Salem State College, MA
Shasta Bible College, CA
Shepherd College, WV
Shimer College, IL
Slippery Rock University of Pennsylvania, PA
State U of NY at Stony Brook, NY
State University of West Georgia, GA
Stonehill College, MA
Teikyo Post University, CT
Tennessee State University, TN
Tennessee Wesleyan College, TN
Union College, KY
The University of Arizona, AZ
University of Hawaii at Manoa, HI
University of Maine at Farmington, ME
University of Maine at Presque Isle, ME
University of Michigan–Flint, MI
University of Minnesota, Morris, MN
University of Missouri–Rolla, MO
The University of Montana–Missoula, MT
University of New Hampshire, NH
University of Oregon, OR
University of Rhode Island, RI
University of Southern Maine, ME
University of Toledo, OH
University of Wisconsin–Eau Claire, WI
University of Wisconsin–La Crosse, WI
University of Wisconsin–Parkside, WI
University of Wisconsin–Superior, WI
Utah State University, UT
Viterbo University, WI
Western Montana College of The U of Montana, MT
Western Oregon University, OR
Xavier University, OH

CHILDREN OF ALUMNI

Albertson College of Idaho, ID
Anna Maria College, MA
Aquinas College, MI
Arkansas State University, AR
Auburn University, AL
Augsburg College, MN
Avila College, MO
Baldwin-Wallace College, OH
Benedictine University, IL
Birmingham-Southern College, AL
Brescia University, KY
Cabrini College, PA
Carthage College, WI
Central Christian College of the Bible, MO
Central Missouri State University, MO
Centre College, KY
Chapman University, CA
Christian Brothers University, TN
Clarke College, IA
Coe College, IA
College of Visual Arts, MN
Columbia College, MO
Crichton College, TN
Culver-Stockton College, MO
Curry College, MA
Daemen College, NY
Delta State University, MS
Detroit College of Business, MI
Detroit College of Business–Flint, MI
Detroit College of Business, Warren Campus, MI
Dominican University, IL
Dordt College, IA
Dowling College, NY
Drake University, IA
D'Youville College, NY
Erskine College, SC
Eureka College, IL
Grace University, NE
Greenville College, IL
Hellenic College, MA
Hillsdale Free Will Baptist College, OK
Huntington College, IN
Huron University, SD
Kansas Wesleyan University, KS
Kentucky Wesleyan College, KY
Lake Superior State University, MI
Lancaster Bible College, PA
Lasell College, MA
Lewis University, IL
LIFE Bible College, CA
Long Island U, Southampton College, NY
Loras College, IA
Louisiana State University and A&M College, LA
Louisiana Tech University, LA
MacMurray College, IL
Maharishi University of Management, IA
Maranatha Baptist Bible College, WI
Marian College, IN
Marymount University, VA
Mercy College, NY
Messiah College, PA
Michigan Technological University, MI
Middlebury College, VT
Minneapolis College of Art and Design, MN
Mississippi State University, MS

Children of Alumni (continued)

Mississippi University for Women, MS
Mississippi Valley State University, MS
Missouri Baptist College, MO
Missouri Valley College, MO
Morningside College, IA
Mount St. Clare College, IA
Mount Union College, OH
Murray State University, KY
Newman University, KS
Northern Michigan University, MI
Northwestern State University of Louisiana, LA
Northwood University, MI
Northwood University, Florida Campus, FL
Northwood University, Texas Campus, TX
Notre Dame College, NH
Ohio Wesleyan University, OH
Oklahoma State U, OK
Oral Roberts University, OK
Paine College, GA
Peirce College, PA
Philadelphia College of Bible, PA
Piedmont Baptist College, NC
Pine Manor College, MA
Practical Bible College, NY
Reinhardt College, GA
Ripon College, WI
Rochester College, MI
Rockhurst University, MO
St. Ambrose University, IA
Saint Francis College, PA
Saint Joseph's College, IN
Saint Mary-of-the-Woods College, IN
St. Thomas University, FL
Shasta Bible College, CA
Sheldon Jackson College, AK
Shimer College, IL
Siena Heights University, MI
Southeastern Bible College, AL
Southern Arkansas University–Magnolia, AR
Southern University and A&M College, LA
Southwestern Oklahoma State University, OK
Spalding University, KY
Tabor College, KS
Thomas More College, KY
Toccoa Falls College, GA
Union College, KY
U of Alaska Fairbanks, AK
University of Detroit Mercy, MI
University of Dubuque, IA
University of Louisiana at Monroe, LA
University of Maine at Presque Isle, ME
University of Mississippi, MS
University of Missouri–Rolla, MO
University of Nevada, Las Vegas, NV
University of Nevada, Reno, NV
University of Oklahoma, OK
University of Rochester, NY
University of St. Francis, IL
University of Saint Francis, IN
University of South Dakota, SD
University of Southern Mississippi, MS
The University of the Arts, PA
University of Wisconsin–Superior, WI
University of Wyoming, WY
Urbana University, OH
Utah State University, UT
Valley City State University, ND
Walsh University, OH
Warner Pacific College, OR
Washington State University, WA
Webber College, FL
Wesleyan College, GA
Western Kentucky University, KY
Westminster College, PA
Whittier College, CA
Whitworth College, WA
Wilkes University, PA
Wilson College, PA
Wittenberg University, OH
Xavier University, OH

ADULT STUDENTS

Albertson College of Idaho, ID
Anderson College, SC
Anderson University, IN
Augustana College, SD
Barton College, NC
Beloit College, WI
Berry College, GA
Bethel College, IN
Bluefield College, VA
Briar Cliff College, IA
Carlow College, PA
Clarke College, IA
Coe College, IA
Coker College, SC
Colby College, ME
College of the Atlantic, ME
The College of West Virginia, WV
Columbia Union College, MD
Converse College, SC
Cornell College, IA
Creighton University, NE
Crichton College, TN
Culver-Stockton College, MO
Dowling College, NY
Drury University, MO
Duquesne University, PA
D'Youville College, NY
Emmanuel College, GA
Faulkner University, AL
Goucher College, MD
Hamilton College, NY
Hastings College, NE
Hillsdale Free Will Baptist College, OK
Huntington College, IN
John Brown University, AR
Juniata College, PA
Lambuth University, TN
Lancaster Bible College, PA
Lynchburg College, VA
Medaille College, NY
Messiah College, PA
Mississippi University for Women, MS
Mount Union College, OH
Nebraska Wesleyan University, NE
Piedmont Baptist College, NC
Pine Manor College, MA
Randolph-Macon Woman's College, VA
Regis University, CO
St. Ambrose University, IA
St. Andrews Presbyterian College, NC
Saint Mary College, KS
Saint Mary's College, IN
Simmons College, MA
Southern Adventist University, TN
State University of West Georgia, GA
Sweet Briar College, VA
Tabor College, KS
Tougaloo College, MS
Trinity College, CT
University of Hawaii at Manoa, HI
University of La Verne, CA
University of Maine at Presque Isle, ME
University of Wisconsin–Superior, WI
Utah State University, UT
Valley Forge Christian College, PA
Washington College, MD
Webber College, FL
Westminster College, PA
Wittenberg University, OH

SENIOR CITIZENS

Albany State University, GA
Albertson College of Idaho, ID
Albertus Magnus College, CT
Albright College, PA
Alvernia College, PA
American International College, MA
American University, DC
Anderson College, SC
Andrews University, MI
Angelo State University, TX
Anna Maria College, MA
Appalachian State University, NC
Arkansas State University, AR
Arkansas Tech University, AR
Armstrong Atlantic State University, GA
Asbury College, KY
Ashland University, OH
Atlanta Christian College, GA
Atlantic Union College, MA
Augsburg College, MN
Augustana College, SD
Augusta State University, GA
Aurora University, IL
Austin Peay State University, TN
Avila College, MO
Baker University, KS
Baltimore Hebrew University, MD
Bartlesville Wesleyan College, OK
Becker College, MA
Belhaven College, MS
Bellarmine College, KY
Belmont Abbey College, NC
Belmont University, TN
Beloit College, WI
Bemidji State University, MN
Benedictine College, KS
Baruch Coll of the City U of NY, NY
Berry College, GA
Bethel College, KS
Bethel College, MN
Black Hills State University, SD
Bloomfield College, NJ
Bluefield College, VA
Bluefield State College, WV
Boise State University, ID
Boston University, MA
Bowie State University, MD
Bowling Green State University, OH
Bradley University, IL
Brescia University, KY
Briar Cliff College, IA
Briarcliffe College, NY
Bryn Mawr College, PA
Burlington College, VT

Cabrini College, PA
Caldwell College, NJ
California Polytechnic State U, San Luis Obispo, CA
California State Polytechnic University, Pomona, CA
California State University, Bakersfield, CA
California State University, Chico, CA
California State University, Fresno, CA
California State University, Hayward, CA
California State University, Long Beach, CA
California State University, Northridge, CA
California State University, Sacramento, CA
California State University, San Marcos, CA
California State University, Stanislaus, CA
Calumet College of Saint Joseph, IN
Cameron University, OK
Campbellsville University, KY
Capital University, OH
Carroll College, MT
Carson-Newman College, TN
Castleton State College, VT
Cedarville College, OH
Centenary College, NJ
Central Bible College, MO
Central Connecticut State University, CT
Central Michigan University, MI
Central Missouri State University, MO
Central Washington University, WA
Chadron State College, NE
Champlain College, VT
Chicago State University, IL
Chowan College, NC
Christopher Newport University, VA
Circleville Bible College, OH
Citadel, The Military Coll of South Carolina, SC
City Coll of the City U of NY, NY
Clarion University of Pennsylvania, PA
Clarke College, IA
Clayton College & State University, GA
Cleary College, MI
Clemson University, SC
Cleveland College of Jewish Studies, OH
Coastal Carolina University, SC
Colby College, ME
College of Charleston, SC
College of Mount St. Joseph, OH
College of Mount Saint Vincent, NY
The College of New Jersey, NJ
The College of New Rochelle, NY
College of Our Lady of the Elms, MA
College of St. Catherine, MN
College of Saint Elizabeth, NJ
College of St. Joseph, VT
College of Saint Mary, NE
The College of St. Scholastica, MN
Coll of Staten Island of the City U of NY, NY
The College of William and Mary, VA
Columbia College, MO
Columbia Union College, MD
Columbus College of Art and Design, OH
Columbus State University, GA
Concordia College, NY
Concordia University, OR
Concordia University at St. Paul, MN
Converse College, SC
Cornell College, IA
Covenant College, GA
Culver-Stockton College, MO
Cumberland University, TN
Curry College, MA
Daemen College, NY
Dakota State University, SD
Dakota Wesleyan University, SD
Dalton State College, GA
Daniel Webster College, NH
Davenport College of Business, Lansing Campus, MI
Defiance College, OH
Delaware State University, DE
Delta State University, MS
Dickinson State University, ND
Doane College, NE
Dominican College of Blauvelt, NY
Dordt College, IA
Dowling College, NY
Drake University, IA
Drew University, NJ
Drexel University, PA
Drury University, MO
Duquesne University, PA
East Carolina University, NC
East Central University, OK
Eastern Connecticut State University, CT
East Stroudsburg University of Pennsylvania, PA
East Tennessee State University, TN
Edinboro University of Pennsylvania, PA
Elmhurst College, IL
Emmanuel College, GA
Emporia State University, KS
Endicott College, MA
Eugene Bible College, OR
Fairleigh Dickinson U, Florham-Madison Campus, NJ
Fairleigh Dickinson U, Teaneck-Hackensack Campus, NJ
Fayetteville State University, NC
Felician College, NJ
Ferrum College, VA
Fitchburg State College, MA
Five Towns College, NY
Florida Agricultural and Mechanical University, FL
Florida Gulf Coast University, FL
Florida Institute of Technology, FL
Florida International University, FL
Florida State University, FL
Fontbonne College, MO
Fort Hays State University, KS
Fort Valley State University, GA
Framingham State College, MA
Francis Marion University, SC
Franklin College of Indiana, IN
Franklin Pierce College, NH
Fresno Pacific University, CA
Friends University, KS
Frostburg State University, MD
Gannon University, PA
George Fox University, OR
George Mason University, VA
Georgia College and State University, GA
Georgian Court College, NJ
Georgia Southern University, GA
Georgia Southwestern State University, GA
Georgia State University, GA
Gonzaga University, WA
Governors State University, IL
Grace Bible College, MI
Graceland College, IA
Grace University, NE
Grambling State University, LA
Grand View College, IA
Greenville College, IL
Gustavus Adolphus College, MN
Hannibal-LaGrange College, MO
Hanover College, IN
Harding University, AR
Henderson State University, AR
Heritage College, WA
Hilbert College, NY
Hillsdale Free Will Baptist College, OK
Hofstra University, NY
Hood College, MD
Hope International University, CA
Houghton College, NY
Houston Baptist University, TX
Howard Payne University, TX
Humboldt State University, CA
Hunter Coll of the City U of NY, NY
Huntington College, IN
Husson College, ME
Idaho State University, ID
Illinois State University, IL
Immaculata College, PA
Indiana University Northwest, IN
Indiana U–Purdue U Fort Wayne, IN
Iona College, NY
Jacksonville State University, AL
James Madison University, VA
Jewish Theological Seminary of America, NY
John Brown University, AR
Johnson State College, VT
Judson College, IL
Kansas Wesleyan University, KS
Kean University, NJ
Kennesaw State University, GA
Kentucky Wesleyan College, KY
King's College, PA
Lake Erie College, OH
Lakeland College, WI
Lake Superior State University, MI
Lamar University, TX
Lambuth University, TN
Lancaster Bible College, PA
Lander University, SC
La Roche College, PA
Lehigh University, PA
Lehman Coll of the City U of NY, NY
Lewis-Clark State College, ID
Lincoln Memorial University, TN
Lincoln University, MO
Linfield College, OR
Long Island U, Brooklyn Campus, NY
Long Island U, Southampton College, NY
Longwood College, VA
Loras College, IA
Louisiana College, LA
Louisiana State University and A&M College, LA
Louisiana State University in Shreveport, LA
Louisiana Tech University, LA
Lourdes College, OH
Loyola University New Orleans, LA
Lynchburg College, VA
Lyndon State College, VT
MacMurray College, IL
Macon State College, GA

Senior Citizens (continued)

Maharishi University of Management, IA
Malone College, OH
Manhattan Christian College, KS
Manhattanville College, NY
Mansfield University of Pennsylvania, PA
Marian College, IN
Marian College of Fond du Lac, WI
Marlboro College, VT
Marquette University, WI
Marymount Manhattan College, NY
Marymount University, VA
Maryville University of Saint Louis, MO
Marywood University, PA
Massachusetts College of Art, MA
Massachusetts College of Liberal Arts, MA
Mayville State University, ND
McNeese State University, LA
McPherson College, KS
Medaille College, NY
Medical College of Georgia, GA
Medical University of South Carolina, SC
Mercy College, NY
Merrimack College, MA
Mesa State College, CO
Messiah College, PA
Methodist College, NC
Metropolitan State College of Denver, CO
Metropolitan State University, MN
Michigan Technological University, MI
MidAmerica Nazarene University, KS
Middle Tennessee State University, TN
Midland Lutheran College, NE
Midway College, KY
Millersville University of Pennsylvania, PA
Minnesota Bible College, MN
Minnesota State University, Mankato, MN
Minnesota State University Moorhead, MN
Mississippi State University, MS
Missouri Baptist College, MO
Missouri Southern State College, MO
Missouri Valley College, MO
Missouri Western State College, MO
Monmouth University, NJ
Montana State U–Billings, MT
Montana State U–Bozeman, MT
Montana State U–Northern, MT
Montana Tech of The University of Montana, MT
Montclair State University, NJ
Montreat College, NC
Morehead State University, KY
Morgan State University, MD
Morningside College, IA
Mount Mary College, WI
Mount Olive College, NC
Mount St. Clare College, IA
Mount Union College, OH
Murray State University, KY
Muskingum College, OH
Nebraska Wesleyan University, NE
New Hampshire College, NH
Newman University, KS
New Mexico Highlands University, NM
New Mexico Institute of Mining and Technology, NM
New York Institute of Technology, NY
North Carolina State University, NC
North Carolina Wesleyan College, NC
North Central College, IL
North Dakota State University, ND
Northeastern Illinois University, IL
Northeastern University, MA
Northern Kentucky University, KY
Northern Michigan University, MI
North Georgia College & State University, GA
Northwest College, WA
Northwestern College, MN
Northwestern Oklahoma State University, OK
Northwest Missouri State University, MO
Ohio Dominican College, OH
The Ohio State University, OH
Ohio University–Chillicothe, OH
Ohio University–Zanesville, OH
Ohio Valley College, WV
Ohio Wesleyan University, OH
Oklahoma Baptist University, OK
Old Dominion University, VA
Oregon Institute of Technology, OR
Ottawa University, KS
Ozark Christian College, MO
Pacific Lutheran University, WA
Pacific Union College, CA
Paier College of Art, Inc., CT
Palm Beach Atlantic College, FL
Park University, MO
Penn State U Abington College, PA
Penn State U Altoona College, PA
Penn State U at Erie, The Behrend College, PA
Penn State U Berks Cmps of Berks-Lehigh Valley Coll, PA
Penn State U Harrisburg Campus of the Capital Coll, PA
Penn State U Lehigh Valley Cmps of Berks-Lehigh Valley Coll, PA
Penn State U Schuylkill Campus of the Capital Coll, PA
Penn State U Univ Park Campus, PA
Pikeville College, KY
Plattsburgh State U of NY, NY
Plymouth State College, NH
Point Loma Nazarene University, CA
Point Park College, PA
Portland State University, OR
Presbyterian College, SC
Presentation College, SD
Puget Sound Christian College, WA
Purchase College, State U of NY, NY
Purdue University, IN
Purdue University Calumet, IN
Purdue University North Central, IN
Queens Coll of the City U of NY, NY
Quincy University, IL
Quinnipiac University, CT
Ramapo College of New Jersey, NJ
Regis University, CO
Reinhardt College, GA
Research College of Nursing, MO
The Richard Stockton College of New Jersey, NJ
Rivier College, NH
Roanoke Bible College, NC
Roanoke College, VA
Robert Morris College, PA
Rochester College, MI
Rockhurst University, MO
Rosemont College, PA
Russell Sage College, NY
Sacred Heart University, CT
St. Ambrose University, IA
Saint Anselm College, NH
St. Bonaventure University, NY
St. Gregory's University, OK
St. John Fisher College, NY
St. John's University, NY
Saint Joseph College, CT
Saint Joseph's College, ME
St. Joseph's College, Suffolk Campus, NY
Saint Mary's College, IN
St. Mary's College of Maryland, MD
St. Thomas Aquinas College, NY
Saint Vincent College, PA
Saint Xavier University, IL
Salem State College, MA
Salem-Teikyo University, WV
Salisbury State University, MD
San Diego State University, CA
San Jose State University, CA
Savannah State University, GA
Seattle Pacific University, WA
Seton Hall University, NJ
Shawnee State University, OH
Shimer College, IL
Shippensburg University of Pennsylvania, PA
Shorter College, GA
Siena College, NY
Siena Heights University, MI
Silver Lake College, WI
Simmons College, MA
Slippery Rock University of Pennsylvania, PA
South Dakota School of Mines and Technology, SD
South Dakota State University, SD
Southeastern Louisiana University, LA
Southeast Missouri State University, MO
Southern Adventist University, TN
Southern Arkansas University–Magnolia, AR
Southern Connecticut State University, CT
Southern Illinois University Carbondale, IL
Southern Nazarene University, OK
Southern Oregon University, OR
Southern Polytechnic State University, GA
Southern Utah University, UT
Southern Vermont College, VT
Southern Wesleyan University, SC
Southwestern College, KS
Southwestern Oklahoma State University, OK
Southwest Missouri State University, MO
Southwest State University, MN
Spalding University, KY
Spring Arbor College, MI
State U of NY at Albany, NY
State U of NY at Farmingdale, NY
State U of NY College at Brockport, NY
State University of West Georgia, GA
Sterling College, KS
Stonehill College, MA
Suffolk University, MA
Sweet Briar College, VA
Tabor College, KS
Tarleton State University, TX
Taylor University, Fort Wayne Campus, IN
Teikyo Post University, CT
Texas A&M International University, TX
Texas A&M University–Commerce, TX
Texas A&M University–Kingsville, TX
Texas A&M University–Texarkana, TX

Texas Woman's University, TX
Thiel College, PA
Thomas University, GA
Toccoa Falls College, GA
Tougaloo College, MS
Towson University, MD
Trevecca Nazarene University, TN
Trinity Christian College, IL
Trinity College of Florida, FL
Trinity College of Vermont, VT
Trinity Lutheran College, WA
Tri-State University, IN
Troy State University Dothan, AL
Truman State University, MO
Union College, KY
Union College, NE
Union College, NY
The University of Akron, OH
U of Alaska Fairbanks, AK
University of Arkansas, AR
University of Arkansas at Little Rock, AR
University of Arkansas at Monticello, AR
University of Arkansas at Pine Bluff, AR
University of Baltimore, MD
University of Bridgeport, CT
U of Calif, Santa Cruz, CA
University of Central Arkansas, AR
University of Central Florida, FL
University of Charleston, WV
University of Colorado at Boulder, CO
University of Dayton, OH
University of Delaware, DE
University of Detroit Mercy, MI
University of Dubuque, IA
The University of Findlay, OH
University of Florida, FL
University of Georgia, GA
University of Great Falls, MT
University of Hartford, CT
University of Hawaii–West Oahu, HI
University of Houston–Clear Lake, TX
University of Houston–Downtown, TX
University of Houston–Victoria, TX
University of Illinois at Chicago, IL
University of Illinois at Urbana–Champaign, IL
University of Indianapolis, IN
University of Kansas, KS
University of Louisiana at Lafayette, LA
University of Louisiana at Monroe, LA
University of Louisville, KY
The University of Maine at Augusta, ME
University of Maine at Farmington, ME
University of Maine at Fort Kent, ME
University of Maine at Machias, ME
University of Maine at Presque Isle, ME
University of Mary, ND
University of Maryland, Baltimore County, MD
University of Maryland, College Park, MD
University of Maryland University College, MD
University of Massachusetts Amherst, MA
University of Massachusetts Boston, MA
University of Massachusetts Dartmouth, MA
University of Massachusetts Lowell, MA
The University of Memphis, TN
University of Michigan, MI
University of Michigan–Dearborn, MI
University of Michigan–Flint, MI
University of Minnesota, Crookston, MN
University of Minnesota, Duluth, MN
University of Minnesota, Twin Cities Campus, MN
University of Mississippi, MS
The University of Montana–Missoula, MT
University of Montevallo, AL
University of Nevada, Las Vegas, NV
University of Nevada, Reno, NV
University of New Hampshire, NH
University of New Hampshire at Manchester, NH
University of New Haven, CT
University of New Mexico, NM
University of New Orleans, LA
The University of North Carolina at Asheville, NC
The University of North Carolina at Chapel Hill, NC
The University of North Carolina at Charlotte, NC
The University of North Carolina at Greensboro, NC
The University of North Carolina at Pembroke, NC
The University of North Carolina at Wilmington, NC
University of North Dakota, ND
University of North Florida, FL
University of North Texas, TX
University of Oklahoma, OK
University of Pittsburgh, PA
University of Rhode Island, RI
University of Saint Francis, IN
University of St. Thomas, MN
University of St. Thomas, TX
University of Science and Arts of Oklahoma, OK
The University of Scranton, PA
University of South Carolina, SC
University of South Carolina Aiken, SC
U of South Carolina Spartanburg, SC
University of South Dakota, SD
University of Southern Colorado, CO
University of Southern Indiana, IN
University of Southern Maine, ME
University of Southern Mississippi, MS
University of South Florida, FL
The University of Tennessee at Chattanooga, TN
The University of Tennessee at Martin, TN
The University of Tennessee Knoxville, TN
The University of Texas at Dallas, TX
University of the District of Columbia, DC
University of the Virgin Islands, VI
University of Toledo, OH
University of Utah, UT
University of Vermont, VT
University of Virginia, VA
University of Virginia's College at Wise, VA
University of West Florida, FL
University of Wisconsin–Eau Claire, WI
University of Wisconsin–Green Bay, WI
University of Wisconsin–La Crosse, WI
University of Wyoming, WY
Urbana University, OH
Ursinus College, PA
Utah State University, UT
Utica College of Syracuse University, NY
Valdosta State University, GA
Virginia Commonwealth University, VA
Virginia State University, VA
Virginia Wesleyan College, VA
Viterbo University, WI
Wagner College, NY
Walla Walla College, WA
Walsh University, OH
Warner Southern College, FL
Wartburg College, IA
Washington State University, WA
Wayne State University, MI
Webber College, FL
Weber State University, UT
Wells College, NY
Wesleyan College, GA
Wesley College, DE
Wesley College, MS
West Chester University of Pennsylvania, PA
Western Carolina University, NC
Western Connecticut State University, CT
Western Illinois University, IL
Western Kentucky University, KY
Western Michigan University, MI
Western Montana College of The U of Montana, MT
Western New England College, MA
Western New Mexico University, NM
Western State College of Colorado, CO
Western Washington University, WA
Westfield State College, MA
West Texas A&M University, TX
Wheeling Jesuit University, WV
Wichita State University, KS
Widener University, PA
Wilkes University, PA
William Jewell College, MO
William Penn University, IA
Williams Baptist College, AR
William Tyndale College, MI
Winona State University, MN
Winston-Salem State University, NC
Winthrop University, SC
Wittenberg University, OH
Worcester State College, MA
Xavier University, OH
Xavier University of Louisiana, LA
Youngstown State University, OH

TUITION PAYMENT ALTERNATIVES

This index lists the colleges that report offering alternative tuition payment plans. *D* (deferred) indicates that a system of deferred payments is a possible option. *G* (guaranteed) indicates that the college offers a plan that guarantees that the tuition rate of an entering student will not increase during the student's entire term of enrollment, from entrance to graduation. *I* (installment) indicates that the school has a plan to permit payment of the tuition in planned installments. *P* (prepayment) means that an entering student may lock in the current tuition rate for the entire term of enrollment by paying the full amount in advance rather than year-by-year.

College	Plans
Abilene Christian University, TX	I,P
Academy of Art College, CA	I
Adams State College, CO	D,I
Adelphi University, NY	D,I,P
Adrian College, MI	I
Agnes Scott College, GA	D,I
Alabama Agricultural and Mechanical University, AL	D
Alabama State University, AL	D,I
Alaska Bible College, AK	I
Albany College of Pharmacy of Union University, NY	I
Albertson College of Idaho, ID	I
Albertus Magnus College, CT	I
Albion College, MI	D
Albright College, PA	I
Al Collins Graphic Design School, AZ	D,I,P
Alfred University, NY	D,I,P
Alice Lloyd College, KY	I
Allegheny College, PA	I,P
Allen College, IA	I
Allentown College of St. Francis de Sales, PA	D,I
Alma College, MI	D,I
Alvernia College, PA	D,I
Alverno College, WI	D,I
American InterContinental University, CA	D,I
American International College, MA	D,I,P
American University, DC	D,I,P
American University of Puerto Rico, PR	G
Amherst College, MA	D,I
Anderson College, SC	I
Anderson University, IN	I
Andrews University, MI	I
Angelo State University, TX	I
Anna Maria College, MA	G,I
Antioch College, OH	I
Antioch Southern California/Santa Barbara, CA	I
Antioch University Seattle, WA	I
Appalachian Bible College, WV	I
Appalachian State University, NC	I
Aquinas College, MI	D,I
Aquinas College, TN	I
Arizona State University West, AZ	I
Arkansas State University, AR	I
Arkansas Tech University, AR	D
Arlington Baptist College, TX	D,I
Art Academy of Cincinnati, OH	I
Art Center College of Design, CA	I
The Art Institute of Colorado, CO	G,I
The Art Institute of Portland, OR	G,I
Art Institute of Southern California, CA	I
Art Institutes International at San Francisco, CA	G,I
Asbury College, KY	D,I
Ashland University, OH	I
Assumption College, MA	I
Atlanta Christian College, GA	I
Atlantic Union College, MA	I
Auburn University Montgomery, AL	D
Audrey Cohen College, NY	G,I
Augsburg College, MN	D,I
Augustana College, IL	I,P
Augustana College, SD	I
Aurora University, IL	D,I
Austin College, TX	I
Austin Peay State University, TN	D,I
Avila College, MO	D,G,I
Azusa Pacific University, CA	I
Babson College, MA	I
Baker University, KS	I
Baldwin-Wallace College, OH	D,I
Ball State University, IN	I
Baltimore Hebrew University, MD	I
Baptist Bible College of Pennsylvania, PA	I
Baptist Missionary Assoc Theol Sem, TX	I
Barat College, IL	D
Barber-Scotia College, NC	I
Barclay College, KS	I
Bard College, NY	I
Barnard College, NY	D,I,P
Barry University, FL	D,I,P
Bartlesville Wesleyan College, OK	D,I
Barton College, NC	I
Bates College, ME	I
Bayamón Central University, PR	D
Baylor University, TX	G,I
Bay Path College, MA	D,I,P
Beaver College, PA	D,I
Becker College, MA	I
Belhaven College, MS	I
Bellarmine College, KY	D,I
Bellevue University, NE	D,I
Bellin College of Nursing, WI	I
Belmont Abbey College, NC	I
Belmont University, TN	D,I
Beloit College, WI	I
Bemidji State University, MN	I
Benedictine College, KS	I
Benedictine University, IL	D,I
Bennett College, NC	D
Bennington College, VT	I
Bentley College, MA	I
Berea College, KY	D
Berklee College of Music, MA	I
Baruch Coll of the City U of NY, NY	D,I
Berry College, GA	I
Bethany College, KS	I
Bethany College, WV	I
Bethel College, IN	I
Bethel College, KS	I
Bethel College, MN	I
Bethel College, TN	I
Beulah Heights Bible College, GA	D,I
Biola University, CA	I
Birmingham-Southern College, AL	I
Blackburn College, IL	I
Black Hills State University, SD	I
Bloomfield College, NJ	D,I
Bluefield College, VA	I,P
Bluefield State College, WV	D
Blue Mountain College, MS	I
Bluffton College, OH	I
Boise Bible College, ID	I
Boise State University, ID	D
Boricua College, NY	D
Boston Architectural Center, MA	D
Boston College, MA	I,P
Boston University, MA	I,P
Bowdoin College, ME	I
Bowie State University, MD	D
Bowling Green State University, OH	I
Bradley University, IL	D,I
Brandeis University, MA	I,P
Brenau University, GA	I
Brescia University, KY	D
Brevard College, NC	I
Briar Cliff College, IA	D
Briarcliffe College, NY	D,I
Bridgewater College, VA	I
Bridgewater State College, MA	I
Brigham Young University–Hawaii Campus, HI	I
Brooks Institute of Photography, CA	D,I
Brown University, RI	D,I,P
Bryant and Stratton College, OH	G
Bryant College, RI	I,P
Bryn Mawr College, PA	D,I,P
Bucknell University, PA	I,P
Buena Vista University, IA	I
Burlington College, VT	I
Butler University, IN	I,P
Cabrini College, PA	I
Caldwell College, NJ	D,I
California Baptist University, CA	D,I
California College of Arts and Crafts, CA	D,I

D = deferred payment system; *G* = guaranteed tuition rate; *I* = installment payments; *P* = prepayment locks in tuition rate

Institution	Option
California Institute of Integral Studies, CA	D
California Institute of Technology, CA	D,I
California Lutheran University, CA	I
California Maritime Academy, CA	I
California Polytechnic State U, San Luis Obispo, CA	I
California State Polytechnic University, Pomona, CA	I
California State University, Bakersfield, CA	I
California State University, Chico, CA	D
California State University, Fullerton, CA	I
California State University, Hayward, CA	I
California State University, Long Beach, CA	I
California State University, Sacramento, CA	I
California University of Pennsylvania, PA	I
Calumet College of Saint Joseph, IN	I
Calvin College, MI	I,P
Cameron University, OK	I
Campbellsville University, KY	D,I
Campbell University, NC	I
Canisius College, NY	D,I
Capital University, OH	I
Capitol College, MD	D,G,I
Cardinal Stritch University, WI	I
Carleton College, MN	I,P
Carlos Albizu University, FL	I
Carlow College, PA	D,I
Carnegie Mellon University, PA	I
Carroll College, MT	I
Carroll College, WI	I
Carson-Newman College, TN	I
Carthage College, WI	I
Case Western Reserve University, OH	I,P
Castleton State College, VT	I
Catawba College, NC	I
The Catholic University of America, DC	D,I
Cazenovia College, NY	I
Cedar Crest College, PA	I
Cedarville College, OH	I
Centenary College, NJ	I
Centenary College of Louisiana, LA	D,G,I
Ctr for Creative Studies—Coll of Art and Design, MI	D,I
Central Bible College, MO	I
Central Christian College of the Bible, MO	D
Central College, IA	I
Central Connecticut State University, CT	D,I
Central Methodist College, MO	I
Central Missouri State University, MO	D,I
Central State University, OH	I
Centre College, KY	I
Chadron State College, NE	I
Chaminade University of Honolulu, HI	D
Champlain College, VT	I
Chapman University, CA	D,I,P
Chatham College, PA	I
Cheyney University of Pennsylvania, PA	D
Chicago State University, IL	D
Chowan College, NC	D,I
Christendom College, VA	I,P
Christian Brothers University, TN	D,I
Christian Heritage College, CA	I
Christopher Newport University, VA	I
Cincinnati Bible College and Seminary, OH	D,I
Circleville Bible College, OH	I
Citadel, The Military Coll of South Carolina, SC	I
City Coll of the City U of NY, NY	D
City University, WA	D
Claflin University, SC	D,I
Claremont McKenna College, CA	I
Clarion University of Pennsylvania, PA	I
Clark Atlanta University, GA	D
Clarke College, IA	D,I
Clarkson College, NE	D,I
Clarkson University, NY	I
Clark University, MA	I,P
Clear Creek Baptist Bible College, KY	I
Clearwater Christian College, FL	I
Cleary College, MI	D,I
Clemson University, SC	D,I
Cleveland College of Jewish Studies, OH	I
Cleveland Institute of Art, OH	I
Cleveland Institute of Music, OH	I
Coastal Carolina University, SC	D,I
Coe College, IA	I
Cogswell Polytechnical College, CA	D
Coker College, SC	I
Colby College, ME	I
Colby-Sawyer College, NH	I
Coleman College, CA	G,I
Colgate University, NY	D,I,P
College Misericordia, PA	D,I
College of Aeronautics, NY	I
College of Charleston, SC	I
College of Insurance, NY	I
College of Mount St. Joseph, OH	I
College of Mount Saint Vincent, NY	I
The College of New Jersey, NJ	D,I
The College of New Rochelle, NY	I,P
College of Notre Dame of Maryland, MD	I
College of Saint Benedict, MN	D,I,P
College of St. Catherine, MN	I
College of Saint Elizabeth, NJ	I
College of St. Joseph, VT	I
College of Saint Mary, NE	D,I
The College of St. Scholastica, MN	I
Coll of Staten Island of the City U of NY, NY	D
College of the Atlantic, ME	I
College of the Holy Cross, MA	I,P
College of the Southwest, NM	D
The College of West Virginia, WV	I
The College of William and Mary, VA	I
The College of Wooster, OH	I
Colorado Christian University, CO	I
The Colorado College, CO	I
Colorado School of Mines, CO	I
Colorado State University, CO	I
Colorado Technical University, CO	I
Colorado Technical University Denver Campus, CO	D,I
Columbia College, MO	D
Columbia College, NY	I,P
Columbia College, SC	I
Columbia College Chicago, IL	D
Columbia College–Hollywood, CA	I
Columbia International University, SC	I
Columbia Union College, MD	D,I
Columbia U, School of General Studies, NY	D,P
Columbia U, School of Engineering & Applied Sci, NY	D,I,P
Columbus College of Art and Design, OH	I
Concord College, WV	D,I
Concordia College, AL	I
Concordia College, MN	I
Concordia College, NY	I
Concordia University, CA	I
Concordia University, IL	I
Concordia University, NE	D,I
Concordia University, OR	I
Concordia University at St. Paul, MN	I
Concordia University Wisconsin, WI	D,G,I
Connecticut College, CT	I
Converse College, SC	I
Coppin State College, MD	D
The Corcoran College of Art and Design, DC	I
Cornell College, IA	I
Cornell University, NY	I,P
Cornerstone University, MI	I
Cornish College of the Arts, WA	I
Covenant College, GA	I
Creighton University, NE	I
The Criswell College, TX	I
Crown College, MN	I
The Culinary Institute of America, NY	I
Culver-Stockton College, MO	I
Cumberland College, KY	I
Cumberland University, TN	I
Curry College, MA	I
Daemen College, NY	D,I
Dakota State University, SD	D
Dakota Wesleyan University, SD	I
Dallas Baptist University, TX	I
Dallas Christian College, TX	I
Daniel Webster College, NH	I
Dartmouth College, NH	I,P
Davenport College of Business, Kalamazoo Campus, MI	D,I
Davenport College of Business, Lansing Campus, MI	I
David Lipscomb University, TN	I
David N. Myers College, OH	D,I
Davidson College, NC	I
Davis & Elkins College, WV	I
Deaconess College of Nursing, MO	D,I
Defiance College, OH	I
Delaware State University, DE	D,I
Delaware Valley College, PA	I
Delta State University, MS	I
Denison University, OH	I,P
DePaul University, IL	D,I
DePauw University, IN	D,I,P
Design Institute of San Diego, CA	I
Detroit College of Business, MI	D,I
Detroit College of Business–Flint, MI	D,I
Detroit College of Business, Warren Campus, MI	D,I
DeVry Institute, NJ	D
DeVry Institute of Technology, AZ	D,I
DeVry Institute of Technology, CA	D,I
DeVry Institute of Technology, CA	I
DeVry Institute of Technology, CA	D,I
DeVry Institute of Technology, CA	I
DeVry Institute of Technology, GA	I

D = deferred payment system; *G* = guaranteed tuition rate; *I* = installment payments; *P* = prepayment locks in tuition rate

DeVry Institute of Technology, GA I
DeVry Institute of Technology, IL I
DeVry Institute of Technology, IL I
DeVry Institute of Technology, MO I
DeVry Institute of Technology, NY I
DeVry Institute of Technology, OH I
DeVry Institute of Technology, TX I
Dickinson College, PA I
Dillard University, LA I
Doane College, NE I
Dominican College of Blauvelt, NY G,I
Dominican University, IL I
Dominican University of California, CA I
Dordt College, IA I
Dowling College, NY D,G,I
Drake University, IA I,P
Drew University, NJ I,P
Drexel University, PA D,I
Drury University, MO D,I,P
Duke University, NC D,I,P
Duquesne University, PA D,I
D'Youville College, NY D,G,I
Earlham College, IN D,I,P
East Carolina University, NC D,I
Eastern Connecticut State University, CT D,I
Eastern Illinois University, IL I
Eastern Kentucky University, KY D
Eastern Mennonite University, VA I
Eastern Michigan University, MI I
Eastern Nazarene College, MA I
Eastern New Mexico University, NM I
Eastern Oregon University, OR I
Eastern Washington University, WA I
East Stroudsburg University of Pennsylvania, PA I
East Tennessee State University, TN D
East Texas Baptist University, TX I
East-West University, IL D,I
Eckerd College, FL I
Edgewood College, WI D,I
Edinboro University of Pennsylvania, PA I
Elizabethtown College, PA I
Elmhurst College, IL D,I
Elmira College, NY I,P
Elon College, NC I
Embry-Riddle Aeronautical University, FL D,I
Emerson College, MA D,P
Emmanuel College, GA I
Emmanuel College, MA D,I
Emmaus Bible College, IA I
Emory & Henry College, VA I
Emory University, GA I,P
Emporia State University, KS D,I
Endicott College, MA I
Erskine College, SC I
Escuela de Artes Plasticas de Puerto Rico, PR D
Eugene Bible College, OR I,P
Eugene Lang College, New School University, NY I
Eureka College, IL I
Evangel University, MO I
The Evergreen State College, WA I
Fairfield University, CT I
Fairleigh Dickinson U, Florham-Madison Campus, NJ D,I
Fairleigh Dickinson U, Teaneck-Hackensack Campus, NJ D,I
Fairmont State College, WV D,I
Faith Baptist Bible Coll and Theological Seminary, IA I
Fashion Institute of Technology, NY I
Faulkner University, AL D,I
Fayetteville State University, NC I
Felician College, NJ D,I
Ferris State University, MI D,I
Ferrum College, VA I
Finch U of Health Sciences/Chicago Medical School, IL I
Finlandia University, MI I
Fisk University, TN I
Fitchburg State College, MA I
Five Towns College, NY D,I
Florida Agricultural and Mechanical University, FL D,P
Florida Atlantic University, FL D,I
Florida Baptist Theological College, FL D
Florida College, FL I
Florida Institute of Technology, FL I
Florida International University, FL P
Florida Metropolitan U-Fort Lauderdale Coll, FL I
Florida Metropolitan U-Orlando Coll, FL D,G,I,P
Florida Metropolitan U-Tampa Coll, FL G,I
Florida Metropolitan U-Tampa Coll, Brandon, FL I
Florida Metropolitan U-Tampa Coll, Lakeland, FL I
Florida Southern College, FL I
Florida State University, FL I,P
Fontbonne College, MO D,I
Fordham University, NY I,P
Fort Hays State University, KS I
Framingham State College, MA I
Franciscan University of Steubenville, OH I
Franklin and Marshall College, PA I
Franklin College of Indiana, IN I
Franklin Pierce College, NH I
Franklin University, OH D,I
Free Will Baptist Bible College, TN D,I
Fresno Pacific University, CA I
Friends University, KS I
Frostburg State University, MD D,I
Furman University, SC I
Gallaudet University, DC I
Gannon University, PA I
Geneva College, PA I
George Fox University, OR I
George Mason University, VA D,I
Georgetown College, KY D
Georgetown University, DC D,I
The George Washington University, DC D,I
Georgia Baptist College of Nursing, GA D,I
Georgian Court College, NJ D,I
Gettysburg College, PA I
Glenville State College, WV I
Goddard College, VT I
Golden Gate University, CA I
Goldey-Beacom College, DE D,I
Gonzaga University, WA D,I
Gordon College, MA I,P
Goucher College, MD I
Governors State University, IL D,I
Grace Bible College, MI I
Grace College, IN I
Graceland College, IA I
Grace University, NE D
Grambling State University, LA I
Grand Canyon University, AZ I
Grand Valley State University, MI D,I
Grand View College, IA D,I
Green Mountain College, VT I
Greensboro College, NC I
Greenville College, IL I
Grinnell College, IA I,P
Guilford College, NC I
Gustavus Adolphus College, MN I,P
Gwynedd-Mercy College, PA I
Hamilton College, NY D,I
Hamilton Technical College, IA G,I
Hamline University, MN I
Hampden-Sydney College, VA I
Hampton University, VA I
Hannibal-LaGrange College, MO D
Hanover College, IN I
Harding University, AR I,P
Hardin-Simmons University, TX D,G,I
Harrington Institute of Interior Design, IL I
Harris-Stowe State College, MO I
Hartwick College, NY I
Harvard University, MA I,P
Harvey Mudd College, CA I
Hastings College, NE D,I
Haverford College, PA I
Hawaii Pacific University, HI I
Heidelberg College, OH D,I
Hendrix College, AR I
Henry Cogswell College, WA D,G,I
Heritage Bible College, NC D,I
Heritage College, WA D,I
Hilbert College, NY D,I
Hillsdale College, MI I
Hillsdale Free Will Baptist College, OK D
Hiram College, OH I
Hobart and William Smith Colleges, NY D,I,P
Hobe Sound Bible College, FL I
Hofstra University, NY D,I
Hollins University, VA I,P
Holy Apostles College and Seminary, CT I
Holy Family College, PA D,I
Holy Names College, CA D,I
Hood College, MD D,I,P
Hope College, MI I
Hope International University, CA I
Houghton College, NY I
Houston Baptist University, TX D,G,I
Howard Payne University, TX I
Humboldt State University, CA I
Humphreys College, CA I,P
Hunter Coll of the City U of NY, NY D
Huntingdon College, AL D
Huntington College, IN G,I
Huron University, SD D,G,I,P
Husson College, ME I,P
Huston-Tillotson College, TX I
Idaho State University, ID D
Illinois College, IL D,I
The Illinois Institute of Art, IL D,I,P
Illinois Institute of Technology, IL I
Illinois State University, IL I
Illinois Wesleyan University, IL I
Immaculata College, PA I

D = deferred payment system; *G* = guaranteed tuition rate; *I* = installment payments; *P* = prepayment locks in tuition rate

Institution	Code
Indiana Institute of Technology, IN	D
Indiana State University, IN	D,I
Indiana University Bloomington, IN	D
Indiana University East, IN	D
Indiana University Northwest, IN	D,I
Indiana University of Pennsylvania, PA	D,I
Indiana U–Purdue U Fort Wayne, IN	D,I
Indiana U–Purdue U Indianapolis, IN	D,I
Indiana University South Bend, IN	D,I
Indiana Wesleyan University, IN	I
Institute for Christian Studies, TX	I
Inter American U of PR, Arecibo Campus, PR	G
Inter American U of PR, Guayama Campus, PR	D
Inter American U of PR, San Germán Campus, PR	D
International Academy of Design, FL	D,G,I
International Acad of Merchandising & Design, Ltd, IL	D,I
International Bible College, AL	D,I
International College, FL	I
Iona College, NY	D,I
Iowa State University of Science and Technology, IA	D,I
Iowa Wesleyan College, IA	D,I
Ithaca College, NY	I
Jacksonville University, FL	I
James Madison University, VA	I
Jamestown College, ND	I
Jarvis Christian College, TX	D,P
Jewish Hospital Coll of Nursing and Allied Health, MO	D,I
Jewish Theological Seminary of America, NY	I
John Brown University, AR	I
John Carroll University, OH	I
Johns Hopkins University, MD	I,P
Johnson & Wales University, RI	G,I
Johnson Bible College, TN	I
Johnson C. Smith University, NC	I
Johnson State College, VT	D,I
John Wesley College, NC	I
Jones International University, CO	G
Judson College, AL	I
Judson College, IL	I
The Juilliard School, NY	I
Juniata College, PA	I
Kalamazoo College, MI	D,I
Kansas State University, KS	D,I
Kansas Wesleyan University, KS	I
Kean University, NJ	D,I
Keene State College, NH	I
Kendall College, IL	I
Kendall College of Art and Design, MI	D,I,P
Kennesaw State University, GA	D
Kent State University, OH	I
Kentucky Christian College, KY	I,P
Kentucky Mountain Bible College, KY	I
Kentucky Wesleyan College, KY	D,I
Kenyon College, OH	I
Kettering University, MI	I
Keuka College, NY	I
King College, TN	G,I,P
King's College, PA	D,I
Knox College, IL	I,P
Kutztown University of Pennsylvania, PA	D,I,P
Laboratory Institute of Merchandising, NY	I
Lafayette College, PA	D,P
LaGrange College, GA	I
Lake Erie College, OH	I
Lake Forest College, IL	I
Lakeland College, WI	I
Lakeview College of Nursing, IL	D,I
Lamar University, TX	I
Lambuth University, TN	D,I
Lancaster Bible College, PA	I
Lander University, SC	I
Lane College, TN	D,I
La Roche College, PA	I
La Salle University, PA	D,I
Lasell College, MA	I
Lawrence Technological University, MI	I
Lawrence University, WI	I
Lees-McRae College, NC	I
Lee University, TN	D
Lehigh University, PA	D,I,P
Lehman Coll of the City U of NY, NY	I
Le Moyne College, NY	D,I
LeMoyne-Owen College, TN	D,I,P
Lesley College, MA	I
LeTourneau University, TX	I
Lewis & Clark College, OR	I
Lewis-Clark State College, ID	D
Lewis University, IL	I
Liberty University, VA	I
LIFE Bible College, CA	I
Limestone College, SC	I
Lincoln Christian College, IL	D,I
Lincoln Memorial University, TN	D,I
Lincoln University, MO	D
Lincoln University, PA	D,I
Linfield College, OR	I
Lock Haven University of Pennsylvania, PA	I
Logan University of Chiropractic, MO	I
Long Island U, Southampton College, NY	D,I
Longwood College, VA	I
Loras College, IA	I
Louisiana State University and A&M College, LA	D
Louisiana State University in Shreveport, LA	D
Lourdes College, OH	D,I
Loyola College in Maryland, MD	G
Loyola Marymount University, CA	I
Loyola University Chicago, IL	I
Loyola University New Orleans, LA	I
Lubbock Christian University, TX	I,P
Luther College, IA	I
Lycoming College, PA	I
Lyme Academy of Fine Arts, CT	I
Lynchburg College, VA	I
Lynn University, FL	D,I
Lyon College, AR	I
Macalester College, MN	I
MacMurray College, IL	I
Madonna University, MI	D
Magnolia Bible College, MS	D
Maharishi University of Management, IA	I
Maine College of Art, ME	D,I
Maine Maritime Academy, ME	I
Malone College, OH	I
Manchester College, IN	D,I
Manhattan Christian College, KS	I
Manhattan College, NY	I
Manhattan School of Music, NY	I
Manhattanville College, NY	D,I
Mannes College of Music, New School University, NY	I
Mansfield University of Pennsylvania, PA	D,I
Maranatha Baptist Bible College, WI	I
Marian College, IN	D,I
Marian College of Fond du Lac, WI	I
Marietta College, OH	I
Marist College, NY	I
Marlboro College, VT	I
Marquette University, WI	I,P
Marshall University, WV	D,I
Mars Hill College, NC	I
Martin Luther College, MN	I
Martin Methodist College, TN	I
Martin University, IN	D,I
Mary Baldwin College, VA	I
Marycrest International University, IA	D,I
Maryland Institute, College of Art, MD	I
Marymount College, NY	D,I
Marymount Manhattan College, NY	I
Marymount University, VA	D,I
Maryville College, TN	D,I
Maryville University of Saint Louis, MO	D,I
Mary Washington College, VA	I
Marywood University, PA	D,I
Massachusetts College of Art, MA	I
Massachusetts College of Liberal Arts, MA	I
Mass Coll of Pharmacy and Allied Health Sciences, MA	I
Massachusetts Institute of Technology, MA	D
The Master's College and Seminary, CA	D,I
The McGregor School of Antioch University, OH	I
McKendree College, IL	I
McMurry University, TX	G,I
McNeese State University, LA	I
MCP Hahnemann University, PA	I
Medaille College, NY	I
Medical University of South Carolina, SC	I
Memphis College of Art, TN	D,I
Menlo College, CA	I
Mercer University, GA	I
Mercy College, NY	D,I
Mercyhurst College, PA	I
Meredith College, NC	I
Merrimack College, MA	D,I
Messenger College, MO	I
Messiah College, PA	I
Methodist College, NC	D,I
Metropolitan State College of Denver, CO	D
Miami University, OH	I
Michigan State University, MI	D,G
Michigan Technological University, MI	I
Mid-America Bible College, OK	I
MidAmerica Nazarene University, KS	I
Middlebury College, VT	I,P
Middle Tennessee State University, TN	D
Midland Lutheran College, NE	I
Midway College, KY	I
Midwestern State University, TX	I
Millersville University of Pennsylvania, PA	I

D = deferred payment system; *G* = guaranteed tuition rate; *I* = installment payments; *P* = prepayment locks in tuition rate

Milligan College, TN I
Millikin University, IL I
Millsaps College, MS I
Mills College, CA I
Milwaukee Institute of Art and Design, WI D
Milwaukee School of Engineering, WI I
Minneapolis College of Art and Design, MN I
Minnesota Bible College, MN I
Minnesota State University, Mankato, MN I
Minnesota State University Moorhead, MN D
Mississippi College, MS D,I
Mississippi University for Women, MS D,I
Mississippi Valley State University, MS I
Missouri Baptist College, MO I
Missouri Southern State College, MO D
Missouri Valley College, MO I
Missouri Western State College, MO D,I
Monmouth College, IL I
Monmouth University, NJ I
Montana State U–Billings, MT I
Montana State U–Bozeman, MT D,I
Montana State U–Northern, MT D
Montana Tech of The University of Montana, MT D
Montclair State University, NJ I
Monterey Institute of International Studies, CA I
Montreat College, NC I
Montserrat College of Art, MA I
Moody Bible Institute, IL I
Moore College of Art and Design, PA I
Moravian College, PA I
Morehead State University, KY D,I
Morgan State University, MD D,I
Morningside College, IA I
Morrison University, NV G,I
Mount Holyoke College, MA I,P
Mount Ida College, MA I
Mount Marty College, SD G,I
Mount Mary College, WI I
Mount Mercy College, IA I
Mount Olive College, NC I
Mount St. Clare College, IA I
Mount Saint Mary College, NY I
Mount St. Mary's College, CA D
Mount Saint Mary's College and Seminary, MD I,P
Mount Senario College, WI I
Mount Union College, OH I,P
Mount Vernon Nazarene College, OH I
Muhlenberg College, PA I,P
Multnomah Bible College and Biblical Seminary, OR I
Murray State University, KY D,I
Muskingum College, OH I
NAES College, IL P
Naropa University, CO D,I,P
National-Louis University, IL D,I
Nazareth College of Rochester, NY I
Nebraska Methodist Coll of Nursing & Allied Health, NE I
Nebraska Wesleyan University, NE I
Neumann College, PA D,I
Newberry College, SC I
New College of the University of South Florida, FL I,P
New England College, NH I
New Hampshire College, NH D,I
New Jersey Institute of Technology, NJ D,I
Newman University, KS D,I
New Mexico Highlands University, NM D
New Mexico Institute of Mining and Technology, NM D
New Sch Bach of Arts, New Sch for Social Research, NY I
Newschool of Architecture, CA D,I,P
New York Institute of Technology, NY I
New York School of Interior Design, NY D,I
New York University, NY D,I,P
Niagara University, NY D,I
Nichols College, MA I
North Carolina Agricultural and Technical State U, NC D
North Carolina Wesleyan College, NC I
North Central College, IL I
North Dakota State University, ND I
Northeastern Illinois University, IL D
Northeastern University, MA D,I
Northern Illinois University, IL I
Northern Kentucky University, KY I
Northern Michigan University, MI I
North Greenville College, SC I
Northland College, WI I,P
Northwest Christian College, OR D,I
Northwest College, WA D,I
Northwest College of Art, WA I
Northwestern College, IA I
Northwestern College, MN I
Northwestern State University of Louisiana, LA I
Northwestern University, IL I
Northwest Missouri State University, MO I
Northwest Nazarene University, ID I,P
Northwood University, MI I
Northwood University, Florida Campus, FL I
Northwood University, Texas Campus, TX I
Norwich University, VT I
Notre Dame College, NH I
Notre Dame College of Ohio, OH I
Nova Southeastern University, FL I
Nyack College, NY I
Oak Hills Christian College, MN I
Oakland City University, IN D,I
Oakland University, MI D,I
Oakwood College, AL I
Oberlin College, OH I
Occidental College, CA I,P
Oglethorpe University, GA I,P
Ohio Dominican College, OH I
Ohio Northern University, OH I
The Ohio State University, OH I
Ohio University, OH I
Ohio University–Chillicothe, OH I
Ohio Valley College, WV I
Ohio Wesleyan University, OH I
Oklahoma Baptist University, OK I
Oklahoma Christian U of Science and Arts, OK P
Oklahoma City University, OK D,I
Oklahoma State U, OK D,I
Old Dominion University, VA D,I
Olivet College, MI I
Olivet Nazarene University, IL I
O'More College of Design, TN D,I
Oral Roberts University, OK I
Oregon College of Art and Craft, OR I
Oregon Health Sciences University, OR D
Oregon Institute of Technology, OR D,I
Oregon State University, OR D
Otis College of Art and Design, CA I
Ottawa University, KS D,I
Otterbein College, OH I
Ouachita Baptist University, AR I
Our Lady of Holy Cross College, LA I
Our Lady of the Lake University of San Antonio, TX I
Ozark Christian College, MO D,I
Pacific Lutheran University, WA I
Pacific Northwest College of Art, OR I
Pacific Oaks College, CA I
Pacific Union College, CA D,G,I
Pacific University, OR D,I
Paier College of Art, Inc., CT I
Paine College, GA I
Palm Beach Atlantic College, FL I
Palmer College of Chiropractic, IA D
Park University, MO I
Parsons School of Design, New School University, NY I
Paul Quinn College, TX I
Peace College, NC I
Peirce College, PA D
Pennsylvania School of Art & Design, PA I
Penn State U Abington College, PA D
Penn State U Altoona College, PA D
Penn State U at Erie, The Behrend College, PA D
Penn State U Berks Cmps of Berks-Lehigh Valley Coll, PA D
Penn State U Harrisburg Campus of the Capital Coll, PA D
Penn State U Lehigh Valley Cmps of Berks-Lehigh Valley Coll, PA D
Penn State U Schuylkill Campus of the Capital Coll, PA D
Penn State U Univ Park Campus, PA D
Pepperdine University, CA D,I,P
Pfeiffer University, NC D,I
Philadelphia College of Bible, PA I
Philadelphia University, PA D,I
Philander Smith College, AR D,I
Piedmont Baptist College, NC I
Piedmont College, GA I
Pikeville College, KY I
Pine Manor College, MA I,P
Pittsburg State University, KS I
Pitzer College, CA D,I
Plattsburgh State U of NY, NY D,I
Plymouth State College, NH I
Point Loma Nazarene University, CA I
Point Park College, PA D,I
Polytechnic U, Brooklyn Campus, NY D,P
Polytechnic University of Puerto Rico, PR D
Pomona College, CA I
Pontifical College Josephinum, OH D,I
Portland State University, OR D,I
Practical Bible College, NY I
Pratt Institute, NY D,I
Presbyterian College, SC I,P
Prescott College, AZ I

D = deferred payment system; *G* = guaranteed tuition rate; *I* = installment payments; *P* = prepayment locks in tuition rate

Presentation College, SD I
Princeton University, NJ D,I
Principia College, IL I
Providence College, RI I
Puget Sound Christian College, WA I,P
Purchase College, State U of NY, NY I
Purdue University, IN I
Purdue University Calumet, IN D
Purdue University North Central, IN D
Queens College, NC I
Queens Coll of the City U of NY, NY I
Quincy University, IL G,I
Quinnipiac University, CT I
Radford University, VA I
Ramapo College of New Jersey, NJ I
Randolph-Macon College, VA I
Randolph-Macon Woman's College, VA I
Reed College, OR I
Reformed Bible College, MI D
Regents College, NY D,I,P
Regis College, MA D,I,P
Regis University, CO D
Reinhardt College, GA I
Rensselaer Polytechnic Institute, NY I
Research College of Nursing, MO D,G,I
Rhode Island School of Design, RI I
Rhodes College, TN I
Rice University, TX I
The Richard Stockton College of New Jersey, NJ I
Rider University, NJ I
Ringling School of Art and Design, FL I
Ripon College, WI G,I
Rivier College, NH D,I
Roanoke Bible College, NC D,I
Roanoke College, VA I
Robert Morris College, IL I
Robert Morris College, PA D,I
Roberts Wesleyan College, NY I
Rochester College, MI I
Rochester Institute of Technology, NY D,I,P
Rockford College, IL D,I
Rockhurst University, MO D,I
Rocky Mountain College, MT I
Rocky Mountain College of Art & Design, CO I
Roger Williams University, RI D,I
Rollins College, FL I,P
Rose-Hulman Institute of Technology, IN I,P
Rosemont College, PA I
Rowan University, NJ D
Rush University, IL D,I
Rust College, MS I
Rutgers, State U of NJ, Camden Coll of Arts & Scis, NJ D
Rutgers, State U of NJ, College of Nursing, NJ D
Rutgers, State U of NJ, College of Pharmacy, NJ D
Rutgers, State U of NJ, Cook College, NJ D
Rutgers, State U of NJ, Douglass College, NJ D
Rutgers, State U of NJ, Livingston College, NJ D
Rutgers, State U of NJ, Mason Gross School of Arts, NJ D
Rutgers, State U of NJ, Newark Coll of Arts & Scis, NJ D
Rutgers, State U of NJ, Rutgers College, NJ I
Rutgers, State U of NJ, College of Engineering, NJ D
Rutgers, State U of NJ, U Coll–Camden, NJ I
Rutgers, State U of NJ, U Coll–Newark, NJ D
Rutgers, State U of NJ, U Coll–New Brunswick, NJ I
Sacred Heart Major Seminary, MI D,I
Sacred Heart University, CT D,I
Saginaw Valley State University, MI I
St. Ambrose University, IA I
St. Andrews Presbyterian College, NC I
Saint Anselm College, NH D,I
Saint Anthony College of Nursing, IL I
Saint Augustine's College, NC I
St. Bonaventure University, NY D,I
St. Charles Borromeo Seminary, Overbrook, PA I
St. Edward's University, TX I
St. Francis College, NY I
Saint Francis College, PA D,I
Saint Francis Medical Center College of Nursing, IL D,I
St. Gregory's University, OK D,I
St. John Fisher College, NY D,I
St. John's College, IL D,I
St. John's College, MD I,P
St. John's College, NM I,P
St. John's Seminary College, CA D,I
Saint John's Seminary College of Liberal Arts, MA I
Saint John's University, MN D,I,P
St. John's University, NY D,G,I
St. John Vianney College Seminary, FL I
Saint Joseph College, CT I
Saint Joseph's College, IN I
Saint Joseph's College, ME I
St. Joseph's College, New York, NY D,I
St. Joseph's College, Suffolk Campus, NY I
Saint Joseph's University, PA D,I
St. Lawrence University, NY D,I
Saint Leo University, FL I
St. Louis Christian College, MO I
St. Louis College of Pharmacy, MO D
Saint Louis University, MO I
Saint Martin's College, WA I
Saint Mary College, KS I
Saint Mary-of-the-Woods College, IN I
Saint Mary's College, IN D,I
Saint Mary's College, MI I
Saint Mary's College of California, CA I,P
St. Mary's University of San Antonio, TX D,I,P
Saint Michael's College, VT I
St. Norbert College, WI D,G,I
St. Olaf College, MN I,P
Saint Peter's College, NJ D,I
St. Thomas Aquinas College, NY D,I
St. Thomas University, FL I
Saint Vincent College, PA D,I
Saint Xavier University, IL I
Salem College, NC I
Salem State College, MA D,I
Salem-Teikyo University, WV I
Salisbury State University, MD I
Sam Houston State University, TX I
Samuel Merritt College, CA D,I
San Diego State University, CA I
San Francisco Art Institute, CA I
San Francisco Conservatory of Music, CA I
San Francisco State University, CA D,I
Santa Clara University, CA D,I,P
Sarah Lawrence College, NY I
Savannah College of Art and Design, GA I
School of the Art Institute of Chicago, IL I
School of the Museum of Fine Arts, MA I
School of Visual Arts, NY I
Schreiner College, TX I
Scripps College, CA I
Seattle Pacific University, WA I
Seattle University, WA I
Seton Hall University, NJ D,I
Seton Hill College, PA I
Shasta Bible College, CA D
Shawnee State University, OH I
Shaw University, NC D,I
Sheldon Jackson College, AK I
Shenandoah University, VA D
Shepherd College, WV I
Shimer College, IL I
Shorter College, GA I
Siena College, NY I
Siena Heights University, MI D,I
Sierra Nevada College, NV D
Silver Lake College, WI I
Simmons College, MA I
Simon's Rock College of Bard, MA I
Simpson College, IA I
Simpson College and Graduate School, CA I
Skidmore College, NY I,P
Slippery Rock University of Pennsylvania, PA I
Smith College, MA I,P
Sojourner-Douglass College, MD D,I
Sonoma State University, CA D
South Dakota School of Mines and Technology, SD I
South Dakota State University, SD D,I
Southeastern Bible College, AL I
Southeastern College of the Assemblies of God, FL I
Southeastern Louisiana University, LA D,I
Southeastern University, DC I
Southeast Missouri State University, MO D,I
Southern Adventist University, TN D,I,P
Southern Arkansas University–Magnolia, AR D,I
Southern Connecticut State University, CT I
Southern Illinois University Carbondale, IL I
Southern Illinois University Edwardsville, IL I
Southern Methodist University, TX I,P
Southern Nazarene University, OK I,P
Southern Oregon University, OR D
Southern Vermont College, VT D,I
Southern Wesleyan University, SC I
Southwest Baptist University, MO I
Southwestern Adventist University, TX I

D = deferred payment system; *G* = guaranteed tuition rate; *I* = installment payments; *P* = prepayment locks in tuition rate

Institution	Alternatives
Southwestern Assemblies of God University, TX	G,I
Southwestern College, KS	I
Southwestern College of Christian Ministries, OK	I
Southwestern Oklahoma State University, OK	I
Southwestern University, TX	D,I,P
Southwest Missouri State University, MO	D
Southwest State University, MN	D,I
Southwest Texas State University, TX	I
Spalding University, KY	I
Spring Arbor College, MI	D,I
Spring Hill College, AL	D
Stanford University, CA	D,I
State U of NY at Albany, NY	I
State U of NY at Binghamton, NY	I
State U of NY at Buffalo, NY	I
State U of NY at Farmingdale, NY	D,I
State U of NY at New Paltz, NY	I
State U of NY at Oswego, NY	D,I
State U of NY at Stony Brook, NY	D,I
State U of NY College at Brockport, NY	D,I
State U of NY College at Buffalo, NY	I
State U of NY College at Cortland, NY	I
State U of NY College at Fredonia, NY	I
State U of NY College at Geneseo, NY	D,I
State U of NY College at Oneonta, NY	I
State U of NY College at Potsdam, NY	I
State U of NY Coll of Environ Sci and Forestry, NY	D,I
State U of NY Institute of Tech at Utica/Rome, NY	I
State U of NY Maritime College, NY	I
State University of New York Upstate Medical University, NY	I
Stephen F. Austin State University, TX	I
Stephens College, MO	I
Sterling College, KS	I
Sterling College, VT	I
Stetson University, FL	I
Stevens Institute of Technology, NJ	I
Stillman College, AL	I
Stonehill College, MA	I,P
Strayer University, DC	I
Suffolk University, MA	D,I
Sullivan College, KY	D,I
Sul Ross State University, TX	I
Susquehanna University, PA	D,I,P
Swarthmore College, PA	I
Sweet Briar College, VA	I
Syracuse University, NY	I,P
Tabor College, KS	I
Talladega College, AL	I
Talmudical Yeshiva of Philadelphia, PA	I
Tarleton State University, TX	I
Taylor University, IN	I
Taylor University, Fort Wayne Campus, IN	I
Teikyo Post University, CT	D,I
Temple University, PA	I
Tennessee State University, TN	D
Tennessee Temple University, TN	I
Tennessee Wesleyan College, TN	D
Texas A&M International University, TX	I
Texas A&M University, TX	I
Texas A&M University at Galveston, TX	I
Texas A&M University–Commerce, TX	I
Texas A&M University–Corpus Christi, TX	D,G,I
Texas A&M University–Kingsville, TX	I
Texas A&M University–Texarkana, TX	I
Texas Chiropractic College, TX	D,I
Texas Christian University, TX	I
Texas Lutheran University, TX	I
Texas Tech University, TX	I
Texas Wesleyan University, TX	D,I
Texas Woman's University, TX	I
Thiel College, PA	I
Thomas Aquinas College, CA	I
Thomas College, ME	I
Thomas Jefferson University, PA	I
Thomas More College, KY	D,I
Thomas More College of Liberal Arts, NH	D,I
Thomas University, GA	D,G,I
Tiffin University, OH	I
Toccoa Falls College, GA	I
Tougaloo College, MS	D,I
Towson University, MD	I
Transylvania University, KY	D,I,P
Trevecca Nazarene University, TN	I
Trinity Baptist College, FL	I
Trinity Bible College, ND	D,I
Trinity Christian College, IL	I
Trinity College, CT	I
Trinity College, DC	D,I
Trinity College of Florida, FL	D
Trinity College of Vermont, VT	D,I
Trinity International U, South Florida Campus, FL	I
Trinity Lutheran College, WA	I
Trinity University, TX	I,P
Tri-State University, IN	I
Troy State University, AL	I
Troy State University Dothan, AL	I
Troy State University Montgomery, AL	D
Truman State University, MO	I
Tufts University, MA	I,P
Tulane University, LA	I
Tusculum College, TN	I
Tuskegee University, AL	I
Union College, KY	I
Union College, NE	I,P
Union College, NY	I
The Union Institute, OH	I
Union University, TN	D,I
United States International University, CA	D,I
Unity College, ME	I
Universidad Adventista de las Antillas, PR	D,I,P
The University of Akron, OH	I
The University of Alabama, AL	D,I
The University of Alabama in Huntsville, AL	D
U of Alaska Fairbanks, AK	D
University of Arkansas, AR	I
University of Arkansas at Little Rock, AR	D
University of Arkansas at Pine Bluff, AR	I
University of Baltimore, MD	D
University of Bridgeport, CT	D,I
U of Calif, Berkeley, CA	I
U of Calif, Irvine, CA	I
U of Calif, Riverside, CA	D,I
U of Calif, San Diego, CA	D
U of Calif, Santa Cruz, CA	D,I
University of Central Arkansas, AR	I
University of Central Florida, FL	D,P
University of Charleston, WV	I
University of Chicago, IL	I,P
University of Cincinnati, OH	I
University of Colorado at Boulder, CO	D
University of Colorado at Colorado Springs, CO	D
University of Colorado at Denver, CO	D,I
University of Connecticut, CT	D,I
University of Dallas, TX	D,I
University of Dayton, OH	D,I
University of Delaware, DE	I,P
University of Detroit Mercy, MI	D,I
University of Dubuque, IA	D,I
The University of Findlay, OH	I
University of Florida, FL	P
University of Great Falls, MT	D
University of Hartford, CT	I,P
University of Houston, TX	I
University of Houston–Clear Lake, TX	I
University of Houston–Downtown, TX	I
University of Houston–Victoria, TX	I,P
University of Idaho, ID	D
University of Illinois at Springfield, IL	I
University of Illinois at Urbana–Champaign, IL	I
University of Indianapolis, IN	D,I
The University of Iowa, IA	I
University of Kansas, KS	I
University of La Verne, CA	D,I
University of Louisiana at Lafayette, LA	D
University of Louisville, KY	I
University of Maine, ME	I
The University of Maine at Augusta, ME	I
University of Maine at Farmington, ME	I
University of Maine at Fort Kent, ME	I
University of Maine at Machias, ME	D,I
University of Maine at Presque Isle, ME	D,I
University of Mary, ND	I
University of Mary Hardin-Baylor, TX	I
University of Maryland, Baltimore County, MD	I
University of Maryland, College Park, MD	D,I
University of Massachusetts Amherst, MA	I
University of Massachusetts Boston, MA	I
University of Massachusetts Dartmouth, MA	I
University of Massachusetts Lowell, MA	I
The University of Memphis, TN	I
University of Miami, FL	I,P
University of Michigan, MI	I
University of Michigan–Dearborn, MI	I
University of Michigan–Flint, MI	D
University of Minnesota, Crookston, MN	G,I
University of Minnesota, Duluth, MN	I
University of Minnesota, Morris, MN	D,I
University of Minnesota, Twin Cities Campus, MN	G,I
University of Mississippi, MS	D,P

D = deferred payment system; *G* = guaranteed tuition rate; *I* = installment payments; *P* = prepayment locks in tuition rate

Institution	Payment
University of Mississippi Medical Center, MS	D,I
University of Missouri–Columbia, MO	I
University of Missouri–Rolla, MO	I
University of Missouri–St. Louis, MO	I
University of Mobile, AL	I
The University of Montana–Missoula, MT	I
University of Montevallo, AL	D
University of Nebraska at Kearney, NE	I
University of Nebraska at Omaha, NE	D
University of Nevada, Las Vegas, NV	D
University of Nevada, Reno, NV	D
University of New England, ME	D,I
University of New Hampshire at Manchester, NH	I
University of New Haven, CT	D,I
University of New Mexico, NM	I
University of New Orleans, LA	D
The University of North Carolina at Asheville, NC	I
The University of North Carolina at Chapel Hill, NC	D
The University of North Carolina at Pembroke, NC	I
The University of North Carolina at Wilmington, NC	I
University of Northern Colorado, CO	D
University of Northern Iowa, IA	I
University of North Florida, FL	D
University of North Texas, TX	I
University of Notre Dame, IN	I
University of Oklahoma, OK	I
University of Oregon, OR	D
University of Pennsylvania, PA	I,P
University of Pittsburgh, PA	D,I
University of Pittsburgh at Bradford, PA	D,I
University of Pittsburgh at Johnstown, PA	D,I
University of Portland, OR	D,I
U of Puerto Rico, Humacao University College, PR	D
U of Puerto Rico Medical Sciences Campus, PR	D
University of Puget Sound, WA	D,I
University of Redlands, CA	I
University of Rhode Island, RI	I
University of Richmond, VA	I
University of Rio Grande, OH	D,I
University of Rochester, NY	I,P
University of St. Francis, IL	I
University of Saint Francis, IN	I
University of St. Thomas, MN	D,I
University of St. Thomas, TX	D,I
University of San Diego, CA	I
University of San Francisco, CA	I
University of Science and Arts of Oklahoma, OK	I
The University of Scranton, PA	I
University of South Carolina, SC	D,I
University of South Carolina Aiken, SC	D
U of South Carolina Spartanburg, SC	D
University of South Dakota, SD	D,I
University of Southern California, CA	I,P
University of Southern Colorado, CO	D,I
University of Southern Indiana, IN	I
University of Southern Maine, ME	I
University of Southern Mississippi, MS	I,P
University of South Florida, FL	I,P
The University of Tampa, FL	I
The University of Tennessee at Chattanooga, TN	D
The University of Tennessee at Martin, TN	D
The University of Tennessee Knoxville, TN	D,I
The University of Tennessee Memphis, TN	I
The University of Texas at Arlington, TX	I
The University of Texas at Austin, TX	I
The University of Texas at Brownsville, TX	I
The University of Texas at Dallas, TX	I
The University of Texas at El Paso, TX	I
The University of Texas at San Antonio, TX	I
The University of Texas at Tyler, TX	I
U of Texas Health Science Center at San Antonio, TX	I
U of Texas-Houston Health Science Center, TX	I
U of Texas Medical Branch at Galveston, TX	I
The University of Texas of the Permian Basin, TX	I
U of Texas Southwestern Medical Center at Dallas, TX	I
The University of the Arts, PA	D,I
University of the District of Columbia, DC	D,I
University of the Incarnate Word, TX	I
University of the Ozarks, AR	I
University of the Pacific, CA	D
University of the Sacred Heart, PR	D
University of the Sciences in Philadelphia, PA	D,I
University of the South, TN	D,I
University of Toledo, OH	I
University of Tulsa, OK	I,P
University of Utah, UT	D,I
University of Vermont, VT	D,I
University of Virginia, VA	I
University of Virginia's College at Wise, VA	I
University of Washington, WA	I
The University of West Alabama, AL	D
University of West Los Angeles, CA	I
University of Wisconsin–Eau Claire, WI	I
University of Wisconsin–Green Bay, WI	I
University of Wisconsin–La Crosse, WI	I
University of Wisconsin–Milwaukee, WI	I
University of Wisconsin–Oshkosh, WI	I
University of Wisconsin–Parkside, WI	I
University of Wisconsin–Platteville, WI	I
University of Wisconsin–River Falls, WI	I
University of Wisconsin–Stevens Point, WI	D
University of Wisconsin–Stout, WI	I
University of Wisconsin–Superior, WI	I
University of Wisconsin–Whitewater, WI	I
University of Wyoming, WY	D,I
Upper Iowa University, IA	I
Urbana University, OH	D,I
Ursinus College, PA	I
Ursuline College, OH	I
Utah State University, UT	D
Utica College of Syracuse University, NY	D
Valley Forge Christian College, PA	I
Valparaiso University, IN	I
Vanderbilt University, TN	D,I,P
Vanguard University of Southern California, CA	I
Vassar College, NY	I
Villanova University, PA	I
Virginia College at Birmingham, AL	G,I
Virginia Commonwealth University, VA	I
Virginia Intermont College, VA	I
Virginia Military Institute, VA	I
Virginia Polytechnic Institute and State U, VA	I
Virginia State University, VA	D
Virginia Union University, VA	D,I
Virginia Wesleyan College, VA	D,I
Viterbo University, WI	I
Voorhees College, SC	D,I
Wabash College, IN	I,P
Wadhams Hall Seminary-College, NY	D,I
Wagner College, NY	I
Wake Forest University, NC	I
Walla Walla College, WA	I
Walsh College of Accountancy and Business Admin, MI	D
Walsh University, OH	D,I
Warner Pacific College, OR	I
Warner Southern College, FL	I
Warren Wilson College, NC	I
Wartburg College, IA	I
Washburn University of Topeka, KS	I
Washington & Jefferson College, PA	D,I
Washington Bible College, MD	D,I
Washington College, MD	I
Washington State University, WA	I,P
Washington University in St. Louis, MO	I,P
Wayland Baptist University, TX	I
Waynesburg College, PA	I
Wayne State College, NE	I
Wayne State University, MI	I
Webber College, FL	I
Weber State University, UT	D,I
Webster University, MO	I
Wellesley College, MA	I,P
Wells College, NY	I
Wentworth Institute of Technology, MA	I
Wesleyan College, GA	I
Wesleyan University, CT	I
Wesley College, DE	I
Wesley College, MS	I
West Chester University of Pennsylvania, PA	D,I,P
Western Baptist College, OR	I
Western Carolina University, NC	I
Western Illinois University, IL	G,I
Western Kentucky University, KY	D,I
Western Maryland College, MD	I,P
Western Michigan University, MI	I
Western Montana College of The U of Montana, MT	D
Western New England College, MA	D,I,P
Western New Mexico University, NM	D
Western Oregon University, OR	D,I
Western State College of Colorado, CO	D,I
Western Washington University, WA	I
Westfield State College, MA	I
West Liberty State College, WV	D,I
Westminster Choir Coll of Rider U, NJ	I
Westminster College, MO	I
Westminster College, PA	I

D = deferred payment system; *G* = guaranteed tuition rate; *I* = installment payments; *P* = prepayment locks in tuition rate

Westminster College, UT D,I
Westmont College, CA D,I
West Texas A&M University, TX I
West Virginia State College, WV I,P
West Virginia University, WV D,I
West Virginia University Institute of Technology, WV I
West Virginia Wesleyan College, WV I
Westwood College of Technology, CO D,I
Wheaton College, IL I
Wheaton College, MA D,I,P
Wheeling Jesuit University, WV G
Wheelock College, MA I
White Pines College, NH I
Whitman College, WA D
Whittier College, CA I
Whitworth College, WA I,P
Wichita State University, KS D
Widener University, PA I
Wilberforce University, OH D,I
Wilkes University, PA I
Willamette University, OR I,P
William Jewell College, MO I,P
William Paterson University of New Jersey, NJ I
William Penn University, IA I
Williams Baptist College, AR I
Williams College, MA I
William Tyndale College, MI D
William Woods University, MO I
Wilmington College, OH I
Wilson College, PA I,P
Wingate University, NC I
Winston-Salem State University, NC I
Winthrop University, SC I
Wisconsin Lutheran College, WI I
Wittenberg University, OH D,I,P
Wofford College, SC I
Woodbury University, CA D,I
Worcester State College, MA D
Xavier University, OH D,I
Xavier University of Louisiana, LA I
Yale University, CT I
Yeshiva Karlin Stolin Rabbinical Institute, NY I
Yeshiva University, NY I
York College, NE I
York College of Pennsylvania, PA I
Youngstown State University, OH I

D = deferred payment system; *G* = guaranteed tuition rate; *I* = installment payments; *P* = prepayment locks in tuition rate